SCOTT

2022 STANDARD POSTAGE STAMP CATALOGUE

ONE HUNDRED AND SEVENTY-EIGHTH EDITION IN SIX VOLUMES

Volume 1B

Austria-B

EDITOR-IN-CHIEF	Jay Bigalke
EDITOR-AT-LARGE	Donna Houseman
CONTRIBUTING EDITOR	Charles Snee
EDITOR EMERITUS	James E. Kloetzel
SENIOR EDITOR /NEW ISSUES AND VALUING	Martin J. Frankevicz
ADMINISTRATIVE ASSISTANT/CATALOGUE LAYOUT	Eric Wiessinger
PRINTING AND IMAGE COORDINATOR	Stacey Mahan
SENIOR GRAPHIC DESIGNER	Cinda McAlexander
SALES DIRECTOR	David Pistello
SALES DIRECTOR	Eric Roth

Released April 2021

Includes New Stamp Listings through the February 2021 Linn's Stamp News Monthly Catalogue Update

AMOS MEDIA

1660 Campbell Road, Suite A, Sidney, OH 45365

Publishers of *Linn's Stamp News, Linn's Stamp News Monthly, Coin World* and *Coin World Monthly.*

Table of contents

See Volumes 1A, 2A through 6B for Countries of the World, United States, United Nations, Abu Dhabi-Australia, C-Z
Volume 1A: United States, United Nations, Abu Dhabi-Australia
Volume 2A: C-Cur; Volume 2B: Cyp-F
Volume 3A: G; Volume 3B: H-I
Volume 4A: J-L; Volume 4B: M
Volume 5A: N-Phil; Volume 5B: Pit-Sam
Volume 6A: San-Tete; Volume 6B: Thai-Z

Scott Catalogue Mission Statement

The Scott Catalogue Team exists to serve the recreational, educational and commercial hobby needs of stamp collectors and dealers.

We strive to set the industry standard for philatelic information and products by developing and providing goods that help collectors identify, value, organize and present their collections.

Quality customer service is, and will continue to be, our highest priority.
We aspire toward achieving total customer satisfaction.

ISBN 978-0-89487-602-8

Library of Congress Card No. 2-3301

AUSTRIA

'os-trē-ə

LOCATION — Central Europe
GOVT. — Republic
AREA — 32,378 sq. mi.
POP. — 8,139,299 (1999 est.)
CAPITAL — Vienna

Before 1867 Austria was an absolute monarchy, which included Hungary and Lombardy-Venetia. In 1867 the Austro-Hungarian Monarchy was established, with Austria and Hungary as equal partners. After World War I, in 1918, the different nationalities established their own states and only the German-speaking parts remained, forming a republic under the name "Deutschosterreich" (German Austria), which name was shortly again changed to "Austria." In 1938 German forces occupied Austria, which became part of the German Reich. After the liberation by Allied troops in 1945, an independent republic was re-established.

60 Kreuzer = 1 Gulden
100 Neu-Kreuzer = 1 Gulden (1858)
100 Heller = 1 Krone (1899)
100 Groschen = 1 Schilling (1925)
100 Cents = 1 Euro (2002)

Catalogue values for unused stamps in this country are for Never Hinged items, beginning with Scott 432 in the regular postage section, Scott B165 in the semi-postal section, Scott C47 in the airpost section, Scott J175 in the postage due section, and Scott 4N1 in the AMG section.

Unused stamps without gum sell for about one-third or less of the values quoted.

Watermarks

Wmk. 91 — "BRIEF-MARKEN" In Double-lined Capitals Across the Middle of the Sheet

Wmk. 140 — Crown

Issues of the Austrian Monarchy (including Hungary)

Coat of Arms — A1

NINE KREUZER

Type I. One heavy line around coat of arms center. On the 9kr the top of "9" is about on a level with "Kreuzer" and not near the top of the label. Each cliche has the "9" in a different position.

Type IA. As type I, but with 1 ¼mm between "9" and "K."

Type II. One heavy line around coat of arms center. On the 9kr the top of "9" is much higher than the top of the word "Kreuzer" and nearly touches the top of the label.

Type III. As type II, but with two, thinner, lines around the center.

The stamps of this issue were at first printed on a rough hand-made paper, varying in thickness and having a watermark in script letters K.K.H.M., the initials of Kaiserlich Königliches Handels-Ministerium (Imperial and Royal Ministry of Commerce), vertically in the gutter between the panes. Parts of these letters show on margin stamps in the sheet. From 1854 a thick, smooth machine-made paper without watermark was used.

Wmk. K.K.H.M. in Sheet or Unwmk.
1850 Typo. *Imperf.*
Thin to Thick Paper

1	A1	1kr yellow	1,650.	115.00
a.		Printed on both sides	*2,000.*	150.00
b.		1kr orange	2,350.	150.00
c.		1kr brown orange	3,475.	625.00
2	A1	2kr black	1,375.	82.50
a.		Ribbed paper	—	4,550.
b.		2kr gray black	2,350.	120.00
d.		Half used as 1kr on cover		*52,500.*
3	A1	3kr red	825.00	4.00
a.		Ribbed paper	*4,000.*	160.00
b.		Laid paper	—	*19,000.*
c.		Printed on both sides		*10,000.*
4	A1	6kr brown	1,000.	6.00
a.		Ribbed paper		*2,450.*
c.		Diagonal half used as 3kr on cover		*20,000.*
5	A1	9kr blue, type II	2,350.	9.00
a.		9kr blue, type I	*2,250.*	10.00
b.		9kr blue, type IA	*15,000.*	*1,250.*
c.		Laid paper, type III		*15,000.*
d.		Printed on both sides, type II		*9,250.*

1854
Machine-made Paper, Type III

1d	A1	1kr yellow	1,450.	100.00
2c	A1	2kr black	1,750.	80.00
3e	A1	3kr red	475.00	4.25
f.		3kr red, type I	4,650.	52.50
4b	A1	6kr brown	975.00	8.25
5e	A1	9kr blue	1,025.	4.25

In 1852-54, Nos. 1-5, rouletted 14, were used in Tokay and Homonna. A 12kr blue exists, but was not issued. Value, $100,000.

The reprints are type III in brighter colors, some on paper watermarked "Briefmarken" in the sheet.

For similar design see Lombardy-Venetia A1.

A2

A3

Emperor Franz Josef — A4

A5

A6

Two Types of Each Value.

Type I. Loops of the bow at the back of the head broken, except the 2kr. In the 2kr, the "2" has a flat foot, thinning to the right. The frame line in the UR corner is thicker than the line below. In the 5kr the top frame line is unbroken.

Type II. Loops complete. Wreath projects further at top of head. In the 2kr, the "2" has a more curved foot of uniform thickness, with a shading line in the upper and lower curves. The frame line UR is thicker than the line below. In the 5kr the top frame line is broken.

1858-59 Embossed *Perf. 14½*

6	A2	2kr yellow, type II	1,225.	55.00
a.		2kr yellow, type I	3,000.	400.00
b.		2kr orange, type II	3,750.	450.00
c.		Half used as 1kr on cover		*41,500.*
7	A3	3kr black, type II	*2,500.*	175.00
a.		3kr black, type I	2,000.	240.00
8	A3	3kr green, type II ('59)	1,350.	140.00
9	A4	5kr red, type II	475.00	2.40
a.		5kr red, type I	2,000.	20.00
b.		5kr red, type II with type I frame	950.00	32.50
10	A5	10kr brown, type II	875.00	4.75
a.		10kr brown, type I	2,400.	24.00
b.		Half used as 5kr on cover		*16,000.*
11	A6	15kr blue, type II	800.00	2.00
a.		Type I	2,400.	24.00
b.		Half used as 7kr on cover		—

The reprints are of type II and are perforated 10½, 11, 12, 12½ and 13. There are also imperforate reprints of Nos. 6 to 8.

For similar designs see Lombardy-Venetia A2-A6.

Franz Josef — A7

1860-61 Embossed *Perf. 14*

12	A7	2kr yellow	450.00	35.00
a.		Half used as 1kr on cover		*25,000.*
13	A7	3kr green	375.00	30.00
14	A7	5kr red	290.00	1.00
15	A7	10kr brown	325.00	3.00
a.		Half used as 5kr on cover		*9,000.*
16	A7	15kr blue	475.00	3.00

The reprints are perforated 9, 9½, 10, 10½, 11, 11½, 12, 12½, 13 and 13½.

There are also imperforate reprints of the 2 and 3kr.

For similar design see Lombardy-Venetia A7.

Coat of Arms — A8

1863

17	A8	2kr yellow	675.00	110.00
a.		Half used as 1kr on cover		—
18	A8	3kr green	525.00	100.00
19	A8	5kr rose	625.00	15.00
20	A8	10kr blue	1,650.	18.50
21	A8	15kr yellow brown	1,650.	18.00

For similar design see Lombardy-Venetia A1.

Wmk. 91, or, before July 1864, Unwmkd.
1863-64 *Perf. 9½*

22	A8	2kr yellow ('64)	190.00	15.00
a.		Ribbed paper		550.00
b.		Half used as 1kr on cover		*27,500.*
23	A8	3kr green ('64)	190.00	15.00
24	A8	5kr rose	55.00	.75
a.		Ribbed paper		775.00
25	A8	10kr blue	250.00	3.50
a.		Half used as 5kr on cover		*22,500.*
26	A8	15kr yellow brown	225.00	2.25
		Nos. 22-26 (5)	910.00	36.50

The reprints are perforated 10½, 11½, 13 and 13½. There are also imperforate reprints of the 2 and 3kr.

Issues of Austro-Hungarian Monarchy

From 1867 to 1871 the independent postal administrations of Austria and Hungary used the same stamps.

A9

A10

5 kr:

Type I. In arabesques in lower left corner, the small ornament at left of the curve nearest the figure "5" is short and has three points at bottom.

Type II. The ornament is prolonged within the curve and has two points at bottom. The corresponding ornament at top of the lower left corner does not touch the curve (1872).

Type III. Similar to type II but the top ornament is joined to the curve (1881). Two different printing methods were used for the 1867-74 issues. The first produced stamps on which the hair and whiskers were coarse and thick, from the second they were fine and clear.

1867-72 Wmk. 91 Typo. *Perf. 9½*
Coarse Print

27	A9	2kr yellow	120.00	3.00
a.		Half used as 1kr on cover		—
28	A9	3kr green	140.00	2.90
29	A9	5kr rose, type II	87.50	.25
a.		5kr rose, type I	95.00	.25
b.		Perf. 10½, type II	190.00	
c.		Cliché of 3kr in plate of 5kr		*37,500.*
30	A9	10kr blue	290.00	2.40
a.		Half used as 5kr on cover		—
31	A9	15kr brown	290.00	6.50
32	A9	25kr lilac	87.50	21.00
b.		25kr brown violet	325.00	65.00
33	A10	50kr light brown	40.00	*130.00*
		Never hinged	70.00	
		On cover		3,000.
a.		50kr pale red brown	500.00	210.00
b.		50kr brownish rose	500.00	325.00
c.		Pair, imperf. btwn., vert. or horizontal	*725.00*	*1,700.*

Issues for Austria only

1874-80 Fine Print *Perf. 9½*

34	A9	2kr yellow ('76)	14.50	.90
35	A9	3kr green ('76)	65.00	.90
36	A9	5kr rose, type III	4.50	.25
37	A9	10kr blue ('75)	160.00	.60
38	A9	15kr brown ('77)	8.75	7.75
39	A9	25kr gray lil ('78)	1.10	*190.00*
40	A10	50kr red brown	14.50	*190.00*

Perf. 9

34a	A9	2kr	250.00	65.00
35a	A9	3kr	225.00	30.00
36a	A9	5kr	87.50	3.50
37a	A9	10kr	440.00	35.00
38a	A9	15kr	625.00	130.00

Perf. 10½

34b	A9	2kr	60.00	4.50
35b	A9	3kr	100.00	2.75
36b	A9	5kr	14.50	.90
37b	A9	10kr	225.00	2.75
38b	A9	15kr	250.00	27.50

Perf. 12

34c	A9	2kr	275.00	160.00
35c	A9	3kr	250.00	27.50
36c	A9	5kr	60.00	5.00
37c	A9	10kr	525.00	130.00
38c	A9	15kr	825.00	190.00
40b	A10	50kr brown ('80)	19.00	*190.00*
c.		Perf. 10½x12	325.00	—

Perf. 13

34d	A9	2kr	325.00	*360.00*
35d	A9	3kr	225.00	36.00
36d	A9	5kr	130.00	21.00
37d	A9	10kr	275.00	100.00
38d	A9	15kr	625.00	475.00
40a	A10	50kr	30.00	*250.00*

Perf. 9x10½

34e	A9	2kr	440.00	87.50
35e	A9	3kr	360.00	77.50
36e	A9	5kr	140.00	18.00
37e	A9	10kr	410.00	105.00

Various compound perforations exist.

Values are for stamps that do not show the watermark. Stamps showing the watermark often sell for more.

For similar designs see Offices in the Turkish Empire A1-A2.

A11

Perf. 9, 9½, 10, 10½, 11½, 12, 12½

1883 Inscriptions in Black

41	A11	2kr brown	6.00	.45
42	A11	3kr green	6.00	.35
43	A11	5kr rose	75.00	.30
a.		Vert. pair, imperf. btwn.	190.00	*425.00*
44	A11	10kr blue	4.50	.35
45	A11	20kr gray	55.00	4.25
46	A11	50kr red lilac, perf 9½	375.00	80.00

The last printings of Nos. 41-46 are watermarked "ZEITUNGS-MARKEN" instead of "BRIEF-MARKEN." Values are for stamps that do not show watermark. Stamps with watermarks that are identifiable as being from "BRIEFMARKEN" sheets often sell for slightly more, while those with watermarks identifying stamps from "ZEITUNGS-MARKEN" sheets sell for significantly more. See the *Scott Classic Specialized Catalogue of Stamps and Covers* for detailed listings.

The 5kr has been reprinted in a dull red rose, perforated 10½.

For similar design see Offices in the Turkish Empire A3.

For surcharges see Offices in the Turkish Empire Nos. 15-19.

A12

A13

Perf. 9 to 13½, also Compound

1890-96 Unwmk. Granite Paper

Numerals in black, Nos. 51-61

51	A12	1kr dark gray	1.50	.30
a.		Pair, imperf. between	225.00	*540.00*
b.		Half used as ½kr on cover		*150.00*
52	A12	2kr light brown	.35	.30
53	A12	3kr gray green	.45	.30
a.		Pair, imperf. between	325.00	*650.00*
54	A12	5kr rose	.45	.30
a.		Pair, imperf. between	260.00	*450.00*
55	A12	10kr ultramarine	1.10	.30
a.		Pair, imperf. between	360.00	*650.00*
56	A12	12kr claret	2.60	.40
a.		Pair, imperf. between	—	800.00
57	A12	15kr lilac	2.60	.40
a.		Pair, imperf. between	475.00	*900.00*
58	A12	20kr olive green	37.50	2.40
59	A12	24kr gray blue	2.25	1.50
a.		Pair, imperf. between	475.00	*700.00*
60	A12	30kr dark brown	2.75	.80
61	A12	50kr violet, perf 10	6.00	*11.00*

Engr.

62	A13	1gld dark blue	3.00	3.00
63	A13	1gld pale lilac ('96)	45.00	4.50
64	A13	2gld carmine	3.25	*24.00*
65	A13	2gld gray green ('96)	15.00	*47.50*
		Nos. 51-65 (15)	123.80	97.00

Nearly all values of the 1890-1907 issues are found with numerals missing in one or more corners, some with numerals printed on the back.

For surcharges see Offices in the Turkish Empire Nos. 20-25, 28-31.

A14

Perf. 9 to 13½, also Compound

1891 Typo. Numerals in black

66	A14	20kr olive green	1.90	.30
67	A14	24kr gray blue	3.25	.95
68	A14	30kr brown	1.90	.30
a.		Pair, imperf. between	275.00	*700.00*
b.		Perf. 9	110.00	55.00
69	A14	50kr violet	1.90	.40
		Nos. 66-69 (4)	8.95	1.95

For surcharges see Offices in the Turkish Empire Nos. 26-27.

A15

A16

A17

A18

Perf. 10½ to 13½ and Compound

1899 Without Varnish Bars

Numerals in black, Nos. 70-82

70	A15	1h lilac	.75	.25
b.		Imperf.	60.00	*150.00*
c.		Perf. 10½	32.50	8.00
d.		Numerals inverted	*2,250.*	*3,400.*
71	A15	2h dark gray	2.75	.65
72	A15	3h bister brown	6.50	.25
b.		"3" in lower right corner sideways		*3,000.*
73	A15	5h blue green	7.25	.25
c.		Perf. 10½	22.50	4.75
74	A15	6h orange	.75	.25
75	A16	10h rose	16.00	.25
b.		Perf. 10½	875.00	210.00
76	A16	20h brown	5.25	.25
77	A16	25h ultramarine	60.00	.35
78	A16	30h red violet	19.00	2.75
b.		Horiz. pair, imperf. btwn.	600.00	—
80	A17	40h green	32.50	3.50
81	A17	50h gray blue	17.50	4.25
b.		All four "50's" parallel		*3,100.*
82	A17	60h brown	50.00	1.25
b.		Horiz. pair, imperf. btwn.	550.00	—
c.		Perf. 10½	105.00	5.40

Engr.

83	A18	1k carmine rose	6.00	.45
a.		1k carmine	6.00	.25
b.		Vert. pair, imperf. btwn.	250.00	*350.00*
84	A18	2k gray lilac	52.50	.45
a.		Vert. pair, imperf. btwn.	440.00	*725.00*
85	A18	4k gray green	10.50	18.00
		Nos. 70-85 (15)	287.25	33.15

For surcharges see Offices in Crete Nos. 1-7, Offices in the Turkish Empire Nos. 32-45.

1901 With Varnish Bars

70a	A15	1h lilac	1.60	.45
71a	A15	2h dark gray	6.50	.40
72a	A15	3h bister brown	.80	.25
73a	A15	5h blue green	.80	.25
74a	A15	6h orange	.80	.25
75a	A16	10h rose	.80	.25
76a	A16	20h brown	.80	.25
77a	A16	25h ultra	.80	.25
78a	A16	30h red violet	3.25	.80
79	A17	35h green	.80	.25
80a	A17	40h green	3.25	*4.75*
81a	A17	50h gray blue	4.75	*11.00*
82a	A17	60h brown	3.25	1.60
		Nos. 70a-78a,79,80a-82a (13)	28.20	20.75

The diagonal yellow bars of varnish were printed across the face to prevent cleaning.

A19

A20

A21

Perf. 12½ to 13½ and Compound

1905-07 Typo.

Without Varnish Bars

Colored Numerals

86	A19	1h lilac	.25	*.35*
87	A19	2h dark gray	.25	.25
88	A19	3h bister brown	.25	.25
89	A19	5h dk blue green	12.00	.25
90	A19	5h yellow grn ('06)	.25	.25
91	A19	6h deep orange	.25	.25
92	A20	10h carmine ('06)	.50	.25
93	A20	12h violet ('07)	1.20	.80
94	A20	20h brown ('06)	4.00	.25
95	A20	25h ultra ('06)	4.00	.40
96	A20	30h red violet ('06)	8.00	.40

Black Numerals

97	A20	10h carmine	16.00	.25
98	A20	20h brown	40.00	1.60
99	A20	25h ultra	40.00	2.40
100	A20	30h red violet	55.00	4.75

White Numerals

101	A21	35h green	2.00	.25
102	A21	40h deep violet	2.00	.80
103	A21	50h dull blue	2.00	*3.50*
104	A21	60h yellow brown	2.00	.80
105	A21	72h rose	2.00	1.75
		Nos. 86-105 (20)	191.95	19.80
		Set, never hinged	650.00	

For surcharges see Offices in Crete Nos. 8-14.

1904 *Perf. 13x13½*

Without Varnish Bars

86a	A19	1h lilac	.35	*.95*
87a	A19	2h dark gray	1.40	.95
88a	A19	3h bister brown	2.00	.25
89a	A19	5h dk blue green	3.25	.25
91a	A19	6h deep orange	8.00	.30
97a	A20	10h carmine	1.75	.25
98a	A20	20h brown	29.00	1.20
99a	A20	25h ultra	29.00	.80
100a	A20	30h red violet	45.00	1.60
101a	A21	35h green	29.00	.55
102a	A21	40h deep violet	27.50	4.00
103a	A21	50h dull blue	29.00	9.50
104a	A21	60h yellow brown	40.00	1.60
105a	A21	72h rose	2.00	2.25
		Nos. 86a-105a (14)	247.25	24.45
		Set, never hinged	875.00	

Stamps of the 1901, 1904 and 1905 issues perf. 9 or 10½, also compound with 12½, were not sold at any post office, but were supplied only to some high-ranking officials. This applies also to the contemporaneous issues of Austrian Offices Abroad.

Karl VI — A22

Franz Josef — A23

Schönbrunn Palace — A24

Franz Josef — A25

Designs: 2h, Maria Theresa. 3h, Joseph II. 5h, 10h, 25h, Franz Josef. 6h, Leopold II. 12h, Franz I. 20h, Ferdinand I. 30h, Franz Josef as youth. 35h, Franz Josef in middle age. 60h, Franz Josef on horseback. 1k, Franz Josef in royal robes. 5k, Hofburg, Vienna.

1908-16 Typo. *Perf. 12½*

Ordinary paper ('08-'13)

110a	A22	1h gray black	.25	.25
111a	A22	2h violet	.25	.25
112	A22	3h magenta	.25	.25
113	A22	5h yellow green	.25	.25
a.		Booklet pane of 6	*27.50*	
114a	A22	6h buff ('13)	.55	.80
115	A22	10h rose	.25	.25
a.		Booklet pane of 6	*82.50*	
116a	A22	12h scarlet	.80	1.20
117a	A22	20h chocolate	4.75	.45
118a	A22	25h deep blue	2.00	.45
119a	A22	30h olive green	9.50	.65
120	A22	35h slate	2.40	.25

Engr.

121	A23	50h dark green	.55	.25
a.		Vert. pair, imperf. btwn.	200.00	*400.00*
b.		Horiz. pair, imperf. btwn.	200.00	*400.00*
122	A23	60h deep carmine	.25	.25
a.		Vert. pair, imperf. btwn.	160.00	*400.00*
b.		Horiz. pair, imperf. btwn.	160.00	*400.00*
123	A23	72h dk brown	1.60	.40
124	A23	1k purple	12.00	.25
a.		Vert. pair, imperf. btwn.	200.00	*350.00*
b.		Horiz. pair, imperf. btwn.	200.00	*350.00*
125	A24	2k lake & olive grn	20.00	.40
126	A24	5k bister & dk vio	40.00	6.00
127	A25	10k blue, bis & dp brn	190.00	65.00
		Nos. 110a-127 (18)	285.65	77.60
		Set, never hinged	875.00	

Definitive set issued for the 60th year of the reign of Emperor Franz Josef.

The 1h-35h exist on both ordinary (1913) and chalk-surfaced (1908) paper. The cheaper varieties are listed above. For detailed listings, see the *Scott Classic Specialized Catalogue of Stamps and Covers.*

All values exist imperforate. They were not sold at any post office, but presented to a number of high government officials. This applies also to all imperforate stamps of later issues, including semi-postals, etc., and those of the Austrian Offices Abroad.

Litho. forgeries of No. 127 exist.

For overprint and surcharge see #J47-J48.

For similar designs see Offices in Crete A5-A6, Offices in the Turkish Empire A16-A17.

Birthday Jubilee Issue

No. 144

Similar to 1908 Issue, but designs enlarged by labels at top and bottom bearing dates "1830" and "1910"

1910 Typo.

128	A22	1h gray black	4.00	*8.00*
129	A22	2h violet	4.75	*16.00*
130	A22	3h magenta	4.00	*12.00*
131	A22	5h yellow green	.25	.35
132	A22	6h buff	3.25	*12.00*
133	A22	10h rose	.25	.35
134	A22	12h scarlet	3.25	*12.00*
135	A22	20h chocolate	3.25	*12.00*
136	A22	25h deep blue	1.60	*2.40*
137	A22	30h olive green	3.25	*12.00*
138	A22	35h slate	3.25	*12.00*

Engr.

139	A23	50h dark green	5.50	*12.00*
140	A23	60h deep car	5.50	*12.00*
141	A23	1k purple	5.50	*16.00*
142	A24	2k lake & ol grn	140.00	*225.00*

143	A24	5k bister & dk vio	110.00	*225.00*
144	A25	10k blue, bis & dp brn	175.00	*325.00*
		Nos. 128-144 (17)	472.60	*914.10*
		Set, never hinged	1,050.	

80th birthday of Emperor Franz Josef.
All values exist imperforate.
Litho. forgeries of Nos. 142-144 exist.

Austrian Crown — A37

Franz Josef — A38

A39

Coat of Arms — A40

Two sizes of Type A40:
Type I: 25x30mm
Type II: 26x29mm

1916-18 **Typo.**

145	A37	3h brt violet	.25	.25
146	A37	5h lt green	.25	.25
a.		Booklet pane of 6	*15.50*	
b.		Booklet pane of 4 + 2 labels	*30.00*	
147	A37	6h deep orange	.25	*.80*
148	A37	10h magenta	.25	.25
a.		Booklet pane of 6	*30.00*	
149	A37	12h light blue	.25	*.90*
150	A38	15h rose red	.40	.25
a.		Booklet pane of 6	*16.50*	
151	A38	20h chocolate	4.00	.25
152	A38	25h blue	4.00	.80
153	A38	30h slate	6.50	.65
154	A39	40h olive green	.25	.25
155	A39	50h blue green	.25	.25
156	A39	60h deep blue	.25	.25
157	A39	80h orange brown	.25	.25
158	A39	90h red violet	.25	.25
159	A39	1k car, *yel* ('18)	.25	.25

Engr.

160	A40	2k dark blue	4.00	.40
161	A40	3k claret	24.00	1.20
162	A40	4k deep green	8.00	2.40
163	A40	10k deep violet	27.50	*52.50*
		Nos. 145-163 (19)	81.15	62.40
		Set, never hinged	240.00	

Stamps of type A38 have two varieties of the frame. Stamps of type A40 have various decorations about the shield.

Nos. 145-163 exist imperf. Value set, $475 hinged, $875 never hinged.

1917 **Ordinary Paper**

164	A40	2k lt blue	2.00	.80
165	A40	3k car rose	47.50	.80
166	A40	4k yel grn	3.25	1.25
167	A40	10k violet	140.00	110.00
		Nos. 164-167 (4)	192.75	112.85
		Set, never hinged	475.00	

Nos. 164-167 exist imperf. Value set, $325 unused, $650 never hinged.

See Nos. 172-175 (granite paper). For overprints and surcharges see Nos. 181-199, C1-C3, J60-J63, N1-N5, N10-N19, N33-N37, N42-N51; Czechoslovakia B1-B6, B11-B23; Western Ukraine 1-3, 6-13, 17-28, 64-71, 74, 76-80, 85-94, N1, N6-N8, N13.

Emperor Karl I — A42

1917-18 **Typo.**

168	A42	15h dull red	.40	.40
a.		Booklet pane of 6	*16.50*	
169	A42	20h dk green ('18)	.40	.40
a.		20h green ('17)	.80	.65
170	A42	25h blue	.40	.40
171	A42	30h dull violet	2.00	.40
		Nos. 168-171 (4)	3.20	1.60
		Set, never hinged	13.50	

Nos. 168-171 exist imperf. Value set, $160 unused, $400 never hinged.

For overprints and surcharges see Nos. N6-N9, N20, N38-N41, N52, N64. Czechoslovakia B7-B10; Western Ukraine 4-5, 14-16, 72-73, 81-84, N2-N5.

1918-19 **Engr.** **Granite Paper**

172	A40	2k lt blue	1.20	*.45*
a.		Perf. 11½	725.00	*1,200.*
173	A40	3k car rose	.40	*.80*
174	A40	4k yel grn ('19)	4.00	*20.00*
175	A40	10k lt vio ('19)	8.00	*32.50*
		Nos. 172-175 (4)	13.60	*53.75*
		Set, never hinged	40.00	

Issues of the Republic

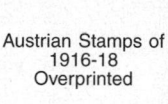

Austrian Stamps of 1916-18 Overprinted

1918-19 **Unwmk.** ***Perf. 12½***

181	A37	3h bright violet	.25	.25
182	A37	5h light green	.25	.25
183	A37	6h deep orange	.80	*3.25*
184	A37	10h magenta	.25	.25
185	A37	12h light blue	.40	*2.40*
186	A42	15h dull red	.80	*2.00*
187	A42	20h deep green	.40	.25
188	A42	25h blue	.80	.25
189	A42	30h dull violet	.80	.25
190	A39	40h olive green	.80	.25
191	A39	50h deep green	.80	*2.00*
192	A39	60h deep blue	1.20	*2.00*
193	A39	80h orange brown	.40	.80
a.		Inverted overprint	275.00	*325.00*
194	A39	90h red violet	1.20	.80
195	A39	1k carmine, *yel*	1.40	.80
196	A40	2k lt blue	.25	.25
a.		Horiz. pair, imperf. between	240.00	
b.		Vert. pair, imperf. between	400.00	
c.		Perf. 11½	95.00	*110.00*
197	A40	3k car rose	.35	*.80*
198	A40	4k yel grn	1.60	*3.25*
a.		Perf. 11½	16.00	35.00
199	A40	10k deep vio	9.50	*20.00*
		Nos. 181-199 (19)	22.25	*40.10*
		Set, never hinged	62.50	

Nos. 181, 182, 184, 187-191, 194, 197 and 199 exist imperforate.

Post Horn — A43

Coat of Arms — A44

Allegory of New Republic — A45

1919-20 **Typo.** ***Perf. 12½***
Ordinary Paper

200	A43	3h gray	.25	.25
201	A44	5h yellow green	.25	.25
202	A44	5h gray ('20)	.25	.25
203	A43	6h orange	.25	*.50*
204	A44	10h deep rose	.25	.25
205	A44	10h red ('20)	.25	.25
a.		Thick grayish paper ('20)	.25	.40
206	A43	12h grnsh blue	.25	*4.00*
207	A43	15h bister ('20)	.35	*.80*
a.		Thick grayish paper ('20)	.25	.40
208	A45	20h dark green	.25	.25
a.		20h yellow green	.25	.25
b.		As "a," thick grysh paper ('20)	1.60	*4.00*
209	A44	25h blue	.25	.25
210	A43	25h violet ('20)	.25	.25
211	A45	30h dark brown	.25	.25
212	A45	40h violet	.25	.25
213	A45	40h lake ('20)	.25	.25
214	A44	45h olive green	.30	*.80*
215	A45	50h dark blue	.25	.25
a.		Thick grayish paper ('20)	.40	*.95*
216	A43	60h ol grn ('20)	.25	.25
217	A44	1k carmine, *yel*	.25	.25
218	A44	1k light blue ('20)	.25	.25
		Nos. 200-218 (19)	4.90	9.85
		Set, never hinged	4.00	

All values exist imperf. (For regularly issued imperfs, see Nos. 227-235.)

For overprints and surcharge see Nos. B11-B19, B30-B38, J102, N21, N27, N53, N58, N65, N71.

Parliament Building A46

1919-20 **Engr.** ***Perf. 12½, 11½***
Granite Paper

219	A46	2k ver & blk	.25	*.80*
a.		Center inverted	*2,750.*	
		Never hinged	*6,500.*	
b.		Perf. 11½	1.60	*3.25*
220	A46	2½k ol bis ('20)	.30	*.25*
221	A46	3k bl & blk brn	.25	.25
a.		Perf. 11½	5.75	*20.00*
222	A46	4k car & blk	.25	.25
a.		Center inverted	*2,100.*	*3,250.*
		Never hinged	*2,750.*	
b.		Perf. 11½	2.00	*6.50*
223	A46	5k black ('20)	.25	.25
a.		Perf. 11½x12½	55.00	*87.50*
		Never hinged	160.00	
b.		Perf. 11½	2.75	*7.25*
224	A46	7½k plum	.30	*.40*
a.		Perf. 11½	120.00	*240.00*
		Never hinged	290.00	
b.		Perf. 11½x12½	80.00	*240.00*
225	A46	10k olive grn & blk brn	.30	*.40*
a.		Perf. 11½x12½	160.00	*300.00*
		Never hinged	475.00	
b.		Perf. 11½	13.50	*30.00*
		Never hinged	32.50	
226	A46	20k lil & red ('20)	.25	*.40*
a.		Center inverted	*60,000.*	*40,000.*
b.		Perf. 11½	72.50	175.00
		Never hinged	175.00	
		Nos. 219-226 (8)	2.15	*3.00*
		Set, never hinged	6.75	

Nos. 220-222, 225-226 exist imperforate between. Values, per pair: unused $200-$350; never hinged $400-$725.

See No. 248. For overprints and surcharge see Nos. B23-B29, B43-B49.

1920 **Typo.** ***Imperf.***
Ordinary Paper

227	A44	5h yellow green	.35	*.95*
228	A44	5h gray	.25	.25
229	A44	10h deep rose	.25	.25
230	A44	10h red	.25	.25
231	A43	15h bister	.25	.25
232	A43	25h violet	.25	.25
233	A45	30h dark brown	.25	.25
234	A45	40h violet	.25	*.25*
235	A43	60h olive green	.25	*.25*
		Nos. 227-235 (9)	2.35	2.95
		Set, never hinged	3.15	

Arms

A47 A48

1920-21 **Typo.** ***Perf. 12½***
White Paper

238	A47	80h rose	.25	.25
239	A47	1k black brown	.25	.25
241	A47	1½k green ('21)	.30	.25
242	A47	2k blue	.25	.30
243	A48	3k yel grn & dk grn ('21)	.25	*.30*
244	A48	4k red & clar ('21)	.25	.25

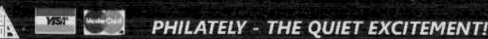

245 A48 5k vio & clar ('21) .25 .25
246 A48 7½k yel & brn ('21) .25 *.30*
247 A48 10k ultra & bl ('21) .25 *.25*
Nos. 238-247 (9) 2.30 2.40
Set, never hinged 4.75

Nos. 238-245, 247 exist on white paper of good quality and on thick grayish paper of inferior quality; No. 246 exists only on white paper. Values are for the cheaper varieties. See the *Scott Classic Specialized Catalogue of Stamps and Covers* for detailed listings.

For overprints and surcharges see Nos. B20-B22, B39-B42.

1921 **Engr.**

248 A46 50k dk violet, *yel* .95 *1.60*
Never hinged 1.60
a. Perf. 11½ 14.50 *77.50*
Never hinged 23.00

Symbols of Agriculture A49

Symbols of Labor and Industry A50

1922-24 **Typo.** ***Perf. 12½***

250 A49 ½k olive bister .25 *.65*
251 A50 1k brown .25 .25
252 A50 2k cobalt blue .25 .25
253 A49 2½k orange brown .25 .25
254 A50 4k dull violet .25 *1.00*
255 A50 5k gray green .25 .25
256 A49 7½k gray violet .25 .25
257 A50 10k claret .25 .25
258 A49 12½k gray green .25 .25
259 A49 15k bluish green .25 .25
260 A49 20k dark blue .25 .25
261 A49 25k claret .25 .25
262 A50 30k pale gray .25 .25
263 A50 45k pale red .25 .25
264 A50 50k orange brown .25 .25
265 A50 60k yellow green .25 .25
266 A50 75k ultramarine .25 .25
267 A50 80k yellow .25 .25
268 A49 100k gray .25 .25
269 A49 120k brown .25 .25
270 A49 150k orange .25 .25
271 A49 160k light green .25 .25
272 A49 180k red .25 .25
273 A49 200k pink .25 .25
274 A49 240k dark violet .25 .25
275 A49 300k light blue .25 .25
276 A49 400k deep green 1.20 .80
a. 400k gray green .90 .40
277 A49 500k yellow .25 .25
278 A49 600k slate .25 .25
279 A49 700k brown ('24) 2.40 .25
280 A49 800k violet ('24) 1.60 *2.10*
281 A50 1000k violet ('23) 2.40 .25
282 A50 1200k car rose ('23) .80 .50
283 A50 1500k orange ('24) 2.00 .25
284 A50 1600k slate ('23) 3.25 *3.25*
285 A50 2000k dp bl ('23) 4.75 2.75
286 A50 3000k lt blue ('23) 12.00 2.40
287 A50 4000k dk bl, *bl* ('24) 6.00 2.75
Nos. 250-287 (38) 43.40 23.45
Set, never hinged 175.00

Nos. 250-287 exist imperf. Value set, $600 unused, $1,200 never hinged.

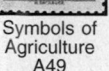

Symbols of Art and Science — A51

1922-24 **Engr.** ***Perf. 12½***

288 A51 20k dark brn, 26x29mm .25 .25
289 A51 25k blue, 26x29mm .25 .25
290 A51 50k brown red, 26x29mm .25 .25
b. Vert. pair, imperf. btwn. 250.00 *350.00*
f. brown red, 25x29½mm .25 .25
291 A51 100k green, 26x29mm 2.50 .25
b. Vert. pair, imperf. btwn. — *475.00*
e. green, 25x29½mm .25 .25
292 A51 200k dk violet, 26x29mm 1.50 .25
b. Vert. pair, imperf. btwn. 250.00
c. dk violet, 25x29½mm .50 .25
293 A51 500k dp orange, 25x29½mm .25 *.25*
a. dp orange, 26x29mm 15.00 15.00
294 A51 1000k blk vio, *yel*, 25x29½mm .25 .25
b. Vert. pair, imperf. btwn. 360.00
c. Horiz. pair, imperf. btwn. 360.00
295 A51 2000k ol grn, *yel*, 25x29½mm .25 .25
a. Vert. pair, imperf. btwn. 360.00
296 A51 3000k clar brn, 25x29½mm ('23) 10.00 .40
297 A51 5000k gray blk, 25x29½mm ('23) 6.50 .80

Granite Paper

298 A51 10,000k red brn, 26x29mm ('24) 4.50 *4.50*
Nos. 288-298 (11) 26.50 7.70
Set, never hinged 72.50

1922-24 ***Perf. 11½***

288a A51 20k dk brown, 26x29mm 1.60 1.60
289a A51 25k blue, 26x29mm 1.25 1.25
290a A51 50k brown red, 26x29mm 1.60 1.60
291a A51 100k green, 26x29mm 4.75 4.75
i. green, 25x29½mm 15.00 15.00
292a A51 200k dk violet, 26x29mm 5.50 5.50
294a A51 1000k bk violet, 25x29½mm 240.00 240.00

Nos. 288-298 come in two design sizes: 25x29½mm and 26x29mm.

On Nos. 281-287, 291-298 "kronen" is abbreviated to "k" and transposed with the numerals.

Nos. 288-298 exist imperf. Value set, $410 hinged, $750 never hinged.

Numeral A52

Fields Crossed by Telegraph Wires A53

Golden Eagle — A54

Church of Minorite Friars — A55

1925-32 **Typo.** ***Perf. 12***

303 A52 1g dark gray .40 .25
304 A52 2g claret .40 .25
305 A52 3g scarlet .40 .25
306 A52 4g grnsh blue ('27) 1.20 .25
307 A52 5g brown orange 1.60 .25
308 A52 6g ultramarine 1.60 .25
309 A52 7g chocolate 1.60 .25
310 A52 8g yellow green 4.00 .25
311 A53 10g orange .80 .25
313 A53 15g red lilac .80 .25
314 A53 16g dark blue .80 .25
315 A53 18g olive green 1.20 *.80*
316 A54 20g dark violet 1.20 .25
317 A54 24g carmine 1.20 .40
318 A54 30g dark brown 1.20 .25
319 A54 40g ultramarine 1.20 .25
320 A54 45g yellow brown 1.60 .25
321 A54 50g gray 1.60 .30
322 A54 80g turquoise blue 3.50 *4.50*

Perf. 12½

Engr.

323 A55 1s deep green 20.00 1.60
a. 1s light green 375.00 24.00
Never hinged 1,750.
b. As "a," pair, imperf between 925.00
324 A55 2s brown rose 8.00 *10.50*
Nos. 303-324 (21) 54.30 *21.85*
Set, never hinged 225.00

Nos. 303-324 exist imperf. Value, set unused $475; never hinged $2,000.

For type A52 surcharged see No. B118.

Güssing — A56

National Library, Vienna — A57

15g, Hochosterwitz. 16g, 20g, Durnstein. 18g, Traunsee. 24g, Salzburg. 30g, Seewiesen. 40g, Innsbruck. 50g, Worthersee. 60g, Hohenems. 2s, St. Stephen's Cathedral, Vienna.

1929-30 **Typo.** ***Perf. 12½***

Size: 25½x21½mm

326 A56 10g brown orange .65 .25
327 A56 10g bister ('30) .65 .25
328 A56 15g violet brown .65 *1.40*
329 A56 16g dark gray .25 .25
330 A56 18g blue green .40 .50
331 A56 20g dark gray ('30) .80 .25
332 A56 24g maroon 6.50 *8.00*
333 A56 24g lake ('30) 6.50 .50
334 A56 30g dark violet 6.50 .25
335 A56 40g dark blue 8.00 .25
336 A56 50g gray violet ('30) 27.50 .25
337 A56 60g olive green 17.50 .25

Engr.

Size: 21x26mm

338 A57 1s black brown 8.00 .25
a. Horiz. pair, imperf. btwn. 260.00
Never hinged 450.00
b. Vert. pair, imperf. btwn. 260.00
Never hinged 450.00
339 A57 2s dark green 16.00 12.00
Never hinged 65.00
a. Horiz. pair, imperf. btwn. 325.00
Nos. 326-339 (14) 99.90 24.65
Set, never hinged 675.00

Nos. 326, 328-330 and 332-339 exist imperf. Values, set of 12 unused hinged $1,450, never hinged $2,000.

Type of 1929-30 Issue

Designs: 12g, Traunsee. 64g, Hohenems.

1932 ***Perf. 12***

Size: 21x16½mm

340 A56 10g olive brown .80 .25
341 A56 12g blue green 1.60 .25
342 A56 18g blue green 1.60 *3.25*
343 A56 20g dark gray .80 .25
344 A56 24g carmine rose 8.00 .25
345 A56 24g dull violet 4.75 .25
346 A56 30g dark violet 20.00 .25
347 A56 30g carmine rose 8.00 .25
a. Vert. pair, imperf. btwn. 45.00
Never hinged, #347a 60.00
348 A56 40g dark blue 24.00 1.60
349 A56 40g dark violet 8.00 .40
350 A56 50g gray violet 24.00 .40
351 A56 50g dull blue 8.00 .40
352 A56 60g gray green 65.00 4.00
353 A56 64g gray green 24.00 .40
Nos. 340-353 (14) 198.55 12.20
Set, never hinged 750.00

For overprints and surcharges see Nos. B87-B92, B119-B121.

Nos. 340-353 exist imperf. Values, set unused hinged, $575, never hinged $1,200.

Used values for Nos. 354-389 are for stamps with philatelic favor cancels. Values for postally used examples are 50%-100% more.

Burgenland A67

Tyrol A68

Costumes of various districts: 3g, Burgenland. 4g, 5g, Carinthia. 6g, 8g, Lower Austria. 12g, 20g, Upper Austria. 24g, 25g, Salzburg. 30g, 35g, Styria. 45g, Tyrol. 60g, Vorarlberg bridal couple. 64g, Vorarlberg. 1s, Viennese family. 2s, Military.

1934-35 **Typo.** ***Perf. 12***

354 A67 1g dark violet .25 .25
355 A67 3g scarlet .25 .25
356 A67 4g olive green .25 .25
357 A67 5g red violet .25 .25
358 A67 6g ultramarine .25 .25
359 A67 8g green .25 .25
360 A67 12g dark brown .25 .25
361 A67 20g yellow brown .25 .25
362 A67 24g grnsh blue .25 .25
363 A67 25g violet .25 .25
364 A67 30g maroon .25 .25
365 A67 35g rose carmine .35 *.35*

Perf. 12½

366 A68 40g slate gray .30 .25
367 A68 45g brown red .30 .25
368 A68 60g ultramarine .55 .40
369 A68 64g brown .80 .25
370 A68 1s deep violet 1.20 .65
371 A68 2s dull green 45.00 *45.00*

Designs Redrawn

Perf. 12 (6g), 12½ (2s)

372 A67 6g ultra ('35) .25 .25
373 A68 2s emerald ('35) 3.50 *3.50*
Nos. 354-373 (20) 55.00 53.65
Set, never hinged 200.00

The design of No. 358 looks as though the man's ears were on backwards, while No. 372 appears correctly.

On No. 373 there are seven feathers on each side of the eagle instead of five.

Nos. 354-373 exist imperf. Values, set unused hinged $410, never hinged $700.

For surcharges see Nos. B128-B131.

Dollfuss Mourning Issue

Engelbert Dollfuss — A85

1934-35 **Engr.** ***Perf. 12½***

374 A85 24g greenish black .35 *.35*
Never hinged 1.60
375 A85 24g indigo ('35) .80 *.80*
Never hinged 3.25

Nos. 374-375 exist imperf. Value, each unused hinged $200, never hinged $400.

"Mother and Child," by Joseph Danhauser A86

1935, May 1

376 A86 24g dark blue .80 .35
Never hinged 2.00
a. Vert. pair, imperf. btwn. 300.00
Never hinged 425.00
b. Horiz. pair, imperf. btwn. 275.00
Never hinged 400.00

Mother's Day. No. 376 exists imperf. Value, unused hinged $200, never hinged $475.

"Madonna and Child," after Painting by Dürer — A87

1936, May 5 **Photo.**

377 A87 24g violet blue .65 *.55*
Never hinged 1.75

Mother's Day. No. 377 exists imperf. Value, unused hinged $250, never hinged $400.

Farm Workers — A88

Design: 5s, Construction workers.

1936, June **Engr.** ***Perf. 12½***

378 A88 3s red orange	13.50	13.50
Never hinged	32.50	
379 A88 5s brown black	32.50	*32.50*
Never hinged	52.50	

Nos. 378-379 exist imperf. Values, set unused hinged $350, never hinged $800.

Engelbert Dollfuss — A90

1936, July 25

380 A90 10s dark blue	725.00	*725.00*
Never hinged	1,100.	

Second anniv. of death of Engelbert Dollfuss, chancellor.
Value, used, is for CTO examples.
Exists imperf. Value, $1,900, never hinged $3,250.

Mother and Child — A91

1937, May 5 **Photo.** ***Perf. 12***

381 A91 24g henna brown	.65	*.80*
Never hinged	1.60	

Mother's Day. Exists imperf. Values, unused hinged $200, never hinged $325.

S.S. Maria Anna A92

Steamships: 24g, Uranus, 64g, Oesterreich.

1937, June 9

382 A92 12g red brown	1.10	.55
383 A92 24g deep blue	1.10	.55
384 A92 64g dark green	1.10	*.55*
Nos. 382-384 (3)	3.30	*1.65*
Set, never hinged	14.50	

Centenary of steamship service on Danube River. Exist imperf. Value, set never hinged $3,500.

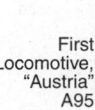

First Locomotive, "Austria" A95

Designs: 25g, Modern steam locomotive. 35g, Modern electric train.

1937, Nov. 22

385 A95 12g black brown	.25	.25
386 A95 25g dark violet	.65	*.65*
387 A95 35g brown red	2.00	*2.00*
Nos. 385-387 (3)	2.90	*2.90*
Set, never hinged	15.00	

Centenary of Austrian railways. Exist imperf. Value, set never hinged $325.

Rose and Zodiac Signs — A98

1937 **Engr.** ***Perf. 13x12½***

388 A98 12g dark green	.25	*.25*
389 A98 24g dark carmine	.25	.25
Set, never hinged	1.60	

Nos. 388-389 exist imperf. Value, set never hinged $275.

Used values for Nos. 390-454 are for stamps with philatelic favor cancels. Postally used examples sell for substantially more.

German stamps were in use in Austria until mid-1945, when they were replaced by issues of the Russian (May) and American-British-French (June) occupation authorities.

For Use in Vienna, Lower Austria and Burgenland

Germany Nos. 509-511 and 511B Overprinted in Black

a

b

1945 **Unwmk.** ***Perf. 14***

390 A115(a) 5pf dp yellow green	.25	*.85*
391 A115(b) 6pf purple	.25	*.85*
392 A115(a) 8pf red	.25	*.45*
393 A115(b) 12pf carmine	.25	*.45*
Nos. 390-393 (4)		*2.60*
Set, never hinged	1.00	

Nos. 390-393 exist with overprint inverted or double.

Germany No. 507, the 3pf, with overprint "a" was prepared, not issued, but sold to collectors after the definitive Republic issue had been placed in use. Values, $30 hinged, $65 never hinged.

German Semi-Postal Stamps, #B207, B209, B210, B283 Surcharged in Black

c

d

1945 ***Perf. 14, 14x13½, 13½x14***

394 SP181(c) 5pf on 12pf + 88pf	.25	*2.00*
395 SP184(d) 6pf on 6pf + 14pf	3.00	*17.50*
396 SP242(d) 8pf on 42pf + 108pf	.40	*3.50*
397 SP183(d) 12pf on 3pf + 7pf	.25	*2.00*
Nos. 394-397 (4)	3.90	*25.00*
Set, never hinged	9.75	

The surcharges are spaced to fit the stamps.

Stamps of Germany, Nos. 509 to 511, 511B, 519 and 529 Overprinted

e

f

1945 **Typo.** ***Perf. 14***
Size: 18½x22½mm

398 A115(e) 5pf dp yel grn	.85	*8.00*
399 A115(f) 5pf dp yel grn	3.50	*27.50*
400 A115(e) 6pf purple	.30	*3.50*
401 A115(e) 8pf red	.30	*3.50*
402 A115(e) 12pf carmine	.85	*4.00*

Engr.
Size: 21½x26mm

403 A115(e) 30pf olive green	6.00	
a. Thin bar at bottom	15.00	
Never hinged	47.50	
404 A118(e) 42pf brt green	20.00	
a. Thin bar at bottom	9.00	
Never hinged	50.00	
Nos. 398-404 (7)	31.80	*46.50*
Set, never hinged	98.00	

On Nos. 403a and 404a, the bottom bar of the overprint is 2½mm wide, and, as the overprint was applied in two operations, "Osterreich" is usually not exactly centered in its diagonal slot. On Nos. 403 and 404, the bottom bar is 3mm wide, and "Osterreich" is always well centered.

Germany Nos. 524-527 (the 1m, 2m, 3m and 5m), overprinted with vertical bars and "Osterreich" similar to "e" and "f," were prepared, not issued, but sold to collectors after the definitive Republic issue had been placed in use. Value for set, $70 hinged, $150 never hinged.

Counterfeits exist of Nos. 403-404, 403a-404a and 1m-5m overprints.

For Use in Styria

Germany Nos. 506 to 511, 511A, 511B, 514 to 523 and 529 Ovptd. in Black

1945 **Unwmk.** **Typo.** ***Perf. 14***
Size: 18½x22½mm

405 A115 1pf gray black	1.25	*8.00*
406 A115 3pf lt brown	.75	*8.00*
407 A115 4pf slate	4.50	*27.50*
408 A115 5pf dp yel grn	1.00	*8.00*
409 A115 6pf purple	.25	*1.60*
410 A115 8pf red	.25	*2.50*
411 A115 10pf dark brown	1.00	*8.00*
412 A115 12pf carmine	.25	*2.50*

Engr.

413 A115 15pf brown lake	.40	*4.00*
414 A115 16pf pck green	10.00	*65.00*
415 A115 20pf blue	1.00	*6.50*
416 A115 24pf org brn	10.00	*65.00*

Size: 22½x26mm

417 A115 25pf brt ultra	1.25	*8.00*
418 A115 30pf olive green	1.25	*8.00*
419 A115 40pf brt red violet	1.25	*8.00*
420 A118 42pf brt green	2.00	*16.00*
421 A115 50pf myrtle green	1.75	*12.00*
422 A115 60pf dk red brown	1.75	*12.00*
423 A115 80pf indigo	1.50	*12.00*
Nos. 405-423 (19)	41.40	*282.60*
Set, never hinged	130.00	

Overprinted on Nos. 524-527

Perf. 12½, 14

424 A116 1m dk slate grn	6.50	*50.00*
a. Perf. 12½	*2,000.*	
Never hinged	*6,500.*	
425 A116 2m violet	6.50	*50.00*
a. Perf. 14	25.00	*80.00*
426 A116 3m copper red	40.00	*150.00*
427 A116 5m dark blue	150.00	*1,200.*
Nos. 424-427 (4)	203.00	*1,450.*
Set, never hinged	650.00	

On the preceding four stamps the innermost vertical lines are 11.1-11.4mm apart; on the pfennig values 6½mm apart.

Counterfeits exist of Nos. 405-427 overprints.

Germany Nos. 524 to 527 Overprinted in Black

Perf. 14

428 A116 1m dk slate grn	9.00	*50.00*
429 A116 2m violet	12.50	*60.00*

Perf. 12½

430 A116 3m copper red	15.00	*90.00*
431 A116 5m dark blue	100.00	*650.00*
Nos. 428-431 (4)	136.50	*850.00*
Set, never hinged	400.00	

On the preceding four stamps, "Osterreich" is thinner, measuring 16mm. On the previous set of 23 values it measures 18mm.

Counterfeits exist of Nos. 428-431 overprints.

Catalogue values for unused stamps in this section, from this point to the end of the section, are for Never Hinged items.

For Use in Vienna, Lower Austria and Burgenland

Coat of Arms
A99 A100

Typographed or Lithographed
1945, July 3 **Unwmk.** ***Perf. 14x13½***
Size: 21x25mm

432 A99 3pf brown	.25	.25
433 A99 4pf slate	.25	.25
434 A99 5pf dark green	.25	.25
435 A99 6pf deep violet	.25	.25
436 A99 8pf orange brown	.25	.25
437 A99 10pf deep brown	.25	.25
438 A99 12pf rose carmine	.25	.25
439 A99 15pf orange red	.25	.25
440 A99 16pf dull blue green	.25	.25

Perf. 14

Size: 24x28½mm

441	A99	20pf light blue	.25	.25
442	A99	24pf orange	.25	.25
443	A99	25pf dark blue	.25	.25
444	A99	30pf deep gray grn	.25	.25
445	A99	38pf ultramarine	.25	.25
446	A99	40pf brt red vio	.25	.25
447	A99	42pf sage green	.25	.25
448	A99	50pf blue green	.25	.25
449	A99	60pf maroon	.25	.25
450	A99	80pf dull lilac	.25	.30

Engr. ***Perf. 14x13½***

451	A100	1m dark green	.25	.25
452	A100	2m dark purple	.25	.25
453	A100	3m dark violet	.25	.25
454	A100	5m brown red	.30	.30
		Nos. 432-454 (23)	5.80	5.85

Nos. 432, 433, 437, 439, 440, 443, 446, 448, 449 are typographed. Nos. 434, 435, 441. 442 are lithographed; the other values exist both ways.

For overprint see No. 604.

For General Use

Lermoos, Winter Scene — A101

The Prater Woods, Vienna — A105

Wolfgang See, near Salzburg A106

Lake Constance A110

Dürnstein, Lower Austria A124

Designs: 4g, Eisenerz surface mine. 5g, Leopoldsberg, near Vienna. 6g, Hohensalzburg, Salzburg Province. 10gr, Hochosterwitz, Carinthia. 15g, Forchtenstein Castle, Burgenland. 16g, Gesäuse Valley. 24g, Höldrichs Mill, Lower Austria. 25g, Oetz Valley Outlet, Tyrol. 30g, Neusiedler Lake, Burgenland. 35g, Belvedere Palace, Vienna. 38g, Langbath Lake. 40g, Mariazell, Styria. 42g, Traunkirchen. 45g, Hartenstein Castle. 50g, Silvretta Mountains, Vorarlberg. 60g, Railroad viaducts near Semmering.

70g, Waterfall of Bad-Gastein, Salzburg. 80g, Kaiser Mountains, Tyrol. 90g, Wayside Shrine, Tragöss, Styria. 2s, St. Christof am Arlberg, Tyrol. 3s, Heiligenblut, Carinthia. 5s, Schönbrunn, Vienna.

Perf. 14x13½

1945-46 **Photo.** **Unwmk.**

455	A101	3g sapphire	.25	.25
456	A101	4g dp orange ('46)	.25	.25
457	A101	5g dk carmine rose	.25	.25
458	A101	6g dk slate green	.25	.25
459	A105	8g golden brown	.25	.25
460	A106	10g dark green	.25	.25
461	A106	12g dark brown	.25	.25
462	A106	15g dk slate bl ('46)	.25	.25
463	A106	16g chnt brn ('46)	.25	.25

Perf. 13½x14

464	A110	20g dp ultra ('46)	.25	.25
465	A110	24g dp yellow grn ('46)	.25	.25
466	A110	25g gray black ('46)	.25	.25
467	A110	30g dark red	.25	.25
468	A110	35g brown red ('46)	.25	.25
469	A110	38g brn olive ('46)	.25	.25
470	A110	40g gray	.25	.25
471	A110	42g brn org ('46)	.25	.25
472	A110	45g dark blue ('46)	.35	*1.60*
473	A110	50g dark blue	.25	.25
474	A110	60g dark violet	.25	.25
a.		Imperf., pair	75.00	*85.00*
475	A110	70g Prus blue ('46)	.25	*.40*
476	A110	80g brown	.35	*.55*
477	A110	90g Prussian green	.80	2.40
478	A124	1s dk red brn ('46)	.80	.80
479	A124	2s blue gray ('46)	2.40	*4.50*
480	A124	3s dk slate grn ('46)	1.00	*5.00*
481	A124	5s dark red ('46)	1.60	*4.00*
		Nos. 455-481 (27)	12.30	24.00

See Nos. 482, 486-488, 496-515. For overprints and surcharges see Nos. 492-493, B166, B280, B287.

No. 461 Overprinted in Carmine

1946, Sept. 26

482	A106	12g dark brown	.30	.60

Meeting of the Soc. for Cultural and Economic Relations with the USSR, Vienna, Sept. 26-29.

City Hall Park, Vienna A128

Hochosterwitz, Carinthia A129

Perf. 14x13½

1946-47 **Photo.** **Unwmk.**

483	A128	8g deep plum	.25	.25
484	A128	8g olive brown	.25	.25
a.		8g dark olive green	.25	.25
485	A129	10g dk brn vio ('47)	.25	.25

Perf. 13½x14

486	A110	30g blue gray ('47)	.35	.35
487	A110	50g brown violet ('47)	.70	.70
488	A110	60g violet blue ('47)	2.50	2.50
		Nos. 483-488 (6)	4.30	4.30

See No. 502.

Franz Grillparzer A130

1947 **Engr.** ***Perf. 14x13½***

489	A130	18g chocolate	.30	.30

Photo.

490	A130	18g dk violet brn	.50	.50

Death of Grillparzer, dramatic poet, 75th anniv.

A second printing of No. 490 on thicker paper was made in June 1947. It has a darker frame and clearer delineation of the portrait.

Issue dates: No. 489, Feb. 10; No. 490, Mar. 31.

Franz Schubert — A131

1947, Mar. 31 **Engr.**

491	A131	12g dark green	.30	*.60*

150th birth anniv. of Franz Schubert, musician and composer.

Nos. 469 and 463 Surcharged in Brown

1947, Sept. 1 **Photo.** ***Perf. 14***

492	A110	75g on 38g brown ol	.25	*1.20*
493	A106	1.40s on 16g chnt brn	.25	*1.20*

The surcharge on No. 493 varies from brown to black brown.

Symbols of Global Telegraphic Communication A132

1947, Nov. 5 **Engr.** ***Perf. 14x13½***

495	A132	40g dark violet	.30	.60

Centenary of the telegraph in Austria.

Scenic Type of 1946

1946, Aug. **Photo.** ***Perf. 13½x14***

496	A124	1s dark brown	1.60	4.00
497	A124	2s dark blue	9.50	4.00
498	A124	3s dark slate green	3.25	4.25
499	A124	5s dark red	40.00	20.00
		Nos. 496-499 (4)	54.35	32.25

On Nos. 478 to 481 the upper and lower panels show a screen effect. On Nos. 496 to 499 the panels appear to be solid color.

Scenic Types of 1945-46

1947-48 **Photo.** ***Perf. 14x13½***

500	A101	3g bright red	.25	.25
501	A101	5g bright red	.25	.25
502	A129	10g bright red	.25	.25
503	A106	15g brt red ('48)	2.00	1.75

Perf. 13½x14

504	A110	20g bright red	.40	.25
505	A110	30g bright red	.40	.25
506	A110	40g bright red	.40	.25
507	A110	50g bright red	.70	.25
508	A110	60g brt red ('48)	12.00	2.00
509	A110	70g brt red ('48)	4.00	.25
510	A110	80g brt red ('48)	4.00	.25
511	A110	90g brt red ('48)	4.75	.80
512	A124	1s dark violet	1.60	.25
513	A124	2s dark violet	1.20	.25
514	A124	3s dk violet ('48)	24.00	2.00
515	A124	5s dk violet ('48)	24.00	2.00
		Nos. 500-515 (16)	80.20	11.30
		Set, hinged	16.00	

Carl Michael Ziehrer (1843-1922), Composer A133

Designs: No. 517, Adalbert Stifter (1805-68), novelist. No. 518, Anton Bruckner (1824-96), composer. 60g, Friedrich von Amerling (1803-87), painter.

1948-49 **Engr.**

516	A133	20g dull green	.40	.25
517	A133	40g chocolate	8.00	4.50
518	A133	40g dark green	8.00	8.00
519	A133	60g rose brown	8.00	.35
		Nos. 516-519 (4)	16.80	13.10

Issue dates: 20g, Jan. 21, No. 517, Sept. 6, No. 518, Sept. 3, 1949, 60g, Jan. 26.

Vorarlberg, Montafon Valley — A134

Costume of Vienna, 1850 — A135

Austrian Costumes: 3g, Tyrol, Inn Valley. 5g, Salzburg, Pinzgau. 10g, Styria, Salzkammergut. 15g, Burgenland, Lutzmannsburg. 25g, Vienna, 1850. 30g, Salzburg, Pongau. 40g, Vienna, 1840. 45g, Carinthia, Lesach Valley. 50g, Vorarlberg, Bregenzer Forest. 60g, Carinthia, Lavant Valley. 70g, Lower Austria, Wachau. 75g, Styria, Salzkammergut. 80g, Styria, Enns Valley. 90g, Central Styria. 1s, Tyrol, Puster Valley. 1.20s, Lower Austria, Vienna Woods. 1.40s, Upper Austria, Inn District. 1.45s, Wilten. 1.50s, Vienna, 1853. 1.60s, Vienna, 1830. 1.70s, East Tyrol, Kals. 2s, Upper Austria. 2.20s, Ischl, 1820. 2.40s, Kitzbuhel. 2.50s, Upper Steiermark, 1850. 2.70s, Little Walser Valley. 3s, Burgenland. 3.50s, Lower Austria, 1850. 4.50s, Gail Valley. 5s, Ziller Valley. 7s, Steiermark, Sulm Valley.

Perf. 14x13½

1948-52 **Unwmk.** **Photo.**

On Toned Paper, with Glossy Yellowish Gum

520	A134	3g gray ('50)	.60	.70
521	A134	5g dk grn ('49)	.25	.25
522	A134	10g deep blue	.25	.25
523	A134	15g brown	.35	.25
524	A134	20g yellow green	.25	.25
525	A134	25g brown ('49)	.25	.25
526	A134	30g dk car rose	3.50	.25
527	A134	30g dk vio ('50)	.75	.25
528	A134	40g violet	3.00	.25
529	A134	40g green ('49)	.60	.25
530	A134	45g violet blue	3.00	.40
531	A134	50g org brn ('49)	.90	.25
532	A134	60g scarlet	.40	.25
533	A134	70g brt bl grn ('49)	.40	.25
534	A134	75g blue	5.00	.40
535	A134	80g car rose ('49)	.85	.25
536	A134	90g brn vio ('49)	40.00	.35
537	A134	1s ultramarine	15.00	.25
538	A134	1s rose red ('50)	100.00	.25
539	A134	1s dk grn ('51)	.60	.25
540	A134	1.20s violet ('49)	.85	.25
541	A134	1.40s brown	2.10	.25
542	A134	1.45s dk car ('51)	3.00	.25
543	A134	1.50s ultra ('51)	1.75	.25
544	A134	1.60s org red ('49)	.60	.25
545	A134	1.70s vio bl ('50)	3.00	.65
546	A134	2s blue green	1.10	.25
547	A134	2.20s slate ('52)	5.00	.25
548	A134	2.40s blue ('51)	1.75	.25
549	A134	2.50s brown ('52)	5.00	3.00
550	A134	2.70s dk brn ('51)	.70	1.40
551	A134	3s brn car ('49)	3.00	.25
552	A134	3.50s dull grn ('51)	21.00	.25
553	A134	4.50s brn vio ('51)	.70	1.40
554	A134	5s dark red vio	1.10	.25
555	A134	7s olive ('52)	4.25	2.40

Engr.

556	A135	10s gray ('50)	35.00	5.50
b.		Flat white gum	275.00	17.50
		Nos. 520-556 (37)	265.85	22.95
		Set, hinged	62.50	

1958-59

On White Paper, with Flat White Gum

521a	A134	5g dk grn	.25	.25
522a	A134	10g deep blue	.25	.25
524a	A134	20g dp yel grn	.25	.25
525a	A134	25g dk brown ('59)	.55	.55
527a	A134	30g dk vio	.80	.25
529a	A134	40g dp bl grn	.65	.25
531a	A134	50g org brn	.95	.25
532a	A134	60g scarlet	.95	.65
533a	A134	70g brt bl grn	.95	.25
535a	A134	80g car rose	.95	.25
540a	A134	1.20s violet	1.60	.65
542a	A134	1.45s dk car	3.25	.65
543a	A134	1.50s ultramarine	4.00	.45
544a	A134	1.60s brn org	4.00	3.00
547a	A134	2.20s slate	6.50	.25
548a	A134	2.40s blue	2.00	.90
549a	A134	2.50s brown	6.50	3.25
551a	A134	3s brn car	4.00	.25
552a	A134	3.50s dull grn	24.00	.25
554a	A134	5s dark red vio ('59)	1.60	.25
555a	A134	7s olive ('59)	4.75	2.40
		Nos. 521a-555a (21)	68.75	15.50
		Set, hinged	15.00	

Designs of the 1958-59 printing are clearer and on most values appear sharper than on the 1948-52 printings.

Pres. Karl Renner — A136

1948, Nov. 12 ***Perf. 14x13½***
557 A136 1s deep blue 2.00 1.50

Founding of the Austrian Republic, 30th anniv. See Nos. 573, 636.

Franz Gruber and Josef Mohr A137

1948, Dec. 18 ***Perf. 13½x14***
558 A137 60g red brown 6.00 4.50

130th anniv. of the hymn "Silent Night, Holy Night".

Symbolical of Child Welfare — A138

1949, May 14 **Photo.** ***Perf. 14x13½***
559 A138 1s bright blue 12.00 3.25

1st year of activity of UNICEF in Austria.

Johann Strauss, the Younger — A139

Designs: 30g, Johann Strauss, the elder. No. 561, Johann Strauss, the younger. No. 562, Karl Millöcker.

1949 **Engr.**
560 A139 30g violet brown 1.60 2.00
561 A139 1s dark blue 3.25 2.25
562 A139 1s dark blue 16.00 12.50
Nos. 560-562 (3) 20.85 16.75

Johann Strauss, the elder (1804-49), Johann Strauss, the younger (1825-99), and Karl Millöcker (1842-1899), composers. See No. 574.

Issue dates: No. 560, 9/24; No. 561, 6/3; No. 562, 12/31.

Esperanto Star, Olive Branches — A140

1949, June 25 **Photo.**
563 A140 20g blue green .95 .95

Austrian Esperanto Congress at Graz.

St. Gebhard — A141

1949, Aug. 6 **Engr.**
564 A141 30g dark violet 1.60 1.60

St. Gebhard (949-995), Bishop of Vorarlberg.

Letter, Roses and Post Horn A142

UPU, 75th Anniv.: 60g, Plaque. 1s, "Austria," wings and monogram.

1949, Oct. 8 ***Perf. 13½x14***
565 A142 40g dark green 4.00 4.00
566 A142 60g dk carmine 4.00 3.25
567 A142 1s dk violet blue 8.00 7.25
Nos. 565-567 (3) 16.00 14.50

Alexander Girardi — A143

Moritz Michael Daffinger — A144

Andreas Hofer — A144a

Josef Madersperger — A144b

Designs: 30g, Alexander Girardi (1850-1918), actor. No. 569, Moritz Michael Daffinger (1790-1849), painter. No. 570, Andreas Hofer (1767-1810), patriot. No. 571, Josef Madersperger (1768-1850), inventor.

1950 **Unwmk.** ***Perf. 14x13½***
568 A143 30g dark blue 1.60 1.20
569 A144 60g red brown 8.00 6.50
570 A144a 60g dull violet 13.00 9.50
571 A144b 60g dark violet 7.25 4.00
Nos. 568-571 (4) 29.85 21.20

Issue dates: 30g, Dec. 5; No. 569, Jan. 25; No. 570, Feb. 20; No. 571, Oct. 2.

Austrian Stamp of 1850 — A146

1950, May 20 ***Perf. 14½***
572 A146 1s black, *straw* 2.00 1.60

Centenary of Austrian postage stamps.

Renner Type of 1948
Frame and Inscriptions Altered

1951, Mar. 3
573 A136 1s black, *straw* 1.20 .45

In memory of Pres. Karl Renner, 1870-1950.

Strauss Type of 1949
Portrait: 60g, Joseph Lanner.

1951, Apr. 12
574 A139 60g dk blue green 4.75 2.40

Joseph Lanner (1801-43), composer.

Martin Johann Schmidt — A147

1951, June 28 **Engr.** ***Perf. 14x13½***
575 A147 1sh brown red 6.50 2.40

150th death anniv. of Martin Johann Schmidt, painter.

7th World Scout Jamboree A148

1951, Aug. 3 **Engr. and Litho.**
576 A148 1sh dk grn, ocher & pink 4.75 4.75

Bad Ischl-St. Wolfgang, Aug. 3-13, 1951.

Wilhelm Kienzl — A149

Josef Schrammel A150

Design: 1s, Karl von Ghega.

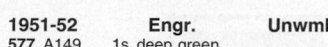

1951-52 **Engr.** **Unwmk.**
577 A149 1s deep green ('52) 6.00 .80
578 A149 1.50s indigo 3.00 1.50
579 A150 1.50s violet blue ('52) 6.00 1.75
Nos. 577-579 (3) 15.00 4.05

Ghega (1802-60), civil engineer; Kienzl (1857-1941), composer; Schrammel (1852-95), composer. See No. 582.

Issued: 1s, 3/2; No. 578, 10/3; No. 579, 3/3.

Breakfast Pavilion, Schönbrunn A151

1952, May 24 ***Perf. 13½x14***
580 A151 1.50s dark green 6.50 2.00

Vienna Zoological Gardens, 200th anniv.

Globe as Dot Over "i" — A152

1952, July 1 ***Perf. 14x13½***
581 A152 1.50s dark blue 5.50 1.00

Formation of the Intl. Union of Socialist Youth Camp, Vienna, July 1-10, 1952.

Type Similar to A150
Portrait: 1s, Nikolaus Lenau.

1952, Aug. 13
582 A150 1s deep green 5.50 1.25

Nikolaus Lenau, pseudonym of Nikolaus Franz Niembsch von Strehlenau (1802-50), poet.

School Girl — A153

1952, Sept. 6
583 A153 2.40s dp violet blue 12.00 2.40

Issued to stimulate letter-writing between Austrian and foreign school children.

Hugo Wolf — A154

1953, Feb. 21 **Engr.** ***Perf. 14x13½***
587 A154 1.50s dark blue 6.00 1.60

Hugo Wolf, composer, 50th death anniv.

Pres. Theodor Körner — A155

1953, Apr. 24
588 A155 1.50s dk violet blue 6.00 1.20

80th birthday of Pres. Theodor Körner. See Nos. 591, 614.

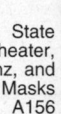

State Theater, Linz, and Masks A156

1953, Oct. 17 ***Perf. 13½x14***
589 A156 1.50s dark gray 15.00 2.40

State Theater at Linz, 150th anniv.

Child and Christmas Tree — A157

1953, Nov. 30 ***Perf. 14x13½***
590 A157 1s dark green 1.00 .50

See No. 597.

Type Similar to A155

Portrait: 1.50s, Moritz von Schwind.

1954, Jan. 21 ***Perf. 14x13½***
591 A155 1.50s purple 11.00 2.25

Moritz von Schwind, painter, 150th birth anniv.

Karl von Rokitansky A158

1954, Feb. 19
592 A158 1.50s purple 12.50 2.25

Karl von Rokitansky, physician, 150th birth anniv. See No. 595.

Esperanto Star and Wreath A159

Engr. and Photo.

1954, June 5 ***Perf. 13½x14***
593 A159 1s dk brown & emer 3.50 .50

Esperanto movement in Austria, 50th anniv.

A160

1954, Aug. 4 Engr. *Perf. 14x13½*
594 A160 1s dark blue green 11.00 2.50

300th birth anniv. of Johann Michael Rottmayr von Rosenbrunn, painter.

Type Similar to A158

Portrait: 1.50s, Carl Auer von Welsbach.

1954, Aug. 4
595 A158 1.50s violet blue 21.00 2.50

25th death anniv. of Carl Auer von Welsbach (1858-1929), chemist.

2nd Intl. Congress for Catholic Church Music, Vienna, Oct. 4-10 — A161

Organ, St. Florian Monastery and Cherub.

1954, Oct. 2 **Unwmk.**
596 A161 1s brown 2.40 .40

Christmas Type of 1953

1954, Nov. 30
597 A157 1s dark blue 4.00 .55

Arms of Austria and Official Publication A162

1954, Dec. 18 **Engr.**
598 A162 1s salmon & black 2.25 .40

Austria's State Printing Plant, 150th anniv., and Wiener Zeitung, government newspaper, 250th year of publication.

Parliament Building A163

Designs: 1s, Western railroad station, Vienna. 1.45s, Letters forming flag. 1.50s, Public housing, Vienna. 2.40s, Limberg dam.

1955, Apr. 27 ***Perf. 13½x14***

599 A163	70g	rose violet	1.20	.70
600 A163	1s	deep ultra	4.25	.25
601 A163	1.45s	scarlet	8.25	2.40
602 A163	1.50s	brown	21.00	.35
603 A163	2.40s	dk blue green	8.25	4.75
		Nos. 599-603 (5)	42.95	8.45

10th anniv. of Austria's liberation.

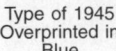

Type of 1945 Overprinted in Blue

1955, May 15 ***Perf. 14x13½***
604 A100 2s blue gray 2.25 .55

Signing of the state treaty with the US, France, Great Britain and Russia, 5/15/55.

Workers of Three Races Climbing Globe A164

1955, May 20 ***Perf. 13½x14***
605 A164 1s indigo 2.25 1.75

4th congress of the Intl. Confederation of Free Trade Unions, Vienna, May.

Burgtheater, Vienna A165

Design: 2.40s, Opera House, Vienna.

1955, July 25
606 A165 1.50s light sepia 3.75 .35
607 A165 2.40s dark blue 4.25 2.10

Re-opening of the Burgtheater and Opera House in Vienna.

Symbolic of Austria's Desire to Join the UN — A166

1955, Oct. 24 **Unwmk.**
608 A166 2.40s green 11.50 2.75

Tenth anniversary of UN.

Wolfgang Amadeus Mozart, Birth Bicent. — A167

1956, Jan. 21 ***Perf. 14x13½***
609 A167 2.40s slate blue 4.25 1.00

Symbolic of Austria's Joining the UN — A168

1956, Feb. 20
610 A168 2.40s chocolate 9.00 1.50

Austria's admission to the UN.

Globe Showing Energy of the Earth A169

1956, May 8 ***Perf. 13½x14***
611 A169 2.40s deep blue 9.00 2.00

Fifth Intl. Power Conf., Vienna, June 17-23.

Map of Europe and City Maps — A170

Photo. and Typo.

1956, June 8 ***Perf. 14x13½***
612 A170 1.45s lt grn blk & red 3.25 .80

23rd Intl. Housing and Town Planning Congress, Vienna, July 22-28.

J.B. Fischer von Erlach, Architect, 300th Birth Anniv. — A171

1956, July 20 **Engr.**
613 A171 1.50s brown .80 .80

Körner Type of 1953

1957, Jan. 11
614 A155 1.50s gray black 1.75 1.60

Death of Pres. Theodor Körner.

Dr. Julius Wagner-Jauregg, Psychiatrist, Birth Cent. — A172

1957, Mar. 7 ***Perf. 14x13½***
615 A172 2.40s brn violet 3.50 2.25

Anton Wildgans, Poet, 25th Death Anniv. — A173

1957, May 3 **Unwmk.**
616 A173 1s violet blue .55 .55

Old and New Postal Motor Coach A174

1957, June 14 ***Perf. 13½x14***
617 A174 1s black, *yellow* .55 .55

Austrian Postal Motor Coach Service, 50th anniv.

Gasherbrum II and Glacier A175

1957, July 27
618 A175 1.50s gray blue .55 .65

Austrian Karakoram Expedition, which climbed Mount Gasherbrum II on July 7, 1956.

A176

A177

Designs: 20g, Farmhouse at Mörbisch. 50g, Heiligenstadt, Vienna. 1s, Mariazell. 1.40s, County seat, Klagenfurt. 1.50s, Rabenhof Building, Erdberg, Vienna. 1.80s, The Mint, Hall, Tyrol. 2s, Christkindl Church. 3.40s, Steiner Gate, Krems. 4s, Vienna Gate, Hainburg. 4.50s, Schwechat Airport, Vienna. 5.50s, Chur Gate, Feldkirch. 6s, County seat, Graz. 6.40s, "Golden Roof," Innsbruck. 10s, Heidenreichstein Castle.

1957-61 Litho. *Perf. 14x13½*
Size: 20x25mm

618A A176 20g violet blk ('61) .25 .25
619 A176 50g bluish blk ('59) .40 .25

Engr.

620 A176 1s chocolate 1.60 .55

Typo.

621 A176 1s chocolate 1.60 .65

Litho.

622 A176 1s choc ('59) .40 .25
622A A176 1.40s brt greenish bl ('60) .40 .25
623 A176 1.50s rose lake ('58) .40 .25
624 A176 1.80s brt ultra ('60) .40 .25
625 A176 2s dull blue ('58) 3.00 .25
626 A176 3.40s yel grn ('60) 1.60 1.20
627 A176 4s brt red lil ('60) 1.75 .25
627A A176 4.50s dl green ('60) 2.00 1.20
628 A176 5.50s grnsh gray ('60) 1.60 1.20
629 A176 6s brt vio ('60) 1.60 .80
629A A176 6.40s brt blue ('60) 2.75 2.75

Engr.
Size: 22x28mm

630 A177 10s dk bl grn 2.75 1.00
Nos. 618A-630 (16) 22.50 11.35

Of the three 1s stamps above, Nos. 620 and 621 have two names in imprint (designer H. Strohofer, engraver G. Wimmer). No. 622 has only Strohofer's name.

Values for Nos. 618A-624, 626-630 are for stamps on white paper. Most denominations also come on grayish paper with yellowish gum.

See Nos. 688-702.

1960-65 Photo. *Perf. 14½x14*
Size: 17x21mm

630A A176 50g slate ('64) .25 .25

Size: 18x21½mm

630B A176 1s chocolate .25 .25

Size: 17x21mm

630C A176 1.50s dk car ('65) .35 .25
Nos. 630A-630C (3) .85 .75

Nos. 630A-630C issued in sheets and coils.

Graukogel, Badgastein A180

1958, Feb. 1 Engr. *Perf. 14x13½*
631 A180 1.50s dark blue .30 .30

Intl. Ski Federation Alpine championships, Badgastein, Feb. 2-7.

Plane over Map of Austria A181

1958, Mar. 27 *Perf. 13½x14*
632 A181 4s red .80 .30

Re-opening of Austrian Airlines.

Mother and Daughter — A182

1958, May 8 Unwmk. *Perf. 14x13½*
633 A182 1.50s dark blue .30 .30

Issued for Mother's Day.

Walther von der Vogelweide A183

1958, July 17 Litho. and Engr.
634 A183 1.50s multicolored .55 .30

3rd Austrian Song Festival, Vienna, 7/17-20.

Oswald Redlich (1858-1944), Historian — A184

1958, Sept. 17 Engr.
635 A184 2.40s ultramarine .75 .45

Renner Type of 1948

1958, Nov. 12
636 A136 1.50s deep green .75 .75

Austrian Republic, 40th anniv.

Giant "E" on Map — A185

1959, Mar. 9
637 A185 2.40s emerald *1.10 .50*

Idea of a United Europe.

Cigarette Machine and Trademark of Tobacco Monopoly — A186

1959, May 8 Unwmk. *Perf. 13½*
638 A186 2.40s dark olive bister .55 .45

Austrian tobacco monopoly, 175th anniv.

Archduke Johann — A187

1959, May 11 *Perf. 14x13½*
639 A187 1.50s deep green .30 .30

Archduke Johann of Austria, military leader and humanitarian, death cent.

Capercaillie A188

Animals: 1.50s, Roe buck. 2.40s, Wild boar. 3.50s, Red deer, doe and fawn.

1959, May 20 Engr.
640 A188 1s rose violet .25 .25
641 A188 1.50s blue violet .50 .50
642 A188 2.40s dk bl green .75 .75
643 A188 3.50s dark brown .75 .75
Nos. 640-643 (4) 2.25 2.25

Congress of the Intl. Hunting Council, Vienna, May 20-24.

Joseph Haydn (1732-1809), Composer A189

1959, May 30 Unwmk.
644 A189 1.50s violet brown .55 .25

Coat of Arms, Tyrol — A190

1959, June 13 *Perf. 14x13½*
645 A190 1.50s rose red .30 .25

Fight for liberation of Tyrol, 150th anniv.

Antenna, Zugspitze — A191

1959, June 19 *Perf. 13½*
646 A191 2.40s dk bl grn .55 .25

Inauguration of Austria's relay system.

Field Ball Player — A192

1s, Runner. 1.80s, Gymnast on vaulting horse. 2s, Woman hurdler. 2.20s, Hammer thrower.

1959-70 Engr. *Perf. 14x13½*
647 A192 1s lilac .30 .25
648 A192 1.50s blue green .55 .45
648A A192 1.80s carmine ('62) .35 .35
648B A192 2s rose lake ('70) .25 .25
648C A192 2.20s bluish blk ('67) .35 .35
Nos. 647-648C (5) 1.80 1.65

Orchestral Instruments A193

Litho. and Engr.

1959, Aug. 19 *Perf. 14x13½*
649 A193 2.40s dull bl & blk .55 .45

World tour of the Vienna Philharmonic Orchestra.

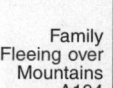

Family Fleeing over Mountains A194

1960, Apr. 7 Engr. *Perf. 13½x14*
650 A194 3s Prussian green .55 .30

WRY, July 1, 1959-June 30, 1960.

President Adolf Schärf — A195

1960, Apr. 20 ***Perf. 14x13½***

651 A195 1.50s gray olive .55 .25

Pres. Adolf Scharf, 70th birthday.

Young Hikers and Hostel A196

1960, May 20 ***Perf. 13½x14***

652 A196 1s carmine rose .30 .25

Youth hiking; youth hostel movement.

Anton Eiselsberg, Surgeon, Birth Cent. — A197

Litho. and Engr.

1960, June 20 ***Perf. 14x13½***

653 A197 1.50s buff & dk brn .65 .25

Gustav Mahler (1860-1911), Composer A198

1960, July 7 **Engr.**

654 A198 1.50s chocolate .65 .25

Jakob Prandtauer, Architect, 300th Birth Anniv. — A199

1960, July 16 **Unwmk.**

655 A199 1.50s Melk Abbey .75 .25

Gross Glockner Mountain Road, 25th Anniv. — A200

1960, Aug. 3

656 A200 1.80s dark blue 1.25 .40

Ionic Capital — A201

1960, Aug. 29 ***Perf. 14x13½***

657 A201 3s black *1.25 .85*

Europa: Idea of a United Europe.

Griffen, Carinthia A202

1960, Oct. 10 **Engr.** ***Perf. 13½x14***

658 A202 1.50s slate green .55 .40

40th anniv. of the plebiscite which kept Carinthia with Austria.

Flame and Broken Chain — A203

1961, May 8 **Unwmk.** ***Perf. 14x13½***

659 A203 1.50s scarlet .30 .25

Victims in Austria's fight for freedom.

First Austrian Mail Plane, 1918 A204

1961, May 15 ***Perf. 13½x14***

660 A204 5s violet blue 1.10 1.10

Airmail Phil. Exhib., LUPOSTA 1961, Vienna, May.

Transportation by Road, Rail and Waterway A205

Engraved and Typographed

1961, May 29 ***Perf. 13½***

661 A205 3s rose red & olive .80 .55

13th European Conference of Transportation ministers, Vienna, May 29-31.

Society of Creative Artists, Künstlerhaus, Vienna, Cent. — A206

Designs: 1s, Mountain Mower, by Albin Egger-Lienz. 1.50s, The Kiss, by August von Pettenkofen. 3s, Girl, by Anton Romako. 5s, Ariadne's Triumph, by Hans Makart.

1961, June 12 **Engr.** ***Perf. 13½x14***

Inscriptions in Red Brown

662	A206	1s	rose lake	.25	.25
663	A206	1.50s	dull violet	.40	.25
664	A206	3s	olive green	.80	.95
665	A206	5s	blue violet	1.40	.65
			Nos. 662-665 (4)	2.85	2.10

Sonnblick Mountain and Observatory A207

1961, Sept. 1 ***Perf. 14x13½***

666 A207 1.80s violet blue .55 .25

Sonnblick meteorological observatory, 75th anniv.

Mercury and Globe — A208

1961, Sept. 18

667 A208 3s black .55 .45

Intl. Banking Congress, Vienna, Sept. 1961. English inscription listing UN financial groups.

Coal Mine Shaft — A209

Designs: 1.50s, Generator. 1.80s, Iron blast furnace. 3s, Pouring steel. 5s, Oil refinery.

1961, Sept. 15 **Engr.** ***Perf. 14x13½***

668	A209	1s	black	.25	.25
669	A209	1.50s	green	.25	.25
670	A209	1.80s	dark car rose	.55	.45
671	A209	3s	bright lilac	.65	.55
672	A209	5s	blue	.80	.75
			Nos. 668-672 (5)	2.50	2.25

15th anniversary of nationalized industry.

Arms of Burgenland A210

1961, Oct. 9 **Engr. and Litho.**

673 A210 1.50s blk, yel & dk red .30 .25

Burgenland as part of the Austrian Republic, 40th anniv.

Franz Liszt (1811-86), Composer A211

1961, Oct. 20 **Engr.**

674 A211 3s dark brown .80 .45

Parliament A212

1961, Dec. 18 ***Perf. 13½x14***

675 A212 1s brown .25 .25

Austrian Bureau of Budget, 200th anniv.

Kaprun-Mooserboden Reservoir — A213

Hydroelectric Power Plants: 1.50s, Ybbs-Persenbeug dam and locks. 1.80s, Lünersee dam and reservoir. 3s, Grossraming dam. 4s, Bisamberg transformer plant. 6.40s, St. Andrä power plant.

1962, Mar. 26 **Unwmk.**

676	A213	1s	violet blue	.25	.25
677	A213	1.50s	red lilac	.30	.25
678	A213	1.80s	green	.50	.40
679	A213	3s	brown	.50	.40
680	A213	4s	rose red	.60	.40
681	A213	6.40s	gray	1.10	1.10
			Nos. 676-681 (6)	3.25	2.80

Nationalization of the electric power industry, 15th anniv.

Johann Nestroy — A214

1962, May 25 ***Perf. 14x13½***

682 A214 1s violet .30 .25

Johann Nepomuk Nestroy, Viennese playwright, author and actor, death cent.

Friedrich Gauermann (1807-1862), Landscape Painter — A215

1962, July 6 **Engr.**

683 A215 1.50s intense blue .30 .25

Scout Emblem and Handshake A216

1962, Oct. 5

684	A216	1.50s dark green	.55	.25

Austria's Boy Scouts, 50th anniv.

Lowlands Forest A217

1.50s, Deciduous forest. 3s, Fir & larch forest.

1962, Oct. 12 ***Perf. 13½x14***

685	A217	1s	greenish gray	.45	.40
686	A217	1.50s	reddish brown	.45	.45
687	A217	3s	dk slate green	1.10	1.10
			Nos. 685-687 (3)	2.00	1.95

Buildings Types of 1957-61

Designs: 30g, City Hall, Vienna. 40g, Porcia Castle, Spittal on the Drau. 60g, Tanners' Tower, Wels. 70g, Residenz Fountain, Salzburg. 80g, Old farmhouse, Pinzgau. 1s, Romanesque columns, Millstatt Abbey. 1.20s, Kornmesser House, Bruck on the Mur. 1.30s, Schatten Castle, Feldkirch, Vorarlberg. 2s, Dragon Fountain, Klagenfurt. 2.20s, Beethoven House, Vienna. 2.50s, Danube Bridge, Linz. 3s, Swiss Gate, Vienna. 3.50s, Esterhazy Palace, Eisenstadt. 8s, City Hall, Steyr. 20s, Melk Abbey.

1962-70 Litho. *Perf. 14x13½*

Size: 20x25mm

688	A176	30g	greenish gray	.40	.25
689	A176	40g	rose red	.25	.25
690	A176	60g	violet brown	.40	.25
691	A176	70g	dark blue	.40	.25
692	A176	80g	yellow brown	.25	.25
693	A176	1s	brown ('70)	.35	.25
694	A176	1.20s	red lilac	.40	.25
695	A176	1.30s	green ('67)	.40	.40
696	A176	2s	dk blue ('68)	.40	.30
697	A176	2.20s	green	.80	.30
698	A176	2.50s	violet	.80	.30
699	A176	3s	bright blue	.90	.25
700	A176	3.50s	rose carmine	1.20	.25
701	A176	8s	claret ('65)	1.60	.55

Perf. 13½

Engr.

Size: 28x36½mm

702	A177	20s	rose claret ('63)	3.50	2.00
			Nos. 688-702 (15)	12.05	6.10

Values for Nos. 688-702 are for stamps on white paper. Some denominations also come on grayish paper with yellowish gum.

Electric Locomotive and Train of 1837 — A218

Lithographed and Engraved

1962, Nov. 9 ***Perf. 13½x14***

703	A218	3s buff & black	1.20	1.20

125th anniversary of Austrian railroads.

Postilions and Postal Clerk, 1863 — A219

1963, May 7 Photo. *Perf. 14x13½*

704	A219	3s dk brn & citron	.75	.55

First Intl. Postal Conference, Paris, cent.

Hermann Bahr, Writer, Birth Cent. — A220

Lithographed and Envraved

1963, July 19 ***Perf. 14x13½***

705	A220	1.50s blue & black	.30	.25

St. Florian Statue, Kefermarkt, Contemporary and Old Fire Engines — A221

1963, Aug. 30 Unwmk.

706	A221	1.50s brt rose & blk	.55	.25

Austrian volunteer fire brigades, cent.

Factory, Flag and "ÖGB" on Map of Austria A222

1963, Sept. 23 Litho. *Perf. 13½x14*

707	A222	1.50s gray, red & dk brn	.30	.25

5th Congress of the Austrian Trade Union Federation (ÖGB), Sept. 23-28.

Arms of Austria and Tyrol A223

1963, Sept. 27 Unwmk.

708	A223	1.50s tan, blk, red & yel	.30	.25

Tyrol's union with Austria, 600th anniv.

Prince Eugene of Savoy (1663-1736), Austrian General — A224

1963, Oct. 18 Engr. *Perf. 14x13½*

709	A224	1.50s violet	.30	.25

Intl. Red Cross, Cent. — A225

1963, Oct. 25 Engr. and Photo.

710	A225	3s blk, sil & red	.55	.25

Slalom A226

Sports: 1.20s, Biathlon (skier with rifle). 1.50s, Ski jump. 1.80s, Women's figure skating. 2.20s, Ice hockey. 3s, Tobogganing. 4s, Bobsledding.

Photo. and Engr.

1963, Nov. 11 ***Perf. 13½x14***

711	A226	1s	multi	.25	.25
712	A226	1.20s	multi	.25	.25
713	A226	1.50s	multi	.35	.35
714	A226	1.80s	multi	.35	.35
715	A226	2.20s	multi	.45	.45
716	A226	3s	multi	.55	.55
717	A226	4s	multi	.55	.55
			Nos. 711-717 (7)	2.75	2.75

9th Winter Olympic Games, Innsbruck, Jan. 29-Feb. 9, 1964.

Baroque Creche by Josef Thaddäus Stammel — A227

1963, Nov. 29 Engr. *Perf. 14x13½*

718	A227	2s dark Prus green	.55	.25

Flowers A228

1964, Apr. 17 Litho. *Perf. 14*

719	A228	1s	Nasturtium	.25	.25
720	A228	1.50s	Peony	.25	.25
721	A228	1.80s	Clematis	.25	.25
722	A228	2.20s	Dahlia	.55	.25
723	A228	3s	Morning glory	.75	.55
724	A228	4s	Hollyhock	1.10	.55
			Nos. 719-724 (6)	3.15	2.10

Vienna Intl. Garden Show, Apr. 16-Oct. 11.

St. Mary Magdalene and Apostle — A229

1964, May 21 Engr. *Perf. 13½*

725	A229	1.50s bluish black	.30	.25

Romanesque art in Austria. The 12th century stained-glass window is from the Weitensfeld Church, the bust of the Apostle from the portal of St. Stephen's Cathedral, Vienna.

Pallas Athena and National Council Chamber — A230

Engr. and Litho.

1964, May 25 ***Perf. 14x13½***

726	A230	1.80s black & emer	.30	.25

2nd Parliamentary and Scientific Conf., Vienna.

The Kiss, by Gustav Klimt A231

1964, June 5 Litho. *Perf. 13½*

727	A231	3s multicolored	1.00	1.00

Re-opening of the Vienna Secession, a museum devoted to early 20th century art (art nouveau).

Brother of Mercy and Patient — A232

1964, June 11 Engr. *Perf. 14x13½*

728	A232	1.50s dark blue	.30	.25

Brothers of Mercy in Austria, 350th anniv.

"Bringing the News of Victory at Kunersdorf" by Bernardo Bellotto — A233

"The Post in Art": 1.20s, Changing Horses at Relay Station, by Julius Hörmann. 1.50s, The Honeymoon Trip, by Moritz von Schwind. 1.80s, After the Rain, by Ignaz Raffalt. 2.20s, Mailcoach in the Mountains, by Adam Klein. 3s, Changing Horses at Bavarian Border, by Friedrich Gauermann. 4s, Postal Sleigh (Truck) in the Mountains, by Adalbert Pilch. 6.40s, Saalbach Post Office, by Adalbert Pilch.

1964, June 15 ***Perf. 13½x14***

729	A233	1s	rose claret	.25	.25
730	A233	1.20s	sepia	.25	.25
731	A233	1.50s	violet blue	.25	.25
732	A233	1.80s	brt violet	.25	.25
733	A233	2.20s	black	.25	.25
734	A233	3s	dl car rose	.55	.55
735	A233	4s	slate green	.55	.55
736	A233	6.40s	dull claret	1.10	1.10
			Nos. 729-736 (8)	3.45	3.45

15th UPU Cong., Vienna, May-June 1964.

Workers — A234

1964, Sept. 4 *Perf. 14x13½*
737 A234 1s black .25 .25

Centenary of Austrian Labor Movement.

Common Design Types pictured following the introduction.

Europa Issue, 1964
Common Design Type

1964, Sept. 14 Litho. *Perf. 12*
Size: 21x36mm
738 CD7 3s dark blue *1.10 .25*
Nos. 738 (1) 1.10 .25

Emblem of Radio Austria and Transistor Radio Panel A235

1964, Oct. 1 Photo. *Perf. 13½*
739 A235 1s black brn & red .25 .25

Forty years of Radio Austria.

6th Congress of the Intl. Graphic Federation, Vienna, Oct. 12-17 — A236

Litho. and Engr.
1964, Oct. 12 *Perf. 14x13½*
740 A236 1.50s Old printing press .30 .25

Dr. Adolf Schärf (1890-1965), Pres. of Austria (1957-65) A237

Pres. Adolf Schärf, Schärf Student Center.

Typo. and Engr.
1965, Apr. 20 *Perf. 12*
741 A237 1.50s bluish black .30 .25

Ruins and New Buildings — A238

1965, Apr. 27 Engr. *Perf. 14x13½*
742 A238 1.80s carmine lake .30 .25

Twenty years of reconstruction.

Oldest Seal of Vienna University — A239

Photo. and Engr.
1965, May 10 *Perf. 14x13½*
743 A239 3s gold & red .55 .25

University of Vienna, 600th anniv.

St. George, 16th Century Wood Sculpture A240

1965, May 17 **Engr.**
744 A240 1.80s bluish black .50 .25

Art of the Danube Art School, 1490-1540, exhibition, May-Oct. 1965. The stamp background shows an engraving by Albrecht Altdorfer.

ITU Emblem, Telegraph Key and TV Antenna — A241

1965, May 17 **Unwmk.**
745 A241 3s violet blue .55 .25

ITU, cent.

Dr. Ignaz Philipp Semmelweis A242

Ferdinand Raimund — A242a

Portraits: No. 747, Bertha von Suttner. No. 749, Ferdinand Georg Waldmüller.

1965 Engr. *Perf. 14x13½*

746 A242	1.50s violet		.30	.25
747 A242	1.50s bluish black		.30	.25
748 A242a	3s dark brown		.55	.25
749 A242a	3s greenish blk		.55	.25
	Nos. 746-749 (4)		1.70	1.00

Semmelweis (1818-65), who discovered the cause of puerperal fever and introduced antisepsis into obstetrics (No. 746). 60th anniv. of the awarding of the Nobel Prize for Peace to von Suttner (1843-1914), pacifist and author (No. 747). Raimund (1790-1836), actor and playwright (No. 748). Waldmüller (1793-1865), painter (No. 749).

Issued: No. 746, Aug. 13; No. 747, Dec. 1; No. 748, June 1; No. 749, Aug. 23.

4th Gymnaestrada, Intl. Athletic Meet, Vienna, July 20-24 — A243

1.50s, Male gymnasts with practice bars. 3s, Dancers with tambourines.

1965, July 20 Photo. and Engr.
750 A243 1.50s gray & black .25 .25
751 A243 3s bister & blk .50 .25

Red Cross and Strip of Gauze — A244

1965, Oct. 1 Litho. *Perf. 14x13½*
752 A244 3s black & red .55 .25

20th Intl. Red Cross Conference, Vienna.

Austrian Flag and Eagle with Mural Crown — A245

1965, Oct. 7 Photo. and Engr.
753 A245 1.50s gold, red & blk .30 .25

50th anniv. of the Union of Austrian Towns.

Austrian Flag, UN Headquarters and Emblem A246

Lithographed and Engraved
1965, Oct. 25 Unwmk. *Perf. 12*
754 A246 3s blk, brt bl & red .55 .25

Austria's admission to the UN, 10th anniv.

University of Technology, Vienna A247

1965, Nov. 8 Engr. *Perf. 13½x14*
755 A247 1.50s violet .30 .25

Vienna University of Technology, 150th anniv.

Map of Austria with Postal Zone Numbers — A248

1966, Jan. 14 Photo. *Perf. 12*
756 A248 1.50s yel, red & blk .30 .25

Introduction of postal zone numbers, 1/1/66.

PTT Building, Emblem and Churches of Sts. Maria Rotunda and Barbara — A249

Lithographed and Engraved
1966, Mar. 4 *Perf. 14x13½*
757 A249 1.50s blk, *dull yellow* .30 .25

Headquarters of the Post and Telegraph Administration, cent.

Maria von Ebner Eschenbach (1830-1916), Novelist, Poet — A250

1966, Mar. 11 **Engr.**
758 A250 3s plum .55 .25

Ferris Wheel, Prater — A251

1966, Apr. 19 Engr. *Perf. 14x13½*
759 A251 1.50s slate green .30 .25

Opening of the Prater (park), Vienna, to the public by Emperor Joseph II, 200th anniv.

Josef Hoffmann (1870-1956), Architect A252

1966, May 6 Unwmk. *Perf. 12*
760 A252 3s dark brown .55 .25

Wiener Neustadt Arms — A253

Photo. and Engr.

1966, May 27 *Perf. 14*

761 A253 1.50s multicolored .30 .25

Wiener Neustadt Art Exhib., centered around the time and person of Frederick III (1440-93).

Austrian Eagle and Emblem of National Bank A254

1966, May 27 *Perf. 14*

762 A254 3s gray grn, dk brn & dk green .55 .25

Austrian National Bank, 150th anniv.

Puppy — A255

Litho. and Engr.

1966, June 16 *Perf. 12*

763 A255 1.80s yellow & black .30 .25

120th anniv. of the Vienna Humane Society.

Alpine Flowers — A256

1.50s, Columbine. 1.80s, Turk's cap. 2.20s, Wulfenia carinthiaca. 3s, Globeflowers. 4s, Fire lily. 5s, Pasqueflower.

1966, Aug. 17 Litho. *Perf. 13½*

Flowers in Natural Colors

764	A256	1.50s dark blue	.30	.30
765	A256	1.80s dark blue	.30	.30
766	A256	2.20s dark blue	.35	.35
767	A256	3s dark blue	.50	.50
768	A256	4s dark blue	.50	.50
769	A256	5s dark blue	.85	.85
		Nos. 764-769 (6)	2.80	2.80

Fair Building A257

1966, Aug. 26 Engr. *Perf. 13½x13*

770 A257 3s violet blue .55 .25

First International Fair at Wels.

Peter Anich (1723-1766), Tirolean Cartographer and Books — A258

1966, Sept. 1 *Perf. 14x13½*

771 A258 1.80s black .30 .25

Sick Worker and Health Emblem — A259

1966, Sept. 19 Engr. and Litho.

772 A259 3s black & vermilion .55 .25

15th Occupational Medicine Congress, Vienna, Sept. 19-24.

Theater Collection: "Eunuchus" by Terence from a 1496 Edition A260

Designs: 1.80s, Map Collection: Title page of Geographia Blavania (Cronus, Hercules and celestial sphere). 2.20s, Picture Archive and Portrait Collection: View of Old Vienna after a watercolor by Anton Stutzinger. 3s, Manuscript Collection: Illustration from the 15th century "Livre du Cuer d'Amours Espris" of the Duke René d'Anjou.

Photogravure and Engraved

1966, Sept. 28 *Perf. 13½x14*

773	A260	1.50s multicolored	.30	.35
774	A260	1.80s multicolored	.30	.35
775	A260	2.20s multicolored	.30	.35
776	A260	3s multicolored	.50	.70
		Nos. 773-776 (4)	1.40	1.75

Austrian National Library.

Young Girl — A261

Litho. and Engr.

1966, Oct. 3 *Perf. 14x13½*

777 A261 3s light blue & black .55 .25

"Save the Child" society, 10th anniv.

Strawberries — A262

1966, Nov. 25 Photo. *Perf. 13½x13*

778	A262	50g shown	.25	.25
779	A262	1s Grapes	.25	.25
780	A262	1.50s Apple	.30	.30
781	A262	1.80s Blackberries	.35	.35
782	A262	2.20s Apricots	.45	.45
783	A262	3s Cherries	.50	.50
		Nos. 778-783 (6)	2.10	2.10

Coat of Arms of University of Linz — A263

Photo. and Engr.

1966, Dec. 9 *Perf. 14x13½*

784 A263 3s multi .55 .25

Inauguration of the Universary of Linz, Oct. 8, 1966.

Vienna Ice Skating Club, Cent. — A264

Photo. and Engr.

1967, Feb. 3 *Perf. 14x13½*

785 A264 3s Skater, 1866 .55 .25

Ballet Dancer — A265

1967, Feb. 15 Engr. *Perf. 11½x12*

786 A265 3s deep claret .30 .25

a. Perf. 12 2.40 2.40

"Blue Danube" waltz by Johann Strauss, cent.

Dr. Karl Schönherr (1867-1943), Poet, Playwright and Physician — A266

1967, Feb. 24 Engr. *Perf. 14x13½*

787 A266 3s gray brown .55 .25

Ice Hockey Goalkeeper A267

Photogravure and Engraved

1967, Mar. 17 *Perf. 13½x14*

788 A267 3s pale grn & dk bl .55 .65

Ice Hockey Championships, Vienna, Mar. 18-29.

Violin, Organ and Laurel — A268

1967, Mar. 28 Engr. *Perf. 13½*

789 A268 3.50s indigo .55 .25

Vienna Philharmonic Orchestra, 125th anniv.

Motherhood, Watercolor by Peter Fendi — A269

1967, Apr. 28 Litho. *Perf. 14*

790 A269 2s multicolored .30 .25

Mother's Day.

Gothic Mantle Madonna A270

1967, May 19 Engr. *Perf. 13½x14*

791 A270 3s slate .55 .25

"Austrian Gothic," art exhibition, Krems, 1967. The Gothic wood carving is from Frauenstein in Upper Austria.

Medieval Gold Cross — A271

Litho. and Engr.

1967, June 9 *Perf. 13½*

792 A271 3.50s Prus grn & multi .55 .25

Salzburg Treasure Chamber; exhibition at Salzburg Cathedral, June 12-Sept. 15.

Swan, Tapestry by Oscar Kokoschka — A272

1967, June 9 **Photo.**

793 A272 2s multicolored .30 .25

Nibelungen District Art Exhibition, Pöchlarn, celebrating the 700th anniversary of Pöchlarn as a city. The design is from the border of the Amor and Psyche tapestry at the Salzburg Festival Theater.

View and Arms of Vienna A273

Engraved and Photogravure

1967, June 12 *Perf. 14x13½*

794 A273 3s black & red .55 .25

10th Europa Talks, "Science and Society in Europe," Vienna, June 13-17.

Prize Bull "Mucki" A274

1967, Aug. 28 **Engr.** ***Perf. 13½***
795 A274 2s deep claret .30 .25

Centenary of the Ried Festival and the Agricultural Fair.

Potato Beetle A275

Engraved and Photogravure

1967, Aug. 29 ***Perf. 13½x14***
796 A275 3s black & multi .55 .25

6th Intl. Congress for Plant Protection, Vienna.

First Locomotive Used on Brenner Pass A276

1967, Sept. 23 **Photo.** ***Perf. 12***
797 A276 3.50s tan & slate grn .75 .25

Centenary of railroad over Brenner Pass.

Christ in Glory — A277

1967, Oct. 9 ***Perf. 13½***
798 A277 2s multicolored .30 .25

Restoration of the Romanesque (11th century) frescoes in the Lambach monastery church.

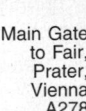

Main Gate to Fair, Prater, Vienna A278

1967, Oct. 24 **Photo.** ***Perf. 13½x14***
799 A278 2s choc & buff .25 .35

Congress of Intl. Trade Fairs, Vienna, Oct., 1967.

Medal Showing Minerva and Art Symbols — A279

Litho. & Engr.

1967, Oct. 25 ***Perf. 13½***
800 A279 2s dk brn, dk bl & yel .25 .25

Vienna Academy of Fine Arts, 275th anniv. The medal was designed by Georg Raphael Donner (1693-1741) and is awarded as an artist's prize.

Frankfurt Medal for Reformation, 1717 — A280

1967, Oct. 31 **Engr.** ***Perf. 14x13½***
801 A280 3.50s blue black .55 .25

450th anniversary of the Reformation.

Mountain Range and Stone Pines A281

1967, Nov. 7 ***Perf. 13½***
802 A281 3.50s green .55 .25

Centenary of academic study of forestry.

Land Survey Monument, 1770 — A282

1967, Nov. 7 **Photo.**
803 A282 2s olive black .25 .25

150th anniversary of official land records.

St. Leopold, Window, Heiligenkreuz Abbey — A283

1967, Nov. 15 **Engr. & Photo.**
804 A283 1.80s multicolored .25 .25

Margrave Leopold III (1075-1136), patron saint of Austria.

Tragic Mask and Violin — A284

1967, Nov. 17 ***Perf. 13½***
805 A284 3.50s bluish lil & blk .55 .55

Academy of Music and Dramatic Art, 150th anniv.

Nativity from 15th Century Altar — A285

1967, Nov. 27 **Engr.** ***Perf. 14x13½***
806 A285 2s green .30 .25

Christmas.

The design shows the late Gothic carved center panel of the altar in St. John's Chapel in Nonnberg Convent, Salzburg.

Innsbruck Stadium, Alps and FISU Emblem — A286

1968, Jan. 22 **Engr.** ***Perf. 13½***
807 A286 2s dark blue .30 .25

Winter University Games under the auspices of FISU (Fédération Internationale du Sport Universitaire), Innsbruck, Jan. 21-28.

Camillo Sitte (1843-1903), Architect, City Planner — A287

1968, Apr. 17 ***Perf. 13½***
808 A287 2s black brown .25 .25

Mother and Child — A288

1968, May 7
809 A288 2s slate green .25 .25

Mother's Day.

Cup and Serpent Emblem — A289

1968, May 7 **Photo.**
810 A289 3.50s dp plum, gray & gold .55 .25

Bicentenary of the Veterinary College.

Bride with Lace Veil — A290

1968, May 24 **Engr.** ***Perf. 12***
811 A290 3.50s blue black .55 .25

Embroidery industry of Vorarlberg, cent.

Horse Race A291

1968, June 4 ***Perf. 13½***
812 A291 3.50s sepia .55 .40

Centenary of horse racing at Freudenau, Vienna.

Dr. Karl Landsteiner A292

1968, June 14 ***Perf. 14x13½***
813 A292 3.50s dark blue .55 .25

Birth cent. of Dr. Karl Landsteiner (1868-1943), pathologist, discoverer of the four main human blood types.

Peter Rosegger (1843-1918), Poet and Writer — A293

1968, June 26
814 A293 2s slate green .25 .25

Angelica Kauffmann, Self-portrait A294

1968, July 15 **Engr.** ***Perf. 14x13½***
815 A294 2s intense black .25 .25

"Angelica Kauffmann and her Contemporaries," art exhibitions, Bregenz, July 28-Oct. 13, and Vienna, Oct. 22, 1968-Jan. 6, 1969.

Bronze Statue of Young Man, 1st Century B.C. — A295

1968, July 15 **Litho. & Engr.**
816 A295 2s grnsh gray & blk .25 .25

20 years of excavations on Magdalene Mountain, Carinthia.

Bishop, Romanesque Bas-relief — A296

1968, Sept. 20 Engr. ***Perf. 14x13½***

817 A296 2s blue gray .25 .25

Graz-Seckau Bishopric, 750th anniv.

Koloman Moser (1868-1918), Stamp Designer, Painter — A297

Engr. & Photo.

1968, Oct. 18 ***Perf. 12***

818 A297 2s black brn & ver .25 .25

Intl. Human Rights Year — A298

1968, Oct. 18 Photo. ***Perf. 14x13½***

819 A298 1.50s gray, dp car & dk green .55 .25

Republic of Austria, 50th Anniv. — A299

Designs: No. 820, Pres. Karl Renner and States' arms. No. 821, Coats of arms of Austria and Austrian states. No. 822, Article I of Austrian Constitution and States' coats of arms.

Engr. & Photo.

1968, Nov. 11 ***Perf. 13½***

820 A299 2s black & multi .30 .30

821 A299 2s black & multi .30 .30

822 A299 2s black & multi .30 .30

Nos. 820-822 (3) .90 .90

Hymn "Silent Night, Holy Night," 150th Anniv. — A300

Crèche, Memorial Chapel, Oberndorf-Salzburg.

1968, Nov. 29 Engr. ***Perf. 14x13½***

823 A300 2s slate green .25 .25

Christmas.

Angels, from Last Judgment by Troger (Röhrenbach-Greillenstein Chapel) — A301

Baroque Frescoes: No. 825, Vanquished Demons, by Paul Troger, Altenburg Abbey. No. 826, Sts. Peter and Paul, by Troger, Melk Abbey. No. 827, The Glorification of Mary, by Franz Anton Maulbertsch, Maria Treu Church, Vienna. No. 828, St. Leopold Carried into Heaven, by Maulbertsch, Ebenfurth Castle Chapel. No. 829, Symbolic figures from The Triumph of Apollo, by Maulbertsch, Halbthurn Castle.

Engr. & Photo.

1968, Dec. 11 ***Perf. 13½x14***

824 A301 2s multicolored .55 .55

825 A301 2s multicolored .55 .55

826 A301 2s multicolored .55 .55

827 A301 2s multicolored .55 .55

828 A301 2s multicolored .55 .55

829 A301 2s multicolored .55 .55

Nos. 824-829 (6) 3.30 3.30

St Sebastian — A302

Statues in St. Stephen's Cathedral, Vienna: No. 831, St. Paul. No. 832, Mantle Madonna. No. 833, St. Christopher. No. 834, St. George and the Dragon. No. 835, St Stephen.

1969, Jan. 28 Engr. ***Perf. 13½***

830 A302 2s black .45 .45

831 A302 2s rose claret .45 .45

832 A302 2s gray blue .45 .45

833 A302 2s slate blue .45 .45

834 A302 2s green .45 .45

835 A302 2s dk red brn .45 .45

Nos. 830-835 (6) 2.70 2.70

500th anniversary of Diocese of Vienna.

Parliament and Pallas Athena Fountain, Vienna A303

1969, Apr. 8 Engr. ***Perf. 13½***

836 A303 2s greenish black .25 .25

Interparliamentary Union Conf., Vienna, 4/7-13.

Europa Issue, 1969

Common Design Type

1969, Apr. 28 Photo. ***Perf. 12***

837 CD12 2s gray grn, brick red & blue .55 .25

Nos. 837 (1) .55 .25

Council of Europe Emblem A304

1969, May 5

838 A304 3.50s gray, ultra, blk & yel .55 .25

20th anniversary of Council of Europe.

Frontier Guards — A305

Engr. & Photo.

1969, May 14 ***Perf. 12***

839 A305 2s sepia & red .25 .25

Austrian Federal Army.

Don Giovanni, by Mozart — A306

Cent. of Vienna Opera House: a, Don Giovanni, Mozart. b, Magic Flute, Mozart. c, Fidelio, Beethoven. d, Lohengrin, Wagner. e, Don Carlos, Verdi. f, Carmen, Bizet. g, Rosencavalier, Richard Strauss. h, Swan Lake, Ballet by Tchaikovsky.

1969, May 23 ***Perf. 13½***

840 A306 Sheet of 8 4.75 4.75

a.-h. 2s, any single .50 .50

Centenary of Vienna Opera House.

No. 840 contains 8 stamps arranged around gold and red center label showing Opera House. Printed in sheets containing 4 Nos. 840 with wide gutters between.

Emperor Maximilian I Exhibition, Innsbruck, May 30-Oct. 5 — A307

Gothic armor of Maximilian I.

1969, June 4 Engr.

841 A307 2s bluish black .25 .25

19th Cong. of the Intl. Org. of Municipalities, Vienna — A308

Oldest Municipal Seal of Vienna.

1969, June 16 Photo. ***Perf. 13½***

842 A308 2s tan, red & black .25 .25

SOS Children's Villages in Austria, 20th Anniv. — A309

Girl's head and village house.

Engraved and Photogravure

1969, June 16 ***Perf. 13½x14***

843 A309 2s yel grn & sepia .25 .25

ILO, 50th Anniv. — A310

Hands holding wrench, and UN emblem.

1969, Aug. 22 Photo. ***Perf. 13x13½***

844 A310 2s deep green .25 .25

Year of Austrians Living Abroad, 1969 — A311

Austria's flag and shield circling the world.

Engraved and Lithographed

1969, Aug. 22 ***Perf. 14x13½***

845 A311 3.50s slate & red .55 .25

Etching Collection in the Albertina, Vienna, Bicent. — A312

Etchings: No. 846, Young Hare, by Dürer. No. 847, El Cid Killing a Bull, by Francisco de Goya. No. 848, Madonna with the Pomegranate, by Raphael. No. 849, The Painter, by Peter Brueghel. No. 850, Rubens' Son Nicolas, by Rubens. No. 851, Self-portrait, by Rembrandt. No. 852, Lady Reading, by Francois Guerin. No. 853, Wife of the Artist, by Egon Schiele.

Engraved and Photogravure

1969, Sept. 26 ***Perf. 13½***

Gray Frame, Buff Background

846 A312 2s black & brown .45 .45

847 A312 2s black .45 .45

848 A312 2s black .45 .45

849 A312 2s black .45 .45

850 A312 2s black & salmon .45 .45

851 A312 2s black .45 .45

852 A312 2s black & salmon .45 .45

853 A312 2s black .45 .45

Nos. 846-853 (8) 3.60 3.60

President Franz Jonas — A313

1969, Oct. 3
854 A313 2s gray & vio blue .25 .25

70th birthday of Franz Jonas, Austrian Pres.

Post Horn, Globe and Lightning A314

1969, Oct. 17 ***Perf. 13½x14***
855 A314 2s multicolored .25 .25

Union of Postal and Telegraph employees, 50th anniv.

Savings Box, about 1450 — A315

1969, Oct. 31 Photo. ***Perf. 13x13½***
856 A315 2s silver & slate green .25 .25

The importance of savings.

Madonna, by Albin Egger-Lienz A316

Engr. & Photo.

1969, Nov. 24 ***Perf. 12***
857 A316 2s dp claret & pale yel .25 .25

Christmas.

Josef Schöffel — A317

1970, Feb. 6 Engr. ***Perf. 14x13½***
858 A317 2s dull purple .25 .25

60th death anniv. of Josef Schöffel, (1832-1910), who saved the Vienna Woods.

St. Klemens M. Hofbauer — A318

Engraved and Photogravure

1970, Mar. 13 ***Perf. 14x13½***
859 A318 2s dk brn & lt tan .25 .25

150th death anniv. St. Klemens Maria Hofbauer (1751-1820); Redemptorist preacher in Poland and Austria, canonized in 1909.

Chancellor Leopold Figl — A319

Belvedere Palace, Vienna — A320

1970, Apr. 27 Engr. ***Perf. 13½***
860 A319 2s dark olive gray .25 .25
861 A320 2s dark rose brown .25 .25

25th anniversary of Second Republic.

European Nature Conservation Year, 1970 — A321

1970, May 19 Engr. ***Perf. 13½***
862 A321 2s Krimml waterfalls .25 .25

Leopold Franzens University, Innsbruck, 300th Anniv. — A322

St. Leopold on oldest seal of Innsbruck University.

Litho. & Engr.

1970, June 5 ***Perf. 13½***
863 A322 2s red & black .25 .25

Organ, Great Hall, Music Academy — A323

Photo. & Engr.

1970, June 5 ***Perf. 14***
864 A323 2s gold & deep claret .25 .25

Vienna Music Academy Building, cent.

Tower Clock, 1450-1550 A324

Old Clocks from Vienna Horological Museum: No. 866, Lyre clock, 1790-1815. No. 867, Pendant clock 1600-50. No. 868, Pendant watch, 1800-30. No. 869, Bracket clock, 1720-60. No. 870, French column clock, 1820-50.

1970

865	A324	1.50s	cream & sepia	.25	.25
866	A324	1.50s	greenish & grn	.25	.35
867	A324	2s	pale bl & dk bl	.25	.25
868	A324	2s	pale rose & lake	.25	.25
869	A324	3.50s	buff & brown	.70	.70
870	A324	3.50s	pale lil & brn vio	.55	.55
			Nos. 865-870 (6)	2.25	2.35

Issued: Nos. 865, 867, 869, 6/22; others, 10/23.

The Beggar Student, by Carl Millöcker — A325

Operettas: No. 872, Fledermaus, by Johann Strauss. No. 873, The Dream Waltz, by Oscar Straus. No. 874, The Bird Seller, by Carl Zeller. No. 875, The Merry Widow, by Franz Lehar. No. 876, Two Hearts in Three-quarter Time, by Robert Stolz.

1970 Photo & Engr. ***Perf. 13½***

871	A325	1.50s	pale grn & grn	.25	.25
872	A325	1.50s	yel & vio blue	.25	.25
873	A325	2s	pale rose & vio brn	.55	.55
874	A325	2s	pale grn & sep	.25	.25
875	A325	3.50s	pale bl & ind	.70	.70
876	A325	3.50s	beige & slate	.55	.55
			Nos. 871-876 (6)	2.55	2.55

Issued: Nos. 871, 873, 875, 7/3; others 9/11.

Bregenz Festival Stage — A326

1970, July 23 ***Photo.***
877 A326 3.50s dark blue & buff .55 .40

25th anniversary of Bregenz Festival.

Salzburg Festival Emblem — A327

1970, July 27 ***Perf. 14***
878 A327 3.50s blk, red, gold & gray .55 .25

50th anniversary of Salzburg Festival.

A328

1970, Aug. 31 ***Engr.***
879 A328 3.50s dark gray .55 .25

13th General Assembly of the World Veterans Federation, Aug. 28-Sept. 4. The head of St. John is from a sculpture showing the Agony in the Garden in the chapel of the Parish Church in Ried. It is attributed to Thomas Schwanthaler (1634-1702).

Thomas Koschat (1845-1914), Carinthian Song Composer A329

1970, Sept. 16 ***Perf. 14x13½***
880 A329 2s chocolate .25 .25

Mountain Scene A330

1970, Sept. 16 Photo. ***Perf. 14x13½***
881 A330 2s vio bl & pink .25 .25

Hiking and mountaineering in Austria.

Alfred Cossmann (1870-1951), Engraver — A331

1970, Oct. 2 Engr. ***Perf. 14x13½***
882 A331 2s dark brown .25 .25

Arms of Carinthia — A332

Photo. & Engr.

1970, Oct. 2 ***Perf. 14***
883 A332 2s ol, red, gold, blk & sil .25 .25

Carinthian plebiscite, 50th anniversary.

UN Emblem A333

1970, Oct. 23 Litho. ***Perf. 14x13½***
884 A333 3.50s lt blue & blk .55 .25

25th anniversary of the United Nations.

Adoration of the Shepherds, Carving from Garsten Vicarage A334

1970, Nov. 27 Engr. *Perf. 13½x14*
885 A334 2s dk violet blue .25 .25

Christmas.

Karl Renner (1870-1950), Austrian Pres. — A335

1970, Dec. 14 Engr. *Perf. 14x13½*
886 A335 2s deep claret .25 .25

Beethoven, by Georg Waldmüller A336

Photo. & Engr.
1970, Dec. 16 *Perf. 13½*
887 A336 3.50s black & buff .55 .40

Ludwig van Beethoven (1770-1827), composer, birth bicentenary.

Enrica Handel-Mazzetti (1871-1955), Novelist, Poet A337

1971, Jan. 11 Engr. *Perf. 14x13½*
888 A337 2s sepia .25 .25

"Watch Out for Children!" A338

1971, Feb. 18 Photo. *Perf. 13½*
889 A338 2s blk, red brn & brt grn .25 .25

Traffic safety.

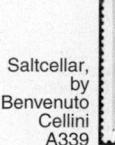

Saltcellar, by Benvenuto Cellini A339

Art Treasures: 1.50s, Covered vessel, made of prase, gold and precious stones, Florentine, 1580. 2s, Emperor Joseph I, ivory statue by Matthias Steinle, 1693.

Photo. & Engr.
1971, Mar. 22 *Perf. 14*
890 A339 1.50s gray & slate grn .55 .25
891 A339 2s gray & dp plum .55 .25
892 A339 3.50s gray, blk & bister .75 .55
Nos. 890-892 (3) 1.85 1.05

Emblem of Austrian Wholesalers' Organization A340

1971, Apr. 16 Photo. *Perf. 13½*
893 A340 3.50s multicolored .55 .25

Intl. Chamber of Commerce, 23rd Congress, Vienna, Apr. 17-23.

Jacopo de Strada, by Titian — A341

Paintings in Vienna Museum: 2s, Village Feast, by Peter Brueghel, the Elder. 3.50s, Young Venetian Woman, by Albrecht Dürer.

1971, May 6 Engr. *Perf. 13½*
894 A341 1.50s rose lake .25 .25
895 A341 2s greenish black .25 .25
896 A341 3.50s deep brown .55 .55
Nos. 894-896 (3) 1.05 1.05

Seal of Paulus of Franchenfordia, 1380 — A342

Photo. & Engr.
1971, May 6 *Perf. 13½x14*
897 A342 3.50s dk brn & bister .55 .25

Congress commemorating the centenary of the Austrian Notaries' Statute, May 5-8.

St. Matthew — A343

1971, May 27 *Perf. 12½x13½*
898 A343 2s brt rose lil & brn .25 .25

Exhibition of "1000 Years of Art in Krems." The statue of St. Matthew is from the Lentl Altar, created about 1520 by the Master of the Pulkau Altar.

August Neilreich — A344

1971, June 1 Engr. *Perf. 14x13½*
899 A344 2s brown .25 .25

August Neilreich (1803-71), botanist.

Singer with Lyre — A345

Photo. & Engr.
1971, July 1 *Perf. 13½x14*
900 A345 4s lt bl, vio bl & gold .55 .50

Intl. Choir Festival, Vienna, July 1-4.

Coat of Arms of Kitzbuhel — A346

1971, Aug. 23 *Perf. 14*
901 A346 2.50s gold & multi .25 .25

700th anniversary of the town of Kitzbuhel.

Vienna Stock Exchange — A347

1971, Sept. 1 Engr. *Perf. 13½x14*
902 A347 4s reddish brown .25 .35

Bicentenary of the Vienna Stock Exchange.

First and Latest Exhibition Halls A348

1971, Sept. 6 Photo. *Perf. 13½x13*
903 A348 2.50s dp rose lilac .25 .25

Vienna Intl. Fair, 50th anniv.

Trade Union Emblem — A349

1971, Sept. 20 *Perf. 14x13½*
904 A349 2s gray, buff & red .25 .25

Austrian Trade Union Assoc., 25th anniv.

Arms of Burgenland A350

1971, Oct. 1
905 A350 2s dk bl, gold, red & blk .25 .25

50th anniv. of Burgenland joining Austria.

Marcus Car — A351

Photo. & Engr.
1971, Oct. 1 *Perf. 14*
906 A351 4s pale green & blk .55 .40

Austrian Automobile, Motorcycle and Touring Club, 75th anniv.

Europa Bridge — A352

1971, Oct. 8 Engr. *Perf. 14x13½*
907 A352 4s violet blue .55 .40

Opening of highway over Brenner Pass.

Styria's Iron Mountain A353

Designs: 2s, Austrian Nitrogen Products, Ltd., Linz. 4s, United Austrian Iron and Steel Works, Ltd. (VÖEST), Linz Harbor.

1971, Oct. 15 *Perf. 13½*
908 A353 1.50s reddish brown .25 .25
909 A353 2s bluish black .25 .25
910 A353 4s dk slate grn .75 .75
Nos. 908-910 (3) 1.25 1.25

25 years of nationalized industry.

High-speed Train on Semmering A354

1971, Oct. 21 *Perf. 14*
911 A354 2s claret .25 .25

Inter-city rapid train service.

Trout Fisherman A355

1971, Nov. 15 ***Perf. 13½***
912 A355 2s dark red brn .25 .25

Dr. Erich Tschermak-Seysenegg (1871-1962), Botanist — A356

Photo. & Engr.

1971, Nov. 15 ***Perf. 14x13½***
913 A356 2s pale ol & dk pur .25 .25

Infant Jesus as Savior, by Dürer — A357

1971, Nov. 26 ***Perf. 13½***
914 A357 2s gold & multi .25 .25

Christmas.

Franz Grillparzer, by Moritz Daffinger — A358

Litho. & Engr.

1972, Jan. 21 ***Perf. 14x13½***
915 A358 2s buff, gold & blk .25 .25

Death cent. of Franz Grillparzer (1791-1872), dramatic poet.

Fountain, Main Square, Friesach — A359

Designs: 2s, Fountain, Heiligenkreuz Abbey. 2.50s, Leopold Fountain, Innsbruck.

1972, Feb. 23 **Engr.** ***Perf. 14x13½***
916 A359 1.50s rose lilac .25 .25
917 A359 2s brown .25 .25
918 A359 2.50s olive .55 .55
Nos. 916-918 (3) 1.05 1.05

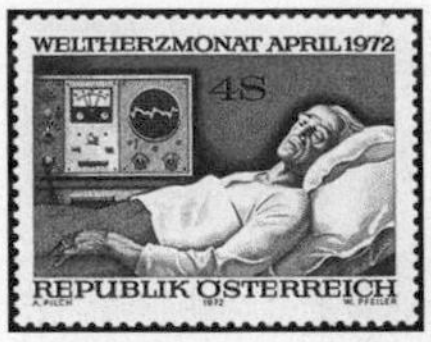

Cardiac Patient and Monitor A360

1972, Apr. 11 ***Perf. 13½x14***
919 A360 4s violet brown .65 .40

World Health Day.

Conference of European Post and Telecommunications Ministers, Vienna, Apr. 11-14 — A361

St. Michael's Gate, Royal Palace, Vienna.

1972, Apr. 11 ***Perf. 14x13½***
920 A361 4s violet blue .75 .40

Gurk (Carinthia) Diocese, 900th Anniv. — A362

Photo. & Engr.

1972, May 5 ***Perf. 14***
921 A362 2s Sculpture, Gurk Cathedral .25 .25

The design is after the central column supporting the sarcophagus of St. Hemma in Gurk Cathedral.

City Hall, Congress Emblem A363

1972, May 23 **Litho. & Engr.**
922 A363 4s red, blk & yel .75 .40

9th Intl. Congress of Public and Cooperative Economy, Vienna, May 23-25.

Power Line in Carnic Alps — A364

2.50s, Power Station, Semmering. 4s, Zemm Power Station (lake in Zillertaler Alps).

1972, June 28 ***Perf. 13½x14***
923 A364 70g gray & violet .25 .25
924 A364 2.50s gray & red brn .50 .25
925 A364 4s gray & slate .75 .55
Nos. 923-925 (3) 1.50 1.05

Nationalization of the power industry, 25th anniv.

Runner with Olympic Torch — A365

Engr. & Photo.

1972, Aug. 21 ***Perf. 14x13½***
926 A365 2s sepia & red .25 .25

Olympic torch relay from Olympia, Greece, to Munich, Germany, passing through Austria.

St. Hermes, by Conrad Laib — A366

1972, Aug. 21 **Engr.**
927 A366 2s violet brown .25 .25

Exhibition of Late Gothic Art, Salzburg.

Pears A367

1972, Sept. ***Perf. 14***
928 A367 2.50s dk blue & multi .50 .25

World Congress of small plot Gardeners, Vienna, Sept. 7-10.

Souvenir Sheet

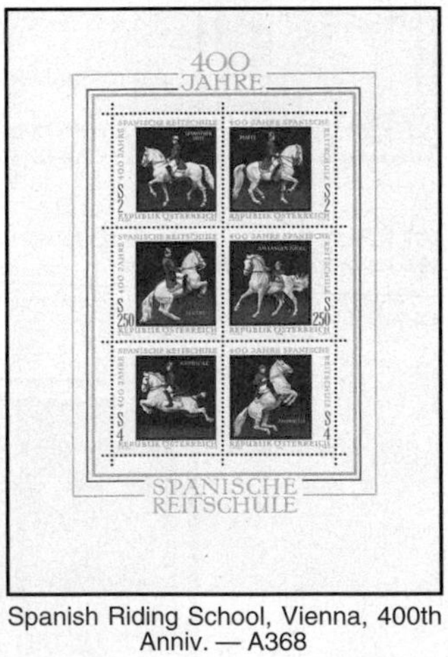

Spanish Riding School, Vienna, 400th Anniv. — A368

1972, Sept. 12 ***Perf. 13½***
929 A368 Sheet of 6 2.75 4.00
a. 2s Spanish walk .25 .25
b. 2s Piaffe .25 .25
c. 2.50s Levade .40 .25
d. 2.50s On long rein .40 .25
e. 4s Capriole .65 .55
f. 4s Courbette .65 .55

Arms of University of Agriculture A369

Photo. & Engr.

1972, Oct. 17 ***Perf. 14x13½***
930 A369 2s black & multi .25 .25

University of Agriculture, Vienna, cent.

Church and Old University — A370

1972, Nov. 7 **Engr.**
931 A370 4s red brown .75 .50

Paris Lodron University, Salzburg, 350th anniv.

Carl Michael Ziehrer — A371

1972, Nov. 14
932 A371 2s rose claret .25 .25

50th death anniv. of Carl Michael Ziehrer (1843-1922), composer.

Virgin and Child, Wood, 1420-30 A372

Photo. & Engr.

1972, Dec. 1 ***Perf. 13½***
933 A372 2s olive & chocolate .25 .25

Christmas.

Racing Sleigh, 1750 A373

Designs: 2s, Coronation landau, 1824. 2.50s, Imperial state coach, 1763.

1972, Dec. 12
934 A373 1.50s pale gray & brn .25 .25
935 A373 2s pale gray & sl grn .50 .40
936 A373 2.50s pale gray & plum .50 .40
Nos. 934-936 (3) 1.25 1.05

Collection of historic state coaches and carriages in Schönbrunn Palace.

Map of Austrian Telephone System A374

1972, Dec. 14 **Photo.** ***Perf. 14***
937 A374 2s yellow & blk .25 .25

Completion of automation of Austrian telephone system.

"Drugs are Death" A375

1973, Jan. 26 Photo. ***Perf. 13½x14***
938 A375 2s scarlet & multi .25 .25

Fight against drug abuse.

Alfons Petzold (1882-1923), Poet — A376

1973, Jan. 26 Engr. ***Perf. 14x13½***
939 A376 2s reddish brn .25 .25

Theodor Körner (1873-1957), Austrian Pres. — A377

Photo. & Engr.

1973, Apr. 24 ***Perf. 14x13½***
940 A377 2s gray & deep claret .25 .25

Douglas DC-9 A378

1973, May 14 ***Perf. 13½x14***
941 A378 2s vio bl & rose red .25 .25

First intl. airmail service, Vienna to Kiev, Mar. 31, 1918, 55th anniv.; Austrian Aviation Corporation, 50th anniv.; Austrian Airlines, 15th anniv.

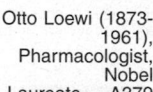

Otto Loewi (1873-1961), Pharmacologist, Nobel Laureate — A379

1973, June 4 Engr. ***Perf. 14x13½***
942 A379 4s deep violet .75 .40

"Support" — A380

1973, June 25
943 A380 2s dark blue .25 .25

Federation of Austrian Social Insurance Institutes, 25th anniv.

Europa Issue

Post Horn and Telephone A381

1973, July 9 Photo. ***Perf. 14***
944 A381 2.50s ocher, blk & yel .75 .25

Dornbirn Fair Emblem A382

1973, July 27 ***Perf. 13½x14***
945 A382 2s multicolored .25 .25

Dornbirn Trade Fair, 25th anniversary.

23rd Intl. Military Pentathlon Championships, Wiener Neustadt, Aug. 13-18 — A383

1973, Aug. 13 Engr. ***Perf. 14x13½***
946 A383 4s Hurdles .65 .40

Leo Slezak (1873-1946), Operatic Tenor — A384

1973, Aug. 17 ***Perf. 14***
947 A384 4s dark brown .65 .25

Gate, Vienna Hofburg, and ISI Emblem — A385

Photogravure and Engraved

1973, Aug. 20 ***Perf. 14x13½***
948 A385 2s gray, dk brn & ver .25 .25

39th Congress of Intl. Statistical Institute, Vienna, Aug. 20-30.

Tegetthoff off Franz Josef Land, by Julius Payer A386

1973, Aug. 30 Engr. ***Perf. 13½x14***
949 A386 2.50s Prussian grn .25 .25

Discovery of Franz Josef Land by an Austrian North Pole expedition, cent.

Academy of Science, by Canaletto A387

1973, Sept. 4
950 A387 2.50s violet .25 .25

World Meteorological Organization, cent.

Arms of Viennese Tanners — A388

Photo. & Engr.

1973, Sept. 4 ***Perf. 14***
951 A388 4s red & multi .55 .25

13th Congress of the Intl. Union of Leather Chemists' Societies, Vienna, Sept. 1-7.

Max Reinhardt (1873-1943), Theatrical Director — A389

1973, Sept. 7 Engr. ***Perf. 13x13½***
952 A389 2s rose magenta .25 .25

Trotter A390

1973, Sept. 28 ***Perf. 13½***
953 A390 2s green .25 .25

Centenary of Vienna Trotting Association.

Ferdinand Hanusch (1866-1923), Secretary of State — A391

1973, Sept. 28 ***Perf. 14x13½***
954 A391 2s rose brown .25 .25

Police Radio Operator A392

1973, Oct. 2 ***Perf. 13½x14***
955 A392 4s violet blue .55 .25

50th anniv. of Intl. Criminal Police Org. (INTERPOL).

Josef Petzval's Photographic Lens — A393

Litho. & Engr.

1973, Oct. 8 ***Perf. 14***
956 A393 2.50s blue & multi .25 .25

EUROPHOT Photographic Cong., Vienna.

Emperor's Spring, Hell Valley A394

Photo. & Engr.

1973, Oct. 23 ***Perf. 13½x14***
957 A394 2s sepia, blue & red .25 .25

Vienna's first mountain spring water supply system, cent.

Almsee, Upper Austria — A395

Hofburg and Prince Eugene Statue, Vienna — A395a

Designs: 50g, Farmhouses, Zillertal, Tirol. 1s, Kahlenbergerdorf. 1.50s, Bludenz, Vorarlberg. 2s, Inn Bridge, Alt Finstermunz. 2.50s, Murau, Styria. 3s, Bischofsmütze, Salzburg. 3.50s, Easter Church, Oberwart. 4.50s, Windmill, Retz. 5s, Aggstein Castle, Lower Austria. 6s, Lindauer Hut, Vorarlberg. 6.50s, Holy Cross Church, Villach, Carinthia. 7s, Falkenstein Castle, Carinthia. 7.50s, Hohensalzburg. 8s, Votive column, Reiteregg, Styria. 10s, Lake Neusiedl, Burgenland. 11s, Old Town, Enns. 16s, Openair Museum, Bad Tatzmannsdorf. 20s, Myra waterfalls.

Photo. & Engr.

1973-78 ***Perf. 13½x14***

Size: 23x29mm

958	A395	50g	gray & slate green	.25	.25
959	A395	1s	brn & dk brown	.30	.25
960	A395	1.50s	rose & brown	.40	.25
961	A395	2s	gray bl & dk blue	.50	.25
962	A395	2.50s	vio & dp violet	.55	.25
963	A395	3s	lt ultra & vio blue	.65	.25
963A	A395	3.50s	dl org & brown	.75	.25
964	A395	4s	brt lil & pur	.65	.25
965	A395	4.50s	brt grn & bl green	.80	.25
966	A395	5s	lilac & vio	.80	.25
967	A395	6s	dp rose & dk violet	1.20	.25
968	A395	6.50s	bl grn & indigo	1.20	.30
969	A395	7s	sage grn & sl green	1.60	.25
970	A395	7.50s	lil rose & claret	2.00	.25
971	A395	8s	dl red & dp brown	1.75	.25
972	A395	10s	gray grn & dk green	2.10	.25
973	A395	11s	ver & dk carmine	2.00	.25
974	A395	16s	bister & brown	3.25	.35

975	A395	20s ol bis & ol grn	4.00	.40
976	A395a	50s gray vio & vio bl	8.00	2.40
		Nos. 958-976 (20)	32.75	7.45

Issued: Nos. 960-963, 1974; Nos. 958-959, 967, 976, 1975; Nos. 965, 971, 973, 1976; Nos. 968, 970, 974-975, 1977; No. 963A, 1978. See Nos. 1100-1109.

Nativity — A396

1973, Nov. 30 ***Perf. 14***
977 A396 2s multicolored .25 .25

Christmas. Design from 14th century stained-glass window.

Pregl — A397

1973, Dec. 12 Engr. ***Perf. 14x13½***
978 A397 4s deep blue .75 .45

50th anniv. of the awarding of the Nobel prize for chemistry to Fritz Pregl (1869-1930).

Radio Austria, 50th Anniv. — A398

1974, Jan. 14 Photo. ***Perf. 14x13½***
979 A398 2.50s Telex Machine .55 .25

Hugo Hofmannsthal (1874-1929), Poet and Playwright A399

1974, Feb. 1 Engr. ***Perf. 14***
980 A399 4s violet blue .75 .50

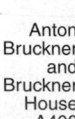

Anton Bruckner and Bruckner House A400

1974, Mar. 22 Engr. ***Perf. 14***
981 A400 4s brown .75 .50

Founding of Anton Bruckner House (concert hall), Linz, and birth of Anton Bruckner (1824-1896), composer, 150th anniv.

Vegetables A401

Photo. & Engr.

1974, Apr. 18 ***Perf. 14***

982	A401	2s shown	.25	.25
983	A401	2.50s Fruits	.55	.25
984	A401	4s Flowers	.75	.75
		Nos. 982-984 (3)	1.55	1.25

Intl. Garden Show, Vienna, Apr. 18-Oct. 14.

Seal of Judenburg A402

1974, Apr. 24 Photo. ***Perf. 14x13½***
985 A402 2s plum & multi .25 .25

750th anniversary of Judenburg.

Karl Kraus (1874-1936), Poet and Satirist — A403

1974, Apr. 6 **Engr.**
986 A403 4s dark red .75 .55

St. Michael, by Thomas Schwanthaler A404

1974, May 3
987 A404 2.50s slate green .50 .25

Exhibition of the works by the Schwanthaler Family of sculptors, (1633-1848), Reichersberg am Inn, May 3-Oct. 13.

A405

Europa: King Arthur, from tomb of Maximilian I

1974, May 8 ***Perf. 13½***
988 A405 2.50s ocher & slate blue .65 .40

Austrian Automobile Assoc., 75th Anniv. — A406

De Dion Bouton motor tricycle.

Photo. & Engr.

1974, May 17 ***Perf. 14x13½***
989 A406 2s gray & vio brn .25 .25

Satyr's Head, Terracotta A407

1974, May 22 ***Perf. 13½x14***
990 A407 2s org brn, gold & blk .25 .25

Exhibition, "Renaissance in Austria," Schallaburg Castle, May 22-Nov. 14.

Road Transport Union Emblem — A408

1974, May 24 Photo. ***Perf. 14x13½***
991 A408 4s deep orange & blk .65 .40

14th Congress of the Intl. Road Transport Union, Innsbruck.

Franz Anton Maulbertsch (1724-96), Painter — A409

1974, June 7 Engr. ***Perf. 14x13½***
992 A409 2s Self-portrait .25 .25

Gendarmes, 1824 and 1974 A410

1974, June 7 Photo. ***Perf. 13½x14***
993 A410 2s red & multi .25 .25

125th anniversary of Austrian gendarmery.

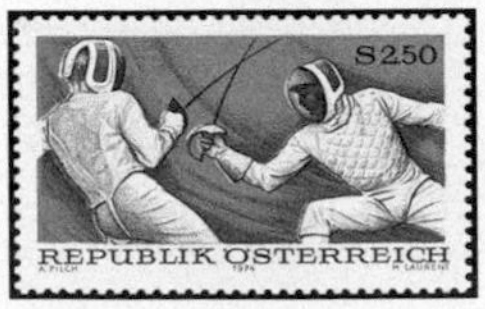
Fencing A411

Photo. & Engr.

1974, June 14 ***Perf. 13½***
994 A411 2.50s red org & blk .25 .25

Transportation Symbols — A412

1974, June 18 Photo. ***Perf. 14x13½***
995 A412 4s lt ultra & multi .65 .40

European Conference of Transportation Ministers, Vienna, June 18-21.

St. Virgil, Sculpture from Nonntal Church — A413

1974, June 28 Engr. ***Perf. 13½x14***
996 A413 2s violet blue .25 .25

Consecration of the Cathedral of Salzburg by Scotch-Irish Bishop Feirgil (St. Virgil), 1200th anniv. Salzburg was a center of Christianization in the 8th century.

Franz Jonas and Austrian Eagle — A414

1974, June 28
997 A414 2s black .25 .25

Jonas (1899-1974), Austrian Pres., 1965-1974.

Franz Stelzhamer A415

1974, July 12 Engr. ***Perf. 14x13½***
998 A415 2s indigo .25 .25

Franz Stelzhamer (1802-1874), poet who wrote in Upper Austrian vernacular, death cent.

Diver — A416

Photo. & Engr.

1974, Aug. 16 ***Perf. 13x13½***
999 A416 4s blue & sepia .65 .40

13th European Swimming, Diving and Water Polo Championships, Vienna, Aug. 18-25.

Ferdinand Ritter von Hebra — A417

1974, Sept. 10 Engr. ***Perf. 14x13½***
1000 A417 4s brown .65 .40

30th Meeting of the Assoc. of German-speaking Dermatologists, Graz, Sept. 10-14. Dr. von Hebra (1816-1880) was a founder of modern dermatology.

Arnold Schonberg A418

1974, Sept. 13 ***Perf. 13½x14***
1001 A418 2.50s purple .40 .25

Schönberg (1874-1951), composer.

Radio Station, Salzburg A419

1974, Oct. 1 Photo. ***Perf. 13½x14***
1002 A419 2s multicolored .25 .25

50th anniversary of Austrian broadcasting.

Edmund Eysler (1874-1949), Composer A420

1974, Oct. 4 Engr. ***Perf. 14x13½***
1003 A420 2s dark olive .25 .25

Mailman, Mail Coach and Train, UPU Emblem A421

4s, Mailman, jet, truck, 1974, & UPU emblem.

1974, Oct. 9 Photo. ***Perf. 13½***
1004 A421 2s deep claret & lil .25 .25
1005 A421 4s dark blue & gray .65 .40

Centenary of Universal Postal Union.

Gauntlet Protecting Rose A422

1974, Oct. 23 Photo. ***Perf. 13½x14***
1006 A422 2s multicolored .25 .25

Environment protection.

Austrian Sports Pool Emblem A423

1974, Oct. 23 Photo. ***Perf. 13½x14***
1007 A423 70g multicolored .25 .25

Austrian Sports Pool (lottery), 25th anniv.

Carl Ditters von Dittersdorf (1739-1799), Composer A424

1974, Oct. 24 Engr. ***Perf. 14x13½***
1008 A424 2s Prussian green .25 .25

Virgin and Child, Wood, c. 1600 — A425

1974, Nov. 29 Photo. & Engr.
1009 A425 2s brown & gold .25 .25

Christmas.

Franz Schmidt (1874-1939), Composer A426

1974, Dec. 18
1010 A426 4s gray & black .65 .40

European Architectural Heritage Year — A427

Photo. & Engr.

1975, Jan. 24 ***Perf. 13½***
1011 A427 2.50s St. Christopher .45 .25

The design shows part of a wooden figure from central panel of the retable in the Kefermarkt Church, 1490-1497.

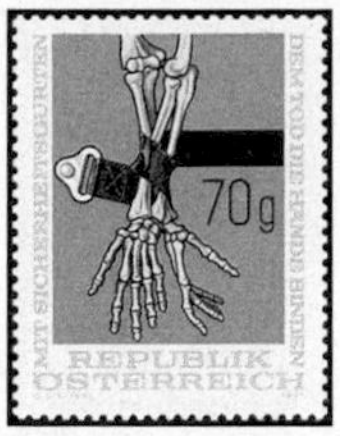

Safety Belt and Skeleton Arms — A428

1975, Apr. 1 Photo. ***Perf. 14x13½***
1012 A428 70g violet & multi .25 .25

Introduction of obligatory use of automobile safety belts.

Stained Glass Window, Vienna City Hall — A429

1975, Apr. 2 ***Perf. 14***
1013 A429 2.50s multicolored .25 .25

11th meeting of the Council of European Municipalities, Vienna, Apr. 2-5.

Austria as Mediator A430

1975, May 2 Litho. ***Perf. 14***
1014 A430 2s blk, gray & ol brn .25 .25

2nd Republic of Austria, 30th anniv.

National Forests, 50th Anniv. — A431

1975, May 6 **Engr.**
1015 A431 2s green .25 .25

Europa Issue

High Priest, by Michael Pacher — A432

Photo. & Engr.

1975, May 27 ***Perf. 14x13½***
1016 A432 2.50s multicolored .45 .25

Design is detail from painting "The Marriage of Joseph and Mary," by Michael Pacher (c. 1450-1500).

Gosaukamm Funicular — A433

1975, June 23 ***Perf. 14x13½***
1017 A433 2s slate & red .25 .25

4th Intl. Funicular Cong., Vienna, 6/23-27.

Josef Misson and Mühlbach am Manhartsberg — A434

1975, June 27 ***Perf. 13½x14***
1018 A434 2s choc & redsh brn .25 .25

Josef Misson (1803-1875), poet who wrote in Lower Austrian vernacular, death cent.

Setting Sun and "P" — A435

1975, Aug. 27 Litho. ***Perf. 14x13½***
1019 A435 1.50s org, blk & bl .25 .25

Austrian Assoc. of Pensioners 25th anniv. meeting, Vienna, Aug. 1975.

Ferdinand Porsche (1875-1951), Engineer, Auto Maker A436

Photo. & Engr.

1975, Sept. 3 ***Perf. 13½x14***
1020 A436 1.50s gray & purple .25 .25

Leo Fall (1873-1925), Composer A437

1975, Sept. 16 Engr. ***Perf. 14x13½***
1021 A437 2s violet .25 .25

10th World Judo Championships, Vienna — A438

1975, Oct. 20 Photo. ***Perf. 14x13½***
1022 A438 2.50s Judo Throw .45 .25

Heinrich Angeli (1840-1925), Painter — A439

1975, Oct. 21 Engr. ***Perf. 14x13½***
1023 A439 2s rose lake .25 .25

Johann Strauss and Dancers A440

Photo. & Engr.
1975, Oct. 24 ***Perf. 13½x14***
1024 A440 4s ocher & sepia .65 .40

Johann Strauss (1825-1899), composer.

Stylized Musician Playing a Viol — A441

1975, Oct. 30 ***Perf. 14x13½***
1025 A441 2.50s silver & vio bl .25 .25

Vienna Symphony Orchestra, 75th anniv.

Symbolic House — A442

1975, Oct. 31 Photo.
1026 A442 2s multicolored .25 .25

Austrian building savings societies, 50th anniv.

Fan with "Hanswurst" Scene, 18th Century A443

1975, Nov. 14 Photo. ***Perf. 13½x14***
1027 A443 1.50s green & multi .25 .25

Salzburg Theater bicentenary.

Virgin and Child, from 15th Century Altar — A444

Photo. & Engr.
1975, Nov. 28 ***Perf. 13x13½***
1028 A444 2s gold & dull purple .25 .25

Christmas.

"The Spiral Tree," by Hundertwasser A445

Photo., Engr. & Typo.
1975, Dec. 11 ***Perf. 13½x14***
1029 A445 4s multicolored .25 .35

Austrian modern art. Friedenstreich Hundertwasser is the pseudonym of Friedrich Stowasser (1928-2000).

Old Burgtheater A446

No. 1030b, Grand staircase, new Burgtheater.

Perf. 14 (pane), 13½x14 (stamps)
1976, Apr. 8 Engr.

1030	Pane of 2 + label	1.20	1.40
a.	A446 3s violet blue	.65	.25
b.	A446 3s deep brown	.65	.25

Bicentenary of Vienna Burgtheater. Label (head of Pan) and inscription in vermilion.

Dr. Robert Barany (1876-1936), Winner of Nobel Prize for Medicine, 1914 — A447

Photo. & Engr.
1976, Apr. 22 ***Perf. 14x13½***
1031 A447 3s blue & brown .55 .25

Ammonite A448

1976, Apr. 30 Photo. ***Perf. 13½x14***
1032 A448 3s red & multi .55 .25

Vienna Museum of Natural History, Centenary Exhibition.

Carinthian Dukes' Coronation Chair — A449

Photo. & Engr.
1976, May 6 ***Perf. 14x13½***
1033 A449 3s grnsh blk & org .55 .25

Millennium of Carinthia.

Siege of Linz, 17th Century Etching — A450

1976, May 14
1034 A450 4s blk & gray grn .75 .45

Upper Austrian Peasants' War, 350th anniv.

Skittles A451

1976, May 14 ***Perf. 13½x14***
1035 A451 4s black & org .55 .25

11th World Skittles Championships, Vienna.

Duke Heinrich II, Stained-glass Window — A452

1976, May 14 ***Perf. 14***
1036 A452 3s multicolored .55 .25

Babenberg Exhibition, Lilienfeld.

St. Wolfgang, from Pacher Altar — A453

1976, May 26 Engr. ***Perf. 13½***
1037 A453 6s bright violet 1.10 .55

Intl. Art Exhibition at St. Wolfgang.

Europa Issue

Tassilo Cup, Kremsmunster, 777 — A454

Photo. & Engr.
1976, Aug. 13 ***Perf. 14x13½***
1038 A454 4s ultra & multi .55 .25

Timber Fair Emblem — A455

1976, Aug. 13 Photo.
1039 A455 3s green & multi .55 .25

Austrian Timber Fair, Klagenfurt, 25th anniv.

Constantin Economo, M.D. (1876-1931), Neurologist A456

1976, Aug. 23 Engr.
1040 A456 3s dark red brown .55 .25

Administrative Court, by Salomon Klein — A457

1976, Oct. 25 Engr. ***Perf. 13½x14***
1041 A457 6s deep brown 1.10 .55

Austrian Central Administrative Court, cent.

Souvenir Sheet

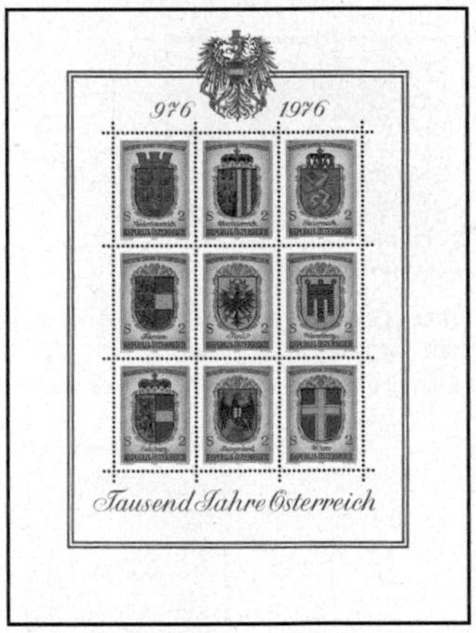

Coats of Arms of Austrian Provinces — A458

Millennium of Austria: a, Lower Austria. b, Upper Austria. c, Styria. d, Carinthia. e, Tyrol. f, Voralberg. g, Salzburg. h, Burgenland. i, Vienna.

Photo. & Engr.
1976, Oct. 25 ***Perf. 14***

1042	A458 Sheet of 9	3.25	4.50
a.-i.	2s any single	.35	.50

"Cancer" A459

1976, Nov. 17 Photo. ***Perf. 14x13½***
1043 A459 2.50s multicolored .55 .25

Fight against cancer.

UN Emblem and Bridge — A460

1976, Nov. 17
1044 A460 3s blue & gold .55 .25

UN Industrial Development Org. (UNIDO), 10th anniv.

Punched Tape, Map of Europe A461

1976, Nov. 17 ***Perf. 14***

1045 A461 1.50s multicolored .25 .25

Austrian Press Agency (APA), 30th anniv.

Viktor Kaplan, Kaplan Turbine A462

Photo. & Engr.

1976, Nov. 26 ***Perf. 13½x14***

1046 A462 2.50s multicolored .25 .25

Viktor Kaplan (1876-1934), inventor of Kaplan turbine, birth centenary.

Nativity, by Konrad von Friesach, c. 1450 A463

1976, Nov. 26 ***Perf. 13½***

1047 A463 3s multicolored .55 .25

Christmas.

Augustin, the Piper — A464

Photo. & Engr.

1976, Dec. 29 ***Perf. 13½***

1048 A464 6s multicolored 1.10 .55

Modern Austrian art.

Rainer Maria Rilke (1875-1926), Poet — A465

1976, Dec. 29 Engr. ***Perf. 14x13½***

1049 A465 3s deep violet .55 .25

Vienna City Synagogue — A466

1976, Dec. 29 Photo. ***Perf. 13½***

1050 A466 1.50s multicolored .25 .25

Sesquicentennial of Vienna City Synagogue.

Nikolaus Joseph von Jacquin (1727-1817), Botanist — A467

1977, Feb. 16 Engr. ***Perf. 14x13½***

1051 A467 4s chocolate .75 .45

Oswald von Wolkenstein (1377-1445), Poet — A468

Photo. & Engr.

1977, Feb. 16 ***Perf. 14***

1052 A468 3s multicolored .55 .25

Handball A469

1977, Feb. 25 Photo. ***Perf. 13½x14***

1053 A469 1.50s multicolored .25 .25

World Indoor Handball Championships, Austria, Feb. 5-Mar. 6.

Alfred Kubin (1877-1959), Illustrator and Writer — A470

1977, Apr. 12 Engr. ***Perf. 14x13½***

1054 A470 6s dk violet blue 1.10 .55

Great Spire, St. Stephen's Cathedral A471

Designs: 3s, Heathen Tower and Frederick's Gable. 4s, Interior view with Albertinian Choir.

1977, Apr. 22 Engr. ***Perf. 13½***

1055 A471 2.50s dark brown .55 .30

1056 A471 3s dark blue .65 .40

1057 A471 4s rose lake .80 .55

Nos. 1055-1057 (3) 2.00 1.25

Restoration and re-opening of St. Stephen's Cathedral, Vienna, 25th anniversary.

Fritz Hermanovsky-Orlando (1877-1954), Poet and Artist — A472

Photo. & Engr.

1977, Apr. 29 ***Perf. 13½x14***

1058 A472 6s Prus green & gold .90 .55

Intl. Atomic Energy Agency (IAEA), 20th Anniv. — A473

1977, May 2 Photo. ***Perf. 14***

1059 A473 3s IAEA Emblem .55 .25

Schwanenstadt, 350th Anniv. — A474

1977, June 10 Photo. ***Perf. 14x13½***

1060 A474 3s Town arms .55 .25

Europa Issue

Attersee, Upper Austria — A475

1977, June 10 Engr. ***Perf. 14***

1061 A475 6s olive green 1.20 .55

Globe, by Vincenzo Coronelli, 1688 — A476

Photo. & Engr.

1977, June 29 ***Perf. 14***

1062 A476 3s black & buff .55 .25

5th Intl. Symposium of the Coronelli World Fed. of Friends of the Globe, Austria, June 29-July 3.

Kayak Race A477

1977, July 15 Photo. ***Perf. 13½x14***

1063 A477 4s multicolored .55 .25

3rd Kayak Slalom White Water Race on Lieser River, Spittal.

The Good Samaritan, by Francesco Bassano A478

1977, Sept. 16 Photo. & Engr.

1064 A478 1.50s brown & red .25 .25

Workers' Good Samaritan Org., 50th anniv.

Papermakers' Coat of Arms — A479

1977, Oct. 10 ***Perf. 14x13½***

1065 A479 3s multicolored .55 .25

17th Conf. of the European Committee of Pulp and Paper Technology (EUCEPA), Vienna.

Man with Austrian Flag Lifting Barbed Wire — A480

1977, Nov. 3 ***Perf. 14***

1066 A480 2.50s slate & red .30 .25

Honoring the martyrs for Austria's freedom.

"Austria," First Steam Locomotive in Austria — A481

Designs: 2.50s, Steam locomotive 214. 3s, Electric locomotive 1044.

Photo. & Engr.

1977, Nov. 17 ***Perf. 13½***

1067 A481 1.50s multicolored .30 .25

1068 A481 2.50s multicolored .55 .25

1069 A481 3s multicolored .90 .25

Nos. 1067-1069 (3) 1.75 .75

140th anniversary of Austrian railroads.

Christmas — A482

Virgin and Child, wood statue, Mariastein, Tyrol.

1977, Nov. 25 ***Perf. 14x13½***

1070 A482 3s multicolored .55 .25

Modern Austrian Art — A483

The Danube Maiden, by Wolfgang Hutter.

1977, Dec. 2 ***Perf. 13½x14***

1071 A483 6s multicolored 1.10 .55

Egon Friedell (1878-1938), Writer and Historian A484

1978, Jan. 23 **Photo. & Engr.**
1072 A484 3s lt blue & blk .55 .25

Subway Train A485

1978, Feb. 24 **Photo.** ***Perf. 13½x14***
1073 A485 3s multicolored .75 .25

New Vienna subway system.

Biathlon Competition A486

1978, Feb. 28 **Photo. & Engr.**
1074 A486 4s multicolored .60 .25

Biathlon World Championships, Hochfilzen, Tyrol, Feb. 28-Mar. 5.

Leopold Kunschak (1871-1953), Political Leader — A487

1978, Mar. 13 **Engr.** ***Perf. 14x13½***
1075 A487 3s violet blue .55 .25

Coyote, Aztec Feather Shield A488

1978, Mar. 13 **Photo.** ***Perf. 13½x14***
1076 A488 3s multicolored .55 .25

Ethnographical Museum, 50th anniv. exhibition.

Alpine Farm, Woodcut by Suitbert Lobisser — A489

1978, Mar. 23 **Engr.** ***Perf. 13½***
1077 A489 3s dark brown, *buff* .55 .25

Lobisser (1878-1943), graphic artist.

Capercaillie, Hunting Bag, 1730, and Rifle, 1655 — A490

Photo. & Engr.

1978, Apr. 28 ***Perf. 13½***
1078 A490 6s multicolored .90 .60

Intl. Hunting Exhibition, Marchegg.

Europa Issue

Riegersburg, Styria — A491

1978, May 3 **Engr.**
1079 A491 6s deep rose lilac *1.60 .55*

Parliament, Vienna, and Map of Europe — A492

1978, May 3 **Photo.** ***Perf. 14x13½***
1080 A492 4s multicolored .75 .45

3rd Interparliamentary Conference for European Cooperation and Security, Vienna.

Admont Pietà, c. 1410 — A493

1978, May 26 **Photo. & Engr.**
1081 A493 2.50s ocher & black .55 .25

Gothic Art in Styria Exhibition, St. Lambrecht, 1978.

Ort Castle, Gmunden — A494

1978, June 9
1082 A494 3s multicolored .55 .25

700th anniversary of Gmunden City.

Child with Flowers and Fruit — A495

Photo. & Engr.

1978, June 30 ***Perf. 14x13½***
1083 A495 6s gold & multi 1.10 .55

25 years of Social Tourism.

Lehar and his Home, Bad Ischl — A496

1978, July 14 **Engr.** ***Perf. 14x13½***
1084 A496 6s slate 1.10 .55

International Lehar Congress, Bad Ischl. Franz Lehar (1870-1948), operetta composer.

Congress Emblem A497

1978, Aug. 21 **Photo.** ***Perf. 13½x14***
1085 A497 1.50s black, red & yel .25 .25

Cong. of Intl. Fed. of Building Construction and Wood Workers, Vienna, Aug. 20-24.

Ottokar of Bohemia and Rudolf of Hapsburg A498

1978, Aug. 25 **Photo. & Engr.**
1086 A498 3s multicolored .55 .25

Battle of Durnkrut and Jedenspeigen (Marchfeld), which established Hapsburg rule in Austria, 700th anniversary.

First Documentary Reference to Villach, "ad pontem uillah" — A499

1978, Sept. 8 **Litho.** ***Perf. 13½x14***
1087 A499 3s multicolored .55 .25

1100th anniversary of Villach, Carinthia.

Seal of Graz, 1440 — A500

Photo. & Engr.

1978, Sept. 13 ***Perf. 14x13½***
1088 A500 4s multicolored .75 .45

850th anniversary of Graz.

Emperor Maximilian Fishing — A501

1978, Sept. 15 ***Perf. 14x13½***
1089 A501 4s multicolored .60 .25

World Fishing Championships, Vienna, Sept. 1978.

"Aid to the Handicapped" — A502

1978, Oct. 2 **Photo.** ***Perf. 13½x14***
1090 A502 6s orange brn & blk .90 .55

Symbolic Column — A503

1978, Oct. 9 **Photo.** ***Perf. 13½***
1091 A503 2.50s orange, blk & gray .30 .25

9th Intl. Congress of Concrete and Prefabrication Industries, Vienna, Oct. 8-13.

Grace, by Albin Egger-Lienz A504

1978, Oct. 27 ***Perf. 13½x14***
1092 A504 6s multicolored 1.10 .55

European Family Congress, Vienna, Oct. 26-29.

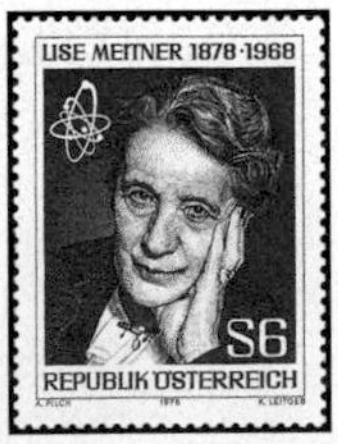

Lise Meitner (1878-1968), Physicist, and Atom Symbol — A505

1978, Nov. 7 **Engr.** ***Perf. 14x13½***
1093 A505 6s dark violet .90 .55

Viktor Adler, by Anton Hanak A506

Photo. & Engr.

1978, Nov. 10 ***Perf. 13½x14***
1094 A506 3s vermilion & black .55 .25

Viktor Adler (1852-1918), leader of Social Democratic Party, 60th death anniversary.

Franz Schubert, by Josef Kriehuber A507

1978, Nov. 17 **Engr.** ***Perf. 14***
1095 A507 6s reddish brown 1.25 .55

Franz Schubert (1797-1828), composer.

Virgin and Child, Wilhering Church — A508

Photo. & Engr.

1978, Dec. 1 ***Perf. 12½x13½***
1096 A508 3s multicolored .55 .25

Christmas.

Archduke Johann Shelter, Grossglockner — A509

1978, Dec. 6 ***Perf. 13½x14***
1097 A509 1.50s gold & dk vio bl .25 .25

Austrian Alpine Club, centenary.

Modern Austrian Art — A510

Adam, by Rudolf Hausner.

1978, Dec. 6 **Photo.** ***Perf. 13½x14***
1098 A510 6s multicolored 1.10 .55

Universal Declaration of Human Rights, 30th Anniv. — A511

1978, Dec. 6 ***Perf. 14x13½***
1099 A511 6s Bound Hands .90 .55

Type of 1973

Designs: 20g, Freistadt, Upper Austria. 3s, Bishofsmutze, Salzburg. 4.20s, Hirschegg, Kleinwalsertal. 5.50s, Peace Chapel, Stoderzinken. 5.60s, Riezlern, Kleinwalsertal. 9s, Asten Carinthia. 12s, Kufstein Fortress. 14s, Weiszsee, Salzburg.

Photo. & Engr.

1978-83 ***Perf. 13½x14***

Size: 23x29mm

1100 A395 20g vio bl & dk bl .50 .25

Size: 17x21mm

1102 A395 3s lt ultra & vio bl .55 .25

Size: 23x29mm

1104 A395 4.20s blk & grysh bl .95 .40
1105 A395 5.50s lilac & pur 1.50 .50
1106 A395 5.60s yel grn & ol grn 1.50 .70
1107 A395 9s rose & car 2.10 .40
1108 A395 12s ocher & vio brn 2.40 .35
1109 A395 14s lt green & green 3.25 .25
Nos. 1100-1109 (8) 12.75 3.10

Issued: 3s, 12/7/78; 4.20s, 6/22/79; 20g, 6/27/80; 12s, 10/3/80; 14s, 1/27/82; 5.50s, 5.60s, 7/1/82; 9s, 2/9/83.

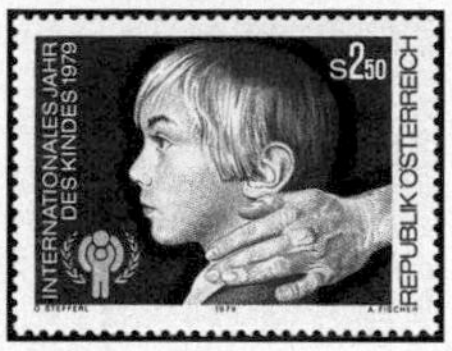

Child and IYC Emblem A512

Photo. & Engr.

1979, Jan. 16 ***Perf. 14***
1110 A512 2.50s multicolored .35 .25

International Year of the Child.

CCIR Emblem A513

1979, Jan. 16 **Photo.** ***Perf. 13½x14***
1111 A513 6s multicolored .80 .60

Intl. Radio Consultative Committee (CCIR) of the ITU, 50th anniv.

Air Rifle, Air Pistol and Club Emblem A514

Photo. & Engr.

1979, Mar. 7 ***Perf. 13½***
1112 A514 6s multicolored .95 .55

Austrian Shooting Club, cent., and European Air Rifle and Air Pistol Championships, Graz.

Figure Skater — A515

1979, Mar. 7 **Photo.** ***Perf. 14x13½***
1113 A515 4s multicolored .75 .40

World Ice Skating Championships, Vienna.

Steamer Franz I A516

Designs: 2.50s, Tugboat Linz. 3s, Passenger ship Theodor Körner.

1979, Mar. 13 **Engr.** ***Perf. 13½***
1114 A516 1.50s violet blue .35 .25
1115 A516 2.50s sepia .50 .35
1116 A516 3s magenta .80 .25
Nos. 1114-1116 (3) 1.65 .85

1st Danube Steamship Company, 150th anniv.

Fashion Design, by Theo Zasche, 1900 — A517

Photo. & Engr.

1979, Mar. 26 ***Perf. 13x13½***
1117 A517 2.50s multicolored .50 .25

50th Intl. Fashion Week, Vienna.

Wiener Neustadt Cathedral, 700th Anniv. — A518

1979, Mar. 27 **Engr.** ***Perf. 13½***
1118 A518 4s violet blue .65 .40

Teacher and Pupils, by Franz A. Zauner — A519

Photo. & Engr.

1979, Mar. 30 ***Perf. 14x13½***
1119 A519 2.50s multicolored .50 .25

Education of the deaf in Austria, 200th anniv.

Population Chart and Baroque Angel — A520

1979, Apr. 6
1120 A520 2.50s multicolored .50 .25

Austrian Central Statistical Bureau, 150th anniv.

Europa Issue

Laurenz Koschier — A521

1979, May 4
1121 A521 6s ocher & purple *1.20 .55*

Diesel Motor — A522

1979, May 4 **Photo.**
1122 A522 4s multicolored .75 .40

13th CIMAC Congress (Intl. Org. for Internal Combustion Machines).

Arms of Ried, Schärding and Braunau — A523

Photo. & Engr.

1979, June 1 ***Perf. 14x13½***
1123 A523 3s multicolored .55 .25

200th anniversary of Innviertel District.

Stream and City — A524

1979, June 1 ***Perf. 13½x14***
1124 A524 2.50s multicolored .35 .25

Control and eliminate water pollution.

Arms of Rottenmann A525

Photo. & Engr.

1979, June 22 ***Perf. 14x13½***
1125 A525 3s multicolored .60 .25

700th anniversary of Rottenmann.

Jodok Fink (1853-1929), Governor of Vorarlberg A526

1979, June 29 **Engr.** ***Perf. 14***
1126 A526 3s brown carmine .55 .25

Arms of Wels, Returnees' Emblem, "Europa Sail" — A527

1979, July 6 Photo. ***Perf. 14x13½***
1127 A527 4s yellow grn & blk .75 .45

5th European Meeting of the Intl. Confederation of Former Prisoners of War, Wels, July 6-8.

Symbolic Flower, Conference Emblem — A528

1979, Aug. 20 Litho. ***Perf. 14x13½***
1128 A528 4s turq blue .75 .45

UN Conf. for Science and Technology, Vienna, Aug. 20-31.

Donaupark, UNIDO and IAEA Emblems A529

1979, Aug. 24 Engr. ***Perf. 13½x14***
1129 A529 6s grayish blue 1.10 .55

Opening of the Donaupark Intl. Center in Vienna, seat of the UN Industrial Development Org. (UNIDO) and the Intl. Atomic Energy Agency (IAEA).

Diseased Eye and Blood Vessels A530

1979, Sept. 10 Photo. ***Perf. 14***
1130 A530 2.50s multicolored .50 .25

10th World Congress of Intl. Diabetes Federation, Vienna, Sept. 9-14.

View of Stanz Valley through East Portal of Arlberg Tunnel A531

1979, Sept. 14 Photo. & Engr.
1131 A531 4s multicolored .75 .45

16th World Road Cong., Vienna, 9/16-21.

Steam Printing Press A532

Photo. & Engr.
1979, Sept. 18 ***Perf. 13½x14***
1132 A532 3s multicolored .50 .25

Austrian Government Printing Office, 175th anniv.

Richard Zsigmondy (1865-1929), Chemist — A533

1979, Sept. 21 Engr. ***Perf. 14x13½***
1133 A533 6s multicolored .90 .55

"Save Energy" A534

1979, Oct. 1 Photo. ***Perf. 14x13½***
1134 A534 2.50s multicolored .50 .25

Festival and Convention Center, Bregenz (Model) — A535

1979, Oct. 1 Engr. ***Perf. 14***
1135 A535 2.50s purple .50 .25

Lions International Emblem A536

1979, Oct. 11 Photo. & Engr.
1136 A536 4s multicolored .75 .45

25th Lions Europa Forum, Vienna, 10/11-13.

A537

Photo. & Engr.
1979, Oct. 19 ***Perf. 13½x14***
1137 A537 2.50s Wilhelm Exner .50 .25

Centenary of Technological Handicraft Museum, founded by Wilhelm Exner.

Modern Austrian Art — A538

The Compassionate Christ, by Hans Fronius.

1979, Oct. 23 Litho. ***Perf. 13½x14***
1138 A538 4s olive & ol blk .75 .45

Locomotive and Arms — A539

1979, Oct. 24 Photo. ***Perf. 13½x14***
1139 A539 2.50s multicolored .55 .25

Raab-Odenburg-Ebenfurt railroad, cent.

August Musger — A540

Photo. & Engr.
1979, Oct. 30 ***Perf. 14x13½***
1140 A540 2.50s bl gray & blk .50 .25

August Musger (1868-1929), developer of slow-motion film technique.

Nativity, St. Barbara's Church A541

1979, Nov. 30 ***Perf. 13½x14***
1141 A541 4s multicolored .75 .45

Christmas.

Arms of Baden — A542

1980, Jan. 25 ***Perf. 14***
1142 A542 4s multicolored .75 .45

Baden, 500th anniversary.

Fight Rheumatism A543

1980, Feb. 21 ***Perf. 13½***
1143 A543 2.50s red & aqua .50 .25

Austrian Exports — A544

1980, Feb. 21 Photo. ***Perf. 14x13½***
1144 A544 4s dark blue & red .50 .25

Austrian Red Cross Centenary A545

1980, Mar. 14 Photo. ***Perf. 13½x14***
1145 A545 2.50s multicolored .50 .25

Rudolph Kirchschlager A546

Photo. & Engr.
1980, Mar. 20 ***Perf. 14x13½***
1146 A546 4s sepia & red .75 .45

Robert Hamerling (1830-1889), Poet — A547

1980, Mar. 24 Engr. ***Perf. 13½x14***
1147 A547 2.50s olive green .40 .25

Seal of Hallein — A548

Photo. & Engr.
1980, Apr. 30 ***Perf. 14x13½***
1148 A548 4s red & black .65 .40

Hallein; 750th anniversary.

Empress Maria Theresa (1717-80) A549

Paintings by: 2.50s, Andreas Moller. 4s, Martin van Meytens. 6s, Josef Ducreux.

1980, May 13 Engr. ***Perf. 13½***
1149 A549 2.50s violet brown .65 .25
1150 A549 4s dark blue .90 .40
1151 A549 6s rose lake 1.50 .80
Nos. 1149-1151 (3) 3.05 1.45

Flags of Austria and Four Powers A550

1980, May 14 Photo. ***Perf. 13½x14***
1152 A550 4s multicolored .55 .25

State Treaty, 25th anniversary.

St. Benedict, by Meinrad Guggenbichler A551

1980, May 16 Engr. *Perf. 14½*
1153 A551 2.50s olive green .45 .25

Congress of Benedictine Order of Austria.

Hygeia by Gustav Klimt — A552

1980, May 20 Photo. *Perf. 14*
1154 A552 4s multicolored .65 .40

Academic teaching of hygiene, 175th anniv.

Aflenz Ground Satellite Receiving Station Inauguration A553

1980, May 30 Photo. *Perf. 14*
1155 A553 6s multicolored .90 .55

Steyr, Etching, 1693 A554

Photo. & Engr.

1980, June 4 *Perf. 13½*
1156 A554 4s multicolored .65 .40

Millennium of Steyr.

Worker, Oil Drill Head — A555

1980, June 12
1157 A555 2.50s multicolored .25 .25

Austrian oil production, 25th anniversary.

Seal of Innsbruck, 1267 A556

1980, June 23 *Perf. 13½x14½*
1158 A556 2.50s multicolored .25 .25

Innsbruck, 800th anniversary.

Duchy of Styria, 800th Anniv. — A557

Perf. 14½x13½

1980, June 23 Photo.
1159 A557 4s Duke's hat .65 .40

Leo Ascher (1880-1942), Composer A558

1980, Aug. 18 Engr. *Perf. 14*
1160 A558 3s dark purple .40 .25

Bible Illustration, Book of Genesis — A559

1980, Aug. 25 *Perf. 13½*
1161 A559 4s multicolored .40 .25

10th Intl. Cong. of the Org. for Old Testament Studies.

Europa Issue

Robert Stolz (1880-1975), Composer A560

1980, Aug. 25 Engr. *Perf. 14x13½*
1162 A560 6s red brown 1.00 .50

Old and Modern Bridges A561

1980, Sept. 1 Photo. *Perf. 13½*
1163 A561 4s multicolored .65 .40

11th Congress of the Intl. Assoc. for Bridge and Structural Engineering, Vienna.

Moon Figure, by Karl Brandstätter A562

Photo. & Engr.

1980, Oct. 10 *Perf. 14x13½*
1164 A562 4s multicolored .65 .40

Customs Service, Sesquicentennial A563

1980, Oct. 13 Photo.
1165 A563 2.50s multicolored .40 .25

Gazette Masthead, 1810 A564

1980, Oct. 23 Photo. *Perf. 13½*
1166 A564 2.50s multicolored .40 .25

Official Gazette of Linz, 350th anniversary.

Waidhofen Town Book Title Page, 14th Century — A565

Photo. & Engr.

1980, Oct. 24 *Perf. 14*
1167 A565 2.50s multicolored .40 .25

Waidhofen on Thaya, 750th anniversary.

Federal Austrian Army, 25th Anniversary A566

1980, Oct. 24 Photo. *Perf. 13½x14*
1168 A566 2.50s grnsh black & red .40 .25

Alfred Wegener A567

1980, Oct. 31 Engr.
1169 A567 4s violet blue .50 .25

Alfred Wegener (1880-1930), scientist, formulated theory of continental drift.

Robert Musil (1880-1942), Writer — A568

1980, Nov. 6 *Perf. 14x13½*
1170 A568 4s dark red brown .65 .40

Christmas — A569

Nativity, stained glass window, Klagenfurt.

Photo. & Engr.

1980, Nov. 28 *Perf. 13½*
1171 A569 4s multicolored .65 .40

25th Anniversary of Social Security A570

1981, Jan. 19 Litho. *Perf. 13½x14*
1172 A570 2.50s multicolored .25 .25

Niebelungen Saga, 1926, by Dachauer — A571

1981, Apr. 6 Engr. *Perf. 14x13½*
1173 A571 3s sepia .40 .25

Wilhelm Dachauer (1881-1951), artist and engraver.

Machinist in Wheelchair A572

1981, Apr. 6 Photo. & Engr.
1174 A572 6s multicolored .80 .55

Rehabilitation Intl., 3rd European Regional Conf.

Sigmund Freud (1856-1939), Psychoanalyst A573

1981, May 6 Engr.
1175 A573 3s rose violet .25 .25

Heating Engineers Union Congress, Vienna — A574

1981, May 11 Photo.
1176 A574 4s multicolored .55 .40

Kuenringer Exhibition, Zwettl Monastery
A575

Azzo (founder of House of Kuenringer) and his followers, bear-skin manuscript.

1981, May 15 **Photo. & Engr.**
1177 A575 3s multicolored .40 .25

Europa — A576

1981, May 22 **Photo.**
1178 A576 6s Maypole 1.00 .50

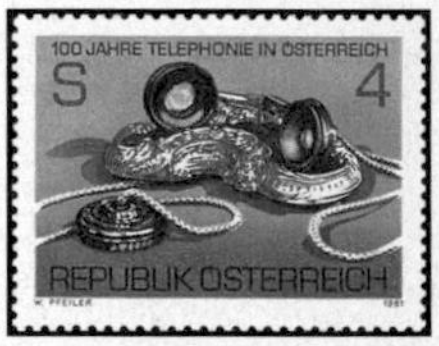

Telephone Service Centenary
A577

Photo. and Engr.

1981 May 29 ***Perf. 13½x14***
1179 A577 4s multicolored .55 .40

Seibersdorf Research Center, 25th Anniv. — A578

1981, June 29 **Photo.** ***Perf. 13½***
1180 A578 4s multicolored .55 .25

The Frog King (Child's Drawing)
A579

1981, June 29 ***Perf. 13½x14***
1181 A579 3s multicolored .40 .25

Town Hall and Town Seal of 1250
A580

Photo. & Engr.

1981, July 17 ***Perf. 13½x14***
1182 A580 4s multicolored .55 .40

St. Veit an der Glan, 800th anniv.

Johann Florian Heller (1813-1871), Pioneer of Urinalysis — A581

1981, Aug. 31 ***Perf. 14x13½***
1183 A581 6s red brown .80 .55

11th Intl. Clinical Chemistry Congress.

Ludwig Boltzmann (1844-1906), Physicist — A582

1981, Sept. 4 **Engr.** ***Perf. 14x13½***
1184 A582 3s dark green .25 .25

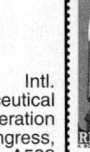

Intl. Pharmaceutical Federation World Congress, Vienna — A583

Photo. & Engr.

1981, Sept. 7 ***Perf. 14***
1185 A583 6s Scale .80 .55

Otto Bauer, Politician, Birth Centenary
A584

1981, Sept. 7 **Photo.** ***Perf. 14x13½***
1186 A584 4s multicolored .55 .40

Escher's Impossible Cube — A585

1981, Sept. 14
1187 A585 4s dk blue & brt blue .55 .40

10th Intl. Mathematicians' Cong., Innsbruck.

Kneeling Virgin, Detail of Coronation of Mary Altarpiece, St. Wolfgang, 500th Anniv. — A586

1981, Sept. 25 **Engr.** ***Perf. 14x13½***
1188 A586 3s dark blue .40 .25

South-East Fair, Graz, 75th Anniv.
A587

1981, Sept. 25 **Photo.** ***Perf. 13½x14***
1189 A587 4s multicolored .55 .25

Holy Trinity, 12th Cent. Byzantine Miniature
A588

1981, Oct. 5
1190 A588 6s multicolored .80 .55

16th Intl. Byzantine Congress.

Hans Kelsen (1881-1973), Co-author of Federal Constitution
A589

1981, Oct. 9 **Engr.**
1191 A589 3s dark carmine .40 .25

Edict of Tolerance Bicen. — A590

Photo. & Engr.

1981, Oct. 9 ***Perf. 14***
1192 A590 4s Joseph II .55 .40

World Food Day
A591

1981, Oct. 16 **Photo.** ***Perf. 13½***
1193 A591 6s multicolored .80 .55

Between the Times, by Oscar Asboth
A592

1981, Oct. 22 **Litho.** ***Perf. 13½x14***
1194 A592 4s multicolored .55 .25

Intl. Catholic Workers' Day — A593

Photo. & Engr.

1981, Oct. 23 ***Perf. 14x13½***
1195 A593 3s multicolored .40 .25

Baron Josef Hammer-Purgstall, Founder of Oriental Studies, 125th Death Anniv. — A594

Photo. & Engr.

1981, Nov. 23 ***Perf. 14***
1196 A594 3s multicolored .40 .25

Julius Raab (1891-1964), Politician
A595

1981, Nov. 27 **Engr.** ***Perf. 13½***
1197 A595 6s rose lake .75 .55

Nativity, Corn Straw Figures
A596

1981, Nov. 27 **Photo. & Engr.**
1198 A596 4s multicolored .50 .25

Christmas.

Stefan Zweig (1881-1942), Writer — A597

1981, Nov. 27 **Engr.** ***Perf. 14x13½***
1199 A597 4s dull violet .50 .40

800th Anniv. of St. Nikola on the Danube
A598

1981, Dec. 4 **Photo. & Engr.**
1200 A598 4s multicolored .50 .40

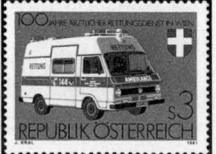

Vienna Emergency Medical Service Centenary
A599

1981, Dec. 9 **Photo.** ***Perf. 13½x14***
1201 A599 3s multicolored .25 .25

Schladming-Haus Alpine World Skiing Championship — A600

1982, Jan. 27 ***Perf. 14***
1202 A600 4s multicolored .50 .25

Dorotheum (State Auction Gallery), 275th Anniv. — A601

Photo. & Engr.

1982, Mar. 12 ***Perf. 14***
1203 A601 4s multicolored .50 .25

Water Rescue Service, 25th Anniv. — A602

1982, Mar. 19 Photo. ***Perf. 14x13½***
1204 A602 5s multicolored .55 .40

St. Severin and the End of the Roman Era Exhibition — A603

Photo. & Engr.

1982, Apr. 23 ***Perf. 14x13½***
1205 A603 3s St. Severin .50 .25

Intl. Kneipp Hydropathy Congress, Vienna — A604

1982, May 4 ***Perf. 14***
1206 A604 4s multicolored .50 .40

Printing in Austria, 500th Anniv. — A605

1982, May 7
1207 A605 4s Printers' guild arms .50 .25

5th European Urology Soc. Cong., Vienna — A606

Design: Urine analysis, Canone di Avicenna manuscript.

1982, May 12 **Photo.**
1208 A606 6s multicolored .75 .55

St. Francis of Assisi, 800th Birth Anniv. — A607

1982, May 14 **Photo. & Engr.**
1209 A607 3s multicolored .50 .25

Haydn and His Time Exhibition, Rohrau — A608

1982, May 19 Engr. ***Perf. 13½***
1210 A608 3s olive green .50 .25

25th World Milk Day — A609

1982, May 25 Photo. ***Perf. 14x13½***
1211 A609 7s multicolored .95 .65

800th Anniv of Gfohl (Market Town) — A610

Photo. & Engr.

1982, May 28 ***Perf. 14***
1212 A610 4s multicolored .50 .40

Tennis Player and Austrian Tennis Federation Emblem — A611

1982, June 11
1213 A611 3s multicolored .40 .25

900th Anniv. of City of Langenlois A612

Photo. & Engr.

1982, June 11 ***Perf. 13½x14***
1214 A612 4s multicolored .50 .35

800th Anniv. of City of Weiz — A613

1982, June 18 Photo. ***Perf. 14x13½***
1215 A613 4s Arms 1.10 .25

Ignaz Seipel (1876-1932), Statesman A614

1982, July 30 Engr. ***Perf. 14x13½***
1216 A614 3s brown violet .25 .25

Europa Issue

Sesquicentennial of Linz-Freistadt-Budweis Horse-drawn Railroad — A615

1982, July 30 ***Perf. 13½***
1217 A615 6s brown *1.60 .55*

Mail Bus Service, 75th Anniv. — A616

1982, Aug. 6 Photo. ***Perf. 14x13½***
1218 A616 4s multicolored .50 .40

Rocket Lift-off — A617

1982, Aug. 9 ***Perf. 14***
1219 A617 4s multicolored .50 .40

2nd UN Conference on Peaceful Uses of Outer Space, Vienna, Aug. 9-21.

Geodesists' Day — A618

Photo. & Engr.

1982, Sept. 1 ***Perf. 13½x14***
1220 A618 3s Tower, Office of Standards .40 .25

Protection of Endangered Species — A619

1982, Sept. 9 ***Perf. 14***
1221 A619 3s Bustard .40 .40
1222 A619 4s Beaver .55 .55
1223 A619 6s Capercaillie .80 .80
Nos. 1221-1223 (3) 1.75 1.75

10th Anniv. of Intl. Institute for Applied Systems Analysis, Vienna A620

1982, Oct. 4 **Photo.**
1224 A620 3s Laxenburg Castle .50 .25

St. Apollonia (Patron Saint of Dentists) A621

1982, Oct. 11 **Photo. & Engr.**
1225 A621 4s multicolored .50 .25

70th Annual World Congress of Dentists.

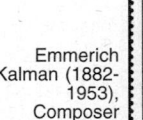

Emmerich Kalman (1882-1953), Composer A622

1982, Oct. 22 Engr. ***Perf. 13½***
1226 A622 3s dark blue .40 .25

Max Mell (1882-1971), Poet — A623

1982, Nov. 10 Photo. ***Perf. 14x13½***
1227 A623 3s multicolored .40 .25

Christmas
A624

Design: Christmas crib, Damuls Church, Vorarlberg, 1630.

Photo. & Engr.

1982, Nov. 25 *Perf. 13½*
1228 A624 4s multicolored .50 .40

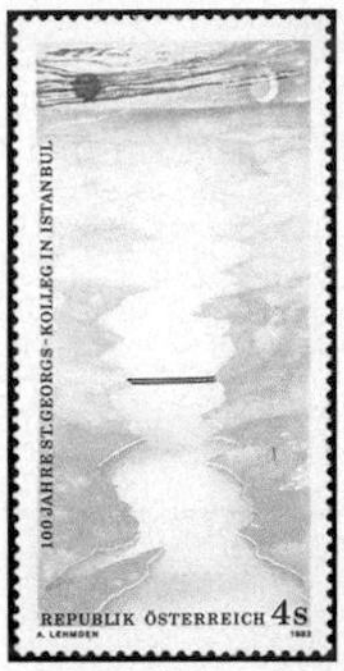

Centenary of St. George's College, Istanbul — A625

1982, Nov. 26 **Litho.** *Perf. 14*
1229 A625 4s Bosporus .50 .40

Portrait of a Girl, by Ernst Fuchs — A626

1982, Dec. 10 **Photo. & Engr.**
1230 A626 4s multicolored .50 .40

Postal Savings Bank Centenary
A627

Photo. & Engr.

1983, Jan. 12 *Perf. 14*
1231 A627 4s Bank .50 .40

Hildegard Burjan (1883-1933), Founder of Caritas Socialis
A628

1983, Jan. 28 **Engr.**
1232 A628 4s rose lake .50 .40

World Communications Year — A629

1983, Feb. 18 **Photo.** *Perf. 13½x14*
1233 A629 7s multicolored .90 .55

75th Anniv. Children's Friends Org. — A630

Photo. & Engr.

1983, Feb. 23 *Perf. 14x13½*
1234 A630 4s multicolored .50 .40

Josef Matthias Hauer (1883-1959), Composer
A631

1983, Mar. 18 **Engr.** *Perf. 14*
1235 A631 3s deep lilac rose .25 .25

25th Anniv. of Austrian Airlines
A632

1983, Mar. 31 **Photo.** *Perf. 13½x14*
1236 A632 6s multicolored .75 .55

Work Inspection Centenary
A633

1983, Apr. 8 **Photo.** *Perf. 13½*
1237 A633 4s multicolored .50 .40

Upper Austria Millennium Provincial Exhibition — A634

3s, Wels Castle, by Matthaus Merian.

1983, Apr. 28 **Photo.** *Perf. 13½*
1238 A634 3s multicolored .25 .25

Gottweig Monastery, 900th Anniv. — A635

Photo. & Engr.

1983, Apr. 29 *Perf. 13½*
1239 A635 3s multicolored .40 .25

7th World Pacemakers Symposium
A636

1983, Apr. 29 **Photo.** *Perf. 14x13½*
1240 A636 4s multicolored .50 .25

Catholic Students' Org.
A637

1983, May 20 **Photo.** *Perf. 14*
1241 A637 4s multicolored .50 .25

Weitra, 800th Anniv.
A638

Photo. & Engr.

1983, May 20 *Perf. 13½*
1242 A638 4s multicolored .50 .40

Granting of Town Rights to Hohenems, 650th Anniv. — A639

1983, May 27 **Photo.** *Perf. 14*
1243 A639 4s multicolored .50 .40

25th Anniv. of Stadthall, Vienna
A640

1983, June 24 **Photo.** *Perf. 14*
1244 A640 4s multicolored .50 .40

Viktor Franz Hess (1883-1964), 1936 Nobel Prize Winner in Physics — A641

1983, June 24 **Engr.** *Perf. 14x13½*
1245 A641 6s dark green 1.20 .55

Europa.

Kiwanis Intl. Convention, Vienna — A642

1983, July 1 **Photo.** *Perf. 13½*
1246 A642 5s multicolored .50 .40

7th World Congress of Psychiatry, Vienna — A643

4s, Emblem, St. Stephen's Cathedral.

1983, July 11 **Photo.** *Perf. 14*
1247 A643 4s multicolored .50 .25

Baron Carl von Hasenauer (1833-1894), Architect
A644

3s, Natural History Museum, Vienna.

1983, July 20 **Engr.** *Perf. 13½x14*
1248 A644 3s chocolate .25 .25

27th Intl. Chamber of Commerce Professional Competition, Linz — A645

1983, Aug. 16 **Photo.**
1249 A645 4s Chamber building .55 .40

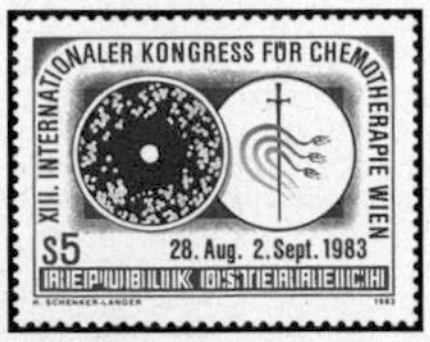

13th Intl. Chemotherapy Congress, Vienna, Aug. 28-Sept. 2 — A646

5s, Penicillin test on cancer.

1983, Aug. 26
1250 A646 5s multicolored .55 .50

Catholics' Day — A647

1983, Sept. 9 Photo. ***Perf. 14x13½***
1251 A647 3s multicolored .25 .25

Visit of Pope John Paul II — A648

Photo. & Engr.
1983, Sept. 9 ***Perf. 13½***
1252 A648 6s multicolored .85 .55

Souvenir Sheet

Battle of 1683 to Relieve Vienna, by Frans Geffel — A649

1983, Sept. 9 ***Perf. 14***
1253 A649 6s multicolored .95 1.20

300th anniv. of Vienna's relief from Turkish siege.

Vienna Rathaus Centenary A650

1983, Sept. 23 ***Perf. 13½x14***
1254 A650 4s multicolored .55 .25

Karl von Terzaghi (1883-1963), Founder of Soil Mechanics A651

1983, Oct. 3 **Engr.**
1255 A651 3s dark blue .40 .25

10th Trade Unions Federal Congress, Oct. 3-8 A652

1983, Oct. 3 Photo. ***Perf. 13½***
1256 A652 3s black & red .40 .25

Evening Sun in Burgenland, by Gottfried Kumpf — A653

Photo. & Engr.
1983, Oct. 7 ***Perf. 13½x14***
1257 A653 4s multicolored .50 .25

Modling-Hinterbruhl Electric Railroad Centenary — A654

1983, Oct. 21 **Photo.**
1258 A654 3s multicolored .50 .25

Provincial Museum of Upper Austria Sesquicentennial — A655

4s, Francisco-Carolinum Museum.

1983, Nov. 4 **Photo. & Engr.**
1259 A655 4s multicolored .55 .25

Creche, St. Andreas Parish Church, Kitzbuhel A656

1983, Nov. 25 ***Perf. 14***
1260 A656 4s multicolored .50 .40

Christmas.

Parliament Bldg. Vienna, 100th Anniv. — A657

1983, Dec. 2 **Engr.**
1261 A657 4s slate blue .55 .25

Altar Picture, St. Nikola/Pram Church — A658

1983, Dec. 6 Photo. ***Perf. 14x13½***
1262 A658 3s multicolored .40 .25

Wolfgang Pauli (1900-58), Physicist, Nobel Laureate — A659

1983, Dec. 15 Engr. ***Perf. 14½x13½***
1263 A659 6s dark red brn .80 .55

Gregor Mendel (1822-1884), Genetics Founder — A660

Photo. & Engr.
1984, Jan. 5 ***Perf. 13½***
1264 A660 4s multicolored .50 .40

Anton Hanak (1875-1934), Sculptor — A661

1984, Jan. 5
1265 A661 3s red brown & blk .25 .25

50th Anniv. of 1934 Uprising — A662

4.50s, Memorial, Woellersdorf.

1984, Feb. 10 Photo. ***Perf. 14***
1266 A662 4.50s black & red .55 .25

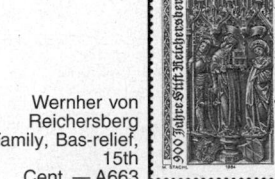

Wernher von Reichersberg Family, Bas-relief, 15th Cent. — A663

Photo. & Engr.
1984, Apr. 25 ***Perf. 14x13½***
1267 A663 3.50s brown & blue .25 .25

900th anniv. of Reichersberg Monastery.

Tobacco Monopoly Bicentenary A665

4.50s, Cigar wrapper, tobacco plant.

1984, May 4 ***Perf. 13½***
1269 A665 4.50s multicolored .55 .40

1200th Anniv. of Kostendorf Municipality A666

1984, May 4
1270 A666 4.50s View, arms .55 .40

Automobile Engineers World Congress A667

5s, Wheel bearing cross-section.

1984, May 4 Photo. ***Perf. 13½x14***
1271 A667 5s multicolored .65 .40

Europa (1959-1984) A668

1984, May 4 ***Perf. 13½***
1272 A668 6s multicolored 1.40 .50

Archduke Johann (1782-1859), by S. von Carolsfeld A669

Photo. & Engr.
1984, May 11 ***Perf. 14***
1273 A669 4.50s multicolored .55 .25

Ore and Iron Provincial Exhibition A670

1984, May 11 ***Perf. 13½***
1274 A670 3.50s Aragonite .50 .25

Era of Emperor Francis Joseph Exhibition A671

Design: Cover of Viribus Unitis, publ. by Max Herzig, 1898.

1984, May 18
1275 A671 3.50s red & gold .50 .25

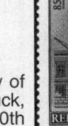

City of Vocklabruck, 850th Anniv. — A672

Photo. & Engr.

1984, May 30 ***Perf. 14x13½***
1276 A672 4.50s Tower, arms .55 .40

Museum of Carinthia, Cent. — A673

Dionysius, Virinum mosaic.

1984, June 1 ***Perf. 13½***
1277 A673 3.50s multicolored .40 .25

Erosion Prevention Systems Centenary A674

4.50s, Stone reinforcement wall.

1984, June 5 **Engr.** ***Perf. 14***
1278 A674 4.50s grnish black .55 .25

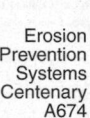

Tyrol Provincial Celebration, 1809-1984 A675

Art Exhibition: Meeting of Imperial Troops with South Tyrolean Reserves under Andreas Hofer near Sterzing in April 1809, by Ludwig Schnorr von Carolsfeld, 1830.

Photo. & Engr.

1984, June 5 ***Perf. 14x13½***
1279 A675 3.50s multicolored .25 .25

Ralph Benatzky (1884-1957), Composer A676

1984, June 5 **Engr.**
1280 A676 4s violet brown .50 .40

Christian von Ehrenfels (1859-1932), Philosopher A677

1984, June 22 **Photo.** ***Perf. 14***
1281 A677 3.50s multicolored .25 .25

25th Anniv. of Minimundus (Model City) A678

4s, Eiffel Tower, Tower of Pisa, ferris wheel.

1984, June 22 ***Perf. 13½x14***
1282 A678 4s multicolored .50 .40

Blockheide Eibenstein Nature Park A679

1984 **Photo. & Engr.**
1283 A679 4s shown .50 .40
1284 A679 4s Lake Neusiedl .50 .40

Issued: No. 1283, June 29; No. 1284, Aug. 13.

See Nos. 1349-1354, 1492-1499, 1744, 1777, 1813, 1843.

Monasteries and Abbeys — A679a

Designs: 3.50s, Geras Monastery, Lower Austria. 4s, Stams. 4.50s, Schlagl. 5s, Benedictine Abbey of St. Paul, Levanttal. 6s, Rein-Hohenfurth.

1984-85			***Perf. 14***	
1285	A679a	3.50s multi	.80	.25
1286	A679a	4s multi	.80	.25
1287	A679a	4.50s multi	.80	.25
1288	A679a	5s multi	.80	.25
1288A	A679a	6s multi	1.10	.25
		Nos. 1285-1288A (5)	4.30	1.25

Issued: 3.50s, 4/27/84; 4s, 9/28/84; 4.50s, 5/18/84; 5s, 9/27/85; 6s, 10/4/84.

See Nos. 1361-1365, 1465-1472.

Schanatobel Railroad Bridge — A680

Railroad Anniversaries: 3.50s, Arlberg centenary. 4.50s, Falkenstein Bridge, Tauern, 75th.

1984, July 6 ***Perf. 14***
1289 A680 3.50s shown .65 .40
1290 A680 4.50s multicolored .80 .50

Balloon Flight in Austria Bicent. — A681

6s, Johan Stuwer's balloon.

1984, July 6 **Photo.**
1291 A681 6s multicolored .75 .55

Intl. Lawyers' Congress, Vienna — A682

7s, Vienna Palace of Justice, emblem.

1984, Aug. 31 **Photo. & Engr.**
1292 A682 7s multicolored .95 .75

7th European Anatomy Congress, Innsbruck — A683

6s, Josef Hyrtl, anatomist.

1984, Sept. 3 **Photo.**
1293 A683 6s multicolored .80 .50

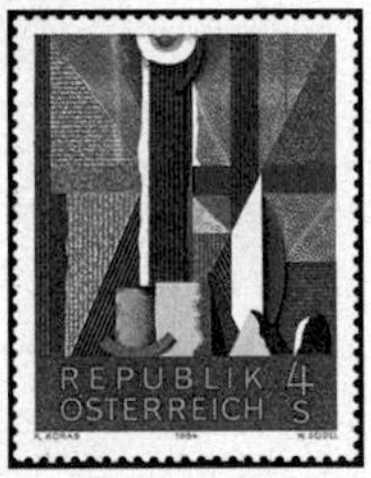

Window, by Karl Korab — A684

1984, Oct. 12
1294 A684 4s multicolored .50 .25

Johannes of Gmunden, Mathematician, 600th Birth Anniv. — A685

3.50s, Clock (Immset Uhr), 1555.

1984, Oct. 18
1295 A685 3.50s multicolored .40 .25

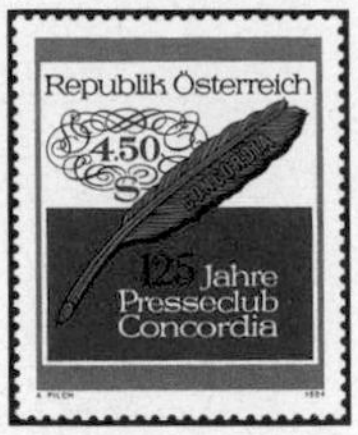

Concordia Press Club, 125th Anniv. — A686

1984, Nov. 9 **Photo.** ***Perf. 13½***
1296 A686 4.50s Quill .55 .25

Fanny Eissler, Dancer, Death Centenary — A687

1984, Nov. 23 **Photo. & Engr.**
1297 A687 4s multicolored .55 .25

Christmas A688

Design: Christ is Born, Aggsbacher Altar, Herzogenburg Monastery.

1984, Nov. 30 ***Perf. 14***
1298 A688 4.50s multicolored .55 .40

Karl Franzens University, Graz, 400th Anniv. — A689

1985, Jan. 4 ***Perf. 14x13½***
1299 A689 3.50s Seal .40 .25

Dr. Lorenz Bohler, Surgeon, Birth Cent. — A690

1985, Jan. 15 **Engr.**
1300 A690 4.50s dk rose lake .55 .25

Nordic Events, Ski Championships, Seefeld — A691

4s, Ski jumper, cross country racer.

1985, Jan. 17 **Photo.** ***Perf. 13½***
1301 A691 4s multicolored .55 .25

Linz Diocese Bicentenary A692

4.50s, Linz Cathedral interior.

1985, Jan. 25
1302 A692 4.50s gold & multi .55 .40

Alban Berg (1885-1935), Composer A693

1985, Feb. 8 **Engr.**
1303 A693 6s bluish black .80 .55

Vocational Training Inst., 25th Anniv. A694

1985, Feb. 15 Photo. ***Perf. 13½x14***
1304 A694 4.50s multicolored .55 .40

City of Bregenz, Bimillennium A695

1985, Feb. 22 ***Perf. 14x13½***
1305 A695 4s multicolored .50 .25

Austrian Registration Labels Cent. A696

1985, Mar. 15 ***Perf. 13½x14***
1306 A696 4.50s Label, 1885 .55 .40

Josef Stefan (1835-1893), Physicist — A697

Photo. & Engr.
1985, Mar. 22 ***Perf. 14x13½***
1307 A697 6s buff, dl red brn & dk brn .80 .55

St. Leopold Exhibition, Klosterneuberg A698

St. Leopold 16th-17th cent. embroidery.

1985, Mar. 29
1308 A698 3.50s multicolored .25 .25

Liberation From German Occupation, 40th Anniv. — A699

1985, Apr. 26 **Photo.**
1309 A699 4.50s multicolored .55 .40

Painter Franz von Defregger (1835-1921) A700

3.50s, Fairy tale teller.

1985, Apr. 26
1310 A700 3.50s gold & multi .40 .25

Europa Issue

Johann Joseph Fux (1660-1741), Composer, Violin and Trombone A701

Photo. & Engr.
1985, May 3 ***Perf. 13½***
1311 A701 6s lil gray & dk brn 1.40 .55

Boheimkirchen (Market Town) Millennium — A702

4.50s, View, coat of arms.

1985, May 10 ***Perf. 14***
1312 A702 4.50s gold & multi .55 .25

European Free Trade Assoc., 25th Anniv. — A703

Mercury staff, flags of member and affiliate nations.

1985, May 10 **Photo.** ***Perf. 13½***
1313 A703 4s multicolored .50 .40

St. Polten Diocese, Bicent. — A704

Episcopal residence gate, St. Polten diocese arms.

1985, May 15 **Photo. & Engr.**
1314 A704 4.50s multicolored .55 .40

The Gumpp Family of Builders, Innsbruck — A705

Perf. 14½x13½
1985, May 17 **Photo.**
1315 A705 3.50s multicolored .40 .25

Garsten Market Town Millennium A706

Design: 17th century engraving by George Matthaus Fischer (1628-1696).

Photo. & Engr.
1985, June 7 ***Perf. 13½x14***
1316 A706 4.50s multicolored .55 .40

UN, 40th Anniv. A707

Perf. 13½x14½
1985, June 26 **Photo.**
1317 A707 4s multicolored .55 .25

Austrian membership, 30th anniv.

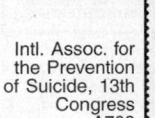

Intl. Assoc. for the Prevention of Suicide, 13th Congress A708

Photo. & Engr.
1985, June 28 ***Perf. 14***
1318 A708 5s brn, lt ap grn & yel .65 .50

Souvenir Sheet

Year of the Forest — A709

6s, Healthy and damaged woodland.

1985, June 28 ***Perf. 13½***
1319 A709 6s multicolored 1.10 1.10

Kurhaus, Bad Ischl Operetta Activities Emblem A710

1985, July 5 ***Perf. 14***
1320 A710 3.50s multicolored .50 .25

Bad Ischl Festival, 25th anniv.

Intl. Competition of Fire Brigades, Vocklabruck A711

4.50s, Fireman, emblem.

1985, July 18 **Photo.** ***Perf. 14x13½***
1321 A711 4.50s multicolored .80 .25

Grossglockner Alpine Motorway, 50th Anniv. — A712

4s, View of Fuschertorl.

Photo. & Engr.
1985, Aug. 2 ***Perf. 13½***
1322 A712 4s multicolored .50 .40

World Chess Federation Congress, Graz — A713

4s, Checkered globe, emblem.

1985, Aug. 28 **Photo.** ***Perf. 13½***
1323 A713 4s multicolored .50 .40

The Legendary Foundation of Konigstetten by Charlemagne, by Auguste Stephan, c. 1870 — A714

Photo. & Engr.

1985, Aug. 30 *Perf. 14*

1324 A714 4.50s multicolored .55 .40

Konigstetten millennium.

Hofkirchen-Taufkirchen-Weibern Municipalities, 1200th Anniv. — A715

4.50s, View of Weiburn, municipal arms.

1985, Aug. 30 *Perf. 13½x14*

1325 A715 4.50s multi .55 .40

Dr. Adam Politzer (1835-1923), Physician A716

1985, Sept. 12 **Engr.** *Perf. 14*

1326 A716 3.50s blue violet .50 .25

Politzer pioneered aural therapy for auditory disorders.

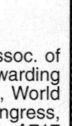

Intl. Assoc. of Forwarding Agents, World Congress, Vienna — A717

1985, Oct. 7 **Photo.** *Perf. 13½*

1327 A717 6s multicolored .80 .55

Carnival Figures Riding High Bicycles, By Paul Flora A718

Photo. & Engr.

1985, Oct. 25 *Perf. 14*

1328 A718 4s multicolored .55 .25

St. Martin on Horseback A719

1985, Nov. 8 **Photo.**

1329 A719 4.50s multicolored .55 .40

Eisenstadt Diocese, 25th anniv.

Creche, Marble Bas-relief, Salzburg — A720

Photo. & Engr.

1985, Nov. 29 *Perf. 13½*

1330 A720 4.50s gold, dl vio & buff .55 .25

Christmas.

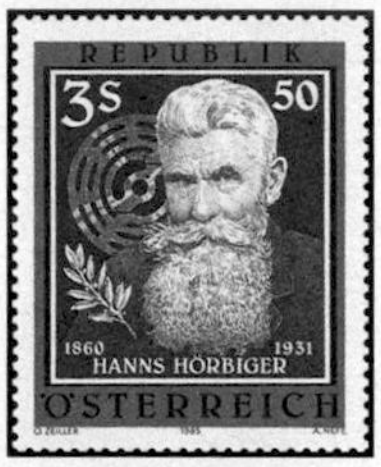

Hanns Horbiger (1860-1931), Inventor A721

1985, Nov. 29 *Perf. 14*

1331 A721 3.50s gold & sepia .40 .25

Aqueduct, Hundsau Brook, Near Gostling A722

1985, Nov. 29 *Perf. 13½x14½*

1332 A722 3.50s red, bluish blk & brt ultra .40 .25

Vienna Aqueduct, 75th anniv.

Chateau de la Muette, Paris Headquarters — A723

1985, Dec. 13

1333 A723 4s sep, rose lil & gold .50 .25

Org. for Economic Cooperation and Development, 25th anniv.

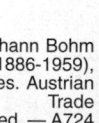

Johann Bohm (1886-1959), Pres. Austrian Trade Fed. — A724

1986, Jan. 24 **Photo.** *Perf. 14*

1334 A724 4.50s blk, ver & gray-ish black .55 .45

Intl. Peace Year — A725

Perf. 13½x14½

1986, Jan. 24 **Photo.**

1335 A725 6s multicolored .75 .50

Digital Telephone Service Introduction A726

5s, Push-button keyboard.

1986, Jan. 29 **Photo.**

1336 A726 5s multicolored .55 .40

Johann Georg Albrechtsberger (b. 1736), Composer — A727

3.50s, Klosterneuberg organ.

Photo. & Engr.

1986, Jan. 31 *Perf. 13½x14½*

1337 A727 3.50s multicolored .40 .25

Korneuburg, 850th Anniv. — A728

1986, Feb. 7 **Photo.** *Perf. 14*

1338 A728 5s multicolored .65 .40

Self-portrait, by Oskar Kokoschka (b.1886) — A729

Perf. 14½x13½

1986, Feb. 28 **Photo.**

1339 A729 4s multicolored .55 .25

Admission to Council of Europe, 30th Anniv. — A730

1986, Feb. 28 **Photo.** *Perf. 13x13½*

1340 A730 6s multicolored .80 .55

Clemens Holzmeister (b. 1886), Architect, Salzburg Festival Theater, 1926 — A731

Photo. & Engr.

1986, Mar. 27 *Perf. 13½*

1341 A731 4s sepia & redsh brn .50 .40

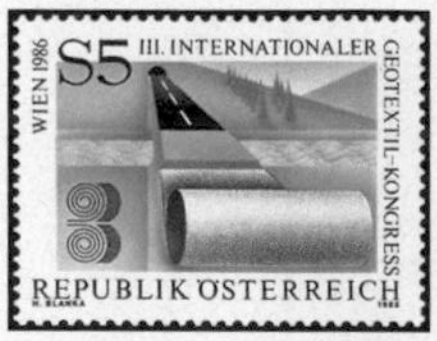

3rd Intl. Geotextile Congress, Vienna A732

1986, Apr. 7 **Photo.** *Perf. 13½x14½*

1342 A732 5s multicolored .65 .25

Prince Eugen and Schlosshof Castle A733

Photo. & Engr.

1986, Apr. 21 *Perf. 14*

1343 A733 4s multicolored .50 .40

Prince Eugen Exhibition, Schlosshof and Niederweiden.

St. Florian Monastery, Upper Austria A734

1986, Apr. 24

1344 A734 4s multicolored .50 .40

The World of Baroque provincial exhibition, St. Florian.

Herberstein Castle, Arms of Styria A735

1986, May 2 *Perf. 13½x14½*

1345 A735 4s multicolored .50 .40

Pasque Flower — A736

1986, May 2 *Perf. 13½*

1346 A736 6s multicolored 1.60 .55

Europa 1986.

Wagner, Scene from Opera Lohengrin — A737

1986, May 21

1347 A737 4s multicolored .50 .25

Intl. Richard Wagner Congress, Vienna.

Antimonite A738

1986, May 23 *Perf. 13½x14½*
1348 A738 4s multicolored .50 .25

Burgenland Provincial Minerals Exhibition.

Scenery Type of 1984

No. 1349, Martinswall, Tyrol. No. 1350, Tschauko Falls, Carinthia. No. 1351, Dachstein Ice Caves. No. 1352, Gauertal, Montafon. No. 1353, Krimmler Waterfalls. No. 1354, Lusthauswasser.

1986-89 Photo. & Engr. *Perf. 14*

1349	A679	5s multicolored	.75	.50
1350	A679	5s multicolored	.65	.50
1351	A679	5s multicolored	.65	.40
1352	A679	5s multicolored	.65	.40
1353	A679	5s multicolored	.65	.50
1354	A679	5s multicolored	.65	.40
		Nos. 1349-1354 (6)	4.00	2.70

Issued: No. 1349, 6/13/86; No. 1350, 7/4/86; No. 1351, 6/11/87; No. 1352, 8/21/87; No. 1353, 8/19/88; No. 1354, 9/1/89.

Waldhofen on Ybbs Township, 800th Anniv. — A739

1986, June 20 Photo. *Perf. 13½*
1355 A739 4s multicolored .55 .40

Salzburg Local Railway, Cent. A740

1986, Aug. 8 Photo. *Perf. 14*
1356 A740 4s multicolored .55 .40

Seals of Dukes Leopold Of Austria, Otakar of Styria, and Georgenberg Church — A741

1986, Aug. 14 Photo. & Engr.
1357 A741 5s multicolored .65 .50

Georgenberg Treaty, 800th anniv.

Julius Tandler (1869-1936), Social Reformer A742

1986, Aug. 22
1358 A742 4s multicolored .50 .40

Sonnblick Observatory, Cent. A743

4s, Observatory, 1886.

Photo. & Engr.
1986, Sept. 5 *Perf. 13½x14½*
1359 A743 4s multicolored .50 .40

Discovery of Mandrake Root — A744

1986, Sept. 8 *Perf. 14½x13½*
1360 A744 5s multicolored .65 .40

European Assoc. for Anesthesiology, 7th cong.

Monasteries and Abbeys Type of 1984

Designs: 5.50s, St. Gerold's Provostry, Vorarlberg. 7s, Loretto Monastery, Burgenland. 7.50s, Dominican Convent, Vienna. 8s, Zwettl Monastery. 10s, Wilten Monastery.

1986-88 Photo. & Engr. *Perf. 14*

1361	A679a	5.50s multicolored	1.10	.25
1362	A679a	7s multicolored	1.60	.25
1363	A679a	7.50s multicolored	1.60	.25
1364	A679a	8s multicolored	1.60	.25
1365	A679a	10s multicolored	1.90	.25
		Nos. 1361-1365 (5)	7.80	1.25

Issued: 5.50s, 9/12/86; 7.50s, 10/3; 7s, 8/14/87; 8s, 5/27/88; 10s, 3/18/88.

Otto Stoessl (d. 1936), Writer — A745

Photo. & Engr.
1986, Sept. 19 *Perf. 14*
1366 A745 4s multicolored .50 .25

Vienna Fire Brigade, 300th Anniv. — A746

1986, Sept. 19 Photo.
1367 A746 4s Fireman, 1686 .80 .25

Silk Viennese Hunting Tapestry A747

Photo. & Engr.
1986, Sept. 19 *Perf. 14*
1368 A747 5s multicolored .65 .50

Intl. conf. on Oriental Carpets, Vienna, Budapest.

Minister at Pulpit — A748

Photo. & Engr.
1986, Oct. 10 *Perf. 14*
1369 A748 5s blk & rose lilac .65 .50

Protestant Act, 25th anniv., and Protestant Patent of Franz Josef I ensuring religious equality, 125th anniv.

Disintegration, by Walter Schmogner A749

1986, Oct. 17 *Perf. 13½x14*
1370 A749 4s multicolored .55 .25

Franz Liszt, Composer, and Birthplace, Burgenland A750

1986, Oct. 17 *Perf. 13½*
1371 A750 5s green & sepia .55 .25

Souvenir Sheet

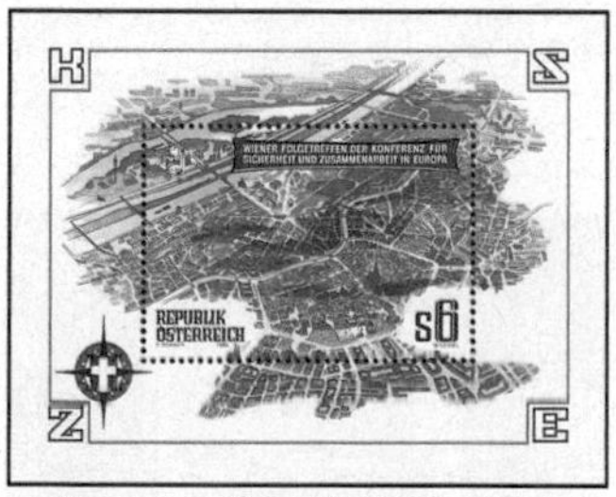

European Security Conference, Vienna — A751

1986, Nov. 4 *Perf. 13½x14*
1372 A751 6s Vienna .90 1.20

Strettweg Cart, 7th Cent. B.C. A752

Photo. & Engr.
1986, Nov. 26 *Perf. 14*
1373 A752 4s multicolored .50 .25

Joanneum Styrian Land Museum, 175th anniv.

Christmas A753

Design: The Little Crib, bas-relief by Schwanthaler (1740-1810), Schlierbach Monastery.

1986, Nov. 28
1374 A753 5s gold & rose lake .65 .50

Federal Chamber of Commerce, 40th Anniv. — A754

1986, Dec. 2 Photo.
1375 A754 5s multicolored .65 .50

Industry A755

No. 1376, Steel workers. No. 1377, Office worker, computer. No. 1378, Lab assistant. No. 1379, Textile worker. No. 1380, Bricklayer.

1986-91 *Perf. 14x13½*

1376	A755	4s multicolored	.50	.40
1377	A755	4s multicolored	.55	.40
1378	A755	4s multicolored	.55	.35
1379	A755	4.50s multicolored	.55	.40
1380	A755	5s multicolored	.65	.50
		Nos. 1376-1380 (5)	2.80	2.05

Issued: No. 1376, 12/4/86; No. 1377, 10/5/87; No. 1378, 10/21/88; 5s, 10/10/89; 4.50s, 10/11/91.

The Educated Eye, by Arnulf Rainer — A756

1987, Jan. 22 Photo. *Perf. 13½x14*
1386 A756 5s multicolored .65 .50

Adult education in Vienna, cent.

The Large Blue Madonna, by Anton Faistauer (1887-1970) — A757

Paintings: 6s, Self-portrait, 1922, by A. Paris Gutersloh (1887-1973).

1987, Feb. 13 *Perf. 14*
1387 A757 4s multicolored .60 .25
1388 A757 6s multicolored .90 .60

Hundertwasser House — A758

Photo. & Engr.

1987, Apr. 6 *Perf. 13½x14*
1389 A758 6s multicolored 1.75 .80

Europa 1987.

World Ice Hockey Championships, Vienna — A759

Perf. 13½x14½

1987, Apr. 17 **Photo.**
1390 A759 5s multicolored .90 .60

Opening of the Austria Center, Vienna A760

1987, Apr. 22
1391 A760 5s multicolored .90 .60

Salzburg City Charter, 700th Anniv. A761

1987, Apr. 24
1392 A761 5s multicolored .90 .60

Work-Men-Machines, Provincial Exhibition, Upper Austria — A762

Photo. & Engr.

1987, Apr. 29 *Perf. 14*
1393 A762 4s Factory, 1920 .60 .25

Equal Rights for Men and Women — A763

1987, Apr. 29 **Photo.** *Perf. 13½*
1394 A763 5s multicolored .80 .60

Adele Bloch-Bauer I, Abstract by Gustav Klimt — A764

Photo. & Engr.

1987, May 8 *Perf. 13½*
1395 A764 4s multicolored .60 .25

The Era of Emperor Franz Joseph, provincial exhibition, Lower Austria.

Arthur Schnitzler (1862-1931), Poet — A765

1987, May 15 *Perf. 14½x13½*
1396 A765 6s multicolored .90 .60

Von Raitenau, View of Salzburg A766

1987, May 15 *Perf. 14*
1397 A766 4s multicolored .60 .50

Prince Archbishop Wolf Dietrich von Raitenau, patron of baroque architecture in Salzburg, provincial exhibition.

Lace, Lustenau Municipal Arms A767

1987, May 22
1398 A767 5s multicolored .80 .60

Lustenau, 1100th anniv.

Souvenir Sheet

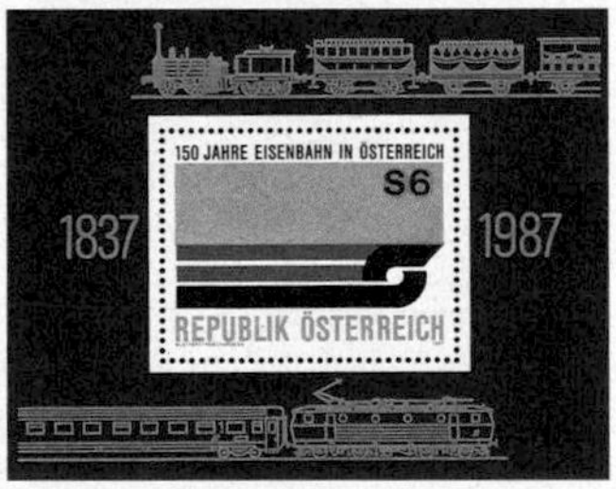

Austrian Railways Sesquicentenary — A768

1987, June 5 **Photo.** *Perf. 13½*
1399 A768 6s multicolored 1.10 1.10

8th Intl. Congress of Engravers, Vienna A769

Photo. & Engr.

1987, June 17 *Perf. 14*
1400 A769 5s gray, gray brn & dull rose .80 .50

Dr. Karl Josef Bayer (1847-1904), Chemist — A770

1987, June 22 *Perf. 14x13½*
1401 A770 5s multicolored .60 .60

Eighth Intl. Light Metals Congress, June 22-26, Leoben and Vienna; Bayer Technique for producing aluminum oxide from bauxite, cent.

Shipping on Achensee, Cent. — A771

1987, June 26 **Photo.**
1402 A771 4s multicolored .60 .50

Ombudsmen's Office, 10th Anniv. — A772

5s, Palais Rottal, Vienna.

1987, July 1
1403 A772 5s multicolored .80 .60

Dr. Erwin Schrodinger (1887-1961), 1933 Nobel Laureate in Physics — A773

1987, Aug. 11 **Photo. & Engr.**
1404 A773 5s dull olive bister, choc & buff .80 .60

Freistadt Exhibitions, 125th Anniv. A774

1987, Aug. 11 *Perf. 14x14½*
1405 A774 5s multicolored .60 .50

Arbing, 850th Anniv. — A775

1987, Aug. 21 *Perf. 13½*
1406 A775 5s multicolored .80 .60

1987 World Cycling Championships, Villach to Vienna — A776

1987, Aug. 25 *Perf. 14*
1407 A776 5s multicolored .80 .60

World Congress of Savings Banks, Vienna A777

Perf. 13½x14½

1987, Sept. 9 **Photo.**
1408 A777 5s multicolored .60 .50

Johann Michael Haydn (1737-1806), Composer A778

Perf. 13½x14½

1987, Sept. 14 **Engr.**
1409 A778 4s dull violet .60 .50

Paul Hofhaymer (1459-1537), Composer A779

Photo. & Engr.

1987, Sept. 11 *Perf. 14*
1410 A779 4s gold, blk & ultra .60 .25

Bearded Vulture — A780

1987, Sept. 25
1411 A780 4s multicolored .60 .25

Innsbruck Zoo, 25th anniv.

Baumgottinnen, by Arnulf Neuwirth — A781

1987, Oct. 9 *Perf. 14x13½*
1412 A781 5s multicolored .80 .50

Modern Art.

Gambling Monopoly, 200th Anniv. — A782

Perf. 14½x13½

1987, Oct. 30 **Photo.**
1413 A782 5s Lottery drum .80 .50

Christoph Willibald Gluck (1714-1787), Composer A784

Photo. & Engr.

1987, Nov. 13 ***Perf. 14***
1415 A784 5s cream & blk .80 .60

Oskar Helmer (b. 1887), Politician — A785

1987, Nov. 13
1416 A785 4s multicolored .60 .50

Joseph Mohr (1792-1848) and Franz Gruber (1787-1863), Opening Bars of "Silent Night, Holy Night" — A786

1987, Nov. 27
1417 A786 5s multicolored 1.20 .60

Christmas.

Intl. Education Congress of Salesian Fathers — A787

5s, St. John Bosco, children.

Photo. & Engr.

1988, Jan. 12 ***Perf. 13½***
1418 A787 5s multicolored .80 .60

Ernst Mach (1838-1916), Physicist — A788

Photo. & Engr.

1988, Feb. 19 ***Perf. 14½x13½***
1419 A788 6s multicolored .90 .60

Village with Bridge (1904), by Franz von Zulow (1883-1963), Painter — A789

1988, Feb. 25 **Photo.** ***Perf. 14½x14***
1420 A789 4s multicolored .60 .50

Biedermeier Provincial Exhibition, Vormarz in Vienna — A790

Painting: Confiscation, by Ferdinand Georg Waldmuller (1793-1865).

Photo. & Engr.

1988, Mar. 11 ***Perf. 14***
1421 A790 4s multicolored .60 .50

Anschluss of March 11, 1938 — A791

1988, Mar. 11 **Photo.** ***Perf. 13½***
1422 A791 5s gray olive, brn blk & ver .60 .25

No. 2 Aigen Steam Locomotive, 1887 A792

5s, Electric train, Josepsplatz.

1988, Mar. 22 ***Perf. 13½x14½***
1423 A792 4s shown .80 .50
1424 A792 5s multicolored .80 .50

Muhlkreis Railway, cent. (4s); Vienna Local Railway, cent. (5s).

World Wildlife Fund — A793

Photo. & Engr.

1988, Apr. 15 ***Perf. 13½x14***
1425 A793 5s Bee eater .90 .60

Styrian Provincial Exhibition on Glass and Coal, Barnbach A794

1988, Apr. 29 ***Perf. 13½***
1426 A794 4s Frosted glass .60 .50

Intl. Red Cross, 125th Anniv. — A795

1988, May 6 **Photo.** ***Perf. 14***
1427 A795 12s grn, brt red & blk 1.25 .90

Gothic Silver Censer — A796

1988, May 6 **Photo. & Engr.**
1428 A796 4s multicolored .60 .50

Art and Monasticism at the Birth of Austria, lower Austrian provincial exhibition, Seltenstetten.

Europa 1988 A797

Communication and transportation.

1988, May 13 **Photo.**
1429 A797 6s multicolored 1.20 .50

Mattsee Monastery and Lion of Alz — A798

1988, May 18 **Photo. & Engr.**
1430 A798 4s multicolored .60 .50

Provincial exhibition at Mattsee Monastery: Bavarian Tribes in Salzburg.

Weinberg Castle A799

Perf. 13½x14½

1988, May 20 **Photo.**
1431 A799 4s multicolored .60 .50

Upper Austrian provincial exhibition: Weinberg Castle.

Odon von Horwath (1901-1938), Dramatist — A800

Photo. & Engr.

1988, June 1 ***Perf. 14½x13½***
1432 A800 6s olive bis & slate grn .90 .60

Stockerau Festival, 25th Anniv. — A801

5s, Stockerau Town Hall.

1988, June 17 ***Perf. 14***
1433 A801 5s multicolored .80 .50

Tauern Motorway Opening — A802

1988, June 24 **Photo.** ***Perf. 13½x14***
1434 A802 4s multicolored .60 .50

Brixlegg, 1200th Anniv. A803

Photo. & Engr.

1988, July 1 ***Perf. 13½x14½***
1435 A803 5s multicolored .90 .50

View of Klagenfurt, Engraving by Matthaus Merian (1593-1650) — A804

Photo. & Engr.

1988, Aug. 12 ***Perf. 14***
1436 A804 5s multicolored .80 .60

Carinthian Postal Service, 400th Anniv.

Brixen-im-Thale, 1200th Anniv. — A805

1988, Aug. 12
1437 A805 5s multicolored .60 .25

Feldkirchen, 1100th Anniv. — A806

1988, Sept. 2 ***Perf. 13½***
1438 A806 5s multicolored .80 .50

Feldbach, 800th Anniv. A807

1988, Sept. 15 **Photo. & Engr.**
1439 A807 5s multicolored .60 .60

Ansfelden, 1200th Anniv. — A808

1988, Sept. 23 ***Perf. 14***
1440 A808 5s multicolored .60 .25

Exports A809

1988, Oct. 18 **Photo.** ***Perf. 14x13½***
1441 A809 8s multicolored 1.75 1.75

No. 1441 has a holographic image. Soaking in water may affect the hologram.

Vienna Concert Hall, 75th Anniv. A810

Photo. & Engr.

1988, Oct. 19 ***Perf. 13½***
1442 A810 5s multicolored .60 .60

The Watchmen, by Giselbert Hoke — A811

1988, Oct. 21 ***Perf. 14***
1443 A811 5s multicolored .80 .60

Social Democrats Unification Party Congress, Cent. — A812

1988, Nov. 11 **Photo.** ***Perf. 14½x14***
1444 A812 4s multicolored .60 .60

Leopold Schonbauer (1888-1963), Physician — A813

Photo. & Engr.

1988, Nov. 11 ***Perf. 14½x13½***
1445 A813 4s multicolored .65 .50

Christmas A814

Nativity painting from St. Barbara's Church.

1988, Nov. 25 ***Perf. 14***
1446 A814 5s multicolored .60 .60

Benedictine Monastery, Melk, 900th Anniv. — A815

Design: Fresco by Paul Troger.

1989, Mar. 17 **Photo. & Engr.**
1447 A815 5s multicolored .60 .25

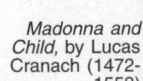

Madonna and Child, by Lucas Cranach (1472-1553) A816

1989, Mar. 17 ***Perf. 14½x13½***
1448 A816 4s multicolored .60 .50

Diocese of Innsbruck, 25th anniv.

Marianne Hainisch (1839-1936), Women's Rights Activist — A817

1989, Mar. 24 ***Perf. 14x13½***
1449 A817 6s multicolored 1.00 .70

Glider Plane and Parachutist A818

1989, Mar. 31 **Photo.** ***Perf. 14***
1450 A818 6s multicolored 1.00 .70

World Gliding Championships, Wiener Neustadt, and World Parachuting Championships, Damuls.

Bruck an der Leitha Commune, 750th Anniv. — A819

Painting by Georg Matthaus Vischer (1628-1696).

1989, Apr. 21
1451 A819 5s multicolored .30 .50

Die Malerei, 1904, by Rudolf Jettmar (1869-1939) A820

Perf. 14½x13½

1989, Apr. 21 **Photo.**
1452 A820 5s multicolored .80 .50

Holy Trinity Church, Stadl-Paura A821

1989, Apr. 26 **Photo. & Engr.**
1453 A821 5s multicolored .70 .30

Michael Prunner (1669-1739), baroque architect.

Eduard Suess (1831-1914), Structural Geologist and Map — A822

Portrait by J. Krieher (1800-1876).

1989, Apr. 26
1454 A822 6s multicolored .70 .30

Ludwig Wittgenstein (1889-1951), Philosopher A823

1989, Apr. 26
1455 A823 5s multicolored .90 .50

Styrian Provincial Exhibition, Judenburg A824

Design: Judenburg, 17th cent., an engraving by Georg Matthaus Vischer.

1989, Apr. 28 ***Perf. 14x13½***
1456 A824 4s multicolored .70 .50

Industrial Technology Exhibition, Pottenstein — A825

1989, Apr. 28 **Photo.** ***Perf. 13½***
1457 A825 4s Steam engine .70 .50

Radstadt Township, 700th Anniv. A826

1989, May 3 **Photo.** ***Perf. 13½x14½***
1458 A826 5s multicolored .80 .50

Toy Boat A827

1989, May 5
1459 A827 6s multicolored 1.20 .50

Europa 1989.

Monastery Church at Lambach, 900th Anniv. — A828

Photo. & Engr.

1989, May 19 ***Perf. 14***
1460 A828 4s multicolored .70 .50

Paddle Steamer *Gisela* A829

1989, May 19 **Photo.** ***Perf. 13½***
1461 A829 5s multicolored 1.25 .60

Shipping on the Traunsee, 150th anniv.

St. Andra im Lavanttal, 650th Anniv. A830

Period cityscape by Matthaus Merian.

1989, May 26 **Photo. & Engr.**
1462 A830 5s multicolored .80 .60

Richard Strauss (1864-1949), Composer A831

Photo. & Engr.

1989, June 1 ***Perf. 14½x13½***
1463 A831 6s dark brn, gold & red brn 1.00 .60

Achensee Railway, Cent. A832

1989, June 8 **Photo.** ***Perf. 13½***
1464 A832 5s multicolored .90 .30

Monastery Type of 1984

Design: 50g, Vorau Abbey, Styria. 1s, Monastery of Mehrerau, Vorarlberg. 1.50s, Monastery of the German Order in Vienna. 2s, Bendictine Monastery, Michaelbeuern. 11s, Engelszell Abbey. 12s, Monastery of the Hospitalers, Eisenstadt. 17s, St. Peter, Salzburg. 20s, Wernberg Monastery.

1989-92 **Photo. & Engr.** ***Perf. 14***

1465	A679a	50g multi	.25	.25
1466	A679a	1s multi	.25	.25
1467	A679a	1.50s multi	.25	.25
1468	A679a	2s multi	.50	.25
1469	A679a	11s multi	2.50	.50
1470	A679a	12s multi	4.00	.90
1471	A679a	17s multi	4.50	.90
1472	A679a	20s multi	6.00	.60
		Nos. 1465-1472 (8)	18.25	3.90

Issued: 1s, 9/1/89; 17s, 6/29/89; 11s, 3/9/90; 50g, 10/12/90; 20s, 5/3/91; 2s, 9/27/91; 1.50s, 10/23/92; 12s, 6/17/92.

Interparliamentary Union, Cent. — A833

Photo. & Engr.

1989, June 30 ***Perf. 14***
1475 A833 6s Parliament, Vienna .90 .60

Social Security in Austria, Cent. — A834

1989, Aug. 1 **Photo.**
1476 A834 5s multicolored .80 .50

UN Offices in Vienna, 10th Anniv. A835

1989, Aug. 23
1477 A835 8s multicolored 1.25 .60

Wildalpen, 850th Anniv. A836

5s, Foundry, coat of arms.

Photo. & Engr.

1989, Sept. 15 ***Perf. 13½x14***
1478 A836 5s multicolored .70 .60

33rd Congress of the Association for Quality Assurance (EOQC) — A837

1989, Sept. 18 **Photo.** ***Perf. 14x13½***
1479 A837 6s multicolored .60 .70

14th World Congress of the Soc. for Criminal Law (AIDP) A838

6s, Justice Palace, Vienna.

Photo. & Engr.

1989, Oct. 2 ***Perf. 13½***
1480 A838 6s multicolored .90 .60

Lebensbaum, by Ernst Steiner — A839

1989, Oct. 10 ***Perf. 13½x14***
1481 A839 5s multicolored .60 .60

Georg Trakl (1887-1914), Expressionist Poet — A840

1989, Nov. 6 **Photo.** ***Perf. 14½x13½***
1482 A840 4s Trakl .70 .50
1483 A840 4s Anzengruber .70 .50

Ludwig Anzengruber (1839-1889), playwright and novelist.

Alfred Fried (1864-1921), Pacifist, Publisher and 1911 Nobel Laureate — A841

1989, Nov. 10 **Photo. & Engr.**
1484 A841 6s multicolored .90 .60

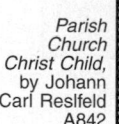

Parish Church Christ Child, by Johann Carl Reslfeld A842

1989, Dec. 1 ***Perf. 13½x14½***
1485 A842 5s multicolored .70 .60

Christmas.

Postal Communications in Europe, 500th Anniv. — A843

The Young Post Rider, an Engraving by Albrecht Dürer

Photo. & Engr.

1990, Jan. 12 ***Perf. 14***
1486 A843 5s choc, gray brn, beige 1.00 .60

See Belgium No. 1332, Germany No. 1592, Berlin No. 9N584 and German Democratic Republic No. 2791.

Hahnenkamm Alpine Competition, Kitzbuhel, 50th Anniv. — A844

Perf. 13½x14½

1990, Jan. 12 **Photo.**
1487 A844 5s multicolored .70 .60

Salomon Sulzer (1804-90), Cantor and Composer A845

Perf. 14½x13½

1990, Jan. 17 **Photo.**
1488 A845 4.50s multicolored .60 .30

Friedrich Emich (1860-1940), Chemist — A846

1990, Jan. 22 **Photo. & Engr.**
1489 A846 6s claret & pale green .90 .60

Miniature from the *Market Book of Grein,* by Ulrich Schreier, c. 1490 A847

1990, Mar. 9 ***Perf. 14***
1490 A847 5s multicolored .90 .65

City of Linz, 500th anniv.

University Seals — A848

1990, Apr. 6
1491 A848 5s multicolored .90 .60

625th Anniv. of Vienna University and 175th anniv. of Vienna Technical University.

Scenery Type of 1984

No. 1492, Styrian Vineyards. No. 1493, Obir Caverns. No. 1494, Natural Bridge, Vorarlberg. No. 1495, Wilder Kaiser Mountain, Tyrol. No. 1496, Peggau Cave, Styria. No. 1497, Moorland, swamp, Heidenreichstein. No. 1498, Hohe Tauern Natl. Park. No. 1499, Nussberg Vineyards.

1990-97 ***Perf. 14***

1492	A679	5s multicolored	.90	.60
1493	A679	5s multicolored	.90	.60
1494	A679	5s multicolored	.90	.60
1495	A679	6s multicolored	1.00	.80
1496	A679	6s multicolored	1.00	.75
1497	A679	6s multicolored	1.00	.55
1498	A679	6s multicolored	1.00	.60
1499	A679	6s multicolored	1.10	1.10
		Nos. 1492-1499 (8)	7.80	5.60

Issued: No. 1492, 4/27; No. 1493, 3/26/91; No. 1494, 2/5/92; No. 1495, 2/19/93; No. 1496, 4/29/94; No. 1497, 5/19/95; No. 1498, 3/29/96; No. 1499, 2/21/97.

Anthering, 1200th Anniv. — A849

Church and municipal arms.

1990, Apr. 27 Photo. ***Perf. 14x13½***
1500 A849 7s multicolored .90 .60

Labor May Day, Cent. — A850

1990, Apr. 30 Photo. ***Perf. 13½***
1501 A850 4.50s multicolored .60 .60

Seckau Abbey, 850th Anniv. — A851

1990, May 4 Engr. ***Perf. 14x13½***
1502 A851 4.50s bluish black .60 .30

Ebene Reichenau Post Office A852

1990, May 4 Photo. ***Perf. 13½x14***
1503 A852 7s multicolored 1.75 .90

Europa.

Hans Makart (1840-84), Self-Portrait A853

Self Portrait: 5s, Egon Schiele (1890-1918).

Photo. & Engr.
1990, May 29 ***Perf. 14***
1504 A853 4.50s multicolored .60 .60
1505 A853 5s multicolored .90 .90

Ferdinand Raimund (1790-1836), Actor — A854

1990, June 1 Photo. ***Perf. 14x13½***
1506 A854 4.50s multicolored .60 .60

Christ Healing the Sick by Rembrandt A855

Photo. & Engr.
1990, June 5 ***Perf. 14***
1507 A855 7s multicolored .90 .60

2nd Intl. Christus Medicus Cong., Bad Ischl.

Hardegg, 700th Anniv. — A856

Photo. & Engr.
1990, June 8 ***Perf. 13½x14***
1508 A856 4.50s multicolored .60 .60

Oberdrauburg, 750th Anniv. — A857

1990, June 8 **Photo.**
1509 A857 5s multicolored .90 .60

Gumpoldskirchen, 850th Anniv. — A858

Photo. & Engr.
1990, June 15 ***Perf. 13½***
1510 A858 5s multicolored .90 .60

Mathias Zdarsky (1856-1940), Alpine Skier — A859

1990, June 20 ***Perf. 14x13½***
1511 A859 5s multicolored .90 .60

Telegraph, 1880, Anton Tschechow, 1978 — A860

1990, June 28 Photo. ***Perf. 14***
1512 A860 9s multicolored 1.25 .90

Modern shipbuilding in Austria, 150th anniv.

Joseph Friedrich Perkonig (1890-1959), Novelist — A861

Photo. & Engr.
1990, Aug. 3 ***Perf. 14x13½***
1513 A861 5s gold & brown .90 .60

Herr des Regenbogens, by Robert Zeppel-Sperl A862

Photo. & Engr.
1990, Aug. 30 ***Perf. 13½x14***
1514 A862 5s multicolored .90 .60

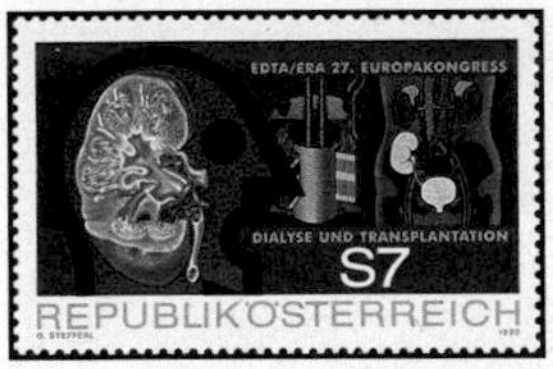

European Dialysis and Transplantation Society, 27th Congress — A863

1990, Sept. 4 Photo. ***Perf. 14***
1515 A863 7s multicolored .90 .60

Franz Werfel (1890-1945), Writer — A864

Photo. & Engr.
1990, Sept. 11 ***Perf. 14x13½***
1516 A864 5s multicolored .90 .60

Austrian Forces in UN Peace Keeping Forces, 30th Anniv. A865

1990, Sept. 20 Photo. ***Perf. 13½***
1517 A865 7s multicolored .90 .60

Federal and State Arms A866

1990, Sept. 24 **Photo. & Engr.**
1518 A866 5s multicolored .60 .30

Federalism in Austria.

Mining Univ., Leoben, 150th Anniv. — A867

Photo. & Engr.
1990, Oct. 22 ***Perf. 14***
1519 A867 4.50s blk, bl grn & red .60 .30

Karl Freiherr von Vogelsang (1818-90), Politician — A868

Photo. & Engr.
1990, Nov. 8 ***Perf. 14x13½***
1520 A868 4.50s multicolored .60 .30

Metalworkers and Miners Trade Union, Cent. — A869

1990, Nov. 16 ***Perf. 14***
1521 A869 5s multicolored .90 .60

3rd World Curling Championships A870

1990, Nov. 23 Photo. ***Perf. 14x13½***
1522 A870 7s multicolored .90 .60

Palmhouse at Schonbrunn — A871

1990, Nov. 30 ***Perf. 14***
1523 A871 5s multicolored .90 .60

Christmas A872

Altar in Klosterneuburg Abbey by the Master from Verdun.

Photo. & Engr.
1990, Nov. 23 ***Perf. 13½***
1524 A872 5s multicolored .60 .30

Franz Grillparzer (1791-1872), Dramatic Poet — A873

Photo. & Engr.

1991, Jan. 15 *Perf. 14x13½*
1525 A873 4.50s multicolored .60 .30

A874

1991, Jan. 21 *Perf. 13½*
1526 A874 5s multicolored .90 .60

Alpine Skiing World Championship, Saalbach-Hinterglemm.

Bruno Kreisky (1911-90), Chancellor A875

1991, Jan. 21 Photo. *Perf. 14x13½*
1527 A875 5s multicolored .90 .60

Friedrich Freiherr von Schmidt (1825-1891), Architect — A876

1991, Jan. 21 *Perf. 14*
1528 A876 7s multicolored 1.25 .90

Visual Arts A877

Designs: 4.50s, Donner Fountain, Vienna, by Raphael Donner (1693-1741), sculptor. 5s, Kitzbuhel in Winter, by Alfons Walde (1891-1958), painter. 7s, Vienna Stock Exchange, Theophil Hansen (1813-1891), architect.

1991, Feb. 8
1529 A877 4.50s multicolored .60 .60
1530 A877 5s multicolored .90 .90
1531 A877 7s multicolored .90 .90
Nos. 1529-1531 (3) 2.40 2.40

See No. 1543.

Marie von Ebner Eschenbach (1830-1916), Novelist A878

1991, Mar. 12 Engr. *Perf. 13½x14½*
1532 A878 4.50s rose violet .60 .60

Miniature Sheet

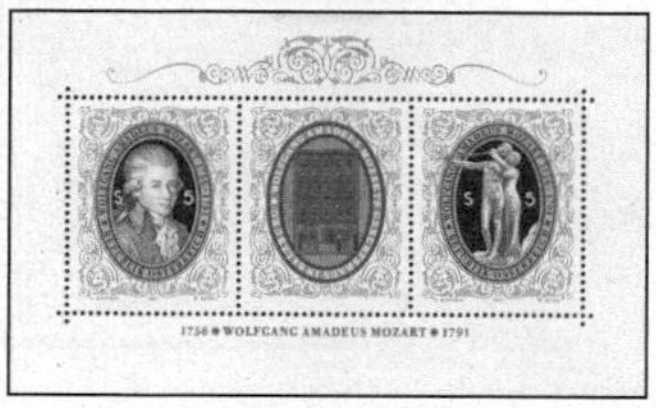

A879

Design: a, Wolfgang Amadeus Mozart (1756-1791), Composer. b, Magic Flute Fountain, Vienna.

Photo. & Engr.

1991, Mar. 22 *Perf. 13½*
1533 A879 Sheet of 2 + label 2.00 2.00
a.-b. 5s any single .60 .60

Spittal an der Drau, 800th Anniv. A880

1991, Apr. 11 *Perf. 14*
1534 A880 4.50s multicolored .60 .60

Europa A881

1991, May 3 Photo. *Perf. 14*
1535 A881 7s ERS-1 satellite 2.25 .90

Garden Banquet by Anthony Bays A882

1991, May 10 Photo. *Perf. 13½*
1536 A882 5s multicolored .60 .60

Vorarlberg Provincial Exhibition, Hohenems.

Museum of Military History, Cent. A883

7s, Interior of Museum of Art History.

Photo. & Engr.

1991, May 24 *Perf. 13½*
1537 A883 5s multicolored .60 .60
1538 A883 7s multicolored 1.25 1.25

Museum of Art History, Cent. (No. 1538).

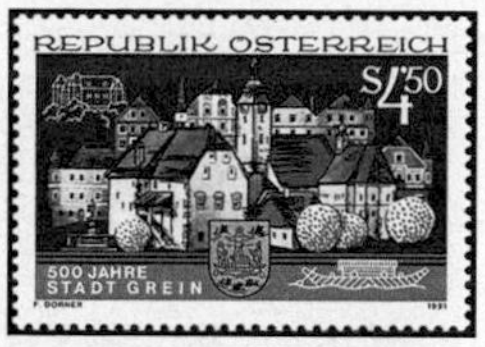

Grein, 500th Anniv. A884

1991, May 24 Photo. *Perf. 14*
1539 A884 4.50s multicolored .60 .60

Tulln, 1200th Anniv. A885

1991, May 24 *Perf. 13½x14*
1540 A885 5s multicolored .90 .60

Completion of Karawanken Tunnels — A886

1991, May 31 *Perf. 14x13½*
1541 A886 7s multicolored .90 .90

5th Anniv. of St. Polten as Provincial Capital of Lower Austria A887

1991, July 5 Photo. *Perf. 14*
1542 A887 5s multicolored .90 .60

Visual Arts Type of 1991

Design: 4.50s, Karlsplatz Station of Vienna Subway by Otto Wagner (1841-1918), Architect.

1991, July 12 Photo. & Engr.
1543 A877 4.50s multicolored .60 .60

Rowing and Junior Canoeing World Championships, Vienna — A888

1991, Aug. 20 Photo. *Perf. 13½x14*
1544 A888 5s multicolored .90 .60

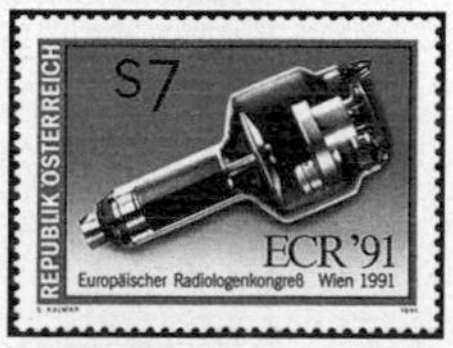

European Congress of Radiologists — A889

1991, Sept. 13 *Perf. 14*
1545 A889 7s multicolored .90 .90

Paracelsus (1493-1541), Physician — A890

1991, Sept. 27 *Perf. 14x13½*
1546 A890 4.50s multicolored .60 .60

Joint Austrian-Soviet Space Mission A891

1991, Oct. 2 *Perf. 14*
1547 A891 9s multicolored 1.25 .90

Austrian Folk Festivals A892

4.50s, Almabtrieb, Tyrol. 5s, Winzerkrone, Vienna. 7s, Ernte-Monstranz, Styria.

1991, Oct. 4 Photo. & Engr.
1548 A892 4.50s multicolored .60 .60
1549 A892 5s multicolored .90 .60
1550 A892 7s multicolored .90 .60
Nos. 1548-1550 (3) 2.40 1.80

See Nos. 1577-1579, 1619-1621, 1633-1635, 1671-1673, 1694, 1705-1706, 1714, 1730, 1741, 1752-1753, 1762, 1778, 1799-1800, 1805-1806, 1824, 1836-1838, 1954, 2020, 2050.

The General by Rudolph Pointner A893

Photo. & Engr.

1991, Oct. 11 *Perf. 13½x14*
1551 A893 5s multicolored .90 .60

Birth of Christ, Baumgartenberg Church — A894

1991, Nov. 29
1552 A894 5s multicolored .90 .30

Christmas.

Julius Raab, Politician, Birth Cent. — A895

1991, Nov. 29 ***Perf. 14x13½***
1553 A895 4.50s red brn & brn .60 .60

1992 Winter and Summer Olympic Games A897

1992, Jan. 14 **Photo.** ***Perf. 14***
1555 A897 7s multicolored .90 .90

Trade Union of Clerks in Private Enterprises, Cent. — A898

1992, Jan. 14
1556 A898 5.50s multicolored .90 .80

8th Natural Run Toboggan World Championships A899

1992, Jan. 29 ***Perf. 14x13½***
1557 A899 5s multicolored .90 .60

George Saiko, Writer, Birth Cent. — A900

1992, Feb. 5 **Engr.** ***Perf. 14x13½***
1558 A900 5.50s brown .90 .60

Worker's Sports, Cent. — A901

1992, Feb. 5 **Photo.** ***Perf. 14***
1559 A901 5.50s multicolored .90 .60

Souvenir Sheet

Vienna Philharmonic Orchestra, 150th Anniv. — A902

Photo. & Engr.
1992, Mar. 27 ***Perf. 14***
1560 A902 5.50s multicolored 1.00 1.25

Scientists A903

Designs: 5s, Franz Joseph Muller von Reichenstein (1742-1825), discoverer of tellurium. 5.50s, Dr. Paul Kitaibel (1757-1817), botanist. 6s, Christian Johann Doppler (1803-1853), physicist. 7s, Richard Kuhn (1900-1967), chemist.

1992, Mar. 27 **Photo.**
1561 A903 5s multicolored .90 .60
1562 A903 5.50s multicolored .90 .60
1563 A903 6s multicolored .90 .90
1564 A903 7s multicolored .90 .90
Nos. 1561-1564 (4) 3.60 3.00

Railway Workers Union, Cent. A904

1992, Apr. 2 ***Perf. 14x13½***
1565 A904 5.50s black & red .90 .60

Norbert Hanrieder (1842-1913), Poet — A905

Photo. & Engr.
1992, Apr. 30 ***Perf. 14x13½***
1566 A905 5.50s purple & buff .90 .60

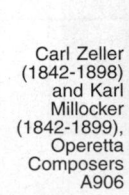

Carl Zeller (1842-1898) and Karl Millocker (1842-1899), Operetta Composers A906

Photo. & Engr.
1992, Apr. 30 ***Perf. 14***
1567 A906 6s multicolored .90 .60

LD Steel Mill, 40th Anniv. A907

1992, May 8 **Photo.** ***Perf. 14x13½***
1568 A907 5s multicolored .60 .60

Discovery of America, 500th Anniv. A908

Photo. & Engr.
1992, May 8 ***Perf. 14***
1569 A908 7s multicolored *2.00* .90

Europa.

Austro-Swiss Treaty on Regulation of Rhine River, Cent. — A909

1992, May 8 **Photo.** ***Perf. 13½x14***
1570 A909 7s multicolored 1.25 .90

Protection of the Alps — A910

1992, May 22 ***Perf. 14x13½***
1571 A910 5.50s multicolored .90 .60

See Switzerland No. 916.

Dr. Anna Dengel (1892-1980), Physician — A911

1992, May 22 **Photo. & Engr.**
1572 A911 5.50s multicolored .90 .60

Sebastian Rieger (1867-1953), Poet — A912

1992, May 22 **Engr.**
1573 A912 5s red brown .90 .60

Lienz, 750th Anniv. A913

1992, June 17 **Photo.** ***Perf. 14x13½***
1574 A913 5s Town Hall .90 .60

Intl. Congress of Austrian Society of Surgeons A914

Photo. & Engr.
1992, June 17 ***Perf. 14***
1575 A914 6s multicolored .90 .90

Dr. Kurt Waldheim, President of Austria, 1986-92 — A915

1992, June 22 ***Perf. 14x13½***
1576 A915 5.50s multicolored .90 .90

Folk Festivals Type of 1991

Designs: 5s, Marksman's target, Lower Austria. 5.50s, Peasant's chest, Carinthia. 7s, Votive icon, Vorarlberg.

Photo. & Engr.
1992, Sept. 18 ***Perf. 14***
1577 A892 5s multicolored .60 .60
1578 A892 5.50s multicolored .90 .90
1579 A892 7s multicolored .90 .90
Nos. 1577-1579 (3) 2.40 2.40

Marchfeld Canal — A917

1992, Oct. 9 **Photo.** ***Perf. 13½x14***
1580 A917 5s multicolored .90 .60

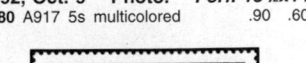

5th Intl. Ombudsman Conference, Vienna — A918

Photo & Engr.
1992, Oct. 9 ***Perf. 14***
1581 A918 5.50s multicolored .90 .60

The Clearance of Seawater, by Peter Pongratz A919

1992, Oct. 9
1582 A919 5.50s multicolored .90 .60

Academy of Fine Arts, 300th Anniv. — A920

Photo. & Engr.
1992, Oct. 23 ***Perf. 14***
1583 A920 5s red & blue .90 .60

Birth of Christ, by Johann Georg Schmidt A921

1992, Nov. 27 ***Perf. 14x13½***
1584 A921 5.50s multicolored .90 .60

Christmas.

Veit Koniger, Sculptor, Death Bicent. A922

Photo. & Engr.
1992, Nov. 27 ***Perf. 14***
1585 A922 5s multicolored .60 .60

Herman Potocnik, Theoretician of Geosynchronous Satellite Orbit, Birth Cent. — A923

1992, Nov. 27 **Photo.**
1586 A923 10s multicolored 1.25 1.25

Famous Buildings A924

5s, Statues & dome of Imperial Palace, Vienna, designed by Joseph Emanuel Fischer von Erlach. 5.50s, Kinsky Palace, designed by Lukas von Hildebrandt. 7s, Vienna State Opera, designed by Eduard van der Null & August Siccard von Siccardsburg.

1993, Jan. 22 **Photo. & Engr.**
1587 A924 5s multicolored .90 .60
1588 A924 5.50s multicolored .90 .60
1589 A924 7s multicolored 1.25 .90
Nos. 1587-1589 (3) 3.05 2.10

Joseph Emanuel Fischer von Erlach, 300th birth anniv. (No. 1587). Johann Lukas von Hildebrandt, 325th birth anniv. (No. 1588). Eduard van der Null, August Siccard von Siccardsburg, 125th death anniv. (No. 1589).

Radio Dispatched Medical Service, 25th Anniv. — A925

1993, Feb. 19 **Photo.**
1590 A925 5s multicolored .90 .60

Typewriter Made by Peter Mitterhofer (1822-1893) A926

1993, Feb. 19 ***Perf. 13½x14***
1591 A926 17s multicolored 3.50 1.25

Popular Entertainers — A927

Strada del Sole, by Rainhard Fendrich.

1993, Mar. 19 **Photo.** ***Perf. 14***
1592 A927 5.50s multicolored .90 .60

See Nos. 1626, 1639.

Charles Sealsfield (1793-1864), Writer A928

Photo. & Engr.
1993, Mar. 19 ***Perf. 13½x14***
1593 A928 10s multicolored 1.25 .90

Rights of the Child — A930

1993, Apr. 16 **Photo.** ***Perf. 13½x14***
1595 A930 7s multicolored 1.25 .90

Flying Harlequin, by Paul Flora A931

1993, Apr. 16 **Photo. & Engr.**
1596 A931 7s multicolored 3.00 .60

Europa.

Monastery of Admont — A932

Designs: 1s, Detail of abbesse's crosier, St. Gabriel Abbey, Styria. 5.50s, Death, wooden statue by Josef Stammel (1695-1765). 6s, Stained glass, Mariastern-Gwiggen Monastery. 7s, Marble lion, Franciscan Monastery, Salzburg. 7.50s, Cupola fresco, by Paul Troger, Monastery of Altenburg. 8s, Gothic entry, Wilhering Monastery, Upper Austria. 10s, Altarpiece, St. Peregrinus praying, Maria Luggau Monastery. 20s, Crosier, Fiecht Monastery. 26s, Sculpture of Mater Dolorosa, Franciscan Monastery, Schwaz, Tirol. 30s, Madonna of Scottish Order, Schottenstift Monastery, Vienna.

Photo. & Engr.
1993-95 ***Perf. 13¾x14***

1599	A932	1s	multicolored	.25	.25
1600	A932	5.50s	multicolored	2.00	.25
1601	A932	6s	multicolored	1.25	.25
1602	A932	7s	multicolored	1.75	.25
1603	A932	7.50s	multicolored	2.00	.55
1604	A932	8s	multicolored	2.25	.65
1605	A932	10s	multicolored	2.50	.50
1606	A932	20s	multicolored	5.00	.55
1607	A932	26s	multicolored	6.00	.75
1608	A932	30s	multicolored	8.00	1.25
	Nos. 1599-1608 (10)			31.00	5.25

Issued: 5.50s, 4/16; 6s, 9/17; 20s, 10/8; 7.50s, 4/4/94; 10s, 8/26/94; 30s, 10/7/94; 7s, 11/18/94; 8s, 9/15/95; 26s, 10/6/95; 1s, 4/28/95.

Peter Rosegger (1843-1918), Poet — A933

1993, May 5 **Photo.** ***Perf. 14x13½***
1617 A933 5.50s green & black .90 .60

Lake Constance Steamer Hohentwiel A934

1993, May 5 **Photo.** ***Perf. 14***
1618 A934 6s multicolored .90 .60

See Germany No. 1786, Switzerland No. 931.

Folk Festivals Type of 1991

Designs: 5s, Corpus Christi Day Procession, Upper Austria. 5.50s, Blockdrawing, Burgenland. 7s, Cracking whip when snow is melting, Salzburg.

Photo. & Engr.
1993, June 11 ***Perf. 14***
1619 A892 5s multicolored .90 .60
1620 A892 5.50s multicolored .90 .60
1621 A892 7s multicolored .90 .90
Nos. 1619-1621 (3) 2.70 2.10

UN Conference on Human Rights, Vienna A935

1993, June 11 **Photo.**
1622 A935 10s multicolored 1.25 .90

Franz Jagerstatter (1907-1943), Conscientious Objector — A936

1993, Aug. 6 **Photo.** ***Perf. 14x13½***
1623 A936 5.50s multicolored .90 .60

Schafberg Railway, Cent. A937

1993, Aug. 6 ***Perf. 13½x14***
1624 A937 6s multicolored .90 .60

Self-portrait with Puppet, by Rudolf Wacker (1893-1939) A938

Photo. & Engr.
1993, Aug. 6 ***Perf. 14***
1625 A938 6s multicolored .60 .60

Popular Entertainers Type of 1993

Design: 5.50s, Granny, by Ludwig Hirsch.

1993, Sept. 3 **Photo.** ***Perf. 14***
1626 A927 5.50s multicolored .90 .60

Vienna Mens' Choral Society, 150th Anniv. A940

1993, Sept. 17 **Photo.** ***Perf. 14***
1627 A940 5s multicolored .60 .60

Easter, by Max Weiler — A941

Photo. & Engr.
1993, Oct. 8 ***Perf. 13½x14***
1628 A941 5.50s multicolored .90 .60

99 Heads, by Hundertwasser A942

1993, Oct. 8

1629 A942 7s multicolored 2.00 .90

Council of Europe Conference, Vienna.

Austrian Republic, 75th Anniv. — A943

Design: 5.50s, Statue of Pallas Athena.

Photo. & Engr.

1993, Nov. 12 ***Perf. 13½x14***

1630 A943 5.50s multicolored .90 .60

Trade Unions in Austria, Cent. A944

1993, Nov. 12 Photo. ***Perf. 14***

1631 A944 5.50s multicolored .60 .60

Birth of Christ, by Master of the Krainburger Altar — A945

Photo. & Engr.

1993, Nov. 26 ***Perf. 13½x14***

1632 A945 5.50s multicolored .90 .60

Christmas.

Folklore and Customs Type of 1991

Antiques: 5.50s, Dolls, cradle, Vorarlberg. 6s, Sled, Steiermark. 7s, Godparent's bowl, Upper Austria.

Photo. & Engr.

1994, Jan. 28 ***Perf. 14***

1633 A892 5.50s multicolored .90 .60
1634 A892 6s multicolored .90 .90
1635 A892 7s multicolored .90 .90
Nos. 1633-1635 (3) 2.70 2.40

1994 Winter Olympics, Lillehammer, Norway — A946

1994, Feb. 9

1636 A946 7s multicolored .90 .90

Vienna Mint, 800th Anniv. A947

1994, Feb. 18

1637 A947 6s multicolored .60 .60

Lying Lady, by Herbert Boeckl (1894-1966) — A948

1994, Mar. 18 Photo. ***Perf. 14x13½***

1638 A948 5.50s multicolored .90 .90

Popular Entertainers Type of 1993

Design: 6s, Rock Me Amadeus, by Falco.

1994, Mar. 18 ***Perf. 14***

1639 A927 6s multicolored .90 .60

Wiener Neustadt, 800th Anniv. — A949

1994, Mar. 18

1640 A949 6s multicolored .90 .60

Lake Rudolph, Teleki-Hohnel Expedition — A950

Photo. & Engr.

1994, May 27 ***Perf. 14x13½***

1641 A950 7s multicolored 1.40 1.00

Europa.

Daniel Gran, 300th Birth Anniv. A951

Fresco: 20s, Allegory of Theology, Jurisprudence and Medicine.

1994, May 27

1642 A951 20s multicolored 3.75 2.00

Carinthian Summer Festival, 25th Anniv. — A952

Design: 5.50s, Scene from The Prodigal Son.

Photo. & Engr.

1994, June 17 ***Perf. 14***

1643 A952 5.50s lake & gold .90 .60

Railway Centennials — A953

1994 Photo. & Engr. ***Perf. 14***

1647 A953 5.50s Gailtal .90 .60
1648 A953 6s Murtal 1.25 .60

Issued: 5.50s, 6s, 6/17/94.

Hermann Gmeiner, 75th Birth Anniv. — A954

1994, June 17 ***Perf. 14x13½***

1656 A954 7s multicolored .90 .90

Karl Seitz (1869-1950) Politician A955

1994, Aug. 12 Photo. ***Perf. 14***

1657 A955 5.50s multicolored .90 .60

Karl Bohm (1894-1981), Conductor A956

Photo. & Engr.

1994, Aug. 26 ***Perf. 14x13½***

1658 A956 7s gold & dk blue .90 .60

Ethnic Minorities in Austria A957

1994, Sept. 9 Photo. ***Perf. 13½***

1659 A957 5.50s multicolored .60 .60

Franz Theodor Csokor (1885-1969), Writer — A958

7s, Joseph Roth (1894-1939), writer.

1994, Sept. 9 ***Perf. 14x13½***

1660 A958 6s multicolored .60 .60
1661 A958 7s multicolored .90 .60

Savings Banks in Austria, 175th Anniv. — A959

Photo. & Engr.

1994, Oct. 7 ***Perf. 14x13½***

1662 A959 7s Coin bank .90 .60

Modern Art — A960

Design: 6s, "Head," by Franz Ringel.

1994, Oct. 7 ***Perf. 13½x14***

1663 A960 6s multicolored .90 .60

Austrian Working Environment — A961

1994, Nov. 18 Photo. ***Perf. 14***

1664 A961 6s Stewardess, child .90 .60

See Nos. 1690, 1703, 1736, 1773, 1828, 1859.

Richard Coudenhove Kalergi, Founder of PanEuropean Union, Birth Cent. — A962

Photo. & Engr.

1994, Nov. 18 ***Perf. 13½***

1665 A962 10s multicolored 1.25 .90

Birth of Christ, by Anton Wollenek A963

1994, Nov. 25 ***Perf. 14***

1666 A963 6s multicolored .90 .60

Christmas.

Membership in European Union — A964

1995, Jan. 13 **Photo.** ***Perf. 14***
1667 A964 7s multicolored .90 .90

Adolf Loos (1870-1933), Architect A965

1995, Jan. 13
1668 A965 10s House, Vienna 1.25 .90

Official Representation for Workers, 75th Anniv. — A966

1995, Feb. 24 ***Perf. 14x13½***
1669 A966 6s multicolored .90 .60

Austrian Gymnastics and Sports Assoc., 50th Anniv. — A967

1995, Feb. 24
1670 A967 6s multicolored .90 .60

Folklore and Customs Type of 1991

Designs: 5.50s, Belt, Gailtal, Carinthia. 6s, Vineyard watchman's costume, Vienna. 7s, Bonnet, Wachau, Lower Austria.

Photo. & Engr.
1995, Mar. 24 ***Perf. 14***
1671 A892 5.50s multicolored .90 .60
1672 A892 6s multicolored .90 .60
1673 A892 7s multicolored 1.25 .60
Nos. 1671-1673 (3) 3.05 1.80

Second Republic, 50th Anniv. — A968

1995, Apr. 27
1674 A968 6s State seal .90 .60

History of Mining & Industry A969

Design: Blast furnaces, old Heft ironworks.

1995, Apr. 28 ***Perf. 13½x14***
1675 A969 5.50s multicolored .90 .60

Carinthian Provincial Exhibition.

Nature Lovers Club, Cent. — A970

1995, Apr. 28 ***Perf. 14***
1676 A970 5.50s multicolored .90 .60

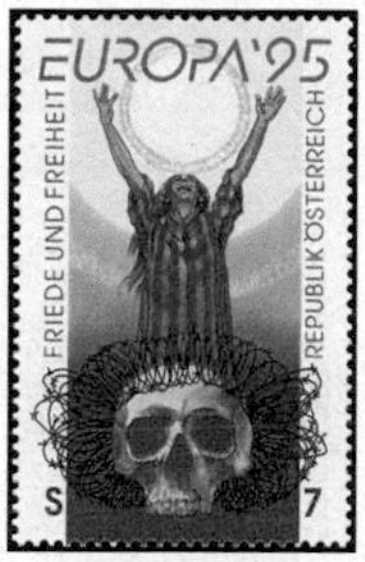

Europa — A971

1995, May 19 ***Perf. 14***
1677 A971 7s multicolored *1.50 .90*

1995 Conference of Ministers of Transportation, Vienna — A972

1995, May 26 **Photo.** ***Perf. 14***
1678 A972 7s multicolored .90 .60

Bregenz Festival, 50th Anniv. A973

1995, June 9
1679 A973 6s multicolored .90 .60

St. Gebhard (949-995) A974

Stained glass window, by Martin Hausle.

1995, June 9
1680 A974 7.50s multicolored .90 .60

UN, 50th Anniv. — A975

1995, June 26 **Photo.** ***Perf. 14***
1681 A975 10s multicolored 1.25 .60

Josef Loschmidt (1821-95), Chemist — A976

Photo. & Engr.
1995, June 26 ***Perf. 14x13½***
1682 A976 20s multicolored 4.50 1.25

Salzburg Festival, 75th Anniv. — A977

Photo. & Engr.
1995, Aug. 18 ***Perf. 13½x14***
1683 A977 6s multicolored .60 .30

Kathe Leichter, Resistance Member, Birth Cent. — A978

1995, Aug. 18 ***Perf. 14x13½***
1684 A978 6s buff, black & red .90 .60

Europaisches Landschaftsbild, by Adolf Frohner — A979

1995, Aug. 18
1685 A979 6s multicolored .90 .60

Operetta Composers A980

Designs: 6s, Franz von Suppe (1819-95), scene from "The Beautiful Galathea." 7s, Nico Dostal (b. 1895), scene from "The Hungarian Wedding."

1995, Sept. 15 ***Perf. 14***
1686 A980 6s multicolored .90 .60
1687 A980 7s multicolored .90 .60

See Croatia No. 253.

University of Klagenfurt, 25th Anniv. — A981

1995, Oct. 6 **Photo.** ***Perf. 14***
1688 A981 5.50s multicolored .60 .30

Carinthian Referendum, 75th Anniv. — A982

1995, Oct. 6 **Photo. & Engr.**
1689 A982 6s multicolored .60 .30

Austria Working Environment Type of 1994

1995, Oct. 20
1690 A961 6s Post office official .90 .30

Composers A983

6s, Anton von Webern (1883-1945). 7s, Ludwig van Beethoven (1770-1827).

1995, Oct. 20 ***Perf. 13½x14***
1691 A983 6s orange & blue .90 .60
1692 A983 7s orange & red .90 .60

Christmas A984

Photo. & Engr.
1995, Dec. 1 ***Perf. 13½***
1693 A984 6s Christ Child .90 .60

Folklore and Customs Type of 1991

Design: Roller and Scheller in "Procession of Masked Groups in Imst," Tyrol.

Photo. & Engr.
1996, Feb. 9 ***Perf. 14***
1694 A892 6s multicolored .90 .30

Maria Theresa Academy, 250th Anniv. — A985

1996, Feb. 9
1695 A985 6s multicolored .90 .30

1996 World Ski Jumping Championships
A986

1996, Feb. 9 **Photo.**
1696 A986 7s multicolored .90 .60

New Western Pier, Vienna Intl. Airport
A987

1996, Mar. 28 **Photo.** ***Perf. 14***
1697 A987 7s multicolored .90 .60

A988

6s, Mother with Child, by Peter Fendi (1796-1842). 7s, Self-portrait, by Leopold Kupelwieser (1795-1862).

1996, Mar. 29
1698 A988 6s multicolored .90 .30
1699 A988 7s multicolored .90 .30

Anton Bruckner (1824-96), Composer, Organist
A989

Photo. & Engr.

1996, Apr. 26 ***Perf. 14***
1700 A989 5.50s Organ, music .90 .60

Georg Matthäus Vischer, 300th Death Anniv.
A990

1996, Apr. 26
1701 A990 10s Kollmitz Castle 1.25 .90

City of Klagenfurt, 800th Anniv. — A991

1996, May 3
1702 A991 6s Ancient square .90 .30

Austrian Working Environment Type of 1994

1996, May 17
1703 A961 6s Chef, waitress .90 .30

Paula von Preradovic, Author
A992

1996, May 17 ***Perf. 13½x14***
1704 A992 7s black, gray & buff 1.25 .90

Europa.

Folklore and Customs Type of 1991

Designs: 5.50s, Corpus Christi poles, Salzburg. 7s, Tyrolian riflemen.

Photo. & Engr.

1996, June 21 ***Perf. 14***
1705 A892 5.50s multicolored .90 .60
1706 A892 7s multicolored .90 .60

1996 Summer Olympic Games, Atlanta — A993

1996, June 21
1707 A993 10s multicolored 1.25 .90

Burgenland Province, 75th Anniv. — A994

1996, Sept. 20
1708 A994 6s multicolored .90 .30

Austrian Mountain Rescue Service, Cent. — A995

1996, Sept. 27
1709 A995 6s multicolored .90 .30

Austria Millennium
A996

Designs: a, Deed by Otto III. b, Empress Maria Theresa, Josef II. c, Duke Henry II. d, 1848 Revolution. e, Rudolf IV. f, Dr. Karl Renner, 1st Republic. g, Emperor Maximilian I. h, State Treaty of 1955, 2nd Republic. i, Imperial Crown of Rudolf II. j, Austria, Europe.

Photo. & Engr.

1996, Oct. 25 ***Perf. 14***
1710 Sheet of 10 19.00 20.00
a.-b. A996 6s any single .90 .90
c.-f. A996 7s any single .90 .90
g.-h. A996 10s any single 1.25 1.25
i.-j. A996 20s any single 3.00 3.00

Power Station, by Reinhard Artberg
A997

1996, Nov. 22
1711 A997 7s multicolored .90 .60

UNICEF, 50th Anniv. — A998

1996, Nov. 22 **Photo.**
1712 A998 10s multicolored 1.25 .90

Christmas
A999

1996, Nov. 29 **Photo. & Engr.**
1713 A999 6s multicolored .90 .60

Folklore and Customs Type of 1991

Epiphany Carol Singers, Burgenland.

Photo. & Engr.

1997, Jan. 17 ***Perf. 14***
1714 A892 7s multicolored .90 .60

Theodor Kramer, Poet, Birth Cent. — A1000

1997, Jan. 17 **Engr.**
1715 A1000 5.50s deep blue .90 .60

Austrian Academy of Sciences, 150th Anniv. — A1001

1997, Feb. 21 **Photo.** ***Perf. 14***
1716 A1001 10s multicolored 1.25 .90

Austrian Electricity Board, 50th Anniv.
A1002

1997, Mar. 21
1717 A1002 6s multicolored .90 .60

The Cruel Lady of Forchtenstein Castle, Burgenland
A1003

Photo. & Engr.

1997, Mar. 21 ***Perf. 14***
1718 A1003 7s multicolored 1.75 .30

See Nos. 1731, 1733, 1745-1746, 1763, 1775, 1794, 1802, 1804, 1810-1811.

Erich Wolfgang Korngold (1897-1957), Composer
A1004

Design: Scene from opera, "The Dead City."

1997, Mar. 21
1719 A1004 20s bl, blk & gold 4.50 2.00

Vienna Rapid, Austrian Soccer Champions — A1005

1997, Apr. 25 **Photo.** ***Perf. 14***
1720 A1005 7s multicolored .90 .60

See Nos. 1754, 1779, 1807, 1839.

Deer Feeding in Wintertime
A1006

1997, Apr. 25
1721 A1006 7s multicolored .90 .60

See Nos. 1747, 1782, 1808, 1835.

St. Peter Canisius (1521-97)
A1007

1997, Apr. 25 *Photo. & Engr.*
1722 A1007 7.50s Canisius Altar, Innsbruck 1.25 .60

Composers — A1008

Designs: 6s, Johannes Brahms (1833-1897). 10s, Franz Schubert (1797-1828).

1997, May 9
1723 A1008 6s gold & vio bl .90 .60
1724 A1008 10s purple & gold 1.75 .90

Stamp Day — A1009

1997, May 9 *Perf. 13½*
1725 A1009 7s "A" and "E" .90 .60

See Nos. B357-B362, 1765, 1791, 1818. The 1st letters spell "Briefmarke," the 2nd "Philatelie."

Child's View of "Town Band of Bremen" A1010

1997, May 23 **Photo.**
1726 A1010 7s multicolored *1.50* .90

Europa.

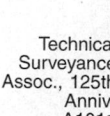

Technical Surveyance Assoc., 125th Anniv. A1011

1997, June 13 **Photo.** *Perf. 14*
1727 A1011 7s multicolored 1.25 .60

Railways A1012

Designs: 6s, Hochschneeberg Cog Railway. 7.50s, Wiener Neustadt-Odenburg Railway.

1997, June 13 **Photo. & Engr.**
1728 A1012 6s multicolored .90 .30
1729 A1012 7.50s multicolored 1.25 .60

Folklore and Customs Type of 1991

6.50s, Marching band, Tyrol.

Photo. & Engr.
1997, July 11 *Perf. 14*
1730 A892 6.50s multicolored .90 .60

Stories and Legends Type of 1997

Design: Dragon of Klagenfurt.

1997, July 11
1731 A1003 6.50s multicolored 1.25 .60

Karl Heinrich Waggerl, Birth Cent. — A1013

1997, July 11
1732 A1013 7s multicolored 1.25 .60

Stories and Legends Type of 1997

Design: Danube water nymph rescuing ferryman, Upper Austria.

Photo. & Engr.
1997, Sept. 19 *Perf. 14*
1733 A1003 14s multicolored 3.25 1.25

1997 Orthopedics Congress, Vienna — A1014

1997, Sept. 19 **Photo.** *Perf. 14*
1734 A1014 8s Adolph Lorenz 1.25 .60

Vienna Agricultural University, 125th Anniv. A1015

1997, Sept. 19
1735 A1015 9s multicolored 1.25 .90

Austrian Working Environment Type of 1994

Photo. & Engr.
1997, Oct. 17 *Perf. 14*
1736 A961 6.50s Nurse, patient .90 .60

"House in Wind," by Helmut Schickhofer — A1016

1997, Oct. 17
1737 A1016 7s multicolored .90 .60

Blind Persons Assocs. in Austria, Cent. — A1017

Photo. & Embossed
1997, Oct. 17
1738 A1017 7s multicolored .90 .60

No. 1738 has embossed Braille inscription.

Dr. Thomas Klestil, Pres. of Austria, 65th birthday — A1018

Photo. & Engr.
1997, Oct. 31 *Perf. 14x13½*
1739 A1018 7s multicolored 1.25 .60

Oskar Werner (1922-84), Actor — A1019

1997, Oct. 31 *Perf. 14*
1740 A1019 7s multicolored 1.25 .60

Folklore and Customs Type of 1991

Upper Austria tower wind players, Steyr.

Photo. & Engr.
1997, Nov. 21 *Perf. 14*
1741 A892 6.50s multicolored .90 .60

Light Into Darkness Relief Organization, 25th Anniv. — A1020

1997, Nov. 28 **Photo.** *Perf. 14*
1742 A1020 7s multicolored .90 .60

Christmas A1021

7s, Mariazell Madonna.

Photo. & Engr.
1997, Nov. 28 *Perf. 14*
1743 A1021 7s multicolored 1.25 .60

Scenery Type of 1984

Kalkalpen Natl. Park, Upper Austria.

Photo. & Engr.
1998, Jan. 23 *Perf. 14*
1744 A679 7s multicolored .90 .60

Stories and Legends Type of 1997

Designs: 9s, The Charming Augustin. 13s, Pied Piper from Korneuburg.

1998, Jan. 23
1745 A1003 9s multicolored 1.75 .90
1746 A1003 13s multicolored 3.25 1.25

Hunting and Environment Type

1998, Feb. 6 **Photo.**
1747 A1006 9s Black cocks .90 .90

1998 Winter Olympic Games, Nagano — A1022

1998, Feb. 6 **Photo. & Engr.**
1748 A1022 14s multicolored 2.50 1.60

Lithographic Printing, Bicent. A1023

Portrait of Aloys Senefelder (1771-1834), inventor of lithography, on printing stone.

1998, Mar. 13 **Litho.** *Perf. 13½*
1749 A1023 7s multicolored 1.25 .60

Joseph Binder (1898-1972), Graphic Artist — A1024

1998, Mar. 13 **Photo.** *Perf. 14*
1750 A1024 7s Poster 1.25 .60

Wiener Secession, Cent. (Assoc. of Artists in Austria-Viennese Secession) A1025

1998, Mar. 13 **Photo. & Engr.**
1751 A1025 8s multicolored 1.25 .90

Folklore and Customs Type of 1991

6.50s, Fiacre, Vienna. 7s, Christ figure, Palm Sunday Donkey Procession, Tyrol.

1998, Apr. 3
1752 A892 6.50s multicolored 1.25 .95
1753 A892 7s multicolored 1.25 1.00

Soccer Champions Type of 1997

7s, Austria-Memphis Club.

1998, Apr. 17 **Photo.**
1754 A1005 7s multicolored 1.25 .60

Salzburg Archdiocese, 1200th Anniv. A1026

1998, Apr. 17 **Photo. & Engr.**
1755 A1026 7s multicolored 1.25 .90

St. Florian, Patron Saint of Fire Brigades A1027

1998, Apr. 17 **Photo.**
1756 A1027 7s multicolored .90 .60

Railway Centennials A1028

No. 1757, Ybbs Railway. No. 1758, Pöstlingberg Railway. No. 1759, Pinzgau Railway.

1998 **Photo. & Engr.** ***Perf. 14***
1757 A1028 6.50s multicolored .90 .60
1758 A1028 6.50s multicolored .90 .60
1759 A1028 6.50s multicolored .90 .60
Nos. 1757-1759 (3) 2.70 1.80

Issued: No. 1757, 5/15; No. 1758, 6/12; No. 1759, 7/17.

Ferdinandeum, Federal Museum of Tyrol, 175th Anniv. A1029

1998, May 15
1760 A1029 7s multicolored .90 .90

Vienna Festival Weeks — A1030

1998, May 15
1761 A1030 7s Townhall *1.60 .60*
Europa.

Folklore and Customs Type of 1991

Samson figure & the Zwergin, Lungau district, Salzburg.

1998, June 5
1762 A892 6.50s multicolored .90 .60

Stories and Legends Type of 1997

Design: 25s, Saint Konrad collecting spring water in his handkerchief, Ems Castle.

1998, June 5
1763 A1003 25s multicolored 6.00 2.50

Christine Lavant, Poet, 25th Death Anniv. A1031

1998, June 5 **Photo.**
1764 A1031 7s multicolored .90 .60

Stamp Day Type of 1997

Photo. & Engr.

1998, June 12 ***Perf. 13½***
1765 A1009 7s "R" and "L" 1.25 .60

See Nos. 1725, 1791,1818, B357-B362. The 1st letters spell "Briefmarke," the 2nd "Philatelie."

Austrian Presidency of the European Union — A1032

1998, July 1 **Photo.** ***Perf. 13½x14***
1766 A1032 7s multicolored 1.25 .60

The People's Opera, Vienna, Centennial & Franz Lehar (1870-1948), Composer — A1033

1998, Sept. 10 **Photo.** ***Perf. 14***
1767 A1033 6.50s multicolored .90 .60

Elizabeth, Empress of Austria (1837-98) A1034

1998, Sept. 10 **Photo. & Engr.**
1768 A1034 7s multicolored 1.25 .60

Vienna University for Commercial Sudies, Cent. — A1035

1998, Sept. 10 **Photo.**
1769 A1035 7s multicolored 1.40 .60

Hans Kudlich, Emancipator of Peasants, 175th Birth Anniv. A1036

Photo. & Engr.

1998, Oct. 23 ***Perf. 14***
1770 A1036 6.50s multicolored 1.25 .60

"My Garden," by Hans Staudacher A1037

1998, Oct. 23
1771 A1037 7s multicolored 1.25 .60

City of Eisenstadt, 350th Anniv. — A1038

1998, Oct. 23
1772 A1038 7s multicolored .90 .60

Austrian Working Environment Type of 1994

6.50s, Reporter, photographer.

Photo. & Engr.

1998, Nov. 6 ***Perf. 14***
1773 A961 6.50s multicolored .90 .60

Christmas A1039

1423 Fresco from Tainach/Tinje Church, Carinthia.

1998, Nov. 27
1774 A1039 7s multicolored 1.25 .60

Stories and Legends Type of 1997

The Dark Maiden of Hardegg Castle.

Photo. & Engr.

1999, Feb. 19 ***Perf. 14***
1775 A1003 8s multicolored 1.75 .90

1999 Nordic Skiing World Championships, Mt. Dachstein, Ramsau A1040

1999, Feb. 19
1776 A1040 7s multicolored 1.25 .60

Scenery Type of 1984

Bohemian Forest, Upper Austria.

Photo. & Engr.

1999, Mar. 19 ***Perf. 14***
1777 A679 7s multicolored 1.25 .60

Folklore and Customs Type of 1991

Traditional walking pilgrimage to Mariazell.

1999, Mar. 19
1778 A892 6.50s multicolored .90 .60

Soccer Champions Type of 1997

Design: Soccer Club SK Puntigamer Sturm Graz.

1999, Apr. 16 **Photo.** ***Perf. 14***
1779 A1005 7s multicolored .90 .60

Schönnbrun Palace, UNESCO World Heritage Site — A1041

Photo. & Engr.

1999, Apr. 16 ***Perf. 14***
1780 A1041 13s multicolored 2.25 1.50

See Nos. 1826, 1845, 1928.

Austrian Patent Office, Cent. — A1042

1999, Apr. 16
1781 A1042 7s multicolored 1.25 .60

Hunting and Environment Type of 1997

1999, May 7 **Litho.** ***Perf. 14***
1782 A1006 6.50s Partridges .90 .60

Austrian General Sport Federation, 50th Anniv. — A1043

1999, May 7 **Engr.** ***Perf. 14***
1783 A1043 7s multicolored 1.25 .60

Council of Europe, 50th Anniv. A1044

1999, May 7 **Photo.** ***Perf. 13½x14***
1784 A1044 14s multicolored 1.25 .60

Karl Jenschke (1899-1969), Automobile Designer A1045

1999, May 28
1785 A1045 7s Steyr automobile 1.25 .60

Marble Relief of St. Martin A1046

Design: 9s, St. Anne, Mary and Jesus.

1999 Photo. & Engr. *Perf. 14*
1786 A1046 8s multicolored 1.25 .90

Perf. 13¾
1787 A1046 9s multicolored 1.25 .90

Issued: 8s, 5/28; 9s, 9/17.
See Nos. 1817, 1830, 1851-1852.

Austrian Social Welfare Service, 125th Anniv. A1047

1999, June 4 Litho. *Perf. 13¾*
1788 A1047 7s multicolored .90 .60

Johann Strauss, the Younger (1825-99), Composer A1048

8s, Johann Strauss, the Elder (1804-49).

1999, June 4 Photo. & Engr.
1789 A1048 7s multicolored 1.25 .60
1790 A1048 8s multicolored 1.25 .60

Stamp Day Type of 1997

1999, June 18 *Perf. 13½*
1791 A1009 7s "K" and "I" 1.25 .60

See Nos. 1725, 1765, 1818, B357-B362. The 1st letters spell "Briefmarke," the 2nd "Philatelie."

Donau-Auen Natl. Park — A1049

1999, June 18 *Perf. 13¾*
1792 A1049 7s multicolored 1.25 .60

Europa.

Natl. Gendarmery, 150th Anniv. — A1050

1999, June 18
1793 A1050 7s multicolored .90 .60

Stories and Legends Type of 1997

Design: The Holy Notburga.

Photo. & Engr.
1999, Aug. 27 *Perf. 13¾x14*
1794 A1003 20s multicolored 5.00 2.50

Graz Opera House, 100th Anniv. — A1051

Photo. & Engr.
1999, Sept. 17 *Perf. 13¾*
1795 A1051 6.50s multicolored 1.25 .60

International Year of Older Persons — A1052

1999, Sept. 17 Photo. *Perf. 13¾*
1796 A1052 7s multicolored 1.25 .60

Federation of Austrian Trade Unions, 14th Congress A1053

1999, Oct. 15 Litho. *Perf. 13¾*
1797 A1053 6.50s multicolored 1.25 .60

"Caffee Girardi," by Wolfgang Herzig — A1054

Photo. & Engr.
1999, Oct. 22 *Perf. 13¾x14*
1798 A1054 7s multicolored .90 .60

Folklore & Customs Type of 1991

7s, The Pummerin, Bell in St. Stephen's Cathedral, Vienna. 8s, Pumpkin Festival, Lower Austria.

1999 Photo. & Engr. *Perf. 13¾*
1799 A892 7s multicolored 1.25 .60
1800 A892 8s multicolored 1.25 .90

Issued: 8s, 10/22; 7s, 11/12.

National Institute of Geology, 150th Anniv. A1055

Photo. & Engr.
1999, Nov. 12 *Perf. 13¾x14*
1801 A1055 7s multicolored 1.25 .60

Stories & Legends Type of 1997

Design: 32s, Discovery of Erzberg.

Photo. & Engr.
1999, Nov. 12 *Perf. 13¾x14*
1802 A1003 32s multicolored 9.50 4.00

Christmas A1056

Photo. & Engr.
1999, Nov. 26 *Perf. 13¾*
1803 A1056 7s Pinkafeld creche 1.25 .60

Stories & Legends Type of 1997

Design: 10s, House of the Basilisk, Vienna.

Photo. & Engr.
2000, Jan. 21 *Perf. 13¾x14*
1804 A1003 10s multi 2.50 1.25
a. Souvenir sheet of 1 35.00 35.00

No. 1804a was sold only with the purchase of an 80s ticket to the Vienna Intl. Philatelic Exhibition.

Folklore & Customs Type of 1991

Designs: 6.50s, Schleicherlaufen Festival, Telfs. 7s, Carrying miniature churches, Bad Eisenkappel.

2000 Photo. & Engr. *Perf. 13¾*
1805 A892 6.50s multi .90 .90
1806 A892 7s multi .90 .90

Issued: 6.50s, 2/11; 7s, 1/21.

Soccer Champions Type of 1997

Design: Tirol Soccer Club.

2000, Mar. 3 Photo. *Perf. 13¾*
1807 A1005 7s multi 1.25 1.00

Hunting and Environment Type of 1997

2000, Mar. 3 *Perf. 14x14¼*
1808 A1006 7s Ibex 1.25 1.00

Intl. Gardening Exhibition, Graz — A1057

Photo. & Embossed
2000, Mar. 3 *Perf. 13½x13¾*
1809 A1057 7s multi 1.25 1.25

Stories & Legends Type of 1997

Designs: 22s, The Witch's Ride. 23s, The Bread Loaf Monument.

2000 Photo. & Engr. *Perf. 13¾x14*
1810 A1003 22s multi 4.50 4.50
1811 A1003 23s multi 4.50 6.00

Issued: 22s, 4/28. 23s, 6/16.

First Ascent of Grossglockner, Bicent. A1058

2000, Apr. 28 *Perf. 13¾*
1812 A1058 7s multi 1.25 1.00

Scenery Type of 1984

Design: Sonnblick Glacier, Granatspitze, Weisssee, Salzburg.

2000, May 9 *Perf. 13¾x14*
1813 A679 7s multi 1.25 1.25

Europa, 2000
Common Design Type

2000, May 9 Photo. *Perf. 14¼x13½*
1814 CD17 7s multi 1.25 1.25
Nos. 1814 (1) 1.25 1.25

Klagenfurt Airport, 75th Anniv. A1059

2000, May 19 *Perf. 13¾*
1815 A1059 7s multi 1.25 1.25

Protection of Historical Monuments, 150th Anniv. — A1060

Photo. & Engr.
2000, May 19 *Perf. 14x13¼*
1816 A1060 8s multi 1.25 1.25

Religious Art Type of 1999

Design: 9s, Illustration of St. Malachy from book, *The Life of Bishop Malachy.*

2000, May 19 *Perf. 13¾*
1817 A1046 9s multi 1.25 1.25

Stamp Day Type of 1997

2000, May 30 *Perf. 13½*
1818 A1009 7s "E" and "E" 1.25 1.25

See Nos. 1725, 1765, 1791, B357-B362. The 1st letters spell "Briefmarke," the 2nd "Philatelie."

Austrian Postage Stamps, 150th Anniv. A1061

2000, May 30 *Perf. 13¾*
1819 A1061 7s Nos. 5, 1818 1.25 .90

Children's Television Character, Confetti A1062

2000, May 31
1820 A1062 7s multi .90 .90

See Nos. 1841, 1893, 1914.

Blue Blues, by Friedensreich Hundertwasser (1928-2000), Artist — A1063

Colors of seven solid vertical panels at top: a, Silver. b, Red. c, Red violet. d, Black.

2000, June 2
1821 Sheet of 4 10.00 10.00
a.-d. A1063 7s Any single 1.25 .90

Discovery of Human Blood Types, Cent. A1064

Perf. 13¾x13½

2000, June 16 **Photo.**
1822 A1064 8s multi 1.25 1.25

Scheduled Motorized Vehicle Passenger Transportation, Cent. — A1065

Photo. & Engr.

2000, June 16 ***Perf. 14***
1823 A1065 9s multi 1.25 1.25

Folklore & Customs Type of 1991

7s, Intl. meeting of rafters, Carinthia.

Photo. & Engr.

2000, Aug. 25 ***Perf. 13¾***
1824 A892 7s multi .90 .90

Vienna Symphony, Cent. — A1066

2000, Sept. 15
1825 A1066 7s multi 1.25 1.25

World Heritage Site Type of 1999

Hallstatt-Dachstein and Salzkammergut

2000, Sept. 15
1826 A1041 7s multi 1.25 1.25

2000 Summer Olympics, Sydney — A1068

2000, Sept. 15 ***Perf. 14x13¾***
1827 A1068 9s multi 1.25 1.25

Working Environment Type of 1994

6.50s, Papermaker, printer.

2000, Sept. 29
1828 A961 6.50s multi .90 .90

Turf Turkey, by Ida Szigethy A1069

2000, Oct. 13 ***Perf. 13¾***
1829 A1069 7s multi 1.25 1.25

Religious Art Type of 1999

Design: 8s, Illuminated text, Codex 965.

2000, Oct. 13
1830 A1046 8s multi 1.25 1.25

Association of Austrian Adult Education Centers, 50th Anniv. A1070

Photo. & Engr.

2000, Nov. 24 ***Perf. 13¾***
1831 A1070 7s multi 1.25 1.25

Vaccinations in Austria, Bicent. — A1071

2000, Nov. 24 ***Perf. 14¼x13½***
1832 A1071 7s multi 1.25 1.25

Christmas A1072

Altar sidewing, St. Martin's Church, Ludesch.

2000, Dec. 1 ***Perf. 13¾***
1833 A1072 7s multi 1.25 1.25

2001 Alpine Skiing World Championships, St. Anton am Arlberg — A1073

2000, Dec. 15 ***Perf. 14x13¾***
1834 A1073 7s multi .90 .90

Hunting & Environment Type of 1997

2001, Feb. 16 **Photo.** ***Perf. 14x14¼***
1835 A1006 7s Ducks 1.25 1.25

Folklore & Customs Type of 1991

Designs: No. 1836, Lenten altar cloths, Eastern Tyrol. No. 1837, Water disk shooting, Prebersee. No. 1838, Boat Mill, Mureck.

2001 **Photo. & Engr.** ***Perf. 13¾***
1836 A892 7s multi 1.25 1.25
1837 A892 7s multi 1.25 1.25
1838 A892 8s multi 1.25 1.25
Nos. 1836-1838 (3) 3.75 3.75

Issued: No. 1836, 5/4/01. No. 1838, 3/30/01. No. 1837, 8/24/01.

Soccer Champions Type of 1997

7s, Wustenrot Salzburg.

2001, Mar. 30 **Photo.** ***Perf. 13¾***
1839 A1005 7s multi 1.25 1.25

Zilltertal Railway, Cent. A1074

Photo. & Engr.

2001, Mar. 30 ***Perf. 13¾***
1840 A1074 7s multi .90 .90

Children's Television Character Type of 2000

2001, Apr. 20 **Photo.** ***Perf. 13¾***
1841 A1062 7s Rolf Rüdiger 1.25 1.25

Salzburg Airport, 75th Anniv. A1075

Photo. & Engr.

2001, Apr. 20 ***Perf. 13½x14¼***
1842 A1075 14s multi 2.50 1.75

Scenery Type of 1984

Design: Bärenschützkamm, Styria.

Photo. & Engr.

2001, May 4 ***Perf. 13¾***
1843 A679 7s multi 1.25 1.25

Europa A1076

2001, May 18 **Photo.** ***Perf. 13¾***
1844 A1076 15s multi *2.50 2.50*

UNESCO World Heritage Type of 1999

Design: Semmering Railway.

Photo. & Engr.

2001, June 8 ***Perf. 13¾***
1845 A1041 35s multi 7.50 7.50

Austrian Aero Club, Cent. — A1077

2001, June 8 ***Perf. 13¾x14***
1846 A1077 7s multi .90 .90

UN High Commissioner for Refugees, 50th Anniv. — A1078

2001, June 8 ***Perf. 14x13¾***
1847 A1078 21s multi 3.75 3.75

7th IVV Hiking Olympics A1079

2001, June 22 **Photo.** ***Perf. 13¾***
1848 A1079 7s multi 1.25 1.25

Military Post Offices Abroad A1080

2001, June 22
1849 A1080 7s multi 1.25 1.25

Conversion of East-West Railway to Four Tracks A1081

Photo. & Engr.

2001, Aug. 31 ***Perf. 13¾***
1850 A1081 7s multi 1.25 1.25

Religious Art Type of 1999

Designs: 7s, Church vestment cut from Turkish tent, 1683. 10s, Pluvial.

2001 **Photo. & Engr.** ***Perf. 13¾***
1851 A1046 7s multi 1.25 1.25
1852 A1046 10s multi 1.25 1.25

Issued: 7s, 10/5; 10s, 9/14.

Johann Nestroy (1801-62), Playwright A1082

2001, Sept. 14
1853 A1082 7s multi .90 .90

The Continents (Detail), by Helmut Leherb — A1083

2001, Sept. 14
1854 A1083 7s multi 1.25 1.25

Joseph Ritter von Führich (1800-76), Painter — A1084

2001, Sept. 14 ***Perf. 14***
1855 A1084 8s multi 1.25 1.25

Leopold Ludwig Döbler (1801-64), Magician A1085

2001, Oct. 5
1856 A1085 7s multi 1.25 1.25

Meteorology and Geodynamics Institute, 150th Anniv. — A1086

2001, Oct. 5
1857 A1086 12s multi 2.00 2.00

Cat King, by Manfred Deix — A1087

2001, Oct. 5 ***Perf. 13¾***
1858 A1087 19s multi 3.75 3.75

See No. 1903.

Working Environment Type of 1994

2001, Oct. 16 ***Perf. 14***
1859 A961 7s Public servants .90 .90

Christmas A1088

Photo. & Engr.

2001, Nov. 30 ***Perf. 14***
1860 A1088 7s multi .90 .90

100 Cents = 1 Euro (€)

Introduction of the Euro — A1089

Photo. & Embossed with Foil Application

2002, Jan. 1 ***Perf. 13½x13¾***
1861 A1089 €3.27 multi 7.00 7.00

Austrian Scenes — A1090

Designs: 4c, Schönlaterngasse, Vienna. 7c, Stations of the Cross, Lower Austria Province. 13c, Cow in pasture, Tyrol Province. 17c, Street, Hadres. 20c, Sailboats on Wörther See, Carinthia. 25c, Rock with crosses, Mondsee, Upper Austria. 27c, Farmhouse, Salzburg Province. 45c, St. Martin's Chapel, Kleinwalser Valley, Vorarlberg. 51c, Schönlaterngasse, Vienna. 55c, Houses, Steyr. 58c, Street, Hadres. 73c, Farmhouse, Salzburg Province. 75c, Ship in Lake Constance (Bodensee), Vorarlberg Province. 87c, Cow in pasture, Tyrol Province. €1, Farmhouse, Rossegg. €1.25, Wine press house, Eisenberg. €2.03, Stations of the Cross, Lower Austria Province. €3.75, Roadside shrine, Carinthia Province.

2002-03 **Photo.** ***Perf. 13¾x14***

1862	A1090	4c multi	.25	.25
1863	A1090	7c multi	.25	.25
1863A	A1090	13c multi	.35	.35
1864	A1090	17c multi	.45	.45
1865	A1090	20c multi	.55	.50
1865A	A1090	25c multi	.65	.50
1866	A1090	27c multi	.70	.50
1866A	A1090	45c multi	1.25	1.25
1867	A1090	51c multi	1.40	.70
1868	A1090	55c multi	1.50	1.40
1869	A1090	58c multi	1.50	.70
1872	A1090	73c multi	1.90	.90
1873	A1090	75c multi	2.00	1.40
1875	A1090	87c multi	2.25	1.10
1876	A1090	€1 multi	2.75	2.10
1877	A1090	€1.25 multi	3.25	2.50
1879	A1090	€2.03 multi	5.25	2.50
1880	A1090	€3.75 multi	9.75	8.50
	Nos. 1862-1880 (18)		36.00	25.85

Issued: 51c, 58c, 73c, 87c, €2.03, 1/1/02. 4c, 7c, 13c, 17c, 27c, 6/2/03; 55c, 75c, €1, €1.25, €3.75, 5/30/03. 20c, 25c, 7/18/03. 45c, 12/5/03.

For surcharges see Nos. 1969, 1979-1986, 2047, B376.

2002 Winter Olympics, Salt Lake City — A1091

Photo. & Engr.

2002, Feb. 8 ***Perf. 14x13¾***
1882 A1091 73c multi 1.50 1.50

Love — A1092

2002, Feb. 14 **Photo.** ***Perf. 14¼x14***
1883 A1092 87c multi 1.75 1.75

Intl. Women's Day — A1093

2002, Mar. 8 ***Perf. 13¾***
1884 A1093 51c multi 1.25 1.25

Promotion of Youth Philately — A1094

Cartoon characters: No. 1885, Girls Mel and Lucy. No. 1886, Sisco and Mauritius (boy and dog). No. 1887, Edison and Gogo (girl and boy).

2002 **Photo.** ***Perf. 14x13¾***

1885	A1094	58c multi	1.50	1.50
1886	A1094	58c multi	1.50	1.50
1887	A1094	58c multi	1.50	1.50
	Nos. 1885-1887 (3)		4.50	4.50

Issued: No. 1885, 4/5. No. 1886, 5/10. No. 1887, 11/22.

Roses — A1095

2002, Apr. 5 **Photo.** ***Perf. 14x13¾***
1888 A1095 58c multi 1.25 1.25

80th Anniversary of Marianneum, by Alfred Kubin — A1096

2002, Apr. 10 ***Perf. 13½x13¾***
1889 A1096 87c black & buff 2.00 2.00

Caritas — A1097

2002, Apr. 26
1890 A1097 51c multi 1.25 1.25

Europa A1098

2002, May 3 ***Perf. 13¾***
1891 A1098 87c multi 2.00 2.00

Lilienfeld Monastery, 800th Anniv. A1099

Photo. & Engr.

2002, May 17 ***Perf. 13¾***
1892 A1099 €2.03 multi 4.50 4.50

Children's Television Character Type of 2000

2002, May 23 **Photo.** ***Perf. 13¾***
1893 A1062 51c Mimi 1.25 1.25

Souvenir Sheet

Schönnbrunn Zoo, 250th Anniv. — A1100

No. 1894: a, Orangutan, leopard, lioness, zebras. b, Various birds. c, Lion, antelope, turtle, crocodile, jellyfish. d, Antelope, elephant, birds, jellyfish, fish, ray.

Photo. & Engr.

2002, June 3 ***Perf. 13½x14¼***

1894	A1100	Sheet of 4	8.00	8.00
a.		51c multi	1.25	1.25
b.		58c multi	2.00	2.00
c.		87c multi	2.00	2.00
d.		€1.38 multi	3.00	3.00

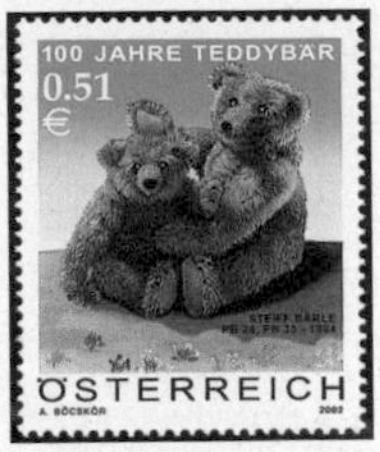

Teddy Bears, Cent. — A1101

2002, June 4 Photo. ***Perf. 14¼x14***
1895 A1101 51c multi 1.25 1.25

Crystal Cup from Innsbruck Glassworks A1102

Photo. & Engr.
2002, June 21 ***Perf. 13¾***
1896 A1102 €1.60 multi 3.50 3.50

Traditional arts and crafts.

Chair by Michael Thonet, 1860 — A1103

2002, June 21 Photo.
1897 A1103 €1.38 multi 3.00 3.00

Austrian design.

Museum of Contemporary Art, Vienna — A1104

2002, Sept. 4 Photo. ***Perf. 14x13¾***
1898 A1104 58c multi 1.25 1.25

Austrians Living Abroad — A1105

Photo. & Engr.
2002, Sept. 5 ***Perf. 13¾x14***
1899 A1105 €2.47 multi 6.00 6.00

Clown Doctor A1106

2002, Sept. 10 Photo. ***Perf. 13¾***
1900 A1106 51c multi 1.25 1.25

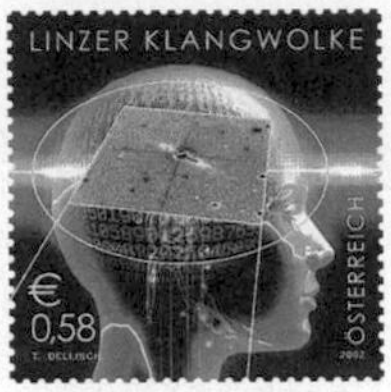

Linz "Sound Cloud" A1107

2002, Sept. 13
1901 A1107 58c multi 1.25 1.25

OAF Gräf & Stift Type 40/45 Automobile A1108

2002, Sept. 27
1902 A1108 51c multi 1.25 1.25

See No. 1925.

Pet Type of 2001

Design: Dog King, by Manfred Deix.

2002, Oct. 4 Photo. ***Perf. 13¾***
1903 A1087 51c multi 1.25 1.25

Train at Vienna South Railway Station A1109

2002, Oct. 4 Photo. & Engr.
1904 A1109 51c multi 1.25 1.25

See Nos. 1921, 1958, 2023, 2059, 2105, 2114, 2166, 2171, 2215, 2249, 2279, 2330, 2337, 2521, 2582, 2634, 2682, 2687, 2761, 2811, 2819, 2871.

Schützenhaus, by Karl Goldammer A1110

2002, Oct. 11
1905 A1110 51c multi 1.25 1.25

Souvenir Sheet

National Lottery, 250th Anniv. — A1111

2002, Oct. 17 Photo. ***Perf.***
1906 A1111 87c multi 2.25 2.25

Thayatal Natl. Park A1112

Photo. & Engr.
2002, Oct. 25 ***Perf. 13¾***
1907 A1112 58c multi 1.25 1.25

Puch 175 SV Motorcycle A1113

2002, Nov. 8 Photo. ***Perf. 14x13¾***
1908 A1113 58c multi 1.25 1.25

One Eye, by Wolfgang Homola A1114

2002, Nov. 15 ***Perf. 13¾***
1909 A1114 €1.38 multi 3.00 3.00

Austrian design.

Christmas — A1115

Photo. & Engr.
2002, Nov. 29 ***Perf. 14x14¼***
1910 A1115 51c multi 1.25 1.25

A1115a

2003, Jan. 22 Litho. ***Perf. 13¾x14***
1910A A1115a 45c multi 6.00 6.00

Graz, 2003 European Cultural Capital A1116

Perf. 13½x14¼
2003, Mar. 14 Photo.
1911 A1116 58c multi 1.40 1.40

Heart, Wedding Rings and Pigeons — A1117

2003, Mar. 21 ***Perf. 14¼x13½***
1912 A1117 58c multi 1.25 1.25

Billy Wilder (1906-2002), Movie Director — A1118

2003, Mar. 21
1913 A1118 58c gray black 1.50 1.50

Children's Television Character Type of 2000

2003, Apr. 11 Photo. ***Perf. 13¾***
1914 A1062 51c Kasperl 1.40 1.40

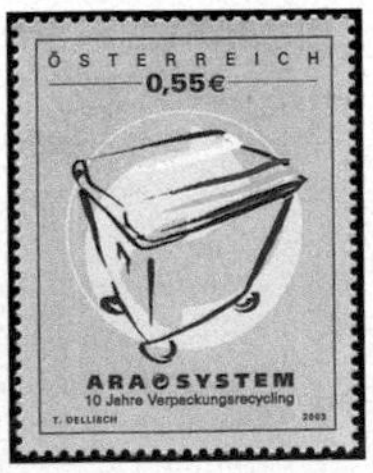

Implementation of Waste Recycling System, 10th Anniv. — A1119

2003, Apr. 11
1915 A1119 55c multi 1.25 1.25

Bar Service No. 248, Glassware by Adolf Loos — A1120

2003, Apr. 11
1916 A1120 €1.38 multi 3.25 3.25

Austrian design.

Souvenir Sheet

Panda Research in Austria — A1121

2003, Apr. 14 *Perf. 14x14¼*

1917 A1121 Sheet of 2 4.00 3.00
a. 75c Two pandas 1.50 1.50
b. €1 Two pandas, diff. 2.00 1.50

No. 1917b is 38mm in diameter.

St. Georgen am Längsee Convent, 1000th Anniv. A1122

2003, Apr. 25 *Perf. 13¾*

1918 A1122 87c multi 2.00 2.00

Souvenir Sheet

Marcel Prawy (1911-2003), Musical Impresario — A1123

2003, Apr. 25

1919 A1123 €1.75 multi 4.00 4.00

Europa A1124

2003, May 9

1920 A1124 €1.02 multi 2.50 2.50

Railways Type of 2002

75c, OEBB Series 5045.

Photo. & Engr.

2003, June 6 *Perf. 13¾*

1921 A1109 75c multi 1.50 1.50

Salzach River Bridge, Laufen, Germany — Oberndorf, Austria — A1125

Photo. & Engr.

2003, June 12 *Perf. 13½*

1922 A1125 55c multi 1.25 1.25

See Germany No. 2245.

Souvenir Sheet

Ford Motor Company, Cent. — A1126

No. 1923: a, Model T. b, Henry Ford (1863-1947). c, 2003 Ford Streetka.

Perf. 13½x14¼

2003, June 16 **Photo.**

1923 A1126 Sheet of 3 + label 5.00 5.00
a.-c. 55c Any single 1.50 1.50

Souvenir Sheet

Rolling Stones — A1127

No. 1924: a, Guitarist Keith Richards. b, Singer Mick Jagger. c, Drummer Charlie Watts. d, Guitarist Ron Wood smoking cigarette.

2003, June 18 *Perf. 14x13½*

1924 A1127 Sheet of 4 5.00 5.00
a.-d. 55c Any single 1.10 1.10

Vehicle Type of 2002

Design: Rosenbauer Panther 8x8 airport fire engine.

2003, June 20 *Perf. 13¾*

1925 A1108 55c multi 1.50 1.50

Bible Year — A1128

2003, June 20

1926 A1128 55c multi 1.40 1.40

Prenez le Temps d'Aimer, by Kiki Kogelnik (1935-97) A1129

2003, July 3 **Photo. & Engr.**

1927 A1129 55c multi 1.25 1.25

UNESCO World Heritage Type of 1999

Design: Neusiedler See.

Photo. & Engr.

2003, July 11 *Perf. 13¾*

1928 A1041 €1 multi 2.50 2.50

Samurai and Geisha A1130

2003, July 19 **Photo.** *Perf. 13¾*

1929 A1130 55c multi 1.25 1.25

Exhibition of Japanese Shogun Era Culture, Leoben Kunsthalle, Vienna.

Performance of Turandot at St. Margarethen Opera Festival — A1131

2003, July 24 *Perf. 14x13¾*

1930 A1131 55c multi 1.25 1.25

Children's Welfare — A1132

2003, Sept. 12 **Photo.** *Perf. 13x13½*

1931 A1132 55c multi 1.25 1.25

Water Tower, Wiener Neustadt A1133

2003, Sept. 18 *Perf. 13¾*

1932 A1133 55c multi 1.25 1.25

50th Austrian Local Government Conference.

Thank You A1134

2003, Sept. 19

1933 A1134 55c multi 1.25 1.25

Mail Order Business A1135

2003, Sept. 24 *Perf. 13¾x14*

1934 A1135 55c multi 1.25 1.25

Werner Schlager, 2003 Table Tennis World Champion — A1136

2003, Sept. 25 *Perf. 14x13¾*

1935 A1136 55c multi 1.40 1.40

Jugend-Phila Graz '03 Youth Philatelic Exhibition — A1137

2003, Sept. 26

1936 A1137 55c multi 1.25 1.25

Performance of Musical "Elisabeth," Theater an der Wien, Vienna — A1138

2003, Oct. 1

1937 A1138 55c multi 1.25 1.25

Souvenir Sheet

Judith I, by Gustav Klimt — A1139

Photo. & Engr.

2003, Oct. 10 *Perf. 13½x13¾*

1938 A1139 €2.10 multi 5.50 5.50

Licht Ins Dunkel Fund-Raising Campaign for the Handicapped, 30th Anniv. — A1140

Perf. 13¾x13½

2003, Nov. 11 **Photo.**

1939 A1140 55c multi 1.25 1.25

Bösendorfer Piano A1141

Jazz Pianist Oscar Peterson and Bösendorfer Piano — A1142

Photo. & Engr.

2003, Nov. 19 ***Perf. 13¾***

1940 A1141 75c multi 1.75 1.75

Photo.

Perf. 13½x12¾

1941 A1142 €1.25 multi 3.00 3.00

Bösendorfer pianos, 175th anniv.

Christmas A1143

Photo. & Engr.

2003, Nov. 28 ***Perf. 13¾x14***

1942 A1143 55c multi 1.25 1.25

A1144

Personalized Stamps A1145

2003, Dec. 5 **Photo.** ***Perf. 13¾***

1943 A1144 55c multi 1.25 1.25

1944 A1145 55c multi 1.25 1.25

Stamp vignettes could be personalized by customers, presumably for an extra fee.

A quantity of Nos. 1943 and 1944 were later imprinted with various commercial themes and offered by Austria Post in full panes at a premium over face value. Only examples as illustrated, bearing generic vignettes, were sold at the face value shown on the stamp. In 2006, Nos. 1943 and 1944 were offered with other denominations that lacked the euro sign. Stamps with similar frames in colors other than yellow and blue, as seen on No. 2036, and stamps with country names and denominations in white were created starting in 2013.

2004 New Year's Concert with Conductor Riccardo Muti — A1146

2004, Jan. 1 **Photo.** ***Perf. 13¾***

1945 A1146 €1 multi 2.25 2.25

Seiji Ozawa, Conductor of Vienna State Opera A1147

2004, Jan. 16 **Photo.** ***Perf. 13¾***

1946 A1147 €1 multi 2.25 2.25

José Carreras, 30th Anniv. at Vienna State Opera A1148

2004, Feb. 23 **Photo.** ***Perf. 13¾***

1947 A1148 €1 multi 2.25 2.25

Austrian Soccer Association, Cent. — A1149

No. 1948: a, Gerhard Hanappi. b, Mathias Sindelar. c, Soccer ball, centenary emblem. d, Bruno Pezzey. e, Ernst Ocwirk. f, Walter Zeman. g, Herbert Prohaska. h, Hans Krankl. i, Andreas Herzog. j, Anton Polster.

2004, Mar. 18

1948 A1149 Sheet of 10 13.00 13.00

a.-j. 55c Any single 1.25 1.25

Easter — A1150

2004, Mar. 26

1949 A1150 55c multi 1.40 1.40

Life Ball, Charity Ball for AIDS Research — A1151

2004, Mar. 29 ***Perf. 14x13¾***

1950 A1151 55c multi 1.25 1.25

Franz Cardinal König (1905-2004) A1152

Photo. & Engr.

2004, Mar. 30 ***Perf. 14¼***

1951 A1152 €1 multi 2.50 2.50

Souvenir Sheet

Wedding of Emperor Franz Joseph and Empress Elizabeth von Wittelsbach, 150th Anniv. — A1153

No. 1952: a, Emperor and Empress on honeymoon in Laxenburg (29x36mm). b, Wedding procession (29x36mm). c, Emperor and Empress (31x38mm).

2004, Apr. 23 ***Perf. 14¼x14***

1952 A1153 Sheet of 3 12.50 12.50

a. €1.25 multi 2.50 2.50

b. €1.50 multi 3.00 3.00

c. €1.75 multi 3.50 3.50

Souvenir Sheet

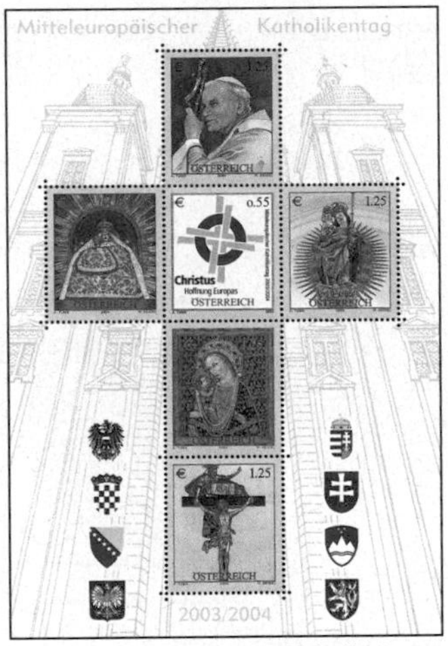

Central European Catholics' Day — A1154

No. 1953: a, Catholics' Day emblem. b, Pope John Paul II. c, Madonna and Child, Mariazell Basilica (silver panel at bottom). d, Mother of God on the Column of the Blessed Virgin, Mariazell Basilica. e, Virgin Mary and Child, Mariazell Basilica (gold frame). f, Altar crucifix, Mariazell Basilica.

Photo. (55c), Photo. & Engr.

2004, Apr. 28 ***Perf. 14***

1953 A1154 Sheet of 6 17.50 17.50

a. 55c multi 1.50 1.50

b.-f. €1.25 Any single 3.25 3.25

Folklore & Customs Type of 1991

Design: Barrel sliding, Klosterneuburg.

Photo. & Engr.

2004, May 8 ***Perf. 13¾***

1954 A892 55c multi 1.40 1.40

Joe Zawinul, Jazz Musician A1155

2004, May 24 **Photo.** ***Perf. 13¾***

1955 A1155 55c multi 1.25 1.25

Europa A1156

2004, June 4 ***Perf. 13¾x14***

1956 A1156 75c multi 1.75 1.75

Papal Order of the Holy Sepulchre of Jerusalem A1157

Photo. & Engr.

2004, June 4 ***Perf. 13¾***

1957 A1157 125c multi 2.50 2.50

Railways Type of 2002

55c, Engerth locomotive.

Photo. & Engr.

2004, June 19 ***Perf. 13¾***

1958 A1109 55c multi 1.25 1.25

21st Danube Island Festival, Vienna A1158

2004, June 25 **Photo.** ***Perf. 13¾x14***

1959 A1158 55c multi 1.25 1.25

Theodor Herzl (1860-1904), Zionist Leader A1159

2004, July 6 ***Perf. 13¾***

1960 A1159 55c multi 1.25 1.25

See Hungary No. 3903, Israel No. 1566.

Arnold Schwarzenegger, Governor of California, Actor — A1160

Perf. 13½x14¼

2004, July 30 **Photo.**
1961 A1160 100c multi 2.25 2.25

Ernst Happel (1925-92), Soccer Coach — A1161

2004, Aug. 17 *Perf. 14x13½*
1962 A1161 100c red & black 2.00 2.00

Winning Entry in Tom Turbo Television Show Children's Stamp Design Contest A1162

2004, Sept. 9 **Photo.** *Perf. 13¾*
1963 A1162 55c multi 1.40 1.40

Tom Tom, Tom Tomette and Schneckodemus, Cartoon by Thomas Kostron — A1163

2004, Sept. 10 *Perf. 14¼x14*
1964 A1163 55c multi 1.25 1.25

Incorporation of Floridsdorf into Vienna, Cent. — A1164

Photo. & Engr.

2004, Sept. 17 *Perf. 14x13¾*
1965 A1164 55c multi 1.25 1.25

Souvenir Sheet

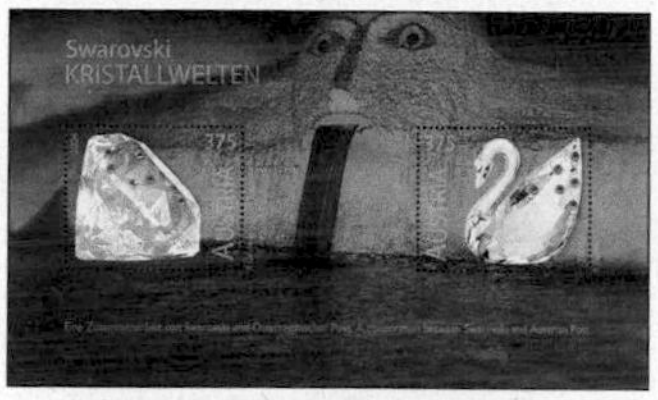

Swarovski Crystal — A1165

No. 1966: a, Crystal. b, Swan.

Photo. With Glass Crystals Affixed

2004, Sept. 20 *Perf. 14x14¼*
1966 A1165 Sheet of 2 20.00 20.00
a.-b. 375c Either single 10.00 10.00

Six crystals are affixed to each stamp. Sheet was sold with a protective sleeve.

Hermann Maier, Skier — A1166

2004, Sept. 25 **Photo.** *Perf. 14x13¾*
1967 A1166 55c multi 1.40 1.40

Kaspar's Winter Scene, by Josef Bramer A1167

Photo. & Engr.

2004, Oct. 8 *Perf. 13½x13¾*
1968 A1167 55c multi 1.25 1.25

No. 1867 Surcharged

2004, Oct. 13 **Photo.** *Perf. 13¾x14*
1969 A1090 55c on 51c #1867 1.50 1.50

Woman Waiting, by Silvia Gredenberg A1168

2004, Oct. 15 **Photo.** *Perf. 13¾x14*
1970 A1168 55c multi 1.50 1.50

Souvenir Sheet

Young Sunflower, by Max Weiler — A1169

Photo. & Engr.

2004, Oct. 18 *Perf. 13¾*
1971 A1169 210c multi 5.00 5.00

Poster for Danube Meadows National Park, by Friedensreich Hundertwasser A1170

Photo. & Engr.

2004, Oct. 22 *Perf. 13½x13¾*
1972 A1170 55c multi 1.25 1.25

Federal Army, 50th Anniv. — A1171

2004, Oct. 26 **Photo.** *Perf. 13¾*
1973 A1171 55c multi 1.25 1.25

Nikolaus Harnoncourt, Conductor, 75th Birthday — A1172

2004, Oct. 29
1974 A1172 100c multi 2.50 2.50

Christmas A1173

Photo. & Engr.

2004, Nov. 26 *Perf. 13½x13¾*
1975 A1173 55c multi 1.25 1.25

2005 New Year's Concert With Conductor Lorin Maazel A1174

2005, Jan. 1 **Photo.** *Perf. 13¾*
1976 A1174 €1 multi 2.50 2.50

Herbert von Karajan Center, 10th Anniv. A1175

2005, Jan. 14 *Perf. 14x14¼*
1977 A1175 55c multi 1.25 1.25

Examples of No. 1977 with a lighter background were given away as gifts to standing order customers.

Stephan Eberharter, Skier — A1176

2005, Jan. 20 *Perf. 14x13¾*
1978 A1176 55c multi 1.50 1.50

Nos. 1862, 1863A, 1864, 1866, 1869, 1872, 1875 and 1879 Surcharged

g

h

i

j

k

l

m

n

2005 **Photo.** *Perf. 13¾x14*
1979 A1090(g) 55c on 13c multi 1.50 1.50
1980 A1090(h) 55c on 17c multi 1.50 1.50
1981 A1090(i) 55c on 27c multi 1.50 1.50
1982 A1090(j) 55c on 4c multi 1.50 1.50
1983 A1090(k) 55c on 58c multi 1.50 1.50
1984 A1090(l) 55c on 73c multi 1.50 1.50
1985 A1090(m) 55c on 87c multi 1.50 1.50
1986 A1090(n) 55c on €2.03 multi 1.50 1.50
Nos. 1979-1986 (8) 12.00 12.00

Issued: Nos. 1979, 1980, 2/11; Nos. 1981, 1986, 2/18; Nos. 1982, 1983, 2/4; Nos. 1984, 1985, 1/25.

Rotary International, Cent. — A1177

2005, Feb. 23 **Photo.** *Perf. 14x14¼*
1987 A1177 55c multi 1.25 1.25

Max Schmeling (1905-2005), Boxer A1178

Photo. & Engr.

2005, Mar. 1 *Perf. 13¾x14*

1988 A1178 100c multi 2.50 2.50

Venus at a Mirror, by Peter Paul Rubens A1179

2005, Mar. 7 *Perf. 13¾*

1989 A1179 125c multi 3.00 3.00

See Liechtenstein No. 1314.

Souvenir Sheet

Carl Djerassi, Chemist and Novelist — A1180

2005, Mar. 8 **Photo.** *Perf. 14*

1990 A1180 100c multi 2.50 2.50

Pope John Paul II (1920-2005) A1181

Photo. & Engr.

2005, Apr. 14 *Perf. 13½x14¼*

1991 A1181 €1 multi 2.50 2.50

Zodiac A1182

New Year 2005 (Year of the Rooster) A1183

Die Cut Perf. 14 Syncopated

2005-06 **Self-Adhesive** **Photo.**

Booklet Stamps

1992	A1182	55c	Taurus	4.00	4.00
1993	A1182	55c	Gemini	4.00	4.00
1994	A1182	55c	Cancer	4.00	4.00
1995	A1183	55c	Red rooster	4.00	4.00
a.			Booklet pane, 2 each #1992-1995	35.00	
1996	A1182	55c	Leo	4.00	4.00
1997	A1182	55c	Virgo	4.00	4.00
1998	A1182	55c	Libra	4.00	4.00
1999	A1183	55c	Yellow rooster	4.00	4.00
a.			Booklet pane, 2 each #1996-1999	35.00	
2000	A1182	55c	Scorpio	4.00	4.00
2001	A1182	55c	Sagittarius	4.00	4.00
2002	A1182	55c	Capricorn	4.00	4.00
2003	A1183	55c	Orange rooster	4.00	4.00
a.			Booklet pane, 2 each #2000-2003	35.00	
2004	A1182	55c	Aquarius	4.00	4.00
2005	A1182	55c	Pisces	4.00	4.00
2006	A1182	55c	Aries	4.00	4.00
2007	A1183	55c	Red dog	4.00	4.00
a.			Booklet pane, 2 each #2004-2007	35.00	

Issued: Nos. 1992-1995, 4/21. Nos. 1996-1999, 7/22; 2000-2003, 10/24; Nos. 2004-2007, 1/20/06.

Austrian Imperial Post Office, Jerusalem A1184

Photo. & Engr.

2005, Apr. 22 *Perf. 13¾*

2008 A1184 100c multi 2.50 2.50

Patron Saints of Austrian Regions A1185

Designs: No. 2009, St. Florian, patron saint of Upper Austria. No. 2010, St. Joseph, patron saint of Styria.

2005 **Photo. & Engr.** *Perf. 13½x14*

2009 A1185 55c multi 1.50 1.50

2010 A1185 55c multi 1.50 1.50

Issued: No. 2009, 5/4; No. 2010, 6/10.

See Nos. 2053, 2062, 2089, 2120, 2162, 2187, 2232.

Liberation of Mauthausen Concentration Camp, 60th Anniv. — A1186

2005, May 6 *Perf. 13¾*

2011 A1186 55c multi 1.50 1.50

Souvenir Sheet

Second Republic, 60th Anniv. — A1187

No. 2012: a, Heraldic eagle and "60" (35x35mm). b, Signatures on State Treaty (42x35mm).

2005, May 15 *Perf. 13¾*

2012 A1187 Sheet of 2 3.00 3.00

a.-b. 55c Either single 1.50 1.50

Heidi Klum, 2005 Life Ball Attendee — A1188

2005, May 20 **Photo.** *Perf. 14x13¾*

2013 A1188 75c multi 2.00 2.00

Europa A1189

2005, May 28 *Perf. 13¾*

2014 A1189 75c multi 1.50 1.50

Jochen Rindt, Formula I Race Car Driver — A1190

2005, June 11 **Photo.** *Perf. 14x13¾*

2015 A1190 55c multi 1.50 1.50

Niki Lauda, Formula I Race Car Driver — A1191

2005, Sept. 13 **Photo.** *Perf. 14x13¾*

2016 A1191 55c multi 1.50 1.50

A €1.25 stamp picturing the Dalai Lama exists. Advance complimentary examples were sent out before the issue was canceled. It is believed approximately 30 examples are extant. An auction sale in 2008 realized €5,683 for the first public sale of the stamp.

Premiere of Animated Movie "Madagascar" A1192

2005, July 7 **Photo.** *Perf. 14*

2017 A1192 55c multi 1.50 1.50

Inachis Io — A1193

Photo. & Engr.

2005, July 15 *Perf. 13½x14¼*

2018 A1193 55c multi 1.50 1.50

Edelweiss A1194

2005, July 19 **Embroidered** *Imperf.*

Self-Adhesive

2019 A1194 375c green & white 11.00 11.00

Folklore & Customs Type of 1991

Design: Frankenburger Dice Game, Upper Austria.

Photo. & Engr.

2005, July 29 *Perf. 13¾*

2020 A892 55c multi 1.50 1.50

Halloween A1195

2005, Sept. 16 **Photo.** *Perf. 13¾*

2021 A1195 55c multi 1.50 1.50

Souvenir Sheet

Row of Houses, by Egon Schiele (1890-1918) — A1196

Photo. & Engr.

2005, Sept. 21 *Perf. 13¾*

2022 A1196 210c multi 5.50 5.50

Railways Type of 2002

55c, Montafon Railway ET 10.103.

2005, Sept. 30

2023 A1109 55c multi 1.50 1.50

Montafon Railway, cent.

Landhaus, Klagenfurt A1197

Photo. & Engr.

2005, Oct. 7 ***Perf. 13¾x13½***
2024 A1197 75c multi 2.00 2.00

Master of Woods, by Karl Hodina A1198

2005, Oct. 14 ***Perf. 13½x13¾***
2025 A1198 55c multi 1.50 1.50

Adalbert Stifter (1805-68), Writer — A1199

2005, Oct. 21 **Photo.** ***Perf. 13¾***
2026 A1199 55c multi 1.50 1.50

Souvenir Sheet

Reopening of National Theater and State Opera House, 50th Anniv. — A1200

No. 2027: a, National Theater. b, State Opera House.

2005, Oct. 25 **Engr.** ***Perf. 13½x14¼***
2027 A1200 Sheet of 2 + central label 3.00 3.00
a.-b. 55c Either single 1.50 1.60

Souvenir Sheet

Cyclorama of Salzburg, by Johann Sattler — A1201

No. 2028: a, Denomination at left. b, Denomination at right.

Photo. & Engr.

2005, Oct. 26 ***Perf. 13¾x13½***
2028 A1201 Sheet of 2 8.00 8.00
a.-b. 125c Either single 3.75 3.75

Expectation, by Veronika Zillner — A1202

Perf. 13½x13¾

2005, Oct. 28 **Photo.**
2029 A1202 55c multi 1.50 1.50

Opening of Film, *The Chronicles of Narnia: The Lion, the Witch and the Wardrobe* A1203

2005, Nov. 8 ***Perf. 13¾***
2030 A1203 55c multi 1.50 1.50

Visitation of Mary Chapel, by Reinhold Stecher A1204

2005, Nov. 14 ***Perf. 13¾x14***
2031 A1204 55c multi 1.50 1.50

Advent and Christmas.

Teutonic Order in Austria, 800th Anniv. A1205

Photo. & Engr.

2005, Nov. 18 ***Perf. 14***
2032 A1205 55c multi 1.50 1.50

Christmas A1206

2005, Nov. 25 **Photo.** ***Perf. 14x14¼***
2033 A1206 55c multi 1.50 1.50

2006 New Year's Concert With Conductor Mariss Jansons A1207

2006, Jan. 1 **Photo.** ***Perf. 13¾x14***
2034 A1207 75c multi 1.75 1.75

Austrian Presidency of European Union A1208

Photo. & Engr.

2006, Jan. 1 ***Perf. 14x14¼***
2035 A1208 75c multi 2.25 2.25

Personalized Stamp — A1209

2006, Jan. 1 **Photo.** ***Perf. 14x13¾***
2036 A1209 55c multi 1.50 1.50

Stamp vignettes could be personalized by customers, presumably for an extra fee.

A quantity of No. 2036 was later imprinted with various commercial themes and offered by Austria Post in full panes at a substantial premium over face value.

Other denominations could be ordered, as well as stamps with vertically oriented frames, but the example of No. 2036 shown is the only stamp with a "generic" vignette that sold for the face value shown on the stamp.

See note after No. 1944.

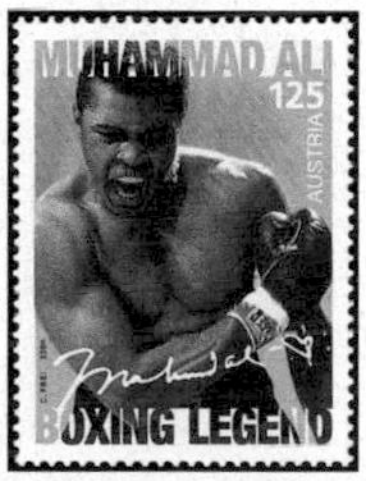

Muhammad Ali, Boxer — A1211

2006, Jan. 14 **Photo.** ***Perf. 13¾x14***
2038 A1211 125c multi 3.00 3.00

Wolfgang Amadeus Mozart (1756-91), Composer A1212

Photo. & Embossed

2006, Jan. 27 ***Perf. 13½x13¾***
2039 A1212 55c multi 1.50 1.50

Europa Stamps, 50th Anniv. — A1213

2006, Mar. 3 **Photo.** ***Perf. 14***
2040 A1213 125c multi 3.25 3.25

Lost in Her Dreams, by Friedrich von Amerling A1214

Photo. & Engr.

2006, Mar. 6 ***Perf. 13¾***
2041 A1214 125c multi 3.25 3.25

See Liechtenstein No. 1342.

Souvenir Sheet

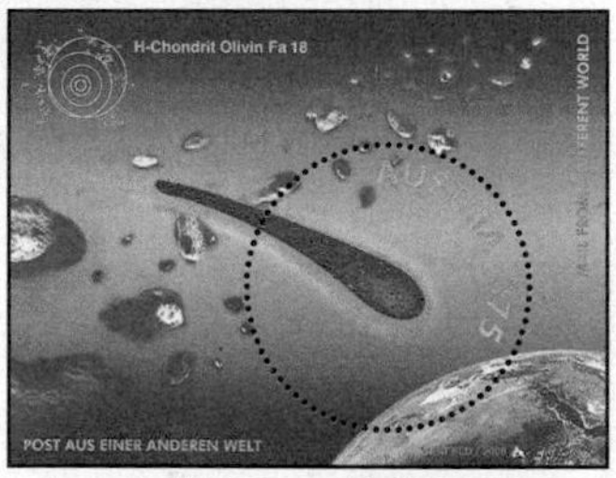

Meteor — A1215

2006, Mar. 24 **Photo.** ***Perf.***
2042 A1215 375c multi 9.00 9.00

Meteorite particles are embedded in the ink used on the meteor.

Karlheinz Böhm, Founder of Menschen für Menschen Foundation, and His Wife, Almaz A1216

2006, Mar. 30 ***Perf. 14***
2043 A1216 100c multi 2.50 2.50

Menschen für Menschen Foundation, 25th anniv.

Souvenir Sheet

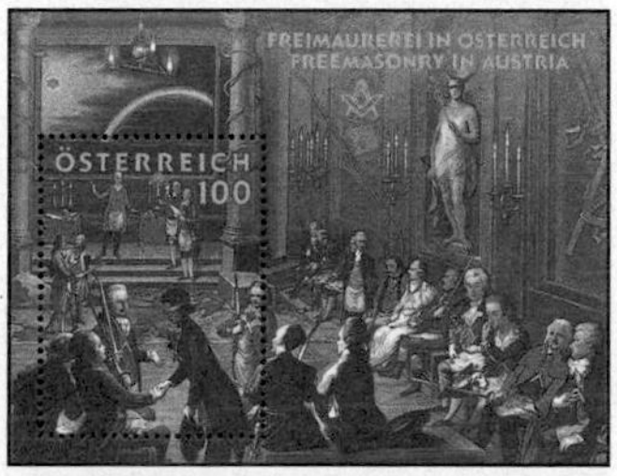

Freemasonry in Austria — A1217

2006, Apr. 6 **Photo. & Engr.**
2044 A1217 100c multi 3.00 3.00

Couch of Sigmund Freud (1856-1939), Psychoanalyst A1218

2006, Apr. 10 **Photo.**
2045 A1218 55c multi 1.25 1.25

Franz Beckenbauer, by Andy Warhol
A1219

2006, Apr. 12 *Perf. 13¾*
2046 A1219 75c multi 2.25 2.25

No. 1863 Surcharged

2006, May 15 Photo. *Perf. 13¾x14*
2047 A1090 55c on 7c #1863 1.40 1.40

Falco (Hans Hölzl, 1957-98), Rock Musician — A1220

Photo. & Engr.
2006, May 18 *Perf. 14¼x13½*
2048 A1220 55c multi 1.40 1.40

Naomi Campbell, 2006 Life Ball Attendee — A1221

2006, May 20 Photo. *Perf. 14x13¾*
2049 A1221 75c multi 2.00 2.00

Folklore & Customs Type of 1991

Design: Kranzelreiten, Weitensfeld.

Photo. & Engr.
2006, June 4 *Perf. 13¾*
2050 A892 55c multi 1.40 1.40

Miniature Sheet

Formula I Race Car Drivers — A1222

No. 2051: a, Jim Clark (1936-68). b, Jacky Ickx. c, Jackie Stewart. d, Alain Prost. e, Stirling Moss. f, Mario Andretti. g, Bruce McLaren (1937-70). h, Jack Brabham.

2006, June 7 Photo. *Perf. 14x13¾*

2051	A1222 Sheet of 8	15.00	15.00
a.-d.	55c Any single	1.25	1.10
e.-f.	75c Either single	1.75	1.50
g.	100c multi	2.50	2.00
h.	125c multi	3.00	2.50

Compare with types A1190-A1191.

Initial Stock Offering of Austria Post — A1223

2006, June 8 *Perf. 13¾*
2052 A1223 55c multi 1.40 1.40

Patron Saints Type of 2005

Design: St. Hemma, patron saint of Carinthia.

Photo. & Engr.
2006, June 27 *Perf. 13¾*
2053 A1185 55c multi 1.40 1.40

Federal Chamber of Industry and Commerce, 60th Anniv. — A1224

2006, June 28 Photo. *Perf. 14*
2054 A1224 55c sil, blk & red 1.40 1.40

Wolfgang Amadeus Mozart and Salzburg — A1225

2006, June 30
2055 A1225 55c multi 1.60 1.60

Activities in Salzburg commemorating 250th anniv. of the birth of Mozart.

Ottfried Fischer, Television Actor — A1226

2006, July 1 *Perf. 13¾x14*
2056 A1226 55c multi 1.40 1.40

Europa
A1227

2006, July 1 *Perf. 14*
2057 A1227 75c multi 1.75 1.75

St. Anne's Column, Innsbruck, 300th Anniv. — A1228

Photo. & Engr.
2006, July 26 *Perf. 14*
2058 A1228 55c multi 1.40 1.40

Railways Type of 2002

55c, Pyhrn Railway locomotive.

2006, Aug. 19 *Perf. 13¾*
2059 A1109 55c multicolored 1.60 1.60

Pyhrn Railway, cent.

Souvenir Sheet

Fireworks — A1229

No. 2060: a, Fireworks over Hong Kong Harbor. b, Fireworks over Prater Ferris wheel, Vienna.

Photo. With Glass Beads Affixed
2006, Aug. 22 *Perf. 14*

2060	A1229 Sheet of 2	20.00	20.00
a.-b.	375c Either single	7.50	7.50
c.	Sheet, Austria #2060b, Hong Kong #1208a	40.00	40.00

See Hong Kong Nos. 1206-1208. No. 2060c, sold for €12.40 in Austria and for $120 in Hong Kong and is identical to Hong Kong No. 1208c.

Lynx Lynx
A1230

Photo. & Engr.
2006, Aug. 25 *Perf. 13½x14¼*
2061 A1230 55c multi 1.40 .140

Patron Saints Type of 2005

Design: St. Gebhard, patron saint of Vorarlberg.

Photo. & Engr.
2006, Sept. 1 *Perf. 13¾*
2062 A1185 55c multi 1.40 1.40

Steyr 220 Automobile — A1231

2006, Sept. 9 **Photo.**
2063 A1231 55c multi 1.40 1.40

KTM R 125 Tarzan Motorcycle
A1232

2006, Sept. 10 *Perf. 14¼*
2064 A1232 55c multi 1.40 1.40

Benjamin Raich, Skier — A1233

2006, Sept. 23 *Perf. 14*
2065 A1233 55c multi 1.40 1.40

Musical Instruments
A1234

Designs: No. 2066, Seven-stringed qin, China. No. 2067, Bösendorfer piano, Austria.

2006, Sept. 26 *Perf. 13½x14¼*
2066 A1234 55c multi 1.40 1.40
2067 A1234 55c multi 1.40 1.40

See People's Republic of China Nos. 3531-3532.

Youngboy Vienna Austria 2005, by Cornelia Schlesinger — A1235

2006, Sept. 29 *Perf. 14x14¼*
2068 A1235 55c multi 1.40 1.40

Homo Sapiens, by Valentin Oman — A1236

Photo. & Engr.
2006, Oct. 9 *Perf. 13¾x14*
2069 A1236 55c multi 1.40 1.40

Wildlife — A1237

Designs: No. 2070, Emys orbicularis. No. 2071, Geronticus eremita. No. 2072, Ursus arctos.

Die Cut Perf. 13¾x13½
2006, Nov. 6 Coil Stamp Photo.
Self-Adhesive
2070 A1237 55c multi 1.40 1.40

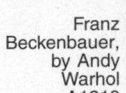

Booklet Stamps
Size: 32x27mm
Die Cut Perf. 14 Syncopated

2071 A1237 55c multi 1.40 1.40
2072 A1237 55c multi 1.40 1.40
a. Booklet pane, 5 each #2071-2072 14.00
Nos. 2070-2072 (3) 4.20 4.20

See Nos. 2092-2094, 2122, 2140-2141, 2154-2155, 2164-2165, 2216-2217, 2235-2237, 2259-2260.

Holy Family at Rest, by Franz Weiss — A1238

Christkindl Pilgrimage Church, by Bishop Reinhold Stecher — A1239

2006 ***Perf. 14x14¼***
2073 A1238 55c multi 1.40 1.40

Perf. 14¼x13½
2074 A1239 55c multi 1.40 1.40

Christmas. Issued: No. 2073, 11/10; No. 2074, 11/24.
1,000 imperf examples of No. 2074 were sold to benefit a charity.

Lviv, Ukraine, 750th Anniv. — A1240

Photo. & Engr.
2006, Dec. 1 ***Perf. 14x13¾***
2075 A1240 55c multi 1.40 1.40

No. 2075 was printed in sheets of 10 stamps and 5 labels. See Ukraine No. 651.

Michael Schumacher, Formula I Race Car Driver — A1241

2006, Dec. 4 Photo. ***Perf. 13½x14***
2076 A1241 75c multi 2.00 2.00

Compare with No. 2103A.

Austrian Stamp and Coin Dealers Association, Cent. — A1242

Photo. & Engr.
2006, Dec. 8 ***Perf. 13¾***
2077 A1242 55c Type N1 1.40 1.40

2007 New Year's Concert With Conductor Zubin Mehta A1243

2007, Jan. 1 Photo. ***Perf. 13¾***
2078 A1243 75c multi 2.00 2.00

Flowers — A1244

Designs: 55c, Alpine rose, edelweiss, and blue gentian. 75c, Christmas rose. 125c, Liverwort, tall cowslip, and daphne.

2007, Jan. 26 ***Perf. 13¾x14***
2079 A1244 55c multi 1.40 1.40
2080 A1244 75c multi 2.00 2.00
2081 A1244 125c multi 2.75 2.75
Nos. 2079-2081 (3) 6.15 6.15

See Nos. 2096-2101, 2130, 2169.

"Mankind and Technology" A1245

Serpentine Die Cut 13¾x14
2007, Feb. 15 Litho.
Coil Stamp
Self-Adhesive
2082 A1245 55c multi 1.40 1.40

Lower Austria Fire and Earth Exhibition — A1246

2007, Feb. 16 Litho. ***Perf. 13¾***
2083 A1246 55c multi 1.40 1.40

Miniature Sheet

Scouting, Cent. — A1247

No. 2084: a, Scout. b, Campfire. c, Tent. d, Guitar.

2007, Feb. 22
2084 A1247 Sheet of 4 5.50 5.50
a.-d. 55c Any single 1.25 1.25

Roe Deer — A1248

2007, Feb. 23 Photo. ***Perf. 14¼x14***
2085 A1248 75c multi 2.00 2.00

Portrait of a Lady, by Bernardino Zaganelli da Cotignola A1249

Photo. & Engr.
2007, Mar. 5 ***Perf. 13¾x13½***
2086 A1249 125c multi 3.00 3.00

Printed in sheets of 8. See Liechtenstein No. 1370.

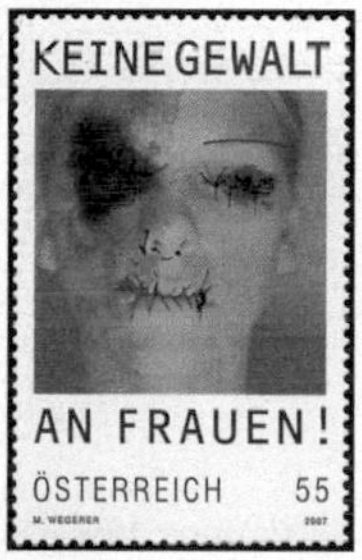

Campaign to End Violence Against Women A1250

2007, Mar. 8 Litho. ***Perf. 13¾x14***
2087 A1250 55c multi 1.40 1.40

Easter Rattles A1251

2007, Mar. 9 ***Perf. 13¾***
2088 A1251 55c multi 1.40 1.40

Patron Saints Type of 2005

Design: St. Klemens Maria Hofbauer, patron saint of Vienna.

Photo. & Engr.
2007, Mar. 15 ***Perf. 13¾x14***
2089 A1185 55c multi 1.40 1.40

Roses — A1252

2007, Mar. 17 Litho. ***Perf. 14***
2090 A1252 (55c) multi 1.40 1.40

Congratulations — A1253

2007, Mar. 30 ***Perf. 13¾***
2091 A1253 (55c) multi 1.40 1.40

Wildlife Type of 2006

Designs: No. 2092, Myotis brandtii. No. 2093, Salamandra salamandra. No. 2094, Astacus astacus.

Serpentine Die Cut 13½
2007 Self-Adhesive Photo.
Coil Stamp
2092 A1237 55c multi 1.40 1.40

Booklet Stamps
Size: 32x27mm
Die Cut Perf. 14 Syncopated
2093 A1237 55c multi 1.40 1.40
2094 A1237 55c multi 1.40 1.40
a. Booklet pane, 5 each #2093-2094 16.00

Issued: No. 2092, 4/20; Nos. 2093-2094, 3/31.

Pope Benedict XVI, 80th Birthday — A1254

2007, Apr. 12 Photo. ***Perf. 14***
2095 A1254 100c multi 2.50 2.50

Flowers Type of 2004

Designs: 4c, Dandelions (Löwenzahn). 10c, Scotch laburnum (Alpen-goldregen). 65c, Guelder rose (Gewöhnlicher schneeball). 100c, Violets (veilchen). 115c, Gentian (Fransenenzian). 140c, Clematis (Waldrebe).

2007 ***Perf. 13¾x14***
2096 A1244 4c multi .25 .25
2097 A1244 10c multi .30 .25
2098 A1244 65c multi 1.50 1.50
2099 A1244 100c multi 2.50 2.50
2100 A1244 115c multi 2.50 2.50
2101 A1244 140c multi 3.25 3.25
Nos. 2096-2101 (6) 10.30 10.25

Issued: 100c, 4/27. 4c, 10c, 65c, 115c, 140c, 8/25.

Austrian Workers' Samaritan Federation, 80th Anniv. A1255

Photo. & Engr.
2007, May 18 ***Perf. 13¾***
2102 A1255 55c multi 1.40 1.40

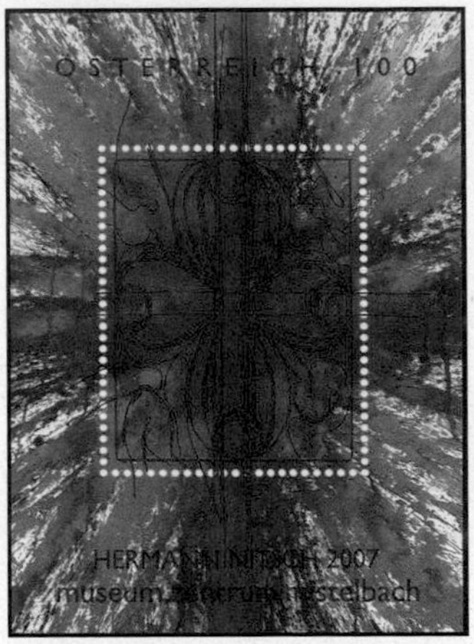

Opening of Hermann Nitsch Museum, Mistelbach — A1256

2007, May 25 *Imperf.*
2103 A1256 100c multi 2.50 2.50

Michael Schumacher Type of 2006 Redrawn

2007, May 29 Photo. *Perf. 13¾x14*
2103A A1241 75c multi 4.00 4.00

No. 2076 is inscribed "Weltmeister 1994 1995." No. 2103A is inscribed "Weltmeister 1995 1996," and has a thicker signature and grayer hair.

Miniature Sheet

Formula I Race Car Drivers — A1257

No. 2104: a, Phil Hill. b, Clay Regazzoni (1939-2006). c, Gerhard Berger. d, Juan Manuel Fangio (1911-95). e, John Surtees. f, Mika Häkkinen. g, Graham Hill (1929-75). h, Emerson Fittipaldi.

2007, May 29 Litho. *Perf. 14*
2104 A1257 Sheet of 8 13.00 13.00
a.-h. 55c Any single 1.40 1.40

Railroads Type of 2002

55c, Mariazell Railway locomotive.

Photo. & Engr.

2007, May 31 *Perf. 13¾*
2105 A1109 55c multi 1.40 1.40

Mariazell Railway, cent.

Mariazell Basilica, 850th Anniv. A1258

2007, June 1 **Litho.**
2106 A1258 55c multi 1.40 1.40

Souvenir Sheet

UEFA European Soccer Championships, Austria and Switzerland — A1259

No. 2107 — Mascots Trix and Flix: a, Chasing ball. b, Holding trophy. c, Running toward each other. d, Celebrating.

2007, June 5 *Perf. 13¼x12¾*
2107 A1259 Sheet of 4 3.00 3.00
a. 20c multi .45 .45
b. 25c multi .60 .60
c. 30c multi .70 .70
d. 35c multi .80 .80

Souvenir Sheet

Self-Portrait of Angelika Kauffmann — A1260

Photo. & Engr.

2007, June 15 *Perf. 13½*
2108 A1260 210c multi 5.50 5.50

Europa A1261

2007, June 16 Litho. *Perf. 14¼x14*
2109 A1261 55c multi 1.40 1.40

Ignaz Joseph Pleyel (1757-1831), Composer A1262

Photo. & Engr.

2007, June 17 *Perf. 14*
2110 A1262 €1 multi 2.50 2.50

Premiere of Animated Movie, "Shrek the Third" — A1263

Perf. 13½x13¾

2007, June 21 **Litho.**
2111 A1263 55c multi 1.40 1.40

Essl Museum, Klosterneuberg A1264

Serpentine Die Cut 13½

2007, July 2 Coil Stamp Photo.

Self-Adhesive

2112 A1264 55c multi 1.40 1.40

Wilhelm Kienzl (1857-1941), Composer — A1265

2007, July 13 Photo. *Perf. 13¾*
2113 A1265 75c multi 2.00 2.00

Railways Type of 2002

75c, Bregenz Forest Railway.

Photo. & Engr.

2007, Aug. 4 *Perf. 13¾*
2114 A1109 75c multi 2.00 2.00

Man, by Astrid Bernhart A1266

2007, Aug. 24 Photo. *Perf. 13¾*
2115 A1266 55c multi 1.40 1.40

Haliaeetus Albicilla A1267

2007, Sept. 7
2116 A1267 55c multi 1.40 1.40

Printed in sheets of 8 + central label. See Serbia No. 399.

Necklace by Josef Hoffmann (1870-1956) — A1268

Litho. & Embossed With Foil Application

2007, Sept. 14 *Imperf.*
2117 A1268 265c multi 6.50 6.50

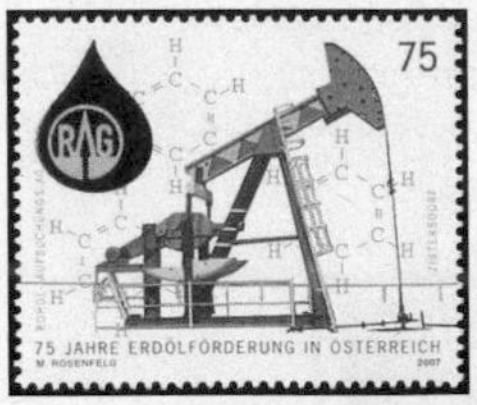

Oil Production in Austria, 75th Anniv. A1269

2007, Sept. 17 Litho. *Perf. 14x13¾*
2118 A1269 75c multi 1.80 1.80

Portions of the design were applied by a thermographic process producing a shiny, raised effect.

Deer, by Friedrich Gauermann (1807-62) — A1270

2007, Sept. 20 **Photo. & Engr.**
2119 A1270 55c multi 1.40 1.40

Patron Saints Type of 2005

Design: St. Rupert, patron saint of Salzburg.

2007, Sept. 24 *Perf. 13¾x14*
2120 A1185 55c multi 1.40 1.40

Niki Hosp, Skier — A1271

2007, Sept. 29 Litho. *Perf. 14x13¾*
2121 A1271 55c multi 1.40 1.40

Wildlife Type of 2006

Serpentine Die Cut 13½

2007, Oct. 10 Coil Stamp Photo.

Self-Adhesive

2122 A1237 75c Lucanus cervus 2.00 2.00

Linz Cathedral Key, Carved by Michael Blümelhuber (1865-1936) A1272

Photo. & Engr.

2007, Oct. 12 *Perf. 13¾x14*
2123 A1272 75c multi 1.75 1.75

Christiane Hörbiger, Actress — A1273

2007, Oct. 13 Litho. *Perf. 14x13¾*
2124 A1273 55c multi 1.40 1.40

Vienna State Opera's Performance of Queen of Spades, by P. I. Tchaikovsky — A1274

2007, Oct. 28 ***Perf. 13¾***
2125 A1274 55c multi 1.40 1.40

Nativity Scene, Chapel of Sts. Peter and Paul, Oberwöllan A1275

Nativity Scene, St. Barbara's Church, Vienna — A1276

2007 **Photo.** ***Perf. 13¾***
2126 A1275 55c multi 1.40 1.40

Perf. 14¼x14
2127 A1276 65c multi 1.50 1.50

Christmas. Issued: 55c, 11/23; 65c, 11/9.

House of the Sea Aquarium, Vienna — A1277

Perf. 13½x13¼
2007, Nov. 29 **Litho.**
2128 A1277 55c multi 1.40 1.40

Portions of the design were applied by a thermographic process, producing a shiny, raised effect.

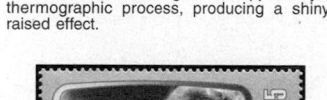

Thomas Gottschalk, Television Personality — A1278

2007, Dec. 8 ***Perf. 13½x13¾***
2129 A1278 65c multi 1.50 1.50

Flowers Type of 2004

Design: 15c, Lady's slippers (Frauenschuh).

2008, Jan. 15 **Photo.** ***Perf. 13¾x14***
2130 A1244 15c multi .45 .45

Miniature Sheet

Venues of UEFA Euro 2008 Soccer Championships — A1279

No. 2131: a, Vienna. b, Salzburg. c, Klagenfurt. d, Innsbruck-Tirol. e, Zurich. f, Basel. g, Bern. h, Geneva.

2008, Jan. 17 **Litho.** ***Perf. 14***
2131 A1279 Sheet of 8 12.00 12.00
a.-d. 55c Any single 1.40 1.40
e.-h. 65c Any single 1.60 1.60

Mascots Trix and Flix A1280

Emblem A1281

Serpentine Die Cut 13¾
2008, Jan. 22 **Coil Stamps** **Photo.**
Self-Adhesive
2132 A1280 55c multi 1.50 1.50
2133 A1281 65c multi 1.75 1.75

UEFA Euro 2008 Soccer Championships, Austria and Switzerland.

Martina, by Hans Robert Pippal (1915-98) A1282

2008, Jan. 31 **Photo.** ***Perf. 13¾x14***
2134 A1282 65c multi 1.75 1.75

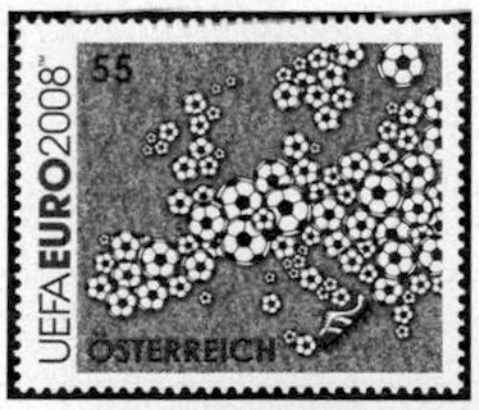

A1283

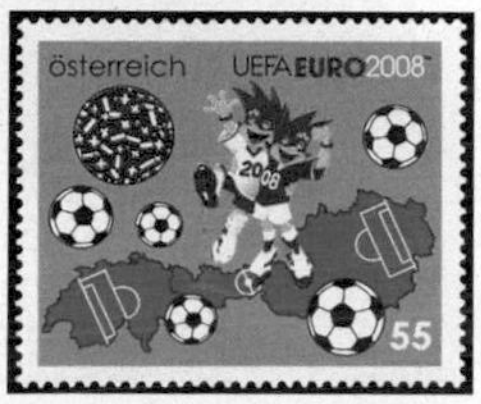

Children's Art A1284

2008, Feb. 4 **Litho.** ***Perf. 13¾***
2135 A1283 55c multi 1.40 1.40
2136 A1284 55c multi 1.40 1.40

UEFA Euro 2008 Soccer Championships, Austria and Switzerland.

Vienna Landmarks Type of Semi-Postals
Souvenir Sheet

2008, Feb. 15 **Photo.** ***Perf. 13¾***
2137 Sheet of 3 + 2 labels 5.50 5.50
a. SP209 55c multi 1.75 1.75
b. SP211 55c multi 1.75 1.75
c. SP213 65c multi 2.00 2.00

2008 Vienna Intl. Stamp Exhibition (WIPA).

Children's Art A1285

2008, Feb. 19 **Litho.** ***Perf. 13¾***
2138 A1285 65c multi 1.50 1.50

UEFA Euro 2008 Soccer Championships, Austria and Switzerland.

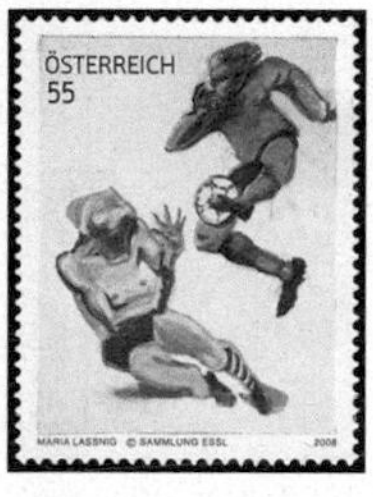

Defense, by Maria Lassnig A1286

2008, Feb. 21
2139 A1286 55c multi 1.40 1.40

UEFA Euro 2008 Soccer Championships, Austria and Switzerland.

Wildlife Type of 2006

Designs: No. 2140, Hyla arborea. No. 2141, Alcedo atthis.

Die Cut Perf. 14 Syncopated
2008, Feb. 25 **Photo.**
Booklet Stamps
Self-Adhesive
Size: 32x27mm
2140 A1237 65c multi 1.75 1.75
2141 A1237 65c multi 1.75 1.75
a. Booklet pane of 10, 5 each #2140-2141, + 10 etiquettes 17.50

Austrian Airlines, 50th Anniv. — A1287

Litho. With Foil Application
2008, Feb. 28 ***Perf. 14***
2142 A1287 140c multi 3.50 3.50

Vienna State Opera Production of "The Force of Destiny," by Giuseppe Verdi A1288

2008, Mar. 1 **Litho.** ***Perf. 13¾***
2143 A1288 55c multi 1.40 1.40

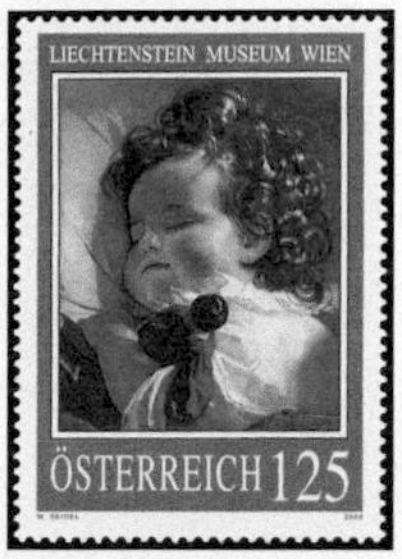

Sleeping Princess Maria Franziska, by Friedrich von Amerling A1289

Photo. & Engr.
2008, Mar. 3 ***Perf. 13¾x13½***
2144 A1289 125c multi 3.00 3.00

See Liechtenstein No. 1407.

Painting by Soshana A1290

2008, Mar. 7 **Photo.** ***Perf. 13½x13¾***
2145 A1290 55c multi 1.40 1.40

Soccer Ball — A1291

Silk-screened
2008, Mar. 12 ***Die Cut***
Self-Adhesive
2146 A1291 375c multi 9.50 9.50

No. 2146 is printed on the same polyurethane foam material used to make soccer balls for the UEFA Euro 2008 Soccer Championships.

Soccer Player, Ball and Field — A1292

2008, Mar. 20 **Litho.** ***Perf. 14***
2147 A1292 55c multi 1.40 1.40

UEFA Euro 2008 Soccer Championships, Austria and Switzerland.

Children's Art A1293

2008, Apr. 2 **Litho.** ***Perf. 13¾***
2148 A1293 125c multi 3.00 3.00

UEFA Euro 2008 Soccer Championships, Austria and Switzerland.

Wachau UNESCO World Heritage Site A1294

2008, Apr. 9 **Photo. & Engr.**

2149 A1294 100c multi 2.50 2.50

A1295

Children's Art — A1296

2008 **Litho.**

2150 A1295 55c multi 1.40 1.40
2151 A1296 100c multi 2.50 2.50

Issued: 55c, 4/18; 100c, 4/19. UEFA 2008 Soccer Championships, Austria and Switzerland.

Tyrolean Federation of Traditional Provincial Costumes, Cent. — A1297

2008, Apr. 26 ***Perf. 14x13¾***

2152 A1297 75c multi 2.00 2.00

Miniature Sheet

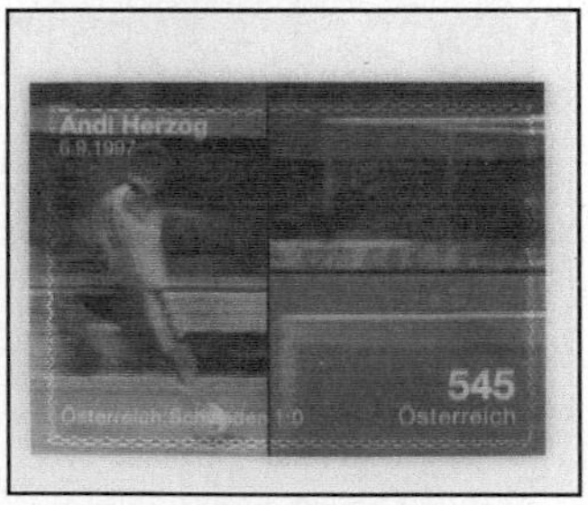

Goal by Andreas Herzog Against Sweden In 1997 World Cup Qualifying Match — A1298

Litho. With Three-Dimensional Plastic Affixed

2008, May 5 ***Serpentine Die Cut 9***

Self-Adhesive

2153 A1298 545c multi 14.00 14.00

UEFA 2008 Soccer Championships, Austria and Switzerland.

Wildlife Type of 2006

Designs: No. 2154, Erinaceus concolor. No. 2155, Lepus europaeus.

Die Cut Perf. 14 Syncopated

2008, May 5 **Photo.**

Booklet Stamps

Self-Adhesive

Size: 32x27mm

2154 A1237 55c multi 1.40 1.40
2155 A1237 55c multi 1.40 1.40
a. Booklet pane of 10, 5 each #2154-2155 14.00

Federal Stud Farm, Piber — A1299

2008, May 9 **Litho.** ***Perf. 14***

2156 A1299 55c multi 1.40 1.40

Grass of Soccer Field — A1300

2008, May 10 ***Perf. 13¾***

2157 A1300 75c multi 2.00 2.00

UEFA 2008 Soccer Championships, Austria and Switzerland.

Soccer Ball and Chairs A1301

2008, May 16

2158 A1301 55c multi 1.40 1.40

UEFA 2008 Soccer Championships, Austria and Switzerland.

Miniature Sheets

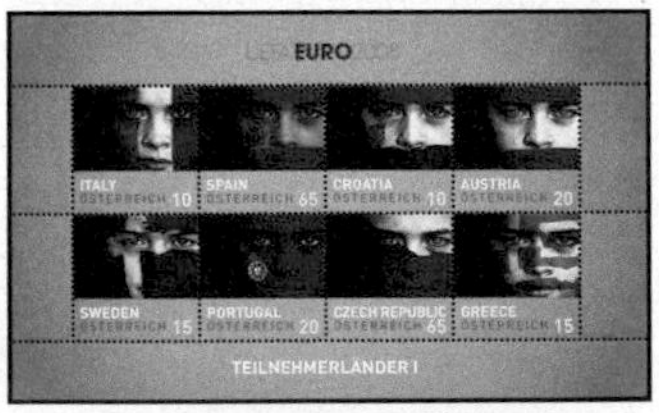

Face Painted with Flags of Countries — A1302

No. 2159: a, Italy. b, Croatia. c, Sweden. d, Greece. e, Austria. f, Portugal. g, Spain. h, Czech Republic.

No. 2160: a, Switzerland. b, Germany. c, Romania. d, Turkey. e, Netherlands. f, Poland. g, Russia. h, France.

2008, May 16 ***Perf. 14***

2159 A1302 Sheet of 8 6.00 6.00
a.-b. 10c Either single .30 .30
c.-d. 15c Either single .30 .30
e.-f. 20c Either single .50 .50
g.-h. 65c Either single 1.40 1.40
2160 A1302 Sheet of 8 7.50 7.50
a.-b. 25c Either single .50 .50
c.-d. 30c Either single .60 .60
e.-f. 35c Either single .80 .80
g.-h. 55c Either single 1.25 1.25

UEFA 2008 Soccer Championships, Austria and Switzerland.

Souvenir Sheet

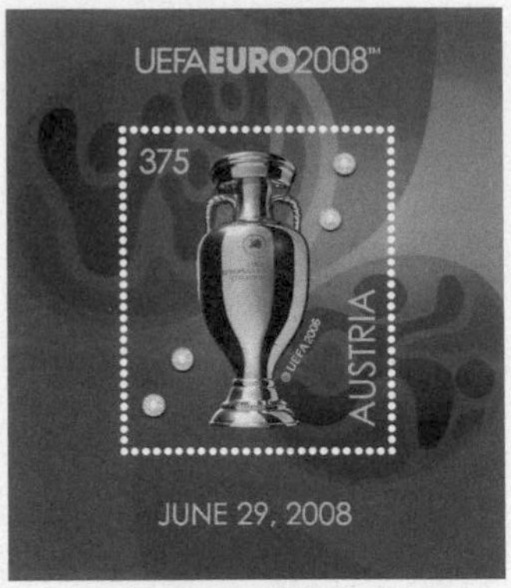

Henri Delaunay Cup — A1303

Photo. With Synthetic Crystals Affixed

2008, June 5 ***Perf. 13¾***

2161 A1303 375c multi 10.00 10.00

UEFA 2008 Soccer Championships, Austria and Switzerland.

Patron Saints Type of 2005

Design: St. Notburga, patron saint of Tyrol.

2008, June 6 **Photo. & Engr.**

2162 A1185 55c multi 1.40 1.40

Europa A1304

2008, June 6 **Photo.**

2163 A1304 65c multi 1.40 1.40

Wildlife Type of 2006

Designs: No. 2164, Upupa epops. No. 2165, Hemaris fuciformis.

Booklet Stamps

Self-Adhesive

Die Cut Perf. 14 Syncopated

2008, June 13 **Size: 32x27mm**

2164 A1237 75c multi 2.00 2.00
2165 A1237 75c multi 2.00 2.00
a. Booklet pane of 10, 5 each #2164-2165 20.00

Railways Type of 2002

75c, Vienna Urban Railway locomotive.

Photo. & Engr.

2008, June 20 ***Perf. 13¾***

2166 A1109 75c multi 2.00 2.00

Vienna Urban Railway, 110th anniv.

Letterbox, by Josef Maria Olbrich (1867-1908) — A1305

2008, Aug. 5 **Litho.** ***Perf. 14***

2167 A1305 65c multi 1.75 1.75

Souvenir Sheet

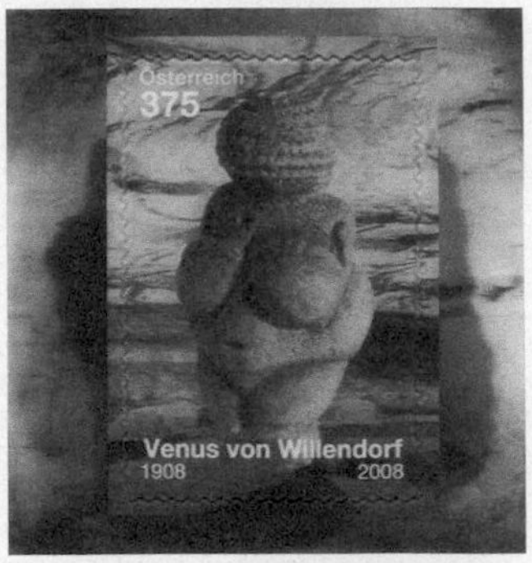

Willendorf Venus — A1306

Litho. with Three-Dimensional Plastic Affixed

2008, Aug. 8 ***Serpentine Die Cut 9¼***

2168 A1306 375c multi 11.50 11.50

This stamp was a gift for standing order customers. It was not made available for sale. Value, $17.50.

Flowers Type of 2004

Design: 50c, Columbine (Akelei).

2008, Sept. 1 **Photo.** ***Perf. 13¾***

2169 A1244 50c multi 1.25 1.25

Vienna Skyline — A1307

Coil Stamp

Photo. With Foil Application

Serpentine Die Cut 13½x14

2008, Sept. 2 **Self-Adhesive**

2170 A1307 55c multi 1.40 1.40

2008 Vienna Intl. Stamp Exhibition (WIPA).

Railways Type of 2002

100c, Princess Elizabeth Western Railway train.

Photo. & Engr.

2008, Sept. 10 ***Perf. 13¾***

2171 A1109 100c multi 2.50 2.50

Princess Elizabeth Western Railway, 150th anniv.

Souvenir Sheet

Mail Coach — A1308

2008, Sept. 12

2172 A1308 265c multi 6.50 6.50

Praga 2008 Intl. Stamp Exhibition, Prague, and 2008 Vienna Intl. Stamp Exhibition. See Czech Republic No. 3398.

Miniature Sheet

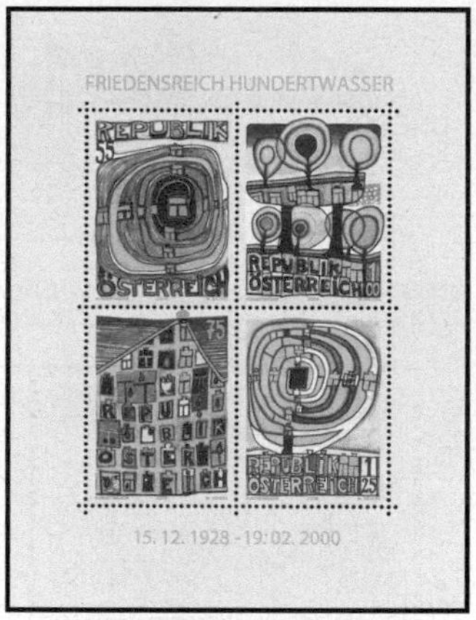

Art by Friedensreich Hundertwasser (1928-2000) — A1309

Various unnamed works of art.

2008, Sept. 18 ***Perf. 13¾x14***

2173	A1309 Sheet of 4	9.00	9.00
a.	55c multi	1.25	1.25
b.	75c multi	1.50	1.50
c.	€1 multi	2.25	2.25
d.	€1.25 multi	2.50	2.50

Nude Woman, by Dina Larot — A1310

2008, Sept. 19 Litho. ***Perf. 13¾x14***
2174 A1310 55c multi 1.40 1.40

Gentian Flower A1311

Embroidered
2008, Sept. 19 ***Imperf.***
Self-Adhesive
2175 A1311 375c tan & dark blue 9.50 9.50

Maximilian Schell, Actor A1312

2008, Sept. 20 Litho. ***Perf. 13¾***
2176 A1312 100c multi 2.50 2.50

Romy Schneider (1938-82), Actress A1313

2008, Sept. 21 **Photo.**
2177 A1313 100c multi 2.50 2.50

Spain, UEFA Euro 2008 Soccer Champions — A1314

2008, Sept. 27 **Litho.**
2178 A1314 65c multi 1.60 1.60

Markus Rogan, Swimmer A1315

2008. Sept. 27
2179 A1315 100c multi 2.50 2.50

Thomas Morgenstern, Skier — A1316

2008, Sept. 27 ***Perf. 14x13¾***
2180 A1316 100c multi 2.50 2.50

70th Birthday of Pres. Heinz Fischer — A1317

2008, Oct. 7 Litho. ***Perf. 14¼x13½***
2181 A1317 55c multi 1.40 1.40

Advertising Art for Manner Neapolitan Wafers A1318

2008, Oct. 16 ***Perf. 13¾***
2182 A1318 55c multi 1.40 1.40

Koloman Moser (1868-1918), Artist — A1319

2008, Oct. 31 ***Perf. 14¼x13½***
2183 A1319 130c multi 3.00 3.00

Lobby of Imperial Post Office, Trieste A1320

2008, Nov. 3 ***Perf. 13¾***
2184 A1320 65c multi 1.50 1.50

Adoration of the Magi, by Unknown Artist A1321

The First Christmas Tree in Ried, by Felix Ignaz Pollinger A1322

2008 **Photo.**
2185 A1321 55c multi 1.40 1.40
2186 A1322 65c multi 1.50 1.50

Issued: 55c, 11/21; 65c, 11/5.

Patron Saints Type of 2005

Design: St. Martin, patron saint of Burgenland.

2008, Nov. 7 **Photo. & Engr.**
2187 A1185 55c multi 1.40 1.40

70th Birthday of Karl Schranz, Olympic Skier A1323

2008, Nov. 11 **Litho.**
2188 A1323 65c multi 1.50 1.50

Souvenir Sheet

Salt and Pepper Shaker by Benvenulto Cellini — A1324

No. 2189: a, Female figure. b, Male figure.

Litho. & Embossed
2009, Jan. 24 ***Perf. 14***

2189	A1324 Sheet of 2	10.00	10.00
a.-b.	210c Either single	5.00	5.00

Landskron Castle — A1325

Serpentine Die Cut 13¾x13½
2009, Jan. 30 Coil Stamp Photo.
Self-Adhesive
2190 A1325 55c multi 1.40 1.40

Advertising Art for Pez Candy A1326

2009, Feb. 6 Litho. ***Perf. 13¾***
2191 A1326 55c multi 1.40 1.40

Imperial Post Office, Cracow A1327

2009, Feb. 13
2192 A1327 100c multi 2.50 2.50

Raimondo Montecuccoli (1609-80), Military Leader A1328

2009, Feb. 20
2193 A1328 130c multi 3.00 3.00

SOS Children's Villages, 60th Anniv. — A1329

2009, Mar. 6 Litho. ***Perf. 14x13¾***
2194 A1329 55c multi 1.40 1.40

Lewis Hamilton, 2008 Formula 1 Racing Champion — A1330

2009, Mar. 17
2195 A1330 100c multi 2.60 2.60

Mercedes Silver Arrow at Vienna Technical Museum — A1331

Litho. With Three-Dimensional Plastic Affixed

Serpentine Die Cut 9¼

2009, Mar. 17 **Self-Adhesive**

2196 A1331 265c multi 6.75 6.75

Schönbrunn Palace, Vienna — A1332

2009, Mar. 20 Litho. ***Perf. 13½x13***

2197 A1332 65c multi 1.50 1.50

Preservation of Polar Regions and Glaciers A1333

2009, Mar. 26 ***Perf. 14¼***

2198 A1333 65c multi 1.50 1.50

Steyr-Daimler-Puch Haflinger, 50th Anniv. — A1334

2009, Mar. 27 ***Perf. 13¾***

2199 A1334 55c multi 1.40 1.40

Joseph Haydn (1732-1809), Composer A1335

2009, Mar. 31

2200 A1335 65c multi 1.50 1.50

Tyto Alba — A1336

Serpentine Die Cut 13½

2009, Apr. 5 Coil Stamp Litho.

Self-Adhesive

2201 A1336 55c multi 1.40 1.40

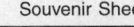

Souvenir Sheet

Art By Christo — A1337

No. 2202: a, Drawing of wrapped Flak Tower. b, Model of building with tower.

2009, Apr. 15 ***Perf. 14***

2202 A1337 Sheet of 2 3.00 3.00

a.-b. 55c Either single 1.40 1.40

Fred Zinnemann (1907-97), Film Director A1338

2009, Apr. 29 ***Perf. 13¾***

2203 A1338 55c multi 1.40 1.40

St. Pölten, 850th Anniv. A1339

2009, May 2 Litho. ***Perf. 13¼x13¾***

2204 A1339 55c multi 1.40 1.40

Vienna State Opera Production of *The Ring of the Nibelungen* A1340

2009, May 2 ***Perf. 13½x13¾***

2205 A1340 100c multi 2.50 2.50

Propeller Steamer Thalia, Cent. — A1341

2009, May 7 ***Perf. 14x13¼***

2206 A1341 55c multi 1.40 1.40

Baptismal Font, Old Cathedral, Linz — A1342

Litho. & Engr.

2009, May 8 ***Perf. 13¾***

2207 A1342 55c multi 1.40 1.40

Vienna State Opera House, 140th Anniv. — A1343

2009, May 25 Litho. ***Perf. 14x13¼***

2208 A1343 100c multi 2.50 2.50

Miniature Sheet

Formula 1 Personalities — A1344

No. 2209: a, Wolfgang Graf Berghe von Trips (1928-61), race car driver. b, Gilles Villeneuve (1950-82), race car driver. c, James Hunt (1947-93), race car driver. d, Bernie Ecclestone, president of Formula One Management.

2009, May 27 ***Perf. 14x13¾***

2209 A1344 Sheet of 4 6.00 6.00

a.-d. 55c Any single 1.40 1.40

Souvenir Sheet

Battle of Aspern and Essling, Bicent. — A1345

2009, June 4 Litho. ***Perf. 14***

2210 A1345 110c multi 3.00 3.00

Europa A1346

2009, June 5 ***Perf. 13¾***

2211 A1346 65c multi 1.75 1.75

Intl. Year of Astronomy.

Graz Historic Center UNESCO World Heritage Site A1347

2009, June 12 **Photo. & Engr.**

2212 A1347 100c multi 2.50 2.50

Wiener Neustadt Airfield, Cent. — A1348

2009, June 12 Litho. ***Perf. 14***

2213 A1348 140c multi 3.50 3.50

Rosalia Alpina — A1349

Serpentine Die Cut 13½x14

2009, June 19 Coil Stamp Photo.

Self-Adhesive

2214 A1349 75c multi 1.75 1.75

Railways Type of 2002

75c, Wachau Railway train.

Photo & Engr.

2009, June 20 ***Perf. 13¾***

2215 A1109 75c multi 2.10 2.10

Wachau Railway, cent.

Wildlife Type of 2006

Designs: No. 2216, Apis mellifera. No. 2217, Merops apiaster.

Die Cut Perf. 14 Syncopated

2009, Aug. 28 **Photo.**

Booklet Stamps

Self-Adhesive

Size: 32x27mm

2216 A1237 55c multi 1.40 1.40

2217 A1237 55c multi 1.40 1.40

a. Booklet pane of 10, 5 each #2216-2217 14.00

This stamp, released Sept. 1, 2009, was a gift for standing order customers. It was not made available for sale. Value, $17.50.

Premiere of Movie, *The Third Man*, 60th Anniv. — A1350

2009, Sept. 2 Litho. *Perf. 14*
2218 A1350 65c multi 1.60 1.60

Opening of Border Between Austria and Hungary, 20th Anniv. A1351

2009, Sept. 10 *Perf. 12*
2219 A1351 65c multi 1.60 1.60

See Germany No. 2548, Hungary No. 4136.

Souvenir Sheet

Archaeological Excavations of Roman Military Camps — A1352

Litho. & Engr.
2009, Sept. 11 *Perf. 13¾x14*
2220 A1352 Sheet of 2 3.00 3.00
a. 55c Carnuntum 1.40 1.40
b. 65c Gerulata 1.60 1.60

See Slovakia No. 579.

Bertha von Suttner (1843-1914), Novelist, 1905 Nobel Peace Laureate A1353

2009, Sept. 12 Litho. *Perf. 14¼x14*
2221 A1353 55c multi 1.40 1.40

Souvenir Sheet

Rosary Triptych, by Ernst Fuchs — A1354

No. 2222: a, Glorious Rosary. b, Joyful Rosary. c, Sorrowful Rosary.

Litho. & Engr.
2009, Sept. 18 *Perf. 14x13¾*
2222 A1354 Sheet of 3 6.00 6.00
a. 55c multi 1.40 1.40
b. 75c multi 1.75 1.75
c. 100c multi 2.50 2.50

Gregor Schlierenzauer, Ski Jumper — A1355

Wolfgang Loitzl, Ski Jumper — A1356

2009, Sept. 26 Litho. *Perf. 14x13¼*
2223 A1355 100c multi 2.50 2.50
2224 A1356 100c multi 2.50 2.50

Drösing-Zistersdorf Local Railway, 120th Anniv. — A1357

2009, Oct. 4 Litho. *Perf. 13¼x13¾*
2225 A1357 100c multi 2.50 2.50

Woman Rocking on a Chair, by Leander Kaiser — A1358

2009, Oct. 9 *Perf. 13¾*
2226 A1358 55c multi 1.40 1.40

Souvenir Sheet

Austria — Japan Year — A1359

No. 2227 — Paintings: a, Portrait of Emilie Flöge, by Gustav Klimt. b, Autumn Clothing, by Shoen Uemura.

2009, Oct. 16 *Perf. 13½*
2227 A1359 Sheet of 2 6.50 6.50
a.-b. 140c Either single 3.00 3.00

See Japan No. 3166.

Souvenir Sheet

Paintings by Diego Velázquez — A1360

No. 2228: a, The Royal Family of Felipe IV. b, The Infanta Margarita Teresa in a Blue Dress.

2009, Oct. 22 Photo. *Perf. 14x13¾*
2228 A1360 Sheet of 2 3.00 3.00
a. 55c multi 1.25 1.25
b. 65c multi 1.50 1.50

See Spain No. 3677.

A1361

Christmas A1362

2009 Litho. *Perf. 14x13¾*
2229 A1361 55c multi 1.40 1.40
Perf. 14
2230 A1362 65c multi 1.50 1.50

Issued: No. 2229, 11/20; No. 2230, 11/6.

Advertising Art for Palmers Underwear A1363

2009, Nov. 12 *Perf. 13¾*
2231 A1363 55c multi 1.40 1.40

Patron Saint Type of 2005

Design: St. Leopold, patron saint of Lower Austria.

Photo. & Engr.
2009, Nov. 13 *Perf. 13½x14*
2232 A1185 55c multi 1.40 1.40

Essl Museum, 10th Anniv. A1364

2009, Nov. 21 Litho. *Perf. 14*
2233 A1364 55c multi 1.40 1.40

Souvenir Sheet

Charles Darwin (1809-82), Naturalist — A1365

No. 2234: a, Monkey with book. b, Boy and mirror held by monkey. c, Monkey with arm extended.

Photo. & Engr.
2009, Nov. 24 *Perf. 14¼x13½*
2234 A1365 Sheet of 3 4.50 4.50
a.-c. 55c Any single 1.40 1.40

Wildlife Type of 2006

Designs: 65c, Felis silvestris. No. 2236, Lutra lutra. No. 2237, Salmo trutta fario.

Coil Stamp
Serpentine Die Cut 13½x14
2010 Litho. Self-Adhesive
2235 A1237 65c multi 1.50 1.50

Booklet Stamps
Size: 32x27mm
Die Cut Perf. 14 Syncopated
2236 A1237 75c multi 1.75 1.75
2237 A1237 75c multi 1.75 1.75
a. Booklet pane of 10, 5 each #2236-2237 21.00

Issued: Nos. 2236-2237, 1/8; No. 2235, 1/13.

Salzburg Old Town Center UNESCO World Heritage Site A1366

Photo. & Engr.
2010, Jan. 29 *Perf. 13¾*
2238 A1366 100c multi 2.50 2.50

Otto Preminger (1905-86), Film Director A1367

2010, Feb. 5 Litho. *Perf. 13¾*
2239 A1367 55c multi 1.40 1.40

Roger Federer, Tennis Player
A1368

2010, Feb. 8 ***Perf. 14x13¾***
2240 A1368 65c multi 1.50 1.50

Annual Rings of Scent and Bliss, by Helmut Kand — A1369

2010, Feb. 10 ***Perf. 13¾***
2241 A1369 55c multi 1.40 1.40

Prince Eugene of Savoy (1663-1736)
A1370

2010, Feb. 12
2242 A1370 65c multi 1.50 1.50

Advertising Art for Kleinbahn
A1371

2010, Feb. 16
2243 A1371 55c multi 1.40 1.40

Souvenir Sheet

The Tyrolean Land Army - Year Nine, by Joseph Anton Koch — A1372

2010, Feb. 19 ***Perf. 14***
2244 A1372 175c multi 4.25 4.25

Andreas Hofer (1767-1810), leader of 1809 Tyrolean Uprising.

Vienna State Opera Production of "Medea," by Aribert Reimann
A1373

2010, Feb. 24 ***Perf. 14x13¾***
2245 A1373 100c multi 2.50 2.50

Soon the Sun Will Rise, by Max Weiler (1910-2001)
A1374

2010, Mar. 18 **Litho.** ***Perf. 14***
2246 A1374 75c multi 1.75 1.75

Lady in Yellow, by Max Kurzweil (1867-1916)
A1375

2010, Mar. 19 ***Perf. 14x13½***
2247 A1375 65c multi 1.50 1.50

Belvedere Castle, Vienna
A1376

2010, Mar. 24 ***Perf. 13½x12¾***
2248 A1376 65c multi 1.50 1.50

Railways Type of 2002

100c, Graz-Köflacher Railway train.

Photo. & Engr.

2010, Apr. 10 ***Perf. 13¾***
2249 A1109 100c multi 2.50 2.50

Graz-Köflacher Railway, 150th anniv.

Hradcany Castle, Prague
A1377

2010, Apr. 16 **Litho.**
2250 A1377 65c multi 1.50 1.50

Souvenir Sheet

Empress Elizabeth, by F. X. Winterhalter — A1378

2010, Apr. 30 ***Perf. 13¼x14***
2251 A1378 55c multi 1.50 1.50

Expo 2010, Shanghai.

Mendel Funicular Railway
A1379

2010, May 8 ***Perf. 13¾***
2252 A1379 65c multi 1.50 1.50

Austria Post Collection Box on Postman's Legs
A1380

2010, May 10 **Litho.** ***Perf. 13¾***
2253 A1380 55c multi 1.40 1.40

Hof Palace — A1381

2010, May 13 **Litho.** ***Perf. 14x13¼***
2254 A1381 55c multi 1.40 1.40

Maria Taferl, 350th Anniv.
A1382

2010, May 16 ***Perf. 13¾***
2255 A1382 55c multi 1.40 1.40

Gustav Mahler (1860-1911), Composer — A1383

2010, May 18 ***Perf. 14x13¾***
2256 A1383 100c multi 2.60 2.60

Salzburg Festival, 90th Anniv.
A1384

2010, May 20 ***Perf. 13¾***
2257 A1384 55c multi 1.40 1.40

Crozier of Archbishop Gebhard of Salzburg
A1385

2010, May 28 **Photo. & Engr.**
2258 A1385 75c multi 1.90 1.90

Wildlife Type of 2006

Designs: 55c, Coracias garrulus. 75c, Aquila chrysaetos.

Self-Adhesive

Serpentine Die Cut 13½x14

2010, May 28 **Coil Stamps** **Litho.**
2259 A1237 55c multi 1.40 1.40
2260 A1237 75c multi 1.90 1.90

Europa
A1386

2010, June 11 **Litho.** ***Perf. 13¾***
2261 A1386 65c multi 1.60 1.60

Self-portrait, by Egon Schiele (1890-1918) — A1387

2010, June 12 **Photo. & Engr.**
2262 A1387 140c multi 3.00 3.00

Second Viennese Mountain Spring Pipeline, Cent. — A1388

2010, June 14 **Litho.** ***Perf. 14x13½***
2263 A1388 55c multi 1.40 1.40

Simon Wiesenthal (1908-2005), Hunter of Nazi War Criminals — A1389

2010, June 14 ***Perf. 12½x12¾***
2264 A1389 75c multi 1.75 1.75

The Star of David is made up of tiny holes made by a laser. See Israel No. 1820.

Ioan Holender, Vienna State Opera Director, 75th Birthday — A1390

2010, June 20 ***Perf. 14x13¾***
2265 A1390 100c multi 2.50 2.50

Palatinate Church, Karnburg A1391

2010, June 25 Litho. ***Perf. 13¾***
2266 A1391 100c multi 2.50 2.50

Johann Joseph Fux (1660-1741), Composer — A1392

2010, June 26 ***Perf. 14***
2267 A1392 100c multi 2.50 2.50

Grete Rehor (1910-87), Politician — A1393

2010, June 29 ***Perf. 13¾***
2268 A1393 55c multi 1.40 1.40

Vienna Rainbow Parade, 15th Anniv. A1394

2010, July 3 ***Perf. 14x14¼***
2269 A1394 55c multi 1.40 1.40

Spielfeld Strass - Bad Radkersburg Railway, 125th Anniv. — A1395

2010, July 10 ***Perf. 13¾***
2270 A1395 65c multi 1.50 1.50

Grafenegg Castle — A1396

Coil Stamp

Serpentine Die Cut 13¾

2010, July 17 Self-Adhesive
2271 A1396 55c multi 1.40 1.40

La Plume, by Alphonse Mucha (1860-1939), Illustrator A1397

2010, July 23 ***Perf. 13¾***
2272 A1397 115c multi 2.75 2.75

Diocese of Elsenstadt, 50th Anniv. — A1398

2010, Aug. 12 Litho. ***Perf. 13¾***
2273 A1398 55c multi 1.40 1.40

Mother Teresa (1910-97), Humanitarian — A1399

2010, Aug. 26 ***Perf. 14***
2274 A1399 130c multi 3.00 3.00

This stamp, released Sept. 3, 2010, was a gift for standing order customers. It was not made available for sale. Value, $10.

Souvenir Sheet

Orient Express — A1400

No. 2275 — Locomotives and views of: a, Sinaia, Romania. b, Salzburg, Austria.

2010, Sept. 6 Litho. ***Perf. 14x14¼***
2275 A1400 Sheet of 2 3.50 3.50
a.-b. 65c Either single 1.75 1.75

See Romania Nos. 5205-5206.

Crucifix by Jakob Adlhart, St. Peter's Archabbey, Salzburg A1401

Photo. & Engr.

2010, Sept. 14 ***Perf. 13¾***
2276 A1401 100c multi 2.50 2.50

Organization of Petroleum Exporting Countries, 50th Anniv. A1402

2010, Sept. 14 Litho. ***Perf. 13¾***
2277 A1402 140c multi 3.50 3.50

Petit Point Embroidery — A1403

Litho. With Embroidery Affixed

2010, Sept. 17 ***Imperf.***
2278 A1403 265c multi 6.50 6.50

Railways Type of 2002

100c, Wechsel Railway train.

Photo. & Engr.

2010, Sept. 19 ***Perf. 13¾***
2279 A1109 100c multi 2.50 2.50

Wechsel Railway, cent.

Andreas and Wolfgang Linger, Lugers — A1404

2010, Sept. 25 Litho. ***Perf. 14x13¾***
2280 A1404 100c multi 2.50 2.50

Modern Furniture by Peter Zuchi A1405

2010, Oct. 1 Litho. ***Perf. 13¾***
2281 A1405 65c multi 1.50 1.50

Archduchess Maria Theresa (1717-80) A1406

2010, Oct. 8
2282 A1406 65c multi 1.50 1.50

Souvenir Sheet

Weather Stations in Austria and Argentina — A1407

No. 2283 — Weather station in: a, Stadtpark, Vienna. b, Buenos Aires Botanical Garden.

2010, Oct. 13
2283 A1407 Sheet of 2 5.75 5.75
a. 65c multi 1.50 1.50
b. 140c multi 3.50 3.50

See Argentina No. 2596.

Ornithopter of Jakob Degen (1760-1848), Inventor A1408

2010, Oct. 15
2284 A1408 125c multi 3.00 3.00

Missions Abroad for Austrian Armed Forces, 50th Anniv. — A1409

2010, Oct. 26 ***Perf. 14x13½***
2285 A1409 65c multi 1.50 1.50

Historic Center of Vienna UNESCO World Heritage Site A1410

Photo. & Engr.

2010, Nov. 5 *Perf. 13¾*

2286 A1410 100c multi 2.50 2.50

Nativity A1411

Innsbruck Buildings, Christmas Tree — A1412

Adoration of the Magi — A1413

2010 Litho. *Perf. 14¼*

2287 A1411 55c multi 1.40 1.40

Perf. 13¾x14

2288 A1412 65c multi 1.50 1.50

Coil Stamp

Self-Adhesive

Serpentine Die Cut 13¾x13½

2289 A1413 (55c) multi 1.40 1.40

Christmas. Issued: No. 2287, 11/19; No. 2288, 11/11; No. 2289, 11/12.

Emperor Franz Josef and Dr. Anton Freiherr von Eiselsberg A1414

2011, Jan. 21 Litho. *Perf. 13¾x14*

2290 A1414 55c multi 1.40 1.40

Austria Cancer Aid, cent.

Imperial Post Office, Maribor A1415

2011, Jan. 21 *Perf. 13¾*

2291 A1415 65c multi 1.50 1.50

Violin and Bow A1416

2011, Jan. 21 *Perf. 13½x14¼*

2292 A1416 75c multi 1.75 1.75

Chancellor Bruno Kreisky (1911-90) A1417

2011, Jan. 22 *Perf. 13¾*

2293 A1417 55c multi 1.40 1.40

Miniature Sheet

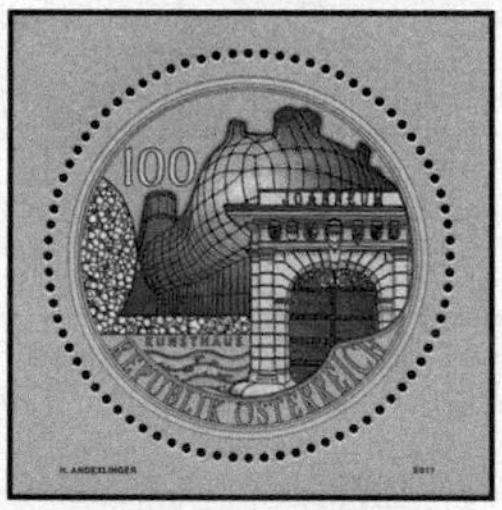

Joanneum, Graz, Bicent. — A1418

2011, Jan. 26 *Perf.*

2294 A1418 100c multi 2.50 2.50

Franz Liszt (1811-86), Composer A1419

2011, Jan. 29 *Perf. 13½x14*

2295 A1419 65c multi 1.50 1.50

Hedy Lamarr (1914-2000), Actress A1420

2011, Feb. 4 *Perf. 13¾*

2296 A1420 55c multi 1.40 1.40

Advertising Art for Schweden-Bomben Confections — A1421

2011, Feb. 15 *Perf. 13¾*

2297 A1421 55c multi 1.40 1.40

Austria Wien Soccer Team, Cent. A1422

2011, Mar. 15 Litho. *Perf. 13¾x14*

2298 A1422 65c multi 1.60 1.60

KTM 125 D.O.H.C. Apfelbeck Motorcycle — A1423

2011, Mar. 15 *Perf. 14x13¾*

2299 A1423 75c multi 2.00 2.00

Puch 500 Automobile — A1424

2011, Mar. 17

2300 A1424 65c multi 1.60 1.60

Karl Gölsdorf (1861-1916), Locomotive Designer — A1425

2011, Mar. 22 *Perf. 13¼x13¾*

2301 A1425 65c multi 1.60 1.60

Vienna Kunsthaus, 20th Anniv. — A1426

Photo. & Engr.

2011, Apr. 8 *Perf. 13¾*

2302 A1426 175c multi 4.50 4.50

Café Hewelka, Vienna A1427

2011, Apr. 11 **Litho.**

2303 A1427 62c multi 1.60 1.60

Manned Space Flight, 50th Anniv. A1428

2011, Apr. 12 *Perf. 13¼x13¾*

2304 A1428 65c multi 1.60 1.60

2011 Lower Austrian Regional Exhibition A1429

2011, Apr. 16 *Perf. 13¾x14*

2305 A1429 62c multi 1.50 1.50

Architecture A1430

Designs: 7c, Ars Electronica Center, Linz. No. 2307, Kunsthaus and Universal Museum Joanneum, Graz. No. 2308, Lentos Kunstmuseum, Linz. No. 2309, Forum Stadtpark, Graz. No. 2310, Museum Moderner Kunst Stiftung Ludwig (Ludwig Foundation Museum of Modern Art), Vienna. No. 2311, Kunsthaus, Bregenz, vert. No. 2312, Kunsthalle, Krems, vert. No. 2313, Museum der Moderne Mönchsberg (Mönchsberg Museum of Modern Art), Salzburg. No. 2314, Essl Museum Klosterneuburg. 145c, Project Space Karlsplatz, Kunsthalle, Vienna. 170c, MAK Center Schindler Chase House, Los Angeles. 340c, Austrian Cultural Forum, New York City, vert.

Die Cut Perf. 13¼

2011, May 1 Coil Stamps Litho.

Self-Adhesive

Background Color

Without Name of Architect

2306 A1430 7c gray .25 .25
2307 A1430 62c light blue 1.75 1.75
2308 A1430 70c yel org 2.00 2.00
2309 A1430 90c lilac 2.60 2.60
Nos. 2306-2309 (4) 6.60 6.60

Booklet Stamps

2310 A1430 62c light blue 1.75 1.75
a. Booklet pane of 4 7.00
2311 A1430 62c light blue 1.75 1.75
2312 A1430 62c light blue 1.75 1.75
a. Booklet pane of 10, 5 each #2311-2312 17.50
2313 A1430 70c yel org 2.00 2.00
a. Booklet pane of 4 + 4 etiquettes 8.00
2314 A1430 90c lilac 2.60 2.60
a. Booklet pane of 4 10.50
2315 A1430 145c blue green 4.25 4.25
a. Booklet pane of 4 17.00
2316 A1430 170c pale orange 5.00 5.00
a. Booklet pane of 4 + 4 etiquettes 20.00
2317 A1430 340c yellow 9.75 9.75
a. Booklet pane of 4 39.00
Nos. 2310-2317 (8) 28.85 28.85

See Nos. 2325, 2357-2364, 2393-2394.

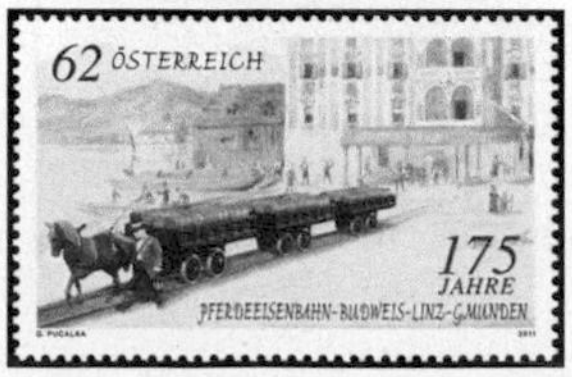

Budweis-Linz-Gmunden Horse-Drawn Railway, 175th Anniv. — A1431

2011, May 1 Litho. *Perf. 14x13¾*

2318 A1431 62c multi 1.60 1.60

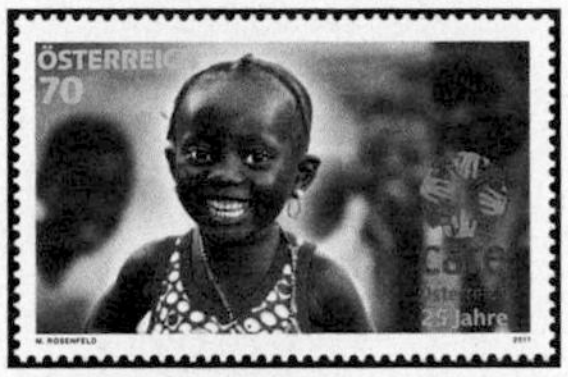

CARE Austria, 25th Anniv. — A1432

2011, May 1
2319 A1432 70c multi 2.00 2.00

Mekhitarists In Vienna, 200th Anniv. A1433

2011, May 1 ***Perf. 14¼x14***
2320 A1433 90c multi 2.25 2.25

Pöllauberg Pilgrimage Church — A1434

2011, May 20 ***Perf. 14x13¾***
2321 A1434 62c multi 1.60 1.60

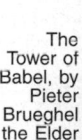

The Tower of Babel, by Pieter Brueghel the Elder A1435

Photo. & Engr.
2011, June 11 ***Perf. 13¾***
2322 A1435 145c multi 3.50 3.50

Souvenir Sheet

Paintings by Hans Makart (1840-84) — A1436

No. 2323: a, Portrait of Dora Fournier-Gabillon. b, The Triumph of Ariadne.

2011, June 9 **Litho.** ***Perf. 14***
2323 A1436 Sheet of 2 6.00 6.00
a. 70c multi 1.75 1.75
b. 170c multi 4.00 4.00

Miniature Sheet

Austria, Country of Forests A1437

2011, June 15 ***Perf.***
2324 A1437 90c multi 2.60 1.25

Values are for stamp with surrounding selvage.

Architecture Type of 2011

Design: Liaunig Museum, Neuhaus.

2011, June 20 **Litho.** ***Perf. 14x13¾***
2325 A1430 5c black .25 .25

Austrian Military Aviation, Cent. A1438

2011, July 1 **Litho.** ***Perf. 14***
2326 A1438 62c multi 1.60 1.60

Tassilo Chalice, Kremsmünster Monastery A1439

Photo. & Engr.
2011, July 1 ***Perf. 13¾***
2327 A1439 145c multi 3.50 3.50

St. Christopher Brotherhood, 625th Anniv. — A1440

2011, July 9 **Litho.** ***Perf. 14***
2328 A1440 62c multi 1.60 1.60

Organization for Economic Cooperation and Development, 50th Anniv. A1441

2011, July 11 ***Perf. 13¾***
2329 A1441 70c multi 1.75 1.75

Railways Type of 2002

90c, Stammersdorf Railway train.

2011, July 15 **Photo. & Engr.**
2330 A1109 90c multi 2.25 2.25

Stammersdorf Local Railway, cent.

Bronze Relief by Ulrich Henn, Rankweil Basilica A1442

Photo. & Engr.
2011, Sept. 2 ***Perf. 13¾***
2331 A1442 90c multi 2.25 2.25

Ferdinand Raimund (1790-1836), Playwright — A1443

2011, Sept. 4 **Litho.** ***Perf. 14x13¾***
2332 A1443 62c multi 1.60 1.60

Austrian Soccer Championships, Cent. — A1444

2011, Sept. 6 ***Perf. 13¼x13¾***
2333 A1444 62c multi 1.60 1.60

Künstlerhaus, Vienna, Cent. — A1445

2011, Sept. 7 ***Perf. 14x13¾***
2334 A1445 62c multi 1.60 1.60

Souvenir Sheet

Austrian Lotto, 25th Anniv. — A1446

2011, Sept. 7 ***Perf.***
2335 A1446 145c multi 3.50 3.50

The top of No. 2335, separated by a row of rouletting, serves as a voucher for a free bet in the Austrian Lotto.

Souvenir Sheet

Europa — A1447

2011, Sept. 8 ***Perf. 13¾***
2336 A1447 170c multi 4.50 4.50

Intl. Year of Forests. No. 2336 is an envelope containing spruce seeds. Rouletting around the souvenir sheet allows it to be removed from the rest of the envelope. Unused values are for the complete envelope with seeds.

Railways Type of 2002

90c, Erzberg Railway train.

Photo. & Engr.
2011, Sept. 10 ***Perf. 13¾***
2337 A1109 90c multi 2.25 2.25

Erzberg Railway, 120th anniv.

Carbon Dioxide Neutral Delivery of Mail — A1448

2011, Sept. 10 **Litho.**
2338 A1448 62c multi 1.75 1.75

Portrait of Walburga Neuzil, by Egon Schiele A1449

2011. Sept. 23 ***Perf. 13¾***
2339 A1449 62c multi 1.60 1.60

Leopold Museum, Vienna, 10th anniv.

Elisabeth Görgl, 2011 Women's Super-G Skiing World Champion — A1450

2011, Sept. 24 ***Perf. 14x13¾***
2340 A1450 62c multi 1.60 1.60

Angst, Painting by Arnulf Rainer — A1451

O.T. 014, 2003, Photograph by Eva Schlegel A1452

2011, Oct. 1 **Litho.** ***Perf. 13¾***

2341 A1451 62c multi 1.60 1.60
2342 A1452 70c multi 1.75 1.75

Trademark Austria A1453

2011, Oct. 4 ***Perf. 14***

2343 A1453 62c multi 1.60 1.60

Loisium Wine Center, Langenlois — A1454

2011, Oct. 7 ***Perf. 14x13¾***

2344 A1454 62c multi 1.60 1.60

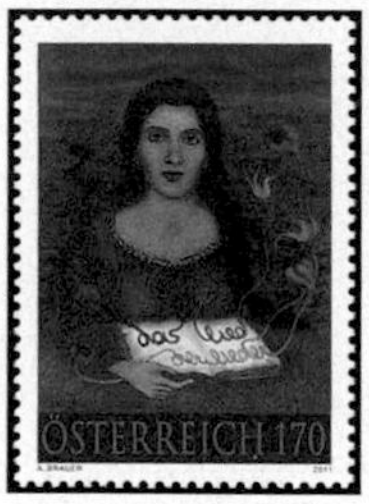

The Song of Songs, Painting by Arik Brauer — A1455

Photo. & Engr.

2011, Oct. 14 ***Perf. 13½***

2345 A1455 170c multi 4.25 4.25

Burgenland Statehood, 90th Anniv. — A1456

2011, Oct. 21 **Litho.** ***Perf. 13¾***

2346 A1456 90c multi 2.50 2.50

Nativity, by Unknown Artist — A1457

Chapel of St. Quirinus A1458

Madonna and Child — A1459

2011 **Litho.** ***Perf. 13¾x14***

2347 A1457 62c multi 1.60 1.60
2348 A1458 70c multi 1.75 1.75

Coil Stamp
Self-Adhesive
Die Cut Perf. 13½x13¼

2349 A1459 62c multi 1.60 1.60

Christmas. Issued: No. 2347, 11/25; No. 2348, 11/11; No. 2349, 11/18.

Reopening of Vienna Western Railway Station — A1460

2011, Nov. 23 ***Perf. 14x13¾***

2350 A1460 70c multi 1.75 1.75

Wolfgang Amadeus Mozart (1756-91), Composer A1461

2011, Dec. 5 ***Perf. 13½x14***

2351 A1461 70c multi 1.75 1.75

Miniature Sheet

Vienna Music Association, Bicent. — A1462

2012, Jan. 1 **Litho.** ***Perf.***

2352 A1462 90c multi 2.25 2.25

1959 Lohner L 125 Scooter A1463

2012, Jan. 2 ***Perf. 13¾***

2353 A1463 145c multi 3.25 3.25

Carl Ritter von Ghega (1802-60), Railway Builder, and Kalte Rinne Viaduct — A1464

2012, Jan. 10 ***Perf. 13½x13¾***

2354 A1464 70c multi 1.75 1.75

Kalte Rinne Viaduct, 160th anniv.

Alpine Association, 150th Anniv. — A1465

2012, Jan. 12 ***Perf. 14x13¾***

2355 A1465 62c multi 1.60 1.60

Vienna Rapid Transit Railway, 50th Anniv. A1466

2012, Jan. 17 ***Perf. 14x14¼***

2356 A1466 62c multi 1.60 1.60

Architecture Type of 2011 With Names of Architects Added

Designs: No. 2357, Like #2307, Spacelab Cook-Fournier architect. No. 2358, Like #2308, Weber Hofer Partner AG architect. No. 2359, Like #2309, Giselbrecht & Zinganel architect. No. 2360, Frauenmuseum (Women's Museum), Hittisau, Cukrowicz Nachbaur Architekten architect. No. 2361, Like #2311, Peter Zumthor architect, vert. No. 2362, Like #2310, Ortner & Ortner architect. No. 2363, Like #2313, Friedrich Hoff Zwink architect. No. 2364, Like #2316, Rudolph M. Schindler architect.

2012 **Litho.** ***Die Cut Perf. 13¼***

Self-Adhesive
Coil Stamps
Background Color

2357 A1430 62c light blue 1.75 1.75
2358 A1430 70c yel org 1.90 1.90
2359 A1430 90c lilac 2.40 2.40
2360 A1430 145c blue green 3.75 3.75
a. Booklet pane of 4 15.00
Nos. 2357-2360 (4) 9.80 9.80

Booklet Stamps

2361 A1430 62c light blue 1.75 1.75
a. Booklet pane of 10 17.50
2362 A1430 62c light blue 1.60 1.60
a. Booklet pane of 4 6.50
2363 A1430 70c yel org 1.90 1.90
a. Booklet pane of 4 + 4 etiquettes 7.75
2364 A1430 170c pale orange 4.50 4.50
a. Booklet pane of 4 + 4 etiquettes 18.00
Nos. 2361-2364 (4) 9.75 9.75

Issued: Nos. 2357, 2361, 2/3; No. 2358, 1/30; Nos. 2359, 2360, 2363, 4/27; Nos. 2360a, 2364, 1/18; No. 2362, 5/18.

This stamp, released Feb. 15, 2012, was a gift for standing order customers. It was not made available for sale. Value, $5.

2012 Vienna Opera Ball — A1467

2012, Feb. 16 **Litho.** ***Perf. 13¾***

2365 A1467 70c multi 1.75 1.75

Stöckl, Photograph by Elfie Semotan — A1468

2012, Feb. 24 ***Perf. 14x13¾***

2366 A1468 70c multi 1.75 1.75

Steyr XII Taxi-Landaulet — A1469

2012, Mar. 26 ***Perf. 13¾***

2367 A1469 70c multi 1.75 1.75

Viennese Oboe A1470

2012, Mar. 26 ***Perf. 13½x14¼***

2368 A1470 90c multi 2.25 2.25

Character From Children's Book "I Am Me," by Mira Lobe A1471

2012, Mar. 27 ***Perf. 13¾***

2369 A1471 62c multi 1.50 1.50

Turhan Bey, Actor
A1472

2012, Mar. 30 **Litho.**
2370 A1472 70c multi 1.75 1.75

Enns, 800th Anniv. — A1473

Litho. & Engr.
2012, Apr. 22 ***Perf. 13¾x14***
2371 A1473 145c multi 3.50 3.50

Bavaria-Upper Austria Provincial Exhibition — A1474

2012, Apr. 26 **Litho.** ***Perf. 13½x14¼***
2372 A1474 70c multi 1.75 1.75

Herzogenburg Priory, 900th Anniv. — A1475

2012, May 5 ***Perf. 13¾***
2373 A1475 90c multi 2.25 2.25

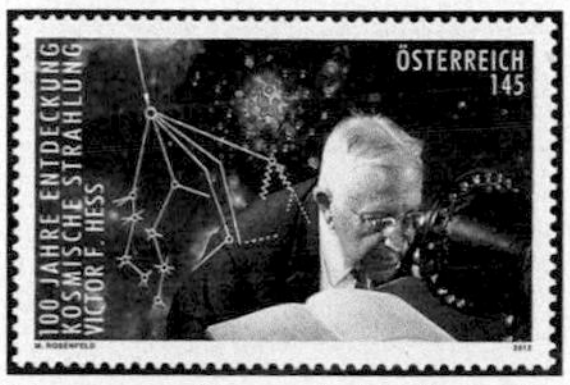

Discovery of Cosmic Radiation by Victor F. Hess (1883-1964) — A1476

Litho. With Foil Application
2012, May 5 ***Perf. 14x13¾***
2374 A1476 145c multi 3.50 3.50

SV Ried Soccer Team, Cent. — A1477

2012, May 6 **Litho.** ***Perf. 13¾***
2375 A1477 62c multi 1.50 1.50

Souvenir Sheet

Prater Ferris Wheel, Vienna — A1478

2012, May 11 ***Perf. 13½x14¼***
2376 A1478 70c multi 2.25 2.25

Europa.

Paddlewheel Steamship Schönbrunn, Cent.
A1479

2012, May 12 ***Perf. 13¾***
2377 A1479 90c multi 2.25 2.25

Johann Nepomuk Nestroy (1801-62), Playwright and Actor — A1480

2012, May 24 **Litho. & Engr.**
2378 A1480 145c multi 3.50 3.50

Self-portrait, by Anton Faistauer (1887-1930)
A1481

2012, June 2 **Litho.** ***Perf. 13¾***
2379 A1481 70c multi 1.75 1.75

Stockerau, 1000th Anniv.
A1482

2012, June 3
2380 A1482 62c multi 1.60 1.60

Stained-Glass Window, Lilienfeld Monastery
A1483

2012, June 8 **Photo. & Engr.**
2381 A1483 145c multi 3.50 3.50

Johann Puch (1862-1914), Bicycle Manufacturer
A1484

2012, June 27 **Litho.** ***Perf. 13¾x14***
2382 A1484 145c multi 3.50 3.50

Caritas Austria Charity Anti-Hunger Campaign — A1485

2012, July 2 ***Perf. 14x14¼***
2383 A1485 62c multi 1.60 1.60

A1486

A1487

Austria on Maps
A1488

2012, June 6 ***Die Cut Perf. 13¼***
Coil Stamps
Self-Adhesive

2384	A1486	(62c) multi		1.60	1.60
2385	A1487	(70c) multi		1.75	1.75
2386	A1488	(€1.70) multi		4.25	4.25
		Nos. 2384-2386 (3)		7.60	7.60

Wolkenturm Open-air Stage, Grafenegg
A1489

2012, July 14 ***Perf. 13¾***
2387 A1489 70c multi 1.75 1.75

Portrait of Fritza Riedler, by Gustav Klimt (1862-1918)
A1490

2012, July 14
2388 A1490 170c multi 4.00 4.00

Imperial Post Office, Zagreb
A1491

2012, July 17
2389 A1491 70c multi 1.75 1.75

Votive Church, Vienna, Painting by Rudolf von Alt (1812-1905)
A1492

Litho. & Engr.
2012, Aug. 23 ***Perf. 13¾***
2390 A1492 170c multi 4.25 4.25

Gmundner Ceramics
A1493

2012, Aug. 24 **Litho.**
2391 A1493 62c multi 1.60 1.60

Steigl Brewery, Salzburg, Horse-drawn Barrel Cart and Beer Stein — A1494

2012, Aug. 26
2392 A1494 62c multi 1.60 1.60

Architecture Type of 2011 With Names of Architects Added

Designs: No. 2393, Like #2314, Heinz Tesar architect. No. 2394, Like #2317, Raimund Abraham architect.

Die Cut Perf. 13¼

2012, Sept. 14 **Litho.**

Self-Adhesive
Booklet Stamps
Background Color

2393 A1430 90c lilac 2.25 2.25
a. Booklet pane of 4 9.00
2394 A1430 340c yellow 8.75 8.75
a. Booklet pane of 4 35.00

Vulpes Vulpes A1495

2012, Sept. 14 Litho. ***Perf. 14x14¼***
2395 A1495 90c multi 2.25 2.25

St. Stephan's Church, Baden, 700th Anniv. A1496

2012, Sept. 16 ***Perf. 13¾x14***
2396 A1496 90c multi 2.25 2.25

Alpenzoo, Innsbruck, 50th Anniv. — A1497

2012, Sept. 22 ***Perf. 13¼x14***
2397 A1497 70c multi 1.90 1.90

Gerlinde Kaltenbrunner, Mountaineer — A1498

2012, Sept. 29 ***Perf. 14x13¾***
2398 A1498 62c multi 1.60 1.60

St. Michael From Mondsee Basilica Altarpiece A1499

Litho. & Engr.

2012, Sept. 29 ***Perf. 13¾***
2399 A1499 145c multi 3.50 3.50

Mittenwald Railway, Cent. — A1500

2012, Sept. 29 ***Perf. 14x13¾***
2400 A1500 145c multi 3.50 3.50

Miniature Sheet

Characters From Movie *Madagascar 3: Europe's Most Wanted* — A1501

No. 2401: a, Penguin lighting fuse of cannon, mouth of Alex the Lion. b, Marty the Zebra, and Gloria the Hippo, in cannon. c, Penguins, part of head of Alex the Lion. d, Part of head of Alex the Lion, Melman the Giraffe.

Serpentine Die Cut 14

2012, Oct. 5 Litho. Self-Adhesive
2401 A1501 Sheet of 4 6.50 6.50
a.-b. 62c Either single 1.40 1.40
c. 70c multi 1.60 1.60
d. 90c multi 2.25 2.25

Sleeping Child, by Bernardo Strozzi A1502

Litho. & Engr.

2012, Oct. 6 ***Perf. 13¾***
2402 A1502 170c multi 4.00 4.00

Souvenir Sheet

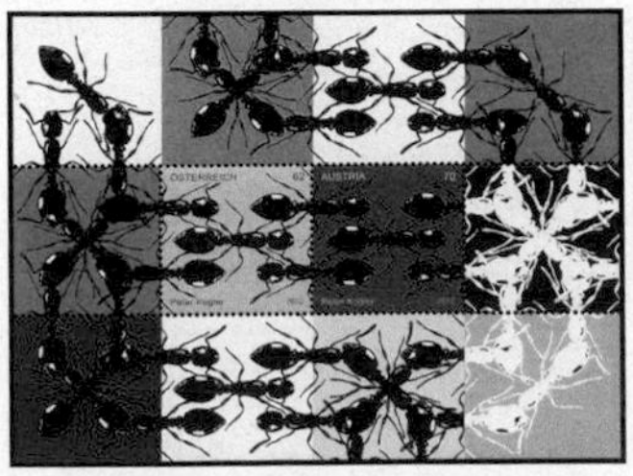

Ants, Painting by Peter Kogler — A1503

2012, Oct. 6 Litho. ***Perf. 14***
2403 A1503 Sheet of 2 3.50 3.50
a. 62c gray, brt org red & blk 1.60 1.60
b. 70c brt org red, gray & blk 1.90 1.90

Self-Portrait With Red Hat, by Marie-Louise von Motesiczky A1504

2012, Oct. 10 ***Perf. 13¾x14***
2404 A1504 62c multi 1.60 1.60

Carl Auer von Welsbach (1858-1929), Inventor, and Gas Lamp — A1505

2012, Oct. 13 ***Perf. 13¼x14***
2405 A1505 62c multi 1.60 1.60

Concession for Raab-Oedenberg-Ebenfurth Railroad, 140th Anniv. — A1506

2012, Oct. 15 ***Perf. 14x13¼***
2406 A1506 62c multi 1.60 1.60

Wine Glass, Wine, Grapes and Windmill A1507

2012, Oct. 19 ***Perf. 13¼x14***
2407 A1507 62c multi 1.60 1.60

Vienna International Film Festival, 50th Anniv. — A1508

2012, Oct. 25 ***Perf. 14x13¾***
2408 A1508 70c multi 1.75 1.75

Souvenir Sheet

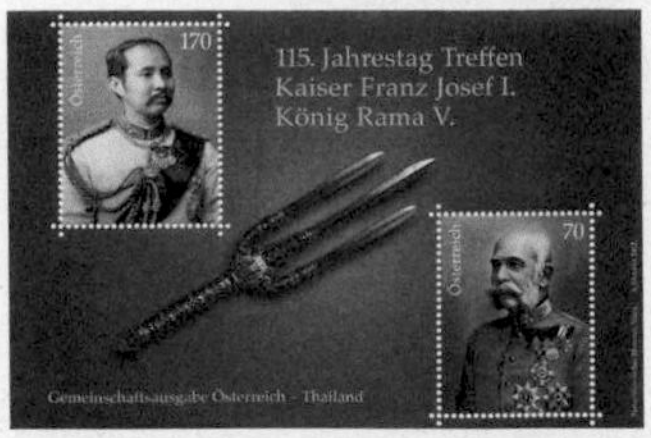

Meeting of Emperor Franz Josef and King Chulalongkorn of Thailand, 115th Anniv. — A1509

No. 2409: a, Emperor Franz Josef. b, King Chulalongkorn.

Perf. 14¼x13½

2012, Nov. 10 **Litho.**
2409 A1509 Sheet of 2 5.50 5.50
a. 70c multi 1.60 1.60
b. 170c multi 4.00 4.00

See Thailand No. 2714.

Arndorfer Altar, Maria Saal Cathedral A1510

Church of St. George, Kals am Grossglockner A1511

Hunters in Snow, by Pieter Breughel, the Elder A1512

Adoration of the Magi, by Jacopo Bassano A1513

2012 ***Perf. 13¾***
2410 A1510 62c multi 1.60 1.60

Perf. 13¾x14
2411 A1511 70c multi 1.90 1.90

Coil Stamps
Self-Adhesive

Die Cut Perf. 13
2412 A1512 62c multi 1.60 1.60
2413 A1513 70c multi 1.90 1.90

Christmas. Issued: Nos. 2410, 2412, 11/30; Nos. 2411, 2413, 11/16.

Lenz Moser Wines A1514

2012, Nov. 17 *Perf. 13¾x14*
2414 A1514 62c multi 1.60 1.60

Railways in Austria, 175th Anniv. — A1515

2012, Nov. 23 *Perf. 14x13¾*
2415 A1515 90c multi 2.40 2.40

2013 World Alpine Skiing Championships, Schladming A1516

Paintings by Christian Ludwig Attersee: 62c, Freedom in the Snow. 70c, Styrian Heart. 90c, Slalom Dance.

2013, Jan. 2 **Litho.** *Perf. 13¾x14*

Panel Color

2416 A1516 62c orange 1.60 1.60
2417 A1516 70c dark red 1.75 1.75
2418 A1516 90c yel green 2.25 2.25
Nos. 2416-2418 (3) 5.60 5.60

Bergisel Ski Jump, Innsbruck A1517

2013, Jan. 4 *Perf. 13¾*
2419 A1517 62c multi 1.60 1.60

Diversity in Unity A1518

2013, Jan. 21
2420 A1518 70c multi 1.75 1.75

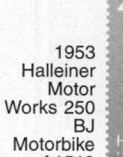

1953 Halleiner Motor Works 250 BJ Motorbike A1519

2013, Jan. 21
2421 A1519 220c multi 6.00 6.00

This stamp, released Feb. 13, 2013, was a gift for standing order customers. It was not made available for sale. Value, $5.

Best Wishes A1520

2013, Feb. 20 **Litho.** *Perf. 14*
2422 A1520 (62c) multi 1.50 1.50

Salzburg Marionette Theater, Cent. — A1521

2013, Feb. 27 *Perf. 13¾x14*
2423 A1521 62c multi 1.50 1.50

1948 Porsche 356 No. 1 Roadster A1522

2013, Feb. 28 *Perf. 13¾*
2424 A1522 70c multi 1.90 1.90

Valie Export - Smart Export, Photograph by Valie Export A1523

2013, Mar. 13
2425 A1523 70c black 1.90 1.90

Bruck Locomotive at Baden Station, c. 1846 — A1524

2013, Mar. 13 *Perf. 14x13¾*
2426 A1524 145c multi 4.00 4.00

Rupicapra Rupicapra A1525

Litho. & Engr.

2013, Mar. 14 *Perf. 14x14¼*
2427 A1525 90c multi 2.40 2.40

Page Illumination, St. Florian Monastery A1526

Photo. & Engr.

2013, Mar. 15 *Perf. 13¾*
2428 A1526 90c multi 2.25 2.25

Senta Berger, Actress A1527

2013, Mar. 22 **Litho.**
2429 A1527 70c multi 1.75 1.75

Preseren Square, Ljubljana, Slovenia A1528

2013, Apr. 6
2430 A1528 62c multi 1.60 1.60

Souvenir Sheet

Underground Post Office in Postojna Cave, Slovenia — A1529

2013, Apr. 6 *Perf. 13¾*
2431 A1529 70c multi 1.90 1.90

See Slovenia No. 982.

Music Theater at Landestheater, Linz — A1530

2013, Apr. 11
2432 A1530 62c multi 1.60 1.60

Landhaus Bacher Restaurant, Mautern — A1531

2013, Apr. 11
2433 A1531 62c multi 1.60 1.60

30th Vienna City Marathon — A1532

2013, Apr. 14 *Perf. 14*
2434 A1532 62c multi 1.60 1.60

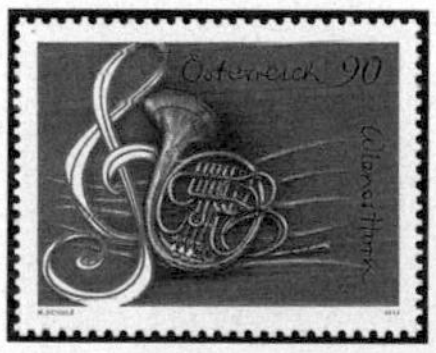

Vienna Horn A1533

2013, Apr. 15 *Perf. 13½x14¼*
2435 A1533 90c multi 2.25 2.25

Julius Lott (1836-83), Builder of Arlberg Railroad A1534

2013, Apr. 17 *Perf. 13¼x13¾*
2436 A1534 70c multi 1.75 1.75

Toboggan Ride, Wurstelprater Amusement Park, Vienna, Cent. — A1535

2013, Apr. 19 *Perf. 13¾*
2437 A1535 62c multi 1.60 1.60

Souvenir Sheet

Attersee Area Transportation Centenaries — A1536

No. 2438: a, Shipping on Attersee, cent. b, Attergau Railway, cent.

2013, Apr. 19 *Perf. 14x13¾*

2438 A1536 Sheet of 2 3.50 3.50
 a. 62c multi 1.60 1.60
 b. 70c multi 1.90 1.90

Hohentwiel Paddle-wheeled Steamer, Cent. — A1537

2013, May 4 **Litho.** *Perf. 13¾*

2439 A1537 62c multi 1.75 1.75

Austrian Open-Air Museum, Stübing, 50th Anniv. A1538

2013, May 5 *Perf. 14x14¼*

2440 A1538 70c multi 1.90 1.90

Souvenir Sheet

Europa — A1539

2013, May 6 *Die Cut*

Self-Adhesive

2441 A1539 70c multi 1.90 1.90

International Red Cross, 150th Anniv. — A1540

2013, May 8 *Perf. 14*

2442 A1540 62c multi 1.75 1.75

Vienna Concert House, Cent. — A1541

2013, May 11 **Litho.**

2443 A1541 90c multi 2.40 2.40

Robert Jungk (1913-94), Journalist A1542

2013, May 13 *Perf. 13¾*

2444 A1542 90c multi 2.40 2.40

Franz West (1947-2012), Artist — A1543

2013, May 14

2445 A1543 70c black 1.90 1.90

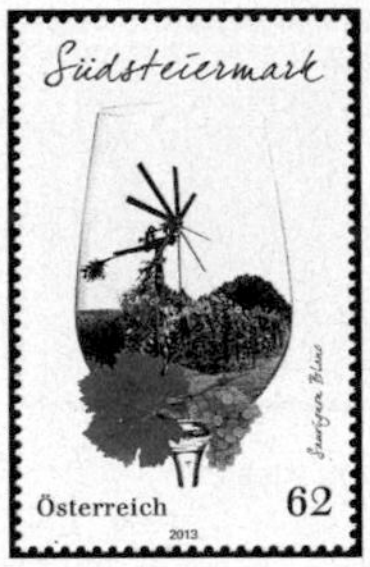

South Styrian Wine Region — A1544

2013, May 24 *Perf. 13¼x14*

2446 A1544 62c multi 1.75 1.75

St. Theodul, Patron Saint of the Walsers A1545

Litho. & Engr.

2013, May 29 *Perf. 13¾*

2447 A1545 145c multi 4.00 4.00

Walser settlements in Vorarlberg, 700th anniv.

Souvenir Sheet

Pilgrimage to Maria Luggau, 500th Anniv. — A1546

2013, May 31 **Litho.** *Perf. 13x13¼*

2448 A1546 170c multi 4.75 4.75

St. Anna's Children's Cancer Research Institute, 25th Anniv. — A1547

2013, June 6 **Litho.** *Perf. 14*

2449 A1547 62c multi 1.75 1.75

Austrian Nature Protection League, Cent. — A1548

2013, June 7

2450 A1548 90c multi 2.40 2.40

Fairtrade Austria, 20th Anniv. — A1549

2013, June 21 *Perf. 13¾*

2451 A1549 62c multi 1.60 1.60

Lorenz I. Bordogna von Taxis (1510-59), Tyrolean Postmaster A1550

2013, June 25 **Litho. & Engr.**

2452 A1550 145c multi 3.75 3.75

Self-portrait, by Richard Gerstl (1883-1908) A1551

2013, June 27 **Litho.** *Perf. 14*

2453 A1551 62c multi 1.60 1.60

Vorau Monastery, 850th Anniv. — A1552

Perf. 13¾x13½

2013, June 28 **Litho. & Engr.**

2454 A1552 145c brown & blk 3.75 3.75

Wacker Soccer Team, Innsbruck, Cent. — A1553

2013, July 5 **Litho.** *Perf. 13¾*

2455 A1553 62c multi 1.60 1.60

Ausserfern Railway, Cent. A1554

2013, July 6 *Perf. 13½x14¼*

2456 A1554 70c multi 1.90 1.90

Traditional Women's Clothing From Gmunden A1555

2013, Aug. 23 **Litho.** *Perf. 13¼x14*

2457 A1555 62c multi 1.75 1.75

Volunteer Fire Departments in Austria, 150th Anniv. A1556

Perf. 13½x14¼

2013, Sept. 7 **Litho. & Engr.**

2458 A1556 90c multi 2.40 2.40

Stylized Landmarks A1557

Austrian flag and: No. 2459, Lindwurm Fountain, Brunnen. No. 2460, Hohensalzburg Fortress, Salzburg. No. 2461, Pöstlingberg Church, Linz. No. 2462, Goldenes Dachl (Golden Roof), Innsbruck, vert. No. 2463, St. Martin's Tower, Bregenz, vert. No. 2464, Bergkirche, Eisenstadt, vert. No. 2465, Landhaus, St. Pölten, vert.

Die Cut Perf. 14

2013, Sept. 12 **Litho.**

Coil Stamps

Self-Adhesive

2459 A1557 62c multi 1.75 1.75
2460 A1557 90c multi 2.40 2.40
2461 A1557 145c multi 4.00 4.00
 Nos. 2459-2461 (3) 8.15 8.15

Booklet Stamps

2462 A1557 62c multi 1.75 1.75
 a. Booklet pane of 4 7.00
2463 A1557 62c multi 1.75 1.75
 a. Booklet pane of 10 17.50
2464 A1557 90c multi 2.40 2.40
 a. Booklet pane of 4 9.75

2465 A1557 145c multi 4.00 4.00
a. Booklet pane of 4 16.00
Nos. 2462-2465 (4) 9.90 9.90

See Nos. 2488-2491.

Souvenir Sheet

Holiday Travel with the Express Mail, Painting by Karl Schnorpfeil (1875-1937) — A1558

2013, Sept. 12 *Perf. 14*
2466 A1558 70c multi 1.90 1.90

Helene Winterstein-Kamberesky (1900-66), Inventor of Waterproof Mascara — A1559

2013, Sept. 13 *Perf. 13¼x14*
2467 A1559 70c multi 1.90 1.90

Advertising Art for Engelhofer Bonbons A1560

2013, Sept. 13 *Perf. 13¾x14*
2468 A1560 70c multi 1.90 1.90

Icon of St. Nicholas of Myra, Russian Orthodox Cathedral, Vienna A1561

Photo. & Engr.

2013, Sept. 20 *Perf. 13¾*
2469 A1561 145c multi 4.00 4.00

Madonna and Child, Painting by Lorenzo Lotto (1480-1557) — A1562

2013, Sept. 26
2470 A1562 170c multi 4.75 4.75

Tyrolean Ski Federation, Cent. — A1563

2013, Oct. 11 **Litho.** *Perf. 14*
2471 A1563 62c multi 1.75 1.75

St. Martin's Church, Linz — A1564

2013, Oct. 11 **Litho.** *Perf. 14*
2472 A1564 62c multi 1.75 1.75

Burgtheater, Vienna, 125th Anniv. — A1565

2013, Oct. 11 **Litho.** *Perf. 13¾*
2473 A1565 70c multi 1.90 1.90

Scene From "Orient, 1st Part," Video Art by Markus Schinwald A1566

2013, Oct. 14 **Litho.** *Perf. 14*
2474 A1566 145c multi 4.00 4.00

Miniature Sheet

Halloween — A1567

No. 2475 — Haunted house and: a, Ghost, witch on broom, spider. b, Bats, vampire. c, Skeleton, graveyard. d, Jack o'lanterns.

Serpentine Die Cut 14¼

2013, Oct. 14 **Litho.**

Self-Adhesive

2475 A1567 Sheet of 4 7.00 7.00
a.-d. 62c Any single 1.75 1.75

Adoration of the Shepherds from Altarpiece of St. Michael's Church, Lungau A1568

St. Georgenberg-Fiecht Abbey — A1569

Franz Xaver Gruber (1787-1863), Composer of "Silent Night," and Silent Night Chapel, Oberndorf — A1570

The Nativity, Painting by Joos van Cleve — A1571

2013 **Litho.** *Perf. 13¾x14*
2476 A1568 62c multi 1.75 1.75
2477 A1569 70c multi 2.00 2.00

Coil Stamps
Self-Adhesive

Die Cut Perf. 14x14¼

2478 A1570 62c multi 1.75 1.75

Die Cut Perf. 13x13½

2479 A1571 70c multi 2.00 2.00

Christmas. No. 2479 lacks country name. Issued: Nos. 2476, 2478, 11/29; Nos. 2477, 2479, 11/15.

E.V.A., by Franz Graf — A1572

2013, Dec. 5 **Litho.** *Perf. 13¾x14*
2480 A1572 145c black 4.00 4.00

Colorable Stamp A1573

2014, Jan. 22 **Litho.** *Perf. 13¾x13¼*
2481 A1573 62c multi 1.75 1.75

No. 2481 was pritned in sheets of 6.

Austro Daimler ADR 22/70 A1574

2014, Jan. 22 **Litho.** *Perf. 14¼*
2482 A1574 170c multi 4.75 4.75

KTM Ponny II Motorcycle A1575

2014, Jan. 31 **Litho.** *Perf. 14¼*
2483 A1575 145c multi 4.00 4.00

This stamp, released Feb. 7, 2014, was a gift for standing order customers. It was not made available for sale. Value, $3.

Romy Awards, 25th Anniv. — A1576

Litho. & Embossed With Foil Application

2014, Feb. 7 *Perf. 14x13¾*
2484 A1576 145c multi 4.00 4.00

Imperial Post Office, Gablonz (Jablonec), Bohemia A1577

2014, Feb. 28 **Litho.** *Perf. 14¼*
2485 A1577 62c multi 1.75 1.75

Hospital of the Brothers of Charity, Vienna, 400th Anniv.
A1578

2014, Mar. 8 Litho. ***Perf. 14¼***
2486 A1578 62c multi 1.75 1.75

Vienna Double Bass — A1579

Litho. & Engr.
2014, Mar. 13 ***Perf. 14***
2487 A1579 175c multi 4.75 4.75

Stylized Landmarks Type of 2013

Designs: No. 2488, Schönbrunn Castle, Vienna. No. 2489, St. Stephen's Cathedral, Vienna, vert. 170c, Riesenrad (Ferris Wheel), Vienna, vert. 340c, Clock tower, Graz, vert.

Die Cut Perf. 14
2014, Mar. 19 **Litho.**

Coil Stamp
Self-Adhesive

2488 A1557 70c multi 2.00 2.00

Booklet Stamps

2489 A1557 70c multi 2.00 2.00
a. Booklet pane of 4 + 4 etiquettes 8.00
2490 A1557 170c multi 4.75 4.75
a. Booklet pane of 4 + 4 etiquettes 19.00
2491 A1557 340c multi 9.50 9.50
a. Booklet pane of 4 38.00
Nos. 2488-2491 (4) 18.25 18.25

Rose — A1580

Silk-Screened on Porcelain Tile
2014, Mar. 20 ***Imperf.***
Self-Adhesive

2492 A1580 590c multi 16.50 16.50

European Organization for Nuclear Research (CERN), 60th Anniv. — A1581

2014, Apr. 4 Litho. ***Perf. 14***
2493 A1581 90c multi 2.50 2.50

Zum Schwarzen Kameel (Black Camel) Restaurant, Vienna — A1582

2014, Apr. 10 Litho. ***Perf. 14¼***
2494 A1582 70c multi 2.00 2.00

Eric Pleskow, Movie Producer
A1583

2014, Apr. 12 Litho. ***Perf. 13¾x13½***
2495 A1583 70c multi 2.00 2.00

Charlie Chaplin (1889-1977), Film Actor — A1584

2014, Apr. 12 Litho. ***Perf. 13¾x14***
2496 A1584 90c gray & blk 2.50 2.50

Klosterneuberg Monastery, 900th Anniv. — A1585

Litho. & Engr.
2014, Apr. 24 ***Perf. 14x13¾***
2497 A1585 145c multi 4.00 4.00

Wachau Wine Region — A1586

2014, May 3 Litho. ***Perf. 13¾x14***
2498 A1586 62c multi 1.75 1.75

Zither — A1587

2014, May 9 Litho. ***Perf. 13½***
2499 A1587 70c multi 1.90 1.90

Europa.

Scolopax Rusticola
A1588

Litho. & Engr.
2014, May 16 ***Perf. 14x14¼***
2500 A1588 170c multi 4.75 4.75

Steamboats on Traunsee, 175th Anniv.
A1589

2014, May 17 Litho. ***Perf. 14¼x14***
2501 A1589 62c multi 1.75 1.75

Erzberg Motorcycle Rodeo, 19th Anniv. — A1590

2014, May 29 Litho. ***Perf. 13¾x14***
2502 A1590 62c multi 1.75 1.75

Souvenir Sheet

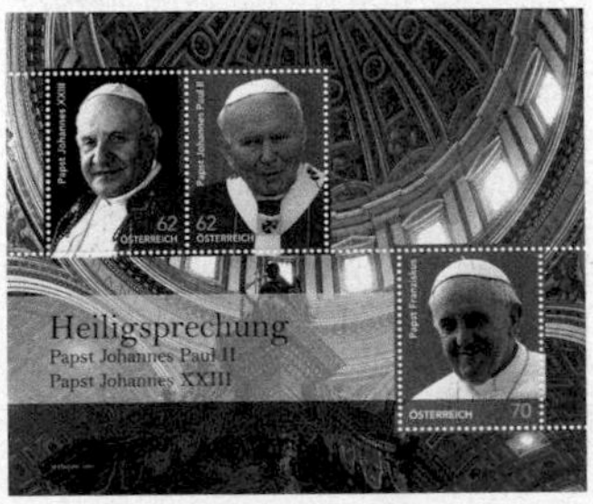

Popes — A1591

No. 2503: a, St. John XXIII. b, St. John Paul II. c, Pope Francis.

2014, June 5 Litho. ***Perf. 13x13½***
2503 A1591 Sheet of 3 5.50 5.50
a.-b. 62c Either single 1.75 1.75
c. 70c multi 1.90 1.90

Canonization of Popes John XXIII and John Paul II.

Josef Madersperger (1768-1850), and His Sewing Machine
A1592

2014, June 6 Litho. ***Perf. 13¾x14***
2504 A1592 70c multi 1.90 1.90

Museum of Applied Arts (MAK), Vienna, 150th Anniv. — A1593

2014, June 10 Litho. ***Perf. 14x13¾***
2505 A1593 62c multi 1.75 1.75

Hans Moser (1880-1964), Actor — A1594

2014, June 10 Litho. ***Perf. 13¼x13***
2506 A1594 70c multi 1.90 1.90

Richard Strauss (1864-1949), Composer — A1595

2014, June 11 Litho. ***Perf. 14x13¾***
2507 A1595 62c multi 1.75 1.75

Austrian Referendum on Joining the European Union, 20th Anniv. — A1596

2014, June 12 Litho. ***Perf. 13¾***
2508 A1596 62c multi 1.75 1.75

Dormition Icon, Hochfeistritz Fortress Church
A1597

Photo. & Engr.
2014, June 13 ***Perf. 13¾***
2509 A1597 90c multi 2.50 2.50

Souvenir Sheet

June 28, 1914 Royal Assassinations — A1598

No. 2510: a, Archduke Franz Ferdinand (1863-1914). b, Duchess Sophie of Hohenberg (1868-1914).

2014, June 28 Litho. *Perf. 13¼x14*

2510 A1598	Sheet of 2	3.75	3.75
a.	62c multi	1.75	1.75
b.	70c multi	1.90	1.90

Traditional Clothing of Ausseerland A1599

2014, July 18 Litho. *Perf. 13¾x14*

2511 A1599 70c multi 1.90 1.90

Miniature Sheet

Characters From *Maya the Bee* Animated Television Show — A1600

No. 2512: a, Willy the Bee. b, Maya the Bee. c, Thekla the Spider. d, Flip the Grasshopper.

Serpentine Die Cut 14

2014, Aug. 29 Litho.

Self-Adhesive

2512 A1600	Sheet of 4	6.50	6.50
a.-d.	62c Any single	1.60	1.60

Museum Angerlehner, Thalheim bei Wels — A1601

2014, Sept. 12 Litho. *Perf. 14¼*

2513 A1601 62c multi 1.60 1.60

Mariatrost Basilica, Graz, 300th Anniv. A1602

2014, Sept. 19 Litho. *Perf. 14¼*

2514 A1602 62c multi 1.60 1.60

Austrian Horse-Drawn Parcel Post Carriage, c. 1830 — A1603

2014, Sept. 20 Litho. *Perf. 14x13¾*

2515 A1603 90c multi 2.25 2.25

Souvenir Sheet

Steyr Valley Railway, 125th Anniv. — A1604

Perf. 13¾x13¼

2014, Sept. 20 Litho.

2516 A1604 145c multi 3.75 3.75

Map of Trans-Alpine Route of Fussach Messenger Courier Service A1605

Litho. & Engr.

2014, Sept. 27 *Perf. 13¾*

2517 A1605 90c multi 2.25 2.25

Vienna Sales Board, 150th Anniv. A1606

2014, Oct. 1 Litho. *Perf. 14¼*

2518 A1606 62c multi 1.60 1.60

Portrait of Isabella Reisser, by Anton Romako A1607

2014, Oct. 10 Litho. *Perf. 14*

2519 A1607 62c multi 1.60 1.60

Opening of Vienna Central Railroad Station — A1608

2014, Oct. 10 Litho. *Perf. 14*

2520 A1608 90c multi 2.25 2.25

Railways Type of 2002

Perf. 13¾x13½

2014, Oct. 10 Litho. & Engr.

2521 A1109 145c Murtal Railway train 3.75 3.75

Murtal Railway, 120th anniv.

Udo Jürgens, Singer, 80th Birthday — A1609

2014, Oct. 18 Litho. *Perf. 14*

2522 A1609 70c multi 1.75 1.75

1656 Portrait of Infanta Margarita Teresa in a White Dress, by Diego Velazquez A1610

Litho. & Engr.

2014, Oct. 18 *Perf. 13¾*

2523 A1610 145c multi 3.75 3.75

Interiors, Film by Ursula Mayer A1611

2014, Oct. 22 Litho. *Perf. 14¼*

2524 A1611 90c black 2.25 2.25

Mona Lisa, by Gelatin Art Collective A1612

2014, Oct. 22 Litho. *Perf. 14*

2525 A1612 170c multi 4.25 4.25

Media Poet, Film by Peter Weibel — A1613

2014, Oct. 25 Litho. *Perf. 14¼x14½*

2526 A1613 62c multi 1.60 1.60

Souvenir Sheet

Vienna Philharmonic Gold Coins, 25th Anniv. — A1614

2014 coin: a, Obverse (pipe organ). b, Reverse (various musical instruments).

Litho. & Embossed With Foil Application

2014, Nov. 5 *Perf.*

2527 A1614	Sheet of 2	4.00	4.00
a.	70c blue & gold	1.75	1.75
b.	90c maroon & gold	2.25	2.25

Hirschegg Parish Church Altarpiece Detail Depicting Adoration of the Magi — A1615

Madonna of Krumlov, c. 1400 — A1616

Adoration of the Magi, by Jan Brueghel the Elder (1568-1625) A1617

Winter Landscape, by Lucas I. van Valckenborch (c. 1535-97) — A1618

2014 Litho. *Perf. 13¾x14*

2528 A1615 62c multi 1.60 1.60
2529 A1616 70c multi 1.75 1.75

Coil Stamps
Self-Adhesive

Die Cut Perf. 13½x13¾

2530 A1617 62c multi 1.60 1.60

Die Cut Perf. 13¼

2531 A1618 70c multi 1.75 1.75

Christmas. Issued: Nos. 2528, 2530, 11/28; Nos. 2529, 2531, 11/14.

Travel Poster by Arthur Zelger (1914-2004), Graphic Designer A1619

2014, Dec. 5 Litho. *Perf. 13¼x14*

2532 A1619 170c multi 4.25 4.25

Souvenir Sheet

Skiing — A1620

No. 2533: a, Toni Sailer, skier. b, Trophy for Hahnenkamm Races.

2015, Jan. 20 Litho. *Perf. 13¾x13½*

2533 A1620 Sheet of 2 3.00 3.00
a. 62c multi 1.40 1.40
b. 70c multi 1.60 1.60

Toni Sailer, 80th birthday; Hahnenkamm Races, 75th anniv.

"Osterreich 62 Cent" — A1621

2015, Jan. 21 Litho. *Perf. 13¾*

2534 A1621 62c red 1.40 1.40

Timpani Drums — A1622

Litho. & Engr.

2015, Jan. 21 *Perf. 14*

2535 A1622 145c multi 3.25 3.25

Austrian Landmarks A1623

Part of map of Austria and: 6c, Riesenrad, Vienna. 10c, Bergkirche, Eisenstadt. 20c, Statue of Athena, Parliament, Vienna. 40c, Sailboarder, Neusiedler See, Burgenland. No. 2540, Clock tower, Graz. No. 2541, Goldenes Dachl (Golden Roof), Innsbruck. No. 2542, Martinsturm, Bregenz. No. 2543, Grossglockner, Hohe Tauern Range.

No. 2544, Heidentor, Carnuntum. No. 2545, Hohensalzburg Castle, Salzburg. No. 2546, St. Stephen's Cathedral, Vienna. No. 2547, Pöstlingberg Church, Linz. 150c, Lindwurm (Dragon Fountain), Klagenfurt. No. 2549, Murinsel, Graz. 170c, Bergisel Ski Jump, Innsbruck. 400c, Forchtenstein Castle.

Die Cut Perf. 13¾

2015, Mar. 1 Litho.

Coil Stamps
Self-Adhesive

2536	A1623	6c	multi	.25	.25
2537	A1623	10c	multi	.25	.25
2538	A1623	20c	multi	.45	.45
2539	A1623	40c	multi	.90	.90
2540	A1623	68c	multi	1.50	1.50
2541	A1623	80c	multi	1.75	1.75
2542	A1623	100c	multi	2.25	2.25
2543	A1623	160c	multi	3.50	3.50
	Nos. 2536-2543 (8)			10.85	10.85

Booklet Stamps

2544	A1623	68c	multi	1.50	1.50
a.	Booklet pane of 4			6.00	
2545	A1623	68c	multi	1.50	1.50
a.	Booklet pane of 10			15.00	
2546	A1623	80c	multi	1.75	1.75
a.	Booklet pane of 4			7.00	
2547	A1623	100c	multi	2.25	2.25
a.	Booklet pane of 4			9.00	
2548	A1623	150c	multi	3.50	3.50
a.	Booklet pane of 4			14.00	
2549	A1623	160c	multi	3.50	3.50
a.	Booklet pane of 4			14.00	
2550	A1623	170c	multi	3.75	3.75
a.	Booklet pane of 4			15.00	
2551	A1623	400c	multi	9.00	9.00
a.	Booklet pane of 4			36.00	
	Nos. 2544-2551 (8)			26.75	26.75

A self-adhesive sheet of four containing die cut examples of Nos. 2536-2539 and a self-adhesive sheet of 11 containing die cut examples of Nos. 2540-2551 were given away to standing order customers. The stamps in the sheets were not valid for postage.

Advertising Art for Schartner Bombe Beverages A1624

2015, Mar. 1 Litho. *Perf. 13¾*

2552 A1624 68c multi 1.50 1.50

Joseph Hardtmuth (1758-1816), Pencil Manufacturer A1625

2015, Mar. 1 Litho. *Perf. 14*

2553 A1625 80c multi 1.75 1.75

1953 Delta-Gnom LM 125 Motorcycle — A1626

2015, Mar. 7 Litho. *Perf. 13¾*

2554 A1626 220c multi 5.00 5.00

Miniature Sheet

Easter — A1627

No. 2555: a, Purple rabbit pointing to Easter eggs in tower. b, Brown and gray rabbits on blanket. c, Yellow rabbit and two mice. d, Pink rabbit and Easter eggs.

Serpentine Die Cut 14

2015, Mar. 7 Litho.

Self-Adhesive

2555 A1627 Sheet of 4 6.00
a.-d. 68c Any single 1.50 1.50

This stamp, released Mar. 7, 2015, was a gift for standing order customers. It was not made available for sale. Value, $3.

University of Vienna, 650th Anniv. — A1628

2015, Mar. 13 Litho. *Perf. 13¾*

2556 A1628 100c multi 2.25 2.25

St. Teresa of Avila (1515-82) A1629

Litho. & Engr.

2015, Mar. 28 *Perf. 13¾*

2557 A1629 170c multi 3.75 3.75

Literature Museum of the Austrian National Library, Vienna — A1630

2015, Apr. 18 Litho. *Perf. 13¾x14*

2558 A1630 68c multi 1.60 1.60

Maria Schell (1926-2005), Actress A1631

2015, Apr. 24 Litho. *Perf. 13½*

2559 A1631 68c multi 1.60 1.60

2015 Eurovision Song Contest, Vienna — A1632

2015, Apr. 24 Litho. *Perf. 14x13¾*

2560 A1632 80c multi 1.90 1.90

Museum Liaunig, Neuhaus A1633

2015, Apr. 26 Litho. *Perf. 14x13¾*

2561 A1633 68c multi 1.60 1.60

Traditional Tyrolean Costumes A1634

2015, May 2 Litho. *Perf. 13¾x14*

2562 A1634 68c multi 1.60 1.60

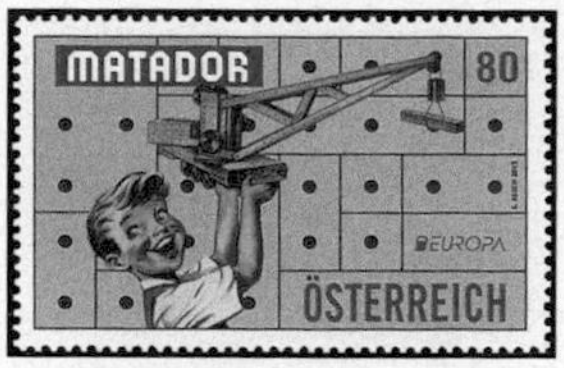

Europa — A1635

2015, May 7 Litho. *Perf. 14x13¾*
2563 A1635 80c multi 1.75 1.75

Souvenir Sheet

After the Rain, by Hubert Schmalix — A1636

2015, May 7 Litho. *Perf. 14*
2564 A1636 100c multi 2.25 2.25

Souvenir Sheet

Penny Black, 175th Anniv. — A1637

2015, May 7 Litho. *Perf. 14¼x14*
2565 A1637 220c multi 5.00 5.00

Steyr Puch IMP 700 GT Coupe A1638

2015, May 29 Litho. *Perf. 13¾*
2566 A1638 100c multi 2.25 2.25

Congress of Vienna, 200th Anniv. A1639

2015, June 9 Litho. *Perf. 13¾*
2567 A1639 68c black 1.50 1.50

Chalice Veil, Diocesan Museum of St. Polten A1640

Photo. & Engr.

2015, June 19 *Perf. 13¾*
2568 A1640 100c multi 2.25 2.25

Lepus Europaeus A1641

Litho. & Engr.

2015, June 19 *Perf. 14x14¼*
2569 A1641 160c multi 3.50 3.50

Spanish Riding School, Vienna, 450th Anniv. A1642

2015, June 26 Litho. *Perf. 13¾*
2570 A1642 80c multi 1.75 1.75

Rankweil Basilica A1643

2015, Aug. 21 Litho. *Perf. 13¾*
2571 A1643 68c multi 1.50 1.50

Souvenir Sheet

Horse-Drawn Mail Wagon — A1644

2015, Aug. 27 Litho. *Perf. 13¼x13*
2572 A1644 100c multi 2.25 2.25

Lady With a Dark Hat, by Anton Faistauer A1645

2015, Aug. 28 Litho. *Perf. 13¾*
2573 A1645 68c multi 1.50 1.50

Carnuntum Wine Region — A1646

2015, Sept. 5 Litho. *Perf. 14*
2574 A1646 80c multi 1.90 1.90

St. John Bosco (1815-88), Founder of Salesians Society A1647

2015, Sept. 12 Litho. *Perf. 13¾*
2575 A1647 150c multi 3.50 3.50

Alpine-Adriatic Philately, 20th Anniv. — A1648

2015, Sept. 18 Litho. *Perf. 14x13¼*
2576 A1648 80c multi 1.90 1.90

Haas House, Vienna, 25th Anniv. A1649

2015, Sept. 19 Litho. *Perf. 13¾*
2577 A1649 68c multi 1.60 1.60

Vexations, Photograph by Gregor Schmoll — A1650

Perf. 14¼x13½

2015, Sept. 19 Litho.
2578 A1650 68c black 1.60 1.60

Friedrich Kiesler (1890-1965), Architect — A1651

2015, Sept. 22 Litho. *Perf. 14x14¼*
2579 A1651 80c multi 1.90 1.90

Lederhosen A1652

Embossed on Brown Leather With Glass Crystals Affixed

Serpentine Die Cut 7¾

2015, Sept. 24 Self-Adhesive
2580 A1652 630c black 14.50 14.50

Univerity of Leoben, 175th Anniv. — A1653

Litho. With Foil Application

2015, Oct. 2 *Perf. 13¾x14¼*
2581 A1653 80c multi 1.90 1.90

Railways Type of 2002

Perf. 13¾x13½

2015, Oct. 3 Litho. & Engr.
2582 A1109 160c Semmerling Railway train 3.75 3.75

Schiebel Camcopter S-100 — A1654

2015, Oct. 17 Litho. *Perf. 14*
2583 A1654 68c multi 1.60 1.60

Painting by Svenja Deininger A1655

2015, Oct. 21 Litho. *Perf. 13¾*
2584 A1655 80c multi 1.75 1.75

Susanna and the Elders, by Tintoretto A1656

Litho. & Engr.

2015, Oct. 21 *Perf. 13¾*
2585 A1656 160c multi 3.50 3.50

Vienna University of Technology, 200th Anniv. — A1657

2015, Nov. 6 Litho. *Perf. 13¾x14*
2586 A1657 68c multi 1.50 1.50

Rotes Haus Restaurant, Dornbirn — A1658

2015, Nov. 6 Litho. *Perf. 13¾*
2587 A1658 150c multi 3.25 3.25

Nativity, by Master of Liefering A1659

Stylized Christmas Tree — A1660

Reindeer A1661

Madonna and Child, Gampern Triptych A1662

2015 Litho. *Perf. 14x13¾*
2588 A1659 68c multi 1.50 1.50

Perf. 13¾x13½
2589 A1660 80c multi 1.75 1.75

Coil Stamps
Self-Adhesive
Die Cut Perf. 14
2590 A1661 68c multi 1.50 1.50

Die Cut Perf. 13¼
2591 A1662 80c multi 1.75 1.75

Christmas. Issued: Nos. 2588, 2590, 11/27; Nos. 2589, 2591, 11/13.

Austrian National Bank, 200th Anniv. A1663

Litho. & Embossed With Foil Application
2016, Jan. 18 *Perf. 13¾*
2592 A1663 100c multi 2.25 2.25

Austrian Automobile, Motorcycle and Touring Club, 120th Anniv. — A1664

2016, Jan. 20 Litho. *Perf. 14¼x14*
2593 A1664 68c multi 1.50 1.50

Turmhutfrau, Digital Painting by Dorothee Golz — A1665

2016, Jan. 28 Litho. *Perf. 14*
2594 A1665 68c multi 1.50 1.50

Future Factor, by Anna Liska and Andreas Wesle A1666

Litho. & Embossed
2016, Jan. 28 *Perf. 14¼x13¾*
2595 A1666 80c gray & white 1.75 1.75

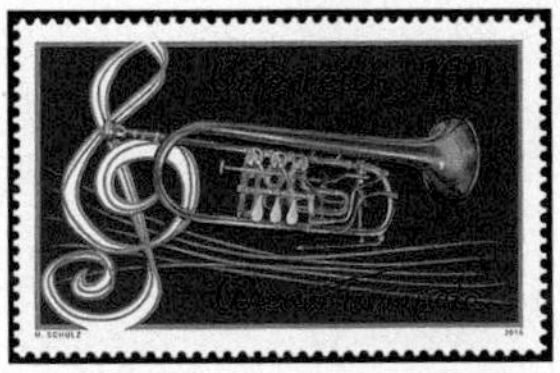

Viennese Trumpet — A1667

Litho. & Embossed
2016, Jan. 28 *Perf. 14*
2596 A1667 160c multi 3.50 3.50

Advertising Art for Fritze Lacquer A1668

2016, Feb. 18 Litho. *Perf. 14*
2597 A1668 100c multi 2.25 2.25

Josef Ressel (1793-1857), Inventor of Ship Propeller A1669

2016, Feb. 19 Litho. *Perf. 14*
2598 A1669 80c multi 1.75 1.75

Crown of the Archduke of Austria, 400th Anniv. — A1670

2016, Mar. 4 Litho. *Perf. 14x13¼*
2599 A1670 150c multi 3.50 3.50

This stamp, released Mar. 5, 2016, was a gift for standing order customers. It was not made available for sale. Value, $1.75.

Dog and Marie von Ebner-Eschenbach (1830-1916), Writer — A1671

Litho. & Engr.
2016, Mar. 5 *Perf. 13¾*
2600 A1671 160c multi 3.75 3.75

Kunsthistorisches Museum, Vienna, 125th Anniv. — A1672

2016, Mar. 8 Litho. *Perf. 13¾*
2601 A1672 100c multi 2.25 2.25

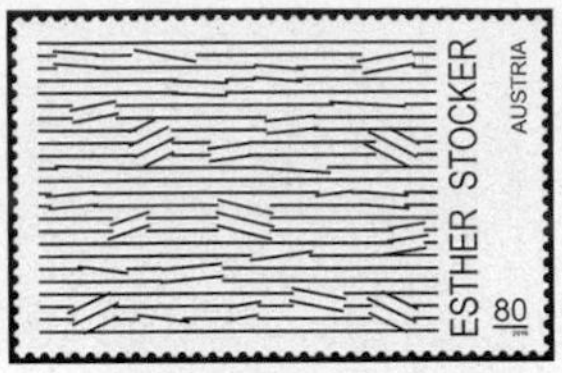

Untitled Art by Esther Stocker — A1673

2016, Mar. 16 Litho. *Perf. 14*
2602 A1673 80c black 1.90 1.90

Untitled Art from Fundraising Series, by Martha Jungwirth — A1674

2016, Mar. 6 Litho. *Perf. 14*
2603 A1674 100c multi 2.25 2.25

Cross From Melk Abbey A1675

Photo. & Engr.
2016, Mar. 17 *Perf. 13¾*
2604 A1675 170c multi 4.00 4.00

1923 Puch 125 LM Motorcycle — A1676

2016, Mar. 23 Litho. *Perf. 14¼x14*
2605 A1676 220c multi 5.00 5.00

Postal Agreement of 1516, 500th Anniv. A1677

2016, Apr. 2 Litho. *Perf. 13¾*
2606 A1677 68c multi 1.60 1.60

Souvenir Sheet

Stamps of 1850 — A1678

No. 2607: a, Lombardy-Venetia #4b. b, Austria #2.

2016, Apr. 2 Litho. *Perf. 13*
2607 A1678 Sheet of 2 6.75 6.75
a. 68c multi 1.60 1.60
b. 220c multi 5.00 5.00

Michael Haneke, Movie Director A1679

2016, Apr. 4 Litho. *Perf. 13½*
2608 A1679 68c multi 1.60 1.60

Untitled Painting by Erwin Bohatsch A1680

2016, Apr. 4 Litho. *Perf. 13¾*
2609 A1680 80c multi 1.90 1.90

Prater Park, Vienna, 250th Anniv. — A1681

2016, Apr. 9 Litho. *Perf. 14*
2610 A1681 80c multi 1.90 1.90

Traditional Clothing of Montafon A1682

2016, Apr. 30 Litho. *Perf. 14*
2611 A1682 68c multi 1.60 1.60

Return of Salzburg to Austria, 200th Anniv. A1683

2016, Apr. 30 Engr. *Perf. 13¾*
2612 A1683 100c multi 2.40 2.40

Mariazell Basilica A1684

2016, May 12 Litho. *Perf. 14*
2613 A1684 80c multi 1.90 1.90

Europa — A1685

2016, May 14 Litho. *Perf. 14*
2614 A1685 80c multi 1.90 1.90

Think Green Issue.

Postcrossing A1686

2016, May 21 Litho. *Perf. 13¾*
2615 A1686 80c multi 1.90 1.90

Traditional Clothing of Schärding A1687

2016, May 29 Litho. *Perf. 14*
2616 A1687 68c multi 1.60 1.60

International Day of United Nations Peacekeepers A1688

2016, May 29 Litho. *Perf. 14*
2617 A1688 68c multi 1.60 1.60

Schärding, 700th Anniv. — A1689

2016, June 4 Litho. *Perf. 14*
2618 A1689 80c multi 1.90 1.90

2016 European Soccer Championships, France — A1690

2016, June 10 Litho. *Perf. 14*
2619 A1690 80c multi 1.90 1.90

Pieta — A1691

Screen Printed on Back of Piece of Glass

2016, June 10 *Imperf.*

Self-Adhesive

2620 A1691 630c multi 20.00 20.00

Concrete Boat, Sculpture by Michael Schuster — A1692

2016, June 15 Litho. *Perf. 14*
2621 A1692 68c multi 1.50 1.50

Madonna and Child Stained-Glass Window From Parish Church, Steyr — A1693

Photo. & Engr.

2016, June 17 *Perf. 13¾*
2622 A1693 100c multi 2.25 2.25

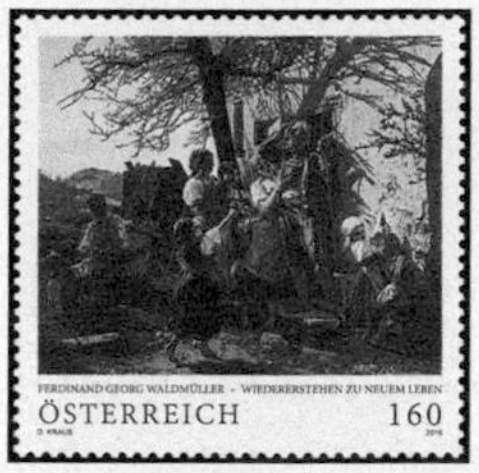

Revival to New Life, by Ferdinand Georg Waldmüller (1793-1865) — A1694

Litho. & Engr.

2016, July 13 *Perf. 13¾*
2623 A1694 160c multi 3.75 3.75

Post Office Savings Bank, Vienna, Designed by Otto Wagner (1841-1918) A1695

2016, July 13 Litho. *Perf. 13¾x14¼*
2624 A1695 170c multi 3.75 3.75

Mittelburgenland Wine Region — A1696

2016, July 16 Litho. *Perf. 14*
2625 A1696 80c multi 1.90 1.90

Souvenir Sheet

Postman on Tricycle — A1697

2016, Aug. 25 Litho. *Perf. 13¼x14*
2626 A1697 100c multi 2.25 2.25

Denzel WD Super 1300 A1698

Perf. 13½x13¾

2016, Aug. 26 Litho.
2627 A1698 100c multi 2.25 2.25

Emperor Franz Joseph I (1830-1916) A1699

2016, Aug. 27 **Litho.** ***Perf. 13¾***
2628 A1699 80c multi 1.90 1.90

Liebespaar, by Koloman Moser (1868-1918) A1700

2016, Sept. 7 **Litho.** ***Perf. 14***
2629 A1700 68c multi 1.60 1.60

Lentia Chair, by March Gut — A1701

2016, Sept. 16 **Litho.** ***Perf. 13½***
2630 A1701 68c multi 1.60 1.60

Flower and "Thank You" A1702

2016, Sept. 22 **Litho.** ***Perf. 14x13¼***
2631 A1702 (68c) multi 1.60 1.60

Dirndl — A1703

Embroidered

2016, Sept. 22 ***Imperf.***

Self-Adhesive

2632 A1703 630c multi 15.00 15.00

Maria Locherboden Church, Mötz — A1704

2016, Sept. 23 **Litho.** ***Perf. 14x13¼***
2633 A1704 68c multi 1.60 1.60

Railways Type of 2002

Design: Gleichenberger Railway train.

Perf. 13¾x13½

2016, Oct. 7 **Litho. & Engr.**
2634 A1109 170c multicolored 3.75 3.75

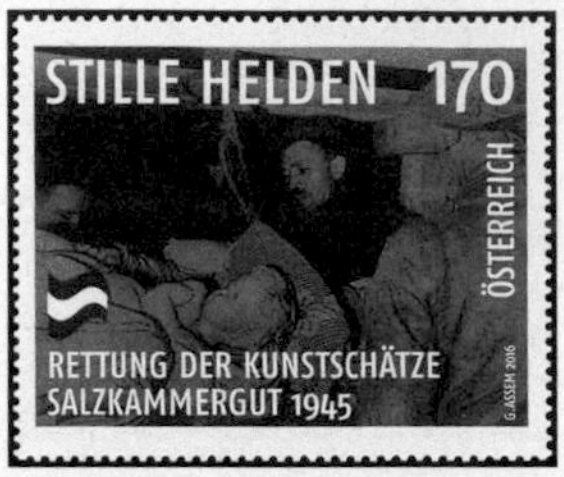

1945 Rescue of Art Treasures from Salt Mines — A1705

2016, Oct. 12 **Litho.** ***Perf. 14x14¼***
2635 A1705 170c multi 3.75 3.75

Souvenir Sheet

Stamps of 1858 — A1706

No. 2636: a, Lombardy-Venetia #8. b, Austria #9.

2016, Oct. 12 **Litho.** ***Perf. 13¼x13***
2636 A1706 Sheet of 2 6.50 6.50
a. 68c multi 1.50 1.50
b. 220c multi 5.00 5.00

Institute for High Energy Physics, 50th Anniv. — A1707

2016, Oct. 19 **Litho.** ***Perf. 14***
2637 A1707 80c multi 1.75 1.75

T-Center, Vienna A1708

2016, Oct. 19 **Litho.** ***Perf. 13¼x13¾***
2638 A1708 80c multi 1.75 1.75

Meles Meles A1709

Litho. & Engr.

2016, Oct. 22 ***Perf. 14x14¼***
2639 A1709 160c multi 3.75 3.75

Gasthof Post Hotel, Lech am Arlberg A1710

2016, Nov. 7 **Litho.** ***Perf. 13¼x13¾***
2640 A1710 68c multi 1.50 1.50

Silent Night, Hymn by Joseph Mohr and Franz Gruber, 200th Anniv. A1711

Symbols of Christmas A1712

Adoration of the Magi, Painting by Unknown Artist, Mariapfarr Church A1713

Nativity, by Master of Raigern A1714

Christmas — A1715

No. 2645: a, Girl behind chair, denomination at LR. b, Boy behind chair, denomination at LL. c, Angel. d, Santa Claus.

2016 **Litho.** ***Perf. 13½***
2641 A1711 68c multi 1.50 1.50
2642 A1712 80c red 1.75 1.75

Coil Stamps
Self-Adhesive
Die Cut Perf. 13¼

2643 A1713 68c multi 1.50 1.50

Die Cut Perf. 14

2644 A1714 80c multi 1.75 1.75

Miniature Sheet
Serpentine Die Cut 14

2645 A1715 Sheet of 4 6.50
a.-b. 68c Either single 1.50 1.50
c.-d. 80c Either single 1.75 1.75

Issued: Nos. 2641, 2643, 11/25; Nos. 2642, 2644, 2645, 11/11.

Helicopter Police Force, 60th Anniv. A1716

2016, Nov. 16 **Litho.** ***Perf. 13¾***
2646 A1716 170c multi 3.75 3.75

Details From State Coats of Arms — A1717

Designs: 25c, Salzburg (lion's feet). No. 2648, Lower Austria (Niederösterreich, eagle's head). No. 2649, Burgenland (eagle's head and tongue). No. 2650, Tyrol (Tirol, crowned eagle). No. 2651, Styria (Steiermark, panther's head). No. 2652, Lower Austria (eagle). No. 2653, Carinthia (Kärnten, lion). No. 2654, Salzburg (lion's head). No. 2655, Upper Austria (Oberösterreich, eagle's head). 170c, Burgenland (eagle feathers). 175c, Tyrol (eagle tail and claws). 210c, Styria (panther's claws). No. 2659, Vorarlberg (rings and banner). No. 2660, Vienna (Wien, cross). 400c, Vorarlberg (banner fringes).

Die Cut Perf. 13½

2017, Jan. 1 **Litho.**

Coil Stamps

2647 A1717 25c multi .55 .55
2648 A1717 68c multi 1.40 1.40

Booklet Stamps

2649 A1717 68c multi 1.40 1.40
a. Booklet pane of 4 5.75
2650 A1717 68c multi 1.40 1.40
a. Booklet pane of 10 14.00
2651 A1717 68c multi 1.40 1.40
a. Booklet pane of 25 35.00
2652 A1717 80c multi 1.75 1.75
a. Booklet pane of 4 7.00
2653 A1717 80c multi 1.75 1.75
a. Booklet pane of 50 87.50
2654 A1717 125c multi 2.60 2.60
a. Booklet pane of 4 10.50
2655 A1717 125c multi 2.60 2.60
a. Booklet pane of 50 130.00
2656 A1717 170c multi 3.50 3.50
a. Booklet pane of 4 14.00
2657 A1717 175c multi 3.75 3.75
a. Booklet pane of 4 15.00
2658 A1717 210c multi 4.50 4.50
a. Booklet pane of 4 18.00
2659 A1717 250c multi 5.25 5.25
a. Booklet pane of 4 21.00
2660 A1717 250c multi 5.25 5.25
a. Booklet pane of 25 135.00
2661 A1717 400c multi 8.25 8.25
a. Booklet pane of 4 33.00
Nos. 2649-2661 (13) 43.40 43.40

Villach Carnival, 150th Anniv. — A1718

2017, Jan. 7 **Litho.** ***Perf. 14x14¼***
2662 A1718 80c multi 1.75 1.75

Staples Repairing Tear A1719

2017, Jan. 18 **Litho.** ***Perf. 14¼x14***
2663 A1719 68c multi 1.50 1.50

Protestant Reformation, 500th Anniv. — A1720

2017, Jan. 24 Litho. *Perf. 14*
2664 A1720 68c multi 1.50 1.50

Photograph of Hochtannberg, by Margherita Spiluttini — A1721

2017, Feb. 8 Litho. *Perf. 14x13½*
2665 A1721 80c black 1.75 1.75

Falco (1957-98), Rock Musician A1722

2017, Feb. 19 Litho. *Perf. 13¼x14*
2666 A1722 80c multi 1.75 1.75

Peter Mitterhofer (1822-93), and His Vienna Typewriter A1723

2017, Feb. 22 Litho. *Perf. 14*
2667 A1723 80c multi 1.75 1.75

Harp and G Clef — A1724

Photo. & Engr.
2017, Feb. 22 *Perf. 13¾*
2668 A1724 210c multi 4.50 4.50

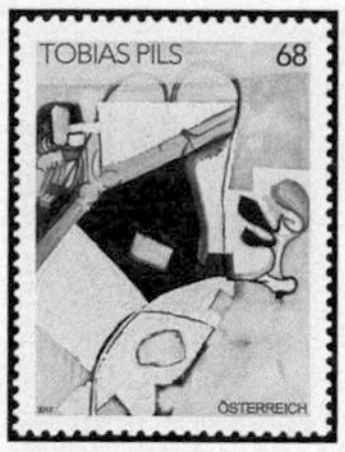

Untitled (Autumn), by Tobias Pils — A1725

2017, Mar. 3 Litho. *Perf. 13¼x14*
2669 A1725 68c multi 1.50 1.50

Miniature Sheet

Birthday Party — A1726

No. 2670: a, Boy and dog. b, Boy, girl, cake with candles. c, Girl holding gift. d, Boy and piece of cake.

Serpentine Die Cut 14
2017, Mar. 4 Litho.
Self-Adhesive

2670	A1726	Sheet of 4	6.00 6.00
a.-d.		68c Any single	1.50 1.50

This stamp, released Mar. 4, 2017, was a gift for standing order customers. It was not made available for sale. Value, $1.75.

Vienna Wine Region — A1727

2017, Mar. 15 Litho. *Perf. 14*
2671 A1727 68c multi 1.50 1.50

Crafts and Trade Code for Goldsmiths and Silversmiths, 650th Anniv. A1728

Litho. With Foil Application
2017, Apr. 12 *Perf. 13¼x14*
2672 A1728 175c multi 4.00 4.00

Souvenir Sheet

Stamps of 1860-62 — A1729

No. 2673: a, Lombardy-Venetia #14. b, Austria #16.

2017, Apr. 12 Litho. *Perf. 13*

2673	A1729	Sheet of 2	6.25 6.25
a.		68c multi	1.50 1.50
b.		220c multi	4.75 4.75

Traditional Clothing of Pöttsching A1730

2017, Apr. 19 Litho. *Perf. 14*
2674 A1730 68c multi 1.50 1.50

Emblem of Schlierbach Cheese A1731

2017, Apr. 28 Litho. *Perf. 13¾*
2675 A1731 68c multi 1.50 1.50

Schönbrunn Palace, Vienna — A1732

2017, May 9 Litho. *Perf. 14¼x13¾*
2676 A1732 68c multi 1.50 1.50

Europa.

Souvenir Sheet

Holy Roman Empress Maria Theresa (1717-80) — A1733

Litho. With Foil Application
2017, May 13 *Perf. 14x13¼*
2677 A1733 170c multi 4.00 4.00

See Croatia No. 1038, Hungary No. 4433, Slovenia No. 1219, Ukraine No. 1093.

Lions Clubs International, Cent. — A1734

2017, May 19 Litho. *Perf. 13¾x14¼*
2678 A1734 80c multi 1.90 1.90

Puch Vehicles A1735

Designs: 68c, 1919-20 Alpenwagen XII. 220c, 1961 150 SR motor scooter.

2017 Litho. *Perf. 13½x13¾*
2679 A1735 68c multi 1.60 1.60
2680 A1735 220c multi 5.00 5.00

Issued: 68c, 5/20; 220c, 5/19.

Vienna Philharmonic Orchestra, 175th Anniv. — A1736

2017, May 25 Litho. *Perf. 14*
2681 A1736 80c multi 1.90 1.90

Railways Type of 2002
2017, May 28 Litho. *Perf. 13¾x13½*
2682 A1109 125c Stainzerbahn train 2.75 2.75

White Act, by Herbert Boeckl (1894-1966) — A1737

2017, June 7 Litho. ***Perf. 13½x13¾***
2683 A1737 68c multi 1.60 1.60

Untitled Painting by Walter Vopava A1738

2017, July 1 Litho. ***Perf. 13¼x14***
2684 A1738 125c multi 3.00 3.00

Christoph Waltz, Actor — A1739

2017, July 12 Litho. ***Perf. 13½***
2685 A1739 80c multi 1.90 1.90

St. Thomas Touching Christ, by Thomas von Villach, St. Andrew Parish Church, Thörl-Maglern A1740

Photo. & Engr.
2017, July 14 ***Perf. 13¾***
2686 A1740 170c silver & multi 4.00 4.00

Railways Type of 2002
2017, July 15 Litho. ***Perf. 13½x13¾***
2687 A1109 175c Brennerbahn train 4.25 4.25

Oak Tree — A1741

Silk-Screened on Wood Veneer
2017, July 28 ***Laser Cut***
Self-Adhesive
2688 A1741 690c multi 16.50 16.50

Souvenir Sheet

19th Century Horse-drawn Post Wagon — A1742

2017, Aug. 24 Litho. ***Perf. 13¼x14***
2689 A1742 210c multi 5.00 5.00

Souvenir Sheet

1867 Stamps of the Austro-Hungarian Empire — A1743

No. 2690: a, 68c, Austria #29. b, 220c, Austria #33.

2017, Aug. 25 Litho. ***Perf. 13¼x13***
2690 A1743 Sheet of 2 7.00 7.00
a. 68c multi 1.75 1.75
b. 220c multi 5.25 5.25

See Hungary No. 4441.

Maria Kirchental, St. Martin bei Lofer — A1744

Perf. 13¾x13¼
2017, Sept. 10 Litho.
2691 A1744 80c multi 1.90 1.90

New Austria Post Headquarters, Vienna — A1745

Perf. 13¼x13¾
2017, Sept. 21 Litho.
2692 A1745 80c multi 1.90 1.90

Coffee House Table Setting A1746

Dürnstein Abbey A1747

Schafberg Railway A1748

Ibex in Dachstein Mountains A1749

Die Cut Perf. 13¼ Syncopated
2017, Sept. 25 Litho.
Coil Stamps
Self-Adhesive
2693 A1746 68c multi —
2694 A1747 80c multi —
2695 A1748 125c multi —
2696 A1749 250c multi 6.00 6.00

Girl with a Fan, by Peter Paul Rubens (1577-1640) A1750

Perf. 13¾x13¼
2017, Oct. 7 Litho. & Engr.
2697 A1750 210c multi 5.00 5.00

Traditional Clothing of Grinzing A1751

2017, Oct. 11 Litho. ***Perf. 14***
2698 A1751 80c multi 1.90 1.90

Feather Bust of Hawaiian Deity A1752

Litho. & Engr.
2017, Oct. 11 ***Perf. 13¼x14***
2699 A1752 175c multi 4.25 4.25

Reopening of World Museum, Vienna.

Cervus Elephus A1753

Litho. & Engr.
2017, Oct. 14 ***Perf. 13½***
2700 A1753 250c multi 6.00 6.00

Adi Ubleis, Harness Racing Driver, 80th Birthday — A1754

2017, Nov. 10 Litho. ***Perf. 14***
2701 A1754 68c multi 1.60 1.60

University of Applied Arts, Vienna, 150th Anniv. — A1755

Perf. 13¾x13¼
2017, Nov. 10 Litho.
2702 A1755 170c multi 4.00 4.00

Adoration of the Magi Stained-Glass Window, St. Maximilian Church, Altschwendt A1756

Items on Advent Calendar A1757

Snowflakes and Swarovski Crystal — A1758

Dolls in Wheelbarrow and Two Girls — A1759

Virgin Mary with Child, by Carlo Maratta (1625-1713) — A1760

Litho., Litho With Affixed Crystal (250c)

2017 *Perf. 14*
2703 A1756 68c multi 1.60 1.60

Perf. 13¾x13¼

2704 A1757 80c multi 1.90 1.90

Perf. 13½

2705 A1758 250c blue 6.00 6.00
Nos. 2703-2705 (3) 9.50 9.50

Coil Stamps Self-Adhesive

Die Cut Perf. 13

2706 A1759 68c multi 1.60 1.60
2707 A1760 80c multi 1.90 1.90

Christmas. Issued: Nos. 2703, 2706, 2707, 12/1; No. 2704, 11/17; No. 2705, 11/13

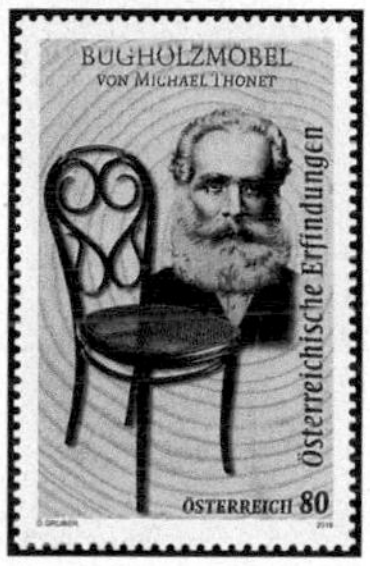

Michael Thonet (1796-1871), and Bentwood Chair — A1761

2018, Jan. 22 **Litho.** *Perf. 14*
2708 A1761 80c multi 2.00 2.00

Viennese Tuba — A1762

Perf. 13¾x14¼

2018, Jan. 22 **Litho. & Engr.**
2709 A1762 210c multi 5.25 5.25

Steyr 50 "Baby" A1763

2018, Jan. 27 **Litho.** *Perf. 13¼x13¾*
2710 A1763 125c multi 3.25 3.25

Faces of Young and Old Woman A1764

2018, Feb. 15 **Litho.** *Perf. 14¼x14*
2711 A1764 68c red 1.75 1.75

Sculpture of Head by Joannis Avramidis (1922-2016) A1765

2018, Feb. 22 **Litho.** *Perf. 14*
2712 A1765 68c multi 1.75 1.75

Still Life, Breakfast with Champagne Glass and Pipe, by Jan Davidzoon de Heem (1606-83) — A1766

Litho. & Engr.

2018, Feb. 22 *Perf. 14¼x14*
2713 A1766 210c multi 5.25 5.25

Souvenir Sheet

Stamps of 1863-64 — A1767

No. 2714: a, Lombardy-Venetia #22. b, Austria #20.

2018, Mar. 3 **Litho.** *Perf. 13*
2714 A1767 Sheet of 2 7.25 7.25
a. 68c multi 1.75 1.75
b. 220c multi 5.50 5.50

This stamp, released Mar. 3, 2018, was a gift for standing order customers. It was not made available for sale. Value, $1.75.

KTM Grand Tourist 125 Motorcycle A1768

Perf. 14¼x13¾

2018, Mar. 17 **Litho.**
2715 A1768 220c multi 5.50 5.50

2018 UCI Road Cycling Championships, Innsbruck — A1769

2018, Apr. 13 **Litho.** *Perf. 13½*
2716 A1769 80c multi 1.90 1.90

Self-Portrait of Martin Johann "Kremser" Schmidt (1718-1801) — A1770

2018, Apr. 13 **Litho.** *Perf. 14¼x13¾*
2717 A1770 80c multi 1.90 1.90

Altar, Holy Spirit Church, Vienna A1771

Photo. & Engr.

2018, Apr. 14 *Perf. 13¾*
2718 A1771 175c multi 4.25 4.25

Sacher Hotel, Vienna, Sachertorte and Coffee Cup — A1772

2018, Apr. 20 **Litho.** *Perf. 14¼x13¾*
2719 A1772 170c multi 4.25 4.25

Austrian National Library, 650th Anniv. — A1773

2018, May 6 **Litho.** *Perf. 14*
2720 A1773 175c multi 4.25 4.25

Schemerl Bridge, Nussdorf A1774

2018, May 9 **Litho.** *Perf. 14¼x13¾*
2721 A1774 80c multi 1.90 1.90

Europa.

Souvenir Sheet

Creation of District Commissions, 150th Anniv. — A1775

No. 2722: a, Emperor Franz Joseph I. b, Arms of Styrian District Commission.

2018, May 18 **Litho.** *Perf. 14x13¼*
2722 A1775 Sheet of 2 3.25 3.25
a.-b. 68c Either single 1.60 1.60

Körbersee A1776

Heuriger A1777

Falkenstein Castle A1778

Eisriesenwelt Ice Cave, Werfen — A1779

Die Cut Perf. 13¼ Syncopated

2018, Feb. 16 **Litho.**

Coil Stamps Self-Adhesive

2723 A1776 68c multi 1.75 1.75
2724 A1777 80c multi 2.00 2.00
2725 A1778 125c multi 3.00 3.00
2726 A1779 250c multi 6.00 6.00
Nos. 2723-2726 (4) 12.75 12.75

Water Sports — A1780

Designs: 68c, Waterskiing. 80c, Kitesurfing. 170c, Sailing, Roman Hagara and Hans-Peter Steinacher, Olympic gold medalists in sailing.

2018, May 25 Litho. ***Perf. 14x13¾***

2727 A1780 68c multi 1.60 1.60
2728 A1780 80c multi 1.90 1.90
2729 A1780 170c multi 4.00 4.00
Nos. 2727-2729 (3) 7.50 7.50

Graz-Seckau Diocese, 800th Anniv. — A1781

2018, June 8 Litho. ***Perf. 13¾x14***

2730 A1781 80c multi 1.90 1.90

Traditional Costumes From Thaya Valley Region — A1782

2018, June 24 Litho. ***Perf. 14***

2731 A1782 80c multi 1.90 1.90

Devices From State and Municipal Coats of Arms — A1783

Designs: 10c, Vorarlberg (rings and banner). 12c, Salzburg State (lion). No. 2734, Bregenz coat of arms. No. 2735, Styria (Steiermark, lion). No. 2736, Klagenfurt (dragon). No. 2737, City of Salzburg (castle). No. 2738, Lower Austria (Nieder Österreich, five eagles). No. 2739, Vienna (Wien, shield with cross). No. 2740, Upper Austria (Ober Osterreich, eagle). No. 2741, Graz (lion). 180c, Burgenland (eagle on rock). No. 2743, Tyrol (Tirol, eagle). No. 2744, St. Pölten (wolf). 420c, Carinthia (Kärnten, three lions).

Die Cut Perf. 13½
2018, June 23 Litho.
Coil Stamps
Self-Adhesive

2732 A1783 10c multi .25 .25
2733 A1783 12c multi .30 .30
2734 A1783 80c multi 1.90 1.90
Nos. 2732-2734 (3) 2.45 2.45

Booklet Stamps

2735 A1783 80c multi 1.90 1.90
a. Booklet pane of 4 7.75
2736 A1783 80c multi 1.90 1.90
a. Booklet pane of 10 19.00
2737 A1783 80c multi 1.90 1.90
a. Booklet pane of 25 47.50
2738 A1783 90c multi 2.10 2.10
a. Booklet pane of 4 8.50
2739 A1783 90c multi 2.10 2.10
a. Booklet pane of 50 105.00
2740 A1783 135c multi 3.25 3.25
a. Booklet pane of 4 13.00
2741 A1783 135c multi 3.25 3.25
a. Booklet pane of 50 165.00
2742 A1783 180c multi 4.25 4.25
a. Booklet pane of 4 17.00
2743 A1783 270c multi 6.25 6.25
a. Booklet pane of 4 25.00
2744 A1783 270c multi 6.25 6.25
a. Booklet pane of 25 160.00
2745 A1783 420c multi 9.75 9.75
a. Booklet pane of 4 39.00
Nos. 2735-2745 (11) 42.90 42.90

Peter Rosegger (1843-1918), Writer — A1784

Perf. 13¾x14¼
2018, June 26 Litho.

2746 A1784 230c multi 5.50 5.50

Austrian Presidency of the Council of the European Union — A1785

Litho. With Foil Application
2018, June 29 ***Perf. 14x13¾***

2747 A1785 135c gold & multi 3.25 3.25

Leonard Bernstein (1918-90), Conductor A1786

2018, July 6 Litho. ***Perf. 14x13½***

2748 A1786 90c multi 2.10 2.10

Big Es, by Hubert Scheibl — A1787

2018, July 6 Litho. ***Perf. 14x13¾***

2749 A1787 180c multi 4.25 4.25

Rosenbauer Heros-Titan Helmet A1788

2018, July 20 Litho. ***Perf. 13½***

2750 A1788 270c multi 6.50 6.50

Republic of Austria, Cent. — A1789

2018, Aug. 23 Litho. ***Perf. 13¼x14***

2751 A1789 80c multi 1.90 1.90

Souvenir Sheet

Horse-drawn Coach — A1790

2018, Aug. 24 Litho. ***Perf. 13¼x14***

2752 A1790 210c multi 5.00 5.00

Miniature Sheet

Paintings — A1791

No. 2753: a, Spring, by Koloman Moser (1868-1918). b, Death and Life, by Gustav Klimt (1862-1918). c, Vienna Metropolitan Railway Station, designed by Otto Wagner (1841-1918). d, Self-portrait with Physalis, by Egon Schiele (1890-1918).

2018, Aug. 24 Litho. ***Perf. 13¾***

2753 A1791 Sheet of 4 7.75 7.75
a.-d. 80c Any single 1.90 1.90

Basilica of the Nativity of Mary, Frauenkirchen — A1792

2018, Sept. 8 Litho. ***Perf. 13¾x13¼***

2754 A1792 80c multi 1.90 1.90

Klaus Maria Brandauer, Actor and Director A1793

2018, Sept. 20 Litho. ***Perf. 13½***

2755 A1793 80c multi 1.90 1.90

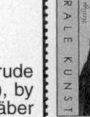

St. Erentrude (?-718), by Georg Stäber A1794

Photo. & Engr.
2018, Sept. 21 ***Perf. 13¾***

2756 A1794 175c sil & multi 4.00 4.00

Styrian Hat A1795

Embroidered
2018, Sept. 22 ***Imperf.***
Self-Adhesive

2757 A1795 690c multi 16.00 16.00

Head of Bear and Emblem of Four Paws International — A1796

2018, Oct. 12 Litho. ***Perf. 14x13½***

2758 A1796 90c multi 2.10 2.10

Flower Bouquet A1797

2018, Oct. 14 Litho. ***Perf. 14***

2759 A1797 (80c) multi 1.90 1.90

Western Styrian Wine Region — A1798

2018, Oct. 18 Litho. ***Perf. 14***

2760 A1798 90c multi 2.10 2.10

Railways Type of 2002

Design: 135c, Crown Prince Rudolf Railway, 150th anniv.

2018, Oct. 20 Litho. ***Perf. 14¼x13¾***

2761 A1109 135c multi 3.25 3.25

Lacquered Teacup A1799

2018, Oct. 24 Litho. *Perf. 14x13¼*

2762 A1799 420c multi 9.75 9.75

Viennese porcelain, 300th anniv.

Stork Over Seewinkel, Lake Neuseidl — A1800

Kufstein Fortress A1801

Roman Arch, Carnuntum — A1802

Apricot Dumplings A1803

Die Cut Perf. 13¼ Syncopated

2018, July 1 Litho.

Coil Stamps
Self-Adhesive

2763	A1800	80c multi	1.90	1.90
2764	A1801	90c multi	2.10	2.10
2765	A1802	135c multi	3.25	3.25
2766	A1803	270c multi	6.25	6.25
		Nos. 2763-2766 (4)	13.50	13.50

Südbahn Hotel, Semmering — A1804

Lebkuchen A1805

Mittenwald Railway A1806

Krimml Waterfalls A1807

Die Cut Perf. 13¼ Syncopated

2018, Oct. 31 Litho.

Coil Stamps
Self-Adhesive

2767	A1804	80c multi	1.90	1.90
2768	A1805	90c multi	2.10	2.10
2769	A1806	135c multi	3.25	3.25
2770	A1807	270c multi	6.25	6.25
		Nos. 2767-2770 (4)	13.50	13.50

Vienna University of Economics and Business Library A1808

2018, Nov. 9 Litho. *Perf. 14¼x13¾*

2771 A1808 270c multi 6.25 6.25

Schlägl Abbey, 800th Anniv. — A1809

Perf. 13¾x13¼

2018, Nov. 11 Litho.

2772 A1809 80c multi 1.90 1.90

The Birth of Christ, Maria Rast am Hainzenberg Church — A1810

Silent Night Memorial Chapel, Obendorf bei Salzburg A1811

Girl With Cat A1812

Christmas Tree A1813

2018 Litho. *Perf. 13½*

2773 A1810 80c multi 1.90 1.90

Perf. 13¾x14¼

2774 A1811 90c multi 2.10 2.10

Self-Adhesive
Die Cut Perf. 13¼x13

2775	A1812	80c multi	1.90	1.90
2776	A1813	90c multi	2.10	2.10

Christmas, Christmas hymn *Silent Night*, 200th anniv. (No. 2774). Issued: Nos. 2773, 2775, 11/30; No. 2774, 11/23; No. 2776, 11/16.

University of Innsbruck, 350th Anniv. — A1814

2019, Jan. 18 Litho. *Perf. 14*

2777 A1814 90c multi 2.10 2.10

Austro Fiat Type 1C A1815

2019, Jan. 30 Litho. *Perf. 14¼x13¾*

2778 A1815 135c multi 3.25 3.25

Lohner Sissy Moped A1816

2019, Jan. 31 Litho. *Perf. 14¼x13¾*

2779 A1816 230c multi 5.25 5.25

Carrier Pigeon A1817

Perf. 14¼x13¾

2019, Feb. 13 Litho.

2780 A1817 80c brt green 1.90 1.90

Fat House, Sculpture by Erwin Wurm — A1818

2019, Feb. 13 Litho. *Perf. 14x13¼*

2781 A1818 175c multi 4.00 4.00

Opening of House of Austrian History, Vienna A1819

2019, Feb. 19 Litho. *Perf. 13¼x14*

2782 A1819 270c red & black 6.25 6.25

Vienna State Opera House, 150th Anniv. — A1820

2019, Feb. 28 Litho. *Perf. 14*

2783 A1820 90c multi 2.10 2.10

This stamp, released Mar. 9, 2019, was a gift for standing order customers. It was not made available for sale. Value, $1.90.

David with the Head of Goliath, by Caravaggio (1567-1610) — A1821

Perf. 14¼x13¾

2019, Mar. 9 Litho. & Engr.

2784 A1821 180c multi 4.00 4.00

Viennese Zither — A1822

Litho. & Engr.

2019, Mar. 20 *Perf. 14x13¾*
2785 A1822 210c multi 4.75 4.75

Many Colorful Trojans and Acorn-Shaped Worms, by Markus Huemer A1823

2019, Mar. 21 Litho. *Perf. 13½x14*
2786 A1823 80c multi 1.90 1.90

Sus Scrofa A1824

Litho. & Engr.

2019, Mar. 29 *Perf. 13½*
2787 A1824 270c multi 6.00 6.00

Viktor Kaplan (1876-1934), Inventor of Kaplan Turbine A1825

2019, Mar. 30 Litho. *Perf. 14*
2788 A1825 80c multi 1.90 1.90

Lambach Abbey A1826

Ringwarte Observation Tower, Hartberg A1827

Kanisfluh A1828

Viennese Waltz Dancers A1829

Die Cut Perf. 13¼ Syncopated

2019, Apr. 1 **Litho.**

Coil Stamps Self-Adhesive

2789 A1826 80c multi 1.90 1.90
2790 A1827 90c multi 2.00 2.00
2791 A1828 135c multi 3.00 3.00
2792 A1829 270c multi 6.00 6.00
Nos. 2789-2792 (4) 12.90 12.90

Holy Roman Emperor Maximilian I (1459-1519) A1830

2019, Apr. 11 Litho. *Perf. 14*
2793 A1830 80c multi 1.90 1.90

Miniature Sheet

Stamp Day — A1831

No. 2794: a, Boy writing letter. b, Boy putting letter in mailbox. c, Mail van. d, Delivery of letter.

Serpentine Die Cut 14

2019, Apr. 24 **Litho.**

Self-Adhesive

2794 A1831 Sheet of 4 7.75
a.-d. 80c Any single 1.90 1.90

Souvenir Sheet

Love — A1832

No. 2795: a, Wreath and heart. b, Birds and hearts.

Litho. With Foil Application

2019, Apr. 24 *Perf. 13¼x14*
2795 A1832 Sheet of 2 2.25 2.25
a. 10c multi .25 .25
b. 80c multi 1.90 1.90

White-tailed Eagle — A1833

2019, May 9 Litho. *Perf. 13¾x14¼*
2796 A1833 90c multi 2.10 2.10

Europa.

Martin Luther Protestant Church, Hainburg A1834

2019, May 14 Litho. *Perf. 14x14¼*
2797 A1834 270c multi 6.00 6.00

Hochriegl Sparkling Wine — A1835

2019, May 15 Litho. *Perf. 14*
2798 A1835 90c multi 2.10 2.10

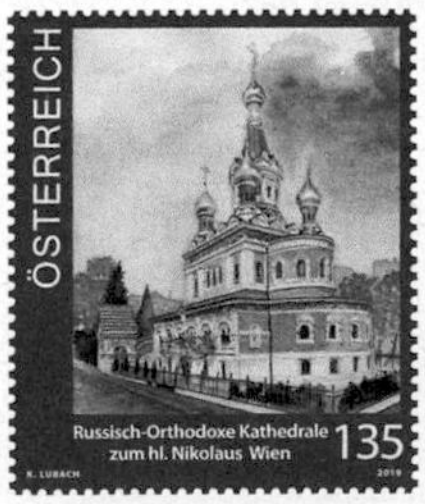

St. Nicholas Russian Orthodox Cathedral, Vienna A1836

2019, May 17 Litho. *Perf. 13¾x13¼*
2799 A1836 135c multi 3.00 3.00

Souvenir Sheet

Austrian Stamps of 1883 — A1837

No. 2800: a, Austria #46. b, Austria #43.

2019, May 17 Litho. *Perf. 13¼x13*
2800 A1837 Sheet of 2 7.25 7.25
a. 80c multi 1.90 1.90
b. 230c multi 5.25 5.25

Unicorn and QR Code — A1838

2801 A1838 690c black & silver + label — —

No. 2801 has a detachable label at right with scratch-off panels. Scanning the QR code into a smartphone or entering code on the label on the website post.at/cryptostamp connects the physical stamp with a virtual stamp that has one of five different colors - black (most common), green, blue, yellow and red (scarcest). The scrach-off panels conceal codes for transferring the virtual stamp to a virtual wallet.

Angel from Admont Abbey A1839

Photo. & Engr.

2019, June 15 *Perf. 13¾*
2802 A1839 135c multi 3.25 3.25

Traditional Women's Clothing From Carinthia A1840

2019, June 27 Litho. *Perf. 14*
2803 A1840 80c multi 1.90 1.90

Stollen and Zauner Konditerei, Bad Ischl A1841

Perf. 14¼x13¾

2019, June 29 **Litho.**
2804 A1841 180c multi 4.25 4.25

Assorted Foods — A1842

Moosham Castle A1843

Houses in Schärding
A1844

Lakeside Promenade, Bregenz
A1845

Die Cut Perf. 13¼ Syncopated

2019, July 1 **Litho.**

Coil Stamps
Self-Adhesive

2805	A1842	80c multi		1.90	1.90
2806	A1843	90c multi		2.10	2.10
2807	A1844	135c multi		3.25	3.25
2808	A1845	270c multi		6.25	6.25
	Nos. 2805-2808 (4)			13.50	13.50

MAM Baby Pacifier
A1846

2019, July 15 **Litho.** ***Perf. 13¾x13½***

2809	A1846	230c multi		5.25	5.25

Souvenir Sheet

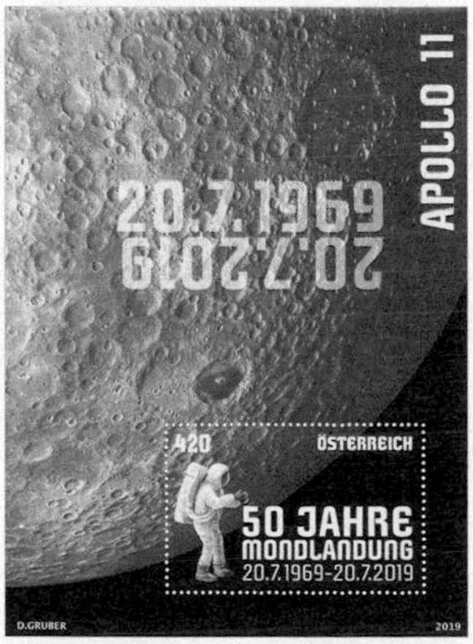

First Man on the Moon, 50th Anniv. — A1847

2019, July 20 **Litho.** ***Perf. 14***

2810	A1847	420c multi		9.50	9.50

Grit is affixed to parts of the design.

Railways Type of 2002

Design: 270c, Gmunden Tramway, 125th anniv.

Litho. & Engr.

2019, Aug. 2 ***Perf. 14***

2811	A1109	270c multi		6.00	6.00

Souvenir Sheet

Royal and Imperial Express Mail Coach, c. 1852 — A1848

2019, Aug. 24 **Litho.** ***Perf. 13¼x14***

2812	A1848	210c multi		4.75	4.75

2019 World Rowing Championships, Linz and Ottensheim — A1849

2019, Aug. 26 **Litho.** ***Perf. 13½x14***

2813	A1849	90c multi		2.00	2.00

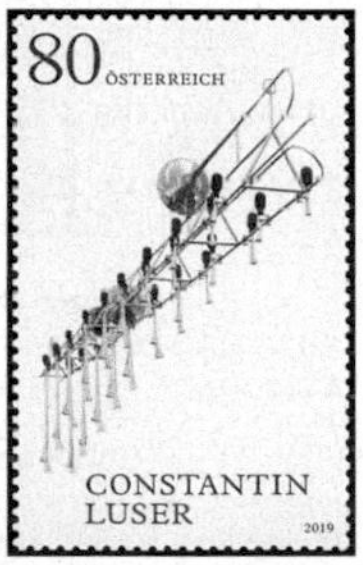

Stille Post, Sculpture by Constantin Luser — A1850

2019, Aug. 27 **Litho.** ***Perf. 13¾***

2814	A1850	80c multi		1.90	1.90

Abbot's Staff From St. Lambrecht's Abbey
A1851

Photo. & Engr.

2019, Sept. 13 ***Perf. 13¾***

2815	A1851	175c multi		4.00	4.00

Kamptal Controlled District Wine Region — A1852

2019, Sept. 19 **Litho.** ***Perf. 13¾x14***

2816	A1852	80c multi		1.75	1.75

Good Times, Bad Times, Photograph by Anna Jermolaewa — A1853

2019, Sept. 27 **Litho.** ***Perf. 14x13¼***

2817	A1853	90c multi		2.00	2.00

Souvenir Sheet

Stamps of 1890 — A1854

No. 2818: a, Austria #53. b, Austria #64.

2019, Sept. 27 **Litho.** ***Perf. 13***

2818	A1854	Sheet of 2		6.75	6.75
a.		80c multi		1.75	1.75
b.		230c multi		5.00	5.00

Railways Type of 2002

Mariazell Railway Himmelstreppe train.

Photo. & Engr.

2019, Oct. 12 ***Perf. 14¼x14***

2819	A1109	230c multi		5.25	5.25

Souvenir Sheet

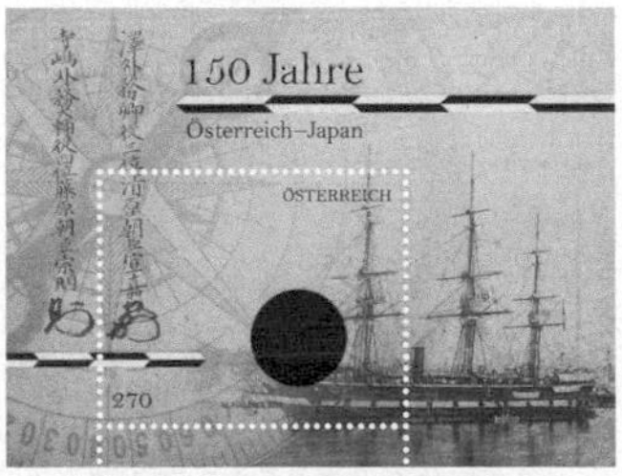

Diplomatic Relations With Japan, 150th Anniv. — A1855

2019, Oct. 15 **Litho.** ***Perf. 14x13¼***

2820	A1855	270c multi		6.00	6.00

Aerial Sports — A1856

Designs: 80c, Paragliding. 90c, Skydiving. 180c, Gliding.

2019, Oct. 19 **Litho.** ***Perf. 14x13½***

2821	A1856	80c multi		1.90	1.90
2822	A1856	90c multi		2.00	2.00
2823	A1856	180c multi		4.00	4.00
	Nos. 2821-2823 (3)			7.90	7.90

Traditional Costumes From Flachgau
A1857

2019, Oct. 25 **Litho.** ***Perf. 13¾x14¼***

2824	A1857	80c multi		1.90	1.90

Klosterneuburg Monastery — A1858

Men Harvesting Hay
A1859

Rappottenstein Castle — A1860

Cattle of Pinzgau Region
A1861

Die Cut Perf. 13¼ Syncopated

2019, Oct. 1 **Litho.**

Coil Stamps
Self-Adhesive

2825	A1858	80c multi		1.75	1.75
2826	A1859	90c multi		2.00	2.00
2827	A1860	135c multi		3.00	3.00
2828	A1861	270c multi		6.00	6.00
	Nos. 2825-2828 (4)			12.75	12.75

Souvenir Sheet

Reign of Charles V (1500-58) as Archduke of Austria and His Selection as Holy Roman Emperor, 500th Anniv. — A1862

Litho. With Foil Application

2019, Nov. 8 *Perf. 13*

2829 A1862 175c gold & multi 4.00 4.00

See Luxembourg No. 1530.

Christkindl Post Office, 70th Anniv. A1863

Goldener Sams Nativity Figures A1864

Christmas Tree — A1865

Children, Christmas Tree and Sled A1866

Christkindl Post Office, 70th Anniv. A1867

2019 **Litho.** *Perf. 13½x14*

2830 A1863 80c gold & multi 1.75 1.75

Perf. 13½

2831 A1864 90c multi 2.00 2.00

Litho. With Crystal Affixed

2832 A1865 270c multi 6.00 6.00

Nos. 2830-2832 (3) 9.75 9.75

Coil Stamps
Self-Adhesive

Die Cut Perf. 13¼

2833 A1866 80c multi 1.75 1.75

2834 A1867 90c gold & multi 2.00 2.00

Christmas. Issued: Nos. 2830, 2833, 11/29; No. 2831, 11/22; No. 2832, 11/8; No. 2834, 11/15.

Salzburg Festival, Cent. — A1868

2020, Jan. 21 **Litho.** *Perf. 14x14¼*

2835 A1868 270c multi 6.00 6.00

Frequency Hopping Spread Spectrum Technology, Invented by Hedy Lamarr (1914-2000) A1869

2020, Jan. 22 **Litho.** *Perf. 14*

2836 A1869 90c multi 2.00 2.00

Austrian Entry into the European Union, 25th Anniv. A1870

Litho. With Foil Application

2020, Jan. 22 *Perf. 13¼x13¾*

2837 A1870 210c gold & multi 4.75 4.75

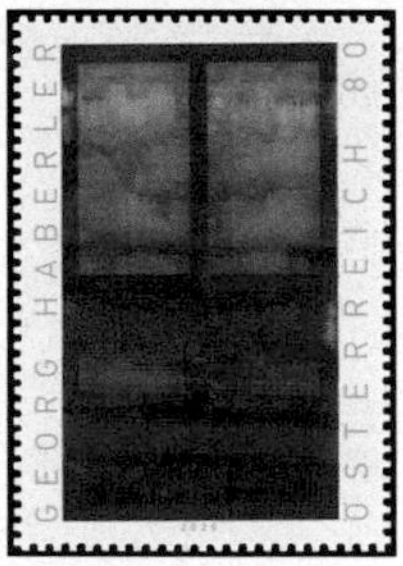

Untitled Painting by Georg Haberler A1871

2020, Jan. 28 **Litho.** *Perf. 13¼x14*

2838 A1871 80c sil & multi 1.75 1.75

Map of Countries in European Union as of January 31, 2020 — A1872

2020, Jan. 31 **Litho.** *Perf. 13½*

2839 A1872 180c multi — —

No, 2839 was prepared for issue on Mar. 29, 2019, when the United Kingdom had originally planned to leave the European Union. After the United Kingdom's new exit date of Jan. 31, 2020 was confirmed, the stamps were overprinted with this date. No. 2839 was not issued without the overprint.

Laurin & Klement Type A Voiturette A1873

Perf. 13¼x13¾

2020, Feb. 12 **Litho.**

2840 A1873 135c multi 3.00 3.00

Consumption Monster Eating Earth — A1874

Perf. 14¼x13¾

2020, Feb. 19 **Litho.**

2841 A1874 80c multi 1.75 1.75

Red Noses Clown Doctors International, 25th Anniv. — A1875

2020, Feb. 25 **Litho.** *Perf. 13¼*

2842 A1875 90c multi 2.00 2.00

Relief on Gilt Copper Depicting Jesus Found in St. Aegidius Church, Vöcklabruck A1876

Litho. & Engr.

2020, Mar. 6 *Perf. 13¾*

2843 A1876 135c sil & multi 3.00 3.00

Souvenir Sheet

Stamps of 1891-06 — A1877

No. 2844: a, Austria #69. b, Austria #65.

2020, Mar. 7 **Litho.** *Perf. 13*

2844 A1877 Sheet of 2 7.00 7.00

a. 85c multi 1.90 1.90

b. 230c multi 5.00 5.00

This stamp, released Mar. 7, 2020, was a gift for standing order customers. It was not made available for sale.

Opportunity, Light Installation by Brigitte Kowanz A1878

2020, Mar. 17 **Litho.** *Perf. 14x14¼*

2845 A1878 180c multi 4.00 4.00

Double Bass — A1879

2020, Mar. 18 **Litho.** *Perf. 14*

2846 A1879 100c multi 2.25 2.25

Wool Cap, Seewinkel A1880

Bonnet, Lake Constance Region A1881

Bridal Wreath, Stinatz A1882

Pocket Watch and Chain, Montafon A1883

Hat, Ausseerland A1884

Bowler Hat and Horse Whip, Vienna A1885

Leather Bag, Salzburg A1886

Choker, Innviertel A1887

Boots, Gail Valley — A1888

Pocket Knife With Deer Antler Handle, Ybbs Valley — A1889

Embroidery, East Tyrol — A1890

Socks, Enns Valley — A1891

Feathered Hat, Pitz Valley A1892

Jacket Pocket Stitching, Salzkammergut A1893

Hunting Knife With Deer Antler Handle, Innergebirg Region A1894

Hat Ornament, Aussee Region A1895

Die Cut Perf. 13½

2020, Apr. 1 Litho.

Coil Stamps
Self-Adhesive

2847	A1880	5c multi	.25	.25
2848	A1881	10c multi	.25	.25
2849	A1882	85c multi	1.90	1.90
		Nos. 2847-2849 (3)	2.40	2.40

Booklet Stamps

2850	A1883	85c multi	1.90	1.90
a.		Booklet pane of 4	7.75	
2851	A1884	85c multi	1.90	1.90
a.		Booklet pane of 10	19.00	
2852	A1885	85c multi	1.90	1.90
a.		Booklet pane of 25	47.50	
2853	A1886	100c multi	2.25	2.25
a.		Booklet pane of 4	9.00	
2854	A1887	100c multi	2.25	2.25
a.		Booklet pane of 50	115.00	
2855	A1888	135c multi	3.00	3.00
a.		Booklet pane of 4	12.00	
2856	A1889	135c multi	3.00	3.00
a.		Booklet pane of 50	150.00	
2857	A1890	175c multi	3.75	3.75
a.		Booklet pane of 4	15.00	
2858	A1891	180c multi	4.00	4.00
a.		Booklet pane of 4	16.00	
2859	A1892	210c multi	4.50	4.50
a.		Booklet pane of 4	18.00	
2860	A1893	275c multi	6.00	6.00
a.		Booklet pane of 4	24.00	
2861	A1894	275c multi	6.00	6.00
a.		Booklet pane of 25	150.00	
2862	A1895	430c multi	9.25	9.25
a.		Booklet pane of 4	37.00	
		Nos. 2850-2862 (13)	49.70	49.70

Water Tower, Floridsdorf A1896

Grünberg Cable Car, Gmunden A1897

Danube-Auen National Park — A1898

Cheese Spaetzle A1899

Die Cut Perf. 13¼ Syncopated

2020, Apr. 1 Litho.

Coil Stamps
Self-Adhesive

2863	A1896	85c multi	1.90	1.90
2864	A1897	100c multi	2.25	2.25
2865	A1898	135c multi	3.00	3.00
2866	A1899	275c multi	6.00	6.00
		Nos. 2863-2866 (4)	13.15	13.15

Traditional Women's Clothing From Wachau Valley — A1900

2020, Apr. 3 Litho. *Perf. 14*

2867	A1900	85c multi	1.90	1.90

Statue of Artemis — A1901

Litho. With Foil Application

2020, Apr. 17 *Perf. 14*

2868	A1901	210c multi	4.75	4.75

Austrian-funded archaeological excavations in Ephesus, Turkey, 125th anniv.

Auer Candies, Cent. — A1902

2020, Apr. 24 Litho. *Perf. 13¼*

2869	A1902	275c multi	6.00	6.00

Post Rider Near Fugger Palace, Innsbruck A1903

2020, May 8 Litho. *Perf. 13¼x13¾*

2870	A1903	100c multi	2.25	2.25

Europa.

Railways Type of 2002

Graz-Köflach Railway "Roter Blitz."

Perf. 14¼x13¾

2020, May 8 Litho. & Engr.

2871	A1109	230c multi	5.25	5.25

Amnesty International Austria, 50th Anniv. — A1904

2020, May 15 Litho. *Perf. 14*

2872	A1904	135c multi	3.00	3.00

Linz Gate, Freistadt, 800th Anniv. — A1905

2020, May 23 Litho. *Perf. 14*

2873	A1905	85c multi	1.90	1.90

Freistadt, 800th Anniv.

Untitled Painting by Herbert Brandl A1906

2020, June 25 Litho. *Perf. 13¼x14*

2874	A1906	85c multi	1.90	1.90

Giant Panda — A1907

Llama — A1908

Honey Badger — A1909

Dog — A1910

Litho. With Foil Application

2020, June 25 *Die Cut*

Self-Adhesive

2875	A1907	700c multi	—	—
2876	A1908	700c multi	—	—
2877	A1909	700c multi	—	—
2878	A1910	700c multi	—	—

Narcissus Festival A1912

Open-Air Museum, Gerersdorf A1913

Highline 179 Suspension Footbridge, Reutte — A1914

Gerlos Pass A1915

Die Cut Perf. 13¼ Syncopated

2020, July 1 **Litho.**

Coil Stamps

Self-Adhesive

2880	A1912	85c multi	1.90	1.90
2881	A1913	100c multi	2.25	2.25
2882	A1914	135c multi	3.00	3.00
2883	A1915	275c multi	6.25	6.25
		Nos. 2880-2883 (4)	13.40	13.40

Lippizaner Stud Farm, Piber, Cent. — A1916

2020, July 4 **Litho.** ***Perf. 14***

2884	A1916	100c multi	2.40	2.40

Schweizerhaus Restaurant, Vienna — A1917

2020, July 11 **Litho.** ***Perf. 14¼x14***

2885	A1917	175c multi	4.25	4.25

Franz Lehár (1870-1948), Composer A1918

2020, July 11 **Litho.** ***Perf. 13½***

2886	A1918	275c multi	6.50	6.50

Swarovski Crystal Business, 125th Anniv. — A1919

Litho. With Foil Application

2020, July 18 ***Perf. 13¼***

2887	A1919	430c sil & multi	10.00	10.00

SEMI-POSTAL STAMPS

Issues of the Monarchy

Emperor Franz Josef — SP1

Perf. 12½

1914, Oct. 4 **Typo.** **Unwmk.**

B1	SP1	5h green	.40	*.80*
B2	SP1	10h rose	.80	*1.60*
		Set, never hinged	2.75	

Nos. B1-B2 were sold at an advance of 2h each over face value. Exist imperf.; value, set $120.

The Firing Step — SP2

Designs: 5h+2h, Cavalry. 10h+2h, Siege gun. 20h+3h, Battleship. 35h+3h, Airplane.

1915, May 1

B3	SP2	3h + 1h violet brn	1.20	*.40*
B4	SP2	5h + 2h green	.25	.25
B5	SP2	10h + 2h deep rose	.25	.25
B6	SP2	20h + 3h Prus blue	4.00	*2.40*
B7	SP2	35h + 3h ultra	6.50	*5.50*
		Nos. B3-B7 (5)	12.20	*8.80*
		Set, never hinged	35.00	

Exist imperf. Value, set $325 hinged and $525 never hinged.

Issues of the Republic

Types of Austria, 1919-20, Overprinted in Black

1920, Sept. 16 ***Perf. 12½***

B11	A44	5h gray, *yellow*	.55	*1.60*
B12	A44	10h red, *pink*	.55	*1.25*
B13	A43	15h bister, *yel*	.25	*.80*
B14	A45	20h dark grn, *bl*	.25	*.65*
B15	A43	25h violet, *pink*	.25	*.75*
B16	A45	30h brown, *buff*	1.40	*2.90*
B17	A45	40h carmine, *yel*	.25	*.80*
B18	A45	50h dark bl, *blue*	.25	*.65*
B19	A43	60h ol grn, *azure*	1.40	*2.75*
B20	A47	80h red	.35	*.75*
B21	A47	1k orange brown	.35	*.80*
B22	A47	2k pale blue	.35	*.80*

Granite Paper

Imperf

B23	A46	2½k brown red	.40	*1.00*
B24	A46	3k dk blue & green	.50	*1.25*
B25	A46	4k carmine & violet	.65	*1.50*
B26	A46	5k blue	.55	*1.25*
B27	A46	7½k yellow green	.55	*1.25*
B28	A46	10k gray grn & red	.55	*1.40*
B29	A46	20k lilac & orange	.75	*1.75*
		Nos. B11-B29 (19)	10.15	*23.90*
		Set, never hinged	26.00	

Carinthia Plebiscite. Sold at three times face value for the benefit of the Plebiscite Propaganda Fund.

Nos. B11-B19 exist imperf. Values, set unused hinged $290, never hinged $400.

Types of Regular Issues of 1919-21 Overprinted

1921, Mar. 1 ***Perf. 12½***

B30	A44	5h gray, *yellow*	.25	*.80*
B31	A44	10h orange brown	.25	*.80*
B32	A43	15h gray	.25	*.80*
B33	A45	20h green, *yellow*	.25	*.80*
B34	A43	25h blue, *yellow*	.25	*.80*
B35	A45	30h violet, *bl*	.50	*1.60*
B36	A45	40h org brn, *pink*	.55	*2.00*
B37	A45	50h green, *blue*	1.25	*3.25*
B38	A43	60h lilac, *yellow*	.50	*1.60*
B39	A47	80h pale blue	.50	*1.60*
B40	A47	1k red org, *blue*	.40	*1.60*
B41	A47	1½k green, *yellow*	.25	*.80*
B42	A47	2k lilac brown	.25	*.80*

Overprinted

B43	A46	2½k light blue	.25	*.80*
B44	A46	3k ol grn & brn red	.25	*.80*
B45	A46	4k lilac & orange	.80	*2.75*
B46	A46	5k olive green	.25	*1.60*
B47	A46	7½k brown red	.30	*1.60*
B48	A46	10k blue & olive grn	.30	*1.60*
B49	A46	20k car rose & vio	.50	*2.40*
		Nos. B30-B49 (20)	8.10	*28.80*
		Set, never hinged	18.00	

Nos. B30-B49 were sold at three times face value, the excess going to help flood victims. Exists imperf. Values, set unused hinged $300, never hinged $525.

Nos. B50-B76, B93-B98, B112-B117, B122-B127, B132-B137 and B146-B164 exist imperf, on handmade paper, printed in black or in colors other than those of the issued stamps. These are proofs.

Franz Joseph Haydn — SP9

Musicians: 5k, Mozart. 7½k, Beethoven. 10k, Schubert. 25k, Anton Bruckner. 50k, Johann Strauss (son). 100k, Hugo Wolf.

1922, Apr. 24 **Engr.** ***Perf. 12½***

B50	SP9	2½k brn, perf. 11½	7.25	7.25
a.		Perf. 12½	11.00	*12.00*
		Never hinged	30.00	
B51	SP9	5k dark blue	1.25	1.25
B52	SP9	7½k black	2.00	2.00
a.		Perf. 11½	110.00	110.00
		Never hinged	240.00	
B53	SP9	10k dark violet	2.75	2.40
a.		Perf. 11½	3.25	3.25
		Never hinged	16.00	
B54	SP9	25k dark green	4.75	*4.75*
a.		Perf. 11½	4.75	4.75
		Never hinged	16.00	
B55	SP9	50k claret	2.40	2.40
B56	SP9	100k brown olive	8.00	*8.00*
a.		Perf. 11½	10.50	10.50
		Never hinged	47.50	
		Nos. B50-B56 (7)	28.40	*28.05*
		Set, never hinged	72.50	

These stamps were sold at 10 times face value, the excess being given to needy musicians.

Used values are for examples with philatelic favor cancels. Postally used stamps are worth 50%-100% more.

All values exist imperf. Values, set unused hinged $900, never hinged $1,750.

A 1969 souvenir sheet without postal validity contains reprints of the 5k in black, 7½k in claret and 50k in dark blue, each overprinted "NEUDRUCK" in black at top. It was issued for the Vienna State Opera Centenary Exhibition.

View of Bregenz — SP16

Designs: 120k, Mirabelle Gardens, Salzburg. 160k, Church at Eisenstadt. 180k, Assembly House, Klagenfurt. 200k, "Golden Roof," Innsbruck. 240k, Main Square, Linz. 400k, Castle Hill, Graz. 600k, Abbey at Melk. 1000k, Upper Belvedere, Vienna.

Various Frames

1923, May 22 ***Perf. 12½***

B57	SP16	100k dk green	4.00	*4.00*
B58	SP16	120k deep blue	4.00	*4.00*
B59	SP16	160k dk violet	4.00	*4.00*
B60	SP16	180k red violet	4.00	*4.00*
B61	SP16	200k lake	4.00	*4.00*
B62	SP16	240k red brown	4.00	*4.00*
B63	SP16	400k dark brown	4.00	*4.00*
B64	SP16	600k olive brn	4.00	*4.00*
B65	SP16	1000k black	4.00	*4.00*
		Nos. B57-B65 (9)	36.00	*36.00*
		Set, never hinged	100.00	

Nos. B57-B65 were sold at five times face value, the excess going to needy artists.

Used values are for examples with philatelic favor cancels. Values for postally used: Nos. B57-B64, each $8; No. B65 $14.

All values exist imperf. on both regular and handmade papers. Values, set hinged $700, never hinged $1,000.

Feebleness — SP25

Designs: 300k+900k, Aid to industry. 500k+1500k, Orphans and widow.

600k+1800k, Indigent old man. 1000k+3000k, Alleviation of hunger.

1924, Sept. 6 **Photo.**

B66	SP25	100k + 300k yel grn	4.00	*4.00*
B67	SP25	300k + 900k red brn	4.00	*4.00*
B68	SP25	500k + 1500k brn vio	4.00	*4.00*
B69	SP25	600k + 1800k pck bl	8.00	*6.50*
B70	SP25	1000k + 3000k brn org	9.50	*8.00*
		Nos. B66-B70 (5)	29.50	*26.50*
		Set, never hinged	67.50	

The surtax was for child welfare and anti-tuberculosis work.

Used values are for examples with philatelic favor cancels. Values for postally used are 2-2.5 times values shown.

Set exists imperf. Values, set unused hinged $350, never hinged $525.

Siegfried Slays the Dragon — SP30

Designs: 8g+2g, Gunther's voyage to Iceland. 15g+5g, Brunhild accusing Kriemhild. 20g+5g, Nymphs telling Hagen the future. 24g+6g, Rudiger von Bechelaren welcomes the Nibelungen. 40g+10g, Dietrich von Bern vanquishes Hagen.

1926, Mar. 8 **Engr.**

B71	SP30	3g + 2g olive blk	.95	.80
B72	SP30	8g + 2g indigo	.40	.40
B73	SP30	15g + 5g dk claret	.35	.35
B74	SP30	20g + 5g olive grn	.50	.50
B75	SP30	24g + 6g dk violet	.50	.50
B76	SP30	40g + 10g red brn	2.40	2.40
		Nos. B71-B76 (6)	5.10	4.95
		Set, never hinged	15.00	

Nibelungen issue. The surtax was for child welfare.

Nos. B71-B76 were printed in two sizes: 27 ½x28 ½mm and 28 ½x27 ½mm.

Used values are for examples with philatelic favor cancels. Values for postally used are 1.5 times values shown.

Nos. B71-B76 exist imperf. Values, set unused hinged $350, never hinged $500.

Pres. Michael Hainisch — SP36

1928, Nov. 5

B77	SP36	10g dark brown	5.50	4.75
B78	SP36	15g red brown	5.50	4.75
B79	SP36	30g black	5.50	4.75
B80	SP36	40g indigo	5.50	4.75
		Nos. B77-B80 (4)	22.00	*19.00*
		Set, never hinged	37.50	

Tenth anniversary of Austrian Republic. Sold at double face value, the premium aiding war orphans and children of war invalids.

Used values are for examples with philatelic favor cancels. Values for postally used are 2.5 times values shown.

Set exists imperf, without gum. Value, set $625.

Pres. Wilhelm Miklas — SP37

1930, Oct. 4

B81	SP37	10g light brown	7.25	*7.25*
B82	SP37	20g red	7.25	*7.25*
B83	SP37	30g brown violet	7.25	*7.25*
B84	SP37	40g indigo	7.25	*7.25*
B85	SP37	50g dark green	7.25	*7.25*
B86	SP37	1s black brown	7.25	*7.25*
		Nos. B81-B86 (6)	43.50	*43.50*
		Set, never hinged	125.00	

Nos. B81-B86 were sold at double face value. The excess aided the anti-tuberculosis campaign and the building of sanatoria in Carinthia.

Used values are for examples with philatelic favor cancels. Values for postally used are 3 times values shown.

Set exists imperf, without gum. Value, set $950.

Regular Issue of 1929-30 Overprinted in Various Colors

1931, June 20

B87	A56	10g bister (Bl)	27.50	*27.50*
B88	A56	20g dk gray (R)	27.50	*27.50*
B89	A56	30g dk violet (Gl)	27.50	*27.50*
B90	A56	40g dk blue (Gl)	27.50	*27.50*
B91	A56	50g gray vio (O)	27.50	*27.50*
B92	A57	1s black brn (Bk)	27.50	*27.50*
		Nos. B87-B92 (6)	165.00	*165.00*
		Set, never hinged	550.00	

Rotary convention, Vienna.

Nos. B87 to B92 were sold at double their face values. The excess was added to the beneficent funds of Rotary International.

Used values are for examples with philatelic favor cancels. Values for postally used are 2 times values shown.

Ferdinand Raimund — SP38

Poets: 20g, Franz Grillparzer. 30g, Johann Nestroy. 40g, Adalbert Stifter. 50g, Ludwig Anzengruber. 1s, Peter Rosegger.

1931, Sept. 12

B93	SP38	10g dark violet	13.50	*11.00*
B94	SP38	20g gray black	13.50	*11.00*
B95	SP38	30g orange red	13.50	*11.00*
B96	SP38	40g dull blue	13.50	*11.00*
B97	SP38	50g gray green	13.50	*11.00*
B98	SP38	1s yellow brown	13.50	*11.00*
		Nos. B93-B98 (6)	81.00	*66.00*
		Set, never hinged	160.00	

Nos. B93-B98 were sold at double face value. The surtax aided unemployed young people.

Used values are for examples with philatelic favor cancels. Values for postally used are 3 times values shown.

Set exists imperf, without gum. Value, set $950.

Chancellor Ignaz Seipel — SP44

1932, Oct. 12 ***Perf. 13***

B99	SP44	50g ultra	12.00	*9.50*
		Never hinged	27.50	

Msgr. Ignaz Seipel, Chancellor of Austria, 1922-29. Sold at double face value, the excess aiding wounded veterans of World War I.

Used value is for a cancelled-to-order example. Value for postally used $27.50.

Exists imperf, without gum. Value $800.

Ferdinand Georg Waldmüller SP45

Artists: 24g, Moritz von Schwind. 30g, Rudolf von Alt. 40g, Hans Makart. 64g, Gustav Klimt. 1s, Albin Egger-Lienz.

1932, Nov. 21

B100	SP45	12g slate green	20.00	*16.00*
B101	SP45	24g dp violet	20.00	*16.00*
B102	SP45	30g dark red	20.00	*16.00*
B103	SP45	40g dark gray	20.00	*16.00*
B104	SP45	64g dark brown	20.00	*16.00*
B105	SP45	1s claret	20.00	*16.00*
		Nos. B100-B105 (6)	120.00	*96.00*
		Set, never hinged	260.00	

Nos. B100 to B105 were sold at double their face values. The surtax was for the assistance of charitable institutions.

Used values are for examples with philatelic favor cancels. Values for postally used, each $60.

Set exists imperf, without gum. Value, set $1,200.

Mountain Climbing SP51

Designs: 24g, Ski gliding. 30g, Walking on skis. 50g, Ski jumping.

1933, Jan. 9 **Photo.** ***Perf. 12½***

B106	SP51	12g dark green	6.50	*6.50*
B107	SP51	24g dark violet	95.00	*75.00*
B108	SP51	30g brown red	12.00	*12.00*
B109	SP51	50g dark blue	95.00	*75.00*
		Nos. B106-B109 (4)	208.50	*168.50*
		Set, never hinged	525.00	

Meeting of the Intl. Ski Federation, Innsbruck, Feb. 8-13.

These stamps were sold at double their face value. The surtax was for the benefit of "Youth in Distress."

Used values are for examples with philatelic favor cancels. Values for postally used, 25%-80% higher.

Set exists imperf, without gum. Value, set $4,000.

Stagecoach, after Painting by Moritz von Schwind — SP55

1933, June 23 **Engr.** ***Perf. 12½***

Ordinary Paper

B110	SP55	50g dp ultra	150.00	150.00
		Never hinged	260.00	
	a.	Granite paper	325.00	325.00
		Never hinged	600.00	

Sheets of 25.

Used values are for examples with philatelic favor cancels. Values for postally used, 50% higher.

Nos. B110 and B110a exist imperf. Value, No. B110 unused hinged, $2,400.

Souvenir Sheet

Perf. 12

Granite Paper

B111	Sheet of 4	2,500.	2,400.
	Never hinged	3,050.	
a.	SP55 50g deep ultra	475.00	475.00
	Never hinged	650.00	

Intl. Phil. Exhib., Vienna, 1933. In addition to the postal value of 50g the stamp was sold at a premium of 50g for charity and of 1.60s for the admission fee to the exhibition.

Size of No. B111: 126x103mm.

Used values are for examples with philatelic favor cancels. Values for postally used, 35% higher.

A 50g dark red in souvenir sheet, with dark blue overprint ("NEUDRUCK WIPA 1965"), had no postal validity.

Sheet margins of No. B111 are uniformly gummed. When sold at the WIPA exhibition, each example of No. B111 was affixed to a heavy dark bluish gray folder with 3 dabs of water soluable glue. When removed these glue spots appear similar to hinge marks. Some consider No. B111 to be never hinged if no additional hinge marks appear beyond the three dissolved glue spots.

No. B111 exists imperf.

St. Stephen's Cathedral in 1683 — SP56

Marco d'Aviano, Papal Legate — SP57

Designs: 30g, Count Ernst Rudiger von Starhemberg. 40g, John III Sobieski, King of Poland. 50g, Karl V, Duke of Lorraine. 64g, Burgomaster Johann Andreas von Liebenberg.

1933, Sept. 6 **Photo.** ***Perf. 12½***

B112	SP56	12g dark green	24.00	*20.00*
B113	SP57	24g dark violet	20.00	*16.00*
B114	SP57	30g brown red	20.00	*16.00*
B115	SP57	40g blue black	32.50	*20.00*
B116	SP57	50g dark blue	20.00	*16.00*
B117	SP57	64g olive brown	27.50	*16.00*
		Nos. B112-B117 (6)	144.00	*104.00*
		Set, never hinged	350.00	

Deliverance of Vienna from the Turks, 250th anniv., and Pan-German Catholic Congress, Sept. 6, 1933.

The stamps were sold at double their face value, the excess being for the aid of Catholic works of charity.

Used values are for examples with philatelic favor cancels. Values for postally used, 2-3 times values shown.

Types of Regular Issue of 1925-30 Surcharged

a

b

c

1933, Dec. 15

B118	A52(a)	5g + 2g ol grn	.25	*.25*
B119	A56(b)	12g + 3g lt blue	.25	*.25*
B120	A56(b)	24g + 6g brn org	.25	*.25*
B121	A57(c)	1s + 50g org red	35.00	*32.50*
		Nos. B118-B121 (4)	35.75	*33.25*
		Set, never hinged	75.00	

Winterhelp.

Used values are for examples with philatelic favor cancels. Values for postally used, 2-3 times values shown.

Anton Pilgram — SP62

Architects: 24g, J. B. Fischer von Erlach. 30g, Jakob Prandtauer. 40g, A. von Siccardsburg & E. van der Null. 60g, Heinrich von Ferstel. 64g, Otto Wagner.

1934, Dec. 2 **Engr.** ***Perf. 12½***

Thick Yellowish Paper

B122	SP62	12g black	9.50	8.00
B123	SP62	24g dull violet	9.50	8.00
B124	SP62	30g carmine	9.50	8.00
B125	SP62	40g brown	9.50	8.00
B126	SP62	60g blue	9.50	8.00
B127	SP62	64g dull green	9.50	8.00
		Nos. B122-B127 (6)	57.00	*48.00*
		Set, never hinged	120.00	

Used values are for examples with philatelic favor cancels. Values for postally used, each $20.

Exist imperf. Values, set unused hinged $650, never hinged $850.

Nos. B124-B127 exist in horiz. pairs imperf. between. Value, each $250-$325.

These stamps were sold at double their face value. The surtax on this and the following issues was devoted to general charity.

Types of Regular Issue of 1934 Surcharged in Black

c

d

1935, Nov. 11 ***Perf. 12, 12½***

B128	A67(d)	5g + 2g emerald	.50	*.80*
B129	A67(d)	12g + 3g blue	.95	.95
B130	A67(d)	24g + 6g lt brown	.50	*.80*
B131	A68(c)	1s + 50g ver	32.50	32.50
		Nos. B128-B131 (4)	34.45	35.05
		Set, never hinged	80.00	

Winterhelp. Set exists imperf. Values, set unused hinged $175, never hinged $260.

Set without surcharge unused hinged $250, never hinged $325.

Prince Eugene of Savoy — SP68

Military Leaders: 24g, Field Marshal Laudon. 30g, Archduke Karl. 40g, Field Marshal Josef Radetzky. 60g, Admiral Wilhelm Tegetthoff. 64g, Field Marshal Franz Conrad Hotzendorff.

1935, Dec. 1 ***Perf. 12½***

B132	SP68	12g brown	10.50	9.50
B133	SP68	24g dark green	10.50	9.50
B134	SP68	30g claret	10.50	9.50
B135	SP68	40g slate	10.50	9.50
B136	SP68	60g deep ultra	10.50	9.50
B137	SP68	64g dark violet	10.50	9.50
		Nos. B132-B137 (6)	63.00	57.00
		Set, never hinged	125.00	

These stamps were sold at double their face value.

Used values are for examples with philatelic favor cancels. Values for postally used, each $20.

Set exists imperf. Values, set unused hinged $650, never hinged $850.

Slalom Turn — SP74

Designs: 24g, Jumper taking off. 35g, Slalom turn. 60g, Innsbruck view.

1936, Feb. 20 **Photo.**

B138	SP74	12g Prus green	1.60	1.60
B139	SP74	24g dp violet	2.40	2.40
B140	SP74	35g rose car	24.00	24.00
B141	SP74	60g sapphire	24.00	24.00
		Nos. B138-B141 (4)	52.00	52.00
		Set, never hinged	130.00	

Ski concourse issue. These stamps were sold at twice face value.

Used values are for examples with philatelic favor cancels. Value for postally used set, $110.

Set exists imperf. Values, set unused hinged $600, never hinged $750.

St. Martin of Tours — SP78

Designs: 12g+3g, Medical clinic. 24g+6g, St. Elizabeth of Hungary. 1s+1s, "Flame of Charity."

1936, Nov. 2 **Unwmk.**

B142	SP78	5g + 2g dp green	.25	.25
B143	SP78	12g + 3g dp violet	.25	.25
B144	SP78	24g + 6g dp blue	.35	.35
B145	SP78	1s + 1s dk car	7.50	7.50
		Nos. B142-B145 (4)	8.35	8.35
		Set, never hinged	14.00	

Winterhelp.

Used values are for examples with philatelic favor cancels. Values for postally used: Nos. B142-B144, each 80¢; No. B145, $19.

Set exists imperf. Values, set unused hinged $400, never hinged $500.

Josef Ressel — SP82

Inventors: 24g, Karl von Ghega. 30g, Josef Werndl. 40g, Carl Auer von Welsbach. 60g, Robert von Lieben. 64g, Viktor Kaplan.

1936, Dec. 6 **Engr.**

B146	SP82	12g dk brown	2.75	2.75
B147	SP82	24g dk violet	2.75	2.75
B148	SP82	30g dp claret	2.75	2.75
B149	SP82	40g gray violet	2.75	2.75
B150	SP82	60g vio blue	2.75	2.75
B151	SP82	64g dk slate green	2.75	2.75
		Nos. B146-B151 (6)	16.50	16.50
		Set, never hinged	47.50	

These stamps were sold at double their face value.

Used values are for examples with philatelic favor cancels. Values for postally used: each $6.75.

Exists imperf, without gum. Value, set unused hinged $800, never hinged $1,000.

Nurse and Infant — SP88

12g+3g, Mother and child. 24g+6g, Nursing the aged. 1s+1s, Sister of Mercy with patient.

1937, Oct. 18 **Photo.**

B152	SP88	5g + 2g dk green	.30	.25
B153	SP88	12g + 3g dk brown	.30	.25
B154	SP88	24g + 6g dk blue	.30	.25
B155	SP88	1s + 1s dk carmine	4.00	3.50
		Nos. B152-B155 (4)	4.90	4.25
		Set, never hinged	11.00	

Winterhelp.

Used values are for examples with philatelic favor cancels. Values for postally used: Nos. B152-B154, each 40c; No. B155, $13.50.

Set exists imperf. Values, set unused hinged $125, never hinged $160.

Gerhard van Swieten — SP92

Physicians: 8g, Leopold Auenbrugger von Auenbrugg. 12g, Karl von Rokitansky. 20g, Joseph Skoda. 24g, Ferdinand von Hebra. 30g, Ferdinand von Arlt. 40g, Joseph Hyrtl. 60g, Theodor Billroth. 64g, Theodor Meynert.

1937, Dec. 5 **Engr.** ***Perf. 12½***

B156	SP92	5g choc	2.40	2.00
B157	SP92	8g dk red	2.40	2.00
B158	SP92	12g brown blk	2.40	2.00
B159	SP92	20g dk green	2.40	2.00
B160	SP92	24g dk violet	2.40	2.00
B161	SP92	30g brown car	2.40	2.00
B162	SP92	40g dp olive grn	2.40	2.00
B163	SP92	60g indigo	2.40	2.00
B164	SP92	64g brown vio	2.40	2.00
		Nos. B156-B164 (9)	21.60	18.00
		Set, never hinged	52.50	

These stamps were sold at double their face value.

Used values are for examples with philatelic favor cancels. Values for postally used: each $5.25.

Set exists imperf, without gum. Value, set $2,250.

Catalogue values for unused stamps in this section, from this point to the end of the section, are for Never Hinged items.

The Dawn of Peace — SP101

1945, Sept. 10 **Photo.** ***Perf. 14***

B165	SP101	1s + 10s dk green	1.25	.80

Used value is for examples with philatelic favor cancels. Postally used value $2.40.

No. 467 Surcharged in Black

1946, June 25

B166	A110	30g + 20g dk red	2.50	2.50

First anniversary of United Nations.

Used value is for examples with philatelic favor cancels. Postally used value $4.75.

Pres. Karl Renner SP102

1946 **Engr.** ***Perf. 13½x14***

B167	SP102	1s + 1s dk slate grn	4.00	.80
B168	SP102	2s + 2s dk blue vio	4.00	.80
B169	SP102	3s + 3s dk purple	4.00	.80
B170	SP102	5s + 5s dk vio brn	4.00	.80
		Nos. B167-B170 (4)	16.00	3.20

Used values are for examples with philatelic favor cancels. Postally used values, each $8.

See Nos. B185-B188.

Nazi Sword Piercing Austria — SP103

Sweeping Away Fascist Symbols — SP104

Designs: 8g+6g, St. Stephen's Cathedral in Flames. 12g+12g, Pleading hand in concentration camp. 30g+30g, Hand choking Nazi serpent. 42g+42g, Hammer breaking Nazi pillar. 1s+1s, Oath of allegiance. 2s+2s, Austrian eagle and burning swastika.

Unwmk.

1946, Sept. 16 **Photo.** ***Perf. 14***

B171	SP103	5g + (3g) sepia	.40	.40
B172	SP104	6g + (4g) dk slate grn	.25	.25
B173	SP104	8g + (6g) orange red	.25	.25
B174	SP104	12g + (12g) slate blk	.25	.25
B175	SP104	30g + (30g) violet	.25	.25
B176	SP104	42g + (42g) dull brn	.25	.25
B177	SP104	1s + 1s dk red	.40	.40
B178	SP104	2s + 2s dk car rose	.80	.80
		Nos. B171-B178 (8)	2.85	2.85

Anti-fascist propaganda.

Used values are for examples with philatelic favor cancels. Postally used values approx. 2-3 times values shown.

A 5g + 3g black olive brown stamp showing SS lightning bolt striking map of Austria and 12g + 12g black gray blue depicting skull with Hitler mask were prepared but not issued. Value, each $1,050.

Race Horse with Foal SP111

Various Race Horses.

1946, Oct. 20 **Engr.** ***Perf. 13½x14***

B179	SP111	16g + 16g rose brown	1.60	1.60
B180	SP111	24g + 24g dk purple	1.60	1.60
B181	SP111	60g + 60g dk green	1.60	1.60
B182	SP111	1s + 1s dk blue gray	1.60	1.60
B183	SP111	2s + 2s yel brown	5.75	4.00
		Nos. B179-B183 (5)	12.15	10.40

Austria Prize race, Vienna.

Used values are for examples with philatelic favor cancels. Postally used values 2-2.5 times values shown.

St. Ruprecht's Church, Vienna — SP116

1946, Oct. 30 ***Perf. 14x13½***

B184	SP116	30g + 70g dark red	.40	.40

Founding of Austria, 950th anniv. The surtax aided the Stamp Day celebration.

Used value is for examples with philatelic favor cancels. Postally used value $2.

Renner Type of 1946
Souvenir Sheets

1946, Sept. 5 ***Imperf.***

B185	Sheet of 8	500.00	450.00
a.	SP102 1s+1s dk slate grn	62.50	32.50
B186	Sheet of 8	500.00	450.00
a.	SP102 2s+2s dk blue vio	62.50	32.50
B187	Sheet of 8	500.00	450.00
a.	SP102 3s+3s dark purple	62.50	32.50
B188	Sheet of 8	500.00	450.00
a.	SP102 5s+5s dk vio brown	62.50	32.50

First anniv. of Austria's liberation. Sheets of 8 plus center label showing arms.

Values for used examples are for those with philatelic favor cancels. Postally used values: singles, each $275; sheets, each $3,250.

Statue of Rudolf IV the Founder — SP118

Designs: 5g+20g, Tomb of Frederick III. 6g+24g, Main pulpit. 8g+32g, Statue of St. Stephen. 10g+40g, Madonna of the Domestics statue. 12g+48g, High altar. 30g+1.20s, Organ, destroyed in 1945. 50g+1.80s, Anton Pilgram statue. 1s+5s, Cathedral from northeast. 2s+10s, Southwest corner of cathedral.

1946, Dec. 12 Engr. *Perf. 14x13½*

B189 SP118 3g + 12g brown .25 .25
B190 SP118 5g + 20g dk vio brown .25 .25
B191 SP118 6g + 24g dk blue .25 .25
B192 SP118 8g + 32g dk grn .25 .25
B193 SP118 10g + 40g dp blue .25 .25
B194 SP118 12g + 48g dk vio .25 .25
B195 SP118 30g + 1.20s car 1.25 1.25
B196 SP118 50g + 1.80s dk bl 1.60 1.60
B197 SP118 1s + 5s brn vio 2.00 2.00
B198 SP118 2s + 10s vio brn 4.00 4.00
Nos. B189-B198 (10) 10.35 10.35

The surtax aided reconstruction of St. Stephen's Cathedral, Vienna.

Values for used examples are for those with philatelic favor cancels. Postally used value, set $24.

Reaping Wheat — SP128

Designs: 8g+2g, Log raft. 10g+5g, Cement factory. 12g+8g, Coal mine. 18g+12g, Oil derricks. 30g+10g, Textile machinery. 35g+15g, Iron furnace. 60g+20g, Electric power lines.

1947, Mar. 23 *Perf. 14x13½*

B199 SP128 3g + 2g yel brown .40 .30
B200 SP128 8g + 2g dk bl grn .40 .30
B201 SP128 10g + 5g slate blk .40 .30
B202 SP128 12g + 8g dark pur .40 .30
B203 SP128 18g + 12g ol green .40 .30
B204 SP128 30g + 10g deep cl .40 .30
B205 SP128 35g + 15g crimson .40 .30
B206 SP128 60g + 20g dk blue .40 .30
Nos. B199-B206 (8) 3.20 2.40

Vienna International Sample Fair, 1947.

Values for used examples are for those with philatelic favor cancels. Postally used value, set $8.

Race Horse and Jockey SP136

1947, June 29 *Perf. 13½x14*

B207 SP136 60g + 20g dp bl, *pale pink* .40 .40

Value for used is for examples with philatelic favor cancels. Postally used value $1.25.

Cup of Corvinus SP137

Designs: 8g+2g, Statue of Providence, Vienna. 10g+5g, Abbey at Melk. 12g+8g, Picture of a Woman, by Kriehuber. 18g+12g, Children at the Window, by Waldmuller. 20g+10g, Entrance, Upper Belvedere Palace. 30g+10g, Nymph Egeria, Schönbrunn Castle. 35g+15g, National Library, Vienna. 48g+12g, "Workshop of a Printer of Engravings," by Schmutzer. 60g+20g, Girl with Straw Hat, by Amerling.

1947, June 20 *Perf. 14x13½*

B208 SP137 3g + 2g brown .40 .30
B209 SP137 8g + 2g dk blue grn .40 .30
B210 SP137 10g + 5g dp claret .40 .30
B211 SP137 12g + 8g dk purple .40 .30
B212 SP137 18g + 12g golden brn .40 .30
B213 SP137 20g + 10g sepia .40 .30
B214 SP137 30g + 10g dk yel grn .40 .30
B215 SP137 35g + 15g deep car .40 .30
B216 SP137 48g + 12g dk brn vio .65 .50
B217 SP137 60g + 20g dp blue .65 .50
Nos. B208-B217 (10) 4.50 3.40

Values for used examples are for those with philatelic favor cancels. Postally used value, double values shown.

Prisoner of War — SP147

12g+8g, Prisoners' Mail, 18g+12g, Prison camp visitor. 35g+15g, Family reunion. 60g+20g, "Industry" beckoning. 1s+40g, Sower.

1947, Aug. 30

B218 SP147 8g + 2g dk green .25 .25
B219 SP147 12g + 8g dk vio brn .25 .25
B220 SP147 18g + 12g black brn .25 .25
B221 SP147 35g + 15g rose brn .25 .25
B222 SP147 60g + 20g dp blue .25 .25
B223 SP147 1s + 40g redsh brn .25 .25
Nos. B218-B223 (6) 1.50 1.50

Values for used examples are for those with philatelic favor cancels. Postally used value, set $5.50.

Olympic Flame and Emblem — SP153

1948, Jan. 16 Engr.

B224 SP153 1s + 50g dark blue .55 .55

The surtax was used to help defray expenses of Austria's 1948 Olympics team.

Laabenbach Bridge Neulengbach SP154

Designs: 20g+10g, Dam, Vermunt Lake. 30g+10g, Danube Port, Vienna. 40g+20g, Mining, Erzberg. 45g+20g, Tracks, Southern Railway Station, Vienna. 60g+30g, Communal housing project, Vienna. 75g+35g, Gas Works, Vienna. 80g+40g, Oil refinery. 1s+50g, Gesäuse Highway, Styria. 1.40s+70g, Parliament Building, Vienna.

1948, Feb. 18 *Perf. 14x13½*

B225 SP154 10g + 5g slate blk .25 .25
B226 SP154 20g + 10g lilac .25 .25
B227 SP154 30g + 10g dull grn .50 .50
B228 SP154 40g + 20g ol brn .25 .25
B229 SP154 45g + 20g dk blue .25 .25
B230 SP154 60g + 30g dk red .25 .25
B231 SP154 75g + 35g dk vio brn .25 .25
B232 SP154 80g + 40g vio brn .25 .25
B233 SP154 1s + 50g dp blue .25 .25
B234 SP154 1.40s + 70g dp car .50 .50
Nos. B225-B234 (10) 3.00 3.00

The surtax was for the Reconstruction Fund.

Violet — SP155

Designs: 20g+10g, Anemone. 30g+10g, Crocus. 40g+20g, Yellow primrose. 45g+20g, Pasqueflower. 60g+30g, Rhododendron. 75g+35g, Dogrose. 80g+40g, Cyclamen. 1s+50g, Alpine Gentian. 1.40s+70g, Edelweiss.

1948, May 14 Engr. & Typo.

B235 SP155 10g + 5g multi .35 .35
B236 SP155 20g + 10g multi .25 .25
B237 SP155 30g + 10g multi 3.25 3.00
B238 SP155 40g + 20g multi .65 .40
B239 SP155 45g + 20g multi .25 .25
B240 SP155 60g + 30g multi .25 .25
B241 SP155 75g + 35g multi .25 .25
B242 SP155 80g + 40g multi .25 .25
B243 SP155 1s + 50g multi .35 .35
B244 SP155 1.40s + 70g multi 1.60 1.60
Nos. B235-B244 (10) 7.45 6.95

Hans Makart — SP156

Designs: 20g+10g, Künstlerhaus, Vienna. 40g+20g, Carl Kundmann. 50g+25g, A. S. von Siccardsburg. 60g+30g, Hans Canon. 1s+50g, William Unger. 1.40s+70g, Friedrich von Schmidt.

1948, June 15 Unwmk. Engr.

B245 SP156 20g + 10g dp yel green 12.00 8.00
B246 SP156 30g + 15g dark brown 2.50 2.50
B247 SP156 40g + 20g ind 3.25 *3.25*
B248 SP156 50g + 25g dk vio 4.00 4.00
B249 SP156 60g + 30g dk red 4.00 4.00
B250 SP156 1s + 50g dk blue 4.00 4.00
B251 SP156 1.40s + 70g red brown 8.00 16.00
Nos. B245-B251 (7) 37.75 41.75

Kunstlerhaus, home of the leading Austrian Artists Association, 80th anniv.

St. Rupert — SP157

Designs: 30g+15g, Cathedral and Fountain. 40g+20g, Facade of Cathedral. 50g+25g, Cathedral from South. 60g+30g, Abbey of St. Peter. 80g+40g, Inside Cathedral. 1s+50g, Salzburg Cathedral and Castle. 1.40s+70g, Madonna by Michael Pacher.

1948, Aug. 6 *Perf. 14x13½*

B252 SP157 20g + 10g dp grn 8.00 8.00
B253 SP157 30g + 15g red brn 2.50 *3.25*
B254 SP157 40g + 20g sl blk 2.75 *3.25*
B255 SP157 50g + 25g choc .40 .80
B256 SP157 60g + 30g dk red .40 .80
B257 SP157 80g + 40g dk brn vio .40 .80
B258 SP157 1s + 50g dp blue .80 .80
B259 SP157 1.40s + 70g dk grn 2.50 3.25
Nos. B252-B259 (8) 17.75 20.95

The surtax was to aid in the reconstruction of Salzburg Cathedral.

Easter — SP158

Designs: 60g+20g, St. Nicholas Day. 1s+25g, Birthday. 1.40s+35g, Christmas.

Inscribed: "Gluckliche Kindheit"

1949, Apr. 13 Unwmk.

B260 SP158 40g + 10g brn vio 15.00 15.00
B261 SP158 60g + 20g brn red 15.00 15.00
B262 SP158 1s + 25g dp ultra 15.00 15.00
B263 SP158 1.40s + 35g dk grn 15.00 15.00
Nos. B260-B263 (4) 60.00 60.00

The surtax was for Child Welfare.

Arms of Austria, 1230 — SP159

1949, Aug. 17 Engr. & Photo.

B264 SP159 40g + 10g 1230 9.00 9.00

Engraved and Typographed

B265 SP159 60g + 15g 1450 7.50 7.50
B266 SP159 1s + 25g 1600 7.50 7.50
B267 SP159 1.60s + 40g 1945 11.00 11.00
Nos. B264-B267 (4) 35.00 35.00

Surtax was for returned prisoners of war.

SP160

Laurel Branch, Stamps and Magnifier

1949, Dec. 3 Engr.

B268 SP160 60g + 15g dark red 3.00 2.50

Stamp Day, Dec. 3-4.

Arms of Austria and Carinthia SP161

Carinthian with Austrian Flag — SP162

Design: 1.70s+40g, Casting ballot.

1950, Oct. 10 Photo. *Perf. 14x13½*

B269 SP161 60g + 15g 30.00 25.00
B270 SP162 1s + 25g 35.00 30.00
B271 SP162 1.70s + 40g 40.00 30.00
Nos. B269-B271 (3) 105.00 85.00

Plebiscite in Carinthia, 30th anniv.

Collector Examining Cover — SP163

1950, Dec. 2 Engr.

B272 SP163 60g + 15g blue grn 9.00 7.50

Stamp Day.

Miner and Mine — SP164

60g+15g, Mason holding brick and trowel. 1s+25g, Bridge builder with hook and chain. 1.70s+40g, Electrician, pole and insulators.

1951, Mar. 10 Unwmk.

B273 SP164 40g + 10g dark brown 16.00 14.50
B274 SP164 60g + 15g dk grn 12.00 14.50
B275 SP164 1s + 25g red brown 12.00 14.50
B276 SP164 1,70s + 40g vio bl 16.00 14.50
Nos. B273-B276 (4) 56.00 58.00

Issued to publicize Austrian reconstruction.

Laurel Branch and Olympic Circles SP165

1952, Jan. 26 *Perf. 13½x14*

B277 SP165 2.40s + 60g grnsh black 20.00 20.00

The surtax was used to help defray expenses of Austria's athletes in the 1952 Olympic Games.

Cupid as Postman SP166

1952, Mar. 10 *Perf. 14x13½*

B278 SP166 1.50s + 35g dark brn car 17.50 15.00

Stamp Day.

Sculpture, "Christ, The Almighty" SP167

1952, Sept. 6 *Perf. 13½x14*

B279 SP167 1s + 25g grnsh gray 10.00 11.00

Austrian Catholic Conv., Vienna, 9/11-14.

Type of 1945-46 Ovptd. in Gold

1953, Aug. 29 Unwmk.

B280 A124 1s + 25g on 5s dl bl 2.50 2.50

60th anniv. of labor unions in Austria.

Bummerlhaus Steyr — SP168

Designs: 1s+25g, Johannes Kepler. 1.50s+40g, Lutheran Bible, 1st edition. 2.40s+60g, Theophil von Hansen. 3s+75g, Reconstructed Lutheran School, Vienna.

1953, Nov. 5 Engr. *Perf. 14x13½*

B281 SP168 70g + 15g vio brn .25 .25
B282 SP168 1s + 25g dk gray blue .25 .25
B283 SP168 1.50s + 40g choc .80 .80
B284 SP168 2.40s + 60g dk grn 3.25 3.25
B285 SP168 3s + 75g dk pur 6.50 6.50
Nos. B281-B285 (5) 11.05 11.05

The surtax was used toward reconstruction of the Lutheran School, Vienna.

Globe and Philatelic Accessories SP169

1953, Dec. 5

B286 SP169 1s + 25g chocolate 6.50 6.50

Stamp Day.

Type of 1945-46 with Denomination Replaced by Asterisks

Overprinted in Brown

1954, Feb. 19 *Perf. 13½x14*

B287 A124 1s + 20g blue gray .40 .50

Surtax for aid to avalanche victims.

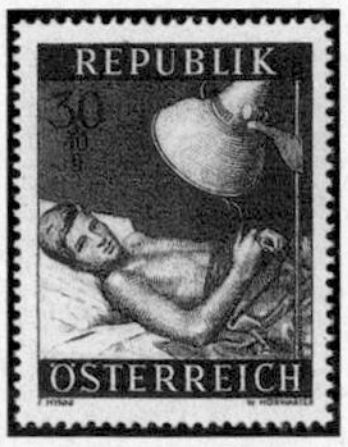
Patient Under Sun Lamp — SP170

Designs: 70g+15g, Physician using microscope. 1s+25g, Mother and children. 1.45s+35g, Operating room. 1.50s+35g, Baby on scale. 2.40s+60g, Nurse.

1954 Engr. *Perf. 14x13½*

B288 SP170 30g + 10g pur 1.25 1.60
B289 SP170 70g + 15g dk brn .25 .25
B290 SP170 1s + 25g dk bl .25 .25
B291 SP170 1.45s + 35g dk bl green .55 .35
B292 SP170 1.50s + 35g dk red 5.50 5.50
B293 SP170 2.40s + 60g dk red brown 6.50 8.00
Nos. B288-B293 (6) 14.30 15.95

The surtax was for social welfare.

Early Vienna-Ulm Ferryboat SP171

1954, Dec. 4 *Perf. 13½x14*

B294 SP171 1s + 25g dk gray grn 6.50 6.50

Stamp Day.

"Industry" Welcoming Returned Prisoner of War SP172

1955, June 29

B295 SP172 1s + 25g red brn 2.50 2.50

Surtax for returned prisoners of war and relatives of prisoners not yet released.

Collector Looking at Album — SP173

1955, Dec. 3 *Perf. 14x13½*

B296 SP173 1s + 25g vio brn 3.50 3.50

Stamp Day. The surtax was for the promotion of Austrian philately.

Ornamental Shield and Letter — SP174

1956, Dec. 1 Engr.

B297 SP174 1s + 25g scarlet 3.00 3.00

Stamp Day. See note after No. B296.

Arms of Austria, 1945 — SP175

Engr. & Typo.

1956, Dec. 21 *Perf. 14x13½*

B298 SP175 1.50s + 50g on 1.60s + 40g gray & red .65 .65

The surtax was for Hungarian refugees.

New Post Office, Linz 2 SP176

Design: 2.40s+60g, Post office, Kitzbuhel.

1957-58 Engr. *Perf. 13½x14*

B299 SP176 1s + 25g dk sl grn 2.40 3.25
B300 SP176 2.40s + 60g blue .95 .95

Stamp Day. See note after B296. Issue dates: 1s, Nov. 30, 1957. 2.40s, Dec. 6, 1958. See No. B303.

Roman Carriage from Tomb at Maria Saal SP177

Litho. & Engr.

1959, Dec. 5 *Perf. 13½x14*

B301 SP177 2.40s + 60g pink & blk .80 1.00

Stamp Day.

Progressive Die Proof under Magnifying Glass SP178

1960, Dec. 2 Engr. *Perf. 13½x14*

B302 SP178 3s + 70g vio brn .95 .95

Stamp Day.

Post Office Type of 1957

Design: 3s+70g, Post Office, Rust.

1961, Dec. 1 Unwmk. *Perf. 13½*

B303 SP176 3s + 70g dk bl grn .95 .95

Stamp Day. See note after No. B296.

Hands of Stamp Engraver at Work SP179

1962, Nov. 30 *Perf. 13½x14*

B304 SP179 3s + 70g dull pur 1.25 1.25

Stamp Day.

Railroad Exit, Post Office Vienna 101 SP180

1963, Nov. 29 Litho. & Engr.

B305 SP180 3s + 70g tan & blk .65 .65

Stamp Day.

View of Vienna, North SP181

Designs: Various view of Vienna with compass indicating direction.

1964, July 20 Litho. *Perf. 13½x14*

B306	SP181	1.50s + 30g ("N")	.35	.40
B307	SP181	1.50s + 30g ("NO")	.35	.40
B308	SP181	1.50s + 30g ("O")	.35	.40
B309	SP181	1.50s + 30g ("SO")	.35	.40
B310	SP181	1.50s + 30g ("S")	.35	.40
B311	SP181	1.50s + 30g ("SW")	.35	.40
B312	SP181	1.50s + 30g ("W")	.35	.40
B313	SP181	1.50s + 30g ("NW")	.35	.40
		Nos. B306-B313 (8)	2.80	3.20

Vienna Intl. Phil. Exhib. (WIPA 1965).

Post Bus Terminal, St. Gilgen, Wolfgangsee — SP182

1964, Dec. 4 Unwmk. *Perf. 13½*

B314 SP182 3s + 70g multi .55 .55

Stamp Day.

Wall Painting, Tomb at Thebes — SP183

Development of Writing: 1.80s+50g, Cuneiform writing on stone tablet and man's head from Assyrian palace. 2.20s+60g, Wax tablet with Latin writing, Corinthian column. 3s+80g, Gothic writing on sealed letter, Gothic window from Munster Cathedral. 4s+1s, Letter with seal and postmark and upright desk. 5s+1.20s, Typewriter.

Litho. & Engr.

1965, June 4 *Perf. 14x13½*

B315	SP183	1.50s + 40g multi	.35	.35
B316	SP183	1.80s + 50g multi	.35	.35
B317	SP183	2.20s + 60g multi	.50	.50
B318	SP183	3s + 80g multi	.55	.55
B319	SP183	4s + 1s multi	.65	.65
B320	SP183	5s + 1.20s multi	.95	.95
		Nos. B315-B320 (6)	3.35	3.35

Vienna Intl. Phil. Exhib., WIPA, June 4-13.

Mailman Distributing Mail SP184

1965, Dec. 3 Engr. *Perf. 13½x14*

B321 SP184 3s + 70g blue grn .50 .80

Stamp Day.

Letter Carrier, 16th Century — SP185

Litho. & Engr.

1966, Dec. 2 *Perf. 13½*

B322 SP185 3s + 70g multi .55 .55

Stamp Day. Design is from Ambras Heroes' Book, Austrian National Library.

Letter Carrier, 16th Century Playing Card — SP186

Engr. & Photo.

1967, Dec. 1 *Perf. 13x13½*

B323 SP186 3.50s + 80g multi .55 .80

Stamp Day.

Mercury, Bas-relief from Purkersdorf SP187

1968, Nov. 29 Engr. *Perf. 13½*

B324 SP187 3.50s + 80g slate green .55 .80

Stamp Day.

Unken Post Station Sign, 1710 — SP188

Engr. & Photo.

1969, Dec. 5 *Perf. 12*

B325 SP188 3.50s + 80g tan, red & blk .55 1.20

Stamp Day. Design is from a watercolor by Friedrich Zeller.

Saddle, Bag, Harness and Post Horn — SP189

Engr. & Litho.

1970, Dec. 4 *Perf. 13½x14*

B326 SP189 3.50s + 80g gray blk & yel .55 1.20

Stamp Day.

"50 Years" SP190

Engr. & Photo.

1971, Dec. 3 *Perf. 13½*

B327 SP190 4s + 1.50s gold & red brn .75 1.20

50th anniversary of the Federation of Austrian Philatelic Societies.

Local Post Carrier — SP191

1972, Dec. 1 Engr. *Perf. 14x13½*

B328 SP191 4s + 1s olive green .75 .65

Stamp Day.

Gabriel, by Lorenz Luchsperger, 15th Century — SP192

1973, Nov. 30

B329 SP192 4s + 1s maroon .65 1.10

Stamp Day.

Mail Coach Leaving Old PTT Building — SP193

1974, Nov. 29 Engr. *Perf. 14x13½*

B330 SP193 4s + 2s violet blue .75 .75

Stamp Day.

Alpine Skiing, Women's SP194

Designs: 1.50s+70g, Ice hockey. 2s+90g, Ski jump. 4s+1.90s, Bobsledding.

1975, Mar. 14 Photo. *Perf. 13½x14*

B331	SP194	1s + 50g multi	.25	.25
B332	SP194	1.50s + 70g multi	.25	.25
B333	SP194	2s + 90g multi	.40	.40
B334	SP194	4s + 1.90s multi	.80	.80
		Nos. B331-B334 (4)	1.70	1.70

1975, Nov. 14

Designs: 70g+30g, Figure skating, pair. 2s+1s, Cross-country skiing. 2.50s+1s, Luge. 4s+2s, Biathlon.

B335	SP194	70g + 30g multi	.25	.40
B336	SP194	2s + 1s multi	.40	.65
B337	SP194	2.50s + 1s multi	.40	.65
B338	SP194	4s + 2s multi	.75	1.20
		Nos. B335-B338 (4)	1.80	2.90

12th Winter Olympic Games, Innsbruck, Feb. 4-15, 1976.

Austria Nos. 5, 250, 455 — SP195

Photo. & Engr.

1975, Nov. 28 *Perf. 14*

B339 SP195 4s + 2s multi .75 1.20

Stamp Day; 125th anniv. of Austrian stamps.

Postilion's Gala Hat and Horn SP196

1976, Dec. 3 *Perf. 13½x14*

B340 SP196 6s + 2s blk & lt vio 1.10 1.00

Stamp Day.

Emanuel Herrmann SP197

1977, Dec. 2 *Perf. 14x13½*

B341 SP197 6s + 2s multi 1.25 1.10

Stamp Day. Emanuel Herrmann (1839-1902), economist, invented postal card. Austria issued first postal card in 1869.

Post Bus, 1913 SP198

1978, Dec. 1 Photo. *Perf. 13½x14*

B342 SP198 10s + 5s multi 2.00 1.20

Stamp Day.

Heroes' Square, Vienna SP199

Photo. & Engr.

1979, Nov. 30 *Perf. 13½*

B343 SP199 16s + 8s multi 3.00 2.40

No. B343 Inscribed "2. Phase"

1980, Nov. 21

B344 SP199 16s + 8s multi 3.25 2.40

Souvenir Sheet

1981, Feb. 20

B345 SP199 16s + 8s multi 2.75 2.75

WIPA 1981 Phil. Exhib., Vienna, May 22-31. No. B345 contains one stamp. No. B345 without denomination and inscribed WIPA in the top banner were issued in limited quantities and were not valid for postage.

Mainz-Weber Mailbox, 1870 — SP200

1982, Nov. 26 Photo. & Engr.

B346 SP200 6s + 3s multi 1.40 1.25

Stamp Day.

Boy Examining Cover
SP201

Photo. & Engr.

1983, Oct. 21 *Perf. 14*

B347 SP201 6s + 3s multi 1.40 1.00

Stamp Day. See Nos. B349-B352, B354-B355.

World Winter Games for the Handicapped — SP202

1984, Jan. 5 **Photo.** *Perf. 13½x13*

B348 SP202 4s + 2s Downhill skier .75 .75

Stamp Day Type of 1983

Designs: No. B349, Seschemnofer III burial chamber detail, pyramid of Cheops, Gizeh. No. B350, Roman messenger on horseback. No. B351, Nuremberg messenger, 16th cent. No. B352, *The Postmaster* (detail), 1841, lithograph by Carl Schuster.

1984-87 **Photo. & Engr.** *Perf. 14*

B349 SP201 6s + 3s multi 1.40 1.40
B350 SP201 6s + 3s multi 1.40 1.40
B351 SP201 6s + 3s multi 1.40 1.40
B352 SP201 6s + 3s multi 1.40 1.40
Nos. B349-B352 (4) 5.60 5.60

Issued: No. B349, 11/30/84; No. B350, 11/28/85; No. B351, 11/28/86; No. B352, 11/19/87.

4th World Winter Sports Championships for the Disabled, Innsbruck — SP203

1988, Jan. 15 **Photo.** *Perf. 13½*

B353 SP203 5s + 2.50s multi 1.40 1.10

Stamp Day Type of 1983

Designs: No. B354, Railway mail car. No. B355, Hansa-Brandenburg CI mail plane.

1988-89 **Photo. & Engr.** *Perf. 14*

B354 SP201 6s +3s multi 1.75 1.40
B355 SP201 6s +3s multi 1.75 1.40

Issued: No. B354, Nov. 17; No. B355, May 24, 1989.

Stamp Day — SP204

1990, May 25 **Photo.** *Perf. 13½*

B356 SP204 7s +3s multi 1.75 1.40

SP205

1991, May 29 **Photo. & Engr.**

B357 SP205 7s +3s B & P 1.75 1.75

1992, May 22

B358 SP205 7s +3s R & H 1.75 1.75

1993, May 5

B359 SP205 7s +3s I & I 1.75 1.75

1994, May 27

B360 SP205 7s +3s E & L 1.90 1.90

SP205a

1995, May 26

B361 SP205a 10s +5s F & A 2.40 2.40

1996, May 17

B362 SP205a 10s +5s M & T 2.60 2.60
Nos. B357-B362,1725,1765,1791 (9) 16.05 14.95

Stamp Day. The 1st letters spell "Briefmarke," the 2nd "Philatelie."
For "A" & "E," see No. 1725; "R" & "L," No. 1765; "K" & "I," No. 1791; "E" & "E," No. 1818.

Special Olympics Winter Games
SP206

1993, Mar. 19 **Photo.** *Perf. 13½x14*

B367 SP206 6s +3s multi 1.90 1.90

Vienna Intl. Postage Stamp Exhibition (WIPA), 2000 — SP207

Designs: No. B368, #5, postman on bicycle. No. B369, #339, early mail truck. No. B370, #525, airplane, service vehicles.

1997-2000 **Photo. & Engr.** *Perf. 14*

B368 SP207 27s +13s multi 7.00 7.00
B369 SP207 32s +13s multi 8.00 8.00
B370 SP207 32s +16s multi 9.00 9.00
a. Souvenir sheet, #B368-B370 + label 30.00 30.00
Nos. B368-B370 (3) 24.00 24.00

Stamps from No. B370a are dated "2000."
Issued: No. B368, 5/23; No. B369, 11/6/98; No. B370, 9/17/99. No. B370a, 2000.

Stamp Day — SP208

Designs: No. B372, 1919 Mail car. No. B373, Siemens M 320 mail wagon, 1987. No B374, Oeffag C II mail plane. No. B375, Junkers F13 airplane.

Photo. & Engr.

2001, May 18 *Perf. 13¾*

B371 SP208 20s +10s multi + label 7.50 7.50

2002, May 24

B372 SP208 €1.60 +80c multi + label 5.50 5.50

2003, May 23

B373 SP208 €2.54 +€1.26 multi + label 10.00 10.00

2004, May 7

B374 SP208 €2.65 +€1.30 multi + label 10.00 10.00

2005, May 27

B375 SP208 265c +130c multi + label 10.00 10.00

See No. B377.

No. 1865A Surcharged

2006, Apr. 21 **Photo.** *Perf. 13¾x14*

B376 A1090 75c +425c on 25c #1865A 9.00 9.00

Surtax was for flood relief. Standing order customers were able to purchase this stamp for the 75c franking value.

Stamp Day Type of 2001

Design: Airbus A310-300.

Photo. & Engr.

2006, July 2 *Perf. 13¾*

B377 SP208 265c +130c multi + label 9.00 9.00

Printed in sheets of 5 stamps + 5 labels.

Ferris Wheel, Vienna
SP209

2006, Aug. 26 **Photo.** *Perf. 13¾*

B378 SP209 55c +20c multi 2.25 2.25
a. Inscribed "ÖSTERREICH" (from #B382a) 2.25 2.25

2008 Vienna Intl. Stamp Exhibition (WIPA), Vienna. See No. 2137a.
No. B378 is inscribed "Osterrreich."

German and Austrian Philatelic Exhibition, Bad Reichenhall
SP210

2006, Oct. 6 **Photo.** *Perf. 14¼x14*

B379 SP210 55c +20c multi 2.00 2.00

Gloriette, Schönbrunn Palace — SP211

2007, Mar. 16 **Photo.** *Perf. 13¾*

B380 SP211 55c +20c multi 2.25 2.25

2008 Vienna Intl. Stamp Exhibition (WIPA). See No. 2137b.

Steamer Wien
SP212

2007, June 15

B381 SP212 265c +130c multi 10.00 10.00

Stamp Day.

St. Stephen's Cathedral, Vienna — SP213

2008, Jan. 18 **Photo.** *Perf. 13¾*

B382 SP213 55c +20c multi 2.25 2.25
a. Souvenir sheet, #B378, B380, B382 7.25 7.25

2008 Vienna Intl. Stamp Exhibition (WIPA). See No. 2137c.
No. B382a issued 9/18.

Paddle-wheel Steamer Schönbrunn — SP214

2008, Sept. 18 **Photo.** *Perf. 13¾*

B383 SP214 265c +130c multi 9.00 9.00

Stamp Day.

MS Osterreich
SP215

2009, Sept. 11 **Litho.** *Perf. 13¾*

B384 SP215 265c +130c multi 9.50 9.50

Stamp Day.

Gmunden
SP216

2010, Aug. 27 Litho. ***Perf. 13¾***
B385 SP216 265c +130c multi 9.00 9.00

Stamp Day.

Graz
SP217

2011, May 13 ***Perf. 13¾***
B386 SP217 272c+136c multi 9.50 9.50

Stamp Day.

Federation of Austrian Philatelist Societies, 90th Anniv. — SP218

2011, Sept. 10 ***Perf. 14¼x14***
B387 SP218 62c+20c multi 2.00 2.00

Breast Cancer Research
SP219

2011, Sept. 28 ***Perf. 13¾***
B388 SP219 90c+10c multi 2.25 2.25

Surtax for Austrian Cancer Aid Society.

Karlsplatz
SP220

2012, May 11
B389 SP220 272c +136c multi 9.00 9.00

Stamp Day.

Winning Drawing in "Children for Integration" Stamp Design Contest
SP221

2012, Aug. 31
B390 SP221 62c +20c multi 2.00 2.00

Winning Art in "Protection of Nature" Children's Stamp Design Contest
SP222

2013, June 13
B391 SP222 62c +20c multi 2.00 2.00

Salzburg
SP223

2013, Aug. 22
B392 SP223 282c+141c multi 10.00 10.00

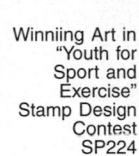

Stamp Day.

Winniing Art in "Youth for Sport and Exercise" Stamp Design Contest
SP224

2014, June 26 Litho. ***Perf. 14¼***
B393 SP224 62c+20c multi 2.25 2.25

Irises and Basilica of Rankweil
SP225

2014, Sept. 26 Litho. ***Perf. 14¼***
B394 SP225 282c +141c multi 11.00 11.00

Stamp Day.

Winning Art in "Healthy Eating" Children's Stamp Design Contest
SP226

2015, June 3 Litho. ***Perf. 13¾***
B395 SP226 68c +20c multi 2.00 2.00

Surtax for promotion of youth philately.

Tulln an der Donau
SP227

2015, June 18 Litho. ***Perf. 13¾***
B396 SP227 288c +144c multi 9.50 9.50

Stamp Day.

Child — SP228

2016, Feb. 18 Litho. ***Perf. 14***
B397 SP228 68c +232c multi 6.50 6.50

Surtax was for UNICEF refugee assistance projects in Syria.

Szombathely, Hungary to Pinkafelder, Austria Train and Stations — SP229

2016, Oct. 21 Litho. ***Perf. 13¾***
B398 SP229 288c +144c multi 9.75 9.75

Stamp Day. Surtax was for promotion of philately.

Theuerdank, Poem by Emperor Maximilian I, 500th Anniv. — SP230

2017, Oct. 6 Litho. ***Perf. 14¼x13¾***
B399 SP230 288c +144c multi 10.00 10.00

Stamp Day. Surtax was for the promotion of philately.

St. Mary's Church and Pyramidenkogel, Maria Wörth, Wörthersee Steamer DS Thalia — SP231

2018, May 25 Litho. ***Perf. 14***
B400 SP231 288c +144c multi 10.00 10.00

Stamp Day. Surtax was for the promotion of philately.

Souvenir Sheet

Airmail Flights in Austria, Cent. — SP232

2018, Oct. 6 Litho. ***Perf. 14***
B401 SP232 90c+45c sil & multi 3.25 3.25

SOS Children's Villages, 70th Anniv. — SP233

Perf. 13½x13¾

2019, Feb. 21 Litho.
B402 SP233 80c +10c multi 2.10 2.10

Souvenir Sheet

Woman Suffrage in Austria, Cent. — SP234

2019, Sept. 17 Litho. ***Perf. 14x13¾***
B403 SP234 90c +45c multi 3.00 3.00

Theresian Military Academy, Wiener Neustadt
SP235

2019, Oct. 18 Litho. ***Perf. 14x13¾***
B404 SP235 310c +155c multi 10.50 10.50

Stamp Day.

AIR POST STAMPS

Issues of the Monarchy

Types of Regular Issue of 1916 Surcharged

1918, Mar. 30 Unwmk. ***Perf. 12½***

C1	A40 1.50k on 2k lilac	1.60	*7.50*
C2	A40 2.50k on 3k ocher	10.50	*32.50*
a.	Inverted surcharge	*1,200.*	
	Never hinged	2,400.	
b.	Perf. 11½	725.00	*1,100.*
	Never hinged	1,600.	
c.	Perf. 12½x11½	65.00	*140.00*
	Never hinged	160.00	

Overprinted

C3	A40 4k gray	4.75	*20.00*
	Nos. C1-C3 (3)	16.85	*60.00*
	Set, never hinged	40.00	

Exist imperf, without gum. Value, set $450.

Nos. C1-C3 also exist without surcharge or overprint. Values, set perf unused hinged $475, never hinged $1,050. Values, set imperf, unused hinged $425, never hinged $850.

Nos. C1-C3 were printed on grayish and on white paper. See the *Scott Classic Specialized*

Catalogue of Stamps and Covers for detailed listing.

A 7k on 10k red brown was prepared but not regularly issued. Values: perf, $650 unused hinged, $1,600 never hinged; imperf, without gum, $1,050.

Issues of the Republic

Hawk — AP1

Wilhelm Kress — AP2

1922-24 Typo. *Perf. 12½*

C4	AP1	300k claret	.35	.35
C5	AP1	400k green ('24)	5.00	4.75
C6	AP1	600k bister	.25	.25
C7	AP1	900k brn orange	.25	.25

Engr.

C8	AP2	1200k brn violet	.25	.25
C9	AP2	2400k slate	.25	.25
C10	AP2	3000k dp brn ('23)	3.25	2.75
C11	AP2	4800k dark bl ('23)	2.75	2.75
		Nos. C4-C11 (8)	12.35	11.60
		Set, never hinged	29.00	

Values for used are for stamps with philatelic favor cancels. Postally used value, set $45.

Set exists imperf. Values, set unused hinged $350, never hinged $500.

Plane and Pilot's Head — AP3

Airplane Passing Crane — AP4

1925-30 Typo. *Perf. 12½*

C12	AP3	2g gray brown	.40	.40
C13	AP3	5g red	.40	.40
a.		Horiz. pair, imperf. btwn.	800.00	
		Never hinged	1,250.	
C14	AP3	6g dark blue	.80	.80
C15	AP3	8g yel green	.80	.80
C16	AP3	10g dp org ('26)	.80	.80
a.		Horiz. pair, imperf. btwn.	800.00	
		Never hinged	1,250.	
C17	AP3	15g red vio ('26)	.40	.40
a.		Horiz. pair, imperf. btwn.	800.00	
		Never hinged	1,250.	
C18	AP3	20g org brn ('30)	11.00	11.00
C19	AP3	25g blk vio ('30)	4.75	4.75
C20	AP3	30g bister ('26)	8.00	8.00
C21	AP3	50g bl gray ('26)	13.50	13.50
C22	AP3	80g dk grn ('30)	2.40	2.40

Photo.

C23	AP4	10g orange red	.80	.80
a.		Horiz. pair, imperf. btwn.	800.00	
		Never hinged	1,250.	
C24	AP4	15g claret	.80	.80
C25	AP4	30g brn violet	.80	.80
C26	AP4	50g gray black	.80	.80
C27	AP4	1s deep blue	8.00	8.00
C28	AP4	2s dark green	1.60	1.60
a.		Vertical pair, imperf. btwn.	800.00	
		Never hinged	1,250.	
C29	AP4	3s red brn ('26)	52.50	52.50
C30	AP4	5s indigo ('26)	13.50	13.50

Size: 25½x32mm

C31	AP4	10s blk brown, *gray* ('26)	8.00	8.00
		Nos. C12-C31 (20)	130.05	130.05
		Set, never hinged	325.00	

Values for used are for stamps with philatelic favor cancels. Postally used value, set $200.

Exists imperf. Values, set unused hinged $850, never hinged $1,100.

Airplane over Güssing Castle — AP5

Airplane over the Danube — AP6

Designs (each includes plane): 10g, Maria-Worth. 15g, Durnstein. 20g, Hallstatt. 25g, Salzburg. 30g, Upper Dachstein and Schladminger Glacier. 40g, Lake Wetter. 50g, Arlberg. 60g, St. Stephen's Cathedral. 80g, Church of the Minorites. 2s, Railroad viaduct, Carinthia. 3s, Gross Glockner mountain. 5s, Aerial railway. 10s, Seaplane and yachts.

1935, Aug. 16 Engr. *Perf. 12½*

C32	AP5	5g rose violet	.25	.25
C33	AP5	10g red orange	.25	.25
C34	AP5	15g yel green	.80	.80
C35	AP5	20g gray blue	.25	.25
C36	AP5	25g violet brn	.25	.25
C37	AP5	30g brn orange	.25	.25
C38	AP5	40g gray green	.25	.25
C39	AP5	50g light sl bl	.25	.25
C40	AP5	60g black brn	.35	.35
C41	AP5	80g light brown	.40	.40
C42	AP6	1s rose red	.35	.35
C43	AP6	2s olive green	2.40	2.00
C44	AP6	3s yellow brn	12.00	8.00
C45	AP6	5s dark green	4.00	2.75
C46	AP6	10s slate blue	52.50	52.50
		Nos. C32-C46 (15)	74.55	68.90
		Set, never hinged	150.00	

Values for used are for stamps with philatelic favor cancels. Postally used value, set $175.

Set exists imperf. Values, set unused hinged $375, never hinged $475.

Catalogue values for unused stamps in this section, from this point to the end of the section, are for Never Hinged items.

Windmill, Neusiedler Lake Shore — AP20

1s, Roman arch, Carnuntum. 2s, Town Hall, Gmund. 3s, Schieder Lake, Hinterstoder. 4s, Praegraten, Eastern Tyrol. 5s, Torsäule, Salzburg. 10s, St. Charles Church, Vienna.

1947 Unwmk. *Perf. 14x13½*

C47	AP20	50g black brown	.40	.40
C48	AP20	1s dark brn vio	.40	.40
C49	AP20	2s dark green	.40	.40
C50	AP20	3s chocolate	2.40	2.40
C51	AP20	4s dark green	2.00	2.00
C52	AP20	5s dark blue	2.00	2.00
C53	AP20	10s dark blue	.80	.80
		Nos. C47-C53 (7)	8.40	8.40

Used values for examples with philatelic favor cancels. Postally used value, set $27.50.

Rooks AP27

Birds: 1s, Barn swallows. 2s, Blackheaded gulls. 3s, Great cormorants. 5s, Buzzard. 10s, Gray heron. 20s, Golden eagle.

1950-53 *Perf. 13½x14*

C54	AP27	60g dark bl vio	1.40	1.40
C55	AP27	1s dark vio blue ('53)	15.00	15.00
C56	AP27	2s dark blue	11.00	11.00
C57	AP27	3s dk slate green ('53)	90.00	90.00
C58	AP27	5s red brn ('53)	90.00	90.00
C59	AP27	10s gray vio ('53)	50.00	42.50
C60	AP27	20s brn blk ('52)	10.00	8.50
		Nos. C54-C60 (7)	267.40	258.40
		Set, hinged	150.00	

Value at lower left on Nos. C59 and C60.

No. C60 exists imperf.

Etrich "Dove" AP28

Designs: 3.50s, Twin-engine jet airliner. 5s, Four-engine jet airliner.

1968, May 31 Engr. *Perf. 13½x14*

C61	AP28	2s olive bister	.35	.35
C62	AP28	3.50s slate green	.55	.65
C63	AP28	5s dark blue	1.10	1.40
		Nos. C61-C63 (3)	2.00	2.40

IFA WIEN 1968 (International Air Post Exhibition), Vienna, May 30-June 4.

POSTAGE DUE STAMPS

Issues of the Monarchy

D1

Perf. 10 to 13½

1894-95 Typo. Wmk. 91

J1	D1	1kr brown	2.00	1.25
a.		Perf. 13½	45.00	62.50
b.		Half used as ½kr on cover		80.00
J2	D1	2kr brown ('95)	2.75	2.40
a.		Pair, imperf. btwn.	200.00	300.00
b.		Half used as 1kr on cover		200.00
J3	D1	3kr brown	3.25	1.25
a.		Half used as 1½kr on cover		160.00
J4	D1	5kr brown	3.25	.80
a.		Perf. 13½	25.00	25.00
b.		Pair, imperf. btwn.	160.00	*250.00*
J5	D1	6kr brown ('95)	2.75	*6.50*
a.		Half used as 3kr on cover		200.00
J6	D1	7kr brown ('95)	.80	*6.00*
a.		Vert. pair, imperf. btwn.	275.00	*550.00*
b.		Horiz. pair, imperf. btwn.	275.00	*550.00*
J7	D1	10kr brown	4.75	.95
a.		Half used as 5kr on cover		140.00
J8	D1	20kr brown	.80	*6.00*
J9	D1	50kr brown	35.00	72.50
		Nos. J1-J9 (9)	55.35	97.65

Values for Nos. J1-J9 are for stamps that do not show the watermark. Stamps showing the watermark often sell for more.

See Nos. J204-J231.

D2

1899-1900 *Imperf.*

J10	D2	1h brown	.25	*.40*
J11	D2	2h brown	.25	*.55*
J12	D2	3h brown ('00)	.25	*.40*
J13	D2	4h brown	2.00	2.00
J14	D2	5h brown ('00)	1.60	*1.25*
J15	D2	6h brown	.25	*.50*
J16	D2	10h brown	.25	*.50*
J17	D2	12h brown	.35	*2.40*
J18	D2	15h brown	.35	*1.60*
J19	D2	20h brown	24.00	4.75
J20	D2	40h brown	2.40	*2.60*
J21	D2	100h brown	4.75	3.25
		Nos. J10-J21 (12)	36.70	20.20

Perf. 10½, 12½, 13½ and Compound

J22	D2	1h brown	.55	.25
J23	D2	2h brown	.40	.25
J24	D2	3h brown ('00)	.40	.25
J25	D2	4h brown	.65	.25
J26	D2	5h brown ('00)	.55	.25
J27	D2	6h brown	.40	.25
J28	D2	10h brown	.55	.25
J29	D2	12h brown	.55	.75
J30	D2	15h brown	.80	.80
J31	D2	20h brown	.95	.25
J32	D2	40h brown	1.25	.75
J33	D2	100h brown	24.00	2.00
		Nos. J22-J33 (12)	31.05	6.30

Nos. J10-J33 exist on unwmkd. paper.

For surcharges see Offices in the Turkish Empire Nos. J1-J5.

D3

Ordinary Thin Paper

1910-13 Unwmk. *Perf. 12½*

J34	D3	1h carmine	.80	*1.60*
J35	D3	2h carmine	.50	.35
d.		Half used as 1h on cover		95.00
J36	D3	4h carmine	.50	.25
c.		Half used as 2h on cover		95.00
J37	D3	6h carmine	.50	.25
J38	D3	10h carmine	.50	.25
c.		Half used as 5h on cover		47.50
J39	D3	14h carmine ('13)	4.00	2.75
J40	D3	20h carmine	8.00	.25
c.		Half used as 10h on cover		95.00
J41	D3	25h carmine ('10)	8.00	6.50
J42	D3	30h carmine	8.00	.35
J43	D3	50h carmine	12.00	.40
J44	D3	100h carmine	16.00	.80
		Never hinged	65.00	
		Nos. J34-J44 (11)	58.80	13.75

All values exist on ordinary paper, Nos. J34-J38, J40, J42-J44 on chalky paper and Nos. J34-J38, J40, J44 on thin ordinary paper. In most cases, values are for the least expensive stamp of the types. Some of the expensive types sell for considerably more.

All values exist imperf.

See Offices in the Turkish Empire type D3.

For overprint on J41, see Western Ukraine N10.

1911, July 16

J45	D3	5k violet	80.00	12.50
J46	D3	10k violet	240.00	4.00

Nos. J45-J46 exist imperf. Value set: unused hinged $900; never hinged $1,200.

Regular Issue of 1908 Overprinted or Surcharged in Carmine or Black

No. J47

No. J48

1916, Oct. 21

J47	A22	1h gray (C)	.25	.25
a.		Pair, one without overprint	210.00	
		Never hinged	300.00	
J48	A22	15h on 2h vio (Bk)	.25	*.55*
a.		Inverted surcharge	400.00	
		Never hinged	750.00	
		Set, never hinged	1.60	

D4

D5

Perf. 12½, 12½x13 (#J57-J59)

1916, Oct. 1

J49	D4	5h rose red	.25	.25
J50	D4	10h rose red	.25	.25
a.		Half used as 5h on cover		65.00
J51	D4	15h rose red	.25	.25
J52	D4	20h rose red	.25	.25
J53	D4	25h rose red	.25	*.95*
J54	D4	30h rose red	.25	*.40*
a.		Half used as 15h on cover		160.00
J55	D4	40h rose red	.25	*.40*
a.		Half used as 20h on cover		140.00
J56	D4	50h rose red	.95	*3.25*
J57	D5	1k ultramarine	.25	*.40*
a.		Horiz. pair, imperf. btwn.	250.00	*550.00*
		Never hinged	550.00	

J58 D5 5k ultramarine 2.75 *3.25*
J59 D5 10k ultramarine 3.50 1.60
Nos. J49-J59 (11) 9.20 *11.25*
Set, never hinged 32.50

Exists imperf. Value set: unused hinged $150, never hinged $400.

For overprints see J64-J74, Western Ukraine Nos. N9, N11-N12. Poland Nos. J1-J10. Western Ukraine Nos. N9, N11-N12.

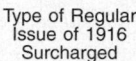

Type of Regular Issue of 1916 Surcharged

1917
J60 A38 10h on 24h blue 1.60 .55
J61 A38 15h on 36h violet .50 .25
J62 A38 20h on 54h orange .25 *.40*
J63 A38 50h on 42h chocolate .35 .35
Nos. J60-J63 (4) 2.70 1.55
Set, never hinged 14.00

All values of this issue are known imperforate, also without surcharge, perforated and imperforate. Values, set imperf unused hinged $160, never hinged $250. Value of set without surcharge imperf unused hinged $200, never hinged $350. Same values for set without surcharge, perf 12½.

For surcharges see Poland Nos. J11-J12

Issues of the Republic

Postage Due Stamps of 1916 Overprinted

1919
J64 D4 5h rose red .25 .25
a. Inverted overprint 250.00 325.00
Never hinged 325.00
J65 D4 10h rose red .25 .25
J66 D4 15h rose red .25 *.40*
J67 D4 20h rose red .25 *.40*
J68 D4 25h rose red 8.00 *27.50*
J69 D4 30h rose red .25 *.40*
J70 D4 40h rose red .25 *.80*
J71 D4 50h rose red .30 *1.25*
J72 D5 1k ultramarine 4.50 *16.00*
J73 D5 5k ultramarine 8.75 *16.00*
J74 D5 10k ultramarine 10.50 4.00
Nos. J64-J74 (11) 33.55 *67.25*
Set, never hinged 100.00

Nos. J64, J65, J67, J70 exist imperf. Value, 4 values hinged $325.

D6

D7

1920-21 *Perf. 12½*
J75 D6 5h bright red .25 *.35*
J76 D6 10h bright red .25 .25
J77 D6 15h bright red .25 *1.60*
J78 D6 20h bright red .25 .25
J79 D6 25h bright red .25 *1.60*
J80 D6 30h bright red .25 *.35*
J81 D6 40h bright red .25 *.35*
J82 D6 50h bright red .25 *.35*
J83 D6 80h bright red .25 *.45*
J84 D7 1k ultramarine .25 .35
J85 D7 1½k ultra ('21) .25 .35
J86 D7 2k ultra ('21) .25 .35
J87 D7 3k ultra ('21) .25 *.95*
J88 D7 4k ultra ('21) .25 *.95*
J89 D7 5k ultramarine .25 .35
J90 D7 8k ultra ('21) .25 *.95*
J91 D7 10k ultramarine .25 *.45*
J92 D7 20k ultra ('21) .30 *2.00*
Nos. J75-J92 (18) *12.25*
Set, never hinged 4.75

Nos. J84-J92 exist on white paper and on grayish white paper. Values are for the cheaper varieties. See the *Scott Classic Specialized Catalogue* for detailed listings.

Nos. J84 to J92 exist imperf. Values, set unused hinged $150, never hinged $250.

Imperf
J93 D6 5h bright red .25 *.65*
J94 D6 10h bright red .25 *.40*
J95 D6 15h bright red .25 *1.60*
J96 D6 20h bright red .25 *.40*
J97 D6 25h bright red .25 *1.60*
J98 D6 30h bright red .25 *1.25*
J99 D6 40h bright red .25 *.65*
J100 D6 50h bright red .25 *1.10*
J101 D6 80h bright red .25 *.85*
Nos. J93-J101 (9) *8.50*
Set, never hinged 3.25

No. 207a Surcharged in Dark Blue

1921, Dec. *Perf. 12½*
J102 A43 7½k on 15h bister .25 *.25*
Never hinged .25
a. Inverted surcharge 450.00 *500.00*

D8

1922
J103 D8 1k reddish buff .25 *.35*
J104 D8 2k reddish buff .25 *.40*
J105 D8 4k reddish buff .25 *.65*
J106 D8 5k reddish buff .25 *.35*
J107 D8 7½k reddish buff .25 *1.20*
J108 D8 10k blue green .25 *.50*
J109 D8 15k blue green .25 *.75*
J110 D8 20k blue green .25 *.55*
J111 D8 25k blue green .25 *1.25*
J112 D8 40k blue green .25 *.40*
J113 D8 50k blue green .25 *1.25*
Nos. J103-J113 (11) *7.65*
Set, never hinged 5.25

Issue date: Nos. J108-J113, June 2.

D9

D10

1922-24
J114 D9 10k cobalt blue .25 *.40*
J115 D9 15k cobalt blue .25 *.55*
J116 D9 20k cobalt blue .25 *.55*
J117 D9 50k cobalt blue .25 *.55*
J118 D10 100k plum .25 .25
J119 D10 150k plum .25 .25
J120 D10 200k plum .25 .25
J121 D10 400k plum .25 .25
J122 D10 600k plum ('23) .25 *.40*
J123 D10 800k plum .25 .25
J124 D10 1,000k plum ('23) .25 .25
J125 D10 1,200k plum ('23) 1.00 *4.75*
J126 D10 1,500k plum ('24) .25 *.80*
J127 D10 1,800k plum ('24) 3.25 *12.00*
J128 D10 2,000k plum ('23) .40 *1.60*
J129 D10 3,000k plum ('24) 5.50 *24.00*
J130 D10 4,000k plum ('24) 3.25 *20.00*
J131 D10 6,000k plum ('24) 3.25 *27.50*
Nos. J114-J131 (18) 19.65 *94.60*
Set, never hinged 70.00

J103-J131 sets exist imperf. Values, both sets unused hinged $450, never hinged $650.

D11

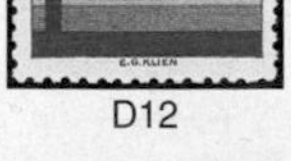
D12

1925-34 *Perf. 12½*
J132 D11 1g red .25 .25
J133 D11 2g red .25 .25
J134 D11 3g red .25 .25
J135 D11 4g red .25 .25
J136 D11 5g red ('27) .25 .25
J137 D11 6g red .25 *.25*
J138 D11 8g red .25 .25
J139 D11 10g dark blue .25 .25
J140 D11 12g dark blue .25 .25
J141 D11 14g dark blue ('27) .25 .25
J142 D11 15g dark blue .25 .25
J143 D11 16g dark blue ('29) .25 .25
J144 D11 18g dark blue ('34) 1.25 *2.75*
J145 D11 20g dark blue .25 .25
J146 D11 23g dark blue .40 .25
J147 D11 24g dark blue ('32) 1.60 .25
J148 D11 28g dark blue ('27) 1.60 .25
J149 D11 30g dark blue .25 .25
J150 D11 31g dark blue ('29) 1.25 .25
J151 D11 35g dark blue ('30) 1.25 .25
J152 D11 39g dark blue ('32) 1.60 .25
J153 D11 40g dark blue 2.00 *2.50*
J154 D11 60g dark blue 2.00 2.00
J155 D12 1s dark green 2.75 1.25
J156 D12 2s dark green 25.00 4.00
J157 D12 5s dark green 87.50 45.00
J158 D12 10s dark green 35.00 8.00
Nos. J132-J158 (27) 166.70 70.50
Set, never hinged 575.00

Issues of 1925-27 exist imperf. Values, set of 18 unused hinged $600, never hinged $800.

Issued: 3g, 2s-10s, Dec; 5g, 28g, 1/1; 14g, June; 31g, 2/1; 35g, Jan; 24g, 39g, Sept; 16g, May; 18g, 6/25; others, 6/1.

Coat of Arms
D13 D14

1935, June 1
J159 D13 1g red .25 .25
J160 D13 2g red .25 .25
J161 D13 3g red .25 .25
J162 D13 5g red .25 .25
J163 D13 10g blue .25 .25
J164 D13 12g blue .25 .25
J165 D13 15g blue .25 *.50*
J166 D13 20g blue .25 .25
J167 D13 24g blue .25 .25
J168 D13 30g blue .25 .25
J169 D13 39g blue .35 .25
J170 D13 60g blue .50 *1.25*
J171 D14 1s green .80 .35
J172 D14 2s green 1.50 1.00
J173 D14 5s green 3.00 *4.00*
J174 D14 10s green 4.75 .65
Nos. J159-J174 (16) 13.40 10.25
Set, never hinged 55.00

On Nos. J163-J170, background lines are horiz.

Nos. J159-J174 exist imperf. Values, set unused hinged $160, never hinged $350.

Catalogue values for unused stamps in this section, from this point to the end of the section, are for Never Hinged items.

D15

1945 Unwmk. Typo. *Perf. 10½*
J175 D15 1g vermilion .25 *.25*
J176 D15 2g vermilion .25 *.25*
J177 D15 3g vermilion .25 .25
J178 D15 5g vermilion .25 .25
J179 D15 10g vermilion .25 .25
J180 D15 12g vermilion .25 .25
J181 D15 20g vermilion .25 .25
J182 D15 24g vermilion .25 *.40*
J183 D15 30g vermilion .25 *.40*
J184 D15 60g vermilion .25 *.40*
J185 D15 1s violet .25 *.40*
J186 D15 2s violet .25 *.80*
J187 D15 5s violet .25 *.80*
J188 D15 10s violet .25 *.80*
Nos. J175-J188 (14) 3.50 *5.75*

Issued: 1g-60g, Sept. 10; 1s-10s, Sept. 24.

Occupation Stamps of the Allied Military Government Overprinted in Black

1946 *Perf. 11*
J189 OS1 3g deep orange .25 .25
J190 OS1 5g bright green .25 .25
J191 OS1 6g red violet .25 .25
J192 OS1 8g rose pink .25 .25
J193 OS1 10g light gray .25 .25
J194 OS1 12g pale buff brown .25 .25
J195 OS1 15g rose red .25 .25
J196 OS1 20g copper brown .25 .25
J197 OS1 25g deep blue .25 .25
J198 OS1 30g bright violet .25 .25
J199 OS1 40g light ultra .25 .25
J200 OS1 60g light olive grn .25 .25
J201 OS1 1s dark violet .25 .25
J202 OS1 2s yellow .50 *.80*
J203 OS1 5s deep ultra .50 *.80*
Nos. J189-J203 (15) 4.25 4.85

Nos. J189-J203 were issued by the Renner Government. Inverted overprints exist on about half of the denominations.

Issued: 3g-60g, Apr. 23; 1s-5s, May 20.

Type of 1894-95
Inscribed "Republik Osterreich"

1947 Typo. *Perf. 14*
J204 D1 1g chocolate .25 .40
J205 D1 2g chocolate .25 .40
J206 D1 3g chocolate .25 .40
J207 D1 5g chocolate .25 .25
J208 D1 8g chocolate .25 .25
J209 D1 10g chocolate .25 .40
J210 D1 12g chocolate .25 .25
J211 D1 15g chocolate .25 .25
J212 D1 16g chocolate .30 *.95*
J213 D1 17g chocolate .30 *.95*
J214 D1 18g chocolate .30 *.95*
J215 D1 20g chocolate .75 .25
J216 D1 24g chocolate .35 *.95*
J217 D1 30g chocolate .25 *.25*
J218 D1 36g chocolate .75 *1.40*
J219 D1 40g chocolate .25 .25
J220 D1 42g chocolate .80 *1.40*
J221 D1 48g chocolate .80 *1.40*
J222 D1 50g chocolate .75 .35
J223 D1 60g chocolate .25 *.35*
J224 D1 70g chocolate .25 .35
J225 D1 80g chocolate 4.50 1.60
J226 D1 1s blue .25 .35
J227 D1 1.15s blue 3.25 .50
J228 D1 1.20s blue 3.25 1.25
J229 D1 2s blue .35 .35
J230 D1 5s blue .35 .35
J231 D1 10s blue .40 .40
Nos. J204-J231 (28) 20.45 17.20

Issue dates: 1g, 20g, 50g, 80g, 1.15s, 1.20s, Sept. 25, others, Aug. 14.

D16

1949-57
J232 D16 1g carmine .35 .25
J233 D16 2g carmine .35 .25
J234 D16 4g carmine ('51) .50 .35
J235 D16 5g carmine 1.90 .40
J236 D16 8g carmine ('51) 1.90 1.60
J237 D16 10g carmine .35 .25
J238 D16 20g carmine .35 .25
J239 D16 30g carmine .35 .25
J240 D16 40g carmine .35 .25
J241 D16 50g carmine .35 .25
J242 D16 60g carmine ('50) 10.50 .40
J243 D16 63g carmine ('57) 4.75 3.50
J244 D16 70g carmine .40 .25
J245 D16 80g carmine .35 .25
J246 D16 90g carmine ('50) .55 .25
J247 D16 1s purple .40 .25
J248 D16 1.20s purple .55 .40
J249 D16 1.35s purple .40 .35
J250 D16 1.40s purple ('51) .40 .40
J251 D16 1.50s purple ('53) .40 .25
J252 D16 1.65s purple ('50) .40 .40
J253 D16 1.70s purple .40 .40
J254 D16 2s purple 1.40 .25
J255 D16 2.50s purple ('51) .75 .25
J256 D16 3s purple ('51) .80 .25
J257 D16 4s purple ('51) 1.00 1.00
J258 D16 5s purple 1.25 .25
J259 D16 10s purple 2.40 .25
Nos. J232-J259 (28) 33.85 13.45

Issued: 60g, 90g, 1.65s, 8/7; 4g, 8g, 1.40s, 2.50s-4s, 12/4; 1.50s, 2/18; 63g, 4/30; others, 11/17.

D17

1985-89 Photo. *Perf. 14*

Background Color

J260	D17	10g brt yel ('86)	.25	.25
J261	D17	20g pink ('86)	.25	.25
J262	D17	50g orange ('86)	.25	*.25*
J263	D17	1s lt blue ('86)	.25	*.35*
J264	D17	2s pale brn ('86)	.25	*.50*
J265	D17	3s violet ('86)	.40	*.55*
J266	D17	5s ocher	.85	.65
J267	D17	10s pale grn ('89)	1.75	1.75
		Nos. J260-J267 (8)	4.25	4.55

Issue dates: 5s, Dec. 12. 20g, 1s, 3s, Mar. 19. 10g, 50g, 2s, Oct. 3. 10s, June 30.

MILITARY STAMPS

Issues of the Austro-Hungarian Military Authorities for the Occupied Territories in World War I

See Bosnia and Herzegovina for similar designs inscribed "MILITARPOST" instead of "FELDPOST."

Stamps of Bosnia of 1912-14 Overprinted

1915 Unwmk. *Perf. 12½*

M1	A23	1h olive green	.25	*.40*
M2	A23	2h bright blue	.25	*.40*
M3	A23	3h claret	.25	*.40*
M4	A23	5h green	.25	*.25*
M5	A23	6h dark gray	.25	*.40*
M6	A23	10h rose carmine	.25	*.25*
M7	A23	12h deep ol grn	.25	*.80*
M8	A23	20h orange brn	.35	*.80*
M9	A23	25h ultramarine	.25	*.80*
M10	A23	30h orange red	3.25	*6.50*
M11	A24	35h myrtle grn	2.50	*4.75*
M12	A24	40h dark violet	2.50	*4.75*
M13	A24	45h olive brown	2.50	*4.75*
M14	A24	50h slate blue	2.50	*4.75*
M15	A24	60h brn violet	.40	*.80*
M16	A24	72h dark blue	2.50	*4.75*
M17	A25	1k brn vio, *straw*	2.50	*4.75*
M18	A25	2k dk gray, *blue*	2.50	*4.75*
M19	A26	3k car, *green*	20.00	*47.50*
M20	A26	5k dk vio, *gray*	20.00	*40.00*
M21	A25	10k dk ultra, *gray*	150.00	*300.00*
		Nos. M1-M21 (21)	213.50	*432.55*
		Set, never hinged	420.00	

Exists imperf. Values, set unused hinged $450, never hinged $875.

Nos. M1-M21 also exist with overprint double, inverted and in red. These varieties were made by order of an official but were not regularly issued. Values, each set: unused $325; never hinged $650.

M1

M2

Design: Emperor Franz Josef.

Perf. 11½, 12½ and Compound

1915-17 Engr.

M22	M1	1h olive green	.25	*.25*
M23	M1	2h dull blue	.25	*.35*
M24	M1	3h claret	.25	*.25*
M25	M1	5h green	.25	*.25*
a.		Perf. 11½	100.00	*150.00*
		Never hinged	200.00	
b.		Perf. 11½x12½	150.00	*240.00*
		Never hinged	325.00	
c.		Perf. 12½x11½	200.00	*325.00*
		Never hinged	400.00	
M26	M1	6h dark gray	.25	*.35*
M27	M1	10h rose carmine	.25	*.25*
M28	M1	10h gray bl ('17)	.25	*.35*
M29	M1	12h deep olive grn	.25	*.40*
M30	M1	15h car rose ('17)	.25	*.40*
a.		Perf. 11½	8.00	*27.50*
		Never hinged	27.50	
M31	M1	20h orange brn	.35	*.40*
M32	M1	20h ol green ('17)	.25	*.50*
M33	M1	25h ultramarine	.25	*.35*
M34	M1	30h vermilion	.35	*.50*
M35	M1	35h dark green	.35	*.65*
M36	M1	40h dark violet	.35	*.65*
M37	M1	45h olive brown	.35	*.65*
M38	M1	50h myrtle green	.35	*.65*
M39	M1	60h brown violet	.35	*.65*
M40	M1	72h dark blue	.35	*.65*
M41	M1	80h org brn ('17)	.35	.35
M42	M1	90h magenta ('17)	.80	*1.25*
M43	M2	1k brn vio, *straw*	1.60	*2.50*
M44	M2	2k dk gray, *blue*	.80	1.60
M45	M2	3k car, *green*	.80	*6.50*
M46	M2	4k dk vio, *gray* ('17)	.80	*8.00*
M47	M2	5k dk vio, *gray*	20.00	*37.50*
M48	M2	10k dk ultra, *gray*	4.00	*16.00*
		Nos. M22-M48 (27)	34.70	*82.20*
		Set, never hinged	125.00	

Nos. M22-M48 exist imperf. Values, set unused hinged $250, never hinged $475.

For overprints see Montenegro Nos. 1N1-1N4.

Emperor Karl I

M3 M4

1917-18 *Perf. 12½*

M49	M3	1h grnsh blue ('18)	.25	.25
a.		Perf. 11½	5.50	*16.00*
		Never hinged	16.00	
M50	M3	2h red org ('18)	.25	*.25*
M51	M3	3h olive gray	.25	*.25*
a.		Perf. 11½	20.00	*47.50*
		Never hinged	47.50	
b.		Perf. 11½x12½	32.50	*80.00*
		Never hinged	80.00	
M52	M3	5h olive green	.25	*.25*
M53	M3	6h violet	.25	*.25*
M54	M3	10h orange brn	.25	*.25*
M55	M3	12h dp blue	.25	*.25*
a.		Perf. 11½	4.00	*12.00*
		Never hinged	12.00	
M56	M3	15h bright rose	.25	*.25*
M57	M3	20h red brown	.25	*.25*
M58	M3	25h ultramarine	.25	*.55*
M59	M3	30h grnsh slate	.25	.25
M60	M3	40h olive bister	.25	*.25*
a.		Perf. 11½	2.50	*6.50*
		Never hinged	6.50	
M61	M3	50h deep green	.25	*.25*
a.		Perf. 11½	8.00	*32.50*
		Never hinged	32.50	
M62	M3	60h car rose	.25	*.40*
M63	M3	80h dull blue	.25	*.25*
M64	M3	90h dk violet	.35	*.80*
M65	M4	2k rose, *straw*	.25	*.25*
a.		Perf. 11½	4.00	*12.00*
		Never hinged	12.00	
M66	M4	3k green, *blue*	1.25	*2.75*
M67	M4	4k rose, *green*	16.00	*24.00*
a.		Perf. 11½	40.00	*80.00*
		Never hinged	80.00	
M68	M4	10k dl vio, *gray*	1.25	*8.00*
a.		Perf. 11½	16.00	*47.50*
		Never hinged	47.50	
		Nos. M49-M68 (20)	22.85	*40.00*
		Set, never hinged	87.50	

Nos. M49-M68 exist imperf. Values, set unused hinged $160, never hinged $325. Also exist in pairs, imperf between. Values, each: unused $60, never hinged $120.

See No. M82. For surcharges and overprints see Italy Nos. N1-N19, N33, Western Ukraine Nos. 44-63, 75, 95-101, Poland Nos. 30-40, Romania Nos. 1N1-1N17.

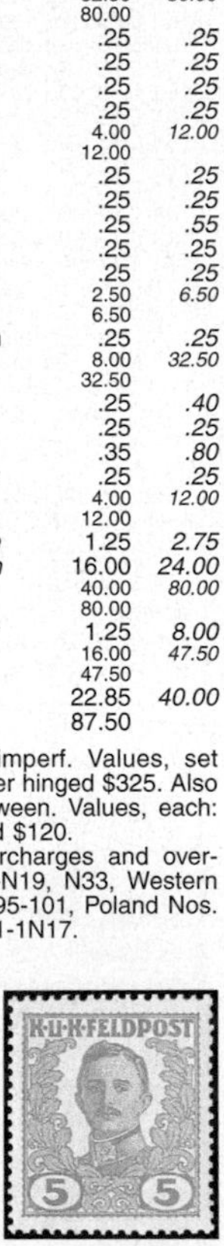

Emperor Karl I — M5

1918 Typo. *Perf. 12½*

M69	M5	1h grnsh blue	24.00
M70	M5	2h orange	9.50
M71	M5	3h olive gray	9.50
M72	M5	5h yellow green	.40
M73	M5	10h dark brown	.40
M74	M5	20h red	.80
M75	M5	25h blue	.80
M76	M5	30h bister	95.00
M77	M5	45h dark slate	95.00
M78	M5	50h deep green	47.50
M79	M5	60h violet	95.00
M80	M5	80h rose	65.00
M81	M5	90h brown violet	1.60

Engr.

M82	M4	1k ol bister, *blue*	.40
		Nos. M69-M82 (14)	444.90
		Set, never hinged	1,050.

Nos. M69-M82 were on sale at the Vienna post office for a few days before the Armistice signing. They were never issued at the Army Post Offices. They exist imperf. Values, set unused hinged $800, never hinged $1,600.

For surcharges see Italy Nos. N20-N33, Romania 1N35-1N47.

MILITARY SEMI-POSTAL STAMPS

Emperor Karl I — MSP7

Empress Zita — MSP8

Perf. 12½x13

1918, July 20 Unwmk. Typo.

MB1	MSP7	10h gray green	.40	*.80*
MB2	MSP8	20h magenta	.40	*.80*
MB3	MSP7	45h blue	.40	*.80*
		Nos. MB1-MB3 (3)	1.20	*2.40*
		Set, never hinged	3.00	

These stamps were sold at a premium of 10h each over face value. The surtax was for "Karl's Fund."

For overprints see Western Ukraine Nos. 31-33.

Exist imperf. Values, set hinged unused $95, never hinged $240.

MILITARY NEWSPAPER STAMPS

Mercury — MN1

1916 Unwmk. Typo. *Perf. 12½*

MP1	MN1	2h blue	.25	*.35*
a.		Perf. 11½	1.25	*2.00*
		Never hinged	3.25	
b.		Perf. 12½x11½	240.00	240.00
		Never hinged	450.00	
MP2	MN1	6h orange	.50	*1.50*
MP3	MN1	10h carmine	.55	*1.50*
MP4	MN1	20h brown	1.25	*1.50*
a.		Perf. 11½	4.00	*8.00*
		Never hinged	8.00	
		Nos. MP1-MP4 (4)	2.55	*4.85*
		Set, never hinged	8.00	

Exist imperf. Values, Nos. MP2-MP3, unused hinged each $1.60, never hinged $6.50; Nos. MP1, MP4, unused hinged each $40, never hinged $120.

For surcharges see Italy Nos. NP1-NP4.

NEWSPAPER STAMPS

From 1851 to 1866, the Austrian Newspaper Stamps were also used in Lombardy-Venetia.

Values for unused stamps 1851-67 are for fine examples with original gum. Examples without gum sell for about a third or less of the figures quoted.

Issues of the Monarchy

Mercury — N1

Three Types

Type I — The "G" has no crossbar.

Type II — The "G" has a crossbar.

Type IIa — as type II but the rosette is deformed. Two spots of color in the "G."

1851-56 Unwmk. Typo. *Imperf.*

Machine-made Paper

P1	N1	(0.6kr) bl, type IIa	175.00	110.00
a.		Blue, type I	250.00	130.00
b.		Ribbed paper	625.00	240.00
c.		Blue, type II	600.00	250.00
P2	N1	(6kr) yel, type I	*31,000.*	*10,000.*
P3	N1	(30kr) rose, type I	—	*13,000.*
P4	N1	(6kr) scar, type II ('56)	*85,000.*	*13,500.*

From 1852 No. P3 and from 1856 No. P2 were used as 0.6 kreuzer values.

Values for Nos. P2-P3 unused are for stamps without gum. Pale shades sell at considerably lower values.

Originals of Nos. P2 and P3 are usually in pale colors and poorly printed. Values are for stamps clearly printed and in bright colors. Numerous reprints of Nos. P1 to P4 were made between 1866 and 1904. Those of Nos. P2 and P3 are always well printed and in much deeper colors. All reprints are in type I, but occasionally show faint traces of a crossbar on "G" of "ZEITUNGS."

N2

Two Types of the 1858-59 Issue

Type I — Loops of the bow at the back of the head broken.

Type II — Loops complete. Wreath projects further at top of head.

1858-59 Embossed

P5	N2	(1kr) blue, type I	650.00	625.00
P6	N2	(1kr) lilac, type II ('59)	875.00	300.00

N3

1861

P7	N3	(1kr) gray	175.00	175.00
a.		(1kr) gray lilac	625.00	240.00
b.		(1kr) deep lilac	2,500.	800.00

The embossing on the reprints of the 1858-59 and 1861 issues is not as sharp as on the originals.

N4

Wmk. 91, or, before July 1864, Unwmkd.

1863

P8	N4	(1.05kr) gray	45.00	16.50
a.		Tete beche pair	*125,000.*	
b.		(1.05kr) gray lilac	100.00	20.00

Values are for stamps that do not show the watermark. Stamps showing the watermark often sell for more.

The embossing of the reprints is not as sharp as on the originals.

Mercury — N5

Three Types

Type I — Helmet not defined at back, more or less blurred. Two thick short lines in front of wing of helmet. Shadow on front of face not separated from hair.

Type II — Helmet distinctly defined. Four thin short lines in front of wing. Shadow on front of face clearly defined from hair.

Type III — Outer white circle around head is open at top (closed on types I and II). Greek border at top and bottom is wider than on types I and II.

Coarse Print

1867-73 Typo. Wmk. 91
P9 N5 (1kr) vio, type I 75.00 8.50
a. (1kr) violet, type II ('73) 225.00 25.00

1874-76 Fine Print
P9B N5 (1kr) vio, type III ('76) .55 .40
c. (1kr) gray lilac, type I ('76) 225.00 32.50
d. (1kr) violet, type II 65.00 8.50
e. Double impression, type III 175.00

Stamps of this issue, except No. P9Bc, exist in many shades, from gray to lilac brown and deep violet. Stamps in type III exist also privately perforated or rouletted.

Mercury — N6

1880
P10 N6 ½kr blue green 8.50 1.25

Nos. P9B and P10 also exist on thicker paper without sheet watermark and No. P10 exists with unofficial perforation.

N7

Without Varnish Bars

1899 Unwmk. *Imperf.*
P11 N7 2h dark blue .25 .25
P12 N7 6h orange 1.60 *2.00*
P13 N7 10h brown 1.60 .95
P14 N7 20h rose 1.60 2.00
Nos. P11-P14 (4) 5.05 5.20

1901 With Varnish Bars
P11a N7 2h dark blue 2.40 .25
P12a N7 6h orange 16.00 24.00
P13a N7 10h brown 16.00 8.00
P14a N7 20h rose 20.00 *65.00*
Nos. P11a-P14a (4) 54.40 97.25

Nos. P11-P14 were re-issued in 1905. They exist privately perforated.

Mercury — N8

Ordinary Paper

1910 *Imperf.*
P15b N8 2h dark blue .50 .25
P16b N8 6h orange 4.00 .35
P17b N8 10h carmine rose 4.00 .35
P18b N8 20h brown 4.50 .30

All values are found on chalky (1908), ordinary (1910), and thin paper (1909). They exist privately perforated. For detailed listings, see Scott *Classic Specialized Catalogue of Stamps and Covers 1840-1940.*

Mercury — N9

1916 *Imperf.*
P19 N9 2h brown .25 *.40*
P20 N9 4h green .35 *1.25*
P21 N9 6h dark blue .55 *1.25*
P22 N9 10h orange .60 *1.25*
P23 N9 30h claret .55 *1.60*
Nos. P19-P23 (5) 2.30 5.75
Set, never hinged 9.50

Nos. P19-P23 exist privately perforated.

Issues of the Republic

Newspaper Stamps of 1916 Overprinted

1919
P24 N9 2h brown .25 *.80*
P25 N9 4h green .40 *6.50*
P26 N9 6h dark blue .25 *8.00*
P27 N9 10h orange .40 *9.50*
P28 N9 30h claret .25 *16.00*
Nos. P24-P28 (5) 1.55 *40.80*
Set, never hinged 3.25

Nos. P24-P28 exist privately perforated.

Mercury — N10

1920-21 *Imperf.*
P29 N10 2h violet .25 .25
P30 N10 4h brown .25 *.25*
P31 N10 5h slate .25 .25
P32 N10 6h turq blue .25 .25
P33 N10 8h green .25 *.40*
P34 N10 9h yellow ('21) .25 .25
P35 N10 10h red .25 .25
P36 N10 12h blue .25 *.40*
P37 N10 15h lilac ('21) .25 *.25*
P38 N10 18h blue grn ('21) .25 *.25*
P39 N10 20h orange .25 *.25*
P40 N10 30h yellow brn ('21) .25 .25
P41 N10 45h green ('21) .25 *.40*
P42 N10 60h claret .25 .25
P43 N10 72h chocolate ('21) .25 *.40*
P44 N10 90h violet ('21) .25 *.80*
P45 N10 1.20k red ('21) .25 *.80*
P46 N10 2.40k yellow grn ('21) .25 *.80*
P47 N10 3k gray ('21) .25 *.80*
Nos. P29-P47 (19) 7.55
Set, never hinged 4.00

Nos. P37-P40, P42, P44 and P47 exist also on thick grayish paper. Values are for the cheaper varieties. See the *Scott Classic Specialized Catalogue* for detailed listings.
Nos. P29-P47 exist privately perforated.

Mercury — N11

1921-22
P48 N11 45h gray .25 .25
P49 N11 75h brown org ('22) .25 .25
P50 N11 1.50k ol bister ('22) .25 .25
P51 N11 1.80k gray blue ('22) .25 .25
P52 N11 2.25k light brown .25 .25
P53 N11 3k dull green ('22) .25 .25
P54 N11 6k claret ('22) .25 *.25*
P55 N11 7.50k bister .25 *.40*
Nos. P48-P55 (8) *2.15*
Set, never hinged 4.75

Used values are for cancelled-to-order stamps. Postally used examples are worth much more.
Nos. P48-P55 exist privately perforated.

NEWSPAPER TAX STAMPS

> Values for unused stamps 1853-59 are for examples in fine condition with gum. Examples without gum sell for about one-third or less of the figures quoted.

Issues of the Monarchy

NT1

Unwmk.
1853, Mar. 1 Typo. *Imperf.*
PR1 NT1 2kr green 1,800. 57.50

The reprints are in finer print than the more coarsely printed originals, and on a smooth toned paper.

Values for Nos. PR2-PR9 are for stamps that do not show the watermark. Stamps showing the watermark often sell for more.

NT2

Two Types.
Type I — The banderol on the Crown of the left eagle touches the beak of the eagle.
Type II — The banderol does not touch the beak.

Wmk. 91, or, before July 1864, Unwmkd.

1858-59
PR2 NT2 1kr blue, type II ('59) 50.00 5.50
a. 1kr blue, type I 1,225. 190.00
b. Printed on both sides, type II —
PR3 NT2 2kr brn, type II ('59) 47.50 6.75
a. 2kr red brown, type II 600.00 240.00
PR4 NT2 4kr brn, type I 425.00 *1,100.*

Nos. PR2a, PR3a, and PR4 were printed only on unwatermarked paper. Nos. PR2 and PR3 exist on unwatermarked and watermarked paper.
Nos. PR2 and PR3 exist in coarse and (after 1874) in fine print, like the contemporary postage stamps.
The reprints of the 4kr brown are of type II and on a smooth toned paper.
Issue date: 4kr, Nov. 1.
See Lombardy-Venetia for the 1kr in black and the 2kr, 4fk in red.

NT3

1877 Redrawn
PR5 NT3 1kr blue 12.50 1.40
a. 1kr pale ultramarine *2,900.*
PR6 NT3 2kr brown 14.00 6.75

In the redrawn stamps the shield is larger and the vertical bar has eight lines above the white square and nine below, instead of five.
Nos. PR5 and PR6 exist also watermarked "WECHSEL" instead of "ZEITUNGS-MARKEN."

NT4

1890, June 1
PR7 NT4 1kr brown 9.00 1.00
PR8 NT4 2kr green 10.00 1.50

Nos. PR5-PR8 exist with private perforation.

NT5

1890, June 1 Wmk. 91 *Perf. 12½*
PR9 NT5 25kr carmine 95.00 *200.00*

Nos. PR1-PR9 did not pay postage, but were a fiscal tax, collected by the postal authorities on newspapers.

SPECIAL HANDLING STAMPS

(For Printed Matter Only)
Issues of the Monarchy

Mercury SH1

1916 Unwmk. *Perf. 12½*
QE1 SH1 2h claret, *yellow* 1.20 *4.00*
QE2 SH1 5h dp green, *yellow* 1.20 *4.00*
Set, never hinged 6.50

SH2

1917 *Perf. 12½*
QE3 SH2 2h claret, *yellow* .25 *.40*
a. Pair, imperf. between 325.00 *650.00*
Never hinged 650.00
b. Perf. 11½x12½ 150.00 *260.00*
Never hinged 800.00
c. Perf. 12½x11½ 225.00 *325.00*
Never hinged 950.00
d. Perf. 11½ 1.60 *4.00*
Never hinged 4.00
QE4 SH2 5h dp grn, *yel* .25 *.40*
a. Pair, imperf. between 325.00 *650.00*
Never hinged 650.00
b. Perf. 11½x12½ 120.00 *150.00*
Never hinged 800.00
c. Perf. 12½x11½ 190.00 *260.00*
Never hinged 950.00
d. Perf. 11½ 1.60 *4.00*
Never hinged 4.00
Set, never hinged 1.60

Nos. QE1-QE4 exist imperforate.

Issues of the Republic

Nos. QE3 and QE4 Overprinted

1919
QE5 SH2 2h claret, *yellow* .35 .25
a. Inverted overprint 325.00
Never hinged 650.00
b. Perf. 11½x12½ 6.00 *12.00*
Never hinged 10.50
c. Perf. 12½x11½ 110.00 *290.00*
Never hinged 325.00
d. Perf. 11½ .40 *1.25*
Never hinged 1.25
QE6 SH2 5h dp grn, *yel* .35 *.25*
a. Perf. 11½x12½ 1.60 *4.50*
Never hinged 4.00
b. Perf. 12½x11½ 40.00 *95.00*
Never hinged 87.50
c. Perf. 11½ .35 *.80*
Never hinged .80
Set, never hinged 1.60

Nos. QE5 and QE6 exist imperforate. Value, set unused hinged $175; never hinged $360.

No. QE3 Surcharged in Dark Blue

1921
QE7 SH2 50h on 2h claret, *yel* .25 *.80*
Never hinged .80

SH4

1922 *Perf. 12½*
QE8 SH4 50h lilac, *yellow* .25 *.25*
Never hinged .40

Nos. QE5-QE8 exist in vertical pairs, imperf between. No. QE8 exists imperf. Value: unused hinged $125; never hinged $250.

OCCUPATION STAMPS

Issued under Italian Occupation

Issued in Trieste

Austrian Stamps of 1916-18 Overprinted

1918 Unwmk. Perf. 12½

N1	A37	3h bright vio	1.60	1.60
a.		Double overprint	57.50	57.50
b.		Inverted overprint	57.50	57.50
N2	A37	5h light grn	1.60	1.60
a.		Inverted overprint	57.50	57.50
c.		Double overprint	—	57.50
N3	A37	6h dp orange	2.50	2.50
N4	A37	10h magenta	25.00	4.00
a.		Inverted overprint	57.50	57.50
N5	A37	12h light bl	3.25	3.25
a.		Double overprint	57.50	57.50
N6	A42	15h dull red	1.60	1.60
a.		Inverted overprint	57.50	57.50
b.		Double overprint	57.50	57.50
N7	A42	20h dark green	1.60	1.60
a.		Inverted overprint	57.50	57.50
c.		Double overprint	140.00	
N8	A42	25h deep blue	12.50	12.50
a.		Inverted overprint	225.00	225.00
N9	A42	30h dl violet	3.25	3.25
N10	A39	40h olive grn	275.00	*290.00*
N11	A39	50h dark green	12.50	12.50
N12	A39	60h deep blue	29.00	29.00
N13	A39	80h orange brn	20.00	20.00
a.		Inverted overprint	—	
N14	A39	1k car, *yel*	20.00	20.00
a.		Double overprint	130.00	
N15	A40	2k light bl	450.00	*500.00*
		Never hinged	900.00	
N16	A40	4k yellow grn	1,050.	*1,250.*
		Never hinged	2,600.	

Handstamped

N17	A40	10k dp violet	*30,000.*	*52,000.*
		Never hinged	*45,000.*	

Granite Paper

N18	A40	2k light blue	675.00	
		Never hinged	1,350.	
N19	A40	3k car rose	650.00	*700.00*
		Never hinged	1,300.	
		Nos. N1-N14 (14)	409.40	403.40
		Set, never hinged	975.00	

Some authorities question the authenticity of No. N18.

Counterfeits of Nos. N10, N15-N19 are plentiful.

A variety of N19 exists on ordinary paper. Only 50 examples are known. Values, $8,250 unused, $12,250 never hinged.

A 90h stamp was printed but not issued because the Austrian stamps were replaced by Italian stamps. Only 50 90h were printed. Values, $4,100 unused, $8,000 never hinged.

Italian Stamps of 1901-18 Overprinted

Wmk. 140 Perf. 14

N20	A42	1c brown	3.25	*8.25*
a.		Inverted overprint	32.50	32.50
N21	A43	2c orange brn	3.25	*8.25*
a.		Inverted overprint	29.00	29.00
N22	A48	5c green	2.50	2.50
a.		Inverted overprint	57.50	57.50
b.		Double overprint	140.00	
N23	A48	10c claret	2.50	2.50
a.		Inverted overprint	85.00	*85.00*
b.		Double overprint	140.00	
N24	A50	20c brn orange	2.50	*3.25*
a.		Inverted overprint	110.00	110.00
b.		Double overprint	130.00	130.00
N25	A49	25c blue	2.50	*4.00*
a.		Double overprint	—	
b.		Inverted overprint	130.00	130.00
N26	A49	40c brown	16.00	*29.00*
a.		Inverted overprint	—	
N27	A45	45c olive grn	6.50	*10.00*
a.		Inverted overprint	160.00	160.00
N28	A49	50c violet	12.50	12.50
N29	A49	60c brown car	85.00	*160.00*
a.		Inverted overprint	—	
b.		Double overprint	375.00	
N30	A46	1 l brn & green	40.00	*57.50*
a.		Inverted overprint	—	
		Nos. N20-N30 (11)	176.50	*297.75*
		Set, never hinged	525.00	

Italian Stamps of 1901-18 Surcharged

N31	A48	5h on 5c green	1.60	*3.25*
		Never hinged	4.00	
a.		"5" omitted	125.00	125.00
b.		Inverted surcharge	125.00	125.00
N32	A50	20h on 20c brn org	1.60	3.25
		Never hinged	4.00	
a.		Double surcharge	125.00	125.00

Issued in the Trentino

Austrian Stamps of 1916-18 Overprinted

1918 Unwmk. Perf. 12½

N33	A37	3h bright vio	12.50	12.50
a.		Double overprint	130.00	130.00
b.		Inverted overprint	125.00	125.00
N34	A37	5h light grn	10.00	5.00
a.		"8 nov. 1918"	*3,400.*	
b.		Inverted overprint	125.00	125.00
N35	A37	6h dp orange	125.00	110.00
N36	A37	10h magenta	10.00	8.25
a.		"8 nov. 1918"	250.00	250.00
N37	A37	12h light blue	325.00	290.00
N38	A42	15h dull red	12.50	10.00
N39	A42	20h dk grn	8.25	8.25
a.		"8 nov. 1918"	325.00	325.00
b.		Double overprint	130.00	130.00
c.		Inverted overprint	57.50	57.50
		Never hinged	*1,900.*	
N40	A42	25h deep blue	75.00	65.00
N41	A42	30h dl violet	29.00	25.00
		Never hinged	42.50	
N42	A39	40h olive grn	100.00	90.00
N43	A39	50h dk grn	65.00	50.00
a.		Inverted overprint	325.00	325.00
N44	A39	60h deep blue	110.00	90.00
a.		Double overprint	325.00	325.00
N45	A39	80h org brn	160.00	130.00
N46	A39	90h red violet	2,250.	3,100.
N47	A39	1k car, *yel*	150.00	125.00
N48	A40	2k light blue	750.00	*900.00*
N49	A40	4k yel green	*3,400.*	*4,100.*
N50a	A40	10k dp vio, gray ovpt.	*25,000.*	*25,000.*

Granite Paper

N51	A40	2k light blue	*1,650.*	*2,250.*
		Never hinged	*3,300.*	

Counterfeits of Nos. N33-N51 are plentiful.

Italian Stamps of 1901-18 Overprinted

Wmk. 140 Perf. 14

N52	A42	1c brown	4.00	*11.50*
a.		Inverted overprint	110.00	110.00
b.		Double overprint	125.00	
N53	A43	2c orange brn	4.00	*11.50*
a.		Inverted overprint	110.00	110.00
N54	A48	5c green	4.00	*11.50*
a.		Inverted overprint	110.00	110.00
b.		Double overprint	125.00	125.00
N55	A48	10c claret	4.00	*11.50*
a.		Inverted overprint	160.00	160.00
b.		Double overprint	125.00	125.00
N56	A50	20c brn orange	4.00	*11.50*
a.		Inverted overprint	160.00	160.00
N57	A49	40c brown	130.00	85.00
N58	A45	45c olive grn	65.00	85.00
a.		Double overprint	375.00	*375.00*
N59	A49	50c violet	65.00	*85.00*
N60	A46	1 l brn & green	65.00	*85.00*
a.		Double overprint	375.00	*375.00*
		Nos. N52-N60 (9)	345.00	397.50

Italian Stamps of 1906-18 Surcharged

N61	A48	5h on 5c green	2.50	*4.00*
N62	A48	10h on 10c claret	2.50	*4.00*
a.		Inverted overprint	110.00	*110.00*
N63	A50	20h on 20c brn org	2.50	*4.00*
a.		Double surcharge	110.00	*110.00*
		Nos. N61-N63 (3)	7.50	*12.00*

General Issue

Italian Stamps of 1901-18 Surcharged

1919

N64	A42	1c on 1c brown	1.60	*4.00*
a.		Inverted surcharge	25.00	25.00
N65	A43	2c on 2c org brn	1.60	*4.00*
a.		Double surcharge	375.00	
b.		Inverted surcharge	20.00	20.00
N66	A48	5c on 5c green	1.60	1.60
a.		Inverted surcharge	65.00	65.00
b.		Double surcharge	125.00	
N67	A48	10c on 10c claret	1.60	1.60
a.		Inverted surcharge	65.00	65.00
b.		Double surcharge	125.00	125.00
N68	A50	20c on 20c brn org	1.60	1.60
a.		Double surcharge	160.00	*160.00*
b.		Half used as 10c on cover		400.00
N69	A49	25c on 25c blue	1.60	*2.50*
a.		Double surcharge	160.00	
N70	A49	40c on 40c brown	1.60	*4.00*
a.		"ccrona"	150.00	150.00
N71	A45	45c on 45c ol grn	1.60	*4.00*
a.		Inverted surcharge	180.00	180.00
N72	A49	50c on 50c violet	1.60	*4.00*
N73	A49	60c on 60c brn car	1.60	*4.00*
a.		"00" for "60"	180.00	*180.00*

Italian No. 87 Surcharged

N74	A46	1cor on 1 l brn & green	5.00	*10.00*
		Nos. N64-N74 (11)	21.00	41.30

Surcharges similar to these but differing in style or arrangement of type were used in Dalmatia.

OCCUPATION SPECIAL DELIVERY STAMPS

Issued in Trieste

Special Delivery Stamp of Italy of 1903 Overprinted

1918 Wmk. 140 Perf. 14

NE1	SD1	25c rose red	75.00	130.00
a.		Inverted overprint	400.00	400.00

General Issue

Special Delivery Stamps of Italy of 1903-09 Surcharged

1919

NE2	SD1	25c on 25c rose	2.50	*3.25*
a.		Double surcharge	130.00	130.00
NE3	SD2	30c on 30c bl & rose	4.00	*6.50*
a.		Pair, one stamp without surcharge		*1,500.*

OCCUPATION POSTAGE DUE STAMPS

Issued in Trieste

Postage Due Stamps of Italy, 1870-94, Overprinted

1918 Wmk. 140 Perf. 14

NJ1	D3	5c buff & mag	1.60	1.60
a.		Inverted overprint	29.00	29.00
b.		Double overprint	260.00	
NJ2	D3	10c buff & mag	1.60	1.60
a.		Inverted overprint	110.00	110.00
NJ3	D3	20c buff & mag	3.25	3.25
a.		Double overprint	260.00	
b.		Inverted overprint	110.00	*110.00*
NJ4	D3	30c buff & mag	6.50	6.50
NJ5	D3	40c buff & mag	50.00	*60.00*
a.		Inverted overprint	375.00	375.00
NJ6	D3	50c buff & mag	110.00	*160.00*
a.		Inverted overprint	450.00	450.00
NJ7	D3	1 l bl & mag	250.00	*500.00*
		Nos. NJ1-NJ7 (7)	422.95	732.95

General Issue

Postage Due Stamps of Italy, 1870-1903 Surcharged

1919 Buff & Magenta

NJ8	D3	5c on 5c	2.50	2.50
a.		Inverted overprint	37.50	37.50
NJ9	D3	10c on 10c	2.50	2.50
a.		Center and surcharge invtd.	260.00	260.00
NJ10	D3	20c on 20c	4.00	2.50
a.		Double overprint	260.00	260.00
NJ11	D3	30c on 30c	4.00	*5.00*
NJ12	D3	40c on 40c	4.00	*5.00*
NJ13	D3	50c on 50c	6.50	*8.25*

Surcharged

NJ14	D3	1cor on 1 l bl & mag	6.50	*12.50*
NJ15	D3	2cor on 2 l bl & mag	75.00	*160.00*
NJ16	D3	5cor on 5 l bl & mag	75.00	*160.00*
		Nos. NJ8-NJ16 (9)	180.00	358.25

A. M. G. ISSUE FOR AUSTRIA

Catalogue values for unused stamps in this section are for Never Hinged items.

Issued jointly by the Allied Military Government of the US and Great Britain, for civilian use in areas under American, British and French occupation. (Upper Austria, Salzburg, Tyrol, Vorarlberg, Styria and Carinthia).

OS1

1945 Unwmk. Litho. Perf. 11

4N1	OS1	1g aquamarine	.25	*.25*
4N2	OS1	3g deep orange	.25	*.25*
4N3	OS1	4g buff	.25	*.25*
4N4	OS1	5g bright green	.25	*.25*
4N5	OS1	6g red violet	.25	*.25*
4N6	OS1	8g rose pink	.25	*.25*
4N7	OS1	10g light gray	.25	.25
4N8	OS1	12g pale buff brown	.25	.25
4N9	OS1	15g rose red	.25	.25
4N10	OS1	20g copper brown	.25	.25
4N11	OS1	25g deep blue	.30	*.30*
4N12	OS1	30g bright violet	.30	*.30*
4N13	OS1	40g light ultra	.30	*.30*
4N14	OS1	60g light olive grn	.40	.40
4N15	OS1	1s dark violet	.40	*.40*
4N16	OS1	2s yellow	.95	*.95*
4N17	OS1	5s deep ultra	.95	*.95*
		Nos. 4N1-4N17 (17)	6.10	6.10

Used values are for examples with philatelic favor cancels. Postally used are worth much more.

For Nos. 4N2, 4N4-4N17 overprinted "PORTO" see Nos. J189-J203.

AUSTRIAN OFFICES ABROAD

These stamps were on sale and usable at all Austrian post-offices in Crete and in the Turkish Empire.

100 Centimes = 1 Franc

OFFICES IN CRETE

Used values are italicized for stamps often found with false cancellations.

Stamps of Austria of 1899-1901 Issue, Surcharged in Black

a

b

c

d

On Nos. 73a, 75a, 77a, 81a
Granite Paper
With Varnish Bars

1903-04 Unwmk. *Perf. 12½, 13½*

1 A15(a) 5c on 5h blue green 1.10 *3.25*
2 A16(b) 10c on 10h rose .50 *4.25*
3 A16(b) 25c on 25h ultra 42.50 27.00
4 A17(c) 50c on 50h gray blue 8.50 *110.00*

On Nos. 83, 83a, 84, 85
Without Varnish Bars

5 A18(d) 1fr on 1k car rose 1.35 *87.50*
a. 1fr on 1k carmine 8.50 *87.50*
b. Horiz. pair, imperf. btwn. *230.00* —
c. Vert. pair, imperf. btwn. — —
6 A18(d) 2fr on 2k ('04) 8.00 *325.00*
7 A18(d) 4fr on 4k ('04) 11.50 *600.00*
Nos. 1-7 (7) 73.45 1,157.

Surcharged on Austrian Stamps of 1904-05
On Nos. 89, 97

1905 Without Varnish Bars

8a A19(a) 5c on 5h blue green 52.50 47.50
9 A20(b) 10c on 10h car 1.10 *12.00*

On Nos. 89a, 97a, 99a, 103a
With Varnish Bars

8 A19(a) 5c on 5h bl grn 3.25 6.25
9a A20(b) 10c on 10h carmine 32.50 32.50
10 A20(b) 25c on 25h ultra 1.10 *115.00*
11 A21(b) 50c on 50h dl bl 2.75 *475.00*

Surcharged on Austrian Stamps and Type of 1906-07
Without Varnish Bars

1907 *Perf. 12½, 13½*

12 A19(a) 5c on 5h yel green (#90) 1.10 *3.25*
13 A20(b) 10c on 10h car (#92) 1.50 *22.00*
14 A20(b) 15c on 15h vio 1.75 *25.00*
Nos. 12-14 (3) 4.35 *50.25*

A5

A6

1908 Typo. *Perf. 12½*

15 A5 5c green, *yellow* .35 *1.25*
a. Imperf. pair 80.00
16 A5 10c scarlet, *rose* .40 *1.25*
a. Imperf. pair 80.00
17 A5 15c brown, *buff* .45 *4.75*
a. Imperf. pair 80.00
18 A5 25c dp blue, *blue* 15.00 3.75
b. As "#18", imperf. pair 80.00

Engr.

19 A6 50c lake, *yellow* 2.75 *32.50*
a. Imperf. pair 80.00
20 A6 1fr brown, *gray* 6.75 *60.00*
a. Vert pair, imperf. btwn. *225.00*
b. As "#20", imperf. pair 80.00
Nos. 15-20 (6) 25.70 *103.50*

Nos. 15-18 are on paper colored on the surface only. All values exist imperforate. Value, each pair $75.

60th year of the reign of Emperor Franz Josef, for permanent use.

Paper Colored Through

1914 Typo.

21 A5 10c rose, *rose* 1.25 *2,000.*
a. Imperf. pair 80.00
22 A5 25c ultra, *blue* 2.25 *150.00*
a. Imperf. pair 80.00

Nos. 21 and 22 exist imperforate. Value, each pair $75.

OFFICES IN THE TURKISH EMPIRE

From 1863 to 1867 the stamps of Lombardy-Venetia (Nos. 15 to 24) were used at the Austrian Offices in the Turkish Empire.

100 Soldi = 1 Florin
40 Paras = 1 Piaster

Values for unused stamps are for examples with gum. Examples without gum sell for about one-third or less of the figures quoted. Used values are italicized for stamps often found with false cancellations.

For similar designs in Kreuzers, see early Austria.

A1

A2

Two different printing methods were used, as in the 1867-74 issues of Austria. They may be distinguished by the coarse or fine lines of the hair and whiskers and by the paper, which is more transparent on the later issue.

1867 Typo. Wmk. 91 *Perf. 9½*
Coarse Print

1 A1 2sld orange 2.40 *27.50*
a. 2sld yellow 65.00 80.00
2 A1 3sld green 150.00 67.50
a. 3sld dark green 325.00 200.00
3 A1 5sld red 240.00 14.00
a. 5sld carmine 325.00 40.00
b. 5sld red lilac 275.00 24.00
4 A1 10sld blue 200.00 2.40
a. 10sld light blue 275.00 3.25
b. 10sld dark blue 240.00 3.25
5 A1 15sld brown 24.00 8.00
a. 15sld dark brown 95.00 65.00
b. 15sld reddish brown 40.00 16.00
c. 15sld gray brown 80.00 16.00
6 A1 25sld violet 24.00 *40.00*
a. 25sld brown violet 40.00 *60.00*
b. 25sld gray lilac 120.00 47.50
7 A2 50sld brn, perf. 10½ 1.25 *65.00*
a. Perf. 12 100.00 *110.00*
b. Perf. 13 325.00 —
k. Perf. 9 27.50 *140.00*
l. 50sld pale red brn, perf. 12 160.00 160.00
m. Vert. pair, imperf. btwn. 300.00 *550.00*
n. Horiz. pair, imperf. btwn. 300.00 *550.00*
o. Perf. 10½x9 85.00 *160.00*

Perf. 9, 9½, 10½ and Compound

1876-83 Fine Print

7C A1 2sld yellow ('83) .40 *3,000.*
7D A1 3sld green ('78) 1.20 27.50
7E A1 5sld red ('78) .40 *24.00*
7F A1 10sld blue 100.00 1.25
7I A1 15sld org brn ('81) 12.00 *160.00*
7J A1 25sld gray lil ('83) .80 *360.00*
Nos. 7C-7J (6) 114.80 3,573.

The 10 soldi was reprinted in deep dull blue, perforated 10½. Value, $6.50.

A3

1883 *Perf. 9½*

8 A3 2sld brown .25 *190.00*
9 A3 3sld green 1.20 *35.00*
10 A3 5sld rose .25 *20.00*
11 A3 10sld blue .80 .80
12 A3 20sld gray, perf. 10 6.50 *600.00*
a. Perf. 9½ 1.60 *9.50*
13 A3 50sld red lilac 1.25 *20.00*
Nos. 8-13 (6) 10.25 865.80

No. 9 Surcharged

10 PARAS ON 3 SOLDI:
Type I — Surcharge 16½mm across. "PARA" about ½mm above bottom of "10." 2mm space between "10" and "P"; 1½mm between "A" and "10." Perf. 9½ only.
Type II — Surcharge 15¼ to 16mm across. "PARA" on same line with figures or slightly higher or lower. 1½mm space between "10" and "P"; 1mm between "A" and "10." Perf. 9½ and 10.

1886 *Perf. 9½, 10*

14 A4 10pa on 3sld grn, type II, perf. 10 .35 *8.00*
a. 10pa on 3sld green, type I 200.00 500.00
b. Inverted surcharge, type I *2,000.*

Surcharged on Austria Nos. 42-46

1888

15 A11 10pa on 3kr grn 4.00 12.00
a. "01 PARA 10" *1,200.*
16 A11 20pa on 5kr rose .40 *12.00*
a. Double surcharge 400.00
Never hinged 1,200.
17 A11 1pi on 10kr blue 65.00 1.60
a. Perf. 13½ 800.00
b. Double surcharge —
18 A11 2pi on 20kr gray 1.60 *6.50*
19 A11 5pi on 50kr vio 2.00 *20.00*
Nos. 15-19 (5) 73.00 52.10

Austria Nos. 52-55, 58, 61 Surcharged

1890-92 Unwmk. *Perf. 9 to 13½*
Granite Paper

20 A12 8pa on 2kr brn ('92) .25 *.65*
a. Perf. 9½ 12.00 16.00
21 A12 10pa on 3kr green .55 .65
a. Pair, imperf. between *550.00*
22 A12 20pa on 5kr rose .35 *.65*
23 A12 1pi on 10kr ultra .40 .25
a. Pair, imperf. between *550.00*
24 A12 2pi on 20kr ol grn 8.00 *32.50*
25 A12 5pi on 50kr vio 12.00 *72.50*
Nos. 20-25 (6) 21.55 *107.20*

See note after Austria No. 65 on missing numerals, etc.

Austria Nos. 66, 69 Surcharged

1891 *Perf. 10 to 13½*

26 A14 2pi on 20kr green 6.50 1.60
a. Perf. 9¼ 200.00 160.00
27 A14 5pi on 50kr violet 3.25 3.25

Two types of the surcharge on No. 26 exist.

Austria Nos. 62-65 Surcharged

1892 *Perf. 10½, 11½*

28 A13 10pi on 1gld blue 12.00 *32.50*
29 A13 20pi on 2gld car 16.00 *60.00*
a. Double surcharge —

1896 *Perf. 10½, 11½, 12½*

30 A13 10pi on 1gld pale lil 18.50 *22.50*
31 A13 20pi on 2gld gray grn 37.50 *75.00*

Austria Nos. 73, 75, 77, 81, 83-85 Surcharged

#32-35

#36-38

Perf. 10½, 12½, 13½ and Compound

1900 Without Varnish Bars

32 A15 10pa on 5h bl grn 4.75 .80
33 A16 20pa on 10h rose 5.50 .80
b. Perf. 12½x10½ 400.00 350.00
34 A16 1pi on 25h ultra 3.25 .40
35 A17 2pi on 50h gray bl 8.00 4.00
36 A18 5pi on 1k car rose .55 .40
a. 5pi on 1k carmine .80 *1.20*
b. Horiz. or vert. pair, imperf. btwn. 160.00
37 A18 10pi on 2k gray lil 2.00 *3.50*
38 A18 20pi on 4k gray grn 1.60 *8.00*
Nos. 32-38 (7) 25.65 *17.90*

In the surcharge on Nos. 37 and 38 "piaster" is printed "PIAST."

1901 With Varnish Bars

32a A15 10pa on 5h blue green 1.60 2.75
33a A16 20pa on 10h rose 2.40 *400.00*
34a A16 1pi on 25h ultra 1.20 .80
35b A17 2pi on 50h gray blue 2.75 8.00
Nos. 32a-35b (4) 7.95 411.55

A4

A5

A6

1906 *Perf. 12½ to 13½*
Without Varnish Bars

39 A4 10pa dark green 12.00 4.00
40 A5 20pa rose .80 *1.20*
41 A5 1pi ultra .80 .40
42 A6 2pi gray blue .80 *1.20*
Nos. 39-42 (4) 14.40 6.80

1903 With Varnish Bars

39a A4 10pa dark green 4.75 2.00
40a A5 20pa rose 3.25 .80
41a A5 1pi ultra 2.40 .40
42a A6 2pi gray blue 160.00 3.25
Nos. 39a-42a (4) 170.40 6.45

1907 Without Varnish Bars

43 A4 10pa yellow green .55 *2.00*
45 A5 30pa violet .55 *4.00*

A7

A8

1908 Typo. *Perf. 12½*

46	A7	10pa green, *yellow*	.25	*.40*
47	A7	20pa scarlet, *rose*	.25	*.40*
48	A7	30pa brown, *buff*	.40	*2.00*
49	A7	1pi deep bl, *blue*	14.50	.25
50	A7	60pa vio, *bluish*	.65	*5.50*

Engr.

51	A8	2pi lake, *yellow*	.65	.25
52	A8	5pi brown, *gray*	.65	*.95*
53	A8	10pi green, *yellow*	.95	*2.40*
54	A8	20pi blue, *gray*	2.40	*4.75*
		Nos. 46-54 (9)	20.70	*16.90*

Nos. 46-50 are on paper colored on the surface only. 60th year of the reign of Emperor Franz Josef I, for permanent use.

Nos. 46-50 exist imperforate. Values, set: unused $275, never hinged $650.

Paper Colored Through

1913-14 Typo.

57	A7	20pa rose, *rose* ('14)	.55	*650.00*
58	A7	1pi ultra, *blue*	.35	*.55*

Nos. 57 and 58 exist imperforate.

POSTAGE DUE STAMPS

Type of Austria D2 Surcharged in Black

1902 Unwmk. *Perf. 12½, 13½*

J1	D2	10pa on 5h gray green	1.60	*8.00*
J2	D2	20pa on 10h gray green	1.60	*12.00*
J3	D2	1pi on 20h gray green	1.60	*12.00*
J4	D2	2pi on 40h gray green	1.60	*12.00*
J5	D2	5pi on 100h gray green	1.60	*8.00*
		Nos. J1-J5 (5)	8.00	*52.00*

Shades of Nos. J1-J5 exist, varying from yellowish to dark green.

D3

1908 Typo. *Perf. 12½*
Chalky Paper

J6	D3	¼pi pale green	3.25	*13.50*
J7	D3	½pi pale green	2.00	*11.00*
J8	D3	1pi pale green	2.40	*8.00*
J9	D3	1½pi pale green	1.20	*24.00*
J10	D3	2pi pale green	1.60	*20.00*
J11	D3	5pi pale green	2.40	*14.50*
J12	D3	10pi pale green	16.00	*150.00*
J13	D3	20pi pale green	11.00	*160.00*
J14	D3	30pi pale green	16.00	14.50
		Nos. J6-J14 (9)	55.85	*415.50*

Nos. J6-J14 exist in distinct shades of green and on thick chalky, regular and thin ordinary paper. Values are for the least expensive variety. For comprehensive listings, see Scott Classic Specialized Catalogue.

No. J6-J14 exist imperforate.

Forgeries exist.

DANUBE STEAM NAVIGATION COMPANY

The Danube Steam Navigation Co. was formed in 1830, servicing Austrian public, military and consular post offices in and in the area of the Ottoman Empire. In 1846 the company became the official carrier for the Austrian Post Office, while continuing their private mail service. In 1866, on the authority of the Austrian Post Office, the company began the use of its own adhesive stamps. For a detailed listing, see Scott *Classic Specialized Catalogue of Stamps and Covers 1840-1940.*

LOMBARDY-VENETIA

Formerly a kingdom in the north of Italy forming part of the Austrian Empire. Milan and Venice were the two principal cities. Lombardy was annexed to Sardinia in 1859, and Venetia to the kingdom of Italy in 1866.

100 Centesimi = 1 Lira
100 Soldi = 1 Florin (1858)

Unused examples without gum of Nos. 1-24 are worth approximately 20% of the values given, which are for stamps with original gum as defined in the catalogue introduction.

For similar designs in Kreuzers, see early Austria.

Coat of Arms — A1

15 CENTESIMI:
Type I — "5" is on a level with the "1." One heavy line around coat of arms center.
Type II — As type I, but "5" is a trifle sideways and is higher than the "1."
Type III — As type II, but two, thinner, lines around center.
30 CENTESIMI:
Type I — Lower ball of "3" is oblong, squashed
Type II — Lower ball of "3" is circular
45 CENTESIMI:
Type I — Lower part of "45" is lower than "Centes." One heavy line around coat of arms center. "45" varies in height and distance from "Centes."
Type II — One heavy line around coat of arms center. Lower part of "45" is on a level with lower part of "Centes."
Type III — As type II, but two, thinner, lines around center.

Wmk. K.K.H.M. in Sheet or Unwmkd.

1850 Typo. *Imperf.*
Thick to Thin Paper

1	A1	5c buff	4,600.	150.00
		On cover, single franking		425.00
a.		Printed on both sides	*22,750.*	625.00
b.		5c yellow	*8,550.*	460.00
c.		5c orange	5,000.	175.00
d.		5c lemon yellow	—	*1,850.*
3	A1	10c black	5,750.	150.00
a.		10c gray black	5,750.	150.00
4	A1	15c red, type III	2,600.	6.00
b.		15c red, type I	*3,750.*	25.00
c.		Ribbed paper, type II	—	750.00
d.		Ribbed paper, type I	*31,500.*	200.00
f.		15c red, type II	*3,500.*	23.00
5	A1	30c brown, type II	7,250.	25.00
a.		Ribbed paper, type I	13,000.	160.00
6	A1	45c blue, type III	*23,000.*	57.50
a.		45c blue, type I	*25,750.*	57.50
b.		Ribbed paper, type I	—	630.00
c.		45c blue, type II	*205,000.*	72.50

1854
Machine-made Paper, Types II or III

3c	A1	10c black	*15,000.*	450.00
4g	A1	15c pale red	*2,600.*	5.00
5b	A1	30c brown, type II ('55)	*9,250.*	20.00
6d	A1	45c blue	*20,000.*	70.00

See note about the paper of the 1850 issue of Austria. *The reprints are type III, in brighter colors.*

A2

A3

A4

A5

A6

Two Types of Each Value.
Type I — Loops of the bow at the back of the head broken.
Type II — Loops complete. Wreath projects further at top of head.

1858-62 Embossed *Perf. 14½*

7	A2	2s yel, type II	2,275.	125.00
a.		2s yellow, type I	11,500.	800.00
8	A3	3s black, type II	18,250.	160.00
a.		3s black, type I	8,750.	300.00
b.		Perf. 16, type I	—	1,850.
c.		Perf. 15x16 or 16x15, type I	*11,500.*	575.00
9	A3	3s grn, type II ('62)	1,250.	120.00
10	A4	5s red, type II	575.00	9.25
a.		5s red, type I	2,850.	45.00
b.		Printed on both sides, type II		*5,250.*
11	A5	10s brn, type II	8,000.	21.00
a.		10s brown, type I	1,250.	130.00
12	A6	15s blue, type II	8,750.	115.00
		No gum	2,150.	
a.		15s blue, type I	16,000.	240.00
b.		Printed on both sides, type II		*14,250.*

The reprints are of type II and are perforated 10½, 11, 11½, 12, 12½ and 13. There are also imperforate reprints of Nos. 7-9.

A7

1861-62 *Perf. 14*

13	A7	5s red	6,850.	8.00
14	A7	10s brown ('62)	13,750.	57.50

The reprints are perforated 9, 9 ½, 10½, 11, 12, 12½ and 13. There are also imperforate reprints of the 2 and 3s.

The 2, 3 and 15s of this type exist only as reprints.

A8

1863

15	A8	2s yellow	325.00	175.00
16	A8	3s green	5,750.	100.00
17	A8	5s rose	7,400.	35.00
18	A8	10s blue	15,000.	75.00
19	A8	15s yellow brown	11,500.	285.00

1864-65 Wmk. 91 *Perf. 9½*

20	A8	2s yellow ('65)	525.00	*750.00*
21	A8	3s green	57.50	50.00
22	A8	5s rose	14.50	9.00
23	A8	10s blue	105.00	20.00
24	A8	15s yellow brown	940.00	200.00

Nos. 15-24 reprints are perforated 10½ and 13. There are also imperforate reprints of the 2s and 3s.

NEWSPAPER TAX STAMPS

From 1853 to 1858 the Austrian Newspaper Tax Stamp 2kr green (No. PR1) was also used in Lombardy-Venetia, at the value of 10 centesimi.

NT1

Type I — The banderol of the left eagle touches the beak of the eagle.
Type II — The banderol does not touch the beak.

1858-59 Unwmk. Typo. *Imperf.*

PR1	NT1	1kr black, type I ('59)	8,000.	*6,750.*
PR2	NT1	2kr red, type II ('59)	1,000.	85.00
a.		Watermark 91	1,300.	100.00
PR3	NT1	4kr red, type I	*200,000.*	*6,250.*

The reprints are on a smooth toned paper and are all of type II.

AZERBAIJAN

ˌa-zər-ˌbī-ˈjän

(Azerbaidjan)

LOCATION — Southernmost part of Russia in Eastern Europe, bounded by Georgia, Dagestan, Caspian Sea, Iran and Armenia
GOVT. — A Soviet Socialist Republic
AREA — 33,430 sq. mi.
POP. — 7,908,224 (1999 est)
CAPITAL — Baku

With Armenia and Georgia, Azerbaijan made up the Transcaucasian Federation of Soviet Republics.

Stamps of Azerbaijan were replaced in 1923 by those of Transcaucasian Federated Republics.

With the breakup of the Soviet Union on Dec. 26, 1991, Azerbaijan and ten former Soviet republics established the Commonwealth of Independent States.

100 Kopecks = 1 Ruble
100 Giapiks = 1 Manat (1992)

Catalogue values for unused stamps in this country are for Never Hinged items, beginning with Scott 350 in the regular postage section, and Scott C1 in the air post section.

Forgeries of No. 1-333 abound. Values are for genuine stamps.

National Republic

Standard Bearer — A1

Farmer at Sunset — A2

Baku — A3

Temple of Eternal Fires — A4

1919 Unwmk. Litho. *Imperf.*

On White Paper

1	A1	10k multicolored	2.00	*2.75*
2	A1	20k multicolored	2.00	*2.75*
3	A2	40k green, yellow & blk	1.40	*2.75*
4	A2	60k red, yellow & blk	1.40	*2.75*
5	A2	1r blue, yellow & blk	2.50	*4.00*
6	A3	2r red, bister & blk	2.50	*4.00*
7	A3	5r blue, bister & blk	2.00	*4.00*
8	A3	10r olive grn, bis & blk	2.50	*4.00*
9	A4	25r blue, red & black	5.50	*8.50*
10	A4	50r ol grn, red & black	3.50	*7.00*
		Nos. 1-10 (10)	25.30	*42.50*

For surcharges see Nos. 57-64, 75-80.

1920

On Grayish Paper

1A	A1	10k multicolored	1.00	*2.00*
2A	A1	20k multicolored	1.00	*2.00*
3A	A2	40k green, yellow & blk	1.00	*2.00*
4A	A2	60k red, yellow & blk	1.00	*2.00*
5A	A2	1r blue, yellow & blk	1.00	*2.00*
6A	A3	2r red, bister & blk	1.25	*2.50*
7A	A3	5r blue, bister & blk	1.00	*2.00*
8A	A3	10r olive grn, bis & blk	1.25	*2.50*
9A	A4	25r blue, red & black	2.25	*5.00*
10A	A4	50r ol grn, red & black	1.00	*2.00*
		Nos. 1A-10A (10)	11.75	*24.00*

Used values for Nos. 1-10A are for stamps with average cancellations or favor cancellations. Examples showing the city and date of use sell for much higher prices.

Soviet Socialist Republic

Symbols of Labor — A5

Oil Well — A6

Bibi Eibatt Oil Field — A7

Khan's Palace, Baku — A8

Globe and Workers — A9

Maiden's Tower, Baku — A10

Goukasoff House A11

Blacksmiths — A12

Hall of Judgment, Baku — A13

1922

15	A5	1r gray green	.60	
16	A6	2r olive black	.40	
17	A7	5r gray brown	.40	
18	A8	10r gray	.40	
19	A9	25r orange brown	.60	
20	A10	50r violet	.60	*4.00*
21	A11	100r dull red	1.00	*4.00*
22	A12	150r blue	.75	*2.50*
23	A9	250r violet & buff	.75	*3.50*
24	A13	400r dark blue	.75	*4.00*
25	A12	500r gray vio & blk	.60	*3.50*
26	A13	1000r dk blue & rose	.75	*2.50*
27	A8	2000r blue & black	.40	*1.25*
28	A7	3000r brown & blue	.40	*1.25*
a.		Tete beche pair	20.00	
29	A11	5000r black, *ol grn*	.60	*1.75*
		Nos. 15-29 (15)	9.00	*28.25*

Used values are for favor-canceled stamps. Postally used examples sell for much higher prices.

For overprints and surcharges see Nos. 32-41, 43, 45-55, 65-72, 300-304, 307-333.

Nos. 15, 17, 23, 28, 27 Handstamped from Metal Dies in a Numbering Machine

1922

32	A5	10,000r on 1r	30.00	25.00
33	A7	15,000r on 5r	20.00	*27.50*
34	A9	33,000r on 250r	20.00	20.00
35	A7	50,000r on 3000r	20.00	20.00
36	A8	66,000r on 2000r	35.00	25.00
		Nos. 32-36 (5)	125.00	117.50

Same Surcharges on Regular Issue and Semi-Postal Stamps of 1922

1922-23

36A	A7	500r on 5r	250.00	
37	A6	1000r on 2r	25.00	*25.00*
38	A8	2000r on 10r	18.00	*20.00*
39	A8	5000r on 2000r	12.00	4.00
40	A11	15,000r on 5000r	50.00	10.00
41	A5	20,000r on 1r	100.00	30.00
42	SP1	25,000r on 500r	*100.00*	—
43	A7	50,000r on 5r	100.00	60.00
44	SP2	50,000r on 1000r	*150.00*	—
45	A11	50,000r on 5000r	25.00	25.00
45A	A8	60,000r on 2000r	120.00	*225.00*
46	A11	70,000r on 5000r	200.00	75.00
47	A6	100,000r on 2r	25.00	18.00
48	A8	200,000r on 10r	20.00	15.00
49	A9	200,000r on 25r	20.00	15.00
50	A7	300,000r on 3000r	50.00	50.00
51	A8	500,000r on 2000r	30.00	30.00

Regular Issue Stamps of 1922-23 Surcharged

52	A7	500r on #33	*650.00*	*700.00*
53	A11	15,000r on #46	*650.00*	*700.00*
54	A7	300,000r on #35	*750.00*	*800.00*
55	A8	500,000r on #36	*650.00*	*750.00*

The surcharged semi-postal stamps were used for regular postage.

Same Surcharges on Stamps of 1919

57	A1	25,000r on 10k	2.00	*3.50*
58	A1	50,000r on 20k	2.00	*3.50*
59	A2	75,000r on 40k	2.00	*5.00*
60	A2	100,000r on 60k	2.00	*3.50*
61	A2	200,000r on 1r	2.00	*5.00*
62	A3	300,000r on 2r	2.00	*5.00*
63	A3	500,000r on 5r	2.00	*7.00*
64	A2	750,000r on 40k	20.00	
		Nos. 57-64 (8)	34.00	*32.50*

Handstamped from Settings of Rubber Type in Black or Violet

Nos. 65-66, 72-80

Nos. 67-70

On Stamps of 1922

65	A6	100,000r on 2r	100.00	—
66	A8	200,000r on 10r	100.00	*100.00*
67	A8	200,000r on 10r (V)	50.00	50.00
68	A9	200,000r on 25r (V)	80.00	80.00
a.		Black surcharge	80.00	*80.00*
69	A7	300,000r on 3000r (V)	50.00	50.00
70	A8	500,000r on 2000r (V)	72.50	72.50
a.		Black surcharge	90.00	*90.00*
72	A11	1,500,000r on 5000r (V)	140.00	140.00
a.		Black surcharge	120.00	120.00

On Stamps of 1919

75	A1	50,000r on 20k	4.00
76	A2	75,000r on 40k	4.00
77	A2	100,000r on 60k	4.00
78	A2	200,000r on 1r	4.00
79	A3	300,000r on 2r	4.00
80	A3	500,000r on 5r	4.00

Inverted and double surcharges of Nos. 32-80 sell for twice the normal price.

Counterfeits exist of Nos. 32-80.

Baku Province

Regular and Semi-Postal Stamps of 1922 Handstamped in Violet or Black

The overprint reads "Bakinskoi P(ochtovoy) K(ontory)," meaning Baku Post Office.

1922 Unwmk. *Imperf.*

300	A5	1r gray green	*100.00*	
301	A7	5r gray brown	*100.00*	*200.00*
302	A12	150r blue	*100.00*	*150.00*
303	A9	250r violet & buff	*100.00*	*200.00*
304	A13	400r dark blue	*75.00*	*100.00*
305	SP1	500r bl & pale bl	*100.00*	*150.00*
306	SP2	1000r brown & bis	*100.00*	
307	A8	2000r blue & black	*120.00*	*150.00*
308	A7	3000r brown & blue	*100.00*	250.00
309	A11	5000r black, *ol grn*	*120.00*	
		Nos. 300-309 (10)	*1,015.*	

Stamps of 1922 Handstamped in Violet

БАКИНСКАГО Г-П-Т.О.№1

Ovpt. reads: Baku Post, Telegraph Office No. 1.

1924 Overprint 24x2mm

312	A12	150r blue	*65.00*
313	A9	250r violet & buff	*65.00*
314	A13	400r dark blue	*65.00*
317	A8	2000r blue & black	*65.00*
318	A7	3000r brn & blue	*65.00*
319	A11	5000r black, *ol grn*	*200.00*

Overprint 30x3½mm

323	A12	150r blue		100.00	125.00
324	A9	250r violet & buff		100.00	
325	A13	400r dark blue		100.00	100.00
328	A8	2000r blue & black		100.00	100.00
329	A7	3000r brn & blue		100.00	150.00
330	A11	5000r black, *ol grn*		100.00	

Overprinted on Nos. 32-33, 35

331	A5	10,000r on 1r	500.00	
332	A7	15,000r on 5r	500.00	
333	A7	50,000r on 3000r	500.00	
		Nos. 312-333 (15)	2,625.	

The overprinted semipostal stamps were used for regular postage.

A 24x2mm handstamp on #17, B1-B2, and 30x3½mm on Nos. 15, 17, B1-B2, was of private origin.

A set of five pictorial labels featuring different scenes, purportedly an unissued set from Azerbaijan, is a private production, likely created by an Italian stamp dealer in 1921 or 1922. The labels are of nominal value. Forgeries exist. Both the original set and the forgeries exist perforated and imperforate.

Catalogue values for unused stamps in this section, from this point to the end of the section, are for Never Hinged items.

Flag, Map — A20

Unwmk.

1992, Mar. 26 Litho. *Perf. 14*

350 A20 35k multicolored 1.50 1.50

For surcharge, see No. 733.

Caspian Sea — A21

1992, May 7 *Perf. 12*

351	A21 25g on 15k multi		.40	.40
a.	Booklet pane of 12		5.00	
	Complete booklet, #351a		6.00	
352	A21 35g on 15k multi		.50	.50
353	A21 50g on 15k multi		.65	.65
354	A21 1.50m on 15k multi		2.25	2.25
355	A21 2.50m on 15k multi		3.50	3.50
	Nos. 351-355 (5)		7.30	7.30

Nos. 351-355 are sucharged on the Azerbaijan value of a National Park series featuring one stamp for each republic, prepared by the Soviet Union but not issued. Value for the unoverprinted Azerbaijan stamp, $1.25.

For additional surcharges see Nos. 435, 501-504.

Iran-Azerbaijan Telecommunications — A21a

1993 Photo. *Perf. 13x13½*

355A A21a 15g multicolored 1.25 1.25

See Iran No. 2544.
For surcharges see Nos. 403-406.

Horses A22

1993, Feb. 1 Litho. *Perf. 13*

356	A22	20g shown	.25	.25
357	A22	30g Kabarda	.25	.25
358	A22	50g Qarabair	.25	.25
359	A22	1m Don	.25	.25
360	A22	2.50m Yakut	.40	.40
361	A22	5m Orlov	.80	.80
362	A22	10m Diliboz	1.75	1.75
		Nos. 356-362 (7)	3.95	3.95

Perf. 12½

Souvenir Sheet

362A A22 8m Qarabag 1.50 1.50

For overprints see Nos. 629-636.

Maiden's Tower — A23

1992-93 Litho. *Perf. 12½x12*

363	A23	10g blk & blue grn	.25	.25
365	A23	20g black & red	.25	.25
367	A23	50g black & blue grn	.25	.25
368	A23	50g black & yellow	.50	.50
370	A23	1m black & rose lilac	.25	.25
372	A23	1.50m black & blue	1.00	1.00
373	A23	2.50m black & yellow	.50	.50
374	A23	5m black & green	.75	.75
		Nos. 363-374 (8)	3.75	3.75

Issued: 10g, 20g, 1.50m, No. 367, Dec. 20; No. 368, 1m, 2.50m, 5m, June 20, 1993.
For surcharges see Nos. 550-557, 757.

Government Building — A24

1993, Oct. 12 Litho. *Perf. 12½*

375	A24	25g yellow & black	.30	.30
376	A24	30g green & black	.30	.30
377	A24	50g blue & black	.40	.40
378	A24	1m red & black	.80	.80
		Nos. 375-378 (4)	1.80	1.80

For surcharges see No. 407-414.

Flowers — A25

25g, Tulipa eichleri. 50g, Puschkinia scilloides. 1m, Iris elegantissima. 1.50m, Iris acutiloba. 5m, Tulipa florenskyii. 10m, Iris reticulata.

No. 385, Muscari elecostomum.

1993, Aug. 12 Litho. *Perf. 12½*

379	A25	25g multi	.25	.25
380	A25	50g multi	.25	.25
381	A25	1m multi	.25	.25
382	A25	1.50m multi	.35	.35
383	A25	5m multi	.85	.85
384	A25	10m multi	1.60	1.60
		Nos. 379-384 (6)	3.55	3.55

Souvenir Sheet

Perf. 13

385 A25 10m multi 1.75 1.75

No. 385 contains one 32x40mm stamp.
For surcharge, see No. 809.

Fish A26

25g, Acipenser guldenstadti. 50g, Acipenser stellatus. 1m, Rutilus frisii kutum. 1.50m, Rutilus rutilus caspicus. 5m, Salmo trutta caspius. No. 391, Alosa kessleri. No. 392, Huso huso.

1993, Aug. 27 *Perf. 12½*

386	A26	25g multicolored	.25	.25
387	A26	50g multicolored	.25	.25
388	A26	1m multicolored	.25	.25
389	A26	1.50m multicolored	.35	.35
390	A26	5m multicolored	.85	.85
391	A26	10m multicolored	1.60	1.60
		Nos. 386-391 (6)	3.55	3.55

Souvenir Sheet

Perf. 13

392 A26 10m multicolored 1.75 1.75

No. 392 contains one 40x32mm stamp.
For surcharges, see Nos. 810, 813.

Pres. Heydar A. Aliyev — A27

Design: No. 394, Map of Nakhichevan.

1993, Sept. 12 Litho. *Perf. 12½x13*

393	A27	25m multicolored	2.00	1.60
394	A27	25m multicolored	2.00	1.60
a.		Pair, #393-394	4.25	4.25
b.		Souv. sheet, #393-394, perf. 12	*90.00*	
c.		Souv. sheet, #393-394, perf. 12	15.00	

Name on map spelled "Naxcivan" on No. 394c. It is spelled "Haxcivan" on Nos. 394-394b.

No. 394c issued Sept. 20, 1993.

Shirvanshah's Palace, UNESCO World Heritage Site, Baku — A28

Style of tombs: 2m, Shirvanshah's Palace, 13th-14th cent. 4m, Turbe mausoleum, 15th cent. 8m, Divan-Khana, 15th cent.

1994, Jan. 17 Litho. *Perf. 11*

395	A28	2m red, silver & black	.25	.25
396	A28	4m green, silver & black	.35	.35
397	A28	8m blue, silver & black	.75	.75
		Nos. 395-397 (3)	1.35	1.35

For surcharges, see Nos. 753, 758-759, 808.

A29

5m, Natl. Colors, Star, Crescent. 8m, Natl. coat of arms.

1994, Jan. 17 *Perf. 12½*

398	A29	5m multicolored	.45	.45
399	A29	8m multicolored	.80	.80

For surcharges, see Nos. 816, 817.

A30

1994, Jan. 17 *Perf. 12½*

400 A30 10m multi + label .75 .75

Mohammed Fizuli (1494-1556), poet.

Mammed Amin Rasulzade (1884-1955), 1st President — A31

Jalil Mamedkulizade, Writer, 125th Birth Anniv. — A32

1994, May 21 *Perf. 12½, 13 (#402)*

401	A31	15m blk, yel & brown	1.25	1.25
402	A32	20m black, blue & gold	1.25	1.25

No. 402 printed se-tenant with label.
For surcharges, see Nos. 814, 867.

No. 355A Surcharged

1994, Jan. 18 Photo. *Perf. 13x13½*

403	A21a	2m on 15g	.50	.50
404	A21a	20m on 15g	1.00	1.00
405	A21a	25m on 15g	1.50	1.50

406 A21a 50m on 15g 3.00 3.00
a. Vert. strip of 4, #403-406 *5.00 5.00*
Nos. 403-406 (4) 6.00 6.00

Nos. 375-378 Surcharged

1994, Feb. 22 Litho. *Perf. 12½*
407 A24 5m on 1m #375 .50 .50
408 A24 10m on 30g #377 .50 .50
409 A24 15m on 30g #377 .50 .50
a. Pair, #408-409 1.25 1.25
410 A24 20m on 50g #378 .50 .50
411 A24 25m on 1m #375 .60 .60
a. Pair, #407, 411 1.40 1.40
412 A24 40m on 50g #378 1.10 1.10
a. Pair, #410, 412 1.75 1.75
413 A24 50m on 25g #376 1.50 1.50
414 A24 100m on 25g #376 2.25 2.25
a. Pair, #413-414 4.00 4.00
Nos. 407-414 (8) 7.45 7.45

Baku Oil Fields — A33

Designs: 15m, Temple of Eternal Fires. 20m, Oil derricks. 25m, Early tanker. 50m, Ludwig Nobel, Robert Nobel, Petr Bilderling, Alfred Nobel.

1994, June 10 Photo. *Perf. 13*
415 A33 15m multicolored .30 .30
416 A33 20m multicolored .30 .30
417 A33 25m multicolored .40 .40
418 A33 50m multicolored 1.00 1.00
a. Souvenir sheet of 1 1.50 1.50
Nos. 415-418 (4) 2.00 2.00

See Turkmenistan Nos. 39-43.

Minerals — A34

1994, June 15 Litho. *Perf. 13¼x13*
419 A34 5m Laumontite .30 .30
420 A34 10m Epidot calcite .50 .50
421 A34 15m Andradite .75 .75
422 A34 20m Amethyst 1.00 1.00
a. Souvenir sheet, #419-422 + 2 labels, perf. 12 2.50 2.50
Nos. 419-422 (4) 2.55 2.55

For surcharges, see Nos. 760, 762-764.

Posthorn — A35

1994, June 28 Litho. *Perf. 12½*
426 A35 5m black & red .25 .25
427 A35 10m black & green .25 .25
428 A35 20m black & blue .40 .40
429 A35 25m black & yellow .40 .40
431 A35 40m black & brown .75 .75
Nos. 426-431 (5) 2.05 2.05

For surcharges see Nos. 487-489A, 752, 761, 765, 811.

No. 351 Surcharged

Unwmk.
1994, Oct. 17 Litho. *Perf. 12*
435 A21 400m on 25g multi 2.50 2.50

Souvenir Sheet

Pres. Heydar A. Aliyev — A36

1994, Oct. 28 Litho. *Perf. 14*
436 A36 150m multicolored 3.00 3.00

Ships of the Caspian Sea A37

Designs: a, Tugboat, "Captain Racebov." b, "Azerbaijan." c, Balt Ro Ro line, "Merkuri I." d, Tanker, "Tovuz." e, Tanker.

1994, Oct. 28
437 A37 50m Strip of 5, #a.-e. 1.75 1.75

Issued in sheets of 15 stamps. The background of the sheet shows a nautical chart, giving each stamp a different background. Value $7.

1994 World Cup Soccer Championships, U.S. — A38

Various soccer plays. Denominations: 5m, 10m, 20m, 25m, 30m, 50m, 80m.

1994, June 17 Litho. *Perf. 13*
438-444 A38 Set of 7 3.50 3.50

Souvenir Sheet

445 A38 100m multicolored 1.75 1.75

No. 445 contains one 32x40mm stamp and is a continuous design.

Dinosaurs — A39

Designs: 5m, Coelophysis, segisaurus. 10m, Pentaceratops, tyrannosaurids. 20m, Segnosaurus, oviraptor. 25m, Albertosaurus, corythosaurus. 30m, Iguanodons. 50m, Stegosaurus, allosaurus. 80m, Tyrannosaurus, saurolophus.
100m, Phobetor.

1994, Sept. 15
446-452 A39 Set of 7 3.25 3.25

Souvenir Sheet
Perf. 12½

453 A39 100m multicolored 2.10 2.10

No. 453 contains one 40x32mm stamp and is a continuous design.

Lyrurus Mlokosiewickzi — A40

a, 50m, Female on nest. b, 80m, Female on mountain cliff. c, 100m, 2 males. d, 120m, Male.

1994, Dec. 15 Litho. *Perf. 12½*
454 A40 Block of 4, #a.-d. 5.00 5.00

World Wildlife Fund.

Raptors A41

10m, Haliaeetus albicilla. 15m, Aguila heliaca. 20m, Aguila rapax. 25m, Gypaetus barbatus, vert. 50m, Falco cherrug, vert.
100m, Aguila chrysaetos.

1994, Nov. 15 Litho. *Perf. 13*
458-462 A41 Set of 5 3.25 3.25

Souvenir Sheet
Perf. 12½

463 A41 100m multicolored 1.75 1.75

No. 463 contains one 40x32mm stamp and is a continuous design.

Cats A42

Designs: 10m, Felis libica, vert. 15m, Felis otocolobus, vert. 20m, Felis lyns, vert. 25m, Felis pardus. 50m, Panthera tigrus.
100m, Panthera tigrus adult and cub, vert.

1994, Dec. 14 *Perf. 13*
464-468 A42 Set of 5 3.25 3.25

Souvenir Sheet

469 A42 100m multicolored 1.75 1.75

No. 469 contains one 32x40mm stamp and is a continuous design.
For overprints see Nos. 637-642.

Butterflies A43

Designs: 10m, Parnassius apollo. 25m, Zegris menestho. 50m, Manduca atropos. 60m, Pararge adrastoides.

1995, Jan. 23 Litho. *Perf. 14*
470 A43 10m multicolored .30 .30
471 A43 25m multicolored .65 .65
472 A43 50m multicolored 1.15 1.15
473 A43 60m multicolored 1.50 1.50
a. Souvenir sheet of 4, #470-473 4.00 4.00
Nos. 470-473 (4) 3.60 3.60

For surcharges, see Nos. 783-786a.

Intl. Olympic Committee, Cent. — A44

Designs: No. 474, Pierre de Coubertin. No. 475, Discus. No. 476, Javelin.

1994, Dec. 15 Litho. *Perf. 12*
474-476 A44 100m Set of 3 2.00 2.00

A45

1994 Winter Olympic medalists, Lillehammer: 10m, Aleksei Urmanov, Russia, figure skating, 25, Nancy Kerrigan, US, figure skating. 40m Bonnie Blair, US, speed skating, horiz. 50m, Takanori Kano, Japan, ski jumping, horiz. 80m, Philip LaRouche, Canada, freestyle skiing. 100m, Four-man bobsled, Germany.
200m, Katja Seizinger, skiing, Germany, vert.

1995, Feb. 10 Litho. *Perf. 14*
478-483 A45 Set of 6 3.50 3.50

Souvenir Sheet

484 A45 200m multicolored 3.25 3.25

Miniature Sheet

A46

No. 485, 100m: a, Mary Cleave, U.S. b, Valentina Tereshkova, Russia. c, Tamara Jernigan, U.S. d, Wendy Lawrence, U.S.
No. 486, 100m: a, Mae Jemison, U.S. b, Catherine Coleman, U.S. c, Ellen Shulman, U.S. d, M.E. Weber, U.S.

1995, Feb. 21
485-486 A46 Set of 2, #a-d 6.00 6.00

First manned moon landing, 25th anniv. (in 1994).

Nos. 426-428 Surcharged

1995 Litho. *Perf. 12½*
487 A35 100m on 5m #426 .25 .25
488 A35 250m on 10m #427 .40 .40
488A A35 400m on 25m No. 429 .75 .75
489 A35 500m on 20m #428 .65 .65
489A A35 900m on 40m No. 431 1.75 1.75
Nos. 487-489A (5) 3.80 3.80

Issued: No. 488A, 7/7; Nos. 487-488, 489, 2/28.

Mushrooms — A47

Designs: 100m, Gymnopilus spectabilis. 250m, Fly agaris. 300m, Lepiota procera. 400m, Hygrophorus spectosus.
500m, Fly agaris, diff.

1995, Sept. 1 Litho. *Perf. 14*
490-493 A47 Set of 4 3.75 3.75

Souvenir Sheet

494 A47 500m multicolored 2.25 2.25

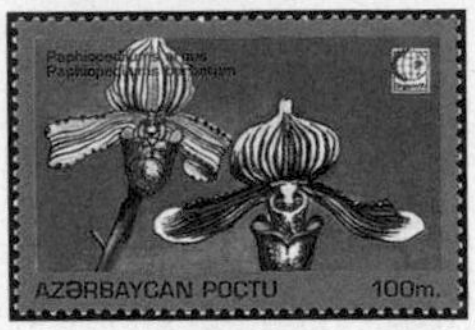

Singapore '95 — A48

Orchids: 100m, Paphiopedilum argus, paphiopedilum barbatum. 250m, Maxillaria picta. 300m, Laeliocattleya. 400m, Dendrobium nobile.
500m, Cattleya gloriette.

1995, Sept. 1

495-498 A48	Set of 4	3.75	3.75

Souvenir Sheet

499 A48	500m multicolored	2.25	2.25

UN, 50th Anniv. A49

Design: 250m, Azerbaijan Pres. Heydar A. Aliyev, UN Sec. Gen. Boutros Boutros-Ghali.

1995, Sept. 15

500 A49	250m multicolored	2.50	2.50

Nos. 352-355 Surcharged

1995 Litho. *Perf. 12*

501 A21	200m on 2.50m #355	.50	.50
502 A21	600m on 35g #352	1.50	1.50
503 A21	800m on 50q #353	2.00	2.00
504 A21	1000m on 1.50m #354	2.50	2.50
	Nos. 501-504 (4)	6.50	6.50

Uzeyir Hacibeyov (1885-1948) A50

400m, Ali Aga Iskenderov (1895-1965).

1995, June 30 Litho. *Perf. 12x12½*

505 A50	250m silver gray & black	.40	.40
506 A50	400m gold bister & brn	.85	.85

Balloons and Airships A51

100m, First hydrogen balloon, 1784. 150m, 1st motorized balloon, 1883. 250m, First elliptical balloon, 1784. 300m, 1st Scott Baldwin dirigible, 1904. 400m, US Marine balloon, 1917. 500m, Pedal-powered dirigible, 1909.
800m, 1st rigid dirigible designed by Hugo Eckener, 1924.

1995, July 20 Litho. *Perf. 13*

507 A51	100m multi, vert.	.25	.25
508 A51	150m multi, vert.	.35	.35
509 A51	250m multi	.50	.50
510 A51	300m multi	.60	.60
511 A51	400m multi	.90	.90
512 A51	500m multi	1.25	1.25
	Nos. 507-512 (6)	3.85	3.85

Souvenir Sheet

513 A51	800m multicolored	2.75	2.75

Marine Life A52

50m, Loligo vulgaris. 100m, Orchistoma pileus. 150m, Pegea confoederata. 250m, Polyorchis karafutoensis. 300m, Agalma okeni.
500m, Corolla spectabillis.

1995, June 2 Litho. *Perf. 13*

514 A52	50m multi	.25	.25
515 A52	100m multi	.45	.45
516 A52	150m multi	.60	.60
517 A52	250m multi, vert.	1.10	1.10
518 A52	300m multi, vert.	1.25	1.25
	Nos. 514-518 (5)	3.65	3.65

Souvenir Sheet

519 A52	500m multicolored	2.50	2.50

Turtles A53

Designs: 50m, Chelus fimbriatus. 100m, Caretta caretta. 150m, Geochelone pardalis. 250m, Geochelone elegans. 300m, Testudo hermanni.
500m, Macroclemys temmincki.

1995, June 12 Litho. *Perf. 13*

520 A53	50m multicolored	.25	.25
521 A53	100m multicolored	.45	.45
522 A53	150m multicolored	.60	.60
523 A53	250m multicolored	1.10	1.10
524 A53	300m multicolored	1.25	1.25
	Nos. 520-524 (5)	3.65	3.65

Souvenir Sheet

525 A53	500m multicolored	2.50	2.50

1998 World Cup Soccer Championships, France — A54

Various soccer plays.

1995, Sept. 30 Litho. *Perf. 12½*

526 A54	100m orange & multi	.40	.40
527 A54	150m green & multi	.55	.55
528 A54	250m yel org & multi	.80	.80
529 A54	300m yellow & multi	1.00	1.00
530 A54	400m blue & multi	1.40	1.40
	Nos. 526-530 (5)	4.15	4.15

Souvenir Sheet

Perf. 13

531 A54	600m multicolored	2.25	2.25

Domestic Cats — A55

100m, Persian. 150m, Chartreux. 250m, Somali. 300m, Longhair Scottish fold. 400m, Cumric. 500m, Turkish angora.
800m, Birman.

1995, Oct. 30 *Perf. 12½*

532 A55	100m multicolored	.35	.35
533 A55	150m multicolored	.50	.50
534 A55	250m multicolored	.65	.65
535 A55	300m multicolored	.80	.80
536 A55	400m multicolored	1.00	1.00
537 A55	500m multicolored	1.25	1.25
	Nos. 532-537 (6)	4.55	4.55

Souvenir Sheet

538 A55	800m multicolored	2.00	2.00

No. 538 contains one 32x40mm stamp.

Fauna and Flora — A56

Designs: 100m, Horse. 200m, Muscari elecostomum, vert. 250m, Huso huso. 300m, Aquila chrysaetos. 400m, Panthera tigrus. 500m, Lyrurus miokosiewickzi, facing right. 1000m, Lyrurus miokosiewickzi, facing left.

1995, Nov. 30

539 A56	100m multicolored	.25	.25
540 A56	200m multicolored	.50	.50
541 A56	250m multicolored	.60	.60
542 A56	300m multicolored	.75	.75
543 A56	400m multicolored	1.00	1.00
544 A56	500m multicolored	1.50	1.50
545 A56	1000m multicolored	2.50	2.50
	Nos. 539-545 (7)	7.10	7.10

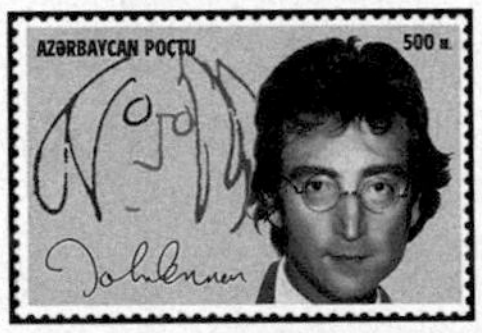

John Lennon (1940-80) A57

1995, Dec. 8 *Perf. 14½*

546 A57	500m multicolored	1.60	1.60

Issued in sheet of 16 plus label.

Miniature Sheet

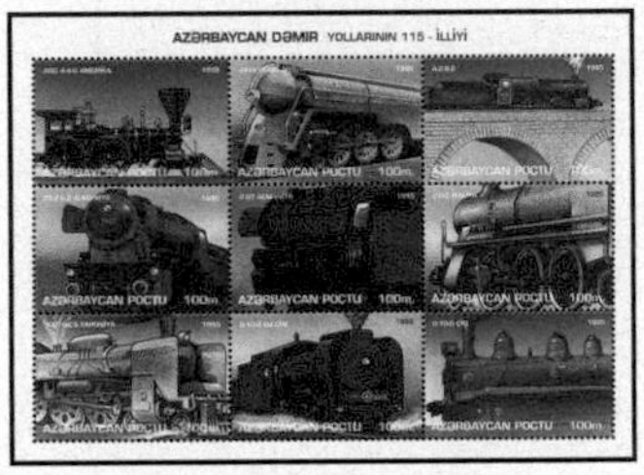

Locomotives — A58

Designs: No. 547a, 4-4-0, America. b, J3 Hudson, US. c, 2-8-2. d, 2-6-2, Germany. e, 2-8-2, Germany. f, 2-6-2, Italy. g, G-C5, Japan. h, 2-10-2 QJ, China. i, 0-10-0, China.
500m, Electric passenger train, vert.

1996, Feb. 1 *Perf. 14*

547 A58	100m Sheet of 9, #a.-i.	6.50	6.50

Souvenir Sheet

548 A58	500m multicolored	3.25	3.25

Dr. M. Topchibashev, Surgeon — A59

1996, Feb. 1

549 A59	300m multicolored	1.25	1.25

Nos. 363, 365, 367-368, 370, 372-374 Surcharged

1995, Jan. 4 Litho. *Perf. 12½x12*

550 A23	250m on 10g #363	.75	.75
551 A23	250m on 20g #365	.75	.75
552 A23	250m on 50g #368	.75	.75
553 A23	250m on 1.50m #372	.75	.75
554 A23	500m on 50g #367	1.50	1.50
555 A23	500m on 1m #370	1.50	1.50
556 A23	500m on 2.50m #373	1.50	1.50
557 A23	500m on 5m #374	1.50	1.50
	Nos. 550-557 (8)	9.00	9.00

1996 Olympic Games, Atlanta A60

50m, Carl Lewis. 100m, Muhammed Ali. 150m, Li Ning. 200m, Said Aouita. 250m, Olga Korbut. 300m, Nadia Comaneci. 400m, Greg Louganis.
500m, Nazim Hüseynov, vert.

1996, Apr. 9 Litho. *Perf. 14*

568 A60	50m multicolored	.25	.25
569 A60	100m multicolored	.40	.40
570 A60	150m multicolored	.40	.40
571 A60	200m multicolored	.55	.55
572 A60	250m multicolored	.70	.70
573 A60	300m multicolored	.90	.90
574 A60	400m multicolored	1.00	1.00
	Nos. 568-574 (7)	4.20	4.20

Souvenir Sheet

575 A60	500m multicolored	1.90	1.90

Husein Aliyev (1911-91), Artist A61

Paintings: 100m, Water bird, swamp. 200m, Landscape.

1996, Apr. 16 Litho. *Perf. 14*

576 A61	100m multicolored	1.00	1.00
577 A61	200m multicolored	1.50	1.50
a.	Pair, #576-577 + label	2.50	2.50

No. 577a issued in sheets of 6 stamps.

Resid Behbudov (1915-89), Singer — A62

1996, Apr. 22 *Perf. 12½*

578 A62	100m multicolored	1.30	1.30

Novruz Bayrami, Natl. Holiday — A63

1996, Mar. 20

579 A63	250m multicolored	1.25	1.25

Independence, 5th Anniv. — A64

1996, May 28 Litho. *Perf. 14*

580 A64	250m multicolored	1.25	1.25

A65

1996, Apr. 22 Litho. *Perf. 12½*
581 A65 100m multicolored 1.25 1.25

Yusif Memmedeliyev (1905-95), chemist.

A66

Jerusalem, 3000th Anniv.: a, 100m, Wailing Wall. b, 250m, Inside cathedral. c, 300m, Dome of the Rock.
500m, Windmill.

1996, June 7 *Perf. 14*
582 A66 Sheet of 3, #a.-c. 4.00 4.00

Souvenir Sheet

583 A66 500m multicolored 3.00 3.00

For overprints see Nos. 643-644.

Dogs
A67

Designs: 50m, German shepherd. 100m, Basset hound. 150m, Collie. 200m, Bull terrier. 300m, Boxer. 400m, Cocker spaniel.
500m, Sharpei.

1996, June 18 *Perf. 13*
584-589 A67 Set of 6 3.75 3.75

Souvenir Sheet

590 A67 500m multicolored 2.00 2.00

Birds — A68

Designs: 50m, Tetraenura regia. 100m, Coliuspasser macrourus. 150m, Oriolus xanthornus. 200m, Oriolus oriolus. 300m, Sturnus vulgaris. 400m, Serinus mozambicus.
500m, Merops apiaster.

1996, June 19 *Perf. 13*
591-596 A68 Set of 6 3.75 3.75

Souvenir Sheet

597 A68 500m multicolored 2.00 2.00

Roses — A69

Designs: 50m, Burgundy. 100m, Virgo. 150m, Rose gaujard. 200m, Luna. 300m, Lady rose. 400m, Landora.
500m, Lougsor, horiz.

1996, June 19
598-603 A69 Set of 6 3.75 3.75

Souvenir Sheet

604 A69 500m multicolored 2.00 2.00

UNICEF, 50th Anniv. — A70

1996, July 8 Litho. *Perf. 14*
605 A70 500m multicolored 1.00 1.00

A71

Competing teams: 100m, Spain, Bulgaria. 150m, Romania, France. 200m, Czech Republic, Germany. 250m, England, Israel. 300m, Croatia, Turkey. 400m, Italy, Russia.
500m, Trophy cup.

1996, July 22
606-611 A71 Set of 6 4.00 4.00

Souvenir Sheet

612 A71 500m multicolored 2.00 2.00

Euro '96, European Soccer Championships, Great Britain.

Ships
A72

Ship, home country: 100m, Chinese junk. 150m, Danmark, Denmark. 200m, Nippon Maru, Japan. 250m, Mircea, Romania. 300m, Kruzenshtern, Russia. 400m, Ariadne, Germany.
500m, Tovarishch, Russia, vert.

1996, Aug. 26 Litho. *Perf. 14*
613-618 A72 Set of 6 4.50 4.50

Souvenir Sheet

619 A72 500m multicolored 3.00 3.00

For overprints see Nos. 645-651.

Bahram Gur Kills a Dragon, Sculpture — A73

1997, Mar. 6 Litho. *Perf. 13½x13*
620 A73 250m black & yellow .35 .35
621 A73 400m black & vermilion .55 .55
622 A73 500m black & green .75 .75
623 A73 1000m black & purple 1.50 1.50
Nos. 620-623 (4) 3.15 3.15

See No. 671.

Famous Personalities — A74

No. 624, Aziz Mamed-Kerim Ogli Aliyev (1897-1962), politician. No. 625, Illyas Efendiyev (1914-96), writer. No. 626, Fatali Khan-Khoyski (1875-1920), politician. No. 627, Nariman Narimanov (1870-1925), politician, writer.

1997, Mar. 25 Litho. *Perf. 14*

Background Color

624 A74 250m tan .80 .80
625 A74 250m gray blue .80 .80
626 A74 250m pale red .80 .80
627 A74 250m pale olive .80 .80
Nos. 624-627 (4) 3.20 3.20

Qobustan Prehistoric Art — A75

Rock carvings: a, Oxen. b, Large horned animals. c, Six figures.

1997, May 19 Litho. *Perf. 14*
628 A75 500m Sheet of 3, #a.-c. 3.50 3.50

For overprint see No. 674.

#356-362A, 464-469 Ovptd. in Red

1997, June 2 Litho. *Perf. 13*

Denominations as Before

629-635 A22 Set of 7 9.00 9.00

Souvenir Sheet

636 A22 8m multicolored 4.00 4.00

Location of overprint varies. No. 636 is ovptd. both on stamp and in sheet margin.

1997, June 2

Denominations as Before

637-641 A42 Set of 5 6.00 6.00

Souvenir Sheet

642 A42 100m multicolored 4.50 4.50

Location of overprint varies. No. 642 is ovptd. both on stamp and in sheet margin.

Nos. 582-583, 613-619 Ovptd.

1997, June 2 *Perf. 14*
643 A66 Sheet of 3, #a.-c. 5.00 5.00

Souvenir Sheet

644 A66 500m multicolored 5.00 5.00

Size and location of overprint varies. Overprint appears both on stamp and in sheet margin.

1997, June 2 *Perf. 14*

Denominations as Before

645-650 A72 Set of 6 5.00 5.00

Souvenir Sheet

651 A72 500m multicolored 5.00 5.00

Location of overprint varies. No. 651 is ovptd. both on stamp and in sheet margin.

Grimm's Fairy Tales — A76

The Town Musicians of Bremen: No. 652: a, Dog. b, Dancing donkey, cat. c, Rooster.
500m, Animals looking through window at treaure chest, man.

1997, July 1 *Perf. 13½x14*
652 A76 250m Sheet of 3, #a.-c. 4.50 4.50

Souvenir Sheet

653 A76 500m multicolored 3.50 3.50

Caspian Seals A77

Designs: a, Seal looking right. b, Mountain top, seal looking forward. c, Seal, seagull. d, Seal looking left. e, Seal looking forward. f, Small seal.
500m, Mother nursing pup.

1997, July 1
654 A77 250m Sheet of 6, #a.-f. 4.50 4.50

Souvenir Sheet

655 A77 500m multicolored 3.50 3.50

Traditional Musical Instruments — A77a

1997, Aug. 4 Litho. *Perf. 14*
656 A77a 250m Qaval .90 .90
657 A77a 250m Tanbur .90 .90
658 A77a 500m Cenq 1.75 1.75
Nos. 656-658 (3) 3.55 3.55

A78

Azerbaijan Oil Industry: a, Early oil derricks, building. b, Off-shore oil drilling platform.

1997, Aug. 18 *Perf. 14½*

Souvenir Sheet

659 A78 500m Sheet of 2, #a.-b. 3.25 3.25

Hagani Shirvany, Poet — A79

1997, Sept. 12 *Perf. 14x13½*
660 A79 250m multicolored 1.00 1.00

Issued in sheets of 4 + 5 labels. Value $5.

Mosques A80

No. 661, Ashaqi Qovgar-agi, Shusha, 1874-75. No. 662, Momuna-Zatun, Naxcivan, 1187. No. 663, Taza-pir, Baku (1905-14).

1997, Sept. 18 **Litho.** *Perf. 14*
661 A80 250m multicolored 1.00 1.00
662 A80 250m multicolored 1.00 1.00
663 A80 250m multicolored 1.00 1.00
Nos. 661-663 (3) 3.00 3.00

H.C. Rasulbekov (1917-1984), Communications Official — A81

1997, Oct. 6 **Litho.** *Perf. 14*
664 A81 250m multicolored .90 .90

1998 World Cup Soccer Championships, France — A82

Winning team photos: No. 665: a, Italy, 1938. b, Argentina, 1986. c, Uruguay, 1930. d, Brazil, 1994. e, England, 1966. f, Germany, 1990.
1500m, Tofiq Bahramov, "Golden Whistle" prize winner, 1966, vert.

1997, Oct. 15
665 A82 250m Sheet of 6, #a.-f. 4.00 4.00

Souvenir Sheet

666 A82 1500m multicolored 3.50 3.50

A83

Figure skaters: No. 667: a, Katarina Witt, Germany. b, Elvis Stojko, Canada. c, Midori Ito, Japan. d, Silhouettes of various winter sports against natl. flag. e, Hand holding Olympic torch. f, Kristi Yamaguchi, US. g, John Curry, England. h, Lu Chen, China.
No. 668, Gordeyeva and Grinkov, Russia.

1998, Jan. 13 **Litho.** *Perf. 14*
667 A83 250m Sheet of 8, #a.-h. 4.50 4.50

Souvenir Sheet

668 A83 500m multicolored 3.50 3.50

1998 Winter Olympic Games, Nagano.

A84

Diana, Princess of Wales (1961-97): No. 669, Wearing black turtleneck. No. 670, Wearing violet dress.

1998, Feb. 4 *Perf. 13½*
669 A84 400m multicolored .70 .70
670 A84 400m multicolored .70 .70

Nos. 669-670 were each issued in sheets of 6. Value, set of 2 sheets $10.

Sculpture Type of 1997

1998, Mar. 23 **Litho.** *Perf. 13½x13*
671 A73 100m blk & bright pink 1.00 1.00

Hasan Aliyev, Ecologist, 90th Birth Anniv. A85

1998, Apr. 3 *Perf. 14*
672 A85 500m multicolored 1.00 1.00

Souvenir Sheet

Pres. Heydar Aliyev, 75th Birthday — A86

1998, May 10 *Perf. 13½*
673 A86 500m multicolored 3.00 3.00

No. 628 Ovptd.

1998, May 13 *Perf. 14*
674 A75 500m Sheet of 3, #a.-c. 8.00 8.00

Additional inscription in sheet margin reads "ISRAEL 98 — WORLD STAMP EXHIBITION / TEL-AVIV 13-21 MAY 1998."

Artists A87

No. 675, Gara Garayev, composer. No. 676, Ashug Alesker, folk musician, poet. No. 677, Mohammad-Hossein Shahriar, poet.

1998, June 7 **Litho.** *Perf. 14*
675 A87 250m multicolored .90 .90
676 A87 250m multicolored .90 .90
677 A87 250m multicolored .90 .90
Nos. 675-677 (3) 2.70 2.70

Bul-Bul, Singer, Birth Cent. — A88

1998, July 7
678 A88 500m multicolored 1.00 1.00

Disney Characters at World Rapid Chess Championship — A89

Designs: 250m, Minnie, Mickey.
No. 679: a, Minnie, Mickey. b, Goofy. c, Donald. d, Pluto. e, Minnie. f, Daisy. g, Goofy, Donald. h, Mickey.
No. 680, 4000m, Donald, Mickey. No. 681, 4000m, Minnie, Mickey.

1998 *Perf. 13½*
678A A89 250m multicolored *4.50 4.50*

Perf. 13½x14

679 A89 500m Sheet of 8, #a.-h. *32.50 32.50*

Souvenir Sheets

680-681 A89 Set of 2 *50.00 50.00*

Issued: 250m, 12/28; others, 11/13.

New Year Holiday A90

Europa: 1000m, Woman rolling dough. 3000m, Men performing at holiday festival.

1998, Dec. 29 **Litho.** *Perf. 13x12½*
682 A90 1000m multicolored *1.50 1.50*
683 A90 3000m multicolored *3.50 3.50*

Nos. 682-683 Ovptd.

1999, Apr. 27 **Litho.** *Perf. 13x12½*
684 A90 1000m on #682 *1.50 1.50*
685 A90 3000m on #683 *3.50 3.50*

A91

Europa: 1000m, Rose flamingo, Gizilagach Natl. Park. 3000m, Deer, Girkan Natl. Park.

1999, Apr. 28 *Perf. 12½x12¾*
686 A91 1000m multicolored *1.75 1.75*
687 A91 3000m multicolored *3.75 3.75*

A92

Towers: 1000m, Dord Kundge, 14th cent. 3000m, Danravy, 13th cent.

1999, Aug. 3 **Litho.** *Perf. 11¼x11¾*
688 A92 1000m black & blue .75 .75
689 A92 3000m black & red 2.00 2.00

See Nos. 701-702, 717-718, 731-732, 744, 754.
For surcharge, see No. 812, 815.

A93

Naxçivan Autonomous Republic, 75th anniv.: a, Pres. Heydar Aliyev, flag. b, Map of Naxçivan.

1999, Oct. 9 *Perf. 12*
690 A93 1000m Pair, #a.-b. 3.00 3.00
c. Souvenir sheet, pair, #a.-b. 3.00 3.00

A94

1999, Oct. 20 *Perf. 12½x12*
691 A94 250m multicolored 1.10 1.10

Jafar Jabbarly (1899-1934), playwright.

Souvenir Sheet

A95

80th anniv. of Azerbaijan postage stamps: a, #1. b, #3. c, #7. d, #10. b-d horiz.

Perf. 14¾x14½ (a), 14½x13¾ (b-d)

1999, Oct. 30
692 A95 500m Sheet of 4, #a.-d. 3.50 3.50

Exists imperf. Value, $20.

Baku Caravansary — A96

No. 693, Inner courtyard. No. 694, Facade, camels.

1999, Dec. 29 Litho. *Perf. 13*
693-694 A96 500m Set of 2 3.50 3.50

A97

1999, Dec. 29 *Perf. 12*
695 A97 1000m multi 1.75 1.75

Council of Europe, 50th anniv.

UPU, 125th Anniv. — A98

Azerbaijan flag, UPU emblem and: a, 250m, Dove. b, 3000m, Computer, satellite.

1999, Dec. 29
696 A98 Pair, #a.-b. 3.50 3.50

Souvenir Sheet

Epic Legend Kitabi Dede Gorgud, 1300th Anniv. — A99

Designs: a, Beyrek fights with camel. b, Wounded Tural on horseback. c, Gazan Khan sleeping, horse.

1999, Dec. 29 *Perf. 12¼x11¾*
697 A99 1000m Sheet of 3, #a.-c. 3.50 3.50

Europa, 2000
Common Design Type

2000, Feb. 7 Litho. *Perf. 12¾x13*
698 CD17 1000m multi *1.00 1.00*
699 CD17 3000m multi *5.00 5.00*

Souvenir Sheet

Baku Transportation — A100

Designs: a, Phaeton. b, Horse-drawn tram. c, Electric tram. d, Trolleybus.

2000, Feb. 15 Litho. *Perf. 12½x12*
700 A100 500m Sheet of 4, #a-d 4.50 4.50

Tower Type of 1999

100m, Ramany Castle, 14th cent, horiz. 250m, Nardaran Castle, 14th cent., horiz.

2000, May 5 Litho. *Perf. 11¾x11¼*
701 A92 100m black & orange .35 .35
702 A92 250m black & green .85 .85

World Meteorological Organization, 50th Anniv. — A101

2000, May 5 *Perf. 12*
703 A101 1000m multi 1.00 1.00

Worldwide Fund for Nature — A102

Aythya nyroca: a, One in flight. b, Two on rocks, three in water. c, One on rocks, three in water. d, One in water, three in flight.

2000, May 5 *Perf. 12½x12*
704 A102 500m Block of 4, #a-d 3.50 3.50

2000 Summer Olympics, Sydney — A103

Designs: a, Wrestling. b, Weight lifting. c, Boxing. d, Running.

2000, May 5 *Perf. 12x12½*
705 A103 500m Block of 4, #a-d 5.00 5.00

Souvenir Sheet

Phasianus Colchicus — A104

2000, June 21 Litho. *Perf. 13½x13*
706 A104 2000m multi 4.00 4.00

Fruit A105

No. 707: a, Cydonia oblonga. b, Punica granatum. c, Persica L. d, Ficus carica.

2000, June 21 *Perf. 13x13¼*
707 Sheet of 4 4.50 4.50
a.-d. A105 500m Any single 1.10 1.10

Rasul Rza (1911-81), Poet A106

2000, Sept. 28 Litho. *Perf. 13x13¼*
708 A106 250m multi 1.00 1.00

Reptiles A107

No. 709: a, Vipera lebetina. b, Laserta saxcola. c, Vipera xanthina. d, Phrynocephalus mystaceus.

No. 710, Natrix tessellata, Phrynocephalus helioscopus, vert.

2000, Sept. 28 *Perf. 13½x13*
709 Sheet of 4 6.50 6.50
a.-d. A107 500m Any single 1.50 1.50

Souvenir Sheet
Perf. 13x13½
710 A107 500m multi 3.00 3.00

Sabit Rahman (1910-70), Writer A108

2000, Nov. 17 *Perf. 13x13¼*
711 A108 1000m multi 1.60 1.60

Intl. Year for the Culture of Peace — A109

2000, Nov. 17 *Perf. 13¼x13*
712 A109 3000m multi 3.50 3.50

Souvenir Sheet

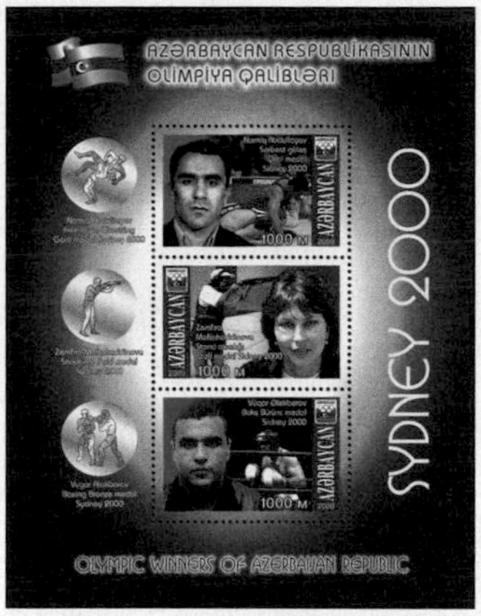

2000 Olympic Medalists — A110

No. 713: a, Namig Abdullaev, 54kg freestyle wrestling gold medalist. b, Zemfira Meftahaddinova, women's skeet shooting gold medalist. c, Vugar Alakbarov, middleweight boxing bronze medalist.

2001, Jan. 26 Litho. *Perf. 13½x13¾*
713 A110 1000m Sheet of 3, #a-c 4.50 4.50

Dated 2000.

Europa — A111

Caspian Sea and: 1000m, Seal. 3000m, Sturgeon, crab, jellyfish.

Perf. 13½x13¼

2001, Mar. 28 Litho.
714-715 A111 Set of 2 *6.00 6.00*
715a Pane, 4 each #714-715 *32.50*

Stamps in the middle two columns of No. 715a are tete beche. No. 715a was sold with booklet cover, but unattached to it.

Admission of Azerbaijan to Council of Europe A112

2001, Apr. 25 *Perf. 13¼x13½*
716 A112 1000m multi 1.75 1.75

Tower Type of 1999

Designs: 100m, Sheki, 18th cent., horiz. 250m, Sheki, 12th-13th cent., horiz.

2001, July 27 *Perf. 14x13¾*
717 A92 100m black & lilac .45 .45
718 A92 250m black & yellow 1.00 1.00

Souvenir Sheet

UN High Commissioner for Refugees, 50th Anniv. — A113

2001, Aug. 22 *Perf. 13¼x13½*
719 A113 3000m multi 3.50 3.50

Souvenir Sheet

Nasir ad-Din at-Tusi (1201-74), Scientist — A114

2001, Sept. 7 ***Perf. 13¼***
720 A114 3000m multi 3.50 3.50

Commonwealth of Independent States, 10th Anniv. — A115

2001, Oct. 8 Litho. ***Perf. 13½x13¼***
721 A115 1000m multi 1.60 1.60

Souvenir Sheet

First Manned Space Flight, 40th Anniv. — A116

2001, Nov. 6 ***Perf. 13¼x13½***
722 A116 3000m multi 3.50 3.50

Independence, 10th Anniv. — A117

Litho. & Embossed with Foil Application

2001, Dec. 1 ***Perf. 13¼***
723 A117 5000m gold & multi 10.00 10.00

Owls — A118

No. 724: a, Asio flammeus. b, Strix aluco. c, Otus scops. d, Asio otus. e, Bubo bubo, wings at side. f, Athene noctua.
No. 725, Bubo bubo, wings extended.

2001, Dec. 1 Litho. ***Perf. 13¼x13***
724 A118 1000m Sheet of 6, #a-f 6.50 6.50

Souvenir Sheet

725 A118 1000m shown 3.50 3.50

Visit of Russian Pres. Vladimir Putin A119

2001, Dec. 20 ***Perf. 13***
726 A119 1000m multi 1.50 1.50

Natl. Olympic Committee, 10th Anniv. — A120

2002, Mar. 6 ***Perf. 13¼x13½***
727 A120 3000m multi 3.00 3.00

Europa — A121

Designs: 1000m, Tight rope walker, musicians, strong man, acrobat. 3000m, Trapeze artist, juggler, horse trainer.

2002, Mar. 11 ***Perf. 13½x13¼***
728-729 A121 Set of 2 5.50 5.50
729a Booklet pane, 2 each #728-729, perf. 13½x13¼ on 3 sides 11.00 —
Complete booklet, #729a 11.00

Azerbaijan — People's Republic of China Diplomatic Relations, 10th Anniv. A122

2002, Mar. 28 Litho. ***Perf. 12***
730 A122 1000m multi 1.20 1.20

Tower Type of 1999

Designs: 100m, Molla Panah Vagif Mausoleum, Shusha. 250m, Mosque, Agdam.

2002, Apr. 23 ***Perf. 13½x14***
731 A92 100m blk & ol grn .30 .30
732 A92 250m blk & tan .60 .60

For surcharge, see No. 812.

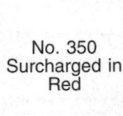

No. 350 Surcharged in Red

Method & Perf. As Before

2002, May 8
733 A20 1000m on 35k multi 1.20 1.20

New Azerbaijan Party, 10th Anniv. — A123

2002, June 1 ***Perf. 13½***
734 A123 3000m multi 3.00 3.00

Butterflies — A124

No. 735: a, Danaus chrysippus. b, Papilio orientalis. c, Thaleropis jonia. d, Vanessa atalanta. e, Argynnis alexandra. f, Brahmaea christophi.

2002, June 19 ***Perf. 13***
735 A124 1000m Sheet of 6, #a-f 7.50 7.50

In Remembrance of Sept. 11, 2001 Terrorist Attacks — A125

2002, Sept. 18 ***Perf. 13½x13¼***
736 A125 1500m multi 1.50 1.50

Printed in sheets of 3. Value $4.50.

Baku Telegraph Office, 70th Anniv. — A126

2002, Sept. 18 ***Perf. 14¼x14***
737 A126 3000m multi 3.00 3.00

Rauf Gadjiev, Composer, 80th Anniv. of Birth A127

2002, Sept. 18 ***Perf. 14x14¼***
738 A127 5000m multi 3.50 3.50

Souvenir Sheet

Visit of Pope John Paul II — A128

2002, Sept. 18 ***Perf. 13¼x13½***
739 A128 1500m multi 3.00 3.00

Souvenir Sheet

European Junior Chess Championships — A129

Baku skyline and stylized chess pieces: a, King, queen, pawns. b, Knights, pawn. c, Two elephants, rook, pawn. d, King, queen, rook, pawn.

2002, Sept. 18 ***Perf. 12¾x13¼***
740 A129 1500m Sheet of 4, #a-d 7.00 7.00

Souvenir Sheet

Turkey's Third Place Finish in 2002 World Cup Soccer Championships — A130

2002, Oct. 16 ***Perf. 13¼x13***
741 A130 5000m multi 4.50 4.50

Women for Peace — A131

2002, Nov. 1 ***Perf. 14¼x14***
742 A131 3000m multi 3.00 3.00

Souvenir Sheet

Aquarium Fish — A132

No. 743: a, Betta splendens. b, Symphysodon aequifasciatus. c, Pterophylium scalare. d, Carassius auratus auratus. e, Melanotaenia boesemani. f, Cichlasoma meeki.

2002, Dec. 27 Litho. ***Perf. 13½***
743 A132 1000m Sheet of 6, #a-f 6.50 6.50

Tower Type of 1999

Design: Askeran Towers, 18th cent., horiz.

2003, Jan. 8 ***Perf. 14x13½***
744 A92 250m black & lt blue .60 .60

Europa A133

Posters: 1000m, Stop Terrorism. 3000m, Sport is the Health of the Nation

2003, Mar. 12 ***Perf. 13½***
745-746 A133 Set of 2 6.00 6.00
746a Booklet pane, 2 each #745-746, perf. 13½ on 3 sides 12.00 12.00

No. 746a was sold with booklet cover, but unattached to it.

Admission to UPU, 10th Anniv. — A134

2003, Apr. 8 ***Perf. 14¼x14***
747 A134 3000m multi 3.00 3.00

Nakhichevan — A135

2003, Apr. 8 ***Perf. 14x14¼***
748 A135 3000m multi 2.75 2.75

For surcharge see No. 851.

Baku — Tbilisi — Ceyhan Oil Pipeline — A136

2003, Apr. 8 ***Perf. 13¾x14¼***
749 A136 3000m multi 3.00 3.00

Zarifa Aliyeva (1923-85), Ophthalmologist — A137

2003, Apr. 28 ***Perf. 14x14¼***
750 A137 3000m multi 2.75 2.75

Souvenir Sheet

Pres. Heydar Aliyev, 80th Birthday — A138

Litho. With Foil Application
2003, May 2 ***Perf. 11½***
751 A138 10,000m multi 9.00 9.00

Nos. 397, 429 Surcharged

Methods and Perfs As Before
2003, May 27
752 A35 500m on 25m #429 .70 .70
753 A28 1000m on 8m #397 1.30 1.30

Towers Type of 1999

Design: 1000m, Ganja Doors on tower walls, Shusha.

2003, Aug. 13 Litho. ***Perf. 13¾***
754 A92 1000m black 1.00 1.00

Souvenir Sheet

Automobiles — A139

No. 755: a, QAZ-11-73. b, QAZ-M-20 Pobeda. c, QAZ-12 Zim. d, QAZ-21 Volqa.

2003, Aug. 13 ***Perf. 11½***
755 A139 500m Sheet of 4, #a-d 3.00 3.00

Arshin Mal Alan, Musical Comedy by Uzeyir Hadjibekov, 90th Anniv. — A140

2003, Nov. 21 Litho. ***Perf. 14¼x14***
756 A140 10,000m multi 7.00 7.00

Nos. 757-759, 761, 765 Surcharged

Nos. 760, 762-764 Surcharged

Methods and Perfs as Before
2003, Dec. 11
757 A23 500m on 50g #367 .75 .75
758 A28 500m on 2m #395 .75 .75
759 A28 500m on 4m #396 .75 .75
760 A34 500m on 5m #419 .75 .75
761 A35 500m on 5m #426 .75 .75
762 A34 500m on 10m #420 .75 .75
763 A34 500m on 15m #421 .75 .75
764 A34 500m on 20m #422 .75 .75
a. On #422a 4.75 4.75
765 A35 500m on 40m #431 .75 .75
Nos. 757-765 (9) 6.75 6.75

Souvenir Sheet

Sheki National Park — A141

No. 766: a, Bear. b, Raccoon. c, Boar. d, Fox.

2003, Dec. 30 Litho. ***Perf. 11½***
766 A141 3000m Sheet of 4, #a-d 9.00 9.00

Nakhichevan Autonomous Republic, 80th Anniv. — A142

2004, Jan. 3 ***Perf. 14¼x14***
767 A142 3000m multi 2.25 2.25

For surcharge see No. 852.

Dove of Peace Monument, Sumgayit — A143

2004, Jan. 31 ***Perf. 13¼x13¾***
768 A143 500m blk & blue .80 .80

See No. 788.

Europa A144

Designs: 1000m, Geygel Lake. 3000m, Baku.

2004, Mar. 16 ***Perf. 13¼x13½***
769-770 A144 Set of 2 4.50 4.50
770a Booklet pane, 2 each #769-770, perf. 13¼x13½ on 3 sides 12.00 —

No. 770a was sold with booklet cover, but unattached to it.

Molla Juma, Poet, 150th Anniv. of Birth A145

2004, Mar. 25 ***Perf. 14x14¼***
771 A145 500m multi 1.25 1.25

2004 Summer Olympics, Athens — A146

No. 772: a, Pole vault. b, Wrestling. c, Running. d, Greek amphora.

2004, Apr. 15 ***Perf. 14¼x14***
772 A146 500m Block of 4, #a-d 4.00 4.00

FIFA (Fédération Internationale de Football Association), Cent. — A147

No. 773 — Soccer stadium, FIFA emblem and: a, World Cup. b, Player wearing jersey #11. c, Player wearing jersey #9. d, Goalie.

2004, Apr. 15 ***Perf. 14x14¼***
773 A147 500m Block of 4, #a-d 4.00 4.00

Pres. Heydar Aliyev (1923-2003) A148

2004, May 10 Litho. ***Perf. 14¼x14***
774 A148 500m multi .95 .95

See Nos. 794, 818.

Great Silk Way — A149

2004, June 7
775 A149 3000m multi 2.75 2.75

Costumes of the 19th Century — A150

Man and woman from: No. 776, 500m, Baku (Baki). No. 777, 500m, Karabakh (Qarabag). No. 778, 500m, Nakhichevan (Naxçivan). No. 779, 500m, Shemakha (Samaxi).

2004, July 8

776-779 A150 Set of 4 4.25 4.25
779a Miniature sheet, 2 each #776-779 8.50 8.50

Internet, 35th Anniv. A151

2004, Sept. 29 Litho. ***Perf. 14x14¼***

780 A151 3000m multi 2.75 2.75

Souvenir Sheet

Pres. Heydar Aliyev (1923-2003) — A152

2004, Dec. 10 ***Perf. 11½***

781 A152 10,000m multi 6.00 6.00

Worldwide Fund for Nature (WWF) — A153

No. 782 — Panthera pardus ciscaucasica: a, Adult on tree branch. b, Two cubs behind branch. c, Adult with mouth open. d, Adult and cub.

2005, Jan. 7 ***Perf. 14x14¼***

782 A153 1000m Block of 4, #a-d 3.25 3.25

Nos. 470-473, 473a Surcharged in Red

2005, Feb. 1 Litho. ***Perf. 14***

783 A43 1000m on 10m #470 .90 .90
784 A43 1000m on 25m #471 .90 .90
785 A43 1000m on 50m #472 .90 .90
786 A43 1000m on 60m #473 .90 .90
a. Souvenir sheet, #783-786 3.50 3.50
Nos. 783-786 (4) 3.60 3.60

Taxation Ministry, 5th Anniv. — A154

2005, Feb. 5 ***Perf. 14¼x14***

787 A154 3000m multi 2.75 2.75

Local Monuments Type of 2004

Design: Observatory, Samaxi.

2005, Mar. 10 ***Perf. 13¼x13¾***

788 A143 500m blk & red vio .75 .75

Orchids — A155

Designs: 500m, Cephalanthera rubra. 1000m, Orchis papilionacea. 1500m, Epipactis atrorubens. 3000m, Orchis purpurea.

2005, Mar. 10 ***Perf. 13¼x13***

789-792 A155 Set of 4 6.50 6.50
a. Souvenir sheet, #789-792 6.50 6.50

End of World War II, 60th Anniv. A156

2005, Apr. 6 ***Perf. 14x14¼***

793 A156 1000m multi 1.50 1.50

Pres. Aliyev Type of 2004

2005, Apr. 18 ***Perf. 14¼x14***

794 A148 1000m bl grn & multi 1.50 1.50

Europa A157

Designs: 1000m, Plov. 3000m, Dolma.

2005, Apr. 18 ***Perf. 13¾x14***

795-796 A157 Set of 2 *5.00 5.00*

Booklet Stamps

797 A157 1000m Like #795 *1.50 1.50*
798 A157 3000m Like #796 *4.50 4.50*
a. Booklet pane of 4, 2 each #797-798 *12.00* —
b. Booklet pane of 6, 3 each #797-798 *18.00* —
Complete booklet, #798a-798b *30.00*

For surcharges see Nos. 838-839.

National Academy of Sciences, 60th Anniv. A158

2005, May 5 Litho. ***Perf. 14x14¼***

799 A158 1000m multi 1.50 1.50

Souvenir Sheet

First Spacewalk, 40th Anniv. — A159

2005, June 1 ***Perf. 11½***

800 A159 3000m multi 4.00 4.00

World Summit on the Information Society, Tunis A160

2005, June 24 ***Perf. 14x14¼***

801 A160 1000m multi 1.50 1.50

Pope John Paul II (1920-2005) — A161

2005, June 24

802 A161 3000m multi 3.00 3.00

For surcharge see No. 853.

Souvenir Sheet

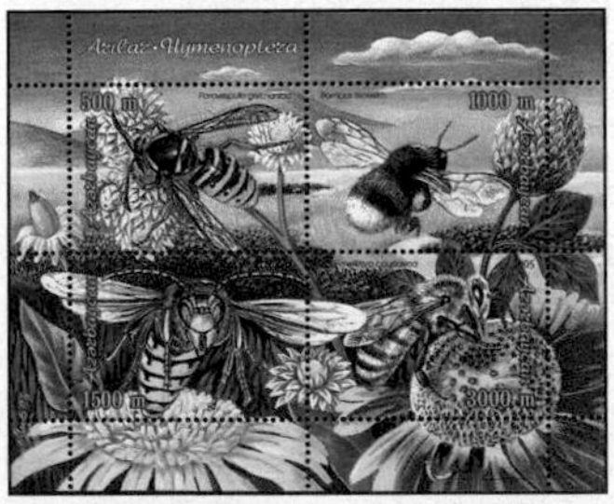

Bees — A162

No. 803: a, 500m, Paravespula germanica. b, 1000m, Bombus terrestris. c, 1500m, Vespa crabro. d, 3000m, Apis mellifera caucasica.

2005, July 27

803 A162 Sheet of 4, #a-d 5.50 5.50

European Philatelic Cooperation, 50th Anniv. (in 2006) — A163

Emblem and vignettes of Europa stamps: No. 804, France #805, Germany #748. No. 805, Azerbaijan #682-683. No. 806, Azerbaijan #698-699. No. 807, Stamps similar to Azerbaijan #745-746.

2005, Oct. 25 ***Perf. 12¾x13***

Background Color

804 A163 3000m gray green *1.75 1.75*
a. Souvenir sheet of 1 *1.75 1.75*
b. Pair, imperf. *4.00 4.00*
805 A163 3000m tan *1.75 1.75*
a. Souvenir sheet of 1 *1.75 1.75*
b. Pair, imperf. *4.00 4.00*
806 A163 3000m yel green *1.75 1.75*
a. Souvenir sheet of 1 *1.75 1.75*
b. Pair, imperf. *4.00 4.00*
807 A163 3000m red orange *1.75 1.75*
a. Souvenir sheet of 1 *1.75 1.75*
b. Pair, imperf. *4.00 4.00*
Nos. 804-807 (4) *7.00 7.00*

For surcharges see Nos. 854-857.

Nos. 381, 387-388, 395, 398-399, 402, 429, 689, and 731 Srchd. in Black, Blue or Red

Methods and Perfs As Before

2006, Jan. 1

808 A28 5g on 8m #395 .35 .35
809 A25 10g on 1m #381 .35 .35
810 A26 10g on 1m #388 .35 .35
811 A35 10g on 25m #429 .35 .35
812 A92 10g on 100m #731 .35 .35
813 A26 20g on 50g #387 .85 .85
814 A32 20g on 20m #402 (Bl) .85 .85
815 A92 20g on 3000m #689 .85 .85
816 A29 60g on 5m #398 (R) 3.25 3.25
817 A29 60g on 8m #399 (R) 3.25 3.25
Nos. 808-817 (10) 10.80 10.80

Pres. Aliyev Type of 2004

2006, Jan. 1 Litho. ***Perf. 14¼x14***

818 A148 60g multi 2.50 2.50

Mosque, Länkäran — A164

2006, Jan. 1 Litho. ***Perf. 13½x14***

819 A164 10g blk & blue .40 .40

Fortress, Lachin — A165

2006, Jan. 1 Litho. ***Perf. 13½x14***

820 A165 20g blk & bister 1.00 1.00

OPEC Intl. Development Fund, 30th Anniv. — A166

2006, Jan. 30 Litho. ***Perf. 14¼x14***

821 A166 5g multi .85 .85

Europa — A167

Monuments and: 20g, Hands, circle of stars. 60g, Dancers, man at computer, oil well, globes.

2006, Mar. 1 ***Perf. 13½x13¼***

822-823 A167 Set of 2 5.00 5.00
823a Booklet pane, 2 each #822-823, perf. 13½x13¾ on 3 sides 22.50 22.50

No. 823a was sold with booklet cover, but unattached to it. The middle columns of the booklet are tete-beche.

2006 World Cup Soccer Championships, Germany — A168

No. 824 — Soccer players and: a, 20g, 2006 World Cup emblem. b, 60g, Emblem, map of Germany.

2006, Mar. 14 ***Perf. 13½***

824 A168 Horiz. pair, #a-b 3.50 3.50

Poets A169

Designs: 10g, Samed Vurgun. 20g, Suleyman Rustam.

2006, Mar. 16 ***Perf. 14x14¼***

825-826 A169 Set of 2 1.40 1.40

Russia Year in Azerbaijan — A170

No. 827: a, 10g, St. Basil's Cathedral, Moscow, Russian flag and arms. b, 20g, Taza Pir Mosque, Azerbaijani flag and arms. c, 30g, Maiden Tower, Azerbaijani flag and arms. d, 60g, Kremlin, Moscow, Russian flag and arms.

2006, Apr. 17 ***Perf. 14x14¼***

827 A170 Block of 4, #a-d 4.00 4.00

Printed in sheets containing two each of Nos. 827a-827d, and 2 labels.

Gulistan Mausoleum, Nakhichevan A171

2006, May 22 Litho. ***Perf. 14¼x14***

828 A171 20g multi .85 .85

World Information Organization Day — A172

2006, June 12

829 A172 1m multi 3.25 3.25

Karabakh Horses A173

Designs: Nos. 830, 834a, 20g, Khan, 1867. Nos. 831, 834b, 20g, Zaman, 1952. Nos. 832, 834c, 20g, Sarvan, 1987. Nos. 833, 834d, 20g, Qar-qar, 2001.
60g, Aliyetmaz, 1867, vert.

2006, June 27 ***Perf. 14x14¼***

Size: 40x28mm

830-833 A173 Set of 4 3.50 3.50

Miniature Sheet

Stamp Size: 52x37mm

Perf. 13½

834 A173 20g Sheet of 4, #a-d 3.50 3.50

Souvenir Sheet

Stamp Size: 28x40mm

Perf. 14¼x14

835 A173 60g multi 2.75 2.75

Summuqqala Tower, Qax — A174

Mausoleum of Nezami, Gäncä — A175

2006, Aug. 3 ***Perf. 13½x14***

836 A174 10g blk & lilac .40 .40
837 A175 20g blk & rose .85 .85

Nos. 797-798 Surcharged

Methods and Perfs As Before

2006, Sept. 28 **Size: 45x35mm**

838 A157 20g on 1000m #797 *1.25 1.25*
839 A157 60g on 3000m #798 *3.00 3.00*
a. Sheet of 4, 2 each #838-839 *8.50 8.50*
b. Sheet of 6, 3 each #838-839 *17.00 17.00*

Nos. 839a-839b were not sold in a booklet, like the unsurcharged stamps. The margins of Nos. 839a-839b, have an overprint commemorating the 50th anniversary of Europa stamps.

Regional Communications Commonwealth, 15th Anniv. — A176

2006, Oct. 9 Litho. ***Perf. 14x14¼***

840 A176 20g multi 1.20 1.20

Independence, 15th Anniv. — A177

2006, Oct. 18

841 A177 20g multi 1.20 1.20

Miniature Sheet

Fire Trucks — A178

No. 842: a, 10g, AMO-F15, 1926. b, 20g, PMQ-1, 1932. c, 60g, PMQ-9, 1950. d, 1m, ATS 2, 5-40, 1998.

2006, Dec. 28

842 A178 Sheet of 4, #a-d 5.50 5.50

Pigeons — A179

No. 843, horiz.: a, Three pigeons. b, Sogani and Qara Ebres pigeons. c, Qirmizi and Qirmizi Cep pigeons. d, Ag Dugus and Qarabas pigeons. e, Two Qara pigeons. f, Qara and Qirmizi Cil pigeons.
1m, Ag Leleyli pigeon.

2007, Jan. 24 ***Perf. 14x14¼***

843 A179 20g Sheet of 6, #a-f 5.00 5.00

Souvenir Sheet

Perf. 14¼x14

844 A179 1m multi 3.00 3.00

Customs Service Buidings — A180

No. 845 — Building for: a, 20g, Baku Customs. b, 60g, Azerbaijan Customs.

2007, Jan. 30 ***Perf. 14¼x14***

845 A180 Horiz. pair, #a-b, + central label 3.75 3.75

Souvenir Sheet

Fall of Khojali, 15th Anniv. — A181

2007, Feb. 26 Litho. ***Perf. 14¼x14***

846 A181 1m multi + 2 labels 3.50 3.50

Europa — A182

Scouting emblem and: 20g, Dove, tents. 60g, Scout, kite.

2007, Apr. 2 ***Perf. 13½x13¼***

847-848 A182 Set of 2 *5.50 5.50*
848a Booklet pane, 4 each #847-848, perf. 13½x13¼ on 3 sides *21.00 21.00*

Scouting, cent. No. 848a was sold with booklet cover, but unattached to it. The middle columns of the booklet are tete-beche.

Friendship Between Azerbaijan and Japan A183

2007, Apr. 5 ***Perf. 14x14¼***

849 A183 1m multi 3.50 3.50

Mosque, Goyçay — A184

2007, Apr. 20 ***Perf. 14x13½***

850 A184 10g blk & yellow .40 .40

Nos. 748, 767, 802, 804-807 Surcharged in Black or Red

Methods and Perfs As Before

2007, Apr. 20

851 A135 60g on 3000m #748 *2.25 2.25*
852 A142 60g on 3000m #767 (R) *2.25 2.25*
853 A161 60g on 3000m #802 *2.40 2.40*
854 A163 60g on 3000m #804 (R) *2.00 2.00*
a. Pair, imperf. *4.00 4.00*
855 A163 60g on 3000m #805 (R) *2.00 2.00*
a. Pair, imperf. *4.00 4.00*
856 A163 60g on 3000m #806 (R) *2.00 2.00*
a. Pair, imperf. *4.00 4.00*
857 A163 60g on 3000m #807 (R) *2.00 2.00*
a. Pair, imperf. *4.00 4.00*
Nos. 851-857 (7) *14.90 14.90*

Dog Fight, by Azim Azimade A185

Wedding, by Azim Azimade A186

2007, June 5 Litho. *Perf. 14x14¼*

858 Horiz. pair with central label *2.10 2.10*
a. A185 20g multi *1.00 1.00*
b. A186 20g multi *1.00 1.00*

Azermarka, 15th Anniv. — A187

2007, July 14 *Perf. 14¼x14*

859 A187 50g multi *2.75 2.75*

Knut, Polar Bear Cub Born in Berlin Zoo A188

2007, Aug. 15 *Perf. 13x13¼*

860 A188 60g shown *3.00 3.00*
a. Souvenir sheet of 4 *12.00 12.00*

Souvenir Sheet

861 A188 1m Knut, vert. *5.00 5.00*

No. 861 contains one 30x38mm stamp.

Flowers — A189

No. 862: a, 10g, Gagea alexeenkoana. b, 20g, Centaurea ficher. c, 40g, Galanthus caucasicus. d, 60g, Ophrys caucasica.
1m, Ophrys caucasica, diff.

2007, Aug. 20 *Perf. 14x14¼*

862 A189 Sheet of 4, #a-d *3.50 3.50*

Souvenir Sheet

863 A189 1m multi *3.00 3.00*

Hüseyn Cavid (1882-1941), Writer — A190

2007, Sept. 19

864 A190 20g multi *1.20 1.20*

Bridges — A191

No. 865: a, 10g, Xudaferin Bridge. b, 20g, Qazançi Bridge. c, 30g, Qudyalçay Bridge. d, 50g, Gancaçay Bridge.
60g, Xudaferin Bridge, diff.

2007, Nov. 1 Litho. *Perf. 14x14¼*

865 A191 Sheet of 4, #a-d *4.25 4.25*

Souvenir Sheet

866 A191 60g multi *2.50 2.50*

No. 401 Surcharged

Methods and Perfs As Before

2007, Nov. 28

867 A31 10g on 15m #401 .40 .40

Xudaferin Bridge, Jabrayil — A192

Fortress, Kalbacar — A193

2007, Nov. 28 Litho. *Perf. 14x13½*

868 A192 10g blk & pale org .50 .50
869 A193 20g blk & green .90 .90

Souvenir Sheet

Launch of Sputnik 1, 50th Anniv. — A194

2007, Nov. 28 *Perf. 14¼x14*

870 A194 1m multi 4.50 4.50

Souvenir Sheet

Lt. Gen. Karim Karimov (1917-2003), USSR Space Flight Commission Chairman — A195

2007, Dec. 30

871 A195 1m multi 4.25 4.25

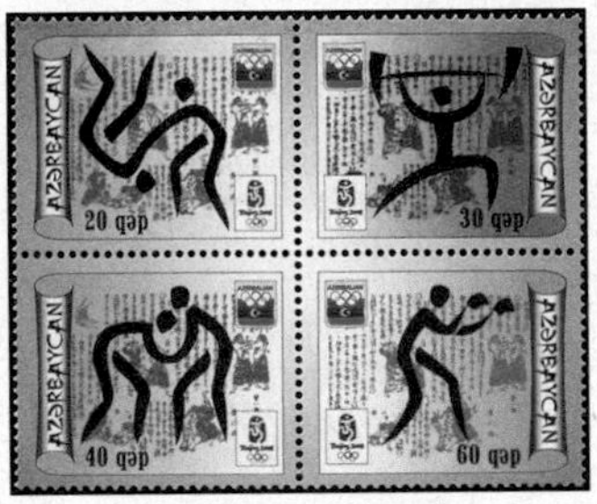

2008 Summer Olympics, Beijing — A196

No. 872: a, 20g, Judo. b, 30g, Weight lifting. c, 40g, Wrestling. d, 60g, Boxing.

2008, Feb. 25 *Perf. 14x14¼*

872 A196 Block of 4, #a-d *5.50 5.50*

Europa — A197

Designs: 20g, Open envelope. 60g, Computer monitor.
1m, Dove.

2008, Mar. 13 Litho. *Perf. 13½*

873-874 A197 Set of 2 5.50 5.50
874a Booklet pane, 4 each #873-874, perf. 13½ on 3 sides 22.00 22.00

Souvenir Sheet

Perf. 13¼x13¾

875 A197 1m multi 5.50 5.50

No. 874a was sold with booklet cover, but unattached to it. The middle columns of the booklet are tete-beche.
No. 875 contains one 18x25mm stamp.

Tower, Qazak — A198

2008, Apr. 8 *Perf. 13½x14*

876 A198 10g blk & sal pink .40 .40

Nakhichevan Drama Theater, 125th Anniv. — A199

2008, Apr. 9 *Perf. 14x14¼*

877 A199 20g multi 1.20 1.20

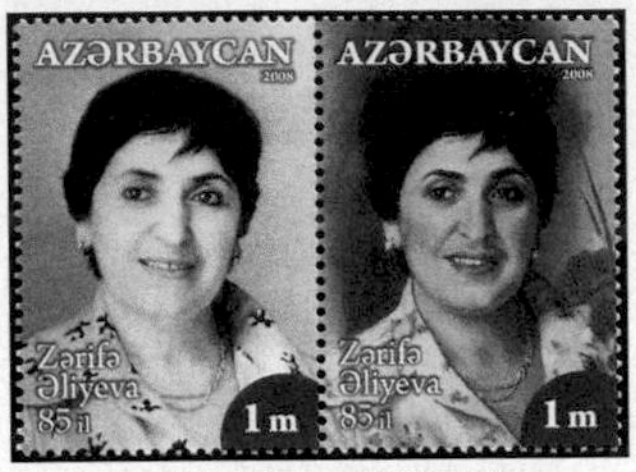

Zarifa Aliyeva (1923-85), Ophthalmologist, Wife of Pres. Heydar Aliyev — A200

Pres. Heydar Aliyev (1923-2003) — A201

No. 878 — Mrs. Aliyeva: a, Plain background. b, Flower in background.
No. 879 — Pres. Aliyev: a, And Azerbaijan flag. b, Blue and green background.

2008 Litho. *Perf. 14¼x14*

878 A200 1m Pair, #a-b 7.50 7.50
879 A201 1m Pair, #a-b 7.50 7.50

Issued: No. 878, 4/28; No. 879, 5/2. Nos. 878 and 879 were each printed in sheets containing four of each stamp of that particular pair and a central label.

Azerbaijan Republic, 90th Anniv. A202

2008, May 28 *Perf. 14x14¼*

880 A202 20g multi 1.20 1.20

Mikayil Müsfiq (1908-39), Poet A203

2008, June 6

881 A203 20g multi 1.20 1.20

Physicists A204

Designs: No. 882, 20g, Lev Landau (1908-68). No. 883, 20g, Hasan Abdullayev (1918-93).

2008, July 21 Litho. *Perf. 14x14¼*

882-883 A204 Set of 2 2.50 2.50

Miniature Sheet

Caspian Shipping Company, 150th Anniv. — A205

No. 884: a, 20g, Tanker Heydar Aliyev. b, 30g, Ferry Azerbaijan. c, 50g, Cargo ship Bestekar Qara Qarayev. d, 60g, Cargo ship Maestro Niyaz. e, 1m, Tanker Vandal.

2008, Sept. 21 ***Perf. 13½***
884 A205 Sheet of 5, #a-e, + 4 labels 9.00 9.00

Jewelry — A206

No. 885: a, Earring 12th-13th cent. b, Pendant, 19th cent.

2008, Sept. 18 ***Perf. 11½***
885 A206 60g Horiz. pair, #a-b, + central label 5.25 5.25

See Ukraine No. 742.

Khanagah Mausoleum, Culfa A207

Garabaghla Mausoleum, Sarur A208

2008, Oct. 3 **Litho.** ***Perf. 14x13½***
886 A207 10g blk & brown .40 .40

Perf. 13½x14
887 A208 20g blk & gray .85 .85

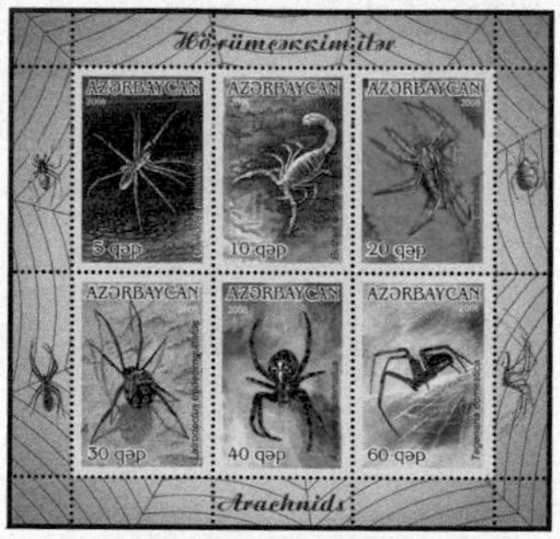

Arachnids — A209

No. 888: a, 5g, Galeodes araneoides. b, 10g, Buthus occitanus. c, 20g, Pisaura mirabilis. d, 30g, Latrodectus tredecimguttatus. e, 40g, Araneus diadematus. f, 60g, Tegenaria domestica.
1m, Argyroneta aquatica.

2008, Dec. 2 ***Perf. 14¼x14***
888 A209 Sheet of 6, #a-f 6.00 6.00

Souvenir Sheet

889 A209 1m multi 4.00 4.00

Mir Jalal (1908-78), Writer — A210

2008, Dec. 17
890 A210 60g multi 2.25 2.25

Azerbaijan postal authorities declared as illegal miniature sheets dated 2008 depiciting the Pope and Princess Diana, Mushrooms, Dinosaurs, Horses, Dogs, Animals and Cats.

Miniature Sheet

Nakhichevan Autonomous Republic, 85th Anniv. — A211

No. 891 — Buildings: a, H. Javid Mausoleum (white building with steps at left). b, Heydar Aliyev School (with curved front, flowers at right). c, Nakhichevan Ministry of Economy building (with island gardens). d, Library, Nakhichevan State University (with red roof and striped curbs). e, Conservatory, Nakhichevan State University (with striped curbs). f, Physiotherapy Center (with curved front and circular garden). g, Tebriz Hotel (with dome at right). h, Medical Center of Nakhichevan (with curved front with brown vertical lines on wings).

2009, Feb. 7
891 A211 20g Sheet of 8, #a-h, + central label 6.50 6.50

Baku, Center of Islamic Culture — A212

Designs: 10g, Emblem. 20g, Emblem and Maiden Tower, Baku.

2009, Feb. 18 ***Perf. 13½x14***
892-893 A212 Set of 2 1.25 1.25

Souvenir Sheet

Preservation of Polar Regions and Glaciers — A213

No. 894 — Emblem and map of: a, Antarctica. b, Greenland and Arctic region.

2009, Mar. 3 ***Perf. 13¾x13½***
894 A213 1m Sheet of 2, #a-b 7.00 7.00

10th Economic Cooperation Organization Summit, Tehran — A214

2009, Apr. 2 ***Perf. 14¼x14***
895 A214 1m multi 3.50 3.50

See Iran 2981, compare with Pakistan 1111.

Europa — A215

Designs: 20g, Nasir ad-Din at-Tusi (1201-74), scientist. 60g, Samaxi Observatory and Moon.
1m, Earth, Moon, telescope of Galileo.

2009, Apr. 13 ***Perf. 13½x13¼***
896-897 A215 Set of 2 5.50 5.50
897a Booklet pane of 8, 4 each #896-897, perf. 13½x13¼ on 3 sides 22.00 —

Souvenir Sheet

898 A215 1m multi 5.50 5.50

Intl. Year of Astronomy. No. 897a was sold with booklet cover, but unattached to it. The middle columns of the booklet pane are tete-beche.

Azerbaijan's Cooperation With NATO, 15th Anniv. — A216

2009, May 4 **Litho.** ***Perf. 14x14¼***
899 A216 20g multi .85 .85

Printed in sheets of 8 + 2 labels.

European Council, 60th Anniv. A217

2009, May 5
900 A217 60g multi 2.75 2.75

European Court of Human Rights, 50th Anniv. A218

2009, May 5
901 A218 60g multi 2.75 2.75

Sumqayit, 60th Anniv. — A219

2009, June 1 ***Perf. 13½x14***
902 A219 10g multi .75 .75

Butterflies — A220

Designs: 10g, Vanessa atalanta. 20g, Papilio alexanor orientalis.

2009, June 1
903-904 A220 Set of 2 1.25 1.25

See Nos.913-914, 928-929, 939.

Diplomatic Service, 90th Anniv. — A221

2009, July 9 **Litho.** ***Perf. 14¼x14***
905 A221 60g multi 2.50 2.50

Printed in sheets of 8 + central label.

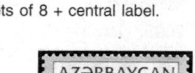

Jalil Mammadguluzadeh (1869-1932), Writer — A222

2009, July 10
906 A222 20g multi 1.25 1.25

Leyla Mammadbeyova (1909-89), Test Pilot — A223

2009, Sept. 19 **Litho.** ***Perf. 14x14¼***
907 A223 20g multi 1.00 1.00

State Oil Fund, 10th Anniv. — A224

2009, Oct. 8 ***Perf. 14¼x14***
908 A224 60g multi 2.00 2.00

Printed in sheets of 8 + central label.

Universal Postal Union, 135th Anniv. A225

No. 909 — Background color: a, 20g, Pale orange. b, 60g, Rose pink.

2009, Oct. 9 ***Perf. 14x14¼***
909 A225 Pair, #a-b 3.25 3.25

Miniature Sheet

Birds — A226

No. 910: a, 10g, Platalea leucorodia. b, 20g, Phalacrocorax pygmaeus. c, 60g, Numenius tenuirostris. d, 1m, Porphyrio porphyrio.

2009, Oct. 19 **Litho.**
910 A226 Sheet of 4, #a-d 6.50 6.50

Souvenir Sheet

Azerbaijan, 2009 European Chess Champions — A227

No. 911 — Chess pieces and map of: a, 50g, Europe. b, 1m, Azerbaijan.

2009, Oct. 8 ***Perf. 14¼x14***
911 A227 Sheet of 2, #a-b 5.00 5.00

Miniature Sheet

Paintings by Sattar Bahlulzadeh (1909-74) — A228

No. 912: a, Qedim Samaxi (Ancient Shamakhi). b, Zeferanla Narlar (Saffron with Pomegranates). c, Buzovna Sahil (Buzovna Shore). d, Menzere (View). e, Laleler (Poppies). f, Qirmizi Menzere (Red View).

2009, Dec. 15 ***Perf. 14x14¼***
912 A228 20g Sheet of 6, #a-f, + 3 central labels 5.50 5.50

Butterflies Type of 2009

Designs: 10g, Thaleropis jonia. 20g, Danaus chrysippus.

2010, Jan. 11 ***Perf. 13½x14***
913-914 A220 Set of 2 1.25 1.25

Souvenir Sheet

January 20, 1990 Baku Massacre — A229

2010, Jan. 20 ***Perf. 14¼x14***
915 A229 1m multi + 2 labels 3.50 3.50

Ministry of Taxation, 10th Anniv. A230

2010, Feb. 11 ***Perf. 14x14¼***
916 A230 60g multi 2.25 2.25

New Year 2010 (Year of the Tiger) — A231

Litho. With Foil Application

2010, Mar. 1 ***Perf. 14¼x14***
917 A231 60g multi 2.25 2.25

Azerbaijan Red Crescent Society, 90th Anniv. A232

2010, Mar. 10 **Litho.** ***Perf. 14x14¼***
918 A232 60g multi 2.25 2.25

Europa — A233

Characters from children's stories: 20g, Boy, dog and bear. 60g, Lion, wolf, duck, fox. 1m, Ogre and children.

2010, Mar. 16 ***Perf. 13x13¼***
919-920 A233 Set of 2 5.00 5.00
920a Booklet pane of 8, 4 each #919-920, perf. 13 on 3 sides 20.00 —

Souvenir Sheet

Perf. 13

921 A233 1m multi 6.00 6.00

No. 920a was sold with booklet cover, but unattached to it. The middle columns of the booklet pane are tete-beche.

Peonies — A234

No. 922 — Flower color: a, Yellow. b, Pink. c, White. d, Red.
20g, Peonies in vase.

2010, Apr. 10 ***Perf. 13¼***
922 A234 10g Sheet of 4, #a-d 2.50 2.50

Souvenir Sheet

923 A234 20g multi 1.50 1.50

Victory in World War II, 65th Anniv. — A235

No. 924 — 65th anniversary emblem and: a, 10g, Soviet soldiers in front of statue in Berlin. b, 20g, Soviet soldiers raising Soviet flag over Reichstag building, Berlin. c, 60g, Soviet airplane, rail tanker.

2010, Apr. 20 **Litho.** ***Perf. 14¼x14***
924 A235 Horiz. strip of 3 3.50 3.50

Printed in sheets containing two strips separated by a horizontal strip of three labels.

2010 World Cup Soccer Championships, South Africa — A236

No. 925 — Soccer player and 2010 World Cup: a, 20g, Emblem. b, 60g, Mascot.

2010, May 18 ***Perf. 14x14¼***
925 A236 Pair, #a-b 3.25 3.25

Souvenir Sheet

Azerbaijan Pavilion, Expo 2010, Shanghai — A237

2010, May 18 ***Perf. 13¼***
926 A237 60g multi 2.50 2.50

Alesker Alekberov (1910-63), Actor A238

2010, June 18 ***Perf. 14x14¼***
927 A238 20g multi 1.25 1.25

Butterflies Type of 2009

Designs: 10g, Argynnis alexandra. 20g, Brahmaea christophi.

2010, July 15 ***Perf. 13½x14***
928-929 A220 Set of 2 1.25 1.25

Mausoleum of Noah, Nakhichevan A239

2010, July 19 ***Perf. 14¼x14***
930 A239 60g multi 2.50 2.50

Buildings in Baku's Old City — A240

No. 931: a, 10g, Shirvanshah Palace, 12th-15th cent. b, 20g, Bazaar Square, 15th cent. c, 30g, Fortress archways, 19th cent. d, 40g, Came Mosque, 14th cent. e, 50g, Qasim Bey Bathhouse, 15th cent. f, 60g, Multam and Bukhara Caravansaries, 15th cent.

No. 932, vert.: a, 10g, Maiden Tower, 6th cent. b, 20g, Muhammad Mosque, 11th cent. c, 30g, Fortress walls, 12th cent. d, 40g, Palace Mosque, 15th cent. e, 50g, Shirvanshah Tomb, 15th cent. f, 60g, Divankhana, 15th cent.

1m, Shirvanshah Palace complex, 12th-15th cent.

2010, July 26 ***Perf. 13½***

Sheets of 6, #a-f

931-932 A240 Set of 2 *17.00 17.00*

Souvenir Sheet

Perf. 14¼x14

933 A240 1m multi 5.00 5.00

No. 933 contains one 56x40mm stamp.

Souvenir Sheet

Temples — A241

No. 934: a, Ateshgah, Baku, Azerbaijan. b, Pyramid of the Sun, Teotihuacan, Mexico.

2010, Oct. 12 **Litho.** ***Perf. 14x14¼***
934 A241 60g Sheet of 2 5.00 5.00

See Mexico No. 2699.

Shafaat Mehdiyev (1910-93), Geologist A242

2010, Nov. 5 ***Perf. 14x14¼***
935 A242 60g multi 2.25 2.25

Cats — A243

No. 936: a, 10g, Scottish fold cat. b, 2g, Persian cat. c, 30g, Somali cat. d, 40g, British shorthaired cat. e, 50g, Burmese cat. f, 60g, Maine Coon cat.
1m, Angora cat.

2010, Nov. 8 ***Perf. 14¼x14***
936 A243 Sheet of 6, #a-f 7.00 7.00

Souvenir Sheet

937 A243 1m multi 3.50 3.50

Birds of the Caspian Sea — A244

No. 938: a, Ardeola ralloides. b, Phoenicopterus roseus.

2010, Nov. 24 ***Perf. 14¼x14***
938 A244 60g Pair, #a-b 4.00 4.00

See Kazakhstan No. 632.

Butterflies Type of 2009

2010, Dec. 15 ***Perf. 13½x14***
939 A220 10g Parnassius apollo .90 .90

Flowers — A245

Designs: 20g, Centaurea fischeri. 50g, Gagea alexeenkoana.

2011, Mar. 10 ***Perf. 13½x14***
940-941 A245 Set of 2 2.50 2.50

See Nos. 951-952.

Novruz Festival — A246

2011, Mar. 18 Litho. ***Perf. 14¼x14***
942 A246 30g multi 1.25 1.25

New Year 2011 (Year of the Rabbit) — A247

Litho. With Foil Application

2011, Mar. 18
943 A247 1m multi 3.50 3.50

Admission of Azerbaijan to European Council, 10th Anniv. — A248

2011, Mar. 18 Litho. ***Perf. 14x14¼***
944 A248 1m multi 3.50 3.50

Europa A249

Designs: 20g, Ulmus densa. 60g, Platanus orientalis.
1m, Parrotia persica.

2011, Apr. 8 ***Perf. 13¼x13***
945 A249 20g multi 1.00 1.00
a. Perf. 13 on 3 sides 1.00 1.00
946 A249 60g multi 4.00 4.00
a. Perf. 13 on 3 sides 4.00 4.00
b. Booklet pane of 8, 4 each #945a-946a 20.00 —

Souvenir Sheet

947 A249 1m multi 5.50 5.50

Intl. Year of Forests. No. 946b was sold with booklet cover, but unattached to it. The middle columns of the booklet pane are tete-beche.

Souvenir Sheet

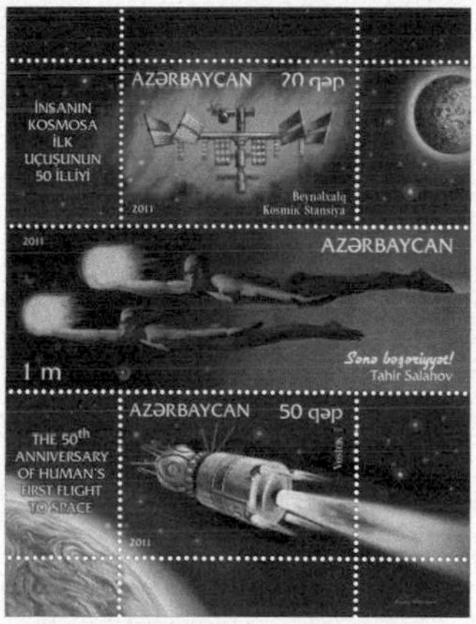

First Manned Space Flight, 50th Anniv. — A250

No. 948: a, 20g, International Space Station (40x28mm). b, 50g, Vostok 1 (40x28mm). c, 1m, To You Mankind, painting by Tahir Salakhov (79x28mm).

Perf. 14x14¼, 14 Horiz. (1m)

2011, Apr. 12
948 A250 Sheet of 3, #a-c 6.00 6.00

Huseyn Aliyev (1911-91), Painter — A251

2011, Apr. 22 ***Perf. 14¼x14***
949 A251 60g multi 2.25 2.25

Musical Instruments — A252

No. 950: a, Hurdy-gurdy (tekerli lira), Belarus. b, Tar, Azerbaijan.

2011, May 25 Litho. ***Perf. 14x14¼***
950 A252 50g Pair, #a-b 3.50 3.50

See Belarus No. 770.

Flowers Type of 2011

Designs: 10g, Ophrys caucasica. 30g, Galanthus caucasicus.

2011, June 20 ***Perf. 13½x14***
951-952 A245 Set of 2 1.75 1.75

Souvenir Sheet

Victory of Eldar Qasimov and Nigar Camal in 2011 Eurovision Song Contest — A253

2011, July 5 ***Perf. 14¼x14***
953 A253 1m multi 3.75 3.75

Heydar Aliyev Palace, Nakhchivan — A254

2011, July 15 ***Perf. 14x14¼***
954 A254 60g multi 2.00 2.00

A255

No. 955: a, Behbud Aga Sahtaxtinski (1881-1924), Minister of State Control. b, Map of Azerbaijan at 1921 signing of Treaty of Kars.

2011, July 15
955 A255 60g Horiz. pair, #a-b 4.00 4.00

Chrysanthemums — A256

No. 956 — Chrysanthemums at: a, 10g, Right. b, 20g, Left.

2011, Aug. 3 ***Perf. 12¾x13***
956 A256 Horiz. pair, #a-b 1.25 1.25

Printed in sheets containing 3 pairs.

Miniature Sheet

Medals and Orders of Azerbaijan — A257

No. 957: a, Order of Heydar Aliyev. b, Gold Star medal. c, Order of Independence (Istiqlal). d, Order of Shah Ismail (Sah Ismayil). e, Order of the Azerbaijani Flag (Azerbaycan Bayragi). f, Order of Honor (Seref). g, Order of Glory (Söhret). h, Order of Friendship (Dostluq). i, Order of Service to the Motherland (Vetene Xidmete Göre).

2011, Sept. 5 ***Perf. 13½***
957 A257 60g Sheet of 9, #a-i 17.50 17.50

Miniature Sheets

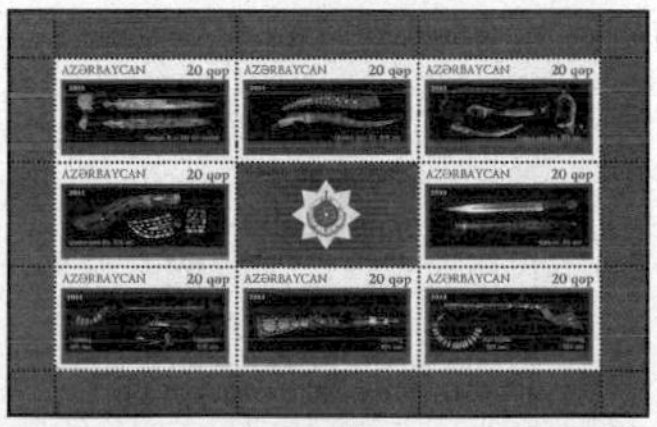

A258

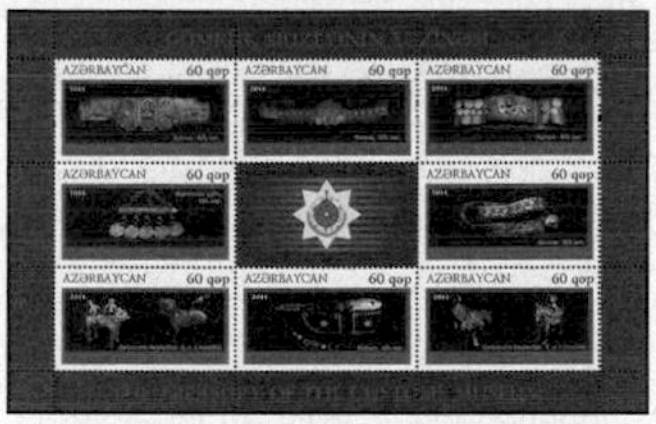

Items in Customs Museum — A259

No. 958: a, Two daggers, 12th-7th cent. B.C. b, Curved dagger with thin blade and scabbard, 19th cent. c, Curved sword, scabbard, sword handle, 19th cent. d, Dagger with wide blade and scabbard, 19th cent. e, Straight dagger and scabbard, 20th cent. f, Rifle and pistol, 19th cent. g, Rifle, 19th cent. h, Rifle and powder horn, 19th cent.

No. 959: a, Belt with oval and rectanuglar panels, 19th cent. b, Belt with loops at bottom and oval buckle, 19th cent. c, Belt with round buttons, 19th cent. d, Cylindrical case with chain and pendants, 19th cent. e, Belt with loops at bottom and round buckle, 19th cent. f, Decorative statues depicting people on amimals, 1st cent. B.C. g, Rübab, 19th cent. h, Decorative statues depicting two-headed animal and horseman, 1st cent. B.C.

2011, Sept. 5
958 A258 20g Sheet of 8, #a-h, + central label 5.00 5.00
959 A259 60g Sheet of 8, #a-h, + central label 15.00 15.00

Nizami Ganjavi (1141-1209), Poet — A260

No. 960 — Ganjavi facing: a, Right. b, Left.

2011, Sept. 21 **Litho.**
960 A260 30g Horiz. pair, #a-b, + central label 2.50 2.50

Regional Communications Commonwealth, 20th Anniv. — A261

2011, Sept. 23 ***Perf. 14x14¼***
961 A261 50g multi 2.00 2.00

Commonwealth of Independent States, 20th Anniv. — A262

2011, Sept. 23
962 A262 60g multi 2.50 2.50

Independence, 20th Anniv. — A263

No. 963: a, Azerbaijan coat of arms. b, Azerbaijan flag. c, Azerbaijan national anthem. d, Azerbaijan map.
No. 964, 2m, Flag and map of Azerbaijan. No. 965, 2m, Pres. Heydar Aliyev and flag.

Litho. & Embossed With Foil Application

2011, Oct. 11 ***Perf. 13½x13***
963 A263 1m Sheet of 4, #a-d 12.50 12.50

Souvenir Sheets

964-965 A263 Set of 2 12.50 12.50

Azerbaijan's Candidacy for Seat on United Nations Security Council — A264

2011, Oct. 21 **Litho.** ***Perf. 14x14¼***
966 A264 60g multi 2.25 2.25

Worldwide Fund for Nature (WWF) — A265

No. 967 — Circaetus gallicus: a, 20g, Two birds in flight. b, 30g, Two adults and chick. c, 50g, Two adults. d, 60g, One adult attacking prey.

2011, Oct. 28
967 A265 Block of 4, #a-d 5.00 5.00
e. Souvenir sheet of 4, #967a-967d 5.00 5.00
f. Souvenir sheet of 8, 2 separated vertical rows of #967a-967d 10.00 10.00

Flag Day — A266

2011, Nov. 9 ***Perf. 14¼x14***
968 A266 30g multi 1.25 1.25

Karabakh Horses — A267

Various horses: 10g, 20g, 30g, 50g.

2011, Nov. 16 ***Perf. 14x13½***
969-972 A267 Set of 4 3.75 3.75

Abbas Zamanov (1911-93), Literary Critic — A268

2011, Dec. 1 ***Perf. 14¼x14***
973 A268 60g multi 2.25 2.25

First Use of Telephone in Azerbaijan, 130th Anniv. A269

2011, Dec. 6 ***Perf. 14x14¼***
974 A269 1m multi 3.00 3.00

Dogs — A270

No. 975: a, 10g, Shar Pei. b, 20g, Dalmatian. c, 30g, Labrador retriever. d, 40g, Doberman Pinscher. e, 50g, Chow Chow. f, 60g, German Shepherd.
1m, Caucasian Shepherds, horiz.

2011, Dec. 10 ***Perf. 14¼x14***
975 A270 Sheet of 6, #a-f 6.50 6.50

Souvenir Sheet

Perf. 14x14¼

976 A270 1m multi 3.00 3.00

Souvenir Sheet

World Championship of Rabita Baku Women's Volleyball Team — A271

2011, Dec. 26 ***Perf. 14¼x14***
977 A271 1m multi 3.75 3.75

New Year 2012 (Year of the Dragon) A272

2012, Jan. 5 **Litho.** ***Perf. 13¼***
978 A272 20g multi .90 .90

Central Bank of Azerbaijan, 20th Anniv. A273

2012, Feb. 12 ***Perf. 14x14¼***
979 A273 50g multi 2.10 2.10

Bahruz Kengerli (1892-1922), Painter — A274

2012, Mar. 15 ***Perf. 14¼x14***
980 A274 20g multi 1.00 1.00

Europa A275

Designs: 20g, Beach on Caspian Sea, airplane, sailboat. 60g, Skier and chairlift.
1m, Baku International Airport, vert.

2012, Mar. 15 ***Perf. 13¼x13***
981-982 A275 Set of 2 5.00 5.00
982a Booklet pane of 8, 4 each #981-982, perf. 13 on 3 sides 20.00 —

Souvenir Sheet

Perf. 13x13¼

983 A275 1m multi 6.00 6.00

No. 982a was sold with, but unattached to, a booklet cover.

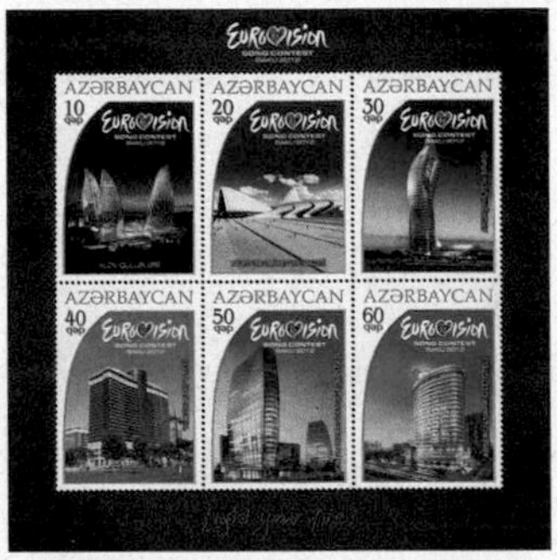

A276

A277

2012 Eurovision Song Contest, Baku — A278

No. 984: a, 10g, Flame Towers. b, 20g, Heydar Aliyev Center. c, 30g, SOCAR (State Oil Company of Azerbaijan) Tower. d, 40g, Baku Hilton Hotel. e, 50g, Port Baku Residences. f, 60g, Absheron Marriott Hotel.
No. 985: a, 10g, Heydar Aliyev Palace. b, 20g, Opera and Ballet Theater. c, 30g, Philharmonic Hall. d, 40g, Green Theater. e, 50g, Mugam Center. f, 60g, Rashid Behbudov State Song Theater.
No. 986: a, 10g, Shirvansahlar Palace. b, 20g, Government House. c, 30g, Baku City Hall. d, 40g, Nizami Museum of Azerbaijani Literature. e, 50g, Heydar Aliyev Foundation Building. f, 60g, Presidium of Azerbaijan National Academy of Sciences.
No. 987, Eurovision Song Contest emblem, Shirvansahlar Palace. No. 988, Flame, Eurovision Song Contest emblem.

Litho. & Embossed With Foil Application

2012, May 14

984 A276 Sheet of 6, #a-f 6.00 6.00
985 A277 Sheet of 6, #a-f 6.00 6.00
986 A278 Sheet of 6, #a-f 6.00 6.00
Nos. 984-986 (3) 18.00 18.00

Souvenir Sheets

987 A278 60g multi 2.00 2.00
988 A278 60g multi 2.00 2.00

Diplomatic Relations Between Azerbaijan and People's Republic of China, 20th Anniv. A279

2012, June 13 Litho. ***Perf. 14x14¼***
989 A279 50g multi 2.00 2.00

Mirza Fatali Axundzade (1812-78), Writer — A280

2012, June 30 ***Perf. 14¼x14***
990 A280 20g multi 1.20 1.20

Mirza Alakbar Sabir (1862-1911), Philosopher A281

2012, July 10
991 A281 20g multi 1.20 1.20

Souvenir Sheet

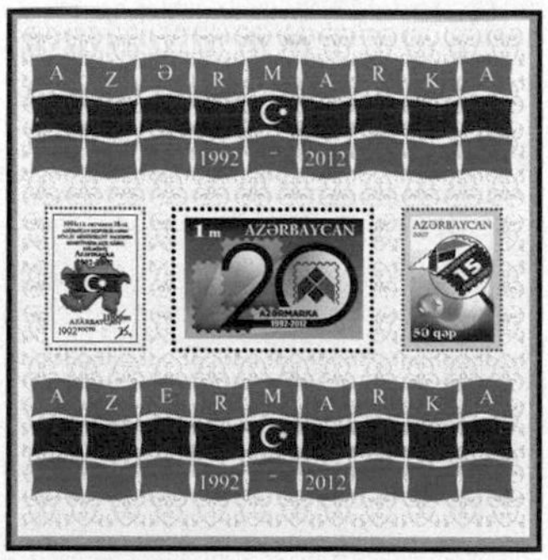

Azermarka, 20th Anniv. — A282

2012, July 14 ***Perf. 14x14¼***
992 A282 1m multi 3.50 3.50

Mammed Said Ordubadi (1872-1950), Writer — A283

2012, Aug. 17 ***Perf. 14¼x14***
993 A283 50g multi 1.75 1.75

Müslüm Magomayev (1942-2008), Singer — A284

2012, Aug. 17
994 A284 50g multi 1.75 1.75

Aythya Nyroca — A285

Various depictions of Aythya nyroca.

2012, Sept. 12 ***Perf. 14x13½***

Frame Color

995 A285 10g yellow .40 .40
996 A285 20g rose lilac .75 .75
997 A285 50g light blue 1.75 1.75
Nos. 995-997 (3) 2.90 2.90

Baku and Arms — A286

National Flag and Symbol — A287

2012, Apr. 6 ***Perf. 14xx14¼***
998 A286 60g multi + label 2.00 2.00

Perf. 14¼x14

999 A287 60g multi + label 2.00 2.00

Souvenir Sheet

Diplomatic Relations Between Azerbaijan and Egypt, 20th Anniv. — A288

No. 1000: a, Maiden's Tower, Azerbaijan. b, Sphinx and Pyramids, Egypt.

2012, June 13 ***Perf. 14x14¼***
1000 A288 60g Sheet of 2, #a-b 4.25 4.25

Huseyn Javid (1882-1941), Poet — A289

2012, Oct. 24 ***Perf. 14¼x14***
1001 A289 20g multi 1.00 1.00

Souvenir Sheet

Karabakh Costumes of the 19th Century — A290

No. 1002 — Emblem of Regional Communications Commonwealth and: a, Woman and girl. b, Man and boy.

2012, Oct. 29
1002 A290 50g Sheet of 2, #a-b 3.50 3.50

Souvenir Sheet

Diplomatic Relations Between Azerbaijan and Poland, 540th Anniv. — A291

No. 1003: a, Sultan Uzun Hasan (1423-78). b, King Casimir IV of Poland (1427-92).

2012, Oct. 29
1003 A291 60g Sheet of 2, #a-b 4.00 4.00

Birds — A292

No. 1004: a, 10g, Goose. b, 20g, Turkey. c, 30g, Chicken. d, 40g, Guinea fowl. e, 50g, Duck. f, 60g, Quail.
1m, Rooster, hen and chick.

2012, Nov. 5
1004 A292 Sheet of 6, #a-f 7.00 7.00

Souvenir Sheet

1005 A292 1m multi 3.00 3.00

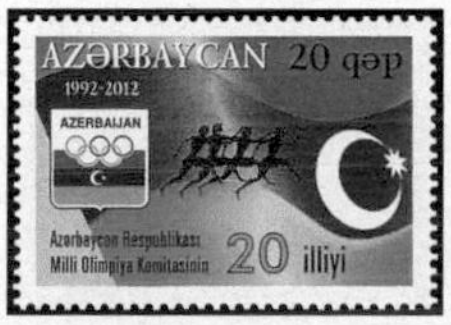

Azerbaijan Olympic Committee, 20th Anniv. A293

2012, Nov. 7 ***Perf. 14x14¼***
1006 A293 20g multi 1.00 1.00

Souvenir Sheet

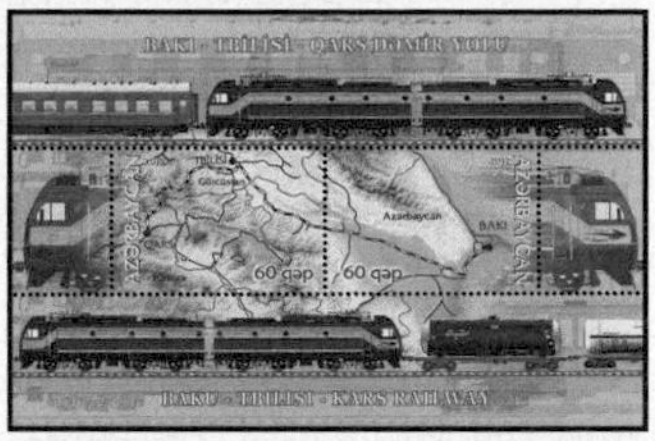

Baku-Tbilisi-Kars Railway — A294

No. 1007 — Map of: a, Western Azerbaijan showing Kars and Tbilisi. b, Eastern Azerbaijan showing Baku.

2012, Nov. 12
1007 A294 60g Sheet of 2, #a-b 4.50 4.50

Developmental Partnership With World Bank, 20th Anniv. — A295

2012, Dec. 14
1008 A295 50g multi 1.75 1.75

Souvenir Sheet

First Azerbaijan Telecommunications Satellite — A296

2013, Jan. 15 ***Perf. 12x12¼***
1009 A296 1m multi 3.50 3.50

Miniature Sheet

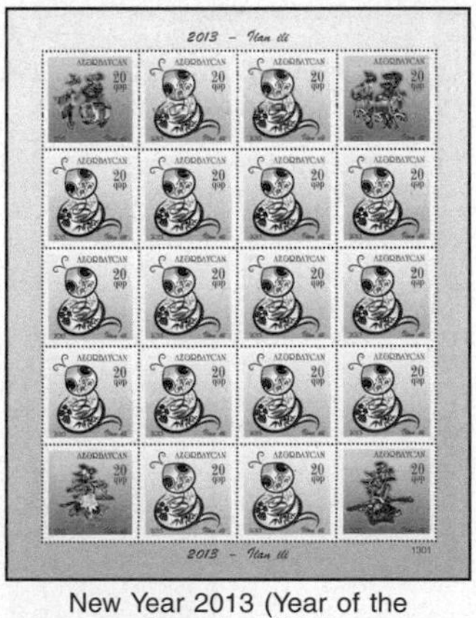

New Year 2013 (Year of the Snake) — A297

No. 1010: a, Fish on Chinese character. b, Deer on Chinese character. c, Cranes on Chinese character. d, Bird on Chinese character. e, Snake.

2013, Jan. 23 ***Perf. 13¼***
1010 A297 20g Sheet of 20, #1010a-1010d, 16 #1010e 12.50 12.50

Europa
A298

Postal vehicles: 20g, Truck. 60g, Van. 1m, Horse-drawn carriage.

2013, Feb. 25 ***Perf. 13¼x13***

1011-1012 A298 Set of 2 5.00 5.00
1012a Booklet pane of 8, 4 each #1011-1012, perf. 13 on 3 sides 20.00 20.00

Souvenir Sheet

1013 A298 1m multi 5.00 5.00

No. 1012a was sold with, but unattached to, a booklet cover. The two different stamps are found tete-beche within the booklet.

Intl. Association of Academies of Science, 20th Anniv. — A299

2013, Apr. 10 ***Perf. 14¼x14***

1014 A299 20g multi .90 .90

Miniature Sheet

Lighthouses — A300

No. 1015: a, Süvelan Lighthouse. b, Amburan Lighthouse. c, Böyük Zire Lighthouse. d, Abseron Lighthouse. e, Cilov Lighthouse.

2013, Apr. 11 ***Perf. 12***

1015 A300 50g Sheet of 5, #a-e, + label 7.75 7.75

Islam Safarli (1923-74), Poet — A301

Alimardan Topchubashov (1863-1934), Politician — A302

Hokuma Gurbanova (1913-88), Actress
A303

Nigar Rafibeyli (1913-81), Writer
A304

2013, Apr. 19 ***Perf. 14¼x14***

1016 A301 20g multi .75 .75

Perf. 14x14¼

1017 A302 20g multi .75 .75
1018 A303 20g multi .75 .75
1019 A304 20g multi .75 .75
Nos. 1016-1019 (4) 3.00 3.00

Souvenir Sheet

Dancers — A305

No. 1020: a, Terekeme dancers, Azerbaijan. b, Kryzhachok dancers, Belarus.

2013, Apr. 24 ***Perf. 13½x13***

1020 A305 50g Sheet of 2, #a-b 3.25 3.25

See Belarus No. 855.

Souvenir Sheet

Zarifa Aliyeva (1923-85), Ophthalmologist, Wife of Pres. Heydar Aliyev — A306

Litho. & Embossed With Foil Application

2013, Apr. 28

1021 A306 1m multi 3.25 3.25

Pres. Heydar Aliyev (1923-2003), Order of St. Andrew the Apostle — A307

2013, May 6 **Litho.** ***Perf. 13½***

1022 A307 50g multi 1.90 1.90

See Russia No. 7442.

A308

A309

Pres. Heydar Aliyev (1923-2003) — A310

No. 1023 — Pres. Aliyev: a, As young man in suit and tie. b, As young man in army uniform. c, As older man, wearing medals. d, Waving. e, Behind microphone, with hand on book. f, With soldiers, holding binoculars.

No. 1024 — Pres. Aliyev with: a, Turkish Pres. Süleyman Demirel, seated on red chairs. b, U.S. Pres. Bill Clinton. c, German Chancellor Helmut Kohl, paneled wall in background. d, Russian Pres. Vladimir Putin, picture frame behind Putin's head. e, French Pres. Jacques Chirac, seated on sofa. f, People's Republic of China Pres. Jiang Zemin.

1m, Pres. Aliyev and flag of Azerbaijan.

Litho. & Embossed With Foil Application

Perf. 13½x13, 13x13½ (#1024)

2013, May 10

1023 A308 50g Sheet of 6, #a-f 9.50 9.50
1024 A309 50g Sheet of 6, #a-f 9.50 9.50

Souvenir Sheet

1025 A310 1m multi 3.25 3.25

Mahsati Ganjavi (c. 1089-1159), Poet — A311

2013, May 14 **Litho.** ***Perf. 14¼x14***

1026 A311 60g multi 2.00 2.00

Souvenir Sheet

Diplomatic Relations Between Belarus and Azerbaijan, 20th Anniv. — A312

Litho. (Sheet Margin Litho. With Foil Application)

2013, June 11 ***Perf. 12***

1027 A312 1m multi 3.00 3.00

See Belarus No. 862.

Souvenir Sheet

Fabric Designs Depicting Peacocks — A313

No. 1028 — Peacock from: a, Hungarian embroidered pillow cover (white background). b, Azeri woven horse blanket (tan background).

2013, June 15 **Litho.** ***Perf. 14x14¼***

1028 A313 60g Sheet of 2, #a-b 3.50 3.50

See Hungary No. 4287.

Souvenir Sheet

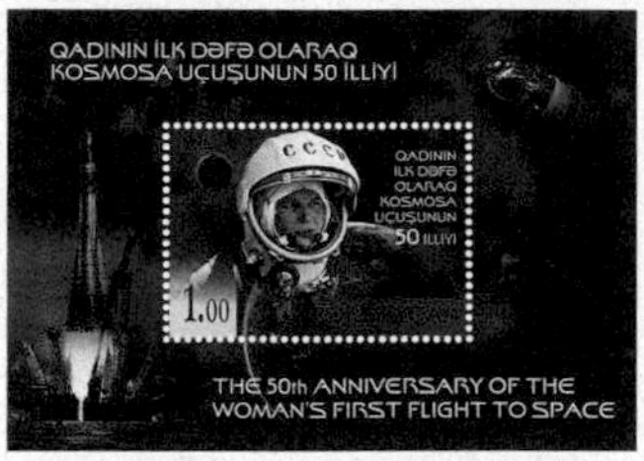

Space Flight of Valentina Tereshkova, First Woman in Space, 50th Anniv. — A314

2013, June 16

1029 A314 1m multi 3.25 3.25

Souvenir Sheet

Armed Forces of Azerbaijan, 95th Anniv. — A315

2013, June 26 ***Perf. 14¼x14***

1030 A315 1m multi 3.25 3.25

Birds — A316

Designs: 10g, Merops persicus. 20g, Coracias garrulus. 30g, Alcedo atthis. 50g, Upupa epops. 60g, Garrulus glandarius.

2013, July 16 **Litho.** ***Perf. 13x13¼***

1031 A316 10g multi .35 .35
1032 A316 20g multi .70 .70
1033 A316 30g multi 1.10 1.10

1034 A316 50g multi 1.75 1.75
1035 A316 60g multi 2.10 2.10
Nos. 1031-1035 (5) 6.00 6.00

State Management of Radio Frequencies, 45th Anniv. — A317

2013, Sept. 3 Litho. *Perf. 13*
1036 A317 60g multi 2.10 2.10

State Committee for Securities, 15th Anniv. A318

2013, Sept. 6 Litho. *Perf. 14x14¼*
1037 A318 60g multi 2.10 2.10

Memmed Araz (1933-2004), Poet — A319

2013, Sept. 10 Litho. *Perf. 14¼x14*
1038 A319 20g multi .85 .85

Souvenir Sheet

Communications — A320

No. 1039: a, Building, people in office, wagon. b, Transmission tower, satellite, satellite dish, women at computers.

2013, Sept. 17 Litho. *Perf. 14¼x14*
1039 A320 50g Sheet of 2, #a-b 3.50 3.50

Miniature Sheets

Wildlife in Hirkan National Park — A321

No. 1040: a, 20g, Cervus nippon. b, 30g, Capreolus. c, 50g, Lynx lynx. d, 60g, Martes foina.
No. 1041: a, 20g, Dendrocopos major. b, 30g, Ciconia nigra. c, 50g, Pelecanus crispus. d, 60g, Marmaronetta angustirostris.

2013, Nov. 15 Litho. *Perf. 12*
Sheets of 4, #a-d
1040-1041 A321 Set of 2 10.00 10.00

Mehdi Huseynzade (1918-44), Soldier — A322

2013, Dec. 12 Litho. *Perf. 14¼x14*
1042 A322 60g multi 2.10 2.10

See Slovenia No. 1022.

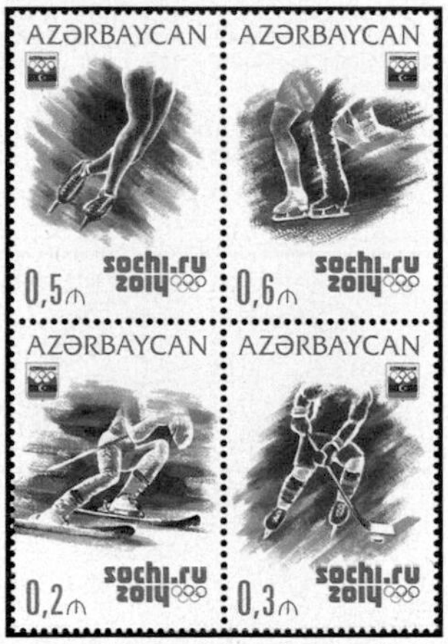

2014 Winter Olympics, Sochi, Russia — A323

No. 1043: a, 20g, Alpine skiing. b, 30g, Ice hockey. c, 50g, Speed skating. d, 60g, Pairs figure skating.

2014, Jan. 15 Litho. *Perf. 14¼x14*
1043 A323 Block or horiz. strip of 4, #a-d 5.50 5.50

Miniature Sheet

New Year 2014 (Year of the Horse) — A324

No. 1044: a, Yellow rocking horse facing right. b, Yellow rocking horse facing left. c, Blue rocking horse facing left. d, Blue rocking horse facing right.

2014, Jan. 16 Litho. *Perf. 14x14¼*
1044 A324 20g Sheet of 4, #a-d 2.75 2.75

Souvenir Sheet

Azerbaijan's Chess Team's Victory at 2013 European Championships — A325

2014, Jan. 16 Litho. *Perf. 14x14¼*
1045 A325 1m multi 3.25 3.25

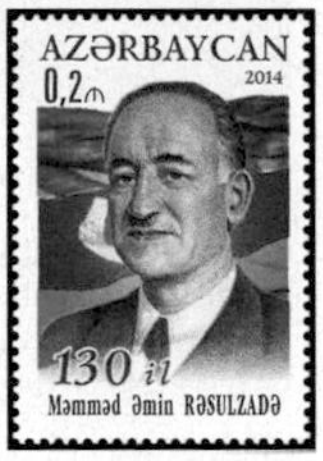

Mammad Amin Rasulzade (1884-1955), President of Democratic Republic of Azerbaijan — A326

2014, Jan. 31 Litho. *Perf. 14¼x14*
1046 A326 20g multi .85 .85

Europa A327

Musical instruments: 20g, Zurna, tar and balaban. 60g, Kamança, qaval and tütak. 1m, Man playing qaval, vert.

2014, Feb. 17 Litho. *Perf. 14x14¼*
1047-1048 A327 Set of 2 5.00 5.00
1048a Booklet pane of 8, 4 each #1047-1048, perf. 14x14¼ on 3 sides 20.00 20.00

Souvenir Sheet
Perf. 14¼x14
1049 A327 1m multi 5.00 5.00

No. 1048a was sold with, but unattached to, a booklet cover. The two different stamps are found tete-beche within the booklet pane.

Heydar Aliyev Memorial, Sumgayit A328

2014, Mar. 7 Litho. *Perf. 14x14¼*
1050 A328 20g multi .85 .85

Sumgayit, 65th anniv.

Souvenir Sheet

Nakhchivan Autonomous Republic, 90th Anniv. — A329

2014, Mar. 7 Litho. *Perf. 14x14¼*
1051 A329 60g multi 2.00 2.00

Cats — A330

Designs: 10g, Tabby cat. 20g, British Shorthair cat. 30g, Maine Coon cat. 50g, Scottish Fold cat. 60g, Birman cat.

2014, Apr. 8 Litho. *Perf. 13¼x13*
1052 A330 10g multi .35 .35
1053 A330 20g multi .65 .65
1054 A330 30g multi 1.00 1.00
1055 A330 50g multi 1.60 1.60
1056 A330 60g multi 1.90 1.90
Nos. 1052-1056 (5) 5.50 5.50

International Dialogue for Environmental Action — A331

No. 1057: a, 10g, Gazella subgutturosa. b, 20g, Panthera pardus. c, 30g, Aquila heliaca. d, 50g, Ursus arctos. e, 60g, Canis lupus.
1m, Hands holding seedling, vert.

2014, May 7 Litho. *Perf. 14x14¼*
1057 A331 Sheet of 5, #a-e, + label 5.75 5.75

Souvenir Sheet
Perf. 14¼x14
1058 A331 1m multi 3.25 3.25

Ilyas Afandiyev (1914-96), Writer A332

2014, May 26 Litho. *Perf. 14x14¼*
1059 A332 20g multi 1.00 1.00

Roses — A333

No. 1060 — Color of rose: a, Pink. b, Pinkish orange. c, Red. d, White.
1m, Red roses, vert.

2014, July 25 Litho. *Perf. 14¼*
1060 A333 30g Sheet of 4, #a-d 4.00 4.00

Souvenir Sheet
Perf. 14¼x14
1061 A333 1m multi 3.00 3.00

No. 1061 contains one 28x40mm stamp.

Dogs — A334

Puppies of various breeds.

2014, Aug. 27 Litho. *Perf. 13¼x13*
1062 A334 10g multi .30 .30
1063 A334 20g multi .65 .65
1064 A334 30g multi .95 .95
1065 A334 50g multi 1.50 1.50
1066 A334 60g multi 1.90 1.90
Nos. 1062-1066 (5) 5.30 5.30

Souvenir Sheet

Butterflies — A335

No. 1067: a, Heodes vigaureae. b, Polyommatus icarus.

2014, Aug. 27 Litho. *Perf. 13¼*
1067 A335 60g Sheet of 2, #a-b 4.00 4.00

Souvenir Sheet

"Contract of the Century" Oil Production Contract, 20th Anniv. — A336

2014, Sept. 20 Litho. *Perf. 14¼x14*
1068 A336 1m multi 3.25 3.25

Souvenir Sheet

Winter Sports — A337

No. 1069: a, Snowboarding. b, Skiing.

2014, Oct. 24 Litho. *Perf. 14¼x14*
1069 A337 50g Sheet of 2, #a-b 4.00 4.00

First Global Forum on Youth Policies, Baku A338

2014, Oct. 28 Litho. *Perf. 14x14¼*
1070 A338 60g multi 2.00 2.00

Souvenir Sheets

Venues of 2015 European Games, Baku — A339

No. 1071, 60g: a, National Stadium. b, Tofiq Bahramov Stadium. c, National Gymnastics Arena.

No. 1072, 60g: a, Crystal Hall. b, Baku Aquatics Center. c, Heydar Aliyev Arena.

2014, Nov. 19 Litho. *Perf. 12*
Sheets of 3, #a-c
1071-1072 A339 Set of 2 12.00 12.00

Miniature Sheets

Famous People — A340

Historic Buildings — A341

No. 1073: a, Molla Panah Vagif (1717-97), poet. b, Khurshidbanu Natavan (1832-97), poet. c, Bulbul (1897-1961), singer. d, Uzeyir Hajibeyov (1885-1948), composer. e, Khan Shushinski (1901-79), singer. f, Abdurrahim Hagverdiyev (1870-1933), writer.

No. 1074: a, Khotavang Christian complex, 6th-13th cent. b, Ganzanar Christian complex, 13th cent. c, Malik Azdhar Mausoleum, 14th cent. d, Ashaga Govhar Agha Mosque, 1874-75. e, Allah-Allah Mausoleum, Barda, 1322. f, Mosque, Agdam, 1868-70.

2014, Nov. 25 Litho. *Perf. 14x14¼*
1073 A340 50g Sheet of 6, #a-f 8.50 8.50
Perf. 14¼x14
1074 A341 50g Sheet of 6, #a-f 8.50 8.50

Souvenir Sheet

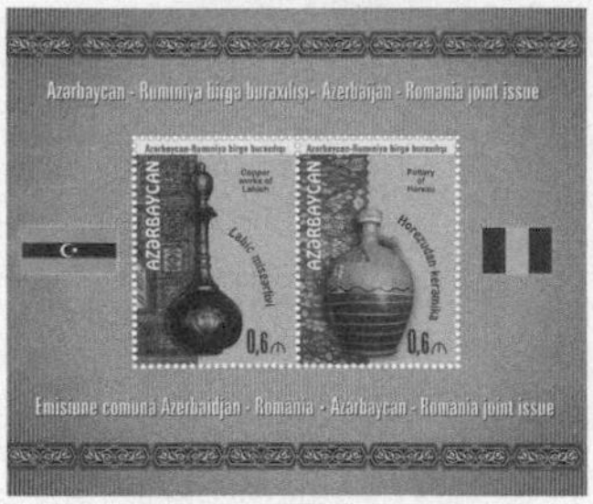

Handicrafts — A342

No. 1075: a, Copper vessel from Lahich, Azerbaijan. b, Pottery jug from Horezu, Romania.

2014, Dec. 19 Litho. *Perf. 14¼x14*
1075 A342 60g Sheet of 2, #a-b 4.25 4.25

See Romania Nos. 5640-5641.

New Year 2015 (Year of the Goat) — A343

No. 1076 — Head of goat facing: a, Left. b, Right.

2015, Jan. 12 Litho. *Perf. 14x14¼*
1076 A343 20g Pair, #a-b 1.60 1.60

Printed in sheets containing two pairs.

Europa — A344

Designs: 20g, Teddy bear, tower of rings, ball. 60g, Blocks, wooden train.
1m, Stuffed rabbit in toy car.

2015, Mar. 6 Litho. *Perf. 14¼x14*
1077-1078 A344 Set of 2 4.75 4.75
1078a Booklet pane of 8, 4 each #1077-1078, perf. 14¼x14 on 3 sides 19.00 —

Souvenir Sheet
1079 A344 1m multi 5.75 5.75

No. 1078a was sold with, but unattached to, a booklet cover. The two different stamps are found tete-beche within the booklet pane.

Aziz Sharif (1895-1988), Writer — A345

2015, Mar. 29 Litho. *Perf. 14¼x14*
1080 A345 50g multi 1.50 1.50

Penny Black, 175th Anniv. — A346

2015, Apr. 1 Litho. *Perf. 14x14¼*
1081 A346 20g multi *.70 .70*

No. 1081 was printed in sheets of 4.

Marmara Group Foundation, 30th Anniv. A347

2015, Apr. 7 Litho. *Perf. 14x14¼*
1082 A347 50g multi *1.50 1.50*

Miniature Sheets

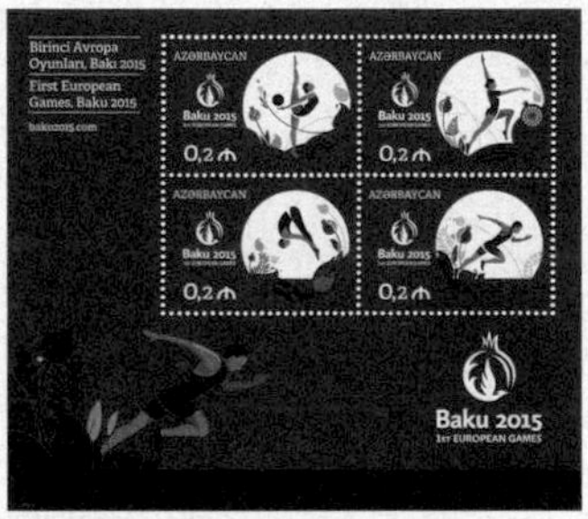

A348

Sports of 2015 European Games, Baku — A349

No. 1083 (purple background): a, Rhythmic gymnastics (gymnast holding ball). b, Aerobic gymnastics (gymnast running with arm raised). c, Trampoline (athlete flipping in air). d, Track (athlete running).

No. 1084 (blue background): a, Swimming. b, Boxing. c, Fencing. d, Diving.

No. 1085 (red background): a, Kayaking. b, Shooting. c, Triathlon. d, Mountain biking.

No. 1086 (green background): a, Archery. b, Wrestling. c, Badminton. d, Table tennis.

No. 1087: a, Artistic gymnastics (gymnast leaping). b, Volleyball. c, BMX cycling. d, Sambo.

2015, Apr. 23 Litho. *Perf. 12*
1083 A348 20g Sheet of 4, #a-d 3.00 3.00
1084 A348 20g Sheet of 4, #a-d 3.00 3.00
1085 A348 20g Sheet of 4, #a-d 3.00 3.00
1086 A348 20g Sheet of 4, #a-d 3.00 3.00
1087 A349 20g Sheet of 4, #a-d 3.00 3.00
Nos. 1083-1087 (5) 15.00 15.00

Victory in World War II, 70th Anniv. A350

2015, May 9 Litho. *Perf. 12*
1088 A350 20g multi *.95 .95*

Intl. Telecommunication Union, 150th Anniv. — A351

2015, May 17 Litho. ***Perf. 14x14¼***
1089 A351 50g multi *1.60 1.60*

Jamshid Nakhchivanski (1895-1938), Military Commander A352

2015, July 16 Litho. ***Perf. 14¼x14***
1090 A352 50g multi *1.60 1.60*

Souvenir Sheet

2015 Chess World Cup, Baku — A353

2015, Sept. 10 Litho. ***Perf. 14¼x14***
1091 A353 1m multi *3.00 3.00*

Architecture A354

No. 1092: a, Maiden's Tower, Baku (denomination at LL). b, Kremlin, Moscow (denomination at LR).

2015, Sept. 22 Litho. ***Perf. 13***
1092 A354 60g Pair, #a-b *3.75 3.75*

Printed in sheets of 4 pairs + central label. See Russia No. 7677.

National Academy of Sciences, 70th Anniv. — A355

2015, Oct. 1 Litho. ***Perf. 14¼x14***
1093 A355 30g multi *1.00 1.00*

Dancers — A356

No. 1094: a, Dancers from Azerbaijan (denomination at LL). b, Dancers from Moldova (denomination at UR).

2015, Oct. 16 Litho. ***Perf. 13¼x13***
1094 Horiz. pair *3.00 3.00*
a.-b. A356 50g Either single *1.50 1.50*

See Moldova No. 883.

United Nations. 70th Anniv. A357

2015, Oct. 24 Litho. ***Perf. 14x14¼***
1095 A357 50g multi *1.60 1.60*

National Flag Square — A358

2015, Nov. 9 Litho. ***Perf. 14¼x14***
1096 A358 50g multi *1.60 1.60*

Book of Dede Korkut — A359

2015, Nov. 16 Litho. ***Perf. 14¼x14***
1097 A359 50g multi *1.60 1.60*

Souvenir Sheet

Buildings on Nizami Street, Baku — A360

No. 1098 — Various buildings with denomination at: a, LL. b, LR.

2015, Nov. 16 Litho. ***Perf. 14¼x14***
1098 A360 50g Sheet of 2, #a-b, + central label *3.75 3.75*

Souvenir Sheet

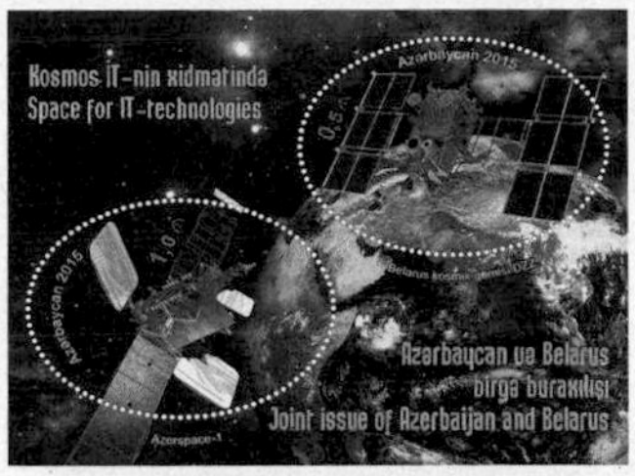

Satellites — A361

No. 1099: a, 50g, DZZ satellite, Belarus. b, 1m, Azerspace-1 satellite, Azerbaijan.

Litho., Sheet Margin Litho. With Foil Application

2015, Dec. 3 ***Perf.***
1099 A361 Sheet of 2, #a-b *4.75 4.75*

See Belarus No. 967.

Rashid Behbudov (1915-89), Singer and Actor A362

2015, Dec. 14 Litho. ***Perf. 14x14¼***
1100 A362 50g multi *1.40 1.40*

Miniature Sheet

New Year 2016 (Year of the Monkey) — A363

No. 1101 — Monkey facing: a, Right, denomination at LL. b, Left, denomination at LR. c, Left, denomination at LL. d, Right, denomination at LR.

2016, Jan. 12 Litho. ***Perf. 14x14¼***
1101 A363 20g Sheet of 4, #a-d *3.00 3.00*

Europa A364

Frame color: 20g, Bluish gray. 60g, Apple green.
1m, No frame.

2016, Jan. 25 Litho. ***Perf. 14x14¼***
1102-1103 A364 Set of 2 *5.00 5.00*
1103a Booklet pane of 8, 4 each #1102-1103, perf. 14x14¼ on 3 sides *20.00 20.00*

Souvenir Sheet

1104 A364 1m multi *5.75 5.75*

Think Green Issue.

No. 1103a was sold with, but unattached to, a booklet cover. Tete-beche pairs of Nos. 1102-1103 are found in No. 1103a.

Broadcasting Anniversaries A365

2016, Feb. 22 Litho. ***Perf. 14¼x14***
1105 A365 50g multi *1.60 1.60*

Radio broadcasting in Azerbaijan, 90th anniv.; television broadcasting, 60th anniv.

Regional Communications Commonwealth, 25th Anniv. — A366

2016, Mar. 2 Litho. ***Perf. 14¼x14***
1106 A366 50g multi *1.60 1.60*

Eynali bey Sultanov (1866-1935), Writer — A367

2016, May 5 Litho. ***Perf. 14¼x14***
1107 A367 20g multi *.60 .60*

Architects and Their Buildings — A368

Union of Architects 80th Anniv. Emblem — A369

No. 1108, 50g: a, Ajami Nakhchivani (12th-13th cent.). b, Ustad Mahmud ibn Saad (13th-14th cent.). c, Karbalayi Safikhan Karabakhi (1817-1910). d, Zivar bey Ahmadbeyov (1873-1925).

No. 1109, 50g: a, I. V. Qoslavskiy (1865-1904). b, I. K. Plosko (1866-1931). c, M. C. Hasinski (1875-1931). d, N. A. fon der Nonne (1836-1906).

No. 1110, 50g: a, Sadig Dadashov (1905-46). b, Mikayil Huseynov (1905-92), c, Enver Kasim-zade (1912-69). d, Hasan Mejidov (1914-78).

2016, May 6 Litho. *Perf. 14x14¼*
Sheets of 4, #a-d

1108-1110 A368 Set of 3 *14.50 14.50*

Souvenir Sheet

1111 A369 1m multi *2.40 2.40*

See Nos. 1131-1133.

Eagles — A370

No. 1112: a, Aquila chrysaetos. b, Aquila nipalensis.

2016, May 12 Litho. *Perf. 14x14¼*

1112 A370 60g Pair, #a-b *3.00 3.00*

See Belarus No. 984.

A371

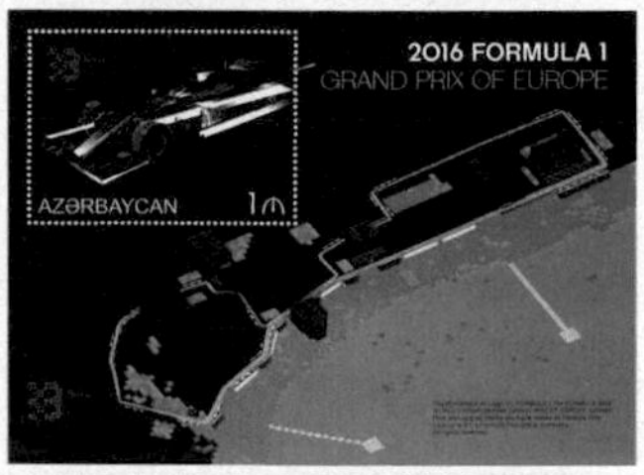

2016 Formula 1 Grand Prix Races, Baku — A372

No. 1113: a, Red car, front view. b, Blue car, front view. c, Dark blue car, front and side view. d, Orange car, rear view.
1m, Red car, emblem of Baku City Circuit.

2016, June 10 Litho. *Perf. 14x14¼*

1113 A371 50g Block of 4, #a-d *5.00 5.00*

Souvenir Sheet
Perf. 14¼x14

1114 A372 1m multi *2.40 2.40*

2016 Summer Olympics, Rio de Janeiro — A373

No. 1115: a, Boxing. b, Weight lifting. c, Wrestling, country name at left. d, Wrestling, country name ar right.

2016, Aug. 1 Litho. *Perf. 14x14¼*

1115 A373 50g Block of 4, #a-d *5.00 5.00*

Miniature Sheet

42nd Chess Olympiad, Baku — A374

No. 1116 — Chess pieces: a, Seated swordsman, rook. b, Swordsman on elephant. c, Kneeling and standing swordsmen. d, Man on horseback. e, Seated and standing swordsmen.

2016, Sept. 1 Litho. *Perf. 14¼x14*

1116 A374 50g Sheet of 5, #a-e *6.00 6.00*

Worldwide Fund for Nature (WWF) — A375

No. 1117 — Manul: a, One animal, country name at left. b, One animal, country name at right. c, Two animals. d, Three animals.

2016, Sept. 5 Litho. *Perf. 14x14¼*

1117 A375 50g Block of 4, #a-d *4.00 4.00*
e Souvenir sheet of 4, #1117a-1117d *4.00 4.00*

Independence, 25th Anniv. — A376

2016, Nov. 15 Litho. *Perf. 14x14¼*

1118 A376 10g multi *.25 .25*

Souvenir Sheet

Restoration of Trapezitsa Architectural Museum Reserve, Veliko Tarnovo, Bulgaria — A377

2016, Nov. 22 Litho. *Perf. 13¼x13*

1119 A377 1.50m multi *3.50 3.50*

See Bulgaria No. 4774.

Telephone Communication in Azerbaijan, 135th Anniv. — A378

2016, Dec. 6 Litho. *Perf. 14x14¼*

1120 A378 10g multi *.25 .25*

Souvenir Sheet

Visit of Pope Francis to Azerbaijan — A379

2016, Dec. 20 Litho. *Perf. 14x14¼*

1121 A379 1.50m multi *3.75 3.75*

Souvenir Sheet

National Cuisine — A380

No. 1122: a, Piti. b, Dolma.

2016, Dec. 22 Litho. *Perf. 14¼x14*

1122 A380 50g Sheet of 2, #a-b *2.75 2.75*

Ganja, 2016 European Youth Capital A381

2017, Jan. 30 Litho. *Perf. 14x14¼*

1123 A381 30g multi *.60 .60*

New Year 2017 (Year of the Rooster) — A382

No. 1124: a, Head of rooster. b, Rooster.

2017, Apr. 14 Litho. *Perf. 14x14¼*

1124 A382 30g Pair, #a-b *1.60 1.60*

Printed in sheets containing two pairs.

Novruz Festival — A383

No. 1125: a, Lake and mountain. b, Fire. c, Mountain. d, Flowers.

2017, Apr. 14 Litho. *Perf. 14¼x14*

1125 A383 30g Block of 4, #a-d *3.25 3.25*

Khojaly Massacre, 25th Anniv. A384

2017, Apr. 14 Litho. *Perf. 14x14¼*

1126 A384 10g multi *.25 .25*

Europa A385

Designs: 20g, Mardakan Castle. 60g, Ramana Castle.
1m, Maiden's Tower, Baku.

2017, Apr. 14 Litho. *Perf. 14x14¼*

1127-1128 A385 Set of 2 *5.25 5.25*
1128a Booklet pane of 8, 4 each #1127-1128, perf. 14x14¼ on 3 sides *21.00 —*

Souvenir Sheet

1129 A385 1m multi *6.25 6.25*

No. 1128a was sold with, but unattached to, a booklet cover. Tete-beche pairs of Nos. 1127-1128 are found in No. 1128a.

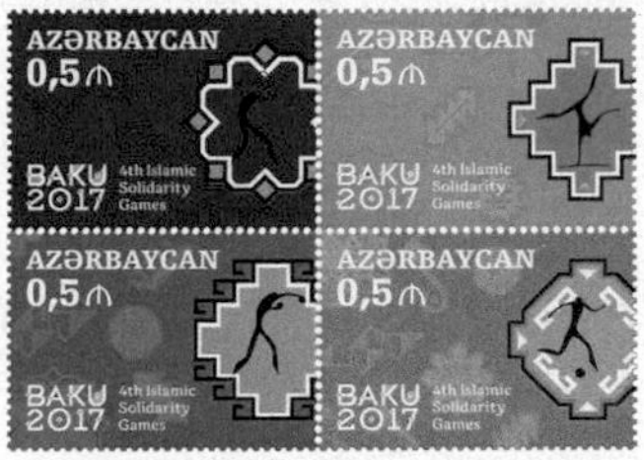

4th Islamic Solidarity Games, Baku — A386

No. 1130: a, Tennis. b, Gymnastics. c, Boxing. d, Soccer.

2017, May 5 Litho. *Perf. 14x14¼*

1130 A386 50g Block of 4, #a-d *4.25 4.25*

Architects and Their Buildings Type of 2016
Miniature Sheets

No. 1131, 50g: a, Qasim bey Hajibababeyov (1811-74). b, Adolf V. Eichler (1869-1911). c, Lev V. Rudnev (1885-1956). d, Alexander A. Vesnin (1883-1959) and Viktor A. Vesnin (1882-1950).
No. 1132, 50g: a, Anvar A. Ismayilov (1916-88). b, Hanifa A. Alasgarov (1912-91). c, Tahir A. Abdullayev (1915-2004). d, Ghazanfar M. Ali-zadeh (1910-94).
No. 1133, 50g: a, Talat A. Khanlarov (1927-2004). b, Juzef I. Gadimov (1928-2012). c, Konstantin I. Senchikhin (1905-85). d, Shafiga M. Zeynalova (1922-78).

2017, June 22 Litho. *Perf. 14x14¼*
Sheets of 4, #a-d

1131-1133 A368 Set of 3 *13.50 13.50*

Emblem of Azerbaijan — A387

2017, July 12 Litho. *Perf. 13¼x13¾*
Background Color

1134 A387 10g white *.25 .25*
1135 A387 20g dull green *.45 .45*
1136 A387 30g salmon *.65 .65*
1137 A387 50g light blue *1.10 1.10*
Nos. 1134-1137 (4) 2.45 2.45

2017 Scouting Events in Azerbaijan — A388

No. 1138: a, 13th World Scout Youth Forum, Gabala. b, 41st World Scout Conference, Baku.

2017, Aug. 14 Litho. ***Perf. 14¼x14***
1138 A388 20g Pair, #a-b *1.10 1.10*

Souvenir Sheet

Azermarka (Printer of Azerbaijan Postage Stamps), 25th Anniv. — A389

2017, Aug. 22 Litho. ***Perf. 14x14¼***
1139 A389 1m multi *2.75 2.75*

Partnership for Development Between Azerbaijan and World Bank — A390

2017, Sept. 19 Litho. ***Perf. 12x12¼***
1140 A390 50g multi *1.10 1.10*

Souvenir Sheet

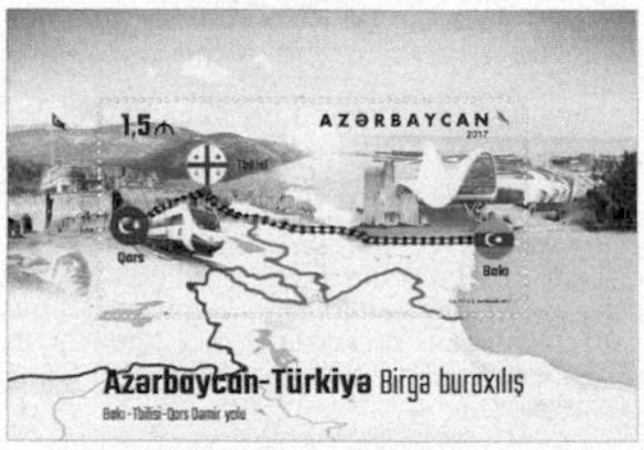

Baku-Tblisi-Kars Railway — A391

2017, Oct. 30 Litho. ***Perf. 13***
1141 A391 1.50m multi *4.00 4.00*

Joint Issue between Azerbaijan and Turkey. See Turkey No. 3572.

Tofig Guliyev (1917-2000), Composer — A392

2017, Dec. 4 Litho. ***Perf. 14x14¼***
1142 A392 50g multi *1.25 1.25*

Miniature Sheet

International Year of Sustainable Tourism for Development — A393

Emblem and various abstract designs, as shown.

2017, Dec. 4 Litho. ***Perf. 12***
1143 A393 50g Sheet of 6, #a-f *7.00 7.00*

Religion in Azerbaijan — A394

No. 1144: a, Fresco depicting Jesus in Orthodox church. b, Imamzadeh Sanctuary (mosque and minarets). c, Stained-glass window depicting crucifixion of Jesus from Catholic church. d, Clock tower of German Lutheran Church. e, Fire Temple. f, Interior of synagogue.

2017, Dec. 6 Litho. ***Perf. 13½x13***
1144 A394 20g Sheet of 6, #a-f *2.75 2.75*

Land of Tolerance.

Poerty of Nizami Ganjavi (1141-1209) — A395

No. 1145: a, Portrait of Nizami Ganjavi. b, Ilustration from *The Seven Beauties* (Yeddi Gözel). c, Illlustration from *Eskandar-nama* (Izgendername). d, Illustration from *Layla and Majnun* (Leyli ve Mecnun). e, Illustration from *The Treasure of Secrets* (Sirler Xezinesi). f, Illustration from *Khosrow and Shirin* (Xosrov ve Sirin).

2017, Dec. 6 Litho. ***Perf. 13½x13***
1145 A395 20g Sheet of 6, #a-f *2.75 2.75*

Miniature Sheet

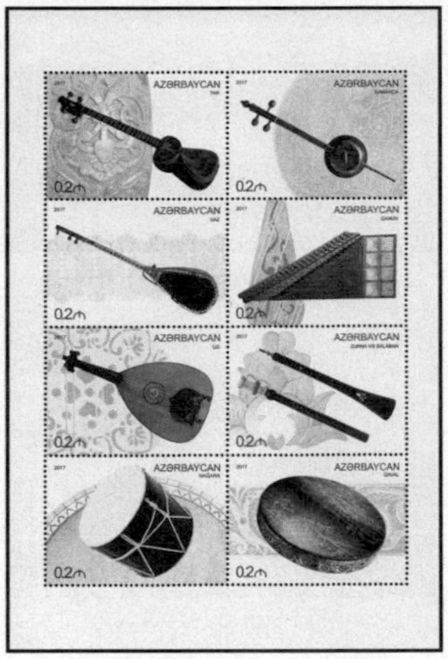

Musical Instruments — A396

No. 1146: a, Tar. b, Kamança. c, Saz. d, Qanun. e, Ud. f, Zurna and Balaban. g, Nagara. h, Qaval.

2017, Dec. 6 Litho. ***Perf. 13x13½***
1146 A396 20g Sheet of 8, #a-h *3.75 3.75*

Miniature Sheet

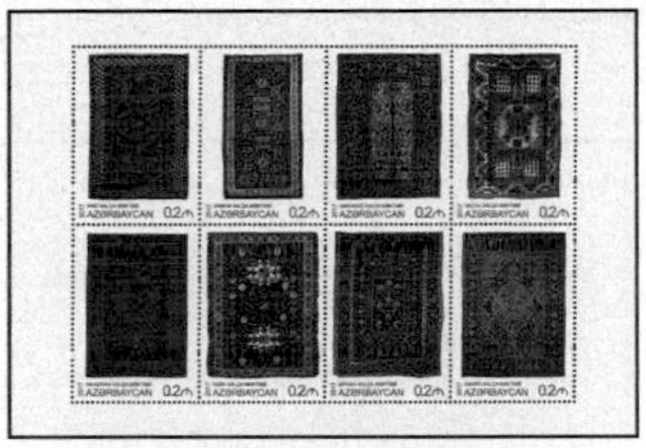

Carpets — A397

No. 1147 — Carpet style: a, Baku (Baki). b, Ganja (Gence). c, Karabakh (Qarabag). d, Kazakh (Qazak). e, Nakhchivan (Naxçivan). f, Quba. g, Shirvan (Sirvan). h, Tabriz (Tebriz).

2017, Dec. 6 Litho. ***Perf. 13½x13***
1147 A397 20g Sheet of 8, #a-h *3.75 3.75*

Miniature Sheet

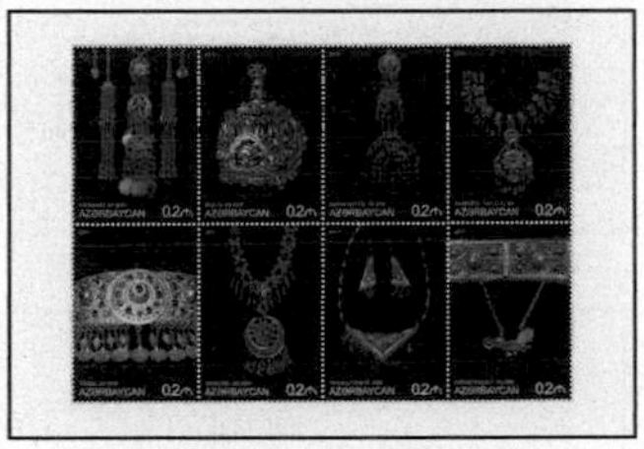

Jewelry — A398

No. 1148: a, Necklace and pendants, 20th cent. b, Ornament, 19th cent. c, Pendant, 20th cent. d, Necklace, 1990. e, Belt with pendants, 20th cent. f, Necklace with pendants, 19th cent. g, Necklace and earrings, 2005. h, Necklace with bird pendant, 20th cent.

2017, Dec. 6 Litho. ***Perf. 13½x13***
1148 A398 20g Sheet of 8, #a-h *3.75 3.75*

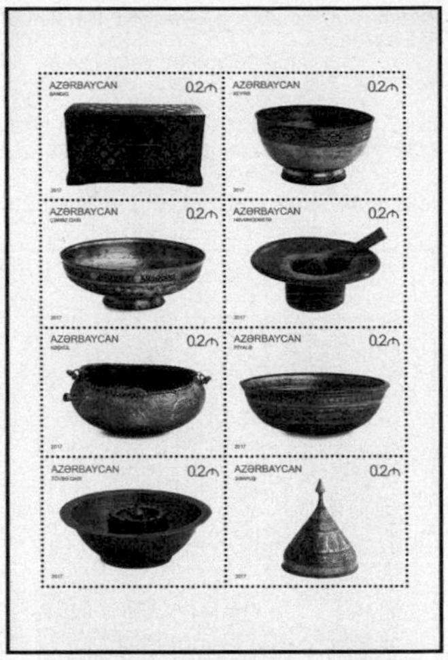

Household Objects — A399

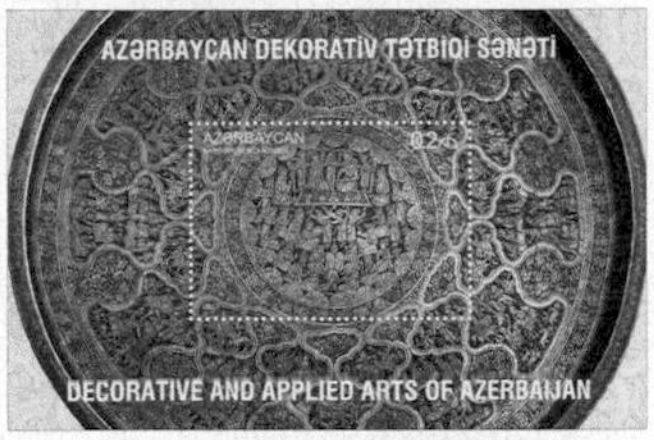

Plate — A400

Plate and Pitcher — A401

No. 1149: a, Chest (sandiq). b, Bowl (xeyre). c, Bowl (çerez qabi). d, Mortar and pestle (hevengdeste). e, Bowl with spout (kesküI). f, Bowl (piyale). g, Bowl with raised center (tövbe qabi). h, Pointed container (serpus).

2017, Dec. 6 Litho. ***Perf. 13x13½***
1149 A399 20g Sheet of 8, #a-h *3.75 3.75*

Souvenir Sheets

1150 A400 20g multi *.50 .50*

Perf. 13½x13

1151 A401 50g multi *1.25 1.25*

Flora — A402

No. 1152: a, Ophrys caucasica. b, Galanthus caucasicus. c, Crocuses. d,

Platanus orientalis. e, Parrotia persica. f, Pinus eldarica.

No. 1153, 50g, Galanthus caucasicus, diff. No. 1154, 50g, Pinus eldarica, diff.

2017, Dec. 6 Litho. *Perf. 13½x13*

1152	A402	20g Sheet of 6, #a-f	*2.75*	*2.75*

Souvenir Sheets

1153-1154	A402	Set of 2	*2.50*	*2.50*

Fauna — A403

No. 1155: a, Horse. b, Canis lupus. c, Ursus arctos. d, Gazella subgutturosa. e, Aquila chrysaetos. f, Phoenicopterus roseus. g, Phoca caspica. h, Panthera pardus ciscaucasica.

No. 1156, 50g, Gazella subgutturosa, diff. No. 1157, 50g, Aquila chrysaetos, diff.

2017, Dec. 6 Litho. *Perf. 13x13½*

1155	A403	20g Sheet of 8, #a-h	*3.75*	*3.75*

Souvenir Sheets

1156-1157	A403	Set of 2	*2.50*	*2.50*

Landscapes — A404

Mount Ilandaq — A405

Lake Goygol — A406

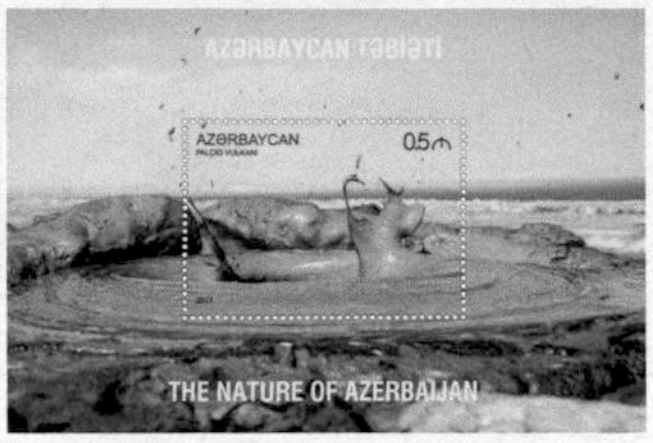

Mud Volcano — A407

No. 1158: a, Khizi Mountains (Xizi Dalgari). b, Mount Bazardüzü. c, Mount Ilandag. d, Lake Goygol. e, Flowers, Lala Duzu. f, Mount Tufandag. g, Mud volcano. h, Valley in autumn (Qizil Payiz).

2017, Dec. 6 Litho. *Perf. 13x13½*

1158	A404	20g Sheet of 8, #a-h	*3.75*	*3.75*

Souvenir Sheets

1159	A405	50g multi	*1.25*	*1.25*
1160	A406	50g multi	*1.25*	*1.25*
1161	A407	50g multi	*1.25*	*1.25*
		Nos. 1159-1161 (3)	*3.75*	*3.75*

Sport Venues — A408

Modern Architecture — A409

Ancient Architecture — A410

Baku Boulevard — A411

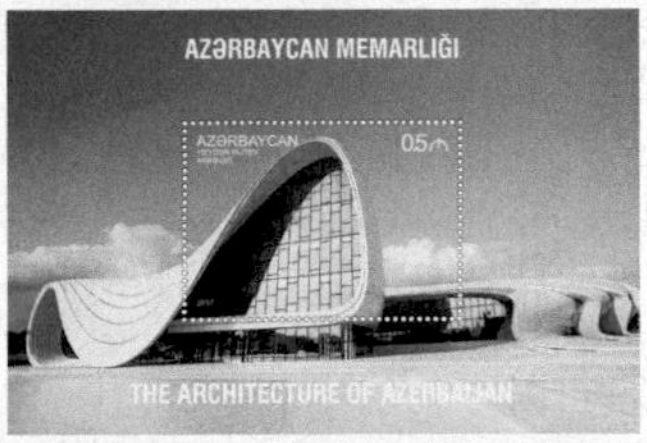

Heydar Aliyev Center, Baku — A412

Flame Towers, Baku — A413

Chirag Gala — A414

Ganjasar Monastery — A415

Juma Mosque, Shamakhi — A416

Heydar Mosque, Baku — A417

No. 1162: a, Baku Olympic Stadium (Baki Olympiya Stadionu). b, Skier, Shahdag Mountain Resort. c, Cyclists at Velopark. d, Heydar Aliyev Sports and Concert Complex (Heyder Eliyev Adina Idman Konsert Kompleksi). e, Azerbaijan Boxing Federation Building (Azerbaycan Boks Federasiyasi). f, Rowers at Kür Olympic Training Center. g, National Gymnastics Arena (Milli Gimnastika Arenasi). h, Baku Aquatic Center (Baki su Idmani Sarayi).

No. 1163: a, State Oil Company of the Azerbaijan Republic Building (ARDNS), and Azersu Office Tower (AZERSU). b, Heydar Aliyev Center (Heyder Eliyev Merkezi). c, Azerbaijan Carpet Museum (Azerbaycan Xalça Muzeyi). d, International Mugham Center (Beynelxalq Mugam Merkezi). e, Flame Towers (Alov Qülleleri). f, National Flag Square (Dövlet Bayragi Meydani). g, Heydar Aliyev International Airport (Heyder Eliyev Beynelxalq Hava Limani). h, Baku Boulevard (Baki Bulvari).

No. 1164: a, Ganja Gate, Shusha Fortress (Susa Qalasi, Gence Qapisi). b, Momine Khatun Mausoleum (Mömine Xatun Türbesi). c, Church of Kish (Kis Mebedi). d, Chirag Gala (Ciraqqala). e, Maiden Tower, Baku (Qiz Qalasi). f, Gobustan Rock Paintings (Qobustan Qayaüstü Resmleri). g, Ganjasar Monastery (Genceser Monastiri). h, Palace of the Sirvanshahs Complex (Sirvansahlar Sarayi Kompleksi).

2017, Dec. 6 Litho. *Perf. 13x13½*

1162	A408	20g Sheet of 8, #a-h	*3.75*	*3.75*
1163	A409	20g Sheet of 8, #a-h	*3.75*	*3.75*
1164	A410	20g Sheet of 8, #a-h	*3.75*	*3.75*
		Nos. 1162-1164 (3)	*11.25*	*11.25*

Souvenir Sheets

1165	A411	50g multi	*1.25*	*1.25*
1166	A412	50g multi	*1.25*	*1.25*
1167	A413	50g multi	*1.25*	*1.25*
1168	A414	50g multi	*1.25*	*1.25*
1169	A415	50g multi	*1.25*	*1.25*
1170	A416	50g multi	*1.25*	*1.25*

Perf. 13½x13

1171	A417	50g multi	*1.25*	*1.25*
		Nos. 1165-1171 (7)	*8.75*	*8.75*

Miniature Sheet

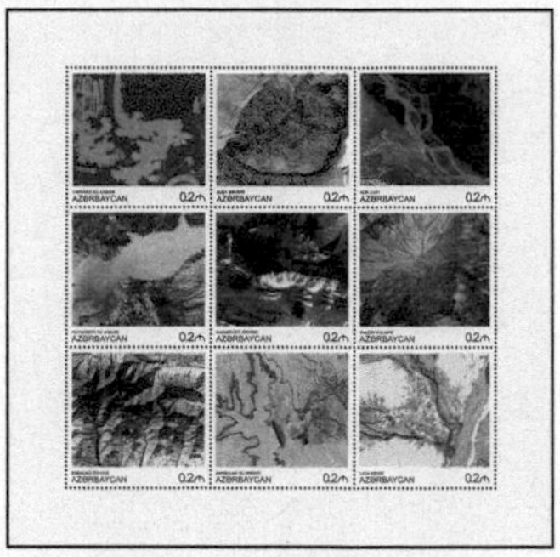

Photographs of Azerbaijan Taken From Outer Space — A418

No. 1172: a, Varvara Reservoir (Varvara su Anbari). b, Shusha (Susa Seheri). c, Kur River (Kür Cayi). d, Xudaferin Reservoir (Xudaferin su Anbari). e, Mount Bazardüzü (Bazardüzü Zirvesi). f, Mud Volcano (Palçiq Vulkani). g, Mount Babadag (Babadag Zirvesi). h, Xanbulan Reservoir (Xanbulan su Anbari). i, Laza (Laza Kendi).

2017, Dec. 6 Litho. *Perf. 13*

1172 A418 20g Sheet of 9, #a-i *4.25 4.25*

Miniature Sheets

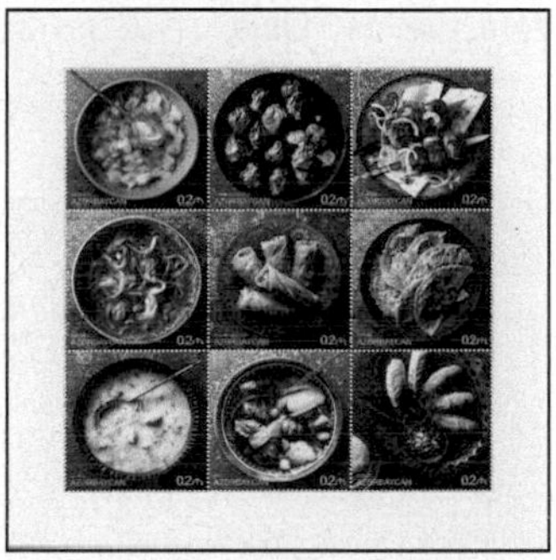

A419

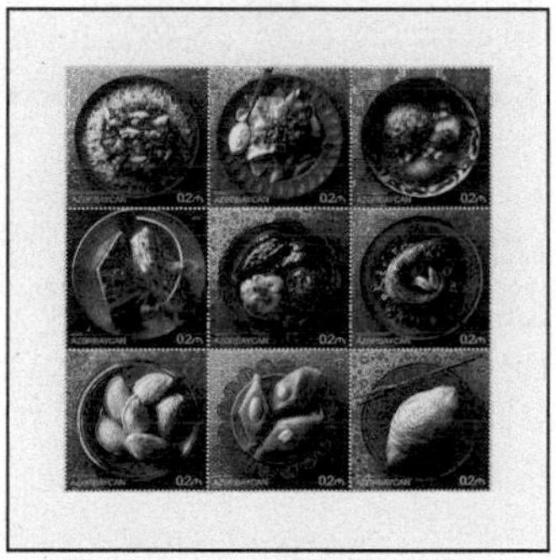

Cuisine of Azerbaijan — A420

No. 1173: a, Dusbere (dumplings). b, Yarpaq dolmasi (stuffed grape leaves). c, Xan kababi (meat kebabs). d, Xemirasi (noodle soup). e, Kelem dolmasi (stuffed cabbage). f, Qutab (stuffed dough pockets). g, Dovga (yogurt soup). h, Piti (soup). i, Gürze (lamb dumplings).

No. 1174: a, Sebzi qovurma plov (vegetable pilaf). b, Xengel (pasta with ground beef). c, Küfte bozbas (meatball soup). d, Kükü (omelette). e, Dolma (stuffed grape leaves). f, Baliq levengisi (fish stuffed with walnuts). g, Sekerbura (nut-filled pastry). h, Paxlava (baklava). i, Badambura (almond pastry).

2017, Dec. 6 Litho. *Perf. 13*

1173 A419 20g Sheet of 9, #a-i *4.25 4.25*
1174 A420 20g Sheet of 9, #a-i *4.25 4.25*

Muslim Magomayev (1942-2008), Opera Singer — A421

2017, Dec. 21 Litho. *Perf. 14¼x14*

1175 A421 50g pale org & blk *1.25 1.25*

Souvenir Sheet

National Crafts — A422

No. 1176: a, Pottery (saxsi dolça). b, Copper pot with handle (mis qab).

2017, Dec. 21 Litho. *Perf. 14¼x14*

1176 A422 50g Sheet of 2, #a-b *2.50 2.50*

Nakhchivan, 2018 Capital of Islamic Culture — A423

2018, Jan. 30 Litho. *Perf. 14x14¼*

1177 A423 50g multi *1.25 1.25*

Architecture
A424 A425

2018, Feb. 1 Litho. *Perf. 13¼x13*

1178 A424 10g Prus blue & tan *.25 .25*
1179 A425 20g Prus blue & tan *.50 .50*

Souvenir sheets of four 60g stamps dated 2017 depicting Dogs, Cats, Butterflies, and Birds, and souvenir sheets of six 60g stamps dated 2017 depicting Pandas, Dogs, Cats, Tigers, Horses, Elephants, dolphins, Owls, Parrots, Fish, Butterflies, Turtles and Dinosaurs were declared to be "fake" by Azerbaijan postal authorities.

March 31, 1918 Baku Massacre, Cent. A426

2018, Mar. 31 Litho. *Perf. 12*

1180 A426 50g multi *1.10 1.10*

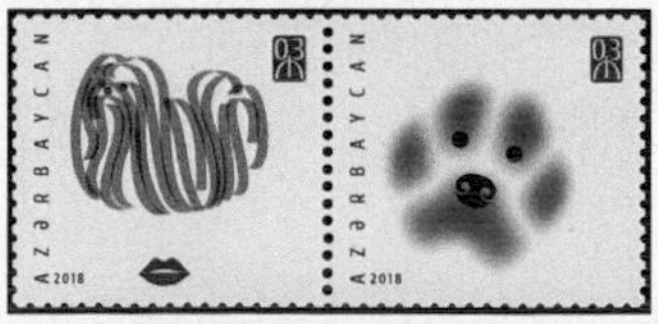

New Year 2018 (Year of the Dog) — A427

No. 1181: a, Lips and stylized dog. b, Dog's eyes and nose in paw print.

2018, Apr. 27 Litho. *Perf. 12*

1181 A427 30g Pair, #a-b *1.40 1.40*

Printed in sheets containing two each Nos. 1181a-1181b.

Qara Qarayev (1918-82), Composer A428

2018, Apr. 27 Litho. *Perf. 12*

1182 A428 50g multi *1.10 1.10*

Souvenir Sheet

Novruz — A429

No. 1183: a, Woman and flowers. b, Two women near fire. c, Woman holding objects in hands.

2018, Apr. 27 Litho. *Perf. 12*

1183 A429 60g Sheet of 3, #a-c *4.25 4.25*

Souvenir Sheets

Pres. Heydar Aliyev (1923-2003) — A430

Zarifa Aliyev (1923-85), Ophthalmologist, and Wife of Pres. Aliyev — A431

2018, May 16 Litho. *Perf. 13x13½*

1184 A430 1.50m gold & multi *3.25 3.25*
1185 A431 1.50m gold & multi *3.25 3.25*

Woman Suffrage in Azerbaijan, Cent. — A432

2018, May 28 Litho. *Perf. 13x13½*

1186 A432 50g multi *1.10 1.10*

A433

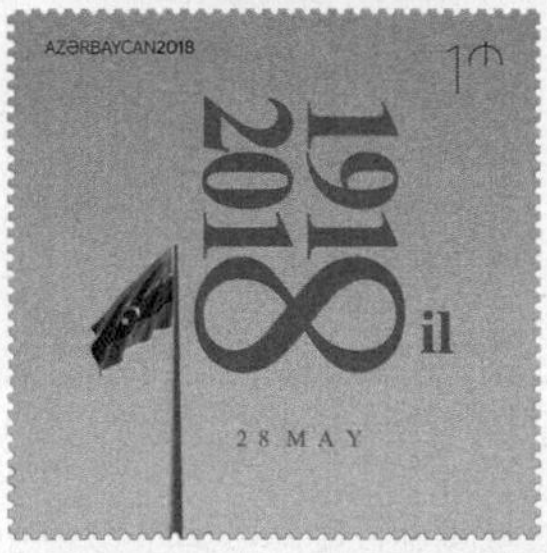

A434

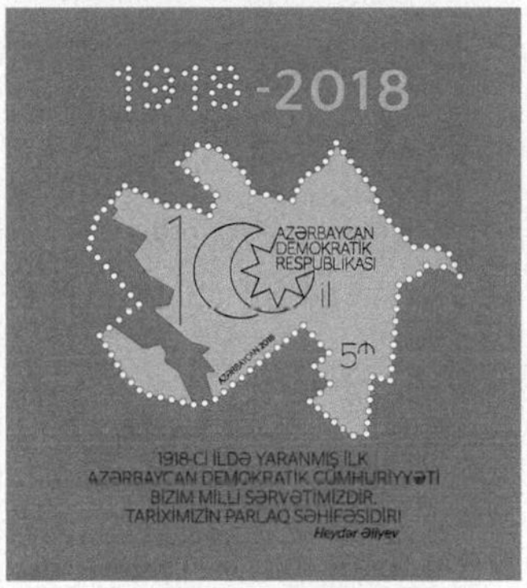

Azerbaijan Democratic Republic, Cent. — A435

2018, May 28 Litho. *Perf. 13x13½*

1187 A433 1m multi *2.25 2.25*

Perf. 13

1188 A434 1m multi *2.25 2.25*

Souvenir Sheet

Litho. With Foil Application

Perf.

1189 A435 5m sil & multi *11.00 11.00*

2018 BMX World Championships, Baku — A436

2018, June 5 Litho. *Perf. 13x13½*

1190 A436 60g multi *1.40 1.40*

Europa A437

Bridge in: 40g, Tovuz. 60g, Gadabay. 1m, Bridge in Culfa.

2018, June 5 Litho. *Perf. 12*

1191-1192 A437 Set of 2 *2.25 2.25*
1192a Booklet pane of 8, 4 each # 1191-1192, perf. 12 on 3 sides *18.00* —

Souvenir Sheet

1193 A437 1m multi *2.25 2.25*

No. 1192a was sold with, but unattached to, a booklet cover. Tete-beche pairs of Nos. 1191-1192 are found in No. 1192a.

Souvenir Sheet

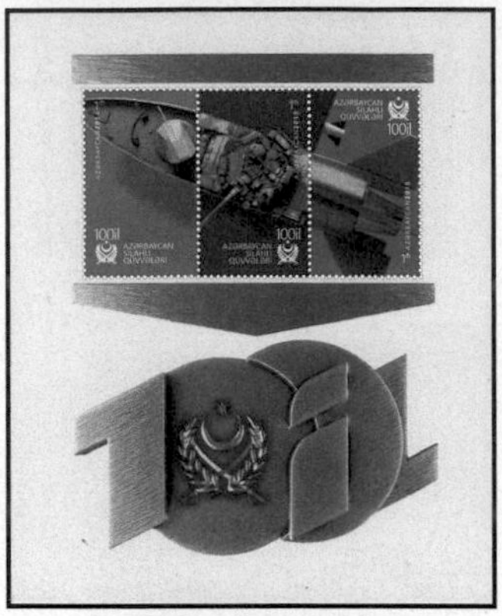

Azerbaijan Armed Forces, Cent. — A438

No. 1194: a, Ship. b, Tank. c, Tail of Fighter Jet.

2018, June 26 Litho. *Perf. 13¼x13*
1194 A438 1m Sheet of 3, #a-c *6.75 6.75*

Souvenir Sheet

2018 World Cup Soccer Championships, Russia — A439

2018, Aug. 24 Litho. *Perf.*
1195 A439 1m multi *3.25 3.25*

2018 World Judo Championships, Baku — A440

2018, Aug. 27 Litho. *Perf. 13*
1196 A440 50g multi *1.60 1.60*

Liberation of Baku, 100th Anniversary A441

2018, Sept. 27 Litho. *Perf. 13¼*
1197 A441 30g multi *1.10 1.10*

Mikayil Mushfig (1908-38), Poet — A442

2018, Nov. 7 Litho. *Perf. 13½x13¼*
1198 A442 30g silver & blk *1.10 1.10*

Flag of Azerbaijan, 110th Anniv. — A443

2018, Nov. 8 Litho. *Perf. 13*
1199 A443 50g multi *1.60 1.60*

Diplomatic Relations Between Azerbaijan and Belarus, 25th Anniversary A444

Litho. With Foil Application
2018, Nov. 19 *Perf. 12*
1200 A444 50g multi *1.50 1.50*

See Belarus No. 1120.

Azerbaijan Post, 100th Anniversary A445

2018, Dec. 4 Litho. *Perf. 13¼*
1201 A445 60g blue *2.10 2.10*

An oblong hole was laser-cut between "1918" and "2018" in the design.

Baku Architecture — A446

Designs: No. 1202, a, Lion and snake facing right. b, Stag. c, Lion and snake facing left.

No. 1203, Stone clock face, vert. No. 1204, Coat of arms of Baku, vert. No. 1205, Lion's head.

2018, Dec. 4 Litho. *Perf. 12*
1202 A446 60g Sheet of 3, #a-c *5.00 5.00*

Souvenir Sheets
Perf. 12¼x12
1203 A446 1m multi *2.75 2.75*
Perf. 13½x13¼
1204 A446 1m multi *2.75 2.75*
Perf.
1205 A446 1m multi *2.75 2.75*
Nos. 1203-1205 (3) 8.25 8.25

No. 1203 contains one 29x41mm stamp. No. 1204 contains one 38x52mm stamp. No. 1205 contains one 40mm diameter stamp.

National Assembly, 100th Anniv. — A447

2018, Dec. 7 Litho. *Perf. 14x14¼*
1206 A447 60g dk red & gray *2.10 2.10*

UNICEF in Azerbaijan, 25th Anniv. — A448

2018, Dec. 11 Litho. *Perf. 13x13¼*
1207 A448 50g brt blue *1.60 1.60*

Souvenir Sheet

Lauch of Azerspace-2 — A449

2018, Dec. 11 Litho. *Perf. 13x13½*
1208 A449 1m multi *3.25 3.25*

Elza Ibrahimova (1938-2012), Composer A450

2018, Dec. 20 Litho. *Perf. 14x14½*
1209 A450 20g multi *.65 .65*

Hassan Abdullayev (1918-1993), Physicist — A451

2018, Dec. 25 Litho. *Perf. 12*
1210 A451 30g multi *1.75 1.75*

Architects — A452

No. 1211, 50g: a, Ilham Aliyev (1934-2002). b, Vadim Shulgin (1926-74). c, Sanan Sultanov (1947-97). d, Parviz Huseynov (1933-2002).

No. 1212, 50g: a, Hajimurad Shugayev (1940-2011). b, Avrora Salamova (1933-86). c, Fira Rustambeyova (1923-99) d, Abram Surkin (1922-2012).

No. 1213, 50g: a, Abdulvahab Salamzadeh (1916-83). b, Davud Akhundov (1918-2003). c, Talat Dadashov (1923-94). d, Boris Revazov (1897-1974).

2018, Dec. 25 Litho. *Perf. 13x13½*
Sheets of 4, #a-d
1211-1213 A452 Set of 3 *13.00 13.00*

Miniature Sheet

Birds of Gara-Yaz State Reserve — A453

No. 1214: a, 20g, Picoides scalaris. b, 20g, Sturnus vulgaris. c, 30g,True thrush. d, 30g, Phasianus. e, 60g, Lamprotornis hildebrandti. f, 60g, Upupa epops.

2018, Dec. 27 Litho. *Perf. 13¼x13*
1214 A453 Sheet of 6, #a-f *5.50 5.50*

Souvenir Sheet

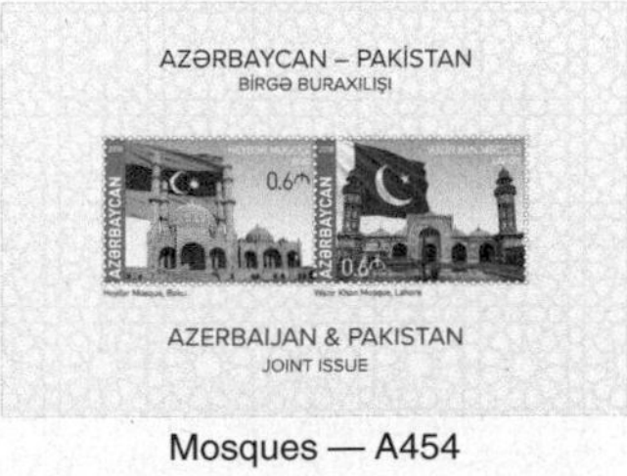

Mosques — A454

Designs: a, Heydar Mosque, Baku, flag of Azerbaijan. b, Wazir Khan Mosque, Lahore, Pakistan, flag of Pakistan.

2018, Dec. 27 Litho. *Perf. 12*
1215 A454 60g Sheet of 2, #a-b *3.25 3.25*

Joint Issue between Azerbaijan and Pakistan. See Pakistan No. 1262.

Souvenir Sheet

New Year 2019 (Year of the Pig) — A455

2019, Mar. 7 **Litho.** ***Perf. 13***
1216 A455 1m multi *2.75 2.75*

Miniature Sheet

Novruz — A456

No. 1217: a, 30g, Girl with jug. b, 30g, Bird, man jumping over fire. c, 50g, Girl with flowers. d, 50g, Man playing music. e, 60g, Girl rolling lavash. f, 60g, Man with crook.

2019, Mar. 19 **Litho.** ***Perf. 12***
1217 A456 Block of 6, #a-f *6.50 6.50*

Retaking of Lala Tapa, 3rd Anniv. A457

2019, Apr. 3 **Litho.** ***Perf. 12***
1218 A457 60g multi *1.75 1.75*

Towers
A458 A459

2019, Apr. 19 **Litho.** ***Perf. 13***
1219 A458 10g gray & gold *.30 .30*
1220 A459 20g magenta & sil *.55 .55*
1221 A458 30g sil & black *.80 .80*
1222 A459 50g gold *1.40 1.40*
Nos. 1219-1222 (4) *3.05 3.05*

Azerbaijan Formula 1 Grand Prix — A460

Formula 1 car: 60g, Front view. 3m, Aerial view.

2019, Apr. 19 **Litho.** ***Perf. 13¼***
1223 A460 60g multi *1.75 1.75*

Souvenir Sheet

Perf. 13½

1224 A460 3m multi *7.75 7.75*

No. 1224 contains one 40x40mm stamp.

Final Match of 2019 Europa League Soccer Championships, Baku — A461

No. 1225 — Soccer player and Olympic Stadium, Baku, at: a, Right. b, Left.

2019, May 29 **Litho.** ***Perf. 12***
1225 A461 60g Horiz. pair, #a-b *3.25 3.25*

Miniature Sheet

Buildings in Baku Designed by Polish Architects — A462

No. 1226: a, City Council Building (with spire), by Józef Goslawski. b, Taghiyev School for Girls (with balcony), by Goslawski. c, Mukhtarov Palace, by Józef Ploszko. d, House of Agabala Guliyev, by Eugeniusz Skibinski.

Perf. 11¼ Syncopated

2019, May 31 **Litho.**
1226 A462 60g Sheet of 4, #a-d *6.50 6.50*

See Poland No. 4421.

Miniature Sheet

Children's Art — A463

No. 1227 — Art by: a, 20g, Elcamal Pasayev. b, 30g, Aylin Eliyeva. c, 50g, Ziya Abdurrehimli, vert. d, 60g, Eli Asimli, vert.

Perf. 13x13½, 13½x13

2019, June 1 **Litho.**
1227 A463 Sheet of 4, #a-d, + central label *4.50 4.50*

Union of International Associations Forum at Heydar Aliyev Center, Baku — A464

2019, June 7 **Litho.** ***Perf. 13***
1228 A464 1m multi *2.60 2.60*

Mohandas K. Gandhi (1869-1948), Indian Nationalist Leader — A465

2019, July 26 **Litho.** ***Perf. 12***
1229 A465 60g multi *1.75 1.75*

Souvenir Sheet

31st International Olympiad in Informatics, Baku — A466

2019, Aug. 10 **Litho.** ***Perf. 13½x13***
1230 A466 1.50m multi *4.00 4.00*

Souvenir Sheet

Azerbaijan Border Guards, Cent. — A467

No. 1231: a, Two medals. b, Three badges. c, Border guard with binoculars.

2019, Aug. 20 **Litho.** ***Perf. 13***
1231 A467 3m Sheet of 3, #a-c *22.00 22.00*

No. 1231c has two hemispheres of soft plastic affixed as the lenses of the binoculars.

State Oil Fund, 20th Anniv. — A468

2019, Sept. 9 **Litho.** ***Perf. 12***
1232 A468 60g multi *1.75 1.75*

Emblem of Azerbaijan International Operating Company A469

Baku-Ceyhan Pipeline, 25th Anniv. — A470

Petroleum Drilling and Distribution Facilities A471

No. 1233: c, Ciraq Oil Platform. d, Merkezi Azeri Oil Platform. e, Sengecal Oil Terminal. f, Serqi Azeri Oil Platform. g, Qerbi Ciraq Oil Platform. h, Derinsulu Günesli Oil Platform. i, Qerbi Azeri Oil Platform. j, Unconnected pipes of Baku-Tbilisi-Ceyhan Pipeline. k, Ceyhan Oil Terminal.

2019, Sept. 20 **Litho.** ***Perf. 12***
1233 Sheet of 20, #1233a, 1233c-1233k, 10 #1233b *21.50 21.50*
a. A469 20g multi *.50 .50*
b. A470 30g multi *.75 .75*
c.-k. A471 60g Any single *1.50 1.50*

Souvenir Sheet

International Civil Aviation Organization, 75th Anniv. — A472

Litho. & Embossed

2019, Sept. 24 ***Perf. 13½x13***
1234 A472 2m multi *5.25 5.25*

A473

Europa — A474

Birds: 50g, Common rosefinch. 60g, Alectoris chukar. 1.50m, Upupa epops, vert.

Perf. 14½x14¼

2019, Sept. 27 **Litho.**

1235-1236 A473 Set of 2 *3.00 3.00*

1236a Booklet pane of 8, 4 each Nos. 1235-1236, perf. 14½x14¼ on 3 sides *12.00* —

Souvenir Sheet

Perf. 14¼x14½

1237 A474 1.50m multi *4.00 4.00*

Souvenir Sheet

Central Bank, Cent. — A475

No. 1238: a, Gold coin, denomination at UR. b, Silver coin, denomination at LR.

Litho. & Embossed With Foil Application

2019, Sept. 30 ***Perf. 13½***

1238 A475 5m Sheet of 2, #a-b *26.00 26.00*

Souvenir Sheet

Imadaddin Nasimi (1369-1417), Poet — A476

No. 1239: a, Head of Nasimi. b, Quill pen.

2019, Oct. 1 **Litho.** ***Perf. 13¼***

1239 A476 60g Sheet of 2, #a-b *4.25 4.25*

Miniature Sheet

Famous Lawyers — A477

No. 1240: a, Alimardan Bey Topchubashov (1863-1934. b, Fatali Khan Khoyski (1875-1920). c, Rustam Khan Khoyski (1888-1948). d, Khalil Bey Khasmammadov (1873-1947). e, Ismail Khan Ziyadkhanov (1867-1920). f, Rashid Bey Akhundzade (1880-1940).

2019, Oct. 4 **Litho.** ***Perf. 12***

1240 A477 60g Sheet of 6, #a-f *9.50 9.50*

Universal Postal Union, 145th Anniv. A478

2019, Oct. 9 **Litho.** ***Perf. 12***

1241 A478 60g multi *1.60 1.60*

7th Turkic Council Summit, Baku — A479

2019, Oct. 15 **Litho.** ***Perf. 12***

1242 A479 60g multi *1.60 1.60*

A480 A481

A482 A483

A484 A485

The Oil Epic, by Sabina Shikhlinskaya

A486 A487

2019, Nov. 19 **Litho.** ***Perf. 13¼***

1243 Sheet of 8 *13.00 13.00*

a. A480 60g multi *1.60 1.60*
b. A481 60g multi *1.60 1.60*
c. A482 60g multi *1.60 1.60*
d. A483 60g multi *1.60 1.60*
e. A484 60g multi *1.60 1.60*
f. A485 60g multi *1.60 1.60*
g. A486 60g multi *1.60 1.60*
h. A487 60g multi *1.60 1.60*

Sumqayit, 70th Anniv. A488

2019, Nov. 21 **Litho.** ***Perf. 13¼x13***

1244 A488 60g multi *1.60 1.60*

A489

Baku University, Cent. — A490

No. 1245: a, Pres. Heydar Aliyev (1923-2003). b, University building. c, Seal of the university.

No. 1246: a, Open book, truncated page at right. b, Open book.

2019, Nov. 26 **Litho.** ***Perf. 13x13¼***

1245 A489 60g Sheet of 3, #a-c *5.00 5.00*

Souvenir Sheet

1246 A490 60g Sheet of 2, #a-b *3.25 3.25*

Melikmamed (Azerbaijan Folk Tale) — A491

The Golden Bird (Belarussian Folk Tale) — A492

Litho. With Foil Application

2019, Dec. 3 ***Perf. 12***

1247 A491 60g gold & multi *1.60 1.60*

1248 A492 60g gold & multi *1.60 1.60*

a. Souvenir sheet of 4, 2 each #1247-1248 *6.50 6.50*

Joint Issue between Azerbaijan and Belarus. See Belarus Nos. 1163-1164.

Stained Glass Window, Juma Mosque, Ordubad A493

Gazanchi Bridge A494

Ilandag Mountain — A495

Landscapes — A496

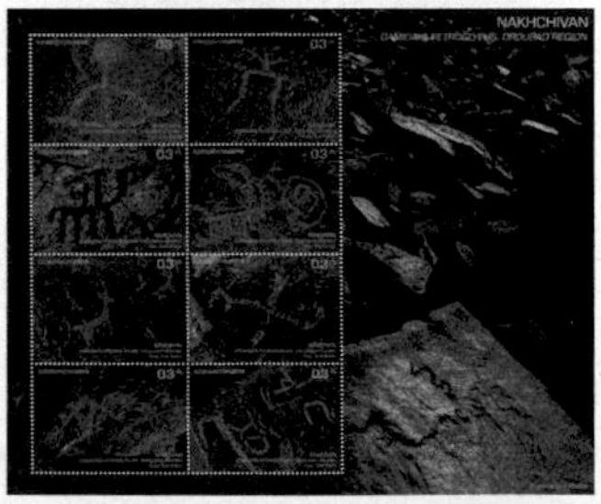

Gamigaya Petroglyphs — A497

Flowers — A498

Religious Sanctuaries — A499

Garabaghlar Mausoleum — A500

Momine Khatun Mausoleum — A501

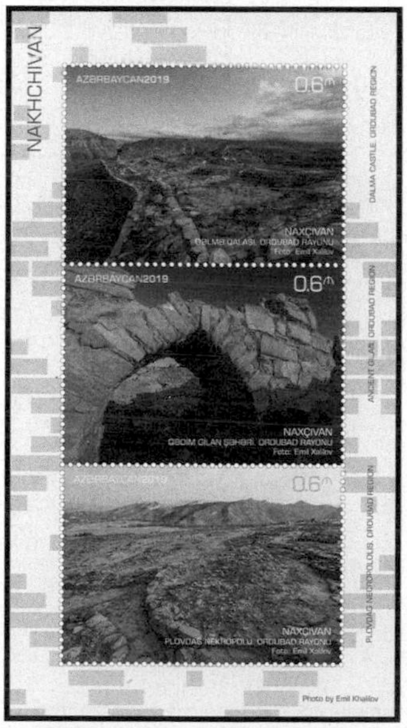

Ordubad Region Archaeological Sites — A502

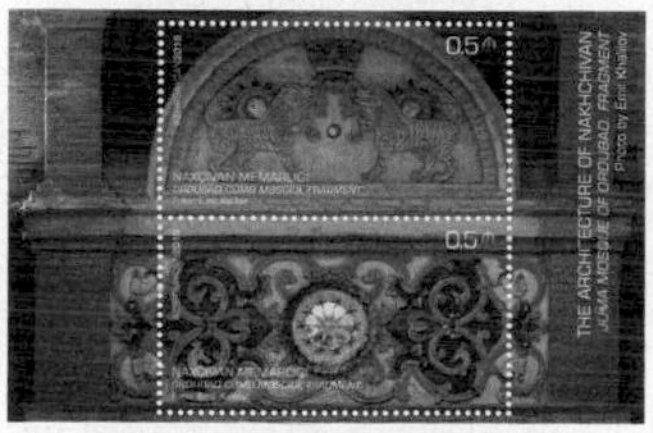

Decorations, Juma Mosque, Ordubad — A503

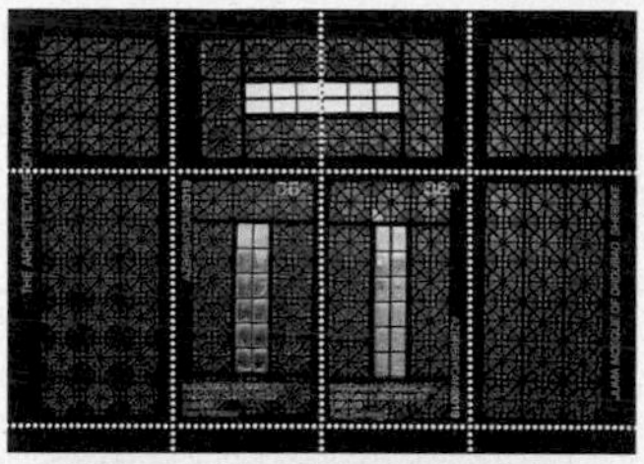

Stained Glass Windows, Juma Mosque, Ordubad — A504

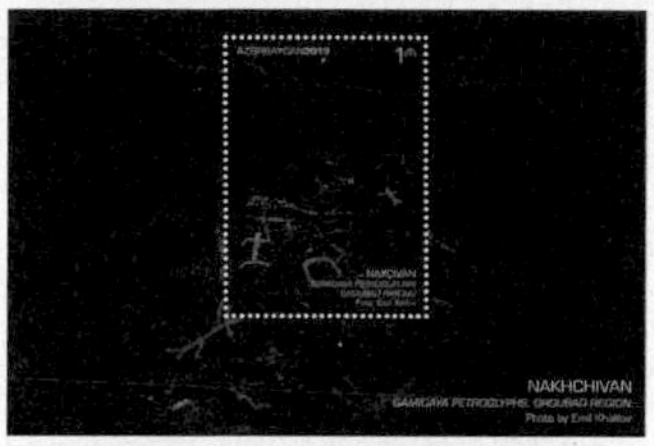

Gamigaya Petroglyph — A505

Detail From Gulustan Mausoleum — A506

White Stork — A507

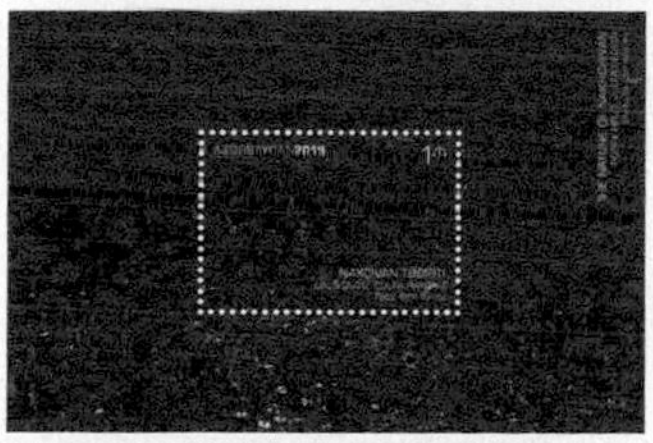

Poppy Field, Julfa Region — A508

Solenanthus Circinnatus — A509

Goygol Lake — A510

Leketag Bridge — A511

Yusif Ibn Kuseyir Mausoleum — A512

No. 1252: a, Ilandag Mountain. b, Mountainside trees in autumn. c, Daridag Mountain. d, Tree in field of dandelions. e, Batabat Lake. f, Mountainside in winter. g, Mountain and field in spring. h, Alinja Fortress. i, Babak Castle. j, Lake Goygol.

No. 1253: a, Head and arms of person. b, Legs and arms of person. c, Animal. d, Two petroglyphs, one circular. e, Two deer, f, Cross with circles on opposite sides. g, Hunter and prey. h, Group of petroglyphs.

No. 1254: a, Nonea pulla. b, Inula aspera. c, Verbascum pyramidatum. d, Gentiana angulosa. e, Aster alpinus. f, Stipa lessingiana.

No. 1255: a, Imamzadeh Mosque. b, Tomb of Prophet Noah, vert. c, Khanogah of Alinjachay and stone cylinders, vert. d, Ashabi-Kahf Cave.

No. 1256: a, Mosque (52x37mm). b, Doorway (40x28mm). c, Detail of archway insets (40x28mm). d, Detail of curved outer walls (40x28mm).

No. 1257: a, Wall detail with blue octagon mosaic (40x28mm). b, Wall detail with blue star mosaic (40x28mm). c, Mausoleum (30x52mm).

No. 1258: a, Ruins of Dalma Castle. b, Arch, Ancient Gilan. c, Plovdag Necropolis.

No. 1259: a, Lions under arch. b, Peacock's head arabasque with stars in central circle.

No. 1260: a, Stained glass window with buildings visible in clear windows. b, Stained glass window with street scene and automobile visible in clear windows.

Perf. 13¼ (#1249), 13½x13 (#1250, 1257c, 1260-1261, 1263, 1268), 13x13½ (#1251, 1253-1255, 1256a, 1258-1259, 1266-1267), 12 (#1252, 1256b-1256d, 1257a-1257b, 1262, 1264-1265)

2019, Dec. 4 **Litho.**

1249	A493	10g multi	.25	.25
1250	A494	1m multi	2.75	2.75
1251	A495	1m multi	2.75	2.75
		Nos. 1249-1251 (3)	5.75	5.75

Miniature Sheets

1252	A496	60g Sheet of 10, #a-j	16.00	16.00
1253	A497	30g Sheet of 8, #a-h	6.50	6.50
1254	A498	60g Sheet of 6, #a-f	9.50	9.50
1255	A499	60g Sheet of 4, #a-d, + central label	6.50	6.50
1256	A500	60g Sheet of 4, #a-d	6.50	6.50
1257	A501	50g Sheet of 3, #a-c	4.00	4.00
1258	A502	60g Sheet of 3, #a-c	4.75	4.75
1259	A503	50g Sheet of 2, #a-b	2.75	2.75
1260	A504	60g Sheet of 2, #a-b	3.25	3.25
		Nos. 1252-1260 (9)	59.75	59.75

Souvenir Sheets

1261	A505	1m multi	2.75	2.75
1262	A506	1m multi	2.75	2.75
1263	A507	1m multi	2.75	2.75
1264	A508	1m multi	2.75	2.75
1265	A509	1m multi	2.75	2.75
1266	A510	1m multi	2.75	2.75
1267	A511	1m multi	2.75	2.75
1268	A512	1.50m multi	4.00	4.00
		Nos. 1261-1268 (8)	23.25	23.25

Nakhichevan Autonomous Republic.

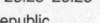

Partnership Between Azerbaijan and European Union, 10th Anniv. A513

2019, Dec. 13 **Litho.** ***Perf. 12***

1269 A513 50g multi *1.50 1.50*

Souvenir Sheet

Azerbaijan Independence Museum, Baku, Cent. — A514

No. 1270: a, 1918 Declaration of Independence. b, National emblem. c, 1919 50-ruble and 100-ruble banknotes.

2019, Dec. 25 **Litho.** ***Perf. 12***

1270 A514 60g Sheet of 3, #a-c *5.00 5.00*

Abbasgulu Bakikhanov (1794-1847), Writer — A515

2019, Dec. 30 **Litho.** ***Perf. 12***

1271 A515 50g multi *1.40 1.40*

Miniature Sheet

First Azerbaijan Postage Stamps, Cent. — A516

No. 1272: a, Azerbaijan #1. b, Azerbaijan #3. c, Azerbaijan #6. d, Azerbaijan #9.

2019, Dec. 30 **Litho.** ***Perf. 12***

1272 A516 60g Sheet of 4, #a-d *6.75 6.75*

Souvenir Sheet

National Commission for UNESCO — A517

2019, Dec. 30 **Litho.** ***Perf. 13x13½***

1273 A517 1.50m multi *4.25 4.25*

New Year 2020 (Year of the Rat) — A518

No. 1274: a, 50g, Rats, bowl and rat trap. b, 60g, Rat with roses and rat with tail as maze.

2020, Feb. 1 Litho. *Perf. 13x13½*

1274	A518	Pair, #a-b	*3.00*	*3.00*

SEMI-POSTAL STAMPS

Carrying Food to Sufferers SP1

1922 Unwmk. *Imperf.*

B1	SP1	500r blue & pale blue	2.00	*8.00*

For overprint and surcharge see Nos. 42, 305.

Widow and Orphans — SP2

1922

B2	SP2	1000r brown & bister	2.00	*8.00*

Counterfeits exist.

For overprint and surcharge see Nos. 44, 306.

Used values for Nos. B1 and B2 are for favor-canceled stamps. Postally used examples sell for much higher prices.

AIR POST STAMP

Catalogue values for all stamps in this section are for never hinged items.

Eagle — AP1

1995, Oct. 16 Litho. *Perf. 14*

C1	AP1	2200m multicolored	4.00	4.00

AZORES

ˈā-ˌzōrz

LOCATION — Group of islands in the North Atlantic Ocean, due west of Portugal
AREA — 922 sq. mi.
POP. — 253,935 (1930)
CAPITAL — Ponta Delgada

Azores stamps were supplanted by those of Portugal in 1931.

In 1934-45, #RA5-RA11, RAJ1-RAJ4, and many stamps between #155-223 were used for regular postage in Portugal.

The Azores were declared an autonomous, or self-governing, region of Portugal in 1976. See Portugal for issues since 1980.

1000 Reis = 1 Milreis
100 Centavos = 1 Escudo (1912)

Stamps of Portugal Overprinted in Black or Carmine

A second type of this overprint has a broad "O" and open "S."

1868 Unwmk. *Imperf.*

1	A14	5r black	*3,500.*	*2,400.*
2	A14	10r yellow	*13,750.*	*10,000.*
3	A14	20r bister	200.00	175.00
4	A14	50r green	200.00	175.00
5	A14	80r orange	240.00	180.00
6	A14	100r lilac	240.00	180.00

The reprints are on thick chalky white wove paper, ungummed, and on thin ivory paper with shiny white gum. Value $35-42.50 each.

1868-70 *Perf. 12½*

5 REIS:
Type I — The "5" at the right is 1mm from end of label.
Type II — The "5" is 1½mm from end of label.

7	A14	5r black, type I (C)	75.00	72.50
a.		Type II	70.00	70.00
8	A14	10r yellow	120.00	40.00
a.		Inverted overprint	*250.00*	*150.00*
9	A14	20r bister	75.00	65.00
10	A14	25r rose	75.00	11.00
a.		Inverted overprint	—	—
11	A14	50r green	210.00	190.00
12	A14	80r orange	210.00	190.00
13	A14	100r lilac ('69)	210.00	190.00
14	A14	120r blue	180.00	120.00
15	A14	240r violet	650.00	400.00

The reprints are on thick chalky white paper ungummed, perf 13½, and on thin ivory paper with shiny white gum, perf 13½. Value $30 each.

Overprint Type B

1871-75 *Perf. 12½*

21	A15	5r black (C)	15.00	9.75
a.		Inverted overprint	*52.50*	*42.50*
23	A15	10r yellow	32.00	25.00
a.		Inverted overprint	—	—
b.		Double overprint	60.00	47.50
24	A15	20r bister	37.50	30.00
25	A15	25r rose	17.00	4.25
a.		Inverted overprint	—	—
b.		Double overprint	*40.00*	
c.		Perf. 14	190.00	85.00
d.		Dbl. impression of stamp	—	—
26	A15	50r green	85.00	42.50
27	A15	80r orange	125.00	67.50
28	A15	100r lilac	100.00	60.00
a.		Perf. 14	195.00	150.00
29	A15	120r blue	180.00	125.00
a.		Inverted overprint	—	—
30	A15	240r violet	900.00	675.00

Nos. 21-29 exist with overprint "b."

The reprints are of type "b." All values exist are on thick chalky white paper ungummed, perf 13½ (value, each $29) and also on thin white paper with shiny white gum and perforated 13½ (value, each $30). The 5r, 10r, 15r, 50r and 120r also exist on thick chalky white paper ungummed, perf 12½. Value, each $80.

Overprinted in Black — c

15 REIS:
Type I — The figures of value, 1 and 5, at the right in upper label are close together.
Type II — The figures of value at the right in upper label are spaced.

1875-80 *Perf. 13½*

31	A15	10r blue green	175.00	145.00
32	A15	10r yellow green	120.00	87.50
33b	A15	15r lilac brown	20.00	16.50
a.		Inverted overprint	*135.00*	*82.50*
34	A15	50r blue	160.00	87.50
35	A15	150r blue	180.00	175.00
36	A15	150r yellow	230.00	175.00
37	A15	300r violet	95.00	65.00

The reprints have the same papers, gum and perforations as those of the preceding issue.

Black Overprint

1880 *Perf. 12½*

38	A17	25r bluish gray	150.00	42.50
39	A18	25r red lilac	60.00	9.50
b.		25r gray	—	—
d.		As "c," double overprint		

Overprint in Carmine or Black

1881-82

40	A16	5r black (C)	26.00	12.00
41	A23	25r brown ('82)	52.50	8.00
a.		Double overprint		
42	A19	50r blue	175.00	42.50
		Nos. 40-42 (3)	253.50	62.50

Reprints of Nos. 38, 39, 39a, 40 and 42 have the same papers, gum and perforations as those of preceding issues.

Overprinted in Red or Black — d

15, 20 REIS:
Type I — The figures of value are some distance apart and close to the end of the label.
Type II — The figures are closer together and farther from the end of the label. On the 15 reis this is particularly apparent in the upper right figures.

1882-85 *Perf. 12½*

43	A16	5r black (R)	28.00	15.00
44	A21	5r slate	19.00	4.50
a.		Double overprint	—	
c.		Inverted overprint	—	45.00
45	A15	10r green	82.50	67.50
a.		Inverted overprint	—	—
46	A22	10r green ('84)	30.00	14.00
a.		Double overprint	—	
47	A15	15r lilac brn	67.50	52.50
b.		Inverted overprint	—	—
48	A15	20r bister	110.00	80.00
a.		Inverted overprint	—	—
49	A15	20r car ('85)	.14000	115.00
a.		Double overprint	190.00	150.00
50	A23	25r brown	30.00	4.50
51	A15	50r blue	*875.00*	*725.00*
52	A24	50r blue	42.50	4.50
a.		Double overprint	—	—
53	A15	80r yellow	80.00	62.50
a.		80r orange	120.00	102.50
b.		Double overprint		
54	A15	100r lilac	120.00	87.50
55	A15	150r blue	*900.00*	*750.00*
56b	A15	150r yellow	60.00	52.50
57b	A15	300r violet	87.50	72.50
58	A21	5r slate (R)	25.00	6.00
59	A24a	500r black	175.00	150.00
60	A15	1000r black (R)	140.00	125.00

This set was issued on both ordinary and enamel surfaced papers. Nos. 51 and 55 exist only on ordinary paper, Nos. 44, 46, 49 and 53 only on surfaced paper, and the other values on both types of paper. Values for Nos. 56b and 57b are for stamps printed on surfaced paper. Stamps on ordinary paper are worth more.

For specialized listings of this issue and other early Azore stamps, see the *Scott Classic Specialized Catalogue.*

Reprints of the 1882-85 issues have the same papers, gum and perforations as those of preceding issues.

1887 Black Overprint *Perf. 11½*

61	A25	20r pink	40.00	17.50
a.		Inverted overprint	115.00	75.00
b.		Double overprint	—	—
62	A26	25r lilac rose	45.00	3.00
a.		Inverted overprint	—	—
b.		Double ovpt., one invtd.	—	—
63	A26	25r red violet	45.00	3.00
a.		Double overprint	—	—
64	A24a	500r red violet	175.00	97.50
a.		Perf. 13½	325.00	240.00
		Nos. 61-64 (4)	305.00	121.00

Nos. 58-64 inclusive have been reprinted on thin white paper with shiny white gum and perforated 13½. Value: Nos. 58, 61-64, each $22.50; No. 59, $85; No. 60, $50.

Prince Henry the Navigator Issue

Portugal Nos. 97-109 Overprinted

1894, Mar. 4 *Perf. 14*

65	A46	5r orange yel	4.50	3.00
a.		Inverted overprint	*60.00*	*60.00*
66	A46	10r violet rose	4.50	3.00
a.		Double overprint	—	—
b.		Inverted overprint	—	—
67	A46	15r brown	5.25	4.00
68	A46	20r violet	6.75	4.25
a.		Double overprint	—	—
69	A47	25r green	6.75	4.50
a.		Double overprint	*75.00*	*75.00*
b.		Inverted overprint	*75.00*	*75.00*
70	A47	50r blue	12.50	7.50
71	A47	75r dp carmine	26.00	9.50
72	A47	80r yellow grn	30.00	11.50
73	A47	100r lt brn, *pale buff*	30.00	9.75
a.		Double overprint	—	—
74	A48	150r lt car, *pale rose*	37.50	19.00
75	A48	300r dk bl, *sal buff*	45.00	27.00
76	A48	500r brn vio, *pale lil*	82.50	45.00
77	A48	1000r gray blk, *yelsh*	160.00	70.00
a.		Double overprint	700.00	500.00
		Nos. 65-77 (13)	451.25	218.00

St. Anthony of Padua Issue

Portugal Nos. 132-146 Overprinted in Red or Black

No. 78

No. 79

1895, June 13 *Perf. 12*

78	A50	2½r black (R)	3.00	1.50
79	A51	5r brown yel	9.50	3.00
80	A51	10r red lilac	9.50	4.50
81	A51	15r red brown	14.50	7.00
82	A51	20r gray lilac	16.00	11.50
83	A51	25r grn & vio	11.50	3.75
84	A52	50r blue & brn	32.50	15.00
85	A52	75r rose & brn	47.50	40.00
86	A52	80r lt grn & brn	52.50	47.50
87	A52	100r choc & blk	50.00	40.00
88	A53	150r vio rose & bis	105.00	100.00
89	A53	200r blue & bis	115.00	100.00
90	A53	300r slate & bis	140.00	102.50
91	A53	500r vio brn & grn	200.00	150.00
92	A53	1000r vio & grn	325.00	225.00
		Nos. 78-92 (15)	1,132.	851.25

7th cent. of the birth of Saint Anthony of Padua.

Common Design Types pictured following the introduction.

Vasco da Gama Issue

Common Design Types

1898, Apr. 1 *Perf. 14, 15*

93	CD20	2½r blue green	3.00	1.50
94	CD21	5r red	3.00	1.50
95	CD22	10r gray lilac	7.00	3.00
96	CD23	25r yel grn	7.00	3.00
97	CD24	50r dark blue	9.00	9.50
98	CD25	75r vio brn	19.50	13.00
99	CD26	100r bis brn	25.00	14.00
100	CD27	150r bister	40.00	28.00
		Nos. 93-100 (8)	113.50	73.50

For overprints and surcharges see Nos. 141-148.

King Carlos — A28

1906 **Typo.** ***Perf. 11½x12***

No.	Type	Description	Unused	Used
101	A28	2½r gray	.75	.75
a.		Inverted overprint	35.00	35.00
102	A28	5r orange yel	.75	.75
a.		Inverted overprint	35.00	35.00
103	A28	10r yellow grn	.75	.75
104	A28	20r gray vio	.70	.75
105	A28	25r carmine	.70	.75
106	A28	50r ultra	6.00	4.75
107	A28	75r brown, *straw*	2.10	1.50
108	A28	100r dk blue, *bl*	2.10	1.40
109	A28	200r red lilac, *pnksh*	2.25	1.40
110	A28	300r dk blue, *rose*	6.75	5.75
111	A28	500r black, *blue*	16.00	14.00
		Nos. 101-111 (11)	38.85	32.55

"Acores" and letters and figures in the corners are in red on the 2½, 10, 20, 75 and 500r and in black on the other values.

King Manuel II — A29

1910, Apr. 1 ***Perf. 14x15***

No.	Type	Description	Unused	Used
112	A29	2½r violet	.75	.75
113	A29	5r black	.75	.75
114	A29	10r dk green	.75	.75
115	A29	15r lilac brn	.75	.75
116	A29	20r carmine	.75	.75
117	A29	25r violet brn	.75	.75
a.		Perf. 11½	7.50	3.75
118	A29	50r blue	3.00	1.60
119	A29	75r bister brn	3.00	1.60
120	A29	80r slate	3.00	1.60
121	A29	100r brown, *lt grn*	4.50	3.75
122	A29	200r green, *sal*	4.50	3.75
123	A29	300r black, *blue*	3.00	2.75
124	A29	500r olive & brown	9.50	9.00
125	A29	1000r blue & black	21.00	19.00
		Nos. 112-125 (14)	56.00	47.55

The errors of color 10r black, 15r dark green, 25r black and 50r carmine are considered to be proofs.

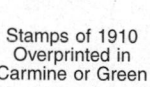

Stamps of 1910 Overprinted in Carmine or Green

1910

No.	Type	Description	Unused	Used
126	A29	2½r violet	.75	.75
a.		Inverted overprint	12.50	12.50
127	A29	5r black	.75	.75
a.		Inverted overprint	12.50	12.50
128	A29	10r dk green	.75	.75
a.		Inverted overprint	12.50	12.50
129	A29	15r lilac brn	2.25	1.40
a.		Inverted overprint	12.50	12.50
130	A29	20r carmine (G)	2.25	1.40
a.		Inverted overprint	22.50	22.50
b.		Double overprint	22.50	22.50
131	A29	25r violet brn	.75	.75
a.		Perf. 11½	65.00	57.50
132	A29	50r blue	1.40	1.50
133	A29	75r bister brn	1.40	.75
a.		Double overprint	12.50	12.50
134	A29	80r slate	1.40	.75
135	A29	100r brown, *grn*	1.50	.75
136	A29	200r green, *sal*	1.50	.75
137	A29	300r black, *blue*	3.50	2.25
138	A29	500r olive & brn	4.50	3.00
139	A29	1000r blue & blk	11.00	7.00
		Nos. 126-139 (14)	33.70	22.55

Vasco da Gama Issue Overprinted or Surcharged in Black

e

f

g

1911 ***Perf. 14, 15***

No.	Type	Description	Unused	Used
141	CD20(e)	2½r blue green	.75	.75
142	CD21(f)	15r on 5r red	.75	.75
143	CD23(e)	25r yellow grn	.75	.75
144	CD24(e)	50r dk blue	2.25	1.40
145	CD25(e)	75r violet brn	2.25	1.50
146	CD27(f)	80r on 150r bister	2.25	1.50
147	CD26(e)	100r yellow brn	3.00	2.25
a.		Double surcharge	26.00	24.00
148	CD22(g)	1000r on 10r lil	20.00	15.00
		Nos. 141-148 (8)	32.00	23.90

Postage Due Stamps of Portugal Overprinted or Surcharged in Black

1911 ***Perf. 12***

No.	Type	Description	Unused	Used
149	D1	5r black	1.50	1.50
150	D1	10r magenta	2.75	1.50
a.		"Acores" double	26.00	19.00
151	D1	20r orange	5.25	3.75
152	D1	200r brn, *buff*	5.25	3.75
a.		"Acores" inverted	100.00	
153	D1	300r on 50r slate	22.00	19.00
154	D1	500r on 100r car, *pink*	22.00	18.00
		Nos. 149-154 (6)	58.75	47.50

Ceres Issue of Portugal Overprinted in Black or Carmine

With Imprint

Chalky Paper

1912-21 ***Perf. 15x14***

No.	Type	Description	Unused	Used
155	A64	¼c olive brown	2.60	.80
156	A64	½c black (C)	2.60	.80
157	A64	1c dp grn ('13)	3.00	.80
158	A64	1½c choc ('13)	4.00	2.50
159	A64	2c car ('13)	6.00	2.60
160	A64	2½c violet	4.50	1.00
161	A64	5c dp blue ('13)	4.50	1.00
162	A64	7½c yel brn ('13)	12.00	6.50
163	A64	8c slate ('13)	12.00	6.50
164	A64	10c org brn ('13)	13.00	7.50
165	A64	15c plum ('13)	17.00	7.50
166	A64	20c vio brn, *grn* ('13)	12.00	7.00
167	A64	30c brn, *pink* ('13)	80.00	60.00
168	A64	30c brn, *yel* ('19)	3.00	2.40
169	A64	50c org, *sal* ('13)	8.00	2.75
170	A64	50c org, *yel* ('13)	7.50	2.75
171	A64	1e dp grn, *bl* ('13)	7.00	6.00
		Nos. 155-171 (17)	196.70	118.40
		Set, never hinged	302.00	

Nos. 155 and 160 also exist on glazed non-chalky paper. Value each, $17 never hinged, $11 unused, and $8.50 used.

Perf. 12x11½

No.	Type	Description	Unused	Used
172	A64	14c dk bl, *yel* ('21)	3.00	2.40
		Nos. 155-172 (18)	199.70	120.80

Ordinary Paper

1917-21 ***Perf. 15x14***

No.	Type	Description	Unused	Used
173	A64	¼c olive brown	.70	.40
a.		Inverted overprint	12.50	9.50
174	A64	½c black (C)	.70	.40
175	A64	1c deep green	1.50	.80
a.		Inverted overprint	12.50	
176	A64	1c dp brn ('18)	.70	.60
a.		Inverted overprint	17.50	
177	A64	1½c choc	1.50	.80
a.		Inverted overprint	13.00	
178	A64	1½c dp grn ('18)	.70	.50
a.		Inverted overprint	17.50	
179	A64	2c carmine	1.15	.60
a.		Inverted overprint	20.00	
180	A64	2c orange ('19)	.70	.50
a.		Inverted overprint	25.00	
181	A64	2½c violet	1.15	.60
182	A64	3c rose ('18)	.70	.60
183	A64	3½c lt grn ('18)	.70	.50
184	A64	4c lt grn ('19)	.70	.60
185	A64	5c deep blue	1.20	.65
186	A64	5c yel brn ('21)	.90	.65
187	A64	6c dull rose ('20)	.70	.60
188	A64	7½c yellow brown	7.50	4.50
189	A64	7½c dp bl ('19)	1.90	1.75
190	A64	8c slate	1.20	.70
191	A64	10c orange brown	8.00	3.00
192	A64	15c plum	.85	.60
193	A64	30c gray brn ('21)	3.75	3.00
194	A64	60c blue ('21)	3.75	3.00
		Never hinged	5.25	
		Nos. 173-194 (22)	40.65	25.35

Examples of thick carton paper varieties exist. See *Scott Classic Specialized Catalogue of Stamps & Covers 1840-1940* for listings.

1918-26 ***Perf. 12x11½***

No.	Type	Description	Unused	Used
195	A64	¼c olive brown	.70	.55
196	A64	½c black (R)	.70	.60
197	A64	1c deep brown	.55	.55
198	A64	1½c deep green	1.05	.70
199	A64	2c org ('19)	.55	.50
a.		Inverted overprint	24.00	
200	A64	3c rose	.70	.60
201	A64	3c dull ultra ('25)	.40	.30
202	A64	4c lt grn ('19)	.70	.60
a.		Inverted overprint	21.00	
203	A64	5c ol brn ('21)	.55	.50
204A	A64	6c dull rose ('20)	.55	.50
204	A64	6c choc ('25)	.55	.50
205	A64	7½c dp bl ('19)	90.00	67.50
206	A64	8c bl grn ('24)	.80	.55
207	A64	8c org ('25)	1.00	.95
208	A64	10c org brn	1.50	.90
209	A64	12c bl gray ('20)	2.75	2.25
210	A64	12c dp grn ('22)	.85	.75
a.		Inverted overprint	20.00	
211	A64	13½c chlky bl ('20)	2.75	2.25
212	A64	15c blk (R) ('24)	.55	.50
213	A64	16c brt ultra ('26)	.95	.90
214	A64	20c choc ('21)	.85	.75
215	A64	20c dp grn ('24)	1.25	.95
a.		Double overprint	22.50	22.50
216	A64	20c gray ('24)	.80	.60
217	A64	24c grnsh bl ('21)	.85	.75
218	A64	25c sal ('23)	.70	.50
219	A64	30c gray brn ('21)	1.90	1.60
220	A64	32c dp grn ('26)	2.75	2.40
221	A64	36c red ('21)	.75	.65
222	A64	40c dp bl ('23)	1.00	.70
223	A64	40c blk brn ('24)	1.90	1.00
224	A64	48c brt rose ('26)	5.00	3.00
225	A64	50c yellow ('23)	1.75	1.50
226	A64	60c blue ('21)	1.75	1.50
227	A64	64c pale ultra ('26)	5.00	2.25
228	A64	75c dull rose ('24)	5.00	4.00
229	A64	80c dull rose ('21)	2.50	2.10
230	A64	80c violet ('24)	2.50	1.90
231	A64	90c chlky bl ('21)	2.50	2.10
232	A64	96c dp rose ('26)	2.75	2.25
233	A64	1e violet ('21)	2.50	2.10
234	A64	1.10e yel brn ('21)	2.75	2.10
235	A64	1.20e yel grn ('22)	4.50	2.10
236	A64	2e slate grn ('22)	12.00	6.50
		Nos. 195-236 (42)	170.85	125.25

Examples of thick carton paper and other varieties exist. See *Scott Classic Specialized Catalogue of Stamps & Covers 1840-1940* for listings.

1924-30 ***Perf. 12x11½***

Glazed Paper

No.	Type	Description	Unused	Used
237	A64	1e gray vio	3.75	3.00
237A	A64	1.20e buff	7.50	6.00
237B	A64	1.50e blk vio	8.25	6.25
237C	A64	1.50e lilac ('25)	9.75	6.00
237D	A64	1.60e dp bl ('25)	8.50	6.50
237E	A64	2.40e apple grn ('30)	70.00	45.00
237F	A64	3e lil pink ('28)	80.00	45.00
237G	A64	3.20e gray grn ('26)	9.00	9.50
237H	A64	5e emer ('25)	19.00	10.00
237I	A64	10e pink ('25)	50.00	27.50
237J	A64	20e pale turq ('25)	115.00	77.50
		Nos. 237-237J (11)	380.75	242.25

For same overprint on surcharged stamps, see Nos. 300-306. For same design without imprint see Nos. 307-313.

Castello-Branco Issue

Stamps of Portugal, 1925, Overprinted in Black or Red

1925, Mar. 29 ***Perf. 12½***

No.	Type	Description	Unused	Used
238	A73	2c orange	.25	.25
239	A73	3c green	.25	.25
240	A73	4c ultra (R)	.25	.25
241	A73	5c scarlet	.25	.25
242	A74	10c pale blue	.25	.25
243	A74	16c red orange	.35	.30
244	A75	25c car rose	.35	.30
245	A74	32c green	.50	.45
246	A75	40c grn & blk (R)	.50	.45
247	A74	48c red brn	1.10	1.10
248	A76	50c blue green	1.10	1.00
249	A76	64c orange brn	1.10	1.00
250	A76	75c gray blk (R)	1.10	1.00
251	A75	80c brown	1.10	1.00
252	A76	96c car rose	1.30	1.10
253	A77	1.50e dk bl, *bl* (R)	1.30	1.10
254	A75	1.60e indigo (R)	1.50	1.30
255	A77	2e dk grn, *grn* (R)	2.50	2.10
256	A77	2.40e red, *org*	3.25	3.00
257	A77	3.20e blk, *grn* (R)	7.50	6.75
		Nos. 238-257 (20)	25.80	23.20

First Independence Issue

Stamps of Portugal, 1926, Overprinted in Red

1926, Aug. 13 ***Perf. 14, 14½***

Center in Black

No.	Type	Description	Unused	Used
258	A79	2c orange	.30	.45
259	A80	3c ultra	.30	.45
260	A79	4c yellow grn	.30	.45
261	A80	5c black brn	.30	.45
262	A79	6c ocher	.30	.45
263	A80	15c dk green	.75	1.15
264	A81	20c dull violet	.75	1.15
265	A82	25c scarlet	.75	1.15
266	A81	32c deep green	.75	1.15
267	A82	40c yellow brn	.75	1.15
268	A82	50c olive bis	1.60	2.00
269	A82	75c red brown	1.90	2.10
270	A83	1e black violet	2.50	3.00
271	A84	4.50e olive green	10.50	11.50
		Nos. 258-271 (14)	21.75	26.60

The use of these stamps instead of those of the regular issue was obligatory on Aug. 13 and 14, Nov. 30 and Dec. 1, 1926.

Centering is vital to the value of Nos. 258-299. Stamps in grades of less than VF sell at significant discounts from the values here.

Second Independence Issue

Same Overprint on Stamps of Portugal, 1927, in Red

1927, Nov. 29 **Center in Black**

No.	Type	Description	Unused	Used
272	A86	2c lt brown	.30	.40
273	A87	3c ultra	.30	.40
274	A86	4c orange	.30	.40
275	A88	5c dk brown	.30	.40
276	A89	6c orange brn	.30	.45
277	A87	15c black brn	.30	.45
278	A86	25c gray	1.25	1.50
279	A89	32c blue grn	1.25	1.50
280	A90	40c yellow grn	1.00	1.00
281	A90	96c red	3.00	3.25
282	A88	1.60e myrtle grn	5.00	6.75
283	A91	4.50e bister	10.50	12.00
		Nos. 272-283 (12)	23.80	28.50

Third Independence Issue

Same Overprint on Stamps of Portugal, 1928, in Red

1928, Nov. 27 **Center in Black**

No.	Type	Description	Unused	Used
284	A93	2c lt blue	.40	.45
285	A94	3c lt green	.40	.45
286	A95	4c lake	.40	.45
287	A96	5c olive grn	.40	.45
288	A97	6c orange brn	.40	.45
289	A94	15c slate	.85	1.00
290	A95	16c dk violet	.75	1.00
291	A93	25c ultra	.75	1.00

292 A97 32c dk green .80 1.00
293 A96 40c olive brn .80 1.00
294 A95 50c red orange 1.60 2.00
295 A94 80c lt gray 1.60 2.00
296 A97 96c carmine 3.25 4.00
297 A96 1e claret 3.25 4.00
298 A93 1.60e dk blue 3.25 4.00
299 A98 4.50e yellow 11.50 13.50
Nos. 284-299 (16) 30.40 36.75

Types of Portugal Nos. 285, 296 & 298F Overprinted & Surcharged in Black

1929-30 ***Perf. 12x11½, 15x14***

300 A64 4c on 25c pink ('30) .75 .75
301 A64 4c on 60c dp blue 1.40 1.30
a. Perf. 15x14 7.50 6.00
302 A64 10c on 25c pink 1.50 1.30
303 A64 12c on 25c pink 1.40 1.30
304 A64 15c on 25c pink 1.40 1.30
305 A64 20c on 25c pink 2.50 2.40
306 A64 40c on 1.10e yel brn 6.75 5.25
Nos. 300-306 (7) 15.70 13.60

Portugal Nos. 400-401, 403-404, 408, 412, 416 Overprinted in Black or Red

1930 ***Perf. 14***

Without Imprint at Foot

307 A85 4c orange .85 .70
308 A85 5c dp brown 3.75 3.25
309 A85 10c orange red 1.50 1.10
310 A85 15c black (R) 1.50 1.10
311 A85 40c brt green 1.40 .85
312 A85 80c violet 15.00 12.00
313 A85 1.60e dk blue 4.50 3.00
Nos. 307-313 (7) 28.50 22.00

Black or Red Overprint

1930-31 ***Perf. 12x11½***

With Imprint at Foot

313A A64 4c orange 3.00 2.40
313B A64 5c blk brn ('31) 4.50 3.25
313C A64 6c red brn ('31) .40 .30
313D A64 15c black (R) .95 .70
313E A64 16c dp blue ('31) 2.75 1.75
313F A64 32c deep green 2.60 1.75
313G A64 40c brt grn ('31) 1.35 .75
313H A64 48c dull pink ('31) 3.50 2.60
313I A64 50c bister ('31) 5.25 3.50
313J A64 50c red brn ('31) 5.25 3.50
313K A64 64c brn rose ('31) 5.25 3.50
313L A64 75c car rose ('31) 5.25 3.50
313M A64 80c dk grn ('31) 5.25 3.00
313N A64 1e brn lake 40.00 27.50
313O A64 1.25e dk blue 2.75 2.25
Nos. 313A=313O (15) 88.05 60.25

The original stamps (Portugal Nos. 496A-496R) were printed at the Lisbon Mint from new plates produced from the original dies. The paper is whiter than the paper used for earlier Ceres stamps. The gum is white.

POSTAGE DUE STAMPS

Portugal Nos. J7-J13 Overprinted in Black

1904 **Unwmk.** ***Perf. 12***

J1 D2 5r brown 1.15 1.00
a. Inverted overprint 3.50 3.50
J2 D2 10r orange 1.30 1.00
J3 D2 20r lilac 2.10 1.00
J4 D2 30r gray green 2.25 2.00
a. Double overprint
J5 D2 40r gray violet 4.00 2.40
J6 D2 50r carmine 7.50 4.25
J7 D2 100r dull blue 8.50 8.25
Nos. J1-J7 (7) 26.80 19.90

Same Overprinted in Carmine or Green (Portugal Nos. J14-J20)

1911

J8 D2 5r brown .75 .60
J9 D2 10r orange .75 .60
J10 D2 20r lilac 1.15 .75
J11 D2 30r gray green 1.15 .75
J12 D2 40r gray violet 1.50 1.10
J13 D2 50r carmine (G) 7.75 7.50
J14 D2 100r dull blue 2.75 2.75
Nos. J8-J14 (7) 15.80 14.05

Portugal Nos. J21-J27 Overprinted in Black

1918

J15 D3 ½c brown .75 .75
a. Inverted overprint 6.00
b. Double overprint 6.00
J16 D3 1c orange .75 .75
a. Inverted overprint 6.00
b. Double overprint 6.00
J17 D3 2c red lilac .85 .75
a. Inverted overprint 4.00
b. Double overprint 6.00
J18 D3 3c green .75 .75
a. Inverted overprint 6.00
b. Double overprint 6.00
J19 D3 4c gray .75 .75
a. Inverted overprint 6.00
b. Double overprint 6.00
J20 D3 5c rose .75 .75
b. Double overprint 6.00
J21 D3 10c dark blue .75 .75
Nos. J15-J21 (7) 5.35 5.25

Stamps and Type of Portugal Postage Dues, 1921-27, Overprinted in Black

1922-24 ***Perf. 11½x12***

J30 D3 ½c gray green ('23) .35 .35
J31 D3 1c gray green ('23) .55 .45
J32 D3 2c gray green ('23) .55 .45
J33 D3 3c gray green ('24) .85 .45
J34 D3 8c gray green ('24) .85 .45
J35 D3 10c gray green ('24) .85 .45
J36 D3 12c gray green ('24) .85 .45
J37 D3 16c gray green ('24) .95 .45
J38 D3 20c gray green .95 .45
J39 D3 24c gray green .95 .45
J40 D3 32c gray green ('24) .95 .45
J41 D3 36c gray green .95 .60
J42 D3 40c gray green ('24) .95 .60
J43 D3 48c gray green ('24) .95 .60
J44 D3 50c gray green .95 .60
J45 D3 60c gray green 1.00 .70
J46 D3 72c gray green 1.00 .70
J47 D3 80c gray green ('24) 5.00 4.25
J48 D3 1.20e gray green 6.50 5.75
Nos. J30-J48 (19) 25.95 18.65

NEWSPAPER STAMPS

Newspaper Stamps of Portugal, Nos. P1, P1a, Overprinted Types c & d in Black or Red and

N3

Perf. 12½, 13½ (#P4)

1876-88 **Unwmk.**

P1 N1 (c) 2½r olive 13.00 5.50
a. Inverted overprint
P2 N1 (d) 2½r olive ('82) 5.75 1.50
a. Inverted overprint — —
b. Double overprint — —
P3 N3 2r black ('85) 6.00 3.00
a. Inverted overprint 65.00 34.00
b. Double overprint, one inverted —
P4 N1 (d) 2½r bister ('82) 5.75 1.50
a. Double overprint 9.00
P5 N3 2r black (R) ('88) 19.00 16.00
Nos. P1-P5 (5) 49.50 27.50

Reprints of the newspaper stamps have the same papers, gum and perforations as reprints of the regular issues. Value $2 each.

PARCEL POST STAMPS

Portugal Nos. Q1-Q17 Ovptd. in Black or Red

1921-22 **Unwmk.** ***Perf. 12***

Q1 PP1 1c lilac brown .50 .45
a. Inverted overprint 6.00
Q2 PP1 2c orange .50 .45
a. Inverted overprint 6.00
Q3 PP1 5c light brown .50 .45
a. Inverted overprint 6.00
b. Double overprint 6.00
Q4 PP1 10c red brown .75 .45
a. Inverted overprint 6.00
b. Double overprint 6.00
Q5 PP1 20c gray blue .75 .45
a. Inverted overprint 6.00
b. Double overprint 6.00
Q6 PP1 40c carmine .75 .45
a. Double overprint 8.00
Q7 PP1 50c black (R) 1.45 .95
Q8 PP1 60c dark blue (R) 1.50 .95
Q9 PP1 70c gray brown 2.50 2.25
a. Double overprint 6.00
Q10 PP1 80c ultra 2.50 2.25
Q11 PP1 90c light violet 2.50 2.25
Q12 PP1 1e light green 2.50 2.25
Q13 PP1 2e pale lilac 4.50 3.25
Q14 PP1 3e olive 7.50 3.50
Q15 PP1 4e ultra 9.00 3.50
Q16 PP1 5e gray 9.00 7.25
Q17 PP1 10e chocolate 40.00 22.00
Nos. Q1-Q17 (17) 86.70 53.10

POSTAL TAX STAMPS

These stamps represent a special fee for the delivery of postal matter on certain days in the year. The money derived from their sale is applied to works of public charity.

Nos. 128 and 157 Overprinted in Carmine

1911-13 **Unwmk.** ***Perf. 14x15***

RA1 A29 10r dark green 1.50 1.10

The 20r of this type was for use on telegrams. Value $2.25 unused, $1.90 used.

Perf. 15x14

RA2 A64 1c deep green 5.00 3.75

The 2c of this type was for use on telegrams. Value $8.25 unused, $4.50 used.

Portugal No. RA4 Overprinted in Black

1915 ***Perf. 12***

RA3 PT2 1c carmine .75 .35

The 2c of this type was for use on telegrams. Value $1.10 unused, 75c used.

Postal Tax Stamp of 1915 Surcharged

1924

RA4 PT2 15c on 1c rose 1.10 *.85*

The 30c on 2c of this type was for use on telegrams. Value $3.75 unused, $1.75 used.

Comrades of the Great War Issue

Postal Tax Stamps of Portugal, 1925, Overprinted

1925, Apr. 8 ***Perf. 11***

RA5 PT3 10c brown 1.10 1.10
RA6 PT3 10c green 1.10 1.10
RA7 PT3 10c rose 1.10 1.10
RA8 PT3 10c ultra 1.10 1.10
Nos. RA5-RA8 (4) 4.40 4.40

The use of Nos. RA5-RA11 in addition to the regular postage was compulsory on certain days. If the tax represented by these stamps was not prepaid, it was collected by means of Postal Tax Due Stamps.

Pombal Issue

Common Design Types

1925 ***Perf. 12½***

RA9 CD28 20c dp grn & blk 1.10 1.10
RA10 CD29 20c dp grn & blk 1.10 1.10
RA11 CD30 20c dp grn & blk 1.10 1.10
Nos. RA9-RA11 (3) 3.30 3.30

POSTAL TAX DUE STAMPS

Portugal No. RAJ1 Ovptd. in Black

1925, Apr. 8 **Unwmk.** ***Perf. 11x11½***

RAJ1 PTD1 20c brown orange 1.10 .95

See note after No. RA8.

Pombal Issue

Common Design Types

1925, May 8 ***Perf. 12½***

RAJ2 CD28 40c dp grn & blk 1.10 1.10
RAJ3 CD29 40c dp grn & blk 1.10 1.10
RAJ4 CD30 40c dp grn & blk 1.10 1.10
Nos. RAJ2-RAJ4 (3) 3.30 3.30

See note after No. RA8.

BAHAMAS

bə-'hä-məs

LOCATION — A group of about 700 islands and 2,000 rocks in the West Indies, off the coast of Florida. Only 30 islands are inhabited.
GOVT. — Independent state in British Commonwealth
AREA — 5,382 sq. mi.
POP. — 283,705 (1999 est.)
CAPITAL — Nassau

The principal island, on which the capital is located, is New Providence. The Bahamas obtained internal self-government on January 7, 1964, and independence on July 10, 1973.

12 Pence = 1 Shilling
20 Shillings = 1 Pound
100 Cents = 1 Dollar (1966)

Catalogue values for unused stamps in this country are for Never Hinged items, beginning with Scott 130, and Scott C1 in the air post section.

Values for unused stamps are for examples with original gum as defined in the catalogue introduction. Very fine examples of Nos. 2-26 will have perforations touching the design or frameline on at least one side due to the narrow spacing of the stamps on the plates. Stamps with perfs clear of the design or framelines on all four sides are extremely scarce and will command higher prices.

Pen cancellations usually indicate revenue use. Such stamps sell for much less than postally canceled examples. Beware of stamps with revenue or pen cancellations removed and forged postal cancellations added.

Queen Victoria — A1

1859-60 Unwmk. Engr. *Imperf.*

1	A1	1p dull lake, thin paper ('60)	75.00	*1,900.*
a.		1p reddish lake, thick paper	*6,000.*	*2,850.*
b.		1p brownish lake, thick paper	*6,000.*	*2,850.*

Most unused examples of No. 1 are remainders, and false cancellations are plentiful.

Queen Victoria — A2

1861 *Rough Perf. 14 to 16*

2	A1	1p lake	925.	425.
a.		Clean-cut perf. ('60)	7,250.	950.
3	A2	4p dull rose	1,800.	500.
a.		Imperf. between, pair	*40,000.*	
4	A2	6p gray lilac	5,500.	800.
a.		Pale lilac	4,250.	650.

No. 2 exists perf 11 to 12½. This is a trial perforation by Perkins, Bacon and was not sent to the colony. Value, $2,850.

1862 *Perf. 11½, 12*

5	A1	1p lake	1,250.	225.
a.		Pair, imperf. between	*6,250.*	
6	A2	4p dull rose	4,500.	500.
7	A2	6p gray violet	13,500.	625.

No.5a was not issued in the Bahamas. It is unique and faulty.

Nos. 5-7 exist with perf. 11½ or 12 compound with 11. See the *Scott Classic Specialized Catalogue.*

Perf. 13

8	A1	1p brown lake	950.	175.
a.		1p carmine lake	1,150.	200.
9	A2	4p rose	3,500.	475.
10	A2	6p gray violet	4,250.	600.
a.		6p dull violet	3,500.	575.

Queen Victoria — A3

Engr., Typo. (A3)

1863-65 Wmk. 1 *Perf. 12½*

11	A1	1p lake	140.00	90.00
a.		1p brown lake	120.00	85.00
b.		1p rose lake	160.00	95.00
c.		1p rose red	75.00	55.00
d.		1p red	75.00	55.00
12	A1	1p vermilion	90.00	57.50
13	A2	4p rose	375.00	75.00
a.		4p rose lake	575.00	100.00
b.		4p bright rose	375.00	75.00
14	A2	6p dk violet	200.00	85.00
a.		6p violet	325.00	115.00
b.		6p rose lilac	*8,500.*	*3,500.*
c.		6p lilac	475.00	90.00
15	A3	1sh green ('65)	3,250.	375.00

For surcharge see No. 26.

1863-81 Engr., Typo. (A3) *Perf. 14*

16	A1	1p vermilion	75.00	20.00
17	A1	1p car lake (anil.)	1,500.	
18	A2	4p rose	525.00	50.00
a.		4p deep rose ('76)	550.00	50.00
b.		4p dull rose	1,900.	50.00
19	A3	1sh green ('80)	10.00	*12.00*
a.		1sh dark green	400.00	50.00

Some examples of No. 16 show a light aniline appearance and care should be taken not to confuse these with No. 17. All known used examples of No. 17 bear fiscal cancels.

Engr., Typo. (A3)

1882-98 Wmk. 2

20	A1	1p vermilion	575.00	75.00
21	A2	4p rose	1,500.	75.00
22	A3	1sh green	50.00	18.00
23	A3	1sh blue grn ('98)	45.00	*50.00*

Perf. 12

24	A1	1p vermilion	60.00	22.50
25	A2	4p rose	925.00	60.00

No. 14a Surcharged in Black

1883 Engr. Wmk. 1 *Perf. 12½*

26	A2	4p on 6p violet	725.	500.
a.		Inverted surcharge	*25,000.*	*12,000.*

The surcharge, being handstamped, is found in various positions. Counterfeit surcharges exist.

Queen Victoria — A5

1884-90 Typo. Wmk. 2 *Perf. 14*

27	A5	1p carmine rose	9.00	3.25
a.		1p pale rose	95.00	16.00
b.		1p car (aniline)	6.25	*8.50*
28	A5	2½p ultra	17.00	3.00
a.		2½p dull blue	95.00	22.50
b.		2½p bright blue	55.00	9.50
29	A5	4p yellow	12.50	5.00
30	A5	6p violet	7.50	*40.00*
31	A5	5sh olive green	90.00	*100.00*
32	A5	£1 brown	350.00	*275.00*
		Revenue cancellation		*55.00*
		Nos. 27-32 (6)	*486.00*	*426.25*

Cleaned fiscally used examples of No. 32 are often found with forged postmarks of small post offices added, especially dated "AU 29 94."

Queen's Staircase — A6

1901-03 Engr. Wmk. 1

33	A6	1p carmine & blk	15.00	*4.00*
34	A6	5p org & blk ('03)	11.00	*65.00*
35	A6	2sh ultra & blk ('03)	35.00	*65.00*
36	A6	3sh green & blk ('03)	50.00	*75.00*
		Nos. 33-36 (4)	111.00	*209.00*

See Nos. 48, 58-62, 71, 78, 81-82.

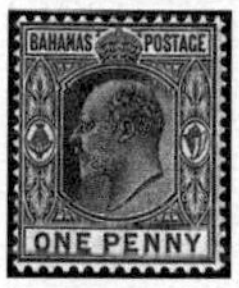

Edward VII — A7

1902 Wmk. 2 Typo.

37	A7	1p carmine rose	2.00	*3.25*
38	A7	2½p ultra	12.50	1.75
39	A7	4p orange	20.00	*77.50*
40	A7	6p bister brn	8.50	*37.50*
41	A7	1sh gray blk & car	26.00	*65.00*
42	A7	5sh violet & ultra	85.00	*110.00*
43	A7	£1 green & blk	325.00	*425.00*
		Nos. 37-43 (7)	479.00	*720.00*

Beware of forged postmarks, especially dated "2 MAR 10."

1906-11 Wmk. 3

44	A7	½p green	6.25	4.00
45	A7	1p car rose	32.50	1.75
46	A7	2½p ultra ('07)	32.50	32.50
47	A7	6p bister brn ('11)	25.00	*60.00*
		Nos. 44-47 (4)	96.25	*98.25*

1911-19 Engr.

48	A6	1p red & gray blk ('16)	6.00	3.25
a.		1p carmine & black ('11)	27.50	3.50

For overprints see Nos. B1-B2.

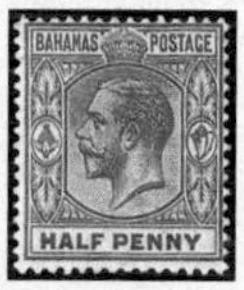

George V — A8

1912-19 Typo.

49	A8	½p green	1.00	*12.50*
50	A8	1p car rose (aniline)	4.50	.45
50A	A8	2p gray ('19)	3.00	*3.75*
51	A8	2½p ultra	6.00	*35.00*
52	A8	4p orange	3.25	*22.50*
53	A8	6p bister brown	2.25	*9.25*

Chalky Paper

54	A8	1sh black & car	2.25	*11.50*
55	A8	5sh violet & ultra	50.00	*90.00*
56	A8	£1 dull grn & blk	250.00	*425.00*
		Nos. 49-56 (9)	322.25	*609.95*

1917-19 Engr.

58	A6	3p reddish pur, *buff*	7.75	13.50
59	A6	3p brown & blk ('19)	4.00	*5.00*
60	A6	5p violet & blk	3.50	*9.00*
61	A6	2sh ultra & black	37.50	*70.00*
62	A6	3sh green & black	82.50	70.00
		Nos. 58-62 (5)	135.25	*167.50*

Peace Commemorative Issue

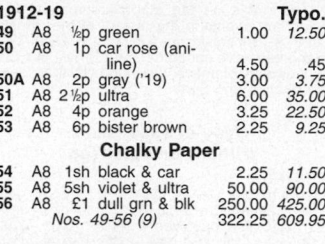

King George V and Seal of Bahamas — A9

1920, Mar. 1 Engr. *Perf. 14*

65	A9	½p gray green	1.25	*7.00*
66	A9	1p deep red	3.50	1.25
67	A9	2p gray	3.50	*9.50*
68	A9	3p brown	3.50	*11.50*
69	A9	1sh dark green	22.50	*45.00*
		Nos. 65-69 (5)	34.25	*74.25*

Types of 1901-12

Typo., Engr. (A6)

1921-34 Wmk. 4

70	A8	½p green ('24)	.65	.50
71	A6	1p car & black	3.50	*4.75*
72	A8	1p car rose	1.25	.25
73	A8	1½p fawn ('34)	13.00	1.25
74	A8	2p gray ('27)	1.90	*3.00*
75	A8	2½p ultra ('22)	1.25	*3.00*
76	A8	3p violet, *yel* ('31)	8.25	*20.00*
77	A8	4p yellow ('24)	1.90	*5.25*
78	A6	5p red vio & gray blk ('29)	5.50	*57.50*
79	A8	6p bister brn ('22)	1.25	*3.00*
80	A8	1sh blk & red ('26)	9.75	7.25
81	A6	2sh ultra & blk ('22)	30.00	27.50
82	A6	3sh grn & blk ('24)	60.00	*82.50*
83	A8	5sh vio & ultra ('24)	45.00	*85.00*
84	A8	£1 grn & blk ('26)	215.00	*425.00*
		Nos. 70-84 (15)	398.20	*725.75*

The 3p, 1sh, 5sh and £1 are on chalky paper.

Seal of Bahamas — A10

1930, Jan. 2 Engr. *Perf. 12*

85	A10	1p red & black	4.25	*3.50*
86	A10	3p dp brown & blk	5.50	*19.00*
87	A10	5p dk vio & blk	5.50	*19.00*
88	A10	2sh ultra & black	22.50	*62.50*
89	A10	3sh dp green & blk	52.50	*110.00*
		Nos. 85-89 (5)	90.25	*214.00*

The dates on the stamps commemorate important events in the history of the colony. The 1st British occupation was in 1629. The Bahamas were ceded to Great Britain in 1729 and a treaty of peace was signed by that country, France and Spain.

Type of 1930 Issue Without Dates at Top

1931-46

90 A10 2sh ultra & black 15.00 9.00
a. 2sh ultra & slate purple 30.00 *37.50*
91 A10 3sh dp green & blk 10.00 7.00
a. 3sh deep grn & slate purple 37.50 35.00

Nos. 90a-91a are on thicker paper with yellowish gum. Later printings are on thinner white paper with colorless gum.
For overprints see Nos. 126-127.

Common Design Types pictured following the introduction.

Silver Jubilee Issue
Common Design Type

1935, May 6 ***Perf. 13½x14***

92 CD301 1½p car & blue 1.25 *4.00*
93 CD301 2½p blue & brn 6.25 *10.00*
94 CD301 6p ol grn & lt bl 8.75 *16.50*
95 CD301 1sh brt vio & ind 8.75 *15.50*
Nos. 92-95 (4) 25.00 *46.00*
Set, never hinged 35.00

Flamingos in Flight A11

1935, May 22 ***Perf. 12½***

96 A11 8p car & ultra 7.25 4.25
Never hinged 10.00

Coronation Issue
Common Design Type

1937, May 12 ***Perf. 13½x14***

97 CD302 ½p dp green .25 .25
98 CD302 1½p brown .30 *1.40*
99 CD302 2½p brt ultra .50 *1.40*
Nos. 97-99 (3) 1.05 *3.05*
Set, never hinged 1.50

George VI — A12

Sea Gardens, Nassau A13

Fort Charlotte A14

Flamingos in Flight A15

1938-46 Typo. Wmk. 4 ***Perf. 14***

100 A12 ½p green 1.00 *1.60*
101 A12 1p carmine 7.00 4.50
Complete booklet, 12 #101 in blocks of 6 and 8 #102 in folded block —
101A A12 1p pale gray ('41) .50 *.90*
102 A12 1½p red brown 1.25 1.60
103 A12 2p gray 14.00 5.75
103B A12 2p carmine ('41) .85 .85
c. "TWO PENCE" double *15,000.*
104 A12 2½p ultra 2.75 *1.90*
104A A12 2½p lt violet ('43) 1.10 1.60
b. "2½ PENNY" double *3,250.* —
105 A12 3p lt violet 13.00 5.00
105A A12 3p ultra ('43) .50 *1.60*

Engr.
Perf. 12½

106 A13 4p red org & blue .80 *1.25*
107 A14 6p blue & ol grn .65 *1.25*
108 A15 8p car & ultra 7.25 3.25

Typo.
Perf. 14

109 A12 10p yel org ('46) 2.25 .55
110 A12 1sh blk & brt red 11.50 1.00
112 A12 5sh pur & ultra 17.50 17.50
113 A12 £1 bl grn & blk 45.00 *60.00*
Nos. 100-113 (17) 126.90 *110.10*
Set, never hinged 190.00

Nos. 110-113 printed on chalky and ordinary paper.
See the *Scott Classic Specialized Catalogue of Stamps & Covers* for listings of shades.
See Nos. 154-156. For overprints see Nos. 116-125, 128-129.

No. 104 Surcharged in Black

1940, Nov. 28 ***Perf. 14***

115 A12 3p on 2½p ultra 1.10 *3.25*
Never hinged 1.75

Stamps of 1931-42 Overprinted in Black

1942, Oct. 12 ***Perf. 14, 12½, 12***

116 A12 ½p green .25 .75
117 A12 1p gray .25 .75
118 A12 1½p red brn .35 .75
119 A12 2p carmine .40 .80
120 A12 2½p ultra .40 .80
121 A12 3p ultra .25 .80
122 A13 4p red org & blue .35 1.10
123 A14 6p blue & ol grn .35 2.10
124 A15 8p car & ultra 1.10 .85
125 A12 1sh blk & car (#110c) 6.50 11.00
126 A10 2sh dk ultra & blk 6.75 *11.50*
127 A10 3sh dp grn & sl pur (#91a) 6.50 *8.00*
128 A12 5sh lilac & ultra (#112a) 17.50 *16.00*
129 A12 £1 grn & blk 22.50 *27.50*
Nos. 116-129 (14) 63.45 *82.70*
Set, never hinged 95.00

450th anniv. of the discovery of America by Columbus.
Nos. 125, 128-129 printed on chalky and original paper.
Two printings of the basic stamps were overprinted, the first with dark gum, the second with white gum.
For shades, see the *Scott Classic Catalogue.*

Catalogue values for unused stamps in this section, from this point to the end of the section, are for Never Hinged items.

Peace Issue
Common Design Type
Perf. 13½x14

1946, Nov. 11 Engr. Wmk. 4

130 CD303 1½p brown .25 .70
131 CD303 3p deep blue .25 .70

Infant Welfare Clinic A16

Designs: 1p, Modern agriculture. 1½p, Sisal. 2p, Native straw work. 2½p, Modern dairying. 3p, Fishing fleet. 4p, Out island settlement. 6p, Tuna fishing. 8p, Paradise Beach. 10p, Modern hotel. 1sh, Yacht racing. 2sh, Water skiing. 3sh, Shipbuilding. 5sh, Modern transportation. 10sh, Modern salt production. £1, Parliament Building.

1948, Oct. 11 Unwmk. ***Perf. 12***

132 A16 ½p orange .40 *1.75*
133 A16 1p olive green .40 .45
134 A16 1½p olive bister .40 *1.00*
135 A16 2p vermilion .40 .50
136 A16 2½p red brown .85 *1.00*
137 A16 3p brt ultra 3.25 1.10
138 A16 4p gray black .75 .90
139 A16 6p emerald 2.75 1.00
140 A16 8p violet 1.25 .90
141 A16 10p rose car 1.25 .75
142 A16 1sh olive brn 3.00 1.25
143 A16 2sh claret 6.25 *11.00*
144 A16 3sh brt blue 12.50 *11.00*
145 A16 5sh purple 20.00 6.50
146 A16 10sh dk gray 15.00 13.00
147 A16 £1 red orange 16.50 *18.00*
Nos. 132-147 (16) 84.95 *70.10*

300th anniv., in 1947, of the settlement of the colony.

Silver Wedding Issue
Common Design Type
Perf. 14x14½

1948, Dec. 1 Wmk. 4 Photo.

148 CD304 1½p red brown .25 .30

Engr.; Name Typo.
Perf. 11½x11

149 CD305 £1 gray green 45.00 40.00

UPU Issue
Common Design Types
Engr.; Name Typo. on #151 & 152

1949, Oct. 10 ***Perf. 13½, 11x11½***

150 CD306 2½p violet .45 *.80*
151 CD307 3p indigo 2.75 *3.75*
152 CD308 6p blue gray .90 *3.50*
153 CD309 1sh rose car 1.25 1.25
Nos. 150-153 (4) 5.35 9.30

George VI Type of 1938
Perf. 13½x14

1951-52 Wmk. 4 Typo.

154 A12 ½p claret ('52) 1.25 *3.75*
a. Wmk. 4a (error) *4,750.* *3,250.*
Lightly hinged 3,250.
155 A12 2p green 2.00 1.00
156 A12 3p rose red ('52) 1.00 *4.00*
Nos. 154-156 (3) 4.25 *8.75*

Coronation Issue
Common Design Type

1953, June 3 Engr. ***Perf. 13½x13***

157 CD312 6p blue & black 1.40 .75

Infant Welfare Clinic A17

Designs: 1p, Modern Agriculture. 1½p, Out island settlement. 2p, Native strawwork. 3p, Fishing fleet. 4p, Water skiing. 5p, Modern dairying. 6p, Modern transportation. 8p, Paradise Beach. 10p, Modern hotels. 1sh, Yacht racing. 2sh, Sisal. 2sh6p, Shipbuilding. 5sh, Tuna fishing. 10sh, Modern salt production. £1, Parliament Building.

1954, Jan. 1 ***Perf. 11x11½***

158 A17 ½p red org & blk .25 *1.75*
159 A17 1p org brn & ol grn .25 *.35*
160 A17 1½p black & blue .25 *.60*
161 A17 2p dk grn & brn org .25 *.35*
Complete booklet, 8 each #159, 160, 161, in blocks of 4 30.00
162 A17 3p dp car & blk .60 *.75*
163 A17 4p lil rose & bl green .30 .30
164 A17 5p dp ultra & brn 1.60 *2.40*
165 A17 6p blk & aqua 2.00 .25
166 A17 8p rose vio & blk .75 .40
Complete booklet, 4 each #163, 165, 166, in blocks of 4 40.00
167 A17 10p ultra & blk .35 .25
168 A17 1sh ol brn & ultra 1.35 .25
169 A17 2sh blk & brn org 2.25 .60
170 A17 2sh6p dp bl & blk 4.00 2.40
171 A17 5sh dp org & emer 20.00 .75
172 A17 10sh grnsh blk & black 27.00 3.50
173 A17 £1 vio & grnsh black 25.00 8.50
Nos. 158-173 (16) 86.20 23.40

See No. 203. For types overprinted or surcharged see Nos. 181-182, 185-200, 202.

Queen Elizabeth II — A18

Wmk. 314

1959, June 10 Engr. ***Perf. 13***

174 A18 1p dk red & black .30 .25
175 A18 2p green & black .30 .25
176 A18 6p blue & black .50 .50
177 A18 10p brown & black .80 .80
Nos. 174-177 (4) 1.90 1.80

Cent. of the 1st postage stamp of Bahamas.

Christ Church Cathedral, Nassau — A19

Perf. 14x13

1962, Jan. 30 Photo. Unwmk.

178 A19 8p shown .55 .55
179 A19 10p Public library .60 .60

Centenary of the city of Nassau.

Freedom from Hunger Issue
Common Design Type
Perf. 14x14½

1963, June 4 Wmk. 314

180 CD314 8p sepia .65 .65
a. "8d," "BAHAMAS" omitted 1,200. *2,000.*

Nos. 166-167 Overprinted: "BAHAMAS TALKS/ 1962"
Perf. 11x11½

1963, July 15 Engr. Wmk. 4

181 A17 8p rose vio & black .65 .65
182 A17 10p ultra & black .65 .65

Meeting of Pres. Kennedy and Prime Minister Harold Macmillan, Dec. 1962.

Red Cross Centenary Issue
Common Design Type
Wmk. 314

1963, Sept. 2 Litho. ***Perf. 13***

183 CD315 1p black & red .30 .30
184 CD315 10p ultra & red 2.00 *2.50*

Type of 1954 Overprinted: "NEW CONSTITUTION/ 1964"

Designs as Before

Perf. 11x11½

1964, Jan. 7 Engr. Wmk. 314

185 A17 ½p red org & blk .30 *1.40*
186 A17 1p org brn & ol grn .30 .30
187 A17 1½p black & blue .90 *1.40*
188 A17 2p dk grn & brn org .30 .30
189 A17 3p dp car & blk 1.75 1.75
190 A17 4p lil rose & bl grn .50 *.70*
191 A17 5p dp ultra & brn .50 *1.75*
192 A17 6p blk & aqua 2.40 .40
193 A17 8p rose vio & blk .90 .40
194 A17 10p ultra & black .40 .30
195 A17 1sh ol brn & ultra 1.40 .30
196 A17 2sh blk & brn org 1.75 1.75
197 A17 2sh6p dp bl & blk 3.00 3.00
198 A17 5sh dp org & emer 7.00 3.25
199 A17 10sh grnsh blk & black 7.25 5.50
200 A17 £1 vio & grnsh black 8.50 *25.00*
Nos. 185-200 (16) 37.15 47.50

Shakespeare Issue
Common Design Type
Perf. 14x14½

1964, Apr. 23 Photo. Wmk. 314

201 CD316 6p greenish blue .60 .35

Type of 1954 Surcharged with Olympic Rings, New Value and Bars

Perf. 11x11½

1964, Oct. 1 Engr. Wmk. 314
202 A17 8p on 1sh ol brn & ultra .90 .90

18th Olympic Games, Tokyo, Oct. 10-25.

Queen Type of 1954

1964, Oct. 6 Wmk. 314
203 A17 2p dk grn & brn org 1.10 .50

Colony Badge A21

Designs: 1p, Out Island Regatta. 1½p, Princess Margaret Hospital. 2p, High School. 3p, Flamingo. 4p, Liner "Queen Elizabeth." 6p, Island development. 8p, Yachting. 10p, Public Square, Nassau. 1sh, Sea Garden, Nassau. 2sh, Cannons at Fort Charlotte. 2sh6p, Sea plane and jetliner. 5sh, 1914 Williamson film project and 1939 underwater post office. 10sh, Conch shell. £1, Columbus' flagship.

Engr. and Litho.

1965, Jan. 7 *Perf. 13½x13*
204 A21 ½p multi, *bluish* .25 *2.00*
205 A21 1p multi .25 *1.10*
206 A21 1½p multi .25 *3.00*
207 A21 2p multi .25 .25
Complete booklet, 8 each #205, 206, 207, in blocks of 4 22.50
208 A21 3p multi 2.00 .25
209 A21 4p multi 2.50 *3.00*
210 A21 6p multi .30 .25
211 A21 8p multi .40 .40
Complete booklet, 4 each #209, 210, 211, in blocks of 4 22.50
212 A21 10p multi .30 .25
213 A21 1sh multi, *grnsh* .40 .25
214 A21 2sh multi, *grnsh* .90 *1.40*
215 A21 2sh6p multi 2.25 *3.75*
216 A21 5sh multi 2.25 1.10
217 A21 10sh multi 14.00 4.00
218 A21 £1 multi 15.00 11.00
Nos. 204-218 (15) 41.30 32.00

Booklet panes were issued Mar. 23, 1965.
See Nos. 252-266. For surcharges see Nos. 221, 230-244.

ITU Issue

Common Design Type

Perf. 11x11½

1965, May 17 Litho. Wmk. 314
219 CD317 1p emerald & org .25 .25
220 CD317 2sh lilac & olive 1.10 *1.25*

No. 211 Surcharged

Engr. & Litho.

1965, July 12 *Perf. 13½x13*
221 A21 9p on 8p multi .45 .30

Intl. Cooperation Year Issue

Common Design Type

Wmk. 314

1965, Oct. 25 Litho. *Perf. 14½*
222 CD318 ½p blue grn & clar .25 *1.25*
223 CD318 1sh lt violet & grn .40 .65

Churchill Memorial Issue

Common Design Type

1966, Jan. 24 Photo. *Perf. 14*
224 CD319 ½p multicolored .25 .25
225 CD319 2p multicolored .45 .25
226 CD319 10p multicolored .80 *1.10*
227 CD319 1sh multicolored .80 *1.60*
Nos. 224-227 (4) 2.30 *3.20*

Royal Visit Issue

Common Design Type Inscribed "Royal Visit / 1966"

1966, Feb. 4 Litho. *Perf. 11x12*
228 CD320 6p violet blue .80 .80
229 CD320 1sh dk car rose 2.25 2.25

Nos. 204-218 Surcharged

Engr. & Litho.

Perf. 13½x13

1966, May 25 Wmk. 314
230 A21 1c on ½p multi .25 .25
231 A21 2c on 1p multi .25 .25
232 A21 3c on 2p multi .25 .25
233 A21 4c on 3p multi .25 .25
234 A21 5c on 4p multi .25 .25
a. Surch. omitted, vert. strip of 7-10 *3,250.*
235 A21 8c on 6p multi .25 .25
236 A21 10c on 8p multi .25 .25
237 A21 11c on 1½p multi .45 .25
238 A21 12c on 10p multi .50 .30
239 A21 15c on 1sh multi .60 .35
240 A21 22c on 2sh multi .75 .40
241 A21 50c on 2sh6p multi 1.60 1.35
242 A21 $1 on 5sh multi 3.00 2.75
243 A21 $2 on 10sh multi 6.50 5.50
244 A21 $3 on £1 multi 9.50 8.00
Nos. 230-244 (15) 24.65 20.65

The denominations are next to the bars instead of below on Nos. 232, 235-240; the length of the bars varies to cover old denomination.

No. 234a, if single, is identical with No. 209, but distinguishable if in vertical strip of 7 to 10. No. 234 was printed in sheets of 100 (10x10); No. 209 in sheets of 60 (10x6).

World Cup Soccer Issue

Common Design Type

1966, July 1 Litho. *Perf. 14*
245 CD321 8c multicolored .25 .25
246 CD321 15c multicolored .40 .40

WHO Headquarters Issue

Common Design Type

1966, Sept. 20 Litho. *Perf. 14*
247 CD322 11c multicolored .30 .30
248 CD322 15c multicolored .50 .50

UNESCO Anniversary Issue

Common Design Type

1966, Dec. 1 Litho. *Perf. 14*
249 CD323 3c "Education" .25 .25
250 CD323 15c "Science" .35 .35
251 CD323 $1 "Culture" 1.75 1.75
Nos. 249-251 (3) 2.35 2.35

Type of 1965

Values in Cents and Dollars

1c, Colony badge. 2c, Out Island Regatta. 3c, High School. 4c, Flamingo. 5c, Liner "Oceanic." 8c, Island development. 10c, Yachting. 11c, Princess Margaret Hospital. 12c, Public Square, Nassau. 15c, Sea Garden, Nassau. 22c, Cannon at Fort Charlotte. 50c, Sea plane, jetliner. $1, 1914 Williamson film project, 1939 underwater post office. $2, Conch shell. $3, Columbus' flagship.

Engr. & Litho.

1967, May 25 *Perf. 13½x13*

Toned Paper

252 A21 1c brown & multi .30 *4.00*
253 A21 2c grn, slate & bl .30 *1.00*
254 A21 3c grn, indigo & vio .30 .35
255 A21 4c ultra, blue & red 4.25 .80
256 A21 5c pur, bl & indigo 1.10 *4.50*
257 A21 8c dk brn, bl & dl grn .30 .35
258 A21 10c car rose, bl & pur .35 *1.10*
259 A21 11c bl, grn & rose red .30 *1.40*
260 A21 12c ol grn, bl & lt brn .30 .35
261 A21 15c rose & multi .65 .35
262 A21 22c rose red, brn & bl .75 *1.10*
263 A21 50c emer, ol & bl 2.25 1.25
264 A21 $1 sep, brn org & dk blue 2.25 1.10
265 A21 $2 green & multi 14.00 5.00
266 A21 $3 pur, bl & brn org 4.25 3.00
Nos. 252-266 (15) 31.65 25.65

1970-71 White Paper
252a A21 1c brown & multi .50 *4.25*
253a A21 2c grn, slate & bl 1.60 *10.00*
254a A21 3c grn, indigo & vio 55.00 6.00
255a A21 4c ultra, blue & red 14.00 *22.50*
256a A21 5c pur, bl & indigo 1.60 *9.50*
257a A21 8c dk brn, bl & dl grn 190.00 20.00
258a A21 10c car rose, bl & pur 1.10 *5.00*
259a A21 11c bl, grn & rose red .95 *3.00*
260a A21 12c ol grn, bl & lt brn ('71) 14.00 *30.00*
261a A21 15c rose & multi 220.00 26.00
262a A21 22c rose red, brn & bl 1.60 *9.50*
263a A21 50c emer, ol & bl 2.50 *6.00*
264a A21 $1 sep, brn org & dk blue ('71) 22.00 *70.00*
265a A21 $2 green & multi ('71) 32.50 *92.50*
266a A21 $3 pur, bl & brn org ('71) 32.50 *92.50*
Nos. 252a-266a (15) 589.85 *406.75*

Nos. 252-266 are on off-white toned paper. Nos. 252a-266a are on very white, untinted paper. Because of the difference in papers and the use of some new plates, there are noticeable differences in shade on most values.

Seal of Bahamas, Queen Elizabeth II and Lord Baden-Powell — A22

60th anniv. of world Scouting: 15c, Scout emblem and portraits as on 3c.

Perf. 14x13½

1967, Sept. 1 Photo. Wmk. 314
267 A22 3c multicolored .25 .25
268 A22 15c multicolored .60 .25

Human Rights Flame and Globe A23

Intl. Human Rights Year: 12c, Human rights flame and scales of justice. $1, Human rights flame and Seal of Bahamas.

1968, May 13 Litho. *Perf. 14*
269 A23 3c multicolored .25 .25
270 A23 12c multicolored .30 .30
271 A23 $1 multicolored .90 .90
Nos. 269-271 (3) 1.45 1.45

Golf — A24

Tourist Publicity: 11c, Yachting. 15c, Horse racing. 50c, Water skiing.

1968, Aug. 20 Unwmk. *Perf. 13½*
272 A24 5c multicolored 2.00 2.00
273 A24 11c multicolored 2.00 2.00
274 A24 15c multicolored 2.50 2.50
275 A24 50c multicolored 3.50 3.50
Nos. 272-275 (4) 10.00 10.00

Olympic Monument and Sailboat — A25

Olympic Monument, San Salvador Island, Bahamas, and: 11c, Long jump. 50c, Running. $1, Sailing.

1968, Sept. 30 Photo. *Perf. 14½x14*
276 A25 5c multicolored .45 .45
277 A25 11c multicolored .75 .75
278 A25 50c multicolored 1.00 1.00
279 A25 $1 multicolored 2.50 2.50
Nos. 276-279 (4) 4.70 4.70

19th Olympic Games, Mexico City, 10/12-27.

Legislative Building — A26

Designs: 10c, Bahamas mace and Big Ben, London, vert. 12c, Local straw market, vert. 15c, Horse-drawn surrey.

Perf. 14½

1968, Nov. 1 Unwmk. Litho.
280 A26 3c brt blue & multi .25 .25
281 A26 10c yel, blk & blue .25 .25
282 A26 12c brt rose & multi .25 .25
283 A26 15c green & multi .25 .25
Nos. 280-283 (4) 1.00 1.00

14th Commonwealth Parliamentary Conf., Nassau, Nov. 1-8.

$100 Coin with Queen Elizabeth II and Landing of Columbus — A27

Gold Coins with Elizabeth II on Obverse: 12c, $50 coin and Santa Maria flagship. 15c, $20 coin and Nassau Harbor Lighthouse. $1, $10 coin and Fort.

Engr. on Gold Paper

1968, Dec. 2 Unwmk. *Perf. 13½*
284 A27 3c dark red .55 .55
285 A27 12c dark green .90 .90
286 A27 15c lilac 1.10 1.10
287 A27 $1 black 2.75 2.75
Nos. 284-287 (4) 5.30 5.30

First gold coinage in the Bahamas.

Bahamas Postal Card and Airplane Wing — A28

Design: 15c, Seaplane, 1929.

Perf. 14½x14

1969, Jan. 30 Litho. Unwmk.
288 A28 12c multicolored .75 .75
289 A28 15c multicolored .90 .90

50th anniv. of the 1st flight from Nassau, Bahamas, to Miami, Fla., Jan. 30, 1919.

Game Fishing Boats A29

Designs: 11c, Paradise Beach. 12c, Sunfish sailboats. 15c, Parade on Rawson Square.

1969, Aug. 26 Litho. Wmk. 314
290 A29 3c multicolored .25 .25
291 A29 11c multicolored .55 .55
292 A29 12c multicolored .60 .60
293 A29 15c multicolored .75 .75
a. Souvenir sheet of 4, #290-293 4.00 4.00
Nos. 290-293 (4) 2.15 2.15

Tourist publicity.

Holy Family, by Nicolas Poussin — A30

Paintings: 3c, Adoration of the Shepherds, by Louis Le Nain. 12c, Adoration of the Kings, by Gerard David. 15c, Adoration of the Kings, by Vincenzo Foppa.

1969, Oct. 15 Photo. *Perf. 12*

294	A30	3c red & multi	.25	.25
295	A30	11c emerald & multi	.25	.25
296	A30	12c ultra & multi	.30	.30
297	A30	15c multicolored	.40	.40
		Nos. 294-297 (4)	1.20	1.20

Christmas.

Girl Guides, Globe and Flags A31

Designs: 12c, Yellow elder and Brownie emblem. 15c, Ranger emblem.

1970, Feb. 23 Wmk. 314 *Perf. 14½*

298	A31	3c vio blue, yel & red	.25	.25
299	A31	12c dk brn, grn & yel	.50	.50
300	A31	15c vio bl, bluish grn & yel	.70	.70
		Nos. 298-300 (3)	1.45	1.45

60th anniversary of the Girl Guides.

Opening of UPU Headquarters, Bern — A32

1970, May 20 Litho. *Perf. 14½*

301	A32	3c vermilion & multi	.25	.25
302	A32	15c orange & multi	.35	.35

Bus and Globe A33

Globe and: 11c, Train. 12c, Sailboat and ship. 15c, Plane.

1970, July 14 *Perf. 13½x13*

303	A33	3c orange & multi	.85	.85
304	A33	11c emerald & multi	1.75	1.75
305	A33	12c multicolored	1.75	1.75
306	A33	15c blue & multi	1.75	1.75
a.		Souvenir sheet of 4, #303-306	11.50	11.50
		Nos. 303-306 (4)	6.10	6.10

Issued to promote good will through world-wide travel and tourism.

People, Palms and Flamingo — A34

15c, Red Cross Headquarters, Nassau & marlin.

1970, Aug. 18 *Perf. 14x14½*

307	A34	3c multicolored	1.00	.65
308	A34	15c multicolored	1.00	*1.60*

Centenary of British Red Cross Society.

Nativity by G. B. Pittoni — A35

Christmas: 11c, Holy Family, by Anton Raphael Mengs. 12c, Adoration of the Shepherds, by Giorgione. 15c, Adoration of the Shepherds, School of Seville.

Perf. 12½x13

1970, Nov. 3 Litho. Wmk. 314

309	A35	3c multicolored	.25	.25
310	A35	11c red org & multi	.30	.30
311	A35	12c emerald & multi	.30	.30
312	A35	15c blue & multi	.45	.45
a.		Souv. sheet of 4, #309-312 + 3 labels	2.25	2.25
		Nos. 309-312 (4)	1.30	1.30

International Airport A36

2c, Breadfruit. 3c, Straw market. 4c, 6c, Hawksbill turtle. 5c, Grouper. 7c, 12c, Hibiscus. 8c, Yellow elder. 10c, Bahamian sponge boat. 11c, Flamingos. 15c, Bonefish. 18c, 22c, Royal poinciana. 50c, Post office, Nassau. $1, Pineapple, vert. $2, Crayfish, vert. $3, "Junkanoo" (costumed drummer), vert.

Wmk. 314 Upright (Sideways on $1, $2, $3)

1971 *Perf. 14½x14, 14x14½*

313	A36	1c blue & multi	.25	.30
314	A36	2c red & multi	.25	.35
315	A36	3c lilac & multi	.25	.30
316	A36	4c brown & multi	1.75	*10.00*
317	A36	5c dp org & multi	.70	.55
318	A36	6c brown & multi	.45	1.10
319	A36	7c green & multi	1.90	*4.25*
320	A36	8c yel & multi	.65	*1.40*
321	A36	10c red & multi	.60	.30
322	A36	11c red & multi	2.40	*3.00*
323	A36	12c green & multi	1.90	*2.75*
324	A36	15c gray & multi	.60	.35
325	A36	18c multicolored	.70	.55
326	A36	22c green & multi	2.90	*15.00*
327	A36	50c multicolored	1.40	*1.50*
328	A36	$1 red & multi	6.50	2.25
329	A36	$2 blue & multi	4.75	5.75
330	A36	$3 vio bl & multi	3.75	*9.00*
		Nos. 313-330 (18)	31.70	*58.70*

See Nos. 398-401, 426-443.

Wmk. 314 Sideways (Upright on $1, $2, $3)

1973

317a	A36	5c	17.50	*24.00*
320a	A36	8c	4.25	*6.75*
327a	A36	50c	3.25	*5.00*
328a	A36	$1	3.25	*5.00*
329a	A36	$2	3.25	*5.00*
330a	A36	$3	4.50	*7.25*
		Nos. 317a-330a (6)	36.00	53.00

1976 Wmk. 373

313a	A36	1c	.25	.25
314a	A36	2c	.25	.25
315a	A36	3c	.25	.25
317b	A36	5c	.25	.25
320b	A36	8c	.25	.25
321a	A36	10c	.25	.25
327b	A36	50c	3.25	*4.25*
328b	A36	$1	6.75	*8.75*
329b	A36	$2	13.50	*16.00*
330b	A36	$3	20.00	*26.00*
		Nos. 313a-330b (10)	45.00	56.50

Snowflake with Peace Signs A37

Christmas: 11c, "Peace on Earth" with doves. 15c, Christmas wreath around old Bahamas coat of arms. 18c, Star of Bethlehem over palms.

Perf. 14x14½

1971 Photo. Wmk. 314

331	A37	3c dp lil rose, gold & org	.25	.25
332	A37	11c violet & gold	.30	.30
333	A37	15c gold embossed & multi	.30	.30
334	A37	18c brt bl, gold & vio bl	.35	.35
a.		Souv. sheet, #331-334, perf 15	2.25	2.25
		Nos. 331-334 (4)	1.20	1.20

High Jump, Arms of Bahamas — A38

Olympic Rings, Compass, Arms of Bahamas and: 11c, Bicycling. 15c, Running. 18c, Sailing.

1972, June 27 Litho. *Perf. 13x13½*

335	A38	10c lt violet & multi	.50	.50
336	A38	11c ocher & multi	.65	.65
337	A38	15c yel green & multi	.90	.90
338	A38	18c blue & multi	1.30	1.30
a.		Souvenir sheet of 4, #335-338	5.50	5.50
		Nos. 335-338 (4)	3.35	3.35

20th Olympic Games, Munich, 8/26-9/10.

Shepherd and Star of Bethlehem — A39

Designs: 6c, Bells. 15c, Holly and monstrance. 20c, Poinsettia.

1972, Oct. 3 Wmk. 314 *Perf. 14*

339	A39	3c gold & multi	.25	.25
340	A39	6c black & multi	.25	.25
341	A39	15c black & multi	.30	.30
342	A39	20c gold & multi	.50	.50
a.		Souvenir sheet of 4, #339-342	2.50	2.50
		Nos. 339-342 (4)	1.30	1.30

Christmas. Gold on 15c is embossed.

Souvenir Sheet

Map of Bahama Islands — A40

1972, Nov. 1 Litho. *Perf. 15*

343	A40	Sheet of 4	6.25	6.25
a.		11c blue & multi	.50	.50
b.		15c blue & multi	.75	.75
c.		18c blue & multi	.90	.90
d.		50c blue & multi	2.75	2.75

Tourism Year of the Americas.

Silver Wedding Issue, 1972

Common Design Type

Design: Queen Elizabeth II, Prince Philip, mace and galleon.

Perf. 14x14½

1972, Nov. 13 Photo. Wmk. 314

344	CD324	11c car rose & multi	.25	.25
345	CD324	18c violet & multi	.35	.35

Weather Satellite, WMO Emblem A41

1973, Apr. 3 Litho. *Perf. 14*

346	A41	15c shown	.55	.45
347	A41	18c Weather radar	.75	.65

Intl. meteorological cooperation, cent.

Clarence A. Bain — A42

Independence: 11c, New Bahamian coat of arms. 15c, New flag and Government House. $1, Milò B. Butler, Sr.

1973 Wmk. 314 *Perf. 14½x14*

348	A42	3c lilac & multi	.25	.25
349	A42	11c lt blue & multi	.35	.35
350	A42	15c lt green & multi	.60	.60
351	A42	$1 yel & multi	1.25	1.25
a.		Souvenir sheet of 4, #348-351	3.00	3.00
		Nos. 348-351 (4)	2.45	2.45

Issued: Nos. 348-350, 7/10; Nos. 351, 351a, 8/1.

Virgin in Prayer, by Sassoferrato A43

Christmas: 11c, Virgin and Child with St. John, by Filippino Lippi. 15c, Choir of Angels, by Marmion. 18c, The Two Trinities, by Murillo.

1973, Oct. 16 Litho. *Perf. 14*

352	A43	3c blue & multi	.25	.25
353	A43	11c multicolored	.30	.30
354	A43	15c gray grn & multi	.30	.30
355	A43	18c lil rose & multi	.40	.40
a.		Souvenir sheet of 4, #352-355	1.50	*2.00*
		Nos. 352-355 (4)	1.25	1.25

Agriculture, Science and Medicine — A44

18c, Symbols of engineering, art, and law.

1974, Feb. 5 Litho. *Perf. 13½x14*

356	A44	15c dull grn & multi	.35	.35
357	A44	18c multicolored	.50	.50

University of the West Indies, 25th anniv.

UPU Emblem A45

Designs: 13c, UPU emblem, vert. 14c, UPU emblem. 18c, UPU monument, Bern, vert.

1974, Apr. 23 *Perf. 14*
358 A45 3c multicolored .25 .25
359 A45 13c multicolored .30 .30
360 A45 14c olive bis & multi .30 .30
361 A45 18c multicolored .35 .35
a. Souvenir sheet of 4, #358-361 1.30 *2.00*
Nos. 358-361 (4) 1.20 1.20

Centenary of Universal Postal Union.

Roseate Spoonbills, Trust Emblem — A46

Protected Birds (National Trust Emblem and): 14c, White-crowned pigeons. 21c, White-tailed tropic birds. 36c, Bahamian parrot.

1974, Sept. 10 Litho. *Perf. 14*
362 A46 13c multicolored 1.50 .65
363 A46 14c multicolored 1.50 .55
364 A46 21c multicolored 2.00 1.00
365 A46 36c multicolored 2.50 *4.25*
a. Souvenir sheet of 4, #362-365 11.00 11.00
Nos. 362-365 (4) 7.50 6.45

Bahamas National Trust, 15th anniv.

Holy Family, by Jacques de Stella A47

Christmas: 10c, Virgin and Child, by Girolamo Romanino. 12c, Virgin and Child with St. John and St. Catherine, by Andrea Previtali. 21c, Virgin and Child with Angels, by Previtali.

1974, Oct. 29 Wmk. 314 *Perf. 13*
366 A47 8c black & multi .25 .25
367 A47 10c green & multi .30 .30
368 A47 12c red & multi .30 .30
369 A47 21c ultra & multi .40 .40
a. Souvenir sheet of 4, #366-369 1.75 *2.25*
Nos. 366-369 (4) 1.25 1.25

Anteos Maerula A48

14c, Eurema nicippe. 18c, Papilio andraemon. 21c, Euptoieta hegesia.

1975, Feb. 4 Litho. *Perf. 14x13½*
370 A48 3c shown .50 .30
371 A48 14c multicolored 1.40 .75
372 A48 18c multicolored 1.50 .95
373 A48 21c multicolored 1.75 1.40
a. Souvenir sheet of 4, #370-373 11.00 11.00
Nos. 370-373 (4) 5.15 3.40

Sheep Raising A49

Designs: 14c, Electric reel fishing, vert. 18c, Growing food. 21c, Crude oil refinery, vert.

Unwmk.

1975, May 27 Litho. *Perf. 14*
374 A49 3c dull grn & multi .25 .25
375 A49 14c green & multi .25 .25
376 A49 18c brown & multi .25 .25
377 A49 21c vio bl & multi .80 .45
a. Souvenir sheet of 4, #374-377 1.40 1.40
Nos. 374-377 (4) 1.55 1.20

Economic diversification.

Rowena Rand, Staff and Chrismon — A50

Plant and IWY Emblem — A51

Wmk. 373

1975, July 22 Litho. *Perf. 14*
378 A50 14c multicolored .30 *.40*
379 A51 18c multicolored .35 *.60*

International Women's Year.

Adoration of the Shepherds, by Perugino — A52

Christmas: 8c, 18c, Adoration of the Kings, by Ghirlandaio. 21c, like 3c.

1975, Dec. 2 Litho. *Perf. 13½*
380 A52 3c dk green & multi .25 .25
381 A52 8c dk violet & multi .25 .25
382 A52 18c purple & multi .65 .65
383 A52 21c maroon & multi .70 .70
a. Souvenir sheet of 4, #380-383 *2.50* *3.00*
Nos. 380-383 (4) 1.85 1.85

Telephones, 1876 and 1976 — A53

Designs: 16c, Radio-telephone link, Deleporte, Nassau (radar). 21c, Alexander Graham Bell. 25c, Communications satellite.

1976, Mar. 23 Litho. *Perf. 14*
384 A53 3c multicolored .25 .25
385 A53 16c multicolored .35 .35
386 A53 21c multicolored .50 .50
387 A53 25c multicolored .60 .60
Nos. 384-387 (4) 1.70 1.70

Centenary of first telephone call by Alexander Graham Bell, Mar. 10, 1876.

Bicycling and Olympic Rings — A54

Olympic Rings and: 16c, Long jump. 25c, Sailing. 40c, Boxing.

1976, July 13 Litho. *Perf. 14*
388 A54 8c magenta & blue 1.75 .30
389 A54 16c orange & brn .50 .40
390 A54 25c magenta & blue .65 .65
391 A54 40c orange & brn .80 1.00
a. Souvenir sheet of 4, #388-391 4.00 4.00
Nos. 388-391 (4) 3.70 2.35

21st Olympic Games, Montreal, Canada, July 17-Aug. 1.

John Murray, Earl of Dunmore A55

Design: 16c, Map of US and Bahamas.

1976, June 1 Wmk. 373 *Perf. 14*
392 A55 16c multicolored .45 .45
393 A55 $1 multicolored 1.75 1.75
a. Souvenir sheet of 4, #393 8.25 *9.25*

American Bicentennial.

Virgin and Child, Filippo Lippi — A56

Christmas: 21c, Adoration of the Shepherds, School of Seville. 25c, Adoration of the Kings, by Vincenzo Foppa. 40c, Virgin and Child, by Vivarini.

1976, Oct. 19 Litho. *Perf. 14½x14*
394 A56 3c brt blue & multi .25 .25
395 A56 21c dp org & multi .25 .25
396 A56 25c emerald & multi .25 .25
397 A56 40c red lilac & multi .40 .40
a. Souvenir sheet of 4, #394-397 1.75 1.75
Nos. 394-397 (4) 1.15 1.15

Type of 1971

16c, Hibiscus. 21c, Breadfruit. 25c, Hawksbill turtle. 40c, Bahamian sponge boat.

1976, Nov. 2 Litho. Wmk. 373
398 A36 16c emerald & multi 1.40 *1.75*
399 A36 21c vermilion & multi 1.75 *4.25*
400 A36 25c brown & multi 2.00 *2.10*
401 A36 40c vermilion & multi 6.00 3.25
Nos. 398-401 (4) 11.15 11.35

Elizabeth II Seated under Gold Canopy — A57

16c, Coronation. 21c, Taking and signing of oath. 40c, Queen holding orb and scepter.

1977, Feb. 7 *Perf. 12*
402 A57 8c silver & multi .25 .25
403 A57 16c silver & multi .25 .25
404 A57 21c silver & multi .25 .25
405 A57 40c silver & multi .30 .30
a. Souvenir sheet of 4, #402-405 1.25 *2.00*
Nos. 402-405 (4) 1.05 1.05

Reign of Queen Elizabeth II, 25th anniv.
For surcharges see Nos. 412-415.

Featherduster — A58

Marine Life: 8c, Porkfish. 16c, Elkhorn coral. 21c, Soft coral and sponge.

1977, May 24 Litho. *Perf. 13½*
406 A58 3c multicolored .65 .40
407 A58 8c multicolored 1.10 .55
408 A58 16c multicolored 1.25 .85
409 A58 21c multicolored 1.40 1.10
a. Souv. sheet, #406-409, perf 14½ 5.50 5.50
Nos. 406-409 (4) 4.40 2.90

Campfire and Shower A59

1977, Sept. 27 Litho. Wmk. 373
410 A59 16c shown .65 .55
411 A59 21c Boating 1.00 .70

6th Caribbean Jamboree, Kingston, Jamaica, Aug. 5-14.

Nos. 402-405a Overprinted "Royal Visit / October 1977"

1977, Oct. 19 Litho. *Perf. 12*
412 A57 8c silver & multi .25 .25
413 A57 16c silver & multi .25 .25
414 A57 21c silver & multi .25 .25
415 A57 40c silver & multi .35 .35
a. Souvenir sheet of 4 1.50 *2.00*
Nos. 412-415 (4) 1.10 1.10

Caribbean visit of Queen Elizabeth II, Oct. 19-20.

Virgin and Child — A60

Creche Figurines: 16c, Three Kings. 21c, Adoration of the Kings. 25c, Three Kings.

1977, Oct. 25 Litho. *Perf. 13½*
416 A60 3c gold & multi .25 .25
417 A60 16c gold & multi .25 .25
418 A60 21c gold & multi .25 .25
419 A60 25c gold & multi .30 .30
a. Souv. sheet, #416-419, perf 14½ 1.60 *3.25*
Nos. 416-419 (4) 1.05 1.05

Christmas.

Nassau Public Library — A61

Architectural Heritage: 8c, St. Matthew's Church. 16c, Government House. 18c, The Hermitage, Cat Island.

1978, Mar. 28 Litho. *Perf. 14½x14*
420 A61 3c black & yel green .25 .25
421 A61 8c black & lt blue .25 .25
422 A61 16c black & lilac rose .25 .25
423 A61 18c black & salmon .25 .25
a. Souvenir sheet of 4, #420-423 1.00 *1.60*
Nos. 420-423 (4) 1.00 1.00

Scepter, St. Edward's Crown, Orb — A62

Perf. 14x13½

1978, June 27 Litho. Wmk. 373
424 A62 16c shown .25 .25
425 A62 $1 Elizabeth II 1.00 .55
a. Souvenir sheet of 2, #424-425 1.75 1.75

Coronation of Queen Elizabeth II, 25th anniv.

Type of 1971

Designs as before and: 16c, Hibiscus. 25c, Hawksbill turtle.

Perf. 14½x14, 14x14½

1978, June **Unwmk.**

426	A36	1c blue & multi	1.25	1.40
430	A36	5c dp org & multi	1.90	2.10
436	A36	16c brt grn & multi	2.50	3.00
439	A36	25c brown & multi	10.50	13.50
440	A36	50c lemon & multi	4.50	5.75
441	A36	$1 lemon & multi	4.50	5.75
442	A36	$2 blue & multi	7.50	10.00
443	A36	$3 vio bl & multi	7.50	10.00
		Nos. 426-443 (8)	40.15	51.50

Angels and Palms A63

Christmas: 5c, Coat of arms within wreath, and sailing ships.

Perf. 14x14½

1978, Nov. 14 **Litho.** **Wmk. 373**

444	A63	5c car, pink & gold	.25	.25
445	A63	21c ultra, dk bl & gold	.30	.30
a.		Souvenir sheet of 2, #444-445	4.00	4.00

Baby Walking, IYC Emblem — A64

IYC Emblem and: 16c, Children playing leapfrog. 21c, Girl skipping rope. 25c, Building blocks with "IYC" and emblem.

Perf. 13½x13

1979, May 15 **Litho.** **Wmk. 373**

446	A64	5c multicolored	.25	.25
447	A64	16c multicolored	.30	.30
448	A64	21c multicolored	.50	.50
449	A64	25c multicolored	.60	.60
a.		Souv. sheet, #446-449, perf 14	2.00	2.00
		Nos. 446-449 (4)	1.65	1.65

International Year of the Child.

Rowland Hill and Penny Black — A65

21c, Stamp printing press, 1840, Bahamas #7. 25c, Great Britain #27 with 1850's Nassau cancellation, Great Britain #29. 40c, Early mailboat, Bahamas #1.

1979, Aug. 14 ***Perf. 13½x14***

450	A65	10c multicolored	.50	.30
451	A65	21c multicolored	.65	.50
452	A65	25c multicolored	.65	.65
453	A65	40c multicolored	.70	.70
a.		Souvenir sheet of 4, #450-453	2.75	2.75
		Nos. 450-453 (4)	2.50	2.15

Sir Rowland Hill (1795-1879), originator of penny postage.

Commonwealth Plaque over Map of Bahamas — A66

Designs: 21c, Parliament buildings. 25c, Legislative chamber. $1, Senate chamber.

1979, Sept. 27 **Litho.** ***Perf. 13½***

454	A66	16c multicolored	.30	.30
455	A66	21c multicolored	.35	.35
456	A66	25c multicolored	.35	.35
457	A66	$1 multicolored	1.40	1.40
a.		Souvenir sheet of 4, #454-457	3.50	3.50
		Nos. 454-457 (4)	2.40	2.40

Parliament of Bahamas, 250th anniv.

Headdress A67

Christmas: Goombay Carnival costumes.

1979, Nov. 6 **Litho.** ***Perf. 13***

458	A67	5c multicolored	.25	.25
459	A67	10c multicolored	.25	.25
460	A67	16c multicolored	.25	.25
461	A67	21c multicolored	.25	.25
462	A67	25c multicolored	.30	.25
463	A67	40c multicolored	.45	.40
a.		Souv. sheet, 458-463, perf 13½	2.50	*3.75*
		Nos. 458-463 (6)	1.75	1.65

Columbus' Landing, 1492 A68

3c, Blackbeard. 5c, Articles, 1647, Eleuthera map. 10c, Ceremonial mace. 12c, Col. Andrew Deveaux. 15c, Slave trading, Vendue House. 16c, Shipwreck salvage, 19th cent. 18c, Blockade runner, 1860s. 21c, Bootlegging, 1919-1929. 25c, Pineapple cultivation. 40c, Sponge clipping. 50c, Victoria & Colonial Hotels. $1, Modern agriculture. $2, Ship, jet. $3, Central Bank, Arms. $5, Prince Charles, Prime Minister Pindling.

1980, July 9 **Litho.** ***Perf. 15***

464	A68	1c shown	.60	2.40
465	A68	3c multicolored	.25	2.40
466	A68	5c multicolored	.25	1.25
467	A68	10c multicolored	.25	.40
468	A68	12c multicolored	.25	1.90
469	A68	15c multicolored	1.75	1.25
470	A68	16c multicolored	.30	1.25
471	A68	18c multicolored	.35	2.40
472	A68	21c multicolored	.40	2.40
473	A68	25c multicolored	.45	2.40
474	A68	40c multicolored	.70	1.90
475	A68	50c multicolored	.95	1.40
476	A68	$1 multicolored	1.75	4.00
477	A68	$2 multicolored	3.50	5.50
478	A68	$3 multicolored	5.50	3.75
479	A68	$5 multicolored	9.00	5.75
		Nos. 464-479 (16)	26.25	*40.35*

For overprints and surcharges see Nos. 496-499, 532-535.

1985, Nov. 6 **Wmk. 384**

464a	A68	1c	3.75	2.50
465a	A68	3c	5.00	3.50
467a	A68	10c	5.50	4.00
473a	A68	25c	11.00	9.00
		Nos. 464a-473a (4)	25.25	19.00

Virgin and Child, Straw Figures — A69

1980, Oct. 28 **Litho.** ***Perf. 14½***

480	A69	5c shown	.25	.25
481	A69	21c Three kings	.25	.35
482	A69	25c Angel	.30	.25
483	A69	$1 Christmas tree	1.00	.90
a.		Souvenir sheet of 4, #480-483	1.75	*2.50*
		Nos. 480-483 (4)	1.80	1.75

Christmas.

Man with Crutch, Sun Rays A70

1981, Feb. 10 **Litho.** ***Perf. 14½***

484	A70	5c shown	.25	.25
485	A70	$1 Man in wheelchair	1.25	1.25
a.		Souvenir sheet of 2, #484-485	1.75	*2.50*

International Year of the Disabled.

Grand Bahama Tracking Station A71

Satellite Views: 20c, Bahamas. 25c, Eleuthera. 50c, Andros and New Providence.

Wmk. 373

1981, Apr. 21 **Litho.** ***Perf. 13½***

486	A71	10c multi	.25	.25
487	A71	20c multi, vert.	.40	.40
488	A71	25c multi	.60	.60
489	A71	50c multi, vert.	1.25	1.25
a.		Souvenir sheet of 4, #486-489	2.75	2.75
		Nos. 486-489 (4)	2.50	2.50

Prince Charles and Lady Diana — A72

$2, Charles, Prime Minister.

Wmk. 373

1981, July 22 **Litho.** ***Perf. 14½***

490	A72	30c shown	.40	.25
491	A72	$2 multicolored	3.75	1.75
a.		Souvenir sheet of 2, #490-491	7.25	3.25

Royal wedding.

Bahama Ducks A73

20c, Reddish egrets. 25c, Brown boobies. $1, West Indian tree ducks.

Wmk. 373

1981, Aug. 25 **Litho.** ***Perf. 14***

492	A73	5c shown	1.40	.75
493	A73	20c multicolored	2.50	1.00
494	A73	25c multicolored	2.50	1.25
495	A73	$1 multicolored	4.50	4.50
a.		Souvenir sheet of 4, #492-495	11.00	11.00
		Nos. 492-495 (4)	10.90	7.50

See Nos. 514-517.

Nos. 466-467, 473, 475 Overprinted: "COMMONWEALTH FINANCE MINISTERS' MEETING 21-23 SEPTEMBER 1981"

1981, Sept. **Litho.** ***Perf. 15***

496	A68	5c multicolored	.35	.35
497	A68	10c multicolored	.35	.35
498	A68	25c multicolored	.60	.60
499	A68	50c multicolored	1.25	1.25
		Nos. 496-499 (4)	2.55	2.55

World Food Day A74

Perf. 13x13½

1981, Oct. 16 **Wmk. 373**

500	A74	5c Chickens	.25	.25
501	A74	20c Sheep	.30	.30
502	A74	30c Lobster	.50	.50
503	A74	50c Pigs	1.00	1.00
a.		Souvenir sheet of 4, #500-503	3.25	3.25
		Nos. 500-503 (4)	2.05	2.05

Christmas — A75

Wmk. 373

1981, Nov. 23 **Litho.** ***Perf. 14***

504	A75	Sheet of 9	7.25	7.25
a.		5c Father Christmas	.50	.50
b.		5c shown	.50	.50
c.		5c St. Nicholas, Holland	.50	.50
d.		25c Lussibruden, Sweden	.75	.75
e.		25c Mother and child	.75	.75
f.		25c King Wenceslas, Czechoslovakia	.75	.75
g.		30c Mother and child	.75	.75
h.		30c Mother and child standing	.75	.75
i.		$1 Christkindl angel, Germany	1.60	1.60

TB Bacillus Centenary A76

1982, Feb. 3 **Litho.** ***Perf. 14***

505	A76	5c Koch	.70	.70
506	A76	16c X-ray	1.40	1.40
507	A76	21c Microscopes	1.60	1.60
508	A76	$1 Mantoux test	3.25	3.25
a.		Souv. sheet, #505-508, perf 14½	7.50	7.50
		Nos. 505-508 (4)	6.95	6.95

Flamingoes A77

Designs: a, Females. b, Males. c, Nesting. d, Juvenile birds. e, Immature birds. No. 509 in continuous design.

Wmk. 373

1982, Apr. 28 **Litho.** ***Perf. 14***

509		Strip of 5	12.00	12.00
a.-e.		A77 25c any single	2.25	2.25

Princess Diana Issue
Common Design Type

1982, July 1 **Litho.** ***Perf. 14***

510	CD333	16c Arms	.55	.25
511	CD333	25c Diana	1.10	.60
512	CD333	40c Wedding	1.60	1.00
513	CD333	$1 Portrait	2.75	2.00
		Nos. 510-513 (4)	6.00	3.85

Bird Type of 1981

Wmk. 373

1982, Aug. 18 Litho. *Perf. 14*

514 A73 10c Bat 1.00 .35
515 A73 16c Hutia 1.40 .45
516 A73 21c Racoon 1.60 .90
517 A73 $1 Dolphins 4.25 2.40
a. Souvenir sheet of 4, #514-517 8.50 8.50
Nos. 514-517 (4) 8.25 4.10

28th Commonwealth Parliamentary Conference A78

Perf. 14x13½

1982, Oct. 16 Litho. Wmk. 373

518 A78 5c Plaque .25 .25
519 A78 25c Assoc. arms .65 .65
520 A78 40c Natl. arms 1.00 1.00
521 A78 50c House of Assembly 1.25 1.25
Nos. 518-521 (4) 3.15 3.15

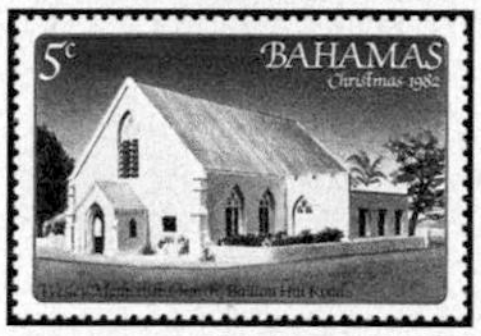

Christmas A79

Designs: 5c, Wesley Methodist Church, Baillou Hill Road. 12c, Centerville Seventh Day Adventist Church. 15c, Church of God of Prophecy, East Street. 21c, Bethel Baptist Church, Meeting Street. 25c, St. Francis Xavier Catholic Church, West Hill Street. $1, Holy Cross Anglican Church, Highbury Park.

1982, Nov. 3 *Perf. 14*

522 A79 5c multicolored .25 .25
523 A79 12c multicolored .25 .25
524 A79 15c multicolored .30 .30
525 A79 21c multicolored .40 .40
526 A79 25c multicolored .40 .40
527 A79 $1 multicolored 1.40 1.40
Nos. 522-527 (6) 3.00 3.00

A80

1983, Mar. 14 Litho.

528 A80 5c Lynden O. Pindling .25 .25
529 A80 25c Flags .50 .50
530 A80 35c Map .50 .50
531 A80 $1 Ocean liner 1.35 1.35
Nos. 528-531 (4) 2.60 2.60

Commonwealth Day.

Nos. 469-472 Surcharged

1983, Apr. 5 Litho. *Perf. 15*

532 A68 20c on 15c multi .60 .60
533 A68 31c on 21c multi .70 .70
534 A68 35c on 16c multi 1.50 1.50
535 A68 80c on 18c multi 2.10 2.10
Nos. 532-535 (4) 4.90 4.90

30th Anniv. of Customs Cooperation Council — A81

Perf. 14x13½

1983, May 31 Wmk. 373

536 A81 31c Officers, ship 1.75 .55
537 A81 $1 Officers, jet 3.50 2.40

10th Anniv. of Independence A82

1983, July 6 Litho. *Perf. 14*

538 A82 $1 Flag raising 1.50 1.50
a. Souvenir sheet, perf. 12 2.25 2.25

Local Butterflies A83

5c, Carters skipper. 25c, Giant southern white. 31c, Large orange sulphur. 50c, Flambeau.

1983, Aug. 24 *Perf. 14½x14*

539 A83 5c multicolored 1.40 .30
540 A83 25c multicolored 2.60 .55
541 A83 31c multicolored 2.60 .85
542 A83 50c multicolored 2.75 1.40
a. Souvenir sheet of 4 10.00 10.00
Nos. 539-542 (4) 9.35 3.10

No. 542a contains Nos. 539-542, perf. 14 and perf. 14½x14.

American Loyalists Arrival Bicentenary — A84

Paintings by Alton Lowe: 5c, Loyalist Dreams, vert. 31c, New Plymouth, Abaco. 35c, New Plymouth Hotel. 50c, Island Hope, vert.

1983, Sept. 28 *Perf. 14*

543 A84 5c multicolored .25 .25
544 A84 31c multicolored .55 .55
545 A84 35c multicolored .65 .65
546 A84 50c multicolored .90 .90
a. Souvenir sheet of 4, #543-546 2.25 2.25
Nos. 543-546 (4) 2.35 2.35

Christmas — A85

Children's designs: 5c, Christmas Bells, by Monica Pinder. 20c, The Flamingo by Cory Bullard. 25c, The Yellow Hibiscus with Christmas Candle by Monique A. Bailey. 31c, Santa goes a Sailing by Sabrina Seiler, horiz. 35c, Silhouette scene with palm trees by James Blake. 50c, Silhouette scene with Pelicans, by Erik Russell, horiz.

1983, Nov. 1 *Perf. 14*

547 A85 5c multicolored .25 .25
548 A85 20c multicolored .40 .40
549 A85 25c multicolored .50 .50
550 A85 31c multicolored .65 .65
551 A85 35c multicolored .75 .75
552 A85 50c multicolored .90 .90
Nos. 547-552 (6) 3.45 3.45

125th Anniv. of Bahamas Stamps — A86

1984, Feb. 22 Litho. *Perf. 14*

553 A86 5c No. 3 .25 .25
554 A86 $1 No. 1 2.25 2.25

Lloyd's List Issue

Common Design Type

5c, Trent. 31c, Orinoco. 35c, Nassau Harbor. 50c, Container ship Oropesa.

Wmk. 373

1984, Apr. 25 Litho. *Perf. 14½*

555 CD335 5c multicolored .50 .25
556 CD335 31c multicolored .90 .60
557 CD335 35c multicolored 1.15 .70
558 CD335 50c multicolored 1.60 1.40
Nos. 555-558 (4) 4.15 2.95

1984 Summer Olympics A87

1984, June 20 Litho. *Perf. 14x14½*

559 A87 5c Running .30 .30
560 A87 25c Discus .60 .60
561 A87 31c Boxing .60 .60
562 A87 $1 Basketball 4.25 4.25
a. Souvenir sheet of 4, #559-562 6.50 6.50
Nos. 559-562 (4) 5.75 5.75

Flags of Bahamas and Caribbean Community — A88

Wmk. 373

1984, July 4 Litho. *Perf. 14*

563 A88 50c multicolored 1.15 1.15

Conference of Heads of Government of Caribbean Community, 5th Meeting.

Allen's Cay Iguana A89

25c, Curly-tailed lizard. 35c, Greenhouse frog. 50c, Atlantic green turtle.

1984, Aug. 15 *Perf. 14*

564 A89 5c shown .45 .25
565 A89 25c multicolored 2.10 .75
566 A89 35c multicolored 2.60 1.10
567 A89 50c multicolored 2.75 2.75
a. Souvenir sheet of 4, #564-567 8.75 8.75
Nos. 564-567 (4) 7.90 4.85

25th Anniv. of Natl. Trust — A90

Wildlife: a, Calliphlox evelynae. b, Megaceryle alcyon, Eleutherodactylus planirostris. c, Phoebis sennae, Phoenicopterus ruber, Himantopus himantopus, Phoebus sennae. d, Urbanus proteus, Chelonia mydas. e, Pandion haliaetus.

Continuous design.

1984, Aug. 15 Litho. *Perf. 14*

568 Strip of 5 19.00 19.00
a.-e. A90 31c any single 3.75 3.75

Christmas — A91

Madonna and Child Paintings.

1984, Nov. 7 Litho. *Perf. 13½x13*

569 A91 5c Titian .50 .40
570 A91 31c Anais Colin 1.40 1.25
571 A91 35c Elena Caula 1.60 1.40
a. Souvenir sheet of 3, #569-571 2.50 2.50
Nos. 569-571 (3) 3.50 3.05

Girl Guides, 75th Anniv., Intl. Youth Year A92

1985, Feb. 22 Litho. *Perf. 14*

572 A92 5c Brownies .70 .40
573 A92 25c Camping 1.40 .85
574 A92 31c Girl Guides 1.75 1.10
575 A92 35c Rangers 2.25 1.60
a. Souvenir sheet of 4, #572-575 6.75 6.75
Nos. 572-575 (4) 6.10 3.95

Audubon Birth Bicentenary — A93

5c, Killdeer. 31c, Mourning dove, vert. 35c, Mourning doves, diff., vert. $1, Killdeers, diff.

Wmk. 373

1985, Apr. 24 Litho. *Perf. 14*

576 A93 5c multicolored 1.10 .85
577 A93 31c multicolored 2.50 .85
578 A93 35c multicolored 2.50 1.00
579 A93 $1 multicolored 4.75 4.75
Nos. 576-579 (4) 10.85 7.45

Queen Mother 85th Birthday

Common Design Type

5c, Portrait, 1927. 25c, At christening of Peter Phillips. 35c, Portrait, 1985. 50c, Holding Prince Henry.

$1.25, In a pony and trap.

Perf. 14½x14

1985, June 7 Litho. Wmk. 384

580 CD336 5c multicolored .40 .25
581 CD336 25c multicolored .80 .45
582 CD336 35c multicolored .90 .65
583 CD336 50c multicolored 1.60 1.60
Nos. 580-583 (4) 3.70 2.95

Souvenir Sheet

584 CD336 $1.25 multicolored 4.00 3.50

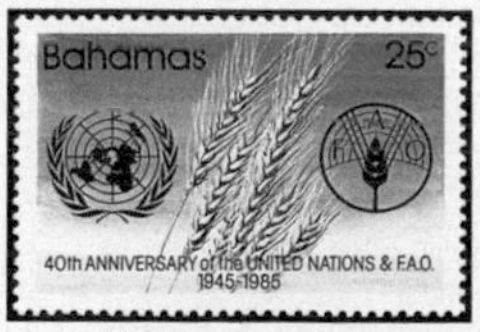

UN and UN Food and Agriculture Org., 40th Annivs. — A94

Wmk. 373

1985, Aug. 26 Litho. *Perf. 14*

585	A94	25c Wheat, emblems	1.10	1.10

Commonwealth Heads of Government Meeting, 1985 — A95

31c, Queen Elizabeth II. 35c, Flag, Commonwealth emblem.

1985, Oct. 16 Wmk. 373 *Perf. 14½*

586	A95	31c multicolored	3.00	3.00
587	A95	35c multicolored	3.00	3.00

Christmas A96

Paintings by Alton Roland Lowe: 5c, Grandma's Christmas Bouquet. 25c, Junkanoo Romeo and Juliet, vert. 31c, Bunce Girl, vert. 35c, Home for Christmas.

1985, Nov. 5 *Perf. 13*

588	A96	5c multicolored	.70	.40
589	A96	25c multicolored	1.60	1.10
590	A96	31c multicolored	1.90	1.40
591	A96	35c multicolored	1.90	1.90
a.		Souv. sheet, #588-591, perf 14	5.50	5.50
		Nos. 588-591 (4)	6.10	4.80

Queen Elizabeth II 60th Birthday
Common Design Type

Designs: 10c, Age 1, 1927. 25c, Coronation, Westminster Abbey, 1953. 35c, Giving speech, royal visit, Bahamas. 40c, At Djakova, Yugoslavia, state visit, 1972. $1, Visiting Crown Agents, 1983.

1986, Apr. 21 Wmk. 384 *Perf. 14½*

592	CD337	10c scar, blk & sil	.25	*.30*
593	CD337	25c ultra & multi	.30	*.40*
594	CD337	35c green & multi	.45	*.60*
595	CD337	40c violet & multi	.50	*.65*
596	CD337	$1 rose vio & multi	1.25	*1.75*
		Nos. 592-596 (5)	2.75	*3.70*

AMERIPEX '86 — A97

1986, May 19 *Perf. 14*

597	A97	5c Nos. 464, 471	1.10	.45
598	A97	25c Nos. 288-289	2.40	.45
599	A97	31c No. 392	2.60	.60
600	A97	50c No. 489a	3.50	3.00
601	A97	$1 Statue of Liberty, vert.	4.25	*4.75*
a.		Souvenir sheet of one	8.00	8.00
		Nos. 597-601 (5)	13.85	9.25

Statue of Liberty, cent.

Royal Wedding Issue, 1986
Common Design Type

Designs: 10c, Formal engagement. $1, Andrew in dress uniform.

1986, July 23 *Perf. 14½x14*

602	CD338	10c multicolored	.25	.25
603	CD338	$1 multicolored	2.50	2.50

Fish A98

5c, Rock beauty. 10c, Stoplight parrotfish. 15c, Jacknife fish. 20c, Flamefish. 25c, Swissguard basslet. 30c, Spotfin butterflyfish. 35c, Queen triggerfish. 40c, Four-eyed butterflyfish. 45c, Fairy basslet. 50c, Queen angelfish. 60c, Blue chromis. $1, Spanish hogfish. $2, Harlequin bass. $3, Blackbar soldierfish. $5, Pygmy angelfish. $10, Red hind.

1986-87 Wmk. 384 *Perf. 14*

604	A98	5c multi	1.10	.60
605	A98	10c multi	1.10	.65
606	A98	15c multi	1.90	1.40
607	A98	20c multi	1.75	1.40
608	A98	25c multi	2.10	1.40
609	A98	30c multi	1.50	1.40
610	A98	35c multi	1.75	*2.10*
611	A98	40c multi	1.75	1.50
612	A98	45c multi	1.90	1.25
613	A98	50c multi	2.75	*2.75*
614	A98	60c multi	3.00	*4.25*
615	A98	$1 multi	3.75	3.00
616	A98	$2 multi	4.00	*6.75*
617	A98	$3 multi	7.75	6.00
618	A98	$5 multi	8.75	7.75
618A	A99	$10 multi ('87)	21.00	19.00
		Nos. 604-618A (16)	65.85	61.20

Issue dates: $10, Jan. 2, others, Aug. 5.

1988, Aug. 15 Inscribed "1988"

611a	A98	40c	2.50	2.50
615a	A98	$1	5.50	5.50
616a	A98	$2	25.00	*20.00*
		Nos. 611a-616a (3)	33.00	28.00

1990, Aug. Inscribed "1990"

605b	A98	10c	2.00	*2.50*
608b	A98	25c	2.25	*2.50*
611b	A98	40c	—	—
612b	A98	45c	2.75	*3.00*
613b	A98	50c	3.50	*3.00*
615b	A98	$1	—	—
617b	A98	$3	8.00	*15.00*
618b	A98	$5	11.00	*16.00*
		Nos. 605b-618b (6)	29.50	*42.00*

1987, June 25 Wmk. 373
Inscribed "1987"

604c	5c	.80	1.00
d.	Inscribed "1989"	—	
605c	10c	.90	.45
d.	Inscribed "1988"	—	
606c	15c	1.00	.60
611c	40c	2.50	1.25
612c	45c	3.00	1.75
613c	50c	3.25	2.00
614c	60c	3.75	2.25
615c	$1	6.50	4.25
616c	$2	12.00	8.00
	Nos. 604c-616c (9)	33.70	21.55

Christ Church Cathedral — A99

Wmk. 373

1986, Sept. 16 Litho. *Perf. 14½*

619	A99	10c View, 19th cent.	.45	.40
620	A99	40c View, 1986	1.00	.90
a.		Souvenir sheet of 2, #619-620	5.00	5.00

City of Nassau, Diocese of Nassau and the Bahamas and Christ Church, 125th anniv.

Christmas, Intl. Peace Year A100

10c, Nativity. 40c, Flight to Egypt. 45c, Children praying. 50c, Exchanging gifts.

Wmk. 384

1986, Nov. 4 Litho. *Perf. 14*

621	A100	10c multicolored	.45	.25
622	A100	40c multicolored	1.30	1.00
623	A100	45c multicolored	1.50	1.40
624	A100	50c multicolored	1.90	*2.25*
a.		Souvenir sheet of 4, #621-624	10.00	10.00
		Nos. 621-624 (4)	5.15	4.90

Pirates of the Caribbean — A101

A102

10c, Anne Bonney. 40c, Blackbeard (d. 1718). 45c, Capt. Edward England. 50c, Capt. Woodes Rogers (c. 1679-1732).
$1.25, Map of the Bahamas.

Wmk. 373

1987, June 2 Litho. *Perf. 14½*

625	A101	10c multi	3.50	1.60
626	A101	40c multi	7.75	7.75
627	A101	45c multi	7.75	5.00
628	A101	50c multi	8.25	8.25
		Nos. 625-628 (4)	27.25	22.60

Souvenir Sheet

629	A102	$1.25 multi	16.00	16.00

Paintings of Lighthouses by Alton Roland Lowe A103

1987, Mar. 31 Wmk. 384

630	A103	10c Great Isaac	4.25	1.25
631	A103	40c Bird Rock	7.50	1.75
632	A103	45c Castle Is.	8.25	1.90
633	A103	$1 Hole in the Wall	12.50	12.50
		Nos. 630-633 (4)	32.50	17.40

Tourist Transportation A104

Ships: No. 634a, Cruise ship, sailboat. b, Cruise ships, tugboat, speedboat. c, Pleasure boat leaving harbor, sailboat. d, Pleasure boat docked, sailboats. e, Sailboats.
Aircraft: No. 635a, Bahamasair plane. b, Bahamasair and Pan Am aircraft. c, Aircraft, radar tower. d, Control tower, aircraft. e, Helicopter, planes.

1987, Aug. 26 Wmk. 373 *Perf. 14*

634		Strip of 5	13.50	13.50
a.-e.	A104	40c any single	2.50	2.50
635		Strip of 5	13.50	13.50
a.-e.	A104	40c any single	2.50	2.50

Orchids Painted by Alton Roland Lowe A105

10c, Cattleyopis lindenii. 40c, Encyclia lucayana. 45c, Encyclia hodgeana. 50c, Encyclia lleidae.

1987, Oct. 20 Wmk. 384 *Perf. 14½*

636	A105	10c multicolored	2.25	.85
637	A105	40c multicolored	4.25	1.40
638	A105	45c multicolored	4.25	1.40
639	A105	50c multicolored	4.25	4.25
a.		Souvenir sheet of 4, #636-639	15.00	15.00
		Nos. 636-639 (4)	15.00	7.90

Christmas.

Discovery of America, 500th Anniv. (in 1992) — A106

10c, Ferdinand & Isabella. 40c, Columbus before the Talavera Committee. 45c, Lucayan village. 50c, Lucayan potters. $1.50, Map, c. 1500.

Perf. 14x14½

1988, Feb. 23 Litho. Wmk. 373

640	A106	10c multicolored	1.40	1.00
641	A106	40c multicolored	2.50	2.50
642	A106	45c multicolored	3.00	3.00
643	A106	50c multicolored	3.00	3.00
		Nos. 640-643 (4)	9.90	9.50

Souvenir Sheet

644	A106	$1.50 multicolored	11.00	11.00

See Nos. 663-667, 688-692, 725-729, 749-753, 762.

World Wildlife Fund A107

Whistling ducks, Dendrocygna arborea: 5c, Ducks in flight. 10c, Among marine plants. 20c, Adults, ducklings. 45c, Wading.

1988, Apr. 29 *Perf. 14½*

645	A107	5c multi	3.25	1.25
646	A107	10c multi	3.75	1.25
647	A107	20c multi	6.00	1.50
648	A107	45c multi	9.25	2.75
		Nos. 645-648 (4)	22.25	6.75

Abolition of Slavery, 150th Anniv. A108

10c, African hut. 40c, Basket weavers in hut, Grantstown.

1988, Aug. 9 *Perf. 14*

649	A108	10c multicolored	.75	.50
650	A108	40c multicolored	2.00	1.40

1988 Summer Olympics, Seoul A109

Games emblem and details of painting by James Martin: 10c, Olympic flame, high jump, hammer throw, basketball and gymnastics. 40c, Swimming, boxing, weight lifting, archery and running. 45c, Gymnastics, shot put and javelin. $1, Running, cycling and gymnastics.

Wmk. 384

1988, Aug. 30 Litho. *Perf. 14*

651	A109 10c multicolored		.90	.40
652	A109 40c multicolored		1.25	.55
653	A109 45c multicolored		1.25	.55
654	A109 $1 multicolored		4.50	4.50
a.	Souvenir sheet of 4, #651-654		8.75	8.75
	Nos. 651-654 (4)		7.90	6.00

Lloyds of London, 300th Anniv.

Common Design Type

Designs: 10c, Lloyds List No. 560, 1740. 40c, Freeport Harbor, horiz. 45c, Space shuttle over the Bahamas, horiz. $1, Supply ship Yarmouth Castle on fire.

1988, Oct. 4 Wmk. 373

655	CD341 10c multicolored	.65	.45
656	CD341 40c multicolored	2.25	.75
657	CD341 45c multicolored	2.25	.75
658	CD341 $1 multicolored	3.75	3.00
	Nos. 655-658 (4)	8.90	4.95

Christmas Carols — A110

Designs: 10c, O' Little Town of Bethlehem. 40c, Little Donkey. 45c, Silent Night. 50c, Hark! The Herald Angels Sing.

1988, Nov. 21 Wmk. 384 *Perf. 14½*

659	A110 10c multicolored	.80	.30
660	A110 40c multicolored	2.10	.75
661	A110 45c multicolored	2.25	.90
662	A110 50c multicolored	2.50	2.50
a.	Souvenir sheet of 4, #659-662	5.50	5.50
	Nos. 659-662 (4)	7.65	4.45

Discovery of America Type

Design: 10c, Columbus as chartmaker. 40c, Development of the caravel. 45c, Navigational tools. 50c, Arawak artifacts. $1.50, Caravel under construction, an illumination from the Nuremburg Chronicles, 15th cent.

Perf. 14½x14

1989, Jan. 25 Litho. Wmk. 373

663	A106 10c multicolored	2.40	.65
664	A106 40c multicolored	3.50	1.25
665	A106 45c multicolored	3.50	1.25
666	A106 50c multicolored	3.50	3.50
	Nos. 663-666 (4)	12.90	6.65

Souvenir Sheet

667	A106 $1.50 multicolored	6.75	6.75

Hummingbirds A111

10c, Cuban emerald. 40c, Ruby-throated. 45c, Bahama woodstar. 50c, Rufous.

Wmk. 384

1989, Mar. 29 Litho. *Perf. 14½*

668	A111 10c multi	3.00	1.60
669	A111 40c multi	4.50	2.50
670	A111 45c multi	5.00	2.50
671	A111 50c multi	6.00	6.00
	Nos. 668-671 (4)	18.50	12.60

Intl. Red Cross and Red Crescent Organizations, 125th Annivs. — A112

1989, May 31 *Perf. 14x14½*

672	A112 10c Water safety	2.50	.85
673	A112 $1 Dunant, Battle of Solferino	5.75	3.50

Moon Landing, 20th Anniv.

Common Design Type

Apollo 8: 10c, Apollo Communications System, Grand Bahama Is. 40c, James Lovell Jr., William Anders and Frank Borman. 45c, Mission emblem. $1, The Rising Earth (photograph). $2, Astronaut practicing lunar surface activities at Manned Spacecraft Center, Houston, in training for Apollo 11 mission.

1989, July 20 *Perf. 14x13½*

Size of Nos. 674-675: 29x29mm

674	CD342 10c multicolored	1.60	.65
675	CD342 40c multicolored	2.40	1.40
676	CD342 45c multicolored	2.75	1.40
677	CD342 $1 multicolored	4.25	4.25
	Nos. 674-677 (4)	11.00	7.70

Souvenir Sheet

678	CD342 $2 multicolored	12.00	12.00

Christmas A113

Designs: 10c, Church of the Nativity, Bethlehem. 40c, Basilica of the Annunciation, Nazareth. 45c, By the Sea of Galilee, Tabgha. $1, Church of the Holy Sepulcher, Jerusalem.

Perf. 14½x14

1989, Oct. 16 Wmk. 373

679	A113 10c multicolored	1.25	.35
680	A113 40c multicolored	2.10	.65
681	A113 45c multicolored	2.10	.65
682	A113 $1 multicolored	5.25	5.25
a.	Souvenir sheet of 4, #679-682	12.00	12.00
	Nos. 679-682 (4)	10.70	6.90

World Stamp Expo '89 A114

Expo emblem and: 10c, Earth, #359. 40c, UPU Headquarters, #301. 45c, US Capitol, #601. $1, Passenger jet, #150. $2, Washington, DC, on map.

1989, Nov. 17 Wmk. 384 *Perf. 14*

683	A114 10c multicolored	.90	.40
684	A114 40c multicolored	2.10	.70
685	A114 45c multicolored	2.10	.75
686	A114 $1 multicolored	7.00	7.00
	Nos. 683-686 (4)	12.10	8.85

Souvenir Sheet

Perf. 14½x14

687	A114 $2 multicolored	12.50	12.50

No. 687 contains one 31x38mm stamp.

Discovery of America Type of 1988

10c, Caravel launch. 40c, Provisioning ships. 45c, Shortening sails. 50c, Lucayan fishermen. $1.50, Columbus's fleet departing from Cadiz.

Perf. 14½x14

1990, Jan. 24 Litho. Wmk. 373

688	A106 10c multicolored	2.25	.85
689	A106 40c multicolored	2.25	1.60
690	A106 45c multicolored	2.75	1.60
691	A106 50c multicolored	2.75	*3.50*
	Nos. 688-691 (4)	10.00	*7.55*

Souvenir Sheet

692	A106 $1.50 multicolored	9.00	9.00

Organization of American States, Cent. — A115

1990, Mar. 14 Wmk. 384 *Perf. 14*

693	A115 40c multicolored	3.25	3.25

Souvenir Sheet

Stamp World London '90 — A116

Aircraft: a, Spitfire I. b, Hurricane IIc.

1990, May 3 Wmk. 384

694	A116 Sheet of 2	14.00	14.00
a.-b.	$1 any single	4.75	4.75

For surcharge see No. B3.

Intl. Literacy Year A117

10c, Teacher helping student. 40c, Children reading to each other. 50c, Children reading aloud.

1990, June 27 Wmk. 384 *Perf. 14*

695	A117 10c multicolored	2.00	.45
696	A117 40c multicolored	2.50	1.40
697	A117 50c multicolored	2.50	*4.50*
	Nos. 695-697 (3)	7.00	6.35

Queen Mother, 90th Birthday

Common Design Types

40c, Portrait, c. 1938. $1.50, At garden party, 1938.

1990, Aug. 4 *Perf. 14x15*

698	CD343 40c multicolored	1.25	1.25

Perf. 14½

699	CD344 $1.50 multicolored	4.00	4.00

Bahamian Parrot — A118

40c, In flight. 45c, Head. 50c, On branch. $1.50, On branch with flowers.

1990, Sept. 26 Wmk. 373 *Perf. 14*

700	A118 10c shown	1.75	.60
701	A118 40c multicolored	3.25	1.25
702	A118 45c multicolored	3.50	1.25
703	A118 50c multicolored	4.00	4.00
	Nos. 700-703 (4)	12.50	7.10

Souvenir Sheet

704	A118 $1.50 multicolored	13.00	13.00

Christmas A119

10c, Angel appears to Mary. 40c, Nativity. 45c, Angel appears to shepherds. $1, Three kings.

Wmk. 373

1990, Nov. 5 Litho. *Perf. 13½*

705	A119 10c multi	1.00	.55
706	A119 40c multi	1.60	.65
707	A119 45c multi	1.60	.65
708	A119 $1 multi	4.50	4.50
a.	Souvenir sheet of 4, #705-708	16.00	16.00
	Nos. 705-708 (4)	8.70	6.35

Birds — A120

5c, Green heron. 10c, Turkey vulture. 15c, Osprey. 20c, Clapper rail. 25c, Royal tern. 30c, Key West quail dove. 40c, Smooth-billed ani. 45c, Burrowing owl. 50c, Hairy woodpecker. 55c, Mangrove cuckoo. 60c, Bahama mockingbird. 70c, Red-winged blackbird. $1, Thick-billed vireo. $2, Bahama yellowthroat. $5, Stripe-headed tanager. $10, Greater Antillean bullfinch.

Wmk. 384

1991, Feb. 4 Litho. *Perf. 14*

709	A120 5c multi	1.90	1.90
710	A120 10c multi	2.25	2.25
711	A120 15c multi	1.75	.70
712	A120 20c multi	2.25	.80
713	A120 25c multi	1.40	.70
714	A120 30c multi	3.75	.80
715	A120 40c multi	4.00	.70
716	A120 45c multi	6.00	.80
717	A120 50c multi	4.75	.80
718	A120 55c multi	4.00	.80
719	A120 60c multi	4.50	.80
720	A120 70c multi	4.50	1.75
721	A120 $1 multi	5.25	1.50
722	A120 $2 multi	11.50	8.25
723	A120 $5 multi	14.50	10.50
724	A120 $10 multi	27.50	17.00
	Nos. 709-724 (16)	99.80	50.05

Issued: $10, 7/1/91; others, 2/4/91.

1993 Dated "1993" Wmk. 373

710a	10c multicolored	.45	.45
713a	25c multicolored	1.10	1.10
714a	30c multicolored	1.40	1.40
715a	40c multicolored	1.75	1.75
718a	55c multicolored	2.50	2.50
723a	$5 multicolored	22.50	22.50
	Nos. 710a-723a (6)	29.70	29.70

Issued: 40c, 12/31/93; others, 9/23/93.

1995 Dated "1995"

711b	15c multicolored	1.75	.75
713b	25c multicolored	1.10	1.10
715b	40c multicolored	2.50	2.50
718b	55c multicolored	2.50	2.50
723b	$5 multicolored	14.50	14.50
	Nos. 711b-723b (5)	22.35	21.35

Discovery of America Type

Designs: 15c, Columbus practices celestial navigation. 40c, The fleet in rough seas. 55c, Natives on the beach. 60c, Map of voyage. $1.50, Pinta's crew sights land.

Perf. 14½x14

1991, Apr. 9 Litho. Wmk. 384

725	A106 15c multicolored	1.90	.80
726	A106 40c multicolored	3.25	2.00
727	A106 55c multicolored	3.50	2.40
728	A106 60c multicolored	4.25	4.25
	Nos. 725-728 (4)	12.90	9.45

Souvenir Sheet

729	A106 $1.50 multicolored	13.00	13.00

Elizabeth & Philip, Birthdays
Common Design Types
Wmk. 384
1991, June 17 Litho. *Perf. 14½*
730 CD346 15c multicolored 1.25 1.25
731 CD345 $1 multicolored 2.75 2.75
a. Pair, #730-731 + label 4.00 4.00

Hurricane Awareness — A121

Designs: 15c, Weather radar image of Hurricane Hugo. 40c, Anatomy of hurricane rotating around eye. 55c, Flooding caused by Hurricane David. 60c, Lockheed WP-3D Orion.

1991, Aug. 28 *Perf. 14*
732 A121 15c multicolored 1.75 .55
733 A121 40c multicolored 2.60 1.50
734 A121 55c multicolored 3.25 2.40
735 A121 60c multicolored 4.00 4.00
Nos. 732-735 (4) 11.60 8.45

Christmas A122

Designs: 15c, The Annunciation. 55c, Mary and Joseph traveling to Bethlehem. 60c, Angel appearing to shepherds. $1, Adoration of the Magi.

1991, Oct. 28 Wmk. 373 *Perf. 14*
736 A122 15c multicolored .80 .30
737 A122 55c multicolored 2.10 .90
738 A122 60c multicolored 2.25 1.25
739 A122 $1 multicolored 3.50 3.50
a. Souvenir sheet of 4, #736-739 11.00 11.00
Nos. 736-739 (4) 8.65 5.95

Majority Rule, 25th Anniv. A123

Designs: 15c, First Progressive Liberal Party cabinet. 40c, Signing of Independence Constitution. 55c, Handing over constitutional instrument, vert. 60c, First Bahamian Governor-General, Sir Milo Butler, vert.

Wmk. 373
1992, Jan. 10 Litho. *Perf. 14*
740 A123 15c multicolored 1.00 .55
741 A123 40c multicolored 2.00 1.60
742 A123 55c multicolored 2.10 2.10
743 A123 60c multicolored 2.50 *3.00*
Nos. 740-743 (4) 7.60 7.25

Queen Elizabeth II's Accession to the Throne, 40th Anniv.
Common Design Type
Wmk. 373
1992, Feb. 6 Litho. *Perf. 14*
744 CD349 15c multicolored .75 .30
745 CD349 40c multicolored 1.25 .55
746 CD349 55c multicolored 1.25 .70
747 CD349 60c multicolored 1.75 1.25
748 CD349 $1 multicolored 1.90 1.90
Nos. 744-748 (5) 6.90 4.70

Discovery of America Type

Designs: 15c, Lucayans first sight of fleet. 40c, Approaching Bahamas coastline. 55c, Lucayans about to meet Columbus. 60c, Columbus gives thanks for safe arrival. $1.50, Monument to Columbus' landing.

Perf. 14½x14
1992, Mar. 17 Litho. Wmk. 384
749 A106 15c multicolored 1.50 .80
750 A106 40c multicolored 2.10 1.60
751 A106 55c multicolored 2.25 2.10
752 A106 60c multicolored 2.50 3.25
Nos. 749-752 (4) 8.35 7.75

Souvenir Sheet
753 A106 $1.50 multicolored 6.00 6.00

Templeton, Galbraith and Hansberger Ltd. Building — A124

Wmk. 384
1992, Apr. 22 Litho. *Perf. 14½*
754 A124 55c multicolored 2.25 2.25

Templeton Prize for Progress in Religion, 20th Anniv.

1992 Summer Olympics, Barcelona A125

Perf. 14½x14
1992, June 2 Wmk. 373
755 A125 15c Pole vault .75 .35
756 A125 40c Javelin 1.10 .90
757 A125 55c Hurdling 1.40 1.40
758 A125 60c Basketball 6.75 6.00
Nos. 755-758 (4) 10.00 8.65

Souvenir Sheet
759 A125 $2 Sailing 9.50 9.50

Intl. Conference on Nutrition — A126

15c, Drought-affected earth, starving child. 55c, Hand holding plant, stalks of grain.

Perf. 14½x13
1992, Aug. 11 Litho. Wmk. 373
760 A126 15c multicolored 1.40 1.10
761 A126 55c multicolored 3.00 2.75

Discovery of America Type
Souvenir Sheet
Perf. 14x13½
1992, Oct. 12 Litho. Wmk. 384
762 A106 $2 Coming ashore 7.50 7.50

Christmas A127

15c, The Annunciation. 55c, Nativity Scene. 60c, Angel, shepherds. 70c, The Magi.

1992, Nov. 2 Wmk. 373 *Perf. 14*
763 A127 15c multicolored .80 .30
764 A127 55c multicolored 2.00 .90
765 A127 60c multicolored 2.25 1.25
766 A127 70c multicolored 2.50 2.50
a. Souvenir sheet of 4, #763-766 9.00 9.00
Nos. 763-766 (4) 7.55 4.95

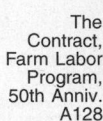

The Contract, Farm Labor Program, 50th Anniv. A128

Bahamian, American flags and: 15c, Silhouette of worker's head. 55c, Onions. 60c, Citrus fruits. 70c, Apples.

Perf. 14x14½
1993, Mar. 16 Litho. Wmk. 384
767 A128 15c multicolored 1.90 .75
768 A128 55c multicolored 2.75 1.50
769 A128 60c multicolored 2.75 2.50
770 A128 70c multicolored 3.50 3.50
Nos. 767-770 (4) 10.90 8.25

Royal Air Force, 75th Anniv.
Common Design Type

Designs: 15c, Westland Wapiti. 40c, Gloster Gladiator. 55c, DeHavilland Vampire. 70c, English Electric Lightning.

No. 775a, Avro Shackleton. b, Fairey Battle. c, Douglas Boston. d, DeHavilland DH9a.

Wmk. 373
1993, Apr. 1 Litho. *Perf. 14*
771 CD350 15c multicolored 1.90 .85
772 CD350 40c multicolored 2.75 1.60
773 CD350 55c multicolored 3.25 2.25
774 CD350 70c multicolored 4.25 4.25
Nos. 771-774 (4) 12.15 8.95

Souvenir Sheet of 4
775 CD350 60c #a.-d. 12.50 12.50

Coronation of Queen Elizabeth II, 40th Anniv. A129

Wmk. 373
1993, June 2 Litho. *Perf. 13½*
776 A129 15c Nos. 424-425 .90 .65
777 A129 55c No. 157 2.25 2.25
778 A129 60c Nos. 402-403 2.40 2.40
779 A129 70c Nos. 404-405 2.75 2.75
Nos. 776-779 (4) 8.30 8.05

A130

Natl. symbols: 15c, Lignum vitae. 55c, Yellow elder. 60c, Blue marlin. 70c, Flamingo.

1993, July 8 Litho. *Perf. 14*
780 A130 15c multicolored .60 .35
781 A130 55c multicolored 1.75 1.75
782 A130 60c multicolored 2.10 2.10
783 A130 70c multicolored 3.00 3.00
Nos. 780-783 (4) 7.45 7.20

Independence, 20th anniv.

A131

Wildflowers: 15c, Cordia. 55c, Seaside morning glory. 60c, Poinciana. 70c, Spider lily.

1993, Sept. 8 Litho. *Perf. 14*
784 A131 15c multicolored 1.60 .55
785 A131 55c multicolored 3.75 1.60
786 A131 60c multicolored 4.00 2.50
787 A131 70c multicolored 4.25 4.25
Nos. 784-787 (4) 13.60 8.90

Christmas A132

15c, Angel, Mary. 55c, Shepherds, angel. 60c, Holy family. 70c, Three wise men. $1, Madonna and Child.

1993, Nov. 1 Litho. *Perf. 14*
788 A132 15c multi 1.25 .55
789 A132 55c multi 2.75 1.90
790 A132 60c multi 3.50 3.25
791 A132 70c multi 4.00 4.00
Nos. 788-791 (4) 11.50 9.70

Souvenir Sheet
792 A132 $1 multi 8.50 8.50

Intl. Year of the Family A133

55c, Children studying. 60c, Son, father fishing. 70c, Children, grandmother.

Wmk. 384
1994, Feb. 18 Litho. *Perf. 13½*
793 A133 15c shown 1.25 .45
794 A133 55c multi 2.50 1.40
795 A133 60c multi 3.50 2.10
796 A133 70c multi 4.25 *4.50*
Nos. 793-796 (4) 11.50 8.45

Hong Kong '94.

Royal Visit — A134

Designs: 15c, Bahamas, United Kingdom flags. 55c, Royal Yacht Britannia. 60c, Queen Elizabeth II. 70c, Prince Philip, Queen.

Perf. 14x13½
1994, Mar. 7 Wmk. 373
797 A134 15c multicolored 1.10 .35
798 A134 55c multicolored 3.25 1.60
799 A134 60c multicolored 3.25 1.90
800 A134 70c multicolored 3.25 3.25
Nos. 797-800 (4) 10.85 7.10

Natl. Family Island Regatta, 40th Anniv. A135

Designs: 15c, 55c, 60c, 70c, Various sailing boats at sea. $2, Beached yacht, vert.

Wmk. 373
1994, Apr. 27 Litho. *Perf. 14*
801 A135 15c multicolored 1.00 .35
802 A135 55c multicolored 2.25 1.10
803 A135 60c multicolored 2.25 2.25
804 A135 70c multicolored 4.00 4.00
Nos. 801-804 (4) 9.50 7.70

Souvenir Sheet
805 A135 $2 multicolored 11.00 11.00

Intl. Olympic Committee, Cent. — A136

Flag, Olympic rings, and: 15c, Nos. 276-279, horiz. 55c, Nos. 388-391. 60c, Nos. 559-562, horiz. 70c, Nos. 755-758.

Wmk. 373

1994, May 31 Litho. *Perf. 14*

806	A136	15c multicolored	2.00	.60
807	A136	55c multicolored	3.25	1.40
808	A136	60c multicolored	3.25	3.25
809	A136	70c multicolored	3.75	3.75
		Nos. 806-809 (4)	12.25	9.00

Souvenir Sheet

First Recipients of the Order of the Caribbean Community — A137

Perf. 13x14

1994, July 5 Litho. Wmk. 373

810	A137	$2 multicolored	8.00	8.00

A138

Butterfly, flower: 15c, Canna skipper, canna. 55c, Cloudless sulphur, cassia. 60c, White peacock, passion flower. 70c, Devillier's swallowtail, calico flower.

1994, Aug. 16 Litho. *Perf. 14*

811	A138	15c multicolored	1.60	.40
812	A138	55c multicolored	3.00	1.25
813	A138	60c multicolored	3.00	3.00
814	A138	70c multicolored	3.50	3.50
		Nos. 811-814 (4)	11.10	8.15

A139

Marine Life: a, Cuban hogfish, Spanish hogfish. b, Tomate, squirrelfish. c, French angelfish. d, Queen angelfish. e, Rock beauty.
$2, Rock beauty, queen angelfish.

1994, Sept. 13 *Perf. 13½x14*

815	A139	40c Strip of 5, #a.-e.	8.25	8.25

Souvenir Sheet

816	A139	$2 multicolored	9.00	9.00

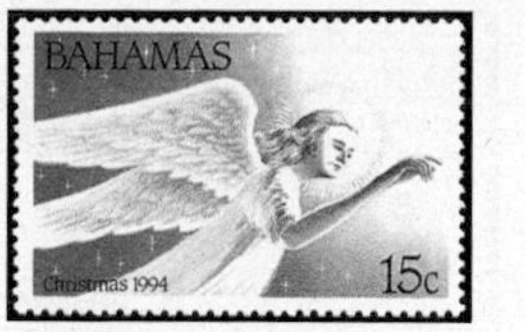

Christmas — A140

Wmk. 384

1994, Oct. 31 Litho. *Perf. 14*

817	A140	15c Angel	.45	.30
818	A140	55c Holy family	1.40	1.40
819	A140	60c Shepherds	1.60	1.60
820	A140	70c Magi	2.10	2.10
		Nos. 817-820 (4)	5.55	5.40

Souvenir Sheet

821	A140	$2 Christ Child, vert.	6.00	6.00

College of the Bahamas, 20th Anniv. — A141

Designs: 15c, Lion. 70c, Queen Elizabeth II, college facade.

Wmk. 373

1995, Feb. 8 Litho. *Perf. 14*

822	A141	15c multicolored	.35	.35
823	A141	70c multicolored	2.10	2.10

End of World War II, 50th Anniv.

Common Design Types

Designs: 15c, Bahamian soldiers on parade. 55c, Neutrality patrols flown by PBY-5A flying boats. 60c, Bahamian women in all three services. 70c, B-24 Liberator, Bahamians in RAF.
$2, Reverse of War Medal 1939-45.

Wmk. 373

1995, May 8 Litho. *Perf. 13½*

824	CD351	15c multicolored	1.25	.45
825	CD351	55c multicolored	3.75	1.25
826	CD351	60c multicolored	3.75	3.75
827	CD351	70c multicolored	4.75	4.75
		Nos. 824-827 (4)	13.50	10.20

Souvenir Sheet

Perf. 14

828	CD352	$2 multicolored	8.50	8.50

Kirtland's Warbler — A142

No. 829, 15c, Female at nest. No. 829A, 15c Singing male. No. 829B, 25c, Female feeding young. No. 829C, 25c, Immature bird feeding, prior to migration.
$2, Female on branch overlooking lake.

Wmk. 373

1995, June 7 Litho. *Perf. 13½*

829	A142	15c multi	1.25	1.25
829A	A142	15c multi	1.25	1.25
829B	A142	25c multi	1.25	1.25
829C	A142	25c multi	1.25	1.25
d.		Strip of 4, as #829-829C, wmk. inverted	5.25	5.25

Souvenir Sheet

Perf. 13

830	A142	$2 multicolored	10.00	10.00

World Wildlife Fund (No. 829).
Nos. 829-829C were printed both in individual sheets of 50, with watermark upright, and in sheets of 16, containing four No. 829d.
No. 830 contains one 42x28mm stamp and has continuous design.

Tourism A143

Designs: 15c, Eleuthera Cliffs. 55c, Clarence Town, Long Island. 60c, Albert Lowe Museum. 70c, Yachting.

Wmk. 384

1995, July 18 Litho. *Perf. 14½*

831	A143	15c multicolored	1.10	.60
832	A143	55c multicolored	2.75	1.25
833	A143	60c multicolored	3.25	3.25
834	A143	70c multicolored	4.00	4.00
		Nos. 831-834 (4)	11.10	9.10

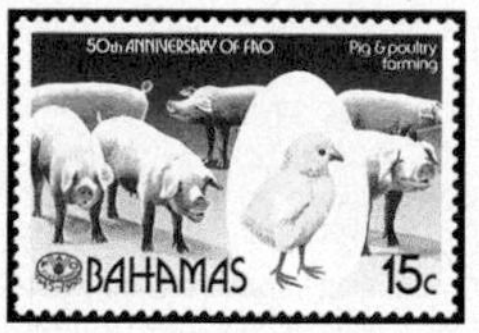

FAO, 50th Anniv. A144

Designs: 15c, Pig, poultry farming. 55c, Horticultural methods. 60c, Healthy eating. 70c, Sustainable fishing.

Perf. 13½x13

1995, Sept. 5 Litho. Wmk. 373

835	A144	15c multicolored	1.00	.35
836	A144	55c multicolored	2.00	1.00
837	A144	60c multicolored	2.50	2.50
838	A144	70c multicolored	3.50	3.50
		Nos. 835-838 (4)	9.00	7.35

UN, 50th Anniv.

Common Design Type

Designs: 15c, Sikorsky S-55, UNEF, Sinai, 1957. 55c, Ferret armored car, UNEF, Sinai, 1957. 60c, Fokker F-27, UNAMIC/UNTAC, Cambodia, 1991-93. 70c, Lockheed Hercules.

Wmk. 373

1995, Oct. 25 Litho. *Perf. 14*

839	CD353	15c multicolored	.90	.40
840	CD353	55c multicolored	2.00	1.75
841	CD353	60c multicolored	2.00	2.00
842	CD353	70c multicolored	2.25	2.25
		Nos. 839-842 (4)	7.15	6.40

Christmas — A145

Designs: 15c, St. Agnes Anglican Church. 55c, Church of God. 60c, Sacred Heart Roman Catholic Church. 70c, Salem Union Baptist Church.

1995, Nov. 17

843	A145	15c multicolored	.50	.40
844	A145	55c multicolored	1.75	1.75
845	A145	60c multicolored	1.75	1.75
846	A145	70c multicolored	2.10	*2.40*
		Nos. 843-846 (4)	6.10	6.30

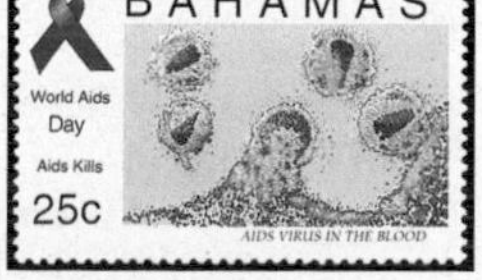

World AIDS Day A146

1995, Dec. 1

847	A146	25c Virus in blood	.90	.90
848	A146	70c Scientific research	2.00	2.00

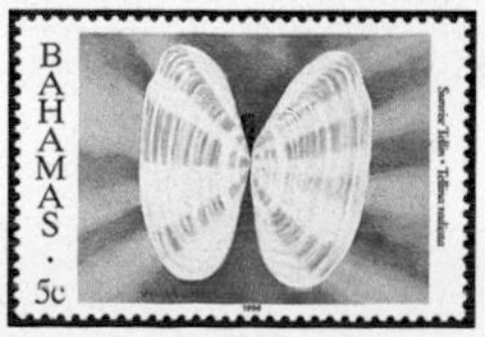

Shells A147

Designs: 5c, Sunrise tellin. 10c, Queen conch. 15c, Angular triton. 20c, True tulip. 25c, Reticulated cowrie-helmet. 30c, Sand dollar. 40c, Lace short-frond murex. 45c, Inflated sea biscuit. 50c, West Indian top shell (magpie). 55c, Spiny oyster. 60c, King helmet. 70c, Lion's paw. $1, Crown cone. $2, Atlantic partridge tun. $5, Wide-mouthed purpura. $10, Triton's trumpet.

Wmk. 373 sideways

1996 Litho. *Perf. 14*

849	A147	5c multicolored	.25	.25
850	A147	10c multicolored	.30	.25
851	A147	15c multicolored	.40	.35
852	A147	20c multicolored	.65	.45
853	A147	25c multicolored	.70	.50
854	A147	30c multicolored	2.10	.55
855	A147	40c multicolored	1.25	.55
856	A147	45c multicolored	2.75	.60
857	A147	50c multicolored	1.40	.60
858	A147	55c multicolored	3.25	.75
859	A147	60c multicolored	1.75	.75
860	A147	70c multicolored	2.10	.95
a.		Souvenir sheet of 1	4.00	4.00
861	A147	$1 multicolored	3.50	1.00
a.		Souvenir sheet of 1	4.00	4.00
862	A147	$2 multicolored	7.25	1.90
863	A147	$5 multicolored	14.50	4.00
864	A147	$10 multicolored	29.00	9.50
		Nos. 849-864 (16)	71.15	22.95

Issued: $10, 7/1; others, 1/2.
No. 860a issued 6/20/97 for return of Hong Kong to China.
No. 861a issued 2/3/97 for Hong Kong '97.
See Nos. 962-964.

1997 Wmk. 373 upright

Inscribed "1997"

849b	A147	5c multicolored	1.50	*1.20*
850b	A147	10c multicolored	.90	*.80*
851b	A147	15c multicolored	1.50	.30
852b	A147	20c multicolored	1.50	.55
853b	A147	25c multicolored	1.75	.50
854b	A147	30c multicolored	1.75	.65
855b	A147	40c multicolored	2.75	.85
856b	A147	45c multicolored	2.50	1.25
857b	A147	50c multicolored	2.75	1.00
858b	A147	55c multicolored	2.75	1.25
859b	A147	60c multicolored	3.75	1.25
860b	A147	70c multicolored	3.75	1.90
861b	A147	$1 multicolored	5.00	2.50
862b	A147	$2 multicolored	9.00	6.25
863b	A147	$5 multicolored	16.00	*13.00*
864b	A147	$10 multicolored	30.00	*24.00*
		Nos. 849b-864b (16)	87.15	*57.25*

Issued: Nos. 861b-864b, 7/1; Nos. 849b-860b, 9/22.

1999 Inscribed "1999"

849c	A147	5c multicolored	1.50	*1.20*
850c	A147	10c multicolored	.90	*.80*
851c	A147	15c multicolored	1.50	.30
852c	A147	20c multicolored	1.50	.55
853c	A147	25c multicolored	1.75	.50
855c	A147	40c multicolored	2.75	.85
857c	A147	50c multicolored	2.75	1.00
859c	A147	60c multicolored	3.75	1.25
860c	A147	70c multicolored	3.75	1.90
861c	A147	$1 multicolored	5.00	2.50
862c	A147	$2 multicolored	9.00	6.25
863c	A147	$5 multicolored	16.00	*13.00*
864c	A147	$10 multicolored	30.00	*24.00*
		Nos. 849c-864c (13)	80.15	*54.10*

2000 Inscribed "2000"

849d	A147	5c multicolored	1.10	*1.20*
851d	A147	15c multicolored	1.10	.30
853d	A147	25c multicolored	1.35	.50
857d	A147	50c multicolored	2.25	1.00
859d	A147	60c multicolored	—	—
860d	A147	70c multicolored	3.00	1.90
862d	A147	$2 multicolored	7.00	6.25
		Nos. 849d-862d (6)	15.80	*11.15*

2001 Inscribed "2001"

851e	A147	15c multicolored	1.50	.30
853e	A147	25c multicolored	1.75	.50
857e	A147	50c multicolored	2.75	1.00
861e	A147	$1 multicolored	5.00	2.50
862e	A147	$2 multicolored	9.00	6.25
		Nos. 851e-862e (5)	20.00	10.55

Radio, Cent. A148

Designs: 15c, East Goodwin Lightship, Marconi apparatus suspended from masthead. 55c, Arrest of Dr. Crippen, newspaper headline telling of wireless message from SS Montrose. 60c, SS Philadelphia, first readable transatlantic messages. 70c, Yacht Elettra, Guglielmo Marconi.
$2, SS Titantic, SS Carpathia.

1996, Feb. 4 Litho. *Perf. 13½*

865	A148	15c multicolored	2.00	.50
866	A148	55c multicolored	2.75	1.50
867	A148	60c multicolored	3.00	2.75
868	A148	70c multicolored	3.25	3.75
		Nos. 865-868 (4)	11.00	8.50

Souvenir Sheet

869	A148	$2 multicolored	10.00	10.00

A149

Wmk. 384

1996, June 25 Litho. *Perf. 13½*

870	A149	15c Swimming	.60	.40
871	A149	55c Track	1.25	1.00
872	A149	60c Basketball	2.50	1.75
873	A149	70c Long jump	1.90	*2.40*
		Nos. 870-873 (4)	6.25	5.55

Souvenir Sheet

874	A149	$2 Javelin, 1896	6.00	6.00

Modern Olympic Games, cent.

A150

Reptiles: 15c, Green anole. 55c, Fowl snake. 60c, Inagua freshwater turtle. 70c, Acklins rock iguana.

Wmk. 384

1996, Sept. 3 Litho. *Perf. 14*

875	A150	15c multicolored	.90	.90
876	A150	55c multicolored	1.75	1.75
877	A150	60c multicolored	2.50	2.50
878	A150	70c multicolored	3.00	3.00
a.		Souvenir sheet, #875-878	8.25	8.25
		Nos. 875-878 (4)	8.15	8.15

Environmental protection.

Christmas A151

Designs: 15c, Angel Gabriel and Mary. 55c, Mary and Joseph. 60c, Shepherds. 70c, Magi. $2, Presentation at the Temple.

Wmk. 373

1996, Nov. 4 Litho. *Perf. 14*

879	A151	15c multicolored	1.10	.40
880	A151	55c multicolored	2.75	.90
881	A151	60c multicolored	3.00	1.40
882	A151	70c multicolored	3.25	3.25
		Nos. 879-882 (4)	10.10	5.95

Souvenir Sheet

883	A151	$2 multicolored	5.50	5.50

Archives Dept., 25th Anniv. — A152

Perf. 14½x14

1996, Dec. 9 Litho. Wmk. 384

884	A152	55c shown	2.25	2.25

Souvenir Sheet

Perf. 14x13½

885	A152	$2 Building, horiz.	6.50	6.50

Queen Elizabeth II and Prince Philip, 50th Wedding Anniv. — A153

Designs: No. 886, Queen. No. 887, Grenadier Guards. No. 888, Prince Philip. No. 889, Queen reviewing Grenadier Guards. No. 890, Prince holding trophy, Queen opening jewel box. No. 891, Prince on polo pony.

$2, Queen, Prince riding in open carriage, horiz.

Wmk. 373

1997, July 9 Litho. *Perf. 13*

886	A153	50c multicolored	2.00	2.00
887	A153	50c multicolored	2.00	2.00
a.		Pair, #886-887	4.25	4.25
888	A153	60c multicolored	2.40	2.40
889	A153	60c multicolored	2.40	2.40
a.		Pair, #888-889	5.00	5.00
890	A153	70c multicolored	2.50	2.50
891	A153	70c multicolored	2.50	2.50
a.		Pair, #890-891	5.25	5.25
		Nos. 886-891 (6)	13.80	13.80

Souvenir Sheet

892	A153	$2 multicolored	8.00	8.00

Intl. Year of the Reefs A154

Various pictures of marine life and coral.

Perf. 14x14½

1997, Sept. 3 Litho. Wmk. 384

893	A154	15c multicolored	1.25	.55
894	A154	55c multicolored	2.75	1.25
895	A154	60c multicolored	2.75	1.75
896	A154	70c multicolored	3.25	3.25
		Nos. 893-896 (4)	10.00	6.80

Christmas — A155

15c, Angel. 55c, Madonna & Child. 60c, Shepherd. 70c, Magi.

$2, Christ Child.

Perf. 13x13½

1997, Oct. 6 Litho. Wmk. 373

897	A155	15c multi	1.25	.30
898	A155	55c multi	2.50	.95
899	A155	60c multi	2.75	1.60
900	A155	70c multi	3.50	3.50
		Nos. 897-900 (4)	10.00	6.35

Souvenir Sheet

901	A155	$2 multi	10.00	10.00

Diana, Princess of Wales (1961-97)

Common Design Type

Various portraits: 902: a, 55c. b, 60c. c, 70c.

Perf. 14½x14

1998, Mar. 31 Litho. Wmk. 373

901A	CD355	15c multicolored	.80	.80

Sheet of 4

902	CD355	#a.-c., 901A	4.50	4.50

Organization of American States, 50th Anniv. — A156

Map of North and South America, national flags, and: 15c, "New Vision" paper. 55c, Building.

1998, Apr. 14 *Perf. 13½x14*

903	A156	15c multicolored	.40	.40
904	A156	55c multicolored	2.00	2.00

University of the West Indies, 50th Anniv. — A157

1998, Apr. 14

905	A157	55c multicolored	2.00	2.00

Universal Declaration of Human Rights, 50th Anniv. — A158

1998, Apr. 14

906	A158	55c multicolored	2.25	2.25

Royal Air Force, 80th Anniv.

Common Design Type of 1993 Re-Inscribed

Designs: 15c, Handley Page Hyderabad. 55c, Hawker Demon. 60c, Gloster Meteor F.8. 70c, Lockheed Neptune MR.1.

No. 911: a, Sopwith Camel. b, Short 184. c, Supermarine Spitfire PR.19. d, North American Mitchell III.

1998, Apr. 1

907	CD350	15c multicolored	.80	.55
908	CD350	55c multicolored	1.80	1.10
909	CD350	60c multicolored	1.75	1.75
910	CD350	70c multicolored	2.25	2.25
		Nos. 907-910 (4)	6.60	5.65

Souvenir Sheet

911	CD350	50c Sheet of 4, #a.-d.	7.00	7.00

Independence, 25th Anniv. — A159

15c, Supreme Court Building. 55c, Nassau Library. 60c, Government House. 70c, Gregory Arch.

$2, Exuma-Family Island Regatta, George Town.

Wmk. 373

1998, July 10 Litho. *Perf. 13½*

912	A159	15c multicolored	1.00	.75
913	A159	55c multicolored	2.10	1.50
914	A159	60c multicolored	2.25	2.25
915	A159	70c multicolored	2.75	2.75
		Nos. 912-915 (4)	8.10	7.25

Souvenir Sheet

916	A159	$2 multicolored	7.00	7.00

Castaway Cay, Disney Cruise Lines A160

1998, Aug. 1 *Perf. 14*

917	A160	55c Daytime	2.25	2.25
918	A160	55c Nighttime	2.25	2.25
a.		Pair, #917-918	4.50	4.50
b.		Bklt. pane, 5 each #917-918	22.50	
		Complete booklet, #918b	25.00	

MS Ryndam, Half Moon Cay — A161

1998, Aug. 19 *Perf. 13½x13*

919	A161	55c multicolored	5.25	2.50

Roses A162

Wmk. 373

1998, Sept. 8 Litho. *Perf. 14*

920	A162	55c Yellow cream	1.90	1.90
921	A162	55c Big red	1.90	1.90
922	A162	55c Seven sisters	1.90	1.90
923	A162	55c Barrel pink	1.90	1.90
924	A162	55c Island beauty	1.90	1.90
a.		Bklt. pane, 2 each #920-924	19.00	
		Complete booklet, #924a	19.00	
		Nos. 920-924 (5)	9.50	9.50

Souvenir Sheet

925	A162	55c like #924	2.75	2.75

No. 925 has parts of other roses extending into center left and upper left area of stamp.

Intl. Year of the Ocean — A163

Wmk. 373

1998, Nov. 24 Litho. *Perf. 14*

926	A163	15c Killer whale	1.25	.75
927	A163	55c Tropical fish	2.00	2.00

Christmas A164

15c, The Annunciation. 55c, Shepherds, star. 60c, Magi. 70c, Flight into Egypt.

$2, Nativity scene.

1998, Dec. 11

928	A164	15c multicolored	.75	.40
929	A164	55c multicolored	1.60	.70
930	A164	60c multicolored	1.90	1.60
931	A164	70c multicolored	2.25	2.25
		Nos. 928-931 (4)	6.50	4.95

Souvenir Sheet

932	A164	$2 multicolored	6.00	6.00

Timothy Gibson, Composer of Natl. Anthem A165

1998 Litho. Wmk. 373 *Perf. 13½*
933 A165 60c multicolored 1.75 1.75

Independence, 25th anniv.

National Trust, 40th Anniv. — A166

Flamingos on the beach: a, One chick, adults. b, Two chicks, adults. c, One chick spreading wings, adults. d, Six in flight over others. e, Three ascending into flight.

Wmk. 384
1999, Feb. 9 Litho. *Perf. 14*
934 A166 55c Strip of 5, #a.-e. 9.25 9.25

No. 934 is a continuous design.
See Nos. 940, 961, 969.

Australia '99, World Stamp Expo A167

Maritime history: 15c, Arawak Indians. 55c, Santa Maria. 60c, Blackbeard's ship, Queen Anne's Revenge. 70c, Banshee running Union blockade, US Civil War.
$2, American invasion of Fort Nassau, 1776.

Perf. 14x14½
1999, Mar. 9 Wmk. 373
935 A167 15c multicolored .50 .45
936 A167 55c multicolored 1.90 1.60
937 A167 60c multicolored 2.50 1.90
938 A167 70c multicolored 2.75 2.75
Nos. 935-938 (4) 7.65 6.70

Souvenir Sheet
939 A167 $2 multicolored 7.00 7.00

National Trust, 40th Anniv. Type

Marine life: a, Dolphin. b, Large fish, four in background. c, Several fish, coral. d, Turtle, fish, coral. e, Lobster, coral.

Wmk. 384
1999, Apr. 6 Litho. *Perf. 14*
940 A166 55c Strip of 5, #a.-e. 11.00 11.00

No. 940 is a continuous design.

Bahamas Historical Society, 40th Anniv. A168

1999, June 9 Litho. *Perf. 13*
941 A168 $1 multicolored 2.00 2.00

1st Manned Moon Landing, 30th Anniv.
Common Design Type

15c, Ascent module in assembly area. 65c, Apollo command & service module. 70c, Descent stage. 80c, Module turns to dock with service module.
$2, Looking at earth from moon.

Perf. 14x13¾
1999, July 20 Litho. Wmk. 384
942 CD357 15c multicolored .80 .80
943 CD357 65c multicolored 2.10 2.10
944 CD357 70c multicolored 2.10 2.10
945 CD357 80c multicolored 2.10 2.10
Nos. 942-945 (4) 7.10 7.10

Souvenir Sheet
Perf. 14
946 CD357 $2 multicolored 7.00 7.00

No. 946 contains one 40mm circular stamp 40mm.

UPU, 125th Anniv. A170

15c, Mail Packet Delaware. 65c, S.S. Atlantis. 70c, M.V. Queen of Bermuda. 80c, USS Saufley.

Wmk. 384
1999, Aug. 17 Litho. *Perf. 13½*
947 A170 15c multi 1.10 .65
948 A170 65c multi 2.50 1.75
949 A170 70c multi 3.00 2.00
950 A170 80c multi 3.25 3.25
Nos. 947-950 (4) 9.85 7.65

Queen Mother's Century
Common Design Type

Queen Mother: 15c, At Hertfordshire Hospital. 65c, With Princess Elizabeth. 70c, With Prince Andrew. 80c, With Irish Guards.
$2, With brother David and 1966 British World Cup team members.

Wmk. 373
1999, Aug. Litho. *Perf. 13½*
951 CD358 15c multicolored .75 .50
952 CD358 65c multicolored 2.25 1.40
953 CD358 70c multicolored 2.25 2.25
954 CD358 80c multicolored 2.25 2.25
Nos. 951-954 (4) 7.50 6.40

Souvenir Sheet
955 CD358 $2 multicolored 6.25 6.25

Environmental Protection — A171

15c, Turtle pond. 65c, Green turtles, limestone cliffs. 70c, Barracudas. 80c, Sea fans on reef.
$2, Atlantic bottlenose dolphin.

Wmk. 373
1999, Sept. 21 Litho. *Perf. 13¾*
956 A171 15c multicolored .75 .50
957 A171 65c multicolored 1.75 1.50
958 A171 70c multicolored 2.25 2.25
959 A171 80c multicolored 2.50 2.50
Nos. 956-959 (4) 7.25 6.75

Souvenir Sheet
960 A171 $2 multicolored 7.00 7.00

National Trust Type of 1999

Designs: a, Tern. b, Heron, c, Hummingbird, orange flower. d, Duck. e, Parrot.

Wmk. 384
1999, Oct. 8 Litho. *Perf. 14¼*
961 A166 65c Strip of 5, #a.-e. 11.00 11.00

Shell Type of 1996
1999 Litho. Wmk. 373 *Perf. 14*
962 A147 35c Like #854 1.50 1.50
963 A147 65c Like #856 6.00 2.75
a. Inscribed "2001" — —
964 A147 80c Like #858 3.75 3.75
Nos. 962-964 (3) 11.25 8.00

Christmas A172

People in various Junkanoo costumes.

Perf. 14½x14¼
1999, Oct. 25 Litho. Wmk. 373
965 A172 15c multicolored .50 .50
966 A172 65c multicolored 1.25 1.25
967 A172 70c multicolored 2.25 2.25
968 A172 80c multicolored 2.50 2.50
Nos. 965-968 (4) 6.50 6.50

National Trust Type of 1999

Designs: a, Orchid. b, Rodent. c, Hummingbird, red flowers. d, Lizard. e, Hibiscus.

Wmk. 384
1999, Oct. 8 Litho. *Perf. 14¼*
969 A166 65c Strip of 5, #a.-e. 13.50 13.50

Historic Fishing Villages A173

15c, New Plymouth. 65c, Cherokee Sound. 70c, Hope Town. 80c, Spanish Wells.

Perf. 13¼x13
2000, Jan. 25 Litho. Wmk. 373
970 A173 15c multi 1.00 .65
971 A173 65c multi 2.40 1.50
972 A173 70c multi 3.25 3.25
973 A173 80c multi 3.75 3.75
Nos. 970-973 (4) 10.40 9.15

Souvenir Sheet

1999 World Champions in Women's 4x100-Meter Relay Race — A174

Wmk. 373
2000, Feb. 22 Litho. *Perf. 14½*
974 A174 $2 multi 4.50 4.50

Bush Medicine Plants A175

Perf. 14¼x14½
2000, May 2 Litho. Wmk. 373
975 A175 15c Prickly pear .65 .65
976 A175 65c Buttercup 1.50 1.50
977 A175 70c Shepherd's needle 1.90 1.90
978 A175 80c Five fingers 2.25 2.25
Nos. 975-978 (4) 6.30 6.30

See Nos. 1040-1043, 1076-1079, 1131-1134.

The Stamp Show 2000, London A176

Battle of Britain, 60th anniv.: 15c, Quick turnaround, rearm and refuel. 65c, Squadron leader R. Stanford-Tuck in Hurricane 1. 70c, Melee. 80c, Tally ho.
$2, Airplanes in flight.

2000, May 22 *Perf. 13¼x13½*
979 A176 15c multi 1.00 .75
980 A176 65c multi 2.10 2.10
981 A176 70c multi 2.25 2.25
982 A176 80c multi 2.25 2.25
Nos. 979-982 (4) 7.60 7.35

Souvenir Sheet
983 A176 $2 multi 6.75 6.75

Souvenir Sheet

Bahamas Cooperatives — A177

2000, June 27 Litho. *Perf. 14*
984 A177 $2 multi 6.00 6.00

2000 Summer Olympics, Sydney A178

15c, Swimming. 65c, Triple jump. 70c, Women's 4x100 meter relay. 80c, Yachting.

2000, July 17 *Perf. 14¼x14½*
985-988 A178 Set of 4 5.75 5.75

Christmas A179

Orchids: 15c, Cockle-shell orchid. 65c, Pleated encyclia. 70c, Pine pink. 80c, Graceful encyclia.

2000, Nov. 7 *Perf. 14½x14¼*
989-992 A179 Set of 4 7.75 7.75

Bahamas Humane Society, 76th Anniv. A180

Designs: 15c, Education. 65c, Fund raising. 70c, Veterinary care. 80c, Animal rescue.

Wmk. 373
2000, Dec. 12 Litho. *Perf. 14*
993-996 A180 Set of 4 10.00 10.00

Early Settlements A181

Designs: 15c, Meadow St., Inagua. 65c, Bain Town. 70c, Hope Town, Abaco. 80c, The Blue Hills.

Wmk. 373
2001, Feb. 6 Litho. *Perf. 14¼*
997-1000 A181 Set of 4 6.75 6.75

Sir Lynden Pindling (1930-2000), Prime Minister — A182

Pindling and: 15c, Microphone. 65c, Flag.

2001, Mar. 22 ***Perf. 14½x14¼***

1001-1002	A182	Set of 2	2.25	2.25
1001a		Inscribed "10th July, 1973"	1.25	1.25

No. 1001 is inscribed "10th July, 1972." Issued: No. 1001a, 8/6/01.

Edible Wild Fruits A183

Designs: 15c, Cocoplum. 65c, Guana berry. 70c, Mastic. 80c, Seagrape.

2001, May 15 ***Perf. 14¼x14½***

1003-1006	A183	Set of 4	6.50	6.50

Birds and Eggs A184

Designs: 5c, Reddish egret. 10c, Purple gallinule. 15c, Antillean nighthawk. 20c, Wilson's plover. 25c, Killdeer. 30c, Bahama woodstar. 40c, Bahama swallow. 50c, Bahama mockingbird. 60c, Black-cowled oriole. 65c, Great lizard cuckoo. 70c, Audubon's shearwater. 80c, Gray kingbird. $1, Bananaquit. $2, Yellow warbler. $5, Antillean bullfinch. $10, Roseate spoonbill.

Wmk. 373

2001, July 1 **Litho.** ***Perf. 14***

Inscribed "2001"

1007	A184	5c multi		.25	.25
1008	A184	10c multi		.25	.25
1009	A184	15c multi		.50	.50
1010	A184	20c multi		.65	.65
1011	A184	25c multi		.80	.80
1012	A184	30c multi		1.00	1.00
1013	A184	40c multi		1.25	1.25
1014	A184	50c multi		1.60	1.60
1015	A184	60c multi		2.00	2.00
1016	A184	65c multi		2.00	2.00
1017	A184	70c multi		2.25	2.25
1018	A184	80c multi		2.50	2.50
1019	A184	$1 multi		3.25	3.25
1020	A184	$2 multi		6.50	6.50
1021	A184	$5 multi		16.00	16.00
1022	A184	$10 multi		32.50	32.50
	Nos. 1007-1022 (16)			73.30	73.30

Name of Bird in Black

Inscribed "2004"

1022A	A184	25c multi	*7.50*	*7.50*

Issued: Nos. 1007-1022 7/1/01; No. 1022A, 9/04.

Name of bird on No. 1011 is in brown.

2002 **Inscribed "2002"**

1010a	A184	20c multi	.65	.65
1011a	A184	25c multi	.80	.80
1013a	A184	40c multi	1.25	1.25
1022b	A184	$10 multi	32.50	32.50
	Nos. 1010a-1022b (4)		35.20	35.20

2005 **Inscribed "2005"**

1022Aa	A184	25c multi	*8.50*	*8.50*

Visits of Royal Navy Ships A185

HMS: 15c, Norfolk, 1933. 25c, Scarborough, 1930s. 50c, Bahamas, 1944. 65c, Battleaxe, 1979. 70c, Invincible, 1997. 80c, Norfolk, 2000.

Wmk. 373

2001, Aug. 21 **Litho.** ***Perf. 14***

1023-1028	A185	Set of 6	13.00	13.00

Christmas — A186

Paintings: 15c, The Adoration of the Shepherds, by Peter Paul Rubens. 65c, Adoration of the Magi, by Rubens and Anthony Van Dyck. 70c, The Holy Virgin in the Wreath of Flowers, by Rubens and Jan Breughel. 80c, The Holy Virgin Adored by Angels, by Rubens.

2001, Nov. 6

1029-1032	A186	Set of 4	7.00	7.00

Reign Of Queen Elizabeth II, 50th Anniv. Issue

Common Design Type

Designs: Nos. 1033, 1037a, 15c, Princess Elizabeth, 1946. Nos. 1034, 1037b, 65c, In 1992. Nos. 1035, 1037c, 70c, With Prince Edward, 1965. Nos. 1036, 1037d, 80c, In 1996. No. 1037e, $2, 1955 portrait by Annigoni (38x50mm).

Perf. 14¼x14½, 13¾ (#1037e)

2002, Feb. 6 **Litho.** **Wmk. 373**

With Gold Frames

1033	CD360	15c multicolored	.50	.50
1034	CD360	65c multicolored	1.00	1.00
1035	CD360	70c multicolored	1.75	1.75
1036	CD360	80c multicolored	2.00	2.00
	Nos. 1033-1036 (4)		5.25	5.25

Souvenir Sheet

Without Gold Frames

1037	CD360	Sheet of 5, #a-e	10.00	10.00

Souvenir Sheet

Avard Moncur, Runner — A187

Perf. 14x13¾

2002, Apr. 16 **Litho.** **Wmk. 373**

1038	A187	$2 multi	5.25	5.25

In Remembrance of Sept. 11, 2001 Terrorist Attacks — A188

Wmk. 373

2002, May 14 **Litho.** ***Perf. 13¾***

1039	A188	$1 multi	4.50	4.50

Printed in sheets of four.

Bush Medicine Plants Type of 2000

Designs: 15c, Wild sage (lantana). 65c, Seaside maho. 70c, Sea ox-eye. 80c, Mexican poppy thistle.

Perf. 14¼x14½

2002, July 2 **Litho.** **Wmk. 373**

1040-1043	A175	Set of 4	7.50	7.50

Queen Mother Elizabeth (1900-2002)

Common Design Type

Designs: 15c, Wearing hat and maple leaf brooch. 65c, Wearing black hat.

No. 1046: a, 70c, Wearing flowered hat. b, 80c, Wearing light blue hat.

Wmk. 373

2002, Aug. 5 **Litho.** ***Perf. 14¼***

With Purple Frames

1044	CD361	15c multicolored	.50	.50
1045	CD361	65c multicolored	2.60	2.60

Souvenir Sheet

Without Purple Frames

Perf. 14½x14¼

1046	CD361	Sheet of 2, #a-b	6.00	6.00

Flora and Fauna — A189

Plates from *The Natural History of Carolina, Florida and the Bahama Islands,* by Mark Catesby: 15c, Rice birds and rice. 25c, Alligator and red mangrove. 50c, Parrotfish. 65c, Ilatehera duck and sea oxeye. 70c, Flamingo and gorgonian coral. 80c, Crested bittern and inkberry.

Wmk. 373

2002, Oct. 1 **Litho.** ***Perf. 14¼***

1047-1052	A189	Set of 6	11.00	11.00

Christmas A190

Carols: 15c, While Shepherds Watched Their Flocks. 65c, We Three Kings of Orient Are. 70c, Once in Royal David's City. 80c, I Saw Three Ships.

2002, Oct. 29 ***Perf. 14¼x14½***

1053-1056	A190	Set of 4	8.00	8.00

Inagua National Park A191

Photos of various birds by: 15c, Alexander Sprunt IV. 25c, Mrs. Lynn Holowesko. 50c, Bahamas National Trust. 65c, Terra Aqua. 70c, Terra Aqua, diff. 80c, Henry Nixon.

Wmk. 373

2003, Feb. 18 **Litho.** ***Perf. 14***

1057-1062	A191	Set of 6	8.50	8.50

Pirates — A192

Designs: 15c, Capt. Edward Teach ("Blackbeard"). 25c, Capt. John Rackham ("Calico Jack"). 50c, Anne Bonney. 65c, Capt. Woodes Rogers. 70c, Sir John Hawkins. 80c, Capt. Bartholomew Roberts ("Black Bart").

2003, Mar. 18

1063-1068	A192	Set of 6	12.00	12.00

50th Natl. Family Island Regatta — A193

Arms, birds and various sailors and sailboats: 15c, 65c, 70c, 80c.

2003, Apr. 30 ***Perf. 13¾***

1069-1072	A193	Set of 4	8.25	8.25

Coronation of Queen Elizabeth II, 50th Anniv.

Common Design Type

Designs: Nos. 1073, 65c, 1075a, 15c, Queen with crown, orb and scepter. Nos. 1074, 80c, 1075b, 70c, Queen and family on Buckingham Palace balcony.

Perf. 14¼x14½

2003, June 2 **Litho.** **Wmk. 373**

Vignettes Framed, Red Background

1073	CD363	65c multicolored	2.75	2.75
1074	CD363	80c multicolored	3.75	3.75

Souvenir Sheet

Vignettes Without Frame, Purple Panel

1075	CD363	Sheet of 2, #a-b	6.50	6.50

Bush Medicine Plants Type of 2000

Designs: 15c, Asystasia. 65c, Cassia. 70c, Lignum vitae. 80c, Snowberry.

Wmk. 373

2003, July 8 **Litho.** ***Perf. 13¾***

1076-1079	A175	Set of 4	7.25	7.25

Powered Flight, Cent. — A194

Designs: 15c, Piper Cub. 25c, DH Tiger Moth. 50c, Lockheed SR-71A Blackbird. 65c, Supermarine S6B. 70c, North American "Miss America" P-51D Mustang. 80c, Douglas DC3 Dakota.

Perf. 13¼x13¾

2003, Sept. 16 **Litho.**

Stamps + Label

1080-1085	A194	Set of 6	10.50	10.50

Christmas A195

St. Matthew's Anglican Church, Nassau: 15c, Altar. 65c, Altar, horiz. 70c, Exterior, horiz. 80c, Exterior.

Perf. 14¾x14, 14x14¾

2003, Oct. 28 **Litho.** **Wmk. 373**

1086-1089	A195	Set of 4	7.00	7.00

Waters of Life — A196

Paintings by Alton Roland Lowe: 15c, Crawfishin'. 65c, Summer. 70c, The Whelkers. 80c, Annual Visit.

2003, Nov. 24 *Perf. 13¾*
1090-1093 A196 Set of 4 7.25 7.25

Harrold and Wilson Ponds A197

Designs: 15c, Birds on and near dead tree. 25c, Bird in water, bird on branch. 50c, Kayakers. 65c, Birds in water. 70c, Birds in water, diff. 80c, Bird watchers.

Wmk. 373
2004, Feb. 24 Litho. *Perf. 13¾*
1094-1099 A197 Set of 6 9.75 9.75

John Wesley (1703-91), Religious Leader A198

Designs: 15c, Methodist Church, Cupid's Bay, Governor's Harbor. 25c, Methodist Church, Grants Town, Nassau. 50c, Chapel, Marsh Harbor, vert. 65c, Ebeneezer Methodist Church. 70c, Trinity Methodist Church. 80c, Portrait of Wesley, by Antonius Roberts.

Wmk. 373
2004, Apr. 27 Litho. *Perf. 13¾*
1100-1105 A198 Set of 6 9.25 9.25

Royal Horticultural Society, Bicent. — A199

Flowers: 15c, Cattleya orchid. 65c, Hibiscus. 70c, Canna lily. 80c, Thunbergia.

Wmk. 373
2004, May 25 Litho. *Perf. 14*
1106-1109 A199 Set of 4 9.25 9.25
1109a Sheet, 5 each #1106-1109, + 5 labels 47.50 47.50

Lighthouses A200

Designs: 15c, Elbow Reef. 50c, Great Stirrup. 65c, Great Isaac. 70c, Hole in the Wall. 80c, Hog Island.

Wmk. 373
2004, July 7 Litho. *Perf. 14*
1110-1114 A200 Set of 5 10.50 10.50

See Nos. 1154-1158.

2004 Summer Olympics, Athens — A201

Designs: 15c, Boxing. 50c, Swimming. 65c, Tennis. 70c, Track.

Perf. 13½x13¼
2004, Aug. 24 Litho. Wmk. 373
1115-1118 A201 Set of 4 8.75 8.75

Children's Junkanoo and Christmas — A202

Designs: 15c, Anticipation. 25c, First time. 50c, On the move, vert. 65c, I'm ready, vert. 70c, Trumpet player, vert. 80c, Drummer boy, vert.

Wmk. 373
2004, Oct. 26 Litho. *Perf. 14*
1119-1124 A202 Set of 6 8.25 8.25

Merchant Ships A203

Designs: 15c, RMS Mauretania. 25c, MV Adonia. 50c, MS Royal Princess. 65c, SS Queen of Nassau. 70c, RMS Transvaal Castle. 80c, SS Norway.

Wmk. 373
2004, Dec. 7 Litho. *Perf. 13¼*
1125-1130 A203 Set of 6 12.50 12.50

Bush Medicine Plants Type of 2000

Designs: 15c, Aloe. 25c, Red stopper. 50c, Blue flower. 65c, Bay lavender.

2005, Feb. 8 *Perf. 13¾*
1131-1134 A175 Set of 4 4.25 4.25

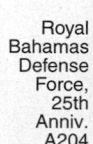

Royal Bahamas Defense Force, 25th Anniv. A204

Designs: 15c, Soliders training in camouflage uniforms. 25c, HMBS Abaco. 50c, HMDS Bahamas. 65c, Six defense force members in various uniforms.

2005, Mar. 29 *Perf. 14*
1135-1138 A204 Set of 4 5.50 5.50

Connections Between Bahamas and Key West, Florida — A205

Paintings by Alton Roland Lowe: 15c, William Curry. 25c, Captain John Bartlum's House, horiz. 50c, Captain John Bartlum. 65c, Captain Tuggy Roberts' House, horiz.

2005, Apr. 26
1139-1142 A205 Set of 4 5.50 5.50

Battle of Trafalgar, Bicent. — A206

Designs: 15c, 1801 RN Pattern Tower Sea Service pistols. 25c, Royal Marine, 1805. 50c, HMS Boreas off Bahamas, 1787, horiz. 65c, The death of Nelson, horiz. 70c, HMS Victory, horiz. 80c, The Achille surrendering to HMS Polyphemus, horiz.

No. 1149: a, Admiral Cuthbert Collingwood. b, HMS Polyphemus.

Wmk. 373, Unwmkd. (70c)
2005, Apr. 29 *Perf. 13¼*
1143-1148 A206 Set of 6 12.00 12.00

Souvenir Sheet
1149 A206 $1 Sheet of 2, #a-b 8.25 8.25

No. 1147 has particles of wood from the HMS Victory embedded in areas covered by a thermographic process that produces a raised, shiny effect.

European Philatelic Cooperation, 50th Anniv. (in 2006) — A207

Flags of Bahamas and European Union, seascape, map of Europe in: 15c, Blue violet 25c, Dull blue green. 50c, Yellow bister. $5, Green.

Unwmk.
2005, June 1 Litho. *Perf. 14*
1150-1153 A207 Set of 4 18.00 18.00
1153a Souvenir sheet, #1150-1153 18.00 18.00

Europa stamps, 50th anniv. (in 2006).

Lighthouses Type of 2004

Designs: 15c, Bird Rock. 50c, Castle Island. 65c, San Salvador. 70c, Great Inagua. 80c, Cay Lobos.

Wmk. 373
2005, July 6 Litho. *Perf. 14*
1154-1158 A200 Set of 5 10.50 10.50

Pope John Paul II (1920-2005) A208

Wmk. 373
2005, Aug. 18 Litho. *Perf. 14*
1159 A208 $1 multi 4.00 4.00

Souvenir Sheet

College of the Bahamas, 30th Anniv. — A209

Wmk. 373
2005, Oct. 18 Litho. *Perf. 14*
1160 A209 $2 multi 7.00 7.00

Christmas — A210

Stories by Hans Christian Andersen (1805-75): 15c, The Little Fir Tree. 25c, The Princess and the Pea. 50c, The Tin Soldier. 65c, Thumbelina.

2005, Nov. 8
1161-1164 A210 Set of 4 5.00 5.00

BirdLife International A211

Various depictions of Bahama nuthatch: 15c, 25c, 50c, 65c, 70c, 80c.

Wmk. 373
2006, Mar. 28 Litho. *Perf. 13¾*
1165-1170 A211 Set of 6 12.00 12.00
1170a Souvenir sheet, #1165-1170 14.00 14.00

Queen Elizabeth II, 80th Birthday A212

Queen Elizabeth II: 15c, As child. 25c, Wearing tiara. 50c, Wearing blue hat. 65c, Wearing white hat.

No. 1175: a, Like 25c. b, Like 50c.

2006, Apr. 21 *Perf. 14*
1171-1174 A212 Set of 4 5.25 5.25

Souvenir Sheet
1175 A212 $1.50 Sheet of 2, #a-b 8.50 8.50

ZNS Broadcasting Network, 70th Anniv. — A213

Designs: 15c, Map of Bahamas, Harcourt R. Bethel, ZNS General Manager. 25c, Map of Bahamas, ZNS Network emblem. 50c, ZNS building. 65c, ZNS building and tower. 70c, Map of Bahamas and radio antenna. 80c, Map of Bahamas, ZNS Radio emblem and microphone.

2006, May 26

1176-1181 A213 Set of 6 8.00 8.00

Flowers A214

Designs: 5c, Amaryllis. 10c, Barleria. 15c, Yesterday, today and tomorrow. 25c, Desert rose. 35c, Poor man's orchid. 40c, Frangipani. 55c, Herald's trumpet. 65c, Oleander. 75c, Bird of paradise. 80c, Plumbago. 90c, Rose. $1, Rubber vine. $2, Star of Bethlehem. $5, Angel's trumpet. $10, Wine lily.

Wmk. 373

2006, July 3 Litho. *Perf. 14*

Inscribed "2006"

1182	A214	5c	multi	.30	.30
1183	A214	10c	multi	.30	.30
1184	A214	25c	multi	.70	.70
1185	A214	35c	multi	.95	.95
1186	A214	40c	multi	1.10	1.10
1187	A214	55c	multi	1.50	1.50
1188	A214	65c	multi	1.75	1.75
1189	A214	75c	multi	1.90	1.90
1190	A214	80c	multi	1.50	1.50
1191	A214	90c	multi	2.50	2.50
1192	A214	$1	multi	2.75	2.75
1193	A214	$2	multi	5.50	5.50
1194	A214	$5	multi	13.00	13.00
1195	A214	$10	multi	27.50	27.50
	Nos. 1182-1195 (14)			61.25	61.25

Dated "2009"

Wmk. 406

1195B A214 15c multi *1.40 1.40*

2007 Wmk. 373 Inscribed "2007"

1182a	A214	5c	multi	*2.50*	*2.50*
1183a	A214	10c	multi	*2.50*	*2.50*

2008 Wmk. 373 Inscribed "2008"

1192b	A214	$1	multi	2.00	2.00
1193b	A214	$2	multi	4.00	4.00
1194b	A214	$5	multi	10.00	10.00
1195c	A214	$10	multi	20.00	20.00
	Nos. 1192b-1195c (4)			36.00	36.00

2008, Aug. Wmk. 406

1182b	5c	.25	.25
1183b	10c	.25	.25
1186a	40c	.80	.80
1187a	55c	1.10	1.10
1188a	65c	1.40	1.40
1189a	75c	1.50	1.50
1190a	80c	1.60	1.60
1191a	90c	1.90	1.90
1192a	$1	2.00	2.00
1193a	$2	4.00	4.00
1194a	$5	10.00	10.00
1195a	$10	20.00	20.00
Nos. 1182b-1195a (12)		44.80	44.80

Dated "2009"

Wmk. 406

1182c	5c multi	*1.00*	*1.00*
1183c	10c multi	*1.00*	*1.00*

Issued: 15c, 2009.

Flowering Vines A215

Designs: 15c, Blue pea. 50c, Allamanda. 65c, Morning glory. 70c, Sky vine.

Perf. 12½x13

2006, Oct. 31 Litho. Wmk. 373

1196-1199 A215 Set of 4 5.25 5.25

Christmas A216

Designs: 15c, Christmas Sunday. 25c, Christmas dinner. 50c, Bay Street shopping. 65c, Boxing Day Junkanoo. 70c, Watch Night service. 80c, New Year's Day Junkanoo.

2006, Nov. 28 *Perf. 13x13¼*

1200-1205 A216 Set of 6 7.75 7.75

Worldwide Fund for Nature (WWF) — A217

Blaineville's beaked whales: 15c, Whale breaching surface of water. 25c, Three whales. 50c, One whale underwater. 60c, Three whales, diff.

Wmk. 373

2007, Jan. 23 Litho. *Perf. 14*

1206-1209 A217 Set of 4 4.50 4.50

1209a Miniature sheet, 4 each #1206-1209 19.00 19.00

Wedding of Queen Elizabeth II and Prince Philip, 60th Anniv. — A218

Designs: 15c, Portrait of couple. 25c, Couple in coach. 50c, Couple on balcony. 65c, Couple passing line of people.
$5, Color portrait of couple.

Wmk. 373

2007, June 1 Litho. *Perf. 13¾*

1210-1213 A218 Set of 4 4.25 4.25

Souvenir Sheet

Perf. 14

1214 A218 $5 multi 13.00 13.00

No. 1214 contains one 43x57mm stamp.

Scouting, Cent. A219

Designs: 15c, Two Scouts at church service, hands of bugler. 25c, Scout on rope, hands tying knot. 50c, Scouts at campfire, hand holding compass. 65c, Scouts at attention, hand giving salute.

No. 1219, vert.: a, 70c, Scouts playing baseball. b, 80c, Lord Robert Baden-Powell.

2007, July 9 *Perf. 13¾*

1215-1218 A219 Set of 4 5.00 5.00

Souvenir Sheet

1219 A219 Sheet of 2, #a-b 3.25 3.25

Governor General's Youth Award, 20th Anniv. — A220

Designs: 15c, Youths building walkway. 25c, Youths painting. 50c, Youths in kayak. 65c, Youths on hike. 70c, Award emblem.

Perf. 12½x13

2007, Sept. 18 Litho. Wmk. 373

1220-1224 A220 Set of 5 6.00 6.00

Christmas — A221

Various Christmas ornaments made of seashells with background colors of: 15c, Purple. 25c, Red violet. 50c, Orange. 65c, Red brown. 70c, Lemon. 80c, Green.

2007, Nov. 13 *Perf. 14*

1225-1230 A221 Set of 6 7.25 7.25

Rev. Charles Wesley (1707-88), Hymn Writer A222

Designs: 15c, Church choir, cross. 50c, Stained glass window showing Charles Wesley and brother, John, vert. 65c, Charles Wesley and frontispiece of *Hymns and Sacred Poems in Two Volumes,* vert. 70c, Harbour Island Methodist Church.

Perf. 12½x13¼, 13¼x12½

2007, Dec. 13

1231-1234 A222 Set of 4 5.75 5.75

Butterflies A223

Designs: 15c, Zebra longwing. 25c, Julia. 50c, Cloudless sulphur. 65c, Queen. 70c, Long-tailed skipper. 80c, Gulf fritillary.

Wmk. 373

2008, Feb. 18 Litho. *Perf. 14*

1235-1240 A223 Set of 6 8.00 8.00

1240a Miniature sheet, #1235-1240 8.00 8.00

Military Uniforms — A224

Designs: 15c, His Majesty's Independent Company. 25c, 47th Regiment of Foot. 50c, 99th Regiment of Foot. 65c, Royal Artillery. 70c Black Garrison Companies.

2008, Mar. 20

1241-1245 A224 Set of 5 6.00 6.00

2008 Summer Olympics, Beijing A225

Designs: 15c, Bamboo, runner. 50c, Dragon, high jump. 65c, Lanterns, javelin. 70c, Fish, runner.

Wmk. 373

2008, Apr. 30 Litho. *Perf. 13½*

1246-1249 A225 Set of 4 5.00 5.00

Royal Bank of Canada in the Bahamas, Cent. A226

Designs: 15c, Anniversary emblem. 25c, Regional head office. 50c, Main branch office, Nassau, early 1900s. 65c, New Carmichael Road office. 70c, Bankers Ross McDonald and Nathaniel Beneby Jr.

Perf. 12½x13¼

2008, Sept. 22 Litho. Wmk. 406

1250-1254 A226 Set of 5 6.50 6.50

National Aeronautics and Space Administration, 50th Anniv. — A227

Designs: 15c, Launch of Space Shuttle Discovery. 25c, Apollo 16 over Moon. 50c, Skylab 3. 65c, Hubble Space Telescope. 70c, Swan Nebula. 80c, Carina Nebula.

Wmk. 373

2008, Oct. 1 Litho. *Perf. 13¾*

1255-1260 A227 Set of 6 7.50 7.50

Christmas A228

Paintings by Leonhard Diefenbach: 15c, Adoration of the Magi. 50c, Magi at the Court of King Herod. 65c, Shepherds. 70c, Adoration of the Shepherds.

Perf. 12½x13

2008, Nov. 11 Litho. Wmk. 406

1261-1264 A228 Set of 4 6.00 6.00

University of the West Indies, 60th Anniv. A229

Anniversary emblem and: 15c, Men and women in doctor's jackets. 25c, Plaque honoring renaming of Clinical Training Program. 65c, Arms and diploma.

2008, Nov. 25

1265-1267 A229 Set of 3 3.00 3.00

Treaty of Paris, 225th Anniv. A230

Designs: 15c, Battle of Lexington. 50c, Washington Crossing the Delaware. 65c, Signatories of the Treaty of Paris, by Benjamin West. 70c, Signed treaty.

2008, Dec. 9

1268-1271 A230 Set of 4 4.50 4.50

Rare Birds — A231

Designs: 15c, Bahamas oriole. 50c, Rose-throated parrot. 65c, Great lizard cuckoo. 70c, Audubon's shearwater.

Wmk. 373

2009, Jan. 6 Litho. *Perf. 13¾*

1272-1275	A231	Set of 4	6.50	6.50

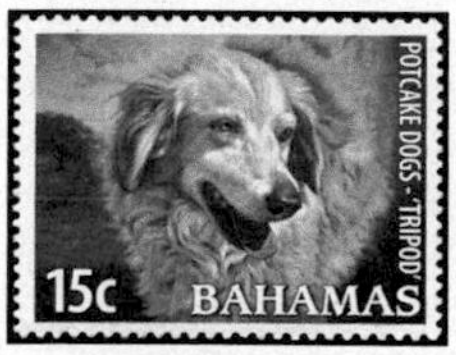

Potcake Dogs A232

Dogs named: 15c, Tripod. 50c, Amigo. 65c, Turtle. 70c, Oreo.

Perf. 12½x13¼

2009, May 1 Wmk. 406

1276-1279	A232	Set of 4	6.50	6.50

Miniature Sheet

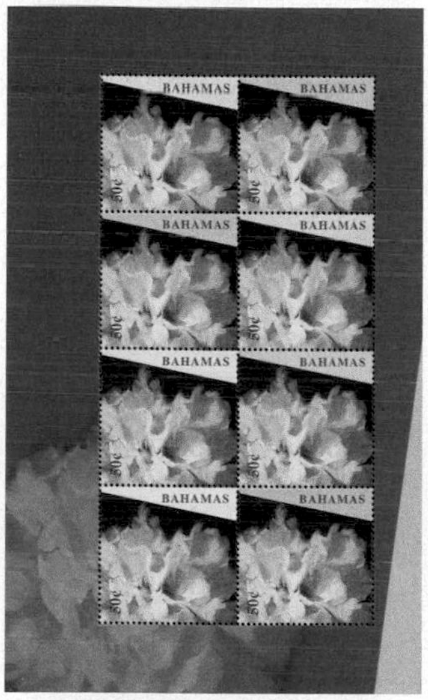

Peonies — A233

No. 1280 — Panel color: a, Pale yellow. b, White. c, Pink. d, Pale blue. e, Pale orange. f, Light green. g, Light yellow. h, Bluish gray.

Perf. 13¼

2009, Apr. 10 Litho. Unwmk.

1280	A233 50c Sheet of 8, #a-h		9.00	9.00

First Bahamas Postage Stamp, 150th Anniv. — A234

No. 1281 — Bahamas #1b with background color of: a, Pink. b, Light blue. c, Light green. d, Lilac.

2009, May 26 Wmk. 406 *Perf. 13*

1281	A234 15c Block of 4, #a-d		1.50	1.50
e.	Souvenir sheet, #1281		1.50	1.50

Naval Aviation, Cent. A235

Royal Navy airplanes: 15c, Hawker Sea Hurricane. 65c, Hawker Sea Fury. 70c, Fairey Gannet. 80c, De Havilland Sea Vampire.

$2, Airplane on Merchant Aircraft Carrier MV Empire MacKendrick.

2009, June 16 Wmk. 406 *Perf. 14*

1282-1285	A235	Set of 4	5.00	5.00

Souvenir Sheet

1286	A235 $2 multi		4.50	4.50

Nos. 1282-1285 each were printed in sheets of 8 + central label.

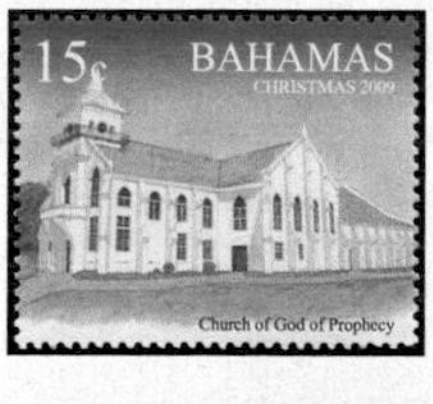

Christmas A236

Designs: 15c, Church of God of Prophecy. 25c, Mission Baptist Church. 50c, Grant's Town Seventh-Day Adventist Church. 65c, Wesley Methodist Church. 70c, St. Francis Xavier Cathedral. 80c, St. Ambrose Anglican Church.

Wmk. 406

2009, Nov. 18 Litho. *Perf. 13¾*

1287-1292	A236	Set of 6	6.75	6.75

Souvenir Sheet

British Commonwealth, 60th Anniv. — A237

2009, Nov. 24

1293	A237 $2 multi		4.50	4.50

Friends of the Environment — A238

Designs: 15c, Whale, dolphin. 50c, Parrot, conch. 65c, Lizard, turtle. 70c, Stork, tree.

2010, Mar. 3 *Perf. 12¾x13*

1294-1297	A238	Set of 4	4.25	4.25

Battle of Britain, 70th Anniv. — A239

Various photographs of Sir Winston Churchill and words from his speeches: 15c, "We shall never surrender." 25c, "The Battle of Britain is about to begin." 50c, "Never in the field of human conflict was so much owed by so many to so few." 65c, "This was their finest hour." 70c, "Upon this battle depends the survival of Christian civilization." 80c, "We shall fight on the beaches."

$2, Sir Douglas Bader.

2010, June 18 *Perf. 12¾*

1298-1303	A239	Set of 6	6.75	6.75

Souvenir Sheet

1303A	A239 $2 black & gray		4.50	4.50

Hurricane Awareness A240

Designs: 15c, Palm trees in hurricane. 50c, Map of hurricane track. 65c, Hurricane, reconnaissance airplane. 70c, National Emergency Management Agency emblem as eye of hurricane.

Perf. 12½x13

2010, Sept. 28 Wmk. 406

1304-1307	A240	Set of 4	7.00	7.00

Christmas — A241

Fireworks and: 15c, Palm tree, cruise ship. 50c, Atlantis Hotel. 65c, Tail of jet airplane. 70c, Fort Fincastle, Water Tower.

Unwmk.

2010, Nov. 10 Litho. *Perf. 14*

1308-1311	A241	Set of 4	7.00	7.00

Sir Victor Sassoon Heart Foundation — A242

Designs: 15c, Heart Ball. 50c, Doctor examining child. 65c, Doctor examining child, diff. 70c, Sir Victor Sassoon (1881-1961), businessman.

Unwmk.

2011, Feb. 12 Litho. *Perf. 14*

1312-1315	A242	Set of 4	4.00	4.00

Service of Queen Elizabeth II and Prince Philip — A243

Designs: 15c, Queen Elizabeth II. 50c, Queen and Prince Philip. 65c, Queen and Prince Philip, diff. 70c, Queen and Prince Philip, diff. $1, Queen and Prince Philip, diff. $2, Prince Philip.

$2.50, Queen and Prince Philip, diff.

2011, Mar. 23 Litho. *Perf. 13¼*

1316-1321	A243	Set of 6	10.00	10.00
1321a	Sheet of 6, #1316-1321, + 3 labels		10.00	10.00

Souvenir Sheet

1322	A243 $2.50 multi		5.00	5.00

Wedding of Prince William and Catherine Middleton — A244

Couple: 15c, In 2008. 50c, At St. James's Palace. 65c, Kissing on Buckingham Palace balcony after wedding.

$5, After wedding at Westninster Abbey, vert.

2011, June 21 *Perf. 14*

1323-1325	A244	Set of 3	2.60	2.60

Souvenir Sheet

Perf. 14¾x14¼

1326	A244 $5 multi		10.00	10.00

No. 1326 contains one 29x46mm stamp.

Establishment of City of Nassau and Anglican Diocese, 150th Anniv. — A245

Designs: 15c, Christ Church Cathedral. 50c, Rawson Square. 65c, Government House. 70c, Bay Street. $1, Bishop Charles Caulfield. $2, Royal Governor Charles Bayley.

2011, Sept. 12 *Perf. 12½x13*

1327-1332	A245	Set of 6	10.00	10.00

Christmas A246

Angel and: 15c, Virgin Mary. 25c, Mary and Joseph. 50c, Magi. 65c, Infant Jesus and lambs. 70c, Shepherds. 80c, Mary and Jesus.

2011, Nov. 17 *Perf. 13½x13¼*

1333-1338	A246	Set of 6	6.25	6.25

Marine Life A247

Designs: 5c, Sea fan. 10c, Christmas tree worm. 15c, Elkhorn coral. 20c, Cushion sea star. 25c, Queen conch. 30c, Hawksbill turtle. 40c, Green moray eel. 50c, Bonefish. 60c, Spidder crab. 65c, Spiny lobster. 70c, Nassau grouper. 80c, Yellowtail snapper. $1, Great barracuda. $2, Spotted eagle ray. $5, Caribbean reef shark. $10, Bottlenose dolphin.

2012, Jan. 3 ***Perf. 13¼x13½***

1339	A247	5c multi	.25	.25
1340	A247	10c multi	.25	.25
1341	A247	15c multi	.30	.30
1342	A247	20c multi	.40	.40
1343	A247	25c multi	.50	.50
1344	A247	30c multi	.60	.60
1345	A247	40c multi	.80	.80
1346	A247	50c multi	1.00	1.00
1347	A247	60c multi	1.25	1.25
1348	A247	65c multi	1.40	1.40
1349	A247	70c multi	1.40	1.40
1350	A247	80c multi	1.60	1.60
1351	A247	$1 multi	2.00	2.00
1352	A247	$2 multi	4.00	4.00
1353	A247	$5 multi	10.00	10.00
1354	A247	$10 multi	20.00	20.00
		Nos. 1339-1354 (16)	45.75	45.75

Worldwide Fund for Nature (WWF) — A248

Caribbean flamingo: Nos. 1355, 1359a, 15c, Head. Nos. 1356, 1359b, 50c, Chick and egg. Nos. 1357, 1359c, 65c, Adults feeding. Nos. 1358, 1359d, 70c, Adults standing, facing right.

$5, Adults standing, facing left.

2012, Mar. 21 ***Perf. 14***

Stamps With White Frames

1355-1358 A248 Set of 4 4.00 4.00

Stamps Without White Frames

1359 A248 Horiz. strip of 4, #a-d 4.00 4.00

Souvenir Sheet

1360 A248 $5 multi 10.00 10.00

2012 Summer Olympics, London — A249

Emblem of 2012 Summer Olympics and: 15c, Boxing, Houses of Parliament. 50c, High jump, Nelson's Column. 65c, Swimming, Tower Bridge. 70c, Runner, Olympic Stadium.

2012, July 11 **Litho.** ***Perf. 13½***

1361-1364 A249 Set of 4 4.00 4.00

Royal Visit of Prince Harry — A250

Diamond and: 15c, Prince Harry in uniform. 50c, Prince Harry holding Bahamian flags. 65c, Prince Harry and young girl. 70c, Queen Elizabeth II.

2012, Aug. 16 **Litho.** ***Perf. 14***

1365-1368 A250 Set of 4 4.00 4.00

Reign of Queen Elizabeth II, 60th anniv.

Woman Suffragists — A251

Designs: 15c, Mary Ingraham (1901-82). 25c, Georgianna Symonette (1902-65). 50c, Mabel Walker (1902-87). 65c, Eugenia Lockhart (1908-89). 70c, Dame Albertha Isaacs (1900-97). 80c, Dr. Doris Johnson (1921-83).

2012, Oct. 10

1369-1374 A251 Set of 6 6.25 6.25

Christmas A252

Designs: 15c, Annunciation. 25c, Mary and Joseph arrive in Bethlehem. 50c, Holy Family. 65c, Shepherds. 70c, Magi. 80c, Flight into Egypt.

2012, Nov. 1 ***Perf. 13½***

1375-1380 A252 Set of 6 6.25 6.25

Items Produced for Coronations — A253

Coronation of Queen Elizabeth II, 60th Anniv. — A254

Items produced for coronation of: 65c, Queen Victoria. 70c, King Edward VII. 80c, King George V. $1, King George VI. $2, Queen Elizabeth II.

2013, Feb. 6 ***Perf. 14***

1381-1385 A253 Set of 5 10.50 10.50

Souvenir Sheet

Perf. 14¾x14

1386 A254 $3 multi 6.00 6.00

Nos. 1381-1385 each were printed in sheets of 8 + label.

Royal Bahamas Police Force Band, 120th Anniv. A255

Designs: 15c, Sir William Murphy presenting gallantry medal to Constable Fred Neville Seymour (first conductor of band), 1948. 25c, Band greeting Royal Yacht Britannia, 1975. 50c, Band, building in background. 65c, Band, water and buildings in background. 70c, Drummer. 80c, Band passing under arch.

2013, May 15

1387-1392 A255 Set of 6 6.25 6.25

Independence, 40th Anniv. — A256

Designs: 15c, Bahamas Independence Conference. 25c, Sir Milo Butler (1906-79), Governor-General, Butler inspecting troops. 50c, Sir Lynden Pindling (1930-2000), Prime Minister, arms of Bahamas. 65c, HMBS Flamingo and four crewmen killed in 1980 sinking of ship by Cuban Air Force. 70c, Rhodes Scholars Christian Campbell, Desiree Cox and Myron Rolle.

2013, July 8

1393-1397 A256 Set of 5 4.50 4.50

Bahamas Reef Environment Educational Foundation, 20th Anniv. — A257

No. 1398: a, Foundation emblem. b, Angelfish and coral.

No. 1399: a, Diver photographing sea turtle. b, Sea turtle.

No. 1400: a, Diver feedding fish. b, Fish and coral.

No. 1401: a, Diver and shark. b, Hammerhead shark.

2013, Oct. 29 **Litho.** ***Perf. 12½***

1398		Horiz. pair + central label	.60	.60
a.-b.	A257	15c Either single	.30	.30
1399		Horiz. pair + central label	2.00	2.00
a.-b.	A257	50c Either single	1.00	1.00
1400		Horiz. pair + central label	2.60	2.60
a.-b.	A257	65c Either single	1.30	1.30
1401		Horiz. pair + central label	2.80	2.80
a.-b.	A257	70c Either single	1.40	1.40
		Nos. 1398-1401 (4)	8.00	8.00

Christmas A258

Inscriptions: 15c, Gabriel Visits Mary. 25c, The Road to Bethlehem. 50c, No Room at the Inn. 65c, Jesus in a Manger. 70c, The Angel Visits the Shepherds. 80c, The Three Kings.

Perf. 13¼x12½

2013, Nov. 19 **Litho.**

1402-1407 A258 Set of 6 6.25 6.25

Royal Christenings A259

Photograph from christening of: 15c, Queen Elizabeth II, 1926. 50c, Prince Charles, 1948. 65c, Prince William, 1982. 70c, Prince George, 2013.

2014, May 21 **Litho.** ***Perf. 13¼x13***

1408-1411 A259 Set of 4 4.00 4.00

Bahamas National Geographic Information Systems Center, 10th Anniv. — A260

Emblem and: 15c, Map of Bahamas with delineated maritime boundaries. 50c, 1960-2012 hurricane distribution map. 65c, Surveyors verifying maritime boundaries. 70c, Data collection on Inagua Island.

2014, July 21 **Litho.** ***Perf. 12¾x13***

1412-1415 A260 Set of 4 4.00 4.00

World's First Undersea Post Office, 75th Anniv. — A261

Inscriptions: 15c, The 1914 Williamson Photosphere Film Project (observation chamber under boat). 50c, Underwater photography (film, photographer, octopus). 65c, The Williamson Photosphere (fish near observation chamber). 70c, John Ernest Williamson (1881-1966), Bahamas #106.

Perf. 12¾x13¼

2014, Aug. 16 **Litho.**

1416-1419 A261 Set of 4 4.00 4.00

Ministry of Tourism. 50th Anniv. A262

Hotels: No. 1420, 50c, Peace & Plenty Hotel, Exuma. No. 1421, 50c, Princess Resort & Casino, Freeport. No. 1422, 50c, Baha Mar Hotel, Nassau. No. 1423, 50c, Atlantis Hotel, Paradise Island.

2014, Oct. 27 **Litho.** ***Perf. 14***

1420-1423 A262 Set of 4 4.00 4.00

Christmas — A263

Inscriptions: 15c, "Peace on Earth." 50c, "Tidings of Great Joy." 65c, "A Time for Giving." 70c, "A Saviour is Born."

Perf. 14¼x14¾

2014, Nov. 11 **Litho.**

1424-1427 A263 Set of 4 4.00 4.00

World Day of Prayer — A264

Art: 15c, Never Forget How to Serve, by Jessica Colebrooke. 50c, Blessed, by Chantal Bethel. 65c, The Master Key, by Tyrone Ferguson.

2015, Mar. 6 **Litho.** ***Perf. 14***

1428-1430 A264 Set of 3 2.60 2.60

Magna Carta, 800th Anniv. A265

Designs: 15c, King John examining Magna Carta. 50c, Bahamas Supreme Court, Nassau. 65c, Bahamas House of Assembly, Nassau. 70c, King John on coin.

Perf. 13¼x13½

2015, June 15 **Litho.**
1431-1434 A265 Set of 4 4.00 4.00

Queen Elizabeth II, Longest-Reigning British Monarch — A266

Queen Elizabeth II and events during her reign: 15c, Bahamas #157 and cover with coronation cachet. 50c, Visit of Princess Margaret to Bahamas General Hospital, 1966. 65c, Meeting with Governor-General Sir Milo Butler, 1975. 70c, Prince Harry meeting with Boy Scouts, 2012.

2015, Sept. 9 **Litho.** ***Perf. 14***
1435-1438 A266 Set of 4 4.00 4.00

Bahamas Girl Guides, Cent. A267

Emblem and: 15c, Rangers, Guides, Brownies and Sunflower at Camp Discovery. 25c, Patrol pitching camp tent at Gwen French site. 50c, Guides building campfire. 65c, Rangers in kayaks. 70c, Brownies with grandmother. 80c, Four early Girl Guide Commissioners.

2015, Oct. 1 **Litho.** ***Perf. 14***
1439-1444 A267 Set of 6 6.25 6.25

Christmas — A268

Designs: 15c, Holy Family. 50c, Shepherds. 65c, Magi. 70c, Infant Jesus in manger.

Perf. 13½x13¼

2015, Nov. 19 **Litho.**
1445-1448 A268 Set of 4 4.00 4.00

Bahamas Marine Mammal Research Organization, 25th Anniv. — A269

Designs: 15c, Pantropical spotted dolphins. 50c, Bottlenose dolphins. 65c, Atlantic spotted dolphin. 70c, Rough-toothed dolphin.

2016, Mar. 31 **Litho.** ***Perf. 14***
1449-1452 A269 Set of 4 4.00 4.00

See Nos. 1466-1469, 1487-1490.

Queen Elizabeth II, 90th Birthday — A270

Photographs of Queen Elizabeth II from: 15c, 1965. 50c, 1961. 65c, 2007. 70c, 1992. $4, Queen Elizabeth II in 1966.

2016, Apr. 21 **Litho.** ***Perf. 14***
1453-1456 A270 Set of 4 4.00 4.00

Souvenir Sheet

1457 A270 $4 multi 8.00 8.00

2016 Summer Olympics, Rio de Janeiro A271

Designs: 15c, High jump. 50c, Sprinter. 65c, Relay race. 70c, Triple jump.

2016, Aug. 10 **Litho.** ***Perf. 13¼***
1458-1461 A271 Set of 4 4.00 4.00

Christmas A272

Designs: 15c, Adoration of the Shepherds. 50c, Holy Family at manger. 65c, Adoration of the Magi. 70c, Holy Family in stable.

2016, Nov. 14 **Litho.** ***Perf. 13¼***
1462-1465 A272 Set of 4 4.00 4.00

Bahamas Marine Mammal Research Organization Type of 2016

Designs: 15c, Sperm whale. 50c, Short-finned pilot whale. 65c, Blainville's beaked whales. 70c, Dwarf sperm whale.

2017, Apr. 10 **Litho.** ***Perf. 13¼***
1466-1469 A269 Set of 4 4.00 4.00

Christmas A273

Designs: 15c, Caribbean pine. 50c, Holly. 65c, Poinsettia. 70c, Ivy.

2017, Oct. 30 **Litho.** ***Perf. 13***
1470-1473 A273 Set of 4 4.00 4.00

70th Wedding Anniversary of Queen Elizabeth II and Prince Philip A274

Photograph of Queen Elizabeth II and Prince Philip taken in: 15c, 1947. 50c, 1958. 65c, 1977. 70c, 2007.

Perf. 13¼x12½

2017, Nov. 20 **Litho.**
1474-1477 A274 Set of 4 4.00 4.00

Wedding of Prince Harry and Meghan Markle A275

Designs: 15c, Engagement photograph. 50c, Couple at choir performance. 65c, Couple sitting in carriage. 70c, Couple leaving St. George's Chapel after wedding.
$2, Couple during wedding ceremony, vert.

Perf. 13¼x13½

2018, Aug. 15 **Litho.**
1478-1481 A275 Set of 4 4.00 4.00

Souvenir Sheet

Perf. 13½x13¼

1482 A275 $2 multi 4.00 4.00

Christmas A276

Churches and words from "Silent Night": 15c, Bethel Baptist Church, Nassau, "Silent Night." 25c, St. Agnes Anglican Church, Grants Town, "Holy Night." 50c, Church of God, Nassau, "All is Calm." 65c, Hillview Seventh Day Adventist Church, Nassau, "All is Bright."

2018, Nov. 29 **Litho.** ***Perf. 13½***
1483-1486 A276 Set of 4 3.25 3.25

Bahamas Marine Mammal Research Organization Type of 2016

Designs: 15c, Melon-headed whale. 50c, West Indian manatee. 65c, Killer whale. 70c, Cuvier's beaked whale.

2019, Apr. 18 **Litho.** ***Perf. 13¼x13½***
1487-1490 A269 Set of 4 4.00 4.00

Native Plants A277

Designs: 5c, Harrisia brookii. 10c, Agave inaguensis. 15c, Euphorbia gymnonota. 20c, Euphorbia longinsulicola. 25c, Encyclia fehlingii. 30c, Pavonia bahamensis. 40c, Lepidaploa arbuscula. 50c, Clematis plukenetii. 60c, Galactia bahamensis. 65c, Wedelia bahamensis. 70c, Cyperus correllii. 80c, Ernodea gigantea. $1, Symphiotrichum lucayanum. $2, Anastraphia pauciflоscula. $5, Nashia inaguensis. $10, Tolumnia sasseri.

2019, Sept. 5 **Litho.** ***Perf. 13¼x13***

1491	A277	5c	multi	.25	.25
1492	A277	10c	multi	.25	.25
1493	A277	15c	multi	.30	.30
1494	A277	20c	multi	.40	.40
1495	A277	25c	multi	.50	.50
1496	A277	30c	multi	.60	.60
1497	A277	40c	multi	.80	.80
1498	A277	50c	multi	1.00	1.00
1499	A277	60c	multi	1.25	1.25
1500	A277	65c	multi	1.30	1.30
1501	A277	70c	multi	1.40	1.40
1502	A277	80c	multi	1.60	1.60
1503	A277	$1	multi	2.00	2.00
1504	A277	$2	multi	4.00	4.00
1505	A277	$5	multi	10.00	10.00
1506	A277	$10	multi	20.00	20.00
	Nos. 1491-1506 (16)			45.65	45.65

Bahamas National Trust, 60th Anniv. — A278

Designs: 15c, Bahama parrot. 50c, Queen conch, horiz. 65c, Exuma Cays Land and Sea Park, horiz. 70c, Flamingos.

Perf. 13½x13¼, 13¼x13½

2019, Oct. 10 **Litho.**
1507-1510 A278 Set of 4 4.00 4.00

Christmas A279

Designs: 15c, Hands holding bells. 25c, Bells with ribbons. 50c, Bell. 65c, Hands holding bells, diff.

2019, Dec. 5 **Litho.** ***Perf. 13¼***
1511-1514 A279 Set of 4 3.25 3.25

SEMI-POSTAL STAMPS

No. 48 Overprinted in Red

1917, May 18 **Wmk. 3** ***Perf. 14***
B1 A6 1p car & black .50 *2.50*

Type of 1911 Overprinted in Red

1919, Jan. 1
B2 A6 1p red & black .40 *3.25*
a. Double overprint *2,750.*

This stamp was originally scheduled for release in 1918.

No. 694 Surcharged Souvenir Sheet

Wmk. 384

1992, Nov. 16 **Litho.** ***Perf. 14***
B3 A116 Sheet of 2, #a.-b. 19.00 19.00

AIR POST STAMPS

Catalogue values for all unused stamps in this section are for Never Hinged items.

Manned Flight Bicentenary — AP1

Airplanes — 10c, Consolidated Catalina. 25c, Avro Tudor IV. 31c, Avro Lancastrian. 35c, Consolidated Commodore.

Wmk. 373

1983, Oct. 13 Litho. ***Perf. 14***

C1	AP1	10c multicolored	.65	.25
a.		Without emblem ('85)	3.00	.50
b.		Without emblem, wmk. 384 ('86)	2.50	1.00
C2	AP1	25c multicolored	.85	.40
a.		Without emblem ('85)	6.00	1.00
b.		Without emblem, wmk. 384 ('86)	5.00	2.00
C3	AP1	31c multicolored	1.00	.55
a.		Without emblem ('85)	1.75	.55
C4	AP1	35c multicolored	.80	.60
a.		Without emblem ('85)	3.25	.65
		Nos. C1-C4 (4)	3.30	1.80

Aircraft AP2

15c, Bahamasair Boeing 737. 40c, Eastern Boeing 757. 45c, Pan Am Airbus A300 B4. 50c, British Airways Boeing 747.

1987, July 7

C5	AP2	15c multicolored	3.50	2.50
C6	AP2	40c multicolored	4.50	3.00
C7	AP2	45c multicolored	4.50	3.00
C8	AP2	50c multicolored	4.50	4.50
		Nos. C5-C8 (4)	17.00	13.00

SPECIAL DELIVERY STAMPS

No. 34 Overprinted

1916 Wmk. 1 ***Perf. 14***

E1	A6	5p orange & black	7.50	*47.50*
a.		Double overprint	*1,000.*	*1,500.*
b.		Inverted overprint	*1,750.*	*1,800.*
c.		Double ovpt., one invtd.	*1,550.*	*1,750.*
d.		Pair, one without overprint	*35,000.*	*50,000.*

The No. E1 overprint exists in two types. Type I (illustrated) is much scarcer. Type II shows "SPECIAL" farther right, so that the letter "I" is slightly right of the vertical line of the "E" below it.

Type of Regular Issue of 1903 Overprinted

1917, July 2 Wmk. 3

E2	A6	5p orange & black	.80	*11.00*

No. 60 Overprinted in Red

1918

E3	A6	5p violet & black	.60	*4.25*

WAR TAX STAMPS

Stamps of 1912-18 Overprinted

1918, Feb. 21 Wmk. 3 ***Perf. 14***

MR1	A8	½p green	14.00	*55.00*
a.		Double overprint	*1,000.*	—
b.		Inverted overprint	—	—
MR2	A8	1p car rose	1.25	*1.00*
a.		Double overprint	—	—
b.		Inverted overprint	—	—
MR3	A6	3p brown, *yel*	3.75	*3.50*
a.		Inverted overprint	*1,400.*	*1,500.*
b.		Double overprint	2,000.	*2,150.*
MR4	A8	1sh black & red	125.00	*175.00*
a.		Double overprint	—	—
		Nos. MR1-MR4 (4)	144.00	*234.50*

Same Overprint on No. 48a

1918, July 10

MR5	A6	1p car & black	4.75	*11.00*
a.		Double overprint	2,150.	*2,400.*
b.		Double ovpt., one invtd.	1,100.	—
c.		Inverted overprint	*1,900.*	*2,000.*

Nos. 49-50, 54 Overprinted in Black or Red

MR6	A8	½p green	2.25	2.25
MR7	A8	1p car rose	4.50	.65
a.		Watermarked sideways	*400.00*	
MR8	A8	1sh black & red (R)	14.00	7.50
		Nos. MR6-MR8 (3)	20.75	10.40

Nos. 58-59 Overprinted

1918-19

MR9	A6	3p brown, *yel*	1.00	*3.25*
MR10	A6	3p brown & blk ('19)	2.25	*7.00*

Nos. 49-50, 54 Overprinted in Red or Black

1919, July 14

MR11	A8	½p green (R)	.40	*1.60*
MR12	A8	1p car rose	1.90	*2.25*
MR13	A8	1sh blk & red (R)	27.50	*60.00*
		Nos. MR11-MR13 (3)	29.80	*63.85*

No. 59 Overprinted

MR14	A6	3p brn & blk	2.00	*10.00*

BAHRAIN

bä-'rān

LOCATION — An archipelago in the Persian Gulf, including the islands of Bahrain, Muharraq, Sitra, Nebi Saleh, Kasasifeh and Arad.
GOVT. — Constitutional monarchy
AREA — 255 sq. mi.
POP. — 629,090 (1999 est.)
CAPITAL — Manama

Bahrain was a British-protected territory until it became an independent state on August 15, 1971.

12 Pies = 1 Anna
16 Annas = 1 Rupee
100 Naye Paise = 1 Rupee (1957)
1000 Fils = 1 Dinar (1966)

Catalogue values for unused stamps in this country are for Never Hinged items, beginning with Scott 62.

Indian Postal Administration

Stamps of India, 1926-32, Overprinted in Black — a

Wmk. Multiple Stars (196)

1933, Aug. 10 ***Perf. 14***

1	A46	3p gray	4.50	1.00
2	A47	½a green	12.00	5.50
3	A68	9p dark green	5.00	6.00
4	A48	1a dark brown	14.00	4.00
5	A69	1a3p violet	19.00	6.00
6	A60	2a vermilion	12.00	*25.00*
7	A51	3a blue	22.50	*85.00*
8	A70	3a6p deep blue	7.00	.85
9	A61	4a olive green	20.00	*87.50*
10	A54	8a red violet	10.00	.65
11	A55	12a claret	9.00	3.75

Overprinted in Black — b

12	A56	1r green & brown	20.00	18.00
13	A56	2r brn org & car rose	37.50	55.00
14	A56	5r dk violet & ultra	300.00	260.00
		Nos. 1-14 (14)	492.50	558.25

No. 14 is more common with an inverted watermark. Value $175.

Stamps of India, 1926-32, Overprinted Type "a" in Black

1934

15	A72	1a dark brown	15.00	.70
a.		Complete booklet, containing 16 #15, wmk inverted, in four blocks of 4	*1,500.*	
16	A51	3a carmine rose	8.50	.90
17	A52	4a olive green	9.75	.80
		Nos. 15-17 (3)	33.25	2.40

The cover of No. 15a is red and black on tan, with Mysore Sandal Soap advertisement on front.

India Nos. 138, 111, 111a Overprinted Type "a" in Black

1935-37 ***Perf. 13½x14, 14***

18	A71	½a green	10.00	2.25
19	A49	2a vermilion	70.00	11.00
a.		Small die ('37)	110.00	.50

India Stamps of 1937 Overprinted Type "a" in Black

1938-41 Wmk. 196 ***Perf. 13½x14***

20	A80	3p slate	12.00	9.00
21	A80	½a brown	7.00	.35
22	A80	9p green	9.00	*16.00*
23	A80	1a carmine	8.00	.35
24	A81	2a scarlet	4.00	7.00
26	A81	3a yel grn ('41)	8.00	14.00
27	A81	3a6p ultra	4.00	*12.00*
28	A81	4a dk brn ('41)	130.00	95.00
30	A81	8a bl vio ('40)	190.00	45.00
31	A81	12a car lake ('40)	110.00	60.00

Overprinted Type "b" in Black

32	A82	1r brn & slate	4.75	3.00
33	A82	2r dk brn & dk vio	12.00	12.00
34	A82	5r dp ultra & dk grn	10.00	*17.50*
35	A82	10r rose car & dk vio ('41)	60.00	65.00
36	A82	15r dk grn & dk brn ('41)	60.00	97.50
37	A82	25r dk vio & bl vio ('41)	95.00	*120.00*
		Nos. 20-37 (16)	723.75	573.70
		Set, never hinged	1,000.	

India Stamps of 1941-43 Overprinted Type "a" in Black

1942-44 Wmk. 196 ***Perf. 13½x14***

38	A83	3p slate	2.00	2.75
39	A83	½a rose vio ('44)	3.00	*4.75*
40	A83	9p lt green ('43)	11.00	*27.50*
41	A83	1a car rose ('44)	5.00	1.25
42	A84	1a3p bister ('43)	6.50	*25.00*
43	A84	1½a dk pur ('43)	4.25	*9.00*
45	A84	2a scarlet ('43)	4.25	2.25
46	A84	3a violet ('43)	14.00	8.50
47	A84	3½a ultra	4.50	*30.00*
48	A85	4a chocolate	3.00	.275
49	A85	6a peacock blue	14.00	*13.50*
50	A85	8a blue vio ('43)	7.00	4.75
51	A85	12a car lake	10.00	6.75
		Nos. 38-51 (13)	88.50	*136.28*
		Set, never hinged	135.00	

British Postal Administration

See Oman (Muscat) for similar stamps with surcharge of new value only.

Great Britain Nos. 258 to 263, 243 and 248 Surcharged in Black — c

1948-49 Wmk. 251 ***Perf. 14½x14***

52	A101	½a on ½p green	.50	*1.75*
53	A101	1a on 1p vermilion	.50	*3.50*
54	A101	1½a on 1½p lt red brn	.50	*4.75*
55	A101	2a on 2p lt orange	.50	.30
56	A101	2½a on 2½p ultra	.75	*7.00*
57	A101	3a on 3p violet	.50	.30
58	A102	6a on 6p rose lilac	.50	.30
59	A103	1r on 1sh brown	1.25	.35

Great Britain Nos. 249A, 250 and 251A Surcharged in Black

Wmk. 259 ***Perf. 14***

60	A104	2r on 2sh6p yel grn	4.50	*8.00*
61	A104	5r on 5sh dull red	4.75	*8.50*
61A	A105	10r on 10sh ultra	65.00	*70.00*
		Nos. 52-61A (11)	79.25	*104.75*

Surcharge bars at bottom on No. 61A.

Issued: 10r, 7/4/49; others, 4/1/48.

Catalogue values for unused stamps in this section, from this point to the end of the section, are for Never Hinged items.

Silver Wedding Issue

Great Britain Nos. 267 and 268 Surcharged in Black

Perf. 14½x14, 14x14½

1948, Apr. 26 **Wmk. 251**

62	A109	2½a on 2½p	1.00	*2.75*
63	A110	15r on £1	37.50	*55.00*

Three bars obliterate the original denomination on No. 63.

Olympic Issue

1948, July 29 ***Perf. 14½x14***

64	A113	2½a on 2½p brt ultra	1.40	*4.75*
a.		Double surcharge	3,500.	*4,250.*
65	A114	3a on 3p dp vio	1.10	*4.25*
66	A115	6a on 6p red vio	1.75	*4.25*
67	A116	1r on 1sh dk brn	2.75	*4.25*
		Nos. 64-67 (4)	7.00	*17.50*

A square of dots obliterates the original denomination on No. 67.

UPU Issue

Great Britain No. 276 Srchd. in Black

Great Britain Nos. 277-279 Srchd. in Black

1949, Oct. 10 **Photo.** ***Perf. 14½x14***

68	A117	2½a on 2½p brt ultra	.90	*3.50*
69	A118	3a on 3p brt vio	1.10	*5.25*
70	A119	6a on 6p red vio	1.00	*3.75*
71	A120	1r on 1sh brown	1.75	*4.00*
		Nos. 68-71 (4)	4.75	*16.50*

Great Britain Nos. 280-285 Surcharged Type "c" in Black

1950-51 **Wmk. 251**

72	A101	½a on ½p lt org	3.00	3.00
73	A101	1a on 1p ultra	3.50	.35
74	A101	1½a on 1½p green	3.50	*20.00*
75	A101	2a on 2p lt red brn	2.00	.35
76	A101	2½a on 2½p ver	3.75	*17.50*
77	A102	4a on 4p ultra	5.00	1.90

Great Britain Nos. 286-288 Surcharged in Black

Type I

Three types of surcharge on No. 78: Type I, "2" level with "RUPEES;" Type II, "2" raised higher than "RUPEES," 15mm between "BAHRAIN" and "2 RUPEES;" Type III, as type II, but 16mm between "BAHRAIN" and "2 RUPEES."

Perf. 11x12

Wmk. 259

78	A121	2r on 2sh6p green, type I ('51)	45.00	17.50
a.		2r on 2sh6p, type II ('53)	140.00	55.00
b.		2r on 2sh6p, type III ('55)	1,750.	150.00
79	A121	5r on 5sh dl red	17.50	7.00
80	A122	10r on 10sh ultra	42.50	12.00
		Nos. 72-80 (9)	125.75	*79.60*

Longer bars, at lower right, on No. 80.

Issued: 4a, Nov. 2, 1950; others, May 3, 1951.

Great Britain 1952-54 Stamps Surcharged in Black or Dark Blue

1952-54 **Wmk. 298** ***Perf. 14½x14***

81	A126	½a on ½p red org ('53)	.25	.25
a.		"½" omitted	*225.00*	*400.00*
82	A126	1a on 1p ultra	.45	.25
83	A126	1½a on 1½p grn	.45	.25
84	A126	2a on 2p red brn	.45	.25
85	A127	2½a on 2½p scar	.60	*1.75*
86	A127	3a on 3p dk pur (Dk Bl)	1.25	.25
87	A128	4a on 4p ultra	6.75	.50
88	A129	6a on 6p lil rose	6.00	.45
89	A132	12a on 1sh3p dk grn	6.00	.75
90	A131	1r on 1sh6p dk bl	6.00	1.00
		Nos. 81-90 (10)	28.20	5.70

Issued: Nos. 83, 85, 12/5; Nos. 81-82, 84, 8/31/53; Nos. 87, 89-90, 11/2/53; Nos. 86, 88, 1/18/54.

Six stamps of this design picturing Sheik Sulman bin Hamad Al Kalifah were for local use in 1953-57. Value, mint set $30.

Six stamps of similar design (same sheik, "Bahrain" vertical at left) were issued in 1961 for local use. Value, mint set, $12.50.

Coronation Issue

Great Britain Nos. 313-316 Surcharged "BAHRAIN" and New Value in Black

Perf. 14½x14

1953, June 3 **Wmk. 298**

92	A134	2½a on 2½p scar	1.25	1.00
93	A135	4a on 4p brt ultra	2.00	5.00
94	A136	12a on 1sh3p dk grn	5.75	4.50
95	A137	1r on 1sh6p dk bl	6.25	2.25
		Nos. 92-95 (4)	15.25	12.75

Squares of dots obliterate the original denominations on Nos. 94-95.

Great Britain Nos. 309-311 Surcharged "BAHRAIN" and New Value in Black

1955 **Wmk. 308** **Engr.** ***Perf. 11x12***

96	A133	2r on 2sh6p dk brn	5.50	2.00
97	A133	5r on 5sh crimson	8.75	3.00
98	A133	10r on 10sh brt ultra	22.50	3.00
		Nos. 96-98 (3)	36.75	8.00

Three slightly different types of surcharge are found on the 2r; two on 5r and 10r.

Great Britain Nos. 317, 323, 325, 332-333 Surcharged "BAHRAIN" and New Value

Perf. 14½x14

1956-57 **Wmk. 308** **Photo.**

99	A126	½a on ½p red org	.55	.25
100	A128	4a on 4p ultra	6.50	*23.50*
101	A129	6a on 6p lil rose	1.00	.80
102	A132	12a on 1sh3p dk green	7.75	*13.00*
103	A131	1r on 1sh6p dk bl ('57)	11.50	.25
		Nos. 99-103 (5)	27.30	*37.80*

No. 103 exists with double surcharge. Value $5,000.

Great Britain Nos. 317-325, 328, 332 Surcharged "BAHRAIN" and New Value

1957, Apr. 1

104	A129	1np on 5p lt brown	.25	.25
105	A126	3np on ½p red org	.50	*3.00*
106	A126	6np on 1p ultra	.50	*3.00*
107	A126	9np on 1½p green	.50	*3.00*
108	A126	12np on 2p red brn	.35	*.70*
109	A127	15np on 2½p scar, type I	.40	.25
a.		Type II	1.10	*6.00*
110	A127	20np on 3p dk pur	.25	.25
111	A128	25np on 4p ultra	1.00	*2.50*
112	A129	40np on 6p lil rose	.75	.25
113	A130	50np on 9p dp ol grn	3.75	*4.50*
114	A132	75np on 1sh3p dk grn	2.50	.60
		Nos. 104-114 (11)	10.75	*18.30*

The arrangement of the surcharge varies on different values: there are three bars through value on No. 113.

Jubilee Jamboree Issue

Great Britain Nos. 334-336 Surcharged "BAHRAIN," New Value and Square of Dots in Black

Perf. 14½x14

1957, Aug. 1 **Photo.** **Wmk. 308**

115	A138	15np on 2½p scar	.35	.35
116	A138	25np on 4p ultra	.50	.50
117	A138	75np on 1sh3p dk grn	.75	.75
		Nos. 115-117 (3)	1.60	1.60

Great Britain No. 357 Surcharged "BAHRAIN/ NP 15 NP" in Black

1960 **Wmk. 322** ***Perf. 14½x14***

118	A127	15np on 2½p scar, type II	5.00	*12.00*

A1

Sheik Sulman bin Hamad Al Khalifah — A2

Perf. 14½x14

1960, July 1 **Photo.** **Unwmk.**

119	A1	5np lt ultra	.25	.25
120	A1	15np orange	.25	.25
121	A1	20np lt violet	.25	.25
122	A1	30np olive bister	.25	.25
123	A1	40np gray	.25	.25
124	A1	50np emerald	.25	.25
125	A1	75np red brown	.35	.25

Engr.

Perf. 13x13½

126	A2	1r gray	2.50	.35
127	A2	2r carmine	3.50	2.50
128	A2	5r ultra	5.50	3.50
129	A2	10r olive green	15.50	6.00
		Nos. 119-129 (11)	28.85	14.10

Sheik Isa bin Sulman Al Khalifah A3

Bahrain Airport A4

Designs: 5r, 10r, Deep water jetty.

1964, Feb. 22 **Photo.** ***Perf. 14½x14***

130	A3	5np ultra	.25	.25
131	A3	15np orange	.25	.25
132	A3	20np brt purple	.25	.25
133	A3	30np brown olive	.25	.25
134	A3	40np slate	.25	.25
135	A3	50np emerald	.25	*.90*
136	A3	75np chestnut	.30	.25

Engr.

Perf. 13½x13

137	A4	1r black	9.00	2.40
138	A4	2r rose red	11.00	3.00
139	A4	5r violet blue	15.00	15.00
140	A4	10r dull green	19.00	20.00
		Nos. 130-140 (11)	55.80	42.80

Bahrain Postal Administration

Sheik Isa bin Sulman Al Khalifah — A5

Sheik and Bahrain International Airport — A6

Pearl Divers — A7

Bab al Bahrain, Suq Al-Khamis Mosque, Sheik, Emblem, etc. — A8

Designs: 50f, 75f, Pier, Mina Sulman harbor. 200f, Falcon and horse race. 500f, "Hospitality," pouring coffee and Sheik's Palace.

Perf. 14½x14

1966, Jan. 1 **Photo.** **Unwmk.**

141	A5	5f green	.50	.35
142	A5	10f dark red	.50	.35
143	A5	15f ultra	.50	.35
144	A5	20f magenta	.50	.35

Perf. 13½x14

145	A6	30f green & black	.60	.35
146	A6	40f blue & black	.70	.35
147	A6	50f dp car rose & blk	.80	.55
148	A6	75f violet & black	1.00	.70

Perf. 14½x14

149	A7	100f dk blue & yel	3.25	1.25
150	A7	200f dk green & org	14.00	2.75
151	A7	500f red brown & yel	12.00	5.00
152	A8	1d multicolored	21.00	10.00
		Nos. 141-152 (12)	55.35	22.35

Produce, Date Palm, Ship, Truck and Plane — A9

1966, Mar. 28 Litho. *Perf. 13x13½*

153	A9	10f red & blue green	.80	.35
154	A9	20f green & vio	1.25	.75
155	A9	40f olive bis & lt bl	2.75	1.50
156	A9	200f vio blue & pink	11.00	9.00
		Nos. 153-156 (4)	15.80	11.60

6th Bahrain Trade Fair & Agricultural Show.

Map of Bahrain and WHO Emblem — A10

1968, June Unwmk. *Perf. 13½x14*

157	A10	20f gray & black	.90	.60
158	A10	40f blue grn & black	3.00	1.75
159	A10	150f dp rose & black	12.00	6.00
		Nos. 157-159 (3)	15.90	8.35

20th anniv. of the WHO.

Isa Town A11

1968, Nov. 18 Litho. *Perf. 14½*

160	A11	50f shown	5.00	2.00
161	A11	80f Market	7.50	2.75
162	A11	120f Stadium	12.00	5.00
163	A11	150f Mosque	13.50	7.25
		Nos. 160-163 (4)	38.00	17.00

Education Symbol — A12

1969, Apr. Litho. *Perf. 13*

164	A12	40f multicolored	1.90	1.40
165	A12	60f multicolored	4.00	2.25
166	A12	150f multicolored	9.25	4.75
		Nos. 164-166 (3)	15.15	8.40

50th anniversary of education in Bahrain.

Map of Arabian Gulf, Radar and Emblem A13

Designs: 40f, 150f, Radar installation and emblem of Cable & Wireless Ltd., vert.

Perf. 14x13½, 13½x14

1969, July 14 Litho.

167	A13	20f lt green & multi	3.00	.85
168	A13	40f vio blue & multi	5.50	2.00
169	A13	100f ocher & multi	12.00	5.25
170	A13	150f rose lilac & multi	20.00	8.50
		Nos. 167-170 (4)	40.50	16.60

Opening of the satellite earth station (connected through the Indian Ocean satellite Intelsat III) at Ras Abu Jarjur, July 14.

Municipal Building, Arms and Map of Bahrain A14

1970, Feb. 23 Litho. *Perf. 12x12½*

171	A14	30f blue & multi	3.00	3.00
172	A14	150f multicolored	14.50	14.50

2nd Conf. of the Arab Cities' Org.

Copper Bull's Head A15

Conf. Emblem and: 80f, Gateway to Qalat al Bahrain, 7th cent. B.C. 120f, Aerial view of grave mounds, Bahrain. 150f, Dilmun seal, 2000 B.C.

1970, Mar. 1 Photo. *Perf. 14½*

173	A15	60f multicolored	5.00	2.25
174	A15	80f multicolored	7.00	2.50
175	A15	120f multicolored	8.50	4.00
176	A15	150f multicolored	10.00	4.75
		Nos. 173-176 (4)	30.50	13.50

3rd Intl. Asian Archaeological Conf., Bahrain.

Vickers VC 10, Big Ben and Minaret A16

1970, Apr. 5 Litho. *Perf. 14½x14*

177	A16	30f multicolored	4.25	.90
178	A16	60f multicolored	7.50	2.00
179	A16	120f multicolored	13.00	6.25
		Nos. 177-179 (3)	24.75	9.15

1st flight to London from the Arabian Gulf Area by Gulf Aviation Company.

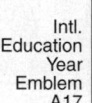

Intl. Education Year Emblem A17

120f, Education Year emblem & students.

1970, Nov. 1 Litho. *Perf. 14½x14*

180	A17	60f blk, blue & org	6.00	3.50
181	A17	120f multicolored	11.50	7.00

Independent State

Declaration of Bahrain Independence, Aug. 15, 1971 — A18

Designs: 30f, "Freedom" with dove and torch, and globe. 60f, Government House, Manama. 120f, 150f, Bahrain coat of arms.

1971, Oct. 2 Photo. *Perf. 14½x14*

182	A18	30f gold & multi	2.80	1.25
183	A18	60f gold & multi	5.00	2.75
184	A18	120f gold & multi	11.00	6.00
185	A18	150f gold & multi	15.00	7.50
		Nos. 182-185 (4)	33.80	17.50

UN Emblem and Sails — A19

30f, 60f, Dhow with sails showing UN and Arab League emblems, horiz. 150f, as 120f.

Perf. 14x14½, 14½x14

1972, Feb. 1 Litho.

186	A19	30f multicolored	5.50	5.00
187	A19	60f red, gray & multi	9.00	8.50
188	A19	120f dull blue & multi	12.00	11.00
189	A19	150f multicolored	22.00	21.00
		Nos. 186-189 (4)	48.50	45.50

Bahrain's admission to the Arab League and the United Nations.

"Your Heart is your Health" — A20

1972, Apr. 7 Litho. *Perf. 14½x14*

190	A20	30f black & multi	6.00	6.00
191	A20	60f gray & multi	11.00	11.00

World Health Day.

UN and FAO Emblems A21

1973, May 12 Litho. *Perf. 12½x13*

192	A21	30f org red, pur & grn	5.75	5.25
193	A21	60f ocher, brn & grn	9.75	9.50

World Food Programs, 10th anniversary.

People of Various Races, Human Rights Flame — A22

1973, Nov. Litho. *Perf. 14x14½*

194	A22	30f blue, blk & brn	5.75	5.75
195	A22	60f lake, blk & brn	10.00	10.00

25th anniversary of the Universal Declaration of Human Rights.

Flour Mill A23

60f, Intl. Airport. 120f, Sulmaniya Medical Center. 150f, ALBA aluminum smelting plant.

1973, Dec. 16 Photo. *Perf. 14½*

196	A23	30f multicolored	2.00	1.25
197	A23	60f multicolored	3.00	2.00
198	A23	120f multicolored	6.00	4.25
199	A23	150f multicolored	6.50	5.00
		Nos. 196-199 (4)	17.50	12.50

National Day.

Letters and UPU Emblem — A24

Carrier Pigeon and UPU Emblem A25

60f, UPU emblem & letters. 150f, Like 120f.

1974, Feb. 4 Litho. *Perf. 13½*

200	A24	30f blue & multi	2.00	2.00
201	A24	60f emerald & multi	3.50	3.50

Perf. 12½x13½

202	A25	120f ultra & multi	3.75	3.75
203	A25	150f yellow & multi	5.50	5.50
		Nos. 200-203 (4)	14.75	14.75

Bahrain's admission to UPU.

Traffic Signals — A26

1974, May 4 Litho. *Perf. 14½*

204	A26	30f org brown & multi	4.00	4.00
205	A26	60f brt blue & multi	8.00	8.00

International Traffic Day.

Jet, Globe, Mail Coach and UPU Emblem — A27

1974, Sept. 1 Photo. *Perf. 14x14½*

206	A27	30f multicolored	1.00	1.00
207	A27	60f multicolored	1.50	1.50
208	A27	120f multicolored	3.75	3.75
209	A27	150f multicolored	4.50	4.50
		Nos. 206-209 (4)	10.75	10.75

Centenary of Universal Postal Union.

National Day Emblem, Sitra Power Station — A28

National Day: 120f, 150f, Bahrain dry dock.

1974, Dec. 16 Litho. *Perf. 14½*

210 A28	30f blue & multi	.90	.90
211 A28	60f green & multi	2.40	2.40
212 A28	120f lil rose & multi	4.00	4.00
213 A28	150f ver & multi	5.25	5.25
	Nos. 210-213 (4)	12.55	12.55

Woman's Silk Gown — A29

Various women's costumes.

Photo.; Gold Embossed

1975, Feb. 1 *Perf. 14½x14*

214 A29	30f blue grn & multi	.95	.95
215 A29	60f vio blue & multi	1.75	1.75
216 A29	120f rose red & multi	3.75	3.75
217 A29	150f multicolored	4.50	4.50
	Nos. 214-217 (4)	10.95	10.95

Pendant — A30

Designs: Various jewelry.

1975, Apr. 1 Photo. *Perf. 14½x14*

218 A30	30f olive & multi	1.10	1.10
219 A30	60f dp pur & multi	2.50	2.50
220 A30	120f dp car & multi	4.25	4.25
221 A30	150f dp blue & multi	5.50	5.50
	Nos. 218-221 (4)	13.35	13.35

Woman Planting Flower, IWY Emblem — A31

60f, Educated woman holding IWY emblem.

1975, July 28 Litho. *Perf. 14½*

222 A31	30f multicolored	2.25	2.25
223 A31	60f multicolored	5.50	5.50

International Women's Year.

Miniature Sheet

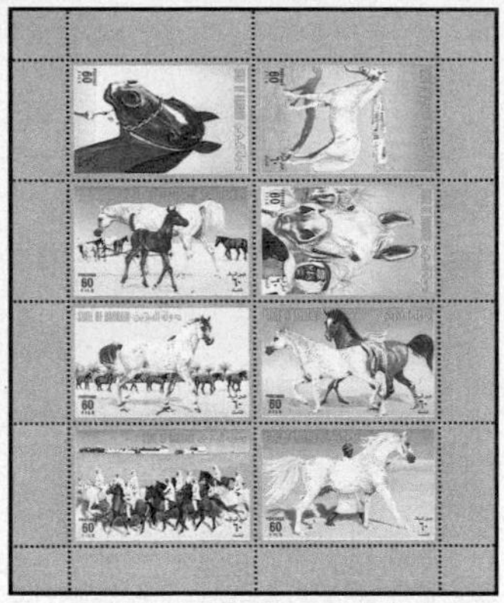

Arabian Stallion — A32

No. 224 — Arabian horses: a, Brown head. b, White mare. c, Mare and foal. d, White head. e, White mare. f, Mare and stallion. g, Bedouins on horseback. Nos. 224a, 224b, 224d are vert.

Perf. 14x14½, 14½x14

1975, Sept. 1 Photo.

224 A32	Sheet of 8	62.50	62.50
a.-h.	60f any single	6.25	6.25

Flag of Bahrain — A33

Map of Bahrain — A34

Sheik Isa — A35

1976-2000 Litho. *Perf. 14½*

225 A33	5f red & ultra	.35	.35
a.	Perf. 14½x13½	—	—
226 A33	10f red & green	.35	.35
a.	Perf. 14½x13½	—	—
227 A33	15f red & black	.35	.35
a.	Perf. 14½x13½	—	—
228 A33	20f red & brown	.55	.35
b.	Perf. 14½x13½	.65	.35
228A A34	25f gray & blk ('79)	.65	.35
229 A34	40f blue & black	.65	.45
229A A34	50f yel grn & blk ('79)	.65	.55
b.	Bold imprint ('88)	4.25	.90
230 A34	60f dl grn & blk ('77)	1.15	.65
231 A34	80f rose lil & blk	1.75	.80
a.	Bold imprint ('88)	4.25	1.50
232 A34	100f lt red brn & blk ('77)	1.75	.95
a.	Bold imprint ('88)	4.25	2.00
233 A34	150f org & black	3.25	1.60
a.	Bold imprint ('88)	4.25	3.75
234 A34	200f yel & black	4.00	1.75
a.	Bold imprint ('88)	4.25	4.25

Engr.

Perf. 12x12½

235 A35	300f lt grn & grn	4.50	2.50
a.	Perf. 13½x14 ('90)	6.00	2.75
236 A35	400f pink & red brn	6.50	4.00
a.	Perf. 13½x14 ('90)	8.00	4.50
b.	Perf. 14½ ('94)	67.50	45.00
237 A35	500f lt bl & dk bl	9.00	4.25
a.	Perf. 13½x14 ('90)	9.75	5.25
238 A35	1d gray & sepia	14.50	7.50
a.	Perf. 13½x14 ('90)	16.50	8.50
b.	1d cream & sepia ('93)	37.50	25.00
c.	As b, perf. 13½x14 ('90)	15.50	8.00
d.	1d pale grn & sepia ('00)	37.50	25.00
239 A35	2d rose & vio ('80)	22.50	10.00
a.	Perf. 13½x14 ('96)	23.00	12.50
240 A35	3d buff & brn ('80)	40.00	20.00
a.	Perf. 13½x14 ('96)	45.00	21.00
	Nos. 225-240 (18)	112.45	56.75

Nos. 229Ab, 231a-234a have printer's imprint in bold in bottom margin, with narrower spacing, and a hyphen after "PRESS."

The 300f-1d stamps were reprinted in slightly different shades with new denominations (2d-3d) in 1980. All are on thicker paper with matte gum; original printings have shiny gum. Values, each: $22 unused, and $11 used.

Concorde at London Airport — A36

Designs: No. 245, Concorde at Bahrain Airport. No. 246, Concorde over London to Bahrain map. No. 247, Concorde on runway at night.

1976, Jan. 22 Photo. *Perf. 13x14*

244 A36	80f gold & multi	3.75	2.50
245 A36	80f gold & multi	3.75	2.50
246 A36	80f gold & multi	3.75	2.50
247 A36	80f gold & multi	3.75	2.50
a.	Souvenir sheet of 4	17.00	17.00
b.	Block of 4, #244-247	16.00	15.00

1st commercial flight of supersonic jet Concorde, London to Bahrain, Jan. 21. No. 247a contains 4 stamps with simulated perfs.

Soldier, Flag and Arms of Bahrain — A37

1976, Feb. 5 Litho. *Perf. 14½*

248 A37	40f yellow & multi	3.00	3.00
249 A37	80f lt blue & multi	5.00	5.00

Defense Force Day.

Sheik Isa, King Khalid, Bahrain and Saudi Flags A38

1976, Mar. 23 Litho. *Perf. 14½*

250 A38	40f gold & multi	3.00	1.50
251 A38	80f silver & multi	5.50	2.75

Visit of King Khalid of Saudi Arabia.

New Housing, Housing Ministry's Seal — A39

1976, Dec. 16 Litho. *Perf. 14½*

252 A39	40f rose & multi	2.25	1.20
253 A39	80f blue & multi	4.50	2.25

National Day.

APU Emblem A40

1977, Apr. 12 Litho. *Perf. 14½*

254 A40	40f silver & multi	1.80	1.50
255 A40	80f rose & multi	4.50	3.25

Arab Postal Union, 25th anniversary.

Miniature Sheet

Saluki dogs — A41

No. 256 — Saluki dogs: a, Dogs on Beach and Dhow. b, Dog and camels. c, Dog and gazelles. d, Dog and Ruler's Palace. e, Dog's head. f, Heads of two dogs. g, Dog in dunes. h, Playing dogs.

1977, July Photo. *Perf. 14x14½*

256 A41	Sheet of 8	35.00	20.00
a.-h.	80f any single	3.50	2.25

Students and Candle A42

1977, Sept. 8 Litho. *Perf. 14½*

257 A42	40f multicolored	2.00	2.00
258 A42	80f multicolored	4.50	4.50

International Literacy Day.

Shipyard and Flags A43

1977, Dec. 16 Litho. *Perf. 14½*

259 A43	40f multicolored	2.00	1.50
260 A43	80f multicolored	4.50	3.00

Inauguration of Arab Shipbuilding and Repair Yard Co.

Antenna, ITU Emblem A44

1978, May 17 Litho. *Perf. 14½*

261 A44	40f yellow & multi	2.00	1.75
262 A44	80f silver & multi	4.25	3.50

10th World Telecommunications Day.

Ghanja Dhow — A45

Dhows of the Arabian Gulf. Nos. 267-270 vertical.

Perf. 14x14½, 14½x14

1979, June 16			**Photo.**		
263	A45	100f	shown	6.00	6.00
264	A45	100f	Zarook	6.00	6.00
265	A45	100f	Shu'ai	6.00	6.00
266	A45	100f	Jaliboot	6.00	6.00
267	A45	100f	Baghla	6.00	6.00
268	A45	100f	Sambuk	6.00	6.00
269	A45	100f	Boom	6.00	6.00
270	A45	100f	Kotia	6.00	6.00
a.			Block of 8, #263-270	75.00	75.00

Learning to Walk — A46

IYC Emblem and: 100f, Hands surrounding girl, UN emblem.

1979		**Litho.**	*Perf. 14½*		
271	A46	50f	multicolored	2.00	1.50
272	A46	100f	multicolored	4.50	3.00

International Year of the Child.

Hegira, 1,500th Anniv. — A47

1980		**Photo.**	*Perf. 13x13½*		
273	A47	50f	multicolored	.95	.65
274	A47	100f	multicolored	1.90	1.35
a.			Miniature sheet of 1	10.50	10.50
275	A47	150f	multicolored	2.25	1.60
276	A47	200f	multicolored	3.50	2.40
			Nos. 273-276 (4)	8.60	6.00

Falcon A48

Various falcons.

Perf. 13½x14, 14x13½

1980, Nov. 1		**Photo.**		
277		Block of 8	35.00	20.00
a.-h.	A48	100f any single	4.00	2.00

IYD Emblem, Sheik Isa A49

1981, Mar. 21		**Litho.**	*Perf. 14½*		
278	A49	50f	multicolored	2.75	1.50
279	A49	100f	multicolored	5.25	3.50

International Year of the Disabled.

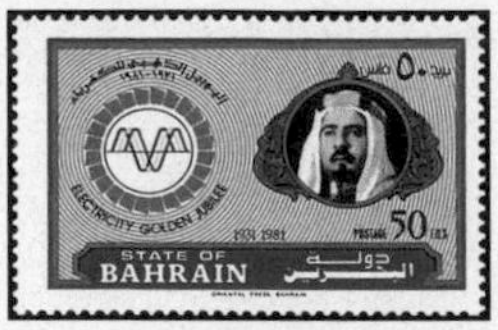
50th Anniversary of Electricity in Bahrain — A50

1981, Apr. 26		**Litho.**	*Perf. 14½*		
280	A50	50f	multicolored	2.75	1.40
281	A50	100f	multicolored	5.25	3.00

Stone Cutting — A51

1981, July 1		**Photo.**	*Perf. 14x13½*		
282	A51	50f	shown	1.25	.65
283	A51	100f	Pottery	1.75	1.20
284	A51	150f	Weaving	3.00	2.50
285	A51	200f	Basket making	3.75	3.00
			Nos. 282-285 (4)	9.75	7.35

Hegira (Pilgrimage Year) — A52

Various mosques.

1981, Oct. 1		**Photo.**	*Perf. 14x13½*		
286	A52	50f	multicolored	1.25	.65
287	A52	100f	multicolored	2.00	1.25
288	A52	150f	multicolored	2.25	2.00
289	A52	200f	multicolored	3.75	2.75
			Nos. 286-289 (4)	9.25	6.65

Sheik Isa, 20th Anniv. of Coronation A53

1981, Dec. 16		**Photo.**	*Perf. 14x13½*		
290	A53	15f	multicolored	.65	.55
291	A53	50f	multicolored	1.20	1.00
292	A53	100f	multicolored	2.00	1.75
293	A53	150f	multicolored	3.25	3.00
294	A53	200f	multicolored	4.00	3.50
			Nos. 290-294 (5)	11.10	9.80

Wildlife in al Areen Park — A54

No. 295: a, Gazelle. b, Oryx. c, Dhub lizard. d, Arabian hares. e, Oryxes. f, Reems.

1982, Mar. 1		**Photo.**	*Perf. 13½x14*	
295		Sheet of 6	16.50	16.50
a.-f.	A54	100f any single	2.50	2.50

Nos. 295a-b and 295e-f exist with blue omitted.

3rd Session of Gulf Supreme Council, Nov. — A55

1982, Nov. 9		**Litho.**	*Perf. 14½*		
296	A55	50f	blue & multi	1.00	1.00
297	A55	100f	green & multi	2.75	2.75

Opening of Madinat Hamad Housing Development — A56

1983, Dec. 1		**Litho.**	*Perf. 14½*		
298	A56	50f	multicolored	1.75	.90
299	A56	100f	multicolored	4.00	2.75

Al Khalifa Dynasty Bicentenary — A57

No. 300 — Sheiks or emblems: a, 500fr, Isa bin Sulman. b, Emblem (tan & multi). c, Isa bin Ali, 1869-1932. d, Hamad bin Isa, 1932-42. e, Sulman bin Hamad, 1942-61. f, Emblem (pale green & multi). g, Emblem (lemon & multi). h, Emblem (light blue & multi). i, Emblem (gray & multi).

1983, Dec. 16		**Litho.**	*Perf. 14½*	
300		Sheet of 9	14.00	14.00
a.-i.	A57	100f any single	1.35	1.35

Souvenir Sheet

301	A57	500f multicolored	12.00	12.00

No. 301 contains one stamp 60x38mm.

Gulf Co-operation Council Traffic Week — A58

1984, Apr. 30		**Litho.**	*Perf. 14½*		
302	A58	15f	multicolored	.60	.45
303	A58	50f	multicolored	1.45	1.00
304	A58	100f	multicolored	2.50	2.00
			Nos. 302-304 (3)	4.55	3.45

1984 Summer Olympics A59

1984, Sept. 15			*Perf. 14½*		
305	A59	15f	Hurdles	.30	.30
306	A59	50f	Equestrian	1.00	1.00
307	A59	100f	Diving	2.00	2.00
308	A59	150f	Fencing	2.50	2.50
309	A59	200f	Shooting	4.00	4.00
			Nos. 305-309 (5)	9.80	9.80

Postal Service Cent. A60

1984, Dec. 8		**Photo.**	*Perf. 12x11½*		
310	A60	15f	multicolored	.55	.55
311	A60	50f	multicolored	1.75	1.75
312	A60	100f	multicolored	3.00	3.00
			Nos. 310-312 (3)	5.30	5.30

Miniature Sheet

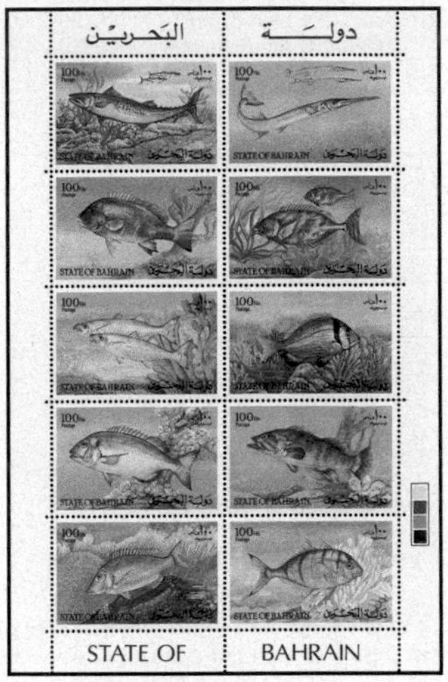
Coastal Fish — A61

Various fish.

1985, Feb. 10		**Photo.**	*Perf. 13½x14*	
313	A61	Sheet of 10	25.00	25.00
a.-j.		100f any single	2.00	2.00

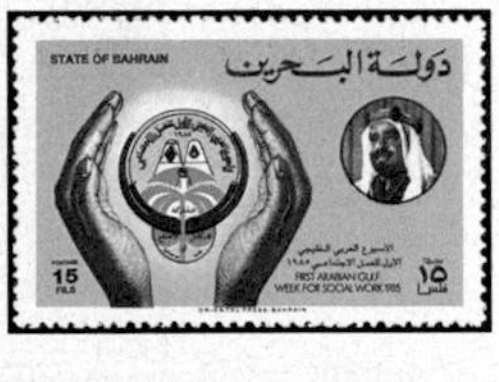
1st Arab Gulf States Week for Social Work A62

1985, Oct. 15		**Litho.**	*Perf. 14½*		
314	A62	15f	multicolored	.55	.45
315	A62	50f	multicolored	1.35	1.35
316	A62	100f	multicolored	3.50	3.00
			Nos. 314-316 (3)	5.40	4.80

Intl. Youth Year A63

1985, Nov. 16					
317	A63	15f	multicolored	.45	.30
318	A63	50f	multicolored	1.20	1.10
319	A63	100f	multicolored	3.50	2.25
			Nos. 317-319 (3)	5.15	3.65

Bahrain-Saudi Arabia Causeway Opening — A64

15f, Causeway, aerial view. 50f, Island. 100f, Causeway.

1986, Nov.		**Litho.**	*Perf. 14½*		
320	A64	15f	multicolored	.55	.55
321	A64	50f	multicolored	1.45	1.45
322	A64	100f	multicolored	2.50	2.50
			Nos. 320-322 (3)	4.50	4.50

Sheik Isa, 25th Anniv. as the Emir — A65

1986, Dec. 16

323	A65 15f multicolored	.50	.50
324	A65 50f multicolored	1.30	1.30
325	A65 100f multicolored	2.25	2.25
a.	Souvenir sheet of 3, #323-325	8.25	8.25
	Nos. 323-325 (3)	4.05	4.05

WHO, 40th Anniv. A66

1988, Apr. 30 Litho. *Perf. 14½*

326	A66 50f multicolored	.80	.80
327	A66 150f multicolored	2.25	2.25

Opening of Ahmed Al Fateh Islamic Center A67

1988, June 2 Litho. *Perf. 14½*

328	A67 50f multicolored	.80	.80
329	A67 150f multicolored	2.25	2.25

1988 Summer Olympics, Seoul — A68

1988, Sept. 17 Litho. *Perf. 14½*

330	A68 50f Running	.50	.50
331	A68 80f Equestrian	.90	.90
332	A68 150f Fencing	1.75	1.75
333	A68 200f Soccer	3.00	3.00
	Nos. 330-333 (4)	6.15	6.15

Gulf Cooperation Council Supreme Council 9th Regular Session, Bahrain — A69

1988, Dec. 19 Litho. *Perf. 14½*

334	A69 50f multicolored	.80	.80
335	A69 150f multicolored	2.25	2.25

Miniature Sheets

Camels — A70

No. 336: a, Close-up of head, rider in background. b, Camel kneeling at rest. c, Two adults, calf. d, Three adults. e, Camel facing right. f, Mount and rider (facing left).

No. 337, vert.: a, Man walking in front of camel, oil well. b, Man walking in front of camel. c, Oil well, camel's head. d, Mount and rider (facing forward). e, Mount and rider (facing right). f, Two dromedaries at a run.

Perf. 13½x14, 14x13½

1989, June 15

336	A70 Sheet of 6	11.00	11.00
a.-f.	150f any single	1.40	1.40
337	A70 Sheet of 6	11.00	11.00
a.-f.	150f any single	1.40	1.40

Sheik Isa — A71

1989, Dec. 16 Litho. *Perf. 13½x14*

338	A71 25f multicolored	.40	.25
339	A71 40f multicolored	.45	.25
340	A71 50f multicolored	.50	.25
341	A71 60f multicolored	.55	.25
342	A71 75f multicolored	.65	.30
343	A71 80f multicolored	.65	.30
344	A71 100f multicolored	.85	.40
345	A71 120f multicolored	1.00	.45
346	A71 150f multicolored	1.30	.60
347	A71 200f multicolored	1.50	.85
a.	Souv. sheet of 10, #338-347	9.00	9.00
	Nos. 338-347 (10)	7.85	3.90

Houbara (Bustard) — A72

No. 348: a, Two birds facing right. b, Two birds facing each other. c, Chicks. d, Adult, chick. e, Adult, facing right, vert. f, In flight. g, Adult facing right. h, Chick, facing left, vert. i, Adult facing left. j, Adult male, close-up. k, Courtship display. l, Two birds facing left.

1990, Feb. 17 Photo. *Perf. 14*

348	Sheet of 12	18.00	18.00
a.-l.	A72 150f any single	1.30	1.30

Gulf Air, 40th Anniv. A73

1990, Mar. 24 Litho. *Perf. 14½*

360	A73 50f multicolored	.50	.50
361	A73 80f multicolored	.80	.80
362	A73 150f multicolored	1.60	1.60
363	A73 200f multicolored	2.40	2.40
	Nos. 360-363 (4)	5.30	5.30

Chamber of Commerce, 50th Anniv. — A74

1990, May 26

364	A74 50f multicolored	.50	.50
365	A74 80f multicolored	.75	.75
366	A74 150f multicolored	1.50	1.50
367	A74 200f multicolored	1.90	1.90
	Nos. 364-367 (4)	4.65	4.65

Intl. Literacy Year A75

1990, Sept. 8 Litho. *Perf. 14½*

368	A75 50f multicolored	.45	.45
369	A75 80f multicolored	.70	.70
370	A75 150f multicolored	1.35	1.35
371	A75 200f multicolored	1.75	1.75
	Nos. 368-371 (4)	4.25	4.25

Miniature Sheet

Indigenous Birds — A76

No. 372: a, Galerida cristata. b, Upupa epops. c, Pycnonotus leucogenys. d, Streptopelia turtur. e, Streptopelia decaocto. f, Falco tinnunculus. g, Passer domesticus, horiz. h, Lanius excubitor, horiz. i, Psittacula krameri.

1991, Sept. 15 Litho. *Perf. 14½*

372	A76 Sheet of 9	20.00	20.00
a.-i.	150f any single	1.80	1.80

See Nos. 382, 407.

A77

Coronation of Sheik Isa, 30th Anniv. — A77a

Litho. & Embossed

1991, Dec. 16 *Perf. 14½*

373	A77 50f multicolored	.45	.45
374	A77a 50f multicolored	.45	.45
375	A77 80f multicolored	.70	.70
376	A77a 80f multicolored	.70	.70
377	A77 150f multicolored	1.50	1.50
378	A77a 150f multicolored	1.50	1.50
379	A77 200f multicolored	2.10	2.10
380	A77a 200f multicolored	2.10	2.10
	Nos. 373-380 (8)	9.50	9.50

Souvenir Sheet

Perf. 14x14½

381	Sheet of 2	11.00	11.00
a.	A77a 500f multicolored	5.25	5.25
b.	A77 500f multicolored	5.25	5.25

No. 381 contains 41x31mm stamps.

Indigenous Birds Type of 1991

Miniature Sheet

No. 382: a, Ciconia ciconia. b, Merops apiaster. c, Sturnus vulgaris. d, Hypocolius ampelinus. e, Cuculus canorus. f, Turdus viscivorus. g, Coracias garrulus. h, Carduelis carduelis. i, Lanius collurio. j, Turdus iliacus, horiz. k, Motacilla alba, horiz. l, Oriolus oriolus, horiz. m, Erithacus rubecula. n, Luscinia luscinia. o, Muscicapa striata. p, Hirundo rustica.

1992, Mar. 21 Litho. *Perf. 14½*

382	Sheet of 16	25.00	25.00
a.-p.	A76 150f any single	1.25	1.25

Miniature Sheet

Horse Racing — A78

No. 383: a, Horses leaving starting gate. b, Trainers leading horses. c, Horses racing around turn. d, Horses in stretch racing by flags. e, Two horses racing by grandstand. f, Five horses galloping. g, Two brown horses racing. h, Black horse, gray horse racing.

1992, May 22

383	A78 Sheet of 8	12.50	12.50
a.-h.	150f any single	1.20	1.20

1992 Summer Olympics, Barcelona — A79

1992, July 25 Litho. *Perf. 14½*

384	A79 50f Equestrian	.50	.50
385	A79 80f Running	.90	.90
386	A79 150f Judo	1.50	1.50
387	A79 200f Cycling	2.10	2.10
	Nos. 384-387 (4)	5.00	5.00

Bahrain Intl. Airport, 60th Anniv. A80

1992, Oct. 27 Litho. *Perf. 14½*

388	A80 50f multicolored	.40	.40
389	A80 80f multicolored	.60	.60
390	A80 150f multicolored	1.50	1.50
391	A80 200f multicolored	2.00	2.00
	Nos. 388-391 (4)	4.50	4.50

Children's Art — A81

Designs: 50f, Girl jumping rope, vert. 80f, Women in traditional dress, vert. 150f, Women stirring kettle. 200f, Fishermen.

1992, Nov. 28 Litho. *Perf. 14½*
392 A81 50f multicolored .35 .35
393 A81 80f multicolored .55 .55
394 A81 150f multicolored 1.10 1.10
395 A81 200f multicolored 1.75 1.75
Nos. 392-395 (4) 3.75 3.75

Inauguration of Expansion of Aluminum Bahrain — A82

50f, Ore funicular. 80f, Smelting pot. 150f, Mill. 200f, Cylindrical aluminum ingots.

1992, Dec. 16
396 A82 50f multicolored .45 .45
397 A82 80f multicolored .80 .80
398 A82 150f multicolored 1.50 1.50
399 A82 200f multicolored 2.00 2.00
Nos. 396-399 (4) 4.75 4.75

Bahrain Defense Force, 25th Anniv. A83

Designs: 50f, Artillery forces, vert. 80f, Fighters, tanks, and ship, vert. 150f, Frigate. 200f, Jet fighter.

Perf. 13½x13, 13x13½
1993, Feb. 5 Litho.
400 A83 50f multicolored .45 .45
401 A83 80f multicolored .65 .65
402 A83 150f multicolored 1.35 1.35
403 A83 200f multicolored 1.75 1.75
Nos. 400-403 (4) 4.20 4.20

World Meteorology Day — A84

Designs: 50f, Satellite image of Bahrain, vert. 150f, Infrared satellite map of world. 200f, Earth, seen from space, vert.

1993, Mar. 23 Litho. *Perf. 14½*
404 A84 50f multicolored .65 .65
405 A84 150f multicolored 1.75 1.75
406 A84 200f multicolored 2.60 2.60
Nos. 404-406 (3) 5.00 5.00

Bird Type of 1991
Miniature Sheet

No. 407: a, Ardea purpurea. b, Gallinula chloropus. c, Phalacrocorax nigrogularis. d, Dromas ardeola. e, Alcedo atthis. f, Vanellus vanellus. g, Haematopus ostralegus, horiz. h, Nycticorax nycticorax. i, Sterna caspia, horiz. j, Arenaria interpres, horiz. k, Rallus aquaticus, horiz. l, Anas platyrhychos, horia. m, Larus fuscus, horiz.

1993, May 22 Litho. *Perf. 14½*
407 Sheet of 13 + 2 labels 24.00 24.00
a.-m. A76 150f any single 1.75 1.75

Gazella Subgutturosa Marica — A85

1993, July 24 Litho. *Perf. 14½*
408 A85 25f Calf 1.20 1.20
409 A85 50f Female standing 2.25 2.25
410 A85 50f Female walking 2.25 2.25
411 A85 150f Male 6.25 6.25
Nos. 408-411 (4) 11.95 11.95

World Wildlife Federation.

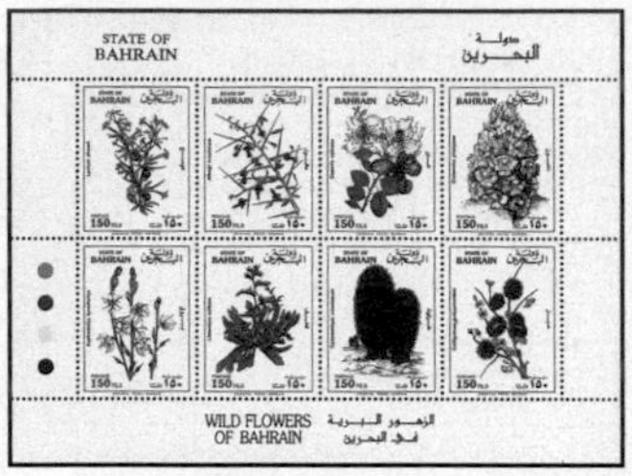

Wild Flowers — A86

Designs: a, Lycium shawii. b, Alhagi maurorum. c, Caparis spinosa. d, Cistanche phelypae. e, Asphodelus tenuifolius. f, Limonium axillare. g, Cynomorium coccineum. h, Calligonum polygonoides.

1993, Oct. 16 Litho. *Perf. 13½x13*
412 A86 150f Sheet of 8, #a.-h. 9.00 9.00

A87

1994, Jan. 22 Litho. *Perf. 14½*
Background Color
413 A87 50f yellow .50 .50
414 A87 80f blue green .75 .75
415 A87 150f purple 1.50 1.50
416 A87 200f blue 2.25 2.25
Nos. 413-416 (4) 5.00 5.00

Intl. Year of the Family.

Butterflies — A88

No. 417: a, Lepidochrysops arabicus. b, Ypthima bolanica. c, Eurema brigitta. d, Precis limnoria. e, Aglais urticae. f, Colotis protomedia. g, Salamis anacardii. h, Byblia ilithyia.

No. 418: a, Papilio machaon. b, Agrodiaetus loewii. c, Vanessa cardui. d, Papilio demoleus. e, Hamanumida daedalus. f, Funonia orithya. g, Funonia chorimine. h, Colias croceus.

Perf. 13½x13, 13x13½
1994, Mar. 21 Litho.
417 A88 50f Sheet of 8, #a.-h. 3.75 3.75
418 A88 150f Sheet of 8, #a.-h. 11.00 11.00

No. 418 is horiz.

A89

1994, May 8 Litho. *Perf. 14½*
419 A89 50f lilac & multi .50 .50
420 A89 80f yellow & multi .80 .80
421 A89 150f salmon & multi 1.50 1.50
422 A89 200f green blue & multi 2.00 2.00
Nos. 419-422 (4) 4.80 4.80

Intl. Red Cross & Red Crescent Societies, 75th anniv.

1994 World Cup Soccer Championships, US — A90

Designs: 50f, Goalkeeper. 80f, Heading ball. 150f, Dribbling ball. 200f, Slide tackle.

1994, June 17 Litho. *Perf. 14*
423 A90 50f multicolored .55 .55
424 A90 80f multicolored .75 .75
425 A90 150f multicolored 1.40 1.40
426 A90 200f multicolored 2.10 2.10
Nos. 423-426 (4) 4.80 4.80

Bahrain's First Satellite Earth Station, 25th Anniv. — A91

1994, July 14
427 A91 50f blue & multi .75 .75
428 A91 80f yellow & multi 1.00 1.00
429 A91 150f violet & multi 1.75 1.75
430 A91 200f pink, yellow & multi 2.25 2.25
Nos. 427-430 (4) 5.75 5.75

Education in Bahrain, 75th Anniv. — A92

1994, Nov. 19 Litho. *Perf. 14½*
431 A92 50f yellow & multi .55 .55
432 A92 80f buff & multi .85 .85
433 A92 150f salmon & multi 1.60 1.60
434 A92 200f pink & multi 2.25 2.25
Nos. 431-434 (4) 5.25 5.25

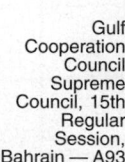

Gulf Cooperation Council Supreme Council, 15th Regular Session, Bahrain — A93

1994, Dec. 19 *Perf. 14*
435 A93 50f blue green & multi .50 .50
436 A93 80f brown & multi .80 .80
437 A93 150f lilac rose & multi 1.50 1.50
438 A93 200f blue & multi 2.25 2.25
Nos. 435-438 (4) 5.05 5.05

Date Palm A94

Designs: 80f, Flowering stage. 100f, Dates beginning to ripen. 200f, Dates up close. 250f, Trees from distance.
500f, Pitcher, basket of dates.

1995, Mar. 21 Litho. *Perf. 14*
439 A94 80f multicolored .75 .75
440 A94 100f multicolored .80 .80
441 A94 200f multicolored 1.75 1.75
442 A94 250f multicolored 2.00 2.00
Nos. 439-442 (4) 5.30 5.30

Souvenir Sheet
443 A94 500f multicolored 4.25 4.25

No. 443 contains one 65x48mm stamp.

Fight Against Polio A95

1995, Apr. 22 Litho. *Perf. 13x13½*
444 A95 80f pink & multi .55 .55
445 A95 200f blue & multi 1.50 1.50
446 A95 250f lt brown & multi 2.10 2.10
Nos. 444-446 (3) 4.15 4.15

World Health Day.

1st Natl. Industries Exhibition A96

1995, May 15
447 A96 80f blue green & multi .60 .60
448 A96 200f lilac & multi 1.75 1.75
449 A96 250f lt brown & multi 2.25 2.25
Nos. 447-449 (3) 4.60 4.60

FAO, 50th Anniv. A97

Fields of various crops.

1995, June 17 Litho. *Perf. 14*
450 A97 80f lilac & multi .60 .60
451 A97 200f blue & multi 1.90 1.90
452 A97 250f lt pink & multi 2.50 2.50
Nos. 450-452 (3) 5.00 5.00

Arab League, 50th Anniv. — A98

1995, Sept. 14 Litho. *Perf. 14½*
453 A98 80f pink & multi .60 .60
454 A98 200f blue & multi 1.75 1.75
455 A98 250f yellow & multi 2.50 2.50
Nos. 453-455 (3) 4.85 4.85

UN, 50th Anniv. A99

1995, Oct. 24 Litho. *Perf. 14½*

456	A99	80f yellow & multi	.55	.55
457	A99	100f green & multi	.90	.90
458	A99	200f pink & multi	1.75	1.75
459	A99	250f blue & multi	2.40	2.40
		Nos. 456-459 (4)	5.60	5.60

Miniature Sheet

Traditional Architecture — A100

No. 460 — Example of architecture, detail: a, Tower with balcony. b, Arched windows behind balcony. c, Double doors under arch. d, Four rows of square windows above row of arched windows. e, Door flanked by two windows. f, Three windows.

1995, Nov. 20 Litho. *Perf. 14½*

460	A100	200f Sheet of 6, #a.-f.	9.00	9.00

National Day — A101

1995, Dec. 16 Litho. *Perf. 14½*

461	A101	80f blue & multi	.60	.60
462	A101	100f green & multi	.90	.90
463	A101	200f violet & multi	2.00	2.00
464	A101	250f blue grn & multi	2.25	2.25
		Nos. 461-464 (4)	5.75	5.75

Public Library, 50th Anniv. — A102

1996, Mar. 23 Litho. *Perf. 14*

465	A102	80f pink & multi	.70	.70
466	A102	200f green & multi	2.00	2.00
467	A102	250f blue & multi	2.40	2.40
		Nos. 465-467 (3)	5.10	5.10

Pearl Diving — A103

Designs: 80f, Group of divers on ship, three in water. 100f, Five divers in water, ship. 200f, Diver underneath water. 250f, Diver being pulled up, underwater scene.

500f, Lantern, weight, scales, pearls, knife.

1996, May 8 Litho. *Perf. 14*

468	A103	80f multicolored	.65	.65
469	A103	100f multicolored	.90	.90
470	A103	200f multicolored	1.90	1.90
471	A103	250f multicolored	2.10	2.10
		Nos. 468-471 (4)	5.55	5.55

Souvenir Sheet

Perf. 14½

472	A103	500f multicolored	6.00	6.00

No. 472 contains one 70x70mm stamp.

1996 Summer Olympics, Atlanta — A104

1996, July 19 Litho. *Perf. 14*

473	A104	80f olive & multi	.70	.70
474	A104	100f pink & multi	.90	.90
475	A104	200f blue grn & multi	2.00	2.00
476	A104	250f orange & multi	2.40	2.40
		Nos. 473-476 (4)	6.00	6.00

Interpol, Intl. Criminal Police Organization — A105

1996, Sept. 25 Litho. *Perf. 14*

477	A105	80f blue & multi	.75	.75
478	A105	100f yellow & multi	1.00	1.00
479	A105	200f pink & multi	2.00	2.00
480	A105	250f green & multi	2.75	2.75
		Nos. 477-480 (4)	6.50	6.50

Aluminum Production in Bahrain, 25th Anniv. — A106

1996, Nov. 20 Litho. *Perf. 14*

481	A106	80f bister & multi	.65	.65
482	A106	100f orange & multi	.80	.80
483	A106	200f blue & multi	2.00	2.00
484	A106	250f green & multi	2.50	2.50
		Nos. 481-484 (4)	5.95	5.95

Accession to the Throne by Sheik Isa Bin Salman Al Khalifa, 35th Anniv. — A107

1996, Dec. 16

485	A107	80f gray & multi	.55	.55
486	A107	100f green & multi	.80	.80
487	A107	200f pink & multi	1.75	1.75
488	A107	250f blue & multi	2.25	2.25
		Nos. 485-488 (4)	5.35	5.35

Bahrain Refinery, 60th Anniv. — A108

1997, Jan. 15 Litho. *Perf. 14*

489	A108	80f red & multi	.80	.80
490	A108	200f blue & multi	2.25	2.25
491	A108	250f yellow & multi	2.50	2.50
		Nos. 489-491 (3)	5.55	5.55

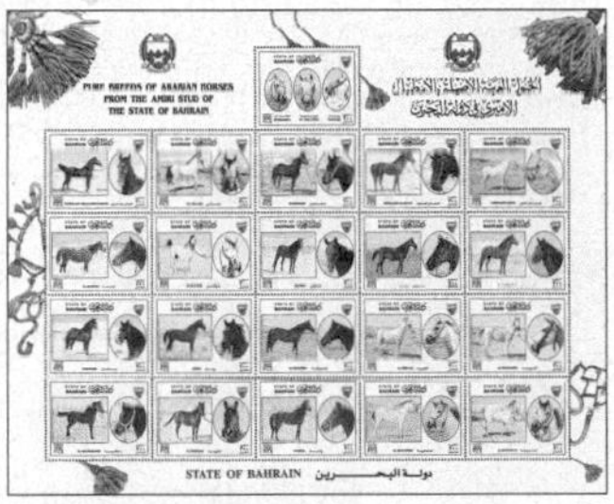

Pure Strains of Arabian Horses, Amiri Stud — A109

No. 492: a, Musannaan, Al-Jellabieh, Rabdaan. b, Kuheilaan weld umm zorayr. c, Al-Jellaby. d, Musannaan. e, Kuheilaan aladiyat. f, Kuheilaan aafas. g, Al-Dhahma. h, Mlolshaan. i, Al-Kray. j, Krush. k, Al Hamdaany. l, Hadhfaan. m, Rabda. n, Al-Suwaitieh. o, Al-Obeyah. p, Al-Shuwaimeh. q, Al-Ma'anaghieh. r, Al-Tuwaisah. s, Wadhna. t, Al-Saqlawieh. u, Al-Shawafah.

1997, Apr. 23 Litho. *Perf. 14x14½*

492	A109	200f Sheet of 21, #a.-u.	32.50	32.50

9th Men's Junior World Volleyball Championship — A110

1997, Aug. 21 Litho. *Perf. 14x14½*

493	A110	80f brown & multi	.70	.70
494	A110	100f green & multi	.90	.90
495	A110	200f gray brn & multi	1.75	1.75
496	A110	250f blue & multi	1.90	1.90
		Nos. 493-496 (4)	5.25	5.25

Montreal Protocol on Substances that Deplete Ozone Layer, 10th Anniv. — A111

1997, Sept. 16 Litho. *Perf. 14½*

497	A111	80f yellow & multi	.60	.60
498	A111	100f purple & multi	.80	.80
499	A111	200f red & multi	1.60	1.60
500	A111	250f green & multi	2.00	2.00
		Nos. 497-500 (4)	5.00	5.00

Sheikh Isa Bin Salman Bridge A112

Designs: 80f, Pylon, supports. 200f, Center of bridge. 250f, 500f, Entire span.

1997, Dec. 28 Litho. *Perf. 13x13½*

501	A112	80f multicolored	.75	.75
502	A112	200f multicolored	2.00	2.00

Size: 76x26mm

503	A112	250f multicolored	2.25	2.25
		Nos. 501-503 (3)	5.00	5.00

Souvenir Sheet

504	A112	500f multicolored	4.50	4.50

Inuaguration of Urea Plant, GPIC (Refinery) Complex — A113

Designs: 80f, View of plant from Persian Gulf. 200f, Plant facilities. 250f, Aerial view.

1998, Mar. 3 Litho. *Perf. 13x13½*

505	A113	80f multicolored	.60	.60
506	A113	200f multicolored	1.90	1.90
507	A113	250f multicolored	2.50	2.50
		Nos. 505-507 (3)	5.00	5.00

World Health Organization, 50th Anniv. — A114

1998, May 11 Litho. *Perf. 14*

508	A114	80f orange & multi	.55	.55
509	A114	200f green & multi	1.75	1.75
510	A114	250f gray & multi	2.50	2.50
		Nos. 508-510 (3)	4.80	4.80

1998 World Cup Soccer Championships, France — A115

Designs: 200f, Soccer balls, world maps, vert. 250f, Players, globe, vert.

1998, June 10

511	A115 80f multicolored	.60	.60
512	A115 200f multicolored	1.90	1.90
513	A115 250f multicolored	2.50	2.50
	Nos. 511-513 (3)	5.00	5.00

14th Arabian Gulf Soccer Cup, Bahrain A116

Design: 200f, 250f, Soccer ball.

1998, Oct. 30 Litho. *Perf. 14*

514	A116 80f shown	.60	.60
515	A116 200f pale violet & multi	1.90	1.90
516	A116 250f bister & multi	2.50	2.50
	Nos. 514-516 (3)	5.00	5.00

Grand Competition for Holy Koran Recitation A117

1999, Jan. 9 Litho. *Perf. 14*

517	A117 100f gray olive & multi	1.00	1.00
518	A117 200f yellow & multi	2.00	2.00
519	A117 250f green & multi	2.25	2.25
	Nos. 517-519 (3)	5.25	5.25

Isa Bin Salman Al-Khalifa (1933-99), Emir of Bahrain — A118

Natl. flag, map and: 100f, 500f, Emir holding sword, vert. 250f, Portrait up close, vert.

Perf. 13¼ (#520, 522), 14¼ (#521)

1999, June 5 Litho.

520	A118 100f multicolored	1.10	1.10
521	A118 200f multicolored	2.00	2.00
522	A118 250f multicolored	2.25	2.25
	Nos. 520-522 (3)	5.35	5.35

Souvenir Sheet

Perf. 14½x13

523	A118 500f multicolored	4.75	4.75

Nos. 520, 522 are 31x50mm. No. 523 contains one 67x102mm stamp.

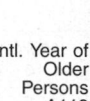

Intl. Year of Older Persons A119

1999, Oct. 9 Litho. *Perf. 13x13½*

524	A119 100f multi	1.00	1.00
525	A119 200f multi, diff.	2.00	2.00
526	A119 250f multi, diff.	2.25	2.25
	Nos. 524-526 (3)	5.25	5.25

Bahrain Stock Exchange, 10th Anniv. — A120

Design: 200f, Pearl Monument, bridge. 250f, Globe.

1999, Nov. 24 Litho. *Perf. 14¼*

527	A120 100f shown	.80	.80
528	A120 200f multicolored	1.60	1.60
529	A120 250f multicolored	1.75	1.75
	Nos. 527-529 (3)	4.15	4.15

Hamad Bin Isa Al-Khalifa, Emir of Bahrain — A121

Emir Hamad: 100f, 500f, Receiving flag from late Emir. 200f, And flag. 250f, And map.

1999, Dec. 16 Litho. *Perf. 14½*

531	A121 100f multi	.90	.90
532	A121 200f multi	2.00	2.00
533	A121 250f multi	2.10	2.10
	Nos. 531-533 (3)	5.00	5.00

Souvenir Sheet

Perf. 13¼x12¾

534	A121 500f multi	4.50	4.50

Dilmun Culture Exhibition A122

Map of Bahrain and: 100f, Bull's head, seal. 200f, Bull's head. 250f, Seal.

2000, Feb. 26 Litho. *Perf. 14¼*

535	A122 100f multi	.80	.80
536	A122 200f multi	1.75	1.75
537	A122 250f multi	2.00	2.00
	Nos. 535-537 (3)	4.55	4.55

Gulf Air, 50th Anniv. A123

Map of Bahrain and: 100f, Emblem, world map. 200f, Emblem. 250f, Birds.

2000, Mar. 24

538	A123 100f multi	1.25	1.25
539	A123 200f multi	2.50	2.50
540	A123 250f multi	2.75	2.75
	Nos. 538-540 (3)	6.50	6.50

Made in Bahrain Exhibition — A124

2000, May 9 *Perf. 14½*

541	A124 100f shown	1.35	1.35
542	A124 200f Emblem, diff.	2.75	2.75
543	A124 250f Oil refinery	3.50	3.50
	Nos. 541-543 (3)	7.60	7.60

Souvenir Sheet

Passage Through Time — A125

No. 544: a, Minarets, fort, flag on dhow's stern. b, Dhows, oil refinery. c, Minaret, date picker. d, Satellite dishes, fort, flag. e, Bridge, pool. f, Woman, jar, dhows. g, Dhows, coffee pot. h, Man with falcon, horse and rider. i, Pearl divers. j, Oyster shuckers. k, Men casting nets. l, Men repairing nets.

Litho. with Foil Application

2000, Oct. 9 *Perf. 14¼*

544	A125 Sheet of 12	24.00	24.00
a.-d.	100f Any single	1.00	1.00
e.-h.	200f Any single	2.00	2.00
i.-l.	250f Any single	2.50	2.50

21st Supreme Council Session of the Gulf Co-operation Council — A126

Designs: 100f, Emblem. 200f, Flags.

2000, Dec. 30 Litho. *Perf. 14¼*

545-546	A126 Set of 2	3.75	3.75

Beit al-Quran, Manama — A127

Designs: 100f, Stained-glass window. 200f, Building illuminated at dusk. 250f, Building during day.

500f, Building during day, stained-glass window, building illuminated at dusk.

2001, Feb. 18 Litho. *Perf. 14¼*

547-549	A127 Set of 3	5.00	5.00

Size: 170x80mm

Imperf

550	A127 500f multi	5.00	5.00

Housing and Agriculture Ministry, 25th Anniv. — A128

Various buildings: 100f, 150f, 200f, 250f.

2001, Apr. 28 *Perf. 14¼*

551-554	A128 Set of 4	6.00	6.00

Intl. Volunteers Year — A129

Emblem and: 100f, Stylized people with arms raised, vert. 150f, Clasped hands. 200f, Stars. 250f, Stylized people holding hands.

2001, Sept. 29 Litho. *Perf. 14¼*

555-558	A129 Set of 4	7.25	7.25

Day of the Arab Woman A130

Designs: 100f, Emblem. 200f, Emblem and rings. 250f, Women, horiz.

2002, Feb. 1 Litho. *Perf. 14¼*

559-561	A130 Set of 3	5.75	5.75

Souvenir Sheet

2002 World Cup Soccer Championships, Japan and Korea — A131

No. 562: a, 100f. b, 200f, c, 250f.

2002, May 31

562	A131 Sheet of 3, #a-c	6.50	6.50

King Hamad — A132

2002, July 15 Litho. *Perf. 13½x13¾*

Background Color

563	A132	25f gray	.25	.25
564	A132	40f brt purple	.25	.25
565	A132	50f dark gray	.30	.30
566	A132	60f dk bl green	.50	.50
567	A132	80f blue	.60	.60
568	A132	100f orange brown	.85	.85
569	A132	125f cerise	.95	.95
570	A132	150f pinkish orange	1.25	1.25
571	A132	200f olive green	1.75	1.75
572	A132	250f rose pink	2.10	2.10
573	A132	300f tan	2.40	2.40
574	A132	400f dull green	3.00	3.00

Size: 26x36mm

Perf. 13¼x13

575	A132	500f rose violet	4.00	4.00
a.		Perf. 13¼x13x13¼x14	4.00	4.00
576	A132	1d dull orange	7.75	7.75
577	A132	2d gray blue	16.00	16.00
578	A132	3d brown violet	24.00	24.00
a.		Souvenir sheet, #563-574, 575a, 576-578	67.50	67.50
		Nos. 563-578 (16)	65.95	65.95

World Teachers' Day — A133

Background color: 100f, Gray green. 200f, Gray.

2002, Oct. 5 Litho. *Perf. 13¼x13*
579-580 A133 Set of 2 2.25 2.25

Parliamentary Elections — A134

Designs: 100f, Flag. 200f, Hand placing ballot in box, vert.

2002, Oct. 24 *Perf. 13x13¼, 13¼x13*
581-582 A134 Set of 2 2.25 2.25

National Day — A135

King Hamad, flag and background color of: 100f, Gray. 200f, Brown violet, vert. 250f, Dark red, vert.

Perf. 13x13¼, 13¼x13
2002, Dec. 16 Litho.
583-585 A135 Set of 3 4.50 4.50

Arab Summit Conference 2003
A136

No. 586: a, Bahrain. b, Sudan. c, Saudi Arabia. d, Djibouti. e, Algeria. f, Tunisia. g, United Arab Emirates. h, Jordan. i, Comoro Islands. j, Qatar. k, Palestine. l, Oman. m, Iraq. n, Somalia. o, Syria. p, Yemen. q, Mauritania. r, Morocco. s, Egypt. t, Libya. u, Lebanon. v, Kuwait.
500f, Montage of scenes.

Litho. With Foil Application
2003, Mar. 1 *Perf. 13*

586	Sheet of 22	32.50	32.50
a.-h.	A136 100f Any single	.65	.65
i.-o.	A136 200f Any single	1.30	1.30
p.-v.	A136 250f Any single	1.60	1.60

Size: 120x103mm
Imperf
587 A136 500f multi 3.75 3.75

World Health Day
A137

UN and Healthy Environments for Children Emblems and: 100f, Children, flowers. 200f, Stylized children.

2003, Apr. 7 Litho. *Perf. 14¼*
588-589 A137 Set of 2 2.75 2.75

World Environment Day — A138

No. 590: a, Swan. b, Peacock. c, Flamingo. d, Ostrich. e, Rumex vesicarius. f, Arnebia hispidissima. g, Capparis spinosa. h, Cassia italica. i, Crab. j, Turtle. k, Sting ray. l, Shark.

2003, June 5 *Perf. 13*

590	A138 Sheet of 12	20.00	20.00
a.-d.	100f Any single	.75	.75
e.-h.	200f Any single	1.50	1.50
i.-l.	250f Any single	2.00	2.00

Intl. Children's Day — A139

No. 591, vert.: a, 100f, Child reading book. b, 150f, Child looking at flowers.
No. 592: a, 200f, Children in field. b, 250f, Children in classroom.

2003, Nov. 20 Litho. *Perf. 14¼*
Vert. Pairs, #a-b
591-592 A139 Set of 2 6.00 6.00

Printed in sheets containing four of each pair.

National Day — A140

King Hamad on horse with panel color of: 100f, Bronze. 200f, Gold. 250f, Silver.
500f, No panel.

Litho. with Foil Application
2003, Dec. 16 *Perf. 14½*
593-595 A140 Set of 3 4.00 4.00

Souvenir Sheet
596 A140 500f multi 3.75 3.75

No. 596 contains one 55x95mm stamp.

Mother's Day
A141

Designs: 100f, Mother and infant. 200f, Mother reading to child.

2004, Mar. 21 Litho. *Perf. 13x13¼*
597-598 A141 Set of 2 2.25 2.25

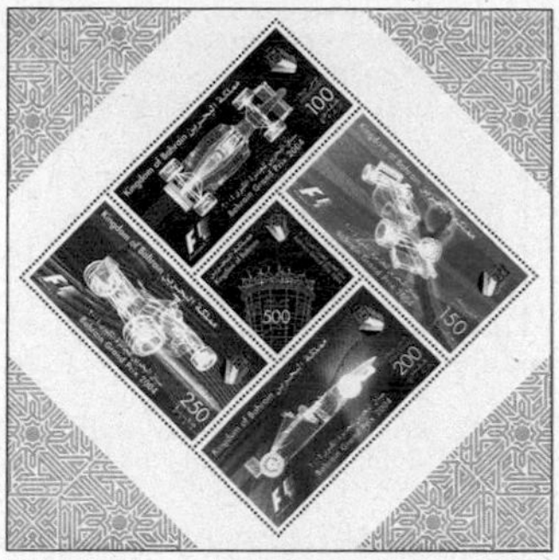

Bahrain Formula 1 Grand Prix — A142

No. 599: a, 100f, Race car, red background (76x36mm). b, 150f, Race car, green background (76x36mm). c, 200f, Race car, blue background (76x36mm). d, 250f, Race car, orange background (76x36mm). e, 500f, Race tower (51x51mm).

2004, Apr. 4 Litho. *Perf. 13*
599 A142 Sheet of 5, #a-e 9.00 9.00

Intl. Day Against Drugs
A143

UN emblem and: 100f, People reaching out to addict. 150f, Addict's arm. 200f, Addict and snake-like needles. 250f, Arms reaching out.

2004, June 24 *Perf. 14¼*
600-603 A143 Set of 4 4.75 4.75

2004 Summer Olympics, Athens — A144

No. 604: a, 100f, Track. b, 150f, Swimming. c, 200f, Sailboarding. d, 250f, Shooting.

2004, Aug. 13
604 A144 Sheet of 4, #a-d 4.25 4.25

Gulf Cooperation Council, 25th Regular Session
A145

Emblem and: 100f, Hands. 200f, Draped flags. 250f, Circle of flags.
500f, Bridge, boats and buildings.

2004, Dec. 20 Litho. *Perf. 14¼*
605-607 A145 Set of 3 3.00 3.00

Souvenir Sheet
Perf. 13¼
608 A145 500f multi 2.75 2.75

No. 608 contains one 175x54mm stamp.

Bahrain Garden Fair
A146

Emblem and various flowers: 100f, 200f, 250f.

2005, Mar. 3 *Perf. 13x13¼*
609-611 A146 Set of 3 3.00 3.00

Inauguration of Constitutional Court — A147

Background colors: 100f, Brown black. 200f, Orange brown. 250f, Blue.

2005, Apr. 18 *Perf. 14½*
612-614 A147 Set of 3 3.75 3.75

Discovery of Artifacts of Dilmon Civilization, 50th Anniv. — A148

Designs: No. 615, 100f, Figurine of human. No. 616, 100f, Sculpted discs. No. 617, 100f, Equestrian statue. No. 618, 200f, Overturned jar and artifacts. No. 619, 200f, Two jars. No. 620, 200f, Jar and lidded jar. No. 621, 250f, Wall, horiz. No. 622, 250f, Steps, horiz. No. 623, 250f, Aerial view of archaeological site, horiz.
500f, Wall, Arab and Western men, horiz.

2005, Apr. 27 Litho. *Perf. 14¼*

615-623	A148 Set of 9	7.75	7.75
623a	Miniature sheet, #615-623	12.00	12.00

Souvenir Sheet
Perf. 14½
624 A148 500f multi 3.75 3.75

No. 624 contains one 88x58mm stamp.

National Day
A149

King Hamad and various buildings: 100f, 200f, 250f. 200f is vert.

2005, Dec. 16 Litho. *Perf. 14¼*
625-627 A149 Set of 3 3.00 3.00

A150

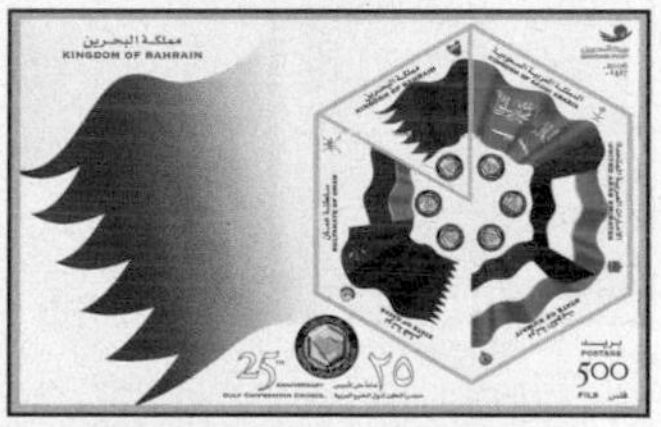

Gulf Cooperation Council, 25th Anniv. — A151

Litho. With Foil Application

2006, May 25 ***Perf. 14***
628 A150 100f multi 2.25 2.25

Imperf

Size: 165x105mm

629 A151 500f multi 7.50 7.50

See Kuwait Nos. 1646-1647, Oman Nos. 477-478, Qatar Nos. 1107-1108, Saudi Arabia No. 1378, and United Arab Emirates Nos. 831-832.

2006 World Cup Soccer Championships, Germany — A152

Emir Hamad and: 100f, Emblem. 200f, Emblem, globe, soccer ball, spheres. 250f, Emblem, globe.

2006, June 9 **Litho.** ***Perf. 14¼***
630-632 A152 Set of 3 3.50 3.50

National Day — A153

King Hamad: 100f, Holding flag and book. 200f, With crown above head. 250f, With crown above head, profile portrait. 500f, Like 100f (36x50mm).

Perf. 14¼, 14 (500f)

2006, Dec. 16 **Litho.**
633-636 A153 Set of 4 5.75 5.75

Gulf Cooperation Council Consumer Protection Day — A154

Designs: 100f, Gulf Cooperation Council emblem, people under umbrella. 200f, People under umbrella of Gulf Cooperation Council flags.

2007, Mar. 1 ***Perf. 13x13¼***
637-638 A154 Set of 2 1.75 1.75

Each stamp printed in sheet of 20 + 5 labels.

National Day — A155

King Hamad: 100f, And crown. 200f, Waving, horiz. 250f, With men, boats, horsemen, horiz.

2007, Dec. 16 **Litho.** ***Perf. 14¼***
639-641 A155 Set of 3 3.00 3.00
640a Souvenir sheet, 2 each #639-640, perf. 13¼ 3.25 3.25

Arab Productive Families Day — A156

Hands of: 100f, Wood carver and basket weaver. 200f, Decoration nailer and seamstress.

2008, Mar. 15 ***Perf. 13¼***
642-643 A156 Set of 2 1.90 1.90

Intl. Nurses Day A157

Designs: 100f, Operating room. 200f, Nurses and child.

2008, May 12 ***Perf. 14¼***
644-645 A157 Set of 2 1.75 1.75

Third Session of Ministerial Meeting of Arab-Chinese Cooperation Forum, Manama — A158

Emblem, Great Wall of China and: 100f, Arch. 200f, Building.

2008, May 21 ***Perf. 13***
646-647 A158 Set of 2 1.75 1.75

"Business Friendly" Advertising Campaign — A159

Text "Business Friendly" in various styles: 100f, 200f.

2008, Aug. 1 **Litho.** ***Perf. 13¼x13***
648-649 A159 Set of 2 2.10 2.10

Souvenir Sheet

2008 Summer Olympics, Beijing — A160

No. 650: a, 100f, Runner crossing finish line. b, 200f, Equestrian.

2008, Aug. 8 ***Perf. 14x13***
650 A160 Sheet of 2, #a-b 2.10 2.10

Miniature Sheets

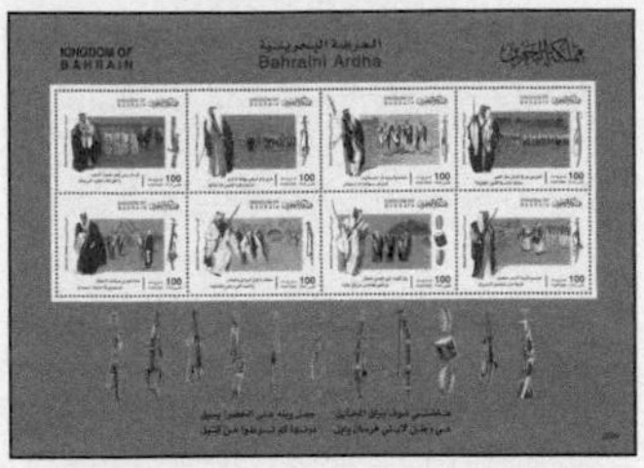

A161

Bahraini Ardha — A162

No. 651 — Color of sky: a, Purple. b, Red brown. c, Blue gray. d, Red violet. e, Gray. f, Yellow orange. g, Blue green. h, Dull brown.

No. 652 — Man in foreground: a, Carrying flag. b, In white robes. c, In red orange robes holding sword.

2008, Dec. 16 ***Perf. 13¼x13***
651 A161 100f Sheet of 8, #a-h 6.50 6.50

Perf. 14

652 A162 200f Sheet of 3, #a-c 3.50 3.50

First Gulf Cooperation Council and Association of South East Asian Nations Ministerial Meeting, Manama A163

Emblems and: 100f, Dhow. 200f, Dhow, diff.

2009, June 29 **Litho.** ***Perf. 14¼***
653-654 A163 Set of 2 2.00 2.00

Souvenir Sheet

Arab Postal Day — A164

No. 655 — Emblem and: a, World map, pigeon. b, Camel caravan.

Litho. With Foil Application

2009, Aug. 3 ***Perf. 13¼***
655 A164 500f Sheet of 2, #a-b 6.50 6.50

Palm Tree Symposium — A165

2009, Nov. 10 **Litho.** ***Perf. 14¼***
656 A165 100f multi .75 .75

A166

Bahraini Women's Day A167

2009, Dec. 1 ***Perf. 13x13¼***
657 A166 100f multi .75 .75
658 A167 200f multi 1.25 1.25

Miniature Sheet

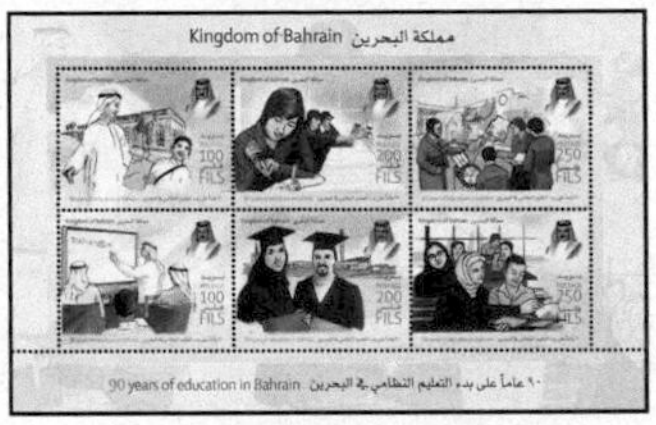

Education in Bahrain, 90th Anniv. — A168

No. 659: a, 100f, Boys outside of school building. b, 100f, Students in math class. c, 200f, Student holding soldering iron. d, 200f, Graduates. e, 250f, Teacher pointing to diagram. f, 250f, Students seated in class.

2009, Dec. 14 ***Perf. 13¼x14¼***
659 A168 Sheet of 6, #a-f 6.75 6.75

National Day A169

Designs: 100f, Flag, map, King Hamad with crown above head, brown background at UL. 200f, As 100f, with blue background at UL. 250f, King Hamad with other sheikhs, buildings, map, horsemen, and flag.
500f, As 250f.

Litho. With Foil Application

2009, Dec. 16 ***Perf. 14¼***
660-662 A169 Set of 3 3.75 3.75

Size: 126x101mm

Imperf

663 A169 500f multi 5.75 5.75

Bahrain Intl. Airshow A170

Airshow emblem and: 100f, King Hamad, airplanes. 200f, Curved red lines.

2010, Jan. 21 **Litho.** ***Perf. 13¼x13***
664-665 A170 Set of 2 1.90 1.90

2010 World Cup Soccer Championships, South Africa — A171

2010 World Cup: 100f, Emblem. 200f, Mascot. 250f, Soccer ball, globe, horiz. (36x26mm).

Perf. 13, 13x13¼ (250f)

2010, June 11 **Litho.**

666-668 A171 Set of 3 3.50 3.50

World Post Day — A172

2010, Oct. 9 ***Perf. 13***

669 A172 250f multi 1.75 1.75

National Day — A173

King Hamad and stylized dove: 100f, Holding ballot above ballot box. 200f, Holding scales of justice. 250f, Writing, vert.

2010, Dec. 16 ***Perf. 14¼***

670-672 A173 Set of 3 3.00 3.00

Bahraini Women's Day — A174

King Hamad and: 100f, Round Supreme Council for Women 10th anniversary emblem. 200f, Rectangular emblem with circles.
500f, King Hamad and buildings.

2011, Dec. 1 ***Perf. 14¼***

673-674 A174 Set of 2 1.60 1.60

Souvenir Sheet

Perf. 13¼x13

675 A174 500f multi 2.75 2.75

No. 675 contains one 90x35mm stamp.

National Day — A175

King Hamad and: 100f, People, heart with Arabic inscription. 200f, Stylized bird over map of Bahrain. 250f, Stylized boat on water, vert.

2011, Dec. 16 ***Perf. 14¼***

676-678 A175 Set of 3 3.00 3.00

Discovery of Oil in Bahrain, 80th Anniv. — A176

Designs: 100f, Airplane over Bahrain Petroleum Company building. 150f, Bahrain Petroleum Company Center of Excellence. 200f, Bridge, man, boy, dhow. 250f, Oil tanks, solar energy facility.

2012, June 17

679-682 A176 Set of 4 3.75 3.75

Royal Charity Organization, 10th Anniv. — A177

2012, July 31

683 A177 250f multi 1.40 1.40

Arab Postal Day — A178

2012, Aug. 3 ***Perf. 12¾x13¼***

684 A178 250f multi 1.40 1.40

6th World Urban Forum, Naples, Italy A179

Emblem and: No. 685, 200f, United Nations Secretary-General Ban Ki-Moon giving award to King Hamad. No. 686, 200f, Bridge, city skyline. No. 687, 200f, Building with wind turbines.

2012, Sept. 1

685-687 A179 Set of 3 3.25 3.25

687a Souvenir sheet of 3, #685-687, perf. 13½x13 4.75 4.75

No. 687a sold for 900f.

Manama, 2012 Capital of Arab Culture A180

2012, Sept. 27 ***Perf. 14¼***

688 A180 200f multi 1.10 1.10

World Habitat Day A181

Designs: No. 689, 100f, Building, denomination in black. No. 690, 100f, Building, diff., denomination in white. No. 691, 100f, Buildings around pond.

2012, Oct. 1 ***Perf. 14¼***

689-691 A181 Set of 3 1.60 1.60

A souvenir sheet containing perf. 13½x13 examples of Nos. 689-691 sold for 900f.

Opening of National Theater, Manama A182

2012, Nov. 12

692 A182 250f multi 1.40 1.40

A183

33rd Supreme Council Summit of the Gulf Cooperation Council A184

Litho. With Foil Application

2012, Dec. 24

693 A183 200f multi 1.10 1.10

694 A184 200f multi 1.10 1.10

Miniature Sheet

33rd Supreme Council Summit of the Gulf Cooperation Council — A185

No. 695 — Various buildings, flag of: a, United Arab Emirates, Sheikh Khalifa. b, Saudi Arabia, King Abdullah. c, Bahrain, King Hamad. d, Kuwait, Sheikh Sabah. e, Qatar, Sheikh Hamad. f, Oman, Sultan Qaboos.

Litho. With Foil Application

2012, Dec. 24 ***Perf. 13½x13***

695 A185 100f Sheet of 6, #a-f 5.50 5.50

No. 695 sold for 1d.

King Hamad, 1 ¼-Anna Local Stamp of 1953 — A186

Designs: 200f, With decorative border and white frame. 500f, Without decorative border and white frame.

2013, Feb. 15 **Litho.** ***Perf. 14¼***

Granite Paper

696 A186 200f multi 1.10 1.10

Souvenir Sheet

Perf. 13¼

697 A186 500f multi 2.75 2.75

First postage stamps of Bahrain, 60th anniv.

Insurance Day — A187

Bahrain Insurance Association emblem and: 100f, Dhows and stylized city skyline. 200f, House, automobile, airplane, medical bag, stethoscope. 250f, Insurance Day emblem.

2013, Mar. 26 **Litho.** ***Perf. 14¼***

698-700 A187 Set of 3 3.00 3.00

Sheikh Isa Award for Service to Humanity A188

Color of geometric pattern in background: 100f, Red brown. 200f, Olive brown.

2013, May 26 **Litho.** ***Perf. 13***

701-702 A188 Set of 2 1.60 1.60

Miniature Sheet

National Day — A189

No. 703 — King Hamad and people carrying flag of Bahrain: a, 200f, Woman wearing headdress and glasses. b, 250f, Woman with stethoscope. c, 300f, Man wearing headdress. d, 400f, Man wearing hard hat.

2013, Dec. 16 **Litho.** ***Perf. 14½***

703 A189 Sheet of 4, #a-d 6.25 6.25

Annual Fine Arts Exhibition, 40th Anniv. — A190

2014, Jan. 15 **Litho.** ***Perf. 14¼***

704 A190 200f multi 1.10 1.10

Third Bahrain International Airshow — A191

Various airshow performers: 200f, 300f, 400f.

2014, Jan. 16 Litho. *Perf. 14¼*
705-707 A191 Set of 3 4.75 4.75

Bahrain Grand Prix, 10th Anniv. A192

Victorious drivers and their cars: 100f, Michael Schumacher, 2004. 150f, Fernando Alonso, 2005, 2006, 2010. 200f, Felipe Massa, 2007, 2008. 250f, Jenson Button, 2009. 500f, Sebastian Vettel, 2012, 2013.

2014, Apr. 6 Litho. *Perf. 14¼*
708-712 A192 Set of 5 6.50 6.50

All Civilizations in Service to Humanity International Interfaith Dialogue — A193

Designs: 200f, Entire tree in green, with world map in white. 250f, Close-up of green tree. 300f, White tree and silhouette of face.

2014, May 5 Litho. *Perf. 13*
713-715 A193 Set of 3 4.00 4.00

Bahrain Bourse, 25th Anniv. — A194

2014, June 16 Litho. *Perf. 14¼*
716 A194 200f multi 1.10 1.10

2014 World Cup Soccer Championships. Brazil — A195

Silhouettes of various people, arm extended on person in: 200f, Orange. 250f, Green and blue, vert. 300f, Red violet.

2014, June 12 Litho. *Perf. 14¼*
717-719 A195 Set of 3 4.00 4.00

National Day — A196

Designs: 200f, Man and woman holding rope on flagpole with Bahrain flag. 300f, Clasped hands on map of Bahrain. 400f, Doves and map of Bahrain.

2014, Dec. 16 Litho. *Perf. 14¼*
720-722 A196 Set of 3 4.75 4.75

Souvenir Sheet

National Initiative for Agricultural Development — A197

No. 723: a, Sheikhs and children. b, Sheikh, army officer, crowd of people, sign.

Perf. 12¾x13¼

2015, Feb. 26 Litho.
723 A197 500f Sheet of 2, #a-b 5.50 5.50

Miniature Sheet

Bahrain Garden Club, 50th Anniv. — A198

No. 724 — Photographs from Garden Club events dated: a, 200f, 1967 (50x60mm). b, 200f, 1989 (50x30mm). c, 200f, 1990 (50x60mm). d, 200f, 1978 (50x60mm). e, 200f, 1992 (50x30mm). f, 300f, 1990 (50x60mm). g, 300f, 1993 (50x30mm). h, 300f, 1994 (50x30mm). i, 400f, 1996 (50x30mm). j, 400f, 2004 (50x60mm). k, 400f, 1997 (50x30mm). l, 400f, 1998 (Sheikhs, women, vegetables, 50x30mm). m, 400f, 2014 (50x60mm). n, 400f, 1998 (Sheikh and children, 50x30mm). o, 500f, 1988 (100x60mm).

Perf. 12¾x13¼

2015, Feb. 26 Litho.
724 A198 Sheet of 15, #a-o 25.50 25.50

Manama, 2015 Capital of Arab Youth — A199

King Hamad, emblems and: 200f, Manama 2015 emblem. 300f, Young men holding flag with Manama 2015 emblem.

2015, Dec. 3 Litho. *Perf. 14¼*
725-726 A199 Set of 2 2.75 2.75

National Day A200

King Hamad, various buildings and people: 200f, 300f, 400f, 1d.

2015, Dec. 16 Litho. *Perf. 14¼*
727-729 A200 Set of 3 4.75 4.75

Size: 202x92mm

Imperf

730 A200 1d multi 5.50 5.50

Bahraini Currency, 50th Anniv. — A201

No. 731 — Obverse and reverse of: a, Half-dinar banknote, 10-fils coin. b, Quarter-dinar banknote, 5-fils coin. c, 100-fils banknote, 1-fils coin. d, 10-dinar banknote, 100-fils coin. e, 5-dinar banknote, 50-fils coin. f, 1-dinar banknote, 25-fils coin.

2015, Dec. 30 Litho. *Perf. 14¼*
731 A201 300f Block of 6, #a-f 9.50 9.50
g. Souvenir sheet of 6, #731a-731f, perf, 13¼ 13.50 13.50

No. 731g sold for 2.50d.

Arab Postal Day — A202

No. 732 — Globe at: a, 200f, Left. b, 300f, Right.

2016, Aug. 3 Litho. *Perf. 14*
732 A202 Horiz. pair, #a-b 2.75 2.75

Relationship Between Bahrain and United Kingdom, 200th Anniv. — A203

200th anniv. emblem and various Bahraini and British buildings: 200f, 500f.

2016, Nov. 10 Litho. *Perf. 14¼*
733-734 A203 Set of 2 3.75 3.75

Supreme Council for Women, 15th Anniv. — A204

2016, Dec. 1 Litho. *Perf. 13*
735 A204 500f multi 2.75 2.75

Gulf Cooperation Council Summit 37th Regular Session — A205

Color behind denomination: 250f, White. 500f, Gold.

2016, Dec. 6 Litho. *Perf. 13*
736-737 A205 Set of 2 4.00 4.00

Miniature Sheet

University of Bahrain, 30th Anniv. — A206

No. 738: a, Building and tower. b, Aerial view of campus. c, Aerial view of courtyard with palm trees, curved building at right. d, Aerial view of building, two buses in foreground. e, Aerial view of plaza with covered walkways. f, Building and large 30th anniv. emblem.

2016, Dec. 29 Litho. *Perf. 14¼*
738 A206 500f Sheet of 6, #a-f 16.00 16.00

Miniature Sheet

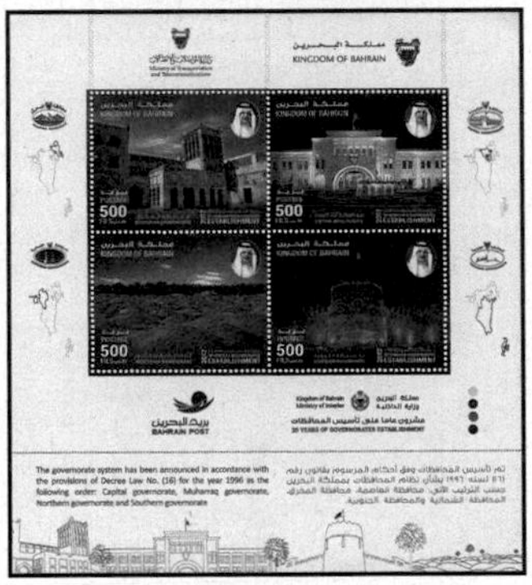

Governates of Bahrain, 20th Anniv. — A207

No. 739: a, Sheikh Isa bin Ali Al Khalifa House, Muharraq Governate. b, Bahrain Gate, Capital Governate. c, Dilmun Burial Grounds, Northern Governate. d, Riffa Fort, Southern Governate.

2017, May 17 Litho. *Perf. 14¼*
739 A207 500f Sheet of 4, #a-d 11.00 11.00

National Day A208

Litho. With Foil Application

2017, Dec. 16 *Perf. 14¼*
740 A208 500f gold & multi 2.75 2.75

Bahrain Defense Force, 50th Anniv. A209

50th anniversary emblem and: 200f, Tanks, King Hamad. 250f, Bahrain Air Force jet, King Hamad. 300f, Ships, King Hamad. 400f, King Hamad seated, vert.
1d, King Hamad, 50th anniversary emblem, arms of Bahrain.

Litho. With Foil Application

2018, Feb. 5 *Perf. 14*
741-744 A209 Set of 4 6.25 6.25

Litho. & Embossed With Foil Application

Size: 153x103mm

Imperf

745 A209 1d multi 5.50 5.50

2017 Discovery of Bahrain's Largest Oil Field in Khalij Al-Bahrain Basin — A210

Designs: 200f, Oil worker and burn-off flame. 250f, Space photograph of Khalij Al-Bahrain Oil Field, vert. 500f, Khalij Al-Bahrain oil platform, 1932 Awali Field oil well.

2018, May 31 **Litho.** *Perf. 14¼*
746-748 A210 Set of 3 5.00 5.00
748a Souvenir sheet of 3, #746-748, perf. 13¼ 5.50 5.50

No. 748a sold for 1d.

Victory of Sheikh Nasser Bin Hamad Al Khalifa in 2018 Ironman Triathlon World Championships — A211

2018, Nov. 8 **Litho.** *Perf. 14¼*
749 A211 400f multi 2.10 2.10

First Flight to Bahrain, Cent. A212

2018, Nov. 13 **Litho.** *Perf. 14¼*
750 A212 400f multi 2.10 2.10

National Day A213

Arabic text and: 200f, Map of Bahrain. 250f, King Hamad, Prince Khalifa and Crown Prince Salman. 500f, King Hamad.

2018, Dec. 16 **Litho.** *Perf. 14¼*
751-753 A213 Set of 3 5.00 5.00
753a Souvenir sheet of 3, #751-753 5.50 5.50

No. 753a sold for 1d.

Reign of King Hamad, 20th Anniv. — A214

2019, Apr. 21 **Litho.** *Perf. 14¼x14½*
754 A214 500f multi 2.75 2.75

Souvenir Sheet

Perf. 14

755 A214 1d King Hamad, diff. 5.50 5.50

No. 755 contains one 120x90mm stamp.

Bahrain Police, Cent. — A215

No. 756: a, Two flag bearers on horseback near Police Fort. b, Cannons in front of Police Fort. c, Policemen on camels. d, Three flag bearers on horseback.
500f, Fag bearers on horseback, cannons and Police Fort (90x70mm).

2019, Dec. 4 **Litho.** *Perf. 14¼*
756 A215 250f Block of 4, #a-d 5.50 5.50
757 A215 500f multi 2.75 2.75

National Day — A216

2019, Dec. 16 **Litho.** *Perf. 14¼*
758 A216 500f gold & multi 2.75 2.75

POSTAL TAX STAMPS

PT1

1973, Oct. 21 **Litho.** *Perf. 14½*
RA1 PT1 5f sky blue *225.00 125.00*

PT2

1974 **Litho.** *Perf. 14½*
RA2 PT2 5f light blue 7.50 .40
a. Perf. 14½x13½ 7.50 .40

No. RA2a was issued around 1988.

PT3

No. RA3 is inscribed "STATE OF BAHRAIN".

2000-02 **Litho.** *Perf. 14½x14*
RA3 PT3 10f green & black 3.00 .40
RA4 PT3 10f green & black ('02) 3.00 .40

No gum examples of RA1-RA4 are considered used.

BANGKOK

'baŋ,käk

LOCATION — Capital of Siam (Thailand)

Stamps were issued by Great Britain under rights obtained in the treaty of 1855. These were in use until July 1, 1885, when the stamps of Siam were designated as the only official postage stamps to be used in the kingdom.

100 Cents = 1 Dollar

Excellent counterfeits of Nos. 1-22 are plentiful.

Stamps of Straits Settlements Overprinted in Black

1882 **Wmk. 1** *Perf. 14*
1 A2 2c brown *4,500. 1,950.*
2 A2 4c rose *4,250. 1,650.*
b. Double overprint *9,750.*
3 A6 5c brown violet *475. 550.*
4 A2 6c violet *325. 150.*
5 A3 8c yel orange *3,750.* 290.
6 A7 10c slate *750. 200.*
7 A3 12c blue *1,500. 600.*
8 A3 24c green *900. 190.*
9 A4 30c claret *57,500. 39,000.*
10 A5 96c olive gray *9,750. 4,000.*

See note after No. 20.

1882-83 **Wmk. 2**
11 A2 2c brown *750.00 450.00*
12 A2 2c rose ('83) *75.00 57.50*
a. Inverted overprint *19,000. 16,500.*
b. Double overprint *3,500. 3,500.*
c. Triple overprint *13,000.*
13 A2 4c rose *900.00 400.00*
14 A2 4c brown ('83) *100.00 90.00*
a. Double overprint 4,500.
15 A6 5c ultra ('83) *425.00 210.00*
16 A2 6c violet ('83) *325.00 170.00*
a. Double overprint *9,000.*
17 A3 8c yel orange *250.00 82.50*
a. Inverted overprint *30,000. 16,000.*
18 A7 10c slate *260.00 110.00*
19 A3 12c violet brn ('83) *450.00 190.00*
20 A3 24c green *8,000. 3,750.*

Double overprints must have two clear impressions. Partial double overprints exist on a number of values of these issues. They sell for a modest premium over catalogue value depending on how much of the impression is present.

1883 **Wmk. 1**
21 A5 2c on 32c pale red *3,500. 3,500.*

On Straits Settlements No. 9

1885 **Wmk. 38**
22 A7 32c on 2a yel (B+B) *45,000.* —

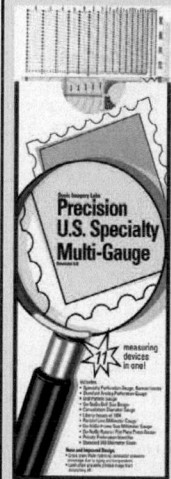

BANGLADESH

ˌbäŋ-glə-ˈdesh

LOCATION — In southern, central Asia, touching India, Burma, and the Bay of Bengal
GOVT. — Republic in the British Commonwealth
AREA — 55,598 sq. mi.
POP. — 127,117,967 (1999 est.)
CAPITAL — Dhaka (Dacca)

Bangladesh, formerly East Pakistan, broke away from Pakistan in April 1971, proclaiming its independence. It consists of 14 former eastern districts of Bengal and the former Sylhet district of Assam province of India.

100 Paisas = 1 Rupee
100 Paisas (Poishas) = 1 Taka (1972)

Catalogue values for all unused stamps in this country are for Never Hinged items.

Various stamps of Pakistan were handstamped locally for use in Bangladesh from March 26, 1971 until April 30, 1973. Thousands of varieties exist.

Map of Bangladesh
A1

Sheik Mujibur Rahman
A2

Designs: 20p, "Dacca University Massacre." 50p, "A Nation of 75 Million People." 1r, Flag of Independence (showing map). 2r, Ballot box. 3r, Broken chain. 10r, "Support Bangladesh" and map.

Perf. 14x14½

1971, July 29 Litho. Unwmk.

1	A1	10p red, dk pur & lt bl	.25	.25
2	A1	20p bl, grn, red & yel	.25	.25
3	A1	50p dp org, gray & brn	.25	.25
4	A1	1r red, emer & yel	.25	.25
5	A1	2r lil rose, lt & dk bl	.40	.40
6	A1	3r blue, emer & grn	.50	.50
7	A2	5r dp org, tan & blk	1.00	1.00
8	A1	10r gold, dk bl & lil rose	1.75	1.75
		Nos. 1-8 (8)	4.65	4.65

A set of 15 stamps of types A1 and A2 in new paisa-taka values and colors was rejected by Bangladesh officials and not issued. Bangladesh representatives in England released these stamps, which were not valid, on Feb. 1, 1972. Value, set $8.

Imperfs of Nos. 1-8 were in the Format International liquidation. They are not errors.

Nos. 1-8 Overprinted in Black or Red

1971, Dec. 20

9	A1	10p multicolored	.25	.25
10	A1	20p multicolored	.20	
11	A1	50p multicolored	.35	
12	A1	1r multicolored	.75	
13	A1	2r multicolored	1.10	
14	A1	3r multicolored	1.50	
15	A2	5r multicolored (R)	2.75	2.75
16	A1	10r multicolored	5.00	*5.00*
		Nos. 9-16 (8)	11.90	

Liberation of Bangladesh.

The 10p, 5r and 10r were issued in Dacca, but Nos. 10-14 were not put on sale in Bangladesh.

Monument — A3

1972, Feb. 21 Litho. *Perf. 13*

32	A3	20p green & rose	.40	.40

Language Movement Martyrs.

"Independence" A4

1972, Mar. 26 Photo. *Perf. 13*

33	A4	20p maroon & red	.30	.25
34	A4	60p dark blue & red	.50	.45
35	A4	75p purple & red	.55	.55
		Nos. 33-35 (3)	1.35	1.25

First anniversary of independence.

Doves of Peace — A5

1972, Dec. 16 Litho. *Perf. 13*

36	A5	20p ocher & multi	.30	.30
37	A5	60p lilac & multi	.45	.45
38	A5	75p yellow green & multi	.50	.50
		Nos. 36-38 (3)	1.25	1.25

Victory Day, Dec. 16.

Flower Growing from Ruin — A6

1973, Mar. 25 Litho. *Perf. 13*

39	A6	20p ocher & multi	.30	.30
40	A6	60p brown & multi	.40	.40
41	A6	1.35t violet blue & multi	.80	.80
		Nos. 39-41 (3)	1.50	1.50

Martyrs of the war of liberation.

Embroidered Quilt — A7

Hilsa — A8

Court of Justice — A9

Designs: 3p, Jute field. 5p, Jack fruit. 10p, Farmer plowing with ox team. 20p, Hibiscus rosenensis. 25p, Tiger. 60p, Bamboo and water lilies. 75p, Women picking tea. 90p, Handicrafts. 2t, Collecting date palm juice, vert. 5t, Net fishing. 10t, Sixty-dome Mosque.

Perf. 14x14½, 14½x14

1973, Apr. 30 Litho.

Size: 21x28mm, 28x21mm

42	A7	2p black	.25	.25
43	A7	3p bright green	.50	.50
44	A7	5p light brown	.50	.25
45	A7	10p black	.30	.25
46	A7	20p olive	.50	.25
47	A7	25p red lilac	3.25	.25
48	A8	50p rose lilac	2.25	.30
49	A7	60p gray	2.25	1.25
50	A7	75p orange	1.25	1.25
51	A7	90p red brown	1.50	2.00

Taka Expressed as "TA"

Size: 35x22mm, 22x35mm

52	A9	1t violet	6.00	.25
53	A9	2t greenish gray	6.00	1.25
54	A9	5t grayish blue	7.50	2.75
55	A9	10t rose	12.00	6.00
		Nos. 42-55 (14)	44.05	16.80

See Nos. 82-85, 95-106, 165-175, 356. For overprints see Nos. O1-O10, O13.

Human Rights Flame — A10

1973, Dec. 10 Litho. *Perf. 13x13½*

56	A10	10p blue & multi	.25	.25
57	A10	1.25t violet & multi	.25	.25

25th anniversary of the Universal Declaration of Human Rights.

Family, Chart, Map of Bangladesh — A11

1974, Feb. 10 Litho. *Perf. 13½*

58	A11	20p blue grn & multi	.25	.25
59	A11	25p brt blue & multi	.25	.25
60	A11	75p red & multi	.25	.25
		Nos. 58-60 (3)	.75	.75

First census in Bangladesh.
For overprints see Nos. 194-196.

Copernicus, Heliocentric System — A12

1974, July 22 Litho. *Perf. 13½*

61	A12	25p violet, blk & org	.25	.25
62	A12	75p emerald, blk & org	.25	.25

Nicolaus Copernicus (1473-1543), Polish astronomer.

Flag and UN Headquarters
A13

1974, Sept. 25 Litho. *Perf. 13½*

63	A13	25p lilac & multi	.25	.25
64	A13	1t blue & multi	.25	.25

Admission of Bangladesh to the UN.

A14

Designs: 25p, 1.75t, UPU emblem. 1.25t, 5t, Mail runner. 25p, 1.25t, country and denomination appear on a yellow background, 1.75t, 5t, blue background.

1974, Oct. 9 *Perf. 13½*

65	A14	25p multicolored	.25	.25
66	A14	1.25t multicolored	.25	.25
67	A14	1.75t multicolored	.25	.25
68	A14	5t multicolored	1.00	1.00
a.		Souv. sheet of 4, #65-68, imperf.	*60.00*	
		Nos. 65-68 (4)	1.75	1.75

A15

1974, Nov. 4 Litho.

69	A15	25p Royal bengal tiger	.85	.25
70	A15	50p Tiger cub	1.10	.75
71	A15	2t Swimming tiger	2.00	2.00
		Nos. 69-71 (3)	3.95	3.00

"Save the Tiger," World Wildlife Fund.

Type of 1973
Taka Expressed in Bengali

1974-75 *Perf. 14½x14, 14x14½*

Size: 35x22mm, 22x35mm

82	A9	1t violet	1.50	.25
83	A9	2t grayish green	3.00	2.00
84	A9	5t grayish blue ('75)	7.00	.75
85	A9	10t rose ('75)	30.00	15.00
		Nos. 82-85 (4)	41.50	18.00

See Nos. 350-356. For overprints see Nos. O11-O12, O14.

Family — A16

Children — A17

Family
A18

1974, Dec. 30 Litho. *Perf. 14*

86	A16	25p ocher & multi	.25	.25
87	A17	70p claret & multi	.25	.25
88	A18	1.25t multicolored	.50	.50
		Nos. 86-88 (3)	1.00	1.00

Family planning. The numerals on No. 87 look like "90" but mean "70."

Betbunia Satellite Earth Station — A19

1975, June 14 Litho. *Perf. 14*

89	A19	25p red, black & silver	.25	.25
90	A19	1t vio blue, blk & silver	.25	.25

Opening of Betbunia Satellite Earth Station.

Allegory, IWY Emblem A20

1975, Dec. 31 Litho. *Perf. 15*

91	A20	50p rose & multi	.25	.25
92	A20	2t lt lilac & multi	.25	.25

International Women's Year.

Types of 1973 Redrawn

1976-77 Litho. *Perf. 15x14½*

Size: 18x23mm, 23x18mm

95	A7	5p green	.25	.25
96	A7	10p black	.25	.25
97	A7	20p olive green	2.00	.25
98	A7	25p rose lilac	7.00	.25
99	A8	50p rose lilac	4.25	.25
100	A7	60p gray	.50	.50
101	A7	75p olive	2.00	2.00
102	A7	90p red brown	.50	.50

Taka Expressed in Bengali

Size: 32x20mm, 20x32mm

103	A9	1t violet	2.50	.25
104	A9	2t greenish gray	2.50	.25
105	A9	5t grayish blue	4.00	3.00
106	A9	10t rose ('77)	15.00	6.00
		Nos. 95-106 (12)	40.75	13.75

For overprints see Nos. O16-O25.

Telephones, 1876 and 1976 — A21

Alexander Graham Bell — A22

1976, Mar. 10 Litho. *Perf. 15*

107	A21	2.25t multicolored	.25	.25
108	A22	5t multicolored	.60	.60

Centenary of first telephone call by Alexander Graham Bell, Mar. 10, 1876.

Eye and Healthful Food A23

1976, Apr. 7 Litho. *Perf. 15*

109	A23	30p yellow & multi	.50	.25
110	A23	2.25t orange & multi	1.25	1.25

World Health Day: Foresight prevents blindness.

Liberty Bell A24

Designs: 2.25t, Statue of Liberty, New York Skyline. 5t, Mayflower. 10t, Mt. Rushmore, presidents' heads.

1976, May 29 Photo. *Perf. 13½x14*

111	A24	30p multicolored	.25	.25
112	A24	2.25t multicolored	.30	.30
113	A24	5t multicolored	.75	.75
114	A24	10t multicolored	.80	.80
a.		Souv. sheet, #111-114, perf 13	4.50	4.50
		Nos. 111-114 (4)	2.10	2.10

American Bicentennial. Sheet exists imperf. Value, $90.

Weaver, Chemist, Farmer, Student and Emblem — A25

1976, July 29 Litho. *Perf. 15*

115	A25	30p multicolored	.25	.25
116	A25	2.25t multicolored	.40	.40

25th anniversary of Colombo Plan. For overprint see No. 252.

Hurdles — A26

Montreal Olympic Emblem and: 30p, Running, horiz. 1t, High jump. 2.25t, Swimming, horiz. 3.50t, Gymnastics. 5t, Soccer.

1976, Nov. 29 Litho. *Perf. 15*

117	A26	25p multicolored	.25	.25
118	A26	30p multicolored	.25	.25
119	A26	1t multicolored	.25	.25
120	A26	2.25t multicolored	.45	.45
121	A26	3.50t multicolored	.75	.75
122	A26	5t multicolored	1.40	1.40
		Nos. 117-122 (6)	3.35	3.35

21st Olympic Games, Montreal, Canada, July 17-Aug. 1.

Coronation Ceremony — A27

Designs: 2.25t, Queen Elizabeth II. 10t, Queen and Prince Philip.

1977, Feb. 7 *Perf. 14x15*

123	A27	30p multicolored	.25	.25
124	A27	2.25t multicolored	.25	.25
125	A27	10t multicolored	.75	.75
a.		Souv. sheet, #123-125, perf 14½	2.00	*2.00*
		Nos. 123-125 (3)	1.25	1.25

25th anniv. of the reign of Elizabeth II. For overprint see No. 228B.

Qazi Nazrul Islam — A28

Nazrul A29

1977, Aug. 29 Litho. *Perf. 14*

126	A28	40p lt green & black	.25	.25
127	A29	2.25t multicolored	.45	.45

Qazi Nazrul Islam (1899-1976), natl. poet.

Pigeon Carrying Letter A30

1977, Sept. 29 Litho. *Perf. 14*

128	A30	30p multicolored	.25	.25
129	A30	2.25t multicolored	.25	.25

Asian-Oceanic Postal Union (AOPU), 15th anniversary.

Leopard A31

40p and 1t are vert.

1977, Nov. 9 Litho. *Perf. 13*

130	A31	40p Asiatic black bear	.25	.25
131	A31	1t Axis deer	.25	.25
132	A31	2.25t shown	.30	.30
133	A31	3.50t Gayal	.30	.30
134	A31	4t Elephant	1.00	1.00
135	A31	5t Bengal tiger	1.40	1.40
		Nos. 130-135 (6)	3.50	3.50

Campfire, Tent, Scout Emblem — A32

Designs: 3.50t, Emblem, first aid, signaling, horiz. 5t, Scout emblem and oath.

1978, Jan. 22 Litho. *Perf. 13*

136	A32	40p multicolored	.25	.25
137	A32	3.50t multicolored	1.00	1.00
138	A32	5t multicolored	1.50	1.50
		Nos. 136-138 (3)	2.75	2.75

1st National Boy Scout Jamboree, Jan. 22. For overprint see No. 269.

Champac — A33

Flowers and Flowering Trees: 1t, Pudding pipe tree. 2.25t, Flamboyant tree. 3.50t, Water lilies. 4t, Butea. 5t, Anthocephalus indicus.

1978, Mar. 31 Litho. *Perf. 13*

139	A33	40p multicolored	.25	.25
140	A33	1t multicolored	.30	.30
141	A33	2.25t multicolored	.35	.35
142	A33	3.50t multicolored	.50	.50
143	A33	4t multicolored	.50	.50
144	A33	5t multicolored	.50	.50
		Nos. 139-144 (6)	2.40	2.40

For overprints see Nos. 259A-259F.

Crown, Scepter and Staff of State — A34

Designs: 3.50t, Royal family on balcony. 5t, Queen Elizabeth II and Prince Philip. 10t, Queen in coronation regalia, Westminster Abbey.

1978, May 20 *Perf. 14*

145	A34	40p multicolored	.25	.25
146	A34	3.50t multicolored	.25	.25
147	A34	5t multicolored	.30	.30
148	A34	10t multicolored	.70	.70
a.		Souv. sheet, #145-148, perf 14½	1.60	1.60
		Nos. 145-148 (4)	1.50	1.50

Coronation of Queen Elizabeth II, 25th anniv.

Alan Cobham's DH50, 1926 — A35

Planes: 2.25t, Capt. Hans Bertram's Junkers W33 Atlantis, 1932-33. 3.50t, Wright brothers' plane. 5t, Concorde.

1978, June 15 Litho. *Perf. 13*

149	A35	40p multicolored	.25	.25
150	A35	2.25t multicolored	.25	.25
151	A35	3.50t multicolored	.50	.50
152	A35	5t multicolored	3.75	3.75
		Nos. 149-152 (4)	4.75	4.75

75th anniversary of powered flight.

Holy Kaaba, Mecca — A37

Design: 3.50t, Pilgrims at Mt. Arafat, horiz.

1978, Nov. 9 Litho. *Perf. 13*

154	A37	40p multicolored	.25	.25
155	A37	3.50t multicolored	.75	.75

Pilgrimage to Mecca.

Jasim Uddin, Poet
A38

1979, Mar. 14 Litho. *Perf. 14*
156 A38 40p multicolored .25 .25

Rowland Hill — A39

Hill and Stamps of Bangladesh: 3.50t, No. 1, horiz. 10t, No. 66, horiz.

1979, Nov. 26 Litho. *Perf. 14*
157 A39 40p multicolored .25 .25
158 A39 3.50t multicolored .35 .35
159 A39 10t multicolored .80 .80
a. Souvenir sheet of 3, #157-159 3.00 3.00
Nos. 157-159 (3) 1.40 1.40

Sir Rowland Hill (1795-1879), originator of penny postage.

Moulana Bhashani — A40

1979, Nov. 17 *Perf. 12½*
160 A40 40p multicolored .25 .25

Moulana Abdul Hamid Khan Bhashani (1880-1976), philosopher and statesman.

A41

IYC Emblem and: 40p, Boys and Hoops. 3.50t, Boys flying kites. 5t, Children jumping.

1979, Dec. 17 Litho. *Perf. 14x14½*
161 A41 40p multicolored .25 .25
162 A41 3.50t multicolored .45 .45
163 A41 5t multicolored .75 .75
a. Souv. sheet, #161-163, perf 14½ 3.00 3.00
Nos. 161-163 (3) 1.45 1.45

International Year of the Child.

Type of 1973

Designs: 5p, Lalbag Fort. 10p, Fenchungan Fertilizer Factory, vert. 15p, Pineapple. 20p, Gas well. 25p, Jute on boat. 30p, Banana tree. 40p, Baitul Mukarram Mosque. 50p, Baitul Mukarram Mosque. 80p, Garh excavations. 1ta, Dotara (musical instrument.) 2t, Karnaphuli Dam.

1979-82 Photo. *Perf. 14½*
Size: 18x23mm, 23x18mm

165 A7 5p brown ('79) .25 .25
166 A7 10p Prus blue .25 .25
167 A7 15p yellow org ('81) .25 .25
168 A7 20p dk carmine ('79) .25 .25
169 A7 25p dk blue ('82) .30 .30
170 A7 30p lt olive grn ('80) 3.00 3.00
171 A9 40p rose magenta ('79) .55 .50
172 A9 50p black & gray ('81) 5.50 5.50
173 A7 80p dk brown ('80) .45 .45
174 A7 1t red lilac ('81) 7.25 7.25
175 A7 2t brt ultra ('81) 3.75 3.75
Nos. 165-175 (11) 21.80 21.75

For overprints see Nos. O27-O36.

A42

Rotary Intl., 75th Anniv.: 40p, Rotary emblem, diff.

1980, Feb. 23 Litho. *Perf. 14*
179 A42 40p multicolored .25 .25
180 A42 5t ultra & gold .70 .70

For overprints see Nos. 285-286.

Canal Digging
A43

1980, Mar. 27 Litho. *Perf. 14*
181 A43 40p multicolored .30 .30

Sher-e-Bangla A.K. Fazlul Huq (1873-1962), Natl. Leader — A44

1980, Apr. 27 Litho. *Perf. 14*
182 A44 40p multicolored .45 .45

Early Mail Transport, London 1980 Emblem — A45

10t, Modern mail transport.

1980, May 5
183 A45 1t shown .25 .25
184 A45 10t multicolored 1.40 1.40
a. Souvenir sheet of 2, #183-184 2.50 *2.50*

London 80 Intl. Stamp Exhib., May 6-14.

Dome of the Rock — A46

1980, Aug. 21 Litho. *Perf. 14½*
185 A46 50p violet rose 1.50 .30

For the families of Palestinians.

A 50p stamp for the Palestinian liberation struggle was prepared for issue on the same day as No. 185, but was not issued because of errors in the Arabic inscription in the design. Value, $10.

Adult Education
A47

1980, Aug. 23 *Perf. 13½*
186 A47 50p multicolored .25 .25

Beach Scene
A48

1980, Sept. 27 Litho. *Perf. 14*
187 A48 50p shown .40 .40
188 A48 5t Beach scene, diff. .85 .85
a. Souvenir sheet of 2, #187-188 1.50 1.50
b. Pair, #187-188 1.25 1.25

World Tourism Conference, Manila, Sept. 27. No. 188b has continuous design.

For overprints see Nos. 243-244.

Hegira (Pilgrimage Year) — A49

1980, Nov. 11 Photo. *Perf. 14*
189 A49 50p multicolored .25 .25

A50

Design: Deer and Boy Scout emblem.

1981, Jan. 1 Litho. *Perf. 14*
190 A50 50p multicolored .30 .25
191 A50 5t multicolored 1.30 1.30

5th Asia-Pacific and 2nd Bangladesh Scout Jamboree, 1980-1981.

For overprint, see No. 321.

A51

1980, Dec. 9 Litho. *Perf. 14*
192 A51 50p multicolored .25 .25
193 A51 2t multicolored .35 .35

Begum Roquiah (1880-1932), educator.

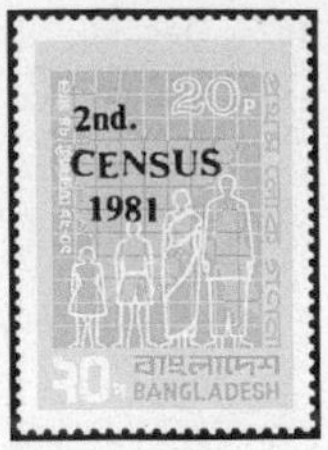

Nos. 58-60 Overprinted

1981, Mar. 6 *Perf. 13½*
194 A11 20p multicolored .25 .25
195 A11 25p multicolored .25 .25
196 A11 75p multicolored .25 .25
Nos. 194-196 (3) .75 .75

A52

1981, Mar. 16 Litho. *Perf. 14*
197 A52 1t multicolored .25 .25
198 A52 15t multicolored 1.75 *1.75*
a. Souvenir sheet of 2, #197-198 2.75 2.75

Queen Mother Elizabeth, 80th birthday (1980).

A53

50p, Citizen Holding Rifle & Flag. 2t, People, map.

1981, Mar. 26
199 A53 50p multicolored .25 .25
200 A53 2t multicolored .25 .25

10th anniversary of independence.

For overprint on 199, see No. 210A.

UN Conference on Least-developed Countries, Paris — A54

1981, Sept. 1 Litho. *Perf. 14x13½*
201 A54 50p multicolored .40 .25

Birth Centenary of Kemal Ataturk (First President of Turkey) — A55

1981, Nov. 10 Litho. *Perf. 14*
202 A55 50p Portrait .50 .50
203 A55 1t Portrait, diff. 1.00 1.00

Intl. Year of the Disabled A56

50p, Sign language, vert. 2t, Amputee.

1981, Dec. 26 Litho. *Perf. 14*

204 A56 50p multicolored .50 .25
205 A56 2t multicolored 1.00 1.00

World Food Day, Oct. 16 — A57

1981, Dec. 31 Litho. *Perf. 13½x14*

206 A57 50p multicolored .60 .60

Boat Hauling Rice Straw — A58

1982, May 22 Litho. *Perf. 13½x14*

207 A58 50p multicolored .50 .50

10th Anniv. of UN Conf. on Human Environment.
For overprint see No. 281.

A59

1982, Oct. 9

208 A59 50p multicolored .55 .55

Dr. Kazi Motahar Hossain, educator and statistician.

Scouting Year A60

1982, Oct. 21 Litho. *Perf. 14*

209 A60 50p Emblem, knots .80 .30
210 A60 2t Baden-Powell, vert. 2.50 2.50

No. 199 Overprinted

1982, Nov. 21 Litho. *Perf. 14*

210A A53 50p multi 4.50 4.50

Armed Forces Day.

Capt. Mohiuddin Jahangir A61

No. 211 — Liberation heroes (tablet color): b, Sepoy Hamidur Rahman (pale green). c, Sepoy Mohammed Mustafa Kamal (rose claret). d, Mohammad Ruhul Amin (yellow). e, M. Matiur Rahman (olive bister). f, Lance-Naik Munshi Abdur Rouf (brown orange). g, Lance-Naik Nur Mouhammad (bright yellow green).

1982, Dec. 16 Litho. *Perf. 14*

211 Strip of 7 2.40 2.40
a.-g. A61 50p multicolored .30 .30

Metric System A62

1983, Jan. 10 Litho. *Perf. 14*

212 A62 50p Mail scale, vert. .60 .60
213 A62 2t Weights, measures 2.00 2.00

TB Bacillus Centenary A63

1983, Feb. 20 Litho. *Perf. 14*

214 A63 50p Koch 1.40 1.40
215 A63 1t Slides, microscope 2.40 2.40

A64

1983, Mar. 14 Litho. *Perf. 14*

216 A64 1t Open stage theater .25 .25
217 A64 3t Boat race .25 .25
218 A64 10t Snake dance .60 .60
219 A64 15t Tea garden 1.00 1.00
Nos. 216-219 (4) 2.10 2.10

Commonwealth Day.

Jnantapash Shahidullah (1885-1969), Educator and Linguist — A65

1983, July 10 Litho. *Perf. 14*

220 A65 50p multicolored .85 .85

Birds A66

Designs: 50p, Copsychus saularis. 2t, Halcyon smyrnensis, vert. 3.75t, Dinopium benghalense, vert. 5t, Carina scutulota.

1983, Aug. 17 Litho. *Perf. 14*

221 A66 50p multi 1.50 1.50
222 A66 2t multi 1.60 1.60
223 A66 3.75t multi 2.25 2.25
224 A66 5t multi 2.60 2.60
a. Souvenir sheet of 4, #221-224 10.00 10.00
Nos. 221-224 (4) 7.95 7.95

No. 224a sold for 13t.

Local Fish A67

50p, Macrobrachium rosengergii. 2t, Stromateus cinereus. 3.75t, Labeo rohita. 5t, Anabas testudineus.

1983, Oct. 31 Litho. *Perf. 14*

225 A67 50p multicolored .75 .75
226 A67 2t multicolored .80 .80
227 A67 3.75t multicolored 1.00 1.00
228 A67 5t multicolored 1.25 *1.25*
a. Souv. sheet of 4, #225-228, imperf. 6.00 6.00
Nos. 225-228 (4) 3.80 3.80

No. 228a sold for 13t.

No. 125 Overprinted in Red

1983, Nov. 14 Litho. *Perf. 14*

228B A27 10t multicolored 15.00 15.00

No. 228B also exists with the overprint reading "Nov. '33" instead of "Nov. '83." Value, $15.

World Communications Year — A68

50p, Messenger, vert. 5t, Jet, train, ship, vert. 10t, Dish antenna, messenger.

1983, Dec. 21 Litho. *Perf. 14*

229 A68 50p multicolored .35 .35
230 A68 5t multicolored 1.50 1.50
231 A68 10t multicolored 2.00 2.00
Nos. 229-231 (3) 3.85 3.85

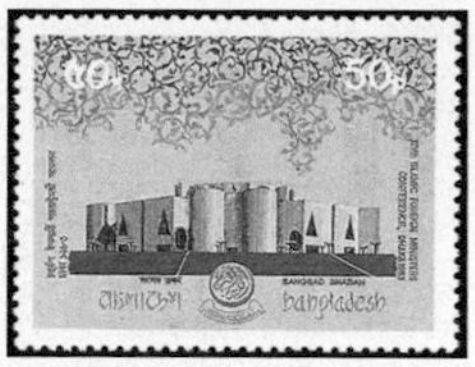

Hall A69

50p, Sangsad Bhaban. 5t, Shait Gumbaz.

1983, Dec. 5 Litho. *Perf. 14*

232 A69 50p multicolored .25 .25
233 A69 5t multicolored 1.75 1.75

14th Islamic Foreign Ministers Conference.

A70

5p, Mailboat. 10p, Dacca P.O. counter. 15p, IWTA Terminal. 20p, Sorting mail. 25p, Mail delivery. 30p, Postman at mailbox. 50p, Mobile post office. 1t, Kamalapur Railway Station. 2t, Zia Intl. Airport. 5t, Khulna G.P.O.

Perf. 11½x12½, 12½x11½

1983, Dec. 21

234 A70 5p multicolored .40 .40
235 A70 10p multicolored .40 .30
236 A70 15p multicolored .50 .30
237 A70 20p multicolored 1.50 .30
238 A70 25p multicolored .75 .30
239 A70 30p multicolored .75 .30
240 A70 50p multicolored 1.50 .30

Size: 30½x18½mm

Perf. 12x11½

241 A70 1t multicolored 1.50 .40
242 A70 2t multicolored 2.25 1.75
242A A70 5t deep magenta 4.00 4.00
Nos. 234-242A (10) 13.55 8.35

Nos. 235-237, 239-242A horiz.
Nos. 234-240 reprinted on cream paper.
See Nos. 270-271. For overprints see Nos. O37-O46, O48, O51-O52.

No. 188b Overprinted in Red in English

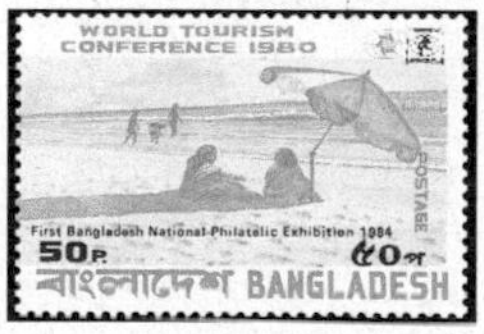

or Bengali

1984, Feb. 1 Litho. *Perf. 14*

243 A48 50p Beach Scene 1.25 1.25
244 A48 5t Beach Scene, diff. 2.00 2.00
a. Pair, #243-244 5.75 5.75

1st Bangladesh Natl. Philatelic Exhibition, 1984. No. 244a has continuous design.

A71

50p, Girl examining stamp album. 7.50t, Boy updating collection.

1984, May 17 *Perf. 14½*

245 50p multicolored .75 .75
246 7.50t multicolored 2.50 2.50
a. Souvenir sheet of 2, #245-246 6.00 6.00
b. A71 Pair, #245-246 3.75 3.75
c. As "a," overprinted *10.00 10.00*

No. 246a sold for 10t.

Overprint in sheet margin of No. 246c reads: "SILVER JUBILEE / BANGLADESH POSTAGE STAMPS 1971-96."

Dacca Zoo — A72

1t, Sarus crane, gavial. 2t, Peafowl, royal Bengal tiger.

1984, July 17 **Litho.** *Perf. 14*

247 A72 1t multicolored 1.75 1.00
248 A72 2t multicolored 3.00 3.00

Postal Life Insurance, Cent. — A73

1984, Dec. 3

249 A73 1t Chicken hawk, hen .75 .25
250 A73 5t Beneficiaries 2.00 2.00

Abbasudin Ahmad, Bengali Singer — A74

1984, Dec. 24

251 A74 3t multicolored 1.00 1.00

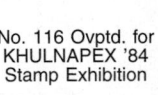

No. 116 Ovptd. for KHULNAPEX '84 Stamp Exhibition

1984, Dec. 29 **Litho.** *Perf. 15*

252 A25 2.25t multicolored 2.00 2.00

1984 Summer Olympics, Los Angeles A75

1984, Dec. 31 *Perf. 14*

253 A75 1t Bicycling 1.50 .30
254 A75 5t Field hockey 2.00 2.00
255 A75 10t Volleyball 2.50 2.50
Nos. 253-255 (3) 6.00 4.80

Islamic Development Bank, 9th Annual Congress, Dacca — A76

1985, Feb. 2

256 A76 1t Farmer .35 .25
257 A76 5t Four Asian races 1.75 1.75

UN Child Survival Campaign A77

1985, Mar. 14

258 A77 1t Breastfeeding .40 .30
259 A77 10t Growth monitoring 2.25 2.25

Nos. 139-144 Ovptd. in Bengali for Local Elections

1985, May 16 **Litho.** *Perf. 14x14½*

259A A33 40p multicolored 1.25 *.50*
259B A33 1t multicolored 1.00 *.40*
259C A33 2.25t multicolored 1.00 *.85*
259D A33 3.50t multicolored 2.00 *1.00*
259E A33 4t multicolored 2.00 *1.00*
259F A33 5t multicolored 4.50 *1.10*
Nos. 259A-259F (6) 11.75 *4.85*

UN Decade for Women — A78

1985, July 18 *Perf. 14*

260 A78 1t shown .25 .25
261 A78 10t Technology 1.75 1.75

UN, 40th Anniv. A79

1985, Sept. 15

262 A79 1t UN building .25 .25
263 A79 10t World map, natl. flag 1.40 1.40

11th anniv. of UN admission.

Intl. Youth Year — A80

1985, Nov. 2 **Litho.** *Perf. 14*

264 A80 1t Scissors, pencil .25 .25
265 A80 5t Hammer, wrenches .40 .40

Seven Doves, Council Emblem — A81

1985, Dec. 8 **Litho.** *Perf. 14*

266 A81 1t shown .40 .40
267 A81 5t Flags, lotus blossom 1.00 1.00

1st South Asian Regional Council Summit, SARC, Dacca.

Shilpacharya Zainul Abedin (1914-1976), Founder, Dacca College of Art — A82

1985, Dec. 28

268 A82 3t multicolored 1.00 .50

No. 138 Overprinted Reading Up

1985, Dec. 29 *Perf. 13*

269 A32 5t multicolored 3.75 3.75

3rd Natl. Scout Jamboree.
The overprint comes in two types.

Postal Services Type of 1983-84

1986-93 **Litho.** *Perf. 12x11½*

Size: 30½x19mm

270 A70 3t Sorting machine 3.50 1.25

Perf. 12x12½

Size: 33½x22½mm

271 A70 4t Chittagong Port 1.25 .75

Issued: 3t, Jan. 11, 1986; 4t, Apr. 22, 1993.
For overprint see No. O46.

Fishing Net, by Safiuddin Ahmed A83

Paintings by Bengali artists: 5t, Happy Return, by Quamrul Hassan. 10t, Levelling the Plowed Field, by Zainul Abedin.

1986, Apr. 6 **Litho.** *Perf. 14*

275 A83 1t multicolored .25 .25
276 A83 5t multicolored .70 .70
277 A83 10t multicolored .85 .85
Nos. 275-277 (3) 1.80 1.80

For overprint see No. 322.

1986 World Cup Soccer Championships, Mexico — A84

1986, June 29 *Perf. 15x14*

278 A84 1t Stealing the ball .50 .25
279 A84 10t Goal 3.50 3.50

Souvenir Sheet

Imperf

279A A84 20t multicolored 8.00 8.00

No. 279A contains one stamp 62x45mm with simulated perfs.

Gen. M.A.G. Osmani (1918-1984), Liberation Forces Commander-in-Chief — A85

1986, Sept. 10 **Litho.** *Perf. 14*

280 A85 3t multicolored 2.00 1.00

No. 207 Ovptd.

1986, Dec. 3 **Litho.** *Perf. 13½x14*

281 A58 50p on #207 3.00 3.00

Intl. Peace Year — A86

A87

1986, Dec. 25 **Litho.** *Perf. 12x12½*

282 A86 1t shown .65 .65
283 A86 10t City ruins, flower 2.50 2.50

Souvenir Sheet

284 A87 20t shown 2.50 2.50

Nos. 179-180 Overprinted or Surcharged

1987, Jan. 12 ***Perf. 14***

285 A42 1t on 40p multicolored	.40	.40
286 A42 5t multicolored	.90	.90

Language Movement, 35th Anniv. — A88

1987, Feb. 21 ***Perf. 12½x12***

287 3t Protestors	1.50	1.50
288 3t Memorial	1.50	1.50
a. A88 Pair, Nos. 287-288	3.50	3.50

World Health Day — A89

1987, Apr. 7 ***Perf. 11½x12***

289 A89 1t Child immunization	2.50	2.50

See No. 318.

Bengali New Year — A90

1t, Bengali script, embroidery.

1987, Apr. 16 ***Perf. 12x12½***

290 A90 1t multicolored	.30	.30
291 A90 10t shown	1.00	1.00

Jute Carpet A91

Exports: 1t, Jute shika (wall hanging, bowl-holder and mats), vert. 10t, Table lamp and shade, vert.

Perf. 12x12½, 12½x12

1987, May 18 **Litho.**

292 A91 1t multicolored	.25	.25
293 A91 5t shown	.50	.50
294 A91 10t multicolored	.75	.75
Nos. 292-294 (3)	1.50	1.50

Ustad Ayet Ali Khan (1884-1967), Composer, and Surbahar A92

1987, Sept. 8 ***Perf. 12x12½***

295 A92 5t multicolored	1.50	1.00

Transportation — A93

1987, Oct. 24 **Litho.** ***Perf. 12½x12***

296 A93 2t Palanquin	.40	.40
297 A93 3t Bicycle rickshaw	1.50	.50
298 A93 5t Paddle steamer	1.75	.75
299 A93 7t Train	4.25	1.75
300 A93 10t Ox cart	1.00	1.00
Nos. 296-300 (5)	8.90	4.40

For overprint see No. 424.

Hossain Shahid Suhrawardy (1893-1963), Politician — A94

1987, Dec. 5 **Litho.** ***Perf. 12x12½***

301 A94 3t multicolored	.70	.70

Intl. Year of Shelter for the Homeless — A95

1987, Dec. 15 ***Perf. 12½x12***

302 5t Homeless people	.60	.60
303 5t Prosperous community	.60	.60
a. A95 Pair, Nos. 302-303	2.75	2.75

Natl. Democracy, 1st Anniv. — A96

Design: Pres. Hossain Mohammed Ershad addressing parliament.

1987, Dec. 31

304 A96 10t multicolored	1.50	1.00

Woman Tending Crop A97

1988, Jan. 26

305 A97 3t shown	.30	.30
306 A97 5t Milking cow, village	.70	.70

Intl. Fund for Agricultural Development (IFAD) Seminar on Loans for Women in Rural Areas.

1988 Summer Olympics, Seoul — A98

No. 307 — Seoul Olympics emblem and: a, Basketball. b, Weight lifting. c, Women's tennis. d, Shooting. e, Boxing.

1988, Sept. 29 **Litho.** ***Perf. 11½***

307 Strip of 5	7.50	7.50
a.-e. A98 5t any single	1.50	1.50

Historical Sites A99

Designs: 1t, Shait Gumbaz Mosque (interior), Bagerhat. 4t, Paharpur Monastery. 5t, Kantanagar Temple, Dinajpur. 10t, Lalbag Fort, Dacca.

1988, Oct. 9 ***Perf. 12½x12***

308 A99 1t multicolored	.65	.65
309 A99 4t multicolored	1.25	1.25
310 A99 5t multicolored	1.25	1.25
311 A99 10t multicolored	2.00	2.00
Nos. 308-311 (4)	5.15	5.15

Qudrat-i-Khuda (1900-1977), Scientist — A100

1988, Nov. 3 ***Perf. 12x12½***

312 A100 5t multicolored	.75	.40

Asia Cup Cricket — A101

1988, Nov. 27

313 Strip of 3	4.00	4.00
a. A101 1t Wicketkeeper	.75	.75
b. A101 5t Batsman	1.50	1.50
c. A101 10t Bowler	2.25	2.25

Intl. Red Cross and Red Crescent Organizations, 125th Annivs. — A102

1988, Oct. 26 **Litho.** ***Perf. 12x12½***

314 A102 5t Emblems, Dunant	1.00	.30
315 A102 10t Blood donation	1.50	1.20

Dacca G.P.O., 25th Anniv. — A103

1988, Dec. 6 ***Perf. 12***

316 A103 1t Exterior	.25	.25
317 A103 5t Sales counter	.60	.40

World Health Day Type of 1987

1988, Jan. 16 **Litho.** ***Perf. 11½x12***

318 A89 25p Oral rehydration	.60	.60

32nd Meeting of the Colombo Plan Consultative Committee, Dacca — A104

1988, Nov. 29 ***Perf. 12x12½***

319 A104 3t multicolored	.25	.25
320 A104 10t multicolored	.65	.65

No. 191 Ovptd.

1988, Dec. 29 **Litho.** ***Perf. 14***

321 A50 5t multicolored	5.25	4.00

5th Natl. Rover Moot (Scouting).

No. 277 Overprinted

1989, Mar. 1

322 A83 10t multicolored	1.30	1.30

4th Asiatic Exposition.

A106

1989, Mar. 13 Litho. *Perf. 12x12½*
324 A106 10t multicolored 1.10 1.10

Police academy, Sardah, 75th anniv.

A107

Modernizing water supply services.

1989, Mar. 7 Litho. *Perf. 12x12½*
325 A107 10t multicolored 1.10 1.10

12th Natl. Science & Technology Week.

A108

French Revolution, Bicent. — A109

Scenes from the revolution: 5t, Close-up of revolutionaries destroying the Bastille, vert. No. 326b, Liberty guiding the people. No. 326c, Women's march on Versailles, vert. No. 327a, Celebration of the Federation on the Champ de Mars. No. 327b, Storming of the Bastille. 25t, Montage of scenes, #326a-326c.

1989, July 12 *Perf. 14*
326 Sheet of 3 + label 2.75 2.75
a. A108 5t multicolored .50 .50
b.-c. A108 10t any single 1.10 1.10

Perf. 14x15
327 Strip of 2 + label 3.00 3.00
a.-b. A109 17t any single 1.25 1.25

Size: 152x88mm

Imperf
328 A108 25t multicolored 3.50 3.50
Nos. 326-328 (3) 9.25 9.25

Labels picture the revolution anniv. emblem.

Rural Development in Asia and the Pacific (CIRDAP), 10th Anniv. — A110

1989, Aug. 10 Litho. *Perf. 12½x12*
329 5t multi .75 .75
330 10t multi .75 .75
a. Pair, Nos. 329-330 1.75 1.75

Child Survival A111

10t, Women and children, diff.

1989, Aug. 22
331 A111 1t shown .25 .25
332 A111 10t multicolored 1.00 1.00

SOS Children's Village, 40th anniv.

Involvement of the Bangladesh Army in UN Peace-keeping Operations, 1st Anniv. — A112

1989, Sept. 12 *Perf. 12x12½*
333 A112 4t shown 1.00 1.00
334 A112 10t Camp, two soldiers 1.25 1.25

2nd Asian Poetry Festival, Dacca — A113

1989, Nov. 17 Litho. *Perf. 12x12½*
335 A113 2t multicolored .25 .25
336 A113 10t multicolored 1.00 1.00

State Printing Office A114

1989, Dec. 7 *Perf. 13½*
337 A114 10t multicolored 1.00 1.00

Bangladesh Television, 25th Anniv. — A115

10t, Emblem, flowers, diff.

1989, Dec. 25 Litho. *Perf. 12½x12*
338 A115 5t shown .60 .60
339 A115 10t multicolored 1.50 1.50

World Wildlife Fund A116

Gavialis gangeticus: 50p, In water. 2p, Gavial's jaws. 4t, Four gavials. 10t, Two gavials resting.

1990, Jan. 31 Litho. *Perf. 14*
340 A116 50p multi .90 .45
341 A116 2t multi 1.15 1.05
342 A116 4t multi 1.75 1.75
343 A116 10t multi 2.25 2.25
a. Block of 4, #340-343 7.00 7.00
Nos. 340-343 (4) 6.05 5.50

Natl. Population Day — A117

1990, Feb. 2 *Perf. 14*
344 A117 6t multicolored 1.00 .55

Penny Black, 150th Anniv. — A118

10t, Penny Black, No. 230.

1990, May 6 *Perf. 14*
345 A118 7t shown 2.00 2.00
346 A118 10t multicolored 2.50 2.50

Justice Syed Mahbub Murshed, (1911-1979) — A119

1990, Apr. 3 Litho. *Perf. 12½x12*
347 A119 5t multicolored 2.25 2.25

Intl. Literacy Year — A120

Design: 10t, Boy teaching girl to write.

1990, Apr. 10 *Perf. 12x12½*
348 A120 6t multicolored 1.10 .50
349 A120 10t multicolored 2.00 1.50

Type of 1973 Redrawn and

Loading Cargo Plane — A121

Curzon Hall — A122

Fertilizer Plant — A123

Postal Academy, Rajshahi A124

Salimullah Hall — A125

Bangla Academy — A126

Designs: No. 356, Sixty-dome Mosque (English inscription at LR).

1989-99 *Perf. 12x11½, 12, 12x12½*
350 A121 3t multicolored 1.00 .50
a. Perf. 14¼x14 2.00 .50
351 A122 5t gray blk & red brn .70 .25
a. Perf. 14¼ .70 .25
352 A123 10t carmine 1.90 1.90
353 A124 20t multicolored 2.25 2.25

Perf. 14½x14
354 A125 6t blue gray & yel 1.10 1.00

Perf. 14x14½
355 A126 2t brown & green .75 .35

Perf. 14¼

Size: 35x22 mm

Taka Expressed in Bengali
356 A9 10t rose 1.00 .75
Nos. 350-356 (7) 8.70 7.00

Issued: 5t, 3/31; 3t, 4/30; 10t, 20t, 7/8; 6t, 1/30/91; 2t, 12/3/93; No. 356, 3/18/99; No. 351a, 8/31/99.

No. 356 is very similar to No. 85 but differs in several ways: the inscription "Sixty-Dome Mosque" has been enlarged and moved from the upper left of the vignette to the lower right; a Bengali inscription has been added in its place at upper left; and the entire design has been lightened condiderably, especially in the skyline of the mosque.

For overprints see Nos. O47A-O47B, O50.

World Cup Soccer Championships, Italy — A133

10t, Soccer player, diff. 25t, Colosseum, soccer ball.

1990, June 12 Litho. *Perf. 14*
362 A133 8t shown 2.50 2.50
363 A133 10t multicolored 3.00 3.00

Size: 115x79mm

Imperf
364 A133 25t multicolored 15.00 15.00
Nos. 362-364 (3) 20.50 20.50

Fruits — A134

1t, Mangifera indica. 2t, Psidium guayava. 3t, Citrullus vulgaris. 4t, Carica papaya. 5t, Artocarpus heterophyllus. 10t, Averrhoa carambola.

1990, July 16 *Perf. 12x12½*
365 A134 1t multicolored .50 .25
366 A134 2t multicolored .50 .25
367 A134 3t multicolored .60 .25
368 A134 4t multicolored .70 .30

369 A134 5t multicolored 1.10 .65
370 A134 10t multicolored 2.10 1.50
Nos. 365-370 (6) 5.50 3.20

UN Conference on Least Developed Nations, Paris — A135

1990, Sept. 3 Litho. *Perf. 14*
371 A135 10t multicolored 2.10 2.10

Asia-Pacific Postal Training Center, 20th Anniv. — A136

1990, Sept. 10 *Perf. 13½x14*
372 2t multicolored 1.00 1.00
373 6t multicolored 1.75 1.75
a. A136 Pair, #372-373 3.50 3.50

No. 373a has continuous design.

11th Asian Games, Beijing A137

1990, Sept. 22 *Perf. 14*
374 A137 2t Rowing 1.00 .30
375 A137 4t Kabaddi 1.25 .30
376 A137 8t Wrestling 1.75 1.50
377 A137 10t Badminton 3.00 2.00
Nos. 374-377 (4) 7.00 4.10

Lalon Shah, Poet — A138

1990, Oct. 17 Litho. *Perf. 14*
378 A138 6t multicolored 1.50 1.00

UN Development Program, 40th Anniv. — A139

1990, Oct. 24 Litho. *Perf. 14*
379 A139 6t multicolored 1.10 .70

A139a

1990, Nov. 29 Litho. *Perf. 14½x14*
379A A139a 2t brown .30 .30

Immunization program. See No. 560.
For surcharge see O47.

A140

Butterflies: No. 380, Danaus chrysippus. No. 381, Precis almana. No. 382, Ixias pyrene. No. 383, Danaus plexippus.

1990, Dec. 24 Litho. *Perf. 13½x12*
380 A140 6t multicolored 2.00 2.00
381 A140 6t multicolored 2.00 2.00
382 A140 10t multicolored 2.25 2.25
383 A140 10t multicolored 2.25 2.25
a. Block of 4, #380-383 10.00 10.00
Nos. 380-383 (4) 8.50 8.50

UN Decade Against Drugs A141

1991, Jan 1 Litho. *Perf. 14x13½*
384 A141 2t Drugs, map 1.25 .50
385 A141 4t shown 2.00 1.25

Third National Census — A142

1991, Mar. 12 Litho. *Perf. 14*
386 A142 4t multicolored 1.75 1.75

Independence, 20th Anniv. — A143

No. 387: a, Invincible Bangla statue. b, Freedom Fighter statue. c, Mujibnagar Memorial. d, Eternal flame. e, National Martyrs' Memorial.

1991, Mar. 26 *Perf. 13½*
387 A143 4t Strip of 5, #a.-e. 6.00 6.00
a.-e. Any single 1.00 1.00

No. 387 printed in continuous design.

A144

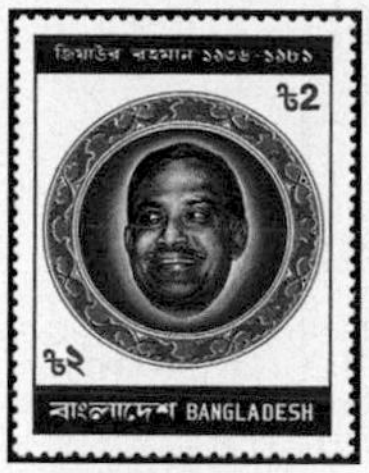

Pres. Ziaur Rahman, 10th Death Anniv. — A145

1991, May 30 *Perf. 14*
388 A144 50p multicolored .50 .50
389 A145 2t multicolored 1.50 1.50
a. Souvenir sheet of 2, #388-389 3.00 3.00

No. 389a sold for 10t.

Endangered Animals — A146

2t, Petaurista petaurista. 4t, Presbytis entellus, vert. 6t, Buceros bicornis, vert. 10t, Manis crassicaudata.

1991, June 16 *Perf. 12*
390 A146 2t multicolored 2.50 2.50
391 A146 4t multicolored 2.50 2.50
392 A146 6t multicolored 2.50 2.50
a. Pair, #391-392 6.00 6.00
393 A146 10t multicolored 2.50 2.50
a. Pair, #390, 393 5.00 5.00
Nos. 390-393 (4) 10.00 10.00

Kaikobad (1857-1951), Poet — A147

1991, July 21 Litho. *Perf. 14*
394 A147 6t multicolored 1.75 1.75

Rabindranath Tagore, Poet, 50th Anniv. of Death — A148

1991, Aug. 7
395 A148 4t multicolored 1.75 1.75

Blood and Eye Donations A149

1991, Sept. 19
396 A149 3t shown 1.25 1.25
397 A149 5t Blind man and eye 1.75 1.75

Sandhani, Medical Students Association, 14th anniversary.

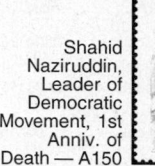

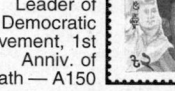

Shahid Naziruddin, Leader of Democratic Movement, 1st Anniv. of Death — A150

1991, Oct. 10
398 A150 2t multicolored 1.10 .60

Shaheed Noor Hossain, 4th Death Anniv. — A151

1991, Nov. 10 Litho. *Perf. 14*
399 A151 2t multicolored 1.10 .60

Archaeological Treasures of Mainamati — A152

No. 400: a, Bronze Stupa with images of Buddha. b, Bowl and pitcher. c, Ruins of Salban Vihara Monastery. d, Gold coins. e, Terra-cotta plaque.

1991, Nov. 26 Litho. *Perf. 13½*
400 A152 4t Strip of 5, #a.-e. 8.50 8.50
a.-e. Any single 1.50 1.50

Mass Uprising, First Anniv. A153

1991, Dec. 6 *Perf. 14*
401 A153 4t multicolored 1.50 1.25

Miniature Sheets

Martyred Intellectuals Who Died in 1971 — A154

No. 402: a, A.N.M. Munier Chowdhury. b, Ghyasuddin Ahmad. c, S.M.A. Rashidul Hasan. d, Muhammad Anwar Pasha. e, Dr. Md. Mortaza. f, Shahid Saber. g, Fazlur Rahman Khan. h, Ranada Prasad Saha. i, Adhyaksha Joges Chandra Ghose. j, Santosh Chandra Bhattacharyya.

No. 403: a, Dr. Gobinda Chandra Deb. b, A.N.M. Muniruzzaman. c, Mufazzal Haider Chaudhury. d, Dr. Abdul Alim Choudhury. e, Sirajuddin Hossain. f, Shahidulla Kaiser. g, Altaf Mahmud. h, Dr. Jyotirmay Guha Thakurta. i, Dr. Md. Abul Khair. j, Dr. Serajul Haque Khan.

No. 404: a, Dr. Mohammad Fazle Rabbi. b, Mir Abdul Quyyum. c, A.N.M. Golam Mostafa. d, Dhirendranath Dutta. e, S.A. Mannan (Ladu Bhai). f, Nizamuddin Ahmad. g, Abul Bashar Chowdhury. h, Selina Parveen. i, Dr. Abul Kalam Azad. j, Saidul Hassan.

No. 404K: l, LCDR. Moazzam Hussain. m, Muhammad Habibur Rahman. n, Khandoker Abu Taleb. o, Moshiur Rahman. p, Md. Abdul Muktadir. q, Nutan Chandra Sinha. r, Syed

Nazmul Haque. s, Dr. Mohammed Amin Uddin. t, Dr. N.A.M. Faizul Mohee. u, Sukha Ranjan Somaddar.

1991-93 Litho. ***Perf. 13½***

402 A154 2t Sheet of 10, #a-j + 5 labels 22.00 15.00
a.-j. Any single .80 .60
403 A154 2t Sheet of 10, #a-j + 5 labels 22.00 15.00
a.-j. Any single .80 .60
404 A154 2t Sheet of 10, #a-j + 5 labels 22.00 15.00
a.-j. Any single .80 .60

Perf. 14½

404K A154 2t Sheet of 10, #l-u + 5 labels 15.00 10.00
l.-u. Any single .60 .40

Independence, 20th anniv. Issued: Nos. 402-404, 12/14/91; No. 404K, 12/14/93.

See Nos. 470-471, 499-500, 534-535, 558-559, 568-569, 595-596, 627-628.

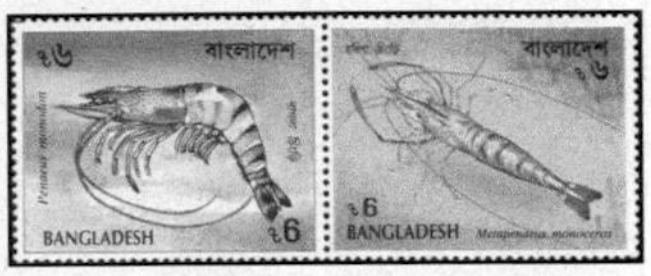

Shrimp — A155

No. 405, Penaeus monodon. No. 406, Metapenaeus monoceros.

1991, Dec. 31 ***Perf. 14***

405 6t multicolored 2.50 2.50
406 6t multicolored 2.50 2.50
a. A155 Pair, #405-406 6.50 6.50

Shaheed Mirze Abu Raihan Jaglu, 5th Death Anniv. A156

1992, Feb. 8 Litho. ***Perf. 14x13½***

407 A156 2t multicolored 1.25 1.10

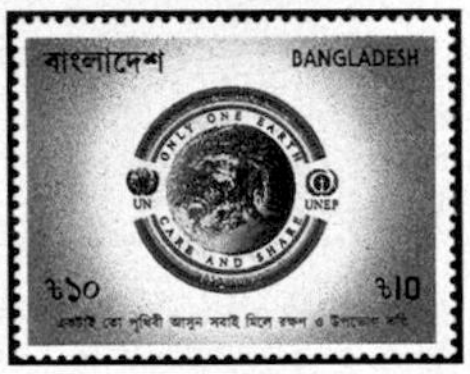

World Environment Day — A157

Design: 4t, Scenes of environmental protection and pollution control, vert.

1992, June 5 Litho. ***Perf. 14***

408 A157 4t multicolored 1.25 1.25
409 A157 10t multicolored 2.50 2.50

Nawab Sirajuddaulah of Bengal (1733-1757) A158

1992, July 2 Litho. ***Perf. 14***

410 A158 10t multicolored 2.00 1.25

Syed Ismail Hossain Sirajee (1880-1931), Writer & Poet — A159

1992, July 17

411 A159 4t multicolored 1.50 1.50

Tree Week — A160

2t, Couple planting tree, horiz. 4t, Birds, trees.

1992, July 17 Litho. ***Perf. 14***

412 A160 2t multicolored 1.50 .80
413 A160 4t multicolored 2.00 1.25

1992 Summer Olympics, Barcelona — A161

No. 414 — Olympic rings and: a, 4t, Rowing. b, 6t, Hands holding Olympic torch. c, 10t, Peace doves. d, 10t, Clasped hands.

1992, July 25 Litho. ***Perf. 14***

414 A161 Block of 4, #a.-d. 7.50 7.50
a.-d. Any single 1.60 1.60

The Star Mosque, 18th Cent. A162

1992, Oct. 29 Litho. ***Perf. 14½x14***

415 A162 10t multicolored 3.00 2.75

Masnad-E-Ala Isa Khan, 393rd Anniv. of Death — A163

1992, Sept. 15 ***Perf. 14x14½***

416 A163 4t multicolored 1.40 .70

7th SAARC Summit, Dacca — A164

1992, Dec. 5

417 A164 6t Flags of members 1.50 1.50
418 A164 10t Emblem 1.90 1.90

1992 Bangladesh Natl. Philatelic Exhibition — A165

No. 419: a, Elephant and mahout, ivory work, 19th cent. b, Post rider, mail box and postman delivering mail to villager.

1992, Sept. 26 ***Perf. 14½x14***

419 A165 10t Pair, #a.-b. + label 3.50 3.50
a.-b. Either single 1.50 1.50
c. Souv. sheet, imperf. *6.00 6.00*

No. 419c contains one strip of No. 419 with simulated perforations and sold for 25t.

1992 Intl. Conference on Nutrition, Rome — A166

1992, Dec. 5

420 A166 4t multicolored 1.75 .95

Meer Nisar Ali Titumeer (1782-1831) — A167

1992, Nov. 19 Litho. ***Perf. 14½x14***

421 A167 10t multicolored 1.75 1.75

Archaeological Relics, Mahasthan — A168

No. 422 — Relics from 3rd century B.C.-15th century A.D.: a, Terracotta seal and head. b, Terracotta hamsa. c, Terracotta Surya image. d, Gupta stone columns.

1992, Nov. 30 Litho. ***Perf. 14½x14***

422 A168 10t Strip of 4, #a.-d. 9.75 9.75
a.-d. Any single 2.00 2.00

Canal Digging — A169

No. 423: a, Workers digging canal. b, Completed project.

1993, Mar. 31 Litho. ***Perf. 14½x14***

423 A169 2t Pair, #a.-b. 2.10 2.10
a.-b. Either single .80 .80

No. 300 Overprinted

1992, Aug. 18 Litho. ***Perf. 12½x12***

424 A93 10t multicolored 3.25 3.25

Syed Abdus Samad (1895-1964), Soccer Player — A170

1993, Feb. 2 ***Perf. 14x14½***

425 A170 2t multicolored 2.00 1.00

A171

1993, Apr. 14

426 A171 2t multicolored 1.10 .55

Completion of 14th cent. Bengali era.

Haji Shariat Ullah (1770-1839), Social Reformer, Religious and Political Leader — A172

1993, Mar. 10 Litho. ***Perf. 14x14½***

427 A172 2t multicolored 1.90 1.25

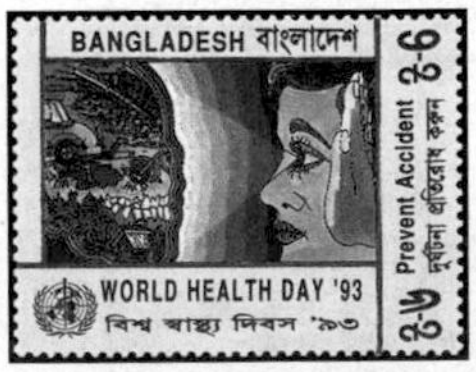

World Health Day A173

6t, Prevent accidents. 10t, Prevent violence, vert.

1993, Apr. 7 ***Perf. 14½x14, 14x14½***

428 A173 6t multicolored 2.50 2.50
429 A173 10t multicolored 3.25 3.25

Compulsory Primary Education — A174

No. 430, Slate, chalk, books. No. 431, Hand writing, children, vert.

1993, May 26
430 A174 2t multicolored 1.25 .80
431 A174 2t multicolored 1.25 .80

Nawab Sir Salimullah (1871-1915), Social Reformer — A175

1993, June 7 Litho. ***Perf. 14½x14***
432 A175 4t multicolored 1.50 1.00

Fishing Industry A176

1993, Aug. 15 Litho. ***Perf. 14½x14***
433 A176 2t multicolored .70 .40

Tomb of Sultan Ghiyasuddin Azam Shah — A177

1993, Dec. 30 Litho. ***Perf. 14½x14***
434 A177 10t multicolored 1.75 1.75

Scenic Views A178

Designs: No. 435, Sunderban. No. 436, Madhabkunda Waterfall, vert. No. 437, River, mountains, vert. No. 438, Beach, Kuakata.

1993, Oct. 30 ***Perf. 14½x14, 14x14½***
435 A178 10t multicolored 1.60 1.60
436 A178 10t multicolored 1.60 1.60
437 A178 10t multicolored 1.60 1.60
438 A178 10t multicolored 1.60 1.60
a. Souv. sheet, #435-438, imperf 6.50 6.50
Nos. 435-438 (4) 6.40 6.40

No. 438a sold for 50t and has simulated perfs.

6th Asian Art Biennial, Bangladesh A179

1993, Nov. 7 Litho. ***Perf. 14x14½***
439 A179 10t multicolored 1.10 1.10

Foy's Lake A180

1993, Nov. 6 ***Perf. 14½x14***
440 A180 10t multicolored 1.50 1.50

Tourism month.

14th Asian Pacific, 5th Bangladesh Natl. Scout Jamboree A181

1994, Jan. 5 ***Perf. 14x14½***
441 A181 2t multicolored .50 .30

Oral Rehydration Solution, 25th Anniv. — A182

1994, Feb. 5 Litho. ***Perf. 13½x14***
442 A182 2t multicolored .75 .75

6th SAF Games, Dhaka A183

1993, Dec. 6 ***Perf. 14x13½, 13½x14***
443 A183 2t Shot put .65 .35
444 A183 4t Runners, vert. .85 .45

Mosques A184

Mosques: 4t, Interior, Chhota Sona, Nawabgonj. No. 446, Exterior, Chhota Sona. No. 447, Exterior, Baba Adam's, Munshigonj.

1994, Mar. 30 Litho. ***Perf. 14x13½***
445 A184 4t multicolored .65 .25
446 A184 6t multicolored .65 .65
447 A184 6t multicolored .65 .65
Nos. 445-447 (3) 1.95 1.55

For overprint see No. 509.

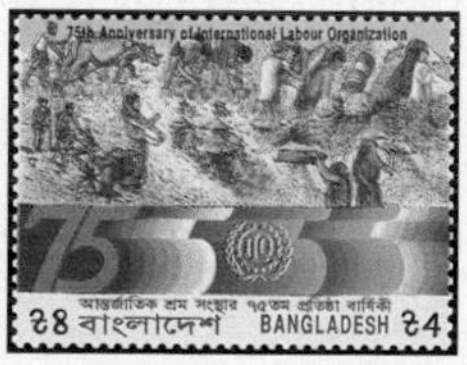
ILO, 75th Anniv. A185

Designs: 4t, People, oxen working in fields. 10t, Man rotating gearwheel, vert.

Perf. 14x13½, 13½x14
1994, Apr. 11 Litho.
448 A185 4t multicolored .30 .25
449 A185 10t multicolored 1.10 1.00

Bangla Era, 15th Cent. — A186

1994, Apr. 14 ***Perf. 13½x14***
450 A186 2t multicolored .75 .40

Traditional Festivals A187

1994, May 12 ***Perf. 14x13½***
451 A187 4t Folk Festival .55 .55
452 A187 4t Baishakhi Festival .60 .60

Intl. Year of the Family — A188

1994, May 15 ***Perf. 13½x14***
453 A188 10t multicolored 1.50 1.50

Tree Planting Campaign A189

4t, Family planting trees. 6t, Hands, seedlings.

1994, June 15 Litho. ***Perf. 13½x14***
454 A189 4t multicolored .55 .55
455 A189 6t multicolored 1.10 1.10

1994 World Cup Soccer Championships, US — A190

Soccer player's uniform colors: a, Red, yellow & blue. b, Yellow, green, & red.

1994, June 17 Litho. ***Perf. 14½***
456 A190 20t Pair, #a.-b. + label 5.00 5.00
a.-b. Either single 2.50 2.50
Complete booklet, #456 *40.00*

No. 456 was printed in panes of 15 (3x5), with each horizontal row containing Nos. 456a and 456b with a connecting label depicting the championship mascot. The booklet contains two No. 456, attached to the booklet cover by sheet selvage.

Jamuna Multi-Purpose Bridge — A191

1994, July 24 ***Perf. 14½x14***
457 A191 4t multicolored 2.50 1.25

Birds — A192

Designs: 4t, Oriolus xanthornus. No. 459, Gallus gallus. No. 460, Dicrurus paradiseus. No. 461, Dendrocitta vagabunda.

1994, Aug. 31 ***Perf. 14x14½***
458 A192 4t multicolored .75 .75
459 A192 6t multicolored 1.00 1.00
460 A192 6t multicolored 1.00 1.00
461 A192 6t multicolored 1.00 1.00
a. Souvenir sheet, #458-461 6.00 6.00
Nos. 458-461 (4) 3.75 3.75

No. 461a sold for 25t.

Dr. Mohammad Ibrahim (1911-89), Pioneer in Treatment of Diabetes — A193

1994, Sept. 6 Litho. ***Perf. 14½x14***
462 A193 2t multicolored .75 .25

Nawab Faizunnessa Chowdhurani (1834-1903), Social Reformer A194

1994, Sept. 23 ***Perf. 14x14½***
463 A194 2t multicolored .50 .25

12th Asian Games, Hiroshima, Japan A195

1994, Oct. 2 ***Perf. 14½x14***
464 A195 4t multicolored .75 .60

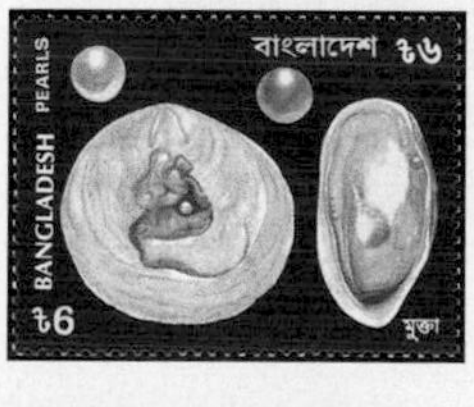
Shells A196

Designs: No. 465, White, pink pearls, oysters. No. 466, Snail, three other shells. No.

467, Scallop, other shells. No. 468, Spiral shaped shells, vert.

Perf. 14½x14, 14x14½

1994, Oct. 30 **Litho.**

465 A196 6t multicolored 1.60 1.60
466 A196 6t multicolored 1.60 1.60
467 A196 6t multicolored 1.60 1.60
468 A196 6t multicolored 1.60 1.60
Nos. 465-468 (4) 6.40 6.40

Democracy Demonstration, Death of Dr. Shamsul Alam Khan Milon, 4th Anniv. — A197

1994, Nov. 27 ***Perf. 14½x14***
469 A197 2t multicolored .50 .25

Martyred Intellectual Type of 1991

No. 470: a, Dr. Harinath Dey. b, Dr. Lt. Col. A.F. Ziaur Rahman. c, Mamum Mahmud. d, Mohsin Ali Dewan. e, Dr. Lt. Col. N.A.M. Jahangir. f, Shah Abdul Majid. g, Muhammad Akhter. h, Meherunnesa.

No. 471: a, Dr. Kasiruddin Talukder. b, Fazlul Haque Choudhury. c, Md. Shamsuzzaman. d, A.K.M. Shamsuddin. e, Lt. Mohammad Anwarul Azim. f, Nurul Amin Khan. g, Mohammad Sadeque. h, Md. Araz Ali.

1994, Dec. 14 ***Perf. 14½***
470 A154 2t Sheet of 8, #a-h + 4 labels 5.00 3.75
a.-h. Any single .40 .35
471 A154 2t Sheet of 8, #a-h + 4 lables 5.50 4.00
a.-h. Any single .40 .35

Vegetables A199

No. 472, Diplazium esculentum. No. 473, Momordica charantia. No. 474, Lagenaria siceraria. No. 475, Trichosanthes dioica. No. 476, Solanum melongena. No. 477, Cucurbita maxima.

1994, Dec. 24 ***Perf. 14x14½, 14½x14***
472 A199 4t multicolored 1.00 .75
473 A199 4t multicolored 1.00 .75
474 A199 6t multicolored 1.25 1.00
475 A199 6t multicolored 1.25 1.00
476 A199 10t multicolored 1.90 1.90
477 A199 10t multicolored 1.90 1.90
Nos. 472-477 (6) 8.30 7.30

Nos. 472-476 are vert.

World Tourism Organization, 20th Anniv. — A200

1995, Jan. 2 ***Perf. 14½x14***
478 A200 10t multicolored 2.50 2.50

Intl. Trade Fair, Dhaka A201

Designs: 4t, Trade products. 6t, Factories, emblems of industry.

1995, Jan. 7 **Litho.** ***Perf. 14x14½***
479 A201 4t multicolored .50 .25
480 A201 6t multicolored .90 .70

Bangladesh Rifles, Bicent. — A202

1995, Jan. 10 **Litho.** ***Perf. 14½x14***
481 A202 2t shown .85 .85
482 A202 4t Building, battalion 1.50 1.50

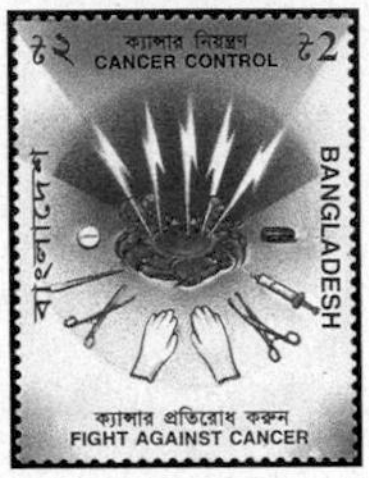

Fight Against Cancer — A203

1995, Apr. 7 **Litho.** ***Perf. 14x14½***
483 A203 2t multicolored .45 .25

Natl. Diabetes Awareness Day — A204

1995, Feb. 28 ***Perf. 14***
484 A204 2t multicolored 1.10 .70

For overprint see No. O49.

Munshi Mohammad Meherullah (1861-1907), Educator A205

1995, June 7 **Litho.** ***Perf. 14x14½***
485 A205 2t multicolored .60 .30

FAO, 50th Anniv. — A206

1995, Oct. 16 **Litho.** ***Perf. 14***
486 A206 10t multicolored .75 .75

UN, 50th Anniv. A207

UN emblem, "50," and: 2t, Dove of peace, UN headquarters. No. 488, "1945," earth from space, "1995." No. 489, Hands of different nationalities clasping, UN headquarters.

1995, Oct. 24 ***Perf. 14½x14***
487 A207 2t multicolored .35 .25
488 A207 10t multicolored .95 .95
489 A207 10t multicolored .95 .95
Nos. 487-489 (3) 2.25 2.15

Flowers — A208

Designs: No. 490, Bombax ceiba. No. 491, Lagerstroemia speciosa. No. 492, Gloriosa superba. No. 493, Canna indica. No. 494, Bauhinia purpurea. No. 495, Passiflora incarnata.

1995, Oct. 9 ***Perf. 14½x14, 14x14½***
490 A208 6t multicolored 1.10 .90
491 A208 6t multi, vert. 1.10 .90
492 A208 10t multi, vert. 1.40 1.40
493 A208 10t multi, vert. 1.40 1.40
494 A208 10t multi, vert. 1.40 1.40
495 A208 10t multi, vert. 1.40 1.40
Nos. 490-495 (6) 7.80 7.40

Shaheed Khandaker Mosharraf Hossain A208a

1995, Oct. 16 **Litho.** ***Perf. 13¾x14¼***
496 A208a 2t multi *90.00 90.00*

No. 496 was removed from sale shortly after release.

18th Eastern Regional Conference on Tuberculosis and Respiratory Diseases, Dhaka — A209

1995, Oct. 29 **Litho.** ***Perf. 14½x14***
497 A209 6t multicolored 2.10 1.00

South Asian Assoc. for Regional Cooperation (SAARC), 10th Anniv. — A210

1995, Dec. 8 **Litho.** ***Perf. 14x14½***
498 A210 2t multicolored 1.75 .75

Martyred Intellectual Type of 1991

No. 499: a, Shaikh Habibur Rahman. b, Dr. Major Naimul Islam. c, Md. Shahidullah. d, Ataur Rahman Khan Khadim. e, A.B.M. Ashraful Islam Bhuiyan. f, Dr. Md. Sadat Ali. g, Sarafat Ali. h, M.A. Sayeed.

No. 500: a, Abdul Ahad. b, Lt. Col. Mohammad Abdul Qadir. c, Mozammel Hoque Chowdhury. d, Rafiqul Haider Chowdhury. e, Dr. Azharul Haque. f, A.K. Shamsuddin. g, Anudwaipayan Bhattacharjee. h, Lutfunnahar Helena.

1995, Dec. 14 **Litho.** ***Perf. 14½x14***
499 A154 2t Sheet of 8, #a-h + 4 labels 6.50 6.50
a.-h. Any single .65 .65
500 A154 2t Sheet of 8, #a-h + 4 labels 6.50 6.50
a.-h. Any single .65 .65

Second Asian Pacific Community Development Scout Camp — A211

1995, Dec. 18 **Litho.** ***Perf. 14x14½***
501 A211 2t multicolored 1.00 .50

Volleyball, Cent. — A212

1995, Dec. 25
502 A212 6t multicolored 1.00 .75

Traditional Costumes — A213

Designs: No. 503, Man in punjabi and lungi, vert. No. 504, Woman in sari, vert. No. 505, Christian bride and groom, vert. No. 506, Muslim bridal couple, vert. No. 507, Hindu bridal couple. No. 508, Buddhist bridal couple.

1995, Dec. 25 ***Perf. 14x14½, 14½x14***
503 A213 6t multicolored 1.10 1.10
504 A213 6t multicolored 1.10 1.10
505 A213 10t multicolored 1.50 1.50
506 A213 10t multicolored 1.50 1.50
507 A213 10t multicolored 1.50 1.50
508 A213 10t multicolored 1.50 1.50
Nos. 503-508 (6) 8.20 8.20

No. 446 Ovptd. in Red

1995, Aug. 23 **Litho.** ***Perf. 14x13½***
509 A184 6t multicolored 2.75 2.75

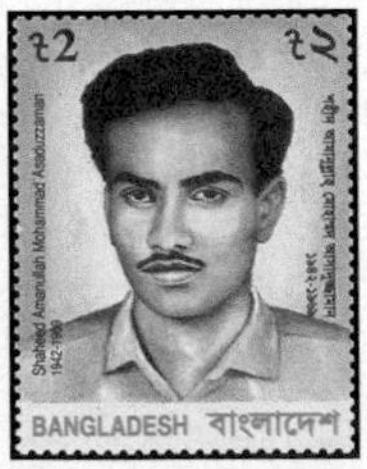

Shaheed Amanullah Mohammad Asaduzzaman (1942-69) A214

1996, Jan. 20 ***Perf. 14x14½***
510 A214 2t multicolored .45 .25

1996 World Cup Cricket Championships — A215

1996, Feb. 14 ***Perf. 14x14½, 14½x14***

511 A215 4t Pitching, vert. 1.40 .60
512 A215 6t At bat, vert. 1.75 .90
513 A215 10t shown 2.50 2.50
Nos. 511-513 (3) 5.65 4.00

Independence, 25th Anniv. — A216

Designs: No. 514, Natl. Martrys' Memorial. No. 515, Industrial development. No. 516, 1971 Destruction of war. No. 517, Educational development. No. 518, Development in communication. No. 519, Development in health.

1996, Mar. 26 **Litho.** ***Perf. 14x14½***

514 A216 4t multicolored .85 .85
515 A216 4t multicolored .85 .85
516 A216 4t multicolored .85 .85
517 A216 4t multicolored .85 .85
518 A216 4t multicolored .85 .85
519 A216 4t multicolored .85 .85
Nos. 514-519 (6) 5.10 5.10

Michael Madhusudan Dutt (1824-73), Writer — A217

1996, June 29 **Litho.** ***Perf. 14x14½***

520 A217 4t multicolored .60 .25

No. 520 exists imperf. Value, $37.50

1996 Summer Olympic Games, Atlanta A218

1996, July 19 **Litho.** ***Perf. 14***

521 A218 4t Gymnast, vert. .35 .25
522 A218 6t Judo, vert. .45 .35
523 A218 10t High jumper .50 .50
524 A218 10t Runners .50 .50
a. Souvenir sheet, #521-524 *2.50 2.50*
Nos. 521-524 (4) 1.80 1.60

No. 524a sold for 50t. Exists imperf. Value, $125.

Sheikh Mujibur Rahman (1920-75), Prime Minister — A219

Design: No. 527, Maulana Mohammad Akrum Khan (1868-1968).

1996 **Litho.** ***Perf. 14x14½***

526 A219 4t multicolored .60 .25
527 A219 4t multicolored .60 .25

Issued: No. 526, 8/15/96, No. 527, 8/18/96.
No. 526 exists imperf. Value, $37.50

Ustad Alauddin Khan (1862-1972), Musician A220

1996, Sept. 6 **Litho.** ***Perf. 14x14½***

528 A220 4t multicolored .75 .25

Children's Paintings A221

Perf. 14x14½, 14½x14

1996, Oct. 9 **Litho.**

529 A221 2t Kingfisher, vert. .60 .45
530 A221 4t River Crossing 1.00 .50

Jailed, 21st Death Anniv. — A222

No. 531: a, Syed Nazrul Islam. b, Tajuddin Ahmad. c, M. Monsoor Ali. d, A.H.M. Quamaruzzaman.

1996, Nov. 3 **Litho.** ***Perf. 14x14½***

531 A222 4t Block of 4, #a.-d. 2.50 2.50

UNICEF, 50th Anniv. — A223

Designs: 4t, Children receiving food, medicine, aid. 10t, Mother holding infant.

1996, Dec. 11

532 A223 4t multicolored .55 .25
533 A223 10t multicolored 1.20 1.20

Martyred Intellectual Type of 1991

No. 534: a, Dr. Jekrul Haque. b, Munshi Kabiruddin Ahmed. c, Md. Abdul Jabbar. d, Mohammad Amir. e, A.K.M. Shamsul Huq Khan. f, Dr. Siddique Ahmed. g, Dr. Soleman Khan. h, S.B.M. Mizanur Rahman.

No. 535: a, Aminuddin. b, Md. Nazrul Islam. c, Zahirul Islam. d, A.K. Lutfor Rahman. e, Afsar Hossain. f, Abul Hashem Mian. g, A.T.M. Alamgir. h, Baser Ali.

1996, Dec. 14 **Litho.** ***Perf. 14½x14***

534 A154 2t Sheet of 8, #a-h + 4 labels 5.50 5.50
535 A154 2t Sheet of 8, #a-h + 4 labels 5.50 3.50

Victory Day, 25th Anniv. A224

Designs: 4t, People celebrating, natl. flag. 6t, Soldiers, monument, vert.

1996, Dec. 16 ***Perf. 14½x14, 14x14½***

536 A224 4t multicolored .50 .50
537 A224 6t multicolored 1.00 1.00

Paul Harris (1868-1947), Founder of Rotary Intl. — A225

1997, Feb. 18 **Litho.** ***Perf. 14x14½***

538 A225 4t multicolored .60 .25

Sheikh Mujibur Rahman's Mar. 7 Speech, 26th Anniv. — A226

1997, Mar. 7 ***Perf. 12½***

539 A226 4t multicolored .75 .25

Sheikh Mujibur Rahman (1920-75) A227

1997, Mar. 17 ***Perf. 14x14½***

540 A227 4t multicolored .90 .25

Independence, 25th Anniv. (in 1996) — A228

1997, Mar. 26 **Litho.** ***Perf. 12½***

541 A228 4t multicolored .60 .25

Heinrich von Stephan (1831-97) A229

1997, Apr. 8 **Litho.** ***Perf. 14x14½***

542 A229 4t multicolored .50 .25

Livestock A230

1997, Apr. 10 **Litho.** ***Perf. 14½x14***

543 A230 4t Goat .95 .90
544 A230 4t Sheep .95 .90
545 A230 6t Cow 1.10 1.00
546 A230 6t Buffalo 1.10 1.00
Nos. 543-546 (4) 4.10 3.80

Paintings — A231

Designs: 6t, "Tilling the Field-2," by S.M. Sultan (1923-94). 10t, "Three Women," by Quamrul Hassan (1921-88).

1997, June 26 **Litho.** ***Perf. 12½***

547 A231 6t multicolored .90 .45
548 A231 10t multicolored 1.50 1.50

6th Intl. Cricket Council Trophy Championship, Malaysia — A232

1997, Sept. 4

549 A232 10t multicolored 2.75 2.75

Ancient Mosques A233

Designs: 4t, Kusumba Mosque, Naogaon, 1558. 6t, Atiya Mosque, Tangail, 1609. 10t, Bagha Mosque, Rajshahi, 1523.

1997, Sept. 4 **Litho.** ***Perf. 14½x14***

550 A233 4t multicolored .75 .40
551 A233 6t multicolored 1.00 .55
552 A233 10t multicolored 1.50 1.50
Nos. 550-552 (3) 3.25 2.45

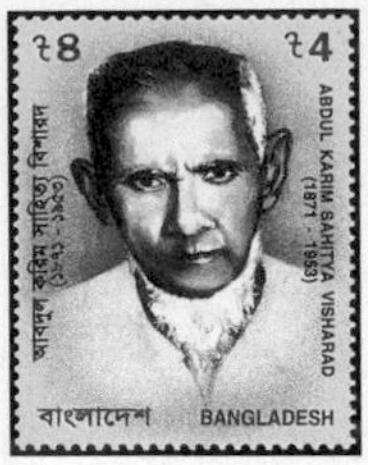

Abdul Karim Sahitya Visharad (1871-1953), Scholar — A234

1997, Oct. 11 *Perf. 14x14½*

553 A234 4t multicolored .50 .25

9th Asia-Pacific, 7th Bangladesh Rover Moot '97 — A235

1997, Oct. 25 *Perf. 14x14½*

554 A235 2t multicolored .60 .25

Armed Forces, 25th Anniv. A236

1997, Nov. 11 *Perf. 14½x14*

555 A236 2t multicolored 2.00 .70

East Bengal Regiment, 50th Anniv. A237

1998, Feb. 15

556 A237 2t multicolored 1.25 .60

Mohammad Mansooruddin (1904-87) A238

1998, Feb. 4 *Perf. 14x14½*

557 A238 4t multicolored 1.75 1.00

Martyred Intellectual Type of 1991

No. 558: a, Dr. Shamsuddin Ahmed. b, Mohammad Salimullah. c, Mohiuddin Haider. d, A.B.M. Abdur Rahim. e, Nitya Nanda Paul. f, Abdul Jabber. g, Dr. A.B.M. Humayun Kabir. h, Khaja Nizamuddin Bhuiyan.

No. 559: a, Gulam Hossain. b, Ali Karim. c, Md. Moazzem Hossain. d, Rafiqul Islam. e, M. Nur Hussain. f, Captain Mahmood Hossain Akonda. g, Abdul Wahab Talukder. h, Dr. Hasimoy Hazra.

1997, Dec. 14

558 A154 2t Sheet of 8, #a-h, + 4 labels 7.00 7.00

559 A154 2t Sheet of 8, #a-h, + 4 labels 7.00 7.00

Immunization Type of 1990

1998, Jan. 22 *Perf. 14½x14*

560 A139a 1t green .25 .25

For overprint see No. O53.

Bulbul Chowdhury (1919-54), Dancer — A239

1998, May 17 *Perf. 14x14½*

561 A239 4t multicolored .50 .25

Opening of the Bangabandhu Bridge — A240

Designs: 4t, East approach road. 6t, West approach road. 8t, River training works. 10t, Bangabandhu Bridge.

1998, June 23 *Perf. 14*

562 A240 4t multicolored .70 .70

563 A240 6t multicolored .85 .85

564 A240 8t multicolored 1.10 1.10

565 A240 10t multicolored 1.40 1.40

Nos. 562-565 (4) 4.05 4.05

1998 World Cup Soccer Championships, France — A241

1998, June 10

566 A241 6t Trophy .90 .30

567 A241 18t Player, trophy 2.10 2.10

Martyred Intellectual Type of 1991

No. 568: a, Md. Khorshed Ali Sarker. b, Abu Yakub Mahfuz. c, S.M. Nurul Huda. d, Nazmul Hoque Sarker. e, Md. Taslim Uddin. f, Gulam Mostafa. g, A. H. Nurul Alam. h, Timir Kanti Dev.

No. 569: a, Altaf Hossain. b, Aminul Hoque. c, S.M. Fazlul Hoque. d, Mozammel Ali. e, Syed Akbar Hossain. f, Sk. Abdus Salam. g, Abdur Rahman. h, Dr. Shyamal Kanti Lala.

1998, Dec. 14 Litho. *Perf. 14½x14*

Sheets of 8, #a-h, + 4 labels

568-569 A154 2t Set of 2 11.50 11.50

Princess Diana (1961-97) — A242

No. 570 — Diana in: a, 8t, Hat. b, 18t, Black dress. c, 22t, Blue dress.

1998, June 6 Litho. *Perf. 14¼*

570 A242 Horiz. strip of 3, #a-c 6.50 6.50

World Solar Program, 1996-2005 A243

Perf. 13¾x14¼

1998, Sept. 24 Litho.

571 A243 10t multicolored 1.25 1.25

World Habitat Day — A244

1998, Oct. 5

572 A244 4t multicolored 1.25 .75

Intl. Fund for Agricultural Development, 20th Anniv. — A245

Sunflower and: 6t, Farmers, "20." 10t, Vegetables, pickers.

1998, Oct. 17

573 A245 6t multicolored .70 .35

574 A245 10t multicolored 1.20 1.20

For overprint see No. 668.

Wills Intl. Cup Cricket Matches A246

1998, Oct. 28

575 A246 6t multicolored 2.00 1.50

Begum Rokeya (1880-1932), Author, Educator — A247

1998, Dec. 9 Litho. *Perf. 14¼x13¾*

576 A247 4t multicolored 1.10 .60

Universal Declaration of Human Rights, 50th Anniv. — A248

1998, Dec. 10 *Perf. 13¾x14¼*

577 A248 10t multi 1.40 1.40

UN Peacekeeping, 50th Anniv. — A249

1998, Dec. 30 *Perf. 13¾x14¼*

578 A249 10t multi 1.40 1.40

Qazi Nazrul Islam (1899-1976), Poet — A250

1998, Dec. 31 *Perf. 14¼*

579 A250 6t multi 1.40 .70

Sixth National Scout Jamboree A251

1999, Feb. 6 *Perf. 13¾x14¼*

580 A251 2t multi 1.00 .50

Surjya Sen (1894-1934), Anti-Colonial Leader — A252

1999, Mar. 22 *Perf. 14¼x13¾*

581 A252 4t multi 1.00 .55

Dr. Fazlur Rahman Khan (1929-82), Architect of Sears Tower, Chicago — A253

1999, Apr. 13 *Perf. 13¾x14¼*

582 A253 4t multi .90 .65

ICC Cricket World Cup, England — A254

Designs: 8t, Emblems. 10t, Bangladesh flag, cricket ball, tiger.

1999, May 11 ***Perf. 13¾x14¼***

583 A254 8t multi 1.75 1.75
584 A254 10t multi 2.50 2.50
a. Souv. sheet, #583-584, perf 14¼ *7.00 7.00*

No. 584a sold for 30t.

Mother Teresa (1910-97) A255

1999, Sept. 5 ***Perf. 13¾x14¼***

585 A255 4t multi 1.50 .90

Admission to UN, 25th Anniv. — A256

1999, Sept. 13

586 A256 8t multi 1.25 .60

Shaheed Mohammad Maizuddin (1930-84) A257

1999, Sept. 27

587 A257 2t multi .60 .30

No. 587 exists imperf. Value, $37.50.

Intl. Year of Older Persons — A258

1999, Oct. 1

588 A258 6t multi 1.00 .70

World Habitat Day A259

1999, Oct. 4 ***Perf. 14¼x13¾***

589 A259 4t multi 1.25 .55

UPU, 125th Anniv. A260

1999, Oct. 9 ***Perf. 14¼x13¾***

590 A260 4t Truck .85 .60
591 A260 4t Motorcycle .85 .60
592 A260 6t Boat 1.25 1.25
593 A260 6t Airplanes 1.25 1.25
a. Souv. sheet, #590-593, perf 14¼ *4.50 4.50*
Nos. 590-593 (4) 4.20 3.70

No. 593a sold for 25t. No. 593a exists imperf. Value, $15.

Sir Jagadis Chandra Bose (1858-1937), Physicist A261

1999, Nov. 5 ***Perf. 13¾x14¼***

594 A261 4t multi 1.50 .75

Martyred Intellectuals Type of 1991

No. 595: a, Dr. Mohammad Shafi. b, Maulana Kasimuddin Ahmed. c, Quazi Ali Imam. d, Sultanuddin Ahmed. e, A.S.M. Ershadullah. f, Mohammad Fazlur Rahman. g, Dr. Capt. A. K. M. Farooq. h, Md. Latafot Hossain Joarder.

No. 596 — Martyred intellectuals who died in 1971: a, Ram Ranjan Bhattacharjya. b, Abani Mohan Dutta. c, Sunawar Ali. d, Abdul Kader Miah. e, Dr. Major Rezaur Rahman. f, Md. Shafiqul Anowar. g, A.A.M. Mozammel Hoque. h, Khandkar Abul Kashem.

1999, Dec. 14 **Litho.** ***Perf. 14¼***

595 A154 2t Sheet of 8, #a-h, + 4 labels 6.00 6.00
596 A154 2r Sheet of 8, #a-h, + 4 labels 6.00 6.00

Millennium — A262

Designs: 4t, Natl. Martyr's Memorial, flag. 6t, Satellite, computer, satellite dish, Bangabandhu Bridge, vert.

Perf. 14¼x13¾, 13¾x14¼

2000, Jan. 1 **Litho.**

597-598 A262 Set of 2 2.50 1.75

Fifth Cub Camporee A263

2000, Feb. 13 ***Perf. 13¾x14¼***

599 A263 2t multi .90 .40

Jibanananda Das (1899-1954), Poet — A264

1999, Nov. 22

600 A264 4t multi .95 .40

Dr. Muhammad Shamsuzzoha (1934-69), Educator A265

2000, Feb. 18

601 A265 4t multi .95 .40

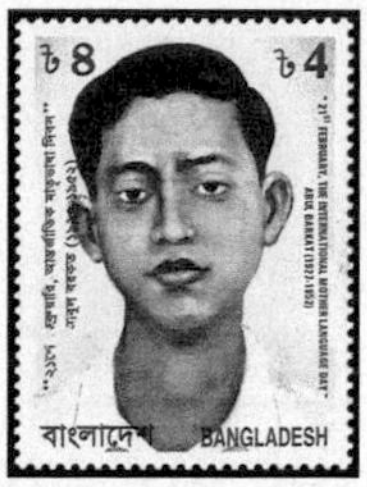

Intl. Mother Language Day — A266

Martyrs: No. 602, 4t, Abul Barkat (1927-52). No. 603, 4t, Abdul Jabbar (1919-52). No. 604, 4t, Shafiur Rahman (1918-52). No. 605, 4t, Rafiq Uddin Ahmad (1926-52).

2000, Feb. 21

602-605 A266 Set of 4 3.00 2.40

World Meteorological Organization, 50th Anniv. — A267

2000, Mar. 23

606 A267 10t multi 2.00 1.50

ICC Cricketnext.com Cricket Week — A268

2000, Apr. 8

607 A268 6t multi 1.50 1.25

Insects — A269

Designs: 2t, Wasp. 4t, Grasshopper. 6t, Apis indica. 10t, Bombyx mori.

2000, May 18 ***Perf. 14¼***

608-611 A269 Set of 4 3.25 3.25

Fauna A270

Designs: No. 612, 4t, Gekko gecko. No. 613, 4t, Hystrix indica. No. 614, 6t, Python molurus. No. 615, 6t, Varanus bengalensis.

2000, May 18 ***Perf. 14¼x13¾***

612-615 A270 Set of 4 3.25 3.25

7th Pepsi Asia Cricket Cup — A271

2000, May 28 ***Perf. 13¾x14¼***

616 A271 6t multi 2.25 1.10

Birds A272

Designs: No. 617, 4t, Amaurornis phoenicurus. No. 618, 4t, Gallicrex cinerea. No. 619, 6t, Phalacrocorax niger, vert. No. 620, 6t, Ardeola grayii, vert.

Perf. 14¼x13¾, 13¾x14¼

2000, July 15

617-620 A272 Set of 4 4.25 4.25

For overprint, see No. 723.

2000 Summer Olympics, Sydney — A273

Shot putters: 6t, Woman. 10t, Man.

2000, Sept. 18 ***Perf. 13¾x14¼***

621-622 A273 Set of 2 2.50 2.00

Bangladesh — People's Republic of China Diplomatic Relations, 25th Anniv. — A274

2000, Oct. 4 **Litho.** ***Perf. 12½***

623 A274 6t multi 2.00 .75

Idrakpur Fort, Munshigonj — A275

Vajrasattva Bhojavihara Mainamati, Comilla — A276

Perf. 14¼x13¾, 13¾x14¼

2000, Nov. 5 **Litho.**

624	A275 4t multi	.80	.60
625	A276 6t multi	1.10	1.00

Intl. Volunteers Year (in 2001) — A277

2000, Dec. 5 Litho. *Perf. 13¾x14¼*

626	A277 6t multi	1.10	.65

Martyred Intellectuals Type of 1991

No. 627, 2t: a, M. A. Gofur. b, Faizur Rahman Ahmed. c, Muslimuddin Miah. d, Sgt. Shamsul Karim Khan. e, Bhikku Zinananda. f, Abdul Jabber. g, Sekander Hayat Chowdhury. h, Chishty Shah Helalur Rahman.

No. 628, 2t: a, Birendra Nath Sarker. b, A. K. M. Nurul Haque. c, Sibendra Nath Mukherjee. d, Zahir Raihan. e, Ferdous Dowla Bablu. f, Capt. A. K. M. Nurul Absur. g, Mizanur Rahman Miju. h, Dr. Shamshad Ali.

2000 Litho. *Perf. 12½*

Sheets of 8, #a-h, + 4 labels

627-628	A154	Set of 2	12.00	12.00

Hason Raza (1854-1922) A278

2000 ? *Perf. 13¾x14¼*

629	A278 6t multi	1.25	.75

2001 Census — A279

2001, Jan. 23 Litho. *Perf. 13¾x14¼*

630	A279 4t multi	1.25	.75

UN High Commissioner for Refugees, 50th Anniv. (in 2001) — A280

Perf. 13¾x14¼

2000, Dec. 14 **Litho.**

631	A280 10t multi	1.50	1.50

Hunger-Free Bangladesh — A281

Perf. 14¼x13¾

2001, Mar. 17 **Litho.**

632	A281 6t multi	1.50	1.00

Peasant Women, by Rashid Chowdhury A282

2001, Apr. 1 Litho. *Perf. 13¾x14¼*

633	A282 10t multi	2.75	2.25

Houses of Worship — A283

No. 634: a, Lalbagh Kella Mosque. b, Uttara Ganabhavan, Natore. c, Armenian Church, Armanitola. d, Panam Nagar, Sonargaon.

2001, Apr. 30 *Perf. 14¼x13¾*

634	A283 6t Block of 4, #a-d	4.50	4.50

World No Tobacco Day A284

2001, May 31 Litho. *Perf. 14¼x13¾*

635	A284 10t multi	2.25	2.25

Artists — A285

No. 636: a, Ustad Gul Mohammad Khan (1876-1979). b, Ustad Khadem Hossain Khan (1923-91). c, Gouhar Jamil (1928-80). d, Abdul Alim (1931-74).

2001, May 31 *Perf. 13¾x14¼*

636	A285 6t Block of 4, #a-d	4.00	4.00

Begum Sufia Kamal (1911-99), Poet — A286

2001, June 20

637	A286 4t multi	.70	.30

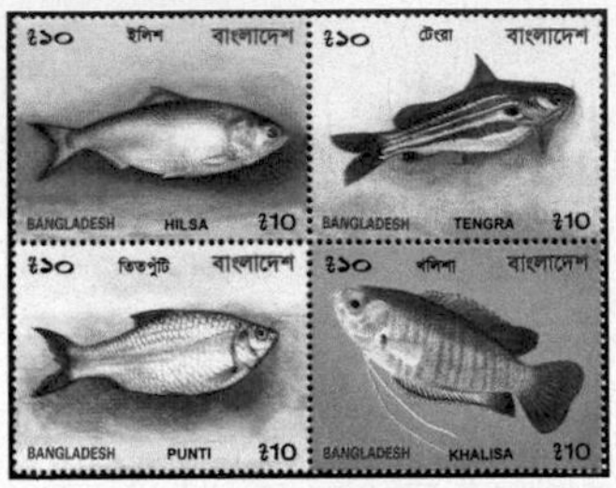

Fish — A287

No. 638: a, Hilsa. b, Tengra. c, Punti. d, Khalisa.

2001, July 9 *Perf. 14¼x13¾*

638	A287 10t Block of 4, #a-d	5.00	4.00

First Completion of Parliamentary Term — A288

2001, July 13

639	A288 10t multi	3.00	2.40

8th Parliamentary Elections — A289

2001, Sept. 30

640	A289 2t multi	.70	.45

Year of Dialogue Among Civilizations A290

2001, Oct. 24 *Perf. 14¼*

641	A290 10t multi	3.00	3.00
a.	Souvenir sheet of 1	5.00	5.00

No. 641a sold for 30t.

Meer Mosharraf Hossain (1847-1912) A291

2001, Nov. 13 *Perf. 13¾x14¼*

642	A291 4t multi	.90	.40

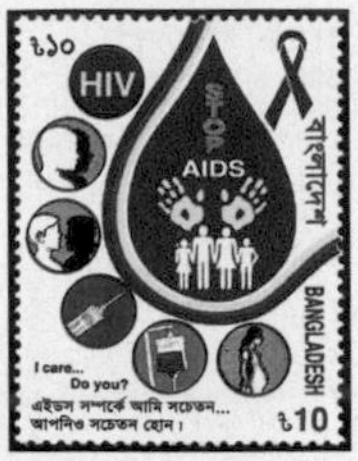

World AIDS Day — A292

2001, Dec. 1

643	A292 10t multi	1.75	1.75

Victory in War of Independence, 30th Anniv. — A293

Medals: a, Bir Bikram. b, Bir Protik. c, Bir Sreshto. d, Bir Uttom.

2001, Dec. 16

644	A293	Horiz. strip of 4	6.00	6.00
a.-d.		10t Any single	1.50	1.50

10th Asian Art Biennale — A294

2002, Jan. 9 Litho. *Perf. 13¾x14¼*

645	A294 10t multi	1.50	1.10

Great Language Movement, 50th Anniv. — A295

No. 646: a, 38 symbols. b, Monument. c, 30 symbols.

30t, Emblem, vert.

2002, Feb. 21 *Perf. 14¼x13¾*

646	A295	Horiz. strip of 3	3.00	3.00
a.-c.		10t Any single	1.00	1.00

Souvenir Sheet

Perf. 14¼

647	A295 30t multi	3.50	3.50

Rokuon-ji Temple, Japan — A296

2002, Apr. 11 Litho. *Perf. 13¾x14¼*

648	A296 10t multi	1.25	1.25

Bangladesh-Japan diplomatic relations, 30th anniv.

Poverty Alleviation Through Goat Production A297

2002, Apr. 27 *Perf. 14¼x13¾*

649	A297 2t multi	.60	.25

United Nations Special Session on Children — A298

2002, Apr. 28 ***Perf. 13¾x14¼***
650 A298 10t multi 1.25 1.25

Mohammad Nasiruddin (1888-1994), Journalist — A299

2002, May 21
651 A299 4t multi 1.00 .50

A300

Tree Planting Campaign — A301

Perf. 14¼x13¾, 13¾x14¼
2002, June 15
652 A300 10t shown 1.00 1.00
653 A300 10t Tree, vert. 1.00 1.00
654 A301 10t shown 1.00 1.00
Nos. 652-654 (3) 3.00 3.00

2002 World Cup Soccer Championships, Japan and Korea — A303

No. 656: a, Flags of participants, trophy in UR. b, World map, soccer field, trophy. c, Flags, trophy in UL.

2002, May 31 Litho. ***Perf. 14¼x13¾***
656 A303 Horiz. strip of 3 4.00 4.00
a.-c. 10t Any single 1.20 1.20

SOS Children's Village, 30th Anniv. — A304

2002, July 9 Litho. ***Perf. 13¾x14¼***
657 A304 6t multi 1.20 .40

World Population Day — A305

2002, July 11
658 A305 6t multi 1.20 .40

Fish — A306

Designs: No. 659, 4t, Labeo gonius. No. 660, 4t, Ompook pabda.

2002, Aug. 10 ***Perf. 14¼x13¾***
659-660 A306 Set of 2 1.60 1.60

Bangladesh - United Kingdom Friendship Bridge — A307

2002, Sept. 10
661 A307 4t multi 1.20 .35

World Habitat Day — A308

2002, Oct. 7 ***Perf. 13¾x14¼***
662 A308 4t multi 1.10 .35

Children's Games — A309

Designs: No. 663, 4t, Dariabandha. No. 664, 4t, Kanamachee.

2002, Nov. 10 ***Perf. 14¼x13¾***
663-664 A309 Set of 2 1.50 1.50

25th Anniversary of Bangladesh National Philatelic Association
For overprint see No. 686.

National Book Year (in 2002) — A310

2003, Jan. 1 Litho. ***Perf. 13¾x14¼***
665 A310 6t multi .50 .35

Jasimuddin (1903-76), Poet — A311

2003, Jan. 1
666 A311 5t multi .65 .35

South Asian Soccer Federation Championships — A312

2003, Jan. 10
667 A312 10t multi 1.50 1.50

No. 574 Overprinted

Perf. 13¾x14¼
2003, Feb. 19 **Litho.**
668 A245 10t multi 3.00 3.00

Shefa-ul-mulk Hakim Habib-ur-Rahman — A313

Perf. 13¾x14¼
2003, Feb. 23 **Litho.**
669 A313 8t multi .65 .65

Pres. Ziaur Rahman (1936-81) — A314

2003, May 29
670 A314 4t multi 1.00 .50

Tree Planting Campaigns — A315

Designs: 6t, Fruit, woman and child planting tree. 8t, Family, hands with seedling, vert. 12t, Tree, fruit, family, vert.

2003 ***Perf. 14¼x13¾, 13¾x14¼***
671-673 A315 Set of 3 3.50 2.75

Issued: 6t, 6/12; 8t, 12t, 6/1.
Fruit tree planting fortnight (No. 671); National tree plantation campaign (Nos. 672-673).

Labeo Calbasu — A316

Perf. 14¼x13¾
2003, Aug. 12 **Litho.**
674 A316 2t multi .75 .65

Inauguration of Rajshahi - Dhaka Rail Link — A317

2003, Aug. 14 ***Perf. 13¾x14¼***
675 A317 10t multi 1.75 1.75

49th Commonwealth Parliamentary Conference — A318

2003, Oct. 7 ***Perf. 14¼x13¾***
676 A318 10t multi 1.25 .80

Eid Mubarak — A319

2003, Nov. 25 ***Perf. 13¾x14¼***
677 A319 4t multi 1.10 .60

Intl. Center for Diarrheal Disease Research, Bangladesh, 25th Anniv. — A320

2003, Dec. 7
678 A320 10t multi 1.10 .55

Rajshahi University, 50th Anniv. — A321

2003, Dec. 21 *Perf. 14¼x13¾*
679 A321 4t multi 1.10 .55

National Library Year (in 2003) A322

2004, Jan. 1 Litho. *Perf. 14¼x13¾*
680 A322 6t multi 1.00 .75

Seventh Bangladesh and Eighth SAARC Scout Jamboree — A323

2004, Jan. 6
681 A323 2t multi 1.25 .75

Sport and the Environment — A324

2004, Jan. 10
682 A324 10t multi 1.50 1.50

11th Asian Art Biennale A325

2004, Jan. 15
683 A325 5t multi .65 .25

National Day A326

2004, Mar. 24
684 A326 5t multi .90 .25

World Health Day A327

2004, Apr. 7
685 A327 6t multi 1.50 1.50

No. 663 Overprinted

2004, May 31
686 A309 4t multi 1.75 1.75

National Tree Plantation Campaign — A328

No. 687: a, Fruit, stylized tree. b, Trees and other plants.

2004, June 1 Litho. *Perf. 13¾x14¼*
687 A328 10t Horiz. pair, #a-b 3.00 3.00

Bangladesh - Iran Friendship — A329

No. 688: a, Tower, Iranian flag, poet Hafez Shirazi. b, Tower, Bangladesh flag, poet Nazrul Islam.

2004, June 3 Litho. *Perf. 14¼x13¾*
688 A329 10t Horiz. pair, #a-b 2.75 2.75

Fruit Tree Planting Fortnight A330

2004, June 6 *Perf. 13¾x14¼*
689 A330 10t multi 1.00 .75

Intl. Year of Rice A331

2004, June 21 *Perf. 14¼x13¾*
690 A331 5t multi .60 .60

World Population Day — A332

2004, July 11 Litho. *Perf. 13¾x14¼*
691 A332 6t multi .60 .30

Bangladesh Partnership With United Nations, 30th Anniv. — A333

2004, Sept. 16 *Perf. 14¼x13¾*
692 A333 4t multi .50 .25

Bhasani Novo Theater, Dhaka A334

2004, Sept. 25
693 A334 4t multi .50 .25

Rotary International, Cent. (in 2005) — A335

2004, Oct. 22 Litho. *Perf. 13¾x14¼*
694 A335 4t multi .50 .25

Miniature Sheet

Flowers — A336

No. 695: a, Argemone mexicana. b, Cyanotis axillaris. c, Thevetia peruvians. d, Pentapetes phoenicea. e, Aegle marmelos. f, Datura stramonium.

2004, Dec. 1 Litho. *Perf. 14¼x12½*
695 A336 5t Sheet of 6, #a-f 4.25 4.25

13th South Asian Association for Regional Cooperation Summit, Dhaka — A337

2004, Dec. 8 *Perf. 13¾x14¼*
696 A337 6t multi .50 .25

Fish — A338

No. 697: a, Sperata aor. b, Notopterus notepterus.

Perf. 14¼x13¾

2004, Dec. 20 **Litho.**
697 A338 10t Horiz. pair, #a-b 2.25 2.25

6th National Cub Scout Camporee A339

Perf. 13¾x14¼

2004, Dec. 26 **Litho.**
698 A339 6t multi 1.00 1.00

Intl. Year of Microcredit — A340

No. 699: a, 4t, Woman with bowl, globe on cart with coin wheels. b, 10t, Woman pushing handle on coin and globe pulley system.

2005, Jan. 15 *Perf. 14¼x13¾*
699 A340 Horiz. pair, #a-b 2.00 2.00

South Asia Tourism Year A341

2005, Feb. 1
700 A341 4t multi .90 .90

Independence Day — A342

2005, Mar. 24
701 A342 10t multi 1.25 .75

Cooperative Movement, Cent. — A343

2005, Mar. 31 *Perf. 13¾x14¼*
702 A343 5t multi .75 .40

National Tree Planting Campaign — A344

No. 703: a, Family planting tree. b, Three trees.

2005, June 1 *Perf. 14¼x13¾*
703 A344 6t Horiz. pair, #a-b 1.50 1.50

Famous Men — A345

No. 704: a, G. A. Mannan (1933-92), choreographer. b, Ustad Phuljhuri Khan (1920-82), musician. c, Usted Abed Hossain Khan (1928-96), musician. d, Ustad Munshi Raisuddin (1901-73), musician.

2005, June 5 *Perf. 13¾x14¼*
704 A345 6t Block of 4, #a-d 2.50 2.50

Nandus Nandus A346

2005, Aug. 7 *Perf. 14¼x13¾*
705 A346 10t multi 1.25 1.25

Dr. Nawab Ali (1902-77), Physician A347

2005, Dec. 4 Litho. *Perf. 13¾x14¼*
706 A347 8t multi 1.00 .75

Science Book Year (in 2005) A348

2006, Jan. 1 *Perf. 14¼x13¾*
707 A348 10t multi 1.10 .75

World Summit on the Information Society, Tunis (in 2005) — A349

2006, Jan. 22
708 A349 10t multi 1.10 .75

OPEC Intl. Development Fund, 30th Anniv. — A350

2006, Jan. 28
709 A350 10t multi 1.10 .75

Diplomatic Relations Between Bangladesh and People's Republic of China, 30th Anniv. — A351

No. 710: a, Tienanmen Square, Beijing. b, National Assembly Building, Dhaka. c, Gabkhan River Bridge, Bangladesh. d, Great Wall of China.

2006, Mar. 6 *Perf. 12*

710	A351 Horiz. strip of 4	3.50	3.50
a.-d.	10t Any single	.35	.30
e.	Souvenir sheet, #710a-710d	6.00	6.00

National Day A352

2006, Mar. 26 *Perf. 14¼x13¾*
711 A352 10t multi 1.25 1.25

World Health Day — A353

2006, July 19 Litho. *Perf. 13¾x14¼*
712 A353 6t multi 1.00 .75

ICC Under 19 World Cricket Cup (in 2004) — A354

2006, July 19
713 A354 10t multi 1.25 1.00

Tree Planting Campaign and Tree Fair — A355

2006, June 5 *Perf. 14¼x13¾*
714 A355 10t multi 1.00 .75

Five Years of Peace and Development A356

2006, Oct. 25 Litho. *Perf. 13¾x14¼*
715 A356 10t multi 1.25 1.00

World AIDS Day — A357

2006, Dec. 6
716 A357 10t multi 1.10 1.00

Mohamed Habibullah Bahar Choudhury (1906-66), Writer — A358

2007, June 25
717 A358 10t multi 1.10 .75

Intl. Women's Day — A359

2007, Mar. 8
718 A359 10t multi 1.10 .80

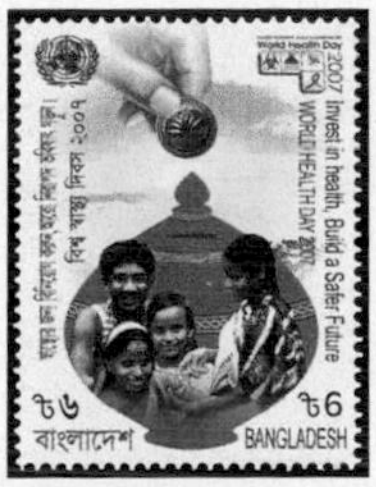

World Health Day — A360

2007, Apr. 7
719 A360 6t multi 1.10 .90

Natl. Tree Planting Campaign A361

2007, June 3
720 A361 10t multi 1.10 .75

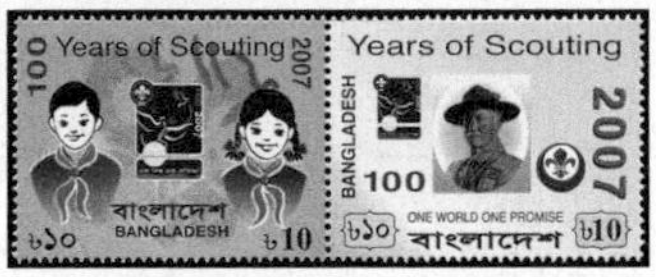

Scouting, Cent. — A362

No. 721 — Scouting Centenary emblem and: a, Scouts. b, Lord Robert Baden-Powell.

2007, July 9 *Perf. 14¼x13¾*
721 A362 10t Horiz. pair, #a-b 2.25 2.25

2007 ICC Cricket World Cup, West Indies — A363

No. 722: a, Cricket World Cup, bowler, tiger, horiz. b, Batsman, Cricket World cup, horiz. c, Cricket players, bails, wickets, glove and balls. d, Players, Cricket World Cup.

Perf. 14¼x13¾ (horiz. stamps), 13¾x14¼

2007, Apr. 19
722 A363 10t Block of 4, #a-d 4.50 4.50

No. 617 Overprinted

Methods and Perfs. As Before

2007, July 29
723 A272 4t multicolored 1.75 1.25

Dr. Muhammad Yunus, 2006 Nobel Peace Prize Winner — A364

Perf. 13¾x14¼

2007, Aug. 29 **Litho.**
724 A364 10t multi *30.00 30.00*

On Sept. 2, 2007 No. 724 was withdrawn from sale because "Muhammad" was abbreviated rather than spelled out, and the Nobel medal shown was for Medicine and not Peace.

Dr. Muhammad Yunus, 2006 Nobel Peace Prize Winner — A365

2007, Sept. 7 **Litho.** ***Perf. 13¾x14¼***
725 A365 10t multi 1.50 1.50

Bangladesh Flood Relief — A366

No. 726: a, Three children standing in flood water. b, People and goats in flood water. c, People on corrugated metal roof. d, Line of people standing in flood water. e, People with food bowls, inundated buildings.

2007, Sept. 13 ***Perf. 13½x12½***
726 Sheet of 5 5.00 5.00
a.-e. A366 2t Any single 1.00 .35

No. 726 was printed as a sheet of six stamps. The upper left stamp, showing Prime Minister Fakhruddin Ahmed, was removed from all sheets prior to sale, because he did not give permission for his image to be used on the stamp.

2007 ICC World Twenty20 Cricket Tournament, South Africa — A367

No. 727: a, Batsman, map of South Africa. b, Cricket match.

2007, Sept. 24 ***Perf. 14¼x13¾***
727 A367 4t Horiz. pair, #a-b 3.00 3.00

Intl. Migrants Day A368

2007, Dec. 18
728 A368 10t multi 1.50 .75

Independence Day — A369

2008, Mar. 25 ***Perf. 13¾x14¼***
729 A369 10t multi 1.50 .75

World Health Day A370

2008, Apr. 7 **Litho.** ***Perf. 14½x13¾***
730 A370 10t multi 1.50 .75

Sundarbans UNESCO World Heritage Site — A371

No. 731: a, Deer. b, River. c, Man in jungle. d, Tiger.

2008, Apr. 18 ***Perf. 14½x13¾***
731 A371 10t Block of 4, #a-d 5.00 5.00
e. Souvenir sheet, #731a-731d, perf. 13¾ 7.50 7.50
f. As "e," imperf. *7.50 7.50*

Nos. 731e and 731f each sold for 50t.

Reign of Aga Khan, 50th Anniv. — A372

Text "Celebrating 50 Years": No. 732, 3t, Against green background. No. 733, 3t, Against red background. No. 734, 6t, In circle, denomination in white. No. 735, 6t, In circle, denomination in gold.

2008, May 19 ***Perf. 13¾x14½***
732-735 A372 Set of 4 2.25 1.50

2008 Summer Olympics, Beijing — A373

No. 736: a, 10t, Runners. b, 15t, Shooting. c, 20t, Mascots of 2008 Summer Olympics. d, 25t, Greece #117, Bangladesh #122, Pierre de Coubertin.

2008, July 6 ***Perf. 14½x13¾***
736 A373 Block of 4, #a-d 5.00 2.50

Stamp Day — A374

2008, July 29 ***Imperf.***
737 A374 50t multi 4.00 2.00

Miniature Sheet

Japan International Cooperation Agency — A375

No. 738: a, 3t, Khepupara Radar Station, Patuakhali. b, 7t, Vocational training program. c, 10t, Jamuna Multi-purpose Bridge. d, 10t, Polio vaccination program.

2008, Sept. 23 ***Perf. 12½x12***
738 A375 Sheet of 4, #a-d 2.50 2.50

Dhaka Chamber of Commerce and Industry, 50th Anniv. — A376

2008, Oct. 23 **Litho.** ***Perf. 13¾x14½***
739 A376 10t multi 1.50 .75

Agriculture Day — A377

2008, Nov. 15
740 A377 4t multi .75 .35

Nimtali Deuri, Dhaka A378

2008, Nov. 28 ***Perf. 14½x13¾***
741 A378 6t multi .80 .35

Dhaka as capital city, 400th anniv.

Beach, Cox's Bazar — A379

2008, Nov. 30 ***Perf. 12½***
742 A379 10t multi 1.25 .60

Intl. Day of Persons with Disabilities A380

2008, Dec. 3 ***Perf. 14½x13¾***
743 A380 3t multi .75 .35

Intl. Year of Sanitation A381

2008, Dec. 24 ***Perf. 13¾x14½***
744 A381 3t multi .90 .45

Souvenir Sheet

Bangladesh No. 32 — A382

2009, Feb. 20 ***Perf. 12½x14½***
745 A382 50t multi 6.00 3.00

Intl. Mother Language Day.

Sheikh Mujibur Rahman (1920-75), President, and Children — A383

2009, Mar. 16 ***Perf. 12½***
746 A383 10t multi 1.25 .60

Children's Day.

National Day — A384

2009, Mar. 25
747 A384 3t multi 1.00 .35

World Health Day — A385

2009, Apr. 7 **Litho.** ***Perf. 13¾x14½***
748 A385 3t multi 1.25 .50

Souvenir Sheet

China 2009 World Stamp Exhibition, Luoyang — A386

No. 749: a, 10t, Exhibition emblem. b, 10t, Exhibition mascot. c, 20t, Ox.

2009, Apr. 10 ***Perf. 14½x12½***
749 A386 Sheet of 3, #a-c, + label 5.00 5.00

No. 749 also was issued in a quantity of 750 with serial numbers. Value, $35.

Shamsun Nahar Mahmud (1908-64), Educator A387

2009, May 26 ***Perf. 13¾x14½***
750 A387 4t multi .75 .40

Natl. Tree Plantation Campaign and Tree Fair — A388

2009, May 31
751 A388 3t multi .50 .30

Daylight Savings Time — A389

2009, June 19 ***Perf. 12x13¾***
752 A389 5t multi .65 .30

World Population Day A390

2009, July 11 ***Perf. 14½x13¾***
753 A390 6t multi .75 .40

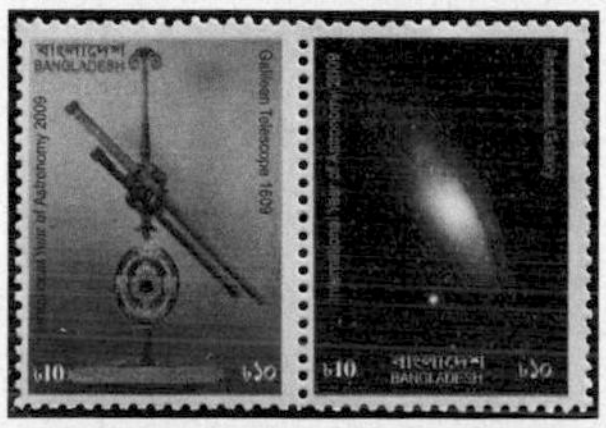

Intl. Year of Astronomy — A391

No. 754: a, Telescope of Galileo Galilei, 1609. b, Andromeda Galaxy.

2009, July 19 ***Perf. 12***
754 A391 10t Pair, #a-b 3.00 3.00

Miniature Sheet

National Mourning Day — A392

No. 755: a, 3t, Begum Fazilatunnessa Mujib. b, 3t, Sheikh Kamal. c, 3t, Sheikh Jamal. d, 3t, Sheikh Russel. e, 3t, Sheikh Abu Naser. f, 3t, Sultana Kamal Khuku. g, 3t, Parveen Jamal Rosy. h, 3t, Abdur Rab Serniabat. i, 3t, Sheikh Fazlul Haque Moni. j, 3t, Begum Arju Moni. k, 3t, Colonel Jamiluddin Ahmed. l, 3t, Baby Serniabat. m, 3t, Arif Serniabat. n, 3t, Sukanto Abullah Babu. o, 3t, Shahid Serniabat. p, 3t, Abdul Nayeem Khan Rintu. q, 15t, Sheikh Mujibur Rahman, President of Bangladesh.

2009, Aug. 12
755 A392 Sheet of 17, #a-q, + label 7.00 7.00

Stamps depict members of family of Sheikh Mujibur Rahman killed in Aug. 15, 1975, army coup.

World Food Day — A393

No. 756: a, Medal. b, Various foods. c, Boat carrying crops. d, Fishing boat, net full of fish.

2009, Oct. 16 **Litho.** ***Perf. 14¼x13¾***
756 A393 3t Block of 4, #a-d 1.75 1.75

Center for the Rehabilitation of the Paralyzed, 30th Anniv. — A394

No. 757: a, Entrance to Center, two women. b, Patients and staff.

2009, Nov. 12 ***Perf. 12¼x12½***
757 A394 7t Horiz. pair, #a-b 1.75 1.75

Prof. Abdul Moktader (1909-93), Educator A395

2009, Dec. 27 ***Perf. 14¼x13¾***
758 A395 4t multi .50 .25

Eighth National Scout Jamboree A396

2010, Jan. 16
759 A396 10t multi 3.25 1.50

Miniature Sheet

Rose Varieties Cultivated in Bangladesh — A397

No. 760: a, Alec's Red. b, Royal Highness. c, Queen Elizabeth. d, Ballerina. e, Alexander. f, Blue Moon. g, Papa Meilland. h, Double Delight. i, Iceberg. j, Sonia. k, Sunblest. l, Picadilly. m, Pascali.

2010, Feb. 11 ***Perf. 12***
760 A397 10t Sheet of 13, #a-m, + label 25.00 25.00

Opening of Intl. Mother Language Institute, Dhaka — A398

2010. Feb. 21
761 A398 15t multi 4.50 3.00

Intl. Women's Day A399

2010, Mar. 3 ***Perf. 14¼x13¾***
762 A399 5t multi 2.00 1.00

A souvenir sheet containing one 10t stamp commemorating National Children's Day sold for 25t. Value, $9.

Miniature Sheet

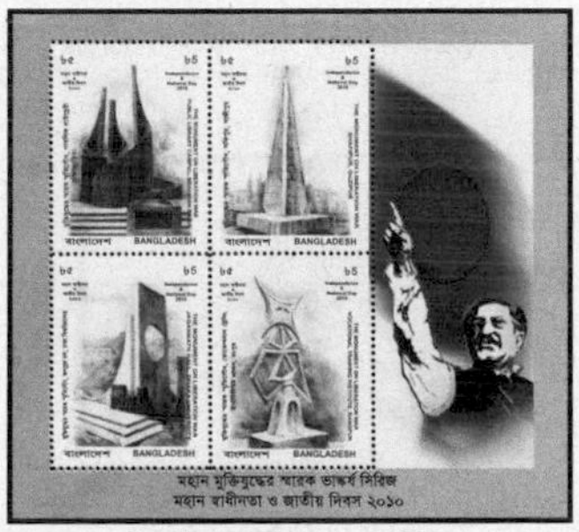

National Day — A400

No. 763 — Liberation War Monuments at: a, Public Library Campus, Brahman Baria. b, Shafipur, Gazipur. c, Jagannath Hall, Dhaka University. d, Vocational Training Institute, Rangpur.

2010, Mar. 26 ***Perf. 14¾x14¼***
763 A400 5t Sheet of 4, #a-d 7.00 7.00

2010 Intl. Cricket Council World Twenty 20 Tournament, West Indies A401

2010, Apr. 22 **Litho.** ***Perf. 13¼***
764 A401 15t multi 4.50 3.00

Souvenir Sheet

Bangabandhu Sheikh Mujib Medical University, 12th Anniv. — A402

2010, May 2 ***Perf. 13¾x12***
765 A402 20t multi 7.50 5.00

Natl. Tree Planting Campaign and Tree Fair A403

2010, June 1 ***Perf. 14¼x14***
766 A403 6t multi 1.50 .75

Dhaka as Capital City, 400th Anniv. — A404

No. 767: a, The Great Katra, Mughal era. b, Buckland Bund on Buriganga River, British era. c, Kamlapur Railway Station, Pakistan era. d, Dhaka in 2008.

2010, June 16 ***Perf. 12x14¼***
767 A404 10t Block of 4, #a-d 12.00 12.00

Intl. Center for Diarrheal Disease Research in Bangladesh, 50th Anniv. A405

2010, June 20 ***Perf. 13½***
768 A405 5t gold & black 1.75 1.00

2010 World Cup Soccer Championships, South Africa — A406

No. 769: a, Two players. b, Three players. c, Mascot.

2010, July 11 ***Perf. 14¼x13¾***

769 Horiz. strip of 3 6.00 6.00
a.-b. A406 10t Either single 1.50 1.50
c. A406 20t multi 1.50 1.50

Souvenir Sheet

Bangkok 2010 Intl. Stamp Exhibition — A407

No. 770: a, Raj Banbihar (Buddhist Monastery), Rangamati, Bangladesh. b, Buddha Dhatu Jadi (Buddhist temple), Bandarban, Bangladesh.

2010, Aug. 2 ***Perf. 12***

770 A407 20t Sheet of 2, #a-b 6.00 6.00

No. 770 also was issued in a quantity of 2,000 with serial numbers. Value, $25.

Miniature Sheet

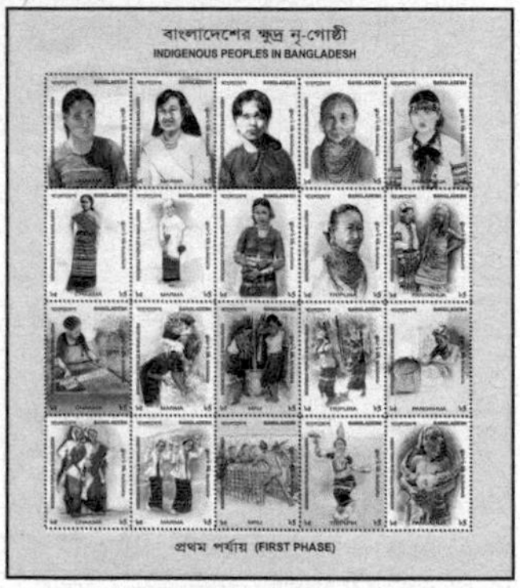

Indigenous People — A408

No. 771: a, Chakma woman with blue and red clothes. b, Chakma woman with sash. c, Chakma woman weaving. d, Two Chakma women. e, Marma woman with flower above ear. f, Marma woman holding bouquet of flowers. g, Marma women picking crops. h, Marma women dancing. i, Mru woman with red blouse. j, Mru woman with bracelets on arms. k, Mru women pounding grain. l, Mru man spearing animal in pen. m, Tripura woman with red clothes. n, Tripura woman with pale pink clothes. o, Tripura women carrying wood. p, Tripura woman dancing. q, Pangkhua woman. r, Pangkhua woman and man. s, Pangkhua man with basket. t, Pangkhua man with bull's skull.

2010, Aug. 2 **Litho.** ***Perf. 12***

771 A408 5t Sheet of 20, #a-t 12.00 12.00

No. 771 also was issued in a quantity of 1,000 inscribed "Bangkok 2010 - 25th Asian International Stamp Exhibition Bangladesh Participation" in the left and right margins. Value, $45.

Birds — A409

No. 772: a, House sparrow. b, Red munia. c, Spotted dove. d, Common myna.

2010, Sept. 27

772 A409 10t Block of 4, #a-d 6.00 6.00

A souvenir sheet containing No. 772 sold for 100t; value, $8. An imperf. souvenir sheet of No. 772 inscribed "Portugal 2010 World Philatelic Exhibition Bangladesh Participation" exists; value, $20. A pane of four No. 772 (16 stamps) inscribed "Portugal 2010 World Philatelic Exhibition Bangladesh Participation" exists; value, $35.

Year of the Tiger — A410

2010, Sept. 28 ***Perf. 13¼x13***

773 A410 50t multi 7.00 7.00

A souvenir sheet containing No. 773 exists. Value, $15.
For overprint, see No. 886.

Abu Nayem Mohammed Nazibudding Khan (1954-71), Fredom Fighter — A411

2010, Dec. 14 ***Perf. 13½***

774 A411 3t multi .40 .30

Population and Housing Census — A412

2011, Jan. 27 ***Perf. 13¾x14¼***

775 A412 3t multi .40 .30

Seventh National Cub Scout Camporee — A413

2011, Feb. 9 ***Perf. 14¼x13¾***

776 A413 10t multi 1.50 .75

1972 Return to Bangladesh of Sheikh Mujibur Rahman (1920-75) — A414

No. 777: a, Rahman and followers. b, Rahman waving to crowd. c, Rahman.

2011, Feb. 10 ***Perf. 13½***

777 A414 Horiz. strip of 3 2.50 2.50
a.-b. 5t Either single .70 .70
c. 10t multi 1.10 1.10

Mahatma Gandhi (1869-1948) — A415

No. 778 — Gandhi: a, At Laksham Railway Station on way to Noakhali. b, With others at Noakhali. c, Alone at Noakhali.

2011, Feb. 10 **Litho.**

778 Horiz. strip of 3 6.00 6.00
a. A415 10t multi 1.50 1.50
b. A415 15t multi 2.00 2.00
c. A415 20t multi 2.25 2.25
d. Sheet of 6, 2 each #778a-778c 3.00 3.00

Indipex 2011 World Philatelic Exhibition, New Delhi

2011 ICC Cricket World Cup Championships, Bangladesh A416

No. 779: a, Bowler. b, Batsman. c, Wicket-keeper. d, Fielder.
50t, Players and umpire, horiz.

2011, Feb. 23 ***Perf. 12½***

779 Horiz. strip of 4 12.00 12.00
a.-d. A416 20t Any single 2.50 2.50

Size: 127x91mm

Imperf

780 A416 50t multi 7.50 7.50

Intl. Anti-Corruption Day (in 2010) — A417

2011, Feb. 24 ***Perf. 12½***

781 A417 5t multi .70 .40

Miniature Sheet

Independence, 40th Anniv. — A418

No. 782: a, 10t, Bangabandhu Square Fountain, Dhaka (32x41mm). b, 10t, Victory of Bangla Monument, Chittagong (32x41mm). c, 10t, Memorial of Liberation War, Rajarbagh Police Line, Dhaka (32x43mm). d, 10t, Invincible Bhoirab, Kishoreganj (32x43mm). e, 20t, Sheikh Mujibur Rahman (1920-75), First President of Bangladesh (32x84mm).

Perf. 12x12x14¼x12 (#782a-782b), 14¼x12x12x12 (#782c-782d), 12

2011, Mar. 26

782 A418 Sheet of 5, #a-e 7.50 7.50

Probashi Kallyan Bank — A419

2011, Apr. 20 ***Perf. 12½***

783 A419 10t multi 1.50 .75

Sir Rabindranath Tagore (1861-1941), Poet — A420

No. 784 — Tagore and: a, Shilaidaha, Kushtia. b, Shahjadpur, Siraganj. c, Dakkhindihi, Khulna. d, Patishar, Naogaon.

2011, May 6 ***Perf. 13½***

784 A420 10t Block of 4, #a-d 6.00 6.00

A souvenir sheet containing a perf. 14¼x13½ example of No. 784 sold for 100t. Value, $10.

National Tree Planting Campaign — A421

2011, June 1 ***Perf. 14¼x13¾***

785 A421 10t multi 1.50 .75

Qazi Nazrul Islam (1899-1976), National Poet — A422

No. 786 — Nazrul Islam and: a, House with red roof. b, House, pond and sign. c, Building with arches. d, Sculpture, Nazrul Museum.

Perf. 13¾x14¼

2011, June 24 **Litho.**
786 A422 10t Block of 4, #a-d 6.00 6.00

Imperforate and Perf. 14¼x13¾ examples of souvenir sheets containing Nos. 786a-786d each sold for 100t. Value, $15.

Rare Turtles — A423

No. 787: a, Hardella thurjii. b, Geoclemys hamiltonii.

2011, July 17 ***Perf. 14¼x13¼***
787 A423 10t Horiz. pair, #a-b 4.00 4.00

A miniature sheet containing four 10t stamps depicting rare animals of Bangladesh sold for 100t. Value, $7.50.

Miniature Sheet

Birds of the Sundarbans World Heritage Site — A424

No. 788: a, Heliopais personata. b, Leptoptilos javanicus. c, Haliaeetus leucogaster. d, Bubo coromandus. e, Pelargopsis amauroptera. f, Halcyon coromanda. g, Alcedo meninting. h, Halcyon pileata. i, Todiramphus chloris. j, Treron bicincta. k, Gorsachius melanolophus. l, Pitta megarhyncha.

2011, July 17 **Litho.** ***Perf. 13¾x12***
788 A424 10t Sheet of 12, #a-l 10.00 10.00

No. 788 exists in a quantity of 3,600 with serial number and inscription for Phila Nippon '11 exhibition; value, $20.

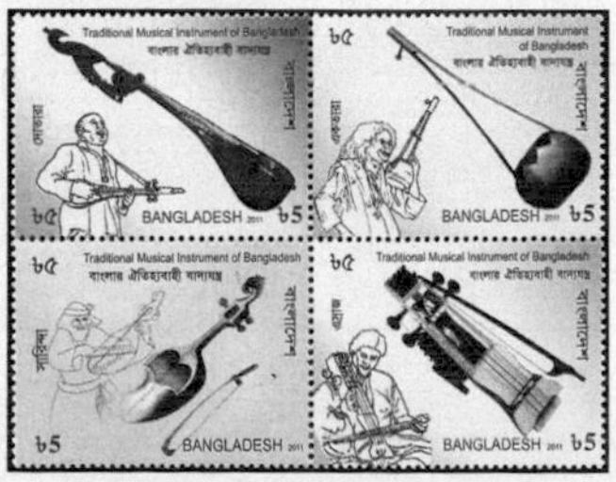

Stringed Instruments — A425

No. 789: a, Dotara (orange background). b, Ektara (green background). c, Sarinda (pale lilac background). d, Sarangi (blue background).

2011, July 21 ***Perf. 14¼x13¾***
789 A425 5t Block of 4, #a-d 1.50 1.50

Miniature Sheet

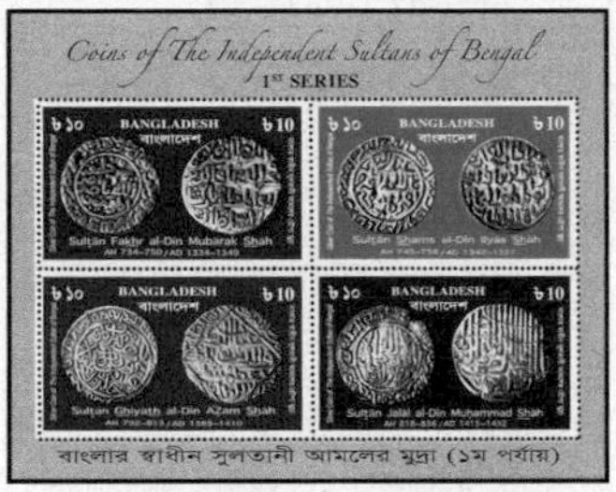

Silver Coins — A426

No. 790 — Silver coins from reign of: a, Sultan Fakhr al-Din Mubarak Shah, 1334-49. b, Sultan Shams al-Din Ilyas Shah, 1342-57. c, Sultan Ghiyath al-Din A'zam Shah, 1389-1410. d, Sultan Jalal al-Din Muhammad Shah, 1415-32.

2011, July 21 ***Perf. 13¾x12***
790 A426 10t Sheet of 4, #a-d 3.00 3.00

Miniature Sheet

PhilaNippon '11 Intl. Philatelic Exhibition, Yokohama — A427

No. 791: a, Imperial Palace, Tokyo. b, Cherry blossoms. c, Mt. Fuji. d, Kiyomizu Temple, Kyoto. e, Sumo wrestling.

2011, July 21 ***Perf. 12x13¾***
791 A427 10t Sheet of 5, #a-d 6.00 6.00

No. 791 sold for 100t.

Dhaka Club, Cent. A428

2011, Aug. 19 ***Perf. 14¼x13¾***
792 A428 3t multi .40 .25

E-Asia 2011 Conference, Dhaka — A429

2011, Dec. 1 **Litho.**
793 A429 10t multi 1.00 .50

Victory in War of Independence, 40th Anniv. — A430

2011, Dec. 16
794 A430 10t multi 1.00 .50

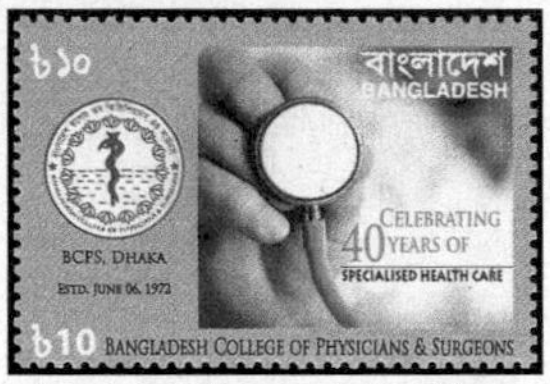

Bangladesh College of Physicians and Surgeons, 40th Anniv. — A431

2011, Dec. 28 ***Perf. 12½***
795 A431 10t multi 1.00 .50

Language Movement, 60th Anniv. — A432

2012, Feb. 28 ***Perf. 13¼x13½***
796 A432 21t multi 1.50 .75

National Day — A433

2012, Mar. 26 ***Perf. 13¾x14¼***
797 A433 26t multi 1.75 1.00

National Plantation Day A434

2012, June 5 ***Perf. 14¼x13¾***
798 A434 10t multi .75 .40

Endangered Animals — A435

No. 799: a, 15t, Gyps bengalensis. b, 25t, Semnopithecus entellus.

2012, June 14
799 A435 Horiz. pair, #a-b 3.00 3.00

A souvenir sheet containing imperforate examples of Nos. 799a and 799b sold for 100t.

Birds — A436

No. 800: a, Ichthyophaga ichthyaetus. b, Centropus bengalensis.

2012, June 14 ***Perf. 13¼***
800 A436 Horiz. pair + central label 3.00 3.00
a.-b. 20t Either single 1.25 1.25

Indonesia 2012 World Stamp Championship, Jakarta. Perf. 12x13½ and imperforate sheets containing four 10t stamps depicting different birds each sold for 100t.

Butterflies — A437

No. 801: a, Leopard lacewing. b, Striped tiger. c, Lemon pansy. d, Knight.

2012, June 14 ***Perf. 12x13¼***
801 A437 10t Block of 4, #a-d 4.75 4.75
e. Block of 4, #801a-801d, perf. 12¾ 3.00 3.00

Birds and Their Nests — A438

No. 802: a, Ploceus philippinus. b, Pycnonotus cafer. c, Orthotomus sutorius. d, Dinopium benghalense. e, Hypothymis azurea. f, Psittacula krameri.

2012, June 14 ***Perf. 13***
802 A438 20t Block of 6, #a-f 8.00 8.00
g. Souvenir sheet of 6, #802a-802f, imperf. 10.00 10.00

No. 802g sold for 150t.

Rotary International in Bangladesh, 75th Anniv. — A439

2012, July 1 ***Perf. 14¼x13¾***
803 A439 10t multi .90 .40

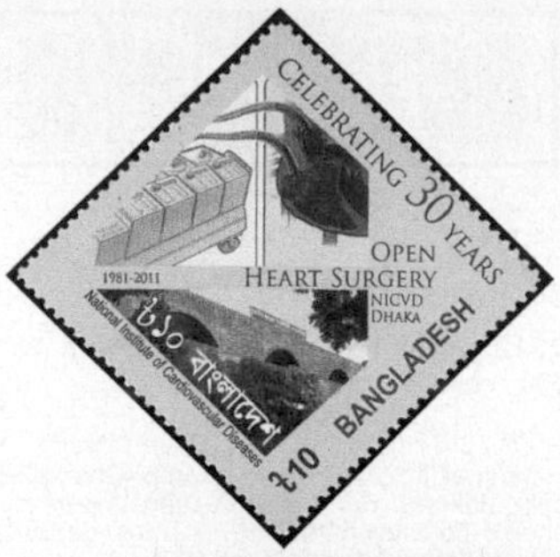

Open Heart Surgery in Bangladesh, 30th Anniv. (in 2011) — A440

2012, Sept. 12 *Perf. 13½*
804 A440 10t multi .85 .40

Intl. Ozone Day A441

2012, Sept. 16 *Perf. 14¼x13¾*
805 A441 10t multi .95 .40

Montreal Protocol, 25th anniv.

24th Asia Pacific Regional Scout Conference A442

2012, Nov. 24 *Perf. 13¾x14¼*
806 A442 20t multi 1.40 .60

Bangladesh Police Academy, Cent. — A443

2012, Dec. 6 *Perf. 14¼x13¾*
807 A443 12t multi 1.00 .50

Asia-Pacific Postal Union, 50th Anniv. (in 2012) — A444

2013, Jan. 13
808 A444 3t multi 1.75 .30

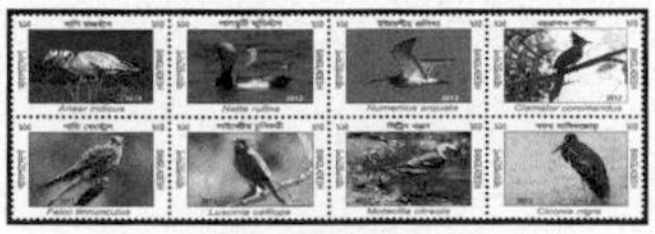

Birds — A445

No. 809: a, Anser indicus. b, Netta rufina. c, Numenius arquata. d, Clamator coromandus. e, Falco tinnunculus. f, Luscinia calliope. g, Motacilla citreola. h, Ciconia nigra.

2013, Jan. 13 **Litho.** *Perf. 12¾*
809 A445 10t Block of 8, #a-h 8.00 8.00
i. Souvenir sheet of 8, #809a-809h, perf. 13¼x12 8.00 8.00
j. As "i," with emblem of 2017 Bandung World Stamp Exhibition overprinted in sheet margin ('17) *2.00 2.00*

SOS Children's Villages in Bangladesh, 40th Anniv. — A446

2013, Jan. 30 **Litho.** *Perf. 13¾x14¼*
810 A446 10t multi 1.25 .50

Audit Day A447

2013, Feb. 7 *Perf. 14¼x13¾*
811 A447 5t multi .75 .30

Sheikh Mujibur Rahman (1920-75), Prime Minister — A448

2013, Mar. 26 *Perf. 13¾x14¼*
812 A448 10t multi .75 .30

Independence, 42nd anniv.

National Tree Planting Campaign A449

2013, June 5 *Perf. 14¼x13¾*
813 A449 10t multi .75 .30

Bangladesh National Museum, Cent. — A450

2013, July 8 *Perf. 12¾*
814 A450 10t multi .75 .30

Statue of Buddha, Dharmarajika Maha Vihara, Dhaka — A451

2013, July 30 *Perf. 13¾x14¼*
815 A451 10t multi 1.50 .75

A souvenir sheet with one perf. 13¼ example of No. 815 sold for 40t. Value, $6.

Flowers — A452

No. 816: a, Mimosa pudica. b, Mesua nagassarium. c, Dillenia indica. d, Wrightia coccinea.

2013, July 30 *Perf. 12x13½*
816 A452 10t Block of 4, #a-d 3.00 3.00
e. Souvenir sheet of 4, #816a-816d, imperf. 4.00 4.00

No. 816e sold for 60t.

Tiger Protection — A453

No. 817: a, Tiger with grass showing above head, Bengali text on top line. b, Two tigers, English text on top line. c, Tiger, English text on top line. d, Tiger with trees and sky above head, Bengali text on top line.

2013, July 30 *Perf. 13¼*
817 A453 10t Block of 4, #a-d 8.50 8.50
e. Souvenir sheet of 4, #817a-817d, perf. 12x13½ 7.50 7.50

No. 817e sold for 80t. An imperforate sheet similar to No. 817e, but with the Bangladesh flag and Thailand 2013 World Stamp Exhibition emblem in the sheet margin, sold for 100t.

Miniature Sheet

Endangered Animals — A454

No. 818: a, 6t, Lutra lutra. b, 8t, Naja naja. c, 10t, Nycticebus bengalensis. d, 12t, Hoolock hoolock.

2013, July 30 *Perf. 13½x13¼*
818 A454 Sheet of 4, #a-d 5.50 5.50
e. Like No. 818, imperf. 5.50 5.50

No. 818 sold for 60t. No. 818e sold for 70t, and has the emblem for the Thailand 2013 World Stamp Exhibition in sheet margin. Value, $9.50.

International Ozone Day — A455

Perf. 14¼x13¾

2013, Sept. 16 **Litho.**
819 A455 10t multi 1.75 .50

Victory Day, 42nd Anniv. — A456

Perf. 13¾x14¼

2013, Dec. 16 **Litho.**
820 A456 10t multi 1.50 .75

National Day A457

Perf. 14¼x13¾

2014, Mar. 26 **Litho.**
821 A457 10t multi 1.50 .50

National Tree Planting Campaign A458

2014, June 5 **Litho.** *Perf. 13¾x14¼*
822 A458 10t multi 1.50 .50

World Population Day A459

Perf. 14¼x14x13¾

2014, July 11 **Litho.**
823 A459 10t multi 1.50 .50

Flowers — A460

No. 824: a, Dendrobium aphyllum. b, Rhyncostylis refusa. c, Nymphaea nouchali. d, Ochna obtusata.

2014, Aug. 4 Litho. ***Perf. 13¼x14¼***
824 A460 10t Block of 4, #a-d 5.00 5.00
e. Souvenir sheet of 4, #824a-824d, perf. 12x13¾ 5.00 5.00

Philakorea 2014 World Stamp Exhibition (No. 824e). No. 824e sold for 60t and exists imperforate.

Bay of Bengal Initiative for Multi-Sectoral Technical and Economic Cooperation Secretariat, Dhaka — A461

Perf. 13¾x14¼
2014, Sept. 13 **Litho.**
825 A461 4t multi .50 .25

Admission of Bangladesh into United Nations, 40th Anniv. — A462

Perf. 13¾x14¼
2014, Sept. 17 **Litho.**
826 A462 5t multi .50 .25

16th Asian Art Biennale, Bangladesh — A463

2014, Dec. 1 Litho. ***Perf. 14¼x13¾***
827 A463 10t multi .50 .25

Bangladesh Betar, 75th Anniv. — A464

Perf. 14¼x13¾
2014, Dec. 15 **Litho.**
828 A464 10t multi .50 .25

Bangaldesh Betar, state-run radio broadcasting organization.

Victory Day, 43rd Anniv. A465

Perf. 14¼x13¾
2014, Dec. 16 **Litho.**
829 A465 10t multi .50 .25

Bangladesh Television, 50th Anniv. — A466

Perf. 13¾x14¼
2014, Dec. 25 **Litho.**
830 A466 10t multi .50 .25

International Customs Day — A467

2015, Jan. 26 Litho. ***Perf. 13¾x14¼***
831 A467 10t multi .50 .25

ICC Cricket World Cup, Australia and New Zealand — A468

2015, Mar. 15 Litho. ***Perf. 12x11¼***
832 A468 10t multi .50 .25

National Day — A469

Perf. 13½x13¼
2015, Mar. 26 **Litho.**
833 A469 10t multi .50 .25

International Telecommunication Union, 150th Anniv. — A470

2015, May 18 Litho. ***Perf. 14¼x13¾***
834 A470 10t multi .50 .25

Stamp Day — A471

2015, July 29 Litho. ***Perf. 13¾x14¼***
835 A471 10t multi .50 .25

Diplomatic Relations Between Bangladesh and People's Republic of China, 40th Anniv. — A472

2015, Oct. 17 Litho. ***Perf. 13¼x13½***
836 A472 10t multi .25 .25

Victory Day — A473

Perf. 13¾x14¼
2015, Dec. 16 **Litho.**
837 A473 10t multi .25 .25

Traditional Boats — A474

No. 838, 10t: a, Saudagari. b, Dingi.
No. 839, 10t, horiz.: a, Kunda. b, Ghasi.

Perf. 13¾x14¼, 14¼x13¾
2015, Dec. 16 **Litho.**
Horiz. Pairs, #a-b
838-839 A474 Set of 2 1.10 1.10

Souvenir Sheet

Traditional Boats — A475

2015, Dec. 16 Litho. ***Imperf.***
840 A475 100t multi 2.60 2.60

Souvenir Sheet

Concert for Bangladesh, 44th Anniv. — A476

Perf. 14¼x13¼
2015, Dec. 16 **Litho.**
841 A476 40t multi 1.60 1.60
a. Imperf. 1.60 1.60

Nos. 841and 841a each sold for 60t.

Indian Ocean Naval Symposium, Dhaka — A477

2016, Jan. 11 Litho. ***Perf. 14¼x13¾***
842 A477 10t multi .25 .25

Scouting in Bangladesh, Cent. — A478

Scouting trefoil and: 10t, Scouts hiking. 20t, Ring of stylized scouts.

2016, Jan. 23 Litho. ***Perf. 13¾x14¼***
843-844 A478 Set of 2 .80 .80

International Customs Day — A479

2016, Jan. 25 Litho. ***Perf. 13¾x14¼***
845 A479 10t multi .25 .25

A480

Muslim Festival A481

2016, Feb. 5 Litho. ***Perf. 13¾x14¼***
846 A480 5t multi .25 .25
Perf. 14¼x13¾
847 A481 10t multi .25 .25

Radharaman Dutta (1833-1915), Poet — A482

Perf. 13¾x14¼
2016, Mar. 14 **Litho.**
848 A482 10t multi .25 .25

National Day
A483

Perf. 14¼x13¾

2016, Mar. 26 **Litho.**
849 A483 10t multi .25 .25

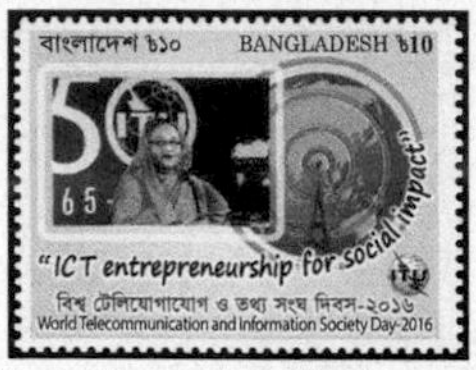

World Telecommunication and Information Society Day — A484

2016, May 18 Litho. ***Perf. 14¼x13¾***
850 A484 10t multi .25 .25

Miniature Sheet

Birds — A485

No. 851: a, Lonchura punctulata. b, Megalaima haemacephala. c, Merops orientalis. d, Aethopyga siparaja. e, Dicaeum cruentatum. f, Chalcophaps indica. g, Pericrocotus flammeus. h, Oriolus xanthornus.

2016, May 28 Litho. ***Perf. 13¼x13***
851 A485 10t Sheet of 8, #a-h 2.10 2.10

2016 World Stamp Show, New York.

Stamp Day — A486

2016, July 29 Litho. ***Perf. 13x13¼***
852 A486 10t multi .25 .25

This sheet of four 10t stamps, released Aug. 10, 2016, sold for 100t.

National Mourning Day
A487

Perf. 14¼x13¾

2016, Aug. 16 **Litho.**
853 A487 10t multi .25 .25

A souvenir sheet containing an imperforate example of No. 853 with simulated perforations sold for 40t.

This souvenir sheet containing one 20t stamp, released Aug. 21, 2016, sold for 80t. It also exists imperforate with simulated perforations.

University of Chittagong, 50th Anniv. — A488

Perf. 13¾x14¼

2016, Nov. 19 **Litho.**
854 A488 10t multi .25 .25

Victory Day — A489

Perf. 13¾x14¼

2016, Nov. 19 **Litho.**
855 A489 16t multi .40 .40

Paintings by Hashem Khan — A490

No. 856 — Various paintings with denomination of: a, 3t. b, 7t. c, 10t, vert. d, 12t.

Perf. 13¼x14¼

2016, Dec. 16 **Litho.**
856 A490 Block of 4, #a-d .85 .85
e. Sheet of 4, #856a-856d, imperf. 1.25 1.25

No. 856e sold for 45t.

11th National Rover Moot — A491

2017, Jan. 26 Litho. ***Perf. 13¾x14¼***
857 A491 10t multi .25 .25

International Customs Day — A492

2017, Jan. 30 Litho. ***Perf. 13¾x14¼***
858 A492 10t multi .25 .25

Children's Day — A493

Perf. 12¾x12½

2017, Mar. 17 **Litho.**
859 A493 10t multi .25 .25

National Day and Independence Day — A494

2017, Mar. 26 **Litho.** ***Perf. 13¾***
860 A494 10t multi .25 .25

136th Assembly of the Inter-Parliamentrary Union, Dhaka — A495

No. 861: a, Sheikh Mujibur Rahman (1920-75) in boat. b, Shaheed Minar Monument, Dhaka. c, National Assembly Building. d, Royal Bengal tiger.

2017, Apr. 1 Litho. ***Perf. 14¼x13¾***
861 A495 10t Block of 4, #a-d 1.00 1.00
e. Souvenir sheet of 4, #861a-861d, perf. 14¼x13½ 1.00 1.00

Hardinge Bridge, Cent. (in 2015) — A496

No. 862: a, Train on bridge. b, Bridge and Padma River.

2017, Apr. 27 Litho. ***Perf. 14¼x13¾***
862 A496 25t Horiz. pair, #a-b 1.25 1.25
c. Souvenir sheet of 2, #862a-862b, imperf. 1.25 1.25

No. 862c has simulated perforations.

Rotary Club of Dhaka, 80th Anniv.
A497

2017, May 8 Litho. ***Perf. 14¼x13¾***
863 A497 15t multi .40 .40

World Telecommunication and Information Society Day — A498

2017, May 17 Litho. ***Perf. 14¼x13¾***
864 A498 10t multi .25 .25

Floating Markets and Agriculture — A499

No. 865 — Various photographs and inscriptions: a, 5t, Floating Market. b, 5t, Floating Agriculture. c, 7t, Floating Agriculture. d, 7t, Floating Market.

2017, June 16 **Litho.** ***Perf. 13¼***
865 A499 Block of 4, #a-d .60 .60
e. Souvenir sheet of 4, #865a-865d .75 .75

No. 865e sold for 30t.

Photographs of 1971 War Crimes — A500

No. 866 — Various photographs of war crimes numbered at UR: a, 1. b, 2. c, 3. d, 4. e, 5. f, 6. g, 7. h, 8. i, 9. j, 10. k, 11. l, 12. m, 13. n, 14. o, 15. p, 15. q, 17. r, 18. s, 19. t, 20. u, 21. v, 22. w, 23. x, 24. y, 25. z, 26. aa, 27. ab, 28. ac, 29. ad, 30. ae, 31. af, 32. ag, 33. ah, 34. ai, 35. aj, 36. ak, 37. al, 38. am, 39. an, 40. ao, 41. ap, 42. aq, 43. ar, 44. as, 45. at, 46. au, 47. av, 48. aw, 49. ax, 50. ay, 51. az, 52. ba, 53. bb, 54. bc, 55. bd, 56. be, 57. bf, 58. bg, 59. bh, 60. bi, 61. bj, 62. bk, 63. bl, 64. bm, 65. bn, 66. bo, 67. bp, 68. bq, 69. br, 70. bs, 71.

2017, July 9 **Litho.** ***Perf. 12½***
866 Sheet of 71 + label 18.00 18.00
a.-bs. A500 10t Any single .25 .25
bt. Sheet of 3, #866a-866c (1-3), + label, imperf. 1.00 1.00

bu.	Sheet of 4, #866d-866g (4-7), imperf.	1.00	1.00
bv.	Sheet of 4, #866h-866k (8-11), imperf.	1.00	1.00
bw.	Sheet of 4, #866l-866o (12-15), imperf.	1.00	1.00
bx.	Sheet of 4, #866p-866s (16-19), imperf.	1.00	1.00
by.	Sheet of 4, #866t-866w (20-23), imperf.	1.00	1.00
bz.	Sheet of 4, #866x-866aa (24-27), imperf.	1.00	1.00
ca.	Sheet of 4, #866ab-866ae (28-31), imperf.	1.00	1.00
cb.	Sheet of 4, #866af-866ai (32-35), imperf.	1.00	1.00
cc.	Sheet of 4, #866aj-866am (36-39), imperf.	1.00	1.00
cd.	Sheet of 4, #866an-866aq (40-43), imperf.	1.00	1.00
ce.	Sheet of 4, #866ar-866au (44-47), imperf.	1.00	1.00
cf.	Sheet of 4, #866av-866ay (48-51), imperf.	1.00	1.00
cg.	Sheet of 4, #866az-866bc (52-55), imperf.	1.00	1.00
ch.	Sheet of 4, #866bd-866bg (56-59), imperf.	1.00	1.00
ci.	Sheet of 4, #866bh-866bk (60-63), imperf.	1.00	1.00
cj.	Sheet of 4, #866bl-866bo (64-67), imperf.	1.00	1.00
ck.	Sheet of 4, #866bp-866bs (68-71), imperf.	1.00	1.00

Nos. 866bt-866ck each have simulated perforations. No. 866bt sold for 40t.

A501

Bengali New Year — A502

No. 867 — Parade with: a, Tiger float at left. b, Mother and child float at center.

2017, Apr. 13 Litho. *Perf. 12½*

867 A501 10t Horiz. pair, #a-b .50 .50

Imperf

868 A502 50t multi 1.25 1.25

Flowers — A503

No. 869: a, Thunbergia grandiflora. b, Eichhornia crassipes.

No. 870: a, Hiptage benghalensis. b, Lippia alba.

2017, Aug. 3 Litho. *Perf. 13½14¼*

869 A503 5t Horiz. pair, #a-b .25 .25

870 A503 7t Horiz. pair, #a-b .35 .35

A souvenir sheet containing perf. 13½x12 examples of Nos. 869a-869b and 870a-870b sold for 50t.

Stamp Day A504

Perf. 14¼x13½

2017, Aug. 10 Litho.

871 A504 7t multi .25 .25

Miniature Sheet

63rd Commonwealth Parliamentary Conference, Dhaka — A505

No. 872: a, Conference emblem. b, Conference emblem, Sheikh Mujibur Rahman, Queen Elizabeth II and Prince Philip. c, Conference emblem, Bangladesh Parliament Building. d, Conference emblem, interior of Bangladesh Parliament Building. e, Conference emblem, National Memorial of Bangladesh. f, Conference emblem, boats.

2017, Nov. 1 Litho. *Perf. 13¼x14¼*

872 A505 10t Sheet of 6, #a-f 1.50 1.50

Start of Construction on Rooppur Nuclear Power Plant — A506

2017, Nov. 30 Litho. *Perf. 12½*

873 A506 10t multi .25 .25

National Victory Day — A507

2017, Dec. 16 Litho. *Perf. 12½*

874 A507 10t multi .25 .25

International Customs Day — A508

2018, Jan. 22 Litho. *Perf. 13¾x14¼*

875 A508 10t multi .25 .25

International Mother Language Day — A509

No. 876 — Emblem and: a, Bangla Academy, Dhaka. b, Muhammad Shahidullah (1885-1969), linguist.

2018, Feb. 21 Litho. *Perf. 13¼*

876 Horiz. pair + central label .50 .50

a. A509 5t multi .25 .25

b. A509 10t multi .25 .25

A souvenir sheet containing Nos. 876a-876b with colored frames sold for 50t.

Addition of March 7, 1971 Speech of Sheikh Mujibur Rahman to UNESCO Memory of the World Register — A510

2018, Mar. 7 Litho. *Perf. 12½*

877 A510 10t multi .25 .25

National Children's Day — A511

2018, Mar. 17 Litho. *Perf. 12½*

878 A511 10t multi .25 .25

Independence and National Day — A512

2018, Mar. 26 Litho. *Perf. 12½*

879 A512 10t multi .25 .25

Sixth National Community Development Camp for Scouts, Haimchar — A513

2018, Mar. 31 Litho. *Perf. 12½*

880 A513 10t multi .25 .25

45th Session of the Organization of Islamic Cooperation Council of Foreign Ministers — A514

2018, May 5 Litho. *Perf. 14¼x13¾*

881 A514 10t multi .25 .25

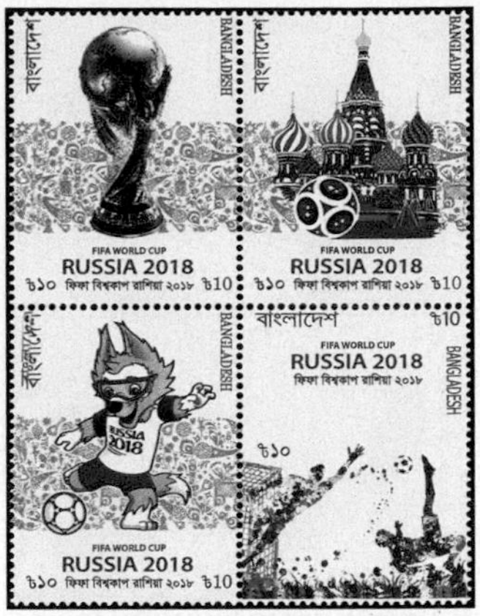

2018 World Cup Soccer Championships, Russia — A515

No. 882: a, World Cup trophy. b, Russian churches and soccer ball. c, 2018 World Cup mascot, Zabivaka. d, Soccer players.

Perf. 13¾x14¼

2018, June 14 Litho.

882 A515 10t Block of 4, #a-d 1.00 1.00

Two perf. 13¼ souvenir sheets having a sheet margin with a pale yellow green background, one containing Nos. 882a and 882b, and the other containing Nos. 883c and 883d, sold for 50t each. Similar souvenir sheets having sheet margins with a pale yellow background, serial numbers and the 2018 Praga Expo show emblem also sold for 50t each.

Change of Bangladesh's United Nations Status to Developing Country from Least Developed Country — A516

2018, June Litho. *Perf. 13½*

883 A516 10t multi .25 .25

This souvenir sheet containing one 10t stamp, released in June 2018, sold for 40t.

Stamp Day — A517

2018, July 29 Litho. *Perf. 13¾x14¼*

884 A517 5t multi .25 .25

Pallas's Fish Eagle — A518

No. 885 — Bird: a, Perched in tree with many branches. b, In flight. c, In flight, carrying nesting material. d, Perched on tree on thick branch.

2018, Aug. **Litho.** ***Perf. 13¼***
885 A518 20t Block of 4, #a-d 1.90 1.90

A souvenir sheet containing one perf. 13½x14¼ example of No. 885a sold for 60t. A similar imperforate souvenir sheet having sheet margins with the flag of Bangladesh, the 2018 Praga Expo show emblem and a serial number sold for 80t.

No. 773 Overprinted

Method and Perf. As Before
2018, Aug.
886 A410 50t on No. 773 1.25 1.25

2016 Asian Art Biennale, Dhaka A519

2018, Aug. **Litho.** ***Perf. 13¼***
887 A519 10t multi .25 .25

Launch of Bangabanhu-1 Satellite — A520

2018, Aug. **Litho.** ***Perf. 12½***
888 A520 10t multi .25 .25

18th Asian Art Biennale — A523

2018, Sept. 1 **Litho.** ***Perf. 14***
894 A523 10t multi .25 .25

Cub Scouts of Bangladesh, Cent. (in 2016) — A524

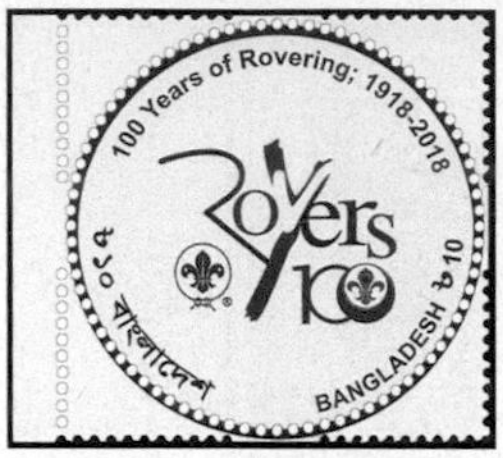

Rover Scouts of Bangladesh, Cent. — A525

Perf. 13 Syncopated
2018, Sept. 24 **Litho.**
895 A524 10t multi .25 .25
896 A525 10t pale yel & multi .25 .25

Souvenir Sheet
Perf.
897 A525 80t lt blue & multi 2.40 2.40

No. 897 sold for 100t. Values for Nos. 895-896 are for stamps with surrounding selvage.

14th Heads of Asian Coast Guard Agencies Meeting, Dhaka A526

2018, Oct. 24 **Litho.** ***Perf. 13¾***
898 A526 10t multi .25 .25

Tourism — A527

No. 899: a, Water lilies, man, and cow, Narsingdi. b, Surfing, Cox's Bazar. c, House, Sajek Valley, Rangamati District. d, Bengali New Year celebration.

2018, Dec. 4 **Litho.** ***Perf. 12½***
899 A527 5t Block of 4, #a-d .50 .50

Digital Bangladesh Day — A528

2018, Dec. 12 **Litho.** ***Perf. 14***
900 A528 10t multi .25 .25

48th Great Victory Day — A529

2018, Dec. 16 **Litho.** ***Perf. 12½***
901 A529 10t multi .25 .25

Shaukat Osman (1917-98), Writer — A530

2019, Jan. 2 **Litho.** ***Perf. 12½***
902 A530 10t multi .25 .25

Sheikh Mujibur Rahman (1920-75), First President of Bangladesh — A531

No. 903: a, Head of Rahman. b, Rahman addressing crowd.

2019, Feb. 23 **Litho.** ***Perf. 13***
903 A531 10t Horiz. pair, #a-b .50 .50

10th Bangladesh Scout Jamboree, Mouchak, Gazipur District — A532

2019, Mar. 14 **Litho.** ***Imperf.***
904 A532 25t multi .60 .60

Independence and National Day — A533

2019, Mar. 26 **Litho.** ***Perf. 12½***
905 A533 10t multi .25 .25

Sheikh Mujibur Rahman (1920-75), First President of Bangladesh A534

2019, Mar. 27 **Litho.** ***Perf. 12½***
906 A534 10t multi .25 .25

Bengali New Year — A535

2019, Apr. 14 **Litho.** ***Perf. 12½***
907 A535 10t multi .25 .25

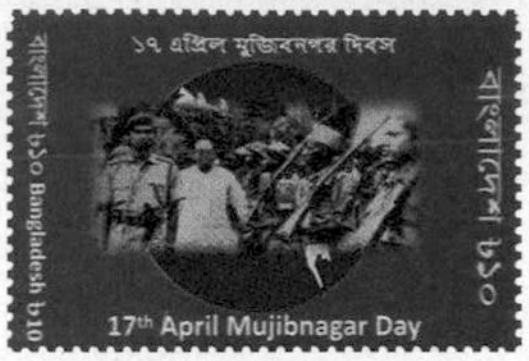

Mujibnagar Day — A536

2019, Apr. 17 **Litho.** ***Perf. 12½***
908 A536 10t multi .25 .25

World Telecommunication and Information Society Day — A537

2019, May 18 **Litho.** ***Perf. 12½***
909 A537 10t multi .25 .25

Launch of Bangabandhu-1 Satellite, 1st Anniv. — A538

2019, May 19 **Litho.** ***Perf. 12½***
910 A538 10t multi .25 .25

2019 ICC Cricket World Cup, England and Wales — A539

Cricket World Cup, emblems and: Nos. 911a, 912a, Bangladeshi batsman. Nos. 911b, 912b, Four Bangladesh players.

2019, June 3 **Litho.** ***Perf. 12½***
911 A539 10t Horiz. pair, #a-b .50 .50

Souvenir Sheet
Imperf
912 A539 10t Sheet of 2, #912a-912b .95 .95

No. 912 sold for 40t and contains two 48x32mm stamps with simulated perforations.

Stamp Day — A541

2019, July 29 Litho. *Perf. 12½*

914	A541	10t multi	.25	.25

Sheikh Mujibur Rahman (1920-75), First President of Bangladesh — A542

2019, Aug. 15 Litho. *Perf. 12½*

915	A542	10t multi	.25	.25

National Mourning Day.

Universal Postal Union, 145th Anniv. — A543

2019, Oct. 9 Litho. *Perf. 13¼*

916	A543	10t multi	.25	.25

Muhammad Hanifuddin Miah (1925-2007), First Bangladeshi Computer Programmer — A544

2019, Oct. 31 Litho. *Perf. 12½*

917	A544	10t multi	.25	.25

OFFICIAL STAMPS

Nos. 42-47, 49-50, 52, 82-84 and 54 Overprinted in Black or Red

Perf. 14x14½, 14½x14

1973-75 Litho.

O1	A7	2p black (R)	*10.00*	*2.10*
O2	A7	3p brt green	*15.00*	*2.10*
O3	A7	5p lt brown	*20.00*	.25
O4	A7	10p black (R)	*25.00*	.25
O5	A7	20p olive	*20.00*	.25
O6	A7	25p red lilac	*25.00*	.25
O8	A7	60p gray (R)	*35.00*	3.25
O9	A7	75p orange ('74)	*40.00*	.40
O10	A9	1t violet (#52)	*50.00*	8.25
O11	A9	1t violet (#82)	7.50	.70
O12	A9	2t grayish grn ('74)	*75.00*	3.25
O13	A9	5t gray blue (#54)	*90.00*	*13.50*
O14	A9	5t grysh bl (#84) ('75)	*17.50*	17.50
		Nos. O1-O14 (13)	*430.00*	52.05

Issue date: Apr. 30, 1973.

Nos. 95-101, 103-105 Overprinted "SERVICE" in Black or Red

1976 Litho. *Perf. 15x14½, 14½x15*

O16	A7	5p green	2.50	1.50
O17	A7	10p black (R)	3.50	1.50
O18	A7	20p olive	4.00	1.50
O19	A7	25p rose	5.50	1.50
O20	A8	50p rose lilac	6.25	.90
O21	A7	60p gray (R)	.65	*3.75*
O22	A7	75p olive	.65	*5.00*

Perf. 15

O23	A9	1t violet	5.00	.70
O24	A9	2t greenish gray	.80	*3.25*
O25	A9	5t grayish blue	.65	*3.25*
		Nos. O16-O25 (10)	29.50	22.85

Nos. 165-175 Ovptd. "SERVICE"

1979-82 Photo. *Perf. 14½*

O27	A7	5p brown	2.40	*3.25*
O28	A7	10p Prussian blue	2.40	*3.50*
O29	A7	15p yellow orange	2.40	*3.25*
O30	A7	20p dk carmine	2.10	*3.25*
O31	A7	25p dk blue ('82)	1.25	*3.25*
O31A	A7	30p lt ol grn ('80)	4.50	3.75
O32	A9	40p rose magenta	3.75	3.25
O33	A9	50p gray ('81)	.60	.25
O34	A7	80p dark brown	3.25	.65
O35	A7	1t red lilac ('81)	.60	.25
O36	A7	2t brt ultra ('81)	.70	*3.50*
		Nos. O27-O36 (11)	23.95	28.15

Nos. 234-242, 242A, 271 Ovptd. "Service" in Red, Diagonally Up on No. O43A, 1t, 2t, 4t, 5t

1983-93 *Perf. 11½x12½, 12½x11½*

O37	A70	5p bluish green	.25	.25
O38	A70	10p deep magenta	.25	.25
O39	A70	15p blue	.25	.25
O40	A70	20p dark gray	.25	.25
O41	A70	25p slate	.25	.25
O42	A70	30p gray brown	5.00	.25
O43	A70	50p yellow brown	.25	.25
O43A	A70	50p yellow brown	.25	.25

Size: 30½x28½mm

Perf. 12x11½

O44	A70	1t ultramarine	1.50	.25
O45	A70	2t Prussian blue	2.50	.25
O45A	A70	5t red violet	5.00	—

Size: 33½x22½mm

Perf. 12

O46	A70	4t blue	2.50	1.00
		Nos. O37-O46 (12)	18.25	3.50

Issued: 4t, 6/28/90; No. O43A, 1993(?); others, 12/21/83. 5t, 7/27/92.

No. 379A Ovptd. in Red

1990 Litho. *Perf. 14½x14*

O47	A139a	2t brown	.75	.75

No. 350 Ovptd. "Service" Diagonally in Red

1994, July 16 Litho. *Perf. 12x11½*

O47A	A121	3t multicolored	*11.50*	*11.50*

No. 354 Ovptd. in Red

1992, Nov. 22 Litho. *Perf. 14½x14*

O47B	A125	6t blue gray & yel	*1.00*	*1.00*

No. 241 Ovptd. in Red

1992, Sept. 16 Litho. *Perf. 12x11½*

O48	A70	1t ultramarine	1.00	1.00

No. 484 Ovptd. in Red

1996 Litho. *Perf. 14*

O49	A204	2t multicolored	*2.75*	*2.75*

No. 351 Ovptd. in Blue

1997? Litho. *Perf. 12*

O50	A122	5t multicolored	*.30*	*.30*
a.		As No. O50, with overprint at left reading bottom to top ('99)		—

Bengali overprint reads from top to bottom.

Nos. 235, 237 Ovptd. in Black or Red

1997? *Perf. 12½x11½*

O51	A70	10p on #235	*.75*	*.75*
O52	A70	20p on #237 (R)	*1.50*	*1.50*

No. 560 Ovptd. in Red

1998 Litho. *Perf. 14½x14*

O53	A139a	1t green	*.25*	*.25*

No. 350a Overprinted Horizontally in Red

2000 ? Litho. *Perf. 14¼x14*

O54	A121	3t multi	—	—

BARBADOS

bär-ˈbā-ˌdōs

LOCATION — A West Indies island east of the Windwards
GOVT. — Independent state in the British Commonwealth
AREA — 166 sq. mi.
POP. — 266,100 (1997 est.)
CAPITAL — Bridgetown

The British colony of Barbados became an independent state on November 30, 1966.

4 Farthings = 1 Penny
12 Pence = 1 Shilling
20 Shillings = 1 Pound
100 Cents = 1 Dollar (1950)

Catalogue values for unused stamps in this country are for Never Hinged items, beginning with Scott 207 in the regular postage section, Scott B2 in the semi-postal section and Scott J1 in the postage due section.

Watermarks

Wmk. 5 — Small Star

Wmk. 6 — Large Star

Values for unused stamps are for examples with original gum as defined in the catalogue introduction. Very fine examples of Nos. 10-42a, 44-59a will have perforations touching the design on at least one side due to the narrow spacing of the stamps on the plates and imperfect perforation methods. Stamps with perfs clear of the design on all four sides are extremely scarce and will command higher prices.

Britannia — A1

1852-55 Unwmk. Engr. *Imperf.*

Blued Paper

1	A1	(½p) deep green	165.00	*375.00*
a.		(½p) yellow green	*9,000.*	800.00
2	A1	(1p) dark blue	45.00	*80.00*
		Pair, on cover		500.00
a.		(1p) blue	65.00	*225.00*
3	A1	(2p) slate blue	30.00	
a.		(2p) grayish slate	325.00	*1,400.*
b.		As "a," vert. half used as 1p on cover		*9,350.*
4	A1	(4p) brn red ('55)	130.00	*325.00*
		Nos. 1-4 (4)	370.00	

No. 3 was not placed in use. Beware of color changelings of Nos. 2-3 that may resemble No. 3a. Certificates of authenticity are required for Nos. 3a and 3b.

Use of No. 3b was authorized from Aug. 4 to Sept. 21, 1854.

1855-58 White Paper

5	A1	(½p) dp grn ('58)	210.00	*230.00*
a.		(½p) yellow green ('57)	600.00	125.00
6	A1	(1p) blue	110.00	70.00
a.		(1p) pale blue	190.00	*80.00*

It is believed that the (4p) brownish red on white paper exists only as No. 17b.

Britannia — A2

1859

8	A2	6p rose red	850.00	140.00
9	A2	1sh black	260.00	85.00

Pin-perf. 14

10	A1	(½p) pale yel grn	3,000.	500.00
11	A1	(1p) blue	2,500.	175.00

Pin-perf. 12½

12	A1	(½p) pale yel grn	10,000.	800.00
12A	A1	(1p) blue	—	1,750.

Pin-perf. 14x12½

12B	A1	(½p) pale yel grn	—	8,500.

1861 *Clean-Cut Perf. 14 to 16*

13	A1	(½p) dark blue grn	200.00	23.00
14	A1	(1p) pale blue	825.00	92.50
a.		(1p) blue	925.00	100.00
b.		Half used as ½p on cover		—

Rough Perf. 14 to 16

15	A1	(½p) green	35.00	47.50
a.		(½p) blue green	62.50	85.00
b.		Imperf., pair	825.00	
16	A1	(1p) blue	87.50	4.25
a.		Diagonal half used as ½p on cover		—
b.		Imperf., pair	875.00	650.00
c.		(1p) deep blue	82.50	4.50
17	A1	(4p) rose red	175.00	77.50
a.		(4p) brown red	210.00	87.50
b.		As "a," imperf., pair	1,750.	
c.		(4p) rose red, imperf., pair	1,200.	
18	A1	(4p) vermilion	350.00	120.00
a.		Imperf., pair	1,650.	
19	A2	6p rose red	400.00	26.00
20	A2	6p orange ver	175.00	37.50
a.		6p vermilion	200.00	32.00
b.		Imperf., pair	825.00	1,100.
21	A2	1sh brnsh blk	82.50	12.00
b.		Horiz. pair, imperf. btwn.	10,000.	
c.		1sh blue (error)	20,000.	

No. 21c was never placed in use. All examples are pen-marked (some have been removed) and have clipped perfs on one or more sides.

Use of No. 14b, 16a was authorized from 4/63-11/66. Only two full covers are known with bisected 1p stamps. The bisected stamps (Nos. 14b, 16a, 33a, 51b) are typically found on fragments or partial covers.

Perf. 11 to 13

22	A1	(½p) deep green	16,500.	
23	A1	(1p) blue	2,500.	

Nos. 22 and 23 were never placed in use.

1870 Wmk. 6 *Rough Perf. 14 to 16*

24	A1	(½p) green	180.00	11.00
a.		Imperf., pair (#24)	1,400.	
b.		(½p) yellow green	240.00	55.00
25	A1	(1p) blue	2,750.	77.50
a.		Imperf., pair	3,000.	
26	A1	(4p) dull red	1,750.	130.00
27	A2	6p vermilion	1,100.	100.00
28	A2	1sh black	500.00	21.00

1871 Wmk. 5

29	A1	(1p) blue	200.00	4.50
30	A1	(4p) rose red	1,425.	77.50
31	A2	6p vermilion	775.00	28.00
32	A2	1sh black	275.00	19.00

1872 *Clean-Cut Perf. 14½ to 16*

33	A1	(1p) blue	350.00	3.25
a.		Diagonal half used as ½p on cover		—
34	A2	6p vermilion	1,050.	92.50
35	A2	1sh black	210.00	19.00

Perf. 11 to 13x14½ to 16

36	A1	(½p) blue green	400.00	70.00
37	A1	(4p) vermilion	875.00	125.00

1873 *Perf. 14*

38	A2	3p claret	375.00	140.00

Wmk. 6
Clean-Cut Perf. 14½ to 16

39	A1	(½p) blue green	500.00	30.00
40	A1	(4p) rose red	1,550.	275.00
41	A2	6p vermilion	1,000.	105.00
a.		Imperf., pair	110.00	1,750.
b.		Horiz. pair, imperf. btwn.	11,000.	
42	A2	1sh black	170.00	24.00
a.		Horiz. pair, imperf. btwn.	10,000.	

Britannia — A3

1873 Wmk. 5 *Perf. 15½x15*

43	A3	5sh dull rose	1,200.	375.00

For surcharged bisects see Nos. 57-59.

1874 Wmk. 6 *Perf. 14*

44	A2	½p blue green	65.00	19.00
45	A2	1p blue	150.00	5.50

Clean-Cut Perf. 14½ to 16

45A	A2	1p blue		25,000.

1875 Wmk. 1 *Perf. 12½*

46	A2	½p yellow green	100.00	9.25
47	A2	4p scarlet	375.00	29.00
48	A2	6p orange	750.00	80.00
49	A2	1sh purple	575.00	5.00
		Nos. 46-49 (4)	1,800.	123.25

1875-79 *Perf. 14*

50	A2	½p yel grn ('76)	29.00	1.00
51	A2	1p ultramarine	150.00	2.25
a.		Half used as ½p on cover		1,350.
b.		1p gray blue	150.00	1.60
c.		Watermarked sideways		1,000.
52	A2	3p violet ('78)	185.00	16.50
53	A2	4p rose red	160.00	15.00
a.		4p scarlet	250.00	5.00
b.		As "a," perf. 14x12½	9,000.	—
54	A2	4p lake	575.00	4.75
55	A2	6p chrome yel	160.00	2.40
a.		6p yellow, wmkd. sideways	400.00	15.00
56	A2	1sh purple ('78)	185.00	9.25
a.		1sh violet ('76)	7,750.	45.00
b.		1sh dull mauve ('79)	575.00	6.00
c.		Half used as 6p on cover		—

Nos. 48, 49, 55, 56 have the watermark sideways.

No. 53b was never placed in use.

No. 43 Surcharged With New Value and Old Denomination Was Cut Off The Bottom of The Stamps

Large Surcharge

Small Surcharge

Large Surcharge, ("1" 7mm High, "D" 2¾mm High)

1878 Wmk. 5 *Perf. 15½x15*
Slanting Serif

57	A3	1p on half of 5sh	6,250.	850.00
a.		Unsevered pair	28,500.	2,750.
b.		Unsevered horiz. pair, #57 + 58		5,500.
d.		Unsevered horiz. pair, #57 + 58, imperf. between		44,000.
e.		Unsevered horiz. pair, #57 + 59	46,000.	9,350.

Straight Serif

58	A3	1p on half of 5sh	8,250.	1,050.
a.		Unsevered pair		4,750.

Small Surcharge, ("1" 6mm, "D" 2½mm High)

59	A3	1p on half of 5sh	10,000.	1,175.
a.		Unsevered pair	42,000.	5,500.

On Nos. 57, 58 and 59 the surcharge is found reading upwards or downwards.

The perforation, which divides the stamp into halves, measures 11½ to 13.

Queen Victoria — A6

1882-85 Typo. Wmk. 2 *Perf. 14*

60	A6	½p green	35.00	2.25
61	A6	1p carmine rose	60.00	1.40
a.		1p rose	90.00	2.75
b.		Half used as ½p on cover		1,900.
62	A6	2½p dull blue	145.00	1.90
a.		2½p ultramarine	125.00	1.90
63	A6	3p magenta	10.00	35.00
a.		3p lilac ('85)	125.00	50.00
64	A6	4p slate	375.00	4.75
65	A6	4p brown ('85)	18.50	2.25
66	A6	6p olive gray	85.00	52.50
67	A6	1sh orange brown	32.50	24.00
68	A6	5sh bister	180.00	215.00
		Nos. 60-68 (9)	941.00	339.05

No. 65 Surcharged in Black

1892

69	A6	½p on 4p brown	2.75	6.50
a.		Without hyphen	21.00	40.00
b.		Double surcharge, one albino		—
c.		Double surch., red & black	950.00	1,275.
d.		As "c," without hyphen	3,750.	4,250.

A8

1892-1903 Wmk. 2

70	A8	1f sl & car ('96)	2.75	.25
71	A8	½p green	2.75	.25
72	A8	1p carmine rose	5.50	.25
73	A8	2p sl & org ('99)	15.00	1.25
74	A8	2½p ultramarine	20.00	.25
75	A8	5p olive brn	8.00	5.25
76	A8	6p vio & car	18.50	3.00
77	A8	8p org & ultra	5.00	32.50
78	A8	10p bl grn & car	13.00	10.00
79	A8	2sh6p slate & org	55.00	70.00
80	A8	2sh6p pur & grn ('03)	160.00	325.00
		Nos. 70-80 (11)	305.50	448.00

See Nos. 90-101. For surcharge see No B1.

Victoria Jubilee Issue

Badge of Colony — A9

1897 Wmk. 1

81	A9	1f gray & car	11.00	1.25
82	A9	½p gray green	11.00	.75
83	A9	1p carmine rose	15.00	.75
84	A9	2½p ultra	18.00	1.50
85	A9	5p dk olive brn	42.50	21.50
86	A9	6p vio & car	50.00	27.50
87	A9	8p org & ultra	25.00	28.50
88	A9	10p bl grn & car	75.00	62.50
89	A9	2sh6p slate & org	115.00	65.00
		Nos. 81-89 (9)	362.50	209.25

Bluish Paper

81a	A9	1f gray & car	32.50	35.00
82a	A9	½p gray green	32.50	35.00
83a	A9	1p carmine rose	45.00	47.50
84a	A9	2½p ultra	45.00	52.50
85a	A9	5p dk olive brn	260.00	300.00
86a	A9	6p vio & car	150.00	165.00
87a	A9	8p org & ultra	160.00	175.00
88a	A9	10p bl grn & car	215.00	275.00
89a	A9	2sh6p slate & org	150.00	150.00
		Nos. 81a-89a (9)	1,090.	1,235.

Badge Type of 1892-1903

1904-10 Wmk. 3

90	A8	1f gray & car	14.00	3.25
91	A8	1f brown ('09)	11.00	.35
92	A8	½p green	27.50	.25
93	A8	1p carmine rose	30.00	.25
94	A8	1p carmine ('09)	32.50	.25
95	A8	2p gray ('10)	13.00	25.00
96	A8	2½p ultramarine	35.00	.35
97	A8	6p vio & car	47.50	40.00
98	A8	6p dl vio & vio ('10)	30.00	42.50
99	A8	8p org & ultra	70.00	135.00
100	A8	1sh blk, *grn* ('10)	20.00	21.00
101	A8	2sh6p pur & green	70.00	160.00
		Nos. 90-101 (12)	400.50	428.20

Nelson Centenary Issue

Lord Nelson Monument — A10

1906 Engr. Wmk. 1

102	A10	1f gray & black	18.00	2.50
103	A10	½p green & black	12.00	.40
104	A10	1p car & black	14.00	.25
105	A10	2p org & black	4.00	5.50
106	A10	2½p ultra & black	4.50	1.50
107	A10	6p lilac & black	22.50	30.00
108	A10	1sh rose & black	26.00	60.00
		Nos. 102-108 (7)	101.00	100.15

See Nos. 110-112.

The "Olive Blossom" A11

1906, Aug. 15 Wmk. 3

109	A11	1p blk, green & blue	20.00	.30

Tercentenary of the 1st British landing.

Nelson Type of 1906

1907, July 6 Wmk. 3

110	A10	1f gray & black	6.25	14.00
111	A10	2p org & black	32.50	47.50
112	A10	2½p ultra & black	10.00	50.00
a.		2½p indigo & black	825.00	1,000.
		Nos. 110-112 (3)	48.75	111.50

A12

A13

King George V — A14

1912 Typo.

116	A12	¼p brown	2.50	1.90
117	A12	½p green	4.75	.25
a.		Booklet pane of 6		
118	A12	1p carmine	12.00	.25
a.		1p scarlet	45.00	4.25
b.		Booklet pane of 6		
119	A12	2p gray	8.00	25.00
120	A12	2½p ultramarine	1.90	1.75
121	A13	3p violet, *yel*	3.00	17.50
122	A13	4p blk & scar, *yel*	5.50	27.50
123	A13	6p vio & red vio	15.00	15.00
124	A14	1sh black, *green*	17.50	29.00
125	A14	2sh vio & ultra, *bl*	65.00	70.00
126	A14	3sh grn & violet	125.00	130.00
		Nos. 116-126 (11)	260.15	318.15

Seal of the Colony — A15

1916-18 Engr.

127	A15	¼p brown	.90	.50
128	A15	½p green	4.50	.25
129	A15	1p red	3.00	.25
130	A15	2p gray	16.00	42.50
131	A15	2½p ultramarine	8.50	3.75
132	A15	3p violet, *yel*	15.00	20.00
133	A15	4p red, *yel*	1.50	17.50
134	A15	4p red & blk ('18)	2.50	4.50
135	A15	6p claret	15.00	10.00
136	A15	1sh black, *green*	17.50	13.50
137	A15	2sh violet, *blue*	22.50	9.25
138	A15	3sh dark violet	75.00	180.00
139	A15	3sh dk vio & grn ('18)	32.50	115.00
a.		3sh bright violet & green ('18)	300.00	450.00
		Nos. 127-139 (13)	214.40	417.00

Nos. 134 and 139 are from a re-engraved die. The central medallion is not surrounded by a line and there are various other small alterations.

Victory Issue

Victory
A16 A17

1920, Sept. 9 **Wmk. 3**
140 A16 ¼p bister & black .35 .85
141 A16 ½p yel grn & blk 2.25 .25
a. Booklet pane of 2
142 A16 1p org red & blk 5.00 .25
a. Booklet pane of 2
143 A16 2p gray & black 3.25 *19.00*
144 A16 2½p ultra & dk bl 3.50 *30.00*
145 A16 3p red lilac & blk 4.50 *8.00*
146 A16 4p gray grn & blk 4.50 *8.75*
147 A16 6p orange & blk 6.50 *27.50*
148 A17 1sh yel grn & blk 22.50 *57.50*
149 A17 2sh brown & blk 52.50 *80.00*
150 A17 3sh orange & blk 57.50 *100.00*

1921, Aug. 22 **Wmk. 4**
151 A16 1p org red & blk 20.00 .35
Nos. 140-151 (12) 182.35 *332.45*

A18

1921-24 **Wmk. 4**
152 A18 ¼p brown .30 .25
153 A18 ½p green 1.90 .50
154 A18 1p carmine 1.00 .25
155 A18 2p gray 2.00 .25
156 A18 2½p ultramarine 1.90 *10.00*
158 A18 6p claret 4.25 *9.00*
159 A18 1sh blk, *emer* ('24) 60.00 *160.00*
160 A18 2sh dk vio, *blue* 12.50 *26.00*
161 A18 3sh dark violet 30.00 *90.00*

Wmk. 3
162 A18 3p violet, *yel* 2.50 *14.00*
163 A18 4p red, *yel* 2.25 *27.50*
164 A18 1sh black, *green* 7.50 *25.00*
Nos. 152-164 (12) 126.10 *362.75*

A19

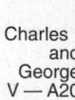

1925-35 **Wmk. 4** ***Perf. 14***
165 A19 ¼p brown .30 .25
166 A19 ½p green .65 .25
a. Perf. 13½x12½ ('32) 12.50 .25
b. Booklet pane of 10
167 A19 1p carmine .65 .25
a. Perf. 13½x12½ ('32) 15.50 .60
b. Booklet pane of 10
168 A19 1½p org, perf. 13½x12½ ('32) 9.00 1.25
a. Booklet pane of 6
b. Perf. 14 17.50 4.00
169 A19 2p gray .80 *4.00*
170 A19 2½p ultramarine .60 *1.00*
a. Perf. 13½x12½ ('32) 22.50 11.00
171 A19 3p vio brn, *yel* 1.25 .55
172 A19 3p red brn, *yel* ('35) 7.50 7.50
173 A19 4p red, *yel* 1.10 *1.90*
174 A19 6p claret 1.25 1.10
175 A19 1sh blk, *emerald* 3.50 *9.25*
a. Perf. 13½x12½ ('32) 75.00 52.50
176 A19 1sh brn blk, *yel grn* ('32) 9.00 *12.50*
177 A19 2sh violet, *bl* 8.75 *10.00*
178 A19 2sh6p car, *blue* ('32) 32.50 *52.50*
179 A19 3sh dark violet 14.00 *25.00*
Nos. 165-179 (15) 90.85 *127.30*

Charles I and George V — A20

1927, Feb. 17 ***Perf. 12½***
180 A20 1p carmine lake 2.00 .90
a. Perf. 12x12½ 5.25 4.00

Tercentenary of the settlement of Barbados.

Common Design Types pictured following the introduction.

Silver Jubilee Issue

Common Design Type

1935, May 6 ***Perf. 11x12***
186 CD301 1p car & dk bl 2.10 .30
187 CD301 1½p blk & ultra 4.50 *8.50*
188 CD301 2½p ultra & brn 2.40 *6.50*
189 CD301 1sh brn vio & ind 21.00 *35.00*
Nos. 186-189 (4) 30.00 50.30
Set, never hinged 45.00

Coronation Issue

Common Design Type

1937, May 14 ***Perf. 13½x14***
190 CD302 1p carmine .25 .25
191 CD302 1½p brown .40 *.80*
192 CD302 2½p bright ultra .45 *.90*
Nos. 190-192 (3) 1.10 1.95
Set, never hinged 2.50

A21

1938-47 ***Perf. 13-14 & Compound***
193 A21 ½p green 5.00 .25
b. Perf. 14 55.00 2.00
c. Booklet pane of 10
193A A21 ½p bister ('42) .25 *.45*
194 A21 1p carmine 14.00 .25
b. Perf. 13½x13 195.00 5.00
c. Booklet pane of 10
194A A21 1p green ('42) .25 .25
d. Perf. 13½x13 3.50 1.00
195 A21 1½p red orange .25 *.65*
c. Perf. 14 4.75 .80
d. Booklet pane of 6
195A A21 2p rose lake ('41) .90 *3.75*
195B A21 2p brt rose red ('43) .50 *1.00*
e. Perf. 14 .50 *2.10*
196 A21 2½p ultramarine .65 *.95*
197 A21 3p brown .65 *4.25*
b. Perf. 14 .25 .75
197A A21 3p deep bl ('47) .65 *2.50*
198 A21 4p black .25 .25
a. Perf. 14 .65 *6.50*
199 A21 6p violet .65 .65
199A A21 8p red vio ('46) .45 *3.25*
200 A21 1sh brn olive 1.40 .25
a. 1sh olive green 12.50 3.00
201 A21 2sh6p brown vio 7.00 2.25
201A A21 5sh indigo ('41) 6.50 *13.00*
Nos. 193-201A (16) 39.35 33.95
Set, never hinged 57.50

For surcharge see No. 209.

Kings Charles I, George VI Assembly Chamber and Mace A22

Perf. 13½x14
1939, June 27 **Engr.** **Wmk. 4**
202 A22 ½p deep green 2.10 1.75
203 A22 1p scarlet 2.10 1.35
204 A22 1½p deep orange 2.25 .65
205 A22 2½p ultramarine 3.25 *9.00*
206 A22 3p yellow brown 3.25 *6.00*
Nos. 202-206 (5) 12.95 *18.75*
Set, never hinged 21.00

Tercentenary of the General Assembly.

Catalogue values for unused stamps in this section, from this point to the end of the section, are for Never Hinged items.

Peace Issue

Common Design Type

1946, Sept. 18
207 CD303 1½p deep orange .25 .55
208 CD303 3p brown .25 .55

Nos. 195e, 195B, Surcharged in Black

1947, Apr. 21 ***Perf. 14***
209 A21 1p on 2p brt rose red 2.40 *6.50*
b. Perf. 13½x13 3.25 *8.00*
c. As "b.," double surcharge 3,250.

Silver Wedding Issue

Common Design Types

Perf. 14x14½
1948, Nov. 24 **Photo.** **Wmk. 4**
210 CD304 1½p orange .35 .55

Engraved; Name Typographed

Perf. 11½x11
211 CD305 5sh dark blue 18.00 13.00

UPU Issue

Common Design Types

1949, Oct. 10 ***Perf. 13½, 11x11½***
212 CD306 1½p red orange .55 *2.10*
213 CD307 3p indigo 2.75 *7.75*
214 CD308 4p gray .55 *3.75*
215 CD309 1sh olive .55 *1.25*
Nos. 212-215 (4) 4.40 *14.85*

Dover Fort — A23

Admiral Nelson Statue — A24

Designs: 2c, Sugar cane breeding. 3c, Public buildings. 6c, Casting net. 8c, Intercolonial schooner. 12c, Flying Fish. 24c, Old Main Guard Garrison. 48c, Cathedral, vert. 60c, Careenage. $1.20, Map, vert. $2.40, Great Seal, 1660.

Perf. 11x11½ (A23), 13x13½ (A24)
1950, May 1 **Engr.** **Wmk. 4**
216 A23 1c slate .35 *4.75*
217 A23 2c emerald .25 *3.25*
218 A23 3c slate & brown 1.25 *4.25*
219 A24 4c carmine .30 .40
220 A23 6c blue .35 *2.50*
221 A23 8c choc & blue 1.60 *4.00*
222 A23 12c olive & aqua 1.25 *2.00*
223 A23 24c gray & red 1.25 .55
224 A24 48c violet 11.00 9.00
225 A23 60c brn car & bl grn 14.00 *15.00*
226 A24 $1.20 olive & car 14.00 5.50
227 A23 $2.40 gray 27.50 *45.00*
Nos. 216-227 (12) 73.10 *96.20*

University Issue

Common Design Types

1951, Feb. 16 ***Perf. 14x14½***
228 CD310 3c turq bl & choc .50 .40
229 CD311 12c ol brn & turq bl 1.25 *2.25*

Stamp of 1852 A25

Perf. 13½
1952, Apr. 15 **Wmk. 4** **Engr.**
230 A25 3c slate bl & dp grn .40 .30
231 A25 4c rose pink & bl .40 *1.25*
232 A25 12c emer & slate bl .40 *1.00*
233 A25 24c gray blk & red brn .80 .80
Nos. 230-233 (4) 2.00 *3.35*

Centenary of Barbados postage stamps.

Coronation Issue

Common Design Type

1953, June 4 ***Perf. 13½x13***
234 CD312 4c red orange & black 1.00 .25

Harbor Police A26

Designs: 1c Dover Fort. 2c, Sugar cane breeding. 3c, Public buildings. 4c, Admiral Nelson Statue, vert. 6c, Casting net. 8c, Intercolonial schooner. 12c, Flying Fish. 24c, Old Main Guard Garrison. 48c, Cathedral, vert. 60c, Careenage. $1.20, Map, vert. $2.40, Great Seal, 1660 ("E II R").

Perf. 11x11½ (horiz.), 13x13½ (vert.)
1953-57 **Engr.**
235 A23 1c slate ('53) .25 *1.00*
236 A23 2c grnsh blue & deep org .25 *1.50*
237 A23 3c emerald & blk 1.75 1.10
238 A24 4c orange & gray .25 .25
239 A26 5c dp car & dp bl 1.75 .75
240 A23 6c red brown .75 .75
241 A23 8c brt blue & blk 1.05 .40
242 A23 12c brn ol & aqua 1.75 .25
243 A23 24c gray & red ('56) 1.05 .25
244 A24 48c violet ('56) 11.00 1.25
245 A23 60c brown car & blue grn ('56) 17.50 5.50
246 A24 $1.20 ol & car ('56) 32.50 6.50
247 A23 $2.40 gray ('57) 2.40 2.25
Nos. 235-247 (13) 72.25 21.75

See Nos. 257-264.

West Indies Federation

Common Design Type

Perf. 11½x11
1958, Apr. 23 **Wmk. 314**
248 CD313 3c green .40 .25
249 CD313 6c blue .60 *2.25*
250 CD313 12c carmine rose .60 .40
Nos. 248-250 (3) 1.60 *2.90*

Deep Water Harbor, Bridgetown A27

1961, May 6 **Engr.** ***Perf. 11x11½***
251 A27 4c orange & black .25 *.50*
252 A27 8c ultra & black .30 *.60*
253 A27 24c black & pink .45 *.60*
Nos. 251-253 (3) 1.00 1.70

Deep Water Harbor at Bridgetown opening.

Scout Emblem and Map of Barbados — A28

Perf. 11½x11
1962, Mar. 9 **Wmk. 314**
254 A28 4c orange & black .60 .25
255 A28 12c gray & blue 1.75 .25
256 A28 $1.20 grnsh gray & car rose 1.75 *3.75*
Nos. 254-256 (3) 4.10 *4.25*

50th anniv. of the founding of the Boy Scouts of Barbados.

Queen Types of 1953-57

Perf. 11x11½, 13x13½
1964-65 **Engr.** **Wmk. 314**
257 A23 1c slate .70 *5.50*
258 A24 4c orange & gray .40 *.60*
259 A23 8c brt bl & blk ('65) .60 .40
260 A23 12c brn ol & aqua ('65) .75
261 A23 24c gray & red .75 *.85*
262 A24 48c violet 3.75 1.50

263	A23	60c brn car & bl grn	13.00	4.00
264	A23	$2.40 gray ('65)	1.75	1.75
		Nos. 257-264 (8)	21.70	
		Nos. 257-259,261-264 (7)		14.60

The 12c was never put on sale in Barbados.

ITU Issue

Common Design Type

Perf. 11x11½

1965, May 17 Litho. Wmk. 314

265	CD317	2c lilac & ver	.25	.25
266	CD317	48c yellow & gray	1.25	1.00

Sea Horse A29

Designs: 1c, Deep sea coral. 2c, Lobster. 4c, Sea urchin. 5c, Staghorn coral. 6c, Butterflyfish. 8c, File shell. 12c, Balloonfish. 15c, Angelfish. 25c, Brain coral. 35c, Brittle star. 50c, Flyingfish. $1, Queen conch shell. $2.50, Fiddler crab.

Wmk. 314 Upright

1965, July 15 Photo. *Perf. 14x13½*

267	A29	1c dk blue, pink & black	.35	.35
268	A29	2c car rose, sepia & org	.30	.25
269	A29	3c org, brn & sep *("Hippocanpus")*	.60	*.60*
270	A29	4c ol grn & dk bl	.30	.35
a.		Imperf., pair	*325.00*	250.00
271	A29	5c lil, brn & pink	.45	.60
272	A29	6c grnsh bl, yel & blk	.55	.50
273	A29	8c ultra, org, red & blk	.45	.35
274	A29	12c rose lil, yel & blk	.50	.35
275	A29	15c red, yel & blk	1.10	.80
276	A29	25c yel brn & ultra	1.40	1.10
277	A29	35c grn, rose brn & blk	2.00	.35
278	A29	50c yel grn & ultra	2.75	.95
279	A29	$1 gray & multi	3.75	2.00
280	A29	$2.50 lt bl & multi	4.00	*8.00*
		Nos. 267-280 (14)	18.50	16.55

1966-69 Wmk. 314 Sideways

$5, "Dolphin" (coryphaena hippurus).

267a	A29	1c	.25	.25
268a	A29	2c ('67)	.30	*1.40*
269A	A29	3c *("Hippocampus")* ('67)	.30	*2.75*
270b	A29	4c	.55	.25
271a	A29	5c	.45	.25
272a	A29	6c ('67)	.70	.25
273a	A29	8c ('67)	.70	.25
274a	A29	12c ('67)	.50	.25
275a	A29	15c	2.10	.25
276a	A29	25c	2.10	.40
277a	A29	35c	2.40	.65
278a	A29	50c	2.10	*4.25*
279a	A29	$1	6.00	1.00
280a	A29	$2.50	7.50	3.00
280B	A29	$5 dk ol & multi ('69)	21.00	20.00
		Nos. 267a-280B (15)	46.95	35.20

For surcharge see No. 327.

Churchill Memorial Issue

Common Design Type

1966, Jan. 24 Wmk. 314 *Perf. 14*

281	CD319	1c multicolored	.30	*3.50*
282	CD319	4c multicolored	.45	.25
283	CD319	25c multicolored	1.00	.50
284	CD319	35c multicolored	1.25	.70
		Nos. 281-284 (4)	3.00	4.95

Royal Visit Issue

Common Design Type

1966, Feb. 4 Litho. *Perf. 11x12*

285	CD320	3c violet blue	.50	.25
286	CD320	35c dark car rose	2.50	1.75

UNESCO Anniversary Issue

Common Design Type

1967, Jan. 6 Litho. *Perf. 14*

287	CD323	4c "Education"	.25	.25
288	CD323	12c "Science"	.85	.55
289	CD323	25c "Culture"	1.25	*1.35*
		Nos. 287-289 (3)	2.35	2.15

Arms of Barbados — A30

Designs: 25c, Hilton Hotel, horiz. 35c, Garfield Sobers, captain of Barbados and West Indies Cricket Team. 50c, Pine Hill Dairy, horiz.

1966, Dec. 2 Unwmk. Photo.

290	A30	4c multicolored	.25	.25
291	A30	25c multicolored	.25	.25
292	A30	35c multicolored	1.78	.80
293	A30	50c multicolored	.75	*1.00*
		Nos. 290-293 (4)	3.03	2.30

Barbados' independence, Nov. 30, 1966.

Policeman and Anchor Monument — A31

Designs: 25c, Policeman with telescope. 35c, Police motor launch, horiz. 50c, Policemen at Harbor Gate.

1967, Oct. 16 Litho. *Perf. 13½x14*

294	A31	4c multicolored	.25	.25
295	A31	25c multicolored	.40	.25
296	A31	35c multicolored	.45	.25
297	A31	50c multicolored	.70	.70
		Nos. 294-297 (4)	1.80	1.45

Centenary of Bridgetown Harbor Police. For surcharge see No. 322.

Independence Arch — A32

1st Anniv. of Independence: 4c, Sir Winston Scott, Governor-General, vert. 35c, Treasury Building. 50c, Parliament Building.

Perf. 14½x14, 14x14½

1967, Dec. 4 Photo. Unwmk.

298	A32	4c multicolored	.25	.25
299	A32	25c multicolored	.25	.25
300	A32	35c multicolored	.30	.30
301	A32	50c multicolored	.40	.40
		Nos. 298-301 (4)	1.20	1.20

UN Building, — A33

1968, Feb. 27 *Perf. 14½x14*

302	A33	15c multicolored	.40	.40

20th anniv. of the UN Economic Commission for Latin America.

Radar Antenna on Top of Old — A34

Designs: 25c, Caribbean Meteorological Institute, Barbados, horiz. 50c, HARP gun used in High Altitude Research Program, at Paragon in Christ Church, Barbados.

Perf. 14x14½, 14½x14

1968, June 4 Photo. Unwmk.

303	A34	3c violet & multi	.25	.25
304	A34	25c vermilion & multi	.25	.25
305	A34	50c orange & multi	.40	.40
		Nos. 303-305 (3)	.90	.90

World Meteorological Day.

Girl Scout at Campfire — A35

Lady Baden-Powell, Queen Elizabeth II and: 25c, Pax Hill Headquarters. 35c, Girl Scout badge.

Perf. 14x14½

1968, Aug. 29 Photo. Unwmk.

306	A35	3c dp ultra, blk & gold	.25	.25
307	A35	25c bluish green, black & gold	.35	.35
308	A35	35c org yel, blk & gold	.65	.65
		Nos. 306-308 (3)	1.25	1.25

Barbados Girl Scouts' 50th anniv.

Human Rights Flame and Escape A36

Designs: 4c, Human Rights flame, hands, and broken chain. 25c, Human Rights flame, family and broken chain.

Perf. 11x11½

1968, Dec. 10 Litho. Unwmk.

309	A36	4c violet, gray grn & red brown	.25	.25
310	A36	25c org, blk & blue	.25	.25
311	A36	35c grnsh blue, blue, blk & org	.25	.25
		Nos. 309-311 (3)	.75	.75

International Human Rights Year.

In the Paddock A37

Horse Racing: 25c, "They're off!" 35c, On the flat. 50c, The Finish.

1969, Mar. 15 Litho. *Perf. 14½*

312	A37	4c multicolored	.25	.25
313	A37	25c multicolored	.25	.25
314	A37	35c multicolored	.30	.30
315	A37	50c multicolored	.40	*2.00*
a.		Souvenir sheet of 4, #312-315	3.25	3.25
		Nos. 312-315 (4)	1.20	2.80

Map of Caribbean — A38

Design: 12c, 50c, "Strength in Unity," horiz.

Perf. 14x14½, 14½x14

1969, May 6 Photo. Wmk. 314

316	A38	5c brown & multi	.25	.25
317	A38	12c ultra & multi	.25	.25
318	A38	25c green & multi	.25	.25
319	A38	50c magenta & multi	.25	.25
		Nos. 316-319 (4)	1.00	1.00

1st anniv. of CARIFTA (Caribbean Free Trade Area).

ILO Emblem A39

Perf. 14x13

1969, Aug. 5 Litho. Unwmk.

320	A39	4c bl grn, brt grn & blk	.25	.25
321	A39	25c red brn, brt mag & red	.25	.25

50th anniv. of the ILO.

No. 294 Surcharged

1969, Aug. 30 *Perf. 13½x14*

322	A31	1c on 4c multicolored	.45	.45

Barbados Boy Scout Emblem — A40

Designs: 25c, Sea Scouts rowing in Bridgetown harbor. 35c, Campfire. 50c, Various Scouts in front of National Headquarters and Training Center, Hazelwood.

Perf. 13½x13

1969, Dec. 16 Litho. Unwmk.

323	A40	5c multicolored	.25	.25
324	A40	25c multicolored	.65	.25
325	A40	35c multicolored	.85	.25
326	A40	50c multicolored	1.25	1.25
a.		Souvenir sheet of 4, #323-326	16.00	16.00
		Nos. 323-326 (4)	3.00	2.00

Attainment of independence by the Barbados Boy Scout Assoc.

No. 271a Surcharged

Wmk. 314 Sideways

1970, Mar. 11 Photo. *Perf. 14x13½*

327	A29	4c on 5c multicolored	.50	.50

This locally applied surcharge exists in several variations: double, triple, on back, in pair with one missing, etc.

Lion at Gun Hill — A41

Barbados Museum A42

2c, Trafalgar Fountain. 3c, Montefiore Drinking Fountain. 4c, St. James' Monument. 5c, St. Ann's Fort. 6c, Old Sugar Mill, Morgan Lewis. 8c, Cenotaph. 10c, South Point Lighthouse. 15c, Sharon Moravian Church. 25c, George Washington House. 35c, St. Nicholas Abbey. 50c, Bowmanston Pumping Station. $1, Queen Elizabeth Hospital. $2.50, Modern sugar factory. $5, Seawell Intl. Airport.

Wmk. 314 Upright (A41), Sideways (A42)

Perf. 12½x13, 13x12½

1970, May 4 **Photo.**

328	A41	1c bl grn & multi	.25	*.80*
329	A41	2c crimson & multi	.25	*.80*
330	A41	3c blue & multi	.25	*.80*
331	A41	4c yellow & multi	.85	.25
332	A41	5c dp org & multi	.25	.25
333	A41	6c dull yel & multi	.30	.30
334	A41	8c dp blue & multi	.25	.25
335	A41	10c red & multi	3.00	.50
336	A42	12c ultra & multi	1.25	.25
337	A42	15c yellow & multi	.25	*.70*
338	A42	25c orange & multi	.25	.25
339	A42	35c pink & multi	.25	*.70*
340	A42	50c bl grn & multi	.40	*1.00*
341	A42	$1 emerald & multi	.55	*2.50*
342	A42	$2.50 ver & multi	1.75	*4.00*
343	A42	$5 yellow & multi	6.00	*11.00*
		Nos. 328-343 (16)	16.10	24.35

Nos. 328-332, 334-343 were reissued in 1971 on glazed paper. Value, set *$50.*

Wmk. 314 Sideways (A41), Upright (A42)

1972-74

331a	A41	4c	2.40	1.75
332a	A41	5c	2.10	1.75
333a	A41	6c	6.00	*11.50*
334a	A41	8c	2.40	1.50
335a	A41	10c ('74)	4.75	*6.75*
336a	A42	12c	2.40	*4.00*
337a	A42	15c	1.25	1.50
338a	A42	25c	4.00	3.00
339a	A42	35c	3.50	.80
340a	A42	50c	4.75	1.75
341a	A42	$1	8.75	3.25
342a	A42	$2.50 ('73)	6.00	*8.25*
343a	A42	$5 ('73)	6.25	5.25
		Nos. 331a-343a (13)	54.55	51.05

For surcharge, see No. 391.

Primary Education, UN and — A43

UN and Education Year Emblems and: 5c, Secondary education (student with microscope). 25c, Technical education (men working with power drill). 50c, University building.

1970, June 26 **Litho.** ***Perf. 14***

344	A43	4c multicolored	.25	.25
345	A43	5c multicolored	.25	.25
346	A43	25c multicolored	.25	.25
347	A43	50c multicolored	.30	.30
		Nos. 344-347 (4)	1.05	1.05

UN, 25th anniv., and Intl. Education Year.

Minnie Root A44

Flowers: 1c, Barbados Easter lily, vert. 10c, Eyelash orchid. 25c, Pride of Barbados, vert. 35c, Christmas hope.

1970, Aug. 24 **Litho.** **Wmk. 314**

348	A44	1c green	.25	.25
349	A44	5c deep magenta	.60	.25
350	A44	10c dark blue	2.10	.40
351	A44	25c brt orange brown	1.60	.95
352	A44	35c blue	1.60	1.10
a.		Souvenir sheet of 5	4.00	4.00
		Nos. 348-352 (5)	6.15	2.95

No. 352a contains 5 imperf. stamps similar to Nos. 348-352 with simulated perforations.

Christ Carrying Cross — A45

Easter: 10c, 50c, Resurrection, by Benjamin West, St. George's Anglican Church. 35c like 4c, Window from St. Margaret's Anglican Church, St. John.

1971, Apr. 7 **Wmk. 314** ***Perf. 14***

353	A45	4c purple & multi	.25	.25
354	A45	10c silver & multi	.25	.25
355	A45	35c brt blue & multi	.25	.25
356	A45	50c gold & multi	.25	.25
		Nos. 353-356 (4)	1.00	1.00

Sailfish Craft A46

Tourism: 5c, Tennis. 12c, Horseback riding. 25c, Water-skiing. 50c, Scuba diving.

1971, Aug. 17 ***Perf. 14x14½***

357	A46	1c multicolored	.25	.25
358	A46	5c multicolored	.40	.25
359	A46	12c multicolored	.65	.25
360	A46	25c multicolored	.40	.25
361	A46	50c multicolored	.55	.55
		Nos. 357-361 (5)	2.25	1.55

Samuel Jackman Prescod — A47

1971, Sept. 26 ***Perf. 14***

362	A47	3c orange & multi	.25	.25
363	A47	35c ultra & multi	.30	.25

Samuel Jackman Prescod (1806-1871), 1st black member of Barbados Assembly.

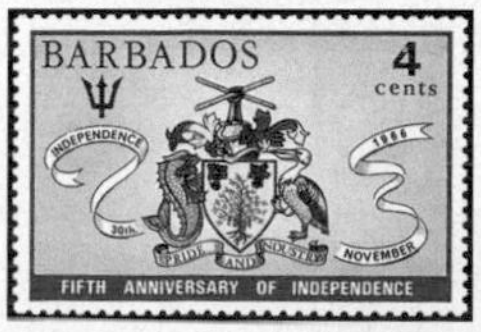

Coat of Arms A48

15c, 50c, Flag and map of Barbados.

1971, Nov. 23

364	A48	4c light blue & multi	.30	.25
365	A48	15c multicolored	.60	.25
366	A48	25c yel green & multi	.60	.25
367	A48	50c blue & multi	1.25	1.25
		Nos. 364-367 (4)	2.75	2.00

5th anniv. of independence.

Telegraphy, 1872 and 1972 — A49

Designs: 10c, "Stanley Angwin" off St. Lawrence Coast. 35c, Earth station and Intelsat 4. 50c, Mt. Misery tropospheric scatter station.

1972, Mar. 28 **Litho.** ***Perf. 14***

368	A49	4c purple & multi	.25	.25
369	A49	10c emerald & multi	.25	.25
370	A49	35c red & multi	.50	.25
371	A49	50c orange & multi	.75	.75
		Nos. 368-371 (4)	1.75	1.50

Centenary of telecommunications to and from Barbados.

Lord Baden-Powell, Charles — A50

5c, Map of Barbados and Combermere School, vert. 25c, Photograph of 1922 troop. 50c, Flags of various Boy Scout troops.

1972, Aug. 1

372	A50	5c ultra & multi	.25	.25
373	A50	15c ultra & multi	.25	.25
374	A50	25c ultra & multi	.55	.25
375	A50	50c ultra & multi	1.00	1.00
		Nos. 372-375 (4)	2.05	1.75

60th anniv. of Barbados Boy Scouts and 4th Caribbean Jamboree.

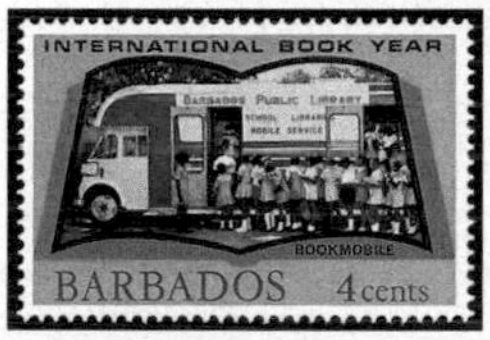

Bookmobile, Open Book — A51

Intl. Book Year: 15c, Visual aids truck. 25c, Central Library, Bridgetown. $1, Codrington College.

1972, Oct. 31 **Litho.** **Wmk. 314**

376	A51	4c brt pink & multi	.30	.25
377	A51	15c dull org & multi	.35	.25
378	A51	25c buff & multi	.35	.25
379	A51	$1 lt violet & multi	1.50	1.50
		Nos. 376-379 (4)	2.50	2.25

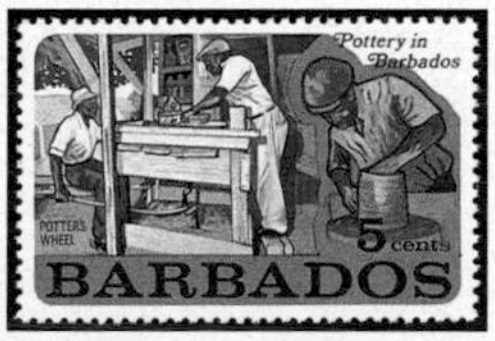

Pottery Wheels A52

Barbados pottery industry: 15c, Kiln. 25c, Finished pottery, Chalky Mount. $1, Pottery on sale at market.

1973, Mar. 1 **Wmk. 314** ***Perf. 14***

380	A52	5c dull red & multi	.25	.25
381	A52	15c olive grn & multi	.25	.25
382	A52	25c gray & multi	.40	.25
383	A52	$1 yellow & multi	1.50	1.50
		Nos. 380-383 (4)	2.40	2.25

First Flight in Barbados, — A53

Aircraft: 15c, First flight to Barbados, De Havilland biplane, 1928. 25c, Passenger plane, 1939. 50c, Vickers VC-10 over control tower, 1973.

1973, July 25 ***Perf. 12½x12***

384	A53	5c blue & multi	.40	.25
385	A53	15c vio blue & multi	1.35	.25
386	A53	25c multicolored	1.60	.30
387	A53	50c blue & multi	2.75	2.50
		Nos. 384-387 (4)	6.10	3.30

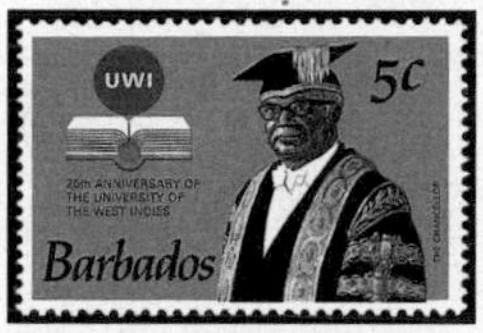

Chancellor Sir Hugh Wooding — A54

Designs: 25c, Sherlock Hall, Cave Hill Campus. 35c, Cave Hill Campus.

1973, Dec. 11 ***Perf. 13x14***

388	A54	5c dp orange & multi	.25	.25
389	A54	25c red brown & multi	.25	.25
390	A54	35c multicolored	.30	.30
		Nos. 388-390 (3)	.80	.80

25th anniv. of the Univ. of the West Indies.

No. 338a Surcharged

1974, Apr. 30 **Photo.** ***Perf. 13x12½***

391	A42	4c on 25c multi	.45	.45
a.		"4c." omitted	19.00	

Old Sailboat A55

Designs: 35c, Rowboat. 50c, Motor-powered fishing boat. $1, Trawler "Calamar."

1974, June 11 **Wmk. 314** ***Perf. 14***

392	A55	15c blue & multi	.25	.25
393	A55	35c multicolored	.30	.25
394	A55	50c vio blue & multi	.35	.35
395	A55	$1 blue & multi	2.75	2.75
a.		Souvenir sheet of 4, #392-395	6.25	6.25
		Nos. 392-395 (4)	3.65	3.60

Fishing boats of Barbados.

Fire Orchid — A56

Orchids: 1c, Cattleya gaskelliana alba. 3c, Rose Marie. 4c, Fiery red orchid. 5c, Schomburgkia humboltii. 8c, Dancing dolls. 10c, Spider orchids. 12c, Dendrobium aggregatum. 15c, Lady slippers. 20c, Spathoglottis. 25c, Eyelash. 35c, Bletia patula. 45c, Sunset Glow. 50c, Sunset Glow. $1, Ascocenda red gem. $2.50, Brassolaeliocattleya nugget. $5, Caularthron bicornutum. $10, Moon orchid.

1c, 20c, 25c, $2.50, $5 horizontal.

Wmk. 314 Sideways; Upright (1c, 20c, 25c, $1, $10)

1974-77 **Photo.** ***Perf. 14***

396	A56	1c multi	.30	*1.75*
397	A56	2c shown	.30	*1.75*
398	A56	3c multi	.50	*1.25*
399	A56	4c multi	2.00	1.10

400	A56	5c	multi	.55	.30
401	A56	8c	multi	1.75	1.10
402	A56	10c	multi	.90	.30
403	A56	12c	multi	.75	*3.25*
404	A56	15c	multi	.75	.75
404C	A56	20c	multi	5.75	5.25
405	A56	25c	multi	.90	.80
406	A56	35c	multi	2.25	2.10
406B	A56	45c	multi	7.50	5.00
407	A56	50c	multi	7.50	5.00

Perf. 14½x14, 14x14½

408	A56	$1	multi	11.00	4.00
409	A56	$2.50	multi	3.00	*5.00*
410	A56	$5	multi	3.00	*7.25*
411	A56	$10	multi	3.00	*16.00*
			Nos. 396-411 (18)	51.70	*61.95*

Issued: 20c, 45c, 5/3/77; others, 9/16/74.
For surcharge see No. B2.

Wmk. 314 Upright; Sideways (1c, 25c, $1)

1976 ***Perf. 14***

396a	A56	1c	multicolored	.90	*4.00*
397a	A56	2c	multicolored	1.10	*4.00*
398a	A56	3c	multicolored	1.25	*4.50*
399a	A56	4c	multicolored	.90	*4.50*
402a	A56	10c	multicolored	1.75	*4.50*
404a	A56	15c	multicolored	1.50	*1.50*
405a	A56	25c	multicolored	3.00	1.50
406a	A56	35c	multicolored	3.25	2.00

Perf. 14½x14

408a	A56	$1	multicolored	9.50	7.00
			Nos. 396a-408a (9)	23.15	33.50

1975 Wmk. 373 ***Perf. 14***

396b	A56	1c	multicolored	.25	*1.60*
397b	A56	2c	multicolored	.25	*1.60*
398b	A56	3c	multicolored	.25	*1.60*
399b	A56	4c	multicolored	.70	*3.50*
400b	A56	5c	multicolored	.45	.25
402b	A56	10c	multicolored	.45	.25
403b	A56	12c	multicolored	10.00	.25
404b	A56	15c	multicolored	.95	.25
405b	A56	25c	multicolored	.95	.25
406c	A56	45c	multicolored	.80	.25
407b	A56	50c	multicolored	8.00	7.25

Perf. 14½x14, 14x14½

408b	A56	$1	multicolored	12.50	*16.00*
409b	A56	$2.50	multicolored	12.50	5.75
410b	A56	$5	multicolored	12.50	9.25
411b	A56	$10	multicolored	15.00	16.00
			Nos. 396b-411b (15)	75.55	*64.05*

UPU Emblem, Barbados No. 64 — A57

Cent. of the UPU: 35c, Letters encircling globe. 50c, Barbados coat of arms. $1, Map of Barbados, sailing ship and jet.

1974, Oct. 9 Litho. ***Perf. 14½***

412	A57	8c	brt rose, org & gray	.25	.25
413	A57	35c	red, blk, & ocher	.25	.25
414	A57	50c	vio blue, bl & sil	.25	.25
415	A57	$1	ultra, blk & brn	.60	.60
a.			Souvenir sheet of 4, #412-415	2.25	2.25
			Nos. 412-415 (4)	1.35	1.35

Yacht Britannia off Barbados — A58

Royal Visit, Feb. 1975: 35c, $1, Palms and sunset.

1975, Feb. 18

416	A58	8c	brown & multi	1.00	.35
417	A58	25c	blue & multi	1.75	.35
418	A58	35c	purple & multi	.80	.40
419	A58	$1	violet & multi	2.00	*4.75*
			Nos. 416-419 (4)	5.55	*5.85*

St. Michael's Cathedral — A59

Designs: 15c, Bishop Coleridge. 50c, All Saints' Church. $1, St. Michael, stained glass window, St. Michael's Cathedral.

Wmk. 314

1975, July 29 Litho. ***Perf. 14***

420	A59	5c	blue & multi	.25	.25
421	A59	15c	lilac & multi	.25	.25
422	A59	50c	green & multi	.50	.50
423	A59	$1	multicolored	.80	.80
a.			Souvenir sheet of 4, #420-423	2.00	*2.25*
			Nos. 420-423 (4)	1.80	1.80

Anglican Diocese in Barbados, sesquicentennial.

Pony Float A60

Designs: 25c, Stiltsman (band and masqueraders). 35c, Maypole dancing. 50c, Cuban dancers.

1975, Nov. 18 Litho. Wmk. 373

424	A60	8c	yellow & multi	.25	.25
425	A60	25c	buff & multi	.25	.25
426	A60	35c	ultra & multi	.25	.25
427	A60	50c	orange & multi	.30	.30
a.			Souvenir sheet of 4, #424-427	1.25	1.25
			Nos. 424-427 (4)	1.05	1.05

Crop-over (harvest) festival.

Sailing Ship, 17th Cent. — A61

350th Anniv. of 1st Settlement: 10c, Bearded fig tree and fruit. 25c, Ogilvy's 17th cent. map. $1, Capt. John Powell.

1975, Dec. 17 Wmk. 373 ***Perf. 13½***

428	A61	4c	lt blue & multi	.55	.25
429	A61	10c	lt blue & multi	.35	.25
430	A61	25c	yellow & multi	1.05	.40
431	A61	$1	dk red & multi	1.05	1.05
a.			Souvenir sheet of 4, #428-431	3.75	3.75
			Nos. 428-431 (4)	3.00	1.95

Coat of Arms — A62

Coil Stamps

1975, Dec. Unwmk. ***Perf. 15x14***

432	A62	5c	light blue	.30	*.75*
433	A62	25c	violet	.40	*1.00*

Map of West Indies, Bats, A63

Prudential Cup — A64

1976, July 7 Litho. ***Perf. 14***

438	A63	25c	lt blue & multi	1.35	1.35
439	A64	45c	lilac rose & black	1.35	1.35

World Cricket Cup, won by West Indies Team, 1975.

Map of South Carolina settled — A65

American Bicentennial: 25c, George Washington and map of Bridge Town area. 50c, Declaration of Independence. $1, Masonic emblem and Prince Hall, founder and Grand Master of African Grand Lodge, Boston, 1790-1807.

1976, Aug. 17 Wmk. 373 ***Perf. 13½***

440	A65	15c	multicolored	.65	.25
441	A65	25c	multicolored	.65	.25
442	A65	50c	multicolored	1.00	1.00
443	A65	$1	multicolored	1.40	1.40
			Nos. 440-443 (4)	3.70	2.90

Mailman with Bicycle A66

PO Act, 125th anniv.: 35c, Mailman on motor scooter. 50c, Cover with Barbados No. 2. $1, Mail truck.

1976, Oct. 19 Litho. ***Perf. 14***

444	A66	8c	rose red, blk & bis	.25	.25
445	A66	35c	multicolored	.25	.25
446	A66	50c	vio blue & multi	.35	.35
447	A66	$1	red & multi	.60	*1.00*
			Nos. 444-447 (4)	1.45	*1.85*

Coast Guard Vessels A67

Designs: 15c, Bank note, reverse, showing Barbados Parliament. 25c, National anthem by Van Roland Edwards (music) and Irvine Burgie (lyrics). $1, Independence Day parade.

1976, Nov. 30 ***Perf. 13x13½***

448	A67	5c	multicolored	.30	.25
449	A67	15c	multicolored	.30	.25
450	A67	25c	yel, brown & blk	.30	.25
451	A67	$1	multicolored	1.25	1.25
a.			Souvenir sheet of 4, #448-451	3.00	3.00
			Nos. 448-451 (4)	2.15	2.00

10th anniv. of independence.

Queen Knighting Garfield — A68

Designs: 50c, Queen arriving at Westminster Abbey. $1, Queen leaving coach.

1977, Feb. 7 ***Perf. 14x13½***

452	A68	15c	silver & multi	.25	.25
453	A68	50c	silver & multi	.40	.40
454	A68	$1	silver & multi	.75	.75
			Nos. 452-454 (3)	1.40	1.40

25th anniv. of the reign of Queen Elizabeth II. See Nos. 467-469.

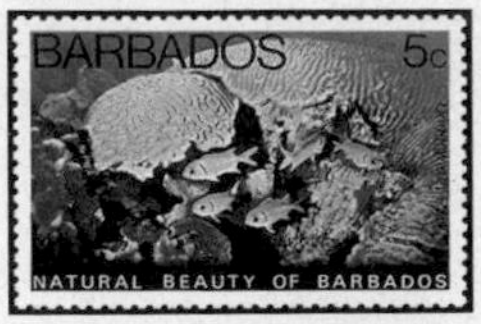

Underwater Park — A69

Beauty of Barbados: 35c, Royal palms, vert. 50c, Underwater caves. $1, Stalagmite in Harrison's Cave, vert.

1977, May 3 Wmk. 373 ***Perf. 14***

455	A69	5c	multicolored	.25	.25
456	A69	35c	multicolored	.50	.25
457	A69	50c	multicolored	.65	.75
458	A69	$1	multicolored	1.25	1.25
a.			Souvenir sheet of 4, #455-458	4.25	4.25
			Nos. 455-458 (4)	2.65	2.50

House of Commons Maces — A70

Designs: 25c, Speaker's chair. 50c, Senate Chamber. $1, Sam Lord's Castle, horiz.

1977, Aug. 2 Litho. ***Perf. 13½***

459	A70	10c	red brown & yel	.25	.25
460	A70	25c	slate grn & org	.25	.25
461	A70	50c	dk brown, brn & yel	.25	.25
462	A70	$1	dk & lt blue & org	.35	.35
			Nos. 459-462 (4)	1.10	1.10

13th Regional Conference of Commonwealth Parliamentary Association.

Charles I Handing Charter — A71

Designs: 12c, Charter scroll. 45c, Charles I and Earl of Carlisle, horiz. $1, Map of Barbados, by Richard Ligon, 1657, horiz.

Perf. 13½x13, 13x13½

1977, Oct. 11 Litho. Wmk. 373

463	A71	12c	buff & multi	.25	.25
464	A71	25c	buff & multi	.25	.25
465	A71	45c	buff & multi	.25	.25
466	A71	$1	buff & multi	.50	.50
			Nos. 463-466 (4)	1.25	1.25

350th anniv. of charter granting Barbados to the Earl of Carlisle.

Silver Jubilee Type, 1977, Inscribed: "ROYAL VISIT"

1977, Oct. 31 Unwmk. ***Roulette 5***

467	A68	15c	silver & multi	.35	.35
468	A68	50c	silver & multi	.25	.25
469	A68	$1	silver & multi	.50	.50
			Nos. 467-469 (3)	1.10	1.10

Caribbean visit of Queen Elizabeth II. Printed on peelable paper backing inscribed in ultramarine multiple rows: "SILVER JUBILEE ROYAL VISIT BARBADOS." Printed with die-cut label inscribed in black "BEND & PEEL" attached at left of stamp. Sheets of 50 stamps and 50 labels.

Gibson's Map of Bridgetown, — A72

25c, Bridgetown, engraving by S. Copens, 1695. 45c, Trafalgar Square, Bridgetown, drawing by J. M. Carter, 1835. $1, The Bridges, 1978.

Wmk. 373

1978, Mar. 1 Litho. *Perf. 14½*
470 A72 12c gold & multi .25 .25
471 A72 25c gold & multi .25 .25
472 A72 45c gold & multi .25 .25
473 A72 $1 gold & multi .25 .25
Nos. 470-473 (4) 1.00 1.00

350th anniv. of founding of Bridgetown.

Elizabeth II Coronation Anniv. Issue
Souvenir Sheet
Common Design Types

1978, Apr. 21 Unwmk. *Perf. 15*
474 Sheet of 6 1.35 1.35
a. CD326 50c Griffin of Edward III .25 .25
b. CD327 50c Elizabeth II .25 .25
c. CD328 50c Pelican .25 .25

No. 474 contains 2 se-tenant strips of Nos. 474a-474c, separated by horizontal gutter with commemorative and descriptive inscriptions and showing central part of coronation with coach.

Freak Bridge Hand
A73

10c, World Bridge Fed. emblem. 45c, Central American and Caribbean Bridge Fed. emblem, $1, Map of Caribbean, cards.

Wmk. 373

1978, June 6 Litho. *Perf. 14½*
475 A73 5c multicolored .25 .25
476 A73 10c multicolored .25 .25
477 A73 45c multicolored .25 .25
478 A73 $1 multicolored .70 .70
a. Souvenir sheet of 4, #475-478 2.40 2.40
Nos. 475-478 (4) 1.45 1.45

7th Regional Bridge Tournament, Dover Centre, Barbados, June 5-14.

Girl Guides' Camp — A74

Designs: 28c, Girl Guides helping children and handicapped. 50c, Badge with "60," vert. $1, Badge with initials, vert.

1978, Aug. 1 Litho. *Perf. 13½*
479 A74 12c multicolored .25 .25
480 A74 28c multicolored .50 .25
481 A74 50c multicolored .75 .40
482 A74 $1 multicolored 1.00 1.00
Nos. 479-482 (4) 2.50 1.90

Girl Guides of Barbados, 60th anniv.

Garment Industry
A75

Industries of Barbados: 28c, Cooper, vert. 45c, Blacksmith, vert. 50c, Wrought iron industry.

1978, Nov. 14 Litho. *Perf. 14*
483 A75 12c multicolored .25 .25
484 A75 28c multicolored .25 .25
485 A75 45c multicolored .35 .35
486 A75 50c multicolored .40 .40
Nos. 483-486 (4) 1.25 1.25

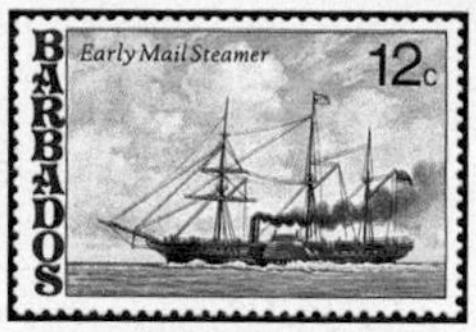

Early Mail Steamer
A76

Ships: 25c, Q.E.II in Deep Water Harbour. 50c, Ra II (raft) nearing Barbados. $1, Early mail steamer.

1979, Feb. 8 Litho. *Perf. 13x13½*
487 A76 12c multicolored .45 .25
488 A76 25c multicolored .65 .25
489 A76 50c multicolored 1.00 1.00
490 A76 $1 multicolored 1.35 1.35
Nos. 487-490 (4) 3.45 2.85

Barbados No. 235
A77

28c, Barbados No. 430, vert. 45c, Penny Black and Maltese postmark, vert. 50c, Barbados No. 21b.

Wmk. 373

1979, May 8 Litho. *Perf. 14*
491 A77 12c multicolored .25 .25
492 A77 28c multicolored .30 .30
493 A77 45c multicolored .40 .40
Nos. 491-493 (3) .95 .95

Souvenir Sheet

494 A77 50c multicolored 1.10 1.10

Sir Rowland Hill (1795-1879), originator of penny postage.

Birds — A78

1c, Grass canaries. 2c, Rain birds. 5c, Sparrows. 8c, Frigate birds. 10c, Cattle egrets. 12c, Green gaulins. 20c, Hummingbirds. 25c, Ground doves. 28c, Blackbirds. 35c, Green-throated caribs. 45c, Wood doves. 50c, Ramiers. 55c, Black-breasted plover. 70c, Yellow breasts. $1, Pee whistlers. $2.50, Christmas birds. $5, Kingfishers. $10, Red-seal coot.

1979-81 Photo. Wmk. 373 *Perf. 14*
495 A78 1c multicolored .25 *1.25*
496 A78 2c multicolored .25 *1.25*
497 A78 5c multicolored .25 *.70*
498 A78 8c multicolored 1.25 *2.25*
499 A78 10c multicolored .25 *.40*
500 A78 12c multicolored .75 *1.50*
501 A78 20c multicolored .30 *.55*
502 A78 25c multicolored .30 *.60*
503 A78 28c multicolored 3.00 2.00
504 A78 35c multicolored 1.10 *.70*
505 A78 45c multicolored 2.25 1.50
506 A78 50c multicolored 2.25 2.00
506A A78 55c multi ('81) 6.00 3.50
507 A78 70c multicolored 3.25 *4.00*
508 A78 $1 multicolored 3.25 1.50
509 A78 $2.50 multicolored 3.25 *6.00*
510 A78 $5 multicolored 4.75 *9.00*
511 A78 $10 multicolored 7.00 *14.00*
Nos. 495-511 (18) 39.70 *52.70*

Issue dates: 55c, Sept. 1; others, Aug. 7.
See Nos. 570-572. For surcharges see No. 563-565

Launcher Transported through — A79

Designs: 10c, Gun on landing craft, Foul Bay, horiz. 20c, Firing of 16-inch launcher by day. 28c, Bath Earth Station and Intelsat IV-A, horiz. 45c, ITOS/NOAA over Caribbean, horiz. 50c, Intelsat IV-A over Atlantic, and globe. $1, Lunar landing module, horiz.

1979, Oct. 9 Photo.
512 A79 10c multicolored .35 .25
513 A79 12c multicolored .35 .25
514 A79 20c multicolored .40 .25
515 A79 28c multicolored .40 .30
516 A79 45c multicolored .65 .55
517 A79 50c multicolored .65 .65
Nos. 512-517 (6) 2.80 2.25

Souvenir Sheet

518 A79 $1 multicolored 2.00 2.00

Space exploration. No. 518 commemorates 10th anniversary of first moon landing.
No. 516 is incorrectly inscribed "Intelsat."

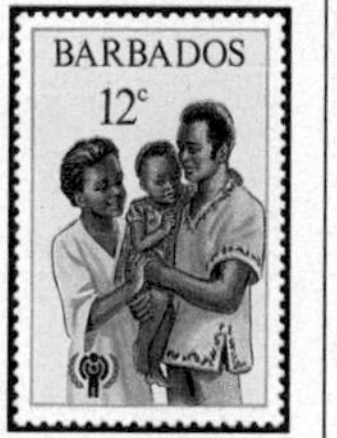

Family, IYC Emblem — A80

IYC Emblem and: 28c, Children holding hands and map of Barbados. 45c, Boy and teacher. 50c, Children playing. $1, Boy and girl flying kite.

1979, Nov. 27 Litho. *Perf. 14*
519 A80 12c multicolored .25 .25
520 A80 28c multicolored .25 .25
521 A80 45c multicolored .25 .25
522 A80 50c multicolored .25 .25
523 A80 $1 multicolored .25 .25
Nos. 519-523 (5) 1.25 1.25

Map of Barbados, Anniversary — A81

Rotary Intl., 75th Anniv.: 28c, Map of district 404. 50c, 75th anniv. emblem. $1, Paul P. Harris, founder.

1980, Feb. 19 Litho. *Perf. 13½*
524 A81 12c multicolored .25 .25
525 A81 28c multicolored .25 .25
526 A81 50c multicolored .25 .25
527 A81 $1 multicolored .30 .30
Nos. 524-527 (4) 1.05 1.05

A82

12c, Regiment volunteer, artillery company, 1909. 35c, Drum major. 50c, Sovereign's, regimental flags. $1, Women's corps.

Wmk. 373

1980, Apr. 8 Litho. *Perf. 14½*
528 A82 12c multicolored .35 .25
529 A82 35c multicolored .45 .35
530 A82 50c multicolored .55 .45
531 A82 $1 multicolored .65 .65
Nos. 528-531 (4) 2.00 1.70

Barbados Regiment, 75th anniv.

Souvenir Sheets

A83

Early mailman, London 1980 emblem. The vignette is a different color for each stamp.

Wmk. 373

1980, May 6 Litho. *Perf. 14*
532 A83 Sheet of 6 1.05 1.05
a.-f. 28c any single .25 .25
533 A83 Sheet of 6 1.20 1.20
a.-f. 50c any single .25 .25

London 80 Intl. Stamp Exhib., May 6-14.

Underwater Scenes — A84

1980, Sept. 30 Litho. *Perf. 13½*
534 A84 12c multicolored .25 .25
535 A84 28c multicolored .60 .35
536 A84 50c multicolored .80 .45
537 A84 $1 multicolored 1.35 1.35
a. Souvenir sheet of 4, #534-537 4.00 4.00
Nos. 534-537 (4) 3.00 2.40

Bathsheba Railroad Station — A85

28c, Cab stand, The Green. 45c, Mule-drawn tram. 70c, Horse-drawn bus. $1, Fairchild St. railroad station.

1981, Jan. 13 Litho. *Perf. 14½*
538 A85 12c shown .25 .25
539 A85 28c multicolored .25 .25
540 A85 45c multicolored .30 .30
541 A85 70c multicolored .50 .50
542 A85 $1 multicolored .75 .75
Nos. 538-542 (5) 2.05 2.05

See Nos. 577-580.

Visually Handicapped Girl — A86

25c, Sign language alphabet, vert. 45c, Blind people crossing street, vert. $2.50, Baseball game.

1981, May 19 Litho. *Perf. 14*
543 A86 10c shown .25 .25
544 A86 25c multicolored .25 .25
545 A86 45c multicolored .40 .40
546 A86 $2.50 multicolored 1.00 1.00
Nos. 543-546 (4) 1.90 1.90

International Year of the Disabled.

Royal Wedding Issue
Common Design Type
Wmk. 373

1981, July 22 Litho. *Perf. 13½*
547 CD331 28c Bouquet .25 .25
548 CD331 50c Charles .25 .25
549 CD331 $2.50 Couple .40 .40
Nos. 547-549 (3) .90 .90

4th Caribbean Arts Festival (CARIFESTA), A87

15c, Landship maneuver. 20c, Yoruba dancer. 40c, Tuk band. 55c, Frank Collymore (sculpture). $1, Barbados Harbor (painting).

1981, Aug. 11 Litho. *Perf. 14½*
550 A87 15c multicolored .25 .25
551 A87 20c multicolored .25 .25
552 A87 40c multicolored .30 .30
553 A87 55c multicolored .45 .45
554 A87 $1 multicolored .70 .70
Nos. 550-554 (5) 1.95 1.95

Hurricane Gladys, View from A88

35c, Satellite view over Barbados. 60c, Police watch. $1, Spotter plane.

1981, Sept. 29 Litho. *Perf. 14*
555 A88 35c multicolored .50 .50
556 A88 50c shown .65 .65
557 A88 60c multicolored 1.00 1.00
558 A88 $1 multicolored 1.35 1.35
Nos. 555-558 (4) 3.50 3.50

Harrison's Cave — A89

10c, Twin Falls. 20c, Rotunda Room Stream. 55c, Rotunda Room formation. $2.50, Cascade Pool.

Perf. 14x14½
1981, Dec. 1 Litho. Wmk. 373
559 A89 10c multicolored .25 .25
560 A89 20c multicolored .25 .25
561 A89 55c multicolored .40 .40
562 A89 $2.50 multicolored 1.60 1.60
Nos. 559-562 (4) 2.50 2.50

Nos. 503, 505, 507 Surcharged

1981, Sept. 1 Photo. *Perf. 14*
563 A78 15c on 28c multi .40 .40
564 A78 40c on 45c multi .50 .50
565 A78 60c on 70c multi .85 .85
Nos. 563-565 (3) 1.75 1.75

Black Belly Sheep A90

1982, Feb. 9 Litho.
566 A90 40c Ram .35 .35
567 A90 50c Ewe .45 .45
568 A90 60c Ewe, lambs .55 .55
569 A90 $1 Pair, map .90 .90
Nos. 566-569 (4) 2.25 2.25

Bird Type of 1979
Wmk. 373

1982, Mar. 1 Photo. *Perf. 14*
570 A78 15c like #503 6.50 5.50
571 A78 40c like #506 6.50 5.50
572 A78 60c like #507 6.50 6.00
Nos. 570-572 (3) 19.50 17.00

Transportation Type of 1981

20c, Lighter. 35c, Rowboat. 55c, Speightstown schooner. $2.50, Inter-colonial schooner.

1982, Apr. 6 Litho. *Perf. 14½*
577 A85 20c multicolored .25 .25
578 A85 35c multicolored .40 .40
579 A85 55c multicolored .60 .60
580 A85 $2.50 multicolored 2.75 2.75
Nos. 577-580 (4) 4.00 4.00

Early marine transport.

Visit of Pres. Ronald Reagan — A92

No. 581, Barbados Flag, arms. No. 582, US Flag, arms.

1982, Apr. 8 Litho. *Perf. 14*
581 20c multicolored .55 .55
582 20c multicolored .55 .55
a. A92 Pair, Nos. 581-582 1.10 1.10
583 55c like #581 .70 .70
584 55c like #582 .70 .70
a. A92 Pair, Nos. 583-584 1.40 1.40
Nos. 581-584 (4) 2.50 2.50

Printed in sheets of 8 with gutter showing Pres. Reagan and Prime Minister Tom Adams.

Princess Diana Issue
Common Design Type

1982, July 1 Litho. *Perf. 14½*
585 CD333 20c Arms .25 .25
586 CD333 60c Diana .55 .40
587 CD333 $1.20 Wedding 1.00 1.00
588 CD333 $2.50 Portrait 1.60 1.60
Nos. 585-588 (4) 3.40 3.25

Scouting Year — A93

15c, Helping woman. 40c, Sign, emblem, flag, horiz. 55c, Religious service, horiz. $1, Flags.
$1.50, Laws.

1982, Sept. 7 Wmk. 373 *Perf. 14*
589 A93 15c multicolored .60 .25
590 A93 40c multicolored 1.90 .40
591 A93 55c multicolored 1.10 .75
592 A93 $1 multicolored 1.70 1.70
Nos. 589-592 (4) 5.30 3.10

Souvenir Sheet

593 A93 $1.50 multicolored 5.25 5.25

Washington's 250th Birth — A94

10c, Arms. 55c, Washington's house, Barbados. 60c, Taking command. $2.50, Taking oath.

1982, Nov. 2 *Perf. 13½x13*
594 A94 10c multicolored .25 .25
595 A94 55c multicolored .40 .40
596 A94 60c multicolored .40 .40
597 A94 $2.50 multicolored 1.20 1.20
Nos. 594-597 (4) 2.25 2.25

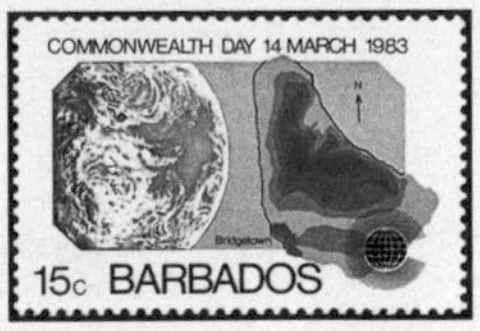

A95

1983, Mar. 14 Litho. *Perf. 14*
598 A95 15c Map, globe .25 .25
599 A95 40c Beach .35 .35
600 A95 60c Sugar cane harvest .45 .45
601 A95 $1 Cricket game 1.70 1.70
Nos. 598-601 (4) 2.75 2.75

Commonwealth Day.

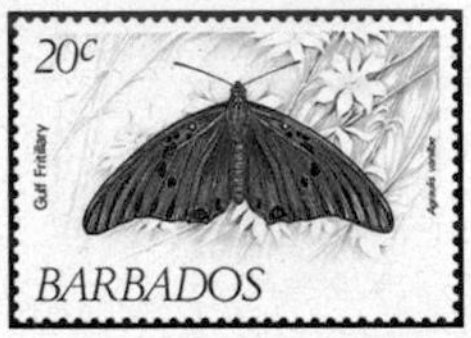

Gulf Fritillary A96

Perf. 13½x13
1983, Feb. 8 Litho. Wmk. 373
602 A96 20c shown 1.75 .50
603 A96 40c Monarch 2.75 .50
604 A96 55c Mimic 2.75 .70
605 A96 $2.50 Hanno Blue 5.75 5.50
Nos. 602-605 (4) 13.00 7.20

Manned Flight Bicentenary — A97

20c, US Navy dirigible. 40c, Douglas DC-3. 55c, Vickers Viscount. $1, Lockheed TriStar.

1983, June 14 Litho. *Perf. 14*
606 A97 20c multi .45 .25
607 A97 40c multi 1.10 .55
608 A97 55c multi 1.20 .70
609 A97 $1 multi 1.75 1.75
Nos. 606-609 (4) 4.50 3.25

Nash 600, 1941 A98

45c, Dodge, 1938. 75c, Ford Model AA, 1930. $2.50, Dodge Four, 1918.

1983, Aug. 9 Litho. *Perf. 14*
610 A98 25c shown .70 .30
611 A98 45c multicolored .80 .45
612 A98 75c multicolored 1.25 1.25
613 A98 $2.50 multicolored 2.60 2.60
Nos. 610-613 (4) 5.35 4.60

A99

20c, Players. 65c, Emblem, map. $1, Cup.

1983, Aug. 30 Litho. *Perf. 14*
614 A99 20c multicolored .45 .30
615 A99 65c multicolored .85 .55
616 A99 $1 multicolored 1.20 1.20
Nos. 614-616 (3) 2.50 2.05

World Cup Table Tennis Championship.

A100

Christmas: 10c, 25c, Angel with lute, painting details. $2, The Virgin and Child, by Masaccio.

1983, Nov. 1 *Perf. 14*
617 A100 10c multicolored .40 .40
618 A100 25c multicolored 1.00 .40

Souvenir Sheet

619 A100 $2 multicolored 3.00 3.00

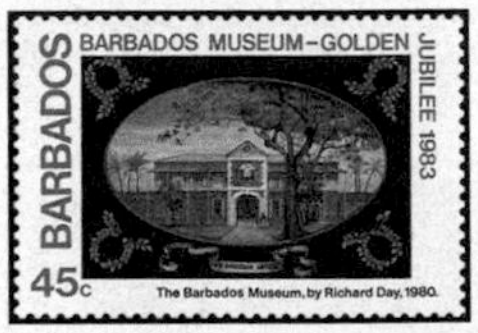

Barbados Museum, Golden A101

Museum Paintings: 45c, by Richard Day. 75c, St. Ann's Garrison in Barbados by W.S. Hedges. $2.50, Needham's Point, Carlisle Bay.

1983, Nov. 1 *Perf. 14*
620 A101 45c multicolored 1.10 .50
621 A101 75c multicolored 1.70 1.70
622 A101 $2.50 multicolored 5.50 5.50
Nos. 620-622 (3) 8.30 7.70

1984 Olympics, Los Angeles A102

1984, Apr. 3 Litho. *Perf. 14*
623 A102 50c Track & field .80 .60
624 A102 65c Shooting 1.00 .75
625 A102 75c Sailing 1.10 1.10
626 A102 $1 Bicycling 3.50 3.50
a. Souvenir sheet of 4, #623-626 8.75 8.75
Nos. 623-626 (4) 6.40 5.95

Lloyd's List Issue
Common Design Type

45c, World map. 50c, Bridgetown Harbor. 75c, Philosopher. $1, Sea Princess.

1984, Apr. 25 Litho. *Perf. 14½*
627 CD335 45c multicolored 1.05 .60
628 CD335 50c multicolored 1.25 .75
629 CD335 75c multicolored 1.90 1.90
630 CD335 $1 multicolored 1.90 1.90
Nos. 627-630 (4) 6.10 5.15

Souvenir Sheet

1984 UPU Congress — A103

1984, June 6 Litho. *Perf. 13½*
631 A103 $2 #213, UPU emblem 4.50 4.50

World Chess Fed., 60th Anniv. A104

1984, Aug. 8 ***Perf. 14x14½***

632	A104	25c	Junior match	1.75	.45
633	A104	45c	Knights	2.00	.75
634	A104	65c	Queens	2.25	2.00
635	A104	$2	Rooks	5.25	5.25
			Nos. 632-635 (4)	11.25	8.45

Christmas — A105

50c, Poinsettia. 65c, Snow-on-the-mountain. 75c, Christmas candle. $1, Christmas hope.

1984, Oct. 24 **Litho.** ***Perf. 14***

636	A105	50c	multicolored	1.80	1.00
637	A105	65c	multicolored	2.00	1.80
638	A105	75c	multicolored	2.25	2.25
639	A105	$1	multicolored	2.50	2.50
			Nos. 636-639 (4)	8.55	7.55

Marine Life A106

1c, Bristle worm. 2c, Spotted trunk fish. 5c, Coney fish. 10c, Pink-tipped anemone. 20c, Christmas tree worm. 25c, Hermit crab. 35c, Animal flower. 40c, Vase sponge. 45c, Spotted moray. 50c, Ghost crab. 65c, Flamingo tongue snail. 75c, Sergeant major fish. $1, Caribbean warty anemone. $2.50, Green turtle. $5, Rock beauty. $10, Elkhorn coral.

1985 **Litho.** **Wmk. 373** ***Perf. 14***

640	A106	1c	multi	.90	.90
641	A106	2c	multi	.90	.90
642	A106	5c	multi	3.00	3.00
643	A106	10c	multi	1.00	1.00
645	A106	20c	multi	2.75	2.75
646	A106	25c	multi	1.90	1.90
648	A106	35c	multi	4.50	4.50
649	A106	40c	multi	4.50	4.50
650	A106	45c	multi	1.90	1.90
651	A106	50c	multi	3.25	3.25
653	A106	65c	multi	3.25	3.25
654	A106	75c	multi	3.25	3.25
656	A106	$1	multi	3.50	3.50
657	A106	$2.50	multi	9.00	9.00
658	A106	$5	multi	10.50	10.50
659	A106	$10	multi	11.50	11.50
			Nos. 640-659 (16)	65.60	65.60

Issued: 10c, 20c, 25c, 50c, $2.50, $5, 2/26; 5c, 35c, 40c, 65c, $10, 4/9; 1c, 2c, 45c, 75c, $1, 5/7.

1987, Sep. 15 **Inscribed "1987"**

640a	A106	1c	4.50	4.50
641a	A106	2c	4.50	4.50
645a	A106	20c	8.00	8.00
651a	A106	50c	9.50	9.50
654a	A106	75c	15.00	15.00
657a	A106	$2.50	16.00	16.00
658a	A106	$5	21.00	21.00
		Nos. 640a-658a (7)	78.50	78.50

Without Imprint

1986, Jan. 6 **Wmk. 384**

642b	A106	5c	1.25	*1.50*
643b	A106	10c	1.25	*1.50*
645b	A106	20c	1.25	*1.50*
646b	A106	25c	3.00	1.75
648b	A106	35c	1.75	1.75
651b	A106	50c	2.50	2.50
657b	A106	$2.50	4.75	4.75
658b	A106	$5	8.25	8.25
659b	A106	$10	10.50	10.50
		Nos. 642b-659b (9)	34.50	34.00

1986 **Inscribed "1986"**

640c	A106	1c	.40	*3.00*
641c	A106	2c	.40	*3.00*
643c	A106	10c	.40	.40
645c	A106	20c	.40	.40
646c	A106	25c	.50	.50
649c	A106	40c	.60	.60
650c	A106	45c	.80	.60
651c	A106	50c	.80	.80
653c	A106	65c	.85	.85
654c	A106	75c	.90	.90
656c	A106	$1	1.10	1.10
657c	A106	$2.50	2.50	*7.50*
658c	A106	$5	5.00	*10.00*
659c	A106	$10	10.00	*10.00*
		Nos. 640c-659c (14)	24.65	*39.65*

Issued: 1c, 2c, 40c, 45c, 7/23. 10c, 25c, 50c-$10, 8/18.

1987 **Inscribed "1987"**

642d	A106	5c	20.00	10.00
643d	A106	10c	.40	.40
646d	A106	25c	.50	.50
648d	A106	35c	20.00	10.00
649d	A106	40c	.60	.60
650d	A106	45c	.80	.60
653d	A106	65c	.85	.85
654d	A106	75c	.90	.90
656d	A106	$1	1.10	1.10
659d	A106	$10	10.00	10.00
		Nos. 642d-659d (10)	55.15	34.95

1988 **Inscribed "1988"**

643e	A106	10c	.40	.40

Queen Mother 85th Birthday
Common Design Type

25c, At Buckingham Palace, 1930. 65c, With Lady Diana, 1981. 75c, At the docks. $1, Holding Prince Henry.
$2, Opening the Garden Center, Syon House.

Perf. 14½x14

1985, June 7 **Litho.** **Wmk. 384**

660	CD336	25c	multi	.35	.30
661	CD336	65c	multi	2.50	1.25
662	CD336	75c	multi	.80	.80
663	CD336	$1	multi	.85	.85
			Nos. 660-663 (4)	4.50	3.20

Souvenir Sheet

664	CD336	$2	multi	3.50	3.50

Audubon Birth Bicentenary — A107

Illustrations of North American bird species: 45c, Falco peregrinus. 65c, Dendroica discolor. 75c, Ardea herodias. $1, Dendroica petechia.
Nos. 666-668 vert.

Wmk. 373

1985, Aug. 6 **Litho.** ***Perf. 14***

665	A107	45c	multicolored	2.50	1.10
666	A107	65c	multicolored	2.60	2.50
667	A107	75c	multicolored	3.00	2.75
668	A107	$1	multicolored	3.25	3.25
			Nos. 665-668 (4)	11.35	9.60

Satellite Orbiting Earth A108

1985, Sept. 10

669	A108	75c	multicolored	1.00	1.00

INTELSAT, Intl. Telecommunications Satellite Consortium, 20th anniv.

Royal Barbados Police, 150th Anniv. — A109

25c, Traffic Department. 50c, Police Band. 65c, Dog Force. $1, Mounted Police.
$2, Band on parade, horiz.

1985, Nov. 19

670	A109	25c	multi	2.25	.75
671	A109	50c	multi	1.60	1.10
672	A109	65c	multi	1.80	1.60
673	A109	$1	multi	2.00	2.00
			Nos. 670-673 (4)	7.65	5.45

Souvenir Sheet

674	A109	$2	multi	3.75	3.75

Queen Elizabeth II 60th Birthday
Common Design Type

Designs: 25c, Age 2. 50c, Senate House opening, University College of the West Indies, Jamaica, 1953. 65c, With Prince Philip, Caribbean Tour, 1985. 75c, Banquet, state visit to Sao Paulo, Brazil, 1968. $2, Visiting Crown Agents, 1983.

Perf. 14x14½

1986, Apr. 21 **Litho.** **Wmk. 384**

675	CD337	25c	scar, blk & sil	.30	.25
676	CD337	50c	ultra & multi	.50	.45
677	CD337	65c	green & multi	.60	.55
678	CD337	75c	violet & multi	.60	.60
679	CD337	$2	rose vio & multi	1.25	1.25
			Nos. 675-679 (5)	3.25	3.10

EXPO '86, Vancouver — A110

50c, Trans-Canada North Star. $2.50, Lady Nelson.

1986, May 2 ***Perf. 14***

680	A110	50c	multicolored	1.25	.80
681	A110	$2.50	multicolored	2.75	2.75

AMERIPEX '86 — A111

$2, Statue of Liberty, NY Harbor.

1986, May 22 **Wmk. 373**

682	A111	45c	No. 441	.95	.50
683	A111	50c	No. 442	1.05	.65
684	A111	65c	No. 558	1.20	1.20
685	A111	$1	Nos. 583-584	1.50	1.50
			Nos. 682-685 (4)	4.70	3.85

Souvenir Sheet

686	A111	$2	multicolored	11.00	11.00

Statue of Liberty, cent.

Royal Wedding Issue, 1986
Common Design Type

Designs: 45c, Informal portrait. $1, Andrew in navy uniform.

Perf. 14½x14

1986, July 23 **Litho.** **Wmk. 384**

687	CD338	45c	multicolored	.75	.50
688	CD338	$1	multicolored	1.25	.75

Electrification of Barbados, A112

10c, Transporting utility poles, 1923. 25c, Heathfield ladder, 1935. 65c, Transport fleet, 1941. $2, Bucket truck, 1986.

Wmk. 384

1986, Sept. 16 **Litho.** ***Perf. 14***

689	A112	10c	multi	.25	.25
690	A112	25c	multi, vert.	.35	.30
691	A112	65c	multi	1.00	.85
692	A112	$2	multi, vert.	2.40	2.40
			Nos. 689-692 (4)	4.00	3.80

Christmas — A113

Church windows and flowers: 25c, Alpinia purpurata. 50c, Anthurium andraeanum. 75c, Heliconia rostrata. $2, Heliconia psittacorum.

1986, Oct. 28 **Wmk. 373**

693	A113	25c	multicolored	.35	.25
694	A113	50c	multicolored	.55	.55
695	A113	75c	multicolored	1.00	1.00
696	A113	$2	multicolored	2.00	2.00
			Nos. 693-696 (4)	3.90	3.80

Natl. Special Olympics, 10th Anniv. A114

1987, Mar. 27 **Wmk. 373** ***Perf. 14***

697	A114	15c	Shot put	.30	.30
698	A114	45c	Wheelchair race	.60	.60
699	A114	65c	Girl's long jump	.85	.85
700	A114	$2	Emblem, creed	2.25	2.25
			Nos. 697-700 (4)	4.00	4.00

CAPEX '87 — A115

25c, Barn swallow. 50c, Yellow warbler. 65c, Audubon's shearwater. 75c, Black-whiskered vireo. $1, Scarlet tanager.

1987, June 12

701	A115	25c	multicolored	2.75	.65
702	A115	50c	multicolored	3.25	1.75
703	A115	65c	multicolored	3.25	1.75
704	A115	75c	multicolored	3.50	3.50
705	A115	$1	multicolored	3.75	3.75
			Nos. 701-705 (5)	16.50	11.40

Natl. Scouting Movement, 75th Anniv. — A116

1987, July 24 ***Perf. 14x14½***

706	A116	10c	Scout sign	.25	.25
707	A116	25c	Campfire	.30	.30
708	A116	65c	Merit badges, etc.	.70	.70
709	A116	$2	Marching band	3.50	3.50
			Nos. 706-709 (4)	4.75	4.75

Bridgetown Synagogue Restoration A117

50c, Exterior. 65c, Interior. 75c, Ten Commandments, vert. $1, Marble laver, vert.

1987, Oct. 6 **Wmk. 384** ***Perf. 14½***

710	A117	50c	multicolored	3.25	2.40
711	A117	65c	multicolored	3.50	3.50
712	A117	75c	multicolored	3.75	3.75
713	A117	$1	multicolored	4.50	4.50
			Nos. 710-713 (4)	15.00	14.15

Natl. Independence, 21st Anniv. — A118

E.W. Barrow (1920-87), Father of Independence — A119

25c, Coat of arms, seal of the colony. 45c, Natl. flag, Union Jack. 65c, Silver dollar, penny. $2, Old and new regimental flags, Queen Elizabeth's colors.

1987, Nov. 24 Litho. *Perf. 14½*

714	A118	25c multicolored	.55	.25
715	A118	45c multicolored	1.35	.45
716	A118	65c multicolored	1.35	.65
717	A118	$2 multicolored	4.50	3.25
		Nos. 714-717 (4)	7.75	4.60

Souvenir Sheet

718	A119	$1.50 multicolored	2.40	2.40

Cricket A120

Bat, wicket posts, ball, 18th cent. belt buckle and batters: 15c, E.A. "Manny" Martindale. 45c, George Challenor. 50c, Herman C. Griffith. 75c, Harold Austin. $2, Frank Worrell.

1988 Litho. Wmk. 373 *Perf. 14*

719	A120	15c multicolored	3.50	1.25
720	A120	45c multicolored	4.25	1.25
720A	A120	50c multicolored	5.00	3.00
721	A120	75c multicolored	5.25	4.50
722	A120	$2 multicolored	6.00	6.00
		Nos. 719-722 (5)	24.00	16.00

The 50c was originally printed with the wrong photograph but was not issued. Examples of the error have appeared on the market.

Issued: No. 720A, July 11; others, June 6.

Lizards — A121

10c, Kentropyx borckianus. 50c, Hemidactylus mabouia. 65c, Anolis extremus. $2, Gymnophthalmus underwoodii.

1988, June 13

723	A121	10c multicolored	2.50	.75
724	A121	50c multicolored	3.50	1.25
725	A121	65c multicolored	4.00	1.75
726	A121	$2 multicolored	8.50	8.50
		Nos. 723-726 (4)	18.50	12.25

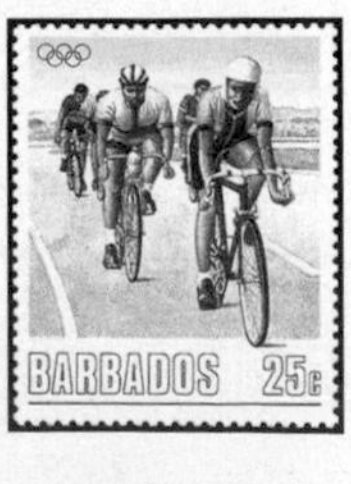

1988 Summer Olympics, Seoul — A122

Wmk. 373

1988, Aug. 2 Litho. *Perf. 14½*

727	A122	25c Cycling	2.25	.60
728	A122	45c Running	.95	.50
729	A122	75c Swimming	1.15	.95
730	A122	$2 Yachting	2.60	2.40
a.		Souvenir sheet of 4, #727-730	7.50	7.50
		Nos. 727-730 (4)	6.95	4.45

Lloyds of London, 300th Anniv.

Common Design Type

40c, Royal Exchange, 1774. 50c, Sugar mill (windmill), horiz. 65c, Container ship Author, horiz. $2, Sinking of the Titanic, 1912.

1988, Oct. 18 Litho. *Perf. 14*

731	CD341	40c multicolored	1.10	.50
732	CD341	50c multicolored	1.40	.60
733	CD341	65c multicolored	2.75	.75
734	CD341	$2 multicolored	7.25	6.50
		Nos. 731-734 (4)	12.50	8.35

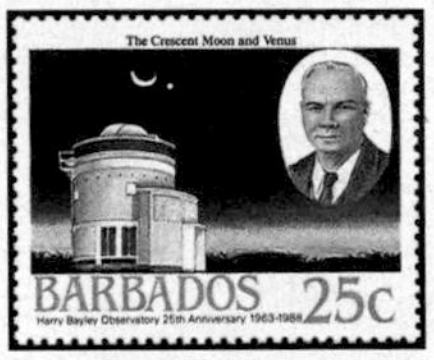

Harry Bayley Observatory, 25th Anniv. A123

Designs: 25c, Observatory, crescent Moon, Venus and Harry Bayley. 65c, Observatory and constellations. 75c, Andromeda Galaxy and telescope. $2, Orion Constellation.

1988, Nov. 28 Wmk. 384 *Perf. 14½*

735	A123	25c multicolored	.90	.35
736	A123	65c multicolored	2.00	.95
737	A123	75c multicolored	2.25	1.25
738	A123	$2 multicolored	4.25	4.25
		Nos. 735-738 (4)	9.40	6.80

Commercial Aviation, 50th Anniv. — A124

Designs: 25c, Caribbean Airline Liat BAe748. 65c, Pan American DC-8. 75c, Two British Airways Concordes, Grantley Adams Intl. Airport. $2, Two Caribbean Air Cargo Boeing 707-351c.

1989, Mar. 20 Litho. *Perf. 14*

739	A124	25c multicolored	3.25	.70
740	A124	65c multicolored	4.75	1.75
741	A124	75c multicolored	4.75	1.75
742	A124	$2 multicolored	7.50	6.75
		Nos. 739-742 (4)	20.25	10.95

Parliament, 350th Anniv. A125

25c, Assembly chamber. 50c, The Speaker. 75c, Parliament, c. 1882. $2.50, Queen in Parliament.

1989, July 19 Litho. *Perf. 13½*

743	A125	25c multicolored	.60	.30
744	A125	50c multicolored	.90	.55
745	A125	75c multicolored	1.75	.80
746	A125	$2.50 multicolored	3.75	3.00
		Nos. 743-746 (4)	7.00	4.65

See No. 752.

Wildlife Preservation — A126

10c, Wild hare, vert. 50c, Red-footed tortoise. 65c, Green monkey, vert. $2, Toad. $1, Mongoose, vert.

1989, Aug. 1 *Perf. 14x13½*

747	A126	10c multicolored	1.00	.50
748	A126	50c multicolored	2.00	1.00
749	A126	65c multicolored	3.00	1.75
750	A126	$2 multicolored	4.75	4.75
		Nos. 747-750 (4)	10.75	8.00

Souvenir Sheet

751	A126	$1 multicolored	2.75	2.75

Parliament Anniv. Type of 1989

Souvenir Sheet

1989, Oct. 9 Wmk. 373 *Perf. 13½*

752	A125	$1 The Mace	2.25	2.25

35th Commonwealth Parliamentary Conf.

Wild Plants — A127

Inscribed "1989"

2c, Bread'n cheese. 5c, Scarlet cordia. 10c, Columnar cactus. 20c, Spiderlily. 25c, Rock balsam. 30c, Hollyhock. 45c, Yellow shakshak. 50c, Whitewood. 55c, Bluebell. 65c, Prickly sage. 70c, Seaside samphire. 80c, Flat-hand dildo. $1.10, Lent tree. $2.50, Rodwood. $5, Cowitch. $10, Maypole.

1989, Nov. 1 Wmk. 373 *Perf. 14½*

753	A127	2c multi	.80	1.60
754	A127	5c multi	1.30	1.50
755	A127	10c multi	1.30	.75
756	A127	20c multi	1.30	.75
757	A127	25c multi	1.30	1.30
758	A127	30c multi	1.90	.60
759	A127	45c multi	1.60	.85
760	A127	50c multi	1.90	.90
761	A127	55c multi	2.60	1.50
762	A127	65c multi	2.00	1.50
763	A127	70c multi	3.25	3.75
764	A127	80c multi	4.50	4.00
765	A127	$1.10 multi	3.75	4.50
766	A127	$2.50 multi	5.25	5.25
767	A127	$5 multi	8.50	11.00
768	A127	$10 multi	16.50	18.50
		Nos. 753-768 (16)	57.75	58.25

35c, Red sage. 90c, Herringbone.

1991-92 Inscribed "1991"

754a	A127	5c	.50	.50
755a	A127	10c	.50	.40
756a	A127	20c	.50	.40
758A	A127	35c multi	1.25	1.00
763a	A127	70c	1.25	1.25
764A	A127	90c multi	1.75	1.75
765a	A127	$1.10	2.00	2.00
		Nos. 754a-765a (7)	7.75	7.30

Nos. 758A and 764A issued June 9, 1992 (inscribed 1991)

For overprints see Nos. 788-790.

Inscribed "1990"

1990 Litho. Wmk. 384

753b	A127	2c	.40	.35
754b	A127	5c	.40	.35
755b	A127	10c	.40	.35
756b	A127	20c	.40	.35
757b	A127	25c	.55	.45
759b	A127	45c	.85	.75
760b	A127	50c	1.00	1.00
762b	A127	65c	1.25	1.25
766b	A127	$2.50	4.50	4.50
767b	A127	$5	9.00	8.75
768b	A127	$10	18.00	17.50
		Nos. 753b-768b (11)	36.75	35.60

World Stamp Expo '89, Washington, DC — A128

Water sports.

1989, Nov. 17 Wmk. 384 *Perf. 14*

769	A128	25c Water skiing	1.75	.55
770	A128	50c Yachting	3.00	1.40
771	A128	65c Scuba diving	3.00	2.00
772	A128	$2.50 Surfing	7.25	7.25
		Nos. 769-772 (4)	15.00	11.20

Horse Racing A129

Wmk. 373

1990, May 3 Litho. *Perf. 14*

773	A129	25c Bugler, jockeys	.70	.40
774	A129	45c Parade ring	1.05	.65
775	A129	75c In the straight	1.50	1.05
776	A129	$2 Winner, vert.	3.75	3.75
		Nos. 773-776 (4)	7.00	5.85

Barbados No. 2 — A130

Stamps on stamps: No. 778, Barbados #61. 65c, Barbados #73. $2.50, Barbados #121. No. 781a, Great Britain #1. No. 781b, Barbados #108.

1990, May 3

777	A130	25c shown	1.75	.55
778	A130	50c multicolored	2.60	1.25
779	A130	65c multicolored	2.75	1.75
780	A130	$2.50 multicolored	6.00	6.00
		Nos. 777-780 (4)	13.10	9.55

Souvenir Sheet

781		Sheet of 2	4.50	4.50
a.-b.		A130 50c any single	1.60	1.60

Stamp World London '90.

Queen Mother, 90th Birthday

Common Design Types

75c, At age 23. $2.50, Engagement portrait, 1923.

1990, Aug. 8 Wmk. 384 *Perf. 14x15*

782	CD343	75c multi	1.00	.70

Perf. 14½

783	CD344	$2.50 gray grn	3.00	3.00

Insects A131

50c, Dragonfly. 65c, Black hardback beetle. 75c, Green grasshopper. $2, God-horse.

Wmk. 373

1990, Oct. 16 Litho. *Perf. 14*

784	A131	50c multicolored	2.00	1.10
785	A131	65c multicolored	2.40	1.25
786	A131	75c multicolored	2.75	1.75
787	A131	$2 multicolored	5.25	5.25
		Nos. 784-787 (4)	12.40	9.35

Nos. 757, 764 and 766 Overprinted

1990, Nov. 21 *Perf. 14½*

788	A127	25c on No. 757	2.40	.75
789	A127	80c on No. 764	4.25	3.00
790	A127	$2.50 on No. 766	10.00	10.00
		Nos. 788-790 (3)	16.65	13.75

Christmas — A132

20c, Christmas star. 50c, Nativity scene. $1, Stained glass window. $2, Angel.

1990, Dec. 4 *Perf. 14*

791	A132	20c multicolored	1.00	.30
792	A132	50c multicolored	1.40	.65
793	A132	$1 multicolored	2.50	1.90
794	A132	$2 multicolored	4.50	4.50
		Nos. 791-794 (4)	9.40	7.35

Yellow Warbler A133

20c, Male, female, nest. 45c, Female, chicks. $1, Male, fledgling.

1991, Mar. 4

795	A133	10c shown	1.75	1.25
796	A133	20c multicolored	3.25	1.25
797	A133	45c multicolored	4.00	1.25
798	A133	$1 multicolored	6.50	6.00
		Nos. 795-798 (4)	15.50	9.75

World Wildlife Fund.

Fishing A134

5c, Daily catch, vert. 50c, Line fishing. 75c, Cleaning fish. $2.50, Game fishing, vert.

Perf. 13½x14, 14x13½

1991, June 18 **Litho.** **Wmk. 373**

799	A134	5c multicolored	.65	.55
800	A134	50c multicolored	2.10	1.00
801	A134	75c multicolored	2.75	1.40
802	A134	$2.50 multicolored	5.50	5.50
		Nos. 799-802 (4)	11.00	8.45

Freemasonry in Barbados, 250th Anniv. — A135

Designs: 25c, Masonic Building, Bridgetown. 65c, Compass and square. 75c, Royal arch jewel. $2.50, Columns, apron and centenary badge.

1991, Sept. 17 *Perf. 14*

803	A135	25c multicolored	2.10	.75
804	A135	65c multicolored	3.25	1.50
805	A135	75c multicolored	3.25	1.50
806	A135	$2.50 multicolored	7.00	7.00
		Nos. 803-806 (4)	15.60	10.75

Butterflies A136

20c, Polydamus swallowtail. 50c, Long-tailed skipper, vert. 65c, Cloudless sulphur. $2.50, Caribbean buckeye, vert. $4, Painted lady.

1991, Nov. 15 **Wmk. 384**

807	A136	20c multicolored	1.50	.55
808	A136	50c multicolored	2.00	.85
809	A136	65c multicolored	2.40	1.25
810	A136	$2.50 multicolored	5.50	5.50
		Nos. 807-810 (4)	11.40	8.15

Souvenir Sheet

811	A136	$4 multicolored	13.00	13.00

Phila Nippon '91.

Independence, 25th Anniv. — A137

Governor-General Dame Nita Barrow and: 10c, Students in classrom. 25c, Barbados Workers Union headquarters. 65c, Building industry. 75c, Agriculture. $1, Inoculations given at health clinic. $2.50, Gordon Greenidge, Desmond Haynes, cricket players (no portrait).

1991, Nov. 20 **Wmk. 373**

812	A137	10c multicolored	.30	.30
813	A137	25c multicolored	.50	.50
814	A137	65c multicolored	1.10	1.10
815	A137	75c multicolored	1.30	1.30
816	A137	$1 multicolored	1.50	1.50
		Nos. 812-816 (5)	4.70	4.70

Souvenir Sheet

817	A137	$2.50 multi, vert.	16.00	16.00

Easter — A138

35c, Christ carrying cross. 70c, Christ on cross. 90c, Christ taken down from cross. $3, Christ risen.

Wmk. 384

1992, Apr. 7 **Litho.** *Perf. 14*

818	A138	35c multicolored	.70	.35
819	A138	70c multicolored	1.25	.85
820	A138	90c multicolored	1.50	1.25
821	A138	$3 multicolored	3.50	3.50
		Nos. 818-821 (4)	6.95	5.95

Flowering Trees — A139

10c, Cannon ball. 30c, Golden shower. 80c, Frangipani. $1.10, Flamboyant.

Perf. 14x13½

1992, June 9 **Litho.** **Wmk. 373**

822	A139	10c multicolored	.85	.55
823	A139	30c multicolored	1.50	.65
824	A139	80c multicolored	3.00	3.00
825	A139	$1.10 multicolored	3.75	3.75
		Nos. 822-825 (4)	9.10	7.95

Orchids A140

Designs: 55c, Epidendrum "Costa Rica." 65c, Cattleya guttaca. 70c, Laeliacattleya "Splashing Around." $1.40, Phalaenopsis "Kathy Saegert."

1992, Sept. 8 *Perf. 13½x14*

826	A140	55c multicolored	1.25	.80
827	A140	65c multicolored	1.75	1.35
828	A140	70c multicolored	1.75	1.35
829	A140	$1.40 multicolored	2.75	2.75
		Nos. 826-829 (4)	7.50	6.25

For overprints see Nos. 838-841.

Transport and Tourism A141

Designs: 5c, Mini Moke, Gun Hill Signal Station, St. George. 35c, Tour bus, Bathsheba Beach, St. Joseph. 90c, BWIA McDonnell Douglas MD 83, Grantley Adams Airport. $2, Cruise ship Festivale, deep water harbor, Bridgetown.

Wmk. 373

1992, Dec. 15 **Litho.** *Perf. 14½*

830	A141	5c multicolored	.75	.75
831	A141	35c multicolored	1.75	.45
832	A141	90c multicolored	3.25	3.25
833	A141	$2 multicolored	5.25	5.25
		Nos. 830-833 (4)	11.00	9.70

Cacti and Succulents A142

10c, Barbados gooseberry. 35c, Night-blooming cereus. $1.40, Aloe. $2, Scrunchineel.

Wmk. 373

1993, Feb. 9 **Litho.** *Perf. 14*

834	A142	10c multicolored	.75	.40
835	A142	35c multicolored	1.80	.50
836	A142	$1.40 multicolored	4.00	4.00
837	A142	$2 multicolored	4.25	4.25
		Nos. 834-837 (4)	10.80	9.15

Nos. 826-829 Ovptd. on 2 or 4 lines

Perf. 13½x14

1993, Apr. 1 **Litho.** **Wmk. 373**

838	A140	55c on #826 multi	1.90	1.90
839	A140	65c on #827 multi	2.25	2.25
840	A140	70c on #828 multi	2.25	2.25
841	A140	$1.40 on #829 multi	3.25	3.25
		Nos. 838-841 (4)	9.65	9.65

Royal Air Force, 75th Anniv.

Common Design Type

Designs: 10c, Hawker Hunter. 30c, Handley Page Victor. 70c, Hawker Typhoon. $3, Hawker Hurricane.

No. 846a, Armstrong Whitworth Siskin 3a. b, Supermarine S.6B. c, Supermarine Walrus. d, Hawker Hart.

1993, Apr. 1 *Perf. 14*

842	CD350	10c multicolored	1.00	.55
843	CD350	30c multicolored	1.40	.55
844	CD350	70c multicolored	2.25	2.25
845	CD350	$3 multicolored	5.00	5.00
		Nos. 842-845 (4)	9.65	8.35

Souvenir Sheet

846	CD350	50c Sheet of 4, #a.-d.	4.50	4.50

Cannon A143

Designs: 5c, 18-pounder Culverin, 1625, Denmark Fort. 45c, 6-pounder Commonwealth gun, 1649-1660, St. Ann's Fort. $1, 9-pounder Demi-culverin, 1691, The Main Guard. $2.50, 32-pounder Demi-cannon, 1693-94, Charles Fort.

Wmk. 373

1993, June 8 **Litho.** *Perf. 13*

847	A143	5c multicolored	.45	.45
848	A143	45c multicolored	1.30	.65
849	A143	$1 multicolored	2.60	2.60
850	A143	$2.50 multicolored	4.00	4.00
		Nos. 847-850 (4)	8.35	7.70

Barbados Museum, 60th Anniv. — A144

Designs: 10c, Shell box, carved figure. 75c, Map, print of three people. 90c, Silver cup, print of soldier. $1.10, Map.

Wmk. 373

1993, Sept. 14 **Litho.** *Perf. 14*

851	A144	10c multicolored	.55	.55
852	A144	75c multicolored	1.80	1.80
853	A144	90c multicolored	2.40	2.40
854	A144	$1.10 multicolored	2.75	2.75
		Nos. 851-854 (4)	7.50	7.50

Prehistoric Aquatic Reptiles — A145

a, Plesiosaurus. b, Ichthyosaurus. c, Elasmosaurus. d, Mosasaurus. e, Archelon. Continuous design.

Wmk. 373

1993, Oct. 28 **Litho.** *Perf. 13*

855	A145	90c Strip of 5, #a.-e.	13.50	13.50

A146

10c, Cricket. 35c, Motor racing. 50c, Golf. 70c, Run Barbados 10k. $1.40, Swimming.

Wmk. 384

1994, Jan. 11 **Litho.** *Perf. 14*

856	A146	10c multi	1.40	.75
857	A146	35c multi	1.50	.55
858	A146	50c multi	2.60	1.80
859	A146	70c multi	2.00	2.00
860	A146	$1.40 multi	2.40	2.40
		Nos. 856-860 (5)	9.90	7.50

Sports & tourism.

Migratory Birds A147

10c, Whimbrel. 35c, American golden plover. 70c, Ruddy turnstone. $3, Tricolored heron.

Wmk. 373

1994, Feb. 18 **Litho.** *Perf. 14*

861	A147	10c multicolored	.70	.70
862	A147	35c multicolored	1.40	.70
863	A147	70c multicolored	2.25	2.25
864	A147	$3 multicolored	5.25	5.25
		Nos. 861-864 (4)	9.60	8.90

Hong Kong '94.

1st UN Conference of Small Island Developing States — A148

10c, Bathsheba. 65c, Pico Tenneriffe. 90c, Ragged Point Lighthouse. $2.50, Consett Bay.

1994, Apr. 25 *Perf. 14x14½*

865	A148	10c	multicolored	.50	.30
866	A148	65c	multicolored	1.75	1.00
867	A148	90c	multicolored	4.25	2.25
868	A148	$2.50	multicolored	4.00	4.00
			Nos. 865-868 (4)	10.50	7.55

Order of the Caribbean Community A149

First award recipients: No. 869, Sir Shridath Ramphal, statesman, Guyana. No. 870, Derek Walcott, writer, Nobel Laureate, St. Lucia. No. 871, William Demas, economist, Trinidad and Tobago.

Wmk. 373

1994, July 4 **Litho.** *Perf. 14*

869	A149	70c	multicolored	1.00	1.00
870	A149	70c	multicolored	1.00	1.00
871	A149	70c	multicolored	1.00	1.00
			Nos. 869-871 (3)	3.00	3.00

Ships A150

Designs: 5c, Dutch Flyut, 1695. 10c, Geestport, 1994. 25c, HMS Victory, 1805. 30c, Royal Viking Queen, 1994. 35c, HMS Barbados, 1945. 45c, Faraday, 1924. 50c, USCG Hamilton, 1974. 65c, HMCS Saguenay, 1939. 70c, Inanda, 1928. 80c, HMS Rodney, 1944. 90c, USS John F. Kennedy, 1982. $1.10, William & John, 1627. $5, USCG Champlain, 1931. $10, Artist, 1877.

Wmk. 373

1994, Aug. 16 **Litho.** *Perf. 14*

872	A150	5c	multicolored	.50	.50
873	A150	10c	multicolored	.50	.50
874	A150	25c	multicolored	.50	.50
875	A150	30c	multicolored	.80	.80
876	A150	35c	multicolored	.95	.95
877	A150	45c	multicolored	1.05	1.05
878	A150	50c	multicolored	1.20	1.20
879	A150	65c	multicolored	1.60	1.60
880	A150	70c	multicolored	1.80	1.80
881	A150	80c	multicolored	2.40	2.40
882	A150	90c	multicolored	2.60	2.60
883	A150	$1.10	multicolored	3.00	3.00
884	A150	$5	multicolored	11.50	11.50
885	A150	$10	multicolored	23.00	23.00
			Nos. 872-885 (14)	51.40	51.40

1997 **Inscribed "1997"**

872a	A150	5c	multicolored	.95	.95
873a	A150	10c	multicolored	.95	.95
874a	A150	25c	multicolored	1.15	.70
875a	A150	30c	multicolored	1.90	.70
876a	A150	35c	multicolored	1.90	.95
877a	A150	45c	multicolored	1.90	.95
880a	A150	70c	multicolored	3.50	.70
882a	A150	90c	multicolored	4.00	2.75
885a	A150	$10	multicolored	13.50	13.50
			Nos. 872a-885a (9)	29.75	22.15

1998 **Inscribed "1998"**

872b	A150	5c	multicolored	.50	.50
873b	A150	10c	multicolored	.50	.50
877b	A150	45c	multicolored	1.10	.75
880b	A150	70c	multicolored	2.60	2.60
			Nos. 872b-880b (4)	4.70	4.35

1999 **Inscribed "1999"**

873c	A150	10c	multicolored	1.80	.85
877c	A150	45c	multicolored	2.60	.65
885c	A150	$10	multicolored	20.00	20.00
			Nos. 873c-885c (3)	24.40	21.50

1996 **Wmk. 384**

872d	A150	5c	.45	.45
873d	A150	10c	.45	.45
875d	A150	30c	.55	.55
876d	A150	35c	.70	.70
877d	A150	45c	1.00	1.00
878d	A150	50c	1.15	1.15
879d	A150	65c	1.30	1.30
880d	A150	70c	1.60	1.60
881d	A150	80c	1.80	1.80
882d	A150	90c	2.25	2.25
883d	A150	$1.10	2.50	2.50
884d	A150	$5	10.50	10.50
		Nos. 872d-884d (12)	24.25	24.25

Inscribed "1996."

Issued: Nos. 875d-877d, 879d-882d, 9/1; others, May 1.

West India Regiment, Bicent. — A151

Designs: 30c, 2nd Regiment, 1860. 50c, 4th Regiment, Light Company, 1795. 70c, 3rd Regiment, drum major, 1860. $1, 5th Regiment, undress, working dress, 1815. $1.10, 1st, 2nd Regiments, Review Order, 1874.

Perf. 15x14

1995, Feb. 21 **Litho.** **Wmk. 373**

886	A151	30c	multicolored	.80	.45
887	A151	50c	multicolored	1.10	.70
888	A151	70c	multicolored	1.50	1.50
889	A151	$1	multicolored	1.75	1.75
890	A151	$1.10	multicolored	2.10	2.10
			Nos. 886-890 (5)	7.25	6.50

End of World War II

Common Design Type

10c, Barbadians serving in the Middle East. 35c, Lancaster bomber. 55c, Spitfire fighter. $2.50, SS Davisian sunk off Barbados, July 10, 1940.
$2, Reverse of War Medal 1939-45.

Wmk. 373

1995, May 8 **Litho.** *Perf. 14*

891	CD351	10c	multicolored	1.10	.70
892	CD351	35c	multicolored	1.60	.70
893	CD351	55c	multicolored	2.00	1.00
894	CD351	$2.50	multicolored	5.50	5.50
			Nos. 891-894 (4)	10.20	7.90

Souvenir Sheet

895	CD352	$2	multicolored	4.00	4.00

Combermere School, 300th Anniv. — A152

Designs: 5c, Scouting, Combermere 1st Barbados, 1912. 20c, Violin, sheet music. 35c, Cricket, Sir Frank Worrell, vert. 90c, Frank Collymore, No. 553. $3, Landscape.

Wmk. 373

1995, July 25 **Litho.** *Perf. 14*

896	A152	5c	multicolored	.45	.45
897	A152	20c	multicolored	.65	.65
898	A152	35c	multicolored	1.90	.65
899	A152	$3	multicolored	2.75	2.75
			Nos. 896-899 (4)	5.75	4.50

Souvenir Sheet

900	Sheet of 5, #896-899, 900a	6.75	6.75
a.	A152 90c multicolored	1.00	1.00

UN, 50th Anniv.

Common Design Type

Designs: 30c, Douglas C-124 Globemaster, Korea 1950-53. 45c, Royal Navy Sea King helicopter. $1.40, Wessex helicopter, UNFICYP, Cyprus 1964. $2, Gazelle helicopter, UNFICYP, Cyprus 1964.

Wmk. 373

1995, Oct. 24 **Litho.** *Perf. 14*

901	CD353	30c	multicolored	1.00	.55
902	CD353	45c	multicolored	1.50	.70
903	CD353	$1.40	multicolored	2.25	2.25
904	CD353	$2	multicolored	2.25	2.25
			Nos. 901-904 (4)	7.00	5.75

Water Lilies — A153

Wmk. 373

1995, Dec. 19 **Litho.** *Perf. 14*

905	A153	10c	Blue beauty	.60	.45
906	A153	65c	White water lily	1.45	1.45
907	A153	70c	Sacred lotus	1.45	1.45
908	A153	$3	Water hyacinth	4.50	4.50
			Nos. 905-908 (4)	8.00	7.85

Barbados Philatelic Society, Cent. A154

Magnifiying glass, tongs, and: 10c, No. 70. 55c, No. 109. $1.10, No. 148. $1.40, No. 192.

Wmk. 373

1996, Jan. 30 **Litho.** *Perf. 14*

909	A154	10c	multicolored	.40	.35
910	A154	55c	multicolored	.75	.55
911	A154	$1.10	multicolored	1.75	1.75
912	A154	$1.40	multicolored	2.10	2.10
			Nos. 909-912 (4)	5.00	4.75

A155

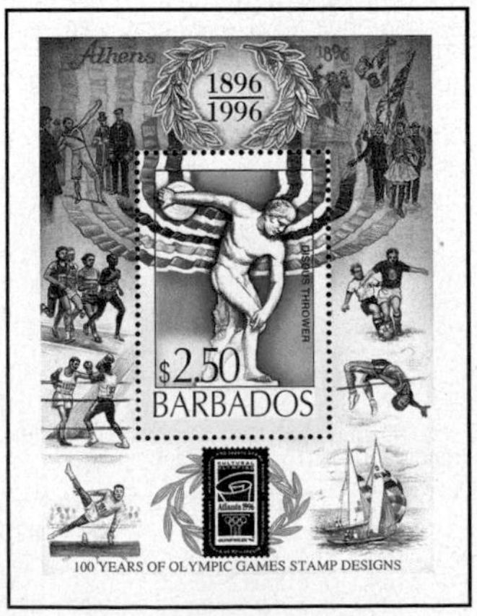

Modern Olympic Games, Cent. — A156

20c, Soccer. 30c, Relay race. 55c, Basketball. $3, Rhythmic gymnastics.
$2.50, Discus thrower.

1996, Apr. 2 **Litho.** *Perf. 14*

913	A155	20c	multicolored	.60	.40
914	A155	30c	multicolored	.65	.40
915	A155	55c	multicolored	2.25	.85
916	A155	$3	multicolored	3.25	3.25
			Nos. 913-916 (4)	6.75	4.90

Souvenir Sheet

917	A156	$2.50	multicolored	3.50	3.50

Olymphilex '96 (No. 917).

CAPEX '96 A157

Transportation links with Canada: 10c, Canadian Airlines DC10. 90c, Air Canada Boeing 767. $1, Air Canada 320 Airbus. $1.40, Canadian Airlines Boeing 767.

Wmk. 373

1996, June 7 **Litho.** *Perf. 14*

918	A157	10c	multicolored	.50	.45
919	A157	90c	multicolored	1.75	1.25
920	A157	$1	multicolored	1.75	1.75
921	A157	$1.40	multicolored	2.25	2.25
			Nos. 918-921 (4)	6.25	5.70

Chattel Houses A158

House features: 35c, Shed roof, lattice work. 70c, Pedimented porch, carved wooden trim. $1.10, Decorative, elegant porch. $2, Hip roof, bell pelmet window hoods.

1996, June 7

922	A158	35c	multicolored	.55	.35
923	A158	70c	multicolored	1.05	.75
924	A158	$1.10	multicolored	1.40	1.40
925	A158	$2	multicolored	2.25	2.25
			Nos. 922-925 (4)	5.25	4.75

Compare with type A239.

Christmas A159

Children's paintings: 10c, Going to Church on Christmas morning. 30c, The Tuk Band. 55c, Caroling on Christmas. $2.50, Decorated houses.

Wmk. 373

1996, Nov. 12 **Litho.** *Perf. 14½*

926	A159	10c	multicolored	.50	.25
927	A159	30c	multicolored	.80	.45
928	A159	55c	multicolored	1.10	.70
929	A159	$2.50	multicolored	2.60	2.60
			Nos. 926-929 (4)	5.00	4.00

UNICEF, 50th anniv.

Hong Kong '97 — A160

Dogs: 10c, Doberman pinscher. 30c, German shepherd. 90c, Japanese akita. $3, Irish red setter.

Perf. 14x14½

1997, Feb. 12 **Litho.** **Wmk. 373**

930	A160	10c	multicolored	.90	.50
931	A160	30c	multicolored	1.70	.50
932	A160	90c	multicolored	2.50	1.45
933	A160	$3	multicolored	5.25	5.25
			Nos. 930-933 (4)	10.35	7.70

Visit of US Pres. Clinton to Barbados, May 1997 A161

35c, Barbados flag, arms. 90c, US flag, arms.

1997, May 9 Litho. *Perf. 14*

934 A161 35c multicolored .95 .95
935 A161 90c multicolored 1.40 1.40
a. Pair, #934-935 2.60 2.60

Issued in sheets of 8 stamps + 2 labels. Sheets exist both with and without a "Pacific '97" overprint in the margin.

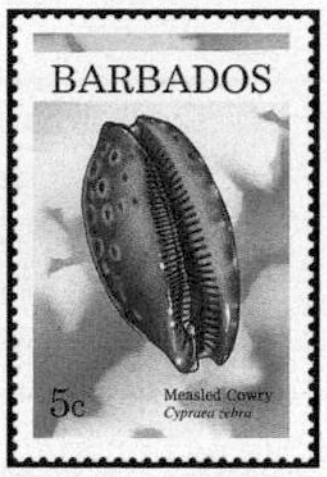

Shells — A162

5c, Measled cowry. 35c, Trumpet triton. 90c, Scotch bonnet. $2, West Indian murex.
$2.50, Sea bottom with miscellaneous shells.

1997, July 29 Litho. *Perf. 14*

936 A162 5c multicolored .40 .40
937 A162 35c multicolored 1.00 .35
938 A162 90c multicolored 1.90 .95
939 A162 $2 multicolored 2.75 2.75
Nos. 936-939 (4) 6.05 4.45

Souvenir Sheet

940 A162 $2.50 multicolored 4.25 4.25

Public Library, 150th Anniv. A163

Designs: 10c, Lucas manuscripts. 30c, Storytelling to children. 70c, Bookmobile. $3, Information technology.

1997, Oct. 1 Litho. *Perf. 14*

941 A163 10c multicolored .35 .25
942 A163 30c multicolored .70 .35
943 A163 70c multicolored 1.60 .70
944 A163 $3 multicolored 3.50 3.50
Nos. 941-944 (4) 6.15 4.80

Fruit — A164

1997, Dec. 16 Litho. *Perf. 14½*

945 A164 35c Barbados cherry .65 .40
946 A164 40c Sugar apple .75 .40
947 A164 $1.15 Soursop 1.75 1.75
948 A164 $1.70 Papaya 2.40 2.40
Nos. 945-948 (4) 5.55 4.95

Souvenir Sheet

Sir Grantley Adams, Birth Cent. — A165

a, Natl. Arms. b, Grantley Adams. c, Natl. flag.

1998, Apr. 27 Litho. *Perf. 13*

949 A165 $1 Sheet of 3, #a.-c. 9.00 9.00

Diana, Princess of Wales (1961-97)

Common Design Type of 1998

Portraits wearing: a, Blue hat. b, Red suit jacket. c, Tiara. d, Black and white.

1998, May *Perf. 14½x14*

950 CD355 $1.15 Sheet of 4, #a.-d. 6.25 6.25

Organization of American States, 50th Anniv. — A166

Designs: 15c, Beach during storm, beach during sunny day. $1, Dancers in native costumes. $2.50, Judge reading at podium, statue of justice.

1998, June 30 Litho. *Perf. 14*

951 A166 15c multicolored .25 .25
952 A166 $1 multicolored 1.00 1.00
953 A166 $2.50 multicolored 2.75 2.75
Nos. 951-953 (3) 4.00 4.00

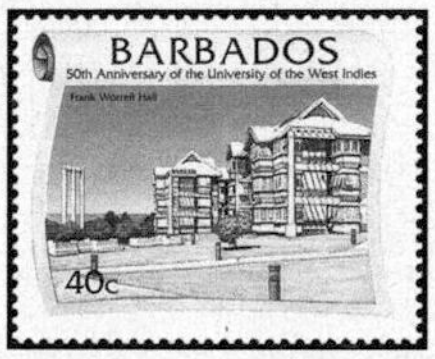

University of West Indies, 50th Anniv. A167

40c, Frank Worrell Hall. $1.15, Graduation. $1.40, Plaque, hummingbird. $1.75, Quadrangle.

1998, July 20 *Perf. 14½*

954 A167 40c multicolored .60 .35
955 A167 $1.15 multicolored 1.60 1.60
956 A167 $1.40 multicolored 2.00 2.00
957 A167 $1.75 multicolored 3.50 3.50
Nos. 954-957 (4) 7.70 7.45

Tourism A168

10c, Catamaran, vert. 45c, Jolly Roger. 70c, Atlantis submarine. $2, MV Harbor Master, vert.

1998, Dec. 1 Litho. *Perf. 14*

958 A168 10c multicolored .35 .35
959 A168 45c multicolored 1.15 .45
960 A168 70c multicolored 1.75 1.25
961 A168 $2 multicolored 3.50 3.50
Nos. 958-961 (4) 6.75 5.55

Australia '99, World Stamp Expo — A169

1999, Mar. 19 Litho. *Perf. 14*

962 A169 $4 Sailboat 5.50 5.50

Piping Plover A170

World Wildlife Fund: 10c, Juvenile in shallow water. 45c, Female with eggs. 50c, Fledglings in nest, male, female. 70c, Male.

1999, Apr. 27 Litho. *Perf. 14*

963 A170 10c multicolored .25 .25
964 A170 45c multicolored 1.00 .75
965 A170 50c multicolored 1.00 1.00
966 A170 70c multicolored 1.30 1.30
Nos. 963-966 (4) 3.55 3.30

1st Manned Moon Landing, 30th Anniv.

Common Design Type

Designs: 40c, Astronaut training. 45c, First stage separation. $1.15, Lunar module. $1.40, Docking with service module.
$2.50, Looking at earth from moon.

Perf. 14x13¾

1999, July 20 Litho. Wmk. 384

967 CD357 40c multicolored .80 .50
968 CD357 45c multicolored .80 .50
969 CD357 $1.15 multicolored 2.10 1.50
970 CD357 $1.40 multicolored 2.25 2.25
Nos. 967-970 (4) 5.95 4.75

Souvenir Sheet

Perf. 14

971 CD357 $2.50 multicolored 3.50 3.50

No. 971 contains one 40mm circular stamp.

Rabbits A171

Designs: a, Rabbit running. b, Rabbit profile. c, Rabbit nursing young. d, Two rabbits leaping. e, Two rabbits at rest.

Perf. 14x14½

1999, Aug. 21 Litho. Wmk. 373

972 A171 70c Strip of 5, #a.-e. 10.00 10.00

China 1999 World Philatelic Exhibition.

UPU, 125th Anniv. A172

1999, Oct. 11 Litho. *Perf. 14*

973 A172 10c Mail coach 1.25 .45
974 A172 45c Mail van 1.75 .55
975 A172 $1.75 Airplane 2.50 2.50
976 A172 $2 Computers 2.75 2.75
Nos. 973-976 (4) 8.25 6.25

Souvenir Sheet

Millennium — A173

Wmk. 373

2000, Feb. 8 Litho. *Perf. 14*

977 A173 $3 multicolored 6.25 6.25

100th Test Cricket Match at Lord's Ground — A174

Designs: 45c, Sir Conrad Hunte. 90c, Malcolm Marshall. $2, Sir Garfield St. A. Sobers.
$2.50, Lord's Ground, horiz.

Wmk. 373

2000, May 22 Litho. *Perf. 14*

978 A174 45c multi 1.30 .55
979 A174 90c multi 2.60 1.10
980 A174 $2 multi 4.75 4.75
Nos. 978-980 (3) 8.65 6.40

Souvenir Sheet

981 A174 $2.50 multi 4.75 4.75

The Stamp Show 2000, London (No. 981).

Sites in Barbados A175

5c, Drax Hall House. 10c, Reaping sugar cane. 40c, Needham's Point Lighthouse. 45c, Port St. Charles. 65c, Synagogue. 70c, Bridgetown port (boats point right). No. 987A, 70c, Bridgetown port (boats point left). 90c, Harrison's Cave. $1.15, Villa Nova. $1.40, Cricket at Kensington Oval. $1.75, Sunbury House. $2, Bethel Methodist Church. $3, Barbados Wildlife Reserve. $5, Royal Westmoreland golf course. $10, Grantley Adams Intl. Airport.

Wmk. 373

2000, May 22 Litho. *Perf. 14*

982 A175 5c multi .30 .55
983 A175 10c multi, vert. .30 .30
a. Inscribed "2002" 2.25 2.25
b. Inscribed "2004" 3.00 3.00
984 A175 40c multi, vert. .55 .55
985 A175 45c multi .65 .65
986 A175 65c multi 1.00 1.00
987 A175 70c multi 1.20 1.20
987A A175 70c multi 1.20 1.20
988 A175 90c multi 1.50 1.50
989 A175 $1.15 multi 2.00 2.00
990 A175 $1.40 multi 2.10 2.10
991 A175 $1.75 multi 2.75 2.75
992 A175 $2 multi 3.25 3.25
993 A175 $3 multi, vert. 4.75 4.75
994 A175 $5 multi, vert. 8.00 8.00
995 A175 $10 multi 14.50 14.50
Nos. 982-995 (15) 44.05 44.05

Nos. 982-987, 988-995 issued 5/22.

World Stamp Expo 2000, Anaheim — A176

25c, Golf equipment. 40c, Golfer on golf ball. $1.40, Golfer at tee. $2, Golfer putting.

Perf. 14½x14¼

2000, July 7 Litho. Wmk. 373

996-999 A176 Set of 4 7.75 7.75

Vintage Cars A177

Designs: 10c, 1947 Bentley Mk VI. 30c, Vanden Plas Princess. 90c, 1952 Austin Atlantic. $3, 1950 Bentley Special.

Perf. 14¼x14½

2000, Nov. 7 Wmk. 373

1000-1003 A177 Set of 4 7.50 7.50

Souvenir Sheet

Hong Kong 2001 Stamp Exhibition — A178

Wmk. 373

2001, Feb. 1 Litho. *Perf. 13¼*

1004 A178 $3 Thread snake 6.00 6.00

Deep Sea Creatures — A179

No. 1005: a, Lizard fish. b, Goldentail moray. c, Blackbar soldierfish. d, Golden zoanthid. e, Sponge brittle star. f, Magnificent feather duster. g, Bearded fireworm. h, Lima shell. i, Yellow tube sponge.

Wmk. 373

2001, May 31 Litho. *Perf. 13½*

1005 A179 45c Sheet of 9, #a-i 8.00 8.00

Phila Nippon '01, Japan A180

Various kites: 10c, 65c, $1.40, $1.75.

2001, Aug. 1 *Perf. 14*

1006-1009 A180 Set of 4 5.00 5.00

George Washington's Visit to Barbados, 250th Anniv. — A181

Designs: 45c, Washington, ship, trunk, dockworker. 50c, Washington, ship, palm trees. $1.15, Washington, Declaration of Independence. $2.50, Fort at Needham's Point.
$3, Portrait of Washington.

Wmk. 373

2001, Nov. 2 Litho. *Perf. 13¼*

1010-1013 A181 Set of 4 7.25 7.25

Souvenir Sheet

1014 A181 $3 multi 4.25 4.25

Independence, 35th Anniv. — A182

Designs: 25c, Bank Holiday Bear. 45c, Tuk band. $1, Landship Movement Maypole dance. $2, National anthem, saxophone and guitar.

2001, Nov. 29 Litho. *Perf. 14*

1015-1018 A182 Set of 4 7.00 7.00

Reign Of Queen Elizabeth II, 50th Anniv. Issue

Common Design Type

Designs: Nos. 1019, 1023a, 10c, Princess Elizabeth. Nos. 1020, 1023b, 70c, Wearing red hat. Nos. 1021, 1023c, $1, Wearing crown. Nos. 1022, 1023d, $1.40, Wearing purple hat. No. 1023e, $3, 1955 portrait by Annigoni (38x50mm).

Perf. 14¼x14½, 13¾ (#1023e)

2002, Feb. 6 Wmk. 373

With Gold Frames

1019 CD360 10c multicolored .40 .40
1020 CD360 70c multicolored 1.40 1.40
1021 CD360 $1 multicolored 1.60 1.60
1022 CD360 $1.40 multicolored 2.25 2.25
Nos. 1019-1022 (4) 5.65 5.65

Souvenir Sheet

Without Gold Frames

1023 CD360 Sheet of 5, #a-e 7.25 7.25

Inland Post, 150th Anniv. A183

Map of Barbados and: 10c, #1. 45c, Early postman. $1.15, Steam packet R.M.S. Esk. $2, BWIA Tristar.

2002, Apr. 15 *Perf. 14*

1024-1027 A183 Set of 4 5.75 5.75

Flowers — A184

Designs: 10c, Red ginger, vert. 40c, Heliconia caribaea, vert. $1.40, Tube rose. $2.50, Anthurium.

Perf. 14¾x14, 14x14¾

2002, May 30 Litho.

1028-1031 A184 Set of 4 5.75 5.75

First Settlement, 375th Anniv. — A185

Designs: 10c, Drax Hall, St. George. 45c, Donkey cart truck. $1.15, Remains of cattle mill, Gibbons. $3, Morgan Lewis, St. Andrew.

Wmk. 373

2002, Sept. 6 Litho. *Perf. 14*

1032-1035 A185 Set of 4 9.00 9.00

Christmas A186

Designs: 45c, Traditional Christmas fare. $1.15, Christmas morning in the park. $1.40, Nativity scene.

2002, Nov. 11

1036-1038 A186 Set of 3 4.00 4.00

Pan-American Health Organization, Cent. — A187

Designs: 10c, AIDS awareness. 70c, Health and longevity. $1.15, Director General Sir George Alleyne. $2, Women's health.

Wmk. 373

2002, Dec. 2 Litho. *Perf. 14*

1039-1042 A187 Set of 4 6.00 6.00

Royal Navy Ships A188

Designs: 10c, HMS Tartar, 1764. 70c, HMS Barbadoes, 1803. $1.15, HMS Valerian, 1926. $2.50, HMS Victorious, 1941.

Wmk. 373

2003, May 26 Litho. *Perf. 14*

1043-1046 A188 Set of 4 8.75 8.75

Settlement Of Bridgetown, 375th Anniv. — A189

Designs: 10c, Broad Street, c. 1900. $1.15, Swan Street, 1900. $1.40, Roebuck Street, c. 1880. $2, Chamberlain Bridge.

Wmk. 373

2003, July 7 Litho. *Perf. 14*

1047-1050 A189 Set of 4 8.00 8.00
1050a Souvenir sheet, #1047-1050 8.25 8.25

Powered Flight, Cent. — A190

Designs: 10c, McDonnell F2H-2 Banshee. 45c, Vickers Viscount 700. 50c, Douglas DC-9-30. $1.15, Short Sunderland MK II. $1.40, North American P-51D Mustang. $2.50, Concorde.

Stamps + Labels

Perf. 13¼x13¾

2003, Sept. 22 Litho. Wmk. 373

1051-1056 A190 Set of 6 9.50 9.50

Festivals — A191

No. 1057: a, Fishermen hauling in catch, Oistins Fish Festival. b, Saxophonist, Barbados Jazz Festival. c, Costumed man and woman, Crop Over Festival. d, Dancers, National Independence Festival of Creative Arts. e, Choir, National Independence Festival of Creative Arts. f, Three people in costume, Crop Over Festival. g, Bassist, Barbados Jazz Festival. h, Fish boning, Oistins Fish Festival.

Wmk. 373

2003, Nov. 24 Litho. *Perf. 13¾*

1057 A191 45c Sheet of 8, #a-h, + central label 10.00 10.00

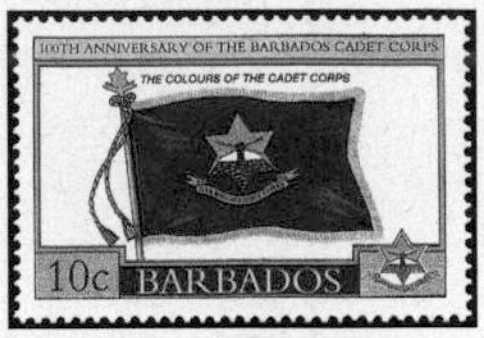

Cadet Corps, Cent. A192

Designs: 10c, Cadet Corps Flag. 25c, Regular Band marching. 50c, Toy Soldier Band. $1, Sea Cadets. $3, Map reading.

Wmk. 373

2004, July 19 Litho. *Perf. 14*

1058-1062 A192 Set of 5 8.00 8.00

2004 Summer Olympics, Athens — A193

Designs: 10, Swimming. 70c, Shooting. $1.15, Running. $2, Judo.

Wmk. 373

2004, Aug. 16 Litho. *Perf. 14*

1063-1066 A193 Set of 4 7.00 7.00

FIFA (Fédération Internationale de Football Association), Cent. — A194

Various soccer players: 5c, 90c, $1.40, $2.50.

Perf. 14x14¾

2004, Oct. 20 Litho. Wmk. 373

1067-1070 A194 Set of 4 7.00 7.00

Corals — A195

No. 1071: a, Brain coral. b, Pillar coral (yellow). c, Pillar coral (tan). d, Fan coral. e, Yellow pencil coral.
$3.50, Maze coral.

2004, Nov. 15 *Perf. 14x14¼*

1071 Horiz. strip of 5 12.50 12.50
a.-e. A195 $1 Any single 2.25 2.25

Souvenir Sheet

Perf. 13¼

1072 A195 $3.50 multi 6.25 6.25

No. 1072 contains one 36x36mm stamp.

Butterflies A196

Designs: 50c, White peacock. $1, Great southern white. $1.40, Orion. $2.50, Mimic. $8, Monarch.

Wmk. 373

2005, Apr. 21 Litho. *Perf. 14*

1073-1076 A196 Set of 4 13.00 13.00

Souvenir Sheet

1077 A196 $8 multi 11.50 11.50

Pacific Explorer 2005 World Stamp Expo, Sydney.

Trees A197

Designs: 5c, Baobab, 10c, African tulip tree. 25c, Rose of Sharon. 45c, Black willow. 50c, Black pearl tree. 75c, Seaside mahoe. 90c, Quickstick. $1, Jerusalem thorn. $1.15, Pink cassia. $1.40, Orchid tree. $1.75, Yellow poui. $2.10, Lignum vitae. $3, Wild cinnamon. $5, Pride of India. $10, Immortelle.

Wmk. 373

2005, July 20 Litho. *Perf. 13¾*

1078	A197	5c	multi	.25	.25
1079	A197	10c	multi	.25	.25
1080	A197	25c	multi	.35	.35
1081	A197	45c	multi	.60	.60
1082	A197	50c	multi	.65	.65
1083	A197	75c	multi	.85	.85
1084	A197	90c	multi	1.00	1.00
1085	A197	$1	multi	1.10	1.10
1086	A197	$1.15	multi	1.60	1.60
1087	A197	$1.40	multi	1.75	1.75
1088	A197	$1.75	multi	2.25	2.25
1089	A197	$2.10	multi	2.75	2.75
1090	A197	$3	multi	3.75	3.75
1091	A197	$5	multi	6.00	6.00
1092	A197	$10	multi	11.50	11.50
	Nos. 1078-1092 (15)			34.65	34.65

Dated "2010"

2010 Wmk. 406 Litho. *Perf. 13¾*

1078a	5c multi	.25	.25
1079a	10c multi	.25	.25
1082a	50c multi	.50	.50
1086a	$1.15 multi	1.25	1.25
1087a	$1.40 multi	1.40	1.40
1088a	$1.75 multi	1.75	1.75
Nos. 1078a-1088a (6)		5.40	5.40

Barbados Fire Service, 50th Anniv. A198

Designs: 5c, Three firefighters. 10c, Parade at firehouse. 90c, Yellow fire truck. $1.15, Old fire trucks. $2.50, Red fire truck.

Wmk. 373

2005, Sept. 26 Litho. *Perf. 14*

1093-1097 A198 Set of 5 12.50 12.50

Extreme Anoles A199

Designs: 10c, Three anoles. 50c, Two anoles. $1.75, One anole. $2, Hatchling and eggs.

Wmk. 373

2005, Nov. 28 Litho. *Perf. 14*

1098-1101 A199 Set of 4 10.50 10.50

Worldwide Fund for Nature (WWF) A200

Queen angelfish and: 10c, Diver. $1.15, Coral. $1.40, Sea floor. $2.10, Coral, diff.

Wmk. 373

2006, Jan. 30 Litho. *Perf. 14*

1102-1105 A200 Set of 4 6.00 6.00

1105a Sheet, 2 each #1102-1105 12.00 12.00

Washington 2006 World Philatelic Exhibition — A201

Children: 10c, Reading. 50c, Playing wheelchair basketball. $2, At computer. $2.50, Playing violins.

Perf. 13¼x13½

2006, May 26 Litho. Wmk. 373

1106-1109 A201 Set of 4 8.50 8.50

Cave Shepherd Store, Cent. A202

Store facades from around: 10c, 1911. 50c, 2000. $1.75, 1975. $2, 1920.

Wmk. 373

2006, Nov. 1 Litho. *Perf. 13¾*

1110-1113 A202 Set of 4 8.50 8.50

Enfranchisement of Free Colored and Black Barbadians, 175th Anniv. — A203

Designs: 10c, Old Town Hall, Coleridge Street. 50c, Samuel Jackman Prescod (1806-71). $1.40, Introduction of ballot box, 1885. $2.50, Sir James Lyon, Governor from 1829-33.

2006, Nov. 27

1114-1117 A203 Set of 4 6.75 6.75

2007 ICC Cricket World Cup — A204

Designs: $1.75, Joel "Big Bird" Garner. $2.10, Old Kensington Oval, horiz. $3, New Kensington Oval, horiz.

$10, ICC Cricket World Cup.

Wmk. 373

2007, Mar. 19 Litho. *Perf. 14*

1118-1120 A204 Set of 3 7.00 7.00

Souvenir Sheet

Litho. & Embossed

1121 A204 $10 multi 10.00 10.00

Abolition of Slavery, Bicent. — A205

Designs: 10c, Sculpture of Bussa, slave revolt leader. $1, William Wilberforce, British abolitionist. $1.75, Slave hut, horiz. $2, Freedom celebration, 1838, horiz.

$3, Slave ship.

Perf. 14¾x14¼, 14¼x14¾

2007, Mar. 26 Litho. Wmk. 373

1122-1125 A205 Set of 4 5.00 5.00

Souvenir Sheet

1126 A205 $3 multi 3.00 3.00

Opening of Jewish Synagogue Museum, Bridgetown A206

Designs: 5c, Interior of synagogue. 10c, Museum building. $1.40, Hanukiah. $2.50, Stained-glass window.

2007, May 15 *Perf. 12½x13*

1127-1130 A206 Set of 4 4.25 4.25

Turtles A207

Turtles: 10c, Green. 50c, Loggerhead. $1, Hawksbill. $2.50, Leatherback.

Perf. 12½x13

2007, Oct. 29 Litho. Unwmk.

1131-1134 A207 Set of 4 4.25 4.25

Algae — A208

Designs: 10c, Padina gymnospora. 50c, Ulva lactuta. $1.75, Sargassum platycarpum. $2, Udotea conglutinata.

Wmk. 373

2008, July 14 Litho. *Perf. 13¾*

1135-1138 A208 Set of 4 4.50 4.50

Barbadians and Aircraft — A209

Designs: 10c, Second Barbados Contingent. 50c, Warren Alleyne, Supermarine Spitfire Mk IX. $1.75, Wing Commander Aubrey Inniss, Bristol Beaufighter Mk VIC. $2, Flying Officer Errol Barrow, Avro Lancaster B Mk 1.

$6, Concorde over Barbados.

Wmk. 373

2008, July 30 Litho. *Perf. 14*

1139-1142 A209 Set of 4 4.50 4.50

Souvenir Sheet

1143 A209 $6 multi 6.00 6.00

Christmas A210

Paintings: 10c, Christmas Moon, by Alison Chapman-Andrews. 50c, Preparing for Christmas, bu Virgil Broodhagen. $1.40, Christmas Candles, by Darla Trotman. $3, Poinsettia and Snow on the Mountain, by Trotman.

2008, Nov. 11 Wmk. 406 *Perf. 13½*

1144-1147 A210 Set of 4 5.00 5.00

Louis Braille (1809-52), Educator of the Blind — A211

Braille and: 50c, Hands of worker using pliers. $1.40, Worker caning chair. $1.75, Student reading Braille text at Braille typewriter. $2, "Louis Braille" in Braille text.

2009, July 6 *Perf. 14*

1148-1151 A211 Set of 4 6.25 6.25

Restructured Criminal Court, 300th Anniv. — A212

Designs: 10c, New Court House. 50c, Handcuffs, seal of the court. $1.40, Judge's robe, wig and gavel. $2.50, Old Court House.

Wmk. 406

2009, Nov. 10 Litho. *Perf. 12½*

1152-1155 A212 Set of 4 5.00 5.00

Queen's Park, Bridgetown, Cent. (in 2009) A213

Designs: 90c, Queen's Park Fountain. $1, Baobab tree. $1.40, Queen's Park House. $2, Band stand.

$4, Band stand at park's opening.

Perf. 12½x13

2010, Jan. 11 Unwmk.

1156-1159 A213 Set of 4 5.50 5.50

Souvenir Sheet

1160 A213 $4 multi 4.50 4.50

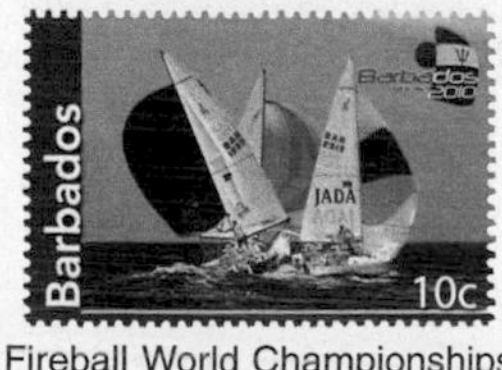

Fireball World Championships Regatta — A214

Various racing sailboats: 10c, 50c, 90c, $1.75, $2.

2010, Apr. 23 Wmk. 406 *Perf. 14*

1161-1165 A214 Set of 5 5.25 5.25

Girl Guides, Cent. A215

Girl Guides: 10c, At camp. 50c, Giving salute. $1, In various uniforms. $2.50, On parade.

$3.50, Centenary emblem, emblems of Girl Guides and Barbados Girl Guides.

Perf. 14¼x14

2010, Sept. 22 Litho. Wmk. 406

1166-1169 A215 Set of 4 4.50 4.50

Souvenir Sheet

1170 A215 $3.50 multi 3.75 3.75

Fruits — A216

Designs: 5c, Golden apples. 10c Coconuts. 35c, Cashews. 40c, Mammy apples. 60c, Barbados cherries. 65c, Sugar apples. 80c, Sea grapes. $1, Tamarinds. $1.25, Carambolas. $1.50, Mangos. $1.80, Bananas. $2.20, Guavas. $2.75, Avocados. $3, Gooseberries. $5, Soursops. $10, Pomegranates.

Unwmk.

2011, Feb. 7 Litho. *Perf. 13*

1171	A216	5c	multi	.25	.25
1172	A216	10c	multi	.25	.25
1173	A216	35c	multi	.35	.35
1174	A216	40c	multi	.40	.40
1175	A216	60c	multi	.60	.60
1176	A216	65c	multi	.65	.65
1177	A216	80c	multi	.80	.80
1178	A216	$1	multi	1.00	1.00
1179	A216	$1.25	multi	1.25	1.25
1180	A216	$1.50	multi	1.50	1.50
1181	A216	$1.80	multi	1.90	1.90
1182	A216	$2.20	multi	2.25	2.25
1183	A216	$2.75	multi	2.75	2.75
1184	A216	$3	multi	3.00	3.00
1185	A216	$5	multi	5.00	5.00
1186	A216	$10	multi	10.00	10.00
	Nos. 1171-1186 (16)			31.95	31.95

Sailor's Valentines (Shell Art) — A217

Designs: 10c, Valentine from 1800s. 65c, "With My Love." $2.20, "Live Today, Hope Tomorrow." $2.75, "Evermore."

Perf. 12½x13

2011, Feb. 14 Wmk. 406

1187-1190 A217 Set of 4 5.75 5.75

Wedding of Prince William and Catherine Middleton — A218

Designs: 15c, Middleton in wedding dress with attendant. 65c, Couple in carriage. $1.80, Couple holding hands, vert. $2.20, Couple waving, vert.

Wmk. 406

2011, Aug. 3 Litho. *Perf. 14*

1191-1194 A218 Set of 4 5.00 5.00

Reign of Queen Elizabeth II, 60th Anniv. A219

Queen Elizabeth II: 10c, Exiting Barbados Parliament, 1989. $1.40, Wearing tiara, 1952. $2.10, Inspecting Barbados soldiers, 1977. $2.50, At Goddard Space Flight Center, Maryland, 2007.

$4, Queen Elizabeth II and Prince Philip at opening of Barbados Parliament, 1987.

2012, Mar. 12 Wmk. 406 *Perf. 13*

1195-1198 A219 Set of 4 6.25 6.25

Souvenir Sheet

Perf. 13½x13

1199 A219 $4 multi 4.00 4.00

No. 1199 contains one 60x40mm stamp.

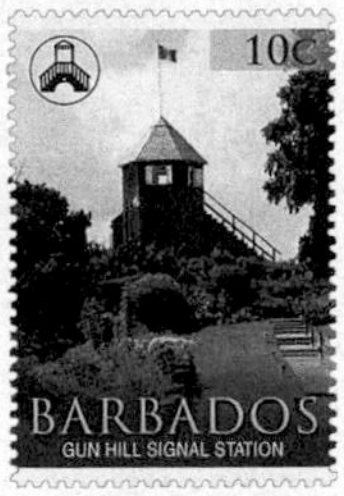

Bridgetown Landmarks A220

Designs: 10c, Gun Hill Signal Station. 65c, Clock tower, Main Guardhouse, Bridgetown Garrison. $2, St. Mary's Church, horiz. $2.75, Public Library, horiz.

2012, July 18 *Perf. 14*

1200-1203 A220 Set of 4 5.50 5.50

National Trust, 50th anniv.

Bridgetown Port, 50th Anniv. (in 2011) — A221

Designs: 10c, Pelican Island. 65c, Lightermen delivering cargo. $1.75, Tugboat Barbados II. $2.80, Aerial view of Bridgetown Port.

2012, Oct. 1

1204-1207 A221 Set of 4 5.50 5.50

Lighthouses A222

Designs: 65c, Harrison Point Lighthouse. $1.50, South Point Lighthouse. $1.80, Needham's Point Lighthouse. $2.20, East Point Lighthouse.

2013, June 13

1208-1211 A222 Set of 4 6.25 6.25

Churches A223

Designs: 10c, Holetown Methodist Church. 65c, Mt. Tabor Moravian Church. $1.80, St. Patrick's Roman Catholic Church. $3, St. John's Anglican Church.

Wmk. 406

2013, Sept. 30 Litho. *Perf. 13¼*

1212-1215 A223 Set of 4 5.75 5.75

Seven Wonders of Barbados — A224

Designs: No. 1216, 65c, Morgan Lewis Windmill. No. 1217, 65c, St. Nicholas Abbey. No. 1218, 65c, Dry Dock, horiz. No. 1219, 65c, Music Rocks, horiz. No. 1220, 65c, Cove Bay, horiz. No. 1221, 65c, Harrison's Cave, horiz. No. 1222, 65c, Lion of Gun Hill, yellow frame, horiz. No. 1223a, Like No. 1222, pale green frame (48x48mm).

Wmk. 406

2014, Feb. 21 Litho. *Perf. 13¼*

1216-1222 A224 Set of 7 4.75 4.75

Miniature Sheet

1223 Sheet of 7, #1216-1221, 1223a 4.75 4.75

a. A224 65c multi .65 .65

Barbados Parliament, 375th Anniv. A225

Designs: 10c, Bust of Sir Conrad Reeves (1821-1902), Chief Justice of Barbados. 65c, Speaker's chair. $1.40, Sir Kenmore Husbands (1905-91), House of Assembly Speaker. $2, House of Assembly stained-glass window depicting King Charles I.

$5, Mace.

Wmk. 406

2014, June 26 Litho. *Perf. 13¾*

1224-1227 A225 Set of 4 4.25 4.25

Souvenir Sheet

1228 A225 $5 multi 5.00 5.00

Panama Canal, Cent. — A226

Designs: 10c, SS Ancon arrives at Cristobal, 1909. 65c, Track shifting gang, 1911, horiz. $1, Rock slide at Gold Hill, 1911, horiz. $2, Workers moving building, 1914, horiz. $3, Floor slab on rock, 1915, horiz.

Wmk. 406

2014, Aug. 15 Litho. *Perf. 14*

1229-1233 A226 Set of 5 6.75 6.75

University of West Indies Branch at Cave Hill, Barbados, 50th Anniv. A227

Designs: 10c, Clock Tower. 65c, Student receiving scroll. $1.40, Golden Stool. $2.50, Standard bearer.

Wmk. 406

2014, Sept. 15 Litho. *Perf. 14*

1234-1237 A227 Set of 4 4.75 4.75

A228

Gardens — A229

Designs: 10c, Gardenia Gardens. 65c, Hunte's Garden. $1.80, Glendale Gardens. $2.20, Eusteen's Gardens.

No. 1242: Various arrangements, as shown.

Perf. 12½x13¼

2014, Dec. 18 Litho. Wmk. 406

1238-1241 A228 Set of 4 4.75 4.75

Miniature Sheet

Perf. 13¼

1242 A229 $1 Sheet of 4, #a-d 4.00 4.00

Windmills — A230

Designs: 10c, Graeme Hall Windmill. 65c, Balls Windmill. $2.20, St. Nicholas Abbey Windmill. $2.50, Morgan Lewis Windmill.

Wmk. 406

2015, June 23 Litho. *Perf. 14*

1243-1246 A230 Set of 4 5.50 5.50

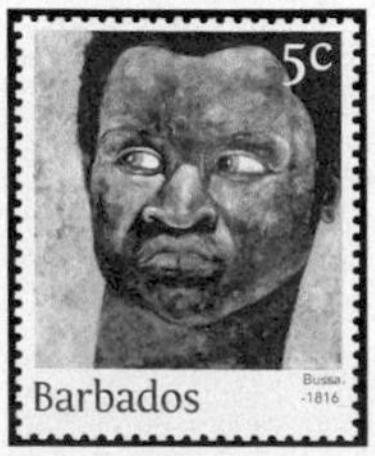

Famous Barbadians A231

Designs: 5c, Bussa (d. 1816), leader of slave rebellion. 10c, Sir Grantley Adams (1898-1971), first Premier of Barbados. 25c, Sir Frank Walcott (1916-99), ambassador to the United Nations. 60c, Sir Hugh Springer

(1913-94), Governor-General. 65c, Daphne Joseph-Hackett (1915-88), actress. $1, Dr. Charles Duncan O'Neal (1879-1936), physician, founder of Democratic League. $1.50, Samuel Jackman Prescod (1806-71), member of Parliament. $1.80, Clement Osbourne Payne (1904-41), trade union leader. $2, Arlington DaCosta Edwards (1933-96), governmental minister, educator. $2.20, Sarah Ann Gill (1795-1866), anti-slavery religious leader. $2.50, Eunice Gibson (1895-1974), founder of Barbados Registered Nurses Association. $3, Errol Walton Barrow (1920-87), first Prime Minister of Barbados. $5, James Arthur Tudor (1892-1985), business leader and politician. $10, Sir Garfield Sobers, cricket player.

Wmk. 406

2016, Jan. 18 Litho. *Perf. 12½*

1247	A231	5c multi	.25	.25
1248	A231	10c multi	.25	.25
1249	A231	25c multi	.25	.25
1250	A231	60c multi	.60	.60
1251	A231	65c multi	.65	.65
1252	A231	$1 multi	1.00	1.00
1253	A231	$1.50 multi	1.50	1.50
1254	A231	$1.80 multi	1.80	1.80
1255	A231	$2 multi	2.00	2.00
1256	A231	$2.20 multi	2.20	2.20
1257	A231	$2.50 multi	2.50	2.50
1258	A231	$3 multi	3.00	3.00
1259	A231	$5 multi	5.00	5.00
1260	A231	$10 multi	10.00	10.00
		Nos. 1247-1260 (14)	31.00	31.00

Landships A232

Designs: 10c, Landship Tuk band, 1970s. 65c, Maypole. $1.80, Landship performance at Crop Over Heritage Gala, 2009. $2.20, Commander Leon Marshall (1906-73).
$5, Lord High Commander Vernon Nathaniel Watson, vert.

Wmk. 406

2016, Aug. 17 Litho. *Perf. 14*
1261-1264 A232 Set of 4 4.75 4.75

Souvenir Sheet

1265 A232 $5 multi 5.00 5.00

Independence, 50th Anniv. — A233

Designs: 10c, Bus. 65c, Samuel Jackman Prescod Polytechnic. $1, Pine Hill Dairy. $1.50, Blenheim Cricket Ground. $1.80, Barbados blackbelly sheep. $2.20, Hilton Barbados Resort.
$8, Prime Minister Errol Walton Barrow on Independence Night, 1966, vert.

Wmk. 406

2016, Nov. 18 Litho. *Perf. 14*
1266-1271 A233 Set of 6 7.25 7.25

Souvenir Sheet

1272 A233 $8 multi 8.00 8.00

Centenarians of Barbados — A234

Designs: No. 1273, 65c, Rev. C. Vincent S. Belle (1915-2016). No. 1274, 65c, Vivian Ursula Blenman (1913-2014). No. 1275, 65c, Beatrice Gertrude Carrington (1912-2012). No. 1276, 65c, Winston Cameron Catline (1915-2015). No. 1277, 65c, Olive Augusta Licorish (1914-2015). No. 1278, 65c, Alma Geraldine Rae (1911-2014). No. 1279, 65c, Rose Adeline Wiltshire (1914-2015). No. 1280, 65c, Aldora Odessa Yearwood (1915-2015). No. 1281, 65c, Francis Medford Clarke. No. 1282, 65c, Vera Elaine Gibbs. No. 1283, 65c, Doris Elese Greaves. No. 1284, 65c, Iona Viola Griffith. No. 1285, 65c, Helen Lizetta Hutchinson. No. 1286, 65c, Constance L. Inniss. No. 1287, 65c, Christopher McDonald Smith. No. 1288, 65c, Rupert Sydney Springer. No. 1289, 65c, Carlotta Elise Strickland. No. 1290, 65c, Alicia Waithe. No. 1291, 65c, Elaine Ometa Walkes. No. 1292, 65c, Edithe Vimetta St. Clair Wilkinson.
No. 1293: a, James Emmanuel Sisnett (1900-2013). b, Emily Clarke (1902-2013). c, Marie Millicent Trotman (1905-2013). d, Millicent Alberta Yearwood. e, Melville Williams. f, Eleise Hortense Rock. g, Sylvia Maughan.

Wmk. 406

2016, Dec. 8 Litho. *Perf. 14*
1273-1292 A234 Set of 20 13.00 13.00

Miniature Sheet

1293 A234 65c Sheet of 7, #a-g, + 2 labels 4.75 4.75

No. 1293b is not inscribed with country name.

Motor Sports A235

Cars, checkered flag and inscriptions: 10c, Triumph TR4, June Rally, 1970. 65c, Mitsubishi Shogun, Mud Dogs, 2011. $1.80, Toyota Starlet, Sprint Event, 1988. $2.20, Subaru Impreza, Sol Rally, 2012.
No. 1298 — Cars, checkered flag and inscriptions: a, Williams Digicel International Race meet, 2011. b, Radical SR3S. c, Big saloons leave the line. d, Bushy Park start, 1994. e, Karting.

Wmk. 406

2017, June 12 Litho. *Perf. 12¾*
1294-1297 A235 Set of 4 4.75 4.75

Miniature Sheet

1298 A235 $1 Sheet of 5, #a-e 5.00 5.00

Renewable Energy — A236

Designs: 10c, Barbados Light & Power Mega Solar Farm. 65c, Solar commercial water heaters on building. $1.80, Bagasse at Portvale Sugar Factory. $2.20, Solar photovoltaic cells on car port roof.

Wmk. 406

2017, Nov. 6 Litho. *Perf. 12¾*
1299-1302 A236 Set of 4 4.75 4.75

Wedding of Prince Harry and Meghan Markle — A237

Designs: 10c, Couple holding hands. 65c, Couple and Archbishop of Canterbury, vert. $1.40, Couple, vert. $2.20, Couple waving.
No. 1307: a, Couple in coach, vert. b, Like 65c. c, Like $1.40.

Wmk. 406

2018, Nov. 21 Litho. *Perf. 13¼*
1303-1306 A237 Set of 4 4.50 4.50

Souvenir Sheet

1307 A237 $3 Sheet of 3, #a-c 9.00 9.00

Royal Commonwealth Society, 150th Anniv. — A238

Designs: 10c, Multi-faith Observance Day service. 65c, Queen's Commonwealth Canopy. $1.40, Christmas in the Square. $2.20, Queen's Commonwealth Essay Competition.
$5, Christmas in the Square, diff.

Perf. 13¼x13

2018, Dec. 20 Litho. Unwmk.
1308-1311 A238 Set of 4 4.50 4.50

Souvenir Sheet

1312 A238 $5 multi 5.00 5.00

Chattel Houses A239

Various chattel houses with denominations the same height as country name: 10c, 65c, $1.80, $2.20.

Perf. 13¼x13

2019, July 16 Litho. Unwmk.
1313-1316 A239 Set of 4 4.75 4.75

Compare with type A158.

SEMI-POSTAL STAMPS

No. 73 Surcharged in Red

Perf. 14

1907, Jan. 25 Typo. Wmk. 2

B1	A8	1p on 2p sl & org	7.00	*13.00*
a.		No period after 1d	70.00	*110.00*
b.		Inverted surcharge	2.00	*7.50*
c.		Inverted surcharge, no period after 1d	47.50	*105.00*
d.		Double surcharge	925.00	*1,000.*
e.		Dbl. surch., both invtd.	925.00	
f.		Dbl. surch., one invtd.	*1,200.*	
g.		Vert. pair, one normal, one surcharge double		*1,200.*
h.		Pair with surcharges tête-bêche	1,800.	

Catalogue values for unused stamps in this section, from this point to the end of the section, are for Never Hinged items.

No. 406 Surcharged

1979, May 29 Photo. Wmk. 314
B2 A56 28c + 4c on 35c multi .70 .70

The surtax was for victims of the eruption of Mt. Soufrière.

POSTAGE DUE STAMPS

Catalogue values for unused stamps in this section are for Never Hinged items.

D1

1934-47 Typo. Wmk. 4 *Perf. 14*

J1	D1	½p green ('35)	1.60	10.00
J2	D1	1p black	2.25	1.75
a.		Half used as ½p on cover		*2,500.*
J3	D1	3p dk car rose ('47)	26.00	24.00
		Nos. J1-J3 (3)	29.85	35.75

A 2nd die of the 1p was introduced in 1947.
Use of #J2a was authorized from Mar. 1934 through Feb. 1935. Some examples have "½d" written on the bisect in black or red ink.

1950

J4	D1	1c green	.30	*3.00*
J5	D1	2c black	1.00	*6.50*
J6	D1	6c carmine rose	1.00	*8.50*
		Nos. J4-J6 (3)	2.30	*18.00*

Values are for 1953 chalky paper printing. Values on ordinary paper, unused $35, used $87.50.

Wmk. 4a (error)

J4a	D1	1c green	450.00	*650.00*
J5a	D1	2c black	800.00	
J6a	D1	6c carmine rose	180.00	
		Nos. J4a-J6a (3)	1,430.	

1965, Aug. 3 Wmk. 314 *Perf. 14*

J7	D1	1c groon	.50	*4.50*
J8	D1	2c black	.60	*5.50*
J9	D1	6c carmine rose	1.50	*13.00*
a.		Wmk. sideways, perf 14x13½	10.50	*20.00*
		Nos. J7-J9 (3)	2.60	*23.00*

Issued: No. J9a, 2/4/74.

Wmk. 314 Sideways

1974, Dec. 4 *Perf. 13x13½*

J8b	D1	2c	8.00	*20.00*
J9b	D1	6c	8.00	*20.00*

D2

Designs: Each stamp shows different stylized flower in background.

Perf. 13½x14

1976, May 12 Litho. Wmk. 373

J10	D2	1c brt pink & mag	.35	.80
J11	D2	2c lt & dk vio blue	.35	.80
J12	D2	5c yellow & brown	.35	.80
J13	D2	10c lilac & purple	.45	1.05
J14	D2	25c yel green & dk grn	1.10	3.00
J15	D2	$1 rose & red	1.10	3.00
		Nos. J10-J15 (6)	3.70	9.45

1985, July *Perf. 15x14*

J10a	D2	1c	.50	.50
J11a	D2	2c	.50	.50
J12a	D2	5c	.50	.50
J13a	D2	10c	.50	.50
J14a	D2	25c	.50	.50
		Nos. J10a-J14a (5)	2.50	2.50

WAR TAX STAMP

No. 118 Overprinted

1917 Wmk. 3 *Perf. 14*

MR1	A12	1p carmine	.55	.25
a.		Imperf., pair	*2,500.*	

BARBUDA

bär-'büd-ə

LOCATION — In northern Leeward Islands, West Indies
GOVT. — Dependency of Antigua
AREA — 63 sq. mi.
POP. — 1,500 (1995 est.)
See Antigua.

12 Pence = 1 Shilling
100 Cents = 1 Dollar (1951)

Catalogue values for unused stamps in this country are for Never Hinged items, beginning with Scott 12 in the regular postage section, and Scott B1 in the semi-postal section.

Watermark

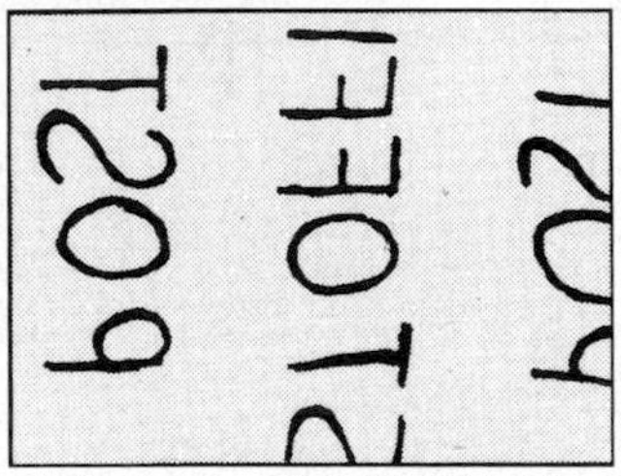

Wmk. 380 — "POST OFFICE"

Leeward Islands Stamps of 1912-22 Ovptd. in Black or Red

Die II

For description of dies I and II, see Dies of British Colonial Stamps in the catalogue introduction.

1922, July 13 Wmk. 4 *Perf. 14*

1	A5	½p	green	1.75	*13.50*
2	A5	1p	rose red	1.75	*13.50*
3	A5	2p	gray	1.75	*7.50*
4	A5	2½p	ultramarine	1.75	*9.00*
5	A5	6p	vio & red vio	2.25	*19.00*
6	A5	2sh	vio & ultra, *bl*	16.00	*55.00*
7	A5	3sh	green & violet	37.50	*82.50*
8	A5	4sh	blk & scar (R)	47.50	*82.50*

Wmk. 3

9	A5	3p	violet, *yel*	2.00	*17.00*
10	A5	1sh	blk, *emer* (R)	1.75	*9.00*
11	A5	5sh	grn & red, *yel*	65.00	*135.00*
			Nos. 1-11 (11)	179.00	*443.50*
			Set, never hinged	300.00	

Beware of forgeries, especially used examples dated June 1, 1923.

Catalogue values for unused stamps in this section, from this point to the end of the section, are for Never Hinged items.

Map — B1

Fish — B2

20c, Great barracuda. 25c, Great amberjack. 35c, French angelfish. 50c, Porkfish. 75c, Striped parrotfish. $1, Long-spine squirrelfish. $2.50, Catalufa. $5, Blue chromis.

1968-70 Litho. Unwmk. *Perf. 14*

12	B1	½c	blk, salmon pink & red brn	.45	*2.75*
13	B1	1c	blk, org & brt org	1.25	.30
14	B1	2c	blk, brt pink & brt rose	1.60	1.25
15	B1	3c	blk, yel & org yel	1.40	.40
16	B1	4c	blk, lt grn & brt grn	2.00	*2.75*
17	B1	5c	blk, bl grn & brt bl grn	1.60	.25
18	B1	6c	blk, lt lil & red lil	1.00	*2.25*
19	B1	10c	blk, lt bl & dk bl	1.40	*1.00*
20	B1	15c	blk, dl grn & grn	1.60	*3.00*
21	B2	20c	multicolored	1.40	*1.40*
22	B2	25c	multicolored	1.10	.30
23	B2	35c	multicolored	1.40	.35
24	B2	50c	multicolored	.70	.55
25	B2	75c	multicolored	.70	.60
26	B2	$1	multicolored	.60	*1.10*
27	B2	$2.50	multicolored	1.00	*.75*
28	B2	$5	multicolored	1.25	*1.60*
			Nos. 12-28 (17)	20.45	20.60

Issued: ½c-15c, 11/19/68; 20c, 7/22/70; 25c-75c, 2/5/69; others, 3/6/69.
For surcharge see No. 80.

1968 Summer Olympics, Mexico City — B3

Designs: 25c, Running, Aztec calendar stone. 35c, High jumping, Aztec statue. 75c, Yachting, Aztec lion mask. $1, Soccer, Aztec carved stone.

1968, Dec. 20

29	B3	25c	multicolored	.40	.25
30	B3	35c	multicolored	.50	.30
31	B3	75c	multicolored	.85	.45
			Nos. 29-31 (3)	1.75	1.00

Souvenir Sheet

32	B3	$1	multicolored	3.00	*3.75*

The Ascension, by Orcagna — B4

1969, Mar. 24

33	B4	25c	blue & black	.25	*.45*
34	B4	35c	dp carmine & blk	.25	*.50*
35	B4	75c	violet & black	.25	*.55*
			Nos. 33-35 (3)	.75	1.50

Easter.

3rd Caribbean Boy Scout Jamboree — B5

1969, Aug. 7

36	B5	25c	Flag ceremony	.50	*.55*
37	B5	35c	Campfire	.60	*.70*
38	B5	75c	Rowing	.80	*.95*
			Nos. 36-38 (3)	1.90	2.20

The Sistine Madonna, by Raphael — B6

1969, Oct. 20

39	B6	½c	multicolored	.25	*.30*
40	B6	25c	multicolored	.25	.25
41	B6	35c	multicolored	.25	.25
42	B6	75c	multicolored	.25	*.40*
			Nos. 39-42 (4)	1.00	1.20

Christmas.

English Monarchs — B7

No. 43, William I. No. 44, William II. No. 45, Henry I. No. 46, Stephen. No. 47, Henry II. No. 48, Richard I. No. 49, John. No. 50, Henry III. No. 51, Edward I. No. 52, Edward II. No. 53, Edward III. No. 54, Richard II. No. 55, Henry IV. No. 56, Henry V. No. 57, Henry VI. No. 58, Edward IV. No. 59, Edward V. No. 60, Richard III. No. 61, Henry VII. No. 62, Henry VIII. No. 63, Edward VI. No. 64, Lady Jane Grey. No. 65, Mary I. No. 66, Elizabeth I. No. 67, James I. No. 68, Charles I. No. 69, Charles II. No. 70, James II. No. 71, William III. No. 72, Mary II. No. 73, Anne. No. 74, George I. No. 75, George II. No. 76, George III. No. 77, George IV. No. 78, William IV. No. 79, Victoria.

1970-71 *Perf. 14½x14*

43-79	B7	35c	Set of 37	8.00	*13.00*

Issued: 1970, No. 43, 2/16; No. 44, 3/2; No. 45, 3/16; No. 46, 4/4; No. 47, 4/15; No. 48, 5/1; No. 49, 5/15; No. 50, 6/1; No. 51, 6/15; No. 52, 7/1; No. 53, 7/15; No. 54, 8/1; No. 55, 8/15; No. 56, 9/1; No. 57, 9/15; No. 58, 10/1; No. 59, 10/15; No. 60, 11/2; No. 61, 11/16; No. 62, 12/1; No. 63, 12/15.

1971; No. 64, 1/2; No. 65, 1/15; No. 66, 2/1; No. 67, 2/15; No. 68, 3/1; No. 69, 3/15; No. 70, 4/1; No. 71, 4/15; No. 72, 5/1; No. 73, 5/15; No. 74, 6/1; No. 75, 6/15; No. 76, 7/1; No. 77, 7/15; No. 78, 8/2; No. 79, 8/16.

See Nos. 622-627 for other Monarchs.

No. 12 Surcharged

1970, Feb. 26 *Perf. 14*

80	B1	20c	on 1/2c multicolored	.40	.40

Easter — B8

1970, Mar. 16

81	B8	25c	Carrying Cross	.25	.30
82	B8	35c	Descent from cross	.25	.30
83	B8	75c	Crucifixion	.25	.35
a.			Strip of 3, #81-83	.70	.70

Charles Dickens B9

1970, July 10

84	B9	20c	Oliver Twist	.30	.30
85	B9	75c	Old Curiosity Shop	.65	.65

Christmas — B10

Designs: 20c, Madonna of the Meadow, by Giovanni Bellini. 50c, Madonna, Child and Angels from Wilton Diptych. 75c, Nativity, by Piero della Francesca.

1970, Oct. 15

86	B10	20c	multicolored	.25	.25
87	B10	50c	multicolored	.25	.30
88	B10	75c	multicolored	.25	.35
			Nos. 86-88 (3)	.75	.90

British Red Cross, Cent. B11

20c, Patient in wheelchair, vert. 75c, Child care.

1970, Dec. 21

89	B11	20c	multicolored	.25	*.40*
90	B11	35c	shown	.25	*.50*
91	B11	75c	multicolored	.40	*.85*
			Nos. 89-91 (3)	.90	*1.75*

Easter — B12

Details from the Mond Crucifixion, by Raphael.

1971, Apr. 7

92	B12	35c	Angel	.25	*.95*
93	B12	50c	Crucifixion	.25	*1.10*
94	B12	75c	Angel, diff.	.30	*1.25*
a.			Strip of 3, #92-94	.85	*3.50*

Martello Tower B13

25c, Sailboats. 50c, Hotel bungalows. 75c, Government House, mystery stone.

1971, May 10

95	B13	20c	shown	.25	*.40*
96	B13	25c	multicolored	.25	*.45*
97	B13	50c	multicolored	.25	*.50*
98	B13	75c	multicolored	.40	*.70*
			Nos. 95-98 (4)	1.15	*2.05*

Christmas — B14

Paintings: ½c, The Granduca Madonna, by Raphael. 35c, The Ansidei Madonna, by Raphael. 50c, The Virgin and Child, by Botticelli. 75c, The Madonna of the Trees, by Bellini.

1971, Oct. 4

99	B14	½c multicolored	.25	.25
100	B14	35c multicolored	.25	.25
101	B14	50c multicolored	.25	*.25*
102	B14	75c multicolored	.25	*.30*
		Nos. 99-102 (4)	1.00	1.05

A set of four stamps for Durer (20c, 35c, 50c, 75c) was not authorized. Value $12.

All stamps are types of Antigua or overprinted on stamps of Antigua unless otherwise specified. Many of the "BARBUDA" overprints are vertical.

Antigua Nos. 321-322 (Wedding of Princess Anne and Mark Phillips) Ovptd. "BARBUDA"

1973, Nov. 14 ***Perf. 13½***

103	A65	35c multicolored	6.00	5.00
104	A65	$2 multicolored	1.50	2.00

Antigua Nos. 313-315a (Butterfly costumes) Ovptd. in Red "BARBUDA"

1973, Nov. 26 ***Perf. 13½x14***

105	A63	20c multicolored	.25	.25
106	A63	35c multicolored	.50	*.60*
107	A63	75c multicolored	.85	.85
		Nos. 105-107 (3)	1.60	1.70

Souvenir Sheet

108		Sheet of 4, #105-107, 108a	1.75	*2.50*
a.		A63 5c multicolored		

Carnival, 1973.

Antigua Nos. 307, 309, 311, 311a (Uniforms) Ovptd. "BARBUDA"

Perf. 14x13½

1973, Nov. 26 **Wmk. 314**

109	A53	½c multicolored	.25	.25
110	A53	20c multicolored	.25	.25
111	A53	75c multicolored	.55	.35
		Nos. 109-111 (3)	1.05	.85

Souvenir Sheet

112		Sheet of 5, #109-111, 112a-112b + label	3.50	3.50
a.		A53 10c multicolored		
b.		A53 35c multicolored		

Antigua Nos. 241a, 242-243, 244a, 245-248, 249a, 250-254, 255a, 256, 256a, 257 Ovptd. "BARBUDA"

Wmk. 314 Sideways, Upright

1973-74 ***Perf. 14***

113	A51	½c multicolored	.30	*.45*
114	A51	1c multicolored	.30	*.45*
115	A51	2c multicolored	.45	*.50*
116	A51	3c multicolored	.45	.45
117	A51	4c multicolored	.60	.50
118	A51	5c multicolored	.80	.80
119	A51	6c multicolored	.80	.80
120	A51	10c multicolored	1.00	*1.00*
121	A51	15c multicolored	1.00	*1.00*
122	A51	20c multicolored	1.00	*1.20*
123	A51	25c multicolored	1.00	*1.20*
124	A51	35c multicolored	1.00	*1.20*
125	A51	50c multicolored	1.00	*1.20*
126	A51	75c multicolored	1.00	*1.20*
127	A51	$1 multicolored	1.00	*1.20*
128	A51	$2.50 multicolored	2.40	*4.25*
a.		Wmk. upright	8.50	9.25
129	A51	$5 multicolored	3.00	*5.50*
		Nos. 113-129 (17)	17.10	*22.90*

Issue dates: ½c, 3c, 15c, $1, $2.50, Feb. 18, 1974. Others, Nov. 26.

Antigua Nos. 316-320a (Christmas) Ovptd. in Silver or Red "BARBUDA"

Perf. 14½

1973, Dec. 11 **Photo.** **Unwmk.**

130	A64	3c multicolored	.25	.25
131	A64	5c multicolored	.25	.25
132	A64	20c multicolored	.25	.25
133	A64	35c multicolored (R)	.25	.25
134	A64	$1 multicolored (R)	.25	.25
		Nos. 130-134 (5)	1.25	1.25

Souvenir Sheet

135		Sheet of 5 + label	5.00	*7.00*
a.		A64 35c multicolored (S)		
b.		A64 $1 multicolored (S)		

No. 135 contains Nos. 130-132, 135a-135b.

Antigua Nos. 323-324a (Visit of Princess Anne and Mark Phillips to Antigua) Ovptd. "BARBUDA"

1973, Dec. 16 **Litho.** ***Perf. 13½***

136	A65	35c multicolored	.25	.25
137	A65	$2 multicolored	1.25	1.25
a.		Souvenir sheet of 2, #136-137	6.00	*7.00*

Antigua Nos. 325-328 (University of West Indies) Ovptd. "BARBUDA"

1974, Feb. 18 **Wmk. 314**

138	A66	5c multicolored	.25	.25
139	A66	20c multicolored	.25	.25
140	A66	35c multicolored	.25	.25
141	A66	75c multicolored	.25	.25
		Nos. 138-141 (4)	1.00	1.00

Antigua Nos. 329-333 (Uniforms) Ovptd. "BARBUDA"

1974, May 1 ***Perf. 14x13½***

142	A53	½c multicolored	.25	.25
143	A53	10c multicolored	.25	.25
144	A53	20c multicolored	.25	.25
145	A53	35c multicolored	.35	.25
146	A53	75c multicolored	.50	*.40*
		Nos. 142-146 (5)	1.60	1.40

No. 333a exists with overprint.

Antigua Nos. 334-340 Ovptd. Type "a" or "b" in Red

a & b

1974, July 15 **Unwmk.** ***Perf. 14½***

Se-tenant Pairs Overprinted Type "a" on Left Stamp, Type "b" on Right Stamp

148	A67	½c multicolored	.25	.25
149	A67	1c multicolored	.25	.25
150	A67	2c multicolored	.40	.25
151	A67	5c multicolored	1.00	.50
152	A67	20c multicolored	.95	*1.50*
153	A67	35c multicolored	3.00	*4.50*
154	A67	$1 multicolored	6.50	*12.00*
		Nos. 148-154 (7)	12.35	*19.25*

Souvenir Sheet

Perf. 13

155		Sheet of 7 + label	7.50	*11.50*
a.		A67 ½c multicolored	.25	*.35*
b.		A67 1c multicolored	.25	*.35*
c.		A67 2c multicolored	.25	*.35*
d.		A67 5c multicolored	.25	*.35*
e.		A67 20c multicolored	1.00	*1.60*
f.		A67 35c multicolored	1.25	*3.25*
g.		A67 $1 multicolored	4.00	*4.75*

UPU, cent.

Antigua Nos. 341-344a (Steel bands - Carnival 1974) Ovptd. "BARBUDA"

1974, Aug. 14 **Wmk. 314** ***Perf. 14***

156	A68	5c multicolored	.25	.25
157	A68	20c multicolored	.25	.25
158	A68	35c multicolored	.25	.25
159	A68	75c multicolored	.25	.25
a.		Souvenir sheet of 4, #156-159	1.00	1.00
		Nos. 156-159 (4)	1.00	1.00

Antigua Nos. 345-348a Overprinted

and

World Cup Soccer Championships — B16

Various soccer plays.

1974, Sept. 2 **Unwmk.** ***Perf. 15, 14***

160	A69	5c multicolored	.25	.25
161	A69	35c multicolored	.25	.25
162	B16	35c multicolored	.25	.25
163	A69	75c multicolored	.25	.25
164	A69	$1 multicolored	.25	.25
a.		Souv. sheet of 4, #160-161, 163-164 + 2 labels, perf. 13½	1.25	1.25
165	B16	$1.20 multicolored	.40	.40
166	B16	$2.50 multicolored	.60	.70
a.		Souv. sheet of 3, #162, 165-166	1.40	1.40
		Nos. 160-166 (7)	2.25	2.35

UPU, Cent. — B17

1974, Sept. 30 ***Perf. 14x13½***

167	B17	35c Ship letter, 1833	.25	.25
168	B17	$1.20 #1, 2 on FDC	.25	.30
169	B17	$2.50 Airplane, map	.40	.50
a.		Souvenir sheet of 3, #167-169	1.90	1.90
		Nos. 167-169 (3)	.90	1.05

Greater Amberjack B18

½c, Oleander, rose bay. 1c, Blue petrea. 2c, Poinsettia. 3c, Cassia tree. 5c, Holy Trinity School. 6c, Snorkeling. 10c, Pilgrim Holiness Church. 15c, New Cottage Hospital. 20c, Post Office & Treasury. 25c, Island jetty & boats. 35c, Martello Tower. 50c, Warden's House. 75c, Inter-island air service. $1, Tortoise. $2.50, Spiny lobster. $5, Frigate birds. $10, Hibiscus.

1974-75 ***Perf. 14x14½, 14½x14***

170	B18	½c multi	.25	*.50*
171	B18	1c multi	.30	*.50*
172	B18	2c multi	.30	*.50*
173	B18	3c multi	.30	*.50*
174	B18	4c shown	2.75	.50
175	B18	5c multi	.35	.25
176	B18	6c multi	.35	*.50*
177	B18	10c multi	.35	.30
178	B18	15c multi	.35	.30
179	B18	20c multi	.35	.30
180	B18	25c multi	.70	.55
181	B18	35c multi	.70	.55

Size: 39x25mm

Perf. 14

182	B18	50c multi	.70	.55
183	B18	75c multi	2.25	1.75
184	B18	$1 multi	1.50	1.40

Size: 45x29mm

Perf. 13½x14

185	B18	$2.50 multi	1.75	*3.50*
186	B18	$5 multi	6.25	5.50
a.		Perf. 14x15	13.50	17.50

Size: 34x47mm

187	B18	$10 multi	4.00	*6.75*
		Nos. 170-187 (18)	23.50	*24.70*

Nos. 170-173, 180, 187 vert.

Issued: 4c, 5c, 6c, 10c, 15c, 20c, 25c, 35c, 75c, 10/15/74; ½c, 1c, 2c, 3c, 50c, $1, $2.50, No. 186, 1/6/75; No. 186a, 7/24/75; $10, 9/19/75.

For overprints see Nos. 213-214.

Antigua Nos. 349-352a Ovptd. in Red

and

Winston Churchill, Birth Cent. — B19

1974 ***Perf. 14½, 13½x14***

188	A70	5c multicolored	.25	.25
189	B19	5c Making broadcast	.25	.25
190	A70	35c multicolored	.30	.25
191	B19	35c Portrait	.25	.25
192	A70	75c multicolored	.50	.50
193	B19	75c Painting	.25	.25
194	A70	$1 multicolored	.85	.80
a.		Souv. sheet of 4, #188, 190, 192, 194	10.50	*20.00*
195	B19	$1 Victory sign	.35	.30
a.		Souv. sheet of 4, #189, 191, 193, 195	1.50	2.00
		Nos. 188-195 (8)	3.00	2.85

Issue dates: Nos. 188, 190, 192, 194, Oct. 15, others, Nov. 20. For overprints see Nos. 213-214.

Antigua Nos. 353-360a (Christmas paintings) Ovptd. "BARBUDA"

1974, Nov. 25 ***Perf. 14½***

196	A71	½c multicolored	.25	.25
197	A71	1c multicolored	.25	.25
198	A71	2c multicolored	.25	.25
199	A71	3c multicolored	.25	.25
200	A71	5c multicolored	.25	.25
201	A71	20c multicolored	.25	.25
202	A71	35c multicolored	.25	.25
203	A71	75c multicolored	.25	.25
a.		Souv. sheet, #200-203, perf 13½	1.10	*1.40*
		Nos. 196-203 (8)	2.00	2.00

Antigua Nos. 369-373a (Nelson's Dockyard) Ovptd. "BARBUDA"

1975, Mar. 17

204	A72	5c multicolored	.25	.25
205	A72	15c multicolored	.45	.35
206	A72	35c multicolored	.55	.45
207	A72	50c multicolored	.65	.65
208	A72	$1 multicolored	.75	.75
a.		Souv. sheet of 5, #204-208 + label, perf. 13½x14	3.00	*4.25*
		Nos. 204-208 (5)	2.65	2.45

Stamps from No. 208a are 43x28mm.

Battle of the Saints B20

1975, May 30 ***Perf. 13½x14***

209	B20	35c shown	.75	.75
210	B20	50c Two ships	1.00	1.00
211	B20	75c Ships firing	1.25	1.25
212	B20	95c Sailors abandoning ship	1.50	1.50
		Nos. 209-212 (4)	4.50	4.50

Barbuda No. 186a Ovptd.

a

b 

1975, July 2 *Perf. 14x15*

213	B18 (a)	$5 multicolored	5.50	*6.50*
214	B18 (b)	$5 multicolored	5.50	*6.50*

Overprint "a" is in 1st and 3rd vertical rows, "b" 2nd and 4th. The 5th row has no overprint. This can be collected se-tenant either as Nos. 213, 214 or 213, 214 and 186a. Value, strip of three, $22.50.

Military Uniforms — B21

Designs: 35c, Officer of 65th Foot, 1763. 50c, Grenadier, 27th Foot, 1701-1710. 75c, Officer of 21st Foot, 1793-1796. 95c, Officer, Royal Regiment of Artillery, 1800.

1975, Sept. 17 *Perf. 14*

215	B21	35c multicolored	.50	.50
216	B21	50c multicolored	.75	.75
217	B21	75c multicolored	1.25	1.25
218	B21	95c multicolored	1.50	1.50
		Nos. 215-218 (4)	4.00	4.00

Barbuda Nos. 189, 191, 193, 195 Ovptd.

1975, Oct. 24 *Perf. 13½x14*

219	B19	5c multicolored	.25	.25
220	B19	35c multicolored	.25	.25
221	B19	75c multicolored	.25	.25
222	B19	$1 multicolored	.30	.25
		Nos. 219-222 (4)	1.05	1.00

Antigua Nos. 394-401a (Christmas) Ovptd. "BARBUDA"

1975, Nov. 17 *Perf. 14*

223	A77	½c multicolored	.25	.25
224	A77	1c multicolored	.25	.25
225	A77	2c multicolored	.25	.25
226	A77	3c multicolored	.25	.25
227	A77	5c multicolored	.25	.25
228	A77	10c multicolored	.25	.25
229	A77	35c multicolored	.25	.25
230	A77	$2 multicolored	.25	.25
a.		Souvenir sheet of 4, #227-230	2.00	2.25
		Nos. 223-230 (8)	2.00	2.00

Antigua Nos. 402-404 (World Cup Cricket) Ovptd. "BARBUDA"

1975, Dec. 15 *Perf. 14*

231	A78	5c multicolored	1.10	1.10
232	A78	35c multicolored	2.10	2.10
233	A78	$2 multicolored	3.75	3.75
		Nos. 231-233 (3)	6.95	6.95

American Revolution, Bicent. — B22

Details from Surrender of Cornwallis at Yorktown, by Trumbull: No. 234a, British officers. b, Gen. Benjamin Lincoln. c, Washington, Allied officers.

The Battle of Princeton: No. 235a, Infantry. b, Battle. c, Cannon fire.

Surrender of Burgoyne at Saratoga by Trumbull: No. 236a, Mounted officer. b, Washington, Burgoyne. c, American officers.

Signing the Declaration of Independence, by Trumbull: No. 237a, Delegates to Continental Congress. b, Adams, Sherman, Livingston, Jefferson and Franklin. c, Hancock, Thomson, Read, Dickinson, and Rutledge. Strips of 3 have continuous designs.

1976, Mar. 8 *Perf. 13½x13*

234	B22	15c Strip of 3, #a.-c.	.25	.25
235	B22	35c Strip of 3, #a.-c.	.80	.80
d.		Souvenir sheet, #234-235	1.20	1.20
236	B22	$1 Strip of 3, #a.-c.	1.00	1.00
237	B22	$2 Strip of 3, #a.-c.	1.75	1.75
d.		Souvenir sheet, #236-237	3.00	3.00

See Nos. 244-247.

Birds B23

35c, Bananaquits. 50c, Blue-hooded euphonia. 75c, Royal tern. 95c, Killdeer. $1.25, Glossy cowbird. $2, Purple gallinule.

1976, June 30 *Perf. 13½x14*

238	B23	35c multicolored	1.00	.65
239	B23	50c multicolored	1.00	.75
240	B23	75c multicolored	1.25	1.00
241	B23	95c multicolored	1.50	1.10
242	B23	$1.25 multicolored	1.50	1.10
243	B23	$2 multicolored	1.50	1.40
		Nos. 238-243 (6)	7.75	6.00

Barbuda #234-237 With Inscription Added at Top Across the Three Stamps in Blue

1976, Aug. 12 *Perf. 13½x14*

Size: 38x31mm

244	B22	15c Strip of 3, #a.-c.	.30	.30
245	B22	35c Strip of 3, #a.-c.	.50	.50
d.		Souvenir sheet of 2, #244-245	1.00	1.00
246	B22	$1 Strip of 3, #a.-c.	.75	.75
247	B22	$2 Strip of 3, #a.-c.	1.25	1.25
d.		Souvenir sheet, #246-247	2.75	2.75

Nos. 244-247 are perforated on outside edges; imperf. vertically within.

Antigua Nos. 448-452 (Christmas) Ovptd. "BARBUDA"

1976, Dec. 2 *Perf. 14*

248	A85	8c multicolored	.25	.25
249	A85	10c multicolored	.25	.25
250	A85	15c multicolored	.25	.25
251	A85	50c multicolored	.25	.25
252	A85	$1 multicolored	.25	.25
		Nos. 248-252 (5)	1.25	1.25

Antigua Nos. 431-437 (Olympic Games) Ovptd. "BARBUDA"

1976, Dec. 28 *Perf. 15*

253	A82	½c yellow & multi	.25	.25
254	A82	1c purple & multi	.25	.25
255	A82	2c emerald & multi	.25	.25
256	A82	15c brt blue & multi	.25	.25
257	A82	30c olive & multi	.25	.25
258	A82	$1 orange & multi	.25	.25
259	A82	$2 red & multi	.25	.25
a.		Souv. sheet, #256-259, perf 13½	2.25	2.25
		Nos. 253-259 (7)	1.75	1.75

Telephone, Cent. — B24

$1.25, Satellite dish, television. $2, Satellites in earth orbit.

1977, Jan. 31 *Perf. 14*

260	B24	75c shown	.25	*.25*
261	B24	$1.25 multicolored	.25	*.35*
262	B24	$2 multicolored	.50	*.60*
a.		Souv. sheet, #260-262, perf 15	1.25	*1.25*
		Nos. 260-262 (3)	1.00	*1.20*

Coronation of Queen Elizabeth II, 25th Anniv. — B25

Designs: Nos. 263a, St. Margaret's Church, Westminster. b, Westminster Abbey entrance. c, Westminster Abbey.

Nos. 264a, Riders on horseback. b, Coronation coach. c, Team of horses. Strips of 3 have continuous designs.

1977, Feb. 7 *Perf. 13½x13*

263	B25	75c Strip of 3, #a.-c.	.35	.35
264	B25	$1.25 Strip of 3, #a.-c.	.55	.55

Souvenir Sheet

265	B25	Sheet of 6	1.25	1.25

Nos. 263a-264c se-tenant with labels. No. 265 contains Nos. 263a-264c with silver borders.

Antigua Nos. 405-422 (1976 Definitives) Ovptd. "BARBUDA"

1977, Apr. 4 *Perf. 15*

266	A79	½c multicolored	.25	.25
267	A79	1c multicolored	.25	.25
268	A79	2c multicolored	.25	.25
269	A79	3c multicolored	.25	.25
270	A79	4c multicolored	.25	.25
271	A79	5c multicolored	.25	.25
272	A79	6c multicolored	.25	.25
273	A79	10c multicolored	.25	.25
274	A79	15c multicolored	.25	.25
275	A79	20c multicolored	.25	.25
276	A79	25c multicolored	.25	.25
277	A79	35c multicolored	.30	.25
278	A79	50c multicolored	.35	.35
279	A79	75c multicolored	.35	.35
280	A79	$1 multicolored	.65	.65

Perf. 13½x14

281	A80	$2.50 multicolored	1.80	2.10
282	A80	$5 multicolored	3.50	4.00
283	A80	$10 multicolored	6.75	7.75
		Nos. 266-283 (18)	16.45	18.20

For overprints see Nos. 506-516.

Antigua Nos. 459-464 (Royal Family) Ovptd. "BARBUDA"

1977, Apr. 4 *Perf. 13½x14, 12*

284	A87	10c multicolored	.25	.25
285	A87	30c multicolored	.25	.25
286	A87	50c multicolored	.25	.25
287	A87	90c multicolored	.25	.35
288	A87	$2.50 multicolored	.50	1.00
		Nos. 284-288 (5)	1.50	2.10

Souvenir Sheet

289	A87	$5 multicolored	1.50	1.50

A booklet of self-adhesive stamps contains one pane of six rouletted and die cut 50c stamps in design of 90c (silver overprint), and one pane of one die cut $5 (gold overprint) in changed colors. Panes have marginal inscriptions.

For overprints see Nos. 312-317.

Antigua Nos. 465-471a (Boy Scouts) Ovptd. "BARBUDA"

1977, June 13 *Perf. 14*

290	A88	½c multicolored	.25	.25
291	A88	1c multicolored	.25	.25
292	A88	2c multicolored	.25	.25
293	A88	10c multicolored	.25	.25
294	A88	30c multicolroed	.50	.50
295	A88	50c multicolored	.70	.70
296	A88	$2 multicolored	1.40	1.40
a.		Souvenir sheet of 3, #294-296	4.00	4.00
		Nos. 290-296 (7)	3.60	3.60

Overprint is slightly smaller on No. 296a.

Antigua Nos. 472-476a (Carnival) Ovptd. "BARBUDA"

1977, Aug. 12

297	A89	10c multicolored	.25	.25
298	A89	30c multicolored	.25	.25
299	A89	50c multicolored	.25	.25
300	A89	90c multicolored	.25	.25
301	A89	$1 multicolored	.25	.30
a.		Souvenir sheet of 4, #298-301	1.90	1.90
		Nos. 297-301 (5)	1.25	1.30

Royal Visit B26

50c, Royal yacht Britannia. $1.50, Jubliee emblem. $2.50, Flags.

1977, Oct. 27 *Perf. 14½*

302	B26	50c multicolored	.25	.25
303	B26	$1.50 multicolored	.25	.25
304	B26	$2.50 multicolored	.40	.50
a.		Souvenir sheet of 3, #302-304	1.50	1.50
		Nos. 302-304 (3)	.90	1.00

Antigua Nos. 483-489 (Christmas) Ovptd. "BARBUDA"

1977, Nov. 15 *Perf. 14*

305	A90	½c multicolored	.25	.25
306	A90	1c multicolored	.25	.25
307	A90	2c multicolored	.25	.25
308	A90	8c multicolored	.25	.25
309	A90	10c multicolored	.25	.25
310	A90	25c multicolored	.25	.25
311	A90	$2 multicolored	.25	.25
a.		Souvenir sheet of 4, #308-311	1.60	1.60
		Nos. 305-311 (7)	1.75	1.75

Antigua Nos. 477-482 (Royal Visit overprints) Ovptd. "BARBUDA" in Black

1977, Dec. 20 *Perf. 12*

312	A87	10c multicolored	.25	.25
313	A87	30c multicolored	.25	.25
314	A87	50c multicolored	.25	.25
315	A87	90c multicolored	.25	.25
316	A87	$2.50 multicolored	.40	.40
		Nos. 312-316 (5)	1.40	1.40

Nos. 312-316 exist with blue overprint.

1977, Nov. 28 *Perf. 13½x14*

312a	A87	10c multicolored	.25	.25
313a	A87	30c multicolored	.25	.25
314a	A87	50c multicolored	.25	.25
315a	A87	90c multicolored	.25	.25
316a	A87	$2.50 multicolored	.40	.40
		Nos. 312a-316a (5)	1.40	1.40

Souvenir Sheet

317	A87	$5 multicolored	1.75	1.75

Overprint of Nos. 312a-316a differs from that on Nos. 312-316.

Anniversaries — B27

First navigable airships, 75th anniv: No. 318a, Zeppelin LZ1. b, German Naval airship L31. c, Graf Zeppelin. d, Gondola on military airship.

Soviet space program, 20th anniv: No. 319a, Sputnik, 1957. b, Vostok rocket, 1961. c, Voskhod rocket, 1964. d, Space walk, 1965.

Lindbergh's Atlantic crossing, 50th anniv: No. 320a, Fueling for flight. b, New York take-off. c, Spirit of St. Louis. d, Welcome in England.

Coronation of Queen Elizabeth II, 25th anniv: No. 321a, Lion of England. b, Unicorn of Scotland. c, Yale of Beaufort. d, Falcon of Plantagenets.

Rubens, 400th birth anniv: No. 322a, Two lions. b, Daniel in the Lion's Den. c, Two lions lying down. d, Lion at Daniel's feet. Block of 4 has continuous design.

1977, Dec. 29 *Perf. 14½x14*

Blocks of 4

318	B27	75c #a.-d.	1.75	1.75
319	B27	95c #a.-d.	2.10	2.10
320	B27	$1.25 #a.-d.	2.40	2.40
321	B27	$2 #a.-d.	3.00	3.00
322	B27	$5 #a.-d.	3.00	*4.00*
e.		Min. sheet, #318-322 + 4 labels	11.00	*18.00*
		Nos. 318-322 (5)	12.25	*13.25*

Antigua Nos. 490-494a (10th Anniversary of Statehood) Ovptd. "BARBUDA"

1978, Feb. 15 *Perf. 13x13½*

323	A91	10c multicolored	.25	.25
324	A91	15c multicolored	.25	.25
325	A91	50c multicolored	1.25	.80
326	A91	90c multicolored	.40	.40
327	A91	$2 multicolored	.55	*.90*
a.		Souv. sheet, #324-327, perf 14	5.00	4.00
		Nos. 323-327 (5)	2.70	2.60

Pieta, by Michelangelo — B28

Works by Michelangelo: 95c, Holy Family. $1.25, Libyan Sibyl. $2, The Flood.

1978, Mar. 23 *Perf. 13½x14*

328	B28	75c multicolored	.25	.25
329	B28	95c multicolored	.25	.25
330	B28	$1.25 multicolored	.25	.25
331	B28	$2 multicolored	.25	.25
a.		Souvenir sheet of 4, #328-331	2.25	2.25
		Nos. 328-331 (4)	1.00	1.00

Antigua Nos. 495-502 (Wright Brothers) Ovptd. "BARBUDA"

1978, Mar. 23 *Perf. 14*

332	A92	½c multicolored	.25	.25
333	A92	1c multicolored	.25	.25
334	A92	2c multicolored	.25	.25
335	A92	10c multicolored	.25	.25
336	A92	50c multicolored	.35	.35
337	A92	90c multicolored	.45	.45
338	A92	$2 multicolored	1.10	1.10
		Nos. 332-338 (7)	2.90	2.90

Souvenir Sheet

339	A92	$2.50 multicolored	2.10	*3.25*

Antigua Nos. 503-507 (Sailing Week) Ovptd. "BARBUDA"

1978, May 22 *Perf. 14½*

340	A93	10c multicolored	.25	.25
341	A93	50c multicolored	.45	.45
342	A93	90c multicolored	.75	.75
343	A93	$2 multicolored	1.40	1.40
		Nos. 340-343 (4)	2.85	2.85

Souvenir Sheet

344	A93	$2.50 multicolored	2.25	*3.00*

Coronation of Queen Elizabeth II, 25th Anniv. — B29

Crowns: No. 345a, St. Edward's. b, Imperial State. No. 346a, Queen Mary's. b, Queen Mother's. No. 347a, Queen Consort's. b, Queen Victoria's.

1978, June 2 *Perf. 15*

Miniature Sheets of Two Each Plus Two Labels

345	B29	75c Sheet of 4	.75	.75
346	B29	$1.50 Sheet of 4	1.25	1.25
347	B29	$2.50 Sheet of 4	2.00	2.00

Souvenir Sheet

Perf. 14½

348	B29	Sheet of 6, #345a-347b	1.50	*2.50*

Antigua Nos. 508-514 (QEII Coronation Anniversary) Ovptd. in Black or Deep Rose Lilac "BARBUDA"

1978 *Perf. 14*

349	A94	10c multicolored	.25	.25
350	A94	30c multicolored	.25	.25
351	A94	50c multicolored	.25	.25
352	A94	90c multicolored	.40	.40
353	A94	$2.50 multicolored	.75	.75
		Nos. 349-353 (5)	1.90	1.90

Souvenir Sheet

354	A94	$5 multicolored	1.60	1.60

Self-adhesive

355		Souvenir booklet	6.50	6.50
a.	A95	Bklt. pane, 3 each 25c and 50c, die cut, rouletted (DRL)	1.50	1.50
b.	A95	$5 Bklt. pane of 1, die cut	5.00	5.00

Issued: Nos. 349-354, June 2; #355, Oct. 12.

Antigua Nos. 515-518 (World Cup Soccer) Ovptd. "BARBUDA"

1978, Sept. 12 *Perf. 15*

356	A96	10c multicolored	.25	.25
357	A96	15c multicolored	.25	.25
358	A96	$3 multicolored	1.00	1.00
		Nos. 356-358 (3)	1.50	1.50

Souvenir Sheet

359		Sheet of 4	1.50	1.50
a.	A96	25c multicolored	.25	.25
b.	A96	30c multicolored	.25	.25
c.	A96	50c multicolored	.25	.25
d.	A96	$2 multicolored	.75	.75

Antigua Nos. 519-523 (Flowers) Ovptd. "BARBUDA"

1978, Nov. 20 *Perf. 14*

360	A97	25c multicolored	.40	.40
361	A97	50c multicolored	.60	.60
362	A97	90c multicolored	.80	*.90*
363	A97	$2 multicolored	1.75	*2.25*
		Nos. 360-363 (4)	3.55	*4.15*

Souvenir Sheet

364	A97	$2.50 multicolored	3.50	3.50

Flora and Fauna B30

25c, Blackbar soldierfish. 50c, Painted lady. 75c, Dwarf poinciana. 95c, Zebra butterfly. $1.25, Bougainvillea.

1978, Nov. 20 *Perf. 15*

365	B30	25c multicolored	2.10	2.10
366	B30	50c multicolored	3.25	3.25
367	B30	75c multicolored	2.50	*3.50*
368	B30	95c multicolored	3.25	*3.50*
369	B30	$1.25 multicolored	2.25	*3.50*
		Nos. 365-369 (5)	13.35	*15.85*

Antigua Nos. 524-527 (Christmas) Ovptd. in Silver "BARBUDA"

1978, Nov. 20 *Perf. 14*

370	A98	8c multicolored	.25	.25
371	A98	25c multicolored	.25	.25
372	A98	$2 multicolored	.75	.75
		Nos. 370-372 (3)	1.25	1.25

Souvenir Sheet

373	A98	$4 multicolored	2.25	2.25

Events and Annivs. B31

Designs: 75c, 1978 World Cup Soccer Championships, vert. 95c, Wright Brothers 1st powered flight, 75th anniv. $1.25, First Trans-Atlantic balloon flight, Aug. 1978. $2, Coronation of Elizabeth II, 25th anniv., vert.

1978, Dec. 20 *Perf. 14*

374	B31	75c multicolored	.55	.55
375	B31	95c multicolored	.65	.65
376	B31	$1.25 multicolored	.95	.95
377	B31	$2 multicolored	1.10	1.10
a.		Souv. sheet, #374-377, imperf	6.50	*7.00*
		Nos. 374-377 (4)	3.25	3.25

No. 377a has simulated perfs.

Nos. 528-532 Overprinted in Bright Blue

and

Sir Rowland Hill, Death Cent. — B32

75c, Sir Rowland Hill, vert. 95c, Mail coach, 1840. $1.25, London's first pillar box, 1855. No. 384, $2, St. Martin's Post Office, London, vert.

1979, Apr. 4

378	A99	25c multicolored	.25	.25
379	A99	50c multicolored	.25	.25
380	B32	75c multicolored	.30	.30
381	B32	95c multicolored	.35	.35
382	A99	$1 multicolored	.45	.45
383	B32	$1.25 multicolored	.50	.50
384	B32	$2 multicolored	.80	.80
a.		Souvenir sheet of 4, #380-381, 383-384, imperf.	2.00	2.00
385	A99	$2 multicolored	1.00	1.00
		Nos. 378-385 (8)	3.90	3.90

Souvenir Sheet

386	A99	$2.50 multicolored	2.00	2.00

No. 384a has simulated perfs.

Antigua Nos. 533-536 (Easter) Ovptd. "BARBUDA"

1979, Apr. 16

387	A100	10c multicolored	.40	.40
388	A100	50c multicolored	.60	.60
389	A100	$4 multicolored	1.50	1.50
		Nos. 387-389 (3)	2.50	2.50

Souvenir Sheet

390	A100	$2.50 multicolored	1.25	*1.50*

Intl. Civil Aviation Organization, 30th Anniv. — B33

75c, Passengers leaving 747. 95c, Air traffic controllers. $1.25, Plane on runway.

1979, May 24 *Perf. 13½x14*

391	B33	75c multicolored	.30	.40
392	B33	95c multicolored	.40	.50
393	B33	$1.25 multicolored	.50	.60
a.		Block of 3, #391-393 + label	1.50	1.50

Antigua Nos. 537-541 (Int'l Year of the Child) Ovptd. "BARBUDA"

1979, May 24 *Perf. 14*

394	A101	25c multicolored	.30	.30
395	A101	50c multicolored	.45	.45
396	A101	90c multicolored	1.00	1.00
397	A101	$2 multicolored	1.25	1.25
		Nos. 394-397 (4)	3.00	3.00

Souvenir Sheet

398	A101	$5 multicolored	2.25	2.25

Antigua Nos. 542-546 (Sport Fish) Ovptd. "BARBUDA"

1979, Aug. 1 *Perf. 14½*

399	A102	30c multicolored	.40	.30
400	A102	50c multicolored	.55	.50
401	A102	90c multicolored	.70	.70
402	A102	$3 multicolored	1.50	*2.00*
		Nos. 399-402 (4)	3.15	*3.50*

Souvenir Sheet

403	A102	$2.50 multicolored	1.75	*2.25*

Antigua Nos. 547-551 (Capt. Cook) Ovptd. "BARBUDA"

1979, Aug. 1 *Perf. 14*

404	A103	25c multicolored	.50	.45
405	A103	50c multicolored	1.25	.60
406	A103	90c multicolored	1.25	.75
407	A103	$3 multicolored	2.40	2.10
		Nos. 404-407 (4)	5.40	3.90

Souvenir Sheet

408	A103	$2.50 multicolored	2.50	2.50

Intl. Year of the Child — B34

Details of the Christ Child from various paintings by Durer: 25c, 1512. 50c, 1516. 75c, 1526. $1.25, 1502.

1979, Sept. 24 *Perf. 14x13½*

409	B34	25c multicolored	.25	.25
410	B34	50c multicolored	.25	.25
411	B34	75c multicolored	.25	.25
412	B34	$1.25 multicolored	.30	.30
a.		Souvenir sheet of 4, #409-412	1.25	1.25
		Nos. 409-412 (4)	1.05	1.05

Antigua Nos. 552-556 (Christmas) Ovptd. "BARBUDA"

1979, Nov. 21 *Perf. 14*

413	A104	8c multicolored	.25	.25
414	A104	25c multicolored	.25	.25
415	A104	50c multicolored	.40	.25
416	A104	$4 multicolored	1.25	1.25
		Nos. 413-416 (4)	2.15	2.00

Souvenir Sheet

Perf. 12x12½

417	A104	$3 multicolored	1.40	1.40

Antigua Nos. 557-561 (Moscow Olympics) Ovptd. "BARBUDA"

1980, Mar. 18

418	A105	10c multicolored	.25	.25
419	A105	25c multicolroed	.25	.25
420	A105	$1 multicolored	.30	.30
421	A105	$2 multicolored	.40	.40
		Nos. 418-421 (4)	1.20	1.20

Souvenir Sheet

422	A105	$3 multicolored	1.75	2.25

Antigua Nos. 571A-571D (London '80 Ovpts.) Overprinted "BARBUDA" in Dark Blue

1980, May 6 *Perf. 12*

423	A99	25c multicolored	.35	.25
424	A99	50c multicolored	.45	.50
425	A99	$1 multicolored	.75	.85
426	A99	$2 multicolored	2.50	1.90
		Nos. 423-426 (4)	4.05	3.50

Nos. 423-426 exist without the "London 1980" overprint.

First Moon Landing, 10th Anniv. — B35

75c, Crew badge. 95c, Plaque left on moon. $1.25, Lunar, command modules. $2, Lunar module.

1980, May 21 *Perf. 13½x14*

427	B35	75c multicolored	.40	.40
428	B35	95c multicolored	.45	.45
429	B35	$1.25 multicolored	.55	.55
430	B35	$2 multicolored	.85	.85
a.		Souvenir sheet of 4, #427-430	2.50	2.50
		Nos. 427-430 (4)	2.25	2.25

American Widgeon B36

2c, Snowy plover. 4c, Rose-breasted grosbeak. 6c, Mangrove cuckoo. 10c, Adelaide's warbler. 15c, Scaly-breasted thrasher. 20c, Yellow-crowned night heron. 25c, Bridled quail dove. 35c, Carib grackle. 50c, Northern pintail. 75c, Black-whiskered vireo. $1, Blue-winged teal. $1.50, Green-throated carib. $2, Red-necked pigeon. $2.50, Stolid flycatcher. $5,

Yellow-bellied sapsucker. $7.50, Caribbean elaenia. $10, Great egret.

1980, June 16 *Perf. 14½x14*

431	B36	1c	shown	.70	.45
432	B36	2c	multicolored	.70	.45
433	B36	4c	multicolored	.80	.45
434	B36	6c	multicolored	.80	.45
435	B36	10c	multicolored	.80	.45
436	B36	15c	multicolored	.80	.45
437	B36	20c	multicolored	1.00	.45
438	B36	25c	multicolored	1.00	.45
439	B36	35c	multicolored	1.00	*1.60*
440	B36	50c	multicolored	1.10	.45
441	B36	75c	multicolored	1.25	.50
442	B36	$1	multicolored	1.40	.85

Perf. 14x14½

443	B36	$1.50	multicolored	2.00	1.10
444	B36	$2	multicolored	3.25	1.60
445	B36	$2.50	multicolored	4.00	1.90
446	B36	$5	multicolored	4.50	3.75
447	B36	$7.50	multicolored	6.25	*6.50*
448	B36	$10	multicolored	8.50	7.75
			Nos. 431-448 (18)	39.85	29.60

Nos. 443-448 vert.

Antigua Nos. 572-578 (Paintings) Ovptd. "BARBUDA"

1980, July 29 *Perf. 13½x14, 14x13½*

449	A106a	10c	multicolored	.25	.25
450	A106a	30c	multicolored	.25	.25
451	A106a	50c	multicolored	.40	.40
452	A106a	90c	multicolored	.50	.50
453	A106a	$1	multicolored	.50	.50
454	A106a	$4	multicolored	2.25	2.25
			Nos. 449-454 (6)	4.15	4.15

Souvenir Sheet

Perf. 14

455	A106a	$5	multicolored	3.50	3.50

Antigua Nos. 579-583 (Rotary Int'l) Ovptd. "BARBUDA"

1980, Sept. 8 *Perf. 14*

456	A107	30c	multicolored	.25	.25
457	A107	50c	multicolored	.25	.25
458	A107	90c	multicolored	.35	.35
459	A107	$3	multicolored	1.00	1.00
			Nos. 456-459 (4)	1.85	1.85

Souvenir Sheet

460	A107	$5	multicolored	2.25	*2.50*

Antigua Nos. 584-586 (Queen Mother) Optd. "BARBUDA"

1980, Oct. 6

461	A108	10c	multicolored	.50	.30
462	A108	$2.50	multicolored	2.50	2.50

Souvenir Sheet

Perf. 12

463	A108	$3	multicolored	3.50	3.50

Antigua Nos. 587-591 (Birds) Ovptd. "BARBUDA"

1980, Dec. 8 *Perf. 14*

464	A109	10c	multicolored	3.25	1.25
465	A109	30c	multicolored	4.00	1.60
466	A109	$1	multicolored	5.00	3.50
467	A109	$2	multicolored	6.00	6.25
			Nos. 464-467 (4)	18.25	12.60

Souvenir Sheet

468	A109	$2.50	multicolored	9.00	7.75

Antigua Nos. 602-606 (Locomotives) Ovptd. "BARBUDA"

1981, Jan. 26

469	A111	25c	multicolored	1.50	.45
470	A111	50c	multicolored	1.75	.55
471	A111	90c	multicolored	2.40	.80
472	A111	$3	multicolored	3.50	1.90
			Nos. 469-472 (4)	9.15	3.70

Souvenir Sheet

473	A111	$2.50	multicolored	3.00	3.00

Famous Women — B37

50c, Florence Nightingale. 90c, Marie Curie. $1, Amy Johnson. $4, Eleanor Roosevelt.

1981, Mar. 9 *Perf. 14x13½*

474	B37	50c	multicolored	.25	.25
475	B37	90c	multicolored	.55	.55
476	B37	$1	multicolored	.50	.50
477	B37	$4	multicolored	.70	.70
			Nos. 474-477 (4)	2.00	2.00

Walt Disney Characters at Sea — B38

10c, Goofy. 20c, Donald Duck. 25c, Mickey Mouse. 30c, Goofy fishing. 35c, Goofy sailing. 40c, Mickey fishing. 75c, Donald Duck boating. $1, Minnie Mouse. $2, Chip 'n Dale.

$2.50, Donald Duck, diff.

1981, May 15 *Perf. 13½x14*

478	B38	10c	multi	1.60	.40
479	B38	20c	multi	1.75	.50
480	B38	25c	multi	2.40	.75
481	B38	30c	multi	2.40	1.00
482	B38	35c	multi	2.40	1.00
483	B38	40c	multi	2.75	1.40
484	B38	75c	multi	3.00	1.75
485	B38	$1	multi	3.75	2.25
486	B38	$2	multi	4.75	3.50
			Nos. 478-486 (9)	24.80	12.55

Souvenir Sheet

487	B38	$2.50	multi	14.00	14.00

Antigua Nos. 618-622 (Picasso) Ovptd. "BARBUDA"

1981, June 9 *Perf. 14*

488	A112	10c	multicolored	.25	.25
489	A112	50c	multicolored	.50	.50
490	A112	90c	multicolored	1.00	1.00
491	A112	$4	multicolored	2.50	2.50
			Nos. 488-491 (4)	4.25	4.25

Souvenir Sheet

Perf. 14x14½

492	A112	$5	multicolored	4.50	4.50

Miniature Sheets

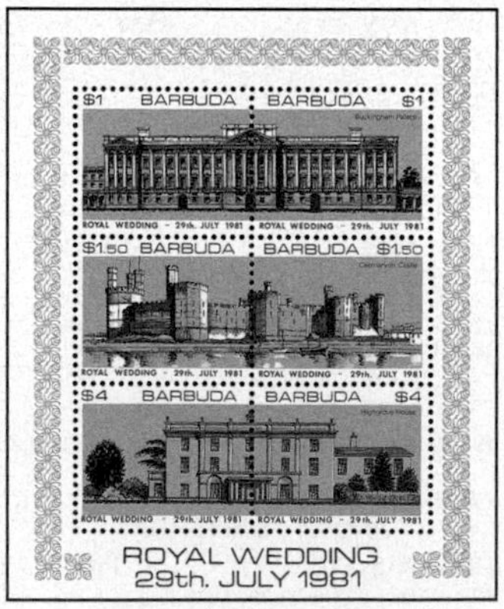

Royal Wedding — B39

a-b, $1, L & R sides of Buckingham Palace. c-d, $1.50, L & R sides of Caernarvon Castle. e-f, $4, L & R sides of Highgrove House.

No. 496, St. Paul's Cathedral, vert.

Sheets of 6, #a-f

1981, July 27 *Perf. 11x11½*

493	B39	blk & salmon	3.00	3.00
494	B39	blk & purple	3.00	3.00
495	B39	blk & gray grn	3.00	3.00

Souvenir Sheet

Perf. 11½x11

496	B39	$5	multicolored	1.25	1.25

Stamps of same denomination have continuous design. For surcharges see Nos. 592-594.

Common Design Types pictured following the introduction.

Antigua Nos. 623-627 (Royal Wedding) Ovptd. in Black or Silver "BARBUDA"

1981, Aug. 14 *Perf. 14*

497	CD331a	25c	multicolored	.25	.25
498	CD331a	50c	multicolored	.25	.25
499	CD331a	$4	multicolored	.70	.70
			Nos. 497-499 (3)	1.20	1.20

Souvenir Sheet

500	CD331	$5	multicolored	1.25	1.25

Self-adhesive

501	CD331	Booklet	8.50	8.50
a.		Pane of 6 (2x25c, 2x$1, 2x$2), Charles, die cut, rouletted (S)	4.00	4.00
b.		Pane of 1, $5 Couple, die cut (S)	4.00	4.00

Issued: Nos. 497-500, Aug. 24; No. 501, Oct. 12.

For surcharge see No. B1.

Intl. Year of the Disabled B40

50c, Travel. 90c, Braille, sign language. $1, Helping hands. $4, Mobility aids.

1981, Sept. 14 *Perf. 14*

502	B40	50c	multicolored	.50	.50
503	B40	90c	multicolored	.50	.50
504	B40	$1	multicolored	.50	.50
505	B40	$4	multicolored	.75	.75
			Nos. 502-505 (4)	2.25	2.25

Antigua Nos. 607-617 (Independence Ovpts.) Ovptd. "BARBUDA"

1981, Nov. 1 *Perf. 15*

506	A79	6c	multicolored	.25	.25
507	A79	10c	multicolored	.25	.25
508	A79	20c	multicolored	.25	.25
509	A79	25c	multicolored	.30	.25
510	A79	35c	multicolored	.40	.30
511	A79	50c	multicolored	.55	.40
512	A79	75c	multicolored	.75	.60
513	A79	$1	multicolored	1.10	.75

Perf. 13½x14

514	A80	$2.50	multicolored	2.75	1.90
515	A80	$5	multicolored	5.00	3.75
516	A80	$10	multicolored	10.00	7.50
			Nos. 506-516 (11)	21.60	16.20

Antigua Nos. 628-632 (Girl Guides) Ovptd. "BARBUDA"

1981, Dec. 14 *Perf. 15*

517	A113	10c	multicolored	.90	.25
518	A113	50c	multicolored	1.50	.55
519	A113	90c	multicolored	2.25	1.00
520	A113	$2.50	multicolored	3.50	2.75
			Nos. 517-520 (4)	8.15	4.55

Souvenir Sheet

521	A113	$5	multicolored	6.00	6.00

Antigua Nos. 643-647 (Int'l Year of the Disabled) Ovptd. "BARBUDA"

1981, Dec. 14

522	A116	10c	multicolored	.25	.25
523	A116	50c	multicolored	.50	.50
524	A116	90c	multicolored	1.00	1.00
525	A116	$2	multicolored	2.00	2.00
			Nos. 522-525 (4)	3.75	3.75

Souvenir Sheet

526	A116	$4	multicolored	3.00	3.00

Antigua Nos. 638-642 (Christmas) Ovptd. in Black or Silver "BARBUDA"

1981, Dec. 22

527	A115	8c	multi	.25	.25
528	A115	30c	multi	.40	.40
529	A115	$1	multi (S)	.50	.50
530	A115	$3	multi	1.60	1.60
			Nos. 527-530 (4)	2.75	2.75

Souvenir Sheet

531	A115	$5	multi	2.25	*2.50*

Birth of Prince William — B41

Various portraits.

1982, June 21 **Wmk. 380** *Perf. 14*

532	B41	$1	buff & multi	.65	.65
533	B41	$2.50	lt pink & multi	1.25	1.25
534	B41	$5	lt lilac & multi	2.75	2.75
			Nos. 532-534 (3)	4.65	4.65

Souvenir Sheet

535	B41	$4	Couple	4.75	4.75

See Nos. 540-543.

The overprint on stamps of Antigua, from here on, read "BARBUDA MAIL" in one or two lines.

Antigua Nos. 672-675 (Royal Baby) Ovptd. in Black or Silver

Perf. 14½x14

1982, Oct. 12 **Unwmk.**

536	CD332	90c	multi	.60	.60
537	CD332	$1	multi (S)	.65	.65
538	CD332	$4	multi (S)	2.75	2.75
			Nos. 536-538 (3)	4.00	4.00

Souvenir Sheet

539	CD332	$5	multi	4.00	4.00

Barbuda Nos. 532-535 Inscribed at Top

Various portraits.

Perf. 14x14½

1982, July 1 **Wmk. 380**

540	B41	$1	lt grn & multi	1.40	.60
541	B41	$2.50	pale sal & multi	2.25	1.50
542	B41	$5	lt bl & multi	3.25	3.00
			Nos. 540-542 (3)	6.90	5.10

Souvenir Sheet

543	B41	$4	Couple	5.00	5.00

Antigua Nos. 663-666 (Diana) Ovptd. in Black or Silver

Perf. 14½x14

1982, Aug. 30 **Unwmk.**

544	CD332	90c	multi	.70	.50
545	CD332	$1	multi (S)	.80	.60
546	CD332	$4	multi	3.25	1.60
			Nos. 544-546 (3)	4.75	2.70

Souvenir Sheet

547	CD332	$5	multi	5.00	5.00

Antigua Nos. 676-683 (Washington/FDR) Overprinted

1982, Dec. 6 *Perf. 15*

551	A121	10c	multicolored	.25	.25
552	A121	25c	multicolored	.40	.25
553	A121	45c	multicolored	1.75	.50
554	A121	60c	multicolored	.50	.50
555	A121	$1	multicolored	2.25	.75
556	A121	$3	multicolored	1.75	1.25
			Nos. 551-556 (6)	6.90	3.50

Souvenir Sheets

557	A121	$4	on #682	3.50	*5.00*
558	A121	$4	on #683	3.50	*5.00*

Antigua Nos. 684-688 (Christmas) Overprinted

1982, Dec. 6 *Perf. 14*

559	A122	10c	multicolored	.25	.25
560	A122	30c	multicolored	.35	.35
561	A122	$1	multicolored	.85	.85
562	A122	$4	multicolored	2.10	2.10
			Nos. 559-562 (4)	3.55	3.55

Souvenir Sheet

563	A122	$5	multicolored	3.00	*4.00*

Antigua Nos. 689-693 (Raphael) Overprinted

1983, Mar. 14 *Perf. 14½*
564 A123 45c multicolored .25 .25
565 A123 50c multicolored .35 .35
566 A123 60c multicolored .35 .35
567 A123 $4 multicolored 2.25 2.25
Nos. 564-567 (4) 3.20 3.20

Souvenir Sheet

568 A123 $5 multicolored 2.50 2.50

Antigua Nos. 694-697 (Commonwealth Day) Overprinted

1983, Mar. 14 *Perf. 14*
569 A124 25c multicolored .60 .60
570 A124 45c multicolored .85 .85
571 A124 60c multicolored 1.40 *1.50*
572 A124 $3 multicolored 3.50 *4.00*
Nos. 569-572 (4) 6.35 *6.95*

Antigua Nos. 698-702 (WCY) Overprinted

1983, Apr. 12
573 A125 15c multicolored 2.50 .30
574 A125 50c multicolored 4.50 1.40
575 A125 60c multicolored 4.00 1.40
576 A125 $3 multicolored 6.25 4.00
Nos. 573-576 (4) 17.25 7.10

Souvenir Sheet

577 A125 $5 multicolored 4.50 *5.75*

First Manned Balloon Flight, Bicent. — B43

$1, Vincenzo Lunardi, 1785. $1.50, Montgolfier brothers, 1783. $2.50, Blanchard & Jeffries, 1785. $5, Graf Zeppelin, 1928.

1983, June 13
578 B43 $1 multicolored .50 .50
579 B43 $1.50 multicolored .75 .75
580 B43 $2.50 multicolored 1.25 1.25
Nos. 578-580 (3) 2.50 2.50

Souvenir Sheet

581 B43 $5 multicolored 4.50 4.75

No. 581 exists imperf. Value, $12.50.

Antigua Nos. 703-707 (Marine Mammals) Overprinted

1983, July 4 *Perf. 15*
582 A126 15c multicolored 2.50 .75
583 A126 50c multicolored 9.00 3.75
584 A126 60c multicolored 10.50 4.00
585 A126 $3 multicolored 14.50 7.00
Nos. 582-585 (4) 36.50 15.50

Souvenir Sheet

586 A126 $5 multicolored 12.50 12.50

Antigua Nos. 726-730 (Flight) Overprinted

1983, Sept. 12
587 A128 30c multicolored 1.75 1.10
588 A128 50c multicolored 2.00 1.40
589 A128 60c multicolored 2.50 1.75
590 A128 $4 multicolored 7.25 7.25
Nos. 587-590 (4) 13.50 11.50

Souvenir Sheet

591 A128 $5 multicolored 6.75 *7.75*

Barbuda Nos. 493-495 Surcharged 45c on $1, 50c on $1.50 & 60c on $4

1983, Oct. 21 *Perf. 11½x11*
592 B39 Sheet of 6, #493 3.50 3.50
593 B39 Sheet of 6, #494 3.50 3.50
594 B39 Sheet of 6, #495 3.50 3.50

Antigua Nos. 708-725 (Definitives) Overprinted

1983, Oct. 28 *Perf. 14*
595 A127 1c multicolored .25 .25
596 A127 2c multicolored .25 .25
597 A127 3c multicolored .25 .25
598 A127 5c multicolored .25 .25
599 A127 10c multicolored .45 .30
600 A127 15c multicolored .80 .30
601 A127 20c multicolored .80 .30
602 A127 25c multicolored .85 .30
603 A127 30c multicolored 1.10 .50
604 A127 40c multicolored 1.25 .70
605 A127 45c multicolored 1.41 .70
606 A127 50c multicolored 1.60 .70
607 A127 60c multicolored 1.90 .90
608 A127 $1 multicolored 2.50 1.75
609 A127 $2 multicolored 3.00 3.50
610 A127 $2.50 multicolored 5.25 5.75
611 A127 $5 multicolored 5.50 6.25
612 A127 $10 multicolored 8.50 *16.00*
Nos. 595-612 (18) 36.01 *38.05*

Antigua Nos. 731-735 (Christmas) Overprinted

1983, Oct. 28 *Perf. 14*
613 A129 10c multicolored .25 .25
614 A129 30c multicolored .25 .25
615 A129 $1 multicolored .85 *.90*
616 A129 $4 multicolored 3.75 *4.00*
Nos. 613-616 (4) 5.10 *5.40*

Souvenir Sheet

617 A129 $5 multicolored 6.00 6.00

Antigua Nos. 736-739 (Methodists) Ovptd. in Black or Silver

1983, Dec. 14 *Perf. 14*
618 A130 15c multicolored (S) .45 .25
619 A130 50c multicolored (S) .75 .50
620 A130 60c multicolored .75 .60
621 A130 $3 multicolored 3.25 3.25
Nos. 618-621 (4) 5.20 4.60

Members of Royal Family — B44

1984, Feb. 14 *Perf. 14½x14*
622 B44 $1 Edward VII .75 *1.50*
623 B44 $1 George V .75 *1.50*
624 B44 $1 George VI .75 *1.50*
625 B44 $1 Elizabeth II .75 *1.50*
626 B44 $1 Prince Charles .75 *1.50*
627 B44 $1 Prince William .75 *1.50*
Nos. 622-627 (6) 4.50 *9.00*

Nos. 740-744 Overprinted

and

1984 Summer Olympics, Los Angeles — B45

$1.50, Olympic Stadium, Athens. $2.50, Olympic Stadium, Los Angeles. $5, Torch bearer.

1984 *Perf. 15, 13½ (B45)*
628 A131 25c multicolored .35 .25
629 A131 50c multicolored .50 .40
630 A131 90c multicolored .60 .45
631 B45 $1.50 multicolored .75 .75
632 B45 $2.50 multicolored 1.50 1.50
633 A131 $3 multicolored 3.00 *2.50*
634 B45 $5 multicolored 3.00 *4.00*
a. Souv. sheet of 1, perf. 15 3.25 *4.00*
Nos. 628-634 (7) 9.70 9.85

Souvenir Sheet

635 A131 $5 multicolored 6.50 *7.25*

Issue dates: A131, Apr. 26, B45, July 27.

Antigua Nos. 755-759 (Flowers) Overprinted

1984, July 12 *Perf. 15*
636 A133 15c multicolored 1.10 .90
637 A133 50c multicolored 1.40 1.60
638 A133 60c multicolored 1.75 1.90
639 A133 $3 multicolored 2.90 *4.00*
Nos. 636-639 (4) 7.15 *8.40*

Souvenir Sheet

640 A133 $5 multicolored 5.50 5.50

Antigua Nos. 745-749 (Ships) Overprinted

1984, July 12
641 A132 45c multicolored 3.25 .85
642 A132 50c multicolored 3.25 1.00
643 A132 60c multicolored 4.25 1.25
644 A132 $4 multicolored 10.00 9.25
Nos. 641-644 (4) 20.75 12.35

Souvenir Sheet

645 A132 $5 multicolored 11.50 10.75

Antigua Nos. 760-767 (U.S. Presidents) Ovptd. in Black or Silver

1984, Oct. 1 *Perf. 14*
646 A134 10c multicolored (S) .25 .25
647 A134 20c multicolored .30 .30
648 A134 30c multicolored .40 .40
649 A134 40c multicolored .65 .65
650 A134 90c multicolored (S) 1.10 1.10
651 A134 $1.10 multicolored (S) 1.10 *1.25*
652 A134 $1.50 multicolored (S) 1.50 *2.00*
653 A134 $2 multicolored 2.00 *2.75*
Nos. 646-653 (8) 7.30 *8.70*

Antigua Nos. 768-772 (Slavery) Overprinted

1984, Oct. 1
654 A135 40c multicolored .65 .65
655 A135 50c multicolored .80 .80
656 A135 60c multicolored 1.10 1.10
657 A135 $3 multicolored 3.25 3.25
Nos. 654-657 (4) 5.80 5.80

Souvenir Sheet

658 A135 $5 multicolored 6.25 6.25

Antigua Nos. 773-778 (Birds) Overprinted

1984, Nov. 21 *Perf. 15*
659 A136 40c multicolored 3.75 1.00
660 A136 50c multicolored 4.25 1.10
661 A136 60c multicolored 4.50 1.25
662 A136 $2 multicolored 6.25 3.00
663 A136 $3 multicolored 6.25 5.00
Nos. 659-663 (5) 25.00 11.35

Souvenir Sheet

664 A136 $5 multicolored 22.50 22.50

Antigua Nos. 782-791 (Paintings) Overprinted in Silver

1984 *Perf. 15*
665 A137a 15c multicolored .25 .25
666 A137a 25c multicolored .40 .40
667 A137a 50c multicolored .80 .50
668 A137a 60c multicolored 1.00 1.00
669 A137a 70c multicolored 1.25 1.25
670 A137a 90c multiclored 1.40 1.40
671 A137a $3 multicolored 2.50 2.50
672 A137a $4 multicolored 3.50 3.50
Nos. 665-672 (8) 11.10 10.80

Souvenir Sheets

673 A137a $5 #790 4.00 *5.00*
674 A137a $5 #791, horiz. 4.00 *5.00*

Issued: Correggio, 11/21; Degas, 11/30.

Antigua Nos. 779-781 (AUSIPEX '84) Overprinted

1984, Nov. 30
675 A137 $1 multicolored 1.00 1.00
676 A137 $5 multicolored 4.00 *5.00*

Souvenir Sheet

677 A137 $5 multicolored 5.00 *6.00*

Antigua Nos. 819-827 (20th Century Leaders) Overprinted

1985, Feb. 18
678 A139 60c multicolored 6.00 6.00
679 A139 60c multicolored 6.00 6.00
680 A139 60c multicolored 6.00 6.00
681 A139 60c multicolored 6.00 6.00
682 A139 $1 multicolored 6.50 6.75
683 A139 $1 multicolored 6.50 6.75
684 A139 $1 multicolored 6.50 6.75
685 A139 $1 multicolored 6.50 6.75
Nos. 678-685 (8) 50.00 51.00

Souvenir Sheet

686 A139 $5 multicolored 13.00 13.00

Queen Mother (Lady Elizabeth Bowes-Lyon), 1907 — B46

45c, Duchess of York, 1926. 50c, Coronation, 1937. 60c, Queen Mother. 90c, Wearing tiara. $2, Wearing blue hat. $3, With children.

1985, Feb. 26 *Perf. 14x14½*
687 B46 15c shown .35 .35
688 B46 45c multicolored .45 .45
689 B46 50c multicolored .45 .45
690 B46 60c multicolored .45 .45
691 B46 90c multicolored .55 .55
692 B46 $2 multicolored .90 .90
693 B46 $3 multicolored 1.25 1.25
Nos. 687-693 (7) 4.40 4.40

For overprints see Nos. 724-728, 733, 735.

Antigua Nos. 828-834 (Statue of Liberty) Overprinted

1985, May 10 *Perf. 15*
694 A140 25c multicolored .40 .40
695 A140 30c multicolored .55 .55
696 A140 50c multicolored .55 .55
697 A140 90c multicolored 1.00 1.00
698 A140 $1 multicolored 1.10 1.10
699 A140 $3 multicolored 3.00 3.00
Nos. 694-699 (6) 6.60 6.60

Souvenir Sheet

700 A140 $5 multicolored 5.50 5.50

Audubon, Birth Bicentenary — B47

45c, Roseate tern. 50c, Mangrove cuckoo. 60c, Yellow-crowned night heron. $5, Brown pelican.

1985, Apr. 4 *Perf. 14*
701 B47 45c multicolored .35 .35
702 B47 50c multicolored .40 .40
703 B47 60c multicolored .45 .45
704 B47 $5 multicolored 3.75 3.75
Nos. 701-704 (4) 4.95 4.95

Antigua Nos. 845-849, 910-913 (Audubon) Ovptd. in Black or Silver

1985-86 *Perf. 15, 12½x12*
705 A143 60c on #910 (S) 9.00 7.00
706 A143 90c on #845 11.00 8.25
707 A143 90c on #911 (S) 11.00 8.25
708 A143 $1 on #846 11.00 8.25
709 A143 $1.50 on #847 11.00 11.00
710 A143 $1.50 on #912 13.50 13.00
711 A143 $3 on #848 22.50 22.50
712 A143 $3 on #913 25.00 25.00
Nos. 705-712 (8) 114.00 103.25

Souvenir Sheet

713 A143 $5 on #849 40.00 40.00

Issue dates: Nos. 706, 708-709, 711, 713, July 18, 1985. Others, Dec. 1986.

Antigua Nos. 850-854 (Butterflies) Overprinted

1985, July 18 *Perf. 14*
714 A144 25c multicolored 9.50 9.00
715 A144 60c multicolored 11.00 10.00
716 A144 95c multicolored 14.00 13.50
717 A144 $4 multicolored 25.00 25.00
Nos. 714-717 (4) 59.50 57.50

Souvenir Sheet

718 A144 $5 multicolored 42.50 42.50

Antigua Nos. 840-844 (Motorcycles) Overprinted

1985, Aug. 2
719 A142 10c multicolored 1.75 1.50
720 A142 30c multicolored 2.75 2.25
721 A142 60c multicolored 3.75 3.50
722 A142 $4 multicolored 12.00 12.00
Nos. 719-722 (4) 20.25 19.25

Souvenir Sheet

723 A142 $5 multicolored 15.00 15.00

Barbuda Nos. 687-693 Overprinted in Silver or Black

Antigua Nos. 866A-870 (Queen Mother) Ovptd. in Silver or Black

Perf. 14, 12x12½ (#729, 731, 736)

1985-86
724 B46 15c multi .40 .40
725 B46 45c multi .55 .55
726 B46 50c multi .70 .70
727 B46 60c multi .90 .90
728 B46 90c multi 1.20 1.20
729 A148 90c multi 1.20 1.20
730 A148 $1 multi (S) 1.40 1.40
731 A148 $1 like #730 1.40 1.40
732 A148 $1.50 multi (S) 2.25 2.25
733 B46 $2 multi 2.60 2.60
734 A148 $2.50 multi 3.50 3.50
735 B46 $3 multi 4.50 4.50
736 A148 $3 multi 4.50 4.50
Nos. 724-736 (13) 25.10 25.10

Souvenir Sheet

737 A148 $5 multi 15.00 15.00

Queen Mother's 85th birthday.
Issue dates: 15c, 45c, 50c, 60c, No. 728, $2, No. 735, Aug. 2. No. 730, $1.50, $2.50, Nov. 8. Others, Dec. 1986. Nos. 729, 731, 736 issued in sheets of 5 plus label.

Antigua Nos. 835-839 (Scenes) Overprinted

1985, Aug. 30 *Perf. 15*
738 A141 15c multicolored .40 .40
739 A141 50c multicolored .65 .65
740 A141 60c multicolored .75 .75
741 A141 $3 multicolored 4.00 4.00
Nos. 738-741 (4) 5.80 5.80

Souvenir Sheet

742 A141 $5 multicolored 6.75 6.75

Antigua Nos. 855-859 (Airplanes) Overprinted

1985, Aug. 30 *Perf. 14*
743 A145 30c multicolored 1.90 1.90
744 A145 90c multicolored 3.25 3.25
745 A145 $1.50 multicolored 4.00 4.00
746 A145 $3 multicolored 5.50 5.50
Nos. 743-746 (4) 14.65 14.65

Souvenir Sheet

747 A145 $5 multicolored 8.50 8.50

Antigua Nos. 860-861 (Maimonides) Overprinted

1985, Nov. 25 *Perf. 14*
748 A146 $2 yellow green 11.50 11.50

Souvenir Sheet

749 A146 $5 deep brown 11.00 11.00

Antigua Nos. 871-875 (Marine Life) Ovptd. in Black or Silver

1985, Nov. 25
750 A149 15c multi (S) 7.50 2.25
751 A149 45c multi 7.50 1.10
752 A149 60c multi 7.50 2.25
753 A149 $3 multi (S) 17.00 8.75
Nos. 750-753 (4) 39.50 14.35

Souvenir Sheet

754 A149 $5 multi 21.00 21.00

Antigua Nos. 862-866 (Youth Year) Overprinted

1986, Feb. 17
755 A147 25c multicolored .30 .30
756 A147 50c multicolored .60 .60
757 A147 60c multicolored .65 .65
758 A147 $3 multicolored 3.25 3.25
Nos. 755-758 (4) 4.80 4.80

Souvenir Sheet

759 A147 $5 multicolored 6.50 6.50

Antigua Nos. 886-889 (Royal Visit) Overprinted

1986, Feb. 17 *Perf. 14½*
760 A152 60c multicolored 3.50 1.10
761 A152 $1 multicolored 3.50 2.40
762 A152 $4 multicolored 9.50 9.75
Nos. 760-762 (3) 16.50 13.25

Souvenir Sheet

763 A152 $5 multicolored 16.00 16.00

Antigua Nos. 876-880 (Bach) Overprinted

1986, Mar. 10 *Perf. 14*
764 A150 25c multicolored 4.00 1.10
765 A150 50c multicolored 4.00 3.00
766 A150 $1 multicolored 5.50 5.75
767 A140 $3 multicolored 10.00 9.50
Nos. 764-767 (4) 23.50 19.35

Souvenir Sheet

768 A150 $5 multicolored 35.00 35.00

Antigua Nos. 881-885 (Girl Guides) Overprinted

1986, Mar. 10 *Perf. 14*
769 A151 15c multicolored 3.00 2.25
770 A151 45c multicolored 5.00 5.00
771 A151 60c multicolored 5.00 5.00
772 A151 $3 multicolored 14.00 14.00
Nos. 769-772 (4) 27.00 26.25

Souvenir Sheet

773 A151 $5 multicolored 45.00 40.00

Antigua Nos. 905-909 (Christmas) Overprinted

1986, Apr. 4 *Perf. 15*
774 A156 10c multicolored .65 .65
775 A156 25c multicolored 1.40 1.40
776 A156 60c multicolored 2.40 2.40
777 A156 $4 multicolored 7.00 7.00
Nos. 774-777 (4) 11.45 11.45

Souvenir Sheet

778 A156 $5 multicolored 8.00 8.00

Queen Elizabeth II, 60th Birthday B48

$1, Shaking hands. $2, Talking with woman. $2.50, With officer.
$5, Portraits.

1986, Apr. 21
779 B48 $1 multi .90 .90
780 B48 $2 multi .90 .90
781 B48 $2.50 multi .90 .90
Nos. 779-781 (3) 2.70 2.70

Souvenir Sheet

Perf. 13½x14

782 B48 $5 multi 7.50 7.50

No. 782 contains one 34x27mm stamp.

Antigua Nos. 925-928 (Queen's Birthday) Overprinted in Silver or Black

1986, Aug. 12
783 CD339 60c multi 1.40 1.40
784 CD339 $1 multi 2.25 2.25
785 CD339 $4 multi 9.00 9.00
Nos. 783-785 (3) 12.65 12.65

Souvenir Sheet

786 CD339 $5 multi (Bk) 10.50 10.50

Nos. 920-924 Overprinted and

Halley's Comet B49

$2.50, Early telescope, dish antenna, vert. $5, World map, comet.

1986 *Perf. 14, 15 (B49)*
787 A158 5c multicolored 2.25 2.25
788 A158 10c multicolored 2.25 2.25
789 A158 60c multicolored 6.25 5.50
790 B49 $1 shown 1.10 1.10
791 B49 $2.50 multicolored 1.60 1.60
792 A158 $4 multicolored 17.00 15.00
793 B49 $5 multicolored 2.75 2.75
Nos. 787-793 (7) 33.20 30.45

Souvenir Sheet

794 A159 $5 multicolored 10.50 10.50

Issued: Nos. 790-791, 793, 7/10; others, 9/22.

Antigua Nos. 901-904 (UN) Overprinted

1986, Aug. 12 *Perf. 13½x14*
795 A155 40c multicolored 3.25 3.25
796 A155 $1 multicolored 4.75 4.75
797 A155 $3 multicolored 8.25 8.25
Nos. 795-797 (3) 16.25 16.25

Souvenir Sheet

Perf. 14x13½

798 A155 $5 multicolored 25.00 25.00

Antigua Nos. 915-919 (World Cup Soccer) Overprinted

1986, Aug. 28 *Perf. 14*
799 A157 30c multicolored 4.25 1.10
800 A157 60c multicolored 6.25 6.00
801 A157 $1 multicolored 6.75 6.50
802 A157 $4 multicolored 12.50 12.50
Nos. 799-802 (4) 29.75 26.10

Souvenir Sheet

803 A157 $5 multicolored 30.00 30.00

See Nos. 848-851.

Antigua Nos. 934-938 (AMERIPEX '86) Overprinted

1986, Aug. 28 **Litho.** *Perf. 15*
804 A161 25c multicolored 5.00 5.00
805 A161 50c multicolored 6.00 6.00
806 A161 $1 multicolored 8.50 8.50
807 A161 $3 multicolored 14.50 14.50
Nos. 804-807 (4) 34.00 34.00

Souvenir Sheet

808 A161 $5 multicolored 20.00 20.00

Antigua Nos. 939-942 (Royal Wedding) Ovptd. in Silver

1986, Sept. 22 *Perf. 14*
809 CD340 45c multicolored .55 .55
810 CD340 60c multicolored .75 .75
811 CD340 $4 multicolored 5.25 5.25
Nos. 809-811 (3) 6.55 6.55

Souvenir Sheet

812 CD340 $5 multicolored 8.00 8.00

Antigua Nos. 943-947 (Conch Shells) Overprinted in Silver or Black

1986, Nov. 10 *Perf. 15*
813 A162 15c multicolored 6.25 6.25
814 A162 45c multicolored 6.50 6.50
815 A162 60c multicolored 9.50 9.50
816 A162 $3 multicolored 20.00 *24.00*
Nos. 813-816 (4) 42.25 *46.25*

Souvenir Sheet

817 A162 $5 multi (Bk) 35.00 35.00

Antigua Nos. 948-957 (Flowers) Overprinted

1986, Nov. 10
818 A163 10c multicolored .45 .45
819 A163 15c multicolored .45 .45
820 A163 50c multicolored .90 .90
821 A163 60c multicolored 1.10 1.10
822 A163 70c multicolored 1.25 1.25
823 A163 $1 multicolored 1.75 1.75
824 A163 $3 multicolored 5.50 5.50
825 A163 $4 multicolored 6.25 6.25
Nos. 818-825 (8) 17.65 17.65

Souvenir Sheets

826 A163 $4 multicolored 22.50 22.50
827 A163 $5 multicolored 22.50 22.50

Antigua Nos. 958-962 (Fungi) Overprinted

1986, Nov. 28
828 A164 10c multicolored 2.25 2.25
829 A164 50c multicolored 8.50 8.50
830 A164 $1 multicolored 13.00 13.00
831 A164 $4 multicolored 24.00 24.00
Nos. 828-831 (4) 47.75 47.75

Souvenir Sheet

832 A164 $5 multicolored 47.50 47.50

Antigua Nos. 929-933 (Boats) Overprinted

1987, Jan. 12 *Perf. 14*
833 A160 30c multicolored 2.10 1.00
834 A160 60c multicolored 3.75 1.75
835 A160 $1 multicolored 5.00 3.00
836 A160 $3 multicolored 9.50 9.50
Nos. 833-836 (4) 20.35 15.25

Souvenir Sheet

837 A160 $5 multicolored 40.00 40.00

Antigua Nos. 968-972A (Classic Cars) Overprinted

1987, Jan. 12
838 A165 10c multicolored .75 .55
839 A165 15c multicolored 1.10 .50
840 A165 50c multicolored 1.25 1.10
841 A165 60c multicolored 1.50 1.40
842 A165 70c multicolored 1.75 1.60
843 A165 $1 multicolored 2.40 2.40
844 A165 $3 multicolored 6.50 6.50
845 A165 $4 multicolored 8.00 8.00
Nos. 838-845 (8) 23.25 22.05

Souvenir Sheets

846 A165 $5 multi (#972) 20.00 20.00
847 A165 $5 multi (#972A) 20.00 20.00

Automobile, cent.

Antigua Nos. 963-966 (World Cup Winners Ovpts.) Overprinted

1987, Mar. 10
848 A157 30c multicolored 3.25 1.60
849 A157 60c multicolored 4.25 2.90
850 A157 $1 multicolored 5.50 4.50
851 A157 $4 multicolored 19.00 19.00
Nos. 848-851 (4) 32.00 28.00

See Nos. 799-802.

Antigua Nos. 1000-1004 (America's Cup) Overprinted

1987, Apr. 23 *Perf. 15*
852 A170 30c multicolored 1.25 .65
853 A170 60c multicolored 1.75 .70
854 A170 $1 multicolored 2.75 1.25
855 A170 $3 multicolored 3.75 3.00
Nos. 852-855 (4) 9.50 5.60

Souvenir Sheet

856 A171 $5 multicolored 9.00 9.00

Antigua Nos. 1005-1014 (WWF) Overprinted

1987, July 1 — *Perf. 14*

857	A172	15c multicolored	*42.50*	*20.00*
858	A173	30c multicolored	*5.75*	*4.00*
859	A172	40c multicolored	*55.00*	*24.00*
860	A173	50c multicolored	*7.50*	*6.50*
861	A172	60c multicolored	*77.50*	*40.00*
862	A172	$1 multicolored	*80.00*	*40.00*
863	A173	$2 multicolored	*15.00*	*15.00*
864	A173	$3 multicolored	*15.00*	*15.00*
		Nos. 857-864 (8)	298.25	164.50

Souvenir Sheets

865	A172	$5 multicolored	*110.00*	*80.00*
866	A173	$5 multicolored	*110.00*	*80.00*

Antigua Nos. 1025-1034 (Transportation) Overprinted

1987, July 28 — *Perf. 15*

867	A175	10c multicolored	3.25	3.25
868	A175	15c multicolored	3.50	2.50
869	A175	30c multicolored	3.75	1.60
870	A175	50c multicolored	4.25	1.60
871	A175	60c multicolored	5.00	2.25
872	A175	70c multicolored	5.50	5.00
873	A175	90c multicolored	6.50	6.25
874	A175	$1.50 multicolored	11.00	11.00
875	A175	$2 multicolored	13.00	14.50
876	A175	$3 multicolored	21.00	21.00
		Nos. 867-876 (10)	76.75	68.95

Marine Life B50

5c, Shore crab. 10c, Sea cucumber. 15c, Stop light parrotfish. 25c, Banded coral shrimp. 35c, Spotted drum. 60c, Thorny starfish. 75c, Atlantic trumpet triton. 90c, Feather-star, yellow beaker sponge. $1, Blue gorgonian, vert. $1.25, Slender filefish, vert. $5, Barred hamlet, vert. $7.50, Fairy basslet, vert. $10, Fire coral, butterfly fish, vert.

1987, July 28

877	B50	5c multicolored	.25	.25
878	B50	10c multicolored	.25	.25
879	B50	15c multicolored	.25	.25
880	B50	25c multicolored	.25	*.30*
881	B50	35c multicolored	.30	*.40*
882	B50	60c multicolored	.35	*.45*
883	B50	75c multicolored	.40	*.90*
884	B50	90c multicolored	.50	1.10
885	B50	$1 multicolored	.60	1.10
886	B50	$1.25 multicolored	.70	1.25
887	B50	$5 multicolored	1.50	8.00
888	B50	$7.50 multicolored	2.75	9.25
889	B50	$10 multicolored	5.00	11.50
		Nos. 877-889 (13)	13.10	*35.00*

For surcharges see Nos. 1133-1134.

Antigua Nos. 1048-1052 (Seoul Olympics) Ovptd. in Silver or Black

1987, Oct. 12 — *Perf. 14*

890	A178	10c multicolored	.75	.75
891	A178	60c multicolored	1.90	1.90
892	A178	$1 multicolored	2.90	2.90
893	A178	$3 multicolored	9.00	9.00
		Nos. 890-893 (4)	14.55	14.55

Souvenir Sheet

894	A178	$5 multi (Bk)	16.00	16.00

1988 Summer Olympics, Seoul.

Antigua Nos. 990-999 (Chagall) Ovptd. in Black or Silver

1987, Oct. 12 — *Perf. 13½x14*

895	A169	10c multicolored	.90	1.10
896	A169	30c multicolored	1.10	.90
897	A169	40c multicolored	1.40	1.10
898	A169	60c multicolored	2.00	1.75
899	A169	90c multicolored	3.25	2.75
900	A169	$1 multicolored (S)	3.50	3.25
901	A169	$3 multicolored	8.50	8.50
902	A169	$4 multicolored	11.00	11.00
		Nos. 895-902 (8)	31.65	30.35

Size: 110x95mm

Imperf

903	A169	$5 multicolored	16.00	16.00
904	A169	$5 multicolored (S)	16.00	16.00

Antigua Nos. 1015-1024 (Statue of Liberty) Ovptd. in Silver or Black

1987, Nov. 5 — *Perf. 14*

905	A174	15c multicolored	.65	.65
906	A174	30c multicolored	.80	.80
907	A174	45c multicolored	1.10	1.10
908	A174	50c multicolored (Bk)	1.25	1.25
909	A174	60c multicolored	1.60	1.60
910	A174	90c multicolored	2.25	2.25
911	A174	$1 multicolored	2.75	2.75
912	A174	$2 multicolored	5.50	5.50
913	A174	$3 multicolored (Bk)	7.50	7.50
914	A174	$5 multicolored	12.50	12.50
		Nos. 905-914 (10)	35.90	35.90

Antigua Nos. 1040-1047 (Entertainers) Ovptd. in Black or Silver

1987, Nov. 5

915	A177	15c multicolored	*4.25*	*1.75*
916	A177	30c multicolored	*9.00*	*3.25*
917	A177	45c multicolored	*4.25*	*1.75*
918	A177	50c multicolored	*4.25*	*2.00*
919	A177	60c multicolored	*14.50*	*3.50*
920	A177	$1 multicolored	*6.75*	*3.50*
921	A177	$2 multicolored	*9.50*	*6.25*
922	A177	$3 multicolored (S)	*29.00*	*12.50*
		Nos. 915-922 (8)	81.50	34.50

Antigua Nos. 1035-1039 (Reptiles & Amphibians) Overprinted

1987, Dec. 8

923	A176	30c multicolored	3.75	2.50
924	A176	60c multicolored	7.75	4.75
925	A176	$1 multicolored	12.00	7.50
926	A176	$3 multicolored	36.00	36.00
		Nos. 923-926 (4)	59.50	50.75

Souvenir Sheet

927	A176	$5 multicolored	40.00	40.00

Antigua Nos. 1063-1067 (Christmas) Overprinted

1988, Jan. 12

928	A181	45c multicolored	.90	.90
929	A181	60c multicolored	1.40	1.40
930	A181	$1 multicolored	2.25	2.25
931	A181	$4 multicolored	8.50	8.50
		Nos. 928-931 (4)	13.05	13.05

Souvenir Sheet

932	A181	$5 multicolored	13.00	13.00

Antigua Nos. 1083-1091 (Salvation Army) Overprinted

1988, Mar. 25

933	A184	25c multicolored	1.40	1.10
934	A184	30c multicolored	1.60	1.10
935	A184	40c multicolored	1.75	1.40
936	A184	45c multicolored	1.75	1.60
937	A184	50c multicolored	1.90	1.75
938	A184	60c multicolored	2.50	2.25
939	A184	$1 multicolored	3.50	3.50
940	A184	$2 multicolored	7.25	7.25
		Nos. 933-940 (8)	21.65	19.95

Souvenir Sheet

941	A184	$5 multicolored	39.00	39.00

Antigua Nos. 1058-1062 (U.S. Constitution) Ovptd. in Silver

1988, May 6

942	A180	15c multicolored	.40	.40
943	A180	45c multicolored	.70	.70
944	A180	60c multicolored	1.00	1.00
945	A180	$4 multicolored	6.00	6.00
		Nos. 942-945 (4)	8.10	8.10

Souvenir Sheet

946	A180	$5 multicolored	7.00	7.00

Antigua Nos. 1068-1072 (Royal Wedding Anniv.) Overprinted

1988, July 4

947	A182	25c multicolored	2.90	1.40
948	A182	60c multicolored	4.25	1.75
949	A182	$2 multicolored	6.00	5.75
950	A182	$3 multicolored	8.50	8.50
		Nos. 947-950 (4)	21.65	17.40

Souvenir Sheet

951	A182	$5 multicolored	20.00	16.00

Antigua Nos. 1073-1082 (Birds) Overprinted

1988, July 4

952	A183	10c multicolored	3.25	2.10
953	A183	15c multicolored	4.00	2.10
954	A183	50c multicolored	4.25	3.50
955	A183	60c multicolored	5.00	4.50
956	A183	70c multicolored	6.25	4.75
957	A183	$1 multicolored	8.00	6.50
958	A183	$3 multicolored	18.00	18.00
959	A183	$4 multicolored	27.50	27.50
		Nos. 952-959 (8)	76.25	68.95

Souvenir Sheets

960	A183	$5 multi (#1081)	27.50	24.00
961	A183	$5 multi (#1082)	27.50	24.00

Antigua Nos. 1092-1101 (Columbus) Overprinted

1988, July 25

962	A185	10c multicolored	3.25	1.10
963	A185	30c multicolored	3.50	1.40
964	A185	45c multicolored	4.25	2.00
965	A185	60c multicolored	4.00	2.90
966	A185	90c multicolored	4.50	3.75
967	A185	$1 multicolored	5.50	4.50
968	A185	$3 multicolored	12.50	12.50
969	A185	$4 multicolored	16.00	16.00
		Nos. 962-969 (8)	53.50	44.15

Souvenir Sheets

970	A185	$5 multi (#1100)	19.00	19.00
971	A185	$5 multi (#1101)	19.00	19.00

Antigua Nos. 1102-1111 (Titian Paintings) Overprinted

1988, July 25 — *Perf. 13½x14*

972	A187	30c multicolored	.90	.70
973	A187	40c multicolored	1.00	.80
974	A187	45c multicolored	1.10	.90
975	A187	50c multicolored	1.25	1.10
976	A187	$1 multicolored	2.00	2.00
977	A187	$2 multicolored	4.75	4.75
978	A187	$3 multicolored	6.00	6.00
979	A187	$4 multicolored	9.00	9.00
		Nos. 972-979 (8)	26.00	25.25

Souvenir Sheets

980	A187	$5 multi (#1110)	13.50	13.50
981	A187	$5 multi (#1111)	13.50	13.50

Antigua Nos. 1053-1057 (Scout Jamboree) Overprinted

1988, Aug. 25 — *Perf. 15*

982	A179	10c multicolored	3.50	2.00
983	A179	60c multicolored	9.00	3.50
984	A179	$1 multicolored	4.50	3.75
985	A179	$3 multicolored	9.00	9.00
		Nos. 982-985 (4)	26.00	18.25

Souvenir Sheet

986	A179	$5 multicolored	24.00	24.00

Antigua Nos. 1112-1116 (Sailboats) Overprinted

1988, Aug. 25

987	A188	30c multicolored	1.60	1.25
988	A188	60c multicolored	2.25	2.25
989	A188	$1 multicolored	3.00	3.00
990	A188	$3 multicolored	8.50	8.50
		Nos. 987-990 (4)	15.35	15.00

Souvenir Sheet

991	A188	$5 multicolored	20.00	17.50

Antigua Nos. 1127-1136 (Flowering Trees) Overprinted

1988, Sept. 16 — *Perf. 14*

992	A190	10c multicolored	.45	.50
993	A190	30c multicolored	.60	.60
994	A190	50c multicolored	.75	.75
995	A190	90c multicolored	1.10	1.10
996	A190	$1 multicolored	1.60	1.60
997	A190	$2 multicolored	3.00	3.00
998	A190	$3 multicolored	4.25	4.25
999	A190	$4 multicolored	5.25	5.25
		Nos. 992-999 (8)	17.00	17.05

Souvenir Sheets

1000	A191	$5 multi (#1135)	9.00	9.00
1001	A191	$5 multi (#1136)	9.00	9.00

Antigua Nos. 1140-1144 (Seoul Olympics) Overprinted

1988, Sept. 16

1002	A192	40c multicolored	2.00	1.10
1003	A192	60c multicolored	2.75	1.75
1004	A192	$1 multicolored	4.00	3.00
1005	A192	$3 multicolored	6.50	6.50
		Nos. 1002-1005 (4)	15.25	12.35

Souvenir Sheet

1006	A192	$5 multicolored	15.00	15.00

Antigua Nos. 1145-1162 (Butterflies) Overprinted

1988-90

1007	A193	1c multicolored	.55	.55
1008	A193	2c multicolored	.55	.55
1009	A193	3c multicolored	.55	.55
1010	A193	5c multicolored	.55	.55
1011	A193	10c multicolored	.55	.55
1012	A193	15c multicolored	.55	.55
1013	A193	20c multicolored	.55	.55
1014	A193	25c multicolored	.55	.55
1015	A193	30c multicolored	.65	.65
1016	A193	40c multicolored	.70	.70
1017	A193	45c multicolored	.90	.90
1018	A193	50c multicolored	1.00	1.00
1019	A193	60c multicolored	1.25	1.25
1020	A193	$1 multicolored	1.90	1.90
1021	A193	$2 multicolored	4.00	4.00
1022	A193	$2.50 multicolored	4.75	4.75
1023	A193	$5 multicolored	10.00	10.00
1024	A193	$10 multicolored	20.00	20.00
1025	A193	$20 multi ('90)	27.50	27.50
		Nos. 1007-1025 (19)	77.05	77.05

Issue dates: $20, May 4, others Dec. 8.

The overprint on No. 1025 is in a thin sans-serif typeface, while Nos. 1007-1024 are overprinted with a thick serif typeface.

Antigua Nos. 1162A-1167 (Kennedy) Overprinted

1989, Apr. 28

1026	A194	1c multicolored	.65	*1.10*
1027	A194	2c multicolored	.65	*1.10*
1028	A194	3c multicolored	.65	*1.10*
1029	A194	4c multicolored	.65	*1.10*
1030	A194	30c multicolored	1.40	.80
1031	A194	60c multicolored	3.50	1.60
1032	A194	$1 multicolored	4.00	2.75
1033	A194	$4 multicolored	10.00	10.00
		Nos. 1026-1033 (8)	21.50	19.55

Souvenir Sheet

1034	A194	$5 multicolored	16.00	16.00

Antigua Nos. 1175-1176 (Arawaks) Overprinted

1989, May 24

1035	A196	$1.50 Strip of 4, #a.-d.	25.00	25.00

Souvenir Sheet

1036	A196	$6 multicolored	15.00	*18.00*

Antigua Nos. 1177-1186 (Jets) Overprinted

1989, May 29

1037	A197	10c multicolored	2.00	1.75
1038	A197	30c multicolored	2.40	1.75
1039	A197	40c multicolored	2.90	2.50
1040	A197	60c multicolored	3.50	3.50
1041	A197	$1 multicolored	4.75	4.75
1042	A197	$2 multicolored	7.50	7.50
1043	A197	$3 multicolored	12.00	12.00
1044	A197	$4 multicolored	18.00	18.00
		Nos. 1037-1044 (8)	53.05	51.75

Souvenir Sheets

1045	A197	$7 multi (#1185)	35.00	27.50
1046	A197	$7 multi (#1186)	35.00	27.50

Antigua Nos. 1187-1196 (Cruise Ships) Overprinted

1989, Sept. 18

1047	A198	25c multicolored	3.50	1.60
1048	A198	45c multicolored	4.25	2.10
1049	A198	50c multicolored	4.25	3.00
1050	A198	60c multicolored	5.50	3.25
1051	A198	75c multicolored	5.50	4.50
1052	A198	90c multicolored	7.25	6.25
1053	A198	$3 multicolored	13.00	13.00
1054	A198	$4 multicolored	17.00	17.00
		Nos. 1047-1054 (8)	60.25	50.70

Souvenir Sheets

1055	A198	$6 multi (#1195)	40.00	35.00
1056	A198	$6 multi (#1196)	40.00	35.00

Antigua Nos. 1197-1206 (Hiroshige Paintings) Overprinted

1989, Dec. 14 — *Perf. 14x13½*

1057	A199	25c multicolored	2.75	1.25
1058	A199	45c multicolored	3.25	1.90
1059	A199	50c multicolored	3.75	2.75
1060	A199	60c multicolored	4.00	3.25
1061	A199	$1 multicolored	4.75	5.00
1062	A199	$2 multicolored	8.00	8.00
1063	A199	$3 multicolored	11.50	11.50
1064	A199	$4 multicolored	16.00	16.00
		Nos. 1057-1064 (8)	54.00	49.65

Souvenir Sheets

1065	A199	$5 multi (#1205)	30.00	27.50
1066	A199	$5 multi (#1206)	30.00	27.50

Antigua Nos. 1217-1222 (World Cup Soccer) Overprinted

1989, Dec. 20 — *Perf. 14*

1067	A201	15c multicolored	1.90	.90
1068	A201	25c multicolored	1.90	.90
1069	A201	$1 multicolored	3.00	3.00
1070	A201	$4 multicolored	11.00	11.00
		Nos. 1067-1070 (4)	17.80	15.80

Souvenir Sheets

1071	A201	$5 multi (#1221)	22.50	22.50
1072	A201	$5 multi (#1222)	22.50	22.50

Antigua Nos. 1264-1273 (Christmas) Overprinted

1989, Dec. 20

1073	A208	10c multicolored	.60	.60
1074	A208	25c multicolored	.60	.60
1075	A208	30c multicolored	.70	.60
1076	A208	50c multicolored	.90	.90
1077	A208	60c multicolored	1.10	1.10
1078	A208	70c multicolored	1.50	1.25
1079	A208	$4 multicolored	5.50	5.50
1080	A208	$5 multicolored	7.00	7.00
		Nos. 1073-1080 (8)	17.90	17.55

Souvenir Sheets

1081	A208	$5 multi (#1272)	15.00	15.00
1082	A208	$5 multi (#1273)	15.00	15.00

Antigua Nos. 1223-1232 (Mushrooms) Overprinted

1990, Feb. 21

1083 A202 10c multicolored 2.50 1.60
1084 A202 25c multicolored 2.50 1.60
1085 A202 50c multicolored 4.00 3.25
1086 A202 60c multicolored 4.25 3.50
1087 A202 75c multicolored 5.50 4.50
1088 A202 $1 multicolored 6.50 6.00
1089 A202 $3 multicolored 18.00 18.00
1090 A202 $4 multicolored 25.00 25.00
Nos. 1083-1090 (8) 68.25 63.45

Souvenir Sheets

1091 A202 $6 multi (#1231) 40.00 35.00
1092 A202 $6 multi (#1232) 40.00 35.00

Antigua Nos. 1233-1237 (Wildlife) Overprinted

1990, Mar. 30

1093 A203 25c multicolored 1.25 .80
1094 A203 45c multicolored 3.25 1.25
1095 A203 60c multicolored 3.00 1.90
1096 A203 $4 multicolored 12.50 12.50
Nos. 1093-1096 (4) 20.00 16.45

Souvenir Sheet

1097 A203 $5 multicolored 30.00 30.00

Antigua Nos. 1258-1262 (Moon Landing) Overprinted

1990, Mar. 30

1098 A206 10c multicolored 1.25 1.25
1099 A206 45c multicolored 1.75 1.75
1100 A206 $1 multicolored 4.50 4.50
1101 A206 $4 multicolored 19.00 19.00
Nos. 1098-1101 (4) 26.50 26.50

Souvenir Sheet

1102 A206 $5 multicolored 29.00 29.00

Antigua Nos. 1275-1284 (America) Overprinted

1990, June 6

1103 A210 10c multicolored 1.60 .65
1104 A210 20c multicolored 1.60 .65
1105 A210 25c multicolored 2.00 .65
1106 A210 45c multicolored 2.25 1.00
1107 A210 60c multicolored 2.50 1.40
1108 A210 $2 multicolored 5.25 5.25
1109 A210 $3 multicolored 7.50 7.50
1110 A210 $4 multicolored 10.00 10.00
Nos. 1103-1110 (8) 32.70 27.10

Souvenir Sheets

1111 A210 $5 multi (#1283) 19.00 19.00
1112 A210 $5 multi (#1284) 19.00 19.00

Antigua Nos. 1285-1294 (Orchids) Overprinted

1990, July 12

1113 A211 15c multicolored 3.25 1.40
1114 A211 45c multicolored 2.50 2.00
1115 A211 50c multicolored 2.75 2.75
1116 A211 60c multicolored 2.90 2.90
1117 A211 $1 multicolored 5.25 5.25
1118 A211 $2 multicolored 10.00 10.00
1119 A211 $3 multicolored 15.00 15.00
1120 A211 $5 multicolored 27.00 27.00
Nos. 1113-1120 (8) 68.65 66.30

Souvenir Sheets

1121 A211 $6 multi (#1293) 27.00 24.00
1122 A211 $6 multi (#1294) 27.00 24.00

Antigua Nos. 1295-1304 (Fish) Overprinted

1990, Aug. 14

1123 A212 10c multicolored 2.75 1.60
1124 A212 15c multicolored 2.75 1.60
1125 A212 50c multicolored 3.00 2.10
1126 A212 60c multicolored 3.75 2.75
1127 A212 $1 multicolored 5.00 4.50
1128 A212 $2 multicolored 8.00 8.00
1129 A212 $3 multicolored 12.50 12.50
1130 A212 $4 multicolored 17.00 17.00
Nos. 1123-1130 (8) 54.75 50.05

Souvenir Sheets

1131 A212 $5 multi (#1303) 27.00 24.00
1132 A212 $5 multi (#1304) 27.00 24.00

Barbuda Nos. 888-889 Surcharged "1st Anniversary / Hurricane Hugo / 16th September, 1989-1990"

1990, Sept. 17 ***Perf. 15***

1133 B50 $5 on $7.50 14.00 14.00
1134 B50 $7.50 on $10 21.00 21.00

Antigua Nos. 1324-1328 (Queen Mother) Overprinted

1990, Oct. 12 ***Perf. 14***

1135 A217 15c multicolored 11.50 2.75
1136 A217 35c multicolored 15.00 2.25
1137 A217 75c multicolored 23.00 5.00
1138 A217 $3 multicolored 40.00 23.00
Nos. 1135-1138 (4) 89.50 33.00

Souvenir Sheet

1139 A217 $6 multicolored 85.00 42.50

Antigua No. 1313 Ovptd. in Silver

Miniature Sheet

1990, Dec. 14

1140 A215 45c Sheet of 20, #a.-t. 85.00 85.00

Antigua Nos. 1360-1369 (Christmas) Overprinted

1990, Dec. 14 ***Perf. 14x13½, 13½x14***

1141 A221 25c multicolored .75 .75
1142 A221 30c multicolored .95 .95
1143 A221 40c multicolored 1.00 1.00
1144 A221 60c multicolored 1.50 1.50
1145 A221 $1 multicolored 2.75 2.75
1146 A221 $2 multicolored 5.25 5.25
1147 A221 $4 multicolored 12.50 12.50
1148 A221 $5 multicolored 12.50 12.50
Nos. 1141-1148 (8) 37.20 37.20

Souvenir Sheets

1149 A221 $6 multi (#1368) 19.00 19.00
1150 A221 $6 multi (#1369) 19.00 19.00

Antigua Nos. 1305-1308 (Penny Black) Overprinted

1991, Feb. 4 ***Perf. 15x14***

1151 A213 45c green 5.00 2.00
1152 A213 60c bright rose 6.00 2.75
1153 A213 $5 bright ultra 24.00 21.00
Nos. 1151-1153 (3) 35.00 25.75

Souvenir Sheet

1154 A213 $6 black 35.00 35.00

Antigua Nos. 1309-1312 (Stamp World London '90) Overprinted

1991, Feb. 4 ***Perf. 13½***

1155 A214 50c red & deep grn 5.25 2.75
1156 A214 75c red & vio brn 6.50 4.00
1157 A214 $4 red & brt ultra 20.00 20.00
Nos. 1155-1157 (3) 31.75 26.75

Souvenir Sheet

1158 A214 $6 red & black 35.00 35.00

Birds — B52

1991, Mar. 25 **Litho.** ***Perf. 14***

1164 B52 60c Troupial 2.40 .95
1168 B52 $2 Christmas bird 3.75 3.25
1169 B52 $4 Rose-breasted grosbeak 6.50 6.50
1171 B52 $7 Stolid flycatcher 10.50 *12.50*
Nos. 1164-1171 (4) 23.15 *23.20*

Antigua Nos. 1329-1333 (Barcelona '92) Overprinted

1991, Apr. 23 **Litho.** ***Perf. 14***

1173 A218 50c multicolored 3.00 1.40
1174 A218 75c multicolored 3.50 2.00
1175 A218 $1 multicolored 4.50 2.50
1176 A218 $5 multicolored 13.50 13.50
Nos. 1173-1176 (4) 24.50 19.40

Souvenir Sheet

1177 A218 $6 multicolored 24.00 24.00

Antigua Nos. 1350-1359 (Birds) Overprinted

1991, Apr. 23

1178 A220 10c multicolored 2.50 1.75
1179 A220 25c multicolored 3.25 1.00
1180 A220 50c multicolored 3.50 2.00
1181 A220 60c multicolored 3.75 2.40
1182 A220 $1 multicolored 4.50 4.25
1183 A220 $2 multicolored 7.75 7.75
1184 A220 $3 multicolored 12.00 12.00
1185 A220 $4 multicolored 13.50 *15.00*
Nos. 1178-1185 (8) 50.75 46.15

Souvenir Sheets

1186 A220 $6 multi (#1358) 25.00 22.00
1187 A220 $6 multi (#1359) 25.00 22.00

Antigua Nos. 1370-1379 (Rubens Paintings) Overprinted

1991, June 21 ***Perf. 14x13½***

1188 A222 25c multicolored .95 .95
1189 A222 45c multicolored 1.60 1.60
1190 A222 50c multicolored 1.75 1.75
1191 A222 60c multicolored 2.00 2.00
1192 A222 $1 multicolored 3.50 3.50
1193 A222 $2 multicolored 6.75 6.75
1194 A222 $3 multicolored 10.00 10.00
1195 A222 $4 multicolored 13.50 13.50
Nos. 1188-1195 (8) 40.05 40.05

Souvenir Sheets

1196 A222 $6 multi (#1378) 20.00 20.00
1197 A222 $6 multi (#1379) 20.00 20.00

Antigua Nos. 1380-1390 (World War II) Overprinted

1991, July 25 **Litho.** ***Perf. 14***

1198 A223 10c multicolored 4.75 1.75
1199 A223 15c multicolored 6.00 1.75
1200 A223 25c multicolored 6.75 1.75
1201 A223 45c multicolored 12.00 3.25
1202 A223 50c multicolored 6.75 3.50
1203 A223 $1 multicolored 15.00 6.75
1204 A223 $2 multicolored 15.00 13.50
1205 A223 $4 multicolored 19.00 19.00
1206 A223 $5 multicolored 19.00 19.00
Nos. 1198-1206 (9) 104.25 70.25

Souvenir Sheets

1207 A223 $6 multi (#1389) 45.00 35.00
1208 A223 $6 multi (#1390) 45.00 35.00

Antigua Scott Nos. 1391-1400 exist overprinted "Barbuda Mail" in two lines. The editors would appreciate receiving any information regarding the circumstances of its issue.

Antigua Nos. 1411-1420 (Voyages) Overprinted

1991, Aug. 26 **Litho.** ***Perf. 14***

1209 A226 10c multicolored 1.75 1.20
1210 A226 15c multicolored 2.00 1.20
1211 A226 45c multicolored 2.40 .80
1212 A226 60c multicolored 2.50 1.75
1213 A226 $1 multicolored 3.25 2.75
1214 A226 $2 multicolored 6.00 5.75
1215 A226 $4 multicolored 15.00 15.00
1216 A226 $5 multicolored 17.00 17.00
Nos. 1209-1216 (8) 49.90 45.45

Souvenir Sheets

1217 A226 $6 multi (#1419) 23.00 21.00
1218 A226 $6 multi (#1420) 23.00 21.00

Antigua Nos. 1401-1410 (Butterflies) Overprinted

1991, Oct. 18

1219 A225 10c multicolored 3.75 1.75
1220 A225 35c multicolored 4.00 2.40
1221 A225 50c multicolored 4.75 2.50
1222 A225 75c multicolored 5.75 2.75
1223 A225 $1 multicolored 6.00 3.50
1224 A225 $2 multicolored 7.50 7.50
1225 A225 $4 multicolored 12.00 12.00
1226 A225 $5 multicolored 13.50 13.50
Nos. 1219-1226 (8) 57.25 45.90

Souvenir Sheets

1227 A225 $6 multi (#1409) 32.50 25.00
1228 A225 $6 multi (#1410) 32.50 25.00

Antigua Nos. 1446-1455 (Royal Family) Overprinted

1991, Nov. 18

1229 CD347 10c multicolored 3.75 2.00
1230 CD347 15c multicolored 4.75 1.50
1231 CD347 20c multicolored 4.75 1.50
1232 CD347 40c multicolored 5.75 1.50
1233 CD347 $1 multicolored 6.00 4.75
1234 CD347 $2 multicolored 7.50 8.25
1235 CD347 $4 multicolored 12.50 17.50
1236 CD347 $5 multicolored 15.00 17.50
Nos. 1229-1236 (8) 60.00 54.50

Souvenir Sheets

1237 CD347 $4 multi (#1454) 32.50 32.50
1238 CD347 $4 multi (#1455) 32.50 32.50

Antigua Nos. 1503-1510 (Christmas) Overprinted

1991, Dec. 24 ***Perf. 12***

1239 A238 10c multicolored 2.50 1.50
1240 A238 30c multicolored 2.75 .80
1241 A238 40c multicolored 3.00 .95
1242 A238 60c multicolored 3.25 1.50
1243 A238 $1 multicolored 3.50 2.25
1244 A238 $3 multicolored 6.00 6.00
1245 A238 $4 multicolored 9.00 9.00
1246 A238 $5 multicolored 11.00 11.00
Nos. 1239-1246 (8) 41.00 33.00

Antigua Nos. 1421-1435 (Van Gogh Paintings) Overprinted

1992, Feb. 20 ***Perf. 13½***

1249 A227 5c multicolored 1.75 1.75
1250 A227 10c multicolored 1.90 1.75
1251 A227 15c multicolored 1.90 .95
1252 A227 25c multicolored 1.90 .95
1253 A227 30c multicolored 2.00 .95
1254 A227 40c multicolored 2.10 .95
1255 A227 50c multicolored 2.10 1.50
1256 A227 75c multicolored 3.50 2.00
1257 A227 $2 multicolored 6.00 2.75
1258 A227 $3 multicolored 7.25 7.25
1259 A227 $4 multicolored 9.00 9.00
1260 A227 $5 multicolored 11.00 11.00
Nos. 1249-1260 (12) 50.40 40.80

Size: 102x76mm

Imperf

1261 A227 $5 multi (#1433) 16.00 16.00
1262 A227 $5 multi (#1434) 16.00 16.00
1263 A227 $6 multi 19.00 19.00

Antigua Nos. 1476-1485 (De Gaulle) Overprinted

1992, Apr. 7 **Litho.** ***Perf. 14***

1264 A231 10c multi 2.75 1.75
1265 A231 15c multi, vert. 3.00 1.75
1266 A231 45c multi, vert. 4.00 1.00
1267 A231 60c multi, vert. 4.50 1.50
1268 A231 $1 multi 5.00 2.75
1269 A231 $2 multi 7.50 7.50
1270 A231 $4 multi 13.50 13.50
1271 A231 $5 multi, vert. 14.50 14.50
Nos. 1264-1271 (8) 54.75 44.25

Souvenir Sheets

1272 A231 $6 multi (#1484) 27.50 25.00
1273 A231 $6 multi (#1485) 27.50 25.00

Antigua Nos. 1551-1560 (Easter) Overprinted

1992, Apr. 16 **Litho.** ***Perf. 14x13½***

1274 A242 10c multicolored 1.90 1.20
1275 A242 15c multicolored 2.10 1.20
1276 A242 30c multicolored 2.25 .85
1277 A242 40c multicolored 2.50 1.20
1278 A242 $1 multicolored 4.00 2.75
1279 A242 $2 multicolored 7.50 7.50
1280 A242 $4 multicolored 10.50 10.50
1281 A242 $5 multicolored 13.50 13.50
Nos. 1274-1281 (8) 44.25 38.70

Souvenir Sheets

1282 A242 $6 multi (#1559) 22.00 22.00
1283 A242 $6 multi (#1560) 22.00 22.00

Antigua Nos. 1489-1492 (Scouts) Overprinted

1992, June 19 **Litho.** ***Perf. 14***

1284 A234 75c multi 3.50 2.10
1285 A234 $2 multi, vert. 3.50 3.50
1286 A234 $3.50 multi 5.00 5.00
Nos. 1284-1286 (3) 12.00 10.60

Souvenir Sheet

1287 A234 $5 multi, vert. 25.00 25.00

Antigua Nos. 1493-1494 (Mozart) Overprinted

1992, June 19

1288 A235 $1.50 multi 10.50 5.75
1289 A235 $4 multi 12.50 12.50

Antigua Nos. 1495-1496 (Glider, Locomotive) Overprinted

1992, June 19

1290 A236 $2 multi 3.50 3.50
1291 A236 $2.50 multi, vert. 10.50 5.75

Antigua Nos. 1499-1502 (Brandenburg Gate) Overprinted

1992, June 19

1292 A237 25c multicolored 1.20 .85
1293 A237 $2 multicolored 3.50 3.50
1294 A237 $3 multicolored 4.00 4.00

Souvenir Sheet

1295 A237 $4 multicolored 27.50 27.50
Nos. 1292-1295 (4) 36.20 35.85

Antigua No. 1488 (Pearl Harbor) Overprinted

1992, Aug. 12 **Litho.** ***Perf. 14½x15***

1295A A233 $1 Sheet of 10, #b-k 105.00 80.00

Antigua Nos. 1571-1578 (America) Overprinted

1992, Oct. 12 **Litho.** ***Perf. 14***

1296 A244 15c multicolored 2.25 1.00
1297 A244 30c multicolored 2.50 1.50
1298 A244 40c multicolored 3.00 1.60
1299 A244 $1 multicolored 4.75 4.25
1300 A244 $2 multicolored 11.00 8.25
1301 A244 $4 multicolored 17.00 17.00
Nos. 1296-1301 (6) 40.50 33.60

Souvenir Sheets

1302 A244 $6 multicolored 21.00 19.00
1303 A244 $6 multicolored 21.00 19.00

Antigua Nos. 1599-1600 (America) Overprinted

1992, Oct. 12 ***Perf. 14½***

1304 A247 $1 multicolored 5.25 4.75
1305 A247 $2 multicolored 9.75 9.00

Antigua Nos. 1513-1518 (QEII Accession) Overprinted

1992, Nov. 3 *Perf. 14*

1306 CD348 10c multicolored 8.00 2.75
1307 CD348 30c multicolored 9.75 1.90
1308 CD348 $1 multicolored 13.50 5.00
1309 CD348 $5 multicolored 24.00 19.00
Nos. 1306-1309 (4) 55.25 28.65

Souvenir Sheets

1310 CD348 $6 multi (#1517) 35.00 27.50
1311 CD348 $6 multi (#1518) 35.00 27.50

Antigua Nos. 1541-1550 (Dinosaurs) Ovptd. "BARBUDA / MAIL"

1992, Dec. 8

1312 A241 10c multicolored 4.00 2.50
1313 A241 15c multicolored 4.75 2.25
1314 A241 30c multicolored 5.75 1.50
1315 A241 50c multicolored 5.75 2.75
1316 A241 $1 multicolored 7.00 4.75
1317 A241 $2 multicolored 11.00 9.75
1318 A241 $4 multicolored 13.50 13.50
1319 A241 $5 multicolored 16.00 16.00
Nos. 1312-1319 (8) 67.75 53.00

Souvenir Sheets

1320 A241 $6 multi (#1549) 35.00 25.00
1321 A241 $6 multi (#1550) 35.00 25.00

Antigua Nos. 1609-1618 (Christmas) Ovptd. "BARBUDA MAIL"

1992, Dec. 8 Litho. *Perf. 13½x14*

1322 A251 10c multicolored 3.50 1.00
1323 A251 25c multicolored 3.50 1.00
1324 A251 30c multicolored 3.50 1.40
1325 A251 40c multicolored 3.75 1.60
1326 A251 60c multicolored 5.00 2.25
1327 A251 $1 multicolored 6.00 2.75
1328 A251 $4 multicolored 14.50 15.00
1329 A251 $5 multicolored 18.00 18.00
Nos. 1322-1329 (8) 57.75 43.00

Souvenir Sheets

1330 A251 $6 multi (#1616) 30.00 30.00
1331 A251 $6 multi (#1617) 30.00 30.00

Antigua No. 1601 (Mega-Event Stamp Show) Ovptd. "BARBUDA MAIL"

1992 Litho. *Perf. 14*

Souvenir Sheet

1332 A248 $6 multicolored 25.00 25.00

Antigua Nos. 1519-1528 (Mushrooms) Ovptd.

1993, Jan. 25 Litho. *Perf. 14*

1333 A239 10c multicolored 2.10 .95
1334 A239 15c multicolored 2.75 .95
1335 A239 30c multicolored 3.50 1.50
1336 A239 40c multicolored 5.00 2.75
1337 A239 $1 multicolored 6.75 4.50
1338 A239 $2 multicolored 12.00 12.00
1339 A239 $4 multicolored 15.00 15.00
1340 A239 $5 multicolored 19.00 19.00
Nos. 1332-1339 (8) 72.10 62.65

Souvenir Sheets

1341 A239 $6 multi (#1527) 35.00 32.50
1342 A239 $6 multi (#1528) 35.00 32.50

Antigua Nos. 1561-1570 (Spanish Art) Ovptd.

1993, Mar. 22 Litho. *Perf. 13*

1343 A243 10c multicolored 2.75 1.75
1344 A243 15c multicolored 3.25 1.75
1345 A243 30c multicolored 3.75 1.75
1346 A243 40c multicolored 4.50 1.75
1347 A243 $1 multicolored 6.00 3.75
1348 A243 $2 multicolored 8.00 8.00
1349 A243 $4 multicolored 12.50 12.50
1350 A243 $5 multicolored 14.50 14.50
Nos. 1343-1350 (8) 55.25 45.75

Imperf

Size: 120x95mm

1351 A243 $6 multi (#1569) 27.50 27.50
1352 A243 $6 multi (#1570) 27.50 27.50

Antigua Nos. 1589-1598 (Nature) Ovptd.

1993, May 10 Litho. *Perf. 14*

1353 A246 10c multicolored 3.25 1.75
1354 A246 25c multicolored 3.50 1.75
1355 A246 45c multicolored 4.00 1.75
1356 A246 60c multicolored 4.25 1.90
1357 A246 $1 multicolored 5.50 3.25
1358 A246 $2 multicolored 7.50 7.50
1359 A246 $4 multicolored 12.50 12.50
1360 A246 $5 multicolored 14.50 14.50
Nos. 1353-1360 (8) 55.00 44.90

Souvenir Sheets

1361 A246 $6 multi (#1597) 25.00 23.00
1362 A246 $6 multi (#1598) 25.00 23.00

Antigua Nos. 1603-1608 (Inventors/Pioneers) Ovptd.

1993, June 29 Litho. *Perf. 14*

1363 A250 10c multicolored 1.00 *1.25*
1364 A250 25c multicolored 3.75 1.20
1365 A250 30c multicolored 2.25 1.20
1366 A250 40c multicolored 3.75 1.20
1367 A250 60c multicolored 6.75 2.25
1368 A250 $1 multicolored 4.75 3.50
1369 A250 $4 multicolored 10.50 10.50
1370 A250 $5 multicolored 12.50 12.50
Nos. 1363-1370 (8) 45.25 33.60

Souvenir Sheets

1371 A250 $6 multi (#1607) 22.00 22.00
1372 A250 $6 multi (#1608) 22.00 22.00

Antigua Nos. 1619-1632 (Anniversaries/Events) Ovptd.

1993, Aug. 16 Litho. *Perf. 14*

1373 A252 10c multi 3.25 1.75
1374 A252 40c multi 5.50 1.50
1375 A253 45c multi 1.20 .85
1376 A252 75c multi 1.75 1.50
1377 A252 $1 multi 3.75 2.50
1378 A252 $1.50 multi 4.75 3.75
1379 A252 $2 multi 17.00 7.75
1380 A253 $2 multi (#1626) 9.75 6.75
1381 A253 $2 multi (#1627) 4.75 4.75
1382 A252 $2.25 multi 4.75 4.75
1383 A252 $3 multi 7.00 7.00
1384 A252 $4 multi (#1630) 9.00 9.00
1385 A252 $4 multi (#1631) 9.00 9.00
1386 A252 $6 multi 10.50 10.50
Nos. 1373-1386 (14) 91.95 71.35

Souvenir Sheets

1387 A252 $6 multi (#1633) *19.00 19.00*
1388 A252 $6 multi (#1634) *19.00 19.00*
1389 A252 $6 multi (#1635) *19.00 19.00*
1390 A252 $6 multi (#1636) *19.00 19.00*
Nos. 1387-1390 (4) *76.00 76.00*

Antigua Nos. 1650-1659 (Flowers) Ovptd.

1993, Sept. 21 Litho. *Perf. 14*

1391 A256 15c multicolored 2.50 1.75
1392 A256 25c multicolored 3.25 1.20
1393 A256 30c multicolored 3.50 1.50
1394 A256 40c multicolored 4.00 1.75
1395 A256 $1 multicolored 4.50 3.50
1396 A256 $2 multicolored 5.50 5.50
1397 A256 $4 multicolored 10.50 10.50
1398 A256 $5 multicolored 12.50 12.50
Nos. 1391-1398 (8) 46.25 38.20

Souvenir Sheets

1399 A256 $6 multi (#1658) 21.00 21.00
1400 A256 $6 multi (#1659) 21.00 21.00

Barbuda Nos. 1164-1171 Overprinted

1993, Oct. 9 Litho. *Perf. 14*

1400A B52 60c multi (#1164) *2.25 2.25*
1400B B52 $2 multi (#1168) *7.50 7.50*
1400C B52 $4 multi (#1169) *15.00 15.00*
1400D B52 $7 multi (#1171) *25.00 25.00*
Nos. 1400A-1400D (4) *49.75 49.75*

Antigua No. 1660-1662 (Endangered Species) Ovptd.

1993, Nov. 11 Litho. *Perf. 14*

1401 A257 $1 Sheet of 12, #a.-l. 85.00 85.00

Souvenir Sheets

1401M A257 $6 multi (#1661) 17.50 17.50
1401N A257 $6 multi (#1662) 17.50 17.50

Antigua Nos. 1647, 1649 (Louvre) Overprinted

1994, Jan. 6 Litho. *Perf. 12*

1401O A255 $1 Sheet of 8, #p-w, + label *45.00 45.00*

Souvenir Sheet

1994, Jan. 6 Litho. *Perf. 14½*

1401X A255 $6 multi (#1649) *37.50 37.50*

Antigua Nos. 1697-1710 (Soccer) Ovptd.

1994, Mar. 3 Litho. *Perf. 14*

1404-1415 A267 $2 Set of 12 65.00 65.00

Souvenir Sheets

1416 A267 $6 multi (#1709) 24.00 24.00
1417 A267 $6 multi (#1710) 24.00 24.00

Antigua Nos. 1676-1678 (Japanese Royal Wedding) Ovptd.

1994, Apr. 21 Litho. *Perf. 14*

1418 A260 40c multicolored 2.10 1.00
1419 A260 $3 multicolored 4.75 4.75

Souvenir Sheet

1420 A260 $6 multicolored 17.00 17.00

Antigua Nos. 1679-1682 (Picasso) Ovptd.

1994, Apr. 21

1421-1423 A261 Set of 3 10.00 8.50

Souvenir Sheet

1424 A261 $6 multicolored 17.00 17.00

Antigua Nos. 1683-1685 (Copernicus) Ovptd.

1994, Apr. 21

1425 A262 40c multicolored 2.10 1.00
1426 A262 $4 multicolored 6.25 6.25

Souvenir Sheet

1427 A262 $5 multicolored 17.00 17.00

Antigua Nos. 1686-1688 (Willy Brandt) Ovptd.

1994, Apr. 21

1428 A263 30c multicolored 2.10 1.00
1429 A263 $4 multicolored 6.25 6.25

Souvenir Sheet

1430 A263 $6 multicolored 15.00 15.00

Antigua Nos. 1692-1693 (Clinton) Ovptd.

1994, Apr. 21

1431 A265 $5 multicolored 6.50 6.50

Souvenir Sheet

1432 A265 $6 multicolored 17.00 17.00

Antigua Nos. 1694-1696 (Lillehammer Olympics) Ovptd.

1994, Apr. 21

1433 A266 15c multicolored 2.25 1.75
1434 A266 $5 multicolored 6.50 6.50

Souvenir Sheet

1435 A266 $6 multicolored 15.00 15.00

Antigua Nos. 1732-1735 (Masons) Ovptd.

1994, Apr. 21

1436-1439 A270 Set of 4 25.00 8.00

Antigua Nos. 1711-1720 (Aviation) Ovptd.

1994, June 15

1440-1446 A268 Set of 7 45.00 45.00

Souvenir Sheets

1447 A268 $6 multi (#1718) 20.00 20.00
1448 A268 $6 multi (#1719) 20.00 20.00
1449 A268 $6 multi (#1720) 20.00 20.00

Antigua Nos. 1736-1741 (Cars) Ovptd.

1994, June 15

1450-1453 A271 30c Set of 4 35.00 35.00

Souvenir Sheets

1454 A271 $6 multi (#1740) 19.00 19.00
1455 A271 $6 multi (#1741) 19.00 19.00

Antigua Nos. 1753-1762 (Fine Art) Overprinted

1994, Aug. 18 Litho. *Perf. 13½x14*

1455A-1455H A273 Set of 8 40.00 40.00

Souvenir Sheets

1455I A273 $6 multi (#1761) *19.00 19.00*
1455J A273 $6 multi (#1762) *19.00 19.00*

Antigua Nos. 1689-1691 (Polska '93) Ovptd.

1994, Sept. 21 Litho. *Perf. 14*

1456 A264 $1 multicolored 7.25 5.75
1457 A264 $3 multicolored 17.50 17.50

Souvenir Sheet

1458 A264 $6 multicolored 20.00 20.00

Antigua Nos. 1786-1795 (Orchids) Ovptd.

1994, Sept. 21 Litho. *Perf. 14*

1459-1466 A279 Set of 8 50.00 50.00

Souvenir Sheets

1467 A279 $6 multi (#1794) 25.00 25.00
1468 A279 $6 multi (#1795) 25.00 25.00

Antigua Nos. 1776-1781 (Sierra Club) Ovptd.

1994, Nov. 3 Litho. *Perf. 14*

1469 A277 $1.50 multi (#1776) 40.00 40.00
1470 A277 $1.50 multi (#1777) 40.00 40.00

Souvenir Sheets

1471 A277 $1.50 multi (#1778) 7.00 7.00
1472 A277 $1.50 multi (#1779) 7.00 7.00
1472A A277 $1.50 multi (#1780) 7.00 7.00
1472B A277 $1.50 multi (#1781) 7.00 7.00

Antigua Nos. 1835-1842 (Soccer) Ovptd.

1995, Jan. 12 Litho. *Perf. 14*

1473-1478 A291 Set of 6 30.00 30.00

Souvenir Sheets

1479 A291 $6 multi (#1841) 15.00 15.00
1480 A291 $6 multi (#1842) 15.00 15.00

Antigua Nos. 1857-1866 (Christmas) Ovptd.

1995, Jan. 12 Litho. *Perf. 14*

1481-1488 A295 Set of 8 30.00 30.00

Souvenir Sheets

Perf. 13½x14

1489 A295 $6 multi (#1865) 15.00 15.00
1490 A295 $6 multi (#1866) 15.00 15.00

Antigua Nos. 1829-1834 (Country Music) Ovptd.

1996, Feb. 14 Litho. *Perf. 14*

1491 A290 75c multi (#1829) 12.50 12.50
1492 A290 75c multi (#1830) 12.50 12.50
1493 A290 75c multi (#1831) 12.50 12.50

Souvenir Sheets

1494 A290 $6 multi (#1832) 14.50 14.50
1495 A290 $6 multi (#1833) 14.50 14.50
1496 A290 $6 multi (#1834) 14.50 14.50

Antigua Nos. 1867-1881 (Birds) Ovptd.

1996 Litho. *Perf. 14½x14*

1497 A296 15c multi (#1867) 1.00 .80
1498 A296 25c multi (#1868) 1.10 .90
1499 A296 35c multi (#1869) 1.25 .90
1500 A296 40c multi (#1870) 1.40 .90
1501 A296 45c multi (#1871) 1.60 .90
1502 A296 60c multi (#1872) 1.60 1.25
1503 A296 65c multi (#1873) 1.60 1.25
1504 A296 70c multi (#1873) 1.75 1.40
1505 A296 75c multi (#1874) 1.90 1.60
1506 A296 90c multi (#1875) 2.00 *3.25*
1507 A296 $1.20 multi (#1876) 2.25 *5.25*
1508 A296 $2 multi (#1877) 3.00 *7.25*
1509 A296 $5 multi (#1878) 6.25 *9.00*
1510 A296 $10 multi (#1879) 12.50 *12.00*
1511 A296 $20 multi (#1880) 19.00 *26.00*
Nos. 1497-1511 (15) 58.20 *72.65*

Antigua Nos. 1806-1808 (Marine Life) Ovptd.

1996, Jan. 22 Litho. *Perf. 14*

1512 A281 50c Sheet of 9, #a.-i. 13.50 13.50

Souvenir Sheets

1513 A281 $6 multi (#1807) 12.50 12.50
1514 A281 $6 multi (#1808) 12.50 12.50

Antigua Nos. 1949-1956 (Christmas) Ovptd.

1996, Jan. 22 *Perf. 13½x14*

1515-1520 A314 Set of 6 19.00 19.00

Souvenir Sheets

1521 A314 $5 multi (#1955) 12.00 12.00
1522 A314 $6 multi (#1956) 13.50 13.50

Antigua Nos. 1763-1765 (Hong Kong '94) Overprinted

1995, Feb. 24 Litho. *Perf. 14*

1523 A274 40c multi (#1763) *7.50 5.75*
1524 A274 40c multi (#1764) *7.50 5.75*
a. Horiz. pair, #1523-1524 *16.00 16.00*

Miniature Sheet

1525 A274 40c Sheet of 6, #a-f (#1765) *16.00 16.00*

Antigua Nos. 1814-1815 (Olympics) Overprinted

1995, Feb. 24 Litho. *Perf. 14*
1526-1527 A284 Set of 2 *12.50 12.50*

An additional item was released in this set. The editors would like to examine it.

Antigua Nos. 1782-1785 (Year of the Dog) Overprinted

1995, Apr. 4 Litho. *Perf. 14*
1529 A278 50c Sheet of 12, #a-l *19.00 19.00*
1530 A278 75c Sheet of 12, #a-l *23.00 20.00*

Souvenir Sheets

1531 A278 $6 multi (#1784) *22.00 17.50*
1532 A278 $6 multi (#1785) *22.00 17.50*

Antigua Nos. 1817-1820 (Cricket) Overprinted

1995, May 18 Litho. *Perf. 14*
1533-1535 A286 Set of 3 *20.00 17.00*

Souvenir Sheet

1535A A286 $3 multi (#1820) *16.00 13.50*

Antigua Nos. 1824-1828 (Philakorea '94) Overprinted

Perf. 14, 13½ (#1494H)

1995, July 12 Litho.
1536-1538 A288 Set of 3 *35.00 35.00*

Miniature Sheet

1539 A289 75c Sheet of 8, #a-h (#1827) *17.00 17.00*

Souvenir Sheet

1540 A288 $4 multi (#1828) *45.00 45.00*

Antigua Nos. 1843-1845 (Caribbean) Overprinted

1995, May 18 Litho. *Perf. 14*
1541-1543 A292 Set of 3 *9.00 9.00*

Antigua No. 1809 (Year Family) Overprinted

1995, July 12 Litho. *Perf. 14*
1543A A282 90c multi *5.25 5.25*

Antigua Nos. 1821-1823 (Moon Landing) Overprinted

1995, July 12 Litho. *Perf. 14*
1544 A287 $1.50 Sheet of 6, #a-f (#1821) *23.00 17.00*
1545 A287 $1.50 Sheet of 6, #a-f (#1822) *23.00 17.00*

Souvenir Sheet

1545G A287 $6 multi (#1823) *30.00 25.00*

Antigua Nos. 1810-1813 (D-Day) Ovptd.

1995, Sept. 29 Litho. *Perf. 14*
1546-1548 A283 Set of 3 *35.00 27.50*

Souvenir Sheet

1549 A283 $6 multi (#1813) *30.00 30.00*

End of World War II, 50th Anniv. — B53

Design: German bombers over St. Paul's Cathedral, London.

1995, Nov. 13 Litho. *Perf. 13*
1550 B53 $8 multicolored 35.00 32.50

For overprints and surcharges see Nos. 1639, B3.

Queen Elizabeth, the Queen Mother, 95th Birthday B54

1995, Nov. 20
1551 B54 $7.50 multicolored 27.50 27.50

For overprints and surcharges see Nos. 1638, B2.

United Nations, 50th Anniv. — B55

1995, Nov. 27
1552 B55 $8 New York City 19.00 19.00

For surcharge see No. B4.

Antigua Nos. 1949-1956 (Christmas) Overprinted

1996, Jan. 22 Litho. *Perf. 13½x14*
1552A-1552F A314 Set of 6 — —

Souvenir Sheets

1552G A314 $5 multi (#1955) *11.00 10.00*
1552H A314 $6 multi (#1956) *12.50 11.00*

Six additional items were issued in this set. The editors would like to examine any examples.

Antigua Nos. 1848, 1850-1851, 1854-1856 (Birds) Ovptd.

1996, Feb. 14 Litho. *Perf. 14*
1553 A294 15c multi (#1848) .75 .75
1553A A294 40c multi (#1850) 2.00 2.00
1554 A294 $1 multi (#1851) 2.75 2.75
1555 A294 $4 multi (#1854) 10.50 10.50
Nos. 1553-1555 (4) 16.00 16.00

Souvenir Sheets

1556 A294 $6 multi (#1855) 15.00 15.00
1557 A294 $6 multi (#1856) 15.00 15.00

Antigua Nos. 1882-1890 (Prehistoric Animals) Ovptd.

1996, June 13 Litho. *Perf. 14*
1558-1563 A297 Set of 6 25.00 25.00
1564 A297 75c Sheet of 12, #a-l 27.50 27.50

Souvenir Sheets

1565 A297 $6 multi (#1889) 19.00 19.00
1566 A297 $6 multi (#1890) 19.00 19.00

Antigua Nos. 1891-1898 (Atlanta Olympics) Ovptd.

1996, July 16 Litho. *Perf. 14*
1567-1572 A298 Set of 6 20.00 20.00

Souvenir Sheets

1573 A298 $6 multi (#1897) 13.50 13.50
1574 A298 $6 multi (#1898) 13.50 13.50

Antigua Nos. 1930-1933 (Boy Scouts) Ovptd.

1996, Sept. 10
1575 A310 $1.20 Strip of 3, #a.-c. (#1930) 12.50 12.50
1576 A310 $1.20 Strip of 3, #a.-c. (#1931) 12.50 12.50

Souvenir Sheets

1577 A310 $6 multi (#1932) 9.50 9.50
1578 A310 $6 multi (#1933) 9.50 9.50

Antigua Nos. 1945-1948 (Nobel Prize) Ovptd.

1996, Oct. 25 Litho. *Perf. 14*
1579 A313 $1 Sheet of 9, #a.-i. (#1945) 13.50 13.50
1580 A313 $1 Sheet of 9, #a.-i. (#1946) 13.50 13.50

Souvenir Sheets

1581 A313 $6 multi (#1947) 12.50 12.50
1582 A313 $6 multi (#1948) 12.50 12.50

Antigua Nos. 2001-2002 (QEII Birthday) Ovptd.

1996, Nov. 14 *Perf. 13½x14*
1583 A323 $2 Strip of 3, #a.-c. 13.50 13.50

Souvenir Sheet

1584 A323 $6 multicolored 15.00 15.00

Antigua Nos. 2018-2025 (Christmas) Ovptd.

1997, Jan. 28 Litho. *Perf. 13½x14*
1585-1590 A328 Set of 6 12.50 12.50

Souvenir Sheets

1591 A328 $6 multi (#2024) 12.50 12.50
1592 A328 $6 multi (#2025) 12.50 12.50

Antigua Nos. 1905-1906 (FAO) Ovptd.

1997, Feb. 24 *Perf. 14*
1593 A301 Strip of 3, #a.-c. 10.50 10.50

Souvenir Sheet

1594 A301 $6 multicolored 13.50 13.50

Antigua Nos. 1907-1908 (Rotary) Ovptd.

1997, Feb. 24
1595 A302 $5 multicolored 13.50 13.50

Souvenir Sheet

1596 A302 $6 multicolored 15.00 15.00

Antigua Nos. 1899-1902 (World War II) Ovptd.

1997, Apr. 4 Litho. *Perf. 14*
1597 A299 $1.20 Sheet of 6, #a.-f. 27.50 27.50
1598 A299 $1.20 Sheet of 8, #a.-h. 20.00 20.00

Souvenir Sheets

1599 A299 $3 multi (#1901) 19.00 19.00
1600 A299 $6 multi (#1902) 20.00 20.00

Antigua Nos. 1903-1904 (UN) Ovptd.

1997 Litho. *Perf. 14*
1601 A300 Strip of 3, #a.-c. 9.00 9.00

Souvenir Sheet

1602 A300 $6 multicolored 12.50 12.50

Antigua Nos. 1909-1910 (Queen Mother) Ovptd.

1997 *Perf. 13½x14*
1603 A303 $1.50 Strip or block of 4, #a.-d. 17.50 17.50

Souvenir Sheet

1604 A303 $6 multicolored 19.00 19.00

Antigua Nos. 1913-1917 (Bees) Ovptd.

1997 Litho. *Perf. 14*
1605-1608 A305 Set of 4 15.00 15.00

Souvenir Sheet

1609 A305 $6 multicolored 15.00 15.00

Antigua Nos. 1918-1919 (Cats) Ovptd.

1997
1610 A306 45c Sheet of 12, #a-l 20.00 20.00

Souvenir Sheet

1611 A306 $6 multicolored 15.00 15.00

Antigua Nos. 1928-1929 (Flowers) Ovptd.

1997
1612 A309 75c Sheet of 12, #a-l 17.00 17.00

Souvenir Sheet

1613 A309 $6 multicolored 15.00 15.00

Antigua Nos. 1934-1942 (Trains) Ovptd.

1997, May 30 Litho. *Perf. 14*
1614-1619 A311 Set of 6 12.00 12.00
1620 A311 $1.20 Sheet of 9, #a.-i. 13.50 13.50

Souvenir Sheets

1621 A311 $6 multi (#1941) 13.50 13.50
1621A A311 $6 multi (#1942) 13.50 13.50

Antigua Nos. 1911-1912 (Ducks) Ovptd.

1997 Litho. *Perf. 14*
1622 A304 75c Sheet of 12, #a-l 21.00 21.00

Souvenir Sheet

1623 A304 $6 multicolored 21.00 21.00

Antigua Nos. 1943-1944 (Birds) Ovptd.

1997
1624 A312 75c Sheet of 12, #a-l 7.50 7.50

Souvenir Sheet

1625 A312 $6 multicolored 8.50 8.50

Antigua Nos. 1967-1970 (Mushrooms) Ovptd.

1997
1626 A317 75c Strips of 4, #a.-d. (#1967) 8.50 8.50
1627 A317 75c Strips of 4, #a.-d. (#1968) 8.50 8.50

Souvenir Sheets

1628 A317 $6 multi (#1969) 12.50 12.50
1629 A317 $6 multi (#1970) 12.50 12.50

Antigua Nos. 1970A-1974 (Ships) Ovptd.

1997, Nov. 3 Litho. *Perf. 14*
1629A-1629F A318 Set of 6 6.00 6.00
1629G A318 $1.20 Sheet of 6, #k-p (#1971) 12.50 12.50
1629H A318 $1.50 Sheet of 6, #q-v (#1972) 12.50 12.50

Souvenir Sheets

1629I A318 $6 multi (#1973) 10.50 10.50
1629J A318 $6 multi (#1974) 10.50 10.50

Antigua Nos. 2111-2118 (Christmas) Ovptd.

1997 Litho. *Perf. 14*
1630-1635 A345 Set of 6 11.50 11.50

Souvenir Sheets

1636 A345 $6 multi (#2117) 9.50 9.50
1637 A345 $6 multi (#2118) 9.50 9.50

Antigua Nos. 2069-2070 (Royal Anniv.) Ovptd.

1997, Nov. 3 Litho. *Perf. 14*
1637A A337 $1 Sheet of 6, #c-h (#2069) 15.00 15.00

Souvenir Sheet

1637B A337 $6 multi (#2070) 20.00 20.00

Nos. 1550-1551 Ovptd. in Gold

1997, July 25 Litho. *Perf. 13*
1638 B54 $7.50 on #1551 15.00 15.00
1639 B53 $8 on #1550 15.00 15.00

Antigua Nos. 1983-1986 (Sea Birds) Ovptd.

1998 Litho. *Perf. 14*
1640 A320 75c Vert. strip, #a.-d. (#1983) 7.25 7.25
1641 A320 75c Vert. strip, #a.-d. (#1984) 7.25 7.25

Souvenir Sheets

1643 A320 $5 multi (#1985) 9.00 9.00
1644 A320 $6 multi (#1986) 9.75 9.75

Antigua Nos. 1975-1982 (Atlanta Olympics) Overprinted

1998, Mar. 25 Litho. *Perf. 14*
1644A-1644D A319 Set of 4 *10.50 10.50*
1644E A319 90c Sheet of 9, #f-n (#1979) *12.50 12.50*

1644O A319 90c Sheet of 9, #p-x (#1980) *12.50 12.50*

Souvenir Sheets

1644Y A319 $5 multi (#1981) *9.50 9.50*
1644Z A319 $6 multi (#1982) *9.50 9.50*

Antigua Nos. 2003-2004 (Cavalry) Ovptd.

1998 Litho. *Perf. 14*

1645 A324 60c Block of 4, #a.-d. 11.50 11.50

Souvenir Sheet

1646 A324 $6 multi 12.50 12.50

Antigua Nos. 2013-2017 (Radio) Overprinted

1998, Mar. 25 Litho. *Perf. 14*

1646A-1646D A327 Set of 4 *12.50 12.50*

Souvenir Sheet

1646E A327 $6 multi *16.00 16.00*

Antigua Nos. 2094-2102 (Soccer) Ovptd.

1998

1647-1652 A342 Set of 6 11.50 11.50
1653 A342 $1 Sheet of 8 + label 19.00 19.00

Souvenir Sheets

1654 A342 $6 multi (#2101) 10.00 10.00
1655 A342 $6 multi (#2102) 10.00 10.00

Antigua Nos. 2005-2008 (UNICEF) Ovptd.

1998 Litho. *Perf. 14*

1656-1658 A325 Set of 3 10.50 10.50

Souvenir Sheet

1659 A325 $6 multicolored 12.50 12.50

Antigua Nos. 2009-2012 (Jerusalem) Ovptd.

1998

1660-1662 A326 Set of 3 11.50 11.50

Souvenir Sheet

1663 A326 $6 multicolored 12.50 12.50

Antigua Nos. 2119-2122 (Diana) Ovptd.

1998 Litho. *Perf. 14*

1664 A346 $1.65 Sheet of 6, #a-f (#2119) 12.50 12.50
1665 A346 $1.65 Sheet of 6, #a-f (#2120) 12.50 12.50

Souvenir Sheets

1666 A346 $6 multi (#2121) 8.50 8.50
1667 A346 $6 multi (#2122) 8.50 8.50

Antigua Nos. 2037-2038 (Broadway) Ovptd.

1998 Litho. *Perf. 14*

1668 A330 $1 Sheet of 9, #a.-i. (#2037) 22.00 22.00

Souvenir Sheet

1669 A330 $6 multi (#2038) 19.00 19.00

Antigua Nos. 2063-2064 (Chaplin) Ovtpd.

1998

1670 A334 $1 Sheet of 9, #a.-i. (#2063) 22.00 22.00

Souvenir Sheet

1671 A334 $6 multi (#2064) 19.00 19.00

Antigua Nos. 2039-2047 (Butterflies) Ovptd.

1998 Litho. *Perf. 14*

1672-1675 A331 Set of 4 12.50 12.50
1676 A331 $1.10 Sheet of 9, #a.-i. (#2043) 17.50 17.50
1677 A331 $1.10 Sheet of 9, #a.-i. (#2044) 17.50 17.50

Souvenir Sheets

1678 A331 $6 multi (#2045) 12.50 12.50
1679 A331 $6 multi (#2046) 12.50 12.50
1680 A331 $6 multi (#2047) 12.50 12.50

Antigua Nos. 2140-2148 (Lighthouses) Ovptd.

1998

1681-1688 A349 Set of 8 23.00 23.00

Souvenir Sheet

1689 A349 $6 multi (#2148) 23.00 23.00

Antigua Nos. 2211-2219 (Christmas) Ovptd.

1998

1690-1696 A366 Set of 7 15.00 15.00

Souvenir Sheets

1697 A366 $6 multi (#2218) 10.00 10.00
1698 A366 $6 multi (#2219) 10.00 10.00

Antigua Nos. 2058-2062 (Animals) Ovptd.

1998 Litho. *Perf. 14*

1699 A333 $1.20 Sheet of 6, #a.-f. (#2058) 13.50 13.50
1700 A333 $1.65 Sheet of 6, #a.-f. (#2059) 16.00 16.00

Souvenir Sheets

1701 A333 $6 multi (#2060) 11.00 11.00
1702 A333 $6 multi (#2061) 11.00 11.00
1703 A333 $6 multi (#2062) 11.00 11.00

Antigua Nos. 2067-2068 (Von Stephan) Ovptd.

1999 Litho. *Perf. 14*

1704 A336 $1.75 Sheet of 3, #a.-c. 15.00 15.00

Souvenir Sheet

1705 A336 $6 multi (#2068) 12.50 12.50

Antigua Nos. 2071-2072 (Fairy Tales) Ovptd.

1999 *Perf. 13½x14*

1706 A338 $1.75 Sheet of 3, #a.-c. 15.00 15.00

Souvenir Sheet

1707 A338 $6 multi (#2072) 12.50 12.50

Antigua Nos. 2084-2093 (Orchids) Ovptd.

1999 Litho. *Perf. 14*

1708-1713 A341 Set of 6 15.00 15.00
1714 A341 $1.65 Sheet of 8, #a.-h. (#2090) 23.00 23.00
1715 A341 $1.65 Sheet of 8, #a.-h. (#2091) 23.00 23.00

Souvenir Sheets

1716 A341 $6 multi (#2092) 14.50 14.50
1717 A341 $6 multi (#2093) 14.50 14.50

Antigua Nos. 2065-2066 (Rotary) Ovptd.

1999 Litho. *Perf. 14*

1718 A335 $1.75 multicolored 11.50 11.50

Souvenir Sheet

1719 A335 $6 multicolored 12.50 12.50

Antigua Nos. 2075-2083 (Mushrooms) Ovptd.

1999

1720-1725 A340 Set of 6 19.00 19.00
1726 A340 $1.75 Sheet of 6, #a.-f. 22.00 22.00

Souvenir Sheets

1727 A340 $6 multi (#2082) 14.50 14.50
1728 A340 $6 multi (#2083) 14.50 14.50

Antigua No. 2184 (Diana) Ovptd.

1999

1729 A358 $1.20 multicolored 5.50 5.50

Antigua Nos. 2268, 2269 (Royal Wedding) Overprinted "BARBOUDA MAIL"

1999, Aug. 12 Litho. *Perf. 13½*

1729A A378 $3 Sheet of 3, #b-d — —
1729E A378 $6 multi *12.50 12.50*

Antigua Nos. 2107-2110 (Trains) Ovptd.

1999 Litho. *Perf. 14*

1730 A344 $1.65 Sheet of 6, #a.-f. (#2107) 11.50 11.50
1731 A344 $1.65 Sheet of 6, #a.-f. (#2108) 11.50 11.50

Souvenir Sheets

1732 A344 $6 brown (#2109) 8.50 8.50
1733 A344 $6 brown (#2110) 8.50 8.50

Antigua Nos. 2133-2139 (Church) Ovptd.

1999

1734-1739 A348 Set of 6 8.00 8.00

Souvenir Sheet

1740 A348 $6 multi (#2139) 9.00 9.00

Antigua Nos. 2155-2161 (High School) Ovptd.

1999

1741-1746 A351 Set of 6 11.00 11.00

Souvenir Sheet

1747 A351 $6 multi (#2161) 10.00 10.00

Antigua Nos. 2295-2301 (Christmas) Ovptd.

1999 *Perf. 13¾*

1748-1753 A383 Set of 6 13.50 13.50

Souvenir Sheet

1754 A383 $6 multi (#2301) 11.50 11.50

Antigua Nos. 2103-2106 (Animals) Ovptd.

2000 Litho. *Perf. 14*

1755 A343 $1.65 Sheet of 6, #a-f (#2103) 19.00 19.00
1756 A343 $1.65 Sheet of 6, #a-f (#2104) 19.00 19.00

Souvenir Sheets

1757 A343 $6 multi (#2105) 16.00 16.00
1758 A343 $6 multi (#2106) 16.00 16.00

Antigua Nos. 2123-2132 (Fish) Ovptd.

2000

1759-1764 A347 Set of 6 13.50 13.50
1765 A347 $1.65 Sheet of 6, #a-f (#2129) 18.00 18.00
1766 A347 $1.65 Sheet of 6, #a-f (#2130) 18.00 18.00

Souvenir Sheets

1767 A347 $6 multi (#2131) 17.00 17.00
1768 A347 $6 multi (#2132) 17.00 17.00

Antigua Nos. 2166-2170 (Ships) Ovptd.

2000 Litho. *Perf. 14x14½*

1769 A353 $1.75 Sheet of 3, #a-c (#2166) 12.50 12.50
1770 A353 $1.75 Sheet of 3, #a-c (#2167) 12.50 12.50

Souvenir Sheets

1771 A353 $6 multi (#2168) 8.50 8.50
1772 A353 $6 multi (#2169) 8.50 8.50
1773 A353 $6 multi (#2170) 8.50 8.50

Antigua Nos. 2172-2175 (Antique Autos) Ovptd.

2000 *Perf. 14*

1774 A355 $1.65 Sheet of 6, #a-f (#2172) 15.00 15.00
1775 A355 $1.65 Sheet of 6, #a-f (#2173) 15.00 15.00

Souvenir Sheets

1776 A355 $6 multi (#2174) 10.00 10.00
1777 A355 $6 multi (#2175) 10.00 10.00

Antigua Nos. 2194-2197 (Scouts) Ovptd.

2000

1778-1780 A361 Set of 3 10.50 10.50

Souvenir Sheet

1781 A361 $6 multi 13.50 13.50

Antigua No. 2198 (OAS) Ovptd.

2000 *Perf. 13½*

1782 A362 $1 multi 6.25 6.25

Antigua Nos. 2176-2179 (Aircraft) Overprinted

2000, Apr. 4 Litho. *Perf. 14*

1783 A356 $1.65 Sheet of 6, #a-f (#2176) *17.00 17.00*
1784 A356 $1.65 Sheet of 6, #a-f (#2177) *17.00 17.00*

Souvenir Sheets

1785 A356 $6 multi (#2178) *12.50 12.50*
1786 A356 $6 multi (#2179) *12.50 12.50*

Antigua Nos. 2373-2374 (Queen Mother) Overprinted

Litho., Margin Embossed

2000, Aug. 4 *Perf. 14*

1787 A404 $2 Sheet of 4, #a-d + label *19.00 19.00*

Souvenir Sheet

Perf. 13¾

1788 A404 $6 multi *15.00 15.00*

Antigua No. 2242 (John Glenn) Overprinted

2000, Nov. 30 Litho. *Perf. 14*

1789 A371 $1.75 Sheet of 4, #a-d *25.00 25.00*

Antigua Nos. 2243-2246 (Space) Overprinted

2000, Nov. 30 Litho. *Perf. 14*

1790 A372 $1.65 Sheet of 6, #a-f (#2243) *12.50 12.50*
1791 A372 $1.65 Sheet of 6, #a-f (#2244) *12.50 12.50*

Souvenir Sheets

1792 A372 $6 multi (#2245) *12.50 12.50*
1793 A372 $6 multi (#2246) *12.50 12.50*

Antigua Nos. 2386-2389 (Battle of Britain) Overprinted

2000, Nov. 30 Litho. *Perf. 14*

1794 A409 $1.20 Sheet of 8, #a-h (#2386) *25.00 25.00*
1795 A409 $1.20 Sheet of 8, #a-h (#2387) *25.00 25.00*

Souvenir Sheets

1796 A409 $6 multi (#2388) *17.00 17.00*
1797 A409 $6 multi (#2389) *17.00 17.00*

Antigua No. 2186, 2189 (Gandhi) Overprinted

2000, Oct. Litho. *Perf. 14*

1810 A359 $1 multi (#2186) — —

Souvenir Sheet

1812 A359 $6 multi (#2189) — —

Three additional stamps exist in this set. The editors would like to examine any examples.

SEMI-POSTAL STAMPS

Catalogue values for unused stamps in this section are for Never Hinged items.

Barbuda No. 501 Crudely Surcharged

1982, June 28 Self-Adhesive

B1 CD331 Booklet 13.50

Nos. 1550-1552 Surcharged in Silver

1995, Nov. Litho. *Perf. 13*

B2	B54	$7.50 +$1 on #1551	6.75	*9.50*
B3	B53	$8 +$1 on #1550	15.00	13.50
B4	B55	$8 +$1 on #1552	6.75	*9.50*
		Nos. B2-B4 (3)	28.50	32.50

BASUTOLAND

bə-ˈsü-tə-ˌland

LOCATION — An enclave in the state of South Africa
GOVT. — British Crown Colony
AREA — 11,716 sq. mi.
POP. — 733,000 (est. 1964)
CAPITAL — Maseru

The Colony, a former independent native state, was annexed to the Cape Colony in 1871. In 1883 control was transferred directly to the British Crown. Stamps of the Cape of Good Hope were used from 1871 to 1910 and those of the Union of South Africa from 1910 to 1933. Basutoland became the independent state of Lesotho on Oct. 4, 1966.

12 Pence = 1 Shilling
100 Cents = 1 Rand (1961)

Catalogue values for unused stamps in this country are for Never Hinged items, beginning with Scott 29 in the regular postage section and Scott J1 in the postage due section.

George V — A1

Crocodile and River Scene

Perf. 12½

1933, Dec. 1 Engr. Wmk. 4

1	A1	½p emerald	1.50	*2.40*
2	A1	1p carmine	1.50	*1.75*
3	A1	2p red violet	1.50	*1.10*
4	A1	3p ultra	1.50	*1.40*
5	A1	4p slate	3.50	*9.00*
6	A1	6p yellow	2.50	*2.40*
7	A1	1sh red orange	4.25	*5.00*
8	A1	2sh6p dk brown	45.00	*57.50*
9	A1	5sh violet	82.50	*95.00*
10	A1	10sh olive green	225.00	*250.00*
		Nos. 1-10 (10)	368.75	*425.55*
		Set, never hinged	750.00	

Common Design Types pictured following the introduction.

Silver Jubilee Issue
Common Design Type

1935, May 4 *Perf. 13½x14*

11	CD301	1p car & blue	1.00	*3.00*
12	CD301	2p gray blk & ultra	1.10	*3.25*
13	CD301	3p blue & brown	4.50	*7.50*
14	CD301	6p brt vio & indigo	5.00	*7.50*
		Nos. 11-14 (4)	11.60	*21.25*
		Set, never hinged	20.00	

Coronation Issue
Common Design Type

1937, May 12 *Perf. 13½x14*

15	CD302	1p carmine	.25	*1.00*
16	CD302	2p rose violet	.40	*1.00*
17	CD302	3p bright ultra	.50	*1.00*
		Nos. 15-17 (3)	1.15	*3.00*
		Set, never hinged	1.75	

George VI — A2

1938, Apr. 1 *Perf. 12½*

18	A2	½p emerald	.25	*1.25*
19	A2	1p rose car	1.25	*.85*
20	A2	1½p light blue	.45	*.65*
21	A2	2p rose lilac	.45	*.80*
22	A2	3p ultra	.50	*1.50*
23	A2	4p gray	1.60	*4.25*
24	A2	6p yel ocher	2.00	*1.75*
25	A2	1sh red orange	3.00	*1.40*
26	A2	2sh6p black brown	14.00	*9.00*
27	A2	5sh violet	30.00	*10.00*
28	A2	10sh olive green	32.50	*24.00*
		Nos. 18-28 (11)	86.00	*55.45*
		Set, never hinged	130.00	

Catalogue values for unused stamps in this section, from this point to the end of the section, are for Never Hinged items.

Peace Issue

South Africa Nos. 100-102 Overprinted

Basic stamps inscribed alternately in English and Afrikaans.

1945, Dec. 3 Wmk. 201 *Perf. 14*

29	A42	1p rose pink & choc, pair	.70	.90
a.		Single, English	.25	.25
b.		Single, Afrikaans	.25	.25
30	A43	2p vio & slate blue, pair	.70	.75
a.		Single, English	.25	.25
b.		Single, Afrikaans	.25	.25
31	A43	3p ultra & dp ultra, pair	.70	.95
a.		Single, English	.25	.25
b.		Single, Afrikaans	.25	.25
		Nos. 29-31 (3)	2.10	2.60

King George VI — A3

King George VI and Queen Elizabeth A4

Princess Margaret Rose and Princess Elizabeth A5

Royal British Family A6

Perf. 12½

1947, Feb. 17 Wmk. 4 Engr.

35	A3	1p red	.25	.25
36	A4	2p green	.25	.25
37	A5	3p ultra	.25	.25
38	A6	1sh dark violet	.25	.25
		Nos. 35-38 (4)	1.00	1.00

Visit of the British Royal Family, Mar. 11-12, 1947.

Silver Wedding Issue
Common Design Types

1948, Dec. 1 Photo. *Perf. 14x14½*

39	CD304	1½p brt ultra	.30	.25

Engr.; Name Typo.
Perf. 11½

40	CD305	10sh dk brn ol	52.50	*55.00*

UPU Issue
Common Design Types

Engr.; Name Typo. on 3p, 6p
Perf. 13½, 11x11½

1949, Oct. 10 Wmk. 4

41	CD306	1½p blue	.50	*1.50*
42	CD307	3p indigo	2.25	*2.00*
43	CD308	6p orange yel	1.25	*5.00*
44	CD309	1sh red brown	.75	*1.50*
		Nos. 41-44 (4)	4.75	*10.00*

Coronation Issue
Common Design Type

1953, June 3 Engr. *Perf. 13½x13*

45	CD312	2p red violet & black	.50	*.60*

Qiloane Hill — A7

Shearing Angora Goats — A8

Designs: 1p, Orange River. 2p, Mosotho horseman. 3p, Basuto household. 4½p, Maletsunyane falls. 6p, Herdboy with lesiba. 1sh, Pastoral scene. 1sh3p, Plane at Lancers Gap. 2sh6p, Old Fort Leribe. 5sh, Mission cave house.

Perf. 13½, 11½ (#56)

1954, Oct. 18 Wmk. 4

46	A7	½p dk brown & gray	.55	.25
47	A7	1p dp grn & gray blk	.50	.25
48	A7	2p org & dp blue	1.00	.25
49	A7	3p car & ol green	2.00	.40
50	A7	4½p dp blue & ind	1.50	.25
51	A7	6p dk grn & org brn	2.50	.25
52	A7	1sh rose vio & dk ol green	2.25	.40
53	A7	1sh3p aqua & brown	27.50	9.00
54	A7	2sh6p lilac rose & dp ultra	29.00	14.00
55	A7	5sh dp car & black	14.00	*12.00*
56	A8	10sh dp cl & black	40.00	27.50
		Nos. 46-56 (11)	120.80	*64.55*

See Nos. 72-82, 87-91. For surcharges see Nos. 57, 61-71.

No. 48 Surcharged

1959, Aug. 1

57	A7	½p on 2p org & dp blue	.30	.25

Chief Moshoeshoe (Moshesh) — A9

Designs: 1sh, Council chamber. 1sh3p, Mosotho on horseback.

Perf. 13x13½

1959, Dec. 15 Wmk. 314

58	A9	3p lt yel, grn & blk	.60	.25
59	A9	1sh green & pink	.60	.25
60	A9	1sh3p orange & ultra	.80	.50
		Nos. 58-60 (3)	2.00	1.00

Institution of the Basutoland National Council.

Nos. 46-56 Surcharged with New Value

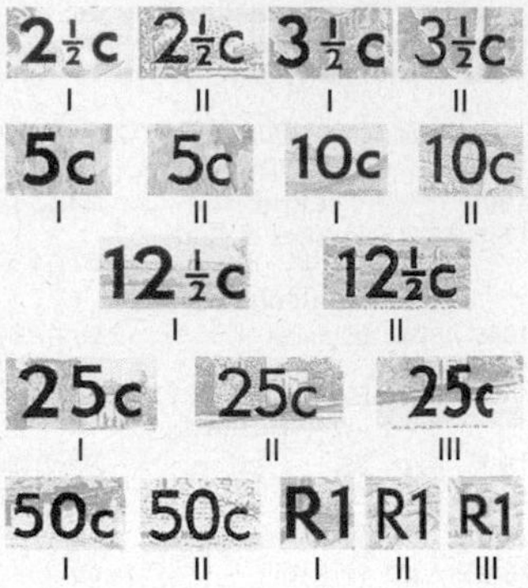

Perf. 13½, 11½ (#71)

1961, Feb. 14 Wmk. 4

61	A7	½c on ½p	.25	.25
a.		Double surcharge	750.00	
62	A7	1c on 1p	.25	.25
63	A7	2c on 2p	1.25	*1.50*
a.		Inverted surcharge	225.00	
64	A7	2½c on 3p (II)	.25	.25
a.		Type I	.25	.25
b.		Inverted surcharge (II)	8,000.	8,000.
65	A7	3½c on 4½p (I)	.35	.25
a.		Type II	4.00	*8.50*
66	A7	5c on 6p (II)	.80	.25
a.		Type I	.40	.25
67	A7	10c on 1sh (I)	.50	.25
a.		Type II	175.00	*180.00*
68	A7	12½c on 1sh3p (II)	13.00	4.75
a.		Type I	6.00	2.25
69	A7	25c on 2sh6p (I)	1.90	.75
a.		Type II	57.50	15.00
b.		Type III	1.90	*2.50*
70	A7	50c on 5sh (II)	4.50	6.00
a.		Type I	8.50	5.50
71	A8	1r on 10sh (III)	32.50	27.50
a.		Type I	67.50	27.50
b.		Type II	32.50	*67.50*
		Nos. 61-71 (11)	55.55	42.00

Surcharge types on Nos. 64-71 are numbered chronologically.

Types of 1954
Value in Cents and Rands

Designs: ½c, Qiloane Hill. 1c, Orange River. 2c, Mosotho horseman. 2½c, Basuto household. 3½c, Maletsunyane Falls. 5c, Herdboy with lesiba. 10c, Pastoral scene. 12½c, Plane at Lancers Gap. 25c, Old Fort Leribe. 50c, Mission cave house. 1r, Shearing Angora goats.

1961-63 Wmk. 4 Engr. *Perf. 13½*

72	A7	½c dk brn & gray ('62)	.25	*.30*
73	A7	1c dp grn & gray blk ('62)	.30	*.40*
74	A7	2c org & dp bl ('62)	3.00	1.50
75	A7	2½c car & ol grn	2.00	.85
76	A7	3½c dp bl & ind ('62)	.80	*1.50*
77	A7	5c dk grn & org brn ('62)	.65	*.70*
78	A7	10c rose vio & dk ol ('62)	.40	*.50*
79	A7	12½c aqua & brn ('62)	25.00	12.00
80	A7	25c lilac rose & dp ultra ('62)	6.50	6.50
81	A7	50c dp car & blk ('62)	20.00	*25.00*

Perf. 11½

82	A8	1r dp cl & blk ('63)	52.50	*27.50*
		Nos. 72-82 (11)	111.40	*76.75*

See Nos. 87-91. For overprints on stamps and types see Lesotho Nos. 5-14, 20a.

Freedom from Hunger Issue
Common Design Type

Perf. 14x14½

1963, June 4 Photo. Wmk. 314

83	CD314	12½c lilac	.50	.25

Red Cross Centenary Issue
Common Design Type

1963, Sept. 2 Litho. *Perf. 13*

84	CD315	2½c black & red	.30	.25
85	CD315	12½c ultra & red	.90	.65

Queen Type of 1961-63

1964 Engr. *Perf. 13½*

87	A7	1c grn & gray blk	.25	*.35*
88	A7	2½c car & ol green	.25	*.30*
89	A7	5c dk green & org brn	.45	*.60*

90 A7 12½c aqua & brown 12.00 2.50
91 A7 50c dp car & black 7.00 *15.00*
Nos. 87-91 (5) 19.95 *18.75*

Mosotho Woman and Child — A10

Designs: 3½c, Maseru border post. 5c, Mountains. 12½c, Legislative Building.

Perf. 14x13½

1965, May 10 Photo. Wmk. 314

97 A10 2½c ultra & multi .25 .25
98 A10 3½c blue & bister .50 .30
99 A10 5c blue & ocher .50 .30
100 A10 12½c lt blue, blk & buff .60 .70
Nos. 97-100 (4) 1.85 1.55

Attainment of self-government.

ITU Issue

Common Design Type

1965, May 17 Litho. *Perf. 11x11½*

101 CD317 1c ver & red lilac .25 .25
102 CD317 20c grnsh bl & org brn .60 .40

Intl. Cooperation Year Issue

Common Design Type

1965, Oct. 25 Wmk. 314 *Perf. 14½*

103 CD318 ½c bluo grn & cl .25 *.50*
104 CD318 12½c lt vio & green .50 .35

Churchill Memorial Issue

Common Design Type

1966, Jan. 24 Photo. *Perf. 14*

Design in Black, Gold and Carmine Rose

105 CD319 1c bright blue .25 *1.00*
106 CD319 2½c green .55 .25
107 CD319 10c brown .75 .50
108 CD319 22½c violet 1.25 *1.50*
Nos. 105-108 (4) 2.80 3.25

POSTAGE DUE STAMPS

Catalogue values for all unused stamps in this section are for Never Hinged items.

D1

1933-52 Wmk. 4 Typo. *Perf. 14*

Chalky Paper

J1 D1 1p dark red ('51) 2.50 *12.00*
a. 1p carmine, ordinary paper 4.50 *17.50*
b. 1p dk car, ordinary paper ('38) 50.00 *60.00*
c. Wmk. 4a (error) 175.00
d. Wmk. 4, crown missing (error) 425.00
J2 D1 2p lt violet ('52) .40 *25.00*
a. 2p lt violet, ordinary paper 12.00 *25.00*
b. Wmk. 4a (error) 190.00
c. Wmk. 4, crown missing (error) 450.00

For surcharge see No. J7.

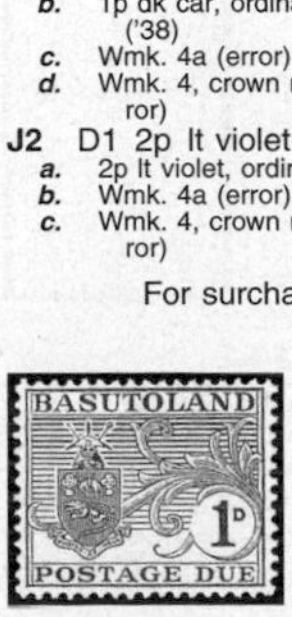
Coat of Arms — D2

1956, Dec. 1

J3 D2 1p carmine .50 *3.00*
J4 D2 2p dark purple .50 *6.00*

Nos. J2-J4 Surcharged

1961

J5 D2 1c on 1p carmine .25 *.40*
J6 D2 1c on 2p dk purple .25 *1.25*
J7 D1 5c on 2p lt violet 1.50 *8.00*
a. Wmk. 4a (error) 375.00
b. Wmk. 4, crown missing (error) 2,000.
J8 D2 5c on 2p dark pur ("5" 7½mm high) .25 .45
a. "5" 3½mm high 17.50 *55.00*
Nos. J5-J8 (4) 2.25 10.10

Value in Cents

1964 Wmk. 314 *Perf. 14*

J9 D2 1c carmine *5.00 26.00*
J10 D2 5c dark purple *5.75 26.00*

For overprints see Lesotho Nos. J1-J2.

OFFICIAL STAMPS

Nos. 1-3 and 6 Overprinted "OFFICIAL"

1934 Wmk. 4 Engr. *Perf. 12½*

O1 A1 ½p emerald *16,500. 8,500.*
O2 A1 1p carmine *6,250. 4,250.*
O3 A1 2p red violet *6,750. 1,500.*
O4 A1 6p yellow *16,500. 5,000.*

Counterfeits exist.

BATUM

bä-'tūm

LOCATION — A seaport on the Black Sea

Batum is the capital of Adzhar, a territory which, in 1921, became an autonomous republic of the Georgian Soviet Socialist Republic.

Stamps of Batum were issued under the administration of British forces which occupied Batum and environs between December, 1918, and July, 1920, following the Treaty of Versailles.

100 Kopecks = 1 Ruble

Counterfeits of Nos. 1-65 abound.

A1

1919 Unwmk. Litho. *Imperf.*

1 A1 5k green 7.00 *27.50*
2 A1 10k ultramarine 5.00 *14.00*
3 A1 50k yellow 7.50 *14.00*
4 A1 1r red brown 12.00 *9.50*
5 A1 3r violet 11.50 *20.00*
6 A1 5r brown 11.00 *42.50*
Nos. 1-6 (6) 54.00 *127.50*

For overprints and surcharges see Nos. 13-20, 51-65.

Nos. 7-12, 21-50: numbers in parentheses are those of the basic Russian stamps.

Russian Stamps of 1909-17 Surcharged

1919 On Stamps of 1917

7 10r on 1k orange (#119) 75.00 *75.00*
8 10r on 3k red (#121) 22.50 *32.50*

On Stamp of 1909-12

Perf. 14x14½

9 10r on 5k claret (#77) 950.00 950.00

On Stamp of 1917

10 10r on 10k on 7k light blue (#117) 975.00 900.00
Nos. 7-10 (4) 2,023. 1,958.

Russian Stamps of 1909-13 Surcharged

1919

11 35k on 4k carmine (#76) *4,000. 6,000.*
12 35k on 4k dull red (#91) *10,000. 13,000.*

This surcharge was intended for postal cards. A few cards which bore adhesive stamps were also surcharged.

Values are for stamps off card and without gum.

Type of 1919 Issue Overprinted

1919 Unwmk. *Imperf.*

13 A1 5k green 22.50 *15.00*
14 A1 10k dark blue 12.00 *18.00*
15 A1 25k orange 21.00 *18.00*
16 A1 1r pale blue 6.00 *18.00*
17 A1 2r salmon pink 1.75 *9.00*
18 A1 3r violet 1.75 *10.00*
19 A1 5r brown 2.00 *10.00*
a. "CCUPATION" *475.00 475.00*
20 A1 7r dull red 5.00 *11.00*
Nos. 13-20 (8) 72.00 *109.00*

Russian Stamps of 1909-17 Surcharged in Various Colors

10r & 50r

15r

On Stamps of 1917

1919-20 *Imperf.*

21 10r on 3k red (#121) 25.00 *27.50*
a. Inverted overprint 500.00
22 15r on 1k org (R) (#119) 50.00 *100.00*
23 15r on 1k org (Bk) (#119) 100.00 *150.00*
a. Inverted overprint 750.00 750.00
24 15r on 1k org (V) (#119) 75.00 *110.00*
25 50r on 1k org (#119) 975.00 *800.00*
26 50r on 2k green (R) (#120) 975.00 *1,100.*

On Stamps of 1909-17

Perf. 14x14½

27 50r on 2k green (#74) 1,000. 850.00
28 50r on 3k red (#75) 1,700. *2,500.*
29 50r on 4k car (#76) 1,500. *1,500.*
30 50r on 5k claret (#77) 975.00 *975.00*
31 50r on 10k dk blue (R) (#79) 3,000. *3,500.*
32 50r on 15k red brn & blue (#81) 700.00 *850.00*

Surcharged

On Stamps of 1909-17

33 25r on 5k cl (Bk) (#77) 100.00 *150.00*
34 25r on 5k cl (Bl) (#77) 100.00 *150.00*
a. Inverted overprint 300.00
35 25r on 10k on 7k lt blue (Bk) (#117) 150.00 *175.00*
36 25r on 10k on 7k lt blue (Bl) (#117) 100.00 *110.00*
37 25r on 20k on 14k bl & rose (Bk) (#118) 100.00 *150.00*
38 25r on 20k on 14k bl & rose (Bl) (#118) 200.00 *200.00*
39 25r on 25k grn & gray vio (Bk) (#83) 160.00 *175.00*
a. Inverted overprint 250.00
40 25r on 25k grn & gray vio (Bl) (#83) 100.00 135.00
41 25r on 50k vio & green (Bk) (#85a) 100.00 *110.00*
a. Inverted overprint 250.00
42 25r on 50k vio & green (Bl) (#85a) 100.00 *150.00*
43 50r on 2k green (#74) 250.00 175.00
44 50r on 3k red (#75) 200.00 175.00
45 50r on 4k car (#76) 200.00 *250.00*
46 50r on 5k claret (#77) 200.00 100.00

On Stamps of 1917

Imperf

47 50r on 2k green (#120) 975.00 *650.00*
48 50r on 3k red (#121) 975.00 *675.00*
49 50r on 5k claret (#123) *1,600. 1,700.*

On Stamp of 1913

Perf. 13½

50 50r on 4k dull red (Bl) (#91) 100.00 *120.00*

Nos. 3, 13 and 15 Surcharged in Black or Blue

No. 51

No. 55

1920 *Imperf.*

51 A1 25r on 5k green 75.00 *100.00*
52 A1 25r on 5k grn (Bl) 250.00 100.00
53 A1 25r on 25k orange 35.00 *45.00*
54 A1 25r on 25k org (Bl) *100.00 140.00*
55 A1 50r on 50k yellow 30.00 *40.00*
56 A1 50r on 50k yel (Bl) 100.00 125.00
Nos. 51-56 (6) 590.00 550.00

The surcharges on Nos. 21-56 inclusive are handstamped and are known double, inverted, etc.

Tree Type of 1919 Overprinted Like Nos. 13-20

1920

57 A1 1r orange brown 2.25 *12.00*
58 A1 2r gray blue 2.25 *12.00*
59 A1 3r rose 2.25 *12.00*
60 A1 5r black brown 2.25 *12.00*
61 A1 7r yellow 2.25 *12.00*
62 A1 10r dark green 2.25 *12.00*
63 A1 15r violet 2.75 *17.50*
64 A1 25r vermilion 2.50 *16.00*
65 A1 50r dark blue 2.75 *20.00*
Nos. 57-65 (9) 21.50 *125.50*

The variety "BPITISH" occurs on Nos. 57-65. Value, about $150 each.

BECHUANALAND

ˌbech-ˈwä-nə-ˌland

(British Bechuanaland)

LOCATION — Southern Africa
GOVT. — A British Crown Colony, which included the area of the former Stellaland, annexed in 1895 to the Cape of Good Hope Colony.
AREA — 51,424 sq. mi.
POP. — 72,700 (1891)
CAPITAL — Vryburg

British Bechuanaland stamps were also used in Bechuanaland Protectorate until 1897.

12 Pence = 1 Shilling
20 Shillings = 1 Pound

Watermarks

Wmk. 29 — Orb

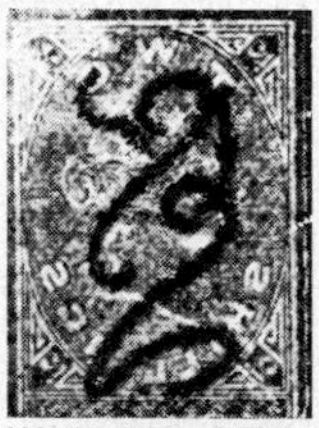

Wmk. 14 — VR in Italics

Cape of Good Hope Stamps of 1871-85 Overprinted

1885-87 Wmk. 1 *Perf. 14*

Black Overprint

1	A6	4p blue ('86)	95.00	*85.00*

Wmk. 2

Black Overprint

3	A6	3p claret	60.00	*70.00*

Red Overprint

4	A6	½p black	40.00	*50.00*
a.		Overprint in lake	5,500.	*10,000.*
b.		Double overprint in lake & blk	900.00	*1,100.*

Wmk. Anchor (16)

Black Overprint

5	A6	½p black ('87)	17.50	*32.50*
a.		"ritish"	2,750.	*2,600.*
b.		Double overprint	4,250.	
6	A6	1p rose	27.50	11.00
a.		"ritish"	*7,500.*	*4,250.*
b.		Double overprint		*2,300.*
7	A6	2p bister	55.00	11.00
a.		"ritish"	9,000.	*5,500.*
b.		Double overprint		2,500.
8	A3	6p violet	220.00	47.50
9	A3	1sh green ('86)	375.00	190.00
a.		"ritish"	*24,000.*	*18,000.*

There is no period after Bechuanaland on the genuine stamps.

Great Britain No. 111 Overprinted in Black

1887 Wmk. 30

10	A54	½p vermilion	2.75	*1.50*
a.		Double overprint	2,700.	

For overprints see Bechuanaland Protectorate Nos. 51-53.

A1

A2

A3

1887 Typo. Wmk. 29

Country Name in Black

11	A1	1p lilac	29.00	5.00
12	A1	2p lilac	125.00	2.75
13	A1	3p lilac	9.00	*9.00*
14	A1	4p lilac	70.00	2.75
15	A1	6p lilac	85.00	3.00

Wmk. 14

16	A2	1sh green	37.50	13.50
17	A2	2sh green	70.00	65.00
18	A2	2sh6p green	85.00	80.00
19	A2	5sh green	140.00	*180.00*
		Pen cancellation		15.00
20	A2	10sh green	275.00	*400.00*
		Pen cancellation		45.00

Wmk. 29

21	A3	£1 lilac	1,100.	*900.00*
		Pen cancellation		65.00
22	A3	£5 lilac	4,000.	*1,900.*
		Pen cancellation		200.00

The corner designs and central oval differs on No. 22.

For overprints see Bechuanaland Protectorate Nos. 54-58, 60-66. For surcharges see Nos. 23-28, 30, AR2, Cape of Good Hope No. 171.

Fiscal cancels can be pen cancellations or ink stampings.

Beware of cleaned pen (fiscal) cancellations and forged postmarks on Nos. 21-22.

Nos. 11-12, 14-16 Surcharged

Black Surcharge

1888 Country Name in Black

23	A1	1p on 1p lilac	9.25	8.50
a.		Double surcharge		
24	A1	6p on 6p lilac	165.00	20.00

Red Surcharge

25	A1	2p on 2p lilac	65.00	4.00
a.		"2" with curved tail	350.00	180.00
26	A1	4p on 4p lilac	450.00	*775.00*

Green Surcharge

27	A1	2p on 2p lilac		*4,000.*
a.		"2" with curved tail		*20,000.*

Blue Surcharge

27A	A1	6p on 6p lilac		*25,000.*

Wmk. 14

Black Surcharge

28	A2	1sh on 1sh green	300.00	100.00

Cape of Good Hope No.41 Overprinted in Green

1889 Wmk. 16

29	A4	½p black	4.00	*40.00*
a.		Double ovpt., one inverted	3,500.	
b.		Double ovpt., one vertical	1,200.	
c.		Pair, one stamp without ovpt.	10,000.	

Exists with "British" missing from shifted overprint.

No. 13 Surcharged in Black

1888 Wmk. 29

30	A1	½p on 3p lilac & blk	275.00	*325.00*

Stamps with errors of spelling in the surcharge are fakes.

Cape of Good Hope Nos. 43-44 Overprinted in Black, Reading Up

1891 Wmk. 16

31	A4	1p rose	14.00	*22.00*
a.		Horiz. pair, one without overprint	*26,000.*	
b.		"British" omitted	4,250.	—
c.		"Bechuanaland" omitted	3,500.	
32	A4	2p bister	8.75	2.75
a.		Without period	325.00	*325.00*

See Nos. 38-39. Only one example of No. 31b exists. It is in the Royal Collection in London.

Stamps of Great Britain Overprinted in Black

1891-94 Wmk. 30

33	A40	1p lilac	7.25	2.00
34	A56	2p green & car	25.00	5.00
35	A59	4p brown & green	4.50	1.10
a.		Half used as 2p on cover		*3,000.*
36	A62	6p violet, *rose*	9.75	2.50
37	A65	1sh green ('94)	16.00	*20.00*
a.		Half used as 6p on cover		—
		Nos. 33-37 (5)	62.50	*30.60*

For surcharges, see Cape of Good Hope Nos. 172, 176-177.

Cape of Good Hope Nos. 43-44 Overprinted, Reading Down

1893-95 Wmk. 16

38	A6	1p rose	5.00	3.00
a.		No dots over both "i" of "British"	160.00	*160.00*
c.		As "a," reading up	*4,500.*	
d.		Pair, one without overprint		
39	A6	2p bister ('95)	16.50	4.25
a.		Double overprint	1,700.	850.00
b.		No dots over both "i" of "British"	275.00	175.00
d.		As "b," reading up	4,750.	

The missing dot-over-i variety exists only on this issue. Nos. 38c and 39d resulted from the sheets being fed into the press upside down.

Nos. 38-39 exist with "British" missing (from shifted overprint).

Cape of Good Hope No. 42 Overprinted

"BECHUANALAND" 16mm Long Overprint Lines 13mm Apart

1897

40	A6	½p light green	3.25	*20.00*

"BECHUANALAND" 15mm Long Overprint Lines 10½mm Apart

41	A6	½p light green	22.50	*75.00*

"BECHUANALAND" 15mm Long Overprint Lines 13½mm Apart

42	A6	½p light green	47.50	*150.00*
		Nos. 40-42 (3)	73.25	*245.00*

Nos. 40-42 actually are issues of Bechuanaland Protectorate.

BECHUANALAND PROTECTORATE

ˌbech-ˈwä-nə-ˌland prə-ˈtek-t̮ə-ˌrət

LOCATION — In central South Africa, north of the Republic of South Africa, east of South West Africa and bounded on the north by the Caprivi Strip of South West Africa and on the east by Southern Rhodesia
GOVT. — British Protectorate
AREA — 222,000 sq. mi.
POP. — 540,400 (1964)
CAPITAL — Vryburg (to 1895), Mafeking (to 1965), Gaberones

Bechuanaland Protectorate became self-governing in 1965 and achieved indepencence as the republic of Botswana, Sept. 30, 1966.

12 Pence = 1 Shilling
20 Shillings = 1 Pound
100 Cents = 1 Rand (1961)

Catalogue values for unused stamps in this country are for Never Hinged items, beginning with Scott 137 in the regular postage section and Scott J7 in the postage due section.

Additional Overprint in Black on Bechuanaland No. 10

a

b

c

1888-90 Wmk. 30 *Perf. 14*

51	A54(a)	½p ver ('90)	275.00	*450.00*
a.		Double overprint	1,800.	*2,200.*
b.		"Protectorrte"		
c.		As "b," double overprint	*20,000.*	
52	A54(b)	½p ver ('88)	13.00	*55.00*
a.		Double overprint	*375.00*	
53	A54(c)	½p ver ('90)	225.00	*250.00*
a.		Inverted overprint	100.00	*130.00*
b.		Double overprint	150.00	*200.00*
c.		As "a," double	750.00	*850.00*
d.		"Portectorate"	—	—
e.		As "a," "Portectorate"	*20,000.*	—

For surcharge see No. 68.

Bechuanaland Nos. 16-20 Overprinted Type "b" in Black

Wmk. 14

Country Name in Black

54	A2	1sh green	150.00	65.00
a.		First "o" omitted	*6,750.*	3,750.
55	A2	2sh green	800.00	*1,200.*
a.		First "o" omitted	*20,000.*	—
56	A2	2sh6p green	650.00	*1,100.*
a.		First "o" omitted	*20,000.*	—
57	A2	5sh green	1,400.	*2,750.*
a.		First "o" omitted	*25,000.*	—
58	A2	10sh green	5,250.	*7,500.*
a.		First "o" omitted	*25,000.*	—

Bechuanaland Nos. 11-15 Ovptd. Type "b" and Srchd. in Black

1888 **Wmk. 29**

Country Name in Black

60 A1 1p on 1p lilac 20.00 *16.00*
a. Short "1" 475.00 *550.00*
61 A1 2p on 2p lilac 50.00 20.00
a. "2" with curved tail 1,000. 550.00
63 A1 3p on 3p reddish lil 225.00 *290.00*
64 A1 4p on 4p lilac 475.00 500.00
a. Small "4" *6,000.* *6,000.*
65 A1 6p on 6p lilac 125.00 55.00

In #60 the "1" is 2½mm high; in #60a, 2mm.

Value Surcharged in Red

66 A1 4p on 4p lilac 160.00 60.00
a. Double overprint *2,750.*

Cape of Good Hope Type of 1886 Overprinted in Green

1889 **Wmk. 16**

67 A6 ½p black 6.50 *62.50*
a. Double overprint 800.00 *800.00*

No. 67 exists with "Bechuanaland" missing and with ovpt. words reversed (from shifted overprint).

Bechuanaland Protectorate No. 52 Surcharged in Black

Wmk. 30

68 A54 4p on ½p ver 52.50 6.25
a. Inverted surcharge *4,500.*
b. "1pence" omitted *7,000.*

Stamps of Great Britain 1881-87, Overprinted in Black

1897, Oct.

69 A54 ½p vermilion 3.00 *2.50*
70 A40 1p lilac 4.50 .85
71 A56 2p green & car 16.00 *4.50*
72 A58 3p violet, *yel* 6.25 *15.00*
73 A59 4p brown & green 29.00 25.00
74 A62 6p violet, *rose* 25.00 16.00
Nos. 69-74 (6) 83.75 63.85

For surcharges see Cape of Good Hope Nos. 167-170, 173-175.

Same on Great Britain No. 125

1902, Feb. 25

75 A54 ½p blue green 1.75 *4.00*

Stamps of Great Britain, 1902, Overprinted in Black

1904-12

76 A66 ½p gray grn ('06) 2.75 *4.50*
77 A66 1p car ('05) 12.00 .50
78 A66 2½p ultra 12.50 11.00
79 A74 1sh scar & grn ('12) 60.00 *170.00*
Nos. 76-79 (4) 87.25 *186.00*

Same on Great Britain No. 143

1908

80 A66 ½p pale yel green 4.00 4.00

Transvaal No. 274 overprinted "Bechuanaland Protectorate," formerly listed as No. 81, now appears as No. AR1 in the Postal-Fiscal Stamps section.

Great Britain No. 154 Overprinted Like Nos. 76-79

1912, Sept. **Wmk. 30** ***Perf. 15x14***

82 A81 1p scarlet 4.00 .90

Great Britain Stamps of 1912-13 Overprinted Like Nos. 76-79

Wmk. Crown and GvR (33)

1913-24

83 A82 ½p green 1.40 *2.00*
84 A83 1p scarlet ('15) 3.25 .85
85 A84 1½p red brn ('20) 7.00 *3.50*
86 A85 2p redsh org (I) 13.00 *4.25*
b. 2p orange (II) ('24) 47.50 4.00
87 A86 2½p ultra 4.00 *27.50*
88 A87 3p bluish violet 6.75 *21.00*
89 A88 4p slate green 7.25 *45.00*
90 A89 6p dull violet 10.00 *32.50*
91 A90 1sh bister 22.50 *45.00*
Nos. 83-91 (9) 75.15 *181.60*

The dies of No. 86 are the same as in Great Britain 1912-13 issue.

Wmk. 34 ***Perf. 11x12***

92 A91 2sh6p dk brn ('15) 150.00 *300.00*
a. 2sh6p light brown ('16) 125.00 *290.00*
93 A91 5sh rose car ('14) 180.00 *450.00*
a. 5sh carmine ('19) 350.00 *500.00*

Nos. 92, 93 were printed by Waterlow Bros. & Layton; Nos. 92a, 93a were printed by Thomas De La Rue & Co.

Same Overprint On Retouched Seahorses Stamps of 1919 (Great Britain Nos. 179, 180)

1920-23

94 A91 2sh6p gray brown 100.00 *200.00*
95 A91 5sh car rose 140.00 *325.00*

Nos. 94-95 measure 22.5-23mm vertically. Most examples have a small dot of color at top center, outside of frameline. Perforation holes are larger and usually are evenly spaced.

Great Britain Stamps of 1924 Overprinted like Nos. 76-79

Wmk. Crown and Block GvR Multiple (35)

1925-27 ***Perf. 15x14***

96 A82 ½p green ('27) 1.65 1.50
97 A83 1p scarlet 2.25 1.00
99 A85 2p deep org (II) 2.50 1.25
101 A87 3p violet ('26) 5.50 *30.00*
102 A88 4p sl grn ('26) 10.00 *55.00*
103 A89 6p dl vio, chalky paper 75.00 *110.00*
104 A90 1sh bister ('26) 11.00 *30.00*
Nos. 96-104 (7) 107.90 *228.75*

George V — A11

Perf. 12½

1932, Dec. 12 **Engr.** **Wmk. 4**

105 A11 ½p green 2.75 .35
a. Horiz. pair, imperf between *32,500.*
106 A11 1p carmine 2.50 .40
107 A11 2p red brown 2.50 .45
108 A11 3p ultra 5.25 *6.00*
109 A11 4p orange 5.25 *15.00*
110 A11 6p red violet 8.00 *9.50*
111 A11 1sh blk & ol grn 7.00 *10.00*
112 A11 2sh blk & org 27.50 *75.00*
113 A11 2sh6p blk & car 29.00 *55.00*
114 A11 3sh blk & red vio 50.00 *65.00*
115 A11 5sh blk & ultra 135.00 *135.00*
116 A11 10sh blk & red brown 350.00 *350.00*
Nos. 105-116 (12) 624.75 *721.70*

Common Design Types pictured following the introduction.

Silver Jubilee Issue

Common Design Type

1935, May 4 ***Perf. 11x12***

117 CD301 1p car & blue 1.75 *6.75*
118 CD301 2p black & ultra 2.50 *6.25*
119 CD301 3p ultra & brown 3.50 *11.00*
120 CD301 6p brown vio & ind 8.00 *12.00*
Nos. 117-120 (4) 15.75 *36.00*
Set, never hinged 24.00

Coronation Issue

Common Design Type

1937, May 12 ***Perf. 13½x14***

121 CD302 1p carmine .25 *.50*
122 CD302 2p brown .30 *1.25*
123 CD302 3p bright ultra .40 *1.60*
Nos. 121-123 (3) .95 3.35
Set, never hinged 1.75

George VI, Cattle and Baobab Tree — A12

1938, Apr. 1 ***Perf. 12½***

124 A12 ½p green 3.00 *3.75*
125 A12 1p rose car .60 .65
126 A12 1½p light blue .75 *1.25*
127 A12 2p brown .60 *.75*
128 A12 3p ultra .75 *3.00*
129 A12 4p orange 1.50 *4.25*
130 A12 6p rose violet 3.25 3.00
131 A12 1sh blk & ol grn 3.50 *9.50*
133 A12 2sh6p black & car 9.00 *20.00*
135 A12 5sh black & ultra 27.50 *32.50*
136 A12 10sh black & brn 19.00 *37.50*
Nos. 124-136 (11) 69.45 *116.15*
Set, never hinged 110.00

Catalogue values for unused stamps in this section, from this point to the end of the section, are for Never Hinged items.

Peace Issue

South Africa Nos. 100-102 Overprinted

Basic stamps inscribed alternately in English and Afrikaans.

1945, Dec. 3 **Wmk. 201** ***Perf. 14***

137 A42 1p rose pink & choc, pair .75 *1.50*
a. Single, English .25 .25
b. Single, Afrikaans .25 .25
138 A43 2p vio & slate blue, pair .55 *1.50*
a. Single, English .25 .25
b. Single, Afrikaans .25 .25
139 A43 3p ultra & dp ultra, pair .75 *1.75*
a. Single, English .25 .25
b. Single, Afrikaans .25 .25
c. Vert. pair, one with overprint omitted 17,000.
Nos. 137-139 (3) 2.05 *4.75*

World War II victory of the Allies.

Royal Visit Issue

Types of Basutoland, 1947

Perf. 12½

1947, Feb. 17 **Wmk. 4** **Engr.**

143 A3 1p red .25 .25
144 A4 2p green .25 .25
145 A5 3p ultra .25 .25
146 A6 1sh dark violet .25 .25
Nos. 143-146 (4) 1.00 1.00

Visit of the British Royal Family, 4/17/47.

Silver Wedding Issue

Common Design Types

1948, Dec. 1 **Photo.** ***Perf. 14x14½***

147 CD304 1½p brt ultra .35 .25

Engr.; Name Typo.

Perf. 11½x11

148 CD305 10sh gray black 42.50 *47.50*

UPU Issue

Common Design Types

Engr.; Name Typo. on 3p and 6p

1949, Oct. 10 ***Perf. 13½, 11x11½***

149 CD306 1½p blue .30 *1.00*
150 CD307 3p indigo 1.50 1.50
151 CD308 6p red lilac .80 *2.75*
152 CD309 1sh olive .75 *2.00*
Nos. 149-152 (4) 3.35 *7.25*

Coronation Issue

Common Design Type

1953, June 3 **Engr.** ***Perf. 13½x13***

153 CD312 2p brown & black .75 .35

Elizabeth II — A13

1955-58 ***Perf. 13x13½***

154 A13 ½p green .60 .35
155 A13 1p rose car 1.00 .25
156 A13 2p brown 1.50 .35
157 A13 3p ultra 3.50 2.50
158 A13 4p orange ('58) *13.00* *13.00*
159 A13 4½p indigo 1.75 1.25
160 A13 6p rose violet 1.50 .90
161 A13 1sh blk & ol grn 1.50 *1.50*
162 A13 1sh3p blk & rose vio 16.00 10.00
163 A13 2sh6p black & car 13.50 10.50
164 A13 5sh black & ultra 20.00 17.50
165 A13 10sh black & brn 42.50 20.00
Nos. 154-165 (12) 116.35 *78.10*

For surcharges see Nos. 169-179.

Victoria, Elizabeth II and Water Hole — A14

Perf. 14½x14

1960, Jan. 21 **Photo.** **Wmk. 314**

166 A14 1p brown & black .50 *.50*
167 A14 3p car rose & black .50 *.50*
168 A14 6p ultra & black .50 *.50*
Nos. 166-168 (3) 1.50 1.50

Proclamation of the Protectorate, 75th anniv.

Nos. 155-165 Surcharged

Elizabeth II, Type I

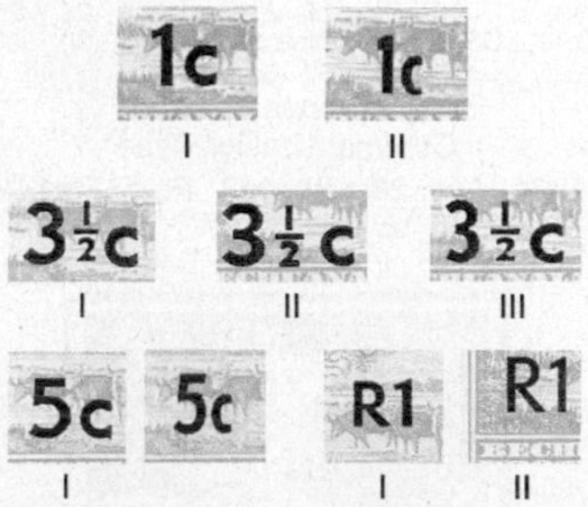

Perf. 13x13½

1961, Feb. 14 **Wmk. 4** **Engr.**

169 1c on 1p (I) .35 .25
a. Type II .45 .25
170 2c on 2p .25 .25
171 2½c on 2p .35 .25
a. Pair, one without surcharge *16,000.*
b. Type II 1.75 3.00
172 2½c on 3p 4.50 *8.00*
173 3½c on 4p (III) .25 .25
a. Type I .60 .60
b. Type II 3.00 *12.00*

174	5c on 6p (II)	.25	.25
a.	Type I	2.25	*3.25*
175	10c on 1sh	.30	.30
a.	Pair, one without surcharge	*20,000.*	
176	12½c on 1sh3p ("12½c" 11¼mm wide)	.65	.35
a.	"12½c" 12½mm wide	.85	.75
177	25c on 2sh6p	1.75	1.00
178	50c on 5sh	2.25	*3.00*
179	1r on 10sh (II, "R1" at lower center)	26.00	*20.00*
a.	Type II, "R1" at lower left	27.50	*30.00*
b.	Type I	375.00	175.00
	Nos. 169-179 (11)	36.90	33.90

Nos. 173a and 173b are found in the same sheet; each comes with "3½c" in both wide and narrow settings.

Surcharge types are numbered chronologically. These and other minor varieties of these overprints are collected by specialists.

African Golden Oriole — A15

Baobab Tree — A16

Designs: 2c, African hoopoe. 2½c, Scarlet-chested sunbird. 3½c, Cape widow bird (Yellow bishop). 5c, Swallow-tailed bee-eater. 7½c, Gray hornbill. 10c, Red-headed weaver. 12½c, Brown-hooded kingfisher. 20c, Woman musician. 35c, Woman grinding corn. 50c, Bechuana ox. 1r, Lion. 2r, Police camel patrol.

Perf. 14x14½, 14½x14

1961, Oct. 2 Photo. Wmk. 314

180	A15	1c lilac, blk & yel	1.75	.55
181	A15	2c pale ol, blk & org	2.25	*4.25*
182	A15	2½c bis, blk, grn & dp car	1.75	.25
183	A15	3½c pink, blk & yel	2.75	*4.75*
184	A15	5c dl org, blk, grn & bl	3.50	1.25
185	A15	7½c yel grn, blk, red & brn	2.25	*2.75*
186	A15	10c aqua & multi	2.25	.75
187	A15	12½c gray, yel, red & blue	19.00	6.00
188	A15	20c gray & brn	4.00	*4.75*
189	A16	25c yel & dk brn	5.00	2.75
190	A15	35c dp org & ultra	4.50	*6.00*
191	A16	50c lt ol grn & sep	2.75	*2.75*
192	A15	1r ocher & black	10.00	3.00
193	A15	2r blue & brn	30.00	12.50
		Nos. 180-193 (14)	91.75	52.30

For overprints see Botswana Nos. 5-18.

Freedom from Hunger Issue

Common Design Type

1963, June 4 ***Perf. 14x14½***

194 CD314 12½c green .50 .50

Red Cross Centenary Issue

Common Design Type

1963, Sept. 2 Litho. ***Perf. 13***

195	CD315	2½c black & red	.25	.25
196	CD315	12½c ultra & red	.70	.60

Shakespeare Issue

Common Design Type

1964, Apr. 23 Photo. ***Perf. 14x14½***

197 CD316 12½c red brown .35 .35

Notwani River Dam, Gaberones Water Supply — A17

Wmk. 314

1965, Mar. 1 Photo. ***Perf. 14½***

198	A17	2½c dark red & gold	.25	.25
199	A17	5c deep ultra & gold	.30	.25
200	A17	12½c brown & gold	.40	.40
201	A17	25c emerald & gold	.50	.50
		Nos. 198-201 (4)	1.45	1.40

Internal self-government, Mar. 1, 1965.

ITU Issue

Common Design Type

Perf. 11x11½

1965, May 17 Litho. Wmk. 314

202	CD317	2½c ver & dl yel	.35	.25
203	CD317	12½c red lil & pale brn	.75	.50

Intl. Cooperation Year Issue

Common Design Type

1965, Oct. 25 ***Perf. 14½***

204	CD318	1c bl grn & claret	.25	*.50*
205	CD318	12½c lt vio & grn	.60	.50

Churchill Memorial Issue

Common Design Type

1966, Jan. 24 Photo. ***Perf. 14***

Design in Black, Gold and Carmine Rose

206	CD319	1c bright blue	.25	*1.20*
207	CD319	2½c green	.45	.25
208	CD319	12½c brown	.85	.40
209	CD319	20c violet	.95	.65
		Nos. 206-209 (4)	2.50	2.50

Haslar Smoke Generator — A18

Wmk. 314

1966, June 1 Photo. ***Perf. 14½***

210	A18	2½c shown	.35	.25
211	A18	5c Bugler	.35	.25
212	A18	15c Gun site	1.00	.35
213	A18	35c Regimental cap badge	.40	.95
		Nos. 210-213 (4)	2.10	1.80

25th anniv. of the Bechuanaland Pioneers and Gunners of World War II.

POSTAL-FISCAL STAMPS

Transvaal No. 274 Overprinted

1910, July Wmk. 3

AR1 A27 6p brn org & blk 190.00 *375.00*

This stamp was issued for fiscal use in January 1907, but the "POSTAGE" inscription was not obliterated, and examples were accepted for postal use during 1910-11.

Bechuanaland No. 16 surcharged "£5"

1918 Wmk. 29

AR2 A2 £5 on 1sh green *92,000.* —

Examples without full gum or with no gum sell for much less than the values for examples with full gum.

The known used examples of AR2 are all fiscally used. Value, $1,400.

South Africa No. 3 Overprinted in two lines

1922 Wmk. 177

AR3 A2 1p rose red 50.00 *155.00*

POSTAGE DUE STAMPS

Postage Due Stamps of Great Britain Overprinted

On Stamp of 1914-22

1926 Wmk. 33 ***Perf. 14x14½***

J1 D1 1p carmine 11.00 *125.00*

On Stamps of 1924-30

Wmk. 35

J2 D1 ½p emerald 11.00 *75.00*

Overprinted

J3	D1	2p black brown	11.00	*100.00*
		Nos. J1-J3 (3)	33.00	*300.00*
		Set, never hinged	52.50	

D2

1932 Wmk. 4 Typo. ***Perf. 14½***

J4	D2	½p olive green	6.75	*60.00*
J5	D2	1p carmine rose	8.00	*10.00*
a.		1p carmine ('58)	1.50	27.50
J6	D2	2p dull violet	10.00	*57.50*
a.		2p violet ('58)	1.75	22.00
c.		As "a," thick "d"	47.50	
b.		As No. J6, thick "d"	120.00	
		Nos. J4-J6 (3)	24.75	*127.50*
		Set, never hinged	40.00	

Nos. J5a, J6a and J6b are on chalky paper. For detailed listings, see the Scott Classic Specialized catalogue.

Catalogue values for unused stamps in this section, from this point to the end of the section, are for Never Hinged items.

Nos. J4-J6 Surcharged

Type I

Type II

1961, Feb. 14 Chalky Paper

J7	D2	1c on 1p car rose, II	.25	*1.75*
a.		Type I	.30	*.60*
b.		Double surcharge, II	375.00	
c.		Ordinary paper, II	20.00	*65.00*
J8	D2	2c on 2p dull vio, II	.25	*2.00*
a.		Thick "d," II	4.75	
b.		Ordinary paper, II	170.00	*180.00*
c.		As "b," thick "d"	*800.00*	
d.		Type I	.35	*1.75*
e.		As "d," thick "d"	7.50	

Ordinary Paper

J9	D2	5c on ½p ol green, I	.50	*.75*
		Nos. J7-J9 (3)	1.00	*4.50*

Denominations in Cents

1961 Wmk. 4 ***Perf. 14***

J10	D2	1c carmine rose	.30	*2.25*
J11	D2	2c dull violet	.30	*2.00*
J12	D2	5c olive green	.50	*2.00*
		Nos. J10-J12 (3)	1.10	*6.25*

BELARUS

ˌbē-lə-ˈrüs

(Byelorussia)

(White Russia)

LOCATION — Eastern Europe, bounded by Russia, Latvia, Lithuania and Poland

GOVT. — Independent republic, member of the Commonwealth of Independent States

AREA — 80,134 sq. mi.

POP. — 10,401,784 (1999 est.)

CAPITAL — Minsk

With the breakup of the Soviet Union on Dec. 26, 1991, Belarus and ten former Soviet republics established the Commonwealth of Independent States.

100 Kopecks = 1 Ruble

Catalogue values for all unused stamps in this country are for Never Hinged items.

Five denominations, perf and imperf, of this design produced in 1920 were not put in use. Value $5. Forgeries abound.

Cross of Ephrosinia of Polotsk — A1

1992, Mar. 20 Litho. ***Perf. 12x12½***

1 A1 1r multicolored .45 .45

For overprint and surcharge see Nos. 17, 230.

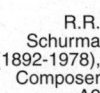

R.R. Schurma (1892-1978), Composer A2

1992, Apr. 10 Photo. ***Perf. 12x11½***

2 A2 20k blue & black .45 .45

For surcharge see No. 203.

Arms of Polotsk — A3

Designs: No. 13, Stag jumping fence. No. 14, Man's head, sword.

1992-94 Photo. ***Perf. 12x11½***

11 A3 2r shown .45 .45

Perf. 12x12½

12 A3 25r Minsk .35 .35
13 A3 700r Grodno .45 .45
14 A3 700r Vitebsk .45 .45
Nos. 11-14 (4) 1.70 1.70

Issued: 2r, 6/9/92; 25r, 11/11/93; Nos. 13, 14, 10/17/94.

National Symbols A4

Designs: No. 15, Natl. arms. No. 16, Map, flag.

1992, Aug. 31 Litho. ***Perf. 12x12½***
15 A4 5r black, red & yellow .65 .65
16 A4 5r multicolored .65 .65

For surcharges see Nos. 55-58, 61-64.

No. 1 Overprinted

Cross of Ephrosinia of Polotsk — A5

1992, Sept. 25 Litho. ***Perf. 12x12½***
17 A1 1r on #1 multi .45 .45

Souvenir Sheet

Perf. 12

18 A5 5r multicolored .80 .80

Orthodox Church in Belarus, 1000th anniv.
No. 18, imperf, was issued Feb. 15, 1993. Value $1.75.
For surcharges see Nos. 59-60, 65-66.

Buildings A6

Designs: No. 19, Church of Boris Gleb, Grodno, 12th cent. No. 20, Mir Castle, 16th cent. No. 21, Nesvizh Castle, 16th-19th cent. No. 22, Kamyanets Tower, 12th-13th cent, vert. No. 23, Church of Ephrosinia of Polotsk, 12th cent., vert. No. 24, Calvinist Church, Zaslaw, 16th cent., vert.

1992, Oct. 15 Litho. ***Perf. 12***
19 A6 2r multicolored .25 .25
20 A6 2r multicolored .25 .25
21 A6 2r multicolored .25 .25
22 A6 2r multicolored .25 .25
23 A6 2r multicolored .25 .25
24 A6 2r multicolored .25 .25
Nos. 19-24 (6) 1.50 1.50

Centuries of construction are in Roman numerals.

Natl. Arms — A7

1992-94 Litho. ***Perf. 12x12½***
25 A7 30k light blue .25 .25
26 A7 45k olive green .25 .25
27 A7 50k green .25 .25
28 A7 1r brown .25 .25
29 A7 2r red brown .25 .25
30 A7 3r org yellow .30 .25
31 A7 5r blue .30 .25
32 A7 10r red .60 .40
33 A7 15r violet .45 .30
34 A7 25r yellow green .60 .45
35 A7 50r bright pink .25 .25
36 A7 100r henna brown .55 .35
37 A7 150r plum .80 .45
38 A7 200r blue green .80 .40
39 A7 300r salmon pink .80 .40
40 A7 600r light lilac .80 .40
40A A7 1000r rose carmine 1.30 .40
40B A7 3000r gray blue 3.00 1.25
Nos. 25-40B (18) 11.80 6.80

Issued: 30k, 45k, 50k, 11/10; 1r-3r, 10r, 1/4/93; 5r, 15r, 25r, 2/9/93; 50r, 100r, 150r, 6/16/93; 200r-3,000r, 12/28/94; others, 1992.
For surcharges see Nos. 72-74, 141-142, 211A-212.

Ceramics A8

Designs: No. 41, Pitcher and bowl. No. 42, Four pieces on tree branches. No. 43, Two large pitchers. No. 44, One large pitcher.

1992, Dec. 24 Litho. ***Perf. 11½***
41 A8 1r multicolored .25 .25
42 A8 1r multicolored .25 .25
43 A8 1r multicolored .25 .25
44 A8 1r multicolored .25 .25
Nos. 41-44 (4) 1.00 1.00

M. I. Garetzky (1893-1938), Writer — A9

1993, June 22 Photo. ***Perf. 12x11½***
45 A9 50r magenta .40 .40

Straw Figures A10

Designs: 5r, Chickens. 10r, Child, mother, vert. 15r, Woman, vert. 25r, Man with scythe, woman with rake, vert.

Perf. 12x11½, 11½x12

1993, Apr. 22 Litho.
47 A10 5r multicolored .30 .30
48 A10 10r multicolored .30 .30
49 A10 15r multicolored .30 .30
50 A10 25r multicolored .50 .50
Nos. 47-50 (4) 1.40 1.40

First World Congress of White Russians — A11

1993, July 8 Litho. ***Perf. 12***
51 A11 50r multicolored .80 .80

Europa — A12

Paintings by Chagall: No. 52, Promenade, vert. No. 53, Man Over Vitebsk. 2500r, Allegory.

1993, Oct. 12 Litho. ***Perf. 14***
52 A12 1500r multicolored *5.00 6.00*
53 A12 1500r multicolored *5.00 6.00*
a. Pair, #52-53 *10.00 12.00*

Souvenir Sheet

54 A12 2500r multicolored *40.00 45.00*

Nos. 15-16, 18 Surcharged

a b

c d

Size and location of surcharge varies.

1993, Oct. 15 Litho. ***Perf. 12x12½***
55 A4(a) 1500r on 5r #15 *4.50 4.50*
56 A4(b) 1500r on 5r #15 *4.50 4.50*
a. Pair, #55-56 *11.50 11.50*
57 A4(c) 1500r on 5r #16 *4.50 4.50*
58 A4(d) 1500r on 5r #16 *4.50 4.50*
a. Pair, #57-58 *11.50 11.50*
Nos. 55-58 (4) *18.00 18.00*

Souvenir Sheets

Perf. 12

Overprints "e" & "f" on No. 18 are slightly different and have the wording at right reading down and Olympic Rings in upper left corner. No. 59 in Belarusian and No. 60 in English.

59 A5(e) 1500r on 5r #18 *10.00 10.00*
60 A5(f) 1500r on 5r #18 *10.00 10.00*

Nos. 59 and 60 exist imperf. Value, each $15. The status of No. 60 is in question.

Nos. 15-16, 18 Surcharged

g h

i j

Size and location of surcharge varies.

1993, Oct. 15 Litho. ***Perf. 12x12½***
61 A4(g) 1500r on 5r #15 *4.50 4.50*
62 A4(h) 1500r on 5r #15 *4.50 4.50*
a. Pair, #61-62 *11.50 11.50*
63 A4(i) 1500r on 5r #16 *4.50 4.50*
64 A4(j) 1500r on 5r #16 *4.50 4.50*
a. Pair, #63-64 *11.50 11.50*
Nos. 61-64 (4) *18.00 18.00*

Souvenir Sheets

Perf. 12

Overprints "k" & "l" on No. 18 are slightly different and have the wording at right reading down. No. 65 in Belarusian and No. 66 in English.

65 A5(k) 1500r on 5r #18 *10.00 10.00*
66 A5(l) 1500r on 5r #18 *10.00 10.00*

The status of Nos. 65-66 are in question. They exist imperf. Value, each $15.

Stansilavski Church A13

1993, Nov. 24 Litho. ***Perf. 12***
67 A13 150r multicolored .50 .50

For surcharge see No. 242.

Famous People A14

Designs: 50r, Kastus Kalinovsky, led 1863 independence movement. No. 69, Prince Rogvold of Polotsk, map of Polotsk. No. 70, Princess Rogneda, daughter of Rogvold, fortress. 100r, Statue of Simon Budny (1530-93), writer and printer, vert.

1993 ***Perf. 12x12½, 12½x12***
68 A14 50r multicolored .30 .30
69 A14 75r multicolored .30 .30
70 A14 75r multicolored .30 .30
71 A14 100r multicolored .30 .30
Nos. 68-71 (4) 1.20 1.20

Issued: 50r, 12/29; 75r, 12/30; 100r, 12/31.

Nos. 27, 29, 30 Surcharged

1994, Feb. 1 Photo. *Perf. 12x12½*

72 A7 15r on 30k light green .30 .30
73 A7 25r on 45k olive green .30 .30
74 A7 50r on 50k green .30 .30
Nos. 72-74 (3) .90 .90

Birds — A15

1994, Jan. 19 Litho. *Perf. 11½*

75 A15 20r Aguila chrysaetos .25 .25
76 A15 40r Cygnus olor .25 .25
77 A15 40r Alcedo atthis .25 .25
a. Block of 3, #75-77 + label .55 .55

See Nos. 87-89. For surcharge see No. 303.

Six World Wildlife Fund labels with 1000r denominations depicting 3 different animals and 3 different birds exist. They were not valid for postage.

Liberation of Soviet Areas, 50th Anniv. A16

No. 78 — Battle maps and: a, Katyusha rockets, liberation of Russia. b, Fighter planes, liberation of Ukraine. c, Combined offensive, liberation of Belarus.

1994, July 3 Litho. *Perf. 12*

78 A16 500r Block of 3 #a.-c. + label .85 .85

See Russia No. 6213, Ukraine No. 195.

1994 Winter Olympics, Lillehammer A17

No. 79, Speed skating. No. 80, Women's figure skating. No. 81, Hockey. No. 82, Cross-country skiing. No. 83, Biathlon.

1994, Aug. 30 Litho. *Perf. 12x12½*

79 A17 1000r multicolored .25 .25
80 A17 1000r multicolored .25 .25
81 A17 1000r multicolored .25 .25
82 A17 1000r multicolored .25 .25
83 A17 1000r multicolored .25 .25
Nos. 79-83 (5) 1.25 1.25

Painters — A18

Designs: No. 84, Farmer, oxen in field, by Ferdinand Rushchyts. No. 85, Knight on horseback, by Jasev Drazdovich. No. 86, Couple walking up path, by Petra Sergievich.

1994, July 18 Litho. *Perf. 12*

84 A18 300r multicolored .25 .25
85 A18 300r multicolored .25 .25
86 A18 300r multicolored .25 .25
Nos. 84-86 (3) .75 .75

For overprint see No. 127.

Bird Type of 1994

1994, Sept. 30 *Perf. 11½*

87 A15 300r like #75 .25 .25
88 A15 400r like #76 .25 .25
89 A15 400r like #77 .25 .25
Nos. 87-89 (3) .75 .75

Ilya Yefimovich Repin (1844-1930), Ukrainian Painter — A19

Designs: No. 90, Self-portrait. No. 91, Repin Museum.

1994, Oct. 31 Litho. *Perf. 12x12½*

90 1000r multicolored .40 .40
91 1000r multicolored .40 .40
a. A19 Pair, #90-91 .80 .80

Churches A20

Designs: No. 92, Sacred Consolidated Church, Sinkavitsch, 16th cent. No. 93, Sts. Peter and Paul Cathedral, Gomel, 19th cent.

1994, Oct. 20 Litho. *Perf. 12*

92 A20 700r multicolored .25 .25
93 A20 700r multicolored .25 .25

Kosciuszko Uprising, Bicent. (in 1994) — A21

Battle scene and: No. 94, Tomasz Vaishetcki (1754-1816). No. 95, Jakov Jasinski (1761-94). No. 96, Tadeusz Kosziuszko (1746-1817). No. 97, Mikhail K. Aginski (1765-1833).

1995, Jan. 11 *Perf. 12½x12*

94 A21 600r multicolored .30 .30
95 A21 600r multicolored .30 .30
96 A21 1000r multicolored .30 .30
97 A21 1000r multicolored .30 .30
Nos. 94-97 (4) 1.20 1.20

End of World War II, 50th Anniv. — A22

1995, May 4 Litho. *Perf. 13½*

98 A22 180r multicolored .25 .25
99 A22 600r multicolored .25 .25

Nos. 98-99 exist imperf. Value, set $125.

Alexander Stepanovich Popov — A23

1995, May 7 *Perf. 14*

100 A23 600r multicolored .40 .40

Radio, cent. Exists imperf. Value, $35.

A24

1995-96 Litho. *Perf. 13x14*

102 A24 180r olive brown & red .25 .25
103 A24 200r gray green & bister .25 .25
105 A24 280r green & blue .25 .25
109 A24 600r plum & bister .35 .35
Nos. 102-109 (4) 1.10 1.10

No. 102 exists imperf. Value, $30.

Issued: 180r, 5/10/95; 280r, 5/18/95; 600r, 8/29/95; 200r, 1/30/96.

For surcharges see Nos. 401-402.

Ivan Chersky (1845-92), Geographer A25

1995, May 15 Litho. *Perf. 13½x14*

113 A25 600r multicolored .40 .40

Exists imperf. Value, $45.

Traditional Costumes — A26

Designs: 600r, Woman wearing shawl, coat, ankle length skirt, man with long coat. 1200r, Woman wearing shawl & apron holding child, man wearing vest, knickers.

1995, July 13 Litho. *Perf. 14½x14*

114 A26 180r multicolored .25 .25
115 A26 600r multicolored .25 .25
116 A26 1200r multicolored .35 .35
Nos. 114-116 (3) .85 .85

See Nos. 164-167, 214-216.

World Wildlife Fund — A27

Various depictions of beaver.

1995, July 20 *Perf. 12*

117 A27 300r multi .30 .30
118 A27 450r multi .30 .30
119 A27 450r multi, horiz. .30 .30
120 A27 800r multi, horiz. .30 .30
Nos. 117-120 (4) 1.20 1.20

Book Fair — A28

1995, Aug. 29 Litho. *Perf. 14*

121 A28 600r multicolored .30 .30

Exists imperf. Value, $50.

A29

1995, Oct. 3 Litho. *Perf. 14*

122 A29 600r Natl. arms .25 .25
123 A29 600r Flag .25 .25

New national symbols. Nos. 122-123 exist imperf. Value, set $100.

UN, 50th Anniv. — A30

1995, Oct. 24 Litho. *Perf. 13½x14*

124 A30 600r bister, black & blue .30 .30

Exists imperf. Value, $40.

Churches A31

Designs: No. 125, Mstislav, 17th-19th cent. No. 126, Kamai, 17th cent.

1995, Nov. 21 *Perf. 14*

125 A31 600r multicolored .25 .25
126 A31 600r multicolored .25 .25

No. 84 Overprinted

1995, Dec. 27 Litho. *Perf. 12*

127 A18 300r multicolored .40 .40

P. V. Sukhi (1895-1975), Airplane Designer A32

1995, Dec. 27 *Perf. 13½*

128 A32 600r multicolored .40 .40

Exists imperf. Value, $45.

Wildlife A33

Designs: 1000r, Lynx lynx. No. 130, Capreolus capreolus. No. 131, Ursus arctos. 3000r, Alces alces. 5000r, Bison bonasus.
10,000r, Cervus elaphus, vert.

1995-96 Litho. *Perf. 14*
129 A33 1000r multi .30 .30
130 A33 2000r multi, vert. .35 .35
131 A33 2000r multi .35 .35
132 A33 3000r multi, vert. .40 .40
133 A33 5000r multi .55 .55
Nos. 129-133 (5) 1.95 1.95

Souvenir Sheet

Imperf

134 A33 10,000r multicolored 2.25 2.25

Issued: Nos. 129-133, 2/6/96; No. 134, 12/29/95.
For surcharge, see No. 607.

Famous People — A34

Designs: 600r, L. Sapega (1557-1633), statesman. 1200r, K. Semyanovitch (1600-51), military scholar. 1800r, S. Polotzki (1629-80), writer.

1995, Dec. 30 Litho. *Perf. 12*
135 A34 600r multicolored .30 .30
136 A34 1200r multicolored .30 .30
137 A34 1800r multicolored .30 .30
Nos. 135-137 (3) .90 .90

Miniature Sheet

Butterflies — A35

No. 138: a, Apatura iris. b, Lopinga achine. c, Callimorpha dominula. d, Catocala fraxini. e, Papilio machaon. f, Parnassius apollo. g, Ammobiota hebe. h, Colias palaeno.
No. 139, Proserpinus proserpina. No. 140, Vacciniina optilete.

1996, Mar. 29 Litho. *Perf. 14*
138 A35 300r Sheet of 8, #a.-h. 6.00 6.00

Souvenir Sheets

139-140 A35 1000r Set of 2 13.50 13.50

Inscribed 1995.

Nos. 28, 34 Surcharged in Green or Red

1996 Litho. *Perf. 12x12½*
141 A7 (B) on 1r #28 (G) .30 .30
142 A7 (A) on 25r #34 (R) .30 .30

Nos. 141-142 were valued at 200r and 400r, respectively, on day of issue.
Issued: No. 141, 2/28; No. 142, 3/13.

Souvenir Sheet

Beaver — A36

1996, Mar. 26 Litho. *Perf. 12½x12*
143 A36 1200r multicolored .45 .45

Kondrat Krapiva (1896-1991), Writer — A37

1996, Mar. 5 Litho. *Perf. 14x14½*
144 A37 1000r multicolored .40 .40

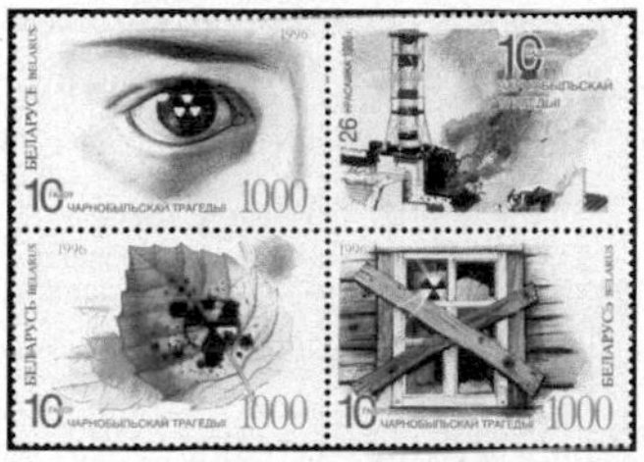

Chernobyl Disaster, 10th Anniv. — A38

No. 145 — Radiation symbol and: a, Eye. b, Leaf showing contamination. c, Boarded-up window.

1996, Apr. 10 Litho. *Perf. 14*
145 A38 1000r Block of 3, #a.-c. + label .55 .55

Coat of Arms — A39

1996, May 6 Litho. *Perf. 13½*
146 A39 100r blue & black .25 .25
147 A39 500r green & black .25 .25
148 A39 600r ver & black .25 .25
149 A39 1000r org & black .25 .25
150 A39 1500r dp lil rose & blk .25 .25
151 A39 1800r violet & black .25 .25
152 A39 2200r rose vio & blk .25 .25
153 A39 3300r yellow & blk .30 .30
154 A39 5000r grn bl & blk .40 .55
155 A39 10,000r ap grn & blk .90 1.10
156 A39 30,000r brn & black 2.75 3.00
157 A39 50,000r red brn & blk 4.50 5.25
Nos. 146-157 (12) 10.60 11.95

See Nos. 182, 196-201. For surcharges see Nos. 395-399.

Agreement with Russia A40

1996, June 14 *Perf. 13½x14*
158 A40 1500r multicolored .40 .40

Exists imperf. Value, $40.

1996 Summer Olympic Games, Atlanta A41

No. 159, Rhythmic gymnastics. No. 160, Discus. No. 161, Wrestling. No. 162, Weight lifting.
5000r, Shooting, vert.

1996, July 15 Litho. *Perf. 14*
159 A41 3000r multicolored .55 .55
160 A41 3000r multicolored .55 .55
161 A41 3000r multicolored .55 .55
162 A41 3000r multicolored .55 .55
Nos. 159-162 (4) 2.20 2.20

Nos. 159-162 exist imperf. Value, set $300.

Souvenir Sheet

Imperf

163 A41 5000r multicolored 1.00 1.00

No. 163 has simulated perforations.

Regional Costume Type of 1995

Couples in traditional 19th cent. costumes: 1800r, Kapiloka-Kletzky region. 2200r, David-Gorodok-Turai region. 3300r, Kobrin region.
5000r, Naralyan region.

1996, Aug. 13 Litho. *Perf. 14*
164 A26 1800r multicolored .30 .30
165 A26 2200r multicolored .35 .35
166 A26 3300r multicolored .40 .40
Nos. 164-166 (3) 1.05 1.05

Souvenir Sheet

Imperf

167 A26 5000r multicolored 1.00 1.00

Medicinal Plants — A42

No. 168, Sanguisorba officinaus. No. 169, Acorus calamus. 2200r, Potentilla erecta. 3300r, Frangula alnus. 5000r, Menyanthes trifoliata.

1996, Aug. 15 *Perf. 14x13½*
168 A42 1500r multicolored .25 .25
169 A42 1500r multicolored .25 .25
170 A42 2200r multicolored .25 .25
171 A42 3300r multicolored .35 .35
Nos. 168-171 (4) 1.10 1.10

Souvenir Sheet

Imperf

172 A42 5000r multicolored .90 .90

Birds — A44

No. 173: a, Ardea cinerea. b, Ciconia nigra. c, Phalacrocorax caroo. d, Ciconia ciconia. e, Larus ridibundus. f, Gallinago gallinago. g, Chlidonias leucopterus. h, Remiz pendulinus. i, Botaurus stellaris. j, Fulica atra. k, Ixobrychus minutus. l, Alcedo atthts.

No. 174: a, Anas crecca. b, Anas strepera. c, Anas acuta. d, Anas platyrhynchos. e, Aythya marila. f, Clangula hyemalis. g, Anas clypeata. h, Anas querquedula. i, Anas penelope. j, Arthya nyroca. k, Bucephala clangula. l, Mergus merganser. m, Mergus albellus. n, Aythya fuligula. o, Mergus serrator. p, Aythya ferina.
Each 1000r: No. 175, Aythya ferina, diff. No. 176, Gallinago gallinago, diff.

1996, Sept. 10 Litho. *Perf. 14*
173 A44 400r Sheet of 12, #a.-l. 6.75 6.75
174 A44 400r Sheet of 16, #a.-p. 6.75 6.75

Souvenir Sheets

175-176 A44 Set of 2 9.00 9.00

Grammar Book, 1596 — A45

1996, Sept. 19 Litho. *Perf. 14x13½*
177 A45 1500r multicolored .45 .45

Exists imperf. Value, $30.

Churches A46

No. 178, Pinsk. No. 179, Mogilev, 17th cent.

1996, Sept. 24 *Perf. 14x14½*
178 A46 3300r multicolored .40 .40
179 A46 3300r multicolored .40 .40

Nos. 178-179 exist imperf.

Mikola Shchakatskin (1896-1940), Art Critic — A47

1996, Oct. 16
180 A47 2000r multicolored .40 .40

Minsk Telephone Station, Cent. A48

1996, Nov. 14
181 A48 2000r multicolored .40 .40

Natl. Arms Type of 1996

1996, Nov. 21 Litho. *Perf. 13½x14*
182 A39 200r gray green & black .40 .40

Pres. Aleksandr G. Lukashenko, Natl. Flag — A49

1996, Dec. 6 Litho. *Perf. 13½*
183 A49 2500r multicolored .45 .45

Famous Men — A50

Designs: No. 184, Kyril Turovski (1130-81), Bishop of Turov. No. 185, Mikola Gusovski (1470-1533), writer. No. 186, Mikolaj Radziwil (1515-65), chancellor of Lithuania.

1996, Dec. 17			*Perf. 13½*	
184	A50	3000r multicolored	.40	.40
185	A50	3000r multicolored	.40	.40
186	A50	3000r multicolored	.40	.40
		Nos. 184-186 (3)	1.20	1.20

New Year — A51

Designs: 1500r, Christmas tree, buildings in Minsk.

1996, Dec. 21			*Perf. 14*	
187	A51	1500r multicolored, vert.	.25	.25
188	A51	2000r multicolored	.30	.30

Nos. 187-188 exist imperf. Value, set $50.

Natl. Museum of Art, Minsk — A52

Icons: No. 189, Madonna and Child, Smolensk, 16th cent. No. 190, Paraskeva, 16th cent. No. 191, Ilya, 17th cent. No. 192, Three saints, 18th cent.

5000r, Birth of Christ, by Peter Yacijevitsch, 1649.

1996, Dec. 26			*Perf. 13½*	
189	A52	3500r multicolored	.40	.40
190	A52	3500r multicolored	.40	.40
191	A52	3500r multicolored	.40	.40
192	A52	3500r multicolored	.40	.40
		Nos. 189-192 (4)	1.60	1.60

Souvenir Sheet

Imperf

193	A52	5000r multicolored	.95	.95

Georgi K. Zhukov (1896-1974), Soviet Marshal A53

1997, Jan. 3			*Perf. 13½*	
194	A53	2000r multicolored	.40	.40

Kupala Natl. Theater, Minsk — A54

1997, Jan. 3			*Perf. 13½x14*	
195	A54	3500r multicolored	.50	.50

Exists imperf.

Coat of Arms Type of 1996

1997		**Litho.**	*Perf. 13½x14*	
196	A39	400r lt brown & black	.30	.30
197	A39	800r dull blue & black	.30	.30
198	A39	1500r brt blue & black	.55	.55
199	A39	2000r apple green & black	.70	.70
200	A39	2500r dk blue & black	.60	.60
201	A39	3000r brown & black	.55	.55
		Nos. 196-201 (6)	3.00	3.00

Issued: 400r, 2000r, 1/9; 1500r, 1/16; 800r, 2500r, 3000r, 9/22.

For surcharge see No. 398.

V.K. Byalynitsky-Birulya (1872-1957), Painter — A55

1997, Feb. 26			*Perf. 14*	
202	A55	2000r multicolored	.40	.40

No. 2 Surcharged in Gray

1997, Mar. 10		**Photo.**	*Perf. 12x11½*	
203	A2	3500r on 20k bl & blk	.50	.50

Fish — A56

Designs: 2000r, Salmo trutta. 3000r, Vimba vimba. No. 206, Thymallus thymallus. No. 207, Barbus barbus.

5000r, Acipenser ruthenus.

1997, Apr. 10		**Litho.**	*Perf. 13½x14*	
204	A56	2000r multicolored	.30	.30
205	A56	3000r multicolored	.40	.40
206	A56	4500r multicolored	.50	.50
207	A56	4500r multicolored	.50	.50
		Nos. 204-207 (4)	1.70	1.70

Souvenir Sheet

208	A56	5000r multicolored	1.00	1.00

Intl. Conference on Sustainable Development of Countries with Economies in Transition — A57

Designs: 3000r, Earth with "SOS" formed in atmosphere. 4500r, Hand above flora and fauna.

1997, Apr. 16			*Perf. 14x14½*	
209	A57	3000r multicolored	.40	.40
210	A57	4500r multicolored	.60	.60
a.		Pair, #209-210 + label	1.00	1.00

Entry into UPU, 50th Anniv. — A58

1997, May 13			*Perf. 14½x14*	
211	A58	3000r multicolored	.50	.50

Nos. 28-29 Surcharged in Violet Blue

1997		**Litho.**	*Perf. 12x12½*	
211A	A7	100r on 1r brown	*8.00*	*8.00*
212	A7	100r on 2r red brn	.25	.25

Issued: 2r, 5/22. No. 211A, surcharged in error, was not regularly issued.

Independence Day, July 3 — A59

1997, June 26			*Perf. 14½x14*	
213	A59	3000r multicolored	.50	.50

Traditional Costume Type

Men and women in 19th cent. costumes, regions: 2000r, Dzisna. 3000r, Navagrudak. 4500r, Byhau.

1997, July 10				
214	A26	2000r multicolored	.25	.25
215	A26	3000r multicolored	.40	.40
216	A26	4500r multicolored	.55	.55
		Nos. 214-216 (3)	1.20	1.20

Book Printing in Belarus, 480th Anniv. — A60

Designs: No. 217, Text, Vilnius period. No. 218, Text, Prague period. 4000r, F. Skorina (1488-1535), Polotsk period. 7500r, F. Skorina, Krakow period.

1997, Sept. 7			*Perf. 13½*	
217	A60	3000r shown	.40	.40
218	A60	3000r gray, black & red	.40	.40
219	A60	4000r gray, black & red	.40	.40
220	A60	7500r gray, black & red	.80	.80
		Nos. 217-220 (4)	2.00	2.00

Pinsk Jesuit College A61

1997, Sept. 13			*Perf. 14x14½*	
221	A61	3000r multicolored	.45	.45

National Library, 75th Anniv. A62

1997, Sept. 15				
222	A62	3000r multicolored	.45	.45

Belarus School for the Blind, Cent. A63

1997, Sept. 28		**Litho.**	*Perf. 14x14¼*	
223	A63	3000r multicolored	.45	.45

Intl. Children's Day — A64

1997, Sept. 28		**Litho.**	*Perf. 14x14½*	
224	A64	3000r multicolored	.45	.45

Fight Against AIDS — A65

1997, Oct. 14			*Perf. 14½x14*	
225	A65	4000r multicolored	.50	.50

Farm Tractors A66

Designs: 3300r, Belarus "1221." 4400r, First wheel tractor, 1953. No. 228, Belarus "952." No. 229, Belarus "680."

1997, Oct. 16			*Perf. 14x14½*	
226	A66	3300r multicolored	.35	.35
227	A66	4400r multicolored	.40	.40
228	A66	7500r multicolored	.65	.65
229	A66	7500r multicolored	.65	.65
a.		Sheet, 2 ea #226-229 + label	4.25	4.25
		Nos. 226-229 (4)	2.05	2.05

No. 1 Surcharged

1997, Dec. 8		**Litho.**	*Perf. 12x12½*	
230	A1	3000r on 1r multi	.45	.45

Holiday Greetings
A68

1997, Dec. 23 Litho. *Perf. 14x14¼*

231 A68 1400r New Year .25 .25
232 A68 4400r Christmas .45 .45

1998 Winter Olympic Games, Nagano — A69

Designs: a, 2000r, Cross country skiing. b, 3300r, Ice hockey. c, 4400r, Biathlon. d, 7500r, Freestyle skiing.

1998, Feb. 3 Litho. *Perf. 13½*

233 A69 Block of 4, #a.-d. 1.40 1.40

P.M. Masherov (1918-80), Politician
A70

1998, Feb. 12 Litho. *Perf. 13½*

234 A70 2500r multicolored .45 .45

Minsk Automobile Plant — A71

Dump trucks: 1400r, 1947 MAZ-205. 2000r, 1968 MAZ-503B. 3000r, 1977 MAZ-5549. 4400r, 1985 MAZ-5551. 7500r, 1994 MAZ-5516.

1998, Apr. 23 Litho. *Perf. 13½*

235 A71 1400r multicolored .40 .40
236 A71 2000r multicolored .40 .40
237 A71 3000r multicolored .50 .50
238 A71 4400r multicolored .70 .70
239 A71 7500r multicolored 1.10 1.10
a. Souvenir sheet, #235-239 + label 2.40 2.40
Nos. 235-239 (5) 3.10 3.10

Europa — A72

1998, May 5 Litho. *Perf. 14*

240 A72 15,000r multicolored *.80 .80*

Town of Nesvizh, 775th Anniv.

A73

1998, May 20 Litho. *Perf. 14*

241 A73 8600r multicolored 1.40 1.40

Adam Mickiewicz (1798-1855), poet.

No. 67 Surcharged in Silver with Post Horn, New Value and Cyrillic Text

1998, May 22 *Perf. 12*

242 A13 8600r on 150r multi .45 .45

St. Petersburt-Mahilyou Post Route, 225th anniv.

A74

Songbirds from Red Book of Belarus: 1500r, Luscinia svecica. 3200r, Remiz pendulinus. 3800r, Acrocephalus paludicola. 5300r, Locustella luscinioides. 8600r, Parus cyanus.

1998, May 29 *Perf. 14*

243 A74 1500r multicolored .30 .30
244 A74 3200r multicolored .35 .35
245 A74 3800r multicolored .35 .35
246 A74 5300r multicolored .50 .50
247 A74 8600r multicolored .65 .65
a. Sheet, 2 each #243-247 4.00 4.00
Nos. 243-247 (5) 2.15 2.15

A75

Designs: 100r, Water-powered mill. 200r, Windmill. 500r, Stork. 1000r, Bison. 2000r, Christmas Star. 3200r, Dulcimer. 5000r, Church, Synkovichy. 5300r, Hurdy-gurdy. 10,000r, Flaming wheel.

1998 *Perf. 13½x14*

248 A75 100r green & black .25 .25
249 A75 200r brown & black .25 .25
250 A75 500r bl, lt blu & blk .25 .25
251 A75 1000r grn, lt grn & blk .25 .25
252 A75 2000r bl, lt bl & blk .25 .25
253 A75 3200r ap grn & blk .50 .50
254 A75 5000r bl, lt bl & blk .25 .25
255 A75 5300r bis, blk & buff .75 .75
256 A75 10,000r org, lt org & blk .30 .30
Nos. 248-256 (9) 3.05 3.05

Issued: 100r, 200r, 7/1; 3200r, 5300r, 6/23; 2000r, 10,000r, 8/5;

See Nos. 282-288, 331-335, 338-339, 361, 363, 409-413. For surcharge see No. 400.

Belarussian Auto Works (BelAZ), 50th Anniv. — A76

Designs: 1500r, Front end loader.

Large quarry truck models: 3200r, #75131. 3800r, #75303. 5300r, #75483. 8600r, #755.

1998, Aug. 12 *Perf. 14x14½*

259 A76 1500r multicolored .25 .25
260 A76 3200r multicolored .25 .25
261 A76 3800r multicolored .25 .25
262 A76 5300r multicolored .25 .25
263 A76 8600r multicolored .25 .25
a. Sheet of 5, #259-263 + label 2.00 2.00
Nos. 259-263 (5) 1.25 1.25

A77

Mushrooms: 2500r, Morchella esculenta. 3800r, Morchella conica. 4600r, Macrolepiota rhacodes. 5800r, Marcrolepiota procera. 9400r, Coprinus comatus.

1998, Sept. 10 Litho. *Perf. 14¼x14*

264 A77 2500r multicolored .25 .25
265 A77 3800r multicolored .25 .25
266 A77 4600r multicolored .25 .25
267 A77 5800r multicolored .25 .25
268 A77 9400r multicolored .25 .25
Nos. 264-268 (5) 1.25 1.25

Tête-bêche pair

264a A77 2500r .45 .45
265a A77 3800r .45 .45
266a A77 4600r .55 .55
267a A77 5800r .65 .65
268a A77 9400r 1.00 1.00

See Nos. 316-320.

Wooden Sculptures — A78

Designs: 3400r, Naversha, 12-13th cent. 3800r, Archangel Michael, 1470-1480. 5800r, Prophet Zacharias, 1642-1646. 9400r, Madonna and Child, 16th cent.

1998, Oct. 6 *Perf. 13½*

269 A78 3400r multicolored .25 .25
270 A78 3800r multicolored .25 .25
271 A78 5800r multicolored .25 .25
272 A78 9400r multicolored .25 .25
Nos. 269-272 (4) 1.00 1.00

World Stamp Day — A79

1998, Oct. 9 *Perf. 14x14½*

273 A79 5500r multicolored .35 .35

Paintings from Natl. Art Museum — A80

3000r, "Kalozha" (church), by V.K. Tsvirko (1913-93). 3500r, "Corner Living Room," by S.U. Zhukovsky (1875-1944). 5000r, "Winter Dream," by V.K. Byalynitsky-Birulya (1872-1957). 5500r, "Portrait of a Girl," by I.I. Alyashkevich (1777-1830). 10,000r, "Woman with a Bowl of Fruit," by I.F. Hrutski (1810-85).

1998, Oct. 20 *Perf. 13½*

274 A80 3000r multi .30 .30
275 A80 3500r multi .30 .30
276 A80 5000r multi .30 .30
277 A80 5500r multi, vert. .30 .30
278 A80 10,000r multi, vert. .30 .30
Nos. 274-278 (5) 1.50 1.50

A81

1998, Nov. 25 *Perf. 14½x14*

279 A81 7100r multicolored .35 .35

Universal Declaration of Human Rights, 50th anniv.

Christmas and New Year — A82

No. 280, Girl wearing short yellow coat, rabbit, log cabin. No. 281, Rabbit, girl wearing long fur-trimmed pink coat, hat.

1998, Nov. 30

280 A82 5500r multicolored .25 .25
281 A82 5500r multicolored .25 .25
a. Pair, #280-281 .40 .40

Type of 1998

Designs: 800r, Church. 1500r, Dulcimer. 3000r, Hurdy-gurdy. 30,000r, Water-powered mill. 50,000r, Windmill. 100,000r, Exhibition center, Minsk, horiz. 500,000r, Dancers.

Perf. 13½x14, 14x13½

1998-99 Litho.

282 A75 800r red lil, pale lil & blk .25 .25
283 A75 1500r golden brn, buff & blk .25 .25
284 A75 3000r yel, pale yel & blk .25 .25
285 A75 30,000r Prus bl, lt bl & blk .30 .30
286 A75 50,000r org, pale org & blk .45 .45
287 A75 100,000r brt pink & blk .70 .70
288 A75 500,000r brn & blk 2.40 2.40
Nos. 282-288 (7) 4.60 4.60

Issued: 800r, 2/5/99; 1500r, 3000r, 12/22/98; 30,000r, 50,000r, 4/14/99; 100,000r, 4/22/99; 500,000r, 6/25/99.

Statues of Aleksander Pushkin and Adam Mickiewicz, St. Petersburg — A95

1999, Jan. 20 Litho. *Perf. 13½*

294 A95 15,300r multi .35 .35

Trucks Made In Minsk — A96

10,000r, Model 8007. 15,000r, Model 543M rocket launcher. No. 297, Model 7907. No. 298, Model 543m with radar.
No. 299: a, 50,000r, Model 7917. b, 150,000r, Model 74135.

1999, Feb. 23

295 A96 10,000r multi .30 .30
296 A96 15,000r multi .30 .30
297 A96 30,000r multi .40 .40
298 A96 30,000r multi .40 .40
Nos. 295-298 (4) 1.40 1.40

Souvenir Sheet

299 A96 Sheet of 6, #295-298, 299a, 299b + 3 labels 2.50 2.50

No. 295 printed in sheets of 8.
See Nos. 322-323.

Glassware in National History and Culture Museum A97

1999, Mar. 4

300 A97 30,000r Goblet .25 .25
301 A97 30,000r Three pieces .25 .25
302 A97 100,000r Lamp .50 .50
Nos. 300-302 (3) 1.00 1.00

No. 77a Surcharged in Red

1999, Apr. 26 Litho. ***Perf. 11½***

303 A15 150,000r on No. 77a 1.10 1.10

Europa — A98

Nature Reserves: No. 304, Berezina, 1925. No. 305, Belovezhskaya Forest, 1939.

1999, Apr. 27 Litho. ***Perf. 13½***

304 A98 150,000r multicolored *1.10 1.10*
305 A98 150,000r multicolored *1.10 1.10*

Regional Architecture — A99

1999, June 10 Litho. ***Perf. 13½***

306 A99 50,000r Well .35 .35
307 A99 50,000r House .35 .35
308 A99 100,000r Windmill .80 .80
Nos. 306-308 (3) 1.50 1.50

No. 306 printed in sheets of 8.

Paintings A100

Designs; 30,000r, Portrait of Y. M. Pen, by A. M. Brazer. 60,000r, St. Anthony's Church, Vitebsk, by S. B. Yudovin. No. 311, Street in Vitebsk, by Y. M. Pen. No. 312, House in Vitebsk, by M. P. Michalap, horiz.
200,000r, Etching by Marc Chagall.

1999, July 2

309 A100 30,000r multi .25 .25
310 A100 60,000r multi .35 .35
311 A100 100,000r multi .50 .50
312 A100 100,000r multi .50 .50
Nos. 309-312 (4) 1.60 1.60

Souvenir Sheet

313 A100 200,000r multi 1.60 1.60

V. M. Karvat (1958-96), Hero — A101

1999, Aug. 12

314 A101 25,000r multi .35 .35

UPU, 125th Anniv. — A102

No. 315: a, Minsk post office, 1954. b, First Minsk post office, 1800.

1999, Aug. 20

315 A102 150,000r Pair, #a.-b. 1.60 1.60

Mushroom Type of 1998

Designs: 30,000r, Flammulina velutipes. 50,000r, Kuehneromyces mutabilis. 75,000r, Lyophyllum connatum. 100,000r, Lyophyllum decastes.
150,000r, Armillariella mellea.

1999, Aug. 21 ***Perf. 14¼x14***

316 A77 30,000r multi .25 .25
a. Tete beche pair .50 .50
317 A77 50,000r multi .40 .40
a. Tete beche pair .80 .80
318 A77 75,000r multi .55 .55
a. Tete beche pair 1.10 1.10
319 A77 100,000r multi .80 .80
a. Tete beche pair 1.60 1.60
Nos. 316-319 (4) 2.00 2.00

Souvenir Sheet

320 A77 150,000r multi 1.40 1.40
a. Tete beche pair 2.75 2.75

Left margin of No. 320 is perforated, and sheet contains two labels.

Re-annexation of Western Belarus from Poland, 60th Anniv. — A103

1999, Sept. 17 Litho. ***Perf. 13½x14***

321 A103 29,000r multi .30 .30

Truck Type of 1999

51,000r, MAZ-6430. 86,000r, MAZ-4370.

1999, Nov. 15 Litho. ***Perf. 13½***

322 A96 51,000r multi .25 .25
323 A96 86,000r multi .35 .35

Children's Art — A104

1999, Nov. 25

324 A104 32,000r shown .25 .25
325 A104 59,000r Girl, vert. .35 .35

New Year — A105

No. 326: a, Bear, snow-covered trees. b, People, snowman.

1999, Nov. 30 ***Perf. 14x14¼***

326 A105 30,000r Pair, #a-b, + central label .35 .35

Christianity, 2000th Anniv. — A106

Designs: 50r, Spaso-Preobrazhenskaya Church, Polotsk. 75r, St. Atistratig Cathedral, Slutsk. 100r, Rev, Serafim Sorovsky Church, Beloozersk.

2000, Jan. 1 ***Perf. 14¼x14***

327 A106 50r multi .35 .35
328 A106 75r multi .60 .60
329 A106 100r multi .90 .90
Nos. 327-329 (3) 1.85 1.85

Souvenir Sheet

Christianity, 2000th Anniversary — A107

No. 330: a, Mother of God mosaic, St. Sofia, Cathedral, Kiev, 11th cent. b, Christ Pantocrator fresco, Church of the Savoior's Transfiguration, Polotsk, 12th cent. c, Volodymyr Madonna, Tretiakov Gallery, Moscow, 12th cent.

2000, Jan. 5 ***Perf. 12x12¼***

330 A107 100r Sheet of 3, #a-c 1.75 1.75

See Ukraine No. 370, Russia No. 6568.

Type of 1998 and

Kryzhachok Dancers — A108

1r, Bison. 2r, Christmas star. 3r, Hurdy-gurdy. 5r, Church, Synkovichy. 10r, Flaming wheel. A, Kupala folk holiday. 20r, Kryzhachok dancers. 30r, Water-powered mill. 50r, Windmill.

2000-02 Litho. ***Perf. 13¼x13¾***

Inscribed "2000"

331 A75 1r multi .25 .25
332 A75 2r multi .25 .25
333 A75 3r multi .25 .25
334 A75 5r multi .25 .25
335 A75 10r multi .25 .25
336 A108 A multi .25 .25
337 A108 20r multi .25 .25
338 A75 30r multi .25 .25
339 A75 50r orange frame .40 .40
Nos. 331-339 (9) 2.40 2.40

Inscribed "2002"

333a A75 3r multi .25 .25
336a A108 A multi .25 .25
337a A108 20r multi .25 .25
339a A75 50r bister brn frame .30 .30
Nos. 333a-339a (4) 1.05 1.05

Booklet Stamp

Self-Adhesive

Serpentine Die Cut 5¾

340 A108 20r red & black .30 .30
a. Booklet pane of 18 3.00
Booklet, #340a 3.00

No. 336 sold for 19r on day of issue.
No. 340 has a line below the country name. Nos. 337 and 364 have lines of microprinting below the country name.
Issued: 1r, 5r, 10r, 1/6; No. 340, 1/14; 2r, 30r, 1/29; 3r, A, No. 337, 3/10; 50r, 4/6; Nos. 333a, 337a, 2/12/02; No. 336a, 4/24/02; No. 339a, 8/8/02.
See Nos. 362, 364-370, 414.

Sukhoi Fighter Aircraft A109

Designs: Nos. 341, 344a, Su-24. Nos. 342, 344b, Su-25. Nos. 343, 344c, Su-27.

2000, Feb. 23 Litho. ***Perf. 14x14¼***

341 A109 50r multicolored .35 .35
342 A109 50r multicolored .35 .35
343 A109 50r multicolored .35 .35
Nos. 341-343 (3) 1.05 1.05

Souvenir Sheet

344 Sheet of 3 + label 1.60 1.60
a.-c. A109 150r Any single .50 .50

See Nos. 383-384.

Birds — A110

Designs: No. 345, Mergellus albelius. No. 346, Burhinus oedicnemus. 75r, Lagopus lagopus. 100r, Aquila pomarina, vert.

Perf. 13½x13¾, 13¾x13½

2000, Mar. 22

345 A110 50r multi .40 .40
346 A110 50r multi .40 .40
347 A110 75r multi .50 .50
348 A110 100r multi .70 .70
Nos. 345-348 (4) 2.00 2.00

Partisan Madonna of Minsk, by M. Savitsky — A111

2000, Apr. 27 ***Perf. 13½***

349 A111 100r multi .50 .50

End of World War II, 55th anniv.

Europa, 2000

Common Design Type

2000, May 9 ***Perf. 14x13½***

350 CD17 250r multi *1.75 1.75*
a. Tete beche pair *4.25 4.25*

Ballet — A112

Designs: 100r, Male dancer lifting female dancer. 150r, Dancer with crown.

2000, May 25 Litho. ***Perf. 13¾x13½***
351 A112 100r multi .60 .60

Souvenir Sheet

352 A112 150r multi + label 1.10 1.10

UN High Commissioner for Refugees, 50th Anniv. — A113

2000, Aug. 23 Litho. ***Perf. 13½x14***
353 A113 50r multi .30 .30

Worldwide Fund for Nature (WWF) — A114

Lynx lynx: No. 354, 100r, Close-up of head. No. 355, 100r, On tree. No. 356, 150r, On snow. No. 357, 150r, Adult and young.

2000, Aug. 25 ***Perf. 14x13½***
354-357 A114 Set of 4 3.00 3.00
357a Sheet, 2 each #354-357 6.25 6.25

Intl. Year of Culture of Peace A115

2000, Sept. 5 Litho. ***Perf. 13½x14***
358 A115 100r multi .50 .50

2000 Summer Olympics, Sydney — A116

No. 359: a, Gymnast on rings. b, Kayak. c, Rhythmic gymnastics.

2000, Sept. 10 Litho. ***Perf. 14x13½***
359 A116 100r Strip of 3, #a-c 1.40 1.40

Souvenir Sheet

360 A116 400r Runner + label 2.50 2.50

Compare Nos. 360 and 382.

Types of 1998 and 2000

Designs: 20r, Kryzhachok dancers. 30r, Water-powered mill. B, Dazhynki Crop Festival. A, Kupala folk holiday. 50r, Windmill. 100r, Exhibition center, Minsk, horiz. 200r, Vitebsk Town Hall. 500r, Dancers.

13¼x14, 14x13¼ (#361), Serpentine Die Cut 5¾ (#364-370)

2000-01 Litho.
361 A75 100r brt pink & blk .45 .45
a. Inscribed "2002" .30 .30
362 A108 200r yel grn & blk ('01) .60 .60
a. Inscribed "2003" .60 .60
363 A75 500r brn & blk ('01) 1.25 1.25
a. Inscribed "2003" 1.50 1.50

Self-Adhesive

364 A108 20r red & black .25 .25
365 A108 30r green & black .25 .25
366 A108 B yel & black .25 .25
367 A108 A blue & black .25 .25
368 A108 50r brown & black .25 .25
369 A108 100r brt pink & blk ('01) .25 .25
370 A108 200r yel grn & blk ('01) .50 .50
Nos. 361-370 (10) 4.30 4.30

Issued: 20r, 30r, B, A, 50r, 11/8/00. No. 362, 500r, 3/19/01; No. 361, 10/18/00; No. 370, 3/29/01.

No. 364 has a line of microprinting below country name, No. 340 has hairline. Nos. 366-367 sold for 34r and 39r respectively on day of issue. Nos. 364-368 each issued in sheets of 24.

Amber — A117

Halite — A118

Flint — A119

Sylvite — A120

2000, Nov. 22 Litho. ***Perf. 14x14¼***
371 A117 200r multi .75 .75
372 A118 200r multi .75 .75
373 A119 200r multi .75 .75
374 A120 200r multi .75 .75
Nos. 371-374 (4) 3.00 3.00

New Year 2001 — A121

2000, Nov. 28 Litho. ***Perf. 14x13½***
375 A121 200r multi 1.00 1.00

Christmas — A122

2000, Dec. 5
376 A122 100r multi .60 .60

A123

Children's Art Contest Winners A124

2000, Dec. 26 ***Perf. 13½***
377 A123 100r multi .35 .35
378 A124 100r multi .35 .35

St. Euphrosyne of Polotsk, 900th Anniv. of Birth — A125

2001, Jan. 5 Litho. ***Imperf.***
379 A125 500r multi 1.50 1.50

Brest Arms — A126

Gomel Arms — A127

2001, Jan. 10 ***Perf. 14¼x14***
380 A126 200r multi .70 .70
381 A127 200r multi .70 .70

Souvenir Sheet

Medal Count From 2000 Summer Olympics, Sydney — A128

Perf. 13¾x13½

2001, Feb. 22 Litho.
382 A128 1000r multi + label 4.50 4.50

Sukhoi Airplane Type of 2000

Designs: No. 383, 250r, RD (ANT-25), 1933. No. 384, 250r, Rodina (ANT-37), 1936.

2001, Feb. 23 Litho. ***Perf. 14x14¼***
383-384 A109 Set of 2 1.75 1.75

Beetles — A130

No. 385: a, Lucanus cervus. b, Oryctes nasicornis.

Perf. 13½x13¾

2001, Mar. 22 Litho.
385 A130 300r Pair, #a-b 1.75 1.75

Flowers — A131

Designs: 200r, Nymphaea alba. 400r, Cypripedium calceolus.

2001, Apr. 25 Litho. ***Perf. 14x14¼***
386-387 A131 Set of 2 2.00 2.00
a. Booklet pane of 12, 6 each #386-387 22.50 —
Booklet, #387a 22.50

The two center vertical pairs in No. 387a are Tête-bêche.

Europa — A132

National Parks: 400r, Prypyatski. 1000r, Narachanski.

2001, May 4 ***Perf. 13¾x13½***
388-389 A132 Set of 2 *5.50 5.50*

Chernobyl Nuclear Disaster, 15th Anniv. — A133

2001, June 9
390 A133 50r multi .30 .30

Native Costumes — A134

Designs: 200r, Woman and children, Slutsk, 19th cent. 1000r, Man, woman and child, Pinsk, 19th cent.

2001, June 15 ***Perf. 14¼x14***
391-392 A134 Set of 2 3.00 3.00
a. Booklet pane of 6, 3 each #391-392 10.00 —
Booklet, #392a 10.00

Independence, 10th Anniv. — A135

Litho. with Hologram Affixed

2001, July 3 ***Perf. 14¼x14***
393 A135 500r multi 1.25 1.25

Commonwealth of Independent States, 10th Anniv. — A136

2001, July 12 **Litho.** ***Perf. 14x13½***
394 A136 195r multi .50 .50

Nos. 102, 105, 146, 148, 150, 153, 198 and 248 Surcharged in Black, Red or Blue

Methods and Perfs as Before

2001

395	A39	400r on 100r #146	.65	.65
396	A39	400r on 600r #148	.65	.65
397	A39	400r on 1500r #150	.65	.65
398	A39	400r on 1500r #198	.65	.65
399	A39	400r on 3300r #153	.65	.65
400	A75	1000r on 100r #248 (R)	2.10	2.10
401	A24	1000r on 180r #102 (Bl)	2.10	2.10
402	A24	1000r on 280r #105	2.10	2.10
		Nos. 395-402 (8)	9.55	9.55

Issued: No. 397, 8/10; others 10/8.

Folktales — A137

Designs: 100r, The Blue Suit Made Inside Out. 200r, Okh and the Golden Snuffbox.

2001, Aug. 24 **Litho.** ***Perf. 13½***
403-404 A137 Set of 2 1.00 1.00

Year of Dialogue Among Civilizations A138

2001, Sept. 5 ***Perf. 14¼x14***
405 A138 400r multi 1.00 1.00
a. Tête-bêche pair 2.75 2.75

Souvenir Sheet

Otto Y. Shmidt (1891-1956), Arctic Explorer — A139

2001, Sept. 30 ***Perf. 14x13½***
406 A139 3000r multi 8.00 8.00

Water Sports — A140

Designs: 200r, Sailboarding. 1000r, Waterskiing.

2001, Oct. 25 ***Perf. 13¾x13½***

407	A140	200r multi	.50	.50
408	A140	1000r multi	2.00	2.00
a.		Booklet pane, 2 each #407-408	5.00	5.00
		Booklet, #408a	5.00	
b.		Souvenir sheet, #408 + 2 labels	2.00	2.00

Types of 1998-2000 Redrawn, Type of 2000 and

A141

Designs: 1r, Bison, with microprinting added in tree branch. 2r, Christmas star, with microprinting replacing line below country name. 5r, Church, Synkovichy, with microprinting replacing lower line in church window. 10r, Flaming wheel, with microprinting replacing line in fire. 30r, Water-powered mill, with microprinting in vertical posts to right of water wheel. B, Dazhynki Crop Festival. H, Church, Polotsk. C, Railway station, Brest. 1000r, Arms of Francis Skaryna, first Belarussian printer. 2000r, City Hall, Minsk. 3000r, City Hall, Nesvizh. 5000r, City Hall, Chechersk.

2001-02 **Litho.** ***Perf. 13¼x14***

409	A75	1r grn, lt grn & blk	.25	.25
410	A75	2r bl, lt bl & blk	.25	.25
411	A75	5r dk bl, lt bl & blk	.25	.25
412	A75	10r org, lt org & blk	.25	.25
413	A75	30r bl grn, lt bl & blk	.25	.25
414	A108	B bister & blk	.25	.25
415	A141	H lt yel, bis & blk	.50	.50
416	A141	C lt yel, ol grn & blk	.60	.60
417	A141	1000r pink, rose & blk	2.00	2.00
418	A141	2000r lt bl, bl & blk	3.25	3.25
a.		Inscribed "2007"	1.60	1.60
419	A141	3000r lt org, org & blk	4.75	4.75
420	A141	5000r lt grn, grn & blk	8.00	8.00
		Nos. 409-420 (12)	20.60	20.60

Nos. 414-416 sold for 55r, 236r and 314r respectively on day of issue. Issued: 1r, 2r, 1/28/02; 5r, 2/1/02; 10r, 2/12/02; 30r, 7/10/02; B, 3/22/02; H, C, 7/16/02, 1000r, 2000r, 3000r, 5000r, 11/16.

See No. 612.

House of Mercy, Minsk A142

2001, Nov. 30 ***Perf. 13¾x14¼***
421 A142 200r multi .50 .50

Christmas A143 New Year's Day A144

2001, Dec. 3 ***Perf. 14¼x14***
422 A143 100r multi .40 .40
423 A144 100r multi .40 .40

Yevgeniy V. Klumov (1876-1944), Surgeon A145

2001, Dec. 16 ***Perf. 13½x14***
424 A145 100r multi .40 .40

Arms of Borisov — A146

2002, Jan. 25 ***Perf. 14¼x14***
425 A146 200r multi .50 .50

2002 Winter Olympics, Salt Lake City — A147

Designs: No. 426, 300r, Slalom. No. 427, 300r, Figure skating. No. 428, 500r, Biathlon. No. 429, 500r, Ski jumping.

2002, Feb. 1 ***Perf. 13½x14***
426-429 A147 Set of 4 3.25 3.25

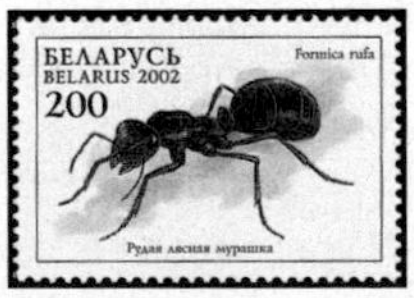

Formica Rufa — A148

2002, Mar. 20

430	A148	200r shown	.50	.50
431	A148	1000r Colony, vert.	2.00	2.00
a.		Booklet pane, 2 #430-431 + 2 labels	7.25	—
		Complete booklet, #431a	7.25	
b.		Souvenir sheet, #431 + 2 labels	2.00	2.00

Souvenir Sheet

Accomplishments of Belarus Winter Olympics Athletes — A149

2002, Apr. 10 ***Perf. 14x13½***
432 A149 2000r multi + 2 labels 3.00 3.00

Europa — A150

Designs: 400r, Clown. 500r, Horse.

2002, Apr. 30
433-434 A150 Set of 2 2.40 2.40

Janka Kupala (1882-1942), Poet — A151 Jakub Kolas (1882-1956), Poet — A152

2002
435 A151 100r multi .45 .45
436 A152 100r multi .45 .45

Souvenir Sheet

437	Sheet of 2 + central label	2.00	2.00
a.	A151 500r red & multi	.90	.90
b.	A152 500r red & multi	.90	.90

Issued: No. 435, 7/6; No. 436, 9/21; No. 437, 6/27.

Flowers — A153

Designs: 30r, Trifolium. 50r, Matricaria. 100r, Pulsatilla patens. 200r, Nuphar lutea. 500r, Chamaenerion angustifolium.
B, Linum. A, Centaurea cyanus. H, Campanula. C, Rhododendron.

2002 **Litho.** ***Serpentine Die Cut 9***

Self-Adhesive

438	A153	30r multi	.25	.25
439	A153	50r multi	.25	.25
440	A153	100r multi	.25	.25
441	A153	200r multi	.35	.35
442	A153	500r multi	.90	.90

Booklet Stamps

443	A153	B multi	.25	.25
a.		Booklet pane of 6	1.75	
		Complete booklet, 4 #443a	10.00	
444	A153	A multi	.30	.30
a.		Booklet pane of 6	2.50	
		Complete booklet, 4 #444a	14.00	
445	A153	H multi	.50	.50
a.		Booklet pane of 6	2.50	
		Complete booklet, 4 #445a	10.00	
446	A153	C multi	.60	.60
a.		Booklet pane of 6	3.50	
		Complete booklet, 4 #446a	14.00	
		Nos. 438-446 (9)	3.65	3.65

Nos. 443-446 sold for 75r, 90r, 236r and 314r respectively on day of issue.
Issued: 200r, 500r, 9/12; B, H, 7/24; A, C, 8/6. 30r, 50r, 100r, 8/28.

Children's Activities A154

Designs: 90r, Go-carting. 230r, Model airplane flying.

2002, July 25 Litho. ***Perf. 13½x14***
447-448 A154 Set of 2 .75 .75

Souvenir Sheet

Bird Life International — A155

No. 449: a, Ciconia ciconia. b, Oriolus oriolus. c, Motacilla alba.

2002, July 30
449 A155 200r Sheet of 3, #a-c, + label 1.75 1.75

Bridges — A156

Designs: 200r, Svisloch River Bridge, Minsk. 300r, Sozh River Bridge, Gomel. 500r, Western Dvina River Bridge, Vitebsk.

2002, Aug. 20 ***Perf. 13½***
450-452 A156 Set of 3 2.50 2.50

Intl. Year of Ecotourism A157

2002, Sept. 10 ***Perf. 13½x14***
453 A157 300r multi 1.00 1.00
a. Booklet pane of 4 + 4 labels 14.00 —
Complete booklet, #453a 14.00

No. 453 printed in sheets of 12 + 8 labels.

Souvenir Sheet

Space Exploration, 45th Anniv. — A158

2002, Nov. 28 Litho. ***Perf. 13½***
454 A158 3000r multi 4.50 4.50

Paintings in National Art Museum — A159

Designs: No. 455, 300r, Battle of Nyemize, by M. Filipovich, 1922. No. 456, 300r, By the Church, by F. Rushchits, 1899, vert.

2002, Nov. 28 Litho. ***Perf. 13½***
455-456 A159 Set of 2 1.25 1.25

Christmas and New Year's Day — A160

Designs: No. 457, 300r, Santa Claus. No. 458, 300r, Angel with bell.

2002, Dec. 5 Litho. ***Perf. 14x13½***
457-458 A160 Set of 2 1.25 1.25

Arms — A161

Designs: No. 459, 300r, Minsk (shown). No. 460, 300r, David-Gorodok.

2003, Jan. 24 ***Perf. 14¼x14***
459-460 A161 Set of 2 1.00 1.00
See Nos. 490-491, 543-545

Souvenir Sheet

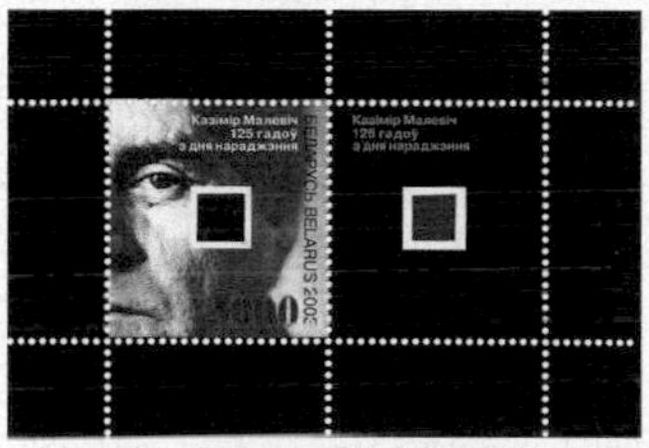

Kasimir S. Malevich (1878-1935), Artist — A162

2003, Feb. 21
461 A162 3000r multi + label 3.50 3.50

Reptiles A163

Designs: 300r, Coronella austriaca. 600r, Emys orbicularis.

2003, Mar. 12 ***Perf. 13½x14***
462-463 A163 Set of 2 1.00 1.00
463a Miniature sheet, 4 each #462-463 5.00 5.00

Intl. Year of Fresh Water — A164

2003, Mar. 25 ***Perf. 14¼x14***
464 A164 370r multi .50 .50

Passer Domesticus — A165

2003, Mar. 31 ***Perf. 14x13½***
465 A165 630r multi .90 .90

Printed in sheets of 7 + label.
See No. 520.

Children's Activities A166

Designs: No. 466, 300r, Rollerblading. No. 467, 300r, Scooter riding, vert.

2003, Apr. 22 ***Perf. 13½x14, 14x13½***
466-467 A166 Set of 2 .80 .80

A167

Europa — A168

2003, Apr. 24
468 A167 400r multi *.50 .50*
a. Booklet pane of 8 *5.00* —
Complete booklet, #468a *7.00*
469 A168 700r multi *1.25 1.25*
a. Booklet pane of 8 *10.00* —
Complete booklet, #469a *12.00*

Endangered Flowers — A169

Designs: 270r, Trollius europaeus. 740r, Iris sibirica.

2003, June 30 ***Perf. 14x13½***
470-471 A169 Set of 2 1.60 1.60
471a Miniature sheet, 4 each #470-471 6.50 6.50

Traditional Clothing — A170

Clothing of: 380r, West Polesye region. 430r, Mogilyov region.

2003, July 10 Litho. ***Perf. 14¼x14***
472-473 A170 Set of 2 1.50 1.50
473a Sheet, 4 each #472-473 + central label 4.50 —

See Nos. 564-565.

Souvenir Sheet

Yachting — A171

No. 474: a, Boat with blue sails. b, Boat with red and white sail, vert.

2003, July 22 Litho. ***Perf. 13½***
474 A171 1000r Sheet of 2, #a-b 2.50 2.50

Souvenir Sheets

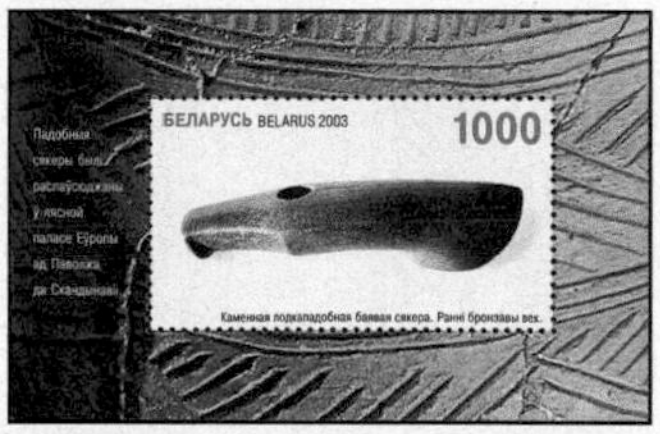

A172

Exhibits at Natl. Museum of History and Culture — A173

Designs: 1000r, Stone ax head, early Bronze Age. No. 476, Ceramic bowl, early Bronze Age. No. 477, Weapon, 14th cent.

2003, Aug. 20
475 A172 1000r multi .90 .90
476 A173 1500r multi + label 1.75 1.75
477 A173 1500r multi + label 1.75 1.75

Wooden Buildings — A174

Designs: 270r, Horse stable, Povitie, 19th cent. 430r, St. George's Church, Sinkevichi, 1724. 740r, Water mill, Volma, 19th-20th cent.

2003, Sept. 18
478-480 A174 Set of 3 1.35 1.35
480a Souvenir sheet, #478-480 1.75 1.75

Dogs — A175

Designs: 270r, Golden retriever. 380r, Mastiff. 430r, German shepherd.

2003, Oct. 14 ***Perf. 14x13½***
481-483 A175 Set of 3 1.50 1.50
483a Souvenir sheet, 2 each #481-483, + 2 labels 3.00 3.00

FIFA (Fédération Internationale de Football Association), Cent. (in 2004) — A176

Designs: No. 484, 380r, Player dribbling ball. No. 485, 380r, Goalie holding ball, vert. 460r, Players, diff. 780r, Goalie holding ball, diff., vert.

Perf. 14x14¼, 14¼x14

2003, Nov. 14 **Litho.**

484-487 A176 Set of 4 2.50 2.50

Christmas and New Year's Day — A177

2003, Nov. 15 ***Perf. 14x13½***

488 A177 380r Angel .45 .45
a. Miniature sheet of 6 2.75 2.75
489 A177 780r Santa Claus 1.00 1.00
a. Miniature sheet of 6 6.00 6.00
b. Booklet pane, 4 each #488-489 5.75 —
Complete booklet, #489b 5.75

Arms Type of 2003

Designs: 460r, Slonim. 780r, Zaslavl.

2004, Jan. 20 ***Perf. 14¼x14***

490-491 A161 Set of 2 1.40 1.40

There Came Spring, by Pavel Maslennikov — A178

2004, Feb. 1 ***Perf. 13½***

492 A178 290r multi .50 .50

Fruit — A179

Designs: 5r, Prunus spinosa. 10r, Vaccinium vitis-idaea. 20r, Vaccinium myrtillus. 30r, Oxycoccus palustris. 50r, Vaccinium uliginosum. 100r, Rubus idaeus. B, Fragaria ananassa. A, Ribes rubrum. 200r, Rubus caesius. H, Ribes nigrum. 300r, Rubus saxatilis. C, Grossularia reclinata. 500r, Fragaria. P, Hippophae rhamnoides. 1000r, Cerasus vulgaris.

2004 ***Perf. 13¼x13¾***

493 A179 5r multi .25 .25
494 A179 10r multi .25 .25
495 A179 20r multi .25 .25
496 A179 30r multi .25 .25
497 A179 50r multi .25 .25
498 A179 100r multi .25 .25
499 A179 B multi .25 .25
500 A179 A multi .25 .25
501 A179 200r multi .25 .25
502 A179 H multi .35 .35
503 A179 300r multi .35 .35
504 A179 C multi .45 .45
505 A179 500r multi .45 .45
506 A179 P multi .70 .70
507 A179 1000r multi .80 .80
a. Miniature sheet, #493-507 6.00 6.00
Nos. 493-507 (15) 5.35 5.35

Issued: 5r, 10r, 20r, 30r, A, P, 2/9; 50r, 100r, B, 200r, H, 300r, C, 500r, 1000r, 2/13. Nos. 499, 500, 502, 504 and 506 each sold for 100r, 120r, 290r, 420r and 780r respectively on day of issue.

St. Valentine's Day — A180

2004, Feb. 14 ***Perf. 13½x13¾***

508 A180 H multi .55 .55
a. Miniature sheet of 7 + label 4.50 4.50

No. 508 sold for 290r on day of issue.

Trees — A181

Designs: 100r, Alnus incana. B, Betula pendula. A, Pinus sylvsetris. 200r, Viburnum opulus. H, Fraxinus excelsior. 300r, Tilia cordata. 400r, Corylus avellana. C, Sorbus aucuparia. 500r, Quercus robur. P, Carpinus betulus. 1000r, Ulmus laevis.

2004, Mar. 23 ***Serpentine Die Cut 9***

Self-Adhesive

509 A181 100r multi .25 .25
510 A181 B multi .25 .25
511 A181 A multi .25 .25
512 A181 200r multi .25 .25
513 A181 H multi .35 .35
514 A181 300r multi .35 .35
515 A181 400r multi .50 .50
516 A181 C multi .55 .55
517 A181 500r multi .65 .65
518 A181 P multi 1.00 1.00
519 A181 1000r multi 1.00 1.00
a. Miniature sheet, #509-519, + label 5.50 5.50
Nos. 509-519 (11) 5.40 5.40

Nos. 510, 511, 513, 516 and 518 each sold for 100r, 120r, 290r, 420r and 780r respectively on day of issue.

Bird Type of 2003

2004, Mar. 31 ***Perf. 13¾x13½***

520 A165 870r Delichon urbica 1.10 1.10

Printed in sheets of 7 + label.

World Under-18 Ice Hockey Championships, Minsk — A182

2004, Apr. 16 **Litho.**

521 A182 320r multi .60 .60

Printed in sheets of 18 + 2 labels.

Europa A183

Designs: 320r, Mushroom picker. 870r, Fisherman.

2004, May 4 ***Perf. 13½x13¾***

522 A183 320r multi .40 .40
a. Booklet pane of 7 + label 2.75 —
Complete booklet, #522a 4.00
523 A183 870r multi 1.10 1.10
a. Booklet pane of 7 + label 7.50 —
Complete booklet, #523a 8.75

Souvenir Sheet

Liberation of Belarus, 60th Anniv. — A184

No. 524: a, 500r, Monument to Soviet Army (30x40mm). b, 1000r, The Parade of Partisans in Minsk, by Y. Zaitsev.

2004, May 4 ***Perf. 13½***

524 A184 Sheet of 2, #a-b 1.75 1.75

Locomotives and Railroad Stations — A185

Designs: 320r, Series D 1-3-0, Mosty Station. 870r, Series A 2-3-0, Vitebsk Station.

2004, May 31 **Litho.** ***Perf. 14x14¼***

525-526 A185 Set of 2 1.50 1.50
526a Sheet of 12, 6 each #525-526 17.00 17.00

Insects A186

Designs: 320r, Polistes gallicus. 505r, Bombus lucorum.
2000r, Apis mellifera.

2004, June 3 ***Perf. 13½x13¾***

527-528 A186 Set of 2 1.00 1.00

Souvenir Sheet

Perf. 13½x13¼

529 A186 2000r multi 2.00 2.00

No. 529 contains one 40x30mm stamp.

Souvenir Sheet

Paintings by Yehuda Pen (1854-1937) — A187

No. 530: a, Self-portrait. b, Watchmaker, horiz.

Perf. 13¼x13½, 13½x13¼ (#530b)

2004, June 5

530 A187 1000r Sheet of 2, #a-b 2.00 2.00

2004 Summer Olympics, Athens A188

Designs: 320r, Cycling. 505r, Hammer throw. 870r, Tennis.

2004, July 13 ***Perf. 14x14¼***

531-533 A188 Set of 3 2.00 2.00

Butterflies — A189

Designs: 300r, Euphydryas maturna. 500r, Pericallia matronula. 800r, Zerynthia polyxena. 1200r, Eudia pavonia.

2004, Sept. 10 ***Perf. 14¼x14***

534-537 A189 Set of 4 3.25 3.25
a. Miniature sheet, 3 each #534-537 + 4 labels *13.00 13.00*

Souvenir Sheet

Gold Medalists at 2004 Summer Olympics — A190

No. 538: a, Yuliya Nesterenko. b, Igor Makarov.

2004, Oct. 7 **Litho.** ***Perf. 14x13½***

538 A190 500r Sheet of 2, #a-b, + central label 1.40 1.40

Horses — A191

No. 539: a, Byelorussian harness horse (UL stamp). b, Andalusian horse (UR stamp). c, Head of Byelorussian harness horse (LL stamp). d, Head of Andalusian horse (LR stamp).

2004, Oct. 27 ***Perf. 12½x12***

539 A191 500r Sheet of 4, #a-d 2.00 2.00

Cats — A192

No. 540: a, 300r, Persian. b, 500r, Thai (denomination at UL). c, 500r, Red Persian (denomination at LR). d, 800r, Mixed breed (denomination at UL). e, 800r, British Shorthair (denomination at LL).

2004, Oct. 29 ***Perf. 13½x14***

540 A192 Sheet of 5, #a-e, + label 2.75 2.75

Happy New Year — A193

2004, Dec. 8 Litho. *Perf. 13¾x13½*

541 A193 320r multi .45 .45

Minsk Metro Stations — A194

No. 542: a, Victory Square Station (gray panel). b, Yakub Kolas Square Station (yellow orange panel).

2004, Dec. 22 *Perf. 13½*

542 Horiz. pair 1.50 1.50
a.-b. A194 560r Either single .75 .75

Arms Type of 2003

Designs: 160r, Dubrovno. 350r, Kamenets. 900r, Mogilyov.

2005, Jan. 25 *Perf. 14¼x14*

543-545 A181 Set of 3 1.50 1.50

Gerasim Bogomolov (1905-81), Hydrologist — A195

2005, Feb. 18 *Perf. 13¾x13½*

546 A195 350r multi .45 .45

Souvenir Sheet

Icons — A196

No. 547: a, Virgin of Vladimir, by Fyodor Povny. b, Nativity, by Georgi Sutulin and Olga Belaya. c, Archangel Michael, by Andrei Kosikov.

Litho. with Foil Application

2005, Mar. 22 *Perf. 11½*

547 A196 1500r Sheet of 3, #a-c *4.25 4.25*

Strix Nebulosa A197

Perf. 13½x13¾

2005, Mar. 31 Litho.

548 A197 900r multi 1.00 1.00

Comes in sheets of 7 + label.

A198

A199

A200

End of World War II, 60th Anniv. A201

No. 553: a, Signing of surrender documents. b, Victory parade (52x30mm).

2005, Apr. 12 *Perf. 13½x13¾*

549	A198	A multi	.30	.30
550	A199	H multi	.35	.35
551	A200	H multi	.35	.35
552	A201	P multi	.90	.90
		Nos. 549-552 (4)	1.90	1.90

Souvenir Sheet

Perf. 13½x13¼, 13½ (#553b)

553 A201 1000r Sheet of 2, #a-b *2.00 2.00*

No. 549 sold for 160r, Nos. 550 and 551 each sold for 360r, and No. 552 sold for 930r on day of issue.

Souvenir Sheet

Fauna — A202

No. 554: a, 500r, Aquila danga. b, 500r, Catocala sponsa. c, 1000r, Castor fiber. d, 1000r, Meles meles.

2005, Apr. 15 *Perf. 12*

554 A202 Sheet of 4, #a-d, + label *3.00 3.00*

See Russia No. 6906.

Europa A203

Designs: 500r, Scallions, carrot, onion, peppers and tomato. 1000r, Bread and hat.

2005, May 4 *Perf. 13½x13¾*

555-556 A203 Set of 2 *1.50 1.50*
555a Booklet pane of 7 + label *3.50* —
Complete booklet, #555a *3.50*
556a Booklet pane of 7 + label *8.50* —
Complete booklet, #556a *8.50*

Stefaniya Stanyuta (1905-2000), Actress — A204

2005, May 13 Litho. *Perf. 13¾x13½*

557 A204 160r multi .40 .40

Printed in sheets of 16 + 4 labels.

Souvenir Sheet

Hans Christian Andersen (1805-75), Author — A205

2005, May 20 *Perf. 13¼x13½*

558 A205 2000r multi 2.00 2.00

Worldwide Fund for Nature (WWF) A206

Ciconia nigra: No. 559, In flight. No. 560, Standing on one leg.

No. 561: a, Head. b, Legs and chicks.

2005, June 2 *Perf. 13½x13¾*

559	A206	500r multi	.50	.50
560	A206	500r multi	.50	.50
561	A206	1000r Vert. pair, #a-b	2.00	2.00
c.		Block of 4, #559, 560, 561a, 561b	3.50	3.50

Harvesting, by Mikhail Sevruk — A207

2005, July 14 *Perf. 13½*

562 A207 170r multi .30 .30

World Summit on the Information Society, Tunis — A208

2005, July 20

563 A208 360r multi .45 .45

Traditional Clothing Type of 2003

Women wearing clothing of: 360r, Mosty region. 570r, Lepel region.

2005, Aug. 18 *Perf. 14¼x14*

564-565 A170 Set of 2 1.00 1.00
565a Sheet of 8, 4 each #564-565, + central label 4.00 4.00

Intl. Year of Sport and Physical Education A209

2005, Aug. 30 *Perf. 13½x13¾*

566 A209 570r multi .60 .60

Volkovysk, 1000th Anniv. — A210

2005, Sept. 2 *Perf. 13½*

567 A210 360r multi .40 .40

Turov Eparchy, 1000th Anniv. — A211

2005, Sept. 17 *Perf. 13¾x13½*

568 A211 360r multi .40 .40

Chess — A212

No. 569 — Background color: a, Dark red. b, Orange brown.

2005, Sept. 23 *Perf. 14x14¼*

569	A212	500r Pair, #a-b	1.00	1.00
c.		Booklet pane, 3 #569a, 4 #569b + label	6.00	—
		Complete booklet, #569c	6.00	
d.		Booklet pane, 3 #569a, 4 #569b + label, imperf.	6.00	—
		Complete booklet, #569d	6.00	

Souvenir Sheet

Castles — A213

No. 570: a, 500r, Vytautas Castle, Grodno. b, 1000r, Lida Castle, Lida.

2005, Nov. 15 *Perf. 13½x14*

570 A213 Sheet of 2, #a-b 2.00 2.00

New Year's Day & Christmas
A214

2005, Dec. 5 Litho. *Perf. 14x14¼*
571 A214 360r multi .80 .80

Printed in sheets of 9 and in sheets of 8 + label.

2006 Winter Olympics, Turin
A215

2006, Jan. 16 *Perf. 13½x14*
572 A215 500r Snowboarding 1.25 1.25

Souvenir Sheet

Perf. 14x13½

573 A215 2000r Freestyle skiing, vert. 2.50 2.50

No. 573 contains one 30x40mm stamp.

Arms of Turov — A216

Arms of Novogrudok
A217

2006, Jan. 30 *Perf. 14¼x14*
574 A216 500r multi .80 .80
575 A217 500r multi .80 .80

Vanellus Vanellus
A218

2006, Apr. 18 *Perf. 13½x14*
576 A218 930r multi .90 .90

Printed in sheets of 7 + label.

Chernobyl Nuclear Accident, 20th Anniv.
A219

2006, Apr. 19
577 A219 360r multi .60 .60

Europa — A220

Children's drawings: 500r, Penguins, by Lina Filippoch. 1000r, Pegasus, by Daria Buneeva, horiz.

2006, May 4 *Perf. 14x13½, 13½x14*
578-579 A220 Set of 2 1.50 1.50
578a Booklet pane of 7 + label 3.75 —
Complete booklet, #578a 3.75
579a Booklet pane of 7 + label 7.25 —
Complete booklet, #579a 7.25

Ivan Shamyakin (1921-2004), Writer — A221

2006, June 2 *Perf. 14x14¼*
580 A221 360r multi .45 .45

Birds — A222

Designs: 10r, Oenanthe oenanthe. 20r, Parus caeruleus. 30r, Ficedula hypoleuca. 50r, Carduelis cannabina. 100r, Sylvia curruca. (160r), Erithacus rubecula. (190r), Phoenicurus ochruros. 200r, Fringilla coelebs. 300r, Passer montanus. (360r), Parus major. 500r, Carduelis chloris. 1000r, Coccothraustes coccothraustes.

2006, June 16 *Perf. 13½x14*
581 A222 10r multi .25 .25
582 A222 20r multi .25 .25
583 A222 30r multi .25 .25
584 A222 50r multi .25 .25
585 A222 100r multi .25 .25
586 A222 (160r) multi .25 .25
587 A222 (190r) multi .25 .25
588 A222 200r multi .25 .25
589 A222 300r multi .25 .25
590 A222 (360r) multi .35 .35
591 A222 500r multi .50 .50
592 A222 1000r multi .85 .85
a. Souvenir sheet, #581-592 4.00 4.00
Nos. 581-592 (12) 3.95 3.95

Bats
A223

Designs: No. 593, 500r, No. 596a, 1000r, Myotis dascyneme. No. 594, 500r, No. 596b, 1000r, Vespertilio murinus. No. 595, 500r, No. 596c, 1000r, Barbastella barbastellus.

2006, June 19 *Perf. 14x14¼*
593-595 A223 Set of 3 1.50 1.50

Souvenir Sheet

Perf. 13½x13¼

596 A223 1000r Sheet of 3, #a-c 3.50 3.50

Souvenir Sheet

Belarus Medals at 2006 Winter Olympics — A224

Perf. 13¾x13½

2006, June 22 Litho.
597 A224 2000r multi + 2 labels 2.25 2.25

Souvenir Sheet

Augustow Canal — A225

2006, Aug. 11 *Perf. 14x14¼*
598 A225 2000r multi 2.25 2.25

Locomotives and Railroad Stations — A226

Designs: No. 599, 1000r, Ov class locomotive, Brest Station (shown). No. 600, 1000r, E class locomotive, Molodechno Station.

2006, Sept. 8
599-600 A226 Set of 2 2.00 2.00
600a Miniature sheet, 4 each #599-600, + central label 7.25 7.25

Orchids
A227

Designs: No. 601, 1000r, Dachylorhiza majalis and insect. No. 602, 1000r, Cephalanthera rubra and dragonfly facing right. No. 603, 1000r, Cephalanthera rubra and dragonfly facing left.

Perf. 13½x13¾

2006, Sept. 16 Litho.
601-603 A227 Set of 3 3.00 3.00
602a Miniature sheet, 4 each #601-602 8.00 8.00

Renewable Energy
A228

Designs: 210r, Wind turbines. 970d, Hydroelectric power station.

2006, Oct. 10 Litho. *Perf. 14x14¼*
604-605 A228 Set of 2 1.25 1.25
605a Miniature sheet, 3 each #604-605 3.75 3.75

Regional Communications Commonwealth, 15th Anniv. — A229

2006, Oct. 13 *Perf. 13½x13¾*
606 A229 410r multi 1.25 1.25

No. 134 Surcharged in Silver and Black

2006, Nov. 10 Litho. *Imperf.*
607 A33 3500r on 10,000r #134 3.75 3.75

Belfila 2006 National Philatelic Exhibition.

Discus Fish — A230

Various discus fish with denominations in: No. 608, 500r, White (shown). No. 609, 500r, White, diff. No. 610, 500r, Blue. No. 611, 500r, Yellow.

2006, Nov. 16 *Perf. 13½x14*
608-611 A230 Set of 4 2.00 2.00
611a Sheet of 8, 2 each #608-611 5.00 5.00

Buildings Type of 2001-02

Perf. 13½x13¾

2006, Dec. 20 Litho.
612 A141 3000r Shklov City Hall 2.50 2.50

New Year 2007 — A231

No. 613 — Tree and stars in: a, Dark blue. b, White.

2006, Dec. 22 *Perf. 13¾x13½*
613 A231 500r Pair, #a-b 1.10 1.10

Printed in sheets containing three of each stamp.

Arms of Krugloe — A232

Arms of Pinsk — A233

2007, Jan. 22 *Perf. 14¼x14*
614 A232 600r multi .85 .85
615 A233 600r multi .85 .85

Napoleon Orda (1807-83), Artist and Musician — A234

Perf. 13¾x13½

2007, Feb. 14 **Litho.**
616 A234 2000r multi + label 3.75 3.75

Printed in sheets of 2 stamps + 2 labels.

Luscinia Luscinia A235

2007, Mar. 26 ***Perf. 13½x13¾***
617 A235 1000r multi 2.75 2.75

Printed in sheets of 7 stamps + label.

Europa — A236

Scouting emblem, "100," and: 500r, Knot. 1000r, Emblem of Natl. Scout Association.

2007, May 4 **Litho.** ***Perf. 14¼x14***
618-619 A236 Set of 2 2.50 2.50
619a Booklet pane, 4 #618, 3 #619, + label 9.25 9.25
Complete booklet, #619a 9.25

Scouting, cent.

Wildlife A237

Designs: No. 620, Vulpes vulpes. No. 621, Mustela putorius. No. 622, Dryomys nitedula. No. 623, Sciurus vulgaris.

Serpentine Die Cut 9¼

2007, June 19 **Self-Adhesive**
620 A237 B multi .30 .30
621 A237 B multi .30 .30
622 A237 A multi .30 .30
623 A237 A multi .30 .30
a. Miniature sheet, 2 each #620-623, + central label 2.50 2.50
Nos. 620-623 (4) 1.20 1.20

On day of issue, Nos. 620 and 621 each sold for 190r, and Nos. 622 and 623 each sold for 220r.

Souvenir Sheet

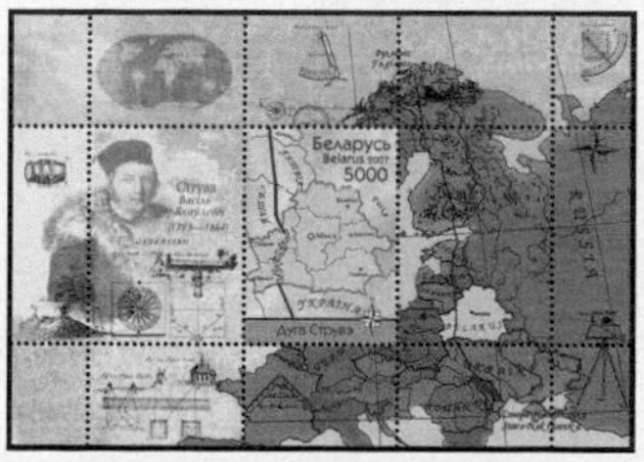

Struve Geodetic Arc — A238

2007, Sept. 20 ***Perf. 14¼x14***
624 A238 5000r multi + 2 labels 5.00 5.00

Birds A239

No. 625 — Birds of the Cepkeliai Nature Reserve, Lithuania, and Katra Sanctuary, Belarus: a, Gallinago media. b, Crex crex.

2007, Oct. 3 **Litho.** ***Perf. 13½x13¾***
625 Horiz. pair + central label 2.00 2.00
a.-b. A239 1000r Either single 1.00 1.00

Printed in sheets of 3 pairs. See Lithuania No. 848.

BirdLife International A240

Birds: No. 626, 500r, Surnia ululu. No. 627, 500r, Nyctea scandiaca. No. 628, 1000r, Glaucidium passerinum. No. 629, 1000r, Asio flammeus.

2007, Nov. 23 ***Perf. 13¾x13½***
626-629 A240 Set of 4 3.50 3.50
629a Miniature sheet, 2 each #626-629 7.00 7.00

Nos. 626-629 each printed in sheets of 7 + label.

Portraits by Unknown Artists in National Museum A241

Designs: Nos. 630a, 631a, Kshishtof Veselovsky, 1636. Nos. 630b, 631b, Griesel Sapega, 1632. Nos. 630c, 631c, Alexandra Marianna Veselovskaya, 1640.

2007, Nov. 28 ***Perf. 13½***
630 Horiz. strip of 3 3.75 3.75
a.-c. A241 1050r Any single 1.20 1.20

Souvenir Sheet

631 Sheet of 3 6.00 6.00
a.-c. A241 1500r Any single 2.00 2.00

No. 630 printed in sheets of 2 strips.

Christmas and New Year's Day — A242

Designs: No. 632, 240r, Children making snowman. No. 633, 240r, Child giving present to another child.

No. 634: a, Boy holding sack. b, Girl holding snowflake.

2007, Dec. 7 ***Perf. 13¾x13½***
632-633 A242 Set of 2 1.25 1.25

Souvenir Sheet

634 Sheet, #632-633, 634a-634b + 2 labels 4.50 4.50
a.-b. A242 1500r Either single 1.90 1.90

Nos. 632-633 were each printed in sheets of 7 + label.

Christmas and New Year's Day — A243

No. 635: a, Christmas tree. b, Candle.

2007, Dec. 7
635 A243 1050r Pair, #a-b 2.40 2.40
c. Souvenir sheet, #635a-635b 3.00 3.00

No. 635 was printed in sheets containing 4 each Nos. 635a-635b.

Church Bells — A244

Various bells from: 600r, 1937. 1000r, 19th cent. 1200r, 1928.
2500r, 18th cent.

2007, Dec. 7 ***Perf. 13½***
636-638 A244 Set of 3 3.00 3.00

Souvenir Sheet

Perf. 14x14¼

639 A244 2500r multi 2.75 2.75

No. 639 contains one 40x28mm stamp.

Weaver — A245

Blacksmith — A246

2007, Dec. 21 ***Perf. 13½***
640 A245 600r multi .70 .70
641 A246 600r multi .70 .70

Nos. 640-641 each printed in sheets of 6.

Farm Animals — A247

Designs: 240r, Sheep. 440r, Ram. 500r, Pig. 1050r, Cows. 1500r, Goats.

2007, Dec. 29 **Litho.**
642-646 A247 Set of 5 4.25 4.25

Nos. 642-646 each printed in sheets of 6.

Hunting — A248

Designs: 440r, Falconry. 1050r, Deer hunt, horiz.

Perf. 13¾x13½, 13½x13¾

2008, Jan. 30
647-648 A248 Set of 2 1.40 1.40

Nos. 647-648 each printed in sheets of 8.

Vincent Dunin-Marcinkevich (1808-84), Writer — A249

2008, Feb. 4 ***Perf. 14¼x14***
649 A249 440r multi .00 .80

Printed in sheets of 8.

Souvenir Sheet

Prince Konstantin Ostrozhsky (1526-1608) — A250

2008, Feb. 17
650 A250 2500r multi + label 2.75 2.75

Egretta Alba — A251

2008, Mar. 13 ***Perf. 13¾x13½***
651 A251 1050r multi 2.00 2.00

Printed in sheets of 7 + label.

Intl. Telecommunications, Information and Bank Technologies Exhibition — A252

2008, Apr. 4 ***Perf. 14x14¼***
652 A252 (440r) multi 1.40 1.40

Printed in sheets of 8.

Europa A253

Designs: No. 653, 1000r, Letter on birch bark. No. 654, 1000r, Computer keyboard, envelopes, "@" symbol.

2008, May 28 Litho. ***Perf. 13½x14***

653-654 A253	Set of 2	2.00	2.00
654a	Booklet pane, 3 each #653-654 + 2 labels	6.75	—
	Complete booklet, #654a	6.75	

Mammals — A254

Designs: 10r, Nyctereutes procyonoides. 200r, Mustela lutreola. 300r, Lepus europaeus. 400r, Canis lupus. 1000r, Martes martes.

2008, June 10 ***Perf. 13½x14***

655 A254	10r multi	.25	.25
656 A254	200r multi	.25	.25
657 A254	300r multi	.35	.35
658 A254	400r multi	.45	.45
659 A254	1000r multi	.90	.90
a.	Miniature sheet, 3 each #655-659	6.25	6.25
	Nos. 655-659 (5)	2.20	2.20

See No. 681.

Flowers — A255

Designs: 20r, Paeonia lactiflora. 30r, Petunia hybrida. 50r, Narcissus hybridus. 100r, Tulipa gesneriana. (200r), Dahlia cultorum. (240r), Rosa hybrida. (440r), Zinnia elegans. 500r, Lilium hybrida.

2008, June 10

660 A255	20r multi	.25	.25
661 A255	30r multi	.25	.25
662 A255	50r multi	.25	.25
663 A255	100r multi	.25	.25
664 A255	(200r) multi	.25	.25
665 A255	(240r) multi	.30	.30
666 A255	(440r) multi	.40	.40
667 A255	500r multi	.50	.50
a.	Miniature sheet, 3 each #660-667	6.00	6.00
	Nos. 660-667 (8)	2.45	2.45

Mushrooms — A256

Designs: 1000r, Cantharellus cibarius. 1500r, Boletus edulis.

2008, July 8 Litho. ***Perf. 14x13½***

668-669 A256 Set of 2 3.50 3.50

2008 Summer Olympics, Beijing A257

2008, Aug. 15 ***Perf. 14x14¼***

670 A257 1000r multi 2.25 2.25

Miniature Sheets

Orders of Belarus — A258

Medals of Belarus — A259

No. 671: a, Order of Exceptional Courage (star in white circle). b, Order of Military Glory (two soldiers in blue laureated circle). c, First, second and third class Orders of the Motherland (three orders with ribbons). d, First, second and third class Orders for Service to the Motherland (three orders without ribbons). e, Order of Friendship of Peoples (Blue violet ribbon). f, Order of Honor (two people in circle within a diamond). g, Order of Francysk Skaryna (red ribbon). h, Order of Mother (light and dark blue ribbon).

No. 672: a, Medal of Note for Military Service (round medal with star, torch, red and green banner). b, Medal of Hero of Belarus (star-shaped medal). c, Medal for Bravery (round medal with airplanes, tank and text). d, Medal for Labor Achievements (round medal with gray and red ribbon). e, First, second and third class medals for Perfect Service (three round medals with green and red ribbons). f, Medal of Note in Guarding the Civil Order (round medal with blue ribbon with red stripes). g, Medal of Note for Guarding the State Border (round medal with border guard and boundary marker). h, Medal of Francysk Skaryna (green and white ribbon).

2008, Aug. 28 ***Perf. 13½***

671 A258 1000r	Sheet of 8, #a-h, + 2 labels	8.00	8.00
672 A259 1000r	Sheet of 8, #a-h, + 2 labels	8.00	8.00

Arms of Orsha — A260

Arms of Vitsebsk — A261

Arms of Nesvizh — A262

2008 ***Perf. 14¼x14***

673 A260	500r multi	.65	.65
674 A261	600r multi	.80	.80
675 A262	1000r multi	1.20	1.20
	Nos. 673-675 (3)	2.65	2.65

Issued: 600r, 9/15; 500r, 1000r, 9/19.

Remembrance of the Holocaust — A263

2008, Oct. 21 ***Perf. 13½x13¾***

676 A263 500r multi 1.50 1.50

Printed in sheets of 8 + label.

Souvenir Sheet

Baptism of Vladimir I (Christianization of Kievan Rus), 1020th Anniv. — A264

No. 677: a, Holy Virgin of Iljinsk and Chernigov. b, Christ Pantocrator. c, Grand Prince Vladimir.

2008, Oct. 25 ***Perf. 13½***

677 A264 1500r Sheet of 3, #a-c 4.50 4.50

Souvenir Sheet

Nesvizh Castle, 425th Anniv. — A265

2008, Dec. 8 Litho. ***Perf. 13½x14***

678 A265 3000r multi + label 3.00 3.00

Christmas and New Year's Day — A266

New Year's Day — A267

2008, Dec. 9 ***Perf. 14x13½***

679 A266 500r multi .50 .50

Perf. 13½

680 A267 1000r multi .90 .90

Mammals Type of 2008

2008, Dec. 10 ***Perf. 13½x14***

681 A254 5000r Bison bonasus 3.50 3.50

BirdLife International A268

Owls: No. 682, 500r, Bubo bubo. No. 683, 500r, Athene noctua. No. 684, 1000r, Otus scops. No. 685, 1000r, Strix uralensis.

2008, Dec. 22 ***Perf. 14x13½***

682-685 A268	Set of 4	3.00	3.00
685a	Sheet of 8, 2 each #682-685	6.50	6.50

Nos. 682-685 each were printed in sheets of 7 + label.

Louis Braille (1809-52), Educator of the Blind — A269

2009, Jan. 4 ***Perf. 13½x14***

686 A269 700r multi .65 .65

Vladimir Muliavin (1941-2003), Folk Singer — A270

2009, Jan. 12 **Litho.**

687 A270 1000r multi + label .90 .90

Withdrawal of Soviet Troops From Afghanistan, 20th Anniv. A271

2009, Jan. 20

688 A271 400r multi .45 .45

Printed in sheets of 8 + central label.

Commonwealth of Independent States Executive Committee Building, Minsk — A272

2009, Feb. 18 ***Perf. 14x14¼***

689 A272 500r multi .55 .55

Miniature Sheet

Folk Holidays — A273

No. 690: a, Kaliady (people walking in snow carrying torches). b, Spring greetings (child in white robe). c, Dazhynki (woman in field of rye). d, Kupalle (woman holding flower).

2009, Mar. 1 ***Perf. 14x13½***
690 A273 500r Sheet of 4, #a-d, + 4 labels 1.75 1.75

Anser Anser A274

2009, Mar. 31 ***Perf. 13½x14***
691 A274 1000r multi .85 .85

Printed in sheets of 7 + label.

Europa A275

Designs: No. 692, 1000r, Armillary sphere, telescope of Galileo. No. 693, 1000r, Moon, dish antenna, satellite.

2009, Apr. 15 ***Perf. 13½x14***
692-693 A275 Set of 2 1.75 1.75
693a Booklet pane of 6, 3 each #692-693, + 2 labels 5.25 —
Complete booklet, #693a 5.25

Intl. Year of Astronomy. Nos. 692-693 each were printed in sheets of 7 + label.

Souvenir Sheet

Year of Native Land — A276

2009, Apr. 21 Litho. ***Perf. 13½x14***
694 A276 2500r multi 2.25 2.25

Poultry — A277

Designs: No. 695, 1000r, Geese. No. 696, 1000r, Ducks.
3000r, Rooster and hen, horiz.

2009, May 5 ***Perf. 14¼x14***
695-696 A277 Set of 2 1.60 1.60

Souvenir Sheet
Perf. 13½x13¾
697 A277 3000r multi + 2 labels 2.75 2.75

Endangered Flora — A278

Designs: No. 698, 1500r, Anemone sylvestris. No. 699, 1500r, Scorzonera glabra.

2009, June 8 ***Perf. 14¼x14***
698-699 A278 Set of 2 2.50 2.50

Nos. 698-699 each were printed in sheets of 5 + label.

Souvenir Sheet

Liberation From Nazi Control, 65th Anniv. — A279

No. 700: a, Victory Square, Minsk. b, Women in Minsk, 1944.

2009, June 26 ***Perf. 14x13½***
700 A279 500r Sheet of 2, #a-b 1.50 1.50

Air Sports A280

Designs: No. 701, 1500r, Two Yak-52 airplanes. No. 702, 1500r, An-2 airplane and skydiver.

2009, July 4 ***Perf. 13½x14***
701-702 A280 Set of 2 2.50 2.50

Nos. 701-702 each were printed in sheets of 5 + label.

Andrei A. Gromyko (1909-89), Foreign Affairs Minister of Soviet Union — A281

2009, July 18 ***Perf. 14x13½***
703 A281 800r multi .65 .65

Holy Virgin of Borkolabovo, 350th Anniv. — A282

2009, July 24 ***Perf. 14¼x14***
704 A282 1380r multi 1.10 1.10

Arms of Smorgon — A283

Arms of Kobrin — A284

2009 **Litho.**
705 A283 1000r multi .85 .85
706 A284 1000r multi .85 .85

Issued: No. 705, 9/6; No. 706, 9/19. Nos. 705-706 each were printed in sheets of 8 + label.

Souvenir Sheet

Belovezhskaya Puscha National Park — A285

No. 707: a, Deer. b, Aurochs. c, Wild boars.

2009, Oct. 3 ***Perf. 14x14¼***
707 A285 1500r Sheet of 3, #a-c 4.50 4.50

A286

2009, Oct. 16 ***Perf. 13½x14***
708 A286 1380r multi 1.10 1.10

First Telegraph Line Between Minsk and Bobruisk, 150th Anniv.
Printed in sheets of 7 + 2 labels.

Galina K. Makarova (1919-93), Actress A287

2009, Oct. 23
709 A287 800r multi .65 .65

Printed in sheets of 5 + label.

Paintings in Natl. Art Museum — A288

Designs: No. 710, 1000r, Sky Blue Day, by Vitaly K. Tsvirko, 1980. No. 711, 1000r, Evening in Minsk Province, by Apollinary G. Goravsky, 1870s.

2009, Nov. 5 Litho. ***Perf. 13½***
710-711 A288 Set of 2 1.75 1.75

Souvenir Sheet

Christmas and New Year's Day — A289

No. 712: a, Decorated tree. b, Angel.

2009, Nov. 12 ***Perf. 13¼x13½***
712 A289 1500r Sheet of 2, #a-b, + central label 2.50 2.50

Souvenir Sheet

Russian Blue Cats — A290

No. 713: a, Head of adult cat. b, Two kittens. c, Three kittens.

2009, Nov. 23 ***Perf. 13½***
713 A290 2500r Sheet of 3, #a-c, + label 5.75 5.75

Sports Facilities in Minsk — A291

No. 714: a, Soccer Stadium (with arched roof). b, Minsk Arena (circular building).

2009, Nov. 30
714 A291 1500r Vert. pair, #a-b 2.50 2.50

Printed in sheets containing 2 pairs and 2 labels.

Souvenir Sheet

Foundation Treaty of the Union State (Economic and Political Confederation With Russia), 10th Anniv. — A292

Litho. With Foil Application
2009, Dec. 8 ***Perf. 14¼x14***
715 A292 4500r multi + 2 labels 4.00 4.00

Souvenir Sheet

2010 Winter Olympics, Vancouver — A293

2010, Jan. 25 Litho. ***Perf. 13½x14***
716 A293 3000r multi + 5 labels 2.50 2.50

Souvenir Sheet

Paintings by Ivan Khrutski (1810-85) — A294

No. 717: a, Self-portrait, 1884. b, Still Life with Dead Game, Vegetables and Mushrooms, 1854.

2010, Feb. 8 ***Perf. 14x14¼***
717 A294 1500r Sheet of 2, #a-b 2.75 2.75

Ivan Naumenko (1925-2006), Writer — A295

2010, Feb. 16 ***Perf. 13½***
718 A295 800r multi .60 .60

Printed in sheets of 5 + label.

Falco Tinnunculus A296

2010, Mar. 19 ***Perf. 13½x13¾***
719 A296 1000r multi .85 .85

Printed in sheets of 7 + label.

Souvenir Sheet

Slutsk Sashes — A297

No. 720: a, Iosif Zhagel wearing sash. b, Slutsk Gate, Nesvizh. c, Detail of Slutsk sash.

2010, Mar. 26 ***Perf. 14x14¼***
720 A297 1000r Sheet of 3, #a-c 2.50 2.50

Europa A298

Designs: No. 721, 1000r, Boy reading book, book characters. No. 722, 1000r, Girl reading book, butterfly.

2010, Mar. 30 ***Perf. 13½x14***
721-722 A298 Set of 2 1.75 1.75
722a Booklet pane of 6, 3 each #721-722, + 2 labels 5.25 —
Complete booklet, #722a 5.25

A299

End of World War II, 65th Anniv. — A300

No. 724: a, 500r, Soldiers at liberation of Minsk. b, 1500r, Berlin Liberation Monument.

2010, Apr. 16 ***Perf. 14x13½***
723 A299 500r multi .40 .40

Souvenir Sheet

724 A300 Sheet of 2, #a-b, + label 1.75 1.75

No. 723 was printed in sheets of 5 + label.

Souvenir Sheet

Intl. Year of Biodiversity — A301

No. 725: a, 300r, Bears. b, 300r, Fish. c, 2400r, Birds, "2010," waves, man, child, tree.

2010, Apr. 23 ***Perf. 13½x14***
725 A301 Sheet of 3, #a-c 2.50 2.50

Expo 2010, Shanghai — A302

2010, May 1 ***Perf. 14x13½***
726 A302 500r multi .40 .40

Postal Agreement With Sovereign Military Order of Malta — A303

2010, June 21 **Litho.** ***Perf. 13½***
727 A303 (920r) multi 1.25 1.25

Sailboats — A304

Designs: 920r, Optimist class. 1420r, Luch class.

2010, June 28 ***Perf. 14¼x14***
728-729 A304 Set of 2 2.00 2.00

Nos. 728-729 each were printed in sheets of 7 + label.

Battle of Grunwald, 600th Anniv. A305

2010, July 15 ***Perf. 14x14¼***
730 A305 1500r multi 1.25 1.25

Printed in sheets of 4.

Darya Domracheva, Bronze Medalist in Biathlon — A306

Sergei Novikov, Silver Medalist in Biathlon — A307

Aleksei Grishin, Gold Medalist in Freestyle Skiing — A308

2010, July 23 ***Perf. 14x13½***
731 A306 (290r) multi .40 .40
732 A307 (920r) multi 1.00 1.00
733 A308 (1420r) multi 1.60 1.60
a. Sheet of 6, 2 each #731-733 + 3 labels 6.00 6.00
Nos. 731-733 (3) 3.00 3.00

Belarussian medalists at 2010 Winter Olympics, Vancouver. Nos. 731-732 each were printed in sheets of 8 + label.

Miniature Sheet

Belarussian Gold Medalists at 2008 Summer Olympics, Beijing — A309

No. 734: a, Men's canoe doubles team. b, Aksana Miankova, women's hammer throw. c, Andrei Aramnau, weightlifting. d, Men's kayak fours team.

2010, July 24 ***Perf. 14¼x14***
734 A309 1000r Sheet of 4, #a-d 3.75 3.75

S Class Locomotive, Vilenski Railroad Station, Minsk — A310

Shch Class Locomotive, Mogilyov Railroad Station — A311

2010, Aug. 2 ***Perf. 12x12¼***
735 A310 1000r multi 1.10 1.10
736 A311 1000r multi 1.10 1.10
a. Sheet of 10, 5 each #735-736, + 2 labels 11.00 11.00

Nos. 735-736 each were printed in sheets of 11 + label.

Worldwide Fund for Nature (WWF) A312

Various depictions of Ophiogomphus cecilia: 900r, 1000r, 1400r, 1500r.

2010, Aug. 10 ***Perf. 13½x14***
737-740 A312 Set of 4 4.00 4.00
740a Sheet of 8, 2 each #737-740 8.00 8.00

Mushrooms — A313

Designs: No. 741, 500r, Clavaridelphus pistillaris and bird. No. 742, 500r, Langermannia gigantea and bird. No. 743, 500r, Hericium coralloides and bird. No. 744, 1000r, Sparassis laminosa and butterfly. No. 745, 1000r, Polyporus umbellatus and rodent.

2010, Aug. 18 ***Perf. 14x13½***
741-745 A313 Set of 5 4.00 4.00

Nos. 741-745 each were printed in sheets of 9 + label.

Arms of Khoiniki — A314

Arms of Lida — A315

2010 **Litho.** ***Perf. 14¼x14***
746 A314 900r multi .75 .75
747 A315 1400r multi 1.25 1.25

Issued: 900r, 9/5; 1400r, 9/24.

Souvenir Sheet

Republican Trade Union Palace of Culture — A316

2010, Sept. 15 ***Perf. 13½***
748 A316 2000r multi + label 1.60 1.60

United Nations, 65th Anniv. A317

2010, Oct. 24 Litho. ***Perf. 13½x13***

749 A317 1000r multi .85 .85

Printed in sheets of 5 + label.

Russian Spaniel — A318 Irish Setter — A319

Russo-European Laika — A320

2010, Nov. 10 ***Perf. 13x13½***

750 A318 1000r multi .75 .75
751 A319 1000r multi .75 .75
752 A320 1000r multi .75 .75
a. Souvenir sheet of 6, 2 each #750-752, + 3 labels 4.50 4.50
Nos. 750-752 (3) 2.25 2.25

New Year 2011 — A321

Christmas — A322

2010, Nov. 12 ***Perf. 13½***

753 A321 1000r multi .85 .85
754 A322 1000r multi .85 .85
a. Souvenir sheet of 4, 2 each #753-754, + 4 labels 3.50 3.50

Nos. 753-754 each were printed in sheets of 7 + label.

2010 Junior Eurovision Song Contest, Minsk A323

2010, Nov. 20 ***Perf. 13½x14***

755 A323 (1010r) multi 1.40 1.40

Printed in sheets of 10 + 2 labels.

Arms of Gantsevichi A324

2010, Nov. 20 ***Perf. 14¼x14***

756 A324 900r multi .70 .70

Souvenir Sheet

Mir Castle — A325

Litho. & Embossed

2010, Dec. 16 ***Perf. 13x13½***

757 A325 5000r multi 4.00 4.00

Primula Elatior — A326

Orchis Ustulata — A327

2011, Jan. 10 Litho. ***Perf. 12¼x12***

758 A326 (1160r) multi 1.25 1.25
759 A327 (1790r) multi 1.90 1.90
a. Souvenir sheet of 4, 2 each #758-759, + 2 labels 6.50 6.50

Endangered flowers.

Preservation of Polar Regions and Glaciers — A328

Designs: 1500r, Map of Antarctica, penguins. 2500r, Map of Arctic region, polar bear.

2011, Feb. 11

760-761 A328 Set of 2 4.50 4.50
761a Tête-bêche pair, #760-761 4.50 4.50
761b Souvenir sheet, 3 #761a 10.50 10.50

Nos. 760-761 each were printed in sheets of 5 + label.

Numenius Arquata A329

Perf. 13½x13¾

2011, Mar. 14 Litho.

762 A329 1500r multi 1.10 1.10

Printed in sheets of 7 + label.

Souvenir Sheets

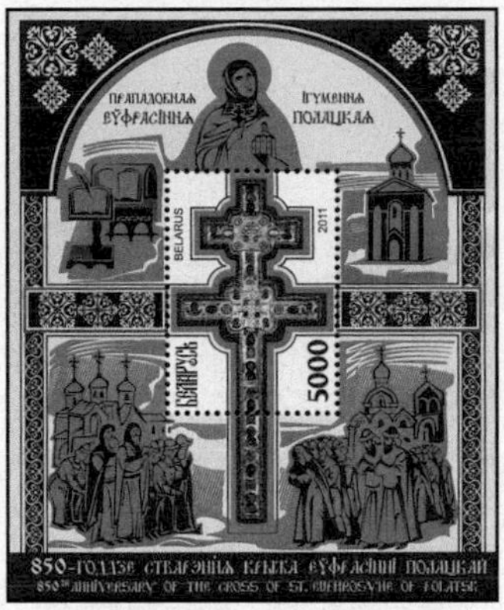

Cross of St. Euphrosyne of Polotsk, 850th Anniv. — A330

Cross with denomination in: 5000r, Red. 10,000r, Gold.

Litho. & Embossed

2011, Mar. 21 ***Perf. 13x13½***

763 A330 5000r multi 4.50 4.50

Litho. & Embossed With Foil Application

764 A330 10,000r multi 8.50 8.50

First Man in Space, 50th Anniv. — A331

2011, Apr. 12 Litho. ***Perf. 13x13½***

765 A331 (1160r) multi 1.25 1.25

Europa — A332

Forest and: 2000r, Buck. 2500r, Bison.

2011, Apr. 14 ***Perf. 12½x12***

766-767 A332 Set of 2 3.00 3.00
767a Sheet of 6, 3 each #766-767 13.00 13.00

Intl. Year of Forests.

Chernobyl Nuclear Disaster, 25th Anniv. A333

2011, Apr. 26 ***Perf. 13½x13***

768 A333 (1330r) multi 1.40 1.40

AIDS Prevention, 30th Anniv. — A334

2011, May 12 ***Perf. 13¾x13½***

769 A334 (1330r) multi 1.40 1.40

Printed in sheets of 8 + central label.

Musical Instruments — A335

No. 770: a, Tar, Azerbaijan. b, Hurdy-gurdy, Belarus.

2011, May 25 ***Perf. 14x14¼***

770 A335 (1330r) Pair, #a-b 2.75 2.75

See Azerbaijan No. 950.

Capitals of Belarus and Armenia — A336

No. 771 Buildings and arms of. a, Minsk, Belarus ("Belarus" at left). b, Yerevan, Armenia ("Belarus" at right).

2011, June 1 ***Perf. 13½***

771 A336 (1330r) Horiz. pair, #a-b 2.75 2.75

See Armenia No. 875.

Commonweath of Independent States, 20th Anniv. — A337

2011, June 28 ***Perf. 13½x13¾***

772 A337 (1330r) multi 1.25 1.25

Souvenir Sheet

Diplomatic Relations Between Belarus and Venezuela, 15th Anniv. — A338

2011, July 5 ***Perf. 12¼x12***

773 A338 3000r multi 1.75 1.75

Slavianski Bazaar Intl. Arts Festival, Vitebsk — A339

No. 774: a, (360r), Stage, Vitebsk coat of arms. b, (1400r), Slavianski Bazaar emblem, Vitebsk Town Hall.

2011, July 8 ***Perf. 13½x13***

774 A339 Horiz. pair, #a-b 1.50 1.50

A340

Equestrian Sports — A341

Designs: No. 775, (1400r), Horse racing. No. 776, (1400r), Dressage. No. 777, (1400r), Jumping.
No. 778, Dressage half-pass, vert.

2011, July 12 *Perf. 12x12¼*
775-777 A340 Set of 3 4.25 4.25

Souvenir Sheet
Perf. 12¼x12

778 A341 (2160r) multi 1.90 1.90

Non-Aligned Movement, 50th Anniv. — A342

2011, Aug. 2 *Perf. 14x13½*
779 A342 (1400r) multi 1.25 1.25

Lota Lota A343

Esox Lucius A344

2011, Aug. 18 *Perf. 14x14¼*
780 A343 (1400r) multi 1.10 1.10
781 A344 (2160r) multi 1.75 1.75
a. Souvenir sheet of 6, 3 each #780-781 10.00 10.00

Regional Communications Commonwealth, 20th Anniv. — A345

2011, Sept. 20 *Perf. 13½x13*
782 A345 (1540r) multi 1.25 1.25

Souvenir Sheet

Buildings in Belarus and Iran — A346

No. 783: a, Mir Castle (building with steeples), Mir, Belarus. b, Arg of Karim Khan (building with round turrets), Shiraz, Iran.

2011, Sept. 28 *Perf. 12x12¼*
783 A346 (2380r) Sheet of 2, #a-b 4.00 4.00

See Iran No. 3046.

Arms of Molodechno A347

2011, Sept. 30 *Perf. 12*
784 A347 (1620r) multi 1.25 1.25

Costumes of Malorita Region — A348

Costumes of Kalinkovichi Region — A349

2011, Oct. 11 *Perf. 14x13½*
785 A348 (1620r) multi 1.25 1.25
786 A349 (2500r) multi 2.25 2.25
a. Souvenir sheet of 8, 4 each #785-786 14.00 14.00

New Year 2012 — A350

Christmas — A351

Litho. & Embossed With Foil Application

2011, Nov. 11 *Perf. 12*
787 A350 (2450r) multi 1.10 1.10
788 A351 (3750r) multi 1.75 1.75

Poster Pigeons A352

Starominsk Stately Piegons A353

Strasser Pigeons A354

2011, Nov. 28 Litho. *Perf. 12x12¼*
789 A352 5000r multi 1.75 1.75
790 A353 5000r multi 1.75 1.75
791 A354 5000r multi 1.75 1.75
a. Souvenir sheet of 6, 2 each #789-791 10.50 10.50
Nos. 789-791 (3) 5.25 5.25

Souvenir Sheet

Diplomatic Relations Between Belarus and People's Republic of China, 20th Anniv. — A355

Litho. & Embossed

2012, Jan. 20 *Perf. 12¼x12*
792 A355 15,000r multi 4.75 4.75

Geometric Designs
A356 A357

2012, Jan. 27 Litho. *Perf. 13½x13*
793 A356 (1100r) gray & red .60 .60
794 A357 (1650r) multi .90 .90

Souvenir Sheet

Orthodox Churches — A358

No. 795: a, St. Sophia Cathedral, Polotsk, and trees. b, All Saints Monument Church, Minsk, and lamp post.

2012, Feb. 22 *Perf. 12¼x12*
795 A358 10,000r Sheet of 2, #a-b 7.00 7.00

A359 A360

Architecture
A361 A362

Designs: 50r, Mahiliou Town Hall. 100r, Kamianets Tower. 200r, Nesvizh Castle, Nesvizh. 500r, Epiphany Church, Polatsk. (500r), Kosava Palace, Kosava. 1000r, Rumyantsev-Paskevich Palace, Homel. 2000r, Mir Castle, Mir. (2450r), Red Church, Minsk. (3750r), Church-fortress, Murovanka. 5000r, Main Post Office, Minsk. 10,000r, Lida Castle, Lida. 20,000r, Bernardine Monastery, Budslau.

2012, Mar. 2 Litho. *Perf. 13½x13*
796 A359 50r multi .25 .25
797 A359 100r multi .25 .25
798 A359 200r multi .25 .25
799 A359 500r multi .25 .25
800 A360 (500r) multi .25 .25
801 A359 1000r multi .40 .40
802 A359 2000r multi .75 .75
803 A361 (2450r) multi .95 .95
804 A362 (3750r) multi 1.50 1.50
805 A359 5000r multi 1.90 1.90
806 A359 10,000r multi 3.75 3.75
807 A359 20,000r multi 7.75 7.75
Nos. 796-807 (12) 18.25 18.25

Self-Adhesive
Die Cut

808 A359 50r multi .25 .25
809 A359 100r multi .25 .25
810 A359 200r multi .25 .25
811 A359 500r multi .25 .25
812 A360 (500r) multi .25 .25
813 A359 1000r multi .40 .40
814 A359 2000r multi .75 .75
815 A361 (2450r) multi .95 .95
816 A362 (3750r) multi 1.50 1.50
817 A359 5000r multi 1.90 1.90
818 A359 10,000r multi 3.75 3.75
819 A359 20,000r multi 7.75 7.75
Nos. 808-819 (12) 18.25 18.25

Europa — A363

No. 820 — People facing: a, Right. b, Left.

2012, Mar. 12 *Perf. 13x13½*
820 A363 5000r Horiz. pair, #a-b 3.00 3.00
c. Souvenir sheet of 6, 3 each #820a-820b 9.00 9.00

Apus Apus — A364

2012, Mar. 22 *Perf. 14x13½*
821 A364 (3750r) multi 2.00 2.00

Printed in sheets of 7 + label.

Costumes From Turov and Mozyr Regions — A365

Costumes From Liahovichi Region — A366

2012, Apr. 12 *Perf. 14¼x14*
822 A365 (2750r) multi 1.25 1.25
823 A366 (4250r) multi 1.75 1.75
a. Souvenir sheet of 8, 4 each #822-823 + label 12.00 12.00

Polypodium Vulgare and Silhouette of Butterfly A367

Salvinia Natans and Silhouette of Fish
A368

Litho. & Embossed

2012, May 3 *Perf. 12x12¼*

824 A367 (2750r) multi 1.25 1.25
825 A368 (4250r) multi 1.75 1.75
a. Souvenir sheet of 8, 4 each #824-825 12.00 12.00

Endangered plants.

Souvenir Sheet

Diplomatic Relations Between Belarus and Cuba, 20th Anniv. — A369

Litho. (Margin Litho. & Embossed)

2012, May 25 *Perf. 12¼x12*

826 A369 15,000r multi 6.00 6.00

Hemiechinus Auritus — A370

Erinaceus Concolor
A371

2012, June 20 Litho. *Perf. 12x12¼*

827 A370 (3300r) multi 1.25 1.25
828 A371 (5100r) multi 1.75 1.75
a. Souvenir sheet of 4, 2 each #827-828 6.00 6.00

See Kazakhstan No. 669.

Triturus Cristatus
A372

Lissotriton Vulgaris
A373

2012, June 25 *Perf. 13*

829 A372 (3300r) multi 1.25 1.25
830 A373 (5100r) multi 1.75 1.75
a. Souvenir sheet of 4, 2 each #829-830 6.00 6.00

See Russia No. 7367.

Souvenir Sheet

Portrait of Marc Chagall, by Yuri Pen — A374

2012, July 7 *Perf. 13½x13*

831 A374 15,000r multi 5.00 5.00

Marc Chagall (1887-1985), painter.

French Invasion, Bicent.
A375

2012, July 10 *Perf. 13½x14*

832 A375 (5100r) multi 2.00 2.00

Printed in sheets of 8 + central label.

Eurasian Economic Community — A376

Litho. & Embossed

2012, July 26 *Perf. 13x13½*

833 A376 (3300r) multi 1.50 1.50

Printed in sheets of 10 + 5 labels.

Belarussian Railway, 150th Anniv. — A377

2012, Aug. 1 **Litho.**

834 A377 (5100r) multi 2.00 2.00

Arms of Glubokoe — A378

Arms of Gorki — A379

2012, Aug. 21 *Perf. 12*

835 A378 (4800r) multi 1.75 1.75
836 A379 (5800r) multi 2.00 2.00

Fire and Rescue Sports in Belarus, 75th Anniv.
A380

2012, Sept. 8 *Perf. 13½x14*

837 A380 5000r multi 1.75 1.75

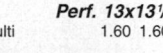

Maxim Tank (1912-95), Poet — A381

2012, Sept. 15 *Perf. 13x13½*

838 A381 (4800r) multi 1.60 1.60

Christmas — A382

New Year's Day — A383

Litho. & Embossed With Foil Application

2012, Nov. 20 *Perf. 12¼x12*

839 A382 (3000r) blue & gold 1.00 1.00
840 A383 (4500r) sil & grn 1.50 1.50

Souvenir Sheet

Diplomatic Relations Between Belarus and Israel, 20th Anniv. — A384

2012, Dec. 18 **Litho.**

841 A384 15,000r multi 5.75 5.75

A385

A386

2012 Summer Olympics, London
A387

2012, Dec. 21 *Perf. 12x12¼*

842 A385 (4500r) bronze & blk 1.75 1.75
843 A386 (5500r) sil & blk 2.10 2.10
844 A387 (5800r) gold & blk 2.25 2.25
Nos. 842-844 (3) 6.10 6.10

2013 World Track Cycling Championships, Minsk — A388

2013, Jan. 28 *Perf. 12*

845 A388 (5500r) multi 2.00 2.00

Botrychium Matricariifolium
A389

Coracias Garrulus
A390

2013, Jan. 31 *Perf. 12¼x12, 12x12¼*

846 A389 (5500r) multi 2.40 2.40
847 A390 (5800r) multi 2.50 2.50
a. Souvenir sheet of 2, #846-847 5.00 5.00

Endangered flora and fauna.

A391

A392

Embroidery
A393

2013, Feb. 12 *Perf. 12*

848 A391 (3000r) multi 1.25 1.25
849 A392 (4500r) multi 1.90 1.90
850 A393 (5500r) multi 2.40 2.40
Nos. 848-850 (3) 5.55 5.55

Upupa Epops
A394

2013, Mar. 12 *Perf. 13½x13*

851 A394 (5800r) multi 2.25 2.25

Khatyn Massacre, 70th Anniv. — A395

2013, Mar. 22

852 A395 (4500r) multi 2.00 2.00

Souvenir Sheet

Belarussian Landscape - Drecheluki Country Estate, by Yuliy Klever — A396

2013, Apr. 10 *Perf. 13x13½*
853 A396 15,000r multi 5.00 5.00

20th Intl. Telecommunications, Information and Banking Technologies Exhibition, Minsk — A397

2013, Apr. 23 *Perf. 12x12¼*
854 A397 (3000r) multi 1.40 1.40

Souvenir Sheet

Dancers — A398

No. 855: a, Kryzhachok dancers, Belarus (man without hat). b, Terekeme dancers, Azerbaijan (man with hat).

2013, Apr. 24 *Perf. 13½x13¼*
855 A398 5000r Sheet of 2, #a-b 3.50 3.50

See Azerbaijan No. 1020.

Peugeot Partner Mail Van A399

MAZ 437143-340 Mail Truck A400

2013, Apr. 29 *Perf. 12x12¼*
856 A399 (5500r) multi 2.25 2.25
857 A400 (5800r) multi 2.25 2.25
a. Souvenir sheet of 4, 2 each #856-857, + label 9.00 9.00

Europa.

Souvenir Sheet

St. Cyril of Turov (1130-82) — A401

Litho. With Foil Application
2013, May 11
858 A401 15,000r multi 5.00 5.00

National Academic Bolshoi Opera and Ballet Theater — A402

2013, May 22 Litho. *Perf. 13x13½*
859 A402 (5500r) multi 2.25 2.25

Souvenir Sheet

Slavonic Alphabet of Saints Cyril and Methodius, 1150th Anniv. — A403

Litho. With Foil Application
2013, May 24 *Perf. 13½x13*
860 A403 15,000r multi 5.25 5.25

2013 Belarussian Presidency of the Commonwealth of Independent States — A404

2013, May 30 **Litho.**
861 A404 (4500r) multi 2.00 2.00

Souvenir Sheet

Diplomatic Relations Between Azerbaijan and Belarus, 20th Anniv. — A405

Litho. (Sheet Margin Litho. With Foil Application)
2013, June 11 *Perf. 12¼x12*
862 A405 15,000r multi 5.25 5.25

See Azerbaijan No. 1027.

Defense of Brest Fortress, 1941 — A406

2013, June 21 Litho. *Perf. 13x13½*
863 A406 (5500r) multi 2.00 2.00

Souvenir Sheet

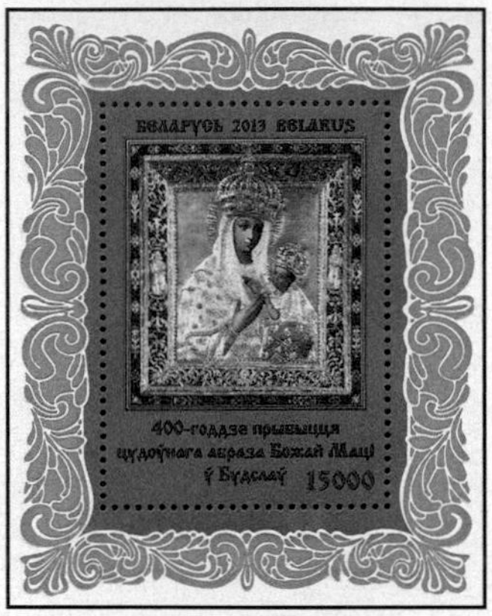

Madonna and Child Icon, National Sanctuary, Budslau, 400th Anniv. — A407

Litho. & Embossed (Sheet Margin Litho. With Foil Application)
2013, July 6 *Perf. 12x12¼*
864 A407 15,000r multi 5.25 5.25

Panthera Pardis Orientalis A408

Ovis Musimon A409

Haliaeetus Pelagicus A410

Panthera Tigris Altaica A411

2013, July 9 Litho. *Perf. 12x12¼*
865 A408 (4000r) multi 1.50 1.50
866 A409 (5500r) multi 2.00 2.00
867 A410 (6500r) multi 2.50 2.50
868 A411 (7000r) multi 2.75 2.75
a. Souvenir sheet of 4, #865-868, + 2 labels 8.75 8.75
Nos. 865-868 (4) 8.75 8.75

Animals in Belarusian zoos.

Belarussian State Puppet Theater, Minsk, 75th Anniv. A412

2013, July 10
869 A412 (5500r) multi 2.00 2.00

Souvenir Sheet

Christianization of Russia, 1025th Anniv. — A413

No. 870 — Icons depicting: a, The Lamentation of Christ, 19th cent. b, Old Testament Trinity, 18th cent. c, Christ Pantocrator, 18th cent.

Litho., Margin Litho. With Foil Application
2013, July 28 *Perf. 13½x13*
870 A413 5000r Sheet of 3, #a-c 5.25 5.25

See Russia No. 7466, Ukraine No. 930.

Tennis Players — A414

No. 871: a, Victoria Azarenka serving. b, Maxim Mirnyi chasing ball.

2013, Aug. 14 Litho. *Perf. 13½x13*
871 A414 (7000r) Pair, #a-b 5.25 5.25

Arms of Bykhov — A415

Arms of Zhlobin — A416

2013 Litho. *Perf. 14¼x14*
872 A415 (6500r) multi 2.25 2.25
873 A416 (6500r) multi 2.25 2.25

Issued: No. 872, 8/20; No. 873, 9/4.

Mushrooms
A417 A418

Designs: No. 874, Hydnum repandum and spider. No. 875, Lactarius torminosus and beetle. No. 876, Cantharellus cinereus and ladybug. No. 877, Rozites caperatus, bird and pine cone.

2013, Sept. 10 Litho. *Perf. 13x13½*
874 A417 (4000r) multi 1.40 1.40
875 A417 (4000r) multi 1.40 1.40
876 A418 (5500r) multi 1.90 1.90
877 A418 (5500r) multi 1.90 1.90
a. Souvenir sheet of 8, 2 each #874-877 13.50 13.50
Nos. 874-877 (4) 6.60 6.60

Historical Means of Communication and Emblem of Regional Communications Commonwealth A419

2013, Oct. 9 Litho. *Perf. 13½x13*

878 A419 (4000r) multi 1.60 1.60

Souvenir Sheet

Diplomatic Relations Between Belarus and Armenia, 20th Anniv. — A420

2013, Oct. 24 Litho. *Perf. 12¼x12*

879 A420 15,000r multi 5.00 5.00

See Armenia No. 952.

Miniature Sheet

Israeli Leaders Born in Belarus — A421

No. 880: a, Yitzhak Shamir (1915-2012), prime minister. b, Chaim Weizmann (1874-1952), president. c, Shimon Peres (born 1923), president. d, Zalman Shazar (1889-1974), president. e, Menachem Begin (1913-92), prime minister.

Litho. With Foil Application

2013, Oct. 30 *Perf. 12x12¼*

880	A421 Sheet of 5 + label	11.00	11.00
a.-b.	(4000r) Either single	1.60	1.60
c.-d.	(5500r) Either single	2.40	2.40
e.	(7000r) multi	3.00	3.00

Miniature Sheet

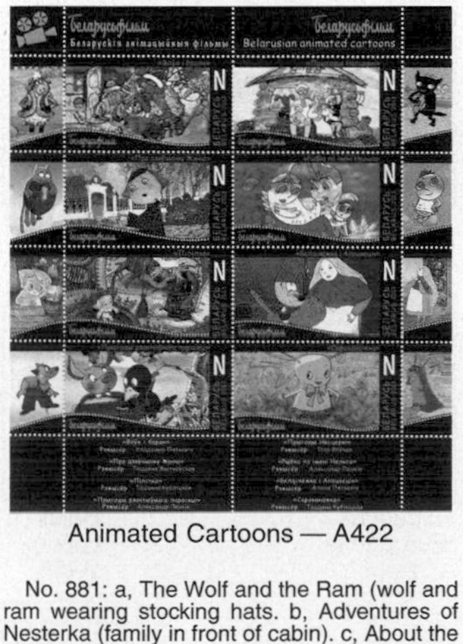

Animated Cartoons — A422

No. 881: a, The Wolf and the Ram (wolf and ram wearing stocking hats. b, Adventures of Nesterka (family in front of cabin). c, About the Girl Zhenya (girl and gate). d, A Small Fish Named Impossible (three fish). e, Pilipka (boy and witch with broom). f, Snow White and Rose Red (Snow White, dwarf and cat). g, Adventures of the Reactive Piglet (piglet and bird looking at book). h, The Centipede (centipede with ribbon).

2013, Nov. 1 Litho. *Perf. 13¼x13½*

881 A422 (4000r) Sheet of 8, #a-h 12.50 12.50

Christmas — A423

New Year 2014 — A424

2013, Nov. 5 Litho. *Perf. 13*

882	A423 (4000r) multi	1.50	1.50
883	A424 (6500r) multi	2.50	2.50
a.	Pair, #882-883	4.00	4.00

Nos. 882-883 were printed in sheets of 6 (3 of each stamp) + 2 labels.

Happy Postcrossing A425

2014, Jan. 2 Litho. *Perf. 12¼x12*

884 A425 (5000r) multi 1.90 1.90

Hoarfrost, Tapestry by G. H. Stasevich A426

Horses, Tapestry by L. N. Gustova A427

2014, Jan. 4 Litho. *Perf. 14x14¼*

885	A426 (1600r) multi	.60	.60
886	A427 (6500r) multi	2.40	2.40

Souvenir Sheet

Belarus Saints, Icon in Memorial Church of All Saints, Minsk — A428

No. 887: a, 30 saints facing right. b, 16 saints and church. c, 30 saints facing left.

Litho. With Foil Application

2014, Jan. 7 *Perf. 13½x13*

887 A428 (8000r) Sheet of 3, #a-c 8.75 8.75

Arkadi Kuleshov (1914-78), Poet — A429

2014, Feb. 6 Litho. *Perf. 13x13½*

888 A429 (1600r) multi .65 .65

Souvenir Sheet

2014 Winter Olympics, Sochi, Russia — A430

2014, Feb. 7 Litho. *Perf. 13x13½*

889 A430 20,000r multi 6.00 6.00

2014 Ice Hockey World Championships, Minsk — A431

2014, Feb. 8 Litho. *Perf. 13x13½*

890 A431 (6500r) multi 2.40 2.40

Surmas and Surma Player A432

Horum and Horum Player A433

2014, Mar. 6 Litho. *Perf. 13½x13*

891	A432 (7500r) multi	2.75	2.75
892	A433 (8000r) multi	3.00	3.00
a.	Souvenir sheet of 6, 3 each #891-892, + 2 labels	17.50	17.50

Europa.

Cuculus Canorus A434

2014, Mar. 11 Litho. *Perf. 13½x13*

893 A434 (5000r) multi 1.90 1.90

Floral Design From Sash Made in Slutsk A435

Litho. & Embossed

2014, Mar. 14 *Perf. 13¼*

894 A435 (5000r) multi 1.90 1.90

Intl. Year of Family Farming A436

2014, Mar. 18 Litho. *Perf. 12*

895 A436 (7500r) multi 2.75 2.75

Miniature Sheet

Space Exploration — A437

No. 896: a, Pyotr Klimuk, first Belarussian cosmonaut in space, space station at left. b, Vladimir Kovalyonok, cosmonaut, space station at right. c, Belarussian satellite over earth. d, Oleg Novitskiy, cosmonaut, rocket launch at left.

2014, Apr. 12 Litho. *Perf. 13½x13*

896 A437 (5000r) Sheet of 4, #a-d 7.25 7.25

Belarus in UNESCO, 60th Anniv. — A438

2014, Apr. 14 Litho. *Perf. 13x13½*

897 A438 (5000r) multi 1.90 1.90

Souvenir Sheet

Liberation of Belarus, Russia and Ukraine From Nazi Occupation, 70th Anniv. — A439

2014, Apr. 18 Litho. *Perf. 13¼x13*

898 A439 15,000r multi 4.75 4.75

See Russia No. 7520.

Trade Unions in Belarus, 110th Anniv. — A440

2014, Apr. 24 Litho. ***Perf. 12x12¼***
899 A440 (1600r) multi .65 .65

No. 899 was printed in sheets of 8 + 4 central labels.

Nadezhda Skardino, Biathlon Bronze Medalist A441

Alla Tsuper, Gold Medalist in Women's Aerial Freestyle Skiing A442

Anton Kushnir, Gold Medalist in Men's Aerial Freestyle Skiing A443

Darya Domracheva, Biathlon Gold Medalist — A444

Litho. & Embossed
2014, May 2 ***Perf. 13½x13***
900 A441 (6500r) multi 2.40 2.40
901 A442 (6500r) multi 2.40 2.40
902 A443 (6500r) multi 2.40 2.40
Nos. 900-902 (3) 7.20 7.20

Souvenir Sheet
Perf.
903 A444 (8000r) multi 3.00 3.00

Souvenir Sheet

Flora and Fauna of Bogs — A445

No. 904: a, Tetrao tetrix. b, Pinus sylvestris, vert.

2014, May 14 Litho. ***Perf. 12***
904 A445 (8000r) Sheet of 2, #a-b 6.00 6.00

Grodno Regional Drama Theater — A446

2014, June 5 Litho. ***Perf. 13x13½***
905 A446 (5000r) multi 1.75 1.75

Yakub Kolas National Academic Drama Theater A447

2014, June 20 Litho. ***Perf. 12x12¼***
906 A447 (5000r) multi 1.75 1.75

Solidago Canadensis A448

Heracleum Sosnowskyi A449

Litho. & Embossed
2014, July 25 ***Perf. 12¼x12***
907 A448 (1600r) multi .60 .60
908 A449 (5000r) multi 1.75 1.75

Flowers in National Academy of Sciences Central Botanical Garden A450

Designs: No. 909, (6500r), Dahlia "Diadema." No. 910, (6500r), Paeonia "Pamyati Gagarina," vert. No. 911, (6500r), Rosa "Gloria Dei," vert. No. 912, (6500r), Lilium "Zorenka."

Perf. 12x12¼, 12¼x12
2014, Aug. 22 **Litho.**
909-912 A450 Set of 4 8.75 8.75
912a Souvenir sheet of 4, #909-912, + central label 8.75 8.75

Nos. 909-912 were each issued in sheets of 4 + central label.

Arms and Tourist Attractions of Zaslawye — A451

2014, Sept. 5 Litho. ***Perf. 13x13½***
913 A451 (6500r) multi 2.25 2.25

Arms of Gorodok — A452

2014, Sept. 19 Litho. ***Perf. 12***
914 A452 (5000r) multi 1.75 1.75

New Year 2015 — A453

Christmas A454

2014, Oct. 2 Litho. ***Perf. 13½x13¼***
915 A453 (1600r) multi .60 .60
916 A454 (7500r) multi 2.75 2.75

Souvenir Sheet

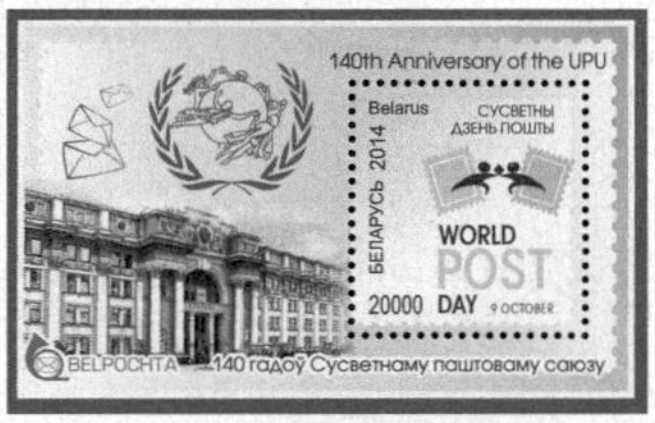

World Post Day — A455

2014, Oct. 9 Litho. ***Perf. 12¼x12***
917 A455 20,000r multi 5.00 5.00

Belarussian Exarchate, 25th Anniv. A456

Litho. With Foil Application
2014, Oct. 11 ***Perf. 13½x13***
918 A456 (7500r) multi 2.75 2.75

National Art Museum, 75th Anniv. — A457

Litho. & Embossed With Foil Application
2014, Nov. 10 ***Perf. 13x13½***
919 A457 (5000r) multi 1.75 1.75

Souvenir Sheet

Diplomatic Relations Between Belarus and Serbia, 20th Anniv. — A458

Litho., Margin Litho. With Foil Application
2014, Nov. 15 ***Perf. 12***
920 A458 20,000r multi 6.00 6.00

Biathlon A459

2014, Nov. 20 Litho. ***Perf. 12x12¼***
921 A459 (6500r) multi 2.25 2.25

A460

A461

A462

Wildlife of Naliboki Forest — A463

2014, Nov. 27 Litho. ***Perf. 12¼x12***
922 Horiz. strip of 4 7.75 7.75
a. A460 (1600r) multi .60 .60
b. A461 (5000r) multi 1.90 1.90
c. A462 (6500r) multi 2.40 2.40
d. A463 (7500r) multi 2.75 2.75
e. Booklet pane of 4, #922a-922d 7.75 —
Complete booklet, #922e 7.75

Nyctereutes Procyonoides A464

Mustela Lutreola A465

Lepus Europaeus A466

Canis Lupus A467

Martes Martes — A468

2014, Dec. 10 Litho. *Die Cut*
Self-Adhesive

923 A464 (1600r) multi		.60	.60
924 A465 (5000r) multi		1.90	1.90
925 A466 (6500r) multi		2.40	2.40
926 A467 (7500r) multi		2.75	2.75
927 A468 (8000r) multi		3.00	3.00
Nos. 923-927 (5)		10.65	10.65

Church of Saints Simon and Helena, Minsk A469

2015, Jan. 23 Litho. *Perf. 13½x13*
928 A469 (5000r) multi 1.90 1.90

MAZ-6440RA Truck — A470

BELAZ-75710 Dump Truck — A471

MZKT-600100 Truck — A472

AMKADOR 732 Backhoe A473

Belarus 2422 Tractor A474

2015, Jan. 30 Litho. *Perf. 14x14¼*

929	Vert. strip of 5	11.50	11.50
a.	A470 (6500r) multi	2.25	2.25
b.	A471 (6500r) multi	2.25	2.25
c.	A472 (6500r) multi	2.25	2.25
d.	A473 (6500r) multi	2.25	2.25
e.	A474 (6500r) multi	2.25	2.25

Souvenir Sheet

New Year 2015 (Year of the Goat) — A475

Litho. & Embossed With Foil Application

2015, Feb. 19 *Perf.*
930 A475 30,000r multi 7.25 7.25

A476

Victory in World War II, 70th Anniv. — A477

Designs: No. 931, Soldiers with captured Nazi flags.

No. 932: a, Soldiers with guns raised in victory. b, Soldiers celebrating in Berlin.

2015, Mar. 10 Litho. *Perf. 12x12¼*
931 A476 (7500r) multi 2.50 2.50

Souvenir Sheet
Litho., Margin Litho. With Foil Application

932	A477	Sheet of 2	5.25	5.25
a.		(7500r) multi	2.50	2.50
b.		(8000r) multi	2.75	2.75

No. 931 was printed in sheets of 8 + label.

Francishak Bahushevich (1840-1900), Poet — A478

2015, Mar. 21 Litho. *Perf. 12x12¼*
933 A478 (5000r) multi 1.90 1.90

Souvenir Sheet

Metropolitan Philaret of Belarus — A479

Litho., Margin Litho. With Foil Application

2015, Mar. 21 *Perf.*
934 A479 30,000r multi 7.00 7.00

20th Belarussian Energy and Ecology Congress, Minsk A480

2015, Mar. 26 Litho. *Perf. 12x12¼*
935 A480 (5000r) multi 1.90 1.90

Asio Otus — A481

2015, Apr. 1 Litho. *Perf. 13x13½*
936 A481 (8000r) multi 2.75 2.75

Rag Dolls — A482

Wooden Toys — A483

2015, Apr. 13 Litho. *Perf. 12¼x12*

937	Horiz. pair	5.25	5.25
a.	A482 (10,500r) multi	2.50	2.50
b.	A483 (12,000r) multi	2.75	2.75
c.	Souvenir sheet of 2, #937a-937b	5.25	5.25

Europa.

Souvenir Sheet

Francysk Skaryna (c. 1490-c.1551), Book Printer — A484

Litho., Margin Litho. With Foil Application

2015, Apr. 16 *Perf. 13x13½*
938 A484 20,000r blk & silver 4.75 4.75

Eurasian Economic Union A485

2015, May 13 Litho. *Perf. 12x12¼*
939 A485 (10,500r) multi 2.50 2.50

Flowers of Central Botanical Garden of the National Academy of Sciences, Minsk A486

Designs: No. 940, (7800r), Philadelphus "Elbrus." No. 941, (7800r), Syringa "Vera Horuzhaya." No. 942, (7800r), Paeonia suffruticosa. No. 943, (7800r), Rhododendron "Akademik Smolskiy."

2015, May 29 Litho. *Perf. 12x12¼*

940-943	A486	Set of 4	7.50	7.50
943a		Souvenir sheet of 4, #940-943	7.50	7.50

Souvenir Sheet

St. Vladimir (c. 958-1015) — A487

Litho. With Foil Application

2015, June 20 *Perf.*
944 A487 30,000r gold & red 7.00 7.00

Arms of Shchuchyn — A488

2015, Aug. 4 Litho. *Perf. 12*
945 A488 (7800r) multi 1.60 1.60

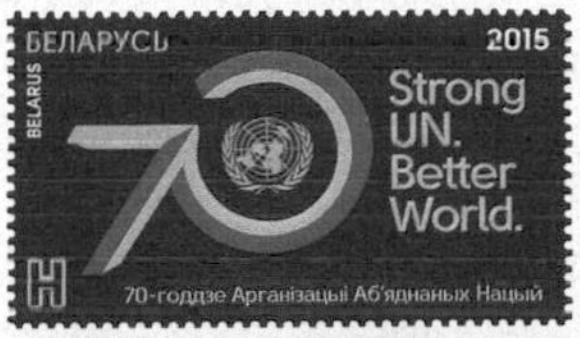

United Nations, 70th Anniv. — A489

Litho. & Embossed

2015, Aug. 11 *Perf. 13x13½*
946 A489 (10,500r) multi 2.10 2.10

Coccinella Septempunctata A490

Psyllobora Vigintiduopunctata — A491

Propylea Quatuordecimpunctata — A492

Calvia Quatuordecimguttata — A493

Litho. & Embossed

2015, Aug. 26 *Perf. 12*

947	A490	(3600r) multi	.70	.70
948	A491	(7800r) multi	1.60	1.60
948	A492	(9600r) multi	1.90	1.90
950	A493	(10,500r) multi	2.10	2.10
a.		Souvenir sheet of 4, #947-950	6.50	6.50
		Nos. 947-950 (4)	6.30	6.30

A494

A495

A496

Spermophilus Suslicus — A497

2015, Sept. 1 **Litho.** *Perf. 12*

951	A494	(3600r) multi	.70	.70
952	A495	(7800r) multi	1.60	1.60
953	A496	(9600r) multi	1.90	1.90
954	A497	(10,500r) multi	2.10	2.10
a.		Souvenir sheet of 4, #951-954	6.50	6.50
		Nos. 951-954 (4)	6.30	6.30

Worldwide Fund for Nature (WWF).

Brest Academic Drama Theater — A498

2015, Sept. 11 **Litho.** *Perf. 13x13½*

955 A498 (3600r) multi .70 .70

Yanka Kupala National Academic Theater — A499

Litho. With Foil Application

2015, Sept. 14 *Perf. 13½x13*

956 A499 (9600r) multi 1.90 1.90

The Lake, by Ossip Zadkine — A500

Landscape with a Red Roof, by Ossip Lubitch — A501

Designs: No. 958, Eva, by Chaim Soutine, vert. No. 960, Lovers, by Marc Chagall, vert.

Perf. 13x13½, 13½x13

2015, Sept. 29 **Litho.**

957	A500	(7800r) multi	1.60	1.60
958	A500	(7800r) multi	1.60	1.60
959	A501	(9600r) multi	1.90	1.90
960	A501	(9600r) multi	1.90	1.90
a.		Souvenir sheet of 4, #957-960	7.00	7.00
		Nos. 957-960 (4)	7.00	7.00

Hyla Arborea A502

Rana Temporaria A503

Rana Lessonae A504

Bombina Bombina A505

2015, Oct. 16 **Litho.** *Perf. 12*

961	A502	(3600r) multi	.70	.70
962	A503	(7800r) multi	1.60	1.60
963	A504	(9600r) multi	1.90	1.90
964	A505	(10,500r) multi	2.10	2.10
a.		Souvenir sheet of 4, #961-964	6.50	6.50
		Nos. 961-964 (4)	6.30	6.30

New Year 2016 A506

Christmas A507

2015, Nov. 3 **Litho.** *Perf. 12*

965	A506	(9600r) multi	1.90	1.90
966	A507	(10,500r) multi	2.10	2.10
a.		Souvenir sheet of 4, 2 each #965-966	8.00	8.00

Souvenir Sheet

Satellites — A508

No. 967: a, DZZ satellite, Belarus. b, Azerspace-1 satellite, Azerbaijan.

Litho., Sheet Margin Litho. With Foil Application

2015, Dec. 3 *Perf.*

967 A508 20,000r Sheet of 2, #a-b 7.75 7.75

See Azerbaijan No. 1099.

Souvenir Sheet

Paintings by Belarussian and Chinese Artists — A509

No. 968: a, Summer (flowers and pots), by Valeriana Zholtok, 1977. b, Flash of Summer Lightning, the Song of Polesye (four birds in flight), by Gavriil Vashchenko, 1968-96. c, Aurochs, by Gennady Loyko, 1968. d, Bull, by Lui Da Wei, 2015. e, Peonies, by Guo Yi Cong, 1984. f, Crane, by Zhan Geng Xi, 2008.

2015, Dec. 15 **Litho.** *Perf. 12*

968	A509	Sheet of 6	10.50	10.50
a.		(3600r) multi	.60	.60
b.		(9300r) multi	1.60	1.60
c.-d.		(11,700r) Either single	1.90	1.90
e.		(12,600r) multi	2.10	2.10
f.		(14,400r) multi	2.40	2.40

Kalduny (Stuffed Dumplings) A510

2016, Jan. 18 **Litho.** *Perf. 13½x13*

969 A510 (12,600r) multi 2.10 2.10

Sarcochilus Sp. — A511

Zygopetalum Maculatum — A512

Dendrobium Unicum A513

Bulbophyllum Ornatissimum — A514

2016, Jan. 28 **Litho.** *Perf. 12*

970	A511	(3600r) multi	.60	.60
971	A512	(9300r) multi	1.60	1.60
972	A513	(11,700r) multi	1.90	1.90
973	A514	(12,600r) multi	2.10	2.10
a.		Souvenir sheet of 4, #970-973	6.25	6.25
		Nos. 970-973 (4)	6.20	6.20

Regional Commmunications Commonwealth, 25th Anniv. — A515

Litho. With Foil Application

2016, Feb. 2 *Perf. 13x13½*

974 A515 (12,600r) multi 2.10 2.10

Carabus Cancellatus A516

Carabus Nitens A517

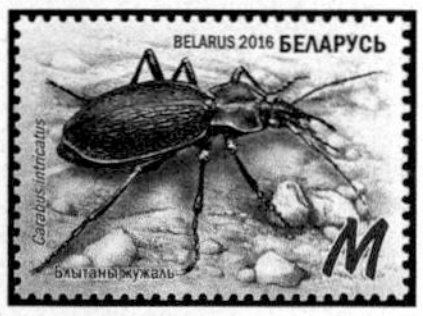

Carabus Intricatus A518

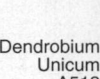

Carabus Clathratus A519

2016, Feb. 16 **Litho.** *Perf. 13½x13*

975	A516	(3600r) multi	.60	.60
976	A517	(9300r) multi	1.60	1.60
977	A518	(11,700r) multi	1.90	1.90
978	A519	(12,600r) multi	2.10	2.10
a.		Souvenir sheet of 4, #975-978	6.25	6.25
		Nos. 975-978 (4)	6.20	6.20

Endangered insects.

Bucephala Clangula A520

2016, Mar. 17 **Litho.** *Perf. 13½x13*

979 A520 (12,600r) multi 2.10 2.10

A521

Europa
A522

2016, Apr. 5 Litho. *Perf. 12*

980 A521 (12,600r) multi 2.25 2.25
981 A522 (14,400r) multi 2.50 2.50
a. Souvenir sheet of 4, 2 each #980-981 9.50 9.50

Think Green Issue.

Belintersat-1 — A523

2016, Apr. 12 Litho. *Perf. 13¼*

982 A523 (12,600r) multi 2.25 2.25

Souvenir Sheet

View With Cypress Trees, by Leon Bakst (1866-1924) — A524

2016, May 11 Litho. *Perf. 13½x13*

983 A524 (14,400r) multi 2.60 2.60

Eagles — A525

No. 984: a, Aquila nipalensis. b, Aquila chrysaetos.

2016, May 12 Litho. *Perf. 12*

984 A525 (12,600r) Pair, #a-b 4.50 4.50

See Azerbaijan No. 1112.

Souvenir Sheet

2016 Summer Olympics, Rio de Janeiro — A526

2016, June 7 Litho. *Perf.*

985 A526 (14,400r) multi 2.60 2.60

Soldiers Defending Brest Fortress — A527

Heroes of the Defense of Brest Fortress — A528

No. 987: a, Ivan M. Zubachov (bald man). b, Piotr M. Gavrilov (wearing medal). c, Andrey M. Kizhevatov (wearing green collar insignia).

Litho. & Embossed With Foil Application

2016, June 22 *Perf. 13x13½*

986 A527 (12,600r) multi 2.25 2.25

Souvenir Sheet

Litho. With Foil Application

Perf. 12

987 A528 Sheet of 3 4.50 4.50
a. (3600r) multi .65 .65
b. (9300r) multi 1.75 1.75
c. (11,700r) multi 2.10 2.10

See Russia No. 7734.

Flag of Belarus A529

Belarus Coat of Arms — A530

Design: (1.44r), Belarus coat of arms, diff.

Litho. With Foil Application

2016, July 3 *Perf. 13½x13*

988 A529 (36k) multi .65 .65

Perf. 13x13½

989 A530 (1.26r) multi 2.25 2.25

Souvenir Sheet

Perf.

990 A530 (1.44r) multi 2.60 2.60

No. 990 contains one 40mm diameter stamp.

Souvenir Sheet

St. Sophia Cathedral, Polotsk — A531

Litho., Sheet Margin Litho & Embossed With Foil Application

2016, July 4 *Perf. 13x13½*

991 A531 (1.44r) multi 2.60 2.60

Belarus Coat of Arms — A532

2016, July 6 Litho. *Die Cut*

Self-Adhesive

Frame Color

992	A532	1k	light blue	.25	.25
993	A532	2k	brown	.25	.25
994	A532	5k	green	.25	.25
995	A532	10k	yellow	.25	.25
996	A532	20k	turquoise	.35	.35
997	A532	30k	rose lilac	.55	.55
998	A532	50k	gray	.90	.90
999	A532	1r	blue	1.75	1.75
1000	A532	2r	red	3.50	3.50
1001	A532	5r	apple green	8.75	8.75
1002	A532	10r	beige	17.50	17.50
1003	A532	20r	violet	35.00	35.00
	Nos. 992-1003 (12)			69.30	69.30

Circus Venues and Performers — A533

No. 1004: a, (36k), Clown juggling balls, Gomel State Circus. b, (1.26r), Horses, Belarusian State Circus.

2016, July 8 Litho. *Perf. 13x13½*

1004 A533 Pair, #a-b 3.00 3.00

Souvenir Sheet

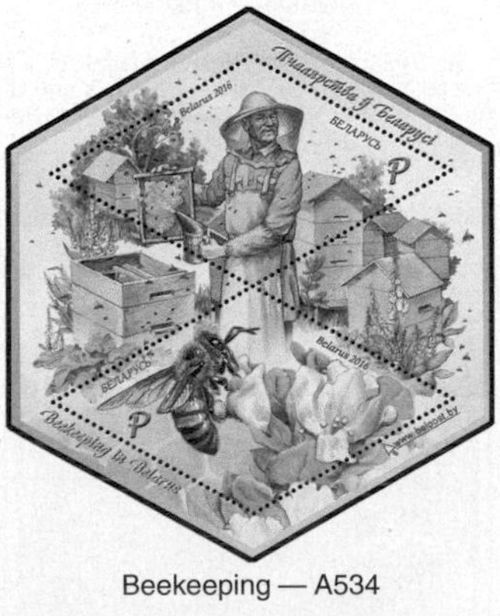

Beekeeping — A534

No. 1005: a, Apiarist and hives. b, Bee and flower.

2016, Aug. 12 Litho. *Perf. 13¼*

1005 A534 (1.44r) Sheet of 2, #a-b 5.25 5.25

Arms of Rahachow — A535

2016, Aug. 16 Litho. *Perf. 14¼x14*

1006 A535 (93k) multi 1.75 1.75

Commonwealth of Independent States, 25th Anniv. — A536

2016, Aug. 30 Litho. *Perf. 12*

1007 A536 (1.44r) multi 2.60 2.60

Day of the Preliminary Investigation Officer — A537

Litho. With Foil Application

2016, Sept. 6 *Perf. 12*

1008 A537 (1.26r) multi 2.10 2.10

No. 1008 was printed in sheets of 8 + central label.

26th Meeting of the Coordination Council of Attorneys General of the Commonwealth of Independent States — A538

No. 1009 — Flag of Belarus and: a, Emblem and office of Belarus Attorney General, date in black. b, Emblem and office of Coordination Council of Commonwealth of Independent States, date in white.

2016, Sept. 7 Litho. *Perf. 12x12¼*

1009 A538 Horiz. pair 2.75 2.75
a. (36k) multi .65 .65
b. (1.26r) multi 2.10 2.10

Woodworking — A539

No. 1010 — Woodworker with mallet and: a, Carving of a bull. b, Wooden flasks.

2016, Sept. 8 Litho. *Perf. 13x13½*

1010 A539 Horiz. pair 2.75 2.75
a. (36k) multi .65 .65
b. (1.26r) multi 2.10 2.10

Joint issue of the Republic of Belarus and the Republic of Moldova.

See Moldova No. 922.

Belarus Customs Service, 25th Anniv. — A540

Litho. & Embossed

2016, Sept. 15 *Perf. 12*

1011 A540 (1.26r) multi 2.10 2.10

Statue of St. Sofia, Buildings and Coat of Arms of Slutsk — A541

2016, Sept. 16 Litho. ***Perf. 13x13½***

1012 A541 (1.17r) multi 2.00 2.00

First mention in writing of Slutsk, 900th anniv.

Souvenir Sheet

Icons — A542

No. 1013: a, Hodegetria from Peter and Paul Church, Halynka, 17th cent. b, St. Anthony of Padua and Jesus, Archangel Michael Church, Miratsichy, 1744.

Litho. & Embossed With Foil Application

2016, Sept. 29 ***Perf. 13½x13***

1013 A542 (1.44r) Horiz. pair, #a-b 5.00 5.00

National Parks of Belarus and Pakistan — A543

No. 1014: a, Narachanski National Park, flag and arms of Belarus. b, Saiful Muluk National Park, flag and arms of Pakistan.

2016, Oct. 5 Litho. ***Perf. 13x13½***

1014 A543 Horiz. pair 2.75 2.75
a. (36k) multi .65 .65
b. (1.26r) multi 2.10 2.10

See Pakistan No. 1238.

Arctia Caja A544

Nymphalis Antiopa A545

Zygaena Filipendulae A546

Smerinthus Ocellata A547

2016, Oct. 19 Litho. ***Perf. 12***

1015 A544 (36k) multi .65 .65
1016 A545 (93k) multi 1.60 1.60
1017 A546 (1.17r) multi 2.00 2.00
1018 A547 (1.26r) multi 2.10 2.10
a. Souvenir sheet of 4, #1015-1018 6.50 6.50
Nos. 1015-1018 (4) 6.35 6.35

Snowflake — A548

Star of Bethlehem, Angels and Church — A549

Litho. With Foil Application

2016, Oct. 27 ***Perf. 13***

1019 A548 (36k) multi .80 .80
1020 A549 (1.26r) multi 3.00 3.00
a. Souvenir sheet of 4, 2 each #1019-1020 7.75 7.75

New Year's Day and Christmas.

Souvenir Sheet

Medalists at 2016 Summer Olympics — A550

No. 1021: a, Seven bronze medalists and bronze medal. b, Four silver medalists and silver medal. c, Uladzislau Hancharou and trampolining gold medal, vert.

Perf. 13½x13, 13x13½

2016, Nov. 30 Litho.

1021 A550 Sheet of 3 8.00 8.00
a. (93k) multi 2.00 2.00
b. (1.26r) multi 2.75 2.75
c. (1.44r) multi 3.25 3.25

Miniature Sheet

Medalists at 2016 Summer Paralympics — A551

No. 1022: a, Aliaksandr Tryputs, javelin bronze medalist (26x30mm). b, Andrei Pranevich, fencing gold medalist holding épée (26x30mm). c, Uladzimir Izotau, swimming gold medalist, holding stuffed mascot (26x30mm). d, Ihar Boki, winner of 6 gold and 1 bronze swimming medals (26x37mm).

2016, Nov. 30 Litho. ***Perf. 13x13½***

1022 A551 Sheet of 4 10.00 10.00
a. (93k) multi 2.00 2.00
b.-c. (1.17r) Either single 2.60 2.60
d. (1.26r) multi 2.75 2.75

UNICEF, 70th Anniv. — A552

2016, Dec. 8 Litho. ***Perf. 13x13½***

1023 A552 (1.26r) multi 2.75 2.75

Maksim Bahdanovich (1891-1917), Writer — A553

2016, Dec. 9 Litho. ***Perf. 13x13½***

1024 A553 (36k) multi .85 .85

Postcrossing A554

2017, Jan. 3 Litho. ***Die Cut***

Self-Adhesive

1025 A554 (1.17r) multi 2.75 2.75

Bengal Cat — A555

Maine Coon Cat — A556

Scottish Fold Cat — A557

British Shorthair Cat — A558

2017, Jan. 18 Litho. ***Perf. 12***

1026 A555 (36k) multi .80 .80
1027 A556 (36k) multi .80 .80
1028 A557 (93k) multi 2.10 2.10
1029 A558 (93k) multi 2.10 2.10
a. Souvenir sheet of 8, 2 each #1026-1029 12.00 12.00
Nos. 1026-1029 (4) 5.80 5.80

A559

Litho. With Foil Application

2017, Jan. 20 ***Perf. 12***

1030 A559 (1.26r) multi 2.75 2.75

Diplomatic Relations Between Belarus and People's Republic of China, 25th Anniv.

French Bulldog — A560

Dachshund A561

Chihuahua A562

American Cocker Spaniel — A563

2017, Jan. 26 Litho. ***Perf. 12***

1031 A560 (36k) multi .80 .80
1032 A561 (36k) multi .80 .80
1033 A562 (93k) multi 2.10 2.10
1034 A563 (93k) multi 2.10 2.10
a. Souvenir sheet of 8, 2 each #1031-1034 12.00 12.00
Nos. 1031-1034 (4) 5.80 5.80

Crafts — A564

No. 1035: a, Woven straw horse. b, Pottery.

2017, Feb. 17 Litho. ***Perf. 12***

1035 A564 Pair + 2 labels 5.00 5.00
a. (93k) multi + label 2.25 2.25
b. (1.26r) multi + label 2.75 2.75

Souvenir Sheet

Belarusian Militia, Cent. — A565

No. 1036: a, Emblem of the Ministry of Internal Affairs (40mm diameter). b, Ministry of Internal Affairs Building (52x37mm).

Perf. (#1036a), Perf. 13x13½
Litho. with Foil Application

2017, Feb. 24
1036 A565 (1.44r) Sheet of 2, #a-b 6.50 6.50

Maskouskaya Metro Station, Minsk — A566

Piatroushchyna Metro Station, Minsk — A567

2017, Feb. 27 Litho. *Perf. 13x13½*
1037 A566 (1.17r) multi 2.60 2.60
1038 A567 (1.17r) multi 2.60 2.60
a. Souvenir sheet of 4, 2 each #1037-1038 10.50 10.50

Souvenir Sheet

First Written Mention of Minsk, 950th Anniv. — A568

Litho. With Foil Application

2017, Mar. 3 *Perf. 13x13½*
1039 A568 5r multi 10.00 10.00

Diplomatic Relations Between Belarus and Poland, 25th Anniv. A569

Litho. With Foil Application

2017, Mar. 15 *Perf. 12*
1040 A569 (1.26r) multi 2.75 2.75

Galerida Cristata A570

2017, Mar. 22 Litho. *Perf. 13½x13*
1041 A570 (1.26r) multi 2.75 2.75

Reconstructed Gate of Ruzhany Palace — A571

Gomel Palace A572

2017, Apr. 20 Litho. *Perf. 12*
1042 A571 (1.38r) multi 3.00 3.00
1043 A572 (1.56r) multi 3.25 3.25
a. Souvenir sheet of 4, 2 each #1042-1043 12.50 12.50

Europa.

Cricetus Cricetus A573

Mustela Erminea A574

Meles Meles A575

Ursus Arctos A576

2017, Apr. 27 Litho. *Perf. 13½x13*
1044 Horiz. strip of 4 8.50 8.50
a. A573 (42k) multi .85 .85
b. A574 (1.02r) multi 2.10 2.10
c. A575 (1.26r) multi 2.60 2.60
d. A576 (1.38r) multi 2.75 2.75

Endangered animals from Red Book of Belarus.

Narcissus "Holiday Sun" — A577

Tulipa "Armani" — A578

2017, May 3 Litho. *Perf. 12*
1045 A577 (1.02r) multi 2.10 2.10
1046 A578 (1.38r) multi 2.75 2.75
a. Souvenir sheet of 4, 2 each #1045-1046 9.75 9.75

Flowers of Central Botanical Garden.

Minsk Horse-Drawn Rail Car in Sabornaya Square — A579

Minsk Horse-Drawn Rail Car — A580

Conductor and Empty Car A581

Minsk Horse-Drawn Rail Car on Zaharyeuskaya Street — A582

2017, May 10 Litho. *Perf. 12*
1047 A579 (42k) multi .75 .75
1048 A580 (1.02r) multi 1.75 1.75
1049 A581 (1.26r) multi 2.10 2.10
1050 A582 (1.38r) multi 2.40 2.40
a. Souvenir sheet of 4, #1047-1050 7.00 7.00
Nos. 1047-1050 (4) 7.00 7.00

Minsk Horse-Drawn Railway, 125th anniv.

Prosecutor's Office, 95th Anniv. — A583

Litho. With Foil Application

2017, June 22 *Perf. 12*
1051 A583 (1.38r) vio bl & gold 2.40 2.40

Horses — A584

No. 1052: a, New Kirgiz horse facing left. b, Trakehner horse facing right.

2017, June 30 Litho. *Perf. 12*
1052 A584 (1.38r) Pair, #a-b 4.75 4.75

See Kyrgyz Express Post No. 56.

World War II Memorial, Lion Statue, Town Hall and Coat of Arms of Mogilev — A585

2017, July 3 Litho. *Perf. 12*
1053 A585 (1.26r) multi 2.25 2.25

Yanka Kupala (1882-1942), Writer A586

Litho. & Embossed With Foil Application

2017, July 7 *Perf. 13½x13*
1054 A586 (1.02r) multi 1.90 1.90

Diplomatic Relations Between Belarus and Latvia, 25th Anniv. A587

Litho. & Embossed With Foil Application

2017, July 19 *Perf. 12*
1055 A587 (1.38r) multi 2.50 2.50

Arms of Polotsk — A588

2017, Aug. 24 Litho. *Perf. 14¼x14*
1056 A588 (1.02r) multi 1.90 1.90

Souvenir Sheet

Book Printing in Belarus, 500th Anniv. — A589

Litho. With Foil Application

2017, Sept. 1 *Perf. 12*
1057 A589 (1.56r) multi 2.75 2.75

Diplomatic Relations Between Belarus and India, 25th Anniv. A590

Litho. & Embossed With Foil Application

2017, Sept. 12 ***Perf. 12***

1058 A590 (1.38r) multi 2.50 2.50

See India No. 2957.

Souvenir Sheet

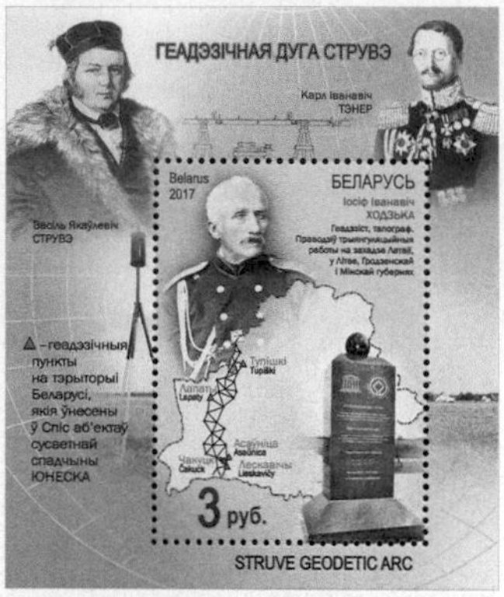

Marker for Struve Geodetic Arc, Map of Triangulation in Belarus, and Józef Chodzko (1800-81), Surveyor — A591

2017, Sept. 14 **Litho.** ***Perf. 12***

1059 A591 3r multi 5.50 5.50

Coat of Arms and Tourist Attractions of Gomel — A592

2017, Sept. 16 **Litho.** ***Perf. 13***

1060 A592 (1.26r) multi 2.40 2.40

Diplomatic Relations Between Belarus and Kazakhstan, 25th Anniv. — A593

2017, Sept. 16 **Litho.** ***Perf. 12***

1061 A593 (1.38r) multi 2.60 2.60

See Kazakhstan No. 825.

Christmas — A594

New Year's Day — A595

2017, Oct. 12 **Litho.** ***Perf. 13¼x13***

1062 A594 (42k) multi .70 .70

1063 A595 (1.26r) multi 2.00 2.00

a. Souvenir sheet of 4, 2 each #1062-1063 5.50 5.50

Souvenir Sheet

Diocese of Polotsk, 1025th Anniv. — A596

No. 1064: a, Annunciation Church, Vitebsk ("P" at LL). b, St. Sophia Cathedral, Polotsk ("P" at LR). c, Transfiguration Church, Polotsk ("P" atUR).

Litho. & Embossed, Sheet Margin Litho. & Embossed With Foil Application

2017, Oct. 26 ***Perf. 12***

1064 A596 (1.56r) Sheet of 3, #a-c 8.75 8.75

Mir Interstate Television and Radio Company, 25th Anniv. A597

Litho. & Embossed

2017, Oct. 31 ***Perf. 13½x13***

1065 A597 (42k) multi .80 .80

See Kazakhstan No. 830, Russia No. 7870.

Yakub Kolas (1882-1956), Poet — A598

Litho. & Embossed With Foil Application

2017, Nov. 2 ***Perf. 13½x13***

1066 A598 (1.02r) gold & multi 1.75 1.75

Russian October Revolution, Cent. — A599

2017, Nov. 3 **Litho.** ***Perf. 13***

1067 A599 (1.38r) gold & multi 2.40 2.40

Souvenir Sheet

Diplomatic Relations Between Belarus and Romania, 25th Anniv. — A600

No. 1068: a, Bread of the New Crop, by Mikhail Savitsky, 1979. b, Rest in the Field, by Corneliu Baba, 1954.

Litho., Sheet Margin Litho. With Foil Application

2017, Nov. 9 ***Perf. 12¾***

1068 A600 (1.56r) Sheet of 2, #a-b 5.50 5.50

Belarus Science Year A601

2017, Nov. 13 **Litho.** ***Perf. 14x14¼***

1069 A601 (42k) multi .75 .75

Diplomatic Relations Between Belarus and Uruguay, 25th Anniv. — A602

No. 1070: a, Bolshoi Theater of Belarusa, Minsk. b, Solís Theater, Montevideo.

Litho. & Embossed With Foil Application

2017, Nov. 15 ***Perf. 12***

1070 A602 (1.38r) Pair, #a-b 5.75 5.75

Printed in sheets containing two pairs. See Uruguay No. 2602.

Diplomatic Relations Between Belarus and Moldova, 25th Anniv. A603

Litho. With Foil Application

2017, Nov. 19 ***Perf. 12***

1071 A603 (1.38r) red & multi 2.40 2.40

Printed in sheets of 8 + central label.

Miniature Sheet

Members of Belarusian National Academy of Sciences — A604

No. 1072: a, Vsevolod M. Ignatovsky (1881-1931), historian. b, Nikolai A. Borisevich (1923-2015), physicist. c, Vasily F. Kuprevich (1897-1969), biologist. d, Pavel O. Gorin (1900-38), historian.

2017, Dec. 7 **Litho.** ***Perf. 12***

1072 A604 (42k) Sheet of 4, #a-d 3.00 3.00

Chicks — A605

Chick of: (42k), Charadrius hiaticula and eggs (inscribed "A"). (1.02r), Sterna hirundo and eggs (inscribed "N"). (1.26r), Tetrastes bonasia (inscribed "M"). (1.38r), Ardea cinerea and eggs (inscribed "H").

2018, Jan. 3 **Litho.** ***Perf. 14x14¼***

1073 A605 (42k) multi .75 .75

1074 A605 (1.02r) multi 1.90 1.90

1075 A605 (1.26r) multi 2.25 2.25

1076 A605 (1.38r) multi 2.50 2.50

a. Souvenir sheet of 8, 2 each #1073-1076 15.00 15.00

Nos. 1073-1076 (4) 7.40 7.40

Border Guard Service, Cent. — A606

Litho. With Foil Application

2018, Jan. 10 ***Perf. 13x13½***

1077 A606 (42k) gold & multi .70 .70

2018 Winter Olympics, PyeongChang, South Korea — A607

2018, Feb. 9 **Litho.** ***Perf. 13½***

1078 A607 (1.68r) multi 3.00 3.00

Internal Troops of the Ministry of Internal Affairs, Cent. — A608

Litho. With Foil Application

2018, Feb. 14 ***Perf. 12***

1079 A608 (1.50r) gold & multi 2.60 2.60

Souvenir Sheet

Icons — A609

No. 1080 — Painting of: a, St. Hilda of Whitby. b, St. Martin of Tours. c, St. Guthlac of Crowland.

Litho., Sheet Margin Litho. With Foil Application

2018, Feb. 18 ***Perf. 13½x13***

1080 A609 (1.68r) Sheet of 3, #a-c 8.50 8.50

Armed Forces of Belarus, Cent. — A610

Litho. With Foil Application

2018, Feb. 19 ***Perf. 13x13½***

1081 A610 (1.50r) gold & multi 2.50 2.50

Souvenir Sheet

Piotr Masherov (1918-80), First Secretary of the Central Committee of the Communist Party of Belarus — A611

Litho. With Foil Application

2018, Feb. 26 ***Perf. 13½x13***

1082 A611 5r gold, sil & multi 7.75 7.75

Fauna of Polesye State Radiation-Ecological Reserve — A612

Fauna of Berezinsky Biosphere Reserve — A613

2018, Mar. 1 Litho. ***Perf. 13x12¾***

1083 A612 (42k) multi .75 .75
1084 A613 (1.50r) multi 2.50 2.50
a. Souvenir sheet of 2, #1083-1084 3.25 3.25

Carduelis Carduelis A614

2018, Mar. 27 Litho. ***Perf. 13½x13***

1085 A614 (1.50r) multi 2.50 2.50

Souvenir Sheet

Belarussian Telegraph Agency, Cent. — A615

Litho. With Foil Application

2018, Apr. 19 ***Perf. 12***

1086 A615 5r sil & multi 8.50 8.50

Disna River Bridge — A616

Island of Courage and Sorrow Bridge, Minsk — A617

2018, Apr. 30 Litho. ***Perf. 13x13½***

1087 A616 (1.50r) multi 2.50 2.50
1088 A617 (1.68r) multi 2.75 2.75
a. Sheet of 2, #1087-1088, + 2 labels 5.25 5.25

Europa.

Early Spring, by Alexey Savrasov (1830-97) A618

Swamp and Cranes, by Ivan Shishkin (1832-98) — A619

Marine Painting, by Ivan Aivazovsky (1817-1900) — A620

Birch Grove, by Arkhip Kuindzhi (c.1842-1910) A621

Perf. 13½x13, 13x13½

2018, May 2 Litho.

1089 A618 (42k) sil & multi .75 .75
1090 A619 (42k) sil & multi .75 .75
1091 A620 (1.50r) sil & multi 2.50 2.50
1092 A621 (1.50r) sil & multi 2.50 2.50
a. Souvenir sheet of 4, #1089-1092 6.50 6.50
b. As "a," litho. with foil application sheet margin 6.50 6.50
Nos. 1089-1092 (4) 6.50 6.50

2017 Telecommunications, Infromation and Bank Technologies Forum (TIBO), Minsk — A622

2018, May 15 Litho. ***Perf. 13x12¾***

1093 A622 (1.50r) multi 2.60 2.60

Hanna Huskova, Freestyle Skiing Gold Medalist — A623

Belarussian Gold Medalist Biathlon Relay Team — A624

Darya Domracheva, Biathlon Silver Medalist — A625

2018, June 20 Litho. ***Perf. 12***

1094 A623 (1.50r) multi 2.60 2.60
1095 A624 (1.50r) multi 2.60 2.60
1096 A625 (1.50r) multi 2.60 2.60
a. Souvenir sheet of 6, 2 each #1094-1096 16.00 16.00
Nos. 1094-1096 (3) 7.80 7.80

Belarussian medalists at 2018 Winter Olympics.

Souvenir Sheet

List of Medalists at 2018 Winter Paralympics — A626

2018, June 20 Litho. ***Perf. 13x13½***

1097 A626 3r multi 5.25 5.25

Coat of Arms and Tourist Attractions of Vitebsk — A627

2018, June 23 Litho. ***Perf. 13x12¾***

1098 A627 (1.38r) multi 2.40 2.40

Vice-Admiral Georgi N. Kholostyakov (1902-83) — A628

Vice-Admiral Yegor A. Tomko (1935-2008) — A629

Vice-Admiral Valentin P. Drozd (1906-43) — A630

Rear Admiral Vladimir N. Dronov A631

2018, July 7 Litho. ***Perf. 12***

1099 A628 (1.38r) multi 2.40 2.40
1100 A629 (1.38r) multi 2.40 2.40
1101 A630 (1.38r) multi 2.40 2.40
1102 A631 (1.38r) multi 2.40 2.40
a. Souvenir sheet of 4, #1099-1102 9.75 9.75
Nos. 1099-1102 (4) 9.60 9.60

2018 Women's Basketball World Cup, Minsk A632

2018, July 19 Litho. ***Perf. 13½x13***

1103 A632 (1.50r) multi 2.50 2.50

Emblem of Ministry of Emergency Situations and Helmet of Belarussian Firefighters A633

2018, July 20 Litho. ***Perf. 12***

1104 A633 (42k) multi .70 .70

Publishing of First Primer, 400th Anniv. A634

Litho. With Foil Application

2018, July 24 ***Perf. 13½x13***

1105 A634 (1.50r) gold & multi 2.50 2.50

Zootoca Vivipara A635

Lacerta Agilis A636

Anguis Fragilis A637

2018, Aug. 13 Litho. *Perf. 13½x13*

1106	A635	(42k) multi	.70	.70
1107	A636	(1.38r) multi	2.25	2.25
1108	A637	(1.50r) multi	2.50	2.50
a.		Souvenir sheet of 3, #1106-1108	5.50	5.50
		Nos. 1106-1108 (3)	5.45	5.45

Nos. 1106-1108 were each printed in sheets of 5 + label.

Arms of Ivanava — A638

2018, Aug. 23 Litho. *Perf. 14¼x14*

1109 A638 (1.14r) multi 1.90 1.90

31st Planetary Congress of the Association of Space Explorers, Minsk — A639

2018, Sept. 13 Litho. *Perf. 13*

1110 A639 (1.50r) multi 2.50 2.50

Arms and Buildings of Hrodna — A640

2018, Sept. 14 Litho. *Perf. 13¼x13*

1111 A640 (1.38r) multi 2.25 2.25

Souvenir Sheet

Paintings of Flowers — A641

2018, Oct. 10 Litho. *Perf. 12¾*

1112	A641	Sheet of 2	5.50	5.50
a.-b.		(1.74r) Either single	2.75	2.75

Diplomatic Relations between Belarus and Armenia, 25th anniv.

No. 1112: a, Winter Roses, by Leonid Shchemeliov, 1973. b, Still Life in a Dark Room, by Pharaon Mirzoyan, 2013.

Inextinguishable Lamp From Crypt of the Memorial Church of All Saints, Minsk — A642

2018, Oct. 14 Litho. *Perf. 13¼x13*

1113 A642 (1.56r) multi 2.50 2.50

Consecration of Memorial Church of All Saints. No. 1113 was printed in sheets of 5 + label.

New Year's Wreath A643

Angel and Wreath A644

Litho. With Foil Application

2018, Oct. 15 *Perf. 13*

1114	A643	(42k) multi	.70	.70
1115	A644	(1.20r) multi	2.00	2.00
a.		Souvenir sheet of 4, 2 each #1114-1115	5.25	5.25

Christmas and New Year's Day.

Diplomatic Relations Between Belarus and Kyrgyzstan, 25th Anniv. A645

Litho. With Foil Application

2018, Oct. 18 *Perf. 12*

1116 A645 (1.56r) multi 2.50 2.50

See Kyrgyz Express Post No. 93.

Portrait of a Student, by V. S. Pratasenia A646

2018, Oct. 25 Litho. *Perf. 13*

1117 A646 (42k) multi .70 .70

All-Union Leninist Young Communist League (Komsomol), cent.

Souvenir Sheet

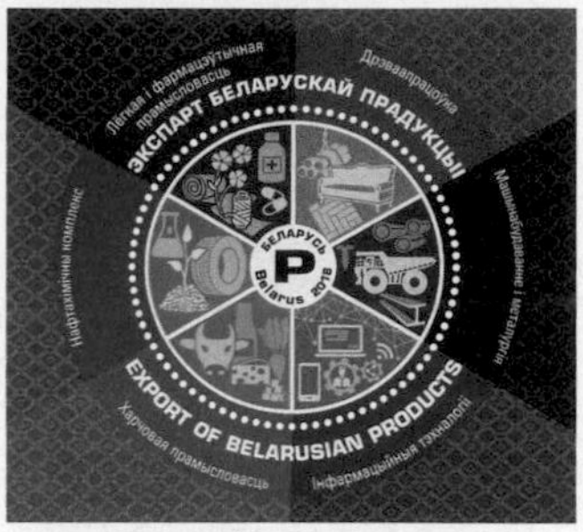

Exportable Products of Belarus — A647

2018, Nov. 2 Litho. *Perf.*

1118 A647 (1.74r) multi 3.00 3.00

Chess Pieces From 11th-14th Centuries A648

No. 1119: a, Two pieces. b, Three pieces.

2018, Nov. 12 Litho. *Perf. 13*

1119	A648	Pair	3.25	3.25
a.		(42k) multi	.70	.70
b.		(1.56r) multi	2.50	2.50

Diplomatic Relations Between Belarus and Azerbaijan, 25th Anniv. A649

Litho. With Foil Application

2018, Nov. 19 *Perf. 12*

1120 A649 (1.56r) multi 2.50 2.50

See Azerbaijan No. 1200.

Diplomatic Relations Between Belarus and Uzbekistan, 25th Anniv. A650

Litho. With Foil Application

2018, Nov. 23 *Perf. 12*

1121 A650 (1.56r) multi 2.50 2.50

See Uzbekistan No. 863.

Finance Ministry of Belarus, Cent. A651

Litho. With Foil Application

2018, Dec. 5 *Perf. 13*

1122 A651 (1.56r) gold multi 2.50 2.50

Byelorussian Soviet Socialist Republic, Cent. — A652

2019, Jan. 2 Litho. *Perf. 13x13½*

1123 A652 (48k) multi .80 .80

Souvenir Sheet

Emblem of Ministry of Emergency Situations — A653

Litho. With Foil Application

2019, Jan. 18 *Perf.*

1124 A653 (1.74r) gold & multi 3.00 3.00

Souvenir Sheet

Belarussian Diplomatic Service, Cent. — A654

Litho. With Foil Application

2019, Jan. 22 *Perf. 13*

1125 A654 (1.74r) sil & multi 3.00 3.00

Cyclist A655

Runner A656

Kayaker A657

Rhythmic Gymnast
A658

2019, Feb. 1 Litho. *Perf. 12*

1126	A655 (48k) multi		.75	.75
1127	A656 (1.20r) multi		2.00	2.00
1128	A657 (1.44r) multi		2.25	2.25
1129	A658 (1.56r) multi		2.50	2.50
a.	Souvenir sheet of 4, #1126-1129		7.50	7.50
	Nos. 1126-1129 (4)		7.50	7.50

2nd European Games, Minsk.

Justice Authorities of Belarus, Cent. — A659

Litho. With Foil Application

2019, Feb. 6 *Perf. 12*

1130	A659 (1.56r) sil & multi	2.60	2.60

No. 1130 was printed in sheets of 6 + label.

Clanga Clanga — A660

2019, Mar. 12 Litho. *Perf. 13x13½*

1131	A660 (1.80r) multi	3.00	3.00

International Year of Indigenous Languages
A661

2019, Mar. 27 Litho. *Perf. 13½x13*

1132	A661 (1.50r) multi	2.40	2.40

Souvenir Sheet

Liberation of Belarus From Nazi Rule, 75th Anniv. — A662

No. 1133: a, Tank carrying partisan soldiers. b, Inhabitants of Minsk greeting tank carrying Soviet soldiers.

Litho., Sheet Margin Litho With Foil Application

2019, Apr. 9 *Perf. 12*

1133	A662 Sheet of 2	5.75	5.75
a.	(1.62r) multi	2.75	2.75
b.	(1.80r) multi	3.00	3.00

Dytiscus Marginalis
A663

Gasterosteus Aculeatus
A664

Astacus Leptodactylus
A665

Viviparus Contectus
A666

2019, Apr. 17 Litho. *Perf. 13½x13*

1134	A663 (48k) multi	.75	.75
1135	A664 (1.26r) multi	2.00	2.00
1136	A665 (1.50r) multi	2.40	2.40
1137	A666 (1.82r) multi	3.00	3.00
a.	Souvenir sheet of 4, #1134-1137	8.25	8.25
	Nos. 1134-1137 (4)	8.15	8.15

Stanislaw Moniuszko (1819-72), Composer — A667

2019, May 4 Litho. *Perf. 13x13½*

1138	A667 (1.50r) multi	2.50	2.50

Ciconia Ciconia and Nest — A668

Ciconia Ciconia — A669

2019, May 9 Litho. *Perf. 12*

1139	A668 (1.62r) multi	2.75	2.75
1140	A669 (1.80r) multi	3.00	3.00
a.	Souvenir sheet of 4, 2 each #1139-1140	11.50	11.50

Europa.

N. N. Alexandrov National Cancer Center of Belarus, 60th Anniv.
A670

Litho. With Foil Application

2019, June 7 *Perf. 12*

1141	A670 (1.62r) multi	3.00	3.00

No. 1141 was printed in sheets of 4 + central label.

Xanthoria Parietina and Fly — A671

Lobaria Pulmonaria and Beetle — A672

Cladonia Floerkeana and Ant — A673

2019, June 27 Litho. *Perf. 13x13½*

1142	A671 (48k) multi	.80	.80
1143	A672 (1.56r) multi	2.60	2.60
1144	A673 (1.68r) multi	3.00	3.00
a.	Souvenir sheet of 6, 2 each #1142-1144	13.00	13.00
	Nos. 1142-1144 (3)	6.40	6.40

Operation Bagration (Belarussian Strategic Offensive Operation), 75th Anniv. — A674

Litho. & Embossed With Foil Application

2019, July 3 *Perf. 13x13½*

1145	A674 (1.68r) gold & multi	3.00	3.00

No. 1145 was printed in sheets of 7 + label. See Russia No. 8036.

Coat of Arms and Tourist Attractions of Slonim — A675

2019, July 10 Litho. *Perf. 13*

1146	A675 (1.56r) multi	2.60	2.60

State Control Committee of Belarus, Cent. — A676

2019, July 29 Litho. *Perf. 13x13½*

1147	A676 (1.68r) multi	3.00	3.00

Eurasian Economic Union, 5th Anniv. — A677

Litho. With Foil Application

2019, Aug. 9 *Perf. 13*

1148	A677 (1.68r) gold & multi	3.00	3.00

No. 1148 was printed in sheets of 5 + label.

Lute
A678

Duda
A679

2019, Aug. 29 Litho. *Perf. 12*

1149	A678 (1.32r) multi	2.25	2.25
1150	A679 (1.56r) multi	2.60	2.60
a.	Souvenir sheet of 4, 2 each #1149-1150	9.75	9.75

Souvenir Sheet

First Written Mention of Brest, 1000th Anniv. — A680

2019, Sept. 4 Litho. *Perf. 13x13½*

1151	A680 (1.86r) multi	3.25	3.25

Coat of Arms and Tourist Attractions of Navahrudak — A681

2019, Sept. 24 Litho. *Perf. 13*

1152	A681 (1.56r) multi	2.75	2.75

Signal Corps of Belarus, Cent. — A682

2019, Oct. 15 Litho. *Perf. 13x13½*

1153	A682 (54k) multi	.95	.95

Kalyady
A683

Christmas
A684

New Year's Day — A685

Litho. With Foil Application

2019, Oct. 30 *Perf. 12*

1154	A683 (54k) sil & multi	.95	.95
1155	A684 (1.56r) sil & multi	2.75	2.75
1156	A685 (1.68r) sil & multi	3.00	3.00
a.	Souvenir sheet of 6, 2 each #1154-1156	13.50	13.50
	Nos. 1154-1156 (3)	6.70	6.70

Diplomatic Relations Between Belarus and Georgia, 25th Anniv. A686

2019, Nov. 1 **Litho.** ***Perf. 12***
1157 A686 (1.68r) multi 3.00 3.00

Belarus Banknotes of 1992-96 A687

Belarus Banknotes of 2000 A688

Belarus Banknotes of 2016 and Coins A689

Litho. With Foil Application

2019, Nov. 4 ***Perf. 12***
1158 A687 (54k) gold & multi .95 .95
1159 A688 (1.32r) gold & multi 2.25 2.25
1160 A689 (1.86r) gold & multi 3.25 3.25
a. Souvenir sheet of 6, 2 each #1158-1160 13.00 13.00
Nos. 1158-1160 (3) 6.45 6.45

Souvenir Sheet

Spring Brook, by Vitold Byalnitsky-Birulya (1872-1957) — A690

Litho. With Foil Application

2019, Nov. 4 ***Perf. 12***
1161 A690 5r sil & multi 8.75 8.75

Diplomatic Relations Between Belarus and Pakistan, 25th Anniv. A691

2019, Nov. 26 **Litho.** ***Perf. 14x14¼***
1162 A691 (1.68r) multi 2.40 2.40

Melikmamed (Azerbaijan Folk Tale) — A692

The Golden Bird (Belarussian Folk Tale) — A693

Litho. With Foil Application

2019, Dec. 3 ***Perf. 12***
1163 A692 (1.32r) gold & multi 1.60 1.60
1164 A693 (1.86r) gold & multi 2.40 2.40
a. Souvenir sheet of 4, 2 each #1163-1164 8.00 8.00

Joint Issue between Belarus and Azerbaijan. See Azerbaijan Nos. 1247-1248.

Souvenir Sheet

Treaty on the Creation of a Union State of Russia and Belarus, 20th Anniv. — A694

No. 1165 — Coat of arms of: a, Belarus. b, Russia.

Litho., Sheet Margin Litho. With Foil Application

2019, Dec. 6 ***Perf.***
1165 A694 (1.86r) Sheet of 2, #a-b 4.75 4.75

Fox Cub — A695

Wolf Cub — A696

Bear Cub — A697

Lynx Kitten — A698

2020, Jan. 9 **Litho.** ***Perf. 12***
1166 A695 (54k) multi .60 .60
1167 A696 (1.32r) multi 1.50 1.50
1168 A697 (1.56r) multi 1.75 1.75
1169 A698 (1.68r) multi 1.90 1.90
a. Souvenir sheet of 8, 2 each #1166-1169 11.50 11.50
Nos. 1166-1169 (4) 5.75 5.75

New Year 2020 (Year of the Rat) — A699

Litho. & Embossed With Foil Application

2020, Jan. 17 ***Perf. 12¼x12***
1170 A699 (1.86r) multi 3.50 3.50

Andrey Makayonak (1920-82), Playwright — A700

2020, Feb. 6 **Litho.** ***Perf. 13x13½***
1171 A700 (1.32r) multi 2.50 2.50

Tetrao Urogallus — A701

2020, Mar. 3 **Litho.** ***Perf. 13x13½***
1172 A701 (1.86r) multi 3.25 3.25

Acyria Globosa A702

Cribraria Purpurea A703

Physarum Album — A704

2020, Apr. 6 **Litho.** ***Perf. 13x13¼***
1173 A702 (54k) multi 1.00 1.00
1174 A703 (1.32r) multi 1.40 1.40
1175 A704 (1.68r) multi 1.75 1.75
a. Souvenir sheet of 6, 2 each #1173-1175 8.50 8.50
Nos. 1173-1175 (3) 4.15 4.15

Souvenir Sheet

End of World War II, 75th Anniv. — A705

2020, Apr. 30 **Litho.** ***Perf. 13***
1176 A705 (1.86r) multi 2.25 2.25

Post Rider and Map of Vilnius-Smolensk Mail Route — A706

Postal Messenger and Map of Cracow-Vilnius Mail Route — A707

2020, May 5 **Litho.** ***Perf. 13x13½***
1177 A706 (1.68r) multi 2.00 2.00

Perf. 13½x13
1178 A707 (1.86r) multi 2.25 2.25
a. Souvenir sheet of 4, 2 each # 1177-1178 8.50 8.50

Souvenir Sheet

End of World War II, 75th Anniv. — A708

Litho., Sheet Margin Litho. With Foil Application

2020, May 8 ***Perf. 13½x13***
1179 A708 (1.86r) multi 2.25 2.25

See Russia No. 8152.

Souvenir Sheet

Appearance of the Zhirovichi Mother of God Icon, 550th Anniv. — A709

Litho. with Foil Application

2020, May 20 ***Perf.***
1180 A709 5r gold & multi 5.25 5.25
a. Imperf. 5.25 5.25

BELGIAN CONGO

'bel-jən 'käŋ-gō

LOCATION — Central Africa
GOVT. — Belgian colony
AREA — 902,082 sq. mi. (estimated)
POP. — 12,660,000 (1956)
CAPITAL — Léopoldville

Congo was an independent state, founded by Leopold II of Belgium, until 1908 when it was annexed to Belgium as a colony. In 1960 it became the independent Republic of the Congo. See Congo Democratic Republic and Zaire.

100 Centimes = 1 Franc

Catalogue values for unused stamps in this country are for Never Hinged items, beginning with Scott 187 in the regular postage section, Scott B32 in the semi-postal section, Scott C17 in the airpost section, and Scott J8 in the postage due section.

Independent State

A1

A2

King Leopold II — A3

1886 Unwmk. Typo. *Perf. 15*

1	A1	5c green	15.00	*26.00*
2	A1	10c rose	5.50	*6.00*
3	A2	25c blue	60.00	47.50
4	A3	50c olive green	9.00	9.00
5	A1	5fr lilac	450.00	350.00
a.		Perf. 14	1,100.	650.00
b.		5fr deep lilac	850.00	525.00
		Nos. 1-5 (5)	539.50	438.50
		Set, never hinged	1,100.	

Counterfeits exist.
For surcharge see No. Q1.

King Leopold II — A4

1887-94

6	A4	5c grn ('89)	1.00	*1.00*
7	A4	10c rose ('89)	1.75	1.75
8	A4	25c blue ('89)	1.75	1.75
9	A4	50c reddish brn	67.50	32.50
10	A4	50c gray ('94)	4.00	*2.50*
11	A4	5fr violet	1,350.	550.00
12	A4	5fr gray ('92)	165.00	130.00
		On portion of parcel wrapper		*1,250.*
13	A4	10fr buff ('91)	625.00	400.00
		Nos. 6-13 (8)	2,216.	1,120.
		Set, never hinged	3,500.	

The 25fr amd 50fr in gray were not issued. Values, each $35.

Counterfeits exist of Nos. 10-13, 25fr and 50fr unused, used, genuine stamps with faked cancels and counterfeit stamps with genuine cancels.

For surcharges, see Nos. Q3-Q6.

Port Matadi — A5

River Scene on the Congo, Stanley Falls — A6

Inkissi Falls — A7

Railroad Bridge on M'pozo River — A8

Hunting Elephants A9

Bangala Chief and Wife — A10

1894-1901 Engr. *Perf. 12½ to 15*

14	A5	5c pale bl & blk	19.00	19.00
15	A5	5c red brn & blk ('95)	4.00	1.75
16	A5	5c grn & blk ('00)	2.00	.70
17	A6	10c red brn & blk	19.00	19.00
18	A6	10c grnsh bl & blk ('95)	4.50	2.00
a.		Center inverted	*3,000.*	*3,000.*
19	A6	10c car & blk ('00)	4.50	1.00
20	A7	25c yel org & blk	5.25	3.25
21	A7	25c lt bl & blk ('00)	5.50	2.00
22	A8	50c grn & blk	2.00	2.00
23	A8	50c ol & blk ('00)	5.50	1.25
24	A9	1fr lilac & blk	30.00	16.00
a.		1fr rose lilac & black	500.00	37.50
25	A9	1fr car & blk ('01)	425.00	9.50
26	A10	5fr lake & blk	57.50	40.00
a.		5fr carmine rose & black	130.00	62.50
		Nos. 14-26 (13)	583.75	117.45
		Set, never hinged	1,100.	

For overprintes see Nos. 31-32, 34, 36-37, 39.

Climbing Oil Palms — A11

Congo Canoe A12

1896

27	A11	15c ocher & blk	5.25	1.00
28	A12	40c bluish grn & blk	5.25	4.00
		Set, never hinged	18.50	

For overprints see Nos. 33, 35.

Congo Village A13

River Steamer on the Congo A14

1898

29	A13	3.50fr red & blk	200.00	145.00
a.		Perf. 14x12	575.00	350.00
30	A14	10fr yel grn & blk	160.00	50.00
a.		Center inverted	*25,000.*	
b.		Perf. 12	800.00	52.50
c.		Perf. 12x14	500.00	—
		As "c," pen canceled		21.00
		Set, never hinged	550.00	

Nos. 29-30 exist imperf. Value, set $850.
For overprints see Nos. 38, 40.

Belgian Congo

Overprinted

1908

31	A5	5c green & blk	8.75	8.00
a.		Handstamped	5.50	3.00
32	A6	10c car & blk	16.00	14.00
a.		Handstamped	5.50	3.00
33	A11	15c ocher & blk	9.25	8.00
a.		Handstamped	8.50	5.00
34	A7	25c lt blue & blk	5.75	3.00
a.		Handstamped	15.00	5.00
c.		Double overprint (#34)	300.00	
35	A12	40c bluish grn & blk	3.25	3.00
a.		Handstamped	16.00	8.75
36	A8	50c olive & blk	6.25	3.00
a.		Handstamped	8.00	5.50
b.		As #36, inverted overprint	775.00	
37	A9	1fr car & blk	27.50	8.50
a.		Handstamped	75.00	17.50
38	A13	3.50fr red & blk	42.50	30.00
a.		Handstamped	450.00	200.00
b.		As #38, inverted overprint	750.00	—
c.		As #38, double overprint	—	—
39	A10	5fr car & blk	75.00	37.50
a.		Handstamped	150.00	77.50
40	A14	10fr yel grn & blk	140.00	35.00
a.		Perf. 14½	375.00	—
b.		Handstamped	275.00	90.00
c.		Handstamped, perf. 14½	575.00	325.00
		Nos. 31-40 (10)	334.25	150.00
		Set, never hinged	800.00	

Most of the above handstamps are also found inverted and double.

There are two types of handstamped overprints, those applied in Brussels and those applied locally. There are eight types of each overprint. Values listed are the lowest for each stamp.

Counterfeits of the handstamped overprints exist.

Imperf examples of No. 37 are proofs.

Port Matadi A15

River Scene on the Congo, Stanley Falls — A16

Climbing Oil Palms — A17

Railroad Bridge on M'pozo River — A18

1909 *Perf. 14*

41	A15	5c green & blk	.75	.75
42	A16	10c carmine & blk	.75	.50
43	A17	15c ocher & blk	37.50	20.00
44	A18	50c olive & blk	3.50	2.25
		Nos. 41-44 (4)	42.50	23.50
		Set, never hinged	200.00	

Port Matadi A19

River Scene on the Congo, Stanley Falls — A20

Climbing Oil Palms — A21

Inkissi Falls — A22

Congo Canoe A23

Railroad Bridge on M'pozo River — A24

Hunting Elephants A25

Congo Village A26

Bangala Chief and Wife — A27

River Steamer on the Congo A28

1910-15 Engr. *Perf. 14, 15*

45	A19	5c green & blk	.60	.25
46	A20	10c carmine & blk	.60	.25
47	A21	15c ocher & blk	.60	.25

48	A21	15c grn & blk ('15)	.50	.25
a.		Booklet pane of 10	25.00	
49	A22	25c blue & blk	1.75	.50
50	A23	40c bluish grn & blk	2.50	2.25
51	A23	40c brn red & blk ('15)	5.50	2.50
52	A24	50c olive & blk	4.00	2.25
53	A24	50c brn lake & blk ('15)	11.00	2.50
54	A25	1fr carmine & blk	4.00	3.25
55	A25	1fr ol bis & blk ('15)	3.00	1.00
56	A26	3fr red & blk	23.00	14.00
57	A27	5fr carmine & blk	35.00	32.50
58	A27	5fr ocher & blk ('15)	2.00	1.00
59	A28	10fr green & blk	29.00	26.00
		Nos. 45-59 (15)	123.05	88.75
		Set, never hinged	400.00	

Nos. 48, 51, 53, 55 and 58 exist imperforate. Value, set $150.

For overprints and surcharges see Nos. 64-76, 81-86, B5-B9.

Port Matadi A29

Stanley Falls, Congo River — A30

Inkissi Falls — A31

TEN CENTIMES.

Type I — Large white space at top of picture and two small white spots at lower edge. Vignette does not fill frame.

Type II — Vignette completely fills frame.

1915

60	A29	5c green & blk	.25	.25
a.		Booklet pane of 10	19.00	
61	A30	10c car & blk (II)	.25	.25
a.		10c carmine & black (I)	.45	.45
d.		Booklet pane of 10 (II)	25.00	
62	A31	25c blue & blk	1.50	.40
a.		Booklet pane of 10	125.00	
		Nos. 60-62 (3)	2.00	.90
		Set, never hinged	6.50	

Nos. 60-62 exist imperforate. Value, set $15.

For surcharges see Nos. 77-80, 87, B1-B4.

For stamps of Belgian Congo overprinted "RUANDA", "URUNDI" or "EST AFRICAIN ALLEMAND OCCUPATION BELGE", see German East Africa.

Stamps of 1910 Issue Surcharged in Red or Black

1921

64	A23	5c on 40c bluish grn & blk (R)	.30	.30
65	A19	10c on 5c grn & blk (R)	.30	.30
66	A24	15c on 50c ol & blk (R)	.30	.30
a.		Inverted surcharge		275.00
67	A21	25c on 15c ocher & blk (R)	2.25	1.25
68	A20	30c on 10c car & blk	.60	.60
69	A22	50c on 25c bl & blk (R)	2.75	1.25
		Nos. 64-69 (6)	6.50	4.00
		Set, never hinged	12.00	

The position of the new value and the bars varies on Nos. 64 to 69.

No. 54 Overprinted

1921

70	A25	1fr carmine & blk	1.25	1.25
a.		Double overprint	125.00	
71	A26	3fr red & blk	4.00	3.50
72	A27	5fr carmine & blk	12.00	11.00
73	A28	10fr green & blk (R)	8.00	5.50
		Nos. 70-73 (4)	25.25	21.25
		Set, never hinged	70.00	

Belgian Surcharges

Nos. 51, 53, 60-62 Surcharged in Black or Red

1922

74	A24	5c on 50c	.50	.50
a.		Inverted surcharge	120.00	120.00
75	A29	10c on 5c (R)	.50	.50
76	A23	25c on 40c (R)	3.00	.50
77	A30	30c on 10c (II)	.30	.30
a.		30c on 10c (I)	.50	.25
b.		Double surcharge	7.50	7.50
c.		Inverted surcharge	190.00	190.00
78	A31	50c on 25c (R)	1.00	.35
a.		Inverted surcharge	190.00	190.00
		Nos. 74-78 (5)	5.30	2.15
		Set, never hinged	15.00	

No. 74 has the surcharge at each side.

Congo Surcharges

Nos. 60, 51 Surcharged in Red or Black

a

b

1922

80	A29	10c on 5c (R)	.50	.50
		Never hinged	1.75	
a.		Inverted surcharge	47.50	37.50
b.		Double surcharge	6.00	
c.		Double surch., one invtd.	50.00	
d.		Pair, one without surcharge	52.50	
e.		On No. 45	325.00	325.00
81	A23	25c on 40c	1.00	.50
		Never hinged	3.50	
a.		Inverted surcharge	47.50	37.50
b.		Double surcharge	6.75	
c.		"25c" double		
d.		25c on 5c, No. 60	225.00	225.00

Nos. 55, 58 Surcharged in Red

1922

84	A25	10c on 1fr (R)	.50	.50
		Never hinged	2.00	
a.		Double surcharge	17.50	
b.		Inverted surcharge	47.50	37.50
85	A27	25c on 5fr	2.00	2.00
		Never hinged	6.50	

Nos. 68, 77 Handstamped

86	A20	25c on 30c on 10c	25.00	22.50
		Never hinged	45.00	
87	A30	25c on 30c on 10c (II)	22.50	22.50
		Never hinged	42.50	

Nos. 86-87 exist with handstamp surcharge inverted.

Counterfeit handstamped surcharges exist.

Headdress — A32

Ubangi Man — A33

Watusi Cattle — A34

Basket Making — A35

Designs: No. 88, Ubangi woman. No. 89, Baluba woman. No. 90, Babuende woman. Nos. 91, 97, 106-108, Ubangi man. Nos. 92, 100-101, Weaving on loom. No. 93, Basket making. Nos. 94-96, 102, Wood carving. Nos. 98-99, Archer. Nos. 103-105, Making pottery. No. 109, Working rubber. No. 110, Making palm oil. No. 111, African elephant. Nos. 112-113, Watussi cattle.

1923-27 Engr. *Perf. 12*

88	A32	5c yellow	.25	.25
89	A33	10c green	.25	.25
90	A33	15c olive brown	.25	.25
91	A33	20c olive grn ('24)	.25	.25
92	A34	20c green ('26)	.25	.25
93	A35	25c red brown	.25	.25
94	A34	30c rose red ('24)	.65	.65
95	A34	30c olive grn ('25)	.25	.25
96	A34	35c green ('27)	.50	.45
97	A33	40c violet ('25)	.50	.25
98	A35	50c gray blue	.25	.25
99	A35	50c buff ('25)	.50	.25
100	A34	75c red orange	.25	.25
101	A34	75c gray bl ('25)	.50	.35
102	A34	75c salmon red ('26)	.25	.25
103	A35	1fr bister brown	.75	.35
104	A35	1fr dl blue ('25)	.50	.25
105	A35	1fr rose red ('27)	1.50	.25
106	A33	1.25fr dl blue ('26)	.75	.50
107	A33	1.50fr dl blue ('26)	.75	.50
108	A33	1.75fr dl blue ('27)	7.50	6.00
109	A35	3fr gray brn ('24)	6.25	3.00
110	A35	5fr gray ('24)	17.50	8.00
111	A35	10fr gray blk ('24)	27.50	20.00

1925-26

112	A34	45c dk vio ('26)	.50	.30
113	A34	60c carmine rose	.50	.25
		Nos. 88-113 (26)	69.15	43.85
		Set, never hinged	250.00	

For surcharges see Nos. 114, 136-138, 157.

No. 107 Surcharged

1927, June 14

114	A32	1.75fr on 1.50fr dl bl	.75	.75
		Never hinged	1.50	

Sir Henry Morton Stanley — A45

1928, June 30 *Perf. 14*

115	A45	5c gray blk	.25	.25
116	A45	10c dp violet	.25	.25
117	A45	20c orange red	.30	.25
118	A45	35c green	1.00	.75
119	A45	40c red brown	.35	.25
120	A45	60c black brn	.50	.25
121	A45	1fr carmine	.45	.25
122	A45	1.60fr dk gray	11.00	9.00
123	A45	1.75fr dp blue	2.00	.75
124	A45	2fr dk brown	1.25	.75
125	A45	2.75fr red violet	11.00	.25
126	A45	3.50fr rose lake	1.40	1.00
127	A45	5fr slate grn	1.25	1.00
128	A45	10fr violet blue	2.25	1.00
129	A45	20fr claret	11.00	7.50
		Nos. 115-129 (15)	44.25	23.50
		Set, never hinged	135.00	

Sir Henry M. Stanley (1841-1904), explorer.

Nos. 115-129 exist in two sizes: 36mm and 37mm high.

Nos. 118, 121-123, 125-126 Surcharged in Red, Blue or Black

1931, Jan. 15

130	A45	40c on 35c	1.25	.60
131	A45	1.25fr on 1fr (Bl)	.75	.25
132	A45	2fr on 1.60fr	1.25	.40
133	A45	2fr on 1.75fr	1.25	.40
134	A45	3.25fr on 2.75fr (Bk)	4.00	3.00
135	A45	3.25fr on 3.50fr (Bk)	8.75	7.50

Nos. 96, 108, 112 Surcharged in Red

Perf. 12½, 12

136	A44	40c on 35c grn	6.50	6.50
137	A44	50c on 45c dk vio	3.75	3.75

No. 108 Surcharged

138	A32	2(fr) on 1.75fr dl bl	20.00	20.00
		Nos. 130-138 (9)	47.50	42.40
		Set, never hinged	140.00	

View of Sankuru River — A46

Flute Players — A50

Designs: 15c, Kivu Kraal. 20c, Sankuru River rapids. 25c, Uele hut. 50c, Musicians of Lake Leopold II. 60c, Batetelas drummers. 75c, Mangbetu woman. 1fr, Domesticated elephant of Api. 1.25fr, Mangbetu chief. 1.50fr, 2fr, Village of Mondimbi. 2.50fr, 3.25fr, Okapi. 4fr, Canoes at Stanleyville. 5fr, Woman preparing cassava. 10fr, Baluba chief. 20fr, Young woman of Irumu.

1931-37 Engr. *Perf. 11½*

139	A46	10c gray brn ('32)	.25	.25
140	A46	15c gray ('32)	.25	.25
141	A46	20c brn lil ('32)	.25	.25
142	A46	25c dp blue ('32)	.25	.25
143	A50	40c dp grn ('32)	.25	.25
144	A46	50c violet ('32)	.25	.25
b.		Booklet pane of 8	7.00	
145	A50	60c vio brn ('32)	.25	.25
146	A50	75c rose ('32)	.25	.25
b.		Booklet pane of 8	5.50	
147	A50	1fr rose red ('32)	.25	.25
148	A50	1.25fr red brown	.25	.25
b.		Booklet pane of 8	5.50	
149	A46	1.50fr dk ol gray ('37)	.25	.25
b.		Booklet pane of 8	9.00	
150	A46	2fr ultra ('32)	.25	.25
151	A46	2.50fr dp blue ('37)	.50	.40
b.		Booklet pane of 8	15.00	
152	A46	3.25fr gray blk ('32)	.65	.65
153	A46	4fr dl vio ('32)	.40	.40
154	A50	5fr dp vio ('32)	1.00	1.00
155	A50	10fr red ('32)	1.40	1.40
156	A50	20fr blk brn ('32)	3.00	3.00
		Nos. 139-156 (18)	9.95	9.85
		Set, never hinged	24.00	

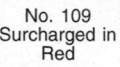

No. 109 Surcharged in Red

1932, Mar. 15 *Perf. 12*

157	A44	3.25fr on 3fr gray brn	9.00	9.00
		Never hinged	30.00	

King Albert Memorial Issue

King Albert — A62

1934, May 7 Photo. *Perf. 11½*

158	A62	1.50fr black	1.00	.75
		Never hinged	2.50	

No. 158 exists imperf. Value, $67.50.

Leopold I, Leopold II, Albert I, Leopold III A63

1935, Aug. 15 Engr. *Perf. 12½x12*

159	A63	50c green	1.50	.85
160	A63	1.25fr dk carmine	1.75	.30
161	A63	1.50fr brown vio	1.75	.30
162	A63	2.40fr brown org	5.50	5.50
163	A63	2.50fr lt blue	5.50	2.00
164	A63	4fr brt violet	5.50	2.75
165	A63	5fr black brn	5.50	3.00
		Nos. 159-165 (7)	27.00	14.70
		Set, never hinged	80.00	

Founding of Congo Free State, 50th anniv.

Nos. 159-165 exist imperf. Value set, $3,500.

For surcharges see Nos. B21-B22.

Molindi River — A64

Bamboos — A65

Suza River — A66

Rutshuru River — A67

Karisimbi A68

Mitumba Forest A69

1937-38 Photo. *Perf. 11½*

166	A64	5c purple & blk	.25	.25
167	A65	90c car & brn	.40	.40
168	A66	1.50fr dp red brn & blk	.30	.30
169	A67	2.40fr ol blk & brn	.30	.30
170	A68	2.50fr dp ultra & blk	.45	.45
171	A69	4.50fr dk grn & brn	.40	.40
172	A69	4.50fr car & sep	.50	.50
		Nos. 166-172 (7)	2.60	2.60
		Set, never hinged	7.50	

National Parks.

Nos. 166-171 were issued Mar. 1, 1938. Exist imperf. Value, set $100.

No. 172 was issued in sheets of four measuring 140x111mm. It was sold by subscription, the subscription closing Dec. 31, 1938. Value: unused $3.75. Exists imperf. Value, $1,250.

See No. B26. For surcharges see Nos. 184, 186.

King Albert Memorial, Leopoldville — A70

1941, Feb. 7 Litho. *Perf. 11*

173	A70	10c lt gray	.40	.25
174	A70	15c brown vio	.45	.25
175	A70	25c lt blue	.50	.35
176	A70	50c lt violet	.40	.25
177	A70	75c rose pink	1.75	.50
178	A70	1.25fr gray	.50	.35
179	A70	1.75fr orange	1.25	.50
180	A70	2.50fr carmine	1.00	.30
181	A70	2.75fr vio blue	1.25	1.00
182	A70	5fr lt olive grn	7.00	7.00
183	A70	10fr rose red	5.50	4.25
		Nos. 173-183 (11)	20.00	15.00
		Set, never hinged	90.00	

Exist imperforate. Value, set hinged, $120, used $55.

For surcharge see No. 185.

Nos. 168, 179, 169 Surcharged in Blue or Black

Nos. 184, 186

No. 185

1941-42 *Perf. 11½, 11*

184	A66	5c on 1.50fr (Bl)	.25	.25
a.		Inverted surcharge	22.50	22.50
185	A70	75c on 1.75fr ('42)	.35	.35
a.		Inverted surcharge	22.50	22.50
186	A67	2.50(fr) on 2.40fr ('42)	1.25	1.25
a.		Double surcharge	22.50	22.50
b.		Inverted surcharge	22.50	22.50
		Nos. 184-186 (3)	1.85	1.85
		Set, never hinged	4.00	

Catalogue values for unused stamps in this section, from this point to the end of the section, are for Never Hinged items.

A71

Oil Palms — A72

Congo Woman — A73

Leopard A74

Askari — A75

Okapi A76

Inscribed "Congo Belge Belgisch Congo"

1942, May 23 Engr. *Perf. 12½*

187	A71	5c red	.25	.25
188	A72	10c olive grn	.25	.25
189	A72	15c brown car	.25	.25
190	A72	20c dp ultra	.25	.25
191	A72	25c brown vio	.25	.25
192	A72	30c blue	.25	.25
193	A72	50c dp green	.25	.25
194	A72	60c chestnut	.25	.25
195	A73	75c dl lil & blk	.35	.25
196	A73	1fr dk brn & blk	.35	.25
197	A73	1.25fr rose red & blk	.35	.25
198	A74	1.75fr dk gray brn	1.25	.90
199	A74	2fr ocher	1.25	.45
200	A74	2.50fr carmine	1.25	.45
201	A75	3.50fr dk ol grn	.60	.25
202	A75	5fr orange	1.25	.25
203	A75	6fr brt ultra	.90	.25
204	A75	7fr black	1.25	.25
205	A75	10fr dp brown	1.25	.35
206	A76	20fr plum & blk	16.00	2.75
		Nos. 187-206 (20)	28.05	8.65

Same Inscribed "Belgisch Congo Congo Belge"

207	A72	10c olive grn	.25	.25
208	A72	15c brown car	.25	.25
209	A72	20c dp ultra	.25	.25
210	A72	25c brown vio	.25	.25
211	A72	30c blue	.25	.25
212	A72	50c dp green	.25	.25
213	A72	60c chestnut	.25	.25
214	A73	75c dl lil & blk	.25	.25
215	A73	1fr dk brn & blk	.35	.25
216	A73	1.25fr rose red & blk	.35	.25
217	A74	1.75fr dk gray brn	1.25	.75
218	A74	2fr ocher	1.25	.25
219	A74	2.50fr carmine	1.25	.25
220	A75	3.50fr dk ol grn	1.25	.25
221	A75	5fr orange	1.00	.25
222	A75	6fr brt ultra	1.00	.25
223	A75	7fr black	.50	.25
224	A75	10fr dp brown	1.00	.25
225	A76	20fr plum & blk	14.00	2.25
		Nos. 207-225 (19)	25.20	7.25

Miniature sheets of Nos. 193, 194, 197, 200, 211, 214, 217 and 219 were printed in 1944 by the Belgian Government in London and given to the Belgian political review, Message, which distributed them to its subscribers, one a month. Values per sheet: with selvage at left, about $120; without selvage at left, $35.

Remainders of these eight miniature sheets received marginal overprints in various colors in 1950, specifying a surtax of 100fr per sheet and paying tribute to the UPU. These sheets, together with four of Ruanda-Urundi, were sold by the Committee of Cultural Works (and not at post offices) in sets of 12 for 1,217.15 francs. Set values: unused $1,750; never hinged $3,000.

Nos. 187-227 imperforate had no franking value. Value, set $275.

For surcharges see Nos. B34-B37.

Congo Woman — A77

Askari — A78

1943, Jan. 1

226	A77	50fr ultra & blk	11.00	4.00
227	A78	100fr car & blk	16.00	5.00

Slaves and Arab Guards A79

Auguste Lambermont A80

Design: 10fr, Leopold II.

Perf. 13x11½, 12½x12

1947 Engr. Unwmk.

228	A79	1.25fr black brown	.30	.25
229	A80	3.50fr dark blue	.45	.25
230	A80	10fr red orange	1.25	.25
		Nos. 228-230 (3)	2.00	.75

50th anniv. of the abolition of slavery in Belgian Congo. See Nos. 261-262.

Baluba Carving of Former King — A82

Carved figures and masks of Baluba tribe: 10c, 50c, 2fr, "Ndoha," figure of tribal king. 15c, 70c, 1.20fr, 2.50fr, "Tshimanyi," an idol. 20c, 75c, 1.60fr, 3.50fr, "Buangakokoma," statue of kneeling beggar. 25c, 1fr, 2.40fr, 5fr, "Mbuta," sacred double cup, carved with two faces, Man and Woman. 40c, 1.25fr, 6fr, 8fr, "Ngadimuashi," female mask. 1.50fr, 3fr, 10fr, 50fr, "Buadi-Muadi," mask with squared features. 6.50fr, 20fr, 100fr, "Mbowa," executioner's mask with buffalo horns.

1947-50 ***Perf. 12½***

231	A82	10c dp org ('48)	.25	.25
232	A82	15c ultra ('48)	.25	.25
233	A82	20c brt bl ('48)	.25	.25
234	A82	25c rose car ('48)	.25	.25
235	A82	40c violet ('48)	.25	.25
236	A82	50c olive brn	.25	.25
237	A82	70c yel grn ('48)	.25	.25
238	A82	75c magenta ('48)	.25	.25
239	A82	1fr yel org & dk vio	2.25	.25
240	A82	1.20fr gray & brn ('50)	.25	.25
241	A82	1.25fr lt bl grn & mag ('48)	.50	.25
242	A82	1.50fr ol & mag ('50)	18.00	7.50
243	A82	1.60fr bl gray & brt bl ('50)	.50	.25
244	A82	2fr org & mag ('48)	.40	.25
245	A82	2.40fr bl grn & dk grn ('50)	.50	.25
246	A82	2.50fr brn red & bl grn	.60	.25
247	A82	3fr lt ultra & ind ('49)	6.50	.25
248	A82	3.50fr lt bl & blk ('48)	6.00	.25
249	A82	5fr bis & mag ('48)	2.00	.25
250	A82	6fr brn org & ind ('48)	2.25	.25
251	A82	6.50fr red org & red brn ('49)	2.75	.25
252	A82	8fr gray bl & dk grn ('50)	3.00	.25
253	A82	10fr pale vio & red brn ('48)	45.00	.25
254	A82	20fr red org & vio brn ('48)	5.00	.25
255	A82	50fr dp org & blk ('48)	7.50	.70
256	A82	100fr crim & blk brn ('48)	10.00	1.10
		Nos. 231-256 (26)	115.00	15.05

Railroad Train and Map — A83

1948, July 1 Unwmk. ***Perf. 13½***

257	A83	2.50fr dp bl & grn	1.00	.40

50th anniv. of railway service in the Congo.

Globe and Ship A84

1949, Nov. 21 ***Perf. 11½***

Granite Paper

258	A84	4fr violet blue	1.00	.50

75th anniv. of the UPU.

Allegorical Figure and Map — A85

1950, Aug. 12 ***Perf. 12x12½***

259	A85	3fr blue & indigo	3.00	.25
260	A85	6.50fr car rose & blk brn	3.00	.25

Establishment of Katanga Province, 50th anniv.

Portrait Type of 1947

Designs: 1.50fr, Cardinal Lavigerie. 3fr, Baron Dhanis.

Perf. 12½x12

1951, June 25 Unwmk.

261	A80	1.50fr purple	2.50	.25
262	A80	3fr black brown	2.50	.25

Littonia — A86

10c, Dissotis. 15c, Protea. 20c, Vellozia. 40c, Ipomoea. 50c, Angraecum. 60c, Euphorbia. 75c, Ochna. 1fr, Hibiscus. 1.25fr, Protea. 1.50fr, Schrizoglossum. 2fr, Ansellia. 3fr, Costus. 4fr, Nymphaea. 5fr, Thunbergia. 6.50fr, Thonningia. 7fr, Gerbera. 8fr, Gloriosa. 10fr, Silene. 20fr, Aristolochia. 50fr, Eulophia. 100fr, Crytosepalum.

Granite Paper

1952-53 Photo. ***Perf. 11½***

Flowers in Natural Colors

Size: 21x25½mm

263	A86	10c multi	.25	.25
264	A86	15c multi	.25	.25
265	A86	20c multi	.25	.25
266	A86	25c shown	.25	.25
267	A86	40c multi	.25	.25
268	A86	50c multi	.25	.25
269	A86	60c multi	.25	.25
270	A86	75c multi	.25	.25
271	A86	1fr multi	.30	.25
272	A86	1.25fr multi ('53)	2.00	.50
273	A86	1.50fr multi	.80	.25
274	A86	2fr multi	.80	.25
275	A86	3fr multi	.80	.25
276	A86	4fr multi	1.10	.25
277	A86	5fr multi	1.60	.25
278	A86	6.50fr multi	1.60	.25
279	A86	7fr multi	2.75	.25
280	A86	8fr multi ('53)	4.25	.30
281	A86	10fr multi ('53)	6.00	.40
282	A86	20fr multi	9.00	.40

Size: 22x32mm

283	A86	50fr multi ('53)	21.00	2.00
284	A86	100fr multi ('53)	27.50	3.50
		Nos. 263-284 (22)	81.50	11.10

Nos. 264, 269 and 270 with additional surcharges are varieties of Congo Democratic Republic Nos. 324, 327 and 328.

St. Francis Xavier — A86a

1953, Jan. 5 Engr. ***Perf. 12½x13***

285	A86a	1.50fr ultra & gray blk	.75	.40

400th death anniv. of St. Francis Xavier.

Canoe on Lake Kivu — A87

1953, Jan. 5 ***Perf. 14***

286	A87	3fr car & blk	3.00	.35
287	A87	7fr dp bl & brn org	3.00	.40

Issued to publicize the Kivu Festival, 1953.

Royal Colonial Institute Jubilee Medal A88

Design: 6.50fr, Same with altered background and transposed inscriptions.

1954, Dec. 27 Photo. ***Perf. 13½***

288	A88	4.50fr indigo & gray	2.00	.50
289	A88	6.50fr dk grn & brn	1.50	.25

25th anniv. of the founding of the Belgian Royal Colonial Institute. Exist imperf. Value, set $45.

King Baudouin and Tropical Scene A89

Designs: King and various views.

Inscribed "Congo Belge-Belgisch Congo"

Engr.; Portrait Photo.

1955, Feb. 15 Unwmk. ***Perf. 11½***

Portrait in Black

290	A89	1.50fr rose car	15.00	2.00
291	A89	3fr green	9.00	1.50
292	A89	4.50fr ultra	9.00	1.00
293	A89	6.50fr dp claret	12.00	.60

Inscribed "Belgisch Congo-Congo Belge"

294	A89	1.50fr rose car	15.00	2.00
295	A89	3fr green	9.00	1.50
296	A89	4.50fr ultra	9.00	1.50
297	A89	6.50fr deep claret	12.00	.50
		Nos. 290-297 (8)	90.00	10.60

Exist imperf. Value, set $325.

Map of Africa and Emblem of Royal Touring Club — A90

1955, July 26 Engr. ***Perf. 11½***

Inscription in French

298	A90	6.50fr vio blue	3.25	.50

Inscription in Flemish

299	A90	6.50fr vio blue	3.25	.50

5th International Congress of African Tourism, Elisabethville, July 26-Aug. 4. Nos. 298-299 printed in alternate rows.

Exist imperf. Value, set $40.

Kings of Belgium A91

1958, July 1 Unwmk. ***Perf. 12½***

300	A91	1fr rose vio	.90	.25
301	A91	1.50fr ultra	.90	.25
302	A91	3fr rose car	.90	.25
303	A91	5fr green	1.50	.45
304	A91	6.50fr brn red	1.25	.25
305	A91	10fr dl vio	1.50	.25
		Nos. 300-305 (6)	6.95	1.70

Belgium's annexation of Congo, 50th anniv. Exist imperf. Value, set $80.

Roan Antelope — A92

Black Buffaloes A93

Designs: 20c, White rhinoceros. 40c, Giraffe. 50c, Thick-tailed bushbaby. 1fr, Gorilla. 2fr, Black-and-white colobus (monkey). 3fr, Elephants. 5fr, Okapis. 6.50fr, Impala. 8fr, Giant pangolin. 10fr, Eland and zebras.

1959, Oct. 15 Photo. ***Perf. 11½***

Granite Paper

306	A92	10c bl & brn	.25	.25
307	A93	20c red org & slate	.25	.25
308	A92	40c brn & bl	.25	.25
309	A93	50c brt ultra, red & sep	.25	.25
310	A92	1fr brn, grn & blk	.25	.25
311	A93	1.50fr blk & org yel	.25	.25
312	A92	2fr crim, blk & brn	.25	.25
313	A93	3fr blk, gray & lil rose	.75	.25
314	A92	5fr brn, dk brn & brt grn	1.00	.25
315	A93	6.50fr bl, brn & org yel	1.25	.45
316	A92	8fr org brn, ol bis & lil	1.25	.45
317	A93	10fr multi	1.25	.45
		Nos. 306-317 (12)	7.25	3.60

Exist imperf. Value, set $100.

Madonna and Child — A94

1959, Dec. 1 Unwmk. ***Perf. 11½***

318	A94	50c golden brn, ocher & red brn	.25	.25
319	A94	1fr dk bl, pur & red brn	.25	.25
320	A94	2fr gray, brt bl & red brn	.35	.25
		Nos. 318-320 (3)	.85	.75

Exist imperf. Value, set $35.

Map of Africa and Symbolic Honeycomb A95

1960, Feb. 19 Unwmk. ***Perf. 11½***

Inscription in French

321	A95	3fr gray & org red	.30	.25

Inscription in Flemish

322	A95	3fr gray & org red	.30	.25

Commission for Technical Co-operation in Africa South of the Sahara (C. C. T. A.), 10th anniv. Exists imperf. Value, set $20.

SEMI-POSTAL STAMPS

Types of 1910-15 Issues Surcharged in Red

1918, May 15 Unwmk. *Perf. 14, 15*

B1 A29 5c + 10c grn & bl .40 .40
B2 A30 10c + 15c car & bl (I) .40 .40
B3 A21 15c + 20c bl grn & bl .40 .40
B4 A31 25c + 25c dp bl & pale bl .40 .40
B5 A23 40c + 40c brn red & bl .60 .60
B6 A24 50c + 50c brn lake & bl .60 .60
B7 A25 1fr + 1fr ol bis & bl 2.25 2.25
B8 A27 5fr + 5fr ocher & bl 17.50 17.50
B9 A28 10fr + 10fr grn & bl 200.00 200.00
Nos. B1-B9 (9) 222.55 *222.55*
Set, never hinged 550.00

The position of the cross and the added value varies on the different stamps.

Nos. B1-B9 exist imperforate without gum. Value, set $600.

Perf 15 examples of Nos. B1-B6 are worth approximately twice the values shown.

For overprints, see German East Africa Nos. NB1-NB9.

SP1

Design: No. B11, Inscribed "Belgisch Congo."

1925, July 8 *Perf. 12½*

B10 SP1 25c + 25c car & blk .30 .30
B11 SP1 25c + 25c car & blk .30 .30
a. Pair, Nos. B10-B11 .75 .75
Never hinged 1.25

Colonial campaigns in 1914-1918.

The surtax helped erect at Kinshasa a monument to those who died in World War I.

Nurse Weighing Child — SP3

First Aid Station SP5

Designs: 20c+10c, Missionary & Child. 60c+30c, Congo hospital. 1fr+50c, Dispensary service. 1.75fr+75c, Convalescent area. 3.50fr+1.50fr, Instruction on bathing infant. 5fr+2.50fr, Operating room. 10fr+5fr, Students.

1930, Jan. 16 Engr. *Perf. 11½*

B12 SP3 10c + 5c ver .75 .75
B13 SP3 20c + 10c dp brn 1.00 1.00
B14 SP5 35c + 15c dp grn 1.50 1.50
B15 SP5 60c + 30c dl vio 1.75 1.75
B16 SP3 1fr + 50c dk car 3.50 3.50
B17 SP5 1.75fr + 75c dp bl 8.75 8.75
B18 SP5 3.50fr + 1.50fr rose lake 12.00 12.00
B19 SP5 5fr + 2.50fr red brn 16.00 16.00
B20 SP5 10fr + 5fr gray blk 19.00 19.00
Nos. B12-B20 (9) 64.25 64.25
Set, never hinged 160.00

The surtax was intended to aid welfare work among the natives, especially the children.

Nos. 161, 163 Surcharged "+50c" in Blue or Red

1936, May 15 *Perf. 12½x12*

B21 A63 1.50fr + 50c (Bl) 8.00 5.75
B22 A63 2.50fr + 50c (R) 3.00 2.00
Set, never hinged 25.00

Surtax was for the King Albert Memorial Fund.

Queen Astrid with Congolese Children — SP12

1936, Aug. 29 Photo. *Perf. 12½*

B23 SP12 1.25fr + 5c dk brn .50 .50
B24 SP12 1.50fr + 10c dull rose .50 .50
B25 SP12 2.50fr + 25c dk blue 1.00 1.00
Nos. B23-B25 (3) 2.00 2.00
Set, never hinged 5.50

Issued in memory of Queen Astrid. The surtax was for the aid of the National League for Protection of Native Children.

Souvenir Sheet

National Parks — SP13

1938, Oct. 3 *Perf. 11½*
Star in Yellow

B26 SP13 Sheet of 6 67.50 67.50
Never hinged 130.00
On first day cover 80.00
a. 5c ultra & light brown 5.00 5.00
b. 90c ultra & light brown 5.00 5.00
c. 1.50fr ultra & light brown 5.00 5.00
d. 2.40fr ultra & light brown 5.00 5.00
e. 2.50fr ultra & light brown 5.00 5.00
f. 4.50fr ultra & light brown 5.00 5.00

Intl. Tourist Cong. A surtax of 3.15fr was for the benefit of the Congo Tourist Service. Exists imperf. Value $1,350.

Marabou Storks and Vultures — SP14

Buffon's Kob — SP15

Designs: 1.50fr+1.50fr, Pygmy chimpanzees. 4.50fr+4.50fr, Dwarf crocodiles. 5fr+5fr, Lioness.

1939, June 6 Photo. *Perf. 14*

B27 SP14 1fr + 1fr dp claret 8.00 *8.00*
B28 SP15 1.25fr + 1.25fr car 8.00 *8.00*
B29 SP15 1.50fr + 1.50fr brt pur 8.00 *8.00*
B30 SP14 4.50fr + 4.50fr sl grn 8.00 *8.00*
B31 SP15 5fr + 5fr brown 8.00 *8.00*
Nos. B27-B31 (5) 40.00 *40.00*
Set, never hinged 85.00

Surtax for the Leopoldville Zoological Gardens. Exists imperf. Value, set $200.

Sold in full sets by subscription.

Catalogue values for unused stamps in this section, from this point to the end of the section, are for Never Hinged items.

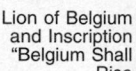

Lion of Belgium and Inscription "Belgium Shall Rise Again" — SP19

1942, Feb. 17 Engr. *Perf. 12½*

B32 SP19 10fr + 40fr brt grn 2.50 2.00
B33 SP19 10fr + 40fr vio bl 2.50 2.00

Nos. 193, 216, 198 and 220 Surcharged in Red

a

b

c

1945

B34 A72 (a) 50c + 50fr 5.50 3.25
B35 A73 (b) 1.25fr + 100fr 5.50 3.25
B36 A74 (c) 1.75fr + 100fr 5.50 3.25
B37 A75 (b) 3.50fr + 100fr 5.50 3.25
Nos. B34-B37 (4) 22.00 *13.00*

The surtax was for the Red Cross.
Sold in full sets by subscription.

Mozart at Age 7 — SP20

Queen Elisabeth and Sonata by Mozart — SP21

Perf. 11½

1956, Oct. 10 Unwmk. Engr.

B38 SP20 4.50fr + 1.50fr brt lil 5.50 2.50
B39 SP21 6.50fr + 2.50fr ultra 7.50 3.50

200th anniv. of the birth of Wolfgang Amadeus Mozart.

The surtax was for the Pro-Mozart Committee.

Exist imperf. Value, set $110.

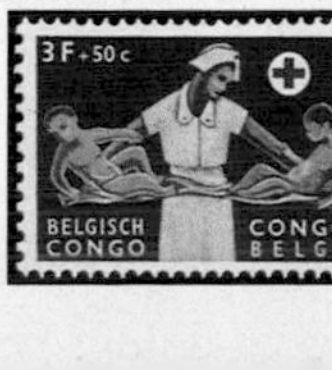

Nurse and Children SP22

Designs: 4.50fr+50c, Patient receiving injection. 6.50fr+40c, Patient being bandaged.

1957, Dec. 10 Photo. *Perf. 13x10½*
Cross in Carmine

B40 SP22 3fr + 50c dk bl 1.25 .50
B41 SP22 4.50fr + 50c dk grn 1.25 .50
B42 SP22 6.50fr + 50c red brn 1.50 .40
Nos. B40-B42 (3) 4.00 1.40

The surtax was for the Red Cross.
Exist imperf. Value, set $100.

High Jump SP23

1960, May 2 Unwmk. *Perf. 13½*

B43 SP23 50c + 25c shown .60 .30
B44 SP23 1.50fr + 50c Hurdles .80 .30
B45 SP23 2fr + 1fr Soccer .80 .30
B46 SP23 3fr + 1.25fr Javelin 1.40 .75
B47 SP23 6.50fr + 3.50fr Discus 1.45 .85
Nos. B43-B47 (5) 5.05 2.50

17th Olympic Games, Rome, Aug. 25-Sept. 11. The surtax was for the youth of Congo. Exist imperf. Value, set $140.

AIR POST STAMPS

Wharf on Congo River AP1

Congo "Country Store" AP2

View of Congo River AP3

Stronghold in the Interior — AP4

Unwmk.

1920, July 1 Engr. *Perf. 12*

C1 AP1 50c orange & blk .60 .25
C2 AP2 1fr dull vio & blk .65 .25
C3 AP3 2fr blue & blk 1.00 .40
C4 AP4 5fr green & blk 1.75 .80
Nos. C1-C4 (4) 4.00 1.70
Set, never hinged 14.00

Kraal AP5

Porters on Safari AP6

1930, Apr. 2

C5	AP5	15fr dk brn & blk	2.75	1.00
C6	AP6	30fr brn vio & blk	3.25	1.50
		Set, never hinged	22.50	

Fokker F VII over Congo AP7

1934, Jan. 22 ***Perf. 13½x14***

C7	AP7	50c gray black	.25	.25
C8	AP7	1fr dk carmine	.50	.25
a.		Booklet pane of 8	8.00	
C9	AP7	1.50fr green	.50	.25
C10	AP7	3fr brown	.25	.25
C11	AP7	4.50fr brt ultra	.50	.25
a.		Booklet pane of 8	14.00	
C12	AP7	5fr red brown	.25	.25
C13	AP7	15fr brown vio	.75	.50
C14	AP7	30fr red orange	1.75	1.50
C15	AP7	50fr violet	5.50	2.75
		Nos. C7-C15 (9)	10.25	6.25
		Set, never hinged	25.00	

The 1fr, 3fr, 4.50fr, 5fr, 15fr exist imperf. Values: 3fr, $35; 5fr, $55; 15fr, $30.

No. C10 Surcharged in Blue with New Value and Bars

1936, Mar. 25

C16	AP7	3.50fr on 3fr brown	.50	.25
		Never hinged	1.00	

Catalogue values for unused stamps in this section, from this point to the end of the section, are for Never Hinged items.

No. C9 Surcharged in Black

1942, Apr. 27

C17	AP7	50c on 1.50fr green	1.00	.30
a.		Inverted surcharge	45.00	15.00

POSTAGE DUE STAMPS

In 1908-23 regular postage stamps handstamped "TAXES" or "TAXE," usually boxed, were used in lieu of postage due stamps.

D1

1923 Typo. Unwmk. ***Perf. 14***

J1	D1	5c black brown	.25	.25
J2	D1	10c rose red	.25	.25
J3	D1	15c violet	.25	.25
J4	D1	30c green	.25	.25
J5	D1	50c ultramarine	.40	.35
J6	D1	50c blue ('29)	.40	.35
J7	D1	1fr gray	.50	.40
		Nos. J1-J7 (7)	2.30	2.10
		Set, never hinged	11.00	

Nos. J1-J7 exist imperf. Value, set $30.

Catalogue values for unused stamps in this section, from this point to the end of the section, are for Never Hinged items.

D2

1943 ***Perf. 14x14½***

J8	D2	10c olive green	.25	.25
J9	D2	20c dark ultramarine	.25	.25
J10	D2	50c green	.25	.25
J11	D2	1fr dark brown	.25	.25
J12	D2	2fr yellow orange	.25	.25
		Nos. J8-J12 (5)	1.25	1.25

1943 ***Perf. 12½***

J8a	D2	10c olive green	.70	.25
J9a	D2	20c dark ultramarine	.70	.25
J10a	D2	50c green	.70	.25
J11a	D2	1fr dark brown	.75	.40
J12a	D2	2fr yellow orange	1.25	.40
		Nos. J8a-J12a (5)	4.10	1.55

D3

1957 Engr. ***Perf. 11½***

J13	D3	10c olive brown	.30	.25
J14	D3	20c claret	.30	.25
J15	D3	50c green	.30	.25
J16	D3	1fr light blue	.45	.25
J17	D3	2fr vermilion	.60	.35
J18	D3	4fr	.70	.50
J19	D3	6fr violet blue	.85	.50
		Nos. J13-J19 (7)	3.50	2.35

Exist imperf. Value, set $20.

PARCEL POST STAMPS

Nos. 5, 11-12 Handstamped Surcharges in Black or Blue

No. Q1

No. Q3

No. Q4

1887-93 Unwmk. ***Perf. 15***

Q1	A1	3.50fr on 5fr lil	1,200.	1,100.
Q3	A4	3.50fr on 5fr vio	1,400.	700.
Q4	A4	3.50fr on 5fr vio ('88)	1,100.	600.
Q6	A4	3.50fr on 5fr gray ('93)	200.	200.
		Never hinged	350.	

Nos. Q1, Q3-Q4, and Q6 are known with inverted surcharge and double surcharge, and No. Q6 in pair with unsurcharged stamp. These varieties sell for somewhat more than the normal surcharges.

Genuine stamps with counterfeit surcharges, counterfeit stamps with counterfeit surcharges, and both with counterfeit cancels exist.

BELGIUM

'bel-jəm

LOCATION — Western Europe, bordering the North Sea
GOVT. — Constitutional Monarchy
AREA — 11,778 sq. mi.
POP. — 10,396,421 (2004)
CAPITAL — Brussels

100 Centimes = 1 Franc
100 Cents = 1 Euro (2002)

Catalogue values for unused stamps in this country are for Never Hinged items, beginning with Scott 322 in the regular postage section, Scott B370 in the semi-postal section, Scott C8 in the airpost section, Scott CB1 in the airpost semi-postal section, Scott F1 in the registration stamp section, Scott J40 in the postage due section, Scott M1 in the military stamp section, Scott O36 in the officials section, and Scott Q267 in the parcel post section.

Watermarks

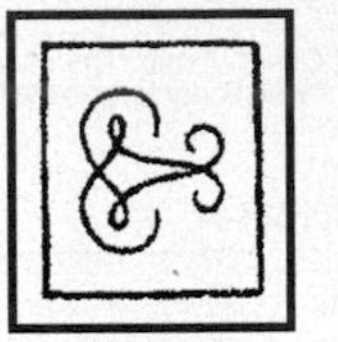

Wmk. 96 (With Frame)

Wmk. 96a (No Frame)

King Leopold I — A1

Wmk. Two "L's" Framed (96)

1849 Engr. ***Imperf.***

1	A1	10c brown	*2,600.*	100.00
a.		10c red brown	*4,300.*	425.00
b.		10c bister brown	*2,900.*	140.00
c.		10c dark brown	*2,650.*	85.00
2	A1	20c blue	*2,650.*	57.50
a.		20c milky blue	*3,700.*	160.00
b.		20c greenish blue	*3,900.*	290.00

The reprints are on thick and thin wove and thick laid paper unwatermarked.

A pale blue shade exists that is often confused with the milky blue.

A souvenir sheet containing reproductions of the 10c, 20c and 40c of 1849-51 with black burelage on back was issued Oct. 17, 1949, for the cent. of the 1st Belgian stamps. It was sold at BEPITEC 1949, an intl. stamp exhib. at Brussels, and was not valid. Value, $15.

King Leopold I — A2

1849-50 **Thin Paper**

3	A2	10c brown ('50)	*2,500.*	100.00
4	A2	20c blue ('50)	*2,200.*	62.50
5	A2	40c carmine rose	*2,000.*	525.00

Nos. 3-5 were printed on both thick and thin paper. See *Scott Classic Specialized Catalog of Stamps & Covers* for detailed listings.

Wmk. Two "L's" Without Frame (96a)

1851-54

6	A2	10c brown	625.00	8.50
a.		Ribbed paper ('54)	1,000.	62.50
7	A2	20c blue	800.00	8.00
a.		Ribbed paper ('54)	1,000.	62.50
8	A2	40c car rose	*4,250.*	110.00
a.		Ribbed paper ('54)	*5,000.*	260.00

Nos. 6-8 were printed on both thin and thick paper. See *Scott Classic Specialized Catalogue of Stamps & Covers* for detailed listings.

Nos. 6a, 7a, 8a must have regular and parallel ribs covering the whole stamp.

1858-61 **Unwmk.**

Stamps 17½x22mm; Oval 17¼high

9	A2	1c green ('61)	*225.00*	125.00
10	A2	10c brown	475.00	9.00
11	A2	20c blue	500.00	9.00
12	A2	40c vermilion	*3,750.*	150.00

Nos. 9 and 13 were valid for postage on newspapers and printed matter only.

Nos. 10-12 were printed in two sizes: 21mm high (with a 16½mm high oval) and 22mm high (with a 17¼mm high oval). The 22mm high stamps were issued in 1861. See *Scott Classic Specialized Catalogue of Stamps & Covers* for detailed listings.

Reprints of Nos. 9 to 12 are on thin wove paper. The colors are brighter than those of the originals. They were made from the dies and show lines outside the stamps.

Values for Nos. 13-16 are for stamps with perfs cutting into the design. Values for perforated stamps from Nos. 17 through 107 are for examples with perforations touching the design on one or two sides. Stamps with all perforations clear are exceptional and command substantial premiums.

1863-65 ***Perf. 14½***

13	A2	1c green	62.50	26.00
14	A2	10c brown	80.00	3.75
15	A2	20c blue	80.00	3.50
16	A2	40c carmine rose	450.00	25.00
		Nos. 13-16 (4)	672.50	58.25

Nos. 13-16 also come perf 12½ and 12½x13½, which were issued in 1863. Values differ. See the *Scott Classic Specialized Catalogue* for detailed listings.

King Leopold I — A3a

A3

A4

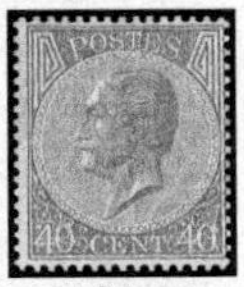

A4a

A5

London Print

1865 Typo. ***Perf. 14***

17	A5	1fr pale violet	1,750.	110.00

Brussels Print

Thick or Thin Paper

1865-67 ***Perf. 15, 14½x14***

18	A3	10c slate ('67)	185.00	2.25
b.		Pair, imperf. between		—
19	A3a	20c blue ('67)	290.00	2.00
20	A4	30c brown ('67)	625.00	11.00
b.		Pair, imperf. between	*2,000.*	
21	A4a	40c rose ('67)	775.00	20.00
22	A5	1fr violet	2,000.	97.50

Nos. 18-22 are valued as perf. 15. Nos. 18-22 also come perf. 14½x14, issued in 1865-66. Values differ. See the *Scott Classic Specialized Catalogue*. Nos. 18b and 20b are from the earlier printings.

The reprints are on thin paper, imperforate and ungummed.

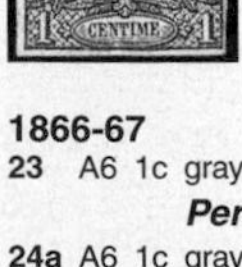

Coat of Arms — A6

1866-67 ***Imperf.***

23	A6	1c gray	250.00	150.00

Perf. 15, 14½x14

24a	A6	1c gray	45.00	16.00
25b	A6	2c blue ('67)	140.00	90.00
26b	A6	5c brown	175.00	90.00
		Nos. 23-26b (4)	610.00	346.00

Nos. 23-26b were valid for postage on newspapers and printed matter only.

Values are for perf. 15 stamps. Values for 14½x14 differ. See the *Scott Classic Specialized Catalogue* for detailed listings.
Counterfeits exist.
Reprints of Nos. 24-26 are on thin paper, imperforate and without gum.

Imperf. varieties of 1869-1912 (between Nos. 28-105) are without gum.

A7

A8

A9

A10

A11

King Leopold II — A12

1869-70 *Perf. 15*

28	A7	1c green	8.25	.40
29	A7	2c ultra ('70)	25.00	1.65
30	A7	5c buff ('70)	62.50	.75
31	A7	8c lilac ('70)	67.50	50.00
32	A8	10c green	27.50	.40
33	A9	20c lt ultra ('70)	125.00	.90
34	A10	30c buff ('70)	80.00	4.00
35	A11	40c brt rose ('70)	135.00	6.50
36	A12	1fr dull lilac ('70)	400.00	17.00
a.		1fr rose lilac	500.00	20.00
		Never hinged	850.00	
		Nos. 28-36 (9)	930.75	81.60

The frames and inscriptions of Nos. 30, 31 and 42 differ slightly from the illustration.
Minor "broken letter" varieties exist on several values.
Nos. 28-30, 32-33, 35-38 also were printed in aniline colors. These are not valued separately.
Nos. 28-36 exist imperforate, without gum. The 1c and 2c are valued from $55 to $85. The 40c and 1fr stamps are scarcer, valued from $500 to $675. Some denominations exist with gum. Pairs command premiums. Large multiples are scarce.
See Nos. 40-43, 49-51, 55.

A13

A14

King Leopold II — A15

1875-78

37	A13	25c olive bister	165.00	1.45
a.		25c ocher	185.00	1.55
38	A14	50c gray	275.00	11.00
		Roller cancel		12.50
a.		50c gray black	325.00	50.00
b.		50c deep black	1,750.	250.00
39	A15	5fr dp red brown	*1,700.*	1,450.
		Roller cancel		700.00
a.		5fr pale brown ('78)	*3,750.*	1,450.
		Roller cancel		700.00

No. 37 exists imperforate, without gum. Value, $250.
Dangerous counterfeits of No. 39 exist.

Printed in Aniline Colors

1881 *Perf. 14*

40	A7	1c gray green	18.00	.85
41	A7	2c lt ultra	19.00	3.00
42	A7	5c orange buff	55.00	1.25
a.		5c red orange	55.00	1.25
43	A8	10c gray green	27.50	1.10
44	A13	25c olive bister	95.00	3.00
		Nos. 40-44 (5)	214.50	9.20

See note following No. 36.

A16

A17

A18

A19

1883

45	A16	10c carmine	27.50	2.50
46	A17	20c gray	175.00	10.00
47	A18	25c blue	360.00	35.00
		Roller cancel		15.00
48	A19	50c violet	325.00	35.00
		Roller cancel		15.00
		Nos. 45-48 (4)	887.50	82.50

A20

A21

A22

1884-85 *Perf. 14*

49	A7	1c olive green	16.00	.75
50	A7	1c gray	4.25	.40
51	A7	5c green	37.50	.40
52	A20	10c rose, *bluish*	12.50	.40
a.		Grayish paper	13.50	.50
c.		Yellowish paper	*225.00*	22.50
53	A21	25c blue, *pink* ('85)	15.00	.75
54	A22	1fr brown, *grnsh*	*750.00*	17.50

The frame and inscription of No. 51 differ slightly from the illustration.
See note after No. 36.
Nos. 50-54 exist imperforate, without gum. The 1c and 10c stamps are valued from $32.50 to $55. The 5c, 25c and 1fr stamps are valued from $160 to $375.

A23

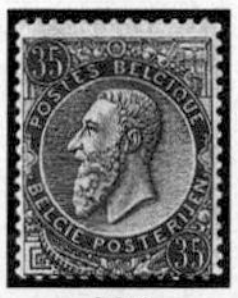
A24

A25

A26

1886-91

55	A7	2c purple brn ('88)	13.50	1.65
56	A23	20c olive, *grnsh*	200.00	1.65
b.		20c deep olive, *grnsh*	210.00	1.90
57	A24	35c vio brn, *brnsh* ('91)	18.00	3.00
58	A25	50c bister, *yelsh*	12.50	2.25
59	A26	2fr violet, *pale lil*	72.50	35.00
		Roller cancel		7.50
		Nos. 55-59 (5)	316.50	43.55

Nos. 56 and 57 exist imperforate, without gum. No. 56 is valued at $275. No. 57 is valued at $55.

Values quoted for Nos. 60-107 are for stamps with label attached. Stamps without label sell for much less.

Coat of Arms
A27

King Leopold
A28

Type A27 has two 1mm high ornamental bands across the top and bottom of the label. These bands do not appear on Type A32.

1893-1900

60	A27	1c gray	1.00	.25
61	A27	2c yellow	1.00	1.10
62	A27	2c violet brn ('94)	1.65	.40
63	A27	2c red brown ('98)	3.00	.90
64	A27	5c yellow grn	9.00	.30
65	A28	10c orange brn	4.00	.30
66	A28	10c brt rose ('00)	3.25	.40
67	A28	20c olive green	15.00	.60
68	A28	25c ultra	10.00	.50
a.		No ball to "5" in upper left corner	32.50	12.50
69	A28	35c violet brn	22.50	1.50
a.		35c red brown	35.00	2.40
70	A28	50c bister	57.50	20.00
71	A28	50c gray ('97)	62.50	2.50
72	A28	1fr car, *lt grn*	80.00	20.00
73	A28	1fr orange ('00)	100.00	5.00
74	A28	2fr lilac, *rose*	80.00	70.00
75	A28	2fr lilac ('00)	160.00	13.50
		Nos. 60-75 (16)	610.40	137.25
		Set, never hinged	1,700.	

Some experts question the existence of No. 61a. The editors would like more information.

Antwerp Exhibition Issue

Arms of Antwerp — A29

1894

76	A29	5c green, *rose*	4.75	3.25
77	A29	10c carmine, *bluish*	3.75	2.50
78	A29	25c blue, *rose*	1.00	1.00
		Nos. 76-78 (3)	9.50	6.75
		Set, never hinged	22.00	

Brussels Exhibition Issue

St. Michael and Satan
A30 A31

1896-97 *Perf. 14x14*

79	A30	5c dp violet	1.00	.60
80	A31	10c orange brown	8.50	3.50
81	A31	10c lilac brown	.50	.35
		Nos. 79-81 (3)	10.00	4.45
		Set, never hinged	25.00	

A32

A33

A34

A35

A36

A37

A38

A39

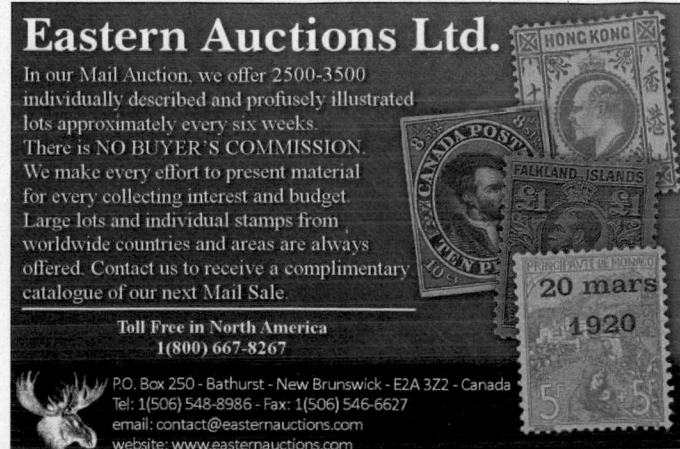

Two types of 1c:
I — Periods after "Dimanche" and "Zondag" in label.
II — No period after "Dimanche." Period often missing after "Zondag."

1905-11 ***Perf. 14***

82	A32	1c gray (I) ('07)	1.50	.25
a.		Type II ('08)	2.00	.60
83	A32	2c red brown ('07)	14.50	5.75
84	A32	5c green ('07)	11.50	.60
85	A33	10c dull rose	1.75	.60
86	A34	20c olive grn	26.00	1.00
87	A35	25c ultra	12.00	.85
a.		25c deep blue ('11)	13.50	2.00
88	A36	35c red brn	27.50	2.40
89	A37	50c bluish gray	95.00	4.00
90	A38	1fr yellow orange	110.00	8.00
91	A39	2fr violet	75.00	22.50
		Bar cancellation		5.00
		Nos. 82-91 (10)	374.75	45.95
		Set, never hinged	800.00	

A40

A41

Lion of Belgium — A42

A43

King Albert I — A44

1912

92	A40	1c orange	.25	.25
93	A41	2c orange brn	.25	.45
94	A42	5c green	.25	.25
95	A43	10c red	.75	.40
96	A43	20c olive grn	16.00	4.00
97	A43	35c bister brn	1.00	.70
98	A43	40c green	16.00	14.50
99	A43	50c gray	1.00	.80
100	A43	1fr orange	4.00	3.00
101	A43	2fr violet	17.50	17.50
102	A44	5fr plum	80.00	25.00
		Nos. 92-102 (11)	137.00	66.85

Counterfeits exist of Nos. 97-102. Those of No. 102 are common.

For overprints see Nos. Q49-Q50, Q52, Q55-Q55A, Q57-Q60.

A45

1912-13 **Larger Head**

103	A45	10c red	.40	.25
a.		Without engraver's name	.25	*.25*
104	A45	20c olive green ('13)	.40	.40
a.		Without engraver's name	2.00	2.00
105	A45	25c ultramarine	4.25	*.30*
a.		Without engraver's name	.25	*.40*
107	A45	40c green ('13)	.50	*.60*
		Nos. 103-107 (4)	5.55	1.55
		Set, never hinged	9.50	

For overprints see Nos. Q51, Q53-Q54, Q56.

Albert I A46

Cloth Hall of Ypres A47

Bridge of Dinant — A48

Library of Louvain — A49

Scheldt River at Antwerp A50

Anti-slavery Campaign in the Congo A51

King Albert I at Furnes A52

Kings of Belgium Leopold I, Albert I, Leopold II A53

1915-20 **Typo.** ***Perf. 14***

108	A46	1c orange	.25	.25
109	A46	2c chocolate	.25	.25
110	A46	3c gray blk ('20)	.30	.25
111	A46	5c green	1.00	.25
112	A46	10c carmine	.90	.25
113	A46	15c purple	1.50	.25
114	A46	20c red violet	3.00	.25
115	A46	25c blue	.50	.40

Engr.

116	A47	35c brown org & blk	.50	.30
117	A48	40c green & black	1.00	.30
a.		Vert. pair, imperf. btwn.		
118	A49	50c car rose & blk	4.50	.30
119	A50	1fr violet	32.50	1.00
120	A51	2fr slate	21.00	2.00
121	A52	5fr dp blue	275.00	125.00
		Telegraph or railroad cancel		55.00
122	A53	10fr brown	20.00	20.00
		Nos. 108-122 (15)	362.20	151.05
		Set, never hinged	1,250.	

Two types each of the 1c, 10c and 20c; three of the 2c and 15c; four of the 5c, differing in the top left corner.

See No. 138. For surcharges see Nos. B34-B47.

Nos. 111-119 were handstamped "T" for local provisional use. For detailed listings see *Scott Classic Specialized Catalogue 1840-1940.*

Perron of Liege (Fountain) — A54

Size: 18¼x28½mm

1919, July 25 ***Perf. 11½***

123	A54	25c blue	2.40	.35
a.		25c deep blue	3.00	.45

Size: 18½x28mm

1919, July 19

123B	A54	25c blue	400.00	400.00
c.		Sheet of 10	6,000.	*6,000.*

No. 123B is the first printing, which was issued in sheets of 10. Nos. 123 and 123a were later printings, issued in sheets of 100.

King Albert in Trench Helmet — A55

Perf. 11, 11½, 11½x11, 11x11½

1919 **Size: 18½x22mm**

124	A55	1c lilac brn	.25	.25
125	A55	2c olive	.25	.25

Size: 22x26mm

126	A55	5c green	.25	.25
127	A55	10c carmine, 22x26¾mm	.25	.25
a.		Size: 22½x26mm	1.00	.60
128	A55	15c gray vio, 22x26¾mm	.30	.30
a.		Size: 22½x26mm	2.40	.60
129	A55	20c olive blk	1.10	1.10
130	A55	25c deep blue	1.60	1.60
131	A55	35c bister brn	3.00	3.00
132	A55	40c red	5.00	5.00
133	A55	50c red brn	9.50	10.00
134	A55	1fr lt orange	40.00	40.00
135	A55	2fr violet	375.00	375.00

Size: 28x33½mm

136	A55	5fr car lake	100.00	100.00
137	A55	10fr claret	110.00	110.00
		Nos. 124-137 (14)	646.50	647.00
		Set, never hinged	1,150.	

Type of 1915 Inscribed: "FRANK" instead of "FRANKEN"

1919, Dec. ***Perf. 14, 15***

138	A52	5fr deep blue	1.75	1.25
		Never hinged	3.00	

Town Hall at Termonde — A56

1920 ***Perf. 11½***

139	A56	65c claret & black, 27x22mm	.75	.25
		Never hinged	1.50	
a.		Center inverted	*67,500.*	
b.		Size: 26¼x22½mm	5.75	2.40
		Never hinged	13.50	

For surcharge see No. 143.

Nos. B48-B50 Surcharged in Red or Black

1921 ***Perf. 12***

140	SP6	20c on 5c + 5c (R)	.60	.25
a.		Inverted surcharge	625.00	625.00
		Never hinged	1,100.	
141	SP7	20c on 10c + 5c	.40	.25
142	SP8	20c on 15c + 15c (R)	.60	.25
a.		Inverted surcharge	625.00	625.00
		Never hinged	1,100.	

No. 139 Surcharged in Red

143	A56	55c on 65c claret & blk	1.50	.35
a.		Pair, one without surcharge	2.25	.85
		Nos. 140-143 (4)	3.10	1.10
		Set, never hinged	8.50	

A58

1922-27 **Typo.** ***Perf. 14***

144	A58	1c orange	.25	.25
145	A58	2c olive ('26)	.25	.25
146	A58	3c fawn	.25	.25
147	A58	5c gray	.25	.25
148	A58	10c blue grn	.25	.25
149	A58	15c plum ('23)	.25	.25
150	A58	20c black brn	.25	.25
151	A58	25c magenta	.25	.25
a.		25c dull violet ('23)	.50	.25
152	A58	30c vermilion	.40	.25
153	A58	30c rose ('25)	.35	.25
154	A58	35c red brown	.35	.30
155	A58	35c blue grn ('27)	.80	.35
156	A58	40c rose	.50	.25
157	A58	50c bister ('25)	.50	.25
158	A58	60c olive brn ('27)	3.75	.25
159	A58	1.25fr dp blue ('26)	1.50	1.25
160	A58	1.50fr brt blue ('26)	2.50	.50
b.		1.50fr intense bright blue ('30)	15.00	4.00
161	A58	1.75fr ultra ('27)	1.75	.25
a.		Tete beche pair	11.00	5.00
c.		Bklt. pane of 4 + 2 labels	40.00	
		Nos. 144-161 (18)	14.40	5.90
		Set, never hinged	32.50	

See Nos. 185-190. For overprints and surcharges see Nos. 191-195, 197, B56, O1-O6.

A59

1921-25 **Engr.**

Perf. 11, 11x11½, 11½, 11½x11, 11½x12, 11½x12½, 12½

162	A59	50c dull blue	.30	.25
163	A59	75c scarlet ('22)	.25	.25
164	A59	75c ultra ('24)	.45	.25
165	A59	1fr black brn ('22)	.80	.25
166	A59	1fr dk blue ('25)	.60	.25
167	A59	2fr dk green ('22)	.90	.25
168	A59	5fr brown vio ('23)	13.50	*15.00*
169	A59	10fr magenta ('22)	9.00	6.50
		Nos. 162-169 (8)	25.80	*23.00*
		Set, never hinged	52.50	

No. 162 measures 18x20¾mm and was printed in sheets of 100.

Philatelic Exhibition Issues

1921, May 26 ***Perf. 11½***

170	A59	50c dark blue	3.50	3.50
		Never hinged	4.75	
a.		Sheet of 25	200.00	175.00
		Never hinged	225.00	

No. 170 measures 17½x21¼mm, was printed in sheets of 25 and sold at the Philatelic Exhibition at Brussels.

The sheet normally has pin holes and a cancellation-like marking in the margin. These are considered unused and the condition valued here.

Souvenir Sheet

1924, May 24 ***Perf. 11½***

171		Sheet of 4	225.00	200.00
		Never hinged	400.00	
a.		A59 5fr red brown	10.00	10.00
		Never hinged	14.00	

Sold only at the Intl. Phil. Exhib., Brussels. Sheet size: 130x145mm.

The sheet normally has pin holes and a cancellation-like marking in the margin. These are considered unused and the condition valued here. Sheets with wrinkles, toning or significant gum skips sell for much less.

Kings Leopold I and Albert I — A60

1925 — *Perf. 14*

172	A60	10c dp green	8.25	8.25
173	A60	15c dull vio	3.75	4.50
174	A60	20c red brown	3.75	4.50
175	A60	25c grnsh black	3.75	4.50
176	A60	30c vermilion	3.75	4.50
177	A60	35c lt blue	3.75	4.50
178	A60	40c brnsh blk	3.75	4.50
179	A60	50c yellow brn	3.75	4.50
180	A60	75c dk blue	3.75	4.50
181	A60	1fr dk violet	7.00	7.50
182	A60	2fr ultra	4.00	4.00
183	A60	5fr blue blk	3.75	4.50
184	A60	10fr dp rose	6.75	8.00
		Nos. 172-184 (13)	59.75	68.25
		Set, never hinged	126.00	

75th anniv. of Belgian postage stamps.

Nos. 172-184 were sold only in sets and only by The Administration of Posts, not at post offices.

A61

1926-27 — **Typo.**

185	A61	75c dk violet	.75	.70
186	A61	1fr pale yellow	.60	.35
187	A61	1fr rose red ('27)	1.50	.25
a.		Tete beche pair	7.50	4.50
c.		Bklt. pane 4 + 2 labels	25.00	
188	A61	2fr Prus blue	3.25	.45
189	A61	5fr emerald ('27)	32.50	1.60
190	A61	10fr dk brown ('27)	70.00	7.75
		Nos. 185-190 (6)	108.60	11.10
		Set, never hinged	249.00	

For overprints and surcharge see Nos. 196, Q174-Q175.

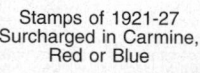

Stamps of 1921-27 Surcharged in Carmine, Red or Blue

1927

191	A58	3c on 2c olive (C)	.25	.25
192	A58	10c on 15c plum (R)	.25	.25
193	A58	35c on 40c rose (Bl)	.40	.25
194	A58	1.75fr on 1.50fr brt bl (C)	1.75	.80
		Nos. 191-194 (4)	2.65	1.55
		Set, never hinged	3.75	

Nos. 153, 185 and 159 Surcharged in Black

1929, Jan. 1

195	A58	5c on 30c rose	.25	.25
196	A61	5c on 75c dk violet	.25	.25
197	A58	5c on 1.25fr dp blue	.25	.25
		Nos. 195-197 (3)	.75	.75
		Set, never hinged	.85	

The surcharge on Nos. 195-197 is a precancelation which alters the value of the stamp to which it is applied.

Values for precanceled stamps in unused column are for those which have not been through the post and have original gum. Values in second column are for postally used, gumless stamps.

A63

1929-32 — **Typo.** — *Perf. 14*

198	A63	1c orange	.25	.25
199	A63	2c emerald ('31)	.45	.45
200	A63	3c red brown	.25	.25
201	A63	5c slate	.25	.25
c.		Bklt. pane of 4 + 2 labels	8.25	
202	A63	10c olive grn	.25	.25
c.		Bklt. pane of 4 + 2 labels	4.50	
203	A63	20c brt violet	1.00	.25
204	A63	25c rose red	.45	.25
c.		Bklt. pane of 4 + 2 labels	8.25	
205	A63	35c green	.50	.25
c.		Bklt. pane of 4 + 2 labels	9.75	
206	A63	40c red vio ('30)	.35	.25
c.		Bklt. pane of 4 + 2 labels	9.75	
207	A63	50c dp blue	.45	.25
c.		Bklt. pane of 4 + 2 labels	8.25	
208	A63	60c rose ('30)	2.25	.25
c.		Bklt. pane of 4 + 2 labels	30.00	
209	A63	70c org brn ('30)	1.10	.25
c.		Bklt. pane of 4 + 2 labels	22.50	
210	A63	75c dk blue ('30)	2.25	.25
b.		75c blue violet	2.40	.25
211	A63	75c dp brown ('32)	6.50	.25
b.		Bklt. pane of 4 + 2 labels	100.00	
		Nos. 198-211 (14)	16.30	3.70
		Set, never hinged	62.50	

For overprints and surcharges see Nos. 225-226, 240-241, 254-256, 309, O7-O15.

Tete Beche Pairs

201a	A63	5c	.60	.60
202a	A63	10c	.30	.30
204a	A63	25c	1.75	1.75
205a	A63	35c	2.75	2.75
206a	A63	40c	2.75	2.75
207a	A63	50c	2.25	2.25
208a	A63	60c	8.00	7.50
209a	A63	70c	6.00	5.00
210a	A63	75c	9.00	8.50
211a	A63	75c	30.00	30.00
		Nos. 201a-211a (10)	63.40	61.40
		Set, never hinged	160.00	

Tete-beche gutter pairs also exist.

A64

1929, Jan. 25 — **Engr.** — *Perf. 14½, 14*

212	A64	10fr dk brown	17.50	4.50
213	A64	20fr dk green	100.00	25.00
214	A64	50fr red violet	17.50	17.50
a.		Perf. 14½	55.00	45.00
215	A64	100fr brownish lake	17.50	17.50
a.		Perf. 14½	50.00	40.00
		Nos. 212-215 (4)	152.50	64.50
		Set, never hinged	276.50	

Peter Paul Rubens — A65

Zenobe Gramme — A66

1930, Apr. 26 — **Photo.** — *Perf. 12½x12*

216	A65	35c blue green	.40	.25
217	A66	35c blue green	.40	.25
		Set, never hinged	2.10	

No. 216 issued for the Antwerp Exhibition, No. 217 the Liege Exhibition.

Leopold I, by Lievin de Winne — A67

Leopold II, by Joseph Leempoels — A68

Design: 1.75fr, Albert I.

1930, July 1 — **Engr.** — *Perf. 11½*

218	A67	60c brown violet	.25	.25
219	A68	1fr carmine	.90	.80
220	A68	1.75fr dk blue	2.25	1.25
		Nos. 218-220 (3)	3.40	2.30
		Set, never hinged	9.60	

Centenary of Belgian independence.
For overprints see Nos. 222-224.

Antwerp Exhibition Issue

Souvenir Sheet

Arms of Antwerp A70

1930, Aug. 9 — *Perf. 11½*

221	A70	4fr Sheet of 1	300.00	250.00
		Never hinged	600.00	
a.		Single stamp	100.00	85.00

Size: 142x141mm. Inscription in lower margin "ATELIER DU TIMBRE-1930-ZEGELFABRIEK." Each purchaser of a ticket to the Antwerp Phil. Exhib., Aug. 9-15, was allowed to purchase one stamp. The ticket cost 6 francs.

The sheet normally has pin holes and a cancellation-like marking in the margin. These are considered unused and the condition valued here. Sheets with wrinkles or toning sell for much less.

Nos. 218-220 Overprinted in Blue or Red

1930, Oct.

222	A67	60c brown vio (Bl)	2.00	2.00
223	A68	1fr carmine (Bl)	8.25	7.75
224	A68	1.75fr dk blue (R)	14.50	14.50
		Nos. 222-224 (3)	24.75	24.25
		Set, never hinged	55.00	

50th meeting of the administrative council of the Intl. Labor Bureau at Brussels.

The names of the painters and the initials of the engraver have been added at the foot of these stamps.

Stamps of 1929-30 Surcharged in Blue or Black

1931, Feb. 20 — *Perf. 14*

225	A63	2c on 3c red brown (Bl)	.25	.25
226	A63	10c on 60c rose (Bk)	.50	.25
		Set, never hinged	3.75	

The surcharge on No. 226 is a precancelation which alters the denomination. See note after No. 197.

King Albert — A71

1931, June 15 — **Photo.**

227	A71	1fr brown carmine	.50	.25
		Never hinged	1.00	

King Albert — A71a

1932, June 1

228	A71a	75c bister brown	1.25	.25
		Never hinged	5.00	
a.		Tete beche pair	6.75	6.75
		Never hinged	17.50	
c.		Bklt. pane 4 + 2 labels	18.00	

See No. 257. For overprint see No. O18.

A72

1931-32 — **Engr.**

229	A72	1.25fr gray black	.75	.50
230	A72	1.50fr brown vio	1.50	.50
231	A72	1.75fr dp blue	.80	.25
232	A72	2fr red brown	1.10	.25
233	A72	2.45fr dp violet	3.00	.40
234	A72	2.50fr black brn ('32)	12.00	.50
235	A72	5fr dp green	25.00	1.10
236	A72	10fr claret	55.00	12.50
		Nos. 229-236 (8)	99.15	16.00
		Set, never hinged	275.00	

Nos. 206 and 209 Surcharged as No. 226, but dated "1932"

1932, Jan. 1

240	A63	10c on 40c red vio	2.75	.35
241	A63	10c on 70c org brn	2.50	.25
		Set, never hinged	22.50	

See note after No. 197.

Gleaner
A73

Mercury
A74

1932, June 1 Typo. *Perf. 13½x14*
245 A73 2c pale green .35 .35
246 A74 5c dp orange .25 .25
247 A73 10c olive grn .25 .25
a. Tete beche pair 4.00 4.00
Never hinged 7.50
c. Bklt. pane 4 + 2 labels 15.00
248 A74 20c brt violet 1.10 .25
249 A73 25c deep red .70 .25
a. Tete beche pair 3.50 3.50
Never hinged 6.50
c. Bklt. pane 4 + 2 labels 15.00
250 A74 35c dp green 2.75 .25
Nos. 245-250 (6) 5.40 1.60
Set, never hinged 14.50

For overprints see Nos. O16-O17.

Auguste Piccard's Balloon — A75

1932, Nov. 26 Engr. *Perf. 11½*
251 A75 75c red brown 3.50 .30
252 A75 1.75fr dk blue 17.50 2.50
253 A75 2.50fr dk violet 20.00 13.50
Nos. 251-253 (3) 41.00 16.30
Set, never hinged 112.50

Issued in commemoration of Prof. Auguste Piccard's two ascents to the stratosphere.

Nos. 206 and 209 Surcharged as No. 226, but dated "1933"

1933, Nov. *Perf. 14*
254 A63 10c on 40c red vio 17.50 3.50
255 A63 10c on 70c org brn 16.00 1.50
Set, never hinged 100.00

No. 206 Surcharged as No. 226, but dated "1934"

1934, Feb.
256 A63 10c on 40c red vio 16.00 1.50
Never hinged 52.50

For Nos. 254 to 256 see note after No. 197.
Regummed examples of Nos. 254-256 are plentiful.

King Albert Memorial Issue
Type of 1932 with Black Margins

1934, Mar. 10 Photo.
257 A71a 75c black .30 .25
Never hinged 1.00

Congo Pavilion — A76

Designs: 1fr, Brussels pavilion. 1.50fr, "Old Brussels." 1.75fr, Belgian pavilion.

1934, July 1 *Perf. 14x13½*
258 A76 35c green .75 .40
259 A76 1fr dk carmine 1.25 .50
260 A76 1.50fr brown 6.00 1.20
261 A76 1.75fr blue 6.00 .40
Nos. 258-261 (4) 14.00 2.50
Set, never hinged 50.00

Brussels Intl. Exhib. of 1935.

King Leopold III
A80 A81

1934-35 *Perf. 13½x14*
262 A80 70c olive blk ('35) .35 .25
a. Tete beche pair 1.50 1.00
c. Bklt. pane 4 + 2 labels 6.25
263 A80 75c brown .60 .25

Perf. 14x13½
264 A81 1fr rose car ('35) 3.00 .35
Nos. 262-264 (3) 3.95 .85
Set, never hinged 11.00

For overprint see No. O19.

Coat of Arms — A82

1935-48 Typo. *Perf. 14*
265 A82 2c green ('37) .25 .25
266 A82 5c orange .25 .25
267 A82 10c olive bister .25 .25
a. Tete beche pair .30 .25
Never hinged .50
b. Bklt. pane 4 + 2 labels 4.50
268 A82 15c dk violet .25 .25
269 A82 20c lilac .25 .25
270 A82 25c carmine rose .25 .25
a. Tete beche pair .30 .40
Never hinged .55
c. Bklt. pane 4 + 2 labels 4.50
271 A82 25c yel org ('46) .25 .25
272 A82 30c brown .25 .25
273 A82 35c green .25 .25
a. Tete beche pair .30 .30
Never hinged .50
c. Bklt. pane 4 + 2 labels 3.00
274 A82 40c red vio ('38) .25 .25
275 A82 50c blue .40 .25
276 A82 60c slate ('41) .25 .25
277 A82 65c red lilac ('46) .25 .25
278 A82 70c lt blue grn ('45) .25 .25
279 A82 75c lilac rose ('45) .25 .25
280 A82 80c green ('48) 4.00 .40
281 A82 90c dull vio ('46) .25 .25
282 A82 1fr red brown ('45) .25 .25
Nos. 265-282 (18) 8.40 4.65
Set, never hinged 17.00

Several stamps of type A82 exist in various shades.
Nos. 265, 361 were privately overprinted and surcharged "+10FR." by the Association Belgo-Americaine for the dedication of the Bastogne Memorial, July 16, 1950. The overprint is in six types. Value $1.50 per set.
See design O1. For overprints and surcharges see Nos. 312-313, 361-364, 390-394, O20-O22, O24, O26-O28, O33.

A83

A83a

Perf. 14, 14x13½, 11½
1936-56 Photo.

Size: 17½x21¾mm
283 A83 70c brown .25 .25
a. Tete beche pair .80 .80
Never hinged 1.25
c. Bklt. pane 4 + 2 labels 7.50

Size: 20¾x24mm
284 A83a 1fr rose car .30 .25
285 A83a 1.20fr dk brown ('51) .60 .25
a. Perf. 11½ ('56) 1.00 .25
Never hinged 2.75
286 A83a 1.50fr brt red vio ('43) .45 .30
287 A83a 1.75fr dp ultra ('43) .25 .25
288 A83a 1.75fr dk car ('50) .25 .25
289 A83a 2fr dk pur ('43) 1.50 1.50
290 A83a 2.25fr grnsh blk ('43) .25 .25
291 A83a 2.50fr org red ('51) 1.75 .30
a. Perf. 11½ ('56) 20.00 .25
Never hinged 65.00
292 A83a 3.25fr chestnut ('43) .25 .25
293 A83a 5fr dp green ('43) 1.50 .50
Nos. 283-293 (11) 7.35 4.35
Set, never hinged 18.00

Nos. 287-288, 290-291, 293 inscribed "Belgie-Belgique."

See designs A85, A91. For overprints and surcharges see Nos. 314, O23, O25, O29, O31, O34.

A84

1936-51 Engr. *Perf. 14x13½*
294 A84 1.50fr rose lilac ('41) .60 .35
295 A84 1.75fr dull blue .25 .25
296 A84 2fr dull vio .40 .30
297 A84 2.25fr gray vio ('41) .25 .25
298 A84 2.45fr black 45.00 .70
299 A84 2.50fr ol blk ('39) 3.00 .25
300 A84 3.25fr org brn ('41) .30 .25
301 A84 5fr dull green 3.00 .50
302 A84 10fr vio brn .60 .25
a. 10fr light brown ('46) 10.00 .25
Never hinged 35.00
303 A84 20fr vermilion 1.00 .30
a. 20fr rose orange ('36) 1.15 .40
Never hinged 4.00

Perf. 11½
304 A84 3fr yel brn ('51) .50 .25
305 A84 4fr bl, *bluish* ('50) 6.00 .25
a. White paper 9.00 .25
Never hinged 14.50
306 A84 6fr brt rose car ('51) 3.00 .25
307 A84 10fr brn vio ('51) .50 .25
308 A84 20fr red ('51) 1.00 .25
Nos. 294-308 (15) 65.40 4.65
Set, never hinged 150.00

See No. 1159. For overprint and surcharges see Nos. 316-317, O32.

No. 206 Surcharged as No. 226, but dated "1937"

1937 Unwmk. *Perf. 14*
309 A63 10c on 40c red vio .25 .25
Never hinged .35

See note after No. 197.

A85

1938-41 Photo. *Perf. 13½x14*
310 A85 75c olive gray .25 .25
a. Tete beche pair 1.00 1.00
Never hinged 1.75
c. Bklt. pane 4 + 2 labels 6.75
311 A85 1fr rose pink ('41) .25 .25
a. Tete beche pair .30 .30
Never hinged .45
b. Booklet pane of 6 2.25
c. Bklt. pane 4 + 2 labels 2.25
Set, never hinged .80

For overprints and surcharges see Nos. 315, O25, O30, O35.

Nos. 272, 274, 283, 310, 299, 298 Srchd. in Blue, Black, Carmine or Red

a

b

c

1938-42
312 A82 (a) 10c on 30c (Bl) .25 .25
313 A82 (a) 10c on 40c (Bl) .25 .25
314 A83 (b) 10c on 70c (Bk) .25 .25
315 A85 (b) 50c on 75c (C) .25 .25
316 A84 (c) 2.25fr on 2.50fr (C) .45 .45
317 A84 (c) 2.50fr on 2.45fr (R) 11.00 .25
Nos. 312-317 (6) 12.45 1.70
Set, never hinged 26.00

Issue date: No. 317, Oct. 31, 1938.

Basilica and Bell Tower — A86

Water Exhibition Buildings — A87

Designs: 1.50fr, Albert Canal and Park. 1.75fr, Eygenbilsen Cut in Albert Canal.

1938, Oct. 31 *Perf. 14x13½, 13½x14*
318 A86 35c dk blue grn .25 .25
319 A87 1fr rose red .30 .30
320 A87 1.50fr vio brn 1.25 .50
321 A87 1.75fr ultra 1.25 .25
Nos. 318-321 (4) 3.05 1.30
Set, never hinged 11.00

Intl. Water Exhibition, Liège, 1939.

Catalogue values for unused stamps in this section, from this point to the end of the section, are for Never Hinged items.

Lion Rampant — A90

1944 Unwmk. Photo. *Perf. 12½*
Inscribed: "Belgique-Belgie"
322 A90 5c chocolate .25 .25
323 A90 10c green .25 .25
324 A90 25c lt blue .25 .25
325 A90 35c brown .25 .25
326 A90 50c lt bl grn .25 .25
327 A90 75c purple .25 .25
328 A90 1fr vermilion .25 .25
329 A90 1.25fr chestnut .25 .25
330 A90 1.50fr orange 1.10 .40
331 A90 1.75fr brt ultra .25 .25
332 A90 2fr aqua 6.25 2.00
333 A90 2.75fr dp mag .25 .25
334 A90 3fr claret .50 .40
335 A90 3.50fr sl blk .50 .40
336 A90 5fr dk olive 13.50 5.00
337 A90 10fr black .90 .60
Nos. 322-337 (16) 25.25 11.30

Inscribed: "Belgie-Belgique"
338 A90 5c chocolate .25 .25
339 A90 10c green .25 .25
340 A90 25c lt bl .25 .25
341 A90 35c brown .25 .25
342 A90 50c lt bl grn .25 .25
343 A90 75c purple .25 .25
344 A90 1fr vermilion .25 .25
345 A90 1.25fr chestnut .25 .25
346 A90 1.50fr orange .30 *.45*
347 A90 1.75fr brt ultra .25 .25
348 A90 2fr aqua 2.50 1.25
349 A90 2.75fr dp magenta .25 .25
350 A90 3fr claret .50 .40
351 A90 3.50fr slate blk .50 .40
352 A90 5fr dark olive 5.25 3.00
353 A90 10fr black .75 *1.00*
Nos. 338-353 (16) 12.30 9.00

Leopold III, Crown and V — A91

1944-57 *Perf. 14x13½*
354 A91 1fr brt rose red .50 .25
355 A91 1.50fr magenta .45 .25
356 A91 1.75fr dp ultra .60 .40
357 A91 2fr dp vio 2.50 .30
358 A91 2.25fr grnsh blk .60 .40
359 A91 3.25fr chnt brn .60 .25

360	A91	5fr dk bl grn	5.50	.25
a.		Perf. 11½ ('57)	200.00	.25
		Nos. 354-360 (7)	10.75	2.10

Nos. 355, 357, 359 inscribed "Belgique-Belgie."

For surcharges see Nos. 365-367 and footnote following No. 367.

Stamps of 1935-41 Overprinted in Red

1944 ***Perf. 14***

361	A82	2c pale green	.25	.25
362	A82	15c indigo	.25	.25
363	A82	20c brt violet	.25	.25
364	A82	60c slate	.25	.25
		Nos. 361-364 (4)	1.00	1.00

See note following No. 282.

Nos. 355, 357, and 360 Srchd. Typographically in Black or Carmine

1946 ***Perf. 14x13½***

365	A91	On 1.50fr magenta	.70	.25
366	A91	On 2fr dp vio (C)	2.00	.70
367	A91	On 5fr dk bl grn (C)	1.75	.30
		Nos. 365-367 (3)	4.45	1.25

To provide denominations created by a reduction in postal rates, the Government produced Nos. 365-367 by typographed surcharge. Also, each post office was authorized on May 20, 1946, to surcharge its stock of 1.50fr, 2fr and 5fr stamps "-10 percent." Hundreds of types and sizes of this surcharge exist, both hand-stamped and typographed. These include the "1,35," "1,80" and "4,50" applied at Ghislenghien.

M. S. Prince Baudouin — A92

2.25fr, S.S. Marie Henriette. 3.15fr, S.S. Diamant.

Perf. 14x13½, 13½x14

1946, June 15 **Photo.** **Unwmk.**

368	A92	1.35fr brt bluish grn	.25	.25
369	A92	2.25fr slate green	.45	.25
370	A92	3.15fr slate black	.50	.25
		Nos. 368-370 (3)	1.20	.75

Centenary of the steamship line between Ostend and Dover.

No. 368 exists in two sizes: 21¼x18¼mm and 21x17mm. Nos. 369-370 are 24½x20mm.

Capt. Adrien de Gerlache — A95

Belgica and Explorers A96

1947, June ***Perf. 14x13½, 11½***

371	A95	1.35fr crimson rose	.25	.25
372	A96	2.25fr gray black	3.50	.75

50th anniv. of Capt. Adrien de Gerlache's Antarctic Expedition.

Joseph A. F. Plateau — A97

1947, June ***Perf. 14x13½***

373	A97	3.15fr deep blue	1.00	.25

Issued to mark the World Film and Fine Arts Festival, Brussels, June, 1947.

Chemical Industry — A98

Industrial Arts — A99

Agriculture A100

Textile Industry A102

Communications Center — A101

Iron Manufacture A103

Photogravure (#374-376, 378), Typographed (#377, 380), Engraved

1948 **Unwmk.** ***Perf. 11½***

374	A98	60c blue grn	.25	.25
375	A98	1.20fr brown	1.90	.25
376	A99	1.35fr red brown	.25	.25
377	A100	1.75fr brt red	.25	.25
378	A99	1.75fr dk gray grn	.60	.25
379	A101	2.25fr gray blue	.75	.50
380	A100	2.50fr dk car rose	7.00	.60
381	A101	3fr brt red vio	12.00	.50
382	A102	3.15fr deep blue	1.00	.60
383	A102	4fr brt ultra	10.00	.40
384	A103	6fr blue green	23.00	.55
385	A103	6.30fr brt red vio	2.75	2.00
		Nos. 374-385 (12)	59.75	6.40

See Nos. O42-O46.

Leopold I — A104

1949, July 1 **Engr.** ***Perf. 14x13½***

386	A104	90c dk green	.55	.30
387	A104	1.75fr brown	.30	.25
388	A104	3fr red	8.00	3.00
389	A104	4fr deep blue	5.50	.85
		Nos. 386-389 (4)	14.35	4.40

Cent. of Belgium's 1st postage stamps. See note on souvenir sheet below No. 2.

Stamps of 1935-45 Precanceled and Surcharged in Black

1949 ***Perf. 14***

390	A82	5c on 15c dk vio	.25	.25
391	A82	5c on 30c brown	.25	.25
392	A82	5c on 40c red vio	.25	.25
393	A82	20c on 70c lt bl grn	.30	.35
394	A82	20c on 75c lil rose	.25	.25

Similar Surcharge and Precancellation in Black on Nos. B455-B458

Perf. 14x13½

395	SP251	10c on #B455	2.25	2.25
396	SP251	40c on #B456	1.10	1.10
397	SP251	80c on #B457	.55	.55
398	SP251	1.20fr on #B458	1.25	1.25
		Nos. 390-398 (9)	6.45	6.50

See note after No. 197.

St. Mary Magdalene, from Painting by Gerard David — A105

1949, July 15 **Photo.** ***Perf. 11***

399	A105	1.75fr dark brown	.70	.30

Gerard David Exhibition at Bruges, 1949.

Allegory of UPU A106

1949, Oct. 1 **Engr.** ***Perf. 11½***

400	A106	4fr deep blue	3.75	2.25

75th anniv. of the UPU.

Symbolical of Pension Fund — A107

Perf. 11½

1950, May 1 **Unwmk.** **Photo.**

401	A107	1.75fr dark brown	.50	.25

General Pension Fund founding, cent.

Lion Rampant — A108

1951, Feb. 15 **Engr.** ***Perf. 11½***

402	A108	20c blue	.25	.25

1951-75 **Typo.** ***Perf. 13½x14***

Size: 17½x21mm

403	A108	2c org brn ('60)	.25	.25
404	A108	3c brt lil ('60)	.25	.25
405	A108	5c pale violet	.25	.25
406	A108	5c brt pink ('74)	.25	.25
407	A108	10c red orange	.25	.25
408	A108	15c brt pink ('59)	.25	.25
409	A108	20c claret	.25	.25
410	A108	25c green	1.50	.25
411	A108	25c lt bl grn ('66)	.25	.25
412	A108	30c gray grn ('57)	.25	.25
413	A108	40c brown olive	.25	.25
414	A108	50c ultra	.25	.25
a.		50c light blue	.25	.25
415	A108	60c lilac rose	.25	.25
416	A108	65c violet brn	11.50	.50
417	A108	75c bluish lilac	.25	.25
418	A108	80c emerald	.75	.25
419	A108	90c deep blue	.75	.25
420	A108	1fr rose	.25	.25
421	A108	2fr emerald ('73)	.25	.25
422	A108	2.50fr brown ('70)	.25	.25
423	A108	3fr brt pink ('70)	.25	.25
424	A108	4fr brt rose lil ('74)	.25	.25
425	A108	4.50fr blue ('74)	.30	.25
426	A108	5fr brt lilac ('75)	.30	.25

Size: 17x20½mm

427	A108	1.50fr dk sl grn ('69)	.25	.25

Perf. 13½x13

428	A108	2fr emerald ('68)	.25	.25

Photo. ***Perf. 11½***

Size: 20½x24mm

429	A108	50c light blue ('61)	.45	.25
430	A108	60c lilac rose ('66)	1.10	.70
431	A108	1fr carmine rose ('59)	.25	.25

Perf. 13½x12½

Size: 17½x22mm

432	A108	50c lt blue ('75)	.25	.25
a.		Booklet pane of 4 (#432, 784 and 2 #785) + labels	1.00	
b.		Booklet pane of 4 (#432 and 3 #787) + labels	1.50	
433	A108	1fr rose ('69)	2.00	.90
434	A108	2fr emerald ('72)	.50	.30
e.		Booklet pane of 6 (4 #434 + 2 #475)	5.50	
f.		Booklet pane of 5 (#434, 4 #476 + label)	8.00	
		Nos. 403-434 (32)	24.65	9.40

Counterfeits exist of No. 416. Nos. 429, 431 also issued in coils with black control number on back of every fifth stamp. Nos. 432-434 issued in booklet panes only. No. 432 has one straightedge, and stamps in the pane are tete-beche. Each pane has 2 labels showing Belgian postal emblem and a large selvage with postal code instructions.

Nos. 433-434 have 1 or 2 straight-edges. Panes have a large selvage with inscription or map of Belgium showing postal zones.

See designs A386, O5. For surcharges see Nos. 477-478, 563-567.

Francois de Tassis (Franz von Taxis) — A109

Portraits: 1.75fr, Jean-Baptiste of Thurn & Taxis. 2fr, Baron Leonard I. 2.50fr, Count Lamoral I. 3fr, Count Leonard II. 4fr, Count Lamoral II. 5fr, Prince Eugene Alexander. 5.75fr, Prince Anselme Francois. 8fr, Prince Alexander Ferdinand. 10fr, Prince Charles Anselme. 20fr, Prince Charles Alexander.

1952, May 14 **Engr.** ***Perf. 11½***

Laid Paper

435	A109	80c olive grn	.25	.25
436	A109	1.75fr red org	.25	.25
437	A109	2fr violet brn	.50	.45
438	A109	2.50fr carmine	.95	.45
439	A109	3fr olive bis	.95	.45
440	A109	4fr ultra	1.00	.45
441	A109	5fr red brn	2.50	1.00
442	A109	5.75fr blue vio	3.50	1.50
443	A109	8fr gray	14.00	3.00
444	A109	10fr rose vio	18.00	5.50
445	A109	20fr brown	80.00	22.50
		Nos. 435-445,B514 (12)	261.90	135.80

13th UPU Cong., Brussels, 1952.

King Baudouin — A110

1952-58 Engr. *Perf. 11½*

Size: 21x24mm

446	A110	1.50fr gray green	1.25	.25
447	A110	2fr crimson	.45	.25
448	A110	4fr ultra	3.75	.25

Size: 24½x35mm

449	A110	50fr gray brn	20.00	.25
a.		50fr violet brown	90.00	.60
450	A110	100fr rose red ('58)	16.00	.25

King Baudouin — A111

1953-72 Photo. *Perf. 11½*

451	A111	1.50fr gray	.25	.25
452	A111	2fr rose carmine	7.25	.25
453	A111	2fr green	.25	.25
454	A111	2.50fr red brn ('57)	.50	.25
a.		2.50fr orange brown ('70)	.25	.25
455	A111	3fr rose lil ('58)	.40	.25
456	A111	3.50fr brt yel grn ('58)	.75	.25
457	A111	4fr brt ultra	.50	.25
458	A111	4.50fr dk red brn ('62)	3.00	.25
459	A111	5fr violet ('57)	1.25	.25
460	A111	6fr dp pink ('58)	.75	.25
461	A111	6.50fr gray ('60)	95.00	15.00
462	A111	7fr blue ('60)	.90	.25
463	A111	7.50fr grysh brn ('58)	87.50	16.00
464	A111	8fr bluish gray ('58)	1.00	.25
465	A111	8.50fr claret ('58)	20.00	.45
466	A111	9fr gray ('58)	95.00	1.90
467	A111	12fr lt bl grn ('66)	13.50	.45
468	A111	30fr red org ('58)	10.00	.25

Redrawn

469	A111	2.50fr org brn ('71)	.35	.25
470	A111	4.50fr brown ('72)	2.25	.60
471	A111	7fr blue ('71)	.60	.25

Perf. 13½x12½

Size: 17½x22mm

472	A111	1.50fr gray ('70)	.60	.30
b.		Bklt. pane of 10	6.50	
c.		Bklt. pane, 3 #472, 3 #475	15.00	
473	A111	2.50fr org brn ('70)	6.00	5.00
h.		Bklt. pane, 1 #473, 5 #475	16.00	
474	A111	3fr lilac rose ('69)	.60	.25
a.		Bklt. pane of 5 + label	25.00	
b.		Bklt. pane, 2 #433, 6 #474	18.00	
475	A111	3.50fr brt yel grn ('70)	.60	.25
476	A111	4.50fr dull red brn ('72)	.60	.35
		Nos. 446-476 (31)	390.85	45.55

Nos. 451, 453, 454a, 455, 456, 458 also issued in coils with black control number on back of every fifth stamp. These coils, except for No. 451, are on luminescent paper.

On Nos. 469-471, the 2, 4 and 7 are 3mm high. The background around the head is white. On Nos. 454, 458, 462 the 2, 4 and 7 are 2½mm high and the background is tinted.

Nos. 472-476 issued in booklets only and have 1 or 2 straight-edges. All panes have a large selvage with inscription or map.

See designs M1, O3.

Luminescent Paper

Stamps issued on both ordinary and luminescent paper include: Nos. 307-308, 430-431, 449-451, 453-460, 462, 464, 467-468, 472, 643-644, 650-651, 837, Q385, Q410.

Stamps issued only on luminescent paper include: Nos. 433, 454a, 472b, 473-474, 649, 652-658, 664-670, 679-682, 688-690, 694-696, 698-703, 705-711, 713-726, 729-747, 751-754, 756-757, 759, 761-762, 764, 766, 769, 772, 774, 778, 789, 791-793, 795, 797-799, 801-807, 809-811, 814-818, 820-834, 836, 838-848.

See note after No. 857.

Nos. 416 and 419 Surcharged and Precanceled in Black

1954, Jan. 1 Unwmk. *Perf. 13½x14*

477	A108	20c on 65c vio brn	1.25	.25
478	A108	20c on 90c dp blue	1.25	.25

See note after No. 197.

Map and Rotary Emblem A112

80c, Mermaid and Mercury holding emblem. 4fr, Rotary emblem and two globes.

1954, Sept. 10 Engr. *Perf. 11½*

479	A112	20c red	.25	.25
480	A112	80c dark green	.40	.25
481	A112	4fr ultra	1.40	.30
		Nos. 479-481 (3)	2.05	.80

5th regional conf. of Rotary Intl. at Ostend. No. 481 for Rotary 50th Anniv. (in 1955).

A souv. sheet containing one each, imperf., was sold for 500 francs. It was not valid for postage. Value, $200.

The Rabot and Begonia — A113

Designs: 2.50fr, The Oudeburg and azalea. 4fr, "Three Towers" and orchid.

1955, Feb. 15 Photo.

482	A113	80c brt carmine	.40	.40
483	A113	2.50fr black brn	7.50	2.00
484	A113	4fr dk rose brn	4.25	.55
		Nos. 482-484 (3)	12.15	2.95

Ghent Intl. Flower Exhibition, 1955.

Homage to Charles V as a Child, by Albrecht de Vriendt A114

Charles V, by Titian — A115

4fr, Abdication of Charles V, by Louis Gallait.

1955, Mar. 25 Unwmk. *Perf. 11½*

485	A114	20c rose red	.25	.25
486	A115	2fr dk gray green	.70	.25
487	A114	4fr blue	3.50	1.00
		Nos. 485-487 (3)	4.45	1.50

Charles V Exhibition, Ghent, 1955.

Emile Verhaeren, by Montald Constant — A116

1955, May 11 Engr.

488	A116	20c dark gray	.25	.25

Birth cent. of Verhaeren, poet.

Allegory of Textile Manufacture A117

1955, May 11

489	A117	2fr violet brown	1.00	.25

2nd Intl. Textile Exhibition, Brussels, June 1955.

"The Foolish Virgin" by Rik Wouters — A118

1955, June 10

490	A118	1.20fr olive green	1.10	.30
491	A118	2fr violet	1.60	.25

3rd biennial exhibition of sculpture, Antwerp, June 11-Sept. 10, 1955.

"Departure of Volunteers from Liege, 1830" by Charles Soubre — A119

1955, Sept. 10 Photo.

492	A119	20c grnsh slate	.25	.25
493	A119	2fr chocolate	.75	.25

Exhibition "The Romantic Movement in Liege Province," Sept. 10-Oct. 31, 1955; and 125th anniv. of Belgium's independence from the Netherlands.

Pelican Giving Blood to Young — A120

1956, Jan. 14 Engr.

494	A120	2fr brt carmine	.30	.25

Blood donor service of the Belgian Red Cross.

Buildings of Tournai, Ghent and Antwerp — A121

1956, July 14 Photo.

495	A121	2fr brt ultra	.25	.25

The Scheldt exhibition (Scaldis) at Tournai, Ghent and Antwerp, July-Sept. 1956.

Europa Issue

"Rebuilding Europe" — A122

1956, Sept. 15 Engr.

496	A122	2fr lt green	*1.25*	.25
497	A122	4fr purple	*7.75*	.25

Issued to symbolize the cooperation among the six countries comprising the Coal and Steel Community.

Train on Map of Belgium and Luxembourg A123

1956, Sept. 29

498	A123	2fr dark blue	.25	.25

Issued to mark the electrification of the Brussels-Luxembourg railroad.

Edouard Anseele — A124

1956, Oct. 27

499	A124	20c violet brown	.25	.25

Cent. of the birth of Edouard Anseele, statesman, and in connection with an exhibition held in his honor at Ghent.

"The Atom" and Exposition Emblem — A125

1957-58 Unwmk.

500	A125	2fr carmine rose	.25	.25
501	A125	2.50fr green ('58)	.35	.25
502	A125	4fr brt violet blue	.50	.25
503	A125	5fr claret ('58)	1.25	.55
		Nos. 500-503 (4)	2.35	1.30

1958 World's Fair at Brussels.

Emperor Maximilian I Receiving Letter — A126

1957, May 19

504	A126	2fr claret	.35	.25

Day of the Stamp, May 19, 1957.

Sikorsky S-58 Helicopter A127

1957, June 15

505 A127 4fr gray grn & brt bl .80 .45

100,000th passenger carried by Sabena helicopter service, June 15, 1957.

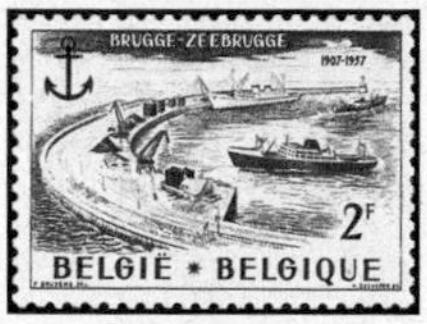

Zeebrugge Harbor A128

1957, July 6

506 A128 2fr dark blue .35 .25

50th anniv. of the completion of the port of Zeebrugge-Bruges.

Leopold I Entering Brussels, 1831 — A129

Leopold I Arriving at Belgian Border A130

1957, July 17 **Photo.**

507 A129 20c dk gray grn .25 .25
508 A130 2fr lilac .55 .25

126th anniv. of the arrival in Belgium of King Leopold I.

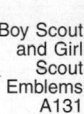

Boy Scout and Girl Scout Emblems A131

Design: 4fr, Robert Lord Baden-Powell, painted by David Jaggers, vert.

Perf. 11½

1957, July 29 **Unwmk.** **Engr.**

509 A131 80c gray .25 .25
510 A131 4fr light green 1.10 .45

Cent. of the birth of Lord Baden-Powell, founder of the Boy Scout movement.

"Kneeling Woman" by Lehmbruck — A132

1957, Aug. 20 **Photo.**

511 A132 2.50fr dk blue grn 1.00 .60

4th Biennial Exposition of Sculpture, Antwerp, May 25-Sept. 15.

"United Europe" — A133

1957, Sept. 16 **Engr.** ***Perf. 11½***

512 A133 2fr dk violet brn *.50* .25
513 A133 4fr dark blue *1.50* *.35*

Europa: United Europe for peace and prosperity.

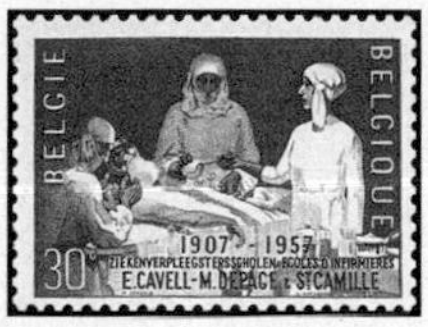

Queen Elisabeth Assisting at Operation, by Allard L'Olivier A134

Perf. 11½

1957, Nov. 23 **Unwmk.** **Engr.**

514 A134 30c rose lilac .25 .25

50th anniv. of the founding of the Edith Cavell-Marie Depage and St. Camille schools of nursing.

Post Horn and Historic Postal Insignia A135

1958, Mar. 16 **Photo.** ***Perf. 11½***

515 A135 2.50fr gray .25 .25

Postal Museum Day.

United Nations Issue

International Labor Organization A136

Allegory of UN — A137

Designs: 1fr, FAO. 2fr, World Bank. 2.50fr, UNESCO. 3fr, UN Pavilion. 5fr, ITU. 8fr, Intl. Monetary Fund. 11fr, WHO. 20fr, UPU.

Perf. 11½

1958, Apr. 17 **Unwmk.** **Engr.**

516 A136 50c gray 2.00 *2.00*
517 A136 1fr claret .30 *.35*
518 A137 1.50fr dp ultra .30 *.35*
519 A137 2fr gray brown .45 *.50*
520 A136 2.50fr olive grn .30 *.45*
521 A136 3fr grnsh blue .50 *.55*
522 A137 5fr rose lilac .35 *.40*
523 A136 8fr red brown .65 *.70*
524 A136 11fr dull lilac 1.25 *1.40*
525 A136 20fr car rose 2.00 *2.25*
Nos. 516-525,C15-C20 (16) 10.45 *10.90*

World's Fair, Brussels, Apr. 17-Oct. 19.

Postally valid only from the UN pavilion at the Brussels Fair. Proceeds went toward financing the UN exhibits.

Eugène Ysaye A138

1958, Sept. 1

526 A138 30c dk blue & plum .25 .25

Ysaye (1858-1931), violinist, composer.

Common Design Types pictured in section at front of book.

Europa Issue, 1958

Common Design Type

1958, Sept. 13 **Photo.**

Size: 24½x35mm

527 CD1 2.50fr brt red & blue *.75* .25
528 CD1 5fr brt blue & red *3.00* *.35*

Issued to show the European Postal Union at the service of European integration.

Universal Declaration of Human Rights, 10th Anniv. — A140

Infant and UN Emblem.

1958, Dec. 10 **Engr.**

529 A140 2.50fr blue gray .30 .25

Charles V , Jean-Baptiste of Thurn and Taxis — A141

1959, Mar. 15 **Unwmk.**

530 A141 2.50fr green .40 .25

Issued for the Day of the Stamp. Design from painting by J.-E. van den Bussche.

NATO Emblem — A142

1959, Apr. 3 **Photo.** ***Perf. 11½***

531 A142 2.50fr dp red & dk bl .40 .25
532 A142 5fr emerald & dk bl 1.10 *.50*

10th anniv. of NATO. See No. 720.

City Hall, Audenarde — A143

1959, Aug. 17 **Engr.**

533 A143 2.50fr deep claret .30 .25

Pope Adrian VI, by Jan van Scorel — A144

1959, Aug. 31 ***Perf. 11½***

534 A144 2.50fr dark red .25 .25
535 A144 5fr Prus blue .35 .25

500th anniv. of the birth of Pope Adrian VI.

Europa Issue, 1959

Common Design Type

1959, Sept. 19 **Photo.**

Size: 24x35½mm

536 CD2 2.50fr dark red *.30* .25
537 CD2 5fr brt grnsh blue *1.25* *.35*

Boeing 707 A146

Engraved and Photogravure

1959, Dec. 1 ***Perf. 11½***

538 A146 6fr dk bl gray & car 1.50 .65

Inauguration of jet flights by Sabena Airlines.

Countess of Taxis — A147

1960, Mar. 21 **Engr.** ***Perf. 11½***

539 A147 3fr dark blue .70 .25

Alexandrine de Rye, Countess of Taxis, Grand Mistress of the Netherlands Posts, 1628-1645, and day of the stamp, Mar. 21, 1960. The painting of the Countess is by Nicholas van der Eggermans.

24th Ghent Intl. Flower Exhibition — A148

40c, Indian azalea. 3fr, Begonia. 6fr, Anthurium, bromelia.

1960, Mar. 28 **Unwmk.**

540 A148 40c multicolored .25 .25
541 A148 3fr multicolored .45 .25
542 A148 6fr multicolored 1.10 .50
Nos. 540-542 (3) 1.80 1.00

Steel Workers, by Constantin Meunier — A149

Design: 3fr, The sower, field and dock workers, from "Monument to Labor," Brussels, by Constantin Meunier, horiz.

Engraved and Photogravure

1960, Apr. 30 *Perf. 11½*

543 A149 40c claret & brt red .25 .25
544 A149 3fr brown & brt red .50 .25

Socialist Party of Belgium, 75th anniv.

Congo River Boat Pilot — A150

Designs: 40c, Medical team. 1fr, Planting tree. 2fr, Sculptors. 2.50fr, Shot put. 3fr, Congolese officials. 6fr, Congolese and Belgian girls playing with doll. 8fr, Boy pointing on globe to independent Congo.

1960, June 30 **Photo.** *Perf. 11½*

Size: 35x24mm

545 A150 10c bright red .25 .25
546 A150 40c rose claret .25 .25
547 A150 1fr brt lilac .40 .25
548 A150 2fr gray green .40 .25
549 A150 2.50fr blue .80 .25
550 A150 3fr dk bl gray .80 .25

Size: 51x35mm

551 A150 6fr violet bl 1.75 .65
552 A150 8fr dk brown 6.00 4.50
Nos. 545-552 (8) 10.65 6.65

Independence of Congo.

Europa Issue, 1960

Common Design Type

1960, Sept. 17

Size: 35x24½mm

553 CD3 3fr claret *.40* .25
554 CD3 6fr gray *.85* *.30*
Nos. 553-554 (2) 1.25 .55

Children Examining Stamp and Globe — A152

1960, Oct. 1 **Photo.** *Perf. 11½*

555 A152 40c bis & blk + label .25 .25

Promoting stamp collecting among children.

H. J. W. Frère-Orban A153

Engraved and Photogravure

1960, Oct. 17 **Unwmk.**

Portrait in Brown

556 A153 10c orange yel .25 .25
557 A153 40c blue grn .25 .25
558 A153 1.50fr brt violet .70 .60
559 A153 3fr red .90 .25
Nos. 556-559 (4) 2.10 1.35

Centenary of Communal Credit Society.

King Baudouin and Queen Fabiola A154

1960, Dec. 13 **Photo.** *Perf. 11½*

Portraits in Dark Brown

560 A154 40c green .25 .25
561 A154 3fr red lilac .75 .25
562 A154 6fr dull blue 1.90 .25
Nos. 560-562 (3) 2.90 .75

Wedding of King Baudouin and Dona Fabiola de Mora y Aragon, Dec. 15, 1960.

Nos. 412, 414 Surcharged

1961-68 **Typo.** *Perf. 13½x14*

563 A108 15c on 30c gray grn .25 .25
564 A108 15c on 50c blue ('68) .25 .25
565 A108 20c on 30c gray grn .25 .25
Nos. 563-565 (3) .75 .75

No. 412 Surcharged and Precanceled

1961

566 A108 15c on 30c gray grn .90 .25
567 A108 20c on 30c gray grn 1.90 1.00

See note after No. 197.

Nicolaus Rockox, by Anthony Van Dyck — A155

Engraved and Photogravure

1961, Mar. 18 *Perf. 11½*

568 A155 3fr bister, blk & brn .35 .25

400th anniv. of the birth of Nicolaus Rockox, mayor of Antwerp.

Seal of Jan Bode, Alderman of Antwerp, 1264 — A156

1961, Apr. 16 **Photo.**

569 A156 3fr buff & brown .35 .25

Issued for Stamp Day, April 16.

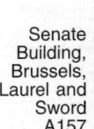

Senate Building, Brussels, Laurel and Sword A157

Engraved and Photogravure

1961, Sept. 14 **Unwmk.** *Perf. 11½*

570 A157 3fr brn & Prus grn .55 .25
571 A157 6fr dk brn & dk car 1.00 .45

50th Conference of the Interparliamentary Union, Brussels, Sept. 14-22.

Europa Issue, 1961

Common Design Type

1961, Sept. 16 **Photo.**

572 CD4 3fr yel grn & dk grn .25 .25
573 CD4 6fr org brn & blk *.50* .25

Atomic Reactor Plant, BR2, Mol — A159

Designs: 3fr, Atomic Reactor BR3, vert. 6fr, Atomic Reactor plant BR3.

1961, Nov. 8 **Unwmk.** *Perf. 11½*

574 A159 40c dk blue grn .25 .25
575 A159 3fr red lilac .25 .25
576 A159 6fr bright blue .45 .35
Nos. 574-576 (3) .95 .85

Atomic nuclear research center at Mol.

Horta Museum — A160

1962, Feb. 15 **Engr.**

577 A160 3fr red brown .30 .25

Baron Victor Horta (1861-1947), architect.

Postrider, 16th Century A161

Engraved and Photogravure

1962, Mar. 25 *Perf. 11½*

Chalky Paper

578 A161 3fr brn & slate grn .30 .25

Stamp Day. See No. 677.

Gerard Mercator (Gerhard Kremer, 1512-1594), Cartographer A162

Engraved and Photogravure

1962, Apr. 14 **Unwmk.**

579 A162 3fr sepia & gray .30 .25

Bro. Alexis-Marie Gochet (1835-1910), Geographer, Educator — A163

Portrait: 3fr, Canon Pierre-Joseph Triest (1760-1836), educator and founder of hospitals and orphanages.

1962, May 19 **Engr.** *Perf. 11½*

580 A163 2fr dark blue .25 .25
581 A163 3fr golden brown .30 .25

Europa Issue, 1962

Common Design Type

1962, Sept. 15 **Photo.**

582 CD5 3fr dp car, citron & blk .25 .25
583 CD5 6fr olive, citron & blk *.40* *.40*

Hand with Barbed Wire and Freed Hand — A165

1962, Sept. 16 **Engr. & Photo.**

584 A165 40c lt blue & blk .25 .25

Issued in memory of concentration camp victims.

Adam, by Michelangelo, Broken Chain and UN Emblem — A166

1962, Nov. 24 *Perf. 11½*

585 A166 3fr gray & blk .25 .25
586 A166 6fr lt redsh brn & dk brn .45 .30

UN Declaration of Human Rights.

Henri Pirenne (1862-1935), Historian — A167

1963, Jan. 15 **Engr.**

587 A167 3fr ultramarine .35 .25

Swordsmen and Ghent Belfry A168

3fr, Modern fencers. 6fr, Arms of the Royal and Knightly Guild of St. Michael, vert.

Engraved and Photogravure

1963, Mar. 23 **Unwmk.** *Perf. 11½*

588 A168 1fr brn red & pale bl .25 .25
589 A168 3fr dk vio & yel grn .25 .25
590 A168 6fr gray, blk, red, bl & gold .65 .35
Nos. 588-590 (3) 1.15 .85

350th anniv. of the granting of a charter to the Ghent guild of fencers.

Stagecoach A169

1963, Apr. 7

591 A169 3fr gray & ocher .25 .25

Stamp Day. See No. 678.

Hotel des Postes, Paris, Stagecoach and Stamp, 1863 A170

Perf. 11½

1963, May 7 Unwmk. Engr.

592 A170 6fr dk brn, gray & yel grn .55 .35

Cent. of the 1st Intl. Postal Conf., Paris, 1863.

"Peace," Child in Rye Field — A171

1963, May 8 Engr. & Photo.

593 A171 3fr grn, blk, yel & brn .30 .25
594 A171 6fr buff, blk, brn & org .75 .30

May 8th Movement for Peace. (On May 8, 1945, World War II ended in Europe).

Allegory and Shields of 17 Member Nations A172

1963, June 13 Unwmk. *Perf. 11½*

595 A172 6fr blue & black .55 .30

10th anniversary of the Conference of European Transport Ministers.

Seal of Union of Belgian Towns — A173

1963, June 17

596 A173 6fr grn, red, blk & gold .55 .35

Intl. Union of Municipalities, 50th anniv.

Caravelle over Brussels National Airport A174

Photogravure and Engraved

1963, Sept. 1 Unwmk. *Perf. 11½*

597 A174 3fr green & gray .30 .25

40th anniversary of SABENA airline.

Europa Issue, 1963

Common Design Type

1963, Sept. 14 Photo.

Size: 35x24mm

598 CD6 3fr blk, dl red & lt brn *.70* .25
599 CD6 6fr blk, lt bl & lt brn *.90* *.30*
Nos. 598-599 (2) 1.60 .55

Jules Destrée A176

Design: No. 601, Henry Van de Velde.

Perf. 11½

1963, Nov. 16 Unwmk. Engr.

600 A176 1fr rose lilac .25 .25
601 A176 1fr green .25 .25

Jules Destrée (1863-1936), statesman and founder of the Royal Academy of French Language and Literature, and of Henry Van de Velde (1863-1957), architect.

No. 600 incorrectly inscribed "1864."

Development of the Mail, Bas-relief — A177

1963, Nov. 23 Engr. & Photo.

602 A177 50c dl red, slate & blk .25 .25

Postal checking service, 50th anniv.

Dr. Armauer G. Hansen A178

Fight Against Leprosy: 2fr, Leprosarium. 5fr, Father Joseph Damien.

1964, Jan. 25 Unwmk. *Perf. 11½*

603 A178 1fr brown org & blk .25 .25
604 A178 2fr brown org & blk .25 .25
605 A178 5fr brown org & blk .45 .35
a. Souvenir sheet of 3, #603-605 3.00 2.75
Nos. 603-605 (3) .95 .85

No. 605a sold for 12fr.

Andreas Vesalius (1514-64), Anatomist — A179

Jules Boulvin (1855-1920), Mechanical Engineer A180

Design: 2fr, Henri Jaspar (1870-1939), statesman and lawyer.

Engraved and Photogravure

1964, Mar. 2 Unwmk. *Perf. 11½*

606 A179 50c pale grn & blk .25 .25
607 A180 1fr pale grn & blk .25 .25
608 A180 2fr pale grn & blk .25 .25
Nos. 606-608 (3) .75 .75

Postilion of Liege, 1830-40 — A181

1964, Apr. 5 Engr. *Perf. 11½*

609 A181 3fr gray black .25 .25

Issued for Stamp Day 1964.

Arms of Ostend A182

1964, May 16 Photo.

610 A182 3fr ultra, ver, gold & blk .25 .25

Millennium of Ostend.

Flame, Hammer and Globe — A183

1fr, "SI" and globe. 2fr, Flame over wavy lines.

1964, July 18 Unwmk. *Perf. 11½*

611 A183 50c dark blue & red .25 .25
612 A183 1fr dark blue & red .25 .25
613 A183 2fr dark blue & red .25 .25
Nos. 611-613 (3) .75 .75

Centenary of the First Socialist International, founded in London, Sept. 28, 1864.

Europa Issue, 1964

Common Design Type

1964, Sept. 12 Photo. *Perf. 11½*

Size: 24x35½mm

614 CD7 3fr yel grn, dk car & gray *.50* .25
615 CD7 6fr car rose, yel grn & bl *.90* .35

Benelux Issue

King Baudouin, Queen Juliana and Grand Duchess Charlotte — A185

1964, Oct. 12

616 A185 3fr olive, lt grn & mar .40 .25

20th anniv. of the customs union of Belgium, Netherlands and Luxembourg.

Hand, Round & Pear-shaped Diamonds — A186

1965, Jan. 23 Unwmk. *Perf. 11½*

617 A186 2fr ultra, dp car & blk .25 .25

Diamond Exhibition "Diamantexpo," Antwerp, July 10-28, 1965.

Symbols of Textile Industry — A187

1965, Jan. 25 Photo.

618 A187 1fr blue, red & blk .25 .25

Eighth textile industry exhibition "Textirama," Ghent, Jan. 29-Feb. 2, 1965.

Vriesia — A188

Designs: 2fr, Echinocactus. 3fr, Stapelia.

1965, Feb. 13 Engr. & Photo.

619 A188 1fr multicolored .25 .25
620 A188 2fr multicolored .25 .25
621 A188 3fr multicolored .25 .25
a. Souvenir sheet of 3, #619-621 1.50 1.50
Nos. 619-621 (3) .75 .75

25th Ghent International Flower Exhibition, Apr. 24-May 3, 1965.

No. 621a was issued Apr. 26 and sold for 20fr.

Paul Hymans (1865-1941), Belgian Foreign Minister, First President of the League of Nations — A189

1965, Feb. 24 Engr. *Perf. 11½*

622 A189 1fr dull purple .25 .25

Peter Paul Rubens — A190

2fr, Frans Snyders. 3fr, Adam van Noort. 6fr, Anthony Van Dyck. 8fr, Jacob Jordaens.

1965, Mar. 15 Photo. & Engr.

Portraits in Sepia

623 A190 1fr carmine rose .25 .25
624 A190 2fr blue green .25 .25
625 A190 3fr plum .25 .25
626 A190 6fr deep carmine .50 .25
627 A190 8fr dark blue .65 .40
Nos. 623-627 (5) 1.90 1.40

Issued to commemorate the founding of the General Savings and Pensions Bank.

Sir Rowland Hill as Philatelist — A191

1965, Mar. 27 Engr. *Perf. 11½*

628 A191 50c blue green .25 .25

Issued to publicize youth philately. The design is from a mural by J. E. Van den Bussche in the General Post Office, Brussels.

Postmaster, c. 1833 — A192

1965, Apr. 26 Unwmk. *Perf. 11½*

629 A192 3fr emerald .25 .25

Issued for Stamp Day.

Telephone, Globe and Teletype Paper — A193

1965, May 8 **Photo.**
630 A193 2fr dull purple & blk .25 .25

Cent. of the ITU.

Staircase, Affligem Abbey — A194

1965, May 27 **Engr.**
631 A194 1fr gray blue .25 .25

St. Jean Berchmans and his Birthplace A195

1965, May 27 **Engr. & Photo.**
632 A195 2fr dk brn & red brn .25 .25

Issued to honor St. Jean Berchmans (1599-1621), Jesuit "Saint of the Daily Life."

TOC H Lamp and Arms of Poperinge — A196

1965, June 19 **Photo.** ***Perf. 11½***
633 A196 3fr ol bis, blk & car .25 .25

50th anniv. of the founding of Talbot House in Poperinge, which served British soldiers in World War I, and where the TOC H Movement began (Christian Social Service; TOC H is army code for Poperinge Center).

Belgian Farmers' Association (Boerenbond), 75th Anniv. — A197

50c, Farmer with tractor. 3fr, Farmer with horse-drawn roller.

Engraved and Photogravure

1965, July 17 **Unwmk.** ***Perf. 11½***
634 A197 50c bl, ol, bis brn & blk .25 .25
635 A197 3fr bl, ol grn, ol & blk .25 .25

Europa Issue, 1965

Common Design Type

1965, Sept. 25 ***Perf. 11½***

Size: 35½x24mm

636 CD8 1fr dl rose & blk .25 .25
637 CD8 3fr grnsh gray & blk .25 .25

Leopold I (1790-1865) A199

1965, Nov. 13 **Engr.**
638 A199 3fr sepia .25 .25
639 A199 6fr bright violet .55 .40

The designs of the vignettes are similar to A4 and A5.

Joseph Lebeau (1794-1865), Foreign Minister — A200

1965, Nov. 13 **Photo.**
640 A200 1fr multicolored .25 .25

Tourist Issue

Grapes and Houses, Hoeilaart A201

Bridge and Castle, Huy A202

No. 643, British War Memorial, Ypres. No. 644, Castle Spontin. No. 645, City Hall, Louvain. No. 646, Ourthe Valley. No. 647, Romanesque Cathedral, gothic fountain, Nivalles. No. 648, Water mill, Kasterlee. No. 649, City Hall, Cloth Guild and Statue of Margarethe of Austria, Malines. No. 650, Town Hall, Lier. No. 651, Castle Bouillon. No. 652, Fountain and Kursaal Spa. No. 653, Windmill, Bokrijk. No. 654, Mountain road, Vielsalm. No. 655, View of Furnes. No. 656, City Hall and Belfry, Mons. No. 657, St. Martin's Church, Aalst. No. 658, Abbey and fountain, St. Hubert.

1965-71 **Engr.** ***Perf. 11½***
641 A201 50c vio bl, lt bl & yel grn .25 .25
642 A202 50c sl grn, lt bl & red brn .25 .25
643 A202 1fr grn, lt bl, sal & brn .25 .25
644 A202 1fr ind, lt bl & ol .25 .25
645 A201 1fr brt rose lil, lt bl & blk .25 .25
646 A202 1fr blk, grnsh bl & ol .25 .25
647 A201 1.50fr sl, sky bl & bis .25 .25
648 A202 1.50fr blk, bl & ol .25 .25
649 A202 1.50fr dk bl & buff .25 .25
650 A201 2fr brn, lt bl & ind .25 .25
651 A202 2fr dk brn, grn & ocher .25 .25
652 A202 2fr bl, brt grn & blk .25 .25
653 A202 2fr blk, lt bl & yel .25 .25
654 A202 2fr blk, lt bl & yel grn .25 .25
655 A202 2fr car, lt bl & dk brn .25 .25
656 A201 2.50fr vio, buff & blk .25 .25
657 A201 2.50fr vio, lt bl, blk & ol .25 .25
658 A201 2.50fr vio bl & yel .25 .25
Nos. 641-658 (18) 4.50 4.50

Issued: Nos. 641-642, 11/13/65; Nos. 643-644, 7/15/67; Nos. 645-646, 12/16/68; Nos. 647-648, 7/6/70; Nos. 649, 656, 12/11/71; Nos. 650-651, 11/11/66; Nos. 652-653, 6/24/68; Nos. 654-655, 9/6/69; Nos. 657-658, 9/11/71.

Queen Elisabeth Type of Semi-Postal Issue, 1956

1965, Dec. 23 **Photo.** ***Perf. 11½***
659 SP305 3fr dark gray .25 .25

Queen Elisabeth (1876-1965).

A dark frame has been added in design of No. 659; 1956 date has been changed to 1965; inscription in bottom panel is Koningin Elisabeth Reine Elisabeth 3F.

"Peace on Earth" A203

Arms of Pope Paul VI — A204

1fr, "Looking toward a Better Future" (family, new buildings, sun & landscape).

1966, Feb. 12 **Photo.** ***Perf. 11½***
660 A203 50c multicolored .25 .25
661 A203 1fr ocher, blk & bl .25 .25
662 A204 3fr gray, gold, car & blk .25 .25
Nos. 660-662 (3) .75 .75

75th anniv. of the encyclical by Pope Leo XIII "Rerum Novarum," which proclaimed the general principles for the organization of modern industrial society.

Rural Mailman, 19th Century — A205

1966, Apr. 17 **Photo.** **Unwmk.**
663 A205 3fr blk, dl yel & pale lil .25 .25

Stamp Day. For overprint see No. 673.

Iguanodon, Natural Science Institute A206

Arend-Roland Comet, Observatory A207

Designs: No. 665, Ancestral head and spiral pattern, Kasai; Central Africa Museum. No. 666, Snowflakes, Meteorological Institute. No. 667, Seal of Charles V, Royal Archives. No. 668, Medieval scholar, Royal Library. 8fr, Satellite and rocket, Space Aeronautics Institute.

1966, May 28 **Engr. & Photo.**
664 A206 1fr green & blk .25 .25
665 A206 2fr gray, blk & brn org .25 .25
666 A206 2fr blue, blk & yel .25 .25
667 A207 3fr dp rose, blk & gold .25 .25
668 A207 3fr multicolored .25 .25
669 A207 6fr ultra, yel & blk .35 .25
670 A207 8fr multicolored .55 .40
Nos. 664-670 (7) 2.15 1.90

National scientific heritage.

Atom Symbol and Retort — A208

Engraved and Photogravure

1966, July 9 **Unwmk.** ***Perf. 11½***
671 A208 6fr gray, blk & red .40 .25

Issued to publicize the European chemical plant, EUROCHEMIC, at Mol.

August Kekulé, Benzene Ring — A209

1966, July 9
672 A209 3fr brt blue & blk .25 .25

August Friedrich Kekule (1829-96), chemistry professor at University of Ghent (1858-67).

No. 663 Overprinted with Red and Blue Emblem

1966, July 11 **Photo.**
673 A205 3fr multicolored .25 .25

19th Intl. P.T.T. Cong., Brussels, July 11-15.

Rik Wouters (1882-1916), Self-portrait A210

1966, Sept. 6 **Photo.** ***Perf. 11½***
674 A210 60c multicolored .25 .25

Europa Issue, 1966

Common Design Type

1966, Sept. 24 **Engr.** ***Perf. 11½***

Size: 24x34mm

675 CD9 3fr brt green .25 .25
676 CD9 6fr brt rose lilac *.55* *.25*

Types of 1962-1963 Overprinted in Black and Red

1966, Nov. 11 **Engr. & Photo.**
677 A161 60c sepia & grnsh gray .25 .25
678 A169 3fr sepia & pale bister .25 .25

75th anniv., Royal Fed. of Phil. Circles of Belgium. Overprint shows emblem of F.I.P.

Lions Emblem — A214

1967, Jan. 14 *Perf. 11½*
679 A214 3fr gray, blk & bl .25 .25
680 A214 6fr lt green, blk & vio .40 .25

Lions Club Intl., 50th anniv.

Pistol by Leonhard Cleuter A215

1967, Feb. 11 **Photo.**
681 A215 2fr dp car, blk & cream .25 .25

Fire Arms Museum in Liege.

International Tourist Year Emblem A216

1967, Feb. 11
682 A216 6fr ver, ultra & blk .50 .25

International Tourist Year, 1967.

Birches and Trientalis A217

Design: No. 684, Dunes, beach grass, privet and blue thistles.

1967, Mar. 11 **Photo.** *Perf. 11½*
683 A217 1fr multicolored .25 .25
684 A217 1fr multicolored .25 .25

Issued to publicize the nature preserves at Hautes Fagnes and Westhoek.

Paul Emile Janson(1872-1944), Lawyer, Statesman — A218

1967, Apr. 15 **Engr.** *Perf. 11½*
685 A218 10fr blue .80 .25

Postilion A219

1967, Apr. 16 **Photo. & Engr.**
686 A219 3fr rose red & claret .25 .25

Issued for Stamp Day, 1967.

Inscribed: "FITCE"

1967, June 24 *Perf. 11½*
687 A219 10fr ultra, sep & emer .80 .45

Issued to commemorate the meeting of the Federation of Common Market Telecommunications Engineers, Brussels, July 3-8.

Europa Issue, 1967
Common Design Type

1967, May 2 **Photo.**
Size: 24x35mm
688 CD10 3fr blk, lt bl & red .25 .25
689 CD10 6fr blk, grnsh gray & yel .80 .30

Flax, Shuttle and Mills — A221

1967, June 3 **Photo.** *Perf. 11½*
690 A221 6fr tan & multi .40 .25

Belgian linen industry.

Old Kursaal, Ostend — A222

1967, June 3 **Engr. & Photo.**
691 A222 2fr dk brn, lt bl & yel .25 .25

700th anniversary of Ostend as a city.

Charles Plisnier and Lodewijk de Haet Foundations A223

Designs: No. 692, Caesar Crossing Rubicon, 15th Century Tapestry. No. 693, Emperor Maximilian Killing a Boar, 16th cent. tapestry.

1967, Sept. 2 **Photo.** *Perf. 11½*
692 A223 1fr multicolored .25 .25
693 A223 1fr multicolored .25 .25

Universities of Ghent and Liège, 150th Anniv. — A224

Arms of Universities: No. 694, Ghent. No. 695, Liege.

Engraved and Photogravure

1967, Sept. 30 *Perf. 11½*
694 A224 3fr gray & multi .25 .25
695 A224 3fr gray & multi .25 .25

Princess Margaret of York — A225

1967, Sept. 30 **Photo.**
696 A225 6fr multicolored .45 .30

British Week, Sept. 28-Oct. 2.

"Virga Jesse," Hasselt — A226

1967, Nov. 11 **Engr.** *Perf. 11½*
697 A226 1fr slate blue .25 .25

Christmas, 1967.

Hand Guarding Worker — A227

1968, Feb. 3 **Photo.** *Perf. 11½*
698 A227 3fr multicolored .25 .25

Issued to publicize industrial safety.

Military Mailman, 1916, by James Thiriar — A228

Engraved and Photogravure

1968, Mar. 17 *Perf. 11½*
699 A228 3fr sepia, lt bl & brn .25 .25

Issued for Stamp Day, 1968.

View of Grammont and Seal of Baudouin VI — A229

Historic Sites: 3fr, Theux-Franchimont fortress, sword and seal. 6fr, Neolithic cave and artifacts, Spiennes. 10fr, Roman oil lamp and St. Medard's Church, Wervik.

1968, Apr. 13 **Photo.** *Perf. 11½*
700 A229 2fr bl, blk, lil & rose .25 .25
701 A229 3fr orange, blk & car .25 .25
702 A229 6fr ultra, ind & bis .40 .25
703 A229 10fr tan, blk, yel & gray .65 .30
Nos. 700-703 (4) 1.55 1.05

Stamp of 1866, No. 23 — A230

1968, Apr. 13 **Engr.** *Perf. 13*
704 A230 1fr black .25 .25

Centenary of the Malines Stamp Printery.

Europa Issue, 1968
Common Design Type

1968, Apr. 27 **Photo.** *Perf. 11½*
Size: 35x24mm
705 CD11 3fr dl grn, gold & blk .30 .25
706 CD11 6fr carmine, sil & blk .95 .25

St. Laurent Abbey, Liège — A232

Designs: 3fr, Gothic Church, Lisseweghe. No. 709. Barges in Zandvliet locks. No. 710, Ship in Neuzen lock, Ghent Canal. 10fr, Ronquieres canal ship lift.

Engraved and Photogravure

1968, Sept. 7 *Perf. 11½*
707 A232 2fr ultra, gray ol & sep .25 .25
708 A232 3fr ol bis, gray & sep .25 .25
709 A232 6fr ind, brt bl & sep .40 .25
710 A232 6fr black, grnsh bl & ol .35 .25
711 A232 10fr bister, brt bl & sep .60 .30
Nos. 707-711 (5) 1.85 1.30

No. 710 issued Dec. 14 for opening of lock at Neuzen, Netherlands.

Christmas Candle — A233

1968, Dec. 7 *Perf. 11½*
712 A233 1fr multicolored .25 .25

Christmas, 1968.

St. Albertus Magnus — A234

1969, Feb. 15 **Engr.** *Perf. 11½*
713 A234 2fr sepia .25 .25

The Church of St. Paul in Antwerp (16th century) was destroyed by fire in Apr. 1968.

Ruins of Aulne Abbey, Gozee — A235

1969, Feb. 15 **Engr. & Photo.**
714 A235 3fr brt pink & blk .25 .25

Aulne Abbey was destroyed in 1794 during the French Revolution.

The Travelers, Roman Sculpture — A236

1969, Mar. 15 Engr. *Perf. 11½*
715 A236 2fr violet brown .25 .25

2,000th anniversary of city of Arlon.

Broodjes Chapel, Antwerp — A237

1969, Mar. 15 Engr. & Photo.
716 A237 3fr gray & blk .25 .25

150th anniv. of public education in Antwerp.

Post Office Train — A238

1969, Apr. 13 Photo. *Perf. 11½*
717 A238 3fr multicolored .25 .25

Issued for Stamp Day.

Europa Issue, 1969
Common Design Type

1969, Apr. 26 Size: 35x24mm
718 CD12 3fr lt grn, brn & blk *.25* .25
719 CD12 6fr sal, rose car & blk *.50* *.25*

NATO Type of 1959 Redrawn and Dated "1949-1969"

1969, May 31 Photo. *Perf. 11½*
720 A142 6fr org brn & ultra .45 .35

20th anniv. of NATO. No. 720 inscribed Belgique-Belgie and OTAN-NAVO.

Construction Workers, by F. Leger — A240

1969, May 31
721 A240 3fr multicolored .25 .25

50th anniversary of the ILO.

World Bicycling Road Championships, Terlaemen to Zolder, Aug. 10. — A241

1969, July 5 Photo. *Perf. 11½*
722 A241 6fr Bicyclist .50 .30

Ribbon in Benelux Colors — A242

1969, Sept. 6 Photo. *Perf. 11½*
723 A242 3fr blk, red, ultra & yel .25 .25

Signing of the customs union of Belgium, Netherlands & Luxembourg, 25th anniv.

Annevoie Garden and Pascali Rose A243

No. 725, Lochristi Garden and begonia.

1969, Sept. 6
724 A243 2fr multicolored .25 .25
725 A243 2fr multicolored .25 .25

Armstrong, Collins, Aldrin and Map Showing Tranquillity Base — A245

1969, Sept. 20 Photo.
726 A245 6fr black .45 .30

See note after Algeria No. 427. See No. B846.

Wounded Veteran — A246

1969, Oct. 11 Engr. *Perf. 11½*
727 A246 1fr blue gray .25 .25

Natl. war veterans' aid organization (O.N.I.G.). The design is similar to type SP10.

Mailman — A247

1969, Oct. 18 Photo.
728 A247 1fr deep rose & multi .25 .25

Issued to publicize youth philately. Design by Danielle Saintenoy, 14.

Kennedy Tunnel Under the Schelde, Antwerp A248

6fr, Three highways crossing near Loncin.

1969, Nov. 8 Engr. *Perf. 11½*
729 A248 3fr multicolored .25 .25
730 A248 6fr multicolored .40 .35

Issued to publicize the John F. Kennedy Tunnel under the Schelde and the Walloon auto route and interchange near Loncin.

Henry Carton de Wiart, by Gaston Geleyn — A249

1969, Nov. 8
731 A249 6fr sepia .50 .35

Count de Wiart (1869-1951), statesman.

The Census at Bethlehem (detail), by Peter Brueghel A250

1969, Dec. 13 Photo.
732 A250 1.50fr multicolored .25 .25

Christmas, 1969.

Symbols of Bank's Activity, 100fr Coin A251

1969, Dec. 13 Engr. & Photo.
733 A251 3.50fr lt ultra, blk & sil .25 .25

50th anniv. of the Industrial Credit Bank (Societe nationale de credit a l'industrie).

Camellia — A252

1970, Jan. 31 Photo. *Perf. 11½*
734 A252 1.50fr shown .25 .25
735 A252 2.50fr Water lily .25 .25
736 A252 3.50fr Azalea .30 .25
a. Souvenir sheet of 3, #734-736 2.00 1.75
Nos. 734-736 (3) .80 .75

Ghent Int'l Flower Exhibition. No. 736a was issued Apr. 25 and sold for 25fr.

Beeches in Botanical Garden — A253

1970, Mar. 7 Engr. & Photo.
737 A253 3.50fr shown .25 .25
738 A253 7fr Birches .50 .30

European Nature Conservation Year.

Youth Stamp Day — A254

1970, Apr. 4 Photo.
739 A254 1.50fr Mailman .25 .25

New UPU Headquarters and Monument, Bern — A255

1970, Apr. 12 Engr. & Photo.
740 A255 3.50fr grn & lt grn .30 .25

Opening of the new UPU Headquarters, Bern.

Europa Issue, 1970
Common Design Type

1970, May 1 Photo. *Perf. 11½*
Size: 35x24mm
741 CD13 3.50fr rose cl, yel & blk *.30* .25
742 CD13 7fr ultra, pink & blk *.80* *.30*

Cooperative Alliance Emblem — A257

1970, June 27 Photo. *Perf. 11½*
743 A257 7fr black & org .50 .25

Intl. Cooperative Alliance, 75th anniv.

Ship in Ghent Terneuzen Lock, Zelzate A258

Design: No. 745, Clock Tower, Virton, vert.

1970, June 27 Engr. & Photo.
744 A258 2.50fr indigo & lt bl .25 .25
745 A258 2.50fr dk pur & ocher .25 .25

King Baudouin — A259

1970-80 Engr. *Perf. 11½*

746	A259	1.75fr	green ('71)	.25	.25
747	A259	2.25fr	gray grn ('72)	.35	.25
748	A259	2.50fr	gray grn ('74)	.25	.25
749	A259	3fr	emerald ('73)	.25	.25
750	A259	3.25fr	violet brn ('75)	.25	.25
751	A259	3.50fr	orange brn	.25	.25
752	A259	3.50fr	brown ('71)	.40	.25
753	A259	4fr	blue ('72)	.35	.25
754	A259	4.50fr	brown ('72)	.30	.25
755	A259	4.50fr	grnsh bl ('74)	.35	.25
756	A259	5fr	lilac ('72)	.40	.25
757	A259	6fr	rose car ('72)	.50	.25
758	A259	6.50fr	vio blk ('74)	.45	.25
759	A259	7fr	ver ('71)	.55	.25
760	A259	7.50fr	brt pink ('75)	.55	.25
761	A259	8fr	black ('72)	.60	.25
762	A259	9fr	ol bis ('71)	.80	.25
763	A259	9fr	red brn ('80)	.75	.25
764	A259	10fr	rose car ('71)	.80	.25
765	A259	11fr	gray ('76)	.85	.25
766	A259	12fr	Prus bl ('72)	.90	.25
767	A259	13fr	slate ('75)	1.00	.25
768	A259	14fr	gray grn ('76)	1.10	.25
769	A259	15fr	lt vio ('71)	1.00	.25
770	A259	16fr	green ('77)	1.75	.25
771	A259	17fr	dull mag ('75)	1.25	.25
772	A259	18fr	steel bl ('71)	1.25	.25

773	A259	18fr grnsh bl ('80)	1.75	.25
774	A259	20fr vio bl ('71)	1.25	.25
775	A259	22fr black ('74)	1.75	1.50
776	A259	22fr lt grn ('79)	1.60	.40
777	A259	25fr lilac ('75)	1.75	.25
778	A259	30fr ocher ('72)	2.00	.25
779	A259	35fr emer ('80)	3.25	.30
780	A259	40fr dk blue ('77)	4.00	.30
781	A259	45fr brown ('80)	4.75	.45

Perf. 12½x13½

Photo.

Size: 22x17mm

782	A259	3fr emerald ('73)	1.10	.75
a.		Booklet pane of 4 (#782 and 3 #783) + labels	10.00	
783	A259	4fr blue ('73)	.50	.50
784	A259	4.50fr grnsh bl ('75)	.40	.30
785	A259	5fr lilac ('73)	.35	.25
a.		Booklet pane of 4 + labels	2.75	
786	A259	6fr carmine ('78)	.40	.25
787	A259	6.50fr dull pur ('75)	.45	.25
788	A259	8fr gray ('78)	.55	.25
		Nos. 746-788 (43)	43.35	13.25

No. 751 issued Sept. 7, 1970, King Baudouin's 40th birthday, and is inscribed "1930-1970." Dates are omitted on other stamps of type A259.

Nos. 754, 756 also issued in coils in 1973 and Nos. 757, 761 in 1978, with black control number on back of every fifth stamp.

Nos. 782-788 issued in booklets only. Nos. 782, 784 have one straight-edge, Nos. 786, 788 have two. The rest have one or two. Stamps in the panes are tete-beche. Each pane has two labels showing Belgian Postal emblem with a large selvage with postal code instructions. Nos. 786, 788 not luminescent.

See designs M2, O4. See Nos. 432a, 432b, 977a, 977b.

UN Headquarters, NY — A260

1970, Sept. 12 **Engr. & Photo.**

789 A260 7fr dk brn & Prus bl .50 .25

25th anniversary of the United Nations.

25th International Fair at Ghent, Sept. 12-27 — A261

1970, Sept. 19

790 A261 1.50fr Fair emblem .25 .25

Queen Fabiola — A262

1970, Sept. 19

791 A262 3.50fr lt blue & blk .25 .25

Issued to publicize the Queen Fabiola Foundation for Mental Health.

The Mason, by Georges Minne — A263

1970, Oct. 17 ***Perf. 11½***

792 A263 3.50fr dull yel & sep .25 .25

50th anniv. of the National Housing Society.

Man, Woman and City — A264

1970, Oct. 17 **Photo.**

793 A264 2.50fr black & multi .25 .25

Social Security System, 25th anniv.

Madonna with the Grapes, by Jean Gossaert — A265

1970, Nov. 14 **Engr.** ***Perf. 11½***

794 A265 1.50fr dark brown .25 .25

Christmas 1970.

Arms of Eupen, Malmédy and Saint-Vith A266

Engraved and Photogravure

1970, Dec. 12 ***Perf. 11½***

795 A266 7fr sepia & dk brn .40 .25

The 50th anniversary of the return of the districts of Eupen, Malmédy and Saint-Vith.

Automatic Telephone — A267

1971, Jan. 16 **Photo.** ***Perf. 11½***

796 A267 1.50fr multicolored .25 .25

Automatization of Belgian telephone system.

50th Automobile Show, Brussels, Jan. 19-31 A268

1971, Jan. 16

797 A268 2.50fr "Auto" .25 .25

Belgian Touring Club, 75th Anniv. — A269

1971, Feb. 13

798 A269 3.50fr Club emblem .25 .25

Tournai Cathedral A270

1971, Feb. 13 **Engr.**

799 A270 7fr bright blue .40 .30

Cathedral of Tournai, 8th centenary.

"The Letter Box," by T. Lobrichon — A271

1971, Mar. 13 **Engr.** ***Perf. 11½***

800 A271 1.50fr dark brown .25 .25

Youth philately.

Albert I, Jules Destrée and Academy — A272

Engraved and Photogravure

1971, Apr. 17 ***Perf. 11½***

801 A272 7fr gray & blk .55 .35

Founding of the Royal Academy of Language and French Literature, 50th anniv.

Stamp Day — A273

1971, Apr. 25

802 A273 3.50fr Mailman .30 .25

Europa Issue, 1971

Common Design Type

1971, May 1 **Photo.**

Size: 35x24mm

803	CD14	3.50fr olive & blk	*.55*	.25
804	CD14	7fr dk ol grn & blk	*.75*	*.30*

Radar Ground Station A275

1971, May 15 **Photo.** ***Perf. 11½***

805 A275 7fr multicolored .55 .35

3rd World Telecommunications Day.

Antarctic Explorer, Ship and Penguins — A276

1971, June 19 **Photo.** ***Perf. 11½***

806 A276 10fr multicolored .60 .45

Tenth anniversary of the Antarctic Treaty pledging peaceful uses of and scientific cooperation in Antarctica.

Abbey of Notre Dame, Orval, 900th Anniv. — A277

1971, June 26 **Engr.** ***Perf. 11½***

807 A277 2.50fr Orval Abbey .25 .25

Georges Hubin (1863-1947), Socialist Leader, Minister of State — A278

1971, June 26 **Engr. & Photo.**

808 A278 1.50fr vio bl & blk .25 .25

Mr. and Mrs. Goliath, the Giants of Ath — A279

View of Ghent A280

1971, Aug. 7 **Photo.**

809 A279 2.50fr multicolored .25 .25

Engr.

810 A280 2.50fr gray brown .25 .25

Test Tubes and Insulin Molecular Diagram — A281

1971, Aug. 7 **Photo.**
811 A281 10fr lt gray & multi .70 .45

50th anniversary of the discovery of insulin.

Family and "50" — A283

1971, Sept. 11 **Photo.**
812 A283 1.50fr green & multi .25 .25

Belgian Large Families League, 50th anniv.

Achaemenidaen Tomb, Buzpar, and Persian Coat of Arms — A284

Engraved and Photogravure

1971, Oct. 2 ***Perf. 11½***
813 A284 7fr multicolored .55 .35

2500th anniversary of the founding of the Persian empire by Cyrus the Great.

Dr. Jules Bordet (1870-1945), Serologist, Immunologist A285

Portrait: No. 815, Stijn Streuvels(1871-1945), Novelist (pen name Frank Lateur).

1971, Oct. 2 **Engr.**
814 A285 3.50fr slate green .25 .25
815 A285 3.50fr dark brown .25 .25

Flight into Egypt, Anonymous A286

1971, Nov. 13 **Photo.**
816 A286 1.50fr multicolored .25 .25

Christmas 1971.

Federation of Belgian Industries (FIB), 25th Anniv. — A287

1971, Nov. 13
817 A287 3.50fr black, ultra & gold .30 .25

International Book Year 1972 — A288

1972, Feb. 19
818 A288 7fr bister, blk & bl .55 .30

Coins of Belgium and Luxembourg A289

1972, Feb. 19 **Engr. & Photo.**
819 A289 1.50fr orange, blk & sil .25 .25

Economic Union of Belgium and Luxembourg, 50th anniversary.

Traffic Signal and Road Signs — A290

1972, Feb. 19 **Photo.**
820 A290 3.50fr blue & multi .25 .25

Via Secura (road safety), 25th anniversary.

Belgica '72 Emblem A291

1972, Mar. 27
821 A291 3.50fr choc, bl & lil .30 .25

International Philatelic Exhibition, Brussels, June 24-July 9.

"Your Heart is your Health" — A292

1972, Mar. 27
822 A292 7fr blk, gray, red & bl .50 .30

World Health Day.

Auguste Vermeylen (1872-1945), Flemish Writer, Educator — A293

Portrait, by Isidore Opsomer.

1972, Mar. 27
823 A293 2.50fr multicolored .25 .25

Stamp Day 1972 — A294

1972, Apr. 23
824 A294 3.50fr Astronaut on Moon .30 .25

Europa Issue 1972

Common Design Type

1972, Apr. 29 **Size: 24x35mm**
825 CD15 3.50fr lt blue & multi *.35* .25
826 CD15 7fr rose & multi *.60* *.30*

"Freedom of the Press" — A296

1972, May 13 **Photo.** ***Perf. 11½***
827 A296 2.50fr multicolored .25 .25

50th anniv. of the BELGA news information agency and 25th Congress of the Intl. Federation of Newspaper Editors (F.I.E.J.), Brussels, May 15-19.

Freight Cars with Automatic Coupling A297

1972, June 3
828 A297 7fr blue & multi .50 .30

Intl. Railroad Union, 50th anniv.

View of Couvin — A298

No. 830, Aldeneik Church, Maaseik, vert.

1972, June 24 **Engr.** ***Perf. 13½x14***
829 A298 2.50fr bl, vio brn & sl grn .25 .25
830 A298 2.50fr dk brown & bl .25 .25

Beatrice, by Gustave de Smet — A299

1972, Sept. 9 **Photo.** ***Perf. 11½***
831 A299 3fr multicolored .30 .25

Youth philately.

Radar Station, Intelsat 4 — A300

1972, Sept. 16
832 A300 3.50fr lt bl, sil & blk .30 .25

Opening of the Lessive satellite earth station.

Frans Masereel(1889-1972), Wood Engraver — A301

1972, Oct. 21
833 A301 4.50fr Self-portrait .35 .25

Adoration of the Kings, by Felix Timmermans A302

1972, Nov. 11 **Photo.** ***Perf. 11½***
834 A302 3.50fr black & multi .30 .25

Christmas 1972.

Maria Theresa, Anonymous A303

1972, Dec. 16 **Photo.** ***Perf. 11½***
835 A303 2fr multicolored .25 .25

200th anniversary of the Belgian Academy of Science, Literature and Art, founded by Empress Maria Theresa.

WMO Emblem, Meteorological Institute, Ukkel — A304

1973, Mar. 24 **Photo.** ***Perf. 11½***
836 A304 9fr blue & multi .70 .35

Cent. of intl. meteorological cooperation.

Natl. Industrial Fire Prevention Campaign — A305

1973, Mar. 24
837 A305 2fr "Fire" .25 .25

Man and WHO Emblem — A306

1973, Apr. 7
838 A306 8fr dk red, ocher & blk .50 .35

25th anniv. of WHO.

Europa Issue 1973
Common Design Type

1973, Apr. 28 Size: 35x24mm
839 CD16 4.50fr org brn, vio bl & yel *.35 .25*
840 CD16 8fr olive, dk bl & yel *.65 .40*

Thurn and Taxis Courier — A308

Engraved and Photogravure
1973, Apr. 28 ***Perf. 11½***
841 A308 4.50fr black & red brn .35 .25

Stamp Day.

Arrows Circling Globe — A309

1973, May 12 Photo.
842 A309 3.50fr dp ocher & multi .30 .25

5th International Telecommunications Day.

Workers' Sports Exhibition Poster, Ghent, 1913 A310

1973, May 12
843 A310 4.50fr multicolored .35 .25

60th anniversary of the International Workers' Sports Movement.

Fair Emblem A311

1973, May 12 Photo. ***Perf. 11½***
844 A311 4.50fr multicolored .35 .25

25th International Fair, Liege, May 12-27.

DC-10 and 1923 Biplane over Brussels Airport — A312

Design: 10fr, Tips biplane, 1908.

1973, May 19 Engr. & Photo.
845 A312 8fr gray bl, blk & ultra .65 .40
846 A312 10fr grn, lt bl & blk .80 .45

50th anniv. of SABENA, Belgian airline (8fr) and 25th anniv. of the "Vieilles Tiges" Belgian flying pioneers' society (10fr).

Adolphe Sax and Tenor Saxophone A313

1973, Sept. 15 Photo.
847 A313 9fr green, blk & bl .60 .30

Adolphe Sax (1814-1894), inventor of saxophone.

Fresco from Bathhouse, Ostend — A314

1973, Sept. 15
848 A314 4.50fr multicolored .35 .25

Year of the Spa.

St. Nicholas Church, Eupen — A315

No. 850, Town Hall, Leau. No. 851, Aarshot Church. No. 852, Chimay Castle. No. 853, Gemmenich Border: Belgium, Germany, Netherlands. No. 854, St. Monan and church, Nassogne. No. 855, Church tower, Dottignes. No. 856, Grand-Place, Sint-Truiden.

1973-75 Engr. ***Perf. 13***
849 A315 2fr plum, sep & lt vio .25 .25
850 A315 3fr black, lt bl & mar .50 .25
851 A315 3fr brn blk & yel .30 .25
852 A315 4fr grnsh blk & grnsh bl .35 .25
853 A315 4fr grnsh blk & bl .40 .25
854 A315 4fr grnsh blk & bl .40 .25
855 A315 4.50fr multicolored .50 .25
856 A315 5fr multicolored .50 .25
Nos. 849-856 (8) 3.20 2.00

Nos. 851, 855 not luminescent. Nos. 850, 852-854, 856 horiz.

Charley, by Henri Evenepoel — A316

1973, Oct. 13 Photo. ***Perf. 11½***
857 A316 3fr multicolored .25 .25

Youth philately.

Luminescent Paper

Starting with No. 858, all stamps are on luminescent paper unless otherwise noted.

Jean-Baptiste Moens — A317

1973, Oct. 13 Engr. & Photo.
858 A317 10fr multi + label .80 .45

50th anniversary of the Belgian Stamp Dealers' Association. Printed in sheets of 12 stamps and 12 labels showing association emblem.

Adoration of the Shepherds, by Hugo van der Goes — A318

1973, Nov. 17 Engr. ***Perf. 11½***
859 A318 4fr blue .30 .25

Christmas 1973.

Louis Pierard, by M. I. Ianchelevici A319

1973, Nov. 17 Engr. & Photo.
860 A319 4fr vermilion & buff .30 .25

Louis Pierard (1886-1952), journalist, member of Parliament.

Highway, Automobile Club Emblem A320

1973, Nov. 17 Photo.
861 A320 5fr yellow & multi .40 .25

Flemish Automobile Club, 50th anniv.

Early Microphone, Emblem of Radio Belgium — A321

1973, Nov. 24 Engr. & Photo.
862 A321 4fr blue & black .35 .25

50th anniversary of Radio Belgium.

Felicien Rops (1833-1898), Painter, Engraver A323

Engraved and Photogravure
1973, Dec. 8 ***Perf. 11½***
863 A323 7fr Self-portrait .55 .25

King Albert, (1875-1934) A324

1974, Feb. 16 Photo. ***Perf. 11½***
864 A324 4fr Prus green & blk .30 .25

Sun, Bird, Flowers and Girl — A325

1974, Mar. 25 Photo. ***Perf. 11½***
865 A325 3fr violet & multi .25 .25

Protection of the environment.

NATO Emblem A326

1974, Apr. 20 Photo. ***Perf. 11½***
866 A326 10fr dp to lt blue .75 .40

25th anniversary of the signing of the North Atlantic Treaty.

Hubert Krains — A327

1974, Apr. 27 **Engr. & Photo.**
867 A327 5fr black & gray .40 .25

Stamp Day.

Europa Issue

"Destroyed City," by Ossip Zadkine — A328

Design: 10fr, Solidarity, by Georges Minne.

1974, May 4

868	A328	5fr black & red	*.65*	.25
869	A328	10fr black & ultra	*.80*	*.40*

Children A329

1974, May 18 **Photo.** ***Perf. 11½***
870 A329 4fr lt blue & multi .30 .25

10th Lay Youth Festival.

Planetarium, Brussels A330

Soleilmont Abbey Ruins — A331

4fr, Pillory, Braine-le-Chateau. 7fr, Fountain, Ghent (procession symbolic of Chamber of Rhetoric). 10fr, Belfry, Bruges, vert.

Engr. and Photo.

1974, June 22 ***Perf. 11½***

871	A330	3fr sky blue & blk	.30	.25
872	A330	4fr lilac rose & blk	.40	.25
873	A331	5fr lt green & blk	.45	.25
874	A331	7fr dull yellow & blk	.55	.25
875	A330	10fr black, blue & brn	.70	.45
		Nos. 871-875 (5)	2.40	1.45

Historic buildings and monuments.

"BENELUX" A332

1974, Sept. 7 **Photo.** ***Perf. 11½***
876 A332 5fr bl grn, dk grn & lt bl .35 .25

30th anniversary of the signing of the customs union of Belgium, Netherlands and Luxembourg.

Jan Vekemans, by Cornelis de Vos — A333

1974, Sept. 14
877 A333 3fr multicolored .25 .25

Youth philately.

Leon Tresignies, Willebroek Canal Bridge A334

1974, Sept. 28 **Engr. & Photo.**
878 A334 4fr brn & ol grn .35 .25

60th death anniversary of Corporal Leon Tresignies (1886-1914), hero of World War I.

Montgomery Blair, UPU Emblem A335

10fr, Heinrich von Stephan, UPU emblem.

1974, Oct. 5 ***Perf. 11½***

879	A335	5fr green & blk	.40	.25
880	A335	10fr brick red & blk	.80	.40

Centenary of Universal Postal Union.

Symbolic Chart — A336

1974, Oct. 12 **Photo.** ***Perf. 11½***
881 A336 7fr multicolored .55 .30

Central Economic Council, 25th anniv.

Rotary Emblem A337

1974, Oct. 19
882 A337 10fr multicolored .75 .35

Rotary International of Belgium, 50th Anniv.

Wild Boar (Regimental Emblem) — A338

1974, Oct. 26
883 A338 3fr multicolored .25 .25

Granting of the colors to the Ardennes Chasseurs Regiment, 40th anniversary.

Angel, by Van Eyck Brothers — A341

1974, Nov. 16 ***Perf. 11½***
884 A341 4fr rose lilac .30 .25

Christmas 1974. The Angel shown is from the triptyque "The Mystical Lamb" in the Saint-Bavon Cathedral, Ghent.

Adolphe Quetelet, by J. Odevaere — A342

1974, Dec. 14 **Engr. & Photo.**
885 A342 10fr black & buff .75 .45

Death centenary of Adolphe Quetelet (1796-1874), statistician, astronomer and Secretary of Royal Academy of Brussels.

Themabelga, International Thematic Stamp Exhibition, Brussels, Dec. 13-21, 1975 — A343

6.50fr, Themabelga emblem.

1975, Feb. 15 **Photo.** ***Perf. 11½***
912 A343 6.50fr multi .50 .25

Ghent Intl. Flower Exhib., Apr. 26-May 5 — A344

4.50fr, Neoregelia carolinae. 5fr, Coltsfoot. 6.50fr, Azalea.

1975, Feb. 22
913 A344 4.50fr multi .35 .25

Photogravure and Engraved

914	A344	5fr multi	.40	.25
915	A344	6.50fr multi	.50	.25
		Nos. 913-915 (3)	1.25	.75

Charles Buls Normal School for Boys, Brussels, Cent. — A345

School emblem, man Leading boy.

1975, Mar. 15 ***Perf. 11½***
916 A345 4.50fr black & multi .35 .25

Davids Foundation Emblem A346

1975, Mar. 22 **Photo.**
917 A346 5fr yellow & multi .40 .25

Centenary of the Davids Foundation, a Catholic organization for the promotion of Flemish through education and books.

King Albert (1875-1934) A347

1975, Apr. 5 **Engr. & Photo.**
918 A347 10fr black & maroon .70 .35

Mailman, 1840, by James Thiriar — A348

1975, Apr. 19 **Engr.** ***Perf. 11½***
919 A348 6.50fr dull magenta .50 .25

Stamp Day 1975.

St. John, from Last Supper, by Bouts — A349

Europa: 10fr, Woman's Head, detail from "Trial by Fire," by Dirk Bouts.

1975, Apr. 26 **Engr. & Photo.**

920	A349	6.50fr black, grn & blue	*.65*	.25
921	A349	10fr black, ocher & red	*.90*	*.45*

Liberation of Concentration Camps, 30th Anniv. — A350

Concentration Camp Symbols: "B" denoted political prisoners, "KG" prisoners of war.

1975, May 3 **Photo.**
922 A350 4.50fr multicolored .35 .25

Hospice of St. John, Bruges A351

Church of St. Loup, Namur — A352

Design: 10fr, Martyrs' Square, Brussels.

1975, May 12 Engr. *Perf. 11½*
926 A351 4.50fr deep rose lilac .40 .25
927 A352 5fr slate green .45 .25
928 A351 10fr bright blue .85 .40
Nos. 926-928 (3) 1.70 .90

European Architectural Heritage Year.

Library, Louvain University, Ryckmans and Cerfaux
A355

1975, June 7 Photo. *Perf. 11½*
931 A355 10fr dull blue & sepia .75 .35

25th anniversary of Louvain Bible Colloquium, founded by Professors Gonzague Ryckmans (1887-1969) and Lucien Cerfaux (1883-1968).

"Metamorphose" by Pol Mara — A356

1975, June 14
932 A356 7fr multicolored .50 .30

Queen Fabiola Mental Health Foundation.

Marie Popelin, Palace of Justice, Brussels — A357

1975, June 21 Engr. & Photo.
933 A357 6.50fr green & claret .55 .25

International Women's Year 1975. Marie Popelin (1846-1913), first Belgian woman doctor of law.

Assia, by Charles Despiau — A358

1975, Sept. 6 *Perf. 11½*
934 A358 5fr yellow grn & blk .35 .25

Middelheim Outdoor Museum, 25th anniv.

Cornelia Vekemans, by Cornelis de Vos — A359

1975, Sept. 20 Photo.
935 A359 4.50fr multicolored .40 .25

Youth philately.

Map of Schelde-Rhine Canal — A360

1975, Sept. 20
936 A360 10fr multicolored .75 .35

Opening of connection between the Schelde and Rhine, Sept. 23, 1975.

National Bank, W. F. Orban, Founder
A361

Photogravure and Engraved

1975, Oct. 11 *Perf. 12½x13*
937 A361 25fr multicolored 2.00 .50

Natl. Bank of Belgium, 125th anniv.

Edmond Thieffry and Plane, 1925
A362

1975, Oct. 18 *Perf. 11½*
938 A362 7fr black & lilac .55 .30

First flight Brussels to Kinshasa, Congo, 50th anniversary.

"Seat of Wisdom" St. Peter's, Louvain — A363

1975, Nov. 8 *Perf. 11½*
939 A363 6.50fr blue, blk & grn .50 .25

University of Louvain, 550th anniversary.

Angels, by Rogier van der Weyden
A364

1975, Nov. 15
940 A364 5fr multicolored .40 .25

Christmas 1975.

Willemsfonds Emblem — A365

1976, Feb. 21 Photo. *Perf. 11½*
941 A365 5fr multicolored .35 .25

Willems Foundation, which supports Flemish language and literature, 125th anniv.

American Bicentennial Emblem — A366

1976, Mar. 13 Photo. *Perf. 11½*
942 A366 14fr multi + label 1.00 .55

American Bicentennial. Black engraved inscription on labels commemorates arrival of first Walloon settlers in Nieu Nederland.

Cardinal Mercier — A367

1976, Mar. 20 Engr.
943 A367 4.50fr brt rose lilac .35 .25

Desire Joseph Cardinal Mercier (1851-1926), professor at Louvain University, spiritual and patriotic leader during World War I.

Flemish Economic Organization (Vlaams Ekonomisch Verbond), 50th Anniv. — A368

1976, Apr. 3 Photo. *Perf. 11½*
944 A368 6.50fr multicolored .50 .25

General Post Office, Brussels
A369

1976, Apr. 24 Engr. *Perf. 11½*
945 A369 6.50fr sepia .50 .25

Stamp Day.

Potter's Hands
A370

Europa: 6.50fr, Basket maker, vert.

1976, May 8 Photo.
946 A370 6.50fr multicolored *.60* .25
947 A370 14fr multicolored *.90* *.40*

Truck on Road
A371

1976, May 8
948 A371 14fr black, yel & red .90 .45

15th Intl. Road Union Cong., Brussels, May 9-13.

Queen Elisabeth (1876-1965)
A372

1976, May 24 *Perf. 11½*
949 A372 14fr green .90 .45

Ardennes Draft Horses
A373

1976, June 19
950 A373 5fr multicolored .40 .30

Ardennes Draft Horses Assoc., 50th anniv.

Souvenir Sheets

King Baudouin — A374

1976, June 26
951 A374 Sheet of 3 2.25 2.25
a. 4.50fr gray .65 .65
b. 6.50fr ocher .65 .65
c. 10fr brick red .65 .65
952 A374 Sheet of 2 4.25 4.25
a. 20fr yellow green 1.40 1.40
b. 30fr Prussian blue 2.00 2.00

25th anniv. of the reign of King Baudouin. No. 951 sold for 30fr, No. 952 for 70fr. The surtax went to a new foundation for the improvement of living conditions in honor of the King.

Electric Train and Society Emblem — A375

1976, Sept. 11 Photo. *Perf. 11½*
953 A375 6.50fr multi .55 .25

Natl. Belgian Railroad Soc., 50th anniv.

William of Nassau, Prince of Orange — A376

1976, Sept. 11 **Engr.**

954 A376 10fr slate green .75 .35

400th anniv. of the pacification of Ghent.

New Subway Train A377

1976, Sept. 18 **Photo.**

955 A377 6.50fr multi .55 .25

Opening of first line of Brussels subway.

Young Musician, by W. C. Duyster — A378

1976, Oct. 2 **Photo.** ***Perf. 11½***

956 A378 4.50fr multi .35 .25

Young musicians and youth philately.

Charles Bernard — A379

St. Jerome in the Mountains, by Le Patinier — A380

Blind Leading the Blind, by Bruegel the Elder A381

No. 958, Fernand Victor Toussaint van Boelaere.

1976, Oct. 16 **Engr.**

957 A379 5fr violet .40 .25
958 A379 5fr red brn & sepia .40 .25
959 A380 6.50fr dark brown .55 .25
960 A381 6.50fr slate green .55 .25
Nos. 957-960 (4) 1.90 1.00

Charles Bernard (1875-1961), French-speaking journalist; Toussaint van Boelaere (1875-1947), Flemish journalist; No. 959, Charles Plisnier Belgian-French Cultural Society. No. 960, Assoc. for Language Promotion.

Remouchamps Caves — A382

Hunnegem Priory, Gramont, and Madonna A383

Designs: No. 963, River Lys and St. Martin's Church. No. 964, Ham-sur-Heure Castle.

1976, Oct. 23 **Engr.** ***Perf. 13***

961 A382 4.50fr multi .40 .25
962 A383 4.50fr multi .40 .25
963 A383 5fr multi .40 .25
964 A383 5fr multi .40 .25
Nos. 961-964 (4) 1.60 1.00

Tourism. Nos. 961-962 are not luminescent.

Nativity, by Master of Flemalle — A384

1976, Nov. 20 ***Perf. 11½***

965 A384 5fr violet .40 .25

Christmas 1976.

Rubens' Monogram — A385

1977, Feb. 12 **Photo. & Engr.**

966 A385 6.50fr lilac & blk .50 .25

Peter Paul Rubens (1577-1640), painter.

Heraldic Lion — A386

1977-85 **Typo.** ***Perf. 13½x14***

Size: 17x20mm

967 A386 50c brn ('80) .25 .25
a. 50c orange brown ('85) .25 .25
968 A386 1fr brt lil .25 .25
a. 1fr bright rose lilac ('84) .25 .25
969 A386 1.50fr gray ('78) .25 .25
970 A386 2fr orange ('78) .25 .25
970A A386 2.50fr yel grn ('81) .30 .25
971 A386 2.75fr Prus bl ('80) .30 .25
972 A386 3fr vio ('78) .30 .25
a. 3fr dull violet ('84) .25 .25
973 A386 4fr red brn ('80) .35 .25
a. 4fr rose brown ('85) .90 .25
974 A386 4.50fr lt ultra .40 .25
975 A386 5fr grn ('80) .40 .25
a. 5fr emerald green ('84) .40 .25
976 A386 6fr dl red brn .50 .25
a. 6fr light red brown ('85) .50 .25
Nos. 967-976 (11) 3.55 2.75

Nos. 967-976 were printed on various papers.

1978, Aug. **Photo.** ***Perf. 13½x12½***

Size: 17x22mm

Booklet Stamps

977 A386 1fr brt lilac .25 .25
a. Bklt. pane, #977-978, 2 #786 1.50
b. Bklt. pane, #977, 979, 2 #788 2.00
978 A386 2fr yellow .30 .30
979 A386 3fr violet .50 .50
Nos. 977-979 (3) 1.05 1.05

Each pane has 2 labels showing Belgian Postal emblem, also a large selvage with zip code instructions. No. 977-979 not luminescent.

See Nos. 1084-1088, design O5.

Anniversary Emblem A387

1977, Mar. 14 **Photo.** ***Perf. 11½***

982 A387 6.50fr sil & multi .50 .25

Royal Belgian Association of Civil and Agricultural Engineers, 50th anniversary.

Birds and Lions Emblem A388

1977, Mar. 28

983 A388 14fr multi 1.00 .30

Belgian District #112 of Lions Intl., 25th anniv.

Pillar Box, 1852 — A389

1977, Apr. 23 **Engr.**

984 A389 6.50fr slate green .55 .25

Stamp Day 1977.

Gileppe Dam, Jalhay A390

Europa: 14fr, War Memorial, Yser at Nieuport.

1977, May 7 **Photo.** ***Perf. 11½***

985 A390 6.50fr multi *.60* .25
986 A390 14fr multi *.80* *.40*

Mars and Mercury Association Emblem — A391

1977, May 14

987 A391 5fr multi .35 .25

Mars and Mercury Association of Reserve and Retired Officers, 50th anniversary.

Prince de Hornes Coat of Arms — A392

Conversion of St. Hubertus — A394

Battle of the Golden Spur, from Oxford Chest — A393

Designs: 6.50fr, Froissart writing book, vert.

1977, June 11 **Engr.** ***Perf. 11½***

988 A392 4.50fr violet .35 .25
989 A393 5fr red .40 .25
990 A393 6.50fr dark brown .45 .25
991 A394 14fr slate green 1.00 .50
Nos. 988-991 (4) 2.20 1.25

300th anniv. of the Principality of Overijse (4.50fr); 675th anniv. of the Battle of the Golden Spur (5f); 600th anniv. of publication of 1st volume of the Chronicles of Jehan Froissart (6.50fr); 1250th anniv. of the death of St. Hubertus (14fr).

Rubens, Self-portrait A395

1977, June 25 **Photo.**

992 A395 5fr multi .40 .25
a. Souvenir sheet of 3 1.25 1.00

Peter Paul Rubens (1577-1640), painter.

Stamps in No. 992a are 37¼mm high, No. 992, 35¼mm. No. 992a sold for 20fr.

Open Book, from The Lamb of God, by Van Eyck Brothers — A396

1977, Sept. 3 **Photo.** ***Perf. 11½***

993 A396 10fr multi .70 .35

Intl. Federation of Library Associations (IFLA), 50th Anniv. Cong., Brussels, Sept. 5-10.

Gymnast and Soccer Player — A397

6.50fr, Fencers in wheelchairs, horiz. 10fr, Basketball players. 14fr, Hockey players.

1977, Sept. 10

994 A397 4.50fr multi .40 .25
995 A397 6.50fr multi .50 .25
996 A397 10fr multi .75 .40
997 A397 14fr multi 1.10 .50
Nos. 994-997 (4) 2.75 1.40

Workers' Gymnastics and Sports Center, 50th anniversary (4.50fr); sport for the Handicapped (6.50fr); 20th European Basketball Championships (10fr); First World Hockey Cup (14fr).

Europalia 77 Emblem — A398

1977, Sept. 17
998 A398 5fr gray & multi .40 .25

5th Europalia Arts Festival, featuring German Federal Republic, Belgium, Oct.-Nov. 1977.

The Egg Farmer, by Gustave De Smet — A399

1977, Oct. 8 **Engr. & Photo.**
999 A399 4.50fr bister & blk .35 .25

Publicity for Belgian eggs.

Mother and Daughter with Album, by Constant Cap A400

1977, Oct. 15 **Engr.**
1000 A400 4.50fr dark brown .35 .25

Youth Philately.

No. 1000 exists in red in a deluxe souvenir sheet. Value, $100.

Bailiff's House, Gembloux — A401

Market Square, St. Nicholas A402

No. 1002, St. Aldegonde Church & Cultural Center. No. 1004, Statue and bridge, Liège.

1977, Oct. 22
1001 A401 4.50fr multi .35 .25
1002 A401 4.50fr multi .35 .25
1003 A402 5fr multi .40 .25
1004 A402 5fr multi .40 .25
Nos. 1001-1004 (4) 1.50 1.00

Tourism. Nos. 1001-1004 not luminescent. See Nos. 1017-1018, 1037-1040.

Nativity, by Rogier van der Weyden — A403

1977, Nov. 11 **Engr.**
1005 A403 5fr rose red .40 .25

Christmas 1977.

Symbols of Transportation and Map — A404

Campidoglio Palace, Rome, and Map — A406

Designs: No. 1007, European Parliament, Strasbourg, Emblem, vert. No. 1009, Paul-Henri Spaak and map of 19 European member countries.

1978, Mar. 18 **Photo.** ***Perf. 11½***
1006 A404 10fr blue & multi .80 .30
1007 A404 10fr blue & multi .80 .30
1008 A406 14fr blue & multi 1.00 .50
1009 A406 14fr blue & multi 1.00 .50
Nos. 1006-1009 (4) 3.60 1.60

European Action: 25th anniversary of the European Transport Ministers' Conference; 1st general elections for European Parliament; 20th anniversary of the signing of the Treaty of Rome; Paul Henri Spaak (1899-1972), Belgian statesman who worked for the establishment of European Community.

Grimbergen Abbey — A407

1978, Apr. 1 **Engr.**
1010 A407 4.50fr red brown .35 .25

850th anniversary of the Premonstratensian Abbey at Grimbergen.

Ostend Chamber of Commerce and Industry, 175th Anniv. — A408

1978, Apr. 8 **Photo.**
1011 A408 8fr Emblem .50 .30

No. 39 with First Day Cancel — A409

1978, Apr. 15
1012 A409 8fr multicolored .55 .25

Stamp Day.

Europa Issue

Pont des Trous, Tournai A410

8fr, Antwerp Cathedral, by Vaclav Hollar.

Photogravure and Engraved

1978, May 6 ***Perf. 11½***
1013 A410 8fr multi, vert. .85 .25
1014 A410 14fr multi 1.10 .40

Virgin of Ghent, Porcelain Plaque — A411

Paul Pastur Workers' University, Charleroi — A412

1978, Sept. 16 **Photo.** ***Perf. 11½***
1015 A411 6fr multicolored .45 .30
1016 A412 8fr multicolored .60 .30

Municipal education in Ghent, 150th anniversary; Paul Pastur Workers' University, Charleroi, 75th anniv. Nos. 1015-1016 are not luminescent.

Types of 1977 and

Tourist Guide, Brussels A413

No. 1017, Jonathas House, Enghien. No. 1018, View of Wetteren and couple in local costume. No. 1020, Prince Carnival, Eupen-St. Vith.

1978, Sept. 25 **Photo. & Engr.**
1017 A401 4.50fr multi .35 .30
1018 A402 4.50fr multi .35 .30
1019 A413 6fr multi .45 .30
1020 A413 6fr multi .45 .30
Nos. 1017-1020 (4) 1.60 1.20

Tourism. Nos. 1017-1020 are not luminescent.

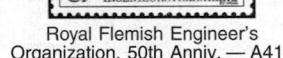

Royal Flemish Engineer's Organization, 50th Anniv. — A414

1978, Oct. 7 **Photo.**
1021 A414 8fr Emblem .50 .25

Young Philatelist A415

1978, Oct. 14 **Engr.** ***Perf. 11½***
1022 A415 4.50fr dk violet .35 .30

Youth philately.

Nativity, Notre Dame, Huy — A416

1978, Nov. 18 **Engr.** ***Perf. 11½***
1023 A416 6fr black .45 .30

Christmas 1978.

Tyll Eulenspiegel, Lay Action Emblem — A417

1979, Mar. 3 **Photo.** ***Perf. 11½***
1024 A417 4.50fr multi .35 .25

10th anniversary of Lay Action Centers.

European Parliament Emblem — A418

1979, Mar. 3
1025 A418 8fr multicolored .60 .25

European Parliament, first direct elections, June 7-10.

St. Michael Banishing Lucifer — A419

1979, Mar. 17 **Photo. & Engr.**
1026 A419 4.50fr rose red & blk .35 .30
1027 A419 8fr brt green & blk .70 .30

Millennium of Brussels.

NATO Emblem and Monument A420

1979, Mar. 31 **Photo.**
1028 A420 3fr multicolored 2.00 .50

NATO, 30th anniv.

Prisoner's Head — A421

1979, Apr. 7 **Photo. & Engr.**
1029 A421 6fr orange & blk .40 .25

25th anniversary of the National Political Prisoners' Monument at Breendonk.

Belgium No. Q2 — A422

1979, Apr. 21 **Photo.** ***Perf. 11½***
1030 A422 8fr multicolored .55 .30

Stamp Day 1979.

Mail Coach and Truck A423

Europa: 14fr, Chappe's heliograph, Intelsat satellite and dish antenna.

1979, Apr. 28 **Photo. & Engr.**

1031	A423 8fr multicolored	*.85*	*.25*
1032	A423 14fr multicolored	*1.60*	*.35*

Chamber of Commerce Emblem — A424

1979, May 19 **Photo.** ***Perf. 11½***

1033	A424 8fr multicolored	.50	.25

Verviers Chamber of Commerce and Industry, 175th anniversary.

"50" Emblem A425

1979, June 9 **Photo.** ***Perf. 11½***

1034	A425 4.50fr gold & ultra	.35	.25

Natl. Fund for Professional Credit, 50th anniv.

Merchants, Roman Bas-relief A426

1979, June 9

1035	A426 10fr multicolored	.65	.30

Belgian Chamber of Trade and Commerce, 50th anniversary.

"Tintin" as Philatelist A427

1979, Sept. 29 **Photo.** ***Perf. 11½***

1036	A427 8fr multicolored	2.25	.70

Youth philately.

Tourism Types of 1977

Designs: No. 1037, Belfry, Thuin. No. 1038, Royal Museum of Central Africa, Tervuren. No. 1039, St. Nicholas Church and cattle, Ciney. No. 1040, St. John's Church and statue of Our Lady, Poperinge.

Perf. 11½ (A401), 13 (A402)

1979, Oct. 22 **Photo. & Engr.**

1037	A401 5fr multicolored	.40	.30
1038	A402 5fr multicolored	.40	.30
1039	A401 6fr multicolored	.50	.30
1040	A402 6fr multicolored	.50	.30
	Nos. 1037-1040 (4)	1.80	1.20

Francois Auguste Gevaert A429

Piano, String Instruments A430

Design: 6fr, Emmanuel Durlet.

1979, Nov. 3 ***Perf. 11½***

1041	A429 5fr brown	.40	.30
1042	A429 6fr brown	.55	.30
1043	A430 14fr brown	.90	.45
	Nos. 1041-1043 (3)	1.85	1.05

Francois Auguste Gevaert (1828-1908), musicologist and composer; Emmanuel Durlet (1893-1977), pianist; Queen Elisabeth Musical Chapel Foundation, 40th anniv.

Virgin and Child, Notre Dame, Foy — A431

1979, Nov. 24 **Photo. & Engr.**

1044	A431 6fr lt grnsh blue	.35	.25

Christmas 1979.

Independence, 150th Anniversary — A432

1980, Jan. 26 **Photo.** ***Perf. 11½***

1045	A432 9fr purple	.60	.25

Frans van Cauwelaert (1880-1961), Minister of State — A433

1980, Feb. 25 **Engr.**

1046	A433 5fr gray	.40	.25

Ghent Flower Show, Apr. 19-27 — A434

5fr, Spring flowers. 6.50fr, Summer flowers. 9fr, Autumn flowers.

1980, Mar. 10 **Photo.**

1047	A434 5fr multi	.40	.30
1048	A434 6.50fr multi	.50	.30
1049	A434 9fr multi	.60	.30
	Nos. 1047-1049 (3)	1.50	.90

P.T.T., 50th Anniv. A435

1980, Apr. 14 **Photo.** ***Perf. 11½***

1050	A435 10fr multicolored	.70	.30

Belgium No. C4 — A436

1980, Apr. 21

1051	A436 9fr multicolored	.65	.30

Stamp Day.

Europa — A437

9fr, St. Benedict, by Hans Memling. 14fr, Margaret of Austria (1480-1530).

1980, Apr. 28

1052	A437 9fr multicolored	*.70*	*.25*
1053	A437 14fr multicolored	*1.10*	*.35*

4th Interparliamentary Conf. for European Cooperation & Security, Brussels, May 12-18 — A438

5fr, Palais des Nations, Brussels.

1980, May 10 **Photo.** ***Perf. 11½***

1054	A438 5fr multicolored	.35	.25

Golden Carriage, 1780, Mons A439

Tourism: No. 1056, Canal landscape, Damme.

1980, May 17

1055	A439 6.50fr multi	.45	.30
1056	A439 6.50fr multi	.45	.30

Souvenir Sheet

Royal Mint Theater, Brussels — A440

Photo. & Engr.

1980, May 31 ***Perf. 11½***

1057	A440 50fr black	4.50	4.50

150th anniv. of independence. Sold for 75fr.

King Baudouin, 50th Birthday — A441

1980, Sept. 6 **Photo.** ***Perf. 11½***

1058	A441 9fr rose claret	.65	.25

View of Chiny A442

Portal and Court, Diest — A443

1980 **Engr.** ***Perf. 13***

1059	A442 5fr multicolored	.40	.30
1060	A443 5fr multicolored	.40	.30

Tourism. Nos. 1059-1060 are not luminescent.

Issued: No. 1059, 9/27; No. 1060, 12/13.

See Nos. 1072-1075, 1120-1125.

Emblem of Belgian Heart League A444

1980, Oct. 4 **Photo.** ***Perf. 11½***

1061	A444 14fr blue & magenta	1.00	.50

Heart Week, Oct. 20-25.

Rodenbach Statue, Roulers — A445

1980, Oct. 11
1062 A445 9fr multicolored .65 .30

Albrecht Rodenbach (1856-1880), poet.

Youth Philately — A446

1980, Oct. 27 Photo. *Perf. 11½*
1063 A446 5fr multicolored .35 .25

National Broadcasting Service, 50th Anniversary A447

1980, Nov. 10
1064 A447 10fr gray & blk .70 .40

Garland and Nativity, by Daniel Seghers, 17th Century A448

1980, Nov. 17
1065 A448 6.50fr multicolored .45 .30

Christmas 1980.

Baron de Gerlache, by F.J. Navez — A449

Leopold I, By Geefs A450

9fr, Baron de Stassart, by F.J. Navez.

1981, Mar. 16 Photo. *Perf. 11½*
1066 A449 6fr multicolored .40 .30
1067 A449 9fr multicolored .60 .30

Photogravure and Engraved

1068 A450 50fr multicolored 3.25 .60

Sesquicentennial of Chamber of Deputies, Senate and Dynasty.

Tchantchès and Op-Signoorke, Puppets — A451

Photogravure and Engraved

1981, May 4 *Perf. 11½*
1069 A451 9fr shown *.80* .25
1070 A451 14fr d'Artagnan and Woltje *1.10* *.45*

Europa.

Impression of M.A. de Cock (Founder of Post Museum) — A452

1981, May 18 Photo.
1071 A452 9fr multicolored .65 .30

Stamp Day.

Tourism Types of 1980

No. 1072, Virgin and Child statue, Our Lady's Church, Tongre-Notre Dame. No. 1073, Egmont Castle, Zottegem. No. 1074, Eau d'Heure River. No. 1075, Tongerlo Abbey, Antwerp.

1981, June 15 Engr. *Perf. 11½*
1072 A442 6fr multi .50 .30
1073 A442 6fr multi .50 .30
1074 A443 6.50fr multi .50 .30
1075 A443 6.50fr multi .50 .30
Nos. 1072-1075 (4) 2.00 1.20

Soccer Player — A453

1981, Sept. 5 Photo. *Perf. 11½*
1076 A453 6fr multicolored .50 .30

Soccer in Belgium centenary; Royal Antwerp Soccer Club.

E. Remouchamps, Founder — A454

1981, Sept. 5 Photo. & Engr.
1077 A454 6.50fr cream & dk brn .45 .30

Walloon Language and Literature Club 125th anniv.

Audit Office Sesquicentennial — A455

1981, Sept. 12 Engr.
1078 A455 10fr dp claret .70 .30

French Horn A456

1981, Sept. 12 Photo.
1079 A456 6.50fr multi .45 .30

Vredekring (Peace Circle) Band of Antwerp centenary.

Souvenir Sheet

Pieta, by Ben Genaux — A457

1981, Sept. 19 Photo. *Perf. 11½*
1080 A457 20fr multicolored 2.00 2.00

Mining disaster at Marcinelle, 25th anniv. Sold for 30fr.

Mausoleum of Marie of Burgundy and Charles the Bold, Bruges — A458

1981, Oct. 10 Photo. & Engr.
1081 A458 50fr multi 3.25 .75

Youth Philately — A459

1981, Oct. 24 Photo.
1082 A459 6fr multi .40 .30

Type of 1977 and

A459a

A460

King Baudouin — A460a

Photo. and Engr.; Photo.

1980-86 *Perf. 13½x14, 11½*
1084 A386 65c brt rose .25 .25
1085 A386 1fr on 5fr grn .25 .25
1086 A386 7fr brt rose .55 .25
1087 A386 8fr grnsh bl .65 .25
1088 A386 9fr dl org .70 .25
1089 A459a 10fr blue .70 .25
1090 A459a 11fr dl red .80 .25
1091 A459a 12fr grn 1.00 .25
1092 A459a 13fr scar 1.00 .25
1093 A459a 15fr red org 1.75 .30
1094 A459a 20fr dk bl 1.75 .25
1095 A459a 22fr lilac 2.50 .60
1096 A459a 23fr gray grn 2.60 .60
1097 A459a 30fr brown 2.10 .25
1098 A459a 40fr red org 3.50 .25
1099 A460 50fr lt grnsh bl & bl 4.75 .30
1100 A460a 50fr tan & dk brn 5.00 .25
1101 A460 65fr pale lil & blk 6.00 .80
1102 A460 100fr lt bis brn & dk bl 9.75 .50
1103 A460a 100fr lt bl & dk bl 13.50 .25
Nos. 1084-1103 (20) 59.10 6.60

Issued: 65c, 4/14/80; 1fr, 5/3/82; 7fr, 5/17/82; 8fr, 5/9/83; 9fr, 2/11/85; 65fr, No. 1099, 1102, 11/5/81; 10fr, 11/15/82; 11fr, 4/5/83; 12fr, 1/23/84; 15fr, 22fr, 30fr, No. 1100, 3/26/84; 20fr, 40fr, No. 1103, 6/12/84; 23fr, 2/25/85; 13fr, 3/10/86. See Nos. 1231-1234.

Printed on various papers.

Max Waller, Movement Founder — A461

Designs: 6.50fr, The Spirit Drinkers, by Gustave van de Woestyne. 9fr, Fernand Severin, poet, 50th death anniv. 10fr, Jan van Ruusbroec, Flemish mystic, 500th birth anniv. 14fr, Thought and Man TV series, 25th anniv.

1981, Nov. 7
1104 A461 6fr multi .40 .30
1105 A461 6.50fr multi .45 .30
1106 A461 9fr multi .60 .30
1107 A461 10fr multi .70 .40
1108 A461 14fr multi 1.10 .50
Nos. 1104-1108 (5) 3.25 1.80

La Jeune Belgique cultural movement cent. (6fr).

Nativity, 16th Cent. Engraving — A466

1981, Nov. 21
1109 A466 6.50fr multi .40 .30

Christmas 1981.

Royal Conservatory of Music Sesquicentennial — A467

Design: 9fr, Judiciary sesquicentennial.

1982, Jan. 25 Photo. *Perf. 11½*
1110 A467 6.50fr multi .40 .30
1111 A467 9fr multi .60 .30

A468

6fr, Cyclotron. 14fr, Galaxy, telescope. 50fr, Koch.

1982, Mar. 1

1112 A468 6fr multicolored .40 .30
1113 A468 14fr multicolored .85 .40
1114 A468 50fr multicolored 3.00 .70
Nos. 1112-1114 (3) 4.25 1.40

Radio-isotope production, Natl. Radio-elements Institute, Fleurus (6fr); Royal Belgian Observatory (14fr); centenary of TB bacillus discovery (50fr).

Joseph Lemaire (1882-1966), Minister of State — A469

1982, Apr. 17 Photo. *Perf. 11½*

1115 A469 6.50fr multi .45 .30

Europa 1982 A470

10fr, Universal suffrage. 17fr, Edict of Tolerance, 1781.

1982, May 1

1116 A470 10fr multicolored *1.00* .25
1117 A470 17fr multicolored *1.75* *.35*

Stamp Day — A471

1982, May 22 Photo. & Engr.

1118 A471 10fr multi .65 .30

67th World Esperanto Congress, Anvers A472

1982, June 7 Photo. *Perf. 11½*

1119 A472 12fr Tower of Babel .80 .35

Tourism Type of 1980

Designs: No. 1120, Tower of Gosselies. No. 1121, Zwijveke Abbey, Dendermonde. No. 1122, Stavelot Abbey. No. 1123, Villers-la-Ville Abbey ruins. No. 1124, Geraardsbergen Abbey entrance. No. 1125, Beveren Pillory.

1982, June 21 Photo. & Engr.

1120 A443 7fr lt bl & blk .55 .30
1121 A443 7fr lt grn & blk .55 .30
1122 A442 7.50fr tan & dk brn .55 .30
1123 A442 7.50fr lt vio & pur .55 .30
1124 A443 7.50fr slate & blk .55 .30
1125 A443 7.50fr beige & blk .55 .30
Nos. 1120-1125 (6) 3.30 1.80

Self Portrait, by L.P. Boon (b. 1912) — A473

Designs: 10fr, Adoration of the Shepherds, by Hugo van der Goes (1440-1482). 12fr, The King on His Throne, carving by M. de Ghelderode (1898-1962). 17fr, Madonna and Child, by Pieter Paulus (1881-1959).

1982, Sept. 13 Photo. *Perf. 11½*

1126 A473 7fr multicolored .40 .30
1127 A473 10fr multicolored .60 .30
1128 A473 12fr multicolored .80 .40
1129 A473 17fr multicolored 1.45 .40
Nos. 1126-1129 (4) 3.25 1.40

Abraham Hans, Writer (1882-1932) A474

1982, Sept. 27

1130 A474 17fr multicolored 1.25 .40

Youth Philately and Scouting A475

1982, Oct. 2 Photo. *Perf. 11½*

1131 A475 7fr multicolored .55 .30

Grand Orient Lodge of Belgium Sesquicentennial A476

1982, Oct. 16 Photo. & Engr.

1132 A476 10fr Man taking oath .65 .25

Cardinal Joseph Cardijn (1882-1967) A477

1982, Nov. 13 Photo.

1133 A477 10fr multicolored .70 .30

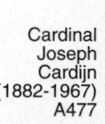

St. Francis of Assisi (1182-1226) A478

1982, Nov. 27

1134 A478 20fr multicolored 1.25 .50

Horse-drawn Trolley A479

1983, Feb. 12 Photo. *Perf. 11½*

1135 A479 7.50fr shown .70 .35
1136 A479 10fr Electric trolley 1.00 .30
1137 A479 50fr Trolley, diff. 3.75 .60
Nos. 1135-1137 (3) 5.45 1.25

Intl. Fed. for Periodical Press, 24th World Congress, Brussels, May 11-13 A480

1983, Mar. 19 Photo. *Perf. 11½*

1138 A480 20fr multicolored 1.30 .50

Homage to Women A481

1983, Apr. 16

1139 A481 8fr Operator .70 .30
1140 A481 11fr Homemaker .80 .30
1141 A481 20fr Executive 1.50 .50
Nos. 1139-1141 (3) 3.00 1.10

Stamp Day — A482

1983, Apr. 23

1142 A482 11fr multicolored .80 .30

Procession of the Precious Blood, Bruges A483

1983, Apr. 30 Photo. *Perf. 11½*

1143 A483 8fr multicolored .55 .25

The design of No. 1143 is continuous, and collectors often prefer pairs to demonstrate this feature. Value, unused or used, $2.

Europa 1983 — A484

Paintings by P. Delvaux. 11fr vert.

1983, May 14

1144 A484 11fr Common Man *.90* .25
1145 A484 20fr Night Train *1.60* *.45*

Manned Flight Bicentenary A485

1983, June 11 Photo. *Perf. 11½*

1146 A485 11fr Balloon over city .75 .30
1147 A485 22fr Country 1.50 .60

Our Lady's Church, Hastiere A486

No. 1149, Landen. No. 1150, Park, Mouscron. No. 1151, Wijnendale Castle, Torhout.

1983, June 25

1148 A486 8fr shown .65 .30
1149 A486 8fr multicolored .65 .30
1150 A486 8fr multicolored .65 .30
1151 A486 8fr multicolored .65 .30
Nos. 1148-1151 (4) 2.60 1.20

Tineke Festival, Heule — A487

1983, Sept. 10 Photo.

1152 A487 8fr multi .55 .30

Enterprise Year Emblem A488

1983, Sept. 24

1153 A488 11fr multicolored .75 .30

European year for small and medium-sized enterprises and craft industry.

Youth Philately — A489

1983, Oct. 10 Photo. *Perf. 11½*

1154 A489 8fr multicolored .55 .30

Belgian Exports A490

No. 1155, Diamond industry. No. 1156, Metallurgy. No. 1157, Textile industry.

1983, Oct. 24 *Perf. 11½*

1155 A490 10fr multicolored .80 .30
1156 A490 10fr multicolored .80 .30
1157 A490 10fr multicolored .80 .30
Nos. 1155-1157 (3) 2.40 .90

See Nos. 1161-1164.

Hendrik Conscience (1812-1883), Novelist — A491

1983, Nov. 7

1158 A491 20fr multicolored 1.40 .40

Leopold III Type of 1936

1983, Dec. 12 Engr. ***Perf. 12x11½***

1159 A84 11fr black .75 .25

Leopold III memorial (1901-1983), King 1934-1951.

Free University of Brussels, Sesqui. — A492

Photogravure and Engraved

1984, Jan. 14 ***Perf. 11½***

1160 A492 11fr multicolored .80 .25

Exports Type of 1983

No. 1161, Chemicals. No. 1162, Food. No. 1163, Transportation equipment. No. 1164, Technology.

1984, Jan. 28 **Photo.**

1161 A490 11fr multicolored .80 .30
1162 A490 11fr multicolored .80 .30
1163 A490 11fr multicolored .80 .30
1164 A490 11fr multicolored .80 .30
Nos. 1161-1164 (4) 3.20 1.20

King Albert I, 50th Death Anniv. — A494

1984, Feb. 11 **Photo. & Engr.**

1165 A494 8fr tan & dk brn .60 .30

1984 Summer Olympic Games — A495

Souvenir Sheet

1984, Mar. 3 **Photo.**

1166 Sheet of 2 2.25 2.25
a. A495 10fr Archery .60 .60
b. A495 24fr Dressage 1.40 1.40

See Nos. B1029-B1030.

Family, Globe, Birds — A496

1984, Mar. 24 Photo. ***Perf. 11½***

1167 A496 12fr multicolored .80 .30

"Movement without a Name" peace org.

St. John Bosco Canonization A497

1984, Apr. 7

1168 A497 8fr multicolored .60 .30

Europa (1959-84) A498

1984, May 5 Photo. ***Perf. 11½***

1169 A498 12fr black & red *.95* .25
1170 A498 22fr black & ultra *1.75* *.30*

Stamp Day — A499

1984, May 19

1171 A499 12fr No. 52 .90 .30

2nd European Parliament Elections A500

1984, May 26

1172 A500 12fr multicolored .90 .30

Royal Military School, 150th Anniv. — A501

1984, June 9 Photo. ***Perf. 11½***

1173 A501 22fr Hat 1.50 .45

Notre-Dame de la Chappelle, Brussels A502

Churches: No. 1175, St. Martin's, Montignyle-Tilleul. No. 1176, Tielt, vert.

Perf. 11½x12, 12x11½

1984, June 23 **Photo. & Engr.**

1174 A502 10fr multicolored .75 .35
1175 A502 10fr multicolored .75 .35
1176 A502 10fr multicolored .75 .35
Nos. 1174-1176 (3) 2.25 1.05

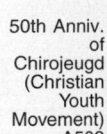

50th Anniv. of Chirojeugd (Christian Youth Movement) A503

1984, Sept. 15 Photo. ***Perf. 11½***

1177 A503 10fr Emblem .75 .35

Affligem Abbey A504

8fr, Averbode, vert. 22fr, Chimay, vert. 24fr, Rochefort, vert.

1984, Oct. 6 **Photo. & Engr.**

1178 A504 8fr tan & black .55 .35
1179 A504 22fr dull mauve & lake brn 1.40 .55
1180 A504 24fr pale blue & indigo 1.50 .55
1181 A504 50fr shown 3.50 .75
Nos. 1178-1181 (4) 6.95 2.20

Youth Philately A505

1984, Oct. 20 **Photo.**

1182 A505 8fr Postman smurf 1.25 .60

Arthur Meulemans (1884-1966), Composer — A506

1984, Nov. 17 **Photo. & Engr.**

1183 A506 12fr multicolored .85 .65

St. Norbert, 850th Death Anniv. — A507

1985, Jan. 14 **Photo. & Engr.**

1184 A507 22fr sepia & beige 1.60 .50

Europalia '85 — A508

1985, Jan. 21 **Photo.**

1185 A508 12fr Virgin of Louvain .85 .30

Belgian Assoc. of Professional Journalists, Cent. A509

1985, Feb. 11 **Photo.**

1186 A509 9fr multicolored .65 .30

Ghent Flower Festival, Orchids — A510

No. 1187, Vanda coerules. No. 1188, Phalaenopsis. No. 1189, Suphrolaelio cattlea riffe.

Photogravure and Engraved

1985, Mar. 18 ***Perf. 11½***

1187 A510 12fr multi .80 .30
1188 A510 12fr multi .80 .30
1189 A510 12fr multi .80 .30
Nos. 1187-1189 (3) 2.40 .90

Visit of Pope John Paul II A511

1985, Apr. 1 **Photo.**

1190 A511 12fr multicolored .80 .30

Belgian Worker's Party Cent. A512

9fr, Chained factory gate. 12fr, Broken wall, red flag.

1985, Apr. 15 **Photo.**

1191 A512 9fr multicolored .60 .40
1192 A512 12fr multicolored .80 .30

Jean de Bast (1883-1975), Engraver A513

1985, Apr. 22 **Engr.**

1193 A513 12fr blue black .80 .30

Stamp Day.

Public Transportation Year — A514

Design: 9fr, Steam tram locomotive Type 18, 1896. 12fr, Locomotive Elephant and tender, 1835. 23fr, Type 23 tank engine, 1904. 24fr, Type I Pacific locomotive, 1935. 50fr, Type 27 electric locomotive, 1975.

1985, May 6 **Photo.**

1194 A514 9fr multicolored .70 .30
1195 A514 12fr multicolored .80 .30
1196 A514 23fr multicolored 1.60 .60
1197 A514 24fr multicolored 1.75 .60
Nos. 1194-1197 (4) 4.85 1.80

Souvenir Sheet

1198 A514 50fr multicolored 4.00 4.00

Europa 1985 A515

12fr, Cesar Franck at organ, 1887. 23fr, Folk figures.

1985, May 13 **Photo.**

1199	A515	12fr multicolored	*.95*	*.25*
1200	A515	23fr multicolored	*1.90*	*.40*

26th Navigation Congress, Brussels A516

No. 1201, Zeebruge Harbor. No. 1202, Projected lock at Strepy-Thieu.

1985, June 10 **Photo.** ***Perf. 11½***

1201	A516	23fr multicolored	1.60	.60
1202	A516	23fr multicolored	1.60	.60

St. Martin's Church, Marcinelle A517

Tourism: No. 1203, Church of the Assumption of Our Lady, Avernas-le-Baudouin, vert. No. 1204, Church of the Old Beguinage, Tongres, vert. No. 1206, Private residence, Puyenbroeck.

1985, June 24 ***Perf. 11½***

1203	A517	12fr multicolored	.80	.30
1204	A517	12fr multicolored	.80	.30
1205	A517	12fr multicolored	.80	.30
1206	A517	12fr multicolored	.80	.30
		Nos. 1203-1206 (4)	3.20	1.20

Queen Astrid (1905-1935) A518

1985, Sept. 2 ***Perf. 11½***

1207	A518	12fr brown	.90	.30

Baking Pies for the Mattetart of Geraardsbergen A519

Folk events: 24fr, Children dancing, centenary of the St. Lambert de Hermalle-Argenteau Les Rouges youth organization.

1985, Sept. 16

1208	A519	12fr multicolored	.85	.30
1209	A519	24fr multicolored	1.75	.50

Liberation from German Occupation, 40th Anniv. — A520

Allegories: 9fr, Dove, liberation of concentration camps. 23fr, Battle of Ardennes. 24fr, Destroyer, liberation of the River Scheldt estuary.

1985, Sept. 30 **Photo.** ***Perf. 11½***

1210	A520	9fr multicolored	.70	.30
1211	A520	23fr multicolored	1.60	.60
1212	A520	24fr multicolored	1.75	.60
		Nos. 1210-1212 (3)	4.05	1.50

Ernest Claes (1885-1968), Author A521

9fr, Portrait, book character.

1985, Oct. 7

1213	A521	9fr multicolored	.65	.30

Intl. Youth Year — A522

9fr, Nude in repose, angel.

1985, Oct. 21

1214	A522	9fr multicolored	.65	.30

King Baudouin & Queen Fabiola, 25th Wedding Anniv. — A523

1985, Dec. 9

1215	A523	12fr multicolored	1.00	.35

Birds — A524

No. 1216, Roitelet huppe. No. 1217, Pic epeichette. No. 1218, Moineau friquet. No. 1219, Gros bec. No. 1220, Bruant des roseaux. No. 1221, Rouge gorge. No. 1222, Gorge bleue. No. 1223, Traquet Patre. No. 1224, Sittele torchepot. No. 1225, Bouvreuil. No. 1226, Mesange bleue. No. 1227, Martin-pecheur. No. 1228, Chardonneret. No. 1229, Grive musicienne. No. 1230, Pinson.

Photo. (50c-2fr, No. 1220, 4.50fr-6fr, No. 1229, 10fr), Typo. (Others)

1985-91 ***Perf. 11½***

1216	A524	50c multicolored	.25	.25
1217	A524	1fr multicolored	.30	.25
1218	A524	2fr multicolored	.25	.25
1219	A524	3fr multicolored	.50	.25
1220	A524	3fr multicolored	.35	.25
1221	A524	3.50fr multicolored	.30	.25
1222	A524	4fr multicolored	.40	.25
1223	A524	4.50fr multicolored	.45	.25
1224	A524	5fr multicolored	.40	.25
1225	A524	6fr multicolored	.60	.25
1226	A524	7fr multicolored	.60	.25
1227	A524	8fr multicolored	.70	.25
1228	A524	9fr multicolored	1.00	.25
1229	A524	9fr multicolored	.70	.25
1230	A524	10fr multicolored	.75	.25
		Nos. 1216-1230 (15)	7.55	3.75

Issued: 7fr, 9/7/87; 5fr, 6fr, 9/12/88; 4fr, 4/17/89; 2fr, 12/4/89; 1fr, 1/8/90; 10fr, 1/15/90; 50c, Nos. 1220, 1229, 9/30/91; others, 9/30/85.

Printed on various papers.

See Nos. 1432-1447, 1627, 1641, 1645, 1651, 1660, 1676, 1696, 1700, 1702-1703, 1714-1715. For stamps denominated in francs and euros, see Nos. 1785-1790A, 1836-1840. For stamps denominated in euros only, see Nos. 1912-1916, 1970-1979, 2071-2076, 2123-2127, 2218-2222, 2278-2280, 2346-2347, 2402-2403, 2409-2411, 2481.

King Type of 1981

1986-90 **Photo.** ***Perf. 11½***

1231	A459a	14fr dark gray	1.00	.25
1232	A459a	24fr dk grysh green	2.00	.40
1233	A459a	25fr blue black	2.10	.25
1234	A460a	200fr sage grn & dl gray grn	29.00	.75
		Nos. 1231-1234 (4)	34.10	1.65

Issued: 24fr, 4/7/86; 200fr, 11/3/86; 14fr, 1/15/90; 25fr, 2/19/90.

Printed on various papers.

Congo Stamp Cent. — A525

10fr, Belgian Congo #3.

1986, Jan. 27 **Photo.** ***Perf. 11½***

1236	A525	10fr multicolored	1.40	.25

No. 1236 is most often collected as a pair. Value never hinged, $8.

See Zaire No. 1230.

Carnival Cities of Aalst and Binche A526

Folklore: masks, giants.

1986, Feb. 3

1237	A526	9fr Aalst Belfry	.60	.35
1238	A526	12fr Binche Gilles	.90	.30

Intl. Peace Year — A527

1986, Mar. 10

1239	A527	23fr Emblem, dove	1.75	.50

Stamp Day — A528

1986, Apr. 21 **Photo.** ***Perf. 11½***

1240	A528	13fr Artifacts	.90	.30

Europa 1986 A529

1986, May 5

1241	A529	13fr Fish	*1.00*	.25
1242	A529	24fr Flora	*2.25*	*.45*

Dogs — A530

9fr, Malines sheepdog. 13fr, Tervueren sheepdog. 24fr, Groenendael sheepdog. 26fr, Flemish cattle dog.

1986, May 26 **Photo.** ***Perf. 11½***

1243	A530	9fr multicolored	.70	.30
1244	A530	13fr multicolored	1.10	.35
1245	A530	24fr multicolored	1.75	.50
1246	A530	26fr multicolored	1.90	.55
		Nos. 1243-1246 (4)	5.45	1.70

St. Ludger's Church, Zele — A531

No. 1248, Waver Town Hall. No. 1249, Nederzwalm Canal. No. 1250, Chapel of Our Lady of the Dunes, Bredene. No. 1251, Licot Castle, Viroinval. No. 1252, Eynenbourg Castle, La Calamine.

1986, June 30 **Photo. & Engr.**

1247	A531	9fr multi	.60	.30
1248	A531	9fr multi	.60	.30
1249	A531	13fr multi, horiz.	.95	.30
1250	A531	13fr multi	.95	.30
1251	A531	13fr multi, horiz.	.95	.30
1252	A531	13fr multi, horiz.	.95	.30
		Nos. 1247-1252 (6)	5.00	1.80

Youth Philately A532

1986, Sept. 1 **Photo.** ***Perf. 11½***

1253	A532	9fr dl ol grn, blk & dk red	.60	.40

Cartoon Exhibition, Knokke.

Famous Men — A533

Designs: 9fr, Constant Permeke, painter, sculptor. 13fr, Baron Michel-Edmond de Selys Longchamps, scientist. 24fr, Felix Timmermans, writer. 26fr, Maurice Careme, poet.

1986, Sept. 29

1254	A533	9fr multicolored	.60	.30
1255	A533	13fr multicolored	1.00	.30
1256	A533	24fr multicolored	1.75	.50
1257	A533	26fr multicolored	1.90	.55
		Nos. 1254-1257 (4)	5.25	1.65

Royal Academy for Dutch Language and Literature, Cent. A534

1986, Oct. 6 **Engr.**
1258 A534 9fr dark blue .60 .30

Natl. Beer Industry A535

13fr, Glass, barley, hops.

Perf. 12½x11½

1986, Oct. 13 **Photo.**
1259 A535 13fr multicolored 1.00 .40

Provincial Law and Councils, 150th Anniv. A536

1986, Oct. 27 ***Perf. 11½***
1260 A536 13fr Stylized map 1.00 .30

Christian Trade Union, Cent. A537

1986, Dec. 13 **Photo.** ***Perf. 11½***
1261 A537 9fr shown .60 .40
1262 A537 13fr design reversed .90 .30

Flanders Technology Intl. — A538

1987, Mar. 2 **Photo.**
1263 A538 13fr multi .90 .30

EUROPALIA '87, Austrian Cultural Events — A539

Design: Woman, detail of a fresco by Gustav Klimt, Palais Stoclet, Brussels.

1987, Apr. 4 **Photo.** ***Perf. 11½***
1264 A539 13fr multicolored .90 .25

Stamp Day 1987 — A540

Portrait: Jakob Wiener (1815-1899), 1st engraver of Belgian stamps.

1987, Apr. 11 **Photo. & Engr.**
1265 A540 13fr grnsh blue & blk grn .90 .30

Folklore A541

9fr, Penitents procession, Veurne. 13fr, Play of John and Alice, Wavre.

1987, Apr. 25 **Photo.**
1266 A541 9fr multicolored .60 .40
1267 A541 13fr multicolored .90 .30

Europa 1987 — A542

Modern architecture: 13fr, Louvain-la-Neuve Church. 24fr, Regional Housing Assoc. Tower, St. Maartensdal at Louvain.

1987, May 9 **Photo.**
1268 A542 13fr multicolored *1.00* .25
1269 A542 24fr multicolored *2.10* *.40*

Statue of Andre-Ernest Gretry (1741-1813), French Composer A543

1987, May 23
1270 A543 24fr multicolored 1.75 .75

Wallonie Royal Opera, Liege, 20th anniv.

Tourism — A544

No. 1271, Statues of Jan Breydel and Pieter de Conin, Bruges. No. 1272, Boondael Chapel, Brussels. No. 1273, Windmill, Keerbergen. No. 1274, St. Christopher's Church, Racour. No. 1275, Virelles Lake, Chimay.

1987, June 13
1271 A544 13fr multicolored .90 .30
1272 A544 13fr multicolored .90 .30
1273 A544 13fr multicolored .90 .30
1274 A544 13fr multicolored .90 .30
1275 A544 13fr multicolored .90 .30
Nos. 1271-1275 (5) 4.50 1.50

Royal Belgian Rowing Assoc., Cent. — A545

European Volleyball Championships A546

1987, Sept. 5
1276 A545 9fr multicolored .60 .40
1277 A546 13fr multicolored .90 .30

Foreign Trade Year — A547

1987, Sept. 12
1278 A547 13fr multi .90 .30

Belgian Social Reform, Cent. A548

1987, Sept. 19
1279 A548 26fr Leisure, by P. Paulus 1.75 .75

Youth Philately A549

1987, Oct. 3
1280 A549 9fr multicolored 1.75 .50

Newspaper Centennials A550

No. 1281, Le Soir. No. 1282, Hett Lattste Nieuws, vert.

1987, Dec. 12
1281 A550 9fr multicolored .70 .30
1282 A550 9fr multicolored .70 .30

The Sea — A551

Designs: a, Lighthouse, trawler, rider and mount. b, Trawler, youths playing volleyball on beach. c, Cruise ship, sailboat, beach and cabana. d, Shore, birds.

1988, Feb. 6 **Photo.** ***Perf. 11½***
1283 Strip of 4 + label 3.00 2.50
a.-d. A551 10fr any single .70 .55

No. 1283 has a continuous design.

Dynamism of the Regions A552

No. 1284, Operation Athena. No. 1285, Flanders Alive Campaign.

1988, Mar. 5 **Photo.** ***Perf. 11½***
1284 A552 13fr multicolored .90 .35
1285 A552 13fr multicolored .90 .35

Stamp Day — A553

Painting: 19th Cent. Postman, by James Thiriar.

1988, Apr. 16 **Photo. & Engr.**
1286 A553 13fr buff & sepia .95 .30

Europa 1988 — A554

Transport and communication: 13fr, Satellite dish. 24fr, Non-polluting combustion engine.

1988, May 9 **Photo.** ***Perf. 11½***
1287 A554 13fr multicolored *1.10* .25
1288 A554 24fr multicolored *1.90* *.75*

Tourism — A555

Designs: No. 1289, Romanesque watchtower, ca. 12th-13th cent., Amay, vert. No. 1290, Our Lady of Hanswijk Basilica, 988, Mechelen, vert. No. 1291, St. Sernin's Church, 16th cent., Waimes. No. 1292, Old Town Hall, 1637, and village water pump, 1761, Peer, vert. No. 1293, Our Lady of Bon-Secours Basilica, 1892, Peruwelz.

Photo. & Engr.

1988, June 20 ***Perf. 11½***
1289 A555 9fr beige & blk .70 .40
1290 A555 9fr lt blue & blk .70 .40
1291 A555 9fr pale blue grn & blk .70 .40
1292 A555 13fr pale pink & blk .90 .30
1293 A555 13fr pale bluish gray & blk .90 .30
Nos. 1289-1293 (5) 3.90 1.80

Our Lady of Hanswijk Basilica millennium (No. 1290); Waimes village, 1100th anniv. (No. 1291).

Jean Monnet (1888-1979), French Economist — A556

1988, Sept. 12 ***Perf. 11½***

1294	A556	13fr black	.95	.35

Tapestry in the Hall of the Royal Academy of Medicine — A557

Academies building and: No. 1296, Lyre, quill pen, open book and atomic symbols.

1988, Sept. 17 **Photo.**

1295	A557	9fr shown	.55	.30
1296	A557	9fr multi	.55	.30

Royal Academy of Medicine (No. 1295); Royal Academy of Science, Literature and Fine Arts (No. 1296).

Cultural Heritage A558

Artifacts: 9fr, Statue and mask in the Antwerp Ethnographical Museum. 13fr, Sarcophagus, St. Martin's Church, Trazegnies. 24fr, Church organ, Geraardsbergen. 26fr, Shrine, St. Hadelin's Church, Vise.

1988, Sept. 24

1297	A558	9fr multi	.70	.30
1298	A558	13fr multi	.90	.25
1299	A558	24fr multi	1.75	.60
1300	A558	26fr multi	1.90	.60
		Nos. 1297-1300 (4)	5.25	1.75

Youth Philately A559

1988, Oct. 10

1301	A559	9fr multi	1.60	.50

Natl. Postal Savings Bank, 75th Anniv. A560

1988, Nov. 7

1302	A560	13fr multi	1.00	.50

Christmas 1988 and New Year 1989 A561

1988, Nov. 21

1303	A561	9fr Winter landscape	.65	.30

Royal Mounted Guard, 50th Anniv. A562

1988, Dec. 12

1304	A562	13fr multi	.95	.35

Printing Presses A563

9fr, J. Moretus I, Antwerp Museum, vert. 24fr, Stanhope, Printing Museum, Brussels, vert. 26fr, Litho Krause, Royal Museum, Mariemont.

1988, Dec. 19 **Engr.**

1305	A563	9fr bl blk & blk	.70	.30
1306	A563	24fr dark red brn	1.60	.55
1307	A563	26fr grn & slate grn	1.75	.50
		Nos. 1305-1307 (3)	4.05	1.35

Lace A564

No. 1308, Marche-en-Famenne. No. 1309, Brussels. No. 1310, Brugge.

1989, Mar. 20 **Photo.**

1308	A564	9fr multi	.70	.35
1309	A564	13fr multi	.90	.25
1310	A564	13fr multi	.90	.25
		Nos. 1308-1310 (3)	2.50	.85

Stamp Day A565

13fr, Mail coach, post chaise.

1989, Apr. 24 **Photo. & Engr.**

1311	A565	13fr multicolored	.95	.35

Europa 1989 — A566

Children's toys.

1989, May 8 **Photo.**

1312	A566	13fr Marbles, horiz.	*1.25*	.30
1313	A566	24fr Jumping-jack	*1.90*	*.70*

Royal Academy of Fine Arts, Antwerp, 325th Anniv. — A567

1989, May 22 ***Perf. 11½***

1314	A567	13fr multi	.85	.30

European Parliament 3rd Elections — A568

1989, June 5 **Photo.**

1315	A568	13fr Brussels	.85	.30

Declaration of Rights of Man and the Citizen, Bicent. — A569

1989, June 12 ***Perf. 11½***

1316	A569	13fr multi + label	1.50	.50

Tourism A570

No. 1317, St. Tillo's Church, Izegem. No. 1318, Logne Castle, Ferrieres. No. 1319, St. Laurentius's Church, Lokeren. No. 1320, Antoing Castle, Antoing.

1989, June 26 **Photo. & Engr.**

1317	A570	9fr multi	.70	.30
1318	A570	9fr multi, vert.	.70	.30
1319	A570	13fr multi, vert.	1.00	.30
1320	A570	13fr multi, vert.	1.00	.30
		Nos. 1317-1320 (4)	3.40	1.20

Ducks — A571

1989, Sept. 4 **Photo.** ***Perf. 12***

Booklet Stamps

1321	A571	13fr Mallard (8a)	1.25	.50
1322	A571	13fr Winter teal (8b)	1.25	.50
1323	A571	13fr Shoveller (8c)	1.25	.50
1324	A571	13fr Pintail (8d)	1.25	.50
a.		Bklt. pane of 4, #1321-1324	5.00	5.00
		Complete booklet, #1324a	5.00	

Shigefusa Uesugi, a Seated Japanese Warrior, 13th Cent. A572

1989, Sept. 18 ***Perf. 11½***

1325	A572	24fr multicolored	1.60	.60

Europalia.

Education League, 125th Anniv. — A573

1989, Sept. 25

1326	A573	13fr multicolored	.85	.30

Treaty of London, 150th Anniv. — A574

13fr, Map of Limburg Provinces.

1989, Oct. 2 **Photo.**

1327	A574	13fr multicolored	.85	.30

See Netherlands No. 750.

Mr. Nibbs — A575

1989, Oct. 9 ***Perf. 11½***

1328	A575	9fr multicolored	1.25	.40

Youth philately promotion.

Christmas, New Year 1990 A576

9fr, Salvation Army band.

1989, Nov. 20 **Photo.**

1329	A576	9fr multicolored	.65	.30

Fr. Damien (1840-89), Missionary, Molokai Is. Leper Colony, Hawaii A577

1989, Nov. 27 **Photo.**

1330	A577	24fr multicolored	1.75	.60

Father Adolf Daens — A578

1989, Dec. 11 **Photo. & Engr.**
1331 A578 9fr pale & dk grn .60 .30

The Young Post Rider, an Engraving by Albrecht Durer — A579

1990, Jan. 12 **Photo. & Engr.**
1332 A579 14fr blksh pur, gray brn, beige 1.00 .30

Postal communications in Europe, 500th anniv.

See Austria No. 1486, Germany No. 1592, Berlin No. 9N584 and German Democratic Republic No. 2791.

Ghent Flower Festival — A580

No. 1333, Iris florentina. No. 1334, Cattleya harrisoniana. No. 1335, Lilium bulbiferum.

1990, Mar. 3 **Photo.**
1333 A580 10fr multicolored .70 .40
1334 A580 14fr multicolored 1.00 .30
1335 A580 14fr multicolored 1.00 .30
Nos. 1333-1335 (3) 2.70 1.00

Intl. Women's Day — A581

25fr, Emilienne Brunfaut.

1990, Mar. 12 **Photo.** ***Perf. 11½***
1336 A581 25fr multicolored 1.75 .75

Wheelchair Basketball — A582

Sports.

1990, Mar. 19
1337 A582 10fr multicolored .65 .40
1338 A582 14fr multicolored 1.00 .30
1339 A582 25fr shown 1.60 .60
Nos. 1337-1339 (3) 3.25 1.30

Special Olympics (10fr); and 1990 World Cup Soccer Championships, Italy (14fr).

Natl. Water Supply Soc., 75th Anniv. A583

1990, Apr. 2
1340 A583 14fr Water means life .95 .35

Postman Roulin, by Van Gogh — A584

1990, Apr. 9
1341 A584 14fr multicolored .95 .30

Stamp Day.

Labor Day, Cent. A585

1990, Apr. 30
1342 A585 25fr multicolored 1.75 .70

Europa 1990 A586

Post offices.

1990, May 7 **Photo. & Engr.**
1343 A586 14fr Ostend 1 *1.10* .25
1344 A586 25fr Liege 1, vert. *2.50* .70

18-Day Campaign, 1940 — A587

14fr, Lys Monument, Courtrai.

1990, May 14 **Photo.** ***Perf. 11½***
1345 A587 14fr multicolored 1.00 .30

Resistance of German occupation.

Stamp Collecting Promotion Type of 1988

Souvenir Sheet

Various flowers from *Sixty Roses for a Queen,* by P.J. Redoute (1759-1840): a, Rose tricolore. b, Belle Rubaree. c, Mycrophylla. d, Amelie rose. e, Adelaide rose. f, Helene rose.

1990, June 2 **Photo. & Engr.**
1346 Sheet of 6 25.00 25.00
a.-c. SP487 14fr any single 3.50 3.50
d.-f. SP487 25fr any single 4.50 4.50

BELGICA '90, Brussels, June 2-10. sold for 220fr.

Battle of Waterloo, 1815 — A588

Design: Marshal Ney leading the French cavalry.

1990, June 18 **Photo.**
1352 A588 25fr multi + label 1.75 1.40

Tourism A589

1990, July 9
1353 A589 10fr Antwerp .80 .40
1354 A589 10fr Dendermonde .80 .40
1355 A589 14fr Gerpinnes, vert. .95 .30
1356 A589 14fr Lommel .95 .30
1357 A589 14fr Watermael .95 .30
Nos. 1353-1357 (5) 4.45 1.70

A590

A590a

King Baudouin A590b

1990-92 **Photo.** ***Perf. 11½***
1364 A590 14fr multicolored 1.10 .25
1365 A590a 15fr rose car 1.25 .25
1366 A590a 28fr blue green 2.00 .55
1367 A590b 100fr slate green 7.50 .50
Nos. 1364-1367 (4) 11.85 1.55

Issue dates: 14fr, Sept. 7; 15fr, Apr. 1; 28fr, Aug. 3, 1992; 100fr, Sept. 14, 1992.

Fish A591

Designs: No. 1383, Perch (Perche). No. 1384, Minnow (Vairon). No. 1385, Bitterling (Bouviere). No. 1386, Stickleback (Epinoche).

1990, Sept. 8 ***Perf. 12***
1383 A591 14fr multicolored 1.75 .60
1384 A591 14fr multicolored 1.75 .60
1385 A591 14fr multicolored 1.75 .60
1386 A591 14fr multicolored 1.75 .60
a. Bklt. pane of 4, #1383-1386 7.00 *7.00*
Complete booklet, #1386a 7.25

Youth Philately A592

1990, Oct. 13 ***Perf. 11½***
1387 A592 10fr multicolored 1.50 .50

St. Bernard, 900th Birth Anniv. — A593

1990, Nov. 5 **Photo & Engr.**
1388 A593 25fr black & buff 1.75 .60

Winter Scene by Jozef Lucas A594

1990, Nov. 12 **Photo.**
1389 A594 10fr multi .70 .30

Christmas.

Self-Portrait A595

Paintings by David Teniers (1610-1690).

1990, Dec. 3
1390 A595 10fr shown .70 .30
1391 A595 14fr Dancers 1.00 .30
1392 A595 25fr Bowlers 1.90 .60
Nos. 1390-1392 (3) 3.60 1.20

A596

Designs: 14fr, The Sower by Constantin Meunier (1831-1905). 25fr, Brabo Fountain by Jef Lambeaux (1852-1908).

Photo. & Engr.

1991, Mar. 18 ***Perf. 11½***
1393 A596 14fr buff & blk 1.00 .30
1394 A596 25fr lt bl & dk bl 1.60 .60

A597

No. 1395, Rhythmic gymnastics. No. 1396, Korfball.

1991, Apr. 8 **Photo.** ***Perf. 11½***
1395 A597 10fr multicolored .65 .30
1396 A597 10fr multicolored .65 .30

No. 1395, European Youth Olympics. No. 1396, Korfball World Championships.

Stamp Printing Office, Mechlin — A598

1991, Apr. 22

1397 A598 14fr multicolored .95 .30

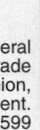

Stamp Day.

Liberal Trade Union, Cent. A599

1991, Apr. 29

1398 A599 25fr blue & lt blue 1.60 .60

Europa A600

14fr, Olympus-1 satellite. 25fr, Hermes space shuttle.

1991, May 6

1399 A600 14fr multicolored *1.25* .25
1400 A600 25fr multicolored *2.50* *.75*

Rerum Novarum Encyclical, Cent. A601

1991, May 13 **Photo.** ***Perf. 11½***

1401 A601 14fr multicolored .90 .30

Princess Isabel & Philip le Bon — A602

1991, May 27 **Photo.** ***Perf. 11½***

1402 A602 14fr multicolored .90 .30

Europalia '91. See Portugal No. 1861.

Tourism A603

Designs: No. 1403, Neptune's Grotto, Couvin. No. 1404, Dieleghem Abbey, Jette. No. 1405, Town Hall, Niel, vert. No. 1406, Nature Reserve, Hautes Fagnes. No. 1407, Legend of giant Rolarius, Roeselare, vert.

1991, June 17 **Photo. & Engr.**

1403 A603 14fr multicolored .90 .30
1404 A603 14fr multicolored .90 .30
1405 A603 14fr multicolored .90 .30
1406 A603 14fr multicolored .90 .30
1407 A603 14fr multicolored .90 .30
Nos. 1403-1407 (5) 4.50 1.50

King Baudouin, Coronation, 40th Anniv. and 60th Birthday A604

1991, June 24 **Photo.**

1408 A604 14fr multicolored 1.90 .30

Royal Academy of Medicine, 150th Anniv. — A605

Photo. & Engr.

1991, Sept. 2 ***Perf. 11½***

1409 A605 10fr multicolored .70 .30

The English Coast at Dover by Alfred W. Finch (1854-1930) A606

1991, Sept. 9 **Photo.**

1410 A606 25fr multicolored 1.75 .65

See Finland Nos. 868-869.

Mushrooms — A607

No. 1411, Amanita phalloides (13A). No. 1412, Amanita rubescens (13B). No. 1413, Boletus erythropus (13C). No. 1414, Hygrocybe persistens (13D).

1991, Sept. 16 **Photo.** ***Perf. 12***

Booklet Stamps

1411 A607 14fr multicolored 1.75 .70
1412 A607 14fr multicolored 1.75 .70
1413 A607 14fr multicolored 1.75 .70
1414 A607 14fr multicolored 1.75 .70
a. Bklt. pane of 4, #1411-1414 7.00 *7.00*
Complete booklet, #1414a 7.25

Doctors Without Borders A608

Design: No. 1415, Amnesty Intl.

1991, Sept. 23 ***Perf. 11½***

1415 A608 25fr multicolored 1.60 .60
1416 A608 25fr multicolored 1.60 .60

Telecom '91 — A609

1991, Oct. 7 **Photo.** ***Perf. 11½***

1417 A609 14fr multicolored .90 .30

6th World Forum and Exposition on Telecommunications, Geneva, Switzerland.

Youth Philately — A610

Cartoon characters: No. 1418, Blake and Mortimer, by Edgar P. Jacobs (16a). No. 1419, Cori the ship boy, by Bob De Moor (16b). No. 1420, Cities of the Fantastic, by Francois Schuiten (16c). No. 1421, Boule and Bill, by Jean Roba (16d).

1991, Oct. 14 ***Perf. 12***

Booklet Stamps

1418 A610 14fr multicolored 1.60 1.25
1419 A610 14fr multicolored 1.60 1.25
1420 A610 14fr multicolored 1.60 1.25
1421 A610 14fr multicolored 1.60 1.25
a. Bklt. pane of 4, #1418-1421 7.00 *7.00*
Complete booklet, #1421a 7.25

Belgian Newspapers, Cent. — A611

No. 1422, Gazet Van Antwerpen. No. 1423, Het Volk.

1991, Nov. 4 **Photo.** ***Perf. 11½***

1422 A611 10fr multicolored .65 .30
1423 A611 10fr multicolored .65 .30

Icon of Madonna and Child, Chevetogne Abbey A612

1991, Nov. 25 **Photo.** ***Perf. 11½***

1424 A612 10fr multicolored .60 .30

Christmas.

Wolfgang Amadeus Mozart, Death Bicent. — A613

1991, Dec. 2 **Photo.** ***Perf. 11½***

1425 A613 25fr multicolored 1.75 .80

Fire Fighting — A614

1992, Feb. 10 **Photo.** ***Perf. 11½***

1426 A614 14fr multicolored .85 .30

Belgian Resistance in WWII — A615

1992, Feb. 24

1427 A615 14fr multicolored .85 .30

Belgian Carpet Industry — A616

Antwerp Diamond Club, Cent. A617

Design: 14fr, Chef's hat, cutlery.

1992, Mar. 9

1428 A616 10fr multicolored .65 .35
1429 A616 14fr multicolored .90 .30
1430 A617 27fr multicolored 1.75 .60
Nos. 1428-1430 (3) 3.30 1.25

Belgian Association of Master Chefs.

Expo '92, Seville A618

1992, Mar. 23

1431 A618 14fr multicolored .90 .30

Bird Type of 1985

No. 1432, Sizerin flamme. No. 1433, Merle noir. No. 1434, Grive mauvis. No. 1435, Gobe mouche noir. No. 1436, Bergeronette grise. No. 1437, Etourneau sansonnet. No. 1438, Hirondelle de cheminee. No. 1439, Geai des chenes. No. 1440, Cincle plongeur. No. 1441, Phragmite des joncs. No. 1442, Loriot. No. 1443, Mesange charbonniere. No. 1444, Verdier. No. 1445, Troglodyte mignon. No. 1446, Moineau domestique. No. 1446A, Pouillot fitis. No. 1447, Jaseur boreal.

1992-96 **Photo.** ***Perf. 11½***

1432	A524	1fr	multicolored	.25	.25
1433	A524	2fr	multicolored	.25	.25
1434	A524	2fr	multicolored	.25	.25
1435	A524	4fr	multicolored	.35	.25
1436	A524	4fr	multicolored	.35	.25
1437	A524	5fr	multicolored	.35	.25
1438	A524	5fr	multicolored	.35	.25
1439	A524	5.50fr	multicolored	.50	.25
1440	A524	6fr	multicolored	.50	.25
1441	A524	6.50fr	multicolored	.50	.30
1442	A524	7fr	multicolored	.60	.25
1443	A524	8fr	multicolored	.60	.25
1444	A524	10fr	multicolored	.75	.25
1445	A524	11fr	multicolored	.80	.25
1446	A524	13fr	multicolored	1.00	.25

1446A A524 14fr multicolored 1.00 .25
1447 A524 16fr multicolored 1.25 .25
Nos. 1432-1447 (17) 9.65 4.30

Issued: 11fr, 4/1/92; 1fr, 2fr, 6fr, 8fr, 10fr, 6/92; 4fr, 5fr, 7fr, 9/7/92; 5.50fr, 9/27/93; 13fr, 16fr, 1/3/94; 6.50fr, 10/3/94; 14fr, 12/18/95; No. 1435A, 5/6/96; No. 1433A, 1434, 7/1/96.
Printed on various papers.
See No. 1838 for similar stamp with additional Euro denomination.

Jean Van Noten (1903-1982), Stamp Designer — A619

Photo. & Engr.

1992, Apr. 13 ***Perf. 11½***
1448 A619 15fr ver & black .85 .30

Stamp Day.

Abstract Painting by Jo Delahaut — A620

No. 1449, Witte Magie No. 6, by Roger Raveel.

1992, Apr. 27 **Photo.** ***Perf. 11½***
1449 A620 15fr multi, vert. .90 .30
1450 A620 15fr multi .90 .30

European Discovery of America, 500th Anniv. — A621

28fr, 500 with globe and astrolabe inside "00" of 500.

1992, May 2
1451 A621 15fr shown *1.25 .30*
1452 A621 28fr multicolored *2.25 .90*

Europa.

Fight Racism — A622

1992, May 18 **Photo.** ***Perf. 11½***
1453 A622 15fr black, gray & pink .85 .30

Paintings from Orsay Museum, Paris — A623

Paintings by Belgian artists: 11fr, The Hamlet, by Jacob Smits. 15fr, The Bath, by Alfred Stevens. 30fr, The Man at the Helm, by Theo Van Rysselberghe.

1992, June 15 **Photo.** ***Perf. 11½***
1454 A623 11fr multicolored .70 .30
1455 A623 15fr multicolored 1.10 .30
1456 A623 30fr multicolored 2.00 .75
Nos. 1454-1456 (3) 3.80 1.35

Tourism — A624

Designs: No. 1457, Manneken Pis Fountain, Brussels. No. 1458, Landcommander Castle Alden Biesen, Bilzen, horiz. No. 1459, Building facade, Andenne. No. 1460, Fools' Monday Carnival, Renaix, horiz. No. 1461, Great Procession, Tournai, horiz.

Photo. & Engr.

1992, July 6 ***Perf. 11½***
1457 A624 15fr multicolored .95 .30
1458 A624 15fr multicolored .95 .30
1459 A624 15fr multicolored .95 .30
1460 A624 15fr multicolored .95 .30
1461 A624 15fr multicolored .95 .30
Nos. 1457-1461 (5) 4.75 1.50

Village of Andenne, 1300th anniv. (No. 1459). Grand Procession of Tournai, 900th anniv. (No. 1461).

Animals — A625

1992, Sept. 7 **Photo.** ***Perf. 12***
Booklet Stamps
1462 A625 15fr Polecat (13a) 1.50 .65
1463 A625 15fr Squirrel (13b) 1.50 .65
1464 A625 15fr Hedgehog (13c) 1.50 .65
1465 A625 15fr Dormouse (13d) 1.50 .65
a. Bklt. pane of 4, #1462-1465 6.00 *6.00*
Complete booklet, #1465a 6.00

Brabant Revolution — A626

Design: 15fr, Troops fighting and Henri Van der Noot, Jean Andre Van der Meersch, and Jean Francois Vonck, rebel leaders.

Photo. & Engr.

1992, Sept. 21 ***Perf. 11½***
1466 A626 15fr multicolored .85 .25

Arms of Thurn and Taxis — A627

1992, Oct. 5 **Photo.** ***Perf. 11½***
1467 A627 15fr multicolored .90 .30

Gaston Lagaffe, by Andre Franquin A628

1992, Oct. 12
1468 A628 15fr multicolored 1.25 .35

Youth philately.

Single European Market — A629

1992, Oct. 26
1469 A629 15fr multicolored .85 .30

Antwerp Zoo, 150th Anniv. — A630

1992, Nov. 16
1470 A630 15fr Okapi .85 .30
1471 A630 30fr Tamarin 2.00 .75

The Brussels Place Royale in Winter, by Luc De Decker A631

1992, Nov. 23
1472 A631 11fr multicolored .65 .30

Christmas.

History A632

Designs: 11fr, Council of Leptines, 1250th anniv. 15fr, 28fr, Missale Romanum of Matthias Corvinus (Matyas Hunyadi, King of Hungary) (diff. details). 30fr, Battles of Neerwinden (1693, 1793).

1993, Mar. 15 **Photo.** ***Perf. 11½***
1473 A632 11fr multicolored .65 .30
1474 A632 15fr multicolored 1.00 .30
1475 A632 30fr multicolored 2.00 .65
Nos. 1473-1475 (3) 3.65 1.25

Souvenir Sheet

1476 A632 28fr multicolored 2.00 2.00

Size of No. 1474, 80x28mm. No. 1476 contains one 55x40mm stamp.
See Hungary No. 3385-3386.

A633

A634

Antwerp, Cultural City of Europe A635

Designs: No. 1477, Panoramic view of Antwerp. No. 1478, Antwerp Town Hall, designed by Cornelis Floris. No. 1479, Woman's Head and Warrior's Torso, by Jacob Jordaens. No. 1480, St. Job's Altar (detail), Schoonbroek. No. 1481, Angels on stained glass window, Mater Dei Chapel of Institut Marie-Josee, by Eugeen Yoors, vert.

1993, Mar. 22
1477 A633 15fr multicolored 1.00 .30
1478 A634 15fr multicolored 1.00 .30
1479 A635 15fr gray & multi 1.00 .30
1480 A635 15fr green & multi 1.00 .30
1481 A635 15fr blue & multi 1.00 .30
Nos. 1477-1481 (5) 5.00 1.50

Antwerp '93.

Stamp Day — A636

1993, Apr. 5
1482 A636 15fr No. 74 .95 .30

Contemporary Paintings — A637

Europa: 15fr, Florence 1960, by Gaston Bertrand. 28fr, De Sjees, by Constant Permeke.

1993, Apr. 26 **Photo.** ***Perf. 11½***
1483 A637 15fr multicolored *1.00 .25*
1484 A637 28fr multicolored *2.00 .60*

Butterflies — A638

1993, May 10

1485 A638 15fr Vanessa atalanta .90 .30
1486 A638 15fr Apatura iris .90 .30
1487 A638 15fr Inachis io .90 .30
1488 A638 15fr Aglais urticae .90 .30
Nos. 1485-1488 (4) 3.60 1.20

Alumni Assoc. (UAE), Free University of Brussels, 150th Anniv. A639

1993, May 17

1489 A639 15fr blue & black .85 .30

No. 1489 is usually collected as a horizontal pair. Value, $5 never-hinged.

Europalia '93 — A640

1993, May 24

1490 A640 15fr Mayan statuette .85 .30

Folklore A641

Designs: 11fr, Ommegang Procession, Brussels. 15fr, Royal Moncrabeau Folk Group, Namur. 28fr, Stilt walkers of Merchtem, vert.

1993, June 7 **Photo.** ***Perf. 11½***

1491 A641 11fr multicolored .75 .35
1492 A641 15fr multicolored .95 .30
1493 A641 28fr multicolored 1.50 .60
Nos. 1491-1493 (3) 3.20 1.25

Tourism A642

Castles: No. 1494, La Hulpe. No. 1495, Cortewalle (Beveren). No. 1496, Jehay. No. 1497, Arenberg (Heverlee), vert. No. 1498, Raeren.

Photo. & Engr.

1993, June 21 ***Perf. 11½***

1494 A642 15fr pale green & blk .95 .30
1495 A642 15fr pale lilac & black .95 .30
1496 A642 15fr pale blue & black .95 .30
1497 A642 15fr pale brn & black .95 .30
1498 A642 15fr pale olive & blk .95 .30
Nos. 1494-1498 (5) 4.75 1.50

Intl. Triennial Exhibition of Tournai A643

1993, July 5 **Photo.** ***Perf. 11½***

1499 A643 15fr black, blue & red .85 .30

Belgian Presidency of European Community Council A644

1993, Aug. 9 **Photo.** ***Perf. 11½***

1500 A644 15fr multicolored .85 .30

Rene Magritte (1898-1967), Artist — A645

1993, Aug. 9

1501 A645 30fr multicolored 1.90 .70

King Baudouin (1930-1993) — A646

1993, Aug. 17 **Photo.** ***Perf. 11½***

1502 A646 15fr black & gray 1.00 .25

European House Cats — A647

1993, Sept. 6 **Photo.** ***Perf. 12***

Booklet Stamps

1503 A647 15fr Brown & white (10a) 1.25 .60
1504 A647 15fr Black & white (10b) 1.25 .60
1505 A647 15fr Gray tabby (10c) 1.25 .60
1506 A647 15fr Calico (10d) 1.25 .60
a. Booklet pane of 4, #1503-1506 5.00 *5.00*
Complete booklet, #1506a 5.00

Publication of De Humani Corporis Fabrica, by Andreas Vesalius, 1543 — A648

1993, Oct. 4 **Photo.** ***Perf. 11½***

1507 A648 15fr multicolored .85 .30

Air Hostess Natacha, by Francois Walthery — A649

1993, Oct. 18

1508 A649 15fr multicolored 1.10 .40

Youth philately.

Publication of "Faux Soir," 50th Anniv. — A650

1993, Nov. 8 **Photo.** ***Perf. 11½***

1509 A650 11fr multicolored .70 .40

Notre-Dame de la Chapelle, Brussels A651

1993, Nov. 22 **Photo.** ***Perf. 11½***

1510 A651 11fr multicolored .60 .30

Christmas, New Year.

Children, Future Decisionmakers — A652

1993, Dec. 13 **Photo.** ***Perf. 11½***

1511 A652 15fr multicolored .85 .30

A653

A654

A655

A655a

King Albert II

1993-98 **Photo.** ***Perf. 11½***

1512 A653 16fr lt gray & multi 1.40 .25
1513 A653 16fr lt & dk bl grn 1.00 .25
1514 A655 16fr multi 1.40 .25
1515 A655 16fr blue .90 .25
1516 A655 17fr blue 1.10 .25
1517 A655 18fr olive black 1.00 .25
1518 A655 19fr dp gray vio 1.20 .30
1519 A653 20fr cream & brn 1.40 .40
1520 A655 20fr brown 1.20 .25
1521 A655 25fr sepia 1.30 .30
1522 A655 28fr claret 1.90 .30
1523 A653 30fr red lilac 1.50 .25
1524 A655 32fr violet blue 1.75 .25
1525 A653 32fr cream & org brn 1.75 .25
1526 A655 34fr dk bl gray 1.50 .50
1527 A655 36fr dk sl bl 1.75 .25
1528 A653 40fr pink & car 2.40 .30
1529 A653 50fr green 4.00 .35
1530 A655 50fr green 3.00 .40
1531 A654 100fr multi 6.00 .35
1532 A654 200fr multi 12.50 2.50
Nos. 1512-1532 (21) 49.95 8.45

Coil Stamp

1536 A655a 19fr deep gray vio 1.50 1.25

Issued: No. 1512, 12/15/93; No. 1513, 1/17/94; 30fr, 2/4/94; No. 1525, 3/7/94; 50fr, 4/18/94; No. 1519, 6/6/94; 40fr, 6/20/94; 100fr, 10/3/94; 200fr, 5/2/95; No. 1514, 6/6/96; No. 1515, 1530, 28fr, 9/2/96; 17fr, 12/16/96; 34fr, 36fr, 2/10/97; 18fr, 4/7/97; No. 1518, 7/7/97; 25fr, 4/20/98; No. 1536, 8/10/98; No. 1520, 10/19/98; No. 1524, 11/9/98.

Paintings A656

Designs: No. 1537, The Malleable Darkness, by Octave Landuyt. No. 1538, Ma Toute Belle, by Serge Vandercam, vert.

1994, Jan. 31 **Photo.** ***Perf. 11½***

1537 A656 16fr multicolored 1.00 .30
1538 A656 16fr multicolored 1.00 .30

Airplanes A657

13fr, Hanriot-Dupont HD-1. 15fr, Spad XIII. 30fr, Schreck FBA-H. 32fr, Stampe-Vertongen SV-4B.

1994, Feb. 28

1539 A657 13fr multicolored .90 .35
1540 A657 15fr multicolored 1.10 .30
1541 A657 30fr multicolored 1.75 .60
1542 A657 32fr multicolored 2.00 .50
Nos. 1539-1542 (4) 5.75 1.75

Daily Newspapers — A658

No. 1543, "Le Jour-Le Courier," cent., vert. No. 1544, "La Wallonie," 75th anniv.

1994, Mar. 21 **Photo.** ***Perf. 11½***

1543 A658 16fr multicolored 1.00 .30
1544 A658 16fr multicolored 1.00 .30

Fall of the Golden Calf (Detail), by Fernand Allard l'Olivier — A659

1994, Mar. 28

1545 A659 16fr multicolored 1.00 .35

Charter of Quaregnon, cent.

Stamp Day — A660

1994, Apr. 11 Photo. *Perf. 11½*

1546 A660 16fr No. 102 1.00 .30

History A661

Scenes from Brabantse Yeesten, 15th cent. illuminated manuscript: 13fr, Reconciliation between John I and Arnold, squire of Wezemaal. 16fr, Tournament at wedding of Charles the Bold and Margaret of York. 30fr, Battle of Woeringen.

1994, Apr. 25

1547 A661 13fr multicolored .80 .35
1548 A661 16fr multicolored 1.00 .30
1549 A661 30fr multicolored 2.00 .70
Nos. 1547-1549 (3) 3.80 1.35

No. 1549 is 81x28mm.

Europa — A662

Designs: 16fr, Abbe Georges Lemaitre (1894-1966), proposed "big-bang" theory of origins of universe. 30fr, Gerardus Mercator (1512-94), cartographer, astronomer.

1994, May 9 Photo. *Perf. 11½*

1550 A662 16fr multicolored *1.10* .25
1551 A662 30fr multicolored *2.25* .80

Papal Visit A663

No. 1552, Father Damien (1840-89). No. 1553, St. Mutien-Marie (1841-1917), Christian educator.

1994, May 16 *Perf. 11½x12*

1552 A663 16fr multicolored 1.00 .30
1553 A663 16fr multicolored 1.00 .30

Tourism A664

Churches: No. 1554, St. Peter's, Bertem. No. 1555, St. Bavo's, Kanegem, vert. No. 1556, Royal St. Mary's, Schaarbeek. No. 1557, St. Gery's, Aubechies. No. 1558, Sts. Peter and Paul, Saint-Severin, Condroz, vert.

1994, June 13 Photo. *Perf. 11½*

1554 A664 16fr multicolored 1.00 .30
1555 A664 16fr multicolored 1.00 .30
1556 A664 16fr multicolored 1.00 .30
1557 A664 16fr multicolored 1.00 .30
1558 A664 16fr multicolored 1.00 .30
Nos. 1554-1558 (5) 5.00 1.50

Guillaume Lekeu (1870-94), Composer A665

Design: No. 1560, Detail of painting by Hans Memling (c.1430-94).

1994, Aug. 16 Photo. *Perf. 11½*

1559 A665 16fr multicolored .90 .30
1560 A665 16fr multicolored .90 .30

Liberation of Belgium, 50th Anniv. — A666

Design: 16fr, General Crerar, Field Marshal Montgomery, Gen. Bradley, Belgium landscape.

1994, Sept. 5 Photo. *Perf. 11x11½*

1561 A666 16fr multicolored 1.10 .30

Wildflowers — A667

Designs: No. 1562, Caltha palustris. No. 1563, Cephalanthera damasonium. No. 1564, Calystegia soldanella. No. 1565, Epipactis helleborine.

1994, Sept. 26 Photo. *Perf. 12*

Booklet Stamps

1562 A667 16fr multi (14a) 1.25 .60
1563 A667 16fr multi (14b) 1.25 .60
1564 A667 16fr multi (14c) 1.25 .60
1565 A667 16fr multi (14d) 1.25 .60
a. Booklet pane of 4, #1562-1565 5.00 *5.00*
Complete booklet, #1565a 5.00
Nos. 1562-1565 (4) 5.00 2.40

Cubitus the Dog, by Luc Dupanloup — A668

1994, Oct. 10 *Perf. 11½*

1566 A668 16fr multicolored 1.25 .40

Youth philately.

Georges Simenon (1903-89), Writer A669

Photo. & Engr.

1994, Oct. 17 *Perf. 11½*

1567 A669 16fr multicolored 1.25 .30

See France No. 2443, Switzerland No. 948.

Christmas A670

1994, Dec. 5 Photo. *Perf. 11½*

1568 A670 13fr multicolored .80 .30

Anniversaries and Events — A671

No. 1569, August Vermeylen Fund, 50th anniv. No. 1570, Belgian Touring Club, cent. No. 1571, Assoc. of Belgian Enterprises, cent. No. 1572, Dept. of Social Security, 50th anniv.

1995, Feb. 13 Photo. *Perf. 11½*

1569 A671 16fr multicolored 1.00 .30
1570 A671 16fr multicolored 1.00 .30
1571 A671 16fr multicolored 1.00 .30
1572 A671 16fr multicolored 1.00 .30
Nos. 1569-1572 (4) 4.00 1.20

Flowers of Ghent A672

13fr, Hibiscus rosa-sinensis. 16fr, Rhododendron simsii. 30fr, Fuchsia hybrida.

1995, Mar. 6

1573 A672 13fr multicolored .75 .40
1574 A672 16fr multicolored 1.00 .30
1575 A672 30fr multicolored 2.00 .60
Nos. 1573-1575 (3) 3.75 1.30

Games — A673

13fr, Crossword puzzles. 16fr, Chess. 30fr, Scrabble. 34fr, Cards.

1995, Mar. 20

1576 A673 13fr multicolored .75 .35
1577 A673 16fr multicolored .95 .30
1578 A673 30fr multicolored 1.90 .60
1579 A673 34fr multicolored 2.00 .75
Nos. 1576-1579 (4) 5.60 2.00

Stamp Day — A674

1995, Apr. 10 Photo. & Engr.

1580 A674 16fr Frans de Troyer 1.00 .30

Peace & Freedom A675

Europa: 16fr, Broken barbed wire, prison guard tower. 30fr, Mushroom cloud, "Never again."

1995, Apr. 24 Photo. *Perf. 11½*

1581 A675 16fr multicolored *1.25* .25
1582 A675 30fr multicolored *2.40* *1.00*

Liberation of concentration camps, 50th anniv. (No. 1581). Nuclear Non-Proliferation Treaty, 25th anniv. (No. 1582).

Battle of Fontenoy, 250th Anniv. — A676

16fr, Irish soldiers, Cross of Fontenoy.

1995, May 15 Photo. *Perf. 11½*

1583 A676 16fr multicolored 1.00 .30

See Ireland No. 967.

UN, 50th Anniv. A677

1995, May 22 Photo. *Perf. 11½*

1584 A677 16fr multicolored 1.00 .30

"Sauvagemont, Maransart," by Pierre Alechinsky — A678

No. 1586: "Telegram-style," by Pol Mara.

1995, June 6

1585 A678 16fr multicolored 1.00 .30
1586 A678 16fr multicolored 1.00 .30

Tourism A679

Architectural designs: No. 1587, Cauchie house, Brussels, by Paul Cauchie (1875-1952). No. 1588, De Viif Werelddelen, corner building, Antwerp, by Frans Smet-Verhas (1851-1925). No. 1589, House, Liege, by Paul Jaspar (1859-1945).

1995, June 26

1587 A679 16fr multicolored 1.00 .30
1588 A679 16fr multicolored 1.00 .30
1589 A679 16fr multicolored 1.00 .30
Nos. 1587-1589 (3) 3.00 .90

Sailing Ships — A680

No. 1590, Mercator. No. 1591, Kruzenstern. No. 1592, Sagres II. No. 1593, Amerigo Vespucci.

Booklet Stamps

1995, Aug. 21 Photo. *Perf. 12*

1590 A680 16fr multicolored	1.20	.60
1591 A680 16fr multicolored	1.20	.60
1592 A680 16fr multicolored	1.20	.60
1593 A680 16fr multicolored	1.20	.60
a. Booklet pane of 4, #1590-1593	5.00	5.00
Complete booklet, #1593a	5.00	
Nos. 1590-1593 (4)	4.80	2.40

Classic Motorcycles A681

13fr, 1908 Minerva. 16fr, 1913 FN, vert. 30fr, 1929 La Mondiale. 32fr, 1937 Gillet, vert.

1995, Sept. 25 Photo. *Perf. 11½*

1594 A681 13fr multi	.75	.40
1595 A681 16fr multi	.90	.30
1596 A681 30fr multi	1.75	.60
1597 A681 32fr multi	2.00	.50
Nos. 1594-1597 (4)	5.40	1.80

Comic Character, Sammy, by Arthur Berckmans A682

1995, Oct. 9 Photo. *Perf. 11½*

1598 A682 16fr multicolored	1.20	.35

Youth philately.

King's Day A683

16fr, King Albert II and Queen Paola.

1995, Nov. 15 Photo. *Perf. 11½*

1599 A683 16fr multicolored	1.00	.30

Christmas — A684

13fr, Nativity scene from "Breviary," book of devotions, c. 1500.

1995, Nov. 20

1600 A684 13fr multicolored	.85	.30

Liberal Party, 150th Anniv. — A685

1996, Mar. 4 Photo. *Perf. 11½*

1601 A685 16fr multicolored	1.00	.30

Portrait of Emile Mayrisch (1862-1928), by Théo Van Rysselberghe (1862-1926) — A686

1996, Mar. 2

1602 A686 (A) multicolored	2.00	.30

No. 1602 was valued at 16fr on day of issue. See Luxembourg No. 939.

Oscar Bonnevalle, Stamp Designer — A687

1996, Apr. 1

1603 A687 16fr multicolored	1.00	.30

Stamp Day.

Insects A688

No. 1604, Sympetrum sanguineum. No. 1605, Bombus terrestris. No. 1606, Lucanus cervus. No. 1607, Melolontha melolontha. No. 1608, Gryllus campestris. No. 1609, Coccinella septempunctata.

1996, Apr. 1 Photo. *Perf. 12*

Booklet Stamps

1604 A688 16fr multicolored	1.00	.75
1605 A688 16fr multicolored	1.00	.75
1606 A688 16fr multicolored	1.00	.75
1607 A688 16fr multicolored	1.00	.75
1608 A688 16fr multicolored	1.00	.75
1609 A688 16fr multicolored	1.00	.75
a. Booklet pane, #1604-1609	6.50	*6.50*
Complete booklet, #1609a	6.50	
Nos. 1604-1609 (6)	6.00	4.50

Famous Women A689

Europa: 16fr, Yvonne Nevejean (1900-87), saved Jewish children during World War II. 30fr, Marie Gevers (1883-1975), poet.

1996, May 6 Photo. *Perf. 11½*

1610 A689 16fr multicolored	*1.00*	.25
1611 A689 30fr multicolored	*2.00*	*1.00*

Tourism — A690

Designs: No. 1612, Grotto of Han-Sur-Lesse, horiz. No. 1613, Village of Begijnendijk as separate community, bicent.

1996, June 10 Photo. *Perf. 11½*

1612 A690 16fr multicolored	1.00	.30
1613 A690 16fr multicolored	1.00	.30

Architecture in Brussels — A691

No. 1614, La Maison du Roi (Grand Place). No. 1615, Galeries Royales Saint-Hubert. No. 1616, Le Palais d'Egmont, Le Petit Sablon, horiz. No. 1617, Le Cinquantenaire, horiz.

1996, June 10

1614 A691 16fr multi (7a)	1.10	.30
1615 A691 16fr multi (7b)	1.10	.30
1616 A691 16fr multi (7c)	1.10	.30
1617 A691 16fr multi (7d)	1.10	.30
Nos. 1614-1617 (4)	4.40	1.20

Auto Races at Spa, Cent. A692

No. 1618, 1900 German 6CV. No. 1619, 1925 Alfa Romeo P2. No. 1620, 1939 Mercedes Benz W154. No. 1621, 1967 Ferrari 330P.

1996, July 1

1618 A692 16fr multicolored	1.00	.30
1619 A692 16fr multicolored	1.00	.30
1620 A692 16fr multicolored	1.00	.30
1621 A692 16fr multicolored	1.00	.30
Nos. 1618-1621 (4)	4.00	1.20

Paintings of Historical Figures — A693

Portraits from town hall triptych, Zierikzee, Netherlands: No. 1622, Philip I, the Handsome (1478-1506). No. 1623, Juana of Castile, the Mad (1479-1555).

1996, Sept. 2 Photo. *Perf. 11½*

1622 A693 16fr multicolored	1.00	.35
1623 A693 16fr multicolored	1.00	.35

Paintings from National Gallery, London — A694

14fr, Reading Man, by Rogier Van Der Weyden (1399-1464). 16fr, Susanna Fourment, by Peter Paul Rubens (1577-1640). 30fr, A Man in a Turban, by Jan Van Eyck (1390-1441).

1996, Sept. 2

1624 A694 14fr multicolored	.90	.30
1625 A694 16fr multicolored	1.10	.30
1626 A694 30fr multicolored	2.25	.50
Nos. 1624-1626 (3)	4.25	1.10

Bird Type of 1985

1996, Oct. 7 Photo. *Perf. 11½*

1627 A524 6fr Tarin des aulnes	.50	.25

Comic Character, Cloro, by Raymond Macherot — A695

1996, Oct. 7

1628 A695 16fr multicolored	1.10	.30

Youth Philately.

Almanac of Mons, by Fr. Charles Letellier, 150th Anniv. A696

1996, Oct. 7

1629 A696 16fr multicolored	1.00	.30

Music and Literature A697

No. 1630, Arthur Grumiaux (1921-86), violinist. No. 1631, Flor Peeters (1903-86), organist. No. 1632, Christian Dotremont (1922-79), poet, artist. No. 1633, Paul Van Ostaijen (1896-1928), writer.

Photo. & Engr.

1996, Oct. 28 *Perf. 11½*

1630 A697 16fr multicolored	1.00	.30
1631 A697 16fr multicolored	1.00	.30
1632 A697 16fr multicolored	1.00	.30
1633 A697 16fr multicolored	1.00	.30
Nos. 1630-1633 (4)	4.00	1.20

Christmas and New Year — A698

Scenes from Christmas Market: a, Decorated trees, rooftops. b, Lighted greeting signs. c, Church. d, Selling desert items. e, Selling Nativity scenes. f, Selling meat. g, Santa ringing bell. h, Man smoking pipe, people with presents. i, People shopping.

1996, Nov. 18 Photo. *Perf. 11½*

1634 A698 Sheet of 9, #a.-i.	7.50	7.50
a.-i. 14fr Any single	.75	.60

Catholic Faculty University, Mons, Cent. A699

1997, Jan. 20 Photo. *Perf. 11½*

1635 A699 17fr multicolored	1.00	.30

Opera at Theatre Royal de la Monnaie, Brussels — A700

No. 1636, Marie Sasse (1834-1907), soprano. No. 1637, Ernest Van Dijck (1861-1923), tenor. No. 1638, Hector Dufranne (1870-1951), baritone. No. 1639, Clara Clairbert (1899-1970), soprano.

1997, Feb. 10
1636 A700 17fr multicolored 1.00 .30
1637 A700 17fr multicolored 1.00 .30
1638 A700 17fr multicolored 1.00 .30
1639 A700 17fr multicolored 1.00 .30
Nos. 1636-1639 (4) 4.00 1.20

Eastern Cantons — A701

1997, Feb. 10 Photo. *Perf. 11½*
1640 A701 17fr multicolored 1.00 .30

Bird Type of 1985

1997, Mar. 10
1641 A524 15fr Mesange boreale .95 .25

UN Peace-Keeping Forces — A702

1997, Mar. 10
1642 A702 17fr multicolored 1.00 .30

Stories and Legends A703

Europa: 17fr, "De Bokkenrijders" (The Goat Riders). 30fr, Jean de Berneau.

1997, Mar. 10 Photo. *Perf. 11½*
1643 A703 17fr multicolored *1.25 .25*
1644 A703 30fr multicolored *2.00 1.00*

Bird Type of 1985

150fr, Pie bavarde, horiz.

1997, Apr. 7 Size: 35x25mm
1645 A524 150fr multicolored 8.00 .25

See No. 1840 for similar stamp with additional Euro denomination.

Constant Spinoy (1924-93), Stamp Engraver — A704

1997, Apr. 7 Photo. & Engr.
1646 A704 17fr multicolored 1.00 .30

Stamp Day.

Intl. Flower Show, Liege — A705

1997, Apr. 21 Photo.
1647 A705 17fr multicolored 1.00 .30

Paintings by Paul Delvaux (1897-1994) A706

Details or entire paintings: 15fr, Woman with garland of leaves in hair. 17fr, Nude, horiz. 32fr, Woman wearing hat, trolley.

1997, Apr. 21
1648 A706 15fr multicolored .85 .40
1649 A706 17fr multicolored 1.10 .30
1650 A706 32fr multicolored 2.10 .60
Nos. 1648-1650 (3) 4.05 1.30

Bird Type of 1985

3fr, Alouette des champs.

1997, May 7 Photo. *Perf. 11½*
1651 A524 3fr multicolored .25 .25

Queen Paola, 60th Birthday A707

1997, May 26
1652 A707 17fr Belvedere Castle 1.10 .30

See Italy No. 2147.

Cartoon Character, "Jommeke," by Jef Nys — A708

1997, May 26
1653 A708 17fr multicolored 1.30 .40

World Congress of Rose Societies — A709

Roses: No. 1654, Rosa damascena coccinea. No. 1655, Rosa sulfurea. No. 1656, Rosa centifolia.

1997, July 7 Photo. *Perf. 11½*
1654 A709 17fr multicolored 1.10 .30
1655 A709 17fr multicolored 1.10 .30
1656 A709 17fr multicolored 1.10 .30
Nos. 1654-1656 (3) 3.30 .90

Churches — A710

No. 1657, Basilica of St. Martin, Halle. No. 1658, Notre Dame Church, Laeken, horiz. No. 1659, Basilica of St. Martin, Liège.

1997, July 7 Photo. & Engr.
1657 A710 17fr multicolored 1.10 .30
1658 A710 17fr multicolored 1.10 .30
1659 A710 17fr multicolored 1.10 .30
Nos. 1657-1659 (3) 3.30 .90

Bird Type of 1985

7fr, Bergeronnette printaniere.

1997, Sept. 1 Photo. *Perf. 11½*
1660 A524 7fr multicolored .55 .30

Bees and Apiculture — A711

No. 1661, Queen, workers. No. 1662, Development of the larvae. No. 1663, Bee exiting cell. No. 1664, Bee collecting nectar. No. 1665, Two bees. No. 1666, Two bees on honeycomb.

1997, Sept. 1 Photo. *Perf. 12*
Booklet Stamps
1661 A711 17fr multi (15a) 1.25 .60
1662 A711 17fr multi (15b) 1.25 .60
1663 A711 17fr multi (15c) 1.25 .60
1664 A711 17fr multi (15d) 1.25 .60
1665 A711 17fr multi (15e) 1.25 .60
1666 A711 17fr multi (15f) 1.25 .60
a. Booklet pane of 6, #1661-1666 7.50 *7.50*
Complete booklet, #1666a 7.50
Nos. 1661-1666 (6) 7.50 3.60

Craftsmen A712

1997, Sept. 1 *Perf. 11½*
1667 A712 17fr Stone cutter 1.10 .30
1668 A712 17fr Mason 1.10 .30
1669 A712 17fr Carpenter 1.10 .30
1670 A712 17fr Blacksmith 1.10 .30
Nos. 1667-1670 (4) 4.40 1.20

Antarctic Expedition by the Belgica, Cent. — A713

1997, Sept. 22 Photo. *Perf. 11½*
1671 A713 17fr multicolored 1.10 .35

Royal Museum of Central Africa, Cent. — A714

No. 1672, Mask, Shaba, Congo. No. 1673, Outside view of museum, horiz. 34fr, Dish Bearer sculpture, Buli area, Congo.

1997, Sept. 22 Photo. *Perf. 11½*
1672 A714 17fr multicolored 1.10 .30
1673 A714 17fr multicolored 1.10 .30
1674 A714 34fr multicolored 2.25 .90
Nos. 1672-1674 (3) 4.45 1.50

No. 1673 is 25x73mm.

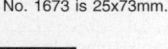

"Fairon," by Pierre Grahame — A715

Christmas.

1997, Oct. 25 Photo. *Perf. 11½*
1675 A715 15fr multicolored 1.00 .30

Bird Type of 1985

15fr, Mesange boreale, horiz.

1997, Dec. 1 Photo. *Perf. 11½*
1676 A524 15fr multicolored 1.15 1.00

No. 1676 issued in coil rolls with every fifth stamp numbered on reverse.
Vert. pairs of No. 1676 exist. Value, $650.

Rhododendron A716

Booklet Stamp
Serpentine Die Cut 13½ on 2 or 3 Sides

1997, Dec. 1 Self-Adhesive
1677 A716 (17fr) multicolored 2.00 .25
a. Booklet pane of 10 22.00 22.00

By its nature, No. 1677a is a complete booklet. The peelable backing serves as a booklet cover.
Compare with design A757.

"Thalys" High Speed Train — A717

1998, Jan. 19 Photo. *Perf. 11½*
1678 A717 17fr multicolored 1.10 .30

Woman Suffrage in Belgium, 50th Anniv. — A718

1998, Jan. 19
1679 A718 17fr multicolored 1.00 .30

Gerard Walschap (1898-1989), Poet, Playwright — A719

No. 1681, Norge (1898-1990), writer

1998, Feb. 16 Photo. *Perf. 11½*
1680 A719 17fr multicolored 1.10 .30
1681 A719 17fr multicolored 1.10 .30

Paintings, by René Magritte (1898-1967) — A720

No. 1682, "La Magie Noire (Black Magic)," nude woman. No. 1683, "La Corde Sensible (Heartstring)," cloud over champagne glass. No. 1684, "Le Chateau des Pyrenees (Castle of the Pyranees)," castle atop floating rock.

1998, Mar. 9 Photo. *Perf. 11½*
1682 A720 17fr multi, vert. 1.10 .30
1683 A720 17fr multi 1.10 .30
1684 A720 17fr multi, vert. 1.10 .30
Nos. 1682-1684 (3) 3.30 .90

Belgian Artists — A721

Details or entire paintings: No. 1685, "La Foire aux Amours," by Félicien Rops (1833-98). No. 1686, "Hospitality for the Strangers," by Gustave van de Woestijne (1881-1947). No. 1687, Self-portrait, "The Man with the Beard," by Felix de Boeck (1898-1995). No. 1688, "Black Writing Mixed with Colors," by Karel Appel & Christian Cotremont of COBRA.

1998, Mar. 9 *Perf. 12*
Booklet Stamps
1685 A721 17fr multicolored 1.10 .75
1686 A721 17fr multicolored 1.10 .75
1687 A721 17fr multicolored 1.10 .75
1688 A721 17fr multicolored 1.10 .75
a. Booklet pane, #1685-1688 5.50 *5.50*
Complete booklet, #1688a 5.50
Nos. 1685-1688 (4) 4.40 3.00

Museum of Fine Arts, Ghent, bicent. (No. 1686). COBRA art movement of painters and poets, 50th anniv. (No. 1688).

Sabena Airlines, 75th Anniv. — A722

1998, Apr. 20 Photo. *Perf. 11½*
1689 A722 17fr multicolored 1.10 .40

Belgian Stamp Dealers' Assoc., 75th Anniv. A723

1998, Apr. 20
1690 A723 17fr multicolored 1.10 .40

"The Return," by René Magritte (1898-1967) — A724

1998, Apr. 20
1691 A724 17fr multicolored 1.10 .40
See France No. 2637.

Wildlife A725

No. 1692, Vulpes vulpes. No. 1693, Cervus elaphus. No. 1694, Sus scrofa. No. 1695, Capreolus capreolus.

1998, Apr. 20
1692 A725 17fr multi 1.10 .40
1693 A725 17fr multi 1.10 .40
1694 A725 17fr multi 1.10 .40
1695 A725 17fr multi 1.10 .40
Nos. 1692-1695 (4) 4.40 1.60

"Souvenir Sheets"

Starting in 1998, items looking like souvenir sheets have appeared in the market. The 1998 item is similar to No. 1695. The 1999 item is similar to No. 1725. The 2000 item is similar to No. 1811. These have no postal value.

Bird Type of 1985

1fr, Mesange huppee.

1998, May 4 Photo. *Perf. 11½*
1696 A524 1fr multicolored .25 .25

Edmund Struyf (1911-96), Founder of Pro-Post, Assoc. for Promotion of Philately — A726

1998, May 4 Photo. & Engr.
1697 A726 17fr multicolored 1.10 .30
Stamp Day.

Natl. Festivals A727

No. 1698, Torhout & Werchter Rock Festival. No. 1699, Wallonia Festival.

1998, May 4 Photo. *Perf. 11½*
1698 A727 17fr multicolored *1.10* .30
1699 A727 17fr multicolored *1.10* .30
Europa.

Bird Type of 1985

7.50fr, Pie-grieche grise.

1998, July 6 Photo. *Perf. 11½*
1700 A524 7.50fr multicolored .45 .25

See No. 1837 for similar stamp with additional Euro denomination.

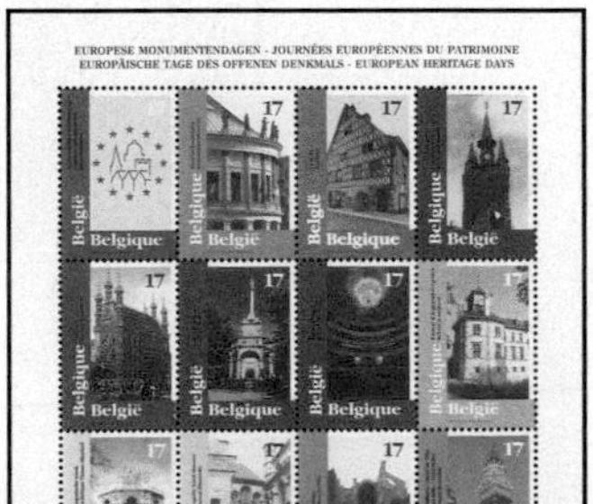
European Heritage Days — A728

a, Logo. b, Bourla Theatre, Antwerp. c, La Halle, Durbuy. d, Halletoren, Kortrijk. e, Louvain Town Hall. f, Perron, Liège. g, Royal Theatre, Namur. h, Aspremont-Lynden Castle, Rekem. i, Neo-Gothic kiosk, Sint-Niklaas. j, Chapelle Saint Vincent, Tournai. k, Villers-la-Ville Abbey. l, Saint Gilles Town Hall, Brussels.

1998, July 6
1701 A728 Sheet of 12 14.00 12.00
a.-l. 17fr Any single 1.10 .45

Bird Type of 1985

1998 Photo. *Perf. 11½*
1702 A524 9fr Pic vert .60 .50
1703 A524 10fr Turtle dove .60 .30
Issued: 9fr, 8/10; 10fr, 9/28/98.

Free Thinking A729

1998, Aug. 10 Photo. *Perf. 11½*
1704 A729 17fr multicolored 1.10 .30

Philips van Marnix van Sint-Aldegonde (1540-98), Author — A730

1998, Aug. 10
1705 A730 17fr multicolored 1.10 .30

Mniszech Palace (Belgian Embassy), Warsaw, Bicent. A731

Photo. & Engr.
1998, Sept. 28 *Perf. 11½*
1706 A731 17fr multicolored 1.10 .30
See Poland No. 3420.

Contemporary Belgium Films — A732

No. 1707, "Le Huitieme Jour". No. 1708, "Daens".

1998, Sept. 28 Photo.
1707 A732 17fr multicolored 1.10 .30
1708 A732 17fr multicolored 1.10 .30

Cartoon Characters, "Chick Bill" and "Ric Hochet" — A733

1998, Oct. 19 Photo. *Perf. 11½*
1709 A733 17fr multicolored 1.10 .60
Youth philately.

Assoc. of Space Explorers, 14th World Congress, Brussels — A734

1998, Oct. 19
1710 A734 17fr multicolored 1.10 .35

World Post Day A735

1998, Oct. 19 Photo. *Perf. 11½*
1711 A735 34fr blue & dark blue 2.25 1.10

World Assoc. for the Development of Philately.

FGTB-ABVV Trade Union, Cent. — A736

Center panel of triptych by Constant Draz (1875-)

1998, Nov. 9 Photo. *Perf. 11½*
1712 A736 17fr multicolored 1.10 .30

Christmas and New Year — A737

1998, Nov. 9
1713 A737 (17fr) multicolored 1.50 .30

Bird Type of 1985

16fr, Mesange noire. 21fr, Grive litorne, horiz.

1998-99 Photo. *Perf. 11½*
1714 A524 16fr multicolored 1.00 .25
1715 A524 21fr multicolored 1.20 .65

No. 1715 also issued in coils with number on reverse of every 5th stamp.
Issued: 16fr, 1/25/99; 21fr, 12/14/98.
See No. 1839 for similar stamp with additional Euro denomination.

A738

Greetings Stamps: No. 1716, Burning candle. No. 1717, Stork carrying a heart. No. 1718, Wristwatch. No. 1719, Four leaf clover with one leaf a heart. No. 1720, Two doves. No. 1721, Heart with arrow through it. No. 1722, Heart-shaped head on woman. No. 1723, Heart-shaped head on man.

1999, Jan. 25 Photo. *Perf. 12*

Booklet Stamps

1716 A738 (17fr) multicolored 1.50 .40
1717 A738 (17fr) multicolored 1.50 .40
1718 A738 (17fr) multicolored 1.50 .40
1719 A738 (17fr) multicolored 1.50 .40
1720 A738 (17fr) multicolored 1.50 .40
1721 A738 (17fr) multicolored 1.50 .40
1722 A738 (17fr) multicolored 1.50 .40
1723 A738 (17fr) multicolored 1.50 .40
a. Booklet pane, #1716-1723 12.00 *12.00*
Complete booklet, #1723a 12.00
Nos. 1716-1723 (8) 12.00 3.20

Nos. 1716-1717, 1719-1720 each also issued in sheets of 20 on July 1. Value, each sheet, $30.

Owls — A739

1999, Feb. 22 Photo. *Perf. 11½*

1724 A739 17fr Tyto alba 1.10 .30
1725 A739 17fr Athene noctua 1.10 .30
1726 A739 17fr Strix aluco 1.10 .30
1727 A739 17fr Asio otus 1.10 .30
Nos. 1724-1727 (4) 4.40 1.20

NATO, 50th Anniv. A740

No. 1728, Leopard tank. No. 1729, F16 fighter. No. 1730, Frigate Wandelaar. No. 1731, Hospital tent. No. 1732, General staff.

1999, Mar. 15

1728 A740 17fr multicolored 1.10 .30
1729 A740 17fr multicolored 1.10 .30
1730 A740 17fr multicolored 1.10 .30
1731 A740 17fr multicolored 1.10 .30
1732 A740 17fr multicolored 1.10 .30
Nos. 1728-1732 (5) 5.50 1.50

UPU, 125th Anniv. A741

1999, Mar. 15

1733 A741 34fr multicolored 2.25 .50

No. 1733 is usually collected as a horizontal pair. Value, $5 never-hinged or used.

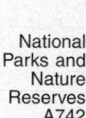

National Parks and Nature Reserves A742

Europa: No. 1734, De Bunt, near town of Hamme. No. 1735, Harchies-Hensies-Pommeroeul.

1999, Apr. 12

1734 A742 17fr multicolored *1.25 .30*
1735 A742 17fr multicolored *1.25 .30*

First Belgian Postage Stamps, 150th Anniv. A743

Photo. & Engr.

1999, Apr. 26 *Perf. 11½*

1736 A743 17fr No. 1 1.10 .25
1737 A743 17fr No. 2 1.10 .25
a. Pair, #1736-1737 3.00 2.50

Painting, "My Favorite Room," by James Ensor (1860-1949) — A744

Designs: No. 1739, Woman Eating Oysters, vert. 30fr, Triumph Over Death, vert. 32fr, Old Lady With Masks, vert.

1999, May 17 Photo. *Perf. 11½*

1738 A744 17fr multicolored 1.10 .30
1739 A744 17fr multicolored 1.10 .30
1740 A744 30fr multicolored 1.75 .60
1741 A744 32fr multicolored 1.75 .60
Nos. 1738-1741 (4) 5.70 1.80

See Israel No. 1365A.

Issued: No. 1738, 5/17; Nos. 1739-1741, 9/11.

Tourism — A745

No. 1742, Giants at Geraardsbergen Fair, vert. No. 1743, Cart d'Or procession of the Confrérie de la Miséracordie, Mons.

1999, June 7 Photo. *Perf. 11½*

1742 A745 17fr multi (10a) 1.10 .30
1743 A745 17fr multi (10b) 1.10 .30

Belgian Chocolate A746

1999, June 7

1744 A746 17fr Bean picker 1.10 .30
1745 A746 17fr Candy maker 1.10 .30
1746 A746 17fr Consumer 1.10 .30
Nos. 1744-1746 (3) 3.30 .90

King Albert and Queen Paola, 40th Wedding Anniv. — A747

1999, July 2 Photo. *Perf. 11½*

1747 A747 17fr multicolored 1.10 .30

Royalty Type of Semi-Postal Stamps

Souvenir Sheet

Kings: a, 50fr, Leopold I. b, 32fr, Leopold II. c, 17fr, Albert I. d, 17fr, Leopold III. e, 32fr, Baudouin. f, 50fr, Albert II.

Photo. & Engr.

1999, Sept. 29 *Perf. 11½*

1748 SP514 Sheet of 6, #a.-f. 20.00 20.00

Bruphila '99. No. 1748 sold for 300fr.

Nobel Laureates in Peace — A750

Designs: 17fr, Henri La Fontaine (1854-1943). 21fr, Auguste Beernaert (1829-1912).

Photo. & Engr.

1999, Sept. 30 *Perf. 11½*

1749 A750 17fr red & gold 1.10 .30
1750 A750 21fr blue & gold 1.25 .70

See Sweden Nos. 2357-2358.

A751

A752

A753

A754

King Albert II

1999-2001 Photo. *Perf. 11¾x11½*

1752 A751 17fr multicolored 1.10 .25
1753 A751 17fr prus blue 1.10 .25
1754 A751 19fr blue 1.25 .40
1755 A751 20fr yel brown 1.25 .30
1756 A752 23fr violet 3.50 3.00
1757 A751 25fr brown 1.75 .40
1758 A751 30fr vio black 1.90 .30
1759 A751 32fr green 2.50 .30
1760 A751 34fr gray blue 2.10 1.75
1761 A751 36fr brown 2.25 .30
Nos. 1752-1761 (10) 18.70 7.25

Engr.

Perf. 11½

1766 A753 50fr blue 3.25 .55

Photo. *Perf. 11½*

1768 A754 100fr multi 6.50 .45

Engr.

1769 A753 200fr claret 13.50 2.75
Nos. 1752-1769 (13) 41.95 11.00

No. 1756 issued in coils. Vert. coil pairs of No. 1756 exist. Value, $600.

Issued: 17fr, 10/4; 19fr, 1/24/00; 30fr, 4/3/00; 32fr, 6/19/00; 23fr, 9/4/00; 50fr, 9/11/00; No. 1753, 11/18/00; 36fr, 12/4/00; 20fr, 25fr, 34fr, 100fr, 200fr, 3/26/01.

Youth Philately — A756

Comic strips: a, Corentin, by Paul Cuvelier (16a). b, Jerry Spring, by Jijé (16b). c, Gil Jourdan, by Maurice Tillieux (16c). d, La Patrouille des Castors, by Mitacq (16d). e, Entrance hall of Belgian Comic Strip Museum (16e). f, Hassan & Kadour, by Jacques Laudy (16f). g, Buck Danny, by Victor Hubinon (16g). h, Tif et Tondu, by Fernand Dineur (16h). i, Les Timour, by Sirius (16i).

1999, Oct. 2 Photo. *Perf. 11½*

1771 A756 Sheet of 9, #a.-i. 12.50 12.50
a.-d. 17fr Any single 1.10 .80
e. 17f 2.00 1.50
f.-i. 17fr Any single 1.10 .80

Geranium — A757

Tulip — A758

Die Cut 10x9¾ on 2 or 3 sides

1999-2000 Self-Adhesive Photo.

Booklet Stamps

1772 A757 (17fr) multi 1.50 .25
a. Complete booklet, 10 #1772 16.00
1773 A758 (21fr) multi 2.25 .35
a. Booklet, 10 #1773 24.00

Die Cut Perf. 11¼

Coil Stamps

Litho.

1774 A757 (17fr) multi 9.00 .35

Photo.

Serpentine Die Cut 13¾

1774A A757 (17fr) multi 12.50 .35
1775 A758 (21fr) multi 6.00 .75

Nos. 1774-1775 are on a waxed backing paper larger than the stamp.

Issued: No. 1773, 4/17/00; No. 1774A, 2/01. others, 11/22/99.

No. 1774A is dated 2000.

Christmas — A762

1999, Nov. 8 Photo. *Perf. 11½*

1776 A762 17fr multi 1.10 .30

Wedding of Prince Philippe and Mathilde d'Udekem d'Acoz, Dec. 4 — A763

1999, Nov. 29

1777 A763 17fr shown 1.25 .40

Souvenir Sheet

1778 A763 21fr Couple, diff. 1.75 1.75

The 20th Century

A764

A764a

A764b

A764c

No. 1779: a, Pope John XXIII. b, King Baudouin. c, Willy Brandt. d, John F. Kennedy. e, Mahatma Gandhi. f, Dr. Martin Luther King, Jr. g, Lenin. h, Che Guevara. i, Golda Meir. j, Nelson Mandela. k, Jesse Owens, Modern Olympic Games. l, Soccer. m, Tour de France. n, Edith Piaf. o, The Beatles. p, Charlie Chaplin. q, Tourism. r, Youth movements. s, Tintin comic strips. t, Philately.

No. 1780: a, Yser front, World War I. b, Concentration camps. c, First atomic bomb. d, Yalta Conference. e, United Nations. f, Decolonization. g, Vietnam War. h, Collapse of the Berlin Wall. i, Peace movements. j, Middle East conflict. k, Rene Magritte, artist. l, Le Corbusier, architect. m, Bertolt Brecht, dramatist. n, James Joyce, novelist. o, Anne Teresa de Keersmaeker, choreographer. p, Bela Bartók, composer. q, Andy Warhol, artist. r, Maria Callas, opera singer. s, Henry Moore, sculptor. t, Toots Thielemans, Charlie Parker, jazz musicians.

No. 1781: a, Ovide Decroly, pedagogue. b, Alternative energy. c, Aviation. d, Sigmund Freud, psychologist. e, Space travel. f, Claude Lévi-Strauss, anthropologist. g, Genetics. h, Pierre Teilhard de Chardin, theologist. i, Max Weber, sociologist, j, Albert Einstein, physicist. k, Penicillin. l, Ilya Prigogine, chemist. m, Roland Barthes, semiotician. n, Simone de Beauvoir, feminist. o, Information. p, John Maynard Keynes, economist. q, Marc Bloch, historian. r, Atomic energy, J. Robert Oppenheimer, physicist. s, Pierre and Marie Curie, physicists. t, Ludwig Josef Wittgenstein, philosopher.

No. 1782: a, Social housing policy. b, May 1968 student protests. c, Telecommunications. d, Wealth and poverty. e, Secularization (laicisation). f, Urbanization. g, Universal suffrage. h, Social security. i, Education (enseignement). j, Aging of the population (vieillissement de la population). k, European Union. l, Universal Declaration of Human Rights. m, Consumer society. n, Women's liberation. o, Deindustrialization. p, Oil crises. q, Mobility. r, Contraception. s, Radio and television. t, Home appliances (appareils menagers).

1999-2002 Photo. *Perf. 11½*

1779	Sheet of 20	25.00	25.00
a.-d.	A764 17fr Any single	1.10	.80
e.	A764 17fr	2.00	1.00
f.-r.	A764 17fr Any single	1.10	.80
s.	A764 17fr	3.00	1.75
t.	A764 17fr	1.10	.80
1780	Sheet of 20	22.00	22.00
a.-t.	A764a 17fr Any single	1.10	.80
1781	Sheet of 20	22.00	22.00
a.-t.	A764b 17fr Any single	1.10	.80
1782	Sheet of 20	22.00	22.00
a.-t.	A764c 41c Any single	1.10	.80
	Nos. 1779-1782 (4)	91.00	91.00

Issued: No. 1779, 12/6/99. No. 1780, 11/20/00. No. 1781, 10/22/01. No. 1782, 10/28/02.

Denominations on No. 1782 are in euros.

Year 2000 A765

2000, Jan. 3 Photo. *Perf. 11¾x11½*

1783	A765 17fr multi	1.10	.30

Brussels, 2000 European City of Culture — A766

Brussels skyline and: a, Seven people. b, Harmonica player, dancer. c, Airplane, train, ships.

2000, Jan. 24 Photo. *Perf. 11½*

1784	Strip of 3 + 2 labels	3.50	*3.50*
a.-c.	A766 17fr any single	1.10	.40

Bird Type of 1985

1fr, Beccroisé des sapins. 2fr, Grimpereau des jardins. 3fr, Pipit parlouse. 5fr, Pinson du nord. 10fr, Pouillot siffleur. No. 1790, 16fr, Pie grièche écorcheur. No. 1790A, 16fr, Pie grièche écoucheur, horiz.

Without "F" and With Euro Denomination

2000 Photo. *Perf. 11¾*

1785	A524	1fr multicolored	.90	.45
1786	A524	2fr multicolored	.25	.25
1787	A524	3fr multicolored	.25	.25
1788	A524	5fr multicolored	.30	.25
1789	A524	10fr multicolored	.65	.30
1790	A524	16fr multicolored	1.00	.45
1790A	A524	16fr multicolored	2.50	2.00
		Nos. 1785-1790A (7)	5.85	3.95

No. 1790A issued in coils.

Issued: No. 1790, 1/24; 1fr, 2fr, 3fr, 5fr, 5/8; 10fr, 9/11; No. 1790A, 9/4.

Holy Roman Emperor Charles V (1500-58) A767

2000, Feb. 21 Photo. *Perf. 11½*

1791	A767 17fr shown	1.10	.30
1792	A767 21fr At age 40	1.25	.60

Souvenir Sheet

1793	A767 34fr In armor	2.25	2.25
a.	Ovptd. in margin	2.25	2.25

No. 1793a was issued 10/6/00 and overprint in margin reads "ESPANA 2000 / Exposición Mundial de Filatelia / Madrid 6-14/X/2000."

See Spain Nos. 3026-3028.

World Mathematics Year — A768

2000, Feb. 21

1794	A768 17fr multi	1.10	.30

Stampin' The Future Children's Stamp Design Contest Winner — A769

2000, Feb. 21

1795	A769 17fr multi	1.10	.30

European Soccer Championships, Belgium and Netherlands — A770

2000, Mar. 27

1796	A770	Pair + label	2.50	2.50
a.		17fr Players	1.10	.40
b.		21fr Ball	1.25	.60

Serpentine Die Cut 10x9¾ on 3 sides

Booklet Stamp

Self-Adhesive

Size: 21x27mm

1797	A770 (17fr) Players, diff.	1.25	.30
a.	Booklet, 10 #1797	16.00	16.00

See Netherlands Nos. 1045-1046.

Worldwide Fund for Nature — A771

Endangered amphibians and reptiles: No. 1798, Vipera berus. No. 1799, Lacerta agilis, vert. No. 1800, Hyla arborea, vert. No. 1801, Salamandra salamandra.

Perf. 11¾x11½, 11½x11¾

2000, Mar. 27 Photo.

1798	A771 17fr multi	1.25	.40
1799	A771 17fr multi	1.25	.40
1800	A771 17fr multi	1.25	.40
1801	A771 17fr multi	1.25	.40
	Nos. 1798-1801 (4)	5.00	1.60

Stamp Day — A772

2000, Apr. 3 Photo. *Perf. 11½*

1802	A772 17fr multi	1.25	.30

Franz von Taxis — A773

2000, Apr. 3

1803	A773 17fr multi + label	1.25	.75

Postal system in Europe, 500th anniv., Belgica 2001 Stamp Exhibition.

Ghent Flower Show A774

Designs: 16fr, Iris spuria. 17fr, Rhododendron, horiz. 21fr, Begonia.

2000, Apr. 17

1804	A774 16fr multi	1.10	.40
1805	A774 17fr multi	1.25	.30
1806	A774 21fr multi	1.50	.75
	Nos. 1804-1806 (3)	3.85	1.45

Prince Philippe's Fund A775

2000, Apr. 17

1807	A775 17fr multi	1.25	.30

2000 Summer Olympics and Paralympics, Sydney A776

Designs: 17fr, Belgian Olympic team emblem. No. 1809, Taekwondo. No. 1810, Wheelchair racer, horiz.

30fr+7fr, Swimmer in triathlon, horiz.

2000, May 8

1808	A776 17fr multi	1.25	.40
1809	A776 17fr +4fr multi	1.50	1.50
1810	A776 17fr +4fr multi	1.50	1.50
	Nos. 1808-1810 (3)	4.25	3.40

Souvenir Sheet

1811	A776 30fr +7fr multi	2.75	2.75

Olymphilex 2000 (No. 1811).

Opening of Musical Instrument Museum, Brussels — A777

No. 1812, Harpsichord (15a). No. 1813, Violin (15b). No. 1814, Lutes (15c). No. 1815, Treble viol (15d). No. 1816, Trumpets (15e). No. 1817, Johann Sebastian Bach (15f).

2000, May 8 Photo. *Perf. 11¾*

Booklet Stamps

1812	A777 (17fr) multi	1.50	1.00
1813	A777 (17fr) multi	1.50	1.00
1814	A777 (17fr) multi	1.50	1.00
1815	A777 (17fr) multi	1.50	1.00
1816	A777 (17fr) multi	1.50	1.00
1817	A777 (17fr) multi	1.50	1.00
a.	Booklet pane, #1812-1817	9.00	*9.00*
	Booklet, #1817a	9.00	
	Nos. 1812-1817 (6)	9.00	6.00

Europa, 2000

Common Design Type

2000, May 9 *Perf. 11½*

1818	CD17 (21fr) multi	*1.40*	.60

UNESCO World Heritage Sites A778

Designs: No. 1819, Flemish Béguinages. No. 1820, Grand-Place, Brussels. No. 1821, Boat lifts, Canal du Centre.

2000, June 19 *Perf. 11½x11¾*

1819	A778 17fr multi	1.25	.30
1820	A778 17fr multi	1.25	.30
1821	A778 17fr multi	1.25	.30
	Nos. 1819-1821 (3)	3.75	.90

Tourism
A779

Churches and their organs: No. 1822, Norbertine Abbey Church, Grimbergen. No. 1823, Collégiale Sainte Waudru, Mons. No. 1824, O.-L.-V. Hemelvaartkerk, Ninove. No. 1825, St. Peter's Church, Bastogne.

2000, June 19 *Perf. 11½*

1822	A779 17fr multi		1.10	.30
1823	A779 17fr multi		1.10	.30
1824	A779 17fr multi		1.10	.30
1825	A779 17fr multi		1.10	.30
	Nos. 1822-1825 (4)		4.40	1.20

A780

2000, Sept. 4 **Photo.** *Perf. 11¾*
1826 A780 17fr multi 5.00 *5.00*

European Postal Services, 500th Anniv., Belgica 2001 Stamp Exhibition.

No. 1826 issued in coils. Vert. coil pairs of No. 1826 exist. Value, $600.

Youth Philately — A781

2000, Sept. 11 *Perf. 11¾x11½*
1827 A781 17fr multi 1.20 .60

Hainault Flower Show
A782

2000, Sept. 11 *Perf. 11½x11¾*
1828 A782 17fr multi 1.20 .30

Violets — A783

Die Cut Perf. 10x9¾ on 2 or 3 Sides
2000, Sept. 11 **Photo.**

Booklet Stamp
Self-Adhesive

1829	A783 (17fr) multi	1.50	.30
a.	Booklet, 10 #1829	16.00	

Contemporary Art — A784

No. 1831, Bing of the Ferro Lusto X, by Panamarenko. No. 1832, Construction, by Anne-Mie Van Kerckhoven. No. 1833, Belgique Eternelle, by J. & L. Charlier. No. 1834, Roses from series "Les Belles de Nuit," by Marie-Jo Lafontaine.

Perf. 11½x11¾, 11¾x11½
2000, Oct. 16 **Photo.**

1831	A784 17fr multi (21a)	1.15	.50
1832	A784 17fr multi (21b), vert.	1.15	.50
1833	A784 17fr multi (21c)	1.15	.50
1834	A784 17fr multi (21d)	1.15	.50
	Nos. 1831-1834 (4)	4.60	2.00

Christmas — A785

2000, Nov. 20 **Photo.** *Perf. 11½*
1835 A785 17fr multi 1.20 .30

Bird Type of 1985

50c, Roitelet huppe. 7.50fr, Pie-grieche grise. 8fr, Mesange charbonniere. 16fr, Sterne pierregarin. 21fr, Grive litorne, horiz. 150fr, Pie bavarde, horiz.

Without F and With Euro Denomination

2000-01 **Photo.** *Perf. 11¾*

1836	A524	50c multi	.25	.25
1837	A524	7.50fr multi	.50	.40
1838	A524	8fr multi	.60	.70
1838A	A524	16fr multi	1.25	.25
1839	A524	21fr multi	1.50	.40

Perf. 11½x11¾
Size: 35x25mm

1840	A524	150fr multi	9.00	.60
		Nos. 1836-1840 (6)	13.10	2.60

Issued: 8fr, 12/4/00. 50c, 7.50fr, 21fr, 150fr, 3/26/01; 16fr, 6/9/01. Numbers have been reserved for additional stamps in this set.

Holy Year 2000 — A786

Photo. & Engr.
2000, Dec. 27 *Perf. 11½*

1841	A786 17fr multicolored	1.10	.30
	With tab	1.25	.50

Royalty Type of Semi-Postal Stamps
Souvenir Sheet

Queens: a, 50fr, Louise-Marie. b, 32fr, Marie-Henriette. c, 17fr, Elisabeth. d, 17fr, Astrid. e, 32fr, Fabiola. f, 50fr, Paola.

Photo. & Engr.
2001, Feb. 12 *Perf. 11½*
1842 SP514 Sheet of 6, #a-f 18.00 18.00

No. 1842 sold for 300fr.

Zénobe Gramme (1826-1901), Electrical Engineer — A787

2001, Mar. 19 **Photo.**
1843 A787 17fr multi 1.25 .30

Catholic University of Louvain, 575th Anniv. — A788

2001, Mar. 19
1844 A788 17fr multi 1.25 .30

Europa — A789

2001, Apr. 23 **Photo.** *Perf. 11½*
1845 A789 21fr multi *1.50* *.60*

Musical and Literary Personalities
A790

Designs: No. 1846, Willem Elsschot (1882-1960), writer. No. 1847, Albert Ayguesparse (1900-96), writer.

21fr, Queen Elisabeth (1876-1965), patron of Queen Elisabeth Intl. Music Competition, horiz.

2001, Apr. 23 **Photo.** *Perf. 11½*

1846	A790 17fr multi	1.25	.30
1847	A790 17fr multi	1.25	.30

Souvenir Sheet

1848 A790 21fr multi 1.75 1.75

Queen Elisabeth Intl. Music Competition, 50th anniv. (No. 1848).

Belgian Natl. Railway Company, 75th Anniv. — A790A

No. 1848A: b, 1938 Type 12 locomotive No. 12004. c, 1971 Series 06 dual engine No. 671. d, 1991 Series 03 threefold engine No. 328.

2001, May 7 **Photo.** *Perf. 11¾x11½*

1848A	Horiz. strip of 3 + 2 labels	4.00	*4.00*
b.-d.	A790A 17fr Any single	1.10	.50

A791

European Posts, 500th Anniv. — A792

Designs: No. 1849, Franz von Taxis, 16th cent. postrider. No. 1850, 17th cent. postman on road near Brussels. No. 1851, 18th cent. postman, quill pen, postal notice. No. 1852, 19th cent. postman, train, Belgium #2 on cover. No. 1853, 20th cent. postman, motorcycle, airplanes, mailboxes.

No. 1854: 150fr, 21st cent. postwoman, Belgica 2001 emblem.

Perf. 11¾x11½
2001, June 9 **Photo.**

Stamp + label

1849	A791 17fr multi	1.25	1.00
1850	A792 17fr multi	1.25	1.00
1851	A792 17fr multi	1.25	1.00
1852	A792 17fr multi	1.25	1.00
1853	A792 17fr multi	1.25	1.00
	Nos. 1849-1853 (5)	6.25	5.00

Souvenir Sheet

1854 A792 150fr multi 16.00 16.00

Nos. 1849 printed in sheets of 10 stamps + 10 labels. For Nos. 1850-1853, each is printed in sheets of 12 stamps + 12 labels.

No. 1854 contains one 38x48mm stamp without an attached label, and sold for 300fr, with the surtax going to Pro Post for the promotion of philately.

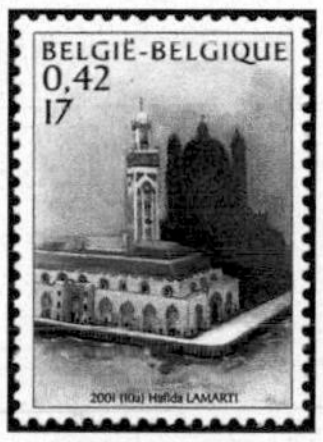

Houses of Worship — A793

Designs: 17fr, Hassan II Mosque, Casablanca, Morocco. 34fr, Koekelberg Basilica.

2001, June 10 **Photo.** *Perf. 11½*

1855	A793 17fr multi	1.10	.30
1856	A793 34fr multi	2.25	1.25

See Morocco Nos. 897-898.

Musées Royaux des Beaux Arts, Brussels, 200th Anniv. — A794

No. 1857: a, Winter Landscape With Skaters, by Pieter Breughel the Elder. b, Study of a Negro's Head, by Peter Paul Rubens. c, Sunday, by Frits Van den Berghe. d, Mussel Triumph II, by Marcel Broodthaers.

2001, June 11 **Photo.** *Perf. 12*

1857	Booklet pane of 4	5.00	5.00
a.-d.	A794 17fr Any single	1.25	.90
	Booklet, #1857	5.25	

Ancient Chinese Receptacles
A795

Designs: 17fr, Earthenware vase. 34fr, Porcelain coffee pot.

2001, June 12 Photo. *Perf. 11½*

1858 A795 17fr multi 1.10 .30
1859 A795 34fr multi 2.25 1.25

See People's Republic of China Nos. 3108-3109.

Youth Philately — A796

2001, June 13

1860 A796 17fr multi 1.10 .60

Belgian Chairmanship of European Union A797

2001, June 15

1861 A797 17fr multi 1.10 .50

Tourism — A798

Town hall belfries: No. 1862, Binche. No. 1863, Dixmude.

2001, Aug. 6 *Perf. 11½x11¾*

1862 A798 17fr multi 1.10 .30
1863 A798 17fr multi 1.10 .30

Farmsteads — A799

2001, Aug. 6 *Perf. 11¾x11½*

1864 A799 17fr Damme 1.10 .30
1865 A799 17fr Beauvechain 1.10 .30
1866 A799 17fr Leuven 1.10 .30
1867 A799 17fr Honnelles 1.10 .30
1868 A799 17fr Hasselt 1.10 .30
Nos. 1864-1868 (5) 5.50 1.50

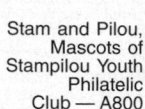

Stam and Pilou, Mascots of Stampilou Youth Philatelic Club — A800

2001, Oct. 8 Photo. *Die Cut*

Self-Adhesive

Booklet Stamp

1869 A800 (17fr) multi 1.50 .50
a. Booklet of 5 + 5 labels 8.00 *8.00*

Stamp Day.

Christmas A801

2001, Nov. 12 Photo. *Perf. 11½*

1870 A801 15fr multi .95 .35

Violets A802

Belgian Post Emblem A802a

Narcissus — A803

Tulips — A804

2001, Dec. 10 Photo. *Perf. 11½*

1871 A802 (17fr) multi 1.75 1.40
1871A A802a (17fr) red 1.75 1.40

Self-Adhesive Booklet Stamps

Die Cut Perf. 10 on 2 or 3 Sides

1872 A803 (17fr) multi 1.50 .35
a. Booklet pane of 10 15.00 *15.00*

Die Cut Perf. 9¾ on 3 Sides

1873 A804 (21fr) multi 2.25 .45
a. Booklet pane of 10 24.00 *24.00*
Nos. 1871-1873 (4) 7.25 3.60

Issued: No. 1871, 10/17; No. 1871A, 12/1. Nos. 1872, 1873, 12/10.

Nos. 1871 and 1871A were each issued in sheets of 15 stamps + 15 labels that could be personalized. The sheets sold for 605fr.

Death Announcement Stamp — A805

2001, Dec. 10 Photo. *Perf. 11½*

1874 A805 (17fr) multi 1.50 .30

See Nos. 1936 and 2035.

Tintin in Africa — A806

Tintin: 17fr, In jungle. 34fr, In automobile.

2001, Dec. 31

1875 A806 17fr multi 1.25 .70

Souvenir Sheet

1876 A806 34fr multi 3.25 *3.25*

No. 1876 contains one 48x37mm stamp. See Democratic Republic of Congo (Zaire) Nos. 1613-1614.

100 Cents = 1 Euro (€)

King Albert II — A807

King Albert II — A808

King Albert II — A809

King Albert II — A810

2002-06 Photo. *Perf. 11½*

1877	A808	7c red & gray bl	.25	.25
1879	A807	42c red	1.00	.30
1881	A807	47c dark green	1.25	1.00
1882	A808	49c red	1.00	.25
1882A	A809	49c red	1.25	1.25
1882B	A809	50c red	1.10	.30
1882C	A810	50c multi	1.25	.30
1883	A807	52c blue	1.25	.85
1884	A810	52c red & car	1.25	.30
1885	A807	59c dk blue	1.50	1.25
1886	A807	60c blue	1.60	.70
1887	A807	60c brt blue + etiquette	1.25	1.00
1888	A807	70c brt blue + etiquette	1.50	1.25
1888A	A810	70c blue	1.75	1.25
1889	A808	79c red & ultra	1.75	1.25
1890	A809	79c red & ultra	2.25	.50
1891	A809	80c red & ultra	1.90	.60
1892	A807	80c ultra + etiquette	1.75	1.40
1893	A810	83c red & bl vio	2.25	.50
1895	A808	€4.21 red & pur	9.00	1.50
		Nos. 1877-1895 (20)	36.10	16.00

Issued: 42c, 52c, 1/1/02. 47c, 5/6/02. 7c, 49c, 59c, No. 1889, 11/4/02. €4.21, 8/11/03. No. 1890, 10/6/03. No. 1882A, 10/27/03; 50c, 60c, 80c, 4/19/04. Nos. 1887, 1892, 9/27/04. 70c, 3/21/05. Nos. 1882C, 1888A, 7/21/05. No. 1884, 1/23/06. No. 1893, 3/20/06.

No. 1888A is inscribed "A Prior" at left.

World Cyclo-Cross and Road Bicycling Championships A811

Royal Belgian Tennis Federation, Cent. — A812

No. 1897: a, Rider looking back. b, Rider with fist in air.

No. 1898: a, Women's tennis. b, Men's tennis.

2002, Jan. 21 Photo. *Perf. 11½*

1897 A811 Vert. pair 2.50 1.10
a.-b. 42c Any single 1.25 .40
1898 A812 Horiz. pair 2.50 1.10
a.-b. 42c Any single 1.25 .55

University of Antwerp, 150th Anniv. A813

2002, Feb. 11 Photo. & Engr.

1899 A813 42c multi 1.10 .35

Bruges, 2002 European Capital of Culture A814

Designs: No. 1900, Restorations and new architecture (4a). No. 1901, Classical and contemporary music (4b). No. 1902, Classical exhibitions and contemporary art (4c).

2002, Mar. 4 Photo.

1900 A814 42c multi 1.10 .35
1901 A814 42c multi 1.10 .35
1902 A814 42c multi 1.10 .35
Nos. 1900-1902 (3) 3.30 1.05

Anna Bijns (1494-1575), Poet — A815

Anna Boch (1848-1936), Painter — A816

2002, Mar. 4

1903 A815 42c multi 1.10 .50
1904 A816 84c multi 2.25 1.25

Stamp Day — A817

2002, Apr. 22 Photo. *Perf. 11½*

1905 A817 47c multi 1.10 .50

Belgian Dog Breeds — A818

Designs: No. 1906, Schipperke. No. 1907, Bouvier des Ardennes. No. 1908, Saint-Hubert. No. 1909, Brussels griffon. No. 1910, Papillon.

2002, Apr. 22 Photo. *Perf. 11½*

Stamp + Label

1906 A818 42c multi 1.10 .90
1907 A818 42c multi 1.10 .90
1908 A818 42c multi 1.10 .90
1909 A818 42c multi 1.10 .90
1910 A818 42c multi 1.10 .90
a. Vert. strip of 5, #1906-1910, + 5 labels 6.50 6.50
Nos. 1906-1910 (5) 5.50 4.50

Europa
A819

2002, May 6

1911 A819 52c multi *1.50* .70

Bird Type of 1985 With Euro Denominations Only

7c, Pigeon colombin. 25c, Huitrier pie. 35c, Pic epeiche. 41c, Tourterelle Turque. 57c, Guifette noire. 70c, Chevalier gambette. €1, Traquet motteux, horiz. €2, Grand gravelot, horiz. €5, Combattant varie, horiz.

2002-03	**Photo.**		***Perf. 11½***	
1912	A524	7c multicolored	.25	.25
1913	A524	25c multicolored	.60	.50
1913A	A524	35c multicolored	.90	.75
1913B	A524	41c multicolored	1.00	.30
1913C	A524	57c multicolored	1.50	.75
1913D	A524	70c multicolored	1.90	.70
		Size:38x27mm		
1914	A524	€1 multicolored	2.50	.50
1915	A524	€2 multicolored	5.00	.60
1916	A524	€5 multicolored	13.00	3.50
		Nos. 1912-1916 (9)	26.65	7.85

Issued: 7c, 5/6. 25c, 7/15. 35c, 3/31/03. 41c, 57c, 70c, €1, €2, €5, 11/4/02.

Leffe Abbey, 850th Anniv. — A820

2002, June 10 Photo. ***Perf. 11½***

1917 A820 42c multi + label 1.25 .45

Castles — A821

No. 1918: a, Chimay. b, Alden Biesen. c, Wissekerke. d, Corroy-le-Château. e, Reinhardstein. f, Loppem. g, Horst. h, Ecaussinnes-Lalaing. i, Ooidonk. j, Modave. Nos. 1918a-1918f are 45x24mm; Nos. 1918g-1918j are 52x21mm.

2002, June 10

1918 A821 Sheet of 10 11.50 *11.50*

a.-j. 42c Any single 1.10 .50

Belgian Post Emblem — A821a

2002, June 15 Photo. ***Perf. 11½***

1918K A821a (42c) red 2.10 2.10

Issued in sheets of 15 stamps + 15 labels that could be personalized. The sheets sold for €16.

Horses
A822

Designs: 40c, Jumping. 42c, Driving, vert. 52c, St. Paul's Horse Procession, Opwijk, cent., vert.

2002, July 1 Photo. ***Perf. 11½***

1919 A822 40c multi 1.00 .50

1920 A822 42c multi 1.10 .50

Souvenir Sheet

1921 A822 52c multi 1.40 1.40

No. 1921 contains one 38x49mm stamp.

Battle of the Courtrai, 700th Anniv. — A823

Designs: 42c, Golden spurs of defeated French knights. 52c, Castle.

57c, Battle scene, horiz.

2002, July 15

1922 A823 42c multi 1.10 .50

1923 A823 52c multi 1.40 1.50

Souvenir Sheet

1924 A823 57c multi 2.00 2.00

No. 1924 contains one 49x38mm stamp.

Windmills — A824

Designs: 42c, Onze-Lieve-Vrouw-Lombeek windmill, Belgium. 52c, Ilha do Faial windmill, Azores.

2002, July 15 Photo. ***Perf. 11½***

1925 A824 42c multi 1.10 .70

1926 A824 52c multi 1.25 1.25

See Portugal Azores Nos. 471-472.

Lace — A825

Lace from: 42c, Liedekerke, Belgium. 74c, Pag Island, Croatia.

2002, July 15

1927 A825 42c multi 1.00 .65

1928 A825 74c multi 1.90 1.25

See Croatia Nos. 497-498.

Youth Philately
A826

2002, July 15 Photo. ***Perf. 11½***

1929 A826 42c multi 1.25 .60

Rights of the Child — A827

2002, Sept. 30 Photo. ***Perf. 11½***

1930 A827 42c multi 1.10 .30

Jean Rey (1902-83), Politician — A828

2002, Sept. 30 Photo. & Engr.

1931 A828 52c dk bl & lt bl 1.50 1.25

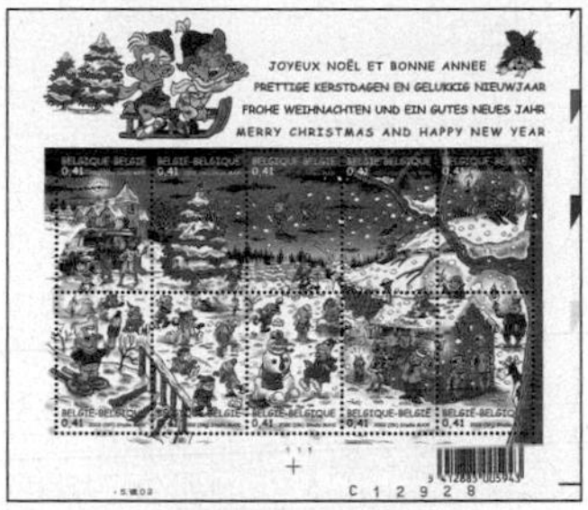

Christmas — A829

No. 1932: a, Family at ice cream truck. b, Ski jumper in Christmas tree. c, Sledder in air, skier in snow. d, Skier on hillside. e, Skiers with torches. f, Boy with ice cream cone. g, Children in snowball fight. h, Children, man and snowman. i, People at snack stand. j, Cow, policeman and burglars.

2002, Oct. 28 Photo.

1932 A829 Sheet of 10 12.50 12.50

a.-j. 41c Any single 1.10 .50

Princess Elizabeth, 1st Birthday A830

Designs: 49c, Princess Elizabeth, vert. 59c, Princesses Elizabeth and Mathilde, Prince Philippe.

84c, Princess Elizabeth, diff.

2002, Nov. 4 Photo. ***Perf. 11½***

1933 A830 49c multi 1.25 .40

1934 A830 59c multi 1.60 1.25

Souvenir Sheet

1935 A830 84c multi 2.75 2.75

No. 1935 contains one 48x37mm stamp. Margins on sheets of No. 1933, inscribed "Prior," served as etiquettes.

Death Announcement Stamp — A831

2002, Nov. 4

1936 A831 (49c) multi 1.40 .30

Compare with type A882.

Crocuses — A832

Booklet Stamp

Die Cut Perf. 10 on 2 or 3 Sides

2002, Nov. 4 Self-Adhesive

1937 A832 (49c) multi 1.50 .30

a. Booklet pane of 10 16.00

Coil Stamp

Serpentine Die Cut 13¼x13½x13¾x14

1938 A832 (49c) multi 1.50 .30

Compare illustration A832 with A859.

80th Birthday of Cartoonist Marc Sleen — A833

Designs: 49c, Nero and Adhemar. 82c, Sleen with cartoon characters.

2002, Dec. 30 ***Perf. 11½***

1939 A833 49c multi 1.25 .50

Souvenir Sheet

1940 A833 82c multi 3.00 3.00

No. 1940 contains one 48x37mm stamp. Margins on sheets of No. 1939, inscribed "Prior," served as etiquettes.

Henry van de Velde (1863-1957), Architect — A834

Designs: 49c, New House, Tervuren, 1927-28 (1a). No. 1942, Paris World's Fair Pavilion, 1937 (1b), vert. No. 1943, Book Tower, Ghent (1c), vert.

84c, Marie Sèthe, wife of van de Velde, on Art Nouveau staircase, vert.

2003, Jan. 27

1941 A834 49c multi 1.25 .40

1942 A834 59c multi 1.60 1.10

1943 A834 59c multi 1.60 1.10

Nos. 1941-1943 (3) 4.45 2.60

Souvenir Sheet

1944 A834 84c multi 2.50 2.50

No. 1944 contains one 37x48mm stamp. Margins on sheets of No. 1941, inscribed "Prior," served as etiquettes.

Love for Service Occupations A835

No. 1945: a, Firefighters. b, Police. c, Civil defense workers. d, Nurses. e, Postal workers. f, Birdcage and hearts.

2003, Jan. 27

1945 Sheet of 10, #1945e-1945f, 2 each #1945a-1945d 12.00 12.00

a.-f. A835 49c Any single 1.25 .65

Margins on sheets, inscribed "Prior," served as etiquettes.

Hector Berlioz (1803-69), Composer A836

2003, Feb. 24

1946	A836	59c multi	1.40	1.25

Traditional Sports A837

Designs: No. 1947, Lawn bowling (4a). No. 1948, Archery (4b).
82c, Pigeon racing, vert.

2003, Feb. 24

1947	A837	49c multi	1.25	.40
1948	A837	49c multi	1.25	.40

Souvenir Sheet

1949	A837	82c multi	2.50	2.50

No. 1949 contains one 37x48mm stamp. Margins on sheets of Nos. 1947-1948, inscribed "Prior," served as etiquettes.

Organization Anniversaries A838

Designs: No. 1950, Association of Engineers of Mons sesquicentennial (5a). No. 1951, Solvay Business School centennial (5b).

2003, Mar. 17

1950	A838	49c multi	1.25	.40
1951	A838	49c multi	1.25	.40

Margins on sheets of Nos. 1950-1951, inscribed "Prior," served as etiquettes.

Liège International Flower Show — A839

2003, Apr. 28 Photo. *Perf. 11½*

1952	A839	49c multi	1.25	.40

Margins on sheets, inscribed "Prior," served as etiquettes.

Georges Simenon (1903-89), Writer — A840

Designs: 49c, Poster for "Maigret Sets a Trap." 59c, Poster for "The Cat."
84c, Simenon at typewriter.

2003, Apr. 28

1953	A840	49c multi	1.25	.60
1954	A840	59c multi	1.60	.90

Souvenir Sheet

1955	A840	84c multi	2.50	2.50

No. 1955 contains one 38x48mm stamp. Margins on sheets of No. 1953, inscribed "Prior," served as etiquettes.

Carillons — A841

No. 1956: a, St. Rombout's Cathedral, Mechelen (denomination at left). b, Sts. Peter and Paul Cathedral, St. Petersburg, Russia (denomination at right).

Photo. & Engr.

2003, May 12 *Perf. 11½*

1956	A841	Horiz. pair	3.25	3.25
a.-b.		59c Either single	1.40	1.25

See Russia No. 6767.

Stamp Day — A842

2003, May 19 Photo. *Perf. 11½*

1957	A842	49c multi	1.10	.40

Margins on sheets, inscribed "Prior," served as etiquettes.

Youth Philately — A843

2003, May 19

1958	A843	49c multi	1.25	.40

Margins on sheets, inscribed "Prior," served as etiquettes.

Belgian Post Emblem — A844

2003 Photo. *Perf. 11½*

1959	A844	49c red	2.00	1.25

Issued in sheets of 15 stamps + 15 labels that could be personalized. The sheets sold for €16.

Minerals A845

No. 1960: a, Calcite (11a). b, Quartz (11b). c, Barite (11c). d, Galena (11d). e, Turquoise (11e).

2003, June 30 Photo. *Perf. 11½*

1960		Vert. strip of 5	6.50	6.50
a.-e.		A845 49c Any single	1.25	.50

Issued in sheets of 2 strips. Margins on sheets, inscribed "Prior," served as etiquettes.

Europa — A846

2003, June 30

1961	A846	59c multi	*1.60*	*1.00*

Tourism — A847

No. 1962: a, La Robe de Mariée, by Paul Delvaux (Koksijde, 13a). b, Tapestry (Oudenaarde, 13b). c, Fist sculpture by Rik Poot, City Hall (Vilvoorde, 13c). d, Royal Castle, playing card suits (Turnhout, 13d). e, Statue of Ambiorix, Gallo-Roman Museum (Tongeren, 13e). f, Fountain by Pol Bury, mineshaft frame (La Louvière, 13f), g, City Hall, lion statue (Braine l'Alleud, 13g). h, Forest, Mardasson Memorial (Bastogne, 13i). i, Büchtelturm, snow-covered tree (Sankt Vith, 13j). j, Saxophone, Citadel (Dinant, 13h).

2003, July 7

1962	A847	Sheet of 10	13.00	13.00
a.-g.		41c Any single	1.10	.65
h.-i.		52c Either single	1.25	.85
j.		57c multi	1.50	.95

Statues and Fountains — A848

Designs: No. 1963, Monument to the Seasonal Worker, Rillaar (14a). No. 1964, La Toinade, Treignes (14b). No. 1965, Hamont Textile Teut, Hamont-Achel (14c). No. 1966, Vaartkapoen, Brussels (14d). No. 1967, Maca, Wavre (14e).

2003, July 7

1963	A848	49c multi	1.25	.40
1964	A848	49c multi	1.25	.40
1965	A848	49c multi	1.25	.40
1966	A848	49c multi	1.25	.40
1967	A848	49c multi	1.25	.40
		Nos. 1963-1967 (5)	6.25	2.00

Margins on sheets, inscribed "Prior," served as etiquettes.

A849

Kings Baudouin and Albert II — A850

2003, Aug. 11

1968	A849	49c multi	1.25	.40

Souvenir Sheet

1969	A850	Sheet of 2	4.50	4.50
a.		59c King Baudouin	1.75	1.25
b.		84c King Albert II	2.50	2.00

Reign of King Albert II, 10th anniv.

Bird Type of 1985 with Euro Denominations Only

1c, Rossignol philoméle. 2c, Becassine des Marais. 40c, Gobemouche gris. 44c, Hirondelle de fenetre. 52c, Huppe fasciée. 55c, Petit gravelot. 65c, Mouette rieuse. 75c, Pluvier doré. €3.72, Poule d'Eau. €4, Hibou grand-duc.

2003-04 Photo. *Perf. 11½*

1970	A524	1c multicolored	.25	.25
1971	A524	2c multicolored	.50	.40
1972	A524	40c multicolored	.90	.75
1973	A524	44c multicolored	1.10	.30
1974	A524	52c multicolored	1.10	1.00
1975	A524	55c multicolored	1.25	1.25
1976	A524	65c multicolored	1.50	1.50
1977	A524	75c multicolored	1.75	1.25

Size: 38x27mm

1978	A524	€3.72 multicolored	9.00	1.25
1979	A524	€4 multicolored	10.00	1.25
		Nos. 1970-1979 (10)	27.35	9.20

Issued: 2c, 52c, 8/11. 1c, 40c, 44c, 55c, 65c, 75c, €4, 4/19/04. €3.72, 10/27.

Europalia Italia Festival, Belgium A851

Designs: 49c, Still Life, by Giorgio Morandi. 59c, 1947 Cisitalia 202, designed by Battista Pininfarina.

2003, Sept. 15 Photo. *Perf. 11½*

1980	A851	49c multicolored	1.30	.45
1981	A851	59c multicolored	1.60	1.10

See Italy Nos. 2568-2569. Margins on sheets of No. 1980, inscribed "Prior," served as etiquettes.

Saint Nicholas — A852

2003, Oct. 27

1982	A852	49c multicolored	1.20	.40

Margins on sheets, inscribed "Prior," served as etiquettes.

Social Cohesion A853

2003, Oct. 27

1983	A853 49c multicolored	1.20	.40

Margins on sheets, inscribed "Prior," served as etiquettes.

Miniature Sheet

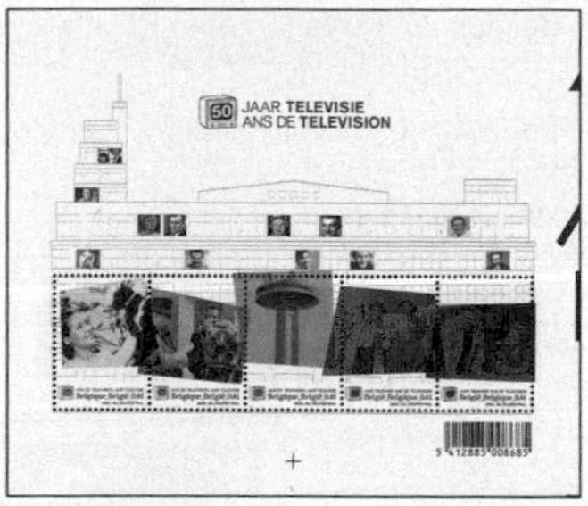

Belgian Television, 50th Anniv. — A854

No. 1984: a, Jardin Extraordinaire (yellow panel, 18a). b, Old camera (blue panel, 18b). c, Broadcasting tower (green panel, 18c). d, Cassiers and Jef Burm (red violet panel, 18d). e, Schipper Naast Mathilde (red panel, 18e).

2003, Nov. 3

1984	A854 Sheet of 5	6.00	6.00
a.-e.	41c Any single	1.10	.80

Books — A855

Books and: No. 1985, Man with apple (19a). No. 1986, Duplicating machine (19b), horiz. No. 1987, Woman reader, cat (19c).

2003, Nov. 12

1985	A855 49c multi	1.10	.40
1986	A855 49c multi	1.10	.40
1987	A855 49c multi	1.10	.40
	Nos. 1985-1987 (3)	3.30	1.20

Margins on sheets, Inscribed "Prior," served as etiquettes.

Authors — A856

Designs: 49c, Maurice Gilliams (1900-82). 59c, Marguerite Yourcenar (1903-87).

2003, Nov. 12

1988	A856 49c brown	1.25	.50
1989	A856 59c org brn & org	1.50	1.00

Margins on sheets of No. 1988, inscribed "Prior," served as etiquettes.

Christmas — A857

2003, Nov. 17

1990	A857 41c multi + label	1.25	.50

Yellow Tulips — A858

Crocuses — A859

Booklet Stamp

Die Cut Perf. 9¾ on 2 or 3 Sides

2003 Photo. Self-Adhesive

1991	A858 (59c) multi	2.25	.50
a.	Booklet pane of 10	24.00	24.00

Coil Stamp

Serpentine Die Cut 13¾x14x13¼x13½

1992	A859 (49c) multi	1.50	.30

Issued: No. 1991, 11/12. Compare illustration A859 with A832.

Tennis Players — A860

Designs: No. 1993, Justine Henin-Hardenne. No. 1994, Kim Clijsters, horiz.

2003, Nov. 24 ***Perf. 11½***

1993	A860 49c multi	1.10	.40
1994	A860 49c multi	1.10	.40

Margins on sheets, inscribed "Prior," served as etiquettes.

Red Carnations A861

Booklet Stamp

Die Cut Perf. 9¾ on 2 or 3 Sides

2004, Jan. 19 Self-Adhesive

1995	A861 (49c) multi	1.40	.30
a.	Booklet pane of 10	14.00	

Miniature Sheet

Art by Fernand Khnopff (1858-1921) — A862

No. 1996: a, Portrait of Marguerite Khnopff (1a, 27x48mm). b, Caresses (1b, 55x24mm). c, Brown Eyes and a Blue Flower (1c, 55x24mm). d, An Abandoned City (1d, 27x48mm).

2004, Jan. 19 ***Perf. 11½***

1996	A862 Sheet of 4	4.50	4.50
a.-d.	41c Any single	1.10	.50

Youth Philately A863

2004, Jan. 19

1997	A863 41c multi	1.10	.60

Miniature Sheet

Famous Belgians — A864

No. 1998: a, Peter Piot, director of UN Program on AIDS (3a). b, Nicole Van Goethem, film director (3b). c, Dirk Frimout and Frank de Winne, astronauts (3c). d, Jacques Rogge, Intl. Olympic Committee President (3d). e, Christian de Duve, 1974 Nobel laureate in Physiology or Medicine (3e). f, Gabrielle Petit, World War II heroine (3f). g, Catherine Verfaille and Christine Van Broeckhoven, medical researchers (3g). h, Jacques Stibbe, philatelist (3h). i, Queen Fabiola (3i). j, Adrien van der Burch, patron of 1935 Brussels Intl. Exhibition (3j).

2004, Feb. 16

1998	A864 Sheet of 10	15.00	15.00
a.-j.	57c Any single	1.40	1.00

Stamp Day A865

2004, Feb. 16

1999	A865 41c multi	1.10	.50

Sugar Industry A866

Designs: No. 2000, Sugar beet (5a). No. 2001, Refinery (5b). No. 2002, Street in Tienen (5c).

2004, Mar. 15

2000	A866 49c multi	1.10	.40
2001	A866 49c multi	1.10	.40
2002	A866 49c multi	1.10	.40
	Nos. 2000-2002 (3)	3.30	1.20

Miniature Sheet

Tintin and the Moon — A867

No. 2003: a, Model of Tintin and rocket (6a). b, Technical sketch of rockets for "Destination Moon" (6b). c, Tintin on spacecraft mattress, from "Destination Moon" (6c). d, Tintin on spacecraft ladder, from "Explorers on the Moon" (6d). e, Tintin on Moon, from "Explorers on the Moon" (6e).

2004, Mar. 15

2003	A867 Sheet of 5	7.50	7.50
a.-e.	41c Any single	1.25	.80

European Parliament Elections A868

2004, Apr. 19

2004	A868 22c multi	.50	.50

Miniature Sheet

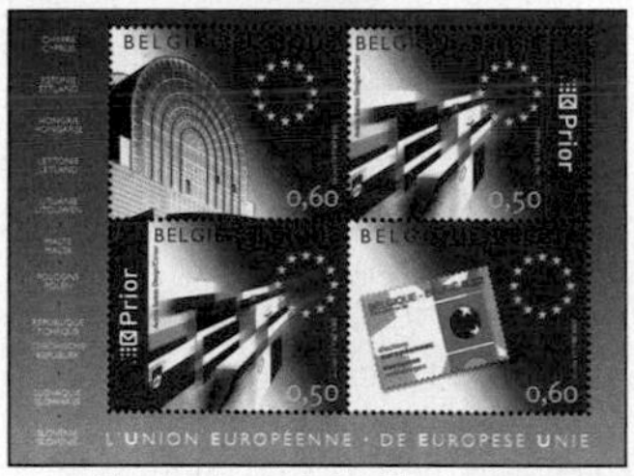

Expansion of the European Union — A869

No. 2005: a, Flags of newly-added countries, "Prior" at right (8bis b). b, As "a," "Prior" at left (8bis c). c, European Parliament, Brussels (8bis a). d, #2004 (8bis d).

2004, Apr. 19 ***Perf. 11½***

2005	A869 Sheet of 4, #a-d	6.50	6.50
a.-b.	50c Either single	1.25	.90
c.-d.	60c Either single	1.50	1.00

Religious Buildings — A870

Designs: No. 2006, Chapel in the Woods, Buggenhout (9a). No. 2007, Sanctuary, Banneaux. (9b). No. 2008, Scherpenheuvel Basilica, Montaigu (9c). No. 2009, Sanctuary, Beauraing, horiz. (9d).

2004, Apr. 19 **Engr.**

2006	A870 49c green	1.10	.65
2007	A870 49c brown	1.10	.65
2008	A870 49c purple	1.10	.65
2009	A870 49c blue	1.10	.65
	Nos. 2006-2009 (4)	4.40	2.60

Margins on sheets, inscribed "Prior," served as etiquettes.

A871

Belgian Post Emblem — A872

2004, Apr. 19 **Photo.**

2010	A871 49c red	1.60	1.00
2011	A872 (49c) red	1.60	.60

Compare illustration A871 with A844.

Liège A873

Designs: No. 2012, Museum of Modern and Contemporary Art, sculpture, by Jef Lambeaux (10a). No. 2013, Bridge designed by Santiago Calatrava (10b).
75c, Steel foundry equipment, vert. (10c).

2004, May 17 Photo. ***Perf. 11½***

2012	A873	44c multi	1.10	.40
2013	A873	44c multi	1.10	.40

Souvenir Sheet

2014	A873	75c multi	2.00	2.00

No. 2014 contains one 38x49mm stamp.

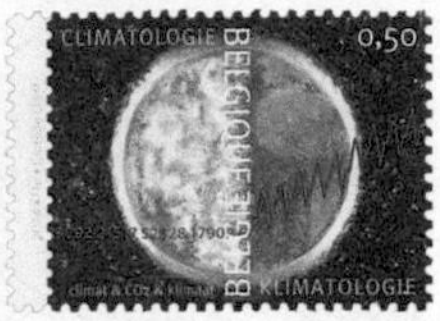

Climatology A874

Designs: 50c, Climate and cabon dioxide (11a). 65c, Relations between Sun and Earth (11b). No. 2017, Earth (11c). No. 2018, Sun (11d).

2004, May 17

2015	A874	50c multi	1.10	.50
2016	A874	65c multi	1.50	.65
2017	A874	80c multi	2.00	.85
2018	A874	80c multi	2.00	.85
		Nos. 2015-2018 (4)	6.60	2.85

Margins on sheets of Nos. 2015 and 2017, inscribed "Prior," served as etiquettes.

Edgar P. Jacobs (1904-87), Cartoonist A875

Blake and Mortimer, by Jacobs — A876

2004, May 24

2019	A875	60c multi	1.40	.75

Souvenir Sheet

2020	A876	€1.20 multi	4.00	4.00

See France No. 3027.

Jazz Musicians A877

Designs: No. 2021, Django Reinhardt (1910-53), guitarist (13a). No. 2022, Fud Candrix (1908-74), saxophonist (13b). No. 2023, René Thomas (1927-75), guitarist (13c). No. 2024, Jack Sels (1922-70), saxophonist (13d). No. 2025, Bobby Jaspar (1926-63), saxophonist (13e).

2004, May 24

2021	A877	50c multi	1.10	.50
2022	A877	50c multi	1.10	.50
2023	A877	50c multi	1.10	.50
2024	A877	50c multi	1.10	.50
2025	A877	50c multi	1.10	.50
		Nos. 2021-2025 (5)	5.50	2.50

Expansion of European Union — A878

No. 2026 — Flags of newly-admitted countries: a, Cyprus. b, Estonia. c, Hungary. d, Latvia. e, Lithuania. f, Malta. g, Poland. h, Czech Republic. i, Slovakia. j, Slovenia.

Die Cut Perf. 10 on 2 or 3 Sides
2004, June 7 Photo.
Self-Adhesive

2026		Booklet pane of 10	12.00	*12.00*
a.-j.		A878 44c Any single	1.10	.80

King Albert II, 70th Birthday A879

2004, June 7 ***Perf. 11½***

2027	A879	50c shown	1.10	.40

Souvenir Sheet

2028	A879	80c Close-up	2.50	2.50

Margins on sheets of No. 2027, inscribed "Prior," served as etiquettes. No. 2028 contains one 38x49mm stamp.

Europa A880

Photography contest winners: No. 2029, The Belgian Coast, by Muriel Vekemans (15a). No. 2030, The Belgian Ardennes, by Freddy Deburghgraeve (15b).

2004, June 7

2029	A880	55c multi	*1.25*	*.60*
2030	A880	55c multi	*1.25*	*.60*

2004 Summer Olympics, Athens A881

Designs: 50c, Women's basketball, vert. 55c, Mountain biking. 60c, Pole vault.
80c, Olympic torch.

2004, July 12

2031	A881	50c multi	1.10	.55
2032	A881	55c multi	1.25	.60
2033	A881	60c multi	1.40	.70
		Nos. 2031-2033 (3)	3.75	1.85

Souvenir Sheet

2034	A881	80c multi	2.40	2.40

Margins on sheets of No. 2031, inscribed "Prior," served as etiquettes. No. 2034 contains one 49x38mm stamp.

Death Announcement Stamp — A882

2004, Sept. 20

2035	A882	(50c) multi	1.25	.40

Compare with type A831.

Sculptures by Idel Ianchelevici (1909-94) — A883

Designs: 50c, L'appel (18a). 55c, Perennis Perdurat Poeta (18b).

2004, Sept. 20

2036	A883	50c multi	1.10	.50
2037	A883	55c multi	1.25	.90

Margins on sheets of No. 2036, inscribed "Prior," served as etiquettes.
See Romania Nos. 4666-4667.

Impatiens — A884

Booklet Stamp
Die Cut Perf. 10x9¾ on 2 or 3 Sides
2004 Photo. Self-Adhesive

2038	A884	(50c) multi	1.40	.30
a.		Booklet pane of 10	16.00	16.00

Coil Stamp
Serpentine Die Cut 13¾x14

2039	A884	(50c) multi	1.40	.30

Issued: No. 2038, 9/27; No. 2039, 12/15.

Belgian World War II Volunteers Medal A885

2004, Sept. 27 Photo. ***Perf. 11½***

2040	A885	50c multi	1.20	.40

Miniature Sheet

Forest Week — A886

No. 2041: a, Squirrel and blackcap. b, Nightingale, robin and red admiral butterfly. c, Bumblebee, vole, flowers, mushrooms, head of weasel. d, Jay, flowers, rear of weasel, left wing of peacock butterfly.

2004, Sept. 27

2041	A886	Sheet of 4	5.00	5.00
a.-d.		44c Any single	1.10	.80

Miniature Sheet

Belgica 2006 World Youth Philatelic Exhibition — A887

No. 2042: a, Pony. b, Robin. c, Kitten. d, Puppy. e, Fish.

2004, Oct. 18

2042	A887	Sheet of 5	14.00	14.00
a.-e.		44c Any single	2.50	2.50

No. 2042 sold for €5, with €2.80 of this going to fund the exhibition.

Halloween — A888

Designs: No. 2043, Witch, bats and black cat. No. 2044, Jack o'lantern and bats.

Booklet Stamp
Die Cut Perf. 10x9¾ on 2 or 3 Sides
2004, Oct. 18 Self-Adhesive

2043	A888	44c multi	1.00	.30
2044	A888	44c multi	1.00	.30
a.		Booklet pane, 5 each #2043-2044	12.50	*12.50*

Writers A889

Designs: 50c, Raymond Jean de Kremer (pen names Jean Ray and John Flanders) (1887-1964). 75c, Johan Daisne (1912-78). 80c, Gérald Bertot (pen name Thomas Owen) (1910-2002), vert.

2004, Nov. 3 ***Perf. 11½***

2045	A889	50c multi	1.25	.50
2046	A889	75c multi	1.75	.75
2047	A889	80c multi	2.00	1.00
		Nos. 2045-2047 (3)	5.00	2.25

Margins on sheets of Nos. 2045 and 2047, inscribed "Prior," served as etiquettes.

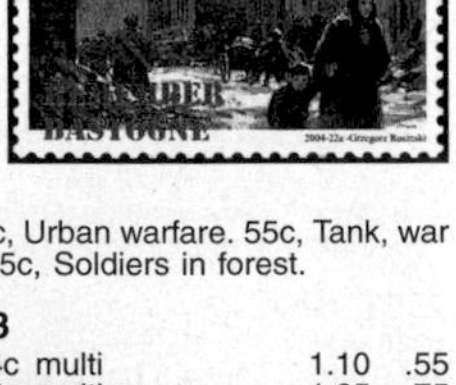

Battle of the Bulge, 60th Anniv. A890

Designs: 44c, Urban warfare. 55c, Tank, war victims, vert. 65c, Soldiers in forest.

2004, Nov. 3

2048	A890	44c multi	1.10	.55
2049	A890	55c multi	1.25	.75
2050	A890	65c multi	1.60	1.00
		Nos. 2048-2050 (3)	3.95	2.30

Christmas A891

Paintings by Peter Paul Rubens: No. 2051, The Flight Into Egypt. Nos. 2052, 2053, Adoration of the Magi.

2004, Nov. 22 *Perf. 11½*

2051	A891	44c tan & multi	1.10	.35
2052	A891	44c blue & multi	1.10	.35

Self-Adhesive
Booklet Stamp
Size: 22x22mm
Die Cut Perf. 10x9¾ on 2 or 3 Sides

2053	A891	44c blue & multi	1.10	.30
a.		Booklet pane of 10	*25.00*	*25.00*

See Germany Nos. B946-B947.

Miniature Sheet

Champion Motocross Riders — A892

No. 2054: a, René Baeton. b, Jacky Martens. c, Georges Jobe. d, Joel Robert. e, Eric Geboers. f, Roger De Coster. g, Stefan Everts. h, Gaston Rahier. i, Joel Smets. j, Harry Everts. k, André Malherbe. l, Steve Ramon.

2004, Nov. 22 *Perf. 11½*

2054	A892	Sheet of 12 + central label and 12 etiquettes	16.50	16.50
a.-l.		50c Any single	1.25	.80

Belgian Post Emblem — A893

2005, Jan. 17

2055	A893	6c red	.25	.25

Women's Council, Cent. — A894

2005, Jan. 17 **Photo.** *Perf. 11½*

2056	A894	50c multi	1.25	.60

Margins on sheets, inscribed "Prior," served as etiquettes.

Michel Vaillant, Comic Strip by Jean Graton A895

2005, Jan. 17 **Photo.** *Perf. 11½*

2057	A895	50c multi	1.25	.50

Website for Belgium's 175th Anniversary Celebrations A896

Die Cut Perf. 10 on 3 Sides
2005, Feb. 14 **Photo.**
Self-Adhesive
Booklet Stamp

2058	A896	(50c) multi	1.25	.30
a.		Booklet pane of 10	15.00	

Rotary International, Cent. — A897

2005, Feb. 14 *Perf. 11½*

2059	A897	80c multi	2.00	1.50

Linguists A898

Designs: No. 2060, Maurice Grevisse (1895-1980), French language grammarian (5a). No. 2061, Johan Hendrik van Dale (1828-72), Dutch language lexicographer (5b).

2004, Feb. 12

2060	A898	55c multi	1.40	.75
2061	A898	55c multi	1.40	.75

Souvenir Sheet

King Albert II and Queen Paola — A899

2005, Feb. 28

2062	A899	75c multi	2.50	2.50

Belgian Independence, 175th anniv.

No. 2062 was later sold in a presentation folder that additionally contained a €4 silver stamp depicting Kings Leopold I and Albert I. This folder sold for €10.

Miniature Sheet

Belgian Independence, 175th Anniv. — A900

No. 2063 — History of Belgium: a, First train (6bis a). b, Bakuba dancer, Belgian Congo (6bis b). c, Teacher in classroom (6bis c). d, Industrialization (6bis d). e, Family (Social progress) (6bis e). f, War (6bis f). g, 1958 World's Fair (6bis g). h, Street sign (Federalism) (6bis h). i, Berlaymont Building (Europe) (6bis i). j, L'Ombre et son Ombre, by René Magritte (Art) (6bis j).

2005, Feb. 28

2063	A900	Sheet of 10	14.00	14.00
a.-j.		44c Any single	1.25	.75

A901

Belgica 2006 World Youth Philatelic Exhibition — A902

Designs: Nos. 2064a, 2065, Space Shuttle (8a). Nos. 2064b, 2067, Airplane (8b). Nos. 2064c, 2066, Train (8c). Nos. 2064d, 2068 Race car (8d). Nos. 2064e, 2069, Motorboat (8e).

2005, Mar. 21 *Perf. 11½*

2064	A901	Sheet of 5	15.00	15.00
a.-e.		44c Any single	2.60	2.60

Booklet Stamps
Self-Adhesive
Die Cut Perf. 10 on 3 Sides

2065	A902	44c multi	1.25	.75
2066	A902	44c multi	1.25	.75
2067	A902	44c multi	1.25	.75
2068	A902	44c multi	1.25	.75
2069	A902	44c multi	1.25	.75
a.		Booklet pane, 2 each #2065-2069	13.00	13.00

No. 2064 sold for €5, with €2.80 of this going to fund the exhibition.

Belgian Post Emblem — A903

2005, Mar. 21 *Perf. 11½*

2070	A903	10c bright blue	.50	.25

Bird Type of 1985 With Euro Denominations Only

3c, Mesange nonnette. 5c, Bruant zizi. 20c, Mouette melanocephale. 44c, Pigeon ramier. 60c, Perdrix grise. 75c, Roitelet triple-bandeau.

2005 **Photo.** *Perf. 11½*

2071	A524	3c multicolored	.25	.25
2072	A524	5c multicolored	.25	.25
2073	A524	20c multicolored	.50	.40
2074	A524	44c multicolored	1.10	.40
2075	A524	60c multicolored	1.40	1.00
2076	A524	75c multicolored	1.75	1.25
		Nos. 2072-2076 (5)	5.00	3.30

Issued: 5c, 20c, 60c, 3/21. 3c, 44c, 75c, 4/4.

Rose Varieties A904

Designs: 44c, Belinda (9a). 70c, Pink Iceberg, vert. (9b). 80c, Old Master (9c).

2005, Apr. 4 **Photo.** *Perf. 11½*

2077	A904	44c multi	1.10	.50
2078	A904	70c multi	1.75	1.00
2079	A904	80c multi	2.00	1.25
		Nos. 2077-2079 (3)	4.85	2.75

2005 Ghent Flower Show. Nos. 2077-2079 are impregnated with a rose scent. Margins on sheets of No. 2079, inscribed "Prior," served as etiquettes.

Europa — A905

No. 2080: a, The Children's Table, by Gustave van de Woestijne (10a). b, Still Life With Oysters, Fruit and Pastry, by Clara Peeters (10b).

2005, Apr. 4

2080	A905	Horiz. pair	*3.25*	*2.25*
a.-b.		60c Either single	*1.50*	*1.00*

Black Stork A906

2005, Apr. 4 **Photo. & Engr.**

2081	A906	€4 multi	10.00	3.50

Stamp Day.

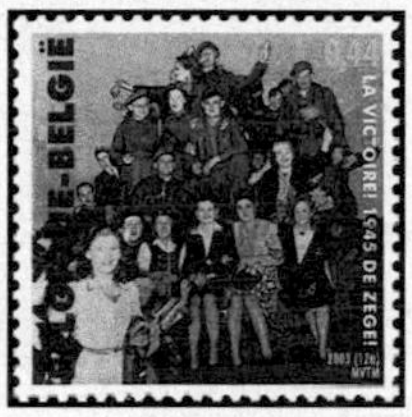

End of World War II, 60th Anniv. A907

Designs: No. 2082, Soldiers and civilians celebrating (12a). No. 2083, Drawing of concentration camp internee, by Wilchar (12b). No. 2084, Photograph of liberated concentration camp internees (12c).

2005, May 9 **Photo.**

2082	A907	44c multi	1.10	.55
2083	A907	44c multi	1.10	.55
2084	A907	44c multi	1.10	.55
		Nos. 2082-2084 (3)	3.30	1.65

Return of Last Belgian Battalion from Korean War, 50th Anniv. — A908

2005, May 9 *Perf. 11½*

2085	A908	44c multi	1.10	.55

Clocks — A909

Designs: No. 2086, Zimmer Tower clock, Lier (14a). No. 2087, Belfry of Mons clock (14b). No. 2088, Mont des Arts clock, Brussels (14c).

2005, May 9 **Engr.**

2086	A909	44c deep blue	1.10	.55
2087	A909	44c dark brown	1.10	.55
2088	A909	44c reddish brown	1.10	.55
		Nos. 2086-2088 (3)	3.30	1.65

Vacations
A910

Designs: No. 2089, Woman on beach, bird (14bis a). No. 2090, Man in Ardennes Forest, deer (14bis b).

2005, May 9 **Photo.**

2089 A910 50c multi + etiquette 1.25 .60
2090 A910 50c multi + etiquette 1.25 .60

Hearts — A911

Darwinhybrid Tulips — A912

Baby Boy — A913

Baby Girl — A914

Doves and Wedding Rings — A915

Wedding Rings — A916

Die Cut Perf. 9¾ on 2 or 3 Sides

2005, May 9 **Photo.**

Booklet Stamps

Self-Adhesive

2091 A911 (50c) multi 1.50 .30
a. Booklet pane of 10 15.00
2092 A912 A multi 2.00 .45
a. Booklet pane of 10 20.00
2093 A913 80c multi 2.00 .50
a. Booklet pane of 10 20.00
2094 A914 80c multi 2.00 .50
a. Booklet pane of 10 20.00
2095 A915 80c multi 2.00 .50
2096 A916 80c multi 2.00 .50
a. Booklet pane of 10, 5 each #2095-2096 20.00
Nos. 2091-2096 (6) 11.50 2.75

No. 2092 sold for 70c on day of issue.

Miniature Sheet

International Judo Champions From Belgium — A917

No. 2097: a, Robert Van de Walle (15a). b, Ingrid Berghmans (15b). c, Ulla Werbrouck (15c). d, Gella Vandecaveye (15d). e, Christel Deliège (15e). f, Johan Laats (15f).

2005, June 20 **Photo.** ***Perf. 11½***

2097 A917 Sheet of 6 10.00 10.00
a.-f. 50c Any single 1.50 .75

Tapestries and Carpets — A918

Designs: 44c, L'humanité Assaillie par les Sept Péchés Capitaux tapestry, Belgium (16a). 60c, Carpet from Hereke region, Turkey (16b).

2005, June 20

2098 A918 44c multi 1.10 .40
2099 A918 60c multi 1.50 1.00

See Turkey Nos. 2943-2944.

National Radio Broadcasting Institute, 75th Anniv. — A919

2005, June 20

2100 A919 50c multi 1.25 .60

Margins on sheets, inscribed "Prior," served as etiquettes.

Souvenir Sheet

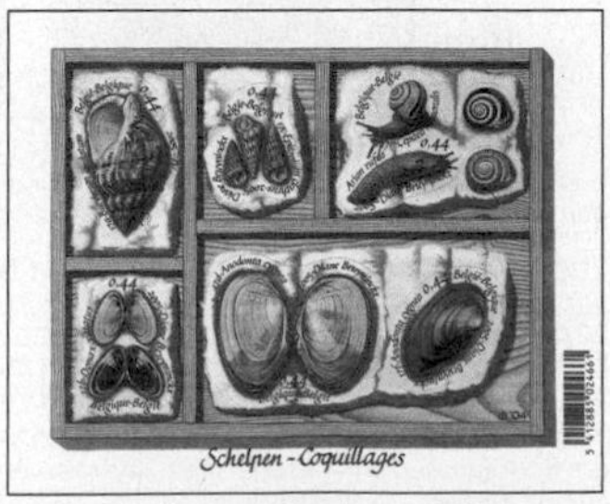

Shells and Snails — A920

No. 2101: a, Buccinum undatum (31x46mm, 17a). b, Donax vittatus (29x38mm, 17b). c, Epitonium clathrus (25x33mm, 17c). d, Interior of Anodonta cygnea (42x48mm, 17d). e, Cepaea nemoralis, Arion rufus (33x40mm, 17e). f, Exterior of Anodonta cygnea (32x34mm, 17f).

2005, July 25 **Photo.** ***Die Cut***

Self-Adhesive

2101 A920 Sheet of 6 9.00 9.00
a.-f. 44c Any single 1.25 .75

Chrysanthemums
A921

Die Cut Perf. 10 on 2 or 3 Sides

2005, Sept. 12 **Photo.**

Self-Adhesive

Booklet Stamp

2102 A921 (50c) multi 1.25 .35
a. Booklet pane of 10 12.50

Shrine of Our Lady, by Nicolas of Verdun, 800th Anniv. A922

2005, Sept. 12 **Photo.** ***Perf. 11½***

2103 A922 75c multi 2.00 1.25

Buildings in Belgium and Singapore — A923

Designs: No. 2104, Belgian Center for Comic Strip Art, Brussels (19a). No. 2105, Museum of Musical Instruments, Brussels (19b). No. 2106, Shops on Bukit Pasoh Road, Singapore (19c). No. 2107, Shop on Kandahar Street, Singapore (19d).

2005, Sept. 12

2104 A923 44c multi 1.10 .55
2105 A923 44c multi 1.10 .55
2106 A923 65c multi 1.60 .80
2107 A923 65c multi 1.60 .80
Nos. 2104-2107 (4) 5.40 2.70

See Singapore Nos. 1160-1163.

Europalia Festival
A924

Paintings by Russian artists: 50c, The Reaper, by Kasimir Malevitch (19bis a). 70c, Allegorical Scene, by Sergei Sudeikin (19bis b).

2005, Sept. 12

2108 A924 50c multi 1.25 .60
2109 A924 70c multi 1.75 .85

Margins on sheets of No. 2108, inscribed "Prior," served as etiquettes.

Miniature Sheet

Asterix in Belgium — A925

No. 2110: a, Asterix (27x27mm, 19 ter a). b, Cacofonix (27x40mm, 19 ter b). c, Getafix (38x28mm, 19 ter c) d, Obelix (38x28mm, 19 ter d). e, Vitalstatistix (27x40mm, 19 ter e). f, Asterix at banquet (38x32mm, 19 ter f).

2005, Sept. 24 **Photo.** ***Perf. 11½***

2110 A925 Sheet of 6 12.00 12.00
a.-f. 60c Any single 1.60 .70

Miniature Sheet

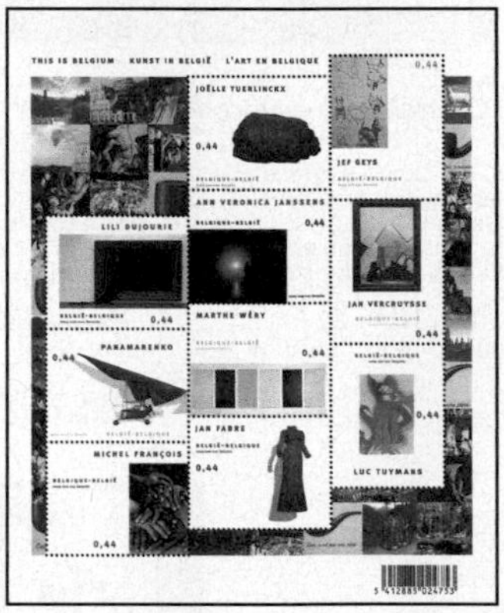

Contemporary Art — A926

No. 2111: a, La Traviata, by Lili Dujourie (20b). b, Donderwalk, by Panamarenko (20h). c, Jeu de Mains, by Michel François (20a). d, OBJET Noir, by Joelle Tuerlinckx (20c). e, Représentation d'un Corps Rond, by Ann Veronica Janssens (20g). f, Tournus, by Marthe Wéry (20e). g, Mur de Montée des Anges, by Jan Fabre (20d). h, ABC Ecole d Paris, by Jef Geys, vert. (20f). i, Portrait of an Artist by Himself (XII), by Jan Vercruysse, vert. (20i). j, Figuur op de Rug Gezien, by Luc Tuymans, vert. (20j).

2005, Oct. 10

2111 A926 Sheet of 10 12.50 12.50
a.-j. 44c multi 1.10 .75

Miniature Sheet

Hans Christian Andersen (1805-75), Author — A927

No. 2112 — Stories by Andersen: a, The Princess and the Pea (21a). b, The Ugly Duckling (21b). c, Thumbelina (21c). d, The Little Mermaid (21d). e, The Emperor's New Clothes (21e).

2005, Oct. 10 Photo. *Perf. 11½*
2112 A927 Sheet of 5 8.00 8.00
a.-e. 50c Any single 1.50 .60

Left margins on No. 2112, inscribed "Prior" served as etiquettes.

Hans Christian Andersen (1805-75), Author — A927a

Nos. 2113: a, The Princess and the Pea, "Prior" at L (21a). b, As "a," "Prior" at R. c, The Ugly Duckling, "Prior" at L (21b). d, As "c," "Prior" at R. e, Thumbelina, "Prior" at L (21c). f, As "e," "Prior" at R. g, The Little Mermaid, "Prior" at L (21d). h, As "g," "Prior" at R. i, The Emperor's New Clothes, "Prior" at L (21d). j, As "i," "Prior" at R.

Die Cut 9¾ on 2 or 3 Sides
2005, Oct. 10 Photo.
Self-Adhesive
2113 Booklet pane of 10 15.00 15.00
a.-j. A927a 50c Any single 1.50 .75

Brass Band Musicians — A928

No. 2114: a, Bass drum (22a). b, Trumpet (22b). c, Sousaphone (22c). d, Clarinet (22d). e, Tuba (22e).

2005, Oct. 31 *Perf. 11½*
2114 Booklet pane of 5+5 etiquettes 7.50 7.50
a.-e. A928 50c Any single 1.50 .60
Complete booklet, #2114 7.50

Writers — A929

No. 2118: a, Maurits Sabbe (1873-1938) (23a). b, Arthur Masson (1896-1970) (23b).

2005, Oct. 31 Photo. *Perf. 11½*
2118 A929 Horiz. pair 2.25 2.25
a.-b. 44c Either single 1.10 .55

Christmas — A930

2005, Oct. 31 Photo. *Perf. 11½*
2119 A930 44c multi 1.10 .40

Christmas Type of 2005
Die Cut Perf. 9¾ on 2 or 3 Sides
2005, Oct. 31 Photo.
Booklet Stamp
Self-Adhesive
Size: 18x26mm
2120 A930 44c multi 1.10 .30
a. Booklet pane of 10 12.00 12.00

Queen Astrid (1905-35) — A931

Queen Astrid: 44c, Wearing tiara (25a). 80c, Holding son (25b).

2005, Oct. 31 Photo. *Perf. 11½*
2121 A931 44c multi 1.25 .55

Souvenir Sheet
2122 A931 80c multi 2.40 2.40

No. 2122 contains one 38x49mm stamp.

Bird Type of 1985 With Euro Denominations Only
2006 Photo. *Perf. 11½*
2123 A524 23c Grebe à cou noir .60 .35
2124 A524 30c Râle des genêts .75 .35
2125 A524 46c Avocette 1.10 .75
2126 A524 78c Barge à queue noire 2.00 1.00

Size: 38x27mm
2127 A524 €4.30 Grebe huppé 12.50 3.00
Nos. 2123-2127 (5) 16.95 5.45

Issued: 30c, 46c, 1/23; 78c, 3/20; €4.30, 5/15. 23c, 6/6.

Wolfgang Amadeus Mozart (1756-91), Composer A932

2006, Jan. 23 Photo. *Perf. 11½*
2128 A932 70c multi 1.75 .85

Playwrights A933

Designs: 52c, Michel de Ghelderode (1898-1962). 78c, Herman Teirlinck (1879-1967).

2006, Jan. 23
2129 A933 52c blk & blue 1.25 .60
2130 A933 78c blk & red vio 2.00 .80

Margins on sheets of No. 2129, inscribed "Prior," served as etiquettes.

Composers of Polyphonic Music — A934

No. 2131: a, Guillaume Dufay (c. 1400-74) and Gilles Binchois (c. 1400-60). b, Johannes Ockeghem (c. 1410-97). c, Jacob Obrecht (c. 1457-1505). d, Adriaan Willaert (c. 1490-1562). e, Orlandus Lassus (1532-94).

2006, Jan. 23
2131 Booklet pane of 5 8.00 8.00
a.-e. A934 60c Any single 1.75 1.00
Complete booklet, #2131 8.00

Farm Animals — A935

No. 2132: a, Donkey. b, Chicken and rooster. c, Two ducks. d, Pig and piglets. e, Cow. f, Goat. g, Two rabbits. h, Two horses. i, Sheep. j, Three geese.

2006, Jan. 23 *Die Cut Perf. 10x9¾*
Self-Adhesive
2132 Booklet pane of 10 14.00 14.00
a.-j. A935 46c Any single 1.25 .55

A936

A937

Designs: 46c, (52c), Crossbowmen.

2006, Feb. 20 *Perf. 11½*
2133 A936 46c multi 1.25 .55

Booklet Stamp
Self-Adhesive
2134 A937 (52c) multi 1.50 .60
a. Booklet pane of 10 15.00

Souvenir Sheet

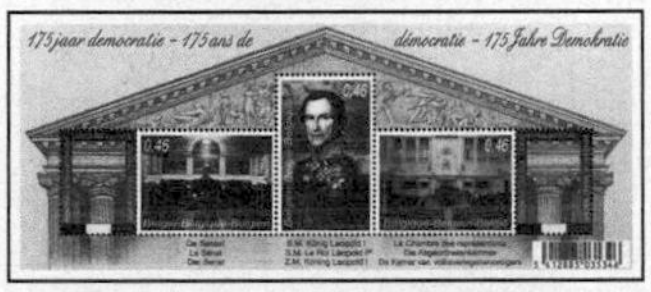

Democracy in Belgium, 175th Anniv. — A938

No. 938: a, Senate chambers (red brown floor). b, King Leopold I, vert. c, Chamber of Representatives (green floor).

2006, Feb. 20
2135 A938 Sheet of 3 + 2 labels 5.00 5.00
a.-c. 46c Any single 1.40 .75

Souvenir Sheet

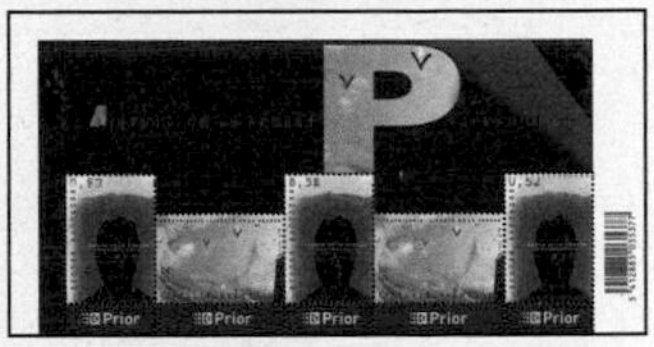

Freedom of the Press — A939

No. 2136: a, Face with open mouth. b, Stylized birds and building, horiz.

2006, Feb. 20
2136 A939 Sheet, 3 #2136a, 2 #2136b + 5 etiquettes 7.50 7.50
a.-b. 52c Either single 1.50 .75

A940

Stamp Festival — A941

2006, Mar. 20 Photo. *Perf. 11½*
2137 A940 46c multi 1.25 .30

Booklet Stamps
Self-Adhesive
2138 A941 (52c) "Prior" at L 1.50 .30
2139 A941 (52c) "Prior" at R 1.50 .60
a. Booklet pane, 5 each #2138-2139 16.00 16.00

Justus Lipsius (1547-1606), Philologist — A942

Photo. & Engr.
2006, Mar. 20 *Perf. 11½*
2140 A942 70c buff & brown 1.75 1.00

Start of Giro d'Italia Cycling Race in Wallonia — A943

2006, Apr. 24 Photo.
2141 A943 52c multi 1.40 .65

Printed in sheets of 5. Margins on sheets, inscribed "Prior," served as etiquettes.

Painting Details — A944

No. 2142 — Paintings by Lambert Lombard (1506-66): a, L'Offrande de Joachim Refusée (six men). b, Auguste et la Sybile de Tibur (four men).

No. 2143 — Paintings by Léon Spilliaert (1881-1946): a, Duizeling (figure on staircase). b, De Dame met de Hoed (woman in hat).

2006, Apr. 24

2142 A944	Vert. pair		4.00	2.00
a.-b.	65c Either single		1.75	1.00
2143 A944	Vert. pair		4.00	2.00
a.-b.	65c Either single		1.75	1.00

Souvenir Sheet

Memorial Van Damme Track and Field Competition — A945

No. 2144 — Runners of the 1970s and 1980s: a, John Walker. b, Alberto Juantorena. c, Ivo Van Damme. d, Sebastian Coe. e, Steve Ovett.

2006, Apr. 24 ***Perf. 11½***

2144 A945	Sheet of 5 + 5 etiquettes	8.00	8.00
a.-e.	52c Any single	1.25	1.00

Miniature Sheet

International Billiards Champions From Belgium — A946

No. 2145: a, Clément Van Hassel. b, Tony Schrauwen. c, Léo Corin. d, Emile Wafflard. e, Ludo Dielis. f, Jos Vervest. g, Frédéric Caudron. h, Laurent Boulanger. i, Paul Stroobants, Eddy Leppens, and Peter De Backer. j, Raymond Ceulemans. k, Raymond Steylaerts. l, Jozef Philipoom.

2006, Apr. 26

2145 A946	Sheet of 12 + label + 12 etiquettes	18.00	18.00
a.-l.	52c Any single	1.25	1.00

Belgica 2006 Intl. Philatelic Exhibition, Brussels
A947 A948

2006, May 15 ***Perf. 11½***

Size:21x25mm

2146	A947	46c multi	1.10	.50

Size:22x26mm

2146A	A947	46c multi	12.00	9.50

Booklet Stamp
Self-Adhesive

Die Cut Perf. 9¾x10 on 2 or 3 Sides

2147 A948	(52c) multi	1.50	.40
a.	Booklet pane of 10	15.00	

No. 2146A was available in sheets with personalizable labels in November and December 2006, and afterwards available without labels.

Red Cross — A949

Booklet Stamp

Die Cut Perf. 10x9¾ on 2 or 3 Sides

2006, May 15 **Self-Adhesive**

Location of "Prior"

2148 A949	(52c) At left	1.50	.40
2149 A949	(52c) At right	1.50	.40
a.	Booklet pane, 5 each #2148-2149	15.00	

See No. B1172.

Lighthouses A950

Photo. & Engr.

2006, May 15 ***Perf. 11½***

2150 A950	46c Blankenberge	1.20	.40
2151 A950	46c Heist	1.20	.40
2152 A950	46c Nieuwpoort	1.20	.40
2153 A950	46c Ostend	1.20	.40
	Nos. 2150-2153 (4)	4.80	1.60

Souvenir Sheet

Fish of the North Sea — A951

No. 2154: a, Petite roussette (dogfish, 50x26mm). b, Cabillaud (cod, 47x26mm). c, Raie bouclée (thornback ray, 50x26mm). d, Hareng (herring, 33x25mm). e, Plie (flounder, 33x25mm).

2006, May 15 **Photo.**

2154 A951	Sheet of 5	7.00	7.00
a.-e.	46c Any single	1.40	.75

Belgian Olympic and Interfederal Committee, Cent. A952

2006, June 6 **Photo.** ***Perf. 11½***

2155 A952	52c multi	1.25	.40

Souvenir Sheet

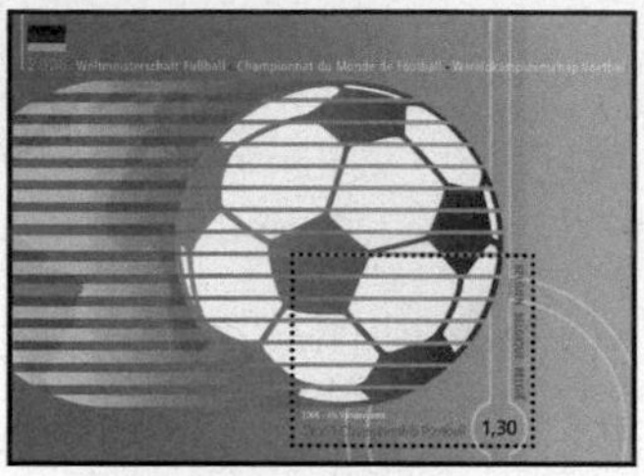

2006 World Cup Soccer Championships, Germany — A953

2006, June 6

2156 A953	€1.30 multi	3.50	3.00

Miniature Sheet

Scenes of Wallonian Villages — A954

No. 2157: a, House and flowers, Deigné. b, Arch, Mélin. c, Statue, Saint-Hadelin Church, Celles. d, Bridge, Lompret. e, Fountain, Ny.

2006, June 6

2157 A954	Sheet of 5	7.50	7.50
a.-e.	52c Any single	1.50	1.00

Centaurea — A955

Booklet Stamp

Die Cut Perf. 9¾ on 2 or 3 Sides

2006, Aug. 7 **Self-Adhesive**

2158 A955	(52c) multi	1.50	.40
a.	Booklet pane of 10	15.00	

Marcinelle Coal Mine Disaster, 50th Anniv. A956

2006, Aug. 7 ***Perf. 11½***

2159 A956	70c multi	2.00	.95

Rembrandt Tulips — A957

Die Cut Perf. 9¾ on 2 or 3 Sides

2006, Sept. 25 **Photo.**

Self-Adhesive
Booklet Stamp

2160 A957	A multi	2.00	1.00
a.	Booklet pane of 10	22.50	22.50

No. 2160 sold for 70c on day of issue.

Institute of Tropical Medicine, Antwerp, Cent. — A958

2006, Sept. 25 ***Perf. 11½***

2161 A958	80c multi	2.00	1.25

Oosterlingenhuis, Bruges — A959 Oosters Huis, Antwerp — A960

2006, Sept. 25

2162 A959	70c multi	1.75	1.00
2163 A960	80c multi	2.00	1.40

Hanseatic League, 650th anniv.

Belgian Philatelic Academy — A961

2006, Oct. 23 **Photo.** ***Perf. 11½***

2164 A961	52c multi	1.25	.60

Printed in sheets of 10. Margins on sheets, inscribed "Prior," served as etiquettes.

Souvenir Sheet

Belgica 2006 Intl. Philatelic Exhibition, Brussels — A962

No. 2165: a, Tennis ball. b, Tulips as stemware. c, Butterflies as four-leaf clover. d, Illuminated tent. e, Vignettes of Nos. 2165a-2165d with speech balloons.

2006, Nov. 16

2165 A962	Sheet of 5	13.50	13.50
a.-e.	46c Any single	2.60	2.60

No. 2165 sold for €5.

Souvenir Sheet

Belgica 2006 Emblem — A963

2006, Nov. 16

2166 A963	€1.95 multi	13.50	13.50

No. 2166 sold for €5.

Europa — A964

No. 2167 — Children's drawings: a, Zebra and cows, by Nassira Tadmiri. b, People and rainbow, by Lize-Maria Verhaeghe.

2006, Nov. 17

2167 A964 Horiz. pair 2.80 2.80
a.-b. 52c Either single 1.40 .60

Printed in sheets of 5 pairs. Margins on sheets, inscibed "Prior," served as etiquettes.

A965

Paintings by COBRA Group Artists — A966

No. 2168: a, New Skin, by Pierre Alechinsky. b, Untitled by Asger Jorn.

2006, Nov. 17 ***Perf. 11½***

Souvenir Sheet

2168 A965 Sheet of 2 3.25 3.25
a. 46c multi 1.25 1.00
b. 70c multi 1.75 1.50

Booklet Stamp
Self-Adhesive
Die Cut Perf. 9¾ on 2 or 3 Sides

2169 A966 (52c) Like #2168a 1.40 .40
a. Booklet pane of 10 15.00 15.00

See Denmark Nos. 1367-1370.

A967

Dance — A968

Designs: Nos. 2170a, 2173, Rock and roll. Nos. 2170b, 2172, Waltz. Nos. 2170c, 2171, Tango. Nos. 2170d, 2174, Cha cha cha. Nos. 2170e, 2175, Samba.

2006, Nov. 18 ***Perf. 11½***

2170 A967 Sheet of 5 8.00 8.00
a.-e. 60c Any single 1.60 1.25

Booklet Stamps
Self-Adhesive
Die Cut Perf. 9¾ on 2 or 3 Sides

2171 A968 (52c) multi 1.40 1.00
2172 A968 (52c) multi 1.40 1.00
2173 A968 (52c) multi 1.40 1.00
2174 A968 (52c) multi 1.40 1.00
2175 A968 (52c) multi 1.40 1.00
a. Booklet pane of 10, 2 each #2171-2175 16.00 16.00

Kramikske, Comic Strip by Jean-Pol Vandenbroeck A969

2006, Nov. 19 ***Perf. 11½***

2176 A969 46c multi 1.25 .60

Youth philately.

Miniature Sheet

Belgian Foods and Beverages — A970

No. 2177: a, Shrimps and tomato. b, Witloof chicory (Belgian endive). c, Eel in green sauce. d, Chocolate. e, Orval beer, vert. f, Gin, vert. g, Ham, sausages, bread and condiments, vert. h, Waffles, vert. i, Mussels, vert. j, Geuze (doubly-fermented beer), vert.

2006, Nov. 19 ***Perf. 11½***

2177 A970 Sheet of 10 12.50 12.50
a.-j. 46c Any single 1.25 .90

Angel Playing Psaltery — A971

Angel Playing Trumpet Marine — A972

Angel Playing Lute — A973

Angel Playing Trumpet — A974

Angel Playing Shawm — A975

Head of Angel — A976

Angels painted by Hans Memling: No. 2179, Head of angel on #2178a. No. 2180, Head of angel on #2178b. No. 2181, Head of angel on #2178c. No. 2182, Head of angel on #2178d. No. 2183, Head of angel on #2178e.

2006, Nov. 20 ***Perf. 12x11¾***

2178 Horiz. strip of 5 6.25 6.25
a. A971 46c multi 1.25 .60
b. A972 46c multi 1.25 .60
c. A973 46c multi 1.25 .60
d. A974 46c multi 1.25 .60
e. A975 46c multi 1.25 .60

Booklet Stamps
Self-Adhesive
Die Cut Perf. 9¾ on 2 or 3 Sides

2179 A976 46c multi 1.25 .40
2180 A976 46c multi 1.25 .40
2181 A976 46c multi 1.25 .40
2182 A976 46c multi 1.25 .40
2183 A976 46c multi 1.25 .40
a. Booklet pane of 10, 2 each #2179-2183 14.00 14.00
Nos. 2179-2183 (5) 6.25 2.00

Christmas.

"Happy Birthday to You" — A977

Birthday Cake — A978

Booklet Stamp
Die Cut Perf. 9¾ on 2 or 3 Sides

2006, Nov. 20 **Self-Adhesive**

2184 A977 (52c) "Prior" at left 1.40 .50
2185 A978 (52c) "Prior" at right 1.40 .50
2186 A978 (52c) "Prior" at left 1.40 .50
2187 A977 (52c) "Prior" at right 1.40 .50
a. Booklet pane of 10, 3 each #2184-2185, 2 each #2186-2187 16.00 16.00
Nos. 2184-2187 (4) 5.60 2.00

Christmas — A979

2006, Nov. 20 **Photo.** ***Perf. 11½***

2188 A979 46c multi 12.00 9.50

No. 2188 was available in sheets with personalizable labels in November and December 2006, and afterwards available without labels. Compare types A979 and A930.

Bicycle — A980

Bowling Ball and Pins — A981

Golf Club and Ball — A982

Bicycle — A983

Bowling Ball and Pins — A984

Golf Club and Ball — A985

2007, Jan. 8 **Photo.** ***Perf. 11½***

2189 A980 46c multi 1.00 .70
2190 A981 60c multi 1.25 1.00
2191 A982 65c multi 1.40 1.20
Nos. 2189-2191 (3) 3.65 2.90

Booklet Stamps
Self-Adhesive
Die Cut Perf. 9¾ on 2 or 3 Sides

2192 A983 (52c) "Prior" at left 1.40 .60
2193 A983 (52c) "Prior" at right 1.40 .60
a. Booklet pane, 5 each #2192-2193 16.00 16.00
2194 A984 (52c) "Prior" at left 1.40 .60
2195 A984 (52c) "Prior" at right 1.40 .60
a. Booklet pane, 5 each #2194-2195 16.00 16.00
2196 A985 (52c) "Prior" at left 1.40 .60
2197 A985 (52c) "Prior" at right 1.40 .60
a. Booklet pane, 5 each #2196-2197 16.00 16.00
Nos. 2192-2197 (6) 8.40 3.60

World Cross-country Cycling Championships, Hooglede-Gits.

King Albert II Type of 2005 and

King Albert II — A986

King Albert II, Numeral on European Union Flag — A987

King Albert II, Numeral on Globe — A988

2007-09 **Photo.** ***Perf. 11½***

2200 A986 1 red & gray 1.50 .25
2202 A810 80c bl, bl gray & blk 2.00 1.00
2203 A987 1 blue & multi 2.25 1.10
2204 A810 90c bl, brn gray & blk 2.00 1.25
2205 A988 1 brn org & multi 2.50 1.25
2206 A986 2 grn & gray 3.25 .75
2210 A986 3 dk bl & gray 4.50 1.10
2211 A987 3 bl grn & multi 6.75 3.50
2213 A986 5 vio & gray 8.50 1.90
2214 A988 3 red vio & multi 7.50 3.75
2216 A986 7 brn & gray 11.00 2.60
Nos. 2200-2216 (11) 51.75 18.45

Issued: Nos. 2202, 2204, 1/29; Nos. 2200, 2206, 2210, 2213, 2216, 10/1, Nos. 2203, 2205, 2211, 2214, 1/2/09.

Nos. 2202 and 2204 are inscribed "A Prior" at left.

Stamps of type A987 were intended for usee to destinations within Europe, and type A988 for use to destinations outside of Europe.

On day of issue, No. 2200 sold for 52c, No. 2203, for 80c, No. 2205, for 90c, No. 2206, for €1.04, No. 2210, for €1.56, No. 2211, for €2.40, No. 2213, for €2.60, No. 2214, for €2.70, and No. 2216, for €3.64.

Bird Type of 1985 With Euro Denominations Only

5c, Sarcelle d'hiver. 6c, Chouette cheveche. 10c, Chouette de Tengmalm. 23c, Choucas des Tours. 40c, Hibou moyen-duc. 70c, Martinet noir. 75c, Faucon crecerelle.

2007 **Photo.** ***Perf. 11½***

2218 A524 5c multicolored .25 .25
2218A A524 6c multicolored .25 .25
2219 A524 10c multicolored .25 .25
2220 A524 23c multicolored .60 .25
2220A A524 40c multicolored 1.00 .30
2221 A524 70c multicolored 1.60 .50
2222 A524 75c multicolored 1.75 .50
Nos. 2218-2222 (7) 5.70 2.30

Issued: 5c, 10c, 2/26; 23c, 3/26; 70c, 75c, 1/29; 6c, 7/9; 40c, 11/12.

Alix, Comic Strip by Jacques Martin
A990

2007, Jan. 29
2223 A990 52c multi 1.40 .60

Youth philately. Printed in sheets of 5. Margins on sheets, inscribed "Prior," served as etiquettes.

Miniature Sheet

Accordions — A991

No. 2224: a, Accordion with piano-like keyboard at left. b, Concertina with hexagonal ends. c, Bohemians accordion. d, Accordion with brown and black trim. e, Accordion with red trim.

2007, Jan. 29
2224 A991 Sheet of 5 + 5 etiquettes 7.00 7.00
a.-e. 52c Any single 1.40 .70

Red Cross Mobile Library for Hospitals — A992

Booklet Stamps
Die Cut Perf. 9¾ on 2 or 3 Sides
2007, Feb. 26 **Self-Adhesive**
2225 A992 (52c) "Prior" at left 1.40 .70
2226 A992 (52c) "Prior" ar right 1.40 .70
a. Booklet pane, 5 each #2225-2226 15.00 15.00

See No. B1175.

Miniature Sheet

Female Writers — A993

No. 2227: a, Julia Tulkens (1902-95), poet. b, Madeleine Bourdouxhe (1906-96), novelist. c, Christine D'haen, poet. d, Jacqueline Harpman, novelist. e, Maria Rosseels (1916-2005), novelist.

2007, Feb. 26 ***Perf. 11½***
2227 A993 Sheet of 5 + 5 etiquettes 7.00 7.00
a.-e. 52c Any single 1.40 .70

Stoclet House, Brussels, Designed by Josef Hoffmann — A994

Designs: 52c, Building interior. 80c, Building exterior.

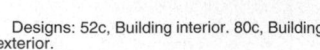

2007, Mar. 26
2228 A994 52c multi 1.25 .70
2229 A994 80c multi 2.00 1.10

Margins of sheets of No. 2228, inscribed "Prior," served as etiquettes. See Czech Republic Nos. 3338-3339.

Souvenir Sheet

Popular Theater — A995

No. 2230: a, Scene from "Tati l'Pèriki." b, Romain Deconinck, actor and impresario, vert. c, Scene from "Le Mariage de Mademoiselle Beulemans."

2007, Mar. 26 **Photo.** ***Perf. 11¾***
2230 A995 Sheet of 3 + 2 labels 4.00 4.00
a.-c. 46c Any single 1.25 .60

European Union, 50th Anniv. — A996

2007, Apr. 30 ***Perf. 11¼x11½***
2231 A996 80c multi 2.00 1.10

Europa — A997

Designs: 46c, Lord Robert Baden-Powell, founder of Scouting movement. 75c, Scouts.

2007, Apr. 30 ***Perf. 11½x11¼***
2232 A997 46c multi 1.25 .65

Souvenir Sheet
Perf. 11½
2233 A997 75c multi 2.10 2.10

Scouting, cent. No. 2233 contains one 38x49mm stamp.

The Adventures of Tintin — A998

No. 2234 — Tintin book covers translated in: a, French (Tintin au Pays des Soviets). b, Danish (Tintin i Congo). c, English (Tintin in America). d, Luxemburgian (Dem Pharao seng Zigaren). e, Chinese (dragon on cover). f, Portuguese (O Idolo Roubado). g, Bengali (Tintin in boat on cover). h, Slovak (Zezlo Král'a Otakara). i, Russian (Tintin and camels on cover). j, Icelandic (Dularfulla Stjarnan). k, Polish (Tajemnica Jednorozca). l, Afrikaans (Die Skat van Rackham die Rooie). m, Tintin author, Hergé. n, Arabic (Tintin and men with man in chair above table on cover). o, Spanish (El Templo del Sol). p, German (Im Reiche des Schwarzend Goldes). q, Finnish (Päämääränä Kuu). r, Swedish (Manen Tur Och Retur). s, Japanese (Tintin and men behind rocks on cover). t, Turkish (Ambardaki Kömür). u, Tibetan (Tintin on snowy mountain). v, Italian (I Gioielli della Castafiore). w, Indonesian (Penerbangan 714). x, Greek (Tintin and Mayan temple on cover). y, Dutch (Kuifje en de Alfa-Kunst).

2007, May 22 ***Perf. 11½***
2234 A998 Sheet of 25 32.00 32.00
a.-y. 46c Any single 1.25 .65

Museums — A999

Designs: 46c, Museum of Fashion, Hasselt. 75c, Notre Dame à la Rose Hospital Museum, Lessines. 92c, Jewish Museum of Belgium, Brussels.

2007, June 18 **Photo.** ***Perf. 11½***
2235 A999 46c multi 1.25 .60
2236 A999 75c multi 1.75 1.10
2237 A999 92c multi 2.50 1.25
Nos. 2235-2237 (3) 5.50 2.95

Souvenir Sheet

Opening of Princess Elisabeth Base, Antarctica — A1000

2007, June 18
2238 A1000 75c multi 2.10 2.10

A1001

Vacations
A1002

Designs: Nos. 2239, 2241, 2242, Woman, man with kite. Nos. 2240, 2243, 2244, People carrying canoe and woman.

2007 **Photo.** ***Perf. 11½***
2239 A1001 52c multi 1.25 .60
2240 A1001 52c multi 1.25 .60

Booklet Stamps
Self-Adhesive
Die Cut Perf. 9¾ on 2 or 3 Sides
2241 A1002 (52c) "Prior" at left 1.50 .75
2242 A1002 (52c) "Prior" at right 1.50 .75
a. Booklet pane of 10, 5 each #2241-2242 15.00
2243 A1002 (52c) "Prior" at left 1.50 .75
2244 A1002 (52c) "Prior" at right 1.50 .75
a. Booklet pane of 10, 5 each #2243-2244 15.00
Nos. 2239-2244 (6) 8.50 4.20

Issued: Nos. 2239-2240, 7/9; Nos. 2241-2244, 6/18. Margins on sheets of Nos. 2239-2240, inscribed "Prior," served as etiquettes.

Tour de France in Belgium — A1003

2007, July 9 ***Perf. 11½***
2245 A1003 52c multi 1.50 .75

Printed in sheets of 5. Margins on sheets, inscribed "Prior," served as etiquettes.

A1004

Port of Zeebrugge, Cent. — A1005

2007, July 9 ***Perf. 11½***
2246 A1004 €1.04 multi 3.00 1.50

Booklet Stamps
Self-Adhesive
Die Cut Perf. 9¾ on 2 or 3 Sides
2247 A1005 (52c) "Prior" at left 1.50 .75
2248 A1005 (52c) "Prior" at right 1.50 .75
a. Booklet pane of 10, 5 each #2247-2248 15.00
Nos. 2246-2248 (3) 6.00 3.00

Margins on sheets of No. 2246, inscribed "Prior," served as etiquettes.

Tourism — A1006

Designs: No. 2249, Athénée François Bovesse, Namur. No. 2250, Collège Saint-Michel, Brussels. No. 2251, Heilig Hart College, Maasmechelen.

Photo. & Engr.
2007, Sept. 3 ***Perf. 11½***
2249 A1006 52c multi 1.50 .75
2250 A1006 52c multi 1.50 .75
2251 A1006 52c multi 1.50 .75
Nos. 2249-2251 (3) 4.50 2.25

Tombeau du Géant, Botassart A1007

2007, Sept. 3 **Photo.**
2252 A1007 52c multi 1.50 .75

Rotunda of Luxembourg Train Station, Luxembourg A1008

2007, Sept. 3 **Photo. & Engr.**
2253 A1008 80c multi 2.00 1.10

See Luxembourg No. 1221.

Miniature Sheet

Scenes From Films By Belgian Directors — A1009

No. 2254: a, Misère au Borinage, by Henri Storck. b, Le Fils, by Jean-Pierre and Luc Dardenne. c, The Man Who Had His Hair Cut Short, by André Delvaux. d, Malpertuis, by Harry Kümel. e, Dust, by Marion Hansel.

2007, Sept. 3 **Photo.**
2254 A1009 Sheet of 5 7.50 7.50
a.-e. 52c Any single 1.50 .75

Souvenir Sheet

Queen Paola, 70th Birthday — A1010

2007, Sept. 3
2255 A1010 €1.04 multi 2.50 2.50

Belgian Post Emblem — A1011

2007, Oct. 1 **Photo.** ***Perf. 11½***
2256 A1011 1 red & black 1.50 .40

Sold for 52c on day of issue.

Fruit — A1012

No. 2257: a, Pears. b, Strawberries. c, Red currants. d, Apples. e, Grapes. f, Cherries. g, Raspberries. h, Peaches. i, Plums. j, Blackberries.

Die Cut Perf. 9¾ on 2 or 3 Sides
2007, Oct. 1 **Photo.**
Self-Adhesive
2257 Booklet pane of 10 15.00 15.00
a.-j. A1012 1 Any single 1.50 .40

Nos. 2257a-2257j each sold for 52c on day of issue.

Mourning Stamp A1013

2007, Oct. 15 ***Perf. 11½***
2258 A1013 1 multi 1.50 .75

Sold for 52c on day of issue.

Miniature Sheet

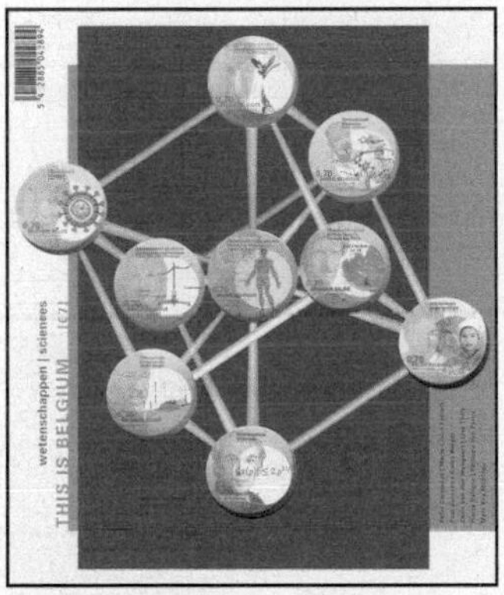

Scientists — A1014

No. 2259 — Scientist and field: a, Marc Van Montagu, molecular genetics. b, Paul Janssen, pharmaceutical entrepreneur. c, Lise Thiry, microbiology. d, Chris Van den Wyngaert, international criminal law. e, Peter Carmeliet, molecular medicine. f, Philippe Van Parijs, social philosophy. g, Marie-Claire Foblets, anthropology. h, André Berger, climatology. i, Pierre Deligne, mathematics.

2007, Oct. 15 ***Die Cut***
Self-Adhesive
2259 A1014 Sheet of 9 16.00 16.00
a.-i. 70c Any single 1.75 1.00

Postage Stamp Festival A1015

Designs: Nos. 2260a, 2261, Man with pipe, book, typewriter. Nos. 2260b, 2262, Woman, hearts, vase, picture frame, typewriter. Nos. 2260c, 2263, Man, musical symbols, typewriter. Nos. 2260d, 2264, Woman in cat costume, typewriter. Nos. 2260e, 2265, Boy at computer.

2007, Oct. 15 ***Perf. 11½***
2260 A1015 Sheet of 5 8.00 8.00
a.-e. 1 Any single 1.50 .75

Booklet Stamps
Self-Adhesive
Size: 28x20mm
Die Cut Perf. 9¾ on 2 or 3 Sides

2261 A1015 1 multi 1.50 .40
2262 A1015 1 multi 1.50 .40
2263 A1015 1 multi 1.50 .40
2264 A1015 1 multi 1.50 .40
2265 A1015 1 multi 1.50 .40
a. Booklet pane of 10, 2 each #2261-2265 15.00
Nos. 2261-2265 (5) 7.50 2.00

On day of issue, Nos. 2260a-2260e, 2261-2265 each sold for 52c.

Dahlias — A1016

Tulips — A1017

Petunias A1018

Coil Stamp
Serpentine Die Cut 13¾x14
2007, Oct. 15 **Self-Adhesive**
2266 A1016 1 multi 1.50 .40

Booklet Stamps
Die Cut Perf. 9¾ on 2 or 3 Sides

2267 A1016 1 multi 1.50 .40
a. Booklet pane of 10 15.00
2268 A1017 A multi 2.40 .60
a. Booklet pane of 10 24.00
2269 A1018 2 multi 3.00 .75
a. Booklet pane of 10 30.00
Nos. 2266-2269 (4) 8.40 2.15

On day of issue, Nos. 2266-2267 each sold for 52c; No. 2268, for 80c; No. 2269, for €1.04.

Les Chemins de la Liberté (Le Voyage), by Thierry Merget A1019

2007, Nov. 12 **Photo.** ***Perf. 11½***
2270 A1019 1 multi 1.60 .80

Miniature Sheet

International Billiards Champions From Belgium — A1020

No. 2271: a, Piet J. Van Duppen. b, Albert Collette. c, Gustaaf Van Belle. d, Piet Sels. e, Gaston De Doncker. f, Théo Moons. g, René Gabriels. h, Victor Luypaerts. i, René Vingerhoedt.

2007, Nov. 12
2271 A1020 Sheet of 9 15.00 15.00
a.-i. 1 Any single 1.60 .80

On day of issue, Nos. 2271a-2271i each sold for 52c.

Bride and Groom A1021

Father and Infant Son A1022

Mother and Infant Daughter — A1023

Booklet Stamps
Die Cut 9¾ on 2 or 3 Sides
2007, Nov. 12 **Self-Adhesive**

2272 A1021 1 multi 1.60 .40
a. Booklet pane of 10 16.00
2273 A1022 1 multi 1.60 .40
a. Booklet pane of 10 16.00
2274 A1023 1 multi 1.60 .40
a. Booklet pane of 10 16.00
Nos. 2272-2274 (3) 4.80 1.20

On day of issue, Nos. 2272-2274 each sold for 52c.

Christmas
A1024 A1025

2007, Nov. 12 ***Perf. 11½***
2275 A1024 1 multi 1.60 .80

Booklet Stamps
Self-Adhesive
Size: 24x29mm
Die Cut Perf. 9¾ on 2 or 3 Sides

2276 A1024 1 multi 1.40 .40
a. Booklet pane of 10 14.00
2277 A1025 A multi 2.10 1.10
a. Booklet pane of 10 21.00

On day of issue, Nos. 2275 and 2276 each had a franking value of 52c, and No. 2277 had a franking value of 80c. On day of issue, No. 2276a sold for €4.68, and No. 2277a sold for €7.20.

Bird Type of 1985 With Euro Denominations Only

10c, Accenteur mouchet. 15c, Cassenoix moucheté. €4.40, Faucon pélerin.

2008, Jan. 21 Photo. *Perf. 11½*
2278 A524 10c multi + etiquette .40 .25
2279 A524 15c multi + etiquette .50 .25

Size: 38x27mm

2280 A524 €4.40 multicolored 10.00 2.50
Nos. 2278-2280 (3) 10.90 3.00

Red Cross Blood Donation — A1026

Die Cut Perf. 9¾ on 2 or 3 Sides
2008, Jan. 21 Photo.

Booklet Stamp
Self-Adhesive

2281 A1026 1 multi 1.60 .80
a. Booklet pane of 10 16.00

See No. B1176. No. 2281 sold for 52c on day of issue.

Miniature Sheet

Paintings by René Magritte (1898-1967) — A1027

No. 2282: a, The Man from the Sea, 1927 (30x40mm). b, Scheherazade, 1950 (30x40mm). c, Midnight Marriage, 1926 (30x40mm). d, Georgette, 1935 (33x40mm). e, The Ignorant Fairy, 1956 (49x37mm).

Perf. 11½, 11¼x11½ (#2282b)
2008, Jan. 21
2282 A1027 Sheet of 5 + 2 labels 8.00 8.00
a.-e. 1 Any single 1.60 .80

Nos. 2282a-2282e each sold for 52c on day of issue. Ungummed imperforate examples of No. 2282 were given as gifts to some standing order subscribers, and were not sold.

Toys — A1028

No. 2283: a, Automobile. b, Baby carriage. c, Doll. d, Airplane. e, Horse. f, Tram. g, Diabolo. h, Teddy bear. i, Top. j, Scooter.

Die Cut Perf. 9¾ on 2 or 3 Sides
2008, Feb. 11 Self-Adhesive
2283 Booklet pane of 10 16.50
a.-j. A1028 1 Any single 1.60 .80

Nos. 2283a-2283j each sold for 54c on day of issue.

Jeremiah, Comic Book Character by Hermann Huppen A1029

2008, Feb. 11 *Perf. 11½*
2284 A1029 1 multi 1.60 .80

No. 2284 sold for 54c on day of issue.

Souvenir Sheet

Floralies of Ghent Flower Show, Bicent. — A1030

2008, Feb. 11
2285 A1030 80c multi 2.00 2.00

Jewish Community in Belgium, Bicent. A1031

2008, Mar. 17 Photo. & Engr.
2286 A1031 90c multi 2.50 1.50

Detective Novels — A1032

No. 2287: a, L'Assassin Habite au 21, by Stanislas-André Steeman. b, De Zaak Alzheimer, by Jef Geeraerts.

2008, Mar. 17 Photo.
2287 A1032 Horiz. pair, #a-b 3.50 1.75
a.-b. 1 Either single 1.75 .85

Nos. 2287a-2287b each sold for 54c on day of issue.

Trams A1033

Designs: 1, Coastal tram. 80c, Charleroi tram. 90c, Brussels tram.

2008, Apr. 14
2288 A1033 1 multi 1.75 .85
2289 A1033 80c multi 2.00 1.25
2290 A1033 90c multi 2.25 1.40
Nos. 2288-2290 (3) 6.00 3.50

No. 2289 sold for 54c on day of issue.

Miniature Sheet

Antverpia 2010 Intl. Philatelic Exhibition — A1034

No. 2291: a, Train, building. b, Buildings, statue. c, Port, cargo containers. d, Models, Flanders Fashion Institute Building. e, Woman wearing necklace, diamonds.

2008, Apr. 14 *Perf. 11½*
2291 A1034 Sheet of 5 15.50 15.50
a.-e. 1 Any single 3.00 3.00

On day of issue, No. 2291 sold for €5 but Nos. 2291a-2291e each had a 54c franking value.

Miniature Sheet

Spirou, Comic Strip by André Franquin — A1035

No. 2292: a, Count of Champignac (with magnifying glass). b, Fantasio. c, Spirou. d, Seccotine (girl). e, Zorglub (bearded man).

2008, Apr. 14
2292 A1035 Sheet of 5 9.00 9.00
a.-e. 1 Any single 1.75 .85

Nos. 2292a-2292e each sold for 54c on day of issue.

Mickey Mouse, 80th Anniv. — A1036

2008, May 19 Photo. *Perf. 11½*
2293 A1036 1 multi 1.75 .85

Sold for 54c on day of issue. Printed in sheets of 5.

Diversity at Work — A1037

2008, May 19
2294 A1037 2 multi 3.50 1.75

Sold for €1.08 on day of issue.

Souvenir Sheet

La Constance and Les Elèves de Thémis Masonic Lodges, Bicent. — A1038

2008, May 19 Litho.
2295 A1038 3 multi 5.25 5.25

Sold for €1.62 on day of issue.

Europa A1039

2008, May 19 Photo. *Perf. 11½*
2296 A1039 80c multi 2.00 1.25

Booklet Stamp
Self-Adhesive
Size: 30x24mm
Die Cut Perf. 9¾ on 2 or 3 Sides

2297 A1039 1 multi 1.75 .85
a. Booklet pane of 10 17.50

No. 2297 sold for 54c on day of issue.

Tagetes Patula — A1040

Orange Favorite Tulips — A1041

Booklet Stamps
Die Cut Perf. 9¾ on 2 or 3 Sides
2008, May 19 Self-Adhesive

2298 A1040 1 multi 1.75 .85
a. Booklet pane of 10 17.50
2299 A1041 A multi 2.60 1.25
a. Booklet pane of 10 26.00

On day of issue, No. 2298 sold for 54c, and No. 2299 sold for 80c. See No. 2316.

Souvenir Sheet

Queen Fabiola, 80th Birthday — A1042

No. 2300: a, Queen Fabiola and King Baudouin, black and white photo. b, Drawing of Queen Fabiola. c, Queen Fabiola and King Baudouin, color photo.

2008, June 11 *Perf. 11½*
2300 A1042 Sheet of 3 6.00 6.00
a.-c. 1 Any single 1.75 .85

Nos. 2300a-2300c each sold for 54c on day of issue.

Sculptures A1043

Designs: 1, La Mer, by George Grard. 80c, Sculpture from Imago series, by Emile Desmedt. 90c, Autoportrait, by Gérald Dederen.

2008, June 11 **Litho.**

2301 A1043 1 multi 1.75 .85
2302 A1043 80c multi 2.00 1.25
2303 A1043 90c multi 2.25 1.40
Nos. 2301-2303 (3) 6.00 3.50

No. 2301 sold for 54c on day of issue.

A1044

Outdoor Activities A1045

Family: Nos. 2304, 2306, Cycling. Nos. 2305, 2307, Walking.

2008, June 11 ***Perf. 11½***

2304 A1044 1 multi 1.75 .85
2305 A1044 1 multi 1.75 .85

Booklet Stamps
Self-Adhesive
Die Cut Perf. 9¾ on 2 or 3 Sides

2306 A1045 1 multi 1.75 .85
a. Booklet pane of 10 17.50
2307 A1045 1 multi 1.75 .85
a. Booklet pane of 10 17.50

On day of issue, Nos. 2304-2307 each sold for 54c.

Folklore and Traditions A1046

Designs: No. 2308, Hopduvelfeesten, Asse. No. 2309, Planting of the Meyboom, Brussels, 700th anniv., vert. No. 2310, Eupen Carnival, vert. No. 2311, Royal Walloon Cabaret Company, Tournai, cent., vert.

Photo. & Engr.

2008 July 14 ***Perf. 11½***

2308 A1046 1 multi 1.75 .85
2309 A1046 1 multi 1.75 .85
2310 A1046 1 multi 1.75 .85
2311 A1046 1 multi 1.75 .85
Nos. 2308-2311 (4) 7.00 3.40

On day of issue Nos. 2308-2311 each sold for 54c.

2008 Summer Olympics, Beijing — A1047

Designs: 1, BMX racer. 90c, Women's relay race, horiz.
2, Tennis, horiz.

2008, July 14 **Photo.**

2312 A1047 1 multi 1.75 .85
2313 A1047 90c multi 2.50 1.50

Souvenir Sheet

2314 A1047 2 multi 3.50 1.75

No. 2314 contains one 48x38mm stamp. On day of issue, Nos. 2312 and 2314 sold for 54c and €1.08, respectively.

Miniature Sheet

Brussels World's Fair, 50th Anniv. — A1048

No. 2315: a, Soviet Union Pavilion and plaza (red panel). b, Thailand Pavilion (yellow panel). c, Hostesses carrying flags (green panel). d, Fair's star emblems (blue panel). e, Atomium (red violet panel).

Perf. 11½ on 3 or 4 Sides

2008, July 14

2315 A1048 Sheet of 5 + 4 labels 8.75 8.75
a.-e. 1 Any single 1.75 .85

On day of issue, Nos. 2315a-2315e each sold for 54c.

Tagetes Patula Type of 2008
Serpentine Die Cut 13¼x13½

2008, Sept. 29 **Photo.**

Coil Stamp
Self-Adhesive

2316 A1040 1 multi 1.50 .40

On day of issue No. 2316 sold for 54c.

St. Gabriel Guild (Religion on Stamps Society), 50th Anniv. A1049

Photo. & Engr.

2008, Sept. 29 ***Perf. 11½***

2317 A1049 1 multi 1.50 .75

Sold for 54c on day of issue.

Miniature Sheet

Photography — A1050

No. 2318 — Photography by: a, Tim Dirven. b, Paul Ausloos. c, Léonard Missone. d, Harry Gruyaert. e, Stephan Vanfleteren.

2008, Sept. 29 **Photo.**

2318 A1050 Sheet of 5 7.50 7.50
a.-e. 80c Any single 1.50 .75

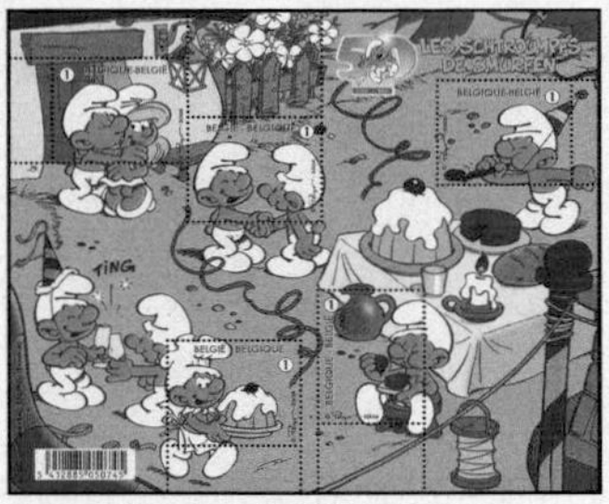

A1051

Smurfs — A1052

No. 2319: a, Smurf and Smurfette kissing. b, Smurfs shaking hands. c, Smurf blowing noisemaker. d, Smurf carrying dessert. e, Smurf eating cake, vert.

No. 2320, Smurf waving, orange background. No. 2321, Smurfette. No. 2322, Papa Smurf. No. 2323, Smurf with drum, horiz. No. 2324, Smurf writing letter. No. 2325, Smurf giggling. No. 2326, Smurf carrying mail bag and letter. No. 2327, Brainy Smurf (with glasses). No. 2328, Gargamel. No. 2329, Smurf with mail bag, letter and posthorn, horiz.

Perf. 11¾x11¼, 11¼(#2319e)

2008, Sept. 29

2319 A1051 Sheet of 5 9.00 9.00
a.-e. 1 Any single 1.75 .75

Booklet Stamps
Self-Adhesive
Die Cut Per. 10 on 2 or 3 Sides

2320 A1052 1 multi 1.50 .75
2321 A1052 1 multi 1.50 .75
2322 A1052 1 multi 1.50 .75
2323 A1052 1 multi 1.50 .75
2324 A1052 1 multi 1.50 .75
2325 A1052 1 multi 1.50 .75
2326 A1052 1 multi 1.50 .75
2327 A1052 1 multi 1.50 .75
2328 A1052 1 multi 1.50 .75
2329 A1052 1 multi 1.50 .75
a. Booklet pane of 10, #2320-2329 16.00 16.00
Nos. 2320-2329 (10) 15.00 7.50

On day of issue, Nos. 2319a-2319e and 2320-2329 each sold for 54c.

A1053

Mustelids A1054

No. 2330: a, Ermine, vert. (hermine, 38x42mm). b, Sable (martre, 48x38mm). c, Marten (fouine, 48x38mm). d, Polecat, vert. (putois, 38x42mm). e, Otter, vert. (38x48mm). f, Badger (blaireau, 48x38mm).

No. 2331, Marten (martre). No. 2332, Marten (fouine). No. 2333, Polecat. No. 2334, Otter. No. 2335, Badger.

Perf. 11½x11¼, 11½ (#2330e, 2330f)

2008, Sept. 29

2330 A1053 Sheet of 6 10.00 10.00
a.-f. 1 Any single 1.60 .75

Booklet Stamps
Self-Adhesive
Die Cut Perf. 10 on 2 or 3 Sides

2331 A1054 1 multi 1.50 .75
2332 A1054 1 multi 1.50 .75
2333 A1054 1 multi 1.50 .75
2334 A1054 1 multi 1.50 .75
2335 A1054 1 multi 1.50 .75
a. Booklet pane of 10, 2 each #2331-2335 15.00
Nos. 2331-2335 (5) 7.50 3.75

On day of issue, Nos. 2330a-2330f and 2331-2335 each sold for 54c.

Belgian Congo, Cent. A1055

Photo. & Engr.

2008, Oct. 20 ***Perf. 11½***

2336 A1055 1 Belgian Congo #37 1.60 .70

On day of issue, No. 2336 sold for 54c.

Museums A1056

Designs: 1, National Footwear Museum, Izegem. No. 2338, Musée en Piconrue, Bastogne. No. 2339, David and Alice van Buuren Museum, Brussels.

2008, Oct. 20 **Litho.**

2337 A1056 1 multi 1.25 .70
2338 A1056 80c multi 2.00 1.10
2339 A1056 80c multi 2.00 1.10
Nos. 2337-2339 (3) 5.25 2.90

On day of issue, No. 2337 sold for 54c.

Souvenir Sheet

End of World War I, 90th Anniv. — A1057

No. 2340: a, Soldiers at Menin Gate, Ypres. b, Statue of King Albert I, Nieuwpoort. c, Poppies.

Perf. 11½x11¼

2008, Oct. 20 **Photo.**

2340 A1057 Sheet of 3 7.00 7.00
a.-c. 90c Any single 2.25 1.10

Universal Declaration of Human Rights, 60th Anniv. — A1058

2008, Nov. 12 ***Perf. 11½***

2341 A1058 90c multi 2.25 1.10

Miniature Sheet

Belgian Music — A1059

No. 2342: a, Queen Elisabeth Competition. b, José Van Dam. c, Rock Werchter. d, Philippe Herreweghe and Collegium Vocale Gent. e, dEUS. f, Conductor Robert Groslot and orchestra. g, Philip Catherine. h, Vaya Con Dios. i, Salvatore Adamo and Will Tura. j, Jacques Brel.

2008, Nov. 12 ***Perf. 11¾x11¼***

2342 A1059 Sheet of 10 + label 21.00 21.00
a.-j. 80c Any single 2.10 1.10

A1060

Christmas
A1061 A1062

No. 2343 — Stained-glass window: a, Désiré Cardinal Mercier. b, St. Francis holding Cross. c, Mary, Joseph and Holy Spirit. d, Franciscan monk. e, Infant Jesus.

2008, Nov. 12 ***Perf. 11¼***

2343 A1060 Sheet of 5 8.00 8.00
a.-e. 1 Any single 1.50 .70

Booklet Stamps

Self-Adhesive

Die Cut Perf. 9¾ on 2 or 3 Sides

2344 A1061 1 multi 1.50 .70
a. Booklet pane of 10 16.00
2345 A1062 (80c) multi 3.00 1.10
a. Booklet pane of 10 30.00

On day of issue, Nos. 2343a-2343e and 2344 each sold for 54c.

Bird Type of 1985 With Euro Denominations Only

27c, Bécasse des bois. €4.60, Pygargue a queue blanche.

2009 **Photo.** ***Perf. 11½***

2346 A524 27c multicolored .75 .35

Size: 31x27mm

2347 A524 €4.60 multicolored 11.00 6.50

Issued: 27c, 4/6; €4.60, 1/2.

Tulipa Bakeri — A1063

Booklet Stamps

Die Cut Perf. 9¾ on 2 or 3 Sides

2009, Jan. 2 **Self-Adhesive**

2348 A1063 1 multi 2.50 1.10
a. Booklet pane of 10 25.00

On day of issue, No. 2348 sold for 80c.

Miniature Sheet

German-speaking Community in Belgium — A1064

No. 2349: a, Marker at border of Belgium, Germany and Netherlands, near Kelmis (30x40mm). b, Jug from Raeren (30x40mm). c, Bütgenbach Lake (30x40mm). d, Eupen Sanitorium (33x40mm). e, Marksman, horiz. (49x37mm).

2009, Jan. 19 ***Perf. 11½***

2349 A1064 Sheet of 5 12.50 12.50
a.-e. 1 Any single 2.10 2.10

On day of issue, Nos. 2349a-2349e each sold for 80c.

Introduction of the Euro, 10th Anniv. — A1065

Booklet Stamps

Die Cut Perf. 9¾ on 2 or 3 Sides

2009, Jan. 19 **Self-Adhesive**

2350 A1065 1 dk blue & blue 1.50 .70
a. Booklet pane of 10 15.00

No. 2350 sold for 54c on day of issue.

Louis Braille (1809-52), Educator of the Blind — A1066

Photo., Engr. & Embossed

2009, Feb. 23 ***Perf. 11½***

2351 A1066 1 multi 1.50 .75

Sold for 59c on day of issue.

River and Canal Barge A1067

2009, Feb. 23 **Photo.**

2352 A1067 2 multi 2.75 1.50

Sold for €1.18 on day of issue.

Postage Stamp Festival — A1068

2009, Mar. 9

2353 A1068 1 multi 1.60 .80

Sold for 59c on day of issue.

Famous Women — A1069

No. 2354: a, Marthe Boel (1877-1956), President of Intl. Council of Women. b, Lily Boeykens (1930-2005), Belgian representative to U.N. Commission on the Status of Women.

2009, Mar. 9 **Litho.**

2354 A1069 Horiz. pair 3.00 1.60
a.-b. 1 Either single 1.60 .80

On day of issue, Nos. 2354a-2354b each sold for 59c.

Souvenir Sheet

Preservation of Polar Regions and Glaciers — A1070

No. 2355: a, Penguins. b, Polar bear.

2009, Mar. 9 ***Perf. 11½***

2355 A1070 Sheet of 2 5.00 5.00
a.-b. 1 Either single 2.75 1.40

On day of issue, Nos. 2355a-2355b each sold for €1.05.

Souvenir Sheet

Europa — A1071

2009, Apr. 6

2356 A1071 1 multi 2.75 2.75

Intl. Year of Astronomy. Sold for 90c on day of issue.

Miniature Sheet

UNESCO World Heritage Sites — A1072

No. 2357: a, Neolithic Flint Mines, Spiennes. b, Notre-Dame Cathedral, Tournai. c, Plantin-Moretus Museum, Antwerp. d, Historic Center of Bruges. e, Town Houses of Architect Victor Horta, Brussels.

2009, Apr. 6 **Photo. & Engr.**

2357 A1072 Sheet of 5 13.00 13.00
a.-e. 1 Any single 2.75 1.40

On day of issue, Nos. 2357a-2357e each sold for €1.05.

A1073 A1074

A1075 A1076

Characters From Animated Movie "Suske en Wiske - De Texas Rakkers" — A1077

Die Cut Perf. 9¾ on 2 or 3 Sides

2009, Apr. 6 **Photo.**

Booklet Stamps

Self-Adhesive

2358 A1073 1 multi 1.40 .80
2359 A1074 1 multi 1.40 .80
2360 A1075 1 multi 1.40 .80
2361 A1076 1 multi 1.40 .80
2362 A1077 1 multi 1.40 .80
a. Booklet pane of 10, 2 each #2358-2362 14.00 14.00
Nos. 2358-2362 (5) 7.00 4.00

On day of issue, Nos. 2358-2362 each sold for 59c.

Miniature Sheet

Antverpia 2010 European Philatelic Championships, Antwerp — A1078

No. 2363: a, Antwerp Museum of Contemporary Art, Flemish Village, by Luc Tuymans. b, Orbino, sculpture by Luc Deleu, Middelheim Museum. c, Actors, Toneelhuis Theater. d, Poster for movie, "Hollywood on the Scheldt," Roma Cinema. e, Writings of Willem Elsschot, sculpture of Elsschot by Wilfried Pas.

2009, May 11 **Photo.** ***Perf. 11½***

2363 A1078 Sheet of 5 15.50 15.50
a.-e. 1 Any single 3.00 3.00

No. 2363 sold for €5.50. Nos. 2363a-2363e each had a franking value of 59c on day of issue.

Composers — A1079

Designs: No. 2364, Henry Purcell (1659-95). No. 2365, Georg Friedrich Handel (1685-1759). No. 2366, Joseph Haydn (1732-1809). No. 2367, Felix Mendelssohn-Bartholdy (1809-47). No. 2368, Clara Schumann (1819-96).

2009, May 11 ***Perf. 11¾x11½***

Booklet Stamps

2364	A1079	1 multi	2.50	1.25
2365	A1079	1 multi	2.50	1.25
2366	A1079	1 multi	2.50	1.25
2367	A1079	1 multi	2.50	1.25
2368	A1079	1 multi	2.50	1.25
a.		Booklet pane of 5, #2364-2368	12.50	—
		Complete booklet, #2368a	12.50	
		Nos. 2364-2368 (5)	12.50	6.25

On day of issue Nos. 2364-2368 each sold for 90c.

Vacations — A1080

Designs: No. 2369, Man with camera. No. 2370, Woman with camera.

Booklet Stamps

Die Cut Perf. 9¾ on 2 or 3 Sides

2009, May 11 **Self-Adhesive**

2369	A1080	1 multi	1.75	.45
2370	A1080	1 multi	1.75	.45
a.		Booklet pane of 10, 5 each #2369-2370	17.50	

On day of issue Nos. 2369-2370 each sold for 59c.

Aviation and Space Exploration Milestones A1081

No. 2371: a, First command of International Space Station by European, 2009. b, Apollo 11 moon landing, 1969. c, First flight of Concorde, 1969. d, Circumnavigational flight of Graf Zeppelin, 1929. e, Flight by Louis Blériot across English Channel, 1909.

Photo. (#2371a), Photo. & Engr.

2009, June 8 ***Perf. 11½***

2371		Vert. strip of 5	8.75	8.75
a.-e.	A1081	1 Any single	1.75	.85

Nos. 2371a-2371e each sold for 59c on day of issue. No. 2371 was printed in sheets containing two strips.

Energy Conservation A1082

Designs: No. 2372, Fluorescent light bulb. No. 2373, Windmill. No. 2374, Bus. No. 2375, Solar energy. No. 2376, Insulated house.

Booklet Stamps

Die Cut Perf. 9¾ on 2 or 3 Sides

2009, June 8 **Self-Adhesive**

2372	A1082	1 multi	1.75	.45
2373	A1082	1 multi	1.75	.45
2374	A1082	1 multi	1.75	.45
2375	A1082	1 multi	1.75	.45
2376	A1082	1 multi	1.75	.45
a.		Booklet pane of 10, 2 each #2372-2376	17.50	
		Nos. 2372-2376 (5)	8.75	2.25

On day of issue Nos. 2372-2376 each sold for 59c.

Yoko Tsuno, Comic Strip by Roger Leloup — A1083

2009, June 29 **Photo.** ***Perf. 11½***

2377	A1083	1 multi	1.75	.85

Sold for 59c on day of issue.

Souvenir Sheet

50th Wedding Anniv. of King Albert II and Queen Paola — A1084

2009, June 29 **Litho.**

2378	A1084	3 multi	5.00	2.50

Sold for €1.77 on day of issue.

Maurice Béjart (1927-2007), Choreographer A1085

2009, Aug. 31 **Litho.**

2379	A1085	1 multi	2.50	1.40

Sold for 90c on day of issue.

1950s Citroen Mail Van A1086

1960s Bedford Mail Van A1087

1970s Renault Mail Van A1088

1980s Renault Mail Van A1089

2009 Citroen Mail Van A1090

2009, Aug. 31 **Photo. & Engr.**

2380	A1086	1 multi	1.75	.85
2381	A1087	1 multi	1.75	.85
2382	A1088	1 multi	1.75	.85
2383	A1089	1 multi	1.75	.85
2384	A1090	1 multi	1.75	.85
a.		Vert. strip of 5, #2380-2384	8.75	4.25
		Nos. 2380-2384 (5)	8.75	4.25

On day of issue, Nos. 2380-2384 each sold for 59c.

Circus Performers — A1091

Designs: No. 2385, Musicians. No. 2386, Bicyclist on tightrope. No. 2387, Magician levitating woman. No. 2388, Human pyramid. No. 2389, Trapeze artists. No. 2390, Clown on ball and acrobat. No. 2391, Acrobats with ball. No. 2392, Magician with doves and rabbit. No. 2393, Acrobat on horseback. No. 2394, Juggler on unicycle.

Die Cut Perf. 10 on 2 or 3 Sides

2009, Aug. 31 **Photo.**

Booklet Stamps

Self-Adhesive

2385	A1091	1 multi	1.75	.45
2386	A1091	1 multi	1.75	.45
2387	A1091	1 multi	1.75	.45
2388	A1091	1 multi	1.75	.45
2389	A1091	1 multi	1.75	.45
2390	A1091	1 multi	1.75	.45
2391	A1091	1 multi	1.75	.45
2392	A1091	1 multi	1.75	.45
2393	A1091	1 multi	1.75	.45
2394	A1091	1 multi	1.75	.45
a.		Booklet pane of 10, #2385-2394	17.50	
		Nos. 2385-2394 (10)	17.50	4.50

On day of issue, Nos. 2385-2394 each sold for 59c.

The Triptych of the Seven Sacraments, Detail of Painting by Rogier van der Weyden — A1092

2009, Sept. 21 **Litho.** ***Perf. 11½***

2395	A1092	2 multi	3.50	1.75

Opening of Leuven Museum exhibition of works by Rogier van der Weyden. Sold for €1.18 on day of issue.

Miniature Sheet

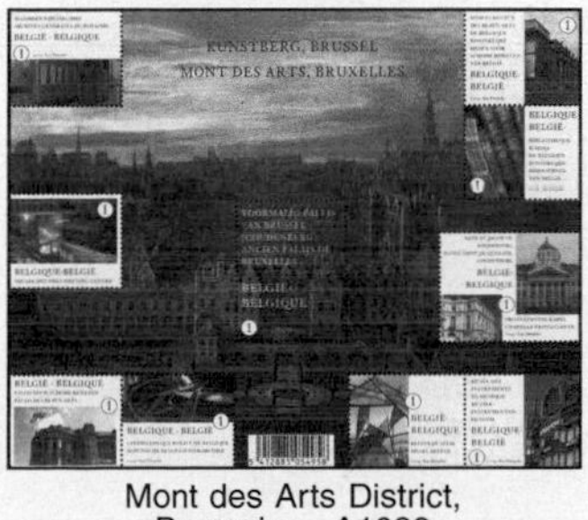

Mont des Arts District, Brussels — A1093

No. 2396: a, General State Archives (40x33mm). b, Royal Museum of Fine Arts of Belgium (40x33mm). c, Royal Library of Belgium (40x33mm). d, Brussels Meeting Center (40x33mm). e, Old Palace of Brussels (38x49mm). f, Saint Jacques-sur-Coudenberg Church, Protestant Chapel (49x38mm). g, Palace of Fine Arts (40x33mm). h, Royal Belgian Film Archive (40x33mm). i, Belvue Museum (40x33mm). j, Musical Instruments Museum (40x33mm).

Perf. 11½ on 2, 3 or 4 Sides

2009, Sept. 21 **Photo.**

2396	A1093	Sheet of 10	17.50	8.75
a.-j.		1 Any single	1.75	.85

Nos. 2396a-2396j each sold for 59c on day of issue.

Chinese Dragon — A1094

Booklet Stamps

Die Cut Perf. 10 on 2 or 3 Sides

2009, Oct. 5 **Self-Adhesive**

2397	A1094	1 multi	1.75	.85
a.		Booklet pane of 10	17.50	

Europalia China Cultural Festival. No. 2397 sold for 59c on day of issue.

Canonization of Father Damien (1840-89) — A1095

2009, Oct. 5 ***Perf. 11½***

2398	A1095	1 multi	2.75	1.40

Sold for 90c on day of issue.

Souvenir Sheet

Comic Strip Museum Festival — A1096

2009, Oct. 5 **Photo.**

2399	A1096	1 multi	3.25	1.60

Sold for €1.05 on day of issue. Imperforate examples were gifts to standing order customers.

Miniature Sheet

Toy Trains — A1097

No. 2400: a, Streamline Mettoy train (blue locomotive and cars). b, Märklin Bavarian locomotive "Aloisus" (locomotive with gold-trimmed window and smokestack). c, Märklin SNCB locomotive tender (locomotive facing left with red trim). d, Märklin Haine-St. Pierre SNCB Diesel locomotive (locomotive with green and yellow trim). e, Märklin Storchenbein locomotive tender replica (locomotive with front wheel in red). f, Märklin Type 16 SNCB locomotives (gray locomotives with yellow and red trim). g, French tin toy train and cars (red locomotive and cars). h, Märklin ICE Deutsches Bahn locomotives (white locomotives with red trim). i, Unpainted French wooden toy train and cars. j, Blue and red Belgian wooden locomotive with pull string.

2009, Oct. 5 ***Perf. 11¾x11¼***

2400 A1097 Sheet of 10 17.50 8.75
a.-j. 1 Any single 1.75 .85

Nos. 2400a-2400j each sold for 59c on day of issue.

Miniature Sheet

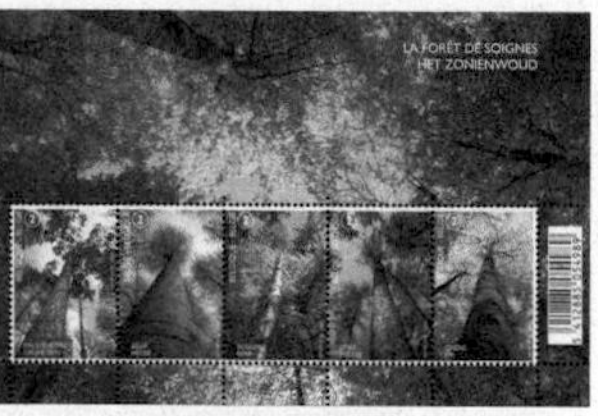

Trees — A1098

No. 2401: a, Scotch pine (pin sylvestre). b, Beech (hêtre). c, Birch (bouleau). d, Larch (mélèze). e, Oak (chêne).

2009, Oct. 5 **Litho.** ***Perf. 11½***

2401 A1098 Sheet of 5 17.50 8.75
a.-e. 2 Any single 3.50 1.75

Nos. 2401a-2401e each sold for €1.18 on day of issue.

Bird Type of 1985 With Euro Denominations Only

2009, Sept. 21 **Litho.** ***Perf. 11½***

2402 A524 1c Pic noir .25 .25
2403 A524 10c Chouette hulotte .30 .25

Miniature Sheet

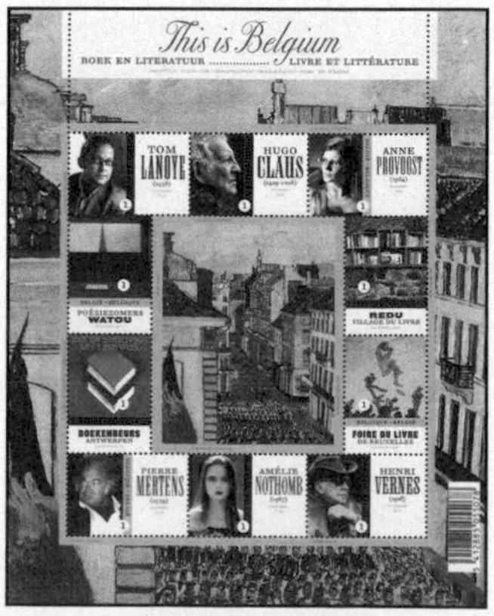

Literature — A1099

No. 2404: a, Tom Lanoye, writer. b, Hugo Claus (1929-2008), writer. c, Anne Provoost, writer. d, Poetry Summers, Watou, vert. e, Redu, town with 22 book stores, vert. f, Boekenbeurs Antwerpen, vert. g, Brussels Book Fair, vert. h, Pierre Mertens, writer. i, Amélie Nothomb, writer. j, Henri Vernes, writer.

2009, Nov. 3 **Photo.** ***Perf. 11½***

2404 A1099 Sheet of 10 17.00 17.00
a.-j. 1 Any single 1.60 .85

Nos. 2404a-2404j each sold for 59c on day of issue.

A1100

Christmas A1101

Yellow panel at: No. 2406, Left. No. 2407, Right.

Booklet Stamps

Die Cut Perf. 9¾ on 2, 3 or 4 Sides

2009, Nov. 3 **Self-Adhesive**

2405 A1100 1 multi 1.75 .45
a. Booklet pane of 10 17.50
2406 A1101 1 multi 2.75 1.40
2407 A1101 1 multi 2.75 1.40
a. Booklet pane of 10, 5 each #2406-2407 27.50
Nos. 2405-2407 (3) 7.25 3.25

On day of issue, No. 2405 sold for 59c and Nos. 2406-2407 each sold for 90c.

Mourning Stamp — A1102

Die Cut Perf. 10 on 2 or 3 Sides

2010, Jan. 4 **Photo.**

Booklet Stamp

Self-Adhesive

2408 A1102 1 multi 1.75 .85
a. Booklet pane of 10 17.50

No. 2408 sold for 59c on day of issue.

Bird Type of 1985 With Euro Denominations Only

5c, Grèbe castagneux. €4.09, Faisan de colchide. €4.60, Chouette effraie.

2010 **Photo.** ***Perf. 11½***

2409 A524 5c multicolored .25 .25

Size: 32x23mm

2410 A524 €4.09 multicolored 9.00 5.25

Size: 27x32mm

2411 A524 €4.60 multicolored 11.00 6.50
Nos. 2409-2411 (3) 20.25 12.00

Issued: 5c, 1/18; €4.09, 6/14; €4.60, 1/4.

Organ Donation A1103

Booklet Stamps

Die Cut Perf. 10 on 2 or 3 Sides

2010, Jan. 18 **Self-Adhesive**

2412 A1103 1 multi 1.75 .85
a. Booklet pane of 10 17.50

No. 2412 sold for 59c on day of issue.

Souvenir Sheet

Paul Otlet (1868-1944), Information Scientist — A1104

2010, Jan. 18 **Litho.** ***Perf. 11½***

2413 A1104 €4.60 multi 13.00 6.50

Miniature Sheet

Antverpia 2010 European Philatelic Championship, Antwerp — A1105

No. 2414: a, Magnifying glass, #2414e, 2414f, emblem of Royal National Association of Belgian Postage Stamp Circles. b, Shopping center, Antwerp. c, Antwerp Zoo. d, Museum aan de Stroom, Antwerp. e, House and self-portrait of Peter Paul Rubens, Antwerp. f, Antwerp City Hall and Cathedral.

2010, Jan. 18

2414 A1105 Sheet of 6 25.00 25.00
a.-f. 1 Any single 4.00 4.00

Royal National Association of Belgian Postage Stamp Circles, 120th anniv. Nos. 2414a-2414f each had a franking value of 59c on the day of issue. No. 2414 sold for €6.50, with the remaining €2.96 going to Antverpia 2010.

Largo Winch, Comic Strip by Philippe Francq A1106

2010, Feb. 22 ***Perf. 11½***

2415 A1106 1 multi 1.75 .80

Sold for 59c on day of issue.

Authors Who Lived in Brussels — A1107

Designs: No. 2416, Paul Verlaine, Arthur Rimbaud. No. 2417, Charles Baudelaire. No. 2418, Multatuli. No. 2419, Charlotte & Emily Bronte. No. 2420, Victor Hugo.

2010, Feb. 22 ***Perf. 11½***

Booklet Stamps

2416 A1107 2 multi 3.25 1.60
2417 A1107 2 multi 3.25 1.60
2418 A1107 2 multi 3.25 1.60
2419 A1107 2 multi 3.25 1.60
2420 A1107 2 multi 3.25 1.60
a. Booklet pane of 5, #2416-2420 17.00 17.00
Complete booklet, #2420a 16.50
Nos. 2416-2420 (5) 16.25 8.00

On day of issue, Nos. 2416-2420 each sold for €1.18.

Ghent Floralies — A1108

No. 2421: a, Nicotiana alata. b, Lychnis coronaria.

2010, Mar. 15 **Photo. & Engr.**

2421 A1108 Vert. pair 3.25 1.60
a.-b. 1 Either single 1.60 .80

On day of issue, Nos. 2421a-2421b each sold for 59c.

Souvenir Sheet

Europa — A1109

No. 2422: a, Boy on books, dog reading book. b, Girl on mushroom, cat reading book.

2010, Mar. 15 **Litho.**

2422 A1109 Sheet of 2 14.50 7.25
a.-b. 3 Either single 7.25 3.50

On day of issue, Nos. 2422a-2422b each sold for €2.70.

Baby Animals A1110

Die Cut Perf. 10 on 2 or 3 Sides

2010, Mar. 15 **Photo.**

Booklet Stamps

Self-Adhesive

2423 A1110 1 Two chicks 1.60 .80
2424 A1110 1 Two rabbits 1.60 .80
2425 A1110 1 Kitten 1.60 .80

2426	A1110	1	Two ducklings	1.60	.80
2427	A1110	1	Colt	1.60	.80
2428	A1110	1	Puppy sitting	1.60	.80
2429	A1110	1	Puppy lying	1.60	.80
2430	A1110	1	Two kittens	1.60	.80
2431	A1110	1	Head of colt	1.60	.80
2432	A1110	1	Two lambs	1.60	.80
a.			Booklet pane of 10, #2423-2432	17.00	17.00
			Nos. 2423-2432 (10)	16.00	8.00

On day of issue, Nos. 2423-2432 each sold for 59c.

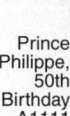

Prince Philippe, 50th Birthday A1111

2010, Apr. 15 Litho. *Perf. 11½*

2433	A1111 2 multi		3.25	1.60

Sold for €1.18 on day of issue.

A1112

No. 2434 — Category and artist: a, Oceans and Seas, by Igor Volt. b, Forests, by Lander Keyaerts. c, Endangered Species, by Eva Sterkens. d, Climate, by Lucie Octave. e, Energy, by Louise Van Goylen.

2010, Apr. 15

2434	Vert. strip of 5	8.00	4.00
a.-e.	A1112 1 Any single	1.60	.80

Winning Designs in "Save the Earth" Children's Stamp Design Contest.

Nos. 2434a-2434e each sold for 59c on day of issue.

Souvenir Sheet

Antverpia 2010 European Philatelic Championship, Antwerp — A1113

2010, Apr. 15

2435	A1113 3 multi	15.00	15.00

No. 2435 sold for €5. The stamp had a franking value of €1.77 on the day of issue, with the remaining €3.23 of the sale price going to Antverpia 2010.

Miniature Sheet

Bird Paintings by André Buzin — A1114

No. 2436: a, Buse variable. b, Faucon hobereau. c, Epervier d'Europe. d, Milan royal. e, Autour des palombes.

2010, Apr. 15

2436	A1114 Sheet of 5	13.50	13.50
a.-e.	1 Any single	2.50	1.50

Use of Buzin's bird paintings on Belgium's definitive stamps, 25th anniv. Nos. 2436a-2436e each sold for 90c on day of issue.

Miniature Sheet

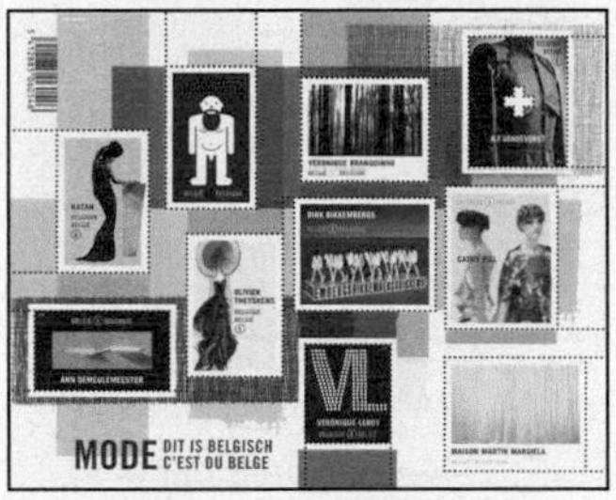

Fashion Houses — A1115

No. 2437: a, Natan (30x48mm). b, Walter Van Beirendonck (30x48mm). c, Veronique Branquinho, horiz. (43x35mm). d, A. F. Vandevorst (33x44mm). e, Olivier Theyskens (32x48mm). f, Dirk Bikkembergs, horiz. (48x38mm). g, Cathy Pill (38x48mm). h, Ann Demeulemeester, horiz. (44x27mm). i, Veronique Leroy (29x33mm). j, Maison Martin Margiela, horiz. (48x38mm).

2010, Apr. 15 Photo.

2437	A1115 Sheet of 10	17.00	17.00
a.-j.	1 Any single	1.60	.80

Nos. 2437a-2437j each sold for 59c on day of issue. No. 2437d has a perforated cross in the vignette.

Belgian Railways, 175th Anniv. A1116

Photo. & Engr.

2010, May 10 *Perf. 11½*

2438	A1116 2 multi	3.25	1.50

Sold for €1.18 on day of issue.

Parties — A1117

Designs: No. 2439, Man and woman with noisemakers. No. 2440, Hands holding gift and bouquet of roses. No. 2441, Man's hand holding Chinese lantern, woman wearing mask. No. 2442, Hands of servers holding trays with birthday cake and drinks. No. 2443, Girl sipping drink, boy holding balloon.

Die Cut Perf. 10 on 2 or 3 Sides

2010, May 10 Photo.

Booklet Stamps

Self-Adhesive

Background Color

2439	A1117	1	green	1.50	.75
2440	A1117	1	red	1.50	.75
2441	A1117	1	violet	1.50	.75
2442	A1117	1	blue	1.50	.75
2443	A1117	1	orange	1.50	.75
a.			Booklet pane of 10, 2 each #2439-2443	17.00	17.00
			Nos. 2439-2443 (5)	7.50	3.75

Nos. 2439-2443 each sold for 59c on day of issue.

2010 World Cup Soccer Championships, South Africa — A1118

2010 Youth Olympics, Singapore A1119

Eddy Merckx, Professional Cyclist — A1120

2010, June 14 Litho. *Perf. 11½*

2444	A1118 1 multi		2.75	1.10
2445	A1119 1 multi		2.75	1.40
2446	A1120 2 multi		3.00	1.50
		Nos. 2444-2446 (3)	8.50	4.00

On day of issue, No. 2444 sold for 90c, No. 2445 sold for €1.05, and No. 2446 sold for €1.18.

Independence of Belgian Congo, 50th Anniv. — A1121

2010, June 14

2447	A1121 1 multi	3.00	1.40

Sold for €1.05 on day of issue.

National Elections — A1122

2010, May 12 Photo. *Perf. 11½*

2448	A1122 1 multi	.80	.35

Sold for 28c on day of issue.

Belgian Presidency of the European Union Council A1123

2010, July 1 Litho. *Perf. 11½*

2449	A1123 1 multi	2.25	1.10

Sold for 90c on day of issue.

Miniature Sheet

High-rise Buildings — A1124

No. 2450: a, Le Tonneau, Brussels. b, Sint-Maartensdal, Louvain. c, Le Fer à Cheval, Brussels. d, Boerentoren, Antwerp. e, La Cité de Droixhe, Liège.

2010, Aug. 30

2450	A1124 Sheet of 5	12.00	6.25
a.-e.	1 Any single	2.40	1.25

Nos. 2450a-2450e each sold for 90c on day of issue. Imperforate sheets were gifts to standing order customers.

Fletsknooppunten A1125

Le Ravel — A1126

Die Cut Perf. 10 on 2 or 3 Sides

2010, Aug. 30 Photo.

Booklet Stamps

Self-Adhesive

2451	A1125 1 multi	1.60	.80
2452	A1126 1 multi	1.60	.80
a.	Booklet pane of 10, 5 each #2451-2452	17.00	17.00

Bicycle paths. Nos. 2451-2452 each sold for 59c on day of issue.

1953 Ford Mail Bus A1127

1931 Mail Train Car A1128

1979 Bedford Mail Truck A1129

1968 Mail Train Car A1130

2009 Volvo Mail Truck A1131

Photo. & Engr.

2010, Aug. 30 *Perf. 11½*

2453	A1127 1 multi		1.60	.80
2454	A1128 1 multi		1.60	.80
2455	A1129 1 multi		1.60	.80
2456	A1130 1 multi		1.60	.80
2457	A1131 1 multi		1.60	.80
a.	Vert. strip of 5, #2453-2457		8.00	4.00
		Nos. 2453-2457 (5)	8.00	4.00

On day of issue, Nos. 2453-2457 each sold for 59c.

De Mena Recreation Center, Rotselaar
A1132

Telematics Center, Marche-en-Famenne — A1133

Wiels Center for Contemporary Art, Brussels — A1134

2010, Sept. 20 **Litho.**

2458 A1132 1 multi	2.10	1.25
2459 A1133 1 multi	2.40	1.50
2460 A1134 2 multi	2.50	1.60
Nos. 2458-2460 (3)	7.00	4.35

Repurposed brewery buildings. On day of issue, No. 2458 sold for 90c; No. 2459, for €1.05; No. 2460, for €1.18.

Miniature Sheet

Hesbaye Region — A1135

No. 2461: a, Blossoming orchard, Sint-Truiden (30x40mm). b, Fruit blossoms (30x40mm). c, Fruit, wine and beer (30x40mm). d, Hélécine (33x40mm). e, Farm, Perwez (49x37mm).

Perf. 11¼x11½ (#a-c), 11½ (#d-e)

2010, Sept. 20 **Photo.**

2461 A1135 Sheet of 5 + 2 labels	11.00	11.00
a.-e. 1 Any single	2.50	1.25

On day of issue, Nos. 2461a-2461e each sold for 90c.

Bpost Emblem — A1136

2010, Oct. 18 **Photo.** ***Perf. 11½***

2462 A1136 1 multi	1.75	.85

Sold for 59c on day of issue.

Tools
A1137

Tools of: No. 2463, Cordonnier (shoemaker). No. 2464, Sabotier (clog maker). No. 2465, Maréchal-ferrant (farrier). No. 2466, Blanchisseuse (washerwoman). No. 2467, Fileuse (spinner).

2010, Oct. 18 **Litho.**

2463 A1137 1 multi	1.75	.85
2464 A1137 1 multi	1.75	.85
2465 A1137 1 multi	1.75	.85
2466 A1137 1 multi	1.75	.85
2467 A1137 1 multi	1.75	.85
a. Vert. strip of 5, #2463-2467	8.75	4.25
Nos. 2463-2467 (5)	8.75	4.25

Nos. 2463-2467 each sold for 59c on day of issue.

Pays de Connaisance
A1138

Voyage Dans la Lune
A1139

Un Cri — A1140

L'Etranger
A1141

La Mer ce Grand Sculpteur
A1142

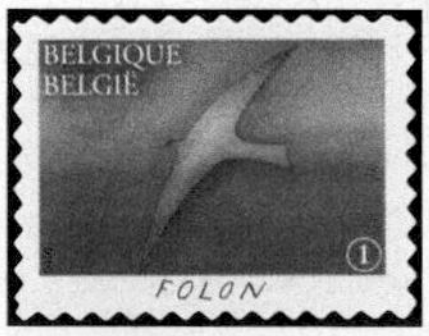

Oiseau
A1143

Waha Church Window — A1144

Pluie — A1145

Un Monde — A1146

L'Aube — A1147

Serpentine Die Cut 8

2010, Oct. 18 **Litho.**

Booklet Stamps
Self-Adhesive

2468 A1138 1 multi	1.75	.85
2469 A1139 1 multi	1.75	.85
2470 A1140 1 multi	1.75	.85
2471 A1141 1 multi	1.75	.85
2472 A1142 1 multi	1.75	.85
2473 A1143 1 multi	1.75	.85
2474 A1144 1 multi	1.75	.85
2475 A1145 1 multi	1.75	.85
2476 A1146 1 multi	1.75	.85
2477 A1147 1 multi	1.75	.85
a. Booklet pane of 10, #2468-2477	17.50	
Nos. 2468-2477 (10)	17.50	8.50

Art of Jean-Michel Folon (1934-2005). Nos. 2468-2477 each sold for 59c on day of issue.

Souvenir Sheet

Primitive Flemish Paintings — A1148

No. 2478: a, Madonna and Child, by Roger de la Pasture. b, Portrait of Laurent Froimont, by Rogier van der Weyden.

2010, Nov. 8 ***Perf. 11½***

2478 A1148 Sheet of 2	15.00	15.00
a.-b. 3 Either single	7.50	3.75

Nos. 2478a-2478b each sold for €2.70 on day of issue. See France No. 3924.

Christmas
A1149

Santa Claus, reindeer and sleigh facing: No. 2479, Left. No. 2480, Right.

Die Cut Perf. 9¾ on 2 or 3 Sides

2010, Nov. 8 **Photo.**

Booklet Stamps
Self-Adhesive

2479 A1149 1 multi	1.50	.75
a. Booklet pane of 10	15.00	15.00
2480 A1149 1 multi	2.10	1.10
a. Booklet pane of 10	21.00	21.00

On day of issue, No. 2479 sold for 59c and No. 2480 sold for 90c.

Bird Type of 1985 With Euro Denominations Only

2011, Jan. 3 **Litho.** ***Perf. 11½***

2481 A524 8c Canard pilet	.25	.25

Liberaliztion of Postal Market — A1150

2011, Jan. 3 **Litho.** ***Perf. 11½***

2482 A1150 1 multi	1.75	.85

Sold for 61c on day of issue.

Intl. Year of Chemistry
A1151

2011, Jan. 17

2483 A1151 1 multi	*10.00*	*4.00*

Sold for 61c on day of issue.

Signs of the Zodiac — A1152

Serpentine Die Cut 7½

2011, Jan. 17 **Self-Adhesive**

2484 A1152 1 multi	1.75	.85

Sold for 61c on day of issue. Printed in sheets of 10 + 12 stickers depicting the Zodiac signs, which could be placed on the stamp.

Homes of Authors
A1153

Designs: No. 2485, La Maison Blanche, home of Maurice Carême, Anderlecht. No. 2486, Domus Erasmi, home of Desiderius Erasmus, Anderlecht. No. 2487, Het Lijsternest, home of Stijn Streuvels, Ingooigem.

2011, Jan. 17

2485 A1153 1 multi	2.50	1.25
2486 A1153 1 multi	2.90	1.50
2487 A1153 2 multi	3.00	1.75
Nos. 2485-2487 (3)	8.40	4.50

On day of issue, No. 2485 sold for 93c; No. 2486, for €1.10; and No. 2487, for €1.22.

G. Dam, Painting by Luc Tuymans
A1154

2011, Feb. 14

2488 A1154 1 multi	1.75	.85

Sold for 61c on day of issue.

European Year of the Volunteer A1155

Die Cut Perf. 9¾ on 2 or 3 Sides

2011, Feb. 14 **Photo.**

Booklet Stamp
Self-Adhesive

2489 A1155 1 multi		1.75	.85
a. Booklet pane of 10		17.50	

No. 2489 sold for 61c on day of issue.

Belgian Art Masterpieces — A1156

Belgian Architecture A1157

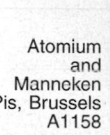

Atomium and Manneken Pis, Brussels A1158

Tank and Mardasson Memorial, Bastogne A1159

Lion's Mound, Waterloo A1160

Serpentine Die Cut 8

2011, Feb. 14 **Litho.**

Booklet Stamps
Self-Adhesive

2490 A1156 1 multi	3.00	1.50
2491 A1157 1 multi	3.00	1.50
2492 A1158 1 multi	3.00	1.50
2493 A1159 1 multi	3.00	1.50
2494 A1160 1 multi	3.00	1.50
a. Booklet pane of 5, #2490-2494	15.00	15.00
Nos. 2490-2494 (5)	15.00	7.50

On day of issue, Nos. 2490-2494 each sold for €1.10.

Bal du Rat Mort, Drawing by James Ensor — A1161

2011, Mar. 7 ***Perf. 11½***

2495 A1161 1 multi	1.75	.85

Cercle Coecilia, 150th anniv. Sold for 61c on day of issue.

Miniature Sheet

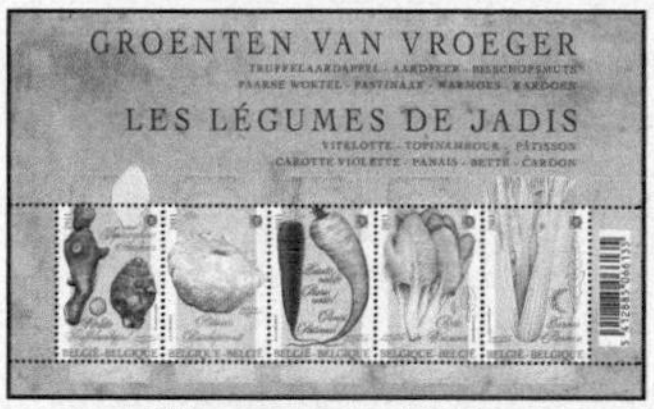

Vegetables — A1162

No. 2496: a, Vitellote (purple potato) and topinambour (Jerusalem artichoke). b, Pâtisson (patty pan squash). c, Carotte violette (purple carrot) and panais (parsnip). d, Bette (chard). e, Cardon (cardoon).

2011, Mar. 7 **Photo.**

2496 A1162 Sheet of 5	15.00	15.00
a.-e. 1 Any single	3.00	1.50

On day of issue, Nos. 2496a-2496e each sold for €1.10.

Miniature Sheet

Mining Heritage of the Campine Region — A1163

No. 2497: a, Miner's housing, Beringen (31x40mm). b, Coal (31x40mm). c, Shaft tower, railway car, As (31x40mm). d, Slagheap and countryside, Zolder (33x40mm). e, People on slagheap, Eisden (49x37mm).

2011, Apr. 4 **Photo.**

2497 A1163 Sheet of 5	12.00	12.00
a.-e. 1 Any single	2.40	1.40

On day of issue, Nos. 2497a-2497e each sold for 93c.

Fair Scenes — A1164

Designs: No. 2498, Flying swings. No. 2499, Fortune-teller. No. 2500, Man and woman on carousel horses. No. 2501, Roller coaster. No. 2502, Ferris wheel. No. 2503, Shooting gallery. No. 2504, Cotton candy vendor. No. 2505, Bumper cars. No. 2506, Boy and carousel. No. 2507, Haunted house.

Die Cut Perf. 9¾ on 2 or 3 Sides

2011, Apr. 4 **Photo.**

Booklet Stamps
Self-Adhesive

2498 A1164 1 multi	1.75	.90
2499 A1164 1 multi	1.75	.90
2500 A1164 1 multi	1.75	.90
2501 A1164 1 multi	1.75	.90
2502 A1164 1 multi	1.75	.90
2503 A1164 1 multi	1.75	.90
2504 A1164 1 multi	1.75	.90
2505 A1164 1 multi	1.75	.90
2506 A1164 1 multi	1.75	.90
2507 A1164 1 multi	1.75	.90
a. Booklet pane of 10, #2498-2507	17.50	17.50
Nos. 2498-2507 (10)	17.50	9.00

On day of issue Nos. 2498-2507 each sold for 61c.

A1165

A1166

A1167

A1168

Mailboxes A1169

Photo. & Engr.

2011, May 16 ***Perf. 11½***

2508 A1165 1 multi	1.60	.80
2509 A1166 1 multi	1.60	.80
2510 A1167 1 multi	1.60	.80
2511 A1168 1 multi	1.60	.80
2512 A1169 1 multi	1.60	.80
a. Horiz. strip of 5, #2508-2512	8.00	8.00
Nos. 2508-2512 (5)	8.00	4.00

On day of issue, Nos. 2518-2512 each sold for 61c.

A1170

A1171

A1172

A1173

Graffiti on De Wand Tram Station Walls, Laeken — A1174

2011, May 16 **Litho.**

2513 Sheet of 5	12.50	12.50
a. A1170 1 multi	2.50	1.25
b. A1171 1 multi	2.50	1.25
c. A1172 1 multi	2.50	1.25
d. A1173 1 multi	2.50	1.25
e. A1174 1 multi	2.50	1.25

On day of issue, Nos. 2513a-2513e each sold for 93c.

Miniature Sheet

Cartoon Art — A1175

No. 2514: a, Head with crown and emoticon face, by Marec (Marc de Cloedt) (27x38mm). b, Laughing baby being held by ankles, by Zak (Jacques Moeraert) (38x33mm). c, Map of Belgium with face and arms, by Kamagurka (Luc Zeebroek) (38x38mm). d, Large man with club and small man sticking out tongue, by Frédéric du Bus (38x38mm). e, Man with pencil for mouth flexing muscles by Clou (Christian Louis) (38x38mm). f, Pencil as gun, by Gal (Gerard Alsteens) (38x33mm). g, Small jester flipping large man off see-saw, by Pierre Kroll (38x38mm). h, Green creature drawing happy face on paper on soldier's back, by Nicolas Vadot (38x38mm). i, Man in superhero costume with dog on leash, by Zaza (Klaas

Storme) (38x38mm). j, Clown lifting barbell, by Cécile Bertrand (38x38mm).

2011, June 27 **Photo.**
2514 A1175 Sheet of 10 17.00 17.00
a.-j. 1 Any single 1.60 .80

On day of issue, Nos. 2514a-2514j each sold for 61c.

Miniature Sheet

Women's Sports — A1176

No. 2515: a, Field hockey. b, Soccer. c, Basketball. d, Volleyball. e, Handball.

2011, June 27 **Litho.**
2515 A1176 Sheet of 5 14.50 14.50
a.-e. 1 Any single 2.75 1.40

On day of issue, Nos. 2515a-2515e each sold for €1.10.

Posters by Henri de Toulouse-Lautrec (1864-1901) A1177

Designs: No. 2516, Confetti. No. 2517, Aristide Bruant Dans son Cabaret. No. 2518, May Milton. No. 2519, Divan Japonais. No. 2520, Reine de Joie. No. 2521, Le Salon des Cent (La Passagère du 54). No. 2522, Caudieux. No. 2523, Jane Avril. No. 2524, Eldorado-Aristide Bruant Dans son Cabaret. No. 2525, Moulin Rouge, La Goulue.

2011, June 27 ***Serpentine Die Cut 8***
Booklet Stamps
Self-Adhesive

2516 A1177 1 multi 1.75 .85
2517 A1177 1 multi 1.75 .85
2518 A1177 1 multi 1.75 .85
2519 A1177 1 multi 1.75 .85
2520 A1177 1 multi 1.75 .85
2521 A1177 1 multi 1.75 .85
2522 A1177 1 multi 1.75 .85
2523 A1177 1 multi 1.75 .85
2524 A1177 1 multi 1.75 .85
2525 A1177 1 multi 1.75 .85
a. Booklet pane of 10, #2516-2525 17.50 17.50
Nos. 2516-2525 (10) 17.50 8.50

On day of issue, Nos. 2516-2525 each sold for 61c.

Miniature Sheet

Courthouses — A1178

No. 2526 — Courthouse in: a, Arlon. b, Ghent. c, Mons. d, Antwerp. e, Charleroi.

2011, Aug. 29 **Litho.** ***Perf. 11½***
2526 A1178 Sheet of 5 17.00 17.00
a.-e. 2 Any single 3.50 1.75

On day of issue, Nos. 2526a-2526e each sold for €1.22.

Miniature Sheet

Tintin — A1179

No. 2527, Scenes from Tintin cartoons, animated and live-action films: a, Tintin and the Crab with the Golden Claws, 1947. b, Tintin and the Crab with the Golden Claws, 1941. c, Black Island (animated), 1961. d, Black Island, 1938. e, Tintin and the Golden Fleece (live-action), 1961. f, Tintin and the Blue Oranges, 1964. g, Tintin and the Sun Temple, 1969. h, Tintin and the Sun Temple, 1949. i, Tintin and the Blue Lotus, 1991. j, Tintin and the Blue Lotus, 1936.

2011, Aug. 29
2527 A1179 Sheet of 10 17.00 17.00
a.-j. 1 Any single 1.60 .85

On day of issue, Nos. 2527a-2527j each sold for 61c. Imperforate sheets were gifts to standing order customers.

Souvenir Sheet

Europa — A1180

No. 2528: a, Eurasian jay. b, Fawn.

2011, Sept. 19
2528 A1180 Sheet of 2 14.00 14.00
a.-b. 3 Either single 7.00 3.75

Intl. Year of Forests. On day of issue, Nos. 2528a-2528b each sold for €2.79.

Bpost Emblem — A1181

Bpost Emblem and Personalizable Image — A1181a

Photo #2529-2532; Litho #2531A
2011-15 ***Perf. 11¾x11½***
2529 A1181 1 multi 1.75 .85
2530 A1181 2 multi 3.50 1.75

Self-Adhesive
Die Cut Perf. 11¾x11½
2531 A1181 1 multi 1.75 .85

Booklet Stamp
Serpentine Die Cut 10
2531A A1181a 1 multi 1.90 1.90
b. Booklet pane of 10 19.00

Die Cut Perf. 11¾x11½
2532 A1181 2 multi 3.50 1.75

Issued: Nos. 2529, 2531, 9/19/11. Nos. 2530, 2532, 3/12/12. No. 2531A, 2015.

On day of issue, Nos. 2529 and 2531 each sold for 61c, and Nos. 2530 and 2532 each sold for €1.30.

No. 2531A has a space to the left of the Bpost emblem and country name where 48x29mm images can be placed. Images can be personalized. The image shown is one of many generic images produced by Belgium Post. Stamps in various printings of No. 2531Ab can have multiple images, different from that shown. Booklets of 10 sold for €8.20. The franking value of stamps was 72c on the day of issue.

Queen Paola and Child — A1182

2011, Oct. 17 **Litho.** ***Perf. 11½***
2533 A1182 1 multi 1.75 .85

No. 2533 sold for 61c on day of issue.

Miniature Sheet

Candies — A1183

No. 2534: a, Babeluttes (wrapped caramel pieces) (25x33mm). b, Cuberdons (chocolate-covered jellies) (26x47mm). c, Caramels (25x33mm). d, Guimauves (marshmallows) (26x50mm). e, Gommes (gummy bears) (26x50mm).

2011, Oct. 17 **Photo.**
2534 A1183 Sheet of 5 12.50 12.50
a.-e. 1 Any single 2.50 1.25

Nos. 2534a-2534e each sold for 93c on day of issue.

Souvenir Sheet

Europalia Intl. Arts Festival, Brazil — A1184

No. 2535 — Brazilian Indians wearing: a, Headdress of feathers. b, Earrings.

2011, Nov. 2 **Litho.**
2535 A1184 Sheet of 2 10.00 10.00
a.-b. 3 Either single 5.00 2.50

Nos. 2535a-2535b each sold for €1.83 on day of issue.

Snowman A1185

Angel — A1186

Die Cut Perf. 9¾ on 2 or 3 Sides
2011, Nov. 2 **Photo.**
Booklet Stamps
Self-Adhesive

2536 A1185 1 multi 1.75 .85
a. Booklet pane of 10 17.50
2537 A1186 1 multi 2.60 1.25
a. Booklet pane of 10 26.00

Christmas. On day of issue, Nos. 2536 and 2537 sold for 61c and 93c, respectively.

Detail From Mayan Calendar A1187

2012, Jan. 16 **Litho.** ***Perf. 11½***
2538 A1187 1 multi 2.75 1.40

No. 2538 sold for €1.19 on day of issue.

Miniature Sheet

Trappist Beer Brands — A1188

No. 2539 — Bottle, cap and goblet of: a, Achel. b, Chimay. c, Orval. d, Rochefort. e, Westmalle. f, Westvleteren.

Perf. 11½ on 3 or 4 Sides
2012, Jan. 16
2539 A1188 Sheet of 6 14.00 14.00
a.-f. 1 Any single 2.25 1.10

Nos. 2539a-2539f each sold for 99c on day of issue.

Mythical Creatures A1189

Designs: No. 2540, Mermaid (sirène). No. 2541, Werewolf (loup-garou). No. 2542, Unicorn (licorne). No. 2543, Dragon. No. 2544, Winged serpent (amphiptère). No. 2545, Pegasus. No. 2546, Griffin (griffon). No. 2547, Centaur. No. 2548, Sphinx. No. 2549, Harpy (harpie).

Die Cut Perf. 9¾ on 2 or 3 Sides
2012, Jan. 16 **Photo.**
Booklet Stamps
Self-Adhesive

2540 A1189 1 multi 1.75 .85
2541 A1189 1 multi 1.75 .85
2542 A1189 1 multi 1.75 .85
2543 A1189 1 multi 1.75 .85
2544 A1189 1 multi 1.75 .85
2545 A1189 1 multi 1.75 .85
2546 A1189 1 multi 1.75 .85

2547 A1189 1 multi 1.75 .85
2548 A1189 1 multi 1.75 .85
2549 A1189 1 multi 1.75 .85
a. Booklet pane of 10, #2540-2549 17.50
Nos. 2540-2549 (10) 17.50 8.50

Nos. 2540-2549 each sold for 65c on day of issue. See Nos. 2608-2617.

Souvenir Sheet

Europa — A1190

No. 2550 — Various Belgian tourist attractions with country name at: a, LL. b, UR.

2012, Feb. 13 Litho. *Perf. 11½*
2550 A1190 Sheet of 2 15.00 15.00
a.-b. 3 Either single 7.50 3.75

Nos. 2550a-2550b each sold for €2.97 on day of issue.

Calligraphy — A1191

Designs: No. 2551, Latin calligraphy. No. 2552, Arabic calligraphy. No. 2553, Chinese calligraphy. No. 2554, Hindi calligraphy. No. 2555, Greek calligraphy.

Perf. 11¼x11¾
2012, Feb. 13 Photo.
Booklet Stamps
2551 A1191 1 multi 3.25 1.60
2552 A1191 1 multi 3.25 1.60
2553 A1191 1 multi 3.25 1.60
2554 A1191 1 multi 3.25 1.60
2555 A1191 1 multi 3.25 1.60
a. Booklet pane of 5, #2551-2555 16.50 16.50
Complete booklet, #2555a 16.50
Nos. 2551-2555 (5) 16.25 8.00

Nos. 2551-2555 each sold for €1.19 on day of issue.

Souvenir Sheet

Cartographers — A1192

No. 2556: a, Gerardus Mercator (1512-94). b, Jodocus Hondius (1563-1612).

Photo. & Engr.
2012, Mar. 12 *Perf. 11½*
2556 A1192 Sheet of 2 19.00 19.00
a.-b. 3 Either single 9.50 4.75

Nos. 2556a-2556b each sold for €3.57 on day of issue.

Cirque du Soleil Performers A1193

Décrocher La Lune A1194

A New Day — A1195

La Rêve A1196

The House of Dancing Water A1197

Serpentine Die Cut 8
2012, Mar. 12 Litho.
Booklet Stamps Self-Adhesive
2557 A1193 1 multi 2.60 1.25
2558 A1194 1 multi 2.60 1.25
2559 A1195 1 multi 2.60 1.25
2560 A1196 1 multi 2.60 1.25
2561 A1197 1 multi 2.60 1.25
a. Booklet pane of 5, #2557-2561 14.00 14.00
Nos. 2557-2561 (5) 13.00 6.25

Scenes from theater productions of director Franco Dragone. Nos. 2557-2561 each sold for 99c on day of issue.

Souvenir Sheet

Sinking of the Titanic, Cent. — A1198

No. 2562 — Stereoptic images of the sinking of the Titanic with top line of smoke from smokestack touching white square around "3": a, At LL corner of square. b, Directly below "3."

2012, Apr. 16 *Perf. 11½*
2562 A1198 Sheet of 2 19.00 19.00
a.-b. 3 Either single 9.50 4.75

Nos. 2562a-2562b each sold for €3.57 on day of issue. See Finland (Aland Islands) No. 328.

Pets — A1199

Designs: No. 2563, Canaries. No. 2564, Guinea pig. No. 2565, Cat. No. 2566, Goldfish. No. 2567, Parakeets. No. 2568, Shetland pony. No. 2569, Chihuahua. No. 2570, Hamsters. No. 2571, Rabbits. No. 2572, Dog with tongue visible.

Die Cut Perf. 9¾ on 2 or 3 Sides
2012, Apr. 16 Photo.
Booklet Stamps Self-Adhesive
2563 A1199 1 multi 1.75 .85
2564 A1199 1 multi 1.75 .85
2565 A1199 1 multi 1.75 .85
2566 A1199 1 multi 1.75 .85
2567 A1199 1 multi 1.75 .85
2568 A1199 1 multi 1.75 .85
2569 A1199 1 multi 1.75 .85
2570 A1199 1 multi 1.75 .85
2571 A1199 1 multi 1.75 .85
2572 A1199 1 multi 1.75 .85
a. Booklet pane of 10, #2563-2572 17.50
Nos. 2563-2572 (10) 17.50 8.50

Nos. 2563-2572 each sold for 65c on day of issue.

Floristan Sunflower, by Jef Geys — A1200

2012, May 21 Litho. *Perf. 11½*
2573 A1200 1 multi 1.75 .85

Exhibition of art by Jef Geys, Royal Museum of Fine Arts, Brussels. No. 2573 sold for 65c on day of issue.

2012 Summer Olympics, London A1201

2012, May 21
2574 A1201 1 multi 3.00 1.50

No. 2574 sold for €1.19 on day of issue.

Independence of Rwanda and Burundi, 50th Anniv. — A1202

Designs: No. 2575, Rwandan basket with lid. No. 2576, Burundian drum.

2012, May 21
2575 A1202 1 yel & multi 3.00 1.50
2576 A1202 1 red & multi 3.00 1.50

Nos. 2575-2576 each sold for €1.19 on day of issue.

Cabaret on the Banks of the River, by Jan Breughel — A1203

2012, June 25
2577 A1203 1 multi 1.75 .80

Exhibition of philatelic collection of Prince Albert II of Monaco, Bruges. No. 2577 sold for 65c on day of issue. See Monaco No. 2681.

Pieris Brassicae A1204

Papilion Machaon A1205

Die Cut Perf. 10 on 2 or 3 Sides
2012, June 25 Photo.
Booklet Stamps Self-Adhesive
2578 A1204 1 multi 1.75 .40
a. Booklet pane of 10 17.50 17.50

Die Cut Perf. 10 on 3 Sides
2579 A1205 1 multi 2.75 .65
a. Booklet pane of 5 13.50 13.50

On day of issue No. 2578 sold for 65c and No. 2579 sold for 99c.

Volcan Ensorcelé A1206

A Propos de Binche A1207

Sans Espoir de Bâtiment Pour Anvers ni Même Pour l'Escault A1208

Parfois, C'est l'Inverse A1209

A la Ligne A1210

Aquarelle Estampillée A1211

Labyrinthe d'Apparat A1212

Encreur A1213

Nuages en Pantalon A1214

Le Dernier Jour A1215

2012, June 25 *Sawtooth Die Cut 8¼*
Booklet Stamps Self-Adhesive
2580 A1206 1 multi 1.75 .85
2581 A1207 1 multi 1.75 .85
2582 A1208 1 multi 1.75 .85

2583	A1209	1	multi	1.75	.85
2584	A1210	1	multi	1.75	.85
2585	A1211	1	multi	1.75	.85
2586	A1212	1	multi	1.75	.85
2587	A1213	1	multi	1.75	.85
2588	A1214	1	multi	1.75	.85
2589	A1215	1	multi	1.75	.85
a.	Booklet pane of 10, #2580-2589			17.50	17.50
	Nos. 2580-2589 (10)			17.50	8.50

Paintings by Pierre Alechinsky. Nos. 2580-2589 each sold for 65c on day of issue.

Zenobe Gramme, by William Vance A1216

2012, Sept. 17 Litho. *Perf. 11½*

2590	A1216	1	multi	1.75	.85

No. 2590 sold for 65c on day of issue.

Miniature Sheet

Comic Strip Characters — A1217

No. 2591: a, Gil and Jo (boy and parrot, yellow green background), by Jef Nys (36x24mm). b, Gaston Lagaffe (light blue background), by André Franquin (27x40mm). c, Bob and Bobette (country name in red), by Willy Vandersteen (38x24mm). d, Jerry Spring (cowboy holding hat), by Jijé (40x27mm). e, Cori le Moussaillon (boy climbing rope ladder on ship's mast), by Bob de Moor (27x40mm). f, Tintin (with dog Snowy), by Hergé (32x36mm). g, Blake and Mortimer (two men, yellow green background), by Edgar P. Jacobs (40x27mm). h, Néro (man walking), by Marc Sleen (27x40mm). i, Lucky Luke (cowboy wearing hat), by Morris (27x40mm). j, The Smurfs, by Peyo (40x27mm).

Perf. 11½, 11¾ (#2591f)

2012, Sept. 17 Photo.

2591	A1217	Sheet of 10	19.00	19.00
a.-j.	1 Any single		1.75	.85

Nos. 2591a-2591j each sold for 65c on day of issue. Imperforate examples of No. 2591 were gifts to standing order customers.

Tree Leaves — A1218

Designs: No. 2592, Acer macrophyllum. No. 2593, Acer palmatum. No. 2594, Morus nigra. No. 2595, Sorbus alnifolia. No. 2596, Ginkgo biloba. No. 2597, Betula pendula. No. 2598, Fagus sylvatica. No. 2599, Aesculus hippocastanum. No. 2600, Euonymus europaeus. No. 2601, Quercus pondaim.

Die Cut Perf. 9¾ on 2 or 3 Sides

2012, Sept. 17 Self-Adhesive

Booklet Stamps

2592	A1218	1	multi	1.75	.85
2593	A1218	1	multi	1.75	.85
2594	A1218	1	multi	1.75	.85
2595	A1218	1	multi	1.75	.85
2596	A1218	1	multi	1.75	.85
2597	A1218	1	multi	1.75	.85
2598	A1218	1	multi	1.75	.85
2599	A1218	1	multi	1.75	.85
2600	A1218	1	multi	1.75	.85
2601	A1218	1	multi	1.75	.85
a.	Booklet pane of 10, #2592-2601			17.50	17.50
	Nos. 2592-2601 (10)			17.50	8.50

Nos. 2592-2601 each sold for 65c on day of issue.

An Offering to Ceres, by Jacob Jordaens — A1219

2012, Oct. 8 Litho. *Perf. 11½*

2602	A1219	1	multi	1.75	.85

No. 2602 sold for 65c on day of issue.

St. Martin Festival — A1220

2012, Oct. 8

2603	A1220	1	multi	1.75	.85

No. 2603 sold for 65c on day of issue.

Miniature Sheet

Condroz Region — A1221

No. 2604: a, Hay rolls in field (30x40mm). b, Fontaine Castle (30x40mm). c, Glasses of regional beers (30x40mm). d, Belgian blue-white cattle grazing (33x40mm). e, Dinant (49x37mm).

Perf. 11¼x11½, 11½ (#2604d, 2604e)

2012, Oct. 8 Photo.

2604	A1221	Sheet of 5 +2 labels	11.00	11.00
a.-e.	1 Any single		1.75	.90

Nos. 2604a-2604e each sold for 99c on day of issue.

Apatura Ilia — A1222

Serpentine Die Cut 13¼x14

2012, Oct. 29 Self-Adhesive

Coil Stamp

2605	A1222	1	multi	1.75	.85

No. 2605 sold for 65c on day of sale.

Christmas

A1223 A1224

Die Cut Perf. 9¾ on 2 or 3 Sides

2012, Oct. 29 Self-Adhesive

Booklet Stamps

2606	A1223	1	multi	1.75	.85
a.	Booklet pane of 10			17.50	
2607	A1224	1	multi	2.60	1.25
a.	Booklet pane of 10			26.00	

On day of issue, No. 2606 sold for 65c; No. 2607, for 99c.

Mythical Creatures Type of 2012

Designs: No. 2608, Devil (diable). No. 2609, Troll. No. 2610, Ghost (fantôme). No. 2611, Magician (magicien). No. 2612, Witch (sorcière). No. 2613, Dwarf (nain). No. 2614, Fairy (fée). No. 2615, Giant (géant). No. 2616, Prince. No. 2617, Elf.

2013, Jan. 21 Self-Adhesive

Booklet Stamps

2608	A1189	1	multi	1.75	.90
2609	A1189	1	multi	1.75	.90
2610	A1189	1	multi	1.75	.90
2611	A1189	1	multi	1.75	.90
2612	A1189	1	multi	1.75	.90
2613	A1189	1	multi	1.75	.90
2614	A1189	1	multi	1.75	.90
2615	A1189	1	multi	1.75	.90
2616	A1189	1	multi	1.75	.90
2617	A1189	1	multi	1.75	.90
a.	Booklet pane of 10, #2608-2617			19.00	19.00
	Nos. 2608-2617 (10)			17.50	9.00

Nos. 2608-2617 each sold for 67c on day of issue.

Black Grouse A1225

2013, Jan. 21 Litho. *Perf. 11¾x11½*

2618	A1225	(40c)	multi	1.00	.50

Princess Mathilde, 40th Birthday — A1226

2013, Jan. 21 *Perf. 11½*

2619	A1226	1	multi	1.90	.95

No. 2619 sold for 67c on day of issue.

Kid Paddle, Animated Cartoon by Midam A1227

2013, Jan. 21

2620	A1227	1	multi	1.75	.85

No. 2620 sold for 67c on day of issue.

Miniature Sheet

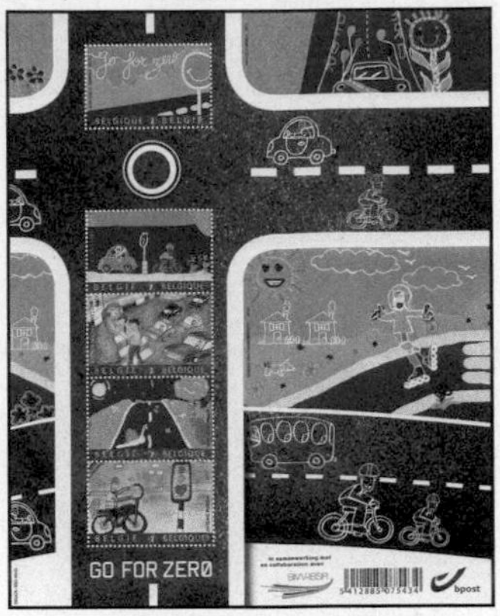

Road Safety — A1228

No. 2621 — Winning designs in stamp design contest: a, Road and sign with smile, by Jean-Louis Rondia. b, Automobile, traffic light, cyclist, flowers, by Ellen Labey. c, Child and woman in crosswalk, by Kiattisak Nulong. d, Snail on road at night, by Jean-Louis Verbaert. e, Cyclist and traffic light, by Antoine Buscemi.

Litho. & Silk-screened

2013, Feb. 11 *Perf. 13¼x13½*

2621	A1228	Sheet of 5	17.50	8.75
a.-e.	2 Any single		3.50	1.75

Nos. 2621a-2621e each sold for €1.34 on day of issue.

Souvenir Sheet

Europa — A1229

No. 2622 — Postal van facing: a, Right. b, Left.

2013, Feb. 11 Litho. *Perf. 11½*

2622	A1229	Sheet of 2	16.00	8.00
a.-b.	3 Either single		8.00	4.00

Nos. 2622a-2622b each sold for €3.09 on day of issue.

Tour des Flandres Bicycle Race, Cent. — A1230

2013, Mar. 25

2623	A1230	1	multi	1.75	.85

No. 2623 sold for 67c on day of issue.

Miniature Sheet

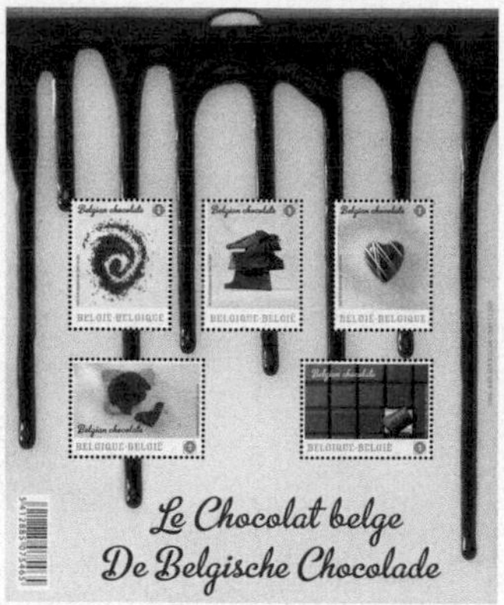

Chocolates — A1231

No. 2624: a, Spiral in chocolate granules. b, Stack of chocolate pieces. c, Heart-shaped candy. d, Cookie with chocolate frosting, horiz. e, Squares of chocolate and piece of candy, horiz.

2013, Mar. 25 ***Perf. 12***

2624	A1231	Sheet of 5	16.50	8.00
a.-e.		1 Any single	3.25	1.60

Nos. 2624a-2624e each sold for €1.24 on day of issue. No. 2624 is impregnated with a chocolate scent.

Bpost Emblem — A1232

Perf. 11¾x11½

2013, Mar. 25 **Photo.**

Self-Adhesive

2625	A1232	1 multi + label	3.50	1.40

No. 2625 sold for €1.03. The label shown is generic, and labels could be personalized for an additional charge. Compare with Type A1181.

Vanessa Atalanta — A1233

Aglais Urticae — A1234

Die Cut Perf. 10 on 3 Sides

2013, Mar. 25 **Self-Adhesive**

Booklet Stamps

2626	A1233	1 multi	3.25	1.60
a.		Booklet pane of 5	16.50	16.50
2627	A1234	2 multi	3.50	1.75
a.		Booklet pane of 5	17.50	17.50

On day of issue No. 2626 sold for €1.24, and No. 2627 sold for €1.34.

Souvenir Sheet

First Airmail Flight in Deperdussin Monoplane, Cent. — A1235

No. 2628 — Monoplane: a, On ground at Saint-Denis-Westrem. b, In air at Berchem-Sainte-Agathe.

Photo. & Engr.

2013, Apr. 15 ***Perf. 11½***

2628	A1235	Sheet of 2	16.50	8.25
a.-b.		3 Either single	8.25	4.00

On day of issue, Nos. 2628a-2628b each sold for €3.09.

The Valley of the Sambre A1236

The Promenade A1237

Summer Afternoon (Tea in the Garden) A1238

Arab Fantasy A1239

Portrait of Marguerite Van Mons A1240

Marie Sèthe at the Harmonium A1241

Bathing Woman A1242

Sisters of the Painter Schlobach A1243

A Reading by Emile Verhaeren A1244

The Artist's Wife and Daughter A1245

Sawtooth Die Cut 8¼

2013, Apr. 15 **Litho.**

Booklet Stamps

Self-Adhesive

2629	A1236	1 multi	1.75	.85
2630	A1237	1 multi	1.75	.85
2631	A1238	1 multi	1.75	.85
2632	A1239	1 multi	1.75	.85
2633	A1240	1 multi	1.75	.85
2634	A1241	1 multi	1.75	.85
2635	A1242	1 multi	1.75	.85
2636	A1243	1 multi	1.75	.85
2637	A1244	1 multi	1.75	.85
2638	A1245	1 multi	1.75	.85
a.		Booklet pane of 10, #2629-2638	17.50	17.50
		Nos. 2629-2638 (10)	17.50	8.50

Paintings by Théo van Rysselberghe (1862-1926). On day of issue, Nos. 2629-2638 each sold for 67c.

Opera Houses and Scenes from Operas by Richard Wagner (1813-83) and Giuseppe Verdi (1813-1901) A1246

Designs: No. 2639, Ghent Opera House, scene from *Das Rheingold,* by Wagner. No. 2640, Antwerp Opera House, scene from *Don Carlos,* by Verdi. No. 2641, Brussels Opera House (at UR), scene from *Macbeth,* by Verdi. No. 2642, Brussels Opera House (at UL), scene from *Parsifal,* by Wagner. No. 2643, Liège Opera House, scene from *Otello,* by Verdi

Photo. & Engr.

2013, May 13 ***Perf. 11½***

Booklet Stamps

2639	A1246	1 multi	2.75	1.40
2640	A1246	1 multi	2.75	1.40
2641	A1246	1 multi	2.75	1.40
2642	A1246	1 multi	2.75	1.40
2643	A1246	1 multi	2.75	1.40
a.		Booklet pane of 5, #2639-2643	14.00	—
		Complete booklet, #2643a	14.00	
		Nos. 2639-2643 (5)	13.75	7.00

On day of issue, Nos. 2639-2643 each sold for €1.03.

Animals in Antwerp Zoo — A1247

Designs: No. 2644, Eyes of owl. No. 2645, Trunk of elephant. No. 2646, Nose and mouth of lion. No. 2647, Heads of two penguins. No. 2648, Head of seal. No. 2649, Head of zebra. No. 2650, Eye of tiger. No. 2651, Eyes of lion tamarin. No. 2652, Head and hindquarters of okapi. No. 2653, Necks of giraffes.

Die Cut Perf. 10 on 2 or 3 Sides

2013, May 13 **Photo.**

Booklet Stamps

Self-Adhesive

2644	A1247	1 multi	1.90	.95
2645	A1247	1 multi	1.90	.95
2646	A1247	1 multi	1.90	.95
2647	A1247	1 multi	1.90	.95
2648	A1247	1 multi	1.90	.95
2649	A1247	1 multi	1.90	.95
2650	A1247	1 multi	1.90	.95
2651	A1247	1 multi	1.90	.95
2652	A1247	1 multi	1.90	.95
2653	A1247	1 multi	1.90	.95
a.		Booklet pane of 10, #2644-2653	19.00	
		Nos. 2644-2653 (10)	19.00	9.50

On day of issue, Nos. 2644-2653 each sold for 67c.

Music Festivals A1248

2013, June 24 **Litho.** ***Perf. 11½***

2654	A1248	1 multi	1.75	.85

No. 2654 sold for 67c on day of issue.

Miniature Sheet

Royal Meteorological Institue, Cent. — A1249

No. 2655: a, Royal Meteorological Institute Building (60x30mm). b, Cloud over Sun, tree in spring (40x30mm). c, Sun over tree in summer (40x30mm). d, Rain cloud over tree in autumn (40x30mm). e, Snow cloud over tree in winter (40x30mm).

Perf. 13¼ (#2655a), 13x13¼

2013, June 24

2655	A1249	Sheet of 5	14.00	7.00
a.-e.		1 Any single	2.75	1.40

On day of issue, Nos. 2655a-2655e each sold for €1.03. The leaves on the trees on Nos. 2655b-2655e are printed in thermochromic ink and change colors when the stamp is warmed.

Souvenir Sheet

Twenty Year Reign of King Albert II — A1250

No. 2656 — King Albert II wearing: a, Uniform and sash. b, Overcoat and scarf.

2013, June 24 ***Perf. 11½***

2656	A1250	Sheet of 2	16.50	16.50
a.-b.		3 Either single	8.25	4.00

On day of issue, Nos. 2656a-2656b each sold for €3.09.

Souvenir Sheet

Belgian Kings — A1251

No. 2657: a, King Philippe (crown at UL). b, King Albert II (crown at UR).

2013, Sept. 2 **Litho.** ***Perf. 11½***

2657	A1251	Sheet of 2	16.50	8.50
a.-b.		3 Either single	8.25	4.25

Abdication of King Albert II and ascension to throne of King Philippe. Nos. 2657a-2657b each sold for €3.09 on day of issue.

Lily — A1252

Die Cut Perf. 9¾ on 2 or 3 Sides

2013, Sept. 13 **Photo.**

Booklet Stamp

Self-Adhesive

2658	A1252	1 multi	1.90	.95
a.		Booklet pane of 10	19.00	

No. 2658 sold for 67c on day of issue.

Good Luck Symbols — A1253

Designs: No. 2659, Hand with crossed fingers. No. 2660, Numeral "7." No. 2661, Horseshoe. No. 2662, Four-leaf clover. No. 2663, Ladybug.

Die Cut Perf. 9¾ on 2 or 3 Sides

2013, Sept. 13 Litho.

Booklet Stamps
Self-Adhesive

2659	A1253	1 multi	1.75	.90
2660	A1253	1 multi	1.75	.90
2661	A1253	1 multi	1.75	.90
2662	A1253	1 multi	1.75	.90
2663	A1253	1 multi	1.75	.90
a.		Booklet pane of 10, 2 each #2659-2663	17.50	17.50
		Nos. 2659-2663 (5)	8.75	4.50

Nos. 2659-2663 each sold for 67c on day of issue.

Souvenir Sheet

Household Items Created by Henry Van de Velde (1863-1957), Interior Designer — A1254

No. 2664: a, Candelabra. b, Chair.

2013, Sept. 13 Litho. *Perf. 13½x14*

2664	A1254	Sheet of 2	16.50	16.50
a.-b.		3 Either single	8.25	4.25

Nos. 2664a-2664b each sold for €3.09 on day of issue.

International Red Cross, 150th Anniv. — A1255

2013, Oct. 28 Litho. *Perf. 11½*

2665	A1255	1 multi	3.50	1.75

No. 2665 sold for €1.24 on day of issue. See Spain No. 3939.

Photograph From Red Star Line Museum, Antwerp A1256

Photograph From War Museum, Bastogne A1257

Photographs From Dossin Barracks Museum of Deportation and Resistance, Mechlin — A1258

2013, Oct. 28 Litho. *Perf. 11½*

2666	A1256	1 multi	1.75	.90
2667	A1257	1 multi	1.75	.90
2668	A1258	1 multi	1.75	.90
		Nos. 2666-2668 (3)	5.25	2.70

Nos. 2666-2668 each sold for 67c on day of issue.

Christmas
A1259 A1260

Die Cut Perf. 9¾ on 2 or 3 Sides

2013, Oct. 28 Photo.

Booklet Stamps
Self-Adhesive

2669	A1259	1 multi	1.75	.90
a.		Booklet pane of 10	17.50	17.50
2670	A1260	1 multi	2.75	1.40
a.		Booklet pane of 10	27.50	27.50

On day of issue No. 2669 sold for 67c and No. 2670 sold for €1.03.

A1261

A1262

King Philippe A1263

Perf. 11¾x11½

2013, Oct. 28 Photo.

2671	A1261	1 multi	1.75	.25
2672	A1262	1 Europe multi	2.75	.75
2673	A1263	1 World multi	3.25	.95
		Nos. 2671-2673 (3)	8.85	2.25

On day of issue, Nos. 2671-2673 sold for 77c, €1.13, and €1.34, respectively, but each stamp sold for 10c less if purchased in quantities of 10.

Compare types A1262-A1263 with types A1361-A1362.

French Bulldog A1264

Bichon Maltese Mix A1265

Belgian Malinois A1266

Golden Retriever A1267

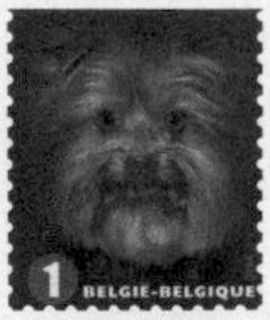

Yorkshire Terrier A1268

Border Collie A1269

Poodle A1270

Cocker Spaniel A1271

Chihuahua A1272

Jack Russell Terrier A1273

Die Cut Perf. 10 on 2 or 3 Sides

2014, Jan. 27 Litho.

Booklet Stamps
Self-Adhesive

2674	A1264	1 multi	1.75	.85
2675	A1265	1 multi	1.75	.85
2676	A1266	1 multi	1.75	.85
2677	A1267	1 multi	1.75	.85
2678	A1268	1 multi	1.75	.85
2679	A1269	1 multi	1.75	.85
2680	A1270	1 multi	1.75	.85
2681	A1271	1 multi	1.75	.85
2682	A1272	1 multi	1.75	.85
2683	A1273	1 multi	1.75	.85
a.		Booklet pane of 10, #2674-2683	17.50	17.50
		Nos. 2674-2683 (10)	17.50	8.50

Nos. 2674-2683 each sold for 70c on day of issue.

Miniature Sheet

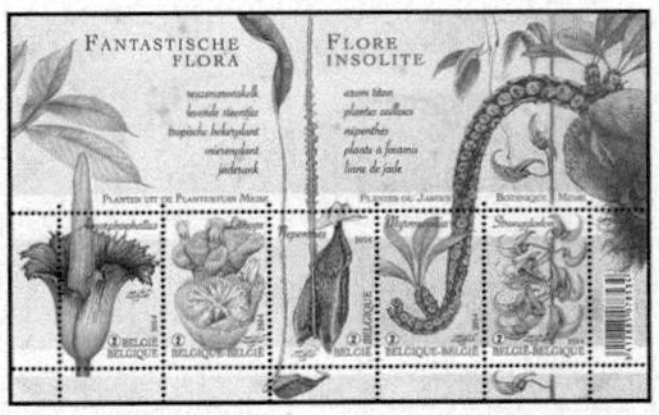

Flora in Meise Botanical Garden — A1274

No. 2684: a, Amorphophallus. b, Lithops. c, Nepenthes. d, Myrmecodia. e, Strongylodon.

2014, Jan. 27 Litho. *Perf. 11½*

2684	A1274	Sheet of 5	19.00	19.00
a.-e.		2 Any single	3.50	1.75

Nos. 2684a-2684e each sold for €1.40 on day of issue.

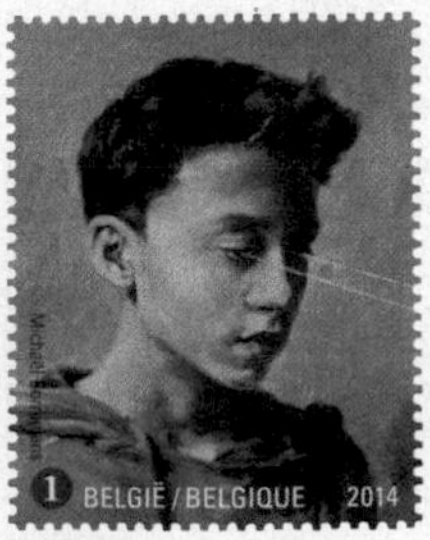

The Son, Painting by Michael Borremans A1275

2014, Feb. 17 Litho. *Perf. 11½*

2685	A1275	1 multi	1.75	.85

No. 2685 sold for 70c on day of issue.

Miniature Sheet

Paintings of Mammals by André Buzin — A1276

No. 2686: a, Lapin de garenne (European rabbits). b, Renard (foxes). c, Lynx. d, Chevreuil (roe deer). e, Sanglier (wild pigs).

2014, Feb. 17 Litho. *Perf. 11½*

2686	A1276	Sheet of 5	17.50	17.50
a.-e.		2 Any single	3.50	1.75

Nos. 2686a-2686e each sold for €1.40 on day of issue.

International Women's Day — A1277

2014, Mar. 10 Litho. *Perf. 11½*

2687	A1277	1 World black	3.25	1.60

No. 2687 sold for €1.29 on day of issue.

Earth Hour — A1278

Litho. & Silk-Screened

2014, Mar. 10 *Perf. 12*

2688	A1278	1 World multi	3.25	1.60

No. 2688 sold for €1.29 on day of issue.

Miniature Sheet

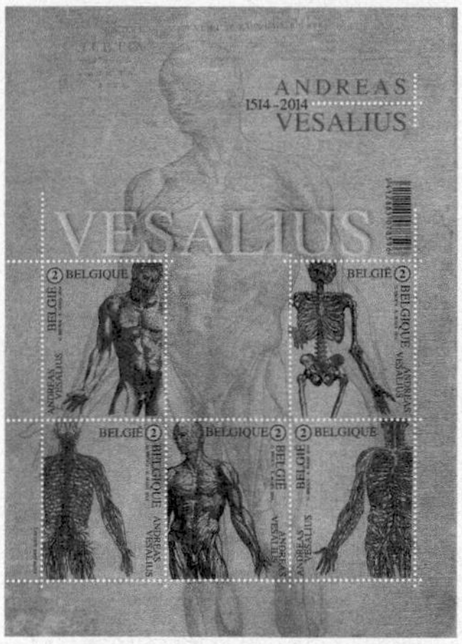

Anatomical Drawings by Andreas Vesalius (1514-64) — A1279

No. 2689: a, Nude man. b, Skeleton. c, Nervous system. d, Muscular system. e, Circulatory system.

Photo. & Engr.

2014, Apr. 22 *Perf. 11½*

2689	A1279	Sheet of 5		17.50	17.50
a.-e.		2 Any single		3.50	1.75

Nos. 2689a-2689e each sold for €1.40 on day of issue. See Portugal No. 3592.

Tintin — A1280

Bianca Castafiore A1281

Thomson and Thompson A1282

Snowy — A1283

Professor Calculus — A1284

Captain Haddock — A1285

Abdullah — A1286

Chang Chong-Chen A1287

General Alcazar — A1288

Nestor — A1289

Die Cut Perf. 10 on 2 or 3 Sides

2014, Apr. 22 **Photo.**

Booklet Stamps
Self-Adhesive

2690	A1280	1	multi	1.75	.90
2691	A1281	1	multi	1.75	.90
2692	A1282	1	multi	1.75	.90
2693	A1283	1	multi	1.75	.90
2694	A1284	1	multi	1.75	.90
2695	A1285	1	multi	1.75	.90
2696	A1286	1	multi	1.75	.90
2697	A1287	1	multi	1.75	.90
2698	A1288	1	multi	1.75	.90
2699	A1289	1	multi	1.75	.90
a.		Booklet pane of 10, #2690-2699		17.50	17.50
		Nos. 2690-2699 (10)		17.50	9.00

Nos. 2690-2699 each sold for 70c on day of issue.

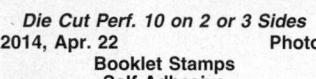

2014 World Cup Soccer Championships, Brazil — A1290

2014, June 10 **Litho.** ***Perf. 12***

2700	A1290	1	Europa multi	2.75	1.40

No. 2700 sold for €1.07 on day of issue.

2014 Men's Field Hockey World Cup, The Hague, Netherlands A1291

2014, June 10 **Litho.** ***Perf. 11½***

2701	A1291	1	World multi	3.25	1.60

No. 2701 sold for €1.29 on day of issue.

Souvenir Sheet

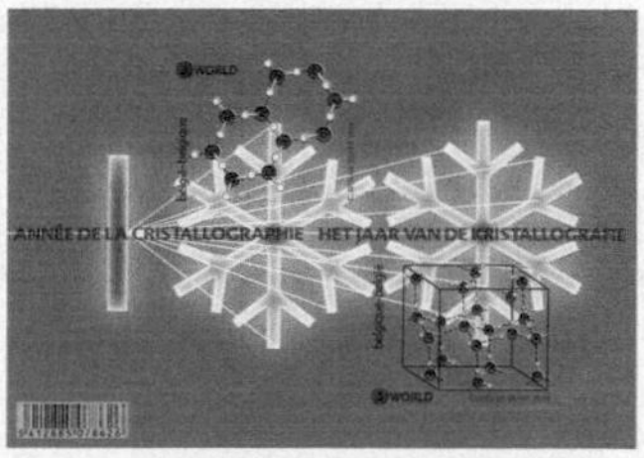

International Year of Crystallography — A1292

No. 2702 — Snowflake and molecular diagrams for ice with: a, 10 red atoms. b, 20 red atoms in cube.

Serpentine Die Cut 8½x9

2014, June 10 **Silk-Screened**
On Polyester Film
Self-Adhesive

2702	A1292	Sheet of 2		19.00	19.00
a.-b.		3 World Either single		9.50	4.75

Nos. 2702a-2702b each sold for €3.07 on day of issue. See Slovenia No. 1050.

Wallonia Mines UNESCO World Heritage Sites — A1293

Photo. & Engr.

2014, July 7 ***Perf. 11½***

2703	A1293	1	World black	3.25	1.60

No. 2703 sold for €1.29 on day of issue. Printed in sheets of 5.

Souvenir Sheet

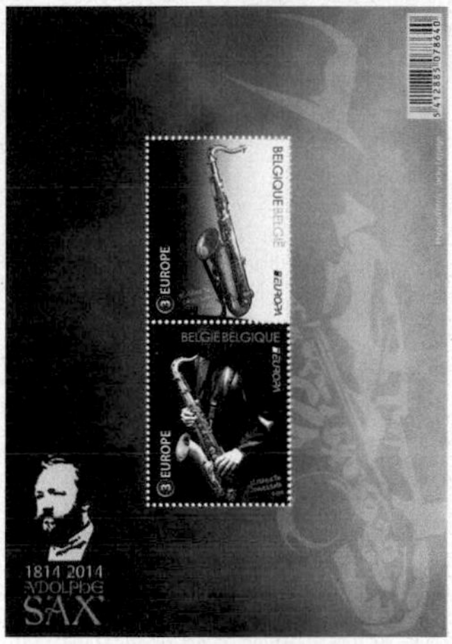

Europa — A1294

No. 2704: a, Saxophone. b, Musician playing saxophone.

Litho. & Embossed (#2704a), Litho. (#2704b)

2014, July 7 ***Perf. 11½***

2704	A1294	Sheet of 2		16.50	16.50
a.-b.		3 Europe Either single		8.25	4.25

Nos. 2704a-2704b each sold for €3.21 on day of issue.

Souvenir Sheet

Panama Canal, Cent. — A1295

No. 2705: a, Construction of Panama Canal. b, Ship passing through Panama Canal.

2014, July 7 **Litho.** ***Perf. 11½***

2705	A1295	Sheet of 2		19.00	19.00
a.-b.		3 World Either single		9.50	4.75

Nos. 2705a-2705b each sold for €3.87 on day of issue.

Blood Will Tell — A1296

Portrait of Adrienne Crowet A1297

The Treachery of Images A1298

Golconda A1299

The Great Family A1300

Discovery A1301

The Domain of Arnheim A1302

The Empire of Lights A1303

Personal Values A1304

The Breast A1305

Sawtooth Die Cut 8¼x8¾, 8¾x8¼

2014, Sept. 8 **Litho.**

Booklet Stamps
Self-Adhesive

2706	A1296	1	multi	1.75	.90
2707	A1297	1	multi	1.75	.90
2708	A1298	1	multi	1.75	.90
2709	A1299	1	multi	1.75	.90
2710	A1300	1	multi	1.75	.90
2711	A1301	1	multi	1.75	.90
2712	A1302	1	multi	1.75	.90
2713	A1303	1	multi	1.75	.90
2714	A1304	1	multi	1.75	.90
2715	A1305	1	multi	1.75	.90
a.		Booklet pane of 10, #2706-2715		17.50	17.50
		Nos. 2706-2715 (10)		17.50	9.00

Paintings by René Magritte (1898-1967). Nos. 2706-2715 each sold for 70c on day of issue.

Le Petit Spirou, Comic Strip by Tome and Janry A1306

2014, Oct. 6 **Litho.** ***Perf. 11½***

2716	A1306	1	multi	1.75	.85

No. 2716 sold for 70c on day of issue.

Locomotives
A1307

2014, Oct. 6 Litho. *Perf. 11½*

2717	A1307	2 multi	3.50	1.75

No. 2717 sold for €1.40 on day of issue and was issued in sheets of 5.

Miniature Sheet

World War I, Cent. — A1308

No. 2718 — War events of 1914: a, Execution of civilians of Dinant (40x30mm). b, Refugees (37x49mm). c, Withdrawal of Belgian forces along the Meuse River (40x30mm). d, Attack of Belgians along Yser Front (40x33mm). e, Destruction of Leuven University Library (40x30mm).

2014, Oct. 16 Photo. *Perf. 11½*

2718	A1308	Sheet of 5 + 2 labels	17.50	8.75
a.-e.		2 Any single	3.50	1.75

On day of issue, Nos. 2718a-2718e each sold for €1.40.

A1309

A1310

A1311

A1312

A1313

A1314

A1315

A1316

A1317

Butterflies
A1318

Serpentine Die Cut 14

2014, Oct. 6 Self-Adhesive Litho.

Coil Stamps

2719	A1309	1 multi	2.00	.85
2720	A1310	1 multi	2.00	.85
2721	A1311	1 multi	2.00	.85
2722	A1312	1 multi	2.00	.85
2723	A1313	1 multi	2.00	.85
2724	A1314	1 multi	2.00	.85
2725	A1315	1 multi	2.00	.85
2726	A1316	1 multi	2.00	.85
2727	A1317	1 multi	2.00	.85
2728	A1318	1 multi	2.00	.85
a.		Horiz. strip of 10, #2719-2728	20.00	20.00
		Nos. 2719-2728 (10)	20.00	8.50

On day of issue, Nos. 2719-2728 each sold for 70c.

Miniature Sheet

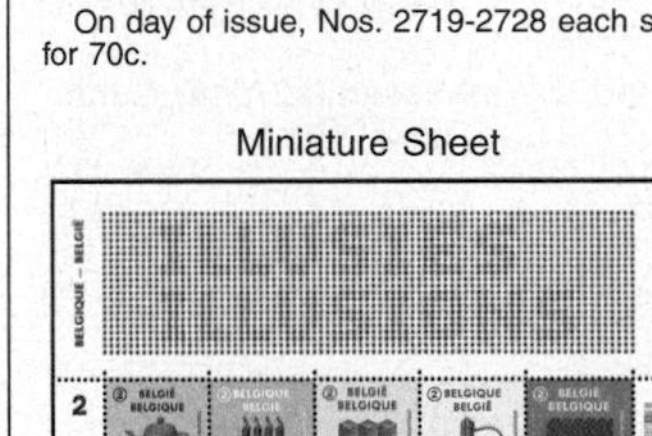

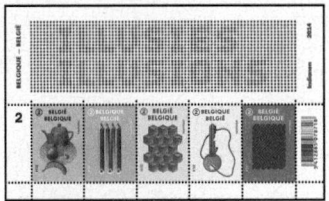

Optical Illusions — A1319

No. 2729: a, Clown's face in tea set and fruit. b, Pencils. c, Cubes. d, Key and silhouette of man. e, "2" hidden in lines.

2014, Oct. 27 Litho. *Perf. 11½*

2729	A1319	Sheet of 5	17.50	8.75
a.-e.		2 Any single	3.50	1.75

Nos. 2729a-2729e each sold for €1.40 on day of issue.

A1320

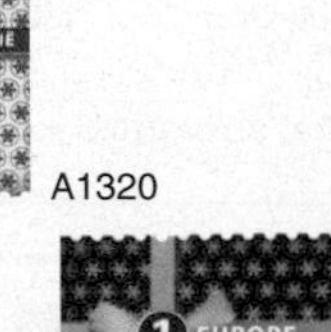

Christmas
A1321

Die Cut Perf. 9¾ on 2 or 3 Sides

2014, Oct. 27 Photo.

Booklet Stamps
Self-Adhesive

2730	A1320	1 multi	1.75	.85
a.		Booklet pane of 10	17.50	17.50
2731	A1321	1 Europe multi	2.75	1.40
a.		Booklet pane of 10	27.50	27.50

On day of issue, No. 2730 sold for 70c and No. 2731 sold for €1.07.

Thorgal, Comic Book Character Drawn by Grzegorz Rosinski
A1322

2015, Jan. 26 Litho. *Perf. 11½*

2732	A1322	2 multi	3.25	1.60

No. 2732 sold for €1.44 on day of issue.

King Philippe — A1323

Die Cut Perf. 10 on 2 or 3 Sides

2015, Jan. 26 Litho.

Booklet Stamps
Self-Adhesive
Background Color

2733	A1323	1 red	1.75	.45
a.		Booklet pane of 10	17.50	17.50
2734	A1323	2 yel orange	3.25	.80
a.		Booklet pane of 5	16.50	16.50

On day of issue, Nos. 2733-2734 sold for 72c and €1.44, respectively. Compare with type A1261. See No. 2883.

A1324

A1325

A1326

A1327

A1328

A1329

A1330

A1331

A1332

A1333

Die Cut Perf. 10x10¼

2015, Jan. 26 Litho.

Booklet Stamps
Self-Adhesive

2735	A1324	1 multi	1.75	.85
2736	A1325	1 multi	1.75	.85
2737	A1326	1 multi	1.75	.85
2738	A1327	1 multi	1.75	.85
2739	A1328	1 multi	1.75	.85
2740	A1329	1 multi	1.75	.85
2741	A1330	1 multi	1.75	.85
2742	A1331	1 multi	1.75	.85
2743	A1332	1 multi	1.75	.85
2744	A1333	1 multi	1.75	.85
a.		Booklet pane of 10, #2735-2744	17.50	17.50
		Nos. 2735-2744 (10)	17.50	8.50

On day of issue, Nos. 2735-2744 each sold for 72c.

Miniature Sheet

Queen Fabiola (1928-2014) — A1334

No. 2795 — Queen Fabiola: a, Wearing tiara (image used for #B729). b, Wearing scarf, with King Baudoin (image used for #2300a). c, Wearing tiara and necklace (image ussed for #B1125). d, With King Baudoin (image used for #B1095). e, Without tiara (image used for #2300b).

2015, Jan. 26 Litho. *Perf. 11½*

2745	A1334	Sheet of 5	17.50	17.50
a.-e.		2 Any single	3.50	1.60

Nos. 2745a-2745e each sold for €1.44 on day of issue.

Miniature Sheet

Tapestries — A1335

No. 2746: a, The Storm, by Liliane Badin, 1963. b, Tantra on Yellow, by Jan Yoors, 1977. c, The Picking, by Edmond Dubrunfaut, 1962. d, History of Jacob: Sharing of the Livestock, by Bernard van Orley and Willem de Kempeneere, 1525-50. e, History of Hercules: Conquest of the Island of Sheep, by unknown creator, 15th cent.

2015, Jan. 26 Litho. *Perf. 11½*

2746	A1335	Sheet of 5	17.50	17.50
a.-e.		2 Any single	3.50	1.60

Nos. 2746a-2746e each sold for €1.44 on day of issue.

Miniature Sheet

Birds and Mammals — A1336

No. 2747: a, Oie cendrée (graylag goose). b, Cygne tuberculé (mute swan). c, Héron cendré (gray heron). d, Grand-duc (Eurasian eagle-owl). e, Foulque macroule (Eurasian coot). f, Cerf rouge (red deer). g, Hermine (ermine). h, Loutre d'Europe (European otter). i, Lièvre brun (brown hare). j, Ecureuil roux (red squirrel).

2015, Mar. 23 Litho. *Perf. 12½*

2747	A1336 Sheet of 10		17.50	17.50
a.-j.	1 Any single		1.75	.80

Nos. 2747a-2747j each sold for 72c on day of issue.

Miniature Sheet

World War I, Cent. — A1337

No. 2748 — Events of 1915: a, Prime Minister Henri Jaspar, health examination of child (40x30mm). b, Red Cross worker serving food to soldiers (37x49mm). c, Food distribution, bag of flour (40x30mm). d, Bread ration ticket, soldier sharing food with child (40x33mm). e, Belgian government officials in exile in Saint-Adresse, France, Ministerial residence, mail box (40x30mm).

2015, Mar. 23 Litho. *Perf. 11½*

2748	A1337 Sheet of 5	15.00	15.00
a.-e.	1 Europe Any single	3.00	1.50

Nos. 2748a-2748e each sold for €1.10 on day of issue. See France No. 4778-4779.

Bpost Emblem — A1338

Perf. 11¾x11½
2015, Apr. 13 Photo.
Self-Adhesive

2749	A1338 1 World multi	3.00	1.50

No. 2749 sold for €1.32 on day of issue.

Souvenir Sheet

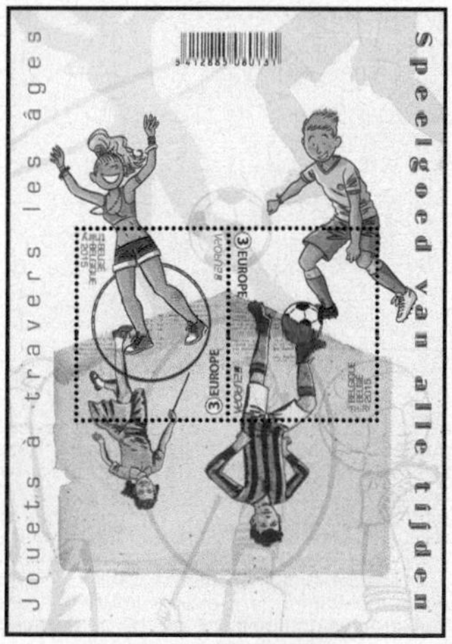

Europa — A1339

No. 2750: a, Girls playing with hoop. b, Boys with soccer ball.

2015, Apr. 13 Litho. *Perf. 11½*

2750	A1339 Sheet of 2	17.00	17.00
a.-b.	3 Europe Either single	8.50	3.75

Nos. 2750a-2750b each sold for €3.30 on day of issue.

Lucky Luke — A1340

Jolly Jumper — A1341

Rantanplan A1342

Joe Dalton A1343

Ma Dalton — A1344

Hank Bully — A1345

Jesse James — A1346

Indian — A1347

Billy the Kid — A1348

Calamity Jane — A1349

Die Cut Perf. 10 on 2 or 3 Sides
2015, Apr. 13 Litho.
Booklet Stamps
Self-Adhesive

2751	A1340 1 multi	1.75	.85
2752	A1341 1 multi	1.75	.85
2753	A1342 1 multi	1.75	.85
2754	A1343 1 multi	1.75	.85
2755	A1344 1 multi	1.75	.85
2756	A1345 1 multi	1.75	.85
2757	A1346 1 multi	1.75	.85
2758	A1347 1 multi	1.75	.85
2759	A1348 1 multi	1.75	.85
2760	A1349 1 multi	1.75	.85
a.	Booklet pane of 10, #2751-2760	17.50	17.50
	Nos. 2751-2760 (10)	17.50	8.50

Lucky Luke cartoon characters, drawn by Morris. Nos. 2751-2760 each sold for 72c on day of issue.

Queen Elisabeth (1876-1965) A1350

Queen Elisabeth: No. 2761, Wearing tiara, 1923. No. 2762, Playing violin, c. 1908.

Photo. & Engr.
2015, May 11 *Perf. 11½*

2761	A1350 1 multi	1.75	.80
2762	A1350 1 multi	1.75	.80

Nos. 2761-2762 were printed in sheets of 10 containing five of each stamp. Each sold for 72c on day of issue. Imperforate sheets of 10 were given as gifts to standing order customers.

Miniature Sheet

Camouflaged Insects — A1351

No. 2763: a, Phromnia rosea on plant stem). b, Gastropacha quercifolia (brown insect on leaf). c, Phyllium giganteum. d, Haaniella dehaanii on stem with thorns. e, Hymenopus coronatus on flower.

2015, May 11 Litho. *Perf. 11½*

2763	A1351 Sheet of 5	17.50	17.50
a.-e.	2 Any single	3.50	1.60

Nos. 2763a-2763e each sold for €1.44 on day of issue.

Miniature Sheet

Battle of Waterloo, 200th Anniv. — A1352

No. 2764: a, Arthur Wellesley, first Duke of Wellington (1769-1852). b, Gebhard Leberecht von Blücher (1742-1819). c, William, Prince of Orange (1792-1849). d, Michel Ney (17691-1815). e, Napoleon Bonaparte (1769-1821).

Photo. & Engr.
2015, June 1 *Perf. 11½*

2764	A1352 Sheet of 5	15.00	15.00
a.-e.	1 Europe Any single	3.00	1.50

Nos. 2764a-2764e each sold for €1.10 on day of issue.

Shrimp Fisherman on Horseback of Oostduinkerke — A1353

2015, June 29 Litho. *Perf. 11½*

2765	A1353 1 World blk & gray	3.00	1.50

No. 2765 sold for €1.32 on day of issue.

Miniature Sheet

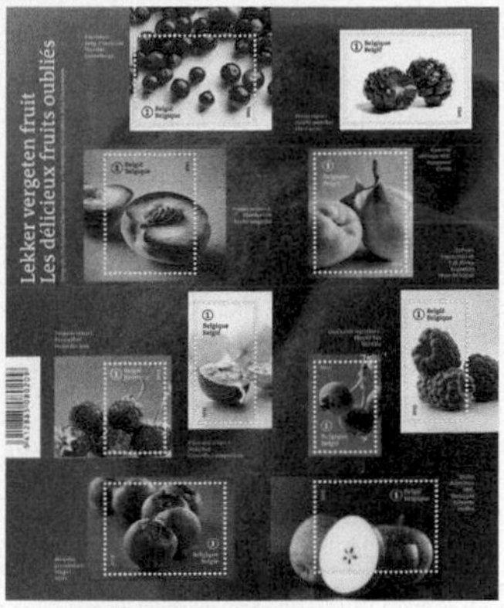

Fruit — A1354

No. 2766: a, Vaccinium oxycoccus (cranberries, 40x30mm). b, Morus nigra (black mulberries, 40x30mm). c, Prunus persica (peaches, 30x40mm). d, Cydonia oblonga (quinces, 30x40mm). e, Ribes uva-crispa (gooseberry, 20x40mm). f, Rubus x loganobacus (loganberries, 20x40mm). g, Fragaria vesca (wild strawberries, 20x30mm). h, Vaccinium myrtillus (European blueberries, 20x30mm). i, Mespilus germanica (medlars, 40x30mm). j, Malus domestica (apples, 40x30mm).

2015, June 29 Litho. *Perf. 12*

2766	A1354 Sheet of 10	17.50	17.50
a.-j.	1 Any single	1.75	.80

Nos. 2766a-2766j each sold for 72c on day of issue.

European Women's Volleyball Championships, Belgium and the Netherlands A1355

2015, Sept. 7 Litho. *Perf. 12*

2767	A1355 1 Europe multi	2.50	1.25

No. 2767 sold for €1.10 on day of issue.

Dinosaurs A1356

Die Cut Perf. 10 on 2 or 3 Sides
2015, Sept. 7 Litho.
Booklet Stamps
Self-Adhesive

2768	A1356 1 Giraffatitan	1.75	.80
2769	A1356 1 Torvosaurus	1.75	.80
2770	A1356 1 Olorotitan	1.75	.80
2771	A1356 1 Deinonychus	1.75	.80
2772	A1356 1 Aurornis	1.75	.80
2773	A1356 1 Ankylosaurus	1.75	.80
2774	A1356 1 Finiosaurus	1.75	.80
2775	A1356 1 Pteranodon	1.75	.80
2776	A1356 1 Iguanodon	1.75	.80
2777	A1356 1 Kentrosaurus	1.75	.80
a.	Booklet pane of 10, #2768-2777	17.50	17.50
	Nos. 2768-2777 (10)	17.50	8.00

On day of issue, Nos. 2768-2777 each sold for 72c.

No. 2774 description is spelled wrong (Finiosaurus), it should be Einiosaurus.

Miniature Sheet

Hot Air Balloons — A1357

No. 2778: a, Orange and red OO-SWF balloon. b, Belgica balloon. c, Le Flesselles balloon. d, Burner firing in gondola under blue balloon. e, Funny Bunny balloon, ballons in background.

Photo. & Engr., Photo. (#2778a, 2778d, 2778e)

2015, Sept. 7 *Perf. 11½*

2778 A1357 Sheet of 5 17.50 17.50
a.-e. 2 Any single 3.50 1.75

On day of issue, Nos. 2778a-2778e each sold for €1.44.

Souvenir Sheet

Manuscript Illuminations Depicting Nativity — A1358

No. 2779 — Illustration from: a, Bible with Raphael d'Urbino illustrations (Mary at right). b, Breviary of Philippe le Bon (Mary at left).

2015, Oct. 26 **Litho.** *Perf. 11½*

2779 A1358 Sheet of 2 16.00 16.00
a.-b. 3 Europe Either single 8.00 4.00

On day of issue, Nos. 2779a-2779b both sold for €3.30.

Christmas
A1359 A1360

Die Cut Perf. 10 on 2 or 3 Sides

2015, Oct. 26 **Litho.**

Booklet Stamps Self-Adhesive

2780 A1359 1 red & multi 1.60 .80
a. Booklet pane of 10 16.00 16.00
2781 A1360 1 Europe green 2.50 1.25
a. Booklet pane of 10 25.00 25.00

On day of issue, No. 2780 sold for 724c; No. 2781, for €1.10.

A1361

King Philippe — A1362

Die Cut Perf. 10 on 3 Sides

2016, Mar. 14 **Litho.**

Booklet Stamps Self-Adhesive

2782 A1361 1 Europe multi 2.60 .65
a. Booklet pane of 5 13.00 13.00
2783 A1362 1 World multi 3.25 .80
a. Booklet pane of 5 16.50 16.50

On day of issue, No. 2782 sold for €1.13 and No. 2783 sold for €1.35. Compare types A1361-A1362 with types A1262-A1263.

A1363

2016, Mar. 14 **Litho.** *Perf. 11½*

2784 A1363 2 multi 3.50 1.75

Cédric, comic strip by Raoul Cauvin and B. D. Laudec, 30th anniv.

No. 2784 sold for €1.48 on day of issue.

Emile Verhaeren (1855-1916), Poet — A1364

2016, Mar. 14 **Litho.** *Perf. 12½*

2785 A1364 2 multi 3.50 1.75

No. 2785 sold for €1.48 on day of issue.

Princess Elisabeth A1365

Prince Gabriel — A1366

Prince Emmanuel A1367

Princess Eléonore A1368

Royal Family — A1369

2016, Mar. 14 **Litho.** *Perf. 12*

2786 A1365 1 multi 1.75 .85
2787 A1366 1 multi 1.75 .85
2788 A1367 1 multi 1.75 .85
2789 A1368 1 multi 1.75 .85
2790 A1369 1 multi 1.75 .85
a. Horiz. strip of 5, #2786-2790 8.75 6.50
Nos. 2786-2790 (5) 8.75 4.25

On day of issue, Nos. 2786-2790 each sold for 74c.

Miniature Sheet

Job Training — A1370

No. 2791: a, Dredge near island, Abu Dhabi (30x40mm). b, Person playing carillon (40x30mm). c, Building under construction and completed building (40x40mm). d, Item made by 3-d printer (40x30mm). e, People painting airplane wing (30x40mm).

2016, Mar. 14 **Litho.** *Perf. 12*

2791 A1370 Sheet of 5 13.00 13.00
a.-e. 1 Europe Any single 2.60 1.40

On day of issue, Nos. 2791a-2791e each sold for €1.13.

Europa A1371

2016, June 13 **Litho.** *Perf. 11½*

2792 A1371 1 Europe multi 2.60 1.40

Think Green Issue.

No. 2792 sold for €1.13 on day of issue.

Miniature Sheet

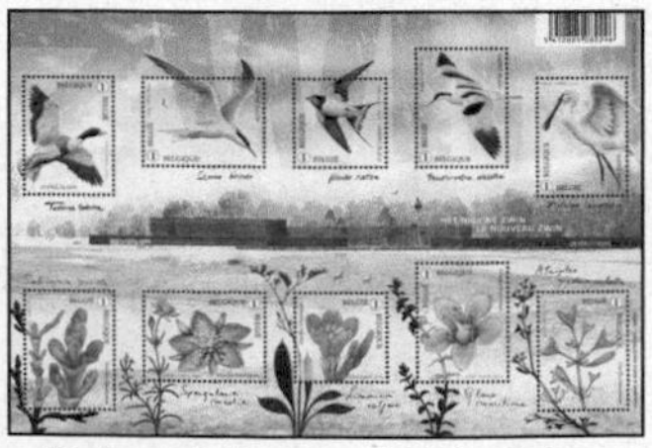

Birds and Flowers of Zwin Nature Park — A1372

No. 2793: a, Tadorna tadorna flying right (30x40mm). b, Sterna hirundo flying right (40x30mm). c, Hirundo rustica flying left (30x30mm). d, Recurvirostra avosetta flying left (30x40mm). e, Platalea leucorodia standing (30x40mm). f, Salicornia pusilla (green & brown rose plant, 30x40mm). g, Spergularia media (purple flower, 40x30mm). h, Limonium vulgare (purple flower, 30x30mm). i, Glaux maritima (pink flower, 30x40mm). j, Atriplex pedunculata (green and brown plant, 30x40mm).

2016, June 13 **Litho.** *Perf. 12*

2793 A1372 Sheet of 10 17.50 17.50
a.-j. 1 Any single 1.75 .85

On day of issue, Nos. 2793a-2793j each sold for 74c.

Miniature Sheet

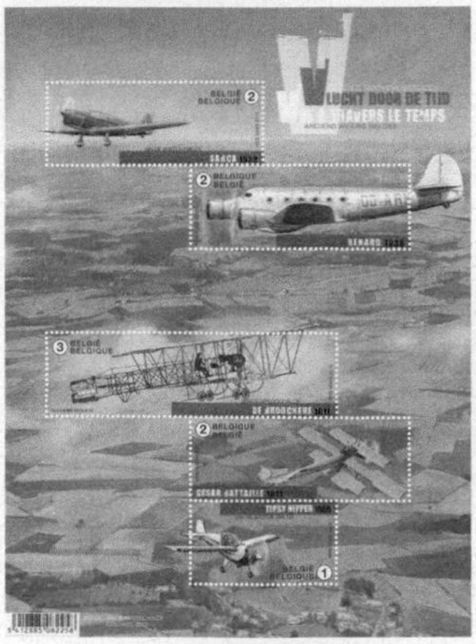

Airplanes — A1373

No. 2794: a, Tipsy Nipper, 1959 (48x28mm). b, Sabca S.40, 1939 (73x28mm). c, Renard R.35 (73x28mm). d, César Bataille, 1911 (73x28mm). e, De Brouckère, 1911 (97x28mm).

Photo., Photo. & Engr. (#2794e)

2016, June 13 *Perf. 11½*

2794 A1373 Sheet of 5 17.50 17.50
a. 1 multi 1.75 .85
b.-d. 2 Any single 3.50 1.75
e. 3 multi 5.25 2.60

On day of issue, No. 2794a sold for 74c, Nos. 2794b-2794d each sold for €1.48, and No. 2794e sold for €2.22.

Miniature Sheet

World War I, Cent. — A1374

No. 2795 — Events of 2016: a, Clandestine publications (40x30mm). b, Gabrielle Petit (1893-1916), spy for Britain executed by Germans, and prison cell (38x49mm). c, Henri Pirenne (1862-1935), historian and arrested resistance leader (40x30mm). d, Commandant Albert De Bueger (1885-1940), Belgian seaplane at Battle of Tabora, German East Africa (40x33mm). e, Belgians forced to work for Germans and political cartoon denouncing forced labor (40x30mm).

2016, June 13 **Photo.** *Perf. 11½*

2795 A1374 Sheet of 5 13.00 13.00
a.-e. 1 Europe Any single 2.60 1.40

On day of issue, Nos. 2795a-2795e each sold for €1.13.

Souvenir Sheet

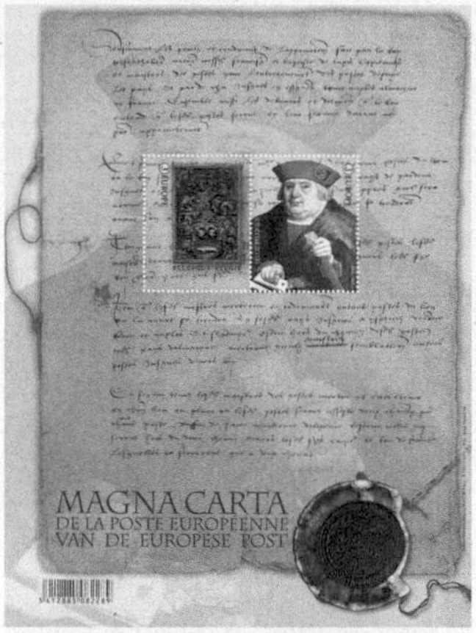

Postal Agreement of 1516, 500th Anniv. — A1375

No. 2796: a, Coat of arms of Jean-Baptiste de Taxis. b, Franz von Taxis (1459-1517), operator of early European postal system.

Litho., Sheet Margin Litho. & Embossed

2016, June 13 *Perf. 11½*

2796 A1375 Sheet of 2 16.00 16.00
a.-b. 3 Europe Either single 8.00 4.00

On day of issue, Nos. 2796a-2796b each sold for €3.39.

Miniature Sheet

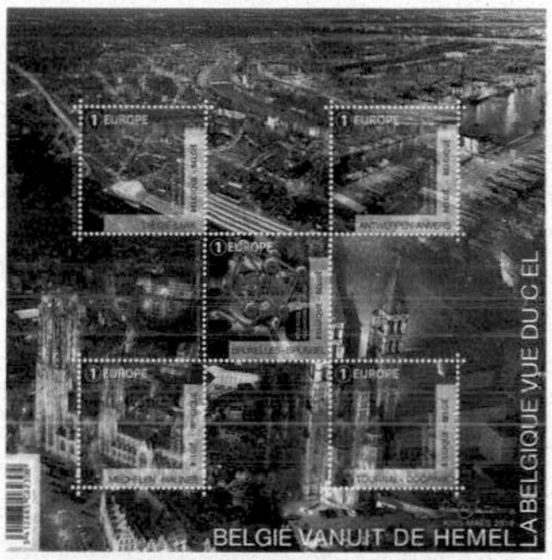

Belgium at Night — A1376

No. 2797: a, Liège-Guillemins Railway Station, Liège. b, Port of Antwerp. c, Atomium, Brussels. d, St. Rombold's Cathedral, Mechelen. e, Notre Dame Cathedral, Tournai.

2016, Aug. 22 Litho. *Perf. 12½*

2797 A1376 Sheet of 5 13.00 13.00
a.-e. 1 Europe Any single 2.60 1.40

Nos. 2797a-2797e each sold for €1.13 on day of issue.

Miniature Sheet

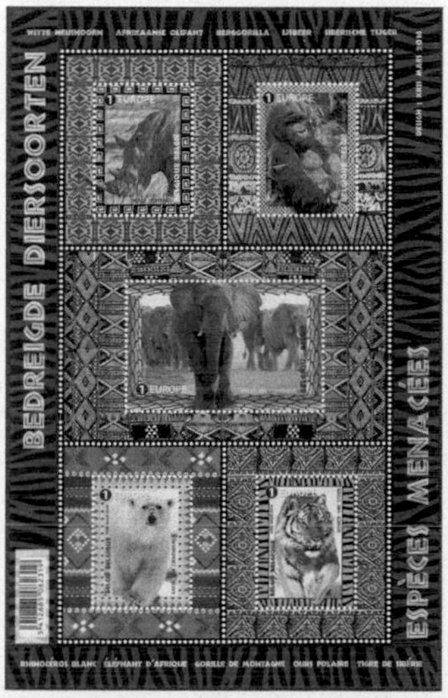

Endangered Animals — A1377

No. 2798: a, White rhinoceros (30x40mm). b, Mountain gorillas (30x40mm). c, African elephants (60x40mm). d, Polar bear (30x40mm). e, Siberian tiger (30x40mm).

2016, Aug. 22 Litho. *Perf. 12*

2798 A1377 Sheet of 5 14.00 14.00
a.-e. 1 Europe Any single 2.75 1.40

Nos. 2798a-2798e each sold for €1.13 on day of issue and are within a perforated frame of sheet margin.

Miniature Sheet

2016 Summer Olympics and Paralympics, Rio de Janeiro — A1378

No. 2799: a, Sailing. b, Rowing. c, Paracycling. d, Wheelchair racing. e, Paraequestrian.

2016, Aug. 22 Litho. *Perf. 12*

2799 A1378 Sheet of 5 15.00 15.00
a.-e. 1 World Any single 3.00 1.50

Nos. 2799a-2799e each sold for €1.35 on day of issue.

Miniature Sheet

Tintin Magazine, 70th Anniv. — A1379

No. 2800 — Magazine cover of: a, French edition, Sept. 26, 1946 (Le Temple du Soleil). b, French edition, Oct. 3, 1946 (Corentin at police call box). c, French edition, Oct. 17, 1946 (Blake and Mortimer on ship). d, Dutch edition, Sept. 20, 1951 (sailing ship). e, Dutch edition, Mar. 24, 1949 (people and house).

2016, Aug. 22 Litho. *Perf. 12*

2800 A1379 Sheet of 5 17.50 17.50
a.-e. 2 Any single 3.50 1.75

Nos. 2800a-2800e each sold for €1.48 on day of issue.

Miniature Sheet

Paintings by Rik Wouters (1882-1916) — A1380

No. 2801: a, Tulips, 1913. b, Woman Reading (Femme lisant), 1913, vert. c, Self-portrait with Cigar, 1913, vert. d, The Ravine, 1913. e, The Ironer, 1912..

2016, Aug. 22 Litho. *Perf. 12*

2801 A1380 Sheet of 5 17.50 17.50
a.-e. 2 Any single 3.50 1.75

Nos. 2801a-2801e each sold for €1.48 on day of issue.

Brussels Chief Rabbi Albert Guigui, Antwerp Bishop Johan Bonny, and Imam Khalid Benhaddou — A1381

2016, Oct. 24 Litho. *Perf. 11½*

2802 A1381 1 multi 1.75 .85

Campaign for religious tolerance. No. 2802 sold for 74c on day of issue.

New NATO Headquarters Building, Brussels — A1382

2016, Oct. 24 Litho. *Perf. 12*

2803 A1382 1 Europe multi 2.75 1.25

No. 2803 sold for €1.13 on day of issue and was printed in sheets of 5.

Begonia A1383

Dahlia A1384

Narcissus A1385

Greek Anemone A1386

Tulip — A1387

Iris — A1388

Amaryllis A1389

Crocus A1390

Lily A1391

Hyacinth A1392

Serpentine Die Cut 14¼x14

2016, Oct. 24 Photo.

Coil Stamps
Self-Adhesive

2804 A1383 1 multi 1.75 .45
2805 A1384 1 multi 1.75 .45
2806 A1385 1 multi 1.75 .45
2807 A1386 1 multi 1.75 .45
2808 A1387 1 multi 1.75 .45
2809 A1388 1 multi 1.75 .45
2810 A1389 1 multi 1.75 .45
2811 A1390 1 multi 1.75 .45
2812 A1391 1 multi 1.75 .45
2813 A1392 1 multi 1.75 .45
a. Vert. strip of 10, #2804-2813 17.50
Nos. 2804-2813 (10) 17.50 4.50

Nos. 2804-2813 each sold for 74c on day of issue.

Miniature Sheet

Belgian Nobel Laureates — A1393

No. 2814: a, Jules Bordet, 1919 Physiology or Medicine laureate. b, Corneille Heymans, 1938 Physiology or Medicine laureate. c, Maurice Maeterlinck, 1911 Literature laureate. d, Albert Claude and Christian de Duve, 1974 Physiology or Medicine laureates. e, François Englert, 2013 Physics laureate, and Robert Brout, physicist. f, Ilya Prigogine, 1977 Chemistry laureate. g, Gustave Rolin-Jaequemyns, honorary president of Institute of International Law, 1904 Peace laureate. h, Auguste Beernaert, 1909 Peace laureate. i, Dominique Pire, 1958 Peace laureate. j, Henri La Fontaine, 1913 Peace laureate.

Photo. & Engr.

2016, Oct. 24 *Perf. 11½*

2814 A1393 Sheet of 10 17.50 17.50
a.-j. 1 Any single 1.75 .85

On day of issue, Nos. 2814a-2814j each sold for 74c.

Miniature Sheet

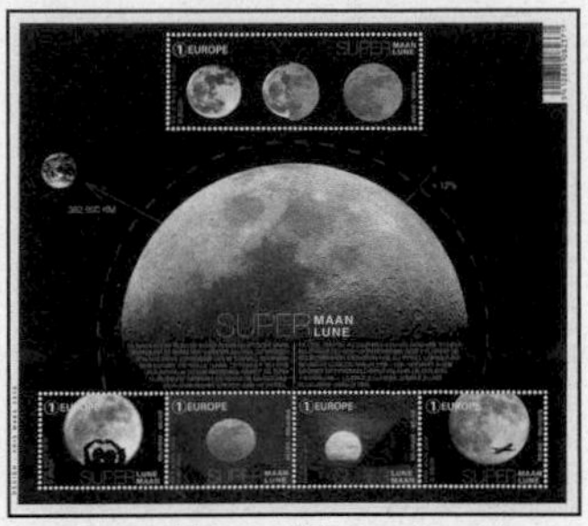

Super Moon of November 14, 2016 — A1394

No. 2815: a, Comparison of normal appearance of Moon with increased apparent size of Super Moon (80x30mm). b, Moon and couple (40x30mm). c, Moon and trees (40x30mm). d, Moon and church steeple (40x30mm). e, Moon and airplane (40x30mm).

2016, Oct. 24 Litho. *Perf. 12*
2815 A1394 Sheet of 5 14.00 14.00
a.-e. 1 Europe Any single 2.75 1.25

On day of issue, Nos. 2815a-2815e each sold for €1.13.

Santa Claus A1395

Reindeer A1396

Die Cut Perf. 10 on 2 or 3 Sides
2016, Oct. 24 Litho.
Booklet Stamps
Self-Adhesive
2816 A1395 1 multi 1.75 .85
a. Booklet pane of 10 17.50 17.50
2817 A1396 1 Europe multi 2.50 1.25
a. Booklet pane of 10 25.00 25.00

On day of issue, No. 2816 sold for 74c and No. 2817 sold for €1.13.

Mother and Child A1397

2017, Jan. 30 Litho. *Perf. 11½*
2818 A1397 1 multi 1.75 .80

No. 2818 sold for 74c on day of issue.

Miniature Sheet

Gaston Lagaffe Comic Strip, by André Franquin, 60th Anniv. — A1398

No. 2819: a, Gaston Lagaffe (40x50mm). b, Aimé De Mesmaeker (30x40mm). c, Léon Prunelle (30x40mm). d, M'oiselle Jeanne (30x40mm). e, Joseph Longtarin (30x40mm).

2017, Jan. 30 Litho. *Perf. 12*
2819 A1398 Sheet of 5 16.50 16.50
a.-e. 2 Any single 3.25 1.60

On day of issue, Nos. 2819a-2819e each sold for €1.48. Black and white imperforate sheets with simulated perforations were given as gifts to standing order customers.

Bpost Emblem — A1399

2017, Mar. 6 Photo. *Perf. 11½*
Self-Adhesive
2820 A1399 1 Europe multi 2.40 1.25

No. 2820 sold for €1.13 on day of issue and could be personalized.

Miniature Sheet

Bluebells in Blue Forest, Halle — A1400

No. 2821: a, Open bluebell and buds (30x30mm). b, Close-up of flower (30x30mm). c, Buds (30x30mm). d, Open flowers (30x30mm). e, Flowers on forest floor, tree trunks (40x30mm).

2017, Mar. 6 Litho. *Perf. 12*
2821 A1400 Sheet of 5 16.50 16.50
a.-e. 2 Any single 3.25 1.60

On day of issue, Nos. 2821a-2821e each sold for €1.48.

Miniature Sheet

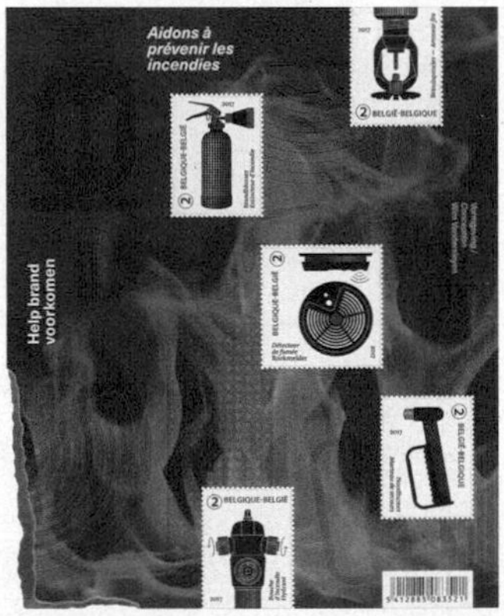

Fire Prevention Equipment — A1401

No. 2822: a, Fire sprinkler head (30x40mm). b, Fire extinguisher (30x40mm). c, Smoke detector (40x40mm). d, Emergency hammer (30x40mm). e, Hydrant (30x40mm).

Perf. 12 on 3 or 4 Sides
2017, Mar. 6 Litho.
2822 A1401 Sheet of 5 16.50 16.50
a.-e. 2 Any single 3.25 1.60

On day of issue, Nos. 2822a-2822e each sold for €1.48.

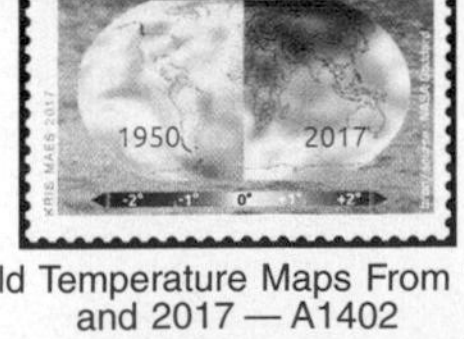

World Temperature Maps From 1950 and 2017 — A1402

Climate Change Goal of Temperature Decrease of 2 Degrees — A1403

Die Cut Perf. 11½
2017, Mar. 6 Litho.
Booklet Stamps
Self-Adhesive
2823 A1402 1 multi 1.60 .80
2824 A1403 1 multi 1.60 .80
a. Booklet pane of 10, 5 each #2823-2824 16.00 16.00

On day of issue, Nos. 2823-2824 each sold for 74c.

Sand Castle A1404

2017, June 12 Litho. *Perf. 12*
2825 A1404 1 Europe multi 2.60 1.40

Europa. No. 2825 sold for €1.13 on day of issue and portions of the design are coated with sand grains.

Miniature Sheet

Belgian Winners of the Tour de France Bicycle Race — A1405

No. 2826: a, Odiel Defraeye, 1912. b, Philippe Thys, 1913, 1914, 1920. c, Firmin Lambot, 1919, 1922. d, Léon Scieur, 1921. e, Lucien Buyze, 1926. f, Maurice De Waele, 1929. g, Romain Maes, 1935. h, Sylvère Maes, 1936, 1939. i, Eddy Merckx, 1969, 1970, 1971, 1972, 1974. j, Lucien Van Impe, 1976.

2017, June 12 Litho. *Perf. 12½*
2826 A1405 Sheet of 10 17.50 17.50
a.-j. 1 Any single 1.75 .85

On day of issue, Nos. 2826a-2826j each sold for 74c. Imperforate sheets of 10 were given as gifts to standing order customers.

Miniature Sheet

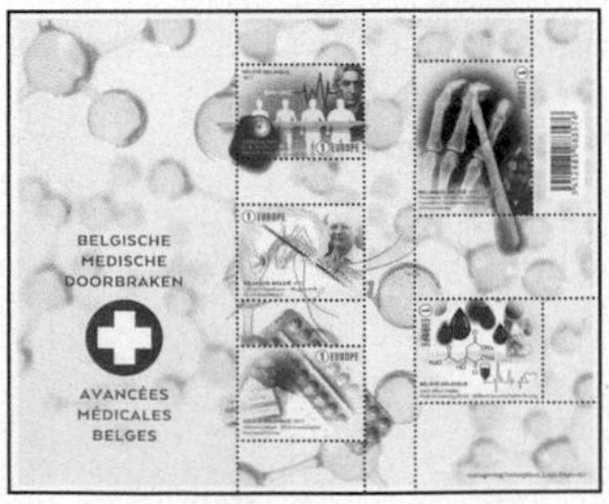

Medical Advances — A1406

No. 2827: a, Adolphe Quetelet (1796-1874), developer of body-mass index (40x30mm). b, Albin Lambotte (1866-1955), developer of surgical treatment of open bone fractures (37x49mm). c, Alfons Vandoninck, developer of mosquito repellent (40x30mm). d, Albert Hustin (1882-1967), developer of blood storage anti-coagulant (37x33mm). e, Ferdinand Peeters (1918-98), developer of birth control pills (40x30mm).

2017, June 12 Photo. *Perf. 11½*
2827 A1406 Sheet of 5 14.00 14.00
a.-e. 1 Europe Any single 2.75 1.40

On day of issue, Nos. 2827a-2827e each sold for €1.13.

Souvenir Sheet

Protestant Reformation, 500th Anniv. — A1407

No. 2828: a, Door of All Saints' Church, Wittenberg, Germany. b, Martin Luther (1483-1546), religious reformer.

Photo. & Engr.
2017, June 12 *Perf. 11½*
2828 A1407 Sheet of 2 17.00 17.00
a.-b. 3 Europe Either single 8.50 4.00

On day of issue, Nos. 2828a-2828b each sold for €3.39.

White Rose — A1408

Die Cut Perf. 10 on 2 or 3 Sides
2017, Aug. 21 Litho.
Booklet Stamp
Self-Adhesive
2829 A1408 1 multi 1.75 .90
a. Booklet pane of 10 17.50

No. 2829 sold for 74c on day of issue.

Kinky and Cosy, Comic Strip Characters by Marnix Verduyn A1409

2017, Aug. 21 Litho. *Perf. 11½*
2830 A1409 2 multi 3.50 1.75

No. 2830 sold for €1.48 on day of issue and was printed in sheets of 5.

Souvenir Sheet

University Bicentennials — A1410

No. 2831: a, University of Liège lecture hall, satellite. b, University of Ghent building, colored chemical reaction in flower.

Photo. & Engr.

2017, Aug. 21 ***Perf. 11½***

2831 A1410 Sheet of 2 9.50 10.00
a.-b. 3 World Either single 9.75 5.00

Nos. 2831a-2831b each sold for €4.05 on day of issue.

Miniature Sheet

Belgian Trains — A1411

No. 2832: a, Type 1935 electric train without identification number, 1935 (40x28mm). b, Type 653 Diesel locomotive 65304, 1936 (40x28mm). c, Type 12 Atlantic steam locomotive and tender (80x28mm). d, Series 54 Diesel locomotive 5404, 1955-57 (40x28mm). e, Desiro electric train 08079, 2008 (40x28mm).

Photo., Photo. & Engr. Sheet Margin

2017, Aug. 21 ***Perf. 11½***

2832 A1411 Sheet of 5 17.50 8.75
a.-e. 2 Any single 3.50 1.75

Nos. 2832a-2832e each sold for €1.48 on day of issue.

Miniature Sheet

Marine Mammals — A1412

No. 2833: a, Dauphin souffleur (bottlenose dolphin) (40x30mm). b, Dauphin à bec blanc (white-beaked dolphin) (40x30mm). c, Baleine à bosse (humpback whale) (40x60mm). d, Phoque gris et veau marin (gray seal and harbor seal) (40x30mm). e, Marsouin (harbor porpoise) (40x30mm).

2017, Aug. 21 **Litho.** ***Perf. 12***

2833 A1412 Sheet of 5 14.00 7.00
a.-e. 1 Europe Any single 2.75 1.40

Nos. 2833a-2833e each sold for €1.13 on day of issue. Animal names are not found on the stamps, but on frames that surround each stamp.

Miniature Sheet

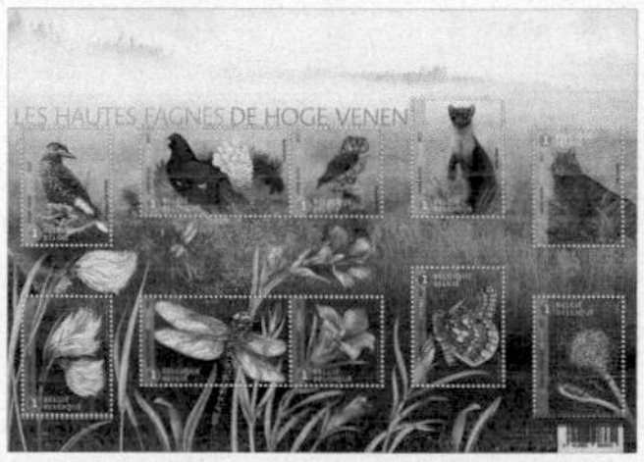

Flora and Fauna of High Fens Nature Reserve — A1413

No. 2834: a, Nucifraga caryocatactes (30x40mm). b, Lyrurus tetrix (50x30mm). c, Aegolius funereus (30x30mm). d, Martes martes (30x40mm). e, Felis silvestris (30x40mm). f, Eriophorum angustifolium (30x40mm). g, Aeshna subarctica (50x30mm). h, Gentiana pneumonanthe (30x30mm). i, Euphydryas aurinia (30x40mm). j, Drosera (30x40mm).

2017, Oct. 23 **Litho.** ***Perf. 12***

2834 A1413 Sheet of 10 17.50 17.50
a.-j. 1 Any single 1.75 .85

Nos. 2834a-2834j each sold for 74c on day of issue.

Miniature Sheet

World War I, Cent. — A1414

No. 2835 — Events of 2017: a, Mail delivery to troops (40x30mm). b, Soldiers and carrier pigeons (38x49mm). c, Soldiers making wireless communications (40x30mm). d, Canadian soldiers at Battle of Passchendaele (40x33mm). e, Baarle-Hertog Post Office and censor examination mark (40x30mm).

2017, Oct. 23 **Photo.** ***Perf. 11½***

2835 A1414 Sheet of 5 13.00 13.00
a.-e. 1 Europe Any single 2.60 1.40

On day of issue, Nos. 2835a-2835e each sold for €1.13.

Miniature Sheet

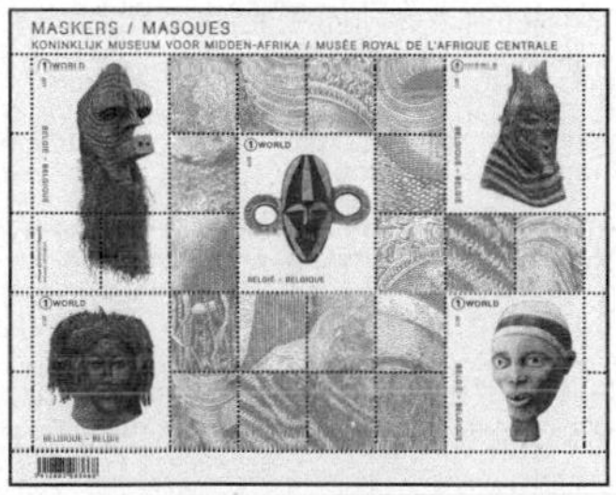

Masks in Royal Museum for Central Africa, Tervuren — A1415

No. 2836: a, Songye mask with rectangular nose. b, Ababua mask with points on top of head. c, Luluwa mask with large round ears. d, Chokwe mask with pierced nose. e, Yombe mask with open mouth with missing teeth.

Photo. & Engr.

2017, Oct. 23 ***Perf. 11½***

2836 A1415 Sheet of 5 + 20 labels 16.50 16.50
a.-e. 1 World Any single 3.25 1.60

On day of issue, Nos. 2836a-2836e each sold for €1.35.

Christmas
A1416 A1417

Die Cut Perf. 10 on 2 or 3 Sides

2017, Oct. 23 **Litho.**

Booklet Stamps
Self-Adhesive

2837 A1416 1 multi 1.75 .85
a. Booklet pane of 10 17.50
2838 A1417 1 Europe multi 2.60 1.40
a. Booklet pane of 10 26.00

On day of issue, No. 2837 sold for 74c; No. 2838, for €1.13.

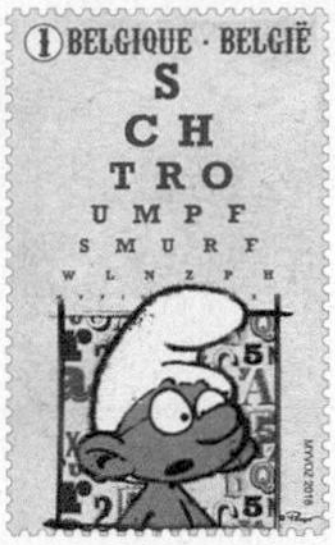

Brainy Smurf — A1418

Grouchy Smurf — A1419

Smurfette A1420

Black Smurf Painting Himself Blue — A1421

Papa Smurf — A1422

2018, Jan. 29 **Litho.** ***Perf. 12***

2839 A1418 1 multi 1.90 .95
2840 A1419 1 multi + label 1.90 .95
2841 A1420 1 multi + label 1.90 .95
2842 A1421 1 multi + label 1.90 .95
2843 A1422 1 multi 1.90 .95
a. Horiz. strip of 5, #2839-2843, + 3 labels 9.50 4.75
Nos. 2839-2843 (5) 9.50 4.75

On day of issue, Nos. 2839-2843 each sold for 74c.

Miniature Sheet

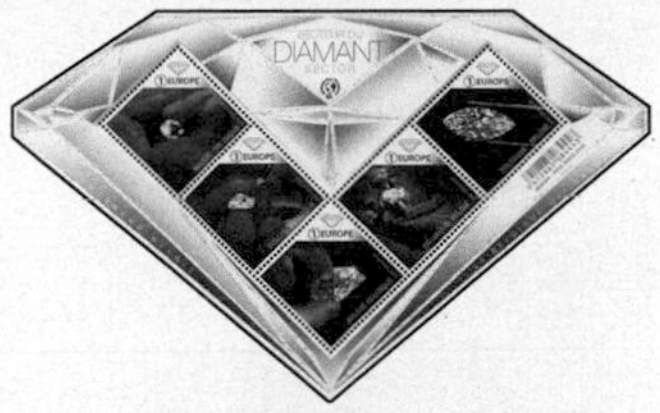

Diamond Cutting — A1423

No. 2844: a, Raw diamond in hand. b, Cut and polished diamond in jeweler's tongs. c, Jeweler marking raw diamond for cutting. d, Diamond in clip being polished. e, Diamond and ore.

2018, Jan. 29 **Litho.** ***Perf. 12½***

2844 A1423 Sheet of 5 15.00 15.00
a.-e. 1 Europe Any single 3.00 1.50

On day of issue, Nos. 2844a-2844e each sold for €1.13.

Miniature Sheet

Beer Culture of Belgium (UNESCO Intangible Cultural Heritage) — A1424

No. 2845: a, Mash tuns (40x30mm). b, Glasses of beer and raw beer ingredients (40x50mm). c, Harvesting of hops (40x30mm). d, Hamburger and beer glasses (40x30mm). e, Beer drinker, bottles and glases (40x30mm).

2018, Jan. 29 **Litho.** ***Perf. 12***

2845 A1424 Sheet of 5 17.50 17.50
a.-e. 1 World Any single 3.50 1.75

On day of issue, Nos. 2845a-2845e each sold for €1.35.

Red-Crested Pochard A1425

2018, Jan. 22 **Litho.** ***Perf. 11½***

2846 A1425 (44c) multi 1.10 .55

Child Focus, Foundation for Missing and Sexually Exploited Children, 20th Anniv. — A1426

2018, Mar. 12 **Litho.** ***Perf. 12***

2847 A1426 1 multi 1.90 .95

No. 2847 sold for 74c on day of issue.

Street Art in Brussels A1427

Street Art in Ghent — A1428

Street Art in Oostende A1429

Street Art in Namur — A1430

Street Art in Liège A1431

2018, Mar. 12 Litho. *Perf. 12*

2848 A1427 1 multi + label 1.90 .95
2849 A1428 1 multi + label 1.90 .95
2850 A1429 1 multi + label 1.90 .95
2851 A1430 1 multi + label 1.90 .95
2852 A1431 1 multi + label 1.90 .95
a. Horiz. strip of 5, #2848-2852, + 5 labels 9.50 4.75
Nos. 2848-2852 (5) 9.50 4.75

On day of issue, Nos. 2848-2852 each sold for 74c.

Miniature Sheet

Paintings by Peter Paul Rubens (1577-1640) — A1432

No. 2853: a, Christ and the Woman Taken into Adultery (28x41mm). b, Venus Frigida (28x41mm). c, Self-portrait (28x41mm). d, The Adoration of the Magi (56x41mm). e, The Miracles of St. Benedict (56x41mm).

2018, Mar. 12 Litho. *Perf. 11½*

2853 A1432 Sheet of 5 19.00 19.00
a.-e. 2 Any single 3.75 1.90

On day of issue, Nos. 2853a-2853e each sold for €1.48.

Miniature Sheet

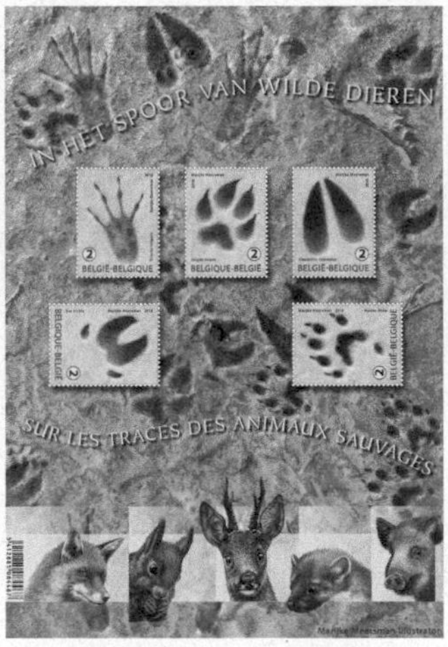

Animal Tracks — A1433

No. 2854 — Track of: a, Sciurus vulgaris. b, Vulpes vulpes. c, Capreolus capreolus. d, Sus scrofa, horiz. e, Martes foina, horiz.

Litho. & Embossed

2018, Mar. 12 *Perf. 12*

2854 A1433 Sheet of 5 19.00 19.00
a.-e. 2 Any single 3.75 1.90

On day of issue, Nos, 2854a-2854e each sold for €1.48.

2018 World Cup Soccer Championships, Russia — A1434

2018, June 11 Litho. *Perf. 12*

2855 A1434 1 Europe multi 3.00 1.50

No. 2855 sold for €1.30 on day of issue.

Youth Philately A1435

Litho. With Foil Application

2018, June 11 *Perf. 12*

2856 A1435 1 World multi 3.50 1.75

No. 2856 sold for €1.52 on day of issue.

Miniature Sheet

Reopening of Africa Museum, Tervuren — A1436

No. 2857: a, Large "A," sculpture by Aimé Mpané. b, Large "F," schistosomiasis parasite. c, Large "R," metal necklace. d, Large "I," new museum pavilion. e, Large "C," malachite.

2018, June 11 Litho. *Perf. 11½*

2857 A1436 Sheet of 5 + 20 labels 15.00 15.00
a.-e. 1 Europe Any single 3.00 1.50

On day of issue, Nos. 2857a-2857e each sold for €1.30.

Miniature Sheet

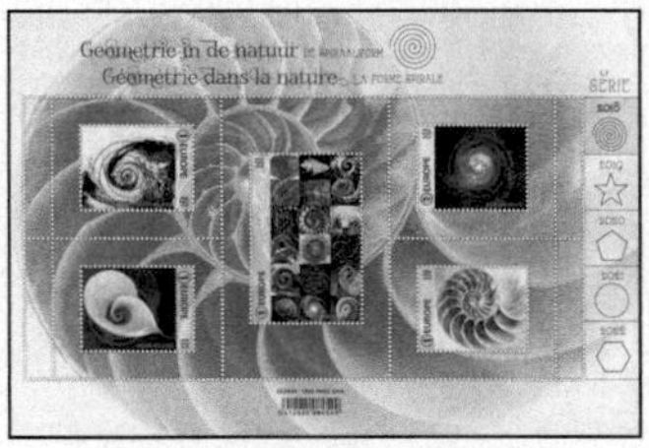

Spirals in Nature — A1437

No. 2858: a, Aerial photograph of hurricane (40x30mm). b, Milky Way galaxy (40x30mm). c, White arum leaf (40x30mm). d, Interior of nautilus shell (40x30mm). e, 18 spirals found in nature (40x60mm).

2018, June 11 Litho. *Perf. 12*

2858 A1437 Sheet of 5 + 4 labels 15.00 15.00
a.-e. 1 Europe Any single 3.00 1.50

On day of issue, Nos. 2858a-28587e each sold for €1.30. Nos. 2858a-2858e are each within a perforated frame of sheet margin.

Souvenir Sheet

Europa — A1438

No. 1438 — Pont des Trous, Tournais, with Europa emblem at: a, UR. b, UL.

Photo. & Engr.

2018, June 11 *Perf. 11½*

2859 A1438 Sheet of 2 18.00 18.00
a.-b. 3 Europe Either single 9.00 9.00

On day of issue, Nos. 2859a-2859b each sold for €3.90.

Fruit — A1439

Serpentine Die Cut 13¾x13½

2018, Aug. 27 Photo.

Coil Stamps
Self-Adhesive

2860 A1439 1 Gooseberry 2.00 2.00
2861 A1439 1 Raspberry 2.00 2.00
2862 A1439 1 Blackberry 2.00 2.00
2863 A1439 1 Blueberry 2.00 2.00
2864 A1439 1 Peach 2.00 2.00
2865 A1439 1 Pear 2.00 2.00
2866 A1439 1 Cherry 2.00 2.00
2867 A1439 1 Apple 2.00 2.00
2868 A1439 1 Strawberry 2.00 2.00
2869 A1439 1 Plum 2.00 2.00
a. Vert. strip of 10, #2860-2869 20.00
Nos. 2860-2869 (10) 20.00 20.00

Nos. 2860-2869 each sold for 84c on day of issue.

Miniature Sheet

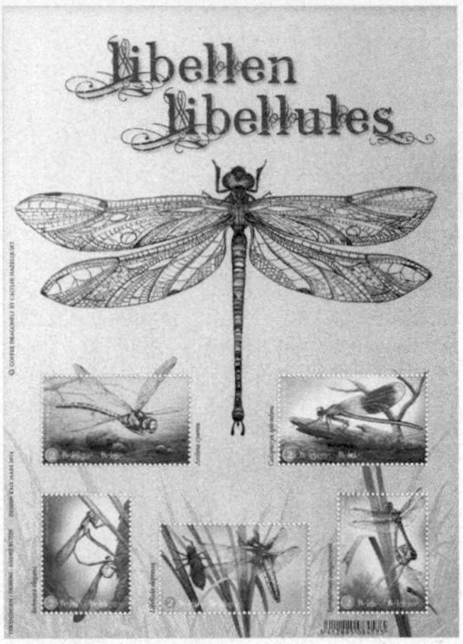

Dragonflies — A1440

No. 2870: a, Aeshna cyanea (50x30mm). b, Calopteryx splendens (50x30mm). c, Ischnura elegans (30x40mm). d, Libellula depressa (50x30mm). e, Sympetrum sanguineum (30x40mm).

2018, Aug. 27 Litho. *Perf. 12*

2870 A1440 Sheet of 5 20.00 20.00
a.-e. 2 Any single 4.00 4.00

On day of issue, Nos. 2870a-2870e each sold for €1.68. Latin names of insects are on sheet margin only.

Prehistoric Animals A1441

Designs: No. 2871, Coelodonta (40x40mm). No. 2872, Megaloceros (40x40mm). No. 2873, Mammuthus (40x40mm). No. 2874, Gastornis (60x60mm). No. 2875, Mosasaurus (60x40mm).

2018, Aug. 27 Litho. *Perf. 12*

2871 A1441 1 multi 2.00 2.00
2872 A1441 1 multi 2.00 2.00
2873 A1441 1 multi 2.00 2.00
2874 A1441 1 multi 2.00 2.00
2875 A1441 1 multi 2.00 2.00
a. Block of 5, #a-e 10.00 10.00
Nos. 2871-2875 (5) 10.00 10.00

On day of issue, Nos. 2871-2875 each sold for 84c.

Miniature Sheet

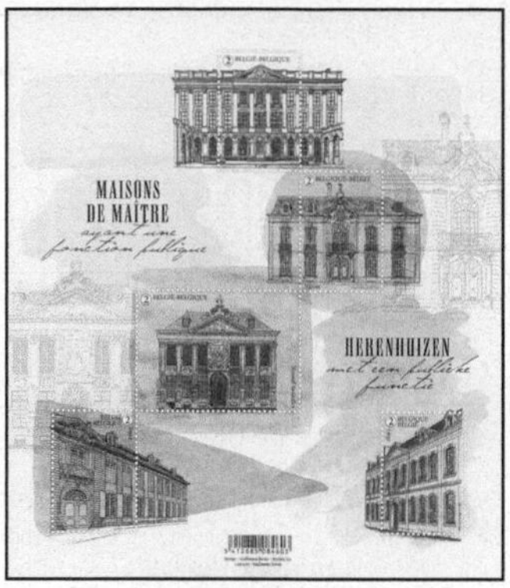

Mansions — A1442

No. 2876: a, Hôtel d'Hane Steenhuyse, Ghent (yellow background, 28x41mm). b, Comtesse d'Arrigade House, Namur (orange yellow background, 28x41mm). c, Bellone House, Brussels (brown ochre background, 56x41mm). d, Meghelynck Museum, Ypres (orange brown background, 28x41mm). e, Ansembourg Museum, Liège (blue violet background, 28x41mm).

Photo. & Engr.

2018, Oct. 22 ***Perf. 11½***

2876 A1442 Sheet of 5 20.00 20.00
a.-e. 2 Any single 4.00 4.00

On day of issue, Nos. 2876a-2876e each sold for €1.68.

Miniature Sheet

World War I, Cent. — A1443

No. 2877 — Events of 2018: a, Liberation (40x30mm). b, Monuments (37x50mm). c, Woman walking with soldier (40x30mm). d, Blinded soldier reading Braille book, wounded soldiers playing instruments (40x33mm). e, Reconstruction of railroad tracks (40x30mm).

2018, Oct. 22 Photo. ***Perf. 11½***

2877 A1443 Sheet of 5 15.00 15.00
a.-e. 1 Europe Any single 3.00 3.00

On day of issue, Nos. 2877a-2877e each sold for €1.30.

Souvenir Sheet

End of World War I, Cent. — A1444

No. 2878 — Poppy in center and: a, Soldiers, Menin Gate list of fallen soldiers and Tyne Cot cemetery. b, Destroyed buildings of Ypres, statue in Vladslo German war cemetery and trench walls.

2018, Oct. 22 Litho. ***Perf. 12***

2878 A1444 Sheet of 2 18.00 18.00
a.-b. 3 Europe Any single 9.00 9.00

On day of issue, Nos. 2878a-2878b each sold for €3.90.

Christmas
A1445 A1446

Die Cut Perf. 9¾x10 on 2 or 3 Sides

2018, Oct. 22 Litho.

Booklet Stamps
Self-Adhesive

2879 A1445 1 multi 1.90 1.90
a. Booklet pane of 10 19.00
2880 A1446 1 Europe multi 3.00 3.00
a. Booklet pane of 10 30.00

On day of issue, No. 2879 sold for 84c, and No. 2880 sold for €1.30.

King Philippe and Data Matrix Code A1447

2019, Jan. 2 Litho. ***Perf. 12***

2881 A1447 (97c) multi 2.25 2.25

Booklet Stamp
Self-Adhesive

Serpentine Die Cut 12¼x12½

2882 A1447 (97c) multi 2.25 2.25
a. Booklet pane of 10 22.50

Matrix codes differ on each stamp.

King Philippe Type of 2015

Die Cut Perf. 9¾x10 on 2 or 3 Sides

2019, Jan. 28 Litho.

Booklet Stamp
Self-Adhesive
Background Color

2883 A1323 1 fawn 2.10 2.10
a. Booklet pane of 10 21.00

No. 2883 sold for 92c on day of issue.

Candles and Data Matrix Code A1448

Serpentine Die Cut 12¼x12½

2019, Jan. 28 Litho.

Booklet Stamp
Self-Adhesive

2884 A1448 (97c) multi 2.25 2.25
a. Booklet pane of 10 22.50

Matrix codes differ on each stamp.

Bank Swallow — A1449

2019, Jan. 28 Litho. ***Perf. 11¾x11½***

2885 A1449 (46c) multi 1.10 1.10

Manneken Pis Statue, Brussels, 400th Anniv. A1450

2019, Jan. 28 Litho. ***Perf. 12½***

2886 A1450 1 World blk & yel 3.75 3.75

No. 2886 sold for €1.62 on day of issue.

Miniature Sheet

Animals at Work — A1451

No. 2887: a, Oxen pulling cart (50x30mm). b, Horse dragging logs (50x30mm). c, Donkey pulling carriage (40x30mm). d, Goat pulling cart (40x30mm). e, Rescue dog (30x40mm).

2019, Jan. 28 Litho. ***Perf. 12***

2887 A1451 Sheet of 5 21.50 21.50
a.-e. 2 Any single 4.25 4.25

Nos. 2887a-2887e each sold for €1.84 on day of issue.

Souvenir Sheet

Awarding of Neutral Moresnet to Belgium, Cent. — A1452

No. 2888: a, Map of Neutral Moresnet, Vieille Montagne Mining Company buildings. b, Privately produced stamps for Neutral Moresnet of 1886, postmarks, and soldiers near border markers.

2019, Jan. 28 Litho. ***Perf. 12***

2888 A1452 Sheet of 2 23.00 23.00
a.-b. 3 World Either single 11.50 11.50

Nos. 2888a-2888b each sold for €4.86 on day of issue.

Belgian Postal Codes, 50th Anniv. A1453

2019, Mar. 18 Litho. ***Perf. 12***

2889 A1453 1 multi 2.10 2.10

No. 2889 sold for 92c on day of issue.

Miniature Sheet

Belgian Participation in Space Exploration — A1454

No. 2890: a, Seven astronomical bodies. b, Mars and curved lines. c, Satellite over Earth, horiz. d, Automated Transfer Vehicle, horiz. e, Weather on other astronomical bodies.

2019, Mar. 18 Litho. ***Perf. 12***

2890 A1454 Sheet of 5 16.50 16.50
a.-e. 1 Europe Any single 3.25 3.25

Nos. 2890a-2890e each sold for €1.40 on day of issue.

Miniature Sheet

Pollinators — A1455

No. 2891: a, Danaus plexippus pollinating Buddleja davidii (40x30mm). b, Leptonycteris yerbabuenae pollinating Carnegiea gigantea (40x30mm). c, Cotinis nitida pollinating Magnolia grandiflora (40x50mm). d, Dasyscolia ciliata pollinating Ophrys speculum (30x40mm). e, Tarsipes rostratus pollinating Eucalyptus caesia (30x40mm).

2019, Mar. 18 Litho. ***Perf. 12***

2891 A1455 Sheet of 5 21.50 21.50
a.-e. 2 Any single 4.25 4.25

Nos. 2891a-2891e each sold for €1.84 on day of issue.

Stamp Printing in Mechelen, 150th Anniv. — A1456

No. 2892: a, Belgium #29. b, Belgium #30. c, Belgium #31,
No. 2893, Belgium #28. No. 2894, Belgium #28-31.

2019, Mar. 18 Litho. ***Perf. 11½***

2892 A1456 Sheet of 3 13.00 13.00
a.-c. 2 Any single 4.25 4.25

Souvenir Sheets
Photo. & Engr.

2893 A1456 2 multi 4.25 4.25

Digital Printing
Perf. 12

2894 A1456 2 multi 4.25 4.25

Nos. 2892a-2892c, 2893 and 2894 each sold for €1.84 on day of issue. No. 2894 contains one 40x40mm stamp.

First Horse-drawn Tram in Brussels, 150th Anniv. — A1457

2019, June 17 Litho. *Perf. 11½*
2895 A1457 2 multi 4.25 4.25

No. 2895 sold for €1.84 on day of issue.

Miniature Sheet

Star-shaped Items in Nature — A1458

No. 2896: a, Star (40x30mm). b, Starfish (40x30mm). c, 15 star-shaped items (40x60mm). d, Starfruit (40x30mm). e, Adenium multiflorum flower (40x30mm).

2019, June 17 Litho. *Perf. 12*
2896 A1458 Sheet of 5 + 4 labels 16.50 16.50
a.-e. 1 Europe Any single 3.25 3.25

Nos. 2896a-2896e each sold for €1.40 on day of issue, and are each within a perforated frame of sheet margin.

Stereotypical Life of Millennials — A1459

No. 2897: a, Hands and protest sign. b, Computer. c, Heart and Millennial woman's torso. d, Welcome mat. e, Smartphone, icons and symbols.

2019, June 17 Litho. *Perf. 12*
2897 A1459 Sheet of 5 21.50 21.50
a.-e. 2 Any single 4.25 4.25

Nos. 2897a-2897e each sold for €1.84 on day of issue.

Souvenir Sheet

Europa — A1460

No. 2898: a, Eurasian jay and nest (country name at bottom). b, Eurasian golden oriole and nest (country name at right).

2019, June 17 Litho. *Perf. 12*
2898 A1460 Sheet of 2 19.00 19.00
a.-b. 3 Europe Either single 9.50 9.50

Nos. 2898a-2898b each sold for €4.20 on day of issue.

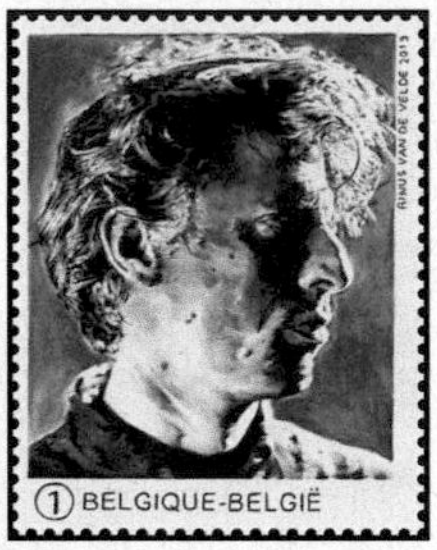

Self-portrait, by Rinus Van de Velde A1461

2019, Aug. 26 Litho. *Perf. 11½*
2899 A1461 1 multi 2.00 2.00

No. 2899 sold for 92c on day of issue.

Drawings of Heads of People, by Charlotte Peys — A1462

2019, Aug. 26 Litho. *Perf. 12*
2900 A1462 2 multi 4.00 4.00

Diversity. No. 2900 sold for €1.84 on day of issue.

Miniature Sheet

Pieter Bruegel the Elder (c.1525-69), Painter — A1463

No. 2901: a, Engraving of Bruegel by Johannes Wierix (1549-c. 1620) (28x41mm). b, Dulle Greit, by Bruegel ("2" at UL, 55x41mm). c, Winter Landscape with Skaters and Bird Trap, by Bruegel (28x41mm). d, The Fall of the Rebel Angels, by Bruegel ("2" at LL, brownish black frame, 55x41mm). e, The Census at Bethlehem, by Bruegel ("2" at LL, orange brown frame, 55x41mm).

Photo. & Engr. (#2901a), Photo. (#2901b-2901e)

2019, Aug. 26 *Perf. 11½*
2901 A1463 Sheet of 5 20.00 20.00
a.-e. 2 Any single 4.00 4.00

On day of issue, Nos. 2901a-2901e each sold for €1.84.

Crown Princess Elisabeth, 18th Birthday — A1464

2019, Oct. 21 Litho. *Perf. 12*
2902 A1464 2 multi 4.25 4.25

No. 2902 sold for €1.84 on day of issue.

Miniature Sheet

Cars of Belgian Winners of the 24 Hours of Le Mans Race — A1465

No. 2903: a, Paul Frère and Olivier Gendebien's 1960 Ferrari 250 TR60 (73x28mm). b, Gendebien's 1958 Ferrari 250 TR58 (49x28mm). c, Lucien Bianchi's 1968 Type Ford GT40 (49x28mm). d, Bertrand Gachot's 1991 Mazda 787B (49x28mm). e, Jacky Ickx's 1982 Porsche 956 (97x28mm).

Litho. & Engr.

2019, Oct. 21 *Perf. 11½*
2903 A1465 Sheet of 5 19.00 19.00
a.-e. 1 World Any single 3.75 3.75

On day of issue, Nos. 2903a-2903e each sold for €1.62.

Miniature Sheet

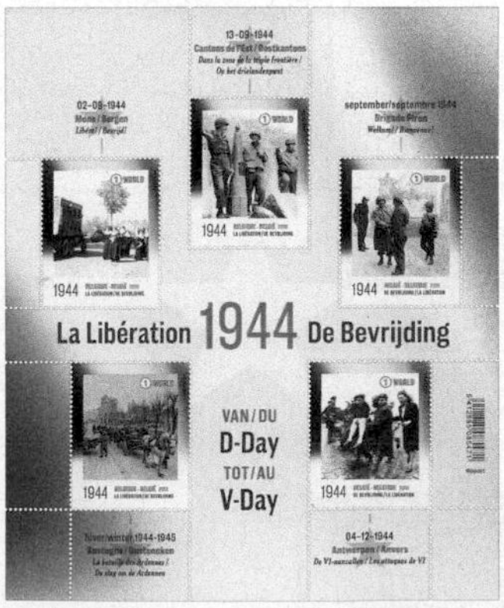

Beginning of Battles to Liberate Belgium, 75th Anniv. — A1466

No. 2904: a, Nuns greeting American soldiers at Mons, Sept. 2, 1944. b, Three soldiers near monuments, Sept. 13, 1944. c, Piron Brigade soldiers and tank, Sept. 1944. d, Civilians with horse-drawn cart fleeing Bastogne, Winter of 1944-45. e, Soldiers carrying woman injured in V-1 attack on Antwerp, Dec. 4, 1944.

2019, Oct. 21 Litho. *Perf. 12*
2904 A1466 Sheet of 5 19.00 19.00
a.-e. 1 World Any single 3.75 3.75

On day of issue, Nos. 2904a-2904e each sold for €1.62.

Christmas
A1467 A1468

Die Cut Perf. 9¾x10 on 2 or 3 Sides
2019, Oct. 21 Litho.
Booklet Stamps
Self-Adhesive

2905 A1467 1 multi 2.10 2.10
a. Booklet pane of 10 21.00
2906 A1468 1 Europe multi 3.25 3.25
a. Booklet pane of 10 32.50

No. 2905 sold for 92c and No. 2906 sold for €1.40 on day of issue.

A1469

A1470

A1471

A1472

Characters from *Bob and Bobette,* Comic Strip by Willy Vandersteen (1913-90) — A1473

2020, Jan. 27 Litho. *Perf. 12*
2907 Horiz. strip of 5 11.50 11.50
a. A1469 1 multi 2.25 2.25
b. A1470 1 multi 2.25 2.25
c. A1471 1 multi 2.25 2.25
d. A1472 1 multi 2.25 2.25
e. A1473 1 multi 2.25 2.25

Bob and Bobette comic strip, 75th anniv.

Miniature Sheet

Old Belgian Stamps — A1474

No. 2908: a, Belgium #1. b, Belgium #135. c, Belgium #139a. d, Belgium #B48. e, Belgium #298.

Photo. & Engr. (#2908c), Photo. (#2908a-2908b, 2908d-2908e)

2020, Jan. 27 ***Perf. 11½***

2908	A1474	Sheet of 5	22.50	22.50
a.-e.		2 Any single	4.50	4.50

On day of issue, Nos. 2908a-2908e each sold for €1.96.

Miniature Sheet

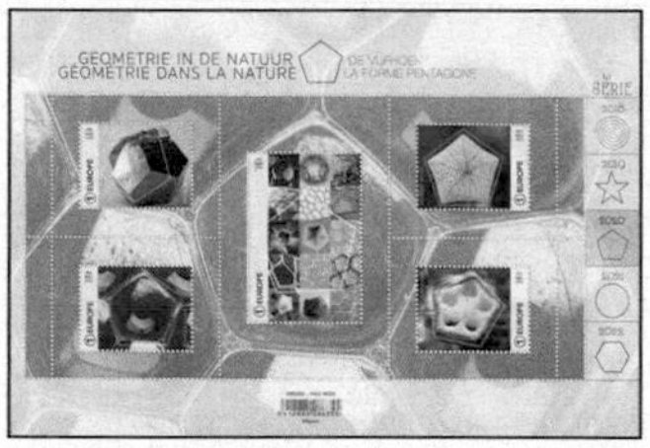

Pentagonal Items in Nature — A1475

No. 2909: a, Pyrite crystal (40x30mm). b, Platycodon grandiflorus (40x30mm). c, 15 pentagonal items (40x60mm). d, Group of connected soap bubbles (40x30mm). e, Sliced okra pod (40x30mm).

2020, Jan. 27 **Litho.** ***Perf. 12***

2909	A1475	Sheet of 5 + 4 labels	17.50	17.50
a.-e.		1 Europe Any single	3.50	3.50

Nos. 2909a-2909e each sold for €1.55 on day of issue, and are each within a perforated frame of sheet margin.

King Philippe, 60th Birthday A1476

2020, Mar. 16 **Litho.** ***Perf. 12½***

2910	A1476	1 multi	2.10	2.10

No. 2910 sold for 98c on day of issue.

United Nations, 75th Anniv. A1477

2020, Mar. 16 **Litho.** ***Perf. 12***

2911	A1477	1 World multi	4.00	4.00

No. 2911 sold for €1.77 on day of issue.

Miniature Sheet

Pigeon Racing — A1478

No. 2912: a, Carrier pigeons and feathers (40x30mm). b, Armando, racing pigeon sold in 2019 for $1,400,000. (40x50mm). c, Soldier on mobile dovecote (40x30mm). d, Prize card (40x30mm). e, Pigeon keeper in window, pigeons on window sills (40x30mm).

2020, Mar. 16 **Litho.** ***Perf. 12***

2912	A1478	Sheet of 5 + 2 labels	20.00	20.00
a.-e.		1 World Any single	4.00	4.00

On day of issue, Nos. 2912a-2912e each sold for €1.77.

Miniature Sheet

Paintings by Jan van Eyck (c. 1390-1441) — A1479

No. 2913: a, God on throne from Ghent Altarpiece (29x40mm). b, Margareta van Eyck (25x38mm). c, Portrait of a Man with a Blue Chaperon (25x38mm). d, Madonna and Child at the Fountain (30x42mm). e, Madonna and Child with Canon Joris van der Paele (30x42mm).

Serpentine Die Cut 19 (#2913a-2913c), Serpentine Die Cut 14¼ (#2913d-2913e)

2020, Mar. 16 **Litho.**

Self-Adhesive

2913	A1479	Sheet of 5	21.50	
a.-e.		2 Any single	4.25	4.25

On day of issue, Nos. 2913a-2913e each sold for €1.96.

"Soccer Unites" — A1480

2020, June 15 **Litho.** ***Perf. 12***

2914	A1480	1 Europe multi	3.50	3.50

No. 2914 sold for €1.55 on day of issue.

2020 Summer Olympics, Tokyo — A1481

2020, June 15 **Litho.** ***Perf. 12***

2915	A1481	1 World multi	4.00	4.00

No. 2915 sold for €1.77 on day of issue. The 2020 Summer Olympics were postponed until 2021 because of the coronavirus pandemic.

Souvenir Sheet

Europa — A1482

No. 2916 — 19th century postal badges depicting: a, Lion. b, Crown and "W."

Litho. & Embossed

2020, June 15 ***Perf. 12***

2916	A1482	Sheet of 2	21.00	21.00
a.-b.		3 Europe Either single	10.50	10.50

On day of issue, Nos. 2916a-2916b each sold for €4.65.

Alzheimer's Disease Awareness A1483

2020, Aug. 31 **Litho.** ***Perf. 12***

2917	A1483	1 multi	2.40	2.40
a.		Tete-beche pair	4.80	4.80

No. 2917 sold for 98c on day of issue.

Hedgehog A1484

Barn Owl A1485

Red Squirrel A1486

Asian Ladybug A1487

Turkish Turtledove A1488

European Rabbit A1489

Green Frog A1490

Honeybee A1491

Gray Mouse A1492

European Robin A1493

Die Cut Perf. 8¾

2020, Aug. 31 **Litho.**

Self-Adhesive

2918	A1484	1 multi	2.40	2.40
2919	A1485	1 multi	2.40	2.40
2920	A1486	1 multi	2.40	2.40
2921	A1487	1 multi	2.40	2.40
2922	A1488	1 multi	2.40	2.40
2923	A1489	1 multi	2.40	2.40
2924	A1490	1 multi	2.40	2.40
2925	A1491	1 multi	2.40	2.40
2926	A1492	1 multi	2.40	2.40
2927	A1493	1 multi	2.40	2.40
a.		Block of 10, #2918-2927	24.00	
		Nos. 2918-2927 (10)	24.00	24.00

On day of issue, Nos. 2918-2927 each sold for 98c. Nos. 2918-2927 were printed in folded sheets of 50 stamps, containing five No. 2927a.

Miniature Sheet

Abbeys — A1494

No. 2928: a, Chevetogne Abbey, Chevetogne. b, Postel Abbey, Mol. c, St. Andrew's Abbey, Zevenkerken. d, Maredsous Abbey, Maredsous. e, Westmalle Abbey, Westmalle.

Photo. & Engr.

2020, Aug. 31 ***Perf. 11½***

2928	A1494	Sheet of 5	24.00	24.00
a.-e.		2 Any single	4.75	4.75

On day of issue, Nos. 2928a-2928e each sold for €1.96.

Miniature Sheet

The Roaring Twenties — A1495

No. 2929: a, Flapper. b, House of Léon Stynen (1899-1990), architect. c, Automobiles. d, Legs of dancing man. e, Toaster.

2020, Aug. 31 Litho. *Perf. 12*

2929	A1495	Sheet of 5	24.00	24.00
a.-e.		2 Any single	4.75	4.75

On day of issue, Nos. 2929a-2929e each sold for €1.96.

Miniature Sheet

European Big Game Animals — A1496

No. 2930: a, European bison (40x60mm). b, Wolverine (glouton) (70x30mm). c, European brown bear (ours brun) (70x40mm). d, Lynx (30x60mm). e, Wolf (30x60mm).

2020, Aug. 31 Litho. *Perf. 12*

2930	A1496	Sheet of 5	24.00	24.00
a.-e.		2 Any single	4.75	4.75

On day of issue, Nos. 2930a-2930e each sold for €1.96.

Walburga, Sculpture by Berlinde De Bruyckere — A1497

2020, Oct. 26 Litho. *Perf. 11½*

2931	A1497	1 multi	2.25	2.25

No. 2931 sold for 98c on day of issue.

Santa Claus-Shaped Speculaas Cookie, Cinnamon Sticks, Star Anise and Cloves — A1498

Santa Claus Stamp for Speculaas Cookie and Cinnamon Sticks — A1499

2020, Oct. 26 Litho. *Perf. 11½*

2932	A1498	1 multi	2.25	2.25
2933	A1499	1 multi	2.25	2.25
a.		Horiz. pair, #2932-2933	4.50	4.50

Printed in sheets of 10 containing five each Nos. 2932-2933. On day of issue, Nos. 2932-2933 each sold for 98c.

Mushrooms A1500

No. 2934: a, Crucibulum crucibuliforme (30x40mm). b, Clathrus ruber (30x40mm). c, Clathrus archeri (50x40mm). d, Geastrum quadrifidum (30x40mm). e, Calocera viscosa (30x40mm).

2020, Oct. 26 Litho. *Perf. 12*

2934		Horiz. strip of 5	11.50	11.50
a.-e.		A1500 1 Any single	2.25	2.25

Printed in sheets containing two horizontal strips. In the horizontal strip of 5, Nos. 2934b and 2934c are placed higher than the other stamps. On day of issue, Nos. 2934a-2934e each sold for 98c.

Miniature Sheet

Sculpture and Grave Markers in Belgian Cemeteries — A1501

No. 2935: a, Grave marker of composer Franz De Vos and his wife, Hortense, Ghent (29x37mm). b, Goblet d'Alviella Mausoleum and Sphinx, Court-Saint Etienne (29x37mm). c, The Thinker, statue by Auguste Rodin, Laeken (29x37mm). d, Grave marker of author Hendrik Conscience (1812-83), Antwerp (29x37mm). e, Cemetery entrance gate, Mons (58x37mm).

Litho. & Engr.

2020, Oct. 26 *Perf. 13x13½*

2935	A1501	Sheet of 5	22.50	22.50
a.-e.		2 Any single	4.50	4.50

On day of issue, Nos. 2935a-2935e each sold for €1.96.

Reindeer

A1502 A1503

Die Cut Perf. 10 on 2 or 3 Sides

2020, Oct. 26 Litho.

Booklet Stamps Self-Adhesive Background Color

2936	A1502	1 red	2.25	2.25
a.		Booklet pane of 10	22.50	
2937	A1503	1 Europe green	3.75	3.75
a.		Booklet pane of 10	37.50	

Christmas. On day of issue, No. 2936 sold for 98c, and No. 2937 sold for €1.55.

SEMI-POSTAL STAMPS

Values quoted for Nos. B1-B24 are for stamps with label attached. Stamps without label sell for one-tenth or less.

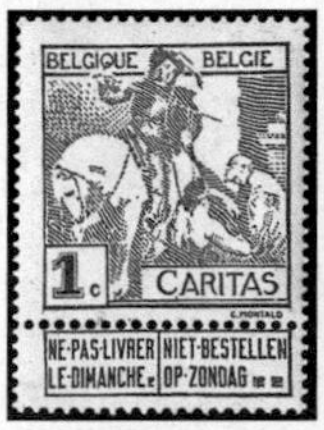

St. Martin of Tours Dividing His Cloak with a Beggar

SP1 SP2

Unwmk.

1910, June 1 Typo. *Perf. 14*

B1	SP1	1c gray	.80	.80
B2	SP1	2c purple brn	8.75	8.75
B3	SP1	5c peacock blue	2.40	2.40
B4	SP1	10c brown red	2.40	2.40
B5	SP2	1c gray green	2.40	2.40
B6	SP2	2c violet brn	6.50	6.50
B7	SP2	5c peacock blue	2.40	2.40
B8	SP2	10c carmine	2.40	2.40
		Nos. B1-B8 (8)	28.05	28.05
		Set, never hinged	85.00	

Overprinted "1911" in Black

1911, Apr. 1

B9	SP1	1c gray	27.50	16.00
a.		Inverted overprint		
B10	SP1	2c purple brn	125.00	72.50
B11	SP1	5c peacock blue	8.00	5.25
B12	SP1	10c brown red	8.00	5.25
B13	SP2	1c gray green	42.50	27.50
B14	SP2	2c violet brn	60.00	32.50
B15	SP2	5c peacock blue	8.00	5.25
B16	SP2	10c carmine	8.00	5.25
		Nos. B9-B16 (8)	287.00	169.50
		Set, never hinged	600.00	

Overprinted "CHARLEROI-1911"

1911, June

B17	SP1	1c gray	4.00	2.50
B18	SP1	2c purple brn	16.00	10.00
B19	SP1	5c peacock blue	9.00	6.50
B20	SP1	10c brown red	9.00	6.50
B21	SP2	1c gray green	4.00	2.50
B22	SP2	2c violet brn	11.00	9.00
B23	SP2	5c peacock blue	9.00	6.50
B24	SP2	10c carmine	9.00	6.50
		Nos. B17-B24 (8)	71.00	50.00
		Set, never hinged	250.00	

Nos. B1-B24 were sold at double face value, except the 10c denominations which were sold for 15c. The surtax benefited the national anti-tuberculosis organization.

King Albert I — SP3

1914, Oct. 3 Litho.

B25	SP3	5c green & red	*3.00*	*3.00*
B26	SP3	10c red	*.35*	*.35*
B27	SP3	20c violet & red	*10.00*	*10.00*
		Nos. B25-B27 (3)	*13.35*	*13.35*
		Set, never hinged	*45.00*	

Counterfeits of Nos. B25-B27 abound. Probably as many as 90% of the stamps on the market are counterfeits. Values are for genuine examples.

Merode Monument — SP4

1914, Oct. 3

B28	SP4	5c green & red	*2.50*	*2.50*
B29	SP4	10c red	*4.00*	*4.00*
B30	SP4	20c violet & red	*50.00*	*50.00*
		Nos. B28-B30 (3)	*56.50*	*56.50*
		Set, never hinged	*160.00*	

Counterfeits of Nos. B28-B30 abound. Probably as many as 90% of the stamps on the market are counterfeits. Genuine stamps have a tail on the "Q" of "BELGIQUE" at the top of the stamp, counterfeits don't have a tail. Values are for genuine examples.

King Albert I — SP5

1915, Jan. 1 *Perf. 12, 14*

B31	SP5	5c green & red	10.00	2.00
a.		Perf. 12x14	40.00	14.00
B32	SP5	10c rose & red	29.00	10.00
B33	SP5	20c violet & red	50.00	16.00
a.		Perf. 14x12	650.00	275.00
b.		Perf. 12	55.00	35.00
		Nos. B31-B33 (3)	89.00	28.00
		Set, never hinged	300.00	

Nos. B25-B33 were sold at double face value. The surtax benefited the Red Cross.

Types of Regular Issue of 1915 Surcharged in Red

Nos. B34-B40

Nos. B41-B43

Nos. B44-B47

1918, Jan. 15 Typo. *Perf. 14*

B34	A46	1c + 1c dp orange	.25	.25
B35	A46	2c + 2c brown	.25	.25
B36	A46	5c + 5c blue grn	1.10	1.10
B37	A46	10c + 10c red	2.50	2.50
B38	A46	15c + 15c brt violet	5.50	5.50
B39	A46	20c + 20c plum	10.00	10.00
B40	A46	25c + 25c ultra	24.00	24.00
		Engr.		
B41	A47	35c + 35c lt vio & blk	10.00	10.00
B42	A48	40c + 40c dull red & blk	10.00	10.00
B43	A49	50c + 50c turq blue & blk	12.00	12.00
B44	A50	1fr + 1fr bluish slate	37.50	37.50
B45	A51	2fr + 2fr dp gray grn	85.00	85.00
B46	A52	5fr + 5fr brown	200.00	200.00
B47	A53	10fr + 10fr dp blue	650.00	650.00
		Nos. B34-B47 (14)	1,048.	1,048.
		Set, never hinged	3,000.	

Discus Thrower — SP6

Racing Chariot — SP7

Runner — SP8

1920, May 20 Engr. *Perf. 12*

B48	SP6	5c + 5c dp green	1.40	1.40
B49	SP7	10c + 5c carmine	1.40	1.40
B50	SP8	15c + 15c dk brown	3.00	3.00
		Nos. B48-B50 (3)	5.80	5.80
		Set, never hinged	20.00	

7th Olympic Games, 1920. Surtax benefited wounded soldiers.

For surcharges see Nos. 140-142.

Allegory: Asking Alms from the Crown — SP9

1922, May 20

B51	SP9	20c + 20c brown	1.40	1.40
		Never hinged	3.00	

Wounded Veteran — SP10

1923, July 5

B52	SP10	20c + 20c slate gray	2.50	2.50
		Never hinged	7.50	

Surtax on Nos. B51-B52 was to aid wounded veterans.

SP11

1925, Dec. 15 **Typo.** ***Perf. 14***

B53	SP11	15c + 5c dull vio & red	.25	.25
B54	SP11	30c + 5c gray & red	.25	.25
B55	SP11	1fr + 10c chalky blue & red	1.25	1.25
		Nos. B53-B55 (3)	1.75	1.75
		Set, never hinged	2.50	

Surtax for the Natl. Anti-Tuberculosis League.

SP12

St. Martin, by Van Dyck
SP13 SP14

1926, Feb. 10

B56	SP12	30c + 30c bluish grn (red surch.)	.50	.50
B57	SP13	1fr + 1fr lt blue	5.50	5.50
B58	SP14	1fr + 1fr lt blue	1.10	1.25
		Nos. B56-B58 (3)	7.10	7.25
		Set, never hinged	16.00	

The surtax aided victims of the Meuse flood.

Lion and Cross of Lorraine — SP15

Queen Elisabeth and King Albert SP16

1926, Dec. 6 **Typo.** ***Perf. 14***

B59	SP15	5c + 5c dk brown	.25	.25
B60	SP15	20c + 5c red brown	.45	.40
B61	SP15	50c + 5c dull violet	.25	.25

Perf. 11½

Engr.

B62	SP16	1.50fr + 25c dk blue	.70	.70
B63	SP16	5fr + 1fr rose red	6.50	6.00
		Nos. B59-B63 (5)	8.15	7.60
		Set, never hinged	16.00	

Surtax was used to benefit tubercular war veterans.

Boat Adrift SP17

1927, Dec. 15 **Engr.** ***Perf. 11½, 14***

B64	SP17	25c + 10c dk brn	.70	.70
B65	SP17	35c + 10c yel grn	.70	.70
B66	SP17	60c + 10c dp vio	.25	.25
B67	SP17	1.75fr + 25c dk blue	1.25	*1.25*
B68	SP17	5fr + 1fr plum	4.50	*4.50*
		Nos. B64-B68 (5)	7.40	*7.40*
		Set, never hinged	16.00	

The surtax on these stamps was divided among several charitable associations.

Ogives of Orval Abbey — SP18

Monk Carving Capital of Column — SP19

Ruins of Orval Abbey SP20

Design: 60c+15c, 1.75fr+25c, 3fr+1fr, Countess Matilda recovering her ring.

1928, Sept. 15 **Photo.** ***Perf. 11½***

B69	SP18	5c + 5c red & gold	.25	.25
B70	SP18	25c + 5c dk vio & gold	.40	.40

Engr.

B71	SP19	35c + 10c dp grn	1.10	1.10
B72	SP19	60c + 15c red brn	.75	.75
B73	SP19	1.75fr + 25c dk blue	3.00	3.00
B74	SP19	2fr + 40c dp vio	27.50	27.50
B75	SP19	3fr + 1fr red	25.00	25.00

Perf. 14

B76	SP20	5fr + 5fr rose lake	16.00	16.00
B77	SP20	10fr + 10fr ol green	16.00	16.00
		Nos. B69-B77 (9)	90.00	90.00
		Set, never hinged	200.00	

Surtax for the restoration of the ruined Orval Abbey.

St. Waudru, Mons — SP22

St. Rombaut, Malines — SP23

Designs: 25c + 15c, Cathedral of Tournai. 60c + 15c, St. Bavon, Ghent. 1.75fr + 25c, St. Gudule, Brussels. 5fr + 5fr, Louvain Library.

1928, Dec. 1 **Photo.** ***Perf. 14, 11½***

B78	SP22	5c + 5c carmine	.25	.25
B79	SP22	25c + 15c ol brn	.25	.25

Engr.

B80	SP23	35c + 10c dp grn	1.25	1.25
B81	SP23	60c + 15c red brn	.45	.45
B82	SP23	1.75fr + 25c vio bl	9.00	9.00
B83	SP23	5fr + 5fr red vio	20.00	20.00
		Nos. B78-B83 (6)	31.20	31.20
		Set, never hinged	65.00	

The surtax was for anti-tuberculosis work.

Nos. B69-B77 with this overprint in blue or red were privately produced. They were for the laying of the 1st stone toward the restoration of the ruined Abbey of Orval. Value, set, $650.

Forgeries of the overprint exist.

Waterfall at Coo — SP28

Bayard Rock, Dinant — SP29

Designs: 35c+10c, Menin Gate, Ypres. 60c+15c, Promenade d'Orleans, Spa. 1.75fr+25c, Antwerp Harbor. 5fr+5fr, Quai Vert, Bruges.

1929, Dec. 2 **Engr.** ***Perf. 11½***

B93	SP28	5c + 5c red brn	.25	.25
B94	SP29	25c + 15c gray blk	1.50	1.50
B95	SP28	35c + 10c green	1.25	1.25
B96	SP28	60c + 15c rose lake	.50	.50
B97	SP28	1.75fr + 25c dp blue	9.00	9.00

Perf. 14

B98	SP29	5fr + 5fr dl vio	35.00	35.00
		Nos. B93-B98 (6)	47.50	47.50
		Set, never hinged	100.00	

Bornhem — SP34

Beloeil — SP35

Gaesbeek SP36

25c + 15c, Wynendaele. 70c + 15c, Oydonck. 1fr + 25c, Ghent. 1.75fr + 25c, Bouillon.

1930, Dec. 1 **Photo.** ***Perf. 14***

B99	SP34	10c + 5c violet	.35	*.35*
B100	SP34	25c + 15c olive brn	1.00	1.00

Engr.

B101	SP35	40c + 10c brn vio	.90	*.90*
B102	SP35	70c + 15c gray blk	.90	.90
B103	SP35	1fr + 25c rose lake	7.50	7.50
B104	SP35	1.75fr + 25c dp bl	5.00	5.00
B105	SP36	5fr + 5fr gray grn	40.00	*40.00*
		Nos. B99-B105 (7)	55.65	*55.65*
		Set, never hinged	150.00	

Philatelic Exhibition Issue

Souvenir Sheet

Prince Leopold — SP41

1931, July 18 **Photo.** ***Perf. 14***

B106	SP41	2.45fr + 55c car brn	225.00	225.00
		Never hinged	650.00	
a.		Single stamp	75.00	75.00

Sold exclusively at the Brussels Phil. Exhib., July 18-21, 1931. Size: 122x159mm. Surtax for the Veterans' Relief Fund.

The sheet normally has pin holes and a cancellation-like marking in the margin. These are considered unused and the condition valued here.

Queen Elisabeth — SP42

1931, Dec. 1 **Engr.**

B107	SP42	10c + 5c red brn	.25	*.25*
B108	SP42	25c + 15c dk vio	1.25	*.50*
B109	SP42	50c + 10c dk grn	.75	*.50*
B110	SP42	75c + 15c blk brn	.85	.25
B111	SP42	1fr + 25c rose lake	8.00	7.00
B112	SP42	1.75fr + 25c ultra	7.00	4.75
B113	SP42	5fr + 5fr brn vio	65.00	65.00
		Nos. B107-B113 (7)	83.10	78.25
		Set, never hinged	175.00	

The surtax was for the National Anti-Tuberculosis League.

Désiré Cardinal Mercier — SP43

Mercier Protecting Children and Aged at Malines — SP44

Mercier as Professor at Louvain University — SP45

Mercier in Full Canonicals, Giving His Blessing SP46

1932, June 10 Photo. ***Perf. 14½x14***
B114 SP43 10c + 10c dk violet .60 *.60*
B115 SP43 50c + 30c brt violet 1.75 *1.75*
B116 SP43 75c + 25c olive brn 1.75 1.75
B117 SP43 1fr + 2fr brown red 7.25 7.25

Engr. ***Perf. 11½***
B118 SP44 1.75fr + 75c dp blue 85.00 *85.00*
B119 SP45 2.50fr + 2.50fr dk brn 85.00 85.00
B120 SP44 3fr + 4.50fr dull grn 85.00 85.00
B121 SP45 5fr + 20fr vio brn 100.00 *100.00*
B122 SP46 10fr + 40fr brn lake 225.00 *225.00*
Nos. B114-B122 (9) 591.35 *591.35*
Set, never hinged 1,050.

Honoring Cardinal Mercier and to obtain funds to erect a monument to his memory.

Belgian Infantryman — SP47

1932, Aug. 4 ***Perf. 14½x14***
B123 SP47 75c + 3.25fr red brn 80.00 80.00
Never hinged 125.00
B124 SP47 1.75fr + 4.25fr dk blue 80.00 80.00
Never hinged 125.00

Honoring Belgian soldiers who fought in WWI and to obtain funds to erect a natl. monument to their glory.

Sanatorium at Waterloo SP48

1932, Dec. 1 Photo. ***Perf. 13½x14***
B125 SP48 10c + 5c dk vio .30 *.90*
B126 SP48 25c + 15c red vio 1.00 *1.25*
B127 SP48 50c + 10c red brn 1.00 *1.25*
B128 SP48 75c + 15c ol brn 1.00 .80
B129 SP48 1fr + 25c dp red 15.00 12.50
B130 SP48 1.75fr + 25c dp blue 11.00 10.00
B131 SP48 5fr + 5fr gray grn 100.00 *100.00*
Nos. B125-B131 (7) 129.30 *126.70*
Set, never hinged 250.00

Surtax for the assistance of the Natl. Anti-Tuberculosis Society at Waterloo.

View of Old Abbey SP49

Ruins of Old Abbey — SP50

Count de Chiny Presenting First Abbey to Countess Matilda SP56

Restoration of Abbey in XVI and XVII Centuries SP57

Abbey in XVIII Century, Maria Theresa and Charles V — SP58

Madonna and Arms of Seven Abbeys SP60

Designs: 25c+15c, Guests, courtyard, 50c+25c, Transept. 75c+50c, Bell Tower. 1fr+1.25fr, Fountain. 1.25fr+1.75fr, Cloisters. 5fr+20fr, Duke of Brabant placing 1st stone of new abbey.

1933, Oct. 15 ***Perf. 14***
B132 SP49 5c + 5c dull grn 70.00 *70.00*
B133 SP50 10c + 15c ol grn 70.00 *70.00*
B134 SP49 25c + 15c dk brn 50.00 *50.00*
B135 SP50 50c + 25c red brn 50.00 *50.00*
B136 SP50 75c + 50c dp grn 50.00 *50.00*
B137 SP50 1fr + 1.25fr cop red 50.00 *50.00*
B138 SP49 1.25fr + 1.75fr gray blk 50.00 *50.00*
B139 SP56 1.75fr + 2.75fr blue 95.00 *50.00*
B140 SP57 2fr + 3fr mag 95.00 *50.00*
B141 SP58 2.50fr + 5fr dull brn 95.00 *50.00*
B142 SP56 5fr + 20fr vio 125.00 *65.00*

Perf. 11½
B143 SP60 10fr + 40fr bl 375.00 *375.00*
Nos. B132-B143 (12) 1,175. *980.00*
Set, never hinged 2,500.

The surtax was for a fund to aid in the restoration of Orval Abbey. Counterfeits exist.

"Tuberculosis Society" — SP61

1933, Dec. 1 Engr. ***Perf. 14x13½***
B144 SP61 10c + 5c blk .75 .75
B145 SP61 25c + 15c vio 2.75 2.75
B146 SP61 50c + 10c red brn 2.50 2.50
B147 SP61 75c + 15c blk brn 35.00 .50
B148 SP61 1fr + 25c cl 18.00 18.00
B149 SP61 1.75fr + 25c vio bl 21.00 21.00
B150 SP61 5fr + 5fr lilac 175.00 140.00
Nos. B144-B150 (7) 255.00 185.50
Set, never hinged 350.00

The surtax was for anti-tuberculosis work.

Peter Benoit — SP62

1934, June 1 **Photo.**
B151 SP62 75c + 25c olive brn 6.00 6.00
Never hinged 15.00

The surtax was to raise funds for the Peter Benoit Memorial.

SP63

King Leopold III — SP64

1934, Sept. 15
B152 SP63 75c + 25c ol blk 17.00 17.00
Never hinged 40.00
a. Sheet of 20 1,200. 1,200.
Never hinged 1,500.
B153 SP64 1fr + 25c red vio 17.00 17.00
Never hinged 40.00
a. Sheet of 20 1,200. 1,200.
Never hinged 1,500.

The surtax aided the National War Veterans' Fund. Sold for 4.50fr a set at the Exhibition of War Postmarks 1914-18, held at Brussels by the Royal Philatelic Club of Veterans. The price included an exhibition ticket. Sold at Brussels post office Sept. 18-22. No. B152 printed in sheets of 20 (4x5) and 100 (10x10). No. B153 printed in sheets of 20 (4x5) and 150 (10x15).

1934, Sept. 24
B154 SP63 75c + 25c violet 3.00 3.00
Never hinged 15.00
B155 SP64 1fr + 25c red brn 7.50 7.50
Never hinged 15.00

The surtax aided the National War Veterans' Fund. No. B154 printed in sheets of 100 (10x10); No. B155 in sheets of 150 (10x15). These stamps remained in use one year.

Crusader SP65

1934, Nov. 17 Engr. ***Perf. 13½x14***
Cross in Red
B156 SP65 10c + 5c blk .25 .25
B157 SP65 25c + 15c brn 3.50 3.50
B158 SP65 50c + 10c dull grn 2.25 2.25
B159 SP65 75c + 15c vio brn 1.25 1.25
B160 SP65 1fr + 25c rose 14.00 14.00
B161 SP65 1.75fr + 25c ultra 12.00 12.00
B162 SP65 5fr + 5fr brn vio 145.00 145.00
Nos. B156-B162 (7) 178.25 178.25
Set, never hinged 550.00

The surtax was for anti-tuberculosis work.

Prince Baudouin, Princess Josephine and Prince Albert SP66

1935, Apr. 10 **Photo.**
B163 SP66 35c + 15c dk grn 1.25 1.10
B164 SP66 70c + 30c red brn 1.25 .90
B165 SP66 1.75fr + 50c dk blue 4.50 *5.25*
Nos. B163-B165 (3) 7.00 *7.25*
Set, never hinged 20.00

Surtax was for Child Welfare Society.

Stagecoach — SP67

1935, Apr. 27
B166 SP67 10c + 10c ol blk .75 .80
B167 SP67 25c + 25c bis brn 2.25 2.10
B168 SP67 35c + 25c dk green 3.00 2.75
Nos. B166-B168 (3) 6.00 5.65
Set, never hinged 15.00

Printed in sheets of 10. Value, set of 3 unused, $150; never hinged, $175.

Souvenir Sheet

Franz von Taxis — SP68

1935, May 25 Engr. ***Perf. 14***
B169 SP68 5fr + 5fr grnsh blk 200.00 200.00
Never hinged 600.00
a. Single stamp 125.00 125.00
Never hinged 150.00

Sheets measure 91½x117mm.
Nos. B166-B169 were issued for the Brussels Philatelic Exhibition (SITEB).
The sheet normally has pin holes and a cancellation-like marking in the margin. These are considered unused and the condition valued here.

Queen Astrid — SP69

1935 Photo. ***Perf. 11½***
Borders in Black
B170 SP69 10c + 5c ol blk .25 .25
B171 SP69 25c + 15c brown .25 *.30*
B172 SP69 35c + 5c dk green .25 *.25*
B173 SP69 50c + 10c rose lil .80 .65
B174 SP69 70c + 5c gray blk .25 .25
B175 SP69 1fr + 25c red 1.00 .85
B176 SP69 1.75fr + 25c blue 2.40 1.75
B177 SP69 2.45fr + 55c dk vio 3.00 *3.25*
Nos. B170-B177 (8) 8.20 7.55
Set, never hinged 25.00

Queen Astrid Memorial issue. The surtax was divided among several charitable organizations.
Issued: No. B174, 10/31; others, 12/1.

Borgerhout Philatelic Exhibition Issue

Souvenir Sheet

Town Hall, Borgerhout
SP70

1936, Oct. 3

B178	SP70	70c + 30c pur brn	90.00	62.50
		Never hinged	275.00	
a.		Single stamp	45.00	
		Never hinged	60.00	

Sheet measures 115x126mm.

The sheet normally has pin holes and a cancellation-like marking in the margin. These are considered unused and the condition valued here.

Town Hall and Belfry of Charleroi
SP71

Charleroi Youth Exhibition

Souvenir Sheet

1936, Oct. 18 **Engr.**

B179	SP71	2.45fr + 55c gray blue	70.00	70.00
		Never hinged	175.00	
a.		Single stamp	45.00	45.00
		Never hinged	60.00	

Sheet measures 95x120mm.

The sheet normally has pin holes and a cancellation-like marking in the margin. These are considered unused and the condition valued here.

Prince Baudouin — SP72

1936, Dec. 1 **Photo.** ***Perf. 14x13½***

B180	SP72	10c + 5c dk brn	.25	.25
B181	SP72	25c + 5c violet	.25	*.25*
B182	SP72	35c + 5c dk green	.25	*.25*
B183	SP72	50c + 5c vio brn	.50	*.50*
B184	SP72	70c + 5c ol grn	.25	.25
B185	SP72	1fr + 25c cerise	1.25	1.25
B186	SP72	1.75fr + 25c ultra	1.90	1.90
B187	SP72	2.45fr + 2.55fr vio rose	5.00	*5.00*
		Nos. B180-B187 (8)	9.65	*9.65*
		Set, never hinged	30.00	

The surtax was for the assistance of the National Anti-Tuberculosis Society.

1937, Jan. 10

B188	SP72	2.45fr + 2.55fr slate	2.25	2.25
		Never hinged	6.00	

Intl. Stamp Day. Surtax for the benefit of the Brussels Postal Museum, the Royal Belgian Phil. Fed. and the Anti-Tuberculosis Soc.

Queen Astrid and Prince Baudouin — SP73

1937, Apr. 15 ***Perf. 11½***

B189	SP73	10c + 5c mag	.25	.25
B190	SP73	25c + 5c ol blk	.25	*.25*
B191	SP73	35c + 5c dk grn	.25	*.25*
B192	SP73	50c + 5c violet	.50	*.50*
B193	SP73	70c + 5c slate	.25	*.30*
B194	SP73	1fr + 25c dk car	1.50	1.50
B195	SP73	1.75fr + 25c dp ultra	2.75	2.75
B196	SP73	2.45fr + 1.55fr dk brn	6.50	6.50
		Nos. B189-B196 (8)	12.25	12.30
		Set, never hinged	45.00	

The surtax was to raise funds for Public Utility Works.

Queen Mother Elisabeth — SP74

1937, Sept. 15 ***Perf. 14x13½***

B197	SP74	70c + 5c int black	.30	.30
B198	SP74	1.75fr + 25c brt ultra	.70	.70
		Set, never hinged	2.00	

Souvenir Sheet

Perf. 11½

B199		Sheet of 4	45.00	45.00
		Never hinged	125.00	
a.		SP74 1.50fr+2.50fr red brn	4.00	4.00
b.		SP74 2.45fr+3.55fr red vio	4.00	4.00

Issued for the benefit of the Queen Elisabeth Music Foundation in connection with the Eugene Ysaye intl. competition.

No. B199 contains two se-tenant pairs of Nos. B199a and B199b. Size: 111x145mm. On sale one day, Sept. 15, at Brussels.

The sheet normally has pin holes and a cancellation-like marking in the margin. These are considered unused and the condition valued here.

Princess Josephine-Charlotte
SP75

1937, Dec. 1 ***Perf. 14x13½***

B200	SP75	10c + 5c sl grn	.25	.25
B201	SP75	25c + 5c lt brn	.25	.25
B202	SP75	35c + 5c yel grn	.25	.25
B203	SP75	50c + 5c ol gray	.35	.35
B204	SP75	70c + 5c brn red	.25	.25
B205	SP75	1fr + 25c red	1.25	1.25
B206	SP75	1.75fr + 25c vio bl	1.50	1.50
B207	SP75	2.45fr + 2.55fr mag	5.00	*5.00*
		Nos. B200-B207 (8)	9.10	*9.10*
		Set, never hinged	30.00	

King Albert Memorial Issue

Souvenir Sheet

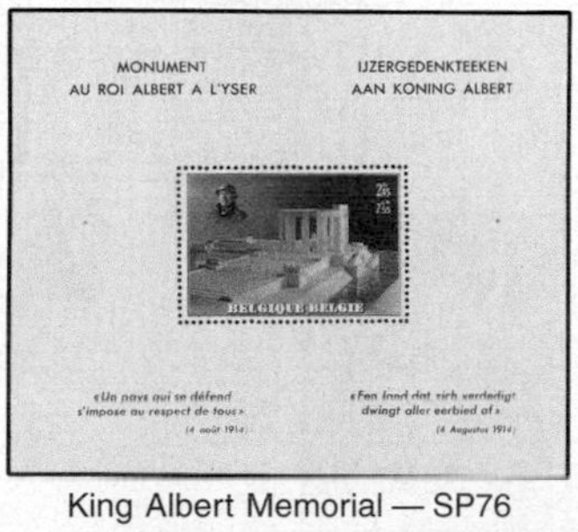

King Albert Memorial — SP76

1938, Feb. 17 ***Perf. 11½***

B208	SP76	2.45fr + 7.55fr brn vio	20.00	20.00
		Never hinged	62.50	
a.		Single stamp	13.00	13.00
		Never hinged	19.00	

Dedication of the monument to King Albert.

The sheet normally has pin holes and a cancellation-like marking in the margin. These are considered unused and the condition valued here. Sheets without the "cancellation" are extremely scarce. Values: unused, $525; never hinged, $1,000.

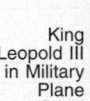

King Leopold III in Military Plane
SP77

1938, Mar. 15

B209	SP77	10c + 5c car brn	.25	*.30*
B210	SP77	35c + 5c dp grn	.35	*.35*
B211	SP77	70c + 5c gray blk	.50	.50
B212	SP77	1.75fr + 25c ultra	3.00	3.00
B213	SP77	2.45fr + 2.55fr pur	4.50	4.50
		Nos. B209-B213 (5)	8.60	8.65
		Set, never hinged	22.50	

The surtax was for the benefit of the National Fund for Aeronautical Propaganda.

Basilica of Koekelberg
SP78

Interior View of the Basilica of Koekelberg
SP79

1938, June 1 **Photo.**

B214	SP78	10c + 5c lt brn	.25	.25
B215	SP78	35c + 5c grn	.25	.25
B216	SP78	70c + 5c gray grn	.25	.25
B217	SP78	1fr + 25c car	.50	.50
B218	SP78	1.75fr + 25c ultra	.50	.50
B219	SP78	2.45fr + 2.55fr brn vio	3.50	*3.50*

Engr.

B220	SP79	5fr + 5fr dl grn	12.50	12.50
		Nos. B214-B220 (7)	17.75	17.75
		Set, never hinged	40.00	

Souvenir Sheet

1938, July 21 **Engr.** ***Perf. 14***

B221	SP79	5fr + 5fr lt vio	16.00	16.00
		Never hinged	25.00	
a.		Single stamp	14.00	14.00
		Never hinged	16.00	

The surtax was for a fund to aid in completing the National Basilica of the Sacred Heart at Koekelberg.

Nos. B214, B216 and B218 are different views of the exterior of the Basilica.

The sheet normally has pin holes and a cancellation-like marking in the margin. These are considered unused and the condition valued here.

Stamps of 1938 Surcharged in Black

Nos. B222-B223

No. B224

1938, Nov. 10 ***Perf. 11½***

B222	SP78	40c on 35c+5c grn	.75	*.75*
B223	SP78	75c on 70c+5c gray grn	.50	*.50*
B224	SP78	2.50 +2.50fr on 2.45+2.55fr	6.75	*6.75*
		Nos. B222-B224 (3)	8.00	*8.00*
		Set, never hinged	19.00	

Prince Albert of Liege — SP81

1938, Dec. 10 **Photo.** ***Perf. 14x13½***

B225	SP81	10c + 5c brown	.25	.25
B226	SP81	30c + 5c mag	.25	*.25*
B227	SP81	40c + 5c olive gray	.25	*.25*
B228	SP81	75c + 5c slate grn	.25	.25
B229	SP81	1fr + 25c dk car	1.25	*1.25*
B230	SP81	1.75fr + 25c ultra	1.25	*1.25*
B231	SP81	2.50fr + 2.50fr dp grn	6.00	*6.00*
B232	SP81	5fr + 5fr brn lake	12.50	12.50
		Nos. B225-B232 (8)	22.00	22.00
		Set, never hinged	70.00	

Henri Dunant
SP82

Florence Nightingale
SP83

Queen Mother Elisabeth and Royal Children — SP84

Queen Astrid — SP86

King Leopold and Royal Children
SP85

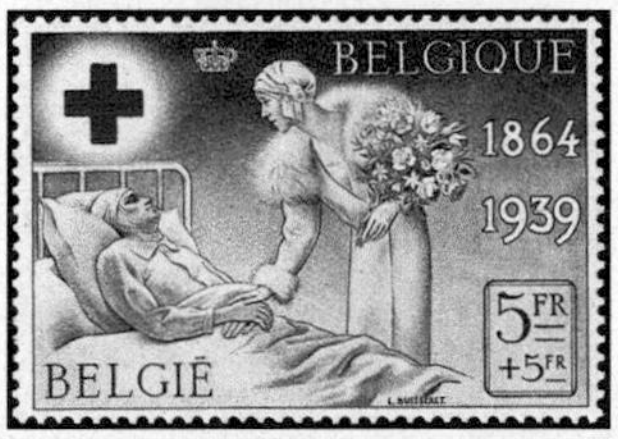

Queen Mother Elisabeth and Wounded Soldier — SP87

1939, Apr. 1 **Photo.** ***Perf. 11½***

Cross in Carmine

B233	SP82	10c + 5c brn	.25	.25
B234	SP83	30c + 5c brn car	.45	.45
B235	SP84	40c + 5c ol gray	.30	*.30*
B236	SP85	75c + 5c slate blk	.60	.25
B237	SP84	1fr + 25c brt rose	3.00	1.60
B238	SP85	1.75fr + 25c brt ultra	1.25	*1.25*
B239	SP86	2.50fr + 2.50fr dl vio	1.75	*1.75*
B240	SP87	5fr + 5fr gray grn	7.00	*7.00*
		Nos. B233-B240 (8)	14.60	*12.85*
		Set, never hinged	42.50	

75th anniversary of the founding of the International Red Cross Society.

In 1941, No. B240 was privately overprinted with a circular red cross overprint and 1941 date. Value, $105.

Rubens' House, Antwerp SP88

"Albert and Nicolas Rubens" — SP89

Arcade, Rubens' House SP90

"Helena Fourment and Her Children" — SP91

Rubens and Isabelle Brandt — SP92

Peter Paul Rubens — SP93

"The Velvet Hat" — SP94

"Descent from the Cross" SP95

1939, July 1

B241	SP88	10c + 5c brn	.25	.25
B242	SP89	40c + 5c brn car	.25	.25
B243	SP90	75c + 5c ol blk	.65	.65
B244	SP91	1fr + 25c rose	2.50	2.50
B245	SP92	1.50fr + 25c sep	2.75	2.75
B246	SP93	1.75fr + 25c dp ultra	4.50	4.50
B247	SP94	2.50fr + 2.50fr brt red vio	15.00	*15.00*
B248	SP95	5fr + 5fr slate gray	19.00	19.00
		Nos. B241-B248 (8)	44.90	44.90
		Set, never hinged	140.00	

Issued to honor Peter Paul Rubens. The surtax was used to restore Rubens' home in Antwerp.

"Martin van Nieuwenhove" by Hans Memling (1430?-1495), Flemish Painter — SP96

1939, July 1

B249	SP96	75c + 75c olive blk	2.75	2.75
		Never hinged	4.50	

Twelfth Century Monks at Work — SP97

Reconstructed Tower Seen through Cloister — SP98

Monks Laboring in the Fields SP99

Orval Abbey, Aerial View SP100

Bishop Heylen of Namur, Madonna and Abbot General Smets of the Trappists — SP101

King Albert I and King Leopold III and Shrine — SP102

1939, July 20

B250	SP97	75c + 75c ol blk	3.50	3.75
B251	SP98	1fr + 1fr rose red	2.25	2.25
B252	SP99	1.50fr + 1.50fr dl brn	2.25	2.25
B253	SP100	1.75fr + 1.75fr saph	2.25	2.25
B254	SP101	2.50fr + 2.50fr brt red vio	9.00	9.00
B255	SP102	5fr + 5fr brn car	10.00	10.00
		Nos. B250-B255 (6)	29.25	29.50
		Set, never hinged	82.50	

The surtax was used for the restoration of the Abbey of Orval.

Bruges SP103

Furnes SP104

Belfries: 30c+5c, Thuin. 40c+5c, Lierre. 75c+5c, Mons. 1.75fr+25c, Namur. 2.50fr+2.50fr, Alost. 5fr+5fr, Tournai.

1939, Dec. 1 Photo. *Perf. 14x13½*

B256	SP103	10c + 5c ol gray	.25	*.25*
B257	SP103	30c + 5c brn org	.30	*.30*
B258	SP103	40c + 5c brt red vio	.50	*.50*
B259	SP103	75c + 5c olive blk	.25	*.25*
		Engr.		
B260	SP104	1fr + 25c rose car	1.25	*1.25*
B261	SP104	1.75fr + 25c dk blue	1.25	*1.25*
B262	SP104	2.50fr + 2.50fr dp red brn	10.00	*10.00*
B263	SP104	5fr + 5fr pur	12.00	*12.00*
		Nos. B256-B263 (8)	25.80	*25.80*
		Set, never hinged	65.00	

Mons SP111

Ghent SP112

Coats of Arms: 40c+10c, Arel. 50c+10c, Bruges. 75c+15c, Namur. 1fr+25c, Hasselt. 1.75fr+50c, Brussels. 2.50fr+2.50fr, Antwerp. 5fr+5fr, Liege.

1940-41 Typo. *Perf. 14x13½*

B264	SP111	10c + 5c multi	.25	.25
B265	SP112	30c + 5c multi	.25	.25
B266	SP111	40c + 10c multi	.25	.25
B267	SP112	50c + 10c multi	.25	.25
B268	SP111	75c + 15c multi	.25	.25
B269	SP112	1fr + 25c multi	.30	.30
B270	SP111	1.75fr + 50c multi	.45	.40
B271	SP112	2.50fr + 2.50fr multi	1.25	1.25
B272	SP111	5fr + 5fr multi	1.50	1.50
		Nos. B264-B272 (9)	4.75	4.70
		Set, never hinged	8.50	

Nos. B264, B269-B272 issued in 1941. Surtax for winter relief. See No. B279.

Queen Elisabeth Music Chapel SP120

Bust of Prince Albert of Liege — SP121

1940, Nov. Photo. *Perf. 11½*

B273	SP120	75c + 75c slate	3.50	3.50
B274	SP120	1fr + 1fr rose red	1.25	1.25
B275	SP121	1.50fr + 1.50fr Prus grn	1.25	1.25
B276	SP121	1.75fr + 1.75fr ultra	1.25	1.25
B277	SP120	2.50fr + 2.50fr brn org	4.00	4.00
B278	SP121	5fr + 5fr red vio	4.00	4.00
		Nos. B273-B278 (6)	15.25	15.25
		Set, never hinged	55.00	

The surtax was for the Queen Elisabeth Music Foundation. Nos. B273-B278 were not authorized for postal use, but were sold to advance subscribers either mint or canceled to order. See Nos. B317-B318.

Arms Types of 1940-41
Souvenir Sheets
Cross and City Name in Carmine
Arms in Color of Stamp
Perf. 14x13½, Imperf.

1941, May Typo.

B279		Sheet of 9	16.00	16.00
		Never hinged	18.00	
a.	SP111	10c + 5c slate	1.10	*1.25*
b.	SP112	30c + 5c emerald	1.10	*1.25*
c.	SP111	40c + 10c chocolate	1.10	*1.25*
d.	SP112	50c + 10c light violet	1.10	*1.25*
e.	SP111	75c + 15c dull purple	1.10	*1.25*
f.	SP112	1fr + 25c carmine	1.10	*1.25*
g.	SP111	1.75fr + 50c dull blue	1.10	*1.25*
h.	SP112	2.50fr + 2.50fr ol gray	1.10	*1.25*
i.	SP111	5fr + 5fr dull violet	4.00	*4.25*

The sheets measure 106x148mm. The surtax was used for relief work.

Painting SP123

Sculpture SP124

Monks Studying Plans of Orval Abbey — SP128

Designs: 40c+60c, 2fr+3.50fr, Monk carrying candle. 50c+65c, 1.75fr+2.50fr, Monk praying. 75c+1fr, 3fr+5fr, Two monks singing.

1941, June Photo. *Perf. 11½*

B281	SP123	10c + 15c brn org	.50	.50
B282	SP124	30c + 30c ol gray	.50	.50
B283	SP124	40c + 60c dp brn	.50	.50
B284	SP124	50c + 65c vio	.50	.50
B285	SP124	75c + 1fr brt red vio	.50	.50
B286	SP124	1fr + 1.50fr rose red	.50	.50
B287	SP123	1.25fr + 1.75fr dp yel grn	.50	.50
B288	SP123	1.75fr + 2.50fr dp ultra	.50	.50
B289	SP123	2fr + 3.50fr red vio	.50	.50
B290	SP124	2.50fr + 4.50fr dl red brn	.50	.50
B291	SP124	3fr + 5fr dk ol grn	.50	.50
B292	SP128	5fr + 10fr grnsh blk	1.50	1.50
		Nos. B281-B292 (12)	7.00	7.00
		Set, never hinged	12.50	

The surtax was used for the restoration of the Abbey of Orval.

Maria Theresa SP129

Charles the Bold SP130

Portraits (in various frames): 35c+5c, Charles of Lorraine. 50c+10c, Margaret of Parma. 60c+10c, Charles V. 1fr+15c, Johanna of Castile. 1.50fr+1fr, Philip the Good. 1.75fr+1.75fr, Margaret of Austria. 3.25fr+3.25fr, Archduke Albert. 5fr+5fr, Archduchess Isabella.

1941-42 **Photo.**

B293 SP129 10c + 5c ol blk .25 .25
B294 SP129 35c + 5c dl grn .25 .25
B295 SP129 50c + 10c brn .25 .25
B296 SP129 60c + 10c pur .25 .25
B297 SP129 1fr + 15c brt car rose .25 .25
B298 SP129 1.50fr + 1fr red vio .25 .25
B299 SP129 1.75fr + 1.75fr ryl bl .25 .25
B300 SP130 2.25fr + 2.25fr dl red brn .30 .30
B301 SP129 3.25fr + 3.25fr lt brn .45 .45
B302 SP129 5fr + 5fr sl grn .90 .90
Nos. B293-B302 (10) 3.40 3.40
Set, never hinged 5.00

Souvenir Sheet

Archduke Albert and Archduchess Isabella — SP139

B302A SP139 Sheet of 2 ('42) 11.00 11.00
Never hinged 14.50
b. 3.25fr+6.75fr turquoise blue 4.50 4.50
c. 5fr+10fr dark carmine 4.50 4.50

The surtax was for the benefit of National Social Service Work among soldiers' families.

Souvenir Sheets

Monks Studying Plans of Orval Abbey — SP140

1941, Oct. **Photo.** ***Perf. 11½***

Inscribed "Belgie-Belgique"

B303 SP140 5fr + 15fr ultra 10.00 10.00
Never hinged 25.00

Inscribed "Belgique-Belgie"

Imperf

B304 SP140 5fr + 15fr ultra 10.00 10.00
Never hinged 25.00

Surtax for the restoration of Orval Abbey.
No. B304 exists perforated.
In 1942 these sheets were privately trimmed and overprinted "1142 1942" and ornament. Values: unused or canceled $500; never hinged $1,000.

St. Martin Statue, Church of Dinant SP141

Lennik, Saint-Quentin SP142

St. Martin's Church, Saint-Trond SP146

Statues of St. Martin: 50c+10c, 3.25fr+3.25fr, Beck, Limburg. 60c+10c, 2.25fr+2.25fr, Dave on the Meuse. 1.75fr+50c, Hal, Brabant.

1941-42 **Photo.** ***Perf. 11½***

B305 SP141 10c + 5c chest .25 .25
B306 SP142 35c + 5c dk bl grn .25 .25
B307 SP142 50c + 10c vio .25 .25
B308 SP142 60c + 10c dp brn .25 .25
B309 SP142 1fr + 15c car .25 .25
B310 SP141 1.50fr + 25c sl grn .25 .25
B311 SP142 1.75fr + 50c dk ultra .30 .30
B312 SP142 2.25fr + 2.25fr red vio .30 .30
B313 SP142 3.25fr + 3.25fr brn vio .40 .40
B314 SP146 5fr + 5fr dk ol grn .75 .75
Nos. B305-B314 (10) 3.25 3.25
Set, never hinged 5.00

Souvenir Sheets

Inscribed "Belgie-Belgique"

B315 SP146 5fr + 20fr vio brn ('42) 22.50 22.50
Never hinged 35.00

Inscribed "Belgique-Belgie"

Imperf

B316 SP146 5fr + 20fr vio brn ('42) 22.50 22.50
Never hinged 35.00

In 1956, the Bureau Europeen de la Jeunesse et de l'Enfance privately overprinted Nos. B315-B316: "Congres Europeen de l'education 7-12 Mai 1956," in dark red and dark green respectively. A black bar obliterates "Winterhulp-Secours d'Hiver."
Values, set of 2 sheets: $40 unused or canceled; $80 never hinged.

Souvenir Sheets

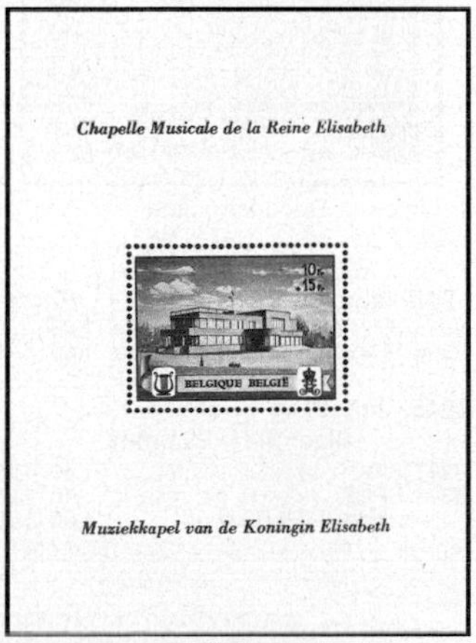

Queen Elisabeth Music Chapel — SP147

1941, Dec. 1 **Photo.** ***Perf. 11½***

Inscribed "Belgique-Belgie"

B317 SP147 10fr + 15fr ol blk 6.50 6.00
Never hinged 9.50

Inscribed "Belgie-Belgique"

Imperf

B318 SP147 10fr + 15fr ol blk 6.50 6.00
Never hinged 9.50

The surtax was for the Queen Elisabeth Music Foundation. These sheets were perforated with the monogram of Queen Elisabeth in 1942. Value, $3 each.
In 1954 Nos. B317-B318 were overprinted for the birth cent. of Edgar Tinel, composer. These overprinted sheets were not postally valid. Value, $4 each.

Jean Bollandus SP148

Christophe Plantin SP156

Designs: 35c+5c, Andreas Vesalius. 50c+10c, Simon Stevinus. 60c+10c, Jean Van Helmont. 1fr+15c, Rembert Dodoens. 1.75fr+50c, Gerardus Mercator. 3.25fr+3.25fr, Abraham Ortelius. 5fr+5fr, Justus Lipsius.

1942, May 15 **Photo.** ***Perf. 14x13½***

B319 SP148 10c + 5c dl brn .25 .25
B320 SP148 35c + 5c gray grn .25 .25
B321 SP148 50c + 10c fawn .25 .25
B322 SP148 60c + 10c grnsh blk .25 .25

Engr.

B323 SP148 1fr + 15c brt rose .25 .25
B324 SP148 1.75fr + 50c dl bl .25 .25
B325 SP148 3.25fr + 3.25fr lil rose .25 .25
B326 SP148 5fr + 5fr vio .25 .25

Perf. 13½x14

B327 SP156 10fr + 30fr red org 1.40 1.40
Nos. B319-B327 (9) 3.40 3.40
Set, never hinged 3.50

The surtax was used to help fight tuberculosis.
No. B327 was sold by subscription at the Brussels Post Office, July 1-10, 1942.

Belgian Prisoner — SP158

1942, Oct. 1 ***Perf. 11½***

B331 SP158 5fr + 45fr olive gray 7.00 7.00
Never hinged 17.00

The surtax was for prisoners of war. Value includes a brown inscribed label which alternates with the stamps in the sheet.

SP159

SP164

SP162

SP168

Various Statues of St. Martin.

1942-43

B332 SP159 10c + 5c org .25 .25
B333 SP159 35c + 5c dk bl grn .25 .25
B334 SP159 50c + 10c dp brn .25 .25
B335 SP162 60c + 10c blk .25 .25
B336 SP159 1fr + 15c brt rose .25 .25
B337 SP164 1.50fr + 25c grnsh blk .25 .25
B338 SP164 1.75fr + 50c dk bl .25 .25
B339 SP162 2.25fr + 2.25fr brn .30 .30
B340 SP162 3.25fr + 3.25fr brt red vio .45 .45
B341 SP168 5fr + 10fr hn brn 1.25 1.25
B342 SP168 10fr + 20fr rose brn & vio brn ('43) 1.10 1.10

Inscribed "Belgique-Belgie"

B343 SP168 10fr + 20fr gldn brn & vio brn ('43) 1.40 1.40
Nos. B332-B343 (12) 6.25 6.25
Set, never hinged 12.50

The surtax was for winter relief.
Issue dates: Nos. B332-B341, Nov. 12, 1942; Nos. B342-B343, Apr. 3, 1943.

Prisoners of War — SP170

No. B345, 2 prisoners with package from home.

1943, May **Photo.** ***Perf. 11½***

B344 SP170 1fr + 30fr ver 2.75 2.75
B345 SP170 1fr + 30fr brn rose 2.75 2.75
Set, never hinged 10.00

The surtax was used for prisoners of war.

Roof Tiler SP172

Coppersmith SP173

Statues in Petit Sablon Park, Brussels: 35c+5c, Blacksmith. 60c+10c, Gunsmith. 1fr+15c, Armsmith. 1.75fr+75c, Goldsmith. 3.25fr+3.25fr, Fishdealer. 5fr+25fr, Watchmaker.

1943, June 1

B346 SP172 10c + 5c chnt brn .25 .25
B347 SP172 35c + 5c grn .25 .25
B348 SP173 50c + 10c dk brn .25 .25
B349 SP173 60c + 10c slate .25 .25
B350 SP173 1fr + 15c dl rose brn .25 .25
B351 SP173 1.75fr + 75c ultra .25 .25
B352 SP173 3.25fr + 3.25fr brt red vio .40 .40
B353 SP173 5fr + 25fr dk pur .90 .90
Nos. B346-B353 (8) 2.80 2.80
Set, never hinged 3.75

Surtax for the control of tuberculosis.

"O" SP180

"ORVAL" — SP185

1943, Oct. 9

B354	SP180	50c + 1fr "O"	.50	.50
B355	SP180	60c + 1.90fr "R"	.30	.25
B356	SP180	1fr + 3fr "V"	.30	.25
B357	SP180	1.75fr + 5.25fr "A"	.30	.25
B358	SP180	3.25fr + 16.75fr "L"	.50	.50
B359	SP185	5fr + 30fr dp brn	.90	.90
		Nos. B354-B359 (6)	2.80	2.65
		Set, never hinged	4.00	

Surtax aided restoration of Orval Abbey.

St. Leonard Church, Leau SP186

St. Martin Church, Courtrai — SP190

Basilica of St. Martin, Angre — SP191

Notre Dame, Hal — SP193

St. Martin SP194

35c+5c, St. Martin Church, Dion-le-Val. 50c+15c, St. Martin Church, Alost. 60c+20c, St. Martin Church, Liege. 3.25fr+11.75fr, St. Martin Church, Loppem. No. B369, St. Martin, beggar & Meuse landscape.

1943-44

B360	SP186	10c + 5c dp brn	.25	.25
B361	SP186	35c + 5c dk bl grn	.25	.25
B362	SP186	50c + 15c ol blk	.25	.25
B363	SP186	60c + 20c brt red vio	.25	.25
B364	SP190	1fr + 1fr rose brn	.30	.30
B365	SP191	1.75fr + 4.25fr dp ultra	.70	.70
B366	SP186	3.25fr + 11.75fr red lil	1.40	1.40
B367	SP193	5fr + 25fr dk bl	2.00	2.00
B368	SP194	10fr + 30fr gray grn ('44)	1.50	1.50
B369	SP194	10fr + 30fr blk brn ('44)	1.50	1.50
		Nos. B360-B369 (10)	8.40	8.40
		Set, never hinged	18.00	

Surtax for winter relief.

Catalogue values for unused stamps in this section, from this point to the end of the section, are for Never Hinged items.

"Daedalus and Icarus" SP196

Sir Anthony Van Dyck, Self-portrait SP200

Paintings by Van Dyck: 50c+2.50fr, "The Good Samaritan." 60c+3.40fr, Detail of "Christ Healing the Paralytic." 1fr+5fr, "Madonna and Child." 5fr+30fr, "St. Sebastian."

1944, Apr. 16 Photo. *Perf. 11½*
Crosses in Carmine

B370	SP196	35c + 1.65fr dk sl grn	.50	.35
B371	SP196	50c + 2.50fr grnsh blk	.50	.35
B372	SP196	60c + 3.40fr blk brn	.50	.35
B373	SP196	1fr + 5fr dk car	.70	.50
B374	SP200	1.75fr + 8.25fr int bl	.75	.50
B375	SP196	5fr + 30fr cop brn	1.25	.75
		Nos. B370-B375 (6)	4.20	2.80

The surtax was for the Belgian Red Cross.

Jan van Eyck — SP202

Godfrey of Bouillon — SP203

Designs: 50c+25c, Jacob van Maerlant. 60c+40c, Jean Joses de Dinant. 1fr+50c, Jacob van Artevelde. 1.75fr+4.25fr, Charles Joseph de Ligne. 2.25fr+8.25fr, Andre Gretry. 3.25fr+11.25fr, Jan Moretus-Plantin. 5fr+35fr, Jan van Ruysbroeck.

1944, May 31

B376	SP202	10c + 15c dk pur	.75	.25
B377	SP203	35c + 15c green	.50	.25
B378	SP203	50c + 25c chnt brn	.50	.25
B379	SP203	60c + 40c ol blk	.50	.25
B380	SP203	1fr + 50c rose brn	.50	.25
B381	SP203	1.75fr + 4.25fr ultra	.50	.25
B382	SP203	2.25fr + 8.25fr grnsh blk	1.10	.70
B383	SP203	3.25fr + 11.25fr dk brn	.50	.35
B384	SP203	5fr + 35fr sl bl	1.60	.70
		Nos. B376-B384 (9)	6.45	3.25

The surtax was for prisoners of war.

Sons of Aymon Astride Bayard SP211

Brabo Slaying the Giant Antigoon SP212

Till Eulenspiegel Singing to Nele SP214

50c+10c, St. Hubert converted by stag with crucifix. 1fr+15fr, St. George slaying the dragon. 1.75fr+5.25fr, Genevieve of Brabant with son & roe-deer. 3.25fr+11.75fr, Tchantches wrestling with the Saracen. 5fr+25fr, St. Gertrude rescuing the knight with the cards.

1944, June 25

B385	SP211	10c + 5c choc	.25	.25
B386	SP212	35c + 5c dk bl grn	.25	.25
B387	SP211	50c + 10c dl vio	.25	.25
B388	SP214	60c + 10c blk brn	.25	.25
B389	SP214	1fr + 15c rose brn	.25	.25
B390	SP214	1.75fr + 5.25fr ultra	.25	*.25*
B391	SP211	3.25fr + 11.75fr grnsh blk	.35	*.35*
B392	SP211	5fr + 25fr dk bl	.45	*.45*
		Nos. B385-B392 (8)	2.30	*2.30*

The surtax was for the control of tuberculosis.

Nos. B385-B389 were overprinted "Breendonk+10fr." in 1946 by the Union Royale Philatelique for an exhibition at Brussels. They had no postal validity. Value same as unused set without overprint.

Union of the Flemish and Walloon Peoples in their Sorrow — SP219

Union in Reconstruction — SP220

Perf. 11½

1945, May 1 Unwmk. Photo.

B395	SP219	1fr + 30fr carmine	1.60	.90
B396	SP220	1¾fr + 30fr brt ultra	1.60	.90

1945, July 21
Size: 34½x23½mm

B397	SP219	1fr + 9fr scarlet	.40	.25
B398	SP220	1fr + 9fr car rose	.40	.25
		Nos. B395-B398 (4)	4.00	2.30

Surtax for the postal employees' relief fund.

Prisoner of War SP221

Reunion SP222

Awaiting Execution SP223

Symbolical Figures "Recovery of Freedom" SP225

Design: 70c+30c, 3.50fr+3.50fr, Member of Resistance Movement.

1945, Sept. 10

B399	SP221	10c + 15c orange	.25	.25
B400	SP222	20c + 20c dp pur	.25	.25
B401	SP223	60c + 25c sepia	.25	.25
B402	SP221	70c + 30c dp yel grn	.25	.25
B403	SP221	75c + 50c org brn	.25	.25
B404	SP222	1fr + 75c brt bl grn	.25	.25
B405	SP223	1.50fr + 1fr brt red	.25	.25
B406	SP221	3.50fr + 3.50fr brt bl	1.75	1.10
B407	SP225	5fr + 40fr brown	2.25	1.25
		Nos. B399-B407 (9)	5.75	4.10

The surtax was for the benefit of prisoners of war, displaced persons, families of executed victims and members of the Resistance Movement.

Arms of West Flanders — SP226

Arms of Provinces: 20c+20c, Luxembourg. 60c+25c, East Flanders. 70c+30c, Namur. 75c+50c, Limburg. 1fr+75c, Hainaut. 1.50fr+1fr, Antwerp. 3.50fr+1.50fr, Liege. 5fr+45fr, Brabant.

1945, Dec. 1

B408	SP226	10c + 15c sl blk & sl gray	.25	.25
B409	SP226	20c + 20c rose car & rose	.25	.25
B410	SP226	60c + 25c dk brn & pale brn	.25	.25
B411	SP226	70c + 30c dk grn & lt grn	.25	.25
B412	SP226	75c + 50c org brn & pale org brn	.25	.25
B413	SP226	1fr + 75c pur & lt pur	.25	.25
B414	SP226	1.50fr + 1fr car & rose	.25	.25
B415	SP226	3.50fr + 1.50fr dp bl & gray bl	.60	.60
B416	SP226	5fr + 45fr dp mag & cer	3.75	2.00
		Nos. B408-B416 (9)	6.10	4.35

The surtax was for tuberculosis prevention.

Father Joseph Damien — SP227

Father Damien Comforting Leper — SP229

Leper Colony, Molokai Island, Hawaii SP228

Perf. 11½

1946, July 15 Unwmk. Photo.

B417	SP227	65c + 75c dk blue	2.00	1.25
B418	SP228	1.35fr + 2fr brown	2.00	1.25
B419	SP229	1.75fr + 18fr rose brn	2.00	1.25

The surtax was for the erection of a museum in Louvain.

Symbols of Wisdom and Patriotism SP230

"In Memoriam" SP232

François Bovesse SP231

1946, July 15

B420	SP230	65c + 75c violet	2.00	1.25
B421	SP231	1.35fr + 2fr dk org brn	2.00	1.25
B422	SP232	1.75fr + 18fr car rose	2.00	1.25

The surtax was for the erection of a "House of the Fine Arts" at Namur.

Emile Vandervelde SP233

Sower SP235

Vandervelde, Laborer and Family — SP234

1946, July 15

B423	SP233	65c + 75c dk sl grn	2.00	1.25
B424	SP234	1.35fr + 2fr dk vio bl	2.00	1.25
B425	SP235	1.75fr + 18fr dp car	2.00	1.25
		Nos. B417-B425 (9)	18.00	11.25

The surtax was for the Emile Vandervelde Institute, to promote social, economic and cultural activities.

For surcharges see Nos. CB4-CB12.

Pepin of Herstal — SP236

1fr+50c, Charlemagne. 1.50fr+1fr, Godfrey of Bouillon. 3.50fr+1.50fr, Robert of Jerusalem. Nos. B430-B431, Baldwin of Constantinople.

1946, Sept. 15 Engr. *Perf. 11½x11*

B426	SP236	75c + 25c grn	.50	.25
B427	SP236	1fr + 50c vio	.75	.30
B428	SP236	1.50fr + 1fr plum	.75	.40
B429	SP236	3.50fr + 1.50fr brt bl	1.00	.60
B430	SP236	5fr + 45fr red vio	13.00	12.00
B431	SP236	5fr + 45fr red org	13.00	11.00
		Nos. B426-B431 (6)	29.00	24.55

The surtax on Nos. B426-B429 was for the benefit of former prisoners of war, displaced persons, the families of executed patriots, and former members of the Resistance Movement.

The surtax on Nos. B430-B431 was divided among several welfare, national celebration and educational organizations.

Issue dates: Nos. B426-B429, Apr. 15; No. B430, Sept. 15; No. B431, Nov. 15.

See Nos. B437-B441, B465-B466, B472-B476.

Malines — SP241

Coats of Arms: 90c+60c, Dinant. 1.35fr+1.15fr, Ostend. 3.15fr+1.85fr, Verviers. 4.50fr+45.50fr, Louvain.

1946, Dec. 2 *Perf. 11½*

B432	SP241	65c + 35c rose car	.55	.25
B433	SP241	90c + 60c lem	.65	.25
B434	SP241	1.35fr + 1.15fr dp grn	.65	.25
B435	SP241	3.15fr + 1.85fr bl	1.00	.40
B436	SP241	4.50fr + 45.50fr dk vio brn	16.00	14.00
		Nos. B432-B436 (5)	18.85	15.15

The surtax was for anti-tuberculosis work. See Nos. B442-B446.

Type of 1946

Designs: 65c+35c, John II, Duke of Brabant. 90c+60c, Count Philip of Alsace. 1.35fr+1.15fr, William the Good. 3.15fr+1.85fr, Bishop Notger of Liege. 20fr+20fr, Philip the Noble.

1947, Sept. 25 Engr. *Perf. 11½x11*

B437	SP236	65c + 35c Prus grn	1.10	.50
B438	SP236	90c + 60c yel grn	1.60	.75
B439	SP236	1.35fr + 1.15fr car	3.00	1.10
B440	SP236	3.15fr + 1.85fr ultra	3.75	1.60
B441	SP236	20fr + 20fr red vio	52.50	42.50
		Nos. B437-B441 (5)	61.95	46.45

The surtax was for victims of World War II.

Arms Type of 1946 Dated "1947"

Coats of Arms: 65c+35c, Nivelles. 90c+60c, St. Trond. 1.35fr+1.15fr, Charleroi. 3.15fr+1.85fr, St. Nicolas. 20fr+20fr, Bouillon.

1947, Dec. 15 *Perf. 11½*

B442	SP241	65c + 35c org	.60	.50
B443	SP241	90c + 60c dp cl	.70	.65
B444	SP241	1.35fr + 1.15fr dk brn	.80	.70
B445	SP241	3.15fr + 1.85fr dp bl	2.75	1.25
B446	SP241	20fr + 20fr dk grn	27.00	17.00
		Nos. B442-B446 (5)	31.85	20.10

The surtax was for anti-tuberculosis work.

St. Benedict and King Totila — SP247

Achel Abbey SP248

3.15fr+2.85fr, St. Benedict, legislator & builder. 10fr+10fr, Death of St. Benedict.

1948, Apr. 5 Photo.

B447	SP247	65c + 65c red brn	1.00	.75
B448	SP248	1.35fr + 1.35fr grnsh blk	1.50	1.00
B449	SP247	3.15fr + 2.85fr dp ultra	3.50	1.25
B450	SP247	10fr + 10fr brt red vio	12.50	10.00
		Nos. B447-B450 (4)	18.50	13.00

The surtax was to aid the Abbey of the Trappist Fathers at Achel.

St. Begga and Chevremont Castle — SP249

Chevremont Basilica and Convent SP250

3.15fr+2.85fr, Madonna of Chevremont & Chapel. 10fr+10fr, Madonna of Mt. Carmel.

1948, Apr. 5 Unwmk.

B451	SP249	65c + 65c bl grn	1.00	.75
B452	SP250	1.35fr + 1.35fr dk car rose	1.60	1.00
B453	SP249	3.15fr + 2.85fr dp bl	3.00	1.25
B454	SP249	10fr + 10fr dp brn	11.00	9.00
		Nos. B451-B454 (4)	16.60	12.00

The surtax was to aid the Basilica of the Carmelite Fathers of Chèvremont.

Anseele Monument Showing French Inscription — SP251

90c+60c, View of Ghent. 1.35fr+1.15fr, Van Artevelde monument, Ghent. 3.15fr+1.85fr, Anseele Monument, Flemish inscription.

1948, June 21 *Perf. 14x13½*

B455	SP251	65c + 35c rose red	2.50	1.25
B456	SP251	90c + 60c gray	3.50	1.90
B457	SP251	1.35fr + 1.15fr hn brn	2.25	1.50
B458	SP251	3.15fr + 1.85fr brt bl	7.50	5.00
a.		Souv. sheet, #B455-B458	200.00	90.00
		Nos. B455-B458 (4)	15.75	9.65

Issued to honor Edouard Anseele, statesman, founder of the Belgian Socialist Party.

No. B458a sold for 50fr.

For surcharges see Nos. 395-398.

Statue "The Unloader" SP252

Underground Fighter SP253

1948, Sept. 4 *Perf. 11½x11*

B460	SP252	10fr + 10fr gray grn	52.50	24.50
B461	SP253	10fr + 10fr red brn	22.50	12.50

The surtax was used toward erection of monuments at Antwerp and Liege.

Portrait Type of 1946 and

Double Barred Cross — SP254

Designs: 4fr+3.25fr, Isabella of Austria. 20fr+20fr, Archduke Albert of Austria.

1948, Dec. 15 Photo. *Perf. 13½x14*

B462	SP254	20c + 5c dk sl grn	.50	.25
B463	SP254	1.20fr + 30c mag	1.50	.50
B464	SP254	1.75fr + 25c red	2.00	.75

Engr. *Perf. 11½x11*

B465	SP236	4fr + 3.25fr ultra	8.50	5.00
B466	SP236	20fr + 20fr Prus grn	42.50	35.00
		Nos. B462-B466 (5)	55.00	41.50

The surtax was divided among several charities.

Souvenir Sheets

Rogier van der Weyden Paintings — SP255

Paintings by van der Weyden (No. B466A): 90c, Virgin and Child. 1.75fr, Christ on the Cross. 4fr, Mary Magdalene.

Paintings by Jordaens (No. B466B): 90c, Woman Reading. 1.75fr, The Flutist. 4fr, Old Woman Reading Letter.

1949, Apr. 1 Photo. *Perf. 11½*

B466A	SP255	Sheet of 3	200.00	175.00
c.		90c deep brown	55.00	50.00
d.		1.75fr deep rose lilac	55.00	45.00
e.		4fr dark violet blue	55.00	45.00
B466B	SP255	Sheet of 3	200.00	175.00
f.		90c dark violet	55.00	50.00
g.		1.75fr red	55.00	45.00
h.		4fr blue	55.00	45.00

The surtax went to various cultural and philanthropic organizations. Sheets sold for 50fr each.

Gum on Nos. B466A-B466B is irregularly applied.

Guido Gezelle — SP256

1949, Nov. 15 Photo. *Perf. 14x13½*

B467 SP256 1.75fr + 75c dk Prus grn 1.75 1.25

50th anniversary of the death of Guido Gezelle, poet. The surtax was for the Guido Gezelle Museum, Bruges.

Portrait Type of 1946 and

Arnica — SP257

Designs: 65c+10c, Sand grass. 90c+10c, Wood myrtle. 1.20fr+30c, Field poppy. 1.75fr+25c, Philip the Good. 3fr+1.50fr, Charles V. 4fr+2fr, Maria-Christina. 6fr+3fr, Charles of Lorraine. 8fr+4fr, Maria-Theresa.

1949, Dec. 20 Typo. *Perf. 13½x14*

B468 SP257 20c + 5c multi .30 .25
B469 SP257 65c + 10c multi 1.25 .40
B470 SP257 90c + 10c multi 1.75 1.00
B471 SP257 1.20fr + 30c multi 2.25 1.00

Engr. *Perf. 11½x11*

B472 SP236 1.75fr + 25c red org 1.00 .35
B473 SP236 3fr + 1.50fr dp claret 11.00 6.00
B474 SP236 4fr + 2fr ultra 11.00 5.00
B475 SP236 6fr + 3fr choc 20.00 11.00
B476 SP236 8fr + 4fr dl grn 22.50 17.50
Nos. B468-B476 (9) 71.05 42.50

The surtax was apportioned among several welfare organizations.

Arms of Belgium and Great Britain — SP258

British Memorial — SP260

Design: 2.50fr+50c, British tanks at Hertain.

Perf. 13½x14, 11½

1950, Mar. 15 Engr.

B477 SP258 80c + 20c grn 1.25 .50
B478 SP258 2.50fr + 50c red 5.50 3.50
B479 SP260 4fr + 2fr dp bl 9.00 6.00
Nos. B477-B479 (3) 15.75 10.00

6th anniv. of the liberation of Belgian territory by the British army.

Hurdling SP261

Relay Race SP262

Designs: 90c+10c, Javelin throwing. 4fr+2fr, Pole vault. 8fr+4fr, Foot race.

Perf. 14x13½, 13½x14

1950, July 1 Engr. Unwmk.

B480 SP261 20c + 5c brt grn .50 .25
B481 SP261 90c + 10c vio brn 4.00 2.00
B482 SP262 1.75fr + 25c car 8.00 2.25
a. Souvenir sheet of 1 80.00 50.00
B483 SP261 4fr + 2fr lt bl 35.00 17.00
B484 SP261 8fr + 4fr dp grn 40.00 27.50
Nos. B480-B484 (5) 87.50 49.00

Issued to publicize the European Athletic Games, Brussels, August 1950.

The margins of No. B482a were trimmed in April, 1951, and an overprint ("25 Francs pour le Fonds Sportif-25e Foire Internationale Bruxelles") was added in red in French and in black in Flemish by a private committee. These pairs of altered sheets were sold at the Brussels Fair.

Values, set of 2 altered sheets: unused or canceled, $17.50; never hinged $35.

Gentian — SP263

Sijsele Sanatorium SP264

Tombeek Sanatorium SP265

Designs: 65c+10c, Cotton Grass. 90c+10c, Foxglove. 1.20fr+30c, Limonia. 4fr+2fr, Jauche Sanatorium.

1950, Dec. 20 Typo. *Perf. 14x13½*

B485 SP263 20c + 5c multi .80 .40
B486 SP263 65c + 10c multi 1.50 .85
B487 SP263 90c + 10c multi 1.60 1.10
B488 SP263 1.20fr + 30c multi 2.75 2.25

Perf. 11½

Engr.

Cross in Red

B489 SP264 1.75fr + 25c car 2.50 1.40
B490 SP264 4fr + 2fr blue 18.00 8.25
B491 SP265 8fr + 4fr bl grn 25.00 17.50
Nos. B485-B491 (7) 52.15 31.75

The surtax was for tuberculosis prevention and other charitable purposes.

Chemist SP266

Allegory of Peace SP268

Colonial Instructor and Class SP267

1951, Mar. 27 Unwmk.

B492 SP266 80c + 20c grn 1.40 1.00
B493 SP267 2.50fr + 50c vio brn 10.00 5.50
B494 SP268 4fr + 2fr dp bl 12.00 6.75
Nos. B492-B494 (3) 23.40 13.25

Surtax for the reconstruction fund of the UNESCO.

Monument to Political Prisoners — SP269

Fort of Breendonk SP270

8fr+4fr, Monument: profile of figure on pedestal.

1951, Aug. 20 Photo. *Perf. 11½*

B495 SP269 1.75fr + 25c blk brn 3.00 .50
B496 SP270 4fr + 2fr bl & sl gray 32.50 17.50
B497 SP269 8fr + 4fr dk bl grn 32.50 20.00
Nos. B495-B497 (3) 68.00 38.00

The surtax was for the erection of a national monument.

Queen Elisabeth — SP271

1951, Sept. 22

B498 SP271 90c + 10c grnsh gray 4.00 .90
B499 SP271 1.75fr + 25c plum 9.00 2.00
B500 SP271 3fr + 1fr grn 32.50 15.00
B501 SP271 4fr + 2fr gray bl 35.00 16.00
B502 SP271 8fr + 4fr sepia 45.00 20.00
Nos. B498-B502 (5) 125.50 53.90

The surtax was for the Queen Elisabeth Medical Foundation.

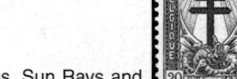

Cross, Sun Rays and Dragon — SP272

Beersel Castle SP273

Horst Castle — SP274

Castles: 4fr+2fr, Lavaux St. Anne. 8fr+4fr, Veves.

1951, Dec. 17 Engr. Unwmk.

B503 SP272 20c + 5c red .35 .25
B504 SP272 65c + 10c dp ultra .85 .30
B505 SP272 90c + 10c sep .90 .35
B506 SP272 1.20fr + 30c rose vio 1.40 .50
B507 SP273 1.75fr + 75c red brn 4.00 1.50
B508 SP274 3fr + 1fr yel grn 14.00 8.25
B509 SP273 4fr + 2fr blue 17.00 9.25
B510 SP274 8fr + 4fr gray 26.50 14.50
Nos. B503-B510 (8) 65.00 34.90

The surtax was for anti-tuberculosis work. See Nos. B523-B526, B547-B550.

Main Altar SP275

Basilica of the Sacred Heart Koekelberg SP276

Procession Bearing Relics of St. Albert of Louvain — SP277

1952, Mar. 1 Photo. *Perf. 11½*

B511 SP275 1.75fr + 25c blk brn 1.50 .50
B512 SP276 4fr + 2fr indigo 16.00 8.00

Engr.

B513 SP277 8fr + 4fr vio brn 25.00 11.50
a. Souv. sheet, #B511-B513 425.00 175.00
Nos. B511-B513 (3) 42.50 20.00

25th anniv. of the Cardinalate of J. E. Van Roey, Primate of Belgium. The surtax was for the Basilica. No. B513a sold for 30fr.

Beaulieu Castle, Malines — SP278

1952, May 14 Engr.

Laid Paper

B514 SP278 40fr + 10fr lt grnsh bl 140.00 100.00

Issued on the occasion of the 13th Universal Postal Union Congress, Brussels, 1952.

August Vermeylen SP279

Portraits: 80c+40c, Karel Van de Woestijne. 90c+45c, Charles de Coster. 1.75fr+75c, M. Maeterlinck. 4fr+2fr, Emile Verhaeren. 8fr+4fr, Hendrik Conscience.

Perf. 11½

1952, Oct. 24 Unwmk. Photo.

B515 SP279 65c + 30c pur 5.75 2.25
B516 SP279 80c + 40c dk grn 6.00 2.75
B517 SP279 90c + 45c sepia 6.25 3.00
B518 SP279 1.75fr + 75c cer 14.50 5.00
B519 SP279 4fr + 2fr bl vio 37.50 17.50

B520	SP279	8fr + 4fr dk brn	45.00	21.00
		Nos. B515-B520 (6)	115.00	51.50

1952, Nov. 15

4fr, Emile Verhaeren. 8fr, Hendrik Conscience.

B521	SP279	4fr (+ 9fr) blue	160.00	70.00
B522	SP279	8fr (+ 9fr) dk car rose	160.00	70.00

On Nos. B521-B522, the denomination is repeated at either side of the stamp. The surtax is expressed on se-tenant labels bearing quotations of Verhaeren (in French) and Conscience (in Flemish). Value is for stamp with label.

A 9-line black overprint was privately applied to these labels: "Conference Internationale de la Musique Bruxelles UNESCO International Music Conference Brussels 1953."

Values: unused or canceled, $75; never hinged $125.

Type of 1951 Dated "1952," and

Arms of Malmédy — SP281

Castle Ruins, Burgreuland SP282

Designs: 4fr+2fr, Vesdre Dam, Eupen. 8fr+4fr, St. Vitus, patron saint of Saint-Vith.

1952, Dec. 15 **Engr.**

B523	SP272	20c + 5c red brn	.50	.50
B524	SP272	80c + 20c grn	.95	.70
B525	SP272	1.20fr + 30c lil rose	2.00	1.10
B526	SP272	1.50fr + 50c ol brn	2.00	1.10
B527	SP281	2fr + 75c car	3.50	3.50
B528	SP282	3fr + 1.50fr choc	22.50	13.50
B529	SP281	4fr + 2fr blue	21.00	12.00
B530	SP281	8fr + 4fr vio brn	22.50	16.00
		Nos. B523-B530 (8)	74.95	48.40

The surtax on Nos. B523-B530 was for anti-tuberculosis and other charitable works.

Walthère Dewé — SP283

1953, Feb. 16 **Photo.**

B531	SP283	2fr + 1fr brn car	2.75	1.75

The surtax was for the construction of a memorial to Walthère Dewé, Underground leader in World War II.

Princess Josephine-Charlotte — SP284

1953, Mar. 14 **Cross in Red**

B532	SP284	80c + 20c ol grn	3.50	1.50
B533	SP284	1.20fr + 30c brn	3.25	1.25
B534	SP284	2fr + 50c rose lake	2.75	1.25
a.		Booklet pane of 8	80.00	65.00
B535	SP284	2.50fr + 50c crim	17.50	10.00
B536	SP284	4fr + 1fr brt blue	19.00	8.75
B537	SP284	5fr + 2fr sl grn	19.00	8.75
		Nos. B532-B537 (6)	65.00	31.50

The surtax was for the Belgian Red Cross.

The selvage of No. B534a is inscribed in French. Value for selvage inscribed in Dutch, $220.

Boats at Dock SP285

Bridge and Citadel, Namur — SP286

Designs: 1.20fr+30c, Bridge at Bouillon. 2fr+50c, Antwerp waterfront. 4fr+2fr, Wharf at Ghent. 8fr+4fr, Meuse River at Freyr.

1953, June 22 **Unwmk.** ***Perf. 11½***

B538	SP285	80c + 20c grn	2.25	1.00
B539	SP285	1.20fr + 30c redsh brn	6.00	2.75
B540	SP285	2fr + 50c sep	6.75	2.75
B541	SP286	2.50fr + 50c dp mag	16.00	8.00
B542	SP286	4fr + 2fr vio bl	26.50	13.00
B543	SP286	8fr + 4fr gray blk	32.50	15.00
		Nos. B538-B543 (6)	90.00	42.50

The surtax was used to promote tourism in the Ardenne-Meuse region and for various cultural works.

Allegory — SP287

1953, Oct. 26 **Engr.**

B544	SP287	80c + 20c grn	5.00	3.00
B545	SP287	2.50fr + 1fr rose car	30.00	20.00
B546	SP287	4fr + 1.50fr blue	32.50	22.50
		Nos. B544-B546 (3)	67.50	45.50

The surtax was for the European Bureau of Childhood and Youth.

Type of 1951 Dated "1953," and

Ernest Malvoz — SP288

Robert Koch SP289

Portraits: 3fr+1.50fr, Carlo Forlanini. 4fr+2fr, Leon Charles Albert Calmette.

1953, Dec. 15

B547	SP272	20c + 5c blue	.60	.55
B548	SP272	80c + 20c rose vio	1.60	.70
B549	SP272	1.20fr + 30c choc	2.50	1.00
B550	SP272	1.50fr + 50c dk gray	3.00	1.25
B551	SP288	2fr + 75c dk grn	4.00	1.75
B552	SP288	3fr + 1.50fr dk red	17.50	9.25
B553	SP288	4fr + 2fr ultra	20.00	11.00
B554	SP289	8fr + 4fr choc	25.00	13.50
		Nos. B547-B554 (8)	74.20	39.00

The surtax was for anti-tuberculosis and other charitable works.

King Albert I Statue — SP290

Albert I Monument, Namur SP291

9fr+4.50fr, Cliffs of Marche-les-Dames.

1954, Feb. 17 **Photo.**

B555	SP290	2fr + 50c chnt brn	10.00	3.75
B556	SP291	4fr + 2fr blue	32.50	14.50
B557	SP290	9fr + 4.50fr ol blk	27.50	15.00
		Nos. B555-B557 (3)	70.00	33.25

20th anniv. of the death of King Albert I. The surtax aided in the erection of the monument pictured on No. B556.

Political Prisoners' Monument SP292

Camp and Fort, Breendonk SP293

Design: 9fr+4.50fr, Political prisoners' monument (profile).

1954, Apr. 1 **Unwmk.** ***Perf. 11½***

B558	SP292	2fr + 1fr red	22.50	11.00
B559	SP293	4fr + 2fr dk brn	50.00	22.50
B560	SP292	9fr + 4.50fr ol grn	52.50	26.50
		Nos. B558-B560 (3)	125.00	60.00

The surtax was used toward the creation of a monument to political prisoners.

Gatehouse and Gateway SP294

Nuns in Courtyard SP295

Our Lady of the Vine SP296

2fr+1fr, Swans in stream. 7fr+3.50fr Nuns at well. 8fr+4fr, Statue above door.

1954, May 15

B561	SP294	80c + 20c dk bl grn	1.00	.75
B562	SP294	2fr + 1fr crim	12.00	1.60
B563	SP295	4fr + 2fr violet	17.00	10.00
B564	SP295	7fr + 3.50fr lil rose	40.00	21.00
B565	SP295	8fr + 4fr brown	40.00	21.00
B566	SP296	9fr + 4.50fr gray bl	65.00	32.50
		Nos. B561-B566 (6)	175.00	86.85

The surtax was for the Friends of the Beguinage of Bruges.

Child's Head — SP297

"The Blind Man and the Paralytic," by Antoine Carte SP298

1954, Dec. 1 **Engr.**

B567	SP297	20c + 5c dk grn	.50	.50
B568	SP297	80c + 20c dk gray	1.00	.90
B569	SP297	1.20fr + 30c org brn	2.00	1.00
B570	SP297	1.50fr + 50c pur	3.50	2.00
B571	SP298	2fr + 75c rose car	8.00	3.75
B572	SP298	4fr + 1fr brt blue	20.00	12.50
		Nos. B567-B572 (6)	35.00	20.65

The surtax was for anti-tuberculosis work.

Ernest Solvay SP299

Jean-Jacques Dony — SP300

Portraits: 1.20fr+30c, Egide Walschaerts. 2fr+50c, Leo H. Baekeland. 3fr+1fr, Jean-Etienne Lenoir. 4fr+2fr, Emile Fourcault and Emile Gobbe.

Perf. 11½

1955, Oct. 22 Unwmk. Photo.

B573	SP299	20c + 5c brn & dk brn	.40	.35
B574	SP300	80c + 20c vio	1.00	.50
B575	SP299	1.20fr + 30c ind	6.25	3.25
B576	SP300	2fr + 50c dp car	5.50	3.00
B577	SP300	3fr + 1fr dk grn	14.50	8.50
B578	SP299	4fr + 2fr brown	14.50	8.50
		Nos. B573-B578 (6)	42.15	24.10

Issued in honor of Belgian scientists.

The surtax was for the benefit of various cultural organizations.

"The Joys of Spring" by E. Canneel SP301

Einar Holböll SP302

Portraits: 4fr+2fr, John D. Rockefeller. 8fr+4fr, Sir Robert W. Philip.

1955, Dec. 5 Unwmk. *Perf. 11½*

B579	SP301	20c + 5c red lil	.70	.30
B580	SP301	80c + 20c grn	1.00	.65
B581	SP301	1.20fr + 30c redsh brn	2.50	.90
B582	SP301	1.50fr + 50c vio bl	3.00	1.10
B583	SP302	2fr + 50c car	9.50	4.75
B584	SP302	4fr + 2fr ultra	26.00	12.00
B585	SP302	8fr + 4fr ol gray	27.50	15.00
		Nos. B579-B585 (7)	70.20	34.70

The surtax was for anti-tuberculosis work.

Palace of Charles of Lorraine — SP303

Queen Elisabeth and Sonata by Mozart — SP304

Design: 2fr+1fr, Mozart at age 7.

1956, Mar. 19 Engr.

B586	SP303	80c + 20c steel bl	1.00	.25
B587	SP303	2fr + 1fr rose lake	4.25	2.50
B588	SP304	4fr + 2fr dull pur	8.00	4.25
		Nos. B586-B588 (3)	13.25	7.00

200th anniversary of the birth of Wolfgang Amadeus Mozart, composer.

The surtax was for the benefit of the Pro-Mozart Committee in Belgium.

Queen Elisabeth — SP305

1956, Aug. 16 Photo.

B589	SP305	80c + 20c slate grn	.50	.35
B590	SP305	2fr + 1fr deep plum	4.00	1.90
B591	SP305	4fr + 2fr brown	5.00	3.00
		Nos. B589-B591 (3)	9.50	5.25

Issued in honor of the 80th birthday of Queen Elisabeth. The surtax went to the Queen Elisabeth Foundation. See No. 659.

Ship with Cross — SP306

Infant on Scales SP307

Rehabilitation SP308

Design: 4fr+2fr, X-Ray examination.

1956, Dec. 17 Engr.

B592	SP306	20c + 5c redsh brn	.25	.25
B593	SP306	80c + 20c grn	.50	.35
B594	SP306	1.20fr + 30c dl lil	1.00	.50
B595	SP306	1.50fr + 50c lt sl bl	1.25	.80
B596	SP307	2fr + 50c ol grn	3.50	2.00
B597	SP307	4fr + 2fr dl pur	13.00	8.00
B598	SP308	8fr + 4fr dp car	15.00	10.00
		Nos. B592-B598 (7)	34.50	21.90

The surtax was for anti-tuberculosis work.

Charles Plisnier and Albrecht Rodenbach SP309

80c+20c, Emiel Vliebergh & Maurice Wilmotte. 1.20fr+30c, Paul Pastur & Julius Hoste. 2fr+50c, Lodewijk de Raet & Jules Destree. 3fr+1fr, Constantin Meunier & Constant Permeke. 4fr+2fr, Lieven Gevaert & Edouard Empain.

Perf. 11½

1957, June 8 Unwmk. Photo.

B599	SP309	20c + 5c brt vio	.25	.25
B600	SP309	80c + 20c lt red brn	.35	.25
B601	SP309	1.20f + 30c blk brn	.75	.60
B602	SP309	2fr + 50c claret	2.00	1.25
B603	SP309	3fr + 1fr dk ol grn	3.00	2.00
B604	SP309	4fr + 2fr vio bl	3.25	2.50
		Nos. B599-B604 (6)	9.60	6.85

The surtax was for the benefit of various cultural organizations.

Dogs and Antarctic Camp SP310

1957, Oct. 18 Engr. *Perf. 11½*

B605	SP310	5fr + 2.50fr gray, org & vio brn	3.25	2.25
a.		Sheet of 4, #B605b	175.00	140.00
b.		Blue, slate & red brown	35.00	29.00

Surtax for Belgian Antarctic Expedition, 1957-58.

Gen. Patton's Grave and Flag SP311

Gen. George S. Patton, Jr. — SP312

Designs: 2.50fr+50c, Memorial, Bastogne. 3fr+1fr, Gen. Patton decorating Brig. Gen. Anthony C. McAuliffe. 6fr+3fr, Tanks of 1918 and 1944.

1957, Oct. 28 Photo.

Size: 36x25mm, 25x36mm

B606	SP311	1fr + 50c dk gray	2.00	1.00
B607	SP311	2.50fr + 50c ol grn	3.00	1.60
B608	SP311	3fr + 1fr red brn	3.75	2.10
B609	SP312	5fr + 2.50fr grysh bl	8.75	5.50

Size: 53x35mm

B610	SP311	6fr + 3fr pale brn car	12.00	8.00
		Nos. B606-B610 (5)	29.50	18.20

The surtax was for the General Patton Memorial Committee and Patriotic Societies.

Adolphe Max — SP313

1957, Nov. 10 Engr.

B611	SP313	2.50fr + 1fr ultra	1.25	.50

18th anniversary of the death of Adolphe Max, mayor of Brussels. The surtax was for the national "Adolphe Max" fund.

"Chinels," Fosses SP314

"Op Signoorken," Malines SP315

Infanta Isabella Shooting Crossbow SP316

Legends: 1.50fr+50c, St. Remacle and the wolf. 2fr+1fr, Longman and the pea soup. 5fr+2fr, The Virgin with Inkwell, vert. 6fr+2.50fr, "Gilles" (clowns), Binche.

1957, Dec. 14 Engr. & Photo.

B612	SP314	30c + 20c	.25	.25
B613	SP315	1fr + 50c	.30	.30
B614	SP314	1.50fr + 50c	.60	.35
B615	SP315	2fr + 1fr	.85	.40
B616	SP316	2.50fr + 1fr	1.90	1.40
B617	SP316	5fr + 2fr	3.50	2.75
B618	SP316	6fr + 2.50fr	5.00	3.50
		Nos. B612-B618 (7)	12.40	8.95

The surtax was for anti-tuberculosis work. See Nos. B631-B637.

Benelux Gate SP317

Designs: 1fr+50c, Civil Engineering Pavilion. 1.50fr+50c, Belgian Congo & Ruanda-Urundi Pavilion. 2.50fr+1fr, Belgium 1900. 3fr+1.50fr, Atomium. 5fr+3fr, Telexpo Pavilion.

Perf. 11½

1958, Apr. 15 Unwmk. Engr.

Size: 35½x24½mm

B619	SP317	30c + 20c multi	.25	.25
B620	SP317	1fr + 50c multi	.25	.25
B621	SP317	1.50fr + 50c multi	.25	.25
B622	SP317	2.50fr + 1fr multi	.30	.25
B623	SP317	3fr + 1.50fr multi	.75	.50

Size: 49x33mm

B624	SP317	5fr + 3fr multi	1.50	1.00
		Nos. B619-B624 (6)	3.30	2.50

World's Fair, Brussels, Apr. 17-Oct. 19.

Marguerite van Eyck by Jan van Eyck — SP318

Christ Carrying Cross, by Hieronymus Bosch SP319

Paintings: 1.50fr+50c, St. Donatien, Jan Gossart. 2.50fr+1fr, Self-portrait, Lambert Lombard. 3fr+1.50fr, The Rower, James Ensor. 5fr+3fr, Henriette, Henri Evenepoel.

1958, Oct. 30 Photo. *Perf. 11½*

Various Frames in Ocher and Brown

B625	SP318	30c + 20c dk ol grn	.45	.25
B626	SP319	1fr + 50c mar	.50	.50
B627	SP318	1.50fr + 50c vio bl	1.00	.75
B628	SP318	2.50fr + 1fr dk brn	2.00	1.60
B629	SP319	3fr + 1.50fr dl red	3.00	2.00
B630	SP318	5fr + 3fr brt bl	5.00	4.50
		Nos. B625-B630 (6)	11.95	9.60

The surtax was for the benefit of various cultural organizations.

Type of 1957

Legends: 40c+10c, Elizabeth, Countess of Hoogstraten. 1fr+50c, Jean de Nivelles. 1.50fr+50c, St. Evermare play, Russon. 2fr+1fr, The Penitents of Furnes. 2.50fr+1fr, Manger and "Pax." 5fr+2fr, Sambre-Meuse procession. 6fr+2.50fr, Our Lady of Peace and "Pax," vert.

Engraved and Photogravure

1958, Dec. 6 Unwmk. *Perf. 11½*

B631	SP314	40c + 10c ultra & brt grn	.25	.25
B632	SP315	1fr + 50c gray brn & org	.30	.30
B633	SP315	1.50fr + 50c cl & brt grn	.55	.30
B634	SP314	2fr + 1fr brn & red	.60	.40
B635	SP316	2.50fr + 1fr vio brn & bl grn	1.75	1.00
B636	SP316	5fr + 2fr cl & bl	3.50	2.75
B637	SP316	6fr + 2.50fr bl & rose red	4.75	4.00
		Nos. B631-B637 (7)	11.70	9.00

The surtax was for anti-tuberculosis work.

"Europe of the Heart" SP320

1959, Feb. 25 Photo. Unwmk.

B638	SP320	1fr + 50c red lil	.40	.30
B639	SP320	2.50fr + 1fr dk grn	.90	.70
B640	SP320	5fr + 2.50fr dp brn	1.25	1.00
		Nos. B638-B640 (3)	2.55	2.00

The surtax was for aid for displaced persons.

Allegory of Blood Transfusion SP321

Henri Dunant and Battlefield at Solferino — SP322

Design: 2.50fr+1fr, 3fr+1.50fr, Red Cross, broken sword and drop of blood, horiz.

1959, June 10 Photo. *Perf. 11½*

B641	SP321	40c + 10c	.30	.30
B642	SP321	1fr + 50c	1.10	.45
B643	SP321	1.50fr + 50c	3.00	1.60
B644	SP321	2.50fr + 1fr	3.50	1.90
B645	SP321	3fr + 1.50fr	6.00	3.50
B646	SP322	5fr + 3fr	12.00	5.50
		Nos. B641-B646 (6)	25.90	13.25

Cent. of the Intl. Red Cross idea. Surtax for the Red Cross and patriotic organizations.

Philip the Good — SP323

Arms of Philip the Good SP324

Designs: 1fr+50c, Charles the Bold. 1.50fr+50c, Emperor Maximilian of Austria. 2.50fr+1fr, Philip the Fair. 3fr+1.50fr, Charles V. Portraits from miniatures by Simon Bening (c. 1483-1561).

1959, July 4 Engr.

B647	SP323	40c + 10c multi	.25	.25
B648	SP323	1fr + 50c multi	.35	.35
B649	SP323	1.50fr + 50c multi	1.25	.80
B650	SP323	2.50fr + 1fr multi	2.25	1.90
B651	SP323	3fr + 1.50fr multi	4.00	3.00
B652	SP324	5fr + 3fr multi	5.50	4.00
		Nos. B647-B652 (6)	13.60	10.30

The surtax was for the Royal Library, Brussels.

Portraits show Grand Masters of the Order of the Golden Fleece.

Whale, Antwerp SP325

Carnival, Stavelot SP326

Designs: 1fr+50c, Dragon, Mons. 2fr+50c, Prince Carnival, Eupen. 3fr+1fr, Jester and cats, Ypres. 6fr+2fr, Holy Family, horiz. 7fr+3fr, Madonna, Liége, horiz.

Engraved and Photogravure

1959, Dec. 5 *Perf. 11½*

B653	SP325	40c + 10c cit, Prus bl & red	.25	.25
B654	SP325	1fr + 50c ol & grn	.35	.25
B655	SP325	2fr + 50c lt brn, org & cl	.45	.30
B656	SP326	2.50fr + 1fr gray, pur & ultra	.70	.30
B657	SP326	3fr + 1fr gray, mar & yel	1.75	1.00
B658	SP326	6fr + 2fr ol, brt bl & hn brn	4.00	3.00
B659	SP326	7fr + 3fr chlky bl & org yel	5.00	4.25
		Nos. B653-B659 (7)	12.50	9.35

The surtax was for anti-tuberculosis work.

Child Refugee — SP327

Designs: 3fr+1.50fr, Man. 6fr+3fr, Woman.

1960, Apr. 7 Engr.

B660	SP327	40c + 10c rose claret	.25	.25
B661	SP327	3fr + 1.50fr gray brn	.50	.25
B662	SP327	6fr + 3fr dk bl	1.00	.90
a.		Souvenir sheet of 3	70.00	60.00
		Nos. B660-B662 (3)	1.75	1.40

World Refugee Year, 7/1/59-6/30/60.

No. B662a contains Nos. B660-B662 with colors changed: 40c+10c, dull purple; 3fr+1.50fr, red brown; 6fr+3fr, henna brown.

Parachutists and Plane SP328

Designs: 2fr+50c, 2.50fr+1fr, Parachutists coming in for landing, vert 3fr+1fr, 6fr+2fr, Parachutist walking with parachute.

Photogravure and Engraved

1960, June 13 *Perf. 11½*

Multicolored

B663	SP328	40c + 10c	.25	.25
B664	SP328	1fr + 50c	1.50	.70
B665	SP328	2fr + 50c	3.25	2.00
B666	SP328	2.50fr + 1fr	5.00	3.00
B667	SP328	3fr + 1fr	5.00	3.00
B668	SP328	6fr + 2fr	6.00	4.00
		Nos. B663-B668 (6)	21.00	12.95

The surtax was for various patriotic and cultural organizations.

Mother and Child, Planes and Rainbow SP329

Designs: 40c+10c, Brussels Airport, planes and rainbow. 6fr+3fr, Rainbow connecting Congo and Belgium, and planes, vert

Perf. 11½

1960, Aug. 3 Unwmk. Photo.

Size: 35x24mm

B669	SP329	40c + 10c grnsh blue	.25	.25
B670	SP329	3fr + 1.50fr brt red	2.25	1.50

Size: 35x52mm

B671	SP329	6fr + 3fr violet	4.50	3.50
		Nos. B669-B671 (3)	7.00	5.25

The surtax was for refugees from Congo.

Infant, Milk Bottle and Mug — SP330

UNICEF: 1fr+50c, Nurse and children of 3 races. 2fr+50c, Refugee woman carrying gift clothes. 2.50fr+1fr, Negro nurse weighing infant. 3fr+1fr, Children of various races dancing. 6fr+2fr, Refugee boys.

Photogravure and Engraved

1960, Oct. 8 *Perf. 11½*

B672	SP330	40c + 10c gldn brn, yel & bl grn	.25	.25
B673	SP330	1fr + 50c ol gray, mar & slate	.75	.50
B674	SP330	2fr + 50c vio, pale brn & brt grn	1.75	1.40
B675	SP330	2.50fr + 1fr dk red, sep & lt bl	2.00	1.40
B676	SP330	3fr + 1fr bl grn, red org & dl vio	2.50	1.60
B677	SP330	6fr + 2fr ultra, emer & brn	4.00	2.50
		Nos. B672-B677 (6)	11.25	7.65

Tapestry SP331

Belgian handicrafts: 1fr+50c, Cut crystal vases, vert. 2fr+50c, Lace, vert. 2.50fr+1fr, Metal plate & jug. 3fr+1fr, Diamonds. 6fr+2fr, Ceramics.

1960, Dec. 5 *Perf. 11½*

Multicolored

B678	SP331	40c + 10c	.25	.25
B679	SP331	1fr + 50c	.75	.75
B680	SP331	2fr + 50c	1.50	1.00
B681	SP331	2.50fr + 1fr	3.00	2.25
B682	SP331	3fr + 1fr	3.50	2.25
B683	SP331	6fr + 2fr	5.00	3.25
		Nos. B678-B683 (6)	14.00	9.75

The surtax was for anti-tuberculosis work.

Jacob Kats and Abbe Nicolas Pietkin SP332

Portraits: 1fr+50c, Albert Mockel and J. F. Willems. 2fr+50c, Jan van Rijswijck and Xavier M. Neujean. 2.50fr+1fr, Joseph Demarteau and A. Van de Perre. 3fr+1fr, Canon Jan-Baptist David and Albert du Bois. 6fr+2fr, Henri Vieuxtemps and Willem de Mol.

1961, Apr. 22 Unwmk. *Perf. 11½*

Multicolored

Portraits in Gray Brown

B684	SP332	40c + 10c	.50	.30
B685	SP332	1fr + 50c	2.25	1.25
B686	SP332	2fr + 50c	3.75	3.00
B687	SP332	2.50fr + 1fr	3.75	3.00
B688	SP332	3fr + 1fr	4.25	3.00
B689	SP332	6fr + 2fr	6.00	4.00
		Nos. B684-B689 (6)	20.50	14.55

The surtax was for the benefit of various cultural organizations.

White Rhinoceros SP333

Animals: 1fr+50c, Przewalski horses. 2fr+50c, Okapi. 2.50fr+1fr, Giraffe, horiz. 3fr+1fr, Lesser panda, horiz. 6fr+2fr, European elk, horiz.

Perf. 11½

1961, June 5 Unwmk. Photo.

Multicolored

B690	SP333	40c + 10c	.25	.25
B691	SP333	1fr + 50c	1.10	.70
B692	SP333	2fr + 50c	1.60	1.40
B693	SP333	2.50fr + 1fr	1.90	1.50
B694	SP333	3fr + 1fr	2.25	1.50
B695	SP333	6fr + 2fr	2.75	2.00
		Nos. B690-B695 (6)	9.85	7.35

The surtax was for various philanthropic organizations.

Antonius Cardinal Perrenot de Granvelle — SP334

Designs: 3fr+1.50fr, Arms of Cardinal de Granvelle. 6fr+3fr, Tower and crosier, symbolic of collaboration between Malines and the Archbishopric.

1961, July 29 Engr.

B696	SP334	40c + 10c mag, car & brn	.25	.25
B697	SP334	3fr + 1.50fr multi	.70	.60
B698	SP334	6fr + 3fr mag pur & bis	1.40	1.10
		Nos. B696-B698 (3)	2.35	1.95

400th anniv. of Malines as an Archbishopric.

Mother and Child by Pierre Paulus — SP335

Plaintings: 1fr+50c, Mother Love, Francois-Joseph Navez. 2fr+50c, Motherhood, Constant Permeke. 2.50fr+1fr, Madonna and Child, Rogier van der Weyden. 3fr+1fr, Madonna with Apple, Hans Memling. 6fr+2fr, Madonna of the Forget-me-not, Peter Paul Rubens.

1961, Dec. 2 Photo. *Perf. 11½*

Gold Frame

B699	SP335	40c + 10c dp brn	.25	.25
B700	SP335	1fr + 50c brt bl	.60	.55
B701	SP335	2fr + 50c rose red	1.10	1.00
B702	SP335	2.50fr + 1fr mag	1.25	1.00
B703	SP335	3fr + 1fr vio bl	1.10	.90

B704 SP335 6fr + 2fr dk sl grn 1.60 1.40
Nos. B699-B704 (6) 5.90 5.10

The surtax was for anti-tuberculosis work.

Castle of the Counts of Male — SP336

Designs: 90c+10c, Royal library, horiz. 1fr+50c, Church of Our Lady, Tongres. 2fr+50c, Collegiate Church, Soignies, horiz. 2.50fr+1fr, Church of Our Lady, Malines. 3fr+1fr, St. Denis Abbey, Broqueroi. 6fr+2fr, Cloth Hall, Ypres, horiz.

1962, Mar. 12 Engr. *Perf. 11½*

B705 SP336 40c + 10c brt grn .25 .25
B706 SP336 90c + 10c lil rose .25 .25
B707 SP336 1fr + 50c dl vio .45 .45
B708 SP336 2fr + 50c violet .85 .85
B709 SP336 2.50fr + 1fr red brn 1.10 1.00
B710 SP336 3fr + 1fr bl grn 1.25 1.00
B711 SP336 6fr + 2fr car rose 2.00 1.75
Nos. B705-B711 (7) 6.15 5.55

The surtax was for various cultural and philanthropic organizations.

Andean Cock of the Rock — SP337

Birds: 1fr+50c, Red lory. 2fr+50c, Guinea touraco. 2.50fr+1fr, Keel-billed toucan. 3fr+1fr, Great bird of paradise. 6fr+2fr, Congolese peacock.

Engraved and Photogravure

1962, June 23 Unwmk. *Perf. 11½*

B712 SP337 40c + 10c multi .25 .25
B713 SP337 1fr + 50c multi .45 .45
B714 SP337 2fr + 50c multi .85 .75
B715 SP337 2.50fr + 1fr multi 1.10 1.00
B716 SP337 3fr + 1fr multi 1.40 1.25
B717 SP337 6fr + 2fr multi 1.75 1.60
Nos. B712-B717 (6) 5.80 5.30

The surtax was for various philanthropic organizations.

Handicapped Child — SP338

Handicapped Children: 40c+10c, Reading Braille. 2fr+50c, Deaf-mute girl with earphones and electronic equipment, horiz. 2.50fr+1fr, Child with ball (cerebral palsy). 3fr+1fr, Girl with crutches (polio). 6fr+2fr, Sitting boys playing ball, horiz.

1962, Sept. 22 Photo.

B718 SP338 40c + 10c choc .25 .25
B719 SP338 1fr + 50c rose red .45 .45
B720 SP338 2fr + 50c brt lil 1.00 .90
B721 SP338 2.50fr + 1fr dl grn 1.00 .90
B722 SP338 3fr + 1fr dk blue 1.00 .90
B723 SP338 6fr + 2fr dk brn 1.50 1.25
Nos. B718-B723 (6) 5.20 4.65

The surtax was for various institutions for handicapped children.

Queen Louise-Marie SP339

Belgian Queens: No. B725, like No. B724 with "ML" initials. 1fr+50c, Marie-Henriette. 2fr+1fr, Elisabeth. 3fr+1.50fr, Astrid. 8fr+2.50fr, Fabiola.

1962, Dec. 8 Photo. & Engr.
Gray, Black & Gold

B724 SP339 40c + 10c ("L") .25 .25
B725 SP339 40c + 10c ("ML") .25 .25
B726 SP339 1fr + 50c .60 .50
B727 SP339 2fr + 1fr 1.25 1.10
B728 SP339 3fr + 1.50fr 1.75 1.40
B729 SP339 8fr + 2.50fr 2.00 1.60
Nos. B724-B729 (6) 6.10 5.10

The surtax was for anti-tuberculosis work.

British War Memorial (Porte de Menin), Ypres SP340

1962, Dec. 26 Engr. *Perf. 11½*

B730 SP340 1fr + 50c multi .40 .40

Millennium of the city of Ypres. Issued in sheets of eight. Value, $6.

Peace Bell Ringing over Globe — SP341

Engraved and Photogravure

1963, Feb. 18 Unwmk. *Perf. 11½*

B731 SP341 3fr +1.50fr multi 1.60 1.60
a. Sheet of 4 7.75 7.75
B732 SP341 6fr +3fr multi .80 .80

The surtax was for the installation of the Peace Bell (Bourdon de la Paix) at Koekelberg Basilica and for the benefit of various cultural organizations.

No. B731 was issued in sheets of 4, No. B732 in sheets of 30.

The Sower by Brueghel — SP342

Designs: 3fr+1fr, The Harvest, by Brueghel, horiz. 6fr+2fr, "Bread," by Anton Carte, horiz.

1963, Mar. 21 *Perf. 11½*

B733 SP342 2fr +1fr multi .25 .25
B734 SP342 3fr +1fr multi .35 .30
B735 SP342 6fr +2fr multi .55 .50
Nos. B733-B735 (3) 1.15 1.05

FAO "Freedom from Hunger" campaign.

Speed Racing — SP343

2fr+1fr, Bicyclists at check point, horiz. 3fr+1.50fr, Team racing, horiz. 6fr+3fr, Pace setters.

Perf. 11½

1963, July 13 Unwmk. Engr.

B736 SP343 1fr + 50c multi .25 .25
B737 SP343 2fr + 1fr bl, car, blk & ol gray .25 .25
B738 SP343 3fr + 1.50fr multi .35 .35
B739 SP343 6fr + 3fr multi .55 .55
Nos. B736-B739 (4) 1.40 1.40

80th anniversary of the founding of the Belgian Bicycle League. The surtax was for athletes at the 1964 Olympic Games.

Princess Paola with Princess Astrid — SP344

Prince Albert and Family — SP345

Designs: 40c+10c, Prince Philippe. 2fr+50c, Princess Astrid. 2.50fr+1fr, Princess Paola. 6fr+2fr, Prince Albert.

1963, Sept. 28 Photo.

B740 SP344 40c + 10c .25 .25
B741 SP344 1fr + 50c .25 .25
B742 SP344 2fr + 50c .35 .35
B743 SP344 2.50fr + 1fr .45 .40
B744 SP345 3fr + 1fr brn & multi .65 .65
B745 SP345 3fr + 1fr yel grn & multi 2.00 2.00
a. Booklet pane of 8 18.00 18.00
B746 SP344 6fr + 2fr 1.75 1.75
Nos. B740-B746 (7) 5.70 5.65

Cent. of the Intl, Red Cross. No. B745 issued in booklet panes of 8, which are in two forms: French and Flemish inscriptions in top and bottom margins transposed. Value the same.

Daughter of Balthazar Gerbier, Painted by Rubens — SP346

Jesus, St. John and Cherubs by Rubens — SP347

Portraits (Rubens' sons): 1fr+40c, Nicolas, 2 yrs. old. 2fr+50c, Franz. 2.50fr+1fr, Nicolas, 6 yrs. old. 3fr+1fr, Albert.

Photogravure and Engraved

1963, Dec. 7 Unwmk. *Perf. 11½*

B747 SP346 50c + 10c .25 .25
B748 SP346 1fr + 40c .25 .25
B749 SP346 2fr + 50c .35 .35
B750 SP346 2.50fr + 1fr .65 .65
B751 SP346 3fr + 1fr .55 .55
B752 SP347 6fr + 2fr 1.00 1.00
Nos. B747-B752 (6) 3.05 3.05

The surtax was for anti-tuberculosis work. See No. B771.

John Quincy Adams and Lord Gambier Signing Treaty of Ghent, by Amédée Forestier — SP348

1964, May 16 Photo. *Perf. 11½*

B753 SP348 6fr + 3fr dk blue .65 .65

Signing of the Treaty of Ghent between the US and Great Britain, Dec. 24, 1814.

Philip van Marnix — SP349

Portraits: 3fr+1.50fr, Ida de Bure Calvin. 6fr+3fr, Jacob Jordaens.

1964, May 30 Engr.

B754 SP349 1fr + 50c blue gray .25 .25
B755 SP349 3fr + 1.50fr rose pink .25 .25
B756 SP349 6fr + 3fr redsh brn .55 .55
Nos. B754-B756 (3) 1.05 1.05

Issued to honor Protestantism in Belgium. The surtax was for the erection of a Protestant church.

Foot Soldier, 1918 — SP350

Designs: 2fr+1fr, Flag bearer, Guides Regiment, 1914. 3fr+1.50fr, Trumpeter of the Grenadiers and drummers, 1914.

1964, Aug. 1 Photo. *Perf. 11½*

B757 SP350 1fr + 50c multi .25 .25
B758 SP350 2fr + 1fr multi .25 .25
B759 SP350 3fr + 1.50fr multi .35 .35
Nos. B757-B759 (3) .85 .85

50th anniversary of the German aggression against Belgium in 1914. The surtax aided patriotic undertakings.

Battle of Bastogne — SP351

6fr+3fr, Liberation of the estuary of the Escaut.

1964, Aug. 1 Unwmk.

B760 SP351 3fr + 1fr multi .25 .25
B761 SP351 6fr + 3fr multi .60 .60

Belgium's Resistance and liberation of World War II. The surtax was to help found an International Student Center at Antwerp and to aid cultural undertakings.

Souvenir Sheets

Rogier van der Weyden Paintings — SP352

Descent From the Cross — SP353

1964, Sept. 19 Photo. *Perf. 11½*

B762 SP352 Sheet of 3 4.25 4.25
- *a.* 1fr Philip the Good 1.10 1.10
- *b.* 2fr Portrait of a Lady 1.10 1.10
- *c.* 3fr Man with Arrow 1.10 1.10

Engr.

B763 SP353 8fr red brown 4.25 4.25

Rogier van der Weyden (Roger de La Pasture, 1400-64). The surtax went to various cultural organizations. No. B762 sold for 14fr, No. B763 for 10fr.

Ancient View of the Pand — SP354

3fr+1fr, Present view of the Pand from Lys River.

1964, Oct. 10 Photo.

B764 SP354 2fr + 1fr blk, grnsh bl & ultra .30 .25
B765 SP354 3fr + 1fr lil rose, bl & dk brn .30 .25

The surtax was for the restoration of the Pand Dominican Abbey in Ghent.

Type of 1963 and

Child of Charles I, Painted by Van Dyck — SP355

Designs: 1fr+40c, William of Orange with his bride, by Van Dyck. 2fr+1fr, Portrait of a small boy with dogs by Erasmus Quellin and Jan Fyt. 3fr+1fr, Alexander Farnese by Antonio Moro. 4fr+2fr, William II, Prince of Orange by Van Dyck. 6fr+3fr, Artist's children by Cornelis De Vos.

1964, Dec. 5 Engr. *Perf. 11½*

B766 SP355 50c + 10c rose clar .25 .25
B767 SP355 1fr + 40c car rose .25 .25
B768 SP355 2fr + 1fr vio brn .25 .25
B769 SP355 3fr + 1fr gray .30 .30
B770 SP355 4fr + 2fr vio bl .35 .35
B771 SP347 6fr + 3fr brt pur .45 .45
Nos. B766-B771 (6) 1.85 1.85

The surtax was for anti-tuberculosis work.

Liberator, Shaking Prisoner's Hand, Concentration Camp — SP356

Designs: 1fr+50c, Prisoner's hand reaching for the sun. 3fr+1.50fr, Searchlights and tank breaking down barbed wire, horiz. 8fr+5fr, Rose growing amid the ruins, horiz.

Engraved and Photogravure

1965, May 8 Unwmk. *Perf. 11½*

B772 SP356 50c + 50c tan, blk & buff .25 .25
B773 SP356 1fr + 50c multi .25 .25
B774 SP356 3fr + 1.50fr dl lil & blk .35 .35
B775 SP356 8fr + 5fr multi .70 .70
Nos. B772-B775 (4) 1.55 1.55

20th anniv. of the liberation of the concentration camps for political prisoners and prisoners of war.

Stoclet House, Brussels SP357

Stoclet House: 6fr+3fr, Hall with marble foundation, vert. 8fr+4fr, View of house from garden.

1965, June 21

B776 SP357 3fr + 1fr slate & tan .35 .35
B777 SP357 6fr + 3fr sepia .60 .60
B778 SP357 8fr + 4fr vio brn & tan .85 .85
Nos. B776-B778 (3) 1.80 1.80

Austrian architect Josef Hoffmann (1870-1956), builder of the art nouveau residence of Adolphe Stoclet, engineer and financier.

Jackson's Chameleon SP358

Animals from Antwerp Zoo: 2fr+1fr, Common iguanas. 3fr+1.50fr, African monitor. 6fr+3fr, Komodo monitor. 8fr+4fr, Nile softshell turtle.

1965, Oct. 16 Photo. *Perf. 11½*

B779 SP358 1fr + 50c multi .25 .25
B780 SP358 2fr + 1fr multi .25 .25
B781 SP358 3fr + 1.50fr multi .35 .35
B782 SP358 6fr + 3fr multi .50 .50
Nos. B779-B782 (4) 1.35 1.35

Miniature Sheet

B783 SP358 8fr + 4fr multi 1.50 1.50

The surtax was for various cultural and philanthropic organizations. No. B783 contains one stamp, size: 52x35mm.

Boatmen's and Archers' Guild Halls SP359

Buildings on Grand-Place, Brussels: 1fr+40c, Brewers' Hall. 2fr+1fr, "King of Spain." 3fr+1.50fr, "Dukes of Brabant." 10fr+4.50fr, Tower of City Hall and St. Michael.

1965, Dec. 4 Engr. *Perf. 11½*

Size: 35x24mm

B784 SP359 50c + 10c ultra .25 .25
B785 SP359 1fr + 40c bl grn .25 .25
B786 SP359 2fr + 1fr rose cl .25 .25
B787 SP359 3fr + 1.50fr violet .35 .35

Size: 24x44mm

B788 SP359 10fr + 4.50fr sep & gray .80 .80
Nos. B784-B788 (5) 1.90 1.90

The surtax was for anti-tuberculosis work.

Souvenir Sheets

Queen Elisabeth — SP360

Design: No. B790, Types of 1931 and 1956.

1966, Apr. 16 Photo. *Perf. 11½*

B789 SP360 Sheet of 2 + label 1.50 1.50
- *a.* SP74 3fr dk brn & gray grn .60 .60
- *b.* SP87 3fr dk brn, yel grn & gold .60 .60

B790 SP360 Sheet of 2 + label 1.50 1.50
- *a.* SP42 3fr dk brn & dl bl .60 .60
- *b.* SP304 3fr dk brn & gray .60 .60

The surtax went to various cultural organizations.
Each sheet sold for 20fr.

Luminescent Paper was used in printing Nos. B789-B790, B801-B806, B808-B809, B811-B823, B825-B831, B833-B835, B837-B840, B842-B846, B848-B850, B852-B854, B856-B863, and from B865 onward unless otherwise noted. In many cases the low value of the set is not on luminescent paper. This will not be noted.

Diver — SP361

Design: 10fr+4fr, Swimmer at start.

1966, May 9 Engr.

B791 SP361 60c + 40c Prus grn, ol & org brn .25 .25
B792 SP361 10fr + 4fr ol grn, org brn & mag .80 .80

Issued to publicize the importance of swimming instruction.

Minorites' Convent, Liège — SP362

Designs: 1fr+50c, Val-Dieu Abbey, Aubel. 2fr+1fr, View and seal of Huy. 10fr+4.50fr, Statue of Ambiorix by Jules Bertin, and tower, Tongeren.

1966, Aug. 27 Engr. *Perf. 11½*

B793 SP362 60c + 40c multi .25 .25
B794 SP362 1fr + 50c multi .25 .25
B795 SP362 2fr + 1fr multi .25 .25
B796 SP362 10fr + 4.50fr multi .75 .75
Nos. B793-B796 (4) 1.50 1.50

The surtax was for various patriotic and cultural organizations.

Surveyor and Dog Team SP363

3fr+1.50fr, Adrien de Gerlache, "Belgica." 6fr+3fr, Surveyor, weather balloon, ship. 10fr+5fr, Penguins, "Magga Dan" (ship used for 1964, 1965 & 1966 expeditions).

1966, Oct. 8 Engr. *Perf. 11½*

B797 SP363 1fr + 50c bl grn .25 .25
B798 SP363 3fr + 1.50fr pale vio .25 .25
B799 SP363 6fr + 3fr dk car .50 .50
Nos. B797-B799 (3) 1.00 1.00

Souvenir Sheet

Engraved and Photogravure

B800 SP363 10fr + 5fr dk gray, sky bl & dk red 1.00 1.00

Belgian Antarctic expeditions. No. B800 contains one 52x35mm stamp.

Boy with Ball and Dog — SP364

Designs: 2fr+1fr, Girl skipping rope. 3fr+1.50fr, Girl and boy blowing soap bubbles. 6fr+3fr, Girl and boy rolling hoops, horiz. 8fr+3.50fr, Four children at play and cat, horiz.

1966, Dec. 3 *Perf. 11½*

B801 SP364 1fr + 1fr pink & blk .25 .25
B802 SP364 2fr + 1fr lt bluish grn & blk .25 .25
B803 SP364 3fr + 1.50fr lt vio & blk .25 .25
B804 SP364 6fr + 3fr pale sal & dk brn .50 .50
B805 SP364 8fr + 3.50fr lt yel grn & dk brn .65 .65
Nos. B801-B805 (5) 1.90 1.90

The surtax was for anti-tuberculosis work.

Souvenir Sheet

Refugees — SP365

1fr, Boy receiving clothes. 2fr, Tibetan children. 3fr, African mother and children.

1967, Mar. 11 Photo. *Perf. 11½*

B806 SP365 Sheet of 3 1.10 1.10
- *a.* 1fr black & yellow .30 .30
- *b.* 2fr black & blue .30 .30
- *c.* 3fr black & orange .40 .40

Issued to help refugees around the world. Sheet has black border with Belgian P.T.T. and UN Refugee emblems. Sold for 20fr.

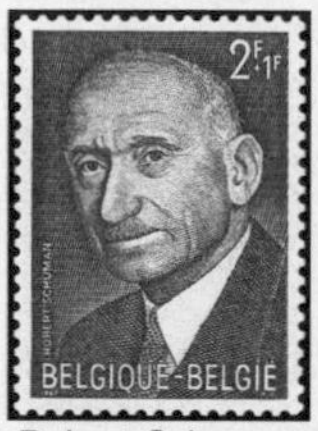

Robert Schuman
SP366

Colonial Brotherhood Emblem
SP368

Kongolo Memorial, Gentinnes
SP367

1967, June 24 Engr. *Perf. 11½*

B807 SP366 2fr + 1fr gray blue .25 .25

Engraved and Photogravure

B808 SP367 5fr + 2fr brn & ol .40 .40
B809 SP368 10fr + 5fr multi .85 .85
Nos. B807-B809 (3) 1.50 1.50

Robert Schuman (1886-1963), French statesman, one of the founders of European Steel and Coal Community, 1st pres. of European Parliament (2fr+1fr); Kongolo Memorial, erected in memory of missionary and civilian victims in the Congo (5fr+2fr); a memorial for African Troops, Brussels (10fr+5fr).

Preaching Fool from "Praise of Folly" by Erasmus
SP369

Erasmus, by Quentin Massys
SP370

Designs: 2fr+1fr, Exhorting Fool from Praise of Folly. 5fr+2fr, Thomas More's Family, by Hans Holbein, horiz. 6fr+3fr, Pierre Gilles (Aegidius), by Quentin Massys.

Photogravure and Engraved (SP369); Photogravure (SP370)

1967, Sept. 2 Unwmk. *Perf. 11*

B810 SP369 1fr + 50c tan, blk, bl & car .25 .25
B811 SP369 2fr + 1fr tan, blk & car .25 .25
B812 SP370 3fr + 1.50fr multi .25 .25
B813 SP369 5fr + 2fr tan, blk & car .45 .45
B814 SP370 6fr + 3fr multi .55 .55
Nos. B810-B814 (5) 1.75 1.75

Issued to commemorate Erasmus (1466(?)-1536), Dutch scholar and his era.

Souvenir Sheet

Pro-Post Association Emblem — SP371

Engraved and Photogravure

1967, Oct. 21 *Perf. 11½*

B815 SP371 10fr + 5fr multi 1.00 1.00

Issued to publicize the POSTPHILA Philatelic Exhibition, Brussels, Oct. 21-29.

Detail from Brueghel's "Children's Games" — SP372

Designs: Various Children's Games. Singles of Nos. B816-B821 arranged in 2 rows of 3 show complete painting by Pieter Brueghel.

1967, Dec. 9 Photo. *Perf. 11½*

B816 SP372 1fr + 50c multi .25 .25
B817 SP372 2fr + 50c multi .25 .25
B818 SP372 3fr + 1fr multi .30 .30
B819 SP372 6fr + 3fr multi .50 .50
B820 SP372 10fr + 4fr multi .85 .85
B821 SP372 13fr + 6fr multi 1.10 1.10
Nos. B816-B821 (6) 3.25 3.25

Queen Fabiola Holding Refugee Child from Congo — SP373

6fr+3fr, Queen Elisabeth & Dr. Depage.

1968, Apr. 27 Photo. *Perf. 11½*

Cross in Red

B822 SP373 6fr + 3fr sepia & gray .65 .65
B823 SP373 10fr + 5fr sepia & gray .95 .95

The surtax was for the Red Cross.

Woman Gymnast and Calendar Stone
SP374

Yachting and "The Swimmer" by Andrien — SP375

Designs: 2fr+1fr, Weight lifter and Mayan motif. 3fr+1.50fr, Hurdler, colossus of Tula and animal head from Kukulkan. 6fr+2fr, Bicyclists and Chichen Itza Temple.

Engraved and Photogravure

1968, May 27 *Perf. 11½*

B824 SP374 1fr + 50c multi .25 .25
B825 SP374 2fr + 1fr multi .25 .25
B826 SP374 3fr + 1.50fr multi .25 .25
B827 SP374 6fr + 2fr multi .55 .55

Photo.

B828 SP375 13fr + 5fr multi 1.10 1.10
Nos. B824-B828 (5) 2.40 2.40

Issued to publicize the 19th Olympic Games, Mexico City, Oct. 12-27.

"Explosion"
SP376

Designs (Paintings by Pol Mara): 12fr+5fr, "Fire." 13fr+5fr, "Tornado."

1968, June 22 Photo.

B829 SP376 10fr + 5fr multi .75 .75
B830 SP376 12fr + 5fr multi 1.00 1.00
B831 SP376 13fr + 5fr multi 1.25 1.25
Nos. B829-B831 (3) 3.00 3.00

The surtax was for disaster victims.

Undulate Triggerfish
SP377

Tropical Fish: 3fr+1.50fr, Angelfish. 6fr+3fr, Turkeyfish (Pterois volitans). 10fr+5fr, Orange butterflyfish.

1968, Oct. 19 Engr. & Photo.

B832 SP377 1fr + 50c multi .25 .25
B833 SP377 3fr + 1.50fr multi .25 .25
B834 SP377 6fr + 3fr multi .55 .55
B835 SP377 10fr + 5fr multi .90 .90
Nos. B832-B835 (4) 1.95 1.95

King Albert and Queen Elisabeth Entering Brussels
SP378

Tomb of the Unknown Soldier and Eternal Flame, Brussels — SP379

Designs: 1fr+50c, King Albert, Queen Elisabeth and Crown Prince Leopold on balcony, Bruges, vert. 6fr+3fr, King and Queen entering Liège.

1968, Nov. 9 Photo. *Perf. 11½*

B836 SP378 1fr + 50c multi .25 .25
B837 SP378 3fr + 1.50fr multi .25 .25
B838 SP378 6fr + 3fr multi .50 .50

Engraved and Photogravure

B839 SP379 10fr + 5fr multi .75 .75
Nos. B836-B839 (4) 1.75 1.75

50th anniv. of the victory in World War I.

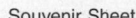

Souvenir Sheet

The Painter and the Amateur, by Peter Brueghel — SP380

1969, May 10 Engr. *Perf. 11½*

B840 SP380 10fr + 5fr sepia 1.10 1.10

Issued to publicize the POSTPHILA 1969 Philatelic Exhibition, Brussels, May 10-18.

Huts, by Ivanka D. Pancheva, Bulgaria — SP381

Children's Drawings and UNICEF Emblem: 3fr+1.50fr, "My Art" (Santa Claus), by Claes Patric, Belgium. 6fr+3fr, "In the Sun" (young boy), by Helena Rejchlova, Czechoslovakia. 10fr+5fr, "Out for a Walk" by Phillis Sporn, US, horiz.

1969, May 31 Photo. *Perf. 11½*

B841 SP381 1fr + 50c multi .25 .25
B842 SP381 3fr + 1.50fr multi .25 .25
B843 SP381 6fr + 3fr multi .55 .55
B844 SP381 10fr + 5fr multi .85 .85
Nos. B841-B844 (4) 1.90 1.90

The surtax was for philanthropic purposes.

Msgr. Victor Scheppers
SP382

1969, July 5 Engr.

B845 SP382 6fr + 3fr rose claret .70 .70

Msgr. Victor Scheppers (1802-77), prison reformer and founder of the Brothers of Mechlin (Scheppers).

Moon Landing Type of 1969

Souvenir Sheet

Design: 20fr+10fr, Armstrong, Collins and Aldrin and moon with Tranquillity Base, vert.

1969, Sept. 20 Photo. *Perf. 11½*

B846 A245 20fr + 10fr indigo 2.75 2.75

See note after No. 726.

Heads from Alexander the Great Tapestry, 15th Century — SP383

Designs from Tapestries: 3fr+1.50fr, Fiddler from "The Feast," c. 1700. 10fr+4fr, Head of beggar from "The Healing of the Paralytic," 16th century.

1969, Sept. 20

B847 SP383 1fr + 50c multi .25 .25
B848 SP383 3fr + 1.50fr multi .40 .40
B849 SP383 10fr + 4fr multi 1.00 1.00
Nos. B847-B849 (3) 1.65 1.65

The surtax was for philanthropic purposes.

Bearded Antwerp Bantam SP384

1969, Nov. 8 **Engr. & Photo.**

B850 SP384 10fr + 5fr multi 1.00 1.00

Angel Playing Lute — SP385

Designs from Stained Glass Windows: 1.50fr+50c, Angel with trumpet, St. Waudru's, Mons. 7fr+3fr, Angel with viol, St. Jacques', Liege. 9fr+4fr, King with bagpipes, Royal Art Museum, Brussels.

1969, Dec. 13 **Photo.**

Size: 24x35mm

B851 SP385 1.50fr + 50c multi .25 .25
B852 SP385 3.50fr + 1.50fr multi .30 .30
B853 SP385 7fr + 3fr multi .65 .65

Size: 35x52mm

B854 SP386 9fr + 4fr multi 1.00 1.00
Nos. B851-B854 (4) 2.20 2.20

The surtax was for philanthropic purposes.

Farm and Windmill, Open-air Museum, Bokrijk SP386

Belgian Museums: 3.50fr+1.50fr, Stage Coach Inn, Courcelles. 7fr+3fr, "The Thresher of Trevires," Gallo-Roman sculpture, Gaumais Museum, Virton. 9fr+4fr, "The Sovereigns," by Henry Moore, Middelheim Museum, Antwerp.

Engraved and Photogravure

1970, May 30 ***Perf. 11½***

B855 SP386 1.50fr + 50c multi .25 .25
B856 SP386 3.50fr + 1.50fr multi .30 .30
B857 SP386 7fr + 3fr multi .60 .60
B858 SP386 9fr + 4fr multi .75 .75
Nos. B855-B858 (4) 1.90 1.90

The surtax went to various culture organizations.

"Resistance" SP387

Design: 7fr+3fr, "Liberation of Camps." The designs were originally used as book covers.

1970, July 4 **Photo.** ***Perf. 11½***

B859 SP387 3.50fr + 1.50fr blk, gray grn & dp car .35 .35
B860 SP387 7fr + 3fr blk, lil & dp car .60 .60

Honoring the Resistance Movement and 25th anniv. of the liberation of concentration camps.

Fishing Rod and Reel SP388

Design: 9fr+4fr, Hockey stick and puck, vert.

1970, Sept. 19 **Engr. & Photo.**

B861 SP388 3.50fr + 1.50fr multi .30 .30
B862 SP388 9fr + 4fr multi .70 .70

Souvenir Sheet

Belgium Nos. 31, 36, 39 — SP389

1970, Oct. 10 ***Perf. 11½***

B863 SP389 Sheet of 3 3.50 3.00
a. 1.50fr + 50c black & dull lilac 1.25 1.00
b. 3.50fr + 1.50fr black & lilac 1.25 1.00
c. 9fr + 4fr black & red brown 1.25 1.00

BELGICA 72 International Philatelic Exhibition, Brussels, June 24-July 9.

Camille Huysmans (1871-1968) SP390

3.50fr+1.50fr, Joseph Cardinal Cardijn (1882-1967). 7fr+3fr, Maria Baers (1883-1959). 9fr+4fr, Paul Pastur (1866-1938).

1970, Nov. 14 ***Perf. 11½***

Portraits in Sepia

B864 SP390 1.50fr + 50c car rose .25 .25
B865 SP390 3.50fr + 1.50fr lilac .30 .30
B866 SP390 7fr + 3fr green .55 .55
B867 SP390 9fr + 4fr blue .75 .75
Nos. B864-B867 (4) 1.85 1.85

"Anxious City" (Detail) by Paul Delvaux — SP391

7fr+3fr, "The Memory," by Rene Magritte.

1970, Dec. 12 **Photo.**

B868 SP391 3.50fr + 1.50fr multi .30 .30
B869 SP391 7fr + 3fr multi .65 .65

Notre Dame du Vivier, Marche-les-Dames — SP392

7fr+3fr, Turnhout Beguinage and Beguine.

1971, Mar. 13 ***Perf. 11½***

B870 SP392 3.50fr + 1.50fr multi .30 .30
B871 SP392 7fr + 3fr multi .60 .60

The surtax was for philanthropic purposes.

Red Cross — SP393

1971, May 22 **Photo.** ***Perf. 11½***

B872 SP393 10fr + 5fr crim & blk .80 .80

Belgian Red Cross.

Discobolus and Munich Cathedral — SP394

1971, June 19 **Engr. & Photo.**

B873 SP394 7fr + 3fr bl & blk .65 .65

Publicity for the 20th Summer Olympic Games, Munich 1972.

Festival of Flanders — SP395

Design: 7fr+3fr, Wallonia Festival.

1971, Sept. 11 **Photo.** ***Perf. 11½***

B874 SP395 3.50fr + 1.50fr multi .30 .30
B875 SP395 7fr + 3fr multi .65 .65

Attre Palace — SP396

Steen Palace, Elewijt — SP397

Design: 10fr+5fr, Royal Palace, Brussels.

1971, Oct. 23 **Engr.**

B876 SP396 3.50fr + 1.50fr sl grn .30 .30
B877 SP397 7fr + 3fr red brn .70 .70
B878 SP396 10fr + 5fr vio bl 1.00 1.00
Nos. B876-B878 (3) 2.00 2.00

Surtax was for BELGICA 72, International Philatelic Exposition.

Ox Fly, tabanus bromius SP398

Insects: 1.50fr+50c, Luna moth, vert. 7fr+3fr, Wasp, polistes gallicus. 9fr+4fr, Tiger beetle, vert.

1971, Dec. 11 **Photo.** ***Perf. 11½***

B879 SP398 1.50fr + 50c multi .25 .25
B880 SP398 3.50fr + 1.50fr multi .30 .30
B881 SP398 7fr + 3fr multi .65 .65
B882 SP398 9fr + 4fr multi .75 .75
Nos. B879-B882 (4) 1.95 1.95

Surtax was for philanthropic purposes.

Leopold I on #1 — SP399

2fr+1fr, Leopold I on #5. 2.50fr+1fr, Leopold II on #45. 3.50fr+1.50fr, Leopold II on #48. 6fr+3fr, Albert I on #135. 7fr+3fr, Albert I on #214. 10fr+5fr, Albert I on #231. 15fr+7.50fr, Leopold III on #290. 20fr+10fr, King Baudouin on #718.

Engraved and Photogravure

1972, June 24 ***Perf. 11½***

B883 SP399 1.50fr + 50c .25 .25
B884 SP399 2fr + 1fr .25 .25
B885 SP399 2.50 + 1fr .30 .30
B886 SP399 3.50fr + 1.50fr .35 .35
B887 SP399 6fr + 3fr .50 .50
B888 SP399 7fr + 3fr .70 .70
B889 SP399 10fr + 5fr .90 .90
B890 SP399 15fr + 7fr 1.25 1.25
B891 SP399 20fr + 10fr 2.00 2.00
Nos. B883-B891 (9) 6.50 6.50

Belgica 72, Intl. Philatelic Exhibition, Brussels, June 24-July 9. Nos. B883-B891 issued in sheets of 10 and of 20 (2 tete beche sheets with gutter between). Sold in complete sets.

Epilepsy Emblem — SP400

1972, Sept. 9 **Photo.** ***Perf. 11½***

B892 SP400 10fr + 5fr multi 1.00 1.00

The surtax was for the William Lennox Center for epilepsy research and treatment.

Gray Lag Goose — SP401

Designs: 4.50fr+2fr, Lapwing. 8fr+4fr, Stork. 9fr+4.50fr, Kestrel, horiz.

1972, Dec. 16 **Photo.** ***Perf. 11½***

B893 SP401 2fr + 1fr multi .25 .25
B894 SP401 4.50fr + 2fr multi .50 .50
B895 SP401 8fr + 4fr multi .80 .80
B896 SP401 9fr + 4.50fr multi .90 .90
Nos. B893-B896 (4) 2.45 2.45

Bijloke Abbey, Ghent — SP402

4.50fr+2fr, St. Ursmer Collegiate Church, Lobbes. 8fr+4fr, Park Abbey, Heverle. 9fr+4.50fr, Abbey, Floreffe.

1973, Mar. 24 **Engr.** ***Perf. 11½***

B897 SP402 2fr + 1fr sl grn .35 .35
B898 SP402 4.50fr + 2fr brown .45 .45
B899 SP402 8fr + 4fr rose lil .75 .75
B900 SP402 9fr + 4.50fr brt bl 1.00 1.00
Nos. B897-B900 (4) 2.55 2.55

Basketball SP403

1973, Apr. 7 **Photo. & Engr.**

B901 SP403 10fr + 5fr multi .90 .90

First World Basketball Championships of the Handicapped, Bruges, Apr. 16-21.

Dirk Martens' Printing Press — SP404

Lady Talbot, by Petrus Christus — SP405

Hadrian and Marcus Aurelius Coins SP406

Council of Malines, by Coussaert — SP407

Designs: 3.50fr+1.50fr, Head of Amon and Tutankhamen's cartouche. 10fr+5fr, Three-master of Ostend Merchant Company.

Photogravure and Engraved; Photogravure (#B906)

1973, June 23 ***Perf. 11½***

B902 SP404 2fr + 1fr multi .25 .25
B903 SP404 3.50fr + 1.50fr multi .30 .30
B904 SP405 4.50fr + 2fr multi .35 .35
B905 SP406 8fr + 4fr multi .65 .65
B906 SP407 9fr + 4.50fr multi .85 .85
B907 SP407 10fr + 5fr multi 1.50 1.50
Nos. B902-B907 (6) 3.90 3.90

500th anniv. of 1st book printed in Belgium (No. B902); 50th anniv. of Queen Elisabeth Egyptological Foundation (No. B903); 500th anniv. of death of painter Petrus Christus (No. B904); Discovery of Roman treasure at Luttre-Liberchies (No. B905); 500th anniv. of Great Council of Malines (No. B906); 250th anniv. of the Ostend Merchant Company (No. B907).

No. B902 is not luminescent.

Queen of Hearts — SP408

Old Playing Cards: No. B909, King of Clubs. No. B910, Jack of Diamonds. No. B911, King of Spades.

1973, Dec. 8 **Photo.** ***Perf. 11½***

B908 SP408 5fr + 2.50fr multi .50 .50
B909 SP408 5fr + 2.50fr multi .50 .50
B910 SP408 5fr + 2.50fr multi .50 .50
B911 SP408 5fr + 2.50fr multi .50 .50
a. Strip of 4, #B908-B911 2.00 2.00

Surtax was for philanthropic purposes.

Symbol of Blood Donations SP409

Design: 10fr+5fr, Traffic lights, Red Cross (symbolic of road accidents).

1974, Feb. 23 **Photo.** ***Perf. 11½***

B912 SP409 4fr + 2fr multi .35 .35
B913 SP409 10fr + 5fr multi .90 .90

The Red Cross as blood collector and aid to accident victims.

Armand Jamar, Self-portrait SP410

Designs: 5fr+2.50fr, Anton Bergmann and view of Lierre. 7fr+3.50fr, Henri Vieuxtemps and view of Verviers. 10fr+5fr, James Ensor, self-portrait, and masks.

1974, Apr. 6 **Photo.** ***Perf. 11½***

Size: 24x35mm

B914 SP410 4fr + 2fr multi .35 .35
B915 SP410 5fr + 2.50fr multi .40 .40
B916 SP410 7fr + 3.50fr multi .55 .55

Size: 35x52mm

B917 SP410 10fr + 5fr multi .85 .85
Nos. B914-B917 (4) 2.15 2.15

Van Gogh, Self-portrait and House at Cuesmes — SP411

1974, Sept. 21 **Photo.** ***Perf. 11½***

B918 SP411 10fr + 5fr multi 1.00 .75

Opening of Vincent van Gogh House at Cuesmes, where he worked as teacher.

Gentian — SP412

Spotted Cat's Ear — SP414

Badger SP413

Design: 7fr+3.50fr, Beetle.

1974, Dec. 8 **Photo.** ***Perf. 11½***

B919 SP412 4fr + 2fr multi .35 .35
B920 SP413 5fr + 2.50fr multi .50 .50
B921 SP413 7fr + 3.50fr multi .60 .60
B922 SP414 10fr + 5fr multi .95 .95
Nos. B919-B922 (4) 2.40 2.40

Pesaro Palace, Venice SP415

St. Bavon Abbey, Ghent SP416

Virgin and Child, by Michelangelo SP417

1975, Apr. 12 **Engr.** ***Perf. 11½***

B923 SP415 6.50fr + 2.50fr brn .55 .55
B924 SP416 10fr + 4.50 vio brn .85 .85
B925 SP417 15fr + 6.50fr brt bl 1.25 1.25
Nos. B923-B925 (3) 2.65 2.65

Surtax was for various cultural organizations.

Frans Hemerijckx and Leprosarium, Kasai — SP418

1975, Sept. 13 **Photo.** ***Perf. 11½***

B926 SP418 20fr + 10fr multi 1.75 1.75

Dr. Frans Hemerijckx (1902-1969), tropical medicine and leprosy expert.

Emile Moyson — SP419

Beheading of St. Dympna — SP420a

Hand Reading Braille SP420

No. B928, Dr. Ferdinand Augustin Snellaert.

1975, Nov. 22 **Engr.** ***Perf. 11½***

B927 SP419 4.50fr + 2fr dp mag .35 .35
B928 SP419 6.50fr + 3fr green .60 .60

Engraved and Photogravure

B929 SP420 10fr + 5fr multi .90 .90

Photo.

B930 SP420a 13fr + 6fr multi 1.10 1.10
Nos. B927-B930 (4) 2.95 2.95

Emile Moyson (1838-1868), freedom fighter for the rights of Flemings and Walloons; Dr. Snellaert (1809-1872), physician and Flemish patriot; Louis Braille (1809-1852), sesquicentennial of invention of Braille system of writing for the blind; St. Dympna, patron saint of Geel, famous for treatment of mentally ill.

The Cheese Vendor — SP421

Designs (THEMABELGA Emblem and): No. B932, Potato vendor. No. B933, Basket carrier. No. B934, Shrimp fisherman with horse, horiz. No. B935, Knife grinder, horiz. No. B936, Milk vendor with dog cart, horiz.

1975, Dec. 13 **Engr. & Photo.**

B931 SP421 4.50fr + 1.50fr multi .35 .35
B932 SP421 6.50fr + 3fr multi .55 .55
B933 SP421 6.50fr + 3fr multi .55 .55
B934 SP421 10fr + 5fr multi .80 .80
B935 SP421 10fr + 5fr multi .80 .80
B936 SP421 30fr + 15fr multi 2.40 2.40
Nos. B931-B936 (6) 5.45 5.45

THEMABELGA Intl. Topical Philatelic Exhib., Brussels, Dec. 13-21. Issued in sheets of 10 (5x2).

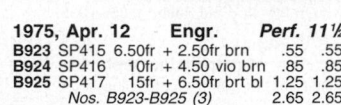

Blackface Fund Collector — SP422

1976, Feb. 14 Photo. *Perf. 11½*

B937 SP422 10fr + 5fr multi 1.00 1.00

"Conservatoire Africain" philanthropic soc., cent., and to publicize the Princess Paola creches.

Swimming and Olympic Emblem SP423

Montreal Olympic Games Emblem and: 5fr+2fr, Running, vert. 6.50fr+2.50fr, Equestrian.

1976, Apr. 10 Photo. *Perf. 11½*

B938 SP423 4.50fr + 1.50fr multi .35 .35
B939 SP423 5fr + 2fr multi .40 .40
B940 SP423 6.50fr + 2.50fr multi .55 .55
Nos. B938-B940 (3) 1.30 1.30

21st Olympic Games, Montreal, Canada, July 17-Aug. 1.

Queen Elisabeth Playing Violin SP424

Engr. & Photo.

1976, May 1 *Perf. 11½*

B941 SP424 14fr + 6fr blk & cl 1.10 1.10

Queen Elisabeth International Music Competition, 25th anniversary.

Souvenir Sheet

Jan Olieslagers, Bleriot Monoplane, Aero Club Emblem — SP425

Engr. & Photo.

1976, June 12 *Perf. 11½*

B942 SP425 25fr + 10fr multi 2.25 2.25

Royal Belgian Aero Club, 75th anniversary, and Jan Olieslagers (1883-1942), aviation pioneer.

Adoration of the Shepherds (detail), by Rubens — SP426

Rubens Paintings (Details): 4.50fr, Descent from the Cross. No. B945, The Virgin with the Parrot. No. B946, Adoration of the Kings. No. B947, Last Communion of St. Francis. 30fr+15fr, Virgin and Child.

1976, Sept. 4 Photo. *Perf. 11½*

Size: 35x52mm

B943 SP426 4.50fr + 1.50fr multi .50 .50

Size: 24x35mm

B944 SP426 6.50fr + 3fr multi .60 .60
B945 SP426 6.50fr + 3fr multi .60 .60
B946 SP426 10fr + 5fr multi 1.00 1.00
B947 SP426 10fr + 5fr multi 1.00 1.00

Size: 35x52mm

B948 SP426 30fr + 15fr multi 2.50 2.50
Nos. B943-B948 (6) 6.20 6.20

Peter Paul Rubens (1577-1640), Flemish painter, 400th birth anniversary.

Dwarf, by Velazquez SP427

1976, Nov. 6 Photo. *Perf. 11½*

B949 SP427 14fr + 6fr multi 1.25 1.25

Surtax was for the National Association for the Mentally Handicapped.

Dr. Albert Hustin SP428

Red Cross and Rheumatism Year Emblem SP429

1977, Feb. 19 Photo. *Perf. 11½*

B950 SP428 6.50fr + 2.50 multi .60 .60
B951 SP429 14fr + 7fr multi 1.10 1.10

Belgian Red Cross.

Bordet Atheneum, Empress Maria Theresa SP430

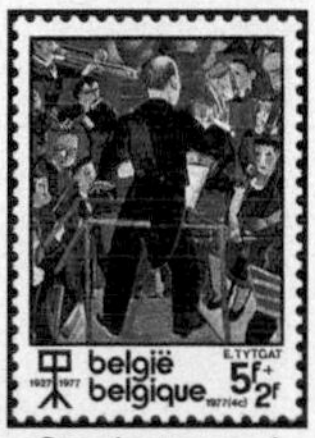

Conductor and Orchestra, by E. Tytgat SP431

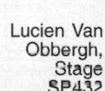

Lucien Van Obbergh, Stage SP432

Humanistic Society Emblem SP433

Camille Lemonnier SP434

Design: No. B953, Marie-Therese College, Herve, and coat of arms.

1977, Mar. 21 Photo. *Perf. 11½*

B952 SP430 4.50fr + 1fr multi .35 .35
B953 SP430 4.50fr + 1fr multi .35 .35
B954 SP431 5fr + 2fr multi .40 .40
B955 SP432 6.50fr + 2fr multi .55 .55
B956 SP433 6.50fr + 2fr blk & red .55 .55

Engr.

B957 SP434 10fr + 5fr slate bl .80 .80
Nos. B952-B957 (6) 3.00 3.00

Bicentenaries of the Jules Bordet Atheneum, Brussels, and the Marie-Therese College, Herve (Nos. B952-B953); 50th anniv. of the Brussels Philharmonic Soc., and Artists' Union (Nos. B954-B955): 25th anniv. of the Flemish Humanistic Organization (No. B956); 75th anniv. of the French-speaking Belgian writers' organization (No. B957).

Young Soccer Players — SP435

1977, Apr. 18 Photo.

B958 SP435 10fr + 5fr multi .90 .90

30th Intl. Junior Soccer Tournament.

Albert-Edouard Janssen, Financier — SP436

Famous Men: No. B960, Joseph Wauters (1875-1929), editor of Le Peuple, and newspaper. No. B961, Jean Capart (1877-1947), Egyptologist, and hieroglyph. No. B962, August de Boeck (1865-1937), composer, and score.

1977, Dec. 3 Engr. *Perf. 11½*

B959 SP436 5fr + 2.50fr brown .40 .40
B960 SP436 5fr + 2.50fr red .40 .40
B961 SP436 10fr + 5fr magenta .80 .80
B962 SP436 10fr + 5fr blue gray .80 .80
Nos. B959-B962 (4) 2.40 2.40

Abandoned Child SP437

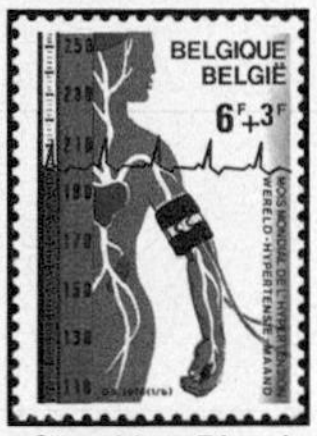

Checking Blood Pressure SP438

De Mick Sanatorium, Brasschaat — SP439

1978, Feb. 18 Photo. *Perf. 11½*

B963 SP437 4.50fr + 1.50fr multi .35 .35
B964 SP438 6fr + 3fr multi .50 .50
B965 SP439 10fr + 5fr multi .80 .80
Nos. B963-B965 (3) 1.65 1.65

Help for abandoned children (No. B963); fight against hypertension (No. B964); fight against tuberculosis (No. B965).

Actors and Theater SP440

Karel van de Woestijne SP441

Designs: No. B967, Harquebusier, Harquebusier Palace and coat of arms. 10fr+5fr, John of Austria and his signature.

Engraved and Photogravure

1978, June 17 *Perf. 11½*

B966 SP440 6fr + 3fr multi .50 .50
B967 SP440 6fr + 3fr multi .50 .50

Engr.

B968 SP441 8fr + 4fr black .65 .65
B969 SP441 10fr + 5fr black .80 .80
Nos. B966-B969 (4) 2.45 2.45

Cent. of Royal Flemish Theater, Brussels (No. B966); 400th anniv. of Harquebusiers' Guild of Vise, Liege (No. 967); Karel van de Woestijne (1878-1929), poet (No. B968); 400th anniv. of signing of Perpetual Edict by John of Austria (No. 969).

Lake Placid '80 and Belgian Olympic Emblems — SP442

Moscow '80 Emblem and: 8fr+3.50fr, Kremlin Towers, Belgian Olympic Committee emblem. 7fr+3fr, Runners from Greek vase, Lake Placid '80 emblem, Olympic rings. 14fr+6fr, Olympic flame, Lake Placid '80, Belgian emblems, Olympic rings.

1978, Nov. 4 Photo. *Perf. 11½*

B970 SP442 6fr + 2.50fr multi .50 .50
B971 SP442 8fr + 3.50fr multi .65 .65

Souvenir Sheet

B972 Sheet of 2 2.00 2.00
a. SP442 7fr + 3fr multi .65 .65
b. SP442 14fr + 6fr multi 1.25 1.25

Surtax was for 1980 Olympic Games.

Great Synagogue, Brussels — SP443

Dancers SP444

Father Pire, African Village SP445

1978, Dec. 2 Engr. *Perf. 11½*

B973 SP443 6fr + 2fr gray grn & sepia .50 .50

Photo.

B974 SP444 8fr + 3fr multi .65 .65
B975 SP445 14fr + 7fr multi 1.25 1.25
Nos. B973-B975 (3) 2.40 2.40

Centenary of Great Synagogue of Brussels; Flemish Catholic Youth Action Organization, 50th anniversary; Nobel Peace Prize awarded to Father Dominique Pire for his "Heart Open to the World" movement, 20th anniversary.

Young People Giving First Aid — SP446

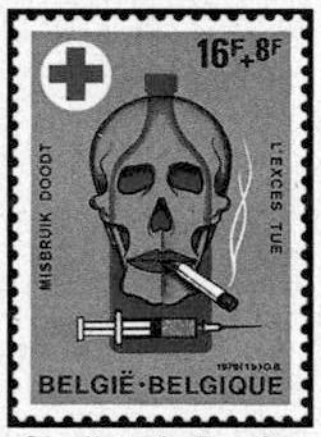

Skull with Bottle, Cigarette, Syringe — SP447

1979, Feb. 10 Photo. *Perf. 11½*

B976 SP446 8fr + 3fr multi .70 .70
B977 SP447 16fr + 8fr multi 1.40 1.40

Belgian Red Cross.

Beatrice Soetkens with Statue of Virgin Mary SP448

Details from Tapestries, 1516-1518, Showing Legend of Our Lady of Sand: 8fr+3fr, Francois de Tassis accepting letter from Emperor Frederick III (beginning of postal service). 14fr+7fr, Arrival of statue, Francois de Tassis and Philip the Fair. No. B981, Statue carried in procession by future Emperor Charles V and his brother Ferdinand. No. B982, Ship carrying Beatrice Soetkens with statue to Brussels, horiz.

1979, May 5 Photo. *Perf. 11½*

B978 SP448 6fr + 2fr multi .50 .50
B979 SP448 8fr + 3fr multi .65 .65
B980 SP448 14fr + 7fr multi 1.25 1.25
B981 SP448 20fr + 10fr multi 1.90 1.90
Nos. B978-B981 (4) 4.30 4.30

Souvenir Sheet

B982 SP448 20fr + 10fr multi 2.00 2.00

The surtax was for festivities in connection with the millennium of Brussels.

Notre Dame Abbey, Brussels — SP449

Designs: 8fr+3fr, Beauvoorde Castle. 14fr+7fr, 1st issue of "Courrier de L'Escaut" and Barthelemy Dumortier, founder. 20fr+10fr, Shrine of St. Hermes, Renaix.

Engraved and Photogravure

1979, Sept. 15 *Perf. 11½*

B983 SP449 6fr + 2fr multi .50 .50
B984 SP449 8fr + 3fr multi .65 .65
B985 SP449 14fr + 7fr multi 1.25 1.25
B986 SP449 20fr + 10fr multi 1.90 1.90
Nos. B983-B986 (4) 4.30 4.30

50th anniv. of restoration of Notre Dame de la Cambre Abbey; historic Beauvoorde Castle, 15th cent. sesquicentennial of the regional newspaper "Le Courrier de L'Escaut"; 850th anniv. of the consecration of the Collegiate Church of St. Hermes, Renaix.

Grand-Hornu Coal Mine — SP450

1979, Oct. 22 Engr. *Perf. 11½*

B987 SP450 10fr + 5fr blk .90 .90

Henry Heyman SP451

Veterans Organization Medal SP452

Boy and IYC Emblem — SP453

1979, Dec. 8 Photo. *Perf. 11½*

B988 SP451 8fr + 3fr multi .65 .65
B989 SP452 10fr + 5fr multi .80 .80
B990 SP453 16fr + 8fr multi 1.25 1.25
Nos. B988-B990 (3) 2.70 2.70

Henri Heyman (1879-1958), Minister of State; Disabled Veterans' Organization, 50th anniv.; Intl. Year of the Child.

Ivo Van Damme, Olympic Rings — SP454

1980, May 3 Photo. *Perf. 11½*

B991 SP454 20fr + 10fr multi 1.75 1.75

Ivo Van Damme (1954-1976), silver medalist, 800-meter race, Montreal Olympics, 1976. Surtax was for Van Damme Memorial Foundation.

Queen Louis-Marie, King Leopold I — SP455

150th Anniversary of Independence (Queens and Kings): 9fr+3fr, Marie Henriette. Leopold II. 14fr+6fr, Elisabeth, Albert I. 17fr+8fr, Astrid, Leopold III. 25fr+10fr, Fabiola, Baudouin.

Photogravure and Engraved

1980, May 31 *Perf. 11½*

B992 SP455 6.50 + 1.50fr multi .55 .55
B993 SP455 9 + 3fr multi .75 .75
B994 SP455 14 + 6fr multi 1.25 1.25
B995 SP455 17 + 8fr multi 1.40 1.40
B996 SP455 25 + 10fr multi 2.10 2.10
Nos. B992-B996 (5) 6.05 6.05

Miner, by Constantine Meunier SP456

Seal of Bishop Notger, First Prince-Bishop — SP457

9fr+3fr, Brewer, 16th century, from St. Lambert's reliquary, vert. 25fr+10fr, Virgin and Child, 13th century, St. John's Collegiate Church, Liege.

1980, Sept. 13 Photo. *Perf. 11½*

B997 SP456 9 + 3fr multi .75 .75
B998 SP456 17 + 6fr multi 1.40 1.40
B999 SP456 25 + 10fr multi 2.10 2.10
Nos. B997-B999 (3) 4.25 4.25

Souvenir Sheet

B1000 SP457 20 + 10fr multi 2.00 2.00

Millennium of the Principality of Liege.

Visual and Oral Handicaps SP458

Intl. Year of the Disabled: 10fr+5fr, Cerebral handicap, vert.

1981, Feb. 9 Photo. *Perf. 11½*

B1001 SP458 10 + 5fr multi 1.00 1.00
B1002 SP458 25 + 10fr multi 2.25 2.25

Dove with Red Cross Carrying Globe SP459

Design: 10fr+5fr, Atomic model, vert.

1981, Apr. 6 Photo. *Perf. 11½*

B1003 SP459 10 + 5fr multi .90 .90
B1004 SP459 25 + 10fr multi 2.10 2.10

Red Cross and: 15th Intl. Radiology Congress, Brussels, June 24-July 1 (No. B1003); intl. disaster relief (No. B1004).

Ovide Decroly SP460

1981, June 1 Photo. *Perf. 11½*

B1005 SP460 35 + 15fr multi 3.00 3.00

Ovide Decroly (1871-1932), developer of educational psychology.

Mounted Police Officer — SP461

Anniversaries: 9fr+4fr, Gendarmerie (State Police Force), 150th. 20fr+7fr, Carabineers Regiment, 150th. 40fr+20fr, Guides Regiment.

1981, Dec. 7 Photo. *Perf. 11½*

B1006 SP461 9 + 4fr multi .85 .85
B1007 SP461 20 + 7fr multi 1.75 1.75
B1008 SP461 40 + 20fr multi 3.50 3.50
Nos. B1006-B1008 (3) 6.10 6.10

Billiards — SP462

1982, Mar. 29 Photo. *Perf. 11½*

B1009 SP462 6 + 2fr shown .80 .80
B1010 SP462 9 + 4fr Cycling 1.10 1.10
B1011 SP462 10 + 5fr Soccer 1.25 1.25
B1012 SP462 50 + 14fr Yachting 3.50 3.50
Nos. B1009-B1012 (4) 6.65 6.65

Souvenir Sheet

B1013 Sheet of 4 7.50 7.50
a. SP462 25fr like #B1009 1.75 1.75
b. SP462 25fr like #B1010 1.75 1.75
c. SP462 25fr like #B1011 1.75 1.75
d. SP462 25fr like #B1012 1.75 1.75

No. B1013 shows designs in changed colors.

Christmas SP463

1982, Nov. 6

B1014 SP463 10 + 1fr multi .80 .80

Surtax was for tuberculosis research.

Belgica '82 Intl. Stamp Exhibition, Brussels, Dec. 11-19
SP464

Messengers (Prints). Nos. B1016-B1018 vert.

Photogravure and Engraved

1982, Dec. 11 *Perf. 11½*

B1015 SP464 7 + 2fr multi .55 .55
B1016 SP464 7.50 + 2.50fr multi .60 .60
B1017 SP464 10 + 3fr multi .80 .80
B1018 SP464 17 + 7fr multi 1.40 1.40
B1019 SP464 20 + 9fr multi 1.60 1.60
B1020 SP464 25 + 10fr multi 2.00 2.00
Nos. B1015-B1020 (6) 6.95 6.95

Souvenir Sheet

B1021 SP464 50 + 25fr multi 5.00 5.00

No. B1021 contains one 48x37mm stamp.

50th Anniv. of Catholic Charities — SP465

1983, Jan. 22 **Photo.** *Perf. 11½*

B1022 SP465 10 + 2fr multi .80 .80

Mountain Climbing — SP466

1983, Mar. 7 **Photo.**

B1023 SP466 12 + 3fr shown 1.00 1.00
B1024 SP466 20 + 5fr Hiking 1.75 1.75

Surtax was for Red Cross.

Madonna by Jef Wauters — SP467

1983, Nov. 21 **Photo.** *Perf. 11½*

B1025 SP467 11 + 1fr multi .80 .80

Rifles Uniform — SP468

No. B1027, Lancers uniform. No. B1028, Grenadiers uniform.

1983, Dec. 5 **Photo.** *Perf. 11½*

B1026 SP468 8 + 2fr shown .75 .75
B1027 SP468 11 + 2fr multi 1.25 1.25
B1028 SP468 50 + 12fr multi 3.75 3.75
Nos. B1026-B1028 (3) 5.75 5.75

Type of 1984 Summer Olympics

No. B1029, Judo, horiz. No. B1030, Wind surfing.

1984, Mar. 3 **Photo.** *Perf. 11½*

B1029 A495 8 + 2fr multi .60 .60
B1030 A495 12 + 3fr multi 1.00 1.00

50th Anniv. of Natl. Lottery
SP469

1984, Mar. 31 **Photo.** *Perf. 11½*

B1031 SP469 12 + 3fr multi 1.00 1.00

Brussels Modern Art Museum Opening
SP470

Paintings: 8fr+2fr, Les Masques Singuliers, by James Ensor. 12fr+3fr, Empire des Lumieres, by Rene Magritte. 22fr+5fr, The End, by Jan Cox. 50fr+13fr, Rhythm No. 6, by Jo Delahaut.

1984, Sept. 1 **Photo.**

B1032 SP470 8 + 2fr multi .75 .75
B1033 SP470 12 + 3fr multi 1.25 1.25
B1034 SP470 22 + 5fr multi 1.75 1.75
B1035 SP470 50 + 13fr multi 4.00 4.00
Nos. B1032-B1035 (4) 7.75 7.75

Child with Parents — SP471

No. B1037, Siblings. No. B1038, Merry-go-round.

1984, Nov. 3 **Photo.**

B1036 SP471 10 + 2fr shown .80 .80
B1037 SP471 12 + 3fr multi 1.00 1.00
B1038 SP471 15 + 3fr multi 1.25 1.25
Nos. B1036-B1038 (3) 3.05 3.05

Surtax was for children's programs.

Christmas 1984
SP472

No. B1039, Three Kings.

1984, Dec. 1

B1039 SP472 12 + 1fr multi 1.00 1.00

Belgian Red Cross Blood Transfusion Service, 50th Anniv. — SP473

1985, Mar. 4 **Photo.** *Perf. 11½*

B1040 SP473 9 + 2fr Tree .80 .80
B1041 SP473 23 + 5fr Hearts 1.90 1.90

Surtax was for the Belgian Red Cross.

Solidarity
SP474

Castles: No. B1042, Trazegnies. No. B1043, Laarne. No. B1044, Turnhout. No. B1045, Colonster.

1985, Nov. 4 **Photo. & Engr.**

B1042 SP474 9 + 2fr multi .80 .80
B1043 SP474 12 + 3fr multi 1.00 1.00
B1044 SP474 23 + 5fr multi 1.75 1.75
B1045 SP474 50 + 12fr multi 3.50 3.50
Nos. B1042-B1045 (4) 7.05 7.05

Christmas 1985, New Year 1986 — SP475

Painting: Miniature from the Book of Hours, by Jean duc de Berry.

1985, Nov. 25 **Photo.**

B1046 SP475 12 + 1fr multi .90 .90

King Baudouin Foundation
SP476

1986, Mar. 24 **Photo.**

B1047 SP476 12 + 3fr Emblem 1.25 1.25

Surtax for the foundation.

Madonna
SP477

Adoration of the Mystic Lamb, St. Bavon Cathedral Altarpiece, Ghent — SP478

Paintings by Hubert van Eyck (c. 1370-1426): No. B1049, Christ in Majesty. No. B1050, St. John the Baptist.

1986, Apr. 5 **Photo.** *Perf. 11½*

B1048 SP477 9 + 2fr shown .75 .75
B1049 SP477 13 + 3fr multi 1.10 1.10
B1050 SP477 24 + 6fr multi 2.00 2.00
Nos. B1048-B1050 (3) 3.85 3.85

Souvenir Sheet

B1051 SP478 50 + 12fr multi 7.00 7.00

Surtax for cultural organizations.

Antique Automobiles
SP479

No. B1052, Lenoir, 1863. No. B1053, Pipe de Tourisme, 1911. No. B1054, Minerva 22 HP, 1930. No. B1055, FN 8 Cylinder, 1931.

1986, Nov. 3 **Photo.**

B1052 SP479 9 + 2fr multi .75 .75
B1053 SP479 13 + 3fr multi 1.10 1.10
B1054 SP479 24 + 6fr multi 2.00 2.00
B1055 SP479 26 + 6fr multi 2.10 2.10
Nos. B1052-B1055 (4) 5.95 5.95

Christmas 1986, New Year 1987
SP480

No. B1056, Village in winter.

1986, Nov. 24 **Photo.**

B1056 SP480 13 + 1fr multi 1.00 1.00

Natl. Red Cross — SP482

Nobel Prize winners for physiology (1938) and medicine (1974): No. B1058, Corneille Heymans (1892-1968). No. B1059, A. Claude (1899-1983).

Photogravure and Engraved

1987, Feb. 16 *Perf. 11½*

B1058 SP482 13 + 3fr dk brn & red 1.25 1.25
B1059 SP482 24 + 6fr dk brn & red 2.25 2.25

European Conservation Year — SP483

No. B1060, Bee orchid. No. B1061, Horseshoe bat. No. B1062, Peregrine falcon.

1987, Mar. 16 **Photo.**

B1060 SP483 9 + 2fr multi .90 .90
B1061 SP483 24 + 6fr multi 2.00 2.00
B1062 SP483 26 + 6fr multi 2.50 2.50
Nos. B1060-B1062 (3) 5.40 5.40

Castles — SP484

No. B1063, Rixensart. No. B1064, Westerlo. No. B1065, Fallais. No. B1066, Gaasbeek.

1987, Oct. 17 **Photo. & Engr.**

B1063 SP484 9 + 2fr multi .75 .75
B1064 SP484 13 + 3fr multi 1.00 1.00
B1065 SP484 26 + 5fr multi 2.00 2.00
B1066 SP484 50 + 12fr multi 3.75 3.75
Nos. B1063-B1066 (4) 7.50 7.50

Christmas 1987 — SP485

Painting: Holy Family, by Rev. Father Lens.

1987, Nov. 14 **Photo.**

B1067 SP485 13 + 1fr multi	1.00	1.00

White and Yellow Cross of Belgium, 50th Anniv. — SP486

1987, Dec. 5

B1068 SP486 9 + 2fr multi	1.00	1.00

Promote Philately — SP487

Various flowers from Sixty Roses for a Queen, by P. J. Redoute (1759-1840).

1988, Apr. 25 **Photo.** ***Perf. 11½***

B1069 SP487 13 + 3fr shown	1.25	1.25
B1070 SP487 24 + 6fr multi, diff.	2.00	2.00

Souvenir Sheet

B1071 SP487 50 + 12fr multi, diff.	7.00	7.00

See Nos. B1081-B1083, B1089-B1091, 1346.

1988 Summer Olympics, Seoul — SP488

No. B1072, Table tennis. No. B1073, Cycling. No. B1074, Marathon runners.

1988, June 6 **Photo.** ***Perf. 11½***

B1072 SP488 9fr + 2fr multi	1.10	1.10
B1073 SP488 13fr + 3fr multi	1.25	1.25

Souvenir Sheet

B1074 SP488 50fr + 12fr multi	7.00	7.00

Solidarity — SP489

No. B1075, Jacques Brel. No. B1076, Jef Denyn. No. B1077, Fr. Ferdinand Verbiest.

1988, Oct. 24 **Photo.** ***Perf. 12x11½***

B1075 SP489 9fr + 2fr multi	1.25	1.25
B1076 SP489 13fr + 3fr multi	1.25	1.25
B1077 SP489 26fr + 6fr multi	2.00	2.00
Nos. B1075-B1077 (3)	4.50	4.50

Belgian Red Cross SP490

Paintings: No. B1078, *Crucifixion of Christ,* by Rogier van der Weyden (c. 1399-1464). No. B1079, *Virgin and Child,* by David (c. 1460-1523). B1089, *The Good Samaritan,* by Denis van Alsloot.

1989, Feb. 20 **Photo.** ***Perf. 11½***

B1078 SP490 9fr + 2fr multi	1.00	1.00
B1079 SP490 13fr + 3fr multi	1.40	1.40
B1080 SP490 24fr + 6fr multi	2.10	2.10
Nos. B1078-B1080 (3)	4.50	4.50

Stamp Collecting Promotion Type of 1988

Various flowers from *Sixty Roses for a Queen,* by P.J. Redoute (1759-1840) and inscriptions: No. B1081, "Centfeuille unique melee de rouge." No. B1082, "Bengale a grandes feuilles." No. B1083, Aeme vibere (tea roses).

1989, Apr. 17

B1081 SP487 13fr + 5fr multi	1.25	1.25
B1082 SP487 24fr + 6fr multi	2.00	2.00

Souvenir Sheet

B1083 SP487 50fr + 17fr multi	7.00	7.00

Solidarity SP491

Royal Greenhouses of Laeken: No. B1084, Exterior. No. B1085, Interior, vert. No. B1086, Dome exterior, vert. No. B1087, Dome interior, vert.

1989, Oct. 23

B1084 SP491 9fr + 3fr multi	1.00	1.00
B1085 SP491 13fr + 4fr multi	1.40	1.40
B1086 SP491 24fr + 5fr multi	1.90	1.90
B1087 SP491 26fr + 6fr multi	2.10	2.10
Nos. B1084-B1087 (4)	6.40	6.40

Queen Elisabeth Chapelle Musicale, 50th Anniv. — SP492

1989, Nov. 6

B1088 SP492 24fr + 6fr G clef	2.00	2.00

Stamp Collecting Promotion Type of 1988

Various flowers from *Sixty Roses for a Queen,* by P.J. Redoute (1759-1840): No. B1089, *Bengale desprez.* No. B1090, *Bengale philippe.* No. B1091, *Maria leonida.*

1990, Feb. 5

B1089 SP487 14fr + 7fr multi	1.50	1.50
B1090 SP487 25fr + 12fr multi	2.50	2.50

Souvenir Sheet

B1091 SP487 50fr + 20fr multi	8.00	8.00

Youth and Music — SP493

14fr+3fr, Beethoven & Lamoraal, Count of Egmont (1522-1568). 25fr+6fr, Joseph Cantre (1890-1957), drawing & sculpture.

1990, Oct. 6

B1092 SP493 10fr + 2fr multi	1.90	1.90
B1093 SP493 14fr + 3fr multi	2.25	2.25
B1094 SP493 25fr + 6fr multi	3.00	3.00
Nos. B1092-B1094 (3)	7.15	7.15

King Baudouin & Queen Fabiola, 30th Wedding Anniv. — SP494

1990, Dec. 10

B1095 SP494 50fr +15fr multi	7.00	7.00

Belgian Red Cross SP495

Details from paintings: No. B1096, The Temptation of St. Anthony by Hieronymus Bosch. No. B1097, The Annunciation by Dirk Bouts.

1991, Feb. 25, **Photo.** ***Perf. 11½***

B1096 SP495 14fr +3fr multi	2.25	2.25
B1097 SP495 25fr +6fr multi	3.25	3.25

Belgian Film Personalities — SP496

10fr+2fr, Charles Dekeukeleire (1905-71), producer. 14fr+3fr, Jacques Ledoux (1921-88), film conservationist. 25fr+6fr, Jacques Feyder (1899-1948), director.

1991, Oct. 28 **Photo.** ***Perf. 11½***

B1098 SP496 10fr +2fr multi	1.00	1.00
B1099 SP496 14fr +3fr multi	1.50	1.50
B1100 SP496 25fr +6fr multi	2.75	2.75
Nos. B1098-B1100 (3)	5.25	5.25

1992 Winter and Summer Olympics, Albertville and Barcelona SP497

No. B1101, Speed skating. No. B1102, Baseball. No. B1103, Women's tennis, horiz. No. B1104, Skeet shooting.

1992, Jan. 20 **Photo.** ***Perf. 11½***

B1101 SP497 10fr +2fr multi	1.10	1.10
B1102 SP497 10fr +2fr multi	1.10	1.10
B1103 SP497 14fr +3fr multi	1.60	1.60
B1104 SP497 25fr +6fr multi	3.00	3.00
Nos. B1101-B1104 (4)	6.80	6.80

Folk Legends SP498

11fr + 2fr, Proud Margaret. 15fr + 3fr, Gustine Maca & the Witches. 28fr + 6fr, Reynard the Fox.

1992, June 22 **Photo.** ***Perf. 11½***

B1105 SP498 11fr +2fr multi	1.25	1.25
B1106 SP498 15fr +3fr multi	1.75	1.75
B1107 SP498 28fr +6fr multi	3.00	3.00
Nos. B1105-B1107 (3)	6.00	6.00

Belgian Red Cross SP499

Paintings: 15fr + 3fr, Man with the Pointed Hat, by Adriaen Brouwer (1605-1638). 28fr + 7fr, Nereid and Triton, by Peter Paul Rubens, horiz.

1993, Feb. 15 **Photo.** ***Perf. 11½***

B1108 SP499 15fr +3fr multi	1.90	1.90
B1109 SP499 28fr +7fr multi	3.75	3.75

Fight Against Cancer SP500

1993, Sept. 20 **Photo.** ***Perf. 11½***

B1110 SP500 15fr +3fr multi	1.50	1.50

Intl. Olympic Committee, Cent. — SP501

No. B1112, Soccer players. No. B1113, Figure skater.

1994, Feb. 14 **Photo.** ***Perf. 11½***

B1111 SP501 16fr +3fr multi	1.75	1.75
B1112 SP501 16fr +3fr multi	1.75	1.75
B1113 SP501 16fr +3fr multi	1.75	1.75
Nos. B1111-B1113 (3)	5.25	5.25

1994 World Cup Soccer Championships, Los Angeles (No. B1112). 1994 Winter Olympics, Lillehammer, Norway (No. B1113).

Porcelain — SP502

Designs: No. B1114, Tournai plate, Museum of Mariemont-Morlanweiz. No. B1115, Etterbeek cup, saucer, Municipal Museum, Louvain. 50fr+11fr, Delft earthenware jars, Pharmacy Museum of Maaseik.

1994, June 27 **Photo.** ***Perf. 11½***

B1114 SP502 16fr +3fr multi	1.50	1.50

B1115 SP502 16fr +3fr multi 1.50 1.50

Souvenir Sheet

B1116 SP502 50fr +11fr multi 7.50 7.50

No. B1116 contains one 49x38mm stamp.

Solidarity SP503

Design: 16fr+3fr, Hearing-impaired person.

1994, Nov. 14 Photo. *Perf. 11½*

B1117 SP503 16fr +3fr multi 1.25 1.25

Museums — SP504

No. B1118, Natl. Flax Museum, Kortrijk. No. B1119, Natl. Water & Fountain Museum, Genval.

34fr+6fr, Intl. Carnival and Mask Museum, Binche.

1995, Jan. 30 Photo. *Perf. 11½*

B1118 SP504 16fr +3fr multi 1.10 1.10
B1119 SP504 16fr +3fr multi 1.10 1.10

Souvenir Sheet

B1120 SP504 34fr +6fr multi 3.00 3.00

Surtax for promotion of philately.

"Souvenir Sheets"

Beginning in 1995 items looking like souvenir sheets have appeared in the market. The 1995 one has the design used for No. B1120. The 1996 one has the design similar to the one used for No. B1128. The 1997 one has the design used for No. B1131. In 2000, the design of No. 1811 was used. These have no postal value.

Royal Belgian Soccer Assoc., Cent. SP505

1995, Aug. 21 Photo. *Perf. 11½*

B1121 SP505 16fr +4fr multi 1.40 1.40

Belgian Red Cross SP506

No. B1122, Princess Astrid, chairwoman of Belgian Red Cross. No. B1123, Wilhelm C. Röntgen (1845-1923), discoverer of the X-ray. No. B1124, Louis Pasteur (1822-95), scientist.

1995, Sept. 11

B1122 SP506 16fr +3fr multi 1.25 1.25
B1123 SP506 16fr +3fr multi 1.25 1.25
B1124 SP506 16fr +3fr multi 1.25 1.25
Nos. B1122-B1124 (3) 3.75 3.75

Solidarity — SP507

1995, Nov. 6 Photo. *Perf. 11½*

B1125 SP507 16fr +4fr multi 1.10 1.10

Surtax for fight against AIDS.

Museums — SP508

No. B1126, Museum of Walloon Life, Liège. No. B1127, Natl. Gin Museum, Hasselt.

34fr+6fr, Butchers' Guild Hall Museum, Antwerp.

1996, Feb. 19 Photo. *Perf. 11½*

B1126 SP508 16fr +4fr multi 1.10 1.10
B1127 SP508 16fr +4fr multi 1.10 1.10

Souvenir Sheet

B1128 SP508 34fr +6fr multi 3.00 3.00

Modern Olympic Games, Cent. SP509

No. B1129, Table tennis. No. B1130, Swimming. No. B1131, High jump.

1996, July 1 Photo. *Perf. 11½*

B1129 SP509 16fr +4fr multi 1.25 1.25
B1130 SP509 16fr +4fr multi 1.25 1.25

Souvenir Sheet

B1131 SP509 34fr +6fr multi 2.75 2.75

No. B1131 contains one 49x38mm stamp.

UNICEF, 50th Anniv. SP510

1996, Nov. 18 Photo. *Perf. 11½*

B1132 SP510 16fr +4fr multi 1.10 1.10

Museums SP511

No. B1133, Deportation and Resistance Museum, Mechlin. No. B1134, Iron Museum, Saint Hubert.

41fr+9fr, Horta Museum, Saint Gilles.

1997, Jan. 20 Photo. *Perf. 11½*

B1133 SP511 17fr +4fr multi 1.25 1.25
B1134 SP511 17fr +4fr multi 1.25 1.25

Souvenir Sheet

B1135 SP511 41fr +9fr multi 4.50 4.50

Surtax for "Pro-Post" association.

Judo — SP512

No. B1136, Men's (10a). No. B1137, Women's (10b).

1997, May 5 Photo. *Perf. 11½*

B1136 SP512 17fr +4fr multi 1.25 1.25
B1137 SP512 17fr +4fr multi 1.25 1.25

Surtax for Belgian Olympic Committee.

Solidarity — SP513

1997, Oct. 25

B1138 SP513 17fr +4fr multi 1.25 1.25

Surtax for Multiple Sclerosis research.

King Leopold III — SP514

32fr+15fr, King Baudouin I. 50fr+25fr, King Albert II.

1998, Feb. 16 Engr. *Perf. 11½*

B1139 SP514 17fr +8fr dk grn 1.40 1.40
B1140 SP514 32fr +15fr dk brn blk 2.50 2.50

Souvenir Sheet

B1141 SP514 50fr +25fr dk vio brn 5.50 5.50

See Nos. B1146-B1148, 1748, B1154-B1156, 1842, B1158-B1160.

Sports SP515

1998, June 8 Photo. *Perf. 11½*

B1142 SP515 17fr +4fr Pelota 1.25 1.25
B1143 SP515 17fr +4fr Handball 1.25 1.25

Souvenir Sheet

B1144 SP515 30fr +7fr Soccer 2.50 2.50

1998 World Cup Soccer Championships, France (No. B1144).

Assist the Blind — SP516

Photo. & Embossed

1998, Nov. 9 *Perf. 11½*

B1145 SP516 17fr +4fr multi 1.25 1.25

Face value is indicated in Braille.

Royalty Type of 1998

Designs: 17fr+8fr, King Albert I. 32fr+15fr, King Leopold II. 50fr+25fr, King Leopold I.

1999, Jan. 25 Engr. *Perf. 11½*

B1146 SP514 17fr +8fr dp grn 1.50 1.50
B1147 SP514 32fr +15fr black 2.50 2.50

Souvenir Sheet

B1148 SP514 50fr +25fr dp brn 4.50 4.50

Motorcycles — SP517

No. B1149, Speed race. No. B1150, Trial, vert. No. B1151, Motocross, vert.

1999, May 17 Photo. *Perf. 11½*

B1149 SP517 17fr +4fr multi 1.25 1.25
B1150 SP517 17fr +4fr multi 1.25 1.25

Souvenir Sheet

B1151 SP517 30fr +7fr multi 2.50 2.50

Solidarity SP518

No. 1152, First aid. No. 1153, Dental care, vert.

1999, Nov. 8 Photo. *Perf. 11½*

B1152 SP518 17fr +4fr multi 1.25 1.25
B1153 SP518 17fr +4fr multi 1.25 1.25

Royalty Type of 1998

Queens: 17fr + 8fr, Astrid (1905-35). 32fr +15fr, Fabiola (b. 1928). 50fr +25fr, Paola (b. 1937).

Photo. & Engr.

2000, Jan. 24 *Perf. 11½*

B1154 SP514 17fr +8fr green 1.50 1.50
B1155 SP514 32fr +15fr black 2.75 2.75

Souvenir Sheet

B1156 SP514 50fr +25fr claret 4.00 4.00

Red Cross/Red Crescent SP519

2000, Mar. 27 Photo. *Perf. 11½*

B1157 SP519 17fr +4fr multi 1.10 1.10

Royalty Type of 1998

Queens: 17fr+8fr, Elisabeth (1876-1965). 32fr+15fr, Marie-Henriette (1836-1902). 50fr+25fr, Louise-Marie (1812-50).

Photo. & Engr.

2001, Feb. 12 *Perf. 11½*

B1158 SP514 17fr +8fr green 1.50 1.50

B1159 SP514 32fr +15fr black 2.75 2.75

Souvenir Sheet

B1160 SP514 50fr +25fr brown 4.00 4.00

Sports SP520

World championship meets: No. B1161, Cycle track racing, Antwerp. No. B1162, Artistic gymnastics, Ghent.

2001, June 14 Photo. ***Perf. 11½***

B1161 SP520 17fr +4fr multi 1.25 1.25
B1162 SP520 17fr +4fr multi 1.25 1.25

Red Cross Volunteers SP521

2001, Sept. 10

B1163 SP521 17fr +4fr multi 1.25 1.25

Winning Drawing in Belgica 2001 Children's Stamp Design Contest SP522

2002, Feb. 11 Photo. ***Perf. 11½***

B1164 SP522 42c +10c multi 1.25 1.25

Red Cross Emergency Aid SP523

2002, June 5 Photo. ***Perf. 11½***

B1165 SP523 84c +12c multi 2.25 2.25

Red Cross — SP524

No. B1166: a, Helicopter and rescue worker (6a). b, Rescue worker on shoulders of another (6b). c, Nurse attending to accident victim (6c).

2003, Mar. 31 Photo. ***Perf. 11½***

B1166 Vert. strip of 3 + 2 labels 4.00 4.00
a.-c. SP524 41c +9c any single 1.25 1.25

Argenteuil, by Edouard Manet — SP525

2003, Sept. 15 Photo. ***Perf. 11½***

B1167 SP525 49c +11c multi 1.40 1.40

Margins on sheets, inscribed "Prior," served as etiquettes.

The Temptation of Saint Anthony, by Salvador Dali SP526

2004, Apr. 19 Photo. ***Perf. 11½***

B1168 SP526 49c +11c multi 1.40 1.40

Margins on sheets, inscribed "Prior," served as etiquettes.

Red Cross Workers SP527

2004, July 12 Photo. ***Perf. 11½***

B1169 SP527 50c +11c multi 1.40 1.40

Margins on sheets, inscribed "Prior," served as etiquettes.

The Violinist, by Kees van Dongen — SP528

2005, Jan. 17 Photo. ***Perf. 11½***

B1170 SP528 50c +12c multi 1.50 1.50

Margins on sheets, inscribed "Prior," served as etiquettes.

Dec. 26, 2004 Tsunami Victim Relief SP529

2005, Feb. 28

B1171 SP529 50c +12c multi 1.75 1.75

Margins on sheets, inscribed "Prior," served as etiquettes. Surtax for Red Cross health care infrastructure relief efforts.

Red Cross SP530

2006, May 15 Photo. ***Perf. 11½***

B1172 SP530 52c +12c multi 1.60 1.60

Margins on sheets, inscribed "Prior," served as etiquettes.

The Kleptomaniac, by Théodore Gericault, and Ghent Museum of Fine Arts — SP531

2006, Oct. 23 Photo. ***Perf. 11½***

B1173 SP531 52c +12c multi 1.60 1.60

Printed in sheets of 5. Margins on sheets, inscibed "Prior," served as etiquettes. Surtax for promotion of philately.

Souvenir Sheet

Seated Nude, by Amedeo Modigliani — SP532

2007, Jan. 8 Photo. ***Perf. 11½***

B1174 SP532 60c +30c multi 4.00 4.00

Surtax for promotion of philately.

Red Cross Mobile Library for Hospitals SP533

2007, Feb. 26

B1175 SP533 52c +25c multi 2.00 2.00

Printed in sheets of 10. Margins on sheets, inscribed "Prior," served as etiquettes.

Red Cross Blood Donation SP534

2008, Jan. 21 Photo. ***Perf. 11½***

B1176 SP534 1 +25c multi 3.00 2.00

No. B1176 sold for 77c on day of issue.

Souvenir Sheet

La Luz que se Apaga, by José Maria Sicilia — SP535

2008, Jan. 21

B1177 SP535 2 +40c multi 4.50 4.50

No. B1177 sold for €1.44 on day of issue.

Red Cross Drinking Water Projects — SP536

2009, Feb. 23 Litho. ***Perf. 11½***

B1178 SP536 1 +25c multi 4.00 3.00

On day of issue, No. B1178 sold for 84c.

Souvenir Sheet

Belgium No. 139a — SP537

2009, Nov. 3 Litho. ***Perf. 11½***

B1179 SP537 (90c) + 40c multi 4.00 4.00

Surtax for promotion of philately.

Miniature Sheet

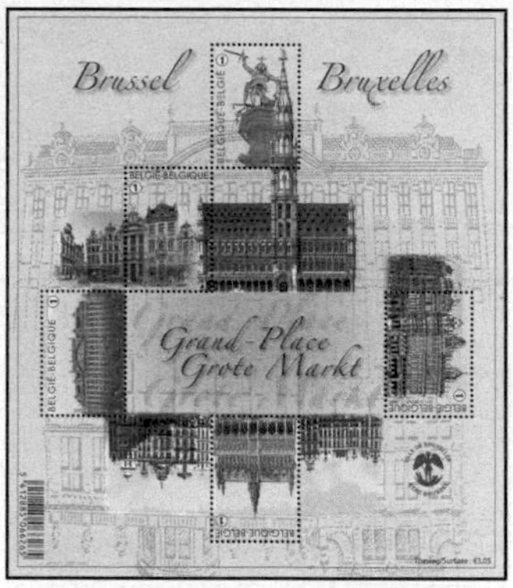

Grand Place, Brussels — SP538

No. B1180: a, Statue of St. Michael, spire of City Hall. b, Star, Swan and Golden Tree Guildhouses. c, House of the Dukes of Brabant (one building), horiz. d, King of Spain, Wheelbarrow, Bag and Claw Guildhouses, horiz. e, Breadhouse (Maison du Roi).

Photo. & Engr.

2011, Sept. 19 *Perf. 11½*

B1180 SP538 Sheet of 5 17.50 17.50
a.-e. 1 + (61c) Any single 3.50 3.50

On day of issue, Nos. B1180a-B1180e each had a franking value of 61c.

Miniature Sheet

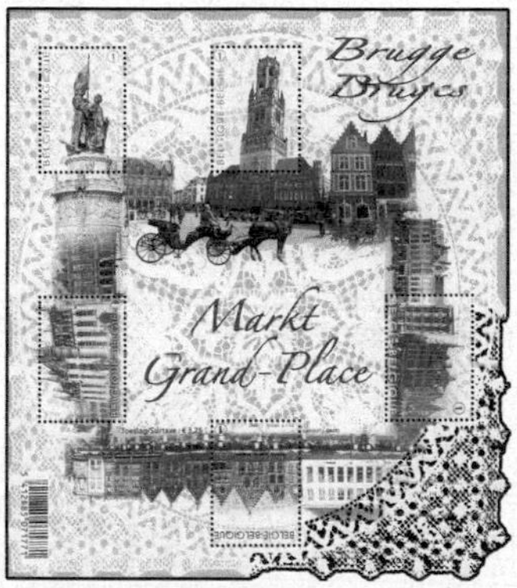

Grand-Place, Bruges — SP539

No. B1181: a, Statue of Jan Breydel and Pieter de Coninck. b, Belfry. c Provincial House, horiz. d, Boechoute, Craenenburg, Die Maene Houses, Pathé Cinema, horiz..e, Spainge, Diephuis and Le Panier d'Or Houses.

2012, Oct. 29

B1181 SP539 Sheet of 5 17.50 17.50
a.-e. SP539 1 + (65c) Any single 3.50 3.50

On day of issue, Nos. B1181a-B1181e each had a franking value of 65c.

Statue of Marie-Christine de Lalaing — SP540

Belfry — SP541

Cloth Hall — SP542

Grange Aux Dimes — SP543

"The Oath" Statue — SP544

Photo. & Engr.

2013, Oct. 28 *Perf. 11½*

B1182 Sheet of 5 17.50 17.50
a. SP540 1+(67c) multi 3.50 3.50
b. SP541 1+(67c) multi 3.50 3.50
c. SP542 1+(67c) multi 3.50 3.50
d. SP543 1+(67c) multi 3.50 3.50
e. SP544 1+(67c) multi 3.50 3.50

Capture of Tournai by King Henry VIII of England, 500th anniv. Nos. B1182a-B1182e each had a franking value of 67c on day of issue.

Miniature Sheet

Grand-Place, Antwerp — SP545

No. B1183: a, Hand from Brabo Fountain (28x40mm). b, Notre-Dame Cathedral (28x40mm) c, Town Hall (56x40mm). d, Guild houses, "1" at LR (28x40mm). e, Guild houses, "1" at UL (28x40mm).

Engr. With Photo. Sheet Margin

2014, Sept. 8 *Perf. 11½*

B1183 SP545 Sheet of 5 17.50 17.50
a.-e. 1+(70c) Any single 3.50 3.50

Nos. B1183a-B1183e each had a franking value of 70c on day of issue. Surtax for the promotion of philately. Photogravure imperforate examples of No. B1183 were given away as gifts to standing-order customers.

Miniature Sheet

Grand-Place, Mons — SP546

No. B1184: a, Hôtel de Blanc Lévrier (woman in LL corner, 28x40mm). b, City Hall (building with tower, 28x40mm). c, St. George's Chapel (building with railing along steps, 28x40mm). d, Hôtel de la Couronne Impériale (building with solid doors, 55x40mm). e, Royal Theater (building with doors with windows, 55x40mm).

Photo. & Engr.

2015, June 1 *Perf. 11½*

B1184 SP546 Sheet of 5 18.50 18.50
a.-e. 1+(72c) Any single 3.75 3.75

Nos. B1184a-B1184e each had a franking value of 72c on day of issue. Surtax was for promotion of philately. A horse hair is affixed to the sheet margin with adhesive tape.

Miniature Sheet

Ghent — SP547

No. B1185: a, Belfry of Ghent. b, St. Nicholas's Church. c, St. Bavo's Cathedral. d, Old City Hall. e, New City Hall.

Photo. & Engr.

2016, Mar. 14 *Perf. 11½*

B1185 SP547 Sheet of 5 + label 18.50 18.50
a.-e. 1+(74c) Any single 3.75 3.75

Nos. B1185a-B1185e each had a franking value of 74c on day of issue. Surtax was for promotion of philately.

Miniature Sheet

Eupen — SP548

No. B1186: a, Franco-German War Memorial, Werthplatz (28x41mm). b, Franciscan Sisters Convent, Marktplatz (28x41mm). c, Merchant's house, Werthplatz (56x41mm). d, St. Nicholas Church, Marktplatz (28x41mm). e, City Hall, Rathausplatz (56x41mm).

Photo. & Engr.

2017, June 12 *Perf. 11½*

B1186 SP548 Sheet of 5 + label 17.50 17.50
a.-e. 1+(74c) Any single 3.50 3.50

Nos. B1186a-B1186e each had a franking value of 74c on day of issue. Surtax was for promotion of philately.

Miniature Sheet

Namur — SP549

No. B1187: a, Statue of angel, Place de l'Ange (28x40mm). b, Belfry of Namur (28x40mm). c, St. Aubin's Cathedral (55x40mm). d, Palais de Congrès and Belfry of Namur (55x40mm). e, Théatre Royal (55x40mm).

Photo. & Engr.

2018, Aug. 27 *Perf. 11½*

B1187 SP549 Sheet of 5 + label 20.00 20.00
a.-e. 1+(84c) Any single 4.00 4.00

Nos. B1187a-B1187e each had a franking value of 84c on day of issue. Surtax was for promotion of philately.

Miniature Sheet

Leuven — SP550

No. B1188: a, City Hall, "Guillaume Broux" inscription at left. b, City Hall, "Przemyslaw Krajewski" inscription at left. c, University Library, horiz. d, University Hall, horiz. e, St. Peter's Church, horiz.

Photo. & Engr.

2019, Aug. 26 *Perf. 12¼*

B1188 SP550 Sheet of 5 20.00 20.00
a.-e. 1+(92c) Any single 4.00 4.00

Nos. B1188a-B1188e each had a franking value of 92c on day of issue. Surtax was for promotion of philately.

Miniature Sheet

Liège — SP551

No. B1189: a, Perron of Liège (28x40mm). b, St. Bartholomew's Church (28x40mm). c, Royal Opera of Wallonia (55x40mm). d, Palace of the Prince-Bishops of Liège (83x40mm). e, City Hall (55x40mm).

Perf. 11¾x11¼

2020, June 15 **Litho. & Engr.**

B1189 SP551 Sheet of 5 22.50 22.50
a.-e. 1+(98c) Any single 4.50 4.50

Nos. B1189a-B1189e each had a franking value of 98c on the day of issue. No. B1189 was sold with a plastic sheet the same size as No. B1189 that depicts the railway station shown on the sheet margin and frames the five stamps. Surtax was for promotion of philately.

AIR POST STAMPS

Fokker FVII/3m over Ostend AP1

Designs: 1.50fr, Plane over St. Hubert. 2fr, over Namur. 5fr, over Brussels.

Perf. 11½

1930, Apr. 30 **Unwmk.** **Photo.**

C1	AP1	50c blue	.45	.25
C2	AP1	1.50fr black brn	2.50	2.50
C3	AP1	2fr deep green	2.00	.90
C4	AP1	5fr brown lake	2.00	1.10
		Nos. C1-C4 (4)	6.95	4.75
		Set, never hinged	22.50	

Nos. C1-C4 exist imperf.

1930, Dec. 5

C5 AP1 5fr dark violet 30.00 30.00
Never hinged 65.00

Issued for use on a mail carrying flight from Brussels to Leopoldville, Belgian Congo, starting Dec. 7.

Exists imperf.

Nos. C2 and C4 Surcharged in Carmine or Blue

1935, May 23

C6 AP1 1fr on 1.50fr (C)	.50	.50
C7 AP1 4fr on 5fr (Bl)	9.00	9.00
Set, never hinged	45.00	

Catalogue values for unused stamps in this section, from this point to the end of the section, are for Never Hinged items.

DC-4 Skymaster, Sabena Airline AP5

1946, Apr. 20 Engr. *Perf. 11½*

C8 AP5 6fr blue	.35	.25
C9 AP5 8.50fr violet brn	.65	.45
C10 AP5 50fr yellow grn	5.50	1.00
a. Perf. 12x11½ ('54)	300.00	1.50
C11 AP5 100fr gray	9.00	2.00
a. Perf. 12x11½ ('54)	100.00	1.50
Nos. C8-C11 (4)	15.50	3.70

Evolution of Postal Transportation — AP6

1949, July 1

C12 AP6 50fr dark brown	52.50	20.00

Centenary of Belgian postage stamps.

Glider — AP7

Design: 7fr, "Tipsy" plane.

1951, June 18 Photo. *Perf. 13½*

C12A Strip of 2 + label	82.50	65.00
b. AP7 6fr dark blue	32.50	20.00
c. AP7 7fr carmine rose	32.50	20.00

For the 50th anniv. of the Aero Club of Belgium. The strip sold for 50fr.

1951, July 25 *Perf. 13½*

C13 AP7 6fr sepia	5.75	.25
C14 AP7 7fr Prus green	5.75	.75

UN Types of Regular Issue, 1958

Designs: 5fr, ICAO. 6fr, World Meteorological Organization. 7.50fr, Protection of Refugees. 8fr, General Agreement on Tariffs and Trade. 9fr, UNICEF. 10fr, Atomic Energy Agency.

Perf. 11½

1958, Apr. 17 Unwmk. Engr.

C15 A137 5fr dull blue	.25	.25
C16 A136 6fr yellow grn	.30	.25
C17 A137 7.50fr lilac	.35	.30
C18 A136 8fr sepia	.40	.30
C19 A137 9fr carmine	.45	.35
C20 A136 10fr redsh brown	.60	.50
Nos. C15-C20 (6)	2.35	1.95

World's Fair, Brussels, Apr. 17-Oct. 19. See note after No. 476.

AIR POST SEMI-POSTAL STAMPS

Catalogue values for unused stamps in this section are for Never Hinged items.

American Soldier in Combat — SPAP1

Perf. 11x11½

1946, June 15 Unwmk. Engr.

CB1 SPAP1 17.50fr + 62.50fr dl brn	1.60	.75
CB2 SPAP1 17.50fr + 62.50fr dl gray grn	1.60	.75

Surtax for an American memorial at Bastogne.

An overprint, "Hommage a Roosevelt," was privately applied to Nos. CB1-CB2 in 1947 by the Association Belgo-Americaine. Values: unused or canceled $5; never hinged $6.

In 1950 another private overprint was applied, in red, to Nos. CB1-CB2. It consists of "16-12-1944, 25-1-1945, Dedication July 16, 1950" and outlines of the American eagle emblem and the Bastogne Memorial. Values: unused or canceled $10; never hinged $20. Similar overprints were applied to Nos. 265 and 361.

Flight Allegory SPAP2

1946, Sept. 7 *Perf. 11½*

CB3 SPAP2 2fr + 8fr brt vio	.55	*.50*

The surtax was for the benefit of aviation.

Nos. B417-B425 Surcharged in Various Arrangements in Red or Dark Blue

Type I

Type II

Type I — Top line "POSTE AERIENNE"
Type II — Top line "LUCHTPOST"

1947, May 18 Photo. *Perf. 11½*

Type I

CB4 SP227 1fr + 2fr (R)	.75	*.65*
CB5 SP228 1.50fr + 2.50fr	.75	*.65*
CB6 SP229 2fr + 45fr	.75	*.65*
CB7 SP230 1fr + 2fr (R)	.75	*.65*
CB8 SP231 1.50fr + 2.50fr	.75	*.65*
CB9 SP232 2fr + 45fr	.75	*.65*
CB10 SP233 1fr + 2fr (R)	.75	*.65*
CB11 SP234 1.50fr + 2.50fr (R)	.75	*.65*
CB12 SP235 2fr + 45fr	.75	*.65*

Type II

CB4A SP227 1fr + 2fr (R)	.75	*.65*
CB5A SP228 1.50fr + 2.50fr	.75	*.65*
CB6A SP229 2fr + 45fr	.75	*.65*
CB7A SP230 1fr + 2fr (R)	.75	*.65*
CB8A SP231 1.50fr + 2.50fr	.75	*.65*
CB9A SP232 2fr + 45fr	.75	*.65*
CB10A SP233 1fr + 2fr (R)	.75	*.65*
CB11A SP234 1.50fr + 2.50fr (R)	.75	*.65*
CB12A SP235 2fr + 45fr	.75	*.65*
Nos. CB4-CB12A (18)	13.50	*11.70*

Issued for CIPEX, NYC. In 1948 Nos. CB4-CB12 and CB4A-CB12A were punched with the letters "IMABA," and the inscription "Imaba du 21 au 29 aout 1948" was applied to the backs.

Values, set: unused or canceled $13.50; never hinged $27.

Helicopter Leaving Airport SPAP3

1950, Aug. 7

CB13 SPAP3 7fr + 3fr blue	8.50	5.25

Surtax for the Natl. Aeronautical Committee.

SPECIAL DELIVERY STAMPS

From 1874 to 1903 certain hexagonal telegraph stamps were used as special delivery stamps.

Town Hall, Brussels — SD1

2.35fr, Street in Ghent. 3.50fr, Bishop's Palace, Liege. 5.25fr, Notre Dame Cathedral, Antwerp.

1929 Unwmk. Photo. *Perf. 11½*

E1 SD1 1.75fr dark blue	.60	.30
E2 SD1 2.35fr carmine	1.75	.45
E3 SD1 3.50fr dark violet	12.00	10.00
E4 SD1 5.25fr olive green	11.00	10.00

Eupen — SD2

1931

E5 SD2 2.45fr dark green	17.00	2.50
Nos. E1-E5 (5)	42.35	23.25
Set, never hinged	125.00	

No. E5 Surcharged in Red

1932

E6 SD2 2.50fr on 2.45fr dk grn	18.00	2.00
Never hinged	65.00	

REGISTRATION STAMPS

Catalogue values in this section are for Never Hinged items.

Osprey — R1

2011, Jan. 3 Litho. *Perf. 11½x11¾*

F1 R1 (€4.70) multi	12.00	2.50

Arctic Tern — R3

2013, Jan. 21 *Perf. 11½x11¾*

F3 R3 (€5.03) multi	12.00	3.00

Northern Shoveler — R5

2015, June 1 Litho. *Perf. 11½*

F5 R5 (€5.13) multi	11.50	3.00

Water Rail — R6

2017, Jan. 30 Litho. *Perf. 11½*

F6 R6 (€5.29) multi	11.50	3.00

Barnacle Goose — R7

2020, Jan. 27 Litho. *Perf. 11¾x11½*

F7 R7 (€5.67) multi	12.50	12.50

REGISTRATION OFFICIAL STAMPS

Catalogue values in this section are for Never Hinged items.

Short-eared Owl — RO1

2012, Feb. 13 Litho. *Perf. 11½*

FO1 RO1 (€4.35) multi	9.00	2.50

Bearded Reedling — RO2

Perf. 11½x11¾

2019, Mar. 18 Litho.

FO2 RO2 (€4.88) multi	11.00	11.00

ACKNOWLEDGMENT OF RECEIPT STAMPS

Lapwing — AR1

2013, Sept. 13 Litho. *Perf. 11½*
H1 AR1 (€1.20) multi 2.50 1.60

Common Goldeneye — AR2

2020, Mar. 16 Litho. *Perf. 11½*
H2 AR2 (€1.35) multi 3.00 3.00

POSTAGE DUE STAMPS

D1

1870 Unwmk. Typo. *Perf. 15*
J1 D1 10c green 3.75 2.00
J2 D1 20c ultra, thin paper 30.00 4.00
Set, never hinged 150.00

In 1909 many bisects of Nos. J1-J2 were created. The 10c bisect used as 5c on piece sells for $3.50.

No. J2 was also printed in aniline ink on thin paper. Value about the same.

D2

1895-09 *Perf. 14*
J3 D2 5c yellow grn .25 .25
J4 D2 10c orange brn 19.00 1.75
J5 D2 10c carmine ('00) .25 .25
J6 D2 20c olive green .25 .25
J7 D2 30c pale blue ('09) .25 .25
J8 D2 50c yellow brn 2.00 5.00
J9 D2 50c gray ('00) .40 .40
J10 D2 1fr carmine 20.00 11.00
J11 D2 1fr ocher ('00) 5.00 5.00
Nos. J3-J11 (9) 47.40 24.15
Set, never hinged 225.00

1916 Redrawn
J12 D2 5c blue grn 40.00 12.00
J13 D2 10c carmine 75.00 20.00
J14 D2 20c dp gray grn 75.00 20.00
J15 D2 30c brt blue 5.00 5.00
J16 D2 50c gray 200.00 75.00
Nos. J12-J16 (5) 395.00 132.00
Set, never hinged 1,500.

In the redrawn stamps the lions have a heavy, colored outline. There is a thick vertical line at the outer edge of the design on each side.

D3

1919 *Perf. 14*
J17 D3 5c green .50 .25
J18 D3 10c carmine 5.00 .25
J19 D3 20c gray green 12.00 1.25
J20 D3 30c bright blue 3.50 .40
J21 D3 50c gray 7.50 1.00
Nos. J17-J21 (5) 28.50 3.15
Set, never hinged 100.00

The 5c, 10c, 20c and 50c values also exist perf 14x15.

Perf. 14x15
J17a D3 5c green 1.75 .25
J18a D3 10c carmine 1.75 .25
J19a D3 20c gray green 6.50 1.00
J21a D3 50c gray 6.00 1.00
Nos. J17a-J19a, J21 (4) 16.00 2.50
Set, never hinged 65.00

D4

1922-32
J22 D4 5c dk gray .25 .25
J23 D4 10c green .25 .25
J24 D4 20c deep brown .25 .25
J25 D4 30c ver ('24) 1.00 .75
a. 30c rose red .70 .50
J26 D4 40c red brn ('25) .25 .25
J27 D4 50c ultra 3.00 .50
J28 D4 70c red brn ('29) .25 .25
J29 D4 1fr violet ('25) .45 .25
J30 D4 1fr rose lilac ('32) .50 .25
J31 D4 1.20fr ol grn ('29) .50 .25
J32 D4 1.50fr ol grn ('32) .55 .45
J33 D4 2fr violet ('29) .55 .25
J34 D4 3.50fr dp blue ('29) .75 .25
Nos. J22-J34 (13) 8.55 4.20
Set, never hinged 20.00

1934-46 *Perf. 14x13½*
J35 D4 35c green ('35) .60 *.60*
J36 D4 50c slate .25 .25
J37 D4 60c carmine ('38) .25 .25
J38 D4 80c slate ('38) .25 .25
J39 D4 1.40fr gray ('35) .55 .45
J39A D4 3fr org brn ('46) 1.00 .50
J39B D4 7fr brt red vio ('46) 1.50 *1.50*
Nos. J35-J39B (7) 4.40 *3.80*
Set, never hinged 8.00

See Nos. J54-J61.

Catalogue values for unused stamps in this section, from this point to the end of the section, are for Never Hinged items.

D5

1945 Typo. *Perf. 12½*
Inscribed "TE BETALEN" at Top
J40 D5 10c gray olive .25 .25
J41 D5 20c ultramarine .25 .25
J42 D5 30c carmine .25 .25
J43 D5 40c black violet .25 .25
J44 D5 50c dl bl grn .25 .25
J45 D5 1fr sepia .25 .25
J46 D5 2fr red orange .25 .25

Inscribed "A PAYER" at Top
J47 D5 10c gray olive .25 .25
J48 D5 20c ultramarine .25 .25
J49 D5 30c carmine .25 .25
J50 D5 40c black vio .25 .25
J51 D5 50c dl bl grn .25 .25
J52 D5 1fr sepia .25 .25
J53 D5 2fr red orange .25 .25
Nos. J40-J53 (14) 3.50 3.50

Type of 1922-32
1949-53 Typo. *Perf. 14x13½*
J54 D4 65c emerald 6.50 3.00
J55 D4 1.60fr lilac rose ('53) 12.50 6.00
J56 D4 1.80fr red 13.00 5.00
J57 D4 2.40fr gray lilac ('53) 8.00 3.00
J58 D4 4fr deep blue ('53) 9.50 .50
J59 D4 5fr red brown 3.00 .25
J60 D4 8fr lilac rose 10.00 8.00
J61 D4 10fr dark violet 6.50 2.50
Nos. J54-J61 (8) 69.00 28.25

D6

Numerals 6½mm or More High
1966-70 Photo.
J62 D6 1fr brt pink .35 .25
J63 D6 2fr blue green .25 .25
J64 D6 3fr blue .35 .25
J65 D6 5fr purple .50 .25
J66 D6 6fr bister brn .75 .25
J67 D6 7fr red org ('70) .60 .30
J68 D6 20fr slate grn 1.20 .50
Nos. J62-J68 (7) 4.00 2.05

Printed on various papers.

Numerals 4½-5½mm High
1985-87 Photo. *Perf. 14x13½*
J69 D6 1fr lilac rose .25 .25
J70 D6 2fr dull blue grn .25 .25
J71 D6 3fr greenish blue .75 .25
J72 D6 4fr green .25 .25
J73 D6 5fr lt violet .25 .25
J73A D6 6fr brown .30 .25
J74 D6 7fr brt orange .40 .40
J75 D6 8fr pale gray .40 .40
J76 D6 9fr rose lake .45 .45
J77 D6 10fr lt red brown .50 .45
J78 D6 20fr lt olive grn 1.00 1.00
Nos. J69-J78 (11) 4.80 4.20

Printed on various papers.

Issue dates: 3fr, 4fr, 8fr-10fr, Mar. 25, 1985. 6fr, 9/5/86. 20fr, 9/8/86. 2fr, 11/12/86. 6fr, 9/5/86. 1fr, 5fr, 7fr, 1987.

MILITARY STAMPS

Catalogue values for unused stamps in this section are for Never Hinged items.

King Baudouin — M1

Unwmk.
1967, July 17 Photo. *Perf. 11*
M1 M1 1.50fr greenish gray .25 .25

King Baudouin — M2

1971-75 Engr. *Perf. 11½*
M2 M2 1.75fr green .30 .30
M3 M2 2.25fr gray green ('72) .25 .25
M4 M2 2.50fr gray green ('74) .25 .25
M5 M2 3.25fr vio brown ('75) .25 .25
Nos. M2-M5 (4) 1.05 1.05

Nos. M1-M3 are luminescent, Nos. M4-M5 are not.

MILITARY PARCEL POST STAMP

Type of Parcel Post Stamp of 1938 Srchd. in Blue

1939 Unwmk. *Perf. 13½*
MQ1 PP19 3fr on 5.50fr copper red .25 .25
Never hinged .50

OFFICIAL STAMPS

For franking the official correspondence of the Administration of the Belgian National Railways.

Most examples of Nos. O1-O25 in the marketplace are counterfeits. Values are for genuine examples.

Regular Issue of 1921-27 Overprinted in Black

1929-30 Unwmk. *Perf. 14*
O1 A58 5c gray .30 .25
O2 A58 10c blue green .30 .25
O3 A58 35c blue green .40 .25
O4 A58 60c olive green .50 .25
O5 A58 1.50fr brt blue 15.00 7.00
O6 A58 1.75fr ultra ('30) 2.00 1.00
Nos. O1-O6 (6) 18.50 9.00
Set, never hinged 75.00

Same Overprint, in Red or Black, on Regular Issues of 1929-30
1929-31
O7 A63 5c slate (R) .25 .25
O8 A63 10c olive grn (R) .25 .25
O9 A63 25c rose red (Bk) 2.00 .40
O10 A63 35c dp green (R) .75 .25
O11 A63 40c red vio (Bk) .75 .25
O12 A63 50c dp blue (R) ('31) .35 .25
O13 A63 60c rose (Bk) 30.00 10.00
O14 A63 70c orange brn (Bk) 3.50 1.25
O15 A63 75c black vio (R) ('31) 7.00 1.00
Nos. O7-O15 (9) 44.85 13.90
Set, never hinged 125.00

Overprinted on Regular Issue of 1932
1932
O16 A73 10c olive grn (R) .75 .50
O17 A74 35c dp green 12.50 .50
O18 A71a 75c bister brn (R) 2.00 .40
Nos. O16-O18 (3) 15.25 1.40
Set, never hinged 55.00

Overprinted on No. 262 in Red
1935 *Perf. 13½x14*
O19 A80 70c olive black 5.00 .35

Regular Stamps of 1935-36 Overprinted in Red
1936-38 *Perf. 13½, 13½x14, 14*
O20 A82 10c olive bister .25 *.25*
O21 A82 35c green .25 *.25*
O22 A82 50c dark blue .45 .45
O23 A83 70c brown 3.50 3.50

Overprinted in Black or Red on Regular Issue of 1938
Perf. 13½x14
O24 A82 40c red violet (Bk) .25 *.25*
O25 A85 75c olive gray (R) .50 .50
Nos. O20-O25 (6) 5.20 5.20
Set, never hinged 12.50

Regular Issues of 1935-41 Overprinted in Red or Dark Blue

1941-44 *Perf. 14, 14x13½, 13½x14*
O26 A82 10c olive bister .25 .25
a. Inverted overprint *65.00 65.00*
O27 A82 40c red violet .25 *.25*
O28 A82 50c dark blue .25 .25
a. Inverted overprint *77.50 77.50*
O29 A83a 1fr rose car (Bl) .25 .25
O30 A85 1fr rose pink (Bl) .45 .45
O31 A83a 2.25fr grnsh blk ('44) .55 *.55*
O32 A84 2.25fr gray violet .65 *.65*
Nos. O26-O32 (7) 2.65 *2.65*
Set, never hinged 3.00

Nos. O21, O23 and O25 Surcharged with New Values in Black or Red

1942

O33	A82	10c on 35c green	.25	.25
O34	A83	50c on 70c brown	.25	.25
O35	A85	50c on 75c ol gray (R)	.45	.45
		Nos. O33-O35 (3)	.95	.95
		Set, never hinged	1.00	

Counterfeits exist of Nos. O26-O35.

Catalogue values for unused stamps in this section, from this point to the end of the section, are for Never Hinged items.

O1

1946-48 Unwmk. *Perf. 14*

O36	O1	10c olive bister	.25	.25
O37	O1	20c brt violet	3.00	.90
O38	O1	50c dk blue	.25	.25
O39	O1	65c red lilac ('48)	4.00	1.10
O40	O1	75c lilac rose	.25	.25
O41	O1	90c brown violet	5.00	.30
		Nos. O36-O41 (6)	12.75	3.05

Types A99, A101 and A102 with "B" Emblem Added to Design

1948 *Perf. 11½*

O42	A99	1.35fr red brown	2.50	.50
O43	A99	1.75fr dk gray green	6.00	.45
O44	A101	3fr brt red violet	27.50	10.00
O45	A102	3.15fr deep blue	11.00	7.00
O46	A102	4fr brt ultra	22.50	12.00
		Nos. O42-O46 (5)	69.50	29.95

O2

1953-66 Typo. *Perf. 13½x14*

O47	O2	10c orange	.35	.25
O48	O2	20c red lilac	3.50	.70
O49	O2	30c gray green ('58)	1.40	.50
O50	O2	40c olive gray	.35	.25
O51	O2	50c light blue	.30	.25
O51A	O2	60c lilac rose ('66)	.75	.25
O52	O2	65c red lilac	30.00	22.50
O53	O2	80c emerald	6.50	1.10
O54	O2	90c deep blue	6.75	1.10
O55	O2	1fr rose	.45	.25
		Nos. O47-O55 (10)	50.35	27.15

See Nos. O66, O68.

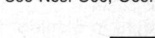

King Baudouin — O3

1954-70 Photo. *Perf. 11½*

O56	O3	1.50fr gray	.30	.25
O57	O3	2fr rose red	40.00	.30
O58	O3	2fr blue grn ('59)	.35	.25
O59	O3	2.50fr red brown ('58)	30.00	.75
O60	O3	3fr red lilac ('58)	1.50	.25
O61	O3	3.50fr yel green ('70)	.75	.25
O62	O3	4fr brt blue	1.00	.25
O63	O3	6fr car rose ('58)	1.50	.60
		Nos. O56-O63 (8)	75.40	2.90

Printed on various papers.

Type of 1953-66 Redrawn

1970-75 Typo. *Perf. 13½x14*

O66	O2	1.50fr grnsh gray ('75)	.25	.25
O68	O2	2.50fr brown	.25	.25

King Baudouin — O4

1971-73 Engr. *Perf. 11½*

O71	O4	3.50fr org brn ('73)	.35	.25
O72	O4	4.50fr brown ('73)	.35	.25
O73	O4	7fr red	.30	.25
O74	O4	15fr violet	.75	.25
		Nos. O71-O74 (4)	1.75	1.00

Nos. O71-O74 were printed on various papers.

1974-80

O75	O4	3fr yellow grn	1.00	.75
O76	O4	4fr blue	1.25	.50
O77	O4	4.50fr grnsh bl ('75)	.25	.25
O78	O4	5fr lilac	.35	.25
O79	O4	6fr carmine ('78)	.35	.25
O80	O4	6.50fr black ('76)	.45	.25
O81	O4	8fr bluish blk ('78)	.50	.25
O82	O4	9fr lt red brn ('80)	.50	.25
O83	O4	10fr rose carmine	.50	.25
O84	O4	25fr lilac ('76)	1.50	.50
O85	O4	30fr org brn ('78)	1.50	.65
		Nos. O75-O85 (11)	8.15	4.15

Heraldic Lion — O5

1977-82 Typo. *Perf. 13½x14*

O87	O5	50c brown ('82)	.25	.25
O92	O5	1fr lilac ('82)	.25	.25
O94	O5	2fr orange ('82)	.25	.25
O95	O5	4fr red brown	.25	.25
O96	O5	5fr green ('80)	.25	.25
		Nos. O87-O96 (5)	1.25	1.25

Nos. O87-O96 were printed on various papers.

NEWSPAPER STAMPS

Most examples of Nos. P1-P40 in the marketplace are counterfeits. Values are for genuine examples.

Parcel Post Stamps of 1923-27 Overprinted

Perf. 14½x14, 14x14½

1928 Unwmk.

P1	PP12	10c vermilion	.45	*.25*
P2	PP12	20c turq blue	.45	*.25*
P3	PP12	40c olive grn	.45	*.25*
P4	PP12	60c orange	.70	*.30*
P5	PP12	70c dk brown	.70	.30
P6	PP12	80c violet	.90	*.45*
P7	PP12	90c slate	9.00	3.00
P8	PP13	1fr brt blue	2.00	.50
a.		1fr ultramarine	4.00	3.00
P10	PP13	2fr olive grn	3.50	.75
P11	PP13	3fr orange red	3.50	.75
P12	PP13	4fr rose	3.50	.75
P13	PP13	5fr violet	3.50	.75
P14	PP13	6fr bister brn	6.50	1.75
P15	PP13	7fr orange	20.00	2.00
P16	PP13	8fr dk brown	12.00	2.00
P17	PP13	9fr red violet	40.00	9.00
P18	PP13	10fr blue green	12.00	2.75
P19	PP13	20fr magenta	40.00	12.50
		Nos. P1-P8,P10-P19 (18)	159.15	38.30
		Set, never hinged	750.00	

Parcel Post Stamps of 1923-28 Overprinted

1929-31

P20	PP12	10c vermilion	.90	.40
P21	PP12	20c turq blue	.45	.45
a.		Inverted overprint	250.00	250.00
P22	PP12	40c olive green	.45	.45
a.		Inverted overprint	250.00	250.00
P23	PP12	60c orange	.65	.40
P24	PP12	70c dk brown	.45	.45
P25	PP12	80c violet	.90	.90
P26	PP12	90c gray	6.25	5.00
P27	PP13	1fr ultra	1.25	.45
a.		1fr bright blue ('31)	6.50	2.50
P28	PP13	1.10fr org brn ('31)	4.50	1.25
P29	PP13	1.50fr gray vio ('31)	4.50	1.25
P30	PP13	2fr olive green	3.00	.90
P31	PP13	2.10fr sl gray ('31)	12.50	9.50
P32	PP13	3fr orange red	3.00	.90
P33	PP13	4fr rose	3.00	.90
P34	PP13	5fr violet	3.00	.90
P35	PP13	6fr bister brn	6.50	1.25
P36	PP13	7fr orange	24.00	1.25
P37	PP13	8fr dk brown	14.00	1.25
P38	PP13	9fr red violet	30.00	16.00
P39	PP13	10fr blue green	18.00	3.50
P40	PP13	20fr magenta	40.00	13.00
		Nos. P20-P40 (21)	177.30	60.35
		Set, never hinged	700.00	

Values of the original 1929 set exist in two formats, differing in the relative placement of the two lines of the overprint. Values are for the less expensive type.

PARCEL POST AND RAILWAY STAMPS

Values for used Railway Stamps (Chemins de Fer) stamps are for copies with railway cancellations. Railway Stamps with postal cancellations sell for twice as much.

Coat of Arms — PP1

1879-82 Unwmk. Typo. *Perf. 14*

Q1	PP1	10c violet brown	110.00	5.75
Q2	PP1	20c blue	275.00	17.50
Q3	PP1	25c green ('81)	375.00	10.00
Q4	PP1	50c carmine	1,750.	10.00
Q5	PP1	80c yellow	2,000.	57.50
Q6	PP1	1fr gray ('82)	275.00	16.00

Used examples of Nos. Q1-Q6 with pinholes, a normal state, sell for approximately 40-60 percent of the values given.

Most of the stamps of 1882-1902 (Nos. Q7 to Q28) are without watermark. Twice in each sheet of 100 stamps they have one of three watermarks: (1) A winged wheel and "Chemins de Fer de l'Etat Belge," (2) Coat of Arms of Belgium and "Royaume de Belgique," (3) Larger Coat of Arms, without inscription.

PP2

1882-94 *Perf. 15½x14¼*

Q7	PP2	10c brown ('86)	20.00	1.50
Q8	PP2	15c gray ('94)	8.75	7.25
Q9	PP2	20c blue ('86)	65.00	7.00
Q10	PP2	25c yel grn ('91)	72.50	4.25
Q11	PP2	50c rose	72.50	2.50
Q12	PP2	80c brnsh buff	72.50	.90
Q13	PP2	80c lemon	75.00	1.60
Q14	PP2	1fr lavender	350.00	3.00
Q15	PP2	2fr yel buff ('94)	210.00	67.50

Counterfeits exist.

PP3

Name of engraver below frame

1895-97

Numerals in Black, except 1fr, 2fr

Q16	PP3	10c red brown ('96)	12.00	.80
Q17	PP3	15c gray	12.00	9.00
Q18	PP3	20c blue	20.00	1.50
Q19	PP3	25c green	20.00	1.50
Q20	PP3	50c carmine	30.00	1.50
Q21	PP3	60c violet ('96)	60.00	1.25
Q22	PP3	80c ol yel ('96)	60.00	1.25
Q23	PP3	1fr lilac brown	225.00	3.50
Q24	PP3	2fr yel buff ('97)	300.00	18.00

Counterfeits exist.

1901-02 Numerals in Black

Q25	PP3	30c orange	25.00	1.75
Q26	PP3	40c green	35.00	1.75
Q27	PP3	70c blue	60.00	1.40
a.		Numerals omitted	*750.00*	
b.		Numerals printed on reverse	*750.00*	
Q28	PP3	90c red	110.00	2.00
		Nos. Q25-Q28 (4)	230.00	6.90

Winged Wheel PP4

Without engraver's name

1902-14 *Perf. 15*

Q29	PP3	10c yel brn & slate	.25	.25
Q30	PP3	15c slate & vio	.25	.25
Q31	PP3	20c ultra & yel brn	.25	.25
Q32	PP3	25c yel grn & red	.25	.25
Q33	PP3	30c orange & bl grn	.25	.25
Q34	PP3	35c bister & bl grn ('12)	.35	.25
Q35	PP3	40c blue grn & vio	.25	.25
Q36	PP3	50c pale rose & vio	.25	.25
Q37	PP3	55c lilac brn & ultra ('14)	.35	.25
Q38	PP3	60c violet & red	.25	.25
Q39	PP3	70c blue & red	.25	.25
Q40	PP3	80c lemon & vio brn	.25	.25
Q41	PP3	90c red & yel grn	.25	.25
Q42	PP4	1fr vio brn & org	.25	.25
Q43	PP4	1.10fr rose & blk ('06)	.25	.25
Q44	PP4	2fr ocher & bl grn	.25	.25
Q45	PP4	3fr black & ultra	.25	.25
Q46	PP4	4fr yel grn & red ('13)	2.00	2.00
Q47	PP4	5fr org & bl grn ('13)	.90	.90
Q48	PP4	10fr ol yel & brn vio ('13)	.90	.90
		Nos. Q29-Q48 (20)	8.25	8.05
		Set, never hinged	16.00	

Regular Issues of 1912-13 Handstamped in Violet

1915 *Perf. 14*

Q49	A42	5c green	*200.00*	—
Q50	A43	10c red	*2,000.*	—
Q51	A45	10c red	*2,150.*	—
a.		With engraver's name	*900.00*	—
Q52	A43	20c olive grn	*2,250.*	—
Q53	A45	20c olive grn	*275.00*	—
a.		With engraver's name	*900.00*	—
Q54	A45	25c ultra	*275.00*	—
a.		With engraver's name	*900.00*	—
Q55	A43	35c bister brn	*400.00*	—
Q55A	A43	40c green	*3,500.*	—
Q56	A45	40c green	*400.00*	—
Q57	A43	50c gray	*400.00*	—
Q58	A43	1fr orange	*375.00*	—
Q59	A43	2fr violet	*1,900.*	—
Q60	A44	5fr plum	*4,000.*	—

Excellent forgeries of this overprint exist.

PP5

PP6

1916 Litho. *Perf. 13½*

Q61	PP5	10c pale blue	1.00	.30
Q62	PP5	15c olive grn	1.25	1.50
Q63	PP5	20c red	2.00	1.00
Q64	PP5	25c lt brown	2.00	1.00
Q65	PP5	30c lilac	1.40	1.00
Q66	PP5	35c gray	1.40	1.00
Q67	PP5	40c orange yel	3.00	2.25
Q68	PP5	50c bister	2.25	.75
Q69	PP5	55c brown	3.00	2.50
Q70	PP5	60c gray vio	2.25	.75
Q71	PP5	70c green	2.25	.75
Q72	PP5	80c red brown	2.25	.75
Q73	PP5	90c blue	2.25	1.00
Q74	PP6	1fr gray	2.25	.75
Q75	PP6	1.10fr ultra *(Franken)*	40.00	25.00
Q76	PP6	2fr red	60.00	1.00
Q77	PP6	3fr violet	60.00	1.00
Q78	PP6	4fr emerald	60.00	2.00
Q79	PP6	5fr brown	125.00	3.00
Q80	PP6	10fr orange	140.00	3.00
		Nos. Q61-Q80 (20)	513.55	50.30
		Set, never hinged	1,700.	

Type of 1916 Inscribed "FRANK" instead of "FRANKEN"

1920

Q81	PP6	1.10fr ultra	4.00	.75

PP7

PP8

1920 *Perf. 14*

Q82	PP7	10c blue grn	1.75	.75
Q83	PP7	15c olive grn	1.75	1.10
Q84	PP7	20c red	1.75	.75
Q85	PP7	25c gray brn	3.00	.75
Q86	PP7	30c red vio	40.00	27.50
Q87	PP7	40c pale org	17.50	1.25
Q88	PP7	50c bister	12.50	1.25
Q89	PP7	55c pale brown	10.00	6.00
Q90	PP7	60c dk violet	18.00	1.00
Q91	PP7	70c green	35.00	1.10
Q92	PP7	80c red brown	65.00	1.50
Q93	PP7	90c dull blue	15.00	1.00
Q94	PP8	1fr gray	125.00	1.50
Q95	PP8	1.10fr ultra	45.00	1.50
Q96	PP8	1.20fr dk green	30.00	1.00
Q97	PP8	1.40fr black brn	30.00	1.00
Q98	PP8	2fr vermilion	175.00	1.25
Q99	PP8	3fr red vio	175.00	.85
Q100	PP8	4fr yel grn	175.00	1.25
Q101	PP8	5fr bister brn	175.00	.75
Q102	PP8	10fr brown org	175.00	1.00
		Nos. Q82-Q102 (21)	1,326.	54.05
		Set, never hinged	4,000.	

PP9

PP10

Types PP7 and PP9 differ in the position of the wheel and the tablet above it.

Types PP8 and PP10 differ in the bars below "FR".

There are many other variations in the designs.

1920-21 Typo.

Q103	PP9	10c carmine	.60	.25
Q104	PP9	15c yel grn	.60	.25
Q105	PP9	20c blue grn	1.10	.25
Q106	PP9	25c ultra	1.10	.25
Q107	PP9	30c chocolate	1.10	.25
Q108	PP9	35c orange brn	1.10	.30
Q109	PP9	40c orange	1.10	.25
Q110	PP9	50c rose	1.10	.25
Q111	PP9	55c yel ('21)	4.50	3.25
Q112	PP9	60c dull rose	1.10	.25
Q113	PP9	70c emerald	4.50	.40
Q114	PP9	80c violet	4.50	.30
Q115	PP9	90c lemon	45.00	32.50
Q116	PP9	90c claret	9.00	.30
Q117	PP10	1fr buff	9.00	.25
Q118	PP10	1fr red brown	8.00	.25
Q119	PP10	1.10fr ultra	3.00	.25
Q120	PP10	1.20fr orange	4.50	.25
Q121	PP10	1.40fr yellow	25.00	2.00
Q122	PP10	1.60fr turq blue	45.00	.50
Q123	PP10	1.60fr emerald	60.00	.70
Q124	PP10	2fr pale rose	50.00	.25
Q125	PP10	3fr dp rose	50.00	.25
Q126	PP10	4fr emerald	50.00	.25
Q127	PP10	5fr lt violet	45.00	.25
Q128	PP10	10fr lemon	260.00	19.00
Q129	PP10	10fr dk brown	70.00	.25
Q130	PP10	15fr dp rose ('21)	70.00	.25
Q131	PP10	20fr dk blue ('21)	650.00	3.00
		Nos. Q103-Q131 (29)	1,476.	66.75
		Set, never hinged	4,500.	

PP11

1922 Engr. *Perf. 11½*

Q132	PP11	2fr black	12.00	.60
Q133	PP11	3fr brown	100.00	.60
Q134	PP11	4fr green	30.00	.60
Q135	PP11	5r claret	35.00	.60
Q136	PP11	10fr yel brown	30.00	.60
Q137	PP11	15fr rose red	30.00	1.20
Q138	PP11	20fr blue	160.00	3.00
		Nos. Q132-Q138 (7)	397.00	7.20
		Set, never hinged	1,500.	

PP12

PP13

Perf. 14x13½, 13½x14

1923-40 Typo.

Q139	PP12	5c red brn	.25	.25
Q140	PP12	10c vermilion	.25	.25
Q141	PP12	15c ultra	.25	.25
Q142	PP12	20c turq blue	.25	.25
Q143	PP12	30c brn vio ('27)	.25	.25
Q144	PP12	40c olive grn	.25	.25
Q145	PP12	50c mag ('27)	.25	.25
Q146	PP12	60c orange	.25	.25
Q147	PP12	70c dk brn ('24)	.25	.25
Q148	PP12	80c violet	.25	.25
Q149	PP12	90c sl ('27)	.65	.25
Q150	PP13	1fr ultra	.45	.25
Q151	PP13	1fr brt blue ('28)	.55	.25
Q152	PP13	1.10fr orange	1.50	.60
Q153	PP13	1.50fr turq blue	1.50	.35
Q154	PP13	1.70fr dp brn ('31)	.40	.40
Q155	PP13	1.80fr claret	2.50	.65
Q156	PP13	2fr ol grn ('24)	.25	.25
Q157	PP13	2.10fr gray grn	4.50	1.00
Q158	PP13	2.40fr dp violet	2.00	1.00
Q159	PP13	2.70fr gray ('24)	35.00	1.25
Q160	PP13	3fr org red	.25	.25
Q161	PP13	3.30fr brn ('24)	60.00	1.25
Q162	PP13	4fr rose ('24)	.25	.25
Q163	PP13	5fr vio ('24)	.40	.25
Q163A	PP13	5fr brn vio ('40)	.45	.40
Q164	PP13	6fr bis brn ('27)	.25	.25
Q165	PP13	7fr org ('27)	.40	.25
Q166	PP13	8fr dp brn ('27)	.40	.25
Q167	PP13	9fr red vio ('27)	1.40	.25
Q168	PP13	10fr blue grn ('27)	.65	.25
Q168A	PP13	10fr blk ('40)	5.75	5.50
Q169	PP13	20fr mag ('27)	.80	.25
Q170	PP13	30fr turq grn ('31)	2.75	.40
Q171	PP13	40fr gray ('31)	55.00	1.20
Q172	PP13	50fr bis ('27)	5.00	.40
		Nos. Q139-Q172 (36)	185.55	20.15
		Set, never hinged	700.00	

See Nos. Q239-Q262. For overprints see Nos. Q216-Q238. Stamps overprinted "Bagages Reisgoed" are revenues.

No. Q158 Srchd.

1924 Green Surcharge

Q173	PP13	2.30fr on 2.40fr vio	5.00	.75
		Never hinged	40.00	

Type of Regular Issue of 1926-27 Overprinted

1928 *Perf. 14*

Q174	A61	4fr buff	6.50	1.10
Q175	A61	5fr bister	6.50	1.25
		Set, never hinged	50.00	

Central P.O., Brussels PP15

1929-30 Engr. *Perf. 11½*

Q176	PP15	3fr black brn	1.50	.25
Q177	PP15	4fr gray	1.50	.25
Q178	PP15	5fr carmine	1.50	.25
Q179	PP15	6fr vio brn ('30)	27.00	27.00
		Nos. Q176-Q179 (4)	31.50	27.75
		Set, never hinged	95.00	

No. Q179 Surcharged in Blue

1933

Q180	PP15	4(fr) on 6fr vio brn	22.50	.25
		Never hinged	90.00	

Modern Locomotive PP16

1934 Photo. *Perf. 13½x14*

Q181	PP16	3fr dk green	10.00	2.50
Q182	PP16	4fr red violet	4.00	.25
Q183	PP16	5fr dp rose	55.00	.25
		Nos. Q181-Q183 (3)	69.00	3.00
		Set, never hinged	225.00	

Modern Railroad Train — PP17

Old Railroad Train — PP18

1935 Engr. *Perf. 14x13½, 13½x14*

Q184	PP17	10c rose car	.45	.30
Q185	PP17	20c violet	.45	.30
Q186	PP17	30c black brn	.50	.30
Q187	PP17	40c dk blue	.50	.30
Q188	PP17	50c orange red	.50	.30
Q189	PP17	60c green	.90	.30
Q190	PP17	70c ultra	1.00	.30
Q191	PP17	80c olive blk	1.00	.30
Q192	PP17	90c rose lake	1.00	.30
Q193	PP18	1fr brown vio	1.00	.30
Q194	PP18	2fr gray blk	2.75	.30
Q195	PP18	3fr red org	2.25	.30
Q196	PP18	4fr violet brn	2.25	.30
Q197	PP18	5fr plum	4.50	.30
Q198	PP18	6fr dp green	6.00	.30
Q199	PP18	7fr dp violet	24.00	.30
Q200	PP18	8fr olive blk	24.00	.30
Q201	PP18	9fr dk blue	24.00	.30
Q202	PP18	10fr car lake	24.00	.30
Q203	PP18	20fr green	50.00	.30
Q204	PP18	30fr violet	110.00	4.25
Q205	PP18	40fr black brn	110.00	4.25
Q206	PP18	50fr rose car	140.00	4.25
Q207	PP18	100fr ultra	275.00	60.00
		Nos. Q184-Q207 (24)	806.05	78.75
		Set, never hinged	3,000.	

Centenary of Belgian State Railway.

Winged Wheel PP19

Surcharged in Red or Blue

1938 Photo. *Perf. 13½*

Q208	PP19	5fr on 3.50fr dk grn	22.50	1.50
Q209	PP19	5fr on 4.50fr rose vio (Bl)	.25	.25
Q210	PP19	6fr on 5.50fr cop red (Bl)	.50	.25
	a.	Half used as 3fr on piece		8.00
		Nos. Q208-Q210 (3)	23.25	2.00
		Set, never hinged	60.00	

Nos. Q208-Q210 exist without surcharge. Value, set, $750.

See Nos. MQ1, Q297-Q299.

Symbolizing Unity Achieved Through Railroads PP20

1939 Engr. *Perf. 13½x14*

Q211	PP20	20c redsh brn	4.00	*4.00*
Q212	PP20	50c vio bl	4.00	*4.00*
Q213	PP20	2fr rose red	4.00	*4.00*
Q214	PP20	9fr slate grn	4.00	*4.00*
Q215	PP20	10fr dk vio	4.00	*4.00*
		Nos. Q211-Q215 (5)	20.00	*20.00*
		Set, never hinged	25.00	

Railroad Exposition and Cong. held at Brussels.

Parcel Post Stamps of 1925-27 Overprinted in Blue or Carmine

Perf. 14½x14, 14x14½

1940			**Unwmk.**	
Q216	PP12	10c vermilion	.25	.25
Q217	PP12	20c turq bl (C)	.25	.25
Q218	PP12	30c brn vio	.25	.25
Q219	PP12	40c ol grn (C)	.25	.25
Q220	PP12	50c magenta	.25	.25
Q221	PP12	60c orange	.60	*.55*
Q222	PP12	70c dk brn	.25	.25
Q223	PP12	80c vio (C)	.25	.25
Q224	PP12	90c slate (C)	.25	.25
Q225	PP13	1fr ultra (C)	.25	.25
Q226	PP13	2fr ol grn (C)	.25	.25
a.		Ovpt. inverted	140.00	75.00
Q227	PP13	3fr org red	.25	.25
Q228	PP13	4fr rose	.25	.25
Q229	PP13	5fr vio (C)	.25	.25
Q230	PP13	6fr bis brn	.35	.25
Q231	PP13	7fr orange	.35	.25
Q232	PP13	8fr dp brn	.35	.25
Q233	PP13	9fr red vio	.35	.25
Q234	PP13	10fr bl grn (C)	.35	.25
Q235	PP13	20fr magenta	.60	.25
Q236	PP13	30fr turq grn (C)	1.10	.75
Q237	PP13	40fr gray (C)	2.25	*2.10*
Q238	PP13	50fr bister	1.60	1.10
		Nos. Q216-Q238 (23)	11.15	9.25
		Set, never hinged	18.00	

Types of 1923-40

1941				
Q239	PP12	10c dl olive	.25	.25
Q240	PP12	20c lt vio	.25	.25
Q241	PP12	30c fawn	.25	.25
Q242	PP12	40c dull blue	.25	.25
Q243	PP12	50c lt grn	.25	.25
Q244	PP12	60c gray	.25	.25
Q245	PP12	70c chalky grn	.25	.25
Q246	PP12	80c orange	.25	.25
Q247	PP12	90c rose lilac	.25	.25
Q248	PP13	1fr lt yel grn	.25	.25
Q249	PP13	2fr vio brn	.40	.25
Q250	PP13	3fr slate	.45	.25
Q251	PP13	4fr dl olive	.50	.25
Q252	PP13	5fr rose lilac	.50	.25
Q253	PP13	5fr black	.85	.30
Q254	PP13	6fr org ver	.75	.30
Q255	PP13	7fr lilac	.75	.25
Q256	PP13	8fr chalky grn	.75	.25
Q257	PP13	9fr blue	.90	.25
Q258	PP13	10fr rose lilac	.90	.25
Q259	PP13	20fr milky blue	2.75	.40
Q260	PP13	30fr orange	5.00	.80
Q261	PP13	40fr rose	6.25	.80
Q262	PP13	50fr brt red vio	10.00	.70
		Nos. Q239-Q262 (24)	33.25	7.80
		Set, never hinged	90.00	

Adjusting Tie Plates — PP21

Engineer at Throttle — PP22

Freight Station Interior — PP23

Signal and Electric Train — PP24

1942	**Engr.**		***Perf. 14x13½***	
Q263	PP21	9.20fr red org	.60	*.60*
Q264	PP22	12.30fr dp grn	.60	*.60*
Q265	PP23	14.30fr dk car	.60	*.60*

Perf. 11½

Q266	PP24	100fr ultra	20.00	20.00
		Nos. Q263-Q266 (4)	21.80	21.80
		Set, never hinged	25.00	

Catalogue values for unused stamps in this section, from this point to the end of the section, are for Never Hinged items.

PP25

PP26

PP27

1945-46	**Photo.**		**Unwmk.**	
Q267	PP25	10c ol blk ('46)	.35	.30
Q268	PP25	20c dp vio	.35	.30
Q269	PP25	30c chnt brn ('46)	.35	.30
Q270	PP25	40c dp bl ('46)	.35	.30
Q271	PP25	50c peacock grn	.35	.30
Q272	PP25	60c blk ('46)	.35	.30
Q273	PP25	70c emer ('46)	.45	.30
Q274	PP25	80c orange	.75	.30
Q275	PP25	90c brn vio ('46)	.35	.30
Q276	PP26	1fr bl grn ('46)	.35	.30
Q277	PP26	2fr blk brn	.35	.30
Q278	PP26	3fr grnsh blk ('46)	2.00	.30
Q279	PP26	4fr dark blue	.45	.30
Q280	PP26	5fr sepia	.50	.30
Q281	PP26	6fr dk ol grn ('46)	2.25	.30
Q282	PP26	7fr dk vio ('46)	.75	.30
Q283	PP26	8fr red org	.75	.30
Q284	PP26	9fr dp bl ('46)	.90	.30
Q285	PP27	10fr dk red ('46)	3.25	.30
Q286	PP27	10fr sepia ('46)	1.90	.30
Q287	PP27	20fr dk yel grn ('46)	1.00	.30
Q288	PP27	30fr dp vio	1.00	.30
Q289	PP27	40fr rose pink	1.00	.30
Q290	PP27	50fr brt bl ('46)	16.00	.70
		Nos. Q267-Q290 (24)	36.10	7.60

Mercury — PP28

1945-46			***Perf. 13½x13***	
Q291	PP28	3fr emer ('46)	.35	.25
Q292	PP28	5fr ultra	.35	.25
Q293	PP28	6fr red	.35	.25

Inscribed "Belgique-Belgie"

Q294	PP28	3fr emer ('46)	.35	.25
Q295	PP28	5fr ultra	.35	.25
Q296	PP28	6fr red	.35	.25
		Nos. Q291-Q296 (6)	2.10	1.50

Winged Wheel Type of 1938

Carmine Surcharge

1946			***Perf. 13½x14***	
Q297	PP19	8fr on 5.50fr brn	.50	.25
Q298	PP19	10fr on 5.50fr dk bl	.75	.25
Q299	PP19	12fr on 5.50fr vio	1.10	.25
		Nos. Q297-Q299 (3)	2.35	.75

Railway Crossing PP29

1947	**Engr.**		***Perf. 12½***	
Q300	PP29	100fr dark green	6.00	.25

Crossbowman with Train — PP30

1947	**Photo.**		***Perf. 11½***	
Q301	PP30	8fr dark olive brn	1.25	.25
Q302	PP30	10fr gray & blue	1.25	.25
Q303	PP30	12fr dark violet	1.60	.45
		Nos. Q301-Q303 (3)	4.10	.95

Nos. Q301-3 Srchd.

1948				
Q304	PP30	9fr on 8fr	1.25	.25
Q305	PP30	11fr on 10fr	1.25	.30
Q306	PP30	13.50fr on 12fr	2.00	.25
		Nos. Q304-Q306 (3)	4.50	.80

Delivery of Parcel PP31

1948				
Q307	PP31	9fr chocolate	6.50	.25
Q308	PP31	11fr brown car	5.50	.25
Q309	PP31	13.50fr gray	9.50	.25
		Nos. Q307-Q309 (3)	21.50	.75

Locomotive of 1835 PP32

Various Locomotives.

Lathe Work in Frame Differs

1949	**Engr.**		***Perf. 12½***	
Q310	PP32	½fr dark brown	.30	.25
Q311	PP32	1fr carmine rose	.40	.25
Q312	PP32	2fr deep ultra	.55	.25
Q313	PP32	3fr dp magenta	1.75	.25
Q314	PP32	4fr blue green	1.25	.25
Q315	PP32	5fr orange red	1.25	.25
Q316	PP32	6fr brown vio	1.75	.30
Q317	PP32	7fr yellow grn	2.75	.25
Q318	PP32	8fr grnsh blue	4.00	.25
Q319	PP32	9fr yellow brn	4.25	.30
Q320	PP32	10fr citron	5.00	.25
Q321	PP32	20fr orange	9.00	.25
Q322	PP32	30fr blue	17.50	.25
Q323	PP32	40fr lilac rose	30.00	.35
Q324	PP32	50fr violet	55.00	.35
Q325	PP32	100fr red	100.00	.70

Engraved; Center Typographed

Q326	PP32	10fr car rose & blk	10.00	1.75
		Nos. Q310-Q326 (17)	244.75	6.50

See No. Q337.

1949			**Engr.**	

Design: Electric locomotive.

Q327	PP32	60fr black brown	22.50	.25

Opening of Charleroi-Brussels electric railway line, Oct. 15, 1949.

Mailing Parcel Post PP33

Sorting PP34

Loading PP35

1950-52			***Perf. 12x12½, 12½***	
Q328	PP33	11fr red orange	4.50	.25
Q329	PP33	12fr red vio ('51)	20.00	1.50
Q330	PP34	13fr dk blue grn	6.00	.25
Q331	PP34	15fr ultra ('51)	15.00	.25
Q332	PP35	16fr gray	5.00	.25
Q333	PP33	17fr brown ('52)	6.50	.25
Q334	PP35	18fr brt car ('51)	13.00	1.00
Q335	PP35	20fr brn org ('52)	6.00	.25
		Nos. Q328-Q335 (8)	76.00	4.00

For surcharges see Nos. Q338-Q340.

Mercury and Winged Wheel — PP36

1951				
Q336	PP36	25fr dark blue	15.00	11.50

25th anniv. of the founding of the Natl. Soc. of Belgian Railroads.

Type of 1949

Design: Electric locomotive.

1952	**Unwmk.**		***Perf. 11½***	
Q337	PP32	300fr red violet	140.00	.65

Nos. Q331, Q328 and Q334 Surcharged with New Value and "X" in Red, Blue or Green

1953			***Perf. 12x12½***	
Q338	PP34	13fr on 15fr (R)	60.00	5.00
Q339	PP33	17fr on 11fr (Bl)	30.00	1.25
Q340	PP35	20fr on 18fr (G)	12.50	2.50
		Nos. Q338-Q340 (3)	102.50	8.75

Electric Train, 1952 PP37

1953			**Engr.**	
Q341	PP37	200fr dk yel grn & vio brn	200.00	3.00
Q342	PP37	200fr dk green	200.00	.75

No. Q341 was issued to commemorate the opening of the railway link connecting Brussels North and South Stations, Oct. 4, 1952.

New North Station, Brussels — PP38

Chapelle Station, Brussels PP39

Designs: No. Q348, 15fr, Congress Station. 10fr, 20fr, 30fr, 40fr, 50fr, South Station. 100fr, 200fr, 300fr, Central Station.

1953-57	**Unwmk.**		***Perf. 11½***	
Q343	PP38	1fr bister	.30	.25
Q344	PP38	2fr slate	.40	.25
Q345	PP38	3fr blue grn	.40	.25
Q346	PP38	4fr orange	.75	.25
Q347	PP38	5fr red brn	2.25	.25
Q348	PP38	5fr dk red brn	9.00	.25

Q349	PP38	6fr rose vio	.95	.25
Q350	PP38	7fr brt green	.95	.25
Q351	PP38	8fr rose red	.95	.25
Q352	PP38	9fr brt grnsh bl	1.40	.25
Q353	PP38	10fr lt grn	1.75	.25
Q354	PP38	15fr dl red	11.00	.25
Q355	PP38	20fr blue	3.00	.25
Q356	PP38	30fr purple	4.50	.25
Q357	PP38	40fr brt purple	6.00	.25
Q358	PP38	50fr lilac rose	7.50	.25
Q359	PP39	60fr brt purple	15.00	.25
Q360	PP39	80fr brown vio	30.00	.35
Q361	PP39	100fr emerald	15.00	.35
Q361A	PP39	200fr brt vio bl	87.50	.65
Q361B	PP39	300fr lilac rose	150.00	1.25
		Nos. Q343-Q361B (21)	348.60	6.85

Issued: #Q347, 20fr, 30fr, 1953; 80fr, 1955; 200fr, 1956; 300fr, 1957; others, 1954.

See Nos. Q407, Q431-Q432.

Electric Train — PP40

1954

Q362	PP40	13fr chocolate	20.00	.25
Q363	PP40	18fr dark blue	20.00	.25
Q364	PP40	21fr lilac rose	20.00	.25
		Nos. Q362-Q364 (3)	60.00	.75

Nos. Q362-Q364 Surcharged with New Value and "X" in Blue, Red or Green

1956

Q365	PP40	14fr on 13fr (B)	7.00	.25
Q366	PP40	19fr on 18fr (R)	7.00	.25
Q367	PP40	22fr on 21fr (G)	7.00	.45
		Nos. Q365-Q367 (3)	21.00	.95

Mercury and Winged Wheel — PP41

1957 Engr. *Perf. 11½*

Q368	PP41	14fr brt green	7.00	.25
Q369	PP41	19fr olive gray	7.00	.25
Q370	PP41	22fr carmine rose	7.00	.30
		Nos. Q368-Q370 (3)	21.00	.80

Nos. Q369-Q370 Surcharged with New Value and "X" in Pink or Green

1959

Q371	PP41	20fr on 19fr (P)	20.00	.25
Q372	PP41	20fr on 22fr (G)	20.00	.25

Old North Station, Brussels PP42

1959 Engr. *Perf. 11½*

Q373	PP42	20fr olive green	12.50	.25

See Nos. Q381, Q383. For surcharges see Nos. Q378, Q382, Q384.

Diesel and Electric Locomotives and Association Emblem PP43

1960 Unwmk. *Perf. 11½*

Q374	PP43	20fr red	40.00	27.50
Q375	PP43	50fr dark blue	40.00	27.50
Q376	PP43	60fr red lilac	40.00	27.50
Q377	PP43	70fr emerald	40.00	27.50
		Nos. Q374-Q377 (4)	160.00	110.00

Intl. Assoc. of Railway Congresses, 75th anniv.

No. Q373 Surcharged with New Value and "X" in Red

1961

Q378	PP42	24fr on 20fr ol grn	45.00	.25

South Station, Brussels — PP44

1962 Unwmk. *Perf. 11½*

Q379	PP44	24fr dull red	5.00	.25

No. Q379 Surcharged with New Value and "X" in Light Green

1963

Q380	PP44	26fr on 24fr dl red	4.50	.25

Type of 1959

Design: 26fr, Central Station, Antwerp.

1963 Engr. *Perf. 11½*

Q381	PP42	26fr blue	4.50	2.50

No. Q381 Surcharged in Red

1964, Apr. 20

Q382	PP42	28fr on 26fr blue	4.50	.25

Type of 1959

Design: 28fr, St. Peter's Station, Ghent.

1965 Engr. *Perf. 11½*

Q383	PP42	28fr red lilac	4.50	1.75

Nos. Q383 Surcharged in Green

1966

Q384	PP42	35fr on 28fr red lil	4.50	.25

Arlon Railroad Station PP45

Perf. 11½

1967, Aug. Unwmk. Engr.

Q385	PP45	25fr bister	8.00	.30
Q386	PP45	30fr blue green	2.00	.30
Q387	PP45	35fr deep blue	2.50	.30
		Nos. Q385-Q387 (3)	12.50	.90

No. Q385 exists on luminescent paper. Value, $500.

See #Q408. For surcharges see #Q410-Q412.

Electric Train PP46

Designs: 2fr, 3fr, 4fr, 5fr, 6fr, 7fr, 8fr, 9fr, like 1fr. 10fr, 20fr, 30fr, 40fr, Train going right. 50fr, 60fr, 70fr, 80fr, 90fr, Train going left. 100fr, 200fr, 300fr, Diesel train.

1968-73 Engr. *Perf. 11½*

Q388	PP46	1fr olive bis	.25	.25
Q389	PP46	2fr slate	.25	.25
Q390	PP46	3fr blue green	.55	.25
Q391	PP46	4fr orange	.55	.25
Q392	PP46	5fr brown	.65	.25
Q393	PP46	6fr plum	.55	.25
Q394	PP46	7fr brt green	.65	.25
Q395	PP46	8fr carmine	.85	.25
Q396	PP46	9fr blue	1.40	.25
Q397	PP46	10fr green	2.75	.25
Q398	PP46	20fr dk blue	1.60	.25
Q399	PP46	30fr dk purple	4.00	.25
Q400	PP46	40fr brt lilac	5.50	.25
Q401	PP46	50fr brt pink	6.75	.25
Q402	PP46	60fr brt violet	8.25	.30
Q402A	PP46	70fr dp bister ('73)	10.00	.30
Q403	PP46	80fr dk brown	6.75	.25
Q403A	PP46	90fr yel grn ('73)	5.50	.30
Q404	PP46	100fr emerald	11.00	.25
Q405	PP46	200fr violet blue	13.00	.50
Q406	PP46	300fr lilac rose	22.50	1.25
		Nos. Q388-Q406 (21)	103.30	6.65

Printed on various papers.

See No. Q409.

Types of 1953-68

10fr, Congress Station, Brussels. 40fr, Arlon Station. 500fr, Electric train going left.

1968, June Engr. *Perf. 11½*

Q407	PP38	10fr gray	1.25	.25
Q408	PP45	40fr vermilion	22.50	.25
Q409	PP46	500fr yellow	32.50	1.90
		Nos. Q407-Q409 (3)	56.25	2.40

Nos. Q385, Q387 and Q408 Surcharged with New Value and "X"

1970, Dec.

Q410	PP45	37fr on 25fr bister	55.00	6.00
Q411	PP45	48fr on 35fr dp bl	5.00	5.00
Q412	PP45	53fr on 40fr ver	5.00	5.00
		Nos. Q410-Q412 (3)	65.00	16.00

No. Q410 was also issued on non-luminescent paper. Value $175.

Ostend Station PP47

1971, Mar. Engr. *Perf. 11½*

Q413	PP47	32fr bis & blk	1.50	1.50
Q414	PP47	37fr gray & blk	10.00	10.00
Q415	PP47	42fr bl & blk	1.50	1.50
Q416	PP47	44fr brt rose & blk	1.50	1.50
Q417	PP47	46fr vio & blk	1.75	1.75
Q418	PP47	50fr brick red & blk	1.50	1.50
Q419	PP47	52fr sep & blk	11.00	11.00
Q420	PP47	54fr yel grn & blk	4.00	4.00
Q421	PP47	61fr grnsh bl & blk	2.50	2.50
		Nos. Q413-Q421 (9)	35.25	35.25

Nos. Q413-Q416, Q419-Q421 Surcharged with New Value and "X"

1971, Dec. 15

Denomination in Black

Q422	PP47	34fr on 32fr bister	1.75	.85
Q423	PP47	40fr on 37fr gray	1.75	.85
Q424	PP47	47fr on 44fr brt rose	2.00	.85
Q425	PP47	53fr on 42fr blue	2.75	.85
Q426	PP47	56fr on 52fr sepia	2.50	.85
Q427	PP47	59fr on 54fr yel grn	2.75	.85
Q428	PP47	66fr on 61fr grnsh blue	2.75	.85
		Nos. Q422-Q428 (7)	16.25	5.95

Track, Underpinning of Railroad Car and Emblems — PP48

1972, Mar. Photo.

Q429	PP48	100fr emer, red & blk	6.50	1.50

Centenary of International Railroad Union.

Congress Emblem PP49

1974, Apr. Photo. *Perf. 11½*

Q430	PP49	100fr yel, blk & red	6.00	2.25

4th International Symposium on Railroad Cybernetics, Washington, DC, Apr. 1974.

Type of 1953-1957

1975, June 1 Engr. *Perf. 11½*

Q431	PP38	20fr emerald	1.75	.40
Q432	PP38	50fr blue	3.50	.60

Railroad Tracks PP50

1976, June 10 Photo. *Perf. 11½*

Q433	PP50	20fr ultra & multi	3.00	.70
Q434	PP50	50fr brt grn & multi	1.75	1.00
Q435	PP50	100fr dp org & multi	4.00	1.50
Q436	PP50	150fr brt lil & multi	6.25	2.25
		Nos. Q433-Q436 (4)	15.00	5.45

Railroad Station — PP51

1977 Photo. *Perf. 11½*

Q437	PP51	1000fr multi	50.00	22.50

Also issued on luminescent paper.

See note following No. Q465.

Freight Car — PP52

Designs: 1fr-9fr, Freight car. 10fr-40fr, Hopper car. 50fr-90fr, Maintenance car. 100fr-500fr, Liquid fuel car.

1980, Dec. 16 Engr. *Perf. 11½*

Q438	PP52	1fr bis brn & blk	.30	.30
Q439	PP52	2fr claret & blk	.30	.30
Q440	PP52	3fr brt bl & blk	.30	.30
Q441	PP52	4fr grnsh blk & blk	.30	.30
Q442	PP52	5fr sepia & blk	.30	.30
Q443	PP52	6fr dp org & blk	.40	.40
Q444	PP52	7fr purple & blk	.50	.50
Q445	PP52	8fr black	.50	.50
Q446	PP52	9fr green & blk	.50	.50
Q447	PP52	10fr yel bis & blk	.50	.50
Q448	PP52	20fr grnsh bl & blk	1.25	.50
Q449	PP52	30fr bister & blk	2.25	.50
Q450	PP52	40fr lt lil & blk	2.50	.50
Q451	PP52	50fr dk brn & blk	2.75	.70
Q452	PP52	60fr olive & blk	3.25	.70
Q453	PP52	70fr vio bl & blk	5.00	5.00
Q454	PP52	80fr vio brn & blk	5.25	1.00
Q455	PP52	90fr lil rose & blk	7.00	7.00
Q456	PP52	100fr crim rose & blk	6.25	1.50
Q457	PP52	200fr brn & blk	12.50	1.75
Q458	PP52	300fr ol gray & blk	18.00	2.50
Q459	PP52	500fr dl pur & blk	32.50	5.25
		Nos. Q438-Q459 (22)	102.40	30.80

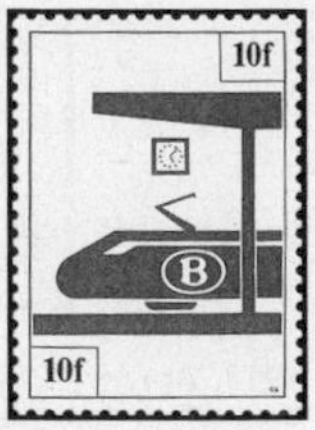

Train in Station — PP53

1982		Engr.	Perf. 11½	
Q460	PP53	10fr red & blk	1.75	.50
Q461	PP53	20fr green & blk	2.00	2.00
Q462	PP53	50fr sepia & blk	3.75	1.00
Q463	PP53	100fr blue & blk	6.50	1.50
		Nos. Q460-Q463 (4)	14.00	5.00

Electric Locomotives PP54

1985, May 3		Photo.	Perf. 11½	
Q464	PP54	250fr BB-150	15.00	12.00
Q465	PP54	500fr BB-120	35.00	17.50

Seven limited edition souvenir sheets exist. These include souvenir sheets of 4 of #Q437, Q464-Q465 with French or Flemish inscriptions, value $2,500, and a bilingual sheet with one each of #Q437, Q464-Q465, value $150.

Stylized Castle, Gabled Station and Electric Rail Car — PP55

1987, Oct. 12		Engr.	Perf. 11½	
Q466	PP55	10fr dk red & blk	1.00	.75
Q467	PP55	20fr dk grn & blk	1.50	1.50
Q468	PP55	50fr dk brn & blk	4.50	2.50
Q469	PP55	100fr dk lil & blk	8.00	4.00
Q470	PP55	150fr dark olive bister & blk	12.50	6.25
		Nos. Q466-Q470 (5)	27.50	15.00

Beginning in 1996, items looking like Parcel Post and Railway stamps have appeared in the market. Though sold by the Philatelic Bureau of the Belgian Post Office, these stamps are part of an ongoing series of Charity items that lack postal validity.

Kilopost — PP56

Maximum package weights: Nos. Q471, Q480, 0.5kg. Nos. Q472, Q481, 1kg. Nos. Q473, Q482, 2kg. Nos. Q474, Q483, 3kg. No. Q475, Q484, 4kg. No. Q476, Q485, 5kg. Nos. Q477, Q486, 10kg. Nos. Q478, Q487, 20kg. No. Q479, Q488, 30kg.

2003-04		Litho.		Perf. 11½	
		Color of Box			
Q471	PP56	(€2.48)	org	18.00	2.00
Q472	PP56	(€3.10)	red	18.00	2.00
Q473	PP56	(€3.72)	blue	18.00	3.00
Q474	PP56	(€5.21)	yel	24.00	3.00
Q475	PP56	(€5.95)	pur	30.00	4.00
Q476	PP56	(€6.69)	grn	25.00	6.00
Q477	PP56	(€7.44)	mar	30.00	9.00
Q478	PP56	(€8.68)	brn	42.00	16.00
Q479	PP56	(€11.16)	aqua	55.00	35.00

Self-Adhesive
Booklet Stamps
Serpentine Die Cut 8 Horiz.

Q480	PP56	(€2.48)	org	12.00	2.00
a.		Booklet pane of 5		60.00	
Q481	PP56	(€3.10)	red	13.00	2.50
a.		Booklet pane of 5		65.00	
Q482	PP56	(€3.72)	blue	15.00	3.00
a.		Booklet pane of 5		75.00	
Q483	PP56	(€5.21)	yel	20.00	1.50
a.		Booklet pane of 5		125.00	
Q484	PP56	(€5.95)	pur	24.00	2.00
a.		Booklet pane of 5		150.00	
Q485	PP56	(€6.69)	grn	26.00	3.00
a.		Booklet pane of 5		175.00	
Q486	PP56	(€7.44)	mar	30.00	6.00
a.		Booklet pane of 5		190.00	
Q487	PP56	(€8.68)	brn	35.00	10.00
a.		Booklet pane of 5		225.00	
Q488	PP56	(€11.16)	aqua	45.00	20.00
a.		Booklet pane of 5		275.00	
		Nos. Q471-Q488 (18)		480.00	130.00

Issued: Nos. Q471-Q482, 11/17. Nos. Q486-Q487, 2004. Nos. Q483-Q485, Q488, 2004.

Kilopost — PP57

Booklet Stamps
Die Cut Perf. 9¾ on 3 Sides

2005-07		Photo.		Self-Adhesive	
		Color of Box			
Q489	PP57	(€3.10)	red	9.00	.50
a.		Booklet pane of 5		45.00	
Q490	PP57	(€13)	blue	32.50	2.00
a.		Booklet pane of 5		165.00	
Q491	PP57	(€2.60)	green ('07)	7.00	.40
a.		Booklet pane of 5		35.00	

Kilopost — PP58

Die Cut Perf. 10 on 3 Sides

2007, Aug. 1			Litho.	
		Booklet Stamps		
		Self-Adhesive		
Q492	PP58	(€3) "Prior" at left	10.00	5.00
Q493	PP58	(€3) "Prior" at right	10.00	5.00
a.		Booklet pane of 5, 3 #Q492, 2 #Q493	50.00	

ISSUED UNDER GERMAN OCCUPATION

German Stamps of 1906-11 Surcharged

Nos. N1-N6

Nos. N7-N9

Wmk. Lozenges (125)

1914-15			Perf. 14, 14½	
N1	A16	3c on 3pf brn	.45	.25
N2	A16	5c on 5pf grn	.40	.25
N3	A16	10c on 10pf car	.50	.25
N4	A16	25c on 20pf ultra	.50	.25
N5	A16	50c on 40pf lake & blk	2.50	1.25
N6	A16	75c on 60pf mag	.90	*1.25*
N7	A16	1fr on 80pf lake & blk, *rose*	2.50	1.75
N8	A17	1fr25c on 1m car	20.00	12.50
N9	A21	2fr50c on 2m gray bl	18.00	15.00
		Nos. N1-N9 (9)	45.75	32.75
		Set, never hinged	160.00	

German Stamps of 1906-18 Surcharged

Nos. N10-N21

No. N22

Nos. N23-N25

1916-18				
N10	A22	2c on 2pf drab	.25	.25
N11	A16	3c on 3pf brn	.35	.25
N12	A16	5c on 5pf grn	.35	.25
N13	A22	8c on 7½pf org	.65	.35
N14	A16	10c on 10pf car	.25	.25
N15	A22	15c on 15pf yel brn	.65	.25
N16	A22	15c on 15pf dk vio	.65	.45
N17	A16	20c on 25pf org & blk, *yel*	.35	.35
N18	A16	25c on 20pf ultra	.35	.25
a.		25c on 20pf blue	.40	.25
N19	A16	40c on 30pf org & blk, *buff*	.40	.30
N20	A16	50c on 40pf lake & blk	.35	.30
N21	A16	75c on 60pf mag	1.00	*12.50*
N22	A16	1fr on 80pf lake & blk, *rose*	2.00	*2.50*
N23	A17	1fr25c on 1m car	2.00	2.00
N24	A21	2fr50c on 2m gray bl	27.50	25.00
a.		2fr50c on 1m car (error)		*3,500.*
N25	A20	6fr25c on 5m sl & car	40.00	37.50
		Nos. N10-N25 (16)	77.10	82.75
		Set, never hinged	145.00	

A similar series of stamps without "Belgien" was used in parts of Belgium and France while occupied by German forces. See France Nos. N15-N26.

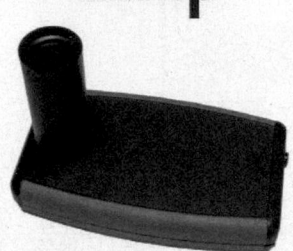

BELIZE

bə-'lēz

LOCATION — Central America bordering on Caribbean Sea to east, Mexico to north, Guatemala to west
GOVT. — Independent state
AREA — 8,867 sq. mi.
POP. — 219,296 (1996 est.)
CAPITAL — Belmopan

Belize was known as British Honduras until 1973. The former British colony achieved independence in September 1981.

100 Cents = 1 Dollar

Catalogue values for all unused stamps in this country are for Never Hinged items.

British Honduras Regular Issue 1968-72 Ovptd. in Black on Silver Panel

Wmk. 314 (½c, 5c, $5), Unwmkd.

1973, June 1 Litho. *Perf. 13x12½*

312	A37	½c	multi (#235)	.25	.25
313	A37	1c	multi (#214)	.25	.25
314	A37	2c	multi (#215)	.25	.25
315	A37	3c	multi (#216)	.25	.25
316	A37	4c	multi (#217)	.25	.25
317	A37	5c	multi (#238)	.25	.25
318	A37	10c	multi (#219)	.25	.25
319	A37	15c	multi (#220)	.25	.25
320	A37	25c	multi (#221)	.45	.45
321	A37	50c	multi (#222)	.85	.85
322	A37	$1	multi (#223)	1.00	*1.40*
323	A37	$2	multi (#224)	1.75	*2.75*
324	A37	$5	multi (#240)	2.00	*5.50*
			Nos. 312-324 (13)	8.05	*12.95*

No. 315 with silver panel omitted exists canceled. Nos. 313 and 319 exist with silver panel double.

Common Design Types pictured following the introduction.

Princess Anne's Wedding Issue
Common Design Type

1973, Nov. 14 Wmk. 314 *Perf. 14*

325	CD325	26c	blue grn & multi	.25	.25
326	CD325	50c	ocher & multi	.25	.25

Crana A50

1c, Jewfish. 2c, White-lipped peccary. 3c, Grouper. 4c, Collared anteater. 5c, Bonefish. 10c, Paca. 15c, Dolphinfish. 25c, Kinkajou. 50c, Muttonfish. $1, Tayra. $2, Great barracudas. $5, Mountain lion.

1974, Jan. 1 Litho. *Perf. 13½*

327	A50	½c	shown	.25	*.70*
328	A50	1c	multicolored	.25	*.40*
329	A50	2c	multicolored	.25	*.40*
330	A50	3c	multicolored	.25	*.30*
331	A50	4c	multicolored	.25	*.40*
332	A50	5c	multicolored	.25	*.30*
333	A50	10c	multicolored	.25	*.30*
334	A50	15c	multicolored	.30	*.30*
335	A50	25c	multicolored	.50	*.50*
336	A50	50c	multicolored	.85	*.90*
337	A50	$1	multicolored	1.00	*1.75*
338	A50	$2	multicolored	1.75	*3.00*
339	A50	$5	multicolored	2.00	*5.50*
			Nos. 327-339 (13)	8.15	*14.75*

Stag, Mayan Pottery A51

Designs: Mayan pottery decorations.

1974, May 1 *Perf. 14½*

340	A51	3c	shown	.25	.25
341	A51	6c	Fire snake	.25	.25
342	A51	16c	Mouse	.25	.25
343	A51	26c	Eagle	.45	.25
344	A51	50c	Parrot	.80	.80
			Nos. 340-344 (5)	2.00	1.80

Parides Arcas A52

Butterflies of Belize: 1c, Thecla regalis. 2c, Colobura dirce. 3c, Catonephele numilia. 4c, Battus belus. 5c, Callicore patelina. 10c, Callicore astala. 15c, Nessaea aglaura. 16c, Prepona pseudojoiceyi. 25c, Papilio thoas. 26c, Hamadryas arethusa. 50c, Thecla bathildis. $1, Caligo uranus. $2, Heliconius sapho. $5, Eurytides philolaus. $10, Philaethria dido.

Wmk. 314 Sideways

1974-77 *Perf. 14*

345	A52	½c	shown	1.15	*5.75*
346	A52	1c	multicolored	1.15	*2.00*
347	A52	2c	multicolored	.60	*.80*
348	A52	3c	multicolored	1.45	.80
349	A52	4c	multicolored	3.50	.35
350	A52	5c	multicolored	3.75	.35
351	A52	10c	multicolored	1.75	.80

Perf. 14x15; 14 (26, 35c)

352	A52	15c	multicolored	1.40	.80
a.			Watermark upright ('75)	.90	2.00
353	A52	16c	multicolored	5.75	*10.00*
354	A52	25c	multicolored	7.50	.45
a.			Watermark upright ('77)	5.00	1.75
355	A52	26c	multicolored	2.25	*5.00*
356	A52	50c	multicolored	3.75	.75
a.			Watermark upright ('77)	5.00	1.75
357	A52	$1	multicolored	7.50	*8.00*
358	A52	$2	multicolored	4.50	1.45
359	A52	$5	multicolored	6.50	*7.00*
a.			Watermark upright ('75)	5.00	8.00
360	A52	$10	multicolored	11.50	4.50
			Nos. 345-360 (16)	64.00	48.80

Issue dates: No. 355A, July 25, 1977; No. 360, Jan. 2, 1975; others Sept. 2, 1974.

For surcharges & overprint see Nos. 380, 386, 395.

1975-78 Wmk. 373

345a	A52	½c	multicolored	2.00	*10.00*
347a	A52	2c	multi ('77)	.50	*.75*
348a	A52	3c	multi ('77)	1.25	.75
349a	A52	4c	multi ('77)	3.00	.35
350a	A52	5c	multi ('77)	3.25	.35
351a	A52	10c	multicolored	3.50	.35
352b	A52	15c	multi ('77)	.75	.70
354b	A52	25c	multi ('78)	6.50	.50
355A	A52	35c	Parides arcas ('77)	13.50	6.25
			Nos. 345a-355A (9)	34.25	20.00

For overprints and surcharges see Nos. 395-396, 424, 426-427.

Churchill and Coronation Coach of Queen Elizabeth II — A53

$1, Churchill & Williamsburg, VA Liberty Bell.

Wmk. 373

1974, Nov. 30 Litho. *Perf. 14*

363	A53	50c	multicolored	.25	.25
364	A53	$1	multicolored	.35	.35

Sir Winston Churchill (1874-1965).

Mayan Urn — A54

Designs: Various Mayan vessels.

1975, June 2 Wmk. 314 *Perf. 14*

365	A54	3c	lt green & multi	.25	.25
366	A54	6c	lt blue & multi	.25	.25
367	A54	16c	dull yel & multi	.30	.25
368	A54	26c	lilac & multi	.45	.25
369	A54	50c	lt brown & multi	.50	*1.75*
			Nos. 365-369 (5)	1.75	2.75

Musicians A55

Christmas: 26c, Nativity (Thatched hut and children). 50c, Drummers, vert. $1, Map of Belize, star, fleeing family, vert.

Perf. 14x14½, 14½x14

1975, Nov. 17 Litho. Wmk. 314

370	A55	6c	multicolored	.25	.25
371	A55	26c	multicolored	.30	.25
372	A55	50c	multicolored	.45	*.55*
373	A55	$1	multicolored	.75	*1.60*
			Nos. 370-373 (4)	1.75	*2.65*

William Wrigley, Jr., Sapodilla Tree — A56

Bicentennial Emblem and: 35c, Charles Lindbergh and "Spirit of St. Louis." $1, John Lloyd Stephens and Mayan temple.

1976, Mar. 29 Wmk. 373 *Perf. 14½*

374	A56	10c	multicolored	.25	.25
375	A56	35c	multicolored	.25	*.40*
376	A56	$1	multicolored	.55	*1.50*
			Nos. 374-376 (3)	1.05	*2.15*

American Bicentennial.

Bicycling A57

Wmk. 373

1976, July 17 Litho. *Perf. 14½*

377	A57	35c	shown	.50	.25
378	A57	45c	Running	.25	.25
379	A57	$1	Shooting	.50	*1.40*
			Nos. 377-379 (3)	1.25	1.90

21st Olympic Games, Montreal, Canada, July 17-Aug. 1.

No. 355 Surcharged

Wmk. 314

1976, Aug. 30 Litho. *Perf. 14*

380	A52	20c	on 26c multi	2.50	2.75

Map of West Indies, Bats, Wicket and Ball — A57a

Prudential Cup — A57b

Unwmk.

1976, Oct. 18 Litho. *Perf. 14*

381	A57a	35c	lt blue & multi	.50	*.60*
382	A57b	$1	lilac rose & blk	1.25	*1.75*

World Cricket Cup, won by West Indies Team, 1975.

Royal Visit, 1975 A58

Designs: 35c, Rose window and Queen's head. $2, Queen surrounded by bishops.

1977, Feb. 7 Litho. *Perf. 13½x14*

383	A58	10c	multicolored	.25	.25
384	A58	35c	multicolored	.25	.25
385	A58	$2	multicolored	.50	*.90*
			Nos. 383-385 (3)	1.00	1.40

25th anniv. of the reign of Elizabeth II.

No. 352 Surcharged

1977 Wmk. 314 *Perf. 14x15*

386	A52	5c	on 15c multi	3.00	3.00

Stamps from the first overprinting process have the "5c" close to the the right edge of the block (varies). Stamps from the second, and more common, overprinting process have about 7mm from the right edge to the "5c."

Red-capped Manakin — A59

Birds of Belize: 10c, Hooded oriole. 25c, Blue-crowned motmot. 35c, Slaty-breasted tinamou. 45c, Ocellated turkey. $1, White hawk.

Wmk. 373

1977, Sept. 3 Litho. *Perf. 14½*

387	A59	8c	shown	.90	.60
388	A59	10c	multicolored	1.10	.35
389	A59	25c	multicolored	1.50	.65
390	A59	35c	multicolored	1.90	.85
391	A59	45c	multicolored	2.10	1.50
392	A59	$1	multicolored	3.75	*6.00*
a.			Souvenir sheet of 6, #387-392	12.00	*14.00*
			Nos. 387-392 (6)	11.25	9.95

See Nos. 398-403, 416-421, 500-501. For overprints and surcharges see No. 502.

Medical Laboratory A60

Design: $1, Mobile medical unit and children receiving treatment.

1977, Dec. 2 *Perf. 13½*

393	A60	35c multicolored	.25	.25
394	A60	$1 multicolored	.70	.70
a.		Souvenir sheet of 2, #393-394	1.50	*1.60*

Pan American Health Org., 75th anniv.

Nos. 351 and 355A Overprinted in Gold: "BELIZE DEFENCE FORCE / 1ST JANUARY 1978"

Wmk. 314, 373

1978, Feb. 15 Litho. *Perf. 14*

395	A52	10c multicolored	1.00	1.00
396	A52	35c multicolored	2.50	2.50

Elizabeth II Coronation Anniversary Issue

Common Design Types

Souvenir Sheet

1978, Apr. 21 Unwmk. *Perf. 15*

397		Sheet of 6	1.40	*1.75*
a.		CD326 75c White lion of Mortimer	.25	.30
b.		CD327 75c Elizabeth II	.25	.30
c.		CD328 75c Jaguar (Maya god)	.25	.30

No. 397 contains 2 se-tenant strips of Nos. 397a-397c, separated by horizontal gutter with commemorative and descriptive inscriptions and showing central part of coronation procession with coach.

Bird Type of 1977

10c, White-crowned parrot. 25c, Crimson-collared tanager. 35c, Citreoline trogon. 45c, Sungrebe. 50c, Muscovy duck. $1, King vulture.

Wmk. 373

1978, July 31 Litho. *Perf. 14½*

398	A59	10c multicolored	.75	.40
399	A59	25c multicolored	1.10	.50
400	A59	35c multicolored	1.50	.75
401	A59	45c multicolored	1.75	1.75
402	A59	50c multicolored	1.90	*2.00*
403	A59	$1 multicolored	2.75	*6.00*
a.		Souvenir sheet of 6, #398-403	11.50	*12.00*
		Nos. 398-403 (6)	9.75	*11.40*

Russelia Sarmentosa A61

Wild Flowers and Ferns: 15c, Lygodium polymorphum. 35c, Heliconia aurantiaca. 45c, Adiantum tetraphyllum. 50c, Angelonia ciliaris. $1, Thelypteris obliterata.

1978, Oct. 16 Litho. *Perf. 14x13½*

404	A61	10c multicolored	.25	.25
405	A61	15c multicolored	.35	.35
406	A61	35c multicolored	.35	.35
407	A61	45c multicolored	.35	.35
408	A61	50c multicolored	.50	.50
409	A61	$1 multicolored	.80	*.95*
		Nos. 404-409 (6)	2.60	2.75

Christmas.

Internal Airmail Service, 1937 — A62

Mail Service: 10c, MV Heron, 1949. 35c, Dugout canoe on river, 1920. 45c, Stann Creek railroad, 1910. 50c, Mounted courier, 1882. $2, RMS Eagle, 1856, and "paid" cancel.

Perf. 13½x14

1979, Jan. 15 Litho. Wmk. 373

410	A62	5c multicolored	.45	.45
411	A62	10c multicolored	.45	.25
412	A62	35c multicolored	.45	.30
413	A62	45c multicolored	.80	.80
414	A62	50c multicolored	.80	.80
415	A62	$2 multicolored	1.50	*2.50*
		Nos. 410-415 (6)	4.45	5.10

Centenary of membership in UPU.

Bird Type of 1977

10c, Boat-billed heron. 25c, Gray-necked wood rail. 35c, Lineated woodpecker. 45c, Blue gray tanager. 50c, Laughing falcon. $1, Long-tailed hermit.

1979, Apr. 16 Unwmk. *Perf. 14½*

416	A59	10c multicolored	.75	.35
417	A59	25c multicolored	1.10	.35
418	A59	35c multicolored	1.25	.60
419	A59	45c multicolored	1.35	.75
420	A59	50c multicolored	1.40	1.25
421	A59	$1 multicolored	2.10	*4.00*
a.		Souvenir sheet of 6, #416-421	8.50	9.00
		Nos. 416-421 (6)	7.95	7.30

Nos. 477, 354b, 595, 355A, 599, 651 Surcharged

No. 422

No. 424

No. 428

1979-83 Litho. *Perf. 14*

422	A67	10c on 15c multi	*7.50*	*5.00*
423	A67	10c on 15c multi	*17.50*	—
424	A52	10c on 25c multi	3.00	2.25
424A	A67	10c on 35c multi	*70.00*	*70.00*
b.		Round obliterator	*300.00*	
425	A76	10c on 35c multi	*60.00*	
426	A52	15c on 35c multi	*100.00*	
427	A52	15c on 35c multi	4.00	2.25
428	A76	$1.25 on $2 multi	30.00	16.00
429	A81	$1.25 on $2 multi	*200.00*	*12.00*

No. 422 has a square the width of the "10c" obliterating the old value. No. 423 has a rectangle that is wider than the "10c."

No. 424A has a square obliterator.

No. 426 has "15c" at top of stamp, No. 427 has "15c" at right of rectangle. Type differs.

No. 429 has rectangular obliterator with new value at top of stamp.

Many errors exist from printer's waste.

Nos. 422 and 427, possibly others, exist fiscally used prior to the stated issue dates.

Issued: No. 426, 3/79; No. 427, 6/79; No. 424, 3/31/80; No. 422, 8/22/81; No. 423, 1/28/83; No. 425, 4/15/83; Nos. 428-429, 6/9/83.

Used Stamps

Postally used stamps are valued the same as unused. Canceled-to-order stamps are of minimal value. Most used stamps from No. 430-679 exist CTO. Most of these appeared on the market after the contract was canceled and were not authorized. The cancellations are printed and the paper differs from the issued stamps.

Imperforate Stamps

Many stamps from No. 430-692 exist imperforate in small quantities. Values up to three times those of perforated stamps.

Queen Elizabeth II, 25th Anniv. of Coronation — A63

Designs: 25c, No. 439, Paslow Bldg., #397c. 50c, Parliament, London, #397a. 75c, Coronation coach. $1, Queen on horseback, vert. $2, Prince of Wales, vert. $3, Queen and Prince Philip, vert. $4, Queen Elizabeth II, portrait, vert. No. 437, St. Edward's Crown, vert. No. 438a, $5, Princess Anne on horseback, Montreal Olympics, vert. No. 438b, $10, Queen, Montreal Olympics, vert.

Unwmk.

1979, May 31 Litho. *Perf. 14*

430	A63	25c multicolored	2.00
431	A63	50c multicolored	2.50
432	A63	75c multicolored	3.25
433	A63	$1 multicolored	4.25
434	A63	$2 multicolored	4.25
435	A63	$3 multicolored	4.25
436	A63	$4 multicolored	4.25
437	A63	$5 multicolored	4.50
		Nos. 430-437 (8)	29.25

Souvenir Sheets

438	A63	Sheet of 2, #a.-b.	19.00
439	A63	$15 multicolored	19.00

Powered Flight, 75th Anniv. — A64

4c, Safety, 1909. 25c, Boeing 707. 50c, Concorde. 75c, Handley Page W8b, 1922. $1, AVRO F, 1912. $1.50, Cody, 1910. $2, Triplane Roe II, 1909. $3, Santos-Dumont, 1906. $4, Wright Brothers Flyer, 1903.

$10, Belize Airways Jet.

1979, July 30

440	A64	4c multicolored	.70
441	A64	25c multicolored	2.10
442	A64	50c multicolored	6.00
443	A64	75c multicolored	2.75
444	A64	$1 multicolored	2.75
445	A64	$1.50 multicolored	3.75
446	A64	$2 multicolored	3.75
447	A64	$3 multicolored	3.25
448	A64	$4 multicolored	4.25
		Nos. 440-448 (9)	29.30

Souvenir Sheets

Perf. 14½

449		Sheet of 2	14.50
a.		A64 $5 Dunne D.5, 1910	7.25
b.		A64 $5 Great Britain #581	7.25
450	A64	$10 multi	14.50

Sir Rowland Hill, death cent., "75th anniv." of ICAO.

1980 Summer Olympics, Moscow — A65

1979, Oct. 10 *Perf. 14*

451	A65	25c Handball	.50
452	A65	50c Weight lifting	.80
453	A65	75c Track	1.10
454	A65	$1 Soccer	1.50
455	A65	$2 Sailing	2.10
456	A65	$3 Swimming	2.50
457	A65	$4 Boxing	3.00
458	A65	$5 Cycling	13.50
		Nos. 451-458 (8)	25.00

Souvenir Sheets

Perf. 14½

459		Sheet of 2	17.00
a.		A65 $5 Track, diff.	6.00
b.		A65 $10 Boxing, diff.	10.00
460	A65	$15 Cycling, diff.	17.00

1980 Winter Olympics, Lake Placid — A66

25c, Torch. 50c, Slalom skiing. 75c, Figure skating. $1, Downhill skiing. $2, Speed skating. $3, Cross country skiing. $4, Biathlon. $5, Olympic medals.

1979, Dec. 4 *Perf. 14*

461	A66	25c multi	.25
462	A66	50c multi	.60
463	A66	75c multi	.85
464	A66	$1 multi	1.05
465	A66	$2 multi	2.10
466	A66	$3 multi	3.25
467	A66	$4 multi	4.00
468	A66	$5 multi	4.75
		Nos. 461-468 (8)	16.85

Souvenir Sheets

Perf. 14½

469		Sheet of 2	13.50
a.		A66 $5 Torch bearers	4.00
b.		A66 $10 Medals, diff.	7.50
470	A66	$15 Torch, diff.	13.50

See Nos. 503-512.

Cypraea Zebra A67

2c, Macrocallista maculata. 3c, Arca zebra, vert. 4c, Chama macerophylla, vert. 5c, Latirus cariniferus. 10c, Conus spurius, vert. 15c, Murex cabritii, vert. 20c, Atrina rigida. 25c, Chlamys imbricata, vert. 35c, Conus granulatus. 45c, Tellina radiata, vert. 50c, Leucozonia nassa. 85c, Tripterotyphis triangularis. $1, Strombus gigas, vert. $2, Strombus gallus, vert. $5, Fasciolaria tulipa. $10, Arene cruentata.

1980, Jan. 7 Litho. *Perf. 14*

Inscribed "1980"

471	A67	1c shown	1.00
472	A67	2c multicolored	1.25
473	A67	3c multicolored	1.40
474	A67	4c multicolored	1.40
475	A67	5c multicolored	1.40
476	A67	10c multicolored	2.10
477	A67	15c multicolored	2.75
478	A67	20c multicolored	2.75
479	A67	25c multicolored	2.75
480	A67	35c multicolored	3.50
481	A67	45c multicolored	4.00
482	A67	50c multicolored	4.00
483	A67	85c multicolored	6.25

484 A67 $1 multicolored 6.75
485 A67 $2 multicolored 9.75
486 A67 $5 multicolored 13.50
487 A67 $10 multicolored 15.50
Nos. 471-487 (17) 80.05

1981 **Inscribed "1981"**

476a A67 10c 12.50
482a A67 50c 12.50
483a A67 85c 12.50
484a A67 $1 17.50
Nos. 476a-484a (4) 55.00

Souvenir Sheets

488 A67 Sheet of 2, 85c, $5 32.50 12.00
489 A67 Sheet of 2, $2, $10 45.00 22.50

Stamps in Nos. 488-489 have different color border and are of a slightly different size than the sheet stamps.

For overprints and surcharges see Nos. 422-423, 424A, 572-589, 592-593.

Intl. Year of the Child — A68

Various children. No. 498a, Three children. No. 498b, Madonna and Child by Durer. No. 499, Children before Christmas tree.

1980, Mar. 15 **Litho.** ***Perf. 14***

490 A68 25c multicolored .75
491 A68 50c multicolored 1.20
492 A68 75c multicolored 1.75
493 A68 $1 multicolored 1.75
494 A68 $1.50 multicolored 2.50
495 A68 $2 multicolored 3.00
496 A68 $3 multicolored 3.75
497 A68 $4 multicolored 4.25
Nos. 490-497 (8) 18.95

Souvenir Sheets

Perf. 13½

498 A68 $5 Sheet of 2, #a.-b. 12.50
499 A68 $10 multicolored 12.50

No. 498 contains two 35x54mm stamps. No. 499 contains one 73x110mm stamp.

Bird Type of 1977

Souvenir Sheets

1980, June 16 **Unwmk.** ***Perf. 13½***

500 Sheet of 6 55.00 55.00
a. A59 10c Jabiru 7.00 7.00
b. A59 25c Barred antshrike 7.50 7.50
c. A59 35c Royal flycatcher 8.25 8.25
d. A59 45c White-necked puffbird 8.25 8.25
e. A59 50c Ornate hawk-eagle 8.50 8.50
f. A59 $1 Golden-masked tanager 8.75 8.75
g. Sheet of 12 150.00 150.00
501 Sheet of 2 42.50 42.50
a. A59 $2 Jabiru 17.00 17.00
b. A59 $3 Golden-masked tanager 23.00 23.00

No. 500g contains 2 each Nos. 500a-500f with gutter between; inscribed "Protection of Environment" and "Wildlife Protection."

No. 500 Surcharged

1980, Oct. 3 **Litho.** ***Perf. 13½***

502 Sheet of 6 80.00 80.00
a. A59 10c multicolored 9.75 9.75
b. A59 25c multicolored 11.00 11.00
c. A59 35c multicolored 11.00 11.00
d. A59 40c on 45c multi 12.00 12.00
e. A59 40c on 50c multi 12.00 12.00
f. A59 40c on $1 multi 12.00 12.00

ESPAMER '80 Stamp Exhibition, Madrid, Spain, Oct. 3-12.

1980 Winter Olympics, Lake Placid — A69

Events and winning country: 25c, Men's speed skating, US. 50c, Ice hockey, US. 75c, No. 512, Men's figure skating, Great Britain. $1, Alpine skiing, Austria. $1.50, Women's giant slalom, Germany. $2, Women's speed skating, Netherlands. $3, Cross country skiing, Sweden. $5, Men's giant slalom, Sweden. Nos. 511a ($5), 511b ($10), Speed skating, US.

1980, Aug. 20 **Litho.** ***Perf. 14***

503 A69 25c multicolored .65
504 A69 50c multicolored 1.10
505 A69 75c multicolored 1.20
506 A69 $1 multicolored 1.60
507 A69 $1.50 multicolored 2.25
508 A69 $2 multicolored 2.60
509 A69 $3 multicolored 3.25
510 A69 $5 multicolored 5.25
Nos. 503-510 (8) 17.90

Souvenir Sheets

Perf. 14½

511 A69 Sheet of 2, #a.-b. 13.50
512 A69 $10 multicolored 13.50

Nos. 503-510 were each issued in sheets of 20 + 10 labels. The 2nd and 5th vertical rows consist of labels.

Intl. Year of the Child — A70

Nos. 513-521: Scenes from Sleeping Beauty. $8, Detail from Paumgartner Family Altarpiece by Albrecht Durer.

1980, Nov. 24 ***Perf. 14***

513 A70 35c multicolored 3.00
514 A70 40c multicolored 3.25
515 A70 50c multicolored 3.75
516 A70 75c multicolored 4.00
517 A70 $1 multicolored 4.00
518 A70 $1.50 multicolored 5.00
519 A70 $3 multicolored 6.00
520 A70 $4 multicolored 6.00
Nos. 513-520 (8) 35.00

Souvenir Sheets

Perf. 14½

521 Sheet of 2 21.00
a. A70 $5 Marriage 7.00
b. A70 $5 Couple on horseback 7.00
522 A70 $8 multicolored 17.00

Nos. 513-520 issued with se-tenent label.

Queen Mother Elizabeth, 80th Birthday — A71

1980, Dec. 12

523 A71 $1 multicolored 3.25

Souvenir Sheet

Perf. 14½

524 A71 $5 multicolored 18.50

No. 524 contains one 46x31mm stamp. No. 523 issued in sheet of 6.

Christmas — A72

25c, Annunciation. 50c, Bethlehem. 75c, Holy Family. $1, Nativity. $1.50, Flight into Egypt. $2, Shepherds. $3, With angel. $4, Adoration.

$5, Nativity. $10, Madonna & Child.

1980, Dec. 30 **Litho.** ***Perf. 14***

525 A72 25c multicolored .85
526 A72 50c multicolored 1.60
527 A72 75c multicolored 2.00
528 A72 $1 multicolored 2.10
529 A72 $1.50 multicolored 2.25
530 A72 $2 multicolored 2.60
531 A72 $3 multicolored 3.00
532 A72 $4 multicolored 3.00
Nos. 525-532 (8) 17.40

Souvenir Sheets

Perf. 14½

533 A72 $5 multicolored 8.00
534 A72 $10 multicolored 17.00

Nos. 525-532 each issued in sheets of 20 + 10 labels. The 2nd and 5th vertical rows consist of labels.

Nos. 529, 532, 534 Surcharged

1981, May 22

535 A72 $1 on $1.50 multi 19.00
536 A72 $2 on $4 multi 20.00

Souvenir Sheet

Perf. 14½

537 A72 $2 on $10 multi 37.50

Location of overprint and surcharge varies.

Intl. Rotary Club — A73

Designs: 25c, Paul P. Harris, founder. 50c, No. 546, Rotary, project emblem. $1, No. 545b, 75th anniv. emblem. $1.50 Diploma, horiz. $2, No. 545a, Project Hippocrates. $3, 75th anniv. project emblems, horiz. No. 544, Hands reach out, horiz.

1981, May 26 ***Perf. 14***

538 A73 25c multicolored 3.00
539 A73 50c multicolored 3.75
540 A73 $1 multicolored 4.50
541 A73 $1.50 multicolored 5.25
542 A73 $2 multicolored 6.00
543 A73 $3 multicolored 8.00
544 A73 $5 multicolored 9.50
Nos. 538-544 (7) 40.00

Souvenir Sheets

Perf. 14½

545 Sheet of 2 45.00
a. A73 $5 multicolored 15.00
b. A73 $10 multicolored 30.00
546 A73 $10 multicolored 30.00

Originally scheduled to be issued Mar. 30, the set was postponed and issued without a 75c stamp. Supposedly some of the 75c were sold to the public. Value $2,500.

For overprints and surcharges see Nos. 563-571, 590-591.

Royal Wedding of Prince Charles and Lady Diana — A74

1981, July 16 ***Perf. 13½x14***

Size: 22.5x38mm

548 A74 50c Coat of Arms .50
549 A74 $1 Prince Charles .90
550 A74 $1.50 Couple 1.25

Size: 25x43mm

With Thin Gold Border

Perf. 13½

551 A74 50c like No. 548 .50
552 A74 $1 like No. 549 .90
553 A74 $1.50 like No. 550 1.25
Nos. 548-553 (6) 5.30

Miniature Sheet

Perf. 14½

554 Sheet of 3, #554a-554c 2.75
a. A74 $3 like No. 550 .90
b. A74 $3 like No. 548 .90
c. A74 $3 like No. 549 .90

Nos. 551-553 issued in sheets of 6 + 3 labels. No. 554 contains three 35x50mm stamps.

For overprints see Nos. 659-665.

1984 Olympics A75

85c, Track. $1, Cycling. $1.50, Boxing. $2, Emblems. $3, Baron Coubertin. $5, Torch, emblems.

1981, Sept. 14 ***Perf. 14***

555 A75 85c multicolored 3.25
556 A75 $1 multicolored 11.00
557 A75 $1.50 multicolored 4.00
558 A75 $2 multicolored 5.25
559 A75 $3 multicolored 6.50
560 A75 $5 multicolored 7.50
Nos. 555-560 (6) 37.50

Souvenir Sheets

Perf. 13½

561 Sheet of 2 40.00
a. A75 $5 like No. 559 10.00
b. A75 $10 like No. 560 30.00

Perf. 14½

562 A75 $15 like No. 558 40.00

No. 561 contains two 35x54mm stamps. No. 562 contains one 46x68mm stamp.

Nos. 561-562 exist with gold background.

Nos. 538-546 Overprinted in Black or Gold

1981, Sept. 21 *Perf. 14*

563 A73 25c multicolored (G) 3.00
564 A73 50c multicolored 4.00
565 A73 $1 multicolored 5.00
566 A73 $1.50 multicolored 6.25
567 A73 $2 multicolored (G) 7.00
568 A73 $3 multicolored 8.25
569 A73 $5 multicolored 10.00
Nos. 563-569 (7) 43.50

Souvenir Sheets

Perf. 14½

570 A73 Sheet of 2, #a.-b. (G) 35.00
571 A73 $10 multicolored 30.00

Size of overprint varies.

Nos. 471-483, 485-489 Ovptd.

1981, Sept. 21

572 A67 1c multicolored 1.90
573 A67 2c multicolored 1.90
574 A67 3c multicolored 1.90
575 A67 4c multicolored 1.90
576 A67 5c multicolored 2.25
577 A67 10c multicolored 3.00
a. Inscribed "1980" *225.00*
578 A67 15c multicolored 4.25
579 A67 20c multicolored 4.25
580 A67 25c multicolored 4.75
581 A67 35c multicolored 4.75
582 A67 45c multicolored 5.50
583 A67 50c multicolored 5.50
584 A67 85c multicolored 8.50
585 A67 $2 multicolored 15.00
586 A67 $5 multicolored 18.50
587 A67 $10 multicolored 22.00
Nos. 572-587 (16) 105.85

Souvenir Sheets

588 A67 Sheet of 2, #488 45.00
589 A67 Sheet of 2, #489 52.50

Size and style of overprint varies, italic on horiz. stamps, upright on vert. stamps and upright capitals on souvenir sheets.
The 10c is dated 1981. Less than 16 sheets dated 1980 were also overprinted.

Nos. 541, 545 Surcharged

1981, Nov. 13 *Perf. 14*

590 A73 $1 on $1.50 multi 24.00

Souvenir Sheet

Perf. 14½

591 Sheet of 2 37.50
a. A73 $1 on $5 multicolored 18.50
b. A73 $1 on $10 multicolored 18.50

Espamer '81.

Nos. 488, 489 Surcharged in Red

1981, Nov. 14 *Perf. 14½*

Souvenir Sheets

592 Sheet of 2 72.50
a. A67 $1 on 85c 27.50
b. A67 $1 on $5 27.50
593 Sheet of 2 72.50
a. A67 $1 on $2 27.50
b. A67 $1 on $10 27.50

Independence — A76

10c, Flag. 35c, Map, vert. 50c, Black orchid, vert. 85c, Tapir. $1, Mahogany tree, vert. $2, Keel-billed toucan.

1981-82 *Perf. 14*

594 A76 10c multicolored 3.75
595 A76 35c multicolored 9.00
596 A76 50c multicolored 12.50
597 A76 85c multicolored 4.25
598 A76 $1 multicolored 3.50
599 A76 $2 multicolored 19.00
Nos. 594-599 (6) 52.00

Souvenir Sheet

Perf. 14½

600 A76 $5 like 10c 40.00

Issued: 50c-$2, 12/18; 10c, 35c, $5, 2/10/82.
For surcharges see Nos. 425, 428, 616.

1982 World Cup Soccer Championships, Spain — A77

10c, Uruguay '30, '50. 25c, Italy '34, '38. 50c, Germany '54, '74. $1, Brazil '58, '62, '70. $1.50, Argentina '78. $2, England '66.
No. 607, Emblem. No. 608, Player.

1981, Dec. 28 *Perf. 14*

601 A77 10c multicolored 2.75
602 A77 25c multicolored 4.00
603 A77 50c multicolored 5.00
604 A77 $1 multicolored 6.25
605 A77 $1.50 multicolored 8.00
606 A77 $2 multicolored 8.75
Nos. 601-606 (6) 34.75

Souvenir Sheets

Perf. 14½

607 A77 $2 multicolored 16.50
608 A77 $3 multicolored 21.00

No. 608 contains one 46x78mm stamp.
For surcharge see No. 617.

Sailing Ships — A78

10c, Man of war, 19th cent. 25c, Madagascar, 1837. 35c, Whitby, 1838. 50c, China, 1838. 85c, Swiftsure, 1850. $2, Windsor Castle, 1857.
$5, 19th cent. ships.

1982, Mar. 15 *Perf. 14*

609 A78 10c multicolored 3.50
610 A78 25c multicolored 5.00
611 A78 35c multicolored 6.00
612 A78 50c multicolored 7.00
613 A78 85c multicolored 8.50
614 A78 $2 multicolored 12.00
Nos. 609-614 (6) 42.00

Souvenir Sheet

Perf. 14½

615 A78 $5 multicolored 45.00

Nos. 599 and 606 Surcharged

1982, Apr. 28

616 A76 $1 on $2 multi 25.00
617 A77 $1 on $2 multi 25.00

Essen '82 Philatelic Exhibition.

Princess of Wales, 21st Birthday — A79

Various portraits.

1982, May 20 *Perf. 13½x14*

618 A79 50c multicolored 1.75
619 A79 $1 multicolored 2.25
620 A79 $1.50 multicolored 2.25
Nos. 618-620 (3) 6.25

Size: 25x42mm

Perf. 13½

621 A79 50c like No. 618 1.75
622 A79 $1 like No. 619 2.25
623 A79 $1.50 like No. 620 2.25
Nos. 621-623 (3) 6.25

Souvenir Sheet

Stamp Size: 31x47mm

Perf. 14½

624 A79 $3 Sheet of 3, #a.-c. like #618-620 10.00

Nos. 618-620 also exist with gold borders, size: 30x45mm. Value, set $16.

Overprinted in Silver

1982, Oct. 21 *Perf. 13½x14*

628 A79 50c multicolored .55
629 A79 $1 multicolored .70
630 A79 $1.50 multicolored .95

Size: 25x42mm

Perf. 13½

631 A79 50c multicolored .55
632 A79 $1 multicolored .70
633 A79 $1.50 multicolored .95
Nos. 628-633 (6) 4.40

Souvenir Sheet

Perf. 14½

634 A79 $3 Sheet of 3, #a.-c. 12.50

Size of overprint varies. The overprint exists on the gold bordered stamps. Value, set $25.
No. 634 exists with a gold overprint. Value $11.

Boy Scouts — A80

10c, Building camp fire. 25c, Bird watching. 35c, Playing guitar. 50c, Hiking. 85c, Flag, scouts. $2, Salute.
No. 644, Scout holding flag, vert. No. 645, Lord Baden Powell, vert.

1982, Aug. 31 *Perf. 14*

638 A80 10c multicolored 1.90
639 A80 25c multicolored 5.50
640 A80 35c multicolored 3.00
641 A80 50c multicolored 3.50
642 A80 85c multicolored 5.00
643 A80 $2 multicolored 5.50
Nos. 638-643 (6) 24.40

Souvenir Sheets

Perf. 14½

644 A80 $2 multicolored 24.00
645 A80 $3 multicolored 24.00

Scouting, 75th anniv. and Lord Baden Powell, 125th birth anniv.
For overprints see Nos. 653-658.

Marine Life — A81

10c, Gorgonia ventalina. 35c, Carpilius corallinus. 50c, Plexaura flexuosa. 85c, Condylactis gigantea. $1, Stenopus hispidus. $2, Abudefduf saxatilis.
$5, Scyllarides aequinoctialis.

1982, Sept. 20 *Perf. 14*

646 A81 10c multicolored 3.50
647 A81 35c multicolored 5.50
648 A81 50c multicolored 6.00
649 A81 85c multicolored 6.25
650 A81 $1 multicolored 8.50
651 A81 $2 multicolored 10.50
Nos. 646-651 (6) 40.25

Souvenir Sheet

Perf. 14½

652 A81 $5 multicolored 55.00

For surcharge see No. 429.

Nos. 638-643 Overprinted in Gold

1982, Oct. 1 *Perf. 14*

653 A80 10c Building camp fire 3.50
654 A80 25c Bird watching 8.50
655 A80 35c Playing guitar 4.50
656 A80 50c Hiking 5.00
657 A80 85c Flag, scouts 12.50
658 A80 $2 Salute 13.50
Nos. 653-658 (6) 47.50

Overprint is different on Nos. 654-655.
Sheets include labels with native Christmas themes.

Nos. 548-554 Overprinted in Gold Similar to Nos. 628-634

1982, Oct. 25 *Perf. 13½x14*

659 A74 50c Coat of Arms 3.50
660 A74 $1 Prince Charles 6.50
661 A74 $1.50 Couple 9.25
Nos. 659-661 (3) 19.25

Size: 25x43mm

Perf. 13½

662	A74	50c like No. 659	.65	
663	A74	$1 like No. 660	.90	
664	A74	$1.50 like No. 661	1.40	
		Nos. 662-664 (3)	2.95	

Miniature Sheet

Perf. 14½

665	Sheet of 3, #665a-665c	9.50	
a.	A74 $3 like No. 661	3.00	
b.	A74 $3 like No. 659	3.00	
c.	A74 $3 like No. 660	3.00	

Nos. 662-664 issued in sheets of 6 plus 3 labels. No. 665 contains three 35x50mm stamps. Size and style of overprint varies.

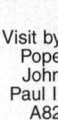

Visit by Pope John Paul II A82

50c, Belize Cathedral.
$2.50, Pope John Paul II.

1983, Mar. 7 ***Perf. 13½***

666 A82 50c multicolored 4.50

Souvenir Sheet

Perf. 14½

667 A82 $2.50 multicolored 32.50

No. 667 contains one 30x47mm stamp. No. 666 issued in sheet of 6.

Commonwealth Day — A83

35c, Map, vert. 50c, Maya Stella. 85c, Supreme Court Building. $2, University Center.

1983, Mar. 14 ***Perf. 13½***

668	A83	35c multicolored	.60	
669	A83	50c multicolored	.65	
670	A83	85c multicolored	.85	
671	A83	$2 multicolored	1.50	
		Nos. 668-671 (4)	3.60	

Issued in miniature sheets of 4. Other formats are suspect.

First Manned Flight, Bicent. — A84

10c, Flying boat, 1670. 25c, Flying machine, 1709. 50c, Airship Guyton de Morveau. 85c, Dirigible. $1, Clement Bayard. $1.50, Great Britain R-34.

No. 678, Nassau Balloon. No. 679, Montgolfier Brothers balloon, vert.

1983, May 16 ***Perf. 14***

672	A84	10c multicolored	3.50	
673	A84	25c multicolored	4.50	
674	A84	50c multicolored	4.75	
675	A84	85c multicolored	5.75	
676	A84	$1 multicolored	6.50	
677	A84	$1.50 multicolored	7.25	
		Nos. 672-677 (6)	32.25	

Souvenir Sheets

Perf. 14½

678	A84	$3 multicolored	20.00	
679	A84	$3 multicolored	20.00	

"Errors"

Many "errors," including imperforates, exist of Nos. 680-898. These unauthorized varieties were printed without the knowledge of the Belize postal service. There may be large quantities of them.

Mayan Monuments — A85

1983, Nov. 14 Litho. ***Perf. 13½x14***

680	A85	10c Altun Ha	.25	.25
681	A85	15c Xunantunich	.25	.25
682	A85	75c Cerros	.55	.55
683	A85	$2 Lamanai	1.25	*1.75*
		Nos. 680-683 (4)	2.30	2.80

Souvenir Sheet

684 A85 $3 Xunantunich, diff. 2.40 2.40

World Communications Year — A86

10c, Belmopan Earth Station. 15c, Telstar 2. 75c, UPU monument. $2, Mail boat.

1983, Nov. 28 ***Perf. 14***

685	A86	10c multicolored	.45	.25
686	A86	15c multicolored	.65	.25
687	A86	75c multicolored	.90	*1.10*
688	A86	$2 multicolored	2.00	*4.50*
		Nos. 685-688 (4)	4.00	*6.10*

Jaguar, World Wildlife Fund Emblem A87

1983, Dec. 9

689	A87	5c Sitting	.55	*.80*
690	A87	10c Standing	.65	.50
691	A87	85c Swimming	2.50	*3.00*
692	A87	$1 Walking	2.60	*3.25*
		Nos. 689-692 (4)	6.30	7.55

Souvenir Sheet

693 A87 $3 Sitting in tree 3.50 3.50

No. 693 contains one stamp 45x28mm.

Christmas — A88

Scenes from mass celebrated by Pope John Paul II during visit, Mar.

1983, Dec. 22

694	A88	10c multicolored	.50	.25
695	A88	15c multicolored	.50	.25
696	A88	75c multicolored	1.00	1.00
697	A88	$2 multicolored	1.50	2.00
		Nos. 694-697 (4)	3.50	3.50

Souvenir Sheet

698 A88 $3 multicolored 3.75 3.75

Foureye Butterflyfish — A89

2c, Cushion star. 3c, Flower coral. 4c, Fairy basslets. 5c, Spanish hogfish. 6c, Star-eyed hermit crab. 10c, Sea fans, fire sponge. 15c, Blueheads. 25c, Blue-striped grunt. 50c, Coral crab. 60c, Tube sponge. 75c, Brain coral. $1, Yellow-tail snapper. $2, Common lettuce slug. $5, Yellow damselfish. $10, Rock beauty.

1984, Feb. 27 ***Perf. 15***

699	A89	1c shown	.60	1.50
700	A89	2c multicolored	.70	1.50
701	A89	3c multicolored	.70	1.50
702	A89	4c multicolored	.85	1.50
703	A89	5c multicolored	.95	1.50
704	A89	6c multicolored	.95	1.75
705	A89	10c multicolored	.95	.35
706	A89	15c multicolored	1.35	.60
707	A89	25c multicolored	1.35	.80
708	A89	50c multicolored	1.35	1.75
709	A89	60c multicolored	1.35	2.00
710	A89	75c multicolored	1.35	1.50
711	A89	$1 multicolored	1.35	1.25
712	A89	$2 multicolored	1.35	.60
713	A89	$5 multicolored	1.75	.75
714	A89	$10 multicolored	2.00	1.15
		Nos. 699-714 (16)	18.90	20.00

Nos. 699-714 exist imperforate, issued at a later date by a liquidator. Value $10 each.

Other denominations, not issued contemporaneously, exist perforated 13½. A 2c stamp perforated 13½ may have been issued in 1988. The editors would like to examine any in period use.

Nos. 709 and 711 exist overprinted "HURRICANE HATTIE". Value $20.

For overprints and surcharge see Nos. 715-716, 762A-762C, 922.

The 50c, 60c, 75c, $1 exist inscribed "1986" in selvage.

1988, July ***Perf. 13½***

705a	A89	10c	.75	.75
706a	A89	15c	1.00	1.00
707a	A89	25c	1.40	1.40
708a	A89	50c	2.10	2.10
709a	A89	60c	2.10	2.10
711a	A89	$1	2.75	2.75
		Nos. 705a-711a (6)	10.10	10.10

Nos. 705, 708 Overprinted: "VISIT OF THE LORD / ARCHBISHOP OF CANTERBURY / 8th-11th MARCH 1984"

1984, Mar. 8

715	A89	10c multicolored	1.40	.70
716	A89	50c multicolored	2.40	*2.75*

1984 Summer Olympics — A90

1984, Apr. 30 ***Perf. 13½x14***

717	A90	25c Shooting	.35	.25
718	A90	75c Boxing	.60	*.75*
719	A90	$1 Running	.70	*1.00*
720	A90	$2 Bicycling	3.00	2.75
		Nos. 717-720 (4)	4.65	4.75

Souvenir Sheet

721 A90 $3 Discus 3.00 3.00

1984 Summer Olympics — A91

1984, Apr. 30 Litho. ***Perf. 14½***

Booklet Stamps

722	A91	5c Running	.50	*.90*
a.		Booklet pane of 4	2.25	
723	A91	20c Javelin	.60	*.90*
a.		Booklet pane of 4	2.75	
724	A91	25c Shot put	.60	*.90*
a.		Booklet pane of 4	2.75	
725	A91	$2 Torch	.80	*1.25*
a.		Booklet pane of 4	4.00	
		Complete booklet, #722a-725a	12.00	
		Nos. 722-725 (4)	2.50	3.95

Ausipex '84 — A92

15c, Br. Honduras #3. 30c, Bath-Bristol mail coach, 1784. 65c, Penny Black, Rowland Hill. 75c, Railroad Pier, Commerce Bight. $2, Royal Exhibition Buildings.

$3, Australia #132, Br. Hond. #3.

1984, Sept. 26 Litho. ***Perf. 15***

726	A92	15c multicolored	.30	.25
727	A92	30c multicolored	.45	.30
728	A92	65c multicolored	.80	.80
729	A92	75c multicolored	.90	*.95*

Perf. 14

730	A92	$2 multicolored	1.25	*2.00*
		Nos. 726-730 (5)	3.70	4.30

Souvenir Sheet

731 A92 $3 multicolored 1.50 1.50

House of Tudor, 500th Anniv. — A93

1984, Oct. 15 ***Perf. 14***

732	A93	50c Queen Victoria	.35	.35
733	A93	50c Prince Albert	.35	.35
a.		Sheet of 4, 2 each, #732-733	1.50	
734	A93	75c King George VI	.40	.55
735	A93	75c Queen Elizabeth	.40	.55
a.		Sheet of 4, 2 each, #734-735	1.75	
736	A93	$1 Prince Charles	.65	.75
737	A93	$1 Princess Diana	.65	.75
a.		Sheet of 4, 2 each, #736-737	2.75	
		Nos. 732-737 (6)	2.80	3.30

Souvenir Sheet

738		Sheet of 2	2.00	2.00
a.		A93 $1.50 Prince Philip	1.00	1.00
b.		A93 $1.50 Queen Elizabeth II	1.00	1.00

Parrots — A94

a, White-fronted Parrot. b, White-capped, horiz. c, Red-lored. d, Mealy, horiz.

$3, Scarlet macaw.

1984, Nov. 1 ***Perf. 11***

739	A94	Block of 4	11.00	11.00
a.-d.		$1 any single	2.50	2.50

Miniature Sheet

Perf. 14

740 A94 $3 multicolored 5.50 5.50

No. 740 contains one 48x32mm stamp.

Mayan Artifacts — A95

25c, Incense holder, 1450. 75c, Cylindrical vase, 675. $1, Tripod vase, 500. $2, Kinich Ahau (sun god).

1984, Nov. 30 ***Perf. 15***

741	A95	25c multicolored	.40	.40
742	A95	75c multicolored	.80	.80
743	A95	$1 multicolored	.85	.85
744	A95	$2 multicolored	1.25	1.25
		Nos. 741-744 (4)	3.30	3.30

Girl Guides 75th Anniv., Intl. Youth Year A96

25c, Gov.-Gen. Gordon. 50c, Camping. 90c, Map reading. $1.25, Students in laboratory. $2, Lady Baden-Powell.

1985, Mar. 15 Litho. *Perf. 15*

745	A96	25c	multicolored	.40	.40
746	A96	50c	multicolored	.60	.60
747	A96	90c	multicolored	.80	.80
748	A96	$1.25	multicolored	.95	.95
749	A96	$2	multicolored	1.20	1.20
			Nos. 745-749 (5)	3.95	3.95

Each stamp shows the scouting and IYY emblems.

For overprints see Nos. 777-781.

Audubon Birth Bicentenary — A97

Illustrations by Audubon: 10c, White-tailed kite. 15c, Cuvier's kinglet. 25c, Painted bunting. 75c, Belted kingfisher. $1, Northern cardinal. $3, Long-billed curlew.

$5, Portrait of Audubon, 1826, by John Syme.

10c, 25c, 75c, $1, $5 vert.

Perf. 14, 15 ($1)

1985, May 30 Litho.

750	A97	10c	multicolored	1.00	1.00
751	A97	15c	multicolored	1.00	1.00
752	A97	25c	multicolored	1.20	1.20
753	A97	75c	multicolored	1.20	1.40
754	A97	$1	multicolored	1.20	1.40
755	A97	$3	multicolored	2.00	2.25
			Nos. 750-755 (6)	7.60	8.25

Souvenir Sheet

Perf. 13½x14

756	A97	$5	multicolored	5.75	5.75

No. 756 contains one 38x51mm stamp. See No. 909A.

Queen Mother, 85th Birthday — A98

Designs: 10c, The Queen Consort and Princess Elizabeth, 1928. 15c, Queen Mother, Elizabeth. 75c, Queen Mother waving a greeting. No. 760, Royal family photograph, christening of Prince Henry. $2, Holding the infant Prince Henry. No. 762, Queen Mother, diff.

1985, June 20

757	A98	10c	shown	.25	.25
758	A98	15c	multicolored	.25	.25
759	A98	75c	multicolored	.70	.70
760	A98	$5	multicolored	2.75	2.75
			Nos. 757-760 (4)	3.95	3.95

Souvenir Sheets

761	A98	$2	multicolored	2.25	2.25
762	A98	$5	multicolored	4.00	4.00

Nos. 761-762 contain one 38x51mm stamp.

For overprints see Nos. 771-776.

Nos. 705-706, 708 Ovptd.

1985, June 24 *Perf. 15*

762A	A89	10c	multicolored	2.00	1.00
762B	A89	15c	multicolored	2.00	1.00
762C	A89	50c	multicolored	3.25	*4.50*
			Nos. 762A-762C (3)	7.25	6.50

Miniature Sheet

Commonwealth Stamp Omnibus, 50th Anniv. — A99

British Honduras Nos. 111-112, 127, 129, 143, 194, 307 and Belize Nos. 326, 385 and 397b on: a, George V and Queen Mary in an open carriage. b, George VI and Queen Consort Elizabeth crowned. c, Civilians celebrating the end of WWII. d, George VI and Queen Consort at mass service. e, Elizabeth II wearing robes of state and the imperial crown. f, Winston Churchill, WWII fighter planes. g, Bridal photograph of Elizabeth II and Prince Philip. h, Bridal photograph of Princess Anne and Capt. Mark Phillips. i, Elizabeth II. j, Imperial crown.

$5, Elizabeth II coronation photograph.

1985, July 25 *Perf. 14½x14*

763	A99		Sheet of 10	6.75	6.75
a.-j.			50c any single	.55	.55

Souvenir Sheet

Perf. 14

764	A99	$5	multicolored	5.00	5.00

No. 764 contains one 38x51mm stamp.

For overprints see Nos. 796-797.

British Post Office, 350th Anniv. A100

10c, Postboy, letters. 15c, Packet, privateer. 25c, Duke of Marlborough. 75c, Diana. $1, Falmouth P.O. packet. $3, S. S. Conway.

1985, Aug. 1 *Perf. 15*

765	A100	10c	multicolored	.45	.45
766	A100	15c	multicolored	.55	.55
767	A100	25c	multicolored	.70	.70
768	A100	75c	multicolored	1.20	1.20
769	A100	$1	multicolored	1.20	1.20
770	A100	$3	multicolored	2.25	2.25
			Nos. 765-770 (6)	6.35	6.35

Nos. 757-762 Overprinted

1985, Sept. 5 Litho. *Perf. 15*

771	A98	10c	multicolored	.50	.40
772	A98	15c	multicolored	.60	.45
773	A98	75c	multicolored	1.25	1.00
774	A98	$5	multicolored	3.25	*3.75*
			Nos. 771-774 (4)	5.60	5.60

Souvenir Sheets

775	A98	$2	multicolored	1.50	1.50
776	A98	$5	multicolored	4.25	4.25

Nos. 745-749 Ovptd.

1985, Sept. 25 *Perf. 15*

777	A96	25c	multicolored	.75	.35
778	A96	50c	multicolored	1.25	.75
779	A96	90c	multicolored	1.75	*1.90*
780	A96	$1.25	multicolored	2.25	*2.50*
781	A96	$2	multicolored	3.00	*3.50*
			Nos. 777-781 (5)	9.00	9.00

Royal Visit — A101

25c, Royal and natl. flags. 75c, Elizabeth II. $4, Britannia.

$5, Elizabeth II, diff.

1985, Oct. 9 *Perf. 15x14½*

782	A101	25c	multicolored	1.10	1.10
783	A101	75c	multicolored	1.40	1.40

Size: 81x38mm

784	A101	$4	multicolored	5.00	5.00
a.			Strip of 3, #782-784	7.75	7.75
			Nos. 782-784 (3)	7.50	7.50

Souvenir Sheet

Perf. 13½x14

785	A101	$5	multicolored	5.25	5.25

No. 785 contains one 38x51mm stamp.

Disneyland, 30th Anniv. A102

Characters from "It's a Small World" — 1c, Royal Canadian Mounted Police. 2c, American Indian. 3c, Inca of the Andes. 4c, Africa. 5c, Far East. 6c, Belize. 50c, Balkans. $1.50, Saudi Arabia. $3, Japan.

$4, Montage.

1985, Nov. 1 *Perf. 11*

786	A102	1c	multicolored	.25	.25
787	A102	2c	multicolored	.25	.25
788	A102	3c	multicolored	.25	.25
789	A102	4c	multicolored	.25	.25
790	A102	5c	multicolored	.25	.25
791	A102	6c	multicolored	.25	.25
792	A102	50c	multicolored	2.00	2.00
793	A102	$1.50	multicolored	3.25	3.25
794	A102	$3	multicolored	4.25	4.25
			Nos. 786-794 (9)	11.00	11.00

Souvenir Sheet

Perf. 14

795	A102	$4	multicolored	8.00	8.00

Christmas.

Nos. 763-764 Overprinted

1985, Dec. 20 *Perf. 14½x14*

796			Sheet of 10	8.75	8.75
a.-j.	A99		50c, any single	.85	.85

Souvenir Sheet

797	A99	$5	multicolored	5.75	5.75

Women in Folk Costumes — A103

1986, Jan. 15 *Perf. 15*

798	A103	5c	India	.90	.35
799	A103	10c	Maya	1.00	.35
800	A103	15c	Garifuna	1.20	.45
801	A103	25c	Creole	1.50	.45
802	A103	50c	China	2.10	1.50
803	A103	75c	Lebanon	2.40	2.40
804	A103	$1	Europe	2.40	*3.00*
805	A103	$2	South America	3.25	*4.50*
			Nos. 798-805 (8)	14.75	13.00

Souvenir Sheet

Perf. 14

806	A103	$5	Maya, So. America	9.25	9.25

No. 806 contains one 38x51mm stamp.

Miniature Sheet

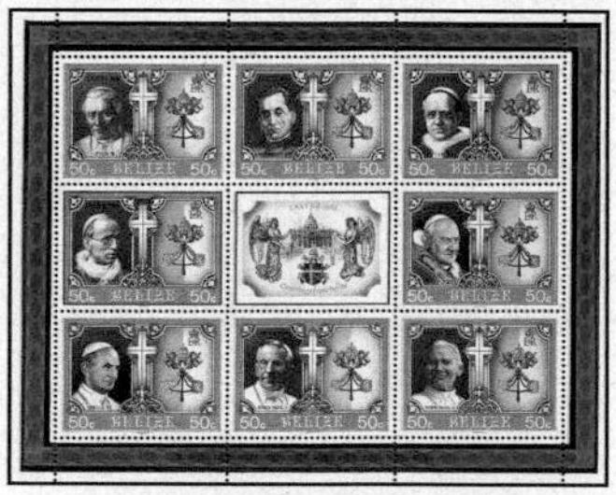

A104

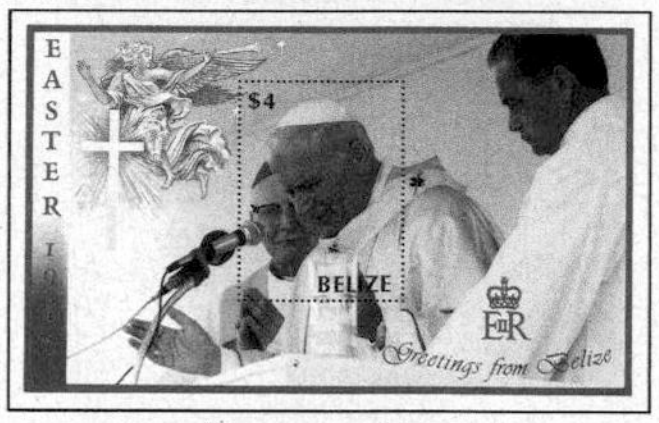

Easter — A105

Papal arms, crucifix and: a, Pius X. b, Benedict XV. c, Pius XI. d, Pius XII. e, John XXIII. f, Paul VI. g, John Paul I. h, John Paul II. No. 573, John Paul II saying mass in Belize.

1986, Apr. 15 Litho. *Perf. 11*

807	A104		Sheet of 8 + label	11.50	11.50
a.-h.			50c, any single	1.25	1.25

Souvenir Sheet

Perf. 14

808	A105	$4	multi	13.00	13.00

No. 807 contains center label picturing the Vatican, and papal crest.

Queen Elizabeth II, 60th Birthday — A106

A107

1986, Apr. 21 *Perf. 14*

809 Strip of 3 1.25 1.25
a. A106 25c Age 2 .25 .25
b. A106 50c Coronation .40 .40
c. A106 75c Riding horse .60 .60
810 A106 $3 Wearing crown jewels 2.40 2.40

Souvenir Sheet

811 A107 $4 Portrait 3.75 3.75

A108

Halley's Comet — A109

1986, Apr. 30

812 Strip of 3 1.90 *3.00*
a. A108 10c Planet-A probe .40 *.80*
b. A108 15c Sighting, 1910 .50 *.95*
c. A108 50c Giotto probe 1.00 1.25
813 Strip of 3 4.60 *5.25*
a. A108 75c Weather bureau 1.00 *1.10*
b. A108 $1 US space telescope, shuttle 1.10 *1.40*
c. A108 $2 Edmond Halley 2.50 *2.75*

Souvenir Sheet

814 A109 $4 Computer graphics 8.50 8.50

Miniature Sheet

A110

US Presidents — A111

1986, May *Perf. 11*

815 A110 Sheet of 6 + 3 labels 4.50 4.50
a. 10c George Washington .25 .25
b. 20c John Adams .25 .25
c. 30c Thomas Jefferson .30 .30
d. 50c James Madison .45 .45
e. $1.50 James Monroe 1.20 1.20
f. $2 John Quincy Adams 1.60 1.60

Souvenir Sheet

Perf. 14

816 A111 $4 Washington 5.25 5.25

No. 815 contains 3 center labels picturing the great seal of the US.

Issue dates: No. 815, May 5; No. 816, May 7.

A112

Statue of Liberty, Cent. — A113

Designs: 25c, Bartholdi, statue. 50c, Statue, US centennial celebration, Philadelphia, 1876. 75c, Statue close-up, flags, 1886 unveiling. $3, Flags, statue close-up. $4, Statue, New York City skyline.

1986, May 15 *Perf. 14*

817 Strip of 3 3.75 3.75
a. A112 25c multicolored .35 .35
b. A112 75c multicolored .80 .80
c. A112 $3 multicolored 2.60 2.60
818 A112 50c multicolored .50 .50

Souvenir Sheet

819 A113 $4 multicolored 5.00 5.00

A114

AMERIPEX '86, Chicago, May 22-June 1 — A115

1986, May 22

820 Strip of 3 2.50 2.50
a. A114 10c British Honduras No. 3 .60 .60
b. A114 15c Stamp of 1981 .75 .75
c. A114 50c US No. C3a 1.20 1.20
821 Strip of 3 3.75 *4.25*
a. A114 75c USS Constitution 1.15 *1.25*
b. A114 $1 Liberty Bell 1.25 *1.40*
c. A114 $2 White House 1.35 *1.60*

Souvenir Sheet

822 A115 $4 Capitol Building 5.00 5.00

For overprints see Nos. 835-837.

1986 World Cup Soccer Championships, Mexico — A116

Designs: 25c, England vs. Brazil. 50c, Mexican player, Mayan statues. 75c, Belize players. $3, Aztec calendar stone, Mexico. $4, Flags composing soccer balls.

1986, June 16 **Litho.** *Perf. 11*

823 A116 25c multicolored 1.75 1.75
824 A116 50c multicolored 2.00 2.00
825 A116 75c multicolored 2.25 2.25
826 A116 $3 multicolored 2.50 2.50
Nos. 823-826 (4) 8.50 8.50

Souvenir Sheet

Perf. 14

827 A116 $4 multicolored 7.50 7.50

Nos. 823-826 printed in sheets of 8 plus label picturing Azteca Stadium, 2 each value per sheet.

Nos. 823-827 Overprinted

1986, Aug. 15

828 A116 25c multicolored 1.75 1.75
829 A116 50c multicolored 2.00 2.00
830 A116 75c multicolored 2.50 2.50
831 A116 $3 multicolored 3.50 3.50
Nos. 828-831 (4) 9.75 9.75

Souvenir Sheet

832 A116 $4 multicolored 9.75 9.75

A117

Wedding of Prince Andrew and Sarah Ferguson A118

1986, July 23 *Perf. 14x14½*

833 Strip of 3 3.50 3.50
a. A117 25c Sarah .75 .50
b. A117 75c Andrew 1.00 1.00
c. A117 $3 Couple 1.75 2.00

Souvenir Sheet

Perf. 14½

834 Sheet of 2 4.75 4.75
a. A118 $1 Sarah, diff. 1.25 1.25
b. A118 $3 Andrew, diff. 3.50 3.50

Size of No. 833c: 92x41mm.

Nos. 820-822 Overprinted

1986, Aug. 28 **Litho.** *Perf. 14*

835 Strip of 3 2.50 2.50
a. A114 10c multicolored .65 .65
b. A114 15c multicolored .85 .85
c. A114 50c multicolored 1.00 1.00
836 Strip of 3 5.00 5.00
a. A114 75c multicolored 1.25 1.25
b. A114 $1 multicolored 1.75 1.75
c. A114 $2 multicolored 2.00 2.00

Souvenir Sheet

837 A115 $4 multicolored 6.75 6.75

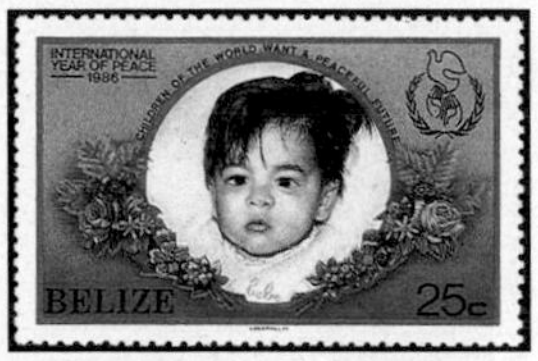

A119

Intl. Peace Year — A120

Children.

1986, Oct. 3 **Litho.** *Perf. 14*

838 A119 25c Infant .80 .80
839 A119 50c Caucasians 1.00 1.00
840 A119 75c Oriental 1.20 1.20
841 A119 $3 Indian, caucasian 2.25 2.25
Nos. 838-841 (4) 5.25 5.25

Souvenir Sheet

842 A120 $4 shown 6.25 6.25

Nos. 838-841 printed se-tenant in sheets of 8 (2 each) plus center label.

Fungi — A121

Toucans — A122

5c, Amanita lilloi. 10c, Keel-billed toucan. 20c, Boletellus cubensis. 25c, Collared aracari. 75c, Psilocybe caerulescens. $1, Emerald toucanet. $1.25, Crimson-rumped toucan. $2, Russula puiggarii.

1986, Oct. 30 *Perf. 14*

843 A121 5c multicolored 1.50 1.50
844 A122 10c multicolored 1.50 1.50
845 A121 20c multicolored 1.75 1.75
846 A122 25c multicolored 1.75 1.75
847 A121 75c multicolored 2.25 2.25
848 A122 $1 multicolored 2.25 2.25
849 A122 $1.25 multicolored 2.50 2.50
850 A121 $2 multicolored 2.50 2.50
Nos. 843-850 (8) 16.00 16.00

Stamps of the same design printed in sheets of 8 plus center label picturing Audubon Society emblem. Value $18 each.

Christmas
A123

Disney characters.

1986, Nov. 14 *Perf. 11*

851 Sheet of 9 12.00 12.00
a. A123 2c Jose Carioca .25 .25
b. A123 3c Carioca, Panchito, Donald .25 .25
c. A123 4c Daisy .25 .25
d. A123 5c Mickey, Minnie .25 .25
e. A123 6c Carioca playing music .25 .25
f. A123 50c Panchito, Donald 1.50 1.50
g. A123 65c Donald, Carioca 1.75 1.75
h. A123 $1.35 Donald 2.75 2.75
i. A123 $2 Goofy 4.00 4.00

Souvenir Sheet

Perf. 14

852 A123 $4 Donald 11.00 11.00

Marriage of Queen Elizabeth II and the Duke of Edinburgh, 40th Anniv. — A124

A125

1987, Oct. 7 **Litho.** *Perf. 15*

853 A124 25c Elizabeth, 1947 .30 .30
854 A124 75c Couple, c. 1980 .55 .55
855 A124 $1 Elizabeth, 1986 .60 .60
856 A124 $4 Wearing robes of Order of the Garter 1.20 1.20
Nos. 853-856 (4) 2.65 2.65

Souvenir Sheet

Perf. 14

857 A125 $6 shown 6.50 6.50

A126

America's Cup 1986-87 — A127

Yachts that competed in the 1987 finals.

1987, Oct. 21 *Perf. 15*

858 A126 25c America II .50 .50
859 A126 75c Stars and Stripes .60 .60
860 A126 $1 Australia II .80 .80
861 A126 $4 White Crusader 1.60 1.60
Nos. 858-861 (4) 3.50 3.50

Souvenir Sheet

Perf. 14

862 A127 $6 Australia II sails 7.00 7.00

Woodcarvings by Sir George Gabb (b. 1928) — A128

A129

25c, Mother and Child. 75c, Standing Form. $1, Love-Doves. $4, Depiction of Music. $6, African Heritage.

1987, Nov. 4 *Perf. 15*

863 A128 25c multicolored .25 .25
864 A128 75c multicolored .55 .55
865 A128 $1 multicolored .60 .60
866 A128 $4 multicolored 1.60 1.60
Nos. 863-866 (4) 3.00 3.00

Souvenir Sheet

Perf. 14

867 A129 $6 multicolored 5.75 5.75

A130

Indigenous Primates — A131

25c, Black spider monkey. 75c, Male black howler. $1, Spider monkeys. $4, Howler monkeys.
$6, Black spider, diff.

1987, Nov. 11 *Perf. 15*

868 A130 25c multicolored .40 .40
869 A130 75c multicolored .70 .70
870 A130 $1 multicolored .75 .75
871 A130 $4 multicolored 1.90 1.90
Nos. 868-871 (4) 3.75 3.75

Souvenir Sheet

Perf. 14

872 A131 $6 multicolored 7.25 7.25

Natl. Girl Guides Movement, 50th Anniv. — A132

Lady Olave Baden-Powell, Founder — A133

25c, Flag-bearers. 75c, Camping. $1, On parade, camp. $4, Olave Baden-Powell.
$6, Lady Olave, diff.

1987, Nov. 25 *Perf. 15*

873 A132 25c multicolored .65 .65
874 A132 75c multicolored 1.00 1.00
875 A132 $1 multicolored 1.35 1.35
876 A132 $4 multicolored 4.00 4.00
Nos. 873-876 (4) 7.00 7.00

Souvenir Sheet

Perf. 14

877 A133 $6 multicolored 6.00 6.00

Intl. Year of Shelter for the Homeless A134

1987, Dec. 3 *Perf. 15*

878 A134 25c Tent dwellings .75 .75
879 A134 75c Urban slum 1.25 1.25
880 A134 $1 Tents, diff. 1.50 1.50
881 A134 $4 Construction 2.75 2.75
Nos. 878-881 (4) 6.25 6.25

Orchids A135

Illustrations from Reichenbachia, published by Henry F. Sander in 1886: 1c, Laelia euspatha. 2c, Cattleya citrina. 3c, Masdevallia bachousiana. 4c, Cypripedium tautzianum. 5c, Trichopilia suavis alba. 6c, Odontoglossum hebraicum. 7c, Cattleya trianaei schroederiana. 10c, Saccolabium giganteum. 30c, Cattleya warscewiczii. 50c, Chysis bractescens. 70c, Cattleya rochellensis. $1, Laelia elegans schilleriana. $1.50, Laelia anceps percivaliana. #895, $3, Laelia gouldiana.
#896, $3, Odontoglossum roezlii. $5, Cattleya dowiana aurea.

1987, Dec. 16 **Litho.** *Perf. 14*

882-895 A135 Set of 14 18.50 18.50

Miniature Sheets

896-897 A135 Set of 2 16.00 16.00

Nos. 882-887 and 889-894 printed in blocks of six. Sheets of 14 contain 2 blocks of Nos. 882-887 plus 2 No. 888 and center label or 2 blocks of Nos. 889-894 plus center strip containing 2 No. 895 and center label. Center labels picture various illustrations from Reichenbachia.
Nos. 896-897 contain one 44x51mm stamp.

Miniature Sheet

Easter — A136

Stations of the Cross (in sequential order): a, Jesus condemned to death. b, Carries the cross. c, Falls the first time. d, Meets his mother, Mary. e, Cyrenean takes up the cross. f, Veronica wipes Jesus's face. g, Falls the second time. h, Consoles the women of Jerusalem. i, Falls the third time. j, Stripped of his robes. k, Nailed to the cross. l, Dies. m, Taken down from the cross. n, Laid in the sepulcher.

1988, Mar. 21 *Perf. 14*

898 A136 Sheet of 14 + label 8.00 8.00
a.-n. 40c, any single .50 .50

A $6 souvenir sheet was prepared but not issued.

1988 Summer Olympics, Seoul — A137

10c, Basketball. 25c, Volleyball. 60c, Table tennis. 75c, Diving. $1, Judo. $2, Field hockey.
$3, Women's gymnastics.

1988, Aug. 15 **Litho.** *Perf. 14*

899 A137 10c multi 3.00 1.00
900 A137 25c multi 1.25 .40
901 A137 60c multi 1.25 .75
902 A137 75c multi 1.25 .95
903 A137 $1 multi 1.40 1.25
904 A137 $2 multi 7.00 5.00
Nos. 899-904 (6) 15.15 9.35

Souvenir Sheet

905 A137 $3 multi 8.00 8.00

Intl. Red Cross, 125th Anniv. A138

60c, Travelling nurse, 1912. 75c, Hospital ship, ambulance boat, 1937. $1, Ambulance, 1956. $2, Ambulance plane, 1940.

1988, Nov. 18 **Litho.** *Perf. 14*

906 A138 60c multicolored 3.50 1.40
907 A138 75c multicolored 3.75 1.60
908 A138 $1 multicolored 4.50 2.25
909 A138 $2 multicolored 6.00 *6.50*
Nos. 906-909 (4) 17.75 11.75

Audubon Type of 1985

Design: 60c, Painted bunting.

1988
909A A97 60c multi *2,000. 750.00*

Indigenous Small Animals — A139

10c, Gibnut (agouti). 25c, Four-eyed opossum, vert. 50c, Ant bear. 75c, Antelope. $2, Peccary.

1989 Litho. Wmk. 384 *Perf. 14*
910 A139 10c multi 4.00 4.00

Unwmk.

911 A139 25c multi 4.00 4.00
a. Wmk. 384 5.50 5.50
912 A139 50c multi 4.75 3.75
913 A139 60c like 10c 4.75 4.00
914 A139 75c multi 4.75 4.00
915 A139 $2 multi 7.75 7.75
Nos. 910-915 (6) 30.00 27.50

Issued: 10c, 7/23; No. 911a, 12/6; others, 2/24.

Moon Landing, 20th Anniv.

Common Design Type

Apollo 9: 25c, Command service and lunar modules docked in space. 50c, Command service module. 75c, Mission emblem. $1, First manned lunar module in space. $5, Apollo 11 command service module.

Perf. 14x13½
1989, July 20 Wmk. 384
Size of Nos. 680-681: 29x29mm

916 CD342 25c multicolored 2.10 .60
917 CD342 50c multicolored 2.50 1.00
918 CD342 75c multicolored 2.75 1.50
919 CD342 $1 multicolored 3.00 2.50
Nos. 916-919 (4) 10.35 5.60

Souvenir Sheet

920 CD342 $5 multi 12.50 12.50

No. 920 Overprinted

1989, Nov. 17 *Perf. 14x13½*
921 CD342 $5 multicolored 13.50 13.50

World Stamp Expo '89.

No. 704 Surcharged

1989, Nov. 15 *Perf. 15*
922 A89 5c on 6c multi *37.50*

Christmas A140

Old churches: 10c, Wesley. 25c, Baptist. 60c, St. John's Cathedral. 75c, St. Andrew's Presbyterian. $1, Holy Redeemer Cathedral.

Wmk. 384
1989, Dec. 13 Litho. *Perf. 14*
927 A140 10c multicolored .40 .25
928 A140 25c multicolored .50 .40
929 A140 60c multicolored 1.00 .90
930 A140 75c multicolored 1.30 1.25
931 A140 $1 multicolored 1.60 *2.00*
Nos. 927-931 (5) 4.80 4.80

A141

Birds and Butterfies: 5c, Piranga leucoptera, Catonephele numilia female. 10c, Ramphastos sulfuratus, Nessaea aglaura. 15c, Fregata magnificens, Eurytides philolaus. 25c, Jabiru mycteria, Heliconius sapho. 30c, Ardea herodias, Colobura dirce. 50c, Icterus galbula, Hamadryas arethusia. 60c, Ara macao, Thecla regalis. 75c, Cyanerpes cyaneus, Callicore patelina. $1, Pulsatrix perspicillata, Caligo uranus. $2, Cyanocorax yncas, Philaethria dido. $5, Cathartes aura, Battus belus. $10, Pandion haliaetus, Papilio thoas.

Wmk. 373
1990, Mar. 1 Litho. *Perf. 14*
932 A141 5c multicolored .85 *1.50*
933 A141 10c multicolored 1.15 1.00
a. Inscribed "1993" 2.00 2.00
934 A141 15c multicolored 1.15 .50
935 A141 25c multicolored 1.15 .50
936 A141 30c multicolored 1.15 .60
937 A141 50c multicolored 1.50 .75
938 A141 60c multicolored 1.75 .90
939 A141 75c multicolored 1.75 .95
940 A141 $1 multicolored 3.25 2.00
941 A141 $2 multicolored 4.00 *4.25*
942 A141 $5 multicolored 6.50 *7.75*
943 A141 $10 multicolored 12.00 *14.50*
Nos. 932-943 (12) 36.20 35.20

For overprints and surcharge see Nos. 944, 1021, 1030.

No. 940 Overprinted

1990, Mar. 1
944 A141 $1 multicolored 6.50 6.50

Turtles A142

10c, Green. 25c, Hawksbill. 60c, Loggerhead. 75c, Loggerhead, diff. $1, Bocatora. $2, Hicatee.

Wmk. 373
1990, Aug. 8 Litho. *Perf. 14*
945 A142 10c multicolored 1.20 .70
946 A142 25c multicolored 1.90 .70
947 A142 60c multicolored 2.75 2.75
948 A142 75c multicolored 3.00 3.00
949 A142 $1 multicolored 3.75 3.75
950 A142 $2 multicolored 5.00 *6.00*
Nos. 945-950 (6) 17.60 16.90

Battle of Britain, 50th Anniv. A143

Aircraft: 10c, Fairey Battle. 25c, Bristol Beaufort. 60c, Bristol Blenheim. 75c, Armstrong-Whitworth Whitley. $1, Vickers-Armstrong Wellington. $2, Handley-Page Hampden.

1990, Sept. 15 Wmk. 384 *Perf. 13½*
951 A143 10c multicolored 2.25 .90
952 A143 25c multicolored 3.00 1.00
953 A143 60c multicolored 4.00 2.00
954 A143 75c multicolored 4.00 2.00
955 A143 $1 multicolored 4.00 2.00
956 A143 $2 multicolored 5.00 4.00
Nos. 951-956 (6) 22.25 11.90

Orchids — A144

25c, Cattleya bowringiana. 50c, Rhyncholaelia digbyana. 60c, Sobralia macrantha. 75c, Chysis bractescens. $1, Vanilla planifolia. $2, Epidendrum polyanthum.

1990, Nov. 1 Wmk. 384 *Perf. 14*
957 A144 25c multicolored 1.40 .30
958 A144 50c multicolored 2.00 .70
959 A144 60c multicolored 2.50 1.60
960 A144 75c multicolored 2.50 1.60
961 A144 $1 multicolored 3.00 3.00
962 A144 $2 multicolored 4.00 4.00
Nos. 957-962 (6) 15.40 11.20

Christmas.

Indigenous Fauna — A145

1991, Apr. 10
963 A145 25c Iguana 1.50 .50
964 A145 50c Crocodile 2.25 1.25
965 A145 60c Manatee 2.75 2.75
966 A145 75c Boa constrictor 3.25 3.25
967 A145 $1 Tapir 3.75 3.75
968 A145 $2 Jaguar 5.00 5.00
Nos. 963-968 (6) 18.50 16.50

Elizabeth & Philip, Birthdays

Common Design Types

1991, June 17 *Perf. 14½*
969 CD345 $1 multicolored 1.50 1.50
970 CD346 $1 multicolored 1.50 1.50
a. Pair, #969-970 + label 3.75 3.75

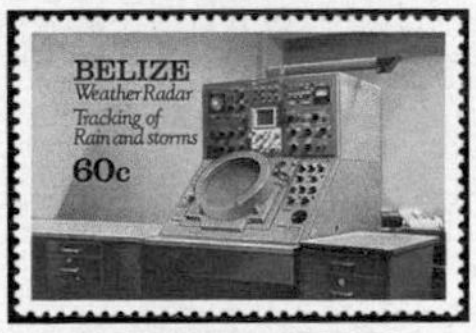

Hurricanes — A146

60c, Weather radar. 75c, Weather observation station. $1, Scene after hurricane. $2, Hurricane Gilbert.

1991, July 31 Wmk. 373 *Perf. 14*
971 A146 60c multicolored 2.40 2.00
972 A146 75c multicolored 2.50 2.25
973 A146 $1 multicolored 2.75 2.75
974 A146 $2 multicolored 4.00 *4.75*
Nos. 971-974 (4) 11.65 11.75

Independence, 10th Anniv. — A147

Famous Men: 25c, Thomas V. Ramos (1887-1955). 60c, Sir Isaiah Morter (1860-1924). 75c, Antonio Soberanis (1897-1975). $1, Santiago Ricalde (1920-1975).

1991, Sept. 4 Wmk. 384
975 A147 25c multicolored .90 .40
976 A147 60c multicolored 1.90 *2.00*
977 A147 75c multicolored 1.90 *2.00*
978 A147 $1 multicolored 2.25 *2.50*
Nos. 975-978 (4) 6.95 *6.90*

Folktales A148

Christmas: 25c, Anansi. 50c, Jack-O-Lantern. 60c, Tata Duende, vert. 75c, Xtabai. $1, Warrie Massa, vert. $2, Old Heg.

Wmk. 373
1991, Nov. 6 Litho. *Perf. 14*
979 A148 25c multicolored 2.00 .45
980 A148 50c multicolored 2.50 .55
981 A148 60c multicolored 2.90 1.25
982 A148 75c multicolored 2.90 1.25
983 A148 $1 multicolored 3.25 2.25
984 A148 $2 multicolored 4.50 *7.00*
Nos. 979-984 (6) 18.05 12.75

See Nos. 999-1002.

Orchids — A149

Easter: 25c, Gongora quinquenervis. 50c, Oncidium sphacelatum. 60c, Encyclia bractescens. 75c, Epidendrum ciliare. $1, Psygmorchis pusilla. $2, Galeandra batemanii.

1992, Apr. 1
985 A149 25c multicolored 1.75 .30
986 A149 50c multicolored 2.40 1.10
987 A149 60c multicolored 2.75 2.50
988 A149 75c multicolored 2.75 2.50
989 A149 $1 multicolored 3.00 *3.00*
990 A149 $2 multicolored 4.75 *7.50*
Nos. 985-990 (6) 17.40 16.90

Famous Belizeans A150

Designs: 25c, Gwendolyn Lizarraga, MBE (1901-75). 60c, Rafael Fonseca, CMG, OBE (1921-78). 75c, Vivian Seay, MBE (1881-1971). $1, Samuel A. Haynes (1898-1971).

1992, Aug. 26 *Perf. 13x12½*
991 A150 25c multicolored .90 .35
992 A150 60c multicolored 1.75 1.75
993 A150 75c multicolored 2.10 2.10
994 A150 $1 multicolored 2.25 2.25
Nos. 991-994 (4) 7.00 6.45

See Nos. 1013-1016.

Discovery of America, 500th Anniv. — A151

Mayan ruins, modern buildings: 25c, Xunantunich, National Assembly. 60c, Altun Ha, Supreme Court Building. 75c, Santa Rita, Tower Hill Sugar Factory. $5, Lamanai, The Citrus Company.

Perf. 13½x14

1992, Oct. 1 Litho. Wmk. 384

995	A151 25c multicolored	1.40	.35
996	A151 60c multicolored	2.10	1.40
997	A151 75c multicolored	2.25	1.75
998	A151 $5 multicolored	11.00	*13.00*
	Nos. 995-998 (4)	16.75	16.50

Folklore Type of 1991

Christmas.

Perf. 13x12½

1992, Nov. 16 Litho. Wmk. 373

999	A148 25c Hashishi Pampi	.45	.30
1000	A148 60c Cadejo	.95	.95
1001	A148 $1 La Sucia, vert.	1.25	1.25
1002	A148 $5 Sisimito	6.25	*6.50*
	Nos. 999-1002 (4)	8.90	9.00

Royal Air Force, 75th Anniv.

Common Design Type

Designs: 25c, Aerospatiale Puma. 50c, British Aerospace Harrier. 60c, DeHavilland Mosquito. 75c, Avro Lancaster. $1, Consolidated Liberator. $3, Short Stirling.

Wmk. 373

1993, Apr. 1 Litho. *Perf. 14*

1003	CD350 25c multicolored	1.90	.90
1004	CD350 50c multicolored	2.25	1.15
1005	CD350 60c multicolored	2.40	1.60
1006	CD350 75c multicolored	2.40	1.60
1007	CD350 $1 multicolored	2.60	2.00
1008	CD350 $3 multicolored	5.00	*9.25*
	Nos. 1003-1008 (6)	16.55	16.50

1993 World Orchid Conference, Glasgow — A152

25c, Lycaste aromatica. 60c, Sobralia decora. $1, Maxillaria alba. $2, Brassavola nodosa.

Perf. 14½x14

1993, Apr. 24 Litho. Wmk. 384

1009	A152 25c multicolored	.70	.45
1010	A152 60c multicolored	1.30	1.30
1011	A152 $1 multicolored	1.75	1.75
1012	A152 $2 multicolored	3.00	*3.25*
	Nos. 1009-1012 (4)	6.75	6.75

Famous Belizeans Type of 1992

Designs: 25c, Herbert Watkin Beaumont (1880-1978). 60c, Dr. Selvyn Walford Young (1899-1977). 75c, Cleopatra White (1898-1987). $1, Dr. Karl Heusner (1872-1960).

Wmk. 384

1993, Aug. 11 Litho. *Perf. 14*

1013	A150 25c multicolored	.55	.35
1014	A150 60c multicolored	1.05	1.00
1015	A150 75c multicolored	1.25	1.25
1016	A150 $1 multicolored	1.50	1.50
	Nos. 1013-1016 (4)	4.35	4.10

Christmas A153

25c, Boom and chime band. 60c, John Canoe dance. 75c, Cortez dance. $2, Maya Musical Group.

Wmk. 373

1993, Nov. 3 Litho. *Perf. 14*

1017	A153 25c multicolored	1.25	.50
1018	A153 60c multicolored	2.25	1.25
1019	A153 75c multicolored	2.25	1.25
1020	A153 $2 multicolored	5.25	8.00
	Nos. 1017-1020 (4)	11.00	11.00

No. 940 Overprinted

Wmk. 373

1994, Feb. 18 Litho. *Perf. 14*

1021	A141 $1 multicolored	4.75	4.25

Royal Visit — A154

Designs: 25c, Belize, United Kingdom Flags. 60c, Queen Elizabeth II wearing hat. 75c, Queen. $1, Queen, Prince Philip.

Perf. 14½x14

1994, Feb. 24 Litho. Wmk. 373

1022	A154 25c multicolored	2.25	.70
1023	A154 60c multicolored	2.90	1.60
1024	A154 75c multicolored	3.25	2.00
1025	A154 $1 multicolored	3.50	3.25
	Nos. 1022-1025 (4)	11.90	7.55

Bats A155

25c, Insect feeder. 60c, Fruit feeder. 75c, Fish feeder. $2, Common vampire.

Wmk. 384

1994, May 30 Litho. *Perf. 14*

1026	A155 25c multicolored	.75	.35
1027	A155 60c multicolored	1.40	1.20
1028	A155 75c multicolored	1.60	1.30
1029	A155 $2 multicolored	3.75	4.50
	Nos. 1026-1029 (4)	7.50	7.35

No. 939 Surcharged

Wmk. 373

1994, Aug. 18 Litho. *Perf. 14*

1030	A141 10c on 75c multi	3.00	3.00

Christmas A156

Orchids: 25c, Cycnoches chlorochilon. 60c, Brassavolas cucullata. 75c, Sobralia mucronata. $1, Nidema Boothii.

1994, Nov. 7 Wmk. 384

1031	A156 25c multicolored	.90	.40
1032	A156 60c multicolored	1.50	1.40
1033	A156 75c multicolored	1.75	1.75
1034	A156 $1 multicolored	2.25	*2.75*
	Nos. 1031-1034 (4)	6.40	6.30

For overprints see Nos. 1051-1054.

Insects A157

5c, Ground beetle. 10c, Harlequin beetle. 15c, Giant water bug. 25c, Peanut-head bug. 30c, Coconut weevil. 50c, Mantis. 60c, Tarantula wasp. 75c, Rhinoceros beetle. $1, Metallic wood borer. $2, Dobson fly. $5, Click beetle. $10, Long-horned beetle.

Wmk. 373

1995, Jan. 11 Litho. *Perf. 14*

Without date imprint

1035	A157 5c multicolored	.60	*1.00*
1036	A157 10c multicolored	.75	*1.00*
1037	A157 15c multicolored	.80	*1.00*
1038	A157 25c multicolored	.95	.30
1039	A157 30c multicolored	.95	.35
1040	A157 50c multicolored	1.10	.40
1041	A157 60c multicolored	1.60	.65
1042	A157 75c multicolored	1.75	.75
1043	A157 $1 multicolored	2.25	1.10
1044	A157 $2 multicolored	4.75	*5.00*
1045	A157 $5 multicolored	9.00	*9.50*
1046	A157 $10 multicolored	13.50	*15.00*
	Nos. 1035-1046 (12)	38.00	*36.05*

For overprints see Nos. 1063-1066.

1996, Oct. 14 Inscribed "1996"

1035a	A157 5c	.60	*1.00*
1036a	A157 10c	.75	*1.00*
1037a	A157 15c	.80	*1.00*
1038a	A157 25c	.95	.30
1039a	A157 30c	.95	.35
1040a	A157 50c	1.10	.40
1041a	A157 60c	1.60	.65
1042a	A157 75c	1.75	.75
1043a	A157 $1	2.25	1.10
1044a	A157 $2	4.75	*5.00*
1045a	A157 $5	8.75	*9.00*
1046a	A157 $10	13.00	*15.00*
	Nos. 1035a-1046a (12)	37.25	*35.55*

End of World War II, 50th Anniv.

Common Design Type

Designs: 25c, War Memorial Cenotaph. 60c, Remembrance Sunday. 75c, British Honduras Forestry Unit. $1, Wellington Bomber.

Wmk. 373

1995, May 8 Litho. *Perf. 13½*

1047	CD351 25c multicolored	.55	.40
1048	CD351 60c multicolored	1.50	1.50
1049	CD351 75c multicolored	1.75	1.75
1050	CD351 $1 multicolored	2.25	2.25
	Nos. 1047-1050 (4)	6.05	5.90

Nos. 1031-1034 Ovptd. in Blue

1995, Sept. 1 Wmk. 384 *Perf. 14*

1051	A156 25c on No. 1031	1.25	.35
1052	A156 60c on No. 1032	1.75	1.10
1053	A156 75c on No. 1033	2.10	2.10
1054	A156 $1 on No. 1034	2.40	*2.75*
	Nos. 1051-1054 (4)	7.50	6.30

UN, 50th Anniv.

Common Design Type

Designs: 25c, M113 Light reconnaissance vehicle. 60c, Sultan, armored command vehicle. 75c, Leyland/DAF 8x4 "Drops" vehicle. $2, Warrior infantry combat vehicle.

Wmk. 384

1995, Oct. 24 Litho. *Perf. 14*

1055	CD353 25c multicolored	.40	.30
1056	CD353 60c multicolored	.95	.90
1057	CD353 75c multicolored	1.10	1.10
1058	CD353 $2 multicolored	2.25	*2.40*
	Nos. 1055-1058 (4)	4.70	4.70

Christmas A158

Doves: 25c, Blue ground. 60c, White-fronted. 75c, Ruddy ground. $1, White-winged.

1995, Nov. 6 Wmk. 373

1059	A158 25c multicolored	.60	.30
1060	A158 60c multicolored	1.20	1.20
1061	A158 75c multicolored	1.45	1.45
1062	A158 $1 multicolored	2.00	*2.25*
	Nos. 1059-1062 (4)	5.25	5.20

Nos. 1037, 1039-1040, 1044 Ovptd.

Wmk. 373

1996, May 17 Litho. *Perf. 14*

1063	A157 15c on #1037	.30	.25
1064	A157 30c on #1039	.65	.50
1065	A157 50c on #1040	.90	.80
1066	A157 $2 on #1044	2.75	*3.00*
	Nos. 1063-1066 (4)	4.60	4.55

CAPEX '96 A159

Trains: 25c, Unloading banana train onto freighter, Commerce Bight Pier. 60c, Engine No. 1, Stann Creek Station. 75c, Mahogany log train, Hunslet 0-6-0 Side Tank Engine No. 4. $3, LMS Jubilee Class 4-6-0 Locomotive No. 5602 "British Honduras."

Perf. 13½x13

1996, June 6 Litho. Wmk. 373

1067	A159 25c multicolored	1.40	.50
1068	A159 60c multicolored	2.00	1.25
1069	A159 75c multicolored	2.00	1.40
1070	A159 $3 multicolored	3.50	5.75
	Nos. 1067-1070 (4)	8.90	8.90

Christmas — A160

Orchids: 25c, Epidendrum stamfordianum. 60c, Oncidium carthagenense. 75c, Oerstedella verrucosa. $1, Coryanthes speciosa.

Wmk. 373

1996, Nov. 6 Litho. *Perf. 14*

1071	A160 25c multicolored	.80	.30
1072	A160 60c multicolored	1.25	.95
1073	A160 75c multicolored	1.40	1.25
1074	A160 $1 multicolored	1.90	*2.00*
	Nos. 1071-1074 (4)	5.35	4.50

Hong Kong '97
A161

Cattle: 25c, Red poll. 60c, Brahman. 75c, Longhorn. $1, Charbray.

Wmk. 373

1997, Feb. 12 Litho. *Perf. 14*

1075	A161 25c multicolored	.75	.30
1076	A161 60c multicolored	1.15	*1.20*
1077	A161 75c multicolored	1.50	*1.60*
1078	A161 $1 multicolored	1.75	*2.00*
	Nos. 1075-1078 (4)	5.15	*5.10*

Snakes — A162

25c, Coral snake. 60c, Green vine snake. 75c, Yellow-jawed tommygoff. $1, Speckled racer.

Wmk. 373

1997, May 28 Litho. *Perf. 14*

1079	A162 25c multicolored	.70	.30
1080	A162 60c multicolored	1.10	1.10
1081	A162 75c multicolored	1.25	1.25
1082	A162 $1 multicolored	1.50	*1.90*
	Nos. 1079-1082 (4)	4.55	4.55

Howler Monkeys — A163

World Wildlife Fund: 10c, Adult male. 25c, Female feeding. 60c, Female with infant. 75c, Juvenile feeding.

Wmk. 373

1997, Aug. 13 Litho. *Perf. 14*

1083	A163 10c multicolored	.40	.25
1084	A163 25c multicolored	.60	.30
1085	A163 60c multicolored	1.00	1.00
1086	A163 75c multicolored	1.20	*1.50*
	Nos. 1083-1086 (4)	3.20	3.05

Christmas A164

Orchids: 25c, Maxillaria elatior. 60c, Dimerandra emarginata. 75c, Macradenia brassavolae. $1, Ornithocephalus gladiatus.

Wmk. 373

1997, Nov. 21 Litho. *Perf. 14*

1087	A164 25c multicolored	.80	.30
1088	A164 60c multicolored	1.30	.80
1089	A164 75c multicolored	1.40	1.30
1090	A164 $1 multicolored	1.90	2.10
	Nos. 1087-1090 (4)	5.40	4.50

Diana, Princess of Wales (1961-97)
Common Design Type

Designs: a, Up close portrait, smiling. b, Wearing evening dress. c, Up close portrait, serious. d, Holding bouquet of flowers.

Perf. 14½x14

1998, Mar. 31 Litho. Wmk. 373

1091	CD355 $1 Sheet of 4, #a.-d.	5.00	5.00

University of West Indies, 50th Anniv. A165

Wmk. 373

1998, July 22 Litho. *Perf. 13*

1092	A165 $1 multicolored	1.45	1.45

Organization of American States, 50th Anniv. A166

Designs: 25c, Children working computers, connecting high schools to the internet. $1, Map of Central America, Inter American Drug Abuse Control Commission.

1998, July 22

1093	A166 25c multicolored	.25	.25
1094	A166 $1 multicolored	1.90	1.90

Battle of St. George's Cay, Bicent. A167

Views of Old Belize from St. George, vert: No. 1095, Woman, child beside small boat. No. 1096, Soldiers at dock, cannon. No. 1097, Cannon balls, cannon, boats in water.

25c, Bayman gun flats. 60c, Bayman sloops. 75c, Schooners. $1, HMS Merlin. $2, Spanish flagship.

1998, Aug. 5 *Perf. 13½*

1095	A167 10c multicolored	.65	*.90*
1096	A167 10c multicolored	.65	*.90*
1097	A167 10c multicolored	.65	*.90*
a.	Strip of 3, #1095-1097	2.00	*3.00*
1098	A167 25c multicolored	.95	.30
1099	A167 60c multicolored	1.35	1.10
1100	A167 75c multicolored	1.50	1.20
1101	A167 $1 multicolored	1.75	1.75
1102	A167 $2 multicolored	2.75	*3.25*
	Nos. 1095-1102 (8)	10.25	10.30

A168

Christmas — Flowers: 25c, Brassia maculata. 60c, Encyclia radiata. 75c, Stanhopea ecornuta. $1, Isochilius carnosiflorus.

1998, Nov. 4 *Perf. 14*

1103	A168 25c multicolored	.55	.30
1104	A168 60c multicolored	.80	.65
1105	A168 75c multicolored	.80	*.85*
1106	A168 $1 multicolored	1.00	*1.25*
	Nos. 1103-1106 (4)	3.15	3.05

A169

Easter — Orchids: 10c, Eucharis grandiflora. 25c, Hippeastrum puniceum. 60c, Zephyranthes citrina. $1, Hymenocallis littoralis.

1999, Mar. 17 *Perf. 13*

1107	A169 10c multicolored	.40	.25
1108	A169 25c multicolored	.55	.30
1109	A169 60c multicolored	.95	.95
1110	A169 $1 multicolored	1.15	*1.50*
	Nos. 1107-1110 (4)	3.05	3.00

UPU, 125th Anniv. A170

1999, Oct. 18 *Perf. 13¼*

1111	A170 25c Bicycle	.65	.40
1112	A170 60c Truck	.80	.65
1113	A170 75c Mailship "Dee"	1.00	.85
1114	A170 $1 Airplane	1.30	*1.50*
	Nos. 1111-1114 (4)	3.75	3.40

Christmas — A171

Designs: 25c, Holy Family with Jesus and St. John, by school of Peter Paul Rubens. 60c, The Holy Family with St. John, by unknown artist. 75c, Madonna with Child, St. John and Angel, by unknown artist. $1, Madonna with Child and St. John by Andrea da Salerno.

1999, Dec. 6 *Perf. 14*

1115	A171 25c multicolored	.40	.20
1116	A171 60c multicolored	.75	.60
1117	A171 75c multicolored	.85	.80
1118	A171 $1 multicolored	1.25	*1.40*
	Nos. 1115-1118 (4)	3.25	3.00

Fauna A172

5c, Iguana. 10c, Gibnut. 15c, Howler monkey. 25c, Ant bear. 30c, Hawksbill turtle. 50c, Antelope. 60c, Jaguar. 75c, Manatee. $1, Crocodile. $2, Tapir. $5, Collared peccary. $10, Boa constrictor.

Wmk. 373

2000, Feb. 15 Litho. *Perf. 14*

Without date imprint

1119	A172 5c multicolored	.25	.60
1120	A172 10c multicolored	.25	.60
1121	A172 15c multicolored	.35	.60
1122	A172 25c multicolored	.50	.25
1123	A172 30c multicolored	.50	.25
1124	A172 50c multicolored	.80	.30
1125	A172 60c multicolored	.95	.35
1126	A172 75c multicolored	1.10	.50
1127	A172 $1 multicolored	1.50	.80
1128	A172 $2 multicolored	2.75	*3.00*
1129	A172 $5 multicolored	6.00	*6.75*
1130	A172 $10 multicolored	12.00	*13.00*
	Nos. 1119-1130 (12)	26.95	27.00

For surcharges see Nos. 1181-1183.

2003, Sept. Inscribed "2003"

1120a	A172 10c	.30	.65
1121a	A172 15c	.40	.65
1122a	A172 25c	.55	.25
1123a	A172 30c	.55	.25
1124a	A172 50c	.85	.35
1125a	A172 60c	1.00	.45
1126a	A172 75c	1.20	.65
1127a	A172 $1	1.50	.80
1128a	A172 $2	3.00	3.00
1129a	A172 $5	7.50	7.75
1130a	A172 $10	13.00	15.00
	Nos. 1120a-1130a (11)	29.85	29.80

Fruits A173

Wmk. 373

2000, Apr. 19 Litho. *Perf. 14*

1131	A173 25c Mango	.50	.25
1132	A173 60c Cashew	.90	.75
1133	A173 75c Papaya	1.20	1.00
1134	A173 $1 Banana	1.40	*2.00*
	Nos. 1131-1134 (4)	4.00	4.00

People's United Party, 50th Anniv. A174

10c, Birth of party politics, 9/29/50. 25c, People gain voting rights, 4/28/54. 60c, Self-government, 1/1/64. 75c, Building the new capital Belmopan, 1967-70. $1, Independence, 9/21/81.

Perf. 13¼x13¾

2000, Sept. 18 Litho. Wmk. 373

1135-1139	A174 Set of 5	4.75	4.75

Christmas A175

Orchids: 25c, Bletia purpurea. 60c, Cyrtopodium punctata. 75c, Cycnoches egertonianum. $1, Catasetum integerrimum.

Perf. 14½x14¼

2000 Litho. Wmk. 373

1140-1143	A175 Set of 4	6.25	6.25

Independence, 20th Anniv. — A176

Designs: 25c, Education. 60c, Shrimp farming. 75c, Privassion Cascade, vert. $2, Map, vert.

Wmk. 373

2001, Oct. 3 Litho. *Perf. 14*

1144-1147	A176 Set of 4	6.75	6.75

Christmas — A177

Orchids: 25c, Sobralia fragrans. 60c, Encyclia cordigera. 75c, Maxillaria fulgens. $1, Epidendrum nocturnum.

Wmk. 373

2001, Dec. 28 Litho. *Perf. 14*

1148-1151	A177 Set of 4	5.25	5.25

Reign Of Queen Elizabeth II, 50th Anniv. Issue
Common Design Type

Designs: Nos. 1152, 1156a, 25c, Princess Elizabeth, 1943. Nos. 1153, 1156b, 60c, In 1952. Nos. 1154, 1156c, 75c, With Prince Charles and Princess Anne. Nos. 1155,

1156d, $1, In 1995. No. 1156e, $5, 1955 portrait by Annigoni (38x50mm).

Perf. 14¼x14½, 13¾ (#1156e)

2002, Feb. 6 Litho. Wmk. 373

With Gold Frames

1152	CD360	25c multicolored	.50	.25
1153	CD360	60c multicolored	.80	.60
1154	CD360	75c multicolored	.95	.85
1155	CD360	$1 multicolored	1.15	*1.30*
		Nos. 1152-1155 (4)	3.40	3.00

Souvenir Sheet

Without Gold Frames

1156	CD360	Sheet of 5, #a-e	9.25	9.25

Christmas — A178

Orchids: 25c, Dichaea neglecta. 50c, Epidendrum hawkesii. 60c, Encyclia belizensis. 75c, Eriopsis biloba. $1, Harbenaria monorrhiza. $2, Mormodes buccinator.

Wmk. 373

2002, Dec. 12 Litho. *Perf. 14*

1157-1162 A178 Set of 6 10.00 10.00

Belize Defense Force, 25th Anniv. A179

Wmk. 373

2003, Jan. 29 Litho. *Perf. 14*

1163 A179 25c multi .55 .55

Powered Flight, Cent. — A180

Designs: 25c, Avro Shackleton Mk 3. 60c, Lockheed L-749 Constellation. 75c, SEPECAT Jaguar GR 1. $3, British Aerospace Harrier GR 3.

$5, Spirit of St. Louis lands in Belize, Dec. 30, 1927.

Wmk. 373

2003, Sept. 17 Litho. *Perf. 14*

Stamps + Label

1164-1167 A180 Set of 4 7.75 7.75

Souvenir Sheet

1168 A180 $5 multi 7.50 7.50

For surcharge see No. 1185.

Christmas A181

Scarlet macaw: 25c, Close-up of head. 60c, Pair on tree. 75c, Three eating clay. $5, Pair in flight.

2003, Nov. 5 *Perf. 13¾*

1169-1172 A181 Set of 4 12.25 12.25

For surcharge see No. 1184.

Whale Shark A182

Various depictions of whale shark: 25c, 60c, 75c, $5.

Wmk. 373

2004, Aug. 16 Litho. *Perf. 13½*

1173-1176 A182 Set of 4 12.00 12.00

Worldwide Fund for Nature (WWF) — A183

Various depictions of Central American wooly opossum with denominations in: 25c, Green, vert. 60c, Blue, vert. 75c, Orange. $5, Red violet.

Perf. 14¼x14, 14x14¼

2004, Nov. 8 Litho. Wmk. 373

1177-1180 A183 Set of 4 11.00 11.00

Nos. 1124-1126 Surcharged

Wmk. 373

2004-2005 Litho. *Perf. 14*

1181	A172	10c on 50c #1124	*1.75*	*1.75*
1182	A172	10c on 60c #1125 ('05)	—	—
1183	A172	15c on 75c #1126	*1.75*	*1.75*

Issued: Nos. 1181, 1183, 10/4/04. No. 1182, 1/31/05.

Nos. 1181 and 1182 exist dated "2003."

No. 1170 Surcharged

Wmk. 373

2005, July 15 Litho. *Perf. 13¾*

1184 A181 10c on 60c #1170 *11.00 11.00*

No. 1165 Surcharged

Wmk. 373

2005, July Litho. *Perf. 14*

1185 A180 10c on 60c #1165 *3.00 3.00*

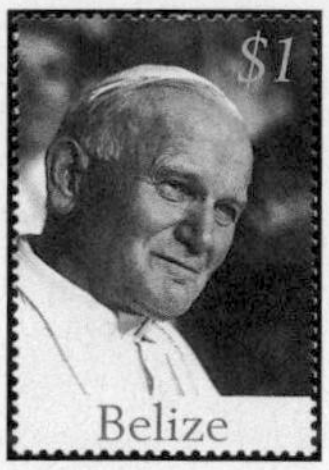

Pope John Paul II (1920-2005) A184

Wmk. 373

2005, Aug. 18 Litho. *Perf. 14*

1186 A184 $1 multi 2.00 2.00

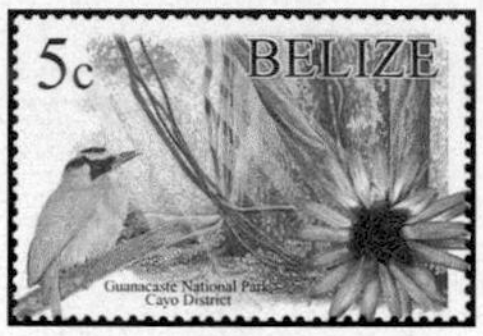

Ecological and Heritage Sites A185

Designs: 5c, Guanacaste National Park. 10c, Government House of Culture. 15c, Lubaantun Archaeological Reserve. 25c, Altun Ha Archaeological Reserve. 30c, Nohoch Che'n Archaeological Reserve. 50c, Goff's Caye. 60c, Nlue Hole Natural Monument. 75c, Lamanai Archaeological Reserve. $1, Half Moon Caye and Lighthouse. $2, Placencia Peninsula. $5, Museum of Belize. $10, Cerros Archaeological Reserve.

2005, Aug. 31 Wmk. 373 *Perf. 14*

1187	A185	5c multi	.25	.25
1188	A185	10c multi	.25	.25
1189	A185	15c multi	.25	.25
1190	A185	25c multi	.30	.30
a.		Wmk. 406	.50	.50
b.		Wmk. 406, dated "2017", perf. 12½x13	.25	.25
1191	A185	30c multi	.35	.35
1192	A185	50c multi	.60	.60
1193	A185	60c multi	.70	.70
1194	A185	75c multi	.85	.85
a.		Wmk. 406, dated "2017", perf. 12½x13	.75	.75
1195	A185	$1 multi	1.10	1.10
1196	A185	$2 multi	2.50	2.50
1197	A185	$5 multi	5.50	5.50
1198	A185	$10 multi	11.00	11.00
		Nos. 1187-1198 (12)	23.65	23.65

Issued: No. 1190a, Feb. 2009.

Europa Stamps, 50th Anniv. A186

Stamps commemorating 125th anniv. of the UPU: 25c, #1111. 75c, #1112. $3, #1113. $5, #1114.

Perf. 13x13¼

2006, Mar. 22 Litho. Unwmk.

1199-1202 A186 Set of 4 16.00 16.00

1202a Souvenir sheet, #1199-1202 15.75 15.75

Independence, 25th Anniv. — A187

Designs: 25c, Prime Minister George Price. 30c, National symbols, horiz. 60c, Map of Belize. $1, 1981 Independence logo. $5, Constitution, horiz.

Perf. 13¼x12½, 12½x13¼

2006, July 3 Litho. Wmk. 373

1203-1207 A187 Set of 5 9.00 9.00

Breast Cancer Research — A188

2006, Oct. 26 Litho. *Perf. 13½x13¼*

1208 A188 $1 multi 2.50 2.50

Art by Belizean Artists — A189

Designs: 25c, Sleeping Giant, sculpture, by George Gabb. 30c, Market Scene, by Louis Belisle, horiz. 60c, The Original Turtle Shell Band, by Pen Cayetano, horiz. 75c, Have Some Coconut Water, by Benjamin Nicholas. $2, Untitled sculpture by Reuben Miguel. $3, Mural at Corozal Town Hall, by Manuel Villamor.

Wmk. 373

2007, May 9 Litho. *Perf. 14*

1209-1214 A189 Set of 6 7.00 7.00

Abolition of the Slave Trade Act, Bicent. — A190

Perf. 12½x13

2007, Sept. 26 Litho. Wmk. 373

1215 A190 $2 multi 2.00 2.00

University of the West Indies, 60th Anniv. A191

Wmk. 373

2008, Nov. 14 Litho. *Perf. 13*

1216 A191 $1 multi 1.50 1.50

Endangered Birds — A192

Designs: 25c, Yellow-headed parrot. 60c, Harpy eagle. $1, Slate-colored seedeater. $2, Green honeycreeper. $5, Great curassow.

Wmk. 406

2009, July 8 Litho. *Perf. 12½*

1217-1221 A192 Set of 5 10.00 10.00

Christmas — A193

Orchids: 25c, Encyclia polybulbon. 60c, Oncidium ensatum. $2, Encyclia livida. $5, Epidendrum difforme.

Wmk. 406

2010, Dec. 8	**Litho.**	***Perf. 12½***
1222-1225 A193	Set of 4	8.00 8.00

Reign of Queen Elizabeth II, 60th Anniv. — A194

Various photographs of Queen Elizabeth II: 25c, 60c, 75c, $1, $2, $5.
$10, Queen Elizabeth II, diff.

Perf. 13¼

2012, Feb. 6	**Litho.**	**Unwmk.**
1226-1231 A194	Set of 6	10.00 10.00
1231a	Sheet of 6, #1226-1231, + 3 labels	10.00 10.00

Souvenir Sheet

1232 A194 $10 multi		10.00 10.00

No. 1188 Surcharged in Black and Silver

Method, Perf. and Watermark As Before

2012, Aug.		
1233 A185 25c on 10c #1188	*15.00*	—

A195

Coronation of Queen Elizabeth II, 60th Anniv. — A196

Various photographs of Queen Elizabeth II: 25c, 60c, 75c, $5.

Perf. 13½x13¼

2013, Apr. 19	**Litho.**	**Wmk. 406**
1234-1237 A195	Set of 4	6.50 6.50

Souvenir Sheet

Perf. 14¾x14¼

1238 A196 $10 multi		10.00 10.00

Pallottine Sisters in Belize, Cent. A197

Designs: 25c, Landing of Sisters at Cayo. 60c, Novitiate Nazareth Chapel, Toledo. $10, Centenary emblem.

Wmk. 406

2013, Oct. 9	**Litho.**	***Perf. 13***
1239-1241 A197	Set of 3	11.00 11.00

Salvation Army in Belize, Cent. — A198

Designs: 25c, Girl putting money in donation bucket. $2, Belize Salvation Army headquarters, horiz.

Wmk. 406

2015, Apr. 8	**Litho.**	***Perf. 14***
1242-1243 A198	Set of 2	2.25 2.25

Diplomatic Relations Between Belize and Mexico, 35th Anniv. A199

Flags of Belize and Mexico and: 25c, Bridge. 60c, Signs on border of Belize and Mexico.

Perf. 13¼x13½

2017, Sept. 27	**Litho.**	**Wmk. 406**
1244-1245 A199	Set of 2	.85 .85

Diplomatic Relations Between Belize and Republic of China A200

Designs: 25c, Flags of Belize and Republic of China. $1, Blue Hole, Belize, and Jade Mountain, Republic of China. $5, Keel-billed toucan and Taiwan blue magpie.

Wmk. 406

2019, Sept. 12	**Litho.**	***Perf. 12¾***
1246 A200 25c multi		.25 .25
1247 A200 $1 multi		1.00 1.00

Souvenir Sheet

1248	Sheet of 2, #1247, 1248a	6.00 6.00
a. A200 $5 multi		5.00 5.00

SEMI-POSTAL STAMPS

World Cup Soccer Championship — SP1

Designs: 20c+10c, 30c+15c, Scotland vs. New Zealand (diff.). 40c+20c, Kuwait vs. France. 60c+30c, Italy vs. Brazil. No. B5, France vs. Northern Ireland. $1.50+75c, Austria vs. Chile. No. B7, Italy vs. Germany, vert. $2+$1, England vs. France, vert.

1982, Dec. 10	**Litho.**	***Perf. 14***	
B1 SP1	20c +10c multi	3.00	1.50
B2 SP1	30c +15c multi	3.00	1.50
B3 SP1	40c +20c multi	3.25	1.50
B4 SP1	60c +30c multi	3.75	1.90
B5 SP1	$1 +50c multi	4.50	2.25
B6 SP1	$1.50 +75c multi	5.25	3.00
	Nos. B1-B6 (6)	22.75	11.65

Souvenir Sheets

Perf. 14½

B7 SP1	$1 +50c multi	13.50	7.25
B8 SP1	$2 +$1 multi	13.50	7.25

Nos. B7-B8 each contain one 50x70mm stamp.

POSTAGE DUE STAMPS

Numeral — D2

Each denomination has different border.

1976, July 1	**Litho.**	**Wmk. 373**	
J6 D2	1c green & red	.25	*1.50*
J7 D2	2c violet & rose lil	.25	*1.50*
J8 D2	5c ocher & brt grn	.25	*1.90*
J9 D2	15c brown org & yel grn	.30	*2.40*
J10 D2	25c slate grn & org	.45	*2.75*
	Nos. J6-J10 (5)	1.50	*10.05*

CAYES OF BELIZE

Catalogue values for all unused stamps in this country are for Never Hinged items.

Spiny Lobster A1

2c, Blue crab. 5c, Red-footed booby. 10c, Brown pelican. 15c, White-tailed deer. 25c, Lighthouse, English Caye. 75c, Spanish galleon, Santa Yaga, c. 1750. $3, Map of Ambergris Caye, vert. $5, Jetty, windsurfers.

Perf. 14½x14, 14x14½

1984, May 30	**Litho.**	**Unwmk.**	
1 A1	1c shown	.25	.25
2 A1	2c multicolored	.25	.25
3 A1	5c multicolored	.25	.25
4 A1	10c multicolored	.25	.25
5 A1	15c multicolored	.25	.25
6 A1	25c multicolored	.25	.25
7 A1	75c multicolored	.85	.85
8 A1	$3 multicolored	4.50	4.50
a.	Souvenir booklet	20.00	
9 A1	$5 multicolored	8.00	8.00
	Nos. 1-9 (9)	14.85	14.85

No. 8a contains four panes. One has one $3 stamp, one has a block of four 25c stamps, two have blocks of four 75c stamps but different text. The stamps are larger than Nos. 6-8, have slightly different colors and are perf. 14½.

The $1 stamp was not issued. Eighteen sheets of 40 were sold for postage by accident.

Lloyd's List Issue

Common Design Type

25c, Queen Elizabeth 2. 75c, Lutine Bell. $1, Loss of the Fishburn. $2, Trafalgar Sword.

1984, June 6		***Perf. 14½x14***	
10 CD335	25c multi	.25	.25
11 CD335	75c multi	.50	.50
12 CD335	$1 multi	.65	.65
13 CD335	$2 multi	1.25	1.25
	Nos. 10-13 (4)	2.65	2.65

1984 Summer Olympics, Los Angeles — A2

1984, Oct. 5		***Perf. 15***	
14 A2	10c Yachting	.25	.25
15 A2	15c Windsurfing	.25	.25
16 A2	75c Swimming	.70	.70
17 A2	$2 Kayaking	1.60	1.60
	Nos. 14-17 (4)	2.80	2.80

No. 17 inscribed Canoeing.

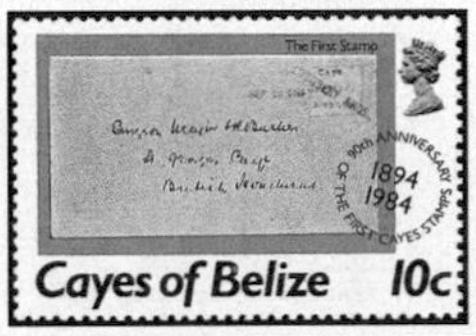

First Cayes Stamps, 90th Anniv. A3

10c, 1895 cover. 15c, Sydney Cuthbert. 75c, Cuthbert's steam yacht. $2, British Honduras #133.

1984, Nov. 5			
18 A3	10c multicolored	.25	.25
19 A3	15c multicolored	.25	.25
20 A3	75c multicolored	.50	.50
21 A3	$2 multicolored	1.75	1.75
	Nos. 18-21 (4)	2.75	2.75

Audubon Birth Bicentenary — A4

Illustrations by Audubon: 25c, Blue-winged teal. 75c, Semipalmated sandpiper. $1, Yellow-crowned night heron, vert. $3, Common gallinule.

1985, May 20 *Perf. 14*

22	A4	25c multicolored	.25	.25
23	A4	75c multicolored	.70	.70
24	A4	$1 multicolored	.85	.85
25	A4	$3 multicolored	2.50	2.50
		Nos. 22-25 (4)	4.30	4.30

Shipwrecks — A5

a, Oxford, c. 1675. b, Santa Yaga, 1780. c, No. 27, Comet, 1822. d, Yeldham, 1800.

1985, June 5 *Perf. 15*

26	A5	$1 Strip of 4 + label	4.25	4.25

Souvenir Sheet

Perf. 13½x14

27	A5	$5 multicolored	4.75	4.75

No. 27 contains one 38x51mm stamp. No. 26 has continuous design.

BENIN

bə-'nin

French Colony

LOCATION — West Coast of Africa
GOVT. — French Possession
AREA — 8,627 sq. mi.
POP. — 493,000 (approx.)
CAPITAL — Benin

In 1895 the French possessions known as Benin were incorporated into the colony of Dahomey and postage stamps of Dahomey superseded those of Benin. Dahomey took the name Benin when it became a republic in 1975.

100 Centimes = 1 Franc

Catalogue values for unused stamps in this country are for Never Hinged items, beginning with Scott 342 in the regular postage section, Scott C240 in the airpost section, Scott J44 in the postage due section, and Scott Q8 in the parcel post section.

Watermark

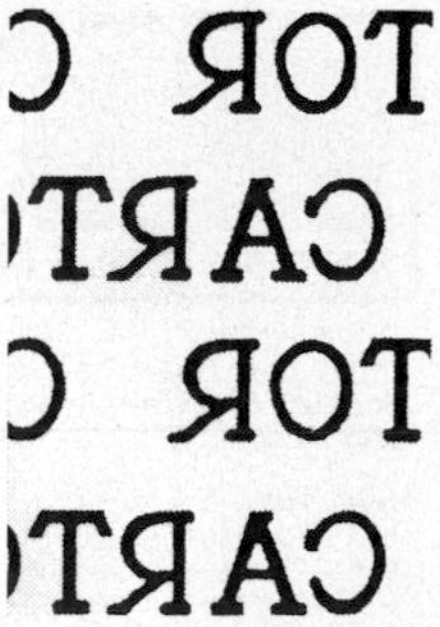

Wmk. 385

Handstamped on Stamps of French Colonies

1892 **Unwmk.** *Perf. 14x13½*

Black Overprint

1	A9	1c blk, *bluish*	200.00	170.00
2	A9	2c brn, *buff*	180.00	150.00
3	A9	4c claret, *lav*	120.00	80.00
4	A9	5c grn, *grnsh*	40.00	32.50
5	A9	10c blk, *lavender*	100.00	80.00
6	A9	15c blue	40.00	32.50
7	A9	20c red, *grn*	250.00	220.00
8	A9	25c blk, *rose*	125.00	80.00
9	A9	30c brn, *yelsh*	225.00	200.00
10	A9	35c blk, *orange*	225.00	200.00
11	A9	40c red, *straw*	200.00	180.00
12	A9	75c car, *rose*	500.00	350.00
13	A9	1fr brnz grn, *straw*	475.00	400.00

Red Overprint

14	A9	15c blue	120.00	100.00

Blue Overprint

15	A9	5c grn, *grnsh*	2,600.	1,200.
15A	A9	15c blue	2,600.	1,200.

For inverted overprints and double overprints and pairs, one without overprint, see the *Scott Classic Specialized Catalogue.*

The overprints of Nos. 1-15A are of four types, three without accent on "E." They exist diagonal.

Counterfeits exist of Nos. 1-19.

Additional Surcharge in Red or Black

1892

16	A9	01c on 5c grn, *grnsh*	360.00	275.00
a.		Double surcharge	1,000.	1,000.
17	A9	40c on 15c blue	225.00	120.00
a.		Double surcharge		*3,800.*
18	A9	75c on 15c blue	1,000.	600.00
19	A9	75c on 15c bl (Bk)	3,500.	2,800.

Counterfeits exist.

Navigation and Commerce — A3

1893 **Typo.** *Perf. 14x13½*

Name of Colony in Blue or Carmine

20	A3	1c blk, *bluish*	5.25	3.25
21	A3	2c brn, *buff*	6.75	4.75
22	A3	4c claret, *lav*	6.75	4.75
23	A3	5c grn, *grnsh*	8.00	5.50
24	A3	10c blk, *lavender*	10.00	6.50
a.		Name of country omitted		*6,500.*
25	A3	15c blue, quadrille paper	40.00	27.50
26	A3	20c red, *grn*	20.00	16.00
27	A3	25c blk, *rose*	52.50	32.50
28	A3	30c brn, *bis*	27.50	21.00
29	A3	40c red, *straw*	8.00	5.50
30	A3	50c car, *rose*	8.00	7.25
31	A3	75c vio, *org*	12.50	12.50
32	A3	1fr brnz grn, *straw*	72.50	72.50
		Nos. 20-32 (13)	277.75	219.50

Perf. 13½x14 stamps are counterfeits.

Navigation and Commerce — A4

1894 *Perf. 14x13½*

33	A4	1c blk, *bluish*	2.50	3.25
34	A4	2c brn, *buff*	4.00	3.25
35	A4	4c claret, *lav*	4.00	3.25
36	A4	5c grn, *grnsh*	6.50	4.00
37	A4	10c blk, *lavender*	7.25	5.50
38	A4	15c bl, quadrille paper	16.00	4.75
39	A4	20c red, *grn*	12.00	9.50
40	A4	25c blk, *rose*	16.00	7.25
41	A4	30c brn, *bis*	12.00	10.50
42	A4	40c red, *straw*	24.00	16.00
43	A4	50c car, *rose*	32.50	16.00
44	A4	75c vio, *org*	32.50	14.50
45	A4	1fr brnz grn, *straw*	8.00	6.50
		Nos. 33-45 (13)	177.25	104.25

Perf. 13½x14 stamps are counterfeits.

PEOPLE'S REPUBLIC OF BENIN

LOCATION — West Coast of Africa
GOVT. — Republic.
AREA — 43,483 sq. mi.
POP. — 6,305,567 (1999 est.)
CAPITAL — Porto Novo (Cotonou is the seat of government)

The Republic of Dahomey proclaimed itself the People's Republic of Benin on Nov. 30, 1975. See Dahomey for stamps issued before then. The country became the Republic of Benin in 1990.

Catalogue values for unused stamps in this section are for Never Hinged items.

Allamanda Cathartica — A83

Flowers: 35fr, Ixora coccinea. 45fr, Hibiscus, 60fr, Phaemeria magnifica.

Unwmk.

1975, Dec. 8 **Photo.** *Perf. 13*

342	A83	10fr lilac & multi	.45	.35
343	A83	35fr gray & multi	1.00	.50
344	A83	45fr multi	1.20	.65
345	A83	60fr blue & multi	1.75	1.00
		Nos. 342-345 (4)	4.40	2.50

For surcharges see Nos. 612, 618, 690B, 719, 723, 788, 1364, 1413, 1416, 1418, 1463, Q18A.

Flag Bearers, Arms of Benin — A84

Design: 60fr, Pres. Kerekou, map with "PRPB," flag and arms of Benin. 100fr, Flag and arms of Benin.

1976, Apr. 30 **Litho.** *Perf. 12*

346	A84	50fr ocher & multi	.70	.35
347	A84	60fr ocher & multi	1.10	.35
348	A84	100fr multi	1.75	.70
		Nos. 346-348 (3)	3.55	1.40

Proclamation of the People's Republic of Benin. Nov. 30, 1975.

For surcharge, see No. Q16A.

A.G. Bell, Satellite and 1876 Telephone — A85

1976, July 9 **Litho.** *Perf. 13*

349	A85	200fr lilac, red & brn	2.50	1.50

Centenary of first telephone call by Alexander Graham Bell, Mar. 10, 1876.

For overprints, see Nos. Q16, Q16A and Q16B.

Dahomey Nos. 277-278 Surcharged

1976, July 19 **Photo.** *Perf. 12½x13*

350	A57	50fr on 1fr multi	.70	.35
351	A57	60fr on 2fr multi	.80	.45

For overprint & surcharge see Nos. 654A, 711.

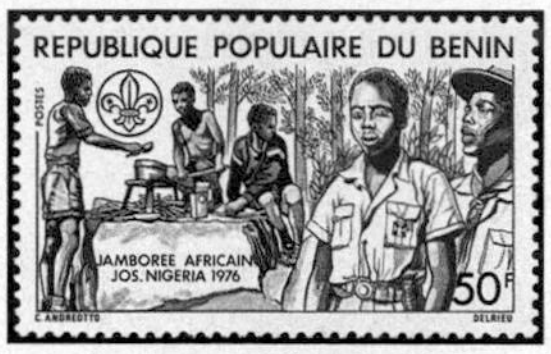

African Jamboree, Nigeria 1976 — A86

1976, Aug. 16 **Litho.** *Perf. 12½x13*

352	A86	50fr Scouts Cooking	.70	.45
353	A86	70fr Three scouts	.90	.50

For surcharge, see No. 446C.

Blood Bank, Cotonou — A87

Designs: 50fr, Accident and first aid station. 60fr, Blood donation.

1976, Sept. 24 **Litho.** *Perf. 13*

354	A87	5fr multicolored	.25	.25
355	A87	50fr multicolored	.55	.35
356	A87	60fr multicolored	1.00	.55
		Nos. 354-356 (3)	1.80	1.15

National Blood Donors Day.

For overprint, see No. Q12.

A88

1976, Oct. 4 **Litho.** *Perf. 13x12½*

357	A88	20fr Manioc	.40	.25
358	A88	50fr Corn	.75	.35
359	A88	60fr Cacao	1.00	.45
360	A88	150fr Cotton	2.25	1.10
		Nos. 357-360 (4)	4.40	2.15

Natl. agricultural production campaign.

For overprint and surcharges see Nos. 565, Q10C, Q19.

Classroom A89

1976, Oct. 25

361 A89 50fr multicolored 1.00 .50

Third anniversary of KPARO newspaper, used in local language studies.

Roan Antelope — A90

Penhari National Park: 30fr, Buffalo. 50fr, Hippopotamus, horiz. 70fr, Lion.

1976, Nov. 8 **Photo.**

362 A90 10fr multicolored .35 .25
363 A90 30fr multicolored .70 .65
364 A90 50fr multicolored 1.60 1.00
365 A90 70fr multicolored 1.75 1.20
Nos. 362-365 (4) 4.40 3.10

For surcharge, see No. Q11A.

Flags, Map of Benin (Bricks), Broken Chains — A91

150fr, Corn, raised hands with weapons.

1976, Nov. 30 **Litho.** ***Perf. 12½***

366 A91 40fr multicolored .50 .25
367 A91 150fr multicolored 1.75 .90

First anniversary of proclamation of the People's Republic of Benin.
For surcharge, see No. Q14.

Table Tennis, Map of Africa (Games' Emblem) — A92

Design: 50fr, Stadium, Cotonou.

1976, Dec. 26 **Litho.** ***Perf. 13***

368 A92 10fr multi .40 .25
369 A92 50fr multi .60 .25

West African University Games, Cotonou, Dec. 26-31.
For overprint, see No. Q25.

Europafrica Issue

Planes over Africa and Europe — A93

1977, May 13 **Litho.** ***Perf. 13***

370 A93 200fr multi 2.50 2.25

For surcharge see No. 590.

Snake A94

1977, June 13 **Litho.** ***Perf. 13x13½***

371 A94 2fr shown .40 .25
372 A94 3fr Tortoise .50 .25
373 A94 5fr Zebus .60 .25
374 A94 10fr Cats 1.00 .25
Nos. 371-374 (4) 2.50 1.00

For surcharges, see Nos. 446A-446B.

Patients at Clinic A95

1977, Aug. 2 **Litho.** ***Perf. 12½***

375 A95 100fr multi 1.75 .80

World Rheumatism Year.
For overprint, see No. Q21.

Karate, Map of Africa — A96

Designs: 100fr, Javelin, map of Africa, Benin Flag, horiz. 150fr, Hurdles.

1977, Aug. 30 **Litho.** ***Perf. 12½***

376 A96 90fr multi 1.20 .60
377 A96 100fr multi 1.20 .80
378 A96 150fr multi 1.90 1.00
a. Souvenir sheet of 3, #376-378 6.25 6.25
Nos. 376-378 (3) 4.30 2.40

2nd West African Games, Lagos, Nigeria.
For surcharges, see Nos. 925, Q20, Q20A, Q33.

Chairman Mao — A97

1977, Sept. 9 **Litho.** ***Perf. 13x12½***

379 A97 100fr multicolored 3.75 2.10

Mao Tse-tung (1893-1976), Chinese communist leader.

Lister and Vaporizer — A98

Designs: 150fr, Scalpels and flames, symbols of antisepsis, and Red Cross.

1977, Sept. 20 **Engr.** ***Perf. 13***

380 A98 150fr multi 1.60 .80
381 A98 210fr multi 2.00 1.40

Joseph Lister (1827-1912), surgeon, founder of antiseptic surgery.
For surcharges see Nos. 560, 566, 919.

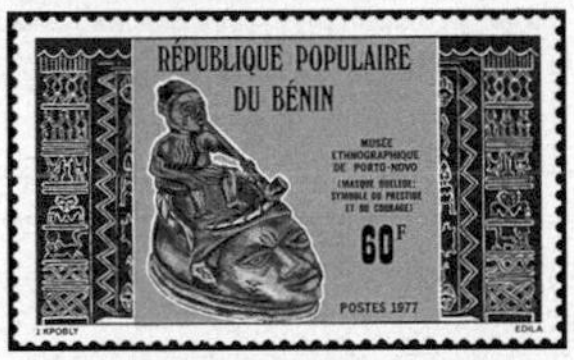
Guelege Mask, Ethnographic Museum, Porto Novo — A99

Designs: 50fr, Jar, symbol of unity, emblem of King Ghezo, Historical Museum, Abomey, vert. 210fr, Abomey Museum.

1977, Oct. 17 ***Perf. 13***

382 A99 50fr red & multi .75 .50
383 A99 60fr blk, bl & bister 1.25 .60
384 A99 210fr multi 3.00 1.40
Nos. 382-384 (3) 5.00 2.50

For surcharge see Nos. 562, 920.

Atacora Falls — A100

Tourist Publicity: 60fr, Pile houses, Ganvie, horiz. 150fr, Round huts, Savalou.

1977, Oct. 24 **Litho.** ***Perf. 12½***

385 A100 50fr multi .60 .35
386 A100 60fr multi .90 .55
387 A100 150fr multi 2.00 1.20
a. Souvenir sheet of 3, #385-387 5.50 5.50
Nos. 385-387 (3) 3.50 2.10

Mother and Child, Owl of Wisdom — A101

150fr, Chopping down magical tree, horiz.

Perf. 12½x13, 13x12½

1977, Dec. 3 **Photo.**

388 A101 60fr multi 1.00 .50
389 A101 150fr multi 2.00 1.00

Campaign against witchcraft.
For surcharge see No. 576.

Battle Scene — A102

1978, Jan. 16 **Litho.** ***Perf. 12½***

390 A102 50fr multi 1.15 .45

Victory of people of Benin over imperialist forces.

Map, People and Houses of Benin — A103

1978, Feb. 1

391 A103 50fr multi .75 .40

General population and dwelling census.

Alexander Fleming, Microscope and Penicillin — A104

1978, Mar. 12 **Litho.** ***Perf. 13***

392 A104 300fr multi 4.00 2.00

Alexnader Fleming (1881-1955), 50th anniversary of discovery of penicillin.

Abdoulaye Issa, Weapons and Fighters A105

1978, Apr. 1 ***Perf. 12½x13***

393 A105 100fr red, blk & gold 1.25 .60

First anniversary of death of Abdoulaye Issa and National Day of Benin's Youth.

El Hadj Omar and Horseback Rider — A106

Design: 90fr, L'Almamy Samory Toure (1830-1900) and horseback riders.

1978, Apr. 10 ***Perf. 13x12½***

394 A106 90fr red & multi 1.25 .50
395 A106 100fr multi 1.25 .60

African heroes of resistance against colonialism.
For surcharge see No. 1008.

ITU Emblem, Satellite, Landscape — A107

1978, May 17 Litho. *Perf. 13*

396	A107	100fr multi	1.50	.80

10th World Telecommunications Day.

Soccer Player, Stadium, Argentina '78 Emblem — A108

Designs (Argentina '78 Emblem and): 300fr, Soccer players and ball, vert. 500fr, Soccer player, globe with ball on map.

1978, June 1 Litho. *Perf. 12½*

397	A108	200fr multi	2.10	1.10
398	A108	300fr multi	2.75	1.60
399	A108	500fr multi	5.00	2.75
a.		Souvenir sheet of 3, perf. 12	13.50	12.50
		Nos. 397-399 (3)	9.85	5.45

11th World Cup Soccer Championship, Argentina, June 1-25. No. 399a contains 3 stamps similar to Nos. 397-399 in changed colors.

For surcharges and overprints see Nos. 591, 593, 595, 1477.

Nos. 397-399a Overprinted in Red Brown

a

b

c

1978, June 25 Litho. *Perf. 12½*

400	A108 (a)	200fr multi	1.75	1.20
401	A108 (b)	300fr multi	2.60	2.00
402	A108 (c)	500fr multi	5.00	3.25
a.		Souvenir sheet of 3	13.50	12.50
		Nos. 400-402 (3)	9.35	6.45

Argentina's victory in 1978 Soccer Championship.

For surcharges and overprints, see Nos. 596, 591A, 1478.

Games' Flag over Africa, Basketball Players — A109

Designs: 60fr, Map of Africa, volleyball players. 80fr, Map of Benin, bicyclists.

1978, July 13 *Perf. 13x12½*

403	A109	50fr lt bl & multi	.55	.25
404	A109	60fr ultra & multi	.80	.45
405	A109	80fr multi	1.00	.55
a.		Souvenir sheet of 3	3.50	3.50
		Nos. 403-405 (3)	2.35	1.25

3rd African Games, Algiers, July 13-28. No. 405a contains 3 stamps in changed colors similar to Nos. 403-405.

Martin Luther King, Jr. — A110

1978, July 30 *Perf. 12½*

406	A110	300fr multi	3.00	1.50

Martin Luther King, Jr. (1929-1968), American civil rights leader.

For surcharge see No. 592.

Kanna Taxi, Oueme A111

60fr Leatherworker & goods. 70fr, Drummer & tom-toms. 100fr, Metalworker & calabashes.

1978, Aug. 26

407	A111	50fr multi	1.10	.30
408	A111	60fr multi	.90	.30
409	A111	70fr multi	1.10	.50
410	A111	100fr multi	1.35	.65
		Nos. 407-410 (4)	4.45	1.75

Getting to know Benin through its provinces.

Map of Italy and Exhibition Poster — A112

1978, Aug. 26 Litho. *Perf. 13*

411	A112	200fr multi	2.25	1.10

Riccione 1978 Philatelic Exhibition.

For overprint see No. 537.

Poultry Breeding — A113

1978 Oct. 5 Photo. *Perf. 12½x13*

412	A113	10fr Turkeys	.35	.25
413	A113	20fr Ducks	.75	.30
414	A113	50fr Chicken	2.10	.70
415	A113	60fr Guinea fowl	2.25	.90
		Nos. 412-415 (4)	5.45	2.15

Royal Messenger, UPU Emblem — A114

UPU Emblem and: 60fr, Boatsman, ship & car. 90fr, Special messenger & plane.

1978, Oct. 16 *Perf. 13x12½, 12½x13*

416	A114	50fr multi	1.10	.35
417	A114	60fr multi, vert.	1.10	.45
418	A114	90fr multi, vert.	1.25	.60
		Nos. 416-418 (3)	3.45	1.40

Centenary of change of "General Postal Union" to "Universal Postal Union."

For surcharge see No. 1009.

Raoul Follereau A115

1978, Dec. 17 Litho. *Perf. 12½*

419	A115	200fr multi	1.75	1.00

Raoul Follereau (1903-1977), apostle to the lepers and educator of the blind.

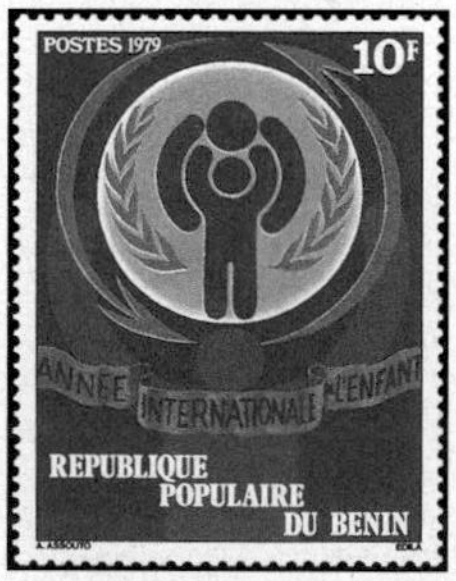

IYC Emblem A116

Intl. Year of the Child: 20fr, Globe as balloon carrying childern. 50fr, Children of various races surrounding globe.

1979, Feb. 20 Litho. *Perf. 12x13*

420	A116	10fr multi	.25	.25
421	A116	20fr multi	.25	.25
422	A116	50fr multi	.40	.25
		Nos. 420-422 (3)	.90	.75

Hydrangea — A117

Flowers: 25fr, Assangokan. 30fr, Geranium. 40fr, Water lilies, horiz.

Perf. 13x12½, 12½x13

1979, Feb. 28 Litho.

423	A117	20fr multi	.25	.25
424	A117	25fr multi	.55	.25
425	A117	30fr multi	.90	.35
426	A117	40fr mutli	1.00	.35
		Nos. 423-426 (4)	2.70	1.20

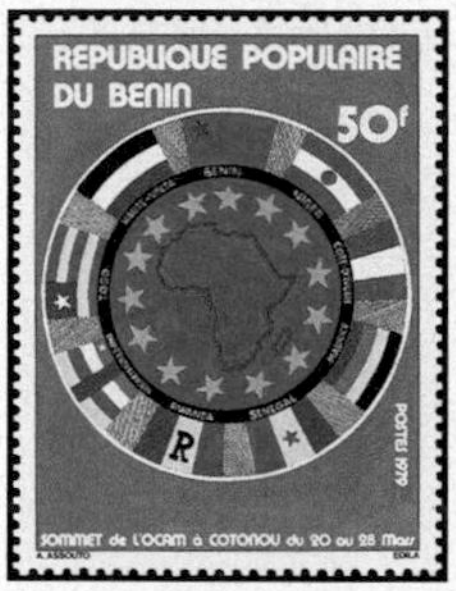

Emblem: Map of Africa and Members' Flags A118

60fr, Map of Benin & flags. 80fr, OCAM flag & map of Africa showing member states.

1979, Mar. 20 Litho. *Perf. 12x13*

427	A118	50fr multi	.50	.25
428	A118	60fr multi	.85	.40
429	A118	80fr multi	1.05	.60
		Nos. 427-429 (3)	2.40	1.25

OCAM Summit Conf., Cotonou, Mar. 20-28.

For overprints see Nos. 434-436.

Tower, Waves, Satellite, ITU Emblem A119

1979, May 17 Litho. *Perf. 12½*

430	A119	50fr multi	.85	.50

World Telecommunications Day.

Bank Building and Sculpture A120

1979, May 26 Litho.

431	A120	50fr multi	1.50	.50

Opening of Headquarters of West African Savings Bank in Dakar.

Guelede Mask, Abomey Tapestry, Malaconotus Bird — A121

Design: 50fr, Jet, canoe, satellite, UPU and exhibition emblems.

1979, June 8 **Litho.** ***Perf. 13***

432 A121 15fr multi 1.75 .80

Engr.

433 A121 50fr multi 1.50 1.00

Philexafrique II, Libreville, Gabon, June 8-17. Nos. 432, 433 each printed in sheets of 10 with 5 labels showing exhibition emblem.

For surcharges, see Nos. 1061A-1061C.

Nos. 427-429 Overprinted

1979, June 26

434 A118 50fr multi .70 .35
435 A118 60fr multi .90 .55
436 A118 80fr multi 1.10 .55
Nos. 434-436 (3) 2.70 1.45

2nd OCAM Summit Conf., June 26-28.

Olympic Flame, and Emblems A122

Pre-Olympic Year: 50fr, High jump.

1979, July 1 **Litho.**

437 A122 10fr multi .25 .25
438 A122 50fr multi 1.00 .45

Antelope A123

Animals: 10fr, Giraffes, map of Benin, vert 20fr, Chimpanzee. 50fr, Elephants, map of Benin, vert.

1979, Oct. 1 **Litho.** ***Perf. 13***

439 A123 5fr multi .35 .25
440 A123 10fr multi .45 .30
441 A123 20fr multi .70 .45
442 A123 50fr multi 1.60 .65
Nos. 439-442 (4) 3.10 1.65

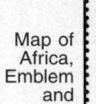

Map of Africa, Emblem and Jet — A124

1979, Dec. 12 **Litho.** ***Perf. 12½***

443 A124 50fr multi .50 .25
444 A124 60fr multi .50 .25

ASECNA (Air Safety Board), 20th anniv.

Mail Services A125

50fr, Post Office and headquarters, vert.

1979, Dec. 19 **Litho.** ***Perf. 13***

445 A125 50fr multi .50 .25
446 A125 60fr multi .50 .25

Office of Posts and Telecommunications, 20th anniversary.

Nos. 353, 371-372 Surcharged

No. 446B

Methods and Perfs As Before

1979

446A A94 50fr on 2fr #371 1.00 40.00
446B A94 50fr on 3fr #372 125.00 40.00
446C A66 50fr on 70fr #353 —

Lenin and Globe — A126

Design: 150fr, Lenin and his published books.

1980, Apr. 22 **Litho.** ***Perf. 12½***

447 A126 50fr shown .65 .25
448 A126 150fr multicolored 1.60 .80

Lenin, 110th birth anniversary.

For surcharge, see No. Q8.

Monument to King Behanzin — A126a

Litho. & Embossed

1980, May 31 ***Perf. 12½***

448A A126a 1000fr gold & multi 9.00 7.00

For overprint see No. Q10A.

Cotonou Club Emlem — A127

200fr, Rotary emblem on globe, horiz.

1980, Feb. 23 **Litho.** ***Perf. 12½***

449 A127 90fr shown .75 .45
450 A127 200fr multicolored 1.75 .95

Rotary International, 75th anniversary.

For surcharge see No. 915.

Galileo, Astrolabe — A128

100fr, Copernicus, solar system.

1980, Apr. 2

451 A128 70fr shown .75 .45
452 A128 100fr multicolored 1.00 .50

Discovery of Pluto, 50th anniversary.

Abu Simbel, UNESCO Emblem — A129

1980, Apr. 15 ***Perf. 13***

453 A129 50fr Column, vert. .60 .25
454 A129 60fr Ramses II, vert. .70 .40
455 A129 150fr shown 1.50 .80
Nos. 453-455 (3) 2.80 1.45

UNESCO campaign to save Nubian monuments, 20h anniversary.

Monument, Martyrs' Square, Cotonou A130

Designs: Various monuments in Martyrs' Square. Cotonou. 60fr, 70fr, 100fr, horiz.

1980, May 2 ***Perf. 12½x13, 13x12½***

456 A130 50fr multi .40 .25
457 A130 60fr multi .50 .25
458 A130 70fr multi .55 .30
459 A130 100fr multi .95 .50
Nos. 456-459 (4) 2.40 1.30

For overprint, see No. Q9. For surcharge see No. 539.

Musical Instruments — A131

5fr, Assan, vert. 10fr, Tinbo. 15fr, Tam-tam sato, vert. 20fr, Kora. 30fr, Gangan. 50fr, Sinhoun.

1980, May 20 ***Perf. 12½***

460 A131 5fr multicolored .25 .25
461 A131 10fr multicolored .30 .25
462 A131 15fr multicolored .45 .25
463 A131 20fr multicolored .45 .25
464 A131 30fr multicolored 1.00 .40
465 A131 50fr multicolored 1.50 .60
Nos. 460-465 (6) 3.95 2.00

First Non-stop Flight, Paris-New York — A132

100fr, Dieudonnée Costes, Maurice Bellonte.

1980, June 2 **Litho.** ***Perf. 12½***

466 A132 90fr shown 1.00 .60
467 A132 100fr multicolored 1.00 .60

For surcharges see Nos. 564, 926.

Lunokhod I on the Moon — A133

1980, June 15 **Engr.** ***Perf. 13***

468 A133 90fr multi .80 .50

Lunokhod I Soviet unmanned moon mission, 10th anniv. See No. C290.

Olympic Flame and Mischa, Moscow '80 Emblem — A134

60fr, Equestrian, vert. 70fr, Judo. 200fr, Flag, sports, globe, vert. 300fr, Weight lifting, vert.

1980, July 16 **Litho.** ***Perf. 12½***

469 A134 50fr shown .50 .25
470 A134 60fr multicolored .50 .35
471 A134 70fr multicolored .70 .45
472 A134 200fr multicolored 1.60 .90
473 A134 300fr multicolored 2.50 1.50
Nos. 469-473 (5) 5.80 3.45

22nd Summer Olympic Games, Moscow, July 19-Aug. 3.

For overprint, see No. Q10. For surcharges see Nos. 559, 561.

Telephone and Rising Sun
A135

World Telecommunications Day: 50fr, Farmer on telephone, vert.

1980, May 17 Litho. *Perf. 12½*
474 A135 50fr multi .50 .30
475 A135 60fr multi .50 .30

Cotonou West African Community Village
A136

Designs: View of Cotonou.

1980, July 26 *Perf. 13x13½*
476 A136 50fr multi .55 .30
477 A136 60fr multi .55 .35
478 A136 70fr multi .85 .70
Nos. 476-478 (3) 1.95 1.35

For surcharges, see Nos. 539A, 540.

Agbadja Dancers — A137

Designs: Dancers and muscians.

1980, Aug. 1 *Perf. 12½*
479 A137 30fr multi .50 .25
480 A137 50fr multi .80 .45
481 A137 60fr multi .80 .50
Nos. 479-481 (3) 2.10 1.20

Fisherman — A138

Designs: 5fr, Throwing net. 15fr, Canoe and shore fishing. 20fr, Basket traps. 50fr, Hauling net. 60fr, River fishing. All horiz.

1980, Sept. 1
482 A138 5fr multi .25 .25
483 A138 10fr multi .40 .25
484 A138 15fr multi .40 .25
485 A138 20fr multi .50 .25
486 A138 50fr multi .90 .45
487 A138 60fr multi 1.10 .45
Nos. 482-487 (6) 3.55 1.90

For surcharge see No. 535.

Philippines under Magnifier — A139

World Tourism Conference, Manila, Sept. 27: 60fr, Emblem on flag, hand pointing to Manila on globe, horiz.

Perf. 13x13½, 13x½x13
1980, Sept. 27
488 A139 50fr multi .50 .25
489 A139 60fr multi .80 .35

For surcharge see No. 557.

A140

40fr, Othreis materna. 50fr, Othreis fullonia. 200fr, Oryctes sp.

1980, Oct. 1 *Perf. 12½*
490 A140 40fr multicolored 1.10 .40
491 A140 50fr multicolored 1.50 .60
492 A140 200fr multicolored 4.50 1.50
Nos. 490-492 (3) 7.10 2.50

A141

1980, Oct. 24 Photo. *Perf. 13½*
493 A141 75fr multi .65 .25

African Postal Union, 5th Anniv.

A142

1980, Nov. 4 *Perf. 12½x13*
494 A142 30fr shown .25 .25
495 A142 50fr Freed prisoner .60 .25
496 A142 60fr Man holding torch .65 .30
Nos. 494-496 (3) 1.50 .80

Declaration of human rights, 30th anniv.
For surcharges, see Nos. Q14A, Q15.

A143

Self-portrait, by Vincent van Gogh, 1888.

1980, Dec. 1 Litho. *Perf. 13*
497 A143 100fr shown 2.75 .80
498 A143 300fr Facteur Roulin 7.00 2.25

Vincent van Gogh (1853-1890), artist.
For surcharge see No. 579.

Offenbach and Scene from Orpheus in the Underworld — A144

1980, Dec. 15 Engr.
499 A144 50fr shown 1.25 .70
500 A144 60fr Paris Life 1.75 .90

Jacques Offenbach (1819-1880), composer.
For surcharges, see Nos. Q13, Q13A.

Kepler and Satellites — A145

50fr, Kepler, diagram, vert.

1980, Dec. 20
501 A145 50fr multicolored .70 .35
502 A145 60fr shown .80 .50

Johannes Kepler (1571-1630), astronomer.

Intl. Year of the Disabled — A146

1981, Apr. 10 Litho. *Perf. 12½*
503 A146 115fr multi 1.10 .60

For surcharge see No. 582.

20th Anniv. of Manned Space Flight — A147

1981, May 30 *Perf. 13*
504 A147 500fr multi 5.00 3.00

For surcharges see Nos. 580, 790.

13th World Telecommunications Day — A148

1981, May 30 Litho. *Perf. 12½*
505 A148 115fr multi 1.10 .50

For surcharge see No. 583.

Amaryllis
A149

20fr, Eichhornia crassipes, vert. 80fr, Parkia biglobosa, vert.

1981, June 20 *Perf. 12½*
506 A149 10fr shown .30 .25
507 A149 20fr multicolored .55 .35
508 A149 80fr multicolored 2.00 .50
Nos. 506-508 (3) 2.85 1.10

For surcharge see No. 542.

Benin Sheraton Hotel
A150

1981, July
509 A150 100fr multi 1.10 .50

For surcharge see No. 541.

Guinea Pig — A151

1981, July 31 *Perf. 13x13½*
510 A151 5fr shown .50 .35
511 A151 60fr Cat 1.25 .60
512 A151 80fr Dogs 1.75 1.00
Nos. 510-512 (3) 3.50 1.95

For surcharges see Nos. 536, 543, 563.

World UPU Day — A152

1981, Oct. 9 Engr. *Perf. 13*
513 A152 100fr red brn & blk .90 .50

25th Intl. Letter Writing Week, Oct. 6-12 — A153

1981, Oct. 15
514 A153 100fr dk bl & pur .90 .50

For surcharge see No. 558.

West African Economic Community
A154

1981, Nov. 20 Litho. *Perf. 12½*
515 A154 60fr multi .75 .30

West African Rice Development Assoc. 10th Anniv. — A155

1981, Dec. 10 *Perf. 13x13½*
516 A155 60fr multi .75 .30

TB Bacillus Centenary A156

1982, Mar. 1 Litho. *Perf. 13*
517 A156 115fr multi 1.50 .75

For surcharge see No. 584.

West African Economic Community, 5th Summit Conference A157

1982, May 27 *Perf. 12½*
518 A157 60fr multi .60 .30

1982 World Cup — A158

1982, June 1 *Perf. 13*
519 A158 90fr Players .80 .45
520 A158 300fr Flags on leg 2.90 1.25

For overprints and surcharges see Nos. 523-524, 594, 789.

France No. B349 Magnified, Map of France — A159

1982, June 11
521 A159 90fr multi .90 .50

For surcharge see No. 916.

PHILEXFRANCE '82 Stamp Exhibition, Paris, June 11-21.

George Washington — A160

200fr, Washington, flag, map.

1982, Mar. 10 Litho. *Perf. 14*
522 A160 200fr multicolored 2.25 1.00

For surcharge see No. 577.

Nos. 519-520 Overprinted

1982, Aug. 16 *Perf. 12½*
523 A158 90fr multi 1.10 .50
524 A158 300fr multi 3.50 1.50

Italy's victory in 1982 World Cup.
For surcharges, see Nos. 594A, 811.

Bluethroat A161

5fr, Daoelo gigas, vert. 15fr, Swallow, vert. 20fr, Kingfisher, weaver bird, vert. 30fr, Great sedge warbler. 60fr, Common warbler. 80fr, Owl, vert. 100fr, Cockatoo, vert.

1982, Sept. 1 *Perf. 14x14½, 14½x14*

525	A161	5fr	multicolored	.95	.45
526	A161	10fr	shown	1.40	.45
527	A161	15fr	multicolored	1.40	.45
528	A161	20fr	multicolored	2.10	.60
529	A161	30fr	multicolored	3.25	.80
530	A161	60fr	multicolored	4.75	1.10
531	A161	80fr	multicolored	8.25	2.50
532	A161	100fr	multicolored	10.50	3.25
			Nos. 525-532 (8)	32.60	9.60

ITU Plenipotentiaries Conference, Nairobi, Sept. — A162

1982, Sept. 26 *Perf. 13*
533 A162 200fr Map 2.00 1.00

For surcharge see No. 585.

13th World UPU Day — A163

1982, Oct. 9 Engr. *Perf. 13*
534 A163 100fr Monument 1.10 .45

Nos. 482, 510, 411 Overprinted in Red or Blue

No. 535

No. 536 — "UAPT 1982" 3mm tall

No. 537

Perf. 13, 12½, 13x13½

1982, Nov. **Litho.**

535	A138	60fr on 5fr multi		8.00	4.00
536	A151	60fr on 5fr multi		4.00	3.00
a.		"UAPT 1982" 2mm tall		*20.00*	*10.00*
537	A112	200fr multi (Bl)		1.75	.75
		Nos. 535-537 (3)		13.75	7.75

Visit of French Pres. Francois Mitterrand A164

1983, Jan. 15 Litho. *Perf. 12½x13*
538 A164 90fr multi 1.50 .75

For surcharge see No. 917.

Nos. 458, 476, 508-509, 512 Surcharged

No. 539

No. 540

No. 541

No. 542

No. 543

Perf. 13x12½, 13x13½, 12½

1983 **Litho.**

539	A130	60fr on 70fr multi	2.00	.70
540	A136	60fr on 50fr multi	2.00	.70
541	A150	60fr on 100fr multi	2.00	.95
542	A149	75fr on 80fr multi	2.00	1.40
543	A151	75fr on 80fr multi	2.00	1.40
		Nos. 539-543 (5)	10.00	5.15

Seme Oil Rig — A165

1983, Apr. 28 Litho. *Perf. 13x12½*
544 A165 125fr multi 1.50 .70

World Communications Year — A166

1983, May 17 Litho. *Perf. 13*
545 A166 185fr multi 1.75 .75

For surcharge see No. 898.

Riccione '83, Stamp Show — A167

1983, Aug. 27 Litho. *Perf. 13*
546 A167 500fr multi 4.50 2.00

For surcharge see No. 922.

Benin Red Cross, 20th Anniv. A168

1983, Sept. 5 Photo. *Perf. 13*
547 A168 105fr multi 1.10 .60

For surcharge see No. 581.

Handicrafts A169

Designs: 75fr, Handcarved lion chairs and table. 90fr, Natural tree table and stools. 200fr, Monkeys holding jar.

1983, Sept. 18 Litho. *Perf. 13*

548	A169	75fr multi	.85	.35
549	A169	90fr multi	1.15	.45
550	A169	200fr multi	1.75	.85
		Nos. 548-550 (3)	3.75	1.65

For surcharge see No. 578.

14th UPU Day — A170

1983, Oct. 9 Engr. *Perf. 13*
551 A170 125fr multi 1.10 .70

For surcharge see No. 575.

Religious Movements A171

1983, Oct. 31 Litho. *Perf. 14x15*

552	A171 75fr Zangbeto	1.00	.50
553	A171 75fr Egoun	1.00	.50

Plaited Hair Styles — A172

1983, Nov. 14

554	A172 30fr Rockcoco	.25	.25
555	A172 75fr Serpent	.65	.50
556	A172 90fr Songas	1.15	.60
	Nos. 554-556 (3)	2.05	1.35

Stamps of 1976-81 Surcharged

No. 557

No. 558

No. 559

No. 560

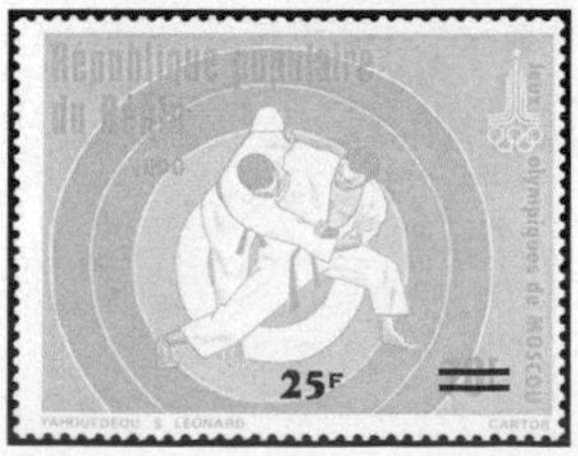

No. 561

No. 562

No. 563

No. 564

No. 565

No. 566

1983, Nov.

557	A139	5fr on 50fr #488	3.00	1.00
558	A153	10fr on 100fr #514	3.00	1.00
559	A134	15fr on 200fr #472	4.00	1.00
560	A98	15fr on 210fr #381	4.00	1.00
561	A134	25fr on 70fr #471	5.00	1.00
562	A99	25fr on 210fr #384	5.00	1.00
563	A151	75fr on 5fr #510	6.00	1.00
564	A132	75fr on 100fr #467	6.00	1.00
565	A88	75fr on 150fr #360	6.00	1.00
566	A98	75fr on 150fr #380	6.00	1.00
		Nos. 557-566 (10)	48.00	10.00

Alfred Nobel (1833-96) A173

1983, Dec. 19 Litho. *Perf. 15x14*

567	A173 300fr multi	3.00	1.40

For surcharge see No. 923.

Council of Unity — A174

1984, May 29 Litho. *Perf. 12*

568	A174 75fr multi	.75	.30
569	A174 90fr multi	.90	.35

For surcharge see No. 918.

1984 UPU Congress A175

1984, June 18 Litho. *Perf. 13*

570	A175 90fr multi	.90	.50

Abomey Calavi Earth Station A176

1984, June 29 Litho. *Perf. 12½x13*

571	A176 75fr Satellite dish	.75	.45

Traditional Costumes A177

1984, July 2 Litho. *Perf. 13½x13*

572	A177 5fr Koumboro	.25	.25
573	A177 10fr Taka	.35	.25
574	A177 20fr Toko	.40	.25
	Nos. 572-574 (3)	1.00	.75

Nos. 389, 498, 503-505, 517, 522, 533, 547, 550 and 551 Surcharged

No. 575

No. 576

No. 577

No. 578

No. 579

No. 580

No. 581

No. 582

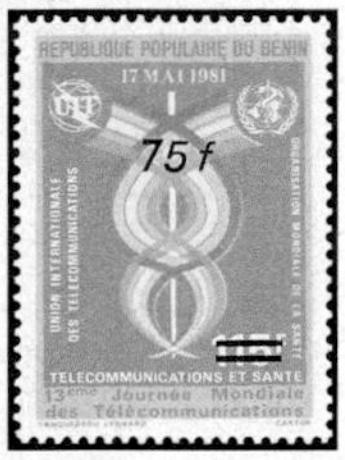

No. 583

No. 584

No. 585

1984, Sept.

575	A170	5fr on 125fr #551	5.00	1.00
576	A101	5fr on 150fr #389	5.00	1.00
577	A160	10fr on 200fr #522	5.00	1.00
578	A169	10fr on 200fr #550	5.00	1.00
579	A143	15fr on 300fr #498	5.00	1.00
580	A147	40fr on 500fr #504	5.00	1.00
581	A168	75fr on 105fr #547	5.00	1.00
582	A146	75fr on 115fr #503	5.00	1.00
583	A148	75fr on 115fr #505	5.00	1.00
584	A156	75fr on 115fr #517	5.00	1.00
585	A162	75fr on 200fr #533	5.00	1.00
		Nos. 575-585 (11)	55.00	11.00

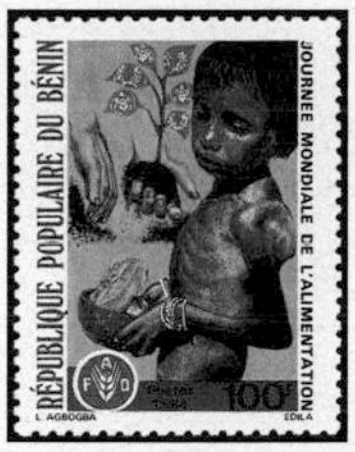

World Food Day — A178

100fr, Malnourished child.

1984, Oct. 16 Litho. *Perf. 12½*
586 A178 100fr multicolored .80 .50

Dinosaurs A179

75fr, Anatosaurus. 90fr, Brontosaurus.

1984, Dec. 14 Litho. *Perf. 13½*
587 A179 75fr multicolored 5.50 1.00
588 A179 90fr multicolored 5.50 1.00

Cultural & Technical Cooperation Agency, 15th Anniv. — A180

300fr, Emblem, globe, hands, book.

1985, Mar 20 Litho. *Perf. 13*
589 A180 300fr multicolored 2.75 1.25

Stamps of 1977-82 Surcharged

No. 590

No. 591

No. 591A

No. 592

No. 593

No. 594

No. 594A

No. 595

No. 596

1985, Mar.

590	A93	75fr on 200fr #370	10.00	2.00
591	A108	75fr on 200fr #397	10.00	2.00
591A	A108(a)	75fr on 200fr #400	*50.00*	*3.00*
592	A110	75fr on 300fr #406	10.00	2.00
593	A108	75fr on 300fr #398	10.00	2.00
594	A158	90fr on 300fr #520	10.00	2.00
594A	A158	90fr on 300fr #524	—	—
595	A108	90fr on 500fr #399	10.00	2.00
596	A108	90fr on 500fr #402	10.00	2.00
		Nos. 590-591,592-596 (7)	70.00	14.00

End of World War II, 40th Anniv. — A180a

1985, May Litho. *Perf. 12*
596A A180a 100fr multicolored 60.00 16.00

Traditional Dances A181

75fr, Teke, Borgou Tribe. 100fr, Tipen'ti, L'Atacora Tribe.

1985, June 1 Litho. *Perf. 15x14½*
597 A181 75fr multicolored 1.00 .50
598 A181 100fr multicolored 1.20 .65

Intl. Youth Year — A182

1985, July 16 *Perf. 13½*
599 A182 150fr multi 1.45 .75

1986 World Cup Soccer Championships, Mexico — A183

1985, July 22 *Perf. 13x12½*
600 A183 200fr multi 1.60 1.00

Beginning with Scott 601, Benin again surcharged stamps of Dahomey with a variety of surcharges. While the listings that follow contain hundreds of surcharged stamps, the Scott editors still need to examine many more other stamps, in order to list all of those that are currently known to exist.

The size and location of the surcharge varies from stamp to stamp. The type face used in the surcharge may also vary from issue to issue.

a

b

c

d

e

f

g

h

i

j

k

Dahomey No. 336 Surcharged with Black Bars and New Value

1985, Aug. ***Perf. 12½***
601 A78(a) 15fr on 40fr multi 4.00 1.00

ASECNA (Air Safety Board), 25th Anniv. — A184

1985, Sept. 16 ***Perf. 13***
602 A184 150fr multi 1.60 .75

UN 40th Anniv. A185

1985, Oct. 24 ***Perf. 12½***
603 A185 250fr multi 2.00 1.00

Benin UN membership, 25th anniv.

ITALIA'85, Rome A186

1985, Oct. 25 ***Perf. 13½***
604 A186 200fr multi 1.60 1.00

PHILEXAFRICA '85, Lome — A187

No. 605, Labor emblem & #569. No. 606, Magnified stamp, #C252 & Gabon #366.

1985, Nov. 16 ***Perf. 13***
605 A187 250fr multi 4.00 2.00
606 A187 250fr multi 3.25 1.75
a. Pair, Nos. 605-606 + label 9.00 9.00

For surcharges, see Nos. 653B-653C.

Audubon Birth Bicent. — A188

1985, Oct. 17 **Litho.** ***Perf. 14x15***
607 A188 150fr Skua gull 3.00 1.50
608 A188 300fr Oyster catcher 7.50 2.50

Mushrooms and Toadstools A189

35fr, Boletus edible. 40fr, Amanite phalloide. 100fr, Brown chanterelle.

1985, Oct. 17
609 A189 35fr multicolored 1.35 .50
610 A189 40fr multicolored 1.75 .90
611 A189 100fr multicolored 4.25 2.00
Nos. 609-611 (3) 7.35 3.40

Dahomey #282, 292, Benin #343 Surcharged

1986, Mar. **Photo.**
612 A83(b) 75fr on 35fr #343 3.75 1.10
613 A57(c) 90fr on 70fr #282 4.50 1.10
614 A60(b) 90fr on 140fr #292 4.50 1.10
Nos. 612-614 (3) 12.75 3.30

African Parliamentary Union, 10th Anniv. — A190

1986, May 8 **Litho.** ***Perf. 13x12½***
615 A190 100fr multi .80 .50

9th Conference, Cotonou, May 8-10.

Halley's Comet — A191

1986, May 30 ***Perf. 12½x12***
616 A191 205fr multi 2.60 1.50

For surcharge see No. 809.

Dahomey No. 283, Benin No. 344 Surcharged

Engraved, Photogravure

1986, June ***Perf. 13***
617 A58(b) 100fr on 40fr #283 3.25 1.00
618 A83(b) 150fr on 45fr #344 3.25 1.00

1986 World Cup Soccer Championships, Mexico — A192

1986, June 29 **Litho.**
619 A192 500fr multi 4.00 2.50

For surcharge see No. 792.

Fight against Desert Encroachment — A193

1986, July 16 ***Perf. 13½***
620 A193 150fr multi 1.40 .75

King Behanzin — A194

Amazon — A194a

1986-88 **Engr.** ***Perf. 13***
621 A194 40fr black .25 .25
622 A194a 100fr brt blue .65 .40
623 A194 125fr maroon .90 .70
624 A194a 150fr violet 1.20 .80
625 A194 190fr dark ultra 1.40 1.00
627 A194 220fr dark grn 1.60 1.25
Nos. 621-627 (6) 6.00 4.40

Issued: 100fr, 150fr, 8/1; others, 10/1/88.
See No. 636. For surcharges see Nos. 787 and 929A.

Flowers — A195

100fr, Haemanthus. 205fr, Hemerocalle, horiz.

Perf. 13x12½, 12½x13

1986, Sept. 1 **Litho.**
631 A195 100fr multi .90 .50
632 A195 205fr multi 2.40 1.10

For surcharge see No. 1061F.

Butterflies A196

No. 633, Day peacock, little tortoiseshell, morio. No. 634, Aurora, machaon and fair lady.

1986, Sept. 15
633 A196 150fr shown 3.25 1.75
634 A196 150fr multi 3.25 1.75

Dahomey Nos. 290, 307 Overprinted Perfs. & Printing Methods as Before

1985, Oct. 15
634A A67(b) 50fr on #307 *47.50 19.00*
634B A60(d) 150fr on 100fr #290 *47.50 19.00*

Statue of Liberty, Cent. — A197

1986, Oct. 28 Litho. *Perf. 12½*
635 A197 250fr multi 2.50 1.25

King Behanzin — A198

1986, Oct. 30 *Perf. 13½*
636 A198 440fr multi 4.50 2.40

Behanzin, leader of resistance movement against French occupation (1886-1894).
For surcharge see Nos. 653A, 921.

Brazilian Cultural Week, Cotonou — A200

1987, Jan. 17 *Perf. 12½*
638 A200 150fr multi 1.25 .75

Rotary Intl. District 910 Conference, Cotonou, Apr. 23-25 — A201

300fr, Center for the Blind, Cotonou.

1987, Apr. 23 Litho. *Perf. 13½*
639 A201 300fr multi 3.00 1.50

Automobile Cent. — A202

Modern car and: 150fr, Steam tricycle, by De Dion-Bouton and Trepardoux, 1887. 300fr, Gas-driven Victoria, by Daimler, 1886.

1987, July 1 *Perf. 12½*
640 A202 150fr multi 1.40 .75
641 A202 300fr multi 3.00 1.50

For surcharge see No. 679B.

Snake Temple Baptism — A203

1987, July 20 *Perf. 13½*
642 A203 100fr multi 1.40 .75

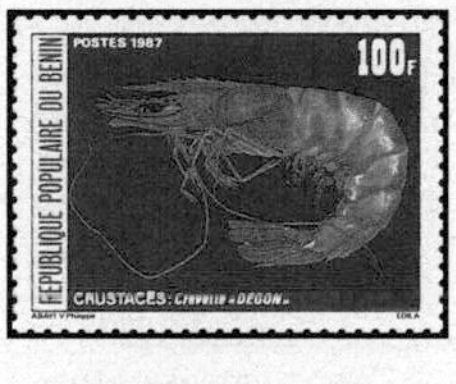

Shellfish A204

1987, July 24 *Perf. 12½*
643 A204 100fr Crayfish 1.50 .80
644 A204 150fr Crab 2.25 1.10

G. Hansen, R. Follereau A205

1987, Sept. 4 *Perf. 13*
645 A205 200fr Cure Leprosy 2.25 1.25

Beginning of Benin Revolution, 15th Anniv. — A205a

1987, Oct. 28 Litho. *Perf. 12x12½*
645A A205a 100fr multi 90.00 3.00

October Revolution, 70th Anniv. — A205b

1987, Nov. 7 Litho. *Perf. 12x12½*
645B A205b 150fr multi 90.00 3.00

Locust Control A206

1987, Dec. 7 Litho. *Perf. 12½x13*
646 A206 100fr multi 1.45 .60

Christmas 1987 A207

1987, Dec. 21 *Perf. 13*
647 A207 150fr multi 1.50 1.00

Dahomey No. 268 overprinted and No. 284 Surcharged

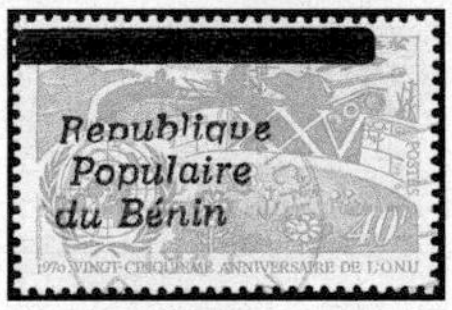

1987 Engr. *Perf. 13*
647A A58(b) 15fr on 100fr #284 50.00 20.00
647B A53(b) 40fr on #268 50.00 16.00

See Nos. C362, C369.

Intl. Red Cross and Red Crescent Organizations, 125th Anniv. — A208

1988, May 25 Litho. *Perf. 13½*
648 A208 200fr multi 1.60 .90

A209

1988, July 11 *Perf. 12½*
649 A209 200fr multi 2.40 1.20

Martin Luther King, Jr. (1929-68), American civil rights leader.

A210

1988, May 25 Litho. *Perf. 13½*
650 A210 125fr multi 1.40 .65

Organization of African Unity, 25th anniv.

WHO, 40th Anniv. — A211

1988, Sept. 1 Litho. *Perf. 13x12½*
651 A211 175fr multi 1.60 .90

Alma Ata Declaration, 10th anniv.; Health Care for All on Earth by the Year 2000.
For surcharge see No. 786.

Ganvie Lake Village — A212

190fr, Boatman, part of boat, village.

1988, Sept. 4 *Perf. 13½*
652 A212 125fr shown 1.00 .60
653 A212 190fr multicolored 1.60 1.00

No. 636 Surcharged

1988 Method and Perf. As Before
653A A198 125fr on 440fr #636 *40.00 15.00*

Benin Nos. 605, 606 Surcharged

1988 Method and Perf. as Before
653B A187 190fr on 250fr #605, "F." in denomination *30.00 12.50*
d. Lowercase "f" in denomination *37.50 17.50*
653C A187 190F on 250fr #606 *30.00 12.50*

No. 653B surcharge has a capital "F." with a period. No. 653Bd has a lower case "f" without a period.

A213

1988, Aug. 14 *Perf. 12½*
654 A213 125fr multi 1.30 1.30

1st Benin Scout Jamboree, Aug. 12-19.

Benin No. 351, Dahomey Nos. 296, 328 Surcharged

1988

Printing Method & Perfs as Before

654A A57(d) 10fr on 60fr on 2fr #351 *50.00 12.50*
654B A62(d) 10fr on 65fr #296 *40.00 25.00*
654E A74(d) 150fr on 200fr #328 *40.00 20.00*

A214

Ritual Offering to Hebiesso, God of Thunder and Lightning.

1988, Dec. 30 Litho. *Perf. 13*
655 A214 125fr multicolored 1.10 .60

Dahomey Nos. 161, 247, 302, 309, 333, 339, 341 Surcharged or Overprinted

1988 Photo. *Perf. 12½x13*
655A A19(d) 5fr on 3fr #161 *50.00 10.00*
655B A68(d) 20fr on 100fr #309 *40.00 14.00*
655C A82(d) 30fr on 150fr #341 *40.00 15.00*
655D A76(d) 25fr on 100fr #333 *50.00 25.00*
655E A45(b) 50fr on 45fr #247 *40.00 35.00*
655F A81(d) 55fr on 200fr #339 *65.00 17.50*
655G A65(b) 65fr on 85fr #302 *80.00 17.00*

No. 380 Overprinted

1989 Engr. *Perf. 13*
655H A98 150fr multi *200.00 200.00*

Rural Development Council, 30th Anniv. — A214a

1989, May 29 Litho. *Perf. 15x14*
655K A214a 75fr multicolored *95.00 18.00*

World Wildlife Fund — A216

Roseate terns, *Sterna dougallii*. 10fr, Three terns. 15fr, Feeding on fish. 50fr, Perched. 125fr, In flight.

1989, Jan. 30 Litho. *Perf. 13*
657 A216 10fr multi 1.00 .50
658 A216 15fr multi 1.00 .50
659 A216 50fr multi 3.00 1.50
660 A216 125fr multi 6.00 3.00
Nos. 657-660 (4) 11.00 5.50

Eiffel Tower Cent. — A217

1989, Apr. 24 Litho. *Perf. 13x12½*
661 A217 190fr multi 2.50 1.25

PHILEXFRANCE '89, French Revolution Bicent. — A218

Design: Bastille, emblems, Declaration of Human Rights and Citizenship, France No. B252-B253.

1989, July 7 *Perf. 13*
662 A218 190fr multicolored 2.50 1.50

Electric Corp. of Benin, 20th Anniv. A219

1989, Oct. Litho. *Perf. 12½x13*
663 A219 125fr multicolored 1.20 .70

Fish A220

1989, Sept. 22 *Perf. 13½*
664 A220 125fr Lote 1.40 .70
665 A220 190fr Pike, salmon 2.50 1.10

Death of King Glele, Cent. — A221

1989, Dec. 16 Litho. *Perf. 13½*
666 A221 190fr multicolored 1.50 .90

Christmas A222

1989, Dec. 25 *Perf. 13*
667 A222 200fr Holy family 1.60 1.00

Benin Posts & Telecommunications, Cent. — A223

1990, Jan. 1 *Perf. 13½*
668 A223 125fr multicolored 1.25 .70

Fruits and Flora A224

60fr, Oranges. 190fr, Kaufmann Tulips, vert. 250fr, Cashews, vert.

1990, Jan. 23 Litho. *Perf. 11½*
669 A224 60fr multi .50 .45
670 A224 190fr multi 2.00 1.25
671 A224 250fr multi 2.25 1.40
Nos. 669-671 (3) 4.75 3.10

Dated 1989.

No. 669 exists with "Populaire" obliterated by black marker.

Moon Landing, 20th Anniv. A225

1990, Jan. 23
672 A225 190fr multicolored 1.60 .90

Dated 1989.

World Cup Soccer Championships, Italy — A226

190fr, Character trademark, vert.

1990, June 8 Litho. *Perf. 12½*
673 A226 125fr shown 1.10 .60
674 A226 190fr multi 1.75 .90

For overprint see No. 676.

Post, Telephone & Telegraph Administration in Benin, Cent. — A227

1990, July 1 *Perf. 13*
675 A227 150fr multicolored 1.40 .70

No. 673 Overprinted

1990 Litho. *Perf. 12½*
676 A226 125fr multicolored 1.10 .65

Charles de Gaulle (1890-1970) — A228

1990, Nov. 22 Litho. *Perf. 13*
677 A228 190fr multicolored 1.90 1.50

See No. 689.

Galileo Probe and Jupiter A229

1990, Dec. 1
678 A229 100fr multicolored .90 .65

For overprint see No. 681.

Christmas A230

1990, Dec. 25 Litho. *Perf. 12½x13*
679 A230 200fr multicolored 2.00 1.25

Benin No. 641 Surcharged

1990

Perf. & Printing Method as Before

679B A202(e) 190fr on 300fr #641 *55.00 17.50*

A230a

1990 Litho. *Perf. 11½x12*

679C A230a 125fr multi *100.00 50.00*

National Conference of Active Forces.

A231

1991, Sept. 3 Litho. *Perf. 13½*

680 A231 125fr multicolored 1.20 .70

Independence, 31st anniv.

No. 678 Ovptd. in Red

1991 *Perf. 13*

681 A229 100fr multicolored 1.00 .75

French Open Tennis Championships, Cent. — A232

1991 *Perf. 13½*

682 A232 125fr multicolored 1.50 1.00

African Tourism Year — A233

1991

683 A233 190fr multicolored 2.00 1.50

Christmas A234

1991, Dec. 2 Litho. *Perf. 13½*

684 A234 125fr multicolored 1.25 .70

Dancer of Guelede — A235

1991, Dec. 2

685 A235 190fr multicolored 2.00 1.00

Wolfgang Amadeus Mozart, Death Bicent. — A236

1991, Dec. 2

686 A236 1000fr multicolored 10.00 6.00

For surcharge see No. 793.

Discovery of America, 500th Anniv. A237

1000fr, Columbus coming ashore, horiz.

1992, Apr. 24 Litho. *Perf. 13*

687 A237 500fr blk, blue & brn 4.25 3.50

688 A237 1000fr multicolored 9.00 5.00

a. Souvenir sheet, #687-688 15.00 14.00

De Gaulle Type of 1990

1992 Litho. *Perf. 13*

689 A228 300fr like #677 3.00 1.90

Intl. Conference on Nutrition, Rome — A238

1992, Dec. 5 Litho. *Perf. 13*

690 A238 190fr multicolored 1.75 1.25

For surcharge see 928.

Dahomey Nos. 160, 266, 303, 311, 325, 327, 331, 334, 338, C161 Surcharged or Overprinted (No. 690A), Benin No. 342 Overprinted (No. 690B)

1992

Perfs. & Printing Methods as Before

690A	A66(e)	5fr on Dah. #303	*60.00*	*25.00*
690B	A83(e)	10fr on #342	*100.00*	*30.00*
690C	A76(e)	25fr on Dah. 331		—
690D	A74(f)	35fr on Dah. #325	*80.00*	*25.00*
690E	A80(f)	35fr on Dah. #338	*50.00*	*16.00*
690F	A19(e)	125fr on 2fr Dah. #160	*80.00*	*13.00*
690G	AP54(f)	125fr on 65fr Dah. #C161	*60.00*	*15.00*
690H	A77(f)	125fr on 65fr Dah. #334 (G)	*100.00*	*25.00*
690I	CD137(e)	125fr on 100fr Dah. #311	*75.00*	*20.00*
690J	A52(f)	190fr on 45fr Dah. #266	*60.00*	*10.00*
690K	A74(f)	125fr on 100fr Dah. #327	*125.00*	*50.00*

Visit of Pope John Paul II, Feb. 3-5 — A239

1993, Feb. 3 Litho. *Perf. 13x12½*

691 A239 190fr multicolored 2.00 1.10

For surcharge, see No. 929.

Dahomey No. 194 Overprinted

1993

Perf. & Printing Method as Before

691A A27(e) 20fr on Dah. #194 75.00 30.00

Ouidah 92, First Festival of Voodoo Culture — A240

1993, Feb. 8 *Perf. 13½*

692 A240 125fr multicolored 1.15 .65

Well of Possotome, Eurystome A241

1993, May 25 Litho. *Perf. 12½*

693 A241 125fr multicolored 2.60 1.00

OAU, 30th Anniv. A242

1993, June 7 Litho. *Perf. 13½*

694 A242 125fr multicolored 1.00 .75

John F. Kennedy — A243

No. 696, Martin Luther King, vert.

1993, June 24 *Perf. 13*

695 A243 190fr shown 1.90 1.00

696 A243 190fr multi 1.90 1.00

Assassinations of Kennedy, 30th anniv. (No. 695), and King, 25th anniv. (No. 696).

For surcharge see No. 1061D.

Dahomey Nos. 161, 173, 175, 277, 312, 317, 335 Overprinted or Surcharged

1993

Perfs. & Printing Methods as Before

697	A21(e)	5fr on #175	*70.00*	*40.00*
698	A69(f)	5fr on #312	*100.00*	*50.00*
699	A71(g)	5fr on #317	*45.00*	*20.00*
700	A19(f)	10fr on 3fr #161	*70.00*	*10.00*
701	A77(f)	10fr on 100fr #335	*45.00*	*17.50*
703	A57(f)	20fr on 1fr #277	*40.00*	*17.50*
704	A21(f)	25fr on 1fr #173	*100.00*	*50.00*

Benin Nos. 343, 345, 350, Dahomey Nos. 169, 177, 221, 226-227, 249, 256, 272, 273, 276, 287, 292, 295, 283, 286, 319, 328, 333 Surcharged or Overprinted (Nos. 708A, 711, 713)

No. 727

1994-95

707	A38(f)	5fr on 1fr Dah. #226	*60.00*	*25.00*
708	A47(e)	10fr on 90fr Dah. #256	*50.00*	*25.00*
708A	A60(f)	25fr on Dah. #287	—	—
709	A71(f)	25fr on Dah. #319	*35.00*	*15.00*
710	A59(e)	40fr on Dah. #286	*60.00*	*35.00*
711	A57(e)	50fr on 1fr #350	*50.00*	*15.00*
712	A58(e)	80fr on 40fr Dah. #283	*35.00*	*15.00*
713	A76(g)	100fr on Dah. #333	*50.00*	*25.00*
715	A38(f)	135fr on 3fr Dah. #227	*75.00*	—
716	A21(e)	135fr on 20fr Dah. #177	—	—

717 A36(e) 135fr on 30fr Dah. #221 45.00 —
718 A62(e) 135fr on 30fr Dah. #295 75.00 —
719 A83(g) 135fr on 35fr #343 75.00 35.00
720 A56(h) 135fr on 40fr Dah. #276 35.00 —
721 A55(e) 135fr on 50fr Dah. #272 35.00 25.00
722 A20(e) 135fr on 60fr Dah. #169 50.00 17.50
723 A83(g) 135fr on 60fr #345 75.00 40.00
724 A55(e) 135fr on 70fr Dah. #273 65.00 35.00
725 A45(e) 200fr on 100fr Dah. #249 60.00 10.00
726 A60(k) 200fr on 140fr Dah. #292 —
727 A74(f) 200fr on Dah. #328 200.00 100.00

UNESCO Conference on The Slave Route — A244

1994 **Litho.** ***Perf. 13x13½***
728 A244 135fr multicolored 40.00 16.00
729 A244 200fr multicolored 65.00 24.00
730 A244 300fr multicolored 40.00 16.00

Natitingou Scout Encampment A245

1994 ***Perf. 12¾x12½***
731 A245 135fr multi 50.00 1.00

Intl. Year of the Family A246

1994 **Litho.** ***Perf. 12½***
732 A246 200fr multicolored 50.00 1.25

1994 World Cup Soccer Championships, US — A247

1994 **Litho.** ***Perf. 13x13½***
733 A247 300fr multicolored 130.00 6.25

1996 Summer Olympics, Atlanta — A248

45fr, Water polo. 50fr, Javelin. 75fr, Weight lifting. 100fr, Tennis. 135fr, Baseball. 200fr, Synchronized swimming.
300fr, Diving.

Perf. 12½x13, 13x12½

1995, Apr. 30 **Litho.**
734 A248 45fr multicolored .25 .25
735 A248 50fr multicolored .30 .30
736 A248 75fr multicolored .50 .50
737 A248 100fr multicolored .60 .60
738 A248 135fr multicolored .80 .80
739 A248 200fr multicolored 1.10 1.10
Nos. 734-739 (6) 3.55 3.55

Souvenir Sheet

740 A248 300fr multicolored *2.50 2.50*

Nos. 735-740 are vert. No. 740 contains one 32x40mm stamp.
For surcharges, see Nos. 1241, 1257.

Dogs A249

40fr, German shepherd. 50fr, Beagle. 75fr, Great dane. 100fr, Boxer. 135fr, Pointer. 200fr, Fox terrier.
300fr, Schnauzer.

1995, Aug. 23 **Litho.** ***Perf. 12½***
741 A249 40fr multi .25 .25
742 A249 50fr multi .35 .35
743 A249 75fr multi .45 .45
744 A249 100fr multi .60 .60
745 A249 135fr multi .80 .80
746 A249 200fr multi 1.10 1.10
Nos. 741-746 (6) 3.55 3.55

Souvenir Sheet

747 A249 300fr multi *3.00 3.00*

For surcharges, see Nos. 1222, 1258.

Ships A250

Designs: 40fr, Steam driven paddle boat, 1788. 50fr, Paddle steamer Charlotte, 1802. 75fr, Transatlantic steamship, Citta de Catania. 100fr, Hovercraft Mountbatten SR-N4. 135fr, QE II. 200fr, Japanese experimental atomic energy ship, Mutsu-NEF.
300fr, Paddle-steamer Savannah, 1819.

1995, May 20
748 A250 40fr multicolored .25 .25
749 A250 50fr multicolored .35 .35
750 A250 75fr multicolored .45 .45
751 A250 100fr multicolored .60 .60
752 A250 135fr multicolored .80 .80
753 A250 200fr multicolored 1.10 1.10
Nos. 748-753 (6) 3.55 3.55

Souvenir Sheet

754 A250 300fr multicolored *2.50 2.50*

No. 754 contains one 40x32mm stamp.
For surcharges, see Nos. 1223, 1259.

Primates A251

50fr, Pan troglodytes. 75fr, Mandrillus sphinx. 100fr, Colobus. 135fr, Macaca sylvanus. 200fr, Comopithecus hamadryas.
300fr, Papio cynocephalus.

1995, June 30
755 A251 50fr multicolored .25 .25
756 A251 75fr multicolored .30 .30
757 A251 100fr multicolored .50 .50
758 A251 135fr multicolored .65 .65
759 A251 200fr multicolored .90 .90
Nos. 755-759 (5) 2.60 2.60

Souvenir Sheet

760 A251 300fr multicolored *3.00 3.00*

No. 760 contains one 32x40mm stamp.
For surcharges, see Nos. 1242, 1260.

Domestic Cats A252

1995, July 30 **Litho.** ***Perf. 12½x13***
761 A252 40fr Shorthair tabby .25 .25
762 A252 50fr Ruddy red .35 .35
763 A252 75fr White longhair .50 .50
764 A252 100fr Seal color point .65 .65
765 A252 135fr Tabby point .80 .80
766 A252 200fr Black shorthair 1.20 1.20
Nos. 761-766 (6) 3.75 3.75

Souvenir Sheet

767 A252 300fr Cat in basket *3.00 3.00*

No. 767 contains one 40x32mm stamp.
For surcharges, see Nos. 1224, 1261.

Flowers — A253

Designs: 40fr, Dracunculus vulgaris. 50fr, Narcissus watieri. 75fr, Amaryllis belladonna. 100fr, Nymphaea capensis. 135fr, Chrysanthemum carinatum. 200fr, Iris tingitana.

1995, Oct. 15 **Litho.** ***Perf. 12½***
768 A253 40fr multicolored .25 .25
769 A253 50fr multicolored .35 .35
770 A253 75fr multicolored .50 .50
771 A253 100fr multicolored .65 .65
772 A253 135fr multicolored .75 .75
773 A253 200fr multicolored 1.10 1.10
Nos. 768-773 (6) 3.60 3.60

For surcharges, see Nos. 1225, 1262.

Wild Animals A254

50fr, Panthera leo. 75fr, Syncerus caffer. 100fr, Pan troglodytes. 135fr, Aepyceros melampus. 200fr, Geosciurus inaurus.
300fr, Loxodonta, vert.

Perf. 13x12½, 12½x13

1995, Sept. 20
774 A254 50fr multicolored .35 .35
775 A254 75fr multicolored .45 .45
776 A254 100fr multicolored .65 .65
777 A254 135fr multicolored .90 .90
778 A254 200fr multicolored 1.20 1.20
Nos. 774-778 (5) 3.55 3.55

Souvenir Sheet

779 A254 300fr multicolored *3.00 3.00*

Nos. 774-777 are vert. No. 779 contains one 32x40mm stamp.
For surcharge, see No. 1263.

Birds Feeding Their Chicks — A255

Designs: 40fr, Coccothraustes coccothraustes. 50fr, Streptopelia chinensis. 75fr, Falco peregrinus. 100fr, Dendroica fusca. 135fr, Larus ridibundus. 200fr, Pelecanus onocrotalus.

1995, Aug. 28 ***Perf. 12½x13***
780 A255 40fr multicolored .25 .25
781 A255 50fr multicolored .35 .35
782 A255 75fr multicolored .50 .50
783 A255 100fr multicolored .65 .65
784 A255 135fr multicolored .70 .70
785 A255 200fr multicolored 1.10 1.10
Nos. 780-785 (6) 3.55 3.55

For surcharges, see Nos. 1226, 1243.

Benin Nos. 344, 504, 519, 619, 627, 651, 686 and Dahomey No. 291 Surcharged

1994-95

Printing Method and Perfs as Before

786 A211 25fr on 175fr #651 *40.00 17.50*
787 A194 50fr on 220fr #627 *25.00 15.00*
788 A83(h) 150fr on 45fr #344 *40.00*
789 A158 150fr on 90fr #519 *60.00 30.00*
790 A147 150fr on 500fr #504 *50.00 15.00*
791 A60(f) 200fr on 135fr #291 *75.00 30.00*
792 A192 200fr on 500fr #619 *60.00 17.50*
793 A236 250fr on 1000fr #686 *60.00 15.00*

Natl. Arms — A256

Denomination 3½mm Wide

1995, Dec. 26 **Litho.** ***Perf. 12½***
793A A256 135fr yellow & multi 1.00 1.00
b. Denomination 3mm wide 6.00 2.50
793B A256 150fr yel grn & multi 1.00 1.00
794 A256 200fr multicolored 1.25 1.10
a. Denomination 3mm wide 6.00 2.50

See Nos. 948-951. For surcharge see No. 1021A.
Nos. 793Ab and 794a issued 8/24/95.

Orchids — A257

Designs: 40fr, Angraecum sesquipedale. 50fr, Polystachya virginea. 75fr, Disa uniflora. 100fr, Ansellia africana. 135fr, Angraecum eichlerianum. 200fr, Jumellea confusa.

1995, Nov. 10 Litho. *Perf. 12½*

795 A257 40fr multicolored .25 .25
796 A257 50fr multicolored .35 .35
797 A257 75fr multicolored .50 .50
798 A257 100fr multicolored .65 .65
799 A257 135fr multicolored .70 .70
800 A257 200fr multicolored 1.10 1.10
Nos. 795-800 (6) 3.55 3.55

For surcharges, see Nos. 1227, 1244.

Butterflies A258

Designs: 40fr, Graphium policenes. 50fr, Vanessa atalanta. 75fr, Polymmatus icarus. 100fr, Danaus chrysipus. 135fr, Cynthia cardui. 200fr, Argus celbulina.
1000fr, Charaxes jasius.

1996, Mar. 10

801 A258 40fr multicolored .30 .30
802 A258 50fr multicolored .30 .30
803 A258 75fr multicolored .60 .60
804 A258 100fr multicolored .70 .70
805 A258 135fr multicolored .90 .90
806 A258 200fr multicolored 1.50 1.50
Nos. 801-806 (6) 4.30 4.30

Souvenir Sheet

807 A258 1000fr multicolored *4.75 4.75*

For surcharge, see No. 1228.

CHINA '96, Beijing — A259

Designs: a, 40fr, Dancer in traditional Chinese costume. b, 50fr, Exhibition emblem. c, 75fr, Water lily. d, 100fr, Temple of Heaven.

1996, Apr. 8

808 A259 Block of 4, #a.-d. 4.00 4.00

Benin Nos. 523, 616 and Dahomey No. 306 Surcharged or Overprinted (No. 810)

1996?

Perfs. & Printing Methods as Before

809 A191 5fr on 205fr #616 *60.00 20.00*
810 A67(g) 35fr on #306 *60.00 15.00*
811 A158 150fr on 90fr #523 *100.00 60.00*

15th Lions Intl. District Convention — A260

1996 Litho. *Perf. 12½*

811A A260 100fr multicolored .40 .40
811B A260 135fr green & multi 1.25 1.25
812 A260 150fr yellow & multi 1.25 1.25
813 A260 200fr red & multi 1.60 1.60
Nos. 811A-813 (4) 4.50 4.50

For surcharge see No. 1021B.
Issued: No. 811A, 12/27; others, 5/2.

La Francophonie Conference A261

1995, Dec. 2 Litho. *Perf. 12½*

814 A261 150fr pink & multi .80 .80
815 A261 200fr blue & multi 1.20 1.00

Cats — A262

1995, Nov. 2 Litho. *Perf. 13*

816 A262 40fr Lynx lynx .30 .30
817 A262 50fr Felis concolor .40 .40
818 A262 75fr Acinonyx jubatus .45 .45
819 A262 100fr Panthera pardus .60 .60
820 A262 135fr Panthera tigris .80 .80
821 A262 200fr Panthera leo 1.20 1.20
Nos. 816-821 (6) 3.75 3.75

For surcharges, see Nos. 1229, 1245, 1264.

1998 World Cup Soccer Championships, France — A263

Various soccer players.

1996, Feb. 10 Litho. *Perf. 13*

822 A263 40fr multicolored .30 .30
823 A263 50fr multicolored .40 .40
824 A263 75fr multicolored .50 .50
825 A263 100fr multicolored .75 .75
826 A263 135fr multicolored .80 .80
827 A263 200fr multicolored 1.25 1.25
Nos. 822-827 (6) 4.00 4.00

Souvenir Sheet

Perf. 12½

828 A263 1000fr multicolored *4.00 4.00*

No. 828 contains one 32x40mm stamp.
For surcharges, see Nos. 1246, 1265

1996 Summer Olympic Games, Atlanta — A264

1996, Jan. 28 Litho. *Perf. 13*

829 A264 40fr Diving .25 .25
830 A264 50fr Tennis .25 .25
831 A264 75fr Running .65 .65
832 A264 100fr Gymnastics .70 .70
833 A264 135fr Weight lifting .90 .90
834 A264 200fr Shooting 1.10 1.10
Nos. 829-834 (6) 3.85 3.85

Souvenir Sheet

835 A264 1000fr Water polo *4.50 4.50*

No. 835 contains one 32x40mm stamp.
For surcharges, see Nos. 1230, 1247, 1266.

Christmas Paintings — A265

Entire paintings or details: 40fr, Holy Family Under the Oak Tree, by Raphael. 50fr, The Holy Family, by Raphael. 75fr, St. John the Baptist as a Child, by Murillo. 100fr, The Virgin of Balances, by Leonardo da Vinci. 135fr, The Virgin and the Infant, by Gerard David. 200fr, Adoration of the Magi, by Juan Bautista Mayno.
1000fr, Rest on the Flight into Egypt, by Murillo.

1996, May 5 Litho. *Perf. 13*

836 A265 40fr multicolored .25 .25
837 A265 50fr multicolored .25 .25
838 A265 75fr multicolored .60 .60
839 A265 100fr multicolored .80 .80
840 A265 135fr multicolored .90 .90
841 A265 200fr multicolored 1.40 1.40
Nos. 836-841 (6) 4.20 4.20

Souvenir Sheet

842 A265 1000fr multicolored *4.00 4.00*

No. 842 contains one 40x32mm stamp.
For surcharges, see Nos. 1231, 1248, 1267.

Wild Cats — A266

Designs: 40fr, Leptailurus serval. 50fr, Profelis temmincki. 75fr, Leopardus pardalis. 100fr, Lynx rufus. 135fr, Prionailurus bengalensis. 200fr, Felis euptilura.
1000fr, Neofelis nebulosa.

1996, June 10 Litho. *Perf. 12x12½*

843 A266 40fr multicolored .25 .25
844 A266 50fr multicolored .25 .25
845 A266 75fr multicolored .45 .45
846 A266 100fr multicolored .55 .55
847 A266 135fr multicolored .80 .80
848 A266 200fr multicolored 1.25 1.25
Nos. 843-848 (6) 3.55 3.55

Souvenir Sheet

Perf. 12½

849 A266 1000fr multicolored *4.00 4.00*

No. 849 contains one 32x40mm stamp.
For surcharges, see Nos. 1232, 1268.

Sailing Ships A267

40fr, Thermopylae. 50fr, 5-masted bark. 75fr, Nightingale. 100fr, Opium clipper. 135fr, The Torrens. 200fr, English clipper.
1000fr, Opium clipper, diff.

1996, May 27 *Perf. 13x12½*

850 A267 40fr multi .25 .25
851 A267 50fr multi .25 .25
852 A267 75fr multi .55 .55
853 A267 100fr multi .55 .55
854 A267 135fr multi 1.00 1.00
855 A267 200fr multi 1.10 1.10
Nos. 850-855 (6) 3.70 3.70

Souvenir Sheet

Perf. 13

856 A267 1000fr multi *4.00 4.00*

No. 856 contains one 32x40mm stamp.
For surcharges, see Nos. 1209, 1249, 1269.

Olymphilex '96 — A268

1996, July 2 *Perf. 13*

857 A268 40fr Running .25 .25
858 A268 50fr Kayaking .25 .25
859 A268 75fr Gymnastics .55 .55
860 A268 100fr Soccer .60 .60
861 A268 135fr Tennis .80 .80
862 A268 200fr Baseball 1.20 1.20
Nos. 857-862 (6) 3.65 3.65

Souvenir Sheet

863 A268 1000fr Basketball *4.00 4.00*

No. 863 contains one 32x40mm stamp.
For surcharges, see Nos. 1233, 1250, 1270.

Modern Olympic Games, Cent. — A269

a, 40fr, Gold medal, woman hurdler. b, 50fr, Runner, Olympic flame. c, 75fr, Pierre de Coubertin, map of US. d, 100fr, Map of US, "1996."

1996, June 20

864 A269 Block of 4, #a.-d. *3.25 3.25*

No. 864 is a continuous design.
For surcharge, see No. 1236.

Horses — A270

Various horses.

1996, Aug. 10 Litho. *Perf. 13*

865 A270 40fr multi, vert. .25 .25
866 A270 50fr multi, vert. .25 .25
867 A270 75fr multi, vert. .50 .50
868 A270 100fr multi, vert. .60 .60
869 A270 135fr multi, vert. .80 .80
870 A270 200fr multicolored 1.20 1.20
Nos. 865-870 (6) 3.60 3.60

For surcharges, see Nos. 1251, 1271.

Flowering Cacti — A271

40fr, Parodia subterranea. 50fr, Astrophytum senile. 75fr, Echinocereus melanocentrus. 100fr, Turbinicarpus kinkerianus. 135fr, Astrophytum capricorne. 200fr, Nelloydia grandiflora.

1996, July 25

871	A271	40fr multicolored	.25	.25
872	A271	50fr multicolored	.25	.25
873	A271	75fr multicolored	.60	.60
874	A271	100fr multicolored	.65	.65
875	A271	135fr multicolored	.80	.80
876	A271	200fr multicolored	1.20	1.20
		Nos. 871-876 (6)	3.75	3.75

For surcharges, see Nos. 1210, 1234, 1272.

Mushrooms A272

Designs: 40fr, Stropharia cubensis. 50fr, Psilocybe zapotecorum. 75fr, Psilocybe mexicana. 100fr, Conocybe siligineoides. 135fr, Psilocybe caerulescens mazatecorum. 200fr, Psilocybe caerulescens nigripes.
1000fr, Psilocybe aztecorum, horiz.

1996, Sept. 30

877	A272	40fr multicolored	.25	.25
878	A272	50fr multicolored	.25	.25
879	A272	75fr multicolored	.55	.55
880	A272	100fr multicolored	.60	.60
881	A272	135fr multicolored	.75	.75
882	A272	200fr multicolored	1.10	1.10
		Nos. 877-882 (6)	3.50	3.50

Souvenir Sheet

Perf. 12½

883	A272	1000fr multicolored	*4.00*	*4.00*

No. 883 contains one 40x32mm stamp.
For surcharge on No. 877, see No. 1235.

Prehistoric Animals — A273

40fr, Longisquama, vert. 50fr, Dimophodon, vert. 75fr, Dunkleosteus. 100fr, Eryops. 135fr, Peloneustes. 200fr, Deinonychus.

1996, Aug. 30 ***Perf. 12½***

884	A273	40fr multicolored	.25	.25
885	A273	50fr multicolored	.25	.25
886	A273	75fr multicolored	.50	.50
887	A273	100fr multicolored	.60	.60
888	A273	135fr multicolored	.80	.80
889	A273	200fr multicolored	1.30	1.30
		Nos. 884-889 (6)	3.70	3.70

For surcharges on No. 886, see Nos. 1236 and 1252.

Birds — A274

Designs: 40fr, Campephilus principalis. 50fr, Picathartes oreas. 75fr, Strigops habroptilus. 100fr, Amazona vittata. 135fr, Nipponia nippon. 200fr, Gymnogyps californianus.
1000fr, Paradisea rudolphi.

1996, Sept. 10

890	A274	40fr multicolored	.25	.25
891	A274	50fr multicolored	.25	.25
892	A274	75fr multicolored	.50	.50
893	A274	100fr multicolored	.60	.60
894	A274	135fr multicolored	.85	.85
895	A274	200fr multicolored	1.25	1.25
		Nos. 890-895 (6)	3.70	3.70

Souvenir Sheet

896	A274	1000fr multicolored	*4.00*	*4.00*

No. 896 contains one 32x40mm stamp.
For surcharges, see Nos. 1253, 1315.

Dahomey No. 235 Overprinted, Benin No. 545 Surcharged

199?

Perfs. & Printing Methods as Before

897	A40(e)	30fr on #235	*27.50*	*20.00*
898	A166	75fr on 185fr #545	*60.00*	*30.00*

Dahomey Nos. 208, 239-241, 257-258, 261, 269, 274, 283, 320, 326, 334-336, 337 Surcharged or Overprinted (No. 899)

1996?

Perfs. & Printing Methods as Before

899	A77(f)	100fr on #335	*60.00*	*20.00*
900	A79(e)	125fr on 150fr #337	*40.00*	*30.00*
901	A77(h)	135fr on 65fr #334	*120.00*	*60.00*
902	A42(e)	150fr on 30fr #239	*20.00*	*20.00*
903	A43(h)	150fr on 30fr #241	*40.00*	
904	A48(h)	150fr on 30fr #257	*20.00*	20.00
905	A50(h)	150fr on 30fr #261	*25.00*	
906	CD132(h)	150fr on 40fr #269	*28.00*	
907	A58(h)	150fr on 40fr #283	*28.00*	28.00
908	A71(e)	150fr on 40fr #320	*28.00*	
909	A74(e)	150fr on 40fr #326	*75.00*	40.00
910	A78(e)	150fr on 40fr #336	*20.00*	20.00
911	A32(e)	150fr on 50fr #208	*60.00*	
912	A42(e)	150fr on 70fr #240	*20.00*	
913	A48(h)	150fr on 70fr #258	*20.00*	20.00
914	A55(h)	150fr on 200fr #274	45.00	

Benin Nos. 381, 384, 449, 521, 538, 546, 567, 569, 636, Surcharged

1996?

Perfs. & Printing Methods as Before

915	A127	10fr on 90fr #449	*40.00*	—
916	A159	10fr on 90fr #521	*50.00*	*25.00*
917	A164	10fr on 90fr #538	*50.00*	*25.00*
918	A174	10fr on 90fr #569	*40.00*	*15.00*
919	A98	40fr on 210fr #381	*40.00*	—
920	A99	40fr on 210fr #384	*70.00*	20.00
921	A198	75fr on 440fr #636	*60.00*	*30.00*
922	A167	100fr on 500fr #546	*60.00*	*17.50*
923	A173	125fr on 300fr #567	*45.00*	*25.00*

Obliterator on No. 922 has either one or two bars. Pairs of No. 922 exist with each stamp having a different obliterator.

Nos. 376, 466, 627, 690, 691 Surcharged

No. 926

1995 Method and Perf. as Before

925	A96	10fr on 90fr #376	*40.00*	*30.00*
926	A132	10fr on 90fr #466	*45.00*	*30.00*
928	A238	150fr on 190fr #690	*20.00*	*25.00*
929	A239	150fr on 190fr #691	—	—
929A	A194	150fr on 220fr #627	—	—

Ungulates — A275

Designs: 40fr, Aepyceros melampus. 50fr, Kobus ellipsiprymnus. 75fr, Caffer caffer. 100fr, Connochaetes taurinus. 135fr, Okapia johnstoni. 200fr, Tragelaphus strepsiceros.

1996, Oct. 15 Litho. ***Perf. 12½x12***

930	A275	40fr multicolored	.25	.25
931	A275	50fr multicolored	.25	.25
932	A275	75fr multicolored	.50	.50
933	A275	100fr multicolored	.60	.60
934	A275	135fr multicolored	.75	.75
935	A275	200fr multicolored	1.10	1.10
		Nos. 930-935 (6)	3.45	3.45

For surcharges, see Nos. 1237, 1254.

Marine Mammals — A276

Designs: 40fr, Delphinapterus leucas. 50fr, Tursiops truncatus. 75fr, Belaenoptera musculus. 100fr, Eubalaena australis. 135fr, Gramphidelphis griseus. 200fr, Orcinus orca.

1996, Nov. 5 ***Perf. 13***

936	A276	40fr multicolored	.25	.25
937	A276	50fr multicolored	.25	.25
938	A276	75fr multicolored	.50	.50
939	A276	100fr multicolored	.60	.60
940	A276	135fr multicolored	.80	.80
941	A276	200fr multicolored	1.25	1.25
		Nos. 936-941 (6)	3.65	3.65

For surcharges, see Nos. 1238, 1255, 1273.

Fish A277

50fr, Pomacanthidae, vert. 75fr, Acanthuridae. 100fr, Carangidae. 135fr, Chaetodontidae. 200fr, Chaetodontidae, diff.
1000fr, Scaridae.

1996, Dec. 4 Litho. ***Perf. 12½***

942	A277	50fr multicolored	.35	.35
943	A277	75fr multicolored	.45	.45
944	A277	100fr multicolored	.65	.65
945	A277	135fr multicolored	.75	.75
946	A277	200fr multicolored	1.25	1.25
		Nos. 942-946 (5)	3.45	3.45

Souvenir Sheet

947	A277	1000fr multicolored	*4.00*	*4.00*

No. 947 contains one 40x32mm stamp.
For surcharges, see Nos. 1256, 1274.

Coat of Arms Type of 1995

1996-97 ***Perf. 12½***

948	A256	100fr multicolored	.50	.50
949	A256	135fr lt yellow & multi	.70	.35
950	A256	150fr lt bl grn & multi	1.10	.70
951	A256	200fr lt orange & multi	1.20	.70
		Nos. 948-951 (4)	3.50	2.25

Nos. 949-951 have "Republique du Benin" at bottom.
Issued: 100fr, 12/27/96; 135fr, 150fr, 200fr, 5/15/97.
For surcharge see No. 1021A.

Military Uniforms — A278

Regiments of European infantry: 135fr, Grenadier, Glassenapp. 150fr, Officer, Von Groben. 200fr, Musketeer, Comte Dohna. 270fr, Bombardier. 300fr, Gendarme. 400fr, Dragoon, Mollendorf.
1000fr, Soldiers, flag, horses, vert.

1997, Feb. 20

952	A278	135fr multicolored	.50	.40
953	A278	150fr multicolored	.75	.40
954	A278	200fr multicolored	.80	.80
955	A278	270fr multicolored	1.00	.90
956	A278	300fr multicolored	1.20	1.20
957	A278	400fr multicolored	1.40	1.40
		Nos. 952-957 (6)	5.65	5.10

Souvenir Sheet

Perf. 13

958	A278	1000fr multicolored	4.00	4.00

No. 958 contains one 32x40mm stamp.
For surcharges, see Nos. 1275, 13354.

Trains A279

135fr, Steam turbine, Reid Maclead, 1920. 150fr, Experimental high speed, 1935. 200fr, Renard Argent, 1935. 270fr, Class No. 21-C-6, 1941. 300fr, Diesel, 1960. 400fr, Diesel, 1960, diff.
1000fr, Coronation Scot, 1937.

1997, Mar. 26 Litho. ***Perf. 13***

959	A279	135fr multicolored	.50	.40
960	A279	150fr multicolored	.75	.50
961	A279	200fr multicolored	.80	.70
962	A279	270fr multicolored	1.00	1.00
963	A279	300fr multicolored	1.20	1.00
964	A279	400fr multicolored	1.40	1.40
		Nos. 959-964 (6)	5.65	5.00

Souvenir Sheet

965	A279	1000fr multicolored	4.00	4.00

No. 965 contains one 40x32mm stamp.
For surcharge on No. 962, see No. 1276.

1998 World Cup Soccer Championship, France — A280

Various soccer plays.

1997, Apr. 9 ***Perf. 12½x13***

966	A280	135fr multicolored	.50	.40
967	A280	150fr multicolored	.60	.40
968	A280	200fr multicolored	.80	.80
969	A280	270fr multicolored	1.00	.90

970 A280 300fr multi, horiz. 1.20 1.20
971 A280 400fr multi, horiz. 1.60 1.60
Nos. 966-971 (6) 5.70 5.30

Souvenir Sheet

972 A280 1000fr multicolored 4.00 4.00

No. 972 contains one 40x32mm stamp.
For surcharge on No. 969, see Nos. 1277 and 1336.

Orchids — A281

Phalaenopsis: 135fr, Penetrate. 150fr, Golden sands. 200fr, Sun spots. 270fr, Fuscata. 300fr, Christi floyd. 400fr, Cayanne. 1000fr, Janet kuhn.

1997, June 9 Litho. *Perf. 12½x13*

973 A281 135fr multicolored .60 .45
974 A281 150fr multicolored .75 .60
975 A281 200fr multicolored .90 .75
976 A281 270fr multicolored 1.00 .90
977 A281 300fr multicolored 1.20 1.20
978 A281 400fr multicolored 1.75 1.50
Nos. 973-978 (6) 6.20 5.40

Souvenir Sheet

Perf. 12½

979 A281 1000fr multicolored 4.00 4.00

No. 979 contains one 32x40mm stamp.
For surcharges, see Nos. 1278, 1337.

Dogs — A282

Designs: 135fr, Irish setter. 150fr, Saluki. 200fr, Doberman pinscher. 270fr, Siberian husky. 300fr, Basenji. 400fr, Boxer. 1000fr, Rhodesian ridgeback.

1997, May 30 *Perf. 13*

980 A282 135fr multicolored .60 .40
981 A282 150fr multicolored .65 .60
982 A282 200fr multicolored .90 .70
983 A282 270fr multicolored 1.00 .90
984 A282 300fr multicolored 1.20 1.10
985 A282 400fr multicolored 1.75 1.25
Nos. 980-985 (6) 6.10 4.95

Souvenir Sheet

Perf. 12½

986 A282 1000fr multicolored 4.00 4.00

No. 986 contains one 32x40mm stamp.
For surcharge on No. 983, see No. 1279.

Antique Automobiles — A283

135fr, 1905 Buick. 150fr, 1903 Ford. 200fr, 1913 Stanley. 270fr, 1911 Stoddar-Dayton. 300fr, 1934 Cadillac. 400fr, 1931 Cadillac. 1000fr, 1928 Ford.

1997, July 5 Litho. *Perf. 13x12½*

987 A283 135fr multi .55 .50
988 A283 150fr multi .65 .60
989 A283 200fr multi .80 .80
990 A283 270fr multi 1.00 .90
991 A283 300fr multi 1.10 1.10
992 A283 400fr multi 1.60 1.50
Nos. 987-992 (6) 5.70 5.40

Souvenir Sheet

Perf. 13

993 A283 1000fr multi 4.00 4.00

No. 993 contains one 40x32mm stamp.
For surcharge on No. 990, see No. 1280.

Songbirds — A284

Designs: 135fr, Pyrrhula pyrrhula. 150fr, Carduelis spinus. 200fr, Turdus torquatus. 270fr, Parus cristatus. 300fr, Nucifraga caryocatactes. 400fr, Luscinia megarhynchos. 1000fr, Motacilla flava.

1997, July 30 *Perf. 13x12½*

994 A284 135fr multicolored .60 .40
995 A284 150fr multicolored .65 .50
996 A284 200fr multicolored .80 .70
997 A284 270fr multicolored 1.00 .90
998 A284 300fr multicolored 1.15 1.00
999 A284 400fr multicolored 1.60 1.50
Nos. 994-999 (6) 5.80 5.00

Souvenir Sheet

Perf. 12½

1000 A284 1000fr multicolored 4.00 4.00

No. 1000 contains one 32x40mm stamp.
For surcharges, see Nos. 1281, 1409.

Flowering Cactus — A285

Designs: 135fr, Faucaria lupina. 150fr, Conophytum bilobun. 200fr, Lithops aucampiae. 270fr, Lithops helmutii. 300fr, Stapelia grandiflora. 400fr, Lithops fulviceps. 1000fr, Pleiospilos willowmorensis.

1997, Aug. 30 Litho. *Perf. 13x12½*

1001 A285 135fr multicolored .60 .40
1002 A285 150fr multicolored .65 .60
1003 A285 200fr multicolored .80 .80
1004 A285 270fr multicolored 1.00 1.00
1005 A285 300fr multicolored 1.15 1.10
1006 A285 400fr multicolored 1.60 1.60
Nos. 1001-1006 (6) 5.80 5.50

Souvenir Sheet

Perf. 12½

1007 A285 1000fr multicolored 4.00 4.00

No. 1007 contains one 32x40mm stamp.
For surcharges, see Nos. 1282, 1339.

Benin No. 394, 418 Surcharged

1995

Perfs. & Printing Methods as Before

1008 A106 10fr on 90fr #394 *80.00 40.00*
1009 A114 10fr on 90fr #418 *80.00 40.00*

Dahomey Nos. 251, 307 Surcharged

1995 Method and Perf. As Before

1011 A67 135fr on 50fr Dahomey #307 *80.00 40.00*
1012 A46(h)135fr on 70fr Dahomey #251 —

Benin Nos. 813, 948 Surcharged

Printing Methods and Perfs as before

1997-99 (?)

1021A A256 135fr on 100fr #948 *40.00 20.00*
1021B A260 135fr on 200fr #813 *40.00 20.00*

Early Locomotives — A286

Designs: 135fr, Puffing Billy, 1813. 150fr, La Fusée, 1829. 200fr, Royal George, 1827. 270fr, Nouveauté, 1829. 300fr, Locomotion, 1825, vert. 400fr, Sans Pareil, 1829, vert. 1000fr, Trevithick locomotive.

1997, Dec. 3 Litho. *Perf. 13*

1022 A286 135fr multicolored .60 .40
1023 A286 150fr multicolored .65 .50
1024 A286 200fr multicolored .80 .70
1025 A286 270fr multicolored 1.00 .90
1026 A286 300fr multicolored 1.15 1.00
1027 A286 400fr multicolored 1.60 1.25
Nos. 1022-1027 (6) 5.80 4.75

Souvenir Sheet

1028 A286 1000fr multicolored 4.00 4.00

No. 1028 contains one 40x32mm stamp.
For surcharge on No. 1025, see Nos. 1283 and 1340.

Mushrooms A287

Designs: 135fr, Amanita caesarea. 150fr, Cortinarius collinitus. 200fr, Amanita bisporigera. 270fr, Amanita rubescens. 300fr, Russula virescens. 400fr, Amanita inaurata. 1000fr, Amanita muscaria.

1997, Nov. 5 Litho. *Perf. 13*

1029 A287 135fr multicolored .60 .40
1030 A287 150fr multicolored .65 .50
1031 A287 200fr multicolored .80 .70
1032 A287 270fr multicolored 1.00 .90
1033 A287 300fr multicolored 1.15 1.00
1034 A287 400fr multicolored 1.60 1.25
Nos. 1029-1034 (6) 5.80 4.75

Souvenir Sheet

1035 A287 1000fr multicolored 4.00 4.00

No. 1035 contains one 32x40mm stamp.
For surcharge on No. 1032, see No. 1284.

Assoc. of African Petroleum Producers, 10th Anniv. — A288

1997, Oct. 20 Litho. *Perf. 13*

1036 A288 135fr green & multi .60 .40
1037 A288 200fr orange & multi .80 .60
1038 A288 300fr blue & multi 1.20 .90
1039 A288 500fr yellow & multi 1.60 1.20
Nos. 1036-1039 (4) 4.20 3.10

For surcharge, see No. 1061E.

Old Sailing Vessels — A289

Designs: 135fr, Egyptian. 150fr, Greek. 200fr, Assyrian-Phoenician. 270fr, Roman. 300fr, Norman. 400fr, Mediterranean. 1000fr, English.

1997, Sept. 10 Litho. *Perf. 12½*

1040 A289 135fr multicolored .60 .40
1041 A289 150fr multicolored .75 .50
1042 A289 200fr multicolored .90 .70
1043 A289 270fr multicolored 1.00 .90
1044 A289 300fr multicolored 1.20 1.00
1045 A289 400fr multicolored 1.60 1.25
Nos. 1040-1045 (6) 6.05 4.75

Souvenir Sheet

1046 A289 1000fr multicolored 4.00 4.00

No. 1046 contains one 32x40mm stamp.
For surcharges, see Nos. 1205, 1341.

Fish A290

Designs: 135fr, Epinephelus fasciatus. 150fr, Apogon victoriae. 200fr, Scarus gibbus. 270fr, Pygoplites diacanthus. 300fr, Cirrhilabrus punctatus. 400fr, Cirrhitichthys oxycephalus. 1000fr, Bodianus bilunulatus.

1997, Sept. 15 Litho. *Perf. 12½*

1047 A290 135fr multicolored .60 .40
1048 A290 150fr multicolored .65 .50
1049 A290 200fr multicolored .80 .70
1050 A290 270fr multicolored 1.00 .90
1051 A290 300fr multicolored 1.15 1.00
1052 A290 400fr multicolored 1.60 1.25
Nos. 1047-1052 (6) 5.80 4.75

Souvenir Sheet

Perf. 13

1053 A290 1000fr multicolored 4.00 4.00

No. 1053 contains one 40x32mm stamp.
For surcharges, see Nos. 1286, 1408.

Arabian Horse — A291

Various horses. Denominations and background colors: d, 135fr, pale green. e, 150fr, orange brown. f, 200fr, yellow. g, 270fr, orange brown. h, 300fr, tan. i, 400fr, pale green.

1997, May 25 Litho. *Perf. 12½*

1053A A291 Pair, #d.-e. 1.25 1.00
1053B A291 Pair, #f.-g. 1.75 1.60
1053C A291 Pair, #h.-i. 3.00 2.25
Nos. 1053A-1053C (3) 6.00 4.85

Souvenir Sheet

1054 A291 1000fr multicolored 4.00 4.00

Dahomey Nos. 242, 243, 263, 266, 296, 340 Surcharged

Methods and Perfs As Before

1997

1054A	A51(h)	35fr on 45fr #263	*30.00*	*30.00*
1054B	A52(h)	35fr on 45fr #266	*50.00*	*50.00*
1054C	AP82(h)	35fr on 50fr #340	*50.00*	*50.00*
1054D	A62(h)	35fr on 65fr #296	*35.00*	*35.00*
1054E	A43(h)	35fr on 100fr #243	—	—
1054F	A43(e)	135fron 450fr #242	—	—

Mushrooms A292

135fr, Tephrocybe carbonaria. 150fr, Suillus luteus. 200fr, Pleurotus ostreatus. 270fr, Hohenbuehelia geogenia. 300fr, Tylopilus felleus. 400fr, Lepiota leucothites.
1000fr, Gymnopilus junonius.

1998, Apr. 28 Litho. *Perf. 12½*

1055	A292	135fr multicolored	.60	.40
1056	A292	150fr multicolored	.65	.50
1057	A292	200fr multicolored	.80	.70
1058	A292	270fr multicolored	1.00	.90
1059	A292	300fr multicolored	1.15	1.00
1060	A292	400fr multicolored	1.60	1.25
		Nos. 1055-1060 (6)	5.80	4.75

Souvenir Sheet

1061	A292	1000fr multicolored	3.75	3.75

For surcharges, see Nos. 1287, 1342.

Nos. 432, 433, 632, 695, 1037 Surcharged or Overprinted

No. 1061F

1998 Method and Perf. as Before

1061A	A121(h)	15fr on #432	*35.00*	*15.00*
1061B	A121(h)	35fr on 50fr #433	*35.00*	*35.00*
1061C	A121(h)	50fr on #433	*37.50*	*20.00*
1061D	A243	50fr on 190fr #695	*300.00*	*150.00*
1061E	A288	135fr on 200fr #1037	*47.50*	*24.00*
1061F	A195(h)	150fr on 205fr #632	*37.50*	*20.00*

Fire Fighting Apparatus — A293

135fr, Philadelphia Double Deck, 1885. 150fr, Veteran, 1850. 200fr, Merry Weather, 1894. 270fr, Horse-drawn wagon, 19th cent. 300fr, 1948 Jeep. 400fr, Chevrolet 6400.
1000fr, 1952 American-La France-Foamite Corp.

1998, Apr. 30 Litho. *Perf. 12¾*

1062	A293	135fr multicolored	.60	.40
1063	A293	150fr multicolored	.65	.50
1064	A293	200fr multicolored	.80	.70
1065	A293	270fr multicolored	1.00	.80
1066	A293	300fr multicolored	1.15	1.00
1067	A293	400fr multicolored	1.60	1.25
		Nos. 1062-1067 (6)	5.80	4.65

Souvenir Sheet

1068	A293	1000fr multicolored	3.75	3.75

No. 1068 contains one 40x32mm stamp.
For surcharges, see Nos. 1288, 1343.

Minerals — A294

No. 1069a, 135fr, Uranifere. No. 1069b, 150fr, Quartz. No. 1070a, 200fr, Aragonite. No. 1070b, 270fr, Malachite. No. 1071a, 300fr, Turquoise. No. 1071b, 400fr, Corundum.
1000fr, Marble.

1998, June 5 Litho. *Perf. 12½*

1069	A294	Pair, #a.-b.	1.20	.90
1070	A294	Pair, #a.-b.	1.75	1.60
1071	A294	Pair, #a.-b.	2.60	2.25
		Nos. 1069-1071 (3)	5.55	4.75

Souvenir Sheet

1072	A294	1000fr multicolored	3.75	3.75

Locomotives — A295

Designs: 135fr, Red 0-6-0. 150fr, 0-4-4. 200fr, Brown 0-6-0. 270fr, Purple 0-6-0. 300fr, Blue 0-6-0. 400fr, "Helvetia" 0-6-0.
1000fr, "Shelby Steel" 0-6-0.

1998, June 30 Litho. *Perf. 12¾*

1073	A295	135fr multicolored	.60	.40
1074	A295	150fr multicolored	.65	.50
1075	A295	200fr multicolored	.80	.70
1076	A295	270fr multicolored	1.00	.90
1077	A295	300fr multicolored	1.15	1.00
1078	A295	400fr multicolored	1.60	1.25
		Nos. 1073-1078 (6)	5.80	4.75

Souvenir Sheet

Perf. 13

1079	A295	1000fr multicolored	3.75	3.75

No. 1079 contains one 40x32mm stamp.
For surcharge on No. 1076, see Nos. 1289 and 1344.

Diana, Princess of Wales (1961-97) — A296

Portraits: a, 135fr. b, 150fr. c, 200fr. d, 270fr. e, 300fr. f, 400fr. g, 500fr. h, 600fr. i, 700fr.

1998, July 10 Litho. *Perf. 12½*

1083	A296	Sheet of 9, #a.-i.	12.00	12.00

Dahomey No. 302 Surcharged

1997?

Perfs. & Printing Method as Before

1084	A65(h)	35fr on 85fr #302	*65.00*	*60.00*

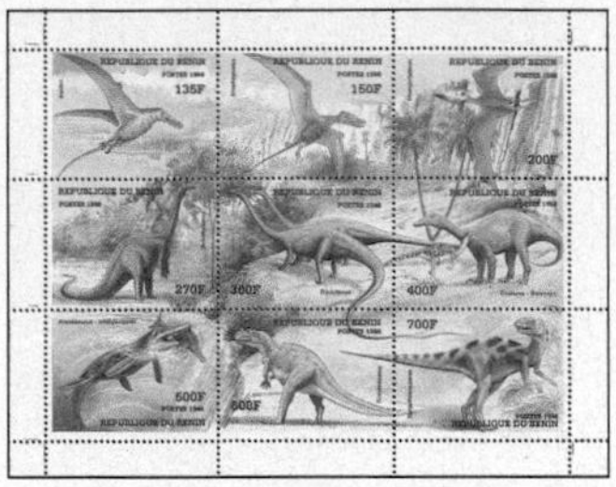

Dinosaurs — A297

No. 1085: a, 135fr, Sordes. b, 150fr, Scaphognatus. c, 200fr, Dsungaripterus. d, 270fr, Brontosaurus. e, 300fr, Diplodocus. f, 400fr, Coelurus, Baryonyx. g, 500fr, Kronosaurus, Ichthyosaurus. h, 600fr, Ceratosaurus. i, 700f, Yangchuansaurus.

1998, July 25 Litho. *Perf. 12¾*

1085	A297	Sheet of 9, #a-i	12.00	12.00

Python Regius A298

Various views of python: a, 135fr. b, 150fr. c, 200fr. d, 2000fr.

1999, Apr. 27 Litho. *Perf. 13*

1086	A298	Strip of 4, #a.-d.	8.00	8.00

World Wildlife Fund.

Dogs — A299

135fr, Beagle. 150fr, Dalmatian. 200fr, Dachshund. 270fr, Cairn terrier. 300fr, Shih Tzu. 400fr, Pug.
1000fr, Springer spaniel, horiz.

1998, July 31 Litho. *Perf. 12¾*

1087	A299	135fr multi	.60	.40
1088	A299	150fr multi	.65	.50
1089	A299	200fr multi	.80	.70
1090	A299	270fr multi	1.00	.90
1091	A299	300fr multi	1.20	1.00
1092	A299	400fr multi	1.60	1.25
		Nos. 1087-1092 (6)	5.85	4.75

Souvenir Sheet

Perf. 13

1093	A299	1000fr multi	3.75	3.25

No. 1093 contains one 40x32mm stamp.
For surcharge on No. 1090, see Nos. 1290 and 1345.

Cats A300

135fr, Abyssinian. 150fr, Striped shorthair. 200fr, Siamese. 270fr, Red striped cat. 300fr, Gray cat with black stripes. 400fr, Manx.
1000fr, Cat with orange, black and white fur.

Perf. 12¼x12½, 12½x12¼

1998, Aug. 10 Litho.

1094	A300	135fr multi, vert.	.50	.40
1095	A300	150fr multi, vert.	.60	.50
1096	A300	200fr multi, vert.	.90	.70
1097	A300	270fr multi	1.00	.90
1098	A300	300fr multi	1.15	1.00
1099	A300	400fr multi	1.40	1.25
		Nos. 1094-1099 (6)	5.55	4.75

Souvenir Sheet

Perf. 13

1100	A300	1000fr multicolored	3.75	3.25

No. 1100 contains one 40x32mm stamp.
For surcharges, see Nos. 1291, 1346.

Antique Automobiles — A301

Designs: 135fr, 1910 Bugatti 13. 150fr, 1903 Clément. 200fr, 1914 Stutz Bearcat. 270fr, 1907 Darracq. 300fr, 1913 Napier. 400fr, 1911 Pierce-Arrow.
1000fr, 1904 Piccolo, vert.

1998, Oct. 12 Litho. *Perf. 12¾*

1101	A301	135fr multi	.60	.40
1102	A301	150fr multi	.65	.50
1103	A301	200fr multi	.80	.70
1104	A301	270fr multi	.95	.90
1105	A301	300fr multi	1.15	1.00
1106	A301	400fr multi	1.50	1.25
		Nos. 1101-1106 (6)	5.65	4.75

Souvenir Sheet

Perf. 12¾x12½

1107	A301	1000fr multi	3.75	3.25

No. 1107 contains one 32x40mm stamp.
For surcharge on No. 1104, see No. 1292.

Butterflies — A301a

Designs: 135fr, Parnassius apollo. 150fr, Anthocharis cardamines. 200fr, Nymphalis antiopa. 250fr, Parage aegeria. 300fr, Palaeochrysophanus hippothoe. 400fr, Carterocephalus palaemon.
1000fr, Aglais urticae.

1998, Dec. 10 Litho. *Perf. 12¾*

1107A-1107F	A301a	Set of 6	5.75	3.75

Souvenir Sheet

Perf. 13

1107G	A301a	1000fr multi	3.75	3.25

No. 1107G contains one 40x32mm stamp.

African Wildlife — A302

Designs: 50fr, Ceratotherium simun. 100fr, Hipotragus niger. No. 1110, Phacochoerus aethiopicus. No. 1111, Hyaena brunnea. No. 1112, Colobus guereza. No. 1113, Hippopotamus amphibius. No. 1114, Cyncerus caffer caffer. No. 1115, Equus zebra. No. 1116, Acinonyx jubatus. No. 1117, Panthera leo leo. 400fr, Lycaon pictus. 500fr, Perodicticus potto.

Perf. 12¼x12½

1999, Mar. 10 Litho.

1108	A302	50fr gray	*1.10*	.25
1109	A302	100fr brt violet	*1.10*	.25
1110	A302	135fr gray green	*1.10*	.30
1111	A302	135fr black	*1.10*	.30
1112	A302	150fr gray blue	*1.10*	.40
1113	A302	150fr emerald	*1.10*	.40
1114	A302	200fr dull brown	*1.40*	.55
1115	A302	200fr blue	*1.40*	.55
1116	A302	300fr henna brown	*1.50*	.75

1117 A302 300fr brown *1.50* .75
1118 A302 400fr red brown *2.25* 1.10
1119 A302 500fr deep bister *3.00* 1.30
Nos. 1108-1119 (12) *17.65* 6.90

Birds — A303

Designs: 135fr, Chloebia gouldiae. 150fr, Sicalis flaveola. 200fr, Quelea quelea. 270fr, Euplectes afer. 300fr, Paroaria coronata. 400fr, Emberiza flaviventris.
1000fr, Mandingoa nitidula.

1999, Jan. 30 Litho. *Perf. 12¾*
1120-1125 A303 Set of 6 5.50 4.00

Souvenir Sheet
Perf. 12½

1126 A303 1000fr multi 3.75 3.25

No. 1126 contains one 32x40mm stamp.
For surcharges, see Nos. 1293, 1410.

Orchids A304

Designs: 50fr, Brassocattleya cliftonii. 100fr, Wilsonara. 150fr, Cypripodium paeony. 300fr, Cymbidium babylon. 400fr, Cattleya. 500fr, Miltonia minx.

1999, Apr. 25 Litho. *Perf. 12¾*
1127 A304 50fr multi .25 .25
1128 A304 100fr multi .40 .35
1129 A304 150fr multi .60 .50
1130 A304 300fr multi 1.15 .90
1131 A304 400fr multi 1.50 1.10
1132 A304 500fr multi 1.75 1.40
Nos. 1127-1132 (6) 5.65 4.50

Souvenir Sheet
Perf. 13

1133 A304 1000fr Miltonia (isis) 3.75 3.25

No. 1133 contains one 28x36mm stamp.
For surcharge, see No. 1239.

Chess Players A305

Designs: 135fr, Mikhail Tal. 150fr, Emanuel Lasker. 200fr, José Raul Capablanca. 270fr, Alexander Alekhine. 300fr, Max Euwe. 400fr, Mikhail Botvinnik.
1000fr, Wilhelm Steinitz.

1999, Mar. 28 Litho. *Perf. 12¾*
1134-1139 A305 Set of 6 5.50 4.00

Souvenir Sheet
Perf. 13

1140 A305 1000fr multi 3.75 3.25

No. 1140 contains one 32x40mm stamp.
For surcharge on No. 1137, see No. 1294.

Ancient Sailing Ships A306

Designs: 135fr, Ceylonese canot. 150fr, Tanka-tim. 200fr, Sampan. 270fr, Polynesian canot. 300fr, Japanese junk. 400fr, Dacca-pulwar.
1000fr, Chinese junk.

1999, Feb. 15 Litho. *Perf. 12¾*
1141-1146 A306 Set of 6 5.50 4.00

Souvenir Sheet
Perf. 12½

1147 A306 1000fr multi 3.75 3.25

No. 1147 contains one 40x32mm stamp.
For surcharge on No. 1144, see No. 1295.

Fish — A307

Designs: 135fr, Notopterus chitala. 150fr, Puntius filamentosus. 200fr, Epalzeorhynchos bicolor. 270fr, Rasbora maculata. 300fr, Pristolepis fasciatus. 400fr, Betta splendens.
1000fr, Trichogaster trichopterus.

1999, May 10 Litho. *Perf. 12½x12¼*
1148 A307 135fr multi .55 .35
1149 A307 150fr multi .65 .40
1150 A307 200fr multi .80 .60
1151 A307 270fr multi .95 .75
1152 A307 300fr multi 1.10 .80
1153 A307 400fr multi 1.60 1.20
Nos. 1148-1153 (6) 5.65 4.10

Souvenir Sheet
Perf. 13x13¼

1154 A307 1000fr multi 3.75 3.25

No. 1154 contains one 40x32mm stamp.
For surcharge, see No. 1347.

Grand Prix de l'Amitie of France Afrique — A308

1999 Litho. *Perf. 13½x13*
1154A A308 135fr multi *50.00* —
1155 A308 150fr multi *50.00 11.00*
1156 A308 200fr multi *50.00 14.00*
1157 A308 300fr multi *50.00 20.00*
1157A A308 500fr multi *50.00 10.00*
b. Souvenir sheet *125.00*
1158 A308 1000fr multi *50.00 14.00*
Nos. 1154A-1158 (6) *300.00 69.00*

Early Steam Vehicles A309

Designs: 135fr, 1786 tricycle made by A. Murdock. 150fr, 1800 locomotive made by Richard Trevithick. 200fr, 1803 locomotive made by Trevithick. 270fr, 1811 locomotive made by John Blenkinsop. 300fr, 1829 locomotive, Stourbridge Lion. 400fr, 1830 locomotive, Tom Thumb.
1000fr, 1760 locomotive made by Isaac Newton, horiz.

1999, June 18 Litho. *Perf. 12¾*
1159-1164 A309 Set of 6 5.50 4.00

Souvenir Sheet
Perf. 13

1165 A309 1000fr multi 3.75 3.25

No. 1165 contains one 40x32 mm stamp.
For surcharge on No. 1162, see No. 1348.

Council of the Entente, 40th Anniv. A310

1999-2001 Litho. *Perf. 13x13¼*
1166 A310 135fr multi, dated "1999" *35.00 20.00*
a. Perf. 13½x13¼, dated "2000" — *15.00*
b. Perf. 13½x13¼, dated "2001" — —
c. Perf. 13, dated "2001" — —
d. Perf. 13x13¼, dated "2000" *45.00* —
e. Perf. 13x13¼, dated "2001" *45.00 25.00*
1167 A310 150fr multi, dated "1999" *35.00 8.00*
a. Perf. 13½x13¼, dated "2001" — *20.00*
b. Perf. 13x13¼, dated "2001" — *15.00*
c. Perf. 13x13¼, dated "2000" *10.00*
d. Perf. 13½x13¼, dated "2000" *45.00 15.00*
1168 A310 200fr multi, dated "1999" *10.00*
a. Perf. 13x13¼, dated "2000" — *11.00*
b. Perf. 13½x13¼, dated "2001" — *16.00*
c. Perf. 13x13¼, dated "2001" *12.00*
d. Perf. 13½x13¼, dated "2000" — *16.00*

Snakes A311

Designs: 135fr, Elaphe longissima. 150fr, Pituophis melanoleucus. 200fr, Natrix natrix. 270fr, Oxybelis fulgidus. 300fr, Epicrates subflavus. 400fr, Crotalus atrox.
1000fr, Vipera berus.

1999, July 18 Litho. *Perf. 12¾*
1170-1175 A311 Set of 6 5.50 4.00

Souvenir Sheet
Perf. 13

1176 A311 1000fr multi 3.75 3.25

No. 1176 contains one 40x32mm stamp.
For surcharge on No. 1173, see No. 1349.

China 1999 World Philatelic Exhibition — A312

No. 1177: a, 50fr, Rocket testing, 14th cent. b, 100fr, Jiuquan space launch center. c, 135fr, DFH-3 communications satellite. d, 150fr, Launch of a foreign satellite. e, 200fr, Long March rocket CZ-2C. f, 300fr, Ship Yuan Wang. g, 400fr, Satellite dish. h, 500fr, Cacheted stamped covers.

1999, Aug. 22 *Perf. 12½*
1177 A312 Sheet of 8, #a-h 7.50 7.50

SOS Children's Villages, 50th Anniv. — A313

Denominations and panel colors: 135fr, Light green. 200fr, Pink. 300fr, Light blue. 500fr, Yellow.

1999, Oct. 15 Litho. *Perf. 12¾*
1178-1181 A313 Set of 4 4.25 4.25

For surcharges, see Nos. 1208, 1240, 1296.

Souvenir Sheet

Manchester United, 1999 English Soccer Champions — A314

No. 1182: a, 135fr, Players celebrating on platform. b, 200fr, Players in action. c, 300fr, Players celebrating. d, 400fr, Stadium. e, 500fr, Trophies. f, 1000fr, Player with trophy.

1999, Oct. 15 *Perf. 13¼*
1182 A314 Sheet of 6, #a-f 9.00 7.25

The sets formerly listed as Nos. 1183-1189 (New Year 2000 - Year of the Dragon) and 1211-1217 (Dogs) were apparently prepared but not issued. These and a set of 12 stamps depicting songbirds were not sold in Benin, and they were not valid for postage. A stamp from the dog set and two stamps from the songbirds set were later surcharged. See Nos. 1351-1353.

Wild Cats A316

Designs: 135fr, Acinonyx jubatus. 150fr, Panthera onca. 200fr, Panthera uncia. 270fr, Panthera pardus. 300fr, Felis concolor. 400fr, Panthera tigris.
1000fr, Panthera leo.

Perf. 12½x12¼
1999, Sept. 28 Litho.
1190-1195 A316 Set of 6 5.50 4.00

Souvenir Sheet

1196 A316 1000fr multi 3.75 3.25

For surcharge, see No. 1350.

Cacti — A317

Designs: 135fr, Mammillaria lenta. 150fr, Oehmea nelsonii. 200fr, Neobesseya rosiflora. 270fr, Opuntia gosseliniana. 300fr, Parodia nivosa. 400fr, Rebutia senilis.
1000fr, Opuntia retrorsa, vert.

1999, Oct. 10 Litho. *Perf. 12¼*

1197-1202 A317 Set of 6 5.50 4.00

Souvenir Sheet

Perf. 12½

1203 A317 1000fr multi 3.75 3.25

No. 1203 contains one 32x40mm rectangular stamp.

Birds — A318

No. 1204: a, 135fr, Estrilda locustella. b, 150fr, Estrilda melanotis.
No. 1205: a, 200fr, Pytelia melba. b, 270fr, Uraeginthus bengalensis.
No. 1206: a, 300fr, Pyromelana orix. b, 400fr, Ploceus cucullatus.
1000fr, Steganura paradisea.

1999, Dec. 7 Litho. *Perf. 12¼*

Pairs, #a-b

1204-1206 A318 Set of 3 5.50 4.00

Souvenir Sheet

1207 A318 1000fr multi 3.75 3.25

Insects — A318a

Designs: 135fr, Zonabris polymorpha. 150fr, Lilioceris lilii. 200fr, Eupholus bennetti. 270fr, Goliathus druryi. 300fr, Leptinotarsa decemlineata. 400fr, Scarabeus sacer.
1000fr, Melasoma populi.

2000 ? Litho. *Perf. 13*

1207A	A318a	135fr multi	—	—
1207B	A318a	150fr multi	—	—
1207C	A318a	200fr multi	—	—
1207D	A318a	270fr multi	—	—
1207E	A318a	300fr multi	—	—
1207F	A318a	400fr multi	—	—

Souvenir Sheet

1207G A318a 1000fr multi — —

Bangkok 2000 Intl. Philatelic Exhibition. Nos. 1207A-1207G were prepared for issue in 2000 but did not go on sale until sometime later. For surcharge, see No. 1354.

No. 1180 Surcharged Method and Perf. as Before

2000 ?

1208 A313 135fr on 300fr #1180 *140.00 50.00*

Nos. 850, 873 Surcharged

Methods and Perfs. as Before

2000 ?

1209 A267 135fr on 40fr #850 *140.00* —
1210 A271 150fr on 75fr #873 75.00 40.00

Lions A319

Designs: 135fr, Lion lying on side. 150fr, Lion walking. 200fr, Lions hunting zebras.

2001 Litho. *Perf. 12*

1211 A319 135fr multi 1.10 1.10
1212 A319 150fr multi 1.20 1.20

Size: 65x22mm

1213 A319 200fr multi 1.75 1.75
Nos. 1211-1213 (3) 4.05 4.05

Three 750fr stamps and a 1500fr souvenir sheet depicting lions and their prey were not authorized by Benin postal officials.

Fire Vehicles — A319a

Designs: 135fr, 1890 hose wagon. 150fr, 1900 fire truck. 200fr, 1903 fire truck. No. 1214C, 750fr, 1913 ladder truck. No. 1214D, 750fr, 1923 ladder truck.

2001 Litho. *Perf. 12*

1214	A319a	135fr multi	*15.00*	—
1214A	A319a	150fr multi	*15.00*	—
1214B	A319a	200fr multi	*15.00*	—
1214C	A319a	750fr multi	*15.00*	—
1214D	A319a	750fr multi	*15.00*	—
		Nos. 1214-1214D (5)	*75.00*	

Benin postal authorities declared a 750fr stamp depicting a 1940 ladder truck and a 1500fr souvenir sheet depicting an 1877 pumper as "not authorized."

A319b

A319c

Primates — A319d

Designs: 150fr, Head of gorilla. 200fr, Gorilla.

2001 Litho. *Perf. 12*

1215	A319b	135fr shown	*15.00*	—
1215A	A319b	150fr multi	*15.00*	—
1215B	A319b	200fr multi	*15.00*	—
1215C	A319c	750fr shown	*15.00*	—
1215D	A319d	750fr shown	*15.00*	—
		Nos. 1215-1215D (5)	*75.00*	

Benin postal authorities declared another 750fr stamp depiciting a primate and a 1500fr souvenir sheet depicting a gorilla as "not authorized."

Abdus Salam, 1979 Nobel Physics Laureate — A320

Abdus Salam and Building A321

2001 Litho. *Perf. 13¼x13*

1218 A320 135fr multi, dated 2001 *7.50 3.00*
a. Dated 2002 *5.00 2.00*
1219 A321 150fr multi, dated 2001 *7.50 3.00*
a. Dated 2002 *5.00 2.00*
1220 A321 200fr multi, dated 2001 — —
a. Dated 2002 *5.00 3.00*
Nos. 1218-1220 (3) 15.00 6.00

Edward Bouchet Abdus Salam Institute Intl. Conference on Physics and High Technology for the Development of Africa, Cotonou. The editors suspect there may be additional stamps in this set and would like to examine any examples. Numbers may change.
For surcharge on No. 1219, see No. 1323.

From this point forward many stamps exist with what appears to be a one-bar obliterator. These are believed to be trial obliterators that were applied to a few rows. The trial sheets were mixed with the other sheets when the surcharging was done, and the two-bar obliterator was applied overtop of the single bar.
When the two-bar obliterator was shifted so that it did not fully cancel the old value, felt pens were frequently used to cross out the old value.

Various Stamps of 1995-99 Surcharged Like No. 1209

No. 1222

No. 1296

Methods and Perfs As Before

2000

1222	A249	135fr on 40fr	#741	*130.00*	*65.00*
1223	A250	135fr on 40fr	#748	*130.00*	*65.00*
1224	A252	135fr on 40fr	#761	*130.00*	*65.00*
1225	A253	135fr on 40fr	#768	*130.00*	*65.00*
1226	A255	135fr on 40fr	#780	*130.00*	*65.00*
1227	A257	135fr on 40fr	#795	*130.00*	*65.00*
1228	A258	135fr on 40fr	#801	*130.00*	*65.00*
1229	A262	135fr on 40fr	#816	*130.00*	*65.00*
1230	A264	135fr on 40fr	#829	*130.00*	*65.00*
1231	A265	135fr on 40fr	#836	*130.00*	*65.00*
1232	A266	135fr on 40fr	#843	*130.00*	*65.00*
1233	A268	135fr on 40fr	#857	*130.00*	*65.00*
1234	A271	135fr on 40fr	#871	*130.00*	*65.00*
1235	A272	135fr on 40fr	#877	*130.00*	*65.00*
1236	A273	135fr on 40fr	#884	*130.00*	*65.00*
1237	A275	135fr on 40fr	#930	*130.00*	*65.00*
1238	A276	135fr on 40fr	#936	*130.00*	*65.00*
1239	A304	135fr on 400fr	#1131	*130.00*	*65.00*
1240	A313	135fr on 500fr	#1181	—	—
1241	A248	150fr on 75fr	#736	*70.00*	*30.00*
1242	A251	150fr on 75fr	#756	*70.00*	*30.00*
1243	A255	150fr on 75fr	#782	*70.00*	*30.00*
1244	A257	150fr on 75fr	#797	*70.00*	*30.00*
1245	A262	150fr on 75fr	#818	*70.00*	*30.00*
1246	A263	150fr on 75fr	#824	*70.00*	*30.00*
1247	A264	150fr on 75fr	#831	*70.00*	*30.00*
1248	A265	150fr on 75fr	#838	*70.00*	*30.00*
1249	A267	150fr on 75fr	#852	*70.00*	*30.00*
1250	A268	150fr on 75fr	#859	*70.00*	*30.00*
1251	A270	150fr on 75fr	#867	*70.00*	*30.00*
1252	A273	150fr on 75fr	#886	*70.00*	*30.00*
1253	A274	150fr on 75fr	#892	*70.00*	*30.00*
1254	A275	150fr on 75fr	#932	*70.00*	*30.00*
1255	A276	150fr on 75fr	#938	*70.00*	*30.00*
1256	A277	150fr on 75fr	#943	*70.00*	*30.00*
1257	A248	150fr on 100fr	#737	*70.00*	*30.00*
1258	A249	150fr on 100fr	#744	*70.00*	*30.00*
1259	A250	150fr on 100fr	#751	*70.00*	*30.00*
1260	A251	150fr on 100fr	#757	*70.00*	*30.00*
1261	A252	150fr on 100fr	#764	*70.00*	*30.00*
1262	A253	150fr on 100fr	#771	*70.00*	*30.00*
1263	A254	150fr on 100fr	#776	*70.00*	*30.00*
1264	A262	150fr on 100fr	#819	*70.00*	*30.00*
1265	A263	150fr on 100fr	#825	*70.00*	*30.00*
1266	A264	150fr on 100fr	#832	*70.00*	*30.00*
1267	A265	150fr on 100fr	#839	*70.00*	*30.00*
1268	A266	150fr on 100fr	#846	*70.00*	*30.00*
1269	A267	150fr on 100fr	#853	*70.00*	*30.00*
1270	A268	150fr on 100fr	#860	*70.00*	*30.00*
1271	A270	150fr on 100fr	#868	*70.00*	*30.00*
1272	A271	150fr on 100fr	#874	*70.00*	*30.00*
1273	A276	150fr on 100fr	#939	*70.00*	*30.00*
1274	A277	150fr on 100fr	#944	*70.00*	*30.00*
1275	A278	150fr on 270fr	#955	*70.00*	*30.00*
1276	A279	150fr on 270fr	#962	*70.00*	*30.00*
1277	A280	150fr on 270fr	#969	*70.00*	*30.00*
1278	A281	150fr on 270fr	#976	*70.00*	*30.00*
1279	A282	150fr on 270fr	#983	*70.00*	*30.00*
1280	A283	150fr on 270fr	#990	*70.00*	*30.00*
1281	A284	150fr on 270fr	#997	*70.00*	*30.00*
1282	A285	150fr on 270fr	#1004	*70.00*	*30.00*
1283	A286	150fr on 270fr	#1025	*70.00*	*30.00*
1284	A287	150fr on 270fr	#1032	*70.00*	*30.00*
1285	A289	150fr on 270fr	#1043	*70.00*	*30.00*
1286	A290	150fr on 270fr	#1050	*70.00*	*30.00*
1287	A292	150fr on 270fr	#1058	*70.00*	*30.00*
1288	A293	150fr on 270fr	#1065	*70.00*	*30.00*

1289 A295 150fr on 270fr #1076 *70.00 30.00*
1290 A299 150fr on 270fr #1090 *70.00 30.00*
1291 A300 150fr on 270fr #1097 *70.00 30.00*
1292 A301 150fr on 270fr #1104 *70.00 30.00*
1293 A303 150fr on 270fr #1123 *70.00 30.00*
1294 A305 150fr on 270fr #1137 *70.00 30.00*
1295 A306 150fr on 270fr #1144 *70.00 30.00*
1296 A313 150fr on 500fr #1181 *70.00 30.00*

From this point forward many stamps exist with what appears to be a one-bar obliterator. These are believed to be trial obliterators that were applied to a few rows. The trial sheets were mixed with the other sheets when the surcharging was done, and the two-bar obliterator was applied overtop of the single bar. No. 1240 exists with surcharge "153F."

Items inscribed "Republique du Benin" that were not authorized by Benin postal officials but which have appeared on the philatelic market include:

Sheet of 15 stamps with various denominations depicting dogs.

Sheet of 9 stamps with various denominations depicting American movie stars, Isabella Rosselini.

Sheets of 6 stamps of various denominations depicting Pope John Paul II, bats, deer, dolphins, frogs, geckos, hares, hummingbirds, kangaroos, lemurs, owls (2 different), pandas, penguins, pigeons, porcupines, rodents, sea gulls, snakes, squirrels, thrushes, toads, turtles.

Souvenir sheets with one 1000fr stamp depicting Isabella Rosselini (2 different), bats, deer, dolphins, frogs, geckos, hares, hummingbirds, kangaroos, lemurs, pigeons, porcupines, rodents, sea gulls, snakes, squirrels, thrushes, toads, turtles.

Sheet of 9 stamps with various denominations depicting Polar bears, Dogs, Wild cats.

Sheet of 8 stamps with various denominations depicting Spiderman, Vin Diesel.

Sheet of 6 stamps with various denominations depicting Lighthouses (2 different), Tigers (2 different), Turtles, Military aircraft.

Sheet of 12 stamps with various denominations depicting Marilyn Monroe (2 different), French firefighters, Carlos Cartagena, Sean Gallimore, Land of the Rising Fun.

Sheets of 10 stamps with various denominations depicting Wolves, Bears, Birds, Elvis Presley.

Sheet of 9 stamps with 100fr denominations depicting Pope John Paul II with Princess Diana.

Sheets of 9 stamps with various denominations depicting Lighthouses (4 different), Windmills (3 different), Looney Tunes characters (3 different), English soccer players and teams (3 different), Paintings of nudes (2 different), Harry Potter (2 different), The Lord of the Rings: The Two Towers (2 different), Terminator 3, Britney Spears, Elvis Presley, Marilyn Monroe, Red Cross, Endangered Animals, Nature Conservancy, Orchids, Gorillas, Cheetahs, Elephants, Lions, Tigers, Horses, Dinosaurs (with Scout emblem), Dinosaurs (without emblems), Trains, Al Buell, Billy DeVorss, Boris Lopez, Edward D'Ancona, Luis Royo Nude Miyazawa, Pearl Frush, Sexy Models, Top Models.

Sheet of 8 stamps with various denominations depicting Horses, Robbie Williams.

Sheet of 6 stamps with 500fr denominations depicting Marilyn Monroe (2 different), Lighthouses, Motorcycles, Trains, Ferrari racing cars, Actresses, Partially nude models.

Sheet of 6 stamps with 300fr denominations depicting Shunga.

Sheets of 6 stamps with 200fr denominations depicting Scenes from Lighthouses, French tales, Wild cats (with scout emblem), Trains.

Sheets of 6 stamps with 100fr denominations depicting Dinosaurs (2 different), Dinosaurs (with Rotary emblem) (2 different), Fire Engines (2 different), Arctic Animals, Lions, Wolves, Prehistoric Elephants, Domestic Cats (with Scout and Rotary emblem), Domestic Cats (without emblems), Dogs, Owls (with Scout emblem), Owls (without emblems), Sparrowhawks, Falcons, Trains, Elvis Presley, Marilyn Monroe, The Beatles.

Sheets of 6 stamps with various denominations depicting Paintings in the Prado (11 differerent), Impressionist Paintings (5 different), Classic Movies (3 different), Marilyn Monroe (3 different), Elvis Presley (perf. and imperf.) (3 different), 75th Academy Awards (2 different), Turtles (2 different), Parrots (with Scout emblem) (2 different), Owl paintings of Pollyanna Pickering (2 different), Trains (2 different), Motorcycles (2 different), Ferrari racing cars, Classic automobiles, Scenes from Japanese tale "Spirited Away," Dogs, Butterflies on Orchids, Dinosaurs, Audubon paintings of animals, Nature Conservancy, James Bond films, Vincent van Gogh, paintings of Nudes, Military aircraft, Pope John Paul II, Elvis Presley, Japanese women, Jazz musicians, Anton Corbijo, Baron Jerry von Lind, Dorian Cleavenger, Drew Posada, Helmut Newton, Matt Hughes, Edvard Runci, Top Models.

Sheet of 4 stamps with 1000fr denominations depicting Winnie the Pooh.

Sheet of 4 stamps with various denominations depicting Madonna, AC/DC, Backstreet Boys, The Beatles, Bee Gees, The Doors, Freddy Mercury, Kiss, Led Zeppelin, Metallica, Mick Jagger, Queen, Bob Hope.

Sheet of 3 stamps with 1000fr denominations depicting Scenes from children's stories.

Sheets of 3 stamps with various denominations depicting Nature Conservancy (2 different), Fighter Air planes, Trains, Automobiles, Pope John Paul II with Mother Teresa and Princess Diana (perf. and imperf.).

Sheets of 2 stamps with 1000fr denominations depicting Nature Conservancy, Pope John Paul II.

Sheets of 2 stamps with 500fr denominations depicting Dinosaurs, Pandas, Chess, Trains, Elvis Presley.

Souvenir sheets of 1 stamp with 3000fr denomination depicting Gullivera Part I, Gullivera Part II.

Souvenir sheets of 1 stamp with 1000fr denomination depicting Disney Characters, Elvis Presley and various scenes from children's stories (15 different), Marilyn Monroe (11 different), Birds (10 different), Elvis Presley (6 different), Windmills (4 different), Aircraft (4 different), Pope John Paul II with Princess Diana (4 different), Lighthouses (3 different); Ricky Carralero (3 different), Pope John Paul II (2 different), Automobiles (2 different), Trains (2 different), Endangered Animals (2 different), Dinosaurs (with Scout emblem) (2 different), Dinosaurs (without emblems) (2 different), Baron Jerry von Lind (2 different), Dorian Cleavenger (2 different), Drew Posada (2 different), Dogs, Penguins, Water Birds, Sea Creatures, Audubon painting of a fox, Nature Conservancy, Madonna, Nadja Auermann, Vincent van Gogh, Painting of a Nude, Japanese Women, Manchester United soccer team, Firefighters, Matt Hughes, Carlos Cartagena, Pope John Paul II with Mother Teresa.

Souvenir sheets of 1 stamp with 500fr denomination depicting James Bond films (3 different), The Beatles (2 different), Owls, Al Buell, Freeman Elliot, Peter Driben, Land of the Rising Fun, Pope John Paul II.

Gate of No Return Slave Route Monument, Ouidah — A322

2003, June 23 Litho. *Perf. 12¾*

1297 A322 135fr multi *3.00 1.50*
1298 A322 150fr multi *3.00 1.50*
1299 A322 200fr multi *3.00 1.50*
1300 A322 300fr multi *3.00 1.50*
1301 A322 1000fr multi *3.00 1.50*

Souvenir Sheet

1301A A322 1000fr Gate, vert. *3.00 1.50*
Nos. 1297-1301A (6) 18.00 9.00

Da Silva Museum of Afro-Brazilian Arts and Culture, Porto-Novo — A323

2003, Nov. 10 Litho. *Perf. 13x13¼*

Panel Color

1302 A323 25fr blue *2.50 1.25*
1303 A323 175fr red violet *2.50 1.25*
1304 A323 250fr green *2.50 1.25*
1305 A323 300fr olive green *2.50 1.25*
1306 A323 500fr blue *2.50 1.25*
1307 A323 1000fr black *2.50 1.25*
Nos. 1302-1307 (6) 15.00 7.50

For surcharges, see Nos. 1355, 1406, 1424.

Cercopithecus Erythrogaster Erythrogaster A324

2003, Dec. 19 Litho. *Perf. 13¼x13*

Panel Color

1308 A324 50fr gray blue *4.00 2.25*
1309 A324 175fr blue *4.00 2.25*
1310 A324 250fr bister *4.00 2.25*
1311 A324 300fr green *4.00 2.25*
1312 A324 400fr brown *4.00 2.25*
1313 A324 500fr orange *4.00 2.25*
1314 A324 600fr dk blue gray *4.00 2.25*
a. Souvenir sheet of 2, #1313-1314 *4.00 2.25*
Nos. 1308-1314 (7) 28.00 15.75

For surcharges, see Nos. 1334, 1356-1361, 1411, 1412, 1427, 1428, 1448.

Nos. 890 and 1167b Surcharged

No. 1316

1000fr surcharges: Type 1, Top serif on "1." Type 2, Top and bottom serif on "1." Type 3, No serifs on "1."

Methods and Perfs. As Before

2003-04 ?

1315 A274 135fr on 40fr #890 — *400.00*
1316 A310 135fr on 150fr #1167b 60.00 30.00
1317 A310 300fr on 150fr #1167b 12.00 8.00
1318 A310 500fr on 150fr #1167b 12.00 8.00
1319 A310 500fr on 150fr #1167b, large "5" — —
1320 A310 1000fr on 150fr #1167b, type 1 — —
1321 A310 1000fr on 150fr #1167b, type 2 — —
1322 A310 1000fr on 150fr #1167b, type 3 — —

No. 1319 has a large "5" with a top line that curves. No. 1318 has a smaller "5" with a top line that is straight but has an upward-pointing serif.

No. 1219a Surcharged

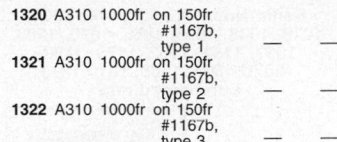

Methods and Perfs As Before

2003 ?

1323 A321 135fr on 150fr multi 15.00 8.00
a. As No. 1323, with wide "F" with short lower bar in surcharge — —

Fight Against Child Trafficking A325

Denomination color: 175fr, Yellow. 250fr, Dark blue. 300fr, White. 400fr, Light blue.

2004, Aug. 31 Litho. *Perf. 13x13¼*

1324-1327 A325 Set of 4 15.00 10.00

For surcharges, see Nos. 1365, 1425, 1446, 1449.

Rotary International, Cent — A326

Denomination color: 50fr, Purple. 175fr, Red. 250fr, Black. 300fr, Brown. 400fr, Green. 500fr, Orange. Inscription on 175fr, 250fr, 300fr reads "ACD / Cotonou du 13 au 16 Avril 2005."

2005, Feb. 1 *Perf. 13¼x13*

1328-1333 A326 Set of 6 13.00 8.00
1333a Souvenir sheet of 1 16.00 —

For surcharges, see Nos. 1407, 1426, 1447, 1450.

Benin postal officials have declared as "not authorized" the following items:

Sheet of 9 stamps with various denominations depicting Harry Potter and the Prisoner of Azkaban, The Lord of the Rings: The Return of the King, Prince William, Princess Diana, Asian lighthouses.

Sheet of 8 stamps with various denominations depicting Marilyn Monroe.

Strip of 8 stamps with various denominations depicting Cats.

Sheet of 6 stamps with various denominations depicting Shells.

Souvenir sheets of one stamp with 1000fr denomination depicting Asian lighthouses (2), Cats.

Benin Nos. 955, 969, 976, 1004, 1025, 1043, 1058, 1065, 1076, 1090, 1097, 1151, 1162, 1173, 1193, 1207D,1305, 1308, 1310-1311 Surcharged and

Carlin — A336a

Hippolais Pallida — A336b

Oenanthe Oenanthe — A336c

No. 1357

Methods and Perfs As Before

2005-08 ?

1334	A324	175fr on 50fr #1308	6.00	5.00
1335	A278	175fr on 270fr #955	—	—
1336	A280	175fr on 270fr #969	45.00	35.00
1337	A281	175fr on 270fr #976	—	—
1339	A285	175fr on 270fr #1004	—	—
1340	A286	175fr on 270fr #1025	45.00	35.00
1341	A289	175fr on 270fr #1043	—	—
1342	A292	175fr on 270fr #1058	—	—
1343	A293	175fr on 270fr #1065	—	—
1344	A295	175fr on 270fr #1076	45.00	35.00
1345	A299	175fr on 270fr #1090	50.00	40.00
1346	A300	175fr on 270fr #1097	—	—
1347	A307	175fr on 270fr #1151	40.00	30.00
1348	A309	175fr on 270fr #1162	40.00	30.00
1349	A311	175fr on 270fr #1173	40.00	30.00
1350	A316	175fr on 270fr #1193	40.00	30.00

Perf. 12¾ (A336a), 12¼x12½ (A336b, A336c)

1351	A336a	175fr on 270fr multi	40.00	30.00
1352	A336b	175fr on 270fr multi	45.00	35.00
1353	A336c	175fr on 270fr multi	45.00	35.00

Methods and Perfs As Before

1354	A318a	175fr on 270fr #1207D	—	—
1355	A323	175fr on 300fr #1305	5.00	5.00
1356	A324	175fr on 300fr #1311	5.00	—
1357	A324	175fr on 250fr #1310	5.00	3.00
1358	A324	200fr on 250fr #1310, thin numerals and "F"	50.00	25.00
1359	A324	200fr on 250fr #1310, thick numerals, "F" with short arms	5.00	3.00
1360	A324	200fr on 250fr #1310, thick numerals and "F"	11.00	6.00
1361	A324	200fr on 250fr #1310, thick numerals and thin "F"	10.00	5.00

Nos. 1351-1353 were not issued without surcharge.

Dahomey Nos. 317, 338, C169 and Benin Nos. 342, 1325 Srchd. or Ovptd.

No. 1364

Methods and Perfs As Before

2008 ?

1362	A80(f)	175fr on 35fr Dahomey #338	45.00	32.50
1363	A71(f)	175fr on 5fr Dahomey #317	40.00	30.00
1364	A83(f)	175fr on 10fr #342	40.00	25.00
1365	A325	175fr on 250fr #1325	4.00	2.50
1366	AP59(f)	250fr on Dahomey #C169	20.00	10.00

Benin postal officials have declared as "illegal" various items commemorating the 50th anniversary of Europa stamps.

Dahomey Nos. 179, 195, 287, 319 and 331 Overprinted Type "g"

Methods and Perfs As Before

2005-09 (?)

1367	A23(g)	25fr multi (#179)	110.00	60.00
1368	A27(g)	25fr multi (#195)	30.00	15.00
1369	A60(g)	25fr multi (#287)	50.00	25.00
1370	A71(g)	25fr multi (#319)	110.00	60.00
1371	A76(g)	25fr multi (#331)	20.00	10.00
		Nos. 1367-1371 (5)	*320.00*	*170.00*

Various Dahomey and Benin Stamps Surcharged With Various Surcharge Types

No. 1373

No. 1381

No. 1450

Methods and Perfs As Before

2005-09 (?)

1372	A21(k)	25fr on 1fr Dah. #173	25.00	12.00
1373	A57(k)	25fr on 1fr Dah. #277	40.00	20.00
a.		With obliterator over "Dahomey" omitted		—
1374	A15(k)	25fr on 3fr Dah. #143	70.00	35.00
1375	A19(k)	25fr on 3fr Dah. #161	20.00	10.00
1376	A38(k)	25fr on 3fr Dah. #227	150.00	75.00
1377	A24(k)	25fr on 4fr Dah. #182	30.00	15.00
1378	A69(k)	25fr on 5fr Dah. #312	175.00	85.00
1379	A71(k)	25fr on 5fr Dah. #317	150.00	75.00
1380	A63(k)	25fr on 10fr Dah. #297	150.00	75.00
1381	A71(k)	25fr on 10fr Dah. #318, obliterator bars evenly spaced	125.00	70.00
a.		Top two bars of obliterator close together		—
1382	A21(k)	25fr on 15fr Dah. #176	40.00	20.00
1383	A69(k)	25fr on 15fr Dah. #313	200.00	100.00
1384	A21(k)	25fr on 20fr Dah. #177	30.00	15.00
1385	A33(k)	25fr on 30fr Dah. #210	20.00	10.00
1386	A41(k)	25fr on 30fr Dah. #237	50.00	25.00
1387	A46(k)	25fr on 30fr Dah. #250	40.00	20.00
1388	A52(k)	25fr on 30fr Dah. #265	50.00	25.00
1389	A62(k)	25fr on 30fr Dah. #295	40.00	20.00
1390	A38(k)	50fr on 30fr Dah. #231	60.00	30.00
1391	A42(k)	50fr on 30fr Dah. #239	40.00	20.00
1392	A43(k)	50fr on 30fr Dah. #241	30.00	15.00
1393	A63(k)	50fr on 35fr Dah. #298	75.00	35.00
1394	A69(k)	50fr on 35fr Dah. #314	75.00	35.00
1395	A74(k)	50fr on 35fr Dah. #325	75.00	35.00
1396	CD132(k)	50fr on 40fr Dah. #269	75.00	35.00
1397	A63(k)	50fr on 40fr Dah. #299	100.00	50.00
1398	A72(k)	50fr on 40fr Dah. #321	50.00	25.00
1399	A74(k)	50fr on 40fr Dah. #326	100.00	50.00
1400	A78(k)	50fr on 40fr Dah. #336	20.00	10.00
1401	A57(f)	175fr on 1fr Dah. #277	15.00	10.00
1402	A38(k)	175fr on 3fr Dah. #227	45.00	30.00
1403	A66(f)	175fr on 5fr Dah. #303	15.00	7.50
1404	A76(f)	175fr on 10fr Dah. #330	—	—
1405	A79(e)	175fr on 150fr Dah. #337	40.00	30.00
1406	A323	175fr on 250fr Ben. #1304	4.50	4.50
1407	A284	175fr on 250fr Ben. #1330	—	—
1408	A290	175fr on 270fr Ben. #1050	200.00	—
1409	A303	175fr on 270fr Ben. #997	—	—
1410	A326	175fr on 270fr Ben. #1123	—	—
1411	A324	175fr on 400fr #1312	4.00	2.50
1412	A324	175fr on 600fr Ben. #1314	—	—
1413	A63(k)	200fr on 35fr Ben. #343	90.00	45.00
1414	A76(k)	200fr on 40fr Dah. #332	30.00	15.00
1415	A45(k)	200fr on 45fr Dah. #247	75.00	35.00
1416	A83(k)	200fr on 45fr Ben. #344	150.00	75.00
1417	A19(k)	200fr on 50fr Dah. #168	120.00	60.00
1418	A83(k)	200fr on 60fr Ben. #345	90.00	45.00
1419	A77(k)	200fr on 65fr Dah. #334	30.00	15.00
1420	A45(k)	200fr on 70fr Dah. #248	75.00	35.00
1421	A45(k)	200fr on 100fr Dah. #249	50.00	25.00
1422	A60(k)	200fr on 100fr Dah. #290	25.00	12.50
1423	A77(k)	200fr on 100fr Dah. #335	25.00	12.50
1424	A323	200fr on 250fr Ben. #1304	—	—
1425	A325	200fr on 250fr Ben. #1325	—	—
1427	A324	200fr on 400fr Ben. #1312	—	—
1428	A324	200fr on 600fr Ben. #1314	—	—
1426	A326	200fr on 250fr #1330	7.00	5.00
1429	A58(k)	300fr on 40fr Dah. #283	40.00	20.00
1430	A59(k)	300fr on 40fr Dah. #286	50.00	25.00
1431	A60(k)	300fr on 40fr Dah. #289	20.00	10.00
1432	A71(k)	300fr on 40fr Dah. #320	75.00	35.00
1433	A52(k)	300fr on 45fr Dah. #266	40.00	20.00
1434	A67(k)	300fr on 50fr Dah. #307	40.00	20.00
1435	A72(k)	300fr on 50fr Dah. #322	85.00	45.00
1436	A82(k)	300fr on 50fr Dah. #340	40.00	20.00

1437 A65(k) 300fr on 85fr Dah. #302 *40.00 20.00*
1438 A47(k) 300fr on 90fr Dah. #256 *90.00 45.00*
1439 A68(k) 300fr on 100fr Dah. #309 *45.00 20.00*
1440 CD137(k) 300fr on 100fr Dah. #311 *35.00 20.00*
1441 A72(k) 300fr on 100fr Dah. #323 *90.00 45.00*
1442 A74(k) 300fr on 100fr Dah. #327 *90.00 45.00*
1443 A76(k) 300fr on 100fr Dah. #333 *40.00 20.00*
1444 A74(f) 300fr on 200fr Dah. #328 *50.00 30.00*
1445 A81(f) 300fr on 200fr Dah. #339 *35.00 25.00*
1446 A325 500fr on 300fr Ben. #1326 *7.50 4.50*
1447 A326 715fr on 250fr Ben. #1330 — —
1448 A324 1000fr on 300fr Ben. #1311 *11.50 11.50*
1449 A325 5000fr on 400fr Ben. #1327 — —
1450 A326 5000fr on 400fr Ben. #1332 — —

Léopold Sédar Senghor (1906-2001), First President of Senegal — A327

Denomination color: 175fr, Red. 300fr, Blue green.

2006 Litho. *Perf. 13x13¼*
1451-1452 A327 Set of 2 4.00 4.00

Benin Coat of Arms — A328

2008, Jan. 1 Litho. *Perf. 13¼x13½*
Denomination Color

1453 A328 25fr blue green *.25 .25*
1454 A328 50fr org brown *.40 .40*
1455 A328 75fr brown *.60 .60*
1456 A328 100fr red *.80 .80*

Size: 36x27mm
Perf. 13x13¼

1457 A328 200fr purple *1.60 1.60*
1458 A328 250fr green *1.90 1.90*
1459 A328 500fr blue gray *4.00 4.00*
1460 A328 5000fr red brown *40.00 40.00*
Nos. 1453-1460 (8) 49.55 49.55

For surcharges see Nos. 1461, 1473-1476.

Benin Coat of Arms Type of 2008

2009 Litho. *Perf. 13¼x13½*
Granite Paper
Denomination Color

1460D A328 200fr green, dated 2017 —

Size: 36x27mm
Perf. 13x13¼

1460E A328 300fr red —
1460F A328 600fr blue —

Nos. 1460E-1460F are dated 2008. Three additional stamps were issued in this set. The editors would like to examine any examples.

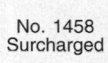

No. 1458 Surcharged

2008 ? Litho. *Perf. 13x13¼*
1461 A328 200fr on 250fr #1458 *65.00 40.00*

Miniature Sheet

2008 Summer Olympics, Beijing — A329

No. 1462: a, Running. b, Taekwondo. c, Swimming. d, Taekwondo, swimming and running.

2008, Oct. 1 Litho. *Perf. 12¾x13½*
1462 A329 200fr Sheet of 4, #a-d *10.00 10.00*

Dahomey Nos. 181, 251, 276, 292, 329, 341 and Benin No. 342 Srchd.

No. 1463

Methods and Perfs As Before
2009

1463 A83(k) 25fr on 10fr Ben. #342 *125.00 65.00*
1464 A56(k) 50fr on 40fr Dah. #276 *25.00 10.00*
1465 A46(k) 300fr on 70fr Dah. #251 *70.00 35.00*
1466 A23(k) 300fr on 100fr Dah. #181 *25.00 10.00*
1467 A60(k) 400fr on 140fr Dah. #292 *25.00 15.00*
1468 A75(k) 1000fr on 35fr Dah. #329 *75.00 35.00*
1469 A82(k) 1000fr on 150fr Dah. #341 *25.00 16.50*
Nos. 1463-1469 (7) 370.00 186.50

Dahomey Nos. 291 and 306 Surcharged
Methods and Perfs As Before
2009

1470 A60(k) 400fr on 135fr Dahomey #291 *60.00 30.00*
1471 A67(k) 1000fr on 35fr Dahomey #306 *45.00 25.00*

Dahomey No. C35 Surcharged With "Poste Aerienne" Obliterated
Method and Perf. As Before
2009 ?

1472 AP15(f) 500fr on 200fr Dah. #C35 *75.00 45.00*

No. 1457 Surcharged

2009 Method and Perf. As Before

1473 A328 250fr on 200fr #1457 *6.00 6.00*
1474 A328 300fr on 200fr #1457 *6.00 6.00*
1475 A328 500fr on 200fr #1457 *6.00 6.00*
1476 A328 600fr on 200fr #1457 *6.00 6.00*
Nos. 1473-1476 (4) 24.00 24.00

Benin Nos. 399a, 402a With "POPULAIRE" Obliterated
Methods and Perfs As Before
2009

1477 A108 On sheet of 3, #a-c (#399a) *27.50 27.50*
1478 A108 On sheet of 3, #a-c (#402a) *32.50 32.50*

Independence, 50th Anniv. — A330

50th anniversary emblem and: 250fr, Dancer. 300fr, Tractor, flags of Benin since 1960. 500fr, Godomey highway interchange.

2010, Aug. 1 Litho. *Perf. 12¾x13*
1479-1481 A330 Set of 3 10.50 10.50

Bernardin Cardinal Gantin (1922-2008) A331

Country name and outline of denomination in: 250fr, Green. 300fr, Red. 600fr, Black.

2011 *Perf. 13¼x13*
1482-1484 A331 Set of 3 *10.00 10.00*

Visit of Pope Benedict XVI to Benin A332

Color of top panel: 250fr, Blue. 300fr, Red violet. 400fr, Purple. 500fr, Red. 1000fr, Bister.

2011, Sept. 22 *Perf. 13x13¼*
1485-1489 A332 Set of 5 *24.00 24.00*

National Day of Traditional Religions — A333

Color of panel at left: 250fr, Blue. 300fr, Light green. 1000fr, Light orange.

2013 Litho. *Perf. 13¼x13*
1490-1492 A333 Set of 3 14.00 14.00

Dr. Boni Yayi, 2012-13 President of the African Union — A334

Denomination color: 300fr, Dark blue green. 1000fr, Green.

2013 Litho. *Perf. 13¼x13*
1493-1494 A334 Set of 2 14.00 14.00

Pres. Sourou-Migan Apithy (1913-89) — A335

2013 Litho. *Perf. 13¼*
1495 A335 50fr multi (16x21mm) —

Perf. 13¼x13

1496 A335 200fr multi —
1497 A335 600fr multi — —
1498 A335 1000fr multi — —

Behanzin High School, Porto-Novo, Cent. A336

2013 Litho. *Perf. 13x13¼*
Denomination Color

1499 A336 200fr green — —
1500 A336 250fr blue 2.25 2.25
1501 A336 600fr magenta 5.50 5.50
1502 A336 1000fr red 9.25 9.25

AIR POST STAMPS

PEOPLE'S REPUBLIC

Catalogue values for unused stamps in this section are for Never Hinged items.

Nativity, by Aert van Leyden — AP84

Christmas: 85fr, Adoration of the Kings, by Rubens, vert. 140fr, Adoration of the Shepherds, by Charles Lebrun. 300fr, The Virgin with the Blue Diadem, by Raphael, vert.

1975, Dec. 19 Litho. *Perf. 13*

C240 AP84 40fr gold & multi .90 .45
C241 AP84 85fr gold & multi 1.25 .80
C242 AP84 140fr gold & multi 2.50 1.10
C243 AP84 300fr gold & multi 5.40 2.75
Nos. C240-C243 (4) 10.05 5.10

For surcharges see Nos. C357C, C362, C367, C379, C407, C407A, C424, C432, C556, C583, C589.

Slalom, Innsbruck Olympic Emblem — AP85

Innsbruck Olympic Games Emblem and: 150fr, Bobsledding, vert. 300fr, Figure skating, pairs.

1976, June 28 Litho. *Perf. 12½*

C244 AP85 60fr multi 1.50 .65
C245 AP85 150fr multi 2.50 1.60
C246 AP85 300fr multi 5.25 3.25
Nos. C244-C246 (3) 9.25 5.50

12th Winter Olympic Games, Innsbruck, Austria, Feb. 4-15.
For surcharge n No. C245, see No. C289C.
For overprint on No. C246, see No. Q22.

Dahomey Nos. C263-C265 Overprinted or Surcharged

No. C247

1976, July 4 Engr. *Perf. 13*

C247 AP86 135fr multi 1.90 1.25
C248 AP86 210fr on 300fr multi 2.75 1.60
C249 AP86 380fr on 500fr multi 5.75 2.75
Nos. C247-C249 (3) 10.40 5.60

The overprint includes a bar covering "DU DAHOMEY" in shades of brown; "POPULAIRE DU BENIN" is blue on Nos. C247-C249, red on No. C249. The surcharge and bars over old value are blue on No. C248, red, brown on No. C249.

Long Jump AP86

Designs (Olympic Rings and): 150fr, Basketball, vert. 200fr, Hurdles.

1976, July 16 Photo. *Perf. 13*

C250 AP86 60fr multi 1.00 .55
C251 AP86 150fr multi 2.25 1.25
C252 AP86 200fr multi 3.00 1.75
a. Souv. sheet of 3, #C250-C252 8.75 8.75
Nos. C250-C252 (3) 6.25 3.55

21st Olympic Games, Montreal, Canada, July 17-Aug 1. For surcharges, see Nos. C289D, C289E.

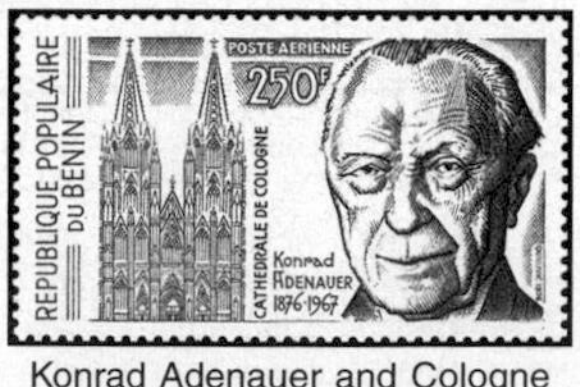

Konrad Adenauer and Cologne Cathedral — AP87

Design: 90fr, Konrad Adenauer, vert.

1976, Aug. 27 Engr. *Perf. 13*

C253 AP87 90fr multi 1.60 .90
C254 AP87 250fr multi 4.75 1.90

Konrad Adenauer (1876-1967), German Chancellor, birth centenary.
For surcharges, see Nos. C289B, Q16C, Q16D, Q17, Q17A, Q26, Q27.

Children's Heads and Flying Fish (Dahomey Type A32) — AP88

210fr, Lion cub's head, Benin design A3, vert.

1976, Sept. 13

C255 AP88 60fr Prus bl & vio bl 1.25 .60
C256 AP88 210fr multi 3.50 1.60

JUVAROUEN 76, Intl. Youth Phil. Exhib., Rouen, France, Apr. 25-May 2.
For surcharges see Nos. C300, C494, C542, C543.

Apollo 14 Emblem and Blast-off — AP89

270fr, Landing craft and man on moon.

1976, Oct. 18 Engr. *Perf. 13*

C257 AP89 130fr multi 1.75 .75
C258 AP89 270fr multi 3.50 1.50

Apollo 14 Moon Mission, 5th anniversary.
For surcharges see Nos. C312, C454, C495, Q23.

Annunciation, by Master of Jativa — AP90

Christmas: 60fr, Nativity, by Gerard David. 270fr, Adoration of the Kings, Dutch School. 300fr, Flight into Egypt, by Gentile Fabriano, horiz.

1976, Dec. 20 Litho. *Perf. 12½*

C259 AP90 50fr gold & multi .95 .50
C260 AP90 60fr gold & multi 1.00 .65
C261 AP90 270fr gold & multi 4.00 2.10
C262 AP90 300fr gold & multi 4.50 2.50
Nos. C259-C262 (4) 10.45 5.75

For surcharges see Nos. C310, C321, C484.

Gamblers and Lottery Emblem — AP91

1977, Mar. 13 Litho. *Perf. 13*

C263 AP91 50fr multi .90 .50

National lottery, 10th anniversary.

Sassenage Castle, Grenoble — AP92

1977, May 16 *Perf. 12½*

C264 AP92 200fr multi 2.75 1.25

10th anniv. of Intl. French Language Council.
For surcharge see No. C334.

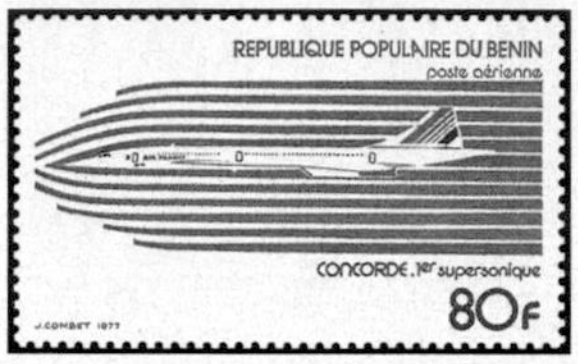

Concorde, Supersonic Plane — AP93

Designs: 150fr, Zeppelin. 300fr, Charles A. Lindbergh and Spirit of St. Louis. 500fr, Charles Nungesser and François Coli, French aviators lost over Atlantic, 1927.

1977, July 25 Engr. *Perf. 13*

C265 AP93 80fr ultra & red 1.00 .50
C266 AP93 150fr multi 2.10 1.00
C267 AP93 300fr multi 3.25 2.10
C268 AP93 500fr multi 6.50 4.00
Nos. C265-C268 (4) 12.85 7.60

Aviation history.
For overprint and surcharges see Nos. C274, C316, C336, C496.

Soccer Player — AP94

200fr, Soccer players and Games' emblem.

1977, July 28 Litho. *Perf. 12½x12*

C269 AP94 60fr multi .95 .55
C270 AP94 200fr multi 2.75 1.90

World Soccer Cup elimination games.
For surcharges see Nos. C289A, C308.

Miss Haverfield, by Gainsborough — AP95

Designs: 150fr, Self-portrait, by Rubens. 200fr, Anguish, man's head by Da Vinci.

1977, Oct. 3 Engr. *Perf. 13*

C271 AP95 100fr sl grn & mar 2.50 .80
C272 AP95 150fr red brn & dk brn 4.00 1.90
C273 AP95 200fr brn & red 5.50 2.50
Nos. C271-C273 (3) 12.00 5.20

For surcharges see Nos. C309, C317.

No. C265 Overprinted

1977, Nov. 22 Engr. *Perf. 13*

C274 AP93 80fr ultra & red 2.00 .90

Concorde, 1st commercial flight, Paris to NY.

Viking on Mars — AP96

150fr, Isaac Newton, apple globe, stars. 200fr, Vladimir M. Komarov, spacecraft and earth. 500fr, Dog Laika, rocket and space.

1977, Nov. 28 Engr. *Perf. 13*

C275 AP96 100fr multi 1.00 .65
C276 AP96 150fr multi 1.90 1.00
C277 AP96 200fr multi 3.00 1.25
C278 AP96 500fr multi 7.00 3.50
Nos. C275-C278 (4) 12.90 6.40

Operation Viking on Mars; Isaac Newton (1642-1727); 10th death anniv. of Russian cosmonaut Vladimir M. Komarov; 20th anniv. of 1st living creature in space.
For surcharges see Nos. C301, C314, C497, Q18.

Monument, Red Star Place, Cotonou AP97

Lithographed; Gold Embossed

1977 Nov. 30 *Perf. 12½*

C279 AP97 500fr multi 6.50 3.00

Suzanne Fourment, by Rubens AP98

380fr, Nicholas Rubens, by Rubens.

1977, Dec. 12 Engr. *Perf. 13*

C280 AP98 200fr multi 3.50 1.50
C281 AP98 380fr claret & ocher 6.00 2.50

For surcharges see Nos. C311, C313, C483.

Parthenon and UNESCO Emblem — AP99

Designs: 70fr, Acropolis and frieze showing Pan-Athenaic procession, vert. 250fr, Parthenon and frieze showing horsemen, vert.

1978, Sept. 22 Litho. *Perf. 12½x12*

C282 AP99 70fr multi .75 .25
C283 AP99 250fr multi 2.75 1.60
C284 AP99 500fr multi 5.50 2.50
Nos. C282-C284 (3) 9.00 4.35

Save the Parthenon in Athens campaign.
For surcharges see Nos. C338, C498.

Philexafrique II — Essen Issue
Common Design Types

Designs: No. C285, Buffalo and Dahomey #C33. No. C286, Wild ducks and Baden #1.

1978, Nov. 1 Litho. *Perf. 12½*

C285 CD138 100fr multi 4.50 1.75
C286 CD139 100fr multi 4.50 1.75
a. Pair, #C285-C286 9.00 8.50

For surcharges, see Nos. C535-C536.

Wilbur and Orville Wright and Flyer — AP100

1978, Dec. 28 Engr. *Perf. 13*

C287 AP100 500fr multi 6.50 3.00

75th anniversary of 1st powered flight.
For surcharges see Nos. C339, C499.

Cook's Ships, Hawaii, World Map — AP101

Design: 50fr, Battle at Kowrowa.

1979, June 1 Engr. *Perf. 13*

C288 AP101 20fr multi .90 .30
C289 AP101 50fr multi 1.10 .50

Capt. James Cook (1728-1779), explorer.

No. C245, C251, C253, C269 Surcharged

No. C289B

No. C289C

1979
Perfs. & Printing Method as Before

C289A AP94 50fr on 60fr #C269 80.00 40.00
C289B AP87 50fr on 90fr #C253 80.00 40.00
C289C AP85 50fr on 150fr #C245 — —
C289D AP86 50fr on 150fr #C251 —

No. C252 Surcharged

1979 Method and Perf. As Before

C289E AP86 50fr on 200fr #C252 —

Lunokhod I — A101a

1980, June 15 Engr. *Perf. 13*
Size: 27x48mm

C290 A101a 210fr multi 3.00 1.40

For surcharges see Nos. C305, C450.

Soccer Players — AP102

1981, Mar. 31 Litho. *Perf. 13*

C291 AP102 200fr Ball, globe 2.00 .80
C292 AP102 500fr shown 5.00 2.00

ESPANA '82 World Soccer Cup eliminations.
For surcharges see Nos. C335, C455, Q10B.

Prince Charles and Lady Diana, London Bridge — AP103

1981, July 29 Litho. *Perf. 12½*

C293 AP103 500fr multi 5.00 2.25

Royal wedding.
For surcharges see Nos. C323, C500.

Three Musicians, by Pablo Picasso (1881-1973) — AP104

Perf. 12½x13, 13x12½

1981, Nov. 2 Litho.

C294 AP104 300fr Dance, vert. 3.25 1.25
C295 AP104 500fr shown 6.00 2.00

For surcharges see Nos. C320, C340.

1300th Anniv. of Bulgaria AP105

1981, Dec. 2 Litho. *Perf. 13*

C296 AP105 100fr multi 1.00 .45

Visit of Pope John Paul II — AP106

1982, Feb. 17 Litho. *Perf. 13*

C297 AP106 80fr multi 2.25 1.00

20th Anniv. of John Glenn's Flight — AP107

1982, Feb. 21 Litho. *Perf. 13*

C298 AP107 500fr multi 6.00 2.50

For surcharge see No. C315.

Scouting Year AP108

1982, June 1 *Perf. 12½*

C299 AP108 105fr multi 1.25 .70

For surcharge see No. C324.

Nos. C256, C275 Surcharged

No. C300

No. C301

1982, Nov. Engr. *Perf. 13*

C300 AP88 50fr on 210fr multi 3.00 3.00
C301 AP96 50fr on 100fr multi 3.00 3.00

(Claude) Monet in His Studio Boat, by (Edouard) Manet — AP109

1982, Dec. 6 Litho. *Perf. 13x12½*

C302 AP109 300fr multi 7.00 2.50

For surcharge see No. C326.

Christmas 1982 AP110

Virgin and Child Paintings: 200fr, Matthias Grunewald. 300fr, Correggio.

1982, Dec. 20 *Perf. 12½x13*

C303 AP110 200fr gold & multi 2.50 1.25
C304 AP110 300fr gold & multi 3.50 1.60

For surcharges see Nos. C325, C337.

No. C290 Surcharged

1983 **Engr.** ***Perf. 13***
C305 A133 75fr on 210fr multi 2.25 1.25

Bangkok '83 Stamp Exhibition AP111

1983, Aug. 4 **Photo.** ***Perf. 13***
C306 AP111 300fr multi 3.25 1.50

For surcharge see No. C322.

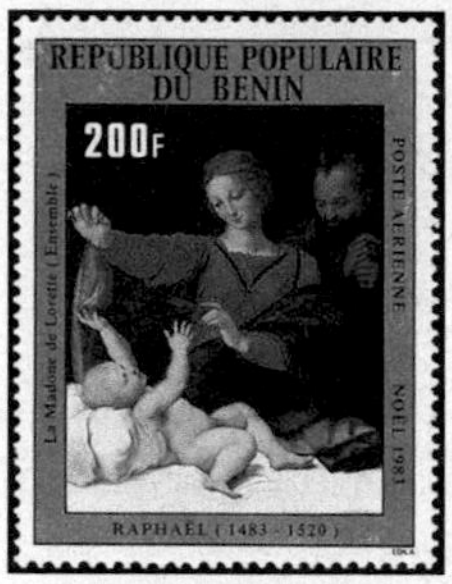

Christmas 1983 AP112

200fr, Loretto Madonna, by Raphael.

1983, Dec. 26 **Litho.** ***Perf. 12½x13***
C307 AP112 200fr multicolored 3.00 1.20

For surcharge see No. C319.

Types of 1976-82 Surcharged

No. C308

No. C309

No. C310

No. C311

No. C312

No. C313

No. C314

No. C315

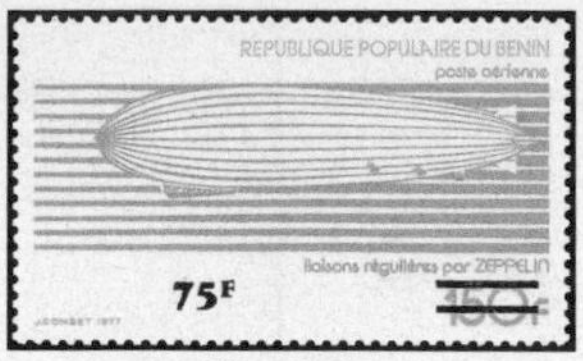

No. C316

No. C317

1983, Nov.

C308 AP94 10fr on 200fr C270 5.00 1.00
C309 AP95 15fr on 200fr C273 5.00 1.00
C310 AP90 15fr on 270fr C261 5.00 1.00
C311 AP98 20fr on 200fr C280 5.00 1.00
C312 AP89 25fr on 270fr C258 5.00 1.00
C313 AP98 25fr on 380fr C281 5.00 1.00
C314 AP96 30fr on 200fr C277 5.00 1.00
C315 AP107 40fr on 500fr C298 5.00 1.00
C316 AP93 75fr on 150fr C266 5.00 1.00
C317 AP95 75fr on 150fr C272 5.00 1.00
Nos. C308-C317 (10) 50.00 10.00

Summer Olympics — AP113

300fr, Sam the Eagle, mascot.

1984, July 16 **Litho.** ***Perf. 13x13½***
C318 AP113 300fr multicolored 3.25 1.50

Nos. C262, C293-C294, C299, C302, C304, C306-C307 Surcharged

No. C319

No. C320

No. C321

No. C322

No. C323

No. C324

No. C325

No. C326

1984, Sept.

C319 AP112 15fr on 200fr #C307 5.00 1.00
C320 AP104 15fr on 300fr #C294 5.00 1.00
C321 AP90 25fr on 300fr #C262 5.00 1.00
C322 AP111 25fr on 300fr #C306 5.00 1.00
C323 AP103 40fr on 500fr #C293 5.00 1.00
C324 AP108 75fr on 105fr #C299 5.00 1.00
C325 AP110 90fr on 200fr #C304 5.00 1.00
C326 AP109 90fr on 300fr #C302 5.00 1.00
Nos. C319-C326 (8) 40.00 8.00

Christmas 1984 AP114

500fr, Virgin and Child, by Murillo.

1984, Dec. 17 Litho. *Perf. 12½x13*

C327 AP114 500fr multicolored 6.00 2.50

For surcharge see No. C486

Ships — AP115

90fr, Sidon merchant ship. 125fr, Wavertree, vert.

1984, Dec. 28 Litho. *Perf. 13*

C328	AP115	90fr	multicolored	1.40	.65
C329	AP115	125fr	multicolored	2.25	.90

Benin-S.O.M. Postal Convention AP116

No. C330, Benin arms. No. C331, Sovereign Order of Malta.

Wmk. 385

1985, Apr. 15 Litho. *Perf. 13½*

C330	AP116	75fr	multicolored	.90	.30
C331	AP116	75fr	multicolored	.90	.30
a.	Pair, #C330-C331			2.40	2.40

PHILEXAFRICA III, Lome — AP117

No. C332, Oil platform. No. C333, Soccer players.

1985, June 24 *Perf. 13*

C332	200fr multicolored		2.50	1.50
C333	200fr multicolored		2.50	1.50
a.	AP117 Pair, #C332-C333 + label		6.00	4.50

For surcharges see Nos. C485-C485A.

Stamps of 1977-82 Surcharged

No. C334

No. C335

No. C336

No. C337

No. C338

No. C339

No. C340

1985, Mar.

C334	AP92	75fr on 200fr #C264		10.00	2.50
C335	AP102	75fr on 200fr #C291		10.00	2.50
C336	AP93	75fr on 300fr #C267		10.00	2.50
C337	AP110	75fr on 300fr #C304		10.00	2.50
C338	AP99	90fr on 500fr #C284		10.00	2.50
C339	AP100	90fr on 500fr #C287		10.00	2.50
C340	AP104	90fr on 500fr #C295		10.00	2.50
	Nos. C334-C340 (7)			70.00	17.50

Dahomey Stamps of 1971-75 Surcharged

No. C341

No. C342

No. C343

No. C343A

No. C344

No. C345

No. C346

No. C347

No. C348

No. C349

No. C350

1985, Aug.

C341	AP87(i)	25fr on 40fr #C266	6.00	1.10
C342	AP49(a)	40fr #C142	6.00	1.10
C343	AP56(i)	75fr on 85fr #C164	6.00	1.10
C343A	AP56(b)(i)	75fr	*75.00*	*2.50*
C344	AP60(a)	75fr on 100fr #C173	6.00	1.10
C345	AP64(i)	75fr on 125fr #C186	6.00	1.10
C346	AP56(i)	90fr on 20fr #C163	6.00	1.10
C347	A61(i)	90fr on 150fr #C153	6.00	1.10
C348	AP49(a)	90fr on 200fr #C143	6.00	1.10
C349	AP78(j)	90fr on 200fr #C237	6.00	1.10
C349A	AP64(f)	125fr on Dahomey #C186	—	—
C350	AP78(j)	150fr #C236	6.00	1.10
	Nos. C341-C350 (11)		135.00	13.50

Christmas — AP118

1985, Dec. 20 Litho. *Perf. 13x12½*
C351 AP118 500fr multi 5.50 3.00

For surcharge see No. C449.

Dahomey Nos. C34-C37, C84, C131 Surcharged or Overprinted

No. C352

No. C353

No. C354

No. C355

No. C356

No. C357

1986 Photo. Perfs. as before

C352	AP33(b)	75fr on 70fr #C84	5.50	1.00
C353	AP14(b)	75fr on 100fr #C34	5.50	1.00
C354	AP15(b)	75fr on 200fr #C35	5.50	1.00
C355	AP15(b)	90fr on 250fr #C36	5.50	1.00
C356	AP45(b)	100fr #C131	5.00	1.00
C357	AP14(b)	150fr on 500fr #C37	5.00	1.00
		Nos. C352-C357 (6)	32.00	6.00

Issued: 75fr, 90fr, Mar; 100fr, 150fr, June.

Dahomey Nos. C82, C139, C141, C146, Benin No. C243 Surcharged

1986

Perfs. & Printing Methods as Before

C357A	AP33(d)	15fr on 45fr Dah. #C82	50.00	25.00
C357B	AP48(d)	25fr on 200fr Dah. #C141 (S)	50.00	25.00
C357C	AP84(d)	30fr on 300fr Benin #C243	40.00	25.00
C357D	AP48(d)	100fr on Dah. #C139	50.00	25.00
C357E	CD135(d)	100fr on Dah. #C146	60.00	25.00

Christmas — AP119

1986, Dec. 24 Litho. *Perf. 13x12½*
C358 AP119 300fr multi 3.50 1.50

Air Africa, 25th Anniv. AP120

1986, Dec. 30 *Perf. 12½*
C359 AP120 100fr multi 1.10 .55

Intl. Agricultural Development Fund (FIDA), 10th Anniv. — AP121

1987, Dec. 14 Litho. *Perf. 13½*
C360 AP121 500fr multi 5.00 2.50

Christmas — AP122

500fr, Adoration of the Magi, storyteller.

1988, Dec. 23 Litho. *Perf. 13x12½*
C361 AP122 500fr multi 5.00 2.40

No. C241 Surcharged

1989, Apr. 24 Litho. *Perf. 13*
C362 AP84(b) 15fr on 85fr multi 30.00 15.00

Dahomey Nos. C37, C53, C138, C152, C156, C165, C175, C182, C186, C234, Benin No. C242 Surcharged or Overprinted

1987

Perfs. & Printing Methods as Before

C363	AP77	20fr on 250fr Dah. #C234	50.00	20.00
C364	AP48(b)	25fr on 150fr Dah. #C175 (S&B)	50.00	20.00
C365	AP63(b)	40fr on 15fr Dah. #C182	42.50	20.00
C366	AP48(b)	40fr on 100fr Dah. #C152	40.00	20.00
C367	AP84(b)	50fr on 140fr Benin #C242	50.00	25.00
C368	AP14(b)	50fr on 500fr Dah. #C37	50.00	25.00
C369	AP22(b)	80fr on Dah. #C53	50.00	25.00
C370	AP56(b)	80fr on 150fr Dah. #C165	50.00	25.00
C371	AP56(c)	80fr on 150fr Dah. #C172	—	—
C372	AP48	100fr on Dah. #C138, "Populaire" same length as "du Benin"	—	—
a.		"Populaire" longer than "du Benin"	—	—
C373	AP52(b)	100fr on Dah. #C156	50.00	20.00

Dahomey Nos. C140, C144, C158, C166, C177, C185, C188 C191, C195, C202, C207, C233, C260, C262, Benin No. C242 Surcharged or Overprinted

No. C376

No. C382

No. C387A

1988-94

Perfs. & Printing Methods as Before

C374	AP50(d)	10fr on 50fr Dah. #C144	50.00	25.00
C375	AP64(d)	10fr on 65fr Dah. #C185	50.00	25.00
C376	AP72(d)	15fr on 150fr Dah. #C207	50.00	25.00
C377	AP67(d)	25fr on 200fr Dah. #C191	50.00	25.00
C378	AP61(d)	40fr on 35fr Dah. #C195	50.00	25.00
C379	AP84(b)	50fr on 140fr #C242	50.00	25.00
C380	AP53(d)	70fr on 250fr Dah. #C158	50.00	25.00
C381	AP48(d)	100fr on Dah. #C140	30.00	15.00
C382	AP65(d)	100fr on Dah #C188	40.00	20.00
C383	AP84(d)	100fr on Dah. #C260	45.00	20.00
C383A	AP61(d)	125fr on Dah. #C177	—	—
C384	AP61(f)	125fr on Dah. #C177	40.00	20.00
C385	AP86(d)	125fr on 75fr Dah. #C262	45.00	20.00
C386	AP57(d)	150fr on 100fr Dah. #C166	50.00	25.00
C387	AP77(d)	190fr on 100fr Dah. #C233	45.00	20.00
C387A	AP70	125fr on Dah. #C202		—

Dahomey Nos. C179, C181, C196, C200, C203, C208 Surcharged in Black or Violet

1988-89

Perfs. & Printing Methods as Before

C388	AP61(d)	25fr on 100fr #C196	60.00	30.00
C389	AP69(d)	25fr on 100fr #C200	—	—
C390	AP62	40fr on 100fr #C181	60.00	30.00
C391	AP73(d)	40fr on 150fr #C208	45.00	25.00
C391A	AP70(j)	125fr on 150fr #C203 (V)	45.00	25.00

C392 AP61(d) 125fr on 250fr #C179 45.00 25.00
C393 AP87(d) 190fr on 250fr #C267 75.00 40.00

Issued: No. C391A, 1989.

Dahomey Nos. C108, C131, C147-C148, C162, C167, C178, C187, C194 Surcharged or Overprinted

No. C394A

1992

Perfs. & Printing Methods as Before

C394 AP51(f) 70fr on #C148 60.00 30.00
C394A AP51(e) 70fr on #C148 60.00 30.00
C395 AP55(e) 100fr on #C162 45.00 25.00
C396 AP68(g) 100fr on #C194 120.00 60.00
C397 AP51(e) 125fr on 40fr #C147 20.00 12.50
C398 A52(f) 125fr on 70fr #C108 60.00 30.00
C399 AP45(f) 125fr on 100fr #C131 —
C400 AP64a(e) 125fr on 100fr #C187 45.00 25.00
C401 AP61(f) 190fr on 140fr #C178 45.00 25.00
C402 AP58(f) 190fr on 150fr #C167 60.00 30.00

Dahomey Nos. C145, C149-C150, C163, C182, C189, C198, C257, C264 Surcharged, Benin No. C241 Surcharged

No. C407A

1993

Perfs. & Printing Methods as Before

C403 AP51(e) 5fr on 100fr #C149 45.00 25.00
C403A AP51(f) 5fr on 100fr #C149 — —
C404 AP50(f) 10fr on 100fr #C145 45.00 25.00
C404A AP56(f) 20fr on #C163 30.00 15.00
C405 AP51(f) 20fr on 200fr #C150 50.00 35.00
C406 AP83(f) 20fr on 500fr #C257 50.00 35.00
C407 AP84(e) 25fr on 85fr #C241 45.00 25.00
C407A AP84(k) 25fr on 85fr #C241 — 25.00
C409 AP63(f) 30fr on 15fr #C182 32.50 15.00
C410 AP61(f) 30fr on 200fr #C198 21.00 12.50
C411 AP66(b) 35fr on #C189 45.00 25.00
C412 AP86(g) 300fr on #C264 50.00 25.00

Dahomey Nos. C14, C31, C33-C34, C46, C54, C58, C101, C110, C128, C144, C151-C153, C155, C168, C179, C191, C196-C198, C203, C222, C234, C236-C237, C250, C253-C256, C261-C262, Benin C240, C242 Surcharged or Overprinted

No. C420

1994-95?

Perfs. & Printing Methods as Before

C413 AP61(g) 10fr on 100fr #C253 85.00 40.00
C414 AP52(e) 15fr on 40fr #C155 45.00 25.00
C415 AP83(f) 25fr on 200fr #C256 50.00 25.00
C416 AP83(f) 35fr on #C255 45.00 25.00
C417 AP49(g) 50fr on #C101 62.50 35.00
C418 AP48(g) 75fr on 40fr #C151 40.00 20.00
C419 AP4(g) 100fr on #C14 40.00 20.00
C420 AP22(h) 100fr on #C54 50.00 25.00
C421 AP50(g) 125fr on 50fr #C144 40.00 20.00
C422 AP75(e) 125fr on 65fr #C222 40.00 20.00
C424 AP84(g) 135fr on 40fr #C240 50.00 —
C425 AP21(f) 135fr on 45fr #C110 62.50 —
C426 AP14(e) 135fr on 50fr #C33 62.50 —
C427 AP21(e) 135fr on 50fr Dah. #C46 — —
C428 AP24(f) 135fr on 70fr #C58 — —
C429 AP43(e) 135fr on 70fr #C128 90.00 —
C429A AP86(k) 135fr on 75fr Dah. #C262 —
C430 AP81(f) 135fr on 250fr #C250 50.00 —
C431 AP61(g) 135fr on 250fr #C254 50.00 25.00
C432 AP84(f) 150fr on 140fr #C242 25.00 15.00
C433 A61(b) 150fr on #C153 75.00 —
C434 AP61(f) 150fr on #C197 50.00 25.00
C434A AP61(g) 190fr on 200fr #C168 50.00 25.00
C435 AP13(e) 200fr on 100fr #C31 125.00 65.00
C436 AP14(e) 200fr on 100fr #C34 50.00 25.00
C437 AP48(e) 200fr on 100fr #C152 45.00 20.00
C438 AP61(f) 200fr on 100fr Dah. #C196 —
C439 AP61(e) 200fr on 100fr #C253 45.00 25.00
C440 AP78(f) 200fr on 150fr #C236 80.00 40.00
C441 AP67(f) 200fr on #C191 60.00 35.00
C442 AP61(g) 200fr on #C198 45.00 20.00
a. "IN" of "BENIN" below obliterator — —
C443 AP78(f) 200fr on Dah. #C237 —
C444 AP61(e) 200fr on 250fr #C179 45.00 —
C445 AP61(e) 200fr on 250fr #C234 75.00
C446 AP61(e) 200fr on 250fr #C254 50.00
C447 AP85(f) 300fr on #C261 65.00 35.00

Benin No. C351 Surcharged

1994-95

Printing Method and Perfs as Before

C449 AP118 200fr on 500fr #C351 60.00 30.00

Benin No. C290 Surcharged, Dahomey Nos. C206, C257 Surcharged

1996?

Perfs. & Printing Methods as Before

C450 A133 40fr on 210fr #C290 60.00 30.00
C451 AP83(f) 200fr on 500fr #C257 65.00 35.00
C452 AP72(d) 1000fr on 150fr #C206 50.00 25.00

Dahomey No. C265 Surcharged, Benin Nos. C258, C292 Surcharged

1996?

Perfs. & Printing Methods as Before

C453 AP86(g) 25fr on 500fr #C265 42.50 25.00
C454 AP89 35fr on 270fr #C258 62.50 —
C455 AP102 100fr on 500fr #C292 62.50 30.00

Dahomey Nos. C61, C74, C85, C88, C94, C106, C109, C111, C113, C115, C120, C124-C125, C130, C135-C136, C138, C142-C143, C150, C157, C204-C205, C207-C208, C260, C263 Surcharged

No. C458

No. C461

No. C464

No. C465

No. C467

No. C469

No. C471

No. C474

No. C475

No. C476

No. C478

No. C479

No. C480

No. C482

1996?

Perfs. & Printing Methods as Before

C456	AP48(e)	70fr on 100fr	#C138	75.00	40.00
C457	AP34(h)	150fr on	#C88	35.00	—
C458	AP21(e)	150fr on	#C115	45.00	—
C459	AP72(e)	150fr on	#C207	35.00	—
C460	AP73(h)	150fr on	#C208	35.00	—
C461	AP34(e)	150fr on 30fr	#C85	40.00	—
C462	AP31(h)	150fr on 30fr	#C74	35.00	—
C463	AP21(e)	150fr on 30fr	#C109	35.00	—
C464	AP40(e)	150fr on 40fr on 30fr	#C120	35.00	—
C465	AP47(e)	150fr on 40fr	#C136	35.00	—
C466	AP49(e)	150fr on 40fr	#C142	35.00	—
C467	CD128(h)	150fr on 50fr	#C94	40.00	—
C468	AP38(h)	150fr on 50fr	#C106	27.50	—
C469	AP71(e)	150fr on 50fr	#C204	35.00	—
C470	AP54(h)	150fr on 70fr	#C124	35.00	—
C471	CD124(h)	150fr on 100fr	#C61	35.00	—
C472	AP21(e)	150fr on 100fr	#C113	35.00	—
C473	AP53(h)	150fr on 100fr	#C157	29.00	—
C474	AP84(h)	150fr on 100fr	#C260	12.50	—
C475	AP21(h)	150fr on 110fr	#C111	35.00	—
C476	AP44(h)	150fr on 110fr	#C130	40.00	—
C477	AP54(h)	150fr on 120fr	#C125	35.00	—
C478	AP86(g)	150fr on 135fr	#C263	62.50	—
C479	AP46(h)	150fr on 200fr	#C135	35.00	—
C480	AP49(e)	150fr on 200fr	#C143	35.00	—
C481	AP51(h)	150fr on 200fr	#C150	35.00	—
C482	AP71(e)	150fr on 200fr	#C205	29.00	—

Benin Nos. C261, C281, C327, C332-C333 Surcharged, Dahomey Nos. C127, C175, C197, C201 Surcharged or Overprinted

No. C483

No. C488

1996-97?

Perfs. & Printing Methods as Before

C483	AP98	30fr on 380fr	#C281	42.50	20.00
C484	AP90	35fr on 270fr	#C261	60.00	35.00
C485	AP117	125fr on 200fr	#C332	35.00	15.00
b.		Lower case"f" in new denomination			—
C485A	AP117	125fr on 200fr	#C333	35.00	15.00
c.		Lower case"f" in new denomination			—
C486	AP114	200fr on 500fr	#C327	60.00	30.00
C487	AP61(h)	150fr on	#C197	—	—
C488	AP43(h)	150fr on 40fr	#C127	22.50	—
C489	AP70(f)	150fr on 50fr	#C201	35.00	15.00
C490	AP48(e)	200fr on 150fr	#C175	62.50	35.00

No. C256, C257, C268, C278, C284, C287 Surcharged

No. C494

No. C497

Method and Perf. as Before

1995-96 ?

C494	AP88	40fr on 210fr	#C256 ('96)	50.00	25.00
C495	AP89	150fr on 130fr	#C257	—	—
C496	AP93	150fr on 500fr	#C268	30.00	15.00
C497	AP96	150fr on 500fr	#C278	22.50	12.00
C498	AP99	150fr on 500fr	#C284	—	—
C499	AP100	150fr on 500fr	#C287	—	—

Benin No. C293 Surcharged, Dahomey Nos. C37, C119, C121, C122, C147, C250 Surcharged

No. C503

1995-97?

Perf. & Printing Methods as Before

C500	AP103	150fr on 500fr	#C293	22.50	—
C502	AP42(k)	135fr on 40fr	Dah. #C121	—	—
C503	AP51(e)	135fr on 40fr	#C147	70.00	35.00
C504	AP42(k)	135fr on 50fr	Dah. #C122	—	—
C509	AP81(f)	150fr on 250fr	#C250	80.00	40.00
C510	AP41(h)	200fr on 100fr	Dah. #C119	—	—
C511	AP15(h)	200fr on 500fr	#C37	—	—

Dahomey Nos. C69, C86, C126, C70 Surcharged

No. C513

1995-99?

Perf. & Printing Methods as Before

C512	AP29(h)	35fr on 45fr	#C69	—	—
C513	AP34(h)	35fr on 45fr	#C86	80.00	40.00
C515	AP42(h)	35fr on 100fr on 200fr	#C126	80.00	40.00
C516	AP29(h)	35fr on 100fr	#C70	50.00	25.00

Dahomey Nos. C28, C47, C72, C92, C93, C105, C112, C114, C116, C133, C134, C139, C141, C168, C177, C202, C223, C264, Benin Nos. C285-C286 Surcharged or Overprinted

No. C523

No. C537

Method and Perf. as Before

1997 ?

C517	AP30(h)	35fr on 55fr	#C72	80.00	40.00
C518	AP46(h)	35fr on 70fr	#C133	—	—
C519	AP10(h)	35fr on 100fr	#C28	—	—
C520	AP21(h)	35fr on 100fr	Dah. #C47	—	—
C522	AP35(h)	35fr on 100fr	#C93	50.00	25.00
C523	A51(h)	35fr on 100fr	#C105	50.00	25.00
C524	AP21(h)	35fr on 100fr	#C114	—	—
C525	AP39(h)	35fr on 100fr	#C116	—	—
C526	AP48(h)	35fr on 100fr	#C139	80.00	40.00
C527	AP46(h)	35fr on 110fr	#C134	—	—
C528	AP61(h)	35fr on 125fr	#C177	—	—
C529	AP70(f)	35fr on 125fr	#C202	—	—
C530	AP75(h)	35fr on 125fr	#C223	80.00	40.00
C531	AP35(h)	35fr on 200fr	#C92	—	—
C532	AP21(h)	35fr on 200fr	#C112	80.00	40.00
C533	AP48(h)	35fr on 200fr	#C141	—	—
C534	AP486(h)	35fr on 300fr	#C264	—	—
C535	CD138(h)	100fr on	#C285	50.00	25.00
C536	CD139(h)	100fr on	#C286	50.00	25.00
C537	AP58	300fr on 200fr	#C168	*30.00*	*20.00*

Dahomey Nos. C15, C172, C206, C224, C256, C257 Surcharged or Overprinted

No. C538

No. C539

No. C540

No. C541

No. C542

No. C543

Method and Perf. as Before

1997 ?

C538 AP56(f) 175fr on 150fr Dahomey #C172 *50.00 35.00*
C539 AP72(f) 175fr on 150fr Dahomey #C206 *50.00 35.00*
C540 AP75(f) 300fr on 200fr Dahomey #C224 *55.00 30.00*
C541 AP4(f) 500fr on Dahomey #C15 *40.00 25.00*
C542 AP63(f) 500fr on 200fr Dahomey #C256 *30.00 20.00*
C543 AP63(f) 500fr on Dahomey #C257 *40.00 25.00*

Benin No. C243, Dahomey Nos. C36, C48, C141, C150, C191, C234, C237, C254, C256, C261, C264, C265, C267 Overprinted Types "f" or "g"

Methods and Perfs As Before

2005-09 (?)

C544 AP21(g) 200fr on Dah. #C48 *50.00 25.00*
C545 AP48(g) 200fr on Dah. #C141 *35.00 15.00*
C546 AP51(g) 200fr on Dah. #C150 *40.00 20.00*
C547 AP67(g) 200fr on Dah. #C191 *40.00 20.00*
C548 AP78(g) 200fr on Dah. #C237 *100.00 50.00*
C549 AP83(g) 200fr on Dah. #C256 *125.00 65.00*
C550 AP15(f) 250fr on Dah. #C36 80.00 40.00
C551 AP61(f) 250fr on Dah. #C234 —
C552 AP61(f) 250fr on Dah. #C254 — —
C553 AP87(f) 250fr on Dah. #C267 — —
C554 AP35(f) 300fr on Dah. #C261 *55.00 30.00*
C555 AP86(f) 300fr on Dah. #C264 *30.00 20.00*
C556 AP84(f) 300fr on Benin #C243 — —
C557 AP86(f) 500fr on Dah. #C265 *35.00 20.00*

Various Stamps of Dahomey and Benin Surcharged Type "f" or "k"

No. C581

Methods and Perfs As Before

2005-09 (?)

C558 AP63(k) 25fr on 15fr Dah. #C182 *125.00 70.00*
C559 AP56(k) 25fr on 20fr Dah. #C163 *40.00 20.00*
C560 AP63(k) 25fr on 20fr Dah. #C183, type 1 surcharge *110.00 60.00*
C561 AP30(k) 50fr on 30fr Dah. #C71 *25.00 12.00*
C562 AP31(k) 50fr on 30fr Dah. #C74 *25.00 12.00*
C563 AP35(k) 50fr on 30fr Dah. #C89 *30.00 15.00*
C564 AP66(k) 50fr on 35fr Dah. #C189 *40.00 20.00*
C565 AP61(k) 50fr on 35fr Dah. #C195 *25.00 12.00*
C566 AP43(k) 50fr on 40fr Dah. #C127 *25.00 12.00*
C567 AP47(k) 50fr on 40fr Dah. #C136 *150.00 75.00*
C568 AP49(k) 50fr on 40fr Dah. #C142 *40.00 20.00*
C569 AP52(k) 50fr on 40fr Dah. #C155 *40.00 20.00*
C570 AP62(k) 50fr on 40fr Dah. #C180 *60.00 30.00*
C571 AP63(k) 50fr on 40fr Dah. #C184 *75.00 40.00*
C572 AP24(f) 175fr on 70fr Dah. #C58 *40.00 20.00*
C573 AP28(f) 175fr on 70fr Dah. #C67 — —
C574 AP32(f) 175fr on 70fr Dah. #C79 *35.00 20.00*
C575 AP28(f) 175fr on 70fr Dah. #C90 — —
C576 AP86(f) 175fr on 135fr Dah. #C263 *17.50 10.00*
C577 AP56(f) 175fr on 150fr Dah. #C165 — —
C578 AP48(f) 175fr on 150fr Dah. #C175 *30.00 20.00*
C579 AP72(f) 175fr on 150fr Dah. #C207 *40.00 25.00*
C580 AP83(k) 200fr on 35fr Dah. #C255 *100.00 50.00*
C581 AP51(k) 200fr on 40fr Dah. #C147 *35.00 17.50*
C582 AP87(k) 200fr on 40fr Dah. #C266 *40.00 20.00*
C583 AP84(k) 200fr on 40fr Ben. #C240 *40.00 20.00*
C584 AP33(k) 200fr on 45fr Dah. #C82 *60.00 30.00*
C585 AP50(k) 200fr on 50fr Dah. #C144 *35.00 17.50*
C586 AP75(k) 200fr on 65fr Dah. #C222 *125.00 70.00*
C587 AP28(k) 200fr on 70fr Dah. #C68 *40.00 20.00*
C588 AP86(k) 200fr on 75fr Dah. #C262 *35.00 17.50*
C589 AP84(k) 200fr on 85fr Ben. #C241 *100.00 50.00*
C590 AP14(k) 200fr on 100fr Dah. #C34 *110.00 60.00*
C591 AP68(k) 200fr on 100fr Dah. #C194 *50.00 25.00*
C592 AP48(k) 300fr on 40fr Dah. #C151 *60.00 30.00*
C593 AP66(k) 300fr on 40fr Dah. #C190 *35.00 17.50*
C594 AP32(k) 300fr on 45fr Dah. #C78 *75.00 40.00*
C595 AP21(k) 300fr on 45fr Dah. #C110 *35.00 17.50*
C596 A49(k) 300fr on 50fr Dah. #C101 *20.00 10.00*
C597 AP70(k) 300fr on 50fr Dah. #C201, type 1 surcharge *35.00 17.50*
a. Type 2 surcharge — —
C598 AP71(k) 300fr on 50fr Dah. #C204 *100.00 50.00*
C599 AP36(k) 300fr on 60fr Dah. #C98 *70.00 35.00*
C600 AP54(k) 300fr on 65fr Dah. #C161 *35.00 17.50*
C601 AP64(k) 300fr on 65fr Dah. #C185 *50.00 25.00*
C602 AP24(k) 300fr on 70fr Dah. #C58 *40.00 20.00*
C603 AP31(k) 300fr on 70fr Dah. #C76 *40.00 20.00*
C604 AP51(k) 300fr on 70fr Dah. #C148 *35.00 17.50*
C605 AP36(k) 300fr on 75fr Dah. #C99 *70.00 35.00*
C606 AP22(k) 300fr on 80fr Dah. #C53 *85.00 42.50*
C607 AP56(b)(k) 300fr on 85fr Dah. #C171 *40.00 20.00*
C608 AP44(k) 300fr on 90fr Dah. #C129 *40.00 20.00*
C609 AP4(k) 300fr on 100fr Dah. #C14 *25.00 12.50*
C610 AP6(k) 300fr on 100fr Dah. #C20 *25.00 12.50*
C611 AP10(k) 300fr on 100fr Dah. #C28 *40.00 20.00*
C612 AP22(k) 300fr on 100fr Dah. #C54 *60.00 30.00*
C613 AP30(k) 300fr on 100fr Dah. #C73 *35.00 17.50*
C614 AP32(k) 300fr on 100fr Dah. #C80 *80.00 40.00*
C615 AP35(k) 300fr on 100fr Dah. #C91 *35.00 17.50*
C616 AP45(k) 300fr on 100fr Dah. #C131 *35.00 17.50*
C617 AP48(k) 300fr on 100fr Dah. #C139 *35.00 17.50*
C618 AP48(k) 300fr on 100fr Dah. #C140 *35.00 17.50*
C619 CD135(k) 300fr on 100fr Dah. #C146 *60.00 30.00*
C620 AP55(k) 300fr on 100fr Dah. #C162 *40.00 20.00*
C621 AP57(k) 300fr on 100fr Dah. #C166 *40.00 20.00*
C622 AP60(k) 300fr on 100fr Dah. #C173 *40.00 20.00*
C623 AP62(k) 300fr on 100fr Dah. #C181 *40.00 20.00*
C624 AP65(k) 300fr on 100fr Dah. #C188 *40.00 20.00*
C625 AP69(k) 300fr on 100fr Dah. #C200 *35.00 17.50*
C626 AP77(k) 300fr on 100fr Dah. #C233 *40.00 20.00*
C627 AP71(f) 300fr on 200fr Dah. #C205 — —
C628 AP61(k) 400fr on 35fr Dah. #C176 *40.00 20.00*
C629 AP35(k) 400fr on 100fr Dah. #C93 *40.00 20.00*
C630 AP50(k) 400fr on 100fr Dah. #C145 *35.00 17.50*
C631 AP51(k) 400fr on 100fr Dah. #C149 *40.00 20.00*
C632 AP70(k) 400fr on 125fr Dah. #C202 *40.00 20.00*
C634 AP70(k) 1000fr on 150fr Dah. #C203 *30.00 15.00*
C635 AP73(k) 1000fr on 150fr Dah. #C208 *70.00 35.00*
C636 AP78(k) 1000fr on 150fr Dah. #C236 *90.00 45.00*

Surcharge types for No. C560: Type 1 - Country name in thick, bold letters, large "f" almost touching "25."

Surcharge types for No. C597: Type 1 - New denomination below "BE" of country name. Type 2 - New denomination below and to the left of country name.

Dahomey Nos. C92, C116, C138, C152, C153, C157, C158, C167, C186, C192, C197, C207, C250 and C253 Surcharged

Methods and Perfs As Before

2009

C637 AP39(k) 400fr on 100fr #C116 *30.00 15.00*
C638 AP48(k) 400fr on 100fr #C138 *40.00 20.00*
C639 AP48(k) 400fr on 100fr #C152 *30.00 15.00*
C640 AP53(k) 400fr on 100fr #C157 *25.00 15.00*
C641 AP61(k) 400fr on 100fr #C253 *40.00 20.00*
C642 AP64(k) 400fr on 125fr #C186 *50.00 25.00*
C643 AP58(k) 400fr on 150fr #C167 *25.00 15.00*
C644 AP68(k) 1000fr on 35fr #C192, type 1 srch. *60.00 30.00*
a. Type 2 surcharge — —
C645 A61(k) 1000fr on 150fr #C153 *40.00 20.00*
C646 AP61(k) 1000fr on 150fr #C197 *40.00 20.00*
C647 AP72(k) 1000fr on 150fr #C207 *90.00 45.00*
C648 AP35(k) 1000fr on 200fr #C92 *25.00 15.00*
C649 AP53(k) 1000fr on 250fr #C158 *25.00 15.00*
C650 AP81(k) 1000fr on 250fr #C250 *40.00 20.00*
Nos. C637-C650 (14) *560.00 290.00*

Surcharge types for No. C644: Type 1 — Denomination closer to thick obliterator over "Dahomey." Type 2 — Denomination closer to two obliterator bars over old denomination.

Dahomey No. C94 Surcharged

2009 **Method and Perf. As Before**

C651 CD128(k) 300fr on 50fr Dah. #C94 — —

Dahomey Nos. C96, and C164 Surcharged

2009 **Method and Perf. As Before**

C651A AP56(k) 300fr on 85fr Dah. #C164 *40.00 20.00*
C651B AP21(k) 400fr on 100fr Dah. #C96 — —

Dahomey No. C177 Surcharged

2009 Method and Perf. As Before

C652 AP61(k) 400fr on 125fr Dahomey #C177 *40.00 20.00*

Dahomey No. C223 Surcharged

2009 Method and Perf. As Before

C653 AP75(k) 400fr on 125fr #C223 *50.00 25.00*

Dahomey No. C206 Surcharged

2009 Method and Perf. As Before

C655 AP72(k) 1000fr on 150fr Dah. #C206 — —

Dahomey No. C224 Overprinted

Method and Perf. As Before

2009 ?

C657 AP75(g) 200fr on Dah. #C224 — —

POSTAGE DUE STAMPS

French Colony

Handstamped in Black on Postage Due Stamps of French Colonies

1894	Unwmk.	*Imperf.*		
J1	D1	5c black	175.00	70.00
J2	D1	10c black	175.00	70.00
J3	D1	20c black	175.00	70.00
J4	D1	30c black	175.00	70.00
		Nos. J1-J4 (4)	700.00	280.00

Nos. J1-J4 exist with overprint in various positions.

Catalogue values for unused stamps in this section are for Never Hinged items.

People's Republic

Pineapples D6

Mail Delivery D7

Designs: 20fr, Cashew, vert. 40fr, Oranges. 50fr, Akee. 80fr, Mail delivery by boat.

1978, Sept. 5	Photo.	*Perf. 13*	
J44 D6	10fr multicolored	.30	.25
J45 D6	20fr multicolored	.55	.45
J46 D6	40fr multicolored	1.00	.65
J47 D6	50fr multicolored	1.40	.90

Engr.

J48 D7	60fr multi	1.10	.65
J49 D7	80fr multi	1.40	.90
	Nos. J44-J49 (6)	5.75	3.80

PARCEL POST STAMPS

Catalogue values for unused stamps in this section are for Never Hinged items.

Nos. 448-448A, 459, 473, C292 Overprinted or Surcharged "Colis Postaux"

No. Q8

No. Q9

No. Q10

No. Q10A

No. Q10B

No. Q9A, As #Q9, with obliterator over "Populaire".

Perfs. and Printing Methods as Before

1982-2002

Q8	A126	100fr on 150fr #448	20.00	12.50
Q9	A130	100fr multi #459	70.00	35.00
Q9A	A130	100fr multi #459	—	—
Q10	A134	300fr multi #473	20.00	12.50
Q10A	A126a	1000fr multi #448A	25.00	12.50
Q10B	AP102	5000fr on 500fr #C292	70.00	35.00
		Nos. Q8-Q10B (5)	205.00	107.50

Issued: No. Q9A, 2002. For overeprint, see No, Q28.

No. 358 Overprinted Vertically Reading Down

Method and Perf as Before

1984 ?

Q10C A88 50fr multi 170.00 85.00

Dahomey No. C205 and Benin No. 362 Surcharged

No. Q11

No. Q11A

1982-89	Photo.	*Perf. 12½x13*		
Q11	AP71	500fr on 200fr Dahomey #C205	25.00	12.50
Q11A	A90	1000fr on 10fr #362	—	—

Dahomey Nos. 336, C223, C224, Benin Nos. 344, 349, 354, 357, 367, 495, 499, C254, C278 Overprinted or Surcharged

No. Q12A

No. Q14

Methods and Perfs as Before

1989-2002

Q12	A87	5fr multi #354	70.00	35.00
Q12A	A78	5fr on 40fr Dahomey #336		—
Q12B	A78	5fr on 40fr As No. Q12A with obliterator over "Populaire"	—	—
Q13	A144	15fr on 50fr #499	35.00	17.50
Q13A	A144	15fr on 50fr As No. Q13 with obliterator over "Populaire"	—	—
Q13B	AP75	50fr on 125fr Dah. #C223	—	—
Q14	A91	60fr on 150fr #367	50.00	25.00
b.		As #Q14, with "Colis Postaux" in serifed type	—	—
Q14A	A142(h)	75fr on 50fr #495	—	—
Q15	A142	75fr on 50fr #495	35.00	17.50
Q16	A85	200fr multi #349	50.00	25.00
Q16A	A85	200fr multi #349	50.00	25.00
Q16B	A85	200fr multi #349	—	—
Q16C	AP87	250fr on #C254	—	—
Q16D	AP87	250fr on #C254	—	—
Q17	AP87	250fr multi #C254	50.00	25.00
Q17A	AP87	250fr multi #C254	50.00	25.00
Q17B	AP75	300fr on 200fr Dahomey #C224	50.00	25.00
Q18	AP96	500fr multi #C278	70.00	35.00
Q18A	A83	500fr on 45fr #344	90.00	45.00

Nos. Q14, Q15 have "Republique de Benin" overprint.

No. Q14 has "Colis Postaux" in sans-serif type.

Nos. Q16 and Q17 have overprint in sans-serif type. Nos. Q16A and Q17A have overprint in serifed type.

Nos. Q16A, Q16B, Q17, Q17A have obliterator over "POPULAIRE." No. Q16B has overprint in sans-serif type. Nos. Q16C, Q16D have no obliterator bar. No. Q16C has "Colis Postaux" in sans-serif type; No. Q16D, in serifed type.

No. 357 Surcharged "COLIS / POSTAUX"

Method and Perf. As Before

1989 ?

Q19 A88 500fr on 20fr #357 —

Nos. 375, 378, C246, C258 Surcharged or Overprinted "Colis Postaux"

Methods and Perfs as Before

1998

Q20	A96	60fr on 150fr #378	50.00	25.00
Q20A	A96	60fr on 150fr #378	—	—
Q21	A95	100fr multi #375	50.00	25.00
Q22	AP85	300fr multi #C246	90.00	45.00
Q23	AP69	5000fr on 270fr #C258	—	—

No. Q20 has "Colis Postaux" in sans-serif type. No. Q20A has obliterator over "Populaire." See No. Q33

Dahomey No. C157, Benin Nos. 368, C254 Overprinted "COLIS / POSTAUX"

1998 ? Method and Perf as Before

Q25	A92	10fr on #368	350.00	225.00
Q25A	AP53	10fr on 100fr Dahomey #C157	175.00	100.00
Q26	AP87	5000fr on 250fr #C254	50.00	25.00
Q27	AP87	5000fr on 250fr #C254	50.00	25.00

No. Q25A has the overprinted word "Populaire" obliterated. No. Q26 has "Colis Postaux" in sans-serif type. Nos. Q27 has "Colis Postaux" in serifed type.

No. Q10 Overprinted

Method and Perf. As Before

1998 ?

Q28 A134(h) 300fr on #Q10 — —

No. 378 Surcharged With "Colis Postaux" in Serifed Type

Method and Perf. As Before

2009 (?)

Q33 A96 60fr on 150fr #378 *50.00 25.00*

No. Q33 With Obliterator Over "Populaire"

Method and Perf. As Before

2009 ?

Q34 A96 60fr on 120fr As #Q33, with obliterator over "Populaire" — —

BERMUDA

ˌbər-ˈmyü-də

LOCATION — A group of about 150 small islands of which only 20 are inhabited, lying in the Atlantic Ocean about 580 miles southeast of Cape Hatteras.
GOVT. — British Crown Colony
AREA — 20.5 sq. mi.
POP. — 62,471 (1999 est.)
CAPITAL — Hamilton

Bermuda achieved internal self-government in 1968.

4 Farthings = 1 Penny
12 Pence = 1 Shilling
20 Shillings = 1 Pound
100 Cents = 1 Dollar (1970)

Catalogue values for unused stamps in this country are for Never Hinged items, beginning with Scott 131.

POSTMASTER STAMPS

PM1

1848-56 Unwmk. *Imperf.*

X1 PM1 1p blk, *bluish* *180,000.*
a. Dated 1849 *200,000.*
X2 PM1 1p red, *bluish* *225,000.*
a. Dated 1854 *400,000.*
X3 PM1 1p red *200,000.*

PM2

Same inscribed "ST GEORGES"

1860

X4 PM2 (1p) red, *yellowish* *100,000.*

Same inscribed "HAMILTON"

1861

X5 PM2 (1p) red, *bluish* 140,000. *130,000.*
X6 PM2 (1p) red *38,500.*

Nos. X1-X3 were produced and used by Postmaster William B. Perot of Hamilton. No. X4 is attributed to Postmaster James H. Thies of St. George's.

Only a few of each stamp exist. Values reflect actual sales figures for stamps in the condition in which they are found.

GENERAL ISSUES

Values for unused stamps are for examples with original gum as defined in the catalogue introduction. Very fine examples of Nos. 1-1a, 2-15b will have perforations touching the design (or framelines where applicable) on at least one side due to the narrow spacing of the stamps on the plates. Stamps with perfs clear of the design on all four sides are scarce and will command higher prices.

Queen Victoria
A1 A2

A3

A4

A5

1865-74 Typo. Wmk. 1 *Perf. 14*

1 A1 1p rose red 110.00 1.75
b. Imperf. *85,000. 27,000.*
2 A2 2p blue ('66) 525.00 40.00
3 A3 3p buff ('73) 600.00 80.00
4 A4 6p brown lilac 2,300. 90.00
5 A4 6p lilac ('74) 30.00 17.00
6 A5 1sh green 450.00 70.00
Nos. 1-6 (6) 4,015. 298.75

See Nos. 7-9, 19-21, 23, 25. For surcharges see Nos. 10-15.

No. 1b is a proof.

1882-1903 *Perf. 14x12½*

7 A3 3p buff 210.00 75.00
8 A4 6p violet ('03) 17.00 *27.50*
9 A5 1sh green ('94) 20.00 *150.00*
a. Vert. strip of 3, perf. all around & imperf. btwn. *13,750.*
Nos. 7-9 (3) 247.00 *252.50*

Handstamped Diagonally

1874 *Perf. 14*

10 A5 3p on 1sh green 1,700. 950.

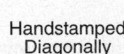

Handstamped Diagonally

11 A1 3p on 1p rose *19,000. 20,000.*
12 A5 3p on 1sh green 2,850. 975.
a. "P" with top like "R" 2,300. 1,100.

No. 11 is stated to be an essay, but a few examples are known used. Nos. 10-12 are found with double or partly double surcharges.

Surcharged in Black

1875

13 A2 1p on 2p blue 875.00 475.00
a. Without period *27,500. 13,250.*
14 A3 1p on 3p buff 550.00 425.00
15 A5 1p on 1sh green 675.00 310.00
a. Inverted surcharge — *50,000.*
b. Without period *40,000. 20,000.*

A6

A7

1880 Wmk. 1

16 A6 ½p brown 8.75 *5.25*
17 A7 4p orange 21.00 2.50

See Nos. 18, 24.

A8

1883-1904 Wmk. 2

18 A6 ½p dp gray grn ('93) 5.00 1.00
a. ½p green ('92) 9.00 4.50
19 A1 1p aniline car ('89) 21.00 .30
a. 1p dull rose 200.00 5.25
b. 1p rose red 100.00 4.00
c. 1p carmine rose ('86) 75.00 1.00
20 A2 2p blue ('86) 75.00 8.25
21 A2 2p brn pur ('98) 6.00 2.75
a. 2p aniline pur ('93) 17.50 6.00
22 A8 2½p ultra ('84) 24.00 .50
a. 2½p deep ultra 37.50 3.75
23 A3 3p gray ('86) 27.50 11.00
24 A7 4p brown org ('04) 37.50 *62.50*
25 A5 1sh ol bis ('93) 19.00 24.00
a. 1sh yellow brown 25.00 24.00
Nos. 18-25 (8) 215.00 *110.30*

A9

1901 Black Surcharge

26 A9 1f on 1sh gray 6.00 1.25

Dry Dock — A10

1902-03

28 A10 ½p gray grn & blk ('03) 15.00 4.50
29 A10 1p car rose & brown 10.00 .35
30 A10 3p ol grn & violet 6.50 *3.50*
Nos. 28-30 (3) 31.50 8.35

1906-10 Wmk. 3

31 A10 ¼p pur & brn ('08) 2.10 1.90
32 A10 ½p gray grn & blk 24.00 1.25
33 A10 ½p green ('09) 25.00 4.50
34 A10 1p car rose & brn 45.00 .25
35 A10 1p carmine ('08) 26.00 .50
36 A10 2p orange & gray 9.25 *13.50*
37 A10 2½p blue & brown 35.00 9.50
38 A10 2½p ultra ('10) 28.00 9.50
39 A10 4p vio brn & blue ('09) 3.75 *20.00*
Nos. 31-39 (9) 198.10 *60.90*

Caravel
A11

King George V
A12

1910-24 Engr. *Perf. 14*

40 A11 ¼p brown ('12) 2.10 *3.00*
a. ¼p pale brown 2.50 *1.75*
41 A11 ½p yel green 3.75 .30
a. ½p dark green ('18) 15.00 1.50
42 A11 1p red (I) 20.00 .35
a. 1p carmine (I) ('19) 67.50 10.00
43 A11 2p gray ('13) 6.50 *21.00*
44 A11 2½p ultra (I) ('12) 4.25 .75
45 A11 3p vio, *yel* ('13) 3.50 *7.50*
46 A11 4p red, *yel* ('19) 14.00 *16.00*
47 A11 6p claret ('24) 12.50 *9.00*
48 A11 1sh blk, *grn* ('12) 6.50 *5.00*
a. 1sh black, *olive* ('25) 6.50 *23.00*

Typographed

Chalky Paper

49 A12 2sh ultra & dl vio, *bl* ('20) 22.50 *62.50*
50 A12 2sh6p red & blk, *bl* 37.50 *100.00*
51 A12 4sh car & blk ('20) 75.00 *200.00*
52 A12 5sh red & grn, *yellow* 75.00 *150.00*
53 A12 10sh red & grn, *green* 225.00 *425.00*
54 A12 £1 blk & vio, *red* 400.00 *700.00*
Nos. 40-54 (15) 908.10 *1,700.*

Types I of 1p and 2½p are illustrated above Nos. 81-97.

The 1p was printed from two plates, the 2nd of which, No. 42a, exists only in carmine on opaque paper with a bluish tinge. Compare No. MR1 (as No. 42) and MR2 (as No. 42a).

Revenue cancellations are found on Nos. 52-54.

See Nos. 81-97.

Seal of the Colony and King George V
A13

1920-21 Wmk. 3 Ordinary Paper

55 A13 ¼p brown 4.00 *28.00*
56 A13 ½p green 9.50 *19.00*
57 A13 2p gray 18.00 *55.00*

Chalky Paper

58 A13 3p vio & dl vio, *yel* 15.00 *55.00*
59 A13 4p red & blk, *yel* 15.00 *42.50*
60 A13 1sh blk, *gray grn* 25.00 *65.00*

Ordinary Paper

Wmk. 4

67 A13 1p rose red 4.50 .35
68 A13 2½p ultra 19.00 20.00

Chalky Paper

69 A13 6p red vio & dl vio 32.50 *95.00*
Nos. 55-60,67-69 (9) 142.50 *379.85*

Issued: 6p, 1/19/21; others, 11/11/20.

King George V
A14

1921, May 12 Engr.

71 A14 ¼p brown 4.25 *4.50*
72 A14 ½p green 3.50 *9.00*
73 A14 1p carmine 12.00 .45

Wmk. 3

74 A14 2p gray 12.00 *55.00*
75 A14 2½p ultra 15.00 7.00
76 A14 3p vio, *orange* 7.00 *20.00*
77 A14 4p scarlet, *org* 20.00 *42.50*
78 A14 6p claret 19.00 *65.00*
79 A14 1sh blk, *green* 29.00 *65.00*
Nos. 71-79 (9) 121.75 *268.45*

Tercentenary of "Local Representative Institutions" (Nos. 55-79).

Types of 1910-20 Issue

Types of 1p

Type I

Type II

Type III

Type I, figure "1" has pointed serifs, scroll at top left very weak.

Type II, thick "1" with square serifs, scroll weak.

Type III, thinner "1" with long square serifs, scroll complete with strong line.

Types of 2½p

Type I

Type II

Type I, small "d," short, thick figures of value.

Type II, larger "d," taller, thinner figures of value.

1922-34 **Wmk. 4**

81	A11	¼p brown ('28)	1.90	*3.75*
82	A11	½p green	1.90	.25
83	A11	1p car, III ('28)	17.00	.35
a.		1p carmine, II ('26)	55.00	8.50
b.		1p carmine, I	21.00	.75
84	A11	1½p red brn ('34)	11.00	.45
85	A11	2p gray ('23)	1.90	1.90
86	A11	2½p ap grn ('23)	3.75	1.90
87	A11	2½p ultra, II ('32)	2.10	.90
a.		2½p ultra, I ('26)	5.50	.60
88	A11	3p ultra ('24)	20.00	*32.50*
89	A11	3p vio, *yel* ('26)	5.00	1.25
90	A11	4p red, *yel* ('24)	2.50	1.25
91	A11	6p claret ('24)	1.50	1.00
92	A11	1sh blk, *emer* ('27)	9.00	*11.00*
93	A11	1sh brn blk, *yel grn* ('34)	42.50	*62.50*

Chalky Paper

94	A12	2sh ultra & vio, *bl* ('27)	55.00	*87.50*
a.		2sh bl & dp vio, *dp bl* ('31)	67.50	*100.00*
95	A12	2sh 6p red & blk, *bl* ('27)	75.00	125.00
a.		2sh6p pale org ver & blk, *gray bl* ('30)	3,500.	3,250.
b.		2sh6p dp ver & blk, *deep blue* ('31)	100.00	*150.00*
96	A12	10sh red & grn, *emer* ('24)	160.00	*300.00*
a.		10sh dp red & pale grn, *dp emer* ('31)	175.00	*350.00*
97	A12	12sh 6p ocher & gray blk ('32)	300.00	*425.00*
		Nos. 81-97 (17)	710.05	*1,057.*

Revenue cancellations are found on Nos. 94-97.

For the 12sh6p with "Revenue" on both sides, see No. AR1.

Common Design Types pictured following the introduction.

Silver Jubilee Issue

Common Design Type

1935, May 6 ***Perf. 11x12***

100	CD301	1p car & dk bl	.55	*2.50*
101	CD301	1½p blk & ultra	.85	*3.50*
102	CD301	2½p ultra & brn	1.40	2.50
103	CD301	1sh brn vio & ind	14.00	*50.00*
		Nos. 100-103 (4)	16.80	*58.50*
		Set, never hinged	32.50	

Hamilton Harbor — A15

South Shore — A16

Yacht "Lucie" — A17

Grape Bay — A18

Typical Cottage — A19

Scene at Par-la-Ville — A20

1936-40 ***Perf. 12***

105	A15	½p blue green	.25	.25
106	A16	1p car & black	.50	.35
107	A16	1½p choc & black	1.15	.60
108	A17	2p lt bl & blk	5.75	2.00
109	A17	2p brn blk & turq bl ('38)	52.50	16.00
109A	A17	2p red & ultra ('40)	1.15	1.25
110	A18	2½p dk bl & lt bl	1.15	.30
111	A19	3p car & black	3.00	2.75
112	A20	6p vio & rose lake	.90	.25
113	A18	1sh deep green	3.75	*23.00*
114	A15	1sh6p brown	.55	.25
		Nos. 105-114 (11)	70.65	47.00
		Set, never hinged	95.00	

No. 108, blue border and black center.
No. 109, black border, blue center.

Coronation Issue

Common Design Type

1937, May 14 ***Perf. 13½x14***

115	CD302	1p carmine	.25	*1.50*
116	CD302	1½p brown	.35	*1.75*
117	CD302	2½p bright ultra	.65	*1.75*
		Nos. 115-117 (3)	1.25	5.00
		Set, never hinged	1.75	

Hamilton Harbor — A21

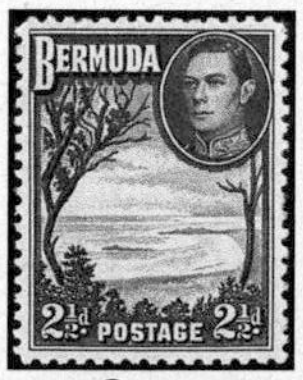

Grape Bay — A22

St. David's Lighthouse A23

King George VI A25

Bermudian Water Scene and Yellow-billed Tropic Bird — A24

1938-51 **Wmk. 4** ***Perf. 12***

118	A21	1p red & blk	.60	.25
a.		1p rose red & black	16.00	1.40
119	A21	1½p vio brn & blue	4.75	1.40
a.		1½p dl vio brn & bl ('43)	4.00	.25
120	A22	2½p blue & lt bl	8.50	1.00
120A	A22	2½p ol brn & lt bl ('41)	2.50	1.25
b.		2½p dk ol blk & pale blue ('43)	2.50	1.40
121	A23	3p car & blk	16.00	2.25
121A	A23	3p dp ultra & blk ('42)	1.40	.25
c.		3p brt ultra & blk ('41)	1.40	.25
		Complete booklet, 6 each #118, 119, 109A, 120Ab, 121Ac	160.00	
		Complete booklet, 6 #121Ac and 18 #112, in blocks of 6, and 12 air mail labels	180.00	
121D	A24	7½p yel grn, bl & blk ('41)	5.00	2.00
122	A22	1sh green	1.60	.55

Typo.

Perf. 13

123	A25	2sh ultra & red vio, *bl* ('50)	13.50	12.00
a.		2sh ultra & vio, *bl*, perf. 14	9.25	3.50
b.		2sh ultra & dl vio, *bl* (mottled paper), perf. 14 ('42)	9.25	3.50
124	A25	2sh 6p red & blk, *bl*	14.50	8.75
a.		Perf. 14	26.00	8.75
125	A25	5sh red & grn, *yel*	17.00	15.00
a.		Perf. 14	60.00	20.00
126	A25	10sh red & grn, *grn* ('51)	40.00	*32.50*
a.		10sh brn lake & grn, *grn*, perf. 14	140.00	100.00
b.		10sh red & grn, *grn*, perf. 14 ('39)	225.00	200.00
127	A25	12sh 6p org & gray blk	87.50	72.50
a.		12sh 6p org & gray, perf. 14	110.00	60.00
b.		12sh 6p yel & gray, perf. 14 ('47)	725.00	600.00
c.		12sh 6p brn org & gray, perf. 14	275.00	100.00

Wmk. 3

128	A25	£1 blk & vio, *red* ('51)	52.50	*62.50*
a.		£1 blk & pur, *red*, perf. 14	300.00	140.00
b.		£1 blk & dk vio, *salmon*, perf. 14 ('43)	87.50	67.50
		Nos. 118-128 (14)	265.35	212.20
		Set, never hinged	450.00	

No. 127b is the so-called "lemon yellow" shade.

Revenue cancellations are found on Nos. 123-128. Stamps with removed revenue cancellations and forged postmarks are abundant.

No. 118a Surcharged in Black

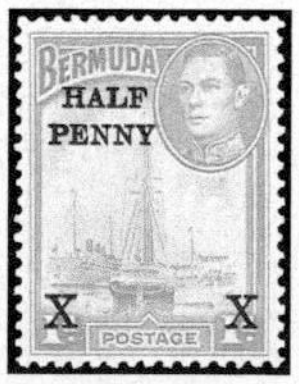

1940, Dec. 20 **Wmk. 4** ***Perf. 12***

129	A21	½p on 1p rose red & blk	.30	*3.00*
		Never hinged	1.00	

Catalogue values for unused stamps in this section, from this point to the end of the section, are for Never Hinged items.

Peace Issue

Common Design Type

Perf. 13½x14

1946, Nov. 6 **Engr.** **Wmk. 4**

131	CD303	1½p brown	.25	.25
132	CD303	3p deep blue	.30	.30

Silver Wedding Issue

Common Design Types

1948, Dec. 1 **Photo.** ***Perf. 14x14½***

133	CD304	1½p red brown	.25	.25

Engr.; Name Typo.

Perf. 11½x11

134	CD305	£1 rose carmine	47.50	*55.00*

Postmaster Stamp of 1848 — A26

1949, Apr. 11 **Engr.** ***Perf. 13x13½***

135	A26	2½p dk brown & dp bl	.25	.25
136	A26	3p dp blue & black	.25	.25
137	A26	6p green & rose vio	.45	.45
		Nos. 135-137 (3)	.95	.95

No. 137 shows a different floral arrangement.
Bermuda's first postage stamp, cent.

UPU Issue

Common Design Types

Engr.; Name Typo.

1949, Oct. 10 ***Perf. 13½, 11x11½***

138	CD306	2½p slate	.50	*2.00*
139	CD307	3p indigo	1.25	1.25
140	CD308	6p rose violet	1.00	.90
141	CD309	1sh blue green	2.00	2.00
		Nos. 138-141 (4)	4.75	6.15

Coronation Issue

Common Design Type

1953, June 4 **Engr.** ***Perf. 13½x13***

142	CD312	1½p dk blue & blk	.85	.50

A27

Easter Lilies — A28

Designs: 1p, 4p, Perot stamp. 2p, Racing dinghy. 2½p, Sir George Somers and "Sea Venture." 3p, 1sh3p, Map. 4½p, 9p, "Sea Venture," boat, hog coin and Perot stamp. 6p, 8p, Yellow-billed tropic bird. 1sh, Hog coins. 2sh, Arms of St. George. 2sh6p, Warwick Fort. 5sh, Hog coin. 10sh, Earliest hog coin. £1, Arms of Bermuda.

1953-58 ***Perf. 13½x13, 13x13½***

143	A27	½p olive green	.50	*3.00*
144	A27	1p rose red & blk	1.25	.55
145	A28	1½p dull green	.30	.25
146	A27	2p red & ultra	.55	.55
147	A27	2½p carmine rose	2.10	.60
148	A27	3p vio *(Sandy's)*	.35	.25
149	A27	3p vio *(Sandys)* ('57)	1.10	.25
150	A27	4p dp ultra & blk	.30	*1.40*
151	A27	4½p green	.55	*1.25*
152	A27	6p dk bluish grn & blk	5.00	.75
153	A27	8p red & blk ('55)	2.50	.45
154	A27	9p violet ('58)	7.25	3.00
155	A27	1sh orange	.55	.25
156	A27	1sh3p blue *(Sandy's)*	3.75	.45
157	A27	1sh3p blue *(Sandys)* ('57)	7.25	.60
158	A27	2sh yellow brown	4.00	1.10
159	A28	2sh6p scarlet	4.75	.70
160	A27	5sh dp car rose	19.50	1.10
161	A27	10sh deep ultra	13.50	9.00

Engr. and Typo.

162	A27	£1 dp ol grn & multi	35.00	24.00
		Nos. 143-162 (20)	110.05	49.50

For overprints, see Nos. 164-167.

Type of 1953 Inscribed "ROYAL VISIT 1953"

Design: 6p, Yellow-billed tropic bird.

1953, Nov. 26 **Engr.**
163 A27 6p dk bluish grn & blk .50 .25

Visit of Queen Elizabeth II and the Duke of Edinburgh, 1953.

Nos. 148 and 156 Overprinted in Violet Blue or Red

1953, Dec. 8 ***Perf. 13½x13***
164 A27 3p violet .25 .25
165 A27 1sh3p blue (R) .25 .25

Three Power Conference, Tucker's Town, December 1953.

Nos. 153 and 156 Overprinted in Black or Red

1956, June 22
166 A27 8p red & black .35 .60
167 A27 1sh3p blue (R) .35 .60

Newport-Bermuda Yacht Race, 50th anniv.

Perot Post Office, Hamilton A29

Perf. 13½x13
1959, Jan. 1 **Engr.** **Wmk. 4**
168 A29 6p lilac & black 1.35 .25

Restoration and reopening of the post office operated at Hamilton by W. B. Perot in the mid-nineteenth century.

Arms of James I and Elizabeth II — A30

Engr. and Litho.
1959, July 29 **Wmk. 314** ***Perf. 13***
Coats of Arms in Blue, Yellow & Red

169 A30 1½p dark blue .35 .35
170 A30 3p gray .40 .40
171 A30 4p rose violet .50 .50
172 A30 8p violet gray .50 .50
173 A30 9p olive green .50 .50
174 A30 1sh3p orange brown .50 .50
Nos. 169-174 (6) 2.75 2.75

350th anniv. of the shipwreck of the "Sea Venture" which resulted in the first permanent settlement of Bermuda.

The Old Rectory, St. George's, 1730 A31

Designs: 2p, Church of St. Peter. 3p, Government House. 4p, Cathedral, Hamilton. 5p, No. 185A, H.M. Dockyard. 6p, Perot's Post Office, 1848. 8p, General Post Office, 1869. 9p, Library and Historical Society. 1sh, Christ Church, Warwick, 1719. 1sh3p, City Hall, Hamilton. 10p, No. 185, Bermuda Cottage, 1705. 2sh, Town of St. George. 2sh3p, Bermuda House, 1710. 2sh6p, Bermuda House, 18th century. 5sh, Colonial Secretariat, 1833. 10sh, Old Post Office, Somerset, 1890. £1, House of Assembly, 1815.

Wmk. 314 Upright
1962-65 **Photo.** ***Perf. 12½***
175 A31 1p org, lil & blk .25 *.75*
176 A31 2p sl, lt vio, grn & yel .25 .25
a. Light vio omitted 1,000. 1,000.
b. Green omitted 7,500.
d. Imperf., pair 2,250.
177 A31 3p lt bl & yel brn .25 .25
178 A31 4p car rose & red brn .25 *.40*
179 A31 5p dk bl & pink 1.50 *3.00*
180 A31 6p emer, lt & dk bl .25 *.30*
181 A31 8p grn, dp org & ultra .30 *.40*
182 A31 9p org brn & grnsh bl .25 *.50*
182A A31 10p brt vio & bis ('65) 8.75 2.00
183 A31 1sh multi .25 .25
184 A31 1sh3p sl, lem & rose car .90 .25
185 A31 1sh6p brt vio & bis 2.50 2.50
186 A31 2sh brn & org 2.75 1.40
187 A31 2sh3p brn & brt yel grn 2.10 *7.00*
188 A31 2sh6p grn, yel & sep .65 .50
189 A31 5sh choc & brt grn 1.10 *1.50*
190 A31 10sh dl grn, buff & rose car 4.50 *7.00*
191 A31 £1 cit, bis, blk & org 14.00 14.00
Nos. 175-191 (18) 40.80 42.25

See No. 252a. For surcharges see Nos. 238-254.

No. 177a, yellow-brown omitted, is no longer listed. All reported examples show traces of the yellow-brown.

1966-69 **Wmk. 314 Sideways**
Unnamed Colors as in 1962-65 Issue

176c A31 2p ('69) 6.50 *8.00*
181a A31 8p ('67) .65 *1.60*
182b A31 10p 1.90 .90
183a A31 1sh ('67) 1.25 *1.40*
185A A31 1sh6p indigo & rose 4.50 *2.75*
186a A31 2sh ('67) 4.50 *5.00*

For surcharges see Nos. 239, 245-246, 248-249.

Freedom from Hunger Issue
Common Design Type

1963, June 4 ***Perf. 14x14½***
192 CD314 1sh3p sepia 1.00 .50

Red Cross Centenary Issue
Common Design Type

Wmk. 314
1963, Sept. 2 **Litho.** ***Perf. 13***
193 CD315 3p black & red .50 .30
194 CD315 1sh3p ultra & red 2.50 2.50

Finn Boat — A32

Wmk. 314
1964, Sept. 28 **Photo.** ***Perf. 13½***
195 A32 3p blue, vio & red .40 .40

18th Olympic Games, Tokyo, Oct. 10-25.

ITU Issue
Common Design Type

Perf. 11x11½
1965, May 17 **Litho.** **Wmk. 314**
196 CD317 3p blue & emerald .65 .50
197 CD317 2sh yel & vio blue 1.50 *1.75*

Scout Badge and Royal Cipher A33

1965, July 24 **Photo.** ***Perf. 12½***
198 A33 2sh multicolored .55 .55

50th anniversary of Scouting in Bermuda.

Intl. Cooperation Year Issue
Common Design Type

1965, Oct. 25 **Litho.** ***Perf. 14½***
199 CD318 4p blue grn & cl .45 .25
200 CD318 2sh6p lt violet & grn 1.60 1.00

Churchill Memorial Issue
Common Design Type

1966, Jan. 24 **Photo.** ***Perf. 14***
Design in Black, Gold and Carmine Rose

201 CD319 3p bright blue .55 .55
202 CD319 6p green .85 .85
203 CD319 10p brown 1.10 1.10
204 CD319 1sh3p violet 1.50 *2.25*
Nos. 201-204 (4) 4.00 *4.75*

World Cup Soccer Issue
Common Design Type

1966, July 1 **Litho.** ***Perf. 14***
205 CD321 10p multicolored .50 .50
206 CD321 2sh6p multicolored 1.25 1.25

UNESCO Anniversary Issue
Common Design Type

1966, Dec. 1 **Litho.** ***Perf. 14***
207 CD323 4p "Education" .45 .40
208 CD323 1sh3p "Science" 1.25 1.25
209 CD323 2sh "Culture" 2.10 *2.25*
Nos. 207-209 (3) 3.80 *3.90*

Post Office, Hamilton A34

Wmk. 314
1967, June 23 **Photo.** ***Perf. 14½***
210 A34 3p vio blue & multi .25 .25
211 A34 1sh orange & multi .25 .25
212 A34 1sh6p green & multi .30 .25
213 A34 2sh6p red & multi .30 *.75*
Nos. 210-213 (4) 1.10 *1.50*

Opening of the new GPO, Hamilton.

Cable Ship Mercury A35

Designs: 1sh, Map of Bermuda and Virgin Islands, telephone and microphone. 1sh6p, Radio tower, television set, telephone and cable. 2sh6p, Cable at sea bottom and ship.

1967, Sept. 14 **Photo.** **Wmk. 314**
214 A35 3p multicolored .25 .25
215 A35 1sh multicolored .30 .30
216 A35 1sh6p multicolored .30 .30
217 A35 2sh6p multicolored .50 *.75*
Nos. 214-217 (4) 1.35 *1.60*

Completion of the Bermuda-Tortola, Virgin Islands, telephone link.

Human Rights Flame, Globe and Doves A36

1968, Feb. 1 **Litho.** ***Perf. 14x14½***
218 A36 3p indigo, lt grn & bl .30 .25
219 A36 1sh brown, lt bl & bl .30 .25
220 A36 1sh6p black, pink & blue .30 .25
221 A36 2sh6p green, yellow & bl .30 .30
Nos. 218-221 (4) 1.20 1.05

International Human Rights Year.

Mace A37

Nos. 224-225, House of Assembly, Bermuda, Parliament, London & royal cipher.

1968, July 1 **Photo.** ***Perf. 14½***
222 A37 3p rose red & multi .30 .25
223 A37 1sh ultra & multi .30 .25
224 A37 1sh6p yellow & multi .30 .25
225 A37 2sh6p multicolored .30 *.50*
Nos. 222-225 (4) 1.20 *1.25*

New constitution.

Olympic Sports and Rings A38

1968, Sept. 24 **Wmk. 314** ***Perf. 12½***
226 A38 3p lilac & multi .25 .25
a. Rose brown omitted ("3d BERMUDA") *4,750.* *5,000.*
227 A38 1sh multi .35 .35
228 A38 1sh6p multi .60 .60
229 A38 2sh6p multi .90 *1.25*
Nos. 226-229 (4) 2.10 *2.45*

19th Olympic Games, Mexico City, 10/12-27.

Girl Guides A39

Designs: 1sh, Like 3p. 1sh6p, 2sh6p, Girl Guides and arms of Bermuda.

1969, Feb. 17 **Litho.** ***Perf. 14***
230 A39 3p lilac & multi .25 .25
231 A39 1sh green & multi .35 .25
232 A39 1sh6p gray & multi .40 .40
233 A39 2sh6p red & multi .60 *1.40*
Nos. 230-233 (4) 1.60 2.30

Bermuda Girl Guides, 50th anniv.

Gold and Emerald Cross — A40

Design: 4p, 2sh, Different background

1969, Sept. 29 **Photo.** ***Perf. 14½x14***
Cross in Yellow, Brown and Emerald

234 A40 4p violet .30 .25
235 A40 1sh3p green .45 .25
236 A40 2sh black .55 *.90*
237 A40 2sh6p carmine rose .60 *1.75*
Nos. 234-237 (4) 1.90 3.15

Treasures salvaged off the coast of Bermuda. The cross shown is from the Tucker treasure from the 16th century Spanish galleon San Pedro.

Buildings Issue and Type of 1962-69 Surcharged with New Value and Bar in Black or Brown

1970, Feb. 6 Wmk. 314 *Perf. 12½*

238	A31	1c on 1p multi	.25	*1.75*
239	A31	2c on 2p multi	.25	.25
a.		Watermark upright	3.00	*6.50*
b.		Light violet omitted	*1,000.*	
c.		Pair, one without surch.	*7,500.*	
240	A31	3c on 3p multi	.25	.25
241	A31	4c on 4p multi (Br)	.25	.25
242	A31	5c on 8p multi	.25	*2.25*
243	A31	6c on 6p multi	.25	*1.75*
244	A31	9c on 9p multi (Br)	.40	*2.75*
245	A31	10c on 10p multi	.40	.25
246	A31	12c on 1sh multi	.40	*1.25*
247	A31	15c on 1sh3p multi	2.00	1.75
248	A31	18c on 1sh6p multi	1.00	.70
249	A31	24c on 2sh multi	1.10	*4.25*
250	A31	30c on 2sh6p multi	1.25	*3.00*
251	A31	36c on 2sh3p multi	2.25	*8.00*
252	A31	60c on 5sh multi	2.90	*4.00*
a.		Surcharge omitted	*1,500.*	
253	A31	$1.20 on 10sh multi	5.25	*13.00*
254	A31	$2.40 on £1 multi	8.00	*17.00*
		Nos. 238-254 (17)	26.45	*62.45*

Watermark upright on 1c, 3c to 9c and 36c; sideways on others. Watermark is sideways on No. 252a, upright on No. 189.

Spathiphyllum — A41

Flowers: 2c, Bottlebrush. 3c, Oleander, vert. 4c, Bermudiana. 5c, Poinsettia. 6c, Hibiscus. 9c, Cereus. 10c, Bougainvillea, vert. 12c, Jacaranda. 15c, Passion flower. 18c, Coralita. 24c, Morning glory. 30c, Tecoma. 36c, Angel's trumpet. 60c, Plumbago. $1.20, Bird of paradise. $2.40, Chalice cup.

Wmk. 314, Sideways on Horiz. Stamps

1970, July 6 *Perf. 14*

255	A41	1c lt grn & multi	.35	*.50*
256	A41	2c pale bl & multi	.60	.50
257	A41	3c yellow & multi	.35	*.50*
258	A41	4c buff & multi	.35	*.50*
259	A41	5c pink & multi	.85	.50
a.		Imperf., pair	1,500.	
260	A41	6c org & multi	.85	.60
261	A41	9c lt grn & multi	.60	.50
262	A41	10c pale sal & multi	.60	.50
263	A41	12c pale yel & multi	2.10	1.75
264	A41	15c buff & multi	2.50	1.50
265	A41	18c pale sal & multi	6.50	2.50
266	A41	24c pink & multi	4.25	4.25
267	A41	30c plum & multi	2.90	1.60
268	A41	36c dk gray & multi	3.50	2.40
269	A41	60c gray & multi	4.75	4.00
270	A41	$1.20 blue & multi	7.75	7.25
271	A41	$2.40 multicolored	15.00	15.00
		Nos. 255-271 (17)	53.80	44.35

See Nos. 322-328. For overprints see Nos. 288-291.

1974-76 Wmk. 314 Upright

259b	A41	5c multicolored	3.25	*3.75*
260a	A41	6c multicolored	7.25	*8.25*
263a	A41	12c multicolored	6.00	*7.00*
267a	A41	30c multicolored ('76)	9.75	*11.00*
		Nos. 259b-267a (4)	26.25	*30.00*

Issued: 30c, June 11; others, June 13.

1975-76 Wmk. 373

256a	A41	2c multicolored	1.75	1.25
260b	A41	6c multicolored	8.00	7.00

Issued: 2c, Dec. 8; 6c, June 11, 1976.

State House, St. George's, 1622-1815 — A42

Designs: 15c, The Sessions House, Hamilton, 1893. 18c, First Assembly House, St. Peter's Church, St. George's. 24c, Temporary Assembly House, Hamilton, 1815-26.

1970, Oct. 12 Litho. *Perf. 14*

272	A42	4c multicolored	.25	.25
273	A42	15c multicolored	.25	.25
274	A42	18c multicolored	.30	.30
275	A42	24c multicolored	.50	*.90*
a.		Souvenir sheet of 4, #272-275	2.25	2.25
		Nos. 272-275 (4)	1.30	1.70

350th anniv. of Bermuda's Parliament.

Street in St. George's A43

"Keep Bermuda Beautiful": 15c, Horseshoe Bay. 18c, Gibb's Hill Lighthouse. 24c, View of Hamilton Harbor.

1971, Feb. 8 Wmk. 314 *Perf. 14*

276	A43	4c multicolored	.25	.25
277	A43	15c multicolored	.70	.70
278	A43	18c multicolored	1.90	2.10
279	A43	24c multicolored	1.50	*1.75*
		Nos. 276-279 (4)	4.35	*4.80*

Building of "Deliverance" — A44

Designs: 15c, "Deliverance" and "Patience" arriving in Jamestown, Va., 1610, vert. 18c, Wreck of "Sea Venture," vert. 24c, "Deliverance" and "Patience" under sail, 1610.

1971, May 10 Litho. Wmk. 314

280	A44	4c multicolored	.80	.30
281	A44	15c brown & multi	2.25	*2.40*
282	A44	18c purple & multi	2.25	*2.40*
283	A44	24c blue & multi	2.50	*2.75*
		Nos. 280-283 (4)	7.80	*7.85*

Voyage of Sir George Somers to Jamestown, Va., from Bermuda, 1610.

Ocean View Golf Course A45

Golf Courses: 15c, Port Royal. 18c, Castle Harbour. 24c, Belmont.

1971, Nov. 1 *Perf. 13*

284	A45	4c multicolored	1.00	.25
285	A45	15c multicolored	1.90	.90
286	A45	18c multicolored	2.00	1.40
287	A45	24c multicolored	2.50	*2.75*
		Nos. 284-287 (4)	7.40	*5.30*

Golfing in Bermuda.

Nos. 258, 264-266 Overprinted: "HEATH-NIXON / DECEMBER 1971"

1971, Dec. 20 Photo. *Perf. 14*

288	A41	4c buff & multi	.25	.25
289	A41	15c buff & multi	.25	.25
290	A41	18c pale sal & multi	.30	*.50*
291	A41	24c pink & multi	.40	*.75*
		Nos. 288-291 (4)	1.20	*1.75*

Meeting of President Richard M. Nixon and Prime Minister Edward Heath of Great Britain, at Hamilton, Dec. 20-21, 1971.

Bonefish A46

1972, Aug. 7 Litho. *Perf. 13½x14*

292	A46	4c shown	.50	.25
293	A46	15c Wahoo	.50	.50
294	A46	18c Yellowfin tuna	.60	*.75*
295	A46	24c Greater amberjack	.65	*1.00*
		Nos. 292-295 (4)	2.25	*2.50*

World fishing records.

Silver Wedding Issue, 1972
Common Design Type

Design: Queen Elizabeth II, Prince Philip, Admiralty oar and mace.

1972, Nov. 20 Photo. *Perf. 14x14½*

296	CD324	4c violet & multi	.25	.25
297	CD324	15c car rose & multi	.25	*.40*

Palmettos — A47

1973, Sept. 3 Wmk. 314 *Perf. 14*

298	A47	4c shown	.40	.25
299	A47	15c Olivewood	1.10	1.10
a.		Brown (Queen's head, "15c") omitted	2,250.	
300	A47	18c Bermuda cedar	1.25	1.25
301	A47	24c Mahogany	1.25	*1.50*
		Nos. 298-301 (4)	4.00	*4.10*

Bermuda National Trust, and "Plant a Tree" campaign.

Princess Anne's Wedding Issue
Common Design Type

1973, Nov. 21 Litho.

302	CD325	15c lilac & multi	.25	.25
303	CD325	18c slate & multi	.25	.25

National Tennis Stadium, Pembroke, 1973 — A48

15c, Bermuda's 1st tennis court, Pembroke, 1873. 18c, Britain's 1st tennis court, Leamington Spa, 1872. 24c, 1t US tennis club, Staten Island, 1874.

1973, Dec. 17 Wmk. 314

304	A48	4c black & multi	.35	.25
305	A48	15c black & multi	.70	.70
306	A48	18c black & multi	.85	*1.25*
307	A48	24c black & multi	1.00	*1.50*
		Nos. 304-307 (4)	2.90	*3.70*

Centenary of tennis in Bermuda.

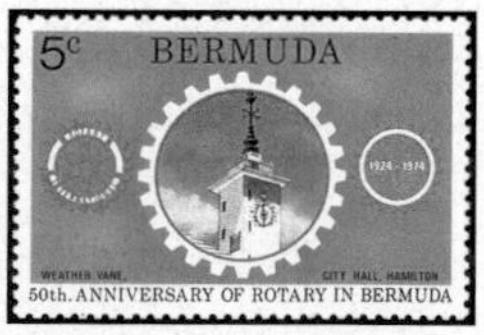

Rotary Emblem, Weather Vane, City Hall, Hamilton A49

Rotary Emblem and: 17c, St. Peter's Church, St. George's. 20c, Somerset Drawbridge, Somerset. 25c, Map of Bermuda on globe, 1626.

1974, June 24 *Perf. 14*

308	A49	5c emerald & multi	.25	.25
309	A49	17c blue & multi	.60	.45
310	A49	20c yel org & multi	.65	*1.25*
311	A49	25c lt violet & multi	.80	*1.75*
		Nos. 308-311 (4)	2.30	*3.70*

50th anniv. of Rotary Intl. in Bermuda.

Jack of Clubs and a Good Bridge Hand — A50

Bermuda Bowl and: 17c, Queen of diamonds. 20c, King of hearts. 25c, Ace of spades.

1975, Jan. 27 Litho. Wmk. 314

312	A50	5c blue & multi	.35	.25
313	A50	17c dull yel & multi	.65	.65
314	A50	20c ver & multi	.75	*1.50*
315	A50	25c lilac & multi	.75	*2.25*
		Nos. 312-315 (4)	2.50	4.65

World Bridge Championship, Bermuda, Jan. 1975.

Queen Elizabeth II and Prince Philip — A51

Perf. 14x14½

1975, Feb. 17 Photo. Wmk. 373

316	A51	17c multicolored	.85	.85
317	A51	20c dk blue & multi	.95	*1.25*

Royal Visit, Feb. 16-18, 1975.

British Cavalier Flying Boat, 1937 A52

17c, U.S. Navy airship "Los Angeles," 1925, flying from Lakehurst, NJ to Hamilton, Bermuda. 20c, Constellation over Kindley Field, 1946. 25c, Boeing 747 on tarmac, 1970.

1975, Apr. 28 Litho. *Perf. 14*

318	A52	5c lt green & multi	.45	.25
319	A52	17c lt ultra & multi	1.75	1.40
320	A52	20c multicolored	1.90	*2.25*
321	A52	25c rose lil & multi	2.25	*2.50*
a.		Souvenir sheet of 4, #318-321	14.00	14.00
		Nos. 318-321 (4)	6.35	*6.40*

Airmail service to Bermuda, 50th anniv.

Flower Type of 1970

1975, June 2 Photo. Wmk. 314

322	A41	17c Passion flower	3.00	*4.00*
323	A41	20c Coralita	3.00	*4.00*
324	A41	25c Morning glory	3.00	*4.00*
325	A41	40c Angel's trumpet	3.00	*4.00*
326	A41	$1 Plumbago	3.50	*4.50*
327	A41	$2 Bird-of-paradise flower	6.00	*7.50*
328	A41	$3 Chalice cup	12.00	*15.00*
		Nos. 322-328 (7)	33.50	*43.00*

Royal Magazine Break-in A54

17c, Sympathizers rowing towards magazine. 20c, Loading gun powder barrels onto ships. 25c, Gun powder barrels on beach.

Perf. 13x13½

1975, Oct. 27 Litho. Wmk. 373

329	A54	5c multicolored	.25	.25
330	A54	17c multicolored	.50	.55
331	A54	20c multicolored	.60	*1.40*

332	A54	25c multicolored	.65	*1.50*
a.		Souv. sheet, #329-332, perf 14	4.50	*7.00*
		Nos. 329-332 (4)	2.00	*3.70*

Gunpowder Plot, 1775, American War of Independence.

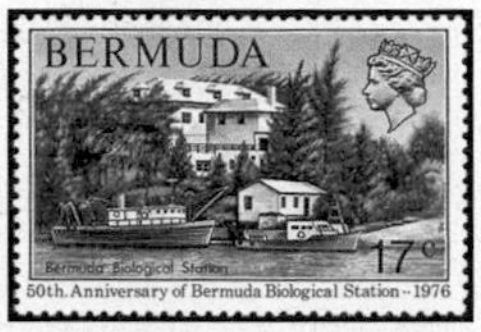

Bermuda Biological Station A55

Designs: 5c, Launching of bathysphere from "Ready," vert. 20c, Sailing ship Challenger, 1873. 25c, Descent of Beebe's bathysphere, 1934, and marine life, vert.

1976, Mar. 29 Litho. *Perf. 14*

333	A55	5c multicolored	.40	.25
334	A55	17c multicolored	.80	.80
335	A55	20c multicolored	.95	*1.50*
336	A55	25c multicolored	1.10	*2.25*
		Nos. 333-336 (4)	3.25	*4.80*

Bermuda Biological Station, 50th anniv.

Christian Radich, Norway A56

Tall Ships: 12c, Juan Sebastian de Elcano, Spain. 17c, Eagle, US. 20c, Sir Winston Churchill, Great Britain. 40c, Kruzenshtern, USSR. $1, Cutty Sark (silver trophy).

1976, June 15 Litho. *Perf. 13*

337	A56	5c lt green & multi	1.10	.25
338	A56	12c violet & multi	1.20	*2.00*
339	A56	17c ultra & multi	1.20	*1.50*
340	A56	20c blue & multi	1.20	*1.50*
341	A56	40c yellow & multi	1.50	*2.25*
342	A56	$1 sl grn & multi	1.90	*5.25*
		Nos. 337-342 (6)	8.10	*12.75*

Trans-Atlantic Cutty Sark International Tall Ships Race, Plymouth, England-New York City (Operation Sail '76).

Silver Cup Trophy and Crossed Club Flags A57

Designs: 17c, St. George's Cricket Club and emblem. 20c, Somerset Cricket Club and emblem. 25c, Cricket match.

1976, Aug. 16 Wmk. 373 *Perf. 14½*

343	A57	5c multicolored	.45	.25
344	A57	17c multicolored	.85	.85
345	A57	20c multicolored	1.10	*1.75*
346	A57	25c multicolored	1.75	*2.75*
		Nos. 343-346 (4)	4.15	*5.60*

St. George's and Somerset Cricket Club matches, 75th anniversary.

Queen's Visit to Bermuda, 1975 — A58

Designs: 20c, St. Edward's Crown. $1, Queen seated in Chair of Estate.

1977, Feb. 7 Litho. *Perf. 14x13½*

347	A58	5c silver & multi	.30	.30
348	A58	20c silver & multi	.30	.30
349	A58	$1 silver & multi	.60	*1.10*
		Nos. 347-349 (3)	1.20	*1.70*

Reign of Queen Elizabeth II, 25th anniv.

Stockdale House, St. George's A59

UPU Emblem and: 15c, Perot Post Office and Perot Stamp. 17c, St. George's Post Office, c. 1860. 20c, Old GPO, Hamilton, c. 1935. 40c, New GPO, Hamilton, 1967.

1977, June 20 Litho. *Perf. 13x13½*

350	A59	5c multicolored	.25	.25
351	A59	15c multicolored	.40	*.45*
352	A59	17c multicolored	.40	*.45*
353	A59	20c multicolored	.45	*.50*
354	A59	40c multicolored	.75	*.85*
		Nos. 350-354 (5)	2.25	*2.50*

Bermuda's UPU membership, cent.

Sailing Ship, 17th Century, Approaching Castle Island — A60

Designs: 15c, King's pilot leaving 18th century naval ship at Murray's Anchorage. 17c, Pilot gigs racing to meet steamship, early 19th century. 20c, Harvest Queen, late 19th century. 40c, Pilot cutter and Queen Elizabeth II off St. David's Lighthouse.

Perf. 13½x14

1977, Sept. 26 Wmk. 373

355	A60	5c multicolored	.60	.25
356	A60	15c multicolored	.90	.90
357	A60	17c multicolored	1.00	.90
358	A60	20c multicolored	1.10	*2.00*
359	A60	40c multicolored	2.00	*3.25*
		Nos. 355-359 (5)	5.60	*7.30*

Piloting in Bermuda waters.

Elizabeth II A61

Designs: 8c, Great Seal of Elizabeth I. 50c, Great Seal of Elizabeth II.

1978, Aug. 28 Litho. *Perf. 14x13½*

360	A61	8c gold & multi	.25	.25
361	A61	50c gold & multi	.35	.35
362	A61	$1 gold & multi	.70	*.80*
		Nos. 360-362 (3)	1.30	*1.40*

25th anniv. of coronation of Elizabeth II.

White-tailed Tropicbird — A62

4c, White-eyed vireo. 5c, Eastern bluebird. 7c, Whistling tree frog. 8c, Cardinal. 10c, Spiny lobster. 12c, Land crab.15c, Skink. 20c, Four-eyed butterflyfish. 25c, Red hind. 30c, Monarch butterfly. 40c, Rock beauty. 50c, Banded butterflyfish. $1, Blue angelfish. $2, Humpback whale. $3, Green turtle. $5, Bermuda Petrel.

Perf. 14; 14x14½ (4c, 5c, $2, $3, $5)

1978-79 Photo. Wmk. 373

363	A62	3c shown	2.25	*2.50*
364	A62	4c multicolored	2.60	*3.00*
365	A62	5c multicolored	1.15	*1.60*
366	A62	7c multicolored	.45	*1.25*
367	A62	8c multicolored	1.25	.45
368	A62	10c multicolored	.25	.25
369	A62	12c multicolored	.30	*.60*
370	A62	15c multicolored	.30	.30
371	A62	20c multicolored	.35	.35
372	A62	25c multicolored	.45	.45
a.		Greenish blue (background) omitted	4,750.	
373	A62	30c multicolored	1.90	*2.00*
374	A62	40c multicolored	.60	*1.50*
375	A62	50c multicolored	.75	*1.25*
376	A62	$1 multicolored	2.10	2.10
377	A62	$2 multicolored	3.00	3.00
378	A62	$3 multicolored	4.50	4.50
379	A62	$5 multicolored	7.75	7.75
		Nos. 363-379 (17)	29.95	32.85

Issued: 3c, 4c, 5c, 8c, $5, 1978; others, 1979.

For surcharge see No. 509.

Map of Bermuda, by George Somers, 1609 — A63

Old Maps of Bermuda: 15c, by John Seller, 1685. 20c, by Herman Moll, 1729, vert. 25c, by Desbruslins, 1740. 50c, by John Speed, 1626.

1979, May 14 Litho. *Perf. 13½*

380	A63	8c multicolored	.25	.25
381	A63	15c multicolored	.30	.25
382	A63	20c multicolored	.35	.30
383	A63	25c multicolored	.40	.40
384	A63	50c multicolored	.55	*.80*
		Nos. 380-384 (5)	1.85	2.00

Bermuda Police Centenary — A64

20c, Traffic direction, horiz. 25c, Water patrol, horiz. 50c, Motorbike and patrol car.

1979, Nov. 26 Wmk. 373 *Perf. 14*

385	A64	8c multicolored	.45	.25
386	A64	20c multicolored	.75	.75
387	A64	25c multicolored	.90	.90
388	A64	50c multicolored	1.15	1.15
		Nos. 385-388 (4)	3.25	3.05

Bermuda No. X1, Penny Black — A65

Bermuda #X1 and: 20c, Hill. 25c, "Paid 1" marking on cover. 50c, "Paid 1" marking.

1980, Feb. 25 Litho. *Perf. 13½x14*

389	A65	8c multicolored	.25	.25
390	A65	20c multicolored	.40	.40
391	A65	25c multicolored	.40	.40
392	A65	50c multicolored	.45	*.90*
		Nos. 389-392 (4)	1.50	*1.95*

Sir Rowland Hill (1795-1879), originator of penny postage.

Tristar-500, London 1980 Emblem — A66

50c, "Orduna," 1926. $1, "Delta," 1856. $2, "Lord Sidmouth," 1818.

1980, May 6 Litho. *Perf. 13x14*

393	A66	25c shown	.40	.25
394	A66	50c multicolored	.65	.50
395	A66	$1 multicolored	1.25	1.25
396	A66	$2 multicolored	1.90	*2.25*
		Nos. 393-396 (4)	4.20	*4.25*

London 1980 Intl. Stamp Exhib., May 6-14.

Gina Swainson, Miss World, 1979-80, Arms of Bermuda — A67

20c, After crowning ceremony. 50c, Welcome home party. $1, In carriage.

1980, May 8 *Perf. 14*

397	A67	8c shown	.30	.30
398	A67	20c multicolored	.40	.40
399	A67	50c multicolored	.70	.70
400	A67	$1 multicolored	1.50	1.50
		Nos. 397-400 (4)	2.90	2.90

Queen Mother Elizabeth Birthday Issue

Common Design Type

1980, Aug. 4 Wmk. 373 *Perf. 14*

401	CD330	25c multicolored	.45	*.75*

Camden, Prime Minister's House A68

8c, View from satellite. 25c, Princess Hotel, Hamilton. 50c, Government House.

1980, Sept. 24 Litho. *Perf. 14*

402	A68	8c multicolored	.25	.25
403	A68	20c shown	.30	.30
404	A68	25c multicolored	.30	*.50*
405	A68	50c multicolored	.60	*1.50*
		Nos. 402-405 (4)	1.45	2.55

Commonwealth Finance Ministers Meeting, Bermuda, Sept.

18th Century Kitchen A69

25c, Gathering Easter lilies. 30c, Fisherman. 40c, Stone cutting, 19th cent. 50c, Onion shipping, 19th cent. $1, Ships, 17th cent.

1981, May 21 Wmk. 373 *Perf. 14*

406	A69	8c shown	.25	.25
407	A69	25c multicolored	.40	.40
408	A69	30c multicolored	.55	.55
409	A69	40c multicolored	.75	.75
410	A69	50c multicolored	.90	.90
411	A69	$1 multicolored	1.75	1.75
		Nos. 406-411 (6)	4.60	4.60

Royal Wedding Issue

Common Design Type

1981, July 22 Wmk. 373 *Perf. 14*

412	CD331	30c Bouquet	.30	.30
413	CD331	50c Charles	.60	.60
414	CD331	$1 Couple	1.10	1.10
		Nos. 412-414 (3)	2.00	2.00

Girl Helping Blind Man Cross Street — A70

25c, Kayaking, Paget Island. 30c, Mountain climbing, St. David's Island. $1, Duke of Edinburgh.

1981, Sept. 28 Litho. *Perf. 14*

415 A70 10c shown .25 .25
416 A70 25c multicolored .30 .30
417 A70 30c multicolored .35 .35
418 A70 $1 multicolored .75 *1.10*
Nos. 415-418 (4) 1.65 *2.00*

Duke of Edinburgh's Awards, 25th anniv.

Conus Species A71

25c, Bursa finlayi. 30c, Sconsia striata. $1, Murex pterynotus lightbourni.

1982, May 13 Wmk. 373 *Perf. 14*

419 A71 10c shown .65 .25
420 A71 25c multicolored 1.25 1.25
421 A71 30c multicolored 1.60 1.60
422 A71 $1 multicolored 4.25 4.25
Nos. 419-422 (4) 7.75 7.35

Bermuda Regiment A72

10c, Color guard. 25c, Queen's birthday parade. 30c, Governor inspecting honor guard. 40c, Beating the retreat. 50c, Ceremonial gunners. $1, Royal visit, 1975.

1982, June 17 Litho. Wmk. 373

423 A72 10c multicolored .75 .25
424 A72 25c multicolored 1.10 .90
425 A72 30c multicolored 1.50 1.50
426 A72 40c multicolored 1.60 1.60
427 A72 50c multicolored 1.60 1.60
428 A72 $1 multicolored 2.75 2.75
Nos. 423-428 (6) 9.30 8.60

Southampton Fort — A73

10c, Charles Fort, vert. 25c, Pembroks Fort, vert. $1, Smiths and Pagets Forts.

1982, Nov. 18 Litho. Wmk. 373

429 A73 10c multicolored .30 .30
430 A73 25c multicolored .80 .80
431 A73 30c shown .90 .90
432 A73 $1 multicolored 1.90 1.90
Nos. 429-432 (4) 3.90 3.90

Arms of Sir Edwin Sandys (1561-1629) A74

Coats of Arms: 25c, Bermuda Company. 50c, William Herbert, 3rd Earl of Pembroke (1584-1630). $1, Sir George Somers (1554-1610).

1983, Apr. 14 Litho. *Perf. 13½*

433 A74 10c multicolored .45 .25
434 A74 25c multicolored 1.40 1.25
435 A74 50c multicolored 2.50 *3.00*
436 A74 $1 multicolored 3.50 *5.00*
Nos. 433-436 (4) 7.85 *9.50*

See Nos. 457-460, 474-477.

Fitted Dinghies — A75

Old and modern boats.

1983, July 21 Wmk. 373 *Perf. 14*

437 A75 12c multicolored .55 .25
438 A75 30c multicolored .75 .75
439 A75 40c multicolored .85 .85
440 A75 $1 multicolored 2.00 *2.75*
Nos. 437-440 (4) 4.15 *4.60*

Manned Flight Bicentenary — A76

Designs: 12c, Curtiss Jenny, 1919 (first flight over Bermuda). 30c, Stinson Pilot Radio, 1930 (first completed US-Bermuda flight). 40c, Cavalier, 1937 (first scheduled passenger flight). $1, USS Los Angeles airship moored to USS Patoka, 1925.

1983, Oct. 13 Litho. *Perf. 14*

441 A76 12c multicolored .80 .30
442 A76 30c multicolored 1.50 1.50
443 A76 40c multicolored 1.75 1.75
444 A76 $1 multicolored 3.00 *4.25*
Nos. 441-444 (4) 7.05 *7.80*

Newspaper and Postal Services, 200th Anniv. — A77

12c, Joseph Stockdale. 30c, First Newspaper. 40c, Stockdale's Postal Service, horiz. $1, "Lady Hammond," horiz.

1984, Jan. 26 Litho. *Perf. 14*

445 A77 12c multicolored .45 .25
446 A77 30c multicolored .75 .75
447 A77 40c multicolored .95 .95
448 A77 $1 multicolored 3.00 3.25
Nos. 445-448 (4) 5.15 5.20

375th Anniv. of Bermuda Settlement — A78

Designs: 12c, Thomas Gates, George Somers. 30c, Jamestown, Virginia, US. 40c, Sea Venture shipwreck. $1, Fleet leaving Plymouth, England.

1984, May 3 Litho. Wmk. 373

449 A78 12c multicolored .25 .25
450 A78 30c multicolored .70 .70
451 A78 40c multicolored 1.25 1.25
452 A78 $1 multicolored 2.75 *5.00*
a. Souv. sheet of 2, #450, 452 5.75 *8.50*
Nos. 449-452 (4) 4.95 *7.20*

1984 Summer Olympics A79

1984, July 19 Litho. *Perf. 14*

453 A79 12c Swimming, vert. .50 .25
454 A79 30c Track & field .95 .95
455 A79 40c Equestrian, vert. 1.60 1.60
456 A79 $1 Sailing 3.25 *5.00*
Nos. 453-456 (4) 6.30 *7.80*

Arms Type of 1983

1984, Sept. 27 Litho. *Perf. 13½*

457 A74 12c Southampton .75 .25
458 A74 30c Smith 1.50 1.25
459 A74 40c Devonshire 1.90 1.90
460 A74 $1 St. George 4.25 4.25
Nos. 457-460 (4) 8.40 7.65

Architecture, Buttery — A80

1985, Jan. 24 Litho. *Perf. 13½x13*

461 A80 12c shown .40 .25
462 A80 30c Rooftops 1.10 1.00
463 A80 40c Chimneys 1.25 1.25
464 A80 $1.50 Archway 4.25 4.25
Nos. 461-464 (4) 7.00 6.75

Audubon Birth Bicentenary — A81

12c, Osprey, vert. 30c, Yellow-crowned night heron, vert. 40c, Great egret. $1.50, Bluebird, vert.

1985, Mar. 21 Wmk. 373 *Perf. 14*

465 A81 12c multicolored 2.75 .85
466 A81 30c multicolored 2.75 1.25
467 A81 40c multicolored 3.25 1.60
468 A81 $1.50 multicolored 5.25 5.25
Nos. 465-468 (4) 14.00 8.95

Queen Mother 85th Birthday Issue
Common Design Type

Designs: 12c, Queen Consort, 1937. 30c, With grandchildren, 80th birthday. 40c, At Clarence House, 83rd birthday. $1.50, Holding Prince Henry. No. 473, In coach with Prince Charles.

Perf. 14½x14

1985, June 7 Wmk. 384

469 CD336 12c gray, bl & blk .35 .35
470 CD336 30c multicolored .70 .70
471 CD336 40c multicolored 1.10 1.10
472 CD336 $1.50 multicolored 3.25 3.25
Nos. 469-472 (4) 5.40 5.40

Souvenir Sheet

473 CD336 $1 multicolored 4.00 4.00

Arms Type of 1983

Coats of Arms: 12c, James Hamilton, 2nd Marquess of Hamilton (1589-1625). 30c, William Paget, 4th Lord Paget (1572-1629). 40c, Robert Rich, 2nd Earl of Warwick (1587-1658). $1.50, Hamilton, 1957.

1985, Sept. 19 Litho. *Perf. 13½*

474 A74 12c multicolored .90 .25
475 A74 30c multicolored 1.75 1.10
476 A74 40c multicolored 2.10 2.10
477 A74 $1.50 multicolored 4.50 4.50
Nos. 474-477 (4) 9.25 7.95

Halley's Comet A82

15c, Bermuda Archipelago. 40c, Nuremberg Chronicles, 1493. 50c, Peter Apian woodcut, 1532. $1.50, Painting by Samuel Scott (c.1702-72).

1985, Nov. 21 Wmk. 384 *Perf. 14½*

478 A82 15c multicolored 1.10 .35
479 A82 40c multicolored 2.10 2.10
480 A82 50c multicolored 2.50 2.50
481 A82 $1.50 multicolored 4.25 *6.00*
Nos. 478-481 (4) 9.95 *10.95*

Shipwrecks — A83

3c, Constellation, 1943. 5c, Early Riser, 1876. 7c, Madiana, 1903. 10c, Curlew, 1856. 12c, Warwick, 1619. 15c, HMS Vixen, 1890. 20c, San Pedro, 1594. 25c, Alert, 1877. 40c, North Carolina, 1880. 50c, Mark Antonie, 1777. 60c, Mary Celestia, 1864. $1, L'Herminie, 1839. $1.50, Caesar, 1818. $2, Lord Amherst, 1778. $3, Minerva, 1849. $5, Caraquet, 1923. $8, HMS Pallas, 1783.

1986 Wmk. 384 *Perf. 14*
Without date imprint

482 A83 3c multicolored .80 *1.75*
483 A83 5c multicolored .30 .30
484 A83 7c multicolored .65 *2.75*
485 A83 10c multicolored .30 .30
486 A83 12c multicolored .65 *.75*
487 A83 15c multicolored .45 *.60*
488 A83 20c multicolored 1.10 .75
489 A83 25c multicolored .75 *3.00*
490 A83 40c multicolored .80 *1.25*
491 A83 50c multicolored 1.60 *3.25*
492 A83 60c multicolored 1.75 1.75
493 A83 $1 multicolored 2.50 *4.25*
494 A83 $1.50 multicolored 6.00 *7.00*
495 A83 $2 multicolored 5.75 *7.50*
496 A83 $3 multicolored 9.25 9.25
497 A83 $5 multicolored 15.00 15.00
498 A83 $8 multicolored 24.00 24.00
Nos. 482-498 (17) 71.65 83.45

See Nos. 545-546. For surcharges see Nos. 598-600.

Inscribed "1989" or "1990"

1989-90

482a A83 3c 1990 1.75 *3.00*
488a A83 20c 1990 3.00 *4.50*
493a A83 $1 1989 1.50 1.50
495a A83 $2 1989 2.50 *4.50*
496a A83 $3 1989 4.50 *8.25*
Nos. 482a-496a (5) 13.25 *21.75*

Issued: Nos. 493a-496a, 7/89; Nos. 482a, 483a, 1/8/90.

Inscribed "1992"

1992 Litho. Wmk. 373 *Perf. 14*

485a A83 10c 2.60 2.60
487a A83 15c 3.25 3.25
488b A83 20c 3.25 3.25
489a A83 25c 3.25 3.25
492a A83 60c 5.50 5.50
497a A83 $5 22.00 22.00
498a A83 $8 32.50 32.50
Nos. 485a-498a (7) 72.35 72.35

Queen Elizabeth II 60th Birthday
Common Design Type

15c, Age 3. 40c, With the Earl of Rosebury, Oaks May Meeting, Epsom, 1954. 50c, With Prince Philip, state visit,1979. 60c, At the British embassy in Paris, state visit, 1972. $1.50, Visiting Crown Agents' offices, 1983.

1986, Apr. 21 Wmk. 384 *Perf. 14½*

499 CD337 15c scar, blk & sil .25 .25
500 CD337 40c ultra & multi .65 .65
501 CD337 50c green & multi .80 .80
502 CD337 60c violet & multi .95 .95
503 CD337 $1.50 rose vio & multi 2.00 *2.50*
Nos. 499-503 (5) 4.65 *5.15*

AMERIPEX '86 — A84

$1.50, Statue of Liberty, S.S. Queen of Bermuda.

1986, May 22 *Perf. 14*

504	A84	15c No. 452a	1.50	.40
505	A84	40c No. 307	2.25	.85
506	A84	50c No. 441	2.25	1.25
507	A84	$1 No. 339	3.75	3.25
		Nos. 504-507 (4)	9.75	5.75

Souvenir Sheet

508	A84	1.50 multi	11.00	11.00

Statue of Liberty, cent.

No. 378 Surcharged

Perf. 14x14½

1986, Dec. 4 Photo. Wmk. 373

509	A62	90c on $3 multi	7.75	7.75

Exists with double surcharge. Value $110.

Transport Railway, c. 1931-1947 — A85

15c, Front Street, c. 1940. 40c, Springfield Trestle. 50c, No. 101, Bailey's Bay Sta. $1.50, No. 31, ship Prince David.

Wmk. 373

1987, Jan. 22 Litho. *Perf. 14*

510	A85	15c multicolored	2.00	.40
511	A85	40c multicolored	2.50	1.40
512	A85	50c multicolored	2.50	1.90
513	A85	$1.50 multicolored	4.00	*5.50*
		Nos. 510-513 (4)	11.00	*9.20*

Paintings by Winslow Homer (1836-1910) A86

15c, Bermuda Settlers, 1901. 30c, Bermuda, 1900. 40c, Bermuda Landscape, 1901. 50c, Inland Water, 1901. $1.50, Salt Kettle, 1899.

1987, Apr. 30 *Perf. 14½*

514	A86	15c multicolored	.80	.40
515	A86	30c multicolored	1.15	.65
516	A86	40c multicolored	1.35	.90
517	A86	50c multicolored	1.60	1.00
518	A86	$1.50 multicolored	3.00	3.00
		Nos. 514-518 (5)	7.90	5.95

Booklet Stamps

519	A86	40c like 15c	1.75	1.75
520	A86	40c like 30c	1.75	1.75
521	A86	40c like No. 516	1.75	1.75
522	A86	40c like 50c	1.75	1.75
523	A86	40c like $1.50	1.75	1.75
a.		Bklt. pane, 2 each #519-523	17.50	
		Complete booklet, #523a	17.50	

Nos. 519-523 printed in strips of 5 within pane. "ER" at lower left.

Intl. Flights Inauguration — A87

15c, Sikorsky S-42B, 1937. 40c, Shorts S-23 Cavalier. 50c, S-42B Bermuda Clipper. $1.50, Cavalier, Bermuda Clipper.

1987, June 18 *Perf. 14*

524	A87	15c multicolored	2.40	.25
525	A87	40c multicolored	3.50	.95
526	A87	50c multicolored	3.75	1.10
527	A87	$1.50 multicolored	6.75	6.75
		Nos. 524-527 (4)	16.40	9.05

Bermuda Telephone Company, Cent. — A88

15c, Telephone poles on wagon. 40c, Operators. 50c, Telephones. $1.50, Satellite, fiber optics, world.

1987, Oct. 1 Litho. Wmk. 384

528	A88	15c multicolored	1.00	.25
529	A88	40c multicolored	2.00	1.00
530	A88	50c multicolored	2.25	1.10
531	A88	$1.50 multicolored	3.75	3.75
		Nos. 528-531 (4)	9.00	6.10

Horse-drawn Commercial Vehicles — A89

15c, Mail wagon, c. 1869. 40c, Open cart, c. 1823. 50c, Closed cart, c. 1823. $1.50, Two-wheel wagon, c. 1930.

1988, Mar. 3 Litho. *Perf. 14*

532	A89	15c multicolored	.40	.25
533	A89	40c multicolored	.90	.90
534	A89	50c multicolored	1.10	1.10
535	A89	$1.50 multicolored	3.50	3.50
		Nos. 532-535 (4)	5.90	5.75

Old Garden Roses A90

15c, Old blush. 30c, Anna Olivier. 40c, Rosa chinensis semperflorens, vert. 50c, Archduke Charles. $1.50, Rosa chinensis viridiflora, vert.

1988, Apr. 21 Wmk. 373

536	A90	15c multicolored	1.25	.40
537	A90	30c multicolored	1.75	.70
538	A90	40c multicolored	1.90	1.25
539	A90	50c multicolored	2.00	1.75
540	A90	$1.50 multicolored	4.00	4.00
		Nos. 536-540 (5)	10.90	8.10

See Nos. 561-575.

Lloyds of London, 300th Anniv.

Common Design Type

18c, Loss of the H.M.S. Lutine, 1799. 50c, Cable ship Sentinel. 60c, The Bermuda, Hamilton, 1931. $2, Valerian, lost during a hurricane, 1926.

1988, Oct. 13 Litho. Wmk. 384

541	CD341	18c multi	1.00	.30
542	CD341	50c multi, horiz.	1.75	.80
543	CD341	60c multi, horiz.	2.00	1.00
544	CD341	$2 multi	3.25	*4.50*
		Nos. 541-544 (4)	8.00	*6.60*

Shipwreck Type of 1986

1988 Litho. Wmk. 384 *Perf. 14*

545	A83	18c like 7c	5.50	4.00
546	A83	70c like $1.50	6.25	*7.00*

Issue dates: 18c, Sept. 22; 70c, Oct. 27.

Military Uniforms — A91

18c, Devonshire Parish Militia, 1812. 50c, 71st Regiment Highlander, 1831-34. 60c, Cameron Highlander, 1942. $2, Troop of Horse, 1774.

1988, Nov. 10 Wmk. 373 *Perf. 14½*

547	A91	18c multicolored	1.60	.40
548	A91	50c multicolored	2.25	1.50
549	A91	60c multicolored	2.50	1.60
550	A91	$2 multicolored	5.25	*7.50*
		Nos. 547-550 (4)	11.60	*11.00*

Ferry Service A92

18c, Corona. 50c, Rowboat ferry. 60c, St. George's Ferry. $2, Laconia.

1989 Litho. Wmk. 384 *Perf. 14*

551	A92	18c multicolored	.60	.40
552	A92	50c multicolored	1.10	1.10
553	A92	60c multicolored	1.25	1.25
554	A92	$2 multicolored	4.00	*4.25*
		Nos. 551-554 (4)	6.95	*7.00*

Photography, Sesquicent. A93

18c, Morgan's Island. 30c, Front Street, Hamilton (cannon in square). 50c, Front Street (seascape). 60c, Crow Lane, Hamilton Harbor. 70c, Hamilton Harbor (shipbuilding). $1, Dockyard.

Perf. 14x14½

1989, May 11 Litho. Wmk. 373

555	A93	18c multicolored	1.10	.40
556	A93	30c multicolored	1.10	.60
557	A93	50c multicolored	1.60	1.60
558	A93	60c multicolored	1.75	1.75
559	A93	70c multicolored	2.10	*2.50*
560	A93	$1 multicolored	2.25	*3.00*
		Nos. 555-560 (6)	9.90	*9.85*

Old Garden Roses Type of 1988

18c, Agrippina. 30c, Smith's Parish. 50c, Champney's pink cluster. 60c, Rosette delizy. $1.50, Rosa bracteata.

1989, July 13 *Perf. 14*

561	A90	18c multicolored	1.25	.40
562	A90	30c multicolored	1.25	.65
563	A90	50c multicolored	1.75	1.60
564	A90	60c multicolored	2.00	1.75
565	A90	$1.50 multicolored	3.25	*5.75*
		Nos. 561-565 (5)	9.50	*10.15*

Nos. 561-562 vert.

Old Garden Roses Type of 1988 with Royal Cipher Instead of Queen's Silhouette

1989, July 13 Booklet Stamps

566	A90	50c like No. 562	2.50	*3.00*
567	A90	50c like No. 540	2.50	*3.00*
568	A90	50c like No. 561	2.50	*3.00*
569	A90	50c like No. 538	2.50	*3.00*
570	A90	50c like No. 563	2.50	*3.00*
571	A90	50c like No. 536	2.50	*3.00*
572	A90	50c like No. 564	2.50	*3.00*
573	A90	50c like No. 537	2.50	*3.00*
574	A90	50c like No. 565	2.50	*3.00*
575	A90	50c like No. 539	2.50	*3.00*
a.		Bklt. pane of 10, #566-575	25.00	
		Complete booklet, #575a	27.50	

Bermuda Library, 150th Anniv. A94

18c, Hamilton Main Library. 50c, St. George's, The Old Rectory. 60c, Springfield, Somerset Library. $2, Cabinet Building.

1989, Sept. 14 *Perf. 13½x14*

576	A94	18c multicolored	.40	.40
577	A94	50c multicolored	1.10	1.10
578	A94	60c multicolored	1.25	1.25
579	A94	$2 multicolored	4.00	*5.50*
		Nos. 576-579 (4)	6.75	*8.25*

Commonwealth Postal Conference — A95

1989, Nov. 3 Wmk. 384 *Perf. 14*

580	A95	18c No. 1	1.25	.40
581	A95	50c No. 2	2.25	1.00
582	A95	60c Type A4	2.50	1.60
583	A95	$2 No. 6	4.00	*5.50*
		Nos. 580-583 (4)	10.00	*8.50*

For overprints see Nos. 594-597.

Fairylands, Bermuda, c. 1890, by Ross Sterling Turner A96

Paintings: 50c, *Shinebone Alley, c. 1953,* by Ogden M. Pleissner. 60c, *Salt Kettle, 1916,* by Prosper Senat. $2, *St. George's, 1934,* by Jack Bush.

1990, Apr. 19

590	A96	18c multicolored	.80	.40
591	A96	50c multicolored	1.50	1.50
592	A96	60c multicolored	1.50	1.50
593	A96	$2 multicolored	4.00	*5.50*
		Nos. 590-593 (4)	7.80	*8.90*

Nos. 580-583 Overprinted

1990, May 3

594	A95	18c multicolored	1.50	.40
595	A95	50c multicolored	2.00	1.75
596	A95	60c multicolored	2.25	2.10
597	A95	$2 multicolored	4.00	*5.50*
		Nos. 594-597 (4)	9.75	*9.75*

Stamp World London '90.

Nos. 486, 491, 494 Surcharged

1990, Aug. 13

598	A83	30c on 12c No. 486	2.50	2.50
599	A83	55c on 50c No. 491	3.25	3.25
600	A83	80c on $1.50 No. 494	4.00	*5.75*
		Nos. 598-600 (3)	9.75	*11.50*

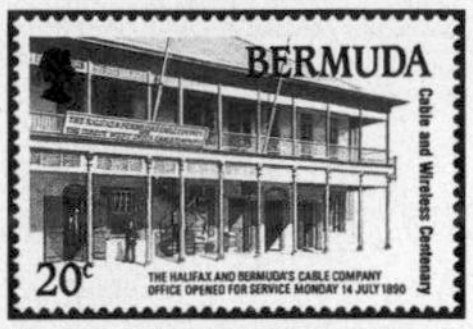

Nova Scotia-Bermuda Cable, Cent. — A97

20c, Office. 55c, Cableship SS Westmeath. 70c, Radio station, 1928. $2, Cableship Sir Eric Sharp.

1990, Oct. 18 Litho. Unwmk.

601	A97	20c multicolored	.80	.40
602	A97	55c multicolored	2.25	1.60
603	A97	70c multicolored	2.25	2.25
604	A97	$2 multicolored	5.75	*7.00*
		Nos. 601-604 (4)	11.05	*11.25*

Nos. 601-602 with Added Inscription "BUSH-MAJOR / 16 MARCH 1991"

1991, Mar. Unwmk. *Perf. 14*

605	A97	20c like #601	2.25	2.00
606	A97	55c like #602	4.25	4.25

Carriages A98

Designs: 20c, Two-seat pony cart, c. 1805. 30c, Varnished rockaway, c. 1830. 55c, Vis-a-Vis Victoria, c. 1895. 70c, Semi-formal phaeton, c. 1900. 80c, Pony runabout, c. 1905. $1, Ladies' phaeton, c. 1910.

Perf. 14x14½

1991, Mar. 21 Litho. Wmk. 373

607	A98	20c green & multi	.80	.40
608	A98	30c bl gray & multi	.90	.85
609	A98	55c dk car & multi	1.75	1.40
610	A98	70c blue & multi	2.50	2.75
611	A98	80c yel org & multi	2.75	*3.50*
612	A98	$1 dk gray & multi	3.00	*4.25*
		Nos. 607-612 (6)	11.70	*13.15*

Paintings A99

Designs: 20c, Bermuda by Prosper Senat, vert. 55c, Bermuda Cottage by Frank Allison. 70c, Old Maid's Lane by Jack Bush, vert. $2, St. George's by Ogden M. Pleissner.

Perf. 14x13½

1991, May 16 Litho. Wmk. 373

613	A99	20c multicolored	1.10	.40
614	A99	55c multicolored	2.25	1.90
615	A99	70c multicolored	2.75	3.25
616	A99	$2 multicolored	6.25	8.00
		Nos. 613-616 (4)	12.35	13.55

Elizabeth & Philip, Birthdays

Common Design Types

1991, June 20 Wmk. 384 *Perf. 14½*

617	CD346	55c multicolored	1.75	*2.00*
618	CD345	70c multicolored	1.75	*2.00*
a.		Pair, #617-618 + label	3.50	*4.00*

Bermuda in World War II A100

Designs: 20c, Floating drydock. 55c, Kindley Air Field. 70c, Trans-atlantic air route, Boeing 314. $2, Censored trans-atlantic mail.

1991, Sept. 19 Wmk. 373 *Perf. 14*

619	A100	20c multicolored	2.00	.45
620	A100	55c multicolored	3.25	2.40
621	A100	70c multicolored	4.00	4.25
622	A100	$2 multicolored	6.75	*8.00*
		Nos. 619-622 (4)	16.00	*15.10*

Queen Elizabeth II's Accession to the Throne, 40th Anniv.

Common Design Type

1992, Feb. 6

623	CD349	20c multicolored	.75	.40
624	CD349	30c multicolored	.90	.75
625	CD349	55c multicolored	1.50	1.40
626	CD349	70c multicolored	2.00	2.25
627	CD349	$1 multicolored	2.25	*2.75*
		Nos. 623-627 (5)	7.40	*7.55*

Age of Exploration — A101

Artifacts: 25c, Rings, medallion. 35c, Ink wells. 60c, Gold pieces. 75c, Bishop button, crucifix. 85c, Pearl earrings and buttons. $1, 8-real coin, jug and measuring cups.

1992, July 23 *Perf. 13½*

628	A101	25c multicolored	1.50	.55
629	A101	35c multicolored	1.60	1.00
630	A101	60c multicolored	2.50	*2.75*
631	A101	75c multicolored	3.00	*3.25*
632	A101	85c multicolored	3.25	*3.75*
633	A101	$1 multicolored	3.50	*4.00*
		Nos. 628-633 (6)	15.35	*15.30*

Stained Glass Windows — A102

Designs: 25c, Ship wreck. 60c, Birds in tree. 75c, St. Francis feeding bird. $2, Seashells.

1992, Sept. 24 *Perf. 14*

634	A102	25c multicolored	1.75	.55
635	A102	60c multicolored	3.25	2.75
636	A102	75c multicolored	4.00	4.00
637	A102	$2 multicolored	8.50	*10.00*
		Nos. 634-637 (4)	17.50	*17.30*

7th World Congress of Kennel Clubs A103

25c, German shepherd. 35c, Irish setter. 60c, Whippet, vert. 75c, Border terrier, vert. 85c, Pomeranian, vert. $1, Schipperke, vert.

Perf. 13½x14, 14x13½

1992, Nov. 12 Litho. Wmk. 373

638	A103	25c multicolored	1.60	.55
639	A103	35c multicolored	2.25	1.10
640	A103	60c multicolored	3.00	2.75
641	A103	75c multicolored	3.00	*3.25*
642	A103	85c multicolored	3.50	*4.00*
643	A103	$1 multicolored	3.75	*4.50*
		Nos. 638-643 (6)	17.10	*16.15*

A104

Tourist Posters — A105

25c, Cyclist, carriage, ship. 60c, Golf course. 75c, Coastline. $2, Dancers.

1993, Feb. 25 Wmk. 373 *Perf. 14*

644	A104	25c multi	2.25	1.00
645	A105	60c multi	3.00	3.00
646	A105	75c multi	2.75	2.75
647	A104	$2 multi	4.75	*6.50*
		Nos. 644-647 (4)	12.75	*13.25*

Royal Air Force, 75th Anniv.

Common Design Type

Designs: 25c, Consolidated Catalina. 60c, Supermarine Spitfire. 75c, Bristol Beaufighter. $2, Handley Page Halifax.

1993, Apr. 1

648	CD350	25c multicolored	.90	.45
649	CD350	60c multicolored	2.00	2.00
650	CD350	75c multicolored	2.50	2.50
651	CD350	$2 multicolored	4.25	*5.50*
		Nos. 648-651 (4)	9.65	*10.45*

Duchesse de Brabant Rose, Bee — A106

1993, Apr. 1 Wmk. 384

Booklet Stamps

652	A106	10c green & multi	.75	*1.60*
653	A106	25c violet & multi	.75	.75
a.		Booklet pane of 5	3.75	
654	A106	50c sepia & multi	2.50	*4.50*
a.		Booklet pane, 2 #652, 3 #654	9.00	
		Complete booklet, #653a, 654a	13.00	
655	A106	60c vermilion & multi	1.75	*1.90*
a.		Booklet pane of 5	8.75	
		Complete booklet, #653a, 655a	18.00	
		Nos. 652-655 (4)	5.75	*8.75*

Hamilton, Bicent. — A107

Designs: 25c, Modern skyline. 60c, Front Street, ships at left. 75c, Front Street, horse carts. $2, Hamilton Harbor, 1823.

Wmk. 373

1993, Sept. 16 Litho. *Perf. 14½*

656	A107	25c multicolored	1.75	.55
657	A107	60c multicolored	3.25	3.25
658	A107	75c multicolored	3.25	3.25
659	A107	$2 multicolored	8.25	8.25
		Nos. 656-659 (4)	16.50	15.30

Furness Lines — A108

25c, Furness Liv-Aboard Bermuda cruises, vert. 60c, SS Queen of Bermuda entering port. 75c, SS Queen of Bermuda, SS Ocean Monarch. $2, Starlit night aboard ship, vert.

Perf. 15x14, 14x15

1994, Jan. 20 Litho. Wmk. 373

660	A108	25c multicolored	.85	.45
661	A108	60c multicolored	2.10	2.10
662	A108	75c multicolored	2.25	2.25
663	A108	$2 multicolored	4.75	*6.00*
		Nos. 660-663 (4)	9.95	*10.80*

Royal Visit — A109

25c, Queen Elizabeth II. 60c, Queen Elizabeth II, Duke of Edinburgh. 75c, Royal yacht Britannia.

Wmk. 373

1994, Mar. 9 Litho. *Perf. 13½*

664	A109	25c multicolored	1.25	.50
665	A109	60c multicolored	3.00	2.75
666	A109	75c multicolored	6.00	5.00
		Nos. 664-666 (3)	10.25	8.25

Flowering Fruits A110

5c, Peach. 7c, Fig. 10c, Calabash, vert. 15c, Natal plum. 18c, Locust & wild honey. 20c, Pomegranate. 25c, Mulberry, vert. 35c, Grape, vert. 55c, Orange, vert. 60c, Surinam cherry. 75c, Loquat. 90c, Sugar apple. $1, Prickly pear, vert. $2, Paw paw. $3, Bay grape. $5, Banana, vert. $8, Lemon.

1994-95 Litho. Wmk. 373 *Perf. 14*

668	A110	5c multi	.40	.40
669	A110	7c multi	.45	.45
670	A110	10c multi	.45	.45
671	A110	15c multi	.70	.40
672	A110	18c multi	4.00	3.00
b.		Inscribed "1996"	1.25	1.25
673	A110	20c multi	.70	.45
674	A110	25c multi	1.00	.60
675	A110	35c multi	1.25	.80
676	A110	55c multi	1.60	1.10
677	A110	60c multi	2.25	1.40
678	A110	75c multi	2.25	2.50
679	A110	90c multi	2.75	2.75
680	A110	$1 multi	3.25	3.25
681	A110	$2 multi	5.00	5.00
682	A110	$3 multi	7.25	7.25
683	A110	$5 multi	9.75	9.75
684	A110	$8 multi	16.00	16.00
		Nos. 668-684 (17)	59.05	55.55

Issued: 5c, 7c, 15c, 20c, $8, 7/14/94; 10c, 25c, 35c, 55c, $1, $5, 10/6/94; 18c, 60c, 75c, 90c, $2, $3, 3/23/95. No. 672a, 9/1/96.

1998, Sept. 1 Wmk. 384

668a	A110	5c	.80	1.25
671a	A110	15c	1.40	.50
672a	A110	18c	1.40	.50
673a	A110	20c	1.40	.60
674a	A110	25c	4.00	.60
678a	A110	75c	4.00	2.00
679a	A110	90c	5.00	2.50
680a	A110	$1	6.00	3.75
		Nos. 668a-680a (8)	24.00	11.70

No. 672a exists dated "1998."

Issued: Nos. 668a, 671a, 673a-674a, 678a-680a, 9/1/98.

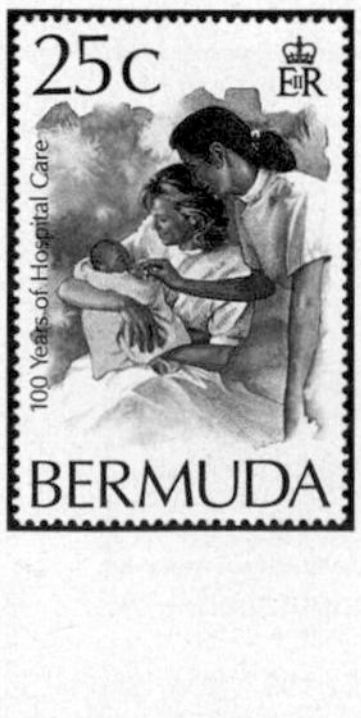

Hospital Care, Cent. — A111

1994, Sept. 15 *Perf. 15x14*

685	A111	25c	Child birth	1.10	.45
686	A111	60c	Dialysis	2.25	2.25
687	A111	75c	Emergency	3.25	3.25
688	A111	$2	Therapy	6.00	*6.75*
			Nos. 685-688 (4)	12.60	*12.70*

Christmas — A112

25c, Gombey dancers. 60c, Carollers. 75c, Marching band. $2, Natl. dance group

1994, Nov. 10 *Perf. 14x15*

689	A112	25c	multi	.80	.45
690	A112	60c	multi	1.50	1.50
691	A112	75c	multi	3.00	2.50
692	A112	$2	multi	5.25	*6.75*
			Nos. 689-692 (4)	10.55	*11.20*

Decimalization, 25th Anniv. — A113

Stamps, 1970 coins: 25c, #255, one cent. 60c, #259, five cents. 75c, #262, ten cents. $2, #324, twenty-five cents.

Wmk. 373

1995, Feb. 6 **Litho.** *Perf. 14*

693	A113	25c	multicolored	.90	.40
694	A113	60c	multicolored	1.50	1.50
695	A113	75c	multicolored	2.00	2.00
696	A113	$2	multicolored	5.50	*6.25*
			Nos. 693-696 (4)	9.90	*10.15*

Outdoor Celebrations — A114

25c, Kite flying. 60c, Majorettes. 75c, Portuguese dancers. $2, Floral float.

Perf. 14x15

1995, May 30 **Litho.** **Wmk. 373**

697	A114	25c	multi	.75	.45
698	A114	60c	multi	2.00	2.00
699	A114	75c	multi	2.25	2.25
700	A114	$2	multi	5.00	*5.75*
			Nos. 697-700 (4)	10.00	*10.45*

Parliament, 375th Anniv. — A115

Designs: 25c, $1, Bermuda coat of arms.

Perf. 14x13½

1995, Nov. 3 **Litho.** **Wmk. 373**

701	A115	25c	blue & multi	1.10	.40
702	A115	$1	green & multi	2.40	*3.00*

See No. 731.

Military Bases A116

Force insignia and: 20c, Ordnance Island Submarine Base. 25c, Royal Naval Dockyard. 60c, Fort Bell and Kindley Field. 75c, Darrell's Island. 90c, US Navy Operating Base. $1, Canadian Forces Station, Daniel's Head.

1995, Dec. 4 *Perf. 14*

703	A116	20c	multicolored	.75	.75
704	A116	25c	multicolored	.90	.45
705	A116	60c	multicolored	1.90	1.90
706	A116	75c	multicolored	2.25	2.25
707	A116	90c	multicolored	2.25	*3.00*
708	A116	$1	multicolored	2.25	*3.00*
			Nos. 703-708 (6)	10.30	*11.35*

Modern Olympic Games, Cent. — A117

Wmk. 384

1996, May 21 **Litho.** *Perf. 14*

709	A117	25c	Track & field	1.10	.60
710	A117	30c	Cycling	4.00	1.60
711	A117	65c	Sailing	2.75	2.75
712	A117	80c	Equestrian	2.75	2.75
			Nos. 709-712 (4)	10.60	7.70

CAPEX '96 A118

Methods of transportation: 25c, Sommerset Express, c. 1900. 60c, Bermuda Railway, 1930's. 75c, First bus, 1946. $2, Early sightseeing bus, c.1947.

Perf. 13½x14

1996, June 7 **Litho.** **Wmk. 373**

713	A118	25c	multicolored	1.50	.60
714	A118	60c	multicolored	3.00	2.00
715	A118	75c	multicolored	3.00	2.40
716	A118	$2	multicolored	5.50	*7.00*
			Nos. 713-716 (4)	13.00	*12.00*

Panoramas of Hamilton and St. George's, by E. J. Holland, 1933 A119

Hamilton, looking across water from Bostock Hill: No. 717, Palm trees, Furness Line ship coming through Two Rock Passage. No. 718, House, buildings on other side. No. 719, Sailboats on water, Princess Hotel. No. 720, Island, Bermudiana Hotel, Cathedral. No. 721, Coral roads on hillside, city of Hamilton.

St. George's, looking across water from St. David's: No. 722, Island, harbor. No. 723, Sailboat, buildings along shore. No. 724, Sailboat, St. George's Hotel, buildings. No. 725, Hillside, ship. No. 726, Homes on hill top, passage out of harbor.

Perf. 14x14½

1996, May 21 **Wmk. 373**

Booklet Stamps

717	A119	60c	multicolored	2.75	2.75
718	A119	60c	multicolored	2.75	2.75
719	A119	60c	multicolored	2.75	2.75
720	A119	60c	multicolored	2.75	2.75
721	A119	60c	multicolored	2.75	2.75
a.			Strip of 5, #717-721	14.00	14.00
722	A119	60c	multicolored	2.75	2.75
723	A119	60c	multicolored	2.75	2.75
724	A119	60c	multicolored	2.75	2.75
725	A119	60c	multicolored	2.75	2.75
726	A119	60c	multicolored	2.75	2.75
a.			Strip of 5, #722-726	14.00	14.00
b.			Booklet pane, #721a, 726a	28.00	
			Complete booklet, #726b	30.00	

Lighthouses A120

Designs: 30c, Hog Fish Beacon. 65c, Gibbs Hill Lighthouse. 80c, St. David's Lighthouse. $2, North Rock Beacon.

Perf. 14x13½

1996, Aug. 15 **Litho.** **Wmk. 373**

727	A120	30c	multicolored	2.10	.85
728	A120	65c	multicolored	2.75	2.25
729	A120	80c	multicolored	3.25	2.75
730	A120	$2	multicolored	5.25	*7.00*
			Nos. 727-730 (4)	13.35	*12.85*

See Nos. 737-740.

Bermuda Coat of Arms Type of 1995

Inscribed "Commonwealth Finance Ministers Meeting"

Perf. 14x13½

1996, Sept. 24 **Litho.** **Wmk. 373**

731	A115	$1	red & multi	3.50	3.50

Queen Elizabeth II — A121

1996, Nov. 7

732	A121	$22	blue & org brn	47.50	*55.00*

Architectural Heritage — A122

30c, Waterville. 65c, Bridge House. 80c, Fannie Fox's Cottage. $2.50, Palmetto House.

Wmk. 384

1996, Nov. 28 **Litho.** *Perf. 14*

733	A122	30c	multicolored	1.10	.55
734	A122	65c	multicolored	1.60	1.60
735	A122	80c	multicolored	2.00	2.00
736	A122	$2.50	multicolored	4.50	*6.50*
			Nos. 733-736 (4)	9.20	10.65

Lighthouse Type of 1996 Redrawn

Wmk. 373

1997, Feb. 12 **Litho.** *Perf. 14*

737	A120	30c	Like #727	2.50	1.10
738	A120	65c	Like #728	3.75	2.75
739	A120	80c	Like #729	4.25	3.25
740	A120	$2.50	Like #730	8.00	*11.00*
			Nos. 737-740 (4)	18.50	*18.10*

Nos. 737-740 each have Hong Kong '97 emblem. No. 738 inscribed "Gibbs Hill Lighthouse c. 1900." No. 739 inscribed "St. David's Lighthouse c. 1900."

Birds A123

Designs: 30c, White-tailed tropicbird. 60c, White-tailed tropicbird, adult, chick, vert. 80c, Cahow, adult, chick, vert. $2.50, Cahow.

Wmk. 384

1997, Apr. 17 **Litho.** *Perf. 14*

741	A123	30c	multicolored	1.10	.75
742	A123	60c	multicolored	2.25	1.90
743	A123	80c	multicolored	3.00	2.75
744	A123	$2.50	multicolored	6.75	*7.50*
			Nos. 741-744 (4)	13.10	12.90

See Nos. 798-801.

Queen Elizabeth II and Prince Philip, 50th Wedding Anniv. A124

Perf. 14x14½

1997, Oct. 9 **Litho.** **Wmk. 373**

745	A124	30c	Queen, crowd	.75	.75
746	A124	$2	Queen, Prince	5.00	5.00
a.			Souvenir sheet of 2, #745-746	6.50	6.50

Education in Bermuda A125

Designs: 30c, Man, children using blocks. 40c, Teacher, students with map. 60c, Boys holding sports trophy. 65c, Students in front of Berkeley Institute. 80c, Students working in lab. 90c, Students in graduation gowns.

Wmk. 384

1997, Dec. 18 **Litho.** *Perf. 14*

747	A125	30c	multicolored	.80	.60
748	A125	40c	multicolored	.90	.90
749	A125	60c	multicolored	1.25	1.25
750	A125	65c	multicolored	1.25	1.25
751	A125	80c	multicolored	1.90	1.90
752	A125	90c	multicolored	2.10	2.10
			Nos. 747-752 (6)	8.20	8.00

Diana, Princess of Wales (1961-97)

Common Design Type

Various portraits: a. 30c. b, 40c. c, 65c. d, 80c.

Perf. 14x14½

1998, Mar. 31 **Litho.** **Wmk. 373**

753	CD355		Sheet of 4, #a.-d.	5.00	5.00

No. 753 sold for $2.15 + 25c, with surtax from international sales being donated to the Princess Diana Memorial Fund and surtax from national sales being donated to designated local charity.

Paintings of the Islands A126

Designs: 30c, Fox's Cottage, St. David's. 40c, East Side, Somerset. 65c, Long Bay Road, Somerset. $2, Flatts Village.

1998, June 4 *Perf. 13½x14*

754	A126	30c	multicolored	1.50	.70
755	A126	40c	multicolored	1.90	1.25
756	A126	65c	multicolored	2.75	2.50
757	A126	$2	multicolored	6.50	*8.50*
			Nos. 754-757 (4)	12.65	12.95

Hospitality for Tourists in Bermuda — A127

Designs: 25c, Carriage ride. 30c, Golfer at registration desk. 65c, Maid leaving flowers on hotel bed. 75c, Chefs preparing food. 80c, Waiter serving couple. 90c, Singer, bartender, guests.

Wmk. 384

1998, Sept. 24 Litho. *Perf. 14½*

758 A127 25c multicolored 1.40 .60
759 A127 30c multicolored 2.10 1.10
760 A127 65c multicolored 2.10 1.75
761 A127 75c multicolored 2.10 2.10
762 A127 80c multicolored 2.25 2.25
763 A127 90c multicolored 2.50 *3.00*
Nos. 758-763 (6) 12.45 *10.80*

Bermuda's Botanical Gardens, Cent. — A128

30c, Agave attenuata. 65c, Bermuda palmetto tree. $1, Banyan tree. $2, Cedar tree.

Wmk. 373

1998, Oct. 15 Litho. *Perf. 14*

764 A128 30c multi 1.75 .70
765 A128 65c multi 2.25 1.25
766 A128 $1 multi 3.50 3.50
767 A128 $2 multi 5.50 *7.50*
Nos. 764-767 (4) 13.00 *12.95*

Christmas A129

Children's paintings: 25c, Lizard in Santa hat stringing Christmas lights, vert. 40c, Stairway, wreath on door.

Wmk. 373

1998, Nov. 26 Litho. *Perf. 14*

768 A129 25c multicolored 1.75 1.40
769 A129 40c multicolored 2.25 2.25

Beaches — A130

30c, Shelly Bay. 60c, Catherine's Bay. 65c, Jobson's Cove. $2, Warwick Long Bay.

Wmk. 373

1999, Apr. 29 Litho. *Perf. 13½*

770 A130 30c multi 1.10 .50
771 A130 60c multi 1.25 1.25
772 A130 65c multi 1.60 1.40
773 A130 $2 multi 4.75 *6.00*
Nos. 770-773 (4) 8.70 *9.15*

Common Design Type and

First Manned Moon Landing, 30th Anniv. A131

30c, Ground station. 60c, Lift-off, vert. 75c, Aerial view of ground station. $2, Moon walk, vert.

65c, Looking at earth from moon.

Wmk. 373

1999, July 20 Litho. *Perf. 13*

774 A131 30c multicolored 1.25 .50
775 A131 60c multicolored 1.90 1.25
776 A131 75c multicolored 2.10 1.75
777 A131 $2 multicolored 4.75 *6.25*
Nos. 774-777 (4) 10.00 *9.75*

Souvenir Sheet

Wmk. 384

Perf. 14

778 CD357 65c multicolored 9.00 9.00

No. 778 contains one 40mm circular stamp.

Mapmaking — A132

30c, Somerset Is., theodolite. 65c, 1901 street map. 80c, Aerial photo, modern street map. $1, Satellite, island.

Wmk. 373

1999, Aug. 19 Litho. *Perf. 14*

779 A132 30c multicolored 1.60 .60
780 A132 65c multicolored 2.75 2.75
781 A132 80c multicolored 3.00 3.00
782 A132 $1 multicolored 3.50 *4.00*
Nos. 779-782 (4) 10.85 *10.35*

Mail Boxes and Stamps — A133

30c, Victoria era, #6. 75c, George V era, #49. 95c, George VI era, #121. $1, Elizabeth II era, #142.

Wmk. 373

1999, Oct. 5 Litho. *Perf. 14¼*

783 A133 30c multicolored 1.75 .80
784 A133 75c multicolored 2.75 2.75
785 A133 95c multicolored 3.00 3.00
786 A133 $1 multicolored 3.00 3.00
Nos. 783-786 (4) 10.50 9.55

Pioneers of Progress — A134

No. 787: a, Dr. E. F. Gordon, labor leader. b, Sir Henry Tucker, banker. c, Gladys Morrell, suffragist.

Perf. 13½x13¼

2000, May 1 Litho. Wmk. 373

787 A134 30c Horiz. strip of 3, #a-c 3.75 3.75

See Nos. 933-937, 963-964.

Sailing Ships — A135

Designs: 30c, Amerigo Vespucci. 60c, Europa. 80c Juan Sebastian de Elcano.

2000, May 23 *Perf. 14*

788 A135 30c multi 1.60 .90
789 A135 60c multi 2.25 2.25
790 A135 80c multi 2.75 *3.25*
Nos. 788-790 (3) 6.60 *6.40*

Royal Family Birthdays — A136

35c, Prince William, 18th. 40c, Prince Andrew, 40th. 50c, Princess Anne, 50th. 70c, Princess Margaret, 70th. $1, Queen Mother, 100th.

2000, Aug. 7

791 A136 35c multi 1.75 .95
792 A136 40c multi 1.90 1.10
793 A136 50c multi 2.10 1.75
794 A136 70c multi 2.25 *2.75*
795 A136 $1 multi 3.00 *3.50*
a. Souvenir sheet, #791-795 12.00 12.00
Nos. 791-795 (5) 11.00 *10.05*

Christmas A137

Children's art: 30c, Santa Claus and Bermuda onion, by Meghan Jones. 45c, Christmas tree, by Carlita Lodge.

Wmk. 384

2000, Sept. 26 Litho. *Perf. 13¾*

796-797 A137 Set of 2 3.25 3.25

Bird Type of 1997 Redrawn with WWF Emblem

Designs: No. 798, 15c, White-tailed tropic bird. No. 799, 15c, Cahow. No. 800, 20c, Cahow, vert. No. 801, 20c, White-tailed tropic bird, vert.

Wmk. 373

2001, Feb. 1 Litho. *Perf. 14*

798-801 A123 Set of 4 4.50 4.50
801a Miniature sheet, 4 each #798-801 19.00 19.00

Hong Kong 2001 Stamp Exhibition (No. 801a).

Historical Tourist Attractions, St. George's A138

Designs: 35c, King's Castle. 50c, Bridge House. 55c, Whitehall. 70c, Fort Cunningham. 85c, St. Peter's Church. 95c, Water Street.

2001, May 1 *Perf. 13¾*

802-807 A138 Set of 6 14.50 14.50

Boer War, Cent. — A139

Designs: 35c, Crowded boat, plow. 50c, Men, boot last. 70c, Man with children, rings and pin. 95c, Men and women, stamped cover.

2001, June 28 *Perf. 14*

808-811 A139 Set of 4 7.75 7.75

Aquarium, Museum and Zoo, 75th Anniv. — A140

Designs: 35c, Child, sea urchins, starfish, vert. 50c, Child, museum display. 55c, Child, tortoise. 70c, Aquarium. 80c, Diver in aquarium tank, vert. 95c, Turtle, vert.

Perf. 14¾x14¼, 14¼x14¾

2001, Aug. 9 Litho. Wmk. 373

812-817 A140 Set of 6 12.00 12.00

Paintings by Charles Lloyd Tucker — A141

Various paintings: 35c, 70c, 85c, $1.

2001, Oct. 9 *Perf. 14¼x14¾*

818-821 A141 Set of 4 11.50 11.50

Reign Of Queen Elizabeth II, 50th Anniv. Issue

Common Design Type

Designs: Nos. 822, 826a, 10c, Princess Elizabeth with dog, 1952. Nos. 823, 826b, 35c, In 1965. Nos. 824, 826c, 70c, Waving. Nos. 825, 826d, 85c, In 1991. No. 826e, $1, 1955 portrait by Annigoni (38x50mm).

Perf. 14¼x14½, 13¾ (#826e)

2002, Feb. 6 Litho. Wmk. 373

With Gold Frames

822 CD360 10c multicolored .50 .50
823 CD360 35c multicolored 1.25 1.25
824 CD360 70c multicolored 2.75 2.75
825 CD360 85c multicolored 3.50 3.50
Nos. 822-825 (4) 8.00 8.00

Souvenir Sheet

Without Gold Frames

826 CD360 Sheet of 5, #a-e 10.00 10.00

Caves A142

Designs: 35c, Fantasy Cave. 70c, Crystal Cave. 80c, Prospero's Cave. $1, Cathedral Cave.

Wmk. 373

2002, May 1 Litho. *Perf. 14*

827-830 A142 Set of 4 11.50 11.50

Cricket Cup Match, Cent. — A143

Details from "One Hundred Up," by Robert D. Bassett: No. 831, 35c, Umpire and fielder. No. 832, 35c, Batsman and wicketkeeper.

$1, Entire painting, horiz.

Wmk. 373

2002, July 4 Litho. *Perf. 14*

831-832 A143 Set of 2 5.00 5.00

Souvenir Sheet

833 A143 $1 multi 6.00 6.00

See Nos. 869-870.

Queen Mother Elizabeth (1900-2002)
Common Design Type

Designs: Nos. 834, 836a, 30c, Without hat (sepia photograph). Nos. 835, 836b, $1.25, Wearing blue hat.

Perf. 13¾x14¼

2002, Aug. 5 Litho. Wmk. 373

With Purple Frames

834	CD361	30c multicolored	1.25	1.25
835	CD361	$1.25 multicolored	4.00	4.00

Souvenir Sheet

Without Purple Frames

Perf. 14½x14¼

836	CD361	Sheet of 2, #a-b	7.00	7.00

Shells — A144

Designs: 5c, Slit worm-shell. 10c, Netted olive. 20c, Angular triton. 25c, Frog shell. 30c, Colorful Atlantic moon. 35c, Noble wentletrap. 40c, Atlantic trumpet triton. 45c, Zigzag scallop. 50c, Bermuda cone. 75c, Very distorted distorsio. 80c, Purple sea snail. 90c, Flame helmet. $1, Scotch bonnet. $2, Gold mouth triton. $3, Bermuda's slit shell. $4, Reticulated cowrie-helmet. $5, Dennison's morum. $8, Sunrise tellin.

2002-03 Litho. Wmk. 373 ***Perf. 14***

837	A144	5c multi	.25	.25
838	A144	10c multi	.30	.30
839	A144	20c multi	.55	.55
840	A144	25c multi	.65	.65
841	A144	30c multi	.75	.75
842	A144	35c multi	.90	.90
a.		Inscribed "2008"	.90	.90
843	A144	40c multi	1.10	1.10
844	A144	45c multi	1.25	1.25
845	A144	50c multi	1.50	1.50
846	A144	75c multi	2.00	2.00
847	A144	80c multi	2.25	*2.75*
848	A144	90c multi	2.50	*2.50*
849	A144	$1 multi	2.50	*3.00*
850	A144	$2 multi	5.25	*6.50*
851	A144	$3 multi	8.00	*8.00*
852	A144	$4 multi	9.00	*10.00*
853	A144	$5 multi	10.00	*11.00*
854	A144	$8 multi	17.00	*18.00*
		Nos. 837-854 (18)	*65.75*	*71.00*

Issued: Nos. 5c, 10c, 35c, 45c, 50c, $8, 9/10/02. 20c, 40c, 80c, 90c, $3, $4, 1/23/03. 25c, 30c, 75c, $1, $2, $5, 3/20/03.

World Peace Day — A145

Dove facing: 35c, Right. 70c, Left.

Wmk. 373

2002, Nov. 7 Litho. ***Perf. 14¼***

855-856	A145	Set of 2	5.25	5.25

Bermuda Biological Station for Research, Cent. A146

Designs: 35c, Biological Station and ship, vert. 70c, Fish. 85c, Researcher probing reef. $1, Shrimp, vert.

Wmk. 373

2003, Feb. 4 Litho. ***Perf. 14***

857-860	A146	Set of 4	9.00	9.00

Items Made in Bermuda — A147

Designs: 35c, Dolls. 70c, Model of ship. 80c, Wooden sculpture. $1, Silver tankard and goblets.

Perf. 14½x14¼

2003, May 15 Litho. Wmk. 373

861-864	A147	Set of 4	7.50	7.50

See Nos. 880-883, 898-901, 925-928.

Head of Queen Elizabeth II
Common Design Type

Wmk. 373

2003, June 2 Litho. ***Perf. 13¾***

865	CD362	$25 multi	50.00	50.00

Coronation of Queen Elizabeth II, 50th Anniv.
Common Design Type

Designs: Nos. 866, 35c, 868a, $1.25, Queen in carriage. Nos. 867, 70c, 868b, $2, Queen with crown at coronation.

Perf. 14¼x14½

2003, June 2 Litho. Wmk. 373

Vignettes Framed, Red Background

866-867	CD363	multicolored	3.25	3.25

Souvenir Sheet

Vignettes Without Frame, Purple Panel

868	CD363	Sheet of 2, #a-b	11.00	11.00

Cricket Cup Type of 2002 with "30th Anniversary CARICOM" Added at Left

Designs: No. 869, 35c, Umpire and fielder. No. 870, 35c, Batsman and wicketkeeper.

Wmk. 373

2003, July 4 Litho. ***Perf. 14***

869-870	A143	Set of 2	4.00	4.00

Poinsettias A148

Bract color: 30c, Red. 45c, White. 80c, Mottled.

Perf. 14½x14¼

2003, Oct. 9 Litho. Wmk. 373

871-873	A148	Set of 3	5.75	5.75

Royal Naval Dockyard — A149

Various views: 25c, 35c, 70c, 85c, 95c, $1.

Wmk. 373

2004, Feb. 19 Litho. ***Perf. 13¾***

874-879	A149	Set of 6	14.00	14.00

Items Made in Bermuda Type of 2003

Designs: 35c, Chair. 70c, Pitcher and plate. 80c, Decorative glassware. $1.25, Quilt.

Wmk. 373

2004, May 15 Litho. ***Perf. 13¾***

880-883	A147	Set of 4	6.25	6.25

Worldwide Fund for Nature (WWF) — A150

Various depictions of school of bluefin tuna: 10c, 35c, 85c, $1.10.

Wmk. 373

2004, Aug. 19 Litho. ***Perf. 14***

884-887	A150	Set of 4	7.25	7.25
887a	A150	Sheetlet, 4 each #884-887	30.00	

Nos. 884-887 were issued issued both in sheets of 50 (with gutter between panes of 25) and in miniature sheets of 16, with 4 se-tenant strips.

Bermuda Orchid Society, 50th Anniv. — A151

Various orchids: 35c, 45c, 85c, $1.10.

Wmk. 373

2004, Nov. 18 Litho. ***Perf. 13¾***

888-891	A151	Set of 4	9.50	9.50

Discovery of Bermuda, 500th Anniv. — A152

Map of Bermuda and: 25c, Compass. 35c, Sextant. 70c, Chronometer. $1.10, Telescope. $1.25, Divider.
$5, Aerial photograph of Bermuda.

Perf. 14x14¾

2005, Jan. 13 Litho. Wmk. 373

892-896	A152	Set of 5	12.50	12.50

Souvenir Sheet

897	A152	$5 multi	14.00	14.00

Items Made in Bermuda Type of 2003

Designs: 35c, Carnival revelor dolls. 70c, Fish and coral sculpture. 85c, Lion and lamb stained glass. $1, Earrings and necklace.

Wmk. 373

2005, May 19 Litho. ***Perf. 13¾***

898-901	A147	Set of 4	8.50	8.50

Battle of Trafalgar, Bicent. — A153

Designs: 10c, HMS Victory. 35c, HMS Pickle under construction in Bermuda. 70c, HMS Pickle picking up survivors from the Achille. 85c, HMS Pickle racing back to England.

Wmk. 373, Unwmkd (10c)

2005, June 23 Litho. ***Perf. 13¼***

902-905	A153	Set of 4	7.25	7.25

No. 902 has particles of wood from the HMS Victory embedded in the areas covered by a thermographic process that produces a shiny, raised effect.

Birds and Habitats A154

Various birds and: 10c, Sandy beach, 25c, Fresh water pond. 35c, Rocky shore. 70c, Upland forest (blue bird). 85c, Upland forest (owl). $1, Mangroves.

2005, Aug. 18 ***Perf. 13¾***

906-911	A154	Set of 6	11.50	11.50

Christmas A155

Light displays: 30c, Christmas tree. 45c, Dolphin. 80c, Snowman.

Wmk. 373

2005, Oct. 27 Litho. ***Perf. 13¾***

912-914	A155	Set of 3	3.75	3.75

Bermuda Electric Light Company, Cent. A156

Designs: 35c, Worker in cherry picker working on overhead electric wires. 70c, Worker in cherry picker. 85c, Worker on elevated walkway near equipment. $1, Building.

2006, Jan. 13 Litho. ***Perf. 13¼x13***

915-918	A156	Set of 4	6.25	6.25

Queen Elizabeth II, 80th Birthday A157

Designs: 35c, As child, with dog. 70c, Wearing tiara and small earrings. 85c, Wearing tiara and large earrings. No. 922, $1.25, Wearing blue hat.
No. 923: a, $1.25, Like 70c. b, $2, Like 85c.

Wmk. 373

2006, Apr. 21 Litho. ***Perf. 14***

With White Frames

919-922	A157	Set of 4	7.00	7.00

Souvenir Sheet

Without White Frames

923	A157	Sheet of 2, #a-b	7.25	7.25

Map of Bermuda A158

2006, May 27 ***Perf. 13¾x13¼***

924	A158	$1.10 multi	2.50	2.50
a.		Souvenir sheet of 1	3.00	3.00

Washington 2006 World Philatelic Exhibition.

Items Made in Bermuda Type of 2003

Designs: 35c, Jar of honey. 70c, Stonecutters, by Sharon Wilson. 85c, I've Caught Some Whoppers, sculpture by Desmond Fountain. $1.25, Bottle of perfume.

2006, June 22 ***Perf. 13x13¼***
925-928 A147 Set of 4 9.00 9.00

Christmas A159

Various wreaths: 30c, 35c, 45c, 80c.

Wmk. 373

2006, Oct. 12 Litho. ***Perf. 13¾***
929-932 A159 Set of 4 6.00 6.00

Pioneers of Progress Type of 2000

Teachers: No. 933, 35c, Millie Neversen (1883-1975). No. 934, 35c, Edith (1880-1978) and Matilda Crawford (1879-1948). No. 935, 35c, May Francis (1899-1985). No. 936, 35c, Francis L. Patton (1843-1932). No. 937, 35c, Adele Tucker (1868-1971).

Perf. 13¾x13½

2007, Feb. 15 Litho. Wmk. 373
933-937 A134 Set of 5 4.00 4.00

Spirit of Bermuda A160

Various views of sloop: 10c, 35c, 70c, 85c, $1.10, $1.25.

Perf. 13¼x13½

2007, May 17 Litho. Wmk. 373
938-943 A160 Set of 6 10.00 10.00

Voyage of Deliverance From Bermuda to Jamestown, Va. — A161

Ship and coastline with panel colors of: 35c, Olive green. $1.10, Blue.

Perf. 12½x12¾

2007, June 21 Litho. Wmk. 373
944-945 A161 Set of 2 5.00 5.00

Jamestown, Va., 400th anniv.

Scouting, Cent. A162

Designs: 35c, 1930 photograph of Bishop's Own Cubs, hand with compass. 70c, 1930 photograph of Lord Robert Baden-Powell inspecting Cubs, hands lashing rope. 85c, 1930 photograph of Scout parade, hands of trumpeter. $1.10, Dance of Kaa, hands tying knot.

No. 950, vert.: a, $1.25, Emblem of Bermuda Scouts. b, $2, Baden-Powell inspecting Cubs.

2007, Aug. 23 ***Perf. 13¾***
946-949 A162 Set of 4 7.00 7.00

Souvenir Sheet

950 A162 Sheet of 2, #a-b 8.00 8.00

Poster Art for Troubador Acts A163

Designs: 35c, Celeste & Harris. 70c, Calypsos Hubert Smith, Sydney Bean, Erskine Zuill, Four Deuces. 85c, Calypso Varieties from Bermuda. $1.10, The Talbot Brothers.

Wmk. 373

2008, Mar. 19 Litho. ***Perf. 13¾***
951-954 A163 Set of 4 7.00 7.00

Bermuda No. X1, 160th Anniv. — A164

Panel color: 35c, Brown. 70c, Gray blue. 85p, Gold. $1.25, Silver

Wmk. 373

2008, Apr. 23 Litho. ***Perf. 13¾***
955-958 A164 Set of 4 8.00 8.00

Local Scenes A165

Designs: (35c), Deep Bay, West Pembroke. (70c), Spanish Point Park. (85c), Flatts Inlet. (95c), Tucker's Town Bay.

Die Cut Perf. 12x12½

2008, May 1 Litho. Unwmk.

Booklet Stamps

Self-Adhesive

959	A165 (35c) multi	.70	.70
a.	Booklet pane of 10	7.00	
960	A165 (70c) multi	1.40	*2.00*
a.	Booklet pane of 10	14.00	
961	A165 (85c) multi	1.75	*2.25*
a.	Booklet pane of 10	17.50	
962	A165 (95c) multi	1.90	*2.75*
a.	Booklet pane of 10	19.00	
	Nos. 959-962 (4)	5.75	*7.70*

No. 959 is inscribed "Postage Paid Local;" No. 960, "Postage Paid Zone 1;" No. 961, "Postage Page Zone 2;" No. 962, "Postage Paid Zone 3."

Pioneers of Progress Type of 2000

Designs: No. 963, 35c, Dr. Pauulu Roosevelt Brown Kamarakafego (1932-2007), political activist. No. 964, 35c, Dame Lois Browne-Evans (1927-2007), attorney general.

Perf. 13¾x13½

2008, June 11 Wmk. 373
963-964 A134 Set of 2 2.00 2.00

2008 Summer Olympics, Beijing A166

Designs: 10c, Running. 35c, Swimming. 70c, Equestrian. 85c, Yachting.

Perf. 12½x13

2008, July 23 Wmk. 373
965-968 A166 Set of 4 5.25 5.25

Lighted Christmas Decorations — A167

Various decorations: 30c, 35c, 45c, 80c.

Wmk. 406

2008, Oct. 1 Litho. ***Perf. 13½***
969-972 A167 Set of 4 4.75 4.75

Settlement of Bermuda, 400th Anniv. — A168

Old and modern: 35c, City photographs. 70c, Harbor scenes. 85c, Harbor scenes, diff. $1.25, Maps.

Perf. 12½x12¾

2009, Jan. 22 Litho. Wmk. 406
973-976 A168 Set of 4 8.75 8.75

First Man on the Moon, 40th Anniv. A169

Designs: 35c, Aerial view of tracking station, Cooper's Island. 70c, Antenna at tracking station, Cooper's Island. 85c, Apollo 11 Lunar Module. 95c, Space Shuttle (STS 126). $1.25, International Space Station.

$1.10, Lunar Module on Moon, vert.

Wmk. 406

2009, Apr. 16 Litho. ***Perf. 13¼***
977-981 A169 Set of 5 10.50 10.50

Souvenir Sheet

Perf. 13x13¼

982 A169 $1.10 multi 3.00 3.00

No. 982 contains one 40x60mm stamp.

Marathon Derby, Cent. A170

Designs: 35c, Athlete with trophy and cup. 70c, Athlete with trophy, window at left. 85c, Motorcyclist following runner. $1.10, Woman racing with men.

2009, May 21 ***Perf. 14***
983-986 A170 Set of 4 7.00 7.00

Atlantic Challenge 2009 Tall Ship Races — A171

Ships: 35c, Concordia. 70c, Picton Castle. 85c, Jolie Brise, horiz. 95c, Tecla. $1.10, Europa. $1.25, Etoile, horiz.

Perf. 13¾x13¼, 13¼x13¾

2009, June 11 Litho. Wmk. 373
987-992 A171 Set of 6 12.50 12.50

Bermuda Theater Boycott, 50th Anniv. A172

Designs: 35c, People. 70c, Stylized people, vert. 85c, Sculpture, vert. $1.25, Photograph of protestors.

2009, July 2 Wmk. 406 ***Perf. 12½***
993-996 A172 Set of 4 8.00 8.00

Christmas — A173

Christmas tree ornaments: 30c, Basket. 35c, Angel. 70c, Basket, diff. 85c, Angel, diff.

Perf. 14x13¾

2009, Sept. 24 Litho. Wmk. 406
997-1000 A173 Set of 4 6.00 6.00

Girl Guides, Cent. — A174

Girl Guides: 35c, At ceremony. 70c, Camping. 85c, Marching. $1.10, With parade float.

$1.25, Bermuda's first black Girl Guides unit.

Perf. 14x14¾

2010, Feb. 18 Litho. Wmk. 406
1001-1004 A174 Set of 4 7.00 7.00

Souvenir Sheet

1005 A174 $1.25 multi 3.50 3.50

African Diaspora Heritage Trail — A175

Designs: 35c, Cobbs Hill Methodist Church. 70c, Bermudian Heritage Museum. 85c, St. Peter's Church. $1.10, Barr's Bay Park.

Perf. 13x12½

2010, May 20 Litho. Wmk. 406
1006-1009 A175 Set of 4 7.75 7.75

Worldwide Fund for Nature (WWF) — A176

Lined seahorse: 35c, Head. 70c, Pair of seahorses. 85c, Pair of seahorses in seaweed. $1.25, Adults and juveniles.

Wmk. 406

2010, June 17 Litho. *Perf. 14*

1010-1013 A176 Set of 4 8.00 8.00
1013a Sheet of 16, 4 each #1010-1013 32.00 32.00

Dockyard Apprentices A177

Designs: 35c, Hull of boat under construction, plumb bob. 70c, Dockyard gates, gears. 85c, Worker and equipment, wooden rudder pattern. $1.10, Apprentices, tools.

Wmk. 406

2010, Sept. 23 Litho. *Perf. 14*

1014-1017 A177 Set of 4 8.00 8.00

Service of Queen Elizabeth II and Prince Philip — A178

Designs: 10c, Queen Elizabeth II. 35c, Queen and Prince Philip. 70c, Queen and Prince Philip, diff. 85c, Queen and Prince Philip, diff. $1.10, Queen and Prince Philip, diff. $1.25, Prince Philip.
$2.50, Queen and Prince Philip, diff.

Perf. 13¼

2011, Mar. 3 Litho. Unwmk.

1018-1023 A178 Set of 6 9.00 9.00
1023a Sheet of 6, #1018-1023, + 3 labels 9.00 9.00

Souvenir Sheet

1024 A178 $2.50 multi 5.25 5.25

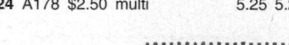

Boat Piloting — A179

Designs: 35c, People dragging boat ashore, nautical chart. 70c, Boats. 85c, Boat, sailor. $1.10, Boat in water, sailors and children on shore.

Perf. 14x14¼

2011, May 19 Wmk. 406

1025-1028 A179 Set of 4 7.00 7.00

Casemate Barracks — A180

Designs: 35c, Casemate Barracks, Great Eastern Storehouse and Commissioner's House, 1857, painting by Gaspard Le Marchant Tupper. 70c, Casemate Barracks and Victualling Yard, 1857, painting by Tupper. 85c, Casemate Barracks and Bermuda Dockyard, 1856, painting by unknown artist. $1.25, 1899 photograph of Casemate Barracks and Lower Ordnance Yard.

Perf. 14¼x14¾

2011, July 21 Wmk. 406

1029-1032 A180 Set of 4 7.00 7.00

Miniature Sheet

Wedding of Prince William and Catherine Middleton — A181

No. 1033 — Couple: a, 35c, Holding hands. b, 70c, Waving in coach, horiz. c, 85c, In automobile, horiz. d, $1.25, Kissing.

2011, Sept. 1 *Perf. 14x14¼*

1033 A181 Sheet of 4, #a-d 7.00 7.00

Reign of Queen Elizabeth II, 60th Anniv. — A182

Various photographs of Queen Elizabeth II: 10c, 35c, 70c, 85c, $1.10, $1.25.
$2.50, Queen Elizabeth II wearing crown.

2012, Feb. 9 Unwmk. *Perf. 13¼*

1034-1039 A182 Set of 6 10.50 10.50
1039a Souvenir sheet of 6, #1034-1039, + 3 labels 10.50 10.50

Souvenir Sheet

1040 A182 $2.50 multi 8.00 8.00

Bermuda Postal Service, 200th Anniv. — A183

Designs: 25c, Postmaster William B. Perot, Bermuda #X1. 35c, Ferry, 1800s, Bermuda #1. 70c, Mail carriage, 1920s, Bermuda #56. 95c, Flying boat, 1930s, Bermuda #109A. $1.10, Mail van, 1960s, Bermuda #225. $1.25, Envelope, binary digits.

2012, Apr. 19 Wmk. 406 *Perf. 13*

1041-1046 A183 Set of 6 11.00 11.00

Paintings — A184

Designs: 35c, South Shore, Bermuda, by Thomas Anschutz. 70c, St. George's, by Ogden Pleissner. 80c, Front Street, 1922, by André Biéler. $1.10, Street Scene, Bermuda (Elliott Street), by Dorothy Austen Stevens. $1.25, La Maison du Gouverneur, by Albert Gleizes, vert. $1.65, The Welcoming Smile, by Frank Small, vert.

Perf. 13¼x13¾, 13¾x13¼

2012, July 12

1047-1052 A184 Set of 6 13.50 13.50

Masterworks Foundation, 25th anniv.

St. Peter's Church, 400th Anniv. — A185

Designs: 35c, Clock tower. 95c, Chandelier and ceiling. $1.10, Bronze plaque for graveyard for blacks and slaves. $1.25, Church exterior.

2012, Oct. 18 *Perf. 13¾x13¼*

1053-1056 A185 Set of 4 8.75 8.75

Items Commemorating British Coronations — A186

Coronation of Queen Elizabeth II, 60th Anniv. — A187

Various items commemorating the coronation of: 10c, Queen Victoria. 35c, King Edward VII. 70c, King George V. 85c, King George VI. $1.10, Queen Elizabeth II.

2013, Feb. 21 *Perf. 14*

1057-1061 A186 Set of 5 7.00 7.00

Souvenir Sheet

Perf. 14¾x14¼

1062 A187 $2.50 multi 5.75 5.75

Beaches — A188

Designs: 35c, Jobson's Cove Beach, Warwick. $1.25, Southlands Beach, Warwick. $1.50, Astwood Park Beach. $1.65, Warwick Long Bay Beach.

2013, May 16 *Perf. 13¾*

1063-1066 A188 Set of 4 10.00 10.00

Gombey Dancers — A189

Various Gombey dancers with frame color of: 35c, Blue. $1.25, Green. $1.50, Red. $1.65, Black.

2013, July 18 *Perf. 14*

1067-1070 A189 Set of 4 11.50 11.50

Mystery Roses — A190

Rose varieties: 35c, Pacific. 70c, Maitland White. 85c, Soncy. $1.10, Spice.

Wmk. 406

2013, Nov. 21 Litho. *Perf. 12½*

1071-1074 A190 Set of 4 7.50 7.50

Eastern Bluebird A191

Eastern bluebird: 35c, Male perched on spruce branch. 85c, Female in nest. $1.10, Male at entrance to birdbox. $1.25, Male and female at birdbox.

Wmk. 406

2014, May 15 Litho. *Perf. 12½*

1075-1078 A191 Set of 4 8.00 8.00

Flowers A192

Designs: 5c, Allamanda cathartica. 10c, Plumeria rubra. 25c, Bougainvillea sp. 35c, Erythrina variegata. $10, Thunbergia grandiflora.

Perf. 13x12¾

2014, July 15 Litho. Wmk. 406

1079-1083 A192 Set of 5 23.00 23.00

See Nos. 1098-1103, 1115-1120.

A193

A194

A195

A196

A197

A198

A199

A200

A201

Roses — A202

Wmk. 406

2014, Dec. 11 Litho. *Perf. 13¾*

1084	Horiz. strip of 5	8.00	8.00
a.	A193 (70c) multi	1.60	1.60
b.	A194 (70c) multi	1.60	1.60
c.	A195 (70c) multi	1.60	1.60
d.	A196 (70c) multi	1.60	1.60
e.	A197 (70c) multi	1.60	1.60
1085	Horiz. strip of 5	8.00	8.00
a.	A198 (70c) multi	1.60	1.60
b.	A199 (70c) multi	1.60	1.60
c.	A200 (70c) multi	1.60	1.60
d.	A201 (70c) multi	1.60	1.60
e.	A202 (70c) multi	1.60	1.60
f.	Booklet pane of 10, #1084a-1084e, 1085a-1085e	16.00	—
	Complete booklet, #1085f	16.00	

Botanical Paintings by Charlotte Anna Lefroy — A203

No. 1086: a, Clematis sp. b, Magnolia grandiflora. c, Cleome speciosa. d, Hibiscus rosa-sinensis. e, Plumeria rubra.

No. 1087: a, Clitoria ternatea. b, Dendrobium moschatum. c, Passiflora edulis. d, Pereskia aculeata and Pereskia bleo. e, Capsicum baccatum.

Wmk. 406

2015, Jan. 15 Litho. *Perf. 14*

1086	Horiz. strip of 5	9.50	9.50
a.-e.	A203 (85c) Any single	1.90	1.90
1087	Horiz. strip of 5	9.50	9.50
a.-e.	A203 (85c) Any single	1.90	1.90
f.	Booklet pane of 10, #1086a-1086e, 1087a-1087e	19.00	—
	Complete booklet, #1087f	19.00	

Nos. 1086a-1086e, 1087a-1087e are each inscribed "Zone 2."

Bermuda Regiment, 50th Anniv. A204

Designs: 35c, Soldier with ear protection crouching. 70c, Soldiers in boat. 80c, Drummers in parade. $1, Queen Elizabeth II inspecting soldiers. $1.25, Soldiers with regimental flags.

Wmk. 406

2015, Apr. 16 Litho. *Perf. 14*

1088-1092 A204 Set of 5 10.00 10.00

Fish A205

Designs: 35c, Bicolor coney. 70c, Blue angelfish. 80c, Gray snapper. 85c, Queen parrotfish. 95c, Yellowhead wrasse.

Wmk. 406

2015, May 21 Litho. *Perf. 14*

1093-1097 A205 Set of 5 8.25 8.25

Flowers Type of 2014

Designs: 50c, Bauhinia variegata. $1, Nerium oleander. $1.15, Macfadyena unguis-cati. $1.20, Hibiscus rosa-sinensis. $1.35, Delonix regia. $1.55, Solanum wendlandii.

Perf. 13x12¾

2015, July 16 Litho. Wmk. 406

1098-1103 A192 Set of 6 15.00 15.00

Bermuda Postage Stamps, 150th Anniv. A206

Designs: 50c, Bermuda #1, hand with quill pen. $1.15, Bermuda #2, hand with fountain pen. $1.20, Bermuda #3, hands at typewriter keys. $1.35, Bermuda #4, hands at computer keyboard. $1.65, Bermuda #6, hands with smartphone.

Wmk. 406

2015, Sept. 17 Litho. *Perf. 14*

1104-1108 A206 Set of 5 13.00 13.00

Bermuda in World War I — A207

Poppy and: 50c, Bermuda Volunteer Rifle Corps awaiting deployment at Hamilton docks, medals. $1, Bermuda members of Royal Garrison Artillery, map of battle engagements. $1.15, Letter to W. F. Anderson of the Lincolnshire Regiment with "Killed in Action" notation. $1.20, Postcard to Bermuda, photograph of Cyril Chesterfield Easton of Bermuda Militia Artillery. $1.35, Recruitment poster for Bermuda Militia Artillery, Royal Garrison Artillery cap badge. $1.55, Cecil Montgomery-Moore and his plane, Royal Flying Corps badge.

Wmk. 406

2016, May 19 Litho. *Perf. 13½*

1109-1114 A207 Set of 6 15.00 15.00

Flowers Type of 2014

Designs: 20c, Datura aurea. 60c, Petrea volubilis. 75c, Cassia javanica. 90c, Lagerstroemia indica. $1.95, Antigonon leptopus. $3, Ipomoea pes-caprae.

Perf. 13¼x13½

2016, Aug. 8 Litho. Wmk. 406

1115-1120 A192 Set of 6 16.50 16.50

Lifecycle of the Monarch Butterfly — A208

Designs: 50c, Caterpillar. $1, Caterpillar and chrysalis. $1.15, Adult with folded wings. $1.35, Adult with open wings.

Wmk. 406

2016, Oct. 20 Litho. *Perf. 13¾*

1121-1124	A208	Set of 4	8.75	8.75
1124a		Souvenir sheet of 4, #1121-1124	8.75	8.75

Queen Elizabeth II — A209

Queen Elizabeth II wearing: 50c, Pale blue hat with pink ribbon. $1.15, Pale orange hat. $1.35, Light blue and white hat.

Wmk. 406

2017, June 29 Litho. *Perf. 13¾*

1125-1127 A209 Set of 3 6.00 6.00

Tall Ships A210

Designs: 50c, STV Spirit of Bermuda. $1.15, Pride of Baltimore II. $1.35, Alexander von Humboldt II. $1.55, Oosterschelde.

Perf. 13¼x13½

2017, Aug. 31 Litho. Wmk. 406

1128-1131 A210 Set of 4 9.25 9.25

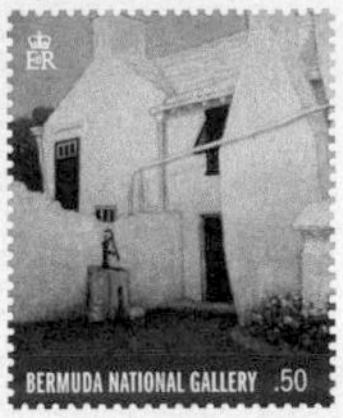

Bermuda National Gallery, 25th Anniv. — A211

Designs: 50c, Old Bermuda House, by William Howe Foote. $1.15, Cerise, by Janet Fish. $1.35, Painting by Sir Joshua Reynolds. $1.55, Bamum wooden mask, Cameroun.

Wmk. 406

2017, Sept. 21 Litho. *Perf. 13¾*

1132-1135 A211 Set of 4 9.25 9.25

Turtles — A212

Designs: 50c, Green turtle. $1.15, Hawksbill turtle. No. 1138, $1.35, Loggerhead turtle. $1.55, Leatherback turtle.

No. 1140 — Head of: a, 10c, Green turtle. b, $1.35, Hawksbill turtle.

Wmk. 406

2018, Mar. 22 Litho. *Perf. 13¼*

1136-1139 A212 Set of 4 9.25 9.25

Souvenir Sheet

1140 A212 Sheet of 2, #a-b 3.00 3.00

Wedding of Prince Harry and Meghan Markle — A213

Various photographs of couple: 50c, $1.15, $1.35.

Perf. 14¼x14

2018, May 21 Litho. Wmk. 406

1141-1143 A213 Set of 3 6.00 6.00

Cedar-Handled Handbags — A214

Various bags with denominations of 50c, $1.20, $1.40, $2.

Wmk. 406

2018, June 21 Litho. *Perf. 14*

1144-1147 A214 Set of 4 10.50 10.50

Royal Air Force, Cent. — A215

Designs: 50c, Lieutenant Rowe Spurling, DeHavilland DH9 light bomber. $1.15, Flight Lieutenant Geoffrey Osborn, Handley Page Halifax heavy bomber. $1.35, Flight Lieutenant Hubert Watlington, Bristol Beaufort torpedo bomber. $1.55, Flight Lieutenant Alan "Smokey" Wingood, Vickers Wellington bomber.

Perf. 14¼x14

2018, Dec. 20 Litho. Wmk. 406

1148-1151 A215 Set of 4 9.25 9.25

Historic Homes A216

Designs: 50c, Waterville. $1.20, Devondale. $1.40, Springfield. $2, Bridge House.

Perf. 14x14¼

2019, Feb. 21 Litho. Wmk. 406

1152-1155 A216 Set of 4 10.50 10.50

Hand-crafted Women's Hats — A217

Various hats: 50c, $1, $1.20, $1.40.

Wmk. 406

2019, May 30 Litho. ***Perf. 14***

1156-1159 A217 Set of 4 8.25 8.25

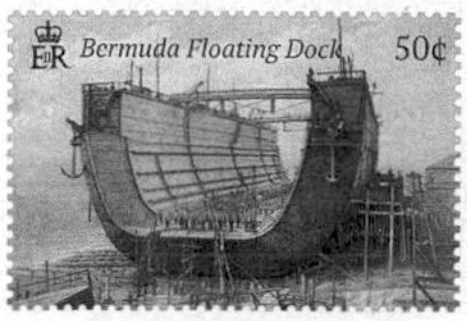

Floating Dock, 150th Anniv. A218

Designs: 50c, Dock under construction in England, 1869. $1, Sailing ship in dock. $1.15, Steamship in dock. $1.35, Empty dock.

Wmk. 406

2019, July 18 Litho. ***Perf. 14***

1160-1163 A218 Set of 4 8.00 8.00

Arrival of Portuguese Immigrants in Bermuda, 170th Anniv. — A219

Designs: 50c, Golden Rule. $2.50, Ship in picture frame.

Wmk. 406

2019, Nov. 1 Litho. ***Perf. 13***

1164-1165 A219 Set of 2 6.00 6.00

Bridges A220

Designs: 50c, Bridge at Norwood. $1.15, Causeway. $1.35, Flatts Bridge. $1.55, Watford Bridge.

Perf. 14x14¼

2020, May 21 Litho. Wmk. 406

1166-1169 A220 Set of 4 9.25 9.25

Bermuda Parliament, 400th Anniv. — A221

Designs: 50c, Sessions House Clock Tower and flag. $1.15, St. Peter's Church, site of first Parliament session, and flag. $1.35, Mace in House of Assembly. $1.55, Gavel.

Perf. 13x12¾

2020, Aug. 6 Litho. Wmk. 406

1170-1173 A221 Set of 4 9.25 9.25

POSTAL-FISCAL STAMP

"Revenue Revenue" — PF1

1936 Typo. Wmk. 4 ***Perf. 14***

Chalky Paper

AR1 PF1 12sh6p org & grayish blk 1,250. *1,750.*

Revenue cancel 75.00

No. AR1 was authorized for postal use from Feb. 1 through May, 1937 and during Nov. and Dec. 1937. Used values are for examples with dated postal cancels indicating usage during the authorized periods. Beware of bogus and improperly dated favor cancels.

WAR TAX STAMPS

No. 42 Overprinted

1918 Wmk. 3 ***Perf. 14***

MR1 A11 1p rose red 1.25 *2.00*

No. 42a Overprinted

1920

MR2 A11 1p carmine 4.00 *3.50*

BHUTAN

bü-'tän

LOCATION — Eastern Himalayas
GOVT. — Kingdom
AREA — 18,000 sq. mi.
POP. — 1,951,965(?) (1999 est.)
CAPITAL — Thimphu

100 Chetrum = 1 Ngultrum or Rupee

Watermark

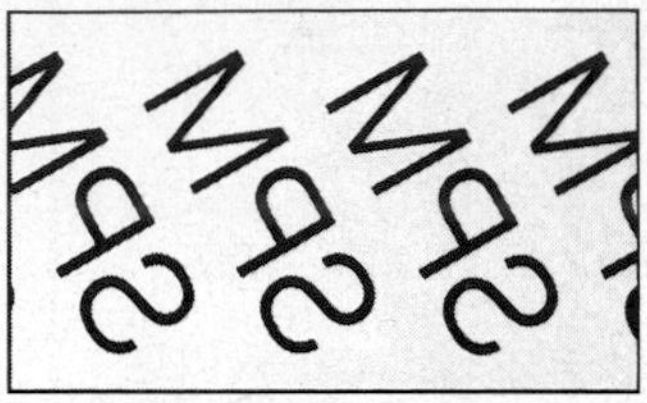

Wmk. 388 — Multiple "SPM"

Catalogue values for all unused stamps in this country are for Never Hinged items.

Postal Runner — A1

Designs: 3ch, 70ch, Archer. 5ch, 1.30nu, Yak. 15ch, Map of Bhutan, portrait of Druk Gyalpo (Dragon King) Ugyen Wangchuk (1867-1902) and Paro Dzong (fortress-monastery). 33ch, Postal runner. All horiz. except 2ch and 33ch.

Perf. 14x14½, 14½x14

1962, Oct. 10 Litho. Unwmk.

1	A1	2ch red & gray	.30	.30
2	A1	3ch red & ultra	.35	.35
3	A1	5ch green & brown	1.90	1.90
4	A1	15ch red, blk & org yel	.30	.30
5	A1	33ch blue grn & lil	.35	.35
6	A1	70ch dp ultra & lt blue	1.00	1.00
7	A1	1.30nu blue & black	2.40	2.40
		Nos. 1-7 (7)	6.60	6.60

Nos. 1-7 were made available to the trade in April 1962, and became valid for postage with the inauguration of the postal service and opening of the first post office on Oct. 10, 1962.

Nos. 1-7 exist in two printings. Slight design differences occur on the 2ch, 5ch, 33ch, 70ch and 1.30nu values.

Imperforates of this issue are from printer's archive.

For overprint & surcharges see Nos. 42, 72-73.

Refugee Year Emblem and Arms of Bhutan A2

1962, Oct. 10 ***Perf. 14½x14***

8	A2	1nu dk blue & dk car rose	1.60	1.60
9	A2	2nu yel grn & red lilac	5.50	5.50

World Refugee Year. Nos. 8-9 exist in various colors, likely originating from printer archives. For surcharges see Nos. 68-69.

Malaria Eradication

A set of three (33ch, 70ch, and 1.30nu) was prepared in 1962 but not issued. All three exist perforated, and the 33ch also exists imperforate. Value, perforated set $275.

Equipment of Ancient Warrior — A3

Perf. 14x14½

1963, May 12 Unwmk.

10	A3	33ch multicolored	.45	.45
11	A3	70ch multicolored	.90	.90
12	A3	1.30nu multicolored	2.25	2.25
		Nos. 10-12 (3)	3.60	3.60

Bhutan's membership in Colombo Plan.
For overprints and surcharges, see B1-3.

Boy Filling Grain Box and Wheat Emblem — A4

1963, July 15 ***Perf. 13½x14***

13	A4	20ch lt blue, yel & red brn	1.00	1.00
14	A4	1.50nu rose lil, bl & red brn	2.10	2.10

FAO "Freedom from Hunger" campaign.
For surcharge see No. 117M.

Masked Dancer — A5

Various Bhutanese Dancers (Five Designs; 2ch, 5ch, 20ch, 1nu, 1.30nu vert.)

1964, Apr. 16 ***Perf. 14½x14, 14x14½***

15	A5	2ch multicolored	.30	.30
16	A5	3ch multicolored	.30	.30
17	A5	5ch multicolored	.30	.30
18	A5	20ch multicolored	.30	.30
19	A5	33ch multicolored	.30	.30
20	A5	70ch multicolored	.30	.30
21	A5	1nu multicolored	1.10	1.10
22	A5	1.30nu multicolored	1.25	1.25
23	A5	2nu multicolored	1.90	1.90
		Nos. 15-23 (9)	6.05	6.05

For surcharges & overprints see nos. 70-71, 74-75, 129A, 129G, C1-C3, C11-C13.

Stone Throwing A6

Sport: 5ch, 33ch, Boxing. 1nu, 3nu, Archery. 2nu, Soccer.

1964, Oct. 10 Litho. ***Perf. 14½***

24	A6	2ch emerald & multi	.30	.30
25	A6	5ch orange & multi	.30	.30
26	A6	15ch brt citron & multi	.30	.30
27	A6	33ch rose lil & multi	.30	.30
28	A6	1nu multicolored	1.00	1.00
29	A6	2nu rose lilac & multi	1.60	1.60
a.		Souv. sheet, #28-29	13.00	13.00
30	A6	3nu lt blue & multi	2.25	2.25
		Nos. 24-30 (7)	6.05	6.05

18th Olympic Games, Tokyo, Oct. 10-25. See No. B4.

Nos. 24-30 exist imperf. Value $17.50. No. 29a exists imperf. Value, $13.

Flags of the World at Half-mast — A7

1964, Nov. 22 Unwmk. ***Perf. 14½***

Flags in Original Colors

31	A7	33ch steel gray	.45	.45
32	A7	1nu silver	1.10	1.10
33	A7	3nu gold	3.00	3.00
a.		Souv. sheet, perf. 13½ or imperf.	7.50	7.50
		Nos. 31-33 (3)	4.55	4.55

Issued in memory of those who died in the service of their country. Nos. 31-33 exist imperf. Value $20.

No. 33a contains 2 stamps similar to Nos. 32-33.

Overprints on No. 31 were not officially issued. For overprints see Nos. 44, 46.

Flowers — A8

1965, Jan. 6 Litho. ***Perf. 13***

34	A8	2ch Primrose	.25	.25
35	A8	5ch Gentian	.25	.25
36	A8	15ch Primrose	.25	.25
37	A8	33ch Gentian	.25	.25
38	A8	50ch Rhododendron	.90	.90
39	A8	75ch Peony	.90	.90
40	A8	1nu Rhododendron	.90	.90
41	A8	2nu Peony	2.25	2.25
		Nos. 34-41 (8)	5.95	5.95

Overprints on No. 37 were not officially issued. For overprints see No. 43, 45, C4-C5, C14-C15.

Nos. 5, 40, 32, 41 and 33 Overprinted "WINSTON CHURCHILL 1874-1965"

1965, Feb. 27

42	A1	33ch bl grn & lilac	.75	.75
43	A8	1nu pink, grn & dk gray	1.25	1.25
44	A7	1nu silver & multi	1.25	1.25
45	A8	2nu sepia, yel & grn	1.75	1.75
46	A7	3nu gold & multi	2.25	2.25
		Nos. 42-46 (5)	7.25	7.25

Issued in memory of Sir Winston Churchill (1874-1965), British statesman. The overprint is in three lines on Nos. 42-43 and 45; in two lines on Nos. 43 and 46.

Nos. 44, 46 exist imperf. Value, both, $4.50.

Nos. 31 and 37 with overprint were prepared but not issued. Value, $62.50 each.

Skyscraper, Pagoda and World's Fair Emblem — A9

Designs: 10ch, 2nu, Pieta by Michelangelo and statue of Khmer Buddha. 20ch, Skyline of NYC and Bhutanese village. 33ch, George Washington Bridge, NY, and foot bridge, Bhutan.

1965, Apr. 21 Litho. ***Perf. 14½***

47	A9	1ch blue & multi	.25	.25
48	A9	10ch green & multi	.25	.25
49	A9	20ch rose lilac & multi	.25	.25
50	A9	33ch bister & multi	.25	.25
51	A9	1.50nu bister & multi	2.00	2.00
52	A9	2nu multicolored	3.00	3.00
a.		Souv. sheet, perf. 13½ or imperf.	8.00	8.00
		Nos. 47-52 (6)	6.00	6.00

Nos. 47-52 exist imperf.; value $5.00.

No. 52a contains two stamps similar to Nos. 51-52.

For overprints see Nos. 87-87B.

Telstar, Short-wave Radio and ITU Emblem — A10

Designs (ITU Emblem and): 2nu, Telstar and Morse key. 3nu, Syncom and ear phones.

1966, Mar. 2 Litho. ***Perf. 14½***

53	A10	35ch multicolored	.25	.25
54	A10	2nu multicolored	.80	.80
55	A10	3nu multicolored	1.40	1.40
		Nos. 53-55 (3)	2.45	2.45

Cent. (in 1965) of the ITU. Souvenir sheets exist containing two stamps similar to Nos. 54-55, perf. 13½ and imperf. Value, 2 sheets, $7.50.

Leopard — A11

Animals: 1ch, 4nu, Asiatic black bear. 2ch, 3nu, Leopard. 4ch, 2nu, Pigmy hog. 8ch, 75ch, Tiger. 10ch, 1.50nu, Dhole (Asiatic hunting dog). 1nu, 5nu, Takin (goat).

1966, Mar. 24 Litho. ***Perf. 13***

56	A11	1ch yellow & blk	.25	.25
57	A11	2ch pale grn & blk	.25	.25
58	A11	4ch lt citron & blk	.25	.25
59	A11	8ch lt blue & blk	.25	.25
60	A11	10ch lt lilac & blk	.35	.35
61	A11	75ch lt yel grn & blk	.50	.50
62	A11	1nu lt green & blk	.85	.85
63	A11	1.50nu lt bl grn & blk	1.10	1.10
64	A11	2nu dull org & blk	1.40	1.40
65	A11	3nu bluish lil & blk	2.00	2.00
66	A11	4nu lt green & blk	2.50	2.50
67	A11	5nu pink & black	3.50	3.50
		Nos. 56-67 (12)	13.20	13.20

Exists imperf, value $25.00.

For surcharges see Nos. 115C, 115E, 115I, 117N, 117P, 129B, 129J. For overprints see Nos. C6-C10, C16-C20.

Nos. 6-9, 20-23 Surcharged

1965 ***Perf. 14½x14, 14x14½***

68	A2	5ch on 1nu	*200.00*	*100.00*
69	A2	5ch on 2nu	*175.00*	*80.00*
70	A5	10ch on 70ch	*100.00*	*14.00*
71	A5	10ch on 2nu	*16.00*	*14.00*
72	A1	15ch on 70ch	*14.00*	*11.00*
73	A1	15ch on 1.30nu	*14.00*	*11.00*
74	A5	20ch on 1nu	*18.00*	*16.00*
75	A5	20ch on 1.30nu	*18.00*	*16.00*
		Nos. 68-75 (8)	*555.00*	*262.00*

The surcharges on Nos. 68-69 contain two bars at left and right obliterating the denomination on both sides of the design. Four bars on Nos. 72-73.

Simtokha Dzong A12

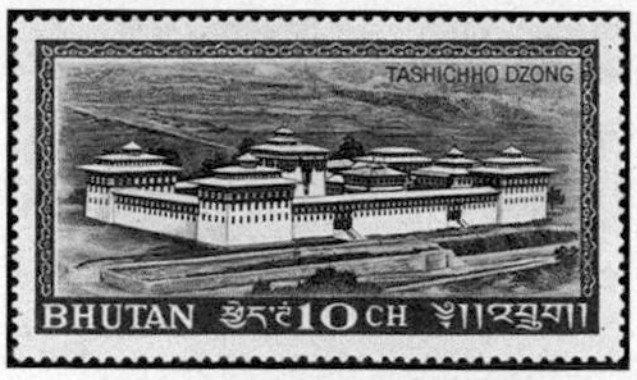

Tashichho Dzong — A13

Daga Dzong
A14

Designs: 5ch, Rinpung Dzong. 50ch, Tongsa Dzong. 1nu, Lhuntsi Dzong.

Perf. 14½x14 (A12), 13½ (A13, A14)

1966-70 **Photo.**

76	A12	5ch orange brn ('67)	*4.00*	*2.40*
77	A13	10ch dk grn & rose vio ('68)	*4.00*	*2.40*
78	A12	15ch brown	*4.00*	*3.25*
79	A12	20ch green	*4.00*	*3.25*
80	A13	50ch blue grn ('68)	*2.00*	*1.75*
81	A14	75ch dk bl & ol gray ('70)	*3.25*	*1.25*
82	A14	1nu dk vio & vio bl ('70)	*3.25*	*1.25*
		Nos. 76-82 (7)	*24.50*	*15.55*

Sizes: 5ch, 15ch, 20ch, 37x20½mm. 10ch, 53½x28½mm. 50ch, 35½x25½mm.

King Jigme Wangchuk — A14a

Coins: 1.30nu, 3nu, 5nu, reverse.

Litho. & Embossed on Gold Foil

1966, July 8 **Die Cut** ***Imperf.***

83	A14a	10ch green	.80	.80
83A	A14a	25ch green	.95	.95
83B	A14a	50ch green	1.40	1.40
83C	A14a	1nu red	2.25	2.25
83D	A14a	1.30nu red	3.00	3.00
83E	A14a	2nu red	3.75	3.75
83F	A14a	3nu red	5.50	5.50
83G	A14a	4nu red	7.00	7.00
83H	A14a	5nu red	8.50	8.50
		Nos. 83-83H (9)	33.15	33.15

Two sets of three dies were used for the embossed coin and show different initials to the lower left of the king's chin, resulting in two types of each of the following: On No. 83: GK or RH; on No. 83A: NR or JM; on No. 83B: JM or AT; on No. 83C: GK or RH, and on No. 83E: NR or JM. Each initialed variety exists in three die types distinguished by the head ornamentation on the right dragons head: Type I left two tendrils of dragons mane short; Type II dragons mane even length, extra horn curled downward; Type III dragons mane even length.

Stamps denominated 15ch, 33ch, and 75ch were prepared but not issued.

For similar designs see Nos. 98-98B, 153-153D, 194-202.

Abominable Snowman — A14b

1966, Oct. 10 **Photo.** ***Perf. 13½***

84	A14b	1ch multicolored	.35	.35
84A	A14b	2ch multi, diff.	.35	.35
84B	A14b	3ch multi, diff.	.35	.35
84C	A14b	4ch multi, diff.	.35	.35
84D	A14b	5ch multi, diff.	.35	.35
84E	A14b	15ch like #84	.35	.35
84F	A14b	30ch like #84A	.35	.35
84G	A14b	40ch like #84B	.35	.35
84H	A14b	50ch like #84C	.35	.35
84I	A14b	1.25nu like #84D	.50	.50
84J	A14b	2.50nu like #84	1.10	1.10
84K	A14b	3nu like #84A	1.20	1.20
84L	A14b	5nu like #84B	2.00	2.00
84M	A14b	6nu like #84C	2.00	2.00
84N	A14b	7nu like #84D	2.00	2.00
		Nos. 84-84N (15)	11.95	11.95

Nos. 84-84N exist imperf. Value, set $25.

For overprints see Nos. 93-93G. For surcharges see Nos. 115D, 115K, 115O, 115P, 117I, 117S.

Flowers
A14c

Designs: 3ch, 50ch, Lilium sherriffiae. 5ch, 1nu, Meconopsis dhwoju. 7ch, 2.50nu, Rhododendron chaetomallum. 10ch, 4nu, Pleione hookeriana. 5nu, Rhododendron giganteum.

1967, Feb. 9 **Litho.** ***Perf. 13***

85	A14c	3ch multicolored	.35	.35
85A	A14c	5ch multicolored	.35	.35
85B	A14c	7ch multicolored	.35	.35
85C	A14c	10ch multicolored	.35	.35

Gray Background

85D	A14c	50ch multicolored	.40	.40
85E	A14c	1nu multicolored	.75	.75
85F	A14c	2.50nu multicolored	1.50	1.50
85G	A14c	4nu multicolored	2.25	2.25
85H	A14c	5nu multicolored	3.00	3.00
		Nos. 85-85H (9)	9.30	9.30

Exists imperf.

For surcharges see Nos. 115F, 115L.

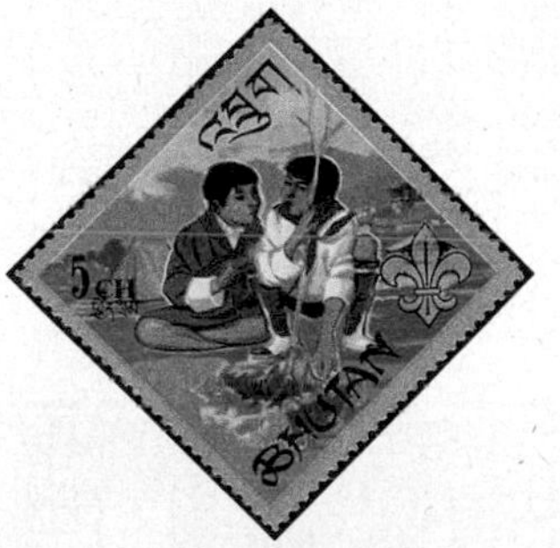

Boy Scouts — A14d

5ch, Planting tree. 10ch, Cooking. 15ch, Mountain climbing.

1967, Mar. 28 **Photo.** ***Perf. 13½***

86	A14d	5ch multi	.35	.35
86A	A14d	10ch multi	.35	.35
86B	A14d	15ch multi	.35	.35

Emblem, Border in Gold

86C	A14d	50ch like #86	.55	.55
86D	A14d	1.25nu like #86A	1.15	1.15
86E	A14d	4nu like #86B	3.25	3.25
f.		Souv. sheet of 2, #86D, 86E	8.00	8.00
		Nos. 86-86E (6)	6.00	6.00

Exist imperf. Value: set $6.50; souvenir sheet $8.

See Nos. 89-89E for overprints. For surcharges see Nos. 115G, 117J, 129K.

Nos. 50-52, 52a Overprinted

Perfs. as Before

1967, May 25 **Litho.**

87	A9	33ch on #50	1.25	1.25
87A	A9	1.50nu on #51	1.40	1.40
87B	A9	2nu on #52	1.75	1.75
c.		Souv. sheet of 2, on #52a	7.50	7.50
		Nos. 87-87B (3)	4.40	4.40

Nos. 87-87B exist imperf. Value: set $8; souvenir sheet $8.

Airplanes — A14f

1967, June 26 **Litho.** ***Perf. 13½***

88	A14f	45ch Lancaster	*.50*	*.50*
88A	A14f	2nu Spitfire	*1.00*	*1.00*
88B	A14f	4nu Hurricane	*2.50*	*2.50*
c.		Souv. sheet of 2, #88A, 88B	*5.25*	*5.25*
		Nos. 88-88B (3)	*4.00*	*4.00*

Churchill and Battle of Britain. Exist imperf. Value: set $6; souvenir sheet $6.

For surcharges see Nos. 117Q, 117T.

Nos. 86-86E, 86Ef Overprinted "WORLD JAMBOREE / IDAHO, U.S.A. / AUG. 1-9,/67"

5ch, Planting tree. 10ch, Cookout. 15ch, Mountain climbing.

1967, Aug. 8 **Photo.** ***Perf. 13½***

89	A14d	5ch multi	.35	.35
89A	A14d	10ch multi	.45	.45
89B	A14d	15ch multi	.50	.50
89C	A14d	50ch like #89	.75	.75
89D	A14d	1.25nu like #89A	1.10	1.10
89E	A14d	4nu like #89B	3.25	3.25
f.		Souv. sheet of 2, #89D, 89E	7.00	7.00
		Nos. 89-89E (6)	6.40	6.40

No. 89Ef sold for 6.25nu. Exist imperf. Value: set $16; souvenir sheet $8.

Girl Scouts — A14g

5ch, Painting. 10ch, Making music. 15ch, Picking fruit.

1967, Sept. 28 **Photo.** ***Perf. 13½***

90	A14g	5ch multi	.25	.25
90A	A14g	10ch multi	.25	.25
90B	A14g	15ch multi	.30	.30

Emblem, Border in Gold

90C	A14g	1.50nu like #90	.85	.85
90D	A14g	2.50nu like #90A	1.75	1.75
90E	A14g	5nu like #90B	4.00	4.00
f.		Souv. sheet of 2, #90D, 90E	8.00	8.00
		Nos. 90-90E (6)	7.40	7.40

Exists imperf. Value: set $7.50; souvenir sheet $10.

For surcharge see No. 266.

Astronaut, Space Capsule — A14h

Astronaut walking in space and: 5ch, 30ch, 4nu, Orbiter, Lunar modules docked. 7ch, 50ch, 5nu, Lunar module. 10ch, 1.25nu, 9nu, Other astronauts.

1967, Oct. 30 **Litho.** ***Imperf.***

91	A14h	3ch multi	.30	.30
91A	A14h	5ch multi	.30	.30
91B	A14h	7ch multi	.30	.30
91C	A14h	10ch multi	.40	.40
m.		Souv. sheet of 4, #91-91C	8.00	8.00
91D	A14h	15ch multi	.50	.50
91E	A14h	30ch multi	1.10	1.10
91F	A14h	50ch multi	1.90	1.90
91G	A14h	1.25nu multi	4.50	4.50
n.		Souv. sheet of 4, #91D-91G	12.00	12.00
91H	A14h	2.50nu multi	2.75	2.75
91I	A14h	4nu multi	4.50	4.50
91J	A14h	5nu multi	5.50	5.50
91K	A14h	9nu multi	9.75	9.75
o.		Souv. sheet of 4, #91H-91K	20.00	20.00
		Nos. 91-91K (12)	31.80	31.80

Nos. 91H-91K are airmail. Nos. 91H-91K exist missing "Air Mail" inscription. Simulated 3-dimensions using a plastic overlay.

For other space issues see designs A15a, A15e.

Nos. 91Cm, 91Gn and 91Ko were officially issued with trial perforations in 10½ and 12. Sets of 3 souvenir sheets exist with multiple parallel lines of perforations of both sizes on one sheet from the postal archives. Set of three perforated souvenir sheets, value $350.

Pheasants — A14i

Designs: 1ch, 2nu, Tragopan satyra. 2ch, 4nu, Lophophorus sclateri. 4ch, 5nu, Lophophorus impejanus. 8ch, 7nu, Lophura leucomelanos. 15ch, 9nu, Crossoptilon crossoptilon.

1968, Jan. 20 **Photo.** ***Perf. 13½***

92	A14i	1ch multicolored	.25	.25
92A	A14i	2ch multicolored	.25	.25
92B	A14i	4ch multicolored	.25	.25
92C	A14i	8ch multicolored	.25	.25
92D	A14i	15ch multicolored	.25	.25

Border in Gold

92E	A14i	2nu multicolored	.75	.75
92F	A14i	4nu multicolored	1.00	1.00
92G	A14i	5nu multicolored	1.25	1.25
92H	A14i	7nu multicolored	1.75	1.75
92I	A14i	9nu multicolored	2.10	2.10
		Nos. 92-92I (10)	8.10	8.10

Unauthorized imperfs exist. Value, $16.

For surcharges see Nos. 115H, 117R, 117V, 129D, 129L.

Nos. 84G, 84I, 84K, 84M Ovptd. in Black on Silver

a

b

Perfs. as Before

1968, Feb. 16 **Photo.**

Overprint Type "a"

93	A14b	40ch on #84G	1.50	1.50
93A	A14b	1.25nu on #84I	1.75	1.75
93B	A14b	3nu on #84K	2.25	2.25
93C	A14b	6nu on #84M	3.00	3.00

Overprint Type "b"

93D	A14b	40ch on #84G	1.50	1.50
93E	A14b	1.25nu on #84I	1.75	1.75
93F	A14b	3nu on #84K	2.25	2.25
93G	A14b	6nu on #84M	3.00	3.00
		Nos. 93-93G (8)	17.00	17.00

Nos. 93-93C and 93D-93G exist imperf. Value, either set $40.

Snow Lion — A14j

Mythological Creatures: 2ch, Elephant. 3ch, Garuda. 4ch, Monastery Tiger. 5ch, Wind Horse. 15ch, Snow Lion.

1968, Mar. 14 Photo. *Perf. 12½*

94	A14j	2ch	multicolored	.35	.35
94A	A14j	3ch	multicolored	.35	.35
94B	A14j	4ch	multicolored	.35	.35
94C	A14j	5ch	multicolored	.35	.35
94D	A14j	15ch	multicolored	.35	.35
94E	A14j	20ch	like #94	.35	.35
94F	A14j	30ch	like #94A	.35	.35
94G	A14j	50ch	like #94B	.35	.35
94H	A14j	1.25nu	like #94C	.45	.45
94I	A14j	1.50nu	like #94	.45	.45
94J	A14j	2nu	like #94D	.80	.80
94K	A14j	2.50nu	like #94A	.80	.80
94L	A14j	4nu	like #94B	1.50	1.50
94M	A14j	5nu	like #94C	2.00	2.00
94N	A14j	10nu	like #94D	3.75	3.75
			Nos. 94-94N (15)	12.55	12.55

Nos. 94I, 94K-94N are airmail. All exist imperf. Value, set $25.

For surcharges see Nos. 115, 115M, 115Q, 117-117E, 129C, C35-C36.

Butterflies A14k

Designs: 15ch, Catagramma sorana. 50ch, Delias hyparete. 1.25nu, Anteos maerula. 2nu, Ornithoptera priamus urvilleanus. 3nu, Euploea mulciber. 4nu, Morpho rhetenor. 5nu, Papilio androgeous. 6nu, Troides magellanus.

1968, May 20 Litho. *Imperf.*

95	A14k	15ch	multi	.85	.85
95A	A14k	50ch	multi	1.20	1.20
95B	A14k	1.25nu	multi	2.40	2.40
95C	A14k	2nu	multi	3.50	3.50
h.			Souv. sheet of 4, #95-95C	15.00	15.00
95D	A14k	3nu	multi	4.00	4.00
95E	A14k	4nu	multi	4.50	4.50
95F	A14k	5nu	multi	5.50	5.00
95G	A14k	6nu	multi	5.75	5.75
i.			Souv. sheet of 4, #95D-95G	22.50	22.50
			Nos. 95-95G (8)	27.70	27.20

Souv. sheets issued Oct. 23. Nos. 95D-95G, 95Gi are airmail. Simulated 3-dimensions using a plastic overlay.

Paintings — A14m

1968 Litho. & Embossed *Imperf.*

96	A14m	2ch	Van Gogh	.25	.25
96A	A14m	4ch	Millet	.25	.25
96B	A14m	5ch	Monet	.25	.25
96C	A14m	10ch	Corot	.25	.25
p.			Souv. sheet of 4, #96-96C	1.60	1.60
96D	A14m	45ch	like #96	.25	.25
96E	A14m	80ch	like #96A	.35	.35
96F	A14m	1.05nu	like #96B	.45	.45
96G	A14m	1.40nu	like #96C	.60	.60
q.			Souv. sheet of 4, #96D-96G	2.40	2.40
96H	A14m	1.50nu	like #96	.65	.65
96I	A14m	2nu	like #96	.85	.85
96J	A14m	2.50nu	like #96A	1.10	1.10
96K	A14m	3nu	like #96A	1.25	1.25
96L	A14m	4nu	like #96B	1.50	1.50
96M	A14m	5nu	like #96C	1.60	1.60
r.			Souv. sheet of 4, #96I, 96K-96M	4.00	4.00
96N	A14m	6nu	like #96B	2.25	2.25
96O	A14m	8nu	like #96C	3.25	3.25
s.			Souv. sheet of 4, #96H, 96J, 96N-96O	8.00	8.00
			Nos. 96-96O (16)	15.10	15.10

Issued: Nos. 96-96G, 96I, 96K-96M, 7/8; Nos. 96Cp, 96Gq, 96Mr, 8/5; others, 8/28.

Nos. 96H, 96J, 96N-96O are airmail.

See Nos. 114-114O, 144-144G.

Summer Olympics, Mexico, 1968 A14n

1968, Oct. 1 Photo. *Perf. 13½*

97	A14n	5ch	Discus	.25	.25
97A	A14n	45ch	Basketball	.25	.25
97B	A14n	60ch	Javelin	.25	.25
97C	A14n	80ch	Shooting	.25	.25
97D	A14n	1.05nu	like #97	.25	.25
97E	A14n	2nu	like #97B	.25	.25
97F	A14n	3nu	like #97C	.45	.45
97G	A14n	5nu	Soccer	.75	.75
h.			Souv. sheet of 2, #97D, 97G	2.50	2.50
			Nos. 97-97G (8)	2.70	2.70

Exist imperf. Values: set $75 unused, $5 used; souvenir sheet $2.75.

For surcharges see Nos. 129E, B5-B7.

Coin Type of 1966 Overprinted

Embossed on Gold Foil

1968, Nov. 12 Die Cut *Imperf.*

98	A14a	15ch	green	2.00	2.00
98A	A14a	33ch	green	3.00	3.00
98B	A14a	9nu	on 75ch green	7.50	7.50
			Nos. 98-98B (3)	12.50	12.50

Human Rights Year.

Nos. 98-98B exist without overprinting. Value, $75.

Nos. 98-98B exist in three die types differentiated by the head ornamentation of the right dragon. See note after No. 83H.

Birds A14p

2ch, 20ch, 1.50nu, Crimson-winged laughing thrush. 3ch, 30ch, 2.50nu, Ward's trogon. 4ch, 50ch, 4nu, Grey peacock-pheasant. 5ch, 1.25nu, 5nu, Rufous necked hornbill. 15ch, 2nu, 10nu, Myzornis.

1968, Dec. 7 Photo. *Perf. 12½*

99	A14p	2ch	multi	.25	.25
99A	A14p	3ch	multi, vert.	.25	.25
99B	A14p	4ch	multi	.25	.25
99C	A14p	5ch	multi, vert.	.25	.25
99D	A14p	15ch	multi	.30	.30
99E	A14p	20ch	multi	.35	.35
99F	A14p	30ch	multi, vert.	.40	.40
99G	A14p	50ch	multi	.40	.40
99H	A14p	1.25nu	multi, vert.	.60	.60
99I	A14p	1.50nu	multi	.75	.75
99J	A14p	2nu	multi	1.00	1.00
99K	A14p	2.50nu	multi, vert.	1.00	1.00
99L	A14p	4nu	multi	1.25	1.25
99M	A14p	5nu	multi, vert.	1.75	1.75
99N	A14p	10nu	multi	3.25	3.25
			Nos. 99-99N (15)	12.05	12.05

1.50nu, 2.50nu, 4nu, 5nu, 10nu are airmail.

Exist imperf. Value $17.50.

For surcharges see Nos. 115A-115B, 115I, 115M, 115R, 117F-117G, 117K, 117O, 129H.

Fish — A14q

1969, Feb. 27 Litho. *Imperf.*

100	A14q	15ch	multicolored	1.60	1.60
100A	A14q	20ch	multi, diff.	2.10	2.10
100B	A14q	30ch	multi, diff.	3.25	3.25
100C	A14q	5nu	multi, diff.	4.25	4.25
100D	A14q	6nu	multi, diff.	5.25	5.25
100E	A14q	7nu	multi, diff.	6.25	6.25
f.			Souv. sheet, #100B-100E	18.00	18.00
			Nos. 100-100E (6)	22.70	22.70

Nos. 100C-100E are airmail. Simulated 3-dimensions using a plastic overlay.

Insects — A14r

1969, Apr. 10 Litho. *Imperf.*

101	A14r	10ch	multi	.90	.90
101A	A14r	75ch	multi, diff.	1.50	1.50
101B	A14r	1.25nu	multi, diff.	2.00	2.00
101C	A14r	2nu	multi, diff.	2.75	2.75
h.			Souv. sheet, #101-101C	22.50	22.50
101D	A14r	3nu	multi, diff.	3.50	3.50
101E	A14r	4nu	multi, diff.	3.75	3.75
101F	A14r	5nu	multi, diff.	4.00	4.00
101G	A14r	6nu	multi, diff.	4.50	4.50
i.			Souv. sheet, #101D-101G	18.50	18.50
			Nos. 101-101G (8)	22.90	22.90

Nos. 101D-101G, 101i are airmail. Simulated 3-dimensions using a plastic overlay.

Admission to UPU — A14s

1969, May 2 Photo. *Perf. 13*

102	A14s	5ch	multi	.25	.25
102A	A14s	10ch	multi	.25	.25
102B	A14s	15ch	multi	.25	.25
102C	A14s	45ch	multi	.25	.25
102D	A14s	60ch	multi	.25	.25
102E	A14s	1.05nu	multi	.30	.30
102F	A14s	1.40nu	multi	.40	.40
102G	A14s	4nu	multi	.90	.90
			Nos. 102-102G (8)	2.85	2.85

Exist imperf. Value $5.50.

For surcharges see Nos. 117H, 117L, 117U, 129.

History of Steel Making — A14t

Designs: 2ch, Pre-biblical. 5ch, Damascus sword. 15ch, 3nu, Saugus Mill. 45ch, Beehive coke ovens. 75ch, 4nu, Bessemer converter. 1.50nu, 5nu, Rolling mill. 1.75nu, Steel mill. 2nu, 6nu, Future applications.

Litho. on Steel Foil

1969, June 2 *Imperf.*

Without Gum

103	A14t	2ch	multicolored	.60	.60
103A	A14t	5ch	multicolored	.60	.60
103B	A14t	15ch	multicolored	.60	.60
m.			Souv. sheet, #103A-103B	2.50	2.50
103C	A14t	45ch	multicolored	.60	.60
n.			Souv. sheet, #103, 103C	2.50	2.50
103D	A14t	75ch	multicolored	.60	.60
103E	A14t	1.50nu	multicolored	1.25	1.25
103F	A14t	1.75nu	multicolored	1.75	1.75
o.			Souv. sheet, #103E-103F	3.00	3.00
103G	A14t	2nu	multicolored	2.50	2.50
p.			Souv. sheet, #103D, 103G	3.00	3.00
103H	A14t	3nu	multicolored	3.00	3.00
103I	A14t	4nu	multicolored	3.50	3.50
103J	A14t	5nu	multicolored	4.00	4.00
q.			Souv. sheet, #103I-103J	8.00	8.00
103K	A14t	6nu	multicolored	5.50	5.50
r.			Souv. sheet, #103H,103K	10.00	10.00
			Nos. 103-103K (12)	24.50	24.50

Nos. 103H-103K, 103q, 103r are airmail. Souv. sheets issued June 30. Stamps from souvenir sheets have inscriptions in either the left or right margin.

Birds — A14u

15ch, Owl. 50ch, Red birds. 1.25nu, Hawk. 2nu, Penguin. 3nu, Macaws. 4nu, Bird of paradise. 5nu, Duck. 6nu, Pheasant.

1969, Aug. 5 Litho. *Imperf.*

104	A14u	15ch	multi	5.50	5.50
104A	A14u	50ch	multi	5.50	5.50
104B	A14u	1.25nu	multi	5.50	5.50
104C	A14u	2nu	multi	5.50	5.50
h.			Souv. sheet, #104-104C	37.50	37.50
104D	A14u	3nu	multi	5.00	5.00
104E	A14u	4nu	multi	3.75	3.75
104F	A14u	5nu	multi	4.00	4.00
104G	A14u	6nu	multi	4.75	4.75
i.			Souv. sheet, #104D-104G	37.50	37.50
			Nos. 104-104G (8)	39.50	39.50

Nos. 104D-104G, 104Gi are airmail. Simulated 3-dimensions using a plastic overlay. Souv. sheets issued Aug. 28.

Buddhist Prayer Banners — A14v

Litho. on Cloth

1969, Sep. 30 *Imperf.*

Self-adhesive

Sizes: 15ch, 75ch, 2nu, 57x57mm, 5nu, 6nu, 70x37mm

105	A14v	15ch	multicolored	13.00	13.00
105A	A14v	75ch	multi, diff.	14.00	14.00
105B	A14v	2nu	multi, diff.	15.00	15.00
105C	A14v	5nu	multi, diff.	16.00	16.00
105D	A14v	6nu	multi, diff.	17.50	17.50
			Nos. 105-105D (5)	75.50	75.50

Souvenir Sheet

105E	Sheet of 3	70.00	70.00

No. 105E shows denominations of 75ch, 5nu, 6nu with design elements of Nos. 105A, 105C, 105D with gray frame. Exists perf. 13½. Value, $70.

Mahatma Gandhi — A15

1969, Oct. 2 Litho. *Perf. 13x13½*

106	A15	20ch light blue & brn	.85	.85
107	A15	2nu lemon & brn olive	4.50	4.50

Mohandas K. Gandhi (1869-1948), leader in India's struggle for independence.

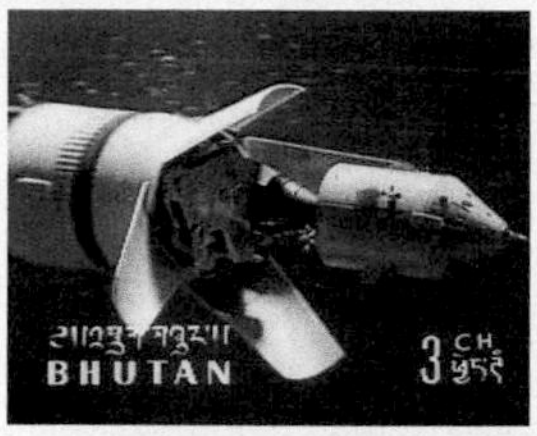

Apollo 11 Moon Landing — A15a

Designs: 3ch, Separation from third stage. 5ch, Entering lunar orbit. 15ch, Lunar module separating from orbiter. 20ch, 3nu, Astronaut standing on lunar module's foot pad. 25ch, Astronaut, lunar module on moon. 45ch, Astronaut, flag. 50ch, 4nu, Setting up experiments. 1.75nu, Lunar module docking with orbiter. 5nu, Lift-off from Cape Canaveral. 6nu, Recovery at sea.

1969 Litho. *Imperf.*

108	A15a	3ch multi	.75	.75
108A	A15a	5ch multi	.75	.75
108B	A15a	15ch multi	.75	.75
108C	A15a	20ch multi	1.00	1.00
m.		Souv. sheet, #108-108C	13.50	13.50
108D	A15a	25ch multi	1.00	1.00
108E	A15a	45ch multi	1.25	1.25
108F	A15a	50ch multi	1.40	1.40
108G	A15a	1.75nu multi	2.50	2.50
n.		Souv. sheet, #108D-100G	18.00	18.00
108H	A15a	3nu multi	3.50	3.50
108I	A15a	4nu multi	4.50	4.50
108J	A15a	5nu multi	5.00	5.00
108K	A15a	6nu multi	5.75	5.75
o.		Souv. sheet, #108H-108K	35.00	35.00
		Nos. 108-108K (12)	28.15	28.15

Nos. 108H-108K, 108Ko are airmail. Simulated 3-dimensions using a plastic overlay.

"Aldrin" misspelled on No. 108Ko.

Issue dates: Nos. 108-108G, Nov. 3; Nos. 108H-108K, Nov. 20; Souv. sheets, Dec. 20.

Paintings A15b

5ch, Clouet. 10ch, van Eyck. 15ch, David. 2.75nu, Rubens. 3nu, Homer. 4nu, Gentileschi. 5nu, Raphael. 6nu, Ghirlandaio.

1970, Jan. 19 Litho. *Imperf.*

109	A15b	5ch multi	1.50	1.50
109A	A15b	10ch multi	1.50	1.50
109B	A15b	15ch multi	1.50	1.50
109C	A15b	2.75nu multi	2.50	2.50
h.		Souv. sheet, #109-109C	13.50	13.50
109D	A15b	3nu multi	2.00	2.00
109E	A15b	4nu multi	2.75	2.75
109F	A15b	5nu multi	3.50	3.50
109G	A15b	6nu multi	4.50	4.50
i.		Souv. sheet, #109D-109G	13.50	13.50
		Nos. 109-109G (8)	19.75	19.75

Nos. 109D-109G, 109Gi are airmail. Simulated 3-dimensions using a plastic overlay. Souv. sheets issued Feb. 25.

Various Forms of Mail Transport, UPU Headquarters, Bern — A15c

1970, Feb. 27 Photo. *Perf. 13½*

110	A15c	3ch ol grn & gold	.50	.50
111	A15c	10ch red brn & gold	.65	.65
112	A15c	20ch Prus bl & gold	.75	.75
113	A15c	2.50nu dp mag & gold	2.00	2.00
		Nos. 110-113 (4)	3.90	3.90

New Headquarters of Universal Postal Union, Bern, Switzerland.

Exist imperf. Value $10.

For surcharge see No. 129I.

Painting Type of 1968

Paintings of flowers.

Litho. & Embossed

1970, May 6 *Imperf.*

114	A14m	2ch Van Gogh	.35	.35
114A	A14m	3ch Redon	.35	.35
114B	A14m	5ch Kuroda	.35	.35
114C	A14m	10ch Renoir	.40	.40
p.		Souv. sheet, #114-114C	2.00	2.00
114D	A14m	15ch Renoir, diff.	.40	.40
114E	A14m	75ch Monet	.40	.40
114F	A14m	80ch like #114	.80	.80
114G	A14m	90ch like #114A	.80	.80
114H	A14m	1nu La Tour	.80	.80
114I	A14m	1.10nu like #114B	.80	.80
114J	A14m	1.40nu Oudot	.80	.80
q.		Souv. sheet, #114D, 114E, 114H, 114J	3.50	3.50
114K	A14m	1.40nu like #114C	.80	.80
r.		Souv. sheet, #114F, 114G, 114I, 114K	5.75	5.75
114L	A14m	1.60nu like #114D	1.20	1.20
114M	A14m	1.70nu like #114E	1.50	1.50
114N	A14m	3nu like #114H	1.60	1.60
114O	A14m	3.50nu like #114J	2.25	2.25
s.		Souv. sheet, #114L-114O	8.00	8.00
		Nos. 114-114O (16)	13.60	13.60

Nos. 114F-114G, 114I, 114K-114O are airmail.

Stamps of 1966-69 Surcharged

1970, June 19

115	A14j	20ch on 2nu, #94J	*4.75*	*4.75*
115A	A14p	20ch on 2nu, #99J	*4.75*	*4.75*
115B	A14p	20ch on 2.50nu, #99K	*4.75*	*4.75*
115C	A11	20ch on 3nu, #65	*4.75*	*4.75*
115D	A14b	20ch on 3nu, #84K	*4.75*	*4.75*
115E	A11	20ch on 4nu, #66	*4.75*	*4.75*
115F	A14c	20ch on 4nu, #85G	*4.75*	*4.75*
115G	A14d	20ch on 4nu, #86E	*20.00*	*20.00*
115H	A14i	20ch on 4nu, #92F	*4.75*	*4.75*
115I	A14p	20ch on 4nu, #99L	*4.75*	*4.75*
115J	A11	20ch on 5nu, #67	*4.75*	*4.75*
115K	A14b	20ch on 5nu, #84L	*4.75*	*4.75*
115L	A14c	20ch on 5nu, #85H	*4.75*	*4.75*
115M	A14j	20ch on 5nu, #94M	*4.75*	*4.75*
115N	A14p	20ch on 5nu, #99M	*4.75*	*4.75*
115O	A14b	20ch on 6nu, #84M	*4.75*	*4.75*
115P	A14b	20ch on 7nu, #84N	*4.75*	*4.75*
115Q	A14j	20ch on 10nu, #94N	*5.00*	*5.00*
115R	A14p	20ch on 10nu, #99N	*5.00*	*5.00*
		Nos. 115-115R (19)	*106.00*	*106.00*

Nos. 115B, 115I, 115M-115N, 115Q-115R are airmail.

Animals — A15d

5ch, African elephant. 10ch, Leopard. 20ch, Ibex. 25ch, Tiger. 30ch, Abominable snowman. 40ch, Water buffalo. 65ch, Rhinoceros. 75ch, Giant pandas. 85ch, Snow leopard. 2nu, Young deer. 3nu, Wild boar, vert. 4nu, Collared bear, vert. 5nu, Takin.

1970, Oct. 15 Litho. *Imperf.*

116	A15d	5ch multi	1.00	1.00
116A	A15d	10ch multi	1.00	1.00
116B	A15d	20ch multi	1.40	1.40
116C	A15d	25ch multi	1.40	1.40
116D	A15d	30ch multi	2.00	2.00
116E	A15d	40ch multi	2.00	2.00
116F	A15d	65ch multi	2.50	2.50
116G	A15d	75ch multi	2.75	2.75
116H	A15d	85ch multi	3.00	3.00
116I	A15d	2nu multi	3.00	3.00
116J	A15d	3nu multi	3.50	3.50
116K	A15d	4nu multi	4.00	4.00
116L	A15d	5nu multi	5.00	5.00
		Nos. 116-116L (13)	32.55	32.55

Nos. 116I-116L are airmail. Simulated 3-dimensions using a plastic overlay.

Stamps of 1963-69 Surcharged

1970, Nov. 2

117	A14j	5ch on 30ch, #94F	*1.75*	*1.75*
117A	A14j	5ch on 50ch, #94G	*1.75*	*1.75*
117B	A14j	5ch on 1.25nu, #94H	*1.75*	*1.75*
117C	A14j	5ch on 1.50nu, #94I	*1.75*	*1.75*
117D	A14j	5ch on 2nu, #94J	*1.75*	*1.75*
117E	A14j	5ch on 2.50nu, #94K	*1.75*	*1.75*
117F	A14p	20ch on 30ch, #99F	*4.75*	*4.75*
117G	A14p	20ch on 50ch, #99G	*4.75*	*4.75*
117H	A14s	20ch on 1.05nu, #102E	*4.75*	*4.75*
117I	A14b	20ch on 1.25nu, #84I	*4.75*	*4.75*
117J	A14d	20ch on 1.25nu, #86D	*4.75*	*4.75*
117K	A14p	20ch on 1.25nu, #99H	*4.75*	*4.75*
117L	A14s	20ch on 1.40nu, #102F	*4.75*	*4.75*
117M	A4	20ch on 1.50nu, #14	*4.75*	*4.75*
117N	A11	20ch on 1.50nu, #63	*4.75*	*4.75*
117O	A14p	20ch on 1.50nu, #99I	*4.75*	*4.75*
117P	A11	20ch on 2nu, #64	*4.75*	*4.75*
117Q	A14f	20ch on 2nu, #88A	*4.75*	*4.75*
117R	A14i	20ch on 2nu, #92E	*4.75*	*4.75*
117S	A14b	20ch on 2.50nu, #84J	*4.75*	*4.75*
117T	A14f	20ch on 4nu, #88B	*4.75*	*4.75*
117U	A14s	20ch on 4nu, #102G	*4.75*	*4.75*
117V	A14i	20ch on 7nu, #92H	*4.75*	*4.75*
		Nos. 117-117V (23)	*91.25*	*91.25*

Nos. 117C, 117E, 117O are airmail.

No. 117C exists with overprint intended for No. 117 (5CH centered to the right of the obliterating bars, rather than adjacent to the lower bar).

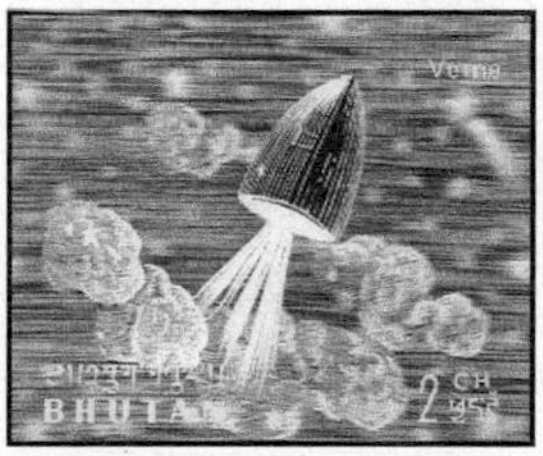

Conquest of Space — A15e

Designs: 2ch, Jules Verne's "From the Earth to the Moon." 5ch, V-2 rocket. 15ch, Vostok. 25ch, Mariner 2. 30ch, Gemini 7. 50ch, Lift-off. 75ch, Edward White during space walk. 1.50nu, Apollo 13. 2nu, View of Earth from moon. 3nu, Another galaxy. 6nu, Moon, Earth, Sun, Mars, Jupiter. 7nu, Future space station.

1970 Litho. *Imperf.*

118	A15e	2ch multi	1.00	1.00
118A	A15e	5ch multi	1.00	1.00
118B	A15e	15ch multi	1.00	1.00
118C	A15e	25ch multi	1.25	1.25
m.		Souv. sheet, #118-118C	10.00	10.00
118D	A15e	30ch multi	1.50	1.50
118E	A15e	50ch multi	2.00	2.00
118F	A15e	75ch multi	2.50	2.50
118G	A15e	1.50nu multi	2.75	2.75
n.		Souv. sheet, #118D-118G	15.00	15.00
118H	A15e	2nu multi	3.25	3.25
118I	A15e	3nu multi	4.00	4.00
118J	A15e	6nu multi	6.00	6.00
118K	A15e	7nu multi	7.00	7.00
o.		Souv. sheet, #118H-118K	30.00	30.00
		Nos. 118-118K (12)	33.25	33.25

Issued: Nos. 118-118G, 11/9; Nos. 118H-118K, 11/30. Souv. sheets, Dec. 18. Nos. 118H-118K are airmail. Simulated 3-dimensions using a plastic overlay.

See Nos. 127-127C. For surcharge see No. 129F.

Wangdiphodrang Dzong and Bridge A15f

1971, Feb. 22 Photo. *Perf. 13½*

119	A15f	2ch gray	1.50	1.50
120	A15f	3ch deep red lilac	1.60	1.60
121	A15f	4ch violet	2.00	2.00
122	A15f	5ch dark green	.65	.65
123	A15f	10ch orange brown	.80	.80
124	A15f	15ch deep blue	1.00	1.00
125	A15f	20ch deep plum	1.40	1.40
		Nos. 119-125 (7)	8.95	8.95

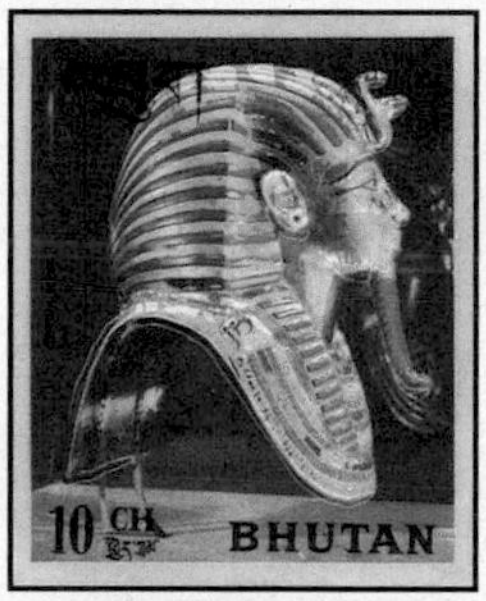

Funeral Mask of King Tutankhamen A15g

History of Sculpture: 75ch, Winged Bull. 1.25nu, Head of Zeus. 2nu, She-wolf Suckling Romulus and Remus, horiz. 3nu, Head of Cicero. 4nu, Head of David, by Michaelangelo. 5nu, Age of Bronze, by Rodin. 6nu, Head of Woman, by Modigliani.

1971, Feb. 27 Litho. *Imperf.*

Self-adhesive

126	A15g	10ch multi	.70	.70
126A	A15g	75ch multi	.85	.85
126B	A15g	1.25nu multi	1.75	1.75
126C	A15g	2nu multi	2.75	2.75
h.		Souv. sheet, #126-126C	6.50	6.50
126D	A15g	3nu multi	4.75	4.75
126E	A15g	4nu multi	5.75	5.75
126F	A15g	5nu multi	7.75	7.75
126G	A15g	6nu multi	5.75	5.75
i.		Souv. sheet, #126D-126G	16.00	16.00
		Nos. 126-126G (8)	30.05	30.05

Stamps are plastic heat molded into three dimensions. Nos. 126D-126G are airmail.

Conquest of Space Type of 1970

Designs: 10ch, 2.50nu, Lunokhod 1. 1.70nu, 4nu, Apollo 15.

1971, Mar. 20 Litho. *Imperf.*

127	A15e	10ch multi	1.40	1.40
127A	A15e	1.70nu multi	2.10	2.10
127B	A15e	2.50nu multi	3.50	3.50
127C	A15e	4nu multi	4.25	4.25
d.		Souv. sheet of 4, #127-127C	22.50	22.50
		Nos. 127-127C (4)	11.25	11.25

Nos. 127B-127C are airmail. Simulated 3-dimensions using a plastic overlay.

No. 127 exists with erroneous surcharge of 90ch that was intended for use on No. 127A to create No. 129F.

Antique Automobiles — A15h

2ch, Mercedes Benz, Germany. 5ch, Ford, US. 10ch, Alfa Romeo, Italy. 15ch, Cord, US. 20ch, Hispano Suiza, Spain. 30ch, Invicta, Britain. 60ch, Renault, France. 75ch, Talbot, Britain. 85ch, Mercer, US. 1nu, Sunbeam, Britain. 1.20nu, Austrian Daimler. 1.55nu, Bugatti, Italy. 1.80nu, Simplex, US. 2nu, Amilcar, France. 2.50nu, Bentley, Britain. 4nu, Morris Garage, Britain. 6nu, Duesenberg, US. 7nu,

Aston Martin, Britain. 9nu, Packard, US. 10nu, Rolls Royce, Britain.

1971 Litho. *Imperf.*

128-128S	A15h	Set of 20	30.00	30.00

Issued: Nos. 128-128F, 5/20; Nos. 128G-128N, 6/10; Nos. 128O-128S, 7/5. Nos. 128O-128S are airmail. Simulated 3-dimensions using a plastic overlay.

"Romeo" misspelled.

Stamps of 1964-71 Surcharged

No. 129F, sans-serif type, 8mm surcharge bars

No. 129F, sans-serif type, 18mm surcharge bars

No. 129F, bold serif type, 18mm surcharge bars

1971, July 1

129	A14s	55ch on 60ch, #102D	2.50	2.50
129A	A5	55ch on 1.30nu, #22	2.50	2.50
129B	A11	55ch on 3nu, #65	2.50	2.50
129C	A14j	55ch on 4nu, #94L	2.50	2.50
129D	A14i	55ch on 5nu, #92G	2.50	2.50
129E	A14n	90ch on 1.05nu, #97D	3.00	3.00
129F	A15e	90ch on 1.70nu, #127A	50.00	50.00
129G	A5	90ch on 2nu, #23	2.50	2.50
129H	A14p	90ch on 2nu, #99J	4.00	4.00
129I	A15c	90ch on 2.50nu, #113	3.00	3.00
129J	A11	90ch on 4nu, #66	3.00	3.00
129K	A14d	90ch on 4nu, #86E	4.00	4.00
129L	A14i	90ch on 9nu, #92I	4.00	4.00
		Nos. 129-129L (13)	86.00	86.00

No. 129C is airmail. No. 129F exists in three varieties: with 90ch surcharge in sans-serif type with bars 8mm or 18mm long, and with surcharge in bold serif type with bars 18mm long. Bold surcharge exists erroneously applied to No. 127.

All values except No. 129F exist with inverted surcharges. Value: each $35, unused or used.

UN Emblem and Bhutan Flag — A16

Designs (Bhutan Flag and): 10ch, UN Headquarters, NY. 20ch, Security Council Chamber and mural by Per Krohg. 3nu, General Assembly Hall.

1971, Sept. 21 Photo. *Perf. 13½*

130	A16	5ch gold, bl & multi	.25	.25
131	A16	10ch gold & multi	.25	.25
132	A16	20ch gold & multi	.25	.25
133	A16	3nu gold & multi	.50	.50
		Nos. 130-133,C21-C23 (7)	3.05	3.05

Bhutan's admission to the UN. Exist imperf. Values, unused or used: set, $6.

For overprints see Nos. 140-143. For surcharge see No. 252.

Boy Scout Crossing Stream in Rope Sling — A17

Emblem & Boy Scouts: 20ch, 2nu, mountaineering. 50ch, 6nu, reading map. 75ch, as 10ch.

1971, Nov. 30 Litho. *Perf. 13½*

134	A17	10ch gold & multi	.25	.25
135	A17	20ch gold & multi	.25	.25
136	A17	50ch gold & multi	.25	.25
137	A17	75ch silver & multi	.50	.50
138	A17	2nu silver & multi	.65	.65
139	A17	6nu silver & multi	2.00	2.00
a.		Souv. sheet of 2, #138-139 + 2 labels	4.50	4.50
		Nos. 134-139 (6)	3.90	3.90

60th anniv. of the Boy Scouts. Exist imperf. Value $7.50. No. 139a imperf., value, *$30.*

For overprint and surcharge see Nos. 253, 383.

Nos. 130-133 Overprinted in Gold

1971, Dec. 23

140	A16	5ch gold & multi	.30	.30
141	A16	10ch gold & multi	.30	.30
142	A16	20ch gold & multi	.30	.30
143	A16	3nu gold & multi	.60	.60
		Nos. 140-143,C24-C26 (7)	4.35	4.35

World Refugee Year. Exist imperf. Values: set, unused $10, used $9.

The Bathing Girl by Renoir A17a

Designs: 20ch, A Bar at the Follies, by Manet, horiz. 90ch, Mona Lisa, by da Vinci. 1.70nu, Cart of Father Juniet, by Rousseau, horiz. 2.50nu, The Gleaners, by Millet, horiz. 4.60nu, White Horse, by Gaugin. 5.40nu, The Dancing Lesson, by Degas. 6nu, After the Rain, by Guillaumin, horiz.

1972 Litho. & Embossed *Imperf.*

144	A17a	15ch multi	.50	.50
144A	A17a	20ch multi	.75	.75
144B	A17a	90ch multi	.85	.85
144C	A17a	1.70nu multi	1.50	1.50
144D	A17a	2.50nu multi	1.50	1.50
h.		Souv. sheet of 4, #144-144B, 144D	7.00	7.00
144E	A17a	4.60nu multi	2.25	2.25
144F	A17a	5.40nu multi	2.75	2.75
144G	A17a	6nu multi	2.75	2.75
i.		Souv. sheet of 4, #144C, 144E-144G	8.00	8.00
		Nos. 144-144G (8)	12.85	12.85

Issued: Nos. 144-144B, 144D, 1/29; others, 2/28.

Nos. 144C, 144E-144G are airmail.

Famous Men A17b

10ch, John F. Kennedy. 15ch, Gandhi. 55ch, Churchill. 2nu, De Gaulle. 6nu, Pope John XXIII. 8nu, Eisenhower.

1972, Apr. 17 Litho. *Imperf.*

Self-adhesive

145	A17b	10ch multi	.60	.60
145A	A17b	15ch multi	.75	.75
145B	A17b	55ch multi	1.10	1.10
145C	A17b	2nu multi	1.25	1.25
145D	A17b	6nu multi	2.00	2.00
145E	A17b	8nu multi	2.75	2.75
f.		Souv. sheet, #145B-145E	7.50	7.50
		Nos. 145-145E (6)	8.45	8.45

Nos. 145C-145E are airmail. Stamps are plastic heat molded into three dimensions.

Book Year Emblem A17c

1972, May 15 Photo. *Perf. 13½x13*

146	A17c	2ch multicolored	.25	.25
146A	A17c	3ch multicolored	.25	.25
146B	A17c	5ch multicolored	.25	.25
146C	A17c	20ch multicolored	.25	.25
		Nos. 146-146C (4)	1.00	1.00

International Book Year.

1972 Summer Olympics, Munich — A17d

1972, June 6 Photo. *Perf. 13½*

147	A17d	10ch Handball	.25	.25
147A	A17d	15ch Archery	.25	.25
147B	A17d	20ch Boxing	.25	.25
147C	A17d	30ch Discus	.25	.25
147D	A17d	35ch Javelin	.25	.25
147E	A17d	45ch Shooting	.25	.25
147F	A17d	1.35nu like #147A	.80	.80
147G	A17d	7nu like #147	1.25	1.25
h.		Souv. sheet of 3, #147D, 147F-147G	3.00	3.00
		Nos. 147-147G (8)	3.55	3.55

Nos. 147D, 147F-147G are airmail and have a gold border.

Exist imperf. Value: set $6; souvenir sheet $6.

For overprint see No. 384.

Apollo 11 Type of 1969

Apollo 16: 15ch, Lift-off, vert. 20ch, Achieving lunar orbit. 90ch, Astronauts Young, Mattingly, Duke, vert. 1.70nu, Lunar module. 2.50nu, Walking on moon. 4.60nu, Gathering rock samples. 5.40nu, Apollo 16 on launch pad, vert. 6nu, Looking at earth, vert.

1972, Sept. 1 Litho. *Imperf.*

148	A15a	15ch multi	1.25	1.25
148A	A15a	20ch multi	1.25	1.25
148B	A15a	90ch multi	1.25	1.25
148C	A15a	1.70nu multi	1.75	1.75
148D	A15a	2.50nu multi	2.25	2.25
h.		Souv. sheet of 4, #148-148B, 148D	17.50	17.50
148E	A15a	4.60nu multi	3.00	3.00
148F	A15a	5.40nu multi	3.50	3.50
148G	A15a	6nu multi	4.75	4.75
i.		Souv. sheet of 4, #148C, 148E-148G	27.50	27.50
		Nos. 148-148G (8)	19.00	19.00

Nos. 148C, 148E-148G are airmail. Simulated 3-dimensions using a plastic overlay.

Dogs A17f

2ch, Pointer. 3ch, Irish Setter. 5ch, Lhasa Apso, vert. 10ch, Dochi. No. 149D, 15ch, Damci. No. 149E, 15ch, Collie. 20ch, Basset hound. 25ch, Damci, diff. 30ch, Fox terrier. 55ch, Lhasa Apso, diff. 99ch, Boxer. 2.50nu, St. Bernard. 4nu, Cocker Spaniel. 8nu, Damci, diff.

18nu, Poodle.

1972-73 Photo. *Perf. 13½*

149	A17f	2ch multi	.25	.25
149A	A17f	3ch multi	.25	.25
149B	A17f	5ch multi	.25	.25
149C	A17f	10ch multi	.25	.25
149D	A17f	15ch multi	.25	.25
149E	A17f	15ch multi	.25	.25
149F	A17f	20ch multi	.25	.25
149G	A17f	25ch multi	.35	.35
149H	A17f	30ch multi	.25	.25
149I	A17f	55ch multi	.35	.35
149J	A17f	99ch multi	.25	.25
149K	A17f	2.50nu multi	.50	.50
149L	A17f	4nu multi	1.50	1.50
o.		Souv. sheet of 3, #149J-149L, perf. 14	6.00	6.00
149M	A17f	8nu multi	2.50	2.50
p.		Souv. sheet of 2, #149I, 149M, perf. 14	5.50	5.50
		Nos. 149-149M (14)	7.45	7.45

Souvenir Sheet

Perf. 14

149N	A17f	18nu multi	8.00	8.00

Issued: Nos. 149B-149D, 149G, 149I, 149M, 149Mp, 10/5; Nos. 149-149A, 149E-149F, 149H, 149J-149L, 149Lo, 1/1/73; No. 149N, 1/15/73. No. 149N is airmail. All exist imperf. Values: set (14), $11; No. 149Lo, $9; 149Mp, $7.50; 149N, $8.

For surcharges & overprints see Nos. 268-269, 385.

Roses — A17g

15ch, Wendy Cussons. 25ch, Iceberg. 30ch, Marchioness of Urquio. 3nu, Pink parfait. 6nu, Roslyn. 7nu, Blue moon.

Scented Paper

1973, Jan. 30 Photo. *Perf. 13½*

150	A17g	15ch multi	.25	.25
150A	A17g	25ch multi	.25	.25
150B	A17g	30ch multi	.25	.25
150C	A17g	3nu multi	.80	.80
150D	A17g	6nu multi	1.00	1.00
150E	A17g	7nu multi	1.60	1.60
f.		Souv. sheet, #150D-150E	3.50	3.50
		Nos. 150-150E (6)	4.15	4.15

Nos. 150D-150E are airmail. Exist imperf. Value: set $10; souvenir sheet $8.

Apollo 11 Type of 1969

Apollo 17: 10ch, Taking photographs on moon. 15ch, Setting up experiments. 55ch, Earth. 2nu, Driving lunar rover. 7nu, Satellite. 9nu, Astronauts Cernan, Evans, Schmitt.

1973, Feb. 28 Litho. *Imperf.*
Size: 50x49mm

151	A15a	10ch multicolored	1.50	1.50
151A	A15a	15ch multicolored	1.50	1.50
151B	A15a	55ch multicolored	2.00	2.00
151C	A15a	2nu multicolored	3.00	3.00
f.		Souv. sheet of 4, #151-151C	12.00	12.00
151D	A15a	7nu multicolored	6.00	6.00
151E	A15a	9nu multicolored	8.00	8.00
g.		Souv. sheet of 2, #151D-151E	*50.00*	*50.00*
		Nos. 151-151E (6)	22.00	22.00

Simulated 3-dimensions using a plastic overlay. Nos. 151D-151E are airmail. No. 151g is circular, 160mm in diameter.

Phonograph Records

A17h

Recordings: 10ch, Bhutanese History. 25ch, Royal Bhutan Anthem. 1.25nu, Bhutanese History (English). 3nu, Bhutanese History (Bhutanese), Folk Song No. 1. 7nu, Folk Song No. 1. 8nu, Folk Song No. 2. 9nu, History in English, Folk Songs Nos. 1 & 2.

Diameter: Nos. 152-152B, 152D-152E, 69mm, Nos. 152C, 152F, 100mm

1973, Apr. 15 Self-adhesive

152	A17h	10ch yel on red	*22.50*	*22.50*
152A	A17h	25ch gold on grn	*34.00*	*34.00*
152B	A17h	1.25nu sil on bl	*45.00*	*45.00*
152C	A17h	3nu sil on pur	*85.00*	*85.00*
152D	A17h	7nu sil on blk	*65.00*	*65.00*
152E	A17h	8nu red on white	*85.00*	*85.00*
152F	A17h	9nu blk on yel	*125.00*	*125.00*
		Nos. 152-152F (7)	*461.50*	*461.50*

Nos. 152C, 152F are airmail. Nos. 152-152F exist in trial colors.
A 6nu stamp, silver on green, exists but was not issued. Value, unused $900.

King Jigme Dorji Wangchuk (d. 1972)
A17i

Embossed on Gold Foil

1973, May 2 Die Cut *Imperf.*

153	A17i	10ch orange	2.00	2.00
153A	A17i	25ch red	2.00	2.00
153B	A17i	3nu green	3.00	3.00
153C	A17i	6nu blue	5.00	5.00
153D	A17i	8nu purple	6.00	6.00
e.		Souv. sheet of 2, #153C-153D	*20.00*	*20.00*
		Nos. 153-153D (5)	18.00	18.00

Nos. 153C-153D are airmail.

Mushrooms — A17j

Different mushrooms.

1973, Sept. 25 Litho. *Imperf.*

154	A17j	15ch multicolored	*.60*	*.60*
154A	A17j	25ch multicolored	*.85*	*.85*
154B	A17j	30ch multicolored	*1.00*	*1.00*
154C	A17j	3nu multicolored	*2.00*	*2.00*
f.		Souv. sheet, #154-154C	*15.00*	*15.00*
154D	A17j	6nu multicolored	*7.50*	*7.50*
154E	A17j	7nu multicolored	*11.00*	*11.00*
g.		Souv. sheet, #154D-154E	*50.00*	*50.00*
		Nos. 154-154E (6)	*22.95*	*22.95*

Simulated 3-dimensions using a plastic overlay. Nos. 154D-154E are airmail.

Bhutanese Mail Service — A17k

Designs: 5ch, 6nu, Letter carrier at mail box. 10ch, 5nu, Postmaster, letter carrier. 15ch, Sacking mail. 25ch, Mailtruck. 1.25nu, Sorting mail. 3nu, Hand-delivered mail.

1973, Nov. 14 Photo. *Perf. 13½*

155	A17k	5ch multi	.25	.25
155A	A17k	10ch multi	.25	.25
155B	A17k	15ch multi	.25	.25
155C	A17k	25ch multi	.25	.25
155D	A17k	1.25nu multi	.25	.25
155E	A17k	3nu multi	.75	.75
155F	A17k	5nu multi	1.25	1.25
155G	A17k	6nu multi	1.50	1.50
h.		Souv. sheet, #155F-155G	5.50	5.50
		Nos. 155-155G (8)	4.75	4.75

Indipex '73. Nos. 155F-155G are airmail. All exist imperf. Values: set $7; souvenir sheet $6.50.
For surcharges and overprint see Nos. 267, 382, C37-C38.

When the printer archives for many sets between 1974 and 1986 were released, numerous unissued imperfs, proofs and trial color proofs made it to the marketplace.

King Jigme Singye Wangchuk and Royal Crest — A18

Designs (King and): 25ch, 90ch, Flag of Bhutan. 1.25nu, Wheel with 8 good luck signs. 2nu, 4nu, Punakha Dzong, former winter capital. 3nu, 5nu, Crown. 5ch, same as 10ch.

1974, June 2 Litho. *Perf. 13½*

157	A18	10ch maroon & multi	.25	.25
158	A18	25ch gold & multi	.25	.25
159	A18	1.25nu multi	.25	.25
160	A18	2nu gold & multi	.40	.40
161	A18	3nu multi	.50	.50
		Nos. 157-161 (5)	1.65	1.65

Souvenir Sheets
Perf. 13½, Imperf.

162		Sheet of 2	3.00	3.00
a.	A18	5ch maroon & multi	.50	
b.	A18	5nu red orange & multi	2.50	
163		Sheet of 2	3.00	3.00
a.	A18	90ch gold & multi	.90	
b.	A18	4nu gold & multi	2.10	

Coronation of King Jigme Singye Wangchuk, June 2, 1974.

Mailman on Horseback
A19

Old and New Locomotives
A20

Designs (UPU Emblem, Carrier Pigeon and): 3ch, Sailing and steam ships. 4ch, Old biplane and jet. 25ch, Mail runner and jeep.

1974, Oct. 9 Litho. *Perf. 14½*

164	A19	1ch grn & multi	.60	.60
165	A20	2ch lilac & multi	.60	.60
166	A20	3ch ocher & multi	.60	.60
167	A20	4ch yel grn & multi	.60	.60
168	A20	25ch salmon & multi	.60	.60
		Nos. 164-168,C27-C29 (8)	5.50	5.50

Centenary of Universal Postal Union. Issued in sheets of 50 and sheets of 5 plus label with multicolored margin. Exist imperf. Values, unused or used: set $6.

Family and WPY Emblem — A21

1974, Dec. 17 *Perf. 13½*

169	A21	25ch bl & multi	.25	.25
170	A21	50ch org & multi	.25	.25
171	A21	90ch ver & multi	.30	.30
172	A21	2.50nu brn & multi	.65	.65
a.		Souvenir sheet, 10nu	2.75	2.75
		Nos. 169-172 (4)	1.45	1.45

For surcharge see No. 254.

Sephisa Chandra — A22

Indigenous butterflies: 2ch, Lethe kansa. 3ch, Neope bhadra. 4ch, Euthalia duda. 5ch, Vindula erota. 10ch, Bhutanitis Lidderdale. 3nu, Limenitis zayla. 5nu, Delis thysbe. 10nu, Dabasa gyas.

1975, Sept. 15 Litho. *Perf. 14½*

173	A22	1ch multicolored	.30	.30
174	A22	2ch multicolored	.30	.30
175	A22	3ch multicolored	.30	.30
176	A22	4ch multicolored	.30	.30
177	A22	5ch multicolored	.30	.30
178	A22	10ch multicolored	.30	.30
179	A22	3nu multicolored	.75	.75
180	A22	5nu multicolored	1.60	1.60
		Nos. 173-180 (8)	4.15	4.15

Souvenir Sheet
Perf. 13

181	A22	10nu multicolored	3.00	3.00

For surcharges see Nos. 255-256.

Apollo and Apollo-Soyuz Emblem — A23

Design: No. 183, Soyuz and emblem.

1975, Dec. 1 Litho. *Perf. 14x13½*

182	A23	10nu multicolored	3.00	3.00
183	A23	10nu multicolored	3.00	3.00
a.		Souvenir sheet of 2, 15nu	6.00	6.00

Apollo Soyuz link-up in space, July 17. Nos. 182-183 printed se-tenant in sheets of 10. Sheets exist imperf. Values: single stamp, $6 each; se-tenant pair $15. No. 183a contains two 15nu stamps similar to Nos 182-183.
For surcharges see Nos. 257-258.

Jewelry — A24

Designs: 2ch, Coffee pot, bell and sugar cup. 3ch, Container and drinking horn. 4ch, Pendants and box cover. 5ch, Painter. 15ch, Silversmith. 20ch, Wood carver with tools. 1.50nu, Mat maker. 5nu, 10nu, Printer.

1975, Dec. 17 *Perf. 14½*

184	A24	1ch multicolored	.30	.30
185	A24	2ch multicolored	.30	.30
186	A24	3ch multicolored	.30	.30
187	A24	4ch multicolored	.30	.30
188	A24	5ch multicolored	.30	.30
189	A24	15ch multicolored	.30	.30
190	A24	20ch multicolored	.30	.30
191	A24	1.50nu multicolored	.35	.35
192	A24	10nu multicolored	2.25	2.25
		Nos. 184-192 (9)	4.70	4.70

Souvenir Sheet
Perf. 13

193	A24	5nu multicolored	4.25	4.25

Handicrafts and craftsmen.
For surcharges see No. 259, 381.

King Jigme Singye Wangchuk
A25

Designs: 25ch, 90ch, 1nu, 2nu, 4nu, like 15ch. 1.30nu, 3nu, 5nu, Coat of arms. Sizes (Diameter): 15ch, 1nu, 1.30nu, 38mm. 25ch, 2nu, 3nu, 49mm. 90ch, 4nu, 5nu, 63mm.

Lithographed, Embossed on Gold Foil

1975, Nov. 11 *Imperf.*

194	A25	15ch emerald	*.65*	*.65*
195	A25	25ch emerald	*.90*	*.90*
196	A25	90ch emerald	*1.40*	*1.40*
197	A25	1nu bright carmine	*1.50*	*1.50*
198	A25	1.30nu bright carmine	*1.90*	*1.90*
199	A25	2nu bright carmine	*2.10*	*2.10*
200	A25	3nu bright carmine	*2.75*	*2.75*
201	A25	4nu bright carmine	*4.75*	*4.75*
202	A25	5nu bright carmine	*6.00*	*6.00*
		Nos. 194-202 (9)	*21.95*	*21.95*

King Jigme Singye Wangchuk's 20th birthday.
Two sets of three dies were used to print Nos. 196, 197, 199, and 201. These stamps exist with either the initials "AT" or "GK" to the left of the king's chin. For more detail on the three die types see note after No. 83H.

Rhododendron Cinnabarinum
A28

Rhododendron: 2ch, Campanulatum. 3ch, Fortunei. 4ch, Red arboreum. 5ch, Pink arboreum. 1nu, Falconeri. 3nu, Hodgsonii. 5nu, Keysii. 10nu, Cinnabarinum.

1976, Feb. 15 Litho. *Perf. 15*

203 A28	1ch rose & multi	.25	.25
204 A28	2ch lt grn & multi	.25	.25
205 A28	3ch gray & multi	.25	.25
206 A28	4ch lil & multi	.25	.25
207 A28	5ch ol gray & multi	.25	.25
208 A28	1nu brn org & multi	.30	.30
209 A28	3nu ultra & multi	.90	.90
210 A28	5nu gray & multi	1.40	1.40
	Nos. 203-210 (8)	3.85	3.85

Souvenir Sheet

Perf. 13½

211 A28	10nu multicolored	3.75	3.75

For surcharge see No. 260.

Slalom and Olympic Games Emblem — A29

Olympic Games Emblem and: 2ch, 4-men bobsled. 3ch, Ice hockey. 4ch, Cross-country skiing. 5ch, Figure skating, women's. 2nu, Downhill skiing. 4nu, Speed skating. 6nu, Ski jump. 10nu, Figure skating, pairs.

1976, Mar. 29 Litho. *Perf. 13½*

212 A29	1ch multicolored	.25	.25
213 A29	2ch multicolored	.25	.25
214 A29	3ch multicolored	.25	.25
215 A29	4ch multicolored	.25	.25
216 A29	5ch multicolored	.25	.25
217 A29	2nu multicolored	.40	.40
218 A29	4nu multicolored	.90	.90
219 A29	10nu multicolored	2.50	2.50
	Nos. 212-219 (8)	5.05	5.05

Souvenir Sheet

220 A29	6nu multicolored	2.75	2.75

12th Winter Olympic Games, Innsbruck, Austria, Feb. 4-15.

For surcharges see Nos. 261-262.

Exist imperf. Values, unused or used: set 7.50; souvenir sheet $7.50.

Ceremonial Masks — A29a

Various masks. Nos. 220E-220K are horiz. stamps.

1976, Apr. 23 Litho. *Imperf.*

220A A29a	5ch multi	.40	.40
220B A29a	10ch multi	.40	.40
220C A29a	15ch multi	.40	.40
220D A29a	20ch multi	.40	.40
220E A29a	25ch multi	.40	.40
220F A29a	30ch multi	.40	.40
220G A29a	35ch multi	.40	.40
220H A29a	1nu multi	2.40	2.40
220I A29a	2nu multi	2.75	2.75
220J A29a	2.50nu multi	2.75	2.75
220K A29a	3nu multi	3.25	3.25
	Nos. 220A-220K (11)	13.95	13.95

Souvenir Sheets

220L A29a	5nu like #220C	5.50	5.00
220M A29a	10nu like #220F	12.50	12.50

Simulated 3-dimensions using a plastic overlay. Nos. 220H-220M are airmail.

Sizes of stamps: No. 220L, 59x70mm, No. 220M, 69x57mm.

Orchid
A30

Designs: Various flowers.

1976, May 29 Litho. *Perf. 14½*

221 A30	1ch multicolored	.25	.25
222 A30	2ch multicolored	.25	.25
223 A30	3ch multicolored	.25	.25
224 A30	4ch multicolored	.25	.25
225 A30	5ch multicolored	.25	.25
226 A30	2nu multicolored	.70	.70
227 A30	4nu multicolored	1.25	1.25
228 A30	6nu multicolored	2.00	2.00
	Nos. 221-228 (8)	5.20	5.20

Souvenir Sheet

Perf. 13½

229 A30	10nu multicolored	4.00	4.00

For surcharges see Nos. 263-264.

Double Carp Design
A31

Designs: Various symbolic designs and Colombo Plan emblem.

1976, July 1 Litho. *Perf. 14½*

230 A31	3ch red & multi	.25	.25
231 A31	4ch ver & multi	.25	.25
232 A31	5ch multicolored	.25	.25
233 A31	25ch bl & multi	.25	.25
234 A31	1.25nu multicolored	.35	.35
235 A31	2nu yel & multi	.60	.60
236 A31	2.50nu vio & multi	.75	.75
237 A31	3nu multicolored	.90	.90
	Nos. 230-237 (8)	3.60	3.60

Colombo Plan, 25th anniversary.

For surcharge see No. 265.

Bandaranaike Conference Hall — A32

1976, Aug. 16 Litho. *Perf. 13½*

238 A32	1.25nu multicolored	.80	.80
239 A32	2.50nu multicolored	1.90	1.90

5th Summit Conference of Non-aligned Countries, Colombo, Sri Lanka, Aug. 9-19.

Elizabeth II — A33

Liberty Bell — A34

Spirit of St. Louis — A35

Bhutanese Archer, Olympic Rings — A36

Designs: No. 242, Alexander Graham Bell. No. 245, LZ 3 Zeppelin docking, 1907. No. 246, Alfred B. Nobel.

1978, Nov. 15 Litho. *Perf. 14½*

240 A33	20nu multicolored	4.00	4.00
241 A34	20nu multicolored	5.25	5.25
242 A33	20nu multicolored	5.25	5.25
243 A35	20nu multicolored	5.25	5.25
244 A36	20nu multicolored	5.25	5.25
245 A35	20nu multicolored	6.75	6.75
246 A33	20nu multicolored	5.75	5.75
	Nos. 240-246 (7)	37.50	37.50

25th anniv. of coronation of Elizabeth II; American Bicentennial; cent. of 1st telephone call by Alexander Graham Bell; Charles A. Lindbergh crossing the Atlantic, 50th anniv.; Olympic Games; 75th anniv. of the Zeppelin; 75th anniv. of Nobel Prize. Seven souvenir sheets exist, each 25nu, commemorating same events with different designs. Size: 103x80mm. Value $50.

Issues of 1967-1976 Surcharged

Perforations and Printing as Before

1978

252 A16	25ch on 3nu (#133)		
253 A17	25ch on 6nu (#139)		
254 A21	25ch on 2.50nu (#172)		
255 A22	25ch on 3nu (#179)		
256 A22	25ch on 5nu (#180)		
257 A23	25ch on 10nu (#182)		
258 A23	25ch on 10nu (#183)		
259 A24	25ch on 10nu (#192)		
260 A28	25ch on 5nu (#210)		
261 A29	25ch on 4nu (#218)		
262 A29	25ch on 10nu (#219)		
263 A30	25ch on 4nu (#227)		
264 A30	25ch on 6nu (#228)		
265 A31	25ch on 2.50nu (#236)		
266 A14g	25ch on 5nu (#90E)		
267 A17k	25ch on 3nu (#155E)		
268 A17f	25ch on 4nu (#149L)		
269 A17f	25ch on 8nu (#149M)		
	Nos. 252-269, C31-C38	120.00	120.00

Mother and Child, IYC Emblem — A37

IYC Emblem and: 5nu, Mother and two children. 10nu, Boys with blackboards and stylus.

1979, June Litho. *Perf. 14x13½*

289 A37	2nu multicolored	.65	.65
290 A37	5nu multicolored	1.75	1.75
291 A37	10nu multicolored	3.00	3.00
a.	Souv. sheet of 3, #289-291 + label, perf. 15x13½	7.00	7.00
	Nos. 289-291 (3)	5.40	5.40

International Year of the Child.

Exist imperf. Values: set $8; souvenir sheet $11.

For overprints see Nos. 761-763.

Conference Emblem and Dove — A38

10nu, Emblem and Bhutanese symbols.

1979, Sept. 3 Litho. *Perf. 14x13½*

292 A38	25ch multicolored	.25	.25
293 A38	10nu multicolored	3.25	3.25

6th Non-Aligned Summit Conference, Havana, August 1979.

Silver Rattle, Dorji
A39

Antiques: 10ch, Silver handbell, Dilbu, vert. 15ch, Cylindrical jar, Jadum, vert. 25ch, Ornamental teapot, Jamjee. 1nu, Leather container, Kem, vert. 1.25nu, Brass teapot, Jamjee. 1.70nu, Vessel with elephant-head legs, Sangphor, vert. 2nu, Teapot with ornamental spout, Jamjee, vert. 3nu, Metal pot on claw-shaped feet, Yangtho, vert. 4nu, Dish inlaid with precious stones, Battha. 5nu, Metal circular flask, Chhap, vert.

1979, Dec. 17 Photo. *Perf. 14*

294 A39	5ch multicolored	.25	.25
295 A39	10ch multicolored	.25	.25
296 A39	15ch multicolored	.25	.25
297 A39	25ch multicolored	.25	.25
298 A39	1nu multicolored	.45	.45
299 A39	1.25nu multicolored	.50	.50
300 A39	1.70nu multicolored	.70	.70
301 A39	2nu multicolored	.90	.90
302 A39	3nu multicolored	1.25	1.25
303 A39	4nu multicolored	1.60	1.60
304 A39	5nu multicolored	2.25	2.25
	Nos. 294-304 (11)	8.65	8.65

For surcharges, see Nos. 1409, 1409A-1409B.

Hill, Rinpiang Dzong — A40

Hill Statue, Stamps of Bhutan and: 2nu, Dzong. 5nu, Ounsti Dzong. 10nu, Lingzi Dzong, Gt. Britain Type 81. 20nu, Rope bridge, Penny Black.

1980, Mar 15 Litho. *Perf. 14x13½*

305 A40	1nu multicolored	.40	.40
306 A40	2nu multicolored	.75	.75
307 A40	5nu multicolored	2.00	2.00
308 A40	10nu multicolored	3.75	3.75
	Nos. 305-308 (4)	6.90	6.90

Souvenir Sheet

309 A40 20nu multicolored 11.00 11.00

Sir Rowland Hill (1795-1879), originator of penny postage.
Exist imperf. Values, unused or used: set $7; souvenir sheet $9.

Kichu Lhakhang Monastery, Phari — A41

Guru Padma Sambhava's Birthday — Monasteries: 1nu, Dungtse, Phari, vert. 2.25nu, Kurjey. 3nu, Tangu, Thimphu. 4nu, Cheri, Thimphu. 5nu, Chorten, Kora. 7nu, Tak-Tsang, Phari, vert.

1981, July 11 Litho. *Perf. 14*

310 A41	1nu multi	.25	.25
311 A41	2nu shown	.40	.40
312 A41	2.25nu multi	.60	.60
313 A41	3nu multi	.70	.70
314 A41	4nu multi	.95	.95
315 A41	5nu multi	1.40	1.40
316 A41	7nu multi	1.75	1.75
	Nos. 310-316 (7)	6.05	6.05

Prince Charles and Lady Diana — A42

1nu, St. Paul's Cathedral.
No 321, Wedding procession.

1981, Sept. 10 Litho. *Perf. 14½*

317 A42	1nu multi	.80	.80
318 A42	5nu like #317	2.00	2.00
319 A42	20nu shown	3.00	3.00
320 A42	25nu like #319	3.25	3.25
	Nos. 317-320 (4)	9.05	9.05

Souvenir Sheet

321 A42 20nu multi 3.00 3.00

Royal wedding. Nos. 318-319 issued in sheets of 5 plus label.
For surcharges see Nos. 471-475.
Exist imperf. Values, unused or used: set $16; souvenir sheet $9.

Orange-bellied Chloropsis — A43

3nu, Monal pheasant. 5nu, Ward's trogon. 10nu, Mrs. Gould's sunbird.
25nu, Maroon oriole.

1982, Apr. 19 Litho. *Perf. 14*

322 A43	2nu shown	.70	.70
323 A43	3nu multi	1.75	1.75
324 A43	5nu multi	2.50	2.50
325 A43	10nu multi	2.75	2.75
	Nos. 322-325 (4)	7.70	7.70

Souvenir Sheet

326 A43 25nu multi 7.50 7.50

1982 World Cup — A44

Designs: Various soccer players.

1982, June 25 Litho. *Perf. 14½x14*

327 A44	1nu multicolored	.25	.25
328 A44	2nu multicolored	.60	.60
329 A44	3nu multicolored	.90	.90
330 A44	20nu multicolored	5.25	5.25
	Nos. 327-330 (4)	7.00	7.00

Souvenir Sheets

331 A44	25nu multicolored	6.00	6.00
331A A44	25nu multicolored	6.00	6.00

Nos. 331-331A have margins continuing design and listing finalists (No. 331, Algeria-Honduras; No. 331A, Hungary-Yugoslavia).
Nos. 327-331A exist imperf.
For surcharges see Nos. 481-485.

21st Birthday of Princess Diana — A45

1nu, St. James' Palace. 10nu, Diana, Charles. 15nu, Windsor Castle. 25nu, Wedding.
20nu, Diana.

1982, Aug.

332 A45	1nu multi	.50	.50
332A A45	10nu multi	4.50	4.50
332B A45	15nu multi	8.00	8.00
333 A45	25nu multi	12.00	12.00
	Nos. 332-333 (4)	25.00	25.00

Souvenir Sheet

334 A45 20nu multi 16.00 7.50

10nu-15nu issued only in sheets of 5 + label.
For overprints and surcharges see Nos. 361-363, 455-459, 476-480.
Exist imperf. Values unused or used: set $25; souvenir sheet $20.

Scouting Year A46

3nu, Baden-Powell, vert. 5nu, Eating around fire. 15nu, Reading map. 20nu, Pitching tents.
25nu, Mountain climbing.

1982, Aug. 23 Litho. *Perf. 14*

335 A46	3nu multi	.80	.80
336 A46	5nu multi	1.50	1.50
337 A46	15nu multi	4.50	4.50
338 A46	20nu multi	5.50	5.50
	Nos. 335-338 (4)	12.30	12.30

Souvenir Sheet

339 A46 25nu multi 8.00 8.00

For surcharges see Nos. 450-454, 559-563.
Exist imperf. Values unused or used: set $25; souvenir sheet $16.

Rama and Cubs with Mowgli — A47

Scenes from Disney's The Jungle Book.
No. 349, Baloo and Mowgli in forest. No. 350, Baloo and Mowgli floating.

1982, Sept. 1 *Perf. 11*

340 A47	1ch multicolored	.25	.25
341 A47	2ch multicolored	.25	.25
342 A47	3ch multicolored	.25	.25
343 A47	4ch multicolored	.25	.25
344 A47	5ch multicolored	.25	.25
345 A47	10ch multicolored	.25	.25
346 A47	30ch multicolored	.25	.25
347 A47	2nu multicolored	.40	.40
348 A47	20nu multicolored	6.00	6.00
	Nos. 340-348 (9)	8.15	8.15

Souvenir Sheets
Perf. 13½

349 A47	20nu multicolored	6.50	6.50
350 A47	20nu multicolored	6.50	6.50

George Washington Surveying — A48

1nu, FDR, Harvard. 2nu, Washington at Valley Forge. 3nu, FDR, family. 4nu, Washington, Battle of Monmouth. 5nu, FDR, White House. 15nu, Washington, Mt. Vernon. 20nu, FDR, Churchill, Stalin.
No. 359, Washington, vert. No. 360, FDR, vert.

1982, Nov. 15 Litho. *Perf. 15*

351 A48	50ch shown	.25	.25
352 A48	1nu multi	.30	.30
353 A48	2nu multi	.35	.35
354 A48	3nu multi	.50	.50
355 A48	4nu multi	.70	.70
356 A48	5nu multi	1.00	1.00
357 A48	15nu multi	2.50	2.50
358 A48	20nu multi	3.25	3.25
	Nos. 351-358 (8)	8.85	8.85

Souvenir Sheets

359 A48	25nu multi	4.50	4.50
360 A48	25nu multi	4.50	4.50

Washington and Franklin D. Roosevelt.
Exist imperf. Values unused or used: set $12; souvenir sheet each $6.

Nos. 332-334 Overprinted: "ROYAL BABY / 21.6.82"

1982, Nov. 19 *Perf. 14½x14*

361 A45	1nu multicolored	.25	.25
361A A45	10nu multicolored	2.50	2.50
361B A45	15nu multicolored	3.50	3.50
362 A45	25nu multicolored	5.75	5.75
	Nos. 361-362 (4)	12.00	12.00

Souvenir Sheet

363 A45 20nu multicolored 7.50 7.50

Birth of Prince William of Wales, June 21.
Exist imperf. Values unused or used: set $17; souvenir sheet $12.

500th Birth Anniv. of Raphael A51

Portraits: 1nu, Angelo Doni. 4nu, Maddalena Doni. 5nu, Baldassare Castiglione. 20nu, La Donna Velata.
No. 379, Expulsion of Heliodorus. No. 380, Mass of Bolsena.

1983, Mar. 23 *Perf. 13½*

375 A51	1nu multi	.30	.30
376 A51	4nu multi	1.10	1.10
377 A51	5nu multi	1.50	1.50
378 A51	20nu multi	6.00	6.00
	Nos. 375-378 (4)	8.90	8.90

Souvenir Sheets

379 A51	25nu multi	8.00	8.00
380 A51	25nu multi	8.00	8.00

Exist imperf. Values unused or used: set $9; souvenir sheets each $6.25.

Nos. 184, 155F, 139, 147G, 149M Srchd. or Ovptd. "Druk Air"

1983, Feb. 11

381 A24	30ch on 1ch multi	2.00	2.00
382 A17k	5nu multicolored	2.75	2.75
383 A17	6nu multicolored	3.00	3.00
384 A17d	7nu multicolored	4.25	4.25
385 A17f	8nu multicolored	4.50	4.50
	Nos. 381-385 (5)	16.50	16.50

Druk Air Service inauguration. Overprint of 8nu all caps. Nos. 382, 384 air mail.

Manned Flight Bicentenary — A52

1983, Aug. 15 Litho. *Perf. 15*

386 A52	50ch Dornier Wal	.25	.25
387 A52	3nu Savoia-Marchetti S-66	.95	.95
388 A52	10nu Hawker Osprey	2.50	2.50
389 A52	20nu Ville de Paris	5.00	5.00
	Nos. 386-389 (4)	8.70	8.70

Souvenir Sheet

390 A52 25nu Balloon Captif 7.50 7.50

Exist imperf. Values unused or used: set $25; souvenir sheet $7.

Buddhist Symbols — A53

25ch, Sacred vase. 50ch, Five Sensory Symbols. 2nu, Seven Treasures. 3nu, Five Sensory Organs. 8nu, Five Fleshes. 9nu, Sacrificial cake.

1983, Aug. 11 Litho. *Perf. 13½*

391 A53	25ch multicolored	.25	.25
392 A53	50ch multicolored	.25	.25
393 A53	2nu multicolored	.40	.40
394 A53	3nu multicolored	.85	.85
395 A53	8nu multicolored	1.90	1.90
396 A53	9nu multicolored	2.50	2.50
a.	Souv. sheet of 6, #391-396	7.50	7.50
	Nos. 391-396 (6)	6.15	6.15

Size of Nos. 393, 396: 45x40mm.

World Communications Year (1983) — A54

Various Disney characters and history of communications.

No. 406, Donald Duck on phone, horiz. No. 407, Mickey Mouse on TV.

1984, Apr. 10 Litho. *Perf. 14½x14*

397 A54 4ch multicolored .25 .25
398 A54 5ch multicolored .25 .25
399 A54 10ch multicolored .25 .25
400 A54 20ch multicolored .25 .25
401 A54 25ch multicolored .25 .25
402 A54 50ch multicolored .25 .25
403 A54 1nu multicolored .50 .50
404 A54 5nu multicolored 1.50 1.50
405 A54 20nu multicolored 4.25 4.25
Nos. 397-405 (9) 7.75 7.75

Souvenir Sheets

Perf. 14x14½

406 A54 20nu multicolored 5.50 5.50
407 A54 20nu multicolored 5.50 5.50

Nos. 397-407 exist imperf.

1984 Winter Olympics — A55

50ch, Skiing. 1nu, Cross-country skiing. 3nu, Speed skating. 20nu, Bobsledding. 25nu, Hockey.

1984, June 16 *Perf. 14*

408 A55 50ch multicolored .30 .30
409 A55 1nu multicolored .40 .40
410 A55 3nu multicolored .75 .75
411 A55 20nu multicolored 4.00 4.00
Nos. 408-411 (4) 5.45 5.45

Souvenir Sheet

412 A55 25nu multicolored 6.25 6.25

Exist imperf. Values unused or used: set $7; souvenir sheet $7.

Golden Langur (WWF) — A56

1nu, Group in tree, horiz. 2nu, Family, horiz. 4nu, Group walking.

No. 417, Snow leopard. No. 418, Yak. No. 419, Blue sheep, horiz.

1984, June 10 Litho. *Perf. 14½*

413 A56 50ch shown .70 .70
414 A56 1nu multicolored .70 .70
415 A56 2nu multicolored 1.75 1.75
416 A56 4nu multicolored 3.25 3.25
Nos. 413-416 (4) 6.40 6.40

Souvenir Sheets

417 A56 20nu multicolored 8.00 8.00
418 A56 25nu multicolored 8.00 8.00
419 A56 25nu multicolored 8.00 8.00

Locomotives A57

50ch, Sans Pareil, 1829. 1nu, Planet, 1830. 3nu, Experiment, 1832. 4nu, Black Hawk, 1835. 5.50nu, Jenny Lind, 1847. 8nu, Semmering-Bavaria, 1851. 10nu, Great Northern #1, 1870. 25nu, German Natl. Tinder, 1880.

No. 428, Darjeeling Himalayan Railway, 1984. No. 429, Sondermann Freight, 1896. No. 430, Crampton's locomotive, 1846. No. 431, Erzsebet, 1870.

1984, July 16

420 A57 50ch multi .25 .25
421 A57 1nu multi .30 .30
422 A57 3nu multi .65 .65
423 A57 4nu multi 1.00 1.00
424 A57 5.50nu multi 1.25 1.25
425 A57 8nu multi 1.75 1.75
426 A57 10nu multi 2.10 2.10
427 A57 25nu multi 5.50 5.50
Nos. 420-427 (8) 12.80 12.80

Souvenir Sheets

428 A57 20nu multi 5.00 5.00
429 A57 20nu multi 5.00 5.00
430 A57 20nu multi 5.00 5.00
431 A57 20nu multi 5.00 5.00

Nos. 424-427 horiz.

Classic Cars A58

50ch, Riley Sprite, 1936. 1nu, Lanchester, 1919. 3nu, Itala, 1907. 4nu, Morris Oxford Bullnose, 1913. 5.50nu, Lagonda LG6, 1939. 6nu, Wolseley, 1903. 8nu, Buick Super, 1952. 20nu, Maybach Zeppelin, 1933.

No. 440, Simplex, 1912. No. 441, Renault, 1901.

1984, Aug. 29 Litho. *Perf. 14*

432 A58 50ch multi .25 .25
433 A58 1nu multi .30 .30
434 A58 3nu multi .70 .70
435 A58 4nu multi 1.00 1.00
436 A58 5.50nu multi 1.25 1.25
437 A58 6nu multi 1.40 1.40
438 A58 8nu multi 1.60 1.60
439 A58 20nu multi 3.75 3.75
Nos. 432-439 (8) 10.25 10.25

Souvenir Sheets

440 A58 25nu multi 5.00 5.00
441 A58 25nu multi 5.00 5.00

Summer Olympic Games — A59

15ch, Women's archery. 25ch, Men's archery. 2nu, Table tennis. 2.25nu, Basketball. 5.50nu, Boxing. 6nu, Running. 8nu, Tennis. 25nu, Archery.

1984, Oct. 27 Litho.

442 A59 15ch multi .25 .25
443 A59 25ch multi .25 .25
444 A59 2nu multi .65 .65
445 A59 2.25nu multi .95 .95
446 A59 5.50nu multi 1.25 1.25
447 A59 6nu multi 1.50 1.50
448 A59 8nu multi 2.25 2.25
Nos. 442-448 (7) 7.10 7.10

Souvenir Sheet

449 A59 25nu multi 6.75 6.75

For overprints see Nos. 537-544.

Exist imperf. Values unused or used: set $8; souvenir sheet $7.

Nos. 335-339 Surcharged with New Values and Bars in Black or Silver

1985 Litho. *Perf. 14*

450 A46 10nu on 3nu multi 2.50 2.25
451 A46 10nu on 5nu multi 2.50 2.25
452 A46 10nu on 15nu multi 2.50 2.25
453 A46 10nu on 20nu multi 2.50 2.25
Nos. 450-453 (4) 10.00 9.00

Souvenir Sheet

454 A46 20nu on 25nu multi 6.00 6.00

Nos. 450-454 exist imperf. Value, set Nos. 450-453: $100.

Nos. 332, 332A, 332B, 333-334 Surcharged with New Values and Bars

1985, Feb. 28

455 A45 5nu on 1nu multi 1.45 1.30
456 A45 5nu on 10nu multi 1.45 1.30
457 A45 5nu on 15nu multi 1.45 1.30
458 A45 40nu on 25nu multi 11.00 11.00
Nos. 455-458 (4) 15.35 14.90

Souvenir Sheet

459 A45 25nu on 20nu multi 11.00 11.00

Nos. 455-459 exist imperf.

50th Anniv. of Donald Duck — A60

4ch, Magician Mickey. 5ch, Slide, Donald, Slide. 10ch, Donald's Golf Game. 20ch, Mr. Duck Steps Out. 25ch, Lion Around. 50ch, Alpine Climbers. 1nu, Flying Jalopy. 5nu, Frank Duck. 20nu, Good Scouts.

No. 469, Three Caballeros. No. 470, Sea Scouts.

1984, Dec. 10 Litho. *Perf. 13½x14*

460 A60 4ch multicolored .25 .25
461 A60 5ch multicolored .25 .25
462 A60 10ch multicolored .25 .25
463 A60 20ch multicolored .25 .25
464 A60 25ch multicolored .25 .25
465 A60 50ch multicolored .25 .25
466 A60 1nu multicolored .25 .25
467 A60 5nu multicolored 1.00 1.00
468 A60 20nu multicolored 4.50 4.50
Nos. 460-468 (9) 7.25 7.25

Souvenir Sheets

469 A60 20nu multicolored 6.00 6.00
470 A60 20nu multicolored 6.00 6.00

Exist imperf. Values unused or used: set $12; souvenir sheets each $7.

Nos. 317-321 Surcharged with New Values and Bars

1985, Feb. 28 Litho. *Perf. 14½*

471 A42 10nu on 1nu multi 4.50 4.00
472 A42 10nu on 5nu multi 4.50 4.00
473 A42 10nu on 20nu multi 4.50 4.00
474 A42 10nu on 25nu multi 4.50 4.00
Nos. 471-474 (4) 18.00 16.00

Souvenir Sheet

475 A42 30nu on 20nu multi 11.00 11.00

Nos. 471-475 exist imperf.

Nos. 361, 361A, 361B, 362-363 Surcharged with New Values and Bars

1985, Feb. 28 *Perf. 14½x14*

476 A45 5nu on 1nu multi 1.45 1.30
477 A45 5nu on 10nu multi 1.45 1.30
478 A45 5nu on 15nu multi 1.45 1.30
479 A45 40nu on 25nu multi 11.00 11.00
Nos. 476-479 (4) 15.35 14.90

Souvenir Sheet

480 A45 25nu on 20nu multi 11.00 9.00

Nos. 476-480 exist imperf.

Nos. 327-331A Surcharged with New Values and Bars in Black or Silver

1985, June

481 A44 5nu on 1nu multi 2.25 2.00
482 A44 5nu on 2nu multi 2.25 2.00
483 A44 5nu on 3nu multi 2.25 2.00
484 A44 5nu on 20nu multi 2.25 2.00
Nos. 481-484 (4) 9.00 8.00

Souvenir Sheets

485 A44 20nu on 25nu multi 4.50 4.25
485A A44 20nu on 25nu multi 4.50 4.25

Nos. 481-485A exist imperf.

Mask Dance of the Judgement of Death — A61

5ch, Shinje Choegyel. 35ch, Raksh Lango. 50ch, Druelgo. 2.50nu, Pago. 3nu, Telgo. 4nu, Due Nakcung. 5nu, Lha Karpo. 5.50nu, Nyalbum. 6nu, Khimda Pelkyi.

1985, Apr. 27 *Perf. 13½*

486 A61 5ch multi .35 .35
487 A61 35ch multi .35 .35
488 A61 50ch multi .35 .35
489 A61 2.50nu multi .50 .50
490 A61 3nu multi .70 .70
491 A61 4nu multi .90 .90
492 A61 5nu multi 1.00 1.00
a. Souv. sheet, #486-487, 491-492 4.50 4.50
493 A61 5.50nu multi 1.25 1.25
494 A61 6nu multi 1.40 1.40
Nos. 486-494 (9) 6.80 6.80

For overprints see Nos. 764-772.

No. 492a was sold by the Bhutan post office uncut, at twice the height of the normal souvenir sheet with the lower half blank. Value, $20.

Monasteries A62

10ch, Domkhar. 25ch, Shemgang. 50ch, Chapcha. 1nu, Tashigang. 2nu, Pungthang Chhug. 5nu, Dechhenphoda.

1984, Dec. 1 Litho. *Perf. 12*

495 A62 10ch chalky blue .30 .30
496 A62 25ch lake brown .30 .30
497 A62 50ch brt violet .30 .30
498 A62 1nu brown .30 .30
499 A62 2nu red .45 .45
500 A62 5nu olive green 1.00 1.00
Nos. 495-500 (6) 2.65 2.65

For surcharges, see Nos. 1344-1347B.

Veteran's War Memorial Building, San Francisco A63

50ch, Flags of Bhutan, UN, vert. 15nu, Headquarters, NY, vert.

25nu, UN Human Rights Declaration.

1985, Oct. 24 Litho. *Perf. 14*

502 A63 50ch multicolored .25 .25
503 A63 15nu multicolored 2.75 2.75
504 A63 20nu shown 3.75 3.75
Nos. 502-504 (3) 6.75 6.75

Souvenir Sheet

505 A63 25nu multicolored 6.50 6.50

UN, 40th anniv.

Audubon Birth Bicentenary — A64

Illustrations of North American bird species by Audubon: 50ch, Anas breweri. 1nu, Lagopus lagopus. 2nu, Charadrius montanus.

3nu, Gavia stellata. 4nu, Canachites canadensis. 5nu, Mergus cucullatus. 15nu, Olor buccinator. 20nu, Bucephala clangula.
No. 514, Accipiter striatus. No. 515, Parus bicolor.

1985

506	A64 50ch multicolored	.25	.25
507	A64 1nu multicolored	.35	.35
508	A64 2nu multicolored	.55	.55
509	A64 3nu multicolored	.60	.60
510	A64 4nu multicolored	.90	.90
511	A64 5nu multicolored	1.00	1.00
512	A64 15nu multicolored	2.50	2.50
513	A64 20nu multicolored	4.00	4.00
	Nos. 506-513 (8)	10.15	10.15

Souvenir Sheets

514	A64 25nu multicolored	5.00	5.00
515	A64 25nu multicolored	5.00	5.00

Issued: Nos. 507, 510-512, 514, 11/15; Nos. 506, 508-509, 513, 515, 12/6.
Exist imperf. Values unused or used: set $20; souvenir sheets, each $7.50.

A Tramp Abroad, by Mark Twain (1835-1910) A65

Walt Disney animated characters.
25nu, Goofy, Mickey Mouse.

1985, Nov. 15

516	A65 50ch multicolored	.30	.25
517	A65 2nu multicolored	.50	.50
518	A65 5nu multicolored	1.10	1.10
519	A65 9nu multicolored	2.00	2.00
520	A65 20nu multicolored	4.25	4.25
	Nos. 516-520 (5)	8.15	8.10

Souvenir Sheet

521	A65 25nu multicolored	6.50	6.50

Intl. Youth Year.
For overprints see Nos. 554, 556-557.
Nos. 516-521 exist imperf.

Rapunzel, by Jacob and Wilhelm Grimm A66

Walt Disney animated characters.

1985, Nov. 15

522	A66 1nu multicolored	.25	.25
523	A66 4nu multicolored	.75	.75
524	A66 7nu multicolored	1.40	1.40
525	A66 8nu multicolored	1.75	1.75
526	A66 15nu multicolored	3.00	3.00
	Nos. 522-526 (5)	7.15	7.15

Souvenir Sheet

527	A66 25nu multicolored	6.50	6.50

No. 525 printed in sheets of 8.
For overprints see Nos. 553, 555, 558.
Nos. 522-527 exist imperf.

First South Asian Regional Cooperation Summit, Dec. 7-8, Dacca, Bangladesh A67

1985, Dec. 8 *Perf. 14*

528	A67 50ch multicolored	.25	.25
529	A67 5nu multicolored	1.00	1.00

Seven Precious Attributes of the Universal King — A68

1986, Feb. 12 Litho. *Perf. 13x12½*

530	A68 30ch Wheel	.25	.25
531	A68 50ch Gem	.25	.25
532	A68 1.25nu Queen	.25	.25
533	A68 2nu Minister	.45	.45
534	A68 4nu Elephant	.80	.80
535	A68 6nu Horse	1.25	1.25
536	A68 8nu General	1.60	1.60
	Nos. 530-536 (7)	4.85	4.85

Nos. 442-443, 445-449 Ovptd. with Medal, Winners' Names and Countries. No. 449 Ovptd. for Men's and Women's Events

15ch, Hyang Soon Seo, So. Korea. 25ch, Darrell Pace, US. 2.25nu, Gold Medal, US. 5.50nu, Mark Breland, US. 6nu, Daley Thompson, Britain. 8nu, Stefan Edberg, Sweden.
No. 543, Hyang Soon Seo. No. 544, Darrel Pace.

1986, May 5 Litho. *Perf. 14*

537	A59 15ch multi	.25	.25
538	A59 25ch multi	.25	.25
539	A59 2.25nu multi	.45	.45
540	A59 5.50nu multi	1.10	1.10
541	A59 6nu multi	1.25	1.25
542	A59 8nu multi	1.60	1.60
	Nos. 537-542 (6)	4.90	4.90

Souvenir Sheets

543	A59 25nu multi	5.00	5.00
544	A59 25nu multi	5.00	5.00

Nos. 537-544 exist imperf.

Kilkhor Mandalas, Deities — A69

Religious art: 10ch, 1nu, Phurpa, ritual dagger. 25ch, 3nu, Amitayus in wrath. 50ch, 5nu, Overpowering Deities. 75ch, 7nu, Great Wrathful One, Guru Rinpoche.

1986, June 17 *Perf. 13½*

545	A69 10ch multicolored	.50	.50
546	A69 25ch multicolored	.50	.50
547	A69 50ch multicolored	.50	.50
548	A69 75ch multicolored	.50	.50
549	A69 1nu multicolored	.50	.50
550	A69 3nu multicolored	.65	.65
551	A69 5nu multicolored	1.10	1.10
552	A69 7nu multicolored	1.60	1.60
	Nos. 545-552 (8)	5.85	5.85

Nos. 525, 519, 526, 520, 521 and 527 Ovptd. with AMERIPEX '86 Emblem

1986, June 16 Litho. *Perf. 14*

553	A66 8nu multi	1.40	1.40
554	A65 9nu multi	2.25	2.25
555	A66 15nu multi	3.50	3.50
556	A65 20nu multi	4.50	4.50
	Nos. 553-556 (4)	11.65	11.65

Souvenir Sheets

557	A65 25nu #521	6.00	6.00
558	A66 25nu #527	6.00	6.00

Nos. 553-558 exist imperf. Value, set Nos. 553-556: $100.

Nos. 335-339 Overprinted

1986, July 23 Litho. *Perf. 14*

559	A46 3nu multi	1.90	1.90
560	A46 5nu multi	3.75	3.75
561	A46 15nu multi	10.00	10.00
562	A46 20nu multi	14.00	14.00
	Nos. 559-562 (4)	29.65	29.65

Souvenir Sheet

563	A46 25nu multi	15.00	15.00

Nos. 559-563 exist imperf. Value, set Nos. 559-562: $100.

A70

A71

Halley's Comet — A72

Designs: 50ch, Babylonian tablet fragments, 2349 B.C. sighting. 1nu, 17th cent. print, A.D. 66 sighting. 2nu, French silhouette art, 1835 sighting. 3nu, Bayeux Tapestry, 1066 sighting. 4nu, Woodblock, 684 sighting. 5nu, Illustration from Bybel Printen, 1650. 15nu, 1456 Sighting, Cancer constellation. 20nu, Delft plate, 1910 sighting. No. 572, Comet over Himalayas. No. 573, Comet over domed temple Dug-gye Jong.

1986, Nov. 4 Litho. *Perf. 15*

564	A70 50ch multicolored	.30	.30
565	A70 1nu multicolored	.30	.30
566	A71 2nu multicolored	.45	.45
567	A70 3nu multicolored	.60	.60
568	A70 4nu multicolored	.90	.90
569	A71 5nu multicolored	1.10	1.10
570	A70 15nu multicolored	3.00	3.00
571	A70 20nu multicolored	4.50	4.50
	Nos. 564-571 (8)	11.15	11.15

Souvenir Sheets

572	A72 25nu multicolored	5.00	5.00
573	A72 25nu multicolored	5.00	5.00

Exist imperf. Values unused or used: set $20; souvenir sheets, each $11.

A73

Statue of Liberty, Cent. — A74

Statue and ships: 50ch, Mircea, Romania. 1nu, Shalom, Israel. 2nu, Leonardo da Vinci, Italy. 3nu, Libertad, Argentina. 4nu, France, France. 5nu, SS United States, US. 15nu, Queen Elizabeth II, England. 20nu, Europa, West Germany. No. 582, Statue. No. 583, Statue, World Trade Center.

1986, Nov. 4

574	A73 50ch multicolored	.25	.25
575	A73 1nu multicolored	.25	.25
576	A73 2nu multicolored	.45	.45
577	A73 3nu multicolored	.65	.65
578	A73 4nu multicolored	.80	.80
579	A73 5nu multicolored	1.10	1.10
580	A73 15nu multicolored	3.00	3.00
581	A73 20nu multicolored	4.50	4.50
	Nos. 574-581 (8)	11.00	11.00

Souvenir Sheets

582	A74 25nu multicolored	5.00	5.00
583	A74 25nu multi, diff.	5.00	5.00

Exist imperf. Values unused or used: set $11; souvenir sheets each $6.

Discovery of America, 500th Anniv. — A75

20ch, Santa Maria. 25ch, Queen Isabella. 50ch, Ship, flying fish. 1nu, Columbus's coat of arms. 2nu, Christopher Columbus. 3nu, Landing in the New World.
No. 590, Pineapple. No. 591, Indian hammock. No. 592, Tobacco plant. No. 593, Flamingo. No. 594, Navigator, astrolabe, 15th cent. No. 595, Lizard. No. 596, Iguana.

1987, May 25 Litho. *Perf. 14*

584	A75 20ch multicolored	.90	.90
585	A75 25ch multicolored	.90	.90
586	A75 50ch multicolored	.90	.90
587	A75 1nu multicolored	1.75	1.75
588	A75 2nu multicolored	3.00	3.00
589	A75 3nu multicolored	4.50	4.50
a.	Miniature sheet of 6, #584-589	16.00	16.00
	Nos. 584-589 (6)	11.95	11.95

Souvenir Sheets

590	A75 20ch multicolored	2.50	2.50
591	A75 25ch multicolored	2.50	2.50
592	A75 50ch multicolored	2.50	2.50
593	A75 1nu multicolored	2.50	2.50
594	A75 2nu multicolored	2.50	2.50
595	A75 3nu multicolored	2.50	2.50
596	A75 5nu multicolored	2.50	2.50

All stamps are vertical except those contained in Nos. 591, 595 and 596. Stamps from No. 589a have white background.
Exist imperf. Values unused or used: set $18; souvenir sheets each $4. Value No. 589a imperf, $40.

CAPEX '87 — A76

Locomotives: 50ch, Canadian Natl. U1-f. 1nu, Via Rail L.R.C. 2nu, Canadian Natl. GM GF-30t. 3nu, Canadian Natl. 4-8-4. 8nu, Canadian Pacific 4-6-2. 10nu, Via Express passenger train. 15nu, Canadian Nat. Turbotrain. 20nu, Canadian Pacific Diesel-Electric Express.
No. 605, Royal Hudson 4-6-4. No. 606, Canadian Natl. 4-8-4, diff.

1987, June 15

597	A76	50ch	multicolored	.25	.25
598	A76	1nu	multicolored	.25	.25
599	A76	2nu	multicolored	.45	.45
600	A76	3nu	multicolored	.75	.75
601	A76	8nu	multicolored	1.75	1.75
602	A76	10nu	multicolored	1.90	1.90
603	A76	15nu	multicolored	2.50	2.50
604	A76	20nu	multicolored	3.25	3.25
			Nos. 597-604 (8)	11.10	11.10

Souvenir Sheet

605	A76	25nu	multicolored	5.50	5.50
606	A76	25nu	multicolored	5.50	5.50

Two Faces, Sculpture by Marc Chagall (1887-1984) A77

Paintings: 1nu, At the Barber's. 2nu, Old Jew with Torah. 3nu, Red Maternity. 4nu, Eve of Yom Kippur. 5nu, The Old Musician. 6nu, The Rabbi of Vitebsk. 7nu, Couple at Dusk. 9nu, The Artistes. 10nu, Moses Breaking the Tablets of the Law. 12nu, Bouquet with Flying Lovers. 20nu, In the Sky of the Opera.

No. 619, Romeo and Juliet. No. 620, Magician of Paris. No. 621, Maternity. No. 622, The Carnival for Aleko: Scene II. No. 623, Visit to the Grandparents. No. 624, The Smolensk Newspaper. No. 625, The Concert. No. 626, Composition with Goat. No. 627, Still Life. No. 628. The Red Gateway. No. 629, Cow with Parasol. No. 630, Russian Village.

1987, Dec. 17 Litho. *Perf. 14*

607-618	A77	Set of 12	20.00	20.00

Size: 110x95mm

Imperf

619-630	A77	25nu Set of 12	65.00	65.00

1988 Winter Olympics, Calgary — A78

Emblem and Disney animated characters as competitors in Olympic events: 50ch, Slalom. 1nu, Downhill skiing. 2nu, Ice hockey. 4nu, Biathlon. 7nu, Speed skating. 8nu, Minnie Mouse(yellow outfit) figure skating. 9nu, Minnie Mouse (red outfit) figure skating. 20nu, Bobsled.

No. 639, Ski jumping. No. 640, Ice dancing.

1988, Feb. 15 Litho. *Perf. 14*

631	A78	50ch	multi	.30	.30
632	A78	1nu	multi	.30	.30
633	A78	2nu	multi	.50	.50
634	A78	4nu	multi	1.00	1.00
635	A78	7nu	multi	1.75	1.75
636	A78	8nu	multi	2.00	2.00
637	A78	9nu	multi	2.40	2.40
638	A78	20nu	multi	5.00	5.00
			Nos. 631-638 (8)	13.25	13.25

Souvenir Sheets

639	A78	25nu	multi	6.25	6.25
640	A78	25nu	multi	6.25	6.25

Nos. 631-640 exist imperf.

Transportation Innovations — A79

50ch, Pullman Pioneer, 1865. 1nu, Stephenson's Rocket, 1829. 2nu, Pierre L'Allement's Velocipede, 1866. 3nu, Benz Velocipede, 1886. 4nu, Volkswagen Beetle, c. 1960. 5nu, Natchez Vs. Robert E. Lee, 1870. 6nu, American La France, 1910. 7nu, USS Constitution, 1787, vert. 9nu, Bell Rocket Belt, 1961, vert. 10nu, Trevithick Locomotive, 1804.

No. 651, Concorde jet. No. 652, Mallard, 1938, vert. No. 653, Shinkansen. No. 654, TGV, 1981.

1988, Mar. 31

641	A79	50ch	multicolored	.25	.25
642	A79	1nu	multicolored	.25	.25
643	A79	2nu	multicolored	.35	.35
644	A79	3nu	multicolored	.50	.50
645	A79	4nu	multicolored	.60	.60
646	A79	5nu	multicolored	.70	.70
647	A79	6nu	multicolored	.90	.90
648	A79	7nu	multicolored	1.00	1.00
649	A79	9nu	multicolored	1.45	1.45
650	A79	10nu	multicolored	1.50	1.50
			Nos. 641-650 (10)	7.50	7.50

Souvenir Sheets

651	A79	25nu	multicolored	6.00	6.00
652	A79	25nu	multicolored	6.00	6.00
653	A79	25nu	multicolored	6.00	6.00
654	A79	25nu	multicolored	6.00	6.00

1988 Summer Olympics, Seoul A80

50ch, Women's gymnastics. 1nu, Tae kwon do. 2nu, Shot put. 4nu, Women's volleyball. 7nu, Basketball. 8nu, Soccer. 9nu, Women's high jump. 20nu, Running.

No. 663, Archery, vert. No. 664, Fencing.

Nos. 7nu-20nu are vertical stamps.

1989, Feb. 15 Litho.

655	A80	50ch	multicolored	.25	.25
656	A80	1nu	multicolored	.25	.25
657	A80	2nu	multicolored	.35	.35
658	A80	4nu	multicolored	.75	.75
659	A80	7nu	multicolored	1.25	1.25
660	A80	8nu	multicolored	1.50	1.50
661	A80	9nu	multicolored	1.75	1.75
662	A80	20nu	multicolored	3.75	3.75
			Nos. 655-662 (8)	9.85	9.85

Souvenir Sheets

663	A80	25nu	multicolored	5.00	5.00
664	A80	25nu	multicolored	5.00	5.00

Exist imperf. Values unused or used: set $10; souvenir sheets each $5.

Paintings by Titian — A81

Designs: 50ch, *Gentleman with a Book.* 1nu, *Venus and Cupid, with a Lute Player.* 2nu, *Diana and Actaeon.* 3nu, *Cardinal Ippolito dei Medici.* 4nu, *Sleeping Venus.* 5nu, *Venus Risen from the Waves.* 6nu, *Worship of Venus.* 7nu, *Fete Champetre.* 10nu, *Perseus and Andromeda.* 15nu, *Danae.* 20nu, *Venus at the Mirror.* 25nu, *Venus and the Organ Player.* No. 677, *The Pardo Venus,* horiz. No. 678, *Venus and Cupid, with an Organist.* No. 679, *Miracle of the Irascible Son.* No. 680, *Diana and Callisto.* No. 681, *Saint John the Almsgiver.* No. 682, *Danae with the Shower of Gold,* horiz. No. 683, *Bacchus and Ariadne.* No. 684, *Venus Blindfolding Cupid.* No. 685, *Portrait of Laura Dianti.* No. 686, *Venus of Urbino.* No. 687, *Portrait of Johann Friedrich.* No. 688, *Mater Dolorosa with Raised Hands.*

Perf. 13½x14, 14x13½

1989, Feb. 15 Litho.

665	A81	50ch	multicolored	.25	.25
666	A81	1nu	multicolored	.30	.30
667	A81	2nu	multicolored	.50	.50
668	A81	3nu	multicolored	.70	.70
669	A81	4nu	multicolored	.85	.85
670	A81	5nu	multicolored	1.25	1.25
671	A81	6nu	multicolored	1.40	1.40
672	A81	7nu	multicolored	1.60	1.60
673	A81	10nu	multicolored	2.10	2.10
674	A81	15nu	multicolored	3.25	3.25
675	A81	20nu	multicolored	4.00	4.00
676	A81	25nu	multicolored	5.00	5.00
			Nos. 665-676 (12)	21.20	21.20

Souvenir Sheets

677-688	A81	25nu Set of 12	60.00	60.00

Mickey Mouse, 60th Anniv. (in 1988) — A82

Movie posters: 1ch, Mickey Mouse, 1930s. 2ch, *Barnyard Olympics,* 1932. 3ch, *Society Dog Show,* 1939. 4ch, *Fantasia,* 1980s re-release. 5ch, *The Mad Dog,* 1932. 10ch, *A Gentleman's Gentleman,* 1941. 50ch, *Symphony hour,* 1942. 10nu, *The Moose Hunt,* 1931. 15nu, *Wild Waves,* 1929. 20nu, *Mickey in Arabia,* 1932. 25nu, *Tugboat Mickey,* 1940. 30nu, *Building a Building,* 1933.

No. 701, *The Mad Doctor,* 1933. No. 702, *The Meller Drammer,* 1933. No. 703, *Ye Olden Days,* 1933. No. 704, *Mickey's Good Deed,* 1932. No. 705, *Mickey's Pal Pluto,* 1933. No. 706, *Trader Mickey,* 1932. No. 707, *Touchdown Mickey,* 1932. No. 708, *Steamboat Willie,* 1928. No. 709, *The Whoopee Party,* 1932. No. 710, *Mickey's Nightmare,* 1932. No. 711, *The Klondike Kid,* 1932. No. 712, *The Wayward Canary,* 1932.

1989, June 20 Litho. *Perf. 13½x14*

689-700	A82	Set of 12	22.50	22.50

Souvenir Sheets

701-712	A82	25nu Set of 12	65.00	65.00

Mushrooms — A83

Designs: 50ch, Tricholoma pardalotum. 1nu, Suillus placidus. 2nu, Boletus regius. 3nu, Gomphidius glutinosus. 4nu, Boletus calopus. 5nu, Suillus grevillei. 6nu, Boletus appendiculatus. 7nu, Lactarius torminosus. 10nu, Macrolepiota rhacodes. 15nu, Amanita rubescens. 20nu, Amanita phalloides. No. 724, Amanita citrina.

No. 725, Russula aurata. No. 726, Gyroporus castaneus. No. 727, Cantharellus cibarius. No. 728, Boletus rhodoxanthus. No. 729, Paxillus involutus. No. 730, Gyroporus cyanescens. No. 731, Lepista nuda. No. 732, Dentinum repandum. No. 733, Lepista saeva. No. 734, Hydnum imbricatum. No. 735, Xerocomus subtomentosus. No. 736, Russula olivacea.

1989, Aug. 22 Litho. *Perf. 14*

713	A83	50ch	multicolored	.25	.25
714	A83	1nu	multicolored	.25	.25
715	A83	2nu	multicolored	.40	.40
716	A83	3nu	multicolored	.65	.65
717	A83	4nu	multicolored	.80	.80
718	A83	5nu	multicolored	1.00	1.00
719	A83	6nu	multicolored	1.10	1.10
720	A83	7nu	multicolored	1.40	1.40
721	A83	10nu	multicolored	2.00	2.00
722	A83	15nu	multicolored	3.00	3.00
723	A83	20nu	multicolored	4.00	4.00
724	A83	25nu	multicolored	5.00	5.00
			Nos. 713-724 (12)	19.85	19.85

Souvenir Sheets

725	A83	25nu	multicolored	5.50	5.50
726	A83	25nu	multicolored	5.50	5.50
727	A83	25nu	multicolored	5.50	5.50
728	A83	25nu	multicolored	5.50	5.50
729	A83	25nu	multicolored	5.50	5.50
730	A83	25nu	multicolored	5.50	5.50
731	A83	25nu	multicolored	5.50	5.50
732	A83	25nu	multicolored	5.50	5.50
733	A83	25nu	multicolored	5.50	5.50
734	A83	25nu	multicolored	5.50	5.50
735	A83	25nu	multicolored	5.50	5.50
736	A83	25nu	multicolored	5.50	5.50
			Nos. 725-736 (12)	66.00	66.00

Intl. Maritime Organization, 30th Anniv. — A84

Ships: 50ch, Spanish galleon *La Reale,* 1680. 1 nu, Submersible *Turtle,* 1776. 2nu, *Charlote Dundas,* 1802. 3nu, *Great Eastern,* c. 1858. 4nu, HMS *Warrior,* 1862. 5nu, Mississippi steamer, 1884. 6nu, *Preussen,* 1902. 7nu, USS *Arizona,* 1915. 10nu, *Bluenose,* 1921. 15nu, Steam trawler, 1925. 20nu, American liberty ship, 1943. No. 748, S.S. *United States,* 1952.

Each 25nu: No. 749, Moran tug, c. 1950. No. 750, Sinking of the *Titanic,* 1912. No. 751, U-boat, c. 1942. No. 752, Japanese warship *Yamato,* 1944. No. 753, HMS *Dreadnought.* No. 754, S.S. *Normandie,* c. 1933, and a Chinese junk. No. 755, HMS *Victory,* 1805. No. 756, USS *Monitor,* 1862. No. 757, *Cutty Sark,* 1869. No. 758, USS *Constitution.* No. 759, HMS *Resolution.* No. 760, Chinese junk.

1989, Aug. 24 Litho. *Perf. 14*

737	A84	50ch	multicolored	.25	.25
738	A84	1nu	multicolored	.40	.40
739	A84	2nu	multicolored	.75	.75
740	A84	3nu	multicolored	1.00	1.00
741	A84	4nu	multicolored	1.25	1.25
742	A84	5nu	multicolored	1.40	1.40
743	A84	6nu	multicolored	1.90	1.90
744	A84	7nu	multicolored	2.00	2.00
745	A84	10nu	multicolored	2.50	2.50
746	A84	15nu	multicolored	3.50	3.50
747	A84	20nu	multicolored	4.25	4.25
748	A84	25nu	multicolored	5.75	5.75
			Nos. 737-748 (12)	24.95	24.95

Souvenir Sheets

749-760	A84	Set of 12	66.00	66.00

Nos. 289-291 Overprinted: WORLD / AIDS DAY

1988, Dec. 1 Litho. *Perf. 14x13½*

761	A37	2nu	multicolored	.60	.60
762	A37	5nu	multicolored	1.40	1.40
763	A37	10nu	multicolored	3.50	3.50
			Nos. 761-763 (3)	5.50	5.50

Nos. 486-494 Ovptd. in Silver: AISA-PACIFIC EXPOSITION / FUKUOKA '89

1989, Mar. 17 *Perf. 13½*

764	A61	5ch	multicolored	.25	.25
765	A61	35ch	multicolored	.25	.25
766	A61	50ch	multicolored	.25	.25
767	A61	2.50nu	multicolored	.45	.45
768	A61	3nu	multicolored	.55	.55
769	A61	4nu	multicolored	.70	.70
770	A61	5nu	multicolored	.95	.95
771	A61	5.50nu	multicolored	1.00	1.00
772	A61	6nu	multicolored	1.10	1.10
			Nos. 764-772 (9)	5.50	5.50

Nos. 764-772 exist overprinted in Japanese. Value, set $125.

Chhukha Hydroelectric Project — A85

1988, Oct. 21 Litho. *Perf. 13½*

773	A85	50ch	multicolored	.50	.50

No. 773 exists imperf. Value, $40.

Jawaharlal Nehru (1889-1964), Indian Prime Minister A85a

1989, Nov. 14 Photo. *Perf. 14*

773A	A85a	100ch olive brown	.40	.40

Denomination is shown as 1.00ch in error.

Birds A86

Designs: 50ch, Larger goldenbacked woodpecker. 1nu, Black-naped monarch. 2nu, White-crested laughing thrush. 3nu, Blood-pheasant. 4nu, Blossom-headed parakeet. 5nu, Rosy minivet. 6nu, Chestnut-headed tit babbler. 7nu, Blue pitta. 10nu, Black-naped oriole. 15nu, Green magpie. 20nu, Indian three-toed kingfisher. No. 785, Ibisbill.

Each 25nu:No. 786, Great pied hornbill. No. 787, Himalayan redbreasted falconet. No. 788, Lammergeier. No. 789, Large racket-tailed drongo. No. 790, Fire-tailed sunbird. No. 791, Indian crested swift. No. 792, White-eared pheasant. No. 793, Satyr tragopan. No. 794, Wallcreeper. No. 795, Fairy bluebird. No. 796, Little spiderhunter. No. 797, Spotted forktail. Nos. 774-779 vert.

1989, Nov. 22 Litho. *Perf. 14*

774	A86	50ch multicolored	.25	.25
775	A86	1nu multicolored	.40	.40
776	A86	2nu multicolored	.75	.75
777	A86	3nu multicolored	1.00	1.00
778	A86	4nu multicolored	1.25	1.25
779	A86	5nu multicolored	1.40	1.40
780	A86	6nu multicolored	1.90	1.90
781	A86	7nu multicolored	2.00	2.00
782	A86	10nu multicolored	2.50	2.50
783	A86	15nu multicolored	3.50	3.50
784	A86	20nu multicolored	4.25	4.25
785	A86	25nu multicolored	5.75	5.75
		Nos. 774-785 (12)	24.95	24.95

Souvenir Sheets

786-797	A86	Set of 12	60.00	60.00

Steam Locomotives — A87

Designs: 50ch, *Best Friend of Charleston,* 1830, US 1nu, Class U, 1949, France. 2nu, *Consolidation,* 1866, US. 3nu, *Luggage Engine,* 1843, Great Britain. 4nu, Class 60-3 Shay, 1913, US. 5nu, *John Bull,* 1831, US. 6nu, *Hercules,* 1837, US. 7nu, Eight-wheel tank engine, 1874, Great Britain. 10nu, *The Illinois,* 1852, US. 15nu, German State 4-6-4, 1935. 20nu, American Standard, 1865. No. 809, Class Ps-4, 1926, US.

Each 25nu: No. 810, *Puffing Billy,* 1814, Great Britain. No. 811, Stephenson's *Rocket,* 1829, Great Britain. No. 812, *Cumberland,* 1845, US, vert. No. 813, *John Stevens,* 1849, US, vert. No. 814, No. 22 Baldwin Locomotive Works, 1873, US, No. 815, *Ariel,* 1877, US. No. 816, 1899 *No. 1301* Webb Compound Engine, Great Britain. No. 817, 1893 *No. 999* Empire State Express, US. No. 818, 1923 Class K-36, US. No. 819, 1935 Class A4, Great Britain. No. 820, 1935 Class A, US. No. 821, 1943 Class P-1, US.

1990, Jan. 30

798	A87	50ch multi	.25	.25
799	A87	1nu multi	.25	.25
800	A87	2nu multi	.40	.40
801	A87	3nu multi	.65	.65
802	A87	4nu multi	.80	.80
803	A87	5nu multi	1.00	1.00
804	A87	6nu multi	1.10	1.10
805	A87	7nu multi	1.40	1.40
806	A87	10nu multi	2.00	2.00
807	A87	15nu multi	3.00	3.00
808	A87	20nu multi	4.00	4.00
809	A87	25nu multi	5.00	5.00
		Nos. 798-809 (12)	19.85	19.85

Souvenir Sheets

810-821	A87	Set of 12	60.00	60.00

Butterflies A88

Designs: 50ch, Charaxes harmodius. 1nu, Prioneris thestylis. 2nu, Sephisa chandra. 3nu, Penthema usarda. 4nu, Troides aecus. 5nu, Polyura eudamippus. 6nu, Polyura dolon. 7nu, Neope bhadra. 10nu, Delias descombesis. 15nu, Childreni childrena. 20nu, Kallima inachus. No. 833, Elymnias malelas.

No. 834, Red lacewing. No. 835, Bhutan glory. No. 836, Great eggfly. No. 837, Kaiser-I-Hind. No. 838, Chestnut tiger. No. 839, Common map. No. 840, Swallowtail. No. 841, Jungle glory. No. 842, Checkered swallowtail. No. 843, Common birdwing. No. 844, Blue banded peacock. No. 845, Camberwell beauty.

1990, Jan. 30 Litho. *Perf. 14*

822	A88	50ch multicolored	.25	.25
823	A88	1nu multicolored	.25	.25
824	A88	2nu multicolored	.45	.45
825	A88	3nu multicolored	.75	.75
826	A88	4nu multicolored	.90	.90
827	A88	5nu multicolored	1.10	1.10
828	A88	6nu multicolored	1.25	1.25
829	A88	7nu multicolored	1.50	1.50
830	A88	10nu multicolored	2.25	2.25
831	A88	15nu multicolored	3.50	3.50
832	A88	20nu multicolored	4.75	4.75
833	A88	25nu multicolored	5.75	5.75
		Nos. 822-833 (12)	22.70	22.70

Souvenir Sheets

834	A88	25nu multicolored	5.00	5.00
835	A88	25nu multicolored	5.00	5.00
836	A88	25nu multicolored	5.00	5.00
837	A88	25nu multicolored	5.00	5.00
838	A88	25nu multicolored	5.00	5.00
839	A88	25nu multicolored	5.00	5.00
840	A88	25nu multicolored	5.00	5.00
841	A88	25nu multicolored	5.00	5.00
842	A88	25nu multicolored	5.00	5.00
843	A88	25nu multicolored	5.00	5.00
844	A88	25nu multicolored	5.00	5.00
845	A88	25nu multicolored	5.00	5.00
		Nos. 834-845 (12)	60.00	60.00

Nos. 822-824, 826-827, 830-831, 834-835, 844-845 are vert.

Paintings by Hiroshige A89

10ch, Plum Estate, Kameido. 20ch, Yatsumi Bridge. 50ch, Ayase River and Kanegafuchi. 75ch, View of Shiba Coast. 1nu, Grandpa's Teahouse, Meguro. 2nu, Kameido Tenjin Shrine. 6nu, Yoroi Ferry, Koami-cho. 7nu, Sakasai Ferry. 10nu, Fukagawa Lumberyards. 15nu, Suido Bridge & Surugadai. 20nu, Meguro Drum Bridge, Sunset Hill. #857, Atagoshita & Yabu Lane.

Each 25nu: No. 858, Towboats Along the Yotsugi-dori Canal. No. 859, Minowa, Kanasugi, Mikawashima. No. 860, Horikiri Iris Garden. No. 861, Fukagawa Susaki & Jumantsubo. No. 862, Suijin Shrine & Massaki on the Sumida River. No. 863, New Year's Eve Foxfires at the Changing Tree, Oji. No. 864, Nihonbashi, Clearing After Snow. No. 865, View to the North from Asukayama. No. 866, Komakata Hall & Azuma Bridge. No. 867, The City Flourishing, Tanabata Festival. No. 868, Suruga-cho. No. 869, Sudden Shower over Shin-Ohashi Bridge & Atake.

1990, May 21 Litho. *Perf. 13½*

846	A89	10ch multicolored	.25	.25
847	A89	20ch multicolored	.25	.25
848	A89	50ch multicolored	.25	.25
849	A89	75ch multicolored	.25	.25
850	A89	1nu multicolored	.25	.25
851	A89	2nu multicolored	.40	.40
852	A89	6nu multicolored	1.40	1.40
853	A89	7nu multicolored	1.50	1.50
854	A89	10nu multicolored	2.25	2.25
855	A89	15nu multicolored	3.50	3.50
856	A89	20nu multicolored	4.50	4.50
857	A89	25nu multicolored	5.25	5.25
		Nos. 846-857 (12)	20.05	20.05

Souvenir Sheets

858-869	A89	Set of 12	62.50	62.50

Hirohito (1901-1989) and enthronement of Akihito as emperor of Japan.

Orchids — A90

Designs: 10ch, Renanthera monachica. 50ch, Vanda coerulea. 1nu, Phalaenopsis violacea. 2nu, Dendrobium nobile. 5nu, Vandopsis lissochiloides. 6nu, Paphiopedilum rothschildianum. 7nu, Phalaenopsis schilleriana. 9nu, Paphiopedilum insigne. 10nu, Paphiopedilum bellatulum. 20nu, Doritis pulcherrima. 25nu, Cymbidium giganteum. 35nu, Phalaenopsis mariae.

No. 882, Vanda coerulescens. No. 883, Vandopsis parishi. No. 884, Dendrobium aphyllum. No. 885, Phalaenopsis amabilis. No. 886, Paphiopedilum haynaldianum. No. 887, Dendrobium loddigesii. No. 888, Vanda alpina. No. 889, Phalaenopsis equestris. No. 890, Vanda cristata. No. 891, Phalaenopsis cornu cervi. No. 892, Paphiopedilum niveum. No. 893, Dendrobium margaritaceum.

1990, Apr. 6 Litho. *Perf. 14*

870	A90	10ch multicolored	.25	.25
871	A90	50ch multicolored	.25	.25
872	A90	1nu multicolored	.25	.25
873	A90	2nu multicolored	.45	.45
874	A90	5nu multicolored	1.00	1.00
875	A90	6nu multicolored	1.25	1.25
876	A90	7nu multicolored	1.40	1.40
877	A90	9nu multicolored	1.75	1.75
878	A90	10nu multicolored	1.90	1.90
879	A90	20nu multicolored	3.50	3.50
880	A90	25nu multicolored	4.25	4.25
881	A90	35nu multicolored	5.75	5.75
		Nos. 870-881 (12)	22.00	22.00

Souvenir Sheets

882	A90	30nu multicolored	6.00	6.00
883	A90	30nu multicolored	6.00	6.00
884	A90	30nu multicolored	6.00	6.00
885	A90	30nu multicolored	6.00	6.00
886	A90	30nu multicolored	6.00	6.00
887	A90	30nu multicolored	6.00	6.00
888	A90	30nu multicolored	6.00	6.00
889	A90	30nu multicolored	6.00	6.00
890	A90	30nu multicolored	6.00	6.00
891	A90	30nu multicolored	6.00	6.00
892	A90	30nu multicolored	6.00	6.00
893	A90	30nu multicolored	6.00	6.00
		Nos. 882-893 (12)	72.00	72.00

EXPO '90 Intl. Garden and Greenery Exposition, Osaka, Apr. 1-Dec. 31.

G.P.O., Thimphu — A90a

1990, May 29 Photo. *Perf. 14*

893A	A90a	1nu multicolored	.75	.75

Penny Black, 150th Anniv. A90b

Penny Black and: 50ch, Bhutan #1. 1nu, Oldenburg #1. 2nu, Bergedorf #3. 4nu, German Democratic Republic #48. 5nu, Brunswick #1. 6nu, Basel #3L1. 8nu, Geneva #2L1. 10nu, Zurich #1L1. No. 902, France #3. 20nu, Vatican City #1. 25nu, Israel #1. No. 905, Japan #1.

Each 15nu: Penny Black and: No. 906a, Mecklenburg-Schwerin #1. b, Mecklenburg-Strelitz #1. No. 907a, Germany #5, #9. b, Prussia #2. No. 908a, Hamburg #1. b, North German Confederation #1, #7. No. 909a, Baden #1. b, Wurttemberg #1. No. 910a, Heligoland #1. b, Hanover #1. No. 911a, Thurn & Taxis #42. b, Thurn & Taxis #3. No. 912a, Schleswig-Holstein #1. b, Lubeck #5.

Each 30nu: No. 913, Saxony #1. No. 914, Berlin #9N1. No. 915, No other stamp. No. 916, US #1. No. 917, Bavaria #1.

1990, Oct. 9 *Perf. 14*

894	A90b	50ch multicolored	.25	.25
895	A90b	1nu multicolored	.25	.25
896	A90b	2nu multicolored	.30	.30
897	A90b	4nu multicolored	.65	.65
898	A90b	5nu multicolored	.80	.80
899	A90b	6nu multicolored	1.00	1.00
900	A90b	8nu multicolored	1.25	1.25
901	A90b	10nu multicolored	1.50	1.50
902	A90b	15nu multicolored	2.50	2.50
903	A90b	20nu multicolored	3.00	3.00
904	A90b	25nu multicolored	3.75	3.75
905	A90b	30nu multicolored	4.75	4.75
		Nos. 894-905 (12)	20.00	20.00

Souvenir Sheets

Sheets of 2 (#906-912) or 1

906-912	A90b	Set of 7	40.00	40.00
913-917	A90b	Set of 5	25.00	25.00

Stamp World London '90.

Panda Bear A91

Tiger A92

Endangered wildlife of Asia: 50ch, Panda sitting up. 1nu, Panda sitting on branch. 2nu, Panda and cub. 4nu, Panda on back eating. 6nu, Adult panda getting food with cub. 7nu, Cub laying on adult panda. 10nu, Elephant. 15nu, Adult panda by fallen tree. 20nu, Barking deer. No. 929, 25nu, Snow leopard.

No. 930, Rhinoceros. No. 931, Clouded leopard. No. 932, Asiatic wild dog. No. 933, Himalayan shou. No. 934, Golden cat. No. 935, Himalayan musk deer. No. 936, Head of panda. No. 937, Asiatic black bear. No. 938, Gaur. No. 939, Pygmy hog. No. 940, Wolf. No. 941, Sloth bear.

1990 *Perf. 14*

918	A91	50ch multi	.30	.25
919	A91	1nu multi	.40	.40
920	A91	2nu multi	.60	.60
921	A91	3nu shown	1.00	1.00
922	A91	4nu multi	1.25	1.25
923	A92	5nu shown	1.40	1.40
924	A91	6nu multi	1.60	1.60
925	A91	7nu multi	1.90	1.90
926	A92	10nu multi	2.50	2.50
927	A91	15nu multi	3.50	3.50
928	A92	20nu multi	4.75	4.75
929	A92	25nu multi	5.75	5.75
		Nos. 918-929 (12)	24.95	24.90

Souvenir Sheets

930	A92	25nu multi	5.50	5.50
931	A92	25nu multi	5.50	5.50
932	A92	25nu multi	5.50	5.50
933	A92	25nu multi	5.50	5.50
934	A92	25nu multi	5.50	5.50
935	A92	25nu multi	5.50	5.50
936	A91	25nu multi	5.50	5.50
937	A92	25nu multi	5.50	5.50
938	A92	25nu multi	5.50	5.50
939	A92	25nu multi	5.50	5.50
940	A92	25nu multi	5.50	5.50
941	A92	25nu multi	5.50	5.50
		Nos. 930-941 (12)	66.00	66.00

Nos. 919-920 and 927 vert.

Buddhist Musical Instruments — A93

1990, Sept. 29 Litho. *Perf. 13½x13*

942	A93	10ch	Dungchen	.25	.25
943	A93	20ch	Dungkar	.25	.25
944	A93	30ch	Roim	.25	.25
945	A93	50ch	Tinchag	.25	.25
946	A93	1nu	Dradu & drilbu	.25	.25
947	A93	2nu	Gya-ling	.40	.40
948	A93	2.50nu	Nga	.50	.50
a.			Souv. sheet, #943, 945, 947-948	*20.00*	*20.00*
949	A93	3.50nu	Kang-dung	.75	.75
a.			Souv. sheet, #942, 944, 946, 949	*50.00*	*50.00*
			Nos. 942-949 (8)	2.90	2.90

Year of the Girl Child — A94

1990, Dec. 8

950	A94	50ch shown	.25	.25
951	A94	20nu Young girl	4.00	4.00

Wonders of the World — A95

Walt Disney characters viewing: 1ch, Temple of Artemis, Ephesus. 2ch, Statue of Zeus, Olympia. 3ch, Egyptian pyramids. 4ch, Lighthouse, Alexandria. 5ch, Mausoleum at Halicarnassus. 10ch, Colossus of Rhodes. 50ch, Hanging gardens of Babylon. 5nu, Mauna Loa volcano, Hawaii. 6nu, Carlsbad Caverns, New Mexico. 10nu, Rainbow Bridge, Utah. 15nu, Grand Canyon of the Colorado, Arizona. 20nu, Old Faithful geyser, Wyoming. 25nu, Giant sequoias, California. 30nu, Crater Lake and Wizard Island, Oregon. 5nu, 6nu, 10nu, 15nu, 20nu, 25nu, 30nu are horiz.

Each 25nu, Walt Disney characters viewing: No. 966, Great Wall of China, horiz. No. 967, Mosque of St. Sophia, Istanbul, Turkey. No. 968, The Leaning Tower of Pisa, Italy. No. 969, Colosseum, Rome. No. 970, Stonehenge, England. No. 971, Catacombs of Alexandria, Egypt. No. 972, Porcelain Tower, Nanking, China, horiz. No. 973, The Panama Canal, horiz. No. 974, Golden Gate Bridge, San Francisco, horiz. No. 975, Sears Tower, Chicago, horiz. No. 976, Gateway Arch, St. Louis. No. 977, Alcan Highway, Alaska and Canada, horiz. No. 978, Hoover Dam, Nevada. No. 979, Empire State Building, New York.

1991, Feb. 2 Litho. *Perf. 14*

952	A95	1ch	multicolored	.25	.25
953	A95	2ch	multicolored	.25	.25
954	A95	3ch	multicolored	.25	.25
955	A95	4ch	multicolored	.25	.25
956	A95	5ch	multicolored	.25	.25
957	A95	10ch	multicolored	.25	.25
958	A95	50ch	multicolored	.25	.25
959	A95	5nu	multicolored	1.40	1.40
960	A95	6nu	multicolored	1.75	1.75
961	A95	10nu	multicolored	2.25	2.25
962	A95	15nu	multicolored	3.00	3.00
963	A95	20nu	multicolored	4.25	4.25
964	A95	25nu	multicolored	4.50	4.50
965	A95	30nu	multicolored	6.00	6.00
			Nos. 952-965 (14)	24.90	24.90

Souvenir Sheets

Perf. 14x13½, 13½x14

966-979	A95	Set of 14	63.00	63.00

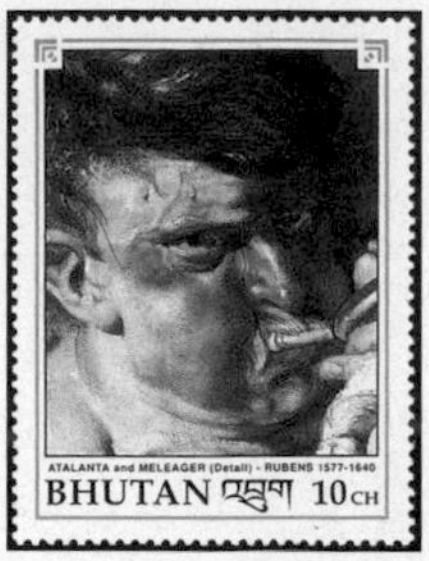

Peter Paul Rubens (1577-1640), Painter A96

Entire paintings or different details from: 10ch, 5nu, 6nu, 10nu, No. 992, Atalanta and Meleager. 50ch, Fall of Phaethon. 1nu, No. 993, Feast of Venus Verticordia. 2nu, Achilles Slaying Hector. 3nu, No. 994, Arachne Punished by Minerva. 4nu, No. 995, Jupiter Receives Psyche on Olympus. 7nu, Venus in Vulcan's Furnace. 20nu, No. 996, Briseis Returned to Achilles. 30nu, No. 997, Mars and Rhea Sylvia. No. 998, Venus Shivering. No. 999, Ganymede and the Eagle. No. 1000, Origin of the Milky Way. No. 1001, Adonis and Venus. No. 1002, Hero and Leander. No. 1003, Fall of the Titans.

Nos. 992-1003, each 25nu.

Nos. 994, 996-997, 1000-1003 are horiz.

1991, Feb. 2

980	A96	10ch	multicolored	.40	.40
981	A96	50ch	multicolored	.40	.40
982	A96	1nu	multicolored	.50	.50
983	A96	2nu	multicolored	.60	.60
984	A96	3nu	multicolored	.90	.90
985	A96	4nu	multicolored	1.15	1.15
986	A96	5nu	multicolored	1.40	1.40
987	A96	6nu	multicolored	1.50	1.50
988	A96	7nu	multicolored	1.60	1.60
989	A96	10nu	multicolored	2.50	2.50
990	A96	20nu	multicolored	3.75	3.75
991	A96	30nu	multicolored	5.50	5.50
			Nos. 980-991 (12)	20.20	20.20

Souvenir Sheets

992-1003	A96	Set of 12	75.00	75.00

Vincent Van Gogh (1853-1890), Painter — A97

Paintings: 10ch, Cottages, Reminiscence of the North. 50ch, Head of a Peasant Woman with Dark Cap. 1nu, Portrait of a Woman in Blue. 2nu, The Midwife. 8nu, Vase with Hollyhocks. 10nu, Portrait of a Man with a Skull Cap. 12nu, Agostina Segatori Sitting in the Cafe du Tambourin. 15nu, Vase with Daisies and Anemones. 18nu, Fritillaries in a Copper Vase. 20nu, Woman Sitting in the Grass. 25nu, On the Outskirts of Paris, horiz. 30nu, Chrysanthemums and Wild Flowers in a Vase.

Each 30nu: No. 1016, Le Moulin de la Galette. No. 1017, Bowl with Sunflowers, Roses and Other Flowers, horiz. No. 1018, Poppies and Butterflies. No. 1019, Trees in the Garden of Saint-Paul Hospital. No. 1020, Le Moulin de Blute Fin. No. 1021, Le Moulin de la Galette, diff. No. 1022, Vase with Peonies. No. 1023, Vase with Zinnias. No. 1024, Fishing in the Spring, Pont de Clichy, horiz. No. 1025, Village Street in Auvers, horiz. No. 1026, Vase with Zinnias and Other Flowers, horiz. No. 1027, Vase with Red Poppies.

1991, July 22 Litho. *Perf. 13½*

1004	A97	10ch	multicolored	.30	.30
1005	A97	50ch	multicolored	.30	.30
1006	A97	1nu	multicolored	.30	.30
1007	A97	2nu	multicolored	.40	.40
1008	A97	8nu	multicolored	1.60	1.60
1009	A97	10nu	multicolored	2.00	2.00
1010	A97	12nu	multicolored	2.50	2.50
1011	A97	15nu	multicolored	3.00	3.00
1012	A97	18nu	multicolored	4.00	4.00
1013	A97	20nu	multicolored	4.25	4.25
1014	A97	25nu	multicolored	5.00	5.00
1015	A97	30nu	multicolored	6.25	6.25
			Nos. 1004-1015 (12)	29.90	29.90

Size: 76x102mm, 102x76mm

Imperf

1016-1027	A97	Set of 12	84.00	84.00

History of World Cup Soccer — A98

Winning team pictures, plays or possible future site: 50ch, Uruguay, 1930. 1nu, Italy, 1934. 2nu, Italy, 1938. 3nu, Uruguay, 1950. 5nu, West Germany, 1954. 10nu, Brazil, 1958. 20nu, Brazil, 1962. 25nu, England, 1966. 29nu, Brazil, 1970. 30nu, West Germany, 1974. 31nu, Argentina, 1978. 32nu, Italy, 1982. 33nu, Argentina, 1986. 34nu, West Germany, 1990. 35nu, Los Angeles Coliseum, 1994.

Players, each 30nu: No. 1043, Claudio Caniggia, Argentina, vert. No. 1044, Salvatore Schillaci, Italy, vert. No. 1045, Roberto Baggio, Italy, vert. No. 1046, Peter Shilton, England, vert. No. 1047, Lothar Matthaus, West Germany, vert. No. 1048, Paul Gascoigne, England, vert.

1991, Aug. 1 Litho. *Perf. 13½*

1028	A98	50ch	multi	.25	.25
1029	A98	1nu	multi	.25	.25
1030	A98	2nu	multi	.35	.35
1031	A98	3nu	multi	.60	.60
1032	A98	5nu	multi	.90	.90
1033	A98	10nu	multi	1.90	1.90
1034	A98	20nu	multi	3.75	3.75
1035	A98	25nu	multi	4.50	4.50
1036	A98	29nu	multi	5.50	5.50
1037	A98	30nu	multi	5.50	5.50
1038	A98	31nu	multi	5.75	5.75
1039	A98	32nu	multi	6.00	6.00
1040	A98	33nu	multi	6.25	6.25
1041	A98	34nu	multi	6.25	6.25
1042	A98	35nu	multi	6.50	6.50
			Nos. 1028-1042 (15)	54.25	54.25

Souvenir Sheets

1043-1048	A98	Set of 6	40.00	40.00

Nos. 1028-1042 and 1043-1048 exist imperf. These were unauthorized but inadvertently sent to Bhutan and distributed. Values, set: $225 and $400, respectively.

Phila Nippon '91 — A99

1991, Nov. 16 *Perf. 13*

1049	A99	15nu multicolored	3.50	3.50

Education in Bhutan A100

1992, Mar. 5 Photo. *Perf. 13½*

1050	A100	1nu multicolored	1.00	1.00

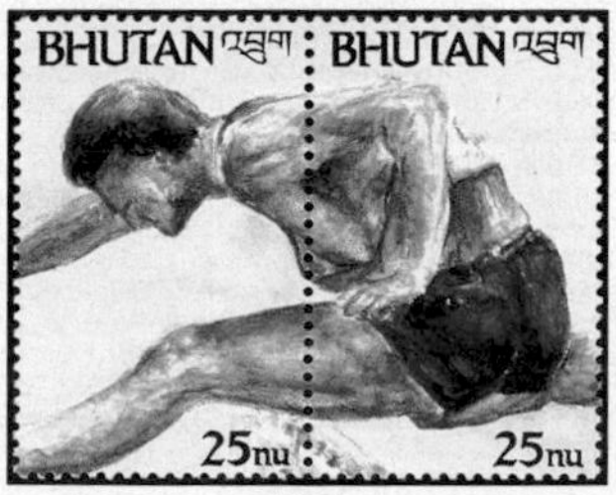

A101

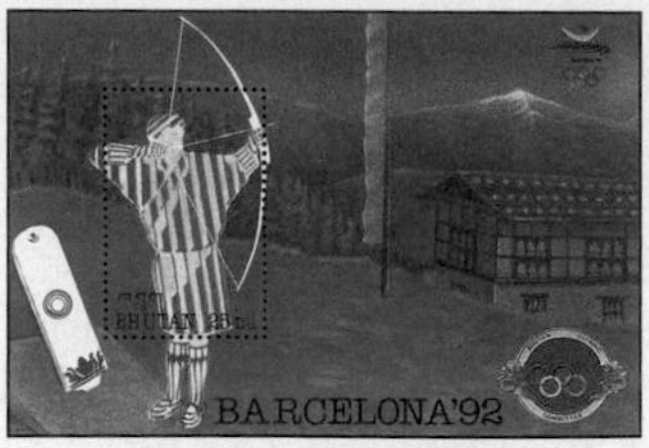

1992 Summer Olympics, Barcelona — A102

1992, July 24 Litho. *Perf. 12*

1051	A101	25nu Pair, #a.-b.	4.50	4.50

Souvenir Sheet

1052	A102	25nu Archer	3.50	3.50

German Reunification — A103

1992, Oct. 3 Litho. *Perf. 12*

1053	A103	25nu multicolored	1.50	1.50

Souvenir Sheet

1054	A103	25nu multicolored	1.50	1.50

Stamp from No. 1054 does not have white inscription or border.

Bhutan Postal Service, 30th Anniv. A104

Designs: 1nu, Mail truck, plane. 3nu, Letter carrier approaching village. 5nu, Letter carrier emptying mail box.

1992, Oct. 9

1055	A104	1nu multicolored	.30	.30
1056	A104	3nu multicolored	.40	.40
1057	A104	5nu multicolored	.75	.75
		Nos. 1055-1057 (3)	1.45	1.45

Environmental Protection — A105

Designs: a, 7nu, Red panda. b, 20nu, Takin. c, 15nu, Black-necked crane, blue poppy. d, 10nu, One-horned rhinoceros.

1993, July 1 Litho. *Perf. 14*

1058	A105	Sheet of 4, #a.-d.	9.00	9.00

No. 1058 was delayed from its originally scheduled release in 1992, although some examples were made available to the trade at that time.

Ship — A106

1992, Sept. 18 ***Perf. 12***

1059 A106 15nu shown		2.50	2.50
1060 A106 20nu Portrait		3.25	3.25

Souvenir Sheet

1061 A106 25nu like #1060	5.00	5.00

Discovery of America, 500th anniv.
Stamp from No. 1061 does not have silver inscription or white border.

A107

Reign of King Jigme Singye Wangchuk, 20th Anniv.: a, 1nu, Man tilling field, factory. b, 5nu, Airplane. c, 10nu, House, well. d, 15nu, King.
20nu, People, flag, King, horiz.

1992, Nov. 11 **Litho.** ***Perf. 12***

1062 A107 Block of 4, #a.-d.	6.00	6.00

Souvenir Sheet

1063 A107 20nu multicolored	6.00	6.00

Intl. Volunteer Day — A108

a, 1.50nu, White inscription. b, 9nu, Green inscription. c, 15nu, Red inscription.

1992, Dec. 5 **Litho.** ***Perf. 14***

1067 A108 Block of 4, #a.-c. + label	5.00	5.00

Medicinal Plants — A109

1.50nu, Meconopsis grandis prain. 7nu, Meconopsis sp. 10nu, Meconopsis wallichii. 12nu, Meconopsis horridula. 20nu, Meconopsis discigera.
25nu, Meconopsis horridula, diff.

1993, Jan. 1 **Litho.** ***Perf. 12***

1068 A109	1.50nu multicolored	.40	.40
1069 A109	7nu multicolored	1.10	1.10
1070 A109	10nu multicolored	1.40	1.40
1071 A109	12nu multicolored	1.90	1.90
1072 A109	20nu multicolored	3.25	3.25
	Nos. 1068-1072 (5)	8.05	8.05

Souvenir Sheet

1073 A109 25nu multicolored	6.00	6.00

Miniature Sheet

Lunar New Year — A110

1993, Feb. 22 **Litho.** ***Perf. 14***

1074 A110 25nu multicolored	7.75	7.75

Exists with overprint "ROCKPEX '93 KAOHSIUNG" in sheet margin.

No. 1074 Surcharged "TAIPEI '93" in Silver and Black

1993, Aug. 14 **Litho.** ***Perf. 14***

1075 A110 30nu on 25nu	7.75	7.75

Paintings A111

Designs: No. 1076, 1ch, No. 1081, 15ch, No. 1086, 1nu, The Love Letter, by Jean-Honoré Fragonard. No. 1077, 2ch, No. 1082, 25ch, No. 1087, 1.25nu, The Writer, by Vittore Carpaccio. No. 1078, 3ch, No. 1083, 50ch, No. 1088, 2nu, Madomoiselle Lavergne, by Jean-Etienne Liotard. No. 1079, 5ch, No. 1084, 60ch, No. 1089, 3nu, Portrait of Erasmus, by Hans Holbein, the Younger. No. 1080, 10ch, No. 1085, 80ch, No. 1090, 6nu, Woman Writing a Letter, by Gerard Terborch.
Color of frames and text outlines: Nos. 1076-1080, bronze, Nos. 1081-1085, silver, Nos. 1086-1090, gold.

1993, May 2 **Photo.** ***Perf. 13½***

1076-1090 A111 Set of 15	8.00	—
1090a Souvenir sheet, #1088-1089, with bronze frames and text outlines, perf.	6.50	—

Nos. 1076-1090, 1090a were prepared and distributed in 1974 but were not made valid until 1993. Nos. 1076-1090 exist imperf. Value, set $15. No. 1090a exists imperf. Value, $6.50. Nos. 1088-1090 are air mail.

Door Gods — A112

1.50nu, Namtheo-Say. 5nu, Pha-Ke-Po. 10nu, Chen-Mi-Jang. 15nu, Yul-Khor-Sung.

1993, Dec. 17 **Litho.** ***Perf. 12***

1091 A112	1.50nu multi	.35	.35
1092 A112	5nu multi	.95	.95
1093 A112	10nu multi	1.90	1.90
1094 A112	15nu multi	2.75	2.75
	Nos. 1091-1094 (4)	5.95	5.95

Flowers — A113

Designs: a, Rhododendron mucronatum. b, Anemone rupicola. c, Polemonium coeruleum. d, Rosa marophylla. e, Paraquilegia microphylla. f, Aquilegia nivalis. g, Geranium wallichianum. h, Rhodendron campanulatum. i, Viola suavis. j, Cyananthus lobatus.
13nu, Red flower, horiz.

1994, Jan. 1 ***Perf. 13***

1095	Strip of 10	10.00	10.00
a.	A113 1nu multicolored	.30	.25
b.	A113 1.5nu multicolored	.30	.25
c.	A113 2nu multicolored	.35	.25
d.	A113 2.5nu multicolored	.35	.25
e.	A113 4nu multicolored	.40	.30
f.	A113 5nu multicolored	.75	.40
g.	A113 6nu multicolored	1.00	.50
h.	A113 7nu multicolored	1.25	.60
i.	A113 9nu multicolored	1.50	.70
j.	A113 10nu multicolored	2.00	1.00

Souvenir Sheet

1096 A113 13nu multicolored	3.50	3.50

New Year 1994 (Year of the Dog) — A114

1994, Feb. 11 **Litho.** ***Perf. 14***

1097 A114 11.50nu multi	1.75	1.75

Souvenir Sheet

1098 A114 20nu like #1097	3.50	3.50

Hong Kong '94.

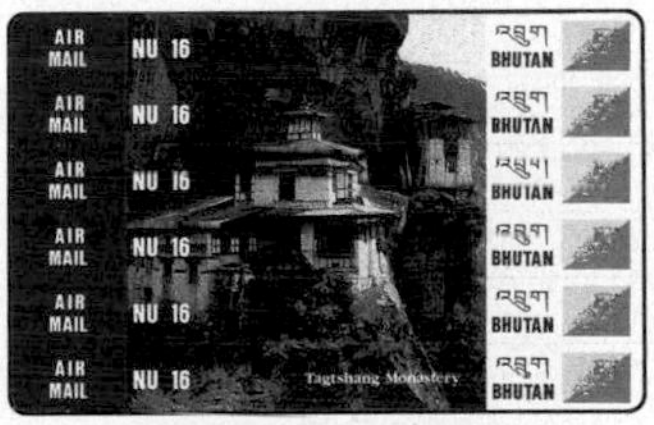

Stamp Cards — A115

Designs: 16nu, Tagtshang Monastery. 20nu, Map of Bhutan.

Roulетted 26 on 2 or 3 Sides

1994, Aug. 15 **Litho.**

Self-Adhesive

Cards of 6 + 6 labels

1099 A115 16nu #a.-f.	12.00	12.00
1100 A115 20nu #a.-f.	13.00	13.00

Individual stamps measure 70x9mm and have a card backing. Se-tenant labels inscribed "AIR MAIL."

Souvenir Sheet

First Manned Moon Landing, 25th Anniv. — A116

a, 30nu, Astronaut on moon. b, 36nu, Space shuttle, earth, moon.

1994, Nov. 11 **Litho.** ***Perf. 14x14½***

1101 A116 Sheet of 2, #a.-b.	12.00	12.00

Nos. 1101a, 1101b have holographic images. Soaking in water may affect the holograms.

Souvenir Sheet

Victory Over Tibet-Mongol Army, 350th Anniv. — A117

Battle scene: a, Mounted officer. b, Hand to hand combat, soldiers in yellow or blue armor. c, Soldier on gray horse. d, Soldiers in red, drummer, horn player.

1994, Dec. 17 **Litho.** ***Perf. 12½***

Granite Paper

1102 A117 15nu Sheet of 4, #a.-d.	6.00	6.00

Souvenir Sheet

Bridges — A118

a, 15nu, Tower Bridge, London, cent. b, 16nu, Wangdue Bridge, Bhutan, 250th anniv.

1994, Nov. 11 ***Perf. 12***

1103 A118 Sheet of 2, #a.-b.	4.50	4.50

1994 World Cup Soccer Championships, US — A119

1994, July 17 **Litho.** ***Perf. 12***

1104 A119 15nu multicolored	2.00	2.00

Souvenir Sheet

World Tourism Year — A120

Scenes of Bhutan: a, 1.50nu, Paro Valley. b, 5nu, Chorten Kora. c, 10nu, Thimphu Tshechu. d, 15nu, Wangdue Tshechu.

1995, Apr. 2 **Litho.** ***Perf. 12***

1105 A120 Sheet of 4, #a.-d.	5.00	5.00

Miniature Sheet

New Year 1995 (Year of the Boar) — A121

Symbols of Chinese Lunar New Year: a, 10ch, Rat. b, 20ch, Ox. c, 30ch, Tiger. d, 40ch, Rabbit. e, 1nu, Dragon. f, 2nu, Snake. g, 3nu, Horse. h, 4nu, Sheep. i, 5nu, Monkey. j, 7nu, Rooster. k, 8nu, Dog. l, 9nu, Boar.
10nu, Wood Hog.

1995, Mar. 2

1106 A121 Sheet of 12, #a.-l. 6.00 6.00

Souvenir Sheet

1107 A121 10nu multicolored 2.00 2.00

No. 1107 is a continuous design.

A122

Flowers: 9nu, Pleione praecox. 10nu, Primula calderina. 16nu, Primula whitei. 18nu, Notholirion macrophyllum.

1995, May 2 Litho. *Perf. 12*

1108-1111 A122 Set of 4 5.50 5.50

A123

UN, 50th Anniv.: a, Human resources development. b, Health & population. c, Water & sanitation. d, Transport & communications. e, Forestry & environment. f, Peace & security. g, UN in Bhutan.

1995, June 26 *Perf. 14*

1112	Strip of 7	8.00	8.00
a.	A123 1.5nu multicolored	.25	.25
b.	A123 9nu multicolored	.35	.35
c.	A123 10nu multicolored	.50	.50
d.	A123 5nu multicolored	.60	.60
e.	A123 16nu multicolored	.75	.75
f.	A123 18nu multicolored	1.00	1.00
g.	A123 11.5nu multicolored	1.25	1.25

Miniature Sheet of 6

Singapore '95 — A124

Birds — No. 1113: a, 1nu, Himalayan pied kingfisher. b, 2nu, Blyth's tragopan. c, 3nu, Long-tailed minivet. d, 10nu, Red junglefowl. e, 15nu, Black-capped sibia. f, 20nu, Red-billed chough.
No. 1114, Black-neck crane.

1995, June 2 Litho. *Perf. 12*

1113 A124 #a.-f. + 3 labels 3.50 3.50

Souvenir Sheet

1114 A124 20nu multicolored 2.50 2.50

Traditional Crafts — A125

1nu, Drying parchment. 2nu, Making tapestry. 3nu, Restoring archaeological finds. 10nu, Weaving textiles. 15nu, Sewing garments. No. 1120, 20nu, Carving wooden vessels.
No. 1121, Mosaic.

1995, Aug. 15 Litho. *Perf. 14*

1115-1120 A125 Set of 6 5.50 5.50

Souvenir Sheet

1121 A125 20nu multicolored 3.25 3.25

New Year 1996 (Year of the Rat) — A126

Designs: a, Monkey. b, Rat, fire. c, Dragon.

1996, Jan. 1 Litho. *Perf. 14*

1122 A126 10nu Sheet of 3, #a.-c. 4.00 4.00

Butterflies A127

a, 2nu, Blue pansy. b, 3nu, Blue peacock. c, 5nu, Great Mormon. d, 10nu, Fritillary. e, 15nu, Blue duke. f, 25nu, Brown Gorgon.
No. 1124, 30nu, Xanthomelas. No. 1124A, 30 nu, Fivebar swordtail.

1996, May 2 Litho. *Perf. 14*

1123 A127 Sheet of 6, #a.-f. 6.00 6.00

Souvenir Sheets

1124-1124A A127 Set of 2 6.50 6.50

1996 Summer Olympic Games, Atlanta A128

5nu, Silver 300n coin, soccer. 7nu, Silver 300n coin, basketball. 10nu, Gold 5s coin, judo. 15nu, Archery.

1996, June 15 Litho. *Perf. 14*

1125-1127 A128 Set of 3 3.00 3.00

Souvenir Sheet

1128 A128 15nu multicolored 3.50 3.50

Olymphilex '96.

Folktales — A129

Designs: a, 1nu, The White Bird. b, 2nu, Sing Sing Lhamo and the Moon. c, 3nu, The Hoopoe. d, 5nu, The Cloud Fairies. e, 10nu, The Three Wishes. f, 20nu, The Abominable Snowman.

1996, Apr. 15 *Perf. 12*

1129 A129 Sheet of 6, #a.-f. 3.00 3.00

Souvenir Sheet

1130 A129 25nu like #1129d 3.00 3.00

Locomotives — A130

No. 1131, each 20nu: a, 0-6-4 Tank engine (Chile). b, First Pacific locomotive in Europe (France). c, 4-6-0 Passenger engine (Norway). d, Atlantic type express (Germany). e, 4-Cylinder 4-6-0 express (Belgium). f, Standard type "4" diesel-electric (England).
No. 1132, each 20nu: a, Standard 0-6-0 Goods engine (India). b, Main-line 1,900 horsepower diesel-electric (Finland). c, 0-8-0 Shunting tank engine (Russia). d, Alco "PA-1" diesel-electric (US). e, "C11" Class 2-6-4 branch passenger tank engine (Japan). f, "Settebello" deluxe high-speed electric train (Italy).
No. 1133, 70nu, Class "KD" 0-6-0 Goods locomotive, 1900 (Sweden). No. 1134, 70nu, Shinkansen "New Railway" series 200 (Japan).

1996, Nov. 25 Litho. *Perf. 14*

Sheets of 6, #a-f

1131-1132 A130 Set of 2 20.00 20.00

Souvenir Sheets

1133-1134 A130 Set of 2 15.00 15.00

Penny Black — A131

Litho. & Embossed

1996, Dec. 17 *Perf. 13½*

1135 A131 140nu black & gold 6.00 6.00

A132

Winter Olympic Medalists: 10nu, Vegard Ulvang, cross-country skiing, 1992. 15nu, Kristi Yamaguchi, figure skating, 1992. 25nu, Markus Wasmeier, giant slalom, 1994. 30nu, Georg Hackl, luge, 1992.
No. 1140: a, Andreas Ostler, 2-man bobsled, 1952. b, Wolfgang Hoppe, 4-man bobsled, 1984. c, Stein Eriksen, giant slalom, 1952. d, Alberto Tomba, giant slalom, 1988.
Each 70nu: No. 1141, Henri Oreiller, downhill, 1948. No. 1142, Eduard Scherrer, 4-man bobsled, 1924.

1997, Jan. 1 *Perf. 14*

1136-1139 A132 Set of 4 7.50 7.50

1140 A132 15nu Strip of 4, #a.-d. 5.50 5.50

Souvenir Sheets

1141-1142 A132 Set of 2 14.50 14.50

No. 1140 was issued in sheets of 8 stamps.

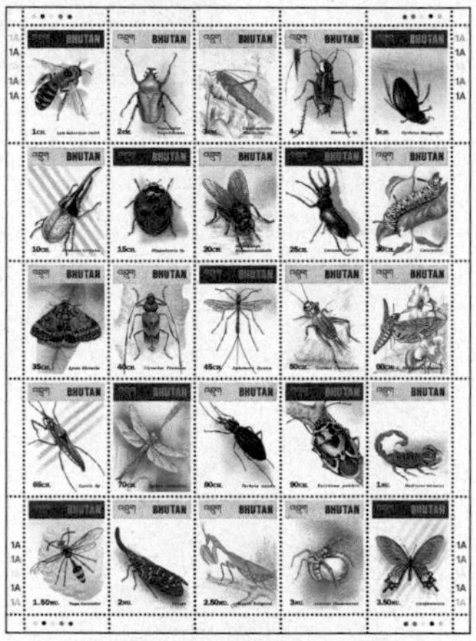

Insects and Arachnids — A133

a, 1ch, Apis laboriosa smith. b, 2ch, Neptunides polychromus. c, 3ch, Conocephalus maculctus. d, 4ch, Blattidae. e, 5ch, Dytiscus marginalis. f, 10ch, Dynastes hercules. g, 15ch, Hippodamia. h, 20ch, Sarcophaga haemorrhoidalis. i, 25ch, Lucanus cervus. j, 30ch, Caterpillar. k, 35ch, Lycia hirtaria. l, 40ch, Clytarlus pennatus. m, 45ch, Ephemera denica. n, 50ch, Gryllus campestris. o, 60ch, Deilephila elpenor. p, 65ch, Gerris. q, 70ch, Agrion splendens. r, 80ch, Tachyta nana. s, 90ch, Eurydema pulchra. t, 1nu, Hadrurus hirsutus. u, 1.50nu, Vespa germanica. v, 2nu, Pyrops. w, 2.50nu, Mantis religiosa. x, 3nu, Araneus diadematus. y, 3.50nu, Atrophaneura.
15nu, Melolontha.

1997, Jan. 15 *Perf. 13*

1143 A133 Sheet of 25, #a.-y. 6.50 6.50

Souvenir Sheet

1144 A133 15nu multicolored 4.00 4.00

Hong Kong '97 — A134

Wildlife: a, Thalarctos maritimus. b, Phascolarctos cinereus. c, Selenarctos thibetanus. d, Ailurus fulgens.
20nu, Ailuropoda melanoleuca.

1997, Feb. 1 Litho. *Perf. 14*

1145 A134 10nu Sheet of 4, #a.-d. 5.50 5.50

Souvenir Sheet

1146 A134 20nu multicolored 3.50 3.50

Signs of the Chinese Zodiac — A135

No. 1147: a, 1ch, Mouse. b, 2ch, Ox. c, 3ch, Tiger. d, 4ch, Rabbit. e, 5nu, Dragon. f, 6nu, Snake. g, 7nu, Horse. h, 8nu, Sheep. i, 90ch, Monkey. j, 10nu, Rooster. k, 11nu, Dog. l, 12nu, Pig.
20nu, Ox, diff.

1997, Feb. 8 Litho. *Perf. 14*

1147	A135	Sheet of 12, #a.-l. + label	9.50 9.50

Souvenir Sheet

1148	A135	20nu multicolored	5.50 5.50

Fauna A136

Cuon alpinus: No. 1149: a, Adult, hind legs off ground. b, Adult walking right. c, Mother nursing young. d, Two seated.
Endangered species: No. 1150: a, Lynx. b, Red panda. c, Takin. d, Musk deer. e, Snow leopard. f, Golden langur. g, Tiger. h, Muntjac. i, Marmot.
No. 1151, 70nu, Pseudois nayaur. No. 1152, 70nu, Ursus thibetanus.

1997, Apr. 24

1149	A136	10nu Block or strip of 4, #a.-d.	5.50 5.50
1150	A136	10nu Sheet of 9, #a.-i.	8.00 8.00

Souvenir Sheets

1151-1152	A136	Set of 2	14.50 14.50

World Wildlife Fund (No. 1149).
No. 1149 issued in sheets of 12 stamps.

UNESCO, 50th Anniv. A137

No. 1153: a, Mount Hungshan, China. b, Mausoleum of first Qin Emperor, China. c, Imperial Bronze Dragon, China. d, Tikal Natl. Park, Guatemala. e, Evora, Portugal. f, Shirakami-Sanchi, Japan. g, Paris, France. h, Valley Below the Falls, Plitvice Lakes Natl. Park, Croatia.
Sites in Germany: No. 1154: a, Cathedral, Bamberg. b, Bamberg. c, St. Michael's Church, Hildesheim. d, Potsdam Palace. e, Potsdam Church. f, Lubeck. g, Quedlinberg. h, Benedictine Church, Lorsch.
No. 1155, 60nu, Goslar, Germany, horiz. No. 1156, 60nu, Cathedral, Comenzada, Portugal, horiz.

1997, May 15 Sheets of 8 + Label

1153	A137	10nu #a.-h.	9.00 9.00
1154	A137	15nu #a.-h.	11.00 11.00

Souvenir Sheets

1155-1156	A137	Set of 2	13.50 13.50

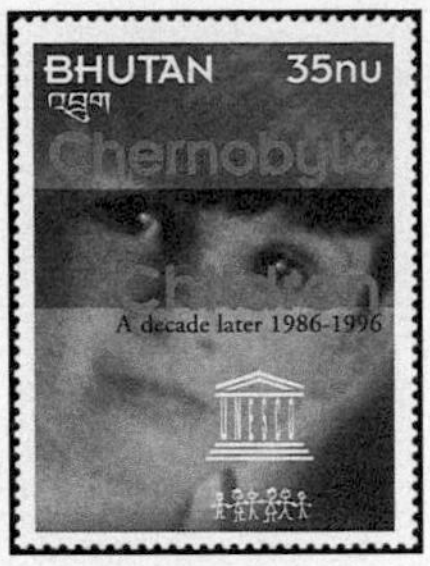

Chernobyl Disaster, 10th Anniv. A138

1997, May 2 Litho. *Perf. 13½x14*

1157	A138	35nu UNESCO	4.75 4.75

Dogs — A139

Designs: 10nu, Dalmatian. 15nu, Siberian husky. 20nu, Saluki. 25nu, Shar pei.
No. 1162: a, Dandie Dinmont terrier. b, Chinese crested. c, Norwich terrier. d, Basset hound. e, Cardigan welsh corgi. f, French bulldog.
60nu, Hovawart.

1997, July 15 *Perf. 14*

1158-1161	A139	Set of 4	5.00 5.00
1162	A139	20nu Sheet of 6, #a.-f.	9.00 9.00

Souvenir Sheet

1163	A139	60nu multicolored	4.50 4.50

Cats — A140

Designs: 10nu, Turkish angora. 15nu, Oriental shorthair. 20nu, British shorthair. 25nu, Burmese.
No. 1168: a, Japanese bobtail. b, Ceylon. c, Exotic. d, Rex. e, Ragdoll. f, Russian blue.
60nu, Tonkinese.

1997, July 15

1164-1167	A140	Set of 4	5.00 5.00
1168	A140	15nu Sheet of 6, #a.-f.	9.00 9.00

Souvenir Sheet

1169	A140	60nu multicolored	4.50 4.50

1998 World Cup Soccer, France A141

English players: 5nu, Pearce. 10nu, Gascoigne. 15nu, Beckham. 20nu, McManaman. 25nu, Adams. 30nu, Ince.
World Cup captains, horiz.: No. 1176: a, Maradona, Argentina, 1986. b, Alberto, Brazil, 1970. c, Dunga, Brazil, 1994. d, Moore, England, 1966. e, Walter, Germany, 1954. f, Matthaus, Germany, 1990. g, Beckenbauer, Germany, 1974. h, Passarella, Argentina, 1978.
Winning teams, horiz.: No. 1177: a, Italy, 1938. b, W. Germany, 1954. c, Uruguay, 1958. d, England, 1966. e, Argentina, 1978. f, Brazil, 1962. g, Italy, 1934. h, Brazil, 1970. i, Uruguay, 1930.
No. 1178, 35nu, Philippe Albert, Belgium. No. 1179, 35nu, Salvatore (Toto) Schillaci, Italy, horiz.

Perf. 13½x14, 14x13½

1997, Oct. 9 Litho.

1170-1175	A141	Set of 6	8.00 8.00

Sheets of 8 or 9

1176	A141	10nu #a.-h. + label	6.25 6.25
1177	A141	10nu #a.-i.	7.00 7.00

Souvenir Sheets

1178-1179	A141	Set of 2	8.75 8.75

Friendship Between India and Bhutan A142

3nu, Jawaharlal Nehru, King Jigme Dorji Wangchuk. 10nu, Rajiv Gandhi, King Jigme Singye Wangchuk.
20nu, Indian Pres. R. V. Venkataraman, King Jigme Singye Wangchuk.

1998 Litho. *Perf. 13x13½*

1180	A142	3nu multicolored	.40 .40
1181	A142	10nu multicolored	.90 .90

Souvenir Sheet

1182	A142	20nu multicolored	2.00 2.00

No. 1182 contains one 76x35mm stamp.

A143

Indepex '97: No. 1183: a, 3nu, Buddha seated with legs crossed. b, 15nu, Buddha seated with legs down. c, 7nu, Gandhi with hands folded. d, 10nu, Gandhi.
No. 1184, 15nu, Buddha. No. 1185, 15nu, Gandhi holding staff.

1998 *Perf. 13½x13*

1183	A143	Sheet of 4, #a.-d.	2.50 2.50

Souvenir Sheets

1184-1185	A143	Set of 2	3.50 3.50

India's independence, 50th anniv.

A144

New Year 1998 (Year of the Tiger): 3nu, Stylized tiger walking right.
Tigers: No. 1187: a, 5nu, Lying down. b, 15nu, Adult walking forward. c, 17nu, Cub walking over rocks.
20nu, Adult up close.

1998, Feb. 28 Litho. *Perf. 14*

1186	A144	3nu multicolored	.25 .25
1187	A144	Sheet of 4, #a.-c., #1186	3.50 3.50

Souvenir Sheet

1188	A144	20nu multicolored	2.40 2.40

WHO, 50th Anniv. A145

1998, Apr. 7 Litho. *Perf. 13½*

1189	A145	3nu multicolored	.25 .25
1190	A145	10nu multicolored	.70 .70

Souvenir Sheet

Perf. 14

1191	A145	15nu Mother, child	1.10 1.10

Safe Motherhood. No. 1191 contains one 35x35mm stamp.

Mother Teresa (1910-97) A146

No. 1191A, Mother Teresa, Princess Diana.
No. 1192: a, Portrait (shown). b, Holding child. c, Holding starving infant. d, Seated among nuns. e, Looking down at sick. f, With hands folded in prayer. g, With Pope John Paul II. h, Portrait, diff.
No. 1193: a, like No. 1191A. b, like No. 1192g.

1998, May 25 Litho. *Perf. 13½*

1191A	A146	10nu multi	4.50 4.50
1192	A146	10nu Sheet of 9, #a.-h., 1191A	9.00 9.00

Souvenir Sheet of 2

1193	A146	25nu #a.-b.	3.00 3.00

No. 1192-1193 exist imperf. Value, $40 and $25, respectively.
No. 1193 contains two 38x43mm stamps.

Birds — A147

No. 1194: a, 10ch, Red-billed chough. b, 30ch, Great hornbill. c, 50ch, Singing lark. d, 70ch, Chestnut-flanked white-eye. e, 90ch, Magpie-robin. f, 1nu, Mrs. Gould's sunbird. g, 2nu, Tailorbird. h, 3nu, Duck. i, 5nu, Spotted cuckoo. j, 7nu, Gold crest. k, 9nu, Common mynah. l, 10nu, Green cochoa.
15nu, Turtle dove.

1998, July 28 Litho. *Perf. 13*

1194	A147	Sheet of 12, #a.-l.	5.00 5.00

Souvenir Sheet

1195	A147	15nu multicolored	2.00 2.00

No. 1195 contains one 40x30mm stamp.

New Year 1999 (Year of the Rabbit) A148

4nu, White rabbit. 15nu, Brown rabbit.
20nu, Rabbit facing forward.

1999, Jan. 1 Litho. *Perf. 13*

1196	A148	4nu multi	.35 .35
1197	A148	16nu multi	1.25 1.25

Souvenir Sheet

Perf. 13½

1198	A148	20nu multi	2.25 2.25

No. 1198 contains one 35x35mm stamp.

King Jigme Singye Wangchuk, 25th Anniv. of Coronation — A149

Various portraits, background color — No. 1199: a, Blue. b, Yellow. c, Orange. d, Green. No. 1200, Bright pink background.

1999, June 2 Litho. *Perf. 12¼*

1199 A149 25nu Sheet of 4, #a.-d. 7.00 7.00

Souvenir Sheet

1200 A149 25nu multicolored 1.90 1.90

Trains A150

Designs: 5nu, Early German steam. 10nu, EID 711 electric. 20nu, Steam engine. 30nu, Trans Europe Express, Germany.

No. 1205: a, Bullet train, Japan, 1964. b, 2-D-2 Class 26, South Africa, 1953. c, Super Chief, US, 1946. d, Magleus Magnet, Japan, 1991. e, The Flying Scotsman, UK, 1922. f, Kodama Train, Japan, 1958. g, Blue Train, South Africa, 1969. h, Inter-City, Germany, 1960. i, High Speed ET 403, Germany, 1973. j, US Standard 4-4-0, 1855. k, Bayer Garratt, South Africa, 1954. l, Settebello train, Italy, 1953.

No. 1206, each 15nu: a, Diesel-electric, France. b, 6-4-4-6 Pennsylvania RR, US. c, 2-8-2 Steam, Germany. d, Amtrak, US. e, GS&W 2-2-2, Britain. f, Class P steam, Denmark. g, French electric. h, First Japanese locomotive. i, 2-8-2 Germany.

No. 1207, each 15nu: a, Pacific Class 01, Germany. b, Neptune Express, Germany. c, 4-4-0 Steam, Britain. d, Shovelnose streamliner, US. e, German electric. f, Early steam, Germany. g, Union Pacific, US. h, Borsig steam, Germany, 1881. i, Borsig 4-6-4, Germany.

No. 1208, 80nu, Union Pacific electric locomotive E2 streamliner, US. No. 1209, 80nu, Great Northern diesel electric streamliner, US.

1999, July 21 *Perf. 14*

1201-1204 A150 Set of 4 4.50 4.50

Sheet of 12

1205 A150 10nu Sheet of 12, #a.-l. 6.00 6.00

Sheets of 9

1206-1207 A150 Set of 2 13.50 13.50

Souvenir Sheets

1208-1209 A150 Set of 2 8.00 8.00

Paintings by Hokusai (1760-1849) A151

Details or entire paintings — No. 1210, each 15nu: a, Suspension Bridge Between Hida and Etchu. b, Drawings of Women (partially nude). c, Exotic Beauty. d, The Poet Nakamaro in China. e, Drawings of Women (clothed). f, Chinese Poet in Snow.

No. 1211, each 15nu: a, Festive Dancers (with umbrella). b, Drawings of Women (holding book). c, Festive Dancers (man wearing checked pattern). d, Festive Dancers (person wearing black outfit). e, Drawings of Women (holding baby). f, Festive Dancers (woman with scarf tied under chin).

No. 1212, horiz., each 15nu: a, Mount Fuji Seen Above Mist on the Tama River. b, Mount Fuji Seen from Shichirigahama. c, Sea Life (turtle). d, Sea Life (fish). e, Mount Fuji Reflected in a Lake. f, Mount Fuji Seen Through the Piers of Mannenbashi.

Each 80nu: No. 1213, The Lotus Pedestal. No. 1214, Kushunoki Masashige. No. 1215, Peasants Leading Oxen.

1999, July 27 *Perf. 13½x14, 14x13½*

Sheets of 6

1210-1212 A151 Set of 3 18.00 18.00

Souvenir Sheet

1213-1215 A151 Set of 3 18.00 18.00

Souvenir Sheet

IBRA '99, Nuremberg A152

a, 35nu, City view. b, 40nu, Show emblem.

1999, Apr. 27 Litho. *Perf. 13¾*

1216 A152 Sheet of 2, #a.-b. 4.50 4.50

Prehistoric Animals — A153

No. 1217, each 10nu: a, Pterodactylus, Brachiosaurus. b, Pteranodon. c, Anurognathus, Tyrannosaurus. d, Brachiosaurus. e, Corythosaurus. f, Iguanodon. g, Lesothosaurus. h, Allosaurus. i, Velociraptor. j, Triceratops. k, Stegosaurus. l, Compsognatus.

No. 1218, each 10nu: a, Tyrannosaurus, black inscriptions b, Dimorphodon. c, Diplodocus. d, Pterodaustro. e, Tyrannosaurus, white inscriptions. f, Edmontosaurus. g, Apatosaurus. h, Deinonychus. i, Hypsilophodon. j, Oviraptor. k, Stegosaurus, diff. l, Triceratops, diff.

No. 1219: a, Moeritherium. b, Platybelodon. c, Wooly mammoth. d, African elephant. e, Deinonychus, diff. f, Dimorphodon, diff. g, Archaeopteryx. h, Ring-necked pheasant.

Each 80nu: No. 1220, Triceratops, vert. No. 1221, Pteranodon. No. 1222, Hoatzin, vert. No. 1223, Ichthyosaur, vert.

1999, Aug. 10 Litho. *Perf. 14*

Sheets of 12

1217-1218 A153 Set of 2 6.00 6.00

Sheet of 8

1219 A153 20nu a.-h. 9.00 9.00

Souvenir Sheets

1220-1223 A153 Set of 4 22.00 22.00

No. 1221 is incorrectly inscribed "Triceratops" instead of "Pteranodon," and No. 1223 is "Present Day Dolphin" instead of "Ichthysoaur."

Fauna — A154

Designs: a, Musk deer. b, Takin. c, Blue sheep. d, Yak. e, Goral.

1999, Aug. 21 Litho. *Perf. 12¾*

1224 A154 20nu Sheet of 5, #a.-e. + label 8.00 8.00

Birds A155

No. 1225, each 15nu: a, Chestnut-bellied chlorophonia. b, Yellow-faced Amazon parrot. c, White ibis. d, Caique. e, Green jay. f, Tufted coquette. g, Common troupial. h, Purple gallinule. i, Copper-rumped hummingbird.

No. 1226, each 15nu: a, Common egret. b, Rufous-browed peppershrike. c, Glittering-throated emerald. d, Great kiskadee. e, Cuban green woodpecker. f, Scarlet ibis. g, Belted kingfisher. h, Barred antshrike. i, Caribbean parakeet.

No. 1227, vert., each 15nu: a, Rufous-tailed jacamar. b, Scarlet macaw. c, Channel-billed toucan. d, Tricolored heron. e, St. Vincent parrot. f, Blue-crowned motmot. g, Horned screamer. h, Black-billed plover. i, Common meadowlark.

Each 80nu: No. 1228, Toco toucan. No. 1229, Red-billed scythebill, vert. No. 1230, Military macaws, vert.

1999, Oct. 17 Litho. *Perf. 14*

Sheets of 9, #a.-i.

1225-1227 A155 Set of 3 27.00 27.00

Souvenir Sheets

1228-1230 A155 Set of 3 16.00 16.00

Butterflies A156

Designs: 5nu, Sara orange tip. 10nu, Pipe-pine swallowtail. 15nu, Longwings. No. 1234, 20nu, Viceroy. 25nu, Silver-spotted skipper, vert. 30nu, Great spangled fritillary, vert. 35nu, Little copper.

No. 1238, each 20nu: a, Frosted skipper. b, Fiery skipper. c, Banded hairstreak. d, Clouded sulphur. e, Milberts tortoise shell. f, Eastern tailed blue.

No. 1239, each 20nu: a, Zebra swallowtail. b, Colorado hairstreak. c, Pink-edged sulphur. d, Fairy yellow. e, Red-spotted purple. f, Aphrodite.

Each 80nu: No. 1240, Checkered white. No. 1241, Gray hairstreak, vert. No. 1242, Gulf fritillary, vert. No. 1243, Monarch, vert.

1999, Oct. 4 Litho. *Perf. 14*

1231-1237 A156 Set of 7 9.50 9.50

Sheets of 6

1238-1239 A156 Set of 2 16.00 16.00

Souvenir Sheets

1240-1243 A156 Set of 4 22.00 22.00

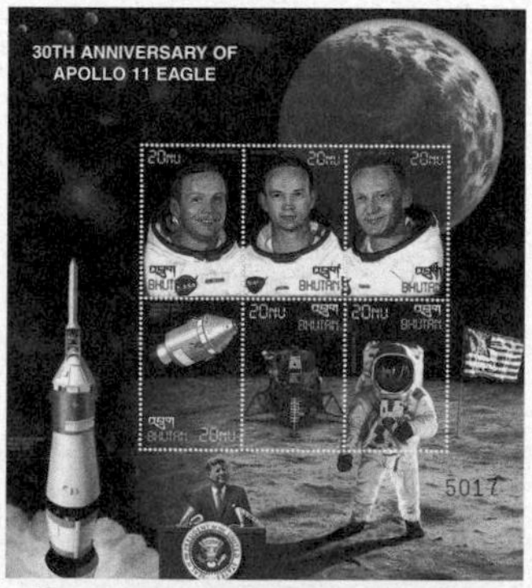

First Manned Moon Landing, 30th Anniv. — A157

No. 1244, each 20nu: a, Neil A. Armstrong (with name patch). b, Michael Collins. c, Edwin E. Aldrin, Jr. d, Command and service modules. e, Lunar module. f, Aldrin on Moon.

No. 1245, each 20nu: a, X-15 rocket. b, Gemini 8. c, Apollo 11 Saturn V rocket. d, Command and service modules (docked with lunar module). e, Lunar module (docked with command and service modules). f, Aldrin on lunar module ladder.

No. 1246, each 20nu: a, Yuri Gagarin. b, Alan B. Shepard, Jr. c, John H. Glenn, Jr. d, Valentina Tereshkova. e, Edward H. White II. f, Armstrong (no name patch).

Each 80nu: No. 1247, Armstrong, diff. No. 1248, Apollo 11 splashdown. No. 1249, Gemini 8 docked with Agena rocket, horiz.

1999, Nov. 1 Litho. *Perf. 14*

Sheets of 6

1244-1246 A157 Set of 3 25.00 25.00

Souvenir Sheets

1247-1249 A157 Set of 3 16.00 16.00

No. 1249 contains one 57x42mm stamp.

Cats, Horses, Dogs A158

Cats: No. 1250, 5nu, Tortoiseshell. No. 1251, 5nu, Woman and cat. 10nu, Chinchilla Golden Longhair.

No. 1253: a, Russian Blue. b, Birman. c, Devon Rex. d, Pewter Longhair. e, Bombay. f, Sorrel Somali. g, Red Tabby Manx. h, Blue Smoke Longhair. i, Oriental Tabby Shorthair. 70nu, Norwegian Shorthair.

1999, Nov. 15 Litho. *Perf. 14*

1250-1252 A158 Set of 3 3.50 3.50

Sheet of 9

1253 A158 12nu #a.-i. 7.00 7.00

Souvenir Sheet

1254 A158 70nu multicolored 5.00 5.00

1999, Nov. 15

Horses: 15nu, Lipizzaner. 20nu, Andalusian.

No. 1257: a, Przewalski. b, Shetland. c, Dutch Gelderlander. d, Shire. e, Arabian. f, Boulonnais. g, Falabella. h, Orlov Trotter. i, Suffolk Punch.

70nu, Connemara.

1255-1256 A158 Set of 2 3.50 3.50

Sheet of 9

1257 A158 12nu #a.-i. 8.00 8.00

Souvenir Sheet

1258 A158 70nu multicolored 5.00 5.00

1999, Nov. 15

Dogs: 25nu, Weimaraner. 30nu, German Shepherd.

No. 1261: a, Australian Silky Terrier. b, Samoyed. c, Basset Bleu de Gascogne. d, Bernese Mountain Dog. e, Pug. f, Bergamasco. g, Basenji. h, Wetterhoun. i, Drever.

70nu, Labrador Retriever.

1259-1260 A158 Set of 2 6.00 6.00

Sheet of 9

1261 A158 12nu #a.-i. 8.00 8.00

Souvenir Sheet

1262 A158 70nu multicolored 5.00 5.00

Birds, Mushrooms, Anilmals A159

No. 1263, each 20nu: a, Crested lark. b, Ferruginous duck. c, Blood pheasant. d, Laughing thrush. e, Golden eagle. f, Siberian rubythroat.

No. 1264, each 20nu: a, Red-crested pochard. b, Satyr tragopan. c, Lammergeier vulture. d, Kalij pheasant. e, Great Indian hornbill. f, Stork.

No. 1265, each 20nu: a, Rufous-necked hornbill. b, Drongo. c, Himalayan monal pheasant. d, Black-necked crane. e, Little green bee-eater. f, Ibis.

Each 100nu: No. 1266, Siberian rubythroat. No. 1267, Black-naped monarch. No. 1268, Mountain peacock pheasant.

1999, Dec. 17 *Perf. 13¾*

Sheets of 6, #a.-f.

1263-1265 A159 Set of 3 27.00 27.00

Souvenir Sheets

1266-1268 A159 Set of 3 20.00 20.00

1999, Dec. 17

No. 1269, each 20nu: a, Boletus frostii. b, Morchella estculenta. c, Hypomyces lactifuorum. d, Polyporus auricularius. e, Cantahrellus lateritius. f, Volvariella pusilla.
No. 1270, each 20nu: a, Microglossum rufum. b, Lactarius hygrophoroides. c, Lactarius speciousus complex. d, Calostoma cinnabarina. e, Clitocybe clavipes. f, Microstoma floccosa.
No. 1271, each 20nu: a, Mutinus elegans. b, Pholiota squarrosoides. c, Coprinus quadrifudus. d, Clavulinopsis fusiformis. e, Spathularia velutipes. f, Ganoderma lucidum.
Each 100nu: No. 1272, Pholiota aurivella. No. 1273, Ramaria grandis. No. 1274, Oudemansiella lucidum.

Sheets of 6, #a.-f.

1269-1271 A159 Set of 3 27.00 27.00

Souvenir Sheets

1272-1274 A159 Set of 3 20.00 20.00

1999, Nov. 24 Litho. *Perf. 13¾*

No. 1275, each 20nu: a, Otter. b, Tibetan wolf. c, Himalayan black bear. d, Snow leopard. e, Flying squirrel. f, Red fox.
No. 1276, each 20nu: a, Bharal. b, Lynx. c, Rat snake. d, Elephant. e, Langur. f, Musk deer.
No. 1277, each 20nu: a, Ibex. b, Takin. c, Agama lizard. d, Marmot. e, Red panda. f, Leopard cat.
Each 100nu: No. 1278, Rhinoceros. No. 1279, Cobra. No. 1280, Tiger.

Sheets of 6, #a-f

1275-1277 A159 Set of 3 27.00 27.00

Souvenir Sheets

1278-1280 A159 Set of 3 20.00 20.00

Millennium
A160

Frame background color: 10nu, Dark blue green. 20nu, Bright violet.

1999, Dec. 15

1281-1282 A160 Set of 2 2.00 2.00

New Year 2000 (Year of the Dragon)
A161

Various dragons. Denominations: 3nu, 5nu, 8nu, 12nu.
15nu, Dragon, vert.

2000

1283-1286 A161 Set of 4 2.50 2.50

Souvenir Sheet

Perf. 12¾

1287 A161 15nu multi 1.50 1.50

No. 1287 contains one 30x40mm stamp.

Space — A162

No. 1288, horiz., each 25nu: a, Victor Patsayev. b, Vladislav Volkov. c, Georgi Dobrovolski. d, Virgil Grissom. e, Roger Chaffee. f, Edward White.
No. 1289, horiz., each 25nu: a, NASA shuttle Challenger. b, X-15. c, Buran. d, Hermes. e, X-33 Venturi Star. f, Hope.
No. 1290, horiz., each 25nu: a, Luna 3. b, Ranger 9. c, Lunar Orbiter. d, Lunar Prospector. e, Apollo 11. f, Selene.
Each 80nu: No. 1291, Challenger. No. 1292, Buran. No. 1293, Astronaut on moon.

2000, May 15 Litho. *Perf. 14*

Sheets of 6, #a-f

1288-1290 A162 Set of 3 30.00 30.00

Souvenir Sheets

1291-1293 A162 Set of 3 15.00 15.00

World Stamp Expo 2000, Anaheim.

First Zeppelin Flight, Cent. — A163

No. 1294, horiz., each 25nu: a, LZ-1 and hills. b, LZ-9. c, LZ-6 in hangar. d, LZ-10. e, LZ-7. f, LZ-11.
No. 1295, horiz., each 25nu: a, LZ-1 and sky. b, LZ-2 and treetops. c, LZ-3 and ground. d, LZ-127. e, LZ-129. f, LZ-130.
No. 1296, horiz., each 25nu: a, LZ-1 and treetops. b, LZ-2 and mountains. c, LZ-3 and sky. d, LZ-4. e, LZ-5. f, LZ-6.
Each 80nu: No. 1297, Ferdinand von Zeppelin, without hat. No. 1298, Zeppelin with white hat. No. 1299, Zeppelin with black hat.

2000, May 15 Sheets of 6, #a-f

1294-1296 A163 Set of 3 30.00 30.00

Souvenir Sheets

1297-1299 A163 Set of 3 16.00 16.00

Souvenir Sheet

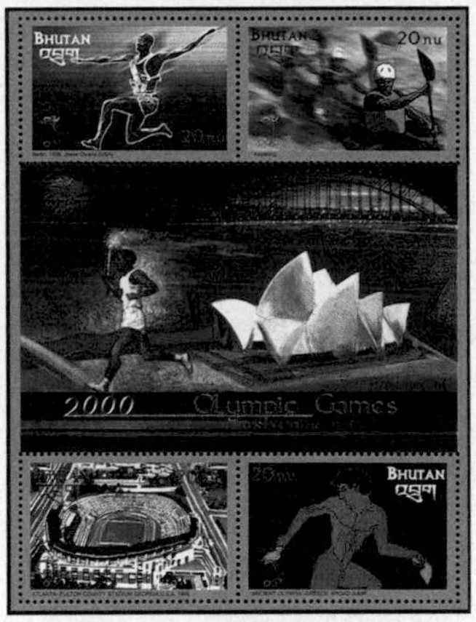

2000 Summer Olympics, Sydney — A164

No. 1300, each 20nu: a, Jesse Owens. b, Kayaking. c, Fulton County Stadium, Atlanta. d, Ancient greek broad jump.

2000, July 24

1300 A164 Sheet of 4, #a-d 5.00 5.00

British Railway System, 175th Anniv. — A165

No. 1301, each 50nu: a, George Stephenson's Rocket. b, London and Birmingham Railway, 1828. c, Northumbrian engine, 1825.
100nu, Stockton and Darlington Railway opening, 1825.

2000, July 31 Litho. *Perf. 14*

1301 A165 Sheet of 3, #a-c 10.00 10.00

Souvenir Sheet

1302 A165 100nu multi 6.50 6.50

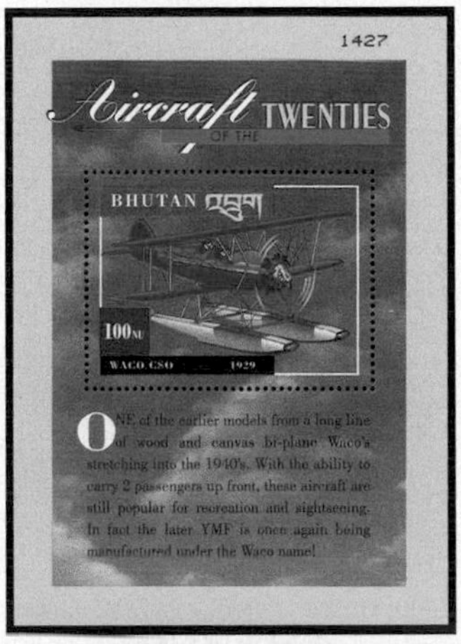

Airplanes — A166

No. 1303, 25nu: a, Laird Commercial. b, Ryan Brougham. c, Cessna AW. d, Travel Air 4000. e, Fairchild F-71. f, Command Aire.
No. 1304, 25nu: a, WACO YMF. b, Piper J4 Cub Coupe. c, Ryan ST-A. d, Spartan Executive. e, Luscombe 8. f, Stinson SR5 Reliant.
No. 1305, 25nu: a, Cessna 195. b, WACO SRE. c, Erco Ercoupe. d, Boeing Stearman. e, Beech Staggerwing. f, Republic Seabee.
No. 1306, 100nu, WACO CSO. No. 1307, 100nu, Curtiss-Wright 19W. No. 1308, 100nu, Grumman G-44 Widgeon.

2000, Aug. 7 *Perf. 13¾*

Sheets of 6, #a-f

1303-1305 A166 Set of 3 26.00 26.00

Souvenir Sheets

1306-1308 A166 Set of 3 18.00 18.00

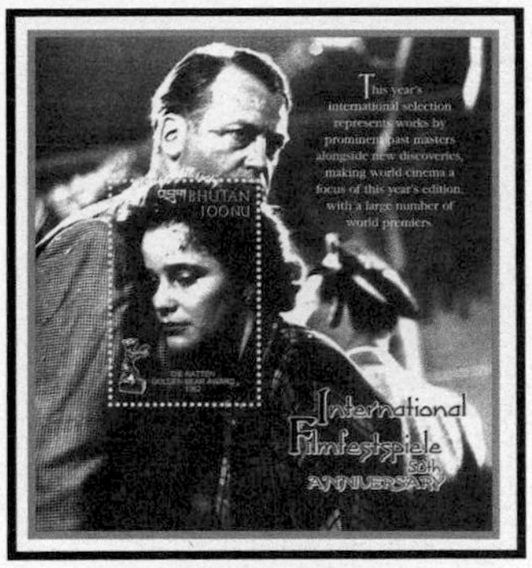

Berlin Film Festival, 50th Anniv. — A167

No. 1309, each 25nu: a, A Kind of Loving. b, Bushido Zankoku Monogatari. c, Hobson's Choice. d, El Lazarillo de Tormes. e, In the Name of the Father. f, Les Cousins.
100nu, Die Ratten.

2000, Aug. 15 *Perf. 14*

1309 A167 Sheet of 6, #a-f 9.00 9.00

Souvenir Sheet

1310 A167 100nu multi 6.50 6.50

Souvenir Sheet

Albert Einstein (1879-1955) — A168

2000, Sept. 1 *Perf. 12x12¼*

1311 A168 100nu multi 7.50 7.50

Flowers — A169

No. 1312, 25nu: a, Crinum amoenum. b, Beaumontia grandiflora. c, Trachelospermum lucidum. d, Curcuma aromatica. e, Barleria cristata. f, Holmskioldia sanguinea.
No. 1313, 25nu: a, Meconopsis villosa. b, Salvia hians. c, Caltha palustris. d, Anemone polyanthes. e, Cypripedium cordigerum. f, Cryptochilus luteus.
No. 1314, 25nu: a, Androsace globifera. b, Tanacetum atkinsonii. c, Aster stracheyi. d, Arenaria glanduligera. e, Sibbaldia purpurea. f, Saxifraga parnassifolia.
No. 1315, 100nu, Dendrobium densiflorum, vert. No. 1316, 100nu, Rhododendron arboreum, vert. No. 1317, Gypsophila cerastioides.

Perf. 14¼x14½, 14½x14¼

2000, Sept. 5

Sheets of 6, #a-f

1312-1314 A169 Set of 3 26.00 26.00

Souvenir Sheets

1315-1317 A169 Set of 3 18.00 18.00

St. Thomas Aquinas (1225-1274) A170

2000, Sept. 18 *Perf. 14x14¾*

1318 A170 25nu multi 1.50 1.50

No. 1318 printed in sheets of 4.

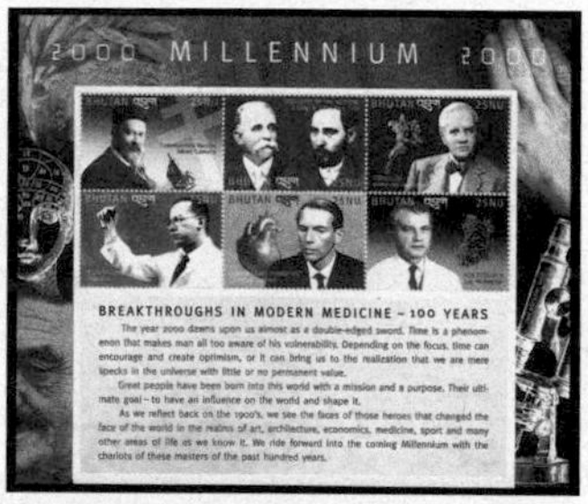

A171

Millennium — A172

Medical pioneers — No. 1319, 25nu: a, Albert Calmette. b, Camillo Golgi and Santiago Ramón y Cajal. c, Alexander Fleming. d, Jonas Salk. e, Christiaan Barnard. f, Luc Montagnier.

Olympic movement — No. 1320, 25nu: a, Baron Pierre de Coubertin. b, 1896 Athens Games. c, Jesse Owens. d, 1972 Munich Games. e, 2000 Sydney Games. f, 2004 Athens Games.

100nu, Paro Taktsang.

2000, Sept. 18 *Perf. 14*

Sheets of 6, #a-f

1319-1320 A171 Set of 2 18.00 18.00

Souvenir Sheet

1321 A172 100nu multi 6.00 6.00

Souvenir Sheets

Explorers — A173

No. 1322, Christopher Columbus. No. 1323, Capt. James Cook.

2000, Sept. 18

1322-1323 A173 100nu Set of 2 12.00 12.00

Expo 2000, Hanover — A174

No. 1324 — Dzongs: a, 3nu, Trashigang. b, 4nu, Lhuentse. c, 6nu, Gasa. d, 7nu, Punakha. e, 10nu, Trashichhoe. f, 20nu, Paro.

No. 1325 — Flora and Fauna, 10nu: a, Snow leopard, b, Raven. c, Golden langur. d, Rhododendron. e, Black-necked crane. f, Blue poppy.

Perf. 13x13¼ (#1324), 12¾

2000, June 1 **Litho.**

Sheets of 6, #a-f

1324-1325 A174 Set of 2 4.75 4.75

Souvenir Sheet

1326 A174 15nu Temple 1.75 1.75

Size of stamps in Nos. 1325-1326: 40x31mm.

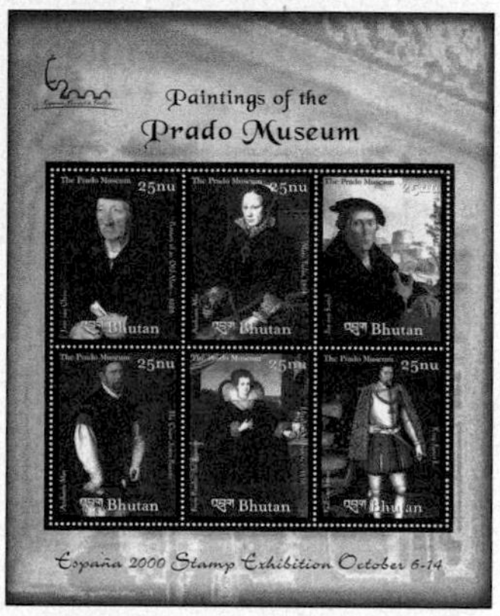

Paintings from the Prado — A175

No. 1327, 25nu: a, Portrait of an Old man, by Joos van Cleve. b, Mary I, by Anthonis Mor. c, Portrait of a Man, by Jan van Scorel. d, The Court Jester Pejerón, by Mor. e, Elizabeth of France, by Frans Pourbus, the Younger. f, King James I, by Paul van Somer.

No. 1328, 25nu: a, Isabella of Portugal, by Titian. b, Lucrecia di Baccia del Fede, the Painter's Wife, by Andrea del Sarto. c, Self-portrait, by Titian. d, Philip II, by Sofonisba Anguisciola. e, Portrait of a Doctor, by Lucia Anguisciola. f, Anna of Austria, by Sofonisba Anguisciola.

No. 1329, 25nu: a, Duchess. b, Child. c, Duke. d, Isidoro Maiquez, by Goya. e, Doña Juana Galarza de Goicoechea, by Goya. f, Ferdinand VII in an Encampment, by Goya. a-c from #1332.

No. 1330, 100nu, Charles V on Horseback at the Battle of Mühlberg. No. 1331, 100nu, The Relief of Genoa, by Antonio de Pereda y Salgado. No. 1332, 100nu, The Duke and Duchess of Osuna With Their Children, by Goya, horiz.

2000, Oct. 6 *Perf. 12x12¼, 12¼x12*

Sheets of 6, #a-f

1327-1329 A175 Set of 3 32.00 32.00

Souvenir Sheets

1330-1332 A175 Set of 3 21.00 21.00

España 2000 Intl. Philatelic Exhibition.

Indepex 2000 Philatelic Exhibition, India — A176

No. 1333: a, 5nu, Butterfly. b, 8nu, Red jungle fowl. c, 10nu, Zinnia elegans. d, 12nu, Tiger.

15nu, Spotted deer.

2000 **Litho.** *Perf. 13¾*

1333 A176 Sheet of 4, #a-d 2.00 2.00

Souvenir Sheet

Perf. 13¼x13½

1334 A176 15nu multi 1.90 1.90

New Year 2001 (Year of the Snake) — A177

Various snakes and flowers with panel colors of: 3nu, Light blue. No. 1337a, 10nu, Dark blue. No. 1337b, 15nu, Green. 20nu, Red.

2001 *Perf. 12¾*

1335-1336 A177 Set of 2 1.50 1.50

Souvenir Sheet

1337 A177 Sheet, #a-b, 1335-1336 3.00 3.00

Souvenir Sheet

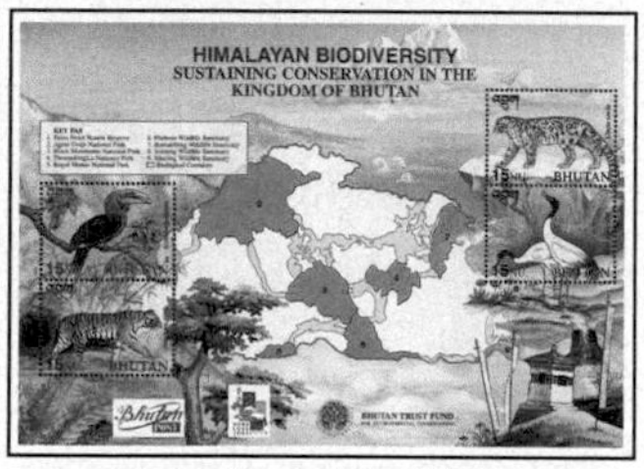

Hong Kong 2001 Stamp Exhibition — A178

No. 1338: a, Uncia uncia. b, Aceros nipalensis. c, Grus nigricollis. d, Panthera tigris.

2001

1338 A178 15nu Sheet of 4, #a-d 4.75 4.75

Intl. Volunteers Year A179

Various children's drawings: 3nu, 4nu, 10nu, 15nu.

2001

1339-1342 A179 Set of 4 2.75 2.75

a. Souvenir sheet, #1339-1342 3.00 3.00

Souvenir Sheet

Choelong Trulsum — A180

No. 1343: a, 10nu, Chenrezig. b, 15nu, Guru Rimpoche. c, 20nu, Sakyamuni.

2001, Sept. 23 **Litho.** *Perf. 13¼*

1343 A180 Sheet of 3, #a-c 3.25 3.25

Nos. 495-498 Surcharged

2001, Oct. 9 **Litho.** *Perf. 11¾*

1344 A62 4nu on 10ch #495 .50 .50
1345 A62 10nu on 25ch #496 1.00 1.00
1346 A62 15nu on 50ch #497 1.60 1.60
1347 A62 20nu on 1nu #498 2.25 2.25
1347A A62 4nu on 10ch #495 *3.00* —
1347B A62 10nu on 25ch #496 *6.00* —
Nos. 1344-1347B (6) 14.35 5.35

Obliterator on Nos. 1347A-1347B has deeper curve than that on Nos. 1344-1345. Two surcharge settings exist on Nos. 1344 and 1345.

Souvenir Sheet

Snow Leopards — A181

No. 1348: a, Face, vert. b, Two leopards. c, Three kittens. d, Leopard walking, vert.

2001, Dec. 17 **Litho.** *Perf. 13½*

1348 A181 10nu Sheet of 8, 2 each #a-d 3.50 3.50

Souvenir Sheet

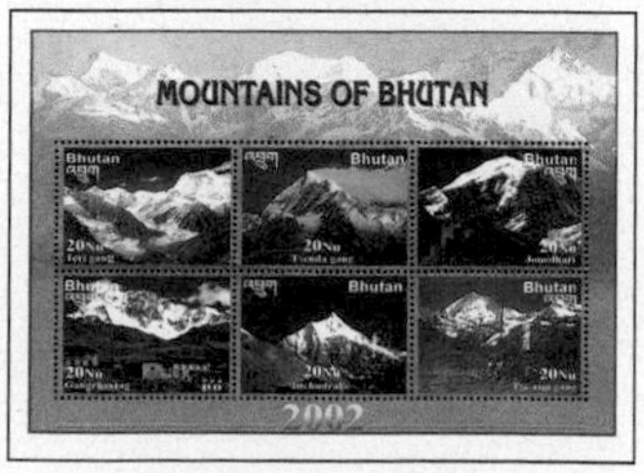

Mountains — A182

No. 1349: a, Teri Gang. b, Tsenda Gang. c, Jomolhari. d, Gangheytag. e, Jitchudrake. f, Tse-rim Gang.

2002, Feb. 5 *Perf. 12¾*

1349 A182 20nu Sheet of 6, #a-f 8.00 8.00

Souvenir Sheet

Orchids — A183

No. 1350: a, Rhomboda lanceolata. b, Odontochilus lanceolatus. c, Zeuxine glandulosa. d, Goodyera schlechtendaliana. e, Anoectochilus lanceolatus. f, Goodyera hipsida.

2002, Apr. 3 ***Perf. 13x13¼***
1350 A183 10nu Sheet of 6 #a-f 4.50 4.50

Souvenir Sheet

Rhododendrons — A184

No. 1351: a, Rhododondron arboreum. b, Rhododendron niveum. c, Rhododendron dalhousiae. d, Rhododendron glaucophyllum. e, Rhododendron barbatum. f, Rhododendron grande.

2002, May 1 ***Perf. 13¾***
1351 A184 15nu Sheet of 6, #a-f, + label 7.50 7.50

New Year 2002 (Year of the Horse) — A185

No. 1352: a, Tan horse. b, White horse.
25nu, Yellow horse, horiz.

2002, Jan. 1 ***Perf. 12¾***
1352 A185 20nu Horiz. pair, #a-b 2.40 2.40

Souvenir Sheet

1353 A185 25nu multi 1.90 1.90

Medicinal Plants — A186

Designs: No. 1354, 10nu, Bombax ceiba. No. 1355, 10nu, Brugmansia suaveolens. No. 1356, 10nu, Podophyllum hexandrum. No. 1357, 10nu, Phytolacca acinosa.

2002, June 2 **Litho.** ***Perf. 12¾***
1354-1357 A186 Set of 4 3.25 3.25
a. Souvenir sheet, #1354-1357 3.50 3.50

United We Stand — A187

2002, Sept. 16 ***Perf. 14***
1358 A187 25nu multi 5.50 5.50

Printed in sheets of 4.

Souvenir Sheet

2002 Winter Olympics, Salt Lake City — A188

No. 1359: a, Ski jumper. b, Cross-country skier.

2002, Sept. 16
1359 A188 50nu Sheet of 2, #a-b 5.50 5.50

Reign of Queen Elizabeth II, 50th Anniv. — A189

No. 1360: a, Wearing blue hat. b, Wearing green and white hat. c, Wearing red violet hat. d, Wearing white hat with blue trim.
90nu, Wearing tiara.

2002, Sept. 16 ***Perf. 14¼***
1360 A189 40nu Sheet of 4, #a-d 7.25 7.25

Souvenir Sheet

1361 A189 90nu multi 6.75 6.75

Intl. Year of Ecotourism — A190

No. 1362: a, Lotus. b, Northern jungle queen butterfly. c, Bengal tiger.
90nu, Peacock.

2002, Oct. 14 ***Perf. 14***
1362 A190 50nu Sheet of 3, #a-c 7.00 7.00

Souvenir Sheet

1363 A190 90nu multi 5.50 5.50

20th World Scout Jamboree, Thailand — A191

No. 1364, horiz.: a, Scout. b, Four scouts. c, Boy saluting, 1908.
90nu, Daniel Beard.

2002, Oct. 14
1364 A191 50nu Sheet of 3, #a-c 7.00 7.00

Souvenir Sheet

1365 A191 90nu multi 5.50 5.50

First Solo Transatlantic Flight, 75th Anniv. — A192

No. 1366: a, Charles Lindbergh and The Spirit of St. Louis. b, Lindbergh.
90nu, Lindbergh, diff.

2002, Oct. 14
1366 A192 75nu Sheet of 2, #a-b 7.00 7.00

Souvenir Sheet

1367 A192 90nu multi 5.00 5.00

2002 World Cup Soccer Championships, Japan and Korea — A193

No. 1368: a, Zinedine Zidane. b, Michael Owen. c, Miyagi Stadium, Japan. d, Cuauhtemoc Blanco. e, Gabriel Batistuta. f, Incheon Stadium, Korea.
150nu, Roberto Carlos.

2002
1368 A193 25nu Sheet of 6, #a-f 7.00 7.00

Souvenir Sheet

1369 A193 150nu multi 7.00 7.00

A194

Flora, Fauna and Mushrooms — A195

No. 1370, 25nu — Flowers: a, Primula cawdoriana. b, Meconopsis aculeata. c, Primula wigramiana. d, Primula stuartii. e, Saxifraga andersonii. f, Rheum nobile.

No. 1371, 25nu — Orchids: a, Coelogyne rhodeana. b, Coelogyne virescens. c, Phalaenopsis schilleriana. d, Angraecum eburneum. e, Dendrobium aureum. f, Dendrobium Caesar x Jag.

No. 1372, 25nu — Mushrooms: a, Entire russula. b, March wax cap. c, Fawn tricholoma. d, Sulfur tuft. e, Poplar tricholoma. f, Annatto-colored cortinarius.

No. 1373, 25nu — Butterflies: a, Dead leaf. b, Troides aeacus. c, Atrophaneura latreillei. d, Teinopalpus imperialis. e, Zeuxidia aurelius. f, Euploea dufresne.

No. 1374, 25nu — Birds: a, Yellow-legged gull. b, Sand martin. c, Asian openbill. d, White stork. e, Eurasian oystercatcher. f, Indian pitta.

No. 1375, 25nu — Animals: a, Gaur. b, Hog badger. c, Indian cobra. d, Leopard gecko. e, Gavial. f, Hispid hare.

No. 1376, 90nu, Paris polyphylla. No. 1377, 90nu, Dendrobium chrysotoxum. No. 1378, 90nu, Red tentacle fungus. No. 1379, 90nu, Portia philota. No. 1380, 90nu, Mandarin duck. No. 1381, 90nu, Estuarine crocodile.

2002, Dec. 16 Litho. *Perf. 14*

Sheets of 6, #a-f

1370-1373 A194 Set of 4 25.00 25.00
1374-1375 A195 Set of 2 12.50 12.50

Souvenir Sheets

1376-1379 A194 Set of 4 15.00 15.00
1380-1381 A195 Set of 2 7.50 7.50

Pres. John F. Kennedy (1917-63) — A196

No. 1382: a, As Choate graduate, 1935. b, With John, Jr. c, As congressman, 1946. d, At White House, 1961. e, With wife at tennis court. f, Wife and children at funeral, 1963.
90nu, Portrait.

2003, Feb. 3

1382 A196 25nu Sheet of 6, #a-f 11.00 11.00

Souvenir Sheet

1383 A196 90nu multi 5.00 5.00

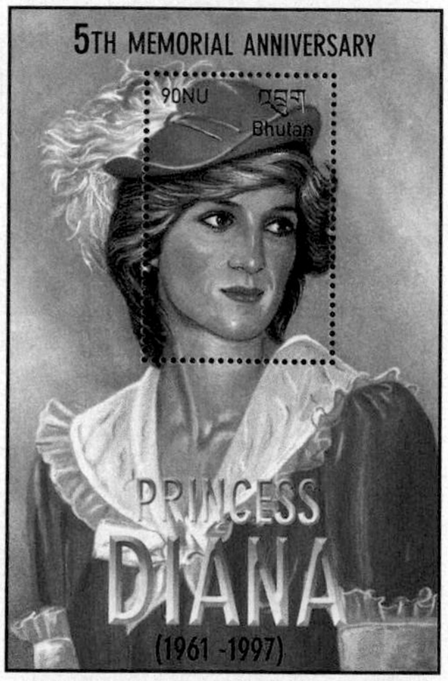

Princess Diana (1961-97) — A197

No. 1384: a, Wearing red dress. b, Wearing blue violet dress. c, Wearing black sweater and blue blouse. d, Wearing tiara and yellow gown.
90nu, Wearing red hat.

2003, Feb. 3

1384 A197 40nu Sheet of 4, #a-d 12.00 12.00

Souvenir Sheet

1385 A197 90nu multi 5.00 5.00

Elvis Presley (1935-77) — A198

No. 1386 — Various photos of Presley with guitar in color of: a, Greenish gray. b, Sepia. c, Bluish gray. d, Lilac.
No. 1387 — Presley without guitar in color of: a, Violet brown. b, Bluish gray. c, Sepia. d, Greenish gray. e, Brown. f, Lilac.

2003, Feb. 3

1386 A198 25nu Sheet of 4, #a-d 6.00 6.00
1387 A198 25nu Sheet of 6, #a-f 9.00 9.00

No. 548 Surcharged

2003, Feb. 25 Litho. *Perf. 13½*

1388 A69 8nu on 75ch multi .60 .60

Souvenir Sheet

New Year 2003 (Year of the Sheep) — A199

No. 1389: a, 15nu, Lambs. b, 20nu, Sheep, vert.

2003, Mar. 3 *Perf. 12½*

1389 A199 Sheet of 2, #a-b 3.00 3.00

Japanese Art — A200

No. 1390, 25nu, vert.: a, Beauty Reading Letter, by Kunisada Utagawa. b, Two Beauties, by Shunsho Katsukawa. c, Beauty Arranging Her Hair, by Doshin Kaigetsudo. d, Dancing, by Kiitsu Suzuki. e, Two Beauties, by Kikumaro Kitagawa. f, Kambun Beauty, by unknown Edo Period artist.
No. 1391, 25nu, vert.: a, Detail of Egret and Willow, by Suzuki. b, Cranes, by Jakuchu Ito. c, Detail of Cranes, by Kiitsu Suzuki. d, Mandarin Ducks Amid Snow-covered Reeds, by Ito. e, Rooster, Hen and Hydrangeas, by Ito. f, Hawk Perched on a Snow-covered Branch, by Zeshin Shibata.
No. 1392, 25nu, vert. — The Thirty-six Poets, by Hoitsu Sakai: a, Poet in black with arms folded. b, Poet in green with object in hand. c, Poet touching head. d, Poets with white, light blue, red and black kimonos. e, Poets with dark blue, black, gray and tan kimonos. f, Poets with white, green, light blue and black kimonos.
No. 1393, 90nu, Detail of Heads of Nine Beauties in a Roundel With Plum Blossom, by Eishi Hosoda. No. 1394, 90nu, Chrysanthemums by a Stream, With Rocks, by Ito. No. 1395, 90nu, Hawk Carrying Off a Monkey, by Shibata.

Perf. 14x14¾, 14¼ (#1392)

2003, Mar. 10

Sheets of 6, #a-f

1390-1392 A200 Set of 3 27.00 27.00

Size: 90x90mm

Imperf

1393-1395 A200 Set of 3 13.50 13.50

Nos. 1390-1391 each contain six 26x77mm stamps; No. 1392 contains six 38x50mm stamps.

Souvenir Sheet

Move for Health Walk — A201

2003, May 19 Litho. *Perf. 13¾*

1396 A201 50nu multi 2.75 2.75

Souvenir Sheet

Education for Every Girl and Boy — A202

No. 1397: a, 5nu, Girl and parrot. b, 5nu, Girl reading book. c, 10nu, Boy and girl. d, 20nu, Girl with soccer ball.

2003, Nov. 11 Litho. *Perf. 12¾*

1397 A202 Sheet of 4, #a-d 2.50 2.50

Souvenir Sheet

Worldwide Fund for Nature (WWF) — A203

No. 1398: a, 2nu, Lophura leucomelanus. b, 5nu, Tragopan blythii. c, 8nu, Tragopan satyra. d, 15nu, Lophophorus impejanus.

2003, Dec. 17

1398 A203 Sheet of 4, #a-d 3.00 3.00

Souvenir Sheet

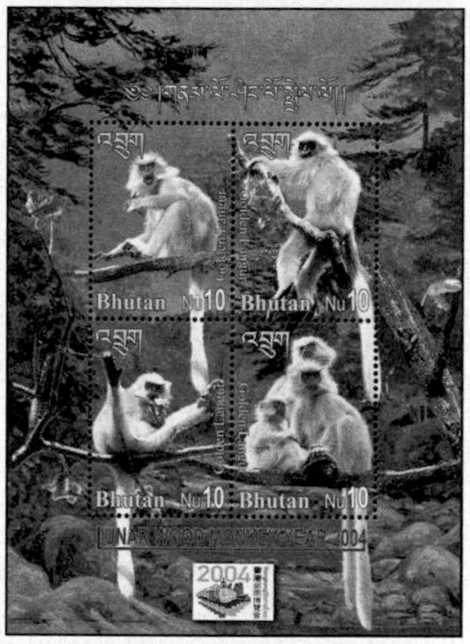

New Year 2004 (Year of the Monkey) — A204

No. 1399 — Golden langurs: a, Langur with elbow on knee. b, Langur on branch, "Golden Langur" at left. c, Langur with legs spread apart. d, Three langurs.

2004, Jan. 30

1399 A204 10nu Sheet of 4, #a-d 4.00 3.25

2004 Hong Kong Stamp Expo.

FIFA (Fédération Internationale de Football Association), Cent. — A205

No. 1400 — World Cup Champions: a, Brazil, 2002. b, France, 1998.

2004 Litho. *Perf. 11¾x12*

1400 A205 10nu Vert. pair, #a-b 1.50 1.50

Expo 2005, Aichi, Japan — A206

No. 1401 — Masked dancers: a, 10nu, Jugging-cham. b, 10nu, Durdhak-cham. c, 20nu, Nga-cham. d, 20nu, Shazam-cham.
30nu, Buddha.

2005, Mar. 25 Litho. *Perf. 13¼*
1401 A206 Sheet of 4, #a-d 4.00 4.00

Souvenir Sheet
Perf. 12

1402 A206 30nu multi 2.00 2.00

No. 1401 contains four 35x70mm stamps.

Souvenir Sheet

Rotary International, Cent. — A207

2005, Aug. 24 *Perf. 12¾*
1403 A207 85nu multi 7.50 7.50

Miniature Sheet

Pope John Paul II (1920-2005) — A208

No. 1404: a, Pink sky showing below LL corner of vignette, purple mountain sloping upward at right. b, Purple mountain at right slightly above top of Pope's shoulder. c, Purple mountain at right below top of Pope's shoulder. d, Pink frame.

2005, Aug. 24
1404 A208 15nu Sheet of 9, #a-c, 6 #d 13.00 13.00

Locomotives — A209

No. 1405, horiz.: a, P36 N0097. b, VIA F 40 6428. c, InterRegio train. d, Amtrak 464.
85nu, P36 N0032.

2005, Aug. 24
1405 A209 30nu Sheet of 4, #a-d 10.00 10.00

Souvenir Sheet

1406 A209 85nu multi 7.50 7.50

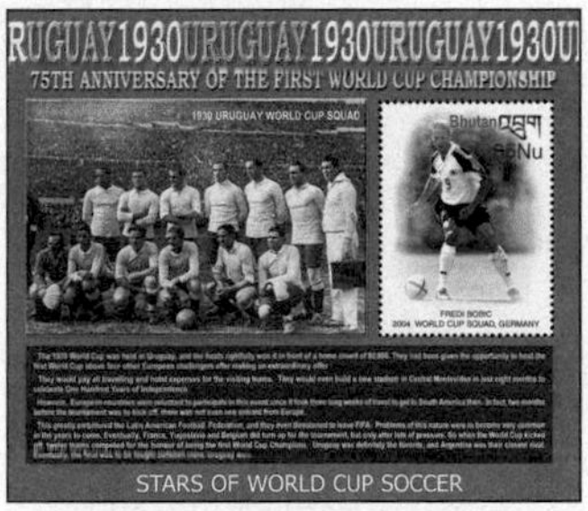

World Cup Soccer Championships, 75th Anniv. — A210

No. 1407: a, Guido Buchwald. b, Mario Basler. c, Torsten Frings.
85nu, Fredi Bobic.

2005, Aug. 24 *Perf. 12¼x12*
1407 A210 40nu Sheet of 3, #a-c 10.00 10.00

Souvenir Sheet

1408 A210 85nu multi 7.50 7.50

No. 298 Surcharged

2005 *Perf. 14*

1409 A39 5nu on 1nu #298	*5.00*	*20.00*
c. No space btwn "Nu5"	*30.00*	*35.00*
1409A A39 5nu on 1.25nu #299	*30.00*	*35.00*
1409B A39 5nu on 1.70nu #300	*30.00*	*35.00*
Nos. 1409-1409B (3)	65.00	90.00

No. 1409 exists with bold sans-serif surcharge. It is not certain whether it was regularly issued. Value unused, *$40.*

No. 1409B exists with inverted surcharges. Value, $70 each.

Souvenir Sheet

New Year 2005 (Year of the Rooster) — A211

No. 1410: a, 15nu, Jungle rooster and hen. b, 20nu, Domestic rooster and hen.

2005 *Perf. 11¾x12*
1410 A211 Sheet of 2, #a-b 2.75 2.75

Japanese Assistance, 20th Anniv. — A212

No. 1411, horiz.: a, Traditional plowing. b, Traditional transplanting. c, Traditional threshing. d, Modern plowing. e, Modern transplanting. f, Modern threshing.
30nu, King Jigme Singye Wangchuk at plow.

2005 *Perf. 11¾x12*
1411 A212 5nu Sheet of 6, #a-f 2.50 2.50

Souvenir Sheet
Perf. 12x11¾

1412 A212 30nu multi 2.50 2.50

Miniature Sheet

My Dream For Peace One Day — A213

No. 1413 — Children's drawings: a, Doves, flags, people, world map. b, Candle, flags. c, Children and jigsaw puzzle. d, Hands, globe, dove. e, Hands, doves, olive branch. f, Globe holding umbrella.

2005, Sept. 21 *Perf. 13¼*
1413 A213 10nu Sheet of 6, #a-f 5.50 5.50

Miniature Sheet

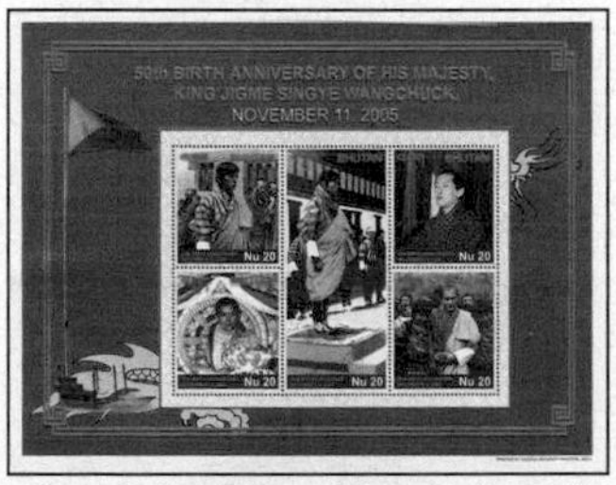

King Jigme Singye Wangchuk, 50th Birthday — A214

No. 1414: a, Standing, with other men. b, At microphone. c, With fruit bowl. d, Shaking hands with man. e, Standing on platform (39x87mm).

2005, Nov. 11 Litho. *Perf. 13¼*
1414 A214 20nu Sheet of 5, #a-e 9.00 9.00

Miniature Sheet

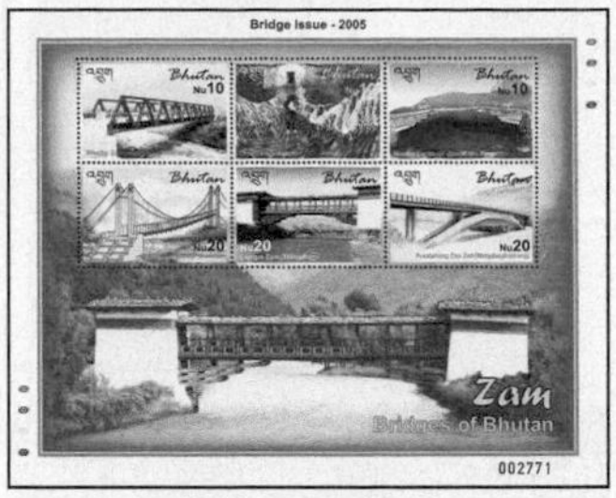

Bridges — A215

No. 1415: a, 10nu, Wachy Bridge. b, 10nu, Chain bridge. c, 10nu, Wooden cantilever bridge. d, 20nu, Mo Chu Bridge. e, 20nu, Langjo Bridge. f, 20nu, Punatshang Chu Bridge.

2005 *Perf. 11¾x12*
1415 A215 Sheet of 6, #a-f 8.00 8.00

New Year 2006 (Year of the Dog) — A216

Designs: Nos. 1416, 1420a, 5nu, St. Bernard. Nos. 1417, 1420b, 10nu, Lhasa Apso. Nos. 1418, 1420c, 15nu, Maltese. Nos. 1419, 1420d, 20nu, Papillon. No. 1420e, 25nu, Husky, vert. (33x68mm).

2006, Feb. 28 Litho. *Perf. 13¼*
Denominations in White or Purple (#1416)

1416-1419 A216 Set of 4 2.50 2.50

Miniature Sheet
Denominations in Yellow

1420 A216 Sheet of 5, #a-e 3.75 3.75

Europa Stamps, 50th Anniv. — A217

Designs: 150nu, Jakar Dzong. 250nu, Archery.

2006 *Perf. 12¾x13½*
1421-1422 A217 Set of 2 20.00 20.00
1422a Souvenir sheet, #1421-1422 20.00 20.00

Nos. 1421-1422, 1422a exist imperf. Values, unused or used: set $25; souvenir sheet $25. Uncut press sheets exist, from which gutter pairs can be cut.

Miniature Sheet

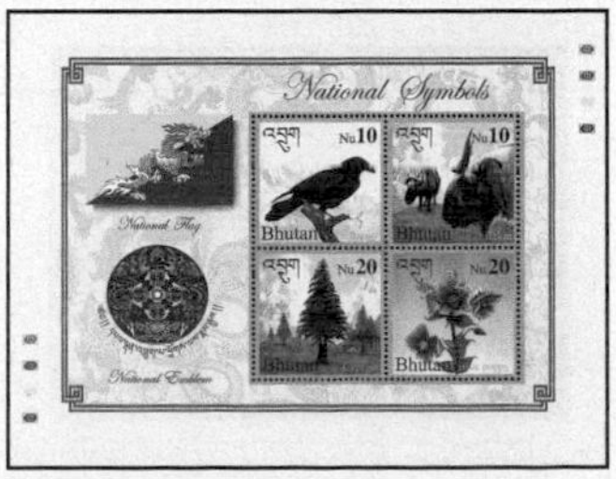

National Symbols — A218

No. 1423: a, 10nu, Raven. b, 10nu, Takins. c, 20nu, Cypress trees. d, 20nu, Blue poppy.

2006 *Perf. 13¼*
1423 A218 Sheet of 4, #a-d 2.75 2.75

A219

New Year 2007 (Year of the Pig) — A220

2007 Litho. *Perf. 12x11¾*

1424 A219 20nu multi 1.00 1.00

Souvenir Sheet

Perf. 13¼

1425 A220 25nu multi 1.25 1.25

Miniature Sheet

Monasteries — A221

No. 1426: a, 8nu, Taktsang Monastery. b, 10nu, Kichu Monastery. c, 15nu, Kurjey Monastery. d, 20nu, Jambay Monastery.

2007 *Perf. 13¼*

1426 A221 Sheet of 4, #a-d — —

A222

New Year 2008 (Year of the Rat) — A223

No. 1428: a, Rat facing right. b, Rat facing left.

2008

1427 A222 20nu multi 1.00 1.00

Souvenir Sheet

Perf. 13½x13¼

1428 A223 20nu Sheet of 2, #a-b 1.75 1.75

Kings — A224

Kings — A225

In Harmony With Nature — A226

No. 1429 — King: a, 5nu, Ugyen Wangchuck. b, 10nu, Jigme Wangchuck. c, 15nu, Jigme Dorji Wangchuck. d, 20nu, Jigme Singye Wangchuck. e, 25nu, Jigme Khesar Namgyel Wangchuck.

2008 Litho. *Perf. 14¼x14½*

1429 A224 Sheet of 5, #a-e, + label 4.25 4.25

Souvenir Sheets

Imperf

Self-Adhesive

1430 A225 225nu multi 15.00 15.00

1431 A226 225nu multi 15.00 15.00

Nos. 1430-1431 are sealed envelopes containing compact discs. Values are for sealed envelopes containing the discs.

Miniature Sheet

2008 Summer Olympics, Beijing — A227

No. 1432: a, 10nu, Archer aiming arrow. b, 15nu, Archer holding bow. c, 25nu, Dragon, denomination in maroon. d, 25nu, Dragon, denomination in white.

2008 *Perf. 13*

1432 A227 Sheet of 4, #a-d 4.25 4.25

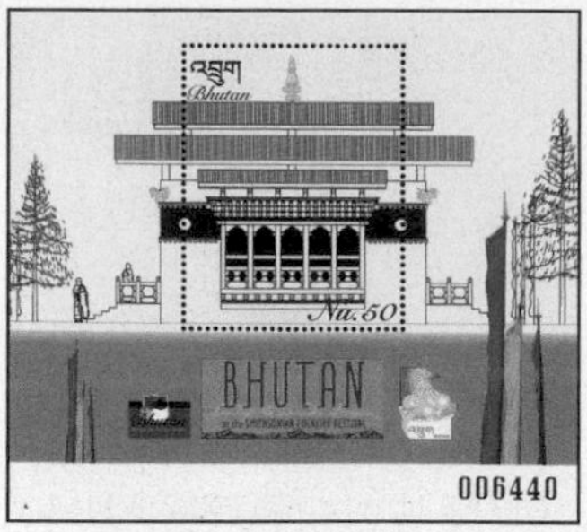

Bhutan at the Smithsonian Folklore Festival — A228

No. 1433: a, Two people wearing Bhutanese masks. b, Archer. c, Farmer plowing. d, Dancers. e, Carver holding knife.

No. 1434, 50nu, Drawing of building. No. 1435, 50nu, Fireworks over building, horiz.

2008 *Perf. 13¼*

1433 A228 20nu Sheet of 5, #a-e 6.00 6.00

Souvenir Sheets

Perf. 14

1434-1435 A228 Set of 2 6.00 6.00

No. 1433 contains five 50x50mm diamond-shaped stamps.

Miniature Sheet

Visit to Bhutan of Indian Prime Minister Manmohan Singh — A229

No. 1436: a, Bhutan Prime Minister Jigme Thinley and Indian Prime Minister Singh shaking hands in front of plaque. b, Thinley and Singh, flags of India and Bhutan. c, Thinley. d, Singh, wearing turban.

2008 Litho. *Perf. 13¼*

1436 A229 25nu Sheet of 4, #a-d 4.75 4.75

Souvenir Sheets

Coronation of King Jigme Khesar Namgyel Wangchuck — A230

Voting for Happiness — A231

2009, Feb. 21 Litho. *Imperf.*

Self-Adhesive

1437 A230 225nu multi 15.00 15.00

1438 A231 225nu multi 15.00 15.00

Nos. 1437-1438 are sealed envelopes containing compact discs. Values are for sealed envelopes containing the discs.

New Year 2009 (Year of the Ox) — A232

Ox with background in: 20nu, Brown. 30nu, Brown black.

2009, Feb. 25 Litho. *Perf. 13*

1439 A232 20nu multi .80 .80

Souvenir Sheet

Perf. 13½

1440 A232 30nu multi 1.25 1.25

No. 1440 contains one 40x30mm stamp.

Punakha Dzong Bridge A233

Designs: 20nu, Entire bridge.

No. 1442: a, Bridge at right. b, Bridge at left.

2009, Mar. 20 *Perf. 12½x12¾*

1441 A233 20nu multi .80 .80

Souvenir Sheet

Perf. 13½x13¼

1442 A233 25nu Sheet of 2, #a-b 2.00 2.00

Souvenir Sheet

July 22, 2009, Total Solar Eclipse — A234

No. 1443 — Solar eclipse, buildings and: a, One man. b, Three men.

2009, June 22 *Perf. 12½*

1443 A234 25nu Sheet of 2, #a-b 2.10 2.10

Miniature Sheet

A235

World Food Program in Bhutan, 35th Anniv. — A236

No. 1444: a, 10nu, Child leading oxen carrying rice bags. b, 10nu, Man near oxen carrying ricebags. c, 10nu, Stacked rice bags and vegetable oil boxes. d, 10nu, Farmer with hoe. e, 10nu, Farmers planting crops. f, 10nu, Men removing rocks near house. g, 20nu, Children eating. h, 20nu, Children on food line. i, 20nu, Children studying.

25nu, People holding cups.

2009, June 27 ***Perf. 13¼***

1444 A235 Sheet of 9, #a-i 5.00 5.00

Souvenir Sheet

Perf. 13

1445 A236 25nu multi 1.10 1.10

Miniature Sheet

Textiles — A237

No. 1446: a, Kushuthara. b, Mentse Mathra. c, Lungserma. d, Yathra.

Perf. 12¾x12½

2009, Sept. 28 Litho. Wmk. 388

1446 A237 20nu Sheet of 4, #a-d 3.50 3.50

Worldwide Fund for Nature (WWF) — A238

No. 1447 — Red panda: a, 20nu, Adult and juvenile. b, 20nu, Adult. c, 25nu, Adult and juvenile, diff. d, 25nu, Adult, diff.

2009, Oct. 9 Unwmk. ***Perf. 13½***

1447 A238 Block of 4, #a-d 4.00 4.00

Souvenir Sheets

New Year 2010 (Year of the Tiger) — A239

No. 1448: a, Tiger at night. b, Tiger in daylight.

50nu, Tiger, vert.

Perf. 12½x12¾

2010, Feb. 14 Wmk. 388

1448 A239 30nu Sheet of 2, #a-b 2.60 2.60

Perf. 13¼x13½

1449 A239 50nu multi 2.25 2.25

Worldwide Fund for Nature (WWF).

World Health Day — A240

No. 1450: a, Memorial Chorten (temple). b, Thimphu buildings, cars on street. c, Aerial view of Thimphu. d, Golfer. e, Cars on highway. f, Building, clock tower and plaza, Thimphu.

25nu, Jigme Dorji Wangchuk National Referral Hospital, Thimphu.

Perf. 12½x12¾

2010, Apr. 7 Litho. Wmk. 388

1450 A240 10nu Sheet of 6, #a-f 2.75 2.75

Souvenir Sheet

Perf. 14

1451 A240 25nu multi 1.25 1.25

No. 1451 contains one 50x39mm stamp.

16th South Asian Association for Regional Cooperation Summit, Thimphu — A241

No. 1452 — Flag of participating nation: a, Afghanistan. b, Bangladesh. c, Bhutan. d, India. e, Maldive Islands. f, Nepal. g, Pakistan. h, Sri Lanka.

25nu, Leaf, flags of the participating nations.

2010, Apr. 23 Unwmk. ***Perf. 13¼***

1452 A241 10nu Sheet of 8, #a-h 3.75 3.75

Souvenir Sheet

1453 A241 25nu multi 1.25 1.25

No. 1452 contains eight 40x30mm stamps.

A242

A243

A244

A245

King Jigme Khesar Namgyel Wangchuck — A246

No. 1454 — King: a, With bow and arrow. b, Throwing dart. c, Playing soccer with children. d, Playing basketball. e, Holding water polo ball. f, Bicycling.

No. 1455 — King: a, Bending with arms out, in front of children. b, Sitting in doorway with children. c, Standing and waving in middle of group of children. d, Standing in front of children. e, Standing, with hands on wall. f, With girl and baby.

No. 1456 — King: a, with Buddhist monk. b, Writing in book. c, Sitting in doorway with children, diff. d, With hands together touching chin. e, Sitting with children. f, Sitting on wall in front of crowd.

No. 1457 — King with background color of: a, Gold. b, Silver. c, Bronze.

Perf. 13½x13¼

2010, Nov. 1 Unwmk.

1454 A242 10nu Sheet of 6, #a-f 2.75 2.75

1455 A243 10nu Sheet of 6, #a-f 2.75 2.75

1456 A244 20nu Sheet of 6, #a-f 5.50 5.50

Perf.

1457 A245 30nu Sheet of 3, #a-c 4.25 4.25

Nos. 1454-1457 (4) 15.25 15.25

Souvenir Sheet

Perf. 13¼x13½

1458 A246 20nu multi .95 .95

Miniature Sheets

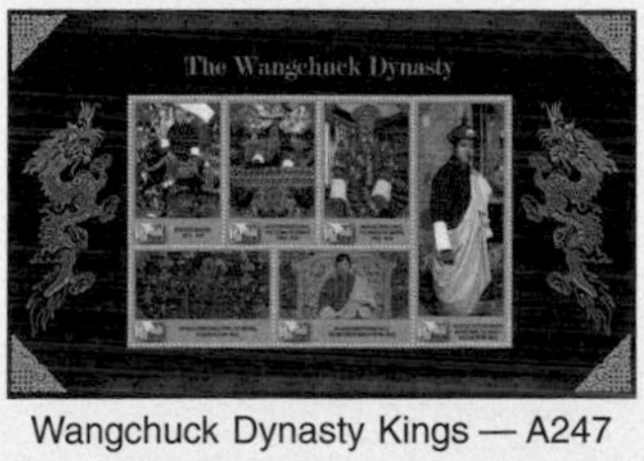

Wangchuck Dynasty Kings — A247

Queens of Bhutan — A248

No. 1459: a, Desi Jigme Namgyel (1825-81) (30x46mm). b, King Ugyen Wangchuck (1826-1926) (30x46mm). c, King Jigme Wangchuck (1905-52) (30x46mm). d, King Jigme Khesar Namgyel Wangchuck (30x76mm). e, King Jigme Dorji Wangchuck (1928-72) (45x30mm). f, King Jigme Singye Wangchuck (45x30mm). No. 1460: a, Queen Ashi Tsendu Lhamo Wangchuck (1886-1922). b, Queen Ashi Phuntsho Choden Wangchuck (1911-2003). c, Queen Ashi Pema Dechen Wangchuck (1918-91). d, Royal Grandmother Ashi Kezang Choeden Wangchuck. e, Queen Mother Ashi Dorji Wangmo Wangchuck. f, Queen Mother Ashi Tshering Pem Wangchuck. g, Queen Mother Ashi Tshering Yangdon Wangchuck. h, Queen Mother Ashi Sangay Choden Wangchuck.

2010, Dec. 17 Unwmk. ***Perf. 14***

1459 A247 15nu Sheet of 6, #a-f 4.00 4.00

Perf. 12¾x12½

Wmk. 388

1460 A248 15nu Sheet of 8, #a-h 5.25 5.25

Souvenir Sheet

New Year 2011 (Year of the Rabbit) — A249

2011, Feb. 3 Wmk. 388 ***Perf. 12¼***

1461 A249 25nu multi 1.10 1.10

Miniature Sheet

Diplomatic Relations Between Bhutan and Japan, 25th Anniv. — A250

No. 1462 — Flags of Bhutan and Japan and: a, Cherry blossoms, Mt. Fuji, flower. b, Bridge in Bhutan. c, Agricultural equipment. d, Farmer inspecting fruit.

Wmk. 388

2011, May 28 Litho. *Perf. 13½*

1462 A250 20nu Sheet of 4, #a-d 3.75 3.75

A251

1958 Visit to Bhutan of Indian Prime Minister Jawaharlal Nehru — A252

No. 1463: a, King Jigme Dorji Wangchuck greeting Nehru. b, Nehru reviewing troops. c, Nehru, King Jigme Dorji Wangchuck and family. d, Meeting.

25nu, Nehru riding ox.

Wmk. 388

2011, Aug. 15 Litho. *Perf. 13½*

1463 A251 10nu Sheet of 4, #a-d 1.75 1.75

Souvenir Sheet

Perf. 13½x14

1464 A252 25nu multi 1.10 1.10

A253

A253a

A253b

A254

Wedding of King Jigme Khesar Namgyel Wangchuk and Jetsun Pema — A254a

No. 1465: a, Couple, white and bister decorative background. b, Bride, white and bister decorative background. c, Couple, foliage in background. d, Bride, dark brown netting in background.

2011, Oct. 9		**Litho.**	***Perf. 13¼***	
1465	A253	25nu Sheet of 4, #a-d	—	—

Souvenir Sheets

1465E	A253a	50nu multi	—	—
1465F	A253b	50nu multi	—	—

Litho. & Embossed

Perf. 13

1466 A254 50nu multi — —

Perf. 13¼

1466A A254a 100nu multi — —

Souvenir Sheet

Wedding of King Jigme Khesar Namgyel Wangchuk and Jetsun Pema — A255

Litho. & Embossed With Foil Application

2011, Oct. 9 *Perf. 13¼*

1467 A255 225nu multi 9.25 9.25

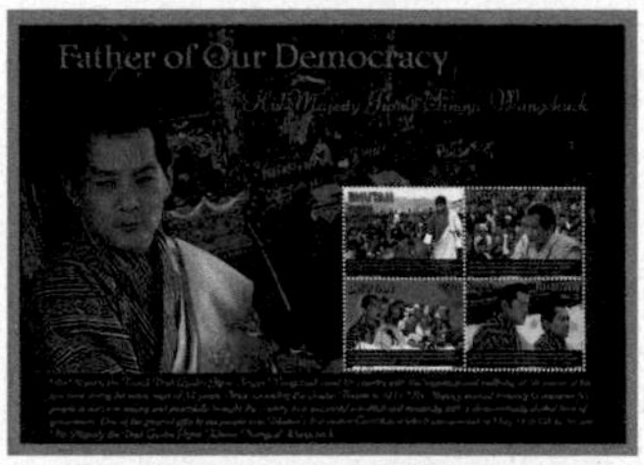

King Jigme Singye Wangchuk — A255a

No. 1467A — King Jigme Singye Wangchuk and: b, Subjects, text starting with "So long as . . ." c, Subjects, text starting with "As a king . . ." d, Subjects, text starting with "One of the most . . ." e, King Jigme Khesar Namgyel Wangchuk, text starting with "It is my wish . . ."

100nu, King Jigme Singye Wangchuk and copy of first Bhutanese constitution.

2011, Nov. Litho. *Perf. 13½x13¼*

1467A A255a 25nu Sheet of 4, #b-e 4.00 4.00

Souvenir Sheet

Perf. 14¼

1467F A255a 100nu multi 4.00 4.00

No. 1467F contains one 45x35mm stamp.

Miniature Sheet

South Asian Association for Regional Cooperation, 25th Anniv. — A255b

No. 1467G — Flags of: h, Bhutan. i, Sri Lanka. j, Afghanistan. k, Pakistan. l, Bangladesh. m, Nepal. n, India. o, Maldive Islands.

2011 Litho. Wmk. 388 *Perf. 14*

1467G A255b 15nu Sheet of 8, #h-o, + central label — —

Education in Bhutan, Cent. (Sherig Century) — A255c

Designs: 10nu, Children and candle.

No. 1467Q: r, School building, candle and ring of text. s, Schooll building, children and candle.

50nu, Like 10nu.

Wmk. 388

2012, May Litho. *Perf. 12½*

1467P	A255c	10nu multi	—	—
1467Q	A255c	30nu Sheet of 2, #r-s	—	—

Souvenir Sheet

Perf. 13½

1467T A255c 50nu multi — —

Bhutan Post, 50th Anniv. — A256

No. 1468: a, Bhutan #4. b, Bhutan #83H. c, Bhutan #84B. d, Bhutan #105B. e, Bhutan #152B. f, Bhutan #153B.

50nu, Postal messenger running.

Perf. 13¼x13

2012, Oct. 10 Litho. Unwmk.

1468 A256 20nu Sheet of 6, #a-f 4.50 4.50

Souvenir Sheet

Perf. 13½

1469 A256 50nu multi 1.90 1.90

No. 1469 contains one 40x40mm stamp.

Souvenir Sheets

A257

A258

A259

A260

A261

Wedding of King Jigme Khesar Namgyel Wangchuk and Jetsun Pema, 1st Anniv. — A262

No. 1470 — Royal couple with: a, Trees with green foliage in background. b, Cherry blossoms in background.

2012, Oct. 13 Litho. *Perf. 13*

1470 A257 50nu Sheet of 2, #a-b, + central label 3.75 3.75

Perf.

1471 A258 100nu multi 3.75 3.75

Perf. 13¼

1472 A259 200nu multi 7.50 7.50
1473 A260 200nu multi 7.50 7.50
1474 A261 200nu multi 7.50 7.50

Perf. 14x14½

1475 A262 200nu multi 7.50 7.50
Nos. 1470-1475 (6) 37.50 37.50

New Year 2012 (Year of the Dragon) A263

2013, Jan. 1 Litho. *Perf. 12½x12¾*

1476 A263 20nu shown .75 .75

Souvenir Sheet

Perf. 12

1477 A263 50nu Dragon, diff. 1.90 1.90

No. 1477 contains one 45x35mm stamp.

New Year 2013 (Year of the Snake) A264

2013, Feb. 11 Litho. *Perf. 13x13¼*

1478 A264 20nu shown .75 .75

Souvenir Sheet

1479 A264 50nu Snake, diff. 1.90 1.90

Eight Manifestations of Guru Padmasambhava — A265

No. 1480: a, Guru Tshokey Dorji. b, Guru Pema Gyalpo. c, Guru Shakya Sengye. d, Guru Loden Chogsey. e, Guru Pema Jungney. f, Guru Nima Yoezer. g, Guru Sengye Dradok. h, Guru Dorji Drolo.
40nu, Guru Padmasambhava.

2013, June 18 Litho. *Perf. 13¼x13*

1480 A265 20nu Sheet of 8, #a-h 5.50 5.50

Souvenir Sheet

Perf. 13¼x13½

1481 A265 40nu multi 1.40 1.40

No. 1481 contains one 42x56mm stamp.

Lama Drukpa Kunley (1455-1529), Buddhist Poet and Teacher — A266

No. 1482 — Drawings on building of: a, Ejaculating penis. b, Penis with white ribbon. c, Penis with eyes and ribbon. d, Penis pointing downward with red and black ribbon.

Perf. 13½x13

2013, Dec. 9 Litho. Unwmk.

1482 A266 20nu Sheet of 4, #a-d 2.60 2.60

Souvenir Sheet

Perf. 13¼x13¾

1483 A266 40nu multi 1.40 1.40

No. 1482 contains four 30x40mm stamps.

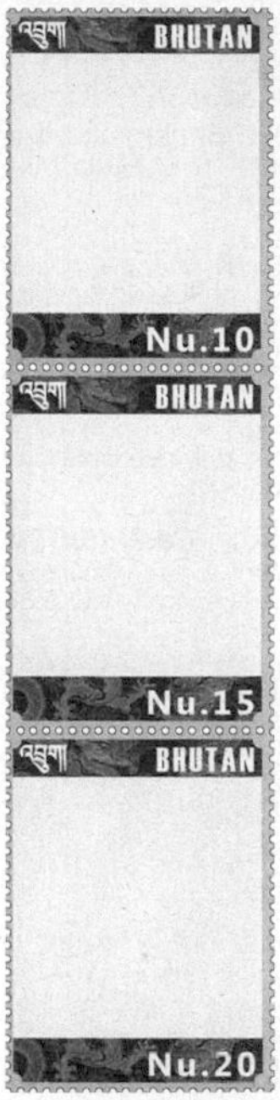

A267

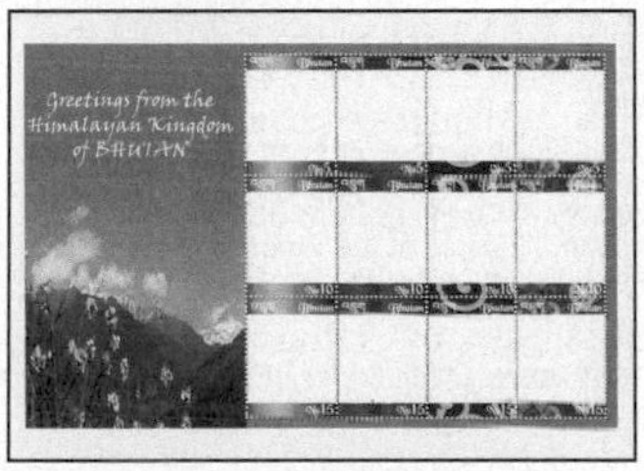

Personalized Stamps — A267a

No. 1485: a, 10nu. b, 15nu. c, 20nu.
No. 1485D: e, 5nu, Spectrum of colors from red to purple in top and bottom panels. f, 5nu, Blue panel at top. g, 5nu, Curved yellow lines on blue background in top and bottom panels. h, 5nu, Circles in top and bottom panels. i, 10nu, Like No. 1485De. j, 10nu, Blue and red in panels. k, 10nu, Like No. 1485Dg. l, 10nu, Like No. 1485Dh. m, 15nu, Like No. 1485De. n, 15nu, Like No. 14895Dj. o, 15nu, Like No. 1485Dg. p, 15nu, Like No. 1485Dh.

2011 ? Litho. *Perf. 13½*

1485 A267 Vert. strip of 3, #a-c — —

Perf. 12

1485D A267a Sheet of 12, #e-p — —

No. 1485 was printed in sheets containing 4 vertical strips. Vignettes on Nos. 1485 and 1485D could be personalized.

New Year 2014 (Year of the Horse) A268

Designs: 10nu, 50nu, Horse.
No. 1487: a, Rat. b, Ox. c, Tiger. d, Rabbit. e, Dragon. f, Snake. g, Horse, diff. h, Sheep. i, Monkey. j, Bird. k, Dog. l, Pig.

2014, Mar. 2 Litho. *Perf. 13x13¼*

1486 A268 10nu multi .35 .35
1487 A268 20nu Sheet of 12, #a-l 7.75 7.75

Souvenir Sheet

1488 A268 50nu multi 1.60 1.60

Chhoetens (Stupas) — A269

No. 1489: a, National Memorial Stupa, Thimphu. b, Khamsum Yuelley Namgyel Stupa, Punakha. c, Kyichu Lhakhang Stupa, Paro. d, Heyjo Stupa, Thimphu. e, Khuruthang Stupa, Punakha. f, Nemizampa Stupa, Paro. g, Druk Wangyel Stupa, Dochula. h, Dechenphodrang Stupa, Thimphu.
No.1490: a, Chorten Kora Stupa, Trashiyangtse. b, Chendebji Stupa, Trongsa.

2014, Apr. 15 Litho. *Perf. 13x13¼*

1489 A269 20nu Sheet of 8, #a-h 5.50 5.50

Souvenir Sheet

1490 A269 25nu Sheet of 2, #a-b 1.75 1.75

A270

Flora and Fauna — A271

No. 1491: a, Rheum nobile. b, Himalayan blue sheep.
No. 1492: a, Melastoma. b, Golden langur. c, Primula. d, Himalayan black bear. e, Red panda. f, Michelia. g, Muntjac. h, Geranium.
50nu, White-bellied heron.

2014, May 10 Litho. *Perf. 13¼x13*

1491 A270 10nu Vert. pair, #a-b .70 .70
1492 A271 20nu Sheet of 8, #a-h 5.50 5.50

Souvenir Sheet

1493 A271 50nu multi 1.75 1.75

A272

A273

Flowers — A274

Designs: 10nu, Primula sikkimensis.
No. 1495: a, Clematis fongulensis. b, Iris goniocarpa. c, Oxygraphis glacialis. d, Rosa macrophylla.
No. 1496: a, Primula griffithii. b, Beaumontia grandiflora. c, Roscoea alpina. d, Lloydia flavonutans. e, Barleria strigosa. f, Primula spathulifolia. g, Curcuma aromatica. h, Rhododendron bhutanense. i, Saxifraga hirculus.

Perf. 13¼x13, 13x13¼ (#1495)

2014, June 15 Litho.

1494 A272 10nu multi .35 .35
1495 A273 10nu Sheet of 4, #a-d 1.40 1.40
1496 A274 20nu Sheet of 9, #a-i 6.00 6.00

Twelve Deeds of Lord Buddha — A275

Shakyamuni Buddha — A276

No. 1497: a, Descent from Tushita Pure Land. b, Entry into his mother's womb. c, Birth in the garden of Lumbini. d, Mastery of arts and skills. e, Marriage and fathering of a child. f, Renunciation of Samsara. g, Practice of austerities for six years. h, Resolve to meditate under the Bodhi tree. i, Conquest of Mara. j, Enlightenment. k, Turning the Wheel of Dharma. l, Mahaparinirvana.

2014, July 31 Litho. *Perf. 13¼x13*

1497 A275 20nu Sheet of 12, #a-l 8.00 8.00

Souvenir Sheet

1498 A276 50nu multi 1.75 1.75

Miniature Sheets

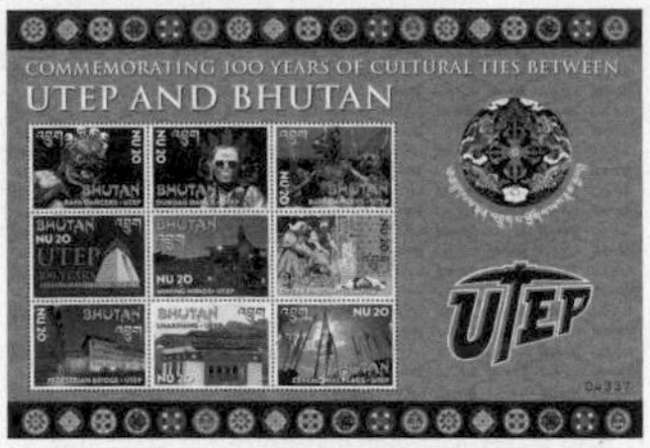

Cultural Ties Between Bhutan and the University of Texas at El Paso, Cent. — A277

No. 1499: a, Rapa dancer, denomination at UR. b, Durdag dance. c, Rapa dancers, denomination at LL. d, University centennial emblem. e, Minding Minds sculpture. f, Opera Bhutan, Thimphu. g, UTEP Pedestrian bridge and campus building. h, Lhakang Building, UTEP. i, Ceremonial flags.
No. 1500: a, Like #1499a. b, Like #1499i. c, Like #1499g. d, Like #1499b.

2014, Aug. 25 Litho. *Perf. 13x13¼*

1499 A277 20nu Sheet of 9, #a-i 6.00 6.00
1500 A277 25nu Sheet of 4, #a-d 3.50 3.50

Diplomatic Relations Between Bhutan and Thailand, 25th Anniv. — A278

No. 1501: a, Meconopsis grandis. b, Khon (Thai mask dance). c, Paro Taktsang, Bhutan. d, Cassia fistula. e, Shawa shachi (mask dance). f, Grand Palace, Bangkok.
80nu, Temple of the Emerald Buddha, Thailand and Punakha Dzong, Bhutan.

2014, Nov. 14 Litho. *Perf. 13x13¼*

1501 A278 20nu Sheet of 6, #a-f 4.00 4.00

Souvenir Sheet

1502 A278 80nu multi 2.60 2.60

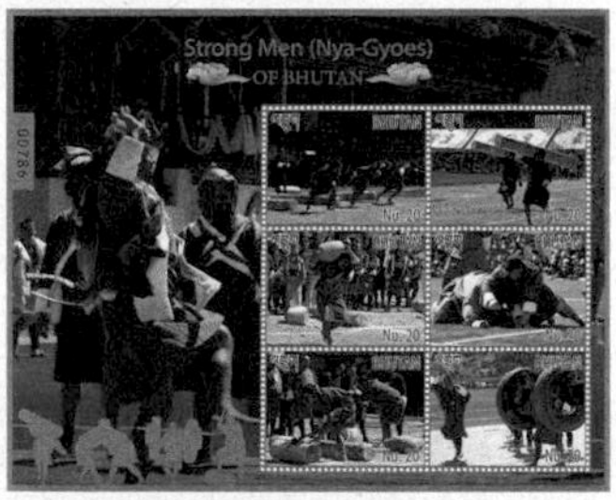

Strong Men — A279

No. 1503: a, Three men dragging logs. b, Two men carrying logs. c, Man carrying sack on shoulder. d, Wrestlers. e, Man cutting log. f, Man lifting tires.
80nu, Man carrying sack on shoulder, vert.

2014, Nov. 17 Litho. *Perf. 13x13¼*

1503 A279 20nu Sheet of 6, #a-f 4.00 4.00

Souvenir Sheet

Perf. 13¼x13

1504 A279 80nu multi 2.60 2.60

Jewelry — A280

No. 1505: a, Brooch necklace. b, Bracelet. c, Necklace. d, Two round brooches. e, Two brooches (connected diamonds). f, Earrings.
80nu, Betel nut container.

2014, Nov. 17 Litho. *Perf. 13x13¼*

1505 A280 20nu Sheet of 6, #a-f 4.00 4.00

Souvenir Sheet

1506 A280 80nu multi 2.60 2.60

Butterflies — A281

No. 1507: a, Orinoma damaris. b, Neurosigma siva. c, Euthalia durga. d, Junonia orithiya.
80nu, Bhutanitis ludlowi.

2014, Nov. 17 Litho. *Perf. 13x13¼*

1507 A281 25nu Sheet of 4, #a-d 3.25 3.25

Souvenir Sheet

1508 A281 80nu multi 2.60 2.60

New Year 2015 (Year of the Sheep) — A282

No. 1509: a, Rat. b, Ox. c, Tiger. d, Rabbit. e, Dragon. f, Snake. g, Horse. h, Sheep. i, Monkey. j, Rooster. k, Dog. l, Pig.
30nu, Sheep, horiz.

2015, Feb. 19 Litho. *Perf. 13¼x13*

1509 A282 10nu Sheet of 12, #a-l 4.00 4.00

Souvenir Sheet

Perf. 13x13¼

1510 A282 30nu multi 1.00 1.00

Drubthop Thangtong Gyalpo (c. 1385-c.1464), Yogi and Bridge Builder — A283

No. 1511: a, Drubthop Thangtong Gyalpo. b, Dungtsi Lhakhang. c, Man on chain bridge. d, Gateway Tschorten. e, Iron Chain Bridge. f, Buddha Sakyamuni. g, Iron chain. h, Aerial view of Iron Chain Bridge.
40nu, Head of Drubthop Thangtong Gyalpo statue.

2015, Apr. 29 Litho. *Perf. 13¼x13*

1511 A283 20nu Sheet of 8, #a-h 5.00 5.00

Souvenir Sheet

1512 A283 40nu multi 1.25 1.25

A284

Atsaras — A285

Designs: 5nu, Two atsaras in purple costumes. 10nu, Two atsaras in orange costumes. 15nu, Atsara. 30nu, Two atsaras in red and orange costumes.
No. 1517: a, Two atsaras, dancer with dragon mask. b, Two atsaras, one crouching. c, Atsara with arm extended, holding phallus near head, dancers in background. d, Two atsaras, one holding phallus. e, Atsara with arms raised, two dancers in background. f, Atsara on back of other atsara.
40nu, Seated atsara holding phallus.

2015, Sept. 10 Litho. *Perf. 13¼x13*

1513-1516 A284 Set of 4 1.90 1.90
1517 A285 20nu Sheet of 6, #a-f 3.75 3.75

Souvenir Sheet

1518 A285 40nu multi 1.25 1.25

Bhutanese Foods — A286

No. 1519: a, Ngya Tshoem. b, Sikam Paa. c, Kewa Datshi. d, Bjasha Maru. e, Haapi Hoentoe. f, Nakey Nosha Paa. g, Nosha Phim. h, Mengay. i, Khuley.
No. 1520: a, Puta. b, Ema Datshi and rice.

2015, Oct. 9 Litho. *Perf. 13x13¼*

1519 A286 15nu Sheet of 9, #a-i 4.25 4.25

Souvenir Sheet

1520 A286 30nu Sheet of 2, #a-b 1.90 1.90

King Jigme Khesar Namgyel Wangchuk — A287

No. 1521: a, Archers (38mm diameter). b, King Jigme Khesar Namgyel Wangchuk greeting crowd (38mm diameter). c, People seated (38mm diameter). d, Crowd (38mm diameter). e, King Jigme Khesar Namgyel, his father, King Jigme Singye Wangchuk, Queen Jetsun (40x30mm). f, King Jigme Khesar Namgyel Wangchuk and women (40x30mm).
No. 1522, King Jigme Khesar Namgyel Wangchuk and man.

Perf. 13x13¼ (#1521e, 1521f, 1522), Perf.

2015, Oct. 9 Litho.

1521 A287 50nu Sheet of 6, #a-f 9.25 9.25

Souvenir Sheet

1522 A287 50nu multi 1.60 1.60

United Nations, 70th Anniv. — A288

No. 1523: a, United Nations Peacekeeper receiving medal. b, Woman writing in book. c, HeForShe campaign. d, Two Bhutanese men.
50nu, People and candles.

2015, Oct. 24 Litho. *Perf. 13x13¼*

1523 A288 30nu Sheet of 4, #a-d 3.75 3.75

Souvenir Sheet

1524 A288 50nu multi 1.60 1.60

Dzongs — A289

No. 1525: a, Rimpung Dzong. b, Semtokha Dzong. c, Punakha Dzong. d, Trongsa Dzong. e, Trashigang Dzong. f, Jakar Dzong.
60nu, Tashichho Dzong.

2015, Nov. 2 Litho. *Perf. 13¼x13*

1525 A289 30nu Sheet of 6, #a-f 5.50 5.50

Souvenir Sheet

1526 A289 60nu multi 1.90 1.90

Monasteries — A290

No. 1527: a, Kurje Lhakhang. b, Jambay Lhakhang. c, Kyichu Lhakhang. d, Changangkha Lhakhang. e, Gangtey Goenpa. f, Tango Monastery.
60nu, Taktshang (Tiger's Nest), vert.

2015, Nov. 3 Litho. *Perf. 13x13¼*

1527 A290 30nu Sheet of 6, #a-f 5.50 5.50

Souvenir Sheet

1528 A290 60nu multi 1.90 1.90

No. 1528 contains one 40x60mm stamp.

A291

A292

A293

A294

A295

A296

King Jigme Singye Wangchuk, 60th Birthday — A297

Various photographs of King Jigme Singye Wangchuk taken during his reign, as shown.

2015, Nov. 7 Litho. *Perf. 13*

1529 A291 15nu Sheet of 4, #a-d 1.90 1.90

1530 A292 15nu Sheet of 4, #a-d 1.90 1.90

1531 A293 15nu Sheet of 4, #a-d 1.90 1.90

1532 A294 15nu Sheet of 4, #a-d 1.90 1.90

1533 A295 15nu Sheet of 4, #a-d 1.90 1.90

Nos. 1529-1533 (5) 9.50 9.50

Souvenir Sheets

Perf. 13¼x13

1534 A296 100nu multi 3.00 3.00

Litho. & Embossed

Perf. 13x13¼

1535 A297 500nu multi 15.00 15.00

Bird Conservation — A298

No., 1536: a, Four black-necked cranes (40x30mm). b, Two black-necked cranes on ground (40x30mm). c, Emblem of Royal Society for Protection of Nature (40x30mm). d, Two black-necked cranes in flight (40x30mm). e, White-bellied heron (40x60mm). f, One black-necked crane in flight (40x30mm). g, Dancers in black-necked crane costumes, Black-necked Crane Festival, Gangtey Goepta (40x30mm). h, Two black-necked cranes and people of Phobji Gewog.
No. 1537: a, Three black-necked cranes in flight (40x30mm). b, White-bellied heron (40x30mm).

2015, Nov. 11 Litho. *Perf. 13x13¼*

1536 A298 15nu Sheet of 8, #a-h 3.75 3.75

Souvenir Sheet

1537 A298 50nu Sheet of 2, #a-b 3.00 3.00

Worldwide Fund for Nature (WWF) — A299

No. 1538: a, Asiatic water buffalo (40x30mm). b, Red panda (40x60mm). c, Snow leopards (40x30mm). d, Golden mahseers (40x30mm). e, Asian elephant (40x30mm). f, White-bellied heron (40x30mm). g, Golden langurs (40x30mm). h, Royal Bengal tiger (40x30mm).
50nu, Himalayan blue sheep.

2015, Nov. 11 Litho. *Perf. 13x13¼*

1538 A299 30nu Sheet of 8, #a-h 7.25 7.25

Souvenir Sheet

1539 A299 50nu multi 1.50 1.50

Royal Visits to Merak and Sakteng — A300

No. 1540: a, King Jigme Khesar Namgyel Wangchuk and crowd of children. b, King Jigme and Queen Jetsun near stove. c, Queen Jetsun. d, Queen Jetsun and crowd of children. e, King Jigme and Queen Jetsun walking. f, King Jigme and Queen Jetsun looking at items on table.
150nu, King Jigme and Queen Jetsun seated.

2015, Nov. 11 Litho. *Perf. 13x13¼*

1540 A300 50nu Sheet of 6, #a-f 9.00 9.00

Souvenir Sheet

1541 A300 150nu multi 4.50 4.50

Traditional Sports — A301

No. 1542: a, Khuru. b, Soksom. c, Bjigdum. d, Dego.
80nu, Archery.

2015, Dec. 17 Litho. *Perf. 13¾x14*

1542 A301 30nu Sheet of 4, #a-d 3.75 3.75

Souvenir Sheet

1543 A301 80nu multi 2.40 2.40

New Year 2016 (Year of the Monkey) — A302

No. 1544: a, Monkey. b, Dragon. c, Rat.
50nu, Four harmonious friends (bird, rabbit, monkey, elephant), vert.

2016, Feb. 9 Litho. *Perf. 13*

1544 A302 30nu Sheet of 3, #a-c 2.75 2.75

Souvenir Sheet

1545 A302 50nu multi 1.50 1.50

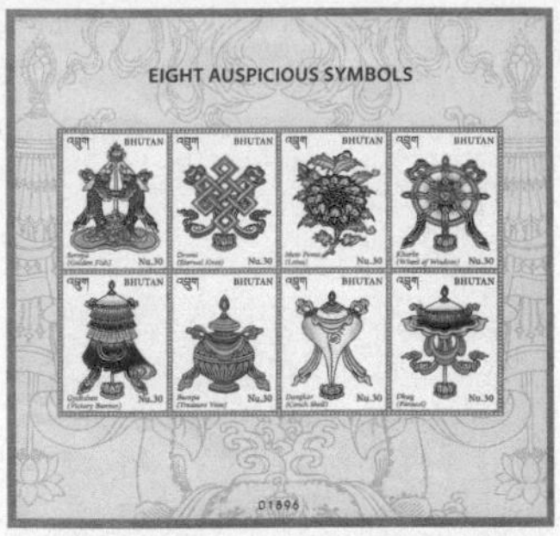

Eight Auspicious Symbols — A303

No. 1546: a, Golden fish. b, Eternal knot. c, Lotus. d, Wheel of wisdom. e, Victory banner. f, Treasure vase. g, Conch shell. h, Parasol.
60nu, Tashi Tagye.

2016, Apr. 16 Litho. *Perf. 13*

1546 A303 30nu Sheet of 8, #a-h 7.25 7.25

Souvenir Sheet

Perf. 13¼

1547 A303 60nu multi 1.90 1.90

No. 1547 contains one 42x70mm stamp.

Birth of Prince Jigme Namgyel Wangchuk — A304

No. 1548 — Inscriptions: a, His Majesty the Fourth Druk Gyalpo. b, His Majesty the King. c, HRH the Gyalsey (King Jigme holding son). d, HRH the Gyalsey (Grandmother, Queen Jetsun and Prince Jigme). e, HRH the Gyalsey (King Jigme, Queen Jestun and Prince Jigme).
200nu, HRH the Gyalsey (Prince Jigme).

Litho. With Foil Application

2016, May 21 *Perf. 13¾x13½*

1548 A304 50nu Sheet of 5, #a-e 7.50 7.50

Souvenir Sheet

1549 A304 200nu multi 6.00 6.00

Four Mythical Animals — A305

No. 1550: a, Tiger. b, Snow lion. c, Garuda. d, Dragon.
80nu, Dragon, diff.

2016, July 18 Litho. *Perf. 14¼*

1550 A305 30nu Sheet of 4, #a-d 3.75 3.75

Souvenir Sheet

1551 A305 80nu multi 2.40 2.40

Miniature Sheet

Diplomatic Relations Between Bhutan and Japan, 30th Anniv. — A306

No. 1552: a, King Jigme Khesar Namgyel Wangchuk, Queen Jetsun Pema, and Empress Michiko of Japan. b, 30th anniv. emblem. c, King and Queen, Japanese Prime Minister Shinzo Abe, soldiers with flags. d, King and Queen with children. e, King and Queen praying with other worshipers. f, Tea ceremony.

2016, Sept. 5 Litho. *Perf. 14¼*

1552 A306 30nu Sheet of 6, #a-f 5.50 5.50

Buddhist Statues and Sites — A307

No. 1553: a, Buddha Dordenma. b, Guru Nangsi Zilnoen. c, Tashichhodzong. d, Lhuntse Dzong.
No. 1554, horiz.: a, Buddha Dordenma, diff. b, Guru Nangsi Zilnoen, diff.

2016, Sept. 6 Litho. *Perf. 14¼*

1553 A307 30nu Sheet of 4, #a-d 3.75 3.75

Souvenir Sheet

Perf. 14x14¼

1554 A307 50nu Sheet of 2, #a-b 3.00 3.00

Miniature Sheet

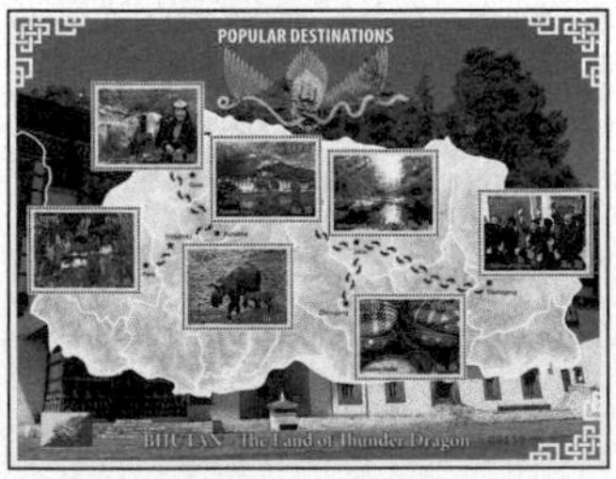

Tourism — A308

No. 1555: a, Layap woman with yak. b, Punakha Dzong. c, Burning Lake. d, Children of Sakteng. e, Tiger's Nest. f, Takins. g, Bamboo baskets.

2016, Oct. 18 Litho. *Perf. 14x14¼*

1555 A308 30nu Sheet of 7, #a-g 6.25 6.25

National Flora and Fauna — A309

No. 1556: a, Raven (national bird). b, Blue poppies (national flower). c, Ludlow's Bhutan swallowtail (national butterfly). d, Takin and cypress tree (national animal and tree).
No. 1557, 60nu, Raven, diff. No. 1558, 60nu, Blue poppies, diff. No. 1559, 60nu, Ludlow's Bhutan swallowtail, diff. No. 1560, 60nu, Takin and cypress tree, diff.

2016, Oct. 18 Litho. *Perf. 14¼x14*

1556 A309 30nu Sheet of 4, #a-d 3.75 3.75

Souvenir Sheets

1557-1560 A309 Set of 4 7.25 7.25

Druk Wangyel Festival — A310

No. 1561: a, Raven-headed deity. b, Jetsun Milarepa. c, Tshering Chednga. d, Combat of the Heroes, mountains in background. e, Gadpo and Ganmo. f, Combat of the Heroes, no mountains. g, Azhe Lhamo. h, Farewell of the Heroes.
40nu, Vision of Bodhisattvas.

2016, Dec. 17 Litho. *Perf. 14¼*

1561 A310 20nu Sheet of 8, #a-h 4.75 4.75

Souvenir Sheet

Perf. 14¼x14

1562 A310 40nu multi 1.25 1.25

No. 1562 contains one 70x46mm stamp.

Prayer Flags — A311

No. 1563: a, Flags above stone monument. b, Flags attached to pole above pile of stones. c, Poles and flags. c, Tree and flags.
40nu, Flags and buildings.

2016, Dec. 17 Litho. *Perf. 14¼*

1563 A311 30nu Sheet of 4, #a-d 3.50 3.50

Souvenir Sheet

1564 A311 40nu multi 1.25 1.25

No. 1564 contains one 40x56mm stamp.

Six Elements of Longevity — A312

No. 1565: a, Old man. b, Tree. c, Cliff. d, Water. e, Bird. f, Deer.
50nu, Old man, vert.

2016, Dec. 17 Litho. *Perf. 14x14¼*

1565 A312 25nu Sheet of 6, #a-f 4.50 4.50

Souvenir Sheet

1566 A312 50nu multi 1.50 1.50

No. 1566 contains one 46x70mm stamp.

Tashigomangs — A313

No. 1567 — Various tashigomangs: a, 9nu. b, 13nu. c, 21nu. d, 37nu.
50nu, Tashigomang, diff.

2016, Dec. 17 Litho. *Perf. 14¼*

1567 A313 Sheet of 4, #a-d 2.40 2.40

Souvenir Sheet

1568 A313 50nu multi 1.50 1.50

New Year 2017 (Year of the Rooster) — A314

No. 1569: a, Rooster. b, Dog. c, Pig. d, Rat. e, Ox. f, Tiger. g, Rabbit. h, Dragon. i, Snake. j, Horse. k, Sheep. l, Monkey.
60nu, Rooster and flames.

Litho. & Embossed

2017, Jan. 1 *Perf. 14¼*

1569 A314 30nu Sheet of 12, #a-l 10.50 10.50

Souvenir Sheet

1570 A314 60nu multi 1.75 1.75

No. 1570 contains one 70x46mm stamp.

Pilgrimage Sites — A315

No. 1571: a, Kyichu Lhakhang. b, Jampa Lhakhang. c, Kurjey Lhakhang. d, Aja Nye. e, The Burning Lake. f, Singye Dzong. g, Tachog Lhakhang. h, Chhorten Kora. i, Dungtse Lhakhang.
100nu, Taktshang.

2017, Mar. 19 Litho. *Perf. 14x14¼*

1571 A315 20nu Sheet of 9, #a-i 5.75 5.75

Souvenir Sheet

1572 A315 100nu multi 3.25 3.25

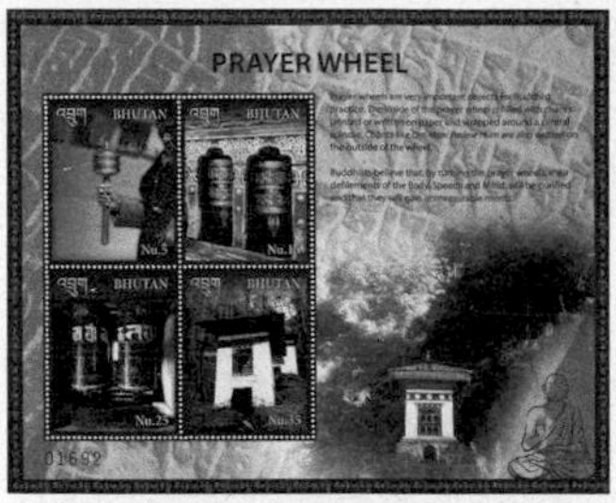

Prayer Wheel — A316

No. 1573: a, 5nu, Buddhist holding prayer wheel. b, 15nu, Prayer wheels in niches. c, 25nu, Prayer wheels on black base. d, 35nu, Temples.
50nu, Buddhists praying.

2017, June 19 Litho. *Perf. 14¼x14*

1573 A316 Sheet of 4, #a-d 2.50 2.50

Souvenir Sheet

Perf. 14x14¼

1574 A316 50nu multi 1.60 1.60

No. 1574 contains one 48x70mm stamp.

Fruits and Nuts — A317

No. 1575: a, Mandarin oranges. b, Bananas. c, Passion fruit. d, Apples. e, Peaches. f, Pears. g, Pineapples. h, Plums.
30nu, Walnuts, vert.

2017, June 19 Litho. *Perf. 14x14¼*

1575 A317 15nu Sheet of 8, #a-h 3.75 3.75

Souvenir Sheet

1576 A317 30nu multi .95 .95

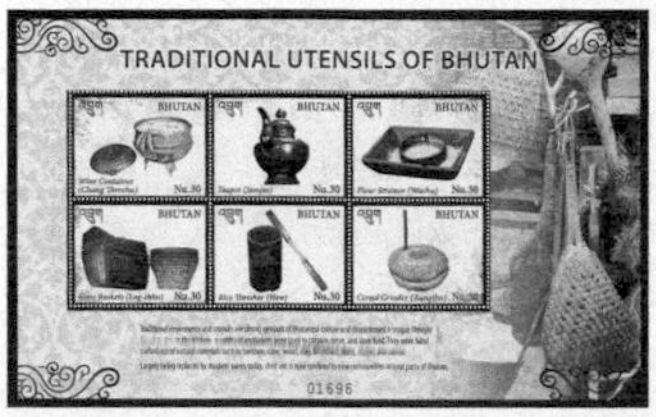

Utensils and Household Items — A318

No. 1577: a, Wine container and lid. b, Teapot. c, Flour strainer. d, Cane baskets. e, Rice thresher. f, Cereal grinder.
50nu, Tea strainer and brass pot.

2017, June 19 Litho. *Perf. 14x14¼*

1577 A318 30nu Sheet of 6, #a-f 5.75 5.75

Souvenir Sheet

Perf. 14¼x14

1578 A318 50nu multi 1.60 1.60

No. 1578 contains one 70x46mm stamp.

Musical Instruments — A319

No. 1579: a, Pod shaker. b, Hammered dulcimer. c, Mouth harp. d, Flute. e, Fiddle. f, Horn.
50nu, Lute, vert.

2017, Sept. 1 Litho. *Perf. 14x14¼*

1579 A319 20nu Sheet of 6, #a-f 3.75 3.75

Souvenir Sheet

Perf. 14¼x14

1580 A319 50nu multi 1.60 1.60

No. 1579b has "Dulcimer" spelled incorrectly on stamp.

Diplomatic Relations Between Bhutan and South Korea, 30th Anniv. — A320

No. 1581: a, Blue flower. b, Puppeteer with puppet. c, Dzong. d, White and red flower. e, Costumed performers and audience. f, Temple and walkway.
60nu, Dzong, temple, flags of Bhutan and South Korea.

2017, Sept. 22 Litho. *Perf. 14x14¼*

1581 A320 30nu Sheet of 6, #a-f 5.75 5.75

Souvenir Sheet

Perf. 14¼

1582 A320 60nu multi 1.90 1.90

No. 1582 contains one 56x40mm stamp.

Blue Poppies — A321

No. 1583: a, Meconopsis sinuata. b, Meconopsis bella. c, Meconopsis merakensis. d, Meconopsis horridula. e, Meconopsis polygaliodes. f, Meconopsis bhutanica. g, Meconopsis elongata. h, Meconopsis simplicifolia.
50nu, Meconopsis gakyidiana, vert.

2017, Oct. 9 Litho. *Perf. 14x14¼*

1583 A321 20nu Sheet of 8, #a-h 5.00 5.00

Souvenir Sheet

Perf. 14¼x14

1584 A321 50nu multi 1.60 1.60

Orchids — A322

No. 1585: a, Epigenium amplum. b, Cypripedium guttatum. c, Dendrobium nobile. d, Esmerelda clarkei. e, Corybas himalaicus. f, Paphiopedilum fairrieanum. g, Odontochilus elwesii. h, Cypripedium tibeticum.
50nu, Bulbophyllum guttulatum.

2017, Oct. 26 Litho. *Perf. 14x14¼*

1585 A322 15nu Sheet of 8, #a-h 3.75 3.75

Souvenir Sheet

1586 A322 50nu multi 1.60 1.60

Rural Bhutan — A323

No. 1587: a, Phobjikha, Wangdiphodrang. b, Yebisa, Punakha. c, Lob Sobtsukha, Punakha. d, Merak, Trashigang.
No. 1588, Ura, Bumthang.

2017, Nov. 1 Litho. *Perf. 13¼x13¾*

1587 A323 30nu Sheet of 4, #a-d 3.75 3.75

Souvenir Sheet

1588 A323 30nu multi .95 .95

Pheasants — A324

No. 1589: a, Blood pheasant. b, Himalayan monal. c, Kalij pheasant. d, Tibetan snowcock. e, Tibetan partridge. f, Snow partridge.
50nu, Satyr tragopan, vert.

2017, Nov. 30 Litho. *Perf. 14¼*

1589 A324 20nu Sheet of 6, #a-f 3.75 3.75

Souvenir Sheet

Perf. 14¼x14

1590 A324 50nu multi 1.60 1.60

Mountain Peaks — A325

No. 1591: a, Jichudrake. b, Gangchen Singye. c, Gangchen Taag. d, Chundugang. e, Jumolhari. f, Masagang. g, Tsherimgang. h, Tarigang.
50nu, Gangkhar Puenseum.

2017, Nov. 30 Litho. *Perf. 14x14¼*

1591 A325 15nu Sheet of 8, #a-h 3.75 3.75

Souvenir Sheet

1592 A325 50nu multi 1.60 1.60

New Year 2018 (Year of the Dog) — A326

No. 1593: a, Horse. b, Dog. c, Tiger.
60nu, Stylized dog.

2018, Jan. 30 Litho. *Perf. 14¼x14*

1593 A326 30nu Sheet of 3, #a-c 3.00 3.00

Souvenir Sheet

Litho. & Embossed

1594 A326 60nu multi 1.90 1.90

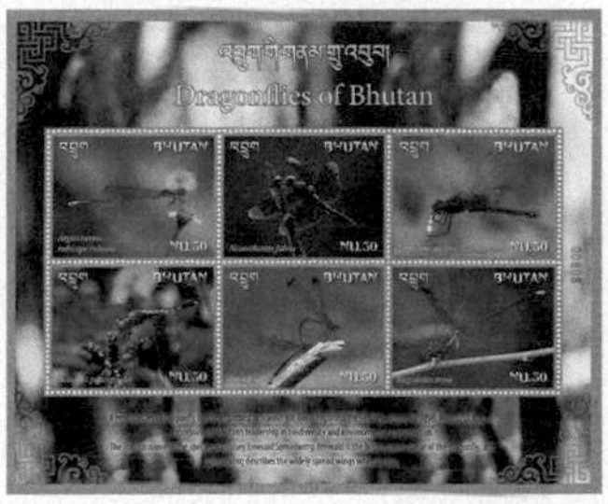

Dragonflies — A327

No. 1595: a, Argiocnemis rubiceps rubeola. b, Neurothemis fulvia. c, Trithemis aurora. d, Acisoma panorpoides. e, Bayadera indica. f, Megalestes irma.
50nu, Gyalsey emerald spreadwing.

2018, Feb. 5 Litho. *Perf. 14x14¼*

1595 A327 30nu Sheet of 6, #a-f 5.50 5.50

Souvenir Sheet

Perf. 14¼x14

1596 A327 50nu multi 1.60 1.60

No. 1596 contains one 56x40mm stamp.

Diplomatic Relations Between Bhutan and India, 50th Anniv. — A328

No. 1597: a, King of Bhutan and Indian officials (black-and-white photograph). b, King of Bhutan reviewing troops. c, King Jigme Khesar Namgyel Wangchuk seated with Indian Prime Minister Narendra Modi, flags in background. d, Modi with King Jigme Khesar Namgyel Wangchuk, Queen Jetsun and Prince Jigme Namgyel Wangchuk. e, King of Bhutan and his wife, holding flowers (black-and-white photograph). f, King of Bhutan and wife seated, reviewing troops (black-and-white photograph). g, King of Bhutan with Indian official and soldier. h, Modi with King Jigme Khesar Namgyel Wangchuk and his father, King Jigme Singye Wangchuk.
50nu, 50th anniversary emblem.

2018, Feb. 21 Litho. *Perf. 14¼*

1597 A328 30nu Sheet of 8, #a-h 7.50 7.50

Souvenir Sheet

Litho. & Embossed

1598 A328 50nu gold & multi 1.60 1.60

No. 1598 contains one 70x46mm stamp.

Global Environment Facility Small Grants Program, 25th Anniv. — A329

No. 1599: a, Solar panels, Jordan. b, Corn harvest, South Africa. c, Gueroba nut harvest, Bento Viana, Brazil. d, Fishing boat, Palau.
30nu, Women winnowing rice, Bhutan.

2018, June 26 Litho. *Perf. 14x14¼*

1599	A329	15nu Sheet of 4, #a-d	1.75	1.75

Souvenir Sheet

1600	A329	30nu multi	.90	.90

Miniature Sheet

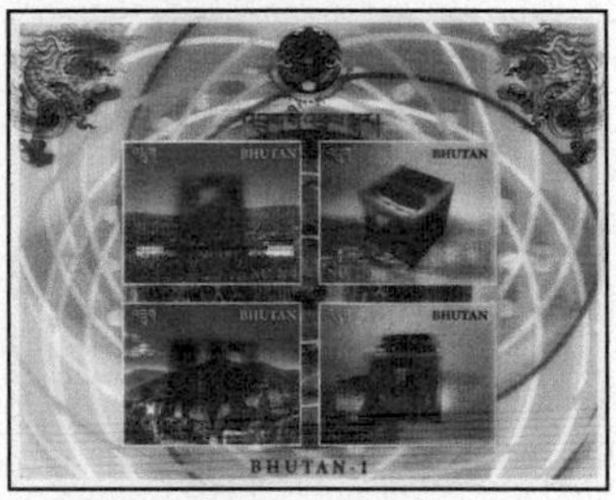

Launch of Bhutan-1 Satellite — A330

No. 1601 — Various depictions of Tashichho Dzong, Thimphu and: a, Front of satellite. b, Top, front and side of satellite. c, Side and front of satellite. d, Top and front of satellite.

Litho. With Lenticular Lens Affixed

2018, Aug. 10 *Imperf.*

1601	A330	250nu Sheet of 4, #a-d	28.00	28.00

Mammals — A331

No. 1602: a, Golden langur. b, Himalayan marmot. c, One-horned rhinoceros. d, Himalayan goral.
40nu, Red panda.

2019, Feb. 1 Litho. *Perf. 14x14¼*

1602	A331	20nu Sheet of 4, #a-d	2.25	2.25

Souvenir Sheet

Perf. 14¼

1603	A331	40nu multi	1.25	1.25

No. 1603 contains one 56x41mm stamp.

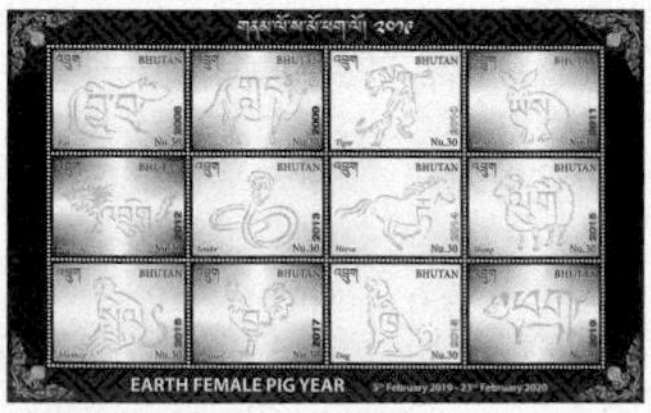

New Year 2019 (Year of the Pig) — A332

No. 1604: a, Rat. b, Ox. c, Tiger. d, Rabbit. e, Dragon. f, Snake. g, Horse. h, Sheep. i, Monkey. j, Rooster. k, Dog. l, Pig.
60nu, Pig and other Chinese Zodiac animals.

Litho. With Foil Application

2019, Feb. 5 *Perf. 14x14¼*

1604	A332	30nu Sheet of 12, #a-l	10.50	10.50

Souvenir Sheet

Litho. & Embossed

Perf. 14¼

1605	A332	60nu multi	1.75	1.75

No. 1605 contains one 70x46mm stamp.

Mohandas K. Gandhi (1869-1948), Indian Nationalist Leader — A333

No. 1606: a, Gandhi. b, Gandhi at spinning wheel.
50nu, Gandhi and followers on Salt March.

2019, May 25 Litho. *Perf. 14x14¼*

1606	A333	30nu Sheet of 2, #a-b	1.75	1.75

Souvenir Sheet

1607	A333	50nu multi	1.50	1.50

Miniature Sheet

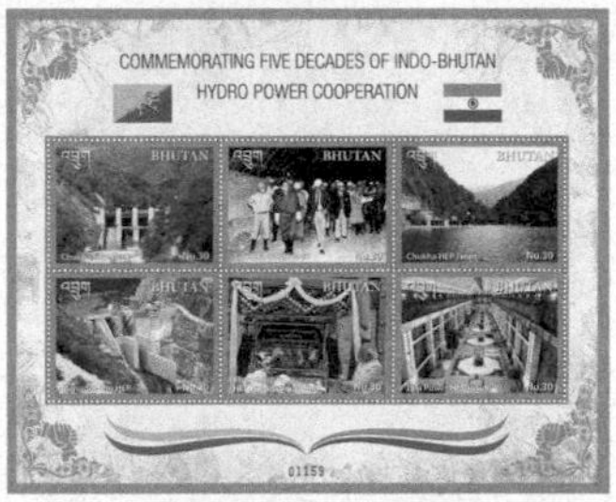

Hydroelectric Power Cooperation Between Bhutan and India, 50th Anniv. — A334

No. 1608: a, Back of Chukha Hydroelectric Project. b, Inspection of Tala Hydroelectric Project. c, Front of Chukha Hydroelectric Project. d, Mangdechhu Hydroelectric Project. e, Foundation stone for Kholongchhu Hydroelectric Project. f, Interior of Tala Hydroelectric Project.

2019, Aug. 17 Litho. *Perf. 14x14¼*

1608	A334	30nu Sheet of 6, #a-f	5.00	5.00

New Year 2020 (Year of the Rat) — A335

No. 1609: a, Rat. b, Ox. c, Tiger. d, Rabbit. e, Dragon. f, Snake. g, Horse. h, Sheep. i, Monkey. j, Rooster. k, Dog. l, Pig.
45nu, Rat, diff.

Litho. With Foil Application

2020, Feb. 7 *Perf. 14x14¼*

1609	A335	30nu Sheet of 12, #a-l	10.00	10.00

Souvenir Sheet

Perf. 14¼x14

1610	A335	45nu multi	1.25	1.25

No. 1610 contains one 70x45mm stamp.

Souvenir Sheet

Sheikh Mujibur Rahman (1920-75), First President of Bangladesh — A336

2020, Mar. 17 Litho. *Perf. 14¼*

1611	A336	30nu multi	.80	.80

SEMI-POSTAL STAMPS

Nos. 10-12 Surcharged

Perf. 14x14½

1964, Mar. Litho. Unwmk.

B1	A3	33ch + 50ch multi	4.00	4.00
B2	A3	70ch + 50ch multi	4.00	4.00
B3	A3	1.30nu + 50ch multi	4.00	4.00
		Nos. B1-B3 (3)	12.00	12.00

9th Winter Olympic Games, Innsbruck, Jan. 29-Feb. 9, 1964.

Olympic Games Type of Regular Issue, 1964

Souvenir Sheet

1964, Oct. 10 *Perf. 13½, Imperf.*

B4	A6	Sheet of 2	20.00	20.00
a.		1nu + 50ch Archery	6.50	6.50
b.		2nu + 50ch Soccer	13.50	13.50

18th Olympic Games, Tokyo, Oct. 10-25.

Nos. 97, 97C, 97E Surcharged

1968, Dec. 7 Photo. *Perf. 13½*

B5	A14n	5ch +5ch	.30	.30
B6	A14n	80ch +25ch	.50	.50
B7	A14n	2nu +50ch	1.25	1.25
		Nos. B5-B7 (3)	2.05	2.05

AIR POST STAMPS

Nos. 19-21, 38-39, 63-67 Ovptd.

a

Perfs. as Before

1967, Jan. 10 Litho.

Overprint "a"

C1	A5	33ch on #19	.30	.30
C2	A5	70ch on #20	.55	.40
C3	A5	1nu on #21	.65	.55
C4	A8	50ch on #38	.40	.30
C5	A8	75ch on #39	.55	.40
C6	A11	1.50nu on #63	1.00	.90
C7	A11	2nu on #64	1.25	1.25
C8	A11	3nu on #65	1.90	1.75
C9	A11	4nu on #66	2.75	2.50
C10	A11	5nu on #67	3.00	2.75

b

Overprint "b"

C11	A5	33ch on #19	.30	.30
C12	A5	70ch on #20	.50	.40
C13	A5	1nu on #21	.65	.55
C14	A8	50ch on #38	.40	.30
C15	A8	75ch on #39	.50	.40
C16	A11	1.50nu on #63	1.00	.90
C17	A11	2nu on #64	1.50	1.25
C18	A11	3nu on #65	1.90	1.75
C19	A11	4nu on #66	2.75	2.50
C20	A11	5nu on #67	3.50	3.40
		Nos. C1-C20 (20)	25.35	22.85

UN Type of Regular Issue

Bhutan Flag and: 2.50nu, UN Headquarters, NYC. 5nu, Security Council Chamber and mural by Per Krohg. 6nu, General Assembly Hall.

1971, Sept. 21 Photo. *Perf. 13½*

C21	A16	2.50nu silver & multi	.40	.40
C22	A16	5nu silver & multi	.60	.60
C23	A16	6nu silver & multi	.80	.80
		Nos. C21-C23 (3)	1.80	1.80

Bhutan's admission to the United Nations. Exist imperf.

Nos. C21-C23 Overprinted in Gold: "UNHCR / UNRWA / 1971" like Nos. 145-145C

1971, Dec. 23 *Perf. 13½*

C24	A16	2.50nu silver & multi	.45	.45
C25	A16	5nu silver & multi	1.00	1.00
C26	A16	6nu silver & multi	1.40	1.40
		Nos. C24-C26 (3)	2.85	2.85

World Refugee Year. Exist imperf.

UPU Types of 1974

UPU Emblem, Carrier Pigeon and: 1nu, Mail runner and jeep. 1.40nu, 10nu, Old and new locomotives. 2nu, Old biplane and jet.

1974, Oct. 9 Litho. *Perf. 14½*

C27	A19	1nu salmon & multi	.35	.35
C28	A20	1.40nu lilac & multi	.90	.90
C29	A20	2nu multicolored	1.25	1.25
		Nos. C27-C29 (3)	2.50	2.50

Souvenir Sheet

Perf. 13

C30	A20	10nu lilac & multi	5.75	5.75

Cent. of the UPU. Nos. C27-C29 were issued in sheets of 50 and sheets of 5 plus label with multicolored margin. Exist imperf.

Issues of 1968-1974 Surcharged 25ch and Bars

1978 Perf. & Printing as Before

C31	A16	25ch on 5nu, #C22	3.00	3.00
C32	A16	25ch on 6nu, #C23	3.00	3.00
C33	A20	25ch on 1.40nu, #C28	4.00	4.00
C34	A20	25ch on 2nu, #C29	4.00	4.00
C35	A14j	25ch on 4nu, #94L	4.00	4.00
C36	A14j	25ch on 10nu, #94N	4.00	4.00
C37	A17k	25ch on 5nu, #155F	4.00	4.00
C38	A17k	25ch on 6nu, #155G	4.00	4.00
		Nos. C31-C38 (8)	30.00	30.00

POSTAL-FISCAL STAMPS

Nos. AR1-AR4 are revenue stamps, authorized for use as postage stamps. After the issue of regular postage stamps in 1962, their use diminished when expansion of the modern postal system made the monastery fortresses' postal runner system obsolete. They were demonitized for postal use in the mid- to late 1980s, but remained on sale in post offices for fiscal use.

2 Shiki = 1 Thala = ½ Rupee (India)

Dorje (thunderbolt) — PF1

Perf. 12½

1955, Sept. 28 Litho. Unwmk.

AR1	PF1	(1sh) blue	1.40	—
AR2	PF1	(2sh) rose red	4.25	—
AR3	PF1	(4sh) green	7.00	—
AR4	PF1	(8sh) orange	19.00	—
		Nos. AR1-AR4 (4)	31.65	

Prior to April 1, 1957, the shiki denominations of Nos. AR1-AR4 equalled 1 anna, 2a, 4a, and 8a, respectively. Beginning April 2, 1957, the denominations equalled ¼ rupee, ½r, 1r, and 5r, respectively.

No. AR1 exists with 10 new paisa and 25np surcharges. There is no official government notice of their issuance.

BIAFRA

bē-af-rə

LOCATION — West Africa on the Gulf of Guinea, between Nigeria and Cameroun.
GOVT. — Republic
AREA — 29,848 sq. mi.
POP. — 13,500,000 (1967 est.)
CAPITAL — Enugu

After independence in 1960, Nigeria was torn by ethnic tensions between the Muslim north and the Christian and Animist south. During 1966, two coups, the first staged by Christian Igbo military officers from the oil-rich southeast (Biafra), with a subsequent counter-coup by Muslim officers, resulted in ethnic riots in which more than 30,000 Igbos were killed. Efforts at reconciliation between the regions failed, and on May 30, 1967, Biafra declared its independence. Hostilities between the central government and Biafra began in July, and after a bitter civil war, Biafra surrendered in Jan. 1970, and the region was reunited with Nigeria. Some 1,000,000 Biafrans died during the hostilities, either in battle or from starvation.

12 Pence = 1 Shilling
20 Shillings = 1 Biafran Pound

Catalogue values for all unused stamps in this country are for Never Hinged items.

Values for used stamps are for favor-canceled examples bearing an UMUAHIA postmark with a four-digit year date, rather than the two-digit date used on normal postal cancels. This device is 31mm in diameter, and the city name is 3mm high, both elements larger than postal cancels. Postally used examples sell for much higher prices.

Map of Biafra — A1

Arms, Flag, Date — A2

Mother and Child — A3

Perf. 12½

1968, Feb. 5 Litho. Unwmk.

1	A1	2p multi	.45	*.80*
2	A2	4p multi	.45	*.80*
3	A3	1s multi	.45	*2.25*
		Nos. 1-3 (3)	1.35	*3.85*

Nigeria Nos. 184-187, 189-197 Overprinted

No. 4

No. 12

Arms in red on Nos. 11-14, 16

1968, Apr. 1

4	A49	½p	multi (#184)	2.00	*6.75*
5	A49	1p	multi (#185)	3.25	*10.00*
6	A49	1½p	multi (#186)	12.00	*20.00*
7	A49	2p	multi (#187)	37.50	*60.00*
8	A49	4p	multi (#189)	19.00	*60.00*
9	A49	6p	multi (#190)	9.50	*18.00*
10	A49	9p	multi (#191)	3.75	*4.50*
11	A49	1sh	multi (#192)	65.00	*135.00*
12	A49	1sh3p	multi (#193)	35.00	*60.00*
13	A49	2sh6p	multi (#194)	4.25	*19.00*
14	A49	5sh	multi (#195)	3.50	*18.50*
15	A49	10sh	multi (#196)	11.00	*47.50*
16	A49	£1	multi (#197)	12.00	*47.50*
			Nos. 4-16 (13)	217.75	*506.75*

Nos. 4-16 were overprinted locally by the Government Printer, Enugu. Overprint errors and varieties exist.

1st Anniv. Indep. — A4

Designs: 4p, Biafran flag, workers, missiles. 1sh, Igbo victim of 1966 Nigerian pogrom. 2sh6p, nurse and refugees. 5sh, Biafran arms, £1 banknote. 10sh, Biafran orphan.

1968, May 30 *Perf. 12½*

17	A4	4p multi	.25	*.25*
18	A4	1sh multi	.35	*.30*
19	A4	2sh6p multi	.85	*3.50*
20	A4	5sh multi	1.00	*4.50*
21	A4	10sh multi	1.60	*5.00*
		Nos. 17-21 (5)	4.05	*13.55*

During 1968 several sets were sold by the Biafran philatelic agents but were not released to post offices within the country and did not perform postal duty: Nigeria Nos. 184 and 185 overprinted "Biafra France Friendship" and surcharged 5sh and £1, respectively. Value, $32.50. Biafra Nos. 17-21 overprinted "Help Biafran Children" and surcharged with additional values. Value, $4. Butterflies and plants, 4 values. Value, $10; later overprinted with Olympic rings and "Mexico Olympics 1968." Value, $14.

2nd Anniv. Indep. — A5

1969, May 30 ***Perf. 13¼x13½***

22	A5	2p multi	1.75	*5.00*
23	A5	4p multi	1.75	*5.00*
24	A5	1sh multi	3.00	*8.00*
25	A5	2sh6p multi	3.50	*16.00*
		Nos. 22-25 (4)	10.00	*34.00*

Souvenir Sheet

26	A5	10sh Biafran children	42.50

No. 26 exists imperf. Value, $65.

No. 26 was numbered on the back. Examples without number are presentation proofs.

Pope Paul VI's Visit to Africa — A6

1969, Aug. 1

27	A6	4p multi, org background	1.25	*3.50*
28	A6	6p multi, blue background	1.40	*9.00*
29	A6	9p multi, green background	1.60	*10.00*
30	A6	3sh multi, rose car background	4.00	*19.00*
a.		Brown background	75.00	
		Nos. 27-30 (4)	8.25	*41.50*

Souvenir Sheet

31	A6	10sh multi, mag background	55.00
a.		Plum background	55.00

In Dec. 1969 and Jan. 1970, as Biafra was collapsing, three sets were issued by Biafra's philatelic agents but were not available within Biafra: Nos. 27-30 overprinted "Christmas 1969 Peace on Earth and Goodwill to All Men." Value, $9. This overprint also was applied to Nos. 31 and 31a, with denomination surcharged to £1; value, each $45. Nos. 22-26 overprinted "Save Biafra 9th Jan. 1970" with added surtax. Values: set $32.50, souvenir sheet $42.50. No. 26 imperf. with this overprint also exists. Nos. 28 and 29 overprinted with UN emblem, "Human Rights" and added surtax. Value, $10.

BOLIVIA

bə-'li-vē-ə

LOCATION — Central South America, separated from the Pacific Ocean by Chile and Peru.
GOVT. — Republic
AREA — 424,165 sq. mi.
POP. — 7,949,933 (1998 est.)
CAPITAL — Sucre (La Paz is the actual seat of government).

100 Centavos = 1 Boliviano
100 Centavos = 1 Peso Boliviano (1963)
100 Centavos = 1 Boliviano (1987)

Catalogue values for unused stamps in this country are for Never Hinged items, beginning with Scott 308 in the regular postage section, Scott C112 in the airpost section, Scott RA5 in the postal tax section, and Scott RAC1 in airpost postal tax section.

On Feb. 21, 1863, the Bolivian Government decreed contracts for carrying the mails should be let to the highest bidder, the service to commence on the day the bid was accepted, and stamps used for the payment of postage. The winner of the contract would be responsible for expenses and would keep the profits. On Mar. 18, the contract was awarded to Sr. Justiniano Garcia and was in effect until Apr. 29, 1863, when it was rescinded. Stamps in the form illustrated above were prepared in denominations of ½, 1, 2 and 4 reales. All values exist in black and in blue. The blue are twice as scarce as the black. Value, black, $75 each.

It is said that used examples exist on covers, but the authenticity of these covers remains to be established.

Condor — A1

A2

A3

72 varieties of each of the 5c, 78 varieties of the 10c, 30 varieties of each of the 50c and 100c.

The plate of the 5c stamps was entirely reengraved 4 times and retouched at least 6 times. Various states of the plate have distinguishing characteristics, each of which is typical of most, though not all the stamps in a sheet. These characteristics (usually termed types) are found in the shading lines at the right side of the globe. a, vertical and diagonal lines. b, diagonal lines only. c, diagonal and horizontal with traces of vertical lines. d, diagonal and horizontal lines. e, horizontal lines only. f, no lines except the curved ones forming the outlines of the globe.

1867-68 Unwmk. Engr. ***Imperf.***

1	A1	5c yel grn, thin paper (a, b)	11.00	*25.00*
a.		5c blue green (a)	11.00	*30.00*
b.		5c deep green (a)	11.00	*30.00*
c.		5c ol grn, thick paper (a)	450.00	450.00
d.		5c yel grn, thick paper (a)	300.00	300.00
e.		5c yel grn, thick paper (b)	300.00	300.00
f.		5c blue green (b)	11.00	*30.00*
2	A1	5c green (d)	10.00	*25.00*
a.		5c green (c)	15.00	*30.00*
b.		5c green (e)	15.00	*30.00*
c.		5c green (f)	15.00	*30.00*
3	A1	5c vio ('68)	375.00	375.00
a.		5c rose lilac ('68)	375.00	375.00
		Revenue cancel		150.00
4	A3	10c brown	400.00	350.00
		Revenue cancel		175.00
5	A2	50c orange	35.00	
		Revenue cancel		15.00

6	A2	50c blue ('68)	*500.00*	
a.		50c dark blue ('68)	*500.00*	
		Revenue cancel		250.00
7	A3	100c blue	80.00	
		Revenue cancel		45.00
8	A3	100c green ('68)	250.00	
a.		100c pale blue grn ('68)	250.00	
		Revenue cancel		175.00

Used values are for postally canceled stamps. Pen cancellations usually indicate that the stamps have been used fiscally and such stamps sell for about one-fifth as much as those with postal cancellations.

The 500c is an essay.

Reprints of Nos. 3,4, 6 and 8 are common. Value, $10 each. Reprints of Nos. 2 and 5 are scarcer. Value, $25 each.

Coat of Arms
A4 A5

1868-69 ***Perf. 12***

Nine Stars

10	A4	5c green	27.50	18.00
11	A4	10c vermilion	45.00	25.00
12	A4	50c blue	70.00	45.00
13	A4	100c orange	80.00	55.00
14	A4	500c black	1,000.	1,000.

Eleven Stars

15	A5	5c green	18.00	12.00
16	A5	10c vermilion	25.00	20.00
a.		Half used as 5c on cover		600.00
17	A5	50c blue	50.00	40.00
18	A5	100c dp orange	60.00	50.00
19	A5	500c black	*3,500.*	*3,500.*

See Nos. 26-27, 31-34.

Arms and "The Law" — A6

1878 Various Frames ***Perf. 12***

20	A6	5c ultra	15.00	7.00
21	A6	10c orange	12.00	6.00
a.		Half used as 5c on cover		250.00
22	A6	20c green	45.00	10.00
a.		Half used as 10c on cover		200.00
23	A6	50c dull carmine	120.00	30.00
		Nos. 20-23 (4)	192.00	53.00

(11 Stars) — A7

Numerals Upright

1887 ***Rouletted***

24	A7	1c rose	4.00	3.00
25	A7	2c violet	4.00	3.00
26	A5	5c blue	14.50	8.00
27	A5	10c orange	14.50	8.00
		Nos. 24-27 (4)	37.00	22.00

See No. 37.

(9 Stars) — A8

1890 ***Perf. 12***

28	A8	1c rose	3.00	2.00
29	A8	2c violet	8.00	4.00
30	A4	5c blue	6.00	2.00
31	A4	10c orange	12.00	3.00
32	A4	20c dk green	25.00	6.00
33	A4	50c red	12.00	8.00
34	A4	100c yellow	25.00	*30.00*
		Nos. 28-34 (7)	91.00	55.00

See Nos. 35-36, 38-39.

1893 Litho. ***Perf. 11***

35	A8	1c rose	6.00	5.00
a.		Imperf. pair	100.00	
b.		Horiz. pair, imperf. vert.	100.00	
c.		Horiz. pair, imperf. btwn.	100.00	
36	A8	2c violet	6.00	5.00
a.		Block of 4 imperf. vert. and horiz. through center	200.00	
b.		Horiz. pair, imperf. btwn.	100.00	
c.		Vert. pair, imperf betwn.	100.00	
37	A7	5c blue	8.00	4.00
a.		Vert. pair, imperf. horiz.	100.00	
b.		Horiz. pair, imperf. btwn.	100.00	
38	A8	10c orange	25.00	8.00
a.		Pair, imperf. btwn., vert. or horiz.	100.00	
39	A8	20c dark green	100.00	45.00
a.		Imperf. pair, vert. or horiz.	200.00	
b.		Pair, imperf. btwn., vert. or horiz.	175.00	
		Nos. 35-39 (5)	145.00	67.00

Coat of Arms — A9

1894 Unwmk. Engr. ***Perf. 14, 14½***

Thin Paper

40	A9	1c bister	1.50	1.25
41	A9	2c red orange	3.00	2.25
42	A9	5c green	1.50	1.25
43	A9	10c yellow brn	1.50	1.25
44	A9	20c dark blue	8.00	8.00
45	A9	50c claret	20.00	20.00
46	A9	100c brown rose	40.00	40.00
		Nos. 40-46 (7)	75.50	74.00

Stamps of type A9 on thick paper were surreptitiously printed in Paris on the order of an official and without government authorization. Some of these stamps were substituted for part of a shipment of stamps on thin paper, which had been printed in London on government order.

When the thick paper stamps reached Bolivia they were at first repudiated but afterwards were allowed to do postal duty. A large quantity of the thick paper stamps were fraudulently canceled in Paris with a cancellation of heavy bars forming an oval. Value of unused set: $5.

To be legitimate, stamps of the thick paper stamps must have genuine cancellations of Bolivia. Value, on cover, each $150.

The 10c blue on thick paper is not known to have been issued.

Some examples of Nos. 40-46 show part of a papermakers' watermark "1011."

For overprints see Nos. 55-59.

President Tomas Frias — A10

President Jose M. Linares — A11

Pedro Domingo Murillo A12

Bernardo Monteagudo A13

Gen. Jose Ballivian — A14

Gen. Antonio Jose de Sucre — A15

Simon Bolivar — A16

Coat of Arms — A17

1897 Litho. ***Perf. 12***

47	A10	1c pale yellow grn	2.00	2.00
a.		Vert. pair, imperf. horiz.	100.00	
b.		Vert. pair, imperf. btwn.	100.00	
48	A11	2c red	3.00	2.00
49	A12	5c dk green	2.00	2.00
a.		Horiz. pair, imperf. btwn.	100.00	
50	A13	10c brown vio	2.00	2.00
a.		Vert. pair, imperf. btwn.	100.00	
51	A14	20c lake & blk	10.00	5.00
a.		Imperf., pair	100.00	
52	A15	50c orange	10.00	10.00
53	A16	1b Prus blue	20.00	20.00
54	A17	2b red, yel, grn & blk	60.00	*90.00*
		Nos. 47-54 (8)	109.00	*133.00*

Excellent forgeries of No. 54, perf and imperf, exist, some postally used.

Reprint of No. 53 has dot in numeral. Same value.

Nos. 40-44 Handstamped in Violet or Blue

1899 ***Perf. 14½***

55	A9	1c yellow bis	30.00	30.00
56	A9	2c red orange	40.00	*50.00*
57	A9	5c green	17.00	17.00
58	A9	10c yellow brn	30.00	30.00
59	A9	20c dark blue	50.00	*75.00*
		Nos. 55-59 (5)	167.00	202.00

The handstamp is found inverted, double, etc. Values twice the listed amounts. Forgeries of this handstamp are plentiful. "E.F." stands for Estado Federal.

The 50c and 100c (Nos. 45-46) were overprinted at a later date in Brazil. Value, $500.

Antonio José de Sucre — A18

Perf. 11½, 12

1899 Engr. Thin Paper

62	A18	1c gray blue	5.00	2.00
63	A18	2c brnsh red	5.00	2.00
64	A18	5c dk green	5.00	2.00
65	A18	10c yellow org	4.00	2.00
66	A18	20c rose pink	5.00	2.00
67	A18	50c bister brn	10.00	5.00
68	A18	1b gray violet	8.00	4.00
		Nos. 62-68 (7)	42.00	19.00

1901

69	A18	5c dark red	3.00	2.00

Col. Adolfo Ballivian A19

Eliodoro Camacho A20

President Narciso Campero A21

Jose Ballivian A22

Gen. Andres Santa Cruz — A23

Coat of Arms — A24

1901-04 **Engr.**

70	A19	1c claret	.85	.30
71	A20	2c green	1.00	.50
73	A21	5c scarlet	1.00	.30
74	A22	10c blue	3.00	.50
75	A23	20c violet & blk	2.00	1.00
76	A24	2b brown	7.00	5.00

Litho.

77	A19	1c claret ('04)	3.00	1.00
		Nos. 70-77 (7)	17.85	8.60

In No. 70 the panel above "CENTAVO" is shaded with continuous lines. In No. 77 the shading is of dots.

Nos. 73-74 exist imperf. Value, pairs, each $50.

See Nos. 103-105, 107, 110.

For surcharges see Nos. 95-96, 193.

Coat of Arms of Dept. of La Paz — A25

Murillo — A26

Jose Miguel Lanza — A27

Ismael Montes — A28

1909 Litho. ***Perf. 11***

78	A25	5c blue & blk	15.00	11.00
79	A26	10c green & blk	15.00	11.00
80	A27	20c orange & blk	15.00	11.00
81	A28	2b red & black	15.00	11.00
		Nos. 78-81 (4)	60.00	44.00

Centenary of Revolution of July, 1809.

Nos. 78-81 exist imperf. and tête bêche. Values: imperf. pairs, each $80; tête bêche pairs, each $95. Nos. 79-81 exist with center inverted. Value, each $95.

Miguel Betanzos A29

Col. Ignacio Warnes A30

Murillo
A31

Monteagudo
A32

Esteban
Arce — A33

Antonio Jose de Sucre — A34

Simon
Bolivar — A35

Manuel
Belgrano — A36

1909 Dated 1809-1825 *Perf. 11½*

82	A29	1c lt brown & blk	1.00	.40
83	A30	2c green & blk	1.50	.60
84	A31	5c red & blk	1.50	.50
85	A32	10c dull bl & blk	2.00	.50
86	A33	20c violet & blk	1.75	.70
87	A34	50c olive bister & blk	2.00	.80
88	A35	1b gray brn & blk	2.50	1.50
89	A36	2b chocolate & blk	2.50	2.00
		Nos. 82-89 (8)	14.75	7.00

War of Independence, 1809-1825.

Nos. 82-89 exist imperf. Value, set of pairs $400.

For surcharge see No. 97.

Warnes
A37

Betanzos
A38

Arce — A39

Dated 1910-1825

1910 *Perf. 13x13½*

92	A37	5c green & black	.50	.30
	a.	Imperf., pair	15.00	
93	A38	10c claret & indigo	.60	.50
	a.	Imperf., pair	50.00	
94	A39	20c dull blue & indigo	1.00	.80
	a.	Imperf., pair	20.00	
		Nos. 92-94 (3)	2.10	1.60

War of Independence.

Nos. 92-94 may be found with parts of a papermaker's watermark: "A I & Co/EXTRA STRONG/9303."

Both perf and imperf exist with inverted centers.

Nos. 71 and 75 Surcharged in Black

1911 *Perf. 11½, 12*

95	A20	5c on 2c green	.75	.30
	a.	Inverted surcharge	10.00	10.00
	b.	Double surcharge	12.00	10.00
	c.	Period after "1911"	4.50	1.50
	d.	Blue surcharge	100.00	80.00
	e.	Double dsurch., one invtd.	20.00	20.00
96	A23	5c on 20c vio & blk	30.00	30.00
	a.	Inverted surcharge	60.00	60.00
	b.	Double surch., one invtd.	80.00	
	c.	Period after "1911"	40.00	40.00

No. 83 Handstamp Surcharged in Green

97	A30	20c on 2c grn & blk	*2,500.*	

This provisional was issued by local authorities at Villa Bella, a town on the Brazilian border. The 20c surcharge was applied after the stamp had been affixed to the cover. Excellent forgeries of No. 96-97 exist.

"Justice"
A40 A41

1912

Black or Dark Blue Overprint On Revenue Stamps

98	A40	2c green (Bk)	.75	.30
	a.	Inverted overprint	15.00	
99	A41	10c ver (Bl)	6.00	1.00
	a.	Inverted overprint	20.00	

A42 A43

Red or Black Overprint

Engr.

100	A42	5c orange (R)	.75	.65
	a.	Inverted overprint	20.00	
	b.	Pair, one without overprint	50.00	
	c.	Black overprint	35.00	

Red or Black Surcharge

101	A43	10c on 1c bl (R)	1.00	.60
	a.	Inverted surcharge	25.00	
	b.	Double surcharge	25.00	
	c.	Dbl. surcharge, one invtd.	40.00	
	d.	Black surcharge	200.00	150.00
	e.	As "d," inverted	250.00	
	f.	As "d," double surcharge	225.00	
	g.	Pair, one without black surch.	800.00	

Fakes of No. 101d are plentiful.

Revenue Stamp Surcharged

Type 1 —Serifed "1"s in date

Type 2 — Sans-serif "1"s in date

1917 Litho.

102	10c on 1c blue, Type 1	*5,000.*	*1,750.*
a.	10c on 1c, Type 2	—	*2,000.*

Design similar to type A43.

1,000 examples of Nos. 102 and 102a were reportedly produced, with 90 percent of the issue being type 1 and the balance type 2. No. 102a also exists with overprint in black. Value, used, $3,500.

Excellent forgeries exist.

Types of 1901 and

Frias — A45

Sucre — A46

Bolivar — A47

1913 Engr. *Perf. 12*

103	A19	1c car rose	.75	.30
104	A20	2c vermilion	.75	.30
105	A21	5c green	1.00	.25
106	A45	8c yellow	1.50	1.00
107	A22	10c gray	1.50	.25
108	A46	50c dull violet	3.00	1.50
109	A47	1b slate blue	6.00	2.00
110	A24	2b black	10.00	5.00
		Nos. 103-110 (8)	24.50	10.60

No. 107, litho., was not regularly issued.

Nine values commemorating the Guaqui-La Paz railroad were printed in 1915 but never issued. Value, set $25.

The original set is engraved. Crude, typographed forgeries exist.

Monolith of
Tiahuanacu
A48

Mt. Potosí
A49

Lake
Titicaca — A50

Mt. Illimani — A51

Legislature
Building — A53

FIVE CENTAVOS.

Type I — Numerals have background of vertical lines. Clouds formed of dots.

Type II — Numerals on white background. Clouds near the mountain formed of wavy lines.

1916-17 Litho. *Perf. 11½*

111	A48	½c brown	.40	.30
	a.	Horiz. pair, imperf. vert.	50.00	40.00
112	A49	1c gray green	.50	.30
	a.	Imperf., pair	40.00	30.00
113	A50	2c car & blk	.50	.30
	a.	Imperf., pair	40.00	30.00
	b.	Vert. pair, imperf. horiz.	40.00	30.00
	c.	Center inverted	*150.00*	*100.00*
	d.	Imperf., center inverted	*250.00*	*150.00*
114	A51	5c dk blue (I)	1.25	.30
	a.	Imperf., pair	40.00	30.00
	b.	Vert. pair, imperf. horiz.	40.00	30.00
	c.	Horiz. pair, imperf. vert.	40.00	30.00
115	A51	5c dk blue (II)	1.00	.50
	a.	Imperf., pair	40.00	30.00
116	A53	10c org & bl	1.00	.30
	a.	Imperf., pair	60.00	40.00
	b.	No period after "Legislativo"	1.00	.30
	c.	Center inverted	*200.00*	*125.00*
	d.	Vertical pair, imperf. between	60.00	50.00
		Nos. 111-116 (6)	4.65	2.00

For surcharges see Nos. 194-196.

Coat of Arms
A54 A55

Printed by the American Bank Note Co.

1919-20 Engr. *Perf. 12*

118	A54	1c carmine	.40	.30
119	A54	2c dk violet	8.00	4.00
120	A54	5c dk green	.75	.30
121	A54	10c vermilion	.75	.30
122	A54	20c dk blue	2.25	.40
123	A54	22c lt blue	1.40	.90
124	A54	24c purple	.90	.60
125	A54	50c orange	7.00	.70
126	A55	1b red brown	9.00	2.50
127	A55	2b black brn	13.50	6.75
		Nos. 118-127 (10)	43.95	16.75

Printed by Perkins, Bacon & Co., Ltd.

1923-27 Re-engraved *Perf. 13½*

128	A54	1c carmine ('27)	.40	.30
129	A54	2c dk violet	.40	.30
130	A54	5c dp green	1.00	.30
131	A54	10c vermilion	25.00	18.00
132	A54	20c slate blue	2.50	.50
135	A54	50c orange	5.50	1.50
136	A55	1b red brown	1.50	1.00
137	A55	2b black brown	2.00	.60
		Nos. 128-137 (8)	38.30	22.50

There are many differences in the designs of the two issues but they are too minute to be illustrated or described.

Nos. 128-137 exist imperf. Value, $50 each pair.

See Nos. 144-146, 173-177. For surcharges see Nos. 138-143, 160, 162, 181-186, 236-237.

Stamps of 1919-20 Surcharged in Blue, Black or Red

1924 *Perf. 12*

138	A54	5c on 1c car (Bl)	.40	.30
	a.	Inverted surcharge	10.00	6.00
	b.	Double surcharge	10.00	6.00
139	A54	15c on 10c ver (Bk)	1.00	.70
	a.	Inverted surcharge	12.00	6.00
	b.	Double surcharge	12.00	6.00
	c.	Double surcharge, one inverted	*12.00*	*6.00*
	d.	Double surcharge, both inverted	*12.00*	*6.00*
140	A54	15c on 22c lt bl (Bk)	1.00	.75
	a.	Inverted surcharge	12.00	6.00
	b.	Double surcharge	16.00	6.00
	c.	Double surcharge, one inverted	*16.00*	*6.00*

No. 140 surcharged in red or blue probably are trial impressions. They appear jointly, and with black in blocks.

Same Surcharge on No. 131
Perf. 13½

142	A54	15c on 10c ver (Bk)	1.00	.30
	a.	Inverted surcharge	12.00	6.00

No. 121 Surcharged

Perf. 12

143	A54	15c on 10c ver (Bk)	1.00	.50
a.		Inverted surcharge	12.00	6.00
b.		Double surcharge	12.00	6.00
		Nos. 138-143 (5)	4.40	2.55

Type of 1919-20 Issue

Printed by Waterlow & Sons

Second Re-engraving

1925 Unwmk. *Perf. 12½*

144	A54	5c deep green	1.00	.50
145	A54	15c ultra	1.00	.50
146	A54	20c dark blue	1.00	.50
		Nos. 144-146 (3)	3.00	1.50

These stamps may be identified by the perforation.

Miner — A56

Sower — A57

Torch of Eternal Freedom — A57a

Kantuta — A57b

Pres. Bautista Saavedra — A57c

Condor Looking Toward the Sea — A57d

Liberty — A57e

Archer on Horse — A57f

Mercury — A57g

Gen. A. J. de Sucre — A57h

1925 Engr. *Perf. 14*

150	A56	1c dark green	1.50	
151	A57	2c rose	1.50	
152	A57a	5c red, *grn*	1.50	.50
153	A57b	10c car, *yel*	2.50	1.00
154	A57c	15c red brown	.80	.50
155	A57d	25c ultra	2.50	1.00
156	A57e	50c dp violet	3.00	1.00
157	A57f	1b red	5.00	2.50
158	A57g	2b orange	6.00	3.00
159	A57h	5b black brn	6.00	3.00
		Nos. 150-159 (10)	30.30	

Cent. of the Republic. The 1c and 2c were not released for general use.

Nos. 150-159 exist imperf. Value, $60 each pair.

For surcharges see Nos. C59-C62.

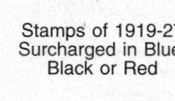

Stamps of 1919-27 Surcharged in Blue, Black or Red

1927

160	A54	5c on 1c car (Bl)	4.50	3.25
a.		Inverted surcharge	15.00	15.00
b.		Black surcharge	40.00	40.00

Perf. 12

162	A54	10c on 24c pur (Bk)	4.50	3.25
a.		Inverted surcharge	50.00	50.00
b.		Red surcharge	70.00	70.00

Coat of Arms — A66

Printed by Waterlow & Sons

1927 Litho. *Perf. 13½*

165	A66	2c yellow	.50	.35
166	A66	3c pink	.90	.90
167	A66	4c red brown	.75	.75
168	A66	20c lt ol grn	1.00	.35
169	A66	25c deep blue	1.00	.50
170	A66	30c violet	1.50	1.50
171	A66	40c orange	2.00	2.00
172	A66	50c dp brown	2.00	1.00
173	A55	1b red	2.50	2.00
174	A55	2b plum	4.00	3.50
175	A55	3b olive grn	4.50	4.50
176	A55	4b claret	7.50	6.00
177	A55	5b bister brn	8.00	6.50
		Nos. 165-177 (13)	36.15	29.85

For overprints and surcharges see Nos. 178-180, 208, 211-212.

Type of 1927 Issue Overprinted

1927

178	A66	5c dark green	.50	.30
179	A66	10c slate	.75	.30
180	A66	15c carmine	.75	.35
		Nos. 178-180 (3)	2.00	.95

Exist with inverted overprint. Value $30 each.

Stamps of 1919-27 Surcharged

1928 *Perf. 12, 12½, 13½*

Red Surcharge

181	A54	15c on 20c #122	15.00	15.00
a.		Inverted surcharge	22.50	22.50
182	A54	15c on 20c #132	15.00	15.00
a.		Inverted surcharge	25.00	25.00
b.		Black surcharge	45.00	
183	A54	15c on 20c #146	250.00	160.00

Black Surcharge

184	A54	15c on 24c #124	2.25	1.25
a.		Inverted surcharge	8.00	8.00
b.		Blue surcharge	75.00	
185	A54	15c on 50c #125	90.00	*400.00*
a.		Inverted surcharge	120.00	
186	A54	15c on 50c #135	1.75	1.25
a.		Inverted surcharge	10.00	10.00
		Nos. 181-186 (6)	374.00	592.50

Condor — A67

Hernando Siles — A68

Map of Bolivia — A69

Printed by Perkins, Bacon & Co., Ltd.

1928 Engr. *Perf. 13½*

189	A67	5c green	1.50	.25
190	A68	10c slate	.50	.25
191	A69	15c carmine lake	3.00	.25
		Nos. 189-191 (3)	5.00	.75

Nos. 104, 111, 113, Surcharged in Various Colors

1930 *Perf. 12, 11½*

193	A20	1c on 2c (Bl)	2.00	2.00
a.		"0.10" for "0.01"	35.00	35.00
194	A50	3c on 2c (Br)	2.00	2.00
195	A48	25c on ½c (Bk)	2.00	2.00
196	A50	25c on 2c (V)	2.00	2.00
		Nos. 193-196 (4)	8.00	8.00

The lines of the surcharges were spaced to fit the various shapes of the stamps. The surcharges exist inverted, double, etc.

Trial printings were made of the surcharges on Nos. 193 and 194 in black and on No. 196 in brown.

Mt. Potosi — A70

Mt. Illimani — A71

Eduardo Abaroa — A72

Map of Bolivia — A73

Sucre — A74

Bolivar — A75

1931 Engr. *Perf. 14*

197	A70	2c green	2.00	1.00
198	A71	5c light blue	2.00	.30
199	A72	10c red orange	2.00	.30
200	A73	15c violet	4.50	.40
201	A73	35c carmine	3.00	1.25
202	A73	45c orange	3.00	1.25
203	A74	50c gray	1.50	1.00
204	A75	1b brown	2.50	1.40
		Nos. 197-204 (8)	20.50	6.90

No. 198 exists imperf.

See Nos. 207, 241. For surcharges see Nos. 209-210.

Symbols of 1930 Revolution — A76

1931 Litho. *Perf. 11*

205	A76	15c scarlet	6.00	1.00
a.		Pair, imperf. between	25.00	
206	A76	50c brt violet	1.50	1.25
a.		Pair, imperf. between	30.00	

Revolution of June 25, 1930.

For surcharges see Nos. 239-240.

Map Type of 1931 Without Imprint

1932 Litho.

207	A73	15c violet	4.00	.35

Stamps of 1927-31 Surcharged

1933 *Perf. 13½, 14*

208	A66	5c on 1b red	1.00	.50
a.		Without period after "Cts"	3.00	3.00
209	A73	15c on 35c car	.50	.50
a.		Inverted surcharge	30.00	20.00
210	A73	15c on 45c orange	.60	.60
a.		Inverted surcharge	30.00	20.00
211	A66	15c on 50c dp brn	2.00	.50
212	A66	25c on 40c orange	1.00	.50
		Nos. 208-212 (5)	5.10	2.60

The hyphens in "13-7-33" occur in three positions: type 1, both hypens in middle (shown); type 2, both hypens on base line of numbers; type 3, left hypen in middle, right hyphen on base line. Values are the same for all types.

Coat of Arms — A77

1933 Engr. *Perf. 12*

213	A77	2c blue green	.50	.30
214	A77	5c blue	.50	.30
215	A77	10c red	1.00	.75
216	A77	15c deep violet	.50	.30
217	A77	25c dark blue	1.50	.75
		Nos. 213-217 (5)	4.00	2.40

For surcharges see Nos. 233-235, 238.

Mariano Baptista — A78

1935

218	A78	15c	dull violet	.75	.50

Map of Bolivia — A79

1935

219	A79	2c	dark blue	.50	.30
220	A79	3c	yellow	.50	.30
221	A79	5c	vermilion	.50	.30
222	A79	5c	blue grn	.50	.30
223	A79	10c	black brn	.50	.30
224	A79	15c	deep rose	.50	.30
225	A79	15c	ultra	.50	.30
226	A79	20c	yellow grn	1.00	.60
227	A79	25c	lt blue	1.50	.30
228	A79	30c	deep rose	1.00	.60
229	A79	40c	orange	2.25	1.00
230	A79	50c	gray violet	2.25	1.00
231	A79	1b	yellow	1.25	.60
232	A79	2b	olive brown	3.00	1.50
			Nos. 219-232 (14)	15.75	7.70

Regular Stamps of 1925-33 Surcharged in Black

1937 *Perf. 11, 12, 13½*

233	A77	5c	on 2c bl grn	.30	.30
234	A77	15c	on 25c dk bl	.50	.50
235	A77	30c	on 25c dk bl	.80	.80
236	A55	45c	on 1b red brn	1.00	1.00
237	A55	1b	on 2b plum	1.00	1.00
a.			"1" missing	15.00	15.00
238	A77	2b	on 25c dk bl	1.00	1.00

"Comunicaciones" on one line

239	A76	3b	on 50c brt vio	2.00	2.00
a.			"3" of value missing	20.00	20.00
240	A76	5b	on 50c brt vio	3.00	3.00
			Nos. 233-240 (8)	9.60	9.60

Exist inverted, double, etc.

President Siles — A80

1937 Unwmk. *Perf. 14*

241	A80	1c	yellow brown	.50	.50

Native School — A81

Oil Wells — A82

Modern Factories A83

Torch of Knowledge A84

Map of the Sucre-Camiri R. R. — A85

Allegory of Free Education — A86

Allegorical Figure of Learning — A87

Symbols of Industry — A88

Modern Agriculture — A89

1938 Litho. *Perf. 10½, 11*

242	A81	2c	dull red	.80	.60
243	A82	10c	pink	.90	.50
244	A83	15c	yellow grn	1.40	.40
245	A84	30c	yellow	1.75	.60
246	A85	45c	rose red	3.00	1.25
247	A86	60c	dk violet	2.50	1.25
248	A87	75c	dull blue	2.00	1.75
249	A88	1b	lt brown	4.50	1.00
250	A89	2b	bister	4.00	1.50
			Nos. 242-250 (9)	20.85	8.85

For surcharge see No. 314.

Llamas — A90

Vicuna — A91

Coat of Arms — A92

Cocoi Herons — A93

Chinchilla — A94

Toco Toucan — A95

Condor — A96

Jaguar — A97

1939, Jan. 21 *Perf. 10½, 11½x10½*

251	A90	2c	green	1.50	.75
252	A90	4c	fawn	1.50	.75
253	A90	5c	red violet	1.50	.75
254	A91	10c	black	1.50	.75
255	A91	15c	emerald	3.00	1.25
256	A91	20c	dk slate grn	3.00	1.25
257	A92	25c	lemon	1.50	.75
258	A92	30c	dark blue	1.50	.75
259	A93	40c	vermilion	2.50	1.00
260	A93	45c	gray	2.50	1.00
261	A94	60c	rose red	2.50	1.00
262	A94	75c	slate blue	2.50	1.00
263	A95	90c	orange	5.00	1.25
264	A95	1b	blue	5.00	1.25
265	A96	2b	rose lake	7.00	1.25
266	A96	3b	dark violet	10.00	1.75
267	A97	4b	brown org	10.00	1.75
268	A97	5b	gray brown	11.50	2.00
			Nos. 251-268 (18)	73.50	20.25

All but 20c exist imperf. Value, each pair $40.

Imperf. counterfeits with altered designs exist of some values.

For surcharges see Nos. 315-317.

Flags of 21 American Republics — A98

1940, Apr. Litho. *Perf. 10½*

269	A98	9b	multicolored	4.50	2.25

Pan American Union, 50th anniversary.

Statue of Murillo — A99

Urns of Murillo and Sagarnaga — A100

Dream of Murillo — A101

Murillo — A102

1941, Apr. 15

270	A99	10c	dull vio brn	.25	.25
271	A100	15c	lt green	.50	.30
a.			Imperf., pair	25.00	
b.			Double impression	8.00	8.00
272	A101	45c	carmine rose	.50	.25
a.			Double impression	10.00	10.00
273	A102	1.05b	dk ultra	.80	.40
			Nos. 270-273 (4)	2.05	1.20

130th anniv. of the execution of Pedro Domingo Murillo (1759-1810), patriot.

For surcharge see No. 333.

First Stamp of Bolivia and 1941 Airmail Stamp — A103

1942, Oct. Litho. *Perf. 13½*

274	A103	5c	pink	1.00	1.00
275	A103	10c	orange	1.00	1.00
276	A103	20c	yellow grn	1.50	1.00
277	A103	40c	carmine rose	1.50	1.00
278	A103	90c	ultra	3.00	2.25
279	A103	1b	violet	5.00	3.75
280	A103	10b	olive bister	20.00	16.00
			Nos. 274-280 (7)	33.00	26.00

1st School Phil. Exposition held in La Paz, Oct., 1941.

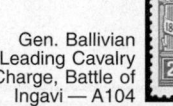

Gen. Ballivian Leading Cavalry Charge, Battle of Ingavi — A104

1943 Photo. *Perf. 12½*

281	A104	2c	lt blue grn	.30	.25
282	A104	3c	orange	.30	.25
283	A104	25c	deep plum	.60	.35
284	A104	45c	ultra	.60	.35
285	A104	3b	scarlet	1.40	.70
286	A104	4b	brt rose lilac	1.50	.80
287	A104	5b	black brown	1.50	.90
			Nos. 281-287 (7)	6.20	3.60

Souvenir Sheets

Perf. 13, Imperf.

288	A104	Sheet of 4	6.00	6.00
289	A104	Sheet of 3	15.00	15.00

Centenary of the Battle of Ingavi, 1841. No. 288 contains 4 stamps similar to Nos. 281-284, No. 289 three stamps similar to Nos. 285-287.

Potosi A107

Quechisla A108

Miner — A109

Dam A110

Mine Interior A111

Chaquiri Dam A112

Entrance to Pulacayo Mine A113

1943 Engr. *Perf. 12½*
290 A107 15c red brown .50 .30
291 A108 45c vio blue .60 .30
292 A109 1.25b brt rose vio 1.00 .50
293 A110 1.50b emerald .80 .50
294 A111 2b brown blk 1.00 .70
295 A112 2.10b lt blue 1.00 .70
296 A113 3b red orange 4.00 1.10
Nos. 290-296 (7) 8.90 4.10

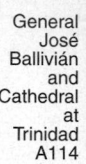

General José Ballivián and Cathedral at Trinidad A114

1943, Nov. 18
297 A114 5c dk green & brn .50 .30
298 A114 10c dull pur & brn .50 .30
299 A114 30c rose red & brn .50 .30
300 A114 45c brt ultra & brn .75 .50
301 A114 2.10b dp org & brn 1.50 1.00
Nos. 297-301,C91-C95 (10) 6.40 4.30

Department of Beni centenary.

"Honor, Work, Law" — A115

"United for the Country" — A116

1944 Litho. *Perf. 13½*
302 A115 20c orange .30 .30
303 A115 90c ultra .30 .30
304 A116 1b brt red vio .30 .30
305 A116 2.40b dull brown .30 .30

1945
306 A115 20c green .30 .30
307 A115 90c dp rose .50 .30
Nos. 302-307,C96-C99 (10) 3.35 2.80

Nos. 302-307 were issued to commemorate the Revolution of Dec. 20, 1943.

Catalogue values for unused stamps in this section, from this point to the end of the section, are for Never Hinged items.

Leopold Benedetto Vincenti, Joseph Ignacio de Sanjines and Bars of Anthem — A117

1946, Aug. 21 Litho. *Perf. 10½*
308 A117 5c rose vio & blk .25 .25
309 A117 10c ultra & blk .25 .25
310 A117 15c blue grn & blk .25 .25
311 A117 30c vermilion & brn .55 .25
a. Souv. sheet of 1, imperf. 2.50 2.50
312 A117 90c dk blue & brn .50 .30
313 A117 2b black & brn 1.20 1.00
a. Souv. sheet of 1, imperf. 4.50 4.50
Nos. 308-313 (6) 3.00 2.30

Adoption of Bolivia's natl. anthem, cent. Nos. 311a and 313a sold for 4b over face.

Nos. 248 and 262 Surcharged in Carmine, Black or Orange

1947, Mar. 12 *Perf. 10½, 11*
314 A87 1.40b on 75c (C) .35 .25
315 A94 1.40b on 75c (Bk) .35 .25
316 A94 1.40b on 75c (C) .35 .25
317 A94 1.40b on 75c (O) .35 .25
Nos. 314-317,C112 (5) 1.75 1.25

People Attacking Presidential Palace — A118

1947, Sept. Litho. *Perf. 13½*
318 A118 20c blue grn .25 .25
319 A118 50c lilac rose .30 .25
320 A118 1.40b grnsh bl .30 .25
321 A118 3.70b dull org 1.00 .30
322 A118 4b violet 1.00 .30
323 A118 10b olive 3.00 1.00
Nos. 318-323,C113-C117 (11) 7.15 3.60

1st anniv. of the Revolution of July 21, 1946. Nos. 318-323 exist imperf. Value, each pair $40.

Arms of Bolivia and Argentina A119

1947, Oct. 23
324 A119 1.40b deep orange .40 .25

Meeting of Presidents Enrique Hertzog of Bolivia and Juan D. Peron of Argentina at Yacuiba on Oct. 23, 1947. Exist imperf.
See No. C118.

Statue of Christ above La Paz — A120

2b, Child kneeling before cross of Golgotha. 3b, St. John Bosco. No. 328, Virgin of Copacabana. No. 329, Pope Pius XII blessing University of La Paz.

1948, Sept. 26 Unwmk. *Perf. 11½*
325 A120 1.40b blue & yel .60 .25
326 A120 2b yel grn & sal .90 .25
327 A120 3b green & gray 1.75 .25
328 A120 5b violet & sal 2.25 .25
329 A120 5b red brn & lt grn 3.00 .60
Nos. 325-329,C119-C123 (10) 14.30 3.50

3rd Inter-American Cong. of Catholic Education.

Map and Emblem of Bolivia Auto Club — A125

1948, Oct. 20
330 A125 5b indigo & salmon 2.50 .60

Intl. Automobile Races of South America, Sept.-Oct. 1948. See No. C124.

Pres. Gregorio Pacheco, Map and Post Horn — A126

1950, Jan. 2 Litho. *Perf. 11½*
331 A126 1.40b violet blue .30 .25
332 A126 4.20b red .50 .25
Nos. 331-332,C125-C127 (5) 1.90 1.25

75th anniv. of the UPU.

No. 273 Surcharged in Black

1950 *Perf. 10½*
333 A102 2b on 1.05b dk ultra .45 .25

Crucifix and View of Potosi — A127

Perf. 11½
1950, Sept. 14 Litho. Unwmk.
334 A127 20c violet .25 .25
335 A127 30c dp orange .25 .25
336 A127 50c lilac rose .25 .25
337 A127 1b carmine .25 .25
338 A127 2b blue .35 .25
339 A127 6b chocolate .35 .25
Nos. 334-339 (6) 1.70 1.50

400th anniv. of the appearance of a crucifix at Potosi. Exist imperf.

Symbols of United Nations — A128

1950, Oct. 24
340 A128 60c ultra 1.40 .25
341 A128 2b green 2.25 .35
Nos. 340-341,C138-C139 (4) 6.65 1.20

5th anniv. of the UN, Oct. 24, 1945.

Gate of the Sun and Llama A129

Church of San Francisco — A130

40c, Avenue Camacho. 50c, Consistorial Palace. 1b, Legislative Palace. 1.40b, Communications Bldg. 2b, Arms. 3b, La Gasca ordering Mendoza to found La Paz. 5b, Capt. Alonso de Mendoza founding La Paz. 10b, Arms; portrait of Mendoza.

1951, Mar. Engr. *Perf. 12½*
Center in Black
342 A129 20c green .25 .25
343 A130 30c dp orange .25 .25
344 A129 40c bister brn .25 .25
345 A129 50c dk red .25 .25
346 A129 1b dp purple .25 .25
347 A129 1.40b dk vio blue .30 .25
348 A129 2b dp purple .40 .25
349 A129 3b red lilac .40 .40
a. Sheet, Nos. 345, 346, 348, 349 3.00 3.00
b. As "a," imperf. 3.00 3.00
350 A129 5b dk red .50 .30
a. Sheet, Nos. 344, 347, 350 3.50 3.50
b. As "a," imperf. 3.50 3.50
351 A129 10b sepia 1.00 .40
a. Sheet, Nos. 342, 343, 351 3.00 3.00
b. As "a," imperf. 3.00 3.00
Nos. 342-351,C140-C149 (20) 9.90 8.65

400th anniv. of the founding of La Paz.
For surcharges see Nos. 393-402.

Boxing A131

Perf. 12½
1951, July 1 Unwmk. Engr.
352 A131 20c shown .35 .25
353 A131 50c Tennis .50 .25
354 A131 1b Diving .50 .25
355 A131 1.40b Soccer .55 .25
356 A131 2b Skiing .75 .40
357 A131 3b Handball 2.50 1.75
a. Sheet, #352-353, 356-357 7.00 7.00
b. As "a," imperf. 7.00 7.00
358 A131 4b Cycling 3.50 2.50
a. Sheet, #354-355, 358 7.00 7.00
b. As "a," imperf. 7.00 7.00
Nos. 352-358,C150-C156 (14) 24.70 12.20

The stamps were intended to commemorate the 5th athletic championship matches held at La Paz, October 1948.

An imperforate souvenir sheet denominated 54b, depicting Nos. 354, 654 and 659 with simulated perforations, was issued March 24, 1982, to celebrate the España '82 World Cup soccer championship games. Value $50.

A souvenir sheet denominated 2b, containing No. 356 perf 14¼, was issued June 15, 1988, to mark the 1988 Calgary Winter Olympic Games. Value $25.

Eagle and Flag of Bolivia A132

1951, Nov. 5 Litho. *Perf. 11½*
Flag in Red, Yellow and Green.
359 A132 2b aqua .25 .25
360 A132 3.50b ultra .25 .25
361 A132 5b purple .25 .25
362 A132 7.50b gray .50 .25
363 A132 15b dp car .65 .30
364 A132 30b sepia 1.40 .65
Nos. 359-364 (6) 3.30 1.95

Cent. of the adoption of Bolivia's natl. flag.

Eduardo Abaroa — A133

1952, Mar. *Perf. 11*
365 A133 80c dk carmine .25 .25
366 A133 1b red orange .25 .25
367 A133 2b emerald .25 .25
368 A133 5b ultra .50 .25
369 A133 10b lilac rose 1.50 .30
370 A133 20b dk brown 2.50 .50
Nos. 365-370,C157-C162 (12) 11.70 4.90

73rd anniv. of the death of Eduardo Abaroa.

Queen Isabella I — A134

1952, July 16 Unwmk. *Perf. 13½*

371	A134	2b vio bl	.45	.25
372	A134	6.30b carmine	.45	.25
		Nos. 371-372,C163-C164 (4)	3.15	1.10

Birth of Isabella I of Spain, 500th anniv.

Columbus Lighthouse — A135

1952, July 16 Litho.

373	A135	2b vio bl, *bl*	.25	.25
374	A135	5b car, *sal*	.80	.50
375	A135	9b emer, *grn*	1.10	1.00
		Nos. 373-375,C165-C168 (7)	3.50	2.75

An imperforate souvenir sheet denominated 1,000,000b, depicting No. 374 with simulated perforations, was issued May 12, 1986, to mark the 500th anniversary of the discovery of America. Value $30.

Miner — A136

1953, Apr. 9

376	A136	2.50b vermilion	.30	.25
377	A136	8b violet	.30	.25

Nationalization of the mines.

Gualberto Villarroel, Victor Paz Estenssoro and Hernan Siles Zuazo A137

1953, Apr. 9 *Perf. 11½*

378	A137	50c rose lil	.25	.25
379	A137	1b brt rose	.25	.25
380	A137	2b vio bl	.30	.25
381	A137	3b lt grn	.30	.25
382	A137	4b yel org	.50	.30
383	A137	5b dl vio	.50	.30
		Nos. 378-383,C169-C175 (13)	5.65	4.30

Revolution of Apr. 9, 1952, 1st anniv.

Map of Bolivia and Cow's Head — A138

25b, 85b, Map and ear of wheat.

1954, Aug. 2 *Perf. 12x11½*

384	A138	5b car rose	.25	.25
385	A138	17b aqua	.25	.25
386	A138	25b chalky blue	.25	.25
387	A138	85b blk brn	.75	.25
		Nos. 384-387,C176-C181 (10)	5.85	2.55

Nos. 384-385 for the agrarian reform laws of 1953-54. Nos. 386-387 for the 1st National Congress of Agronomy. Exist imperf.

Oil Refinery A139

1955, Oct. 9 Unwmk. *Perf. 12x11½*

388	A139	10b ultra & lt ultra	.35	.25
389	A139	35b rose car & rose	.35	.25
390	A139	40b dk & lt yel grn	.35	.25
391	A139	50b red vio & lil rose	.50	.25
392	A139	80b brn & bis brn	.75	.25
		Nos. 388-392,C182-C186 (10)	12.15	4.25

Nos. 388-392 exist imperf. Value, set of pairs $250.

Nos. 342-351, Surcharged with New Values and Bars in Ultramarine

1957, Feb. 14 Engr. *Perf. 12½*

Center in Black

393	A129	50b on 3b red lilac	.25	.25
394	A129	100b on 2b dp pur	.25	.25
395	A129	200b on 1b dp pur	.25	.25
396	A129	300b on 1.40b dk vio bl	.30	.25
397	A129	350b on 20c green	.50	.25
398	A129	400b on 40c bis brn	.60	.25
399	A130	600b on 30c dp org	.50	.30
400	A129	800b on 50c dk red	.75	.30
401	A129	1000b on 10b sepia	.75	.30
402	A129	2000b on 5b dk red	1.25	.50
		Nos. 393-402 (10)	5.40	2.90

See Nos. C187-C196.

CEPAL Building, Santiago de Chile, and Meeting Hall in La Paz — A140

1957, May 15 Litho. *Perf. 13*

403	A140	150b gray & ultra	.25	.25
404	A140	350b bis brn & gray	.30	.25
405	A140	550b chlky bl & brn	.40	.25
406	A140	750b dp rose & grn	.45	.30
407	A140	900b grn & brn blk	1.50	.60
		Nos. 403-407,C197-C201 (10)	10.80	5.20

7th session of the C. E. P. A. L. (Comision Economica para la America Latina de las Naciones Unidas), La Paz. Nos. 403-407 exist imperf. Value, set of pairs $250.

For surcharges see Nos. 482-484,

Presidents Siles Zuazo and Aramburu A141

1957, Dec. 15 Unwmk. *Perf. 11½*

408	A141	50b dp red org & org	.25	.25
409	A141	350b dp blue & blue	.55	.25
410	A141	1000b dp brn & brn rose	1.25	.30
		Nos. 408-410,C202-C204 (6)	5.55	1.80

Opening of the Santa Cruz-Yacuiba Railroad and the meeting of the Presidents of Bolivia and Argentina. Nos. 408-410, C202-C204 exist imperf. Value, set of pairs $160.

For surcharge see No. 699.

Flags of Bolivia and Mexico and Presidents Hernan Siles Zuazo and Adolfo Lopez Mateos A142

1960, Jan. 30 Litho. *Perf. 11½*

411	A142	350b olive	.30	.25
412	A142	600b red brown	.40	.25
413	A142	1500b black brown	1.00	.35
		Nos. 411-413,C205-C207 (6)	6.20	3.10

Issued for an expected visit of Mexico's President Adolfo Lopez Mateos. On sale Jan. 30-Feb. 1, 1960.

Indians and Mt. Illimani A143

1960, Mar. 26 Unwmk.

414	A143	500b olive bister	.75	.40
415	A143	1000b blue	1.50	.60
416	A143	2000b brown	3.75	1.00
417	A143	4000b green	6.00	4.50
		Nos. 414-417,C208-C211 (8)	36.75	18.75

Refugee Children — A144

1960, Apr. 7 *Perf. 11½*

418	A144	50b brown	.25	.25
419	A144	350b claret	.25	.25
420	A144	400b steel blue	.40	.25
421	A144	1000b gray brown	.80	.50
422	A144	3000b slate green	2.00	1.25
		Nos. 418-422,C212-C216 (10)	8.30	5.20

World Refugee Year, 7/1/59-6/30/60.

For surcharges see Nos. 454-458, 529.

Jaime Laredo A145

1960, Aug. 15 Litho. *Perf. 11½*

423	A145	100b olive	.50	.25
424	A145	350b deep rose	.70	.25
425	A145	500b Prus green	1.00	.30
426	A145	1000b brown	1.25	.70
427	A145	1500b violet blue	2.25	1.25
428	A145	5000b gray	5.50	2.25
		Nos. 423-428,C217-C222 (12)	29.45	11.05

Issued to honor violinist Jaime Laredo.

For surcharge see No. 485.

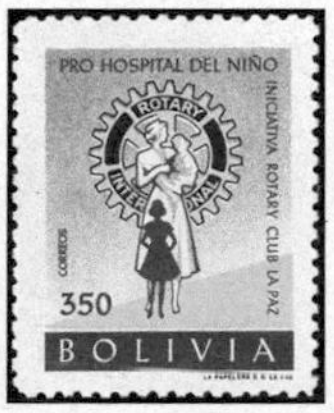

Rotary Emblem and Nurse with Children — A146

1960, Nov. 19 *Perf. 11½*

429	A146	350b multi	.30	.25
430	A146	500b multi	.45	.30
431	A146	600b multi	.75	.30
432	A146	1000b multi	1.00	.50
		Nos. 429-432,C223-C226 (8)	9.90	4.30

Issued for the Children's Hospital, sponsored by the Rotary Club of La Paz.

For surcharges see Nos. 486-487.

A147

A148

Designs from Gate of the Sun — A148a

Designs: Various prehistoric gods and ornaments from Tiahuanacu excavations.

Surcharged in Black or Dark Red Gold Background

1960, Dec. 16 *Perf. 13x12, 12x13*

Sizes: 21x23mm, 23x21mm

433	A147	50b on ½c red	.80	.45
434	A147	100b on 1c red	.50	.25
435	A147	200b on 2c blk	1.60	.25
436	A147	300b on 5c grn (DR)	.35	.25
437	A147	350b on 10c grn	1.25	1.10
438	A148	400b on 15c ind	.50	.25
439	A148	500b on 20c red	.50	.25
440	A148	500b on 50c red	.60	.25
441	A148	600b on 22½c grn	.80	.40
442	A148	600b on 60c vio	.90	.50
443	A148	700b on 25c vio	1.25	.30
444	A148	700b on 1b grn	1.75	1.00
445	A148	800b on 30c red	1.00	.30
446	A148	900b on 40c grn	.75	.40
447	A148	1000b on 2b bl	1.00	.50
448	A148	1800b on 3b gray	10.00	6.00

Perf. 11

Size: 49½x23mm

449	A148	4000b on 4b gray	75.00	60.00

Perf. 11x13½

Size: 49x53mm

450	A148a	5000b on 5b gray	18.00	12.50
a.		Perf. 11¼x11½	—	—
		Nos. 433-450 (18)	116.55	84.95

Nos. 433-450 were not regularly issued without surcharge. Value, set $60.

The decree for Nos. 433-450 stipulated that 7 were for air mail (500b on 50c, 600b on 60c, 700b on 1b, 1000b, 1800b, 4000b and 5000b), but the overprinting failed to include "Aereo."

The 800b surcharge also exists on the 1c red and gold. This was not listed in the decree. Value $20.

An imperforate 1,000,000b souvenir sheet, depicting the 5c and 3b values of the unissued set was issued May 12, 1986, to commemorate Halley's Comet. Value $75.

For surcharges see Nos. 528, 614.

Miguel de Cervantes — A149

1961, Nov. Photo. *Perf. 13x12½*

451	A149	600b ocher & dl vio	.60	.25

Cervantes' appointment as Chief Magistrate of La Paz. See No. C230.

Nuflo de Chaves — A150

1961, Nov. Unwmk.
452 A150 1500b dk bl, *buff* 1.25 .50

Founding of Santa Cruz de la Sierra, 400th anniv. See Nos. 468, C246. For surcharge see No. 533.

People below Eucharist Symbol — A151

1962, Mar. 19 Litho. *Perf. 10½*
453 A151 1000b gray grn, red & yel 1.25 .75

4th Natl. Eucharistic Congress, Santa Cruz, 1961. See No. C231.

Nos. 418-422 Surcharged Horizontally with New Value and Bars or Greek Key Border Segment

No. 454

No. 455

No. 456

Nos. 457-458

1962, June *Perf. 11½*
454 A144 600b on 50b brown .40 .25
455 A144 900b on 350b claret .50 .25
456 A144 1000b on 400b steel blue .60 .25
457 A144 2000b on 1000b gray brn 1.00 .50
458 A144 3500b on 3000b slate grn 1.25 1.00
Nos. 454-458,C232-C236 (10) 10.55 5.45

Old value obliterated with two short bars on No. 454; four short bars on Nos. 455-456 and Greek key border on Nos. 457-458. The Greek key obliteration comes in two positions: two full "keys" on top, and one full and two half keys on top.

Flowers — A152

1962, June 28 Litho. *Perf. 10½*
459 A152 200b Hibiscus .75 .30
460 A152 400b Bicolored vanda 1.25 .30
461 A152 600b Lily 2.00 .40
462 A152 1000b Orchid 2.50 .40
Nos. 459-462,C237-C240 (8) 19.75 6.70

Bolivia's Armed Forces — A153

1962, Sept. 5 *Perf. 11½*
463 A153 400b Infantry .25 .25
464 A153 500b Cavalry .45 .25
465 A153 600b Artillery .40 .30
466 A153 2000b Engineers 1.00 .40
Nos. 463-466,C241-C244 (8) 6.10 3.50

Anti-Malaria Emblem — A154

1962, Oct. 4
467 A154 600b dk & lt vio & yel .50 .30

WHO drive to eradicate malaria. See No. C245.

Portrait Type of 1961

Design: 600b, Alonso de Mendoza.

1962 Photo. *Perf. 13x12½*
468 A150 600b rose vio, *bluish* .50 .30

Soccer and Flags A155

Design: 1b, Goalkeeper catching ball, vert.

1963, Mar. 21 Litho. *Perf. 11½*
Flags in National Colors
469 A155 60c gray .65 .35
470 A155 1b gray 1.00 .45

21st South American Soccer Championships. See Nos. C247-C248.

An imperforate 20b souvenir sheet, depicting Nos. 469 and C247 with simulated perforations, was issued April 28, 1980, to commemorate the Argentina 1978 and España 1982 World Cup championship soccer games. Value $45.

Two imperforate souvenir sheets commemorating España '82 were issued Aug. 11, 1981. One depicts Nos. 469 and 654 with simulated perforations and is denominated 14.80b (value $75). The other depicts No. 470 with simulated perforations (value$45).

Globe and Wheat Emblem A156

1963, Aug. 1 Unwmk. *Perf. 11½*
471 A156 60c dk bl, bl & yel .45 .25

"Freedom from Hunger" campaign of the FAO. See No. C249.

Oil Derrick and Chart — A157

Designs: 60c, Map of Bolivia. 1b, Students.

1963, Dec. 21 Litho. *Perf. 11½*
472 A157 10c green & dk brn .25 .25
473 A157 60c ocher & dk brn .25 .25
474 A157 1b dk blue, grn & yel .35 .25
Nos. 472-474,C251-C253 (6) 3.15 2.30

Revolution of Apr. 9, 1952, 10th anniv.

Flags of Bolivia and Peru A158

1966, Aug. 10 Wmk. 90 *Perf. 13½*
Flags in National Colors
475 A158 10c black & tan .25 .25
476 A158 60c black & lt grn .25 .25
477 A158 1b black & gray .40 .25
478 A158 2b black & rose .70 .60
Nos. 475-478,C254-C257 (8) 4.20 3.50

Marshal Andrés Santa Cruz (1792-1865), president of Bolivia and of Peru-Bolivian Confederation.

Children — A159

Perf. 13½
1966, Dec. 16 Unwmk. Litho.
479 A159 30c ocher & sepia .40 .25

Issued to help poor children. See No. C258.

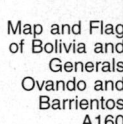

Map and Flag of Bolivia and Generals Ovando and Barrientos A160

1966, Dec. 16 Litho. *Perf. 13½*
Flag in Red, Yellow and Green
480 A160 60c violet brn & tan .45 .25
481 A160 1b dull grn & tan .50 .25

Issued to honor Generals Rene Barrientos Ortuno and Alfredo Ovando C., co-Presidents, 1965-66. See Nos. C259-C260.

Various Issues 1957-60 and Type A161 Surcharged

No. 403 Surcharged

1966, Dec. 21
482 A140 20c on 150b gray & ultra .25 .25

Nos. 405-406 Surcharged

483 A140 30c on 550b chlky bl & brn .35 .25
484 A140 2.80b on 750b dp rose & grn 1.00 .60

No. 424 Surcharged

485 A145 60c on 350b dp rose .65 .25

Nos. 429-430 Surcharged

486 A146 1.60b on 350b multi 1.00 .60
487 A146 2.40b on 500b multi 1.25 .90

Revenue Stamps of 1946 Surcharged

488 A161 20c on 5b red .25 .25

Revenue Stamps of 1946 Surcharged

489 A161 60c on 2b grn .35 .25

Revenue Stamps of 1946 Surcharged

490 A161 1b on 10b brn .60 .25

Revenue Stamps of 1946 Surcharged

491 A161 1.60b on 50c vio .60 .25
Nos. 482-491,C261-C272 (22) 20.35 11.90

For surcharge see No. C272.

Sower — A162

1967, Sept. 20 Litho. *Perf. 13½x13*
492 A162 70c multicolored .40 .25

50th anniv. of Lions Intl. See Nos. C273-C273a.

"Macheteros"
A163

Designs (Folklore characters): 60c, Chunchos. 1b, Wiphala. 2b, Diablada.

1968, June 24 *Perf. 13½x13*
493 A163 30c gray & multi .25 .25
494 A163 60c sky bl & multi .35 .30
495 A163 1b gray & multi .50 .25
496 A163 2b gray ol & multi .80 .25
a. Souvenir sheet of 4, #493-496, imperf 15.00 15.00
Nos. 493-496,C274-C277 (8) 5.10 2.25

Issued to publicize the 9th Congress of the Postal Union of the Americas and Spain.

Arms of
Tarija — A164

1968, Oct. 29 **Litho.** *Perf. 13½x13*
497 A164 20c pale sal & multi .25 .25
498 A164 30c gray & multi .25 .25
499 A164 40c dl yel & multi .25 .25
500 A164 60c lt yel grn & multi .35 .25
Nos. 497-500,C278-C281 (8) 4.25 2.65

Battle of Tablada sesquicentennial.

Pres. Gualberto
Villaroel — A165

1968, Nov. 6 **Unwmk.**
501 A165 20c sepia & org .80 .25
502 A165 30c sepia & dl bl grn .80 .25
503 A165 40c sepia & dl rose .80 .25
504 A165 50c sepia & yel grn .80 .25
505 A165 1b sepia & ol bister .80 .25
Nos. 501-505 (5) 4.00 1.25

4th centenary of the founding of Cochabamba. See Nos. C282-C286.

ITU Emblem
A166

1968, Dec. 3 **Litho.** *Perf. 13x13½*
506 A166 10c gray, blk & yel .25 .25
507 A166 60c org, blk & ol .50 .50

Cent. (in 1965) of the ITU. See Nos. C287-C288.

Polychrome
Painted Clay Cup,
Inca
Period — A167

1968, Nov. 14 *Perf. 13½x13*
508 A167 20c dk bl grn & multi .35 .25
509 A167 60c vio bl & multi .70 .40

20th anniv. (in 1966) of UNESCO. See Nos. C289-C290.

John F.
Kennedy
A168

1968, Nov. 22 *Perf. 13x13½*
510 A168 10c yel grn & blk .25 .25
511 A168 4b vio & blk 2.00 1.90
a. Souvenir sheet of 1, type of #511 2.50 2.50

See Nos. C291-C292.

Tennis
Player — A169

1968, Dec. 10 *Perf. 13x13½*
512 A169 10c gray, blk & lt brn .35 .35
513 A169 20c yel, blk & lt brn .35 .35
514 A169 30c ultra, blk & lt brn .35 .35
a. Souvenir sheet #512-514, imperf 2.50 2.50
Nos. 512-514 (3) 1.05 1.05

32nd South American Tennis Championships, La Paz, 1965. See Nos. C293-C294.

Issue of
1863 — A170

1968, Dec. 23 **Litho.** *Perf. 13x13½*
515 A170 10c yel grn, brn & blk 1.00 .25
516 A170 30c lt bl, brn & blk 1.00 .40
517 A170 2b gray, brn & blk 1.00 .40
a. Souvenir sheet #515-517, imperf 6.00 6.00
Nos. 515-517,C295-C297 (6) 8.45 4.20

Cent. of Bolivian postage stamps. See Nos. C295-C297.

Rifle Shooting
A171

Sports: 50c, Equestrian. 60c, Canoeing.

1969, Oct. 29 **Litho.** *Perf. 13x13½*
518 A171 40c red brn, org & blk .50 .50
519 A171 50c emer, red & blk .50 .50
520 A171 60c bl, emer & blk .50 .50
a. Souvenir sheet #518-520, imperf 6.00 6.00
Nos. 518-520,C299-C301 (6) 5.65 5.00

19th Olympic Games, Mexico City, 10/12-27/68.

Temenis
Laothoe
Violetta
A172

Butterflies: 10c, Papilio crassus. 20c, Catagramma cynosura. 30c, Eunica eurota flora. 80c, Ituna phenarete.

1970, Apr. 24 **Litho.** *Perf. 13x13½*
521 A172 5c pale lil & multi 2.00 1.00
522 A172 10c pink & multi 4.00 2.00
523 A172 20c gray & multi 4.00 2.00
524 A172 30c yel & multi 4.00 2.00
525 A172 80c multicolored 4.00 2.00
a. Souvenir sheet #521-523, imperf 30.00 30.00
Nos. 521-525,C302-C306 (10) 58.00 28.50

A souvenir sheet exists containing 3 imperf. stamps similar to Nos. 521-523. Black marginal inscription. Size: 129½x80mm. Value $45.

Boy Scout — A173

Design: 10c, Girl Scout planting rose bush.

1970, June 17 *Perf. 13½x13*
526 A173 5c multicolored .25 .25
527 A173 10c multicolored .25 .25
Nos. 526-527,C307-C308 (4) 1.25 1.25

Honoring the Bolivian Scout movement.

A 1,000,000b imperforate souvenir sheet, depicting No. 526 with simulated perforations, was issued May 12, 1986, to mark the explosion of the U.S. Space Shuttle Challenger. Value $30.

No. 437 Surcharged
Red

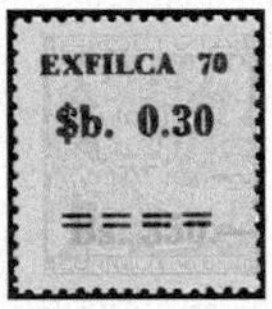

1970, Dec. 6 **Litho.** *Perf. 13x12*
528 A147 30c on 350b on 10c .50 .35

EXFILCA 70, 2nd Interamerican Philatelic Exhib., Caracas, Venezuela, Nov. 27-Dec. 6.

Nos. 455 and 452 Surcharged in Black or Red

1970, Dec. **Photo.** *Perf. 11½*
529 A144 60c on 900b on 350b .35 .25
533 A150 1.20b on 1500b (R) .60 .25

Amaryllis
Yungacensis
A174

Bolivian Flowers: 30c, Amaryllis escobar uriae, horiz. 40c, Amaryllis evansae, horiz. 2b, Gymnocalycium chiquitanum.

Perf. 13x13½, 13½x13

1971, Aug. 9 **Litho.** **Unwmk.**
534 A174 30c gray & multi .35 .25
535 A174 40c multi .35 .25
536 A174 50c multi .50 .25
537 A174 2b multi 1.25 .60
a. Souvenir sheet of 4, #534, 535, C310, C312, imperf 15.00 15.00
b. Souvenir sheet of 4, #536, 537, C311, C313, imperf 15.00 15.00
Nos. 534-537,C310-C313 (8) 8.75 5.80

Sica Sica
Church,
EXFILIMA
Emblem — A175

1971, Nov. 6 *Perf. 14x13½*
538 A175 20c red & multi .45 .25

EXFILIMA '71, 3rd Inter-American Philatelic Exhibition, Lima, Peru, Nov. 6-14.

A176

Design: Pres. Hugo Banzer Suarez.

1972, Jan. 24 **Litho.** *Perf. 13½*
539 A176 1.20b blk & multi 2.00 .25

Bolivia's development, 8/19/71-1/24/72.

A177

Folk Dances: 20c, Chiriwano de Achocalla. 40c, Rueda Chapaca. 60c, Kena-kena. 1b, Waca Thokori.

1972, Mar. 23 **Litho.** *Perf. 13½x13*
540 A177 20c red & multi .25 .25
541 A177 40c rose lil & multi .45 .35
542 A177 60c cream & multi .60 .25
543 A177 1b citron & multi .80 .35
a. Souvenir sheet of 4, #540, 541, C315, imperf 35.00 35.00
b. Souvenir sheet of 4, #542, 543, C314 imperf 35.00 35.00
Nos. 540-543,C314-C315 (6) 3.85 1.70

Madonna and
Child by B.
Bitti — A178

Bolivian paintings: 10c, Nativity, by Melchor Perez de Holguin. 50c, Coronation of the Virgin, by G. M. Berrio. 70c, Harquebusier, anonymous. 80c, St. Peter of Alcantara, by Holguin.

1972 **Litho.** *Perf. 14x13½*
544 A178 10c gray & multi .35 .25
545 A178 50c sal & multi .50 .25
546 A178 70c lt grn & multi .60 .25
547 A178 80c buff & multi .70 .25
548 A178 1b multi 1.00 .25
a. Souvenir sheet of 2, #548, C318, imperf 45.00 45.00
b. Souvenir sheet of 4, #C317, C318 imperf 45.00 45.00
Nos. 544-548,C316-C319 (9) 6.40 2.35

Issue dates: 1b, Aug. 17; others, Dec. 4.

An imperforate 20b souvenir sheet, depicting No. 548 with simulated perforations, was issued March 16, 1979, to mark the International Year of the Child. Value $45.

An imperf 1b souvenir sheet, depicting No. 548 with simulated perforations, was issued Aug. 1, 1982, to celebrate Christmas. Value $65.

A 2b souvenir sheet containing No. 548, perf 13¼ was issued Dec. 16, 1987, for Christmas. Value $30.

Tarija Cathedral, EXFILBRA Emblem — A179

1972, Aug. 26
549 A179 30c multi .45 .25

4th Inter-American Philatelic Exhibition, EXFILBRA, Rio de Janeiro, Brazil, 8/26-9/2.

Echinocactus Notocactus A180

Designs: Various cacti.

1973, Aug. 6	**Litho.**	***Perf. 13½***	
550	A180 20c crim & multi	.55	.30
551	A180 40c multi	.55	.30
552	A180 50c multi	.55	.30
553	A180 70c multi	.60	.40
a.	Souvenir sheet of 2, #553, C321, imperf	40.00	40.00
b.	Souvenir sheet of 4, #551, C323 imperf	40.00	40.00
	Nos. 550-553,C321-C323 (7)	5.75	2.40

Power Station, Santa Isabel A181

Designs: 20c, Tin industry. 90c, Bismuth industry. 1b, Natural gas plant.

1973, Nov. 26	**Litho.**	***Perf. 13½***	
554	A181 10c gray & multi	1.25	.25
555	A181 20c tan & multi	1.25	.25
556	A181 90c lt grn & multi	1.50	.25
557	A181 1b yel & multi	1.50	.25
	Nos. 554-557,C324-C325 (6)	11.75	1.50

Bolivia's development.

Cattleya Nobilior — A182

Orchids: 50c, Zygopetalum bolivianum. 1b, Huntleya melagris.

1974, May 15		***Perf. 13½***	
558	A182 20c gray & multi	1.50	.25
559	A182 50c lt bl & multi	1.50	.25
560	A182 1b cit & multi	1.50	.25
a.	Souvenir sheet of 2, #558, C328, imperf	50.00	20.00
b.	Souvenir sheet of 4, #559, 560 imperf	50.00	20.00
	Nos. 558-560,C327-C330 (7)	27.00	3.60

For surcharge see No. 704.

Four imperforate souvenir sheets were issued May 31, 1974, to publicize 1975-77 Bolivian philatelic expositions. They depict: 14.90b, Nos. 18, 544 and C330; 15.50b, Nos. 18, 545 and C329; 16b, Nos. 18 and C320; 16.70b, Nos. 18, 547 and C327. Value, each $5. These sheets were later (Sept. 21) overprinted for various 1974 special events. Vale, set of 4: unused $275; used $150.

UPU and Philatelic Exposition Emblems — A183

1974, Oct. 9
561 A183 3.50b grn, blk & bl 1.25 .50

Centenary of Universal Postal Union: PRENFIL-UPU Philatelic Exhibition, Buenos Aires, Oct. 1-12; EXPO-UPU Philatelic Exhibition, Montevideo, Oct. 20-27.

Gen. Sucre, by I. Wallpher A184

1974, Dec. 9 **Litho.** ***Perf. 13¾***
562 A184 5b multicolored 1.50 .75

Sesquicentennial of the Battle of Ayacucho.

An imperforate 5b souvenir sheet, depicting No. 562 with simulated perforations, was issued Dec. 31, 1982, to honor Peter Paul Reubens. Value $50.

An imperforate 1,000,000b souvenir sheet, containing No. 562 perf 13¼, was issued Sept. 25, 1986, to mark the Seoul Summer Olympic Games. Value $40.

Lions Emblem and Steles A185

1975, Mar. 17 **Litho.** ***Perf. 13½***
563 A185 30c red & multi .60 .40

Lions Intl. in Bolivia, 25th anniv.

España 75 Emblem A186

1975, Mar.
564 A186 4.50b yel, red & blk 1.00 .45

Espana 75 International Philatelic Exhibition, Madrid, Apr. 4-13.

Emblem A187

1975 **Litho.** ***Perf. 13½***
565 A187 2.50b lil, blk & sil 1.00 .35

First meeting of Postal Ministers, Quito, Ecuador, March 1974, and for the Cartagena Agreement.

Four 20b imperforate souvenir sheets were issued in March 1975 to publicize 1975-77 Bolivian stamp exhibitions. Each depicts No. 14, with Nos. 562, 563, 564 or 565. Value, each $5. These sheets were also overprint to commemorate special events of 1974. Value, set $175.

Two of the unoverprinted 1974 sheets, those depicting Nos. 563 and 564, were overprinted in April 1981 to commemorate the 150th anniv. of the death of Símon Bolívar. Value, each $5. These sheets were also overprinted to mark the 50th anniv. of the first Bolivia-Brazil flight. Value, each $5.

Pando Coat of Arms — A188

Designs: Departmental coats of arms.

1975, July 16	**Litho.**	***Perf. 13½***	
566	A188 20c shown	.45	.25
567	A188 2b Chuquisaca	1.00	.50
568	A188 3b Cochabamba	1.25	.75
	Nos. 566-568,C336-C341 (9)	10.80	5.60

Sesquicentennial of Republic of Bolivia.

Simón Bolívar — A189

Presidents and Statesmen of Bolivia: 30c, Victor Paz Estenssoro. 60c, Tomas Frias. 1b, Ismael Montes. 2.50b, Aniceto Arce. 7b, Bautista Saavedra. 10b, Jose Manuel Pando. 15b, Jose Maria Linares. 50b, Simon Bolivar.

1975		**Litho.**	***Perf. 13½***	
		Size: 24x32mm		
569	A189	30c multi	.25	.25
569A	A189	60c multi	.25	.25
570	A189	1b multi	.25	.25
571	A189	2.50b multi	.75	.25
572	A189	7b multi	1.75	1.00
573	A189	10b multi	3.00	1.50
574	A189	15b multi	4.00	1.75
		Size: 28x39mm		
575	A189	50b multi	15.00	10.00
	Nos. 569-575,C346-C353 (16)		54.90	34.80

Sesquicentennial of Republic of Bolivia.

An imperforate 20b souvenir sheet, depicting No. 575 with simulated perforations, was issued Oct. 13, 1980, to celebrate the 1980 Lake Placid Winter Olympic Games. Value $20.

An imperforate 10b souvenir sheet, depicting No. 573 with simulated perforations, was issued March 24, 1982, to commemorate the España '82 World Cup soccer championship games. Value $35.

"EXFIVIA 75" A190

1975, Dec. 1	**Litho.**	***Perf. 13½***	
576	A190 3b multicolored	1.20	.80
a.	Souvenir sheet	2.50	2.50

EXFIVIA 75, 1st Bolivian Philatelic Exposition. No. 576a contains one stamp similar to #576 with simulated perfs. Sold for 5b.

No. 576a was overprinted in 1981 for EXFIVA 77 and EXFILMAR 79. Value $5.

An imperforate 20b souvenir sheet, depicting No. 576 with simulated perforations, was issued June 1, 1978, commemorating the 75th anniv. of the Nobel Prize (in 1976). Value $85.

A191

Chiang Kai-shek, flags of Bolivia and China.

1976, Apr. 4	**Litho.**	***Perf. 13½***	
577	A191 2.50b multi, red circle	4.50	1.50
578	A191 2.50b multi, bl circle	4.50	1.50

Pres. Chiang Kai-shek of China (1887-1975).

Erroneous red of sun's circle on Chinese flag of No. 577 was corrected on No. 578 with a dark blue overlay.

Navy Day — A192

1976, Apr. **Litho.** ***Perf. 13½***
579 A192 50c Naval insignia .60 .50

Geological Map, Pickax and Lamp — A193

1976, May
580 A193 4b multicolored 1.25 .50

Bolivian Geological Institute.

Lufthansa Jet, Bolivian and German Colors A194

1976, May
581 A194 3b multicolored 1.25 .60

Lufthansa, 50th anniversary.

An imperforate 20b souvenir sheet, depicting No. 581 with simulated perforations, was issued June 1, 1978, to celebrate the Argentina 78 World Cup. Value $35.

Two imperforate 20b souvenir sheets, depicting No. 581 with simulated perforations, were issued Oct. 13, 1980, to celebrate the 50th anniversary of Zeppelin flights to South America.

Boy Scout and Scout Emblem — A195

1976, May **Litho.** ***Perf. 13½***
582 A195 1b multicolored .75 .65

Bolivian Boy Scouts, 60th anniversary.

An imperfoate 125,000b souvenir sheet, depicting Nos. 582 and 683 with simulated perforations, was issued June 24, 1985, to mark the 75th anniv. of the Boy Scouts. Value $10. This sheet was overprinted, surcharged 1,500,000b and reissued Apr. 18, 1986, to honor the 1987/88 World Jamboree in Australia. Value $20.

Battle Scene, US Bicentennial Emblem — A196

1976, May 25

583 A196 4.50b bis & multi		2.00	1.00
a. Souenir sheet of 1		25.00	25.00

American Bicentennial.

No. 583a contains one stamp similar to No. 583 with simulated perforations. Size: 130x80mm.

Three imperforate souvenir sheets, each denominated 20b, depicting No. 583 with simulated perforations and various historic U.S. motifs, were issued Dec. 20, 1976, to commemorate the U.S. Bicentennial. Value, each $6.

Family, Map of Bolivia — A197

1976 *Perf. 13½*

584 A197 2.50b multicolored	.85	.50

National Census 1976.

Vicente Bernedo — A198

1976, Oct.

585 A198 1.50b multicolored	.50	.40

Brother Vicente Bernedo de Potosi (1544-1619), missionary to the Indians.

Four imperforate souvenir sheets, each denominated 20b, depicting No. 585 with simulated perforations were issued Dec. 20, 1976, celebrating various themes. These comprise: 75th anniv. Nobel prize, value $50; 1976 Montreal Summer Olympics, value $25; U.S. Bicentennial / Space, value $35; 100th anniv. telephone, 25th anniv. United Nations, 110th anniv. ITU, value $35.

Policeman with Dog, Rainbow over La Paz — A199

1976, Oct.

586 A199 2.50b multicolored	.80	.80

Bolivian Police, 150 years of service.

Emblem, Bolivar and Sucre A200

1976, Nov. 18 **Litho.** *Perf. 13½*

587 A200 1.50b multicolored	1.00	.50

Intl. Congress of Bolivarian Societies.

Pedro Poveda, View of La Paz — A201

1976, Dec.

588 A201 1.50b multicolored	.50	.25

Pedro Poveda (1874-1936), educator.

A202

1976, Dec. 17 *Perf. 10½*

594 A202	20c brown	.35	.25
595 A202	1b ultra	.65	.25
596 A202	1.50b green	1.10	.60
	Nos. 594-596 (3)	2.10	1.10

Boy and Girl — A203

1977, Feb. 4 **Litho.** *Perf. 13½*

599 A203 50c multicolored	.40	.25

Christmas 1976, and for 50th anniversary of the Inter-American Children's Institute.

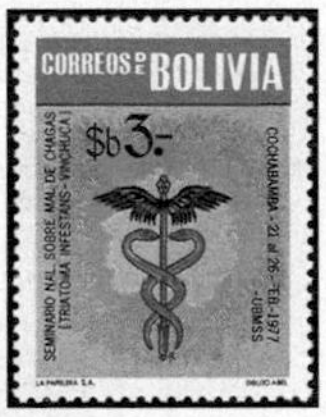

Staff of Aesculapius A204

1977, Mar. 18 **Litho.** *Perf. 13½x13*

600 A204 3b multicolored	1.00	.30

National Seminar on Chagas' disease, Cochabamba, Feb. 21-26.

Supreme Court, Sucre — A205

Designs: 4b, Manuel Maria Urcullu, first President of Supreme Court. 4.50b, Pantaleon Dalence, President 1883-1889.

1977, May 3

601 A205	2.50b multi	.45	.25
602 A205	4b multi	.65	.25
603 A205	4.50b multi	.90	.30
	Nos. 601-603 (3)	2.00	.80

Sesquicentennial of Bolivian Supreme Court.

Newspaper Mastheads — A206

Designs: 2.50b, Alfredo Alexander and Hoy, horiz. 3b, Jose Carrasco and El Diario, horiz. 4b, Demetrio Canelas and Los Tiempos. 5.50b, Frontpage of Presencia.

1977, June **Litho.** *Perf. 13½*

604 A206	1.50b multi	.40	.30
605 A206	2.50b multi	.60	.30
606 A206	3b multi	.60	.30
607 A206	4b multi	.75	.40
608 A206	5.50b multi	1.00	.30
	Nos. 604-608 (5)	3.35	1.60

Bolivian newspapers and their founders.

Map of Bolivia, Tower and Flag — A207

1977, June

609 A207 3b multi	.75	.30

90th anniversary of Oruro Club.

Games' Poster — A208

1977, Oct. 20 **Litho.** *Perf. 13½*

610 A208 5b blue & multi	1.00	.40

8th Bolivian Games, La Paz, Oct. 1977.

Four imperforate souvenir sheets, each denominated 20b, depicting No. 610 with simulated perforations were issued June 1, 1978. Each sheet celebrated an upcoming philatelic exhibition: Honduras '78; Capex '78; Praga '78; and Philaserdica '79. Value, each $15.

Tin Miner and Emblem — A209

1977, Oct. 31 **Litho.** *Perf. 13*

611 A209 3b multicolored	1.00	.30

Bolivian Mining Corp., 25th anniv.

Miners, Globe, Tin Symbol — A210

1977, Nov. 3

612 A210 6b silver & multi	1.50	.60

Intl. Tin Symposium, La Paz, Nov. 14-21.

Two souvenir sheets, denominated 1,000,000b, containing No. 612 perf 13¼, were issued Sept. 25, 1986, to commemorate the Uncia-Antofagasto railway. Value, each $30.

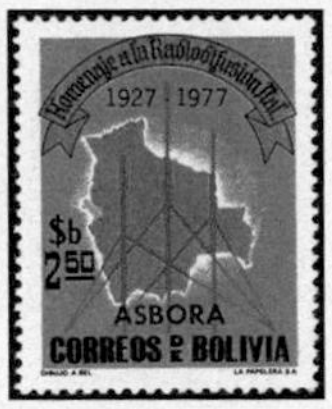

Map of Bolivia, Radio Masts — A211

1977, Nov. 11

613 A211 2.50b blue & multi	.75	.50

Radio Bolivia, ASBORA, 50th anniversary.

No. 450 Surcharged in Black

1977, Nov. 25 **Litho.** *Perf. 11x13½*

614 A147 5b on 5000b on 5b	3.00	2.00

EXFIVIA '77 Philatelic Exhibition, Cochabamba.

Eye, Compass, Book of Law — A212

1978, May 3 **Litho.** *Perf. 13½x13*

615 A212 5b multi	1.10	.30

Audit Department, 50th anniversary.

Mt. Illimani A213

Pre-Columbian Monolith A214

Design: 1.50b, Mt. Cerro de Potosi.

Perf. 11x10½, 10½x11

1978, June 1 **Litho.**

616 A213	50c bl & Prus bl	.30	.25
617 A214	1b brn & lemon	.30	.25
618 A213	1.50b red & bl gray	.50	.35
	Nos. 616-618 (3)	1.10	.85

Andean Countries, Staff of Aesculapius — A215

1978, June 1 *Perf. 10½x11*

626 A215 2b org & blk	.60	.30

Health Ministers of Andean Countries, 5th meeting.

Map of Americas with Bolivia — A216

1978, June 1

627 A216 2.50b brt blue & red .80 .30

World Rheumatism Year.
For surcharges see Nos. 697, 972.

Central Bank Building — A217

1978, July 26 Litho. *Perf. 13½*

628 A217 7b multi 1.75 .40

50th anniversary of Bank of Bolivia.

Jesus and Children — A218

1979, Feb. 20 Litho. *Perf. 13½*

629 A218 8b multicolored 1.50 .50

International Year of the Child.

An imperforate 20b souvenir sheet, depicting No. 629 with simulated perforations, was issued March 16, 1979, for the International Year of the Child. Value $50.

An imperforate 20b souvenir sheet, depicting Nos. 599 and 629 with simulated perforations, was issued April 28, 1980, marking the Year of the Child. Value $25.

Antofagasta Cancel — A219

Eduardo Abaroa, Chain — A220

Designs: 1b, La Chimba cancel. 1.50b, Mejillones cancel. 5.50b, View of Antofagasta. 6.50b, Woman in chains, symbolizing captive province, vert. 8b, Map of Antofagasta Province, 1876, vert. 10b, Arms of province, vert.

1979, Mar. 23 Litho. *Perf. 10½*

630	A219	50e buff & blk	.40	.25
631	A219	1b pink & blk	.60	.40
632	A219	1.50b pale grn & blk	.70	.40

Perf. 13½

633	A220	5.50b multi	1.00	.40
634	A220	6.50b multi	1.20	.40
635	A220	7b multi	1.20	.40
636	A220	8b multi	1.40	.50
637	A220	10b multi	1.75	.50
		Nos. 630-637 (8)	8.25	3.25

Loss of Antofagasta coastal area to Chile, cent.

For surcharge see No. 696.

An imperforate 1000b souvenir sheet, depicting No. 637 with simulated perforations, was issued March 26, 1984, to mark the 1984 World Postal Congress in Hamburg. Value $25.

Emblem and Map of Bolivia — A221

1979, Mar. 26 *Perf. 13½x13*

638 A221 3b multicolored 1.20 .70

Radio Club of Bolivia.

Gymnast — A222

6.50b, Runner and Games emblem, horiz.

1979, Mar. 27 *Perf. 13x13½, 13½x13*

639	A222	6.50b multi	1.25	.25
640	A222	10b multi	2.00	.50
a.		Souvenir sheet of one	5.50	5.50

Southern Cross Sports Games, Bolivia, Nov. 3-12, 1978.

No. 640a contains No. 640 with simulated perforations. Sold for 20b. Size: 80x130mm.

For surcharge see No. 965.

No. 640a was overprinted in two versions in 1981, the first overprint commemorating the 10th anniv. of the Santa Cruz Philatelic Center, the second celebrating the 10th anniv. of the Bolivian Philatelic Federation. Value, each $5.

Two imperforate 20b souvenir sheets, one depicting No. 639, the other No. 640, both with simulated perforations, were issued March 16, 1979, to mark the 1980 Olympic Games. Values, each $30.

Two imperforate souvenir sheets, each denominated 20b, one depicting No. 639, the other No. 640, both with simulated perforations, were issued Oct. 13, 1980, to commemorate the 1980 Moscow Olympic Games. Values, each $75.

Bulgaria No. 1 — A223

1979, Mar. 30 *Perf. 10½*

641 A223 2.50b multi .60 .40

PHILASERDICA '79 International Philatelic Exhibition, Sofia, Bulgaria, May 18-27.

For surcharge see No. 694.

EXFILMAR Emblem — A224

1979, Apr. 2

642 A224 2b multi 2.00 .65

Bolivian Maritime Philatelic Exhibition, La Paz, Nov. 18-28.

For surcharge see No. 698.

OAS Emblem, Map of Bolivia — A226

1979, Oct. 22 Litho. *Perf. 14x13½*

644 A226 6b multi 1.20 .40

Organization of American States, 9th Congress, La Paz, Oct.-Nov.

Franz Tamayo — A227

Bolivian and Japanese Flags, Hospital — A228

UN Emblem and Meeting — A229

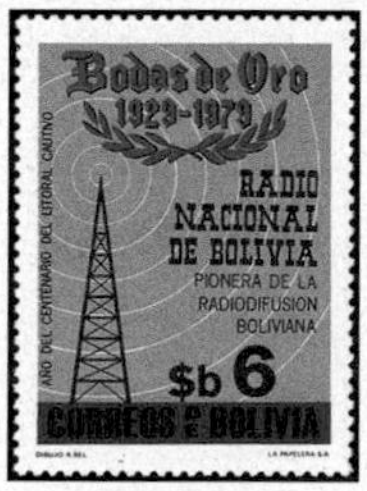

Radio Tower and Waves — A230

1979, Dec.

645	A227	2.80b blk & gray	.60	.50
646	A228	5b multi	1.00	.25
648	A229	5b multi	1.00	.25
649	A230	6b multi	1.25	.50
		Nos. 645-649 (4)	3.85	1.50

Franz Tamayo, lawyer, birth centenary; Japanese-Bolivian health care cooperation; CEPAL, 18th Congress, La Paz, Sept. 18-26; Bolivian National Radio, 50th anniversary.

For surcharge see No. 695.

An imperforate 500,000b souvenir sheet, depicting No. 645 with simulated perforations, was issued Dec. 1985 to mark the 850th anniv. of Malmonides, Jewish philosopher (1135-1204). Value $10.

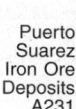

Puerto Suarez Iron Ore Deposits A231

1979 Litho. *Perf. 13½x14*

650 A231 9.50b multi 3.50 .80

Bolivia No. 19, EXFILMAR Emblem, Bolivian Flag — A232

1980 Litho. *Perf. 13½*

651 A232 4b multi 1.25 .40

EXFILMAR, Bolivian Maritime Philatelic Exhibition, La Paz, Nov. 18-28, 1979.

An imperforate 4b souvenir sheet, depicting No. 651 with simulated perforations, was issued Dec. 31, 1982, to commemorate space exploration. Value $75.

Juana Azurduy on Horseback A233

1980 Litho. *Perf. 14x13½*

652 A233 4b multi .80 .40

Juana Azurduy de Padilla, independence fighter, birth bicentenary.

A souvenir sheet containing No. 652 perforated 13¼ was issued Oct. 19, 1990, to commemorate the 700th anniv. of the Swiss Confederation.

La Salle and World Map A234

1980 *Perf. 13½x14*

653 A234 9b multi 1.75 .70

St. Jean Baptiste de la Salle (1651-1719), educator.

For surcharge see No. 966.

"Victory" in Chariot, Madrid, Exhibition Emblem, Flags of Bolivia and Spain A235

1980, Oct. Litho. *Perf. 13½x14*

654 A235 14b multi 2.50 .75

ESPAMER '80 Stamp Exhibition, Madrid.

Map of South America, Flags of Argentina, Bolivia and Peru — A236

1980, Oct. *Perf. 14x13½*

655 A236 2b multi 1.10 .30

Ministers of Public Works and Transport of Argentina, Bolivia and Peru meeting.

Santa Cruz-Trinidad Railroad, Inauguration of Third Section — A237

1980, Oct.

656 A237 3b multi .75 .30

An imperforate 1500b souvenir sheet, depicting No. 656 and the 50c value of the unissued 1915 set, both with simulated perforations, was issued June 20, 1984, to mark the World Postal Congress in Hamburg. Value $30.

Flag on Provincial Map — A238

1b, Soldier, flag, map. 3b, Flag, map. 40b, Soldier, civilians, horiz.

Perf. 14x13½, 13½x14

1981, May 11 **Litho.**

657	A238	1b multi	*25.00*	*30.00*
658	A238	3b multi	*25.00*	*30.00*
659	A238	40b shown	10.00	4.00
660	A238	50b multi	10.00	4.00
		Nos. 657-660 (4)	70.00	68.00

July 17 Revolution memorial.

An imperforate 40b souvenir sheet, depicting No. 659 with simulated perforations, was issued March 24, 1982, to honor Princess Diana. Value $30.

Parrots — A239

4b, Ara macao. 7b, Ara chloroptera. 8b, Ara ararauna. 9b, Ara rubrogenys. 10b, Ara auricollis. 12b, Anodorhynchus hyacinthinus. 15b, Ara militaris. 20b, Ara severa.

1981, May 11 ***Perf. 14x13½***

661	A239	4b multi	.75	.25
662	A239	7b multi	1.40	.25
663	A239	8b multi	1.75	.50
664	A239	9b multi	1.75	.60
665	A239	10b multi	2.00	.60
666	A239	12b multi	2.50	1.00
667	A239	15b multi	3.25	1.20
668	A239	20b multi	4.00	1.50
		Nos. 661-668 (8)	17.40	5.90

Christmas 1981 — A240

1b, Virgin and Child, vert. 2b, Child, star.

1981, Dec. 7 **Litho.** ***Perf. 10½***

669	A240	1b red	.25	.25
670	A240	2b blue, pale blue	.40	.25

American Airforces Commanders' 22nd Conference, Buenos Aires — A241

1982, Apr. 12 **Litho.** ***Perf. 13½***

671	A241	14b multi	2.25	1.25

75th Anniv. of Cobija — A242

1982, July 8 **Litho.** ***Perf. 13½***

672	A242	28b multi	.60	.40

Simon Bolivar Birth Bicentenary (1983) A243

1982, July 12

673	A243	18b multi	.40	.30

1983 World Telecommunications Year — A244

1982, July 15

674	A244	26b Receiving station	.60	.40

An imperforate 1b souvenir sheet, depicting No. 674 with simulated perforations, was issued March 20, 1987, to honor Wernher von Braun. Value $60.

1982 World Cup — A245

100b, Final Act, by Picasso.

1982, July 21 ***Perf. 11***

675	A245	4b shown	.30	.30
676	A245	100b multicolored	2.50	1.50

For surcharge see No. 701.

Two imperforate souvenir sheets, each denominated 104b, were issued Aug. 1, 1982, to celebrate España '82. The first depicts No. 676 with a stamp similar to No. 675, both with simulated perforations. Value $35. The second depicts No. 677 with simulated perforations. Value $65.

Two imperforate souvenir sheets were issued Dec. 31, 1982, to commemorate the victory of the Italian team in the España '82 World Cup games. One depicts Nos. 675 and 676 with simulated perfs and is denominated 104b. The second depicts Nos. 676 and 677 and is denominated 116b. Values, each $30.

Girl Playing Piano — A246

16b, Boy playing soccer, vert.

1982, July 25 ***Perf. 13½***

677	A246	16b multicolored	1.50	.75
678	A246	20b shown	2.00	.75

An imperforate 200b souvenir sheet, depicting Nos. 678 and 629 with simulated perforations, was issued Sept. 16, 1983, for the International Year of the Child. Value $75.

An imperforate 27,500b souvenir sheet, depicting No. 678 with simulated perfs, was issued April 4, 1985, to mark the International Year of the Child. Value $50.

Bolivian-Chinese Agricultural Cooperation, 1972-1982 — A247

1982, Aug. 12

679	A247	30b multi	1.25	.75

A248

1982, Aug. 26

680	A248	22b multi	1.50	.80

First Bolivian-Japanese Gastroenterology Conference, La Paz, Jan.

Stamps — A249

1982, Aug. 31 **Litho.** ***Perf. 14x13½***

681	A249	19b multicolored	1.75	.60

10th Anniv. of Bolivian Philatelic Federation.

A250

1982, Sept. 1

682	A250	20b tan & dk brown	.50	.30

Pres. Hernando Siles, birth centenary.

Scouting Year — A251

1982, Sept. 3 ***Perf. 11***

683	A251	5b Baden-Powell	.40	.30

For surcharge see No. 703.

Cochabamba Philatelic Center, 25th Anniv. — A252

1982, Sept. 14

684	A252	3b multicolored	.40	.30

For surcharge see No. 700.

Cochabamba Superior Court of Justice Sesquicentennial — A253

1982 **Litho.** ***Perf. 13½***

685	A253	10b multicolored	.50	.30

For surcharge see No. 970.

Enthronement of Virgin of Copacabana, 400th Anniv. — A254

1982, Nov. 15 **Litho.** ***Perf. 13½***

686	A254	13b multicolored	.50	.30

For surcharge see No. 971.

Navy Day — A255

14b, Port Busch Naval Base.

1982, Nov. 17

687	A255	14b multicolored	.40	.30

An imperforate 1,000,000b souvenir sheet, depicting No. 687 with simulated perforations, was issued Jan. 5, 1987, to mark the 500th anniv. of Columbus' discovery of America. Value $20.

Christmas — A256

1982, Nov. 19 ***Perf. 11***

688	A256	10b green & gray	.90	.25

For surcharge see No. 702.

An imperforate 1,000,000b souvenir sheet, depicting No. 688 with simulated perforations, was issued Dec.24, 1986, for Christmas. Value $27.50.

A257

1983, Feb. 13 Litho. *Perf. 13½*
689 A257 50b multicolored 1.25 .60

10th Youth Soccer Championship, Jan. 22-Feb. 13.
A 2b souvenir sheet containing Nos. 689 and 726, both perf 13¼, was issued Dec. 15, 1988, to mark the Italia 1990 World Cup. Value $25.

EXFIVIA '83 Philatelic Exhibition A258

1983, Nov. 5 Litho. *Perf. 13½*
690 A258 150b brown carmine 1.50 .75

An imperforate 1000b souvenir sheet, depicting Nos. 690 and 356 with simulated perforations, was issued March 26, 1984, to mark the 1984 Sarajevo Winter Olympic Games. Value $27.50.
An imperforate 500,000b souvenir sheet, depicting No. 690 with simulated perforartions, was issued Dec. 3, 1985, to celebrate Halley's Comet. Value $30.

Visit of Brazilian Pres. Joao Figueiredo, Feb. — A259

1984, Feb. 7 Litho. *Perf. 13½x14*
691 A259 150b multicolored .75 .25

Simon Bolivar Entering La Paz, by Carmen Baptista A260

Paintings of Bolivar: 50b, Riding Horse, by Mulato Gil de Quesada, vert.

Perf. 14x13½, 13½x14
1984, Mar. 30
692 A260 50b multi .30 .25
693 A260 200b multi 1.00 .40

An imperforate 1500b souvenir sheet, depicting No. 692 with simulated perforations, was issued June 20, 1984, to mark the 1984 Los Angeles Summer Olympic Games. Value $20.
A 2b souvenir sheet containing No. 692, perf. 13¼, was issued Dec. 16, 1987, to mark the 1988 Seoul Summer Olympc Games. Value $25.

Types of 1957-79 Surcharged

1984, Mar.
694 A223 40b on 2.50b #641 .30 .25
695 A227 40b on 2.80b #645 .30 .25
696 A219 60b on 1.50b #632 .30 .25
697 A216 60b on 2.50b #627 .30 .25
698 A224 100b on 2b #642 .50 .30
699 A141 200b on 350b #409 1.00 .40
Nos. 694-699 (6) 2.70 1.70

See No. 972 for surcharge similar to No. 697.

Nos. 675, 683-684, 688, C328 Surcharged

1984, June 27 Litho. *Perf. 11*
700 A252 500b on 3b #684 1.25 .50
701 A245 1000b on 4b #675 2.50 1.25
702 A256 2000b on 10b #688 5.00 2.00
703 A251 5000b on 5b #683 12.00 5.00

Perf. 13½
704 A182 10,000b on 3.80b #C328 16.00 10.00
Nos. 700-704 (5) 36.75 18.75

An imperforate 500,000b souvenir sheet, depicting No. 704 with simulated perforations, was issued Dec. 31, 1985, picturing Raphael's *The Three Graces*. Value $20.

Road Safety Education — A261

Cartoons: 80b, Jaywalker. 120b, Motorcycle policeman, ambulance.

1984, Sept. 7 Litho. *Perf. 11*
705 A261 80b multicolored 2.00 .25
706 A261 120b multicolored 2.00 .25

Jose Eustaquio Mendez, 200th Birth Anniv. — A262

Paintings: 300b, Birthplace, by Jorge Campos. 500b, Mendez Leading the Battle of La Tablada, by M. Villegas, horiz.

Perf. 14x13½, 13½x14
1984, Sept. 19
707 A262 300b multi .30 .25
708 A262 500b multi .30 .25

1983 World Cup Soccer Championships, Mexico — A263

Sponsoring shoe-manufacturers' trademarks and: 100b, 200b, Outline map of Bolivia, natl. colors. 600b, World map, soccer ball.

1984, Oct. 26 *Perf. 11*
709 A263 100b multi .50 .25
710 A263 200b multi .50 .25
711 A263 600b multi, horiz. .50 .25
Nos. 709-711 (3) 1.50 .75

An imperforate 125,000b souvenir sheet, depicting No. 711 with simulated perforations, was issued June 24, 1985, to mark the Bolivia's participation in group 3 qualifying round for the World Cup, Mexico 1986.

Chasqui, Postal Runner — A264

1985
712 A264 11000b vio bl 1.00 .30

For surcharge see No. 962.

Intl. Year of Professional Education — A265

2000b, Natl. Manual Crafts emblem.

1985, Apr. 25
713 A265 2000b red, blue .30 .25

For surcharges see Nos. 721-722, 959.

Intl. Anti-Polio Campaign — A266

1985, May 22
714 A266 20000b lt bl & vio .50 .25

Endangered Wildlife — A267

23000b, Altiplano boliviano. 25000b, Sarcorhamphus gryphus. 30000b, Blastocaros dichotomus.

1985, May 22
715 A267 23000b multi 1.50 .60
716 A267 25000b multi .60 .40
717 A267 30000b multi .70 .50
Nos. 715-717 (3) 2.80 1.50

Nos. 716-717 vert.
For surcharge see No. 963.

Dona Vicenta Juaristi Eguino (b. 1785), Independence Heroine — A268

1985, Oct. Litho. *Perf. 13½*
718 A268 300000b multi 1.40 .60

UN, 40th Anniv. — A269

1985, Oct. 24 *Perf. 11*
719 A269 1000000b bl & gold 4.50 .50

For surcharge see No. 964.
A 3b souvenir sheet containing No. 719, perforated 12½x11½, was issued Nov. 30, 1991, to promote world peace. Value $10.

A270

1985, Nov.
720 A270 200000b multi .85 .50

Soccer Team named "The Strongest," 75th anniv.

No. 713 Surcharged

1986 Litho. *Perf. 11*
721 A265 200000b on 2000b .75 .25
722 A265 5000000b on 2000b 8.00 5.00

A271

300000, Emblems, vert. 550000, Pique trademark, vert. 1000000, Azteca Stadium. 2500000, World cup, vert.

1986
723 A271 300000 multi .50 .30
724 A271 550000 multi 1.00 .50
725 A271 1000000 multi 1.50 .80
726 A271 2500000 multi 5.00 2.00
Nos. 723-726 (4) 8.00 3.60

1986 World Cup Soccer Championships.
For surcharges see Nos. 961, 1257-1258.
A 1,000,000b souvenir sheet containing No. 723 perforated 13¼ was issued Sept. 25, 1986, to mark the World Cup finals in Mexico City. Value $30.
A 2b souvenir sheet containing Nos. 723 and 739, perf 13¼ was issued Jan. 25, 1989, to mark the Italia 1990 World Cup championships. Value $25.

Intl. Youth Year
A272 A273

1986
727 A272 150000b brt car rose .40 .30
728 A272 500000b bl grn 1.25 .50
729 A273 3000000b multi 7.50 2.50
Nos. 727-729 (3) 9.15 3.30

Inscribed 1985.
For surcharge see No. 958.

Alfonso Sobieta Viaduct, Carretera Quillacollo, Confital A274

1986 *Perf. 13½*
730 A274 400000 int bl & gray .65 .30

Inter-American Development Bank, 25th anniv.

Admission of Bolivia to the UPU, Cent. — A275

1986, Apr. 3 *Perf. 11*
731 A275 800000 multi 1.60 1.00

A 2b souvenir sheet containing No. 731 perforated 13¼ was issued Dec. 7, 1989, to honor the 500th anniv. of the Imperial Reichspost. Value $50.

Postal Workers Soc., 50th Anniv. — A276

1986, Sept. 5

732 A276 2000000 brn & pale brn 5.50 1.50

For surcharge see No. 967.

Founding of Trinidad, 300th Anniv. A277

No. 733, Bull and Rider, by Vaca.

1986, May 25 ***Perf. 13½x14***

733 A277 1400000 multi 2.50 1.50

For surcharge see No. 960.

Bolivian Philatelic Federation, 15th Anniv. — A278

1986, Nov. 28

734 A278 600000b No. 19 1.00 .50

Death of a Priest, by Jose Antonio Zampa — A279

1986, Nov. 21 ***Perf. 13¾x13½***

735 A279 400000b multi 1.20 .50

Intl. Peace Year — A280

1986, Sept. 16 ***Perf. 11***

736 A280 200000 yel grn & pale grn .60 .30

Natl. Oil Corp. (YPBF), 50th Anniv. — A281

1986, Dec. 22 Litho. ***Perf. 11***

737 A281 1000000b multi 2.25 1.10

For surcharge see No. 1259.

A282

Photograph of a Devil-mask Dancer, by Jimenez Cordero.

Perf. 13¾x13½

1987, Feb. 13 Litho.

738 A282 20c multi 1.10 .30

February 10th Society, cent. (in 1985).

A283

Perf. 13¾x13½

1987, Mar. 20 Litho.

739 A283 30c Crossed flags 1.10 .50

State Visit of Richard von Weizsacker, Pres. of Germany, Mar. 20.

A 2b souvenir sheet containing No. 739 perforated 13¼ was issued Dec. 16, 1987, to commemorate the 750th anniv. of the founding of Berlin. Value $35.

A 2b souvenir sheet containing No. 739 perforated 13¼ was issued March 18, 1990, to promote world peace. Value $15.

State Visit of King Juan Carlos of Spain, May 20 A284

1987, May 20 ***Perf. 13½x13¾***

740 A284 60c Natl. arms 1.50 .60

A 2b souvenir sheet containing No. 740 perforated 13¼ was issued Dec. 15, 1988, to mark the Summer Olympic Games in Seoul (1988) and Barcelona (1992). Value $25.

EXFIVIA '87 — A285

Mount Potosi, 18th cent. engraving.

1987, Oct. Litho. ***Perf. 13½***

741 A285 50c multi 2.50 .60

See No. 750.

Wildlife Conservation A286

1987, Oct.

742	A286 20c Condor		.80	.30
743	A286 20c Tapir		.80	.30
744	A286 30c Vicuna		1.25	.40
745	A286 30c Armadillo		1.25	.40
746	A286 40c Spectacled bears		1.50	.50
747	A286 60c Toucans		2.50	.70
	Nos. 742-747 (6)		8.10	2.60

Wildlife in danger of extinction.

A 2b souvenir sheet containing No. 742 perforated 13½ was issued Dec. 7, 1989, to mark the 20th anniv. of the Apollo XI moon landing. Value $20.

A 3b souvenir sheet containing No. 742 perforated 13x13¾ was issued Nov. 30, 1991, to honor Otto Lilienthal and Lilienthal '91. Value $12.

A 3b souvenir sheet containing No. 742 perforated 13½ was issued July 6, 1992, to mark various aviation anninersaries. Value $15.

ESPAMER '87, La Coruna — A287

No. 748, Nina, stern of Santa Maria. No. 749, Bow of Santa Maria, Pinta.

1987, Oct. Litho. ***Perf. 14x13½***

748	20c multicolored	.60	.30
749	20c multicolored	.60	.30
a.	A287 Pair, #748-749	3.00	3.00

No. 749a has a continuous design.

A 2b souvenir sheet containing No. 749a, perforated 13¼ around and imperforate between, was issued Aug. 15, 1988, to celebrate the 500th anniv. of the discovery of America and the 1992 Barcelona Summer Olympic Games. Value $20.

EXFIVIA Type of 1987

Photograph of Mt. Potosi by Jimenez Cordoro.

1987, Aug. 5 Litho. ***Perf. 13½***

750 A285 40c multi 1.00 .50

Musical Instruments — A288

50c, Zampona and quena (wind instruments). 1b, Charango, vert.

1987, Dec. 3 ***Perf. 13½x14, 14x13½***

751	A288 50c multicolored	1.20	.50
752	A288 1b multicolored	2.50	1.10

A289

State Visit of Pope John Paul II A290

Pontiff, religious architecture and art: No. 753, Cathedral of Kings, Beni. No. 754, Carabuco Church. No. 755, Tihuanacu Church. No. 756, St. Francis's Church, Sucre. No. 757, St. Joseph's of Chiquitos Church. 40c, Cobija Chapel, vert. No. 759, Jayu Kcota Church. No. 760, Cochabamba Cathedral, vert. 60c, St. Francis's Basilica, La Paz, vert. No. 762, Christ of Machaca Church. No. 763, St. Lawrence's Church, Potosi, vert. No. 764, *The Holy Family*, by Rubens, vert. No. 765, *The Virgin of Copacabana*, statue, vert. No. 766, Vallegrande Church. No. 767, Tarija Cathedral, vert. No. 768, Concepcion Church.

1988 Litho. ***Perf. 13½x14, 14x13½***

753	A289 20c multi	.50	.30
754	A289 20c multi	.50	.30
755	A289 20c multi	.50	.30
756	A289 30c multi	.80	.30
757	A289 30c multi	.80	.30
758	A289 40c multi	1.00	.40
759	A289 50c multi	1.50	.40
760	A289 50c multi	1.50	.40
761	A289 60c multi	1.75	.50
762	A289 70c multi	1.90	.50
763	A289 70c multi	1.90	.50
764	A289 80c multi	2.25	.80
765	A289 80c multi	2.25	.80
766	A289 80c multi	2.25	.80
767	A289 1.30b multi	3.25	1.50
768	A289 1.30b multi	3.25	1.50
769	A290 1.50b shown	3.75	1.50
	Nos. 753-769 (17)	29.65	11.10

Issue dates: 1.50b, May 9; others, Mar. 3.

A 2b souvenir sheet containing No. 764 perforated 13¼ was issued July 16, 1989, to honor Peter Paul Reubens. Value $50.

A 2b souvenir sheet containing No. 764 perforated 13¼ was issued June 2, 1990, to mark the 350th anniv. of the death of artist Peter Paul Reubens (1577-1640). Value $35.

An imperforate souvenir sheet depicting Nos. 769 and 901F with simulated perforations was issued Oct. 20, 1994. Value $5.

An imperforate souvenir sheet depicting Nos. 769 and 934 with simulated perforations was issued Nov. 9, 1994, to celebrate Christmas. Value $25.

Visit of Pres. Jose Sarney of Brazil A291

1988, Aug. 2 Litho. ***Perf. 13½x14***

770 A291 50c multi 1.10 .50

St. John Bosco (1815-1888) A292

1988, Aug. 16 ***Perf. 13½***

771 A292 30c multi .80 .30

Bolivian Railways, Cent. — A293

Design: 1b, Steam locomotive from the La Paz-Beni line, made by Marca Shy Ohio, Natl. Railway Museum, Sucre.

1988, Aug. 29

772 A293 1b multi 3.00 1.00

Nataniel Aguirre (b. 1888), Author — A294

1988, Sept. 14 Litho. ***Perf. 13½***

773 A294 1b blk & beige 2.00 1.00

Department of Pando, 50th Anniv. — A295

Designs: 40c, *Columna Porvenir,* memorial to the Battle of Bahio. 60c, Siringuero rubber production (worker sapping latex from *Hevea brasiliensis*).

1988, Sept. 26 ***Perf. 13½***
774 A295 40c multi .90 .50
775 A295 60c multi 1.50 .70

1988 Summer Olympics, Seoul — A296

1988, Sept. 27
776 A296 1.50b multi 3.50 1.75

A 2b souvenir sheet containing No. 776 perforated 13¼ was issued Jan. 25, 1989, to honor the German gold medal winners in the equestrian competition at the 1988 Seoul Summer Olympic Games. Value $20.

An imperforate souvenir sheet depicting Nos. 776 and 85, with simulated perforations, was issued July 4, 1995, to mark the 1996 Atlanta Summer Olympic Games. Value $8.

A297

Designs: 70c, Archbishop Bernardino de Cardenas (1579-1668). 80c, Mother Rosa Gattorno (1831-1900), founder of the Sisters of Santa Ana.

1988
777 A297 70c multi 1.60 .75
778 A297 80c multi 1.75 .80

Issue dates: 70c, Oct. 20, 80c, Oct. 14.

Ministry of Transportation & Communications A298

1988, Oct. 24 Litho. ***Perf. 14x13½***
779 A298 2b dp car, blk & pale ol grn 4.00 2.00

Army Communications, 50th Anniv. (in 1987) — A299

1988, Nov. 29 Litho. ***Perf. 13½***
780 A299 70c multi 1.75 .75

Bolivian Automobile Club, 50th Anniv. A300

1988, Dec. 29 Litho. ***Perf. 13½***
781 A300 1.50b multi 2.75 1.25

An imperforate souvenir sheet depicting No. 781 with simulated perforations was issued July 12, 1995, to mark the first anniv. of the death of Ayrton Senna, Brazilian Formula-1 race driver. Value $8.

Flowering Plants and Emblems A301

50c, Orchid, BULGARIA '89 emblem. 60c, Kantuta blossoms, ITALIA '90 emblem. 70c, *Heliconia humilis,* Albertville '86 emblem. 1b, Hoffmanseggia, Barcelona '92 Games emblem. 2b, Puya raymondi, Seoul '88 Games and five-ring emblems.

1989, Feb. 17 Litho. ***Perf. 13½***
782 A301 50c multi, vert. 1.60 .50
783 A301 60c multi 2.00 .55
784 A301 70c multi, vert. 3.00 1.25
785 A301 1b multi, vert. 4.00 1.50
786 A301 2b multi, vert. 7.00 3.00
Nos. 782-786 (5) 17.60 6.80

A 2b souvenir sheet containing No. 783 perforated 13¼ was issued May 18, 1990, to mark the Italia 1990 World Cup games. Value $20.

A 2b souvenir sheet, containing two No. 783, perforated 13¼ aound and imperforate between, was issued Aug. 2, 1990, marking Italia 1990 and picturing the final Germany-Argentina match. Value $20.

Two 2b souvenir sheets, one containing No. 784 perforated 13¼x13½, the other containing two No. 784, perforated 13¼x13½ around and imperforate between, were issued Dec. 27, 1990, to mark the 1992 Albertville Winter Olympic Games. Value, each $10.

A 3b souvenir sheet containing No. 785 perforated 13¾x13, was issued July 6, 1992, to mark Barcelona 1992, Atlanta 1996 and Berlin 2000 Olympic Games. Value $10.

Radio FIDES, 50th Anniv. A302

1989, Feb. 2
787 A302 80c multi 1.50 .75

Gold Quarto of 1852 A303

1989, Feb. 9 ***Perf. 13½x14***
788 A303 1b multi 2.00 1.00

A 3b souvenir sheet containing No. 788 perforated 11¾x12½, was issued April 30, 1993, to mark the 40th anniv. of silver coinage in the German Federal Republic. Value $10. A second sheet, also denominated 3b, depicting No. 788 in tan, rather than blue, and with different marginal design, was issued July 26. Value $12.

French Revolution, Bicent. — A304

1989, June 23 Litho. ***Perf. 14x13½***
789 A304 70c red, blk & blue 1.75 .70

Uyuni Township, Cent. — A305

1989, July 9 Litho. ***Perf. 14x13½***
790 A305 30c bl, blk & gray 1.00 .35

Noel Kempff Mercado Natl. Park, Santa Cruz — A306

1.50b, Federico Ahlfeld Falls, Pauserna River. 3b, *Ozotoceros bezcarticus* (deer).

1989, Sept. 24 Litho. ***Perf. 13½x14***
791 A306 1.50b multicolored 3.50 1.50
792 A306 3b multicolored 7.00 3.00

UPAEP — A306a

50c, Metalworking. 1b, Temple of Kalasasaya.

1989, Oct. 12 Litho. ***Perf. 13½***
792A A306a 50c multicolored 2.00 .60
792B A306a 1b multicolored 4.00 1.00

See Nos. 808-809

A 2b souvenir sheet containing Nos. 792A and 792B, perforated 13¼ around and imperforate between, was issued June 2, 1990, to celebrate the 500th anniv. of the discovery of America, UPAEP and Expo '92 Sevila. Value $25.

State Visit by Dr. Carlos Andres Perez, Pres. of Venezuela — A306b

1989, Oct. 14
792C A306b 2b multi 3.50 1.50

See Nos. 825-826, 832.

City of Potosi — A306c

1989, Nov. 10 Litho. ***Perf. 13½***
792D A306c 60c Cobija Arch .85 .60
792E A306c 80c Mint 1.25 .90
f. Pair, #792D-792E 3.50 2.50

Christmas — A307

Paintings: 40c, *Andean Stillwaters,* by Arturo Borda. 60c, *The Virgin of the Roses,* anonymous. 80c, *The Conquistador,* by Jorge de la Reza. 1b, *Native Harmony,* by Juan Rimsa. 1.50b, *Woman with Jug,* by Cecilio Guzman de Rojas. 2b, *Bloom of Tenderness,* by Gil Imana. Nos. 794-798 vert.

1989, Dec. 18 ***Perf. 13½x14, 14x13½***
793 A307 40c multicolored 1.00 .30
794 A307 60c multicolored 1.60 .40
795 A307 80c multicolored 2.25 .60
796 A307 1b multicolored 2.50 .70
797 A307 1.50b multicolored 3.75 1.25
798 A307 2b multicolored 4.75 1.50
Nos. 793-798 (6) 15.85 4.75

A 3b souvenir sheet containing No. 797, perforated 12½x11¾, was issued Jan. 27, 19930 to commemorate the 200th anniv. of the Louvre. Value $20.

Fight Against Drug Abuse — A308

1990, Jan. 23 Litho. ***Perf. 13½***
799 A308 80c multicolored 1.50 .75

Penny Black, 150th Anniv. — A309

Great Britain #1, Sir Rowland Hill, Bolivia #1

1990, May 13 ***Perf. 14x13½***
800 A309 4b multicolored 6.00 3.00

World Cup Soccer Championships, Italy — A310

1990, June 16 ***Perf. 13½***
801 A310 2b Stadium, Milan 2.75 1.40
802 A310 6b Game 10.00 4.50

A 3b souvenir sheet containing No. 801 perforated 13x13¾ and 817 perforated 11½x12½ was issued July 6, 1992, to honor World Cup soccer. Value $10.

Organization of American States, Cent. — A311

1990, Apr. 14

803 A311 80c dark bl & brt bl 2.25 .50

A312

1990, Apr. 16

804 A312 1.20b multi 3.00 1.00

Telecommunications — A313

1990 Litho. ***Perf. 14x13½***

805 A313 70c multi 1.25 .90

A 3b souvenir sheet containing No. 805 perforated 12½x11¾ was issued on April 27, 1992, on the theme of the creation of the Milky Way. Value $15.

A 3b souvenir sheet containing No. 805 perforated 12½x11¾ was issued on Feb. 17, 1993, to mark the 450th anniv. of the death of astronomer Nikolaus Kopernikus (1473-1543). Value $12.

National Chamber of Commerce, Cent. — A314

1990, June

806 A314 50c gold, blk & bl 1.00 .60

Cochabamba Social Club, Cent. — A315

1990, Sept. 14 Litho. ***Perf. 13½***

807 A315 40c multicolored .65 .40

UPAEP Type of 1989

80c, Huts. 1b, Mountains, lake, vert.

Perf. 13½x14, 14x13½

1990, Oct. 12 Litho.

808 A306a 80c multicolored 4.50 .80
809 A306a 1b multicolored 6.00 1.00

A317

1990, Oct. 19 ***Perf. 14x13½***

810 A317 1.20b multicolored 1.75 1.00

Magistrate's District of Larecaja, 400th Anniv.

A318

1990, Oct. 12 ***Perf. 14x13½***

811 A318 2b multicolored 2.75 1.50

Discovery of America, 500th anniv. (in 1992).

German Reunification A319

1990, Nov. 19 Litho. ***Perf. 14x13½***

812 A319 2b multicolored 3.50 1.50

An imperforate 5b souvenir sheet depicting No. 812 with simulated perforations was issued Nov. 20, 1990, to celebrate German reunification and the Philatelia '90 philatelic exhibition in Berlin. Exists with either black or red control number. Value, each $15.

A 3b souvenir sheet containing No. 812, perforated 12½x11½ was issued April 27, 1992, to commemorate the 200th anniv. of the port of Brandenburg. Value $12.

Visit of Carlos Salinas de Gortari, Pres. of Mexico A320

Design: 80c, Visit of Rodrigo Borja Cevallos, Pres. of Ecuador.

1990, Dec. 13 Litho. ***Perf. 13½***

813 A320 60c multicolored 2.00 .80
814 A320 80c multicolored 2.25 .80

4th Congress of the Andean Presidents — A321

1990, Nov. 29 ***Perf. 13½x14***

815 A321 1.50b multicolored 2.50 1.00

Exfivia '90 — A322

1990, Dec. 9 ***Perf. 13½***

816 A322 40c dk blue .70 .30

Christmas — A323

1990, Nov. 20 ***Perf. 11***

817 A323 50c multicolored .80 .30

Express Mail Service A324

1990, Dec. 14 ***Perf. 13½x14***

818 A324 1b multicolored 1.50 .50

A 3b souvenir sheet containing No. 818, perforated 11¾x12½ was issued Dec. 31, 1993, honoring Dr. Hermann Oberth. Value $15.

Bolivian Radio Club, 50th Anniv. — A325

1991, Mar. 1 Litho. ***Perf. 14x13½***

819 A325 2.40b multicolored 3.25 1.50

End of Chaco War, 56th Anniv. — A326

Map of Heroes of Chaco Highway.

1991, June 14 Litho. ***Perf. 14x13½***

820 A326 60c multicolored 1.00 .50

National Museums — A327

No. 821, Archaeology. No. 822, Art. No. 823, Ethnology, Folklore.

1991, June 13 ***Perf. 13½***

821 A327 50c multi 1.00 .35
822 A327 50c multi 1.00 .35
823 A327 1b multi 2.00 .60
a. Strip of 3, #821-823 4.00 4.00

Espamer '91.

A328

Our Lady of Peace, Metropolitan Cathedral.

1991, July 15 Litho. ***Perf. 14x13½***

824 A328 1.20b multicolored 2.25 .75

Presidential State Visit Type of 1989

Jaime Paz Zamora, Pres. of Bolivia and: No. 825, Dr. Carlos Saul Menem, Pres. of Argentina. No. 826, Dr. Luis Alberto Lacalle, Pres. of Uruguay.

1991 ***Perf. 13½x14***

825 A306b 1b multicolored 1.50 .50
826 A306b 1b multicolored 1.50 .50

Issue dates: No. 825, Aug. 5; No. 826, Aug. 12.

World Wildlife Fund — A329

Tremarctos ornatus: No. 827, Adult, two cubs. No. 828, Adult's head. No. 829, Adult on tree limb. No. 830, Adult, cubs on tree limb.

1991, May 31 ***Perf. 13½***

827 A329 30c multicolored 2.40 .50
828 A329 30c multicolored 2.40 .50
829 A329 30c multicolored 2.40 .50
830 A329 30c multicolored 2.40 .50
Nos. 827-830 (4) 9.60 2.00

A330

1991, Aug. 21 Litho. ***Perf. 14x13½***

831 A330 70c multicolored 1.25 .50

Bolivian Philatelic Federation, 20th anniv.

Presidential State Visit Type of 1989

Design: 50c, Jaime Paz Zamora, Pres. of Bolivia and Alberto Fujimori, Pres. of Peru.

1991, Aug. 29 ***Perf. 13½x14***

832 A306b 50c multicolored .90 .40

National Census — A331

1991, Nov. 19 Litho. ***Perf. 14x13½***

833 A331 50c multicolored .80 .40

America Issue — A332

UPAEP emblem and: 60c, First Discovery of Chuquiago, 1535, by Arturo Reque M. 1.20c, Founding of the City of La Paz, 1548, by J. Rimsa, vert.

1991, Oct. 12 ***Perf. 13½x14, 14x13½***

834	A332	60c multicolored	2.50	.60
835	A332	1.20b multicolored	5.00	1.10

First National Grand Prix Auto and Motorcycle Race — A332a

1991, Sept. 5 **Litho.** ***Perf. 14x13½***

835A	A332a	50c multicolored	.85	.40

ECOBOL, Postal Security System — A333

1991, Sept. 9 ***Perf. 13½x14***

836	A333	1.40b multicolored	2.00	.75

Simon Bolivar — A334

1992, Feb. 15 **Litho.** ***Perf. 13½***

837	A334	1.20b buff, brn & org brn	2.00	.75

Exfilbo '92.

Scouting in Bolivia, 75th Anniv. (in 1990) and 1992 Andes Jamboree A335

1992, Jan. 13 ***Perf. 13½x14***

838	A335	1.20b multicolored	2.00	1.00

Dated 1991.

An imperforate souvenir sheet, depicting Nos. 838, 936 and type of 683 valued 2b, was issued Nov. 7, 1994. Value $5.

Christmas A336

Paintings: 2b, Landscape, by Daniel Pena y Sarmiento. 5b, Woman with Fruit, by Cecilio Guzman de Rojas. 15b, Native Mother, by Crespo Gastelu.

1991, Dec.19 **Litho.** ***Perf. 13½***

839	A336	2b multicolored	3.25	1.50
840	A336	5b multicolored	7.00	3.00
841	A336	15b multicolored	20.00	9.00
		Nos. 839-841 (3)	30.25	13.50

Pacific Ocean Access Pact Between Bolivia and Peru A337

Designs: 1.20b, Pres. Zamora raising flag, vert. 1.50b, Pres. Jaime Paz Zamora of Bolivia and Pres. Alberto Fujimori, Peru. 1.80b, Shoreline of access zone near Ilo, Peru.

1992, Mar. 23 ***Perf. 14x13½, 13½x14***

842	A337	1.20b multicolored	*1.90*	1.00
843	A337	1.50b multicolored	*2.25*	1.00
844	A337	1.80b multicolored	*2.75*	1.25
		Nos. 842-844 (3)	*6.90*	3.25

Expo '92, Seville A338

1992, Apr. 15 ***Perf. 13½x14***

845	A338	30c multicolored	.85	.30
846	A338	50c Columbus' ships	1.15	.40

Miraflores Rotary Club, District 4690, Mt. Illimani A339

1992, Apr. 30 **Litho.** ***Perf. 13½***

847	A339	90c multicolored	1.40	.70

Prof. Elizardo Perez, Founder of Ayllu of Warisata School, Birth Cent. — A340

1992, June 6 **Litho.** ***Perf. 13½***

848	A340	60c multicolored	.90	.50

Government Palace, Sucre — A341

1992, July 10 **Litho.** ***Perf. 13½x14***

849	A341	50c multicolored	1.50	.50

A342

1992, Sept. 11 ***Perf. 14x13½***

850	A342	50c multicolored	.75	.50

Los Tiempos Newpaper, 25th anniv.

1992 Summer Olympics, Barcelona — A343

Mario Martinez Guzman, tennis player.

1992, Aug. 9 ***Perf. 13½***

851	A343	1.50b multicolored	2.00	1.00

A 3b souvenir sheet containing No. 851, perforated 14x13, was issued Jan. 27, 1993, to mark the Barcelona 1992 and Atlanta 1996 Olympic Games. Value $30.

First Intl. Whitewater Canoe Regatta, Bermejo River A343a

1992, Sept. 17 **Litho.** ***Perf. 13½***

851A	A343a	1.20b multicolored	2.00	1.00

1994 World Cup Soccer Championships, US — A344

1992, Oct. 2 **Litho.** ***Perf. 13½***

852	A344	1.20b multicolored	3.50	1.50

A 3b souvenir sheet containing No. 852, perf 13x13¾, was issued Dec. 31, 1993, to mark the 1994 World Cup. Value $10.

Oruro Technical University, Cent. — A345

1992, Oct. 15 ***Perf. 13½x14***

853	A345	50c multicolored	.85	.50

Interamerican Institute for Agricultural Cooperation, 50th Anniv. — A346

1.20b, Chenopodium quinoa.

1992, Oct. 7 ***Perf. 13½***

854	A346	1.20b multi	2.00	1.00

Discovery of America, 500th Anniv. A347

Paintings: 60c, Columbus departing from Palos, vert. 2b, Columbus with Caribbean natives.

1992, Oct. 1 ***Perf. 14x13½, 13½x14***

855	A347	60c multicolored	1.25	.50
856	A347	2b multicolored	4.50	1.50

Battle of Ingavi, 150th Anniv. (in 1991) A348

1992, Nov. 18 **Litho.** ***Perf. 13½x14***

857	A348	1.20b sepia & black	2.75	.80

12th Bolivian Games, Cochabamba and Santa Cruz — A349

1992, Nov. 13

858	A349	2b multicolored	3.00	1.25

Fauna, Events A350

Event emblem and fauna: 20c, Beni Dept., sesquicentennial, caiman. 50c, Polska '93, paca. 1b, Bangkok '93, chinchilla. 2b, 1994 Winter Olympics, Lillehammer, Norway, anteater. 3b, Brandenburg Gate, jaguar. 4b, Brasiliana '93, hummingbird, vert. 5b, 1994 World Cup Soccer Championships, US, piranhas.

1992, Nov. 18 **Litho.** ***Perf. 13½***

859	A350	20c multicolored	.50	.25
860	A350	50c multicolored	1.00	.40
861	A350	1b multicolored	1.50	.75
862	A350	2b multicolored	3.00	1.25
863	A350	3b multicolored	5.00	2.00
864	A350	4b multicolored	6.00	2.50
865	A350	5b multicolored	8.00	3.50
		Nos. 859-865 (7)	25.00	10.65

A 3b souvenir sheet containing No. 862 perforated 13x13¾ was issued Dec. 31, 1993, to mark the 1994 Lillehammer Winter Olympic Games. Value $30.

A 4b souvenir sheet depicting Nos. 864 and C224 with simulated perforations was issued July 3, 1995, to recognize Rotary International and to promote nature conservation. Value $10.

Christmas — A350a

Designs: 1.20b, Man in canoe, star. 2.50b, Star over churches. 6b, Flowers, church, infant on hay.

1992, Dec. 1 **Litho.** ***Perf. 13½***

865A	A350a	1.20b multi	1.60	.50
865B	A350a	2.50b multi	3.25	1.25
865C	A350a	6b multi	8.75	3.25
		Nos. 865A-865C (3)	13.60	5.00

A351

Nicolaus Copernicus (1473-1543), Polish Astronomer: 50c, Santa Ana Intl. astrometrical observatory, Tarija, horiz.

Perf. 13x13½, 13½x13

1993, Feb. 18 **Litho.**

866	A351	50c multicolored	.70	.30
867	A351	2b black	2.50	.80

An imperforate 3.50b souvenir sheet depicting Nos. 867 and 923 with simulated perforations was issued Oct. 21, 1994. Value $10.

A352

1993, Apr. 14 **Litho.** ***Perf. 13½***

868	A352	60c multicolored	1.10	.40

Beatification of Mother Nazaria.

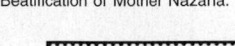

12th Bolivar Games A353

1993, Apr. 24 ***Perf. 13½x14***

869	A353	2.30b multicolored	2.75	1.10

Bolivia #C240, Brazil #3 A354

1993, May 31

870	A354	2.30b multicolored	3.00	1.10

First Brazilian Stamp, 150th anniv.

A355

Eternal Father, by Gaspar de la Cueva.

1993, June 9 **Litho.** ***Perf. 13½***

871	A355	1.80b multicolored	2.75	1.00

Virgin of Urkupina A356

1993, July 31 **Litho.** ***Perf. 14x13½***

872	A356	50c multi	1.20	.35

City of Quillacollo, 400th anniv.

Pedro Domingo Murillo Industrial School A357

1993, Aug. 4 ***Perf. 13½***

873	A357	60c multicolored	.85	.35

Butterflies A358

No. 874, Archaeoprepona demophon. No. 875, Morpho sp. No. 876, Papilio sp. No. 877, Historis odius. No. 878, Euptoieta hegesia. No. 879, Morpho deidamia. No. 880, Papilio thoas. No. 881, Danaus plexippus. No. 882, Caligo sp. No. 883, Anaea marthesia. No. 884, Rothschildia sp. No. 885, Heliconius sp. No. 886, Marpesia corinna. No. 887, Prepona chromus. No. 888, Heliconius sp., diff. No. 889, Siproeta epaphus.

1993, June 4 ***Perf. 13½x14***

874	A358	60c multicolored	1.25	.40
875	A358	60c multicolored	1.25	.40
876	A358	80c multicolored	1.60	.75
877	A358	80c multicolored	1.60	.75
878	A358	80c multicolored	1.60	.75
879	A358	1.80b multicolored	3.50	1.00
880	A358	1.80b multicolored	3.50	1.00
881	A358	1.80b multicolored	3.50	1.00
882	A358	2.30b multicolored	4.75	1.25
883	A358	2.30b multicolored	4.75	1.25
884	A358	2.30b multicolored	4.75	1.25
885	A358	2.70b multicolored	6.00	1.50
886	A358	2.70b multicolored	6.00	1.50
887	A358	2.70b multicolored	6.00	1.50
888	A358	3.50b multicolored	7.50	1.75
889	A358	3.50b multicolored	7.50	1.75
a.		Sheet of 16, #874-889	85.00	85.00
		Nos. 874-889 (16)	65.05	17.80

Pan-American Health Organization, 90th Anniv. — A359

1993, Oct. 13 **Litho.** ***Perf. 13½***

890	A359	80c multicolored	1.00	.50

An imperforate souvenir sheet depicting Nos. 890 and 789 with simulated perforations was issued July 8, 1995, to honor Louis Pasteur. Value $10.

Archaeological Finds — A360

Location of cave paintings: No. 891, Oruro. No. 892, Santa Cruz, vert. No. 893, Beni, vert. No. 894, Chuquisaca, vert. No. 895, Chuquisaca. No. 896, Potosi. No. 897, La Paz, vert. No. 898, Tarija, vert. No. 899, Cochabamba.

1993, Sept. 28

891	A360	80c multicolored	2.25	.40
892	A360	80c multicolored	2.25	.40
893	A360	80c multicolored	2.25	.40
894	A360	80c multicolored	2.25	.40
895	A360	80c multicolored	2.25	.40
896	A360	80c multicolored	2.25	.40
897	A360	80c multicolored	2.25	.40
898	A360	80c multicolored	2.25	.40
899	A360	80c multicolored	2.25	.40
		Nos. 891-899 (9)	20.25	3.60

America Issue — A361

80c, Saimiri sciureus. 2.30b, Felis pardalis.

1993, Oct. 9 **Litho.** ***Perf. 13½***

900	A361	80c multi	1.50	.50
901	A361	2.30b multi	4.50	1.50

Famous People — A361a

Designs: 50c, Yolanda Bedregal, poet. 70c, Simon Martinic, President of Cochabamba Philatelic Center. 90c, Eugenio von Boeck, politician, President of Bolivian Philatelic Federation. 1b, Marina Nunez del Prado, sculptor.

1993, Nov. 17 **Litho.** ***Perf. 11***

901A	A361a	50c sepia	.50	.30
901B	A361a	70c sepia	.80	.30
901C	A361a	90c sepia	1.25	.50
901D	A361a	1b sepia	1.25	.50
		Nos. 901A-901D (4)	3.80	1.60

Christmas — A361b

Paintings: 2.30b, Adoration of the Shepherds, by Leonardo Flores. 3.50b, Virgin with Child and Saints, by unknown artist. 6b, Virgin of the Milk, by Melchor Perez de Holguin.

1993, Dec. 8 ***Perf. 14x13½***

901E	A361b	2.30b multicolored	5.00	1.10
901F	A361b	3.50b multicolored	7.50	1.50
901G	A361b	6b multicolored	12.00	3.00
		Nos. 901E-901G (3)	24.50	5.60

Town of Riberalta, Cent. — A362

1994, Feb. 3 **Litho.** ***Perf. 13½***

902	A362	2b multicolored	2.50	.80

World Population Day — A363

1994, Feb. 17 **Litho.** ***Perf. 13½***

903	A363	2.30b multicolored	3.50	1.25

A364

1994, Feb. 21 ***Perf. 13½***

904	A364	2b buff & multi	2.25	.80
905	A364	2.30b multi	2.75	1.25

Inauguration of Pres. Gonzalo Sanchez de Lozada.

A365

1994 World Cup Soccer Championships, US: 80c, Mascot. 1.80b, Bolivia, Uruguay. 2.30b, Bolivia, Venezuela. No. 909, Part of Bolivian team, goalies in black. No. 910, Part of Bolivian team, diff. 2.70b, Bolivia, Ecuador. 3.50b, Bolivia, Brazil.

1994, Mar. 22

906	A365	80c multicolored	1.00	.40
907	A365	1.80b multicolored	2.00	1.00
908	A365	2.30b multicolored	3.00	1.25
909	A365	2.50b multicolored	3.00	1.25
910	A365	2.50b multicolored	3.00	1.25
a.		Pair, #909-910	8.00	8.00
911	A365	2.70b multicolored	3.25	1.25
912	A365	3.50b multicolored	4.25	1.75
		Nos. 906-912 (7)	19.50	8.15

An imperforate souvenir sheet depicting Nos. 907-908 and 911-912 with simulated perforations was issued May 9, 1994. Value $10. On Sept. 18, this sheet was re-released with the overprint "Brasil Campeon." Value $10.

SOS Children's Village, Bolivia — A366

1994, Apr. 12 **Litho.** ***Perf. 13½***

913	A366	2.70b multicolored	3.00	1.25

Catholic Archdiocese La Paz, 50th Anniv. — A367

Churches, priests: 1.80b, Church of San Pedro, Msgr. Jorge Manrique Hurtado. 2b, Archbishop Abel I. Antezana y Rojas, Church of the Sacred Heart of Mary, vert. 3.50b, Msgr. Luis Sainz Hinojosa, Church of Santo Domingo, vert.

1994, July 12 **Litho.** ***Perf. 13½***

914	A367	1.80b multicolored	2.75	.80
915	A367	2b multicolored	3.25	1.00
916	A367	3.50b multicolored	6.00	1.75
		Nos. 914-916 (3)	12.00	3.55

A368

Design: 2b, Pres. Victor Paz Estenssoro.

1994, Oct. 2 Litho. *Perf. 13½*

917 A368 2b multicolored 2.25 1.00

A369

1994, Oct. 9

918 A369 1.80b No. 46 1.90 .90

Battle of Ft. Boqueron A370

Col. Manuel Marzana Oroza, battle scene.

1994, Oct. 6

919 A370 80c multicolored 1.25 .40

San Borja, 300th Anniv. A371

1994, Oct. 14

920 A371 1.60b Erythrina fusca 1.75 .60

America Issue — A372

Old, new methods of postal transport: 1b, Streetcar, van. 5b, Airplane, ox cart.

1994, Oct. 12

921 A372 1b multicolored 1.25 .40
922 A372 5b multicolored 5.25 2.25

1994 Solar Eclipse — A373

1994 Oct. 21

923 A373 3.50b multicolored 3.75 1.25

Environmental Protection — A374

Trees: 60c, Buddleja coriacea. 1.80b, Bertholletia exelsa. 2b, Schinus molle, horiz. 2.70b, Polylepis racemosa. 3, Tabebuia chrysantha. 3.50b, Erythrina falcata, horiz.

1994, Sept. 21

924	A374	60c multicolored	.75	.25
925	A374	1.80b multicolored	1.60	.75
926	A374	2b multicolored	1.90	.80
927	A374	2.70b multicolored	2.50	1.25
928	A374	3b multicolored	3.25	1.50
929	A374	3.50b multicolored	3.50	1.75
		Nos. 924-929 (6)	13.50	6.30

An imperforate souvenir sheet depicting Nos. 925 and 928 with simulated perforations was issued Nov. 3, 1994. Value $12.

Gen. Antonio Jose de Sucre (1795-1830) A375

1995, Jan. 25 Litho. *Perf. 13½*

930 A375 1.80b shown 2.25 .90
931 A375 3.50b red, yel, grn background 4.00 1.25

Christmas A377

2b, Tarija girl. 5b, High plateau child. 20b, Eastern girl.

1994, Nov. 25 Litho. *Perf. 13½*

933	A377	2b multi	3.25	.80
934	A377	5b multi	8.00	2.25
935	A377	20b multi	30.00	9.00
		Nos. 933-935 (3)	41.25	12.05

A378

1994, Nov. 28 Litho. *Perf. 13½*

936 A378 1.80b multicolored 2.00 1.00

Pan-American Scout Jamboree, Cochabamba

Cathedral of St. Anne — A379

1995, Apr. 21 Litho. *Perf. 13½*

937 A379 1.90b black & multi 2.25 1.00
938 A379 2.90b blue & multi 3.25 1.25

Yacuma-Beni Province, cent.

Franciscans at Copacabana Natl. Sanctuary, Cent. — A380

1995, May 2

939 A380 60c gray & multi 1.00 .30
940 A380 80c bister & multi 1.50 .35

A381

1995 Litho. *Perf. 13½*

941 A381 2b multicolored 2.00 1.00

Peace Between Bolivia and Paraguay. Dated 1994.

A382

1995, July 25

942 A382 2.40b multicolored 2.75 1.10

Andes Development Corporation (CAF), 25th anniv.

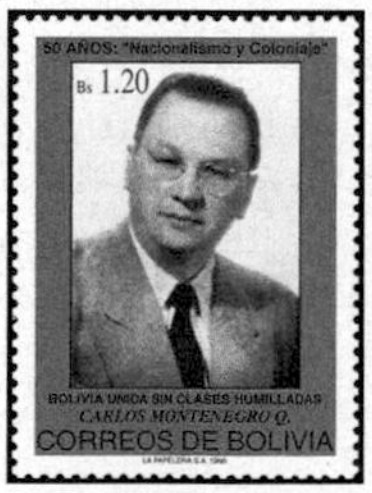

50th Anniv. of Publication of "Nationalism and the Colonial Age," by Carlos Montenegro (1904-53) A383

1995, Aug. 8

943 A383 1.20b pink & black 2.75 .60

FAO, 50th Anniv. — A384

1995, Sept. 26

944 A384 1b multicolored 2.00 .60

UN, 50th Anniv. — A385

1995, Oct. 24 *Perf. 14½*

945 A385 2.90b multicolored 2.25 1.25

America Issue A386

1995, Nov. 21 *Perf. 14*

946	A386	5b Condor	5.00	2.00
947	A386	5b Llamas	5.00	2.00
a.		Pair, #946-947	10.00	10.00

ICAO, 50th Anniv. — A387

1995, Dec. 4 *Perf. 13½x13*

948 A387 50c multicolored 1.25 .40

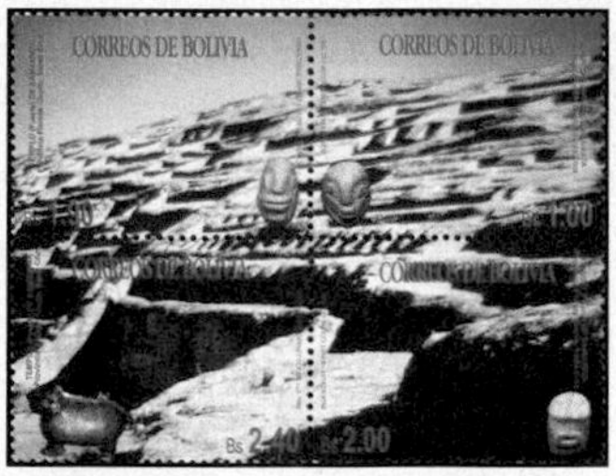

Temple of Samaipata — A388

Archaeological finds and: a, 1.90b, Top of ruins. b, 1b, Top of ruins, diff. c, 2.40b, Lower excavation. d, 2b, Floor, tiers.

1995, Dec. 4 *Perf. 13x13½*

949 A388 Block of 4, #a.-d. 12.50 12.50

No. 949 is a continuous design.

Taquiña Brewery, Cent. — A389

1995, Dec. 8 *Perf. 14*

950 A389 1b multicolored 2.50 .60

Christmas A390

Paintings: 1.20b, The Annunciation, by Cima da Conegliano. 3b, The Nativity, by Hans Baldung. 3.50b, Adoration of the Magi, by Rogier van der Weyden.

1995, Dec. 15 *Perf. 14x13½*

951 A390 1.20b multicolored 1.25 .50
952 A390 3b multicolored 3.00 1.10
953 A390 3.50b multicolored 3.75 1.40
Nos. 951-953 (3) 8.00 3.00

Natl. Anthem, 150th Anniv. — A391

Designs: 1b, J.I. de Sanjines, lyricist. 2b, B. Vincenti, composer.

1995, Dec. 18 **Litho.** *Perf. 13½*

954 1b multicolored 1.40 .70
955 2b multicolored 2.50 1.40
a. A391 Pair, #954-955 5.00 5.00

Decree to Abolish Abuse of Indian Labor, 50th Anniv. — A392

Designs: 1.90b, Modern representations of industry, Gov. Gualberto Villarroel. 2.90, Addressing labor policies, silhouettes of people rejoicing.

1996, Jan. 26 *Perf. 14*

956 1.90b multicolored 2.00 1.00
957 2.90b multicolored 3.00 1.50
a. A392 Pair, #956-957 6.00 5.00

Nos. 639, 653, 685-686, 712-713, 715, 719, 726, 729, 732-733, C332, C348 Srchd.

Perfs. and Printing Methods as Before

1996

958 A273 50c on 3,000,000b #729 .50 .25
959 A265 60c on 2000b #713 .85 .25
960 A277 60c on 1,400,000b #733 .85 .25
961 A271 1b on 2,500,000b #726 .85 .50
962 A264 1.50b on 11,000b #712 1.50 .60
963 A267 2.50b on 23,000b #715 2.25 1.00
964 A269 3b on 1,000,000b #719 2.75 1.25
965 A222 3.50b on 6.50b #639 3.25 1.40
966 A234 3.50b on 9b #653 3.25 1.40
967 A276 3.50b on 2,000,000b #732 3.25 1.40
968 AP67 3.80b on 3.80b #C332 3.25 1.40
969 A189 20b on 3.80b #C348 18.00 8.00
970 A253 20b on 10b #685 18.00 8.00
971 A254 20b on 13b #686 18.00 8.00
Nos. 958-971 (14) 76.55 33.70

Size and location of surcharge varies.

No. 627 Surcharged

1996 **Litho.** *Perf. 10½*

972 A216 60c on 2.50b multi .90 .25

See No. 697 for similar surcharge.

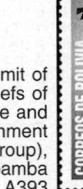

10th Summit of the Chiefs of State and Government (Rio Group), Cochabamba A393

Designs: 2.50b, Stylized person. 3.50b, Stylized globe surrounded by lines.

1996, Sept. 4 *Perf. 14*

973 A393 2.50b multicolored 2.25 .90
974 A393 3.50b multicolored 3.25 1.25

Anniversaries A394

50c, Natl. Bank of Bolivia, 125th anniv. 1b, Joco Joaquin de Lemoine (1776 1851), first postal administrator, vert.

1996, Dec. 8 **Litho.** *Perf. 13½*

975 A394 50c multicolored .50 .25
976 A394 1b multicolored 1.00 .40

Summit of the Americas to Sustain Development A395

1996, Dec. 8 *Perf. 14x13½*

977 A395 2.50b org brn & multi 2.25 1.00
978 A395 5b black & multi 4.50 2.00

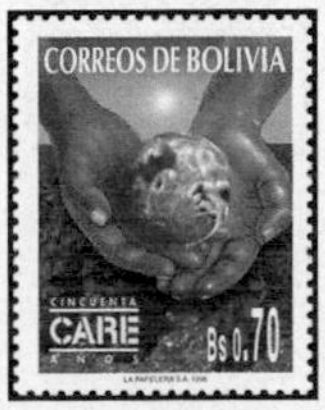

CARE in Bolivia, 20th Anniv. — A396

1996, Dec. 19 *Perf. 13½*

979 A396 60c Family, horiz. .65 .25
980 A396 70c shown .85 .30

Natl. Symphony Orchestra, 50th Anniv. — A397

1.50b, Flute, saxophone. 2b, String instruments.

1996, Dec. 24

981 1.50b multicolored 1.50 .75
982 2b multicolored 1.90 1.10
a. A397 Pair, #981-982 4.00 4.00

No. 982a is a continuous design.

Tourism in Oruro A398

Designs: 50c, Miners' Monument, vert. 60c, Folklore costume, vert. 1b, Virgin of Socavon, vert. 1.50b, Sajama mountains. 2.50b, Chipaya child, building, vert. 3b, Raul Shaw, "Moreno."

1997, Feb. 3 **Litho.** *Perf. 14½*

983 A398 50c multicolored .60 .60
984 A398 60c multicolored .90 .90
985 A398 1b multicolored 1.50 1.50
986 A398 1.50b multicolored 1.50 1.50
987 A398 2.50b multicolored 2.25 2.25
988 A398 3b multicolored 3.25 3.25
Nos. 983-988 (6) 10.00 10.00

Dated 1996.

Tourism in Chuquisaca — A399

Designs: 60c, La Glorieta. 1b, Governor's Palace, vert. No. 991, Dinosaur tracks. No. 992, House of Liberty. 2b, Tarabaqueno, vert. 3b, Statue of Juana Azurduy of Padilla, vert.

1997, Jan. 30 *Perf. 13½x14, 14x13½*

989 A399 60c multicolored .60 .60
990 A399 1b multicolored .90 .90
991 A399 1.50b multicolored 1.75 1.75
992 A399 1.50b multicolored 1.75 1.75
993 A399 2b multicolored 2.25 2.25
994 A399 3b multicolored 3.25 3.25
Nos. 989-994 (6) 10.50 10.50

Dated 1996.

Tourism in Tarija — A400

Designs: 50c, House of Culture, Dorada, vert. 60c, Church of Entre Rios, vert. 80c, San Luis Falls. 1b, Monument to the Chaco War. 3b, Temple, Statue of the Virgin Mary, Chaguaya. 20b, Eustaquio Mendez house, monument.

1997, Jan. 24 *Perf. 14x13½, 13½x14*

995 A400 50c multicolored .50 .30
996 A400 60c multicolored .65 .35
997 A400 80c multicolored .85 .55
998 A400 1b multicolored 1.10 .65
999 A400 3b multicolored 3.25 1.90
1000 A400 20b multicolored 20.00 11.00
Nos. 995-1000 (6) 26.35 14.75

Dated 1996.

Visit of French Pres. Jacques Chirac A401

Design: Bolivian Pres. Gonzalo Sanchez de Lozada, Chirac.

1997, Mar. 15 *Perf. 14*

1001 A401 4b multicolored 4.00 4.00

Salesian Order in Bolivia, Cent. — A402

Designs: 1.50b, St. John Bosco (1815-88), church. 2b, Statue of St. John Bosco talking with boy, church.

1997, Apr. 29 **Litho.** *Perf. 13½*

1002 A402 1.50b multicolored 1.50 1.50
1003 A402 2b multicolored 2.00 2.00

UNICEF, 50th Anniv. A403

Children's drawings: 50c, Houses, children on playground. 90c, Child running, cactus, rock, lake. 1b, Boys, girls arm in arm across globe. 2.50b, Girl on swing, others in background.

1997

1004 A403 50c multicolored .50 .45
1005 A403 90c multicolored .95 .75
1006 A403 1b multicolored 1.20 .75
1007 A403 2.50b multicolored 2.75 2.10
Nos. 1004-1007 (4) 5.40 4.05

Department of La Paz — A404

Tourism: 50c, Mt. Chulumani, Las Yungas, vert. 80c, Inca monolith, vert. 1.50b, City, Mt. Illimani, vert. 2b, Gate of the Sun, Tiwanacu. 2.50b, Traditional dancers, vert. 10b, Virgin of Copacabana, reed boat.

1997, May 28 **Litho.** *Perf. 13½*

1008 A404 50c multicolored .50 .45
1009 A404 80c multicolored .75 .70
1010 A404 1.50b multicolored 1.40 1.25
1011 A404 2b multicolored 1.75 1.60
1012 A404 2.50b multicolored 2.25 2.00
1013 A404 10b multicolored 9.25 8.50
Nos. 1008-1013 (6) 15.90 14.50

1997 America Cup Soccer Championships, Bolivia — A405

1998 World Cup Soccer Championships, France — A406

1997, June 13

1014	A405	3b multicolored	3.00	3.00
1015	A406	5b multicolored	5.00	5.00

National Congress A407

1997, July 8 Litho. *Perf. 13½*

1016	A407	1b multicolored	1.00	.50

America Issue — A408

Women in traditional costumes: 5b, From valley region. 15b, From eastern Bolivia.

1997, July 14 Litho. *Perf. 13½*

1017	A408	5b multicolored	5.00	5.00
1018	A408	15b multicolored	14.00	14.00

Mercosur (Common Market of Latin America) A409

1997, Sept. 26

1019	A409	3b multicolored	2.75	2.00

See Argentina No. 1975, Brazil No. 2646, Paraguay No. 2565, Uruguay No. 1681.

Christmas A410

Paintings: 2b, Virgen del Cerro, by unknown artist. 5b, Virgen de la Leche, by unknown artist. 10b, The Holy Family, by Melchor Pérez de Holguin.

1997, Dec. 19 Litho. *Perf. 13½*

1020	A410	2b multicolored	2.50	1.40
1021	A410	5b multicolored	5.50	3.50
1022	A410	10b multicolored	10.00	5.00
		Nos. 1020-1022 (3)	18.00	9.90

Diana, Princess of Wales (1961-97) A411

1997, Dec. 29

1023	A411	2b Portrait, vert.	2.00	1.40
1024	A411	3b In mine field	2.75	2.10

Visit of Prime Minister of Spain A412

Hugo Banzer Suarez, Pres. of Bolivia and José Maria Aznar.

1998, Mar. 16

1025	A412	6b multicolored	6.00	3.50

Bolivian Society of Engineers, 75th Anniv. A413

1998, Apr. 28

1026	A413	3.50b multicolored	3.00	1.50

Rotary Intl. in Bolivia, 70th Anniv. — A414

1998, Apr. 30 Litho. *Perf. 13½*

1027	A414	5b multicolored	4.00	2.25

A415

America Issue: 4b, Letter Carriers, 1942, horiz.

1998, July 9

1028	A415	3b multicolored	2.50	1.25
1029	A415	4b multicolored	3.50	1.50

Famous Men — A416

1.50b, Werner Guttentag Tichauer, bibliographer. 2b, Dr. Martin Cardenas Hermosa, botanist. 3.50b, Adrian Patiño Carpio, composer.

1998, July 10

1030	A416	1.50b brown	1.00	.50
1031	A416	2b green, vert	1.50	.75
1032	A416	3.50b black, vert	2.40	.90
		Booklet, 4 each #1030-1032	50.00	
		Nos. 1030-1032 (3)	4.90	2.15

Regions in Bolivia A417

Beni: 50c, Victoria regia. 1b, Calliandra. 1.50b, White Tajibo tree, vert. 3.50b, Amazon mask. 5b, Nutria. 7b, King vulture.

1998, Oct. 11 Litho. *Perf. 13½*

1033	A417	50c black & multi	.30	.25
1034	A417	1b black & multi	.95	.40
1035	A417	1.50b black & multi	1.50	.70
1036	A417	3.50b black & multi	3.25	1.50
1037	A417	5b black & multi	4.50	2.00
1038	A417	7b black & multi	6.00	4.00
		Nos. 1033-1038 (6)	16.50	8.85

Pando: 50c, Acre River. 1b, Sloth climbing bamboo tree, vert. 1.50b, Bahia Arroyo, vert. 4b, Boa. 5b, Family of capybaras. 7b, Houses, palm trees, vert.

1039	A417	50c green & multi	.50	.30
1040	A417	1b green & multi	.75	.40
1041	A417	1.50b green & multi	1.25	.70
1042	A417	4b green & multi	3.25	1.75
1043	A417	5b green & multi	4.50	2.00
1044	A417	7b green & multi	6.50	4.00
		Nos. 1039-1044 (6)	16.75	9.15
		Nos. 1033-1044 (12)	33.25	18.00

Women of Bolivia — A418

First Lady Yolanda Prada de Banzer and: 1.50b, Women working in fields, making pottery, weaving. 2b, Women working on computer, standing at blackboard.

1998, Oct. 11

1045	A418	1.50b multicolored	1.50	.75
1046	A418	2b multicolored	2.10	1.00
a.		Pair, #1045-1046	4.50	4.50

America Issue.

City of La Paz, 450th Anniv. A419

2b, Plaza de Laja Church.

1998, Oct. 14

1047	A419	2b multicolored	2.00	1.00

A420

1998, Nov. 6 Litho. *Perf. 13½x13¾*

1048	A420	3.50b blue & yellow	2.75	.75

Organization of American States, 50th anniv.

A421

1998, Nov. 12 *Perf. 13¼x13½*

1049	A421	2b multicolored	1.50	.50

Bolivian Philatelic Federation, 25th anniv., Espamer '98, Buenos Aires.

Christmas — A422

2b, Child's drawing of church. 6b, Pope John Paul II. 7b, John Paul II, Mother Teresa.

Perf. 13¼x13½, 13½x13¼

1998, Nov. 26

1050	A422	2b multi, horiz.	1.60	.50
1051	A422	6b multi	3.75	1.75
1052	A422	7b multi	4.50	2.00
		Nos. 1050-1052 (3)	9.85	4.25

UPU, 125th Anniv. A423

1999, Jan. 26 Litho. *Perf. 13½*

1053	A423	3.50b multicolored	3.00	.70

AFC Soccer Club, 75th Anniv. — A424

1999, Apr. 22 Litho. *Perf. 13½*

1054	A424	5b multicolored	4.50	2.25

Geneva Convention and Bolivian Red Cross, 50th Anniv. A425

1999, May 18

1055	A425	5b multicolored	4.25	1.25

Bernardo Guarachi, First Bolivian to Reach Summit of Mt. Everest A426

1999, May 25

1056	A426	6b multicolored	6.00	3.00

Special Olympics of Bolivia, 30th Anniv. — A427

Designs: 2b, Medalists on podium. 2.50b, Winners of swimming event, running event.

1999

1057	A427	2b multicolored	1.50	.50
1058	A427	2.50b multicolored	1.75	.60

Japanese Immigration to Bolivia, Cent. — A428

Designs: 3b, Golden Pavilion, Kyoto. 6b, Sun setting across water, vert.

1999, June 3

1059	A428	3b multicolored	2.25	.70
1060	A428	6b multicolored	4.50	1.75

Bolivian Cinema, 100th Anniv. A429

No. 1061, Hacia la Gloria, 1932-33. No. 1062, Jonas y la Ballena Rosada, 1995. No. 1063, Wara Wara, 1929. No. 1064, Vuelve Sebastiana, 1953. No. 1065, La Campana del Chaco, 1933. No. 1066, La Vertiente, 1958. No. 1067, Yawar Mallku, 1969. No. 1068, Mi Socio, 1982.

1999 Litho. *Perf. 13½*

1061	A429	50c multi	.35	.25
1062	A429	50c multi	.35	.25
1063	A429	1b multi	.75	.45
1064	A429	1b multi	.75	.45
1065	A429	3b multi	2.60	1.25
1066	A429	3b multi	2.60	1.25
1067	A429	6b multi	5.00	2.50
1068	A429	6b multi	5.00	2.50
a.		Sheet of 8, #1061-1068	17.50	17.50
		Nos. 1061-1068 (8)	17.40	8.90

SOS Children's Village, 50th Anniv. — A430

1999, July 8

1069	A430	3.50b multicolored	2.50	1.40

Intl. Day Against Illegal Drugs A431

Perf. 13¼x13½

1999, June 26 Litho.

1070	A431	3.50b multicolored	2.50	1.40

Completion of Bolivian-Brazilian Gas Pipeline — A432

Designs: 3b, Presidents of Bolivia and Brazil, map of pipeline. 6b, Presidents, gas flame.

1999, July 1 Litho. *Perf. 13½*

1071	A432	3b multicolored	3.50	1.75
1072	A432	6b multicolored	6.00	3.00

La Paz Lions Club, 50th Anniv. — A433

1999 *Perf. 13½x13¼*

1073	A433	3.50b multicolored	2.50	1.40

Cochabamba Tourism — A434

50c, Mt. Tunari. 1b, Cochabamba Valley. 2b, Container from Omerque culture, idol from Pachamama culture. 3b, Totora. 5b, Composer Teofilo Vargas Candia. 6b, Statue of Jesus Christ.

1999 *Perf. 13½x13¾, 13¾x13½*

1074	A434	50c multi	.45	.25
1075	A434	1b multi	.85	.40
1076	A434	2b multi, vert.	1.40	.60
1077	A434	3b multi	1.90	.85
1078	A434	5b multi, vert.	3.00	1.25
1079	A434	6b multi, vert.	3.50	1.50
		Nos. 1074-1079 (6)	11.10	4.85

Potosí Tourism A435

50c, Tarapaya Lake. 1b, Obverse and reverse of 1827 Bolivian coin. 2b, Mt. Chorolque. 3b, Lake, llama, birds. 5b, "Mestizo Woman with a Cigarette Case," by Teofilo Loaiza. 6b, Alfredo Dominguez Romero, musician.

Perf. 13¾x13½, 13½x13¾

1999 Litho.

1080	A435	50c multi, vert.	.45	.25
1081	A435	1b multi	.85	.40
1082	A435	2b multi	1.50	.75
1083	A435	3b multi	2.00	1.00
1084	A435	5b multi, vert.	3.25	1.60
1085	A435	6b multi, vert.	4.00	2.00
		Nos. 1080-1085 (6)	12.05	6.00

America Issue, A New Millennium Without Arms — A436

1999 *Perf. 13½x13¼*

1086	A436	3.50b shown	3.00	1.50
1087	A436	3.50b Globe, flower	3.00	1.50

Christmas A437

2b, Children, Christmas tree. 6b, The Birth of Jesus, by Gaspar Miguel de Berrios. 7b, Our Families of the World, by Omar Medina.

1999 *Perf. 13¼x13½, 13½x13¼*

1088	A437	2b multi	1.30	.65
1089	A437	6b multi, vert.	3.50	1.75
1090	A437	7b multi, vert.	4.50	2.25
		Nos. 1088-1090 (3)	9.30	4.65

Discovery of Brazil, 500th Anniv. A438

2000 Litho. *Perf. 13½x13¾*

1091	A438	5b multi	4.00	2.00

2000 Doble Copacabana Bicycle Race — A439

Various views of racers.

2000

1092	A439	1b multi	.90	.70
1093	A439	3b multi	2.00	1.50
1094	A439	5b multi	4.00	3.00
1095	A439	7b multi	6.00	4.00
		Nos. 1092-1095 (4)	12.90	9.20

Sgt. Maximiliano Paredes Military School, Cent. — A440

2000 Litho. *Perf. 13½x13¾*

1096	A440	2.50b multi	3.00	1.50

Federal Republic of Germany, 50th Anniv. (in 1999) A441

2000

1097	A441	6b multi	4.50	3.25

Paintings of Cecilio Guzmán de Rojas (1900-51) — A442

Designs: 1b, Self-portrait, vert. 2.50b, Triunfo de la Naturaleza. 5b, Andina, vert. 6b, Riña de Estudiantes.

2000 *Perf. 13¾x13½, 13½x13¾*

1098-1101	A442	Set of 4	10.00	7.50

Artifacts from Natl. Archaeological Museum — A443

Artifacts from: No. 1102, 50c, Pando. No. 1103, 50c, Potosí. 70c, Beni. 90c, Tarija. No. 1106, 1b, Chuquisaca. No. 1107, 1b, Oruro. 3b, Cochabamba. 5b, Santa Cruz. 20b, La Paz.

2000 *Perf. 11¼x11*

1102-1110	A443	Set of 9	24.00	18.00

America Issue, Fight Against AIDS — A444

Designs: No. 1111, 3.50b, Symbols for male and female in whirlwind. No. 1112, 3.50b, Man, woman, clouds, brick wall.

2000 *Perf. 13¼x13½*

1111-1112	A444	Set of 2	7.00	5.25

Victor Agustin Ugarte, Soccer Player — A445

2000, Apr. 24 Litho. *Perf. 13½x13¼*

1113	A445	3b multi	2.50	1.90

Santa Cruz Tourism A446

Designs: 50c, Fountains, Parque el Arenal. 1b, Ox cart. 2b, Writers Raúl Otero Reiche, Gabriel René Moreno, Hernando Sanabria Fernández. 3b, Virgin of Cotoca, vert. 5b, Anthropomorphic vessel, vert. 6b, Speothos venaticus.

Perf. 13½x13¾, 13¾x13½

2000, Apr. 28

1114-1119	A446	Set of 6	15.00	11.00

Javier del Granado (1913-96), Writer — A447

2000, May 26 Litho. *Perf. 13¼x13½*

1120	A447	3b multi	3.00	2.25

Millennium — A448

2000 Litho. *Perf. 13½x13¼*

1121	A448	5b multi	3.50	2.60

Sovereign Military Order of Malta, 900th Anniv. — A449

2000 *Perf. 13¾x13½*

1122	A449	6b multi	4.25	1.25

Christmas — A450

Angels from Calamarca Church: 3b, Gabriel. 5b, Angel of Virtue. 10b, Angel with spike of grain.

2000
1123-1125 A450 Set of 3 12.50 4.25

Holy Year 2000 — A451

Holy Year emblem and: 4b, Basilica de San Francisco, La Paz. 6b, Wheat stalks, barbed wire.

2000 **Litho.** ***Perf. 13½x13¼***
1126-1127 A451 Set of 2 8.00 3.00

Promotion of Philately A452

National Symbols A453

Designs: 50c, Man carying first day covers up stairs. 1b, Child, six stamps. 1.50b, Stamp collector. 2b, Child, three stamps. 2.50b, Envelope in bin. 10b, Patuju bandera, current national flower. 20b, La kantuta, previous national flower. 30b, Coat of arms, 1825. 50b, Coat of arms, 1826. 100b, Coat of arms, 1851.

2001 **Litho.** ***Perf. 10½***

1128	A452	50c green	.30	.25
1129	A452	1b green	.70	.30
1130	A452	1.50b green	1.10	.50
1131	A452	2b green	1.40	.70
1132	A452	2.50b green	2.00	.80
a.		Horiz. strip, #1128-1132, + label	6.75	6.75

Perf. 13¾x13½

1133	A453	10b multi	8.00	4.00
1134	A453	20b multi	15.00	8.00
1135	A453	30b multi	22.50	12.00
1136	A453	50b multi	37.50	25.00
1137	A453	100b multi	75.00	40.00
		Nos. 1128-1137 (10)	163.50	91.55

Issued: 50c, 1b, 1.50b, 2b, 2.50b, 6/12; 10b, 6/29; 20b, 6/8; 30b, 5/16; 50b, 3/16; 100b, 4/16.

Bolivia - European Union Cooperation, 25th Anniv. — A454

2001, May 8 **Litho.** ***Perf. 13½x13¾***
1138 A454 6b multi 4.25 1.25

Law and Political Science Faculty of San Andres University, 171st Anniv. — A455

2001, May 18 ***Perf. 13¾x13½***
1139 A455 6b multi 4.25 1.25

Muela del Diablo A457

2001, July 6 **Litho.** ***Perf. 13½x13¾***
1141 A457 1.50b multi 1.25 .40

2001 Census — A458

2001, Aug. 1 ***Perf. 11***

1142		Horiz. strip of 5	9.00	9.00
a.	A458	1b purple & multi	.95	.30
b.	A458	1.50b red & multi	1.40	.40
c.	A458	1.50b green & multi	1.40	.40
d.	A458	2.50b blue & multi	2.25	.65
e.	A458	3b violet & multi	3.00	.70

Butterflies and Insects A459

Butterflies: No. 1143, 1b, Heliconinae. 1.50b, Philaethria dido. No. 1145, 2.50b, Diathria clymene. No. 1146, 5b, Arctiidae. No. 1147, 6b, Morpho godarti. No. 1148, 6b, Caligo idomineus.

Insects: No. 1149, 1b, Orthopteridae. No. 1150, 2.50b, Mantidae. No. 1151, 3b, Tropidacris latreillei. 4b, Pyrrhodae. No. 1153, 5b, Acrocinus longimanus. No. 1154, 5b, Lucanidae.

Perf. 13¼x13½
2001, Aug. 30 **Litho.**
1143-1148 A459 Set of 6 16.50 6.75
1149-1154 A459 Set of 6 16.50 6.75

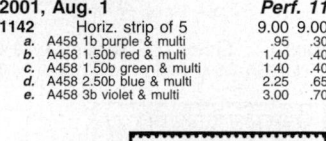

21st Inter-American Scout Conference A460

2001, Sept. 13 ***Perf. 13¾x13½***
1155 A460 3.50b multi 3.00 2.25

America Issue, UNESCO World Heritage Sites — A461

Designs: 1.50b, Door from Church of St. Francis, Potosi. 5b, Tiwanakwu monoliths, horiz.

Perf. 13¾x13½, 13½x13¾
2001, Sept. 26
1156-1157 A461 Set of 2 7.00 4.00

Breast Cancer Prevention A462

2001, Oct. 18 **Litho.** ***Perf. 13¼x13½***
1158 A462 1.50b multi 1.25 1.00

Christmas — A463

Sculptures by Gaspar de la Cueva: 3b, St. Mary Magdalene. 5b, St. Apolonia. 10b, St. Teresa of Avila.

2001, Nov. 15 ***Perf. 13½x13¼***
1159-1161 A463 Set of 3 15.00 9.25

Joaquin Gantier, Historian, and Casa de la Libertad — A464

2001, Nov. 20
1162 A464 4b multi 3.75 2.00

Bolivian-Belgian Cooperation — A465

2001, Nov. 21 ***Perf. 13¼x13½***
1163 A465 6b multi 5.00 2.50

Meeting of Bolivian and Peruvian Presidents A466

Arms of Bolivia and Peru and: 50c, Dam, aerial view of Lake Titicaca. 3b, Bridge, Route from La Paz, Bolivia to Ilo, Peru.

2002, Jan. 26 ***Perf. 13¾x13½***
1164-1165 A466 Set of 2 3.00 1.75

Mauro Nuñez, Composer, Cent. of Birth — A467

No. 1166: a, 1b, Musical score and stringed instruments. b, 6b, Musical score and Nuñez.

2002, Jan. 29
1166 A467 Horiz. pair, #a-b 6.00 4.50

A468

Dances: 50c, Diablada. 1.50b, Morenada. 2.50b, Caporales. 5b, Tobas. No. 1171, 7b, Suri Sikuri, vert. No. 1172, 7b, Pujllay, vert.

Perf. 13¼x13½, 13½x13¼
2002, Feb. 8
1167-1172 A468 Set of 6 20.00 14.00

Naming of Oruro Carnival as UNESCO Masterpiece of Oral and Intangible Heritage of Humanity

Butterfly and insect Type of 2001
Miniature Sheet

No. 1173: a, Urania leilus. b, Tropidacris latreillei. c, Papilio cresphontes. d, Acrocinus longimanus. e, Preponia buckleyana. f, Half of Thysannia agripyna, denomination at left. g, Half of Thysannia agripyna, denomination at right. h, Lucanidae. i, Nymphalidae. j, Dynastidae. k, Nymphalidae-heliconinae. l, Orthopteridae.

2002, Feb. 15 ***Perf. 13¼x13½***
1173 A459 3b Sheet of 12, #a-l 30.00 30.00

3rd Intl. Theater Festival, La Paz — A469

2002, Mar. 21 ***Perf. 13¾x13½***
1174 A469 3b multi 2.50 1.25

Intl. Year of Mountains and Intl. Year of Ecotourism A470

Designs: 80c, Viscachas Mountain, Potosi Department. 1b, Tree, Cochabamba Department, vert. 1.50, Mount Huayna Potosi, La Paz Department. No. 1178, 2.50b, Mt. Sajama, Oruro Department, vert. No. 1179, 2.50b, Mt. Payachatas, Oruro Department.

Perf. 13¼x13½, 13½x13¼
2002, Apr. 2
1175-1179 A470 Set of 5 7.75 3.00

Dr. Gunnar Mendoza, Historian
A471

2002, May 25 ***Perf. 13¼x13½***

1180 A471 4b multi 3.25 2.00

Gen. Germán Busch Military Aviation College, 50th Anniv.
A472

Designs: 4b, Airplane over mountains. 5b, Two airplanes, vert. 6b, Three helicopters.

Perf. 13¼x13½, 13½x13¼

2002, June 14

1181-1183 A472 Set of 3 12.00 8.00

Museo de la Recoleta, Sucre, 400th Anniv. — A473

2002, July 12 ***Perf. 13¾x13½***

1184 A473 4b multi 3.25 2.00

Birds — A474

Designs: 50c, Neochen jubata. 4b, Falco deiroleucus. 6b, Dryocopus schulzi.

2002, July 12 ***Perf. 13½x13¼***

1185-1187 A474 Set of 3 9.00 5.50

Cefilco Philatelic Co., Cochabamba (50c), Bolivian Philatelic Federation, 30th anniv. (4b), Phila Korea 2002 World Stamp Exhibition, Seoul (6b).

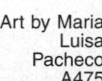

Art by Maria Luisa Pacheco
A475

Designs: 70c, Untitled work, vert. 80c, Cordillera, 1967, vert. 5b, Cerros, 1967.

Perf. 13½x13¼, 13¼x13½

2002, July 29

1188-1190 A475 Set of 3 5.25 3.25

Sculptures by Marina Nuñez del Prado — A476

Designs: 70c, Madona India. 80c Madre India. 5b, Venus Negra.

2002, July 29 **Litho.** ***Perf. 13½x13¼***

1191-1193 A476 Set of 3 5.25 3.25

Armando Alba Zambrana (1901-74), Historian
A477

Perf. 13¼x13½

2002, Aug. 30 **Litho.**

1194 A477 3b multi 2.75 1.75

Pan-American Health Organization, Cent. — A478

2002, Apr. 24 ***Perf. 13½x13¾***

1195 A478 3b multi 2.75 1.75

America Issue, Education
A479

Students: 1b, In classroom. 2.50b, At computer.

2002, Oct. 11 ***Perf. 13¼x13½***

1196-1197 A479 Set of 2 3.50 2.25

Alcide d'Orbigny (1802-57), Naturalist
A480

Designs: 1b, D'orbigny and man and woman in native costumes, vert. 4b, D'Orbigny and boat. 6b, Portrait, vert.

Perf. 13¾x13½, 13½x13¾

2002, Sept. 26

1198-1200 A480 Set of 3 9.00 5.50

Christmas — A481

Designs: 3b, Madonna and Child. 5b, Andean nativity. 6b, Adoration of the Magi.

Perf. 13½x13¼

2002, Nov. 14 **Litho.**

1201-1203 A481 Set of 3 10.00 10.00

Apolinar Camacho (1917-2002), Composer
A482

2003, Jan. 10 ***Perf. 13¾x13½***

1204 A482 2.50b multi 1.50 1.25

Battle of Bahia, Cent. (in 2002) — A483

No. 1205: a, 50c, One statue. b, 1b, Three statues.

2003, May 5 **Litho.** ***Perf. 13½x13¼***

1205 A483 Pair, #a-b 1.50 1.50

Permanent Assembly for Human Rights in Bolivia, 25th Anniv. — A484

2003, June 5

1206 A484 6b blue 4.00 1.50

Central Bank of Bolivia, 75th Anniv. — A485

2003, July 18 ***Perf. 13¾x13½***

1207 A485 4b multi 2.50 1.10

Constitutional Tribunal, 5th Anniv.
A486

2003, July 25 ***Perf. 13¼x13½***

1208 A486 1.50b multi 1.10 .50

Indigenous Flora and Fauna
A487

No. 1209: a, 6b, Quinoa. b, 7b, Llamas.

2003, Sept. 23

1209 A487 Pair, #a-b 9.50 5.00

Republic of Panama, Cent.
A488

2003, Nov. 3 **Litho.** ***Perf. 13½x13¾***

1210 A488 7b multi 3.50 1.50

13th Iberoamerican Heads of State Summit, Santa Cruz de la Sierra — A489

No. 1211: a, Flags, Western hemisphere. b, Flags, Eastern hemisphere.

2003, Nov. 7

1211 A489 6b Horiz. pair, #a-b 8.00 3.00

Porfirio Díaz Machicao (1909-81), Rosendo Villalobos (1859-1932), and Msgr. Juan Quiros (1914-92) — A490

Virgin of Guadalupe
A491

2003 ***Perf. 13½x13¾, 13¾x13½***

1212 A490 6b multi 5.00 1.50

1213 A491 6b multi 5.00 1.50

a. Pair, #1212-1213 12.50 5.00

Bolivian Language Academy, 75th anniv. (No. 1212), La Plata Archdiocese, 450th anniv. (No. 1213).

Issued: No. 1212, 11/12; No. 1213, 11/25.

Christmas
A492

Paintings depicting the Adoration of the Shepherds by: 1.50b, Leonardo Flores, vert. 6b, Bernardo Bitti, vert. 7b, Melchor Pérez de Holguín.

Perf. 13¾x13½, 13½x13¾

2003, Dec. 16

1214-1216 A492 Set of 3 8.00 4.00

Pontificate of Pope John Paul II, 25th Anniv.
A493

Designs: 1b, Pope waving, vert. 1.50b, Painting, vert. 5b, Pope blessing Indians. 6b, Pope waving, diff., vert. 7b, Photograph, vert.

20b, Arms of Bolivia and Vatican City, Pope John Paul II, aerial view of Vartican City, #1013, 1161.

2003 ***Perf. 13¾x13½, 13½x13¾***

1217-1221 A493 Set of 5 12.50 11.50

Imperf

Size: 150x110mm

1222 A493 20b multi 12.50 11.50

Arco Iris Foundation, 10th Anniv. — A494

2004, Apr. 4 Litho. ***Perf. 13¾x13½***
1223 A494 1.80b multi 1.25 .50

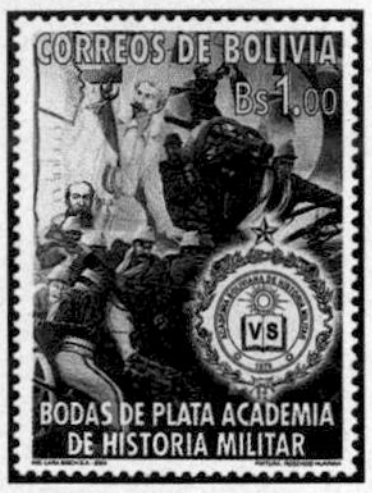

Academy of Military History, 25th Anniv. — A495

2004, Oct. 19 Litho. ***Perf. 13¾x13½***
1224 A495 1b multi .60 .30

2004 Summer Olympics, Athens — A496

Designs: 1.50b, Shooting, gymnastics, judo. 7b, Track, swimming.

2004, Nov. 8
1225-1226 A496 Set of 2 4.00 1.50

Christmas A497

Designs: 1.50b, Nativity. 3b, Shepherd praying. 6b, Candle.

2004, Dec. 16
1227-1229 A497 Set of 3 5.50 2.00

La Paz Journalist's Association, 75th Anniv. — A498

2004, Dec. 23
1230 A498 1.50b multi .85 .50

America Issue - Environmental Protection A499

Designs: 5b, Palm tree. 6b, Parrots.

2004, Dec. 30
1231-1232 A499 Set of 2 6.00 2.75

Rotary International, Cent. — A500

No. 1233 — Emblem of Rotary International and: a, Emblem of PolioPlus, map of Bolivia. b, Paul Harris, flag of Bolivia.

2005, Mar. 4 Litho. ***Perf. 13¼x13½***
1233 A500 3b Horiz. pair, #a-b 4.00 1.25

Projects of Bolivia and the European Union A501

Designs: 5b, PRAS PANDO, Pando water and drainage project. 6b, PRAEDAC, Chapare alternate development program, vert.

Perf. 13¼x13½, 13½x13¼
2005, Mar. 16
1234-1235 A501 Set of 2 6.00 2.00

Textiles — A502

Designs: 50c, Aguayo Calamarca. 1b, Aqsu Bolivar. 1.50b, Incuña Camacho. No. 1239, 6b, Llixlla Challa. No. 1240, 6b, Unku Santo Lago Titicaca, horiz.

Perf. 13½x13¼, 13¼x13½
2005, Apr. 1
1236-1240 A502 Set of 5 7.75 3.25

Marshal Otto Felipe Braun — A503

2005, May 20 ***Perf. 13¾x13½***
1241 A503 6b multi 3.25 1.25

Birds — A504

Designs: 1b, Harpia harpyja. 1.50b, Penelope dabbenei. 7b, Aulacorhynchus coeruleicinctus.

2005, June 28 ***Perf. 13½x13¼***
1242-1244 A504 Set of 3 5.00 1.50

Interexpo '05, Dominican Republic (1b), Bolivian Philatelic Federation, 35th anniv. (1.50b), Washington 2006 Intl. Philatelic Exhibition (7b).

Pope John Paul II (1920-2005) — A505

Pope Benedict XVI — A506

2005, Aug. 1 Litho. ***Perf. 13½x13¾***
1245 A505 5b multi 2.50 1.25

Perf. 13¾x13½
1246 A506 5b multi 2.50 1.25

Pacific War, 125th Anniv. A507

Perf. 13½x13¾
2005, Aug. 17 Litho.
1247 A507 5b multi 3.00 1.25

Publication of *Don Quixote,* by Miguel de Cervantes, 400th Anniv. — A508

2005, Aug. 26
1248 A508 4b multi 2.50 1.00

America Issue — Fight Against Poverty A509

Paintings by Gilka Wara Libermann: 6b, Mother and child. 7b, Sailboat and fish skeleton.

2005, Aug. 26
1249-1250 A509 Set of 2 9.00 3.50

Gen. Ildefonso Murguia and Presidential Escort Regiment A510

2005, Sept. 3 Litho. ***Perf. 13¾x13½***
1251 A510 2b multi 1.25 .50

Presidential Escort Regiment, 184th anniv.

Tourism A511

2005, Sept. 27 ***Perf. 13½x13¾***
1252 A511 6b multi 3.25 1.50

Environmental Protection League — A512

2005, Oct. 5
1253 A512 6b multi 3.25 1.50

Miniature Sheet

Stamp Day — A513

No. 1254: a, 2b, Unissued Bolivian stamps of 1863. b, 2b, Imperf. Bolivia #C7. c, 2b, Brazil #1, stamp similar to Great Britain #1. d, 4b, Bolivia #2-3. e, 4b, Bolivia #C25. f, 4b, Bolivia #740.

2005, Oct. 9 ***Perf. 13¼x13½***
1254 A513 Sheet of 6, #a-f 10.00 10.00

Christmas A514

Designs: 1.50b on 60c, Magi on camels, Star of Bethlehem. 3b on 80c, Holy Family.

2005, Oct. 9 Litho. *Perf. 13¾x13½*
1255-1256 A514 Set of 2 2.50 1.10

Dark gray and dark blue portions of the designs of Nos. 1255-1256 were overprinted on unissued stamps.

Nos. 724, 725, 737 Surcharged

Methods and Perfs As Before

2006, Feb. 12
1257 A271 1b on 1,000,000b #725 .55 .50
1258 A271 2b on 550,000b #724 1.10 1.00
1259 A281 2.50b on 1,000,000b #737 1.40 1.25
Nos. 1257-1259 (3) 3.05 2.75

Size and location of surcharge varies.

National Faculty of Engineering, Cent. — A515

2006, July 4 Litho. *Perf. 13½x13¾*
1260 A515 6b multi 2.25 1.50

Pres. Evo Morales Ayma — A516

President: 1.50b, Waving. 5b, With flag. 6b, Wearing traditional Indian costume.

2006, Aug. 15 *Perf. 13¾x13½*
1261-1263 A516 Set of 3 4.25 3.50

Bolivian Red Cross — A517

2006, Aug. 16
1264 A517 5b multi 1.75 1.00

Bolivia Post Corporation, 15th Anniv. — A518

Incan post runner and envelopes in: 1b, Green. 1.50b, Blue.

Perf. 13½x13¼
2006, Aug. 21 Litho.
1265-1266 A518 Set of 2 1.00 .65

Miniature Sheet

Stamp Day — A519

No. 1267: a, 1.50b, Boy Scouts viewing exhibits at Exfivia 75. b, 1.50b, Stamp collector with open album. c, 1.50b, Bolivia #189, Honduras #C1052i. d, 6b, People viewing exhibits at Exfilmar 80. e, 6b, Bolivia #1247, Iceland #990a. f, 6b, Bolivia #C240, Dominican Republic #1308a.

2006, Aug. 24 *Perf. 13½x13¾*
1267 A519 Sheet of 6, #a-f 9.00 7.50

On Mar. 1, 2018, Supreme Decree 3495 declared that the Postal Company of Bolivia (ECOBOL) was to be closed immediately because of debt. The decree announced the creation of the Agencia Boliviana de Correos to replace the closed Postal Company of Bolivia. When the Agencia Boliviana de Correos opened for business, it handstamped in red stamp stock produced for the Postal Company of Bolivia with the emblem shown above. It is not known currently if the handstamping was done at a central location and overprinted stock was distributed to post offices or if this handstamp was sent to various post offices and the handstamping was done locally. Stamps issued as far back as 2006 (No. 1270) are known to have been overprinted. It is possible that stamps other than the items that are listed below exist with this overprint. The editors would like to examine any examples of stamps bearing this overprint that are not listed.

History of the National Flag — A520

Designs: 1.50b, Legislative Palace and flag of 1851. 5b, Exterior of Casa de la Libertad and flag of 1826. 6b, Interior of Casa de la Libertad, flag of 1825.

2006, Sept. 21 *Perf. 13¾x13½*
1268-1270 A520 Set of 3 4.50 3.50
1270A A520 6b As No. 1270 with red Agencia Boliviana de Correos handstamp ('18) — —

Franciscan Order in Tarija, 400th Anniv. — A521

Designs: No. 1271, 2b, Franciscan monk and donkey. No. 1272, 2b, Exterior of San Francisco Church. No. 1273, 6b, Interior of San Francisco Basilica, vert. No. 1274, 6b, Painting of Virgin Mary and angels, vert.

Perf. 13½x13¾, 13¾x13½
2006, Oct. 2
1271-1274 A521 Set of 4 7.00 4.00
1273A A521 6b As No. 1273, with red Agencia Boliviana de Correos handstamp ('18) — —

Nos. 1271 and 1273 are dated "2005." See note after Nos. 1268-1270.

First Flight of Alberto Santos-Dumont, Cent. — A522

2006, Oct. 23 *Perf. 13½x13¾*
1275 A522 1.50b multi .70 .50

Oruro, 400th Anniv. A523

2006, Oct. 23
1276 A523 4b multi 1.50 1.00

Puerto Bahia, Cent. A524

Designs: 1b, Avenida 9 de Febrero. 1.50b, German Busch Plaza. 2.50b, Chestnut tree, vert. 3b, Potosí Plaza. 4b, Bahía Pando River. 6b, Bolivia-Brazil Friendship Bridge. 7b, Avenida del Puerto, vert.

Perf. 13½x13¾, 13¾x13½
2006, Nov. 24 Litho.
1277-1283 A524 Set of 7 10.00 6.25

America Issue, Energy Conservation A525

Designs: 3b, Fluorescent light bulb on flower stalk, doctor, patient and people. 4b, Light bulb containing money.

2006, Dec. 4 Litho. *Perf. 13¾x13½*
1284-1285 A525 Set of 2 4.50 2.00

Manco Kapac Province, 50th Anniv. A526

Designs: 5b, Ruins of astronomical observatory. 6b, Copacabana Church. 7b, Boat on Lake Titicaca.

2006, Dec. 4 *Perf. 13½x13¾*
1286-1288 A526 Set of 3 7.50 4.00

No. 1288 is dated "2003."

Deserts and Desertification — A527

Designs: 1.50b, Mine degradation in Potosi Department. 2b, Gullies, Tarija Department. 3b, Terraces, La Paz. 4b, Deforested area, Caranavi.

2006, Dec. 4
1289-1292 A527 Set of 4 5.50 3.00

Endangered Animals A528

Designs: 1b, Vicuna. 1.50b, Caiman, horiz. 5b, Caiman, diff., horiz. 7b, Vicuna, horiz.

Perf. 13¾x13½, 13½x13¾
2006, Dec. 4
1293-1296 A528 Set of 4 6.00 4.00

Christmas A529

Designs: 4b, Virgin of Rosario. 5b, Adoration of the Magi. 6b, Adoration of the Shepherds.

2006, Dec. 4 *Perf. 13¾x13½*
1297-1299 A529 Set of 3 5.50 3.50

Birds — A530

Designs: 2.50b, Toucan, Pando Department. 3.50b, Horned curassow, Santa Cruz Department. 6b, Blue bird, Pando Department. 7b, Harpy eagle, Santa Cruz Department.

2006, Dec. 11
1300-1303 A530 Set of 4 7.50 5.00

Dogs — A531

Designs: 1b, Miniature schnauzer. 3b, Husky. 4b, Boxer. 6b, Mixed-breed.

2006, Dec. 21
1304-1307 A531 Set of 4 5.00 3.50

36th Lions International Forum for Latin America and the Caribbean, Cochabamba — A532

2007, Jan. 7 Litho. *Perf. 13½x13¾*
1308 A532 6b multi 2.25 1.40
1308A A532 6b As No. 1308 with red Agencia Boliviana de Correos handstamp ('18) — —

Treaty of Rome, 50th Anniv. — A533

No. 1309: a, 3.50b, Map of Europe. b, 7b, European Union flag.

2007, Mar. 27
1309 A533 Horiz. pair, #a-b 3.50 2.50

Cochabamba Philatelic Center (CEFILCO), 50th Anniv — A534

Designs: 50c, Brochures on philately for young people. 1b, Arnold Glaeser, first President of CEFILCO, Bolivia #C270. 2.50b, Bolivia #901B, 1999 CEFILCO stamp catalogue. 3b, Philatelists Franz Steimbach and Oscar Roca.

No. 1314: a, 3.50b, Cochabamba Cathedral and monument. b, 6b, Sculpture of Christ, Cochabamba Cathedral.

2007, Apr. 18
1310-1313 A534 Set of 4 3.25 1.50
1314 A534 Horiz. pair, #a-b 4.25 2.50
1314C A534 As No. 1314, with red Agencia Boliviana de Correos handstamp ('18) — —
d. 3.50b As No. 1314a, with red Agencia Boliviana de Correos handstamp ('18) — —
e. 6b As No. 1314b, with red Agencia Boliviana de Correos handstamp ('18) — —

See note after Nos. 1268-1270.

Charangos A535

Designs: 4b, Charangos, Bolivian arms. 6b, Charango, mountain, horiz.

Perf. 13¾x13½, 13½x13¾

2007, Apr. 27
1315-1316 A535 Set of 2 3.25 2.75
1316A A535 6b As No. 1316, with red Agencia Boliviana de Correos handstamp ('18) — —

See note after Nos. 1268-1270.

Bolivian Red Cross, 90th Anniv. A536

2007, May 24 *Perf. 13½x13¾*
1317 A536 2.50b multi 1.00 .50

Francis Harrington, Founder of American Institute, La Paz — A537

2007, May 30 Litho.
1318 A537 7.50b multi 2.50 1.75

American Institute, cent.

Natl. Chamber of Industry, 75th Anniv. — A538

No. 1319: a, 9b, Gears, map of Bolivia. b, 12b, Gears.

2007, June 28
1319 A538 Horiz. pair, #a-b 9.00 5.00

Santa Cruz Zoo — A539

Cats: 6b, Jaguar. 9b, Puma.

2007 *Perf. 13¾x13½*
1320-1321 A539 Set of 2 6.00 4.00

Scouting, Cent. A540

Designs: 7.50b, Lord Robert Baden-Powell blowing kudu horn. 8.50b, Scouting emblem, vert.

2007 *Perf. 13½x13¾, 13¾x13½*
1322-1323 A540 Set of 2 6.75 5.00

57th Conference of the Chiefs of American Air Forces, Santa Cruz de la Sierra — A541

2007 *Perf. 13½x13¾*
1324 A541 10.50b multi 6.50 4.00

Birds — A542

Designs: 4b, Opisthocomus hoazin, La Paz Department. No. 1326, 5.50b,Tunqui, La Paz Department, horiz. No. 1327, 5.50b, Ara ararauna, Santa Cruz Department, horiz. 7.50b, Porphyrula martinica, Santa Cruz Department, horiz.

2007 *Perf. 13¾x13½, 13½x13¾*
1325-1328 A542 Set of 4 9.00 6.25

Issued: Nos. 1325-1326, 7/28; Nos. 1327-1328, 7/20.

Birds Type of 2007

Designs: 3.50b, Cyclarhis guyanensis, Tarija Department, horiz. 4b, Egretta alba, Cochabamba Department. 5.50b, Ramphastos toco, Beni Department, horiz. No. 1332, 6.50b, Bubo virginianus, Cochabamba Department. No. 1333, 6.50b, Trogon melanurus, Pando Department. No. 1334, 6.50b, Falco sparverius, Potosí Department, horiz. No. 1335, 6.50b, Hymanotopus mexicanus, Oruro Department. No. 1336, 7.50b, Opisthocomus hoazin, Beni Department, horiz. No. 1337, 7.50b, Platalea ajaja, Oruro Department, horiz. No. 1338, 8.50b, Sarcoramphus papa, Tarija Department, horiz. No. 1339, 8.50b, Momotus momota, Chuquisaca Department, horiz. No. 1340, 9b, Tinamotis pentlandii, Potosí Department. No. 1341, 9b, Chlorostilbon aureoventris, Chuquisaca Department. 10.50b, Ardea cocoi, Pando Department.

Perf. 13½x13¾, 13¾x13½

2008 Litho.
1329-1342 A542 Set of 14 37.50 37.50
1331A A542 5.50b As No. 1331, with red Agencia Boliviana de Correos handstamp ('18) — —
1332A A542 6.50b As No. 1332, with red Agencia Boliviana de Correos handstamp ('18) — —
1333A A542 6.50b As No. 1333, with red Agencia Boliviana de Correos handstamp ('18) — —
1334A A542 6.50b As No. 1334, with red Agencia Boliviana de Correos handstamp ('18) — —
1338A A542 8.50b As No. 1338, with red Agencia Boliviana de Correos handstamp ('18) — —
1339A A542 8.50b As No. 1339, with red Agencia Boliviana de Correos handstamp ('18) — —

Issued: Nos. 1329, 1338, 8/20; Nos. 1330, 1332, 8/21; Nos. 1333, 1342, 8/22; Nos. 1331, 1336, 8/23; Nos. 1334, 1340, 8/24; Nos. 1339, 1341, 8/27; Nos. 1335, 1337, 8/28.

See note after Nos. 1268-1270.

Death of Ernesto "Che" Guevara in Bolivia, 40th Anniv. A543

Designs: 30b, Autograph of Guevara. 50b, Various images of Guevara, vert.

Perf. 13½x13¾, 13¾x13½

2007, Oct. 8
1343-1344 A543 Set of 2 30.00 30.00

Bolivian Air Force, 50th Anniv. A544

Anniversary emblem and: 7.50b, Planes on ground. 9b, Plane in flight.

2007, Oct. 12 *Perf. 13½x13¾*
1345-1346 A544 Set of 2 6.50 6.00

Intl. Civil Aviation Day A545

Airplane and: 6.50b, Globe. 8.50b, World map.

2007, Dec. 10
1347-1348 A545 Set of 2 7.00 6.50

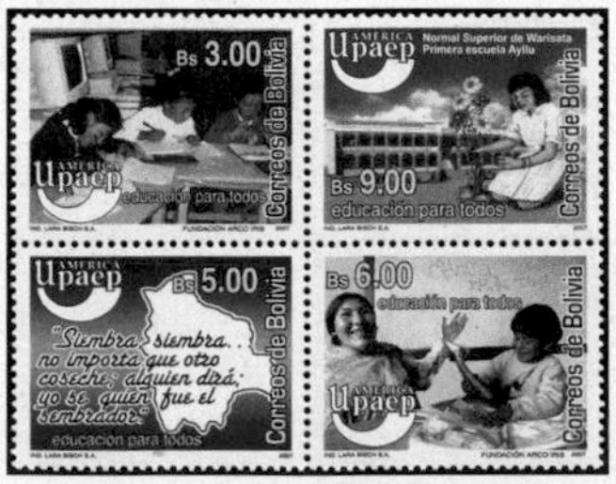

America Issue, Education For All — A546

No. 1349: a, 3b, Three schoolgirls in classroom. b, 5b, Text, map of Bolivia. c, 6b, Teacher and student. d, 9b, School building, girl and flowers.

Perf. 13¼x13½

2007, Dec. 12 Litho.
1349 A546 Block of 4, #a-d 8.50 6.00

Tourism A547

Designs: 2b, Maragua Syncline, Chuquisaca Department. 2.50b, Festuca grass pasturelands, Oruro Department. 3.50b, Lagoon, Pando Department. 5b, Lake on Beni River, Beni Department. No. 1354, Manuripi River, Beni Department. No. 1355, Valley, Tarija Department. No. 1356, Zongo Valley, La Paz Department. No. 1357, Trees along Orthon River, Pando Department. No. 1358, Tornado in Sajama Valley, Oruro Department, vert. No. 1359, Sucre Bridge over Pilcomayo River, Chuquisaca Department. No. 1360, Cactus, Isla del Pescador, Potosí Department, vert. 10b, Chapare River, Cochabamba Department. No. 1362, Trichocereus camarguensis, Tarija Department. No. 1363, Uyuni Salt Flats, Potosí Department. 20b, Lake Caimán, Santa Cruz Department. 30b, Zongo, La Paz Department, vert. 50b, Plaza Sucre, Cochabamba Department. 100b, Arcoiris Waterfall, Santa Cruz Department, vert.

Perf. 13½x13¾, 13¾x13½

2007 **Litho.**

1350	A547	2b	multi	.75	.55
1351	A547	2.50b	multi	.85	.65
1352	A547	3.50b	multi	1.50	.95
1353	A547	5b	multi	2.25	1.40
1354	A547	5.50b	multi	2.40	1.50
1354A	A547	5.50b	As No. 1354, with red Agencia Boliviana de Correos handstamp ('18)	—	—
1355	A547	5.50b	multi	2.40	1.50
1356	A547	5.50b	multi	2.40	1.50
1356A	A547	5.50b	As No. 1356 with red Agencia Boliviana de Correos handstamp ('18)	—	—
1357	A547	7.50b	multi	3.25	2.00
1358	A547	7.50b	multi	3.25	2.00
1359	A547	9b	multi	4.00	2.40
1360	A547	9b	multi	4.00	2.40
1361	A547	10b	multi	4.25	2.60
1362	A547	10.50b	multi	4.25	2.75
1363	A547	10.50b	multi	4.25	2.75
1364	A547	20b	multi	8.50	5.25
1365	A547	30b	multi	12.50	8.00
1366	A547	50b	multi	22.50	16.00
1366A	A547	50b	As No. 1366, with red Agencia Boliviana de Correos handstamp ('18)	—	—
1367	A547	100b	multi	42.50	40.00
1367A	A547	50b	As No. 1367, with red Agencia Boliviana de Correos handstamp ('18)	—	—
	Nos. 1350-1367A (21)			125.80	94.20

Issued: Nos. 1352-1355, 1357, 1362, 12/13; Nos. 1350, 1351, 1356, 1358-1361, 1363-1367, 12/14.

See note after Nos. 1268-1270.

Christmas — A548

No. 1368: a, 3.50b, Holy Family. b, 4b, Adoration of the Shepherds. c, 6.50b, Epiphany.

Perf. 13¾x13½

2007, Dec. 19 **Litho.**

1368 A548 Horiz. strip of 3, #a-c 5.00 5.00

World Post Day — A549

2008, Jan. 15

1369 A549 1b multi .45 .30

Dated 2007.

Bolivian Episcopal Commission of Pastoral Social Charities, 50th Anniv. — A550

Designs: 10b, Jesus, icons, people, map of Bolivia and South America. 15b, Church and indigenous people, vert.

Perf. 13½x13¾, 13¾x13½

2008, Jan. 24

1370-1371 A550 Set of 2 9.50 7.50

Jesuit Church, Santa Cruz A551

Various views of church: 5b, 9b.

2008, Feb. 15 *Perf. 13½x13¾*

1372-1373 A551 Set of 2 5.50 3.75

Dated 2007.

Cochabamba Rotary Club, 80th Anniv. (in 2007) — A552

2008, Mar. 7 *Perf. 13¾x13½*

1374 A552 20b multi 8.50 5.25

Dated 2007.

Superior Court of Oruro, 150th Anniv. (in 2005) — A553

2008, Apr. 5

1375 A553 20b multi 8.50 7.00

Dated 2007.

The Strongest Soccer Team, Cent. — A554

No. 1376: a, 1.50b, Team emblem. b, 2.50b, Team crest. c, 5.50b, Trophy. d, 6.50b, 1908 team.

2008, Apr. 11 *Perf. 13½x13¾*

1376 A554 Block of 4, #a-d 7.00 6.00

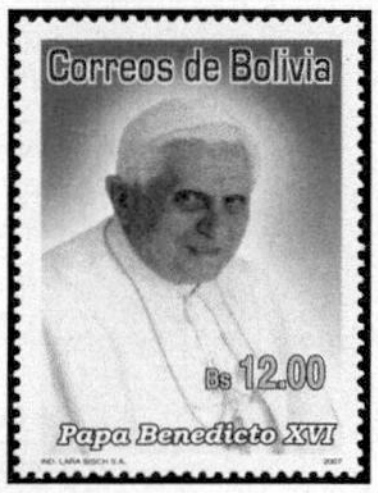

Pope Benedict XVI — A555

Pope Benedict XVI wearing: 12b, White vestments. 15b, Colored vestments.

2008, May 29 **Litho.** *Perf. 13¾x13½*

1377-1378 A555 Set of 2 11.00 9.00

1377A A555 12b As No. 1377, with red Agencia Boliviana de Correos handstamp ('18) — —

Dated 2007. See note after Nos. 1268-1270.

Mountain, Soccer Stadium and Ball A556

2008, June 13 *Perf. 13½x13¾*

1379 A556 3b multi 1.25 1.00

Protest against FIFA proposal to ban international soccer matches at altitudes above 2500 meters.

Sucre Rebellion of May 25, 1809 A557

Designs: 1.50b, Clock tower. 5.50b, Liberty Belltower. 7.50b, Clock tower, building with anniversary banner. 9b, San Francisco Xavier University.

2008, June 18

1380-1383 A557 Set of 4 10.00 8.00

Superintendent of Banks and Financial Institutions, 80th Anniv. — A558

Designs: 3b, Emblem. 7b, Building, vert.

Perf. 13½x13¾, 13¾x13½

2008, July 10

1384-1385 A558 Set of 2 4.25 3.50

Acquisition of MA-60 Airplanes by Bolivian Air Force — A559

Airplane: 1.50b, In flight. 9b, On ground.

2008, Aug. 14 *Perf. 13½x13¾*

1386-1387 A559 Set of 2 4.50 4.00

Intl. Year of the Potato A560

Potato varieties and their blossoms: 1.50b, Luk'i Negra. 5.50b, Sani Imilla. 7.50b, Saq'ampaya. 10.50b, Waych'a.

2008, Oct. 10

1388-1391 A560 Set of 4 12.00 10.00

Map of Bolivia and Envelopes — A561

2009, May 1 **Litho.** *Perf. 13½x13¾*

1392 A561 1.50b multi .75 .60

No. 1392 paid an additional postage fee for mail that was to be handled by private postal services in Bolivia.

Nationalization of Entel, 1st Anniv. — A562

Designs: 2b, Emblem. 3b, Emblem and people, horiz.

Perf. 13¾x13½, 13½x13¾

2009, May 5

1393-1394 A562 Set of 2 2.75 2.25

Rainbow Foundation, 15th Anniv. — A563

2009, May 11 *Perf. 13½x13¾*

1395 A563 5b multi 2.75 2.25

Marshal Sucre National University, Cent. — A564

2009, June 6
1396 A564 3b multi 1.75 1.00

Solidarity With Cuba A565

2009, June 10
1397 A565 7.50b multi 4.00 3.25

Inter-American Development Bank, 50th Anniv. — A566

2009, June 22 ***Perf. 13¾x13½***
1398 A566 5b multi 2.75 2.25

La Paz Revolution, Bicent. — A567

2009, July 14
1399 A567 2b multi 1.10 .90

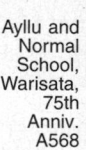

Ayllu and Normal School, Warisata, 75th Anniv. A568

2009, Aug. 2 ***Perf. 13½x13¾***
1400 A568 2.50b multi 1.40 1.10

National Institute of Health Laboratories, Cent. — A569

2009, Aug. 4 ***Perf. 13¾x13½***
1401 A569 1.50b multi .90 .70

Venezuela National High School, Cent. — A570

Designs: 1b, Medals. 3b, School building.

2009, Aug. 10 ***Perf. 13½x13¾***
1402-1403 A570 Set of 2 2.25 1.75

Enrique Lindemann B Educational Unit — A571

2009, Aug. 19 **Litho.**
1404 A571 3.50b multi 2.00 1.50

Conquest of Mt. Everest by Bernardo Guarachi, 10th Anniv. (in 2008) — A572

Guarachi, first Bolivian to reach summit of Mt. Everest wearing: 50c, Ski cap. 7b, Red parka, horiz.

Perf. 13¾x13½, 13½x13¾
2009, Aug. 28
1405-1406 A572 Set of 2 4.00 3.50

San Ramon Home for the Elderly, Cent. A573

2009, Oct. 26 ***Perf. 13½x13¾***
1407 A573 2b multi 1.10 .90

16th Bolivarian Games, Sucre — A574

Designs: 1.50b, Emblem. 9b, Emblem, diff.

2009, Nov. 14 ***Perf. 13¾x13½***
1408-1409 A574 Set of 2 4.50 4.00

America Issue — A575

Children playing with traditional toys: 1b, Top. 7b, Kite.

2009, Nov. 20
1410-1411 A575 Set of 2 3.25 3.00

Japan Intl. Cooperation Agency in Bolivia, 30th Anniv. — A576

Various agency workers with Bolivians: 1b, 1.50b, 3b, 9b.

2009, Dec. 4 ***Perf. 13½x13¾***
1412-1415 A576 Set of 4 6.00 5.50

Dated 2008.

Bolivian Philatelic Federation, 38th Anniv. — A577

2009, Dec. 10
1416 A577 3.50b multi 1.50 1.50

Christmas A578

Designs: 7b, Flight into Egypt. 9b, Jesus in manger.

Perf. 13¾x13½
2009, Dec. 21 **Litho.**
1417-1418 A578 Set of 2 6.50 4.75

Re-election of Pres. Evo Morales Ayma — A579

Pres. Morales: 12.50b, Holding poles. 9b, Waving.

2010, Jan. 20 **Litho.** ***Perf. 13¾x13½***
1419-1420 A579 Set of 2 4.50 3.50

Airplane and Letter to France A580

2010, Mar. 15 ***Perf. 13½x13¾***
1421 A580 9b multi 3.50 3.25

First airmail flight from the Pyrenees to the Andes, 80th anniv.

Global Warming — A581

Mt. Chacaltaya with: 2.50b, Little snow cover. 10b, More snow cover.

2010, Apr. 20
1422-1423 A581 Set of 2 5.00 4.50

Túpac Katari (c. 1750-81), and Wife, Bartolina Sisa (c. 1750-82), Leaders of Rebellion of Indigenous People — A582

2010, Apr. 25 ***Perf. 13¾x13½***
1424 A582 1.50b brown .65 .60

Bolivian Traditions A583

Designs: 1.50b, Items associated with All Saint's Day. 10.50b, Ekeko, god of abundance.

2010, May 10 ***Perf. 13½x13¾***
1425-1426 A583 Set of 2 5.00 5.00

Masks — A584

Designs: 1b, Pepino. 2b, Moreno. 9b, Chuncho. 10b, Kusillo.

2010, May 10 ***Perf. 13¾x13½***
1427-1430 A584 Set of 4 9.00 9.00

Flowers — A585

No. 1431: a, Flowers. b, Flowers and butterfly.

2010, May 27 ***Perf. 13½x13¾***
1431 A585 1.50b Horiz. pair, #a-b 1.50 1.00

Rose, Barbed Wire, Rainer and José Luis Ibsen A586

2010, Aug. 31

1432 A586 3b multi 1.40 1.00

Rainer Ibsen (1949-72), and his father, José Luis (1925-73), were kidnapped and murdered political prisoners of the Banzer regime.

Bolivian Army, 200th Anniv. A587

Flags and: 3.50b, Bulldozer and tank. 9b, Military leaders and battle scene.

2010, Aug. 31

1433-1434 A587 Set of 2 5.00 4.25

2010 Youth Olympics, Singapore — A588

Emblem and: 2b, Soccer player, cyclist. 9b, Swimmer, runner.

2010, Sept. 8 Litho. ***Perf. 13½x13¾***

1435-1436 A588 Set of 2 4.50 3.75

Declaration of Independence of Cochabamba, Bicent. — A589

2010, Sept. 10 ***Perf. 13¾x13½***

1437 A589 9b multi 3.50 3.00

Rebellion Against Spanish Rule of Santa Cruz, Bicent. A590

2010, Sept. 20 ***Perf. 13½x13¾***

1438 A590 5b multi 2.25 1.75

America Issue, National Symbols — A591

No. 1439 — Government Palace, La Paz and: a, 2.50b, Andean condor, Bolivian national bird. b, 5b, Patuju, Bolivian national flower.

2010, Oct. 20

1439 A591 Horiz. pair, #a-b 3.25 2.50

Military Engineering School, 60th Anniv. — A592

2010, Oct. 26

1440 A592 7b multi 2.75 2.75

1440A A592 7b As No. 1440, with red Agencia Boliviana de Correos handstamp ('18) — —

See note after Nos. 1268-1270.

Endangered Species A593

Designs: 1b, Puya raimondii. 2b, Leopardus jacobita, horiz. 2.50b, Atelopus tricolor, horiz. 3.50b, Anairetes alpinus, horiz.

Perf. 13¾x13½, 13½x13¾

2010, Nov. 1

1441-1444 A593 Set of 4 4.50 3.75

Rebellion Against Spanish Rule of Potosí, Bicent. A594

2010, Nov. 10 ***Perf. 13½x13¾***

1445 A594 3.50b multi 1.40 1.10

Zampona, Woodcut by Fausto Aoiz Vilaseca (1908-94) A595

2010, Dec. 13 ***Perf. 13¾x13½***

1446 A595 2b multi 1.10 1.00

Christmas A596

Items in Santa Clara Museum of Religious Art, Sucre: 3b, Archangel Michael, wooden sculpture. 9b, Adoration of the Shepherds, painting, horiz.

Perf. 13¾x13½, 13½x13¾

2010, Dec. 17

1447-1448 A596 Set of 2 5.50 5.00

Jaime Escalante (1930-2010), Bolivian-born American High School Mathematics Teacher — A597

2011, Jan. 20 ***Perf. 13½x13¾***

1449 A597 2b multi 1.10 1.00

Fruits A598

Designs: 1.50b, Oranges (naranja). 5.50b, Mangos. 7.50b, Papayas. 9b, Avocados (palta). 10.50b, Bananas (platano).

2011

1450-1454 A598 Set of 5 13.50 13.50

1450a Dated "2012," oranges in yellow — —

Nos. 1450-1454 paid an additional postage fee for mail that was to be handled by private postal services in Bolivia. See Nos. 1544A-1544B.

Grains — A599

Designs: 1b, Chenopodium quinoa. 2b, Amaranthus. 2.50b, Chenopodium pallidicaule. 5b, Lupinus mutabilis.

2011, July 5 ***Perf. 13¾x13½***

1455-1458 A599 Set of 4 5.50 4.00

Boliviana de Aviación, 4th Anniv. A600

2011, July 22 ***Perf. 13½x13¾***

1459 A600 3b multi 1.75 1.25

Bolivian Cooperation With Cuba — A601

Designs: 2b, Doctor administering eye examination on patient. 2.50b, People in map of bolivia, dove, vert. 3b, Teacher and adult student.

Perf. 13½x13¾, 13¾x13½

2011, Sept. 2

1460-1462 A601 Set of 3 4.00 2.75

Intl. Registry of Bolivian Ships, 10th Anniv. A602

Designs: 1.50b, Barge. 9b, Bolivian Navy boat.

2011, Sept. 2 ***Perf. 13½x13¾***

1463-1464 A602 Set of 2 5.50 4.00

Blood Donation Campaign — A603

2011, Sept. 15

1465 A603 3b multi 1.75 1.25

Postal Union of the Americas, Spain and Portugal (UPAEP), Cent. — A604

2011, Oct. 6 ***Perf. 13¾x13½***

1466 A604 9b multi 5.00 3.25

Endangered Fish — A605

Designs: 1b, Orestias agassii. 1.50b, Cichla pleiozona. 3b, Colossoma macropomum. 9b, Orestias luteus.

2011, Oct. 21 ***Perf. 13½x13¾***

1467-1470 A605 Set of 4 7.50 6.50

National Institute of Statistics, 75th Anniv. A606

2011, Oct. 25

1471 A606 9b multi 5.00 3.25

Mailboxes A607

Designs: 1.50b, Rectangular mailbox. 9b, Mailbox with rounded top.

2011, Dec. 6

1472-1473 A607 Set of 2 5.50 4.00

Christmas
A608

Children's drawings: 1b, Child, star, Christmas tree, gifts, by Sarah Laura Zailes Azeñas. 9b, Children and Christmas tree, by Adriana Nahir Peñaloza Cusi, horiz.

Perf. 13¾x13½, 13½x13¾

2011, Dec. 7

1474-1475 A608 Set of 2 5.50 3.75

Human
Rights
A609

2011, Dec. 9 *Perf. 13½x13¾*

1476 A609 9b multi 5.00 3.25

Intl. Year of
Forests — A610

Emblem and: 2.50b, Bertholletia excelsa. 3b, Swietenia macrophylla.

2011, Dec. 11 *Perf. 13¾x13½*

1477-1478 A610 Set of 2 3.00 2.00

Traditional Cuisine — A611

Designs: 1b, Saice. 1.50b, Majao. 2.50b, Silpancho. 9b, Plato Paceño.

2011, Dec. 16 *Perf. 13½x13¾*

1479-1482 A611 Set of 4 8.00 5.25

Coca Production — A612

Designs: 50c, Coca plantation and products using coca. 9b, Coca leaves and berries, vert.

Perf. 13½x13¾, 13¾x13½

2011, Dec. 19

1483-1484 A612 Set of 2 5.00 3.75

Yacimentos Petroliferos Fiscales Bolivianos Corporation, 75th Anniv. — A613

Designs: 50c, Line of workers. 9b, Dionisio Foianini, nationalizer of Bolivian oil fields, oil derrick, workers with Bolivian flag, vert.

2011, Dec. 21

1485-1486 A613 Set of 2 5.00 3.50

Coin Commemorating New Bolivian Constitution — A614

2012, Jan. 20 *Perf. 13¾x13½*

1487 A614 3b multi 1.75 1.25

Bolivia's
Seacoast
Claim — A615

2012, Mar. 12

1488 A615 5b multi 2.75 2.50

Year Against Violence Towards Children and Adolescents — A616

2012, Apr. 12 *Perf. 13½x13¾*

1489 A616 3.50b multi 1.90 1.50

Workers
A617

Designs: 50c, Sugar cane cutter (zafra). 1b, Seamstresses (fabril). 3b, Miner (minero). 5b, Petroleum worker (petrolero), vert.

Perf. 13½x13¾, 13¾x13½

2012, May 1

1490-1493 A617 Set of 4 5.00 4.00

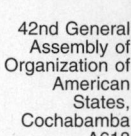

42nd General
Assembly of
Organization of
American
States,
Cochabamba
A618

2012, May 7 *Perf. 13¾x13½*

1494 A618 10b multi 5.50 3.00

World Internet
Day — A619

Designs: 1b, Map of Western Hemisphere, "@." 1.50b, Stylized globe, pointing finger icon. 3b, "@" and emblems of internet websites.

2012, May 17 **Litho.**

1495-1497 A619 Set of 3 3.50 2.50

Heroic
Resistance of
Cochabamba
Women,
Bicent. — A620

2012, May 22 *Perf. 13¾x13½*

1498 A620 1.50b multi 1.00 .75

Domesticated Animals — A621

Designs: 50c, Chickens (gallina). 1b, Burro. 3b, Sheep (oveja). 5b, Rabbit (conejo).

2012, May 28 *Perf. 13½x13¾*

1499-1502 A621 Set of 4 6.00 4.00

Dinosaurs and Their Tracks — A622

Designs: 50c, Theropod. 1.50b, Ankylosaurus. 3b, Sauropod. 5b, Stegosaurus.

2012, June 8 **Litho.**

1503-1506 A622 Set of 4 7.00 3.75

Emblem
of the
Attorney
General
A623

2012, June 25

1507 A623 3.50b multi 2.25 1.50

Minerals
A624

Designs: 1b, Andorite. 1.50b, Bismuthinite. 2b, Amethyst. 5b, Cassiterite.

2012, July 11

1508-1511 A624 Set of 4 6.25 3.75

Folk
Dances — A625

Designs: 50c, Ch'utas. 1b, Llamerada. 1.50b, Kullawada. 2b, Caporales. 10b, Morenada.

2012, July 24 *Perf. 13¾x13½*

1512-1516 A625 Set of 5 10.00 6.00

See Nos. 1569-1572.

Television
Show "La
Bicicleta
de los
Huanca,"
25th
Anniv.
A626

2012, Aug. 17 *Perf. 13½x13¾*

1517 A626 4b multi 2.50 1.75

Bolivian
Dishes
A627

Designs: 50c, Locro de Gallina. 1b, Mondongo. 1.50b, K'ala Phurka. 5b, Charquekan.

2012, Sept. 18

1518-1521 A627 Set of 4 5.25 3.25

Orchids
A628

Designs: 50c, Vasqueziella boliviana. 1.50b, Masdevallia yungasensis. 3b, Cattleya rex. 5b, Restrepia vasquezii.

2012, Sept. 19

1522-1525 A628 Set of 4 6.50 4.00

Congressional Library, Cent. — A629

2012, Sept. 21
1526 A629 3.50b multi 2.25 1.50

Decolonization Day — A630

Designs: 1b, Mother Earth and alignment of planets (end of Mayan calendar cycle). 1.50b, 1492 discovery of America by Christopher Columbus, vert. 2.50b, Amazonian collective marriage ceremony, vert.

Perf. 13½x13¾, 13¾x13½
2012, Oct. 6
1527-1529 A630 Set of 3 3.50 2.00

America Issue — A631

Myths and legends: 1b, La Palliri. 5b, El amor maldito transformalo en culebra (Cursed love transformed into a snake).

2012, Oct. 12 ***Perf. 13¾x13½***
1530-1531 A631 Set of 2 4.00 2.50

Intl. Year of Sustainable Energy For All — A632

Emblem and: 1b, Christ of Peace statue, Cochabamba, wind generators, power lines. 3.50b, Mountain, solar panels.

2012, Oct. 25 **Litho.**
1532-1533 A632 Set of 2 3.00 2.00

Leaders of 1781 Siege of La Paz A633

Designs: 50c, Tupac Katari (c. 1750-81), and torture of prisoner. 1.50b, Micaela Bastidas (1745-81), Bartolina Sisa (c. 1750-82), wife of Katari, vert. 3b, Katari and Sisa.

Perf. 13½x13¾, 13¾x13½
2012, Oct.
1534-1536 A633 Set of 3 3.50 2.00

Mentisan Ointment, 75th Anniv. A634

2012, Nov. 6 ***Perf. 13½x13¾***
1537 A634 30b multi 20.00 12.50

Christmas A635

Children's art: 1.50b, Bolivians and Holy Family, by Wara Bascopé Céspedes. 2.50b, Christmas tree, by Stefany Gissell Robles.

2012, Nov. 12 ***Perf. 13¾x13½***
1538-1539 A635 Set of 2 2.75 1.75

Avelino Siñani - Elizardo Pérez Education Law, 2nd Anniv. A636

2012, Dec. 14 ***Perf. 11¼x11***
1540 A636 2.50b multi 1.60 1.00

Quinoa Cultivation A637

Quinoa seeds and: 1b, Chenopodium quinoa plants. 3.50b, Quinoa harvesters, horiz. 4b, Quinoa plants in field, horiz.

Perf. 13¾x13½, 13½x13¾
2012, Dec. 18
1541-1543 A637 Set of 3 5.50 3.25

Bolivian Private Enterprise Confederation, 50th Anniv. — A638

2012, Dec. 19 Litho. ***Perf. 11x11½***
1544 A638 4b multi 2.60 1.25

Fruit Type of 2011 and

Oranges (Different Type Font) — A638a

2012-13 Litho. ***Perf. 13½x13¾***
1544A A638a 1.50b multi, dated "2012" — —

Size: 34x27mm
Dated "2013"
Perf. 11¼x11
1544B A598 1.50b multi — —

Intl. Day Against Corruption A639

Emblem and: 2b, Man, flag of Bolivia. 3b, Pres. Evo Morales, man, horiz.

Perf. 11x11½, 11½x11
2013, Feb. 27 **Litho.**
1545-1546 A639 Set of 2 3.00 1.50

World Health Day — A640

2013, Apr. 9 Litho. ***Perf. 13¾x13½***
1547 A640 20b multi 12.00 5.75

Bolivian Institute of High Altitude Biology, 50th Anniv. — A641

2013, Apr. 13 Litho. ***Perf. 13¾x13½***
1548 A641 9b multi 6.00 2.60

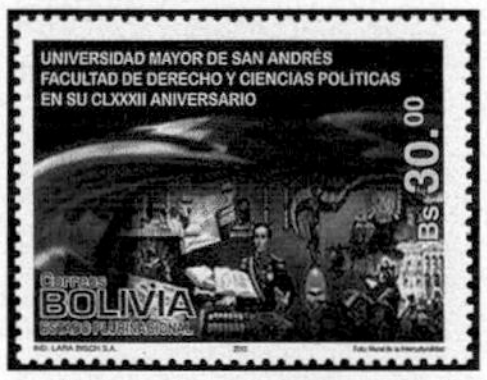

Higher University of San Andrés Law and Political Science Faculty, 182nd Anniv. A642

2013, Apr. 29 Litho. ***Perf. 13½x13¾***
1549 A642 30b multi 20.00 8.75

Oruro Carnaval, Cent. — A643

Designs: 1b, Tobas Fraternity Central Zone costumes. 1.50b, Hijos del Sol Fraternity Inca costumes. 10.50b, Morenada Folklore Team Northern Zone costumes. 12b, Diablada Oruro costumes.

2013, May 17 Litho. ***Perf. 13¾x13½***
1550-1553 A643 Set of 4 15.00 7.25
1552A A643 10.50b As No. 1552 with red Agencia Boliviana de Correos handstamp ('18) — —

Special Anti-Drug Trafficking Police Force, 25th Anniv. A644

2013, May 20 Litho. ***Perf. 13½x13¾***
1554 A644 100b multi 29.00 29.00

Public University of El Alto, 13th Anniv. — A645

2013, May 29 Litho. ***Perf. 13¾x13½***
1555 A645 4b multi 1.25 1.25

World Environment Day — A646

2013, July 9 Litho. ***Perf. 13¾x13½***
1556 A646 15b multi 4.50 4.50

Endangered Animals — A647

Designs: 50c, Hippocamelus antisensis. 1b, Lonchorhina aurita. 9b, Nymphargus pluvialis, horiz. 10.50b, Vultur gryphus, horiz.

Perf. 13¾x13½, 13½x13¾
2013, July 9 **Litho.**
1557-1560 A647 Set of 4 6.25 6.25

Endangered Flora — A648

Designs: 1.50b, Cedrela angustifolia. 2.50b, Parajubaea sunkha. 3b, Trichocereus atacamensis. 10.50b, Azorella compacta.

2013, July 9 Litho. ***Perf. 13½x13¾***
1561-1564 A648 Set of 4 5.25 5.25
1564A A648 10.50b As No. 1564, with red Agencia Boliviana de Correos handstamp ('18) — —

See note after Nos. 1268-1270.

San Ignacio College, La Paz, 50th Anniv. A649

2013, July 25 Litho. ***Perf. 13½x13¾***
1565 A649 4b multi 1.25 1.25

Torotoro Conservation Association, 25th Anniv. — A650

2013, Sept. 6 Litho. ***Perf. 13¾x13½***
1566 A650 1.50b multi .45 .45

Bolivian Migrants A651

Perf. 13½x13¾
2013, Sept. 19 Litho.
1567 A651 50b multi 14.50 14.50

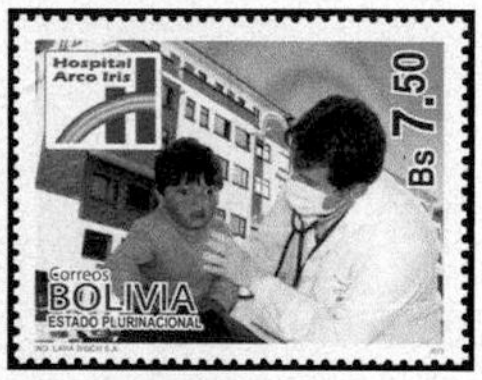

Doctor Examining Child, Arco Iris Hospital — A652

Perf. 13½x13¾
2013, Sept. 28 Litho.
1568 A652 7.50b multi 2.25 2.25

Folk Dances Type of 2012

Designs: 50c, Pujllay. 1.50b, Tinku. 2b, Waka Wakas. 7.50b, Diablada.

2013, Oct. 8 Litho. ***Perf. 13¾x13½***
1569-1572 A625 Set of 4 3.50 3.50

Water and Life — A653

2013, Oct. 14 Litho. ***Perf. 11¼x11***
Granite Paper
1573 A653 10.50b multi 3.00 3.00

Giovanni Boccaccio (1313-75), Writer — A654

2013, Oct. 25 Litho. ***Perf. 13¾x13½***
1574 A654 9b multi 2.60 2.60

Christmas — A655

Designs: 50c, Child holding Christmas gift, line of wagons carrying gifts. 9b, Child holding toy truck, gift distribution volunteers.

2013, Dec. 3 Litho. ***Perf. 13½x13¾***
1575-1576 A655 Set of 2 3.50 3.50

Campaign Against Discrimination — A656

America issue: 50c, Three men. 15b, Red apple and six green apples.

2013, Dec. 6 Litho. ***Perf. 13½x13¾***
1577-1578 A656 Set of 2 5.75 5.75

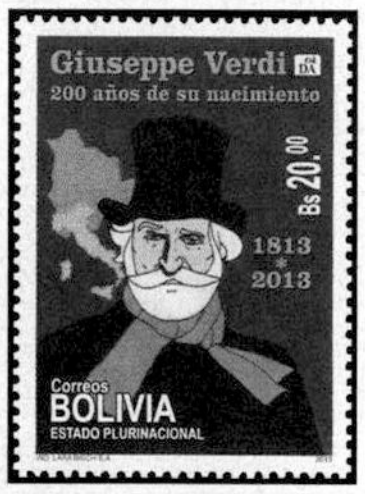

Giuseppe Verdi (1813-1901), Composer A657

Perf. 13¾x13½
2013, Dec. 13 Litho.
1579 A657 20b multi 7.00 7.00

Simón Bolívar (1783-1830), First President of Bolivia — A658

Bolívar and flag of Bolivia: 1.50b, 9b. No. 1581 is vert.

Perf. 13½x13¾, 13¾x13½
2013, Dec. 17 Litho.
1580-1581 A658 Set of 2 4.00 4.00

Tupac Katari Satellite A659

Designs: 1.50b, Pres. Evo Morales. 9b, Emblem of Bolivian Space Agency, vert.

Perf. 13½x13¾, 13¾x13½
2013, Dec. 18 Litho.
1582-1583 A659 Set of 2 4.00 4.00

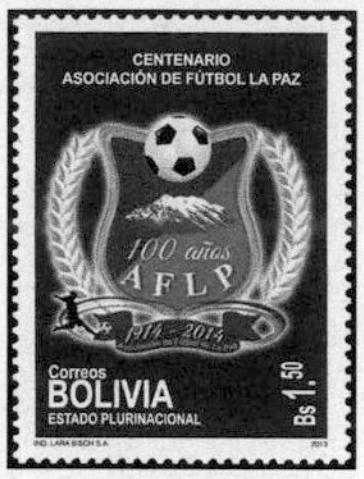

La Paz Soccer Association, Cent. — A660

2014, Jan. 8 Litho. ***Perf. 13¾x13½***
1584 A660 1.50b multi .45 .45

Dated 2013.

2014 Dakar Rally A661

Designs: 10b, Dakar Rally emblem, motorcyclist. 20b, Dakar Rally emblem, Salar de Uyuni, vert.

Perf. 13½x13¾, 13¾x13½
2014, Jan. 12 Litho.
1585-1586 A661 Set of 2 11.00 11.00

Dated 2013.

Map and Flag of Bolivia A662

2014, Feb. 1 Litho. ***Perf. 13½x14***
1587 A662 1.50b multi — —

Regulatory Authority for Telecommunications and Transportation decree No. 29799 concerning operation of express service, courier and mail delivery companies. Compare with illustration A678a.

Map and Flag of Bolivia Type of 2014

2018 Litho. ***Perf. 13½***
1587C A662 1.50b Dated "2015," as No. 1587 with red Agencia Boliviana de Correos handstamp ('18) — —

The editors would like to see any example of No. 1587C without the handstamp and if it exists, any example of No. 1587 with the handstamp.

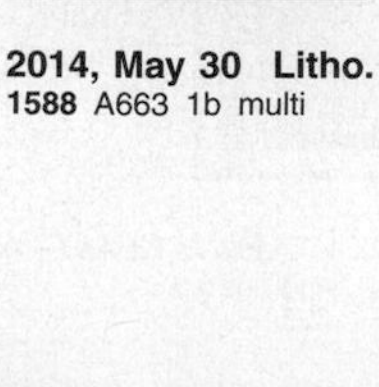

La Paz-El Alto Cable Car — A663

2014, May 30 Litho. ***Perf. 13¾x13½***
1588 A663 1b multi .30 .30

Bolivian Presidency of Group of 77 and China — A664

Perf. 13½x13¾
2014, June 12 Litho.
1589 A664 2b multi .60 .60

2014 World Cup Soccer Championships, Brazil — A665

Perf. 13¾x13½
2014, June 12 Litho.
1590 A665 5b multi 1.50 1.50

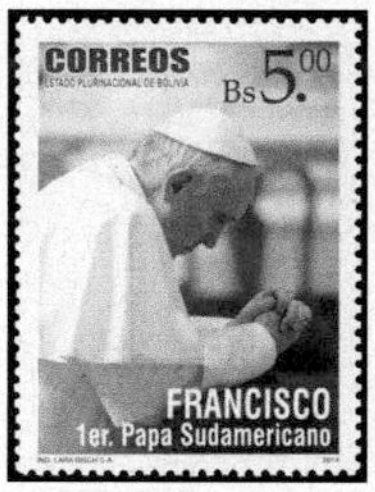

Pope Francis — A666

2014, July 3 Litho. ***Perf. 13¾x13½***
1591 A666 5b multi 1.50 1.50

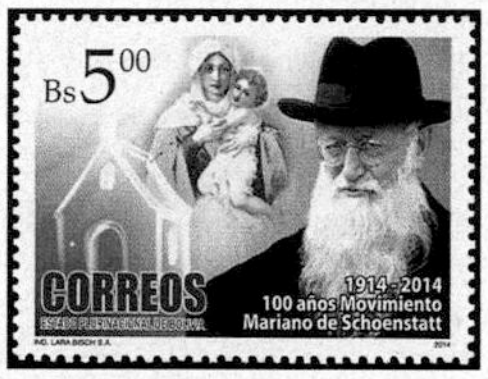

Father Joseph Kentenich (1885-1968), Founder of Schoenstatt Movement and Refuge of Sinners Madonna, by Luigi Crosio — A667

2014, July 6 Litho. ***Perf. 13½x13¾***
1592 A667 5b multi 1.50 1.50

Schoenstatt Movement, cent.

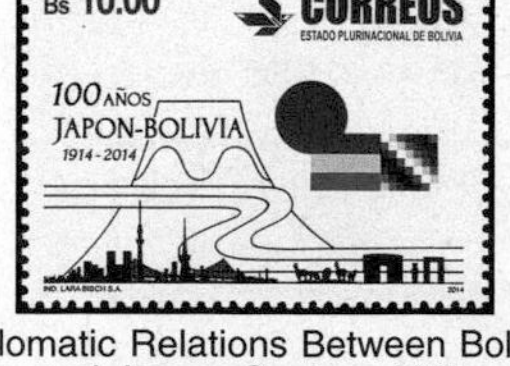

Diplomatic Relations Between Bolivia and Japan, Cent. — A668

2014, July 10 Litho. ***Perf. 13½x13¾***
1593 A668 10b multi 3.00 3.00

America Issue A669

Designs: 1b, Bolivian Pres. Evo Morales, Venezuelan Pres. Hugo Chávez (1954-2013). 25b, Chávez holding map, vert.

Perf. 13½x13¾, 13¾x13½

2014, July 28 **Litho.**

1594-1595 A669 Set of 2 9.00 9.00

Gunnar Mendoza Loza (1914-94), Historian A670

2014, Sept. 3 **Litho.** ***Perf. 13¾x13½***

1596 A670 4b multi 1.25 1.25

Mauricio Otazo, Conductor of National Symphony Orchestra A671

2014, Oct. 24 **Litho.** ***Perf. 13¾x13½***

1597 A671 15b multi 4.50 4.50

St. Francis of Assisi University, La Paz — A672

2014, Oct. 30 **Litho.** ***Perf. 13½x13¾***

1598 A672 2b multi .60 .60

Mountains — A673

No. 1599: a, Mt. Condoriri, mountain climber at left. b, Mt. Condoriri, mountain climber at right.

9b, Mt. Illampu and mountain climber. 23b, Mt. Huayna Potosí and mountain climber.

Perf. 13½x13¾

2014, Dec. 16 **Litho.**

1599 A673 2b Horiz. pair, #a-b 1.25 1.25
1600 A673 9b multi 2.75 2.75
1600A A673 9b As No. 1600, with red Agencia Boliviana de Correos handstamp ('18) — —
1601 A673 23b multi 7.25 7.25
Nos. 1599-1601 (4) 11.25 11.25

See note after Nos. 1268-1270.

Christmas A674

Perf. 13¾x13½

2014, Dec. 17 **Litho.**

1602 A674 15b multi 4.50 4.50

Galaxy and Telescope — A675

2014, Dec. 19 **Litho.** ***Perf. 11x11¼***

1603 A675 100b multi 30.00 30.00
1603A A675 100b As No. 1603, with red Agencia Boliviana de Correos handstamp ('18) — —

Galileo Galilei (1564-1642), astronomer. See note after Nos. 1268-1270.

2015 Dakar Rally — A676

2014, Dec. 31 **Litho.** ***Perf. 11¼x11***

1604 A676 7.50b multi 2.25 2.25

Bolivian Alliance for the Peoples of Our America and Peoples' Trade Agreement, 10th Anniv. — A677

Designs, 1b, Flags wrapped around map of South America. 12b, Flags to right of map of South America.

2015, Feb. 4 **Litho.** ***Perf. 13¾x13½***

1605-1606 A677 Set of 2 3.75 3.75
1606A A677 12b As No. 1606, with red Agencia Bolivi-ana de Corre-os handstamp ('18) — —

See note after Nos. 1268-1270.

Map and Flag of Bolivia — A678a

2018 **Litho.** ***Perf. 11½x11***

Granite Paper
With Red Agencia Boliviana de Correos Handstamp

1607A A678a 1.50b multi — —

Regulatory Authority for Telecommunications and Transportation decree No. 29799 concerning operation of express service, courier and mail delivery companies. Compare with illustration A662.

The editors would like to see any example of No. 1607A without the handstamp. See note after Nos. 1268-1270.

Carnival Dancers — A679

Designs: 1b, Cueca Chapaca. 2b, Llamerada. 2.50b, Tinku.

2015, Apr. 29 **Litho.** ***Perf. 13¾x13½***

1608-1610 A679 Set of 3 1.60 1.60

National Telecommunications Company (ENTEL), 50th Anniv. — A680

2015, Apr. 30 **Litho.** ***Perf. 13¾x13½***

1611 A680 4b multi 1.25 1.25

Endangered Animals — A681

Designs: 5.50b, Fulica cornuta. 9b, Dynastes satanas. 15b, Chaetophractus nationi. 50b, Harpia harpyja.

2015, May 16 **Litho.** ***Perf. 13¾x13½***

1612-1615 A681 Set of 4 23.00 23.00
1612A A681 5.50b As No. 1612, with red Agencia Boliviana de Correos handstamp ('18) — —
1615A A681 50b As No. 1615, with red Agencia Boliviana de Correos handstamp ('18) — —

See note after Nos. 1268-1270.

Diplomatic Relations Between Bolivia and South Korea, 50th Anniv. — A682

No. 1616: a, Mergus squamatus. b, Phibalura flavirostris.

Perf. 13½x13¾

2015, June 25 **Litho.**

1616 A682 2b Horiz. pair, #a-b 1.50 1.50

See South Korea No. 2443.

Visit to Bolivia of Pope Francis — A683

2015, July 2 **Litho.** ***Perf. 13¾x13½***

1617 A683 20b multi 5.75 5.75
1617A A683 20b As No. 1617, with red Agencia Bolivi-ana de Corre-os handstamp ('18) — —

See note after Nos. 1268-1270.

San José de la Recoleta Convent, 90th Anniv. — A684

2015, Aug. 1 **Litho.** ***Perf. 13¾x13½***

1618 A684 3b multi .90 .90

International Telecommunication Union, 150th Anniv. — A685

Perf. 13½x13¾

2015, Aug. 18 **Litho.**

1619 A685 10b multi 3.00 3.00
1619A A685 10b As No. 1619, with red Agencia Bolivi-ana de Corre-os handstamp ('18) — —

See note after Nos. 1268-1270.

La Paz Department Tourism — A686

No. 1620: a, 1b, Thatch house. b, 4b, Indigenous musicians.

Perf. 13½x13¾

2015, Sept. 24 **Litho.**

1620 A686 Horiz. pair, #a-b 1.50 1.50

Bolivia Post Corporation, 25th Anniv. — A687

2015, Oct. 15 **Litho.** ***Perf. 13¾x13½***

1621 A687 2b multi .60 .60

Comprehensive Law 263 Against Human Trafficking A688

2015, Oct. 22 **Litho.** ***Perf. 13¾x13½***

1622 A688 2b multi *.60 .60*

America Issue.

FEMCO, 50th Anniv. — A689

No. 1623 — Half of FEMCO 50th anniversary emblem and: a, Public lighting fixture. b, Shelving unit.

Perf. 13½x13¾

2015, Nov. 19 **Litho.**

1623 A689 2b Horiz. pair, #a-b *1.25 1.25*

Pres. Andrés de Santa Cruz y Calahumana (1792-1865) A690

Perf. 13¾x13½

2015, Nov. 27 **Litho.**

1624 A690 2b multi .60 .60

San Andrés University, 185th Anniv. — A691

Perf. 13½x13¾

2015, Nov. 27 **Litho.**

1625 A691 3b multi .90 .90

Fe y Alegría Foundation in Bolivia, 50th Anniv. — A692

Perf. 13½x13¾

2016, Aug. 16 **Litho.**

1626 A692 100b multi 29.00 29.00

1626A A692 100b As No. 1626, with red Agencia Boliviana de Correos handstamp ('18) — —

See note after Nos. 1268-1270.

Tourism A693

Designs: 2b, Lake Titicaca. 5b, Tower of David rock formation, vert. 15b, Milluni Peak. 20b, Cinti Canyon.

Perf. 13½x13¾, 13¾x13½

2016, Aug. 16 **Litho.**

1627-1630 A693 Set of 4 *12.50 12.50*

Bolivian Cuisine A694

Designs: 3b, Guiso de cumanda. 4b, Majao. 5b, Chairo, vert. 7.50b, Sillp'ancho. 10b, Map of Bolivia's four gastronomic regions, vert.

Perf. 13½x13¾, 13¾x13½

2016, Oct. 15 **Litho.**

1631-1635 A694 Set of 5 8.75 8.75

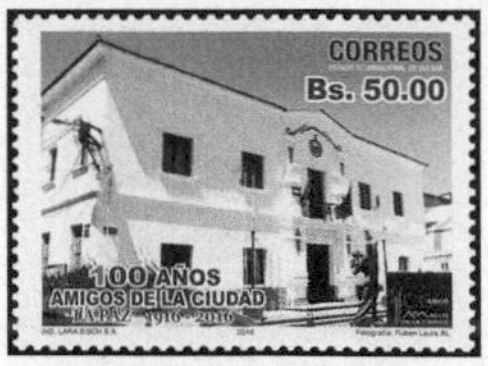

Friends of the City Organization, La Paz, Cent. — A695

2016, Oct. 17 **Litho.** *Perf. 13½x13¾*

1636 A695 50b multi 14.50 14.50

1636A A695 50b As No. 1636, with red Agencia Boliviana de Correos handstamp ('18) — —

See note after Nos. 1268-1270.

Festival of the Santísima Trinidad del Señor Jesús de Gran Poder, La Paz — A696

2016, Dec. 2 **Litho.** *Perf. 13¾x13½*

1637 A696 2b multi *.60 .60*

Christmas A697

Stripes in colors of national flag, stars and: 2b, Map of Bolivia and stylized Christmas tree. 15b, Stylized people and globe.

Perf. 13½x13¾

2016, Dec. 23 **Litho.**

1638-1639 A697 Set of 2 *5.00 5.00*

1639A A697 15b As No. 1639, with red Agencia Boliviana de Correos handstamp ('18) — —

See note after Nos. 1268-1270.

Silala Springs — A698

Designs: 14b, Spring. 18b, Animals near spring, horiz.

Perf. 13¾x13½, 13½x13¾

2016, Dec. 29 **Litho.**

1640-1641 A698 Set of 2 9.50 9.50

1640A A698 14b As No. 1640, with red Agencia Boliviana de Correos handstamp ('18) — —

1641A A698 18b As No. 1641, with red Agencia Boliviana de Correos handstamp ('18) — —

See note after Nos. 1268-1270.

International Court of Justice's 2015 Decision on Bolivia's Claim for Sea Access — A699

2017, Feb. 8 **Litho.** *Perf. 13½x13¾*

1642 A699 1b multi .30 .30

Dated 2016.

Philatelists José Barrientos and Martha V. de Peredo — A700

Perf. 13½x13¾

2017, Aug. 20 **Litho.**

1643 A700 2b multi — —

1643A A700 2b As No. 1643, with red Agencia Boliviana de Correos handstamp ('18) — —

See note after Nos. 1268-1270.

First Bolivian Postage Stamps, 150th Anniv. A701

2017, Oct. 18 **Litho.** *Perf. 13½x13¾*

1644 A701 5b multi — —

1644A A701 5b As No. 1644, with red Agencia Boliviana de Correos handstamp ('18) — —

See note after Nos. 1268-1270.

Phibalura Boliviana A702

Pauxi Unicornis A703

2017, Oct. 18 **Litho.** *Perf. 13¾x13½*

1645 A702 50c multi — —

1645A A702 50c As No. 1645, with red Agencia Boliviana de Correos handstamp ('18) — —

Perf. 13½x13¾

1646 A703 3b multi — —

1646A A703 3b As No. 1646, with red Agencia Boliviana de Correos handstamp ('18) — —

Endangered birds. See note after Nos. 1268-1270.

Goyi Educational Supplement, 50th Anniv. — A704

2017, Oct. 27 **Litho.** *Perf. 13¾x13½*

1647 A704 4b multi — —

1647A A704 4b As No. 1647, with red Agencia Boliviana de Correos handstamp ('18) — —

See note after Nos. 1268-1270.

Símon Bolívar Teacher's Training School, Cent. — A705

2017, Nov. 8 **Litho.** *Perf. 13¾x13½*

1648 A705 10b multi — —

1648A A705 10b As No. 1648, with red Agencia Boliviana de Correos handstamp ('18) — —

See note after Nos. 1268-1270.

Battle of La Tablada de Tolomosa, 200th Anniv. — A706

2017, Nov. 9 **Litho.** *Perf. 13½x13¾*

1649 A706 20b multi — —

1649A A706 20b As No. 1649, with red Agencia Boliviana de Correos handstamp ('18) — —

See note after Nos. 1268-1270.

AIR POST STAMPS

Aviation School
AP1 AP2

1924, Dec. **Unwmk.** **Engr.** *Perf. 14*

C1	AP1	10c ver & blk	1.00	.50
a.		Inverted center	*3,250.*	
C2	AP1	15c carmine & blk	2.00	2.00
C3	AP1	25c dk bl & blk	1.50	1.00
C4	AP1	50c orange & blk	10.00	5.00
C5	AP2	1b red brn & blk	3.00	3.00

C6 AP2 2b blk brn & blk 20.00 10.00
C7 AP2 5b dk vio & blk 25.00 20.00
Nos. C1-C7 (7) 62.50 41.50

Natl. Aviation School establishment.

These stamps were available for ordinary postage. Nos. C1, C3, C5 and C6 exist imperforate. Value, $400. each pair.

Proofs of the 2b with inverted center exist imperforate and privately perforated. Value, *$2,750.*

For overprints and surcharges see Nos. C11-C23, C56-C58.

Emblem of Lloyd Aéreo Boliviano AP3

1928 **Litho.** ***Perf. 11***
C8 AP3 15c green 2.50 1.50
a. Imperf., pair 70.00 60.00
C9 AP3 20c dark blue 4.00 3.25
C10 AP3 35c red brown 3.25 2.50
Nos. C8-C10 (3) 9.75 7.25

No. C8 exists imperf. between. Value, $60 pair.

For surcharges see Nos. C24-C26, C53-C55.

Graf Zeppelin Issues

Nos. C1-C5 Surcharged or Overprinted in Various Colors

Nos. C11, C19

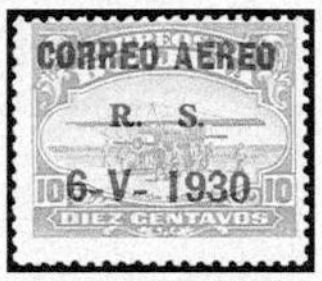

Nos. C12-C18, C20-C23

1930, May 6 ***Perf. 14***
C11 AP1 5c on 10c ver & blk (G) 20.00 20.00
C12 AP1 10c ver & blk (Bl) 20.00 20.00
C13 AP1 10c ver & blk (Brn) *2,500.* *2,500.*
C14 AP1 15c car & blk (V) 20.00 20.00
C15 AP1 25c dk bl & blk (R) 20.00 20.00
C16 AP1 50c org & blk (Brn) 20.00 20.00
C17 AP1 50c org & blk (R) *1,000.* *1,000.*
C18 AP2 1b red brn & blk (gold) 350.00 350.00

Experts consider the 50c with gold or silver overprint and 5c with black to be trial color proofs.

Nos. C11-C18 exist with the surcharges inverted, double, or double with one inverted, but the regularity of these varieties is questioned.

See notes following No. C23.

Surcharged or Overprinted in Bronze Inks of Various Colors

C19 AP1 5c on 10c ver & blk (G) 120.00 *150.00*
a. Inverted surcharge 200.00 —
C20 AP1 10c ver & blk (Bl) 100.00 *150.00*
a. Inverted surcharge 175.00 —
C21 AP1 15c car & blk (V) 100.00 *150.00*
a. Inverted surcharge 175.00 —
C22 AP1 25c dk bl & blk (cop) 100.00 *150.00*
a. Inverted surcharge 175.00 —
C23 AP2 1b red brn & blk (gold) *700.00* *900.00*
a. Inverted surcharge 1,300. —
Nos. C19-C23 (5) 1,120. *1,500.*

Flight of the airship Graf Zeppelin from Europe to Brazil and return via Lakehurst, NJ.

Nos. C19 to C23 were intended for use on postal matter forwarded by the Graf Zeppelin.

No. C18 was overprinted with light gold or gilt bronze ink. No. C23 was overprinted with deep gold bronze ink. Nos. C13 and C17 were overprinted with trial colors but were sold with the regular printings. The 5c on 10c is known surcharged in black and in blue.

No. C8-C10 Surcharged

1930, May 6 ***Perf. 11***
C24 AP3 1.50b on 15c 80.00 80.00
a. Inverted surcharge 300.00 300.00
b. Comma instead of period after "1" 100.00 100.00
C25 AP3 3b on 20c 80.00 80.00
a. Inverted surcharge 350.00 350.00
b. Comma instead of period after "3" 125.00 125.00
C26 AP3 6b on 35c *80.00* *80.00*
a. Inverted surcharge 375.00 375.00
b. Comma instead of period after "6" 125.00 125.00
Nos. C24-C26 (3) 240.00 240.00

Airplane and Bullock Cart — AP6

Airplane and River Boat — AP7

1930, July 24 **Litho.** ***Perf. 14***
C27 AP6 5c dp violet 1.50 1.10
C28 AP7 15c red 1.50 1.10
C29 AP7 20c yellow 1.10 .90
C30 AP6 35c yellow grn 1.00 .75
C31 AP7 50c deep blue 2.50 1.50
C32 AP6 1b lt brown 3.50 1.75
C33 AP7 2b deep rose 4.50 2.50
C34 AP6 3b slate 8.00 6.00
Nos. C27-C34 (8) 23.60 15.60

Nos. C27 to C34 exist imperforate. Value, $60 each pair.

For surcharge see No. C52.

Air Service Emblem AP8

1932, Sept. 16 ***Perf. 11***
C35 AP8 5c ultra 3.25 2.40
C36 AP8 10c gray 2.00 1.50
C37 AP8 15c dark rose 2.00 1.50
C38 AP8 25c orange 2.00 1.50
C39 AP8 30c green 1.25 .80
C40 AP8 50c violet 3.25 2.50
C41 AP8 1b dk brown 3.25 2.50
Nos. C35-C41 (7) 17.00 12.70

Map of Bolivia — AP9

1935, Feb. 1 **Engr.** ***Perf. 12***
C42 AP9 5c brown red .30 .30
C43 AP9 10c dk green .30 .30
C44 AP9 20c dk violet .30 .30
C45 AP9 30c ultra .30 .30
C46 AP9 50c orange .50 .50
C47 AP9 1b bister brn .50 .50
C48 AP9 1½b yellow 1.25 .75
C49 AP9 2b carmine 1.25 1.00
C50 AP9 5b green 1.50 1.25
C51 AP9 10b dk brown 5.00 1.75
Nos. C42-C51 (10) 11.20 6.95

Nos. C1, C4, C10, C30 Srchd. in Red (#C52-C56) or Green (#C57-C58) — c

1937, Oct. 6 ***Perf. 11, 14***
C52 AP6 5c on 35c yel grn .50 .40
a. "Carreo" 30.00 30.00
b. Inverted surcharge 20.00
C53 AP3 20c on 35c red brn .75 .60
a. Inverted surcharge 20.00 20.00
C54 AP3 50c on 35c red brn 1.50 1.00
a. Inverted surcharge 50.00 50.00
C55 AP3 1b on 35c red brn 2.00 1.50
a. Inverted surcharge 25.00 20.00
C56 AP1 2b on 50c org & blk 2.50 2.00
a. Inverted surcharge 20.00 15.00
C57 AP1 12b on 10c ver & blk 15.00 10.00
a. Inverted surcharge 75.00 50.00
C58 AP1 15b on 10c ver & blk 15.00 10.00
a. Inverted surcharge 75.00 30.00

Regular Postage Stamps of 1925 Surcharged in Green or Red — d

Perf. 14
C59 A56 (d) 3b on 50c dp vio (G) 5.00 5.00
C60 A56 (d) 4b on 1b red (G) 5.00 5.00
C61 A57 (c) 5b on 2b org (G) 6.00 6.00
a. Double surcharge 175.00
C62 A56 (d) 10b on 5b blk brn 8.50 7.00
a. Double surcharge 50.00
Nos. C52-C62 (11) 61.75 48.50

No. C59-C62 exist with inverted surcharge, No. C62a with black and black and red surcharges.

Courtyard of Potosi Mint — AP10

Miner — AP11

Emancipated Woman AP12

Pincers, Torch and Good Will Principles AP15

Airplane over Field AP13

Airplanes and Liberty Monument AP14

Airplane over River AP16

Emblem of New Government AP17

Transport Planes over Map of Bolivia AP18

1938, May **Litho.** ***Perf. 10½***
C63 AP10 20c deep rose .60 .30
C64 AP11 30c gray .60 .30
C65 AP12 40c yellow .70 .40
C66 AP13 50c yellow grn .60 .30
C67 AP14 60c dull blue .75 .40
C68 AP15 1b dull red .75 .40
C69 AP16 2b bister 1.50 .50
C70 AP17 3b lt brown 2.25 1.00
C71 AP18 5b dk violet 3.00 1.00
Nos. C63-C71 (9) 10.75 4.60

40c, 1b, 2b exist imperf.

Chalice — AP19

Virgin of Copacabana AP20

Jesus Christ — AP21

Church of San Francisco, La Paz AP22

St. Anthony of Padua — AP23

1939, July 19 **Litho.** ***Perf. 13½, 10½***
C72 AP19 5c dull violet .75 .50
a. Pair, imperf. between 80.00
C73 AP20 30c lt bl grn 1.00 .50
C74 AP21 45c violet bl 1.00 .50
a. Vertical pair, imperf. between 90.00
C75 AP22 60c carmine 1.50 .75
C76 AP23 75c vermilion 1.50 1.25
C77 AP23 90c deep blue 1.50 .60
C78 AP22 2b dull brown 2.50 .50
C79 AP21 4b deep plum 3.00 1.00
C80 AP20 5b lt blue 7.00 .80
C81 AP19 10b yellow 12.00 1.25
Nos. C72-C81 (10) 31.75 7.65

2nd National Eucharistic Congress.

For surcharge see No. C112.

Plane over Lake Titicaca — AP24

Mt. Illimani and Condor — AP25

1941, Aug. 21 *Perf. 13½*

C82 AP24 10b dull green 15.00 2.00
C83 AP24 20b light ultra 7.00 2.50
C84 AP25 50b rose lilac 15.00 5.00
C85 AP25 100b olive bister 25.00 8.00
Nos. C82-C85 (4) 62.00 17.50

Counterfeits exist.

A souvenir sheet containing Nos. C84 and 356, perforated 13¼ and 14¼ respectively, was issued Dec. 16, 1987, to mark the 1988 Calgary Winter Olympic Games. Value $20.

Liberty and Clasped Hands — AP26

1942, Nov. 12

C86 AP26 40c rose lake .50 .50
C87 AP26 50c ultra .50 .50
C88 AP26 1b orange brn 1.50 .75
C89 AP26 5b magenta 2.00 .60
  a. Double impression 90.00
C90 AP26 10b dull brn vio 6.50 3.50
Nos. C86-C90 (5) 11.00 5.85

Conference of Chancellors, Jan. 15, 1942.

Ballivián Type of Regular Issue

General José Ballivián; old and modern transportation.

1943, Nov. 18 Engr. *Perf. 12½*

C91 A114 10c rose vio & brn .30 .25
C92 A114 20c emerald & brn .30 .25
C93 A114 30c rose car & brn .30 .25
C94 A114 3b blue & brn .75 .40
C95 A114 5b black & brn 1.00 .75
Nos. C91-C95 (5) 2.65 1.90

Condor and Sun Rising — AP28

Plane — AP29

1944, Sept. 19 Litho. *Perf. 13½*

C96 AP28 40c red violet .25 .25
C97 AP28 1b blue violet .30 .25
C98 AP29 1.50b yellow green .30 .25
C99 AP29 2.50b dk gray blue .50 .25
Nos. C96-C99 (4) 1.35 1.00

Revolution of Dec. 20, 1943.

Map of Natl. Airways — AP30

1945, May 31 *Perf. 11*

C100 AP30 10c red .30 .25
  a. Imperf., pair 25.00
C101 AP30 50c yellow .30 .25
  a. Imperf., pair 30.00
C102 AP30 90c lt green .40 .30
  a. Imperf., pair 30.00
C103 AP30 5b lt ultra 1.00 .50
C104 AP30 20b deep brown 2.00 1.00
Nos. C100-C104 (5) 4.00 2.30

10th anniversary of first flight, La Paz to Tacna, Peru, by Panagra Airways.

For surcharges see Nos. C128-C129.

Map of Bolivian Air Lines — AP31

1945, Sept. 15 *Perf. 13½*

Centers in Red and Blue

C105 AP31 20c violet .25 .25
C106 AP31 30c orange brn .25 .25
C107 AP31 50c brt blue grn .25 .25
C108 AP31 90c brt violet .25 .25
C109 AP31 2b blue .40 .25
C110 AP31 3b magenta .50 .25
C111 AP31 4b olive bister .90 .50
Nos. C105-C111 (7) 2.80 2.00

Founding of Lloyd Aéreo Boliviano, 20th anniv.

Catalogue values for unused stamps in this section, from this point to the end of the section, are for Never Hinged items.

No. C76 Surcharged in Blue

1947, Mar. 23

C112 AP23 1.40b on 75c ver .35 .25

Mt. Illimani — AP32

1947, Sept. 15 Litho. *Perf. 11½*

C113 AP32 1b rose car .25 .25
C114 AP32 1.40b emerald .25 .25
  a. Imperf, pair 20.00
C115 AP32 2.50b blue .25 .25
  a. Imperf, pair 20.00
C116 AP32 3b dp orange .30 .25
C117 AP32 4b rose lilac .25 .25
Nos. C113-C117 (5) 1.30 1.25

1st anniv. of the Revolution of July 21, 1946.

For surcharge see No. C137.

Bolivia/Argentina Arms Type

1947, Oct. 23 *Perf. 13½*

C118 A119 2.90b ultra .45 .35
  a. Imperf., pair 30.00
  b. Perf. 10½ 7.50 6.00

Statue of Christ Type

Designs: 2.50b, Statue of Christ above La Paz. 3.70b, Child kneeling before cross. No. C121, St. John Bosco. No. C122, Virgin of Copacabana. 13.60b, Pope Plus XII blessing University of La Paz.

1948, Sept. 26 *Perf. 11½*

C119 A120 2.50b ver & yellow .80 .35
C120 A120 3.70b rose & cream 1.00 .50
C121 A120 4b rose lil & gray 1.25 .35
C122 A120 4b lt ultra & sal 1.50 .35
C123 A120 13.60b ultra & lt grn 1.25 .35
Nos. C119-C123 (5) 5.80 1.90

Bolivia Auto Club Type

1948, Oct.

C124 A125 10b emerald & salmon 4.00 .35

Pacheco Type of Regular Issue

1950, Jan. 2 Unwmk.

C125 A126 1.40b orange brown .35 .25
C126 A126 2.50b orange .40 .25
C127 A126 3.30b rose violet .35 .25
Nos. C125-C127 (3) 1.10 .75

75th anniv. of the UPU.

No. C126 exists imperf. Value, pair $25.

Nos. C100 and C104 Surcharged in Black

1950, May 31 *Perf. 11*

C128 AP30 4b on 10c red .25 .25
  a. Inverted surcharge 35.00 35.00
C129 AP30 10b on 20b dp brn .50 .40
  a. Inverted surcharge 35.00 35.00

Panagra air services in Bolivia, 15th anniv.

L. A. B. Plane — AP35

1950, Sept. 15 Litho. *Perf. 13½*

C130 AP35 20c red orange .25 .25
C131 AP35 30c purple .25 .25
C132 AP35 50c green .25 .25
C133 AP35 1b orange .25 .25
C134 AP35 3b ultra .25 .25
C135 AP35 15b carmine .60 .50
C136 AP35 50b chocolate 1.50 1.00
Nos. C130-C136 (7) 3.35 2.75

25th anniv. of the founding of Lloyd Aero Boliviano. 30c, 50c, 15b exist imperforate.

No. C132 exists without imprint at bottom of stamp.

No. C116 Surcharged in Black

1950, Sept. 24 *Perf. 11½*

C137 AP32 1.40b on 3b dp org .30 .25

1st anniv. of the ending of the Civil War of Aug. 24-Sept. 24, 1949.

Exists with inverted and double surcharge.

UN Type of Regular Issue

1950, Oct. 24 Unwmk.

C138 A128 3.60b crimson rose 1.00 .25
C139 A128 4.70b black brown 2.00 .35

La Paz Type of Regular Issue

20c, Gate of the Sun and llama. 30c, Church of Old San Francisco. 40c, Avenue Camacho. 50c, Consistorial Palace. 1b, Legislative Palace. 2b, Communications Bldg. 3b, Arms. 4b, La Gasca ordering Mendoza to found La Paz. 5b, Capt. Alonso de Mendoza founding La Paz. 10b, Arms; portrait of Mendoza.

1951, Mar. 1 Engr. *Perf. 12½*

Center in Black

C140 A129 20c carmine .25 .25
C141 A130 30c dk vio bl .25 .25
C142 A129 40c dark blue .25 .25
C143 A129 50c blue green .30 .30
C144 A129 1b red .50 .30
C145 A129 2b red orange .70 .60
C146 A129 3b deep blue .70 .60
C147 A129 4b vermilion .80 .75
  a. Souvenir sheet of 4 3.00 3.00
  b. As "a," imperf. 3.00 3.00
C148 A129 5b dark green .80 .75
  a. Souvenir sheet of 3 3.00 3.00
  b. As "a," imperf. 3.00 3.00
C149 A129 10b red brown 1.50 1.75
  a. Souvenir sheet of 3 3.00 3.00
  b. As "a," imperf. 3.00 3.00
Nos. C140-C149 (10) 6.05 5.80

Nos. C147a-C147b contain #C143-C145, C147; Nos. C148a-C148b contain #C142, C146, C148; Nos. C149a-C149b contain #C140, C141, C149.

For surcharges see Nos. C187-C196.

Athletic Type of Regular Issue

20c, Horsemanship. 30c, Basketball. 50c, Fencing. 1b, Hurdling. 2.50b, Javelin throwing. 3b, Relay race. 5b, La Paz stadium.

1951, Aug. 23 Unwmk.

Center in Black

C150 A131 20c purple .60 .25
C151 A131 30c rose vio 1.00 .25
C152 A131 50c dp red org 1.10 .25
C153 A131 1b chocolate 1.10 .25
C154 A131 2.50b orange 2.25 .55
C155 A131 3b black brn 4.00 2.00
  a. Souv. sheet, #C153-C155 10.00 10.00
  b. As "a," imperf. 10.00 10.00
C156 A131 5b red 6.00 3.00
  a. Souv. sheet of 4, #C150-C152, C156 17.50 17.50
  b. As "a," imperf. 17.50 17.50
Nos. C150-C156 (7) 16.05 6.55

Eduardo Abaroa Type

1952, Mar. 24 Litho. *Perf. 11*

C157 A133 70c rose red .25 .25
C158 A133 2b orange yel .45 .25
C159 A133 3b yellow green .25 .25
C160 A133 5b blue 1.00 .50
C161 A133 50b rose lilac 1.50 .60
C162 A133 100b gray black 3.00 1.25
  a. Perf. 14 60.00 30.00
Nos. C157-C162 (6) 6.45 3.10

Queen Isabella I Type

1952, July 16 *Perf. 13½*

C163 A134 50b emerald .75 .25
C164 A134 100b brown 1.50 .35

Nos. C163-C164 exist imperforate. Value, $40 each pair.

An imperforate 500,000b souvenir sheet depicting No. C164 with simulated perforations was issued Dec. 31, 1985, to mark the 500th anniv. of the discovery of America. Value $20.

Columbus Lighthouse Type

1952, July 16

C165 A135 2b rose lil, *sal* .25 .25
C166 A135 3.70b blue grn, *bl* .25 .25
C167 A135 4.40b orange, *salmon* .25 .25
C168 A135 20b dk brn, *cream* .60 .25
Nos. C165-C168 (4) 1.35 1.00

No. C168 exists imperforate. Value, $60 pair.

Revolution Type and

Soldiers — AP43

Perf. 13½ (AP43), 11½ (A137)

1953, Apr. 9 Litho.

C169 A137 3.70b chocolate .75 .75
C170 AP43 6b red violet .30 .25
C171 A137 9b brown rose .30 .25
C172 A137 10b aqua .30 .25
C173 A137 16b vermilion .30 .30
C174 AP43 22.50b dk brown 1.00 .60
C175 A137 40b gray .60 .30
Nos. C169-C175 (7) 3.55 2.70

Nos. C169-C170 and C174 exist imperf. Value, $40 each pair.

Map and Peasant Type and

Pres. Victor Paz Estenssoro Embracing Indian — AP45

1954, Aug. 2 *Perf. 12x11½*

C176 AP45 20b orange brn .30 .25
C177 A138 27b brt pink .25 .25
C178 A138 30b red org .30 .25
C179 A138 45b violet brn .50 .25

C180 AP45 100b blue grn 1.00 .25
C181 A138 300b yellow grn 2.00 .30
Nos. C176-C181 (6) 4.35 1.55

AP45 for 3rd Inter-American Indian Cong. A138 agrarian reform laws of 1953-54.
Nos. C176-C180 exist imperf. Value, $25 each pair.
For surcharge see No. C261.

Oil Derricks — AP47

1955, Oct. 9 *Perf. 10½*
C182 AP47 55b dk & lt grnsh bl .35 .25
C183 AP47 70b dk gray & gray .60 .25
C184 AP47 90b dk & lt grn .90 .25
Perf. 13
C185 AP47 500b red lilac 3.00 .75
C186 AP47 1000b blk brn & fawn 5.00 1.50
Nos. C182-C186 (5) 9.85 3.00

For surcharge see No. C262.

Nos. C140-C149 Surcharged in Black or Carmine

1957 **Engr.** *Perf. 12½*
Center in Black
C187 A129 100b on 3b (C) .25 .25
C188 A129 200b on 2b .25 .25
C189 A129 500b on 4b .30 .25
C190 A129 600b on 1b .30 .25
C191 A129 700b on 20c .50 .25
C192 A129 800b on 40c (C) .60 .30
C193 A130 900b on 30c (C) .75 .25
C194 A129 1800b on 50c (C) 1.20 .50
C195 A129 3000b on 5b (C) 1.75 1.00
C196 A129 5000b on 10b (C) 3.00 2.00
Nos. C187-C196 (10) 8.90 5.30

See Nos. 393-402.

Map of South America and Bolivian National Arms — AP48

Unwmk.
1957, May 25 **Litho.** *Perf. 12*
C197 AP48 700b lilac & vio .55 .35
C198 AP48 1200b pale brn .85 .60
C199 AP48 1350b rose car 1.00 .60
C200 AP48 2700b blue grn 2.00 .75
C201 AP48 4000b violet bl 3.50 1.25
Nos. C197-C201 (5) 7.90 3.55

Nos. C197-C201 exist imperf. Value, $50 each pair.
For surcharges see Nos. C263-C265.

Type of Regular Issue, 1957

1957, Dec. 19 *Perf. 11½*
C202 A141 600b dp mag & pink .50 .30
C203 A141 700b vio blue & blue 1.00 .30
C204 A141 900b dk grn & pale grn 2.00 .40
Nos. C202-C204 (3) 3.50 1.00

Type of Regular Issue, 1960

1960, Jan. 30
C205 A142 400b rose claret 1.00 .50
C206 A142 800b slate blue 1.25 .75
C207 A142 2000b slate 2.25 1.00
Nos. C205-C207 (3) 4.50 2.25

Gate of the Sun, Tiahuanacu AP49

1960, Mar. 26 **Litho.** *Perf. 11½*
C208 AP49 3000b gray 3.25 2.00
C209 AP49 5000b orange 4.50 2.00
C210 AP49 10,000b rose cl 7.00 3.25
C211 AP49 15,000b blue violet 10.00 5.00
Nos. C208-C211 (4) 24.75 12.25

Uprooted Oak Emblem — AP50

1960, Apr. 7 *Perf. 11½*
C212 AP50 600b ultra .50 .25
C213 AP50 700b lt red brn .50 .30
C214 AP50 900b dk bl grn .60 .30
C215 AP50 1800b violet 1.25 .60
C216 AP50 2000b gray 1.75 1.25
Nos. C212-C216 (5) 4.60 2.70

WRY, July 1, 1959-June 30, 1960.
No. C215 exists with "1961" overprint in dark carmine, but was not regularly issued in this form.

Jaime Laredo Type

Laredo facing left, Bolivia in color.

Perf. 11½
1960, Aug. 15 **Unwmk.** **Litho.**
C217 A145 600b rose vio 1.25 .45
C218 A145 700b ol gray 1.25 .50
C219 A145 800b vio brn 1.75 .50
C220 A145 900b dk bl 3.00 .60
C221 A145 1800b green 4.00 2.00
C222 A145 4000b dk gray 7.00 2.00
Nos. C217-C222 (6) 18.25 6.05

Issued to honor the violinist Jaime Laredo.
For surcharges see Nos. C266-C267.

Children's Hospital Type of 1960

1960, Nov. 21 *Perf. 11½*
C223 A146 600b multi .75 .35
C224 A146 1000b multi .75 .35
C225 A146 1800b multi 1.40 .75
C226 A146 5000b multi 4.50 1.50
Nos. C223-C226 (4) 7.40 2.95

For surcharges see No. C268-C269.

Pres. Paz Estenssoro and Pres. Getulio Vargas of Brazil AP52

1960, Dec. 14 **Litho.** *Perf. 11½*
C227 AP52 1200b on 10b org & blk 1.00 .75

Exists with surcharge inverted. Value, $75.
No. C227 without surcharge was not regularly issued, although a decree authorizing its circulation was published. Value, $1.
Postally used counterfeits of surcharge exist.

Pres. Paz Estenssoro and Pres. Frondizi of Argentina AP53

4000b, Flags of Bolivia and Argentina.

1961, May 23 *Perf. 10½*
C228 AP53 4000b brn, red, yel, grn & bl 1.25 1.00
C229 AP53 6000b dk grn & blk 2.00 1.25

Visit of the President of Argentina, Dr. Arturo Frondizi, to Bolivia.
For surcharge see No. C309.

Miguel de Cervantes — AP54

1961, Oct. **Photo.** *Perf. 13*
C230 AP54 1400b pale grn & dk ol grn 1.00 .45

Cervantes' appointment as Chief Magistrate of La Paz. See No. 451.

Virgin of Cotoca and Symbol of Eucharist — AP55

1962, Mar. 19 **Litho.** *Perf. 10½*
C231 AP55 1400b brn, pink & yel .80 .35

4th Natl. Eucharistic Cong., Santa Cruz, 1961.

Nos. C212-C216 Surcharged

1962, June **Unwmk.** *Perf. 11½*
C232 AP50 1200b on 600b 1.10 .50
C233 AP50 1300b on 700b 1.10 .50
C234 AP50 1400b on 900b 1.10 .50
C235 AP50 2800b on 1,800b 1.75 .70
C236 AP50 3000b on 2,000b 1.75 1.00
Nos. C232-C236 (5) 6.80 3.20

The overprinted segment of Greek key border on Nos. C232-C236 comes in two positions: two full "keys" on top, and one full and two half keys on top.If at top, the surcharge is inverted.

Flower Type of 1962

Flowers: 100b, 1800b, Cantua buxifolia. 800b, 10,000b, Cantua bicolor.

1962, June 28 **Litho.** *Perf. 10½*
Flowers in Natural Colors
C237 A152 100b dk bl .75 .25
C238 A152 800b green 1.25 .30
C239 A152 1800b violet 2.75 .75
a. Souvenir sheet of 3 12.00 12.00
C240 A152 10,000b dk bl 8.50 4.00
Nos. C237-C240 (4) 13.25 5.30

No. C239a contains 3 imperf. stamps similar to Nos. C237-C239, but with the 1,800b background color changed to dark violet blue.
For surcharges see Nos. C270-C271.

Planes and Parachutes AP56

1200b, 5000b, Plane and oxcart. 2000b, Aerial photography (plane over South America).

1962, Sept. 5 **Litho.** *Perf. 11½*
Emblem in Red, Yellow & Green
C241 AP56 600b blk & bl .50 .25
C242 AP56 1200b multi .60 .30
C243 AP56 2000b multi .90 .50
C244 AP56 5000b multi 2.00 1.25
Nos. C241-C244 (4) 4.00 2.30

Armed Forces of Bolivia.
An imperforate 200b souvenir sheet depicting No. C241 with simulated perforations was issued Sept. 16, 1983, to clebrate 200 years of manned flight. Value $50.

Malaria Type of 1962

Design: Inscription around mosquito, laurel around globe.

1962, Oct. 4
C245 A154 2000b ind, grn & yel 2.00 .50

Type of Regular Issue, 1961

Design: Pedro de la Gasca (1485-1567).

1962 **Unwmk.** **Photo.** *Perf. 13x12½*
C246 A150 1200b brn, *yel* .60 .30

Condor, Soccer Ball and Flags — AP57

1.80b, Map of Bolivia, soccer ball, goal and flags.

1963, Mar. 21 **Litho.** *Perf. 11½*
C247 AP57 1.40b multi 1.50 1.00
C248 AP57 1.80b multi 1.50 1.00

21st South American Soccer Championships.
An imperforate 20b souvenir sheet depicting No. C248 with simulated perforations was issued March 16, 1979 to celebrate the 1979 World Cup soccer championship games. Value $40.
Two imperforate 20b souvenir sheets, one containing No. C247 and the other containing No. C248, both with simulated perforations, were issued Oct. 13, 1980, to mark various World Cup competitions. Value, each $45.

Freedom from Hunger Type

Design: Wheat, globe and wheat emblem.

1963, Aug. 1 **Unwmk.** *Perf. 11½*
C249 A156 1.20b dk grn, bl & yel 1.00 .75

Alliance for Progress Emblem — AP58

1963, Nov. 15 *Perf. 11½*
C250 AP58 1.20b dl yel, ultra & grn 1.25 .75

2nd anniv. of the Alliance for Progress, which aims to stimulate economic growth and raise living standards in Latin America.

Type of Regular Issue, 1963

1.20b, Ballot box and voters. 1.40b, Map and farmer breaking chain. 2.80b, Miners.

1963, Dec. 21 *Perf. 11½*
C251 A157 1.20b gray, dk brn & rose .60 .25
C252 A157 1.40b bister & grn .70 .40
C253 A157 2.80b slate & buff 1.00 .90
Nos. C251-C253 (3) 2.30 1.55

Andrés Santa Cruz — AP59

Perf. 13½

1966, Aug. 10 Wmk. 90 Litho.

C254 AP59 20c dp bl .30 .25
C255 AP59 60c dp grn .30 .30
C256 AP59 1.20b red brn .75 .60
C257 AP59 2.80b black 1.25 1.00
Nos. C254-C257 (4) 2.60 2.15

Cent. (in 1965) of the death of Marshal Andrés Santa Cruz (1792-1865), pres. of Bolivia and of Peru-Bolivia Confederation.

Children Type of 1966

Design: 1.40b, Mother and children.

1966, Dec. 16 Unwmk. *Perf. 13½*

C258 A159 1.40b gray bl & blk 2.25 .50

Co-Presidents Type of Regular Issue

1966, Dec. 16 Litho. *Perf. 12½*

Flag in Red, Yellow and Green

C259 A160 2.80b gray & tan 1.50 .80
C260 A160 10b sep & tan 3.00 1.00
a. Souvenir sheet of 4 9.00 9.00

No. C260a contains 4 imperf. stamps similar to Nos. 480-481 and C259-C260. Dark green marginal inscription. Size: 135x82mm.

Various Issues 1954-62 Surcharged with New Values and Bars

On No. C177

1966, Dec. 21

C261 A138 10c on 27b .30 .30
a. Agraria/Agraria 20.00 10.00

On No. C182

C262 AP47 10c on 55b .30 .30

On No. C199

C263 AP48 60c on 1350b .75 .30

On No. C200

C264 AP48 2.80b on 2700b 3.00 2.25

On No. C201

C265 AP48 4b on 4000b 2.00 1.50

On No. C219

C266 A145 1.20b on 800b 1.50 .30

On No. C222

C267 A145 1.40b on 4,000b 1.10 .75

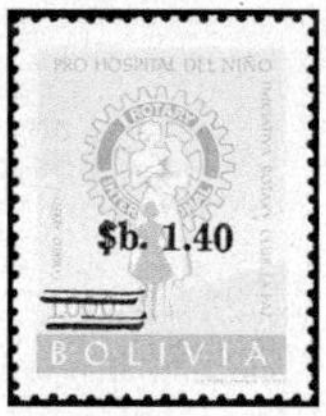

Nos. C224-C225

C268 A146 1.40b on 1,000b .75 .75
C269 A146 1.40b on 1,800b .75 .75

Nos. C238-C239

C270 A152 1.20b on 800b 1.50 .30
C271 A152 1.20b on 1,800b 1.50 .30

Revenue Stamp of 1946 Surcharged

C272 A161 1.20b on 1b dk bl .60 .25
Nos. C261-C272 (12) 14.05 8.05

Lions Emblem and Pre-historic Sculptures AP60

1967, Sept. 20 Litho. *Perf. 13x13½*

C273 AP60 2b red & multi 1.20 .75
a. Souvenir sheet of 2 5.50 5.50

50th anniv. of Lions Intl. No. C273a contains 2 imperf. stamps similar to Nos. 492 and C273.

Folklore Type of Regular Issue

Folklore characters: 1.20p, Pujllay. 1.40p, Ujusiris. 2p, Morenada. 3p, Auki-aukis.

1968, June 24 *Perf. 13½x13*

C274 A163 1.20b lt yel grn & multi .45 .25
C275 A163 1.40b gray & multi .50 .25
C276 A163 2b dk ol bis & multi 1.00 .35
C277 A163 3b sky bl & multi 1.25 .35
a. Souvenir sheet of 4, #C274-C277 imperf 15.00 15.00
Nos. C274-C277 (4) 3.20 1.20

Moto Mendez — AP61

1968, Oct. 29 Litho. *Perf. 13½x13*

C278 AP61 1b multi .40 .25
C279 AP61 1.20b multi .50 .25
C280 AP61 2b multi 1.00 .45
C281 AP61 4b multi 1.25 .70
Nos. C278-C281 (4) 3.15 1.65

Battle of Tablada sesquicentennial.

Pres. Gualberto Villarroel AP62

1968, Nov. 6 *Perf. 13x13½*

C282 AP62 1.40b org & blk .90 .30
C283 AP62 3b lt bl & blk 1.50 .40
C284 AP62 4b rose & blk 2.00 .50
C285 AP62 5b gray grn & blk 2.25 .75
C286 AP62 10b pale pur & blk 4.00 1.40
Nos. C282-C286 (5) 10.65 3.35

4th centenary of Cochabamba.

ITU Type of Regular Issue

1968, Dec. 3 Litho. *Perf. 13x13½*

C287 A166 1.20b gray, blk & yel .75 .40
C288 A166 1.40b bl, blk & gray ol .75 .25

UNESCO Emblem — AP63

1968, Nov. 14 *Perf. 13½x13*

C289 AP63 1.20b pale vio & blk .70 .50
C290 AP63 2.80b yel grn & blk 1.25 .75

20th anniv. (in 1966) of UNESCO.

Kennedy Type of Regular Issue

1968, Nov. 22 Unwmk.

C291 A168 1b grn & blk .35 .25
C292 A168 10b scar & blk 4.00 3.75
a. 7.50 7.50 7.50

No. C292a contains one imperf. stamp similar to No. C291. Dark violet marginal inscription. Size: 131x81½mm.

Tennis Type of Regular Issue

1968, Dec. 10 *Perf. 13x13½*

C293 A169 1.40b org, blk & lt brn 1.25 .45
C294 A169 2.80b sky bl, blk & lt brn 2.00 .75
a. Souvenir sheet of 1 #C293, imperf 15.00 15.00

A 1,000,000b souvenir sheet containing Nos. C294 and 353, perforated 13¼ and 14¼ respectively, was issued Sept. 25, 1986, with a tennis theme. Value $30.

Stamp Centenary Type

Design: 1.40b, 2.80b, 3b, Bolivia No. 1.

1968, Dec. 23 Litho. *Perf. 13x13½*

C295 A170 1.40b org, grn & blk 1.25 .65
C296 A170 2.80b pale rose, grn & blk 2.10 1.25
C297 A170 3b lt vio, grn & blk 2.10 1.25
a. Souvenir sheet of 3, #C295-C297, imperf 6.00 6.00
Nos. C295-C297 (3) 5.45 3.15

An imperforate 20b souvenir sheet depicting No. C297 with simulated perforations was issued March 16, 1979, to mark the 100th anniv. of the death of Sir Rowland Hill (1795-1879), inventor of the postage stamp. Value $50.

Two additional imperforate 20b souvenir sheets, one depicting Nos. C297 and C358, with Bolivia Nos. 14 and 19 and Great Britain No. 1, the other depicting Nos. C297, C11, C12, C17, a trial color surcharge on No. C4, and Great Britain No. 1, were issued April 28, 1980, to mark the 100th anniv. of the death of Sir Rowland Hill. Value, both sheets $60.

Franklin D. Roosevelt — AP64

1969, Oct. 29 Litho. *Perf. 13½x13*

C298 AP64 5b brn, blk & buff 2.00 1.50

Olympic Type of Regular Issue

Sports: 1.20b, Woman runner, vert. 2.80b, Discus thrower, vert. 5b, Hurdler.

Perf. 13½x13, 13x13½

1969, Oct. 29 Litho.

C299 A171 1.20b yel grn, bis & blk .75 .50
C300 A171 2.80b red, org & blk 1.40 1.00
C301 A171 5b bl, lt bl, red & blk 2.00 2.00
a. Souvenir sheet of 3, #C299-C301 imperf 12.50 12.50
Nos. C299-C301 (3) 4.15 3.50

Two imperforate 20b souvenir sheets depicting Nos. C300 and C301 with simulated perforations were issued April 28, 1980, to commemorate the 1980 Moscow Olympics. Value, both sheets $75.

An imperforate 200b souvenir sheet depicting Nos. C300 and 639 with simulated perforations was issued Sept. 16, 1983, to mark the 1983 Los Angeles Summer Olympic Games. Value $25.

An imperforate 27,500b souvenir sheet depicting No. C299 with simulated perforations was issued April 4, 1985, to mark the 1984 Los Angeles Summer Olympic Games. Value $25.

A 2b souvenir sheet containing Nos. C299 and 712, perforated 13¼, was issued April 13, 1987, to mark the 1988 Seoul Summer Olympic Games. Value $20.

An additional 2b souvenir sheet containing No. C300, perforated 13¼, was issued Aug. 15, 1988, to mark the Seoul Olympics. Value $30.

Butterfly Type of Regular Issue

1b, Metamorpha dido wernichei. 1.80b, Heliconius felix. 2.80b, Morpho casica. 3b, Papilio yuracares. 4b, Heliconius melitus.

1970, Apr. 24 Litho. *Perf. 13x13½*

C302 A172 1b sal & multi 4.00 2.00
C303 A172 1.80b lt bl & multi 6.00 3.00
C304 A172 2.80b multi 9.00 4.50
C305 A172 3b multi 9.00 4.50
C306 A172 4b multi 12.00 5.50
a. Souvenir sheet of 3, #C302-C304 25.00 25.00
Nos. C302-C306 (5) 40.00 19.50

A souvenir sheet exists containing 3 imperf. stamps similar to Nos. C302-C304. Black marginal inscription. Size: 129½x80mm.

Scout Type of Regular Issue

Designs: 50c, Boy Scout building brick wall. 1.20b, Bolivian Boy Scout emblem.

1970, June 17 Litho. *Perf. 13½x13*

C307 A173 50c yel & multi .25 .25
C308 A173 1.20b multi .50 .50

No. C228 Surcharged

1970, Dec. Litho. *Perf. 10½*

C309	AP53 1.20b on 4000b multi		.45	.25

Flower Type of Regular Issue

Bolivian Flowers: 1.20b, Amaryllis pseudopardina, horiz. 1.40b, Rebutia kruegeri. 2.80b, Lobivia pentlandii, horiz. 4b, Rebutia tunariensis.

Perf. 13x13½, 13½x13

1971, Aug. 9 Litho. Unwmk.

C310	A174	1.20b multi	.80	.60
C311	A174	1.40b multi	1.00	.75
C312	A174	2.80b multi	2.00	1.10
C313	A174	4b multi	2.50	2.00
		Nos. C310-C313 (4)	6.30	4.45

Folk Dance Type of Regular Issue

1972, Mar. 23 Litho. *Perf. 13½x13*

C314	A177	1.20b Kusillo	.75	.25
a.		Souvenir sheet of 3, #542-543, C314 imperf	40.00	40.00
C315	A177	1.40b Taquirari	1.00	.25
a.		Souvenir sheet of 3, #540-541, C315 imperf	40.00	40.00

Painting Type of Regular Issue

Bolivian Paintings: 1.40b, Portrait of Chola Paceña, by Cecilio Guzman de Rojas. 1.50b, Adoration of the Kings, by G. Gamarra. 1.60b, Adoration of Pachamama (mountain), by A. Borda. 2b, The Kiss of the Idol, by Guzman de Rojas.

1972 Litho. *Perf. 13½*

C316	A178	1.40b multi	.75	.25
C317	A178	1.50b multi	.75	.25
C318	A178	1.60b multi	.75	.25
a.		Souvenir sheet of 2, #548, C318 imperf	50.00	50.00
C319	A178	2b multi	1.00	.35
a.		Souvenir sheet of 2, #C317, C319, imperf	50.00	50.00
		Nos. C316-C319 (4)	3.25	1.10

Issued: 1.40b, Dec. 4; others Aug. 17.

An imperforate 20b souvenir sheet depicting No. C318 with simulated perforations was issued March 16, 1979, to mark the 1980 Olympic Games. Value $25.

An imperforate 1.50b souvenir sheet depicting No. C317 with simulated perforations was issued Aug. 1, 1982, for Christmas 1982. Value $60.

An imperforate 200b souvenir sheet depicting Nos. C318 and 616 with simulated perforations was issued Sept. 16, 1983, to celebrate the 1984 Sarajevo Winter Olympic Games. Value $30.

An imperforate 7500b souvenir sheet depicting No. C319 with simulated perforations was issued Nov. 12, 1984, to honor Peter Paul Reubens (pictures *Diana and Calisto*). Value $50.

An imperforate 1b souvenir sheet depicting No. C319 with simulated perforations was issued March 20, 1987, to honor Peter Paul Reubens (pictures *Juno and Argus*). Value $25.

Bolivian Coat of Arms AP65

1972, Dec. 4 *Perf. 13½x13¾*

C320	AP65	4b lt bl & multi	2.75	.75

An imperforate 20b souvenir sheet depicting Nos. C320 and 651 with simulated perforations was issued Oct. 13, 1980, to celebrate the 1980 Lake Placid Winter Olympic Games. Value $75.

An imperforate 4b souvenir sheet depicting No. C320 with simulated perforations was issued Aug. 11, 1981, to celebrate the wedding of Prince Charles and Lady Diana. Value $25.

An imperforate 4b souvenir sheet depicting No. C320 with simulated perforations was issued March 24, 1982, to honor Princess Diana. Value $25.

An imperforate 7500b souvenir sheet depicting Nos. C320 and 703 with simulated perforations was issued Nov. 12, 1984, to mark the 1984 Sarajevo Winter Olympic Games. Value $50.

An imperforate 500,000b souvenir sheet depicting No. C320 with simulated perforations was issued Dec. 3, 1985, to mark the World Chess Congress. Value $65.

A 1,000,000b souvenir sheet containing Nos. C320 and 616 perforated 13¼ was issued Sept. 25, 1986, to mark the 1988 Calgary Winter Olympic Games. Value $30.

A 2b souvenir sheet containing No. C320 perforated 13¼ was issued April 13, 1987, to mark the 1988 Calgary Winter Olympic Games. Value $27.50.

A 2b souvenir sheet containing No. C320 perforated 13¼ was issued Dec. 16, 1987, to honor U.S. and Soviet space flights. Value $25.

A 2b souvenir sheet containing No. C320 perforated 13¼ was issued July 16, 1989, to commemorate the 200th anniv. of the French Revolution. Value $20.

A 2b souvenir sheet containing No. C320 perforated 13¼ was issued May 18, 1990, to mark the 700th anniv. of the Swiss Confederation. Value $40.

Cactus Type of Regular Issue

Designs: Various cacti.

1973, Aug. 6 Litho. *Perf. 13½*

C321	A180	1.20b tan & multi	.75	.25
C322	A180	1.90b org & multi	1.00	.35
C323	A180	2b multi	1.75	.50
		Nos. C321-C323 (3)	3.50	1.10

Development Type of Regular Issue

1.40b, Highway 1Y4. 2b, Rail car on bridge.

1973, Nov. 26 Litho. *Perf. 13½*

C324	A181	1.40b salmon & multi	2.50	.25
C325	A181	2b multi	3.75	.25

A 2b souvenir sheet containing No. C325 perforated 13¼ was issued June 15, 1988, to mark the 1931 Bentley/Zug auto/train race in England. Value $35.

Santos-Dumont and 14-Bis Plane — AP66

1973, July 20

C326	AP66	1.40b yel & blk	1.00	.40

Alberto Santos-Dumont (1873-1932), Brazilian aviation pioneer.

Orchid Type of 1974

Orchids: 2.50b, Cattleya luteola, horiz. 3.80b, Stanhopaea. 4b, Catasetum, horiz. 5b, Maxillaria.

1974 Litho. *Perf. 13½*

C327	A182	2.50b multi	3.50	.40
C328	A182	3.80b rose & multi	5.00	.65
C329	A182	4b multi	5.00	.80
C330	A182	5b sal & multi	9.00	1.00
		Nos. C327-C330 (4)	22.50	2.85

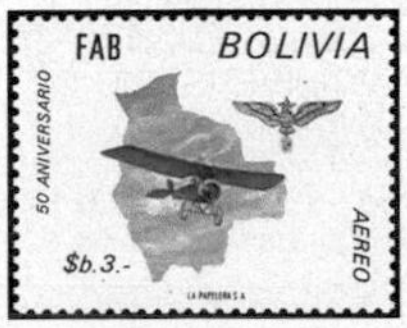

Air Force Emblem, Plane over Map of Bolivia AP67

Designs: 3.80b, Plane over Andes. 4.50b, Triple decker and jet. 8b, Rafael Pabon and double decker. 15b, Jet and "50."

1974 Litho. *Perf. 13x13½*

C331	AP67	3b multi	1.00	.60
C332	AP67	3.80b multi	1.50	1.00
C333	AP67	4.50b multi	1.50	1.00
C334	AP67	8b multi	2.50	2.00
C335	AP67	15b multi	5.00	2.75
		Nos. C331-C335 (5)	11.50	7.35

Bolivian Air Force, 50th anniv. Nos. C331-C335 exist imperf. Value, $40 each pair.

For surcharge see No. 968.

Coat of Arms Type of 1975

Designs: Departmental coats of arms.

1975, July 16 Litho. *Perf. 13½*

C336	A188	20c Beni	.50	.25
C337	A188	30c Tarija	.50	.25
C338	A188	50c Potosi	.70	.30
C339	A188	1b Oruro	1.40	.80
C340	A188	2.50b Santa Cruz	2.50	1.25
C341	A188	3b La Paz	2.50	1.25
		Nos. C336-C341 (6)	8.10	4.10

LAB Emblem — AP68

Bolivia on Map of Americas AP69

Map of Bolivia, Plane and Kyllmann AP70

1975 Litho. *Perf. 13½*

C342	AP68	1b gold, bl & blk	.60	.50
C343	AP69	1.50b multi	.90	.50
C344	AP70	2b multi	1.25	.60
		Nos. C342-C344 (3)	2.75	1.60

Lloyd Aereo Boliviano, 50th anniversary, founded by Guillermo Kyllmann.

Bolivar, Presidents Perez and Banzer, and Flags — AP71

1975, Aug. 4 Litho. *Perf. 13½*

C345	AP71	3b gold & multi	1.00	.75

Visit of Pres. Carlos A. Perez of Venezuela.

Eight imperforate souvenir sheets, each denominated 5.50b, depicting No. 19 with various contemporaneous Bolivian stamps with simulated perforations were issued on Nov. 7, 1975, celebrating various anniversaries and philatelic events. These comprise: No. 345, Innsbruck 1976, value $25; No. C345, Interphil '76, value $6; No. C350, Concorde/Zeppelin, value $50; No. C350, Wien '75, value $6; No. C3251, U.S. Bicentennial, value $30; No. C351, Hafnia '76, value $6; No C352, Montreal Olympics/Argentina '78, value $35; No. C352, Exfilmo '75, value $6. Four of these sheets were overprinted in April 1981 for WIPA 81 (value $5), Espamer 81 (value $5), Philatokyo 81 (value $5) and Philexfrance 1982 (value $12.50).

An imperforate 25b souvenir sheet depicting No. C345 with simulated perforations was issued June 1, 1978, to commemorate the 25th anniv. of the coronation of Queen Elizabeth II. Value $25.

Bolivar Type of 1975

Presidents and Statesmen of Bolivia: 50c, Rene Barrientos O. 2b, Francisco B. O'Connor. 3.80b, Gualberto Villarroel. 4.20b, German Busch. 4.50b, Hugo Banzer Suarez. 20b, José Ballivian. 30b, Andres de Santa Cruz. 40b, Antonio Jose de Sucre.

1975 Litho. *Perf. 13½*

Size: 24x33mm

C346	A189	50c multi	.25	.25
C347	A189	2b multi	1.40	.50
C348	A189	3.80b multi	1.50	.80
C349	A189	4.20b multi	2.00	1.00

Size: 28x39mm

C350	A189	4.50b multi	1.50	1.00

Size: 24x33mm

C351	A189	20b multi	6.00	4.00
C352	A189	30b multi	7.00	5.00
C353	A189	40b multi	10.00	7.00
		Nos. C346-C353 (8)	29.65	19.55

For surcharge see No. 969.

An imperforate 20b souvenir sheet depicting No. C353 with simulated perforations was issued March 16, 1979, to commemorate the 75th anniv. of powered flight. Value $40.

An imperforate 54b souvenir sheet depicting Nos. C346 and C358 with simulated perforations was issued April 28, 1980, to celebrate the 1980 Lake Placid Winter Olympics. Value $25.

UPU Emblem AP72

1975, Dec. 7 Litho. *Perf. 13½*

C358	AP72	25b blue & multi	4.00	3.50
a.		Souvenir sheet of 1, imperf	20.00	20.00

Cent. of UPU (in 1974).

No. C358a contains a single No. C358, imperforate with simulated perforations. Size: 130x80mm.

An imperforate 25b souvenir sheet depicting No. C358 with simulated perforations was issued Jan. 1, 1978, to recognize Charles Lindbergh and Zeppelin flights. Value $100.

POSTAGE DUE STAMPS

D1

1931 Unwmk. Engr. *Perf. 14, 14½*

J1	D1	5c ultra	1.75	*3.50*
J2	D1	10c red	2.50	*3.50*
J3	D1	15c yellow	2.50	*5.00*
J4	D1	30c deep green	2.50	*6.00*
J5	D1	40c deep violet	6.00	*8.00*
J6	D1	50c black brown	12.00	*15.00*
		Nos. J1-J6 (6)	27.25	*41.00*

Symbol of Youth — D2

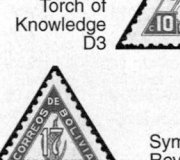

Torch of Knowledge D3

Symbol of the Revolution of May 17, 1936 — D4

1938 Litho. *Perf. 11*

J7	D2	5c deep rose	1.75	1.50
a.		Pair, imperf. between	10.00	
J8	D3	10c green	2.00	1.50
J9	D4	30c gray blue	2.00	1.60
		Nos. J7-J9 (3)	5.75	4.60

POSTAL TAX STAMPS

Worker — PT1

Imprint: "LITO. UNIDAS LA PAZ."

Perf. 13½x10½, 10½, 13½

1939 Litho. Unwmk.

RA1	PT1 5c dull violet	1.00	.50
a.	Double impression	15.00	15.00

Redrawn

Imprint: "TALL. OFFSET LA PAZ."

1940 ***Perf. 12x11, 11***

RA2	PT1 5c violet	.75	.30
a.	Horizontal pair, imperf. between	3.00	2.00
b.	Imperf. horiz., pair	10.00	
c.	Double impression	15.00	10.00

Tax of Nos. RA1-RA2 was for the Workers' Home Building Fund.

Communications Symbols — PT2

1944-45 Litho. ***Perf. 10½***

RA3	PT2 10c salmon	.75	.30
RA4	PT2 10c blue ('45)	.75	.30

A 30c orange inscribed "Centenario de la Creacion del Departmento del Beni" was issued in 1946 and required to be affixed to all air and surface mail to and from the Department of Beni in addition to regular postage. Values: unused $1; used 50¢.Five higher denominations in the same scenic design were used for local revenue purposes.

Catalogue values for unused stamps in this section, from this point to the end of the section, are for Never Hinged items.

Type of 1944 Redrawn

1947-48 Unwmk. ***Perf. 10½***

RA5	PT2 10c carmine	2.50	.25
RA6	PT2 10c org yel ('48)	2.50	.25
RA7	PT2 10c yel brn ('48)	2.50	.25
RA8	PT2 10c emerald ('48)	2.50	.25
	Nos. RA5-RA8 (4)	10.00	1.00

Post horn and envelope reduced in size.

Condor, Envelope and Post Horn — PT3

1951-52

RA9	PT3 20c deep orange	.70	.30
a.	Imperf., pair	25.00	
RA10	PT3 20c green ('52)	.70	.30
a.	Imperf., pair	25.00	
RA11	PT3 20c blue ('52)	.70	.30
a.	Imperf., pair	25.00	
	Nos. RA9-RA11 (3)	2.10	.90

For surcharges see Nos. RA17-RA18.

Communication Symbols — PT4

1952-54 ***Perf. 13½, 10½, 10½x12***

RA12	PT4 50c green	.70	.25
RA13	PT4 50c carmine	1.00	.25
RA14	PT4 3b green	.70	.30
RA15	PT4 3b olive bister	.85	.30
RA16	PT4 5b violet ('54)	2.50	1.00
	Nos. RA12-RA16 (5)	5.75	2.10

For surcharges see Nos. RA21-RA22.

No. RA10 and Type of 1951-52 Surcharged with New Value in Black

1953 ***Perf. 10½***

RA17	PT3 50c on 20c green	.60	.25
RA18	PT3 50c on 20c red vio	.60	.25

Postman Blowing Horn — PT5

1954-55 Unwmk. ***Perf. 10½***

RA19	PT5 1b brown	1.25	.25
RA20	PT5 1b car rose ('55)	1.25	.25

Nos. RA19-RA20 exist imperf. Value, $25 each pair.

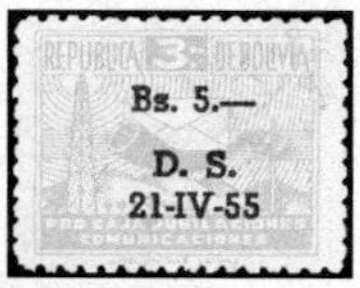

Nos. RA15 and RA14 Surcharged in Black

1955 ***Perf. 10½, 10½x12***

RA21	PT4 5b on 3b olive bister	1.00	.25
RA22	PT4 5b on 3b green	2.00	.30

Tax of Nos. RA3-RA22 was for the Communications Employees Fund.

No. RA21 is known with surcharge in thin type of different font and with comma added after "55." Value, $10.

Plane over Airport — PT6

Planes — PT7

Perf. 10½, 12, 13½

1955 Unwmk. Litho.

RA23	PT6 5b dp ultra	1.00	.30
a.	Vertical pair imperf. between	30.00	

Perf. 11½

RA24	PT7 10b light green	1.00	.30

PT8

PT9

1955 Litho. ***Perf. 10½***

RA25	PT8 5b red	15.00	10.00
a.	Imperf., pair	40.00	

Perf. 12

RA26	PT9 20b dark brown	1.10	.30

Tax of Nos. RA23-RA26 was for the building of new airports.

General Alfredo Ovando and Three Men — PT10

1970, Sept. 26 Litho. ***Perf. 13x13½***

RA27	PT10 20c black & red	.70	.30

See No. RAC1.

Pres. German Busch PT11

1971, May 13 Litho. ***Perf. 13x13½***

RA28	PT11 20c lilac & black	.70	.30

AIR POST POSTAL TAX STAMPS

Catalogue values for unused stamps in this section are for Never Hinged items.

Type of Postal Tax Issue

Design: 30c, General Ovando and oil well.

1970, Sept. 26 Litho. ***Perf. 13x13½***

RAC1	PT10 30c blk & grn	.80	.30

Pres. Gualberto Villarroel, Refinery PTAP1

1971, May 25 Litho. ***Perf. 13x13½***

RAC2	PTAP1 30c lt bl & blk	1.00	.30

Inscribed: "XXV ANIVERSARIO DE SU GOBIERNO"

1975 Litho. ***Perf. 13x13½***

RAC3	PTAP1 30c lt bl & blk	10.00	2.75

BOSNIA & HERZEGOVINA

'bäz-nē-ə and ˌhert-sə-gō-'vē-nə

LOCATION — Between Dalmatia and Serbia

GOVT. — Provinces of Turkey under Austro-Hungarian occupation, 1879-1908; provinces of Austria-Hungary 1908-1918

AREA — 19,768 sq. mi.

POP. — 2,000,000 (approx. 1918)

CAPITAL — Sarajevo

Following World War I Bosnia and Herzegovina united with the kingdoms of Montenegro and Serbia, and Croatia, Dalmatia and Slovenia, to form the Kingdom of Yugoslavia (See Yugoslavia.)

100 Novcica (Neukreuzer) = 1 Florin (Gulden)

100 Heller = 1 Krone (1900)

Watermark

Wmk. 91 — BRIEF-MARKEN or (from 1890) ZEITUNGS-MARKEN in Double-lined Capitals, Across the Sheet

Coat of Arms — A1

Type I — The heraldic eaglets on the right side of the escutcheon are entirely blank. The eye of the lion is indicated by a very small dot, which sometimes fails to print.

Type II — There is a colored line across the lowest eaglet. A similar line sometimes appears on the middle eaglet. The eye of the lion is formed by a large dot which touches the outline of the head above it.

Type III — The eaglets and eye of the lion are similar to type I. Each tail feather of the large eagle has two lines of shading and the lowest feather does not touch the curved line below it. In types I and II there are several shading lines in these feathers, and the lowest feather touches the curved line.

Varieties of the Numerals

2 NOVCICA:
A — The "2" has curved tail. All are type I.
B — The "2" has straight tail. All are type II.

15 NOVCICA:
C — The serif of the "1" is short and forms a wide angle with the vertical stroke.
D — The serif of the "1" forms an acute angle with the vertical stroke.
The numerals of the 5n were retouched several times and show minor differences, especially in the flag.

Other Varieties

½ NOVCICA:
There is a black dot between the curved ends of the ornaments near the lower spandrels.
G — This dot touches the curve at its right. Stamps of this (1st) printing are litho.
H — This dot stands clear of the curved lines. Stamps of this (2nd) printing are typo.

10 NOVCICA:
Ten stamps in each sheet of type II show a small cross in the upper section of the right side of the escutcheon.

Perf. 9 to 13½ and Compound

1879-94 Litho. Wmk. 91

Type I

1	A1	½n blk (type II) ('94)	26.00	*37.50*
2	A1	1n gray	15.00	2.25
c.		1n gray lilac		3.00
4	A1	2n yellow	22.50	1.50
5	A1	3n green	26.00	3.00
6	A1	5n rose red	37.50	.40
7	A1	10n blue	150.00	1.50
8	A1	15n brown (D)	150.00	9.75
a.		15n brown (C)	360.00	50.00
9	A1	20n gray green ('93)	500.00	13.50
10	A1	25n violet	130.00	11.00
		Nos. 1-10 (9)	1,057.	80.40

No. 2c was never issued. It is usually canceled by blue pencil marks and "mint" examples generally have been cleaned.

Perf. 10½ to 13 and Compound

1894-98 Typo.

Type II

1a	A1	½n black	16.50	*22.50*
2a	A1	1n gray	5.25	1.50
4a	A1	2n yellow	3.25	.75
5a	A1	3n green	5.25	1.50
6a	A1	5n rose red	125.00	.75
7a	A1	10n blue	7.50	1.10
b.		Pair, imperf btw, perf 10½ all around		*12,500.*

8b	A1	15n brown	6.75	4.50
9a	A1	20n gray green	7.50	6.00
10a	A1	25n violet	9.00	13.50
		Nos. 1a-10a (9)	186.00	52.10

Type III

6b	A1	5n rose red ('98)	3.75	.75

All the preceding stamps exist in various shades.

Nos. 1a to 10a were reprinted in 1911 in lighter colors, on very white paper and perf. 12½. Value, set $32.50.

A2

A3

Perf. 10½, 12½ and Compound

1900 **Typo.**

11	A2	1h gray black	.25	.25
12	A2	2h gray	.25	.25
13	A2	3h yellow	.25	.25
14	A2	5h green	.25	.25
15	A2	6h brown	.40	.25
16	A2	10h red	.25	.25
17	A2	20h rose	130.00	12.00
18	A2	25h blue	1.10	1.10
19	A2	30h bister brown	130.00	13.00
20	A2	40h orange	190.00	15.00
21	A2	50h red lilac	.75	.75
22	A3	1k dark rose	1.00	.60
23	A3	2k ultra	1.50	*1.90*
24	A3	5k dull blue grn	3.25	*6.00*
		Nos. 11-24 (14)	459.25	51.85

All values of this issue except the 3h exist on ribbed paper.

Nos. 17, 19 and 20 were reprinted in 1911. The reprints are in lighter colors and on whiter paper than the originals. Reprints of Nos. 17 and 19 are perf. 10½ and those of No. 20 are perf. 12½. Value each $5. Reprints also exist imperf.

Numerals in Black

1901-04 ***Perf. 12½***

25	A2	20h pink ('02)	.90	.60
26	A2	30h bistor brn ('03)	.90	.60
27	A2	35h blue	1.40	.90
a.		35h ultramarine	*175.00*	9.00
28	A2	40h orange ('03)	1.10	.90
29	A2	45h grnsh blue ('04)	1.10	.90
		Nos. 25-29 (5)	5.40	3.90

Nos. 11-16, 18, 21-29 exist imperf. Most of Nos. 11-29 exist perf. 6½; compound with 12½; part perf.; in pairs imperf. between. These were supplied only to some high-ranking officials and never sold at any P.O.

For surcharges, see Yugoslavia Nos. 1LJ14-1LJ22.

View of Deboj
A4

The Carsija at Sarajevo — A5

Designs: 2h, View of Mostar. 3h, Pliva Gate, Jajce. 5h, Narenta Pass and Prenj River. 6h, Rama Valley. 10h, Vrbas Valley. 20h, Old Bridge, Mostar. 25h, Bey's Mosque, Sarajevo. 30h, Donkey post. 35h, Jezero and tourists' pavilion. 40h, Mail wagon. 45h, Bazaar at Sarajevo. 50h, Postal car. 2k, St. Luke's Campanile, Jajce. 5k, Emperor Franz Josef.

Perf. 6½, 9½, 10½ and 12½, also Compounds

1906 **Engr.** **Unwmk.**

30	A4	1h black	.25	.25
31	A4	2h violet	.25	.25
32	A4	3h olive	.25	.25
33	A4	5h dark green	.35	.35
34	A4	6h brown	.25	*.35*
a.		Perf. 13½	.75	1.50
35	A4	10h carmine	.45	.35
36	A4	20h dark brown	.75	.75
a.		Perf. 13½	2.10	4.00
37	A4	25h deep blue	1.50	2.25
38	A4	30h green	1.50	1.10
39	A4	35h myrtle green	1.50	1.10
40	A4	40h orange red	1.50	1.10
41	A4	45h brown red	1.50	2.60
42	A4	50h dull violet	2.25	2.60
43	A5	1k maroon	6.00	3.75
44	A5	2k gray green	7.50	*13.00*
45	A5	5k dull blue	4.50	*9.00*
		Nos. 30-45 (16)	30.30	*39.05*

Nos. 30-45 exist imperf. Value, set $91.35 unused, $107 canceled. Many perforation varieties exist. See the *Scott Classic Specialized Catalogue of Stamps and Covers 1840-1940* for detailed listings.

For overprints and surcharges see Nos. 126, B1-B4, Yugoslavia Nos. 1L38, 1LB5-1LB7.

Birthday Jubilee Issue

Designs of 1906 Issue, with "1830-1910" in Label at Bottom

1910 ***Perf. 12½***

46	A4	1h black	.40	.40
47	A4	2h violet	.40	.40
48	A4	3h olive	.40	.40
49	A4	5h dark green	.40	.40
50	A4	6h orange brn	.40	.40
51	A4	10h carmine	.75	.25
52	A4	20h dark brown	1.50	*2.25*
53	A4	25h deep blue	2.25	*3.75*
54	A4	30h green	2.25	*3.75*
55	A4	35h myrtle grn	2.25	*3.75*
56	A4	40h orange red	2.25	*3.75*
57	A4	45h brown red	3.00	*7.50*
58	A4	50h dull violet	3.75	*7.50*
59	A5	1k maroon	4.50	*7.50*
60	A5	2k gray green	15.00	*52.50*
61	A5	5k dull blue	1.50	*9.00*
		Nos. 46-61 (16)	41.00	*103.50*

80th birthday of Emperor Franz Josef. For overprints, see Yugoslavia Nos. 1L1-1L16.

Scenic Type of 1906

Views: 12h, Jaice. 60h, Konjica. 72h, Vishegrad.

1912

62	A4	12h ultra	5.25	*6.75*
63	A4	60h dull blue	3.00	*4.50*
64	A4	72h carmine	11.00	*22.50*
		Nos. 62-64 (3)	19.25	*33.75*

Value, imperf set, $110.

See Austria for similar designs inscribed "FELDPOST" instead of "MILITARPOST."

Emperor Franz Josef
A23 A24

A25

A26

1912-14 **Various Frames**

65	A23	1h olive green	.40	.25
66	A23	2h brt blue	.40	.25
67	A23	3h claret	.40	.25
68	A23	5h green	.40	.25
69	A23	6h dark gray	.40	.25
70	A23	10h rose car	.40	.25
71	A23	12h dp olive grn	.55	.40
72	A23	20h orange brn	2.75	.25
73	A23	25h ultra	1.50	.25
74	A23	30h orange red	1.50	.25
75	A24	35h myrtle grn	1.50	.25
76	A24	40h dk violet	4.50	.25
77	A24	45h olive brn	2.25	.40
78	A24	50h slate blue	2.25	.25
79	A24	60h brown vio	1.50	.25
80	A24	72h dark blue	3.25	*5.25*
81	A25	1k brn vio, *straw*	8.25	.75
82	A25	2k dk gray, *bl*	7.50	.75
83	A26	3k carmine, *grn*	8.25	*11.00*
84	A26	5k dk vio, *gray*	15.00	*30.00*
85	A25	10k dk ultra, *gray* ('14)	90.00	*125.00*
		Nos. 65-85 (21)	152.95	176.80

Value, imperf set, $325.

For overprints and surcharges see Nos. 127, B5-B8, Austria M1-M21.

A27

A28

1916-17 ***Perf. 12½***

86	A27	3h dark gray	.25	*.40*
87	A27	5h olive green	.30	*.60*
88	A27	6h violet	.60	*.75*
89	A27	10h olive brown	2.25	*3.00*
a.		10h bister	2.25	3.75
90	A27	12h blue gray	.75	*1.10*
91	A27	15h car rose	.25	.25
92	A27	20h brown	.75	*1.10*
93	A27	25h blue	.75	*1.10*
94	A27	30h dark green	.75	*1.10*
95	A27	40h vermilion	.75	*1.10*
96	A27	50h green	.75	*1.10*
97	A27	60h lake	.75	*1.10*
98	A27	80h orange brn	3.75	1.50
a.		Perf. 11½	3.75	*7.50*
99	A27	90h dark violet	3.00	*1.90*
a.		Perf. 11½	1,050.	—
101	A28	2k claret, *straw*	1.90	*3.00*
102	A28	3k green, *bl*	2.25	*3.75*
103	A28	4k carmine, *grn*	7.50	*13.50*
104	A28	10k dp vio, *gray*	19.00	*37.50*
		Nos. 86-104 (18)	46.30	*73.85*

Value, imperf set: hinged $260; never hinged $525.

For overprints see Nos. B11-B12.

Emperor Karl I
A29 A30

1917 ***Perf. 12½***

105	A29	3h olive gray	.25	*.30*
a.		Perf. 11½	110.00	*240.00*
b.		Perf. 12½x11½	22.50	*52.50*
106	A29	5h olive green	.25	*.30*
107	A29	6h violet	.40	*.90*
108	A29	10h orange brn	.25	.25
a.		Perf. 11½x12½	190.00	*260.00*
b.		Perf. 11½	260.00	*560.00*
109	A29	12h blue	.40	*.90*
110	A29	15h brt rose	.25	.25
111	A29	20h red brown	.25	.25
112	A29	25h ultra	.75	*.75*
113	A29	30h gray green	.40	*.40*
114	A29	40h olive bis	.40	*.40*
115	A29	50h dp green	.75	*.75*
116	A29	60h car rose	.55	*.75*
a.		Perf. 11½	26.00	*60.00*
117	A29	80h steel blue	.40	*.65*
118	A29	90h dull violet	1.10	*1.90*
119	A30	2k carmine, *straw*	1.50	.75
120	A30	3k green, *bl*	21.00	*24.00*
121	A30	4k carmine, *grn*	7.50	*15.00*
122	A30	10k dp violet, *gray*	3.75	*13.50*
		Nos. 105-122 (18)	40.15	*62.00*

Value, imperf set, $190.

Nos. 47 and 66 Overprinted in Red

1918

126	A4	2h violet	.50	*1.50*
b.		Inverted overprint	37.50	
d.		Double overprint	19.00	
f.		Double overprint, one inverted	30.00	
127	A23	2h bright blue	.50	*1.50*
a.		Pair, one without overprint	—	
b.		Inverted overprint	15.00	
c.		Double overprint	11.00	
d.		Double overprint, one inverted	22.50	

Emperor Karl I — A31

1918 **Typo.** ***Perf. 12½, Imperf.***

128	A31	2h orange	11.00	
129	A31	3h dark green	11.00	
130	A31	5h lt green	11.00	
131	A31	6h blue green	11.00	
132	A31	10h brown	11.00	
133	A31	20h brick red	11.00	
134	A31	25h ultra	11.00	
135	A31	45h dk slate	11.00	
136	A31	50h lt bluish grn	11.00	
137	A31	60h blue violet	11.00	
138	A31	70h ocher	11.00	
139	A31	80h rose	11.00	
140	A31	90h violet brn	11.00	

Engr.

141	A30	1k ol grn, *grnsh*	*1,900.*	
		Nos. 128-140 (13)	143.00	

Nos. 128-141 were prepared for use in Bosnia and Herzegovina, but were not issued there. They were sold after the Armistice at the Vienna post office for a few days.

Nos. 128-141 exist imperf. Value, set $190.

SEMI-POSTAL STAMPS

Nos. 33 and 35 Surcharged in Red

1914, Nov. 1 **Unwmk.** ***Perf. 12½***

B1	A4	7h on 5h dk grn	.40	*.75*
B2	A4	12h on 10h car	.40	*.75*

Three varieties of the surcharge include "4" with open top, narrow "4" and wide "4." See the *Scott Classic Specialized Catalogue of Stamps and Covers* for detailed listings.

Nos. B1-B2 exist with double and inverted surcharges. Values, double surcharge, each: unused $22.50, never hinged $37.50. Values, inverted surcharge, each: unused $26, never hinged $45.

Nos. 33, 35 Surcharged in Red or Blue

1915, July 10 ***Perf. 12½***

B3	A4	7h on 5h (R)	12.00	*19.00*
a.		Perf. 9¼	240.00	*275.00*
B4	A4	12h on 10h (Bl)	.40	*.55*

Nos. B3-B4 exist with double and inverted surcharges. Value about $30 each.

Nos. 68, 70 Surcharged in Red or Blue

1915, Dec. 1

B5 A23 7h on 5h (R) .75 *2.10*
a. "1915" at top and bottom 37.50 *67.50*
B6 A23 12h on 10h (Bl) 1.50 *5.25*
a. Surcharged "7 Heller." 37.50 *75.00*

Nos. B5-B6 are found in four types differing in length of surcharge lines. See the *Scott Classic Specialized Catalogue of Stamps and Covers* for detailed listings.

Nos. B5-B6 exist with double and inverted surcharges. Values, each: unused $22.50, never hinged $37.50.

Nos. B5a and B6a exist double and inverted. Value: each, $750.

Nos. 68, 70 Surcharged in Red or Blue

1916. Feb. 1

B7 A23 7h on 5h (R) .75 .75
B8 A23 12h on 10h (Bl) .75 .75

The overprint on Nos. B7-B8 is found in two types, differing in length of surcharge lines. See the *Scott Classic Specialized Catalogue of Stamps and Covers* for detailed listings.

Nos. B7-B8 exist with double and inverted surcharges. Values: double surcharge, each $19 unused, $37.50 never hinged; inverted surcharge, each $15 unused, $30 never hinged.

Wounded Soldier — SP1

Blind Soldier — SP2

1916, July 10 Engr.

B9 SP1 5h (+ 2h) green .85 *1.90*
B10 SP2 10h (+ 2h) magenta 1.50 *2.60*

Nos. B9-B10 exist imperf. Value, set $110. For overprints, see Yugoslavia Nos. 1LB3-1LB4.

Nos. 89, 89a, 91 Overprinted

1917, May 9

B11 A27 10h bister (#89a) .25 *.25*
B12 A27 15h carmine rose .25 *.50*

Nos. B11-B12 exist imperf. Value set $150.

Nos. B11-B12 exist with double and inverted overprint. Values: double surcharge, each $15 unused, $30 never hinged; inverted surcharge, each $22.50 unused, $45 never hinged.

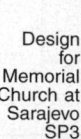

Design for Memorial Church at Sarajevo SP3

Archduke Francis Ferdinand — SP4

Duchess Sophia and Archduke Francis Ferdinand SP5

1917, June 20 Typo. *Perf. 12½*

B13 SP3 10h violet black .35 *.40*
B14 SP4 15h claret .35 *.40*
B15 SP5 40h deep blue .25 *.40*
Nos. B13-B15 (3) .95 1.20

Assassination of Archduke Ferdinand and Archduchess Sophia. Sold at a premium of 2h each, which helped build a memorial church at Sarajevo.

Exist perf 11½. See Scott Classic Specialized catalogue for detailed listings.

Exist imperf. Value set, $35.

Blind Soldier — SP6

Design: 15h, Wounded soldier.

1918, Mar. 1 Engr. *Perf. 12½*

B16 SP6 10h (+ 10h) grnsh bl .65 *1.50*
B17 SP6 15h (+ 10h) red brn .65 *1.50*

Nos. B16-B17 exist imperf. Value, set $67.50. For overprints, see Yugoslavia Nos. 1LB1-1LB2.

Emperor Karl I — SP8

Design: 15h, Empress Zita.

1918, July 20 Typo. *Perf. 12½x13*

B18 SP8 10h gray green .50 *1.25*
B19 SP8 15h brown red .50 *1.25*
B20 SP8 40h violet .50 *1.25*
Nos. B18-B20 (3) 1.50 *3.75*

Sold at a premium of 10h each which went to the "Karl's Fund."

Nos. B18-B20 exist imperf. Value, set: $75.

POSTAGE DUE STAMPS

D1

1904 Unwmk. *Perf. 12½*

J1 D1 1h black, red & yel .75 .30
J2 D1 2h black, red & yel .75 .30
J3 D1 3h black, red & yel .75 .30
J4 D1 4h black, red & yel .75 .30
J5 D1 5h black, red & yel 3.75 .30
J6 D1 6h black, red & yel .75 .30
J7 D1 7h black, red & yel 5.25 *3.75*
J8 D1 8h black, red & yel 5.25 2.25
J9 D1 10h black, red & yel .75 .30
J10 D1 15h black, red & yel .75 .30
J11 D1 20h black, red & yel 6.00 .30
J12 D1 50h black, red & yel 3.00 .40
J13 D1 200h black, red & grn 26.00 3.00
Nos. J1-J13 (13) 54.50 12.10
Set, never hinged 105.00

Nos. J1-J13 exists with a wide variety of perforations. See the *Scott Classic Specialized Catalogue of Stamps and Covers* for detailed listings.

Nos. J1-J13 also exist perf. 10½, 9¼, 6¼, and in various compound combinations.

Value, imperf set: hinged $125; never hinged $300.

For overprints and surcharges see Western Ukraine Nos. 61-72, Yugoslavia Nos. 1LJ23-1LJ26.

D2

1916-18 *Perf. 12½*

J14 D2 2h red ('18) .40 *1.50*
J15 D2 4h red ('18) .25 *1.50*
J16 D2 5h red .40 *1.50*
J17 D2 6h red ('18) .25 *1.50*
J18 D2 10h red .40 *1.50*
J19 D2 15h red 3.00 *9.00*
J20 D2 20h red .40 *1.50*
J21 D2 25h red 1.10 *3.75*
J22 D2 30h red .90 *3.75*
J23 D2 40h red 8.25 *21.00*
J24 D2 50h red 26.00 *62.50*
J25 D2 1k dark blue 3.75 *11.00*
J26 D2 3k dark blue 15.00 *40.00*
Nos. J14-J26 (13) 60.10 *160.00*
Set, never hinged 185.00

Nos. J25-J26 have colored numerals on a white tablet.

Value, imperf. set: unused $135, never hinged $300.

For surcharges see Italy Nos. NJ1-NJ7, Yugoslavia 1LJ1-1LJ13.

NEWSPAPER STAMPS

Bosnian Girl — N1

1913 Unwmk. *Imperf.*

P1 N1 2h ultra .75 *.75*
P2 N1 6h violet 2.25 *3.50*
P3 N1 10h rose 2.60 *3.50*
P4 N1 20h green 3.00 *3.75*
Nos. P1-P4 (4) 8.60 11.50

Used values are for postally used examples. Favor-canceled stamps are valued the same as unused.

After Bosnia and Herzegovina became part of Yugoslavia, stamps of type N1 perf., and imperf. copies surcharged with new values, were used as regular postage stamps. See Yugoslavia Nos. 1L17-1L22, 1L43-1L45.

SPECIAL DELIVERY STAMPS

"Lightning" — SH1

1916 Unwmk. Engr. *Perf. 12½*

QE1 SH1 2h vermilion .25 .75
a. Perf. 11½x12½ 375.00
QE2 SH1 5h deep green .40 1.10
a. Perf. 11½ 15.00 37.50

Nos. QE1-QE2 exist imperf. Values, set: unused $130, never hinged $260.

For surcharges see Italy Nos. NE1-NE2, Yugoslavia Nos. 1LE1-1LE2.

BOSNIA & HERZEGOVINA (BOSNIAK GOVERNMENT)

'bäz-nē-ak

LOCATION — Bordering on Croatia, Seribia & Montenegro.
GOVT. — Republic
CAPITAL — Sarajevo

Formerly part of Yugoslavia. Proclamation of independence in 1992 was followed by protracted civil war that was ended by the Dayton Peace Agreement of Nov. 21, 1995.

While Dinars were the official currency until 6/22/98, a currency pegged to the German mark was in use for some time prior to that. Stamps are denominated in pfennigs and marks in 11/97.

100 Paras = 1 Dinar
100 Pfennig = 1 Mark (6/22/98)

Catalogue values for all unused stamps in this country are for Never Hinged items.

Muslim Government in Sarajevo

Natl. Arms — A50

Denominations: 100d, 500d, 1000d, 5000d, 10,000d, 20,000d, 50,000d.

1993, Oct. 27 Litho. *Imperf.*
Booklet Stamps

200-206 A50 Set of 7 16.00 16.00

Nos. 200-206 each were available in bklts. of 50 (10 strips of 5).

1984 Winter Olympic Games, Sarajevo, 10th Anniv. — A51

No. 207, Games emblem. No. 208a, 100,000d, Four man bobsled. No. 208b, 200,000d, Hockey.

1994, Feb. 8

207 A51 50,000d org & blk 2.50 2.50

Souvenir Sheet

208 A51 Sheet of 2, #a.-b. 11.50 11.50

No. 208 contains 45x27mm stamps.

Souvenir Sheet

Bairam Festival — A52

Various illustrations from Koran: a, 400d. b, 600d.

1995, May 12 *Perf. 14*

209 A52 Sheet of 2, #a.-b. 16.00 16.00

Main Post Office, Sarajevo
A53

Designs: 10d, Facade. 20d, 30d, Demolished interior. 35d, 50d, Pre-civil war exterior. 100d, 200d, Post-war exterior.

1995, June 12

210-216	A53	Set of 7	8.00 8.00
216a		Pane of 7	9.00 9.00

No. 216a sold unattached in booklet covers.

Bosnian History
A54

Designs: 35d, Historical map, 10th-15th cent. 100d, Tomb, vert. 200d, Arms, Kotromanic Dynasty, vert. 300d, Charter by Ban Kulin, 1189.

1995, Aug. 12 ***Perf. 11½***
217-220 A54 Set of 4 9.00 9.00

Peace & Freedom, Europa
A55

1995, Sept. 25
221 A55 200d multicolored *3.50 3.50*

World Post Day — A56

1995, Sept. 25
222 A56 100d multicolored 1.60 1.60

A57

Flowers: No. 223: a, 100d, Simphyandra hofmannii. b, 200d, Lilium bosniacum.

1995, Oct. 12
223 A57 Pair, #a.-b. 4.75 4.75

Fish
A58

No. 224: a, 100d, Aulopyge hugeli. b, 200d, Paraphoxinus alepidotus.

1995, Oct. 12
224 A58 Pair, #a.-b. 4.75 4.75

Children's Week
A59

1995, Oct. 12
225 A59 100d multicolored 1.60 1.60

Electric Tram System, Sarajevo, Cent.
A60

1995, Oct. 12
226 A60 200d multicolored 3.00 3.00

Bridges
A61

Designs: 20d, Kozija, Sarajevo. 30d, Arslanagica, Trebinje. 35d, Latinska, Sarajevo. 50d, Old Bridge, Mostar. 100d, Visegrad.

1995, Dec. 12
227-231 A61 Set of 5 3.75 3.75

Christmas
A62

Designs: 100d, Visiting friends. 200d, Madonna and Child, vert.

1995, Dec. 24
232-233 A62 Set of 2 4.00 4.00

Queen Jelena's Tomb — A63

1995, Dec. 31
234 A63 30d multicolored .50 .50

A64

Design: Husein Gradascevic (1802-33).

1995, Dec. 31
235 A64 35d multicolored .50 .50

Mirza Safvet Basagic (1870-1934) — A65

1995, Dec. 31
236 A65 100d multicolored 1.10 1.10

Religious Diversity
A66

1995, Dec. 31
237 A66 35d multicolored .60 .60

Destruction of Olympic Stadium, Sarajevo — A67

35d, Stadium, various skaters. 100d, Stadium ablaze, vert.

1995, Dec. 31
238-239 A67 Set of 2 2.25 2.25

Famous Women — A68

Europa: 80d, Bahrija Hadzic (1904-93), opera singer. 120d, Nasiha Hadzic (1932-95), writer.

1996, Apr. 15 ***Perf. 15***
240-241 A68 Set of 2 *3.50 3.50*

UNICEF, 50th Anniv. — A69

Designs: a, 50d, Child stepping on land mine. b, 150d, Child's handprint.

1996, Apr. 15 ***Perf. 11½***
242 A69 Pair, #a.-b. 3.25 3.25

Bobovac Castle — A70

1996, May 5 ***Perf. 11½***
243 A70 35d multicolored .55 .55

Bairam Festival — A71

1996, May 5 ***Perf. 14***
244 A71 80d multicolored 1.50 1.50

No. 244 was issued in sheets of 2. Value $3.50.

Sarajevo Town Hall, Cent.
A72

1996, May 5 ***Perf. 11½***
245 A72 80d multicolored 1.10 1.10

Bosnian Journalists Assoc., Cent.
A73

1996, May 5
246 A73 100d multicolored 1.60 1.60

Essen '96, Intl. Philatelic Expo
A74

1996, May 25 ***Perf. 11½***
247 A74 200d multicolored 2.75 2.75

1996 Summer Olympic Games, Atlanta — A75

No. 248: a, 120d, Baron de Coubertin. b, 80d, Olympic Torch. c, 30d, Runners. d, 35d, Atlanta Games emblem.

1996, May 25
248 A75 Block of 4, #a.-d. 4.00 4.00

Background of No. 248 differs with location on sheet.

Alexander Graham Bell's Telephone, 120th Anniv.
A76

1996, July 10 ***Perf. 11½***
249 A76 80d multicolored 1.00 1.00

A77

1996, July 10
250 A77 100d multicolored 1.50 1.50

Extension of Privleges to Dubrovnik by Ban Stepan II, 1333.

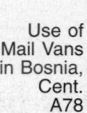

Use of Mail Vans in Bosnia, Cent. A78

1996, July 10
251 A78 120d multicolored 1.50 1.50

Flowers — A79

No. 252: a, 30d, Campanula hercegovina. b, 35d, Iris bosniaca.

1996, July 10
252 A79 Pair, #a.-b. 1.00 1.00

Printed checkerwise on the sheet.

Dogs A80

No. 253: a, 35d, Barak. b, 80d, Tornjak.

1996, July 10
253 A80 Pair, #a.-b. 2.00 2.00

Printed checkerwise on the sheet.

SOS Children's Village, Sarajevo — A81

1996, Sept. 1
254 A81 100d multicolored 1.50 1.50

A83

A84

Traditional costumes — No. 255: a, 50d, Moslem, Bjelasnice. b, 80d, Croatian. c, 100d, Moslem, Sarajevo.

Uniforms — No. 256: a, 35d, Bogomil soldier. b, 80d, Austro-Hungarian rifleman. c, 100d, Turkish light cavalry. d, 120d, Medieval Bosnian king.

1996, Sept. 20
255 A83 Strip of 3, #a.-c. + label 3.00 3.00
256 A84 Strip of 4, #a.-d. 5.00 5.00

Winter Festival, Sarajevo A85

1996, Nov. 25
257 A85 100d multicolored 1.50 1.50

Bosnia Day — A86

1996, Nov. 25
258 A86 120d Map, natl. arms 1.75 1.75

Christmas A87

1996, Dec. 21
259 A87 100d multicolored 1.50 1.50

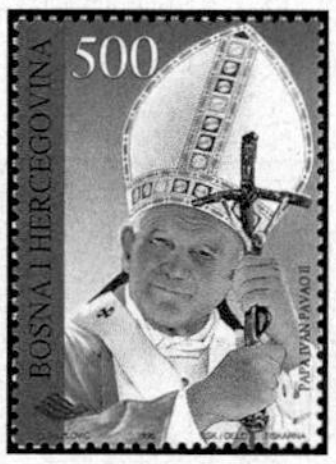

Visit by Pope John Paul II — A88

1996, Dec. 21 *Perf. 14*
260 A88 500d multicolored 8.00 8.00

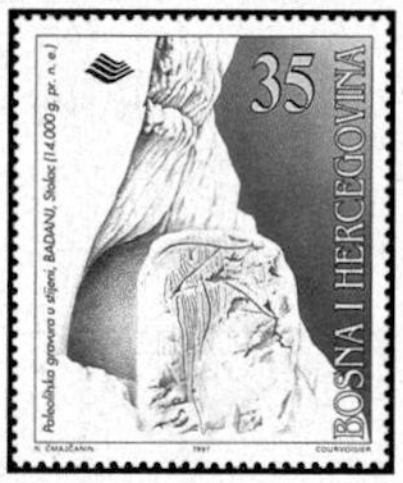

Archaeological Finds — A89

Designs: 35d, Paleolithic rock carving, Badanj. 50d, Neolithic ceramic head, Butmir. 80d, Bronze age bird wagon, Glasinac.

Walls of Daorson, Illyria — No. 264: a, 100d, Walls, rock face at L. b, 120d, Low wall outside city wall.

1997, Mar. 31 *Perf. 15*
261-263 A89 Set of 3 2.25 2.25

Souvenir Sheet

264 A89 Sheet of 2, #a.-b. 3.25 3.25

Children's Week — A90

1997, Apr. 15 *Perf. 11½*
265 A90 100d multicolored 1.50 1.50

Bairam Festival — A91

200d, Ferhad Pasha Mosque.

1997, Apr. 15 *Perf. 11½*
266 A91 200d multi 3.00 3.00

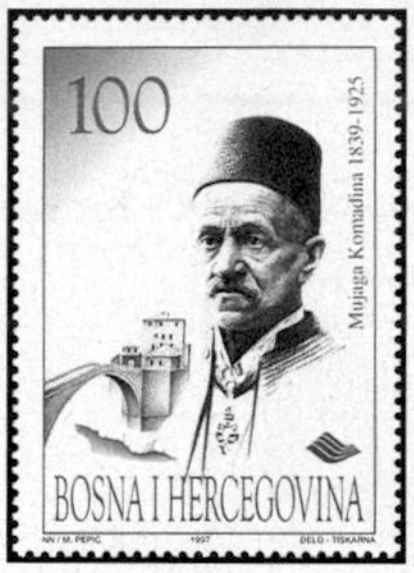

A92

1997, Apr. 25 *Perf. 14*
267 A92 100d multicolored 1.50 1.50

Mujaga Komadina (1839-1925), mayor of Mostar.

A93

Europa (Myths & Legends): 100d, Trojan warriors, map. 120d, Man on prayer mat, castle from The Miraculous Spring of Ajvatovica.

1997, May 3 *Perf. 11½*
268-269 A93 Set of 2 3.50 3.50

Greenpeace, 25th Anniv. — A94

Rainbow Warrior, inscribed: a, 35d, Grace. b, 80d, Dorreboom. c, 100d, Beltra. d, 120d, Morgan.

1997, May 25
270 A94 Block or strip of 4, #a.-d. 6.50 6.50

Third Intl. Film Festival, Sarajevo A95

1997, June 15
271 A95 110d multicolored 1.75 1.75

Mediterranean Games, Bari — A96

Designs: 40d, Games emblem. 130d, Boxing, basketball, kick boxing.

1997, June 15
272-273 A96 Set of 2 2.50 2.50

Discovery of Electrons, Cent. A97

1997, June 25
274 A97 40d multicolored .85 .85

Vasco da Gama's Voyage Around Africa, 500th Anniv. — A98

1997, June 25
275 A98 110d multicolored 1.75 1.75

Stamp Day — A99

1997, June 25
276 A99 130d multicolored 2.00 2.00

Railroads in Bosnia & Herzegovina, 125th Anniv. — A100

1997, June 25
277 A100 150d multicolored 2.25 2.25

Fauna — A101

No. 278: a, 40d, Dinaromys bogdanovi. b, 80d, Triturus alpestris.

No. 279: a, 40d, Oxytropis prenja. b, 110d, Dianthus freynii.

1997, Aug. 25
278 A101 Pair, #a.-b. 2.50 2.50
279 A101 Pair, #a.-b. 2.75 2.75

World Peace Day — A102

a, 50d, Sweden, Switzerland, Australia & other flags. b, 60d, Flags, globe showing Europe, Africa. c, 70d, Flags, globe showing North & South America. d, 110d, US, UK, Canadian & other flags.

1997, Aug. 25
280 A102 Strip of 4, #a.-d. 4.50 4.50

Great Sarajevo Fire, 300th Anniv. — A103

1997, Sept. 15
281 A103 110d multicolored 2.00 2.00

Architecture — A104

Designs: 40d, House with attic. 50d, Tiled stove, door. 130d, Three-storied house.

1997, Sept. 15
282-284 A104 Set of 3 3.00 3.00

Italian Pioneer Corps Aid in Reconstruction of Sarajevo — A105

1997, Nov. 1 ***Perf. 14***
285 A105 1.40m multicolored 2.00 2.00

Famous Men A106

1.30m, Augustin Tin Ujevic (1891-1955), writer. 2m, Zaim Imamovic (1920-94), singer, vert.

1997, Nov. 1 ***Perf. 11½***
286-287 A106 Set of 2 4.50 4.50

Diana, Princess of Wales (1961-97) — A107

1997, Nov. 3 ***Perf. 14***
288 A107 2.50m multicolored 3.50 3.50

Gnijezdo, by Fikret Libovac A108

Sarajevo Library, by Nusret Pasic A109

1997, Nov. 6 ***Perf. 11½***
289 A108 35pf multicolored .50 .50
290 A109 80pf multicolored 1.25 1.25

Samac-Sarajevo Railway, 50th Anniv. — A110

1997, Nov. 17 ***Perf. 14***
291 A110 35pf multicolored .60 .60

Religious Holidays — A111

50pf, Nativity Scene, Orthodox Christmas. No. 293, 1.10m, Wreath on door, Christmas. No. 294, 1.10m, Pupils before teacher, Hagada.

1997, Dec. 22 ***Perf. 11½***
292-294 A111 Set of 3 4.00 4.00

A112

Designs: a, 35pf, Sports. b, 1m, Games emblem.

1998, Jan. 15 ***Perf. 14***
295 A112 Sheet of 2, #a.-b. 2.00 2.00

1998 Winter Olympic Games, Nagano.

Bairam Festival — A113

1998, Jan. 28
296 A113 1m Mosque fountain 1.50 1.50

Ahmed Muradbegovic (1898-1972), Writer — A114

1998, Mar. 20
297 A114 1.50m multicolored 2.25 2.25

Fortified Towns — A115

No. 298: a, 35pf, Zvornik. b, 70pf, Bihac. c, 1m, Pocitelj. d, 1.20m, Gradacac.

1998, Mar. 20
298 A115 Booklet pane of 4, #a.-d. 5.00 5.00
Complete booklet, #298 5.50 5.50

A116

1998, May 5 ***Perf. 11½***
299 A116 1.10m multicolored *3.00 3.00*

Intl. Theater Festival, Sarajevo, Europa.

A117

Former Presidents of Univ. of Arts and Science: 40pf, Branislav Durdev (1908-93). 70pf, Alojz Benac (1914-92). 1.30m, Edhem Camo (1909-96).

1998, May 5
300-302 A117 Set of 3 3.50 3.50

A118

Ciconia Ciconia — No. 303: a, 70pf, Three in water. b, 90pf, Two in flight. c, 1.10m, Two in nest. d, 1.30m, Adult, chicks.

1998, May 5
303 A118 Strip of 4, #a.-d. 6.00 6.00

A119

1998, May 22
304 A119 2m Sheet with 2 labels 3.00 3.00

World Congress of Intl. League of Humanists, Sarajevo.

1998 World Cup Soccer Championships, France — A120

50pf, Soccer balls. 1m, Map, soccer ball 1.50m, Asim Ferhatovic Hase (1934-87), soccer player.

1998, May 22 ***Perf. 14½***
305-307 A120 Set of 3 4.50 4.50

Sarajevo Tunnel, 5th Anniv. — A121

1998, July 20 ***Perf. 11½***
308 A121 1.10m multicolored 1.60 1.60

Mushrooms A122

50pf, Morchella esculenta. 80pf, Cantharellus cibarius. 1.10m, Boletus edulis. 1.35m, Amanita caesarea.

1998, July 30
309-312 A122 Set of 4 5.50 5.50

Paris Subway A123

1998, Aug. 30
313 A123 2m violet blue & green 2.75 2.75

Henri Dunant — A124

1998, Sept. 14 ***Perf. 14***
314 A124 50pf multicolored .85 .85

Intl. Red Cross fight against tuberculosis.

Cities — A125

1998, Sept. 24
315 A125 5pf Travnik .30 .30
316 A125 38pf Sarajevo .45 .45

Chess — A126

Bosnian players — No. 317: a, 20pf, Woman at chess board. b, 40pf, Silver medal team, 31st Chess Olympiad. c, 60pf, Women's team, 32nd Chess Olympiad. d, 80pf, Men, Women's teams, 11th European Chess Championships.

1998, Sept. 24
317 A126 Sheet of 4, #a.-d. 3.00 3.00

World Post Day — A127

1998, Oct. 9 ***Perf. 11½***
318 A127 1m multicolored 1.50 1.50

Musical Instruments A128

1998, Oct. 23
319 A128 80pf multicolored 1.25 1.25

Intl. Day of Disabled Persons A129

1998, Dec. 3
320 A129 1m multicolored 1.50 1.50

Mt. Bjelasnica A130

1998, Dec. 3
321 A130 1m multicolored 1.50 1.50

Universal Declaration of Human Rights, 50th Anniv. — A131

1998, Dec. 10 ***Perf. 14½***
322 A131 1.35m multicolored 2.00 2.00

New Year A132

Christmas — A133

Designs: 1m, Child's drawing. 1.50m, Fr. Andeo Zvizdovic (1420?-98).

1998, Dec. 18 ***Perf. 11½***
323 A132 1m multicolored 1.50 1.50
324 A133 1.50m multicolored 2.25 2.25

School Anniversaries — A134

Designs: No. 325, 40pf, First Sarajevo High School, 120th anniv. No. 326, 40pf, Sarajevo University, 50th anniv., vert.

1999, Apr. 22 **Litho.** ***Perf. 11¾***
325-326 A134 Set of 2 1.20 1.20

Flora and Fauna A135

80pf, Pigeons. 1.10m, Knautia sarajevensis.

1999, Apr. 22 **Litho.** ***Perf. 11¾***
327-328 A135 Set of 2 3.50 3.50

First Manned Moon Landing, 30th Anniv. — A136

1999, May 20 **Litho.** ***Perf. 11¾***
329 A136 2m multicolored 2.75 2.75

Una River — A137

1999, May 20
330 A137 2m multicolored *3.50 3.50*

Europa

Gorazde A137a

1999, June 9 **Litho.** ***Perf. 14x14¼***
330A A137a 40pf multi .60 .60

World Environmental Protection Day — A138

80pf, Buna River Wellspring.

1999, June 15 **Litho.** ***Perf. 11¾***
331 A138 80pf multi 1.25 1.25

Philex France 99 — A139

1999, June 15
332 A139 2m multicolored 2.75 2.75

Special Olympics A140

1999, June 15
333 A140 50pf multicolored .70 .70

Bosnia & Herzegovina Postage Stamps, 120th Anniv. — A141

1999, July 1
334 A141 1m multicolored 1.75 1.75

UPU, 125th Anniv. — A142

1999, July 1 **Litho.** ***Perf. 11¾***
335 A142 1.50m multi 2.25 2.25

Minerals A143

Designs: 40pf, Tuzlite. 60pf, Siderite. 1.20m, Hijelofan. 1.80m, Quartz, vert.

1999, July 27 **Litho.** ***Perf. 11¾***
336-339 A143 Set of 4 6.00 6.00

Dzuzovi Mehmed Pasha Sokolovic Koran Manuscript A144

1999, Sept. 23
340 A144 1.50m multicolored 2.00 2.00

Kursumli Medresa Library, Founded 1537 — A145

1999, Sept. 23
341 A145 1m multicolored 1.40 1.40

Radiology in Bosnia & Herzegovina, Cent. — A146

1999, Oct. 5
342 A146 90pf multicolored 1.40 1.40

Handija Kasevljakovic (1888-1959), Historian — A147

1999, Oct. 5
343 A147 1.30m multicolored 1.75 1.75

25th European Chess Club Cup Finals — A148

1999, Oct. 29 **Litho.** ***Perf. 14***
344 A148 1.10m multicolored 1.75 1.75

Hvalov Zbornik, Book in Glagolitic Text — A149

1999, Sept. 23 **Litho.** ***Perf. 11¾***
345 A149 1.10m multicolored 1.60 1.60

Sarajevo Summit A150

1999, July 29 **Litho.** ***Perf. 14***
346 A150 2m multi 3.00 3.00

Expo 2000, Hanover A151

1999, Nov. 9 **Litho.** ***Perf. 11¾***
347 A151 1m multi 1.40 1.40

Painting by Afan Ramic A152

1999, Nov. 25
348 A152 1.20m multi 1.60 1.60

Birth of Six Billionth Person A153

1999, Nov. 25 ***Perf. 14***
349 A153 2.50m multi 4.00 4.00

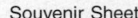

Souvenir Sheet

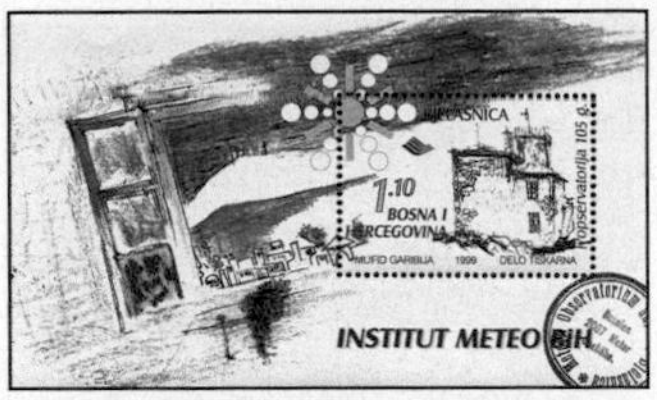

Bjelasnica Weather Observatory, 105th Anniv. — A154

1999, Dec. 15
350 A154 1.10m multi 1.60 1.60

Sarajevo Philharmonic A155

Sarajevo Intl. Music Festival A156

1999, Dec. 20
351 A155 40pf multi .60 .60
352 A156 1.10m multi 1.40 1.40

Mehmed Spaho (1883-1939), Politician — A157

2000, Mar. 15 ***Perf. 11¾***
353 A157 1m multi 1.60 1.60

Bairam Festival — A158

2000, Mar. 15
354 A158 1.10m multi 1.75 1.75

Amateur Radio in Bosnia and Herzegovina, 50th Anniv. — A159

2000, Mar. 15
355 A159 1.50m multi 2.50 2.50

Oriental Institute, Sarajevo, 50th Anniv. — A160

2000, Mar. 15
356 A160 2m multi 3.00 3.00

Souvenir Sheet

2000 Summer Olympics, Sydney — A161

Emblem of Sydney Olympics and map of: a, 1.30m, Bosnia & Herzegovina. b, 1.70m, Australia.

2000, Apr. 10 **Litho.** ***Perf. 14¾***
357 A161 Sheet of 2, #a-b 5.00 5.00

Europa, 2000

Common Design Type

2000, May 9 ***Perf. 11¾***
358 CD17 2m multi *4.75 4.75*

Birds A162

1m, Gyps fulvus. 1.50m, Platalea leucorodia.

2000, May 9 **Litho.** ***Perf. 11¾***
359-360 A162 Set of 2 4.00 4.00

Lake Boracko A163

River Una Emeralds — A164

2000, May 9
361 A163 40pf multi .65 .65
362 A164 1m multi 1.60 1.60

World Environmental Protection Day.

Souvenir Sheet

Greenpeace — A165

a, 50pf, Fish. b, 60pf, Lobster. c, 90pf, Anemones. d, 1.50m, Diver on shipwreck.

2000, May 9 ***Perf. 11¾x11½***
363 A165 Sheet of 4, #a-d 6.00 6.00

First Zeppelin Flight, Cent. A166

2000, June 10 ***Perf. 11¾***
364 A166 1.50m multi 2.25 2.25

Cities — A167

2000, June 9 **Litho.** ***Perf. 14***
365 A167 50pf Zenica .90 .90
366 A167 1m Mostar 1.20 1.20
367 A167 1.10m Bihac 1.40 1.40
368 A167 1.50m Tuzla, vert. 2.00 2.00
Nos. 365-368 (4) 5.50 5.50

Vranduk A168

Kraljeva Sutjeska A169

2000, Sept. 20 ***Perf. 11¾x11½***
369 A168 1.30m multi 1.75 1.75
370 A169 1.50m multi 2.50 2.50

The Adventures of Tom Sawyer, by Mark Twain A170

2000, Sept. 20
371 A170 1.50m multi 2.50 2.50

Souvenir Sheet

Millennium — A171

2000, Sept. 20 ***Perf. 11¾***
372 A171 2m multi 3.00 3.00

No. 372 contains one 29x57mm 80pf "stamp," and one 57x57mm 1.20m "stamp," but both lack the country name, which appears only in the sheet margin.

Intl. Children's Week — A172

2000, Oct. 5 ***Perf. 11½x11¾***
373 A172 1.60m multi 2.50 2.50

Paintings A173

Paintings by: 60pf, J. Mujezinovic. 80pf, I. Seremet.

2000, Oct. 5 ***Perf. 11¾x11½***
374-375 A173 Set of 2 2.25 2.25

UN High Commissioner for Refugees, 50th Anniv. — A174

2000, Dec. 14 ***Perf. 11¾x11½***
376 A174 1m multi 1.50 1.50

Cities — A175

2001, Mar. 22 ***Perf. 14***

377	A175	10pf Tesanj, vert.	.25	.25
378	A175	20pf Bugojno	.30	.30
379	A175	30pf Konjic	.40	.40
380	A175	35pf Zivinice	.80	.80
381	A175	2m Cazin	3.00	3.00
		Nos. 377-381 (5)	4.75	4.75

Animals — A176

No. 382, vert.: a, 90pf, Alcedo atthis. b, 1.10m, Bombycilla garrulus. No. 383: a, 1.10m, Equus caballus facing right. b, 1.90m, Equus caballus facing left.

2001, Mar. 22 Litho. ***Perf. 11¾***
382 A176 Horiz. pair, #a-b 2.50 2.50

Perf. 11¾x11½
383 A176 Horiz. pair, #a-b 3.00 3.00

Walt Disney (1901-66) — A177

Perf. 11½x11¾
2001, Mar. 22 **Litho.**
384 A177 1.10m multi 1.25 1.25

Shell Fossils — A178

Denominations in: a, 1.30m, Blue. b, 1.80m, Black.

2001, Mar. 22 ***Perf. 11¾x11½***
385 A178 Horiz. pair, #a-b 3.50 3.50

Souvenir Sheet

Comic Strips — A179

Inscriptions: a, Ti si moje janje. b, Ti si moj medo. c, Ti si moja maca. d, Ti si moj cvijet. e, Ti si moje pile.

2001, Mar. 22 Litho. ***Perf. 11¾***
Granite Paper
386 A179 30pf Sheet of 5, #a-e 2.50 2.50

See No. 419.

Souvenir Sheet

Europa — A180

2001, Apr. 10 ***Perf. 11½x11¾***
387 A180 2m multi *3.50 3.50*

Souvenir Sheet

Bosnia Institute, Sarajevo — A181

2001, May 25 Litho. ***Perf. 14***
388 A181 1.10m multi 1.90 1.90

Souvenir Sheet

Emir Balic, Mostar Bridge Diver — A182

2001, May 30 ***Perf. 11½x11¾***
389 A182 2m multi 3.50 3.50

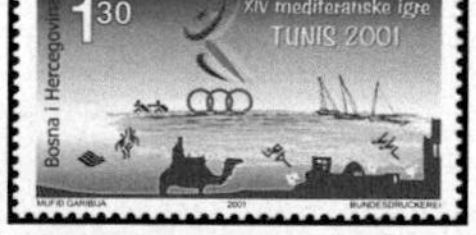

14th Mediterranean Games, Tunis — A183

2001, May 30 Litho. ***Perf. 14x14¼***
390 A183 1.30m multi 2.00 2.00

Ferrari Race Cars — A184

No. 391: a, 40pf, 15954 625 F1. b, 60pf, 1970 312 B. c, 1.30m, 1978 312 T3. d, 1.70m, 1983 126 C3.

2001, June 20 Litho. ***Perf. 14x14¼***
391 A184 Block of 4, #a-d 6.00 6.00

Zeljeznic, Soccer Champions — A185

2001, July 18
392 A185 1m multi 1.50 1.50

Nobel Prizes, Cent. A186

2001, July 18
393 A186 1.50m multi 2.25 2.25

Charlie Chaplin (1889-1977) A187

2001, July 18 ***Perf. 14x13¾***
394 A187 1.60m multi 2.50 2.50

Art by Edin Numankadic — A188

Perf. 12½x12¾
2001, Sept. 10 **Litho.**
395 A188 80pf multi 1.25 1.25

Portions of the design were applied by a thermographic process producing a shiny, raised effect.

David, by Michelangelo, 500th Anniv. — A189

2001, Sept. 10
396 A189 2m multi 3.00 3.00

Portions of the design were applied by a thermographic process producing a shiny, raised effect.

Breastfeeding Week — A190

2001, Oct. 1 Litho. ***Perf. 14***
397 A190 1.10m multi 1.75 1.75

World Post Day — A191

2001, Oct. 9
398 A191 1.30m multi 3.00 3.00

Horse-drawn Mail Delivery Railcar — A192

2001, Oct. 30 Litho. ***Perf. 14¼x14***
399 A192 1.10m multi 1.75 1.75

Alija Bejtic (1920-81), Historian — A193

2001, Nov. 10 Litho. ***Perf. 14***
400 A193 80pf multi 1.25 1.25

Albert Einstein A194

2001, Dec. 14
401 A194 1.50m multi 2.50 2.50

Musical Group "Indexi" A195

2002, Apr. 5 Litho. ***Perf. 14***
402 A195 38pf multi .65 .65

Mustafa Ejubovic (Sejh Jujo, 1651-1707), Writer — A196

2002, Apr. 15 Litho. ***Perf. 13¾x14***
403 A196 1m multi 1.50 1.50

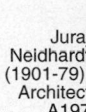

Juraj Neidhardt (1901-79), Architect A197

2002, Apr. 15 ***Perf. 14x13¾***
404 A197 1m multi 1.50 1.50

Dr. Sevala Zildzic-Iblizovic (1903-78) — A198

2002, Apr. 15 ***Perf. 13¾x14***
405 A198 1.30m multi 2.25 2.25

Sarajevo's Candidacy to Host 2010 Winter Olympics — A199

2002, Apr. 15 Litho. ***Perf. 13¾x14***
406 A199 1.50m multi 2.50 2.50

Intl. Earth Day — A200

2002, Apr. 15 Litho. ***Perf. 13¾***
407 A200 2m multi 2.75 2.75

Bosnia & Herzegovina Scouting Organization, 80th Anniv. — A201

2002, Apr. 20 Litho. ***Perf. 14x13¾***
408 A201 1m multi 1.75 1.75

Europa — A202

2002, Apr. 20 ***Perf. 13¾x14***
409 A202 2.50m multi 4.00 4.00

Independence, 10th Anniv. — A203

2002, Apr. 20 ***Perf. 14x13¾***
410 A203 2.50m multi 3.75 3.75

Souvenir Sheet

Sarajevo Fire Fighters — A204

2002, Apr. 20 ***Perf. 13¾x14***
411 A204 2.20m multi 3.50 3.50

Flowers — A205

Designs: 1m, Gentiana dinarica. 1.50m, Aquilegia dinarica.

2002, Apr. 20 Litho. ***Perf. 13¾x14***
412-413 A205 Set of 2 4.00 4.00

Butterflies — A206

Designs: 1.50m, Parnassus apollo. 2.50m, Iphiclides podalirius.

2002, Apr. 20 Litho. ***Perf. 13¾x14***
414-415 A206 Set of 2 6.00 6.00

Traditional Food A207

2002, June 28 Litho. ***Perf. 14***
416 A207 1.10m multi 1.75 1.75

30th Una River Regatta A208

2002, June 28
417 A208 1.30m multi 2.25 2.25

Souvenir Sheet

Ships — A209

No. 418: a, 1.20m, Galley. b, 1.80m, Galleon.

2002, June 28
418 A209 Sheet of 2, #a-b 5.00 5.00

Comic Strips Type of 2001

Inscriptions: a, Ako mi se ne javis! b, Ako me ne volis! c, Ako ti dosadujem! d, Ako me ne odgovoris! e, Ako me foliras.

2002, June 28
419 A179 40pf Sheet of 5, #a-e 3.50 3.50

Napredak, Croatian Cultural Organization, Cent. — A210

Perf. 13¾x13½
2002, Sept. 14 Litho.
420 A210 1m multi 1.60 1.60

Mountaineering, Cent. — A211

2002, Sept. 14 ***Perf. 13½x13¾***
421 A211 1m multi 1.40 1.40

Sarajevo Synagogue, Cent. A212

2002, Sept. 14
422 A212 2m multi 3.50 3.50

Miniature Sheet

Handicrafts — A213

No. 423: a, 80pf, Ironsmithing. b, 1.10m, Basketry. c, 1.20m, Filigree. d, 1.30m, Embroidery.

2002, Oct. 10
423 A213 Sheet of 4, #a-d 7.00 7.00

Bosnia & Herzegovina Flag — A214

2002, Nov. 20
424 A214 1m multi 1.60 1.60

Introduction of Euro Currency in Europe A215

2002, Nov. 20
425 A215 2m multi 3.25 3.25

Campaign Against Drug Abuse — A216

2002, Dec. 10 ***Perf. 14***
426 A216 10pf multi .50 .50

Mother and Child Institute — A217

2002, Dec. 10
427 A217 38pf multi .95 .95

Mak Dizdar (1917-71), Writer — A218

2002, Dec. 10
428 A218 1m multi 1.75 1.75

Coins — A219

Coins from reign of: 20pf, King Tvrtko (1376-91). 30pf, King Stjepan Tomas (1443-61). 50pf, King Stjepan Tomasevic (1461-63).

2002, Dec. 10
429-431 A219 Set of 3 1.50 1.50

Paintings by Mersad Berber (b. 1940) — A220

Designs: 40pf, Horse's head (34x34mm). 1.10m, Portrait of a woman. 1.50m, Angel statue, two women, horiz.

2002, Dec. 10 ***Perf. 13¾ (40pf), 14***
432-434 A220 Set of 3 5.00 5.00

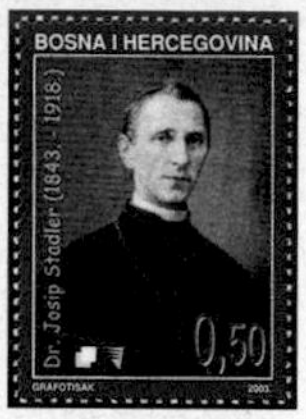

Archbishop Josip Stadler (1843-1918) — A221

2003, Jan. 24 Litho. ***Perf. 14***
435 A221 50pf multi .90 .90

No. 435 was sold by the post offices of the Moslem Administration as well as the Croat Administration.

Preporod, Bosnian Cultural Association, Cent. — A222

2003, Feb. 20 Litho. ***Perf. 13x13¼***
436 A222 1m multi 1.60 1.60

Portions of the design were applied by a thermographic process producing a shiny, raised effect.

2006 European Foresters' Competition in Nordic Skiing, Sarajevo — A223

2003, Feb. 20 ***Perf. 13¼x13½***
437 A223 1m multi 1.60 1.60

Mother and Child, by Omer Mujadzic (1903-91) A224

2003, Mar. 31 ***Perf. 13¼***
438 A224 70pf multi 1.20 1.20

Svetozar Zimonjic (1928-99), Electrical Engineer — A225

2003, Mar. 31 ***Perf. 13½x13¼***
439 A225 90pf multi 1.50 1.50

Bosnian Sitting Volleyball Team, 2002 World Champions — A226

2003, Mar. 31 ***Perf. 13½x13***
440 A226 1m multi 1.60 1.60

Flowers — A227

No. 441: a, Leontopodium alpinum (38mm diameter). b, Gentiana symphyandra.

2003, Mar. 31 ***Perf. 12¾***
441 A227 90pf Pair, #a-b 3.00 3.00

Europa — A228

2003, May 9 ***Perf. 13½x13¼***
442 A228 2.50m multi 4.00 4.00
a. Booklet pane of 4 16.00 —
Complete booklet, #442a 20.00

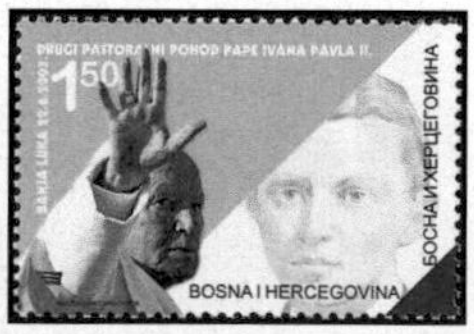

Visit of Pope John Paul II — A229

Perf. 13¼x13½
2003, June 22 Litho.
443 A229 1.50m multi 2.50 2.50

Discovery of Structure of DNA, 50th Anniv. — A230

2003, June 30 ***Perf. 13***
444 A230 50pf multi .90 .90

Souvenir Sheet

San Monstruma, Comic Strip by Enki Bilal — A231

Designs: a, Man on roof of building (30x24mm). b, Hotel and street (30x24mm). c, Man and woman (40x26mm). d, Woman and two men (40x26mm).

Perf. 13¼ (#a, b), 13 (#c, d)
2003, June 30
445 A231 50pf Sheet of 4, #a-d 3.50 3.50

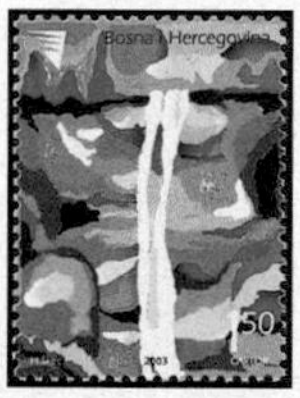

Skakavac Waterfall — A232

2003, Sept. 30 Litho. ***Perf. 13½***
446 A232 1.50m multi 2.50 2.50

Printed in sheets of 8 + 2 labels.

Decorations in Cekrekci Musilhudin Mosque — A233

Decorations in Hajji Sinan Dervish Convent — A234

2003, Sept. 30 ***Perf. 13¼***
447 A233 1m multi 1.50 1.50

Perf. 13¼
448 A234 2m multi 3.50 3.50

Children's Week A235

2003, Oct. 3 ***Perf. 13¼x13½***
449 A235 50pf multi .90 .90

Self-Adhesive

Serpentine Die Cut 12½
450 A235 50pf multi *24.00 24.00*

Souvenir Sheet

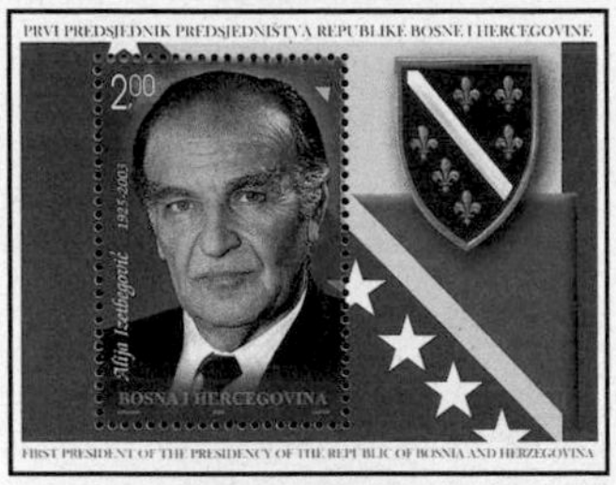

Pres. Alija Izetbegovic (1925-2003) — A236

2003, Nov. 27 *Perf. 13½x13¼*
451 A236 2m multi 3.50 3.50

Souvenir Sheet

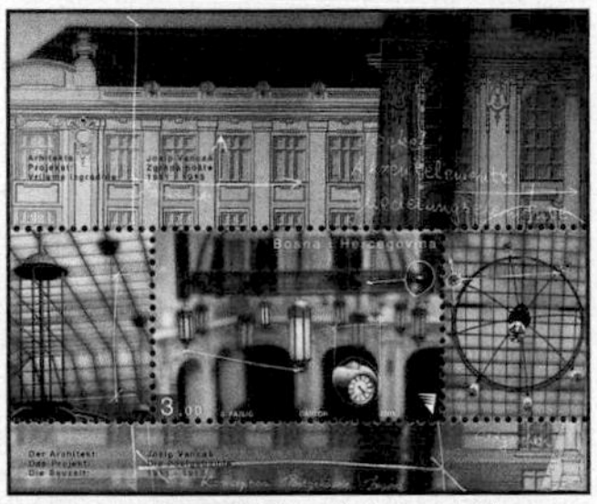

Sarajevo Post Office, by Josip Vancas, 90th Anniv. — A237

2003, Nov. 27 *Perf. 13*
452 A237 3m multi 4.75 4.75

Animals — A238

Designs: 30pf, Rupicapra rupicapra balcanica. 50pf, Ursus arctos bosniensis.

2003, Dec. 9 *Perf. 13¼*
453-454 A238 Set of 2 2.00 2.00

Christmas A239

2003, Dec. 18 **Litho.** *Perf. 13¼*
455 A239 20pf multi .45 .45

Pleminitas II, by Dzevad Hozo — A240

2003, Dec. 18 *Perf. 13½x13¼*
456 A240 10pf multi .25 .25

Painting by Ibrahim Ljubovic — A241

2003, Dec. 20 *Perf. 12½*
457 A241 1.50m multi 2.50 2.50

Powered Flight, Cent. A242

Perf. 13¼x13½

2003, Dec. 20 **Litho.**
458 A242 1m multi 1.75 1.75

Bayram Festival — A243

2004, Jan. 19 **Litho.** *Perf. 13¼*
459 A243 50pf multi .90 .90

Ban Kulin, 800th Anniv. of Death — A244

2004, Jan. 26 *Perf. 12½*
460 A244 50pf multi .90 .90

Love A245

2004, Feb. 2 *Perf. 13*
461 A245 2m multi 3.50 3.50

Values are for stamps with surrounding selvage.

Sarajevo Winter Olympics, 20th Anniv. — A246

2004, Feb. 7 *Perf. 13¼*
462 A241 1.50m multi + 2 flanking labels 2.10 2.10

Cities — A247

Designs: 20pf, Jajce, vert. 50pf, Jablanica. 2m, Stolac. 4m, Gradacac, vert. 5m, Fojnica.

2004 *Perf. 13½x13¼, 13¼x13½*
463 A247 20pf multi .40 .40
464 A247 50pf multi 1.00 1.00
465 A247 2m multi 3.75 3.75
466 A247 4m multi 7.75 7.75
467 A247 5m multi 10.00 10.00
Nos. 463-467 (5) 22.90 22.90

Issued: 20pf, 50pf, 4/5; 2m, 3/15; 4m, 5m, 2/23.

FIFA (Fédération Internationale de Football Association), Cent. — A248

2004, Mar. 31 *Perf. 13*
468 A248 2m multi 3.50 3.50

Flora — A249

No. 469 — Orchids: a, 1.50m, Cattleya intermedia. b, 2m, Brassavola David Sander.
No. 470 — Succulents: a, 1.50m, Aloe barbadensis. b, 2.50, Carnegiea gigantea.

2004, Mar. 31 *Perf. 13½x13¼*
Vert. Pairs, #a-b
469-470 A249 Set of 2 10.00 10.00

Zodiac Signs — A250

Nos. 471 and 472: a, Aries. b, Taurus. c, Gemini. d, Cancer. e, Leo. f, Virgo. g, Libra. h, Scorpio. i, Sagittarius. j, Capricorn. k, Aquarius. l, Pisces.

2004, Apr. 15 *Perf. 13¼*
471 A250 50pf Sheet of 12, #a-l 9.50 9.50

Booklet Stamps
Self-Adhesive
Serpentine Die Cut 12½

472 Booklet of 12 10.00 10.00
a.-l. A250 50pf Any single .75 .75

Europa — A251

No. 473: a, 1m, Clock on skis. b, 1.50m, Clocks at beach.

2004, Apr. 26 *Perf. 13½x13¼*
473 A251 Pair, #a-b 4.00 4.00
c. Booklet pane, 3 each #473a-473b *12.00* 12.00
Complete booklet, #473c *13.00* 13.00

European Youth Peace Summit — A252

2004, Apr. 26 **Litho.**
474 A252 1.50m multi 2.50 2.50

Greetings — A253

2004, May 15 *Perf. 13*
475 Horiz. pair, #a-b, with alternating labels 3.00 3.00
a. A253 50pf Clown and balloons .75 .75
b. A253 1.50m Bride and groom 2.25 2.25

Souvenir Sheet

Bees — A254

No. 476: a, On flower. b, In flight.

2004, May 15 *Perf. 13x13¼*
476 A254 2m Sheet of 2, #a-b 6.00 6.00

Reconstruction of Old Bridge, Mostar — A255

Old Bridge: 50pf, Close-up. 1m, From distance, horiz.

Perf. 13½x13¼, 13¼x13½

2004, June 23

477-478 A255 Set of 2 2.50 2.50
478a Souvenir sheet, #477-478, perf. 13 2.50 2.50

No. 478a is rouletted in five sections with stamps which have printer's inscription at bottom, in the central section.

2004 Summer Olympics, Athens — A256

2004, July 5 *Perf. 13*

479 A256 2m multi 3.50 3.50

10th Sarajevo Film Festival — A257

2004, July 26 *Perf. 13½x13¼*

480 A257 1.50m multi 2.10 2.10

Cities Type of 2004 and

A258

Designs: 10pf, Brcko. 20pf, Livno, vert. 30pf, Visoko. 1m, Sanski Most, vert.

2004, Dec. 31 **Litho.** *Perf. 13*

481 A258 10pf multi .25 .25
482 A247 20pf multi .35 .35
483 A258 30pf multi .40 .40
484 A258 1m multi 1.40 1.40
Nos. 481-484 (4) 2.40 2.40

The New Year, by Adin Hebib — A259

2004, Dec. 31

485 A259 1m multi 1.25 1.25

European Cultural Convention, 50th Anniv. — A260

2004, Dec. 31

486 A260 1.50m multi 2.50 2.50

Windows, by Safet Zec A261

2004, Dec. 31

487 A261 2m multi 2.75 2.75

Nikola Sop (1904-82), Poet — A262

2004, Dec. 31

488 A262 3m multi 4.00 4.00

Family Houses A263

House of: No. 489, 1m, Svrzo family (blue denomination). No. 490, 1m, Despic family (red denomination).

2004, Dec. 31

489-490 A263 Set of 2 2.75 2.75

Chamber Theater 55, Sarajevo, 50th Anniv. A264

2005, Mar. 7 **Litho.** *Perf. 13*

491 A264 40pf multi .65 .65

Jablanica Hydroelectric Plant, 50th Anniv. — A265

2005, Mar. 7

492 A265 60pf multi 1.10 1.10

Electric Lighting and Trams in Sarajevo, 110th Anniv. — A266

2005, Mar. 7

493 A266 2m multi 3.50 3.50

Izet Kiko Sarajlic (1930-2002), Poet — A267

2005, Mar. 10

494 A267 1m multi 1.25 1.25

Hasan Kikic (1905-42), Writer — A268

2005, Mar. 10

495 A268 1.50m multi 2.50 2.50

Europa A269

Designs: No. 496, 2m, Baklava (denomination in black). No. 497, 2m, Stuffed onions (denomination in white).

2005, Apr. 20

496-497 A269 Set of 2 6.50 6.50
a. Souvenir sheet, #496-497 6.50 6.50

Roses — A270

Designs: 80pf, Rosa damascena. 1.20m, Rosa alba.

2005, Apr. 20 **Litho.** *Perf. 13*

498-499 A270 Set of 2 3.50 3.50

Fauna A271

Designs: 2m, Tetrao urogalius. 3m, Castor fiber.

2005, Apr. 20 **Litho.** *Perf. 13*

500-501 A271 Set of 2 8.50 8.50

Nos. 500-501 each printed in sheets of 8 + 2 labels.

Mediterranean Games, Almería, Spain — A272

2005, May 20 **Litho.** *Perf. 13*

502 A272 1m multi 1.75 1.75

Sarajevo Music Academy, 50th Anniv. A273

2005, May 31

503 A273 1m multi 1.75 1.75

Friendship Between Sarajevo and Doha, Qatar A274

2005, June 30

504 A274 2m multi 2.75 2.75

See Qatar No. 1000.

Srebrenica Massacre, 10th Anniv. — A275

2005, July 1 **Litho.** *Perf. 13*

505 A275 1m multi 1.75 1.75

Mail Services A276

Running mailman with letter and: 10pf, Mail van, EMS emblem. 20pf, Printing press. 30pf, Text. 50pf, Bosnia & Herzegovina #327.

2005, Sept. 1

506 A276 10pf multi .25 .25
507 A276 20pf multi .40 .40
508 A276 30pf multi .50 .50
509 A276 50pf multi .80 .80
Nos. 506-509 (4) 1.95 1.95

Fruit — A277

Designs: 1m, Pyrus communis. 1.50m, Orange carica. 2m, Ficus carica. 2.50m, Prunus domestica. 5m, Prunus avium.

2005, Sept. 1

510 A277 1m multi 1.75 1.75
511 A277 1.50m multi 2.60 2.60
512 A277 2m multi 3.50 3.50
513 A277 2.50m multi 4.50 4.50
514 A277 5m multi 8.50 8.50
Nos. 510-514 (5) 20.85 20.85

Aladza Mosque, Foca — A278

2005, Sept. 15 **Litho.** ***Perf. 13***
515 A278 1m multi 1.75 1.75

Zitomislici Moanastery, Mostar — A279

2005, Sept. 15
516 A279 1m multi 1.75 1.75

St. Mark the Evangelist Monastery, Plehan — A280

2005, Sept. 15
517 A280 1m multi 1.75 1.75

The Bay, by Hakija Kulenovic (1905-87) — A281

2005, Sept. 15
518 A281 2m multi 3.50 3.50

Souvenir Sheet

Cartoon Characters — A282

No. 502: a, Girl and dogs. b, Windsurfing hedgehog.

2005, Sept. 15
519 A282 50pf Sheet of 2, #a-b 1.75 1.75

Trade Unions in Bosnia & Herzegovina, Cent. — A283

2005, Sept. 15 **Litho.** ***Perf. 13***
520 A283 1m multi 1.75 1.75

Bogomil Culture A284

Designs: No. 521, 50pf, Ban Kulin (1180-1203). No. 522, 50pf, King Tvrtko I Kotromanic (1353-91). 1m, Stone carving of Bogomil burning at stake. 2m, Bull of Pope Eugene IV.

2005, Oct. 10 ***Perf. 13¾x13¼***
521-524 A284 Set of 4 6.50 6.50

2004 Exhibition at Bosniac Institute, Istanbul — A285

Designs: 70pf, Exhibit hall. 4m, Entryway and exhibits.

2005, Nov. 15 ***Perf. 13***
525-526 A285 Set of 2 7.50 7.50

Nos. 525-526 each printed in sheets of 8 + 2 labels.

Dayton Peace Accords, 10th Anniv. — A286

2005, Nov. 21 ***Perf. 13¾x13¼***
527 A286 1.50m multi 2.50 2.50

Printed in sheets of 8 + label.

End of World War II, 60th Anniv. — A287

2005, Nov. 25
528 A287 1m multi 1.75 1.75

Europa Stamps, 50th Anniv. (in 2006) A288

No. 529: a, Flags and Western Hemisphere. b, Flags and Eastern Hemisphere. c, Map of Europe and 1-euro coin. d, Stars and chess organization emblems.

2005, Nov. 30 ***Perf. 13***
529 Horiz. strip of 4 *18.00 18.00*
a.-d. A288 3m Any single *4.00 4.00*
e. Souvenir sheet, #529a-529d *18.00 18.00*

No. 529e exists imperf. Value $30.

World Vision — A289

2005, Dec. 3 ***Perf. 13¾x13¼***
530 A289 50pf multi 1.60 1.60

Souvenir Sheet

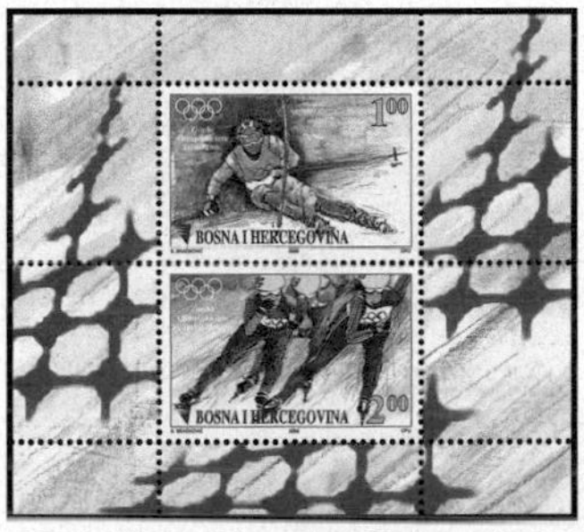

2006 Winter Olympics, Turin — A290

No. 531: a, 1m, Skiing. b, 2m, Speed skating.

2006, Feb. 1 **Litho.** ***Perf. 13***
531 A290 Sheet of 2, #a-b 5.00 5.00

Tourism A291

Designs: No. 532, 1m, Treskavica, Trnovo. No. 533, 1m, Raft in water, Gorazde, vert.

Perf. 13¼x13¾, 13¾x13¼
2006, Mar. 10
532-533 A291 Set of 2 3.50 3.50

Souvenir Sheet

Automobiles — A292

No. 534: a, 50pf, 1935 Mercedes-Benz 500k Cabriolet B. b, 50pf, 1939 Dodge D11 Graber Cabriolet. c, 1m, 1929, Mercedes-Benz SS Schwarzer. d, 2m, 1939 Bugatti T57 Ventoux.

2006, Apr. 5 ***Perf. 13***
534 A292 Sheet of 4, #a-d 7.00 7.00

Europa A293

Designs: No. 535, 2m, Upper arc of circle, denomination at left. No. 536, 2m, Lower arc of circle, denomination at right.

2006, Apr. 5 ***Perf. 13***
535-536 A293 Set of 2 7.00 7.00
536a Souvenir sheet, #535-536 7.00 7.00

Fauna and Fungi — A294

Designs: 1.50m, Formica rufa. 3m, Sarcosphaera crassa.

2006, Apr. 20 ***Perf. 13¾x13¼***
537-538 A294 Set of 2 7.50 7.50

Prisoners of War Association, 10th Anniv. — A295

2006, May 9 ***Perf. 13¼x13¾***
539 A295 1m multi 1.75 1.75

Bosnia & Herzegovina Art Gallery, 60th Anniv. — A296

2006, May 20 ***Perf. 13***
540 A296 1m multi 1.75 1.75

Isak Samokovlija (1889-1955), Writer, and Samuel, the Porter — A297

2006, May 20
541 A297 1m multi 1.75 1.75

Academicians — A298

Designs: No. 542, 1m, Muhamed Kadic (1906-83). No. 543, 1m, Mustafa Kamaric (1906-73).

2006, May 20 **Litho.** ***Perf. 13***
542-543 A298 Set of 2 3.50 3.50

Sarajevo Soccer Team, 60th Anniv. A299

2006, June 10 **Litho.** ***Perf. 13½***
544 A299 1m multi 1.75 1.75
a. Booklet pane of 2 4.50 4.50

A circle of perforations is in the middle of the stamp.

2006 World Cup Soccer Championships, Germany — A300

2006, June 10
545 A300 3m multi 5.00 5.00
a. Booklet pane of 2 10.00 10.00
Complete booklet, #544a, 545a 15.00

A circle of perforations is in the middle of the stamp.

49th European Junior Table Tennis Championships A301

2006, July 5 ***Perf. 13***
546 A301 1m multi 1.75 1.75

Breza Basilica Archaelogical Site — A302

2006, Sept. 10 ***Perf. 13¼x13¾***
547 A302 1m multi 1.75 1.75

Semiz Ali Pasha's Mosque, Praca — A303

2006, Sept. 10 ***Perf. 13¾x13¼***
548 A303 1m multi 1.75 1.75

Souvenir Sheet

Cartoon Characters From "Ptice Kao Mi" — A304

No. 549: a, Red bird. b, Yellow bird.

2006, Sept. 10 **Litho.**
549 A304 50pf Sheet of 2, #a-b 1.75 1.75

Vegetables — A305

Designs: 10pf, Potatoes (Solanum tuberosum). 20pf, Cauliflower (Brassica oleracea var. botrytis). 30pf, Savoy cabbage (Brassica oleracea var. sabauda). 40pf, Cabbage (Brassica oleracea var. capitata). 50pf, Garlic (Allium sativum). 1m, Carrots (Dauctus carota).

2006, Mar. **Litho.** ***Perf. 13½x13¾***
550 A305 10pf multi .25 .25
551 A305 20pf multi .35 .35
552 A305 30pf multi .50 .50
553 A305 40pf multi .85 .85
554 A305 50pf multi .95 .95
555 A305 1m multi 1.75 1.75
Nos. 550-555 (6) 4.65 4.65

Wild Animals A306

Designs: 1.50m, Lepus europaeus. 2m, Capreolus capreolus. 2.50m, Anas sp., horiz. 4m, Vulpes vulpes. 5m, Canis lupus, horiz.

Perf. 13¾x13¼, 13¼x13¾
2006, June 30
556 A306 1.50m multi 2.50 2.50
557 A306 2m multi 3.25 3.25
558 A306 2.50m multi 4.00 4.00
559 A306 4m multi 6.50 6.50
560 A306 5m multi 8.00 8.00
Nos. 556-560 (5) 24.25 24.25

Each stamp printed in sheets of 8 + label.

Children's Week — A307

2006, Oct. 6 ***Die Cut***
Self-Adhesive
561 A307 50pf multi .90 .90

Elci Ibrahim-Pasha Madrassa, Travnik, 300th Anniv. — A308

2006, Oct. 25 ***Perf. 13¼x13¾***
562 A308 1m multi 1.75 1.75

Tuzla University, 30th Anniv. — A309

2006, Oct. 25 ***Perf. 13¾x13¼***
563 A309 1m multi 1.75 1.75

Nobel Laureates A310

Designs: 1m, Vladimir Prelog (1906-98), 1975 Chemistry laureate. 2.50m, Ivo Andric (1892-1975), 1961 Literature laureate.

2006, Oct. 25
564-565 A310 Set of 2 5.50 5.50

Museum Exhibits — A311

2006, Nov. 24 ***Perf. 13***
566 A311 1m multi 1.75 1.75

Trains A312

Designs: 50pf, Steam locomotive. 1m, Electric train.

2006, Nov. 24 **Litho.**
567-568 A312 Set of 2 2.50 2.50

Sarajevo National Opera, 60th Anniv. — A313

2007, Feb. 15 ***Perf. 13¾x13¼***
569 A313 50pf multi .90 .90

Prokos Lake A314

2007, Feb. 15 ***Perf. 13¼x13¾***
570 A314 2.50m multi 4.00 4.00

Europa A315

Scouts and: No. 571, 2m, Backpacks. No. 572, 2m. Tent and campfire.

2007, Feb. 15 ***Perf. 13***
571-572 A315 Set of 2 7.00 7.00
572a Souvenir sheet, #571-572 + 2 labels 7.00 7.00
572b Booklet pane, 2 each #571-572 + label 15.00 —
Complete booklet, #572b 15.00

Scouting, cent. Nos. 571-572 each were printed in sheets of 8 + label.

Domesticated Animals — A316

Designs: 10pf, Ovis aries. 20pf, Capra hircus. 30pf, Bos taurus. 40pf, Equus asinus. 70pf, Equus caballus. 1m, Felis silvestris.

2007, Jan. 31 **Litho.** ***Perf. 13***
573 A316 10pf multi .25 .25
574 A316 20pf multi .30 .30
575 A316 30pf multi .50 .50
576 A316 40pf multi .75 .75

Perf. 13¼x13¾
Size: 40x33mm

577 A316 70pf multi 1.25 1.25
578 A316 1m multi 1.60 1.60
Nos. 573-578 (6) 4.65 4.65

Nos. 573-578 each printed in sheets of 8 + label.

Knautia Travnicensis A317

Sciurus Vulgaris A318

2007, Mar. 15 ***Perf. 13***
579 A317 80pf multi 1.25 1.25
580 A318 1.20m multi 2.25 2.25

Nos. 579-580 each printed in sheets of 8 + label.

Kozarac
A319

2007, Mar. 15 *Perf. 13¾x13¼*
581 A319 1m multi 1.75 1.75

Dr. Abdulah Nakas Hospital, 140th Anniv.
A320

2007, Apr. 10 *Perf. 13¼x13¾*
582 A320 1.50m sil & maroon 2.50 2.50

Madrassa, Cazin, 140th Anniv. — A321

2007, Apr. 10 *Perf. 13*
583 A321 2m multi 3.50 3.50

Fountain, Tuzla — A322

Fountain, Mostar
A323

Fountain, Sanski Most — A324

Fountain, Sarajevo
A325

Fountain Near Bey's Mosque
A326

Perf. 13¾x13¼, 13¼x13¾

2007, Apr. 10

584	A322	1.50m multi	2.25	2.25
585	A323	2m multi	3.00	3.00
586	A324	2.50m multi	4.00	4.00
587	A325	4m multi	6.25	6.25
588	A326	5m multi	7.50	7.50
		Nos. 584-588 (5)	23.00	23.00

Nos. 584-588 each printed in sheets of 8 + label.

Gajret Newspaper, Cent. — A327

2007, Apr. 16 *Perf. 13*
589 A327 1m multi 1.75 1.75

Gazi Husrev-Begova Library — A328

2007, Apr. 16
590 A328 1.50m multi 2.50 2.50

Islamic Sciences Faculty, Sarajevo, 30th Anniv.
A329

2007, Apr. 16
591 A329 2m multi 3.50 3.50

Pocitelj Art Colony
A330

2007, May 4 **Litho.** *Perf. 13¼x13¾*
592 A330 1m multi 1.75 1.75

Painting by Ismet Rizvic
A331

2007, May 4 **Litho.** *Perf. 13*
593 A331 1.50m multi 2.50 2.50

Bear Figurine, 3500 B.C.
A332

2007, June 1 *Perf. 13¼x13¾*
594 A332 1m multi 1.75 1.75

Karel Parik (1857-1942), Architect — A333

2007, June 6 *Perf. 13*
595 A333 2.50m multi 4.00 4.00

Karate — A334

2007, July 2 **Litho.** *Perf. 13*
596 A334 1m multi 1.50 1.50

Zulfikar Zuko Dzumhur (1920-89), Cartoonist
A335

2007, July 2
597 A335 1m multi 1.75 1.75

Sarajevo University Medical Faculty, 61st Anniv.
A336

2007, July 2
598 A336 1m multi 1.75 1.75

Sepp Blatter, Fédération Internationale de Football Association (FIFA) President — A337

Juan Antonio Samaranch, Former Pres. of Intl. Olympic Committee — A338

Perf. 13¼x13¾

2007, Sept. 20 **Litho.**
599 A337 2m multi 3.50 3.50
600 A338 2m multi 3.50 3.50

Honorary Ambassadors of Sport and Culture of Peace.

Fortress, Samobor
A339

Perf. 13¾x13¼

2007, Sept. 28 **Litho.**
601 A339 1m multi 1.75 1.75

Ecology
A340

Children's art by: No. 602, 50pf, Amira Halilovic. No. 603, 50pf, Maida Hasanic.

2007, Sept. 28 *Perf. 13*
602-603 A340 Set of 2 1.75 1.75
603a Souvenir sheet, #602-603 1.75 1.75

Meat Pie
A341

2007, Oct. 1 *Perf. 13½*
604 A341 2m multi 3.50 3.50

Values are for stamps with surrounding selvage.

Stegosaurus — A342

2007, Nov. 15 *Perf. 13¼x13¾*
605 A342 2m multi 3.50 3.50

Space Flight of Dog, Laika, on Sputnik 2, 50th Anniv. — A343

2007, Nov. 15 *Perf. 13¾x13¼*
606 A343 3m multi 5.00 5.00

Bosnian University Sports Association, 60th Anniv. — A344

2007, Dec. 3 ***Perf. 13***
607 A344 50pf multi .90 .90

Printed in sheets of 4.

Bosnian Handball Team, 60th Anniv. — A345

2007, Dec. 31
608 A345 50pf multi .90 .90

Merhamet Charitable Organization, 95th Anniv. — A346

2008, Feb. 15
609 A346 70pf multi 1.20 1.20

Europa A347

Designs: 2m, Letter, candle, quill pen. 3m, Person writing on postcard.

2008, Mar. 8 Litho. ***Perf. 13½x13¾***
610-611 A347 Set of 2 8.50 8.50
611a Souvenir sheet, #610-611 8.50 8.50

University of Sarajevo College of Pharmacy — A348

2008, Feb. 15 Litho. ***Perf. 13***
612 A348 2m multi 3.50 3.50

Local Cuisine A349

Designs: 1m, Shishkebabs. 2m, Apple stuffed with whipped cream.

2008, Feb. 15 ***Perf. 13¼x13¾***
613-614 A349 Set of 2 5.00 5.00

Nos. 613-614 each were printed in sheets of 8 + label.

Blood Transfusion Institute, Sarajevo, 50th Anniv. A350

2008, Mar. 8 ***Perf. 13***
615 A350 1.50m multi 2.50 2.50

Intl. Women's Day — A351

2008, Mar. 8
616 A351 2m multi 3.50 3.50

Printed in sheets of 8 + label.

Bosanska Krupa — A352

Velika Kladusa A353

2008, Mar. 8
617 A352 70pf multi 1.25 1.25
618 A353 1m multi 1.75 1.75

Nos. 617-618 each were printed in sheets of 8 + label.

Sarajevo Shooting Club, 60th Anniv. A354

2008, Apr. 10
619 A354 1.50m multi 2.50 2.50

Universal Esperanto Association, Cent. — A355

2008, Apr. 10
620 A355 1.50m multi 2.50 2.50

2008 Summer Olympics, Beijing A356

Designs: 1m, Judo. 1.50m, Track and field.

2008, May 5 ***Perf. 13¾x13¼***
621-622 A356 Set of 2 3.50 3.50

Nos. 621-622 each were printed in sheets of 8 + label.

Motorcycles A357

Designs: No. 623, 1.50m, Jawa Trail 90. No. 624, 1.50m, Ural-3.

2008, May 5 ***Perf. 13***
623-624 A357 Set of 2 4.50 4.50

Vjetrenica Cave A358

2008, June 10 **Litho.**
625 A358 1m multi 1.75 1.75

Stabilization and Association Agreement with European Union — A359

2008, June 16
626 A359 70pf multi 1.20 1.20

Krivaja House, Zavidovici A360

2008, July 1 ***Perf. 13¾x13¼***
627 A360 2.50m multi 4.00 4.00

Pond Flora and Fauna A361

Designs: 1.50m, Nymphaea alba. 2m, Rana esculenta.

2008, July 1 ***Perf. 13***
628-629 A361 Set of 2 6.00 6.00

Nos. 628-629 each were printed in sheets of 9 + label.

Musalla, Kamengrad A362

Ostrovica A363

2008, July 11
630 A362 1m multi 1.75 1.75
631 A363 1.50m multi 2.50 2.50

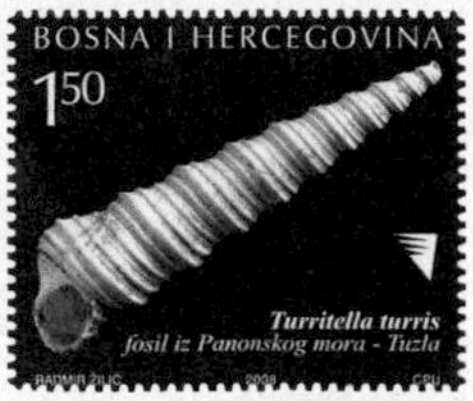

Turritella Turris Fossil Shell A364

2008, Sept. 1 ***Perf. 13¼x13¾***
632 A364 1.50m multi 2.50 2.50

Printed in sheets of 8 + label.

Friendship Between Bosnia and Herzegovina and Kuwait — A365

2008, Sept. 9 ***Perf. 13***
633 A365 3m multi 5.00 5.00

Sarajevo Ski Club, 80th Anniv. A366

2008, Nov. 1 ***Perf. 13¼x13¾***
634 A366 2m multi 3.50 3.50

Printed in sheets of 8 + label.

Fauna — A367

Designs: 5pf, Lynx lynx. 70pf, Accipiter gentilis. 5m, Strigiformes.

2008, Dec. 15 ***Perf. 13¾x13¼***
635-637 A367 Set of 3 7.50 7.50

Douglas Fir A368

Birch A369

Cypress A370

2008, Dec. 15 *Perf. 13¼x13¾*

638 A368 70c multi	.90	.90
639 A369 70c multi	.90	.90
640 A370 70c multi	.90	.90
Nos. 638-640 (3)	2.70	2.70

Europa A371

Designs: 2m, Planets. 3m, Space telescope.

2009, Sept. 10 **Litho.** *Perf. 13*

641-642 A371 Set of 2	8.50	8.50
642a Souvenir sheet of 2, #641-642, + 2 labels	8.50	8.50

Intl. Year of Astronomy.

Intl. Day of Missing Persons A372

2009, Aug. 30 **Litho.** *Perf. 13*
643 A372 20pf multi .40 .40

Hirundo Rustica A373

2009, Sept. 10 *Perf. 13¼x13*
644 A373 70pf multi 1.20 1.20

Printed in sheets of 8 + label.

Historical Archives of Sarajevo Museum — A374

2009, Sept. 10 *Perf. 13*
645 A374 70pf multi 1.10 1.10

Academic Culture Center of Sarajevo University, 60th Anniv. — A375

2009, Sept. 10 *Perf. 13¼x13*
646 A375 1m multi 1.50 1.50

Council of Europe, 60th Anniv. — A376

2009, Sept. 10 *Perf. 13x13¼*
647 A376 1m multi 1.50 1.50

Sarajevo Museum, 60th Anniv. A377

2009, Sept. 10 *Perf. 13*
648 A377 1m multi 1.50 1.50

Bosnian Coffee — A378

2009, Sept. 10 **Litho.**
649 A378 1m multi 1.50 1.50

Printed in sheets of 8 + label.

Charles Darwin (1809-82), Naturalist — A379

2009, Sept. 10 *Perf. 13¼x13*
650 A379 2m multi 3.50 3.50

World Track and Field Championships, Berlin — A380

Designs: 1.50m, Runners. 2m, Stylized runners.

2009, Sept. 10

651-652 A380 Set of 2	5.50	5.50
652a Souvenir sheet, #651-652	5.50	5.50

Children's Week A381

2009, Oct. 1 *Perf. 13*
653 A381 70pf multi 1.20 1.20

Pansies A382

2009, Oct. 9 *Perf. 13¼x13*
654 A382 1m multi 1.50 1.50

Printed in sheets of 8 + label.

Sarajevo Canton Tribunal, 130th Anniv. A383

2009, Oct. 9 *Perf. 13*
655 A383 1m multi 1.75 1.75

Postal Cooperation Between Bosnia & Herzegovina and Turkey — A384

2009, Oct. 9
656 A384 2m multi 2.90 2.90

See Turkey No. 3191.

Strawberries — A385

2009, Oct. 9
657 A385 5m multi 8.50 8.50

Franciscan Theological College, Sarajevo, Cent. — A386

2009, Dec. 7 **Litho.**
658 A386 1m multi 1.50 1.50

Printed in sheets of 8 + label.

Franciscan Order, 800th Anniv. A387

2009, Dec. 7
659 A387 1.50m multi 2.25 2.25

Printed in sheets of 8 + label.

Sign Language A388

2009, Dec. 7 *Perf. 13¼x13*
660 A388 1.50m multi 2.50 2.50

Souvenir Sheet

2010 Winter Olympics, Vancouver — A389

No. 661: a, 1.50m, Skier, ski jumper, speed skater, ice hockey players, biathlete. b, 2m, Figure skater, snowboarder, ice hockey player, bobsledders.

2010, Feb. 12 *Perf. 13x13¼*
661 A389 Sheet of 2, #a-b 6.00 6.00

Old City, Srebrenik A390

Ostrozac Castle A391

2010, Mar. 22 *Perf. 13*

662 A390 70pf multi	1.25	1.25
663 A391 1m multi	1.75	1.75

Nos. 662-663 each were printed in sheets of 8 + label.

Taxus Baccata A392

Aesculus Hippocastanum — A393

Cygnus Olor — A394

2010, Apr. 12 Litho. *Perf. 13*

664 A392 1m multi 1.75 1.75
665 A393 1m multi 1.75 1.75

Souvenir Sheet

666 A394 2m multi 3.50 3.50

Nos. 664-665 each were printed in sheets of 8 + label.

Folk Ballad "Hasanaganica" — A395

2010, Apr. 26 *Perf. 13¼x13*

667 A395 1m multi 1.50 1.50

Printed in sheets of 8 + label.

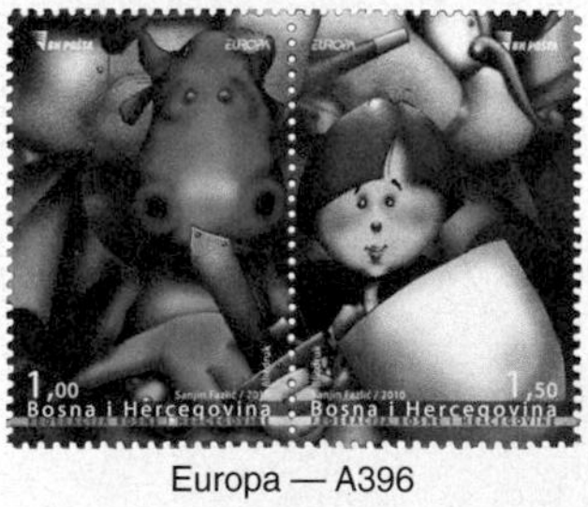

Europa — A396

No. 668: a, 1m, Dragon. b, 1.50m, Little Blu (knight).

2010, Apr. 26 *Perf. 13x13¼*

668 A396 Horiz. pair, #a-b 4.50 4.50
c. Souvenir sheet, #668a-668b 4.50 4.50
d. Booklet pane, 3 each #668a-668b, perf. 13x13¼ on 2 or 3 sides 13.50 —
Complete booklet, #668d 14.00

Ajvatovica, 500th Anniv. — A397

2010, June 15 *Perf. 13*

669 A397 1.50m multi 2.50 2.50

Robert Schumann (1810-56), Composer — A398

Frédéric Chopin (1810-49), Composer — A399

2010, Oct. 18 Litho. *Perf. 13¼x13*

670 A398 1m multi 1.50 1.50
671 A399 1.50m multi 2.50 2.50

Nos. 670-671 each were printed in sheets of 8 + label.

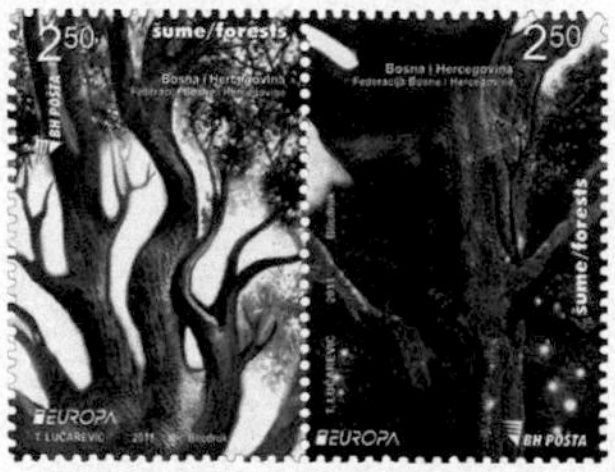

Europa — A400

No. 672 — Tree with denomination at: a, Upper left. b, Upper right.

2011, May 9 *Perf. 13x13¼*

672 A400 2.50m Horiz. pair, #a-b 7.00 7.00
c. Souvenir sheet, #672a-672b 7.00 7.00
d. Booklet pane of 6, 3 each #672a-672b, perf. 13x13¼ on 2 or 3 sides 21.00 —

Intl. Year of Forests. No. 672d was sold with, but not attached to, a booklet cover.

Gentiana Jasnae A401

Passer Domesticus — A402

2011, May 26 *Perf. 13*

673 A401 2m multi 3.25 3.25

Souvenir Sheet

674 A402 2.50m multi 4.00 4.00

No. 673 was printed in sheets of 8 + label.

Apparition of the Virgin Mary at Medjugorje, 30th Anniv. — A403

Litho. With Foil Application

2011, May 26

675 A403 2.50m multi 3.75 3.75

Printed in sheets of 8 + label.

Souvenir Sheet

First Man in Space, 50th Anniv. — A404

2011, May 26 Litho.

676 A404 2m multi 3.00 3.00

Arms of Duke Stjepan Vukcic Kosaca (1404-66) A405

2011, June 6 Litho. *Perf. 13¼x13*

677 A405 1m multi 1.40 1.40

Printed in sheets of 8 + label.

Campaign Against AIDS, 30th Anniv. — A406

2011, June 6 Litho. *Perf. 13*

678 A406 70pf multi 1.00 1.00

Hutovo Blato Nature Park — A407

2011, Sept. 20

679 A407 70pf multi .90 .90

No. 679 was printed in sheets of 8 + label.

Astacus Astacus A408

2011, Sept. 20

680 A408 1.50m multi 2.10 2.10

No. 680 was printed in sheets of 8 + label.

Writers A409

Designs: 1m, Skender Kulenovic (1910-78). 1.50m, Mesa Selimovic (1910-82).

2011, Oct. 7 *Perf. 13¼x13*

681-682 A409 Set of 2 3.50 3.50

Nos. 681-682 each were printed in sheets of 8 + label.

Fridtjof Nansen (1861-1930), Polar Explorer and Diplomat — A410

2011, Oct. 25 *Perf. 13x13¼*

683 A410 1.50m multi 2.25 2.25

Souvenir Sheet

Sinking of the Titanic, Cent. — A411

2012, May 29 Litho. *Perf. 13*

684 A411 2.50m multi 3.75 3.75

Souvenir Sheet

Locomotives — A412

No. 685: a, 1m, Locomotive 55-99. b, 1.50m, Locomotive 83-180.

2012, May 29 *Perf. 13¼x13*

685 A412 Sheet of 2, #a-b 3.75 3.75

Europa — A413

No. 686: a, Sarajevo. b, Mountains, waterfalls, rowboat, monument.

2012, May 29 *Perf. 13x13¼*

686 A413 2.50m Horiz. pair, #a-b 7.50 7.50
c. Souvenir sheet of 2, #686a-686b 7.50 7.50
d. Booklet pane of 6, 3 each #686a-686b, perf. 13x13¼ on 2 or 3 sides 22.50 —
Complete booklet, #686d 22.50

Miniature Sheet

Flowers — A414

No. 687: a, Three Viola odorata. b, Two Primula veris. c, Two Helleborus. d, Two Galanthus. e, Two Crocus sativa. f, Viola odorata and bubbles. g, Cluster of Primula veris and leaves. h, Two Helleborus and leaves. i, Two Galanthus and rock crystal. j, Crocus sativa and rock crystal.

2012, June 7 ***Perf. 13***
687 A414 70pf Sheet of 10, #a-j 10.00 10.00

Rustempasic Castle, Bugojno — A415

2012, June 22
688 A415 2m multi 3.00 3.00

Printed in sheets of 8 + label.

Old Sections of Cities A416

No. 689: a, Tesanj. b, Buzim.

2012, June 25 ***Perf. 13¼x13***
689 A416 20pf Vert. pair, #a-b .70 .70

Sports A417

2012, July 10 ***Perf. 13x13¼***
690 A417 2.50m multi 3.75 3.75

Printed in sheets of 8 + label.

La Benevolencia Jewish Organization, 120th Anniv. — A418

2012, Sept. 10 ***Perf. 13***
691 A418 70pf multi 1.10 1.10

No. 691 was printed in sheets of 8 + label.

Snakes — A419

Designs: 1m, Vipera ammodytes. 1.50m, Vipera berus bosniensis.

2012, Sept. 10
692-693 A419 Set of 2 4.00 4.00

Nos. 692-693 each were printed in sheets of 8 + label.

Children's Week A420

2012, Oct. 1
694 A420 70pf multi 1.10 1.10

Printed in sheets of 8 + label.

Intorduction of Euro Currency in Europe, 10th Anniv. — A421

2012, Oct. 1
695 A421 2m multi 3.00 3.00

Marine Life A422

No. 696: a, Various fish. b, Seahorse and fish. c, Sstarfish. d, Crab and fish. e, Jellyfish and fish.

2012, Nov. 27
696 Horiz. strip of 5 5.75 5.75
a.-e. A422 70pf Any single 1.10 1.10

Souvenir Sheet

Insects — A423

No. 697: a, Chorthippus brunneus. b, Tibicen linnei.

2013, Mar. 15
697 A423 2.50m Sheet of 2, #a-b 7.50 7.50

Old City, Kljuc — A424

2013, Mar. 20
698 A424 70pf multi 1.50 1.50

Europa — A425

No. 699 — Postal van: a, Facing left. b, Facing right.

2013, May 9 ***Perf. 13¼x13***
699 A425 2.50m Horiz. pair, #a-b 7.50 7.50
c. Souvenir sheet of 2, #699a-699b 7.50 7.50
d. Booklet pane of 6, 3 each #699a-699b, perf. 13¼x13 on 2 or 3 sides 22.50 —

No. 699d was sold with, but unattached to, a booklet cover.

Composers A426

Designs: No. 700, 2m, Giuseppe Verdi (1813-1901). No. 701, 2m, Richard Wagner (1813-83).

2013, May 22 ***Serpentine Die Cut 11***
Self-Adhesive
700-701 A426 Set of 2 6.00 6.00

Nos. 700-701 were printed in sheets of 8 + central label.

17th Mediterranean Games, Mersin, Turkey — A427

2013, June 20 ***Perf. 13***
702 A427 1m multi 1.50 1.50

Friends of Nature Postal Workers Lodge, 60th Anniv. A428

2013, July 29 **Litho.** ***Perf. 13***
703 A428 70pf multi .95 .95

Architecture — A429

No. 704: a, Velagicevina guest house, Blagaj. b, Guest house, Fojnica.

2013, July 29 **Litho.** ***Perf. 13***
704 A429 90pf Horiz. pair, #a-b 2.50 2.50

Souvenir Sheet

Seventh World Paragliding Accuracy Championships, Bjelasnica — A430

2013, July 29 **Litho.** ***Perf. 13***
705 A430 1.50m multi 2.10 2.10

Flowers — A431

No. 706: a, Sage (kadulja). b, Acacia (bagrem). c, Dandelion (maslacak). d, Linden (lipa). e, Heather (vrijesak).

2013, Sept. 25 **Litho.** ***Perf. 13¼x13***
706 Horiz. strip of 5 .70 .70
a.-e. A431 10pf Any single .25 .25

Winning Design in Children's Art Contest on Theme of Water Conservation A432

2013, Oct. 9 **Litho.** ***Perf. 13x13¼***
707 A432 1.50m multi 2.10 2.10

QR Code — A433

2013, Oct. 9 **Litho.** ***Perf. 13***
708 A433 1.70m multi 2.40 2.40

Bosnia & Herzegovina Postal Service, 20th anniv.

Statute for First Automobile Club in Bosnia & Herzegovina, Cent. — A434

2013, Nov. 25 **Litho.** ***Perf. 13***
709 A434 1.50m multi 2.10 2.10

Reconstruction of Sarajevo City Hall — A435

2014, May 9 **Litho.** ***Perf. 13x13¼***
710 A435 1.70m multi 2.40 2.40

William Shakespeare (1564-1616), Writer — A436

2014, May 9 **Litho.** ***Perf. 13***
711 A436 2m multi 2.75 2.75

No. 711 was printed in sheets of 8 + central label.

Sarajevo in Winter, by Fuad Arifhodzic (1914-2008) — A437

2014, May 9 Litho. *Perf. 13¼x13*
712 A437 2.50m multi 3.50 3.50

No. 712 was printed in sheets of 8 + central label.

Souvenir Sheet

Paeonia Officinalis — A438

2014, May 9 Litho. *Perf. 13*
713 A438 1.50m multi 2.10 2.10

Europa — A439

No. 714 — Sheet music and: a, Accordion. b, Violin and tambourine.

2014, May 9 Litho. *Perf. 13¼x13*
714 A439 2.50m Horiz. pair, #a-b 7.00 7.00
c. Souvenir sheet of 2, 714a-714b 7.00 7.00
d. Booklet pane of 6, 3 each #714a-714b, perf. 13¼x13 on 2 or 3 sides 21.00 —

No. 714d was sold with, but unattached to, a booklet cover.

Houses of Worship — A440

Designs: 5pf, St. Anthony of Padua Church, Bihac. 10pf, Sava Atik Mosque, Brcko. 20pf, Mosque, Velika Kladusa. 30pf, Synagogue, Zenica. 40pf, Temple of Prophet St. Elias, Maglaj. 50pf, Sultan Mehmid Fatih Mosque, Kraljeva Sutjeska. 2.70m, Heart of Jesus Catholic Cathedral, Sarajevo. 4m, Serbian Orthodox Cathedral, Sarajevo.

2014 Litho. *Perf. 13¼x13*

715 A440	5pf black & gray	.25	.25
716 A440	10pf multi	.25	.25
717 A440	20pf multi	.30	.30
718 A440	30pf multi	.40	.40
719 A440	40pf multi	.55	.55
720 A440	50pf multi	.70	.70
721 A440	2.70m multi	3.75	3.75
722 A440	4m multi	5.50	5.50
	Nos. 715-722 (8)	11.70	11.70

Issued: 5pf, 5/9; 20pf, 5/26; others, 7/31.

Aleksa Santic (1868-1924), Poet — A441

2014, May 26 Litho. *Perf. 13*
723 A441 90c multi 1.25 1.25

Safvet-beg Basagic (1870-1934), Writer — A442

2014, July 31 Litho. *Perf. 13*
724 A442 70pf multi 1.00 1.00

Wind Generators A443

2014, July 31 Litho. *Perf. 13*
725 A443 1.10m multi 1.50 1.50

Bijambare Cave A444

2014, July 31 Litho. *Perf. 13¼x13*
726 A444 3m multi 4.25 4.25

Rubber Duck — A445

2014, Aug. 20 Litho. *Perf. 13*
727 A445 1m multi 1.40 1.40

Cinematography in Bosnia & Herzegovina.

Dzebarska Mosque, Zivinice A446

2014, Aug. 20 Litho. *Perf. 13x13¼*
728 A446 1.30m multi 1.75 1.75

Cyphonethes Tajanus — A447

2014, Sept. 10 Litho. *Perf. 13*
729 A447 90pf multi 1.25 1.25

No. 729 was printed in sheets of 9 + label.

Children's Art A448

2014, Oct. 9 Litho. *Perf. 13¼x13*
730 A448 90pf multi 1.25 1.25

Zepce A449

2014, Oct. 14 Litho. *Perf. 13¼x13*
731 A449 1m multi 1.40 1.40

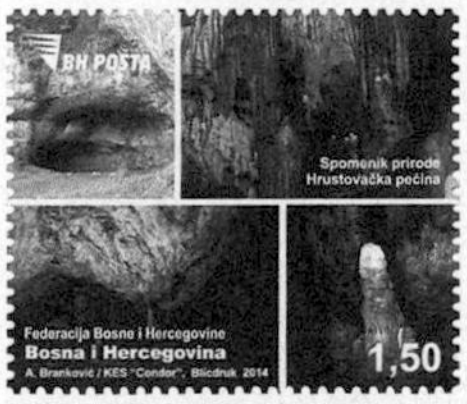

Hrustovo Cave A450

2014, Nov. 20 Litho. *Perf. 13*
732 A450 1.50m multi 3.00 3.00

National Handball Team A451

2015, Feb. 17 Litho. *Perf. 13*
733 A451 2m multi 2.75 2.75

Souvenir Sheet

Coccinellidae — A452

2015, Feb. 27 Litho. *Perf. 13*
734 A452 2m multi 2.75 2.75

United Nations Conference on Disaster Risk Reduction — A453

2015, Mar. 13 Litho. *Perf. 13*
735 A453 90pf multi 1.25 1.25

First Bosniak High School, 20th Anniv. A454

2015, May 6 Litho. *Perf. 13x13¼*
736 A454 1m multi 1.50 1.50

Souvenir Sheet

Pyotr I. Tchaikovsky (1840-93), Composer — A455

2015, May 7 Litho. *Perf. 13*
737 A455 2.50m multi 3.50 3.50

Europa — A456

No. 738: a, Wooden airplane. b, Wooden sled.

2015, May 8 Litho. *Perf. 13*
738 A456 2.50m Horiz. pair, #a-b 6.50 6.50
c. Souvenir sheet of 2, #738a-738b 6.50 6.50
d. Booklet pane of 6, 3 each #738a-738b, perf. 13 on 2 or 3 sides 20.00 —

No. 738d was sold with, but unattached to, a booklet cover.

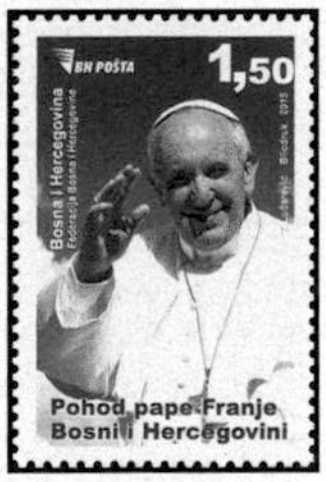

Visit of Pope Francis — A457

2015, June 6 Litho. *Perf. 12¾x13¼*
739 A457 1.50m multi 2.10 2.10

Bosnian Chairmanship of Council of Europe — A458

Perf. 13¼x12¾
2015, June 21 Litho.
740 A458 50pf multi .70 .70

A459

2015, July 1 Litho. *Perf. 13x13¼*
741 A459 1.50m multi 2.00 2.00

Publication of *Alice's Adventures in Wonderland,* by Lewis Carroll, 150th anniv.

No. 741 was printed in sheets of 8 + central label.

Berries A460

Designs: 10pf, Rubus fruticosus. 20pf, Rubus idaeus. 30pf, Ribes nigrum.

2015, Aug. 4 Litho. *Perf. 13*

742 A460 10pf multi + label .25 .25
743 A460 20pf multi + label .25 .25
744 A460 30pf multi + label .35 .35
Nos. 742-744 (3) .85 .85

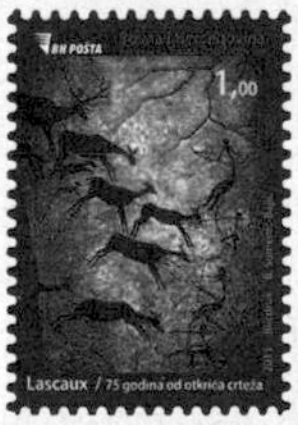

Discovery of Prehistoric Art in Lascaux Caves, 75th Anniv. — A461

Serpentine Die Cut 11

2015, Sept. 10 Litho.

Self-Adhesive

745 A461 1m multi 1.25 1.25

Jewish District in Sarajevo, 450th Anniv. A462

2015, Oct. 1 Litho. *Perf. 13x13¼*

746 A462 40pf multi .50 .50

Children's Drawing by Amina Covrk — A463

2015, Oct. 9 Litho. *Perf. 13x13¼*

747 A463 90pf multi 1.20 1.20

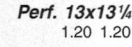

Amel Tuka, Bronze Medalist in 800-Meter Race at 2015 World Track and Field Championships — A464

2015, Oct. 9 Litho. *Perf. 13¼x13*

748 A464 1.30m multi 1.60 1.60

A465

2015, Oct. 9 Litho. *Perf. 13*

749 A465 2.70m multi 3.50 3.50

Victory of Bosnia & Herzegovina under-16 men's basketball team in 2015 European championships.

Souvenir Sheet

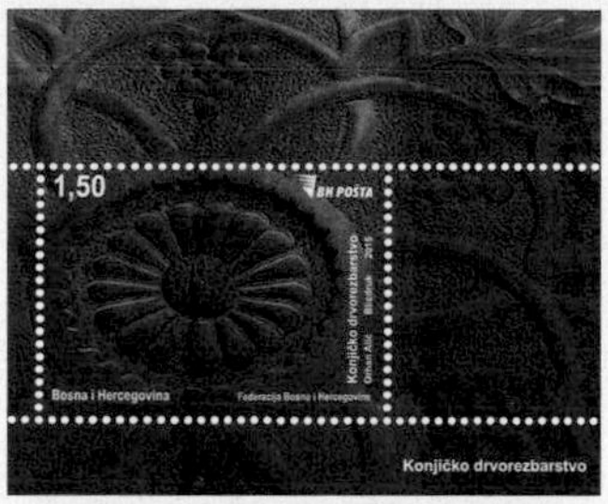

Konjic Woodcarving — A466

Litho. & Embossed

2015, Oct. 9 *Perf. 13x13¼*

750 A466 1.50m multi 2.00 2.00

Old Town of Maglaj A467

2015, Oct. 22 Litho. *Perf. 13*

751 A467 90pf multi 1.20 1.20

Syringa Vulgaris — A468

2015, Nov. 4 Litho. *Perf. 13*

752 A468 1m multi 1.40 1.40

Buildings in Mackovac A469

2015, Nov. 24 Litho. *Perf. 13*

753 A469 70pf multi .80 .80

Ethno Tourism.

Festina Lente Bridge, Sarajevo A470

2015, Nov. 27 Litho. *Perf. 13*

754 A470 2.50m multi 2.75 2.75

Rug Design — A471

2015, Dec. 20 Litho. *Perf. 13*

755 A471 5m multi 5.75 5.75

Old Mosque, Spionica A472

2015, Dec. 22 Litho. *Perf. 13x13½*

756 A472 1.10m multi 1.25 1.25

Carved Tablet and Arch Found Near Zenica A473

2015, Dec. 22 Litho. *Perf. 13*

757 A473 3m multi 3.50 3.50

Panel of the Great Judge Gradesa.

First Newspaper in Bosnia & Herzegovina, 150th Anniv. — A474

2016, May 9 Litho. *Perf. 13½*

758 A474 1.50m multi 1.75 1.75

A475

Europa A476

2016, May 9 Litho. *Perf. 13¼x13¾*

759 A475 2.50m multi 3.00 3.00
760 A476 2.50m multi 3.00 3.00

Think Green Issue.

Souvenir Sheet

Miguel de Cervantes (1547-1616), Writer, and Characters Don Quixote and Sancho Panza — A477

2016, May 9 Litho. *Perf. 13¼x13¾*

761 A477 2m multi 2.40 2.40

Hum Mountain Relay Tower — A478

2016, May 17 Litho. *Perf. 13*

762 A478 70pf multi .80 .80

Halacsya Sendtneri A479

2016, May 25 Litho. *Perf. 13¼x13¾*

763 A479 1m multi 1.25 1.25

Evliya Celebi (1611-82), Explorer A480

2016, May 25 Litho. *Perf. 13*

764 A480 2m multi 2.40 2.40

No. 764 was printed in sheets of 8 + central label.

Souvenir Sheet

Butterflies — A481

No. 765: a, Coenonympha tullia. b, Cupido decolorata.

2016, May 25 Litho. *Perf. 13¼x13¾*

765 A481 2.50m Sheet of 2, #a-b 5.75 5.75
c. Booklet pane of 6, 3 each #765a-765b, perf. 13¼x13¾ on 2 or 3 sides 17.50 —

No. 765c was sold with, but unattached to, a booklet cover.

Painting by Nasuh Matrakci (1480-c. 1564), Statesman A482

2016, July 6 Litho. *Perf. 13¼x13¾*

766 A482 1.50m multi 1.75 1.75

Yellow Fortress, Sarajevo A483

2016, Aug. 5 Litho. *Perf. 13*

767 A483 30pf multi + label .35 .35

Summer Sports and Recreation — A484

2016, Aug. 5 Litho. ***Perf. 13¼x13¾***
768 A484 2.50m multi 3.00 3.00

Winning Design in Children's Stamp Design Contest A485

2016, Oct. 3 Litho. ***Perf. 13¼x13¾***
769 A485 90pf multi 1.10 1.10

Tombstone, Durdevic — A486

Perf. 13¾x13¼
2016, Nov. 24 Litho.
770 A486 1m multi 1.10 1.10

Campaign Against Domestic Violence A487

2016, Dec. 8 Litho. ***Perf. 13¼x13¾***
771 A487 2.50m multi 2.75 2.75

Mosque, Travnik A488

2016, Dec. 15 Litho. ***Perf. 13***
772 A488 1.70m multi 1.90 1.90

Pliva Lakes Waterfalls A489

2016, Dec. 15 Litho. ***Perf. 13½***
773 A489 2.70m multi 3.00 3.00

New Year 2017 A490

2016, Dec. 15 Litho. ***Perf. 13***
774 A490 1.50m multi + label 1.60 1.60

Pannonian Lakes, Tuzla A491

2016, Dec. 21 Litho. ***Perf. 13½***
775 A491 2m multi 2.25 2.25

Matija Divkovic (1563-1631), and His 1611 Book *Christian Doctrine* — A492

2016, Dec. 23 Litho. ***Perf. 13½***
776 A492 90pf multi .95 .95

Karl May (1842-1912), Writer of Novels About American Indians — A493

2017, Apr. 20 Litho. ***Perf. 13***
777 A493 2m multi 2.25 2.25

Souvenir Sheet

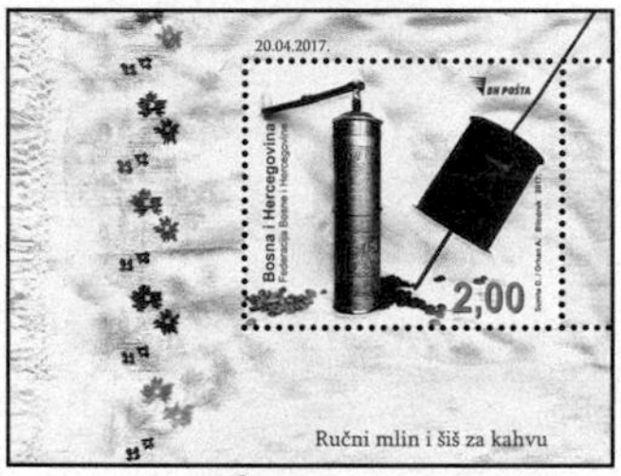

Coffee Grinders — A494

Litho. & Embossed
2017, Apr. 20 ***Perf. 13***
778 A494 2m multi 2.25 2.25

Birds A495

Designs: 90pf, Aquila pomarina. 2.50m, Ardea cinerea.

2017, Apr. 20 Litho. ***Perf. 13x13¼***
779 A495 90pf multi 1.00 1.00

Souvenir Sheet

780 A495 2.50m multi 3.00 3.00

Europa — A496

No. 781: a, Window at Jajce Castle. b, Jajce Castle.

2017, May 9 Litho. ***Perf. 13***
781 A496 2.50m Horiz. pair, #a-b 5.75 5.75
c. Souvenir sheet of 2, #781a-781b 5.75 5.75
d. Booklet pane of 6, 3 each #781a-781b, perf. 13 on 2 or 3 sides 17.50 —

Membership in the Universal Postal Union, 125th Anniv. — A497

Perf. 13¼x12¾
2017, June 27 Litho.
782 A497 1.50m multi 1.75 1.75

Self-portrait, by Mersad Berber (1940-2012) A498

2017, July 6 Litho. ***Perf. 12¾x13¼***
783 A498 1.70m multi 2.10 2.10

Exhibition of paintings by Berber at Sarajevo City Hall.

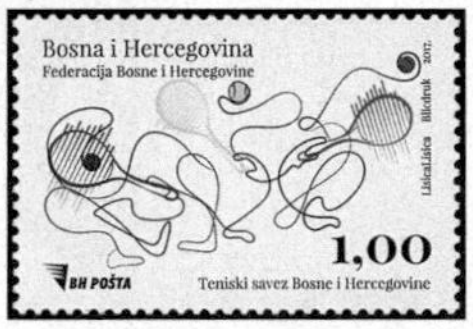

Tennis Association of Bosnia & Herzegovina — A499

Perf. 13¼x12¾
2017, Aug. 22 Litho.
784 A499 1m multi 1.25 1.25

Herbs and Spices A500

No. 785: a, Cimet (cinnamon). b, Bosiljak (basil). c, Kim (caraway seeds). d, Kopar (dill). e, Lovor (bay leaves).

2017, Sept. 11 Litho. ***Perf. 13***
785 Horiz. strip of 5 + 5 labels 5.50 5.50
a.-e. A500 90pf Any single + label 1.10 1.10

Rakitnica River Canyon A501

2017, Sept. 27 Litho. ***Perf. 13x13¼***
786 A501 2.50m multi 3.00 3.00

No. 786 was printed in sheets of 8 + central label.

Behram-Bey Madrasa, Tuzla — A502

2017, Oct. 5 Litho. ***Perf. 13***
787 A502 1.70m multi 2.00 2.00

Opening of House for Parents of Hospitalized Children, 1st Anniv. — A503

2017, Oct. 13 Litho. ***Perf. 13***
788 A503 90pf multi 1.10 1.10

Strbacki Waterfall A504

2017, Oct. 25 Litho. ***Perf. 13x13¼***
789 A504 1.50m multi 1.90 1.90

Souvenir Sheet

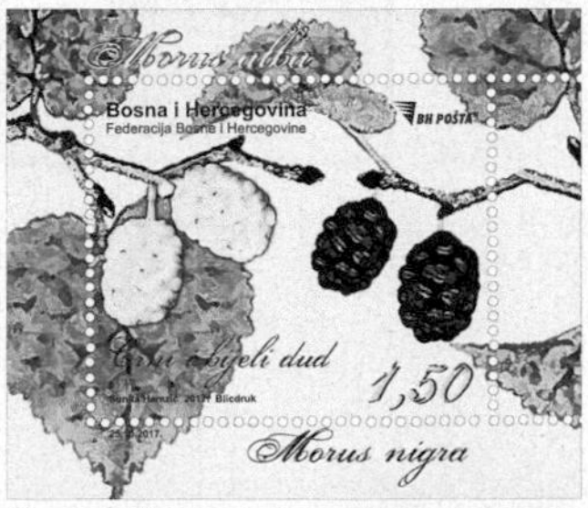

Morus Alba and Morus Nigra — A505

2017, Oct. 25 Litho. ***Perf. 13***
790 A505 1.50m multi 1.90 1.90

Marie Sklodowska Curie (1867-1934), 1903 Nobel Laureate in Physics and 1911 Nobel Laureate in Chemistry — A506

2017, Nov. 7 Litho. ***Perf. 13¼x12¾***
791 A506 1m multi 1.25 1.25

Mt. Maglic A507

2017, Nov. 21 Litho. ***Perf. 13***
792 A507 2m multi 2.50 2.50

Travnik Cheese A508

2017, Nov. 21 Litho. *Perf. 13*
793 A508 1.10m multi + label 1.40 1.40

Mine Safety A509

Perf. 13¼x12¾
2017, Nov. 23 Litho.
794 A509 70pf multi .85 .85

Nikola Tesla (1856-1943), Inventor, and Wireless Electricity Transmission Tower — A510

2018, Jan. 30 Litho. *Perf. 13*
795 A510 2m multi 2.60 2.60

Souvenir Sheet

Sokollu Mehmet Pasha (1506-79), Ottoman Grand Vizier — A511

2018, Feb. 28 Litho. *Perf. 13*
796 A511 2m multi 2.50 2.50

Reopening of Sarajevo Funicular — A512

2018, Mar. 30 Litho. *Perf. 13½x13*
797 A512 90pf multi 1.25 1.25

Souvenir Sheet

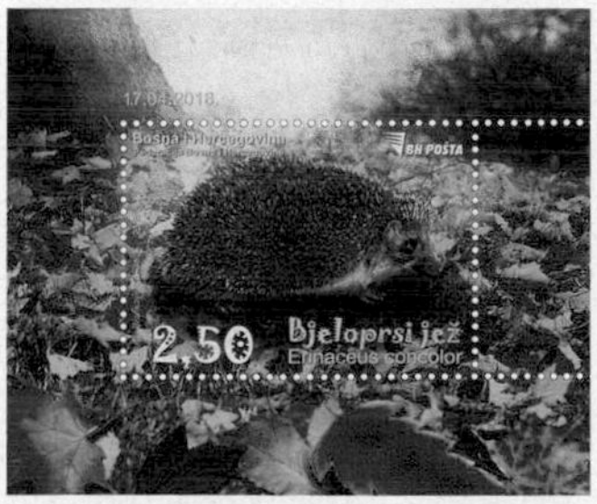

Erinaceus Concolor — A513

2018, Apr. 17 Litho. *Perf. 13x13½*
798 A513 2.50m multi 3.25 3.25

Europa — A514

No. 799: a, Roman bridge over Ilidza River (denomination at LL). b, Seher-Cehaja Bridge, Sarajevo (denomination at LR).

2018, May 9 Litho. *Perf. 13*
799 A514 2.50m Horiz. pair, #a-b 6.00 6.00
c. Souvenir sheet of 2, #799a-799b 6.00 6.00
d. Booklet pane of 6, 3 each #799a-799b, perf. 13 on 2 or 3 sides 18.00 —

No. 799d was sold with, but unattached to, a booklet cover.

A515

Design: Karadoz Bey Mosque and Madrasa, Mostar.

2018, May 4 Litho. *Perf. 13*
800 A515 2.70m multi + label 3.25 3.25

Bosnian Mark, 20th Anniv. A516

Perf. 13½x12¾
2018, June 22 Litho.
801 A516 1.50m multi 1.90 1.90

Mosque, Milodraz A517

2018, Aug. 10 Litho. *Perf. 13*
802 A517 2.70m multi 3.25 3.25

See Turkey No.

Soccer A518

2018, Aug. 22 Litho. *Perf. 13*
803 A518 2m multi 2.40 2.40

Nuts A519

No. 804: a, Ljesnak (hazelnuts). b, Pistaci (pistachios). c, Orah (walnuts). d, Badem (almonds). e, Kikiriki (peanuts).

2018, Sept. 10 Litho. *Perf. 13*
804 Strip of 5 + 5 labels 5.50 5.50
a.-e. A519 90pf Any single + label 1.10 1.10

International Peace Day — A520

2018, Sept. 21 Litho. *Perf. 13x13½*
805 A520 2.50m multi 3.00 3.00

No. 805 was printed in sheets of 8 + cental label.

Bosnian Cuisine A521

No. 806: a, Sarma (stuffed cabbage). b, Hercegovacka japrak sarma (stuffed grape leaves). c, Sogan dolma (stuffed onions). d, Klepe (pierogi). e, Sarena dolma (stuffed vegetables).

2018, Sept. 28 Litho. *Perf. 13x13½*
806 Strip of 5 3.00 3.00
a.-e. A521 50pf Any single .60 .60

Association of Patients with Epidermolysis Bullosa Dystrophica, 10th Anniv. — A522

2018, Oct. 9 Litho. *Perf. 13*
807 A522 90pf multi 1.10 1.10

Dragonfly A523

2018, Oct. 25 Litho. *Perf. 13¼x13*
808 A523 1m multi 1.25 1.25

Souvenir Sheet

Salix Alba — A524

2018, Oct. 25 Litho. *Perf. 13*
809 A524 1.50m multi 1.75 1.75

Desserts A525

No. 810: a, Ruzica. b, Hurmasica. c, Divit baklava. d, Kadaif. e, Tulumba.

2018, Nov. 15 Litho. *Perf. 13½x13*
810 Strip of 5 4.25 4.25
a.-e. A525 70pf Any single .85 .85

Medicinal Herbs — A526

No. 811: a, Brusnica (cranberries). b, Majcina dusica (thyme). c, Kamilica (chamomile). d, Neven (marigolds). e, Sipurak (rose hips).

2018, Nov. 15 Litho. *Perf. 13x13½*
811 Strip of 5 6.25 6.25
a.-e. A526 1.10m Any single 1.25 1.25

Turhan Emin Mosque, Ustikolina A527

2018, Dec. 20 Litho. *Perf. 13*
812 A527 1.50m multi 1.75 1.75

Souvenir Sheet

2019 Winter European Youth Olympic Festival, Sarajevo and East Sarajevo — A528

No. 813 — Festival mascot: a, 1m, Skiing. b, 1.50m, Running.

2019, Feb. 7 Litho. *Perf. 13*
813 A528 Sheet of 2, #a-b 3.00 3.00

Sultan Selim Mosque, Stolac — A529

2019, Mar. 15 Litho. *Perf. 13½x13*
814 A529 2m multi 2.40 2.40

Bliha River Waterfall — A530

2019, Mar. 28 Litho. *Perf. 13x13¼*
815 A530 90pf multi 1.10 1.10

Souvenir Sheet

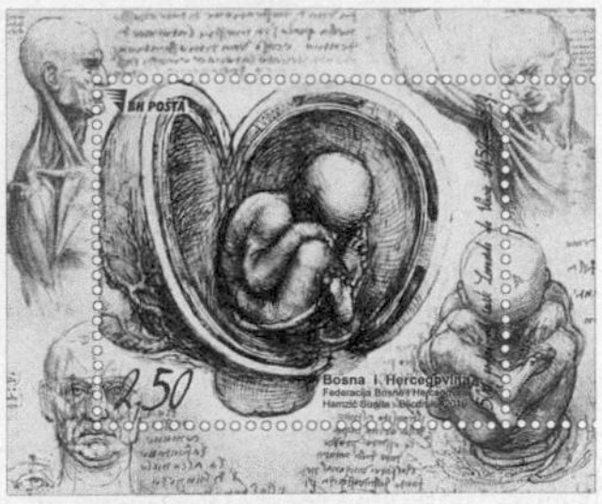

Studies of the Fetus in the Womb, by Leonardo da Vinci (1452-1519) — A531

2019, Apr. 28 **Litho.** ***Perf. 13***
816 A531 2.50m multi 3.00 3.00

Europa — A532

No. 817: a, Vanellus vanellus. b, Eremophila alpestris.

2019, May 9 **Litho.** ***Perf. 13½x13***
817 A532 2.50m Horiz. pair, #a-b 5.75 5.75
c. Souvenir sheet of 2, #817a-817b 5.75 5.75
d. Booklet pane of 6, 3 each #817a-817b, perf. 13½x13 on 2 or 3 sides. 17.50 —

Tree of Life, Photograph by Samir Hadzic — A533

2019, May 17 **Litho.** ***Perf. 13x13¼***
818 A533 20pf multi .25 .25

World Inflammatory Bowel Disease Day. See Bosnia & Herzegovina (Croat) No. 392, Bosnia & Herzegovina (Serb) No. 616.

Aladza Mosque, Foca — A534

2019, May 20 **Litho.** ***Perf. 13***
819 A534 2.70m multi + label 3.25 3.25

Begova Mosque and Sarajevo Clock Tower A535

2019, June 4 **Litho.** ***Perf. 13***
820 A535 1.50m multi 1.75 1.75

Education Builds Bosnia & Herzegovina Association, 25th Anniv. — A536

2019, July 25 **Litho.** ***Perf. 13x13½***
821 A536 1m multi 1.25 1.25

Corn A537

Buckwheat A538

Rice A539

Wheat A540

Oats A541

2019, Sept. 12 **Litho.** ***Perf. 13x13¼***
822 Horiz. strip of 5 .55 .55
a. A537 10pf multi .25 .25
b. A538 10pf multi .25 .25
c. A539 10pf multi .25 .25
d. A540 10pf multi .25 .25
e. A541 10pf multi .25 .25

Cereals.

Wilson's Promenade, Sarajevo — A542

2019, Sept. 12 **Litho.** ***Perf. 13¼x13***
823 A542 90pf multi 1.00 1.00

Souvenir Sheet

The Night Watch, by Rembrandt van Rijn (1606-69) — A543

2019, Oct. 4 **Litho.** ***Perf. 13***
824 A543 1.50m multi 1.75 1.75

Los Rosales Center for Children and Youth With Special Needs, Mostar A544

2019, Oct. 9 **Litho.** ***Perf. 13***
825 A544 90pf multi 1.10 1.10

Travnik Fortress A545

2019, Oct. 15 **Litho.** ***Perf. 13¼x13***
826 A545 2m multi 2.40 2.40

No. 826 was printed in sheets of 8 + central label.

Daphne Blagayana A546

2019, Nov. 27 **Litho.** ***Perf. 13x13¼***
827 A546 1m multi 1.25 1.25

BOSNIA & HERZEGOVINA (CROAT ADMIN)

Bosnian Croat Administration Located In Mostar

(Herceg Bosna)

100 Paras = 1 Dinar (1993)
100 Lipa = 1 Kuna (1994)
100 pfennig = 1 Mark (6/22/98)

Catalogue values for all unused stamps in this country are for Never Hinged items.

A1

1993, May 12 **Litho.** ***Perf. 14***
1 A1 2000d multicolored 1.00 1.00

Our Lady of Peace Shrine, Medjugorje.

A2

Silvije Kranjcevic (1865-1908), poet: 500d, Waterfall, gate at Jajce. 1000d, Old bridge, Mostar, horiz.

1993
2-4 A2 Set of 3 1.50 1.50

Issued: 200d, 5/20; 500d, 5/18; 1000d, 5/15.

Census in Bosnia & Herzegovina, 250th Anniv. — A3

1993, May 24
5 A3 100d Medieval gravestone .30 .30

Madonna of the Grand Duke, by Raphael — A4

1993, Dec. 3
6 A4 6000d multicolored 2.00 2.00

Christmas.

Paintings, by Gabrijel Jurkic (1886-1974) — A5

Europa: a, 3500d, Uplands in Bloom. b, 5000d, Wild Poppy.

1993, Dec. 6
7 A5 Pair, #a.-b. *9.00 9.00*

Kravica Waterfalls A6

1993, Dec. 7
8 A6 3000d multicolored 1.00 1.00

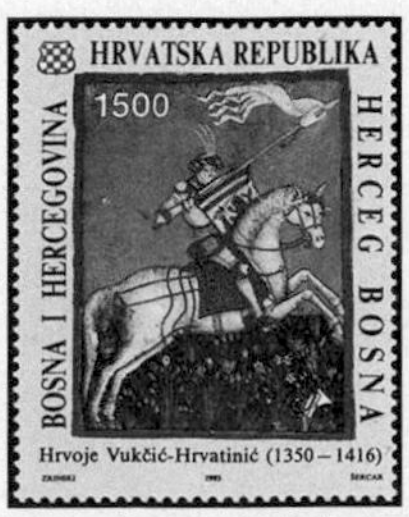

Grand Duke Hrvoje Vukcic-Hrvatinic (1350-1416) — A7

1993, Dec. 8
9 A7 1500d multicolored 1.25 1.25

Pleham Monastery A8

1993, Dec. 15

10 A8 2200d multicolored 1.25 1.25

Formation of Bosnian Croat Administration A9

1994, Feb. 10

11 A9 10,000d multicolored 4.50 4.50

Bronze Cross, Rama A10

1994, Nov. 28

12 A10 2.80k multicolored 1.50 1.50

Flora & Fauna — A11

a, 3.80k, Campanula hercegovina. b, 4k, Dog.

1994, Nov. 30

13 A11 Pair, #a.-b. 4.00 4.00

Hutovo Wetlands A12

1994, Dec. 2

14 A12 80 l multicolored .90 .90

Europa — A13

Transportation: a, 8k, Bicycles, 1885. b, 10k, 1901 Mercedes.

1994, Dec. 5

15 A13 Pair, #a.-b. *10.00 10.00*

City of Ljubuski, 550th Anniv. — A14

1994, Dec. 8

16 A14 1k multicolored .50 .50

Dr. Nikolic Franciscan Hospital, Nova Bila, 2nd Anniv. — A15

1994, Dec. 12

17 A15 5k multicolored 2.40 2.40

UN, 50th Anniv. — A16

1995, Oct. 24 ***Rouletted***

Self-Adhesive

18 A16 1.50k Card of 10 *55.00 55.00*

Color ranges from pale pink at UL of card to dark rose at LR of card. Each stamp is numbered at LR.

Christmas — A17

1995, Dec. 4 ***Perf. 14***

19 A17 5.40k multicolored 2.25 2.25

Kraljeva Sutjeska Monastery A18

1995, Dec. 7

20 A18 3k multicolored 1.20 1.20

Cities — A19

Monasteries: 2k, Srebrenica. 4k, Mostar.

1995

21-22 A19 Set of 2 3.00 3.00

Issued: 2k, 12/20; 4k, 12/12.

Europa — A20

1995, Dec. 28

23 A20 6.50k multicolored *21.00 21.00*

A21

1996, June 24

24	A21 10k multicolored	5.00	5.00
a.	Booklet pane of 4	20.00	
	Complete booklet, #24a	20.00	

Apparitions at Medugorje, 15th anniv.

Europa — A22

1996, July 20

25 A22 2.40k multicolored *2.00 2.00*

Queen Katarina Kosaca Kotromanic.

A23

1996, July 23

26 A23 1.40k multicolored .65 .65

Franciscan Monastery, Siroki Brijeg, 150th anniv.

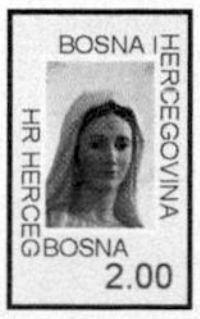

Virgin Mary — A24

1996, Aug. 14 ***Rouletted***

Self-Adhesive

27	A24 2k multicolored	2.75	2.75
a.	Card of 10	27.50	27.50
28	A24 9k multicolored	9.25	9.25
a.	Card of 5 + 5 labels	47.50	47.50

Nos. 27-28 Surcharged

1996, Oct. 21 ***Rouletted***

Self-Adhesive

29	A24 1.10k on 2k multi	*20.00*	—
a.	Card of 10	*165.00*	
30	A24 1.10k on 9k multi	*45.00*	—
a.	Card of 5 + 5 labels	*165.00*	

Taipei '96 Philatelic Exhibition.

Christmas — A25

1996, Dec. 8 **Litho.** ***Perf. 14***

31 A25 2.20k multicolored 1.00 1.00

Europa — A26

Myths & legends: a, 2k, St. George slaying the dragon. b, 5k, Zeus coming to Europa disguised as a bull.

1997, Apr. 4

32 A26 Pair, #a.-b. 4.00 4.00

No. 32b is 39x34mm.

A27

1997, Apr. 12

33	A27 3.60k multicolored	1.60	1.60
a.	Pane of 4	6.50	

Visit of Pope John Paul II.

Samatorje Church — A28

1997, Apr. 20

34 A28 1.40k multi .55 .55

Flora & Fauna — A29

Designs: 1k, Ardea purpurea. 2.40k, Symphyandra hofmannii.

1997

35-36 A29 Set of 2 1.60 1.60

Issued: 1k, 11/19. 2.40k, 11/17.

Christmas A30

1997, Dec. 1
37 A30 1.40k multicolored .65 .65

World Animated Film Festival A31

1998, Apr. 1
38 A31 6.50k multicolored 3.50 3.50

Europa.

Hercegovina, 550th Anniv. — A32

1998, Apr. 8
39 A32 2.30k multicolored .90 .90

City of Livno, 1100th Anniv. — A33

1998, Apr. 9
40 A33 1.20k multicolored .55 .55

Sibiraea Croatica — A34

1998, Nov. 9
41 A34 1.40k multicolored .65 .65

Gyps Fulvus — A35

1998, Nov. 16
42 A35 2.40m multicolored 1.10 1.10

Christmas — A36

1998, Dec. 2
43 A36 5.40k multi 2.75 2.75

Native Attire — A37

1999, Mar. 26 **Litho.** ***Perf. 14***
44 A37 40pf multi .55 .55

A. B. Simic (1898-1925) — A38

1999, Mar. 29
45 A38 30pf multi .45 .45

Bobovac Castle — A39

1999, Mar. 30
46 A39 10pf multi .30 .30

Europa — A40

1999, Mar. 31
47 A40 1.50m Blidinje Park 3.00 3.00

Dianthus Freynii — A41

1999, Oct. 11 **Litho.** ***Perf. 14***
48 A41 80pf multi 1.25 1.25

Martes Martes — A42

1999, Oct. 15
49 A42 40pf multi .60 .60

Stolac Castle — A43

1999, Nov. 3
50 A43 10pf multi .30 .30

Christmas — A44

1999, Nov. 22
51 A44 30pf multi .55 .55

Nikola Sop (1904-82), Writer — A45

2000, Apr. 5 **Litho.** ***Perf. 14***
52 A45 40pf multi .55 .55

World Health Day — A46

2000, Apr. 7
53 A46 40pf multi .55 .55

Europa — A47

2000, May 9
54 A47 1.80m multi *5.25 5.25*

Brother Lovro Karaula (1800-75) — A48

2000, May 19
55 A48 80pf multi 1.00 1.00

Quercus Sessilis — A49

2000, Aug. 16
56 A49 1.50m multi 2.00 2.00

Anguilla Anguilla A50

2000, Aug. 18
57 A50 80pf multi 1.25 1.25

16th European Chess Club Cup — A51

30th Intl. Chess Tournament A52

2000, Sept. 23
58 A51 80pf multi 1.25 1.25
59 A52 80pf multi 1.25 1.25

Tomislavgrad Monastery A53

2000, Sept. 26
60 A53 1.50m multi 2.25 2.25

Woman From Kraljeva Sutjeska — A54

2000, Sept. 27
61 A54 40pf multi .60 .60

Fight Against AIDS — A55

2000, Dec. 1
62 A55 80pf multi 1.25 1.25

Christmas — A56

2000, Dec. 4
63 A56 40pf multi .60 .60

Fish — A57

Designs: 30pf, Chondrostoma phoxinus. 1.50m, Salmo marmoratus.

2001
64-65 A57 Set of 2 2.50 2.50

Europa — A58

Designs: 1.10m, Tihaljina spring. 1.80m, Pliva waterfall.

2001, Mar. 31
66-67 A58 Set of 2 4.50 4.50

Execution of Zrinski and Frankopan, 330th Anniv. — A59

No. 68: a, Petar Zrinski (1621-71). b, Fran Krsto Frankopan (1643-71).

2001, Apr. 30 **Litho.** ***Perf. 14***
68 A59 40pf Vert. pair, #a-b 1.10 1.10

16th Century Galley — A60

2001, June 15
69 A60 1.80m multi 2.25 2.25

Boat From Neretva River Valley — A61

2001, June 20 ***Perf. 14x14¼***
70 A61 80pf multi 1.25 1.25

Souvenir Sheet

Apparition of the Virgin Mary at Medjugorje, 20th Anniv. — A62

2001, June 24
71 A62 3.80m multi 5.00 5.00

Our Lady of Kondzilo — A63

2001, Aug. 15 ***Perf. 14***
72 A63 80pf multi 1.20 1.20

Computers, 50th Anniv. — A64

No. 73: a, Denomination in red. b, Denomination in black and white.

2001, Sept. 9
73 A64 40pf Horiz. pair, #a-b 1.20 1.20

Mars Odyssey Mission — A65

2001, Sept. 9
74 A65 1.50m multi + label 2.00 2.00

Father Slavko Barbaric (1946-2000), Priest at Medjugorje A66

2001, Nov. 24
75 A66 80pf multi 1.20 1.20

Walt Disney (1901-66), Animated Film Producer A67

2001, Dec. 5
76 A67 1.50m multi 2.00 2.00

Christmas A68

2001, Dec. 8
77 A68 40pf multi .60 .60

Nobel Prizes, Cent. — A69

2001, Dec. 10 **Litho.** ***Perf. 14***
78 A69 1.80m multi 2.50 2.50

2002 Winter Olympics, Salt Lake City — A70

2002, Feb. 4 **Litho.** ***Perf. 14***
79 A70 80pf multi 1.20 1.20

Intl. Year of Mountains — A71

2002, Mar. 11 **Litho.** ***Perf. 14***
80 A71 40pf multi + label .60 .60

First Written Record of Mostar, 550th Anniv. — A72

2002, Apr. 3
81 A72 30pf multi .50 .50

Europa — A73

Designs: 80pf, Clown, lion and mouse. 1.50m, Clowns, juggler, circus tent.

2002, Apr. 5
82-83 A73 Set of 2 5.00 5.00

Leonardo da Vinci (1452-1519) — A74

2002, Apr. 15
84 A74 40pf multi 1.00 1.00

2002 World Cup Soccer Championships, Japan and Korea — A75

2002, May 22
85 A75 1.50m multi 2.50 2.50

Father Didak Buntic (1871-1922) — A76

2002, June 5
86 A76 80pf multi 1.20 1.20

Humac Tablet — A77

2002, June 13
87 A77 40pf multi .60 .60

Marilyn Monroe (1926-62), Actress — A78

2002, Aug. 5
88 A78 40pf multi 1.20 1.20

Elvis Presley (1935-77) — A79

2002, Aug. 16
89 A79 1.50m multi 2.50 2.50

Television, 75th Anniv. — A80

2002, Sept. 7
90 A80 1.50m multi 2.00 2.00

Stamp Day — A81

2002, Sept. 9
91 A81 80pf multi 1.10 1.10

Croatian Cultural Association Napredak, Cent. — A82

2002, Sept. 14
92 A82 40pf multi .60 .60

European Bocce Championships, Grude — A83

2002, Oct. 8
93 A83 1.50m multi 2.10 2.10

Viola Beckiana — A84

2002, Oct. 21

94 A84 30pf multi .60 .60

Vanessa Atalanta A85

2002, Oct. 25

95 A85 80pf multi 1.20 1.20

Christmas — A86

2002, Dec. 4

96 A86 40pf multi .60 .60

Archdiocesan Gymnasium, Travnik, 120th Anniv. — A87

2002, Dec. 14

97 A87 80pf multi 1.20 1.20

A 50pf stamp commemorating Archbishop Josip Stadler was jointly issued by the post offices of the Croat Administration and the Muslim Government. It is listed as No. 435 in the listings of the Muslim Government issues.

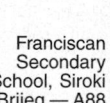

Franciscan Secondary School, Siroki Brijeg — A88

2003, Feb. 26 Litho. *Perf. 14*

98 A88 40pf multi .60 .60

Europa — A89

2003, Apr. 5

99 A89 1.80m multi 3.50 3.50

Printed in sheets of 8 stamps + label.

Abjuration of the Bogomil Heresy at Bilino Polje, 800th Anniv. — A90

2003, Apr. 8

100 A90 50pf multi .70 .70

Post Office of the Croat Administration, 10th Anniv. — A91

2003, May 12

101 A91 80pf multi 1.20 1.20

World Wine Day A92

2003, May 25

102 A92 1.50m multi 2.00 2.00

Flora & Fauna — A93

Designs: 50pf, Oxytropis prenja. 2m, Alectoris graeca.

2003 Litho. *Perf. 14*

103 A93 50pf multi .75 .75

104 A93 2m multi 2.75 2.75

Issued: 50pf, 6/10; 2m, 6/16.

Visit of Pope John Paul II — A94

2003, June 22 *Perf. 13¼x13½*

105 A94 1.50m multi 2.10 2.10

Father Matija Divkovic (1563-1631), First Bosnian Writer — A95

2003, June 24 *Perf. 14*

106 A95 3.80m multi 5.25 5.25

Woman From Rama — A96

Jewelry From Neum — A97

2003, Aug. 20 Litho. *Perf. 14*

107 A96 50pf multi .80 .80

108 A97 70pf multi 1.00 1.00

Cross on Mt. Krizevac, 70th Anniv. — A98

2003, Sept. 14

109 A98 80pf multi 1.25 1.25

Ban Stjepan II Kotromanic, 650th Anniv. of Death — A99

2003, Sept. 28

110 A99 20pf multi .35 .35

Teleprinter, 75th Anniv. A100

2003, Oct. 9 Litho. *Perf. 14*

111 A100 1.50m blk & red brn 2.25 2.25

World Post Day.

Alberto Fortis, Writer of Dalmatian Travelogue, 200th Anniv. of Death — A101

2003, Oct. 21

112 A101 50pf multi .75 .75

Intl. Children's Day — A102

2003, Nov. 20

113 A102 1m multi 1.40 1.40

Christmas A103

2003, Dec. 4

114 A103 50pf multi .90 .90

First Flight, Cent. — A104

2003, Dec. 17

115 A104 2m multi 2.75 2.75

Intl. Investment Conference A105

2004, Jan. 23

116 A105 5m silver 6.75 6.75

St. Valentine's Day — A106

2004, Feb. 14

117 A106 10pf multi .40 .40

Albert Einstein (1879-1955) A107

2004, Mar. 14

118 A107 50pf multi .90 .90

Hand Tattoos A108

2004, Mar. 20

119 A108 50pf multi .90 .90

Flora & Fauna Type of 2003

Designs: 1m, Aquilegia dinarica. 1.50m, Salamandra atra prenjensis.

2004, Mar. 30

120 A93 1m multi 1.25 1.25

121 A93 1.50m multi 2.50 2.50

Europa — A109

No. 122: a, 1.50m, Skis of skier at hill, 2m, Fins of swimmer at beach.

2004, Apr. 5 Litho. *Perf. 14*

122 A109 Horiz. pair, #a-b *8.00 8.00*

Printed in sheets of 4 pairs + 2 labels.

Father Andrija Kacic Miosic (1704-60), Poet — A110

2004, Apr. 17
123 A110 70pf dk ol bis & brn 1.00 1.00

A111

2004, June 12
124 A111 2m multi 2.75 2.75
a. Miniature sheet of 4 11.00 11.00

European Soccer Championships, Portugal.

A112

2004, June 27
125 A112 70pf multi 1.00 1.00

Kocerin Tablet, 600th anniv.

Moon Landing, 35th Anniv. — A113

2004, July 20
126 A113 1m multi 1.50 1.50

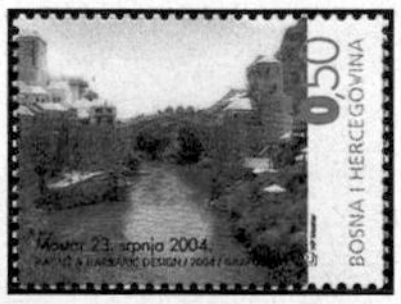

Reconstruction of Old Bridge, Mostar — A114

2004, July 23
127 A114 50pf multi .90 .90

Buna River Water Wheel A115

2004, Sept. 9 Litho. *Perf. 14*
128 A115 1m multi 1.50 1.50

World Post Day — A116

2004, Oct. 9
129 A116 1.50m multi 2.25 2.25

Printed in sheets of 8 + label.

Savings Day — A117

2004, Oct. 31
130 A117 50pf multi .90 .90

Printed in sheets of 8 + label.

Karl Benz (1844-1929), Automobile Manufacturer — A118

2004, Nov. 25
131 A118 1.50m multi 2.25 2.25

Printed in sheets of 8 + label.

Christmas — A119

No. 132: a, 50pf, Journey to Bethlehem. b, 1m, Christmas trees, man with gift.

2004, Dec. 4
132 A119 Horiz. pair, #a-b 2.25 2.25

Woman From Kupres — A120

2005, Feb. 20
133 A120 1.50m multi 2.25 2.25

Birds — A121

No. 134: a, Egretta garzetta. b, Himantopus himantopus. c, Merops apiaster. d, Alcedo atthis.

2005, Mar. 2
134 A121 1m Block of 4, #a-d 6.25 6.25

Flowers — A122

Designs: No. 135, 50pf, Gentiana dinarica. No. 136, 50pf, Petteria ramentacea.

2005, Mar. 2
135-136 A122 Set of 2 1.50 1.50

Zrinjski Soccer Team, Cent. — A123

No. 137: a, Three players, denomination at right. b, Two players, denomination at left.

2005, Mar. 15 Litho. *Perf. 14*
137 A123 3m Pair, #a-b 9.00 9.00

Easter — A124

2005, Mar. 27
138 A124 50pf multi .90 .90

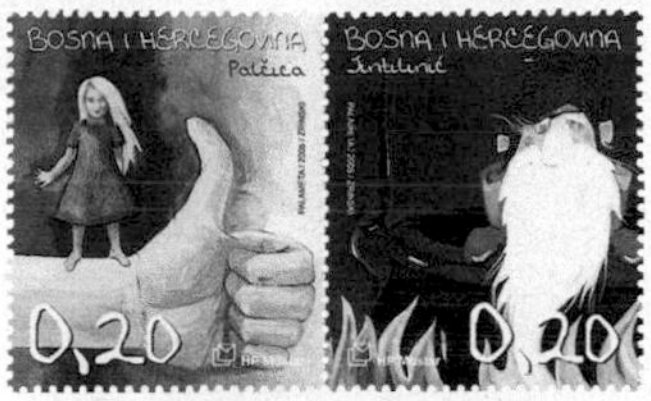

Fairy Tales — A125

No. 139: a, Palcica (Thumbelina, by Hans Christian Andersen). b, Tintilinic, by Ivana Brlic Mazuranic.

2005, Apr. 2
139 A125 20pf Pair, #a-b .90 .90

Europa — A126

No. 140: a, Wine bottle, knife, cutting board, garlic, ham, cheese, and bread. b, Cruet, grapes, bread, nuts and cheese.

2005, Apr. 5
140 Pair 6.00 6.00
a.-b. A126 2m Either single 3.00 3.00
c. Souvenir sheet, 2 each #140a-140b 12.00 12.00

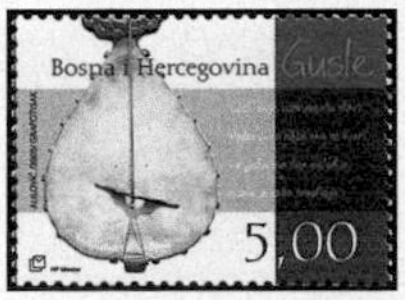

One-string Fiddle — A127

2005, May 10 Litho. *Perf. 14*
141 A127 5m multi 7.50 7.50

Vjetrenica Cave — A128

2005, June 5 Litho. *Perf. 14*
142 A128 1m multi 1.50 1.50

World Environment Day.

Metkovic — Mostar Rail Line — A129

2005, June 14
143 A129 50pf multi .90 .90

Medjugorje Youth Festival A130

2005, July 29 Litho. *Perf. 14*
144 A130 1m multi 1.50 1.50

Father Grgo Martic (1822-1905), Writer — A131

2005, Aug. 30
145 A131 1m multi 1.50 1.50

Trumpet A132

2005, Oct. 1 Litho. *Perf. 14*
146 A132 50pf multi .90 .90

Printed in sheets of 8 + label.

Dayton Peace Accords, 10th Anniv. — A133

2005, Nov. 21
147 A133 1.50m multi 2.25 2.25

Printed in sheets of 8 + label.

Brother Slavko Barbaric (1946-2000) A134

2005, Nov. 24
148 A134 1m multi 1.50 1.50

Printed in sheets of 8 + label.

Christmas — A135

Designs: No. 149, 50pf, Madonna and Child. No. 150, 50pf, Christmas tree.

2005, Dec. 4
149-150 A135 Set of 2 1.50 1.50

Nos. 149-150 each printed in sheets of 8 + label.

Europa Stamps, 50th Anniv. — A136

No. 151: a, Map of Europe, "50." b, Map of Europe in flowers, envelope. c, Map of Europe in examples of #99. d, Flags, flower, "50."

2006, Jan. 15

151	Horiz. strip of 4	12.00	12.00
a.-d.	A136 2m Any single	2.75	2.75
e.	Souvenir sheet, #151a-151d	18.00	18.00

World Wetlands Day — A137

2006, Feb. 2
152 A137 1m multi 1.50 1.50

Printed in sheets of 8 + label.

Europa — A138

No. 153: a, Footprints and "integration." b, Faces.

2006, Apr. 5

153	A138 2m Pair, #a-b	6.00	6.00
c.	Souvenir sheet, 2 each #153a-153b	12.00	12.00

No. 153 printed in sheets containing 4 pairs and 2 labels.

Earth Day — A139

2006, Apr. 22
154 A139 1m multi 1.50 1.50

World Press Freedom Day — A140

2006, May 3
155 A140 50pf multi .90 .90

World Telecommunications Day — A141

2006, May 17
156 A141 1m multi 1.50 1.50

Apparition of the Virgin Mary at Medjugorje, 25th Anniv. — A142

Designs: No. 157, Statue of Virgin Mary, church at night. No. 158, Statue with halo. No. 159, Statue and cross. No. 160, Statue, church and tent. No. 161, People and church.

2006, June 18 Litho. *Perf. 14*
Booklet Stamps

157	A142 1m multi	1.50	1.50
158	A142 1m multi	1.50	1.50
159	A142 1m multi	1.50	1.50
160	A142 1m multi	1.50	1.50
161	A142 1m multi	1.50	1.50
a.	Booklet pane, 2 each #157-161	16.00	—
	Complete booklet, #161a	16.00	

Parish of Uzdol, 150th Anniv. — A143

2006, June 24
162 A143 50pf multi .90 .90

Printed in sheets of 8 + label.

Nikola Tesla (1856-1943), Electrical Engineer — A144

2006, July 9
163 A144 2m multi 3.00 3.00

Medieval Tombstones A145

2006, Sept. 9
164 A145 20pf multi .40 .40

European Car-Free Day — A146

2006, Sept. 22
165 A146 1m multi 1.50 1.50

Printed in sheets of 8 + label.

Women's Jewelry in Franciscan Monastery Museum, Humac — A147

2006, Oct. 9
166 A147 5m multi 8.00 8.00

Flowers — A148

No. 167: a, Cerastium dinaricum. b, Papaver kerneri.

2006, Nov. 1
167 A148 20pf Horiz. pair, #a-b .75 .75

Birds —A148a

Designs: No. 167C, 70pf, Podiceps cristatus. No. 167D, 70pf, Acrocephalus scirpaceus. No. 167E, 70pf, Upupa epops. No. 167F, 70pf, Alauda arvensis.

2006, Nov. 1 Litho. *Perf. 14*
167C-167F A148a Set of 4 4.50 4.50

A148b

Christmas — A148c

2006, Dec. 1 Litho. *Perf. 14*

167G	A148b 50pf multi	.65	.65
167H	A148c 1m multi	1.60	1.60

Nos. 167G-167H each were printed in sheets of 8 + label.

Valentine's Day — A149

2007, Feb. 14 Litho. *Perf. 14*
168 A149 10pf multi .35 .35

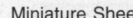

Miniature Sheet

Tornjak Dog — A150

No. 169: a, Head of dog facing right. b, Head of dog facing left. c, Entire dog facing right. d, Entire dog facing left.

2007, Feb. 22
169 A150 70pf Sheet of 4, #a-d 4.50 4.50

Mak Dizdar (1917-71), Poet — A151

2007, Mar. 21
170 A151 1m multi 1.50 1.50

Europa — A152

No. 171: a, Clasped hands. b, Knot.

2007, Apr. 5

171	A152 3m Pair, #a-b	9.00	9.00
c.	Miniature sheet, 2 each #171a-171b	17.50	17.50

Scouting, cent.

Souvenir Sheet

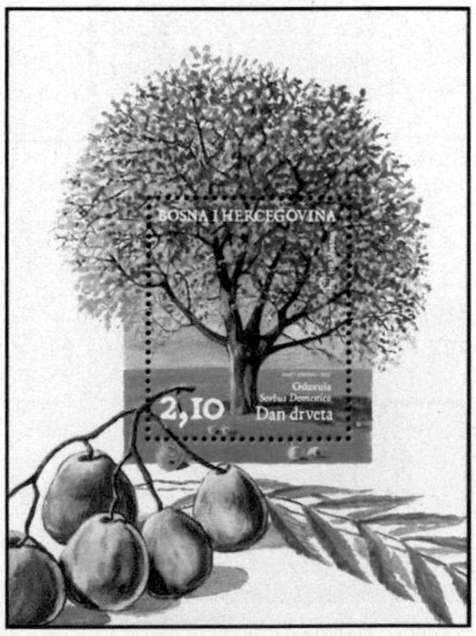

Arbor Day — A153

2007, Apr. 25
172 A153 2.10m multi 3.50 3.50

Gabela Archaeological Site — A154

2007, May 12
173 A154 1.50m multi 2.25 2.25

Iris — A155

Irises and Ship — A156

2007, May 22
174 A155 2m multi 3.50 3.50

Souvenir Sheet

175 A156 3m multi 5.00 5.00

Apparition of the Virgin Mary at Medjugorje, 26th Anniv. — A157

No. 176: a, Statue of Virgin Mary. b, Hands holding rosary. c, People near statue of Virgin Mary. d, Steeple and statue of Virgin Mary. e, Statue of priest holding crucifix.

2007, June 1 **Booklet Stamps**
176 Horiz. strip of 5 7.50 7.50
a.-e. A157 1m Any single 1.50 1.50
f. Booklet pane of 10, 2 each #176a-176e 15.00 —
Complete booklet, #176f 15.00

Bishop Marko Dobretic (c. 1707-84) — A158

2007, June 13
177 A158 60pf multi 1.00 1.00

Boljuni Cemetery — A159

2007, Sept. 23 **Litho.** ***Perf. 14***
178 A159 20pf multi .40 .40
Printed in sheets of 8 + label.

World Bowling Championships, Grude — A160

2007, Sept. 24
179 A160 5m black & red 8.50 8.50
Printed in sheets of 8 + label.

Distaff and Spindle — A161

2007, Oct. 9
180 A161 70pf multi 1.10 1.10
Printed in sheets of 8 + label.

Birds of Hutovo Blato — A162

No. 181: a, Streptopelia turtur. b, Anas crecca. c, Anas platyrhynchos. d, Fulica atra.

2007, Nov. 1
181 A162 2m Block of 4, #a-d 14.00 14.00

Flora of Blidinje Nature Park — A163

Designs: No. 182, Gentiana lutea. No. 183, Vaccinium vitis-idaea.

2007, Nov. 1
182 A163 3m multi 5.00 5.00

Souvenir Sheet

183 A163 3m multi 5.00 5.00

Christmas and New Year's Day — A164

Designs: 50pf, Candles and wreath. 70pf, Christmas tree near steps.

2007, Dec. 1
184-185 A164 Set of 2 2.00 2.00
Nos. 184-185 each printed in sheets of 8 + label.

Bishop Andjeo Kraljevic (1807-79) A165

2007, Dec. 28
186 A165 1m multi 1.50 1.50

Easter — A166

2008, Mar. 23 **Litho.** ***Perf. 14***
187 A166 70pf multi 1.25 1.25

Croatian Cultural Days — A167

2008, Mar. 25
188 A167 10pf multi .35 .35

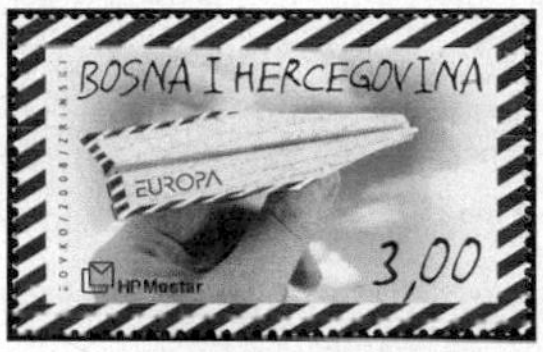

Europa — A168

Designs: No. 189, 3m, Airmail envelope folded into paper airplane. No. 190, 3m, Letter and fountain pen.

2008, Apr. 5
189-190 A168 Set of 2 9.50 9.50
190a Miniature sheet, 2 each #189-190 19.00 19.00

Helmet of Illyrian Warrior — A169

Litho. & Embossed

2008, May 12 ***Perf. 14***
191 A169 2.10m multi 3.00 3.00
Printed in sheets of 8 + 2 labels.

Grave of Rabbi Moshe Danon — A170

2008, May 21
192 A170 1.50m multi 2.00 2.00

Souvenir Sheet

Achillea Millefolium and Andrija Simic (1833-1905), Outlaw — A171

2008, May 22
193 A171 2.90m multi 4.00 4.00

Apparition of the Virgin Mary at Medjugorje, 27th Anniv. — A172

No. 194: a, Dove, cross, cloud. b, Dove, Virgin Mary. c, Bible, crucified Jesus, praying hands. d, Hands, church. e, Virgin Mary, child, dove.

2008, June 1
194 Horiz. strip of 5 8.50 8.50
a.-e. A172 1m Any single 1.60 1.60

Brotnjo Vintage Days — A173

Color of grapes: 50pf, Purple. 70pf, Red.

2008, Sept. 9 **Litho.** ***Perf. 14***
195-196 A173 Set of 2 1.90 1.90

Zaostrog Monastery — A174

2008, Oct. 4
197 A174 1m multi 1.50 1.50

Tobacco Cutter — A175

2008, Oct. 9
198 A175 2m multi 3.00 3.00
Printed in sheets of 8 + label.

Zepce, 550th Anniv. — A176

2008, Oct. 14

199 A176 1.50m multi 2.25 2.25

Intl. Year of the Potato — A177

Solanum tuberosum: 60pf, Plant and tubers. 5m, Flower.

2008, Nov. 1

200 A177 60pf multi .90 .90

Souvenir Sheet

201 A177 5m multi 7.50 7.50

Birds — A178

No. 202: a, Accipiter gentilis. b, Bubo bubo. c, Circaetus gallicus. d, Falco tinnunculus.

2008, Nov. 1

202 A178 1.50m Block of 4, #a-d 9.50 9.50

Father Leo Petrovic (1883-1945), Professor — A179

2008, Nov. 15

203 A179 1m multi 2.10 2.10

Christmas A180

New Year's Day — A181

2008, Dec. 1

204 A180 70pf multi 1.20 1.20
205 A181 70pf multi 1.20 1.20

Siroki Brijeg Soccer Team, 60th Anniv. — A182

Players and team emblem: 70pf, Sepia photograph. 2.10m, Full color and black-and-white photographs.

2008, Dec. 12

206 A182 70pf multi 1.10 1.10

Souvenir Sheet

207 A182 2.10m multi 3.25 3.25

No. 207 contains one 35x30mm stamp.

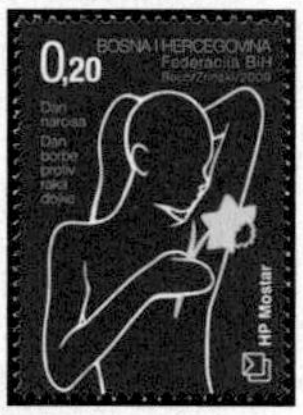

Daffodil Day — A183

2009, Mar. 21 Litho. *Perf. 14*

208 A183 20pf brt pink & yel .35 .35

Campaign against breast cancer.

Intl. Water Day — A184

No. 209: a, Waterfall on Pliva River. b, Mills along river.

2009, Mar. 22

209 A184 70pf Horiz. pair, #a-b 2.00 2.00

Council of Europe, 60th Anniv. — A185

European Court of Human Rights, 50th Anniv. A186

2009, Apr. 1

210 A185 1.50m multi 2.25 2.25
211 A186 1.50m multi 2.25 2.25

Europa A187

No. 212 — Planets and: a, Galileo Galilei (1564-1642), astronomer. b, Telescope.

2009, Apr. 5 Litho. & Embossed

212 A187 3m Vert. pair, #a-b 8.00 9.00

Intl. Year of Astronomy. Printed in sheets containing two pairs.

Seal of Duke Stipan Vukcic Kosaca — A188

2009, May 12 Litho. *Perf. 14*

213 A188 1.50m multi 2.00 2.00

Printed in sheets of 8 + label.

Field of Tanacetum Balsamita — A189

No. 215, Flowers, woman's head.

2009, May 22

214 A189 2.10m shown 2.75 2.75

Souvenir Sheet

215 A189 2.10m multi 2.75 2.75

Guca Gora Franciscan Monastery, 150th Anniv. A190

2009, May 30

216 A190 70pf multi 1.00 1.00

Printed in sheets of 8 + central label.

Apparition of the Virgin Mary at Medjugorje, 28th Anniv. — A191

No. 217: a, Virgin Mary. b, Virgin Mary and church. c, Steeples and hand raising crucifix. d, Cross and path. e, Church.

2009, June 1 *Perf. 14*

Booklet Stamps

217	Horiz. strip of 5	6.00	6.00
a.-e.	A191 1m Any single	1.10	1.10
f.	Booklet pane of 10, 2 each #217a-217e	12.00	—
	Complete booklet, #217f	12.00	

10th Mediterranean Film Festival A192

2009, Sept. 1

218 A192 70pf multi 1.00 1.00

Franciscan Order, 800th Anniv. — A193

No. 219: a, Monk's rope cincture. b, Shrine.

2009, Oct. 4 Litho. *Perf. 14*

219 A193 1m Horiz. pair, #a-b 2.75 2.75

Wooden Hope Chest — A194

2009, Oct. 9

220 A194 70pf multi 1.00 1.00

Gorica Livno Franciscan Monastery, 150th Anniv. — A195

2009, Nov. 1

221 A195 60pf multi .90 .90

Prunus Domestica A196

Prunus domestica: No. 222, Fruit on branch. No. 223, Blossoms and fruit.

2009, Nov. 1

222 A196 5m multi 6.00 6.00

Souvenir Sheet

223 A196 5m multi 6.00 6.00

Birds of Hutovo Blato — A197

No. 224: a, Coturnix coturnix. b, Cuculus canorus. c, Rallus aquaticus. d, Nycticorax nycticorax.

2009, Nov. 1

224 A197 1.50m Block or strip of 4, #a-d 7.50 7.50

Christmas A198

New Year's Day — A199

2009, Dec. 1

225 A198 70pf multi 1.00 1.00
226 A199 70pf multi 1.00 1.00

2010 Winter Olympics, Vancouver A200

Designs: 70pf, Shown. 1.50m, Maple leaf on skis.

2010, Feb. 1

227-228 A200 Set of 2 3.00 3.00

Nos. 227-228 each were printed in sheets of 8 + 2 labels.

Intl. Women's Day — A201

2010, Mar. 8

229 A201 20pf multi .30 .30

Friar Martin Nedic (1810-95), Poet — A202

2010, Apr. 1

230 A202 2.10m multi 2.75 2.75

Europa — A203

Stylized child with: No. 231, 3m, Kite. No. 232, 3m, Pinwheel.

2010, Apr. 5

231-232 A203 Set of 2 8.50 8.50
232a Sheet of 4, 2 each #231-232 17.00 17.00

Ravlica Cave Archaeological Site — A204

2010, May 12 **Litho.** ***Perf. 14***

233 A204 1.50m multi 2.25 2.25

Souvenir Sheet

Linden Tree in Slavic Mythology — A205

2010, May 22

234 A205 5m multi 6.00 6.00

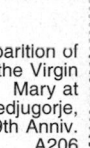

Apparition of the Virgin Mary at Medjugorje, 29th Anniv. A206

No. 235: a, Flags, church and crowd. b, Statue and crowd. c, Hand holding rosary. d, Cross and crowd. e, Statue and crosses on hillside.

2010, June 1 **Booklet Stamps**

235 Vert. strip of 5 7.50 7.50
a.-e. A206 1m Any single 1.50 1.50
f. Booklet pane of 10, 2 each #235a-235e 15.00 15.00
Complete booklet, #235f 15.00 15.00

Matrix Croatica General Assembly, Citluk — A207

2010, June 19

236 A207 1m red & black 1.25 1.25

Printed in sheets of 8 + 2 labels.

Mother Teresa (1910-97), Humanitarian A208

2010, Aug. 27 **Litho.** ***Perf. 14***

237 A208 2.10m blue 3.25 3.25

Intl. Day for Habitat Protection — A209

No. 238: a, Lake Prokosko. b, Lake Prokosko and Triturus alpestris reiseri.

2010, Oct. 6

238 A209 1m Horiz. pair, #a-b 3.00 3.00

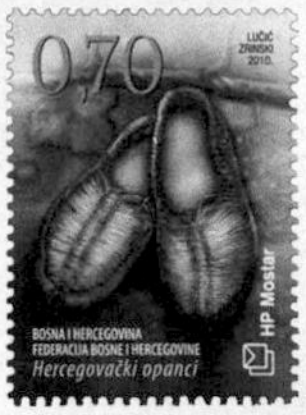

Peasant's Shoes — A210

2010, Oct. 9

239 A210 70pf multi 1.10 1.10

Worldwide Fund for Nature — A211

No. 240 — Lacerta trilineata: a, With black coloring, on rock. b, Climbing tree. c, With green coloring, on rock. d, Head.

2010, Nov. 1

240 A211 50pf Block of 4, #a-d 2.75 2.75

Mushrooms — A212

No. 241: a, Lycoperdon perlatum. b, Amanita muscaria.

2010, Nov. 1

241 A212 2.10m Horiz. pair, #a-b 6.50 6.50

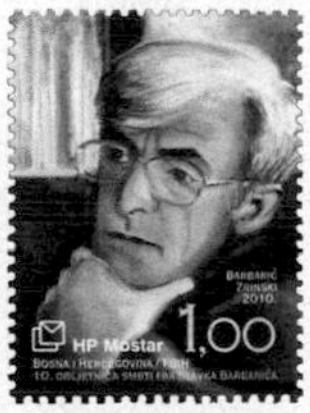

Father Slavko Barbaric (1946-2000), Investigator of Medjugorje Apparitions — A213

2010, Nov. 24

242 A213 1m multi 1.60 1.60

Christmas A214

New Year 2011 — A215

2010, Dec. 1

243 A214 70pf multi 1.10 1.10
244 A215 70pf multi 1.10 1.10

Printing of First Croatian Book in Bosnia & Herzegovina, 400th Anniv. A216

2011, Feb. 21

245 A216 70pf multi .90 .90

World Meteorological Day — A217

2011, Mar. 23

246 A217 20pf multi .30 .30

Easter A218

2011, Apr. 1

247 A218 70pf multi .90 .90

Europa — A219

No. 248 — Forest with: a, Green panels. b, Red panels.

2011, Apr. 5

248 A219 3m Pair, #a-b 8.50 8.50
c. Souvenir sheet of 4, 2 each #248a-248b 17.00 17.00

Intl. Year of Forests. No. 248 was printed in sheets containing four pairs and two central labels.

First Man in Space, 50th Anniv. — A220

2011, Apr. 12

249 A220 10pf multi .35 .35

Diagram of Early Christian Basilica, Cim — A221

2011, May 12

250 A221 1.50m multi 2.25 2.25

Rudjer Boskovic (1711-87), Astronomer A222

2011, May 18

251 A222 2.10m multi 3.25 3.25

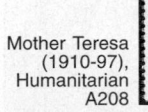

Souvenir Sheet

Hawthorn Branch — A223

2011, May 22
252 A223 5m multi 6.50 6.50

Apparition of the Virgin Mary at Medjugorje, 30th Anniv. — A224

No. 253: a, Wooden cross and rosary beads. b, Church. c, Sculpture of crucified Jesus. d, Statue of Virgin Mary.

Litho. & Embossed

2011, June 1 ***Perf. 14x13¾***
253 A224 1m Block of 4, #a-d 6.00 6.00
e. Souvenir sheet of 4, #253a-253d 6.00 6.00
f. Booklet pane, 2 #253 + 2 labels 12.00 —
Complete booklet, #253f 12.00

St. Anthony of Padua (1195-1231) A225

2011, June 13 **Litho.** ***Perf. 14***
254 A225 1m multi 1.60 1.60

World Bicycle Day — A226

2011, July 16 **Litho.** ***Perf. 14***
255 A226 70pf green .90 .90

Skopaljska Gracanica Parish, Cent. — A227

2011, Aug. 13
256 A227 50pf multi .65 .65

Beatification of the Blessed Martyrs of Drina — A228

2011, Sept. 24
257 A228 70pf multi .90 .90

Fibulae A229

2011, Oct. 9
258 A229 1m multi 1.25 1.25

World Post Day. No. 258 was printed in sheets of 8 + label.

Fridtjof Nansen (1861-1930), Polar Explorer and Diplomat — A230

2011, Oct. 10
259 A230 1.50m multi 1.90 1.90

Fruit — A231

No. 260: a, Punica granatum. b, Ficus carica.

2011, Nov. 1
260 A231 2m Horiz. pair, #a-b 5.00 5.00

Lynx Lynx — A232

No. 261 — Panel color: a, Green. b, Red. c, Orange. d, Blue violet.

2011, Nov. 1
261 A232 3m Block of 4, #a-d 15.00 15.00

Christmas A233

New Year 2012 A234

2011, Dec. 1
262 A233 70pf multi .90 .90
263 A234 70pf multi .90 .90

Latin Grammar Book, by Toma Babic, 300th Anniv. of Publication A235

2012, Feb. 21
264 A235 70pf multi .90 .90

Cheese Produced at Trappist Monasteries A236

2012, Mar. 21
265 A236 2.10m multi 2.50 2.50

Europa — A237

No. 266 — Sites in Mostar: a, Duke Stjepan Kosaca Lodge. b, Old Bridge.

2012, Apr. 5
266 A237 3m Pair, #a-b 8.00 8.00
c. Souvenir sheet of 4, 2 each #266a-266b 16.00 16.00

No. 266 was printed in sheets of 4 pairs + 2 labels.

Intl. Red Cross Day — A238

2012, May 8
267 A238 1m red & black 1.60 1.60

Monument to God Mithra, Konjic A239

2012, May 12
268 A239 70pf multi 1.10 1.10

Souvenir Sheet

Carpinus Betulus — A240

2012, May 22
269 A240 3m multi 3.50 3.50

Nobel Laureates Ivo Andric (1892-1975) and Vladimir Prelog (1906-98) — A241

2012, May 23
270 A241 1.50m multi 1.90 1.90

Apparition of the Virgin Mary at Medjugorje, 31st Anniv. — A242

2012, June 1
271 A242 1m multi 1.50 1.50

Walled Towns — A243

No. 272: a, Visoko. b, Blagaj.

2012, June 22
272 A243 60pf Pair, #a-b 1.50 1.50

Father Nikola Simovic (1839-1912), Vicar General — A244

2012, Sept. 10
273 A244 1m multi 1.40 1.40

Printed in sheets of 8 + central label.

Sargija — A245

2012, Oct. 9
274 A245 20pf multi .30 .30

3rd Cent. B.C. Coins From Daorson — A246

No. 275 — Obverse and reverse of coin: a, With verdigris (green oxidation). b, Without verdigris.

2012, Oct. 31 **Litho. & Embossed**
275 A246 5m Pair, #a-b 12.00 12.00

Savings Day. No. 275 was printed in sheets containing two pairs.

Prunus Avium — A247

Prunus avium: a, Fruit. b, Blossoms.

2012, Nov. 1 **Litho.**
276 A247 50pf Pair, #a-b 1.40 1.40

Printed in sheets containing 4 pairs + 2 labels

Snakes — A248

No. 277: a, Natrix natrix. b, Zamenis longissimus. c, Vipera ammodytes. d, Vipera berus.

2012, Nov. 1 ***Perf. 14***
277 A248 2m Block of 4, #a-d 10.00 10.00

Christmas A249

New Year's Day — A250

2012, Dec. 1
278 A249 70pf multi .95 .95
279 A250 70pf multi .95 .95

Edict of Milan, 1700th Anniv. — A251

2013, Jan. 26
280 A251 90pf multi 1.25 1.25

Printed in sheets of 8 + central label.

New Year 2013 (Year of the Snake) A252

2013, Feb. 10 ***Perf. 14***
281 A252 20pf multi .30 .30

Kulin (1163-1204), Ban of Bosnia — A253

2013, Mar. 1
282 A253 1.50m multi 2.00 2.00

Printed in sheets of 8 + 2 labels.

Europa — A254

No. 283: a, Postal van. b, Postal moped.

2013, Apr. 5 ***Perf. 14¼x14***
283 A254 3m Horiz. pair, #a-b 8.00 8.00
c. Souvenir sheet of 4, 2 each #283a-283b 16.00 16.00

No. 283 was printed in sheets containing 4 pairs + 2 labels.

Intl. Firefighter's Day — A255

2013, May 4 ***Perf. 14***
284 A255 70pf multi .95 .95

Cemetery Stone, Monastery of St. John, Livno — A256

2013, May 12
285 A256 10pf multi .25 .25

Postage Stamps of Croat Administration, 20th Anniv. — A257

Litho. With Foil Application
Perf. 13¾x14 Syncopated

2013, May 12
286 A257 2.10m multi 2.75 2.75

Printed in sheets of 9 + label.

Souvenir Sheet

Quercus Cerris — A258

Perf. 13¾x14 Syncopated

2013, May 22 **Litho.**
287 A258 2m multi 2.50 2.50

Apparition of the Virgin Mary at Medjugorje, 32nd Anniv. A259

2013, June 1 **Litho.** ***Perf. 14***
288 A259 1m multi 1.40 1.40

Friar Radoslav Glavas (1867-1913), Writer — A260

2013, July 20 **Litho.** ***Perf. 14x14¼***
289 A260 1m multi 1.40 1.40

Wooden Plow — A261

2013, Oct. 9 **Litho.** ***Perf. 14x14¼***
290 A261 2.70m multi 3.50 3.50

Giuseppe Verdi (1813-1901), Composer — A262

2013, Oct. 10 **Litho.** ***Perf. 14***
291 A262 1.50m multi 1.90 1.90

No. 291 was printed in sheets of 8 + 2 labels.

Friar Dominik Mandic (1889-1973), Historian — A263

2013, Oct. 24 **Litho.** ***Perf. 14***
292 A263 1.10m multi 1.50 1.50

Celtis Australis — A264

No. 293: a, Tree. b, Leaves and fruit on branch.

2013, Nov. 1 **Litho.** ***Perf. 14x14¼***
293 A264 3.10m Vert. pair, #a-b 8.00 8.00

Lutra Lutra — A265

No. 294 — Otter: a, Head at left, denomination in black. b, Head at right, denomination in white. c, Head at right, denomination in black. d, Head in center, denomination in white.

2013, Nov. 1 **Litho.** ***Perf. 14¼x14***
294 A265 3.10m Vert. strip of 4, #a-d 16.00 16.00

Christmas and New Year's Day — A266

No. 295: a, Christmas (blue frame). b, New Year's Day (red frame).

2013, Dec. 1 **Litho.** ***Perf. 14x14¼***
295 A266 90pf Vert. pair, #a-b 2.40 2.40

Friar Mladen Hrkac (1950-2010) A267

2013, Dec. 20 Litho. *Perf. 14*
296 A267 2.90m multi 3.75 3.75

Intl. Human Solidarity Day. No. 296 was printed in sheets of 8 + central label.

Writers — A268

No. 297: a, Jagoda Truhelka (1864-1957), novelist. b, Anton Gustav Matos (1873-1914), poet. c, Friar Lucijan Kordic (1914-93), historian.

2014, Feb. 21 Litho. *Perf. 14*
297 Horiz. strip of 3 + flanking label 2.40 2.40
a.-c. A268 60pf Any single .75 .75

Intl. Day of the Mother Tongue.

Snowy Idyll, Painting by Gabrijel Jurkic (1886-1974) — A269

2014, Feb. 25 Litho. *Perf. 14*
298 A269 5m multi 6.50 6.50

Europa — A270

No. 299 — Musical instruments: a, Diple. b, Dvojnice.

2014, Apr. 5 Litho. *Perf. 14*
299 A270 3m Pair, #a-b 7.50 7.50
c. Souvenir sheet of 4, 2 each #299a-299b 15.00 15.00

No. 299 was printed in sheets of 8 (4 each Nos. 299a-299b) + 2 central labels.

William Shakespeare (1564-1616), Writer, Scene From *Romeo and Juliet* — A271

2014, Apr. 23 Litho. *Perf. 14*
300 A271 50pf multi .70 .70

15th Century Tombstone, Sluzanj — A272

2014, May 12 Litho. *Perf. 14*
301 A272 90pf multi 1.25 1.25

Souvenir Sheet

Corylus Avellana Leaves and Nuts — A273

2014, May 22 Litho. *Perf. 14*
302 A273 2m multi 2.75 2.75

International Sports Day — A274

2014, May 25 Litho. *Perf. 14x13¾*
303 A274 1m multi 1.40 1.40

Values are for stamps with surrounding selvage. No. 303 was printed in sheets of 8 + central label.

Apparition of the Virgin Mary at Medjugorje, 33rd Anniv. — A275

2014, June 1 Litho. *Perf. 14x13¾*
304 A275 1m multi 1.40 1.40

Values are for stamps with surrounding selvage. No. 304 was impregnated with a rose scent.

Ivan Zovko (1864-1900), Writer and Folklorist — A276

2014, Aug. 20 Litho. *Perf. 14*
305 A276 1.50m multi 2.00 2.00

No. 305 was printed in sheets of 8 + central label.

Victory of Marin Cilic in 2013 U. S. Open Tennis Championships — A277

2014, Sept. 28 Litho. *Perf. 14*
306 A277 1.50m multi 2.00 2.00

No. 306 was printed in sheets of 8 + central label.

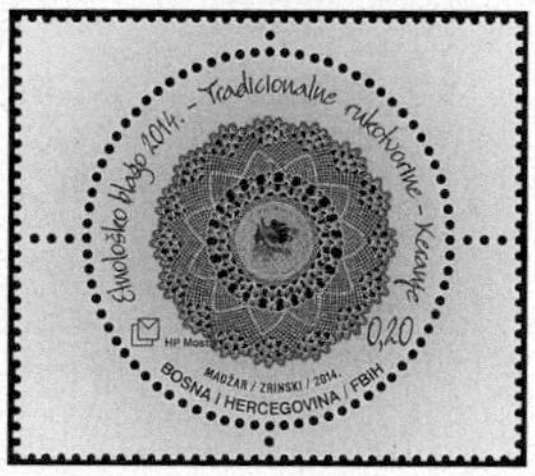

Lace A278

2014, Oct. 9 Litho. *Perf. 14x13¾*
307 A278 20pf multi .25 .25

No. 307 was printed in sheets of 8 + central label. Values are for stamps with surrounding selvage.

Roman Gold Coin Depicting Emperor Nero — A279

Litho. & Embossed

2014, Oct. 31 *Perf. 14*
308 A279 3m multi 4.00 4.00

No. 308 was printed in sheets of 6 + 2 labels.

Flowers — A280

No. 309: a, Helleborus hercegovinus. b, Lilium cattaniae.

2014, Nov. 1 Litho. *Perf. 14*
309 A280 1m Pair, #a-b 2.60 2.60

Farm Animals — A281

No. 310: a, Equus caballus. b, Equus asinus. c, Equus hinnus. d, Equus mulus.

2014, Nov. 1 Litho. *Perf. 14*
310 A281 3m Block of 4, #a-d 15.50 15.50

Christmas and New Year's Day — A282

No. 311: a, Clock and champagne flutes. b, Holy Family, Christmas tree.

2014, Dec. 1 Litho. *Perf. 14*
311 A282 90pf Pair, #a-b 2.40 2.40

Persecution of Franciscans at Siroki Brijeg, 70th Anniv. — A283

2015, Feb. 7 Litho. *Perf. 14*
312 A283 90pf pur & blk 1.10 1.10

No. 312 was printed in sheets of 12 + 4 labels.

Ilija Jakovljevic (1898-1948), Writer — A284

2015, Feb. 21 Litho. *Perf. 14*
313 A284 1.50m tan & blk 1.75 1.75

Father Mihovil Sucic (1820-65), Physician — A285

2015, Mar. 3 Litho. *Perf. 14*
314 A285 1m multi 1.25 1.25

Easter — A286

Litho. With Foil Application

2015, Mar. 25 *Perf. 14*
315 A286 90pf multi 1.10 1.10

No. 315 was printed in sheets of 8 + central label.

Europa — A287

No. 316 — Children and toys: a, Wooden whistle. b, Rocking horse.

2015, Apr. 4 **Litho.** *Perf. 14*
316 A287 3m Horiz. pair, #a-b 6.75 6.75
c. Souvenir sheet of 4, 2 each #316a-316b 13.50 13.50

No. 316 was printed in sheets containing 4 pairs + 2 labels.

International Day of Sports for Development and Peace — A288

2015, Apr. 6 **Litho.** *Perf. 14*
317 A288 5m multi 6.00 6.00

Rivino Archaeological Site — A289

2015, May 12 **Litho.** *Perf. 14*
318 A289 10pf multi .25 .25

Souvenir Sheet

Woman Knitting Shirt From Hemp Fibers — A290

2015, May 22 **Litho.** *Perf. 14*
319 A290 2.90m multi 3.50 3.50

Apparition of the Virgin Mary at Medjugorje, 34th Anniv. — A291

2015, June 1 **Litho.** *Perf. 14*
320 A291 1m multi 1.25 1.25

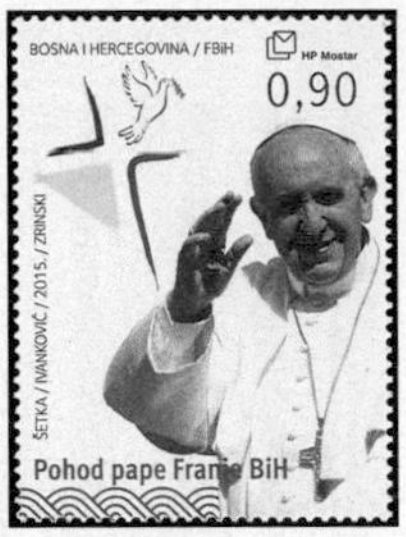

Visit of Pope Francis to Bosnia & Herzegovina A292

2015, June 6 **Litho.** *Perf. 14*
321 A292 90pf multi 1.10 1.10

No. 321 was printed in sheets of 8 + central label.

International Left-Hander's Day — A293

2015, Aug. 13 **Litho.** *Perf. 14*
322 A293 2m multi 2.40 2.40

Lace — A294

Litho. & Embossed

2015, Oct. 9 *Perf. 14*
323 A294 3.60m multi 4.25 4.25

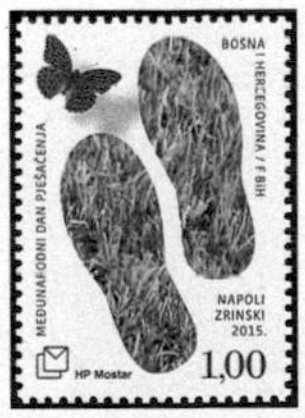

Intl. Day of Hiking — A295

2015, Oct. 15 **Litho.** *Perf. 14*
324 A295 1m multi 1.25 1.25

No. 324 was printed in sheets of 8 + central label.

World Food Day — A296

2015, Oct. 16 **Litho.** *Perf. 14*
325 A296 90pf multi 1.10 1.10

Flowers — A297

No. 326: a, Arum petteri. b, Crocus tommasinianus.

2015, Nov. 1 **Litho.** *Perf. 14*
326 A297 2m Pair, #a-b 5.00 5.00

Mammals — A298

No. 327: a, Canis lupus. b, Vulpes vulpes. c, Canis aureus. d, Ursus arctos.

2015, Nov. 1 **Litho.** *Perf. 14*
327 A298 2m Block or vert. strip of 4, #a-d 10.00 10.00

Christmas and New Year's Day — A299

No. 328: a, Window and ornaments (New Year's Day). b, Nativity scene (Christmas).

Litho. (#328a), Litho. & Embossed (#328b)

2015, Dec. 1 *Perf. 14*
328 A299 90pf Pair, #a-b 2.00 2.00

Publication of General Theory of Relativity, by Albert Einstein, Cent. — A300

2016, Mar. 20 **Litho.** *Perf. 14*
329 A300 90pf multi 1.10 1.10

No. 329 was printed in sheets of 8 + central label.

Europa A301

2016, Apr. 5 **Litho.** *Perf. 14*
330 A301 3m multi 3.50 3.50
a. Souvenir sheet of 2 7.00 7.00

Think Green Issue.
No. 330 was printed in sheets of 8 + 2 labels.

Runners — A302

2016, Apr. 6 **Litho.** *Perf. 14*
331 A302 90pf multi 1.10 1.10

International Day of Sport for Development and Peace.

Roman Empire Courier Service A303

2016, May 12 **Litho.** *Perf. 14*
332 A303 1.50m multi 1.75 1.75

No. 332 was printed in sheets of 8 + central label.

Souvenir Sheet

Cornelian Cherries — A304

2016, May 22 **Litho.** *Perf. 14*
333 A304 5m multi 5.75 5.75

Father Petar Bakula (1816-73), Theologian — A305

2016, May 24 **Litho.** *Perf. 14*
334 A305 90pf multi 1.10 1.10

Apparition of the Virgin Mary at Medjugorje, 35th Anniv. — A306

2016, June 1 **Litho.** *Perf. 14*
335 A306 1m multi 1.25 1.25

Serpentine Die Cut 15¼x14¼ Syncopated

Coil Stamp Self-Adhesive

336 A306 1m multi 1.25 1.25

World Environment Day — A307

2016, June 5 **Litho.** *Perf. 14*
337 A307 90pf multi 1.10 1.10

Serpentine Die Cut 15¼x14¼ Syncopated

Coil Stamp Self-Adhesive

338 A307 90pf multi 1.10 1.10

World Heart Day
A308

2016, Sept. 29 Litho. *Perf. 14*
339 A308 2.70m multi 3.25 3.25

Values are for stamps with surrounding selvage.

Old Agricultural Tools — A309

2016, Oct. 9 Litho. *Perf. 14*
340 A309 1.10m multi 1.25 1.25

Water Lilies — A310

No. 341: a, Nymphaea alba. b, Nymphaea lutea.

2016, Nov. 1 Litho. *Perf. 14*
341 A310 2.70m Pair, #a-b 6.25 6.25

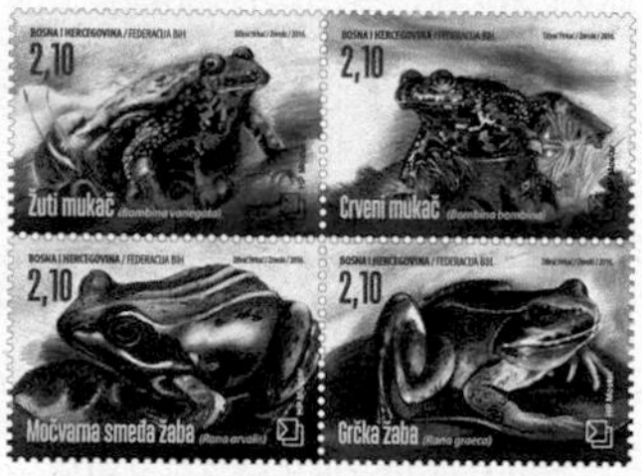

Frogs — A311

No. 342: a, Bombina variegata. b, Bombina bombina. c, Rana arvalis. d, Rana graeca.

2016, Nov. 1 Litho. *Perf. 14*
342 A311 2.10m Block or vert. strip of 4, #a-d 9.50 9.50

Aristotle (384-322 B.C.), Philosopher
A312

2016, Nov. 17 Litho. *Perf. 14*
343 A312 90pf multi 1.00 1.00

International Men's Day — A313

Litho. With Foil Application

2016, Nov. 19 *Perf. 14*
344 A313 5m multi 5.50 5.50

Christmas and New Year's Day — A314

No. 345: a, Snowman in 2017 snow globe. b, Holy Family.

2016, Dec. 1 Litho. *Perf. 14*
345 A314 90pf Pair, #a-b 2.00 2.00

International Water Day — A315

2017, Mar. 22 Litho. *Perf. 14*
346 A315 2.70m multi 3.00 3.00

Reconstruction of Franciscan Monastery, Humac
A316

2017, May 4 Litho. *Perf. 14*
347 A316 60pf multi .70 .70

Europa — A317

No. 348: a, Pocitelj Castle. b, Vranduk Castle.

2017, May 9 Litho. *Perf. 14*
348 A317 3m Pair, #a-b 7.00 7.00
c. Souvenir sheet of 4, 2 each #348a-348b 14.00 14.00

Printed in sheets of 8, containing 4 each Nos. 348a-348b + 2 central labels.

12th Century Tombstone Epitaph for Priest Tjehodraga — A318

2017, May 12 Litho. *Perf. 14*
349 A318 90pf black & red 1.10 1.10

Coil Stamp
Self-Adhesive
Serpentine Die Cut 15¼x14¼
Syncopated

350 A318 90pf black & red 1.10 1.10

Souvenir Sheet

Myth of Narcissus and Echo — A319

2017, May 22 Litho. *Perf. 14*
351 A319 5m multi 5.75 5.75

Apparition of the Virgin Mary at Medjugorje, 36th Anniv. — A320

2017, June 1 Litho. *Perf. 14*
352 A320 1m multi 1.25 1.25

Invention of Draisine, by Karl Drais (1785-1851)
A321

2017, June 12 Litho. *Perf. 14*
353 A321 2.90m multi 3.50 3.50

Radoslav Dodig (1954-2016), Archaeologist — A322

2017, June 17 Litho. *Perf. 14*
354 A322 90pf multi 1.10 1.10

Friar Branko Maric (1896-1974), Ethnomusicologist
A323

2017, June 21 Litho. *Perf. 14*
355 A323 2.70m multi 3.25 3.25

Coil Stamp
Self-Adhesive
Serpentine Die Cut 15½x14
Syncopated

356 A323 2.70m multi 3.25 3.25

World Music Day. No. 355 was printed in sheets of 8 + 2 central labels.

Handball — A324

2017, July 18 Litho. *Perf. 14*
357 A324 3.60m multi 4.50 4.50

Coil Stamp
Self-Adhesive
Serpentine Die Cut 15½x14
Syncopated

358 A324 3.60m multi 4.50 4.50

No. 357 was printed in sheets of 8 + central label.

Painting by Milivoj Uzelac (1897-1977) — A325

2017, July 23 Litho. *Perf. 14*
359 A325 2.90m multi 3.50 3.50

Rescue of Starving Bosnian Children by Father Didak Buntic (1871-1922), Cent. — A326

2017, Sept. 5 Litho. *Perf. 14*
360 A326 1.30m multi 1.60 1.60

Decorated Cane Handle
A327

2017, Oct. 9 Litho. *Perf. 14*
361 A327 1m multi 1.25 1.25

Mary's Meals Charity, 25th Anniv. — A328

2017, Oct. 9 Litho. *Perf. 14*
362 A328 3.10m multi 3.75 3.75

Helichrysum Italicum — A329

No. 363 — Denomination at: a, LL. b, UL.

2017, Nov. 1 Litho. *Perf. 14*
363 A329 2.70m Horiz. pair, #a-b 6.50 6.50

No. 363 is impregnated with the scent of the flower.

Worldwide Fund for Nature (WWF) — A330

No. 364 — Rupricapra rupicapra balcanica: a, One animal with dark brown fur. b, Two animals facing right. c, Heads of two animals. d. One animal with orange brown fur.

2017, Nov. 1 Litho. *Perf. 14*
364 A330 1.50m Block of 4, #a-d 7.25 7.25

Printed in sheets containing two blocks and two central labels.

Christmas — A331

Designs: Nos. 365a, 367, Angel. Nos. 365b, 366, Christmas tree.

2017, Dec. 1 Litho. *Perf. 14*
365 A331 90pf Pair, #a-b 2.25 2.25

Coil Stamps
Self-Adhesive
Serpentine Die Cut 15½x14
Syncopated

366 A331 90pf multi 1.10 1.10
367 A331 90pf multi 1.10 1.10
a. Horiz. coil pair, #366-367 2.20

No. 365 was printed in sheets containing 4 pairs + 2 labels.

100th Birthday of Father Bazilije Pandzic, Historian — A332

2018, Jan. 30 Litho. *Perf. 14*
368 A332 90pf multi 1.25 1.25

World Day of the Sick — A333

2018, Feb. 11 Litho. *Perf. 14*
369 A333 1.10m multi 1.40 1.40

World Down Syndrome Day — A334

2018, Mar. 21 Litho. *Perf. 14*
370 A334 3.10m multi 4.00 4.00

Europa — A335

No. 371 — Roman bridge over: a, Bosnia River (tree in foreground). b, Sujica River.

2018, Apr. 5 Litho. *Perf. 14*
371 A335 3m Pair, #a-b 7.50 7.50
c. Souvenir sheet of 4, 2 each #371a-371b 15.00 15.00

Printed in sheets of 8, containing 4 each #371a-371b + 2 labels.

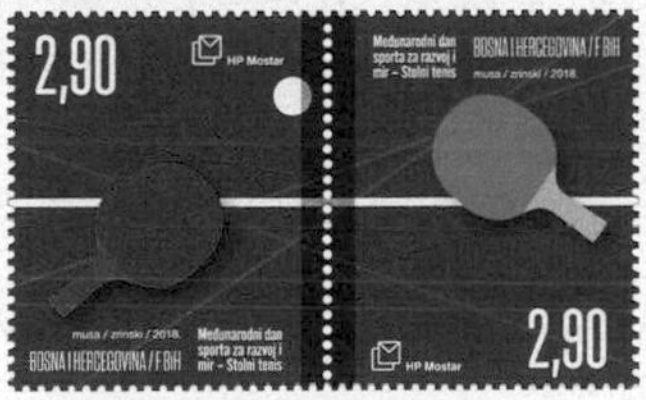

International Day of Sport — A336

No. 372: a, Table tennis ball and red paddle. b, Green paddle.

2018, Apr. 6 Litho. *Perf. 14*
372 A336 2.90m Horiz. pair, #a-b 7.25 7.25

Church Bell, Rosko Polje — A337

2018, May 12 Litho. *Perf. 14*
373 A337 90pf multi 1.10 1.10

No. 373 was printed in sheets of 12 + 4 central labels.

International Day of Families A338

2018, May 15 Litho. *Perf. 14*
374 A338 1.50m multi 1.90 1.90

Souvenir Sheet

Myth of Heather Flowers and Fairy, Vjetrenica — A339

2018, May 22 Litho. *Perf. 14*
375 A339 5m multi 6.00 6.00

Appearance of the Virgin Mary at Medjugorje, 37th Anniv. — A340

2018, June 1 Litho. *Perf. 14*
376 A340 1m multi 1.25 1.25

World Blood Donor Day — A341

2018, June 14 Litho. *Perf. 14*
377 A341 1.10m multi 1.40 1.40

International Coffee Day — A342

No. 378 — Coffee beans with cream in coffee cup depicting: a, Bosnian Croat Postal Service emblem. b, Heart.

2018, Oct. 1 Litho. *Perf. 14*
378 A342 2.90m Pair, #a-b 7.00 7.00

Loom — A343

2018, Oct. 9 Litho. *Perf. 14*
379 A343 90pf multi 1.10 1.10

Coil Stamp
Self-Adhesive
Serpentine Die Cut 15½x14
Syncopated

380 A343 90pf multi 1.10 1.10

World Food Day A344

No. 381: a, Ustipci. b, Cicvara.

Perf. 13¾x14 Syncopated
2018, Oct. 16 Litho.
381 Pair 8.50 8.50
a.-b. A344 3.60m Either single 4.25 4.25

Printed in sheets containing 4 each #381a-381b + 2 central labels.

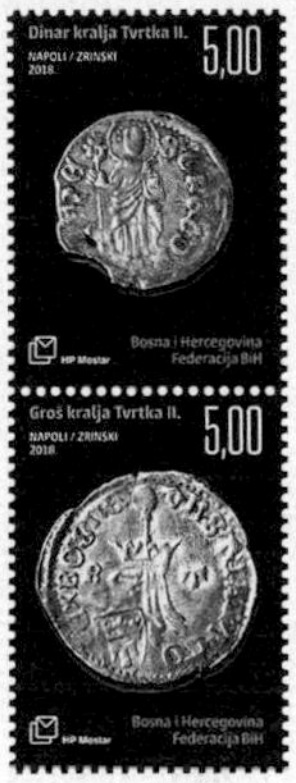

Coins of the Reign of King Tvrtko II — A345

No. 382: a, Dinar (18mm diameter coin). b, Groschen (21mm diameter coin).

Litho. & Embossed
2018, Oct. 31 *Perf. 14*
382 A345 5m Vert. pair, #a-b 12.00 12.00

Flowers — A346

No. 383: a, Daphne blagayana. b, Spiranthes spiralis.

2018, Nov. 1 Litho. *Perf. 14*
383 A346 2m Pair, #a-b 4.75 4.75

Fish — A347

No. 384: a, Salmothymus oxyrhynchus. b, Phoxinellus pseudalepidotus. c, Cobitis herzegoviensis. d, Aulopyge huegelii.

2018, Nov. 1 Litho. *Perf. 14*
384 A347 2.70m Block of 4, #a-d 12.50 12.50

Christmas and New Year's Day — A348

No. 385: a, Angel with horn and sleeping child (Christmas). b, Children dancing and angel (New Year's Day).

2018, Dec. 1 Litho. *Perf. 14*
385 A348 90pf Horiz. pair, #a-b 2.10 2.10

European Data Protection Day — A349

2019, Jan. 28 Litho. *Perf. 14*
386 A349 1.80m yel green & black 2.10 2.10

Toni Pehar (1952-2009), Actor — A350

2019, Apr. 29 Litho. *Perf. 14*
387 A350 90pf multi 1.10 1.10

Europa — A351

No. 388: a, Parus major. b, Parus caeruleus.

2019, Apr. 30 Litho. *Perf. 14*
388 A351 3m Horiz. pair, #a-b 7.00 7.00
c. Souvenir sheet of 2, #388a-388b 7.00 7.00

No. 388 was printed in sheets containing 4 pairs + 2 central labels.

Leonardo da Vinci (1452-1519), Sculptor and Painter A352

No. 389: a, Angel, Madonna Litta. b, Mona Lisa, Lady with an Ermine.

2019, May 2 Litho. *Perf. 14*
389 A352 4m Pair, #a-b 9.25 9.25

No. 389 was printed in sheets containing 4 each #389a-389b + central label.

Catacombs, Jajce — A353

2019, May 12 Litho. *Perf. 14*
390 A353 10pf multi .25 .25

Mother's Day — A354

2019, May 12 Litho. *Perf. 14*
391 A354 1.10m multi 1.25 1.25

Tree of Life, Photograph by Samir Hadzic — A355

2019, May 19 Litho. *Perf. 14*
392 A355 1.80m multi 2.10 2.10

World Inflammatory Bowel Disease Day. See Bosnia & Herzegovina (Bosniak) No. 818, Bosnia & Herzegovina (Serb) No. 616.

Souvenir Sheet

Myth of Cerberus and Wolfbane — A356

2019, May 22 Litho. *Perf. 14x14¼*
393 A356 5m multi 5.75 5.75

World No Tobacco Day — A357

2019, May 31 Litho. *Perf. 14*
394 A357 2.90m multi 3.50 3.50

30th Medjugorje Youth Festival A358

2019, June 1 Litho. *Perf. 14*
395 A358 1.50m multi 1.75 1.75

No. 395 was printed in sheets of 8 + central label.

Mostar Bridges — A359

No. 396: a, Carinski Bridge. b, Lucki Bridge.

2019, July 1 Litho. *Perf. 14*
396 A359 5m Vert. pair, #a-b 11.50 11.50

Printed in sheets of 8 (4 each #396a-396b) + 2 labels.

Volleyball — A360

No. 397 — Volleyball and: a, Two hands. b, Net and five hands.

2019, Sept. 13 Litho. *Perf. 14*
397 A360 3.10m Pair, #a-b 7.00 7.00

Alone with the Wind, by Ivica Vlasic — A361

2019, Sept. 23 Litho. *Perf. 14*
398 A361 2.70m multi 3.00 3.00

Dalmatinski Yatagan A362

2019, Oct. 9 Litho. *Perf. 14*
399 A362 1.10m multi 1.25 1.25

World Food Day — A363

No. 400: a, Pura lucnica (polenta and garlic sauce). b, Pole ispod saca (pan-baked potatoes).

2019, Oct. 16 Litho. *Perf. 14*
400 A363 2.70m Pair, #a-b 6.25 6.25

Fruit — A364

No. 401: a, Arbutus unedo. b, Fragaria vesca.

2019, Nov. 1 Litho. *Perf. 14*
401 A364 2.90m Pair, #a-b 6.75 6.75

Turtles A365

No. 402: a, Testudo hermanni. b, Chelonia mydas. c, Caretta caretta. d, Emys orbicularis.

2019, Nov. 1 Litho. *Perf. 14*
402 Horiz. strip of 4 14.00 14.00
a.-d. A365 3.10m Any single 3.50 3.50

Christmas and New Year's Day — A366

No. 403: a, Open door, gifts and "2020". b, Nativity scene.

2019, Dec. 1 Litho. *Perf. 14*
403 A366 90pf Pair, #a-b 2.10 2.10

Kiluba Language Bible Translated by Father Blago Brkic (1920-2009), Missionary to Africa — A367

2020, Feb. 21 Litho. *Perf. 14*
404 A367 50pf multi .60 .60

No. 404 was printed in sheets of 8 + central label.

Runners in Mostar Half-Marathon A368

2020, Mar. 20 Litho. *Perf. 14*
405 A368 1.50m multi 1.75 1.75

Rama Lake — A369

No. 406: a, Aerial view of Scit Peninsula and Rama Monastery. b, Aerial view of lake and islands.

2020, Mar. 22 Litho. *Perf. 14*
406 A369 1.80m Pair, #a-b 4.00 4.00

World Water Day.

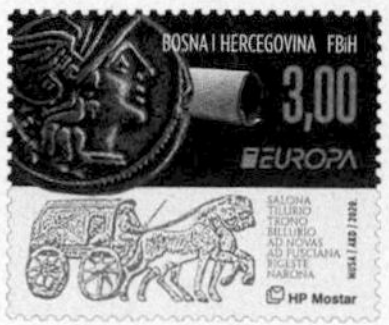

Obverse of Roman Silver Denarius, Scroll and Roman Messenger Cart — A371

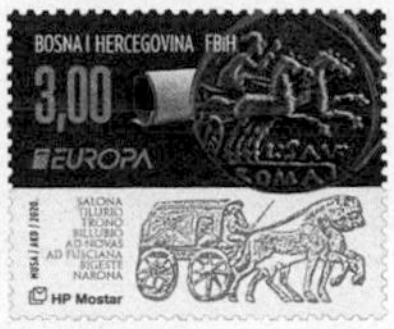

Reverse of Roman Silver Denarius, Scroll and Roman Messenger Cart — A372

2020, Apr. 5 **Litho.** ***Perf. 14***
408 A371 3m gold & multi 3.50 3.50
409 A372 3m gold & multi 3.50 3.50
a. Souvenir sheet of 2, #408-409 7.00 7.00

Europa. Nos. 408-409 were each printed in sheets of 8 + central label.

International Day of Sport for Development and Peace — A373

No. 410 — Judokas with denomination at: a, LL. b, UR.

2020, Apr. 6 **Litho.** ***Perf. 14***
410 A373 3.10m Vert. pair, #a-b 7.00 7.00

Radimlja Necropolis A374

2020, May 12 **Litho.** ***Perf. 14***
411 A374 20pf multi .25 .25

Souvenir Sheet

Dandelions — A375

2020, May 22 **Litho.** ***Perf. 14***
412 A375 5m multi 5.75 5.75

Apparition of the Virgin Mary at Medjugorje, 39th Anniv. — A376

2020, June 1 **Litho.** ***Perf. 14***
413 A376 1.50m multi 1.75 1.75

Architecture — A377

No. 414: a, Windows of Mostar Gymnasium. b, Villa Fessler.

2020, July 1 **Litho.** ***Perf. 14***
414 A377 2.70m Pair, #a-b 6.25 6.25

European Day of Languages A378

2020, Sept. 26 **Litho.** ***Perf. 14***
415 A378 90pf multi 1.10 1.10

Cruciform Fibula — A379

2020, Oct. 9 **Litho.** ***Perf. 14***
416 A379 70pf multi .85 .85

World Food Day — A380

No. 417: a, Smokvenjak (fig cake). b, Cupter (dried grape jelly).

2020, Oct. 14 **Litho.** ***Perf. 14***
417 A380 1.10m Vert. pair, #a-b 2.60 2.60

Flowers A381

No. 418. a, Veronica saturejoides. b, Moltkia petraea.

2020, Nov. 1 **Litho.** ***Perf. 14***
418 A381 2.70m Pair, #a-b 6.50 6.50

Butterflies — A382

No. 419: a, Proterebia afra dalmata. b, Aptura metis. c, Melitaea britomartis. d, Pyrgus sidae.

2020, Nov. 1 **Litho.** ***Perf. 14***
419 A382 2.90m Block of 4, #a-d 14.00 14.00

BOSNIA & HERZEGOVINA (SERB ADMIN)

Bosnian Serb Administration Located In Banja Luka

(Republika Srpska)

100 Paras = 1 Dinar

100 pfennig = 1 mark (6/22/98)

Catalogue values for all unused stamps in this country are for Never Hinged items.

Stamps of Yugoslavia Surcharged

No. 3

No. 3a

No. 4

No. 9

No. 11

1992, Oct. 26 **Litho.** ***Perf. 12½***

1	A559	5d on 10p #2004	1.50	1.50
2	A559	30d on 3d #2015	*160.00*	*160.00*
3	A559	50d on 40p #2007a, perf. 13½	1.50	1.50
a.		Thick bars in obliterator	1.50	1.50
b.		On #2007, perf 12½	100.00	100.00
4	A559	60d on 20p #2005	1.75	1.75
5	A559	60d on 30p #2006	1.75	1.75
6	A559	100d on 1d #2013	1.75	1.75
7	A559	100d on 2d #2014a, perf. 13½	1.75	1.75
a.		On #2014, perf 12½	75.00	75.00
8	A559	100d on 3d #2015	1.75	1.75
9	A621	300d on 5d #2017a, perf. 13½	1.75	1.75
a.		On #2017, perf 12½	30.00	30.00
10	A620	500d on 50p #2008	1.75	1.75
11	A619	500d on 60p #2009	1.75	1.75
a.		On #2009 perf. 13½	*110.00*	*110.00*
		Nos. 1-11 (11)	*177.00*	*177.00*

Obliterator on Nos. 1, 3 and 9 has thin bars.

Musical Instrument — A1

Designs: 10d, 20d, 30d, 5000d, 6000d, 10,000d, Stringed instrument. 50d, 100d, 20,000d, 30,000d, Coat of arms, vert. 500d, 50,000d, Monastery.

1993 ***Perf. 13¼, 12½ (#19)***

12	A1	10d blk & org yel	5.25	5.25
13	A1	20d blk & blue	.25	.25
14	A1	30d blk & salmon	.60	.60
15	A1	50d blk & ver	.60	.60
16	A1	100d blk & ver	1.60	1.60
17	A1	500d blk & blue	3.50	3.50
18	A1	5000d blk & lilac	.30	.30
19	A1	6000d blk & yel	.30	.30
20	A1	10,000d blk & vio bl	3.75	3.75
a.		Perf. 12½	2.75	2.75
21	A1	20,000d blk & ver	1.00	1.00
22	A1	30,000d blk & ver	1.60	1.60
23	A1	50,000d blk & lilac	1.60	1.60
		Nos. 12-23 (12)	20.35	20.35

Nos. 12-17 dated 1992, others dated 1993. Issued: Nos. 12-17, 1/11; others 6/8.

Nos. 13 and 21 with an "A" overprint and stamps of type A1 with an "R" overprint are locals.

For surcharges see Nos. 24-26, 34-36, 41-45, F9.

Nos. 15-16 Surcharged

1993, June 15

24	A1	7500d on 50d #15	2.00	2.00
25	A1	7500d on 100d #16	2.00	2.00
26	A1	9000d on 50d #15	3.00	3.00
		Nos. 24-26 (3)	7.00	7.00

Referendum, May 15-16, 1993.

A2

Symbol of St. John, the Evangelist.

1993, Aug. 16 ***Perf. 13¼***
27 A2 (A) vermilion .70 .70

Icon of St. Stefan — A3

1994, Jan. 9 ***Perf. 14***
28 A3 1d multicolored 7.00 7.00

King Peter I Karageorge A4

1994, May 28
29 A4 80p sepia 3.00 3.00

City of Banja Luka, 500th Anniv. A5

1994, July 18

30 A5 1.20d multicolored 4.00 4.00

Madonna & Child, Cajnica Church — A6

1994, Sept. 1

33 A6 1d multicolored 3.25 3.25

Nos. 18, 20, 23 Surcharged

1994, Nov. 1 ***Perf. 13¼***

34	A1	(A) on 5000d #18	1.60	1.60
35	A1	40p on 10,000d #20	1.60	1.60
a.		On #20a	3.50	3.50
36	A1	2d on 50,000d #23	1.60	1.60
a.		Perf 12½	22.50	22.50
		Nos. 34-36,F9 (4)	6.40	6.40

No. 34 sold for 20p on day of issue.

Mostanica Monastery A7

Designs: 60p, Tavna Monastery, vert. 1.20d, Zitomislic Monastery, vert.

1994 ***Perf. 14***

37-39 A7 Set of 3 9.00 9.00

Issued: 60p, 11/11; 1d, 12/31; 1.20d, 12/28.

Flora & Fauna A8

No. 40: a, Shore lark. b, Dinaromys bogdanovi. c, Edraianthus niveus. d, Aquilegia dinarica.

1996, Mar. 1 ***Perf. 13¾***

40 A8 1.20d Block of 4, #a.-d. 5.25 5.25

Nos. 14-16, 19, 22 Surcharged

1996, July 1 ***Perf. 13¼***

41	A1	70p on 30d #14	.50	.50
42	A1	1d on 100d #16	.70	.70
43	A1	2d on 30,000d #22	1.40	1.40
44	A1	3d on 50d #15	2.25	2.25
		Perf. 12½		
45	A1	5d on 6000d #19	3.75	3.75
		Nos. 41-45 (5)	8.60	8.60

Relay Station, Mt. Kozara — A9

1.20d, Drina River Bridge, Srbinje, horiz. 2d, Mt. Romanija relay station. 5d, Stolice relay station, Mt. Maljevica. 10d, Visegrad Bridge, horiz.

1996, Sept. 20 ***Perf. 14***

46	A9	(A)	multicolored	.25	.25
47	A9	1.20d	multicolored	.60	.60
48	A9	2d	multicolored	1.20	1.20
49	A9	5d	multicolored	2.75	2.75
50	A9	10d	multicolored	5.50	5.50
			Nos. 46-50,F10 (6)	11.05	11.05

No. 46 sold for 30p on day of issue.

Church, Bashcharsi A10

1997, July 7 ***Perf. 13¾***

51 A10 2.50d multicolored 1.75 1.75

Mihailo Pupin (1848-1935), Electrical Engineer A11

1997, July 14

52 A11 2.50d multicolored 1.75 1.75

A12

Flowers: No. 53, Oxytropis compestris. No. 54, Primula kitaibeliana. No. 55, Pedicularis hoermanniana. No. 56, Knautia sarajevensis.

1997, Sept. 12

53-56 A12 3.20d Set of 4 7.00 7.00

A13

Famous Men: A, Branko Copic (1915-85). 1.50d, Mesa Selimovic (1910-82). 3d, Aleksa Santic (1868-1924). 5d, Peter Kocic (1873-1916). 10d, Ivo Andric (1892-1975).

1997, Nov. 1 ***Perf. 13¾***

57	A13	A	multicolored	.35	.35
58	A13	1.50d	multicolored	.55	.55
59	A13	3d	multicolored	1.40	1.40
60	A13	5d	multicolored	2.40	2.40
61	A13	10d	multicolored	4.50	4.50
			Nos. 57-61,F11 (6)	9.95	9.95

No. 57 sold for 60p on day of issue.

A14

2.50d, Lutra lutra. 4.50d, Capreolus capreolus. 6.50d, Ursus arctos.

1997, Nov. 12

62-64 A14 Set of 3 6.00 6.00

Europa — A15

Stories & legends: 2.50d, Two queens. 6.50d, Prince on horseback.

1997, Nov. 12

65-66 A15 Set of 2 22.50 22.50

Diana, Princess of Wales (1961-97) — A16

"Diana" in: a, Roman letters. b, Cyrillic letters.

1997, Dec. 22

67 A16 3.50d Pair, #a.-b. 15.00 15.00

1998 World Cup Soccer Championships, France — A17

Players, country flags (each 90p) — No. 68: a, Brazil. b, Morocco. c, Norway. d, Scotland. e, Italy. f, Chile. g, Austria. h, Cameroun.

No. 69: a, France. b, Saudi Arabia. c, Denmark. d, South Africa. e, Spain. f, Nigeria. g, Paraguay. h, Bulgaria.

No. 70: a, Netherlands. b, Belgium. c, Mexico. d, South Korea. e, Germany. f, US. g, Yugoslavia. h, Iran.

No. 71: a, Romania. b, England. c, Tunisia. d, Colombia. e, Argentina. f, Jamaica. g, Croatia. h, Japan.

1998, May 5 **Sheets of 8 + label**

68-71 A17 Set of 4 60.00 60.00

Europa — A18

Natl. festivals, each 7.50d: No. 72, Instrument at R. No. 73, Instrument at L.

1998, June 9

72-73 A18 Set of 2 *21.00 21.00*

Icons, Chelandari Monastery A19

Various icons: 50p, 70p, 1.70d, 2d.

1998

74-77 A19 Set of 4 9.00 9.00

Buildings — A20

Designs: 15pf, Bijeljina. 20pf, Sokolac. A, Banja Luka. 75pf, Prijedor. 2m, Brcko, vert. 4.50m, Zvornik, vert. 10m, Doboj.

1999, Mar. 15 **Litho.** ***Perf. 13¾***

78-84 A20 Set of 7 27.50 27.50

No. 80 has black "A." It sold for 50pf on day of issue. See No. F12.

Air Srpska Airplanes A21

Airplane: No. 85, 50pf, In clouds. No. 86, 50pf, Over lake. 75pf, Over rocks. 1.50m, Over lake, diff.

1999, Mar. 26 **Litho.** ***Perf. 13¾***

85-88 A21 Set of 4 6.00 6.00

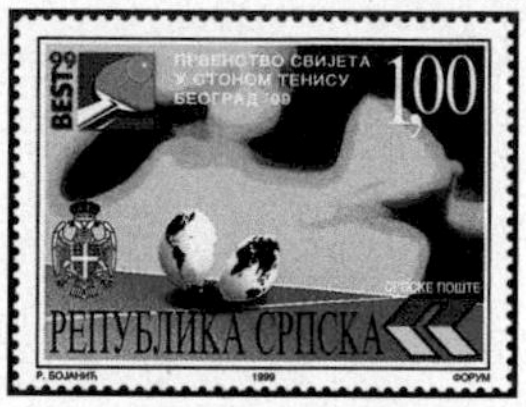

World Table Tennis Championships, Belgrade — A22

Designs: 1m, Cracked globe as ball. 2m, Table, paddle, ball.

1999, Apr. 19

89-90 A22 Set of 2 7.50 7.50

Issued in sheets of 8 + label.

Europa — A23

Natl. Parks: 1.50m, Kozara. 2m, Peruchitsa.

1999, May 4

91-92 A23 Set of 2 *160.00 160.00*

Anniversaries — A24

No. 93, each 50pf: a, Gorazde incorporation document. b, Dobrin Monastery (denomination at UL). c, Illuminated letter. d, Zitomislic

Monastery. e, Gomionica Monastery (2 steeples). f, Madonna and Child icon. g, St. Nicholas icon. h, Holy trinity icon.

1999, May 26 Litho. *Perf. 13¾*

93 A24 Sheet of 8, #a-h, + label 7.00 7.00

Dabrobosanska and Zahumskohercegovacka Archbishopric, 780th anniv., Gorazde Printing Press, 480th anniv.

Fish — A25

No. 94: a, 50pf, Salmo trutta m. fario. b, 50pf, Salmo trutta m. lacustris. c, 75pf, Hucho hucho. d, 1m, Thymallus thymallus.

1999, June 17

94 A25 Horiz. strip of 4, #a-d, + central label 5.25 5.25

Issued in sheets of 5 strips with different labels.

Man on the Moon, 30th Anniv. — A26

Designs: 1m, Equipment on moon. 2m, Astronaut, lunar module.

1999, July 21

95-96 A26 Set of 2 5.25 5.25

Issued in sheets of 8 + 1 label.

UPU, 125th Anniv. — A27

Designs: 75pf, Pencil. 1.25m, Arc and map.

1999, Sept. 9

97-98 A27 Set of 2 3.75 3.75

Issued in sheets of 8 + 1 label.

Icons — A28

No. 99, each 50pf: a, Madonna and Child (black denomination at UL). b, Madonna and Child (white denomination at UL). c, Madonna and Child (white denomination at LR). d, Saint with cross. e, Pieta. f, Christ enters Jerusalem (on donkey). g, St. Jovan (with scroll). h, Sts. Sava and Simeon.

1999, Oct. 29

99 A28 Sheet of 8, #a-h, + label 6.00 6.00

Millennium — A29

a, Egyptians, obelisk. b, Hourglass. c, Iron bell. d, Locomotive, steamship. e, Balloon, airplanes, automobiles. f, Man on the moon.

1999, Nov. 22

100	A29 Booklet pane of 6	13.00	13.00
a.-e.	50pf Any single	1.75	1.75
f.	1m multi	3.00	3.00
	Booklet, #100	14.00	14.00

See No. 126.

Postal Services in Serbian Territory, 135th Anniv. — A30

3m, Postriders on bridge.

1999, Dec. 23

101 A30 50pf shown .85 .85

Souvenir Sheet

102 A30 3m multi 70.00 70.00

Prince Stephen Nemanja — A31

2000, Feb. 29

103 A31 1.50m multi 2.75 2.75

Issued in sheets of 8 + 1 label.

Flora — A32

1m, Prunus domestica. 2m, Corylus avellana.

2000, Mar. 22

104-105 A32 Set of 2 4.00 4.00

Issued in sheets of 8 + 1 label.

Bridges — A33

No. 106, Brod (deer at left). No. 107, Pavlovica (horses and birds). No. 108, Zepce (bird at right). No. 109, Zvornik (bird at left).

2000, Apr. 12

106-109 A33 1m Set of 4 7.00 7.00

Issued in sheets of 8 + 1 label.

Jovan Ducic (1871-1943), Writer — A34

2000, Apr. 26 Litho. *Perf. 13¾*

110 A34 20pf multi .45 .45

Common Design Type and

Europa — A35

2000, May 5 Litho. *Perf. 13¾*

111 CD17 1.50m multi *50.00 50.00*

112 A35 2.50m multi *60.00 60.00*

Banja Luka Province, Cent. — A36

2000, May 26 Litho. *Perf. 13¾*

113 A36 1.50m multi 2.75 2.75

European Soccer Championships A37

Various players. Denominations: 1m, 2m.

2000, June 14

114-115 A37 Set of 2 5.75 5.75

Souvenir Sheet

116 A37 6m Players, map 17.50 17.50

No. 116 contains one 35x42mm stamp.

Nevesinje Rebellion, 125th Anniv. — A38

2000, July 12

117 A38 1.50m multi 2.75 2.75

2000 Summer Olympics, Sydney A39

Map of Australia and: No. 118, 50pf, Handball. No. 119, 50pf, Basketball. No. 120, 50pf, Hurdles. No. 121, 50pf, Volleyball.

2m, Emu, kangaroo, Australian arms.

2000, Sept. 6

118-121 A39 Set of 4 3.50 3.50

Souvenir Sheet

122 A39 2m multi + label 3.50 3.50

No. 122 contains one 42x35mm stamp.

Locomotives A40

No. 123 — Locomotive from: a, 1848. b, 1865. c, 1930. d, 1990.

2000, Oct. 4 Litho. *Perf. 13¾*

123	Horiz. strip of 4 + central label	8.50	8.50
a.-c.	A40 50pf Any single	1.50	1.50
d.	A40 1m multi	3.00	3.00

Protected Species — A41

Designs: 1m, Leontopodium alpinum. 2m, Proteus anguinus, horiz.

2000, Oct. 31

124-125 A41 Set of 2 5.50 5.50

Millennium Type of 1999

No. 126: a, Ship. b, Glassblowers. c, Blacksmith. d, Printers. e, James Watt, steam engine, steam-powered vehicle. f, Satellites. g, People on shore, ships (105x55mm).

2000, Nov. 22

126	Booklet pane of 7 + label	10.00	10.00
a.-f.	A29 50pf Any single	1.00	1.00
g.	A29 3m multi	4.00	4.00
	Booklet, #126	11.00	11.00

Icons — A42

Icons from: No. 127, 50pf, 1577-78. No. 128, 50pf, 1607-08. No. 129, 1m, 1577-78. No. 130, 1m, Unknown year.

2000, Dec. 20

127-130 A42 Set of 4 5.00 5.00

Invention of the Telephone, 125th Anniv. — A43

2001, Feb. 27

131 A43 1m multi 1.75 1.75

Manned Space Flight, 40th Anniv. — A44

Designs: 1m, Yuri Gagarin, Vostok 1. 3m, Gagarin, Earth, rocket lift-off.

2001, Mar. 29

132 A44 1m multi 1.75 1.75

Souvenir Sheet

133 A44 3m multi 7.00 7.00

No. 133 contains one 53x35mm stamp.

Vlado Milosevic, Composer — A45

2001, Apr. 11

134 A45 50pf multi .90 .90

Europa — A46

Designs: Nos. 135, 137a, 1m, Skakavac Waterfall. No. 136, 137b, 2m, Turjanica River.

White Border

2001, May 4 ***Perf. 13¾***

135-136 A46 Set of 2 *6.00 6.00*

Light Blue Border

Perf. 13¾ Vert.

137 A46 Vert. pair, #a-b *15.00 15.00*

No. 137 printed in panes of 3 pairs which were sold with a booklet cover, but unattached to it.

Butterflies — A47

Designs: No. 138, 50pf, Maniola jurtina. No. 139, 50pf, Pyrgus malvae. No. 140, 1m, Papilio machaon. No. 141, 1m, Lycaena pylaeas.

2001, June 19 ***Perf. 13¾***

138-141 A47 Set of 4 5.50 5.50

Kostajnica A48

Srbinje — A49

2001, Sept. 5 **Litho.** ***Perf. 13¾***

142 A48 25pf multi .50 .50

143 A49 1m multi 1.60 1.60

Issued: 25pf, 9/5. 1m, 9/20.

Karate Championships A50

2001, Sept. 5

144 A50 1.50m multi 2.50 2.50

A51

A51a

A51b

A51c Costumes

2001, July 17 **Litho.** ***Perf. 13¾***

145 A51 50pf multi	.75	.75
146 A51a 50pf multi	.75	.75
147 A51b 1m multi	1.75	1.75
148 A51c 1m multi	1.75	1.75
Nos. 145-148 (4)	5.00	5.00

A52

A53

A54

A55

Caves

A56 A57

2001, Sept. 20 ***Perf. 13¾ Vert.***

149	Booklet pane of 6	5.00	
a.	A52 50pf Rastusha Cave	.80	.80
b.	A53 50pf Vaganska Cave	.80	.80
c.	A54 50pf Pavlova Cave	.80	.80
d.	A55 50pf Orlovacha Cave	.80	.80
e.	A56 50pf Ledana Cave	.80	.80
f.	A57 50pf Pod Jelikom Cave	.80	.80

Building Type of 1999 with Red "A"

2001, Oct. 23 **Litho.** ***Perf. 13¾***

150 A20 A Banja Luka .90 .90

No. 150 sold for 50pf on day of issue. "A" on No. 80 is in black.

Nobel Prizes, Cent. — A58

Designs: 1m, Alfred Nobel (1833-96). 2m, Ivo Andric (1892-1975), 1961 Literature laureate.

2001, Oct. 23

151-152 A58 Set of 2 5.00 5.00

Each stamp printed in sheets of 8 + central label.

Bardacha-Srbac — A59

Lake Klinje — A60

2001, Nov. 15

153 A59 1m multi 1.75 1.75

154 A60 1m multi 1.75 1.75

Each stamp printed in sheets of 8 + central label.

Art A61

Designs: No. 155, 50pf, Belgrade Suburb, by Kosta Hakman (1899-1961). No. 156, 50pf, Djerdap, by Todor Shvrakic (1882-1931). No. 157, 50pf, Still Life With Parrot, by Jovan Bijelic (1884-1964), vert. No. 158, 50pf, Adela, by Miodrag Vujacic Mirski (1932-97), vert.

2001, Dec. 5

155-158 A61 Set of 4 3.50 3.50

Each stamp printed in sheets of 8 + central label.

Christmas A62

2001, Dec. 5

159 A62 1m multi 1.75 1.75

Printed in sheets of 8 + central label.

Borac Soccer Team, 75th Anniv. — A63

2001, Dec. 24

160 A63 1.50m multi 2.50 2.50

Printed in sheets of 8 + central label.

A64

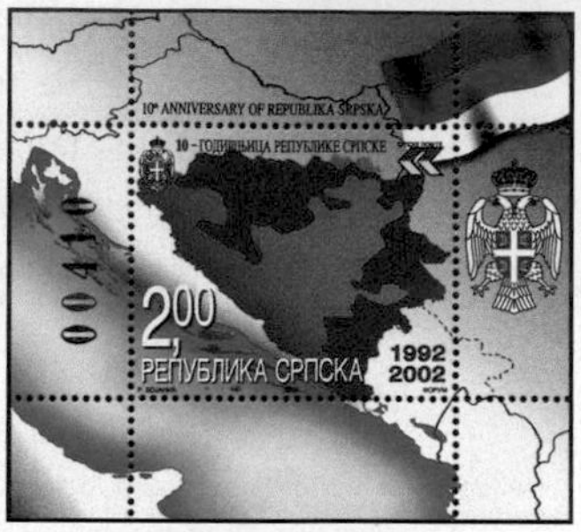

Serb Administration, 10th Anniv. — A65

Designs: 50pf, Arms, vert. 1m, Flag.

2002, Jan. 10

161-162 A64 Set of 2 2.50 2.50

Souvenir Sheet

163 A65 2m multi 3.50 3.50

Nos. 161-162 were each printed in sheets of 8 + central label.

War on Terrorism — A66

Designs: 1m, Hand holding snake. 2m, Globe, eyes, guns.

2002, Jan. 29 **Litho.** ***Perf. 13¾***

164 A66 1m multi 1.60 1.60

Souvenir Sheet

165 A66 2m multi 3.50 3.50

No. 164 printed in sheets of 8 + central label. No. 165 contains one 35x46mm stamp.

2002 Winter Olympics, Salt Lake City — A67

Designs: 50pf, Ski jumper. 1m, Bobsled.

2002, Feb. 13

166-167 A67 Set of 2 2.50 2.50

Each stamp printed in sheets of 8 + label.

Serbian Sarajevo — A68

Serbian Brod — A69

2002

168 A68 50pf multi .85 .85
169 A69 2m multi 3.50 3.50

Issued: 50pf, 3/5. 2m, 4/18.

Education, Cent. — A70

2002, Mar. 5

170 A70 1m multi 1.60 1.60

Printed in sheets of 8 + central label.

Charles Lindbergh's Non-stop Solo Trans-Atlantic Flight, 75th Anniv. — A71

2002, Apr. 11

171 A71 1m multi 1.60 1.60

Printed in sheets of 8 + central label.

Europa — A72

Designs: 1m, Horses and clown. 1.50m, Elephants and clowns.

2002, Apr. 30 Litho. ***Perf. 13¾***

172-173 A72 Set of 2 *5.00 5.00*

Pink Border

173A Vert. pair *9.00 9.00*
b. A72 1m Like #172, imperf. at top *2.50 2.50*
c. A72 1.50m Like #173, imperf. at bottom *5.00 5.00*

No. 173A printed in sheets of 3 pairs which were sold in a booklet cover, but unattached to it.

2002 World Cup Soccer Championships, Japan and Korea — A73

Designs: 50pf, Two players. 1m, Two players, diff.

2002, May 31

174-175 A73 Set of 2 2.50 2.50

Resorts — A74

Designs: 25pf, Banja Slatina. 50pf, Banja Mljechanica. 75pf, Banja Vilina Vlas. 1m, Banja Laktashi. 1.50m, Banja Vruchica. 5m, Banja Dvorovi.

2002, July 5

176-181 A74 Set of 6 14.00 14.00

See No. 225. Compare with Nos. 241-242.

Artifacts A75

Designs: No. 182, 50pf, Greco-Illyrian helmet, 4th-5th cent. No. 183, 50pf, Glassware, 14th cent. No. 184, 1m, Silver snake heads, 4th-5th cent. No. 185, 1m, Inscriptions on stone, 12th cent.

2002, Sept. 5

182-185 A75 Set of 4 4.50 4.50

Mushrooms A76

No. 186: a, Boletus regius. b, Macrolepiota procera. c, Amanita caesarea. d, Craterellus cornucopioides.

2002, Oct. 17 Litho. ***Perf. 13¾***

186 Horiz. strip of 4, #a-d, + central label 4.50 4.50
a.-b. A76 50pf Any single 1.00 1.00
c.-d. A76 1m Any single 1.40 1.40

Nature Protection — A77

Designs: 50pf, Maglic. 1m, Klekovacha.

2002, Nov. 26 Litho. ***Perf. 13¾***

187-188 A77 Set of 2 2.50 2.50

Art — A78

Designs: No. 189, 50pf, Crno Jezero pod Durmitorom, by Lazar Drijaca, 1935. No. 190, 50pf, Petar Popovic Pecija, by Spiro Bocaric, 1933, vert. No. 191, 1m, Zembiljeva Ulica, by Branko Sotra, 1937. No. 192, 1m, Ptice u Pejzazu, by Milan Sovilj, 2000.

2002, Dec. 18

189-192 A78 Set of 4 5.00 5.00

Souvenir Sheet

Showing of First Film in Bosnia, Cent. — A79

2003, Feb. 13 Litho. ***Perf. 13¾***

193 A79 3m multi 5.00 5.00

Alekse Santic (1868-1924), Writer — A80

2003, Mar. 5

194 A80 1m multi 1.60 1.60

Easter — A80a

Designs: 50pf, Crucifixion. 1m, Resurrection of Christ, by Matthias Grünewald.

2003, Mar. 28

195-196 A80a Set of 2 2.50 2.50

Souvenir Sheet

First Ascent of Mt. Everest, 50th Anniv. — A81

No. 197: a, Mt. Everest. b, Mt. Everest and mountain climber.

2003, Apr. 16 Litho. ***Perf. 13¾***

197 A81 1.50m Sheet of 2, #a-b 5.00 5.00

Europa — A82

Designs: 1m, Man affixing poster to wall. 1.50m, Hand and poster.

2003, May 5 ***Perf. 13¾***

198 A82 1m multi *2.50 2.50*
a. Perf. 13¾, imperf. at top *5.50 5.50*
b. Perf. 13¾, imperf. at bottom *6.00 6.00*

199 A82 1.50m multi *3.50 3.50*
a. Perf. 13¾, imperf. at bottom *7.00 7.00*
b. Perf. 13¾, imperf. at top *8.00 8.00*

A sheet of six containing one each of Nos. 198b and 199b and two each of Nos. 198a and 199a was sold in, but unattached to, a booklet cover.

Horses — A83

Designs: No. 200, 50pf, Arabian. No. 201, 50pf, Two Lippizaners. No. 202, 1m, Bosansko-brdski. No. 203, 1m, Two Posavacs.

2003, June 9 ***Perf. 13¾***

200-203 A83 Set of 4 5.00 5.00

A84

Visit of Pope John Paul II — A85

2003, June 22 ***Perf. 13¾***

204 A84 1.50m multi 4.50 4.50

Perf. 13½x13¾

205 A85 1.50m multi 4.50 4.50

No. 204 was printed in sheets of 8 stamps + central label.

Orders — A86

Different orders with background colors of: 50pf, Brown. 1m, Blue.

2003, July 11 ***Perf. 13¾x13***

206-207 A86 Set of 2 2.50 2.50

Fight Against Terrorism — A87

2003, Aug. 14 Litho. ***Perf. 13¾x13***

208 A87 1m multi 1.60 1.60

Leo Tolstoy (1828-1910), Writer — A88

2003, Sept. 25 Litho. ***Perf. 13¾x13***

209 A88 1m multi 1.60 1.60

Printed in sheets of 8 + label.

Nature Protection — A89

Designs: 50pf, Bear eating fish, Ugar River. 1m, Drina River.

2003, Oct. 21

210-211 A89 Set of 2 2.50 2.50

Each stamp printed in sheet of 8 + label.

Icons — A90

No. 212: a, St. Sava and Martyr Barbara (shown). b, St. Lazarus, 1658. c, Crowning of Mary in Heaven, by Dimitrije Bacevic. d, Holy Family.

2003, Nov. 19 *Perf. 13x13¾*

212 Horiz. strip of 4 + central label 5.00 5.00
a.-b. A90 50pf Either single 1.00 1.00
c.-d. A90 1m Either single 1.50 1.50

New Year's Day — A91

Designs: 50pf, Child and snowman. 1m, Santa Claus and reindeer.

2003, Dec. 5 *Perf. 13¾x13*

213-214 A91 Set of 2 2.50 2.50

Each stamp printed in sheet of 8 + label.

Powered Flight, Cent. — A92

Designs: 50pf, Wright Brothers, Wright Flyer. 1m, Count Ferdinand von Zeppelin, Graf Zeppelin.

2003, Dec. 17 *Perf. 13x13¾*

215-216 A92 Set of 2 2.50 2.50

Souvenir Sheet

First Serbian Rebellion, Bicent. — A93

No. 217 — Rebels: a, Denomination at UL. b, Denomination at LR.

2004, Feb. 5 *Perf. 13¾x13*

217 A93 1.50m Sheet of 2, #a-b 5.00 5.00

Souvenir Sheet

2004 Summer Olympics, Athens — A94

No. 218 — Chariot race: a, Denomination at UL. b, Denomination at UR.

2004, Mar. 2 *Perf. 13x13¾*

218 A94 1.50m Sheet of 2, #a-b 5.00 5.00

Albert Einstein (1879-1955) A95

2004, Mar. 12

219 A95 1.50m multi 2.50 2.50

Printed in sheets of 8 + label.

Easter — A96

Paintings by: 50pf, Konstantinos Xenopoulos, 1961. 1m, Eremija Profeta.

2004, Apr. 2

220-221 A96 Set of 2 2.50 2.50

Europa — A97

Designs: Nos. 222, 224a, 224b, 1m, White water rafting. Nos. 223, 224c, 224d, 1.50m, Paragliding.

2004, May 5 Litho. *Perf. 13¾x13*

White Border

222-223 A97 Set of 2 4.00 4.00

Light Blue Border

Perf. 13¾x13 on 3 Sides

224 Sheet of 6, #224b, 224d, 2 each #224a, 224c 16.00 16.00
a. A97 1m Imperf. at top 2.25 2.25
b. A97 1m Imperf. at bottom 2.25 2.25
c. A97 1.50m Imperf. at bottom 3.00 3.00
d. A97 1.50m Imperf. at top 3.00 3.00

Nos. 222-223 each were printed in sheets of 8 + label. No. 224 was sold in booket cover but was not attached to it.

Resorts Type of 2002

2004, May 10 *Perf. 13¾*

225 A74 20pf Kulasi .50 .50
a. Dated "2006" .50 .50

Milutin Milankovic (1879-1958), Astronomer — A98

2004, May 28 *Perf. 13¾x13*

226 A98 1m multi 1.60 1.60

Printed in sheets of 8 + label.

European Soccer Championships, Portugal — A99

2004, June 8 *Perf. 13x13¾*

227 A99 1.50m multi 2.50 2.50

Printed in sheets of 8 + label.

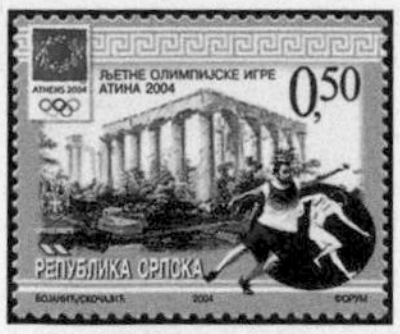

2004 Summer Olympics, Athens A100

Athens Olympics emblem and: No. 228, 50pf, Shot put, Greek ruins. No. 229, 50pf, Hurdle, Greek ruins. No. 230, 1m, Runners, Greek ruins. No. 231, 1m, Runners, horses.

2004, July 12

228-231 A100 Set of 4 3.25 3.25

Nos. 228-230 each were printed in sheets of 8 + label. No. 231 was printed in sheet of 3 + 3 labels.

Nature Protection — A101

Designs: 50pf, Arctostaphylos uva-ursi. 1m, Monticola saxatilis.

2004, Aug. 27 Litho. *Perf. 13¾x13*

232-233 A101 Set of 2 2.50 2.50

Each stamp printed in sheets of 8 + label.

Minerals A102

Designs: No. 234, 50pf, Antimonite (shown). No. 235, 50pf, Pyrite (Prussian blue background). No. 236, 1m, Sphalerite. No. 237, 1m, Quartz, vert.

2004, Sept. 14 *Perf. 13¾*

234-237 A102 Set of 4 4.50 4.50

Each stamp printed in sheets of 8 + label.

Michael Pupin (1858-1935), Physicist — A103

2004, Oct. 9 Litho. *Perf. 13¾x13½*

238 A103 1m multi 1.60 1.60

Printed in sheets of 8 + label.

Fight Against Terrorism — A104

2004, Oct. 21

239 A104 1m multi 1.60 1.60

Printed in sheets of 8 + label.

Flowers — A105

No. 240: a, Digitalis grandiflora. b, Arnica montana. c, Rosa pendulina. d, Gentiana lutea.

2004, Nov. 18 Litho. *Perf. 13¾x13*

240 Horiz. strip of 4 + central label 5.00 5.00
a.-b. A105 50pf Either single .80 .80
c.-d. A105 1m Either single 1.60 1.60

Banja Mljechanica Resort — A106

Banja Laktashi Resort — A107

2004, Dec. 6 *Perf. 13¾*

241 A106 50pf multi .75 .75
242 A107 1m multi 1.75 1.75

Compare No. 241 with No. 177, which has red in sky and a black roof. Compare No. 242 with No. 179, which has a blue sky.

Christmas A108

2004, Dec. 7 *Perf. 13x13¾*

243 A108 1m multi 1.60 1.60

Printed in sheets of 8 + label.

Paintings by Milenko Atanatskovic A109

Designs: 50c, Serbian Farmer, Semberije. 1m, Beledija, Stara Opstina, (house) horiz.

2005, Feb. 7 *Perf. 13¾x13, 13x13¾*

244-245 A109 Set of 2 2.50 2.50

Each stamp printed in sheets of 8 + label.

Janj River Waterfall A110

Perf. 13¼x13¾

2005, Mar. 22 **Litho.**

246 A110 1m multi 1.60 1.60

Printed in sheets of 8 + label.

Europa A111

Designs: Nos. 247, 249a, 249b, 1m, Cooking pots near fire. Nos. 248. 249c, 249d, 1.50m, Food on table.

2005, Apr. 4 ***Perf. 13¼x13¾***

Tan Bottom Panel

247-248 A111 Set of 2 4.50 4.50

Green Bottom Panel

Perf. 13¼x13¾ on 3 Sides

249 Sheet of 6, #249b, 249d, 2 each #249a, 249c 11.00 11.00
- *a.* A111 1m Imperf. at top 1.25 1.25
- *b.* A111 1m Imperf. at bottom 1.25 1.25
- *c.* A111 1.50m Imperf. at top 2.00 2.00
- *d.* A111 1.50m Imperf. at bottom 2.00 2.00

Nos. 247-248 each were printed in sheets of 8 + label. No. 249 was issued with, but not attached to, a booklet cover.

Easter — A112

2005, Apr. 18 ***Perf. 13¾x13¼***

250 A112 50pf multi .80 .80

Printed in sheets of 8 + label.

Pope John Paul II (1920-2005) A113

Pope John Paul II: 1.50m, Praying. 5m, With arms open.

2005, Apr. 21 **Litho.** ***Perf. 13x13¾***

251 A113 1.50m multi 2.50 2.50

Souvenir Sheet

252 A113 5m multi 7.50 7.50

No. 251 printed in sheets of 8 + label.

Vipers — A114

No. 253: a, Vipera berus berus. b, Vipera ursinii. c, Vipera berus bosniensis. d, Vipera ammodytes.

Perf. 13¼x13¾

2005, June 23 **Litho.**

253 Horiz. strip of 4 + central label 5.00 5.00
- *a.-b.* A114 50pf Either single .75 .75
- *c.-d.* A114 1m Either single 1.50 1.50

Disneyland, 50th Anniv. — A115

Designs: 50pf, Sleeping Beauty Castle. 1m, Buildings.

2005, July 15 ***Perf. 13¾x13¼***

254-255 A115 Set of 2 2.50 2.50

Nos. 254-255 each printed in sheets of 8 + label.

Bulls — A116

2005, Aug. 5 **Litho.** ***Perf. 13¼x13¾***

256 A116 1.50m multi 2.50 2.50

Printed in sheets of 8 + label.

European Philatelic Cooperation, 50th Anniv. (in 2006) — A117

Designs: No. 257, 1.95m, Perucica (stream). No. 258, 1.95m, Rafters. No. 259, 1.95m, Old Bridge, Mostar. No. 260, 1.95m, Drina River multi-arch stone bridge.

2005, Aug. 30 ***Perf. 13¾x13¼***

257-260 A117 Set of 4 12.00 12.00
- *260a* Sheet of 4, #257-260 13.00 13.00

Europa stamps, 50th anniv. (in 2006).

Nos. 257-260 each printed in sheets of 8 + label.

2005 European Basketball Championships — A118

No. 261 — Background colors: a, Green. b, Indigo. c, Blue. d, Red. e, Yellow brown.

Perf. 13¼x13¾

2005, Sept. 16 **Litho.**

261 Strip of 5 4.00 4.00
- *a.-e.* A118 50pf Any single .75 .75

Museum of the Serb Republic, 75th Anniv. — A119

National Theater, 75th Anniv. — A120

2005, Sept. 26 ***Perf. 13¾x13¼***

262 A119 1m multi 1.60 1.60

Perf. 13¼x13¾

263 A120 1m multi 1.60 1.60

Nos. 262-263 each printed in sheets of 8 + label.

Souvenir Sheet

Visegrad-Mokra Gora Railroad — A121

No. 264: a, 50pf, Train and tunnel. b, 1m, Train and station.

2005, Oct. 3 ***Perf. 13¼x13¾***

264 A121 Sheet of 2, #a-b 2.50 2.50

Intl. Aeronautics Federation, Cent. — A122

2005, Oct. 14

265 A122 1.50m multi 2.50 2.50

Printed in sheets of 8 + label.

Dayton Peace Accords, 10th Anniv. — A123

2005, Nov. 21 ***Perf. 13¾x13¼***

266 A123 1.50m multi 2.50 2.50

Printed in sheets of 8 + label.

Banja Guber Resort — A124

2005, Nov. 23 ***Perf. 13¾***

267 A124 50pf multi .80 .80

Nature Protection — A125

Birds: 50pf, Crex crex. 1m, Platalea leucorodia.

2005, Nov. 25 ***Perf. 13¾x13¼***

268-269 A125 Set of 2 2.60 2.60

Nos. 268-269 each printed in sheets of 8 + label.

Liberation of Jasenovac Concentration Camp, 60th Anniv. — A126

2005, Dec. 15 ***Perf. 13¼x13¾***

270 A126 50pf multi .80 .80

Printed in sheets of 8 + label.

Wolfgang Amadeus Mozart (1756-91), Composer — A127

2006, Jan. 27 ***Perf. 13¾x13¼***

271 A127 1.50m multi 2.50 2.50

Printed in sheets of 8 + label.

Branka Sotre (1906-60), Painter — A128

2006, Jan. 31

272 A128 1m multi 1.60 1.60

Printed in sheets of 8 + label.

2006 Winter Olympics, Turin — A129

Designs: 50pf, Biathlon. 1m, Alpine skier.

2006, Feb. 10 ***Perf. 13¼x13¾***

273-274 A129 Set of 2 2.50 2.50

Nos. 273-274 each printed in sheets of 8 + label.

Flowers A130

No. 275: a, Saxifraga prenja. b, Asperula hercegovina. c, Oxytropis prenja. d, Campanula hercegovina.

Perf. 13¼x13¾

2006, Mar. 14 **Litho.**

275 Strip of 4 + central label 4.50 4.50
- *a.-b.* A130 50pf Either single .75 .75
- *c.-d.* A130 1m Either single 1.40 1.40

Printed in sheets of 24 containing six of each stamp + a central label.

Europa A131

Designs: Nos. 276, 278a, 278b, 1m, Person crying. Nos. 277, 2778c, 278d, 1.50m, People holding hands.

2006, Apr. 5 ***Perf. 13¼x13¾***

White Top and Bottom Panel

276-277 A131 Set of 2 4.50 4.50

Yellow Backgrounds

Perf. 13¼x13¾ on 3 Sides

278 Sheet of 6, #278a, 278d, 2 each #278b, 278c 14.00 14.00
- *a.* A131 1m Imperf. at top 1.60 1.60
- *b.* A131 1m Imperf. at bottom 1.60 1.60
- *c.* A131 1.50m Imperf. at top 2.75 2.75
- *d.* A131 1.50m Imperf. at bottom 2.75 2.75

Nos. 276-277 each printed in sheets of 8 + label. No. 278 was issued with, but not attached to, a booklet cover.

Easter — A132

2006, Apr. 14 *Perf. 13¼x13¾*
279 A132 70pf multi 1.25 1.25

Printed in sheets of 8 + label.

2006 World Cup Soccer Championships, Germany — A133

No. 280: a, 50pf, Players and soccer ball. b, 1m, Soccer ball, German flag, stadium.
3m, Player and soccer ball.

2006, June 9
280 A133 Pair, #a-b 2.50 2.50

Souvenir Sheet

281 A133 3m multi 4.50 4.50

No. 280 printed in sheets containing 4 of each stamp + label. No. 281 contains one 35x27mm stamp.

Vidovdan Race, Brcko — A134

2006, June 28
282 A134 1m multi 1.60 1.60

Printed in sheets of 8 + label.

Souvenir Sheet

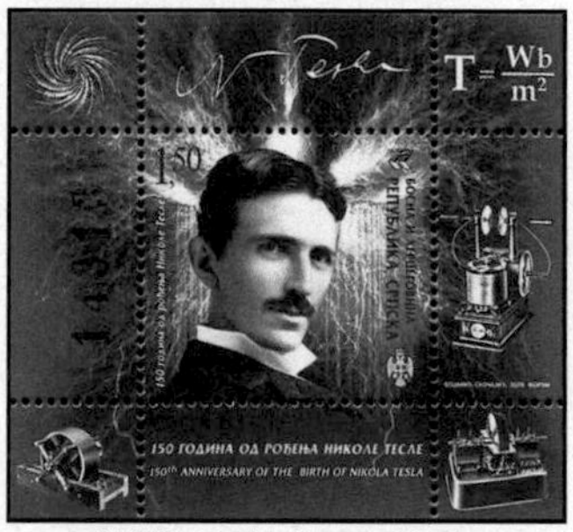

Nikola Tesla (1856-1943), Inventor — A135

2006, July 10
283 A135 1.50m multi 2.50 2.50

See No. 288A.

Nature Protection A136

Designs: 50pf, Tetrao urogallus. 1m, Rupicapra rupicapra.

2006, Sept. 19
284-285 A136 Set of 2 2.60 2.60

Children's Theater, 50th Anniv. — A137

2006, Oct. 14 Litho. *Perf. 13¼x13¾*
286 A137 1m multi 1.60 1.60

Printed in sheets of 8 + label.

A138

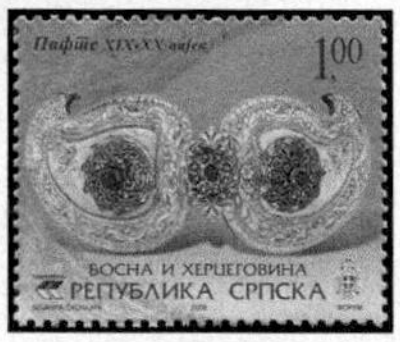

Jewelry A139

2006, Nov. 28
287 A138 1m multi 1.60 1.60
288 A139 1m multi 1.60 1.60

Each stamp printed in sheets of 8 + label.

Tesla Type of 2006

2006, Dec. 29 Litho. *Perf. 13¾*

Size: 25x23mm

288A A135 70pf multi 1.20 1.20

Johann Wolfgang von Goethe (1749-1832), Poet — A140

Perf. 13¼x13¾

2007, Mar. 22 **Litho.**
289 A140 1.50m multi 2.50 2.50

Printed in sheets of 8 + label.

Easter — A141

2007, Apr. 10 *Perf. 13¾x13¼*
290 A141 70pf multi 1.20 1.20

Printed in sheets of 8 + label.

Leonardo da Vinci (1452-1519), Painter — A142

No. 291, 70pf — Head of Isabella d'Este with text in: a, Cyrillic letters. b, Latin letters.
No. 292, 1m — Sketch of St. Peter with text in: a, Cyrillic letters. b, Latin letters.

2007, Apr. 16 *Perf. 13¾x13¼*

Pairs, #a-b

291-292 A142 Set of 2 5.50 5.50

Nos. 291-292 each printed in sheets of 4 pairs + label.

Europa A143

Designs: Nos. 293, 295a, 295b, 1m, Scouts and tents. Nos. 294, 295c, 295d, 1.50m, Scouts on expedition.

2007, May 3 *Perf. 13¼x13¾*

Green Background

293-294 A143 Set of 2 4.50 4.50

Rose Violet Background

Perf. 13¼x13¾ on 3 Sides

295	Sheet of 6, #295a, 295d, 2 each #295b, 295c	15.00	15.00
a.	A143 1m Imperf. at top	2.00	2.00
b.	A143 1m Imperf. at bottom	2.00	2.00
c.	A143 1.50m Imperf. at top	3.00	3.00
d.	A143 1.50m Imperf. at bottom	3.00	3.00

Scouting, cent. Nos. 293-294 were each printed in sheets of 8 + label. No. 295 was issued with, but not attached to, a booklet cover.

Monasteries A144

Designs: 70pf, Liplje Monastery. 1m, Dobricevo Monastery.

2007, June 5 *Perf. 13¼x13¾*
296-297 A144 Set of 2 2.75 2.75

Nos. 296-297 were each printed in sheets of 8 + label.

Post Office and Church, Obudovac A145

Municipal Building, Prijedor A146

Fire House, Kozarac A147

Town Square, Bijeljina A148

Deventa A149

Foca A150

Cultural Club, Laktasi A151

Building, Srebrenica A152

Cultural Club, Sipovo — A153

Municipal Building, Mrkonjic Grad — A154

Old City, Trebinje A155

Zvornik A156

2007		**Litho.**		*Perf. 13¾*	
298	A145	10pf	multi	.50	.50
299	A146	20pf	multi	.50	.50
300	A147	20pf	multi	.50	.50
301	A148	20pf	multi	.50	.50
302	A149	20pf	multi	.50	.50
303	A150	20pf	multi	.50	.50
304	A151	20pf	multi	.50	.50
305	A152	70pf	multi	1.20	1.20
306	A153	1.50m	multi	2.00	2.00
307	A154	1.50m	multi	2.00	2.00
308	A155	2m	multi	3.00	3.00
309	A156	5m	multi	8.50	8.50
	Nos. 298-309 (12)			20.20	20.20

Issued: 10pf, 7/7; 70pf, 6/20; others, 6/9.

A157

A158

A159

Dogs — A160

2007, July 5 *Perf. 13¼x13¾*

310 Horiz. strip of 4 + central label 4.50 4.50
a. A157 70pf multi 1.00 1.00
b. A158 70pf multi 1.00 1.00
c. A159 70pf multi 1.00 1.00
d. A160 70pf multi 1.00 1.00

Ban Svetislav Milosavljevic (1882-1960) A161

2007, Sept. 7 *Perf. 13¾x13¼*

311 A161 1.50m multi 2.50 2.50

Souvenir Sheet

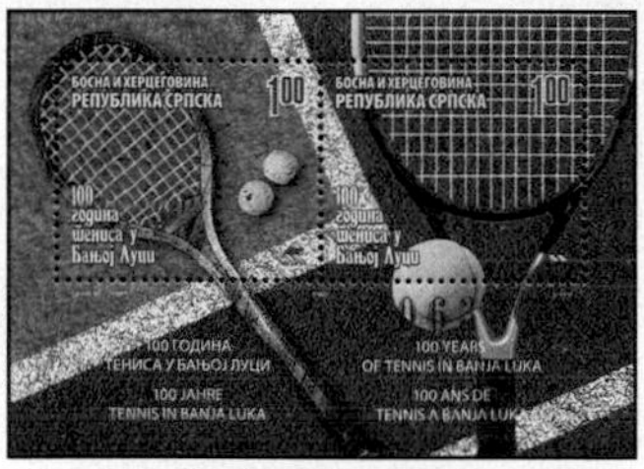

Tennis in Banja Luka, Cent. — A162

No. 312: a, Wooden racquet, old balls. b, Modern racquet and ball.

2007, Sept. 14 *Perf. 13¾*

312 A162 1m Sheet of 2, #a-b 3.00 3.00

Launch of Sputnik 1, 50th Anniv. — A163

2007, Oct. 4 **Litho.** *Perf. 13¾x13¼*

313 A163 1.50m multi 2.50 2.50

Printed in sheets of 8 + label.

Pine Cones — A164

Designs: 70pf, Picea abies. 1m, Picea omorica.

2007, Nov. 9

314-315 A164 Set of 2 2.75 2.75

Nos. 314-315 each printed in sheets of 8 + label.

Filip Visnjic Library, 75th Anniv. — A165

2007, Nov. 26 *Perf. 13¼x13¾*

316 A165 70pf multi 1.20 1.20

Printed in sheets of 8 + label.

New Year 2008 — A166

Designs: No. 317, 70pf, Snowman. No. 318, 70pf, Christmas tree.

Perf. 13¾x13¼

2007, Dec. 10 **Litho.**

317-318 A166 Set of 2 2.25 2.25

Nos. 317-318 were each printed in sheets of 8 + label.

Serb Republic Adminstrative Center — A167

2007, Dec. 20

319 A167 70pf multi 1.20 1.20

Samac Post Office, 125th Anniv. — A168

2008, Feb. 28 **Litho.** *Perf. 14*

320 A168 1.40m multi 2.25 2.25

Printed in sheets of 8 + label.

Self-Portrait of Vincent Van Gogh (1853-90), Painter — A169

2008, Mar. 28 **Litho.** *Perf. 14x14¼*

321 A169 1.50m multi 2.50 2.50

Printed in sheets of 8 + label.

Souvenir Sheet

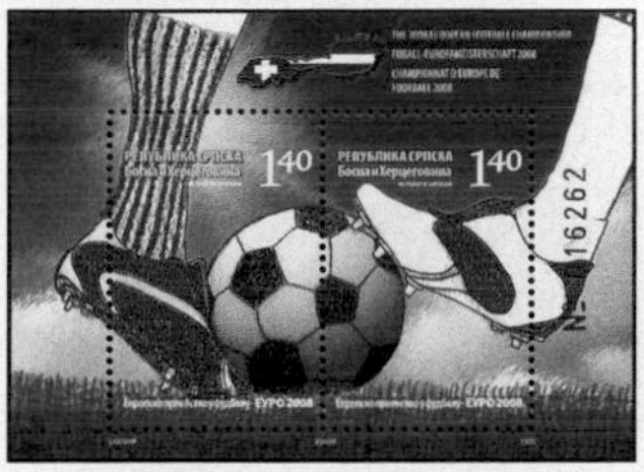

UEFA Euro 2008 Soccer Championships, Austria and Switzerland — A170

No. 322: a, Foot to left of soccer ball. b, Foot to right of soccer ball.

2008, Apr. 18 *Perf. 13x13½*

322 A170 1.40m Sheet of 2, #a-b 4.50 4.50

Europa — A171

Letter and: Nos. 323, 325a, 325b, 1m, Quill pen and inkwell. Nos. 324, 325c, 325d, 2m, Hand with pencil.

2008, Apr. 24 *Perf. 14*

Stamps With White Frames

323-324 A171 Set of 2 5.00 5.00

Stamps With Tan Frames

Perf. 13x13½ on 3 Sides

325 Sheet, #325a, 325d, 2 each #325b-325c 15.00 15.00
a. A171 1m Imperf. at top 1.50 1.50
b. A171 1m Imperf. at bottom 1.50 1.50
c. A171 2m Imperf. at top 3.00 3.00
d. A171 2m Imperf. at bottom 3.00 3.00

Nos. 323-324 each were printed in sheets of 8 + label.

Djurdjevdan Festival A172

2008, May 8 **Litho.** *Perf. 13*

326 A172 1.50m multi 2.50 2.50

Printed in sheets of 8 + label.

A173

A174

A175

Personalized Stamps A176

2008, May 13 *Serpentine Die Cut 10*

Self-Adhesive

327 A173 70pf multi 1.10 1.10
328 A174 70pf multi 1.10 1.10
329 A175 70pf multi 1.10 1.10
330 A176 70pf multi 1.10 1.10
Nos. 327-330 (4) 4.40 4.40

Images shown in frames of Nos. 327-330 are generic and could be personalized.

Banja Luka Carnival — A177

2008, May 15 *Perf. 13*

331 A177 1.50m multi 2.50 2.50

Mushrooms A178

No. 332: a, Gyromitra esculenta. b, Amanita muscaria. c, Amanita pantherina. d, Amanita phalloides.

2008, May 26 *Perf. 13x13¼*

332 Horiz. strip of 4 + central label 4.50 4.50
a.-d. A178 70pf Any single 1.10 1.10

Charles Darwin (1809-82), Naturalist, and Birds — A179

2008, July 1 *Perf. 13*

333 A179 1.50m multi 2.50 2.50

Development by Darwin of theory of evolution, 150th anniv.

Flowers

A180 A181

Designs: 50pf, Gentiana verna. 1.50m, Galanthus nivalis. 2m, Viola odorata. 5m, Centaurea cyanus.

2008, July 7 **Litho.** *Perf. 13*

334 A180 50pf multi .80 .80
335 A181 1.50m multi 2.25 2.25
336 A180 2m multi 3.25 3.25
337 A180 5m multi 8.00 8.00
Nos. 334-337 (4) 14.30 14.30

2008 Summer Olympics, Beijing A182

Map of China and: 70pf, High jump, National Stadium. 2.10m, Swimmer on starting platform, Aquatics Center.
3.10m, Gymnast.

2008, July 16

338-339 A182 Set of 2 4.50 4.50

Souvenir Sheet

340 A182 3.10m multi 4.50 4.50

Nos. 338 and 339 each were printed in sheets of 8 + label.

Birds — A183

Designs: No. 341, 1m, Strix aluco. No. 342, 1m, Ciconia ciconia.

2008, Aug. 12
341-342 A183 Set of 2 3.00 3.00

Nos. 341 and 342 each were printed in sheets of 8 + label.

Monasteries A184

Monastery at: No. 343, 1m, Gracanica (shown). No. 344, 1m, Tvrdos.

2008, Sept. 10
343-344 A184 Set of 2 3.00 3.00

Nos. 343 and 344 each were printed in sheets of 8 + label.

Souvenir Sheet

Bosnian Serb Pres. Milan Jelic (1956-2007) — A185

2008, Sept. 20
345 A185 2.10m multi 3.25 3.25

Orient Express, 125th Anniv. — A186

2008, Oct. 3 Litho. *Perf. 13*
346 A186 1.40m multi 2.25 2.25

Printed in sheets of 8 + label.

Alfred Nobel (1833-96), Inventor and Philanthropist A187

2008, Oct. 21
347 A187 1.50m multi 2.50 2.50

Printed in sheets of 8 + label.

Jovan Jovanovich Zmaj (1833-1904), Poet — A188

2008, Nov. 24
348 A188 1.50m multi 2.50 2.50

Printed in sheets of 8 + label.

Christmas A189

2008, Dec. 26
349 A189 1m multi 1.60 1.60

Printed in sheets of 8 + label.

1984 Sarajevo Winter Olympics, 25th Anniv. — A190

2009, Feb. 13
350 A190 1.50m multi 2.50 2.50

Printed in sheets of 8 + label.

Explorers and Ships — A191

Designs: 70pf, Amerigo Vespucci (1454-1512). 1.50m, Marco Polo (1254-1324).

2009, Mar. 7
351-352 A191 Set of 2 3.50 3.50

Nos. 351-352 each were printed in sheets of 8 + label.

Buildings A192

Designs; 1m, European Court of Human Rights. 1.50m, Council of Europe Building.

2009, Mar. 25
353-354 A192 Set of 2 4.00 4.00

European Court of Human Rights, 50th anniv., Council of Europe, 60th anniv. Nos. 353-354 each were printed in sheets of 8 + label.

Animals — A193

Designs: 20pf, Meles meles. 70pf, Sciurus vulgaris. 1m, Vulpes vulpes.

2009, Apr. 15
355 A193 20pf multi .40 .40
a. Perf. 13¾ .40 .40
356 A193 70pf multi 1.75 1.75
357 A193 1m multi 1.10 1.10
Nos. 355-357 (3) 3.25 3.25

Issued: No. 355a, 12/10.

Dinosaurs A194

Designs: 70pf, Triceratops. 1.50m, Diplodocus.

2009, Mar. 13 Litho. *Perf. 13*
358-359 A194 Set of 2 3.50 3.50

Nos. 358-359 each were printed in sheets of 8 + label.

Europa A195

Designs: Nos. 360, 362a, 362b, 362c, 1m, Observatory. Nos. 361, 362d, 362e, 362f, 2m, Telescope and star chart.

2009, Apr. 23 *Perf. 13*
Stamp Size: 35x26mm
360-361 A195 Set of 2 5.00 5.00

Souvenir Sheet
Stamp Size: 38x27mm
Perf. 13¼x13 on 2 or 3 Sides

362 Sheet of 6 16.00 16.00
a. A195 1m Imperf. at right 1.75 1.75
b A195 1m Imperf. at left 1.75 1.75
c. A195 1m Imperf. at right and bottom 1.75 1.75
d. A195 2m Imperf. at left 3.50 3.50
e. A195 2m Imperf. at right 3.50 3.50
f. A195 2m Imperf. at left and bottom 3.50 3.50

Intl. Year of Astronomy. Nos. 360-361 each were printed in sheets of 8 + label.

Souvenir Sheet

World Rafting Championships, Banja Luka — A196

No. 363 — Rafters with: a, All paddles in water. b, Two paddles out of water.

2009, May 15 *Perf. 13¾*
363 A196 1.50m Sheet of 2, #a-b 5.00 5.00

Paja Jovanovic (1859-1957), Painter — A197

2009, June 16 *Perf. 13¾x13¼*
364 A197 1.40m multi 2.25 2.25

Printed in sheets of 8 + label.

Portraits of Amedeo Modigliani (1884-1920) A198

2009, July 11 *Perf. 13¼x13¾*
365 A198 1.50m multi 2.25 2.25

Printed in sheets of 8 + label.

Cats — A199

No. 366: a, Siamese (shown). b, Tabby (broom in background). c, Russian blue (flower pot with flowers in background). d, Persian (large pot in background).

2009, Aug. 19
366 Horiz. strip of 4 + central label 4.50 4.50
a.-d. A199 70pf Any single 1.00 1.00

Forts — A200

Fort at: 20pf, Doboj. 70pf, Zvornik. 1m, Kastel.

2009 Litho. *Perf. 13¾*
367 A200 20pf multi .30 .30
368 A200 70pf multi 1.10 1.10
369 A200 1m multi 1.60 1.60
Nos. 367-369 (3) 3.00 3.00

Issued: 20pf, 7/23; 70pf, 1m, 9/25.

Insects A201

Designs: No. 370, 1m, Coccinellidae. No. 371, 1m, Odonata. No. 372, 1m, Lucanus cervus.

2009, Sept. 9 Litho. *Perf. 13¼x13¾*
370-372 A201 Set of 3 4.50 4.50

Nos. 370-372 each were printed in sheets of 8 + label.

Skoda 1937 Locomotive A202

Rama Locomotive A203

UNRRA 22 Locomotive A204

JZ 83-056 Locomotive A205

2009, Nov. 10
373 A202 70pf multi 1.10 1.10
374 A203 70pf multi 1.10 1.10
375 A204 80pf multi 1.20 1.20
376 A205 80pf multi 1.20 1.20
Nos. 373-376 (4) 4.60 4.60

Nos. 373-376 each were printed in sheets of 8 + label.

Automobiles A206

Designs: No. 377, 70pf, Red Citroen 2CV. No. 378, 70pf, Yellow Fiat 500. 80pf, Volkswagen Beetle.

2009, Nov. 17

377-379 A206 Set of 3 3.50 3.50

Nos. 377-379 each were printed in sheets of 8 + label.

Christmas and New Year's Day — A207

Designs: No. 380, 60pf, Santa Claus. No. 381, 60pf, Snowman.

2009, Dec. 4 ***Perf. 13¾x13¼***

380-381 A207 Set of 2 2.00 2.00

Nos. 380-381 each were printed in sheets of 8 + label.

Zvornik, 600th Anniv. — A208

2010, Jan. 26 ***Perf. 13¼x13¾***

382 A208 70pf multi 1.10 1.10

Printed in sheets of 8 + label.

2010 Winter Olympics, Vancouver A209

Designs: 70pf, Luge. 1.50m, Figure skating.

2010, Feb. 5

383-384 A209 Set of 2 3.50 3.50

Nos. 383-384 each were printed in sheets of 8 + label.

Frédéric Chopin (1810-49), Composer — A210

2010, Mar. 1 ***Perf. 13¾x13¼***

385 A210 1.50m multi 2.50 2.50

Printed in sheets of 8 + label.

Mesa Selimovic (1910-82), Writer — A211

2010, Apr. 20

386 A211 1m multi 1.50 1.50

Printed in sheets of 8 + label.

Europa A212

Children's books: Nos. 387, 389a, 389b, 389c, 1m, Flying. Nos. 388, 389d, 389e, 389f, 2m, On tree.

2010, May 7 **Litho.** ***Perf. 13x13¾***

387-388 A212 Set of 2 4.00 4.00

Perf. 13x13¾ on 2 or 3 Sides

389	Sheet of 6	12.00	12.00
a.	A212 1m Imperf. at top	1.40	1.40
b.	A212 1m Imperf. at bottom	1.40	1.40
c.	A212 1m Imperf. at bottom and right	1.40	1.40
d.	A212 2m Imperf. at top	2.60	2.60
e.	A212 2m Imperf. at top and right	2.60	2.60
f.	A212 2m Imperf. at bottom	2.60	2.60

Nos. 387-388 each were printed in sheets of 8 + label. No. 389 was sold with, but unattached to, a booklet cover.

2010 World Cup Soccer Championships, South Africa — A213

Designs: No. 390, 1.50m, Player with arms raised. No. 391, 1.50m, Player dribbling ball.

2010, May 25 ***Perf. 13x13¾***

390-391 A213 Set of 2 4.50 4.50

Nos. 390-391 each were printed in sheets of 8 + label.

Animals — A214

2010, May 28 ***Perf. 13¾***

392	A214	10pf Hedgehog	.35	.35
393	A214	50pf Boar	.80	.80
394	A214	90pf Wolf	1.40	1.40
395	A214	1m Bear	1.60	1.60
		Nos. 392-395 (4)	4.15	4.15

Old Weapons — A215

2010, June 15

396	A215	1.80m Knives	2.75	2.75
397	A215	2m Guns	3.00	3.00
398	A215	5m Iron mace	7.25	7.25
		Nos. 396-398 (3)	13.00	13.00

Nos. 396-398 each were printed in sheets of 8 + label.

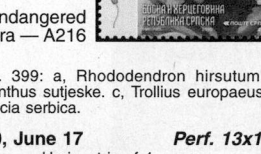

Endangered Flora — A216

No. 399: a, Rhododendron hirsutum. b, Edrainthus sutjeske. c, Trollius europaeus. d, Pancicia serbica.

2010, June 17 ***Perf. 13x13¾***

399	Horiz. strip of 4 + central label	4.50	4.50
a.-d.	A216 70pf Any single	1.00	1.00

Fragments of Roman Monuments A217

Monument fragment showing: 70pf, People. 1.50m, Text.

2010, June 30

400-401 A217 Set of 2 3.50 3.50

Nos. 400-401 each were printed in sheets of 8 + label.

50th Trumpet Festival, Guca, Serbia — A218

2010, Aug. 13 **Litho.** ***Perf. 13x13¾***

402 A218 1.50m multi 2.25 2.25

Printed in sheets of 8 + label. See Serbia No. 516.

Day of Fallen and Missing Persons — A219

2010, Sept. 15 ***Perf. 13¾x13***

403 A219 90pf multi 1.50 1.50

Printed in sheets of 8 + label.

A220

Fish — A221

2010, Sept. 23 ***Perf. 13¼x13¾***

404	A220	1m multi	1.50	1.50
405	A221	1m multi	1.50	1.50

Nos. 404-405 each were printed in sheets of 8 + label.

Serb Republic Museum, Banja Luka, 80th Anniv. — A222

2010, Sept. 24 ***Perf. 13¾x13***

406 A222 90pf multi 1.40 1.40

Printed in sheets of 8 + label.

Banja Luka Gymnasium, 115th Anniv. — A223

2010, Oct. 4 ***Perf. 13x13¾***

407 A223 90pf multi 1.40 1.40

Printed in sheets of 8 + label.

Souvenir Sheet

World Post Day — A224

No. 408: a, 70pf, Detail from Bosnia & Herzegovina #41. b, 1.40m, Marija Zvijezda Trappist Monastery, Banja Luka, detail from Bosnia & Herzegovina #41.

2010, Oct. 9 **Litho.**

408 A224 Sheet of 2, #a-b 3.50 3.50

St. Nicholas and Christmas Stocking A225

2010, Nov. 24

409 A225 1m multi 1.50 1.50

Printed in sheets of 8 + label.

Souvenir Sheet

St. Basil of Ostrog (1610-71) — A226

No. 410: a, 70pf, Ostrog Monastery. b, 1.40m, St. Basil of Ostrog.

2010, Dec. 28 ***Perf. 13¾***

410 A226 Sheet of 2, #a-b 3.25 3.25

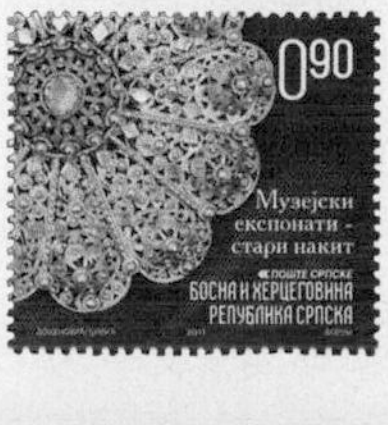

Women's Beaded Headdresses A227

Various headdresses with denomination at: No. 411, 90pf, UR. No. 412, 90pf, UL.

2011, Jan. 24 ***Perf. 13x13¾***
411-412 A227 Set of 2 2.75 2.75

Nos. 411-412 each were printed in sheets of 8 + label.

Milan Budimir (1891-1975), Philosopher A228

2011, Feb. 11 ***Perf. 13¾x13***
413 A228 90pf multi 1.50 1.50

Printed in sheets of 8 + label.

Awarding of Nobel Prize in Chemistry to Marie Curie, Cent. — A229

2011, Mar. 8 Litho. ***Perf. 13¾x13¼***
414 A229 1.50m multi 2.25 2.25

Printed in sheets of 8 + central label.

Europa A230

Forest scene with: Nos. 415, 417a, 417b, 417c, 1m, Deer and rabbit. Nos. 416, 417d, 417e, 417f, 2m, Fox and bear.

2011, Apr. 6 ***Perf. 13x13¾***
415-416 A230 Set of 2 4.50 4.50

Perf. 13x13¾ on 2 or 3 Sides

417	Sheet of 6	18.00	18.00
a.	A230 1m Imperf. at top	2.00	2.00
b.	A230 1m Imperf. at bottom	2.00	2.00
c.	A230 1m Imperf. at bottom and right	2.00	2.00
d.	A230 2m Imperf. at top	4.00	4.00
e.	A230 2m Imperf. at top and right	4.00	4.00
f.	A230 2m Imperf. at bottom	4.00	4.00

Intl. Year of Forests. Nos. 415-416 each were printed in sheets of 8 + label. No. 417 was sold with, but unattached to, a booklet cover.

Animals — A231

2011, Apr. 20 Litho. ***Perf. 13¾***

418	A231 10pf Rabbit	.25	.25
419	A231 20pf Weasel	.35	.35
420	A231 50pf Otter	.80	.80
421	A231 90pf Lynx	1.60	1.60
	Nos. 418-421 (4)	3.00	3.00

Birds — A232

No. 422: a, Aythya ferina. b, Alcedo atthis. c, Cygnus olor. d, Podiceps nigricollis

2011, May 10 ***Perf. 13¼x13¾***
422 Horiz. strip of 4 + central label 5.50 5.50
a.-d. A232 90pf Any single 1.25 1.25

National and University Library, 75th Anniv. — A233

2011, May 17 ***Perf. 13¾x13¼***
423 A233 90pf multi 1.40 1.40

Printed in sheets of 8 + label.

Souvenir Sheet

European Kayak and Canoe Championships, Banja Luka. — A234

No. 424: a, 1.50m, Canoeist. b, 2.30m, Kayaker.

2011, June 7 ***Perf. 13¾***
424 A234 Sheet of 2, #a-b 5.50 5.50

Book Illuminations A235

Various book illuminations.

2011, June 15 ***Perf. 13¾***

Denomination Color

425	A235 1.50m brown	2.25	2.25
426	A235 2.30m blue green	3.50	3.50
427	A235 5m buff	7.25	7.25
a.	Dated "2013"	5.50	5.50
	Nos. 425-427 (3)	13.00	13.00

Issued: No. 427a, 12/5/13.

Intl. Youth Year — A236

2011, June 30 ***Perf. 13¾x13¼***
428 A236 90pf multi 1.40 1.40

Printed in sheets of 8 + label.

Locomotives A237

Designs: No. 429, 90pf, DMV 801. No. 430, 90pf, DMV 802. No. 431, 90pf, DHL 720-001. No. 432, 90pf, DHL 740-108.
3m, DHL L458-096.

2011, July 1 ***Perf. 13¼x13¾***
429-432 A237 Set of 4 5.25 5.25

Souvenir Sheet

Perf. 13¾

433 A237 3m multi 4.50 4.50

Nos. 429-432 each were printed in sheets of 8 + label. No. 433 contains one 35x29mm stamp.

Birds — A238

Designs: 90pf, Buteo buteo. 1.50m, Accipiter gentilis.

2011, Sept. 15 ***Perf. 13¼x13¾***
434-435 A238 Set of 2 3.50 3.50

Fridtjof Nansen (1861-1930), Polar Explorer and Diplomat — A239

2011, Oct. 10 ***Perf. 13¾x13¼***
436 A239 1.50m multi 2.25 2.25

No. 436 was printed in sheets of 8 + central label.

Franz Liszt (1811-86), Composer A240

2011, Oct. 22
437 A240 1.50m multi 2.25 2.25

No. 437 was printed in sheets of 8 + central label.

Novak Djokovic, Tennis Player, and Wimbledon Singles Trophy — A241

2011, Nov. 30
438 A241 90pf multi 3.50 3.50

No. 438 was printed in sheets of 8 + central label.

Ivo Andric (1892-1975), 1961 Nobel Literature Laureate A242

2011, Dec. 10 ***Perf. 13¼x13¾***
439 A242 90pf multi 1.40 1.40

No. 439 was printed in sheets of 8 + central label.

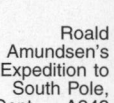

Roald Amundsen's Expedition to South Pole, Cent. — A243

Amundsen and: 1.50m, Expedition member Helmer Hanssen near Norwegian flag at South Pole. 2m, Dog sled, Norwegian flag and map of expedition's route.

2011, Dec. 14 ***Perf. 13¼x13¾***
440 A243 1.50m multi 2.25 2.25

Souvenir Sheet

Perf. 13¾

441 A243 2m multi 3.00 3.00

No. 440 was printed in sheets of 8 + central label. No. 441 contains one 35x29mm stamp.

New Year 2012 (Year of the Dragon) A244

2012, Feb. 14 ***Perf. 13¼x13¾***
442 A244 90pf multi 2.50 2.50

No. 442 was printed in sheets of 8 + central label.

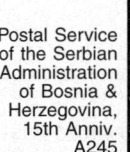

Postal Service of the Serbian Administration of Bosnia & Herzegovina, 15th Anniv. A245

2012, Feb. 23
443 A245 90pf multi 1.40 1.40

No. 443 was printed in sheets of 8 + central label.

A246

A247

A248

Architecture A249

2012, Mar. 9 ***Perf. 13x13¼***

444	Horiz. strip of 4 + central label	5.50	5.50
a.	A246 90pf multi	1.25	1.25
b.	A247 90pf multi	1.25	1.25
c.	A248 90pf multi	1.25	1.25
d.	A249 90pf multi	1.25	1.25

Transportation Disasters A250

Designs: No. 445, 1.50m, Titanic. No. 446, 1.50m, Hindenburg.

2012, Apr. 23 ***Perf. 13¼x13¾***

445-446	A250 Set of 2	4.50	4.50

Sinking of the Titanic, cent.; Burning of the Hindenburg, 75th anniv. Nos. 445-446 each were printed in sheets of 8 + central label.

Europa A251

Forest scene with: Nos. 447, 449a, 449b, 449c, 1m, River rafters. Nos. 448, 449d, 449e, 449f, 2m, Hikers.

2012, Apr. 26 ***Perf. 13x13¾***

447-448	A251 Set of 2	4.00	4.00

Perf. 13x13¾ on 2 or 3 Sides

449	Sheet of 6	12.00	12.00
a.	A251 1m Imperf. at top	1.40	1.40
b.	A251 1m Imperf. at bottom	1.40	1.40
c.	A251 1m Imperf. at top and right	1.40	1.40
d.	A251 2m Imperf. at top	2.60	2.60
e.	A251 2m Imperf. at bottom	2.60	2.60
f.	A251 2m Imperf. at bottom and right	2.60	2.60

Nos. 447-448 each were printed in sheets of 8 + label. No. 449 was sold with, but unattached to, a booklet cover.

Musical Instruments — A252

2012, May 17 ***Perf. 13¾***

450	A252 10pf Dvojnice	.35	.35
451	A252 20pf Rognjaca	.35	.35
452	A252 35pf Gusle	.45	.45
	Nos. 450-452 (3)	1.15	1.15

European Nature Protection A253

No. 453: a, 90pf, Stone pinnacles. b, 1.50m, Janja River waterfalls.

2012, May 29 ***Perf. 13x13¾***

453	A253 Vert. pair, #a-b	4.00	4.00

Printed in sheets containing 4 pairs + 2 labels

Animals — A254

2012, June 12 ***Perf. 13¾***

454	A254 50pf Otter	.75	.75
455	A254 90pf Lynx	1.50	1.50

Trees — A255

No. 456: a, Quercus (oak). b, Fraxinus (ash). c, Tilia (linden). d, Betula (birch).

2012, June 13 ***Perf. 13x13¼***

456	Horiz. strip of 4 + flanking label	5.50	5.50
a.-d.	A255 90pf Any single	1.25	1.25

Slavija Boxing Club, 50th Anniv. — A256

2012, Sept. 15 **Litho.**

457	A256 90pf multi	1.40	1.40

Printed in sheets of 8 + central label.

Airplanes A257

Designs: 90pf, Fizir FN biplane. 1.50m, Ikarus IK 2.

2012, Sept. 19 ***Perf. 13x13¾***

458-459	A257 Set of 2	3.50	3.50

Nos. 458-459 each were printed in sheets of 8 + central label.

Souvenir Sheet

Amateur Film Making in Banja Luka, 75th Anniv. — A258

2012, Oct. 26 ***Perf. 13¾***

460	A258 2.30m multi	3.50	3.50

Vuk Karadzic (1787-1864), Linguist A259

2012, Nov. 7 ***Perf. 13x13¼***

461	A259 1.50m multi	2.25	2.25

Printed in sheets of 8 + central label.

Sub-machine Guns — A260

Designs: 10pf, MP 40. 20pf, PPSh-41. 35pf, Sten Mk II.

2013, Jan. 10 ***Perf. 13¾***

462	A260 10pf multi	.25	.25
463	A260 20pf multi	.30	.30
464	A260 35pf multi	.50	.50
	Nos. 462-464 (3)	1.05	1.05

Chess Pieces — A261

Designs: 50pf, Black rook, White bishop. 90pf, Black knight, White pawn. 2.30m, Black queen, White king.

2013, Jan. 10

465	A261 50pf multi	.60	.60
466	A261 90pf multi	1.10	1.10
467	A261 2.30m multi	2.75	2.75
	Nos. 465-467 (3)	4.45	4.45

JZ 73 Steam Locomotive A262

JZ 85 Steam Locomotive A263

JZ 92 Steam Locomotive A264

Kloze Steam Locomotive A265

2013, Feb. 7 ***Perf. 13¼x13¾***

468	A262 90pf multi	1.25	1.25
469	A263 90pf multi	1.25	1.25
470	A264 90pf multi	1.25	1.25
471	A265 90pf multi	1.25	1.25
	Nos. 468-471 (4)	5.00	5.00

Nos. 468-471 each were printed in sheets of 8 + central label.

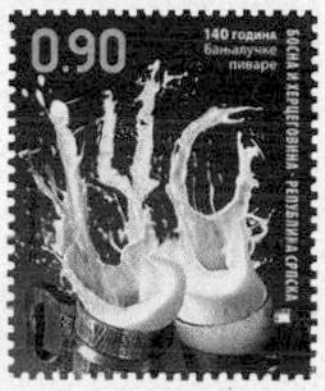

Banja Luka Brewery, 140th Anniv. — A266

2013, Mar. 6 ***Perf. 13¾x13¼***

472	A266 90pf multi	1.40	1.40

No. 472 was printed in sheets of 8 + central label.

Europa A267

Old postal truck: Nos. 473, 475a, 475b, 475c, 1m, Facing right. Nos. 474, 475d, 475e, 475f, 2m, Facing left.

2013, July 12 ***Perf. 13x13¾***

473-474	A267 Set of 2	4.50	4.50

Perf. 13x13¾ on 2 or 3 Sides

475	Sheet of 6	13.00	13.00
a.	A267 1m Imperf. at top	1.50	1.50
b.	A267 1m Imperf. at bottom	1.50	1.50
c.	A267 1m Imperf. at top and right	1.50	1.50
d.	A267 2m Imperf. at top	2.75	2.75
e.	A267 2m Imperf. at bottom	2.75	2.75
f.	A267 2m Imperf. at bottom and right	2.75	2.75

Nos. 473-474 each were printed in sheets of 8 + central label.

Giuseppe Verdi (1813-1901), Composer A268

Richard Wagner (1813-83), Composer A269

2013, July 17 ***Perf. 13x13¾***

476	A268 1.50m multi	2.10	2.10
477	A269 1.50m multi	2.10	2.10

Nos. 476-477 each were printed in sheets of 8 + central label.

Souvenir Sheet

Edict of Milan, 1700th Anniv. — A270

No. 478: a, Bust of Emperor Constantine. b, Chrismon and wreath.

2013, July 19 ***Perf. 13¾***

478	A270 1.50m Sheet of 2, #a-b	4.25	4.25

Glas Newspaper, 70th Anniv. — A271

2013, July 30 ***Perf. 13¾x13***

479	A271 90pf multi	1.40	1.40

No. 479 was printed in sheets of 8 + central label.

Souvenir Sheet

Nevesinje Olympics — A272

No. 480: a, Horse racing. b, Shot put.

2013, Aug. 29 Litho. *Perf. 13¾*

480 A272 1.50m Sheet of 2, #a-b 4.25 4.25

Amphibians A273

Designs: 90pf, Salamandra salamandra. 1.50m, Rana dalmatina.

Perf. 13¼x13¾

2013, Sept. 12 Litho.

481-482 A273 Set of 2 3.50 3.50

482a Vert. pair, #481-482 3.50 3.50

Nos. 481-482 were printed in sheets of 8 (4 of each stamp) + 2 labels

Bats — A274

No. 483: a, Rhinolophus ferrumequinum. b, Myotis myotis. c, Rhinolophus euryale. d, Miniopterus schreibersii.

Perf. 13¼x13¾

2013, Sept. 20 Litho.

483 Horiz. strip of 4 + flanking label 5.25 5.25

a.-d. A274 90pf Any single 1.25 1.25

Traditional Handicrafts A275

No. 484: a, Lid with handle. b, Saddle. c, Harness. d, Knife.

2013, Oct. 18 Litho. *Perf. 13x13¾*

484 A275 Vert. strip of 4 + flanking label 5.25 5.25

a.-d. 90pf Any single 1.25 1.25

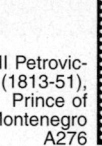

Petar II Petrovic-Njegos (1813-51), Prince of Montenegro A276

Perf. 13¾x13¼

2013, Nov. 13 Litho.

485 A276 1.50m multi 2.10 2.10

No. 485 was printed in sheets of 8 + central label.

Patenting of Turbine Invented by Nikola Tesla, Cent. — A277

Perf. 13¼x13¾

2013, Nov. 29 Litho.

486 A277 90pf multi 1.40 1.40

No. 486 was printed in sheets of 8 + central label.

William Shakespeare (1564-1616), Writer — A278

Galileo Galilei (1564-1642), Astronomer A279

2014, Feb. 5 Litho. *Perf. 13¼x13¾*

487 A278 1.70m multi 2.50 2.50

488 A279 1.70m multi 2.50 2.50

Nos. 487-488 each were printed in sheets of 8 + central label.

Butterflies — A280

Designs: 1.10m, Erebia medusa. 1.70m, Aglais urticae. 2.70m, Melanargia galathea. 4m, Nymphalis antiopa. 5.10m, Iphiclides podalirius.

2014, Feb. 25 Litho. *Perf. 13¾*

489 A280 1.10m multi 1.60 1.60

490 A280 1.70m multi 2.40 2.40

491 A280 2.70m multi 3.75 3.75

492 A280 4m multi 5.75 5.75

493 A280 5.10m multi 7.25 7.25

Nos. 489-493 (5) 20.75 20.75

Borik Sports Arena, Banja Luka, 40th Anniv. — A281

Perf. 13¼x13¾

2014, Mar. 20 Litho.

494 A281 90pf multi 1.40 1.40

No. 494 was printed in sheets of 8 + central label.

Nature Protection A282

Flora: 90pf, Fagus moesiaca. 1.70m, Adiantum capillis-veneris.

Perf. 13¼x13¾

2014, Mar. 20 Litho.

495-496 A282 Set of 2 3.75 3.75

Nos. 495-496 were each printed in sheets of 8 + central label.

Europa A283

Designs: Nos. 497, 499a, 499b, 499c, 1m, Dvojnice (flute). Nos. 498, 499d, 499e, 499f, 2m, Fiddle.

2014, Apr. 25 Litho. *Perf. 13x13¼*

497-498 A283 Set of 2 4.25 4.25

Perf. 13x13¾ on 2 or 3 Sides

499 Sheet of 6 13.00 13.00

a. A283 1m Imperf. at top 1.40 1.40

b. A283 1m Imperf. at bottom 1.40 1.40

c. A283 1m Imperf. at top and right 1.40 1.40

d. A283 2m Imperf. at top 2.75 2.75

e. A283 2m Imperf. at bottom 2.75 2.75

f. A283 2m Imperf. at bottom and right 2.75 2.75

Nos. 497-498 were each printed in sheets of 8 + central label.

Souvenir Sheet

2014 World Cup Soccer Championships, Brazil — A284

2014, May 12 Litho. *Perf. 13¾*

500 A284 5.10m multi 7.25 7.25

Dr. Vaso Butozan Veterinary Institute, 80th Anniv. — A285

2014, May 15 Litho. *Perf. 13x13¾*

501 A285 90pf multi 1.40 1.40

No. 501 was printed in sheets of 8 + central label.

National Library, Srebrenica, 55th Anniv. — A286

2014, June 2 Litho. *Perf. 13x13¾*

502 A286 90pf multi 1.40 1.40

No. 502 was printed in sheets of 8 + central label.

Zmijanje Embroidery — A287

No. 503 — Embroidery designs: a, 90pf. b, 1,70m.

2014, June 5 Litho. *Perf. 13¾x13*

503 A287 Horiz. pair, #a-b 3.75 3.75

No. 503 was printed in sheets of 4 pairs + 2 labels, with stamps of the same denomination arranged tete-beche in relation to each other.

Wooden Churches — A288

Designs: 10pf, Church of the Ascension, Omarska. 20pf, St. Nicholas Church, Romanovci. 75pf, St. Nicholas Church, Jelicka.

2014, July 17 Litho. *Perf. 13¾*

504 A288 10pf multi .25 .25

505 A288 20pf multi .30 .30

506 A288 75pf multi 1.00 1.00

Nos. 504-506 (3) 1.55 1.55

Insects — A289

Designs: 90pf, Mosquito. 1.10m, Ant. 2.70m, Wasp.

2014, July 17 Litho. *Perf. 13¾*

507	A289	90pf	multi	1.25	1.25
508	A289	1.10m	multi	1.50	1.50
509	A289	2.70m	multi	3.75	3.75
	Nos. 507-509 (3)			6.50	6.50

Prijedorska Zelenika Apples — A290

Ilinjaca Apples — A291

Bijelica Apples — A292

Krompirusa Apples — A293

Perf. 13¼x13¾

2014, Sept. 10 Litho.

510	Horiz. strip of 4 + flanking label	5.25	5.25
a.	A290 90pf multi	1.25	1.25
b.	A291 90pf multi	1.25	1.25
c.	A292 90pf multi	1.25	1.25
d.	A293 90pf multi	1.25	1.25

Branislav Nusic (1864-1938), Writer — A294

2014, Oct. 20 Litho. *Perf. 13¼x13¾*

511 A294 90pf multi 1.40 1.40

No. 511 was printed in sheets of 8 + central label.

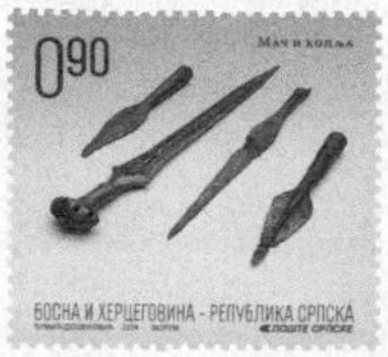

Sword and Spearheads A295

Ceramic Cup — A296

Perf. 13¼x13¾

2014, Nov. 20 Litho.

512	A295	90pf	multi	1.25	1.25
513	A296	1.70m	multi	2.50	2.50

Items from Donja Dolina archaeological site. Nos. 512-513 were printed in sheets of 8 (4 of each stamp) + 2 labels.

Milan Kovacevic (1915-85), Sports Television Broadcaster A297

Branko Copic (1915-84), Writer — A298

2015, Jan. 23 Litho. *Perf. 13¼x13¾*

514	A297	90pf	multi	1.25	1.25
515	A298	1.70m	multi	2.50	2.50

Nos. 514-515 were each printed in sheets of 8 + central label.

International Year of Light — A299

Perf. 13¼x13¾

2015, Feb. 16 Litho.

516 A299 1.70m multi 2.50 2.50

No. 516 was printed in sheets of 8 + central label.

Liberation of Jasenovac Concentration Camp, 70th Anniv. — A300

2015, Apr. 15 Litho. *Perf. 13¾x13¼*

517 A300 90pf multi 1.40 1.40

No. 517 was printed in sheets of 8 + central label.

Europa A301

Old toys: Nos. 518, 520a, 520b, 520c, 90pf, Robot. Nos. 519, 520d, 520e, 520f, 1.70m, Tractor.

2015, Apr. 17 Litho. *Perf. 13¼x13¾*

518-519 A301 Set of 2 4.00 4.00

Perf. 13¼x13¾ on 2 or 3 Sides

520	Sheet of 6	12.00	12.00
a.	A301 90pf Imperf. at top	1.00	1.00
b.	A301 90pf Imperf. at bottom	1.00	1.00
c.	A301 90pf Imperf. at top and right	1.00	1.00
d.	A301 1.70m Imperf. at top	2.00	2.00
e.	A301 1.70m Imperf. at bottom	2.00	2.00
f.	A301 1.70m Imperf. at bottom and right	2.00	2.00

Nos. 518-519 were each printed in sheets of 8 + central label.

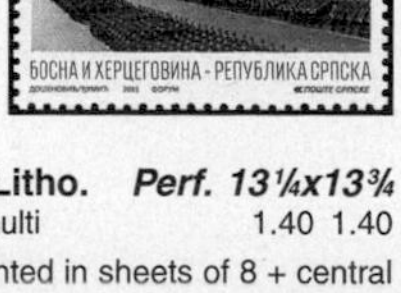

Victory in World War II, 70th Anniv. — A302

2015, May 8 Litho. *Perf. 13¼x13¾*

521 A302 90pf multi 1.40 1.40

No. 521 was printed in sheets of 8 + central label.

Doboj, 600th Anniv. — A303

2015, May 20 Litho. *Perf. 13x13¾*

522 A303 90pf multi 1.40 1.40

No. 522 was printed in sheets of 8 + central label.

Monument to Petar Kocic (1877-1916), Writer — A304

2015, Aug. 21 Litho. *Perf. 13¾x13*

523 A304 2.70m multi 4.00 4.00

50th Kocic Assembly. No. 523 was printed in sheets of 8 + label.

Nuts — A305

Farm Animals — A306

Designs: 10pf, Castanea sativa. 20pf, Corylus avellana. 90pf, Juglans. 1.10m, Bos taurus taurus. 1.70m, Capra hircus. 2.70m, Ovis aries. 5.10m, Equus caballus.

Perf. 13¾x13¼

2015, Aug. 28 Litho.

524	A305	10pf	multi	.25	.25
525	A305	20pf	multi	.25	.25
526	A305	90pf	multi	1.20	1.20
527	A306	1.10m	multi	1.40	1.40
528	A306	1.70m	multi	2.25	2.25
529	A306	2.70m	multi	3.50	3.50
530	A306	5.10m	multi	6.50	6.50
	Nos. 524-530 (7)			15.35	15.35

Souvenir Sheet

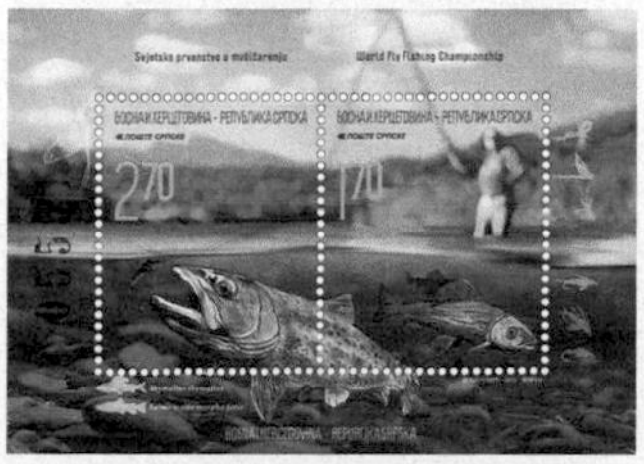

2015 World Fly Fishing Championships, Jajce — A307

No. 531: a, 1.70m, Fisherman and Thymallus thymallus. b, 2.70m, Salmo trutta morpah fario.

2015, Sept. 2 Litho. *Perf. 13¾*

531 A307 Sheet of 2, #a-b 6.50 6.50

Birds — A308

No. 532: a, Alauda arvensis. b, Carduelis carduelis. c, Luscinia megarhynchos. d, Turdus merula.

2015, Sept. 3 Litho. *Perf. 13¼x13¾*

532	Horiz. strip of 4	5.25	5.25
a.-d.	A308 90pf Any single	1.25	1.25

Printed in sheets containing 5 strips + 5 labels at right.

Dayton Peace Accords, 20th Anniv. — A309

Perf. 13¾x13¼

2015, Sept. 17 Litho.

533 A309 90pf multi 1.40 1.40

No. 533 was printed in sheets of 8 + central label.

Nature Protection A310

No. 534: a, 90pf, Nuphar luteum (yellow water lily). b, 1.70m, Urtica kioviensis (swamp nettle).

2015, Sept. 23 Litho. *Perf. 13x13¾*

534 A310 Vert. pair, #a-b 3.75 3.75

No. 534 was printed in sheets containing 4 pairs + 2 labels.

Jovan Cvijic (1865-1927), Geologist A311

2015, Oct. 12 Litho. *Perf. 13¼x13¾*

535 A311 1.70m multi 2.50 2.50

No. 535 was printed in sheets of 8 + central label.

Waterfall and Bridge — A312

Millstone A313

Water Wheel — A314

Mill Exterior A315

Perf. 13¼x13¾

2015, Nov. 27 Litho.

536 Horiz. strip of 4 + label at right 4.00 4.00
- *a.* A312 90pf multi 1.00 1.00
- *b.* A313 90pf multi 1.00 1.00
- *c.* A314 90pf multi 1.00 1.00
- *d.* A315 90pf multi 1.00 1.00

Diana Budisavljevic (1891-1978), Rescuer of Children in Concentration Camps — A316

2016, Jan. 25 Litho. *Perf. 13¾x13¼*

537 A316 1.70m multi 1.90 1.90

No. 537 was printed in sheets of 8 + central label.

Death of Serbian King Stefan Dragutin, 700th Anniv. — A317

Perf. 13¾x13¼

2016, Feb. 10 Litho.

538 A317 90pf multi 1.00 1.00

No. 538 was printed in sheets of 8 + central label.

Fruit — A318

Designs: 90pf, Prunus spinosa. 1.10m, Rubus fruticosus.

2016, Apr. 6 Litho. *Perf. 13¾x13¼*

539-540 A318 Set of 2 2.40 2.40

See No. 549.

A319

Europa A320

2016, Apr. 25 Litho. *Perf. 13¼x13¾*

541 A319 1.50m multi 1.75 1.75
542 A320 1.50m multi 1.75 1.75

Perf. 13¼x13¾ on 2 or 3 Sides

543 Sheet of 4 7.00 7.00
- *a.* A319 1.50m Imperf. at top 1.75 1.75
- *b.* A320 1.50m Imperf. at top and right 1.75 1.75
- *c.* A320 1.50m Imperf. at bottom 1.75 1.75
- *d.* A319 1.50m Imperf. at bottom and right 1.75 1.75

Think Green Issue.

Nature Protection — A321

No. 544: a, 90pf, Ciconia nigra. b, 1.70m, Helichrysum arenarium.

2016, May 16 Litho. *Perf. 13¼x13¾*

544 A321 Pair, #a-b 3.00 3.00

Printed in sheets containing 4 each Nos. 544a-544b + 2 labels.

Children's Day — A322

2016, June 1 Litho. *Perf. 13¾x13¼*

545 A322 1.70m multi 2.00 2.00

No. 545 was printed in sheets of 8 + label.

Souvenir Sheet

Soccer Player and Ball — A323

2016, June 10 Litho. *Perf. 13¾*

546 A323 5.10m multi 6.00 6.00

Miniature Sheet

Summer Sports — A324

No. 547: a, Shot put. b, Judo. c, Running. d, Swimming.

2016, July 7 Litho. *Perf. 13¾*

547 A324 1.70m Sheet of 4, #a-d 7.75 7.75

Miniature Sheet

Gyps Fulvus — A325

No. 548 — Bird: a, 90pf, Perched on rock. b, 90pf, In flight at angle. c, 1.70m, In flight, feet down. d, 1.70m, Perched on tree stump.

2016, Sept. 14 Litho. *Perf. 13¾*

548 A325 Sheet of 4, #a-d 6.00 6.00

Fruit Type of 2016

Perf. 13¾x13¼

2016, Sept. 16 Litho.

549 A318 50pf Comus mas .60 .60

River Fauna — A326

Designs: 10pf, Castor fiber. 20pf, Anas platyrhynchos. 1m, Astacus astacus. 1.70m, Esox lucius. 2.70m, Mauremys rivulata.

2016, Oct. 14 Litho. *Perf. 13¾x13¼*

550-554 A326 Set of 5 6.50 6.50

National Assembly, 25th Anniv. — A327

2016, Oct. 21 Litho. *Perf. 13¾x13¼*

555 A327 90pf multi 1.10 1.10

No. 555 was printed in sheets of 8 + central label.

Mushrooms — A328

No. 556: a, Pleurotus ostreatus (Oyster). b, Cantharellus cibarius (Chanterelle). c, Ganoderma lucidum (Reishi). d, Trametes versicolor (Turkey tail).

Perf. 13¼x13¾

2016, Nov. 25 Litho.

556 A328 90pf Block of 4, #a-d 4.00 4.00

No. 556 was printed in sheets containing 4 each Nos. 556a-556d + 9 labels.

A329

A330

A331

Household Objects A332

2016, Dec. 2 Litho. *Perf. 13¼x13¾*

557 Horiz. strip of 4 + flanking label 4.00 4.00
- *a.* A329 90pf multi 1.00 1.00
- *b.* A330 90pf multi 1.00 1.00
- *c.* A331 90pf multi 1.00 1.00
- *d.* A332 90pf multi 1.00 1.00

Composers — A333

No. 558: a, Sergei Prokofiev (1891-1953). b, Erik Satie (1866-1925). c, Antonín Dvorák (1841-1904).

2016, Dec. 9 Litho. *Perf. 13¾x13¼*

558 A333 1.70m Block of 3, #a-c, + label 5.50 5.50

Printed in sheets of 12 (4 each Nos. 558a-558c) + 4 central labels.

Radio in Banja Luka, 50th Anniv. — A334

2017, Feb. 2 Litho. *Perf. 13¾x13¼*

559 A334 90pf multi 1.00 1.00

No. 559 was printed in sheets of 8 + central label.

Coronation of King Stefan Nemanjic (c. 1165-1228), 800th Anniv. — A335

2017, Mar. 9 Litho. *Perf. 13¼x13¾*

560 A335 1.70m multi 1.90 1.90

No. 560 was printed in sheets of 8 + central label.

Stuplje Monastery A336

Mostanica Monastery A337

Krupa Monastery A338

Gomionica Monastery A339

Perf. 13¾x13¼

2017, Mar. 23 Litho.

561	A336	90pf multi	1.00	1.00
562	A337	1.10m multi	1.25	1.25
563	A338	2m multi	2.25	2.25
564	A339	4m multi	4.50	4.50
		Nos. 561-564 (4)	9.00	9.00

Jovan Ducic (1871-1943), Writer — A340

2017, Apr. 5 Litho. ***Perf. 13¾x13¼***
565 A340 90pf multi 1.00 1.00

No. 565 was printed in sheets of 8 + central label.

Elektrokrajina, 70th Anniv. — A341

2017, Apr. 19 Litho. ***Perf. 13¼x13¾***
566 A341 90pf multi 1.00 1.00

No. 566 was printed in sheets of 8 + central label.

A342

Kastel Fortress, Banja Luka — A343

2017, Apr. 28 Litho. ***Perf. 13¼x13¾***
567 A342 1.70m multi 1.90 1.90
568 A343 1.70m multi 1.90 1.90

Perf. 13¼x13¾ on 2 or 3 Sides

569 Sheet of 4 7.75 7.75
a. A342 1.70m Imperf. at top 1.90 1.90
b. A343 1.70m Imperf. at top and right 1.90 1.90
c. A343 1.70m Imperf. at bottom 1.90 1.90
d. A342 1.70m Imperf. at bottom and right 1.90 1.90

Europa. Nos. 567-568 were each printed in sheets of 8 + central label.

Petar Kocic Theater Festival, 20th Anniv. — A344

2017, May 11 Litho. ***Perf. 13¾x13¼***
570 A344 90pf multi 1.10 1.10

No. 570 was printed in sheets of 8 + central label.

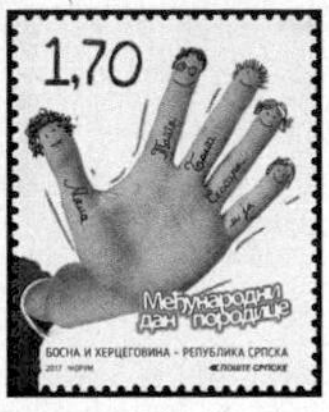
International Family Day — A345

2017, May 15 Litho. ***Perf. 13¾x13¼***
571 A345 1.70m multi 2.00 2.00

No. 571 was printed in sheets of 8 + central label.

Filip Visnjic (1767-1834), Poet and Musician — A346

2017, May 29 Litho. ***Perf. 13¾x13¼***
572 A346 90pf multi 1.10 1.10

No. 572 was printed in sheets of 8 + label.

Battle of Kozara, 75th Anniv. — A347

No. 573: a, Kozara Memorial. b, Woman, children, soldiers.

Perf. 13¾x13¼

2017, June 10 Litho.
573 A347 1.70m Horiz. pair, #a-b 4.00 4.00

Flowers — A348

Designs: 20pf, Cyclamen purpurascens. 1.50m, Scrophularia scopolii. 1.70m, Lilium martagon. 2.70m, Limodorum abortivum. 5.10m, Convallaria majalis.

Perf. 13¾x13¼

2017, June 15 Litho.
574-578 A348 Set of 5 13.00 13.00

Souvenir Sheet

Dayak Boats — A349

2017, July 5 Litho. ***Perf. 13¾***
579 A349 5.10m multi 6.25 6.25

Tombstones — A350

No. 580 — Denominations: a, 90pf. b, 1.70m.

2017, Sept. 7 Litho. ***Perf. 13¾x13¼***
580 A350 Pair, #a-b 3.25 3.25

Printed in sheets containing 4 pairs + 2 central labels.

Flora — A351

No. 581: a, Helianthus annuus. b, Glycine max. c, Linum usitatissimum. d, Cannabis sativa.

Perf. 13¾x13¼

2017, Sept. 21 Litho.
581 A351 90pf Block or vert. strip of 4, #a-d 4.50 4.50

Ivo Andric (1892-1975), 1961 Nobel Laureate in Literature — A352

No. 582 — Andric as: a, Older man. b, Younger man.

2017, Oct. 9 Litho. ***Perf. 13x13¾***
582 A352 90pf Pair, #a-b 2.25 2.25

Banski Dvor Cultural Center, Banja Luka, 85th Anniv. — A353

2017, Nov. 8 Litho. ***Perf. 13¼x13¾***
583 A353 90pf multi 1.10 1.10

No. 583 was printed in sheets of 8 + central label.

Miniature Sheet

Endangered Animals — A354

No. 584: a, 90pf, Ursus arctos. b, 90pf, Lynx lynx. c, 1.70m, Ursus arctos cub. d, 1.70m, Lynx lynx kitten.

2017, Nov. 9 Litho. ***Perf. 13¾***
584 A354 Sheet of 4, 3a-d 6.50 6.50

Souvenir Sheet

Epic Poem, *Marko Kraljevic and Musa Kesedzija* — A355

No. 585: a, 1.70m, Musa Kesedzija. b, 2.70m, Marko Kraljevic.

2017, Dec. 21 Litho. ***Perf. 13¾***
585 A355 Sheet of 2, #a-b 5.50 5.50

Sir Isaac Newton (1643-1727), Mathematician and Astronomer A356

2018, Jan. 25 Litho. ***Perf. 13¼x13¾***
586 A356 1.70m multi 2.25 2.25

No. 586 was printed in sheets of 8 + label.

Art — A357

No. 587 — Art by: a, 90pf, Radenko Milak. b, 1.70m, Mladen Miljanovic.

Perf. 13¼x13¾

2018, Feb. 20 Litho.

587 A357 Vert. pair, #a-b 3.25 3.25

Jedinstvo Singing Society, 125th Anniv. — A358

Perf. 13¼x13¾

2018, Mar. 15 Litho.

588 A358 90pf multi 1.25 1.25

No. 588 was printed in sheets of 8 + label.

Bridge, Trebinje A359

Bridge, Visegrad A360

2018, Apr. 27 Litho. ***Perf. 13¼x13¾***

589 A359 1.70m multi 2.10 2.10

590 A360 1.70m multi 2.10 2.10

Perf. 13¼x13¾ on 2 or 3 Sides

591 Sheet of 4 8.50 8.50

a. A359 1.70m Imperf. at top 2.10 2.10

b. A360 1.70m Imperf. at top and right 2.10 2.10

c. A360 1.70m Imperf. at bottom 2.10 2.10

d. A359 1.70m Imperf. at bottom and right 2.10 2.10

Europa. Nos. 589-590 were each printed in sheets of 8 + label.

Premiere of Children's Play, *The Sad Prince,* 20th Anniv. — A361

2018, Apr. 30 Litho. ***Perf. 13¾x13¼***

592 A361 90pf multi 1.10 1.10

No. 592 was printed in sheets of 8 + label.

Djurdjevdan (St. George's Day) Festival, 25th Anniv. — A362

2018, May 4 Litho. ***Perf. 13¾x13¼***

593 A362 90pf multi 1.10 1.10

No. 593 was printed in sheets of 8 + central label.

Aleksa Santic (1868-1924), Poet — A363

2018, May 25 Litho. ***Perf. 13¼x13¾***

594 A363 90pf multi 1.10 1.10

No. 594 was printed in sheets of 8 + label.

Souvenir Sheet

Rafting — A364

No. 595: a, 1.70m, Log raft. b, 2.70m, Rafters on Drina River.

2018, June 15 Litho. ***Perf. 13¾***

595 A364 Sheet of 2, #a-b 5.25 5.25

Souvenir Sheet

50th International Handball Tournament, Doboj — A365

No. 596: a, Player with ball. b, Player attempting block.

2018, July 5 Litho. ***Perf. 13¾***

596 A365 2.70m Sheet of 2, #a-b 6.50 6.50

Miniature Sheet

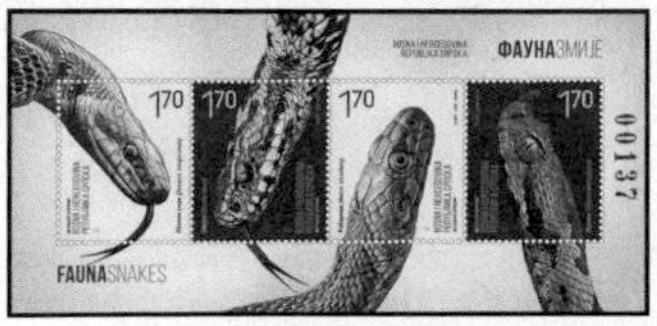

Snakes — A366

No. 597: a, Zamenis longissimus. b, Vipera berus. c, Natrix tessellata. d, Vipera ammodytes.

2018, Sept. 5 Litho. ***Perf. 13¾***

597 A366 1.70m Sheet of 4, #a-d 8.25 8.25

Miniature Sheet

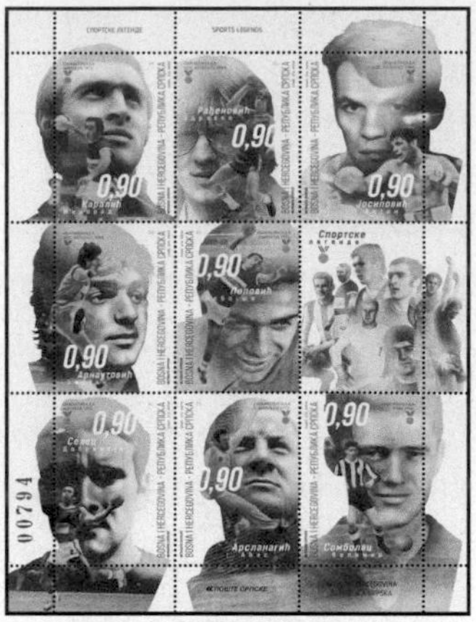

Olympic Gold Medalists — A367

No. 598: a, Milorad Karalic, handball player, 1972. b, Zdravko Radjenovic, handball player, 1984. c, Anton Josipovic, boxer, 1984. d, Zlatan Arnautovic, handball player, 1984. e, Nebojsa Popovic, handball player, 1972. f, Dobrivoje Selec, handball player, 1972. g, Abas Arslanagic, handball player, 1972. h, Velimir Sombolac (1939-2016), soccer player, 1960.

Perf. 13¼x13¾

2018, Sept. 27 Litho.

598 A367 90pf Sheet of 8, #a-h, + label 8.75 8.75

Flowers — A368

No. 599: a, Iris reichenbachii. b, Pimpinella serbica.

2018, Oct. 9 Litho. ***Perf. 13¼x13¾***

599 A368 1.70m Pair, #a-b 4.00 4.00

Nature Protection.

No. 599 was printed in sheets of 8 (4 each Nos. 599a-599b) + 2 labels.

Mail Carrier and Steps of Mail Delivery — A369

2018, Oct. 11 Litho. ***Perf. 13¾x13¼***

600 A369 90pf multi 1.10 1.10

Count Sava Vladislavich-Raguzinsky (1669-1738), Diplomat and Writer — A370

2018, Oct. 26 Litho. ***Perf. 14x13¼***

601 A370 90pf multi 1.10 1.10

Printed in sheets of 8 + label.

Orthodox Monasteries A371

Designs: 90pf, Liplje Monastery, Teslic. 1m, Osovica Monastery, Srbac.

2018, Oct. 30 Litho. ***Perf. 13¼x13¾***

602-603 A371 Set of 2 2.25 2.25

Fruit — A372

Designs: 20pf, Prunus persicus. 2.70m, Prunus armeniaca.

2018, Oct. 30 Litho. ***Perf. 13¼x13¾***

604-605 A372 Set of 2 3.50 3.50

World War II Battles, 75th Anniv. — A373

No. 606 — Monument to: a, Battle of the Neretva River, soldiers and collapsed bridges. b, Battle of the Sutjeska River and soldiers.

2018, Nov. 5 Litho. ***Perf. 13¾x13¼***

606 A373 1.70m Horiz. pair, #a-b 4.00 4.00

Famous Men — A374

No. 607: a, Mihailo Petrovic Alas (1868-1943), mathematician. b, Milos Crnjanski (1893-1977), writer.

Perf. 13¾x13¼

2018, Dec. 10 Litho.

607 A374 1.70m Vert. pair, #a-b 4.00 4.00

Souvenir Sheet

Goradze Printing House, 500th Anniv. — A375

2019, Jan. 28 Litho. *Perf. 13¾*
608 A375 5.10m multi 6.00 6.00

2018 European Youth Olympic Winter Festival, Sarajevo and East Sarajevo — A376

No. 609: a, Mascot on skis. b, Mascot playing five sports.

2019, Feb. 9 Litho. *Perf. 13¼x13¾*
609 A376 2.70m Pair, #a-b 6.75 6.75

Bust of Felix Mendelssohn (1809-47), Composer A377

Perf. 13¾x13¼
2019, Feb. 27 Litho.
610 A377 1.70m multi 2.00 2.00

No. 610 was printed in sheets of 8 + label.

Serbian Orthodox Church, 800th Anniv. — A378

No. 611: a, Church coat of arms and St. Sava Cathedral, Belgrade. b, 800th anniversary emblem, Cathedral of Christ the Savior, Banja Luka.

2019, Mar. 7 Litho. *Perf. 13¾x13¼*
611 A378 1.70m Horiz. pair, #a-b 4.00 4.00

Europa — A379

Designs: Nos. 612, 614a, 614b, 1.80m, Falco peregrinus. Nos. 613, 614c, 614d, 2.70m, Aquila chrysaetos.

2019, Apr. 24 Litho. *Perf. 13¾x13¼*
612-613 A379 Set of 2 5.25 5.25

Perf. 13¾x13¼ on 3 Sides

614 Sheet of 4 10.50 10.50
a. A379 1.80m As No. 612, imperf. at top 2.00 2.00
b. A379 1.80m As No. 612, imperf. at bottom 2.00 2.00
c. A379 2.70m As No. 613, imperf. at top 3.25 3.25
d. A379 2.70m As No. 613, imperf. at bottom 3.25 3.25

Risto Jeremic (1869-1952), Surgeon — A380

2019, May 18 Litho. *Perf. 13¾x13¼*
615 A380 90pf multi 1.10 1.10

No. 615 was printed in sheets of 8 + label.

Tree of Life, Photograph by Samir Hadzic — A381

2019, May 18 Litho. *Perf. 13¾x13¼*
616 A381 1.80m multi 2.10 2.10

World Inflammatory Bowel Disease Day. See Bosnia & Herzegovina (Bosniak) No. 818, Bosnia & Herzegovina (Croat) No. 392.

National Parks — A382

Designs: 90pf, Drina National Park. 1.80m, Cicelj National Park.

2019, June 7 Litho. *Perf. 13¼x13¾*
617-618 A382 Set of 2 3.25 3.25
618a Pair, #617-618 3.25 3.25

Nos. 617-618 were printed in sheets of 8, containing 4 of each stamp, + 2 labels.

Miniature Sheet

Signing of the Treaty of Versailles, Cent. — A383

No. 619: a, Field Marshal Radomir Putnik (1847-1917). b, World War I victory parade in Paris. c, Petar Bojovic (1858-1945), military commander, and Arc de Triomphe, Paris. d, Milunka Savic (1888-1973), heroine, holding rifle. e, Momcilo Gavric (1906-93), youngest World War I soldier, with arm in sling. f, Field Marshal Zivojin Misic (1855-1921), wearing cap (denomination at UR). g, Serbian soldiers in action. h, Stepa Stepanovic (1856-1929), military commander, Serbian soldiers in background.

Perf. 13¼x13¾
2019, June 28 Litho.
619 A383 90pf Sheet of 8, #a-h, + central label 8.50 8.50

Souvenir Sheet

First Man on the Moon, 50th Anniv. — A384

No. 620 — Astronaut on: a, Moon. b, Ladder of Lunar Module.

2019, July 3 Litho. *Perf. 13¾*
620 A384 2.70m Sheet of 2, #a-b 6.25 6.25

Summer Activities on the Vrbas River — A385

2019, July 19 Litho. *Perf. 13¼x13¾*
621 A385 90pf multi 1.10 1.10

No. 621 was printed in sheets of 8 + label.

Motorcycles A386

Designs: 20pf, Tomos A3. 25pf, Vespa 125. 50pf, BMW R75. 1m, Honda ST70. 2m, Harley-Davidson EL.

2019, July 25 Litho. *Perf. 13¼x13¾*

622	A386	20pf multi	.25	.25
623	A386	25pf multi	.30	.30
624	A386	50pf multi	.55	.55
625	A386	1m multi	1.10	1.10
626	A386	2m multi	2.25	2.25
		Nos. 622-626 (5)	4.45	4.45

Iskra House for Parents with Sick Children, Banja Luka — A387

Perf. 13¼x13¾
2019, Sept. 11 Litho.
627 A387 90pf multi 1.00 1.00

No. 627 was printed in sheets of 8 + label.

Filip Visnjic Gymnasium, Bijeljina, Cent. — A388

Perf. 13¾x13¼
2019, Sept. 19 Litho.
628 A388 90pf multi 1.00 1.00

No. 628 was printed in sheets of 8 + central label.

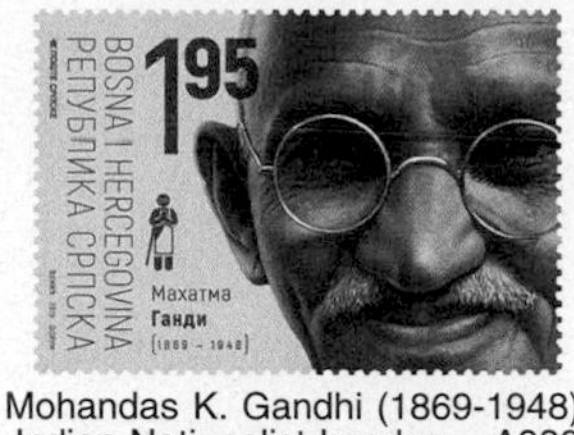

Mohandas K. Gandhi (1869-1948), Indian Nationalist Leader — A389

2019, Oct. 2 Litho. *Perf. 13¾x13*
629 A389 1.95m multi 2.25 2.25

Religious Items — A390

No. 630: a, Madonna and Child icon, 16th cent. b, Kivot, 17th cent.

2019, Nov. 5 Litho. *Perf. 13¾x13¼*
630 A390 90pf Horiz. pair, #a-b 2.10 2.10

Fish — A391

No. 631: a, Barbus barbus. b, Perca fluviatilis. c, Sander lucioperca. d, Silurus glanis.

2019, Dec. 5 Litho. *Perf. 13x13¾*
631 Horiz. strip or block of 4 4.50 4.50
a.-d. A391 90pf Any single 1.10 1.10

No. 631 was printed in sheets of two strips, which are tete-beche in relationship to each other.

Ludwig van Beethoven (1770-1827), Composer — A392

2020, Jan. 29 Litho. *Perf. 13¾x13¼*
632 A392 1.95m multi 2.25 2.25

No. 632 was printed in sheets of 8 + label.

Museum of Semberija and Gradiska, 50th Anniv. — A393

No. 633 — Bronze statuette and inscribed stone with date at lower right of: a, 1301. b, 4th cent.

Perf. 13¼x13¾
2020, Feb. 21 Litho.
633 A393 90pf Horiz. pair, #a-b 2.10 2.10

No. 633 was printed in sheets of 4 pairs + 2 central labels.

Motion Pictures by the Lumière Brothers, 125th Anniv. — A394

Perf. 13¾x13¼

2020, Mar. 19 Litho.

634 A394 1.95m multi 2.25 2.25

No. 634 was printed in sheets of 8 + label.

Souvenir Sheet

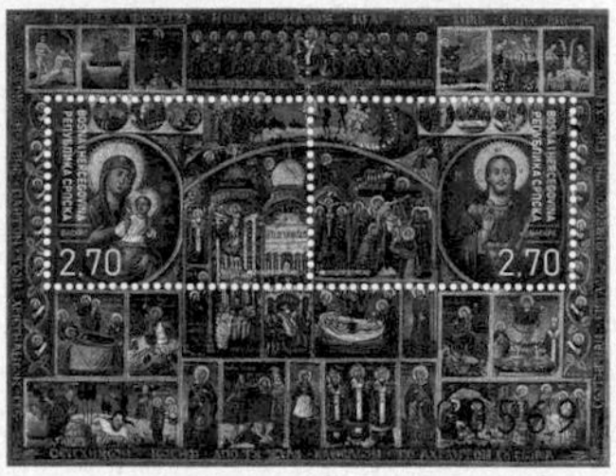

Easter — A395

No. 635 — Icon depicting: a, Madonna and Child in oval at left. b, Jesus Christ in oval at right.

2020, Mar. 27 Litho. *Perf. 13¾*

635 A395 2.70m Sheet of 2, #a-b 6.00 6.00

REGISTRATION STAMPS

No. 19 Surcharged

1994, Nov. 1 Litho. *Perf. 13¼*

F9 A1 (P) on 6,000d #19 1.60 1.60

No. F9 sold for 40p on day of issue.

Relay Station Type of 1996

Kraljica relay station, Mt. Ozren.

1996, Sept. 20 *Perf. 14*

F10 A9 (R) multicolored .75 .75

No. F10 sold for 90p on day of issue.

Famous Men Type of 1997

1997, Nov. 1 *Perf. 13¾*

F11 A13 (R) Jovan Ducic (1871-1943) .75 .75

No. F11 sold for 90p on day of issue.

Building Type of 1999

1999, Mar. 15 Litho. *Perf. 13¾*

F12 A20 (R) Trebinje 2.00 2.00

No. F12 sold for 1m on day of issue.

POSTAL TAX STAMPS

Robert Koch (1843-1910) — PT1

1997, Sept. 14 Litho. *Imperf.*

Self-Adhesive

RA1 PT1 15p red & blue 1.00 1.00

Obligatory on mail 9/14-21.

Red Cross — PT2

1998, May 5 Self-Adhesive

RA2 PT2 90p multicolored 1.00 1.00

Obligatory on mail 5/5-15.

Fight Against Tuberculosis PT3

1998, Sept. 14 *Perf. 10¾*

RA3 PT3 75pf multicolored 1.00 1.00

Obligatory on mail 9/14-21.

Red Cross — PT4

1999, May 8 Litho. *Perf. 10¾*

RA4 PT4 10pf multi 1.00 1.00

Obligatory on mail 5/8-5/15.

Red Cross — PT5

1999, Sept. 14 Litho. *Perf. 10¾*

RA5 PT5 10pf multi .60 .60

Obligatory on mail 9/14-21.

Red Cross — PT6

2000, May 8 Litho. *Perf. 10¾*

RA6 PT6 10pf multi 1.00 1.00

Obligatory on mail 5/8-5/15.

Red Cross — PT7

2000, Sept. 14 Litho. *Perf. 10¾*

RA7 PT7 10pf multi 1.00 1.00

Obligatory on mail 9/14-21.

Red Cross — PT8

2001, May 8 Litho. *Perf. 10¾*

RA8 PT8 10pf multi 1.00 1.00

Obligatory on mail 5/8-5/15.

Anti-Tuberculosis Week — PT9

2001, Sept. 14 Litho. *Perf. 10½*

RA9 PT9 10pf multi 1.00 1.00

Obligatory on mail 9/14-9/21.

Red Cross — PT10

2002, May 8 Litho. *Perf. 10¾*

RA10 PT10 10pf multi .90 .90

Obligatory on mail 5/8-5/15.

Fight Against Tuberculosis — PT11

2002, Sept. 14 Litho. *Perf. 10¾*

RA11 PT11 10pf multi .90 .90

Obligatory on mail 9/14-9/21.

Red Cross — PT12

2003, May 8 Litho. *Perf. 10¾*

RA12 PT12 10pf multi .90 .90

Obligatory on mail 5/8-5/15.

Fight Against Tuberculosis PT13

2003, Sept. 14 Litho. *Perf. 10¾*

RA13 PT13 10pf multi .90 .90

a. Imperf. 1.90 1.90

Obligatory on mail 9/14-9/21.

Red Cross — PT14

2004, May 8 Litho. *Perf. 10¾*

RA14 PT14 10pf multi .75 .75

a. Imperf. 1.75 1.75

Obligatory on mail 5/8-5/15.

Fight Against Tuberculosis PT15

2004, Sept. 14 Litho. *Perf. 10¾*

RA15 PT15 10pf multi .75 .75

a. Imperf. 1.75 1.75

Obligatory on mail 9/14-9/21.

Red Cross — PT16

2005, May 8 Litho. *Imperf.*

Self-Adhesive

RA16 PT16 10pf red & black .80 .80

Obligatory on mail 5/8-5/15.

Fight Against Tuberculosis PT17

Rouletted 16½

2005, Sept. 14 Litho.

RA17 PT17 10pf multi .50 .50

a. Imperf. .75 .75

Obligatory on mail 9/14-9/21.

PT18

2006, May 8 Litho. *Perf. 10*

RA18 PT18 20pf multi .50 .50

a. Imperf. .75 .75

Red Cross. Obligatory on mail 5/8-5/15.

PT19

2006, Sept. 14 *Perf. 10¾*

RA19 PT19 20pf multi .50 .50
a. Imperf. .75 .75

Fight against tuberculosis. Obligatory on mail 9/14-9/21.

PT20

2007, May 8 **Litho.** *Perf. 10*

RA20 PT20 20pf multi .50 .50
a. Imperf. .75 .75

Red Cross. Obligatory on mail May 8-15.

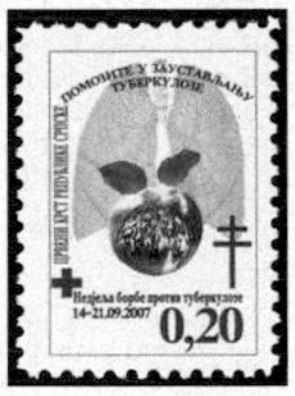

PT21

2007, Sept. 14 *Perf. 10*

RA21 PT21 20pf multi .60 .60
a. Imperf. 1.40 1.40

Fight against tuberculosis. Obligatory on mail Sept. 14-21.

Hands — PT22

2008, May 8 **Litho.** *Perf. 10*

RA22 PT22 20pf multi .60 .60
a. Imperf. .60 .60

Red Cross. Obligatory on mail May 8-15.

PT23

2008, Sept. 14 **Litho.** *Perf. 10*

RA23 PT23 20pf multi .60 .60
a. Imperf. .60 .60

Fight against tuberculosis. Obligatory on mail Sept. 14-21.

PT24

2009, May 8 *Perf. 10¾*

RA24 PT24 20pf multi .60 .60
a. Imperf. .60 .60

Red Cross. Obligatory on mail May 8-15.

Fight Against Tuberculosis PT25

2009, Sept. 14 **Litho.** *Perf. 10¾x11*

RA25 PT25 20pf multi .60 .60
a. Imperf. .60 .60

Obligatory on mail Sept. 14-21.

Red Cross — PT26

2010, May 8 **Litho.** *Perf. 10¾*

RA26 PT26 20pf multi .60 .60
a. Imperf. .60 .60

Obligatory on mail May 8-15.

Fight Against Tuberculosis PT27

2010, Sept. 14 **Litho.** *Perf. 10¾*

RA27 PT27 20pf multi .60 .60
a. Imperf. .60 .60

Obligatory on mail Sept. 14-21.

Red Cross — PT28

2011, May 8 *Perf. 10*

RA28 PT28 20pf multi .60 .60
a. Perf. 10 horiz. .60 .60

Obligatory on mail May 8-15.

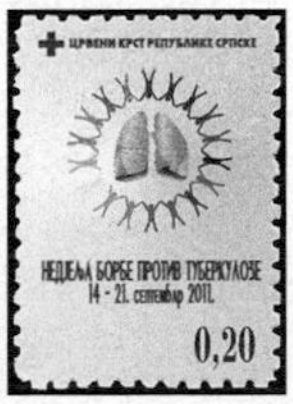

Fight Against Tuberculosis — PT29

2011, Sept. 14

RA29 PT29 20pf multi .60 .60
a. Imperf. .60 .60

Obligatory on mail Sept. 14-21.

Red Cross — PT30

2012, May 8 *Perf. 9*

RA30 PT30 20pf multi .60 .60
a. Imperf. .60 .60

Obligatory on mail May 8-15.

Fight Against Tuberculosis PT31

2012, Sept. 14 **Litho.** *Perf. 9*

RA31 PT31 20pf multi .60 .60
a. Imperf. .60 .60

Obligatory on mail Sept. 14-21.

Red Cross, 150th Anniv. — PT32

2013, May 8 **Litho.** *Perf. 9*

RA32 PT32 20pf multi .60 .60
a. Imperf. .60 .60

Obligatory on mail May 8-15.

Fight Against Tuberculosis — PT33

2013, Sept. 14 **Litho.** *Perf. 9*

RA33 PT33 20pf multi .60 .60
a. Imperf. .60 .60

Obligatory on mail Sept. 14-21.

Red Cross — PT34

2014, May 8 **Litho.** *Perf. 9*

RA34 PT34 20pf red & silver .60 .60
a. Imperf. .60 .60

Obligatory on mail May 8-15.

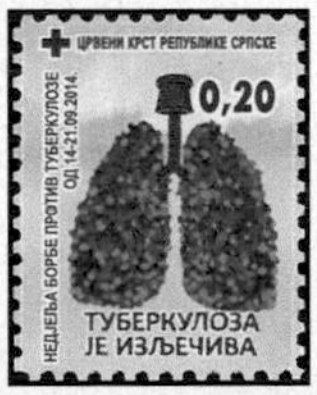

Fight Against Tuberculosis PT35

2014, Sept. 14 **Litho.** *Perf. 9*

RA35 PT35 20pf multi .60 .60
a. Imperf. .60 .60

Obligatory on mail Sept. 14-21.

Red Cross — PT36

2015, May 8 **Litho.** *Perf. 9*

RA36 PT36 20pf red & black .60 .60
a. Imperf. .60 .50

Obligatory on mail May 8-15.

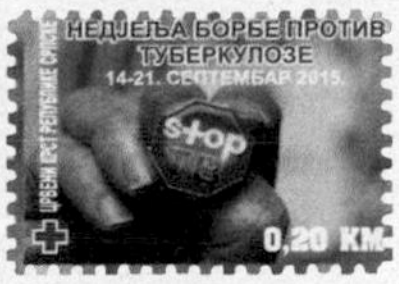

Fight Against Tuberculosis PT37

2015, Sept. 14 **Litho.** *Perf. 9*

RA37 PT37 20pf multi .60 .60
a. Imperf. .60 .60

Obligatory on mail Sept. 14-21.

Red Cross — PT38

2016, May 8 **Litho.** *Perf. 9*

RA38 PT38 20pf red & blue .25 .25
a. Imperf. .25 .25

Obligatory on mail May 8-15.

Fight Against Tuberculosis PT39

2016, Sept. 14 **Litho.** *Perf. 9*

RA39 PT39 20pf multi .25 .25
a. Imperf. .25 .25

Obligatory on mail Sept. 14-21.

Red Cross — PT40

2017, May 8 **Litho.** *Perf. 9*

RA40 PT40 20pf grnsh blue & red .25 .25
a. Imperf. .25 .25

Obligatory on mail May 8-15.

Fight Against Tuberculosis PT41

2017, Sept. 14 **Litho.** *Perf. 10*

RA41 PT41 20pf multi .25 .25
a. Imperf. .25 .25

Obligatory on mail Sept. 14-21.

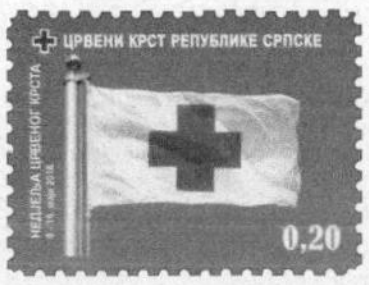

Red Cross Flag — PT42

2018, May 8 **Litho.** *Perf. 10*

RA42 PT42 20pf grnsh blue & red .25 .25
a. Imperf. .25 .25

Obligatory on mail May 8-15.

Fight Against Tuberculosis — PT43

2018, Sept. 14 **Litho.** ***Perf. 9***

RA43	PT43 20pf multi		.25	.25
a.	Imperf.		.25	.25

Obligatory on mail Sept. 14-21.

BOTSWANA

bä-'swä-nə

LOCATION — In central South Africa, north of the Republic of South Africa, east of Namibia and bounded on the north by the Caprivi Strip of Namibia and on the east by Zimbabwe.
GOVT. — Independent republic
AREA — 222,000 sq. mi.
POP. — 1,561,973 (July 2004 est.)
CAPITAL — Gaborone

The former Bechuanaland Protectorate became an independent republic, September 30, 1966, taking the name Botswana.

100 Cents = 1 Rand
100 Thebe = 1 Pula (1976)

Catalogue values for all unused stamps in this country are for Never Hinged items.

National Assembly Building — A1

Designs: 5c, Abattoir, Lobatsi. 15c, Dakota plane. 35c, State House, Gaborone.

Unwmk.
1966, Sept. 30 **Photo.** ***Perf. 14***

1	A1	2½c multicolored	.25	.25
a.		Imperf., pair	*425.00*	
2	A1	5c multicolored	.25	.25
3	A1	15c multicolored	.80	.25
4	A1	35c multicolored	.50	.40
		Nos. 1-4 (4)	1.80	1.15

Establishment of Republic of Botswana.

Bechuanaland Protectorate Nos. 180-193 Overprinted

Perf. 14x14½, 14½x14
1966, Sept. 30 **Wmk. 314**

5	A15	1c multicolored	.45	.25
6	A15	2c multicolored	.50	*1.75*
7	A15	2½c multicolored	.50	.25
8	A15	3½c yel, blk, sep & pink	1.75	.25
9	A15	5c multicolored	2.25	*1.50*
10	A15	7½c multicolored	.75	*1.75*
11	A15	10c multicolored	1.50	.25
12	A15	12½c multicolored	2.75	*4.00*
13	A15	20c gray & brown	.35	*2.00*
14	A15	25c yel & dk brn	.35	*2.50*
15	A15	35c dp org & ultra	.55	*3.00*
16	A15	50c lt ol grn & sep	.55	.95
17	A15	1r ocher & black	.75	*1.25*
18	A15	2r blue & brown	1.75	*3.25*
		Nos. 5-18 (14)	14.75	22.95

European Golden Oriole — A2

Birds: 2c, African hoopoe. 3c, Groundscraper thrush. 4c, Blue waxbill. 5c, Secretary bird. 7c, Yellow-billed hornbill. 10c, Crimson-breasted shrike. 15c, Malachite kingfisher. 20c, Fish eagle. 25c, Gray lourie. 35c, Scimitar bill. 50c, Knob-billed duck. 1r, Crested barbet. 2r, Didrio cuckoo.

Perf. 14x14½
1967, Jan. 3 **Photo.** **Unwmk.**

19	A2	1c gray & multi	.40	.25
20	A2	2c lt blue & multi	.60	.25
21	A2	3c yel green & multi	.75	.25
22	A2	4c salmon & multi	.75	.35
23	A2	5c pink & multi	.75	.40
24	A2	7c slate & multi	.80	.70
25	A2	10c emerald & multi	.80	.80
26	A2	15c lt green & multi	9.00	2.75
27	A2	20c ultra & multi	9.00	1.50
28	A2	25c green & multi	6.50	1.50
29	A2	35c multicolored	9.00	3.00
30	A2	50c dl yel & multi	3.50	3.00
31	A2	1r dl grn & multi	7.50	3.50
32	A2	2r org brn & multi	9.50	*17.50*
		Nos. 19-32 (14)	58.85	35.75

No. 19 exists with Maltese Cross watermark (error). Value, used $1,100.

Nos. 19, 20, 22, 24 and 25 exist with gum Arabic and PVA gum.

University Buildings and Graduates — A3

1967, Apr. 7 ***Perf. 14x14½***

33	A3	3c yel, sepia & dp blue	.25	.25
34	A3	7c blue, sepia & dp bl	.25	.25
35	A3	15c dull rose, sepia & dp bl	.25	.25
36	A3	35c lt vio, sepia & dp bl	.25	.25
		Nos. 33-36 (4)	1.00	1.00

1st conferment of degrees by the University of Botswana, Lesotho and Swaziland at Roma, Lesotho.

Chobe Bush Bucks A4

Designs: 7c, Sable antelopes. 35c, Fishing on the Chobe River.

1967, Oct. 2 **Photo.** ***Perf. 14***

37	A4	3c multicolored	.25	.25
38	A4	7c multicolored	.25	.25
39	A4	35c multicolored	1.35	*1.40*
		Nos. 37-39 (3)	1.85	1.90

Publicity for Chobe Game Reserve.

Human Rights Flame and Arms of Botswana — A5

Design elements rearranged on 15c, 25c.

1968, Apr. 8 **Litho.** ***Perf. 13½x13***

40	A5	3c brown red & multi	.25	.25
41	A5	15c emerald & multi	.30	*.45*
42	A5	25c yellow & multi	.30	*.55*
		Nos. 40-42 (3)	.85	1.25

International Human Rights Year.

Rock Painting A6

Girl Wearing Ceremonial Beads — A7

Designs: 10c, Baobab Trees, by Thomas Baines (34x25mm). 15c, National Museum and Art Gallery (71½x19mm).

Perf. 13x13½ (3c, 10c); Perf. 12½ (7c); Perf. 12½x13 (15c)
1968, Sept. 30 **Litho.**

43	A6	3c multicolored	.25	.25
44	A7	7c multicolored	.35	.40
45	A6	10c multicolored	.35	.35
46	A6	15c multicolored	.55	*1.60*
a.		Souv. sheet of 4, #43-46, perf. 13½	2.00	*3.00*
		Nos. 43-46 (4)	1.50	2.60

Opening of the National Museum and Art Gallery, Gaborone, Sept. 30, 1968.

African Nativity Scene A8

1968, Nov. 11 **Unwmk.** ***Perf. 13x14***

47	A8	1c car & multi	.25	.25
48	A8	2c brown & multi	.25	.25
49	A8	5c green & multi	.25	.25
50	A8	25c dp violet & multi	.25	*.50*
		Nos. 47-50 (4)	1.00	1.25

Christmas.

Boy Scout, Botswana Scout Emblem and Lion — A9

Botswana Boy Scout emblem, lion and: 15c, Boy Scouts cooking, vert. 25c, Boy Scouts around campfire.

1969, Aug. 21 **Litho.** ***Perf. 13½***

51	A9	3c emerald & multi	.60	.30
52	A9	15c lt brown & multi	.70	*1.10*
53	A9	25c dk brown & multi	.70	*1.10*
		Nos. 51-53 (3)	2.00	2.50

22nd World Scouting Conf., Helsinki, Finland, Aug. 21-27.

Mother, Child and Star of Bethlehem — A10

1969, Nov. 6 ***Perf. 14½x14***

54	A10	1c dk brn & lt blue	.25	.25
55	A10	2c dk brn & apple grn	.25	.25
56	A10	4c dk brn & dull yel	.25	.25
57	A10	35c dk brn & vio blue	.25	.25
a.		Souv. sheet, #54-57, perf 14½	1.00	1.00
		Nos. 54-57 (4)	1.00	1.00

Christmas.

Diamond Treatment Plant, Orapa — A11

Designs: 7c, Copper and nickel mining, Selebi-Pikwe. 10c, Copper and nickel mining and metal bars, Selebi-Pikwe, horiz. 35c, Orapa diamond mine and diamonds, horiz.

1970, Mar. 23 ***Perf. 14½x14, 14x14½***

58	A11	3c multicolored	1.00	.30
59	A11	7c multicolored	1.30	.30
60	A11	10c multicolored	1.75	.25
61	A11	35c multicolored	3.75	1.75
		Nos. 58-61 (4)	7.80	2.60

Botswana development program.

Mr. Micawber and Charles Dickens A12

Charles Dickens (1812-70), English novelist and: 7c, Scrooge. 15c, Fagin. 25c, Bill Sykes.

1970, July 7 **Litho.** ***Perf. 11***

62	A12	3c gray green & multi	.30	.25
63	A12	7c multicolored	.30	.25
64	A12	15c brown & multi	.55	.50
65	A12	25c dp violet & multi	.85	.75
a.		Souvenir sheet of 4, #62-65	4.00	4.00
		Nos. 62-65 (4)	2.00	1.75

UN Headquarters, Emblem — A13

1970, Oct. 24 **Litho.** ***Perf. 11***

66	A13	15c ultra, red & silver	.90	.40

United Nations' 25th anniversary.

Toys A14

1970, Nov. 3 **Litho.** ***Perf. 14***

67	A14	1c Crocodile	.25	.25
68	A14	2c Giraffe	.25	.25
69	A14	7c Elephant	.25	.25
70	A14	25c Rhinoceros	.75	.90
a.		Souvenir sheet of 4, #67-70	1.80	1.80
		Nos. 67-70 (4)	1.50	1.65

Christmas.

Sorghum A15

1971, Apr. 6 **Litho.** ***Perf. 14***

71	A15	3c shown	.25	.25
72	A15	7c Millet	.25	.25
73	A15	10c Corn	.25	.25
74	A15	35c Peanuts	1.00	1.00
		Nos. 71-74 (4)	1.75	1.75

Ox Head and Botswana Map — A16

Map of Botswana and: 4c, Cogwheels and waves. 7c, Zebra rampant. 10c, Tusk and corn. 20c, Coat of arms of Botswana.

1971, Sept. 30 ***Perf. 14½x14***

75	A16	3c yel grn, blk & brn	.25	.25
76	A16	4c lt blue, blk & bl	.25	.25
77	A16	7c orange & blk	.25	.25
78	A16	10c yellow & multi	.25	.25
79	A16	20c blue & multi	.70	*2.40*
		Nos. 75-79 (5)	1.70	3.40

5th anniversary of independence.

King Bringing Gift — A17

Christmas: 2c, King bringing gift. 7c, Kneeling King with gift. 20c, Three Kings and star.

1971, Nov. 11 ***Perf. 14***

80	A17	2c brt rose & multi	.25	.25
81	A17	3c lt blue & multi	.25	.25
82	A17	7c brt pink & multi	.25	.25
83	A17	20c vio blue & multi	.25	.60
a.		Souvenir sheet of 4, #80-83	1.25	1.25
		Nos. 80-83 (4)	1.00	1.35

Constellation Orion — A18

Night sky over Botswana: 7c, Scorpio. 10c, Centaur. 20c, Southern Cross.

1972, Apr. 24 **Litho.** ***Perf. 14***

84	A18	3c dp org, bl grn & blk	1.15	.45
85	A18	7c org, blue & blk	1.40	1.00
86	A18	10c org, green & blk	1.60	1.15
87	A18	20c emer, vio bl & blk	2.25	4.00
		Nos. 84-87 (4)	6.40	6.60

Gubulawayo Cancel and Map of Trail — A19

Sections of Mafeking-Gubulawayo Trail and: 4c, Bechuanaland Protectorate No. 65. 7c, Mail runners. 20c, Mafeking 638 killer cancellation.

1972, Aug. 21 ***Perf. 13½x13***

88	A19	3c cream & multi	.30	.25
89	A19	4c cream & multi	.30	.30
90	A19	7c cream & multi	.45	.45
91	A19	20c cream & multi	1.10	1.40
a.		Souvenir sheet of 4	16.00	16.00
		Nos. 88-91 (4)	2.15	2.40

84th anniv. of Mafeking to Gubulawayo runner post. No. 91a contains one each of Nos. 88-91, arranged vertically to show map of trail. No. 91a exists with pale buff background omitted. Value, $700.

Compare with design A89.

Cross, Map of Botswana, Bells — A20

Cross, map of Botswana and: 3c, Candle. 7c, Christmas tree. 20c, Star and holly.

1972, Nov. 6 **Litho.** ***Perf. 14***

92	A20	2c yellow & multi	.25	.25
93	A20	3c pale lilac & multi	.25	.25
94	A20	7c yel green & multi	.25	.25
95	A20	20c pink & multi	.25	.25
a.		Souvenir sheet of 4, #92-95	1.80	1.80
		Nos. 92-95 (4)	1.00	1.00

Christmas.

Chariot of the Sun, Trundholm, Denmark — A21

WMO Emblem and: 3c, Thor, Norse thunder god, vert. 7c, Ymir, Icelandic frost giant, vert. 20c, Odin on 8-legged horse Sleipnir.

1973, Mar. 23 **Litho.** ***Perf. 14***

96	A21	3c orange & multi	.25	.25
97	A21	4c yellow & multi	.35	.25
98	A21	7c ultra & multi	.40	.25
99	A21	20c gold & multi	1.10	1.05
		Nos. 96-99 (4)	2.10	1.80

Intl. meteorological cooperation, cent.

Livingstone and Boat on Lake Ngwami — A22

Design: 20c, Livingstone and his meeting with Henry Stanley.

1973, Sept. 10 **Litho.** ***Perf. 13½x14***

100	A22	3c gray & multi	.25	.25
101	A22	20c yel green & multi	1.20	1.20

Dr. David Livingstone (1813-1873), medical missionary and explorer.

Shepherd and Flock — A23

Christmas: 3c, Ass and foal, African huts, vert. 7c, African mother, child and star, vert. 20c, Tribal meeting (kgotla), symbolic of Wise Men.

1973, Nov. 12 **Litho.** ***Perf. 14½***

102	A23	3c multicolored	.25	.25
103	A23	4c multicolored	.25	.25
104	A23	7c multicolored	.25	.25
105	A23	20c multicolored	.25	*.75*
		Nos. 102-105 (4)	1.00	1.50

Gaborone Campus, Botswana A24

Designs: 7c, Kwaluseni Campus, Swaziland. 20c, Roma Campus, Lesotho. 35c, Map and flags of Botswana, Swaziland & Lesotho.

1974, May 8 **Litho.** ***Perf. 14***

106	A24	3c lt blue & multi	.25	.25
107	A24	7c yel green & multi	.25	.25
108	A24	20c yel green & multi	.25	.25
109	A24	35c brt blue & multi	.25	.25
		Nos. 106-109 (4)	1.00	1.00

10th anniversary of the University of Botswana, Lesotho and Swaziland.

UPU Emblem, Mail Vehicles — A25

UPU, cent.: 3c, Post Office, Palapye, c. 1889. 7c, Bechuanaland police camel post, 1900. 20c, 1920 and 1974 planes.

1974, May 22 **Litho.** ***Perf. 13½x14***

110	A25	2c car & multi	.65	.40
111	A25	3c green & multi	.65	.40
112	A25	7c brown & multi	1.10	.80
113	A25	20c blue & multi	3.00	2.75
		Nos. 110-113 (4)	5.40	4.35

Gems and Minerals A26

1c, Amethyst. 2c, Agate Botswana pink. 3c, Quartz. 4c, Niccolite. 5c, Moss agate. 7c, Agate. 10c, Stilbite. 15c, Moshaneng banded marble. 20c, Gem diamonds. 25c, Chrysotile. 35c, Jasper. 50c, Moss quartz. 1r, Citrine. 2r, Chalcopyrite.

1974, July 1 **Photo.** ***Perf. 14x13***

114	A26	1c multi	.65	*2.50*
115	A26	2c multi	.65	*2.50*
116	A26	3c multi	.70	*.80*
117	A26	4c multi	.80	.60
118	A26	5c multi	.80	*1.00*
119	A26	7c multi	.90	1.25
120	A26	10c multi	1.75	.65
121	A26	15c multi	2.25	*4.00*
122	A26	20c multi	4.50	4.00
123	A26	25c multi	5.50	2.50
124	A26	35c multi	5.50	4.75
125	A26	50c multi	5.00	*5.50*
126	A26	1r multi	8.25	*10.00*
127	A26	2r multi	22.00	20.00
		Nos. 114-127 (14)	59.25	60.05

For surcharges see Nos. 155-168.

Stapelia Variegata — A27

Flowers of Botswana: 7c, Hibiscus lunarifolius. 15c, Ceratotheca triloba. 20c, Nerine laticoma.

1974, Nov. 4 **Litho.** ***Perf. 14***

128	A27	2c multicolored	.40	*.45*
129	A27	7c multicolored	.55	.25
130	A27	15c multicolored	.85	*1.00*
131	A27	20c multicolored	1.15	*1.25*
a.		Souvenir sheet of 4, #128-131	4.00	4.00
		Nos. 128-131 (4)	2.95	2.95

Pres. Sir Seretse Khama — A28

1975, Mar. 24 **Photo.** ***Perf. 13½x13***

132	A28	4c olive & multi	.25	.25
133	A28	10c yellow & multi	.25	.25
134	A28	20c ultra & multi	.25	.25
135	A28	35c brown & multi	.40	.40
a.		Souvenir sheet of 4, #132-135	1.10	*1.25*
		Nos. 132-135 (4)	1.15	1.15

10th anniv. of self-government.

Ostrich and Rock Painting A29

Paintings and animals: 10c, Rhinoceros. 25c, Hyena. 35c, Scorpion.

1975, June 23 **Litho.** ***Perf. 14x14½***

136	A29	4c yel green & multi	1.00	.25
137	A29	10c buff & multi	1.60	.25
138	A29	25c blue & multi	3.25	.60
139	A29	35c lilac & multi	3.25	1.25
a.		Souvenir sheet of 4, #136-139	17.00	17.00
		Nos. 136-139 (4)	9.10	2.35

Rock paintings from Tsodilo Hills.

Map of British Bechuanaland A30

Chiefs Sobele, Bathoen and Khama A31

Design: 10c, Khama the Great, antelope.

Perf. 14½x14, 14x14½

1975, Oct. 31 **Litho.**

140	A30	6c buff & multi	.45	.25
141	A30	10c rose & multi	.55	.25
142	A31	25c lt green & multi	1.15	.80
		Nos. 140-142 (3)	2.15	1.30

Establishment of Protectorate, 90th anniv. (6c); Khama the Great (1828-1923), centenary of his accession as chief (10c); visit of the chiefs of the Bakwena, Bangwaketse and Bamangwato tribes to London, 80th anniv. (25c).

Aloe Marlothii — A32

Christmas: 10c, Aloe lutescens. 15c, Aloe zebrina. 25c, Aloe littoralis.

1975, Nov. 3 **Litho.** ***Perf. 14½x14***

143	A32	3c multicolored	.40	.25
144	A32	10c multicolored	.80	.25
145	A32	15c multicolored	1.20	*1.75*
146	A32	25c multicolored	1.50	*2.75*
		Nos. 143-146 (4)	3.90	5.00

Traditional Musical Instruments — A33

Designs: 4c, Drum. 10c, Hand piano. 15c, Segankuru (violin). 25c, Kudu signal horn.

1976, Mar. 1 Litho. *Perf. 14*

147	A33	4c yellow & multi	.25	.25
148	A33	10c lilac & multi	.25	.25
149	A33	15c dull yel & multi	.35	*.55*
150	A33	25c lt blue & multi	.40	*1.25*
		Nos. 147-150 (4)	1.25	2.30

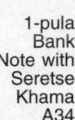

1-pula Bank Note with Seretse Khama A34

Reverse of Bank Notes: 10c, Basket weaver, hut builder. 15c, Antelopes. 25c, National Assembly building.

1976, June 28 Litho. *Perf. 14*

151	A34	4c rose & multi	.25	.25
152	A34	10c brt green & multi	.25	.25
153	A34	15c yel green & multi	.35	.25
154	A34	25c blue & multi	.45	.45
a.		Souvenir sheet of 4, #151-154	2.40	*3.50*
		Nos. 151-154 (4)	1.30	1.20

First national currency.

Nos. 114-127 Surcharged in Black or Gold

Type I

Type II

Type I surcharge: Thick numerals and "t."
Type II surcharge: Thin numerals and "t."

Type I

1976, Aug. 23 Photo. *Perf. 14x13*

155	A26	1t on 1c multi	2.30	.70
156	A26	2t on 2c multi	2.30	1.00
157	A26	3t on 3c multi (G)	1.75	.60
158	A26	4t on 4c multi	2.75	.45
159	A26	5t on 5c multi	2.75	.45
160	A26	7t on 7c multi	1.45	*2.50*
161	A26	10t on 10c multi	1.45	.80
162	A26	15t on 15c multi (G)	5.00	2.75
163	A26	20t on 20c multi	8.50	.80
164	A26	25t on 25c multi	5.75	1.25
165	A26	35t on 35c multi	4.75	4.75
166	A26	50t on 50c multi	6.25	*9.00*
167	A26	1p on 1r multi	7.00	*9.50*
168	A26	2p on 2r multi (G)	9.25	11.50
		Nos. 155-168 (14)	61.25	46.05

1977, July 15 Type II

155a	A26	1t on 1c multi	2.25	.80
156a	A26	2t on 2c multi	2.25	.80
158a	A26	4t on 4c multi	2.60	.80
159a	A26	5t on 5c multi	2.60	.80
162a	A26	15t on 15c multi (G)	6.00	1.50
163a	A26	20t on 20c multi (G)	7.75	1.50
		Nos. 155a-163a (6)	23.45	6.20

The government printer in Pretoria applied the typographed type I surcharge. Enschede applied the lithographed type II surcharge.

1977, Aug. 3 - Oct. 17 Type I
Surcharge at Bottom Right

157b	A26	3t on 3c multi	*60.00*	*17.50*
160b	A26	7t on 7c multi	*70.00*	*22.50*
166b	A26	50t on 50c multi	*300.00*	*75.00*
167b	A26	1p on 1r multi	*90.00*	*45.00*
		Nos. 157b-167b (4)	*520.00*	*160.00*

Cattle Industry A35

Designs: 10t, Antelope, tourism, vert. 15t, Schoolhouse and children, education. 25t, Rural weaving, vert. 35t, Mining industry, vert.

1976, Sept. 30 Litho. *Perf. 14x14½*
Textured Paper

169	A35	4t multicolored	.25	.25
170	A35	10t multicolored	.25	.25
171	A35	15t multicolored	.25	.50
172	A35	25t multicolored	.25	.65
173	A35	35t multicolored	.95	*1.00*
		Nos. 169-173 (5)	1.95	2.65

10th anniversary of independence.

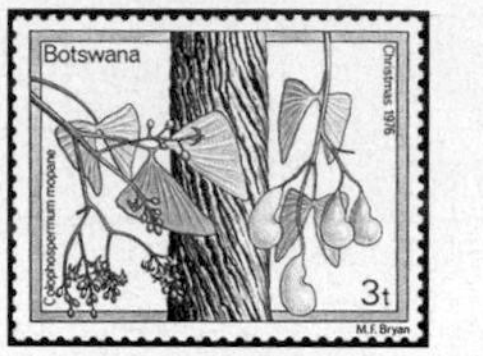

Colophospermum Mopane — A36

Trees: 4t, Baikiaea plurijuga. 10t, Sterculia rogersii. 25t, Acacia nilotica. 40t, Kigelia africana.

1976, Nov. 1 Litho. *Perf. 13*

174	A36	3t multicolored	.30	.25
175	A36	4t multicolored	.30	.25
176	A36	10t multicolored	.40	.25
177	A36	25t multicolored	.90	.90
178	A36	40t multicolored	1.50	1.50
		Nos. 174-178 (5)	3.40	3.15

Christmas.

Pres. Seretse Khama and Elizabeth II — A37

Designs: 25t, Coronation coach in procession. 40t, Recognition scene.

1977, Feb. 7 Litho. *Perf. 12*

179	A37	4t multicolored	.25	.25
180	A37	25t multicolored	.25	.25
181	A37	40t multicolored	.35	.50
		Nos. 179-181 (3)	.85	1.00

Reign of Queen Elizabeth II, 25th anniv.

Clawless Otter — A38

World Wildlife Fund Emblem and: 4t, Serval. 10t, Bat-eared foxes. 25t, Pangolins. 40t, Brown hyena.

1977, June 6 Litho. *Perf. 14*

182	A38	3t multicolored	6.75	.70
183	A38	4t multicolored	6.75	.70
184	A38	10t multicolored	7.75	.70
185	A38	25t multicolored	17.50	3.25
186	A38	40t multicolored	21.00	12.00
		Nos. 182-186 (5)	59.75	17.35

Endangered wildlife.

Khama Memorial A39

Designs: 4t, Gcwihaba Caverns. 15t, Green's (expedition) tree. 20t, Mmajojo ruins. 25t, Ancient morabaraba board. 35t, Matsieng's footprints.

1977, Aug. 22 Litho. *Perf. 14*

187	A39	4t multicolored	.30	.25
188	A39	5t multicolored	.30	.25
189	A39	15t multicolored	.50	.40
190	A39	20t multicolored	.50	.50
191	A39	25t multicolored	.50	.50
192	A39	35t multicolored	.65	.65
a.		Souvenir sheet of 6, #187-192	3.75	3.75
		Nos. 187-192 (6)	2.75	2.55

Historical sites and national monuments.

Lilies — A40

Designs: 3t, Hypoxis Itida. 5t, Haemanthus magnificus. 10t, Boophane disticha. 25t, Vellozia retinervis. 40t, Ammocharis coranica.

1977, Nov. 7 Litho. *Perf. 14*

193	A40	3t sepia & multi	.25	.25
194	A40	5t gray & multi	.25	.25
195	A40	10t multicolored	.25	.25
196	A40	25t multicolored	.50	*.65*
197	A40	40t multicolored	.90	*1.25*
		Nos. 193-197 (5)	2.15	2.65

Christmas.

Birds — A41

1t, Black korhaan. 2t, Marabou storks. 3t, Red-billed hoopoe. 4t, Carmine bee-eaters. 5t, African jacana. 7t, Paradise flycatcher. 10t, Bennett's woodpecker. 15t, Red bishop. 20t, Crowned plovers. 25t, Giant kingfishers. 30t, White-faced ducks. 35t, Green-backed heron. 45t, Black-headed herons. 50t, Spotted eagle owl. 1p, Gabar goshawk. 2p, Martial eagle. 5p, Saddlebill storks.

1978, July 3 Photo. *Perf. 14*

198	A41	1t multicolored	.90	*1.20*
199	A41	2t multicolored	1.20	1.20
200	A41	3t multicolored	.90	.90
201	A41	4t multicolored	2.60	*1.00*
202	A41	5t multicolored	1.30	.40
203	A41	7t multicolored	1.30	*2.75*
204	A41	10t multicolored	2.60	.60
205	A41	15t multicolored	2.00	*2.75*
206	A41	20t multicolored	2.25	2.00
207	A41	25t multicolored	.90	*3.00*
208	A41	30t multicolored	.90	.90
209	A41	35t multicolored	.90	*3.00*
210	A41	45t multicolored	1.30	*2.75*
211	A41	50t multicolored	6.50	4.50
212	A41	1p multicolored	3.25	*4.50*
213	A41	2p multicolored	4.00	*8.00*
214	A41	5p multicolored	7.25	*16.00*
		Nos. 198-214 (17)	40.05	55.45

For surcharges see Nos. 289-290.

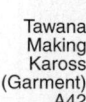

Tawana Making Kaross (Garment) A42

Designs: 5t, Map of Okavango Delta. 15t, Bushman collecting roots. 20t, Herero woman milking cow. 25t, Yei pulling mokoro (boat). 35t, Mbukushu fishing.

1978, Sept. 11 Litho. *Perf. 14*
Textured Paper

215	A42	4t multicolored	.25	*.30*
216	A42	5t multicolored	.25	.25
217	A42	15t multicolored	.25	*.40*
218	A42	20t multicolored	.30	*.65*
219	A42	25t multicolored	.35	*.60*
220	A42	35t multicolored	.60	*1.50*
a.		Souvenir sheet of 6, #215-220	2.25	*3.50*
		Nos. 215-220 (6)	2.00	*3.70*

People of the Okavango Delta.

Caralluma Lutea — A43

Flowers: 10t, Hoodia lugardii. 15t, Ipomoea transvaalensis. 25t, Ansellia gigantea.

1978, Nov. 6

221	A43	5t multicolored	.40	.25
222	A43	10t multicolored	.50	.25
223	A43	15t multicolored	1.10	.60
224	A43	25t multicolored	1.25	.80
		Nos. 221-224 (4)	3.25	1.90

Christmas.

Boy at Sip Well — A44

Water Development: 5t, Watering pit. 10t, Hand-dug well and goats. 25t, Windmill, well and cattle. 40t, Modern drilling rig.

1979, Mar. 30 Litho. *Perf. 14*

225	A44	3t multicolored	.25	.25
226	A44	5t multicolored	.25	.25
227	A44	10t multicolored	.25	.25
228	A44	25t multicolored	.25	.25
229	A44	40t multicolored	.30	.30
		Nos. 225-229 (5)	1.30	1.30

Botswana Pot — A45

Handicrafts: 10t, Clay buffalo. 25t, Woven covered basket. 40t, Beaded bag.

1979, June 11 Litho. *Perf. 14*

230	A45	5t multicolored	.25	.25
231	A45	10t multicolored	.25	.25
232	A45	25t multicolored	.25	.25
233	A45	40t multicolored	.50	.50
a.		Souvenir sheet of 4, #230-233	1.50	1.50
		Nos. 230-233 (4)	1.25	1.25

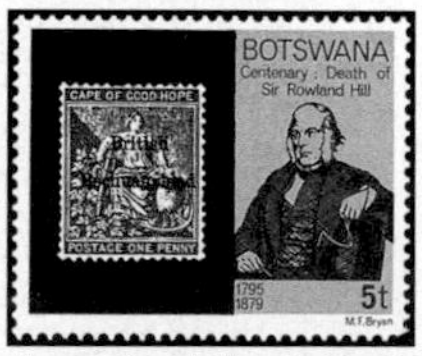

Bechuanaland No. 6, Rowland Hill — A46

Sir Rowland Hill (1795-1879), originator of penny postage, and: 25t, Bechuanaland Protectorate No. 107. 45t, Botswana No. 20.

1979, Aug. 27 Litho. *Perf. 13½*

234	A46	5t rose & black	.25	.25
235	A46	25t multicolored	.35	.35
236	A46	45t multicolored	.50	.50
		Nos. 234-236 (3)	1.10	1.10

Children Playing A47

Design: 10t, Child playing with rag doll, and IYC emblem, vert.

1979, Sept. 24 *Perf. 14*

237	A47	5t multicolored	.25	.25
238	A47	10t multicolored	.25	.25

International Year of the Child.

Ximenia Caffra — A48

Christmas: 10t, Sclerocarya caffra. 15t, Hexalobus monopetalus. 25t, Ficus soldanella.

1979, Nov. 12 **Litho.** *Perf. 14*

239	A48 5t multicolored	.25	.25
240	A48 10t multicolored	.25	.25
241	A48 15t multicolored	.45	.45
242	A48 25t multicolored	.60	.60
	Nos. 239-242 (4)	1.55	1.55

Flap-Necked Chameleon A49

10t, Leopard tortoise. 25t, Puff adder. 40t, White-throated monitor.

1980, Mar. 3 **Litho.** *Perf. 14*

243	A49 5t shown	.80	.25
244	A49 10t multicolored	.80	.30
245	A49 25t multicolored	1.30	1.25
246	A49 40t multicolored	1.60	*3.00*
	Nos. 243-246 (4)	4.50	4.80

Rock Breaking (Early Mining) A50

1980, July 7 **Litho.** *Perf. 13½x14*

247	A50 5t shown	.35	.25
248	A50 10t Ore hoisting	.45	.25
249	A50 15t Ore transport	1.00	.80
250	A50 20t Ore crushing	1.10	1.10
251	A50 25t Smelting	1.15	1.10
252	A50 35t Tools, products	1.45	*1.50*
	Nos. 247-252 (6)	5.50	5.00

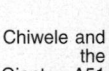

Chiwele and the Giant — A51

Folktales: 10t, Kgori Is Not Deceived. 30t, Nyambi's Wife and Crocodile. 45t, Clever Hare, horiz.

Perf. 14, 14½ (10t, 30t)

1980, Sept. 8

253	A51 5t multicolored	.25	.25

Size: 28x36mm

254	A51 10t multicolored	.25	.25
255	A51 30t multicolored	.50	.50

Size: 44x26mm

256	A51 45t multicolored	.65	.65
	Nos. 253-256 (4)	1.65	1.65

Game Watching — A52

1980, Oct. 6 **Litho.** *Perf. 14*

257	A52 5t multicolored	.70	.40

World Tourism Conf., Manila, Sept. 27.

Christmas — A53

10t, Acacia nilotica. 25t, Acacia erubescens. 40t, Dichrostachys cinerea.

1980, Nov. 3 **Litho.** *Perf. 14*

258	A53 5t shown	.25	.25
259	A53 10t multicolored	.25	.25
260	A53 25t multicolored	.60	.35
261	A53 40t multicolored	.95	.70
	Nos. 258-261 (4)	2.05	1.55

Heinrich von Stephan, Bechuanaland Protectorate No. 150, Botswana No. 111 — A55

Design: 20t, Von Stephan, Bechuanaland Protectorate No. 151, Botswana No. 112.

1981, Jan. 7 *Perf. 14*

266	A55 6t multicolored	.65	.35
267	A55 20t multicolored	1.75	*2.25*

Von Stephan (1831-1897), founder of UPU.

Emperor Dragonfly — A56

7t, Praying mantis. 10t, Elegant grasshopper. 20t, Dung beetle. 30t, Citrus swallowtail butterfly. 45t, Mopane worm.

1981, Feb. 23 **Litho.** *Perf. 14*

268	A56 6t shown	.40	.25
269	A56 7t multicolored	.40	.25
270	A56 10t multicolored	.40	.25
271	A56 20t multicolored	.75	.55
272	A56 30t multicolored	1.00	.75
273	A56 45t multicolored	1.25	1.25
a.	Souv. sheet of 6, #268-273	7.00	7.00
	Nos. 268-273 (6)	4.20	3.30

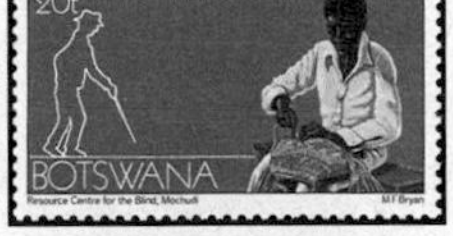

Blind Basket Weaver A57

1981, Apr. 6 **Litho.** *Perf. 14*

274	A57 6t Seamstress	.25	.25
275	A57 20t shown	.65	.35
276	A57 30t Carpenter	.85	.45
	Nos. 274-276 (3)	1.75	1.05

International Year of the Disabled.

Woman Reading Letter (Literacy Campaign) — A58

7t, Man sending telegram. 20t, Boy, newspaper. 30t, Father and daughter reading.

1981, June 8

277	A58 6t shown	.25	.25
278	A58 7t multicolored	.25	.25
279	A58 20t multicolored	.45	.35
280	A58 30t multicolored	.65	.45
	Nos. 277-280 (4)	1.60	1.30

Pres. Seretse Khama (1921-80) and Flag A59

Portrait and various local buildings: 6t, 10t, 45t..

1981, July 13

281	A59 6t multicolored	.25	.25
282	A59 10t multicolored	.25	.25
283	A59 30t multicolored	.45	.45
284	A59 45t multicolored	.55	.55
	Nos. 281-284 (4)	1.50	1.50

Cattle in Agricultural Show — A60

1981, Sept. 21 **Litho.** *Perf. 14½*

285	A60 6t Plowing	.25	.25
286	A60 20t shown	.35	.25
287	A60 30t Meat Commission	.50	.40
288	A60 45t Vaccine Institute	.70	.60
	Nos. 285-288 (4)	1.80	1.50

Nos. 204, 209 Surcharged

1981, Sept. 1 **Photo.** *Perf. 14*

289	A41 25t on 35t multicolored	4.75	3.50
290	A41 30t on 10t multicolored	4.75	3.50

Christmas — A61

Designs: Water lilies.

1981, Nov. 11 **Litho.**

291	A61 6t Nymphaea caerulea	.30	.25
292	A61 10t Nymphoides indica	.35	.25
293	A61 25t Nymphaea lotus	.80	*.90*
294	A61 40t Ottelia kunenensis	1.05	*2.25*
	Nos. 291-294 (4)	2.50	3.65

Children's Drawings — A62

1982, Feb. 15 **Litho.** *Perf. 14½x14*

295	A62 6t Cattle	.50	.25
296	A62 10t Kgotla meeting	.65	.25
297	A62 30t Village	2.25	1.50
298	A62 45t Huts	2.25	2.25
	Nos. 295-298 (4)	5.65	4.25

Traditional Houses — A63

1982, May 3 **Litho.** *Perf. 14*

299	A63 6t Common type	.50	.25
300	A63 10t Kgatleng	.60	.25
301	A63 30t Northeastern	2.25	1.25
302	A63 45t Sarwa	2.25	3.00
	Nos. 299-302 (4)	5.60	4.75

Red-billed Teals — A64

1t, Masked weaver. 2t, Lesser double-collared sunbirds. 3t, White-fronted bee-eaters. 4t, Ostriches. 5t, Grey-headed gulls. 6t, Pygmy geese. 7t, Cattle egrets. 8t, Lanner falcon. 10t, Yellow-billed storks. 20t, Barn owls. 25t, Hamerkops. 30t, Stilts. 35t, Blacksmith plovers. 45t, Wattled plover. 50t, Crowned guinea-fowl. 1p, Cape vultures. 2p, Augur bustards.

Perf. 14x14½, 14½x14

1982, Aug. 2 **Photo.**

303	A64 1t multicolored	.95	*1.75*
304	A64 2t multicolored	1.15	*1.75*
305	A64 3t multicolored	1.40	*1.75*
306	A64 4t multicolored	1.40	*1.75*
307	A64 5t multicolored	1.40	*1.75*
308	A64 6t multicolored	1.40	.45
309	A64 7t multicolored	1.40	.25
310	A64 8t multicolored	3.25	1.60
311	A64 10t multicolored	1.40	.25
312	A64 15t shown	3.25	.30
313	A64 20t multicolored	6.50	3.75
314	A64 25t multicolored	3.75	.85
315	A64 30t multicolored	4.50	1.00
316	A64 35t multicolored	4.50	.90
317	A64 45t multicolored	4.50	2.00
318	A64 50t multicolored	5.50	2.75
319	A64 1p multicolored	10.50	*12.00*
320	A64 2p multicolored	13.00	*17.00*
	Nos. 303-320 (18)	69.75	51.85

Nos. 303-311 vert.

For surcharges see Nos. 401-403.

Christmas — A65

Designs: Mushrooms.

1982, Nov. 2 **Litho.** *Perf. 14½*

321	A65 7t Shaggy mane	2.75	.25
322	A65 15t Orange milk	4.25	.75
323	A65 35t Panther	6.75	2.25
324	A65 50t King boletus	8.50	*9.00*
	Nos. 321-324 (4)	22.25	12.25

A66

7t, Pres. Quett Masire. 15t, Dancers. 35t, Melbourne Conference Center. 45t, Heads of State meeting.

1983, Mar. 14 **Litho.** *Perf. 14*

325	A66 7t multicolored	.25	.25
326	A66 15t multicolored	.25	.25
327	A66 35t multicolored	.60	*.65*
328	A66 45t multicolored	.70	*1.00*
	Nos. 325-328 (4)	1.80	2.15

Commonwealth Day.

Endangered Species — A67

7t, Wattle crane. 15t, Aloe lutescens. 35t, Roan antelope. 50t, Hyphaene ventricosa.

1983, Apr. 19 Litho. *Perf. 14x14½*

329 A67 7t multi	4.00	.50
330 A67 15t multi	3.50	.90
331 A67 35t multi	4.00	3.00
332 A67 50t multi	4.50	5.75
Nos. 329-332 (4)	16.00	10.15

Wooden Spoons — A68

1983, June 18 Litho. *Perf. 14*

333 A68 7t shown	.40	.25
334 A68 15t Jewelry	.75	.30
335 A68 35t Ox-hide milk bag	1.25	.75
336 A68 50t Decorated knives	1.65	1.10
a. Souvenir sheet of 4, #333-336	8.25	8.25
Nos. 333-336 (4)	4.05	2.40

Christmas A69

Dragonflies: 6t, Pantala flavescens. 15t, Anax imperator. 25t, Trithemis arteriosa. 45t, Chlorolestes elegans.

1983, Nov. 7 Litho. *Perf. 14½x14*

337 A69 6t multicolored	1.00	.25
338 A69 15t multicolored	2.25	.40
339 A69 25t multicolored	2.50	.80
340 A69 45t multicolored	3.25	*4.75*
Nos. 337-340 (4)	9.00	6.20

Mining Industry — A70

7t, Diamonds. 15t, Lime. 35t, Copper, nickel, vert. 50t, Coal, vert.

1984, Mar. 19 Litho. *Perf. 14½*

341 A70 7t multi	3.00	.60
342 A70 15t multi	3.00	.85
343 A70 35t multi	4.75	3.50
344 A70 50t multi	5.50	*10.00*
Nos. 341-344 (4)	16.25	14.95

Traditional Transport A71

1984, June 16 Litho. *Perf. 14½x14*

345 A71 7t Man riding ox	.30	.25
346 A71 25t Sled	1.00	.75
347 A71 35t Wagon	1.30	*1.40*
348 A71 50t Cart	1.90	*2.25*
Nos. 345-348 (4)	4.50	*4.65*

Intl. Civil Aviation Org., 40th Anniv. — A72

7t, Avro 504. 10t, Westland Wessex. 15t, Junkers 52-3M. 25t, Dragon Rapide. 35t, DC-3. 50t, F27 Fokker Friendship.

1984, Oct. 8 Litho. *Perf. 14x13½*

349 A72 7t multi	.95	.25
350 A72 10t multi	1.25	.40
351 A72 15t multi	1.75	1.00
352 A72 25t multi	2.50	2.00
353 A72 35t multi	3.00	3.75
354 A72 50t multi	3.25	*7.00*
Nos. 349-354 (6)	12.70	14.40

Butterflies A73

7t, Papilio demodocus. 25t, Byblia acheloia. 35t, Hypolimnas missipus. 50t, Graphium taboranus.

1984, Nov. 5 Litho. *Perf. 14½x14*

355 A73 7t multicolored	2.75	.30
356 A73 25t multicolored	4.25	1.75
357 A73 35t multicolored	4.75	3.25
358 A73 50t multicolored	6.25	*11.00*
Nos. 355-358 (4)	18.00	16.30

Christmas 1984.

Traditional & Exotic Foods — A74

7t, Man preparing seswaa. 15t, Woman preparing bogobe. 25t, Girl eating madilla. 50t, Woman collecting caterpillars.

1985, Mar. 18 Litho. *Perf. 14½*

359 A74 7t multicolored	.65	.30
360 A74 15t multicolored	.90	.55
361 A74 25t multicolored	1.25	1.00
362 A74 50t multicolored	2.10	2.10
a. Souvenir sheet of 4, #359-362	10.50	10.50
Nos. 359-362 (4)	4.90	3.95

Southern African Development Coordination Conference, 5th anniv.

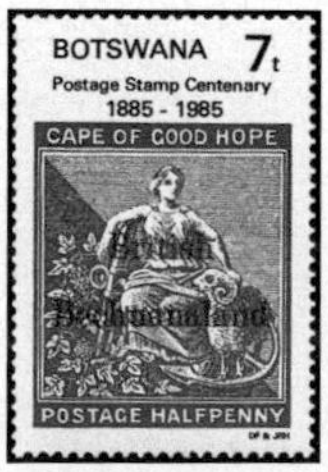

Bechuanaland No. 4 — A75

Postage stamp cent.: 15t, Bechuanaland Protectorate No. 72. 25t, Bechuanaland Protectorate No. 106. 35t, Bechuanaland No. 199, 50t, Botswana No. 1, horiz.

1985, June 24

363 A75 7t multicolored	1.25	.25
364 A75 15t multicolored	2.25	.60
365 A75 25t multicolored	2.75	.85
366 A75 35t multicolored	3.25	2.25
367 A75 50t multicolored	3.50	4.50
Nos. 363-367 (5)	13.00	8.45

Police Centenary A76

Designs: 7t, Bechuanaland Border Police, 1885-95. 10t, Bechuanaland Mounted Police, 1894-1902. 25t, Bechuanaland Protectorate Police, 1903-66. 50t, Botswana Motorcycle Police, 1966-85.

1985, Aug. 5 *Perf. 14½x14*

368 A76 7t multicolored	2.75	.60
369 A76 10t multicolored	3.25	.60
370 A76 25t multicolored	4.50	1.25
371 A76 50t multicolored	7.00	5.75
Nos. 368-371 (4)	17.50	8.20

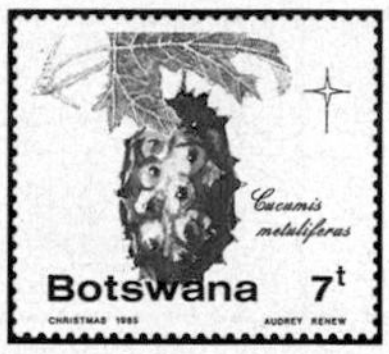

Edible Wild Cucumbers A77

7t, Cucumis metuliferus. 15t, Acanthosicyos naudinianus. 25t, Coccinia sessifolia. 50t, Momordica balsamina.

1985, Nov. 4

372 A77 7t multicolored	2.00	.65
373 A77 15t multicolored	2.00	1.00
374 A77 25t multicolored	3.25	1.90
375 A77 50t multicolored	6.00	6.00
Nos. 372-375 (4)	13.25	9.55

Christmas.

Declaration of Protectorate, Cent. — A78

7t, Heads of state meet. 15t, Declaration reading, 1885. 25t, Mackenzie and Khama. 50t, Map.

1985, Dec. 30 Litho. *Perf. 14x14½*

376 A78 7t multicolored	.50	.25
377 A78 15t multicolored	1.00	.50
378 A78 25t multicolored	1.75	1.25
379 A78 50t multicolored	4.00	*5.25*
a. Souvenir sheet of 4, #376-379	18.00	18.00
Nos. 376-379 (4)	7.25	7.25

Halley's Comet — A79

7t, Comet over Serowe. 15t, Over Bobonong. 35t, Over Gomare swamps. 50t, Over Thamaga, Letlhakeng.

1986, Mar. 24 *Perf. 14½x14*

380 A79 7t multicolored	1.10	.25
381 A79 15t multicolored	2.00	.90
382 A79 35t multicolored	2.75	1.75
383 A79 50t multicolored	3.00	*3.75*
Nos. 380-383 (4)	8.85	6.65

Milk Containers — A80

1986, June 23 *Perf. 14½*

384 A80 8t Leather bag	.40	.25
385 A80 15t Ceramic pots	.50	.40
386 A80 35t Wood pot	1.00	1.00
387 A80 50t Woman, pots	1.40	1.40
Nos. 384-387 (4)	3.30	3.05

Souvenir Sheet

Natl. Independence, 20th Anniv. — A81

No. 388: a, Map of natl. parks and reserves. b, Morupule Power Station. c, Cattle, Kgalagadi. d, Natl. Assembly.

1986, Sept. 30 Litho. *Perf. 14½x14*

388 A81 Sheet of 4	6.00	6.00
a.-d. 20t any single	1.50	1.50

Flowers of the Okavango Swamps — A82

8t, Ludwigia stogonifera. 15t, Sopubia mannii. 35t, Commelina diffusa. 50t, Hibiscus diversifolius.

1986, Nov. 3 Litho. *Perf. 14x14½*

389 A82 8t multicolored	1.50	.25
390 A82 15t multicolored	2.75	1.35
391 A82 35t multicolored	4.50	3.75
392 A82 50t multicolored	5.00	*8.00*
Nos. 389-392 (4)	13.75	13.35

Christmas.

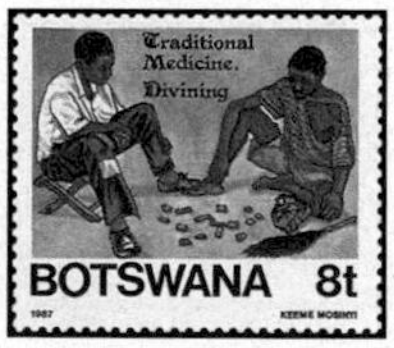

Traditional Medicine A83

8t, Professional diviners. 15t, Lightning prevention. 35t, Rainmaker. 50t, Bloodletting.

1987, Mar. 2 Litho. *Perf. 14½x14*

393 A83 8t multicolored	1.00	.25
394 A83 15t multicolored	1.90	.75
395 A83 35t multicolored	2.75	2.75
396 A83 50t multicolored	3.50	5.00
Nos. 393-396 (4)	9.15	8.75

UN Child Survival Campaign — A84

1987, June 1

397 A84 8t Oral rehydration therapy	.50	.25
398 A84 15t Growth monitoring	.80	.60
399 A84 35t Immunization	1.70	2.00
400 A84 50t Breast-feeding	2.00	3.00
Nos. 397-400 (4)	5.00	5.85

Nos. 308, 311 and 318 Surcharged

Perf. 14x14½,14½x14

1987, Apr. 1 **Photo.**

401	A64	3t on 6t No. 308	2.60	1.25
402	A64	5t on 10t No. 311	2.60	1.75
403	A64	20t on 50t No. 318	4.75	1.60
		Nos. 401-403 (3)	9.95	4.60

Wildlife Conservation — A85

1t, Cape fox. 2t, Lechwe. 3t, Zebra. 4t, Duiker. 5t, Banded mongoose. 6t, Rusty-spotted genet. 8t, Hedgehog. 10t, Scrub hare. 12t, Hippopotamus. 15t, Suricate. 20t, Caracal. 25t, Steenbok. 30t, Gemsbok. 35t, Square-lipped rhino. 40t, Mountain reedbuck. 50t, Rock dassie. 1p, Giraffe. 2p, Tsessebe. 3p, Side-striped jackal. 5p, Hartebeest.

1987, Aug. 3 *Perf. 14*

404	A85	1t multicolored	.25	*1.25*
405	A85	2t multicolored	.75	*1.75*
406	A85	3t multicolored	.25	*1.50*
407	A85	4t multicolored	.25	*1.75*
408	A85	5t multicolored	.30	*1.75*
409	A85	6t multicolored	.30	*1.75*
410	A85	8t multicolored	.45	.25
411	A85	10t multicolored	.45	.25
412	A85	12t multicolored	5.75	4.00
413	A85	15t multicolored	3.50	2.50
414	A85	20t multicolored	1.00	.75
415	A85	25t multicolored	1.00	1.50
416	A85	30t multicolored	2.10	2.00
417	A85	35t multicolored	3.50	3.50
418	A85	40t multicolored	2.50	2.00
419	A85	50t multicolored	1.30	*2.00*
420	A85	1p multicolored	3.50	*3.25*
421	A85	2p multicolored	3.50	*5.50*
422	A85	3p multicolored	5.50	*8.50*
423	A85	5p multicolored	8.50	*10.00*
		Nos. 404-423 (20)	44.65	55.75

For surcharges see Nos. 480-482, 506-509.

Wetland Grasses — A86

8t, Cyperus articulatus. 15t, Miscanthus junceus. 30t, Cyperus alopecuroides. 1p, Typha latifolia.

1987, Oct. 26 *Perf. 14x14½*

424	A86	8t multicolored	.50	.25
425	A86	15t multicolored	.80	.50
426	A86	30t multicolored	1.60	.80
427	A86	1p multicolored	3.25	5.75
a.		Souvenir sheet of 4, #424-427	8.00	8.00
		Nos. 424-427 (4)	6.15	7.30

Christmas, preservation of the Okavango and Kuando-Chobe River wetlands.

Early Cultivation Techniques A87

8t, Digging stick. 15t, Iron hoe. 35t, Wooden plow. 50t, Communal planting, Lesotla.

1988, Mar. 14 **Litho.** *Perf. 14½x14*

428	A87	8t multicolored	.55	.25
429	A87	15t multicolored	.80	.40
430	A87	35t multicolored	1.40	1.40
431	A87	50t multicolored	2.00	2.00
		Nos. 428-431 (4)	4.75	4.05

World Wildlife Fund — A88

Designs: WWF emblem and various red lechwe, Kobus leche.

1988, June 6 **Litho.** *Perf. 14½x14*

432	A88	10t Adult wading	1.20	.25
433	A88	15t Adult, sun	2.40	.75
434	A88	35t Cow, calf	3.25	2.00
435	A88	75t Herd	5.00	*8.50*
		Nos. 432-435 (4)	11.85	11.50

Runner Post, Cent. — A89

Routes and: 10t, Gubulawayo, Bechuanaland, cancellation dated Aug. 21 '88. 15t, Bechuanaland Protectorate No. 65. 30t, Pack traders. 60t, Mafeking killer cancel No. 638.

1988, Aug. 22 **Litho.** *Perf. 14½*

436	A89	10t multicolored	.50	.25
437	A89	15t multicolored	.80	.35
438	A89	30t multicolored	1.40	.85
439	A89	60t multicolored	2.25	*2.75*
a.		Souvenir sheet of 4, #436-439	13.50	13.50
		Nos. 436-439 (4)	4.95	4.20

Printed in a continuous design picturing the Mafeking-Gubulawayo route and part of the Shoshong runner post route.

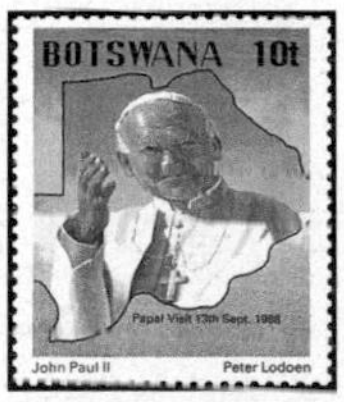

State Visit of Pope John Paul II, Sept. 13 — A90

1988, Sept. 13 **Litho.** *Perf. 14x14½*

440	A90	10t Map, portrait	2.25	.25
441	A90	15t Portrait	2.50	.35
442	A90	30t Map, portrait, diff.	3.25	.85
443	A90	80t Portrait, diff.	4.00	*5.00*
		Nos. 440-443 (4)	12.00	6.45

Natl. Museum and Art Gallery, Gaborone, 20th Anniv. — A91

8t, Museum. 15t, Pottery, c. 400-1300. 30t, Buffalo bellows. 60t, Children, mobile museum.

1988, Sept. 30 *Perf. 14½*

444	A91	8t multicolored	.35	.25
445	A91	15t multicolored	.45	.45
446	A91	30t multicolored	.80	.80
447	A91	60t multicolored	1.60	1.60
		Nos. 444-447 (4)	3.20	3.10

Flowering Plants of Southeastern Botswana — A92

8t, Grewia flava. 15t, Cienfuegosia digitata. 40t, Solanum seaforthianum. 75t, Carissa bispinosa.

1988, Oct. 31 **Litho.** *Perf. 14x14½*

448	A92	8t multicolored	.35	.25
449	A92	15t multicolored	.50	.35
450	A92	40t multicolored	1.00	.75
451	A92	75t multicolored	1.75	1.75
		Nos. 448-451 (4)	3.60	3.10

Christmas.

Traditional Grain Storage — A93

8t, Sesigo basket granary. 15t, Letlole daga granary. 30t, Sefalana bisque granary. 60t, Serala granaries.

1989, Mar. 13 **Litho.** *Perf. 14x14½*

452	A93	8t multicolored	.95	.25
453	A93	15t multicolored	1.50	.50
454	A93	30t multicolored	2.10	.75
455	A93	60t multicolored	3.25	3.00
		Nos. 452-455 (4)	7.80	4.50

Slaty Egrets A94

1989, July 5 *Perf. 15x14*

456	A94	8t Nesting	.80	.25
457	A94	15t Young	1.10	.45
458	A94	30t Adult in flight	1.50	.80
459	A94	60t Two adults	2.10	*3.00*
a.		Souvenir sheet of 4, #456-459	5.50	5.50
		Nos. 456-459 (4)	5.50	4.50

Children's Drawings A95

10t, Ephraim Seeletso. 15t, Neelma Bhatia, vert. 30t, Thabo Habana. 1p, Thabo Olesitse.

1989, Sept. 4 *Perf. 14½x14, 14x14½*

460	A95	10t multicolored	.55	.25
461	A95	15t multicolored	.75	.55
462	A95	30t multicolored	1.15	1.10
463	A95	1p multicolored	3.00	*3.50*
		Nos. 460-463 (4)	5.45	5.40

Star and Orchids — A96

8t, Eulophia angolensis. 15t, Eulophia hereoensis. 30t, Eulophia speciosa. 60t, Eulophia petersii.

1989, Oct. 30 **Litho.** *Perf. 14x14½*

464	A96	8t multicolored	1.15	.25
465	A96	15t multicolored	2.00	.65
466	A96	30t multicolored	2.50	1.15
467	A96	60t multicolored	4.25	*7.75*
		Nos. 464-467 (4)	9.90	9.80

Christmas.

Anniversaries — A97

Designs: 8t, Bechuanaland Protectorate #201. 15t, Voter at ballot box. 30t, Map & flags of nations at SADCC conference. 60t, Great Britain #1.

1990, Mar. 5 **Litho.** *Perf. 14½*

468	A97	8t multicolored	1.75	.25
469	A97	15t multicolored	1.75	.85
470	A97	30t multicolored	3.50	2.40
471	A97	60t multicolored	4.50	*8.00*
		Nos. 468-471 (4)	11.50	11.50

25th anniv. of self government (8t); 1st elections, 25th anniv. (15t); Southern African Development Coordination Conference (SADCC), 10th anniv. (30t); and Penny Black, 150th anniv. (60t).

Stamp World London '90 — A98

Aspects of the telecommunications industry.

1990, May 3

472	A98	8t Training	.65	.25
473	A98	15t Transmission	1.10	.60
474	A98	30t Public telephone	1.80	1.00
475	A98	2p Testing circuitry	4.75	*6.25*
		Nos. 472-475 (4)	8.30	8.10

Traditional Dress — A99

1990, Aug. 1 **Litho.** *Perf. 14*

476	A99	8t Children	.60	.25
477	A99	15t Young woman	1.10	.40
478	A99	30t Man	2.00	.75
479	A99	2p Adult woman	5.00	*7.00*
a.		Souvenir sheet of 4, #476-479	11.25	11.25
		Nos. 476-479 (4)	8.70	8.40

Nos. 404 & 412 Surcharged

No. 409 Surcharged

1990, Apr. 27

480	A85	10t on 1t No. 404	1.00	.25
481	A85	20t on 6t No. 409	1.75	1.00
482	A85	50t on 12t No. 412	5.50	5.50
		Nos. 480-482 (3)	8.25	6.75

Flowering Trees — A100

8t, Acacia nigrescens. 15t, Peltophorum africanum. 30t, Burkea africana. 2p, Pterocarpus angolensis.

1990, Oct. 30 Litho. *Perf. 14*

483	A100	8t multicolored	.80	.25
484	A100	15t multicolored	1.25	.45
485	A100	30t multicolored	2.25	1.00
486	A100	2p multicolored	5.00	*7.50*
		Nos. 483-486 (4)	9.30	9.20

Christmas.

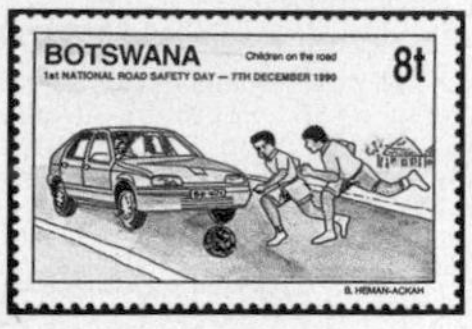

Natl. Road Safety Day A101

8t, Children playing on road. 15t, Accident. 30t, Livestock on road.

1990, Dec. 7 Litho. *Perf. 14½*

487	A101	8t multicolored	3.25	.50
488	A101	15t multicolored	3.75	1.50
489	A101	30t multicolored	4.75	3.75
		Nos. 487-489 (3)	11.75	5.75

Petroglyphs A102

Various petroglyphs.

1991, Mar. 4 Litho. *Perf. 14x14½*

Textured Paper

490	A102	8t multicolored	3.00	.50
491	A102	15t multicolored	3.50	1.00
492	A102	30t multicolored	4.25	1.75
493	A102	2p multicolored	7.50	*13.00*
		Nos. 490-493 (4)	18.25	16.25

Natl. Census — A103

8t, Children playing. 15t, Houses. 30t, Children in schoolyard. 2p, Children, hospital.

1991, June 3 Litho. *Perf. 14*

494	A103	8t multicolored	1.50	.25

Perf. 14½

495	A103	15t multicolored	2.10	.70

Perf. 14x14½

496	A103	30t multicolored	2.40	1.30
497	A103	2p multicolored	9.50	*12.50*
		Nos. 494-497 (4)	15.50	14.75

African Tourism Year A104

8t, Tourists, elephants. 15t, Birds, crocodiles. 35t, Airplane, fish eagles. 2p, Okavango Delta.

1991, Sept. 30 Litho. *Perf. 14*

498	A104	8t multicolored	3.25	1.15
499	A104	15t multicolored	3.75	1.30
500	A104	35t multicolored	7.25	4.75

Size 26x43mm

501	A104	2p multicolored	9.50	*12.00*
		Nos. 498-501 (4)	23.75	19.20

No. 501 incorporates designs of Nos. 498-500.

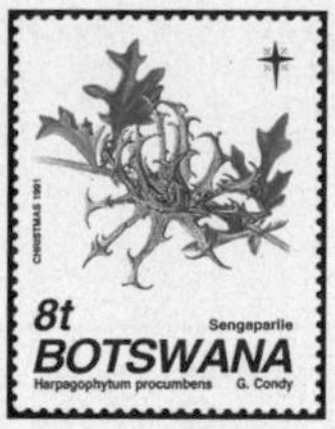

Christmas — A105

Seed pods: 8t, Harpagophytum procumbens. 15t, Tylosema esculentum. 30t, Abrus precatorius. 2p, Kigelia africana.

1991, Nov. 4 Litho. *Perf. 14*

502	A105	8t multicolored	.75	.25
503	A105	15t multicolored	1.25	.50
504	A105	30t multicolored	2.25	1.00
505	A105	2p multicolored	5.50	*8.00*
		Nos. 502-505 (4)	9.75	9.75

Nos. 406, 409 & 412 Surcharged

1992, Mar. 9 Litho. *Perf. 14*

506	A85	8t on 12t No. 412	2.75	1.00
507	A85	10t on 12t No. 412	2.75	1.00
508	A85	25t on 6t No. 409	2.00	2.25
509	A85	40t on 3t No. 406	3.50	*6.00*
		Nos. 506-509 (4)	11.00	10.25

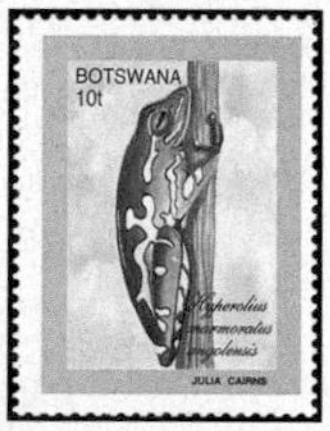

Climbing Frogs — A106

Designs: 8t, Cacosternum boettgeri, horiz. 10t, Hyperolius marmoratus angolensis. 40t, Bufo fenoulheti, horiz. 1p, Hyperolius.

1992, Mar. 23 *Perf. 14½x14, 14x14½*

510	A106	8t multicolored	1.00	.30
511	A106	10t multicolored	1.00	.30
512	A106	40t multicolored	3.00	1.50
513	A106	1p multicolored	6.00	*8.50*
		Nos. 510-513 (4)	11.00	10.60

Botswana Railways A107

Designs: 10t, Deluxe air-conditioned coaches. 25t, BD1 locomotive. 40t, Deluxe coach interio. 2p, Locomotive pulling air-conditioned coaches.

1992, June 29 Litho. *Perf. 14*

514	A107	10t multi	1.75	.50
515	A107	25t multi, vert.	2.25	1.00
516	A107	40t multi, vert.	2.50	1.25
517	A107	2p multi	3.75	*8.50*
a.		Souv. sheet of 4, #514-517 + label	17.00	17.00
		Nos. 514-517 (4)	10.25	11.25

Wild Animals A108

1t, Cheetah. 2t, Spring hares. 4t, Blackfooted cat. 5t, Striped mouse. 10t, Oribi. 12t, Pangolin. 15t, Aardwolf. 20t, Warthog. 25t, Ground squirrels. 35t, Honey badger. 40t, Common mole rat. 45t, Wild dogs. 50t, Water mongoose. 80t, Klipspringer. 1p, Lesser bushbaby. 2p, Bushveld elephant shrew. 5p, Zorilla. 10p, Vervet monkey.

1992, Aug. 3 Litho. *Perf. 14½*

518	A108	1t multicolored	.45	*2.00*
519	A108	2t multicolored	.45	*2.00*
520	A108	4t multicolored	.80	*2.00*
521	A108	5t multicolored	.80	*1.75*
522	A108	10t multicolored	1.10	.30
523	A108	12t multicolored	1.75	*3.00*
524	A108	15t multicolored	1.75	.60
525	A108	20t multicolored	1.75	.50
526	A108	25t multicolored	1.75	.30
527	A108	35t multicolored	2.00	.45
528	A108	40t multicolored	2.00	.45
529	A108	45t multicolored	2.00	.45
530	A108	50t multicolored	2.00	.55
531	A108	80t multicolored	3.50	2.75
532	A108	1p multicolored	3.50	2.75
533	A108	2p multicolored	5.50	5.50
534	A108	5p multicolored	8.00	*8.50*
535	A108	10p multicolored	10.00	*12.00*
		Nos. 518-535 (18)	49.10	45.85

For surcharges see Nos. 594A-597.

A109

1992, Aug. 7 *Perf. 14x15*

536	A109	10t Boxer	.75	.25
537	A109	50t Four sprinters	1.75	.65
538	A109	1p Two boxers	2.50	*3.00*
539	A109	2p Three runners	3.00	*4.25*
a.		Souvenir sheet of 4, #536-539	8.50	8.50
		Nos. 536-539 (4)	8.00	8.15

1992 Summer Olympics, Barcelona.

Ferns — A110

10t, Adiantum incisum. 25t, Actiniopteris radiata. 40t, Ceratopteris cornuta. 1.50p, Pellaea calomelanos.

1992, Nov. 23 Litho. *Perf. 14½*

540	A110	10t multicolored	.70	.25
541	A110	25t multicolored	1.10	.45
542	A110	40t multicolored	1.45	.70
543	A110	1.50p multicolored	4.50	*6.25*
		Nos. 540-543 (4)	7.75	7.65

Christmas.

Organizations A111

10t, Lions Intl., conquering blindness. 15t, Red Cross Society. 25t, Ecumenical Decade, churches in solidarity with women. 35t, Round Table supporting the deaf. 40t, Rotary Intl. 50t, Botswana Christian Council.

1993, Mar. 29 Litho. *Perf. 14*

544	A111	10t multi, vert.	1.00	.25
545	A111	15t multi	1.10	.50
546	A111	25t multi, vert.	1.10	.60
547	A111	35t multi	1.50	1.75
548	A111	40t multi, vert.	1.50	2.00
549	A111	50t multi	2.00	*3.00*
		Nos. 544-549 (6)	8.20	8.10

Botswana Railway, Cent. A112

Designs: 10t, Engine No. 1, 6th class 4-6-0, Bechuanaland Railways. 40t, Engine No. 317, 19th class 4-8-2. 50t, Engine No. 256, 12th class 4-8-2. 1.50p, Engine No. 71, 7th class 4-8-0, Rhodesia Railways.

1993, May 24 Litho. *Perf. 15x14*

550	A112	10t multicolored	1.10	.60
551	A112	40t multicolored	2.10	.85
552	A112	50t multicolored	2.10	1.10
553	A112	1.50p multicolored	3.00	*5.00*
a.		Souvenir sheet of 4, #550-553	8.25	8.25
		Nos. 550-553 (4)	8.30	7.55

Eagles — A113

10t, Long crested eagle. 25t, Snake eagle. 50t, Bateleur eagle. 1.50p, Secretary bird.

1993, Aug. 30 Litho. *Perf. 14½*

554	A113	10t multicolored	1.00	.50
555	A113	25t multicolored	2.00	1.00
556	A113	50t multicolored	2.50	2.50
557	A113	1.50p multicolored	4.00	*5.50*
		Nos. 554-557 (4)	9.50	9.50

Christmas A114

12t, Aloe zebrina. 25t, Croton megalobotrys. 50t, Boophane disticha. 1p, Euphorbia davyi.

1993, Oct. 25 Litho. *Perf. 14x14½*

558	A114	12t multicolored	.60	.25
559	A114	25t multicolored	.90	.30
560	A114	50t multicolored	1.25	.70
561	A114	1p multicolored	1.90	*3.50*
		Nos. 558-561 (4)	4.65	4.75

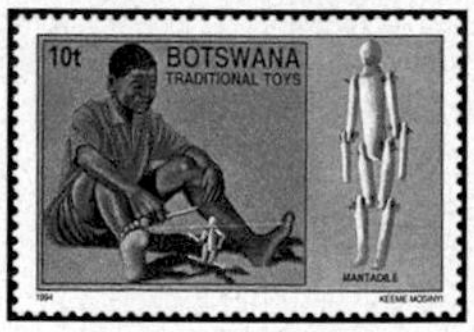

Traditional Children's Toys A115

10t, Mantadile. 40t, Dikgomo tsa mimopa. 50t, Sefuu-fuu. 1p, Mantlwane.

1994, Mar. 28 Litho. *Perf. 14½*

562	A115	10t multicolored	.45	.25
563	A115	40t multicolored	.85	.45
564	A115	50t multicolored	.95	.70
565	A115	1p multicolored	1.75	*2.60*
		Nos. 562-565 (4)	4.00	4.00

ICAO, 50th Anniv. A116

10t, Inside control tower. 25t, Fire engine. 40t, Baggage carts, vert. 50t, Control tower, vert.

Perf. 14½x14, 14x14½

1994, June 30 Litho.

566	A116	10t multicolored	.45	.25
567	A116	25t multicolored	.85	.45
568	A116	40t multicolored	.95	.70
569	A116	50t multicolored	1.75	*2.60*
		Nos. 566-569 (4)	4.00	4.00

A117

Environmental Protection: 10t, Flamingos, Sua Pan, vert. 35t, Makgadikgadi Pan trees. 50t, Zebra, Makgadikgadi Palm trees, vert. 2p, Map of Makgadikgadi Pans.

1994, Sept. 26 Litho. *Perf. 14*

570	A117	10t multicolored	1.90	.50
571	A117	35t multicolored	.85	.50
572	A117	50t multicolored	1.30	1.00
573	A117	2p multicolored	4.50	*6.50*
		Nos. 570-573 (4)	8.55	8.50

Christmas A118

Edible fruits: 10t, Ziziphus mucronata. 25t, Strychnos cocculoides. 40t, Bauhinia petersiana. 50t, Schinziphyton rautaneii.

1994, Oct. 24

574	A118	10t multicolored	.45	.25
575	A118	25t multicolored	.65	.50
576	A118	40t multicolored	1.00	*1.10*
577	A118	50t multicolored	1.15	*1.40*
		Nos. 574-577 (4)	3.25	3.25

See Nos. 587-590.

Traditional Fishing A119

1995, Apr. 3 Litho. *Perf. 14*

578	A119	15t Spear	.60	.30
579	A119	40t Hook	1.15	.60
580	A119	65t Net	1.50	1.60
581	A119	80t Basket	2.00	*2.75*
		Nos. 578-581 (4)	5.25	5.25

UN, 50th Anniv. — A120

20t, FAO. 50t, World Food Program. 80t, Development Plan. 1p, UNICEF.

1995, Oct. 16 Litho. *Perf. 14*

582	A120	20t multicolored	.30	.25
583	A120	50t multicolored	.55	.45
584	A120	80t multicolored	1.50	1.05
585	A120	1p multicolored	1.15	*1.75*
		Nos. 582-585 (4)	3.50	3.50

World Wildlife Fund — A121

No. 586 — Hyaena brunnea: a, 20t, Adult walking right. b, 50t, Two young. c, 80t, Adult finding eggs. d, 1p, Two young, adult resting.

1995, Nov. 6

586	A121	Strip of 4, #a.-d.	5.50	5.50

No. 586 was printed in sheets of 16 containing 4 strips each of 4 stamps.

Christmas Type of 1994

20t, Adenia glauca. 50t, Pterodiscus ngamicus. 80t, Sesamothamnus lugardii. 1p, Fockea multiflora.

1995, Nov. 27 Litho. *Perf. 14*

587	A118	20t multicolored	.50	.25
588	A118	50t multicolored	.90	.45
589	A118	80t multicolored	1.50	1.50
590	A118	1p multicolored	1.60	*2.25*
		Nos. 587-590 (4)	4.50	4.45

Traditional Weapons A122

20t, Spears. 50t, Axes. 80t, Shield, knobkerries. 1p, Knives, cases.

1996, Mar. 25 Litho. *Perf. 14*

591	A122	20t multicolored	.35	.25
592	A122	50t multicolored	.65	.55
593	A122	80t multicolored	1.00	1.00
594	A122	1p multicolored	1.10	*1.30*
		Nos. 591-594 (4)	3.10	3.10

No. 523 Surcharged

Nos. 518-520 Surcharged

1994-96 Litho. *Perf. 14½*

594A	A108	10t on 12t No. 523	18.00	3.00
595	A108	20t on 2t No. 519	1.90	.80
596	A108	30t on 1t No. 518	2.10	1.40
597	A108	70t on 4t No. 520	3.25	*7.00*
		Nos. 594A-597 (4)	25.25	12.20

Issued: No. 594A, 8/1/94; others, 2/12/96.

Radio, Cent. — A123

Designs: 20t, Child listening to early radio. 50t, Mobile unit, transmitter. 80t, Local police. 1p, Radio Botswana at the Kgotila.

1996, June 3 Litho. *Perf. 14*

598	A123	20t multicolored	.30	.25
599	A123	50t multicolored	.50	.45
600	A123	80t multicolored	2.50	1.45
601	A123	1p multicolored	.85	*2.00*
		Nos. 598-601 (4)	4.15	4.15

Modern Olympic Games, Cent. — A124

Designs: 20t, Hand holding torch, laurel wreath, Olympic rings. 50t, Pierre de Coubertin. 80t, Map, flag of Botswana, athletes. 1p, Ruins of original Olympic Stadium, Olympia.

1996, July 19 Litho. *Perf. 14*

602	A124	20t multicolored	.60	.25
603	A124	50t multicolored	.80	.35
604	A124	80t multicolored	2.25	1.50
605	A124	1p multicolored	1.25	*2.00*
		Nos. 602-605 (4)	4.90	4.10

Worthy Causes — A125

Designs: 20t, Family planning education, Welfare Association. 30t, Skills for the blind, Pudulogong Rehabilitation Center. 50t, Collection of seeds, Forestry Association. 70t, Secretarial class, YWCA. 80t, Day care center, Council of Women. 1p, SOS Children's Village, Tlokweng.

1996, Sept. 23 Litho. *Perf. 14*

606	A125	20t multicolored	.35	.25
607	A125	30t multicolored	.35	.25
608	A125	50t multicolored	.50	.50
609	A125	70t multicolored	.70	*.90*
610	A125	80t multicolored	.85	*1.10*
611	A125	1p multicolored	1.00	*1.90*
		Nos. 606-611 (6)	3.75	*4.90*

Adansonia Digitata — A126

1996, Nov. 4 Litho. *Perf. 14*

612	A126	20t Leaf, flower	.40	.25
613	A126	50t Fruit	.65	.40
614	A126	80t Tree in leaf	.95	*1.10*
615	A126	1p Tree without leaves	1.10	*1.75*
		Nos. 612-615 (4)	3.10	*3.50*

Christmas.

Francistown, Cent. — A127

Designs: 20t, Tati Hotel. 50t, Railway station. 80t, Company manager's house. 1p, Monarch Mine.

1997, Apr. 21 Litho. *Perf. 14*

616	A127	20t multicolored	.70	.30
617	A127	50t multicolored	.75	.65
618	A127	80t multicolored	1.25	1.25
619	A127	1p multicolored	1.40	*2.00*
		Nos. 616-619 (4)	4.10	4.20

Birds — A128

Designs: 5t, Pel's fishing owl. 10t, Gymnogene. 15t, Meyers parrot. 20t, Harlequin quail. 25t, Marico sunbird. 30t, Kurrichane thrush. 40t, Redheaded finch. 50t, Buffalo weaver. 60t, Sacred ibis. 70t, Cape shoveller. 80t, Greater honeyguide. 1p, Woodland kingfisher. 1.25p, Purple heron. 1.50p, Yellowbilled oxpecker. 2p, Shafttailed whydah. 2.50p, White stork. 5p, Ovambo sparrowhawk. 10p, Spotted crake.

1997, Aug. 4 Litho. *Perf. 13½*

620	A128	5t multi, vert.	.70	*1.20*
621	A128	10t multi	.70	*1.20*
622	A128	15t multi, vert.	.85	*1.20*
623	A128	20t multi	.85	*1.20*
624	A128	25t multi	.85	*1.20*
625	A128	30t multi	.85	*1.20*
626	A128	40t multi, vert.	1.10	.70
627	A128	50t multi, vert.	1.10	.45
628	A128	60t multi	1.30	.85
629	A128	70t multi	1.30	.85
630	A128	80t multi	1.30	.85
631	A128	1p multi	1.50	.85
632	A128	1.25p multi, vert.	2.10	1.70
633	A128	1.50p multi	2.10	*2.40*
634	A128	2p multi, vert.	2.60	2.60
635	A128	2.50p multi, vert.	3.25	3.25
636	A128	5p multi, vert.	6.00	6.00
637	A128	10p multi, vert.	8.25	8.25
		Nos. 620-637 (18)	36.70	35.95

For surcharge, see No. 935A.

Botswana Railway, Cent. — A129

Designs: 35t, Bechuanaland Rail, 1897. 50t, Elephants on the tracks. 80t, First locomotives in Bechuanaland, Cape of Good Hope 4-6-0. 1p, 4-6-4+4-6-4 Beyer Garratt. 2p, New BD3 locomotive. 2.50p, Fantuzzi Container Stacker.

1997, July 12 Litho. *Perf. 14x14½*

638	A129	35t multicolored	.60	.35
639	A129	50t multicolored	1.00	.50
640	A129	80t multicolored	1.10	.70
641	A129	1p multicolored	1.10	.95
642	A129	2p multicolored	1.40	*1.75*
643	A129	2.50p multicolored	1.50	*2.10*
		Nos. 638-643 (6)	6.70	6.35

A130

Queen Elizabeth II and Prince Philip, 50th wedding anniv.: No. 644, Prince in casual attire. No. 645, Queen wearing white & blue hat. No. 646, Queen with horse. No. 647, Prince with horse. No. 648, Prince, Queen. No. 649, Princess Anne in riding attire.

10p, Queen, Prince riding in open carriage.

Wmk. 373

1997, Sept. 22 Litho. *Perf. 13*

644	A130	35t multicolored	.30	.30
645	A130	35t multicolored	.30	.30
a.		Pair, #644-645	.60	.60
646	A130	2p multicolored	1.50	1.50
647	A130	2p multicolored	1.50	1.50
a.		Pair, #646-647	3.00	3.00
648	A130	2.50p multicolored	1.60	1.60
649	A130	2.50p multicolored	1.60	1.60
a.		Pair, #648-649	3.25	3.25
		Nos. 644-649 (6)	6.80	6.80

Souvenir Sheet

650	A130	10p multicolored	6.00	6.00

A131

Christmas (Combretum):, 35t, Zeyheri. 1p, Apiculatum. 2p, Molle. 2.50p, Imberbe.

1997, Nov. 10 Unwmk. *Perf. 14*

651	A131	35t multicolored	.45	.25
652	A131	1p multicolored	1.10	.50
653	A131	2p multicolored	2.25	2.25
654	A131	2.50p multicolored	2.75	2.75
		Nos. 651-654 (4)	6.55	5.75

Tourism A132

1998, Mar. 23

655	A132	35t	Baobab trees	.35	.25
656	A132	1p	Crocodile	.75	.50
657	A132	2p	Stalactites, vert.	1.25	1.25
658	A132	2.50p	Tourists, vert.	1.75	*2.00*
			Nos. 655-658 (4)	4.10	4.00

Diana, Princess of Wales (1961-97)

Common Design Type

Portraits: 35t, No. 663a, Wearing red (without hat). 1p, No. 663b, Wearing red with hat. 2p, No. 663c, Wearing white (hand on face). No. 662, Greeting people.

1998, June 1 Wmk. 373 ***Perf. 13***

659	CD355	35t	multicolored	.30	.25
660	CD355	1p	multicolored	.50	.45
661	CD355	2p	multicolored	1.00	*1.25*
662	CD355	2.50p	multicolored	1.20	*1.60*
			Nos. 659-662 (4)	3.00	*3.55*

Souvenir Sheet

663	CD355	2.50p	Sheet of 4, #662, 663a-663c	5.25	5.25

Textiles — A133

Designs: 35t, Tapestry of a village. 55t, Woman arranging materials on ground. 1p, Tapestry of African map, animals, huts, people. 2p, Woman seated at loom.

2.50p, Tapestry of elephants and trees, horiz.

Perf. 14x13½

1998, Sept. 28 Litho. Unwmk.

664	A133	35t	multicolored	.55	.30
665	A133	55t	multicolored	.75	.40
666	A133	1p	multicolored	1.50	1.40
667	A133	2p	multicolored	1.75	*2.60*
			Nos. 664-667 (4)	4.55	4.70

Souvenir Sheet

Perf. 13½

668	A133	2.50p	multicolored	3.75	3.75

Christmas — A134

Berries: 35t, Ficus ingens. 55t, Ficus pygmaea. 1p, Ficus abutilifolia. 2.50p, Ficus sycomorus.

1998, Nov. 30 Litho. ***Perf. 13x13½***

669	A134	35t	multicolored	.65	.25
670	A134	55t	multicolored	.80	.25
671	A134	1p	multicolored	1.50	.70
672	A134	2.50p	multicolored	2.50	*3.50*
			Nos. 669-672 (4)	5.45	4.70

Tourism A135

Designs: 35t, Rock paintings. 55t, Salt pan. 1p, Rock paintings, diff. 2p, Baobab tree.

1999, May 24 Litho. ***Perf. 13½x14***

673	A135	35t multi	1.00	.25
674	A135	55t multi	1.50	.40

Perf. 14x13½

675	A135	1p multi, vert.	1.75	1.50
676	A135	2p multi, vert.	1.90	*2.75*
		Nos. 673-676 (4)	6.15	4.90

Souvenir Sheet

Southern African Development Community Day — A136

1999, Aug. 17 Litho. ***Perf. 14¼***

677	A136	5p multi	5.75	5.75

UPU, 125th Anniv. A137

1999, Oct. 9 Litho. ***Perf. 14¼***

678	A137	2p multicolored	2.60	2.60

Mpule Kwelagobe, Miss Universe 1999 — A138

35t, With crown, vert. 1p, With headdress. 2p, In swimsuit, vert. 2.50p, With Botswana sash. 15p, With leopard.

1999, Dec. 1 ***Perf. 14½***

679	A138	35t multi	.60	.25
680	A138	1p multi	1.25	.40
681	A138	2p multi	1.75	.95
682	A138	2.50p multi	1.90	1.00
683	A138	15p multi	10.50	*13.00*
a.		Souvenir sheet of 5, #679-683	16.50	16.50
		Nos. 679-683 (5)	16.00	15.60

River Scenes A139

Designs: 35t, Bird over river. 1p, Hippopotami in river, vert. 2p, Bird, man in canoe. 2.50p, Elephant on shore, vert.

2000, Apr. 5 Litho. ***Perf. 14***

684	A139	35t multi	.70	.25
685	A139	1p multi	1.05	.75
686	A139	2p multi	1.75	1.25
687	A139	2.50p multi	2.00	*2.25*
		Nos. 684-687 (4)	5.50	4.50

Moths A140

Designs: 35t, Mopane. 70t, Wild silk. 1p, Crimson-speckled footman. 2p, African lunar. 15p, Speckled emperor.

2000, July 19 Litho. ***Perf. 12½***

688-692	A140	Set of 5	10.00	*11.00*
692a		Souvenir sheet, #688-692	13.00	*15.00*

Literacy Decade A141

Designs: 35t, Mother and child. 70t, Old men learning to read. 2p, Man unaware of fire danger. 2.50p, Man at ATM machine.

2000, Aug. 23 ***Perf. 12***

693-696	A141	Set of 4 + labels	3.25	3.25

Kings and Presidents A142

Designs: 35t, Sebele I of Bakwena, Bathoen I of Bangwaketse, Khama III of Bangwato (60x40mm). 1p, Sir Seretse Khama. 2p, Sir Ketumile J. Masire. 2.50p, Festus G. Mogae.

Litho. & Embossed

2000, Sept. 29 ***Perf. 14***

697-700	A142	Set of 4	4.00	4.00

Botswana Flying Mission — A143

Designs: 35t, Two men, plane with yellow stripes. 1.75p, Plane, nurses, people. 2p, Plane in air, natives in boats. 2.50p, Plane, donkey cart.

2000, Nov. 3 Litho. ***Perf. 13½***

701-704	A143	Set of 4	4.50	4.50
704a		Horiz. strip of 4, #701-704, + central label	5.75	5.75

Wetlands Fauna A144

Designs: 35t, Hippopotamus. 1p, Tiger fish, tilapia. 1.75p, Wattled crane, painted reed frog, vert. 2p, Vervet monkey, Pels fishing owl, vert. 2.50p, Sitatunga, Nile crocodile, red lechwe.

2000, Dec. 6 Litho. ***Perf. 13¾***

705-709	A144	Set of 5	7.00	7.00
709a		Souvenir sheet, #705-709, perf. 13½	7.50	7.50
709b		As "a," with emblem of Hong Kong 2001 Stamp Exhibition in margin	7.75	7.75

Issued: No. 709b, 1/2/01.

See Nos. 726-730, 761-765, 775-779.

Diamonds — A145

Cut diamond and: 35t, Uncut diamonds. 1.75p, Mine. 2p, Diamond grader. 2.50p, Pendant and ring.

Serpentine Die Cut 10

2001, Feb. 1 Litho.

Self-Adhesive

710-713	A145	Set of 4	8.00	*8.50*

Unused value is for stamps with surrounding selvage. See No. 1013.

Kgalagadi Transfrontier Park A146

Designs: 35t, Pygmy falcons. 1p, Leopard. 2p, Gemsboks, flags of Botswana and South Africa. 2.50p, Bat-eared fox.

2001, May 12 Litho. ***Perf. 13x13¼***

714-717	A146	Set of 4	7.50	7.50
717a		Souvenir sheet #715, 717	4.00	4.00

See South Africa Nos. 1252-1255.

Basketry A147

Designs: 35t, Shown. 1p, Tall basket with triangles and chevrons. 2p, Basket weaver. 2.50p, Spherical basket.

2001, July 30 ***Perf. 13¼***

718-721	A147	Set of 4	3.75	3.75
721a		Souvenir sheet, #718-721	3.75	3.75

Sky Views A148

Natives and pictures of sun on horizon: 50t, 1p, 2p, 10p.

2001, Sept. 28 ***Perf. 13½***

722-725	A148	Set of 4	6.75	6.75

Wetlands Fauna Type of 2000

Designs: 50t, Water monitor, carmine bee-eaters. 1.75p, Buffalos. 2p, Savanna baboons, vert. 2.50p, Lion, vert. 3p, African elephants.

2001, Dec. 12 Litho. ***Perf. 13¾***

726-730	A144	Set of 5	6.50	6.50
730a		Souvenir sheet, #726-730, perf. 13½	6.75	6.75

Snakes A149

Designs: 50t, Black mamba. 1.75p, Spitting cobra, vert. 2.50p, Puff adder. 3p, Boomslang, vert.

2002, Mar. 22 ***Perf. 14x13¼, 13¼x14***

731-734	A149	Set of 4	4.25	*4.50*

Pottery A150

Pots: 50t, Mbukushu. 2p, Sekgatla. 2.50p, Sotswana. 3p, Kalanga.

2002, May 31 Litho. ***Perf. 13¾***
735-738 A150 Set of 4 3.75 3.75

Reign of Queen Elizabeth II, 50th Anniv. — A151

Queen Elizabeth II: 55t, Wearing crown, horiz. 2.75p, Holding flowers.

2002, July 25 ***Perf. 13x13¼, 13¼x13***
739-740 A151 Set of 2 3.00 *3.25*

Mammals — A152

Designs: 5t, Tree squirrel. 10t, Black-backed jackal. 20t, African wild cat. 30t, Slender mongoose, horiz. 40t, African civet, horiz. 55t, Elephant. 90t, Reedbuck. 1p, Kudu. 1.45p, Waterbuck. 1.95p, Sable, horiz. 2.20p, Sitatunga, horiz. 2.75p, Porcupine, horiz. 3.30p, Serval, horiz. 4p, Antbear, horiz. 5p, Bush pig, horiz. 15p, Chakma baboon.

Perf. 13½x13¼, 13¼x13½

2002, Aug. 5 Photo.

741	A152	5t multi	.25	.25
742	A152	10t multi	.25	.25
743	A152	20t multi	.35	.35
744	A152	30t multi	.45	.45
745	A152	40t multi	.60	.50
746	A152	55t multi	1.90	.50
747	A152	90t multi	.85	.50
748	A152	1p multi	.85	.50
749	A152	1.45p multi	1.25	.85
750	A152	1.95p multi	1.75	1.50
751	A152	2.20p multi	2.00	1.50
752	A152	2.75p multi	2.00	1.50
753	A152	3.30p multi	2.10	1.90
754	A152	4p multi	2.50	*2.75*
755	A152	5p multi	2.75	*3.00*
756	A152	15p multi	5.75	*8.25*
		Nos. 741-756 (16)	25.60	24.55

For surcharges see Nos. 813A-813B.

2002-03 AIDS Campaign — A153

Designs: 55t, Voluntary counseling and testing centers. 1.10p, Prevention of mother to child transmission. 2.75p, Stigma and discrimination. 3.30p, Orphan care.

2002, Dec. 1 Litho. ***Perf. 14x14¼***
757-760 A153 Set of 4 5.00 5.00

Wetlands Fauna Type of 2000

Wildlife in the Makgadikgadi Pans: 55t, Aardwolf. 1.10p, Blue wildebeest. 2.50p, Zebras, vert. 2.75p, Flamingos, vert. 3.30p, Pelican.

2002, Dec. 18 ***Perf. 13¾***
761-765 A144 Set of 5 6.75 6.75
765a Souvenir sheet, #761-765, perf. 13½ 7.00 7.00

Tourist Attractions A154

Designs: 55t, Hill of Lovers. 2.20p, Sand dunes, Bokspits. 2.75p, Moremi Waterfalls, vert. 3.30p, Entrance of Gcwihaba Cave.

2003, Mar. 27 Litho. ***Perf. 13¾***
766-769 A154 Set of 4 4.25 4.25

Beetles — A155

Designs: 55t, Ngwale. 2.20p, Kgomo-ya-buru. 2.75p, Kgomo-ya-pula. 3.30p, Lebitse. 5.50p, Kgaladuwa.

2003, Nov. 12 Litho. ***Perf. 13***
770-773 A155 Set of 4 5.00 5.00

Souvenir Sheet

774 A155 5.50p multi 5.50 *5.75*

Wetlands Fauna Type of 2000

Fauna of the Limpopo River Valley: 55t, Giraffe. 1.45p, Black eagle, Nile crocodile, vert. 2.50p, Ostrich, vert. 2.75p, Klipspringer. 3.30p, Serval cat.

2003, Dec. 23 Litho. ***Perf. 13¾***
775-779 A144 Set of 5 7.25 7.25
779a Souvenir sheet, #775-779, perf. 13½ 7.25 7.25

Contemporary Art — A156

Designs: 55t, People and Birds. 1.45p, Stylized trees. 2.75p, Stylized tree. 3.30p, Snake.

2004, Apr. 29 ***Perf. 13¾***
780-783 A156 Set of 4 5.00 5.00

Traditional Lifestyles — A157

Designs: 80t, Masimo. 2.10p, Kgotla. 3.90p, Moraka. 4.70p, Legae.

2004, June 30 Litho. ***Perf. 14***
784-787 A157 Set of 4 6.50 6.50

World Post Day — A158

Designs: 80t, Child placing letter in mail box. 2.10p, Children reading letter. 3.90p, Mailman and car. 4.70p, Woman reading letter.

2004, Oct. 9 Litho. ***Perf. 14x14¾***
788-791 A158 Set of 4 6.50 6.50

Birds A159

Designs: 5p, Cattle egrets, national bird of Botswana.

No. 793: a, 40t, Peregrine falcons, national bird of Angola. b, 50t, African fish eagles, national bird of Zambia. c, 60t, African fish eagles, national bird of Zimbabwe. d, 70t, Bar-tailed trogons. e, 80t, Purple-crested louries, national bird of Swaziland. f, 1p, African fish eagles, national bird of Namibia. g, 2p, Blue cranes, national bird of South Africa.

2004, Oct. 9 Litho. ***Perf. 14***
792 A159 5p multi 2.75 2.75

Miniature Sheet

793 A159 Sheet of 8, #a-g, #792 7.00 7.00

See Namibia No. 1052, South Africa No. 1342, Swaziland Nos. 727-735, Zambia No. 1033, and Zimbabwe No. 975.

Christmas A160

Flowers: 80t, Pterodiscus speciosus. 2.10p, Bulbine narcissifolia. 3.90p, Babiana hypogea. 4.70p, Hibiscus micranthus.

2004, Dec. 8 ***Perf. 13***
794-797 A160 Set of 4 7.00 7.00

Historic Buildings A161

Designs: 80t, Blackbeard's Store, Phalatswe, 1899. 2.10p, Primary School, 1899. 3.90p, Telegraph Office, Phalatswe, 1899. 4.70p, Magistrate's Court, Phalatswe, 1899.

2005, Mar. 21 Litho. ***Perf. 14¾x14***
798-801 A161 Set of 4 6.50 6.50

Food Crops — A162

Designs: 80t, Beans. 2.10p, Millet. 3.90p, Sorghum. 4.70p, Watermelon.

2005, June 15 Litho. ***Perf. 13¾***
802-805 A162 Set of 4 4.75 4.75

Worldwide Fund for Nature (WWF) — A163

Black-footed cat: 80t, With dead bird. 2.10p, Looking left. 3.90p, Adult and kitten. 4.70p, Close-up of head.

2005, Oct. 25 Litho. ***Perf. 13¼x13½***
806-809 A163 Set of 4 5.00 5.00
809a Sheet, 2 each #806-809 10.00 10.00

Christmas A164

Doves and pigeons: 80t, Namaqua dove. 2.10p, Red-eyed dove. 3.90p, Laughing doves. 4.70p, Green pigeons

2005, Dec. 20 ***Perf. 14x14¾***
810-813 A164 Set of 4 5.25 5.25

No. 747 Surcharged

No. 750 Surcharged

Methods and Perfs As Before

2006, Apr. 26
813A A152 80t on 90t #747 *5.25* —
813B A152 2.10p on 1.95p #750 *5.25* —

Fish A165

Designs: 80t, Nembwe. 2.10p, Tiger fish. 3.90p, Pike. 4.70p, Spotted squeaker.

2006, May 30 Litho. ***Perf. 13¼x13¾***
814-817 A165 Set of 4 5.25 5.25

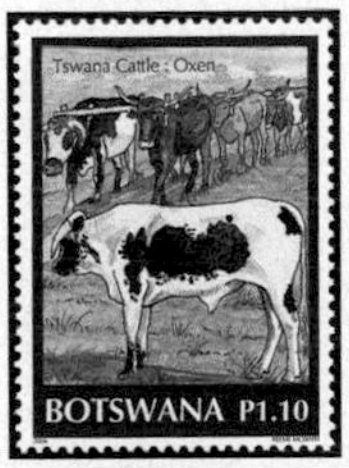

Tswana Cattle — A166

Designs: 1.10p, Oxen. 2.60p, Cows and calves. 4.10p, Bulls. 4.90p, Horn shapes.

2006, Sept. 4 Litho. ***Perf. 13¾x13¼***
818-821 A166 Set of 4 5.25 5.25

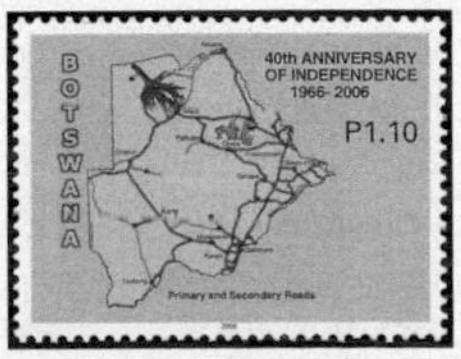

Independence, 40th Anniv. — A167

Maps of Botswana showing: 1.10p, Primary and secondary roads. 2.60p, Population distribution. 4.10p, Mines and coal resources. 4.90p, National parks and reserves.

Perf. 13¼x13¾

2006, Sept. 29 Litho.
822-825 A167 Set of 4 4.00 4.00
825a Souvenir sheet, #822-825 4.00 4.00

Christmas A168

Flora: 1.10p, Hyphaene petersiana tree. 2.60p, Phoenix reclinata tree. 4.10p, Hyphaene petersiana fruit. 4.90p, Phoenix reclinata fruit.

2006, Dec. 1 ***Perf. 13¾x13¼***
826-829 A168 Set of 4 4.00 4.00

Kingfishers A169

Designs: 1.10p, Pied kingfisher. 2.60p, Malachite kingfisher. 4.10p, Woodland kingfisher. 4.90p, Brown-hooded kingfisher.

Perf. 13¾x13¼
2007, Mar. 31 **Litho.**
830-833 A169 Set of 4 4.00 4.00

Mushrooms — A170

Designs: 1.10p, False parasols. 2.60p, Bushveld bolete. 4.10p, Lacquered bracket fungus. 4.90p, Collared earthstars.

2007, July 30 **Litho.** ***Perf. 13½x13¾***
834-837 A170 Set of 4 4.00 4.00

Miniature Sheet

National Animals — A171

No. 838: a, 1.10p, Nyala (Malawi). b, 2.60p, Nyala (Zimbabwe). c, 4.10p, Oryx (Namibia). d, 4.90p, Buffalo (Zambia). e, 5.50p, Buschell's zebra (Botswana).

Litho. With Foil Application
2007, Oct. 9 ***Perf. 13¾***
838 A171 Sheet of 5, #a-e 6.00 6.00

See Malawi No. 752, Namibia Nos. 1141-1142, Zambia Nos. 1097-1101, Zimbabwe Nos. 1064-1068.

University of Botswana, 25th Anniv. A172

Anniversary emblem and: 1.10p, Library. 2.60p, Campus appeal. 4.10p, Okavango research. 4.90p, Old and new infrastructure.

2007, Oct. 13 **Litho.** ***Perf. 14***
839-842 A172 Set of 4 4.50 4.50

Butterflies A173

Designs: 10t, Mimosa sapphire. 20t, Bushveld orange-tip. 30t, African monarch. 40t, Common black-eye. 50t, Brown playboy. 1p, Sapphire. B, Dwarf blue. 2p, Large blue emperor. A, Scarlet tip. 3p, Apricot playboy. 4p, Blue pansy. 5p, Black-striped hairtail. 10p, Natal barred blue. 20p, Foxy charaxes.

2007, Nov. 1 **Litho.** ***Perf. 13½x13¾***

843	A173	10t multi	.30	.30
844	A173	20t multi	.30	.30
845	A173	30t multi	.30	.30
846	A173	40t multi	.30	.30
847	A173	50t multi	.30	.30
848	A173	1p multi	.45	.45
849	A173	B multi	.55	.55
850	A173	2p multi	.90	.90
851	A173	A multi	1.20	1.20
852	A173	3p multi	1.30	1.30
853	A173	4p multi	1.90	1.90
854	A173	5p multi	2.25	2.25
855	A173	10p multi	4.50	4.50
856	A173	20p multi	9.00	9.00
		Nos. 843-856 (14)	23.55	23.55

On day of issue, No. 849 sold for 1.10p; No. 851 for 2.60p.

Art — A174

Designs: 1.10p, Dancer, by Boitshepo Lesego. 2.60p, Baobab Tree, by Philip Huebsch. 4.10p, Child Playing with Dolls, by Giel Kgamane. 4.90p, Donkeys Tired After Hard Work, by Tineni Kepaletswe, horiz. 5.50p, Donkeys in the City, by Andrew Jones, horiz.

2008, Mar. 28 ***Perf. 14***
857-861 A174 Set of 5 6.00 6.00

Elephants A175

Elephants and: 1.10p, Hunters. 2.60p, Tourists in boat. 4.10p, Botswana villagers. 4.90p, Riders.

2008, June 20 **Litho.** ***Perf. 14***
862-865 A175 Set of 4 4.00 4.00

2008 Summer Olympics, Beijing — A176

Designs: 1.10p, Runners. 2.60p, Boxing.

2008, Aug. 8 ***Perf. 14¼***
866-867 A176 Set of 2 1.25 1.25

National Museum, 40th Anniv. A177

Designs: 1.10p, Launch of Pitse Ya Naga (mobile museum), 1978. 2.60p, Opening of Botanical Garden, 1988, vert. 4.10p, Opening of new museum galleries, 2008. 4.90p, Tsodilo Hills rock drawings, 1998. 5.50p, Official opening, 1968, vert.

2008, Sept. 29
868-872 A177 Set of 5 5.50 5.50

Events of 2008 — A178

Designs: 4.10p, Premiere of movie filmed in Botswana, *The No. 1 Ladies Detective Agency*. 4.90p, Launch of Heart Foundation of Botswana, vert. 5.50p, Launch of Diamond Trading Company.

2008, Oct. 30
873-875 A178 Set of 3 3.75 3.75

Beetles A179

Designs: 1.10p, Small green dung beetle. 2.60p, Lunate ladybird. 4.10p, Garden fruit chafer. 4.90p, Darkling beetle.

2008, Dec. 1 ***Perf. 14x13¼***
876-879 A179 Set of 4 3.25 3.25

Endangered Birds — A180

Designs: 1.10p, Lesser flamingos. 2.60p, Gray crowned cranes, horiz. 4.10p, Wattled cranes, horiz. 4.90p, Blue cranes, horiz.

2009, June 5 **Litho.** ***Perf. 14***
880-883 A180 Set of 4 3.75 3.75

Children A181

Inscriptions: 1.10p, Education. 2.60p, Sanitation, vert. 4.10p, Inoculation, vert. 4.90p, Orphan care.

2009, Sept. 11 **Litho.** ***Perf. 14***
884-887 A181 Set of 4 4.00 4.00

Night Sky Over Botswana — A182

Botswana landscapes and: 1.10p, Southern Cross constellation, giraffes. 2.60p, Meteorite, native hunters. 4.10p, Moon, native dancers. 4.90p, Solar eclipse, lions.

2009, Nov. 18 ***Perf. 13½x13¾***
888-891 A182 Set of 4 4.00 4.00

Honey Bees A183

Apis mellifera: 1.10p, Bee at flower. 2.60p, Bees on honeycomb. 4.10p, Beehive. 4.90p, Bees at flower.

2010, Mar. 25 **Litho.** ***Perf. 14x13¼***
892-895 A183 Set of 4 3.75 3.75

2010 World Cup Soccer Championships, South Africa — A184

Soccer players, ball, 2010 World Cup mascot and flag of: Nos. 896, 905a, 1.10p, Botswana. Nos. 897, 905b, 2.60p, Namibia. Nos. 898, 905c, 3p, South Africa. Nos. 899, 905d, 4p, Zimbabwe. Nos. 900, 905e, 4.10p, Malawi. Nos. 901, 905f, 4.90p, Swaziland. Nos. 902, 905g, 5.50p, Mauritius. Nos. 903, 905h, 6.60p, Lesotho. Nos. 904, 905i, 8.20p, Zambia.

2010, Apr. 9 ***Perf. 13¾***
On Plain Paper With Olive Brown Background
896-904 A184 Set of 9 12.00 12.00
On Gold-faced Paper
905 A184 Sheet of 9, #a-i 14.00 14.00

No. 905 exists imperf. Value $800.

See Lesotho No. , Malawi No. 753, Mauritius No. 1086, Namibia No. 1188, South Africa No. 1403, Swaziland Nos. 794-803, Zambia Nos. 1115-1118, and Zimbabwe Nos. 1112-1121.

A single sheetlet of 9 omnibus issues exist containing 905a. See footnote under Namibia 1188.

Energy — A185

Designs: 2.60p, Family watching television. 4.10p, Botswanan with cell phone, solar panel outside of house. 5.50p, Man on locomotive. 6.10p, People and compact fluorescent lightbulb, horiz.

2010, Oct. 8 ***Perf. 14***
906-909 A185 Set of 4 6.00 6.00

Nocturnal Animals — A185a

Designs: 2.60p, Spring hare. 3p, Fruit bat. 4.10p, Pearl spotted owl. 5.50p, Aardwolf, horiz. 5.60p, Porcupine. 6.10p, Civet, horiz.

Perf. 13¼x13, 13x13¼

2010, Dec. 1 **Litho.**

Granite Paper

909A-909F A185a Set of 6 8.25 8.25
909g Souvenir sheet of 6, #909A-909F 8.00 8.00

Flowers — A186

Designs: 2.60p, Ipomoea obscura. 4.10p, Xenostegia tridentata. 5.50p, Ipomoea magnusiana. 6.10p, Ipomoea bolusiana.

2011, Mar. 11 ***Perf. 13¼x13¾***
910-913 A186 Set of 4 6.00 6.00

Worldwide Fund for Nature (WWF) A187

Southern white rhinoceros: 2.60p, One rhinoceros facing left. 4.10p, Two rhinoceroses facing forward. 5.50p, Two rhinoceroses facing left. 6.10p, One rhinoceros facing forward, another facing right.

2011, Nov. 21 ***Perf. 14x13¼***
914-917 A187 Set of 4 5.25 5.25
917a Souvenir sheet of 4, #914-917 5.75 5.75

No. 917a is in the shape of a rhinoceros.

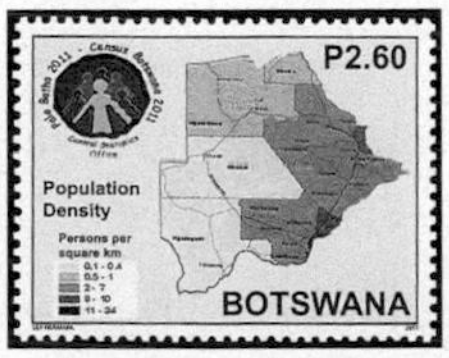

2011 Census A188

Emblem of 2011 Census and: 2.60p, Map of Botswana showing population density. 4.10p, Graduates, road, communications tower. 5.50p, Bar graph showing males and females in age groupings, vert. 6.20p, Population growth graph, vert.

2011, Sept. 9 ***Perf. 14x13¼, 13¼x14***
918-921 A188 Set of 4 5.25 5.25

Malaria Prevention A189

Inscriptions: 2.60p, Spraying of houses. 4.10p, Using anti-malaria medicines. 5.50p, Keeping surroundings clean. 6.10p, Sleeping under treated mosquito nets.

2011, Oct. 25 ***Perf. 13¼x14***
922-925 A189 Set of 4 5.25 5.25

Wild Dogs A190

Designs: 2.60p, One dog. 4.10p, Two dogs. 5.50p, Four dogs. 6.10p, Six dogs.

2011, Dec. 18 **Litho.** ***Perf. 14x13½***
926-929 A190 Set of 4 8.00 8.00

Myths and Legends A191

Designs: 3.20p, Matsieng. 4p, All the Stars in Heaven. 4.10p, Tumtumbolosa, horiz. 4.90p, Kgwanyape, horiz. 5.50p, Nonyane, horiz. 6.60p, How Death Came to the World.

Perf. 13¾x13¼, 13¼x13¾

2012 **Litho.**
930-935 A191 Set of 6 7.75 7.75

No. 625 Surcharged

Method and Perf. As Before

2013, Jan. 11
935A A128 7.30p on 30t #625 3.25 3.25

Save Water — A192

No. 936, 3.20p: a, Water flowing from spigot to bucket. b, Woman carrying water bucket.
No. 937, 4.90p: a, Water flowing from bowl to jar. b, Water cistern.
No. 938, 7.30p: a, Hands collecting water droplets over jar. b, Water pipe and pumping plant.

2013, Apr. 8 **Litho.** ***Perf. 14***

Horiz. pairs, #a-b

936-938 A192 Set of 3 7.75 7.75

Birds A193

Designs: 10t, Harlequin quail. 20t, Burchell's sandgrouse. 50t, Purple gallinule, vert. 1p, Pied avocet, vert. 2p, Kori bustard, vert. 3p, African spoonbill, vert. (3.50p), Southern red bishops, vert. 5p, African skimmer. (5.40p), Blue waxbill. (8p), Paradise flycatcher, vert. 10p, Secretary bird, vert. 20p, Bradfield's hornbill. 30p, Spotted eagle owl, vert. 50p, Southern red bishop, vert.

Perf. 14x13½, 13½x14

2014, May 13 **Litho.**

939	A193	10t	multi	.25	.25
940	A193	20t	multi	.25	.25
941	A193	50t	multi	.25	.25
942	A193	1p	multi	.25	.25
943	A193	2p	multi	.45	.45
944	A193	3p	multi	.70	.70
945	A193	(3.50p)	multi	.80	.80
946	A193	5p	multi	1.10	1.10
947	A193	(5.40p)	multi	1.25	1.25
948	A193	(8p)	multi	1.90	1.90
949	A193	10p	multi	2.25	2.25
950	A193	20p	multi	4.50	4.50
951	A193	30p	multi	6.75	6.75
952	A193	50p	multi	11.50	11.50
	Nos. 939-952 (14)			32.20	32.20

Lions of the Chobe A194

Designs: 3.50p, Male lion facing left. 5.40p, Pride of lions. 7.30p, Lioness facing right. 8p, Two lionesses and cub.

2014, June 20 **Litho.** ***Perf. 13½***
953-956 A194 Set of 4 5.50 5.50
956a Souvenir sheet of 4, #953-956, perf. 14 5.50 5.50
956b As "a," with PhilaKorea 2014 emblem in sheet margin 5.50 5.50

Issued: No. 956b, 8/7.

Domesticated Animals — A195

Designs: 30t, Dogs. 40t, Goats. 3.50p, Cattle. 5.40p, Donkeys. 7.30p, Chickens. 8p, Cats.

2014, Aug. 1 **Litho.** ***Perf. 14***
957-962 A195 Set of 6 5.75 5.75

World Post Day A196

Map of Botswana and: 3.50p, People and stack of papers. 5.40p, Airplane and globe. 7.30p, Elderly people and card reader. 8p, Letter and people in canoe.

Litho. With Foil Application

2014, Oct. 9 ***Perf. 14***
963-966 A196 Set of 4 5.25 5.25

National Flora A197

Designs: 3.50p, Morula tree, Motshikiri grass, Sengaparile flowers. 5.40p, Morula tree and people (44x30mm). 7.30p, Motshikiri grass, grass harvesters (44x30mm). 8p, Sengaparile flowers, hand with seeds (44x30mm).

2014, Nov. 27 **Litho.** ***Perf. 14***
967-970 A197 Set of 4 5.25 5.25

Naming of Okavango Delta as 1000th UNESCO World Heritage Site — A198

Various Okavango Delta animals and inscription: 3.50p, Pristine freshwater systems and biodiversity. 5.40p, Exceptional natural and untouched beauty. 7.30p, Protecting places for posterity. 8p, Significant natural habitat for conservation.

2015, Mar. 10 **Litho.** ***Perf. 14½x14***
971-974 A198 Set of 4 5.00 5.00
974a Souvenir sheet of 4, #971-974 5.00 5.00

Nos. 971-974, 974a have printing on back.

Abstract Art — A199

Designs: 4p, The Drum, by Modirwa Kekwaletswe. 5.90p, Hut, by Reginald Bakwena, horiz. 8p, Untitled, by Isaac Chibua, horiz. 10p, Come Together, by Prince Marokane.

Perf. 14x14¼, 14¼x14

2015, May 20 **Litho.**
975-978 A199 Set of 4 5.75 5.75

Buffalos A200

Designs: 4p, Head of adult buffalo. 5.90p, Two young bulls jousting. 7.80p, Lion and buffalos (The Wall of Horns). 10p, Cow and calf, vert.

Perf. 13¾x13¼, 13¼x13¾

2015, July 22 **Litho.**
979-982 A200 Set of 4 5.50 5.50
982a Souvenir sheet of 4, #979-982, perf. 14 5.50 5.50

Vultures A201

Designs: 4p, Lappet-faced vultures. 5p, White-headed vultures. 5.90p, White-backed vultures. 7.80p, Hooded vultures. 10p, Hooded vultures (60x30mm).

Perf. 13¾x13¼, 14 (10p)

2015, Sept. 28 **Litho.**
983-987 A201 Set of 5 6.25 6.25
987a Souvenir sheet of 5, #983-987, perf. 14 6.25 6.25

Vervet Monkeys — A202

Designs: 4p, Vervet monkey, drawing and paint brush. 5.90p, Vervet monkeys grooming, horiz. 7.80p, Vervet monkeys in trees, horiz. 10p, Mother vervet monkey nurturing juvenile.

2015, Nov. 20 **Litho.** ***Perf. 14***
988-991 A202 Set of 4 5.25 5.25
991a Souvenir sheet of 4, #988-991 5.25 5.25
991b As "a," with Thailand 2016 emblem in sheet margin 5.25 5.25
991c As "a," with Hong Kong 2015 emblem in sheet margin 5.25 5.25

Elephants A203

Elephants: 4p, Foraging. 5.90p, Mother and calf. 7.80p, Cooling down in Okavango Delta. 10p, Herd seeking water.

Perf. 13¾x13½
2016, Mar. 14 **Litho.**
992-995 A203 Set of 4 5.25 5.25
995a Souvenir sheet of 4, #992-995 5.25 5.25
995b As #995a, with Thailand 2016 emblem in sheet margin 5.25 5.25

Issued: No. 995b, 8/10.

Dances A204

Dances: 4p, Diware. 5.90p, Tsutsube. 7.80p, Setapa. 10p, Hosana.

Litho. & Embossed
2016, May 1 ***Perf. 13¾x13½***
996-999 A204 Set of 4 5.25 5.25

50 Years of Progress — A205

Inscriptions: 30t, Health. 40t, Education. 50t, Sports development. 4p, Access to clean water. 5p, Infrastructure communications. 5.90p, Rural development. 7.80p, Infrastructure roads & buildings, vert. 10p, Gender equity, vert.

Perf. 14½x14, 14x14½
2016, Aug. 1 **Litho.**
1000-1007 A205 Set of 8 6.50 6.50

Independence, 50th anniv.

Diamonds Type of 2001 and

Favorite Botswana Stamps — A206

Designs: 50t, Botswana #132. 4p, Botswana #359. 5.90p, Botswana #831. 7.80p, Botswana #490. No. 1012, 10p, Botswana #710.
No. 1013, Cut and uncut diamonds.

2016, Oct. 1 **Litho.** ***Perf. 14x14½***
1008-1012 A206 Set of 5 5.25 5.25

Souvenir Sheet
Self-Adhesive
Litho. With Foil Application
Serpentine Die Cut 10

1013 A145 10p multi 1.90 1.90

People Participating in Kgotlas — A207

Various people participating in kgotla and inscription: 50t, Traditional adjudication. 4p, Information dissemination. 5.90p, Coronation of a chief. 10p, Dikgafela Harvest Celebration.

2016, Dec. 1 **Litho.** ***Perf. 14x13¼***
1014-1017 A207 Set of 4 4.00 4.00

Leopards — A208

Designs: 4p, Female leopard and cub. 5.90p, Male leopard in tree (45x30mm). 8p, Leopard returning from the hunt (45x30mm). 10p, Head of leopard.

Perf. 14¾, 14¼x14 (#1019-1020)
2017, Feb. 28 **Litho.**
1018-1021 A208 Set of 4 5.50 5.50
1021a Souvenir sheet of 4, #1018-1021, perf. 14 5.50 5.50

2017 Netball World Youth Cup, Gaborone A209

Various netball players with frame color of: 40t, Orange. 50t, Red. 4p, Blue. 5.90p, Green. 10p, Magenta (35x70mm).

Perf. 14¼, 14x14¼ (10p)
2017, May 1 **Litho.**
1022-1026 A209 Set of 5 4.00 4.00
1026a Souvenir sheet of 1 1.90 1.90

Endangered Birds — A210

Designs: 50t, Kori bustard and chick. 5p, Black-bellied bustard, vert. 7p, Red-crested korhaan and Northern black korhaan, vert. 9p, Denham's bustard, vert. 10p, Ludwig's bustard, vert.

Perf. 14¼x14, 14x14¼
2017, Aug. 7 **Litho.**
1027-1031 A210 Set of 5 6.25 6.25
1031a Souvenir sheet of 5, #1027-1031 6.25 6.25

River Crossing A211

Designs: 5p, Elephants and ferry crossing Chobe River. 7p, Boat and Hippopotami crossing Limpopo River. 9p, Horses and riders crossing Thamalakane River. 10p, Trucks crossing Molopo River.

2017, Oct. 1 **Litho.** ***Perf. 13½x13¼***
1032-1035 A211 Set of 4 6.00 6.00
1035a Souvenir sheet of 4, #1032-1035 6.00 6.00

Flowers — A212

Designs: 1p, Drimia sanguinea. 5p, Orbea knobelli, horiz. 7p, Hibiscus trionum, horiz. 10p, Hoodia gordonii.

2017, Dec. 5 **Litho.** ***Perf. 13½***
1036-1039 A212 Set of 4 4.75 4.75

Flamingos A213

Designs:, 5p, Heads of greater and lesser flamingos. 7p, Filter feeding. 9p, Greater and lesser flamingos in water. 10p, Crop milk feeding.

2018, Mar. 15 **Litho.** ***Perf. 13½***
1040-1043 A213 Set of 4 6.50 6.50
1043a Block of 4 #1040-1043 6.50 6.50
1043b Souvenir sheet of 4, #1040-1043, perf. 14 6.50 6.50

Sir Ketumile Masire (1925-2017), Second President of Botswana — A214

Masire and: 5p, Students. 7p, Nelson Mandela (1918-2013), President of South Africa. 10p, Tractor.

2018, July 1 **Litho.** ***Perf. 13½***
1044-1046 A214 Set of 3 4.25 4.25

Animals A215

Designs: 10t, Kalahari ground gecko. 20t, Bat-eared fox. 30t, Namaqua sandgrouse, vert. 40t, Bateleur. 50t, Giant African bullfrog. 1p, Black mamba, vert. 2p, Sociable weaver. 3p, Three-spot tilapia. (5p), Springbok. (7p), Small-spotted genet. (8p), Puku. 9p, Blue wildebeest, vert. 10p, Knob-billed duck. 20p, Kalahari tent tortoise. 30p, Chestnut-banded plover.

Perf. 13¾x14¼, 14¼x13¾
2018, Aug. 30 **Litho.**
1047 A215 10t multi .25 .25
1048 A215 20t multi .25 .25
1049 A215 30t multi .25 .25
1050 A215 40t multi .25 .25
1051 A215 50t multi .25 .25
1052 A215 1p multi .25 .25
1053 A215 2p multi .35 .35
1054 A215 3p multi .55 .55
1055 A215 (5p) multi .90 .90
1056 A215 (7p) multi 1.25 1.25
1057 A215 (8p) multi 1.50 1.50
1058 A215 9p multi 1.60 1.60
a. Souvenir sheet of 5, #1048, 1055-1058 5.50 5.50
1059 A215 10p multi 1.90 1.90
1060 A215 20p multi 3.75 3.75
a. Souvenir sheet of 5, #1047, 1051-1052, 1054, 1060 5.25 5.25
1061 A215 30p multi 5.50 5.50
a. Souvenir sheet of 5, #1049, 1050, 1053, 1059, 1061 8.25 8.25
Nos. 1047-1061 (15) 18.80 18.80

No. 1055 is inscribed "STD A"; No. 1056, "STD B", No. 1057, "Postcard Rate."

Big Game Animals A216

Designs: 5p, Rhinoceros. 7p, Lions. 8p, Leopard. 9p, Elephants. 10p, African buffalo.

2018, Nov. 22 **Litho.** ***Perf. 14***
1062-1066 A216 Set of 5 7.50 7.50
1066a Souvenir sheet of 5, #1062-1066 7.50 7.50

No. 1062-1066, 1066a have back printing.

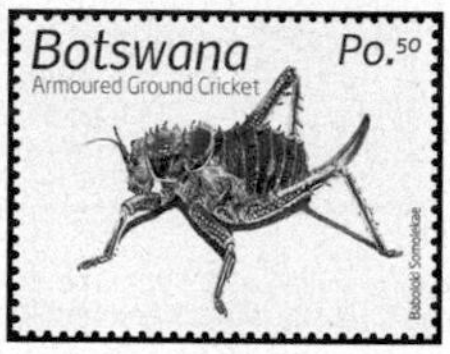

Insects A217

Designs: 50t, Armored ground cricket. 1p, Tiger beetle. 2p, Saw-backed locust. 5p, Robber fly. 7p, Hooked-tailed antlion. 10p, Yellow pansy butterfly.

Perf. 13½x13¼
2019, Feb. 20 **Litho.**
1067-1072 A217 Set of 6 4.75 4.75

Animals of the Nxai Pans — A218

Designs: 50t, Cheetah. 2p, Springboks, vert. 3p, Gemsbok, vert. 5p, Bat-eared foxes. 7p, Lanner falcon.

2019, Aug. 15 **Litho.** ***Perf. 14½***
1073-1077 A218 Set of 5 3.25 3.25
1077a Souvenir sheet of 5, #1073-1077 3.25 3.25

Cranes — A219

Designs: 2p, Blue cranes. 5p, Gray crowned cranes. 7p, Wattled cranes. 10p, Wattled crane and construction crane, horiz. (50x30mm).

Perf. 13½, 14¼ (10p)

2019, Oct. 9 **Litho.**

1078-1081	A219	Set of 4	4.50	4.50
1081a		Souvenir sheet of 1	1.90	1.90

Tourist Attractions — A220

Designs: 2p, Baobab trees at Lekhubu Island. 5p, Buffalos at Sedudu Island. 7p, Gcwihaba Caves and bat. 10p, Moremi Gorge and Broom cluster fig tree.

2019, Dec. 5 **Litho.** ***Perf. 14½x14***

1082-1085	A220	Set of 4	4.50	4.50
1085a		Souvenir sheet of 8, 2 each #1082-1085, + 4 labels	9.00	9.00

Spiders A221

No. 1086: a, Ceratogyrus darlingi. b, Stegodyphus domicola. c, Seothyra fasciata. d, Kima africana. e, Trichonephila senegalensis. f, Ammoxenus psammodromus.

2020, Mar. 7 **Litho.** ***Perf. 14¼***

1086		Horiz. strip of 6	4.75	4.75
a.	A221	50c multi	.25	.25
b.	A221	1p multi	.25	.25
c.	A221	2p multi	.35	.35
d.	A221	5p multi	.85	.85
e.	A221	7p multi	1.25	1.25
f.	A221	10p multi	1.75	1.75
g.		Souvenir sheet of 6, #1086a-1086f	4.75	4.75

African Scops Owl — A222

Owl: 5p, Against tree. 7p, Head, horiz. 9p, In tree hollow, horiz. 10p, At night.

Perf. 13¼x13½, 13½x13¼

2020, June 5 **Litho.**

1087-1090	A222	Set of 4	5.25	5.25
1090a		Souvenir sheet of 4, #1087-1090	5.25	5.25

POSTAGE DUE STAMPS

Bechuanaland Protectorate Nos. J10-J12 Overprinted

Perf. 14

1967, Mar. 1 **Wmk. 4** **Typo.**

J1	D2	1c carmine rose	.30	3.00
J2	D2	2c dull violet	.30	3.00
J3	D2	5c olive green	.40	3.00
		Nos. J1-J3 (3)	1.00	9.00

Elephant — D1

Perf. 13½

1971, June 9 **Litho.** **Unwmk.**

J4	D1	1c carmine rose	1.75	4.50
J5	D1	2c violet blue	2.25	5.00
J6	D1	6c sepia	2.75	7.50
J7	D1	14c green	3.25	10.00
		Nos. J4-J7 (4)	10.00	27.00

Zebra — D2

1978 ***Perf. 12½***

J8	D2	1t red orange & black	1.00	1.75
J9	D2	2t emerald & black	1.00	1.75
J10	D2	4t red & black	1.00	1.75
J11	D2	10t dark blue & black	1.00	1.75
J12	D2	16t brown & black	1.00	1.75
		Nos. J8-J12 (5)	5.00	8.75

1984 ***Perf. 14½x14***

J8a	D2	1t	1.30	2.00
J9a	D2	2t	1.30	2.00
J10a	D2	4t	1.30	2.00
J11a	D2	10t	1.30	2.00
J12a	D2	16t	1.30	2.00
		Nos. J8a-J12a (5)	6.50	10.00

1989, Apr. 1 ***Perf. 14½***

J8b	D2	1t	.50	.65
J9b	D2	2t	.50	.65
J10b	D2	4t	.50	.65
J11b	D2	10t	.50	.65
J12b	D2	16t	.75	1.00
		Nos. J8b-J12b (5)	2.75	3.60

The design is the same size on the 1984 and 1989 issues, but the grass of Nos. J8b-J12b is lower and less defined than on previous issues. The paper is wider on the 1989 issue.

1994, Dec. 1 ***Perf. 14***

J8c	D2	1t	1.00	1.00
J9c	D2	2t	1.00	1.00
J10c	D2	4t	1.00	1.00
J11c	D2	10t	1.00	1.00
J12c	D2	16t	1.00	1.00
		Nos. J8c-J12c (5)	5.00	5.00

See note after No. J12b.

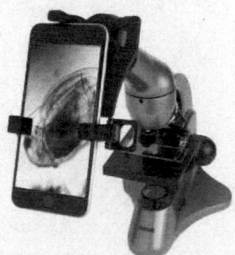

BRAZIL

brə-'zil

Brasil (after 1918)

LOCATION — On the north and east coasts of South America, bordering on the Atlantic Ocean.
GOVT. — Republic
AREA — 3,286,000 sq. mi.
POP. — 157,070,163 (1996)
CAPITAL — Brasilia

Brazil was an independent empire from 1822 to 1889, when a constitution was adopted and the country became officially known as The United States of Brazil.

1000 Reis = 1 Milreis
100 Centavos = 1 Cruzeiro (1942)
100 Centavos = 1 Cruzado (1986)
100 Centavos = 1 Cruzeiro (1990)
(Cruzeiro Real 8/2/93-7/1/94)
100 Centavos = 1 Real (7/1/94)

Catalogue values for unused stamps in this country are for Never Hinged items, beginning with Scott 680 in the regular postage section, Scott B12 in the semi-postal section, Scott C66 in the airpost section, Scott RA2 in the postal tax section, and Scott RAB1 in the postal tax semi-postal section.

Values for unused stamps are for examples with original gum as defined in the catalogue introduction except for Nos. 1-98, which are valued without gum. Nos. 1-52 with original gum command a substantial premium (up to 100%). Nos. 53-78 with original gum command a premium of up to 50%. Nos. 79-98 with original gum command a premium of 10%-25%.

Watermarks

Wmk. 97 — "CORREIO FEDERAL REPUBLICA DOS ESTADOS UNIDOS DO BRAZIL" in Sheet

Wmk. 98 — "IMPOSTO DE CONSUMO REPUBLICA DOS ESTADOS UNIDOS DO BRAZIL" in Sheet

Wmk. 99 — "CORREIO"

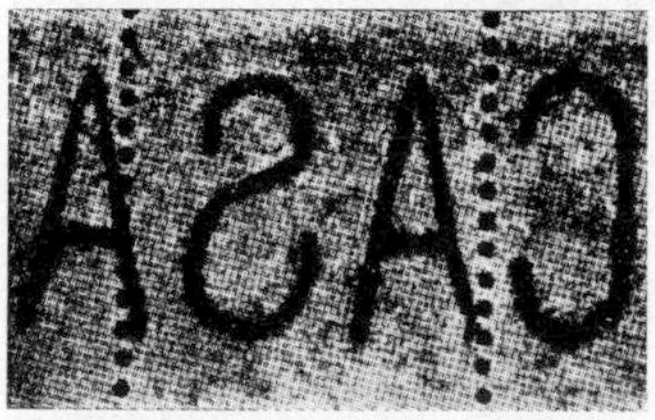

Wmk. 100 — "CASA DA MOEDA" in Sheet

Because of the spacing of this watermark, a few stamps in each sheet may show no watermark. Variations of this watermark occur in some stamps reading 'CASA MOEDA ENTRE ESTRELAS', 'CASA DA MOEDA ENTRE ESTRELAS', or 'CASACASA DA MOEDA ENTRE ESTRALAS.'

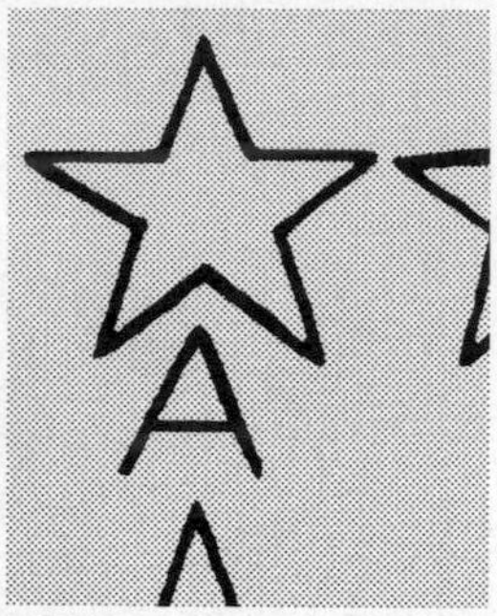

Wmk. 101 — Stars and CASA DA MOEDA

Wmk. 116 — Crosses and Circles

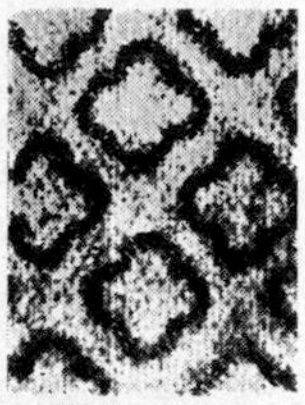

Wmk. 127 — Quatrefoils

Wmk. 193 — ESTADOS UNIDOS DO BRASIL

Wmk. 206 — Star-framed CM, Multiple

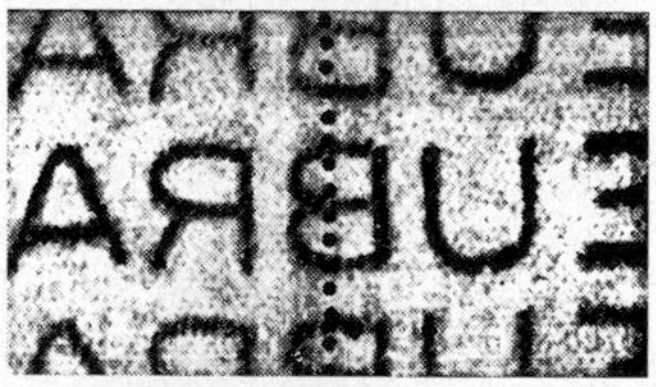

Wmk. 218 — E U BRASIL Multiple, Letters 8mm High

Wmk. 221 — ESTADOS UNIDOS DO BRASIL, Multiple, Letters 6mm High

Wmk. 222 — CORREIO BRASIL and 5 Stars in Squared Circle

Wmk. 236 — Coat of Arms in Sheet

Watermark (reduced illustration) covers 22 stamps in sheet.

Wmk. 245 — Multiple "CASA DA MOEDA DO BRASIL" and Small Formee Cross

Wmk. 249 — "CORREIO BRASIL" multiple

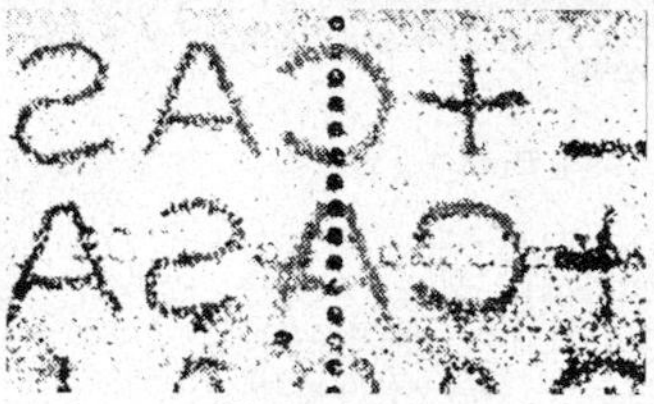

Wmk. 256 — "CASA+DA+MOEDA+DO+BRAZIL" in 8mm Letters

Wmk. 264 — "*CORREIO*BRASIL*" Multiple, Letters 7mm High

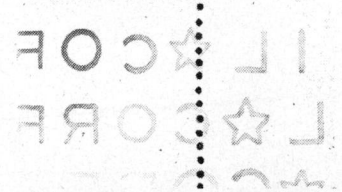

Wmk. 267 — "*CORREIO*BRASIL*" Multiple in Small Letters 5mm High

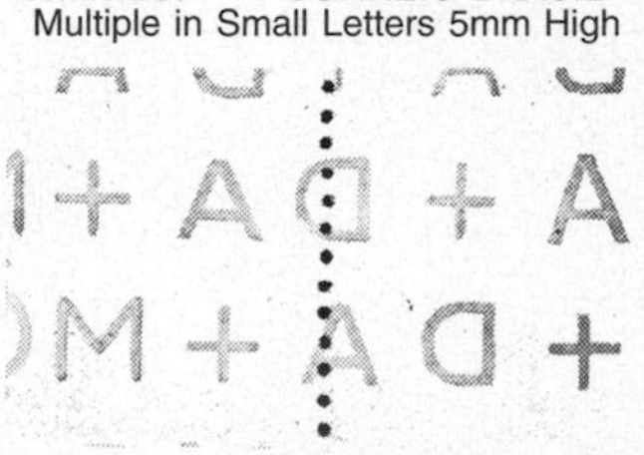

Wmk. 268 — "CASA+DA+MOEDA+DO+BRASIL" in 6mm Letters

Wmk. 270 — Wavy Lines and Seal

Wmk. 271 — Wavy Lines

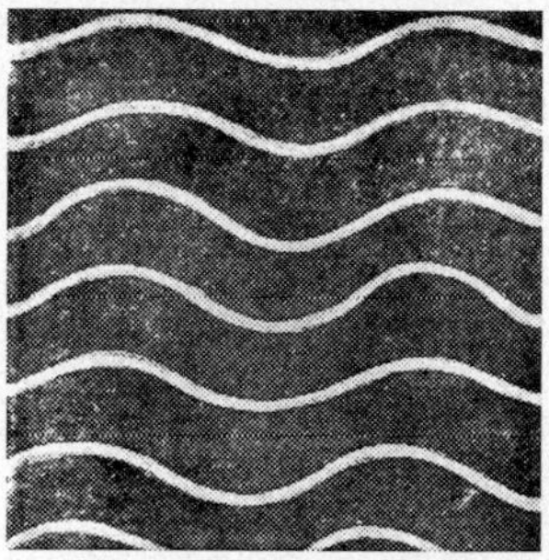

Wmk. 281 — Wavy Lines

ISSUES OF THE EMPIRE

A1

Fine Impressions
Grayish or Yellowish Paper
Unwmk.

1843, Aug. 1 — Engr. — *Imperf.*

1	A1 30r black	4,500.	550.
c.	Pair, #1-2		*950,000.*
2	A1 60r black	825.	275.
3	A1 90r black	4,000.	1,300.

Nos. 1-3 were issued with gum, but very few unused examples retain even a trace of their original gum. Stamps with original gum command substantial premiums.

Fine impressions are true black and have background lathework complete. Intermediate impressions are grayish black and have weaker lathework in the background. These sell for somewhat less than fine impressions. Worn impressions have white areas in the background surrounding the numerals due to plate wear affecting especially the lathework. These examples sell for somewhat less than intermediate impressions.

Most examples of Nos. 1-3 also exist on white paper, usually thin and somewhat translucent. Such examples are scarce and command premiums. For detailed listings, see the Scott Classic Specialized catalogue

A2

Grayish or Yellowish Paper

1844-46

7	A2	10r black	125.00	25.00
8	A2	30r black	145.00	35.00
9	A2	60r black	125.00	25.00
10	A2	90r black	1,000.	120.00
11	A2	180r black	4,500.	1,800.
12	A2	300r black	6,500.	2,000.
13	A2	600r black	6,000.	2,200.

Nos. 8, 9 and 10 exist on thick paper and are considerably scarcer.

A3

Grayish or Yellowish Paper

1850, Jan. 1

21	A3	10r black	30.00	*35.00*
22	A3	20r black	92.50	*120.00*
23	A3	30r black	12.00	3.50
24	A3	60r black	12.00	3.00
25	A3	90r black	110.00	14.50
26	A3	180r black	115.00	65.00
27	A3	300r black	400.00	72.50
28	A3	600r black	500.00	110.00

No. 22 used is generally found precanceled with a single horizontal line in pen or blue crayon or with two diagonal pen lines. Value precanceled without gum, $75.

All values except the 90r were reprinted in 1910 on very thick paper.

1854

37	A3	10r blue	14.50	12.00
c.		Double impression	2,000.	650.00
38	A3	30r blue	40.00	*65.00*

For more complete listings, see Scott *Classic Specialized Catalogue of Stamps and Covers 1840-1940.*

A4

1861

39	A4	280r red	160.00	110.00
40	A4	430r yellow	200.00	160.00

Nos. 39-40 have been reprinted on thick white paper with white gum. They are printed in aniline inks and the colors are brighter than those of the originals.

1866 ***Perf. 13½***

42	A3	10r blue	*300.00*	*150.00*
43	A3	20r black	*1,100.*	*500.00*
44	A3	30r black	*350.00*	*190.00*
45	A3	30r blue	*800.00*	*925.00*
46	A3	60r black	*300.00*	*30.00*
47	A3	90r black	*725.00*	*350.00*
48	A3	180r black	*925.00*	*350.00*
49	A4	280r red	*800.00*	*850.00*
50	A3	300r black	*1,100.*	*425.00*
51	A4	430r yellow	*725.00*	*425.00*
52	A3	600r black	*725.00*	*300.00*

Fraudulent perforations abound. Purchases should be accompanied by certificates of authenticity.

A 10r black is questioned.

A5

A6

A7

A8

A8a

A9

Emperor Dom Pedro — A9a

Types of 100 reis:

Type I — Left frameline weak and incomplete and composed of a single line that never touches the upper or lower ornaments. The upper left ornament is broken. The lower left ornament is vestigial.

Type Ia — Left frameline is incomplete and composed of a single line that does not touch the upper ornaments. The lower left ornament is complete.

Type II — Left frameline incomplete and composed of a double outer line that does not touch the upper ornaments. The lower left ornament is slightly broken.

Type III — Left frameline complete and composed of two continuous outer lines that meet the upper ornaments. The lower left ornament is complete.

Thick or Thin White Wove Paper

1866, July 1 ***Perf. 12***

53	A5	10r vermilion	14.50	5.00
54	A6	20r red lilac	25.00	3.50
56	A7	50r blue	35.00	2.50
57	A8	80r slate violet	92.50	6.00
58	A8a	100r blue green	35.00	1.90
59	A9	200r black	120.00	12.00
a.		Half used as 100r on cover		*1,750.*
60	A9a	500r orange	250.00	35.00
		Nos. 53-60 (7)	572.00	65.90

The 10r and 20r exist imperf. on both white and bluish paper. Some authorities consider them proofs.

Nos. 58 and 65 are found in four types.

1868 **Bluish Paper**

53a	A5	10r	600.00	500.00
54b	A6	20r	190.00	85.00
56a	A7	50r	225.00	30.00
57a	A8	80r	300.00	35.00
58b	A8a	100r Type II	960.00	140.00

1876-77 ***Rouletted***

61	A5	10r vermilion ('77)	72.50	35.00
62	A6	20r red lilac ('77)	85.00	30.00
63	A7	50r blue ('77)	85.00	8.50
64	A8	80r violet ('77)	210.00	20.00
65	A8a	100r green (III)	50.00	1.50
66	A9	200r black ('77)	100.00	9.25
a.		Half used as 100r on cover		*1,000.*
67	A9a	500r orange	225.00	42.50
		Nos. 61-67 (7)	827.50	146.75

A10

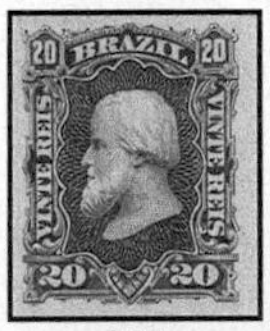
A11

A12

A13

A14

A15

A16

A17

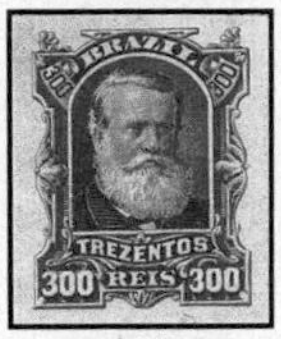
A18

A19

A20

1878-79 ***Rouletted***

68	A10	10r vermilion	14.50	3.50
69	A11	20r violet	19.00	3.00
70	A12	50r blue	30.00	2.00
71	A13	80r lake	35.00	10.00
72	A14	100r green	35.00	1.50
73	A15	200r black	175.00	17.50
a.		Half used as 100r on cover		*1,000.*
74	A16	260r dk brown	100.00	27.50
75	A18	300r bister	100.00	7.25
a.		One-third used as 100r on cover		*10,000.*
76	A19	700r red brown	190.00	100.00
77	A20	1000r gray lilac	225.00	47.50
		Nos. 68-77 (10)	923.50	219.75

1878, Aug. 21 ***Perf. 12***

78	A17	300r orange & grn	100.00	25.00

Nos. 68-78 exist imperforate.

A21

A22

A23

Small Heads
Laid Paper

Perf. 13, 13½ and Compound

1881, July 15

79	A21	50r blue	150.00	24.00
80	A22	100r olive green	600.00	47.50
81	A23	200r pale red brn	600.00	140.00
a.		Half used as 100r on cover		*2,100.*

On Nos. 79 and 80 the hair above the ear curves forward. On Nos. 83 and 88 it is drawn backward. On the stamps of the 1881 issue the beard is smaller than in the 1882-85 issues and fills less of the space between the neck and the frame at the left.

See No. 88.

A24

A25

A26

A27

Type I

Type II

100 REIS and 200 REIS:

Type I — Groundwork formed of diagonal crossed lines and horizontal lines.

Type II — Groundwork formed of diagonal crossed lines and vertical lines.

Larger Heads
Laid Paper

Perf. 12½ to 14 and Compound

1882-84

82	A24	10r black	12.00	*25.00*
83	A25	100r dk grn, type I	50.00	4.50
b.		100r dark green, type II	425.00	14.50
84	A26	200r pale red brn, type I	100.00	30.00
a.		Half used as 100r on cover		*1,300.*
85	A27	200r pale rose, type II	55.00	5.50
a.		Diag. half used as 100r on cover		950.00
		Nos. 82-85 (4)	217.00	65.00

See No. 86.

A28

A29

A30

TYPES OF A29

Type I — Groundwork of horizontal lines.

Type II — Groundwork of diagonal crossed lines.

Type III — Groundwork solid.

Perf. 13, 13½, 14 and Compound

1884-85

86	A24	10r orange	3.00	3.25
87	A28	20r slate green	35.00	3.50
a.		20r olive green	35.00	3.50
b.		Half used as 10r on newspaper		*3,500.*
88	A21	50r bl, head larger	35.00	3.50
90	A29	100r lilac, type I	150.00	3.00
a.		100r lilac, type II	450.00	75.00
b.		100r lilac, type III	325.00	55.00
91	A30	100r lilac	200.00	5.00
		Nos. 86-91 (5)	423.00	18.25

A31

Perf. 13, 13½, 14 and Compound

1885

92	A31	100r lilac	140.00	3.00

Design A31 has a value tablet the color of the stamp. Design A35 has a white value tablet.

A32

Southern Cross — A33

Crown — A34

1887

93	A32	50r chalky blue	35.00	5.00
94	A33	300r gray blue	230.00	30.00
95	A34	500r olive	140.00	14.00
		Nos. 93-95 (3)	405.00	49.00

A35

A36

Entrance to Bay of Rio de Janeiro — A37

1888

96	A35	100r lilac	72.50	1.90
a.		Imperf., pair	150.00	*175.00*
97	A36	700r violet	80.00	*110.00*
98	A37	1000r dull blue	275.00	110.00
		Nos. 96-98 (3)	427.50	221.90

Issues of the Republic

Southern Cross — A38

Wove Paper, Thin to Thick

Perf. 12½ to 14, 11 to 11½, and 12½ to 14x11 to 11½, Rough or Clean-Cut

Engraved; Typographed (#102)

1890-91

99	A38	20r gray green	2.50	1.90
a.		20r blue green	2.50	1.90
b.		20r emerald	19.00	7.00
100	A38	50r gray green	6.25	1.90
a.		50r olive green	14.00	7.00
b.		50r yellow green	14.00	7.00
c.		50r dark slate green	8.25	4.00
d.		Horiz. pair, imperf. btwn.		—
101	A38	100r lilac rose	475.00	6.00
102	A38	100r red lil, redrawn	30.00	1.90
a.		Tete beche pair	*25,000.*	*19,000.*
103	A38	200r purple	10.00	1.90
a.		200r violet	12.00	2.50
b.		200r violet blue	27.50	3.50
c.		Half used as 100r on cover		875.00
104	A38	300r dark violet	90.00	6.00
a.		300r gray	90.00	10.00
b.		300r gray blue	100.00	10.00
c.		300r slate violet	175.00	30.00
105	A38	500r olive bister	21.00	9.50
a.		500r olive gray	21.00	11.50
106	A38	500r slate	21.00	13.50
107	A38	700r fawn	19.00	*19.00*
a.		700r chocolate	24.00	26.00
108	A38	1000r bister	17.50	3.50
a.		1000r yellow buff	35.00	8.50
		Nos. 99-108 (10)	692.25	65.10

The redrawn 100r may be distinguished by the absence of the curved lines of shading in the left side of the central oval. The pearls in the oval are not well aligned and there is less shading at right and left of "CORREIO" and "100 REIS."

A 100 reis stamp of type A38 but inscribed "BRAZIL" instead of "E. U. DO BRAZIL" was not placed in issue but postmarked copies are known. A reprint on thick paper was made in 1910.

No. 101 exists imperf., not regularly issued. For surcharges see Nos. 151-158.

Liberty Head — A39

Perf. 12½ to 14, 11 to 11½ and 12½ to 14x11 to 11½

1891, May 1 **Typo.**

109	A39	100r blue & red	42.50	1.75
a.		Frame inverted	175.00	110.00
b.		Tete beche pair	850.00	*925.00*
c.		100r ultra & red	42.50	1.90

Liberty Head — A40

Perf. 11, 11½, 13, 13½, 14 and Compound

1893, Jan. 18 **Litho.**

111	A40	100r rose	75.00	1.75

A41

A41a

Sugarloaf Mountain

A42

A42a

Liberty Head

Hermes — A43

Perf. 11 to 11½, 12½ to 14 and 12½ to 14x11 to 11½

1894-97 **Unwmk.**

112	A41	10r rose & blue	2.50	.90
113	A41a	10r rose & blue	2.50	.90
114	A41a	20r orange & bl ('97)	1.40	.40
115	A41a	50r dk blue & blue	13.00	1.60
116	A42	100r carmine & blk	5.00	.50
118	A42a	200r orange & blk	1.25	.50
d.		Half used as 100r on cover		850.00
119	A42a	300r green & blk	19.00	.70
120	A42a	500r blue & blk	30.00	2.00
121	A42a	700r light lilac & blk	20.00	2.00
122	A43	1000r green & vio	72.50	2.00
124	A43	2000r blk & gray lil	85.00	20.00
		Nos. 112-124 (11)	252.15	31.50

The head of No. 116 exists in five types. See Nos. 140-150A, 159-161, 166-171d.

1889 Issue of Newspaper Stamps Surcharged (Type N1)

a

b

c

1898		**Green Surcharge**		***Rouletted***
125	(b)	700r on 500r yel	8.50	*12.00*
126	(c)	1000r on 700r yel	42.50	35.00
a.		Surcharged "700r"	850.00	1,000.
127	(c)	2000r on 1000r yel	35.00	18.00
128	(c)	2000r on 1000r brn	25.00	7.25
		Violet Surcharge		
129	(a)	100r on 50r brn yel	2.50	*55.00*
130	(c)	100r on 50r brn yel	90.00	75.00
131	(c)	300r on 200r blk	4.00	1.40
a.		Double surcharge	190.00	325.00

The surcharge on No. 130 is handstamped. The impression is blurred and lighter in color than on No. 129. The two surcharges differ most in the shapes and serifs of the figures "1."

Counterfeits exist of No. 126a.

		Black Surcharge		
132	(b)	200r on 100r vio	4.00	1.40
a.		Double surcharge	95.00	*200.00*
b.		Inverted surcharge	95.00	*200.00*
132C	(b)	500r on 300r car	6.50	3.50
133	(b)	700r on 500r grn	9.50	2.40
		Blue Surcharge		
134	(b)	500r on 300r car	7.50	6.25
		Red Surcharge		
135	(c)	1000r on 700r ultra	27.50	17.00
a.		Inverted surcharge	240.00	—

Surcharged on 1890-94 Issues

d

e

Perf. 11 to 14 and Compound

		Black Surcharge		
136	N3(e)	20r on 10r blue	3.75	7.00
137	N2(d)	200r on 100r red lilac	25.00	17.00
a.		Double surcharge	275.00	300.00

Surcharge on No. 137 comes blue to deep black.

		Blue Surcharge		
138	N3(e)	50r on 20r grn	9.50	11.50
		Red Surcharge		
139	N3(e)	100r on 50r grn	21.00	24.00
a.		Blue surcharge	15.00	.

The surcharge on 139a exists inverted, and in pair, one without surcharge.

Types of 1894-97

1899 ***Perf. 5½-7 and 11-11½x5½-7***

140	A41a	10r rose & bl	6.00	*14.00*
141	A41a	20r orange & bl	9.25	9.25
142	A41a	50r dk bl & lt bl	12.00	*37.50*
143	A42	100r car & blk	20.00	5.50
144	A42a	200r org & blk	12.00	3.50
145	A42a	300r green & blk	75.00	8.75
		Nos. 140-145 (6)	134.25	78.50

Perf. 8½-9½, 8½-9½x11-11½

146	A41a	10r rose & bl	6.00	3.50
147	A41a	20r orange & bl	19.00	3.50
147A	A41a	50r dk bl & bl	160.00	35.00
148	A42	100r car & blk	37.50	1.75
149	A42a	200r org & blk	19.00	1.25
150	A42a	300r green & blk	75.00	6.00
150A	A43	1000r green & vio	160.00	15.00
		Nos. 146-150A (7)	476.50	66.00

Nos. 140-150A are valued with perfs just cut into the design on one or two sides. Expect some irregularity of the perforations.

Issue of 1890-93 Surcharged in Violet or Magenta

Perf. 11 to 11½, 12½ to 14 and Compound

1899, June 25

151	A38	50r on 20r gray grn	2.50	*3.50*
a.		Double surcharge	150.00	150.00
152	A38	100r on 50r gray grn	2.50	*3.50*
b.		Double surcharge	125.00	125.00
153	A38	300r on 200r pur	9.25	*14.50*
a.		Double surcharge	300.00	—
b.		Pair, one without surcharge	500.00	—
154	A38	500r on 300r ultra, perf. 13	22.50	8.75
a.		500r on 300r gray lilac	35.00	10.00
b.		Pair, one without surcharge	500.00	*575.00*
c.		500r on 300r slate violet	45.00	17.00
155	A38	700r on 500r ol bis	30.00	7.00
a.		Pair, one without surcharge	500.00	—
156	A38	1000r on 700r choc	22.50	7.00
157	A38	1000r on 700r fawn	22.50	7.00
a.		Pair, one without surcharge	500.00	*575.00*
158	A38	2000r on 1000r bister (perf 11-11½)	37.50	5.25
a.		2000r on 1000r yel buff (perf 13)	60.00	5.25
b.		Pair, one without surcharge	500.00	*575.00*
		Nos. 151-158 (8)	149.25	56.50

Types of 1894-97

Perf. 11, 11½, 13 and Compound

1900

159	A41a	50r green	13.00	.70
160	A42	100r rose	25.00	.35
a.		Frame around inner oval	125.00	4.75
161	A42a	200r blue	14.50	.40
		Nos. 159-161 (3)	52.50	1.45

Three types exist of No. 161, all of which have the frame around inner oval.

Cabral Arrives at Brazil — A44

Independence Proclaimed — A45

"Emancipation of Slaves" — A46

Allegory, Republic of Brazil — A47

1900, Jan. 1 **Litho.** ***Perf. 12½***

162	A44	100r red	7.25	4.50
a.		Imperf., pair	400.00	500.00

163	A45	200r green & yel	7.25	4.50
164	A46	500r blue	7.25	4.50
165	A47	700r emerald	7.25	4.50
		Nos. 162-165 (4)	29.00	18.00
		Set, never hinged	75.00	

Discovery of Brazil, 400th anniversary.

Types of 1894-97

Wmk. (97? or 98?)

1905 ***Perf. 11, 11½***

166	A41a	10r rose & bl	7.00	4.75
167	A41a	20r org & bl	12.50	2.40
168	A41a	50r green	25.00	3.50
169	A42	100r rose	32.50	1.25
170	A42a	200r dark blue	19.00	1.25
171	A42a	300r grn & blk	65.00	2.40
		Nos. 166-171 (6)	161.00	15.55

Positive identification of Wmk. 97 or 98 places stamp in specific watermark groups below.

Wmk. 97

166b	A41a	10r rose & blue	37.50	19.00
167b	A41a	20r org & blue	37.50	9.50
168b	A41a	50r green	72.50	9.50
169b	A42	100r rose	250.00	35.00
170b	A42a	200r dark blue	150.00	4.75
171b	A42a	300r green & blk	450.00	35.00
171A	A43	1000r grn & vio	350.00	35.00
		Nos. 166b-171A (7)	1,348.	147.75

Wmk. 98

166c	A41a	10r rose & blue	50.00	50.00
167c	A41a	20r org & blue	100.00	24.00
168c	A41a	50r green	200.00	35.00
169c	A42	100r rose	100.00	4.75
170c	A42a	200r dark blue	150.00	4.75
171d	A42a	300r green & blk	350.00	35.00
		Nos. 166c-171d (6)	950.00	153.50

Allegory, Pan-American Congress A48

1906, July 23 **Litho.** **Unwmk.**

172	A48	100r carmine rose	28.00	22.00
173	A48	200r blue	65.00	8.00

Third Pan-American Congress.

Aristides Lobo A48a

Benjamin Constant A49

Pedro Alvares Cabral A50

Eduardo Wandenkolk A51

Manuel Deodoro da Fonseca A52

Floriano Peixoto A53

Prudente de Moraes A54

Manuel Ferraz de Campos Salles A55

Francisco de Paula Rodrigues Alves — A56

Liberty Head — A57

A58

A59

1906-16 **Engr.** ***Perf. 12***

174	A48a	10r bluish slate ('15)	1.10	.25
175	A49	20r aniline violet ('15)	1.50	.25
176	A50	50r green	1.10	.25
a.		Booklet pane of 6 ('08)	50.00	*120.00*
177	A51	100r anil rose	2.50	.25
a.		Imperf. vert., coil ('16)	5.50	.40
b.		Booklet pane of 6 ('08)	120.00	*120.00*
178	A52	200r blue	2.50	.25
a.		Booklet pane of 6 ('08)	85.00	*120.00*
179	A52	200r ultra ('15)	2.50	.25
a.		Imperf. vert., coil ('16)	3.00	.40
180	A53	300r gray blk	4.75	.80
181	A54	400r olive grn	50.00	2.40
182	A55	500r dk violet	7.50	.80
183	A54	600r ol grn ('10)	3.50	1.20
184	A56	700r red brown	7.50	3.50
185	A57	1000r vermilion	45.00	1.25
186	A58	2000r yellow grn	35.00	.80
187	A58	2000r Prus blue ('15)	24.00	1.25
188	A59	5000r car rose	16.50	2.40
		Nos. 174-188 (15)	204.95	15.90

Allegorical Emblems: Liberty, Peace, Industry, etc. — A60

1908, July 14

189	A60	100r carmine	5.00	2.00

National Exhibition, Rio de Janeiro.

Emblems of Peace Between Brazil and Portugal A61

1908, July 14

190	A61	100r red	13.00	1.50

Opening of Brazilian ports to foreign commerce, cent. Medallions picture King Carlos I of Portugal and Pres. Affonso Penna of Brazil.

Bonifacio, Bolivar, Hidalgo, O'Higgins, San Martin, Washington — A62

1909

191	A62	200r deep blue	12.00	1.50

For surcharge see No. E1.

Nilo Peçanha — A63

1910, Nov. 15

192	A63	10,000r brown	10.00	2.50

Baron of Rio Branco — A64

1913-16

193	A64	1000r deep green	4.75	.40
194	A64	1000r slate ('16)	37.50	.80

Cabo Frio — A65

Perf. 11½

1915, Nov. 13 **Litho.** **Wmk. 99**

195	A65	100r dk grn, *yelsh*	6.00	4.50

Founding of the town of Cabo Frio, 300th anniversary.

Bay of Guajara A66

1916, Jan. 5

196	A66	100r carmine	8.00	6.00

City of Belem, 300th anniversary.

Revolutionary Flag — A67

1917, Mar. 6

197	A67	100r deep blue	16.00	8.00

Revolution of Pernambuco, Mar. 6, 1817.

Rodrigues Alves — A68

Unwmk.

1917, Aug. 31 **Engr.** ***Perf. 12***

198	A68	5000r red brown	100.00	12.00

Liberty Head A69 A70

Perf. 12½, 13, 13x13½.

1918-20 **Typo.** **Unwmk.**

200	A69	10r orange brn	.80	.30
201	A69	20r slate	.80	.30
202	A69	25r ol gray ('20)	.80	.30
203	A69	50r green	170.00	4.00
204	A70	100r rose	2.25	.30
a.		Imperf., pair	350.00	
205	A70	300r red orange	40.00	4.00
206	A70	500r dull violet	40.00	4.00
		Nos. 200-206 (7)	254.65	13.20

1918-20 **Wmk. 100**

207	A69	10r red brown	8.00	2.00
a.		Imperf., pair	—	
207B	A69	20r slate	2.00	1.90
c.		Imperf., pair	350.00	
208	A69	25r ol gray ('20)	1.00	.60
209	A69	50r green	1.90	.60
210	A70	100r rose	100.00	.60
a.		Imperf., pair	—	
211	A70	200r dull blue	8.00	.60
212	A70	300r orange	90.00	5.00
213	A70	500r dull violet	90.00	10.00
214	A70	600r orange	3.75	*10.00*
		Nos. 207-214 (9)	304.65	31.30

Because of the spacing of this watermark, a few stamps in each sheet may show no watermark, these are worth considerably more.

The editors would like to see evidence of the existence of Nos. 207a and 210a.

"Education" — A72

1918 **Engr.** ***Perf. 11½***

215	A72	1000r blue	9.00	.30
216	A72	2000r red brown	45.00	13.00
217	A72	5000r dark violet	9.00	9.00
		Nos. 215-217 (3)	63.00	22.30

Watermark note below No. 257 also applies to Nos. 215-217.

See Nos. 233-234, 283-285, 404, 406, 458, 460. For surcharge see No. C30.

Railroad A73

"Industry" A74

"Aviation" A75

Mercury A76

"Navigation" — A77

Perf. 13½x13, 13x13½

1920-22 **Typo.** **Unwmk.**

218	A73	10r red violet	1.50	.50
219	A73	20r olive green	1.50	.50
220	A74	25r brown violet	.50	.50
221	A74	50r blue green	2.00	.50
222	A74	50r org brn ('22)	4.50	.50
223	A75	100r rose red	4.50	.50
224	A75	100r orange ('22)	10.00	.50
225	A75	150r violet ('21)	2.00	.50
226	A75	200r blue	6.00	.50
227	A75	200r rose red ('22)	9.00	.50
228	A76	300r olive gray	17.00	.50
229	A76	400r dull blue ('22)	30.00	3.75
230	A76	500r red brown	24.00	.50
		Nos. 218-230 (13)	112.50	9.75

See Nos. 236-257, 265-266, 268-271, 273-274, 276-281, 302-311, 316-322, 326-340, 431-434, 436-441, 461-463B, 467-470, 472-474, 488-490, 492-494. For surcharges see Nos. 356-358, 376-377.

Nos. 218, 219, and 227 exist on experimental chalky paper. Value $300 each.

Perf. 11, 11½

Engr. **Wmk. 100**

231	A77	600r red orange	2.40	.50
232	A77	1000r claret	4.75	.30
a.		Perf. 8½	150.00	15.00

233	A72	2000r dull violet	27.50	.50
234	A72	5000r brown	21.00	11.00
		Nos. 231-234 (4)	55.65	12.30

Nos. 233 and 234 are inscribed "BRASIL CORREIO." Watermark note below No. 257 also applies to Nos. 231-234.

See No. 282.

King Albert of Belgium and President Epitacio Pessoa
A78

1920, Sept. 19 Engr. *Perf. 11½x11*

235	A78	100r dull red	1.00	*1.75*

Visit of the King and Queen of Belgium.

Types of 1920-22 Issue

Perf. 13x13½, 13x12½

1922-29 Typo. Wmk. 100

236	A73	10r red violet	.75	.35
237	A73	20r olive green	.75	.35
238	A75	20r gray vio ('29)	.50	.50
239	A74	25r brown violet	.75	6.00
240	A74	50r blue grn	4.25	*80.00*
241	A74	50r org brn ('23)	.75	1.50
242	A75	100r rose red	30.00	.50
243	A75	100r orange ('26)	2.00	.50
244	A75	100r turq grn ('28)	1.50	.25
245	A75	150r violet	4.00	.30
246	A75	200r blue	400.00	12.00
247	A75	200r rose red	2.50	.35
248	A75	200r ol grn ('28)	7.00	*9.00*
249	A76	300r olive gray	4.00	.50
250	A76	300r rose red ('29)	2.00	.50
251	A76	400r blue	4.00	.35
252	A76	400r orange ('29)	1.50	*6.00*
253	A76	500r red brown	10.00	.50
254	A76	500r ultra ('29)	16.00	1.40
255	A76	600r brn org ('29)	12.00	3.00
256	A76	700r dull vio ('29)	16.00	1.60
257	A76	1000r turq bl ('29)	16.00	.50
		Nos. 236-257 (22)	536.25	*125.95*

Because of the spacing of the watermark, a few stamps in each sheet show no watermark.

A booklet exists with panes of 6 (2x3), created from the left margin blocks of sheet stamps of Nos. 241, 243, 247, 249 and 253. Once removed from the booklet, they cannot be separately identified.

"Agriculture" — A79

1922 Unwmk. *Perf. 13x13½*

258	A79	40r orange brown	.70	.50
259	A79	80r grnsh blue	.50	*3.00*

See Nos. 263, 267, 275.

No. 259 exists with watermark 100. Value $2500.

Declaration of Ypiranga — A80

Dom Pedro I and Jose Bonifacio — A81

National Exposition and President Pessoa — A82

Unwmk.

1922, Sept. 7 Engr. *Perf. 14*

260	A80	100r ultra	2.40	.75
261	A81	200r red	5.00	.50
262	A82	300r green	5.00	.50
		Nos. 260-262 (3)	12.40	1.75
		Set, never hinged	72.00	

Cent. of independence and Natl. Exposition of 1922.

Agriculture Type of 1922

Perf. 13½x12

1923 Wmk. 100 Typo.

263	A79	40r orange brown	.75	*10.00*

Brazilian Army Entering Bahia — A83

Unwmk.

1923, July 12 Litho. *Perf. 13*

264	A83	200r rose	11.00	7.50

Centenary of the taking of Bahia from the Portuguese.

Types of 1920-22 Issue

Perf. 13x13½

1924 Typo. Wmk. 193

265	A73	10r red violet	10.00	7.00
266	A73	20r olive green	14.00	7.00
267	A79	40r orange brown	8.50	3.00
268	A74	50r orange brown	13.00	*30.00*
269	A75	100r orange	8.50	.75
270	A75	200r rose	13.00	.75
271	A76	400r blue	10.00	6.00
		Nos. 265-271 (7)	77.00	*54.50*

Arms of Equatorial Confederation, 1824 — A84

Unwmk.

1924, July 2 Litho. *Perf. 11*

272	A84	200r bl, blk, yel, & red	3.25	1.75
a.		Red omitted	350.00	350.00

Centenary of the Equatorial Confederation.

Chemically bleached fakes of No. 272a are more common than the genuine error. Expertization is advised.

Types of 1920-22 Issue

Perf. 9½ to 13½ and Compound

1924-28 Typo. Wmk. 101

273	A73	10r red violet	.50	.35
274	A73	20r olive gray	.50	.35
275	A79	40r orange brn	.50	.35
276	A74	50r orange brn	.75	.30
277	A75	100r red orange	2.25	.35
278	A75	200r rose	1.00	.35
279	A76	300r ol gray ('25)	12.00	.50
280	A76	400r blue	6.00	.50
281	A76	500r red brown	25.00	.50

Engr.

282	A77	600r red org ('26)	2.50	.35
283	A72	2000r dull vio ('26)	8.00	.75
284	A72	5000r brown ('26)	22.50	12.50
285	A72	10,000r rose ('28)	30.00	2.00
		Nos. 273-285 (13)	111.50	19.15

Nos. 283-285 are inscribed "BRASIL CORREIO."

Ruy Barbosa — A85

1925 Wmk. 100 *Perf. 11½*

286	A85	1000r claret	10.00	5.00

1925-27 Wmk. 101 *Perf. 11½-11¾*

287	A85	1000r claret	4.00	2.00
a.		Perf. 11-11½ ('25)	100.00	6.50

Watermark of no. 287 reads 'CASA MOEDA ENTRE ESTRELAS' vertically or horizontally.

Watermark on Np. 287a reads 'CASA DA MOEDA ENTRE ESTRELAS' or 'CASACASA DA MOEDA ENTRE ESTRELAS' horizontally, See note below watermark 100.

"Justice" — A86

Scales of Justice and Map of Brazil — A87

Perf. 13½x13

1927, Aug. 11 Typo. Wmk. 206

288	A86	100r deep blue	1.10	.65
289	A87	200r rose	1.05	.65

Founding of the law courses, cent.

Liberty Holding Coffee Leaves — A88

1928, Feb. 5

290	A88	100r blue green	2.00	1.00
291	A88	200r carmine	1.50	.75
292	A88	300r olive black	9.00	.60
		Nos. 290-292 (3)	12.50	2.35

Introduction of the coffee tree in Brazil, bicent.

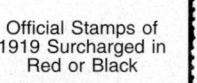

Official Stamps of 1919 Surcharged in Red or Black

Perf. 11, 11½

1928 Wmk. 100 Engr.

293	O3	700r on 500r org	12.00	12.00
a.		Inverted surcharge	450.00	450.00
294	O3	1000r on 100r rose red (Bk)	6.00	.60
295	O3	2000r on 200r dull bl	7.50	1.40
296	O3	5000r on 50r grn	7.50	2.00
a.		Inverted surcharge	450.00	450.00
297	O3	10,000r on 10r ol grn	30.00	2.50
		Nos. 293-297 (5)	63.00	18.50

Nos. 293-297 were used for ordinary postage.

Stamps in the outer rows of the sheets are often without watermark.

Ruy Barbosa — A89

1929 Wmk. 101 *Perf. 11¼x11¾*

300	A89	5000r blue violet	20.00	.50
a.		Perf. 9-9½	30.00	.50

See Nos. 405, 459. For surcharge see No. C29.

Types of 1920-22 Issue

Perf. 13½x12½

1929 Typo. Wmk. 218

302	A75	20r gray violet	.50	.30
303	A75	50r red brown	.50	.30
304	A75	100r turq green	.50	.30
305	A75	200r olive green	30.00	6.00
306	A76	300r rose red	1.50	.30
307	A76	400r orange	1.50	*4.00*
308	A76	500r ultra	15.00	.65
309	A76	600r brown org	20.00	1.50
310	A76	700r dp violet	3.25	.30
311	A76	1000r turq blue	8.00	.30
		Nos. 302-311 (10)	80.75	13.95

Wmk. 218 exists both in vertical alignment and in echelon.

Wmk. in echelon

302a	A75	20r	.50	.40
303a	A75	50r	375.00	240.00
306a	A76	300r	1.50	1.00
308a	A76	500r	450.00	150.00
311a	A76	1000r	17.50	*20.00*

Architectural Fantasies
A90 A91

Architectural Fantasy — A92

Perf. 13x13½

1930, June 20 Wmk. 206

312	A90	100r turq blue	2.00	1.75
313	A91	200r olive gray	4.25	1.00
314	A92	300r rose red	7.00	1.75
		Nos. 312-314 (3)	13.25	4.50

Fourth Pan-American Congress of Architects and Exposition of Architecture.

Types of 1920-22 Issue

1930 Wmk. 221 *Perf. 13x12½*

316	A75	20r gray violet	.60	.35
317	A75	50r red brown	.60	.35
318	A75	100r turq blue	1.50	.35
319	A75	200r olive green	5.00	.75
320	A76	300r rose red	1.25	.35
321	A76	500r ultra	2.50	.35
322	A76	1000r turq blue	35.00	2.00
		Nos. 316-322 (7)	46.45	4.50

A stamp, design A89, 5000r, perforated 11, watermark 221 was prepared but not issued. Value $3750. One is known with a favor cancel.

Imperforates

From 1930 to 1947, imperforate or partly perforated sheets of nearly all commemoratives were obtainable. Additionally many definative issues were available imperforate between 1920 and 1947.

Types of 1920-22 Issue

Perf. 11, 13½x13, 13½x12½, 13x12½

1931-34 Typo. Wmk. 222

326	A75	10r deep brown	.25	.25
327	A75	20r gray violet	.25	.25
328	A74	25r brn vio ('34)	.25	*1.00*
330	A75	50r blue green	.25	.25
331	A75	50r red brown	.25	.25
332	A75	100r orange	.40	.25
334	A75	200r dp carmine	1.00	.40
335	A76	300r olive green	.60	.25
336	A76	400r ultra	2.00	.25
337	A76	500r red brown	4.75	.25
338	A76	600r brown org	12.50	.25
339	A76	700r deep violet	7.50	.25
340	A76	1000r turq blue	18.00	.25
		Nos. 326-340 (13)	48.00	4.15

Getulio Vargas and Joao Pessoa
A93

Vargas and Pessoa
A94

Oswaldo Aranha
A95 A96

Antonio Carlos
A97

Pessoa
A98

Vargas — A99

Unwmk.

1931, Apr. 29 Litho. *Perf. 14*

342 A93 10r + 10r lt bl .25 *20.00*
343 A93 20r + 20r yel brn .25 *14.00*
344 A95 50r + 50r bl grn, red & yel .25 *.25*
a. Red missing at left 1.60 *1.60*
345 A93 100r + 50r orange .70 .45
346 A93 200r + 100r green .55 .45
347 A94 300r + 150r multi .55 .45
348 A93 400r + 200r dp rose 1.00 1.00
349 A93 500r + 250r dk bl 1.00 .50
350 A93 600r + 300r brn vio .95 *17.00*
351 A94 700r + 350r multi .80 .30
352 A96 1000r + 500r brt grn, red & yel 2.00 .30
353 A97 2000r + 1000r gray blk & red 6.00 .80
354 A98 5000r + 2500r blk & red 32.50 13.50
355 A99 10000r + 5000r brt grn & yel 65.00 24.00
Nos. 342-355 (14) 111.80 93.00
Set, Never hinged 210.00

Revolution of Oct. 3, 1930. Prepared as semi-postal stamps, Nos. 342-355 were sold as ordinary postage stamps with stated surtax ignored.

Nos. 306, 320 and 250 Surcharged

Perf. 13½x12½

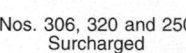

1931, July 20 Wmk. 218

356 A76 200r on 300r rose red 2.50 1.40
a. Wmk. in echelon 30.00 30.00
b. Inverted surcharge 95.00 95.00

Perf. 13x12½

Wmk. 221

357 A76 200r on 300r rose red .50 .25
a. Inverted surcharge 95.00 95.00
b. Double surcharge 80.00 80.00

Perf. 13½x12½

Wmk. 100

358 A76 200r on 300r rose red 120.00 120.00
a. Inverted surcharge 1,200. —

Map of South America Showing Meridian of Tordesillas — A100

Joao Ramalho and Tibiriça
A101

Martim Affonso de Souza
A102

King John III of Portugal
A103

Disembarkation of M. A. de Souza at Sao Vicente — A104

Wmk. 222

1932, June 3 Typo. *Perf. 13*

359 A100 20r dk violet .40 .40
360 A101 100r black .40 .40
361 A102 200r purple .40 .40
362 A103 600r red brown 1.60 2.00

Engr.

Wmk. 101

Perf. 9½, 11, Compound

363 A104 700r ultra 3.00 2.50
Nos. 359-363 (5) 5.80 5.70

1st colonization of Brazil at Sao Vicente, in 1532, under the hereditary captaincy of Martim Affonso de Souza.

Values for No. 363 are for perf. 9½, other varieties are worth more. All nine perforation varieties can be found in a single block of nine. Value $225.

Revolutionary Issue

Map of Brazil — A105

Soldier and Flag — A106

Allegory: Freedom, Justice, Equality
A107

Soldier's Head
A108

"LEX" and Sword
A109

Symbolical of Law and Order — A110

Symbolical of Justice — A111

Perf. 11½

1932, Sept. Litho. Unwmk.

364 A105 100r brown org .60 2.00
365 A106 200r dk car .50 .80
366 A107 300r gray green 1.25 3.75
367 A108 400r dark blue 3.50 *6.00*
368 A105 500r blk brn 3.50 *6.00*
369 A107 600r red 3.50 *6.00*
370 A106 700r violet 2.50 *6.00*
371 A108 1000r orange 1.60 *6.00*
372 A109 2000r dark brn 22.00 *30.00*
373 A110 5000r yellow grn 30.00 *55.00*
374 A111 10000r plum 35.00 *60.00*
Nos. 364-374 (11) 103.95 181.55

Issued by the revolutionary forces in the state of Sao Paulo during the revolt of September, 1932. Subsequently the stamps were recognized by the Federal Government and placed in general use.

Excellent counterfeits of Nos. 373 and 374 exist. Favor cancels, applied at a later date, abound.

City of Vassouras and Illuminated Memorial — A112

Wmk. 222

1933, Jan. 15 Typo. *Perf. 12*

375 A112 200r rose red 1.00 .60

City of Vassouras founding, cent.

Nos. 306, 320 Surcharged

Perf. 13½x12½

1933, July 28 Wmk. 218

376 A76 200r on 300r rose red 2.50 2.50
a. Wmk. 218 in echelon (No. 306a) 30.00 30.00
b. Wmk. 100 (No. 250) 350.00 350.00
d. As "b," inverted surcharge 1,350. —

Perf. 13x12½

Wmk. 221

377 A76 200r on 300r rose red .75 .75
a. Inverted surcharge 100.00 100.00
b. Double surcharge 100.00 100.00

Religious Symbols and Inscriptions — A113

Wmk. 222

1933, Sept. 3 Typo. *Perf. 13*

378 A113 200r dark red 1.00 .80

1st Natl. Eucharistic Congress in Brazil.

"Flag of the Race"
A114

1933, Aug. 18

379 A114 200r deep red 1.25 .80

The raising of the "Flag of the Race" and the 441st anniv. of the sailing of Columbus from Palos, Spain, Aug. 3, 1492.

Republic Figure, Flags of Brazil and Argentina — A115

Wmk. 101

1933, Oct. 7 Engr. *Perf. 11½*

380 A115 200r blue .25 .25

Thick Laid Paper

1933, Dec. Wmk. 236 *Perf. 11, 11½*

381 A115 400r green .60 .60
382 A115 600r brt rose 3.00 3.50
383 A115 1000r lt violet 3.50 3.00
Nos. 380-383 (4) 7.35 7.35

Visit of President Justo of the Argentina to Brazil, Oct. 2-7, 1933.

Allegory: "Faith and Energy" — A116

1933 Typo. Wmk. 222

384 A116 200r dark red .50 .25
385 A116 200r dark violet 1.50 .25

See Nos. 435, 471, 491.

Allegory of Flight — A117

Wmk. 236

1934, Apr. 15 Engr. *Perf. 12*

386 A117 200r blue .80 .25

1st Natl. Aviation Congress at Sao Paulo.

A118

Wmk. 222

1934, May 12 Typo. *Perf. 11*

387 A118 200r dark olive .25 .25
388 A118 400r carmine 1.00 *1.25*
a. Double impression 1,500.
389 A118 700r ultra 1.60 1.60
390 A118 1000r orange 4.75 .80
Nos. 387-390 (4) 7.60 3.90

7th Intl. Fair at Rio de Janeiro.

Christ of Corcovado A119

1934, Oct. 20

392 A119 300r dark red, I	4.25	4.25
a. Tete beche pair	17.00	17.00
393 A119 700r ultra, I	17.00	17.00
a. Tete beche pair	60.00	60.00

The three printings of Nos. 392-393, distinguishable by shades, sell for different prices.

José de Anchieta A120

Thick Laid Paper

Perf. 11, 12, Compound

1934, Nov. 8 **Wmk. 236**

394 A120 200r yellow brown	.90	.40
395 A120 300r violet	.90	.40
396 A120 700r blue	2.00	2.50
397 A120 1000r lt green	4.00	1.25
Nos. 394-397 (4)	7.80	4.55

Jose de Anchieta, S.J. (1534-1597), Portuguese missionary and "father of Brazilian literature."

A121

"Brazil" and "Uruguay" — A122

Wmk. 222

1935, Jan. 8 **Typo.** ***Perf. 11***

398 A121 200r orange	.80	.25
399 A122 300r yellow	.80	*1.25*
400 A122 700r ultra	4.50	10.00
401 A121 1000r dk violet	12.10	8.00
Nos. 398-401 (4)	18.10	19.50

Visit of President Terra of Uruguay.

View of Town of Igarassu A123

1935, July 1

402 A123 200r maroon & brn	1.60	.75
403 A123 300r vio & olive brn	1.60	.60

Captaincy of Pernambuco founding, 400th anniv.

Types of 1918-29

Thick Laid Paper

Perf. 11, 12, Compound

1934-36 **Engr.** **Wmk. 236**

404 A72 2000r violet	50.00	.80
405 A89 5000r blue vio ('36)	100.00	.80
406 A72 10000r claret ('36)	85.00	.80
Nos. 404-406 (3)	235.00	2.40

No. 404 is inscribed "BRASIL CORREIO."

Revolutionist A124

Bento Gonçalves da Silva — A125

Duke of Caxias A126

1935, Sept. 20-1936, Jan.

407 A124 200r black	1.00	.50
408 A124 300r rose lake	1.00	.50
409 A125 700r dull blue	3.25	*4.50*
410 A126 1000r light violet	4.75	1.75
Nos. 407-410 (4)	10.00	7.25

Centenary of the "Ragged" Revolution.

Federal District Coat of Arms A127

Wmk. 222

1935, Oct. 19 **Typo.** ***Perf. 11***

411 A127 200r blue	3.25	3.25

8th Intl. Sample Fair held at Rio de Janeiro.

Coutinho's Ship — A128

Arms of Fernandes Coutinho — A129

1935, Oct. 25

412 A128 300r maroon	2.50	1.25
413 A129 700r turq blue	5.50	3.75

400th anniversary of the establishment of the first Portuguese colony at Espirito Santo by Vasco Fernandes Coutinho.

Gavea, Rock near Rio de Janeiro A130

1935, Oct. 12 **Wmk. 245** ***Perf. 11***

414 A130 300r brown & vio	2.50	1.25
415 A130 300r blk & turq bl	2.50	1.25
416 A130 300r Prus bl & ultra	2.50	1.25
417 A130 300r crimson & blk	2.50	1.25
Nos. 414-417 (4)	10.00	5.00

"Child's Day," Oct. 12.

Viscount of Cairu — A131

Perf. 11, 12x11

1936, Jan. 20 **Engr.** **Wmk. 236**

418 A131 1200r violet	7.50	6.00

Jose da Silva Lisboa, Viscount of Cairu (1756-1835).

View of Cametá A132

1936, Feb. 26 ***Perf. 11, 12***

419 A132 200r brown orange	1.25	1.00
420 A132 300r green	1.25	.85

300th anniversary of the founding of the city of Cameta, Dec. 24, 1635.

Coining Press A133

Thick Laid Paper

1936, Mar. 24 ***Perf. 11***

421 A133 300r pur brn, *cr*	1.00	1.00

1st Numismatic Cong. at Sao Paulo, Mar., 1936.

Carlos Gomes — A134

"Il Guarany" — A135

Thick Laid Paper

1936, July 11 ***Perf. 11, 11x12***

422 A134 300r dull rose	.75	.25
423 A134 300r black brown	.75	.25
424 A135 700r ocher	3.25	1.50
425 A135 700r blue	4.00	2.50
Nos. 422-425 (4)	8.75	4.50

Birth cent. of Antonio Carlos Gomes, who composed the opera "Il Guarany."

Scales of Justice — A136

Wmk. 222

1936, July 4 **Typo.** ***Perf. 11***

426 A136 300r rose	1.00	.65
a. Double impression	525.00	—

First National Judicial Congress.

Federal District Coat of Arms A137

1936, Nov. 13 **Typo.** **Wmk. 249**

427 A137 200r rose red	1.25	.50

Ninth International Sample Fair held at Rio de Janeiro.

Eucharistic Congress Seal — A138

1936, Dec. 17 **Wmk. 245** ***Perf. 11½***

428 A138 300r grn, yel, bl & blk	1.00	.50

2nd Natl. Eucharistic Congress in Brazil.

Botafogo Bay A139

Thick Laid Paper

Wmk. 236

1937, Jan. 2 **Engr.** ***Perf. 11***

429 A139 700r blue	1.25	.65
430 A139 700r black	1.25	.65

Birth cent. of Francisco Pereira Passos, engineer who planned the modern city of Rio de Janeiro.

Types of 1920-22, 1933

Perf. 11, 11½ and Compound

1936-37 **Typo.** **Wmk. 249**

431 A75 10r deep brown	.35	.25
432 A75 20r dull violet	.35	.25
433 A75 50r blue green	.35	.25
434 A75 100r orange	1.00	.25
435 A116 200r dk violet	2.75	.25
436 A76 300r olive green	.75	.25
437 A76 400r blue	1.75	.25
438 A76 500r lt brown	2.40	.25
439 A76 600r brn org ('37)	12.00	.25
440 A76 700r deep violet	4.75	.25
441 A76 1000r turq blue	8.00	.25
Nos. 431-441 (11)	34.45	2.75

Massed Flags and Star of Esperanto A140

1937, Jan. 19

442 A140 300r green	1.00	.75

Ninth Brazilian Esperanto Congress.

Bay of Rio de Janeiro A141

1937, June 9 Unwmk. *Perf. 12½*

443 A141 300r orange red & blk 1.00 .75
444 A141 700r blue & dk brn 2.00 1.00

2nd South American Radio Communication Conf. held in Rio, June 7-19.

Globe — A142

Perf. 11, 12

1937, Sept. 4 Wmk. 249

445 A142 300r green 1.00 .65

50th anniversary of Esperanto.

Monroe Palace, Rio de Janeiro A143

Botanical Garden, Rio de Janeiro — A144

1937, Sept. 30 Unwmk. *Perf. 12½*

446 A143 200r lt brn & bl .75 .50
447 A144 300r org & ol grn .75 .50
448 A143 2000r grn & cerise 8.00 *12.00*
449 A144 10000r lake & indigo 65.00 57.50
Nos. 446-449 (4) 74.50 70.50

Brig. Gen. Jose da Silva Paes — A145

1937, Oct. 11 Wmk. 249 *Perf. 11½*

450 A145 300r blue .75 .50

Bicentenary of Rio Grande do Sul.

Eagle and Shield — A146

1937, Dec. 2 Typo. *Perf. 11*

451 A146 400r dark blue .85 .25

150th anniversary of the US Constitution.

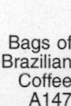

Bags of Brazilian Coffee A147

Frame Engraved, Center Typographed

1938, Jan. 17 Unwmk. *Perf. 12½*

452 A147 1200r multicolored 6.00 .60

Arms of Olinda A148

Perf. 11, 11x11½

1938, Jan. 24 Engr. Wmk. 249

453 A148 400r violet .80 .25

4th cent. of the founding of the city of Olinda.

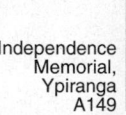

Independence Memorial, Ypiranga A149

1938, Jan. 24 Typo. *Perf. 11*

454 A149 400r brown olive .80 .25

Proclamation of Brazil's independence by Dom Pedro, Sept. 7, 1822.

Iguaçu Falls — A150

Perf. 12½

1938, Jan. 10 Unwmk. Engr.

455 A150 1000r sepia & yel brn 2.50 1.00
456 A150 5000r ol blk & grn 30.00 25.00

Couto de Magalhaes A151

Perf. 11, 11x11½

1938, Mar. 17 Wmk. 249

457 A151 400r dull green .80 .25

General Couto de Magalhaes (1837-1898), statesman, soldier, explorer, writer, developer.

Types of 1918-38

Perf. 11, 12x11, 12x11½, 12

1938 Engr. Wmk. 249

458 A72 2000r blue violet 17.50 .30
459 A89 5000r violet blue 55.00 1.50
460 A72 10000r rose lake 90.00 2.25
Nos. 458-460 (3) 162.50 4.05

No. 458 is inscribed "BRASIL CORREIO."

Types of 1920-22

1938 Wmk. 245 Typo. *Perf. 11*

461 A75 50r blue green 1.40 1.10
462 A75 100r yellow 4.75 1.10
463 A76 300r olive green 1.40 2.50
463A A76 400r ultra 425.00 200.00
463B A76 500r red brown 1.40 *80.00*
Nos. 461-463B (5) 433.95 284.70

National Archives Building A152

1938, May 20 Wmk. 249

464 A152 400r brown .75 .25

Centenary of National Archives.

Souvenir Sheets

Sir Rowland Hill — A153

1938, Oct. 22 *Imperf.*

465 A153 Sheet of 10 18.00 18.00
a. 400r dull green, single stamp 1.70 1.70

Brazilian Intl. Philatelic Exposition (Brapex). Issued in sheets measuring 106x118mm. A few perforated sheets exist.

President Vargas — A154

1938, Nov. 10 *Perf. 11*

Without Gum

466 A154 Sheet of 10 35.00 35.00
a. 400r slate blue, single stamp 1.75 1.75

Constitution of Brazil, set up by President Vargas, Nov. 10, 1937. Size: 113x135½mm.

Types of 1920-33

1939 Typo. Wmk. 256 *Perf. 11*

467 A75 10r red brown 1.50 1.50
468 A75 20r dull violet 2.75 .30
469 A75 50r blue green 2.25 .30
470 A75 100r yellow org 2.25 .30
471 A116 200r dk violet 3.25 .30
472 A76 400r ultra 4.25 .30
473 A76 600r dull orange 6.00 .30
474 A76 1000r turq blue 25.00 .30
Nos. 467-474 (8) 47.25 3.60

View of Rio de Janeiro — A155

1939, June 14 Engr. Wmk. 249

475 A155 1200r dull violet 2.00 .25

View of Santos — A156

1939, Aug. 23

476 A156 400r dull blue .50 .40

Centenary of founding of Santos.

Chalice Vine and Blossoms — A157

1939, Aug. 23

477 A157 400r green 1.00 .35

1st South American Botanical Congress held in January, 1938.

Eucharistic Congress Seal — A158

1939, Sept. 3

478 A158 400r rose red .60 .45

Third National Eucharistic Congress.

Duke of Caxias, Army Patron — A159

1939, Sept. 12 Photo. *Rouletted*

479 A159 400r deep ultra .60 .45

Issued for Soldiers' Day.

A159a

A159b

A159c

A159d

Designs: 400r, George Washington. 800r, Emperor Pedro II. 1200r, Grover Cleveland. 1600r, Statue of Friendship, given by US.

Unwmk.

1939, Oct. 7 Engr. *Perf. 12*

480	A159a	400r yellow orange	.40	.25
481	A159b	800r dark green	.35	.25
482	A159c	1200r rose car	.40	.25
483	A159d	1600r dark blue	.40	.25
		Nos. 480-483 (4)	1.55	1.00

New York World's Fair.

Benjamin Constant A160

Fonseca on Horseback A162

Manuel Deodoro da Fonseca and President Vargas A161

Wmk. 249

1939, Nov. 15 Photo. *Rouletted*

484	A160	400r deep green	.85	.25
485	A161	1200r chocolate	.65	.25

Engr. *Perf. 11*

486	A162	800r gray black	.80	.25
		Nos. 484-486 (3)	2.30	.75

Proclamation of the Republic, 50th anniv.
No. 484 was issued without gum.

President Roosevelt, President Vargas and Map of the Americas A163

1940, Apr. 14

487	A163	400r slate blue	.60	.25

Pan American Union, 50th anniversary.

Types of 1920-33

1940-41 Typo. Wmk. 264 *Perf. 11*

488	A75	10r red brown	.80	.80
489	A75	20r dull violet	.80	*1.50*
489A	A75	50r blue grn ('41)	1.50	*2.25*
490	A75	100r yellow org	2.50	.50
491	A116	200r violet	5.00	.50
492	A76	400r ultra	13.00	.50
493	A76	600r dull org	13.00	.50
494	A76	1000r turq blue	27.50	.50
		Nos. 488-494 (8)	64.10	*7.05*

Map of Brazil — A164

1940, Sept. 7 Engr.

495	A164	400r carmine	.50	.25
a.		Unwmkd.	160.00	100.00
b.		Wmk. 249	1,500.	—

9th Brazilian Congress of Geography held at Florianopolis.

No. 495 exists with papermaker's watermark of a large globe and "American Bank" in sheet. Value $350.

Nos. 495a-b were issued without gum.

Victoria Regia Water Lily — A165

President Vargas — A166

Relief Map of Brazil — A167

1940, Oct. 30 Wmk. 249 *Perf. 11*

Without Gum

496	A165	1000r dull violet	2.25	2.25
a.		Sheet of 10	24.00	*24.00*
497	A166	5000r red	15.00	*18.00*
a.		Sheet of 10	150.00	*200.00*
498	A167	10,000r slate blue	30.00	15.00
a.		Sheet of 10	225.00	*250.00*
		Nos. 496-498 (3)	47.25	*35.25*

New York World's Fair.

All three sheets exist unwatermarked and also with papermaker's watermark of large globe and "AMERICA BANK" in sheet. Value $600 per sheet. A few imperforate sheets also exist.

Nos. 496-498 were issued without gum.

Joaquim Machado de Assis — A168

1940, Nov. 1

499	A168	400r black	.65	.25

Birth centenary of Joaquim Maria Machado de Assis, poet and novelist.

Pioneers and Buildings of Porto Alegre — A169

1940, Nov. 2 Wmk. 264

500	A169	400r green	.45	.25

Colonization of Porto Alegre, bicent.

Proclamation of King John IV of Portugal — A173

1940, Dec. 1 Wmk. 249

501	A173	1200r blue black	1.75	.50

800th anniv. of Portuguese independence and 300th anniv. of the restoration of the monarchy.

No. 501 was also printed on paper with papermaker's watermark of large globe and "AMERICA BANK." Value $375. Unwatermarked stamps are from these sheets. Value of unwatermarked stamps, $150.

Brazilian Flags and Head of Liberty — A175

Wmk. 256

1940, Dec. 18 Engr. *Perf. 11*

502	A175	400r dull violet	.45	.25
b.		Unwmkd.	225.00	225.00

Wmk. 245

502A	A175	400r dull violet	62.50	40.00

10th anniv. of the inauguration of President Vargas.

Calendar Sheet and Inscription "Day of the Fifth General Census of Brazil" — A176

Wmk. 256

1941, Jan. 14 Typo. *Perf. 11*

503	A176	400r blue & red	.40	.25
		Never hinged	.80	

Wmk. 245

504	A176	400r blue & red	2.00	.75
		Never hinged	8.00	

Fifth general census of Brazil.

King Alfonso Henriques A177

Father Antonio Vieira A178

Salvador Corrêia de Sa e Benevides — A179

President Carmona of Portugal and President Vargas A180

Wmk. 264

1940-41 Photo. *Rouletted*

504A	A177	200r pink	.35	.25
505	A178	400r ultra	.35	.25
506	A179	800r brt violet	.40	.25
506A	A180	5400r slate grn	2.50	.40

Wmk. 249

507	A177	200r pink	7.25	2.50
507A	A178	400r ultra	50.00	30.00
508	A180	5400r slate grn	7.25	3.75
		Nos. 504A-508 (7)	68.10	37.40
		Set, never hinged	160.00	

Portuguese Independence, 800th anniv.

For surcharge & overprint see nos. C45, C47.

Jose de Anchieta — A181

Wmk. 264

1941, Aug. 1 Engr. *Perf. 11*

509	A181	1000r gray violet	1.00	.50
		Never hinged	4.00	

Society of Jesus, 400th anniversary.

Amador Bueno — A182

1941, Oct. 20 *Perf. 11½*

510	A182	400r black	.75	.25
		Never hinged	1.25	

300th anniv. of the acclamation of Amador Bueno (1572-1648) as king of Sao Paulo.

Air Force Emblem A183

1941, Oct. 20 *Perf. 11*

511	A183	5400r slate green	3.50	1.00
		Never hinged	12.00	

Issued in connection with Aviation Week, as propaganda for the Brazilian Air Force.

Petroleum A184

Agriculture A185

Steel Industry A186

Commerce A187

Marshal Peixoto A188

Count of Porto Alegre A189

Admiral J. A. C. Maurity A190

"Armed Forces" A191

Vargas — A192

1941-42 Wmk. 264 Typo. *Perf. 11*

512 A184 10r yellow brn .50 .40
513 A184 20r olive grn .50 .40
514 A184 50r olive bis .50 .40
515 A184 100r blue grn .50 .40
516 A185 200r brown org 2.00 .40
517 A185 300r lilac rose .50 .40
518 A185 400r grnsh blue 2.40 .40
519 A185 500r salmon .50 .40
520 A186 600r violet 2.00 .40
521 A186 700r brt rose .50 .40
522 A186 1000r gray 3.75 .40
523 A186 1200r dl blue 4.75 .40
524 A187 2000r gray vio 5.50 .40

Engr.

525 A188 5000r blue 15.00 .40
526 A189 10,000r rose red 18.00 .40
527 A190 20,000r dp brown 22.50 2.00
528 A191 50,000r red ('42) 47.50 13.50
529 A192 100,000r blue ('42) 1.25 *13.50*
Nos. 512-529 (18) 128.15 35.00

Nos. 512 to 527 and later issues come on thick or thin paper. The stamps on both papers also exist with three vertical green lines printed on the back, a control mark.

See Nos. 541-587, 592-593, 656-670.

Bernardino de Campos A193

Prudente de Morais A194

1942, May 25

533 A193 1000r red 1.60 .40
Never hinged 20.00
534 A194 1200r blue 6.00 .25
Never hinged 60.00

100th anniversary of the birth of Bernardino de Campos and Prudente de Morais, lawyers and statesmen of Brazil.

Head of Indo-Brazilian Bull — A195

1942, May 1 Wmk. 264 *Perf. 11½*

535 A195 200r blue .40 .25
Never hinged 1.50
536 A195 400r orange brn .40 .25
Never hinged 1.50
a. Wmk. 267 85.00 85.00
Never hinged 175.00

2nd Agriculture and Livestock Show of Central Brazil held at Uberaba.

Outline of Brazil and Torch of Knowledge — A196

Wmk. 264

1942, July 5 Typo. *Perf. 11*

537 A196 400r orange brn .60 .25
Never hinged 1.50

8th Brazilian Congress of Education.

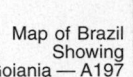

Map of Brazil Showing Goiania — A197

1942, July 5

538 A197 400r lt violet .60 .25
Never hinged 1.50

Founding of Goiania city.

Seal of Congress A198

1942, Sept. 20 Wmk. 264

539 A198 400r olive bister .60 .25
Never hinged 1.25
a. Wmk. 267 30.00 30.00
Never hinged 70.00

4th Natl. Eucharistic Cong. at Sao Paulo.

Types of 1941-42

1942-47 Wmk. 245 *Perf. 11*

541 A184 20r olive green .60 *2.00*
542 A184 50r ol bis .60 .45
543 A184 100r blue grn 3.75 3.75
544 A185 200r brown org 2.00 .50
545 A185 400r grnsh blue 2.00 .50
546 A186 600r lt violet 5.50 .50
547 A186 700r brt rose .60 *2.00*
548 A186 1200r dl blue 5.50 .50
549 A187 2000r gray vio ('47) 14.00 .50

Engr.

550 A188 5000r blue 25.00 .50
551 A189 10,000r rose red 22.50 .75
552 A190 20,000r dp brn ('47) 15.00 2.00
553 A192 100,000r blue 18.00 *22.50*
Nos. 541-553 (13) 115.05 36.45

Types of 1941-42

1941-47 Typo. Wmk. 268 *Perf. 11*

554 A184 20r olive grn .80 .90
555 A184 50r ol bis ('47) 2.00 1.50
556 A184 100r bl grn ('43) 1.25 .45
557 A185 200r brn org ('43) .80 .40
558 A185 300r lil rose ('43) 1.25 .40
559 A185 400r grnsh bl ('42) 1.25 .45
560 A185 500r sal ('43) 1.25 .40
561 A186 600r violet 2.00 .40
562 A186 700r brt rose ('45) 1.25 *5.50*
563 A186 1000r gray 2.40 .40
564 A186 1200r dp bl ('44) 4.00 .45
565 A187 2000r gray vio ('43) 15.00 .40

Engr.

566 A188 5000r blue ('43) 15.00 .40
567 A189 10,000r rose red ('43) 22.50 1.25
568 A190 20,000r dp brn ('42) 60.00 .40
569 A191 50,000r red ('42) 30.00 4.00
a. 50,000r dark brown red ('47) 30.00 15.00
570 A192 100,000r blue 2.00 *5.50*
Nos. 554-570 (17) 162.75 23.20

Nos. 554-570 exist with horizontal and vertical watermarks, coming in two varieties, "CASA+DA+MOEDA+DO+BRAZIL" and "CASA+DA+MOEDA."

Types of 1941-42

1942-47 Typo. Wmk. 267

573 A184 20r ol grn ('43) .60 .40
574 A184 50r ol bis ('43) .60 .40
575 A184 100r bl grn ('43) .60 .40
576 A185 200r brn org ('43) 2.00 .40
577 A185 400r grnsh blue .60 .40
578 A185 500r sal ('43) 175.00 45.00
579 A186 600r violet ('43) 30.00 4.50
580 A186 700r brt rose ('47) 1.25 *45.00*
581 A186 1000r gray ('44) 4.00 .40
582 A186 1200r dl bl 4.00 .40
583 A187 2000r gray vio 7.50 .40

Engr.

584 A188 5000r blue 7.50 .40
585 A189 10,000r rose red ('44) 15.00 2.00
586 A190 20,000r dp brn ('45) 20.00 .90
587 A191 50,000r red ('43) 75.00 18.00
Nos. 573-587 (15) 343.65 119.00

1942 Typo. Wmk. 249

592 A184 100r bl grn 15.00 *20.00*
593 A186 600r violet 4.50 4.50

Map Showing Amazon River — A199

1943, Mar. 19 Wmk. 267 *Perf. 11*

607 A199 40c orange brown .60 .25
Never hinged 1.50

Discovery of the Amazon River, 400th anniv.

Reproduction of Brazil Stamp of 1866 — A200

1943, Mar. 28 Wmk. 267

608 A200 40c violet .60 .60
Never hinged 2.00
a. Wmk. 268 *1,100.*
Never hinged 1,900.

Centenary of city of Petropolis.

Adaptation of 1843 "Bull's-eye" A201

1943, Aug. 1 Engr. *Imperf.*

609 A201 30c black .70 .30
610 A201 60c black .85 .25
611 A201 90c black .70 .30
Nos. 609-611 (3) 2.25 .85
Set, never hinged 7.00

Cent. of the 1st postage stamp of Brazil.

Nos. 609-611 exist unwatermarked. Values $200, $400, and $200 respectively.

Nos. 610 and 611 exist with Globe watermark. See note below No. 501. Value $400 each.

Souvenir Sheet

A202

Wmk. 281 Horizontally or Vertically

1943 Engr. *Imperf.*

Without Gum

612 A202 Sheet of 3 20.00 20.00
a. 30c black 6.00 6.00
b. 60c black 6.00 6.00
c. 90c black 6.00 6.00

No. 612 exists unwatermarked. Value $600. Exists in two sizes. Sheets over 100mm vertically are worth more. Value $250 unused and $35 used.

Ubaldino do Amaral — A203

Perf. 11, 12, Compound

1943, Aug. 27 Typo. Wmk. 264

613 A203 40c dull slate green .30 .25
Never hinged 2.00
a. Wmk. 267 50.00 30.00
Never hinged 100.00

Birth centenary of Ubaldino do Amaral, banker and statesman.

"Justice" — A204

1943, Aug. 30 Wmk. 267

614 A204 2cr bright rose .85 .85
Never hinged 3.50

Centenary of Institute of Brazilian Lawyers.

Indo-Brazilian Bull — A205

1943, Aug. 30 Engr.

615 A205 40c dk red brn .55 .30
Never hinged 2.00

9th Livestock Show at Bahia.

José Barbosa Rodrigues — A206

1943, Nov. 13 Typo.

616 A206 40c bluish grn .40 .25
Never hinged 2.00

Birth cent. of Jose Barbosa Rodrigues, botanist.

Charity Hospital, Santos A207

1943, Nov. 7 Engr.

617 A207 1cr blue .55 .35
Never hinged 2.00

400th anniv. of Charity Hospital, Santos.

Pedro Americo de Figueiredo e Melo (1843-1905), Artist-hero and Statesman — A208

Wmk. 267

1943, Dec. 16 Typo. *Perf. 11*

618 A208 40c brown orange	.40	.25
Never hinged	2.00	

Gen. A. E. Gomes Carneiro A209

1944, Feb. 9 Engr.

619 A209 1.20cr rose	1.00	.25
Never hinged	2.40	

50th anniversary of the Lapa siege.

Statue of Baron of Rio Branco — A210

1944, May 13 Typo.

620 A210 1cr blue	.45	.25
Never hinged	2.40	

Statue of the Baron of Rio Branco unveiling.

Duke of Caxias A211

1944, May 13 Unwmk. *Perf. 12*
Granite Paper

621 A211 1.20cr bl grn & pale org	.60	.25
Never hinged	2.40	

Centenary of pacification of Sao Paulo and Minas Gerais in an independence movement in 1842.

YMCA Seal — A212

1944, June 7 Litho. *Perf. 11*
Granite Paper

622 A212 40c dp bl, car & yel	.25	.25
Never hinged	1.60	

Centenary of Young Men's Christian Assn.

Chamber of Commerce Rio Grande — A213

Wmk. 268

1944, Sept. 25 Engr. *Perf. 12*

623 A213 40c lt yellow brn	.25	.25
Never hinged	1.60	

Centenary of the Chamber of Commerce of Rio Grande.

Martim F. R. de Andrada A214

1945, Jan. 30 *Perf. 11*

624 A214 40c blue	.30	.25
Never hinged	1.60	

Centenary of the death of Martim F. R. de Andrada, statesman.

Meeting of Duke of Caxias and David Canabarro A215

1945, Mar. 19 Photo.

625 A215 40c ultra	.30	.25
Never hinged	1.60	

Pacification of Rio Grande do Sul, cent.

Globe and "Esperanto" — A216

1945, Apr. 16

626 A216 40c lt blue grn	.40	.35
Never hinged	1.60	

10th Esperanto Congress, Rio, Apr. 14-22.

Baron of Rio Branco's Bookplate A217

1945, Apr. 20 Wmk. 268 *Perf. 11*

627 A217 40c violet	.40	.25
Never hinged	1.00	

Cent. of the birth of Jose Maria da Silva Paranhos, Baron of Rio Branco.

Nostalgia A218

Glory — A219

Victory A220

Peace A221

Cooperation — A222

Rouletted 7

1945, May 8 Engr. Wmk. 268

628 A218 20c dk rose vio	.25	.25
629 A219 40c dk carmine	.25	.25
630 A220 1cr dull orange	3.00	3.00
631 A221 2cr steel blue	.55	.45
632 A222 5cr green	2.00	.35
Nos. 628-632 (5)	6.05	4.30
Set, never hinged	17.00	

Victory of the Allied Nations in Europe.

Nos. 628-632 exist on thin card, imperf. and unwatermarked.

Francisco Manoel da Silva (1795-1865), Composer (in 1831) of the National Anthem — A223

Wmk. 245

1945, May 30 Typo. *Perf. 12*

633 A223 40c brt rose	.40	.25
Never hinged	1.50	
a. Wmk. 268	15.00	15.00
Never hinged	35.00	

Bahia Institute of Geography and History A224

1945, May 30 Wmk. 268 *Perf. 11*

634 A224 40c lt ultra	.30	.25
Never hinged	2.25	

50th anniv. of the founding of the Institute of Geography and History at Bahia.

Emblems of 5th Army and B.E.F.
A225 A226

U.S. Flag and Shoulder Patches A227

Brazilian Flag and Shoulder Patches A228

Victory Symbol and Shoulder Patches — A229

1945, July 18 Litho.

635 A225 20c multicolored	.30	.25
636 A226 40c multicolored	.30	.25
637 A227 1cr multicolored	1.15	.35
638 A228 2cr multicolored	1.60	.50
639 A229 5cr multicolored	2.75	.65
Nos. 635-639 (5)	6.10	2.00
Set, never hinged	18.00	

Honoring the Brazilian Expeditionary Force and the US 5th Army Battle against the Axis in Italy.

Radio Tower and Map — A230

1945, Sept. 3 Engr.

640 A230 1.20cr gray	.30	.25
Never hinged	2.00	

Third Inter-American Conference on Radio Communications.

No. 640 was reproduced on a souvenir card with blue background and inscriptions. Size: 145x161mm.

A 40c lilac stamp, picturing the International Bridge between Argentina and Brazil and portraits of Presidents Justo and Vargas, was prepared late in 1945. It was not issued, but later was sold, without postal value, to collectors. Value, 30 cents.

Admiral Luiz Felipe Saldanha da Gama (1846-1895) — A231

1946, Apr. 7
641 A231 40c gray black .30 .95
Never hinged 1.20

Exists unwatermarked. Value $120.

Princess Isabel d'Orleans-Braganca Birth Cent. — A232

1946, July 29 **Unwmk.**
642 A232 40c black .30 5.00
Never hinged 1.20

Post Horn, V and Envelope — A233

Post Office, Rio de Janeiro A234

Bay of Rio de Janeiro and Plane A235

Wmk. 268
1946, Sept. 2 Litho. ***Perf. 11***
643 A233 40c blk & pale org .25 .25

Perf. 12½
Engr. **Unwmk.**
Center in Ultramarine
644 A234 2cr slate .40 .40
645 A234 5cr orange brn .60 .40
646 A234 10cr dk violet 1.00 .40

Center in Brown Orange
647 A235 1.30cr dk green .60 .40
648 A235 1.70cr car rose 2.75 .75
649 A235 2.20cr dp ultra 4.00 .55
Nos. 643-649 (7) 9.60 3.15
Set, never hinged 24.00

5th Postal Union Congress of the Americas and Spain.
No. 643 was reproduced on a souvenir card. Size: 188x239mm. Sold for 10cr.

Liberty — A236

Perf. 11x11½
1946, Sept. 18 **Wmk. 268**
650 A236 40c blk & gray .25 .25
Never hinged .40
a. Unwmkd. 150.00
Never hinged 300.00

Adoption of the Constitution of 1946.

Columbus Lighthouse, Dominican Republic — A237

1946, Sept. 14 Litho. ***Perf. 11***
651 A237 5cr Prus grn 4.00 1.60
Never hinged 20.00

Orchid — A238

1946, Nov. 8 **Wmk. 268**
652 A238 40c ultra, red & yel .25 .25
Never hinged 1.20
a. Unwmkd. 150.00

4th National Exhibition of Orchids, Rio de Janeiro, November, 1946.

Gen. A. E. Gomes Carneiro — A239

Perf. 10½x12
1946, Dec. 6 Engr. **Unwmk.**
653 A239 40c deep green .25 .25
Never hinged .40

Centenary of the birth of Gen. Antonio Ernesto Gomes Carneiro.

Brazilian Academy of Letters A240

1946, Dec. 14 ***Perf. 11***
654 A240 40c blue .25 .25
Never hinged .60

50th anniv. of the foundation of the Brazilian Academy of Letters, Rio de Janeiro.

Antonio de Castro Alves (1847-1871), Poet — A241

1947, Mar. 14 Litho. **Wmk. 267**
655 A241 40c bluish green .25 .25
Never hinged .60

Types of 1941-42, Values in Centavos or Cruzeiros

1947-54 Wmk. 267 Typo. ***Perf. 11***
656 A184 2c olive .30 .25
657 A184 5c yellow brn .30 .25
658 A184 10c green .55 .25
659 A185 20c brown org .55 .25
660 A185 30c dk lil rose 1.25 .25
661 A185 40c blue .55 .25
b. Wmk. 268 3,000. 225.00
661A A185 50c salmon 1.25 .25
662 A186 60c lt violet 1.75 .25
663 A186 70c brt rose ('54) .55 .25
664 A186 1cr gray 3.75 .25
665 A186 1.20cr dull blue 6.00 .25
a. Wmk. 268 300.00 75.00
666 A187 2cr gray violet 7.50 .25

Engr.
667 A188 5cr blue 22.50 .25
a. Perf. 11¾ 70.00 1.75
668 A189 10cr rose red 35.00 .25
669 A190 20cr deep brn 30.00 .25
a. Perf. 13-13½ 60.00 1.75
670 A191 50cr red 60.00 .25
a. Perf. 14-14½ 60.00 7.50
Nos. 656-670 (16) 171.80 4.00

Pres. Gonzalez Videla of Chile A242

1947, June 26 Unwmk. ***Perf. 12x11***
671 A242 40c dk brown orange .25 .25
Never hinged .40

Visit of President Gabriel Gonzalez Videla of Chile, June 1947.
A souvenir folder contains four impressions of No. 671, and measures 6½x8¼ inches.

"Peace" and Western Hemisphere A243

1947, Aug. 15 ***Perf. 11x12***
672 A243 1.20cr blue .30 .25
Never hinged 1.20

Inter-American Defense Conference at Rio de Janeiro, August-September, 1947.

Pres. Harry S. Truman, Map and Statue of Liberty A244

1947, Sept. 1 Typo. ***Perf. 12x11***
673 A244 40c ultra .25 .25
Never hinged .80

Visit of US President Harry S Truman to Brazil, Sept. 1947.

Pres. Eurico Gaspar Dutra — A245

Wmk. 268
1947, Sept. 7 Engr. ***Perf. 11***
674 A245 20c green .25 .25
675 A245 40c rose carmine .25 .25
676 A245 1.20cr deep blue .25 .25
Nos. 674-676 (3) .75 .75
Set, never hinged 2.25

The souvenir sheet containing Nos. 674-676 is listed as No. C73A. See No. 679.

Mother and Child — A246

1947, Oct. 10 Typo. **Unwmk.**
677 A246 40c brt ultra .25 .25
Never hinged .80

Issued to mark Child Care Week, 1947.

Arms of Belo Horizonte — A247

1947, Dec. 12 Engr. **Wmk. 267**
678 A247 1.20cr rose carmine .25 .25
Never hinged .80

50th anniversary of the founding of the city of Belo Horizonte.

Dutra Type of 1947
1948 Engr. **Wmk. 267**
679 A245 20c green 3.75 3.75
Never hinged 8.00

Catalogue values for unused stamps in this section, from this point to the end of the section, are for Never Hinged items.

Globe — A248

1948, July 10 **Litho.**
680 A248 40c dl grn & pale lil .65 .25

International Exposition of Industry and Commerce, Petropolis, 1948.

Arms of Paranagua A249

1948, July 29
681 A249 5cr bister brown 7.50 .65

300th anniversary of the founding of the city of Paranagua, July 29, 1648.

Child Reading Book — A250

1948, Aug. 1
682 A250 40c green .60 .25

National Education Campaign.
No. 682 was reproduced on a souvenir card. Size: 124x157mm.

Tiradentes — A251

1948, Nov. 12
683 A251 40c brown orange .40 .25

200th anniversary of the birth of Joaquim José da Silva Xavier (Tiradentes).

Symbolical of Cancer Eradication A252

1948, Dec. 14
684 A252 40c claret .60 .25

Anti-cancer publicity.

Adult Student A253

1949, Jan. 3 Wmk. 267 ***Perf. 12x11***
685 A253 60c red vio & pink .60 .25

Campaign for adult education.

"Battle of Guararapes," by Vitor Meireles — A254

1949, Feb. 15 ***Perf. 11½x12***
686 A254 60c lt blue 2.50 .30

2nd Battle of Guararapes, 300th anniv.

Church of Sao Francisco de Paula — A255

Perf. 11x12
1949, Mar. 8 Unwmk. Engr.
687 A255 60c dark brown .60 .25
a. Souvenir sheet 75.00 75.00

Bicentenary of city of Ouro Fino, state of Minas Gerais.
No. 687a contains one imperf. stamp similar to No. 687, with dates in lower margin. Size: 70x89mm. Issued without gum.

Manuel de Nobrega — A256

1949, Mar. 29 ***Imperf.***
688 A256 60c violet .60 .25

Founding of the City of Salvador, 400th anniv.

Emblem of Brazilian Air Force and Plane A257

1949, June 18
689 A257 60c blue violet .60 .25

Issued to honor the Brazilian Air Force.

Star and Angel — A258

1949 Wmk. 267 Litho. ***Perf. 11x12***
690 A258 60c pink .60 .25

1st Ecclesiastical Cong., Salvador, Bahia.

Globe A259

1949, Oct. 31 Typo. ***Perf. 12x11***
691 A259 1.50cr blue .75 .25

75th anniv. of the UPU.

Ruy Barbosa A260

Unwmk.
1949, Dec. 14 Engr. ***Perf. 12***
692 A260 1.20cr rose carmine 1.00 .25

Centenary of birth of Ruy Barbosa.

Joaquim Cardinal Arcoverde A. Cavalcanti, Birth Centenary — A261

Perf. 11x12
1950, Feb. 27 Litho. Wmk. 267
693 A261 60c rose .65 .25

Grapes and Factory A262

1950, Mar. 15 ***Perf. 12x11***
694 A262 60c rose lake .60 .25

75th anniversary of Italian immigration to the state of Rio Grande do Sul.

Virgin of the Globe — A263

1950, May 31 ***Perf. 11x12***
695 A263 60c blk & lt bl .60 .25

Establishment in Brazil of the Daughters of Charity of St. Vincent de Paul, cent.

Globe and Soccer Players — A264

1950, June 24
696 A264 60c ultra, bl & gray 1.50 .30

4th World Soccer Championship.

Symbolical of Brazilian Population Growth A265

1950, July 10 Typo. ***Perf. 12x11***
697 A265 60c rose lake .60 .25

Issued to publicize the 6th Brazilian census.

Dr. Oswaldo Cruz — A266

1950, Aug. 23 Litho. ***Perf. 11x12***
698 A266 60c orange brown .65 .25

5th International Congress of Microbiology.

View of Blumenau and Itajai River A267

Perf. 12x11
1950, Sept. 9 Wmk. 267
699 A267 60c bright pink .65 .25

Centenary of the founding of Blumenau.

Amazonas Theater, Manaus A268

1950, Sept. 27
700 A268 60c light brn red .60 .25

Centenary of Amazonas Province.

Arms of Juiz de Fora — A269

1950, Oct. 24 ***Perf. 11x12***
701 A269 60c carmine .60 .25

Centenary of the founding of Juiz de Fora.

Post Office at Recife
A270

1951, Jan. 10 **Typo.** ***Perf. 12x11***

702 A270 60c carmine .60 .25
703 A270 1.20cr carmine .60 .25

Opening of the new building of the Pernambuco Post Office.

Arms of Joinville — A271

1951, Mar. 9 ***Perf. 11x12***

704 A271 60c orange brown .80 .25

Centenary of the founding of Joinville.

Jean-Baptiste de La Salle — A272

1951, Apr. 30 **Litho.**

705 A272 60c blue .80 .25

Birth of Jean-Baptiste de La Salle, 300th anniv.

Heart and Flowers — A273

1951, May 13 **Engr.**

706 A273 60c deep plum .90 .25

Mother's Day, May 14, 1951.

Sylvio Romero — A274

1951, Apr. 21 **Litho.**

707 A274 60c dl vio brn .60 .25

Romero (1851-1914), poet and author.

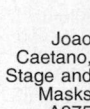

Joao Caetano, Stage and Masks
A275

1951, July 9 ***Perf. 12x11***

708 A275 60c lt gray bl .60 .25

1st Brazilian Theater Cong., Rio, July 9-13, 1951.

Orville A. Derby — A276

1951, July 23 ***Perf. 11x12***

709 A276 2cr slate .70 .25

Centenary of the birth (in New York State) of Orville A. Derby, geologist.

First Mass Celebrated in Brazil — A277

1951, July 25

710 A277 60c dl brn & buff .60 .25

4th Inter-American Congress on Catholic Education, Rio do Janeiro, 1951

Euclides Pinto Martins A278

1951, Aug. 16 ***Perf. 12x11***

711 A278 3.80cr brn & citron 3.50 .30

1st flight from NYC to Rio, 29th anniv.

Monastery of the Rock
A279

1951, Sept. 8

712 A279 60c dl brn & cream .60 .25

Founding of Vitoria, 4th centenary.

Santos-Dumont and Model Plane Contest — A280

Dirigible and Eiffel Tower — A281

Perf. 11x12

1951, Oct. 19 **Wmk. 267** **Litho.**

713 A280 60c salmon & dk brn .80 .25

Unwmk. **Engr.**

714 A281 3.80cr dark purple 2.40 .25

Week of the Wing and 50th anniv. of Santos-Dumont's flight around the Eiffel Tower.

In December 1951, Nos. 713 and 714 were privately overprinted: "Exposicao Filatelica Regional Distrito Federal 15-XII-1951 23-XII-1951." These were attached to souvenir sheets bearing engraved facsimiles of Nos. 38, 49 and 51, which were sold by Clube Filatelico do Brasil to mark its 20th anniversary. The overprinted stamps on the sheets were canceled, but 530 "unused" sets were sold by the club.

Farmers and Ear of Wheat — A282

1951, Nov. 10 **Litho.** **Wmk. 267**

715 A282 60c dp grn & gray .60 .25

Festival of Grain at Bage, 1951.

Map and Open Bible A283

1951, Dec. 9 ***Perf. 12x11***

716 A283 1.20cr brn org 1.25 .25

Issued to publicize the Day of the Bible.

Queen Isabella — A284

1952, Mar. 10 ***Perf. 11x12***

717 A284 3.80cr lt bl 2.00 .30

500th anniversary of the birth of Queen Isabella I of Spain.

Henrique Oswald — A285

1952, Apr. 22

718 A285 60c brown .60 .25

Oswald (1852-1931), composer.

Vicente Licinio Cardoso — A286

1952, May 2

719 A286 60c gray blue .75 .25

4th Brazilian Homeopathic Congress.

Map and Symbol of Labor — A287

1952, Apr. 30

720 A287 1.50cr brnsh pink .75 .25

5th International Labor Organization Conference for American Countries.

Gen. Polidoro da Fonseca — A288

Portraits: 5cr, Baron de Capanema. 10cr, Minister Eusebio de Queiros.

Unwmk.

1952, May 11 **Engr.** ***Perf. 11***

721	A288	2.40cr lt car	.60	.25
722	A288	5cr blue	4.00	.25
723	A288	10cr dk bl grn	4.00	.25
		Nos. 721-723 (3)	8.60	.75

Centenary of telegraph in Brazil.

Luiz de Albuquerque M. P. Caceres — A289

Perf. 11x12

1952, June 8 **Litho.** **Wmk. 267**

724 A289 1.20cr vio bl .60 .25

200th anniversary of the founding of the city of Mato Grosso.

Symbolizing the Glory of Sports — A290

1952, July 21 ***Perf. 12x11***

725 A290 1.20cr dp bl & bl 1.50 .40

Fluminense Soccer Club, 50th anniversary.

José Antonio Saraiva — A291

1952, Aug. 16 *Perf. 11x12*
726 A291 60c lil rose .75 .25

Centenary of the founding of Terezina, capital of Piaui State.

Emperor Dom Pedro — A292

1952, Sept. 3 **Wmk. 267**
727 A292 60c lt bl & blk .75 .25

Issued for Stamp Day and the 2nd Philatelic Exhibition of Sao Paulo.

Flag-encircled Globe — A293

1952, Oct. 24 *Perf. 13½*
728 A293 3.80cr blue 2.50 .40

Issued to publicize United Nations Day.

View of Sao Paulo, Sun and Compasses — A294

1952, Nov. 8 **Litho.** *Perf. 12x11*
729 A294 60c dl bl, yel & gray grn .75 .25

City Planning Day.

Father Diogo Antonio Feijo — A295

1952, Nov. 9 *Perf. 11x12*
730 A295 60c fawn .60 .25

Rodolpho Bernardelli and His "Christ and the Adultress" A297

1952, Dec. 18 *Perf. 12x11*
732 A297 60c gray blue .75 .25

Bernardelli, sculptor and painter, birth cent.

Map of Western Hemisphere and View of Rio de Janeiro — A298

1952, Sept. 20
733 A298 3.80cr vio brn & lt grn 2.00 .35

2nd Congress of American Industrial Medicine, Rio de Janeiro, 1952.

Arms and Head of Pioneer A299

Coffee, Cotton and Sugar Cane — A300

Designs: 2.80cr, Jesuit monk planting tree. 3.80cr, 5.80cr, Spiral, symbolizing progress.

1953, Jan. 25 **Litho.** *Perf. 11*
734 A299 1.20cr ol brn & blk brn 2.00 .25
735 A300 2cr olive grn & yel 3.50 .25
736 A300 2.80cr red brn & dp org 2.25 .25
737 A300 3.80cr dk brn & yel grn 1.90 .25
738 A300 5.80cr int bl & yel grn 1.75 .25
Nos. 734-738 (5) 11.40 1.25

400th anniversary of Sao Paulo.
Used copies of No. 734 exist with design inverted. Value $6,000.

Ledger and Winged Cap A301

1953, Feb. 22 *Perf. 12x11*
739 A301 1.20cr dl brn & fawn 1.00 .25

6th Brazilian Accounting Congress.

Joao Ramalho — A302

Wmk. 264
1953, Apr. 8 **Engr.** *Perf. 11½*
740 A302 60c blue .25 .25

Founding of the city of Santo Andre, 4th cent.

Aarao Reis and Plan of Belo Horizonte A303

1953, May 6 **Photo.**
741 A303 1.20cr red brn .25 .25

Aarao Leal de Carvalho Reis (1853-1936), civil engineer.

Almirante Saldanha — A304

1953, May 16
742 A304 1.50cr royal blue .30 .30

4th globe-circling voyage of the training ship Almirante Saldanha.

A305

Joaquim Jose Rodrigues Torres, Viscount of Itaborai.

1953, July 5 **Photo.**
743 A305 1.20cr violet .25 .25

Centenary of the Bank of Brazil.

Lamp and Rio-Petropolis Highway — A306

1953, July 14
744 A306 1.20cr gray .25 .25

10th Intl. Congress of Nursing, Petropolis, 1953.

Bay of Rio de Janeiro A307

1953, July 15
745 A307 3.80cr dk bl grn .40 .25

Issued to publicize the fourth World Congress of Baptist Youth, July 1953.

Arms of Jau and Map A308

1953, Aug. 15 **Engr.**
746 A308 1.20cr purple .25 .25

Centenary of the city of Jau.

Ministry of Health and Education Building, Rio — A309

1953, Aug. 1
747 A309 1.20cr dp grn .25 .25

Day of the Stamp and the first Philatelic Exhibition of National Education.

Maria Quiteria de Jesus Medeiros — A310

1953, Aug. 21 **Photo.**
748 A310 60c vio bl .25 .25

Centenary of the death of Maria Quiteria de Jesus Medeiros (1792-1848), independence heroine.

Pres. Odria of Peru — A311

1953, Aug. 25
749 A311 1.40cr rose brn .25 .25

Issued to publicize the visit of Gen. Manuel A. Odria, President of Peru, Aug. 25, 1953.

Duke of Caxias Leading his Troops — A312

Designs: 1.20cr, Caxias' tomb. 1.70cr, 5.80cr, Portrait of Caxias. 3.80cr, Arms of Caxias.

Engr. (60c, 5.80cr); Photo.
1953, Aug. 25
750 A312 60c dp grn .30 .25
751 A312 1.20cr dp claret .30 .25
752 A312 1.70cr slate grn .30 .25
753 A312 3.80cr rose brn .50 .25
754 A312 5.80cr gray vio .50 .25
Nos. 750-754 (5) 1.90 1.25

150th anniversary of the birth of Luis Alves de Lima e Silva, Duke of Caxias.

Quill Pen, Map and Tree — A313

1953, Sept. 12 **Photo.**
755 A313 60c ultra .25 .25

5th National Congress of Journalism.

Horacio Hora — A314

1953, Sept. 17 **Litho.** **Wmk. 267**
756 A314 60c org & dp plum .25 .25

Horacio Pinto de Hora (1853-1890), painter.

Pres. Somoza of Nicaragua — A315

1953, Sept. 24 **Photo.** **Wmk. 264**
757 A315 1.40cr dk vio brn .25 .25

Issued to publicize the visit of Gen. Anastasio Somoza, president of Nicaragua.

Auguste de Saint-Hilaire A316

1953, Sept. 30
758 A316 1.20cr dk brn car .25 .25

Centenary of the death of Auguste de Saint-Hilaire, explorer and botanist.

Jose Carlos do Patrocinio — A317

1953, Oct. 9 **Photo.**
759 A317 60c dk slate gray .25 .25

Jose Carlos do Patrocinio, (1853-1905), journalist and abolitionist.

Clock Tower, Crato — A318

1953, Oct. 17
760 A318 60c blue green .25 .25

Centenary of the city of Crato.

Joao Capistrano de Abreu — A319

1953, Oct. 23
761 A319 60c dull blue .25 .25
762 A319 5cr purple 1.30 .25

Joao Capistrano de Abreu (1853-1927), historian.

Allegory: "Justice" — A320

1953, Nov. 17
763 A320 60c indigo .25 .25
764 A320 1.20cr dp magenta .25 .25

50th anniv. of the Treaty of Petropolis.

Farm Worker in Wheat Field — A321

1953, Nov. 29 **Photo.** ***Perf. 11½***
766 A321 60c dk green .25 .25

3rd Natl. Wheat Festival, Erechim, 1953.

Teacher and Pupils — A322

1953, Dec. 14
767 A322 60c red .25 .25

First National Conference of Primary School Teachers, Salvador, 1953.

Zacarias de Gois e Vasconsellos A323

Porters With Trays of Coffee Beans — A323a

1953-54 **Photo.**
768 A323 2cr org brn & blk, *buff* ('54) 1.30 .50
a. White paper 2.00 1.00
769 A323a 5cr dp org & blk 1.00 .40

Centenary of the state of Parana.

Alexandre de Gusmao — A324

1954, Jan. 13
770 A324 1.20cr brn vio .25 .25

Gusmao (1695-1753), statesman, diplomat and writer.

Symbolical of Sao Paulo's Growth — A325

Arms and View of Sao Paulo A326

Designs: 2cr, Priest, settler and Indian. 2.80cr, José de Anchieta.

1954, Jan. 25 ***Perf. 11½x11***
771 A325 1.20cr dk vio brn .50 .25
a. Buff paper 2.50 1.00

Engr.

772 A325 2cr lilac rose .70 .25
773 A325 2.80cr pur gray 1.00 .25

Perf. 11x11½

774 A326 3.80cr dl grn 1.15 .25
a. Buff paper 4.00 .80
775 A326 5.80cr dl red 1.50 .25
a. Buff paper 8.00 .75
Nos. 771-775 (5) 4.85 1.25

400th anniversary of Sao Paulo.

J. Fernandes Vieira, A. Vidal de Negreiros, A. F. Camarao and H. Dias — A327

Perf. 11x11½

1954, Feb. 18 **Photo.** **Unwmk.**
776 A327 1.20cr ultra .25 .25

300th anniversary of the recovery of Pernambuco from the Dutch.

Sao Paulo and Minerva A328

1954, Feb. 24
777 A328 1.50cr dp plum .25 .25

10th International Congress of Scientific Organizations, Sao Paulo, 1954.

Stylized Grapes, Jug and Map — A329

1954, Feb. 27 **Photo.** ***Perf. 11½x11***
778 A329 40c dp claret .25 .25

Grape Festival, Rio Grande do Sul.

Monument of the Immigrants — A330

1954, Feb. 28
779 A330 60c dp vio bl .25 .25

Unveiling of the Monument to the Immigrants of Caxias do Sul.

First Brazilian Locomotive — A331

Perf. 11x11½

1954, Apr. 30 **Unwmk.**
781 A331 40c carmine .35 .25

Centenary of the first railroad engine built in Brazil.

Pres. Chamoun of Lebanon — A332

1954, May 12 Photo. ***Perf. 11½x11***

782 A332 1.50cr maroon .25 .25

Visit of Pres. Camille Chamoun of Lebanon.

Sao Jose College, Rio de Janeiro A333

J. B. Champagnat Marcelin — A334

1954, June 6 ***Perf. 11x11½, 11½x11***

783 A333 60c purple .25 .25
784 A334 120cr vio blue .25 .25

50th anniversary of the founding of the Marist Brothers in Brazil.

Apolonia Pinto — A335

1954, June 21 **Photo.**

785 A335 1.20cr bright green .40 .25

Apolonia Pinto (1854-1937), actress.

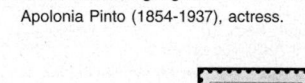

Adm. Margues Tamandare — A336

Portraits: 2c, 5c, 10c, Admiral Margues Tamandare. 20c, 30c, 40c, Oswaldo Cruz. 50c, 60c, 90c, Joaquim Murtinho. 1cr, 1.50cr, 2cr, Duke of Caxias. 5cr, 10cr, Ruy Barbosa. 20cr, 50cr, Jose Bonifacio.

1954-60 Wmk. 267 ***Perf. 11x11½***

786	A336	2c vio blue	.30	.25
787	A336	5c org red	.30	.25
788	A336	10c brt green	.30	.25
789	A336	20c magenta	.50	.25
790	A336	30c dk gray grn	.50	.25
791	A336	40c rose red	1.00	.30
792	A336	50c violet	1.50	.30
793	A336	60c gray grn	.50	.25
794	A336	90c orange ('55)	1.00	.30
795	A336	1cr brown	1.50	.25
796	A336	1.50cr blue	.30	.25
a.		Wmk. 264	50.00	12.50
797	A336	2cr dk bl grn ('56)	2.75	.30
798	A336	5cr rose lil ('56)	9.00	.30
799	A336	10cr lt grn ('60)	4.50	.30
800	A336	20cr crim rose ('59)	9.00	.30
801	A336	50cr ultra ('59)	17.50	.30
		Nos. 786-801 (16)	50.45	4.40

See Nos. 890, 930-933.

Boy Scout Waving Flag (Statue) — A337

1954, Aug. 2 Unwmk. ***Perf. 11½x11***

802 A337 1.20cr vio bl .50 .25

Intl. Boy Scout Encampment, Sao Paulo.

Baltasar Fernandes, Explorer — A338

1954, Aug. 15

803 A338 60c dk red .25 .25

300th anniversary of city of Sorocaba.

Adeodato Giovanni Cardinal Piazza — A339

1954, Sept. 2

804 A339 4.20cr red org .50 .35

Visit of Adeodato Cardinal Piazza, papal legate to Brazil.

Our Lady of Aparecida, Map of Brazil — A340

Virgin Standing on Globe — A340a

1954

805 A340 60c claret .30 .30
806 A340a 1.20cr vio bl .30 .30

No. 805 was issued for the 1st Cong. of Brazil's Patron Saint (Our Lady of Aparecida); No. 806, the cent. of the proclamation of the dogma of the Immaculate Conception. Both stamps also for the Marian Year.

Issue dates: 60c, Sept. 6; 1.20cr, Sept. 8.

Benjamin Constant and Hand Reading Braille A341

1954, Sept. 27 Photo. Unwmk.

807 A341 60c dk grn .25 .25

Centenary of the founding of the Benjamin Constant Institute.

River Battle of Riachuelo — A342

Admiral F. M. Barroso — A343

1954, Oct. 6 ***Perf. 11x11½, 11½x11***

808 A342 40c redsh brown .25 .25
809 A343 60c violet .25 .25

Admiral Francisco Manoel Barroso da Silva (1804-82).

Dr. Christian F. S. Hahnemann — A344

1954, Oct. 8 ***Perf. 11½x11***

810 A344 2.70cr dk green .50 .25

1st World Cong. of Homeopathic Medicine.

Nizia Floresta — A345

1954, Oct. 12

811 A345 60c lilac rose .25 .25

Reburial of the remains of Nizia Floresta (Dio Nizia Pinto Lisboa), writer and educator.

Ears of Wheat — A346

1954, Oct. 22

812 A346 60c olive .25 .25

4th National Wheat Festival, Carazinho.

Basketball Player and Ball-Globe — A347

1954, Oct. 23 **Photo.**

813 A347 1.40cr orange red .50 .25

Issued to publicize the second World Basketball Championship Matches, 1954.

Allegory of the Spring Games — A348

Perf. 11½x11

1954, Nov. 6 **Wmk. 267**

814 A348 60c red brown .45 .25

Issued to publicize the 6th Spring Games.

San Francisco Hydroelectric Plant — A349

1955, Jan. 15 ***Perf. 11x11½***

815 A349 60c brown org .25 .25

Issued to publicize the inauguration of the San Francisco Hydroelectric Plant.

Itutinga Hydroelectric Plant — A350

1955, Feb. 3

816 A350 40c blue .25 .25

Issued to publicize the inauguration of the Itutinga Hydroelectric Plant at Lavras.

Rotary Emblem and Bay of Rio de Janeiro — A351

1955, Feb. 23 ***Perf. 12x11½***

817 A351 2.70cr dp turq grn & dp bluish grn 1.20 .35

Rotary International, 50th anniversary.

Fausto Cardoso Palace
A352

1955, Mar. 17 ***Perf. 11x11½***

818 A352 40c henna brown .25 .25

Centenary of Aracaju.

Aviation Symbols
A353

1955, Mar. 13 **Photo.** ***Perf. 11½***

819 A353 60c dark gray green .25 .25

Issued to publicize the third National Aviation Congress at Sao Paulo, Mar. 6-13.

Arms of Botucatu
A354

1955, Apr. 14

820 A354 60c orange brn .25 .25

821 A354 1.20cr brt green .25 .25

Centenary of Botucatu.

Young Racers at Starting Line
A355

Perf. 11½

1955, Apr. 30 **Photo.** **Unwmk.**

823 A355 60c orange brn .30 .25

5th Children's Games.

Marshal Hermes da Fonseca — A356

1955, May 12 **Wmk. 267**

824 A356 60c purple .25 .25

Marshal Hermes da Fonseca, birth cent.

Congress Altar, Sail and Sugarloaf Mountain — A357

Designs: 2.70cr, St. Pascoal. 4.20cr, Aloisi Benedetto Cardinal Masella.

Granite Paper

Engraved; Photogravure (2.70cr)

1955, July 17 **Unwmk.** ***Perf. 11½***

825 A357 1.40cr green .30 .25

826 A357 2.70cr deep claret .30 .40

827 A357 4.20cr blue .80 .30

Nos. 825-827 (3) 1.40 .95

36th World Eucharistic Cong. in Rio de Janeiro.

Girl Gymnasts
A358

1955, Nov. 12 **Engr.**

Granite Paper

828 A358 60c rose lilac .30 .25

Issued to publicize the 7th Spring Games.

José B. Monteiro Lobato, Author
A359

1955, Dec. 8 **Granite Paper**

829 A359 40c dark green .25 .25

Adolfo Lutz — A360

1955, Dec. 18 **Granite Paper**

830 A360 60c dk green .25 .25

Centenary of the birth of Adolfo Lutz, public health pioneer.

Lt. Col. Vilagran Cabrita — A361

1955, Dec. 22 **Photo.** **Wmk. 267**

831 A361 60c violet blue .25 .25

First Battalion of Engineers, cent.

Salto Grande Hydroelectric Dam
A362

1956, Jan. 15 **Unwmk.** ***Perf. 11½***

Granite Paper

832 A362 60c brick red .25 .25

Arms of Mococa — A363

Wmk. 256

1956, Apr. 17 **Photo.** ***Perf. 11½***

833 A363 60c brick red .25 .25

Centenary of Mococa, Sao Paulo.

"G" and Globe — A364

1956, Apr. 14 **Unwmk.**

Granite Paper

834 A364 1.20cr violet blue .25 .25

18th Intl. Geographic Cong., Rio, Aug. 1956.

Girls' Foot Race
A365

1956, Apr. 28 **Photo.**

Granite Paper

835 A365 2.50cr brt blue .30 .25

6th Children's Games.

Plane over Map of Brazil — A366

1956, June 12 **Wmk. 267** ***Perf. 11½***

836 A366 3.30cr brt vio bl .30 .25

National Airmail Service, 25th anniv.

Fireman Rescuing Child
A367

1956, July 2 **Wmk. 264**

837 A367 2.50cr crimson .40 .25

a. Buff paper .80 .25

Centenary of the Fire Brigade.

Map of Brazil and Open Book
A368

1956, Sept. 8 **Wmk. 267**

838 A368 2.50cr brt vio bl .25 .25

50th anniversary of the arrival of the Marist Brothers in Northern Brazil.

Church and Monument, Franca — A369

1956, Sept. 7 **Engr.**

839 A369 2.50cr dk blue .25 .25

Centenary of city of Franca, Sao Paulo.

Woman Hurdler
A370

1956, Sept. 22 **Photo.** **Unwmk.**

Granite Paper

840 A370 2.50cr dk car .60 .30

Issued to publicize the 8th Spring Games.

Forest and Map of Brazil — A371

1956, Sept. 30 **Wmk. 267** ***Perf. 11½***

841 A371 2.50cr dk green .30 .25

Issued to publicize education in forestry.

Baron da Bocaina
A372

1956, Oct. 8 **Engr.** **Wmk. 268**

842 A372 2.50cr reddish brown .30 .30

Centenary of the birth of Baron da Bocaina, who introduced the special delivery mail system to Brazil.

Marbleized Paper

Paper with a distinct wavy-line or marbleized watermark (which Brazilians call *marmorizado* paper) has been found on many stamps of Brazil, 1956-68, including Nos. 843-845, 847, 851-854, 858-858A, 864, 878, 880, 882, 884, 886-887, 896, 909, 918, 920-921, 925-928, 936-939, 949, 955-958, 960, 962-964, 978-979, 983, 985-987, 997-998, 1002-1003, 1005, 1009-1012, 1017, 1024, 1026, 1055, 1075, 1078, 1082, C82, C82a, C83-C87, C96, C99, C109.

Quantities are much less than those of stamps on regular paper.

Panama Stamp Showing Pres. Juscelino Kubitschek A373

1956, Oct. 12 Photo. Wmk. 267

843 A373 3.30cr green & blk .30 .25

Issued on America Day, Oct. 12, to commemorate the meeting of the Presidents and the Pan-American Conference at Panama City, July 21-22.

Symbolical of Steel Production — A374

Wmk. 267

1957, Jan. 31 Photo. *Perf. 11½*

844 A374 2.50cr chocolate .30 .25

2nd expansion of the National Steel Company at Volta Redonda.

Joaquim E. Gomes da Silva — A375

1957, Mar. 1 Photo. Unwmk.

Granite Paper

845 A375 2.50cr dk bl grn .30 .25

Centenary of the birth (in 1856) of Joaquim E. Gomes da Silva.

Allan Kardec A376

Wmk. 268

1957, Apr. 18 Engr. *Perf. 11½*

846 A376 2.50cr dk brown .25 .25

Issued in honor of Allan Kardec, pen name of Leon Hippolyto Denizard Rivail, and for the centenary of the publication of his "Codification of Spiritism."

Boy Gymnast A377

1957, Apr. 27 Photo. Unwmk.

Granite Paper

847 A377 2.50cr lake .40 .25

7th Children's Games.

Pres. Craveiro Lopes — A378

1957, June 7 Engr. Wmk. 267

848 A378 6.50cr blue .30 .25

Visit of Gen. Francisco Higino Craveiro Lopes, President of Portugal.

Stamp of 1932 — A379

1957, July 9 Photo.

849 A379 2.50cr rose .30 .25

25th anniv. of the movement for a constitution.

St. Antonio Monastery, Pernambuco — A380

1957, Aug. 24 Engr. Wmk. 267

850 A380 2.50cr deep magenta .25 .25

300th anniv. of the emancipation of the Franciscan province of St. Antonio in Pernambuco State.

Volleyball — A381

1957, Sept. 28 Photo. *Perf. 11½*

851 A381 2.50cr dull org red .50 .30

Issued for the 9th Spring Games.

Basketball — A382

1957, Oct. 12

852 A382 3.30cr org & brt grn .40 .30

2nd Women's International Basketball Championship, Rio de Janeiro.

Count of Pinhal and Sao Carlos A383

1957, Nov. 4 Wmk. 267 *Perf. 11½*

853 A383 2.50cr rose .30 .30

Centenary of the city of Sao Carlos and honoring the Count of Pinhal, its founder.

Auguste Comte — A384

1957, Nov. 15

854 A384 2.50cr dk red brn .25 .25

Centenary of the death of Auguste Comte, French mathematician and philosopher.

Radio Station A385

1957, Dec. 10 Wmk. 268

855 A385 2.50cr dk green .25 .25

Opening of Sarapui Central Radio Station.

Admiral Tamandare and Warship — A386

Aircraft Carrier — A386a

1957-58 Photo.

856 A386 2.50cr light blue .25 .25

Engr.

857 A386a 3.30cr green ('58) .25 .25

150th anniversary of the birth of Admiral Joaquin Marques de Tamandare, founder of the Brazilian navy.

Coffee Plant and Symbolic "R" — A387

Wmk. 267

1957-58 Photo. *Perf. 11½*

858 A387 2.50cr magenta .30 .25

Unwmk.

Granite Paper

858A A387 2.50cr magenta ('58) .30 .25

Centenary (in 1956) of the city of Ribeirao Preto in Sao Paulo state.

Dom John VI — A388

1958, Jan. 28 Engr. Wmk. 268

859 A388 2.50cr magenta .25 .25

150th anniversary of the opening of the ports of Brazil to foreign trade.

Bugler A389

1958, Mar. 18 Wmk. 267

860 A389 2.50cr red .25 .25

Brazilian Marine Corps, 150th anniv.

Station at Rio and Locomotive of 1858 — A390

Wmk. 267

1958, Mar. 29 Photo. *Perf. 11½*

861 A390 2.50cr red brn .25 .25

Central Railroad of Brazil, cent.

Court House — A391

1958, Apr. 1 Engr. Wmk. 256

862 A391 2.50cr green .25 .25

150th anniv. of the Military Superior Court.

Emblem and Brazilian Pavilion A392

1958, Apr. 17 Wmk. 267

863 A392 2.50cr dk blue .25 .25

World's Fair, Brussels, Apr. 17-Oct. 19.

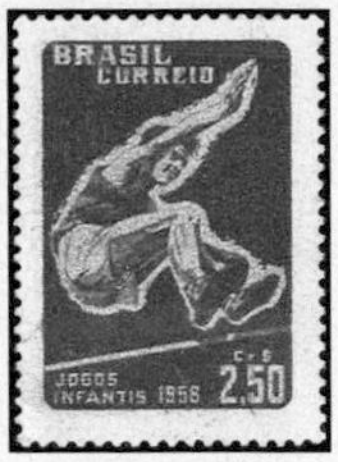

High Jump — A393

1958, Apr. 20 Photo. Unwmk.
Granite Paper

864 A393 2.50cr crimson rose .40 .30

8th Children's Games.

Marshal Mariano da Silva Rondon A394

1958, Apr. 19 Engr. Wmk. 267

865 A394 2.50cr magenta .25 .25

Issued to honor Marshal Mariano da Silva Rondon and the "Day of the Indian."

Hydroelectric Station — A395

1958, Apr. 28 Wmk. 267 *Perf. 11½*

866 A395 2.50cr magenta .25 .25

Opening of Sao Paulo State power plant.

National Printing Plant A396

1958, May 22 Photo.

867 A396 2.50cr redsh brn .25 .25

150th anniversary of the founding of the National Printing Plant.

Marshal Osorio — A397

1958, May 24

868 A397 2.50cr brt violet .25 .25

150th anniversary of the birth of Marshal Manoel Luiz Osorio.

Pres. Ramon Villeda Morales — A398

1958, June 7 Engr. *Perf. 11½*

869 A398 6.50cr dk green 2.00 .40

a. Wmk. 268 12.00 1.25

Visit of Pres. Ramon Villeda Morales of Honduras.

Fountain — A399

1958, June 13

870 A399 2.50cr dk green .25 .25

Botanical Garden, Rio de Janeiro, 150th anniv.

Symbols of Agriculture A400

1958, June 18 Photo.

871 A400 2.50cr rose carmine .25 .25

50th anniv. of Japanese immigration to Brazil.

Prophet Joel — A401

1958, June 21 Engr.

872 A401 2.50cr dk blue .25 .25

Bicentenary of the Cathedral of Bom Jesus at Matosinhos.

Stylized Globe A402

1958, July 10 Photo.

873 A402 2.50cr dk brown .25 .25

Intl. Investment Conference, Belo Horizonte.

Julio Bueno Brandao — A403

1958, Aug. 1 Wmk. 268 *Perf. 11½*

874 A403 2.50cr red brown .25 .25

Centenary of the birth of Julio Bueno Brandao, President of Minas Gerais.

Palacio Tiradentes (House of Congress) A404

1958, July 24 Engr.

875 A404 2.50cr sepia .25 .25

47th Interparliamentary Conference, Rio de Janeiro, July 24-Aug. 1.

Presidential Palace, Brasilia — A405

1958, Aug. 8 Photo. Wmk. 267

876 A405 2.50cr ultra .25 .25

Issued to publicize the construction of Brazil's new capital, Brasilia.

Freighters A406

1958, Aug. 22

877 A406 2.50cr blue .25 .25

Brazilian merchant marine.

Joaquim Caetano da Silva A407

1958, Sept. 2 Unwmk.
Granite Paper

878 A407 2.50cr redsh brn .25 .25

Joaquim Caetano da Silva, scientist & historian.

Giovanni Gronchi — A408

1958, Sept. 4 Engr. Wmk. 268

879 A408 7cr dk blue .50 .25

Visit of Italy's President Giovanni Gronchi to Brazil.

Archers — A409

Perf. 11½

1958, Sept. 21 Photo. Unwmk.
Granite Paper

880 A409 2.50cr red org .50 .25

Issued to publicize the 10th Spring Games.

Elderly Couple — A410

1958, Sept. 27 Wmk. 267

881 A410 2.50cr magenta .25 .25

Day of the Old People, Sept. 27.

Machado de Assis — A411

1958, Sept. 28 Unwmk.

882 A411 2.50cr red brn .25 .25

50th anniversary of the death of Joaquim Maria Machado de Assis, writer.

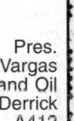

Pres. Vargas and Oil Derrick A412

1958, Oct. 6 Wmk. 268

883 A412 2.50cr blue .25 .25

5th anniv. of Pres. Getulio D. Vargas' oil law.

Globe — A413

Wmk. 267

1958, Nov. 14 Photo. *Perf. 11½*

884 A413 2.50cr blue .30 .25

7th Inter-American Congress of Municipalities.

Gen. Lauro Sodré — A414

1958, Nov. 15 Engr.

885 A414 3.30cr green .25 .25

Cent. of the birth of Gen. Lauro Sodré.

UN Emblem — A415

1958, Dec. 26 Photo. *Perf. 11½*
886 A415 2.50cr brt blue .25 .25

10th anniv. of the signing of the Universal Declaration of Human Rights.

Soccer Player — A416

1959, Jan. 20
887 A416 3.30cr emer & red brn .50 .30

World Soccer Championships of 1958.

Railroad Track and Map — A417

1959, Apr. Wmk. 267 *Perf. 11½*
888 A417 2.50cr dp orange .25 .25

Centenary of the linking of Patos and Campina Grande by railroad.

Pres. Sukarno of Indonesia — A418

1959, May 20
889 A418 2.50cr blue .25 .25

Visit of President Sukarno of Indonesia.

Dom John VI — A419

Perf. 10½x11½
1959, June 12 Wmk. 267
890 A419 2.50cr crimson .30 .25

Boy Polo Players — A420

1959, June 13 *Perf. 11½*
891 A420 2.50cr orange brn .30 .25

9th Children's Games.

Loading Freighter — A421

1959, July 10
892 A421 2.50cr dk green .25 .25

Honoring the merchant marine.

Organ and Emblem — A422

1959, July 16 Photo.
893 A422 3.30cr magenta .25 .25

Bicentenary of the Carmelite Order in Brazil.

Joachim Silverio de Souza — A423

1959, July 20 *Perf. 11½*
894 A423 2.50cr red brown .25 .25

Birth centenary of Joachim Silverio de Souza, first bishop of Diamantina, Minas Gerais.

Symbolic Road — A424

1959, Sept. 27 Wmk. 267
895 A424 3.30cr bl grn & ultra .25 .25

11th International Roadbuilding Congress.

Woman Athlete — A425

1959, Oct. 4
896 A425 2.50cr lilac rose .30 .25

11th Spring Games.

Map of Parana A426

1959, Sept. 27
897 A426 2.50cr dk green .25 .25

Founding of Londrina, Parana, 25th anniv.

Globe and Snipes — A427

1959, Oct. 22 *Perf. 11½*
898 A427 6.50cr dull grn .30 .25

World Championship of Snipe Class Sailboats, Porto Alegre, won by Brazilian yachtsmen.

Cross of Lusitania — A428

1959, Oct. 24 Engr.
899 A428 6.50cr dull blue .25 .25

4th Intl. Conf. on Brazilian-Portuguese Studies, University of Bahia, Aug. 10-20.

Factory Entrance and Order of Southern Cross — A429

1959, Nov. 19 Photo.
900 A429 3.30cr orange red .25 .25

Pres. Vargas Gunpowder Factory, 50th anniv.

Corcovado Christ, Globe and Southern Cross — A430

1959, Nov. 26 *Perf. 11½*
901 A430 2.50cr blue .30 .25

Universal Thanksgiving Day.

Burning Bush A431

1959, Dec. 24 Wmk. 267
902 A431 3.30cr lt grn .25 .25

Centenary of Presbyterian work in Brazil.

Piraja da Silva and Schistosoma Mansoni — A432

1959, Dec. 28
903 A432 2.50cr rose violet .25 .25

25th anniv. of the discovery and identification of schistosoma mansoni, a parasite of the fluke family, by Dr. Piraja da Silva.

Luiz de Matos A433

1960, Jan. 3 Photo.
904 A433 3.30cr red brown .25 .25

Birth centenary of Luiz de Matos.

Zamenhof — A434

1960, Mar. 10 Wmk. 267 *Perf. 11½*
905 A434 6.50cr emerald .25 .25

Lazarus Ludwig Zamenhof (1859-1917), Polish oculist who invented Esperanto in 1887.

Adél Pinto — A435

1960, Mar. 19 Engr. Wmk. 268
906 A435 11.50cr rose red .25 .25

Centenary of the birth of Adél Pinto, civil engineer and railroad expert.

Presidential Palace, Colonnade — A436

Design: 27cr, Plan of Brasilia (like No. C98).

Perf. 11x11½
1960 Photo. Wmk. 267
907 A436 2.50cr brt green .25 .25

Size: 105x46 ½mm
908 A436 27cr salmon 1.75 .60
Nos. 907-908,C95-C98 (6) 3.15 1.85

No. 907 for the inauguration of Brazil's new capital, Brasilia, Apr. 21, 1960.
No. 908 for the birthday of Pres. Juscelino Kubitschek and has a 27cr in design of No. C98, flanked by the chief design features of Nos. 907, C95-C97, with Kubitschek signature below. Issued in sheets of 4 with wide horizontal gutter.
Issued: 2.50cr, 4/21; 27cr, 9/12.

Grain, Coffee, Cotton and Cacao — A437

Perf. 11½x11
1960, July 28 Wmk. 267
909 A437 2.50cr brown .25 .25

Centenary of Ministry of Agriculture.

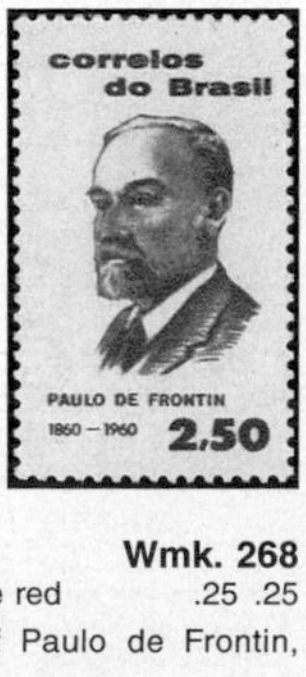

Paulo de Frontin — A438

1960, Oct. 12 Wmk. 268
910 A438 2.50cr orange red .25 .25

Cent. of the birth of Paulo de Frontin, engineer.

Woman Athlete Holding Torch — A439

1960, Oct. 18 *Perf. 11½x11*
911 A439 2.50cr blue grn .25 .25

12th Spring Games.

Volleyball and Net — A440

Perf. 11½x11
1960, Nov. 12 Wmk. 268
912 A440 11cr blue .30 .25

International Volleyball Championships.

Locomotive Wheels — A441

1960, Oct. 15 *Perf. 11½x11*
913 A441 2.50cr ultra .30 .25

10th Pan-American Railroad Congress.

Symbols of Flight A442

1960, Dec. 16 Photo. *Perf. 11½*
914 A442 2.50cr brn & yel .25 .25

Intl. Fair of Industry and Commerce, Rio.

Emperor Haile Selassie — A443

1961, Jan. 31 *Perf. 11½x11*
915 A443 2.50cr dk brown .25 .25

Visit of Emperor Haile Selassie of Ethiopia to Brazil, Dec. 1960.

Map of Brazil, Open Book and Sacred Heart Emblem A444

Perf. 11x11½
1961, Mar. 13 Wmk. 268
916 A444 2.50cr blue .25 .25

50th anniv. of the operation in Brazil of the Order of the Blessed Heart of Mary.

Map of Guanabara — A445

1961, Mar. 27 Wmk. 267
917 A445 7.50cr org brn .35 .25

Promulgation of the constitution of the state of Guanabara.

Arms of Agulhas Negras — A446

Design: 3.30cr, Dress helmet and sword.

Perf. 11½x11
1961, Apr. 23 Wmk. 267
918 A446 2.50cr green .25 .25
919 A446 3.30cr rose car .25 .25

Sesquicentennial of the Agulhas Negras Military Academy.

Brazil and Senegal Linked on Map — A447

1961, Apr. 28 Photo.
920 A447 27cr ultra .30 .25

Visit of Afonso Arinos, Brazilian foreign minister, to Senegal to attend its independence ceremonies.

View of Ouro Preto, 1711 A448

1961, June 6 *Perf. 11x11½*
921 A448 1cr orange .25 .25

250th anniversary of Ouro Preto.

War Arsenal A449

1961, June 20 Wmk. 256
924 A449 5cr dk red brn .30 .25

War Arsenal, Rio de Janeiro, 150th anniv.

Coffee Bean and Branch — A450

Perf. 11½x11
1961, June 26 Wmk. 267
925 A450 20cr redsh brn .60 .25

8th Directorial Committee meeting of the Intl. Coffee Convention, Rio, June 26.

Rabindranath Tagore — A451

1961, July 28 Photo. Wmk. 267
926 A451 10cr rose car .30 .25

Rabindranath Tagore, Indian poet, birth cent.

Stamp of 1861 and Map of English Channel A452

Design: 20cr, 430r stamp of 1861 and map of Netherlands.

1961, Aug. 1 *Perf. 11x11½*
927 A452 10cr rose .40 .25
928 A452 20cr salmon pink 1.60 .25

Centenary of 1861 stamp issue.

Portrait Type of 1954-60
Designs as Before

1961 Wmk. 268 *Perf. 11x11½*
930 A336 1cr brown 1.20 .60
931 A336 2cr dk bl grn 1.80 .60
932 A336 5cr red lilac 5.50 .35
933 A336 10cr emerald 10.00 .35
Nos. 930-933 (4) 18.50 1.90

1cr, 5cr, 10cr have patterned background.

Sun, Clouds, Rain and Weather Symbols — A453

1962, Mar. 23 *Perf. 11½x11*
936 A453 10cr red brown .50 .25

World Meteorological Day, Mar. 23.

Dedo de Deus Peak — A454

1962, Apr. 14 Photo. Wmk. 267

937 A454 8cr emerald .25 .25

50th anniversary of the climbing of Dedo de Deus (Finger of God) peak.

Dr. Gaspar Vianna and Leishmania Protozoa — A455

1962, Apr. 24 ***Perf. 11x11½***

938 A455 8cr blue .25 .25

Discovery by Gaspar Oliveiro Vianna (1885-1914) of a cure for leishmaniasis, 50th anniv.

Henrique Dias A456

1962, June 18 Wmk. 267

939 A456 10cr dk vio brn .25 .25

300th anniversary of the death of Henrique Dias, Negro military leader who fought against the Dutch and Spaniards.

Millimeter Gauge — A457

1962, June 26 ***Perf. 11½x11***

940 A457 100cr car rose .50 .25

Centenary of the introduction of the metric system in Brazil.

Sailboats, Snipe Class — A458

1962, July 21 Photo. Wmk. 267

941 A458 8cr Prus green .30 .25

Commemorating the 13th Brazilian championships for Snipe Class sailing.

Julio Mesquita A459

1962, Aug. 18 ***Perf. 11x11½***

942 A459 8cr dull brown 2.50 .25

Julio Mesquita, journalist and founder of a Sao Paulo newspaper, birth cent.

Empress Leopoldina — A460

1962, Sept. 7 ***Perf. 11½x11***

943 A460 8cr rose claret .25 .25

140th anniversary of independence.

Buildings, Brasilia — A461

Perf. 11x11½

1962, Oct. 24 Wmk. 267

944 A461 10cr orange .25 .25

51st Interparliamentary Conf., Brasilia.

Pouring Ladle — A462

1962, Oct. 26 ***Perf. 11½x11***

945 A462 8cr orange .25 .25

Inauguration of the Usiminas State Iron and Steel Foundry at Belo Horizonte, Minas Gerais.

UPAE Emblem A463

1962, Nov. 19 ***Perf. 11x11½***

946 A463 8cr bright magenta .25 .25

Founding of the Postal Union of the Americas and Spain, UPAE, 50th anniv.

Chimney and Cogwheel Forming "10" — A464

1962, Nov. 26 ***Perf. 11½x11***

947 A464 10cr lt blue grn .25 .25

Natl. Economic and Development Bank, 10th anniv.

Quintino Bocaiuva — A465

Perf. 11½x11

1962, Dec. 27 Photo. Wmk. 267

948 A465 8cr brown org .25 .25

Bocaiuva, journalist, 50th death anniv.

Soccer Player and Globe — A466

1963, Jan. 14

949 A466 10cr blue grn 1.00 .25

World Soccer Championship of 1962.

Carrier Pigeon — A467

1963, Jan. Unwmk. Litho. ***Perf. 14***

950 A467 8cr yel, dk bl, red & grn .30 .25

Souvenir Sheet

Imperf

951 A467 100cr yel, dk bl, red & grn 6.00 1.75

300 years of Brazilian postal service.

Issue dates: 8cr, Jan. 25; 100cr, Jan. 31.

Severino Neiva — A468

Perf. 10½x11½

1963, Jan. 31 Photo. Wmk. 267

952 A468 8cr brt vio .50 .25

Radar Tracking Station and Rockets — A469

Perf. 11½x11

1963, Mar. 15 Wmk. 268

953 A469 21cr lt ultra .25 .25

International Aeronautics and Space Exhibition, Sao Paulo.

"Cross of Unity" — A470

1963 Wmk. 267 ***Perf. 11½x11***

954 A470 8cr red lilac .25 .25

Vatican II, the 21st Ecumenical Council of the Roman Catholic Church.

"ABC" in Geometric Form — A471

1963, Apr. 22 Photo. Wmk. 267

955 A471 8cr brt bl & lt bl .25 .25

Education Week, Apr. 22-27, 3-year alphabetization program.

Basketball Player — A472

1963, May 15

956 A472 8cr dp lilac rose .40 .25

4th International Basketball Championships, Rio de Janeiro, May 10-25, 1963.

Games Emblem — A473

1963, May 22 ***Perf. 11½x11***

957 A473 10cr car rose .40 .25

4th Pan American Games, Sao Paulo.

"OEA" and Map of the Americas — A474

1963, June 6
958 A474 10cr org & dp org .30 .25

15th anniversary of the charter of the Organization of American States.

José Bonifacio de Andrada — A475

1963, June 13
959 A475 8cr dk brown .25 .25

Bicentenary of the birth of José Bonifacio de Andrada e Silva, statesman.

Wheat A476

Perf. 11x11½

1963, June 18 Photo. Wmk. 267
960 A476 10cr blue .30 .25

FAO "Freedom from Hunger" campaign

Centenary Emblem — A477

1963, Aug. 19 ***Perf. 11½x11***
961 A477 8cr yel org & red .25 .25

Centenary of International Red Cross.

Joao Caetano — A478

1963, Aug. 24 ***Perf. 11½x11***
962 A478 8cr slate .25 .25

Death centenary of Joao Caetano, actor.

Symbols of Agriculture, Industry and Atomic Energy — A479

1963, Aug. 28
963 A479 10cr car rose .30 .25

Atomic Development Law, 1st anniv.

Hammer Thrower — A480

1963, Sept. 13
964 A480 10cr gray .40 .25

Intl. College Students' Games, Porto Alegre.

Marshal Tito — A481

1963, Sept. 19
965 A481 80cr sepia .75 .25

Visit of Marshal Tito of Yugoslavia.

Compass Rose, Map of Brazil and View of Rio — A482

1963, Sept. 20
966 A482 8cr lt blue grn .25 .25

8th International Leprology Congress.

Oil Derrick and Storage Tank A483

1963, Oct. 3 ***Perf. 11x11½***
967 A483 8cr dk slate grn .25 .25

Petrobras, the natl. oil company, 10th anniv.

"Spring Games" A484

1963, Nov. 5 Photo. Wmk. 267
968 A484 8cr yel & org .40 .25

1963 Spring Games.

Dr. Borges de Medeiros (1863-1962), Governor of Rio Grande do Sul — A485

1963, Nov. 29 ***Perf. 11½x11***
969 A485 8cr red brown .25 .25

Sao Joao del Rei A486

1963, Dec. 8 ***Perf. 11x11½***
970 A486 8cr violet blue .25 .25

250th anniversary of Sao Joao del Rei.

Dr. Alvaro Alvim A487

1963, Dec. 19
971 A487 8cr dk gray .25 .25

Alvaro Alvim (1863-1928), X-ray specialist and martyr of science.

Viscount de Mauá — A488

1963, Dec. 28 ***Perf. 11½x11***
972 A488 8cr rose car .25 .25

Sesquicentennial of the birth of Viscount de Mauá, founder of first Brazilian railroad.

Mandacaru Cactus and Emblem — A489

1964, Jan. 23 Photo. Wmk. 267
973 A489 8cr dull green .25 .25

Bank of Northeast Brazil, 10th anniv.

Coelho Netto — A490

1964, Feb. 21 ***Perf. 11½x11***
974 A490 8cr brt violet .25 .25

Birth centenary of Coelho Netto, writer.

Lauro Müller — A491

1964, Mar. 8 Wmk. 267
975 A491 8cr dp orange .25 .25

Lauro Siverino Müller, politician and member of the Brazilian Academy of Letters, birth cent.

Child Holding Spoon A492

1964, Mar. 25 ***Perf. 11x11½***
976 A492 8cr yel brn & yel .25 .25

Issued for "School Meals Week."

Chalice Rock — A493

1964, Apr. 9 Engr. ***Perf. 11½x11***
977 A493 80cr red orange .25 .25

Issued for tourist publicity.

Allan Kardec — A494

1964, Apr. 18 Photo.
978 A494 30cr slate green .50 .25

Cent. of "O Evangelho" (Gospel) of the codification of Spiritism.

Heinrich Lübke — A495

Perf. 11½x11

1964, May 8 Photo. Wmk. 267

979 A495 100cr red brown .35 .25

Visit of President Heinrich Lübke of Germany.

Pope John XXIII — A496

1964, June 29 Wmk. 267

980 A496 20cr dk car rose .25 .25
a. Unwmkd. 2.00 .25

Issued in memory of Pope John XXIII.

Pres. Senghor of Senegal — A497

1964, Sept. 19 Wmk. 267

981 A497 20cr dk brown .25 .25

Visit of Leopold Sedar Senghor, President of Senegal.

Botafogo Bay and Sugarloaf Mountain — A498

Designs: 100cr, Our Lady of Penha Church, vert. 200cr, Copacabana beach.

Perf. 11x11½, 11½x11

1964-65 Photo.

983 A498 15cr org & bl .25 .25
984 A498 100cr brt grn & red brn, *yel* .30 .25
985 A498 200cr black & red 1.60 .25
a. Souvenir sheet of 3 ('65) 17.50 17.50
Nos. 983-985 (3) 2.15 .75

4th cent. of Rio de Janeiro.

No. 985a contains three imperf. stamps similar to Nos. 983-985, but printed in brown. Sold for 320cr. Issued Dec. 30, 1965.

A souvenir card containing one lithographed facsimile of No. 984, imperf., exists, but has no franking value. Size: 100x125mm. Sold by P.O. for 250cr.

Pres. Charles de Gaulle — A499

1964, Oct. 13 ***Perf. 11½x11***

986 A499 100cr orange brn .30 .25

Visit of Charles de Gaulle, President of France, Oct. 13-15.

Pres. John F. Kennedy — A500

1964, Oct. 24 Photo. Wmk. 267

987 A500 100cr slate .25 .25

"Prophet" by Lisboa — A501

1964, Nov. 18 ***Perf. 11½x11***

988 A501 10cr slate .25 .25

150th death anniv. of the sculptor Antonio Francisco Lisboa, "O Aleijadinho" (The Cripple).

Antonio Goncalves Dias — A502

Designs: 30cr, Euclides da Cunha. 50cr, Prof. Angelo Moreira da Costa Lima. 200cr, Tiradentes. 500cr, Dom Pedro I. 1000cr, Dom Pedro II.

1965-66 Wmk. 267 ***Perf. 11x11½***

989 A502 30cr brt bluish grn ('66) 4.00 .25
989A A502 50cr dull brn ('66) 3.50 .25
990 A502 100cr blue 1.50 .25
991 A502 200cr brown org 7.00 .25
992 A502 500cr red brown 30.00 .45
992A A502 1000cr sl bl ('66) 60.00 1.60
Nos. 989-992A (6) 106.00 3.05

Statue of St. Sebastian, Guanataro Bay — A503

The Arches A504

Design: 35cr, Estacio de Sa (1520-67), founder of Rio de Janeiro.

1965 Photo. ***Perf. 11½***

Size: 24x37mm

993 A503 30cr bl & rose red .25 .25

Lithographed and Engraved

Perf. 11x11½

994 A504 30cr lt bl & blk .25 .25

Photo. ***Perf. 11½***

Size: 21x39mm

995 A503 35cr blk & org .25 .25
a. Souvenir sheet of 3 5.75 5.75
Nos. 993-995 (3) .75 .75

4th cent. of Rio de Janeiro.

No. 995a contains three imperf. stamps similar to Nos. 993-995, but printed in deep orange. Size: 130x79mm. Sold for 100cr.

Issued: No. 993, 3/5; No. 994, 11/30; No. 995, 7/28; No. 995a, 12/30.

Sword and Cross — A505

1965, Apr. 15 Wmk. 267 ***Perf. 11½***

996 A505 120cr gray .25 .25

1st anniv, of the democratic revolution.

Vital Brazil — A506

1965, Apr. 28 Wmk. 267 ***Perf. 11½***

997 A506 120cr deep orange .40 .25

Centenary of birth of Vital Brazil, M.D.

A souvenir card containing one impression similar to No. 997, imperf., exists, printed in dull plum. Sold by P.O. for 250cr. Size: 114x180mm.

Shah of Iran — A507

1965, May 5 Photo.

998 A507 120cr rose claret .30 .25

Commemorating the visit of Shah Mohammed Riza Pahlavi of Iran.

Marshal Mariano da Silva Rondon — A508

1965, May 7 Engr.

999 A508 30cr claret .30 .25

Marshal Mariano da Silva Rondon (1865-1958), explorer and expert on Indians.

Lions' Emblem — A509

1965, May 14 Photo.

1000 A509 35cr pale vio & blk .25 .25

12th convention of the Lions Clubs of Brazil, Rio de Janeiro, May 11-16.

ITU Emblem, Old and New Communication Equipment — A510

1965, May 21 ***Perf. 11½***

1001 A510 120cr yellow & grn .30 .25

Centenary of the ITU.

Epitácio Pessoa — A511

1965, May 23 Photo.

1002 A511 35cr blue gray .25 .25

Epitácio da Silva Pessoa (1865-1942), jurist, president of Brazil, 1919-22.

Statue of Admiral Barroso — A512

1965, June 11

1003 A512 30cr blue .25 .25

Cent. of the naval battle of Riachuelo.

A souvenir card containing one lithographed facsimile of No. 1003, imperf., exists. Size: 100x139½mm.

José de Alencar and Indian Princess — A513

1965, June 24 ***Perf. 11½x11***

1004 A513 30cr deep plum .25 .25

Centenary of the publication of "Iracema" by Joséde Alencar.

A souvenir card containing one lithographed facsimile of No. 1004, printed in rose red and imperf., exists. Size: 100x141½mm.

Winston Churchill A514

1965, June 25 *Perf. 11x11½*
1005 A514 200cr slate .35 .25

Scout Jamboree Emblem — A515

1965, July 17 **Photo.** *Perf. 11¾*
1006 A515 30cr dull bl grn .35 .25

1st Pan-American Boy Scout Jamboree, Fundao Island, Rio de Janeiro, July 15-25.

ICY Emblem A516

1965, Aug. 25 **Wmk. 267** *Perf. 11½*
1007 A516 120cr dl bl & blk .50 .25

International Cooperation Year, 1965.

Leoncio Correias — A517

1965, Sept. 1 *Perf. 11½x11*
1008 A517 35cr slate grn .25 .25

Leoncio Correias, poet, birth cent.

Emblem — A518

1965, Sept. 4
1009 A518 30cr brt rose .25 .25

Eighth Biennial Fine Arts Exhibition, Sao Paulo, Nov.-Dec., 1965.

Pres. Saragat of Italy — A519

1965, Sept. 11 **Photo.** **Wmk. 267**
1010 A519 100cr slate grn, *pink* .25 .25

Visit of Pres. Giuseppe Saragat of Italy.

Grand Duke and Duchess of Luxembourg — A520

1965, Sept. 17 *Perf. 11x11½*
1011 A520 100cr brn olive .25 .25

Visit of Grand Duke Jean and Grand Duchess Josephine Charlotte of Luxembourg.

Biplane — A521

1965, Oct. 8 **Photo.** *Perf. 11½x11*
1012 A521 35cr ultra .25 .25

3rd Aviation Week Philatelic Exhibition, Rio.

A souvenir card carries one impression of this 35cr, imperf. Size: 102x140mm. Sold for 100cr.

Flags of OAS Members A522

1965, Nov. 17 *Perf. 11x11½*
1013 A522 100cr brt bl & blk .25 .25

2nd meeting of OAS Foreign Ministers, Rio.

King Baudouin and Queen Fabiola of Belgium — A523

1965, Nov. 18
1014 A523 100cr gray .25 .25

Visit of King and Queen of Belgium.

"Coffee Beans" — A524

Perf. 11½x11

1965, Dec. 21 **Photo.** **Wmk. 267**
1015 A524 30cr brown .30 .25

Brazilian coffee publicity.

Conveyor and Loading Crane A525

1966, Apr. 1 *Perf. 11x11½*
1016 A525 110cr tan & dk sl grn .30 .25

Opening of the new terminal of the Rio Doce Iron Ore Company at Tubarao.

Pouring Ladle and Steel Beam — A526

Perf. 11½x11

1966, Apr. 16 **Photo.** **Wmk. 267**
1017 A526 30cr blk, *dp org* .25 .25

25th anniv. of the National Steel Company (nationalization of the steel industry).

Prof. de Rocha Dissecting Cadaver — A527

1966, Apr. 26
1018 A527 30cr brt bluish grn .30 .25

50th anniv. of the discovery and description of Rickettsia Prowazeki, the cause of typhus fever, by Prof. Henrique de Rocha Lima.

Battle of Tuiuti A528

Perf. 11x11½

1966, May 24 **Photo.** **Wmk. 267**
1019 A528 30cr gray grn .30 .25

Centenary of the Battle of Tuiuti.

Symbolic Water Cycle — A529

1966, July 1 *Perf. 11½x11*
1020 A529 100cr lt brn & bl .25 .25

Hydrological Decade (UNESCO), 1965-74.

Pres. Shazar of Israel — A530

1966, July 18 **Photo.** **Wmk. 267**
1021 A530 100cr ultra .30 .25

Visit of Pres. Zalman Shazar of Israel.

Imperial Academy of Fine Arts — A531

Perf. 11x11½

1966, Aug. 12 **Engr.** **Wmk. 267**
1022 A531 100cr red brown 1.00 .25

150th anniversary of French art mission.

Military Service Emblem A532

1966, Sept. 6 **Photo.** *Perf. 11x11½*
1023 A532 30cr yel, ultra & grn .25 .25
a. With commemorative border 3.25 3.25

New Military Service Law.

No. 1023a issued in sheets of 4. It carries at left a 30cr, design A532, in deeper tones of yellow and ultramarine, Wmk. 264. Without gum. Sold for 100cr.

Ruben Dario — A533

Perf. 11½x11

1966, Sept. 20 **Photo.** **Wmk. 267**
1024 A533 100cr brt rose lilac .25 .25

Ruben Dario (pen name of Felix Ruben Garcia Sarmiento (1867-1916), Nicaraguan poet, newspaper correspondent and diplomat.

Ceramic Candlestick from Santarém — A534

1966, Oct. 6 *Perf. 11x11½*
1025 A534 30cr dk brn, *salmon* .25 .25

Centenary of Goeldi Museum at Belem.

Arms of Santa Cruz — A535

Perf. 11½x11

1966, Oct. 15 Photo. Wmk. 267

1026 A535 30cr slate grn .25 .25

1st Natl. Tobacco Exposition, Santa Cruz.

UNESCO Emblem A536

1966, Oct. 24 Engr. *Perf. 11½*

1027 A536 120cr black .40 .25

a. With commemorative border 8.00 8.00

20th anniv. of UNESCO. No. 1027a issued in sheets of 4. It carries at right a design similar to No. 1027. Unwatermarked granite paper, without gum. Sold for 150cr.

Captain Antonio Correia Pinto and Map of Lages — A537

Perf. 11½x11

1966, Nov. 22 Photo. Wmk. 267

1028 A537 30cr salmon pink .25 .25

Arrival of Capt. Antonio Correia Pinto, bicent.

Cross of Lusitania and Southern Cross — A538

1966, Dec. 4 *Perf. 11½*

1029 A538 100cr blue green .30 .25

LUBRAPEX 1966 philatelic exhibition at the National Museum of Fine Arts, Rio.

A539

A540

Madonna and Child — A540a

Perf. 11½x11

1966, Dec. Photo. Wmk. 267

1030 A539 30cr blue green .25 .25

Perf. 11½

1031 A540 35cr salmon & ultra .25 .25

a. A540a 150cr salmon & ultra 4.00 *5.50*

Christmas 1966.

No. 1031a measures 46x103mm and is printed in sheets of 4. Issued without gum.

Issued: 30cr, 12/8; 35cr, 12/22; 150cr, 12/28.

Arms of Laguna A541

1967, Jan. 4 Engr. *Perf. 11x11½*

1032 A541 60cr sepia .25 .25

Centenary of the Post and Telegraph Agency of Laguna, Santa Catarina.

Railroad Bridge A542

1967, Feb. 16 Photo. Wmk. 267

1033 A542 50cr deep orange .35 .25

Centenary of the Santos-Jundiai railroad.

Black Madonna of Czestochowa, Polish Eagle and Cross — A543

1967, Mar. 12 *Perf. 11x11½*

1034 A543 50cr yel, bl & rose red .35 .25

Adoption of Christianity in Poland, 1,000th anniv.

Research Rocket — A544

1967, Mar. 23 *Perf. 11½x11*

1035 A544 50cr blk & brt bl .35 .25

World Meteorological Day, March 23.

Anita Garibaldi — A545

Portraits: 1c, Mother Joana Angelica. 2c, Marilia de Dirceu. 3c, Dr. Rita Lobato. 6c, Ana Neri. 10c, Darcy Vargas.

Perf. 11x11½

1967-69 Photo. Wmk. 267

1036 A545 1c dp ultra .25 .25

1037 A545 2c red brn .25 .25

1038 A545 3c brt grn .25 .25

1039 A545 5c black .25 .25

1040 A545 6c brown .25 .25

1041 A545 10c dk slate grn 1.25 .25

Nos. 1036-1041 (6) 2.50 1.50

Issued: 1c, 5/3; 2c, 8/14; 3c, 6/7; 5c, 4/14; 6c, 5/14/67; 10c, 6/18/69.

VARIG Airlines — A546

1967, May 8 *Perf. 11½x11*

1046 A546 6c brt bl & blk .25 .25

40th anniversary of VARIG Airlines.

Lions Emblem and Globes A547

1967, May 9 Engr. *Perf. 11x11½*

1047 A547 6c green .25 .25

a. Souvenir sheet 7.50 7.50

50th anniv. of Lions Intl. No. 1047a contains one imperf. stamp similar to No. 1047. Sold for 15c.

Madonna and Child, by Robert Feruzzi — A548

1967, May 14 Photo. *Perf. 11½x11*

1048 A548 5c violet .25 .25

a. 15c Souvenir sheet 5.50 2.75

Mother's Day. No. 1048a contains one 15c imperf. stamp in design of No. 1048.

Prince Akihito and Princess Michiko A549

1967, May 25 *Perf. 11x11½*

1049 A549 10c black & pink .55 .25

Visit to Brazil of Crown Prince Akihito and Princess Michiko of Japan.

Carrier Pigeon and Radar Screen — A550

Perf. 11½x11

1967, June 20 Photo. Wmk. 267

1050 A550 10c sl & brt pink .25 .25

Commemorating the opening of the Communications Ministry in Brasilia.

Brother Vicente do Salvador — A551

1967, June 28 Engr.

1051 A551 5c brown .25 .25

400th birth anniv. of Brother Vicente do Salvador (1564-1636), founder of Franciscan convent in Rio de Janeiro, and historian.

Boy, Girl and 4-S Emblem A552

1967, July 12 Photo. *Perf. 11½*

1052 A552 5c green & blk .25 .25

National 4-S (4-H) Day.

Möbius Strip A553

1967, July 21 ***Perf. 11x11½***
1053 A553 5c brt bl & blk .25 .25

6th Brazilian Mathematical Congress.

Fish A554

1967, Aug. 1 ***Perf. 11½***
1054 A554 5c slate .30 .25

Bicentenary of city of Piracicaba.

Golden Rose and Papal Arms — A555

1967, Aug. 15
1055 A555 20c mag & yel .50 .25

Offering of a golden rose by Pope Paul VI to the Virgin Mary of Fatima (Our Lady of Peace), Patroness of Brazil.

General Sampaio — A556

1967, Aug. 25 **Engr.** ***Perf. 11½x11***
1056 A556 5c blue .25 .25

Honoring General Antonio de Sampaio, hero of the Battle of Tutui.

King Olaf of Norway — A557

1967, Sept. 8 **Photo.**
1057 A557 10c brown org .25 .25

Visit of King Olaf of Norway.

Sun over Sugar Loaf, Botafogo Bay — A558

Photogravure and Embossed

1967, Sept. 25 **Wmk. 267** ***Perf. 11½***
1058 A558 10c blk & dp org .35 .25

22nd meeting of the Intl. Monetary Fund, Intl. Bank for Reconstruction and Development, Intl. Financial Corporation and Intl. Development Assoc.

Nilo Peçanha — A559

Perf. 11½x11

1967, Oct. 1 **Photo.** **Wmk. 267**
1059 A559 5c brown violet .25 .25

Peçanha (1867-1924), Pres. of Brazil 1909-10.

Virgin of the Apparition and Basilica of Aparecida — A560

1967, Oct. 11 ***Perf. 11½***
1060 A560 5c ultra & dl yel .25 .25
a. Souvenir sheet of 2 20.00 14.00

250th anniv. of the discovery of the statue of Our Lady of the Apparition, now in the National Basilica of the Apparition at Aparecida do Norte.

No. 1060a contains imperf. 5c and 10c stamps similar to No. 1060. Issued Dec. 27, 1967, for Christmas.

Cockerel, Festival Emblem — A561

Engraved and Photogravure

1967, Oct. 16 ***Perf. 11½x11***
1061 A561 20c black & multi .35 .25

Second International Folksong Festival.

Balloon, Plane and Rocket A562

Perf. 11x11½

1967, Oct. 18 **Photo.** **Unwmk.**
1062 A562 10c blue .35 .25
a. 15c souvenir sheet 37.50 20.00

Week of the Wing, Oct. 18-23. No. 1062a contains one imperf. 15c stamp similar to No. 1062 and was issued Oct. 23.

Pres. Arthur Bernardes — A563

Portraits of Brazilian Presidents: 20c, Campos Salles. 50c, Wenceslau Pereira Gomes Braz. 1cr, Washington Pereira de Souza Luiz. 2cr, Castello Branco.

Perf. 11x11½

1967-68 **Photo.** **Wmk. 267**
1063 A563 10c blue .35 .25
1064 A563 20c dk red brn 2.50 .25

Engr.

1065 A563 50c black ('68) 12.00 .25
1066 A563 1cr lil rose ('68) 18.00 .25
1067 A563 2cr emerald ('68) 3.00 .25
Nos. 1063-1067 (5) 35.85 1.25

Carnival of Rio — A564

1967, Nov. 22 ***Perf. 11½x11***
1070 A564 10c lem, ultra & pink .25 .25
a. 15c souvenir sheet 13.00 8.00

Issued for International Tourist Year, 1967. No. 1070a contains a 15c imperf. stamp in design of No. 1070. Issued Nov. 24.

Ships, Anchor and Sailor — A565

1967, Dec. 6
1071 A565 10c ultra .35 .25

Issued for Navy Week.

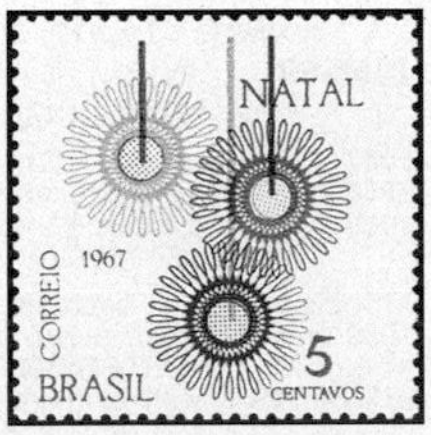

Christmas Decorations A566

1967, Dec. 8 ***Perf. 11½***
1072 A566 5c car, yel & bl .25 .25

Christmas 1967.

Olavo Bilac, Planes, Tank and Aircraft Carrier A567

Perf. 11x11½

1967, Dec. 16 **Photo.** **Wmk. 267**
1073 A567 5c brt blue & yel .25 .25

Issued for Reservists' Day and to honor Olavo Bilac, sponsor of compulsory military service.

Rodrigues de Carvalho — A568

1967, Dec. 18 **Engr.** ***Perf. 11½x11***
1074 A568 10c green .40 .25

Cent. of the birth of Rodrigues de Carvalho, poet and lawyer.

Orlando Rangel A569

1968, Feb. 29 **Photo.** ***Perf. 11x11½***
1075 A569 5c lt grnsh bl & blk .30 .25

Orlando de Fonseca Rangel, pioneer of pharmaceutical industry in Brazil, birth cent.

Virgin of Paranagua and Diver — A570

1968, Mar. 9 ***Perf. 11½x11***
1076 A570 10c dk sl grn & brt yel grn .25 .25

250th anniversary of the first underwater explorations at Paranagua.

Map of Brazil Showing Manaus — A571

1968, Mar. 13 **Photo.** **Wmk. 267**
1077 A571 10c yel, grn & red .30 .25

Free port of Manaus on the Amazon River.

Human Rights Flame — A572

1968, Mar. 21 ***Perf. 11½x11***
1078 A572 10c blue & salmon .25 .25

International Human Rights Year.

Paul Harris and Rotary Emblem — A573

1968, Apr. 19 Litho. Unwmk.
Without Gum

1079 A573 20c grn & org brn .40 .30

Paul Percy Harris (1868-1947), founder of Rotary International.

Pedro Alvares Cabral and his Fleet — A574

Design: 20c, First Mass celebrated in Brazil.

1968 Without Gum *Perf. 11½*

1080 A574 10c multicolored .25 .25
1081 A574 20c multicolored .40 .25

500th anniversary of the birth of Pedro Alvares Cabral, navigator, who took possession of Brazil for Portugal.

Issue dates: 10c, Apr. 22; 20c, July 11.

College Arms — A575

1968, Apr. 22 Photo. Wmk. 267

1082 A575 10c vio bl, red & gold .25 .25

Centenary of St. Luiz College, Sao Paulo.

Motherhood, by Henrique Bernardeli A576

1968, May 12 Litho. Unwmk.
Without Gum

1083 A576 5c multicolored .30 .25

Issued for Mother's Day.

Harpy Eagle A577

Photogravure and Engraved
1968, May 28 Wmk. 267

1084 A577 20c brt bl & blk 1.25 .25

Sesquicentennial of National Museum.

Brazilian and Japanese Women — A578

1968, June 28 Litho. Unwmk.
Without Gum

1085 A578 10c yellow & multi .30 .25

Commemorating the inauguration of Varig's direct Brazil-Japan airline.

Horse Race A579

Perf. 11x11½
1968, July 16 Litho. Unwmk.
Without Gum

1086 A579 10c multicolored .30 .25

Centenary of the Jockey Club of Brazil.

Musician Wren A580

Designs: 10c, Red-crested cardinal, vert. 50c, Royal flycatcher, vert.

Perf. 11½x11, 11x11½
1968-69 Engr. Wmk. in Sheet
Without Gum

1087 A580 10c multi ('69) .35 .25
1088 A580 20c multicolored .50 .25
1089 A580 50c multicolored 1.00 .25
Nos. 1087-1089 (3) 1.85 .75

Some stamps in each sheet of Nos. 1087-1089 show parts of a two-line papermaker's watermark: "WESTERPOST / INDUSTRIA BRASILEIRA" with diamond-shaped emblem between last two words. Entire watermark appears in one sheet margin. Value, set $45.

Issued: 10c, 8/20/69; 20c, 7/9/68; 50c, 8/2/68.

Mailbox and Envelope — A581

Photogravure and Engraved
1968, Aug. 1 Wmk. 267 *Perf. 11*

1091 A581 5c tan, blk & grn .25 .25

Stamp Day, 1968 and for 125th anniv. of the 1st Brazilian postage stamps.

Emilio Luiz Mallet — A582

Perf. 11½x11
1968, Aug. 25 Engr. Wmk. 267

1092 A582 10c pale purple .25 .25

Honoring Marshal Emilio Luiz Mallet, Baron of Itapevi, patron of the marines.

Map of South America — A583

1968, Sept. 5 Photo.

1093 A583 10c deep orange .25 .25

Visit of President Eduardo Frei of Chile.

Seal of Portuguese Literary School — A584

Photogravure and Engraved
1968, Sept. 10 *Perf. 11½*

1094 A584 5c pink & grn .25 .25

Centenary of Portuguese Literary School.

Map of Brazil and Telex Tape A585

1968, Sept. Photo. *Perf. 11x11½*

1095 A585 20c citron & brt grn .50 .25

Linking of 25 Brazilian cities by teletype.

Soldiers' Heads on Medal — A586

Perf. 11½x11
1968, Sept. 24 Litho. Unwmk.
Without Gum

1096 A586 5c blue & gray .25 .25

8th American Armed Forces Conference.

Clef, Notes and Sugarloaf Mountain A587

1968, Sept. 30 *Perf. 11½*
Without Gum

1097 A587 6c blk, yel & red .25 .25

Third International Folksong Festival.

Catalytic Cracking Plant A588

1968, Oct. 4 Without Gum

1098 A588 6c blue & multi .40 .25

Petrobras, the natl. oil company, 15th anniv.

Child Protection — A589

Whimsical Girl — A590

5c, School boy walking toward the sun.

Perf. 11½x11, 11x11½
1968, Oct. 16 Litho. Unwmk.
Without Gum

1099 A590 5c gray & lt bl .25 .25
1100 A589 10c brt bl, dk red & blk .25 .25
1101 A590 20c multicolored .35 .25
Nos. 1099-1101 (3) .85 .75

22nd anniv. of UNICEF.

Children with Books A591

1968, Oct. 23 *Perf. 11x11½*
Without Gum

1102 A591 5c multicolored .25 .25

Book Week.

UN Emblem and Flags — A592

1968, Oct. 24 ***Perf. 11½x11***
Without Gum

1103 A592 20c black & multi .35 .25

20th anniv. of WHO.

Jean Baptiste Debret, Self-portrait — A593

Perf. 11x11½
1968, Oct. 30 **Litho.** **Unwmk.**
Without Gum

1104 A593 10c dk gray & pale yel .25 .25

Jean Baptiste Debret, (1768-1848), French painter who worked in Brazil (1816-31). Design includes his "Burden Bearer."

Queen Elizabeth II A594

1968, Nov. 4 ***Perf. 11½***
Without Gum

1105 A594 70c lt bl & multi .60 .40

Visit of Queen Elizabeth II of Great Britain.

Francisco Braga — A595

Perf. 11½x11
1968, Nov. 19 **Wmk. 267**

1106 A595 5c dull red brn .35 .25

Cent. of the birth of Antonio Francisco Braga, composer of the Hymn of the Flag.

Brazilian Flag — A596

1968, Nov. 19 **Unwmk.** ***Perf. 11½***
Without Gum

1107 A596 10c multicolored .30 .25

Issued for Flag Day.

Clasped Hands and Globe A597

Perf. 11x11½
1968, Nov. 25 **Typo.** **Unwmk.**
Without Gum

1108 A597 5c multicolored .25 .25

Issued for Voluntary Blood Donor's Day.

Old Locomotive — A598

1968, Nov. 28 **Litho.** ***Perf. 11½***
Without Gum

1109 A598 5c multicolored 1.00 .35

Centenary of the Sao Paulo Railroad.

Bell — A599

Santa Claus and Boy — A599a

1968 **Without Gum** ***Perf. 11½x11***

1110 A599 5c multicolored .25 .25
1111 A599a 6c multicolored .25 .25

Christmas 1968.
Issue dates: 5c, Dec. 12; 6c, Dec. 20.

Francisco Caldas, Jr. — A600

1968, Dec. 13 **Without Gum**

1112 A600 10c crimson & blk .25 .25

Cent. of the birth of Francisco Caldas, Jr., journalist and founder of Correio de Povo, newspaper.

Map of Brazil, War Memorial and Reservists' Emblem — A601

Perf. 11x11½
1968, Dec. 16 **Photo.** **Wmk. 267**

1113 A601 5c bl grn & org brn .25 .25

Issued for Reservists' Day.

Radar Antenna — A602

Perf. 11½x11
1969, Feb. 28 **Litho.** **Unwmk.**
Without Gum

1114 A602 30c ultra, lt bl & blk .35 .25

Inauguration of EMBRATEL, satellite communications ground station bringing US television to Brazil via Telstar.

Viscount of Rio Branco — A603

1969, Mar. 16 **Without Gum**

1115 A603 5c black & buff .25 .25

José Maria da Silva Paranhos, Viscount of Rio Branco (1819-1880), statesman.

St. Gabriel — A604

1969, Mar. 24 **Without Gum**

1116 A604 5c multicolored .25 .25

Honoring St. Gabriel as patron saint of telecommunications.

Shoemaker's Last and Globe — A605

Perf. 11x11½
1969, Mar. 29 **Litho.** **Unwmk.**
Without Gum

1117 A605 5c multicolored .25 .25

4th Intl. Shoe Fair, Novo Hamburgo.

Allan Kardec A606

1969, Mar. 31 **Photo.** **Wmk. 267**

1118 A606 5c brt grn & org brn .35 .25

Allan Kardec (pen name of Leon Hippolyto Denizard Rivail, 1803-1869), French physician and spiritist.

Men of 3 Races and Arms of Cuiabá A607

1969, Apr. 8 **Litho.** **Unwmk.**
Without Gum

1119 A607 5c black & multi .25 .25

250th anniversary of the founding of Cuiabá, capital of Matto Grosso.

State Mint — A608

1969, Apr. 11 ***Perf. 11½***
Without Gum

1120 A608 5c olive bister & org .30 .25

Opening of the state money printing plant.

Brazilian Stamps and Emblem A609

Perf. 11x11½
1969, Apr. 30 **Litho.** **Unwmk.**
Without Gum

1121 A609 5c multicolored .30 .25

Sao Paulo Philatelic Society, 50th anniv.

St. Anne, Baroque Statue A610

1969, May 8 ***Perf. 11½***
Without Gum

1122 A610 5c lemon & multi .25 .25

Issued for Mother's Day.

ILO Emblem A611

Perf. 11x11½
1969, May 13 **Photo.** **Wmk. 267**

1123 A611 5c dp rose red & gold .25 .25

50th anniv. of the ILO.

Diving Platform and Swimming Pool — A612

Lithographed and Photogravure
Perf. 11½x11
1969, June 13 **Unwmk.**
Without Gum

1124 A612 20c bis brn, blk & bl grn .35 .25

40th anniversary of the Cearense Water Sports Club, Fortaleza.

Mother and Child at Window — A613

Sculpture, by Felicia Leirner — A613a

"The Sun Sets in Brasilia," by Danilo di Prete — A613b

Angelfish, by Aldemir Martins — A613c

Size: 24x36mm

1969 Litho. ***Perf. 11½***

1125 A613 10c orange & multi .35 .25

Size: 33x34mm

1126 A613a 20c red & multi .35 .25

Size: 33x53mm

1127 A613b 50c yellow & multi 1.50 .50

Without Gum

1128 A613c 1cr gray & multi 2.00 .75
Nos. 1125-1128 (4) 4.20 1.75

10th Biennial Art Exhibition, Sao Paulo, Sept.-Dec. 1969.

Angelfish A614

No. 1130: 10c, Tetra. 15c, Piranha. 20c, Megalamphodus megalopterus. 30c, Black tetra.

Wmk. 267

1969, July 21 Litho. ***Perf. 11½***

1129 A614 20c multicolored .35 .25

Souvenir Sheet

Fish — A615

1969, July 24 Unwmk. ***Imperf.***

1130 A615	Sheet of 4	5.75	5.75
a.	10c yellow & multi	1.25	1.25
b.	15c bright blue & multi	1.25	1.25
c.	20c green & multi	1.25	1.25
d.	30c orange & multi	1.25	1.25

Issued to publicize the work of ACAPI, an organization devoted to the preservation and development of fish in Brazil.

No. 1130 contains four 38½x21mm stamps.

L. O. Teles de Menezes — A616

Perf. 11½x11

1969, July 26 Photo. Wmk. 267

1131 A616 50c dp org & bl grn .75 .75

Centenary of Spiritism press in Brazil.

Mailman — A617

1969, Aug. 1

1132 A617 30c blue .60 .25

Issued for Stamp Day.

Map of Brazil A618

Railroad Bridge A619

Gen. Tasso Fragoso — A620

Without Gum

Perf. 11½

1969, Aug. 25 Unwmk. Litho.

1133 A618 10c lt ultra, grn & yel .25 .25

Perf. 11x11½

1134 A619 20c multicolored .30 .25

With Gum

Perf. 11½x11

Engr. Wmk. 267

1135 A620 20c green .50 .25
Nos. 1133-1135 (3) 1.05 .75

No. 1133 honors the Army as guardian of security; No. 1134, as promoter of development. No. 1135 the birth centenary of Gen. Tasso Fragoso.

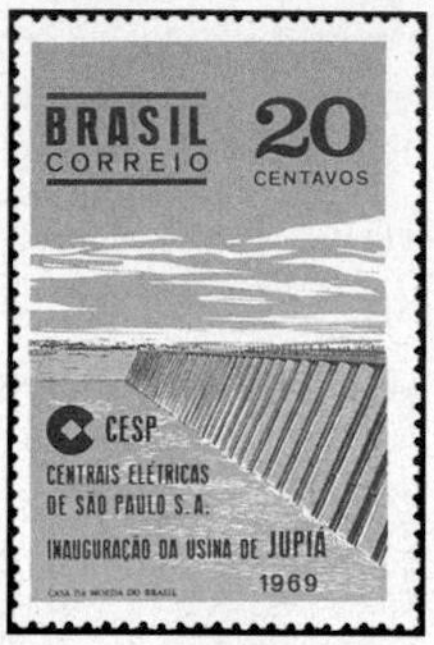

Jupia Dam, Parana River A621

Perf. 11½

1969, Sept. 10 Litho. Unwmk.

Without Gum

1136 A621 20c lt blue & multi .35 .25

Inauguration of the Jupia Dam, part of the Urubupunga hydroelectric system serving Sao Paulo.

Gandhi and Spinning Wheel A622

1969, Oct. 2 ***Perf. 11x11½***

1137 A622 20c yellow & blk .60 .30

Mohandas K. Gandhi (1869-1948), leader in India's fight for independence.

Santos Dumont, Eiffel Tower and Module Landing on Moon — A623

1969, Oct. 17 ***Perf. 11½***

Without Gum

1138 A623 50c dk bl & multi 1.00 1.00

Man's first landing on the moon, July 20, 1969. See note after US No. C76.

Smelting Plant A624

1969, Oct. 26 Unwmk. ***Perf. 11½***

Without Gum

1139 A624 20c multicolored .30 .25

Expansion of Brazil's steel industry.

Steel Furnace A625

1969, Oct. 31 Litho.

Without Gum

1140 A625 10c yellow & multi .30 .25

25th anniversary of Acesita Steel Works.

Water Vendor, by J. B. Debret — A626

Design: 30c, Street Scene, by Debret.

1969-70 Without Gum

1141 A626 20c multicolored .70 .25
1141A A626 30c multicolored .50 .30

Jean Baptiste Debret (1768-1848), painter. Issued: 20c, 11/5/69; 30c, 5/19/70.

Exhibition Emblem — A627

1969, Nov. 15 ***Perf. 11½x11***

Without Gum

1142 A627 10c multicolored .25 .25

ABUEXPO 69 Philatelic Exposition, Sao Paulo, Nov. 15-23.

Plane — A628

1969, Nov. 23 Without Gum

1143 A628 50c multicolored 1.00 .35

Publicizing the year of the expansion of the national aviation industry.

Pelé Scoring
A629

1969-70 Without Gum

1144 A629 10c multicolored .50 *5.00*

Souvenir Sheet

Imperf

1145 A629 75c multi ('70) 6.00 5.00

Commemorating the 1,000th goal scored by Pele, Brazilian soccer player.

No. 1145 contains one imperf. stamp with simulated perforations.

Issued: 10c, 11/28/69; 75c, 1/23/70.

Madonna and Child from Villa Velha Monastery
A630

Perf. 11½

1969, Dec. Unwmk. Litho.

1146 A630 10c gold & multi .30 .25

Souvenir Sheet

Imperf

1147 A630 75c gold & multi *30.00 30.00*

Christmas 1969.

No. 1147 has simulated perforations.

Issue dates: 10c, Dec. 8; 75c, Dec. 18.

Destroyer and Submarine — A631

Perf. 11x11½

1969, Dec. 9 Engr. Wmk. 267

1148 A631 5c bluish gray .35 .25

Issued for Navy Day.

Dr. Herman Blumenau
A632

1969, Dec. 26 *Perf. 11½*

1149 A632 20c gray grn .70 .25

Dr. Herman Blumenau (1819-1899), founder of Blumenau, Santa Catarina State.

Carnival Scene — A633

Sugarloaf Mountain, Mask, Confetti and Streamers
A634

Designs: 5c, Jumping boy and 2 women, vert. 20c, Clowns. 50c, Drummer.

1969-70 Litho. Unwmk.

Without Gum

1150 A633 5c multicolored .50 .25

1151 A633 10c multicolored .50 .25

1152 A633 20c multicolored .50 .25

1153 A634 30c multicolored 1.50 .50

1154 A634 50c multicolored 3.00 .50

Nos. 1150-1154 (5) 6.00 1.75

Carioca Carnival, Rio de Janeiro.

Issued: nos. 1150-1152, 12/29; others, 2/5/70.

Opening Bars of "Il Guarani" with Antonio Carlos Gomes Conducting — A635

1970, Mar. 19 Litho. *Perf. 11½*

Without Gum

1155 A635 20c blk, yel, gray & brn .35 .25

Centenary of the opera Il Guarani, by Antonio Carlos Gomes.

Church of Penha
A636

1970, Apr. 6 Unwmk. *Perf. 11½*

Without Gum

1156 A636 20c black & multi .30 .25

400th anniversary of the Church of Penha, State of Espirito Santo.

Assembly Building
A637

10th anniv. of Brasilia: 50c, Reflecting Pool. 1cr, Presidential Palace.

1970, Apr. 21 Without Gum

1157 A637 20c multicolored .35 .25

1158 A637 50c multicolored 1.20 1.00

1159 A637 1cr multicolored 1.45 1.00

Nos. 1157-1159 (3) 3.00 2.25

Symbolic Water Design
A638

1970, May 5 Unwmk. *Perf. 11½*

Without Gum

1161 A638 50c multicolored .60 .25

Publicizing the Rondon Project for the development of the Amazon River basin.

Marshal Manoel Luiz Osorio and Osorio Arms — A639

1970, May 8 Without Gum

1162 A639 20c multicolored .60 .30

Commemorating the inauguration of the Marshal Osorio Historical Park.

Madonna, from San Antonio Monastery, Rio de Janeiro
A640

1970, May 10 Without Gum

1163 A640 20c multicolored .35 .25

Issued for Mother's Day.

Detail from Brasilia Cathedral — A641

1970, May 27 Engr. Wmk. 267

1164 A641 20c lt yellow grn .30 .25

8th National Eucharistic Congress, Brasilia.

Census Symbol — A642

Perf. 11½

1970, June 22 Unwmk. Litho.

Without Gum

1165 A642 20c green & yel .35 .25

Publicizing the 8th general census.

Soccer Cup, Maps of Brazil and Mexico
A643

Swedish Flag and Player Holding Rimet Cup — A644

Designs: 2cr, Chilean flag and soccer. 3cr, Mexican flag and soccer.

1970 Without Gum

1166 A643 50c blk, lt bl & gold .70 .30

1167 A644 1cr pink & multi 2.00 .60

1168 A644 2cr gray & multi 3.50 1.00

1169 A644 3cr multicolored 3.00 .50

Nos. 1166-1169 (4) 9.20 2.40

9th World Soccer Championships for the Jules Rimet Cup, Mexico City, May 30-June 21. No. 1166 honors Brazil's victory.

Issued: No. 1166, 6/24; Nos. 1167-1169, 8/4.

Corcovado Christ and Map of South America
A645

1970, July 18 Without Gum

1170 A645 50c brn, dk red & bl .50 .25

6th World Cong. of Marist Brothers' Alumni.

Pandia Calogeras, Minister of War — A646

Perf. 11½x11

1970, Aug. 25 Photo. Unwmk.

1171 A646 20c blue green .40 .25

Brazilian Military Emblems and Map — A647

Perf. 11x11½

1970, Sept. 8 Litho. Unwmk.

Without Gum

1172 A647 20c gray & multi .30 .25

25th anniv. of victory in World War II.

Annunciation (Brazilian Primitive Painting)
A648

1970, Sept. 29 ***Perf. 11½***

Without Gum

1173 A648 20c multicolored .40 .25

Issued for St. Gabriel's (patron saint of communications) Day.

Boy in Library — A649

1970, Oct. 23 **Without Gum**

1174 A649 20c multicolored .25 .25

Issued to publicize Book Week.

UN Emblem — A650

1970, Oct. 24 **Without Gum**

1175 A650 50c dk bl, lt bl & sil .40 .25

25th anniversary of the United Nations.

Rio de Janeiro, 1820 — A651

LUBRAPEX 70 Emblem — A651a

Designs: 1cr, Rio de Janeiro with Sugar Loaf Mountain, 1970. No. 1179, like 20c.

1970, Oct. **Without Gum**

1176 A651 20c multicolored .60 .25
1177 A651a 50c yel brn & blk 2.50 .60
1178 A651 1cr multicolored 3.00 1.00
Nos. 1176-1178 (3) 6.10 1.85

Souvenir Sheet

Imperf

1179 A651 1cr multicolored 16.00 12.00

LUBRAPEX 70, 3rd Portuguese-Brazilian Phil. Exhib., Rio de Janeiro, Oct. 24-31.

Issued: Nos. 1176-1178, 10/27; No. 1179, 10/31.

Holy Family by Candido Portinari A652

1970, Dec. **Litho.** ***Perf. 11½***

Without Gum

1180 A652 50c multicolored .50 .30

Souvenir Sheet

Imperf

1181 A652 1cr multicolored 37.50 5.00

Christmas 1970. No. 1181 contains one stamp with simulated perforations.

Issue dates: 50c, Dec. 1; 1cr, Dec. 8.

Battleship — A653

1970, Dec. 11 **Litho.** ***Perf. 11½***

Without Gum

1182 A653 20c multicolored .50 .30

Navy Day.

CIH Emblem — A654

1971, Mar. 28 **Litho.** ***Perf. 11½***

Without Gum

1183 A654 50c black & red .50 .25

3rd Inter-American Housing Cong., 3/27-4/3.

Links Around Globe — A655

1971, Mar. 31 **Litho.** ***Perf. 12½x11***

Without Gum

1184 A655 20c grn, yel, blk & red .30 .25

Intl. year against racial discrimination.

Morpho Melacheilus — A656

Design: 1cr, Papilio thoas brasiliensis.

Perf. 11x11½

1971, Apr. 28 **Litho.** **Unwmk.**

Without Gum

1185 A656 20c multicolored .75 .25
1186 A656 1cr multicolored 3.50 1.00

Madonna and Child — A657

1971, May 9 **Litho.** ***Perf. 11½***

Without Gum

1187 A657 20c multicolored .40 .25

Mother's Day, 1971.

Basketball A658

1971, May 19 **Without Gum**

1188 A658 70c multicolored .75 .40

6th World Women's Basketball Championship.

Map of Trans-Amazon Highway — A659

Perf. 11½

1971, July 1 **Unwmk.** **Litho.**

Without Gum

1189 40c multicolored 5.00 1.00
1190 1cr multicolored 5.00 1.75
a. A659 Pair, #1189-1190 20.00 10.00

Trans-Amazon Highway. No. 1190a printed in sheets of 28 (4x7). Horizontal rows contain 2 No. 1190a with a label between. Each label carries different inscription.

Man's Head, by Victor Mairelles de Lima A661

Stamp Day: 1cr, Arab Violinist, by Pedro Américo.

1971, Aug. 1

1191 A661 40c pink & multi .90 .25
1192 A661 1cr gray & multi 2.50 .80

Duke of Caxias and Map of Brazil A662

1971, Aug. 23 **Photo.**

1193 A662 20c yel grn & red brn .45 .25

Army Week.

Anita Garibaldi — A663

1971, Aug. 30 **Litho.**

Without Gum

1194 A663 20c multicolored .50 .25

Anita Garibaldi (1821-1849), heroine in liberation of Brazil.

Xavante Jet and Santos Dumont's Plane, 1910 — A664

1971, Sept. 6 **Without Gum**

1195 A664 40c yellow & multi .70 .25

First flight of Xavante jet plane.

Flags and Map of Central American Nations — A665

1971, Sept. 15 **Without Gum**

1196 A665 40c ocher & multi .60 .25

Sesquicentennial of the independence of Central American nations.

"71" in French Flag Colors — A666

1971, Sept. 16 **Without Gum**

1197 A666 1.30cr ultra & multi .40 .25

French Exhibition.

Black Mother, by Lucilio de Albuquerque A667

1971, Sept. 28 **Without Gum**

1198 A667 40c multicolored .30 .25

Centenary of law guaranteeing personal freedom starting at birth.

Archangel Gabriel — A668

1971, Sept. 29 *Perf. 11½x11*

Without Gum

1199 A668 40c multicolored .50 .25

St. Gabriel's Day.

Bridge over River A669

Children's Drawings: 35c, People crossing bridge. 60c, Woman with hat.

1971, Oct. 25 *Perf. 11½*

Without Gum

1200 A669 35c pink, bl & blk .60 .25
1201 A669 45c black & multi .60 .25
1202 A669 60c olive & multi .60 .25
Nos. 1200-1202 (3) 1.80 .75

Children's Day.

Werkhäuserii Superba — A670

1971, Nov. 16 **Without Gum**

1203 A670 40c blue & multi .70 .25

In memory of Carlos Werkhauser, botanist.

Greek Key Pattern "25" — A671

1971, Dec. 3 **Without Gum**

1204 20c black & blue 1.25 .25
1205 40c black & org 1.25 .25
a. A671 Pair, #1204-1205 3.50 3.50

25th anniversary of SENAC (national apprenticeship system) and SESC (commercial social service).

Gunboat A672

1971, Dec. 8 *Perf. 11*

Without Gum

1206 A672 20c blue & multi .30 .25

Navy Day.

Cross and Circles — A673

1971, Dec. 11

1207 A673 20c car & blue .60 .25
1208 A673 75c silver & gray .60 .25
1209 A673 1.30cr blk, yel, grn & bl 1.60 .60
Nos. 1207-1209 (3) 2.80 *1.10*

Christmas 1971.

Washing of Bonfim Church, Salvador, Bahia — A674

Designs: 40c, Grape Festival, Rio Grande do Sul. 75c, Festival of the Virgin of Nazareth, Belém. 1.30cr, Winter Arts Festival, Ouro Preto.

1972, Feb. 18 **Litho.** *Perf. 11½x11*

Without Gum

1210 A674 20c silver & multi .55 .25
1211 A674 40c silver & multi .70 .25
1212 A674 75c silver & multi .90 .50
1213 A674 1.30cr silver & multi 3.50 1.10
Nos. 1210-1213 (4) 5.65 2.10

Pres. Lanusse and Flag of Argentina A675

1972, Mar. 13 *Perf. 11x11½*

Without Gum

1214 A675 40c blue & multi .70 .50

Visit of Lt. Gen. Alejandro Agustin Lanusse, president of Argentina.

Presidents Castello Branco, Costa e Silva and Garrastazu Medici — A676

1972, Mar. 29 **Without Gum**

1215 A676 20c emerald & multi .70 .25

Anniversary of 1964 revolution.

Post Office Emblem — A677

Perf. 11½x11

1972, Apr. 10 **Photo.** **Unwmk.**

1216 A677 20c red brown 1.50 .25

No. 1216 is luminescent.

Pres. Thomaz and Portuguese Flag — A678

1972, Apr. 22 **Litho.** *Perf. 11*

Without Gum

1217 A678 75c ol brn & multi .85 .50

Visit of Pres. Americo Thomaz of Portugal to Brazil, Apr. 22-27.

Soil Research (CPRM) A679

40c, Offshore oil rig. 75c, Hydroelectric dam. 1.30cr, Iron ore production.

1972, May 3 *Perf. 11½*

Without Gum

1218 A679 20c shown .50 .25
1219 A679 40c multi .70 .25
1220 A679 75c multi .70 .60
1221 A679 1.30cr multi 1.45 .35
Nos. 1218-1221 (4) 3.35 1.45

Industrial development. Stamps are inscribed with names of industrial firms.
See Nos. 1228-1229.

Souvenir Sheet

Poster for Modern Art Week 1922 — A680

1972, May 5

1222 A680 1cr black & car 50.00 40.00

50th anniversary of Modern Art Week.

Mailman, Map of Brazil and Letters A681

Designs: 45c, "Telecommunications", vert. 60c, Tropospheric scatter system. 70c, Road map of Brazil and worker.

1972, May 26 **Without Gum**

1223 A681 35c blue & multi .70 .25
1224 A681 45c silver & multi .70 .30
1225 A681 60c black & multi .70 .25
1226 A681 70c multicolored 1.00 .25
Nos. 1223-1226 (4) 3.10 1.05

Unification of communications in Brazil.

Development Type of 1972 and

Automobiles — A682

Perf. 11x11½, 11½x11

1972, June 21 **Photo.**

1227 A682 35c shown .60 .25

Litho.

1228 A679 45c Ships .60 .25
1229 A679 70c Ingots .60 .25
Nos. 1227-1229 (3) 1.80 .75

Industrial development. The 35c is luminescent.

Soccer — A683

75c, Folk music. 1.30cr, Plastic arts.

Perf. 11½x11

1972, July 7 **Photo.** **Unwmk.**

1230 A683 20c black & yel .40 .25
1231 A683 75c black & ver .80 .40
1232 A683 1.30cr black & ultra 1.60 .80
Nos. 1230-1232 (3) 2.80 1.45

150th anniv. of independence. No. 1230 publicizes the 1972 sports tournament, a part of independence celebrations. Luminescent.

Souvenir Sheet

Shout of Independence, by Pedro Americo de Figueiredo e Melo — A684

1972, July 19 **Litho.** *Perf. 11½*

Without Gum

1233 A684 1cr multicolored 6.00 *7.00*

4th Interamerican Philatelic Exhibition, EXFILBRA, Rio de Janeiro, Aug 26-Sept. 2.

Figurehead A685

Brazilian folklore: 60c, Gauchos dancing fandango. 75c, Acrobats (capoeira). 1.15cr, Karajá (ceramic) doll. 1.30cr, Mock bullfight (bumba meu boi).

1972, Aug. 6 **Without Gum**

1234 A685 45c multicolored .40 .25
1235 A685 60c org & multi .80 .40
1236 A685 75c gray & multi .40 .25
1237 A685 1.15cr multicolored .40 .25
1238 A685 1.30cr yellow & multi 2.50 .60
Nos. 1234-1238 (5) 4.50 1.75

Map of Brazil, by Diego Homem, 1568
A686

Designs: 1cr, Map of Americas, by Nicholas Visscher, 1652. 2cr, Map of Americas, by Lopo Homem, 1519.

1972, Aug. 26 Litho. *Perf. 11½*
Without Gum

1239	A686	70c multicolored	.80	.25
1240	A686	1cr multicolored	6.00	.70
1241	A686	2cr multicolored	1.50	.60
		Nos. 1239-1241 (3)	8.30	1.55

4th Inter-American Philatelic Exhibition, EXFILBRA, Rio de Janeiro, Aug. 26-Sept. 2.

Dom Pedro Proclaimed Emperor, by Jean Baptiste Debret — A687

Designs: 30c, Founding of Brazil (people with imperial flag), vert. 1cr, Coronation of Emperor Dom Pedro, vert. 2cr, Dom Pedro commemorative medal. 3.50cr, Independence Monument, Ipiranga.

1972, Sept. 4 Litho. *Perf. 11½x11*

1242	A687	30c yellow & grn	.60	.25
1243	A687	70c pink & rose lil	.60	.25
1244	A687	1cr buff & red brn	3.00	.25
1245	A687	2cr pale yel & blk	2.00	.25
1246	A687	3.50cr gray & blk	2.00	.70
		Nos. 1242-1246 (5)	8.20	1.70

Sesquicentennial of independence.

Souvenir Sheet

"Automobile Race" — A688

1972, Nov. 14 *Perf. 11½*

1247	A688	2cr multicolored	8.50	*10.00*

Emerson Fittipaldi, Brazilian world racing champion.

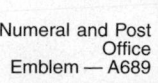

Numeral and Post Office Emblem — A689

Möbius Strip A689a

Perf. 11½x11
1972-75 Unwmk. Photo.

1248	A689	5c orange ('74)	.25	.25
a.		Wmk. 267	.35	.25
1249	A689	10c brown ('73)	.25	.25
a.		Wmk. 267	1.50	.25
1250	A689	15c brt blue ('75)	.35	.25
1251	A689	20c ultra	2.00	.25
1252	A689	25c sepia ('75)	.35	.25
1253	A689	30c dp carmine	1.20	.25
1254	A689	40c dk grn ('73)	.35	.25
1255	A689	50c olive ('74)	1.00	.25
1256	A689	70c red lilac ('75)	.50	.25

Engr. *Perf. 11½*

1257	A689a	1cr lilac ('74)	.50	.25
1258	A689a	2cr grnsh bl ('74)	1.20	.25
1259	A689a	4cr org & vio ('75)	4.50	.25
1260	A689a	5cr brn, car & buff ('74)	3.50	.25
1261	A689a	10cr grn, blk & buff ('74)	6.00	.25
		Nos. 1248-1261 (14)	21.95	3.50

The 5cr and 10cr have beige lithographed multiple Post Office emblem underprint.

Nos. 1248-1261 are luminescent. Nos. 1248a and 1249a are not.

No. 1257 exists unwatermarked. Value $150.

No. 1258 exists with watermark 267. Value $250.

Hand Writing "Mobral" A690

Designs: 20c, Multiracial group and population growth curve. 1cr, People and hands holding house. 2cr, People, industrial scene and upward arrow.

1972, Nov. 28 Litho. *Perf. 11½*
Without Gum

1262	A690	10c black & multi	.40	.25
1263	A690	20c black & multi	.40	.25
1264	A690	1cr black & multi	1.20	.25
1265	A690	2cr black & multi	5.00	.50
		Nos. 1262-1265 (4)	7.00	1.25

Publicity for: "Mobral" literacy campaign (10c); Centenary of census (20c); Housing and retirement fund (1cr); Growth of gross national product (2cr).

Congress Building, Brasilia, by Oscar Niemeyer, and "Os Guerreiros," by Bruno Giorgi — A691

1972, Dec. 4 Without Gum

1266	A691	1cr blue, blk & org	6.00	3.50

Meeting of Natl. Cong., Brasilia, Dec. 4-8.

Holy Family (Clay Figurines) — A692

1972, Dec. 13 Photo. *Perf. 11½x11*

1267	A692	20c ocher & blk	.40	.25

Christmas 1972. Luminescent.

Retirement Plan — A693

Designs: No.1269, School children and traffic lights, horiz. 70c, Dr. Oswaldo Cruz with Red Cross, caricature. 2cr, Produce, fish and cattle, horiz.

Perf. 11½x11, 11x11½
1972, Dec. 20 Litho.
Without Gum

1268	A693	10c blk, bl & dl org	.60	.25
1269	A693	10c orange & multi	.60	.25
1270	A693	70c blk, red & brn	2.25	1.50
1271	A693	2cr green & multi	6.00	3.00
		Nos. 1268-1271 (4)	9.45	5.00

Publicity for: Agricultural workers' assistance program (No. 1268); highway and transportation development (No. 1269); centenary of the birth of Dr. Oswaldo Cruz (1872-1917), Director of Public Health Institute (70c); agricultural and cattle export (2cr). Nos. 1268-1271 are luminescent.

Sailing Ship, Navy A694

Designs: 10c, Monument, Brazilian Expeditionary Force. No. 1274, Plumed helmet, Army. No. 1275, Rocket, Air Force.

Lithographed and Engraved
1972, Dec. 28 *Perf. 11x11½*
Without Gum

1272	A694	10c brn, dk brn & blk	.60	.60
1273	A694	30c lt ultra, grn & blk	.60	.60
1274	A694	30c yel grn, bl grn & blk	.60	.60
1275	A694	30c lilac, mar & blk	.60	.60
a.		Block of 4, #1272-1275	3.50	3.50

Armed Forces Day.

Rotary Emblem and Cogwheels A695

Perf. 11½
1973, Mar. 21 Litho. Unwmk.

1276	A695	1cr ultra, grnsh bl & yel	1.25	.60

Rotary International serving Brazil 50 years.

Swimming — A696

Designs: No. 1278, Gymnastics. No. 1279, Volleyball, vert.

1973 Photo. *Perf. 11x11½, 11½x11*

1277	A696	40c brt bl & red brn	.55	.25
1278	A696	40c green & org brn	1.00	.25
1279	A696	40c violet & org brn	.55	.25
		Nos. 1277-1279 (3)	2.10	.75

Issued: No. 1277, 4/19; No. 1278, 5/22; No.1279, 10/15.

Flag of Paraguay A697

Perf. 11½
1973, Apr. 27 Litho. Unwmk.

1280	A697	70c multicolored	.85	.35

Visit of Pres. Alfredo Stroessner of Paraguay, Apr. 25-27.

"Communications" — A698

Designs: 1cr, Neptune, map of South America and Africa.

1973, May 5 *Perf. 11x11½*

1281	A698	70c multicolored	1.00	.25
1282	A698	1cr multicolored	2.50	.70

Inauguration of the Ministry of Communications Building, Brasilia (70c); and of the first underwater telephone cable between South America and Europe, Bracan 1 (1cr).

Congress Emblem — A699

1973, May 19 *Perf. 11½x11*

1283	A699	1cr orange & pur	2.50	.70

24th Congress of the International Chamber of Commerce, Rio de Janeiro, May 19-26.

Swallowtailed Manakin — A700

Birds: No. 1285, Orange-backed oriole. No. 1286, Brazilian ruby (hummingbird).

1973 Litho. *Perf. 11x11½*

1284	A700	20c multicolored	1.25	.25
1285	A700	20c multicolored	1.25	.25
1286	A700	20c multicolored	1.25	.25
		Nos. 1284-1286 (3)	3.75	.75

Issued: No. 1284, 5/26; No. 1285, 6/6; No. 1286, 6/19.

Tourists A701

1973, June 28 Litho. *Perf. 11x11½*

1287	A701	70c multicolored	.50	.25

National Tourism Year.

Conference at Itu — A702

1973 ***Perf. 11½x11***

1288	A702	20c shown	.60	.25
1289	A702	20c Decorated wagon	.60	.25
1290	A702	20c Indian	.60	.25
1291	A702	20c Graciosa Road	.60	.25
		Nos. 1288-1291 (4)	2.40	1.00

Centenary of the Itu Convention (No. 1288); sesquicentennial of the July 2 episode (No. 1289); 400th anniversary of the founding of Niteroi (No. 1290); centenary of Graciosa Road (No. 1291).

Issue dates: No. 1291, July 29; others July 2.

Satellite and Multi-spectral Image A703

Designs: 70c, Official opening of Engineering School, 1913. 1cr, Möbius strips and "IMPA."

1973, July 11 ***Perf. 11½***

1292	A703	20c black & multi	.40	.25
1293	A703	70c dk blue & multi	1.25	.25
1294	A703	1cr lilac & multi	1.75	.25
		Nos. 1292-1294 (3)	3.40	.75

Institute for Space Research (20c); School of Engineering, Itajubá, 60th anniversary (70c); Institute for Pure and Applied Mathematics (1cr).

Santos-Dumont and 14-Bis Plane — A704

Santos-Dumont and: 70c, No. 6 Balloon and Eiffel Tower. 2cr Demoiselle plane.

Lithographed and Engraved

1973, July 20 ***Perf. 11x11½***

1295	A704	20c lt grn, brt grn & brn	.60	.25
1296	A704	70c yel, rose red & brn	1.25	.50
1297	A704	2cr bl, vio bl & brn	2.50	.50
		Nos. 1295-1297 (3)	4.35	1.25

Centenary of the birth of Alberto Santos-Dumont (1873-1932), aviation pioneer.

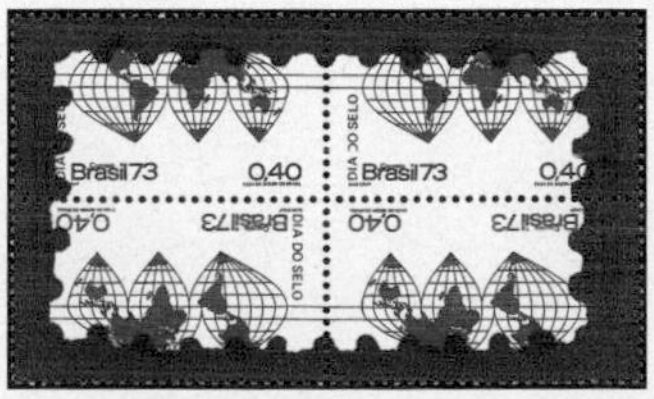

Mercator Map — A705

Designs: No. 1298, "BRASIL" within white background. No. 1299, Right half of "0" in "40" overlays red border. No. 1299A, "B" in "BRASIL" touches red. No. 1299B, Top edge of "0" in "40" overlays red border.

Photogravure and Engraved

1973, Aug. 1 **Wmk. 267**

1298		40c red & black	2.50	2.50
1299		40c red & black	.60	.60
1299A		40c red & black	12.00	7.00
1299B		40c red & black	3.50	3.50
c.		A705 Block of 4, #1298-1299B	25.00	20.00

Stamp Day. Nos. 1298-1299B are printed se-tenant horizontally and tête bêche vertically in sheets of 55.

Gonçalves Dias (1823-1864), Poet — A706

Perf. 11½x11

1973, Aug. 10 **Wmk. 267**

1300	A706	40c violet & blk	.40	.20

Souvenir Sheet

Copernicus and Sun — A707

Perf. 11x11½

1973, Aug. 15 **Litho.** **Unwmk.**

1301	A707	1cr multicolored	12.50	12.50

500th anniversary of the birth of Nicolaus Copernicus (1473-1543), Polish astronomer.

Folklore Festival Banner — A708

1973, Aug. 22 ***Perf. 11½***

1302	A708	40c ultra & multi	.40	.25

Folklore Day, Aug. 22.

Masonic Emblem A709

1973, Aug. 24 **Photo.** ***Perf. 11x11½***

1303	A709	1cr Prus blue	1.50	.65

Free Masons of Brazil, 1822-1973.

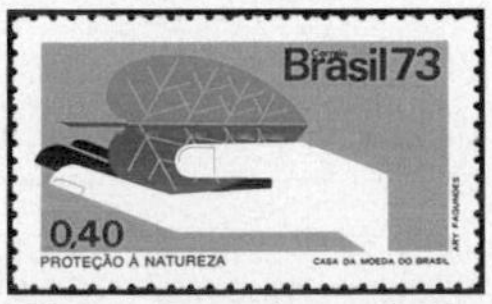

Nature Protection — A710

Designs: No. 1305, Fire protection. No. 1306, Aviation safety. No. 1307, Safeguarding cultural heritage.

1973, Sept. 20 **Litho.** ***Perf. 11x11½***

1304	A710	40c brt grn & multi	.45	.45
1305	A710	40c dk blue & multi	.45	.45
1306	A710	40c lt blue & multi	.45	.45
1307	A710	40c pink & multi	.45	.45
		Nos. 1304-1307 (4)	1.80	1.80

Souvenir Sheet

St. Gabriel and Proclamation of Pope Paul VI — A711

Lithographed and Engraved

1973, Sept. 29 **Unwmk.** ***Perf. 11½***

1308	A711	1cr bister & blk	12.50	5.75

1st National Exhibition of Religious Philately, Rio de Janeiro, Sept. 29-Oct. 6.

St. Teresa — A712

Photogravure and Engraved

Perf. 11½x11

1973, Sept. 30 **Wmk. 267**

1309	A712	2cr dk org & brn	1.25	.75

St. Teresa of Lisieux, the Little Flower (1873-1897), Carmelite nun.

Monteiro Lobato and Emily A713

No. 1311, Aunt Nastacia. No. 1312, Snubnose, Peter and Rhino. No. 1313, Viscount de Sabugosa. No. 1314, Dona Benta.

Perf. 11½

1973, Oct. 12 **Litho.** **Unwmk.**

1310	A713	40c shown	.65	.60
1311	A713	40c multicolored	.65	.60
1312	A713	40c multicolored	.65	.60
1313	A713	40c multicolored	.65	.60
1314	A713	40c multicolored	.65	.60
a.		Block of 5 + label	3.25	3.25

Monteiro Lobato, author of children's books.

Soapstone Sculpture of Isaiah (detail) A714

Baroque Art in Brazil: No. 1316, Arabesque, gilded wood carving, horiz. 70c, Father José Mauricio Nuñes Garcia and music score. 1cr, Church door, Salvador, Bahia. 2cr, Angels, church ceiling painting by Manoel da Costa Athayde, horiz.

1973, Nov. 5

1315	A714	40c multicolored	.55	.25
1316	A714	40c multicolored	.55	.25
1317	A714	70c multicolored	1.25	.65
1318	A714	1cr multicolored	5.00	.90
1319	A714	2cr multicolored	5.00	1.10
		Nos. 1315-1319 (5)	12.35	3.15

Old and New Telephones — A715

1973, Nov. 28 ***Perf. 11x11½***

1320	A715	40c multicolored	.40	.25

50th anniv. of Brazilian Telephone Co.

Symbolic Angel A716

1973, Nov. 30 ***Perf. 11½***

1321	A716	40c ver & multi	.40	.25

Christmas 1973.

River Boats A717

1973, Nov. 30 **Litho.** ***Perf. 11x11½***

1322	A717	40c "Gaiola"	.40	.25
1323	A717	70c "Regatao"	.65	.45
1324	A717	1cr "Jangada"	3.00	1.50
1325	A717	2cr "Saveiro"	2.50	1.05
		Nos. 1322-1325 (4)	6.55	3.25

Nos. 1322-1325 are luminescent.

Scales of Justice A718

1973, Dec. 5 ***Perf. 11½***

1326	A718	40c magenta & vio	.45	.25

To honor the High Federal Court, created in 1891. Luminescent.

José Placido de Castro — A719

Lithographed and Engraved

Perf. 11½x11

1973, Dec. 12 **Wmk. 267**

1327	A719	40c lilac rose & blk	.65	.25

Centenary of the birth of Jose Placido de Castro, liberator of the State of Acre.

Scarlet Ibis and Victoria Regia — A720

Designs: 70c, Jaguar and spathodea campanulata. 1cr, Scarlet macaw and carnauba palm. 2cr, Rhea and coral tree.

Perf. 11½x11

1973, Dec. 28 Litho. Unwmk.

1328 A720 40c brown & multi	.65	.25
1329 A720 70c brown & multi	1.60	.75
1330 A720 1cr bister & multi	1.60	.25
1331 A720 2cr bister & multi	6.25	1.90
Nos. 1328-1331 (4)	10.10	3.15

Nos. 1328-1331 are luminescent.

Saci Perere, Mocking Goblin — A721

Characters from Brazilian Legends: 80c, Zumbi, last chief of rebellious slaves. 1cr, Chico Rei, African king. 1.30cr, Little Black Boy of the Pasture. 2.50cr, Iara, Queen of the Waters.

Perf. 11½x11

1974, Feb. 28 Litho. Unwmk.

Size: 21x39mm

1332 A721 40c multicolored	.55	.25
1333 A721 80c multicolored	1.00	.25
1334 A721 1cr multicolored	1.25	.25

Perf. 11½

Size: 32½x33mm

1335 A721 1.30cr multicolored	2.75	.50
1336 A721 2.50cr multicolored	7.25	1.90
Nos. 1332-1336 (5)	12.80	3.15

Nos. 1332-1336 are luminescent.

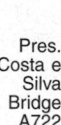

Pres. Costa e Silva Bridge A722

1974, Mar. 11

1337 A722 40c multicolored .65 .25

Inauguration of the Pres. Costa e Silva Bridge, Rio Niteroi, connecting Rio de Janeiro and Guanabara State.

"The Press" A723

1974, Mar. 25 ***Perf. 11½***

1338 A723 40c shown	.40	.25
1339 A723 40c "Radio"	.40	.25
1340 A723 40c "Television"	.40	.25
Nos. 1338-1340 (3)	1.20	.75

Communications Commemorations: No. 1338, bicentenary of first Brazilian newspaper, published in London by Hipolito da Costa; No. 1339, founding of the Radio Sociedade do Rio de Janeiro by Roquette Pinto; No. 1340, installation of first Brazilian television station by Assis Chateaubriand. Luminescent.

"Reconstruction" — A724

1974, Mar. 31

1341 A724 40c multicolored .45 .25

10 years of progress. Luminescent.

Corcovado Christ, Marconi, Colors of Brazil and Italy — A725

1974, Apr. 25 Litho. ***Perf. 11½***

1342 A725 2.50cr multi 5.25 2.75

Guglielmo Marconi (1874-1937), Italian physicist and inventor. Luminescent.

Stamp Printing Press, Stamp Designing A726

1974, May 6

1343 A726 80c multicolored .55 .25

Brazilian mint.

World Map, Indian, Caucasian and Black Men — A727

World Map and: No. 1345, Brazilians. No. 1346, Cabin & German horseback rider. No. 1347, Italian farm wagon. No. 1348, Japanese woman & torii.

1974, May 3 Unwmk.

1344 A727 40c multicolored	.45	.25
1345 A727 40c multicolored	.45	.25
1346 A727 2.50cr multicolored	2.25	.40
1347 A727 2.50cr multicolored	4.75	.40
1348 A727 2.50cr multicolored	2.25	.40
Nos. 1344-1348 (5)	10.15	1.70

Ethnic and migration influences in Brazil.

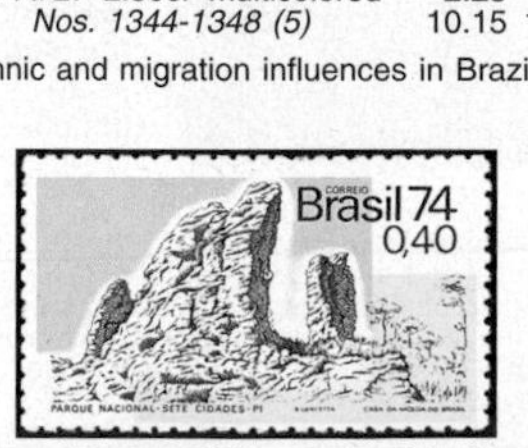

Sandstone Cliffs, Sete Cidades National Park — A728

Tourist publicity: 80c, Ruins of Cathedral of Sao Miguel das Missões.

Lithographed and Engraved

1974, June 8 ***Perf. 11x11½***

1349 A728 40c multicolored	.55	.25
1350 A728 80c multicolored	.55	.25

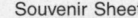

Souvenir Sheet

Soccer — A729

1974, June 20 Litho. ***Perf. 11½***

1351 A729 2.50cr multi 12.50 12.50

World Cup Soccer Championship, Munich, June 13-July 7.

Church and College, Caraça A730

1974, July 6 Litho. ***Perf. 11x11½***

1352 A730 40c multicolored .55 .25

College (Seminary) of Caraça, bicent.

Wave on Television Screen A731

1974, July 15 ***Perf. 11½***

1353 A731 40c black & blue .30 .25

TELEBRAS, Third Brazilian Congress of Telecommunications, Brasilia, July 15-20.

Fernao Dias Paes A732

1974, July 21 ***Perf. 11½***

1354 A732 20c green & multi .30 .25

3rd centenary of the expedition led by Fernao Dias Paes exploring Minas Gerais and the passage from South to North in Brazil.

Mexican Flag — A733

1974, July 24 Litho. ***Perf. 11½***

1355 A733 80c multicolored 1.10 .55

Visit of Pres. Luis Echeverria Alvares of Mexico, July 24-29.

Flags of Brazil and Germany A734

1974, Aug. 5 ***Perf. 11x11½***

1356 A734 40c multicolored .55 .30

World Cup Soccer Championship, 1974, victory of German Federal Republic.

Souvenir Sheet

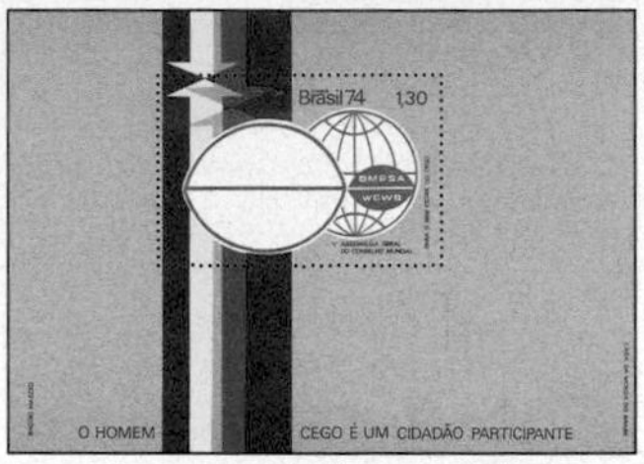

Congress Emblem — A735

1974, Aug. 7 ***Perf. 11½***

1357 A735 1.30cr multi 1.75 1.75

5th World Assembly of the World Council for the Welfare of the Blind, Sao Paulo, Aug. 7-16. Stamp and margin inscribed in Braille with name of Assembly.

Exists imperforate. Value $1300. Exists with the braile missing or duplicated in the margin. Value $600 and $65 respectively.

Raul Pederneiras (1874-1953, Journalist, Professor of Law and Fine Arts), Caricature by J. Carlos — A736

Lithographed and Engraved

1974, Aug. 15 ***Perf. 11½x11***

1358 A736 40c buff, blk & ocher .35 .25

Society Emblem and Landscape — A737

1974, Aug. 19 Litho. ***Perf. 11x11½***

1359 A737 1.30cr multi .50 .30

13th Congress of the International Union of Building and Savings Societies.

Souvenir Sheet

Five Women, by Di Cavalcanti — A738

1974, Aug. 26 Litho. ***Perf. 11½***
1360 A738 2cr multicolored 5.25 5.25

LUBRAPEX 74, 5th Portuguese-Brazilian Phil. Exhib., Sao Paulo, Nov. 26-Dec. 4.

"UPU" and World Map A739

1974, Oct. 9 Litho. ***Perf. 11½***
1361 A739 2.50cr blk & brt bl 4.75 2.50

Centenary of Universal Postal Union.

Hammock (Antillean Arawak Culture) A740

Bilro Lace — A741

Singer of "Cord" Verses — A742

Ceramic Figure by Master Vitalino — A743

1974, Oct. 16 Litho. ***Perf. 11½***
1362 A740 50c deep rose lilac .75 .25
1363 A741 50c lt & dk blue 1.10 .25
1364 A742 50c yel & red brn .65 .25
1365 A743 50c brt yel & dk brn .65 .25
Nos. 1362-1365 (4) 3.15 1.00

Popular Brazilian crafts.

Branch of Coffee A744

1974, Oct. 27 Unwmk. ***Perf. 11***
1366 A744 50c multicolored .40 .25

Centenary of city of Campinas.

Hornless Tabapua A745

Animals of Brazil: 1.30cr, Creole horse. 2.50cr, Brazilian mastiff.

1974, Nov. 10 ***Perf. 11½***
1367 A745 80c multi .75 .30
1368 A745 1.30cr multi .75 .30
1369 A745 2.50cr multi 5.50 1.00
Nos. 1367-1369 (3) 7.00 1.60

Christmas — A746

1974, Nov. 18 ***Perf. 11½x11***
1370 A746 50c Angel .25 .25

Solteira Island Hydroelectric Dam — A747

1974, Nov. 11 ***Perf. 11½***
1371 A747 50c black & yellow .35 .25

Inauguration of the Solteira Island Hydroelectric Dam over Parana River.

The Girls, by Carlos Reis — A748

1974, Nov. 26
1372 A748 1.30cr multi .25 .25

LUBRAPEX 74, 5th Portuguese-Brazilian Phil. Exhib., Sao Paulo, Nov. 26-Dec. 4.

Youths, Judge, Scales A749

1974, Dec. 20 Litho. ***Perf. 11½***
1373 A749 90c yel, red & bl .25 .25

Juvenile Court of Brazil, 50th anniversary.

Long Distance Runner — A750

1974, Dec. 23
1374 A750 3.30cr multi .55 .30

Sao Silvestre long distance running, 50th anniversary.

News Vendor, 1875, Masthead, 1975 A751

1975, Jan. 4
1375 A751 50c multicolored .35 .25

Newspaper "O Estado de S. Paulo," cent.

Sao Paulo Industrial Park A752

Designs: 1.40cr, Natural rubber industry, Acre. 4.50cr, Manganese mining, Amapá.

1975, Jan. 24 Litho. ***Perf. 11x11½***
1376 A752 50c vio bl & yel .50 .25
1377 A752 1.40cr yellow & brn .30 .25
1378 A752 4.50cr yellow & blk 1.50 .25
Nos. 1376-1378 (3) 2.30 .75

Economic development.

Fort of the Holy Cross A753

Colonial forts: No. 1380, Fort of the Three Kings. No. 1381, Fort of Monteserrat. 90c, Fort of Our Lady of Help.

Litho. & Engr.

1975, Mar. 14 ***Perf. 11½***
1379 A753 50c yel & red brn .35 .25
1380 A753 50c yel & red brn .35 .25
1381 A753 50c yel & red brn .35 .25
1382 A753 90c yel & red brn .35 .25
Nos. 1379-1382 (4) 1.40 1.00

House on Stilts, Amazon Region A754

Designs: 50c, Modern houses and plan of Brasilia. 1.40cr, Indian hut, Rondonia. 3.30cr, German-style cottage (Enxaimel), Santa Catarina.

1975, Apr. 18 Litho. ***Perf. 11½***
1383 A754 50c yel & multi 1.25 .75
1384 A754 50c yel & multi 11.00 5.25
a. Pair, #1383-1384 12.50 6.50
1385 A754 1cr yel & multi .40 .30
1386 A754 1.40cr yel & multi 7.00 1.90
1387 A754 1.40cr yel & multi .40 .30
a. Pair, #1386-1387 8.00 2.75
1388 A754 3.30cr yel & multi .40 .30
1389 A754 3.30cr yel & multi 7.00 1.25
a. Pair, #1388-1389 8.00 1.90
Nos. 1383-1389 (7) 27.45 10.05

Brazilian architecture. Nos. 1383, 1386, 1388 have yellow strip at right side, others at left.

Fish — A755

No. 1390, Astronotus ocellatus. No. 1391, Colomesus psitacus. No. 1392, Phallocerus caudimaculatus. No. 1393, Symphysodon discus.

1975, May 2 Litho. ***Perf. 11½***
1390 A755 50c multicolored .40 .25
1391 A755 50c multicolored .40 .25
1392 A755 50c multicolored .40 .25
1393 A755 50c multicolored .40 .25
Nos. 1390-1393 (4) 1.60 1.00

Soldier's Head in Brazil's Colors, Plane, Rifle and Ship — A756

1975, May 8 ***Perf. 11½x11***
1394 A756 50c vio bl & multi .35 .25

In honor of the veterans of World War II, on the 30th anniversary of victory.

Brazilian Otter — A757

Nature protection: 70c, Brazilian pines, horiz. 3.30cr, Marsh cayman, horiz.

1975, June 17 Litho. ***Perf. 11½***
1395 A757 70c bl, grn & blk .75 .40
1396 A757 1cr multi .55 .30
1397 A757 3.30cr multi .55 .30
Nos. 1395-1397 (3) 1.85 1.00

Petroglyphs, Stone of Ingá — A758

Marjoara Vase, Pará — A759

Vinctifer Comptoni, Petrified Fish A760

1975, July 8 Litho. *Perf. 11½*

1398 A758 70c multicolored .55 .25
1399 A759 1cr multicolored .30 .25
1400 A760 1cr multicolored .30 .25
Nos. 1398-1400 (3) 1.15 .75

Archaeological discoveries.

Immaculate Conception, Franciscan Monastery, Vitoria — A761

1975, July 15

1401 A761 3.30cr blue & multi .55 .30

Holy Year 1975 and 300th anniv. of establishment of the Franciscan Province in Southern Brazil.

Post and Telegraph Ministry — A762

1975, Aug. 8 Engr. *Perf. 11½*

1402 A762 70c dk carmine .30 .25

Stamp Day 1975.

Dances A763

Designs: No. 1403, Sword Dance, Minas Gerais. No. 1404, Umbrella Dance, Pernambuco. No. 1405, Warrior's Dance, Alagoas.

1975, Aug. 22 Litho. *Perf. 11½*

1403 A763 70c pale blue & multi .35 .25
1404 A763 70c pink & multi .35 .25
1405 A763 70c yellow & multi .35 .25
Nos. 1403-1405 (3) 1.05 .75

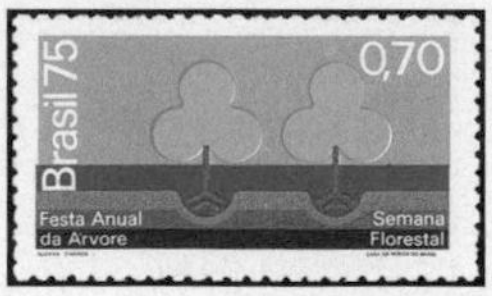

Trees A764

1975, Sept. 15 *Perf. 11x11½*

1406 A764 70c multicolored .25 .25

Annual Tree Festival.

Globe, Radar and Satellite — A765

1975, Sept. 16 *Perf. 11½*

1407 A765 3.30cr multi .50 .30

Inauguration of 2nd antenna of Tangua Earth Station, Rio de Janeiro State.

Woman Holding Flowers and Globe A766

1975, Sept. 23

1408 A766 3.30cr multi .55 .30

International Women's Year 1975.

Tile, Railing and Column, Alcantara A767

Cross and Monastery, Sao Cristovao — A768

Historic cities: No. 1411, Jug and Clock Tower, Goiás, vert.

1975, Sept. 27 Litho. *Perf. 11½*

1409 A767 70c multicolored .30 .25
1410 A768 70c multicolored .30 .25
1411 A768 70c multicolored .30 .25
Nos. 1409-1411 (3) .90 .75

"Books teach how to live" A769

1975, Oct. 23 Litho. *Perf. 11½*

1412 A769 70c multicolored .25 .25

Day of the Book.

ASTA Congress Emblem A770

1975, Oct. 27 *Perf. 11x11½*

1413 A770 70c multicolored .25 .25

American Society of Travel Agents, 45th World Congress, Rio, Oct. 27-Nov. 1.

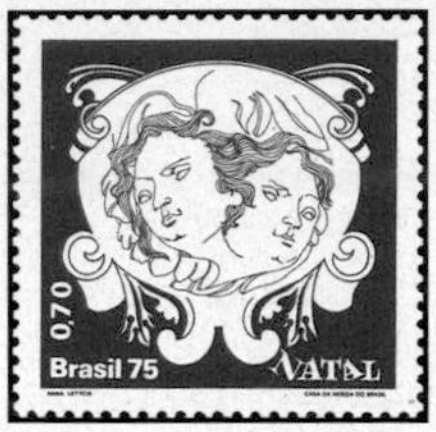

Angels A771

1975, Nov. 11

1414 A771 70c red & brown .25 .25

Christmas 1975.

Map of Americas, Waves — A772

1975, Nov. 19 *Perf. 11½x12*

1415 A772 5.20cr gray & multi 1.50 .75

2nd Interamerican Conference of Telecommunications (CITEL), Rio, Nov. 19-27.

Dom Pedro II — A773

1975, Dec. 2 Engr. *Perf. 12*

1416 A773 70c violet brown .55 .25

Dom Pedro II (1825-1891), emperor of Brazil, birth sesquicentennial.

People and Cross A774

1975, Nov. 27 Litho. *Perf. 11x11½*

1417 A774 70c lt bl & dp bl .25 .25

National Day of Thanksgiving.

Tourism A775

Designs: No. 1418, Guarapari Beach, Espirito Santo. No. 1419, Salt Stone beach, Piaui. No. 1420, Cliffs, Rio Grande Do Sul.

1975, Dec. 19 Litho. *Perf. 11½*

1418 A775 70c multicolored .25 .25
1419 A775 70c multicolored .25 .25
1420 A775 70c multicolored .35 .25
Nos. 1418-1420 (3) .85 .75

Triple Jump, Games Emblem A776

1975, Dec. 22 *Perf. 11x11½*

1421 A776 1.60cr bl grn & blk .25 .25

Triple jump world record by Joao Carlos de Oliveira in 7th Pan-American Games, Mexico City, Oct. 12-26.

UN Emblem and Headquarters — A777

1975, Dec. 29 *Perf. 11½*

1422 A777 1.30cr dp bl & vio bl .25 .25

United Nations, 30th anniversary.

Light Bulbs, House and Sun A778

Energy conservation: No. 1424, Gasoline drops, car and sun.

1976, Jan. 16

1423 A778 70c multicolored .25 .25
1424 A778 70c multicolored .25 .25

Concorde A779

1976, Jan. 21 Litho. *Perf. 11x11½*

1425 A779 5.20cr bluish black .30 .25

First commercial flight of supersonic jet Concorde from Paris to Rio, Jan. 21.

Souvenir Sheet

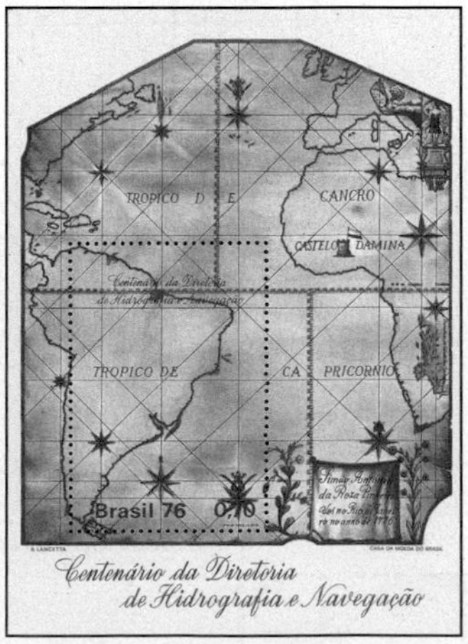

Nautical Map of South Atlantic, 1776 — A780

1976, Feb. 2 *Perf. 11½*

1426 A780 70c salmon & multi .75 .75

Centenary of the Naval Hydrographic and Navigation Institute.

Telephone Lines, 1876 Telephone — A781

1976, Mar. 10 Litho. ***Perf. 11x11½***

1427 A781 5.20cr orange & blue .30 .25

Centenary of first telephone call by Alexander Graham Bell, March 10, 1876.

Eye and Exclamation Point — A782

1976, Apr. 7 Litho. ***Perf. 11½x11***

1428 A782 1cr vio red brn & brn .25 *.55*

World Health Day: "Foresight prevents blindness."

Kaiapo Body Painting — A783

Designs: No. 1430, Bakairi ceremonial mask. No. 1431, Karajá feather headdress.

1976, Apr. 19 Litho. ***Perf. 11½***

1429 A783 1cr light violet & multi .25 .25
1430 A783 1cr light violet & multi .25 .25
1431 A783 1cr light violet & multi .25 .25
Nos. 1429-1431 (3) .75 .75

Preservation of indigenous culture.

Itamaraty Palace, Brasilia A784

1976, Apr. 20

1432 A784 1cr multicolored .25 *.55*

Diplomats' Day. Itamaraty Palace, designed by Oscar Niemeyer, houses the Ministry of Foreign Affairs.

Watering Can over Stones, by José Tarcisio A785

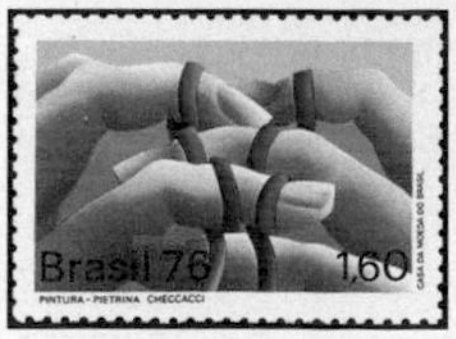

Fingers and Ribbons, by Pietrina Checcacci A786

1976, May 14 Litho. ***Perf. 11½***

1433 A785 1cr multi .25 .25
1434 A786 1.60cr multi .25 .25

Modern Brazilian art.

Basketball — A787

Olympic Rings and: 1.40cr, Yachting. 5.20cr, Judo.

1976, May 21 Litho. ***Perf. 11½***

1435 A787 1cr emerald & blk .25 .25
1436 A787 1.40cr dk blue & blk .25 .25
1437 A787 5.20cr orange & blk .25 .25
Nos. 1435-1437 (3) .75 .75

21st Olympic Games, Montreal, Canada, July 17-Aug. 1.

Orchid — A788

Nature protection: No. 1439, Golden-faced lion monkey.

1976, June 4 ***Perf. 11½x11***

1438 A788 1cr multicolored .25 .25
1439 A788 1cr multicolored .25 .25

Film Camera, Brazilian Colors — A789

1976, June 19

1440 A789 1cr vio bl, brt grn & yel .25 .25

Brazilian film industry.

Bahia Woman — A790

Designs: 10c, Oxcart driver, horiz. 20c, Raft fishermen, horiz. 30c, Rubber plantation worker. 40c, Cowboy, horiz. 50c, Gaucho. 80c, Gold panner. 1cr, Banana plantation worker. 1.10cr, Grape harvester. 1.30cr, Coffee picker. 1.80cr, Farmer gathering wax palms. 2cr, Potter. 5cr, Sugar cane cutter. 7cr, Salt mine worker. 10cr, Fisherman. 15cr, Coconut seller. 20cr, Lacemaker.

Perf. 11½x11, 11x11½

1976-78 Photo.

1441 A790 10c red brn ('77) .25 .25
1442 A790 15c brown .25 .25
1443 A790 20c violet blue .25 .25
1444 A790 30c lilac rose .25 .25
1445 A790 40c orange ('77) .25 .25
1446 A790 50c citron .40 .25
1447 A790 80c slate green 1.25 .25
1448 A790 1cr black .25 .25
1449 A790 1.10cr magenta ('77) .25 .25
1450 A790 1.30cr red ('77) .25 .25
1451 A790 1.80cr dk vio bl ('78) .25 .25

Engr.

1452 A790 2cr brown ('77) 2.75 .25
1453 A790 5cr dk pur ('77) 3.75 .25
1454 A790 7cr violet 7.25 .25
1455 A790 10cr yel grn ('77) 5.25 .25
1456 A790 15cr gray grn ('78) 2.25 .25
1457 A790 20cr blue 4.75 .25
Nos. 1441-1457 (17) 29.90 4.25

See Nos. 1653-1657.

Fish A791

Designs: No. 1460, Hyphessobrycon innesi. No. 1461, Copeina arnoldi. No. 1462, Prochilodus insignis. No. 1463, Crenicichla lepidota. No. 1464, Ageneiosus. No. 1465, Corydoras reticulatus.

1976, July 12 Litho. ***Perf. 11x11½***

1460 A791 1cr multi .40 .35
1461 A791 1cr multi .40 .35
1462 A791 1cr multi .40 .35
1463 A791 1cr multi .40 .35
1464 A791 1cr multi .40 .35
1465 A791 1cr multi .40 .35
a. Block of 6, #1460-1465 2.50 2.50

Santa Marta Lighthouse A792

1976, July 29 Engr. ***Perf. 12x11½***

1466 A792 1cr blue .25 *.35*

300th anniversary of the city of Laguna.

Children on Magic Carpet A793

1976, Aug. 1 Litho. ***Perf. 11½x12***

1467 A793 1cr multicolored .25 .25

Stamp Day.

Nurse's Lamp and Head A794

1976, Aug. 12 Litho. ***Perf. 11½***

1468 A794 1cr multicolored .25 .25

Brazilian Nurses' Assoc., 50th anniv.

Puppet, Soldier — A795

Designs: 1.30cr, Girl's head. 1.60cr, Hand with puppet head on each finger, horiz.

1976, Aug. 20

1469 A795 1cr multi .25 .25
1470 A795 1.30cr multi .25 .25
1471 A795 1.60cr multi .25 .25
Nos. 1469-1471 (3) .75 .75

Mamulengo puppet show.

Winner's Medal — A796

1976, Aug. 21

1472 A796 5.20cr multi .30 .30

27th International Military Athletic Championships, Rio de Janeiro, Aug. 21-28.

Family Protection — A797

1976, Sept. 12

1473 A797 1cr lt & dk blue .25 .25

National organizations SENAC and SESC helping commercial employees to improve their living standard, both commercially and socially.

Dying Tree — A798

1976, Sept. 20 Litho. ***Perf. 11½***

1474 A798 1cr gray & multi .25 .25

Protection of the environment.

Atom Symbol, Electron Orbits A799

1976, Sept. 21

1475 A799 5.20cr multi .25 .25

20th General Conference of the International Atomic Energy Agency, Rio de Janeiro, Sept. 21-29.

Train in Tunnel A800

1976, Sept. 26

1476 A800 1.60cr multi .25 .25

Sao Paulo subway, 1st in Brazil.

St. Francis and Birds A801

1976, Oct. 4

1477 A801 5.20cr multi .30 .25

St. Francis of Assisi, 750th death anniv.

Ouro Preto School of Mining — A802

1976, Oct. 12 Engr. *Perf. 12x11½*

1478 A802 1cr dk vio .25 .75

Ouro Preto School of Mining, centenary.

Three Kings A803

Children's drawings — No. 1480, Santa Claus on donkey. No. 1481, Virgin and Child and Angels. No. 1482, Angels with candle. No. 1483, Nativity.

1976, Nov. 4 Litho. *Perf. 11½*

1479	A803	80c shown	.50	.25
1480	A803	80c multicolored	.50	.25
1481	A803	80c multicolored	.50	.25
1482	A803	80c multicolored	.50	.25
1483	A803	80c multicolored	.50	.25
a.		Strip of 5, #1479-1483	2.50	2.50

Christmas 1976.

Souvenir Sheet

30,000 Reis Banknote — A804

1976, Nov. 5 Litho. *Perf. 11½*

1484 A804 80c multicolored .30 *.75*

Opening of 1000th branch of Bank of Brazil, Barra do Bugres, Mato Grosso.

Exists imperforate. Value $10,000.

Virgin of Monte Serrat, by Friar Agostinho A805

St. Joseph, 18th Century Wood Sculpture — A806

5.60cr, The Dance, by Rodolfo Bernadelli, 19th cent. 6.50cr, The Caravel, by Bruno Giorgi, 20th cent. abstract sculpture.

1976, Nov. 5

1485	A805	80c multi	.25	.25
1486	A806	5cr multi	.30	.30
1487	A805	5.60cr multi	.30	.30
1488	A806	6.50cr multi	.30	.30
		Nos. 1485-1488 (4)	1.15	1.15

Development of Brazilian sculpture.

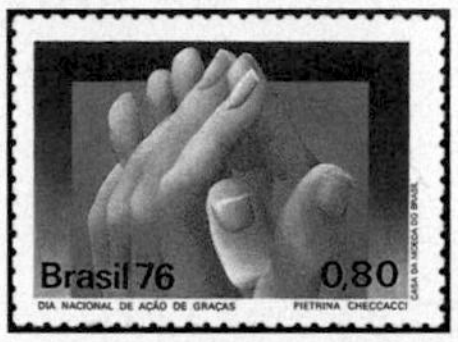

Praying Hands A807

1976, Nov. 25

1489 A807 80c multicolored .25 .25

National Day of Thanksgiving.

Sailor, 1840 — A808

Design: 2cr, Marine's uniform, 1808.

1976, Dec. 13 Litho. *Perf. 11½x11*

1490	A808	80c multicolored	.25	.25
1491	A808	2cr multicolored	.30	.25

Brazilian Navy.

"Natural Resources and Development" — A809

1976, Dec. 17 *Perf. 11½*

1492 A809 80c multicolored .25 .25

Brazilian Bureau of Standards, founded 1940.

Wheel of Life — A810

Designs: 5.60cr, Beggar, sculpture by Agnaldo dos Santos. 6.50cr, Benin mask.

1977, Jan. 14

1493	A810	5cr multi	.30	.25
1494	A810	5.60cr multi	.30	.25
1495	A810	6.50cr multi	.30	.25
		Nos. 1493-1495 (3)	.90	.75

FESTAC '77, 2nd World Black and African Festival, Lagos, Nigeria, Jan. 15-Feb. 12.

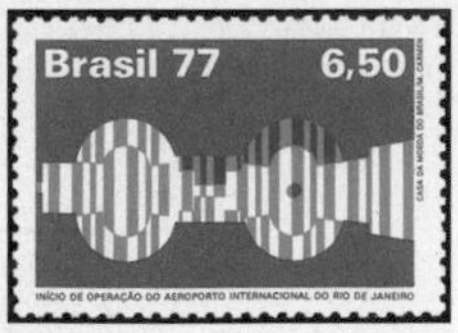

A811

1977, Jan. 20 Litho. *Perf. 11½*

1496 A811 6.50cr bl & yel grn .30 .30

Rio de Janeiro International Airport.

Seminar Emblem with Map of Americas — A812

1977, Feb. 6

1497 A812 1.10cr gray, vio bl & bl .25 .25

6th Inter-American Budget Seminar.

Salicylate, Microphoto A813

1977, Apr. 10 Litho. *Perf. 11½*

1498 A813 1.10cr multi .25 .25

International Rheumatism Year.

Lions International Emblem A814

1977, Apr. 16

1499 A814 1.10cr multi .25 .25

25th anniv. of Brazilian Lions Intl.

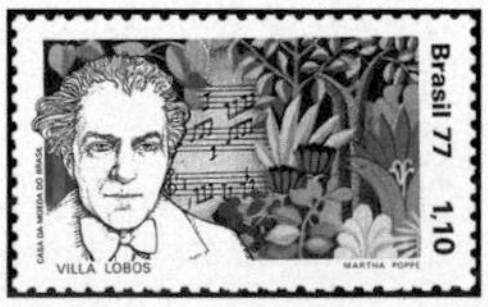

Heitor Villa Lobos A815

No. 1501, Chiquinha Gonzaga. No. 1502, Noel Rosa.

1977, Apr. 26 *Perf. 11x11½*

1500	A815	1.10cr shown	.25	.25
1501	A815	1.10cr multicolored	.25	.25
1502	A815	1.10cr multicolored	.25	.25
		Nos. 1500-1502 (3)	.75	.75

Brazilian composers.

Farmer and Worker — A816

Medicine Bottles and Flask — A817

1977, May 8 Litho. *Perf. 11½*

1503	A816	1.10cr grn & multi	.25	.25
1504	A817	1.10cr lt & dk grn	.25	.25

Support and security for rural and urban workers (No. 1503) and establishment in 1971 of Medicine Distribution Center (CEME) for low-cost medicines (No. 1504).

Churchyard Cross, Porto Seguro — A818

Views, Porto Seguro: 5cr, Beach and boats. 5.60cr, Our Lady of Pena Chapel. 6.50cr, Town Hall.

1977, May 25 Litho. *Perf. 11½*

1505	A818	1.10cr multi	.25	.25
1506	A818	5cr multi	.40	.25
1507	A818	5.60cr multi	.30	.25
1508	A818	6.50cr multi	.30	.25
		Nos. 1505-1508 (4)	1.25	1.00

Cent. of Brazil's membership in UPU.

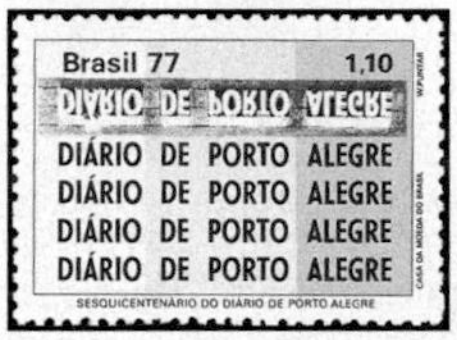

Diario de Porto Alegre A819

1977, June 1

1509 A819 1.10cr multi .25 .25

Diario de Porto Alegre, newspaper, 150th anniv.

Blue Whale A820

1977, June 3

1510 A820 1.30cr multi .30 .25

Protection of marine life.

"Life and Development" A821

1977, June 20

1511 A821 1.30cr multi .25 .25

National Development Bank, 25th anniv.

Train Leaving Tunnel A822

1977, July 8 **Engr.** ***Perf. 11½***

1512	A822	1.30cr black	.25	.25

Centenary of Sao Paulo-Rio de Janeiro railroad.

Shells — A823

Designs: No. 1513, Vasum cassiforme. No. 1514, Strombus goliath. No. 1515, Murex tenuivaricosus.

1977, July 14 **Litho.**

1513	A823	1.30cr blue & multi	.30	.25
1514	A823	1.30cr brown & multi	.30	.25
1515	A823	1.30cr green & multi	.30	.25
		Nos. 1513-1515 (3)	.90	.75

Caduceus, Formulas for Water and Fluoride — A824

1977, July 15 ***Perf. 11½x11***

1516	A824	1.30cr multi	.25	.25

3rd Intl. Odontology Congress, Rio, 7/15-21.

Masonic Emblem, Map of Brazil — A825

1977, July 18 ***Perf. 11½***

1517	A825	1.30cr bl, lt bl & blk	.30	.25

50th anniversary of the founding of the Brazilian Grand Masonic Lodge.

"Stamps Don't Sink or Lose their Way" — A826

1977, Aug. 1

1518	A826	1.30cr multi	.25	.25

Stamp Day 1977.

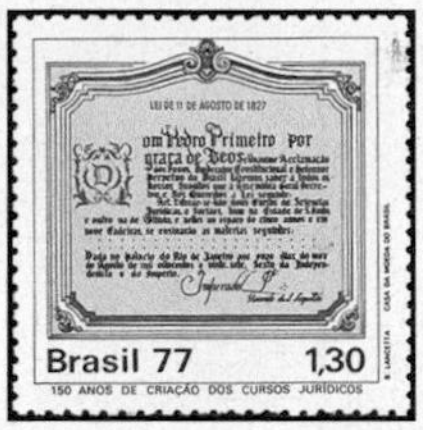

Dom Pedro's Proclamation A827

1977, Aug. 11 **Litho.** ***Perf. 11½***

1519	A827	1.30cr multi	.25	.25

150th anniversary of Brazilian Law School.

Horses and Bulls — A828

Brazilian folklore: No. 1521, King on horseback. No. 1522, Joust, horiz.

Perf. 11½x11, 11x11½ **Litho.**

1977, Aug. 20

1520	A828	1.30cr ocher & multi	.25	.25
1521	A828	1.30cr blue & multi	.25	.25
1522	A828	1.30cr yel & multi	.25	.25
		Nos. 1520-1522 (3)	.75	.75

Brazilian Colonial Coins A829

Designs: No. 1523, 2000-reis doubloon. No. 1524, 640r pataca. No. 1525, 20r copper "vintem."

1977, Aug. 31 ***Perf. 11½***

1523	A829	1.30cr vio bl & multi	.25	.25
1524	A829	1.30cr dk red & multi	.25	.25
1525	A829	1.30cr yel & multi	.25	.25
		Nos. 1523-1525 (3)	.75	.75

Pinwheel — A830

1977, Sept. 1

1526	A830	1.30cr multi	.25	.25

National Week.

Neoregelia Carolinae — A831

1977, Sept. 21 **Litho.** ***Perf. 11½***

1527	A831	1.30cr multi	.25	.25

Nature preservation.

Pen, Pencil, Letters — A832

1977, Oct. 15 **Litho.** ***Perf. 11½***

1528	A832	1.30cr multi	.25	.25

Primary education, sesquicentennial.

Dome and Telescope A833

1977, Oct. 15

1529	A833	1.30cr multi	.25	.25

National Astrophysics Observatory, Brasópolis, sesquicentennial.

"Jahu" Hydroplane (Savoia Marchetti S-55) — A834

Design: No. 1531, PAX, dirigible.

1977, Oct. 17

1530	A834	1.30cr multi	.25	.25
1531	A834	1.30cr multi	.25	.25

50th anniv. of crossing of South Atlantic by Joao Ribeiro de Barros, Genoa-Sao Paulo (No. 1530) and 75th anniv. of the PAX airship (No. 1531).

Il'Guarani — A835

1977, Oct. 24

1532	A835	1.30cr multi	.25	.25

Book Day and to honor Jose Martiniano de Alencar, writer, jurist.

Amateur Radio Operators' Day — A836

1977, Nov. 5 **Litho.** ***Perf. 11½***

1533	A836	1.30cr Waves	.25	.25

Christmas A837

Folk art: 1.30cr, Nativity. 2cr, Annunciation. 5cr, Nativity.

1977, Nov. 10

1534	A837	1.30cr bister & multi	.25	.25
1535	A837	2cr bister & multi	.25	.25
1536	A837	5cr bister & multi	.35	.35
		Nos. 1534-1536 (3)	.85	.85

A838

1977, Nov. 19

1537	A838	1.30cr Emerald	.25	.25
1538	A838	1.30cr Topaz	.25	.25
1539	A838	1.30cr Aquamarine	.25	.25
		Nos. 1537-1539 (3)	.75	.75

PORTUCALE 77, 2nd International Topical Exhibition, Porto, Nov. 19-20.

Angel, Cornucopia A839

1977, Nov. 24 **Litho.** ***Perf. 11½***

1540	A839	1.30cr multicolored	.25	.25

National Thanksgiving Day.

Army's Railroad Construction Battalion — A840

Civilian services of armed forces: No. 1542, Navy's Amazon flotilla. No. 1543, Air Force's postal service (plane).

1977, Dec. 5

1541	A840	1.30cr multi	.25	.25
1542	A840	1.30cr multi	.25	.25
1543	A840	1.30cr multi	.25	.25
		Nos. 1541-1543 (3)	.75	.75

Varig Emblem, Jet A841

1977, Dec. ***Perf. 11x11½***

1544	A841	1.30cr bl & blk	.25	.25

50th anniversary of Varig Airline.

Brazilian Architecture A842

Designs: 2.70cr, Sts. Cosme and Damiao Church, Igaracu. 7.50cr, St. Bento Monastery Church, Rio de Janeiro. 8.50cr, Church of St. Francis of Assisi, Ouro Preto. 9.50cr, St. Anthony Convent Church, Joao Pessoa.

1977, Dec. 8

1545 A842 2.70cr multi .30 .25
1546 A842 7.50cr multi .50 .25
1547 A842 8.50cr multi .55 .25
1548 A842 9.50cr multi .55 .30
Nos. 1545-1548 (4) 1.90 1.05

Woman Holding Sheaf — A843

1977, Dec. 19 ***Perf. 11½***

1549 A843 1.30cr multi .25 .25

Brazilian diplomacy.

Soccer Ball and Foot — A844

Designs: No. 1551, Soccer ball in net. No. 1552, Symbolic soccer player.

1978, Mar. 1 Litho. ***Perf. 11½***

1550 A844 1.80cr multi .25 .25
1551 A844 1.80cr multi .25 .25
1552 A844 1.80cr multi .25 .25
Nos. 1550-1552 (3) .75 .75

11th World Cup Soccer Championship, Argentina, June 1-25.

"La Fosca" on La Scala Stage and Carlos Gomes A845

1978, Feb. 9

1553 A845 1.80cr multi .25 .25

Bicentenary of La Scala in Milan, and to honor Carlos Gomes (1836-1893), Brazilian composer.

Symbols of Postal Mechanization — A846

1978, Mar. 15 Litho. ***Perf. 11½***

1554 A846 1.80cr multi .25 .25

Opening of Postal Staff College.

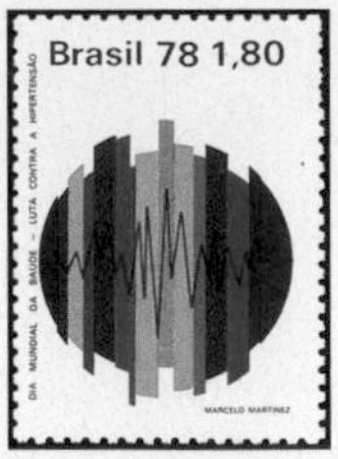

Hypertension Chart — A847

1978, Apr. 4

1555 A847 1.80cr multi .25 .25

World Health Day, fight against hypertension.

Waves from Antenna Uniting World — A848

1978, May 17 Litho. ***Perf. 12x11½***

1556 A848 1.80cr multi .25 .25

10th World Telecommunications Day.

Brazilian Canary A849

Birds: 8.50cr, Cotinga. 9.50cr, Tanager fastuosa.

1978, June 5 ***Perf. 11½x12***

1557 A849 7.50cr multi .55 .40
1558 A849 8.50cr multi .55 .40
1559 A849 9.50cr multi .55 .40
Nos. 1557-1559 (3) 1.65 1.20

Inocencio Serzedelo Correa and Manuel Francisco Correa, 1893 — A850

1978, June 20 Litho. ***Perf. 11x11½***

1560 A850 1.80cr multi .25 .25

85th anniversary of Union Court of Audit.

Post and Telegraph Building A851

1978, June 22 ***Perf. 11½***

1561 A851 1.80cr multi .25 .25

Souvenir Sheet

Imperf

1562 A851 7.50cr multi .65 *1.50*

Inauguration of Post and Telegraph Building (ECT), Brasilia, and for BRAPEX, 3rd Brazilian Philatelic Exhibition, Brasilia, June 23-28 (No. 1562).

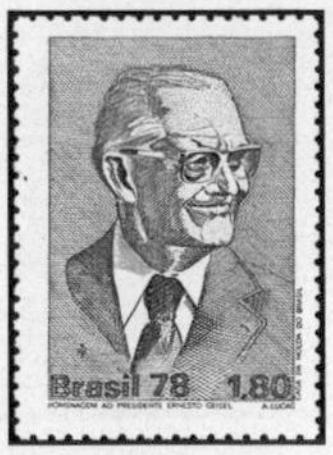

Ernesto Geisel, President of Brazil — A852

1978, June 22 Engr. ***Perf. 11½***

1563 A852 1.80cr dull green .25 .25

Savoia-Marchetti S-64, Map of South Atlantic — A853

1978, July 3 Litho.

1564 A853 1.80cr multi .25 .25

50th anniv. of 1st crossing of South Atlantic by Carlos del Prete and Arturo Ferrarin.

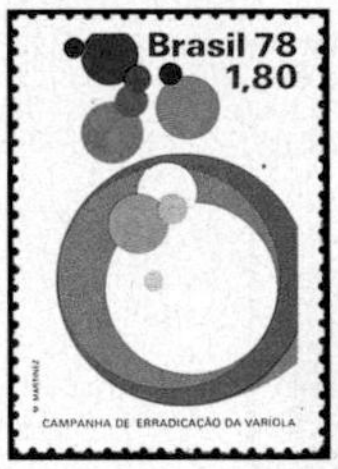

Symbolic of Smallpox Eradication A854

1978, July 25

1565 A854 1.80cr multi .25 .25

Eradication of smallpox.

Brazil No. 68 — A855

1978, Aug. 1

1566 A855 1.80cr multi .25 .25

Stamp Day, centenary of the "Barba Branca" (white beard) issue.

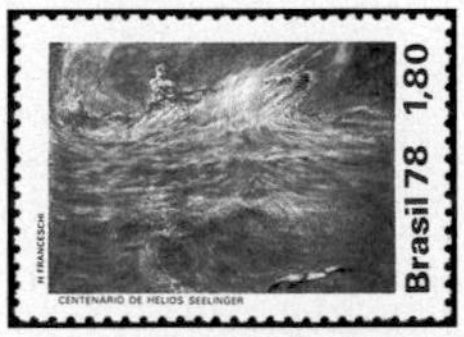

Stormy Sea, by Seelinger A856

1978, Aug. 4

1567 A856 1.80cr multi .25 .25

Helios Seelinger, painter, birth centenary.

Musicians and Instruments A857

Designs: No. 1568, Guitar players. No. 1569, Flutes. No. 1570, Percussion instruments.

1978, Aug. 22 Litho. ***Perf. 11½***

1568 A857 1.80cr multi .25 .25
1569 A857 1.80cr multi .25 .25
1570 A857 1.80cr multi .25 .25
Nos. 1568-1570 (3) .75 .75

Children at Play A858

1978, Sept. 1 Litho. ***Perf. 11½***

1571 A858 1.80cr multi .25 .25

National Week.

Collegiate Church A859

1978, Sept. 6 Engr.

1572 A859 1.80cr red brn .25 .25

Restoration of patio of Collegiate Church, Sao Paulo.

Justice by A. Geschiatti A860

1978, Sept. 18 Litho.

1573 A860 1.80cr blk & olive .25 .25

Federal Supreme Court, sesquicentennial.

Iguacu National Park — A861

Design: No. 1574, Iguacu Falls. No. 1575, Yellow ipe.

1978, Sept. 21

1574 A861 1.80cr multi .25 .25
1575 A861 1.80cr multi .25 .25

Stages of Intelsat Satellite A862

1978, Oct. 9 Litho. ***Perf. 11½***

1576 A862 1.80cr multi .25 .25

Brazilian Flags A863

Designs: No. 1577, Flag of the Order of Christ. No. 1578, Principality of Brazil. No.

1579, United Kingdom. No. 1580, Imperial Brazil. No. 1581, National flag (current).

1978, Oct. 13

1577	A863	1.80cr multi		.30	.30
1578	A863	1.80cr multi		.30	.30
1579	A863	1.80cr multi		.30	.30
1580	A863	8.50cr multi		.30	.30
1581	A863	8.50cr multi		.30	.30
a.	Block of 5, #1577-1581 + label			1.50	1.50
	Nos. 1577-1581 (5)			1.50	1.50

7th LUBRAPEX Philatelic Exhibition, Porto Alegre.

Mail Transportation — A864

Designs: No. 1582, Mail street car. No. 1583, Overland mail truck. No. 1584, Mail delivery truck. 7.50cr. Railroad mail car. 8.50cr, Mail coach. 9.50cr, Post riders.

1978, Oct. 21 ***Perf. 11x11½***

1582	A864	1.80cr multi		.30	.25
1583	A864	1.80cr multi		.30	.25
1584	A864	1.80cr multi		.30	.25
1585	A864	7.50cr multi		.30	.25
1586	A864	8.50cr multi		.30	.25
1587	A864	9.50cr multi		.30	.25
a.	Block of 6, #1582-1587			2.00	2.00

18th UPU Congress, Rio de Janeiro, 1979.

Gaucho Herding Cattle, and Cactus — A865

1978, Oct. 23 ***Perf. 11½x11***

1588	A865	1.80cr multi		.25	.25

Joao Guimaraes Rosa, poet and diplomat, 70th birthday.

Landscape Paintings A866

Designs: No. 1589, St. Anthony's Hill, by Nicholas A. Taunay. No. 1590, Castle Hill, by Victor Meirelles. No. 1591, View of Sabara, by Alberto da Veiga Guignard. No. 1592, View of Pernambuco, by Frans Post.

1978, Nov. 6 **Litho.** ***Perf. 11½***

1589	A866	1.80cr multi		.25	.25
1590	A866	1.80cr multi		.25	.25
1591	A866	1.80cr multi		.25	.25
1592	A866	1.80cr multi		.25	.25
	Nos. 1589-1592 (4)			1.00	1.00

Christmas A867

Angel with: No. 1593, Harp. No. 1594, Lute. No. 1595, Oboe.

1978, Nov. 10

1593	A867	1.80cr multi		.25	.25
1594	A867	1.80cr multi		.25	.25
1595	A867	1.80cr multi		.25	.25
	Nos. 1593-1595 (3)			.75	.75

Symbolic Candles — A868

1978, Nov. 23

1596	A868	1.80cr blk, gold & car		.25	.25

National Thanksgiving Day.

Red Crosses and Activities A869

1978, Dec. 5 **Litho.** ***Perf. 11x11½***

1597	A869	1.80cr blk & red		.25	.25

70th anniversary of Brazilian Red Cross.

Paz Theater, Belem A870

Designs: 12cr, José de Alencar Theater, Fortaleza. 12.50cr, Municipal Theater, Rio de Janeiro.

1978, Dec. 6 ***Perf. 11½***

1598	A870	10.50cr multi		.55	.30
1599	A870	12cr multi		.55	.30
1600	A870	12.50cr multi		.55	.30
	Nos. 1598-1600 (3)			1.65	.90

Subway Trains — A871

1979, Mar. 5 **Litho.** ***Perf. 11½***

1601	A871	2.50cr multi		.25	.25

Inauguration of Rio subway system.

Old and New Post Offices A872

Designs: No. 1603, Old and new mail boxes. No. 1604, Manual and automatic mail sorting. No. 1605, Old and new planes. No. 1606, Telegraph and telex machine. No. 1607, Mailmen's uniforms.

1979, Mar. 20 **Litho.** ***Perf. 11x11½***

1602	A872	2.50cr multi		.35	.25
1603	A872	2.50cr multi		.35	.25
1604	A872	2.50cr multi		.35	.25
1605	A872	2.50cr multi		.35	.25
1606	A872	2.50cr multi		.35	.25
1607	A872	2.50cr multi		.35	.25
a.	Block of 6, #1602-1607			2.10	2.10

10th anniv. of the new Post and Telegraph Dept., and 18th Universal Postal Union Cong., Rio de Janeiro, Sept.-Oct., 1979.

O'Day 23 Class Yacht A873

Yachts and Stamp Outlines: 10.50cr, Penguin Class. 12cr, Hobie Cat Class. 12.50cr, Snipe Class.

1979, Apr. 18 **Litho.** ***Perf. 11x11½***

1608	A873	2.50cr multi		.25	.25
1609	A873	10.50cr multi		.25	.25
1610	A873	12cr multi		.25	.25
1611	A873	12.50cr multi		.25	.25
	Nos. 1608-1611 (4)			1.00	1.00

Brasiliana '79, 3rd World Thematic Stamp Exhibition, Sao Conrado, Sept. 15-23.

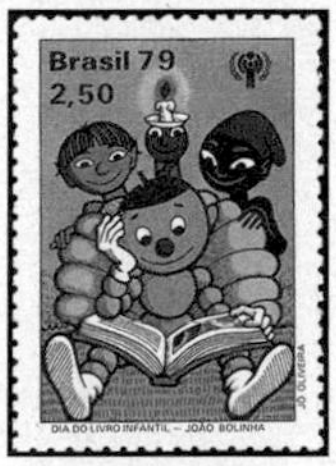

Children, IYC Emblem — A874

1979, May 23 **Litho.** ***Perf. 11½***

1612	A874	2.50cr multi		.25	.25

Intl. Year of the Child & Children's Book Day.

Giant Water Lily — A875

Designs: 12cr, Amazon manatee. 12.50cr, Arrau (turtle).

1979, June 5 **Litho.** ***Perf. 11½***

1613	A875	10.50cr multi		.35	.25
1614	A875	12cr multi		.35	.25
1615	A875	12.50cr multi		.35	.25
	Nos. 1613-1615 (3)			1.05	.75

Amazon National Park, nature conservation.

Bank Emblem A876

1979, June 7

1616	A876	2.50cr multi		.25	.25

Northwest Bank of Brazil, 25th anniversary.

Physician Tending Patient 15th Cent. Woodcut A877

1979, June 30

1617	A877	2.50cr multi		.25	.25

Natl. Academy of Medicine, 150th anniv.

Flower made of Hearts — A878

1979, July 8 **Litho.** ***Perf. 11½***

1618	A878	2.50cr multi		.25	.25

35th Brazilian Cardiology Congress.

Souvenir Sheet

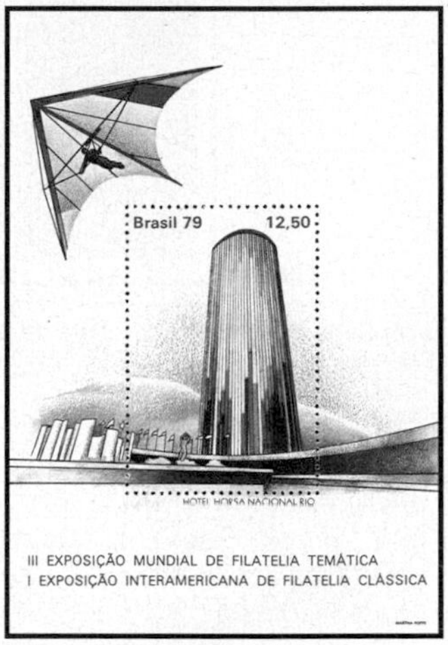

Hotel Nacional, Rio de Janeiro — A879

1979, July 16

1619	A879	12.50cr multi		.65	*1.00*

Brasiliana '79 comprising 1st Inter-American Exhibition of Classical Philately and 3rd World Topical Exhibition, Rio de Janeiro, Sept. 15-23.

Cithaerias Aurora A880

Moths: 10.50cr, Evenus regalis. 12cr, Caligo eurilochus. 12.50cr, Diaethria clymena janeira.

1979, Aug. 1

1620	A880	2.50cr multi		.30	.25
1621	A880	10.50cr multi		.55	.30
1622	A880	12cr multi		.55	.30
1623	A880	12.50cr multi		.75	.40
	Nos. 1620-1623 (4)			2.15	1.25

Stamp Day 1979.

EMB-121 Xingo A881

1979, Aug. 19 **Litho.** ***Perf. 11½***

1624	A881	2.50cr vio blue		.25	.25

Embraer, Brazilian aircraft comp., 10th anniv.

National Week — A882

Natl. emblem over landscape.

1979, Sept. 12

1625	A882 3.20cr multi		.25	.25

A883

1979, Sept. 8 Litho. *Perf. 11½*

1626	A883 2.50cr multi	.25	.25

Statue of Our Lady of the Apparition, 75th anniversary of coronation.

"UPU," Envelope and Mail Transport A884

"UPU" and: No. 1628, Post Office emblems. 10.50cr, Globe. 12cr, Flags of Brazil and UN. 12.50cr, UPU emblem.

1979, Sept. 12 *Perf. 11x11½*

1627	A884	2.50cr multi	.25	.25
1628	A884	2.50cr multi	.25	.25
1629	A884	10.50cr multi	.25	.25
1630	A884	12cr multi	.25	.25
1631	A884	12.50cr multi	.25	.25
		Nos. 1627-1631 (5)	1.25	1.25

18th UPU Cong., Rio, Sept.-Oct. 1979.

Pyramid Fountain, Rio de Janeiro — A885

Fountains: 10.50cr, Facade, Marilia, Ouro Preto, horiz. 12cr, Boa Vista, Recife.

Perf. 12x11½, 11½x12

1979, Sept. 15

1632	A885	2.50cr multi	.25	.25
1633	A885	10.50cr multi	.30	.25
1634	A885	12cr multi	.30	.25
		Nos. 1632-1634 (3)	.85	.75

Brasiliana '79, 1st Interamerican Exhibition of Classical Philately.

Church of the Glory A886

Landscapes by Leandro Joaquim: 12cr, Whale hunting on Guanabara Bay. 12.50cr, Boqueirao Lagoon and Carioca Aqueduct.

1979, Sept. 15 *Perf. 11½*

1635	A886	2.50cr multi	.25	.25
1636	A886	12cr multi	.30	.25
1637	A886	12.50cr multi	.30	.25
		Nos. 1635-1637 (3)	.85	.75

Brasiliana '79, 3rd World Topical Exhibition, Sao Conrado, Sept. 15-23.

World Map A887

1979, Sept. 20

1638	A887 2.50cr multi	.25	.25

3rd World Telecommunications Exhibition, Geneva, Sept. 20-26.

"UPU" and UPU Emblem — A888

1979, Oct. 9 Litho. *Perf. 11½x11*

1639	A888	2.50cr multi	.25	.25
1640	A888	10.50cr multi	.25	.25
1641	A888	12cr multi	.25	.25
1642	A888	12.50cr multi	.25	.25
		Nos. 1639-1642 (4)	1.00	1.00

Universal Postal Union Day.

IYC Emblem, Feather Toy A889

IYC Emblem and Toys: No. 1644, Bumble bee, ragdoll. No. 1645, Flower, top. No. 1646, Wooden acrobat.

1979, Oct. 12 *Perf. 11½*

1643	A889	2.50cr multi	.25	.25
1644	A889	3.20cr multi	.25	.25
1645	A889	3.20cr multi	.25	.25
1646	A889	3.20cr multi	.25	.25
		Nos. 1643-1646 (4)	1.00	1.00

International Year of the Child.

Christmas A890

Designs: No. 1647, Adoration of the Magi. No. 1648, Nativity. No. 1649 Jesus and the Elders in the Temple.

1979, Nov. 12 Litho. *Perf. 11½*

1647	A890	3.20cr multi	.25	.25
1648	A890	3.20cr multi	.25	.25
1649	A890	3.20cr multi	.25	.25
		Nos. 1647-1649 (3)	.75	.75

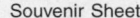

Souvenir Sheet

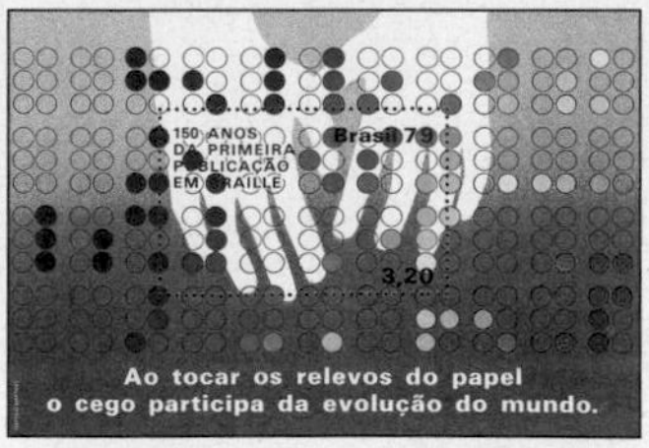

Hands Reading Braille — A891

Lithographed and Embossed

1979, Nov. 20. *Perf. 11½*

1650	A891 3.20cr multi	.55	*.75*

Publication of Braille script, 150th anniversary. Margin shows extension of stamp design with Braille printed and embossed.

Thanksgiving A892

1979, Nov. 22

1651	A892 3.20cr Wheat harvester	.25	.25

Steel Mill — A893

1979, Nov. 23

1652	A893 3.20cr multi	.25	.25

COSIPA Steelworks, Sao Paulo, 25th anniversary.

Type of 1976

Designs: 70c, Women grinding coconuts. 2.50cr, Basket weaver. 3.20cr, River boatman. 21cr, Harvesting ramie (China grass). 27cr, Man leading pack mule. 3.20cr, 27cr, horiz.

Photogravure, Engraved (21cr)

1979 *Perf. 11x11½, 11½x11*

1653	A790	70c gray green	.25	.25
1654	A790	2.50cr sepia	.25	.25
1655	A790	3.20cr blue	.25	.25
1656	A790	21cr purple	1.50	.25
1657	A790	27cr sepia	1.75	.25
		Nos. 1653-1657 (5)	4.00	1.25

A894

Designs: 2cr, Coconuts. 3cr, Mangoes. 4cr, Corn. 5cr,Onions. 7cr, Oranges. 10cr, Maracuja. 12cr, Pineapple. 15cr, Bananas. 17cr, Guarana. 20cr, Sugar cane. 24cr, Beekeeping. 30cr, Silkworm. 34cr, Cacao. 38cr, Coffee. 42cr, Soybeans. 45cr, Mandioca. 50cr, Wheat. 57cr, Peanuts. 66cr, Grapes. 100cr, Cashews. 140cr, Tomatoes. 200cr, Mamona. 500cr, Cotton.

1980-83 Photo. *Perf. 11½x11*

1658	A894	2cr yel brn ('82)	.25	.25
1659	A894	3cr red ('82)	.25	.25
1660	A894	4cr orange	.30	.25
1661	A894	5cr dk pur ('82)	.25	.25
1662	A894	7cr org ('81)	.25	.25
1663	A894	10cr bl grn ('82)	.25	.25
1664	A894	12cr dk grn ('81)	.25	.25
1665	A894	15cr gldn brn ('83)	.25	.25
1666	A894	17cr brn org ('82)	.40	.25
1667	A894	20cr olive ('82)	.25	.25
1668	A894	24cr bis ('82)	.75	.25
1669	A894	30cr blk ('82)	.75	.25
1670	A894	34cr brown	5.50	.55
1671	A894	38cr red ('83)	2.75	.25
1672	A894	42cr green	13.00	.65
1673	A894	45cr sepia ('83)	.25	.25
1674	A894	50cr yel org ('82)	.30	.25
1675	A894	57cr brn ('83)	2.75	.25
1676	A894	66cr pur ('81)	7.50	.30
1677	A894	100cr dk red brn ('81)	.35	.25
1678	A894	140cr red ('82)	7.50	1.60

Engr.

1678A	A894	200cr grn ('82)	1.25	.25
1679	A894	500cr brn ('82)	2.00	.25
		Nos. 1658-1679 (23)	47.35	7.85

See Nos. 1934-1941.

Plant Inside Raindrop — A896

Light bulb containing: 17cr+7cr, Sun. 20cr+8cr, Windmill. 21cr+9cr, Dam.

1980, Jan. 2 Litho. *Perf. 12*

1680	A896	3.20cr multi	.25	.25
1681	A896	24cr (17 + 7)	.25	.25
1682	A896	28cr (20 + 8)	.60	.30
1683	A896	30cr (21 + 9)	.75	.40
		Nos. 1680-1683 (4)	1.85	1.20

Nos. 1681-1683 were originally intended to be sold as semi-postal stamps but were actually issued as regular postage stamps, sold and valid for the combined denominations appearing on each stamp.

Anthracite Industry A897

1980, Mar. 19 Litho. *Perf. 11½*

1684	A897 4cr multi	.25	.25

Map of Americas, Symbols of Development — A898

1980, Apr. 14 Litho. *Perf. 11x11½*

1685	A898 4cr multi	.25	.25

21st Assembly of Inter-American Development Bank Governors, Rio, Apr. 14-16.

Tapirape Mask, Mato Grosso A899

No. 1687, Tukuna mask, Amazonas, vert. No. 1688, Kanela mask, Maranhao, vert.

1980, Apr. 18 *Perf. 11½*

1686	A899	4cr shown	.25	.25
1687	A899	4cr multicolored	.25	.25
1688	A899	4cr multicolored	.25	.25
		Nos. 1686-1688 (3)	.75	.75

Brazilian Television, 30th Anniversary
A900

1980, May 5 Litho. ***Perf. 11½***
1689 A900 4cr multicolored .25 .25

Duke of Caxias, by Miranda — A901

1980, May 7
1690 A901 4cr multicolored .25 .25

Duke of Caxias, death centenary.

The Worker, by Candido Portinari — A902

Paintings: 28cr, Mademoiselle Pogany, by Constantin Brancusi. 30cr, The Glass of Water, by Francisco Aurelio de Figueiredo.

1980, May 18
1691 A902 24cr multi .30 .30
1692 A902 28cr multi .40 .30
1693 A902 30cr multi .65 .40
Nos. 1691-1693 (3) 1.35 1.00

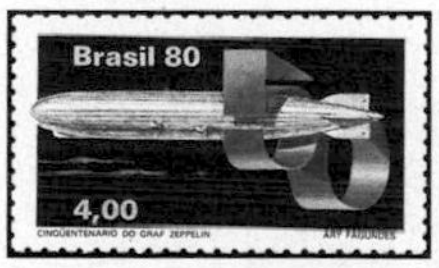

A903

1980, June Litho. ***Perf. 11x11½***
1694 A903 4cr multicolored .25 .25

Graf Zeppelin, 50th Anniversary of Atlantic Crossing.

Pope John Paul II, St. Peter's, Rome, Congress Emblem
A904

Pope, Emblem and Brazilian Churches: No. 1696, Fortaleza, vert. 24cr, Apericida 28cr, Rio de Janeiro. 30cr, Brasilia.

1980, June 24 ***Perf. 12***
1695 A904 4cr multi .25 .25
1696 A904 4cr multi .25 .25
1697 A904 24cr multi .30 .30
1698 A904 28cr multi .30 .30
1699 A904 30cr multi .55 .40
Nos. 1695-1699 (5) 1.65 1.50

Visit of Pope John Paul II to Brazil, June 30-July 12; 10th National Eucharistic Congress, Fortaleza, July 9-16.

1st Airmail Flight across the South Atlantic, 50th Anniv.
A905

1980, June Litho. ***Perf. 11x11½***
1700 A905 4cr multicolored .25 .25

Souvenir Sheet

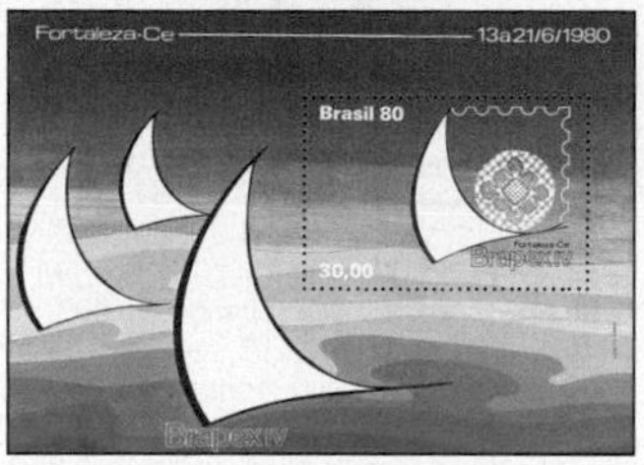

Yacht Sail, Exhibition Emblem — A906

1980, June ***Perf. 11½***
1701 A906 30cr multi .60 .60

Brapex IV Stamp Exhib., Fortaleza, June 13-21.

Rowing, Moscow '80 Emblem
A907

1980, June 30
1702 A907 4cr shown .35 .25
1703 A907 4cr Target shooting .35 .25
1704 A907 4cr Bicycling .35 .25
Nos. 1702-1704 (3) 1.05 .75

22nd Summer Olympic Games, Moscow, July 19-Aug. 3.

Rondon Community Works Project
A908

1980, July 11
1705 A908 4cr multicolored .25 .25

Helen Keller and Anne Sullivan
A909

1980, July 28
1706 A909 4cr multicolored .25 .25

Helen Keller (1880-1968), blind deaf writer and lecturer taught by Anne Sullivan (1867-1936).

Souvenir Sheet

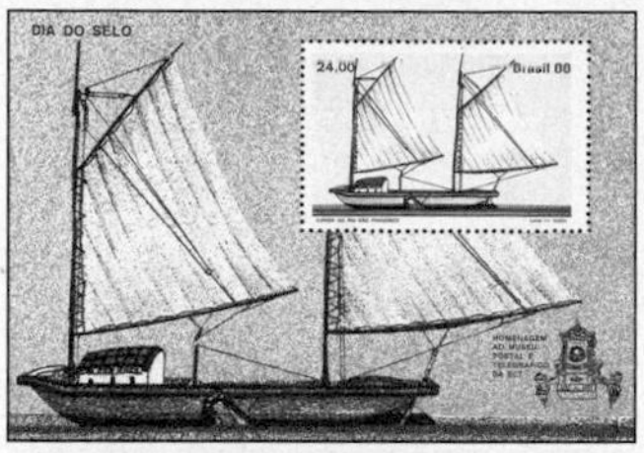

Sáo Francisco River Canoe — A910

1980, Aug. 1 Litho. ***Perf. 11½***
1707 A910 24cr multi .65 .65

Stamp Day.

Microscope, Red Cross, Insects, Brick and Tile Houses — A911

1980, Aug. 5 ***Perf. 11½x11***
1708 A911 4cr multi .25 .25

National Health Day.

EMBRATEL, 15th Anniversary — A912

1980, Sept. 16 Litho. ***Perf. 12***
1709 A912 5cr multi .25 .25

Souvenir Sheet

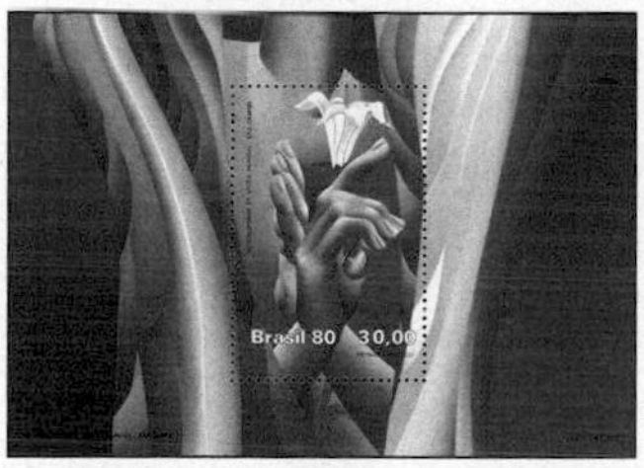

A913

1980, Sept. 29 ***Perf. 11½x12***
1710 A913 30cr multi .60 .60

St. Gabriel World Union, 6th congress.

Orchids
A914

Designs: No. 1711, Cattleya amethystoglossa. No. 1712, Laelia cinnabarina. 24cr, Zygopetalu, crinitum. 28cr, Laelia tenebrosa.

1980, Oct. 3 ***Perf. 11½***
1711 A914 5cr multi .25 .25
1712 A914 5cr multi .25 .25
1713 A914 24cr multi .90 .40
1714 A914 28cr multi .90 .40
Nos. 1711-1714 (4) 2.30 1.30

Espamer 80, American-European Philatelic Exhibition, Madrid, Oct. 3-12.

Parrots — A915

Designs: No. 1715, Amazona brazilensis. No. 1716, Amazona Vinacea. No. 1717, Touit melanonota. No. 1718, Amazona pretrei.

1980, Oct. 18 Litho. ***Perf. 12***
1715 A915 5cr multi .40 .25
1716 A915 5cr multi .40 .25
1717 A915 28cr multi .90 .40
1718 A915 28cr multi .90 .40
Nos. 1715-1718 (4) 2.60 1.30

Lubrapex '80 Stamp Exhib., Lisbon, Oct. 18-26.

Captain Rodrigo, Hero of Erico Verissimo's "O Continento"
A916

1980, Oct. 23
1719 A916 5cr multi .25 .25

Book Day.

Christmas
A917

1980, Nov. 5
1720 A917 5cr Flight into Egypt .25 .25

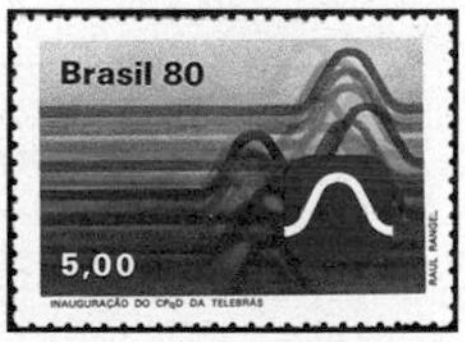

Sound Waves and Oscillator Screen
A918

1980, Nov. 7
1721 A918 5cr multi .25 .25

Telebras Research Center inauguration.

Carvalho Viaduct, Paranagua-Curitiba Railroad — A919

1980, Nov. 10
1722 A919 5cr multi .25 .25

Engineering Club centenary.

Postal Chess Contest
A920

5cr, Portable chess board.

1980, Nov. 18 Litho. *Perf. 11½*
1723 A920 5cr multicolored .25 .25

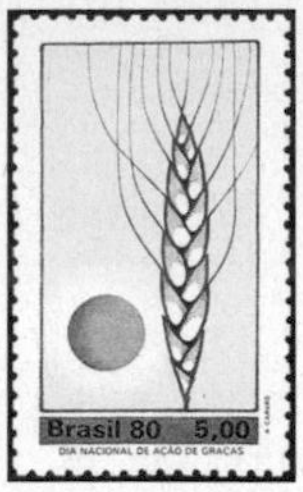

Thanksgiving A921

1980, Nov. 27 *Perf. 11½x11*
1724 A921 5cr Sun, wheat .25 .25

Father Anchieta Writing "Virgin Mary, Mother of God" on Sand of Iperoig Beach — A922

1980, Dec. 8 *Perf. 12*
1725 A922 5cr multi .25 .25

Antonio Francisco Lisboa (O Aleijadinho), 250th Birth Anniv. — A923

No. 1726 — Paintings of the life of Christ: a, Mount of Olives. b, Arrest in the Garden. c, Flagellation. d, Crown of Thorns. e, Christ Carrying the Cross (shown). f, Crucifixion.

1980, Dec. 29
1726 Block of 6 3.50 6.50
a.-f. A923 5cr any single .55 .25

Agricultural Productivity — A924

35cr, Domestic markets. 40cr, Exports.

1981, Jan. 2 Litho. *Perf. 11x11½*
1727 A924 30cr shown .60 .25
1728 A924 35cr multicolored .60 .25
1729 A924 40cr multicolored .60 .25
Nos. 1727-1729 (3) 1.80 .75

Boy Scout and Campfire A925

1981, Jan. 22 Litho. *Perf. 11x11½*
1730 A925 5cr shown .30 .25
1731 A925 5cr Scouts cooking .30 .25
1732 A925 5cr Scout, tents .30 .25
Nos. 1730-1732 (3) .90 .75

4th Pan-American Scout Jamboree.

Souvenir Sheet

Dept. of Posts & Telegraphs, 50th anniv. — A926

1981, Mar. 11 Litho. *Perf. 11*
1733 A926 Sheet of 3 5.00 5.00
a. 30cr Mailman, 1930 1.25 1.25
b. 35cr Mailman, 1981 1.25 1.25
c. 40cr Telegram messenger, 1930 1.25 1.25

Souvenir Sheet

The Hunter and the Jaguar, by Felix Taunay (1795-1881) — A927

1981, Apr. 10 Litho. *Perf. 11*
1734 A927 30cr multi 1.25 1.25

Lima Barreto and Rio de Janeiro, 1900 A928

1981, May 13 Litho. *Perf. 11½*
1735 A928 7cr multi .25 .25

Lima Barreto, writer, birth centenary.

Maraca Indian Funerary Urn — A929

No. 1737, Marajoara triangular jug. No. 1738, Tupi-Guarani bowl.

1981, May 18
1736 A929 7cr shown .25 .25
1737 A929 7cr multicolored .25 .25
1738 A929 7cr multicolored .25 .25
Nos. 1736-1738 (3) .75 .75

Hummingbirds — A930

Designs: No. 1739, Lophornis magnifica. No. 1740, Phaethornis pretrei. No. 1741, Chrysolampis mosquitus. No. 1742, Heliactin cornuta.

1981, May 22 *Perf. 11½*
1739 A930 7cr multi .50 .35
1740 A930 7cr multi .50 .35
1741 A930 7cr multi .50 .35
1742 A930 7cr multi .50 .35
Nos. 1739-1742 (4) 2.00 1.40

Rotary Emblem and Faces A931

1981, May 31
1743 A931 7cr Emblem, hands .35 .25
1744 A931 35cr shown .70 .40

72nd Convention of Rotary Intl., Sao Paulo.

Environmental Protection — A932

1981, June 5 *Perf. 12*
1745 A932 7cr Fish .40 .25
1746 A932 7cr Forest .40 .25
1747 A932 7cr Clouds (air) .40 .25
1748 A932 7cr Village (soil) .40 .25
a. Block of 4, #1745-1748 2.50 2.50

Biplane, 1931 (Airmail Service, 50th Anniv.) A933

1981, June 10 *Perf. 11½*
1749 A933 7cr multi .25 .25

Madeira-Mamore Railroad, 50th Anniv. of Nationalization — A934

1981, July 10 Litho. *Perf. 11x11½*
1750 A934 7cr multi .25 .25

66th Intl. Esperanto Congress, Brasilia A935

1981, July 26 *Perf. 12*
1751 A935 7cr green & blk .25 .25

No. 79 A936

1981, Aug. 1
1752 A936 50cr shown .75 .50
1753 A936 55cr No. 80 .75 .50
1754 A936 60cr No. 81 .75 .50
Nos. 1752-1754 (3) 2.25 1.50

Stamp Day; cent. of "small head" stamps.

Institute of Military Engineering, 50th Anniv. — A937

1981, Aug. 11 Litho. *Perf. 11½*
1755 A937 12cr multi .25 .25

Reisado Dancers A938

1981, Aug. 22
1756 A938 50cr Dancers, diff. .75 .35
1757 A938 55cr Sailors .75 .35
1758 A938 60cr shown .75 .35
Nos. 1756-1758 (3) 2.25 1.05

Intl. Year of the Disabled A939

1981, Sept. 17 Litho. *Perf. 11½*
1759 A939 12cr multi .25 .25

Flowers of the Central Plateau A940

No. 1760, Palicourea rigida. No. 1761, Dalechampia caperonioides. No. 1762, Cassia clausseni, vert. No. 1763, Eremanthus sphaerocephalus, vert.

1981, Sept. 21 Litho. *Perf. 12*
1760 A940 12cr multicolored .30 .25
1761 A940 12cr multicolored .30 .25
1762 A940 12cr multicolored .30 .25
1763 A940 12cr multicolored .30 .25
Nos. 1760-1763 (4) 1.20 1.00

Virgin of Nazareth Statue — A941

1981, Oct. 10 Litho. *Perf. 12*
1764 A941 12cr multi .25 .25

Candle Festival of Nazareth, Belem.

Christ the Redeemer Statue, Rio de Janeiro, 50th Anniv. — A942

1981, Oct. 12
1765 A942 12cr multi .25 .25

World Food Day A943

1981, Oct. 16
1766 A943 12c multi .25 .25

75th Anniv. of Santos-Dumont's First Flight — A944

1981, Oct. 23 Litho. *Perf. 12*
1767 A944 60cr multi 1.25 .40

Father José de Santa Rita Durao, Titlepage of his Epic Poem Caramuru, Diego Alvares Correia (Character) — A945

1981, Oct. 29
1768 A945 12cr multi .25 *.25*

Caramuru publication 200th anniv.; World Book Day.

Christmas A946

Designs: Creches and figurines.

1981, Nov. 10 Litho. *Perf. 12*

1769	A946 12cr multi	.30	.25
1770	A946 50cr multi	.40	.25
1771	A946 55cr multi, vert.	.40	.25
1772	A946 60cr multi, vert.	.65	.25
	Nos. 1769-1772 (4)	1.75	1.00

State Flags A947

No. 1773: a, Alagoas. b, Bahia. c, Federal District. d, Pernambuco. e, Sergipe.

1981, Nov. 19

1773	Block of 5 + label	1.50	2.25
a.-e.	A947 12cr, any single	.30	.25

Label shows arms of Brazil.

See Nos. 1830, 1892, 1962, 2037, 2249, 2726-2727.

Thanksgiving A948

1981, Nov. 26 Litho. *Perf. 11½*
1776 A948 12cr multi .30 .25

Ministry of Labor, 50th Anniv. A949

1981, Nov. 26
1777 A949 12cr multi .25 .25

School of Engineering, Itajuba — A950

1981, Nov. 30 *Perf. 11x11½*
1778 A950 15cr lt grn & pur .25 .25

Theodomiro C. Santiago, founder, birth centenary.

Sao Paulo State Police Sesquicentennial A951

No. 1779, Policeman with saxophone. No. 1780, Mounted policemen.

1981, Dec. 15 Litho. *Perf. 12*

1779	A951 12cr multicolored	.25	.25
1780	A951 12cr multicolored	.25	.25

Army Library Centenary A952

1981, Dec. 17
1781 A952 12cr multi .25 .25

Souvenir Sheet

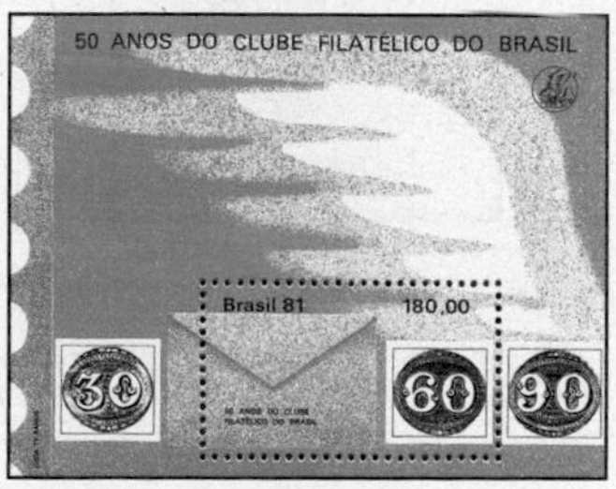

A953

1981, Dec. 18 *Perf. 11*
1782 A953 180cr multi 3.75 3.75

Philatelic Club of Brazil, 50th anniv.

Brigadier Eduardo Gomes A954

1982, Jan. 20 Litho. *Perf. 11x11½*
1783 A954 12cr blue & blk .25 .25

Birth Centenary of Henrique Lage, Industrialist — A956

1982, Mar. 14 Litho. *Perf. 11½*
1785 A956 17cr multi .25 .25

1982 World Cup Soccer A957

Designs: Various soccer players.

1982, Mar. 19

1786	A957 75cr multi	1.25	.60
1787	A957 80cr multi	1.25	.60
1788	A957 85cr multi	1.25	.60
	Nos. 1786-1788 (3)	3.75	1.80

Souvenir Sheet

Imperf

1789	Sheet of 3	7.50	7.50
a.	A957 100cr like #1786	2.00	1.50
b.	A957 100cr like #1787	2.00	1.50
c.	A957 100cr like #1788	2.00	1.50

TB Bacillus Cent. — A958

90cr, Microscope, lung. 100cr, Lung, pills.

1982, Mar. 24 *Perf. 12*

1790	A958 90cr multicolored	2.75	1.25
1791	A958 100cr multicolored	2.75	1.25
a.	Pair, #1790-1791	6.00	2.50

Souvenir Sheet

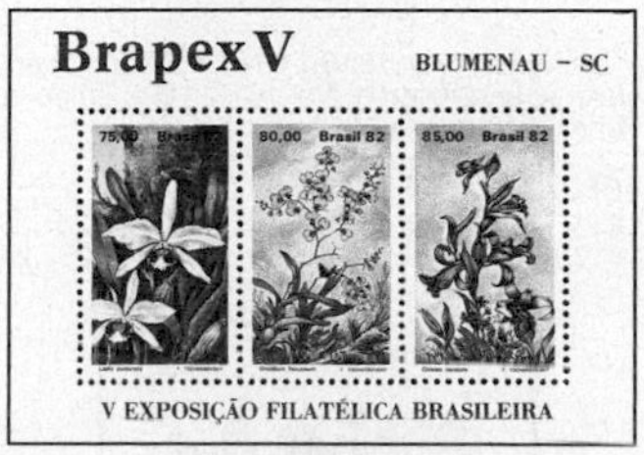

A959

1982, Apr. 17 Litho. *Perf. 11*

1792	A959 Sheet of 3	9.00	9.00
a.	75cr Laelia Purpurata	2.75	2.75
b.	80cr Oncidium flexuosum	2.75	2.75
c.	85cr Cleistes revoluta	2.75	2.75

BRAPEX V Stamp Exhibition, Blumenau.

Oil Drilling Centenary A960

1982, Apr. 18 *Perf. 11½*
1793 A960 17cr multi .25 .25

400th Birth Anniv. of St. Vincent de Paul A961

1982, Apr. 24 Litho. *Perf. 11½*
1794 A961 17cr multi .25 .25

Seven Steps of Guaira (Waterfalls) A962

1982, Apr. 29

1795	A962 17cr Fifth Fall	.25	.25
1796	A962 21cr Seventh Fall	.25	.25

Ministry of Communications, 15th Anniv. — A963

1982, May 15
1797 A963 21cr multi .25 .25

Museology Course, Natl. Historical Museum, 50th Anniv. A964

1982, May 18
1798 A964 17cr blk & sal pink .25 .25

Vale de Rio Doce Mining Co. — A965

1982, June 1
1799 A965 17cr Gears .25 .25

Martin Afonso de Souza Reading Charter to Settlers A966

1982, June 3 Litho. *Perf. 11½*
1800 A966 17cr multi .25 .25

Town of Sao Vincente, 450th anniv.

Armadillo
A967

1982, June 4

1801 A967 17cr shown	.35	.25
1802 A967 21cr Wolves	.55	.25
1803 A967 30cr Deer	1.50	.25
Nos. 1801-1803 (3)	2.40	.75

Film Strip and Award
A968

1982, June 19

1804 A968 17cr multi .25 .25

20th anniv. of Golden Palm award for The Promise Keeper, Cannes Film Festival.

Souvenir Sheet

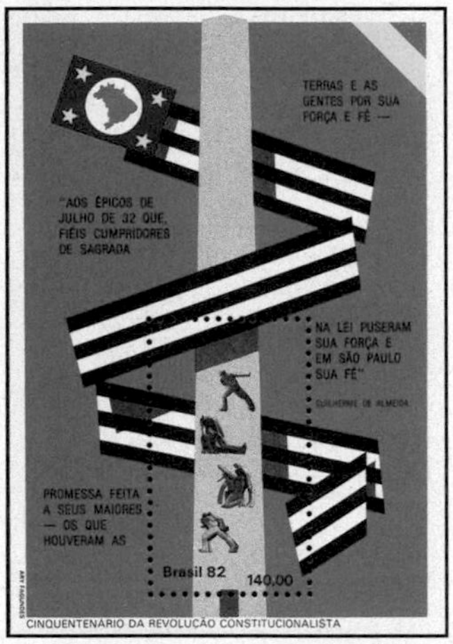

50th Anniv. of Constitutionalist Revolution — A969

1982, July 9 Litho. *Perf. 11*

1805 A969 140cr multi 3.25 3.25

Church of Our Lady of O'Sabara — A970

Baroque Architecture, Minas Gerais State: No. 1807, Church of Our Lady of the Rosary, Diamantina. No. 1808, Town Square, Mariana.

1982, July 16 *Perf. 11½*

1806 A970 17cr multi	.35	.25
1807 A970 17cr multi, horiz.	.35	.25
1808 A970 17cr multi, horiz.	.35	.25
Nos. 1806-1808 (3)	1.05	.75

St. Francis of Assisi, 800th Birth Anniv. — A971

1982, July 24

1809 A971 21cr multi .25 .25

Stamp Day and Centenary of Pedro II "Large Head" Stamps
A972

1982, Aug. 1

1810 A972 21cr No. 82 .25 .25

Port of Manaus Free Trade Zone
A973

1982, Aug. 15 *Perf. 11x11½*

1811 A973 75cr multi .50 .30

Scouting Year — A974

1982, Aug. 21 Litho. *Perf. 11*

1812 A974 Sheet of 2	7.75	7.75
a. 185cr Scout	3.75	3.75
b. 85cr Baden-Powell	3.75	3.75

Orixas Folk Costumes of African Origin
A975

1982, Aug. 21 *Perf. 11½*

1813 A975 20cr Iemanja	.45	.25
1814 A975 20cr Xango	.45	.25
1815 A975 20cr Oxumare	.45	.25
Nos. 1813-1815 (3)	1.35	.75

10th Anniv. of Central Bank of Brazil Currency Museum
A976

Designs: No. 1816, 1645 12-florin coin, obverse and reverse. No. 1817, 1822 Emperor Pedro 6.40-reis coronation coin.

1982, Aug. 31

1816 A976 25cr multi	.25	.25
1817 A976 25cr multi	.25	.25

Dom Pedro Proclaiming Independence — A977

1982, Sept. 1

1818 A977 25cr multi .25 .25

National Week.

Portrait — A978

1982, Oct. 4

1819 A978 85cr multicolored .75 .40

St. Theresa of Avila (1515-1582).

A979

1982, Oct. 15 Litho. *Perf. 11½x11*

1820 A979 75cr Instruments	.75	.40
1821 A979 80cr Dancers	.75	.40
1822 A979 85cr Musicians	.75	.40
Nos. 1820-1822 (3)	2.25	1.20

Souvenir Sheet

Perf. 11

1822A A979 Sheet of 3, #1820-1822	4.75	4.75
b. 75cr Instruments	1.25	1.25
c. 80cr Dancers	1.25	1.25
d. 85cr Musicians	1.25	1.25

Lubrapex 82, 4th Portuguese-Brazilian Stamp Exhibition. Stamps in No. 1822A are without "LUBRAPEX 82".

Aviation Industry Day
A980

24cr, Embraer EMB-312 trainer plane.

1982, Oct. 17 *Perf. 12*

1823 A980 24cr multicolored .25 .25

Bastos Tigre, Poet, Birth Centenary, and "Saudade" Text
A981

1982, Oct. 29

1824 A981 24cr multi .25 .25

Book Day.

10th Anniv. of Brazilian Telecommunications Co. — A982

1982, Nov. 9 Litho. *Perf. 11½*

1825 A982 24cr multi .25 .25

Christmas
A983

Children's Drawings.

1982, Nov. 10

1826 A983 24cr Nativity	.75	.25
1827 A983 24cr Angels	.75	.25
1828 A983 30cr Nativity, diff.	.75	.25
1829 A983 30cr Flight into Egypt	.75	.25
Nos. 1826-1829 (4)	3.00	1.00

State Flags Type of 1981

No. 1830: a, Ceara. b, Espirito Santo. c, Paraiba. d, Grande de Norte. e, Rondonia.

1982, Nov. 19

1830 Block of 5 + label	5.50	10.00
a.-e. A947 24cr any single	1.10	.30

Thanksgiving — A985

1982, Nov. 25

1835 A985 24cr multi .25 .25

Homage to the Deaf — A986

1982, Dec. 1

1836 A986 24cr multi .25 .25

Naval Academy Bicentenary
A987

Training Ships: No. 1837, Brazil. No. 1838, Benjamin Constant. No. 1839, Almirante Saldanha.

1982, Dec. 14

1837 A987 24cr multi	.40	.25
1838 A987 24cr multi	.40	.25
1839 A987 24cr multi	.40	.25
Nos. 1837-1839 (3)	1.20	.75

Souvenir Sheet

No. 12 — A988

1982, Dec. 18 Litho. *Perf. 11*

1840 A988 200cr multi 3.75 3.75

BRASILIANA '83 Intl. Stamp Exhibition, Rio de Janeiro, July 29-Aug. 7.

Brasiliana '83 Carnival
A989

24cr, Samba drummers. 130cr, Street parade. 140cr, Dancer. 150cr, Male dancer.

1983, Feb. 9 Litho. *Perf. 11½*

1841	A989	24cr multi	.65	.25
1842	A989	130cr multi	2.50	.80
1843	A989	140cr multi	2.50	.80
1844	A989	150cr multi	2.50	.80
		Nos. 1841-1844 (4)	8.15	2.65

Antarctic Expedition
A990

150cr, Support ship Barano de Teffe.

1983, Feb. 20 Litho. *Perf. 11½*

1845 A990 150cr multi 1.10 .55

50th Anniv. of Women's Rights — A991

1983, Mar. 8

1846 A991 130cr multi .90 .55

Itaipu Hydroelectric Power Station Opening — A992

1983, Mar. Litho. *Perf. 12*

1847 A992 140cr multi .90 .50

Cancer Prevention
A993

Designs: 30cr, Microscope. 38cr, Antonio Prudente, Paulista Cancer Assoc. founder, Camargo Hospital.

1983, Apr. 18

1848	A993	30cr multi	.85	.50
1849	A993	38cr multi	.85	.50
a.		Pair, #1848-1849	1.75	1.25

Martin Luther (1483-1546)
A994

1983, Apr. 18

1850 A994 150cr pale grn & blk 1.25 .50

Agricultural Research
A995

No. 1851, Chestnut tree. No. 1852, Genetic research. No. 1853, Tropical soy beans.

1983, Apr. 26 Litho. *Perf. 11½*

1851	A995	30cr multi	.30	.25
1852	A995	30cr multi	.30	.25
1853	A995	38cr multi	.30	.25
		Nos. 1851-1853 (3)	.90	.75

Father Rogerio Neuhaus (1863-1934), Centenary of Ordination — A996

1983, May 3 *Perf. 11½x11*

1854 A996 30cr multi .30 .25

30th Anniv. of Customs Cooperation Council — A997

1983, May 5 *Perf. 11x11½*

1855 A997 30cr multi .30 .25

World Communications Year — A998

1983, May 17 Litho. *Perf. 11½*

1856 A998 250cr multi 2.50 .75

Toucans
A999

30cr, Tucanucu. 185cr, White-breasted. 205cr, Green-beaked. 215cr, Black-beaked.

1983, May 21

1857	A999	30cr multicolored	.85	.40
1858	A999	185cr multicolored	3.25	.65
1859	A999	205cr multicolored	3.25	.65
1860	A999	215cr multicolored	3.25	.65
		Nos. 1857-1860 (4)	10.60	2.35

Souvenir Sheet

Resurrection, by Raphael (1483-1517) — A1000

1983, May 25 *Perf. 11*

1861 A1000 250cr multi 3.75 3.75

Hohenzollern 980 Locomotive, 1875 — A1001

Various locomotives: No. 1863, Baldwin #1, 1881. No. 1864, Fowler #1, 1872.

1983, June 12 Litho. *Perf. 11½*

1862	A1001	30cr shown	.65	.30
1863	A1001	30cr multicolored	.65	.30
1864	A1001	38cr multicolored	.65	.30
		Nos. 1862-1864 (3)	1.95	.90

9th Women's Basketball World Championship
A1002

1983, July 24 Litho. *Perf. 11½x11*

1865	A1002	30cr Players, front view	.40	.25
1866	A1002	30cr Players, rear view	.40	.25

Simon Bolivar (1783-1830) — A1003

1983, July 24 *Perf. 12*

1867 A1003 30cr multi .25 .25

Children's Polio and Measles Vaccination Campaign — A1004

1983, July 25

1868	A1004	30cr Girl, measles	.25	.25
1869	A1004	30cr Boy, polio	.25	.25

Goddess Minerva, Computer Tape — A1005

1983, July 28 *Perf. 11½x11*

1870 A1005 30cr multicolored .25 .25

20th Anniv. of Master's program in engineering.

A1006

Guanabara Bay.

1983, July 29 Engr.

1871	A1006	185cr No. 1	1.10	.55
1872	A1006	205cr No. 2	1.25	.55
1873	A1006	215cr No. 3	1.60	.55
		Nos. 1871-1873 (3)	3.95	1.65

Souvenir Sheet

Perf. 11

1874	Sheet of 3	9.00	9.00
a.	A1006 185cr No. 1	2.75	2.75
b.	A1006 205cr No. 2	2.75	2.75
c.	A1006 215cr No. 3	2.75	2.75

BRASILIANA '83 Intl. Stamp Show, Rio de Janeiro, July 29-Aug. 7.

Stamps in No. 1874 have unframed denomination at bottom of the stamps. The background scene is enlarged to cover all 3 stamps in a continuous design.

Souvenir Sheets

A set of five 2000cr souvenir sheets also exist for BRASILIANA '83. These picture early flying attempts, Ademar Ferreira da Silva, Olympic gold medal winner, Soccer, Formula 1 auto racing, and Gold medal winners in Olympic sailing. Value $30 each.

Souvenir Sheet

The First Mass in Brazil, by Vitor Meireles (1833-1903) — A1007

1983, Aug. 18 *Perf. 11*

1875 A1007 250cr multi 3.75 3.75

EMB-120 Brasilia Passenger Plane
A1008

1983, Aug. 19 *Perf. 12*

1876 A1008 30cr multi .35 .30

Vision of Don Bosco Centenary
A1009

1983, Aug. 30
1877 A1009 130cr multi .65 .30

Independence Week — A1010

1983, Sept. 1 Litho. *Perf. 11½*
1878 A1010 50cr multi .30 .25

National Steel Corp., 10th Anniv.
A1011

1983, Sept. 17 Litho. *Perf. 11½*
1879 A1011 45cr multi .30 .25

Cactus
A1012

No. 1880, Pilosocereus gounellei. No. 1881, Melocactus bahiensis. No. 1882, Cereus jamacaru.

1983, Sept. 12 Litho. *Perf. 11½*
1880 A1012 45cr multicolored .50 .25
1881 A1012 45cr multicolored .50 .25
1882 A1012 57cr multicolored .65 .25
Nos. 1880-1882 (3) 1.65 .75

50th Anniv. of the 1st National Eucharistic Congress
A1013

1983, Oct. 12 Litho. *Perf. 11½*
1883 A1013 45cr multi .25 .25

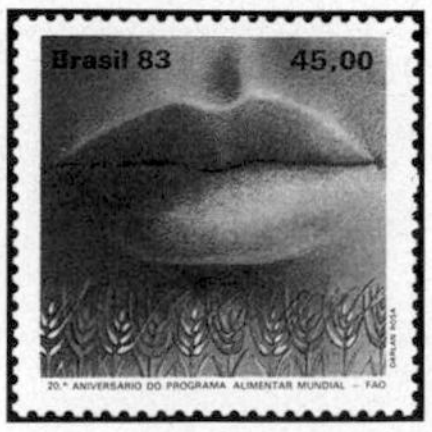

World Food Program
A1014

1983, Oct. 14 Litho. *Perf. 11½*
1884 A1014 45cr Mouth, grain .25 .25
1885 A1014 57cr Fish, sailboat .25 .25

Souvenir Sheet

Louis Breguet, Death Centenary — A1015

376cr, Telegraph transmitter.

1983, Oct. 27 Litho. *Perf. 11*
1886 A1015 376cr multi 7.50 7.50

Christmas 1983
A1016

17th-18th Cent. Statues: 45cr, Our Lady of the Angels. 315cr, Our Lady of the Parturition. 335cr, Our Lady of Joy. 345cr, Our Lady of the Presentation.

1983, Nov. 10 Litho. *Perf. 11½*
1887 A1016 45cr multi .40 .30
1888 A1016 315cr multi 2.00 .75
1889 A1016 335cr multi 2.00 .75
1890 A1016 345cr multi 2.00 .75
Nos. 1887-1890 (4) 6.40 2.55

Marshal Mascarenhas Birth Centenary — A1017

1983, Nov. 13 Litho. *Perf. 11½*
1891 A1017 45cr Battle sites .30 .25

Commander of Brazilian Expeditionary Force in Italy.

State Flags Type of 1981

No. 1892: a, Amazonas. b, Goias. c, Rio. d, Mato Grosso Do Sol. e, Parana.

1983, Nov. 17 Litho. *Perf. 11½*
1892 Block of 5 + label 6.00 12.00
a.-e. A947 45cr any single 1.00 .40

Thanksgiving — A1018

1983, Nov. 24 Litho. *Perf. 12*
1896 A1018 45cr Madonna, wheat .30 .30

Manned Flight Bicentenary
A1019

345cr, Montgolfiere balloon, 1783.

1983, Dec. 15 Litho. *Perf. 12*
1897 A1019 345cr multi 2.75 1.25

Ethnic Groups
A1020

1984, Jan. 20 Litho. *Perf. 12*
1898 A1020 45cr multi .25 .25

50th anniv. of publication of Masters and Slaves, sociological study by Gilberto Freyre.

Centenary of Crystal Palace, Petropolis
A1021

1984, Feb. 2
1899 A1021 45cr multi .25 .25

Souvenir Sheet

Flags (Sculpture with 40 Figures), by Victor Brecheret (b. 1894) — A1022

1984, Feb. 22 Litho. *Perf. 11*
1900 A1022 805cr multi 2.75 2.75

Naval Museum Centenary
A1023

620cr, Figurehead, frigate, 1847.

1984, Mar. 23 Litho. *Perf. 11½*
1901 A1023 620cr multi .90 .25

Slavery Abolition Centenary
A1024

585cr, Broken chain, raft. 610cr, Freed slave.

1984, Mar. 25
1902 A1024 585cr multi .75 .30
1903 A1024 610cr multi .75 .30

Souvenir Sheet

Visit of King Carl XVI Gustaf of Sweden — A1025

1984, Apr. 2 *Perf. 11*
1904 A1025 2105cr multi 6.00 6.00

1984 Summer Olympics
A1026

No. 1905, Long jump. No. 1906, 100-meter race. No. 1907, Relay race. 585cr, Pole vault. 610cr, High jump. 620cr, Hurdles.

1984, Apr. 13 *Perf. 11½*
1905 A1026 65cr multi .85 .30
1906 A1026 65cr multi .85 .30
1907 A1026 65cr multi .85 .30
1908 A1026 585cr multi .85 .30
1909 A1026 610cr multi .85 .30
1910 A1026 620cr multi .85 .30
a. Block of 6, #1905-1910 5.25 5.25

Voters Casting Ballots, Symbols of Labor
A1027

Pres. Getulio Vargas Birth Centenary — Symbols of Development: No. 1912, Oil rig, blast furnace. No. 1913, High-tension towers.

1984, Apr. 19 Litho. *Perf. 11½*
1911 A1027 65cr shown .25 .25
1912 A1027 65cr multi .25 .25
1913 A1027 65cr multi .25 .25
Nos. 1911-1913 (3) .75 .75

Columbus, Espana '84 Emblem — A1028

1984, Apr. 27
1914 A1028 65cr Pedro Cabral .30 .25
1915 A1028 610cr shown .75 .30

Map of Americas, Heads — A1029

1984, May 7 Litho. *Perf. 11½*
1916 A1029 65cr multi .25 .25

Pan-American Association of Finance and Guarantees, 8th Assembly.

Lubrapex '84 — A1030

18th Century Paintings, Mariana Cathedral: 65cr, Hunting scene. 585cr, Pastoral scene. 610cr, People under umbrellas. 620cr, Elephants.

1984, May 8 *Perf. 11½x11*

1917	A1030	65cr multi	.65	.25
1918	A1030	585cr multi	1.25	.40
1919	A1030	610cr multi	1.25	.40
1920	A1030	620cr multi	1.25	.40
		Nos. 1917-1920 (4)	4.40	1.45

Souvenir Sheet

Intl. Fedn. of Soccer Associations, 80th Anniv. — A1031

1984, May 21 *Perf. 11*

1921	A1031	2115cr Globe	6.00	6.00

Exists imperforate. Value $800.

Matto Grosso Lowland Fauna A1032

1984, June 5 **Litho.** *Perf. 11½*

1922		Strip of 3	1.25	1.25
a.	A1032	65cr Deer	.40	.30
b.	A1032	65cr Jaguar	.40	.30
c.	A1032	80cr Alligator	.40	.30

First Letter Mailed in Brazil, by Guido Mondin — A1033

1984, June 8 *Perf. 12x11½*

1923	A1033	65cr multi	.25	.25

Postal Union of Americas and Spain, first anniv. of new headquarters.

Brazil-Germany Air Service, 50th Anniv. — A1034

610cr, Dornier-Wal seaplane. 620cr, Steamer Westfalen.

1984, June 19

1924		610cr multi	1.50	.40
1925		620cr multi	1.50	.40
a.	A1034	Pair, #1924-1925	3.00	.80

Woolly Spider Monkey, World Wildlife Fund Emblem — A1036

1984, July 2 *Perf. 11½*

1926	A1036	65cr Mother, baby	.35	.30
1927	A1036	80cr Monkey	.35	.30

Agriculture Type of 1980

Designs: 65cr, Rubber tree. 80cr, Brazil nuts. 120cr, Rice. 150cr, Eucalyptus. 300cr, Pinha da Parana. 800cr, Carnauba. 1000cr, Babacu. 2000cr, Sunflower.

Photogravure (65, 80, 120, 150cr), Engraved

1984-85 *Perf. 11x11½*

1934	A894	65cr lilac	.25	.25
1935	A894	80cr brn red	.55	.25
1936	A894	120cr dk sl bl	.25	.25
1937	A894	150cr green	.25	.25
1938	A894	300cr rose mag	2.75	.25
1939	A894	800cr grnsh bl	1.25	.25
1940	A894	1000cr lemon	1.25	.25
1941	A894	2000cr yel org ('85)	2.25	.30
		Nos. 1934-1941 (8)	8.00	2.05

Marajo Isld. Buffalo A1037

1984, July 9 **Litho.** *Perf. 12*

1942	A1037	Strip of 3	1.25	1.25
a.		65cr Approaching stream	.40	.30
b.		65cr Standing on bank	.40	.30
c.		80cr Drinking	.40	.30

Continuous design.

Banco Economico Sesquicentenary — A1038

1984, July 13 *Perf. 11½*

1943	A1038	65cr Bank, coins	.25	.25

Historic Railway Stations A1039

No. 1944, Japeri. No. 1945, Luz, vert. No. 1946, Sao Joao del Rei.

1984, July 23 **Litho.** *Perf. 11½*

1944	A1039	65cr multi	.25	.25
1945	A1039	65cr multi	.25	.25
1946	A1039	80cr multi	.25	.25
		Nos. 1944-1946 (3)	.75	.75

Souvenir Sheet

A1040

1984, Aug. 13 *Perf. 11*

1947	A1040	585cr Girl scout	5.50	5.50

Girl Scouts in Brazil, 65th anniv.

Couple Sheltered From Rain — A1041

1984, Aug. 21 **Litho.** *Perf. 11½*

1948	A1041	65cr multicolored	.25	.25

Housing project bank, 20th anniv.

Independence Week — A1042

Children's Drawings: No. 1949, Explorer & ship. No. 1950, Sailing ships. No. 1951, "BRASIL" mural. No. 1952, Children under rainbow.

1984, Sept. 3

1949	A1042	100cr multi	.30	.25
1950	A1042	100cr multi	.30	.25
1951	A1042	100cr multi	.30	.25
1952	A1042	100cr multi	.30	.25
		Nos. 1949-1952 (4)	1.20	1.00

Rio de Janeiro Chamber of Commerce Sesquicentenary — A1043

100cr, Monument, worker silhouette.

1984, Sept. 10

1953	A1043	100cr multi	.25	.25

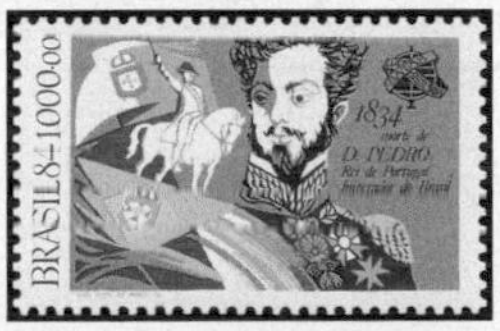

Death Sesquicentenary of Don Pedro I (IV of Portugal) — A1044

1984, Sept. 23 *Perf. 12x11½*

1954	A1044	1000cr Portrait	2.75	.75

Local Mushrooms A1045

120cr, Pycnoporus sanguineus. 1050cr, Calvatia sp. 1080cr, Pleurotus sp, horiz.

1984, Oct. 22 *Perf. 11½*

1955	A1045	120cr multi	.30	.25
1956	A1045	1050cr multi	1.90	.55
1957	A1045	1080cr multi	1.90	.55
		Nos. 1955-1957 (3)	4.10	1.35

Book Day — A1046

120cr, Girl in open book.

1984, Oct. 23 *Perf. 11½*

1958	A1046	120cr multi	.25	.25

New State Mint Opening — A1047

1984, Nov. 1

1959	A1047	120cr multi	.25	.25

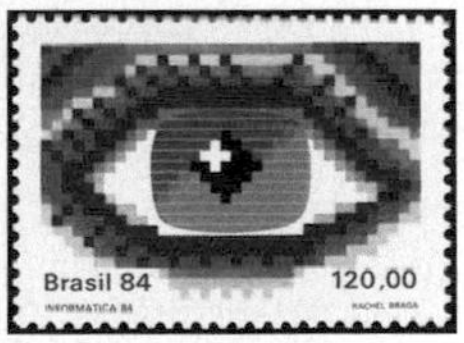

Informatics Fair & Congress A1048

120cr, Eye, computer terminal.

1984, Nov. 5 **Litho.** *Perf. 12*

1960	A1048	120cr multi	.25	.25

Org. of American States, 14th Assembly A1049

1984, Nov. 14

1961	A1049	120cr Emblem, flags	.25	.25

State Flags Type of 1981

No. 1962: a, Maranhao. b, Mato Grosso. c, Minas Gerais. d, Piaui. e, Santa Catarina.

1984, Nov. 19 *Perf. 11½*

1962		Block of 5 + label	3.25	3.25
a.-e.	A947	120cr, any single	.55	.40

Thanksgiving 1984 — A1051

120cr, Bell tower, Brasilia.

1984, Nov. 22
1963 A1051 120cr multicolored .25 .25

Christmas 1984 A1052

Paintings: No. 1964, Nativity, by Djanira. No. 1965, Virgin and Child, by Glauco Rodrigues. No. 1966, Flight into Egypt, by Paul Garfunkel. No. 1967, Nativity, by Di Cavalcanti.

1984, Dec. 3 Litho. ***Perf. 12***

1964	A1052	120cr multi	.30	.30
1965	A1052	120cr multi	.30	.30
1966	A1052	1050cr multi	1.50	.55
1967	A1052	1080cr multi	1.50	.55
		Nos. 1964-1967 (4)	3.60	1.70

40th Anniv., International Civil Aviation Organization — A1053

120cr, Aircraft, Earth globe.

1984, Dec. 7 Litho. ***Perf. 12***
1968 A1053 120cr multi .25 .25

25th Anniv., North-Eastern Development — A1054

1984, Dec. 14 Litho. ***Perf. 12***
1969 A1054 120cr Farmer, field .25 .25

Emilio Rouede A1055

Painting: Church of the Virgin of Safe Travels, by Rouede.

1985, Jan. 22 Litho. ***Perf. 12***
1970 A1055 120cr multi .25 .25

BRASILSAT — A1056

1985, Feb. 8 Litho. ***Perf. 11½x12***
1971 A1056 150cr Satellite, Brazil .25 .25

Metropolitan Railways — A1057

1985, Mar. 2 Litho. ***Perf. 11x11½***
1972 A1057 200cr Passenger trains .25 .25

Brasilia Botanical Gardens A1058

200cr, Caryocar brasiliense.

1985, Mar. 8 Litho. ***Perf. 11½x12***
1973 A1058 200cr multi .25 .25

40th Anniv., Brazilian Paratroops A1059

1985, Mar. 8 Litho. ***Perf. 11½x12***
1974 A1059 200cr Parachute drop .25 .25

Natl. Climate Awareness Program — A1060

1985, Mar. 18 Litho. ***Perf. 11½x12***
1975 A1060 500cr multi .25 .25

Pure Bred Horses A1061

No. 1976, Campolina. No. 1977, Marajoara. No. 1978, Mangalarga marchador.

1985, Mar. 19 Litho. ***Perf. 12***

1976	A1061	1000cr multi	1.10	.55
1977	A1061	1500cr multi	1.10	.55
1978	A1061	1500cr multi	1.10	.55
		Nos. 1976-1978 (3)	3.30	1.65

Ouro Preto — A1062

No. 1980, St. Miguel des Missoes. No. 1981, Olinda.

1985, Apr. 18 Litho. ***Perf. 11½x12***

1979	A1062	220cr shown	.25	.25
1980	A1062	220cr multi	.25	.25
1981	A1062	220cr multi	.25	.25
		Nos. 1979-1981 (3)	.75	.75

Polivolume, by Mary Vieira — A1063

1985, Apr. 20 Litho.
1982 A1063 220cr multi .25 .25

Rio Branco Inst., 40th anniv.

Natl. Capital, Brasilia, 25th Anniv. — A1064

No. 1983, Natl. Theater, acoustic shell. No. 1984, Catetinho Palace, JK Memorial.

1985, Apr. 22 Litho.

1983	A1064	220cr multi	.25	.25
1984	A1064	220cr multi	.25	.25

A1065

A1065a

1985-86 Photo. ***Perf. 11½***

1985	A1065	50cr lake	.25	.25
1986	A1065	100cr dp vio	.25	.25
1987	A1065	150cr violet	.25	.25
1988	A1065	200cr ultra	.25	.25
1989	A1065	220cr green	.35	*5.00*
1990	A1065	300cr royal bl	.25	.25
1991	A1065	500cr olive blk	.25	.25
1992	A1065a	1000cr brn ol ('86)	.25	.25
1993	A1065a	2000cr brt grn ('86)	.25	.25
1994	A1065a	3000cr dl vio	.25	.25
1995	A1065a	5000cr brown	1.25	.25
		Nos. 1985-1995 (11)	3.85	7.50

Marshal Rondon, 120th Birth Anniv. A1066

1985, May 5 ***Perf. 11x11½***
1996 A1066 220cr multi .25 .25

Educator, protector of the Indians, building superintendent of telegraph lines.

Candido Fontoura (1885-1974) A1067

1985, May 14 ***Perf. 12x11½***
1997 A1067 220cr multi .25 .25

Pioneer of the Brazilian pharmaceutical industry.

Brapex VI — A1068

Cave paintings: No. 1998, Deer, Cerca Grande. No. 1999, Lizards, Lapa do Caboclo. No. 2000, Running deer, Grande Abrigo de Santana do Riacho.

1985, May 18 ***Perf. 11½x11***

1998	A1068	300cr multi	.25	.25
1999	A1068	300cr multi	.25	.25
2000	A1068	2000cr multi	.65	.65
		Nos. 1998-2000 (3)	1.15	1.15

Souvenir Sheet

Perf. 10½x11

2000A	A1068	Sheet of 3, #1998-2000	3.50	3.50
b.		300cr multi	.80	.80
c.		300cr multi	.80	.80
d.		2000cr multi	.80	.80

Wildlife Conservation — A1069

Birds in Marinho dos Abrolhos National Park: No. 2001, Fregata magnificens. No. 2002, Sula dactylatra. No. 2003, Anous stolidus. No. 2004, Pluvialis squatarola.

1985, June 5 ***Perf. 11½x12***

2001	A1069	220cr multi	.30	.30
2002	A1069	220cr multi	.30	.30
2003	A1069	220cr multi	.35	.30
2004	A1069	2000cr multi	1.00	.35
		Nos. 2001-2004 (4)	1.95	1.25

A1070

UN infant survival campaign: No. 2005, Mother breastfeeding infant. No. 2006, Hand, eyedropper, children.

1985, June 11 ***Perf. 12x11½***

2005	A1070	220cr multi	.35	.35
2006	A1070	220cr multi	.35	.35
a.		Pair, #2005-2006	.70	.70

Sea Search & Rescue — A1071

1985, June 22 Litho. ***Perf. 11½x11***
2007 A1071 220cr multi .25 .25

Souvenir Sheet

World Cup Soccer, Mexico, 1986 — A1072

1985, June 23 — ***Perf. 11***
2008 A1072 2000cr multi 5.50 5.50

Intl. Youth Year — A1073

1985, June 28 — ***Perf. 12***
2009 A1073 220cr Circle of children .25 .25

11th Natl. Eucharistic Congress A1074

2000cr, Mosaic, Priest raising host.

1985, July 16 — ***Perf. 12x11½***
2010 A1074 2000cr multi .55 .30

Director Humberto Mauro, Scene from Sangue Mineiro, 1929 — A1075

1985, July 27
2011 A1075 300cr multi .25 .25

Cataguases Studios, 60th anniv.

Escola e Sacro Museum, Convent St. Anthony, Joao Pessoa, Paraiba A1076

1985, Aug. 5 — ***Perf. 11½x12***
2012 A1076 330cr multi .25 .25

Paraiba State 400th anniv.

Inconfidencia Museum A1077

No. 2014, Museum of History & Diplomacy.

1985, Aug. 11 — ***Perf. 12x11½***
2013 A1077 300cr shown .25 .25
2014 A1077 300cr multi .25 .25

Revolutionary, by Guido Mondin — A1078

1985, Aug. 14
2015 A1078 330cr multi .25 .25

Cabanagem Insurrection, 150th anniv.

AMX Subsonic Air Force Fighter Plane A1079

1985, Aug. 19 — ***Perf. 11½x12***
2016 A1079 330cr multi .25 .25

AMX Project, joint program with Italy.

16th-17th Century Military Uniforms A1080

No. 2017, Captain, crossbowman. No. 2018, Harquebusier, sergeant. No. 2019, Musketeer, pikeman. No. 2020, Fusilier, pikeman.

1985, Aug. 26 — ***Perf. 12x11½***
2017 A1080 300cr multi .25 .25
2018 A1080 300cr multi .25 .25
2019 A1080 300cr multi .25 .25
2020 A1080 300cr multi .25 .25
Nos. 2017-2020 (4) 1.00 1.00

Bento Goncalves and Insurrectionist Cavalry on Southern Battlefields, by Guido Mondin — A1081

1985, Sept. 20 — ***Perf. 11½x12***
2021 A1081 330cr multi .25 .25

Farrouphilha Insurrection, 150th anniv.

Aparados da Serra National Park A1082

3100cr, Ravine. 3320cr, Mountains. 3480cr, Forest, waterfall.

1985, Sept. 23
2022 A1082 3100cr multi 1.10 .30
2023 A1082 3320cr multi 1.10 .30
2024 A1082 3480cr multi 1.50 .45
Nos. 2022-2024 (3) 3.70 1.05

President-elect Tancredo Neves, Natl. Congress, Alvorada Palace, Supreme Court — A1083

1985, Oct. 10 Litho. — ***Perf. 11x11½***
2025 A1083 330cr multi .25 .25

FEB, Postmark A1084

1985, Oct. 10 — ***Perf. 11½x12***
2026 A1084 500cr multi .25 .25

Brazilian Expeditionary Force Postal Service, 41st anniv.

Rio de Janeiro-Niteroi Ferry Service, 150th Anniv. — A1085

1985, Oct. 14 — ***Perf. 11½x12***
2027 A1085 500cr Segunda .30 .25
2028 A1085 500cr Terceira .30 .25
2029 A1085 500cr Especuladora .30 .25
2030 A1085 500cr Urca .30 .25
Nos. 2027-2030 (4) 1.20 1.00

Muniz M-7 Inaugural Flight, 50th Anniv. — A1086

1985, Oct. 22
2031 A1086 500cr multi .25 .25

UN 40th Anniv. — A1087

1985, Oct. 24 — ***Perf. 11½x11***
2032 A1087 500cr multi .25 .25

Natl. Press System — A1088

1985, Nov. 7
2033 A1088 500cr multi .25 .25

Diario de Pernambuco, newspaper, 160th anniv.

Christmas 1985 A1089

No. 2034, Christ in Manger. No. 2035, Adoration of the Magi. No. 2036, Flight to Egypt.

1985, Nov. 11 — ***Perf. 11½x12***
2034 A1089 500cr multi .30 .25
2035 A1089 500cr multi .30 .25
2036 A1089 500cr multi .30 .25
Nos. 2034-2036 (3) .90 .75

State Flags Type of 1981

No. 2037: a, Para. b, Rio Grande do Sul. c, Acre. d, Sao Paulo.

1985, Nov. 19 — ***Perf. 12***
2037 Block of 4 2.25 *4.00*
a.-d. A947 500cr, any single .55 .30

Thanksgiving Day — A1091

500cr, Child gathering wheat.

1985, Nov. 28 — ***Perf. 12x11½***
2038 A1091 500cr multi .25 .25

Economic Development of Serra dos Carajas Region — A1092

1985, Dec. 11 Litho. — ***Perf. 11½x12***
2039 A1092 500cr multi .25 .25

Fr. Bartholomeu Lourenco de Gusmao (1685-1724), Inventor, the Aerostat — A1093

1985, Dec. 19 Litho. — ***Perf. 11x11½***
2040 A1093 500cr multi .25 .25

A1094

The Trees, by Da Costa E Silva (b. 1885), poet.

1985, Dec. 20 Litho. ***Perf. 12x11½***

2041 A1094 500cr multi .25 .25

Values for used commemoratives issued after 1985 and for used souvenir sheets are for favor-canceled examples. Postally used examples are worth more.

Souvenir Sheet

A1095

1986, Mar. 3 Litho. ***Perf. 11***

2042 A1095 10000cr multi 6.00 6.00

1986 World Cup Soccer Championships, Mexico. LUBRAPEX '86, philatelic exhibition.

Halley's Comet — A1096

1986, Apr. 11 Litho. ***Perf. 11½x12***

2043 A1096 50c multi .25 .25

Commander Ferraz Antarctic Station, 2nd Anniv. — A1097

1986, Apr. 25

2044 A1097 50c multi .30 .25

Labor Day — A1098

1986, May 1 Litho. ***Perf. 12x11½***

2045 A1098 50c multi .25 .25

Maternity, by Henrique Bernardelli (1858-1936) A1099

1986, May 8

2046 A1099 50c multi .25 .25

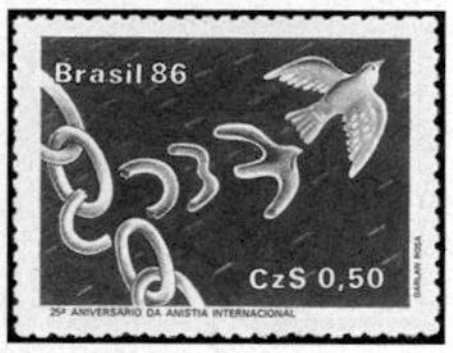

Amnesty Intl., 25th Anniv. A1100

1986, May 28 Litho. ***Perf. 11½x12***

2047 A1100 50c multi .25 .25

Butterflies A1101

No. 2048, Pyrrhopyge ruficauda. No. 2049, Prepona eugenes diluta. No. 2050, Pierriballia mandel molione.

1986, June 5 ***Perf. 12x11½***

2048	A1101	50c multi	.40	.25
2049	A1101	50c multi	.40	.25
2050	A1101	50c multi	.40	.25
		Nos. 2048-2050 (3)	1.20	.75

Score from Opera "Il Guarani" and Antonio Carlos Gomes (1836-1896), Composer — A1102

1986, July 11 ***Perf. 11½x12***

2051 A1102 50c multi .25 .25

Natl. Accident Prevention Campaign — A1103

1986, July 30 Litho. ***Perf. 11½x11***

2052 A1103 50c Lineman .25 .25

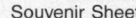

Souvenir Sheet

Stamp Day — A1104

1986, Aug. 1 ***Perf. 11***

2053 A1104 5cz No. 53 2.00 2.00

Brazilian Phil. Soc., 75th anniv., and Dom Pedro II issue, Nos. 53-60, 120th anniv.

Architecture A1105

Designs: 10c, House of Garcia D'Avila, Nazare de Mata, Bahia. 20c, Church of Our Lady of the Assumption, Anchieta Village. 50c, Fort Reis Magos, Natal. 1cz, Pilgrim's Column, Alcantara Village, 1648. 2cz, Cloisters, St. Francis Convent, Olinda. 5cz, St. Anthony's Chapel, Sao Roque. 10cz, St. Lawrence of the Indians Church, Niteroi. 20cz, Principe da Beiro Fort, Mato Dentro. 50cz, Jesus of Matozinhos Church, vert. 100cz, Church of our Lady of Sorrow, Campanha. 200cz, Casa dos Contos, Ouro Preto. 500cz, Antiga Alfandega, Belem, Para.

Perf. 11x10½, 10½x11

1986-88 **Photo.**

2055	A1105	10c sage grn	.25	.25
2057	A1105	20c brt blue	.25	.25
2059	A1105	50c orange	.25	.25
a.		Litho., perf. 13 ('88)	5.50	.30
2064	A1105	1cz golden brn	.25	.25
a.		Litho., perf. 11½x11 ('88)	4.50	.30
2065	A1105	2cz dull rose	.25	.25
a.		Litho., perf. 13 ('88)	.75	.25
b.		Litho., perf. 11½x11 ('88)	1.90	.25
2067	A1105	5cz lt olive grn	.25	.25
a.		Litho., perf. 13 ('88)	2.25	.25
b.		Litho., perf. 11½x11 ('88)	6.00	.25
2068	A1105	10cz slate blue	.25	.25
a.		Litho., perf. 13 ('88)	3.75	.40
b.		Litho., perf. 11½x11 ('88)	4.50	.40
2069	A1105	20cz lt red brn	.25	.25
2070	A1105	50cz brn org	.25	.25
2071	A1105	100cz dull grn	.25	.25
2072	A1105	200cz deep blue	.25	.25
2073	A1105	500cz dull red brn	.25	.25
		Nos. 2055-2073 (12)	3.00	3.00

Nos. 2065-2070 exist in multiple shades.

Issued: 10c, 8/11; 20c, 12/8; 50c, 8/19; 1cz, 11/19; 2cz, 11/9; 5cz, 12/30; 10cz, 6/2/87; 20cz, 50cz, 9/18/87; 100cz, 12/21/87; 200cz, 5/9/88; 500cz, 11/22/88.

A1106

Famous Men — A1106a

Designs: No. 2074, Juscelino Kubitschek de Oliveira, president 1956-61, and Alvorado Palace, Brasilia. No. 2075, Octavio Mangabeira, statesman, and Itamaraty Palace, Rio de Janeiro, horiz.

1986 ***Perf. 12x11½, 11½x12***

2074	A1106	50c multi	.25	.25
2075	A1106a	50c multi	.25	.25

Issued: No. 2074, Aug. 21; No. 2075, Aug. 27.

World Gastroenterology Congress, Sao Paulo — A1107

1986, Sept. 7 ***Perf. 11½x12***

2076 A1107 50c multi .25 .25

Federal Broadcasting System, 50th Anniv. — A1108

1986, Sept. 15 ***Perf. 12x11½***

2077 A1108 50c multi .25 .25

Intl. Peace Year — A1109

Painting (detail): War and Peace, by Candido Portinari.

1986, Sept. 16

2078 A1109 50c multi .25 .25

Ernesto Simoes Filho (b. 1886), Publisher of A Tarde A1110

1986, Oct. 4 Litho. ***Perf. 11½x12***

2079 A1110 50c multi .25 .25

Famous Men — A1111

Designs: No. 2080, Title page from manuscript, c. 1683-94, by Gregorio Mattos e Guerra (b. 1636), author. No. 2081, Manuel Bandeira (1886-1968), poet, text from I'll Go Back to Pasargada.

1986, Oct. 29 *Perf. 11½x11*

2080 A1111 50c lake & beige .25 .25
2081 A1111 50c lake & dl grn .25 .25

Federal Savings Bank, 125th Anniv. — A1112

1986, Nov. 4 *Perf. 12x11½*

2082 A1112 50c multi .25 .25

Flowering Plants — A1113

50c, Urera mitis. 6.50cz, Couroupita guyanensis. 6.90cz, Bauhinia variegata, horiz.

Perf. 12x11½, 11½x12

1986, Sept. 23

2083 A1113 50c multi .25 .25
2084 A1113 6.50cz multi .55 .30
2085 A1113 6.90cz multi .65 .30
Nos. 2083-2085 (3) 1.45 .85

Glauber Rocha, Film Industry Pioneer — A1114

1986, Nov. 20 *Perf. 12x11½*

2086 A1114 50c multi .25 .25

LUBRAPEX '86 — A1115

Cordel Folk Tales: No. 2087, Romance of the Mysterious Peacock. No. 2088, History of the Empress Porcina.

1986, Nov. 21 *Perf. 11x12*

2087 A1115 6.90cz multi .55 .25
2088 A1115 6.90cz multi .55 .25

Souvenir Sheet

Perf. 11

2088A A1115 Sheet of 2, #2087-2088 2.75 2.75
b. 6.90cz multi 1.00 1.00
c. 6.90cz multi 1.00 1.00

Christmas A1116

Birds: 50c, And Christ child. 6.50cz, And tree. 7.30cz, Eating fruit.

1986, Nov. 10 *Perf. 11½x12*

2089 A1116 50c multi .30 .25
2090 A1116 6.50cz multi .55 .30
2091 A1116 7.30cz multi .65 .30
Nos. 2089-2091 (3) 1.50 .85

Military Uniforms, c. 1930 — A1117

Designs: No. 2092, Navy lieutenant commander, dreadnought Minas Gerais. No. 2093, Army flight lieutenant, WACO S.C.O. biplane, Fortaleza Airport.

1986, Dec. 15 *Perf. 12x11½*

2092 A1117 50c multi .25 .25
2093 A1117 50c multi .25 .25

Fortaleza Air Base, 50th anniv. (No. 2093).

Bartolomeu de Gusmao Airport, 50th Anniv. — A1118

1986, Dec. 26

2094 A1118 1cz multi .30 .25

Heitor Villa Lobos (1887-1959), Conductor A1119

1987, Mar. 5 Litho. *Perf. 12x11½*

2095 A1119 1.50cz multi .25 .25

A1120

Design: Natl. Air Force C-130 transport plane, flag, the Antarctic.

1987, Mar. 9 *Perf. 11x11½*

2096 A1120 1cz multi .30 .25

Antarctic Project.

Special Mail Services A1121

1987, Mar. 20 *Perf. 12x11½*

2097 A1121 1cz Rural delivery .25 .25
2098 A1121 1cz Intl. express .25 .25

TELECOM '87, Geneva A1122

2cz, Brasilsat, wave, globe.

1987, May 5 *Perf. 11½x12*

2099 A1122 2cz multi .25 .25

10th Pan American Games, Indianapolis, Aug. 7-25 — A1123

1987, May 20 *Perf. 12x11½*

2100 A1123 18cz multi .25 .25

Natl. Fine Arts Museum, 150th Anniv A1124

1987, Jan. 13 *Perf. 11½x12*

2101 A1124 1cz multi .25 .25

Marine Conservation — A1125

No. 2102, Eubalaena australis. No. 2103, Eretmochelys imbricata.

1987, June 5

2102 A1125 2cz multi .30 .25
2103 A1125 2cz multi .30 .25

Federal Court of Appeal, 40th Anniv. A1126

1987, June 15

2104 A1126 2cz multi .25 .25

Military Club, Cent. — A1127

1987, June 26 *Perf. 12x11½*

2105 A1127 3cz multi .25 .25

Agriculture Institute of Campinas, Cent. A1128

1987, June 27 *Perf. 11½x12*

2106 A1128 2cz multi .25 .25

Entomological Society, 50th Anniv. — A1129

1987, July 17

2107 A1129 3cz Zoolea lopiceps .25 .25
2108 A1129 3cz Fulgora servillei .25 .25

Natl. Tourism Year A1130

Designs: No. 2109, Monuments and Sugarloaf Mountain, Rio de Janeiro. No. 2110, Colonial church, sailboats, parrot, cashews.

1987, Aug. 4

2109 A1130 3cz multicolored .25 .25
2110 A1130 3cz multicolored .25 .25

Royal Portuguese Cabinet of Literature, 150th Anniv. — A1131

1987, Aug. 27 *Perf. 12x11½*

2111 A1131 30cz ver & brt grn .50 .40

Sport Club Intl. — A1132

Championship soccer clubs, Brazil's Gold Cup: b, Sao Paulo. c, Guarani. d, Regatas do Flamengo.

1987, Aug. 29 *Perf. 11½x12*

2112 A1132 Block of 4 1.10 2.00
a.-d. 3cz any single .25 .25

St. Francis Convent, 400th Anniv. A1133

1987, Oct. 4
2113 A1133 4cz multi .25 .25

Jose Americo de Almeida, Author A1134

Design: Characters from romance novel, "A Bagaceira," 1928, and portrait of author.

1987, Oct. 23 Litho. ***Perf. 11x11½***
2114 A1134 4cz multi .25 .25

Spanish Galleons Anchored in Recife Port, 1537 A1135

1987, Nov. 12 Litho. ***Perf. 11½x12***
2115 A1135 5cz Harbor entrance .25 .25

Recife City, 450th anniv.

Thanksgiving A1136

1987, Nov. 26 ***Perf. 12x11½***
2116 A1136 5cz multi .25 .25

Christmas 1987 A1137

No. 2117, Shepherd and flock. No. 2118, Christmas pageant. No. 2119, Six angels.

1987, Nov. 30 ***Perf. 11½x12***
2117 A1137 6cz multi .25 .25
2118 A1137 6cz multi .25 .25
2119 A1137 6cz multi .25 .25
Nos. 2117-2119 (3) .75 .75

Pedro II College, 150th Anniv. — A1138

Gold pen Emperor Pedro II used to sign edict establishing the school, and Senator Bernardo Pereira de Vasconcellos, founder.

1987, Dec. 2
2120 A1138 6cz multi .25 .25

Natl. Orchid Growers' Soc., 50th Anniv. A1139

No. 2121, Laelia lobata veitch. No. 2122, Cattleya guttata lindley.

1987, Dec. 3
2121 A1139 6cz multi .30 .25
2122 A1139 6cz multi .30 .25

Marian Year — A1140

Statue of Our Lady and Basilica at Fatima, Portugal.

1987, Dec. 20 ***Perf. 12x11½***
2123 A1140 50cz multi .45 .25

Exhibit of the Statue of Our Lady of Fatima in Brazil.

Descriptive Treatise of Brazil, by Gabriel S. de Sousa, 400th Anniv. — A1141

1987, Dec. 21 Litho. ***Perf. 11x11½***
2124 A1141 7cz multi .25 .25

Natl. Archives, 150th Anniv. A1142

Design: Text from illuminated Gregorian canticle and computer terminal.

1988, Jan. 5 ***Perf. 11½x12***
2125 A1142 7cz multi .25 .25

Opening of Brazilian Ports to Ships of Friendly Nations, 180th Anniv. A1143

1988, Jan. 28 ***Perf. 11x11½***
2126 A1143 7cz multi .25 .25

Souvenir Sheet

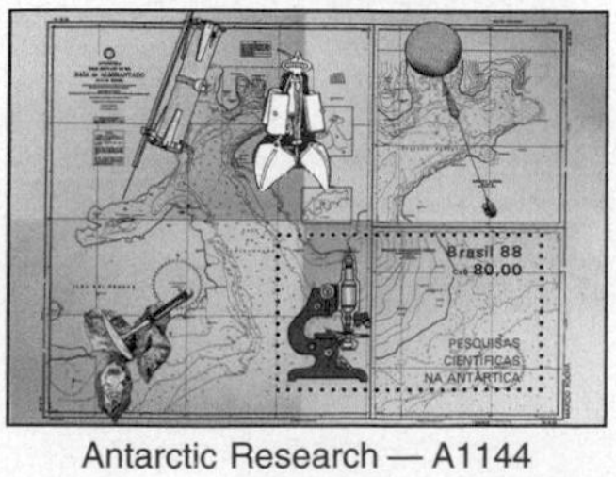

Antarctic Research — A1144

1988, Feb. 9 Litho. ***Perf. 11***
2127 A1144 80cz multi 1.10 1.10

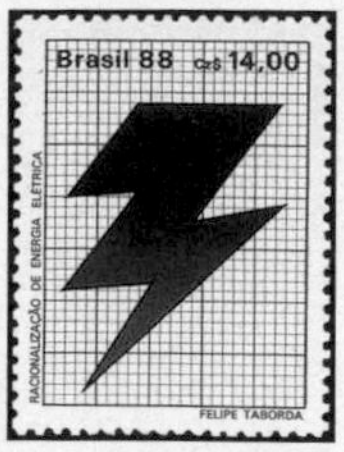

Energy Resources A1145

1988, Mar. 15 Litho. ***Perf. 12x11½***
2128 A1145 14cz Electricity .25 .25
2129 A1145 14cz Fossil fuels .25 .25

Souvenir Sheet

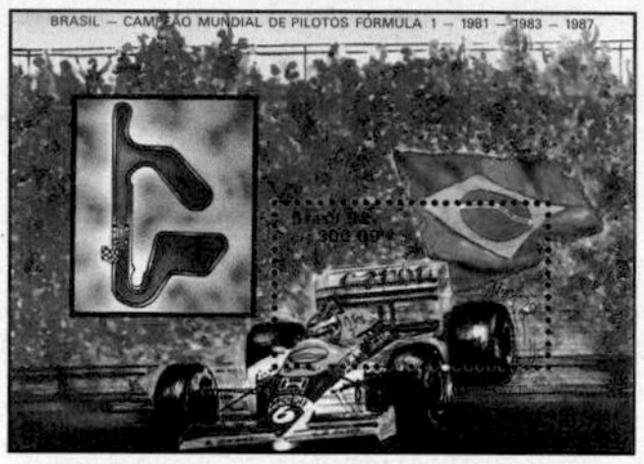

Brazilians as Formula 1 World Champions in 1981, 1983, 1987 — A1146

1988, Mar. 30 ***Perf. 11***
2130 A1146 300cz multi 3.75 3.75

Jose Bonifacio, Armorial and Masonic Emblems A1147

1988, Apr. 6 ***Perf. 12x11½***
2131 A1147 20cz multi .25 .25

Jose Bonifacio de Andrada e Silva (c. 1763-1838), geologist and prime minister under Pedro I who supported the movement for independence from Portugal and was exiled for opposing the emperor's advisors.

Abolition of Slavery, Cent. — A1148

Designs: 20cz, Declaration and quill pen. 50cz, Slave ship and maps of African coastline and slave trade route between Africa and South America.

1988, May 12 Litho. ***Perf. 12x11½***
2132 A1148 20cz multi .25 .25
2133 A1148 50cz multi .25 .25

Telecom '88 — A1149

1988, May 16 ***Perf. 11½x11***
2134 A1149 50cz multi .25 .25

Jesus of Matosinhos Sanctuary A1150

50cz, Pilot plan of Brazilia. 100cz, Salvador historic district.

1988, May 16 ***Perf. 11½x12***
2135 A1150 20cz shown .25 .25
2136 A1150 50cz multi .25 .25
2137 A1150 100cz multi .25 .25
Nos. 2135-2137 (3) .75 .75

LUBRAPEX '88. World heritage list.

Japanese Immigrants in Brazil, 80th Anniv. — A1151

1988, June 18 Litho. ***Perf. 11½x11***
2138 A1151 100cz multi .35 .25

A1152

1988, July 1 Photo. ***Perf. 13***
2139 A1152 (A) brt blue 1.50 .25
a. Perf 11x11½ 1.50 .25

No. 2139 met the first class domestic letter postage rate (28cz).
See Nos. 2201, 2218.

Judo — A1153

1988, July 14 Litho. ***Perf. 12x11½***
2140 A1153 20cz multi .35 .25

1988 Summer Olympics, Seoul.

Wildlife Conservation — A1154

20cz, Myrmecophaga tridactyla. 50cz, Chaetomys subspinosus. 100cz, Speothos venaticus.

1988, July 24 ***Perf. 11½x12***
2141 A1154 20cz multi .30 .25
2142 A1154 50cz multi .30 .25
2143 A1154 100cz multi .45 .25
Nos. 2141-2143 (3) 1.05 .75

Souvenir Sheet

The Mothorland, 1919 by Pedro Bruno — A1155

1988, Aug. 1 Litho. *Perf. 11*
2144 A1155 250cz multi 3.75 3.75

Stamp Day, BRASILIANA '89.

Natl. Confederation of Industries, 50th Anniv. — A1156

1988, Aug. 12 *Perf. 11½x12*
2145 A1156 50cz multi .25 .25

Soccer Clubs A1157

No. 2146, Recife, Pernambuco. No. 2147, Coritiba, Parana. 100cz, Gremio, Porto Alegre, Rio Grande do Sul. 200cz, Fluminense, Rio de Janeiro.

1988, Sept. 29 *Perf. 11½x12*
2146 A1157 50cz multi .35 .35
2147 A1157 50cz multi .35 .35
2148 A1157 100cz multi .35 .35
2149 A1157 200cz multi .35 .35
a. Block of 4, #2146-2149 1.50 3.00

Poems, 1888 A1158

Portraits and text: 50cz, *O Ateneu,* by Raul Pompeia. 100cz, *Poesias,* by Olavo Bilac.

1988, Oct. 28 *Perf. 11x11½*
2150 A1158 50cz multi .25 .25
2151 A1158 100cz multi .25 .25

Souvenir Sheet

1988 Democratic Constitution for the Union of the People and the State — A1159

550cz, Government building.

1988, Oct. 5 Litho. *Perf. 11*
2152 A1159 550cz multi 2.25 2.25

Origami Art A1160

50cz, Abbey, nuns. 100cz, Nativity. 200cz, Santa Claus, presents.

1988, Nov. 11 Litho. *Perf. 11½x12*
2153 A1160 50cz multi .25 .25
2154 A1160 100cz multi .25 .25
2155 A1160 200cz multi .30 .30
Nos. 2153-2155 (3) .80 .80

Christmas.

ARBRAFEX Philatelic Exhibition of Argentina and Brazil — A1161

1988, Nov. 26
2156 A1161 400cz multi 1.50 .75

Fresh-water Fish — A1162

Designs: a, Gasteropelecus. b, Osteoglossum ferreirai. c, Moenkhausia. d, Xavantei. e, Ancistrus hoplogenys. f, Brochis splendens.
Se-tenant in a continuous design.

1988, Nov. 29 Litho. *Perf. 11½x12*
2157 Block of 6 1.25 2.50
a.-f. A1162 55cz any single .25 .25

Souvenir Sheet

BRAPEX '88, Ecological Preservation — A1163

1988, Dec. 10 *Perf. 11*
2158 A1163 Sheet of 3 4.00 4.00
a. 100cz Parrot .50 .50
b. 250cz Plant 1.25 1.25
c. 400cz Egret 2.00 2.00

Satellite Dishes — A1164

1988, Dec. 20 *Perf. 12x11½*
2159 A1164 70cz multi .25 .25

Ansat 10, Earth satellite station communication.

Performing Arts — A1165

1988, Dec. 21
2160 A1165 70cz multi .25 .25

Court of Justice, Bahia, 380th Anniv. A1166

1989, Mar. 10 Litho. *Perf. 11½x12*
2161 A1166 25c multi .25 .25

Public Library Year A1167

25c, Library, Bahia, 1811.

1989, Mar. 13 *Perf. 11½*
2162 A1167 25c multi .25 .25

Brazilian Post & Telegraph Enterprise, 20th Anniv. A1168

No. 2163 — Intl. and domestic postal services: a, Facsimile transmission (Post Grama). b, Express mail (EMS). c, Parcel post (Sedex). d, Postal savings (CEFPostal).

1989, Mar. 20 *Perf. 11½x12*
2163 Block of 4 .85 1.60
a.-d. A1168 25c any single .25 .25

Souvenir Sheet

Ayrton Senna, 1988 Formula 1 World Champion — A1169

1989, Mar. 23
2164 A1169 2cz multi 12.00 12.00

Environmental Conservation A1170

1989, Apr. 6 Litho. *Perf. 12x11½*
2165 A1170 25c multi .25 .25

Mineira Inconfidencia Independence Movement, Bicent. — A1171

Designs: a, Pyramid, hand. b, Figure of a man, houses. c, Destruction of houses.

1989, Apr. 21 *Perf. 11½x12*
2166 A1171 Strip of 3 .65 .50
a.-b. 30c any single .25 .25
c. 40c multi .25 .25

First rebellion against Portuguese dominion.

Military School, Rio de Janeiro, Cent. A1172

1989, May 6 Litho. *Perf. 11½x12*
2167 A1172 50c multi .25 .25

Flowering Plants A1173

Designs: 50c, Pavonia alnifolia. 1cz, Worsleya rayneri. 1.50cz, Heliconia farinosa.

1989, June 5 *Perf. 11½x12, 12x11½*
2168 A1173 50c multi .30 .25
2169 A1173 1cz multi .40 .25
2170 A1173 1.50cz multi .50 .25
Nos. 2168-2170 (3) 1.20 .75

Nos. 2169-2170 vert.

Barreto and Recife Law School, Pedro II Square A1174

1989, June 7 *Perf. 11x11½*
2171 A1174 50c multi .25 .25

Tobias Barreto (b. 1839), advocate of Germanization of Brazil.

Cultura Broadcasting System, 20th Anniv. — A1175

1989, June 27 Litho. *Perf. 11½x12*
2172 A1175 50c multi .25 .25

Aviation
A1176

50c, Ultra-light aircraft. 1.50cz, Eiffel Tower, Demoiselle.

1989, July 7

2173	A1176	50c multi	.35	.25
2174	A1176	1.50cz multi	.35	.25

Flight of Santos-Dumont's *Demoiselle,* 80th anniv (1.50cz).

Indigenous
Flora — A1177

Designs: 10c, Dichorisandra, vert. 20c, Quiabentia zehnteri. 50c, Bougainvillea glabra. 1cz, Impatiens specie. 2cz, Chorisia crispiflora. 5cz, Hibiscus trilineatus.

1989 Photo. ***Perf. 11x11½, 11½x11***

2176	A1177	10c multi	.25	.25
2177	A1177	20c multi	.25	.25
2178	A1177	50c multi	.25	.25
2179	A1177	1cz multi	.25	.25
2180	A1177	2cz multi	.25	.25
2181	A1177	5cz multi	.25	.25
		Nos. 2176-2181 (6)	1.50	1.50

Issued: 10c, July 4; 20c, June 21; 50c, June 26; 1cz, June 19; 2cz, 5cz, Dec. 4.
No. 2181 vert.
See Nos. 2259-2273.

Souvenir Sheet

Largo da Carioca, by Nicolas Antoine Taunay — A1179

1989, July 7 Litho. ***Perf. 11***

2197	A1179	3cz multi	3.25	3.25

PHILEXFRANCE '89, French revolution bicent.
Exists imperforate. Value $550.

Cut and Uncut
Gemstones
A1180

1989, July 12 Litho. ***Perf. 12x11½***

2198	A1180	50c Tourmaline	.30	.25
2199	A1180	1.50cz Amethyst	.30	.25

Souvenir Sheet

Paco Imperial, Rio de Janeiro, and Map — A1181

1989, July 28 ***Perf. 11***

2200	A1181	5cz multi	5.00	5.00

BRASILANA '89.

Type of 1988 Redrawn

1989, July 26 Photo. ***Perf. 13***

2201	A1152 (A)	org & brt blue	1.25	.25
		Complete booklet, strip of 10 #2201	12.50	

Size of type and postal emblem are smaller on No. 2201; "1e PORTE" is at lower left.
No. 2201 met the first class domestic letter postage rate (cz).

Pernambuco Commercial Assoc., 150th Anniv. — A1182

1989, Aug. 1 Litho. ***Perf. 11½x12***

2202	A1182	50c multi	.25	.25

Photography, 150th Anniv. — A1183

1989, Aug. 14

2203	A1183	1.50cz multi	.25	.25

1st Hydroelecric Power Station in South America, Marmelos-o, Cent. — A1184

1989, Sept. 5 Litho. ***Perf. 11½x12***

2204	A1184	50c multi	.25	.25

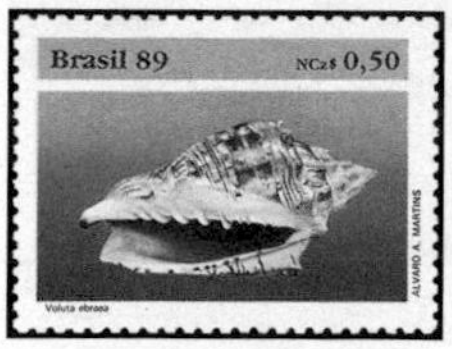

Conchs
Endemic to
the
Brazilian
Coast
A1185

Designs: 50c,Voluta ebraea. 1cz, Morum matthewsi. 1.50cz, Agaronia travassosi.

1989, Sept. 8

2205	A1185	50c multi	.30	.30
2206	A1185	1cz multi	.40	.30
2207	A1185	1.50cz multi	.50	.30
		Nos. 2205-2207 (3)	1.20	.90

Wildlife conservation.

America
Issue
A1186

UPAE emblem and pre-Columbian stone carvings: 1cz, Muiraquita ritual statue, vert. 4cz, Ceramic brazier under three-footed votive urn.

Perf. 12x11½, 11½x12

1989, Oct. 12 Litho.

2208	A1186	1cz multicolored	.25	.25
2209	A1186	4cz multicolored	.25	.30

Discovery of America 500th anniv. (in 1992).

A1187

Hologram and: a. *Lemons,* by Danilo di Prete. b. *O Indio E A Suacuapara,* by sculptor Victor Brecheret. c. Francisco Matarazzo.

1989, Oct. 14 ***Perf. 11***

Souvenir Sheet

2210	A1187	Sheet of 3	2.50	2.50
a.		2cz multicolored	.75	.75
b.		3cz multicolored	.75	.75
c.		5cz multicolored	.75	.75

Sao Paulo 20th intl. art biennial.

A1188

Writers, residences and quotes: No. 2211, Casimiro de Abreu (b. 1839). No. 2212, Cora Coralina (b. 1889). No. 2213, Joaquim Machado de Assis (b. 1839).

1989, Oct. 26 ***Perf. 11½x11***

2211	A1188	1cz multicolored	.25	.25
2212	A1188	1cz multicolored	.25	.25
2213	A1188	1cz multicolored	.25	.25
		Nos. 2211-2213 (3)	.75	.75

Federal Police Department, 25th Anniv. — A1189

1989, Nov. 9 ***Perf. 11½x12***

2214	A1189	1cz multicolored	.25	.25

Christmas
A1190

1989, Nov. 10 ***Perf. 12x11½***

2215	A1190	70c Heralding angel	.25	.25
2216	A1190	1cz Holy family	.25	.25

Thanksgiving
Day — A1191

1989, Nov. 23

2217	A1191	1cz multicolored	.25	.25

Type of 1988 Redrawn

1989, Nov. 6 Photo. ***Perf. 13x13½***

2218	A1152	(B) org & dark red	1.60	.55

Size of type and postal emblem are smaller on No. 2218; "1e PORTE" is at lower left.
No. 2218 met the first class intl. letter postage rate, initially at 9cz.

Souvenir Sheet

Proclamation of the Republic, Cent. — A1192

1989, Nov. 19 Litho. ***Perf. 11***

2225	A1192	15cz multicolored	2.50	2.50

Bahia
Sports
Club, 58th
Anniv.
A1193

1989, Nov. 30 ***Perf. 11½x12***

2226	A1193	50c Soccer	.30	.25

Yellow Man, by
Anita Malfatti
(b. 1889)
A1194

1989, Dec. 2 ***Perf. 12x11½***

2227	A1194	1cz multicolored	.25	.25

Bahia State Public Archives, Cent. — A1195

1990, Jan. 16 Litho. ***Perf. 11½x12***

2228	A1195	2cz multicolored	.25	.25

Brazilian
Botanical
Soc., 40th
Anniv.
A1196

2cz, Sabia, Caatinga. 13cz, Pau, Brazil.

1990, Jan. 21
2229 A1196 2cz multi .25 .25
2230 A1196 13cz multi .25 .25

Churches
A1197

Designs: 2cz, St. John the Baptist Cathedral, Santa Cruz do Sul, vert. 3cz, Our Lady of Victory Church, Oeiras. 5cz, Our Lady of the Rosary Church, Ouro Preto, vert.

1990, Feb. 5 ***Perf. 12x11½, 11½x12***
2231 A1197 2cz multicolored .25 .25
2232 A1197 3cz multicolored .25 .25
2233 A1197 5cz multicolored .25 .25
Nos. 2231-2233 (3) .75 .75

Lloyd's of London in Brazil, Cent.
A1198

1990, Feb. 19 Litho. ***Perf. 11½x12***
2234 A1198 3cz multicolored .25 .25

Souvenir Sheet

Antarctic Research Program — A1199

1990, Feb. 22 Litho. ***Perf. 11***
2235 A1199 20cz Fauna, map 2.50 2.50

Vasco da Gama Soccer Club
A1200

1990, Mar. 5
2236 A1200 10cz multicolored .25 .25

Lindolfo Collor (b. 1890), Syndicated Columnist, and Labor Monument
A1201

1990, Mar. 7
2237 A1201 20cz multicolored .25 .25

Pres. Jose Sarney — A1202

1990, Mar. 8 ***Perf. 12x11½***
2238 A1202 20cz chalky blue .25 .25

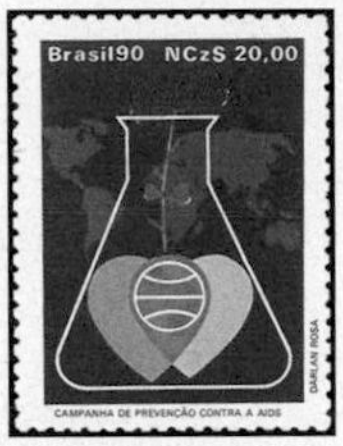
AIDS Prevention
A1203

1990, Apr. 6 ***Perf. 12x11½***
2239 A1203 20cz multicolored .25 .25

Souvenir Sheet

Penny Black, 150th Anniv. — A1204

No. 2240: 20cr, Dom Pedro, Brazil No. 1. 100cr, Queen Victoria, Great Britain No. 1.

1990, May 3 Litho. ***Perf. 11***
2240 A1204 Sheet of 2 2.50 2.50
a. 20cr multicolored .65 .65
b. 100cr multicolored 1.75 1.75

Central Bank, 25th Anniv.
A1205

1990, Mar. 30 Litho. ***Perf. 11½x12***
2241 A1205 20cr multicolored .25 .25

Amazon River Postal Network, 21st Anniv.
A1207

1990, Apr. 20 ***Perf. 11x11½***
2243 A1207 20cr multicolored .25 .25

Souvenir Sheet

World Cup Soccer Championships, Italy — A1208

1990, May 12 Litho. ***Perf. 12x11½***
2244 A1208 120cr multicolored 2.50 2.50

22nd Congress of the Intl. Union of Highway Transportation — A1209

1990. May 14 ***Perf. 11½x12***
2245 A1209 20cr multicolored .55 .55
2246 A1209 80cr multicolored .55 .55
a. Pair, #2245-2246 1.10 1.10

No. 2246a has a continuous design.

Imperial Crown, 18th Cent. — A1210

Designs: No. 2248, Our Lady of Immaculate Conception, 18th cent.

1990, May 18 ***Perf. 12x11½***
2247 A1210 20cr shown .25 .25
2248 A1210 20cr multicolored .25 .25

Imperial Museum, 50th anniv.(No. 2247). Mission Museum, 50th anniv. (No. 2248).

State Flags Type of 1981

1990, May 20 ***Perf. 11½x12***
2249 A947 20cr Tocantins .25 .25

Army Geographical Service, Cent. — A1212

1990, May 30 ***Perf. 11x11½***
2250 A1212 20cr multicolored .25 .25

Film Personalities — A1213

No. 2251, Adhemar Gonzaga. No. 2252, Carmen Miranda. No. 2253, Carmen Santos. No. 2254, Oscarito.

1990, June 19 ***Perf. 11½x12***
2251 A1213 25cr multi 1.50 1.50
2252 A1213 25cr multi 1.50 1.50
2253 A1213 25cr multi 1.50 1.50
2254 A1213 25cr multi 1.50 1.50
a. Block of 4, #2251-2254 6.00 12.00

France-Brazil House, Rio de Janeiro — A1214

1990, July 14 Litho. ***Perf. 11½x11***
2255 A1214 50cr multicolored .55 .55

See France No. 2226.

World Men's Volleyball Chmpships.
A1215

1990, July 28 Litho. ***Perf. 12x11½***
2256 A1215 10cr multicolored .25 .25

CBA 123
A1216

1990, July 30 ***Perf. 11½x12***
2257 A1216 10cr multicolored .25 .25

Intl. Literacy Year — A1217

1990, Aug. 22 ***Perf. 12x11½***
2258 A1217 10cr multicolored .25 .25

Flora Type of 1989

Designs: 1cr, Like #2179. 2cr, Like #2180. 5cr, Like #2181. 10cr, Tibouchina granulosa. 20cr, Cassia macranthera. No. 2264, Clitoria fairchildiana. No. 2265, Tibouchina mutabilis. 100cr, Erythrina crista-galli. 200cr, Jacaranda mimosifolia. 500cr, Caesalpinia peltophoroides. 1000, Pachira aquatica. 2000, Hibiscus pernambucensis. 5000, Triplaris surinamensis. 10,000, Tabebuia heptaphylla. 20,000, Erythrina speciosa.

Perf. 11x11½, 11½x11
1989-93 **Photo.**
2259 A1177 1cr multi .25 .25
2260 A1177 2cr multi .25 .25
2261 A1177 5cr multi .25 .25
2262 A1177 10cr multi .25 .25
2263 A1177 20cr multi .25 .25
2264 A1177 50cr multi .25 .25
2265 A1177 50cr multi .40 .25
2266 A1177 100cr multi, perf. 13 .25 .25
2267 A1177 200cr multi .30 .25
2268 A1177 500cr multi .30 .25
2269 A1177 1000cr multi .25 .25
2270 A1177 2000cr multi .25 .25
2271 A1177 5000cr multi .30 .25
2272 A1177 10,000cr multi .40 .25
2273 A1177 20,000cr multi .30 .25
Nos. 2259-2273 (15) 4.25 3.75

Issued: 1cr, 11/8/90; 2cr, 11/12/90; 5cr, 11/16/90; No. 2264, 6/1/89; 10cr, 4/18/90; 20cr, 5/4/90; 100cr, 8/24/90; 200cr, 6/16/91; 500cr, 5/14/91; 1000cr, 9/2/92; 2000cr, 9/8/92; 5000cr, 10/16/92; 10,000cr, 11/16/92; 20,000cr, 4/25/93; No. 2265, 10/20/93.

Granbery Institute, Cent. A1218

1990, Sept. 8 Litho. ***Perf. 11½x12***

2279 A1218 13cr multicolored .25 .25

18th Panamerican Railroad Congress — A1219

1990, Sept. 9

2280 A1219 95cr multicolored .75 .75

Embratel, 25th Anniv. — A1220

1990, Sept. 21

2281 A1220 13cr multicolored .25 .25

LUBRAPEX '90 A1221

Statues by Ceschiatti and Giorgi (No. 2283): No. 2282, As Banhistas. No. 2283, Os Candangos. No. 2284, Evangelista Sao Joao. No. 2285, A Justica.

1990, Sept. 22

2282 A1221 25cr multi 1.10 1.10
2283 A1221 25cr multi 1.10 1.10
2284 A1221 100cr multi 1.60 1.60
2285 A1221 100cr multi 1.60 1.60
a. Block of 4, #2282-2285 6.00 6.00
b. Souv. sheet of 4, #2282-2285 7.00 7.00

Praia Do Sul Wildlife Reserve A1222

1990, Oct. 12

2286 A1222 15cr Flowers .30 .30
2287 A1222 105cr Shoreline 1.00 1.00
a. Pair, #2286-2287 1.40 1.40

Discovery of America, 500th anniv. (in 1992).

Natl. Library, 180th Anniv. A1223

Writers: No. 2289, Guilherme de Almeida (1890-1969). No. 2290, Oswald de Andrade (1890-1954).

1990, Oct. 29 Litho. ***Perf. 11x11½***

2288 A1223 15cr multicolored .25 .25
2289 A1223 15cr multicolored .25 .25
2290 A1223 15cr multicolored .25 .25
Nos. 2288-2290 (3) .75 .75

Natl. Tax Court, Cent. A1224

1990, Nov. 7 Litho. ***Perf. 11½x12***

2291 A1224 15cr multicolored .25 .25

Christmas A1225

Architecture of Brasilia: No. 2292, National Congress. No. 2293, Television tower.

1990, Nov. 20

2292 A1225 15cr multicolored .25 .25
2293 A1225 15cr multicolored .25 .25

A1226

1990, Dec. 13 Litho. ***Perf. 12x11½***

2294 A1226 15cr multicolored .25 .25

Organization of American States, cent.

A1227

1990, Dec. 14

2295 A1227 15cr multicolored .25 .25

First Flight of Nike Apache Missile, 25th anniv.

Colonization of Sergipe, Founding of Sao Cristovao, 400th Anniv. — A1228

1990, Dec. 18 Litho. ***Perf. 11½x12***

2296 A1228 15cr multicolored .25 .25

World Congress of Physical Education A1229

1991, Jan. 7 ***Perf. 11½x12***

2297 A1229 17cr multicolored .25 .25

Rock in Rio II — A1230

1991, Jan. 9 ***Perf. 12x11½***

2298 A1230 25cr Cazuza .35 .35
2299 A1230 185cr Raul Seixas .35 .35
a. Pair, #2298-2299 .75 .75
Complete booklet, pane of 12 5.00 5.00

Printed in panes of 12.

Ministry of Aviation, 50th Anniv. A1231

1991, Jan. 20 ***Perf. 11x11½***

2300 A1231 17cr multicolored .25 .25

Carnivals A1232

1991, Feb. 8 Litho. ***Perf. 12x11½***

2301 A1232 25cr Olinda .25 .25
2302 A1232 30cr Salvador .25 .25
2303 A1232 280cr Rio de Janeiro .30 .30
Nos. 2301-2303 (3) .80 .80

Visit to Antarctica by Pres. Collor — A1233

1991, Feb. 20

2304 A1233 300cr multicolored .75 .75

Hang Gliding World Championships — A1234

1991, Feb. 24 ***Perf. 11½x12***

2305 A1234 36cr multicolored .25 .25

11th Pan American Games, 25th Summer Olympics A1235

1991, Mar. 30 Litho. ***Perf. 11½x12***

2306 A1235 36cr Sailing .55 .55
2307 A1235 36cr Rowing .55 .55
2308 A1235 300cr Swimming .55 .55
a. Block of 3, #2306-2308 + label 1.75 1.75

Fight Against Drugs — A1236

1991, Apr. 7 Litho. ***Perf. 12x11½***

2309 A1236 40cr Drugs .25 .25
2310 A1236 40cr Alcohol .25 .25
2311 A1236 40cr Smoking .25 .25
Nos. 2309-2311 (3) .75 .75

Yanomami Indian Culture — A1237

1991, Apr. 19 ***Perf. 11½x11, 11x11½***

2312 A1237 40cr shown .25 .25
2313 A1237 400cr Indian, horiz. .65 .65

Journal of Brazil, Cent. A1238

1991, Apr. 8 Litho. ***Perf. 11x11½***

2314 A1238 40cr multicolored .25 .25

Neochen Jubata (Orinoco Goose) — A1239

1991, June 5 Litho. ***Perf. 12x11½***

2315 A1239 45cr multi .25 .25

UN Conference on Development.

Snakes & Dinosaurs A1240

No. 2316, Bothrops jararaca. No. 2317, Corallus caninus. No. 2318, Teropods. No. 2319, Sauropods.

1991, June 6 ***Perf. 11½x12***

2316 A1240 45cr multi .25 .25
2317 A1240 45cr multi .25 .25
a. Pair, #2316-2317 .50 .50
2318 A1240 45cr multi .25 .25
2319 A1240 350cr multi .40 .40
a. Pair, #2318-2319 .65 .65
Nos. 2316-2319 (4) 1.15 1.15

Flag of Brazil — A1241

Perf. 13x13½

1991, June 10-1992, Oct. Photo.

2320 A1241 A multicolored 1.00 .25

Valued at domestic letter rate on day of issue.

No. 2320 exists with a printer's marking on lower right.

Fire Pumper A1242

1991, July 2 Litho. *Perf. 11½x12*

2321 A1242 45cr multicolored .25 .25

Tourism A1243

Map location and: 45cr, Painted stones, Roraima. 350cr, Dedo de Deus Mountain, Rio De Janeiro.

1991, July 6 *Perf. 11x11½*

2322 A1243 45cr multicolored .25 .25
2323 A1243 350cr multicolored .55 .55

Labor Laws, 50th Anniv. A1244

1991, Aug. 11 *Perf. 11½x12*

2324 A1244 45cr multicolored .25 .25

Leonardo Mota, Birth Cent. A1245

1991, Aug. 22

2325 A1245 45cr buff, blk & red .25 .25

Folklore Festival.

Jose Basilio da Gama (1741-1795), Poet — A1246

Designs: No. 2327, Fagundes Varela (b. 1841), poet. No. 2328, Jackson de Figueiredo (b. 1891), writer.

1991, Aug. 29

2326 A1246 45cr multicolored .25 .25
2327 A1246 50cr multicolored .25 .25
2328 A1246 50cr multicolored .25 .25
Nos. 2326-2328 (3) .75 .75

12th Natl. Eucharistic Congress A1247

50cr, Pope John Paul II. 400cr, Map, crosses.

1991, Oct. 6 Litho. *Perf. 12x11½*

2329 A1247 50cr multi .85 .85
2330 A1247 400cr multi 1.40 1.40
a. Pair, #2329-2330 2.50 2.50

Visit by Pope John Paul II.

First Brazilian Constitution, Cent. — A1248

1991, Oct. 7 *Perf. 11½x12*

2331 A1248 50cr multicolored .25 .25

Telecom '91 — A1249

1991, Oct. 8 *Perf. 12x11½*

2332 A1249 50cr multicolored .25 .25

Sixth World Forum and Exposition on Telecommunications, Geneva, Switzerland.

America Issue A1250

UPAEP emblem and explorers: 50cr, Ferdinand Magellan (c. 1480-1521). 400cr, Francisco de Orellana (c. 1490-c. 1546).

1991, Oct. 12 *Perf. 11½x12*

2333 A1250 50cr multicolored .25 .25
2334 A1250 400cr multicolored .55 .55

Discovery of America, 500th anniv. (in 1992).

A1251

BRAPEX VIII (Orchids and Hummingbirds): 50cr, Colibri serrirostris, Cattleya warneri. No. 2336, Chlorostilbon aureoventris, Rodriguezia venusta. No. 2337, Clytolaema rubricauda, Zygopetalum intermedium. No. 2338a, 50cr, Colibri serrirostris. b, 50cr, Chlorostilbon aureoventris. c, 500cr, Clytolaema rubricauda.

1991, Oct. 29 Litho. *Perf. 12x11½*

2335 A1251 50cr multicolored .25 .25
2336 A1251 65cr multicolored .25 .25
2337 A1251 65cr multicolored .25 .25
Nos. 2335-2337 (3) .75 .75

Souvenir Sheet

2338 A1251 Sheet of 3, #a.-c. 8.00 8.00

A1252

1991, Oct. 29 Litho. *Perf. 11½x11*

2339 A1252 400cr multicolored .40 .40

Lasar Segall, artist, birth cent.

Bureau of Agriculture and Provision of Sao Paulo, Cent. — A1253

1991, Nov. 11 *Perf. 12x11½*

2340 A1253 70cr multicolored .25 .25

First Civilian Presidents, Birth Sesquicentennials — A1254

Designs: 70cr, Manuel de Campos Salles. 90cr, Prudente de Moraes Barros.

1991, Nov. 14 *Perf. 11½x12*

2341 A1254 70cr multi .25 .25
2342 A1254 90cr multi .25 .25
a. Pair, #2341-2342 .50 .50

Christmas A1255

1991, Nov. 20 *Perf. 12x11½*

2343 A1255 70cr multicolored .25 .25

Thanksgiving A1256

1991, Nov. 28

2344 A1256 70cr multicolored .25 .25

Military Police A1257

1991, Dec. 1 *Perf. 11½x12*

2345 A1257 80cr multicolored .25 .25

Souvenir Sheet

Emperor Dom Pedro (1825-1891) — A1258

No. 2346: a, 80cr, Older age. b, 800cr, Wearing crown.

Litho. & Engr.

1991, Nov. 29 *Perf. 11*

2346 A1258 Sheet of 2, #a.-b. 3.50 3.50

BRASILIANA 93.

Churches A1259

Designs: No. 2347, Presbyterian Church, Rio de Janeiro. No. 2348, First Baptist Church, Niteroi.

1992, Jan. 12 Litho. *Perf. 12x11½*

2347 A1259 250cr multicolored .25 .25
2348 A1259 250cr multicolored .25 .25

1992 Summer Olympics, Barcelona A1260

Medalists in shooting, Antwerp, 1920: 300cr, Afranio Costa, silver. 2500cr, Guihlherme Paraense, gold.

1992, Jan. 28 *Perf. 11½x12*

2349 A1260 300cr multicolored .25 .25
2350 A1260 2500cr multicolored 1.00 1.00

Port of Santos, Cent. A1261

1992, Feb. 3 Litho. *Perf. 11½*

2351 A1261 300cr multicolored .25 .25

Fauna of Fernando de Noronha Island A1262

400cr, White-tailed tropicbirds. 2500cr, Dolphins.

1992, Feb. 25 Litho. *Perf. 11½x12*

2352 A1262 400cr multi .25 .25
2353 A1262 2500cr multi .75 .75

Earth Summit, Rio de Janeiro.

Yellow Amaryllis — A1263

1992, Feb. 27 Photo. ***Perf. 13½***

2354 A1263 (A) multicolored 3.00 .25

No. 2354 met the second class domestic letter postage rate of 265cr on date of issue.

ARBRAFEX '92, Argentina-Brazil Philatelic Exhibition — A1264

Designs: No. 2355, Gaucho throwing bola at rhea. No. 2356, Man playing accordion, couple dancing. No. 2357, Couple in horse-drawn cart, woman. 1000cr, Gaucho throwing lasso at steer.

No. 2358c, 250cr, like No. 2356. d, 500cr, like No. 2355. e, 1500cr, like No. 2358.

1992, Mar. 20 Litho. ***Perf. 11½x12***

2355 A1264 250cr multi .25 .25
2356 A1264 250cr multi .25 .25
2357 A1264 250cr multi .25 .25
2358 A1264 1000cr multi .55 .55
a. Block of 4, Nos. 2355-2358 1.40 1.40

Souvenir Sheet

2358B A1264 Sheet of 4, #2357, 2358c-2358e 12.00 12.00

1992 Summer Olympics, Barcelona A1265

1992, Apr. 3 ***Perf. 12x11½***

2359 A1265 300cr multicolored .25 .25

Discovery of America, 500th Anniv. A1266

500cr, Columbus' fleet. 3500cr, Columbus, map.

1992, Apr. 24 ***Perf. 11½x12***

2360 A1266 500cr multi .30 .30
2361 A1266 3500cr multi .65 .65
a. Pair, #2360-2361 1.00 1.00

Telebras Telecommunications System — A1267

1992, May 5 ***Perf. 11x11½***

2362 A1267 350cr multicolored .25 .25

Installation of 10 million telephones.

Langsdorff Expedition to Brazil, 170th Anniv. A1268

Designs: No. 2363, Aime-Adrien Taunay, natives. No. 2364, Johann Moritz Rugendas, monkey. No. 2365, Hercule Florence, flowering plant. 3000cr, Gregory Ivanovitch Langsdorff, map.

1992, June 2 ***Perf. 11½x12***

2363 A1268 500cr multicolored .25 .25
2364 A1268 500cr multicolored .25 .25
2365 A1268 500cr multicolored .25 .25
2366 A1268 3000cr multicolored .55 .55
Nos. 2363-2366 (4) 1.30 1.30

UN Conf. on Environmental Development, Rio.

UN Conference on Environmental Development, Rio de Janeiro — A1269

Globe and: No. 2367, Flags of Sweden and Brazil. No. 2368, City, grain, mountain and tree. 3000cr, Map of Brazil, parrot, orchid.

1992, June 3 Litho. ***Perf. 11x11½***

2367 A1269 450cr multicolored .25 .25
2368 A1269 450cr multicolored .25 .25
2369 A1269 3000cr multicolored .75 .75
Nos. 2367-2369 (3) 1.25 1.25

Ecology A1270

Designs: No. 2370, Flowers, waterfall, and butterflies. No. 2371, Butterflies, canoe, and hummingbirds. No. 2372, Boy taking pictures of tropical birds. No. 2373, Armadillo, girl picking fruit.

1992, June 4 ***Perf. 11½x12***

2370 A1270 500cr multicolored .30 .30
2371 A1270 500cr multicolored .30 .30
2372 A1270 500cr multicolored .30 .30
2373 A1270 500cr multicolored .30 .30
a. Strip of 4, #2370-2373 1.25 1.25
Complete booklet, #2373a 1.25

UN Conf. on Environmental Development, Rio.

Floral Paintings by Margaret Mee — A1271

No. 2374, Nidularium innocentii. No. 2375, Canistrum exiguum. No. 2376, Canistrum cyathiforme. No. 2377, Nidularium rubens.

1992, June 5 ***Perf. 12x11½***

2374 A1271 600cr multicolored .30 .25
2375 A1271 600cr multicolored .30 .25
2376 A1271 700cr multicolored .30 .25
2377 A1271 700cr multicolored .30 .25
Nos. 2374-2377 (4) 1.20 1.00

UN Conf. on Environmental Development, Rio.

Souvenir Sheet

Joaquim Jose da Silva Xavier (1748-1792), Patriot — A1272

Litho. & Engr.

1992, Apr. 21 ***Perf. 11***

2378 A1272 3500cr multicolored 2.75 2.75

Souvenir Sheet

A1273

Expedition of Alexandre Rodrigues Ferreira, Bicent.: a, 500cr, Sailing ships, gray and green hulls. b, 1000cr, Sailing ships, red hulls. c, 2500cr, Sailing ship at shore.

1992, May 9 Litho. ***Perf. 11½x12***

2379 A1273 Sheet of 3, #a.-c. 2.75 2.75

Lubrapex '92.

Diabetes Day — A1274

1992, June 5 Litho. ***Perf. 12x11½***

2380 A1274 600cr Hummingbird .25 .25

Volunteer Firemen of Joinville — A1275

1992, July 13 Litho. ***Perf. 11½x11***

2381 A1275 550cr multicolored .30 .25

A1276

Serra da Capivara National Park: No. 2382, Leopard, animals, map of park. No. 2383, Canyon, map of Brazil.

1992, July 17 ***Perf. 12x11½***

2382 550cr multicolored .30 .30
2383 550cr multicolored .30 .30
a. A1276 Pair, #2382-2383 .65 .65

A1277

1992, July 24

2384 A1277 550cr multicolored .25 .25

Financing for studies and projects.

Natl. Service for Industrial Training, 50th Anniv. — A1278

1992, Aug. 5 ***Perf. 11½x12***

2385 A1278 650cr multicolored .25 .25

Fortresses A1279

650cr, Santa Cruz. 3000cr, Santo Antonio.

1992, Aug. 19 Litho. ***Perf. 11½x12***

2386 A1279 650cr multi .25 .25
2387 A1279 3000cr multi .55 .55

Masonic Square, Compass and Lodge A1280

1992, Aug. 20

2388 A1280 650cr multicolored .30 .30

Brazilian Assistance Legion, 50th Anniv. — A1281

1992, Aug. 28 ***Perf. 12x11½***

2389 A1281 650cr multicolored .25 .25

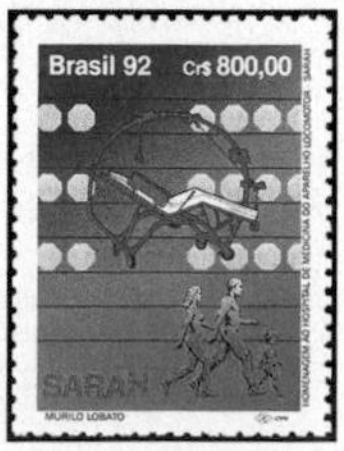

Hospital of Medicine and Orthopedics A1282

1992, Sept. 11

2390 A1282 800cr multicolored .25 .25

Merry Christmas A1283

1992, Nov. 20 *Perf. 11½*
2391 A1283 (1) multicolored 1.50 1.50

No. 2391 met the first class domestic letter postage rate of 1090cr on day of issue.

Writers A1284

Designs: No. 2392, Graciliano Ramos (1892-1953). No. 2393, Menotti del Picchia (1892-1988). 1000cr, Assis Chateaubriand (1892-1968).

Perf. 12x11½, 11½x12
1992, Oct. 29 **Litho.**
2392 A1284 900cr multi, vert. .25 .25
2393 A1284 900cr multi, vert. .25 .25
2394 A1284 1000cr multi .25 .25
Nos. 2392-2394 (3) .75 .75

Expedition of Luis Cruls, Cent. A1285

1992, Nov. 11 *Perf. 11½x12*
2395 A1285 900cr multicolored .25 .25

Brazillian Program for Quality and Productivity A1286

1992, Nov. 12
2396 A1286 1200cr multicolored .25 .25

Souvenir Sheet

Tourism Year in the Americas — A1287

a, 1200cr, Mountains, coastline. b, 9000cr, Sugarloaf Mt., aerial tram, Rio de Janeiro.

1992, Nov. 18 **Litho.** *Perf. 11½x12*
2397 A1287 Sheet of 2, #a.-b. 1.60 1.60

Brasiliana '93

Sister Irma Dulce A1288

1993, Mar. 13 **Litho.** *Perf. 11½x12*
2398 A1288 3500cr multicolored .25 .25

Souvenir Sheet

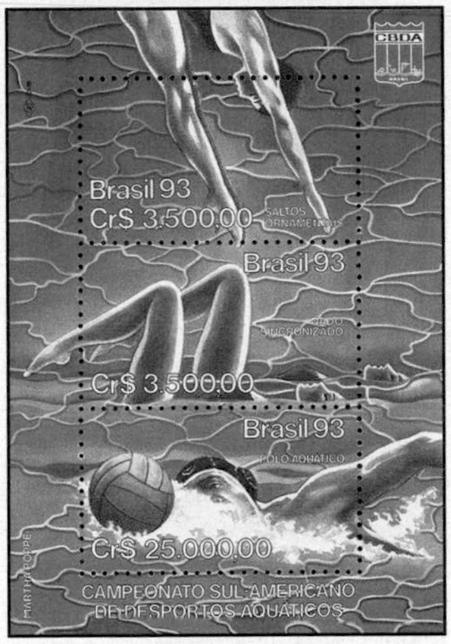

Water Sports Championships of South America — A1289

Designs: a, 3500cr, Diver. b, 3500cr, Synchronized swimmers. c, 25,000cr, Water polo.

1993, Mar. 21 **Litho.** *Perf. 11*
2399 A1289 Sheet of 3, #a.-c. 2.25 2.25

Curitiba, 300th Anniv. A1290

1993, Mar. 29
2400 A1290 4500cr multicolored .25 .25

Health and Preservation of Life — A1291

Red Cross emblem and: No. 2401, Bleeding heart, flowers. No. 2402, Cancer symbol, breast. No. 2403, Brain waves, rainbow emerging from head.

1993, Apr. 7 **Litho.** *Perf. 12x11½*
2401 A1291 4500cr multicolored .40 .40
2402 A1291 4500cr multicolored .40 .40
2403 A1291 4500cr multicolored .40 .40
a. Strip of 3, #2401-2403 1.25 1.25

Pedro Americo, 150th Birth Anniv. — A1292

Paintings: 5500cr, A Study of Love, 1883. No. 2405, David and Abizag, 1879, horiz. No. 2406, Seated Nude, 1882.

1993, Apr. 29 *Perf. 12x11½, 11½x12*
2404 A1292 5500cr multi .25 .25
2405 A1292 36,000cr multi .55 .55
2406 A1292 36,000cr multi .55 .55
Nos. 2404-2406 (3) 1.35 1.35

Natl. Flag — A1292a

1993, May 26 **Litho.** *Die Cut*
Self-adhesive
2407 A1292a A multicolored 1.90 .35

No. 2407 valued at first class domestic letter rate of 9570cr on day of issue.

Beetles A1293

8000cr, Dynastes hercules. 55,000cr, Batus barbicornis.

1993, June 5 **Litho.** *Perf. 11½x12*
2408 A1293 8000cr multi .25 .25
2409 A1293 55,000cr multi .55 .55

3rd Iberian-American Conference of Chiefs of State and Heads of Government, Salvador — A1294

1993, July 15 **Litho.** *Perf. 11x11½*
2410 A1294 12,000cr multi .25 .25

1st Brazilian Postage Stamps, 150th Anniv. — A1295

Litho. & Engr.
1993, July 30 *Perf. 12x11½*
2411 A1295 30,000cr No. 1 .55 .55
2412 A1295 60,000cr No. 2 .55 .55
2413 A1295 90,000cr No. 3 1.25 1.25
a. Souvenir sheet of 3, #2411-2413, wmk. 268 16.00 16.00
Nos. 2411-2413 (3) 2.35 2.35

No. 2413a sold for 200,000cr and was issued without gum. Stamps in No. 2413a do not have imprint at bottom.

Union of Portuguese Speaking Capitals A1296

No. 2414: a, 15,000cr, Brasilia. b, 71,000cr, Rio de Janiero.

1993, July 30 **Litho.** *Perf. 11½x12*
2414 A1296 Pair, #a.-b. 1.00 1.00

No. 2414 printed in continuous design.

Monica & Friends, by Mauricio de Sousa — A1297

Monica, Cebolinha, Cascao, Magali, and Bidu: a, Engraving die. b, Reading proclamation, king, No. 1. c, Writing and sending letter, No. 2. d, Receiving letter, No. 3.

1993, Aug. 1
2415 A1297 (1) Strip of 4, #a.-d. 6.00 6.00
Complete booklet, #2415 6.00

First Brazilian postage stamps, 150th anniv. Nos. 2415a-2415d paid the first class rate (9600cr) on day of issue.

Brazilian Post, 330th Anniv. — A1298

No. 2416 — Postal buildings: a, Imperial Post Office, Rio de Janeiro. b, Petropolis. c, Central office, Rio de Janeiro. d, Niteroi.

1993, Aug. 3 **Litho.** *Perf. 11½x12*
2416 A1298 20,000cr Block of 4, #a.-d. 1.10 1.10

Brazilian Engineering Schools — A1299

Designs: No. 2417, School of Engineering, Federal University, Rio de Janeiro. No. 2418, Polytechnical School, University of Sao Paulo.

1993, Aug. 24 **Litho.** *Perf. 11x11½*
2417 A1299 17cr multicolored .25 .25
2418 A1299 17cr multicolored .25 .25

Preservation of Sambaquis Archaelogical Sites — A1300

1993, Sept. 19 *Perf. 12x11½*
2419 A1300 17cr Two artifacts .25 .25
2420 A1300 17cr Six artifacts .25 .25

Ulysses Guimaraes, Natl. Congress — A1301

1993, Oct. 6 **Litho.** *Perf. 11x11½*
2421 A1301 22cr multicolored .25 .25

A1302

1993, Oct. 8 Litho. *Perf. 12x11½*
2422 A1302 22cr multicolored .25 .25

Virgin of Nazare Religious Festival, bicent.

A1303

Endangered birds (America Issue): 22cr, Anodorhynchus hyacinthinus, anodorhynchus glaucus, anodorhynchus leari. 130cr, Cyanopsitta spixii.

1993, Oct. 13 Litho. *Perf. 11½x11*
2423 A1303 22cr multicolored .30 .30
2424 A1303 130cr multicolored .75 .75

Composers
A1304

No. 2425, Vinicius de Moraes. No. 2426, Pixinguinha.

1993, Oct. 19 Litho. *Perf. 12x11½*
2425 A1304 22cr multi .25 .25
2426 A1304 22cr multi .25 .25

Poets — A1307

No. 2427, Mario de Andrade (1893-1945). No. 2428, Alceu Amoroso Lima (Tristao de Athayde) (1893-1983). No. 2429, Gilka Machado (1893-1980).

1993, Oct. 29 Litho. *Perf. 12x11½*
2427 A1307 30cr multicolored .25 .25
2428 A1307 30cr multicolored .25 .25
2429 A1307 30cr multicolored .25 .25
Nos. 2427-2429 (3) .75 .75

Natl. Book Day.

Brazil-Portugal Treaty of Consultation and Friendship, 40th Anniv. — A1308

1993, Nov. 3 Litho. *Perf. 11½x12*
2430 A1308 30cr multicolored .25 .25

See Portugal No. 1980.

Image of the Republic — A1309

Photo. & Engr.

1993, Nov. 3 *Perf. 13*
2431 A1309 (B) multicolored 3.75 1.50

Valued at first class international letter rate (178.70 cr) on day of issue.

2nd Intl. Biennial of Comic Strips
A1310

Cartoon drawings: No. 2432, Nho-Quim. No. 2433, Benjamin. No. 2434, Lamparina. No. 2435, Reco-Reco, Bolao, Azeitona.

1993, Nov. 11 Litho. *Perf. 11½x12*
2432 A1310 (1) multicolored 1.25 1.25
2433 A1310 (1) multicolored 1.25 1.25
2434 A1310 (1) multicolored 1.25 1.25
2435 A1310 (1) multicolored 1.25 1.25
a. Block of 4, #2432-2435 5.00 5.00

Valued at first class domestic letter rate (30.20 cr) on day of issue.

Launching of First Brazilian-Built Submarine — A1311

1993, Nov. 18 *Perf. 11½*
2436 A1311 240cr multicolored .60 .60

Christmas
A1312

1993, Nov. 20
2437 A1312 (1) multicolored 1.60 1.60

Valued at first class domestic letter rate (30.20 cr) on day of issue.

First Fighter Group, 50th Anniv.
A1313

1993, Dec. 18 Litho. *Perf. 11½*
2438 A1313 42cr multicolored .30 .30

Convent of Merces, 340th Anniv.
A1314

1994, Jan. 31 Litho. *Perf. 11½x12*
2439 A1314 58cr multicolored .25 .25

Mae Menininha of Gantois, Birth Cent. — A1315

1994, Feb. 10 Litho. *Perf. 11x11½*
2440 A1315 80cr multicolored .25 .25

Intl. Olympic Committee, Cent.
A1316

1994, Feb. 17 *Perf. 11½x12*
2441 A1316 (1) multicolored 2.25 2.25

No. 2441 valued at first class international letter rate (446.30 cr) on day of issue.

Natl. Flag — A1317

1994, Jan. 31 Litho. *Die Cut*
Self-Adhesive
2442 A1317 (1) multicolored 1.25 .25

No. 2442 valued at first class domestic letter rate (55.90 cr) on day of issue.

Birds — A1318

Designs: 10cr, Notiochelidon cyanoleuca. 20cr, Buteo magnirostris. 50cr, Turdus rufiventris. 100cr, Columbina talpacoti. 200cr, Vanellus chilensis. 500cr, Zonotrichia capensis.

1994 Photo. *Perf. 11x11½*
2443 A1318 10cr multi .25 .25
2444 A1318 20cr multi .25 .25
2445 A1318 50cr multi .25 .25
2446 A1318 100cr multi .25 .25
2447 A1318 200cr multi .30 .25
2448 A1318 500cr multi .40 .25
Nos. 2443-2448 (6) 1.70 1.50

Issued: 10cr, 3/17; 20cr, 3/9; 50cr, 3/1; 100cr, 200cr, 4/4; 500cr, 4/13.
See Nos. 2484-2494.

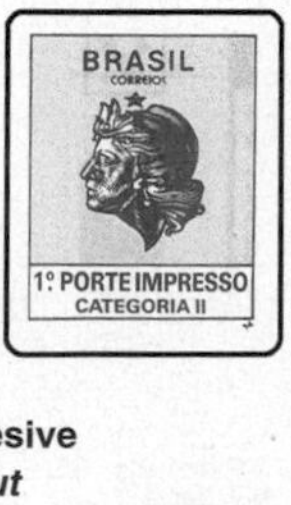

Image of the Republic — A1318a

Self-Adhesive
Die Cut

1994, May 10 Litho.
2449 A1318a (1) blue .80 .25
2450 A1318a (3) claret 1.25 .35

Size: 25x35mm
Perf. 12x11½
2451 A1318a (4) green 1.25 .40
2452 A1318a (5) henna brown 1.50 .65
Nos. 2449-2452 (4) 4.80 1.65

Nos. 2449, 2450, 2451, 2452 valued 131.37cr, 321.14cr, 452.52cr, 905.05cr on day of issue.

Prince Henry the Navigator (1394-1460) — A1319

1994, Mar. 4 Litho. *Perf. 11½x12*
2463 A1319 635cr multicolored .55 .55

See Macao No. 719, Portugal No. 1987.

America Issue
A1320

Postal vehicles: 110cr, Bicycle, country scene. 635cr, Motorcycle, city scene.

1994, Mar. 18
2464 A1320 110cr multicolored .35 .35
2465 A1320 635cr multicolored 1.00 1.00

Father Cicero Romao Batista, 150th Birth Anniv.
A1321

1994, Mar. 24 *Perf. 11x11½*
2466 A1321 (1) multicolored .80 .75

No. 2466 valued at first class domestic letter rate (98.80 cr) on day of issue.

Albert Sabin, Campaign Against Polio
A1322

1994, Apr. 7 *Perf. 11½x12*
2467 A1322 160cr multicolored .35 .35

Carlos Castello Branco, Journalist
A1323

1994, Apr. 14
2468 A1323 160cr multicolored .35 .35

Karl Friedrich Phillip von Martius, Naturalist
A1324

Flowers: No. 2469, Euterpe oleracea. No. 2470, Jacaranda paucifoliolata. No. 2471, Barbacernia tomentosa.

1994, Apr. 24 ***Perf. 12x11½***
2469 A1324 (1) multicolored .90 .90
2470 A1324 (1) multicolored .90 .90
2471 A1324 (1) multicolored 1.50 1.50
Nos. 2469-2471 (3) 3.30 3.30

Nos. 2469-2470 were valued at first class domestic letter rate (144 cr) on day of issue. No. 2471 valued at first class intl. letter rate (860 cr) on day of issue.

Monkeys — A1326

No. 2474, Leontopithecus rosalia. No. 2475, Saguinus imperator. No. 2476, Saguinus bicolor.

1994, May 24
2474 A1326 (1) multicolored .80 .80
2475 A1326 (1) multicolored .80 .80
2476 A1326 (1) multicolored .80 .80
Nos. 2474-2476 (3) 2.40 2.40

Nos. 2474-2476 were valued at first class domestic letter rate (207.03 cr) on day of issue.

1994 World Cup Soccer Championships, US — A1327

1994, May 19 ***Perf. 11½x12***
2477 A1327 (1) multicolored 1.75 1.75

No. 2477 was valued at first class intl. rate (1378.32 cr) on day of issue.
Soccer in Brazil, cent.

Souvenir Sheet

46th Frankfurt Intl. Book Fair — A1328

1994, May 27
2478 A1328 (1) multicolored 2.75 2.75

No. 2478 was valued at first class intl. rate (1523.83 cr) on day of issue.

Natl. Literacy Program — A1329

Designs: No. 2479, Pencil, buildings. No. 2480, Pencil, people on television, people watching. No. 2481, Classroom, pencil. No. 2482, Pencils crossed over fingerprint, map of Brazil.

1994, June 3 **Litho.** ***Perf. 12x11½***
2479 A1329 (1) multicolored .80 .80
2480 A1329 (1) multicolored .80 .80
2481 A1329 (1) multicolored .80 .80
2482 A1329 (1) multicolored .80 .80
Nos. 2479-2482 (4) 3.20 3.20

Nos. 2479-2482 were valued at first class domestic letter rate (233.05 cr) on day of issue.

Souvenir Sheet

Treaty of Tordesillas, 500th Anniv. — A1330

1994, June 7
2483 A1330 (1) multicolored 3.50 3.50

No. 2483 was valued at first class intl. letter rate (1689.02 cr) on day of issue.

Bird Type of 1994 and

A1330a

Designs: 1c, Like No. 2443. 2c, Like No. 2444. 5c, Like No. 2445. 10c, Like No. 2446. 15c, Sicalis flaveola. 20c, Like No. 2447. No. 2490, Tyrannus savana. 50c, Like No. 2448. 1r, Fumarius rufus.
No. 2498, Mylozetestes similis. No. 2499, Volantia jacarina.

Perf. 11x11½, 13 (15c), 12½13 (22c)
1994-2001 **Photo.**
2484 A1318 1c multi .25 .25
2485 A1318 2c multi .25 .25
2486 A1318 5c multi .25 .25
2487 A1318 10c multi .25 .25
2488 A1330a 15c multi .75 .35
2489 A1318 20c multi .50 .40
2490 A1318 22c multi .40 .40
a. Inscribed "1999" 1.00 .45
2491 A1318 50c multi 1.10 1.00
2494 A1318 1r multi 2.00 2.00
Nos. 2484-2494 (9) 5.75 5.15

Size: 21x27mm
Self-Adhesive
Serpentine Die Cut 5¾
2498 A1318 22c multi .85 .30
2499 A1318 (22c) multi 1.25 .55
a. Inscribed "2000" 1.10 1.10

No. 2499 is inscribed "1o PORTE NATIONAL" and was valued at 22c on day of issue.
No. 2490 has 1998 year date; No. 2499 has 1997 year date.
Issued: 1c, 2c, 5c, 20c, 20c, 50c, 1r, 7/1/94; 11/16/95; No. 2490, 10/13/97; No. 2498, 2/16/98; No. 2499, 7/22/97; No. 2490a, 11/99; No. 2499a, 1/01.

Prominent Brazilians A1331

Designs: No. 2504, Edgard Santos (1894-1962), surgeon, educator. No. 2505, Oswaldo Aranha (1894-1960), politician. No. 2507, Otto Lara Resende (1922-92), writer, educator.

1994, July 5 **Litho.** ***Perf. 11½x12***
2504 A1331 (1) multicolored .75 .60
2505 A1331 (1) multicolored .75 .60
2506 A1331 (1) multicolored .75 .60
Nos. 2504-2506 (3) 2.25 1.80

Nos. 2504-2506 were valued at first class domestic letter rate (12c) on day of issue.

Petrobras, 40th Anniv. — A1332

1994, July 15 ***Perf. 12x11½***
2507 A1332 12c multicolored .25 .25

Brazilian State Mint, 300th Anniv. — A1333

Litho. & Engr.
1994, July 26 ***Perf. 11½***
2508 A1333 12c multicolored .25 .25

Campaign Against Famine & Misery A1334

1994, July 27 **Litho.** ***Perf. 11½x12***
2509 A1334 (1) Fish .80 .35
2510 A1334 (1) Bread .80 .35

Nos. 2509-2510 were valued at first class domestic letter rate (12c) on day of issue.

Institute of Brazilian Lawyers, 150th Anniv. A1335

1994, Aug. 11
2511 A1335 12c multicolored .25 .25

Intl. Year of the Family A1336

1994, Aug. 16 ***Perf. 11½***
2512 A1336 84c multicolored 1.10 1.10

Maternity Hospital of Sao Paulo, Cent. A1337

1994, Aug. 26 ***Perf. 11½x12***
2513 A1337 12c multicolored .25 .25

Vincente Celestino (1894-1968), Singer — A1338

1994, Sept. 12
2514 A1338 12c multicolored .25 .25

"Contos da Carochinha," First Brazilian Children's Book, Cent. — A1339

No. 2515: Fairy tales: a, Joao e Maria (Hansel & Gretel). b, Dona Baratinha. c, Puss 'n Boots. d, Tom Thumb.

1994, Oct. 5 **Litho.** ***Perf. 11½x12***
2515 Block of 4 3.00 3.00
a.-b. A1339 12c any single .30 .30
c.-d. A1339 84c any single 1.00 1.00

Brazilian Literature A1340

Portraits: No. 2516, Tomas Antonio Gonzaga (1744-1809?), poet. No. 2517, Fernando de Azevedo (1894-1974), author.

1994, Oct. 5 ***Perf. 11½***
2516 A1340 12c multicolored .25 .25
2517 A1340 12c multicolored .25 .25

St. Clare of Assisi (1194-1253) A1341

1994, Oct. 19 ***Perf. 12x11½***
2518 A1341 12c multicolored .25 .25

Ayrton Senna (1960-1994), Race Car Driver — A1342

No. 2519: a, McClaren Formula 1 race car, Brazilian flag. b, Fans, Senna. c, Flags, race cars, Senna.

1994, Oct. 24 ***Perf. 11½x12***
2519 Triptych 1.75 1.75
a.-b. A1342 12c any single .30 .30
c. A1342 84c multicolored 1.10 1.10

Institute of History & Geography of Sao Paulo, Cent.
A1343

1994, Nov. 1
2520 A1343 12c multicolored .25 .25

Popular Music
A1344

Designs: No. 2521, Music from "The Sea," by Dorival Caymmi. No. 2522, Adoniran Barbosa (1910-82), samba composer.

1994, Nov. 5 ***Perf. 11½***
2521 A1344 12c multicolored .25 .25
2522 A1344 12c multicolored .25 .25

Christmas
A1345

No. 2523 — Folk characters: a, Boy wearing Santa coat, pot on head. b, Worm in apple. c, Man, animals singing. d, Shoe on tree stump, man with pipe holding pen.

1994, Dec. 1 **Litho.** ***Perf. 11½***
2523 Block of 4 1.75 1.75
a. A1345 84c multicolored 1.10 1.10
b.-d. A1345 12c any single .35 .35
e. Booklet pane, #2523 + 4 labels *17.50*
Complete booklet, #2523e *20.00*

Souvenir Sheet

Brazil, 1994 World Cup Soccer Champions — A1346

1994, Dec. 5 ***Perf. 12x11½***
2524 A1346 2.14r multicolored 6.00 6.00

Louis Pasteur (1822-95)
A1347

1995, Feb. 19 **Litho.** ***Perf. 11½x12***
2525 A1347 84c multicolored 1.25 1.25

Historical Events
A1348

Designs: No. 2526, Capture of Monte Castello, 50th anniv. No. 2527, End of the Farroupilha Revolution, 150th anniv.

1995, Feb. 21
2526 A1348 12c multicolored .25 .25
2527 A1348 12c multicolored .25 .25

Pres. Itamar Franco — A1349

1995, Mar. 22 **Litho.** ***Perf. 12x11½***
2528 A1349 12c multicolored .25 .25

FAO, 50th Anniv. — A1350

1995, Apr. 3 ***Perf. 11½x11***
2529 A1350 84c multicolored 1.25 1.25

Famous Men
A1351

Designs: No. 2530, Alexandre de Gusmao (1695-1753), diplomat. No. 2531, Francisco Brandao, Viscount of Jequitinhonha (1794-1870), lawyer, abolitionist. 15c, Jose da Silva Paranhos, Jr., Baron of Rio Branco (1845-1912), politician, diplomat.

1995, Apr. 28 ***Perf. 11½x12***
2530 A1351 12c multicolored .25 .25
2531 A1351 12c multicolored .25 .25
2532 A1351 15c multicolored .25 .25
Nos. 2530-2532 (3) .75 .75

Guglielmo Marconi (1874-1937), Radio Transmitting Equipment — A1352

1995, May 5 **Litho.** ***Perf. 11½x12***
2533 A1352 84c multicolored 1.25 1.25
Radio, cent.

Friendship Between Brazil & Japan
A1353

1995, May 29
2534 A1353 84c multicolored 1.25 1.25

Endangered Birds — A1354

No. 2535, Tinamus solitarius. No. 2536, Mitu mitu.

1995, June 5 ***Perf. 12x11½***
2535 A1354 12c multicolored .50 .30
2536 A1354 12c multicolored .50 .30

June Festivals — A1355

Designs: No. 2537, Couples dancing at Campina Grande, "Greatest St. John's Party of the World." No. 2538, Bride, bridegroom, festivities, Caruaru.

1995, June 11 ***Perf. 11½x12***
2537 A1355 12c multicolored .30 .30
2538 A1355 12c multicolored .30 .30

St. Anthony of Padua (1195-1231) — A1356

1995, June 13
2539 A1356 84c multicolored 1.25 1.25
See Portugal No. 2054.

Souvenir Sheet

Louis and Auguste Lumiere, Camera — A1357

1995, June 21
2540 A1357 2.14r multicolored 6.50 6.50
Motion pictures, cent.

New Currency, The Real, 1st Anniv. — A1358

1995, July 1 **Litho.** ***Perf. 12x11½***
2541 A1358 12c multicolored .30 .30

Volleyball, Cent. — A1359

1995, July 8
2542 A1359 15c multicolored .30 .30

Dinosaurs
A1360

15c, Angaturama limai. 1.50r, Titanosaurus.

1995, July 23 ***Perf. 11½x12***
2543 A1360 15c multi .30 .30
2544 A1360 1.50r multi 1.50 1.50

Traffic Safety Program
A1361

Designs: 12c, Test dummy without seat belt hitting windshield. 71c, Auto hitting alcoholic beverage glass.

1995, July 25
2545 A1361 12c multicolored .30 .30
2546 A1361 71c multicolored 1.25 1.25

Souvenir Sheet

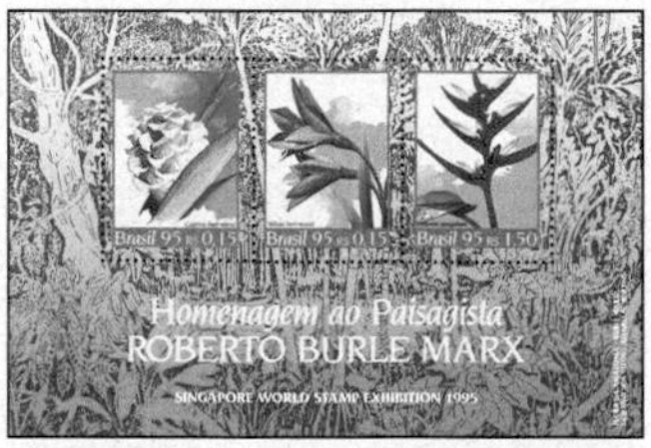

Roberto Burle Marx, Botanist — A1362

No. 2547: a, 15c, Calathea burle-marxii. b, 15c, Vellozia burle-marxii. c, 1.50r, Heliconia aemygdiana.

1995, Aug. 4 **Litho.** ***Perf. 12x11½***
2547 A1362 Sheet of 3, #a.-c. 6.00 6.00
Singapore '95.

Parachute Infantry Brigade, 50th Anniv. — A1363

1995, Aug. 23
2548 A1363 15c multicolored .30 .30

Paulista Museum, Cent. A1364

1995, Sept. 5 *Perf. 11½*

2549 A1364 15c multicolored .30 .30

Lighthouses A1365

No. 2550, Olinda. No. 2551, Sao Joao. No. 2552, Santo Antonio da Barra.

1995, Sept. 28

2550 A1365 15c multi 1.00 .35
2551 A1365 15c multi 1.00 .35
2552 A1365 15c multi 1.00 .35
Nos. 2550-2552 (3) 3.00 1.05

Wilhelm Röntgen (1845-1923), Discovery of the X-Ray, Cent. A1366

1995, Sept. 30

2553 A1366 84c multicolored 1.25 1.25

Wildlife Scene Along Tiete River — A1367

Designs: 15c, No. 2556a, Bird, otter with fish. 84c, No. 2556b, Birds, river boat.

1995, Sept. 30 *Perf. 12x11½*

2554 A1367 15c multicolored .55 .55
2555 A1367 84c multicolored 1.50 1.50

Souvenir Sheet

2556 A1367 1.50r Sheet of 2, #a.-b. 12.00 12.00

Lubrapex '95, 15th Brazilian-Portuguese Philatelic Exhibition.
No. 2556 is a continuous design.

Flamengo Regatta Soccer Club — A1368

1995, Oct. 6 *Perf. 11x11½*

2557 A1368 15c multicolored .55 .35

America Issue — A1369

Outdoor scenes: 15c, Trees, mushrooms, alligator, lake. 84c, Black-neck swans on lake, false swans in air.

1995, Oct. 12 Litho. *Perf. 11½x12*

2558 15c multicolored .30 .30
2559 84c multicolored 1.25 1.25
a. A1369 Pair, #2558-2559 1.75 1.75

UN, 50th Anniv. — A1370

1995, Oct. 24 *Perf. 12x11½*

2560 1.05r multicolored 1.75 1.75
2561 1.05r multicolored 1.75 1.75
a. A1370 Pair, No. 2560-2561 4.00 4.00

Writers — A1372

Designs: No. 2562, Eca de Queiroz (1845-1900), village. No. 2563, Rubem Braga (1913-90), beach, Rio de Janeiro. 23c, Carlos Drummond de Andrade (1902-87), letters.

1995, Oct. 27 *Perf. 12x11*

2562 A1372 15c multicolored .40 .40
2563 A1372 15c multicolored .40 .40
2564 A1372 23c multicolored .60 .60
Nos. 2562-2564 (3) 1.40 1.40

Souvenir Sheet

Death of Zumbi Dos Palmares, Slave Resistance Leader, 300th Anniv. — A1373

1995, Nov. 20 *Perf. 12x11½*

2565 A1373 1.05r multicolored 6.00 6.00

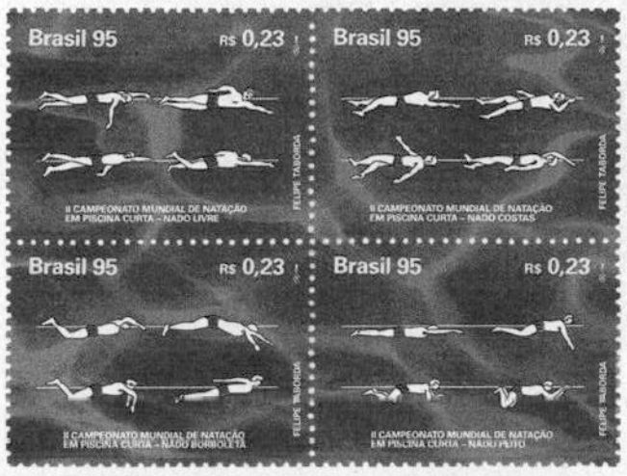

2nd World Short Course Swimming Championships — A1374

No. 2566: a, Freestyle. b, Backstroke. c, Butterfly. d, Breaststroke.

1995, Nov. 30 *Perf. 11½x12*

2566 A1374 23c Block of 4, #a.-d. 3.25 3.25

Christmas — A1375

No. 2567: a, 23c, Cherub looking right, stars. b, 15c, Cherub looking left, stars.

1995, Dec. 1 *Perf. 11½*

2567 A1375 Pair, #a.-b.+2 labels 1.75 1.75

Botafogo Soccer and Regatta Club A1376

1995, Dec. 8 *Perf. 11x11½*

2568 A1376 15c multicolored .40 .35

Diário de Pernambuco Newspaper, 170th Anniv. — A1377

1995, Dec. 14 Litho. *Perf. 12x11½*

2569 A1377 23c multicolored .60 .60

Souvenir Sheet

Amazon Theatre, Cent. — A1378

1996, Feb. 27

2570 A1378 1.23r multicolored 6.00 6.00

Francisco Prestes Maia, Politician, Birth Cent. A1379

1996, Mar. 19 *Perf. 11½x12*

2571 A1379 18c multicolored .60 .40

Ireneu Bornhausen, Governor of Santa Catarina, Birth Cent. — A1380

1996, Mar. 25 *Perf. 11x11½*

2572 A1380 27c multicolored .60 .55

Paintings A1381

Designs: No. 2573, Boat with Little Flags and Birds, by Alfredo Volpi. No. 2574, Ouro Preto Landscape, by Alberto da Veiga Guignard.

1996, Apr. 15 *Perf. 12x11½*

2573 A1381 15c multicolored .75 .30
2574 A1381 15c multicolored .75 .30

UNICEF, 50th Anniv. A1382

1996, Apr. 16 *Perf. 11½*

2575 A1382 23c multicolored .75 .50

Portuguese Discovery of Brazil, 500th Anniv. (in 2000) — A1383

1996, Apr. 22 *Perf. 12x11½*

2576 A1383 1.05r multicolored 2.75 2.25

See No. 2626.

Israel Pinheiro da Silva, Politician, Business Entrepeneur, Birth Cent. — A1384

1996, Apr. 23 *Perf. 11½x12*

2577 A1384 18c multicolored .75 .40

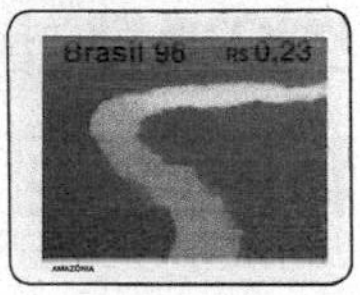

Tourism A1385

Designs: No. 2578, Amazon River. No. 2579, Swampland area. No. 2580, Sail boat, northeastern states. No. 2581, Sugarloaf, Guanabara Bay. No. 2582, Iguacu Falls.

1996, Apr. 24 *Die Cut*

Self-Adhesive

2578 A1385 23c multicolored .75 .30
2579 A1385 23c multicolored .75 .30
2580 A1385 23c multicolored .75 .30
2581 A1385 23c multicolored .75 .30
2582 A1385 23c multicolored .75 .30
a. Strip of 5, #2578-2582 4.00

Hummingbirds — A1386

Espamer '96: 15c, Topaza pella. 1.05r, Stephanoxis lalandi. 1.15r, Eupetomena macroura.

1996, May 4 Litho. *Perf. 11½*

2583 A1386 15c multicolored .75 .50
2584 A1386 1.05r multicolored 4.00 3.00
2585 A1386 1.15r multicolored 4.00 3.00
Nos. 2583-2585 (3) 8.75 6.50

1996 Summer Olympic Games, Atlanta
A1387

No. 2586, Marathon. No. 2587, Gymnastics. No. 2588, Swimming. No. 2589, Beach volleyball.

1996, May 21

2586	A1387	18c multi	.75	.40
2587	A1387	23c multi	1.00	.50
2588	A1387	1.05r multi	3.75	2.00
2589	A1387	1.05r multi	3.75	2.00
	Nos. 2586-2589 (4)		9.25	4.90

Souvenir Sheet

Brazilian Caverns — A1388

1996, June 5 *Perf. 11½x12*
2590 A1388 2.68r multicolored 8.00 8.00

Americas Telecom '96 — A1389

1996, June 10 *Perf. 11½*
2591 A1389 1.05r multicolored 2.75 2.75

Souvenir Sheet

World Day to Fight Desertification — A1390

1996, June 17 *Perf. 12x11½*
2592 A1390 1.23r multicolored 6.00 6.00

Fight Against Drug Abuse
A1391

1996, June 26 *Perf. 11½x12*
2593 A1391 27c multicolored 1.25 .65

Year of Education
A1392

1996, July 10 *Perf. 12x11½*
2594 A1392 23c multicolored 1.25 .55

Princess Isabel, 150th Birth Anniv.
A1393

1996, July 29 *Perf. 11½x12*
2595 A1393 18c multicolored .75 .40

Carlos Gomes (1836-96), Composer
A1394

1996, Sept. 16 *Perf. 11½*
2596 A1394 50c multicolored 1.25 1.25

15th World Orchid Conference
A1395

Designs: No. 2597, Promenaea stapelioides. No. 2598, Cattleya eldorado. No. 2599, Cattleya loddigesii.

1996, Sept. 17

2597	A1395	15c multicolored	1.50	.60
2598	A1395	15c multicolored	1.50	.60
2599	A1395	15c multicolored	1.50	.60
	Nos. 2597-2599 (3)		4.50	1.80

Apparition of Virgin Mary at La Salette, 150th Anniv.
A1396

1996, Sept. 19
2600 A1396 1r multicolored 2.75 2.25

Souvenir Sheet

Popular Legends — A1397

No. 2601: a, 23c, "Cuca" walking from house. b, 1.05r, "Boitatá," snake of life. c, 1.15r, "Caipora," defender of ecology.

1996, Sept. 28 *Perf. 11x10½*
2601 A1397 Sheet of 3, #a.-c. 7.50 7.50

BRAPEX '96.

23rd Sao Paulo Intl. Biennial Exhibition — A1398

No. 2602: a, Marilyn Monroe by Andy Warhol, vert. b, The Scream, by Edvard Munch, vert. c, Abstract, by Louise Bourgeois, vert. d, Woman Drawing, by Pablo Picasso.

1996, Oct. 5 *Perf. 12x11½*
2602 A1398 55c Block of 4, #a.-d. 22.50 22.50

Traditional Costumes
A1400

America issue: 50c, Man dressed as cowboy. 1r, Woman dressed in baiana clothes.

1996, Oct. 12 **Litho.** *Perf. 11½*

2604	A1400	50c multicolored	1.00	1.00
2605	A1400	1r multicolored	3.50	3.50

Christmas
A1401

1996, Nov. 4 **Litho.** *Perf. 12x11½*
2606 A1401 1st multicolored 1.25 .60

No. 2606 was valued at 23c on day of issue.

José Carlos (1884-1950), Caricaturist
A1402

1996, Nov. 22
2607 A1402 1st multicolored 1.25 .60

No. 2607 was valued at 23c on day of issue.

Tourism
A1403

Designs: No. 2608, Ipiranga Monument, Sao Paulo. No. 2609, Hercílio Luz Bridge, Florianópolis. No. 2610, Natl. Congress Building, Brasília. No. 2611, Pelourinho, Salvador. No. 2612, Ver-o-Peso Market, Belém.

Serpentine Die Cut

1996, Dec. 9 **Photo.**

Self-Adhesive

2608	A1403	1st multicolored	.80	.30
2609	A1403	1st multicolored	.80	.30
2610	A1403	1st multicolored	.80	.30
2611	A1403	1st multicolored	.80	.30
2612	A1403	1st multicolored	.80	.30
a.		Strip of 5, #2608-2612	4.00	

Nos. 2608-2612 are inscribed "1o PORTE NACIONAL," and were valued 23c on day of issue. Selvage surrounding each stamp in No. 2612a is rouletted.

Rio de Janeiro, Candidate for 2004 Summer Olympic Games
A1404

1997, Jan. 17 **Litho.** *Perf. 11½*
2613 A1404 1st multicolored 2.75 2.25

No. 2613 is inscribed "1o PORTE INTERNACIONAL" and was valued at 1.05r on day of issue.

The Postman
A1405

1997, Jan. 25
2614 A1405 1st multicolored .80 .75

America issue. No. 2614 is inscribed "1o PORTE NACIONAL" and was valued at 23c on day of issue.

Antonio de Castro Alves (1847-71), Poet A1406

1997, Mar. 14

2615	A1406	15c multicolored	.60	.50

Marquis of Tamandaré, Naval Officer, Death Cent. — A1407

1997, Mar. 19 ***Perf. 11x11½***

2616	A1407	23c multicolored	.65	.50

Stamp Design Contest Winner A1408

1997, Mar. 20 ***Perf. 11½x12***

2617	A1408	15c "Joy Joy"	.75	.35

World Day of Water — A1409

1997, Mar. 22 ***Perf. 12x11½***

2618	A1409	1.05r multicolored	1.90	1.90

Brazilian Airplanes A1410

Designs: No. 2619, EMB-145. No. 2620, AMX. No. 2621, EMB-312 H Super Tucano. No. 2622, EMB-120 Brasilia. No. 2623, EMB-312 Tucano.

1997, Mar. 27 **Litho.** ***Die Cut***

Self-Adhesive

2619	A1410	15c multicolored	.75	.30
2620	A1410	15c multicolored	.75	.30
2621	A1410	15c multicolored	.75	.30
2622	A1410	15c multicolored	.75	.30
2623	A1410	15c multicolored	.75	.30
a.		Strip of 5, #2619-2623	4.00	4.00

Campaign Against AIDS — A1411

1997, Apr. 7 **Litho.** ***Perf. 12x11½***

2624	A1411	23c multicolored	.65	.50

Souvenir Sheet

Indian Culture — A1412

Weapons of the Xingu Indians.

1997, Apr. 16 ***Perf. 11x11½***

2625	A1412	1.15r multicolored	3.00	3.00

Portuguese Discovery of Brazil, 500th Anniv. Type

1997, Apr. 22 ***Perf. 12x11½***

2626	A1383	1.05r like #2576	2.25	2.25

No. 2576 has green background and blue in lower right corner. No. 2626 has those colors reversed and is inscribed "BRASIL 97" at top.

Pixinguinha (1897-1973), Composer, Musician — A1413

1997, Apr. 23

2627	A1413	15c multicolored	.60	.35

Souvenir Sheet

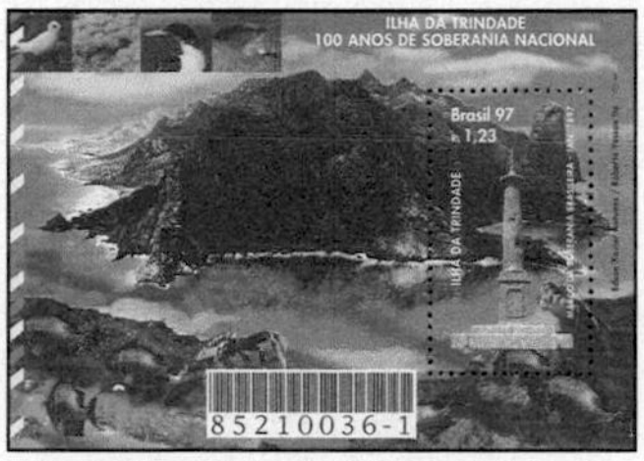

Brazilian Claim to Trindade Island, Cent. — A1414

1997, May 7 ***Perf. 11½x11***

2628	A1414	1.23r multicolored	6.00	6.00

Human Rights — A1415

1997, May 13 ***Perf. 12x11½***

2629	A1415	18c multicolored	.60	.35

Souvenir Sheet

Brazilian Antarctic Program — A1416

1997, May 13

2630	A1416	2.68r multicolored	6.50	6.50

Fruits and Nuts — A1417

Designs: 1c, Oranges. 2c, Bananas. 5c, Papayas. 10c, Pineapple. Nos. 2635, 2636L, Cashews. Nos. 2636, 2636Q, Sugar apple. No. 2636A, Grapes. Nos. 2636B, 2636M, 2636R, Watermelon. 50c, Surinam cherry (pitanga), 51c, Coconuts. 80c, Apples. 82c, Lemons. 1r, Strawberries.

1997-99 **Litho.** ***Serpentine Die Cut***

Self-Adhesive

2631	A1417	1c	multi	.65	.30
2632	A1417	2c	multi	.65	.30
2633	A1417	5c	multi	.65	.30
2634	A1417	10c	multi, vert.	1.50	.65
2635	A1417	20c	multi, vert.	3.00	1.50
2636	A1417	20c	multi, vert.	1.50	.65
2636A	A1417	22c	multi	.65	.30
2636B	A1417	(22c)	multi	2.75	.35
2636C	A1417	50c	multi	.90	.45
2636D	A1417	51c	multi, vert.	2.00	1.50
2636E	A1417	80c	multi, vert.	5.00	3.00
2636F	A1417	82c	multi, vert.	6.50	5.00
2636G	A1417	1r	multi, vert.	2.00	.65
	Nos. 2631-2636G (13)			27.75	14.95

Issued: (22c), 5/28; 1c, 6/97; 2c, 10c, No. 2635, 7/97; 5c, 8/97; 1r, 8/3; 22c, 10/3; No. 2636, 51c, 80c, 82c, 1/15/98; 50c, 11/26/99.

No. 2636B is inscribed "1o PORTE NATIONAL" and was valued at 22c on day of issue.

Fruits and Nuts Type of 1997-99

1998-99 **Litho.** ***Die Cut***

Self-Adhesive

2636H	A1417	1c	multi	.35	.35
2636I	A1417	2c	multi	.50	.50
2636J	A1417	5c	multi	.65	.65
2636K	A1417	10c	multi, vert.	1.50	.65
2636L	A1417	20c	multi, vert.	2.00	.65
2636M	A1417	(22c)	multi	3.25	.35
	Nos. 2636H-2636M (6)			8.25	3.15

Microperfed

Without Gum

2636N	A1417	1c	multi	1.75	1.75
2636O	A1417	5c	multi	8.00	8.00
2636P	A1417	10c	multi, vert.	12.00	12.00
2636Q	A1417	20c	multi, vert.	12.00	12.00
2636R	A1417	(31c)	multi	6.00	6.00
2636S	A1417	51c	multi, vert.	12.00	12.00
2636T	A1417	80c	multi, vert.	20.00	20.00
2636U	A1417	1r	multi, vert.	20.00	20.00
	Nos. 2636N-2636U (8)			91.75	91.75

Issued: 2636H-2636L, 1998. No. 2636M, 1999.

Issued: Nos. 2636N-2636Q, 9/28/99; No. 2636R, 9/12/99; No. 2636S, 9/22/99; Nos. 2636T, 2636U, 9/15/99.

A1418

Amazon Flora and Fauna — A1419

Designs: No. 2637, Swietenia macropylla. No. 2638, Arapaima gigas.

1997, June 5 **Litho.** ***Perf. 11½x12***

2637	A1418	27c multicolored	.75	.40
2638	A1419	27c multicolored	.75	.40

Fr. José de Anchieta (1534-97), Missionary in Brazil — A1420

Design: No. 2640, Fr. António Vieira (1608-97), missionary in Brazil, diplomat.

1997, June 9 ***Perf. 12***

2639	A1420	1.05r multicolored	1.75	1.75
2640	A1420	1.05r multicolored	1.75	1.75

See Portugal Nos. 2168-2169.

Tourism A1421

Designs: No. 2641, Parnaíba River Delta. No. 2642, Lencóis Maranhenses Park.

1997, June 20 ***Perf. 11½x12***

2641	A1421	1st multicolored	2.25	2.00
2642	A1421	1st multicolored	2.25	2.00

Nos. 2641-2642 are inscribed "1o PORTE INTERNACIONAL TAXE PERCUE" and were each valued at on day of issue.

Brazilian Academy of Literature, Cent. A1422

1997, July 20

2643	A1422	22c multicolored	.55	.50

Emiliano de Cavalcanti (1897-1976), Painter A1423

1997, Sept. 16 **Litho.** ***Perf. 11½***

2644	A1423	31c multicolored	.55	.50

2nd World Meeting of the Pope with Families, Rio de Janeiro
A1424

1997, Sept. 22 ***Perf. 11½x12***
2645 A1424 1.20r multicolored 1.75 1.75

A1425

1997, Sept. 26 ***Perf. 12x11½***
2646 A1425 80c multicolored 1.25 1.25

MERCOSUR (Common Market of Latin America). See Argentina #1975, Bolivia #1019, Paraguay #2565, Uruguay #1681.

A1426

1997, Sept. 27
2647 A1426 22c multicolored .75 .75

End of Canudos War, cent.

Integration of MERCOSUR Communications by Telebras, 25th Anniv. — A1427

1997, Oct. 6 ***Perf. 11½***
2648 A1427 80c multicolored 1.25 1.25

Composers — A1428

Designs: No. 2649, Oscar Lorenzo Fernandez (1897-1948). No. 2650, Francisco Mignone (1897-1986).

1997, Oct. 7 ***Perf. 11x11½***
2649 A1428 22c multicolored .65 .45
2650 A1428 22c multicolored .65 .45

Marist Brothers Presence in Brazil, Cent.
A1429

1997, Oct. 22
2651 A1429 22c multicolored .65 .45

Christmas
A1430

1997, Nov. 5 ***Perf. 12x11½***
2652 A1430 22c multicolored .65 .45

Education and Citizenship — A1431

1997, Dec. 10 ***Perf. 11x11½***
2653 A1431 31c blue & yellow .65 .65

City of Belo Horizonte, Cent.
A1432

1997, Dec. 12 ***Perf. 11½x12***
2654 A1432 31c multicolored .65 .65

Citzenship
A1433

Map of Brazil and: No. 2655, Education, stack of books. No. 2656, Employment, worker's papers. No. 2657, Agriculture, oranges. No. 2658, Health, stethoscope, vert. No. 2659, Culture, clapboard with musical notes, artist's paint brush, vert.

1997, Dec. 20 ***Die Cut***
Self-Adhesive
Booklet Stamps

2655 A1433 22c multicolored .90 .45
2656 A1433 22c multicolored .90 .45
2657 A1433 22c multicolored .90 .45
2658 A1433 22c multicolored .90 .45
2659 A1433 22c multicolored .90 .45
a. Bklt. pane, 2 ea #2655-2659 10.00

The peelable paper backing of No. 2659a serves as a booklet cover.

Gems — A1434

No. 2660, Alexandrite. No. 2661, Cat's eye chrysoberyl. No. 2662, Indicolite.

1998, Jan. 22 ***Perf. 12x11½***
2660 A1434 22c multicolored 1.50 .60
2661 A1434 22c multicolored 1.50 .60
2662 A1434 22c multicolored 1.50 .60
a. Strip of 3, #2660-2662 4.50 2.75

Famous Brazilian Women
A1435

America Issue: No. 2663, Elis Regina, singer. No. 2664, Clementina de Jesus, singer. No. 2665, Dulcina de Moraes, actress. No. 2666, Clarice Lispector, writer.

1998, Mar. 11 ***Perf. 11½***
2663 A1435 22c multicolored .70 .45
2664 A1435 22c multicolored .70 .45
2665 A1435 22c multicolored .70 .45
2666 A1435 22c multicolored .70 .45
a. Block of 4, #2663-2666 3.00 3.00

Education — A1436

1998, Mar. 19 ***Perf. 12x11½***
2667 31c Children at desks .65 .65
2668 31c Teacher at blackboard .65 .65
a. A1436 Pair, #2667-2668 1.40 1.40

Cruz e Sousa (1861-98), Poet
A1437

1998, Mar. 19 **Litho.** ***Perf. 11½x12***
2669 A1437 36c multicolored .65 .65

Discovery of Brazil, 500th Anniv. — A1438

Designs: No. 2670, 1519 map showing natives, vegetation, fauna. No. 2671, Caravel from Cabral's fleet.

1998, Apr. 22 ***Perf. 12x11½***
2670 1.05r multicolored 2.75 1.40
2671 1.05r multicolored 2.75 1.40
a. A1438 Pair, #2670-2671 5.50 5.50

Volunteer Work — A1439

Designs: a, Caring for sick man. b, Caring for sick child. c, Fighting forest fire. c, Child's hand holding adult's finger.

1998, May 5 ***Perf. 11½x12***
2672 A1439 31c Block of 4, #a.-d. 2.25 2.25

Brazilian Circus — A1440

No. 2673 — Piolin the clown: a, Looking through circle. b, Standing in ring. c, With outside of tent to the left. d, With inside of tent to the right.

1998, May 18 ***Perf. 12x11½***
2673 A1440 31c Block of 4, #a.-d. 2.25 2.25

Intl. Year of the Ocean — A1441

No. 2674 — Pictures, drawings of marine life: a, Turtle. b, Tail fin of whale. c, Barracuda. d, Jellyfish, school of fish. e, School of fish, diver. f, Dolphins. g, Yellow round fish. h, Two whales. i, Two black-striped butterfly fish. j, Orange & yellow fish. k, Manatee. l, Yellow-striped fish. m, Blue & yellow fish. n, Several striped fish. o, Fish with wing-like fins. p, Manta ray. q, Two fish swimming in opposite directions. r, Long, thin fish, coral. s, Moray eel. t, Yellow & black butterfly fish, coral. u, Starfish, fish. v, Crab, coral. w, Black & orange fish, coral. x, Sea horse, coral.

1998, May 22 ***Perf. 11½x12***
Sheet of 24
2674 A1441 31c #a.-x. 22.00 22.00

Expo '98.

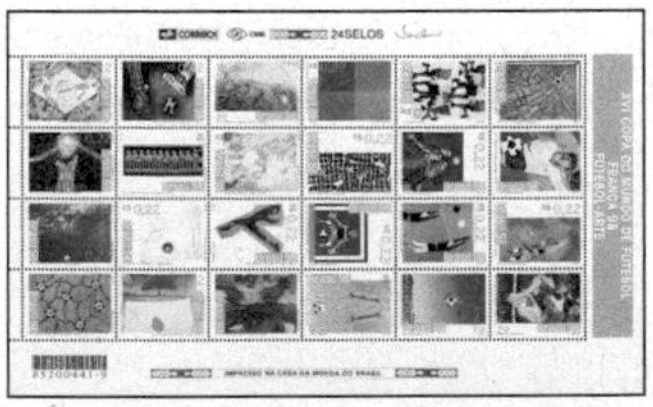

1998 World Cup Soccer Championships, France — A1442

No. 2675 — Paintings by: a, Gregorio Gruber. b, Mario Gruber. c, Maciej Babinski. d, Cildo Meireles, vert. e, Claudio Tozzi, vert. f, Antonio Henrique Amaral, vert. g, Jose Roberto Aguilar. h, Nelson Leirner. i, Wesley Duke Lee. j, Mauricio Nogueira Lima, vert. k, Zelio Alves Pinto, vert. l, Aldemir Martins, vert. m, Ivald Granato. n, Carlos Vergara. o, Joao Camara, vert. p, Roberto Magalhaes, vert. q, Guto Lacaz, vert. r, Glauco Rodrigues, vert. s, Leda Catunda. t, Tomoshige Kusuno. u, Jose Zaragoza. v, Luiz Zerbine, vert. w, Antonio Peticov, vert. x, Marcia Grostein, vert.

1998, May 28 ***Perf. 11½x12, 12x11½***
2675 A1442 22c Sheet of 24, #a.-x. 22.00 22.00

Feijoada, Traditional Cuisine
A1443

1998, June 1 ***Perf. 11½***
2676 A1443 31c multicolored .55 .50

Preservation of Flora and Fauna — A1444

Designs: No. 2677, Araucaria angustifolia. No. 2678, Cyanocorax caeruleus.

1998, June 5 ***Perf. 11½x12***
2677 22c multicolored .60 .60
2678 22c multicolored .60 .60
a. A1444 Pair, #2677-2678 1.40 1.40

Launching of Submarine Tapajó
A1445

1998, June 5
2679 A1445 51c multicolored .75 .75

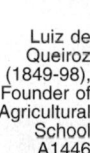

Luiz de Queiroz (1849-98), Founder of Agricultural School
A1446

1998, June 6 ***Perf. 11½***
2680 A1446 36c multicolored .60 .60

Benedictine Monastery, Sao Paulo, 400th Anniv.
A1447

1998, July 10 **Litho.** ***Perf. 11½x12***
2681 A1447 22c multicolored .60 .60

Alberto Santos-Dumont (1873-1932), Aviation Pioneer — A1448

Designs: No. 2682, Balloon "Brazil." No. 2683, Dirigible Nr. 1, Santos-Dumont at controls.

1998, July 18
2682 A1448 31c multicolored .80 .40
2683 A1448 31c multicolored .80 .40
a. Pair, #2682-2683 1.75 1.10

Brazilian Cinema, Cent. (in 1997) — A1449

No. 2684: a, Guanabara Bay, by Lumière, 1897. b, Taciana Reiss in "Limite," by Mário Peixoto, 1931. c, Actors in (Chanchada), from "A Dupla do Barulho," by Carlos Manga, 1953. d, Films produced by Vera Cruz pictures, caricature of Mazzaropi from "The Dream Factory." e, Glauber Rocha's "New Cinema". f, International film festival awards won by Brazilian films.

1998, July 24 ***Perf. 11½***
2684 A1449 31c Block of 6, #a.-f. 3.50 3.50

Rodrigo Melo Franco de Andrade (1898-1969), and Church of Our Lady of the Rosary, Ouro Preto — A1450

1998, Aug. 17 ***Perf. 11x11½***
2685 A1450 51c multicolored .75 .65

Luís da Camara Cascudo (1898-1986), Writer — A1451

1998, Aug. 22
2686 A1451 22c multicolored .55 .40

42nd Aeronautical Pentathlon World Championship — A1452

No. 2687: a, Fencing. b, Running. c, Swimming. d, Shooting. e, Basketball.

1998, Aug. 22 ***Perf. 12x11½***
2687 A1452 22c Strip of 5, #a.-e. 3.50 3.50

Missionary Cross, Ruins of the Church of Sao Miguel das Missoes — A1453

1998, Sept. 17 ***Perf. 11½x12***
2688 A1453 80c multicolored 1.25 1.00

24th Sao Paulo Art Biennial — A1454

No. 2689: a, Biennial emblem, by José Leonilson. b, Tapuia Dance, by Albert von Eckhout. c, The Schoolboy, by Vincent van Gogh. d, Portrait of Michel Leiris, by Francis Bacon. e, The King's Museum, by René Magritte. f, Urutu, by Tarsila do Amaral. g, Facade with Arcs, Circle and Fascia, by Alfredo Volpi. h, The Raft of the Medusa, by Asger Jorn.

1998, Sept. 22
2689 A1454 31c Block of 8, #a.-h. 4.50 4.50

Nos. 2689b, 2689h have horiz. designs placed vert. on stamps.

Child and Citizenship Stamp Design Contest Winner
A1455

1998, Oct. 9
2690 A1455 22c multicolored .35 .30

Reorganization of Maritime Mail from Portugal to Brazil, Bicent. — A1456

1998, Oct. 9
2691 A1456 1.20r multicolored 1.75 1.50

See Portugal Nos. 2271-2272.

Dom Pedro I (1798-1834)
A1457

1998, Oct. 13 ***Perf. 11½***
2692 A1457 22c multicolored .55 .25

Frisco's Mango Refreshment Promotional Stamp — A1458

Serpentine Die Cut

1998, Oct. 15 **Photo.**

Self-Adhesive

2693 A1458 36c multicolored 2.75 2.75

No. 2693 is valid on all mail, but must be used on mail entries to Frisco on Faustao's Truck raffle.

Flowers — A1459

No. 2694: a, Solanum lycocarpum. b, Cattleya walkeriana. c, Kielmeyera coriacea.

1998, Oct. 23 **Litho.** ***Perf. 11½***
2694 A1459 31c Strip of 3, #a.-c. 1.75 1.75

Humanitarians — A1460

No. 2695: a, Mother Teresa (1910-97). b, Friar Galvao (1739-1822). c, Herbert José de Souza "Betinho" (b. 1935). d, Friar Damiao (1898-1997).

1998, Oct. 25
2695 A1460 31c Block of 4, #a.-d. 2.25 2.25

A1461

31c, Sergio Motta, Former Minister of Communications, Natl. Telecommunications Agency Headquarters, Brasilia.

1998, Nov. 5 ***Perf. 12x11½***
2696 A1461 31c multicolored .60 .35

Christmas — A1462

1998, Nov. 19 ***Perf. 11½x12***
2697 A1462 22c multicolored .60 .30

Domestic Animals
A1463

Designs: No. 2698, Moxotó goat. No. 2699, Brazilian donkey. No. 2700, Junqueira ox. No. 2701, Brazilian terrier. No. 2702, Brazilian shorthair cat.

1998, Nov. 20 ***Die Cut***

Booklet Stamps

Self-Adhesive

2698 A1463 22c multi .60 .60
2699 A1463 22c multi .60 .60
2700 A1463 22c multi .60 .60
2701 A1463 22c multi, vert. .60 .60
2702 A1463 22c multi, vert. .60 .60
a. Bklt. pane, 2 ea #2698-2702 6.50

No. 2702a is a complete booklet.

Universal Declaration of Human Rights, 50th Anniv. — A1464

1998, Dec. 9 ***Perf. 12x11½***
2703 A1464 1.20r multicolored 1.25 1.25

Natal, 400th Anniv. A1465

No. 2704, Wise Men's Fortress. No. 2705, Mother Luiza Lighthouse, vert.

Perf. 11x11½, 11½x11

1999, Jan. 6 **Litho.**

2704 A1465 31c multicolored .45 .40
2705 A1465 31c multicolored .45 .40

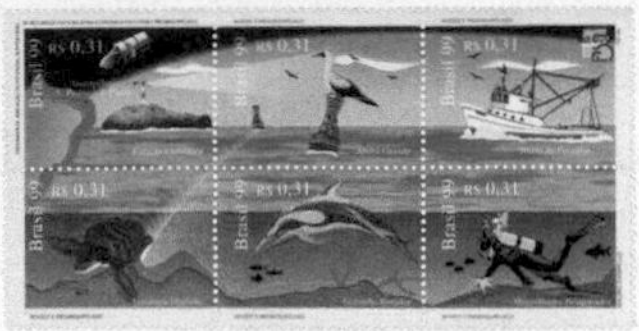

Program for Evaluating Resources in Brazil's Exclusive Economic Zone — A1466

No. 2706: a, Satellite, St. Peter and St. Paul Archipelago. b, Bird on buoy. c, Fishing boat. d, Sea turtle. e, Dolphin. f, Diver.

1999, Mar. 5 ***Perf. 11½x12***

2706 A1466 31c Block of 6, #a.-f. 2.50 2.50

Australia '99 World Stamp Expo.

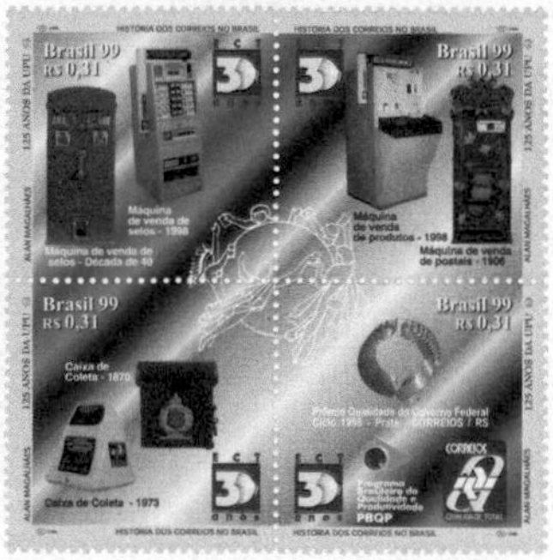

UPU, 125th Anniv. — A1467

No. 2707: a, Stamp vending machines from 1940s and 1998. b, Vending machines, 1906, 1998. c, Collection boxes, 1870, 1973. d, Federal Government's 1998 Quality Award.

1999, Mar. 19 ***Perf. 11½***

2707 A1467 31c Block of 4, #a.-d. 1.75 1.75

Reorganization of Brazilian Posts and Telegraphs, 30th anniv.

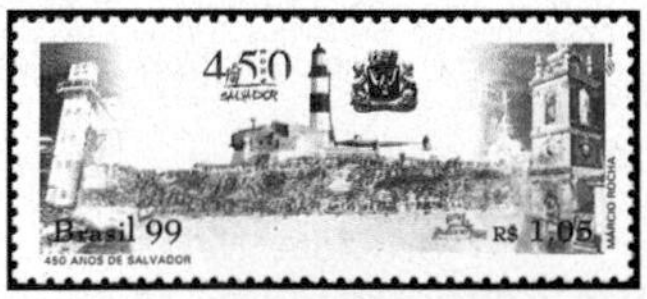

City of Salvador, 450th Anniv. — A1468

1999, Mar. 29 **Litho.** ***Perf. 11½x12***

2708 A1468 1.05r multi 1.50 1.50

Dinosaurs' Valley A1469

1999, Apr. 17 **Litho.** ***Perf. 11½x12***

2709 A1469 1.05r multicolored 1.25 1.25

Fort of Santo Amaro da Barra Grande — A1470

1999, Apr. 21 **Litho.** ***Perf. 11½x12***

2710 A1470 22c multicolored .45 .25

Souvenir Sheet

Discovery of Brazil, 500th Anniv. (in 2000) — A1471

1999, Apr. 22 **Litho.** ***Perf. 11½x11***

2711 A1471 2.68r multi 4.50 4.50

Lubrapex 2000.

6th Air Transportation Squadron, 30th Anniv. — A1472

1999, May 12 **Litho.** ***Perf. 11x11½***

2712 A1472 51c multicolored .65 .50

Holy Spirit Feast, Planaltina — A1473

1999, May 21 ***Perf. 12x11½***

2713 A1473 22c multicolored .45 .25

Historical and Cultural Heritage — A1474

No. 2714 — Views of cities: a, Ouro Preto. b, Olinda. c, Sao Luís.

1999, June 2 ***Perf. 11½x11***

2714 A1474 1.05r Sheet of 3, #a.-c. 3.75 3.75

PhilexFrance '99, World Philatelic Exhibition.

Sao Paolo State Institute for Technological Research, Cent. — A1475

1999, June 24 **Litho.** ***Perf. 11½x12***

2715 A1475 36c multicolored .60 .40

Flight of Alberto Santos-Dumont's Dirigible No. 3, Cent. — A1476

1999, July 20

2716 A1476 1.20r multicolored 1.75 1.75

Forest Fire Prevention A1477

No. 2717: a, Anteater. b, Flower. c, Leaf. d, Burnt trunk.

Serpentine Die Cut 6

1999, Aug. 1 **Litho.**

Self-Adhesive

2717 Block of 4 3.25 3.25
a.-d. A1477 51c Any single .75 .75

No. 2717 is printed on recycled paper impregnated with burnt wood odor.

Souvenir Sheet

America Issue, A New Millennium Without Arms — A1478

No. 2718: a, Hands of adult and child drawing dove. b, Overturned tank.

1999, Aug. 6 **Litho.** ***Perf. 12x11½***

2718 A1478 90c Sheet of 2, #a.-b. 1.75 1.75

Issued with rouletted tab at right showing Universal Product Code.

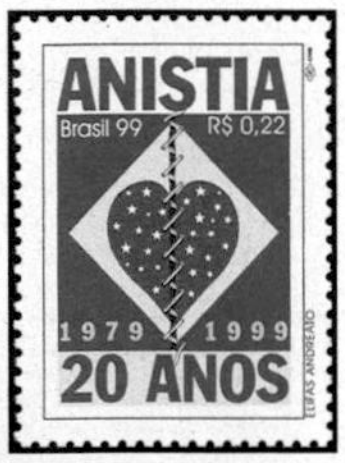

Political Amnesty, 20th Anniv. — A1479

1999, Aug. 18

2719 A1479 22c multicolored .45 .25

Famous Brazilians — A1480

Designs: 22c, Joaquim Nabuco (1849-1910), politician and diplomat. 31c, Ruy Barbosa (1849-1923), politician and justice for International Court.

1999, Aug. 19 **Litho.** ***Perf. 11½x12***

2720 A1480 22c multicolored .45 .25
2721 A1480 31c multicolored .45 .35

Fish — A1481

No. 2722: a, 22c, Salminus maxillosus. b, 31c, Brycon microlepsus. c, 36c, Acestrorhynchus pantaneiro. d, 51c, Hyphessobrycon eques. e, 80c, Rineloricaria. f, 90c, Leporinus macrocephalus. g, 1.05r, Abramites. h, 1.20r, Ancistrus.

1999, Aug. 20 **Litho.** ***Perf. 11½x12***

2722 A1481 Sheet of 8, #a.-h. 8.00 8.00

China 1999 World Philatelic Exhibition. No. 2722h has a holographic image. Soaking in water may affect hologram.

Mercosur Cultural Heritage Day A1482

1999, Sept. 17 **Litho.** ***Perf. 11½x12***

2723 A1482 80c multi .75 .75

Water Resources — A1483

No. 2724: a, Ecological station, Aguas Emendadas. b, House on water's edge, boat. c, Cedro Dam. d, Orós Dam.

1999, Oct. 21
2724 A1483 31c Block of 4, #a.-d. 1.75 1.75

National Library of Rio de Janeiro Bookplate A1484

1999, Oct. 29 Litho. ***Perf. 12x11½***
2725 A1484 22c multi .45 .25

State Flag Type of 1981

1999, Nov. 19 Litho. ***Perf. 11½x12***
2726 A947 31c Amapá .45 .35
2727 A947 36c Roraima .45 .35

Antonio Carlos Jobim (1927-94), Composer A1485

1999, Nov. 22
2728 A1485 31c multi .45 .35

Christianity, 2000th Anniv. — A1486

No. 2729: a, The Annunciation. b, Birth of Jesus and adoration of the Magi. c, Presentation of Jesus in the temple. d, Baptism of Jesus by John the Baptist. e, Evangelization of Jesus and Apostles. f, Death of Jesus and resurrection.

1999, Nov. 26 Litho. ***Perf. 11½***
2729 A1486 22c Block of 6, #a-f 2.50 2.50

New Middle School Education System — A1487

1999, Dec. 2 ***Perf. 11x11½***
2730 A1487 31c multi .45 .35

Itamaraty Palace, Rio A1488

Litho. & Engr.

1999, Dec. 6 ***Perf. 11½x12***
2731 A1488 1.05r pale yel & brn 1.25 1.25

New Year 2000 — A1489

2000, Jan. 1 Litho.
2732 A1489 90c multi .75 .75

National School Book Program A1490

2000, Feb. 7 ***Perf. 11x11½***
2733 A1490 31c multi .45 .35

Aviatrixes — A1491

No. 2734: a, Ada Rogato (1920-86). b, Thereza de Marzo (1903-86). c, Anésia Pinheiro (1904-99).

2000, Mar. 8 ***Perf. 11½x12***
2734 A1491 22c Horiz. strip of 3, #a-c .80 .80

Regional Cuisine — A1492

a, Moqueca Capixaba. b, Moqueca Baiana.

2000, Mar. 24
2735 A1492 1.05r Pair, #a-b 2.00 2.00

Gilberto Freyre (1900-87), Sociologist — A1493

2000, Mar. 24
2736 A1493 36c multi .45 .40

UIT Telecom A1494

2000, Apr. 9 Litho. ***Perf. 11½***
2737 A1494 51c multi .60 .55

Discovery of Brazil, 500th anniv.

Discovery of Brazil, 500th Anniv. — A1495

No. 2738: a, Two sailors, three natives, parrot. b, Sailor, ships, four natives. c, Sailors, natives, sails. d, Sailor and natives inspecting tree.

2000, Apr. 11 Litho. ***Perf. 11½x12***
2738 A1495 31c Block of 4, #a-d 2.25 2.25

See Portugal Nos. 2354-2357.

Discovery of Brazil, 500th Anniv. — A1496

2000, Apr. 11 Litho. ***Perf. 11½***
2739 A1496 31c multi + label 8.00 8.00

Printed in sheets of 9 stamps + 9 labels that could be personalized. Sheets sold for 5r.

Discovery of Brazil, 500th Anniv. — A1497

No. 2740: a, Brazilian flag as sails of ship. b, Man with pineapple, telephone dial, horn. c, Parrot and ships. d, Ship, map of Brazil, children. e, Race car driver Ayrton Senna. f, Flora and fauna. g, Map of Brazil, compass roses. h, Dove. i, Native with decorated face. j, Stylized "500." k, Native with feathered headdress. l, Children's drawing. m, Aviator Alberto Santos Dumont. n, Ship, manuscript. o, World Cup trophies, soccer player and ball, map. p, Fiber optic cables, street lights. q, Bull with Brazilian flag. r, Parrot. s, Native masks. t, Ship, Brazil highlighted on globe.

2000, Apr. 22 Litho. ***Perf. 11½***
2740 A1497 45c Sheet of 20, #a-t, + 4 labels 22.50 22.50

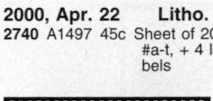

Brazil Trade Net Website, 2nd Anniv. A1498

2000, May 11 Litho. ***Perf. 11½***
2741 A1498 27c multi .45 .30

National Coastal Management Program — A1499

2000, May 16 Litho. ***Perf. 11½***
2742 A1499 40c multi .45 .40

Souvenir Sheet

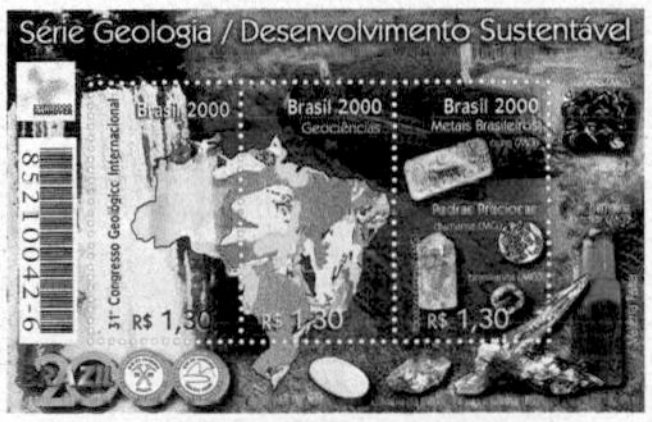

Expo 2000, Hanover — A1500

No. 2743: a, Map of Western Brazil. b, Map of Eastern Brazil. c, Gold and gemstones.

2000, May 19 Litho. ***Perf. 10¾x11***
2743 A1500 1.30r #a-c 5.00 5.00

Oswaldo Cruz Foundation, Cent. — A1501

2000, May 25 ***Perf. 11½x12***
2744 A1501 40c multicolored .45 .40

Africa Day A1502

2000, May 25 ***Perf. 11½***
2745 A1502 1.10r multi .75 .75

Sailing Feats of Amyr Klink A1503

No. 2746: a, First crossing of South Atlantic by rowboat, 1984. b, Solo circumnavigation of Antarctica, 1999.

2000, May 27
2746 A1503 1r Vert. pair, #a-b 2.75 2.75

Juiz de Fora, 150th Anniv. — A1504

2000, May 31 ***Perf. 11½x12***
2747 A1504 60c multi .60 .60

Sports — A1505

No. 2748, Hanggliding. No. 2749, Surfing. No. 2750, Mountain climbing. No. 2751, Skateboarding.

Serpentine Die Cut 5¾
2000 Self-Adhesive Photo.
2748 A1505 27c multi .35 .25
2749 A1505 27c multi .30 .25
2750 A1505 40c multi .50 .25
2751 A1505 40c multi .45 .25
Nos. 2748-2751 (4) 1.60 1.00

Issued: Nos. 2748, 2750, 6/1; No. 2749, 8/1; No. 2751, 7/1.

Environmental Protection — A1506

No. 2752: a, Trees. b, Trees, Felis tigrina in background. c, Heads of two Felis tigrina, two white flowers. d, Felis tigrina, one white flower.

2000, June 5 ***Perf. 11½***
2752 A1506 40c Block of 4, #a-d 3.00 3.00

Ships — A1507

No. 2753: a, Cisne Branco. b, Brasil.

2000, June 11 Litho. ***Perf. 11x11½***
2753 A1507 27c Pair, #a-b .85 .60

Souvenir Sheets

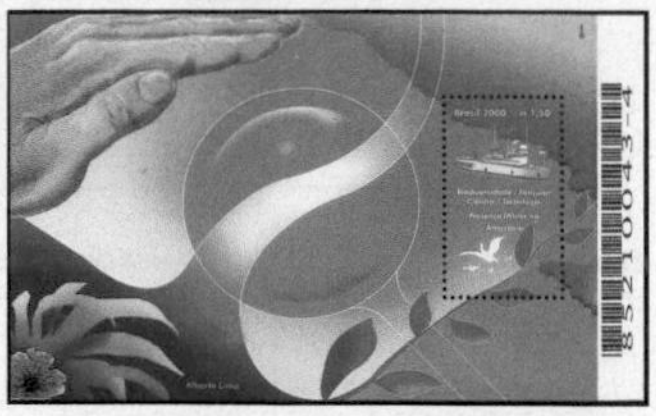

Military Presence in Amazonia — A1508

2000, June 11 Litho. ***Perf. 11½x11***
2754 A1508 1.50r multi 1.25 1.25

Barcode is separated from the sheet margin by a row of microperfs.

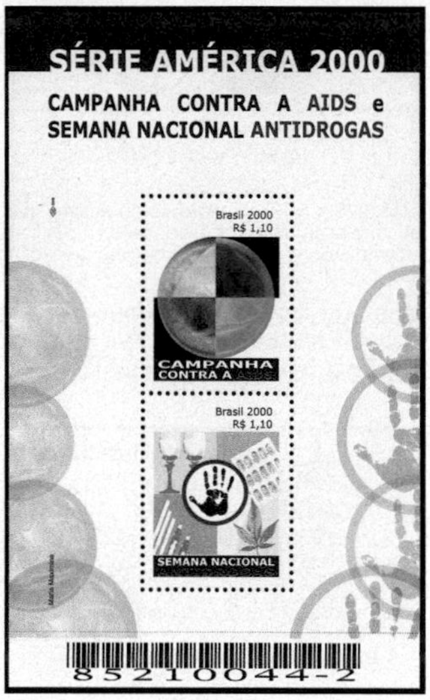

America Issue — A1509

No. 2755: a, Campaign against AIDS. b, Natl. anti-drug week.

2000, June 19 ***Perf. 12x11½***
2755 A1509 1.10r Sheet of 2, #a-b 2.25 2.25

Barcode is separated from the sheet margin by a row of microperfs.

Anísio Teixeira (1900-71), Educator — A1510

2000, July 12 Litho. ***Perf. 11½x12***
2756 A1510 45c multi .45 .45

Children's and Teenagers Statute, 10th Anniv. — A1511

2000, July 13 ***Perf. 12x11½***
2757 A1511 27c multi .30 .30

Natl. Movement of Street Boys and Girls, 15th Anniv. — A1512

2000, July 13
2758 A1512 40c multi .45 .45

Gustavo Capanema (1900-54), Politician — A1513

2000, Aug. 10 Litho. ***Perf. 11½x12***
2759 A1513 60c multi .60 .60

Milton Campos, Politician — A1514

2000, Aug. 16
2760 A1514 1r multi .75 .75

World Ozone Layer Protection Day — A1515

2000, Sept. 16 ***Perf. 12x11½***
2761 A1515 1.45r multi 1.25 1.25

Fruit — A1516

Serpentine Die Cut 5¾
2000, Sept. 21 Litho.
Self-Adhesive
2762 A1516 27c Cupuacu .65 .35
2763 A1516 40c Soursop 1.00 .55

2000 Summer Olympics, Sydney — A1517

No. 2764: a, Pommel horse. b, Weight lifting. c, Discus. d, Men's rings. e, Sprinting. f, Javelin. g, Rhythmic gymnastics. h, Field hockey. i, Volleyball. j, Synchronized swimming. k, Judo. l, Wrestling. m, Cycling. n, Rowing. o, Parallel bars. p, Equestrian. q, Pole vault. r, Fencing. s, Shooting. t, Taekwondo.

No. 2765: a, Archery. b, Beach volleyball. c, Boxing. d, Soccer. e, Canoeing. f, Handball. g, Diving. h, Rhythmic gymnastics. i, Badminton. j, Swimming. k, Hurdles. l, Pentathlon. m, Basketball. n, Tennis. o, Marathon. p, High jump. q, Long jump. r, Triple jump. s, Triathlon. t, Yachting.

2000, Sept. 23 Litho. ***Perf. 11½x12***
2764 Sheet of 20 + 4 labels 26.00 26.00
a.-t. A1517 40c Any single 1.25 1.25
2765 Sheet of 20 + 4 labels 26.00 26.00
a.-t. A1517 40c Any single 1.25 1.25

Organ Donation and Transplantation — A1519

No. 2766: a, Doctor holding heart. b, Heart, hands, body with organs outlined.

2000, Sept. 27
2766 A1519 1.50r Horiz. pair, #a-b 2.50 2.50

Masks and Puppets A1520

Designs: No. 2767, 27c, Chinese puppet. No. 2768, 27c, Brazilian mask.

2000, Oct. 9
2767-2768 A1520 Set of 2 .60 .60

Brazil-People's Republic of China diplomatic relations, 25th anniv. See People's Republic of China Nos. 3053-3054.

Race Car Drivers A1521

Designs: 1.30r, Francisco "Chico" Landi (1907-89). 1.45r, Ayrton Senna (1960-94).

2000, Oct. 12 ***Perf. 11x11½***
2769-2770 A1521 Set of 2 2.50 2.50

Telecourse 2000 Project A1522

2000, Oct. 13 Litho. ***Perf. 11½x12***
2771 A1522 27c multi .30 .30

Airplanes A1523

No. 2772: a, EMB 145 AEW. b, Super Tucano. c, AMX-T. d, ERJ 135. e, ERJ 170. f, ERJ 145. g, ERJ 190. h, EMB 145 RS/MP. i, ERJ 140. j, EMB 120.

2000, Oct. 23 Litho. ***Die Cut***
Self-Adhesive
2772 Pane of 10 6.00 6.00
a.-j. A1523 27c Any single .30 .30

Christmas — A1524

No. 2773: a, Hand of Jesus, star of Bethlehem. b, Mary, baby Jesus. c, Hand of Jesus, fish, boats on Sea of Galilee. d, Jesus, Sea of Galilee. e, Hand of Jesus, mountain, trees, Earth. f, Jesus, Earth.

2000, Nov. 23 ***Perf. 11½***
2773 A1524 Block of 6 2.25 2.25
a.-f. 27c Any single .35 .35

Light and Sound Project — A1525

2000, Dec. 2 ***Perf. 12x11½***
2774 A1525 1.30r multi 1.00 1.00

Settlement of Brazil-French Guiana Border Dispute, Cent. — A1526

2000, Dec. 12 ***Perf. 11½x12***
2775 A1526 40c multi .40 .40

Advent of New Millennium — A1527

Designs: Nos. 2776, 2779a, 40c, Chalice and eucharist. Nos. 2777, 2779b, 1.30r, Star of David, menorah, Torah, tablets. Nos. 2778, 2779c, 1.30r, Minaret, dome of mosque, Holy Ka'aba.

2001, Jan. 1 ***Perf. 11x11½***
2776-2778 A1527 Set of 3 2.50 2.50

Souvenir Sheet

2779 A1527 Sheet of 3, #a-c 3.25 3.25

Nos. 2779a-2779c lack white border. On No. 2779, barcode is separated from sheet margin by a row of rouletting.

Pan-American Scout Jamboree, Foz do Iguaçu — A1528

No. 2780: a, Flags, map, emblems. b, Scouts in canoe, waterfall.

2001, Jan. 7 ***Perf. 12x11½***
2780 A1528 1.10r Horiz. pair, #a-b 1.90 1.90

New Year 2001 (Year of the Snake) — A1529

Litho. & Embossed

2001, Jan. 24 ***Perf. 11½***
2781 A1529 1.45r multi 1.25 1.25

Hong Kong 2001 Stamp Exhibition.

Venomous Animals A1530

No. 2782: a, Dirphya sp. b, Megalopyge sp. c, Phoneutria sp. d, Tityus bahiensis. e, Crotalus durissus. f, Micrurus corallinus. g, Lachesis muta. h, Bothrops jararaca.

2001, Feb. 23 **Litho.** ***Perf. 11½x12***
2782 Shoot of 8 4.50 4.50
a.-h A1530 40c Any single .55 .40

Butantan Institute, cent.

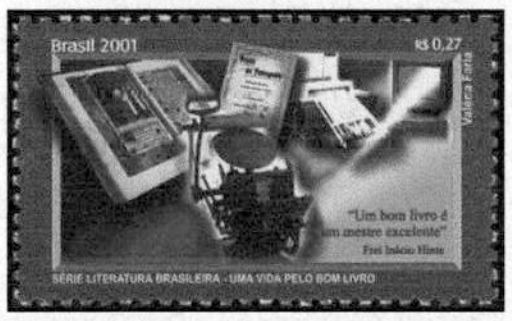

Brazilian Publishing Industry — A1531

2001, Mar. 5 ***Perf. 11x11½***
2783 A1531 27c multi .30 .30

Special Exports Program — A1532

2001, Mar. 5 ***Perf. 11½x12***
2784 A1532 1.30r multi 1.00 1.00

National Library, 190th Anniv. — A1533

Litho. & Engr.

2001, Mar. 26 ***Perf. 11½x12***
2785 A1533 27c multi .30 .25

Council for Scientific and Technical Development — A1534

2001, Apr. 17
2786 A1534 40c blue .40 .40

Soccer Teams — A1535

Designs: No. 2787, Regatas Vasco da Gama. No. 2788, Palmeiras. No. 2789, Gremio. No. 2790, Sao Paolo. No. 2791, Santos. No. 2792, Regatas do Flamengo.

2001 **Litho.** ***Perf. 12x11½***

2787	A1535	70c multi	1.10	1.10
2788	A1535	70c multi	1.10	1.10
2789	A1535	70c multi	1.10	1.10
2790	A1535	70c multi	1.10	1.10
2791	A1535	1r multi	1.10	1.10
2792	A1535	1r multi	1.10	1.10
	Nos. 2787-2792 (6)		6.60	6.60

Issued: No. 2787, 8/21; No. 2788, 8/26; No. 2789, 9/10; No. 2790, 12/16; No. 2791, 4/20. No. 2792, 11/28.

Intl. Culture of Peace Year — A1536

2001, May 3 **Litho.** ***Perf. 12x11½***
2794 A1536 1.10r multi .90 .90

Murilo Mendes (1901-75), Poet — A1537

2001, May 13 ***Perf. 11x11½***
2795 A1537 40c multi .40 .35

Minas Commercial Association, Cent. A1538

2001, May 16 ***Perf. 11½***
2796 A1538 40c multi .40 .35

World Tobacco-free Day — A1539

2001, May 31 ***Perf. 12x11½***
2797 A1539 40c multi .40 .35

José Lins do Rego (1901-87), Writer — A1540

2001, May 31 ***Perf. 11x11½***
2798 A1540 60c multi .45 .45

Souvenir Sheet

Worldwide Fund for Nature (WWF) — A1541

Parrots: a, Anodorhynchus hyacinthinus. b, Aratinga solstitialis auricapilla. c, Pyrrhura cruentata. d, Amazona xanthops.

2001, June 3 ***Perf. 11½***
2799 A1541 1.30r Sheet of 4, #a-d 6.50 6.50

Barbosa Lima Sobrinho (1897-2000), Journalist A1542

2001, June 6
2800 A1542 40c multi .35 .35

Beaches A1543

No. 2801: a, Jericoacoara. b, Ponta Negra. c, Rosa.

2001, June 13 ***Perf. 11x11½***
2801 Horiz. strip of 3 1.40 1.40
a.-c. A1543 40c Any single .45 .45

Issued in sheets of 25 stamps containing 10 each of Nos. 2801a-2801b and 5 of No. 2801c.

Souvenir Sheet

Automobiles — A1544

No. 2802: a, 1959 Romi Isetta. b, 1965 DKW Vemag. c, 1962 Renault Gordini. d, 1959 Volkswagen 1200. e, 1964 Simca Chambord. f, 1961 Aero-Willys.

2001, June 16 ***Perf. 11½x12***
2802 A1544 1.10r Sheet of 6, #a-f 7.25 7.25

Bernardo Sayao (1901-59), Politician A1545

2001, June 18 ***Perf. 11½***
2803 A1545 60c multi .55 .50

Eleazar de Carvalho (1912-96), Composer A1546

2001, July 1
2804 A1546 45c multi .35 .35

Souvenir Sheet

Third French Tennis Open Victory of Gustavo Kuerten — A1547

2001, July 10
2805 A1547 1.30r multi 1.75 1.75

Academic Qualifications Coordinating Institution, 50th Anniv. — A1548

2001, July 11 ***Perf. 11x11½***
2806 A1548 40c multi .35 .35

Pedro Aleixo, Politician, Cent. of Birth A1549

2001, Aug. 1 ***Perf. 11½***
2807 A1549 55c multi .55 .50

Solidarity Community Programs — A1550

No. 2808: a, Map on man. b, Man on map.

2001, Aug. 25
2808 A1550 55c Horiz. pair, #a-b .60 .60

World Conference Against Racism, Durban, South Africa — A1551

2001, Aug. 30 ***Perf. 12x11½***
2809 A1551 1.30r multi 1.00 1.00

See South Africa Nos. 1261-1262.

Musical Instruments A1552

Designs: 1c, Drum (Tambourin). 5c, Saxophone. 10c, Ukulele. 40c, Flute. 50c, Rebec. 55c, Guitar. 60c, Drum. 70c, Guitar (viola caipira). 1r, Trombone.

2001 Litho. ***Serpentine Die Cut 5¾***
Self-Adhesive

2810	A1552	1c multi	.30	.25
2811	A1552	5c multi	.45	.25
2812	A1552	10c multi	.45	.25
2813	A1552	40c multi	.60	.25
2814	A1552	50c multi	.60	.25
2815	A1552	55c multi	.60	.25
2816	A1552	60c multi	.80	.30
2817	A1552	70c multi	.80	.30
2818	A1552	1r multi	1.25	.30
		Nos. 2810-2818 (9)	5.85	2.40

Booklet Stamp
Self-Adhesive
Die Cut

2818A	A1552	40c multi	.65	.65
b.		Booklet pane of 5	6.50	

Issued: Nos. 2810-2818, 9/20. No. 2818A, 10/15.

Clóvis Beviláqua (1859-1944), Writer of Civil Law Code A1553

2001, Oct. 4 Litho. ***Perf. 11½***
2819 A1553 55c multi .50 .50

Year of Dialogue Among Civilizations A1554

2001, Oct. 9 ***Perf. 12x11½***
2820 A1554 1.30r multi 1.00 1.00

Souvenir Sheet

Commercial Aircraft — A1555

No. 2821: a, Junkers F-13. b, Douglas C-47. c, Dornier Wal. d, Lockheed Constellation. e, Convair 340. f, Caravelle.

2001, Oct. 23 Litho. ***Perf. 11½x12***
2821 A1555 55c Sheet of 6, #a-f 4.75 4.75

Barcode is separated from sheet margin by a row of rouletting.

Cecília Meireles (1901-64), Poet — A1556

2001, Nov. 7 Litho. ***Perf. 11x11½***
2822 A1556 55c multi .75 .50

America Issue - Bom Jesus de Matosinhos Sanctuary, UNESCO World Heritage Site — A1557

2001, Nov. 9 ***Perf. 11½x12***
2823 A1557 1.30r multi 1.00 1.00

Madalena Caramuru, First Literate Woman in Brazil A1558

2001, Nov. 14
2824 A1558 55c multi .50 .50

National Day of Black Consciousness — A1559

2001, Nov. 20
2825 A1559 40c multi .35 .35

Pantanal Flora A1560

No. 2826: a, Caiman crocodilus yacare, Plataleia ajaja. b, Anhinga anhinga. c, Ardea cocoi. d, Jabiru mycteria. e, Pseudoplatystoma fasciatum. f, Leporinus macrocephalus. g, Hydrochoerus hydrochoeris. h, Nasua nasua, Casmerodius albus. i, Eichornia crassipes. j, Porphyrula martinica.

2001, Nov. 20 ***Die Cut Perf. 6¼***
Self-Adhesive

2826		Booklet of 10	7.50	
a.-j.	A1560 55c Any single		.50	.50

See No. 2832.

Christmas A1561

2001, Nov. 23 ***Perf. 11½x12***
2827 A1561 40c multi .35 .35

Souvenir Sheet

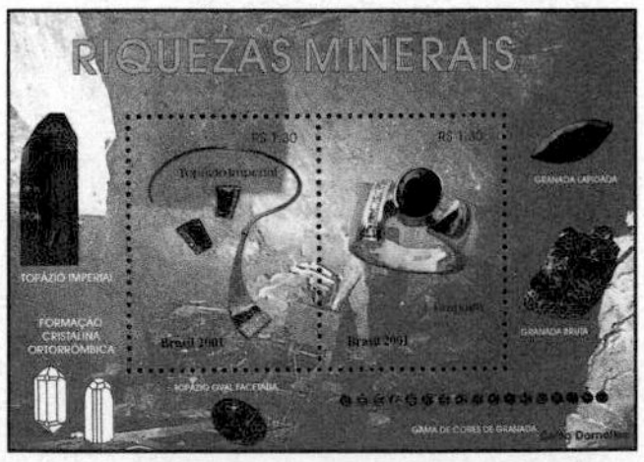

Minerals — A1562

No. 2828: a, Topaz jewelry. b, Garnet ring.

2001, Nov. 30 ***Perf. 12x11½***
2828 A1562 1.30r Sheet of 2, #a-b 2.75 2.75

Intl. Day of Disabled Persons — A1563

2001, Dec. 3 ***Perf. 11½***
2829 A1563 1.45r multi 1.25 1.25

Coffee
A1564

2001, Dec. 7 ***Perf. 11½x12***
2830 A1564 1.30r multi 1.00 1.00

No. 2830 is impregnated with a coffee scent.

Merchant Ships — A1565

No. 2831: a, Copacabana. b, Flamengo.

2001, Dec. 13 ***Perf. 11x11½***
2831 A1565 55c Horiz. pair, #a-b 1.50 1.50

Pantanal Flora Type of 2001 With "MERCOSUR" Inscription Added

1r, Eichornia crassipes.

2001, Dec. 21 ***Perf. 11½x12***
2832 A1560 1r multi .75 .75

Kahal Zur Israel, First Synagogue in the Americas A1566

2001, Oct. 21 Litho. ***Perf. 11½x12***
2833 A1566 1.30r multi 1.00 1.00

New Year 2002 (Year of the Horse) — A1567

Litho. With Foil Application

2002, Jan. 25 ***Perf. 11½***
2834 A1567 1.45r multi 1.25 1.25

2002 Winter Olympics, Salt Lake City — A1568

No. 2835: a, Alpine skiing. b, Cross-country skiing. c, Luge. d, Bobsled.

2002, Feb. 4 Litho. ***Perf. 11½x12***
2835 A1568 1.10r Block of 4, #a-d 3.50 3.50

Lucio Costa (1902-98), Architect A1569

2002, Feb. 27
2836 A1569 55c multi .50 .50

Intl. Women's Day — A1570

2002, Mar. 8 ***Perf. 11½***
2837 A1570 40c multi .35 .35

Sao José do Rio Preto, 150th Anniv. A1571

2002, Mar. 19 ***Perf. 11½x12***
2838 A1571 40c multi .35 .35

Pres. Juscelino Kubitschek (1902-76) — A1572

2002, Apr. 21 **Litho.**
2839 A1572 55c multi .50 .45

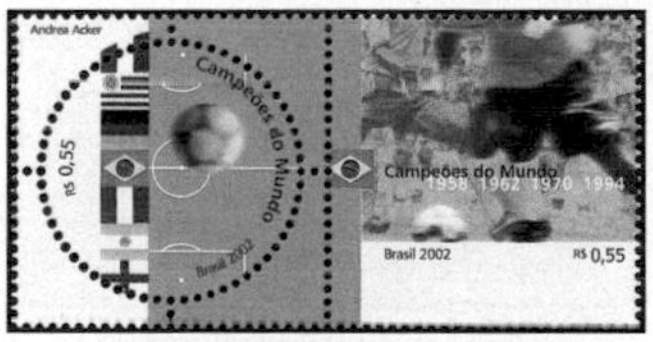

2002 World Cup Soccer Championships, Japan and Korea — A1573

No. 2840: a, Flags, soccer ball, and field (28mm diameter). b, Soccer players, years of Brazilian championships.

2002, Apr. 22 Photo. ***Perf. 13¾***
2840 A1573 55c Horiz. pair, #a-b 1.10 1.10

See Argentina No. 2184, France No. 2891, Germany No. 2163, Italy No. 2526, and Uruguay No. 1946.

Progress in Brazilian Education — A1574

No. 2841: a, Children in classroom, globe, letters "a-d." b, Computer, globe, letters "e-h."

2002, Apr. 28 Litho. ***Perf. 11½x12***
2841 A1574 40c Horiz. pair, #a-b .75 .70

St. Josemaría Escrivá de Balaguer (1902-75) — A1575

2002, May 1
2842 A1575 55c multi .50 .45

Souvenir Sheet

Brazilian Air Force's Esquadrilha da Fumaça Aerobatics Team — A1576

No. 2843: a, T-6 North American. b, T-24 Super Fouga Magister. c, T-25 Universal. d, Two T-27 Tucanos, one flying upside-down. e, T-27 Tucanos, heart-shaped smoke design. f, Blue, green and yellow T-27 Tucano.

2002, May 17
2843 A1576 55c Sheet of 6, #a-f 3.75 3.75

Barcode is separated from sheet margin by a row of rouletting.

Children's Cavalhadinha of Pirenópolis — A1577

No. 2844: a, Procession of virgins and stick-pony riders. b, Stick-pony combat. c, Children wearing masks. d, Musicians and vendor.

2002, May 19 ***Perf. 11x11½***
2844 A1577 40c Block of 4, #a-d 2.25 2.25

Couroupita Guianensis A1578

Serpentine Die Cut 12¾x13

2002, May 20 Coil Stamp Photo.

Self-Adhesive

2845 A1578 55c multi 1.10 1.00

Souvenir Sheet

Coral Reefs — A1579

No. 2846 — Coral and: a, Orange fish, school of fish. b, Seahorse. c, Orange fish. d, Orange fish, starfish.

2002, June 5 ***Perf. 11½***
2846 A1579 40c Sheet of 4, #a-d 2.75 2.75

Philakorea 2002 World Stamp Exhibition, Seoul. Barcode is separated from sheet margin by a row of rouletting.

Charity Hospital of Curitiba, 150th Anniv. A1580

2002, June 9 Litho. ***Perf. 11x11½***
2847 A1580 70c multi .60 .50

Brazil's Fifth World Cup Soccer Championship A1581

2002, July 2 Litho. ***Perf. 12x11½***
2848 A1581 55c multi .60 .50

Souvenir Sheet

Preservation of Caatinga Nordestina — A1582

2002, July 14 Litho. ***Perf. 10¾x11***
2849 A1582 1.10r multi 1.75 1.75

Fluminense Soccer Team, Cent. — A1583

2002, July 17 Litho. ***Perf. 12x11½***

2850 A1583 55c multi .60 .40

Souvenir Sheet

Alberto Santos-Dumont's House, Encantada — A1584

No. 2851: a, House. b, Santos-Dumont and stairway.

2002, July 19 Litho. ***Perf. 11¾***

2851 A1584 1r Sheet of 2, #a-b 2.75 2.75

System for the Vigilance of the Amazon Project — A1585

2002, July 27 ***Perf. 11½x12***

2852 A1585 1.10r multi 1.00 .75

Jorge Amado (1912-2001), Writer — A1586

2002, Aug. 5 ***Perf. 11x11½***

2853 A1586 40c multi .40 .30

Plácido de Castro and Rio Branco Palace A1587

2002, Aug. 6 Litho. ***Perf. 11½x12***

2854 A1587 50c multi .40 .35

Acre Revolution, cent.

Souvenir Sheet

Protected Area for Whales — A1588

2002, Sept. 14 Litho. ***Perf. 12x11½***

2855 A1588 1.30r multi 1.75 1.75

Confluence of Rio Solimoes and Rio Negro A1589

2002, Sept. 27 ***Perf. 11½***

2856 A1589 45c multi .40 .25

Adhemar Ferreira da Silva (1927-2001), 1952 and 1956 Olympic Triple Jump Gold Medalist — A1590

2002, Sept. 28 ***Perf. 11x11½***

2857 A1590 40c multi .40 .25

Motorcycles — A1591

No. 2858: a, YZF-R1. b, CG125 Titan. c, GSX-R1000. d, Daytona 955i Centennial Edition. e, BMW R32 and BMW R 1200 C. f, V-ROD.

2002, Sept. 29 Litho. ***Perf. 11½x12***

2858 A1591 60c Sheet of 6, #a-f 8.00 8.00

Locomotives — A1592

No. 2859, Zezé Leoni. 2860, Baroneza.

2002, Sept. 30

2859 55c multicolored .65 .65

2859A 55c multicolored .65 .65

a. A1592 Pair, #2859-2859A 3.75 3.75

Tourism in Bonito A1593

2002, Oct. 2 Litho. ***Perf. 11½x12***

2860 A1593 1r multi .75 .55

Carlos Drummond de Andrade (1902-87), Writer — A1594

2002, Oct. 25 ***Perf. 11x11½***

2861 A1594 55c multi .50 .30

America Issue - Youth, Education and Literacy — A1595

2002, Nov. 14 Litho. ***Perf. 11½x12***

2862 A1595 1.30r multi 1.00 .95

National Archives — A1596

2002, Nov. 20

2863 A1596 40c multi .40 .30

Sergio Motta Cultural Center A1597

2002, Nov. 24

2864 A1597 45c multi .45 .30

Christmas A1598

2002, Nov. 29

2865 A1598 45c multi .45 .30

Social Security in Brazil, 80th Anniv. A1599

2002, Dec. 3

2866 A1599 45c multi .45 .30

Ethnographic Paintings of Albert Eckhout — A1600

No. 2867: a, Group of natives. b, Woman with basket of flowers. c, Native man with headdress and spears. d, Man with bow and arrows. e, Man with spears. f, Woman with child and basket. g, Woman with headdress and child. h, Man with gun.

2002, Dec. 3 ***Perf. 11½***

2867 A1600 45c Block of 8, #a-h 8.00 8.00

Brazil — Iran Diplomatic Relations, Cent. A1601

Flags of Brazil and Iran, and pottery and rug from: No. 2868, 60c, Brazil. No. 2869, 60c, Iran.

2002, Dec. 15 ***Perf. 11½x12***

2868-2869 A1601 Set of 2 1.25 .80

See Iran No. 2844.

Musical Instruments — A1602

Designs: 1c, Drum (Atabaque). 5c, Snare drum (Caixa clara). 10c, Trumpet. 20c, Clarinet. 45c, Mandolin (Bandolim). 50c, Tambourine (Pandeiro). 60c, Accordion. 70c, Maraca (Cholcalho). 80c, Xylophone. 1r, Berimbau.

Serpentine Die Cut 5¾

2002-05 **Photo.**

Self-Adhesive

2869A A1602 1c multi .25 .25

2870 A1602 5c multi .25 .25

2871 A1602 10c multi .25 .25

2872 A1602 20c multi .25 .25

2873 A1602 45c multi .50 .25

2874 A1602 50c multi .50 .25
2875 A1602 60c multi .55 .25
2876 A1602 70c multi .60 .25
2877 A1602 80c multi .80 .25
2877A A1602 1r multi 1.10 .55

Die Cut Perf. 12x12¼

2877B A1602 1c like #2869A 1.00 .30
2877C A1602 5c like #2870 .30 .30
2877D A1602 10c like #2871 .30 .30
2877E A1602 20c like #2872 .30 .30
2877K A1602 1r like #2877A .90 .60
Nos. 2869A-2877K (14) 7.55 4.30

Issued: Nos. 2869A-2877A, 2002; Nos. 2877B-2877D, 2877K, 5/2005; 2877E, 2005.

Rotary Intl. in Brazil, 80th Anniv. — A1603

2003, Feb. 26 Litho. ***Perf. 12x11½***
2878 A1603 60c multi .60 .35

Waterfalls A1604

Waterfalls: No. 2879, Itiquira. No. 2880, Rio Preto.

2003, Mar. 22
2879 A1604 45c multi .40 .40
2880 A1604 45c multi .40 .40
a. Pair, #2879-2880 1.25 1.25

Souvenir Sheet

Coffee Plantations — A1605

No. 2881: a, Pau d'Alho. b, Ponte Alta.

2003, Apr. 15 ***Perf. 11½***
2881 A1605 1r Sheet of 2, #a-b 2.75 2.75

Independence of East Timor — A1606

2003, May 20 ***Perf. 11½x12***
2882 A1606 1.45r multi 1.40 1.10

America Issue — Medicinal Plants — A1607

No. 2883: a, Macrosiphonia velame. b, Lychnophora ericoides. c, Lafoensia pacari. d, Tabebuia impetiginosa. e, Xylopia aromatica. f, Himatanthus obovatus.

2003, June 2 ***Perf. 11½***
2883 A1607 60c Sheet of 6, #a-f 4.75 4.75

Art Made From Recycled Material — A1608

No. 2884: a, Glass bottles. b, Paper. c, Plastic. d, Metal.

2003, June 5
2884 A1608 60c Block of 4, #a-d 4.00 4.00

Santo Inácio College, Cent. A1609

2003, July 1 ***Perf. 11½x12***
2885 A1609 60c multi .60 .45

Pluft, the Ghost, and Maribel A1610

2003, July 12
2886 A1610 80c multi .70 .55

Ceará State, 400th Anniv. A1611

2003, July 15
2887 A1611 70c multi .70 .50

Souvenir Sheet

Stamp Collecting — A1612

No. 2888: a, Collector's album, Brazil #2 in tongs. b, Portugal #2 in tongs.

2003, Aug. 1 ***Perf. 11½***
2888 A1612 1.30r Sheet of 2, #a-b 3.25 3.25

First Portuguese stamp, 150th anniv., Lubrapex 2003 Philatelic Exhibition.

Souvenir Sheet

Dolphins — A1613

Litho. with Hologram Applied
2003, Aug. 10 ***Perf. 11½***
2889 A1613 2.90r multi 3.75 3.75

Bangkok 2003 Intl. Philatelic Exhibition.

Barnabite Order in Brazil, Cent. A1614

2003, Aug. 22 Litho. ***Perf. 11½x12***
2890 A1614 45c multi .50 .35

A1615

60c, Luis Alves de Lima y Silva, Duque de Caxias (1803-80), Soldier and Politician.

2003, Aug. 25
2891 A1615 60c multi .60 .45

Self-Portrait, by Candido Portinari (1903-62) A1616

2003, Sept. 4 Litho. ***Perf. 12x11½***
2892 A1616 80c multi .75 .55

Courtesy on Mass Transit — A1617

Designs: No. 2893, "No Drinking." No. 2894, "Be Peaceful" (dove in triangle).

Serpentine Die Cut 5¾
2003, Sept. 5 Photo.
Self-Adhesive
2893 A1617 (50c) multi .55 .25
2894 A1617 (74c) multi .85 .25

Grémio Soccer Team, Cent. — A1618

2003, Sept. 18 Litho. ***Perf. 12x11½***
2895 A1618 60c multi .55 .45
a. Sheet of 12 + 12 labels 65.00 65.00

No. 2895a sold for 21r. Labels could be personalized.

Antonina - Morretes Railway A1619

2003, Sept. 30 Litho. ***Perf. 11½***
2896 A1619 74c multi .75 .75

Children's Games — A1620

No. 2897: a, Kite flying (Pipa). b, Cricket (Bete). c, Rope jumping (Pula corda). d, Hula hoop (Bambole).

2003, Oct. 4
2897 A1620 50c Block of 4, #a-d 4.00 4.00

Program Against Hunger
A1621

2003, Oct. 9 ***Perf. 11½x12***

2898 A1621 50c multi .50 .50

Souvenir Sheet

Export Products — A1622

2003, Oct. 29 ***Perf. 11½***

2899 A1622 1.30r multi 1.75 1.75

Christmas — A1623

Frame color: No. 2900, 50c, Green. No. 2901, 50c, Gold.

2003, Oct. 31 ***Die Cut Perf. 12***

Self-Adhesive

2900-2901 A1623 Set of 2 1.50 1.50

Marcantonio Vilaça Cultural Space — A1624

2003, Nov. 5 **Litho.** ***Perf. 11½x12***

2902 A1624 74c multi .75 .75

Ary Barroso (1903-64), Songwriter, Television Personality — A1625

2003, Nov. 7

2903 A1625 1.50r multi 1.25 1.25

Congress, 180th Anniv.
A1626

2003, Nov. 13

2904 A1626 74c multi .75 .75

Brazil — Lebanon Diplomatic and Cultural Relations
A1627

2003, Nov. 21 **Litho.** ***Perf. 12x11½***

2905 A1627 1.75r multi 1.25 1.25

Fight Against AIDS
A1628

2003, Dec. 1 **Litho.** ***Perf. 11***

2906 A1628 74c multi .75 .75

Values are for stamps with surrounding selvage.

Paragliding
A1629

2003, Dec. 6 ***Perf. 11½x12***

2907 A1629 75c multi .65 .65

Capistrano de Abreu (1853-1927), Ethnographer — A1630

2003, Dec. 9

2908 A1630 50c multi .40 .40

Fernando Henrique Cardoso, President from 1995-2002
A1631

2003, Dec. 20 ***Perf. 11½***

2909 A1631 74c multi .65 .65

Paintings by Candido Portinari — A1632

Designs: 74c, Boy from Brodowski. 75c, Cowboy.

2003 **Litho.** ***Die Cut Perf. 12x12¼***

Self-Adhesive

2910 A1632 74c black .75 .75

2911 A1632 75c black .75 .75

Festivals — A1633

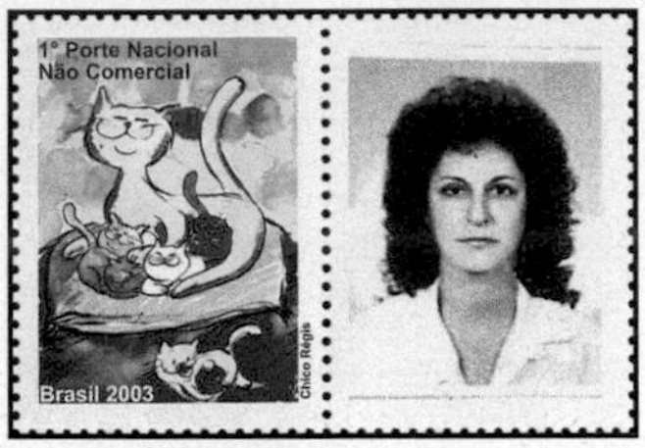

Cats — A1634

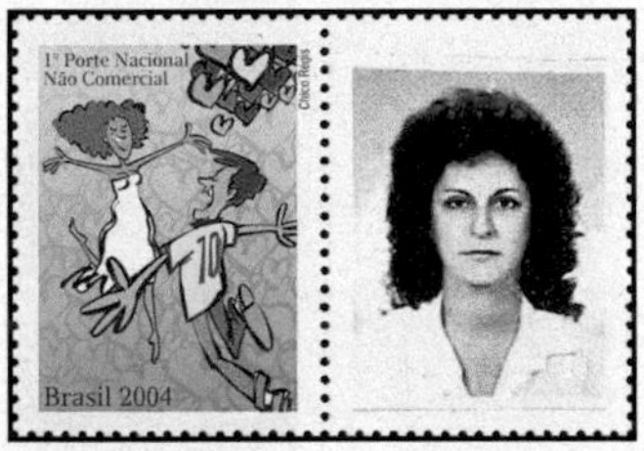

Romance — A1635

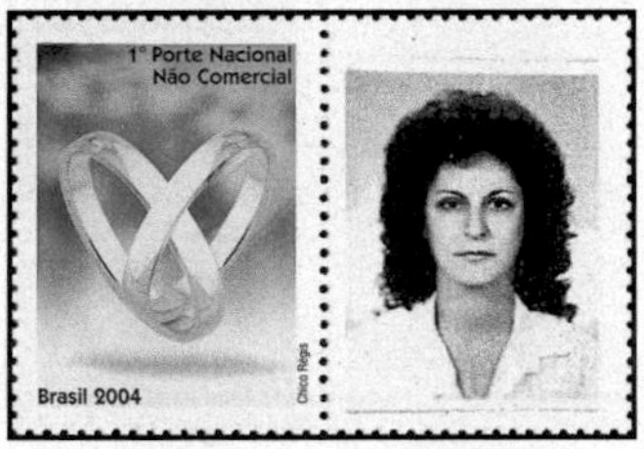

Wedding Rings — A1636

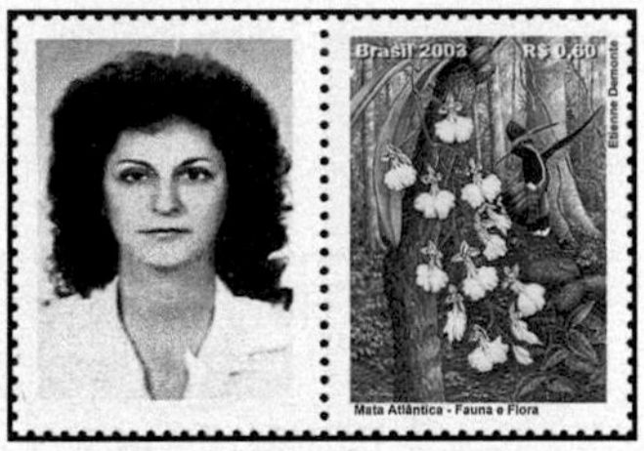

Mata Atlantica — A1637

2003-04 **Litho.** ***Perf. 12x11½***

2912 A1633 45c multi + label 6.00 6.00

2913 A1634 (50c) multi + label 1.75 1.75

2914 A1635 (50c) multi + label 2.50 2.50

2915 A1636 (50c) multi + label 1.75 1.75

2916 A1637 60c multi + label 6.00 6.00

Nos. 2912-2916 (5) 18.00 18.00

Issued: Nos. 2912, 2916, 2003; Nos. 2913-2915, 2004. Nos. 2912-2916 each were printed in sheets of 12 stamps + 12 labels that could be personalized. Each sheet sold for 21r.

Souvenir Sheet

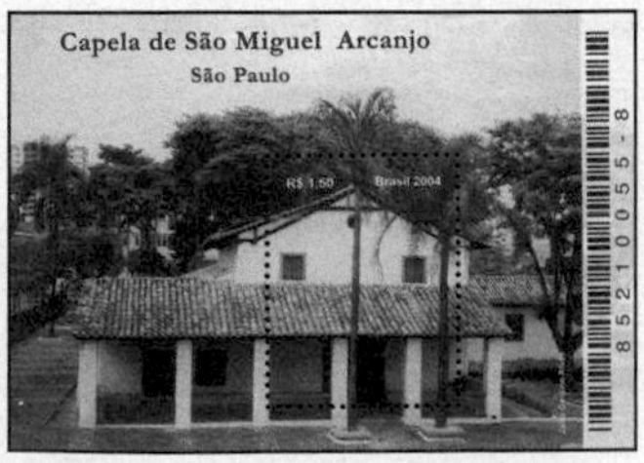

Sao Miguel Arcanjo Chapel, Sao Paolo — A1638

2004, Jan. 17 **Litho.** ***Perf. 12x11½***

2917 A1638 1.50r multi 1.50 1.50

Sao Paolo, 450th Anniv. — A1639

No. 2918: a, Faces. b, Buildings, road. c, Buildings, trees. d, "450."

2004, Jan. 23 ***Perf. 11½x12***

2918 Block of 4 2.50 2.50

a.-d. A1639 74c Any single .60 .50

Vicente Scherer (1903-96), Monk, Educator
A1640

2004, Feb. 5

2919 A1640 50c multi .40 .40

Bairro da Lapa — A1641

2004, Feb. 19 ***Perf. 12x11½***

2920 A1641 75c multi .60 .60

Eudocimus Ruber
A1642

2004, Feb. 20 ***Perf. 11½x12***

2921 A1642 74c multi .60 .60

2921a Sheet of 12 + 12 labels 37.50 37.50

No. 2921a sold for 21r. Labels could be personalized.

Potable Water — A1643

2004, Mar. 22 ***Perf. 12x11½***

2922 A1643 1.20r multi 1.00 1.00

Orlando Villas Bôas (1914-2002), Advocate of Indian Rights — A1644

2004, Apr. 19

2923 A1644 74c multi .60 .60

FIFA (Fédération Internationale de Football Association), Cent. A1645

2004, May 21 *Perf. 11½*
2924 A1645 1.60r multi 1.25 1.25

92nd Intl. Labor Organization Conference — A1646

2004, June 1 *Perf. 11½x12*
2925 A1646 50c multi .40 .40

Preservation of Mangrove Swamps and Tidal Zones — A1647

No. 2926: a, Ajaja ajaja. b, Pitangus sulphuratus. c, Chasmagnathus granulata. d, Aramides mangle. e, Goniopsis cruentata.

2004, June 5
2926 A1647 1.60r Sheet of 5, #a-e 7.50 7.50

2004 Summer Olympics, Athens — A1648

No. 2927: a, Torch bearer, Rio de Janeiro. b, 2004 Athens Olympics emblem. c, Sailing. d, Track and field.

2004, June 12 *Perf. 11½*
2927 A1648 1.60r Block of 4, #a-d 2.25 2.25

Bonfim Basilica, 250th Anniv. A1649

2004, June 18 *Perf. 11½x12*
2928 A1649 74c multi .60 .60

Folk Festivals — A1650

No. 2929: a, Caprichoso. b, Garantido.

2004, June 28
2929 A1650 74c Horiz. pair, #a-b .85 .85

Brazilian Inventions A1651

Designs: No. 2930, Telephone card. No. 2931, Artificial heart valve. No. 2932, Caller identification system for telephones.

2004, July 15 *Perf. 11½*
2930 A1651 50c multi .40 .40
2931 A1651 50c multi .40 .40
2932 A1651 50c multi .40 .40
a. Strip of 3, #2930-2932 3.00 3.00

Nos. 2930-2932 were printed in sheets containing eight of each stamp.

CBERS-2 Satellite A1652

2004, Aug. 9 **Litho.** *Perf. 11½x12*
2933 A1652 1.75r multi 1.40 1.40

Masonic Traditions — A1653

No. 2934 — Masonic emblem and: a, Pillars. b, Mason with hammer and chisel. c, Book, ladder and symbols. d, Tools.

2004, Aug. 20 **Litho.** *Perf. 11½*
2934 A1653 50c Block of 4, #a-d 3.50 3.50

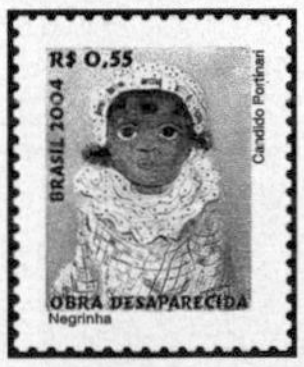

Paintings by Candido Portinari — A1654

Designs: 55c, Negrinha. 80c, Duas Crianças. 95c, Seated Child with Sheep. 1.15r, Group of Women and Child. 1.50r, Marcel Gontrau.

2004, May 26 *Die Cut Perf. 12x12¼*
Self-Adhesive
2935 A1654 55c multi .40 .25
2936 A1654 80c multi .55 .25
2937 A1654 95c multi .70 .30
2938 A1654 1.15r black .85 .30
2939 A1654 1.50r multi 1.10 .40
a. Die cut perf. 12x12¼ syncopated ('11) .65 .65
Nos. 2935-2939 (5) 3.60 1.50

Flag and Sculptures — A1655

Chiroxiphia Caudata — A1656

Tourism — A1657

2004 **Litho.** *Perf. 11½x12*
2940 A1655 (80c) multi + label 2.25 2.25
2941 A1656 (80c) multi + label 2.25 2.25
2942 A1657 (80c) multi + label 2.25 2.25
Nos. 2940-2942 (3) 6.75 6.75

Issued: No. 2940, 8/3; No. 2941, 9/22; No. 2942, 10/15. Labels could be personalized.

Nelson Rodrigues (1912-80), Playwright — A1658

2004, Aug. 23 **Litho.** *Perf. 11½x12*
2943 A1658 50c multi .60 .60

Brazil in World War II — A1659

No. 2944: a, Airplane. b, Ship. c, Troops in action. d, Soldier reading letter.

2004, Aug. 25 *Perf. 11½*
2944 A1659 50c Block of 4, #a-d 3.50 3.50

Coronation of Our Lady of Aparecida, Cent. — A1660

2004, Sept. 8 *Perf. 12x11½*
2945 A1660 74c multi .60 .60

Allan Kardec (1804-69), Writer A1661

2004, Oct. 3 *Perf. 11½x12*
2946 A1661 1.60r multi 1.25 1.25

Christmas A1662

2004, Oct. 28 *Die Cut*
Self-Adhesive
2947 A1662 (55c) multi .75 .75
a. Booklet pane of 10 12.00

Porto Alegre Post Office A1663

2004, Oct. 29 *Perf. 11½x12*
2948 A1663 50c multi .40 .40

Cyperus Articulatus A1664

2004, Nov. 23 *Perf. 12x11½*
2949 A1664 1.60r multi 1.40 1.40

Pampulha Architectural Complex — A1665

2004, Dec. 12 *Perf. 11½x12*
2950 A1665 80c multi .65 .65

Nise da Silveira (1905-99), Psychiatrist — A1666

2005, Feb. 15 **Litho.**
2951 A1666 55c multi .45 .45

Rotary International, Cent. — A1667

2005, Mar. 23 ***Perf. 11½***
2952 A1667 1.45r multi 1.10 1.10

Souvenir Sheet

Theobroma Grandiflorum — A1668

No. 2953: a, Fruit on tree. b, Fruit cut open.

2005, Mar. 15
2953 A1668 1.90r Sheet of 2, #a-b 3.50 3.50

Pacific Explorer 2005 World Stamp Expo, Sydney.

Lebanese Immigration to Brazil — A1669

2005, Mar. 31 ***Perf. 11½x12***
2954 A1669 1.75r multi 1.50 1.50

Oscar Niemeyer Museum A1670

2005, Apr. 25
2955 A1670 80c multi .65 .65

Pope John Paul II (1920-2005) A1671

2005, May 18 ***Perf. 11½x11***
2956 A1671 80c multi .70 .70

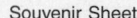

Souvenir Sheet

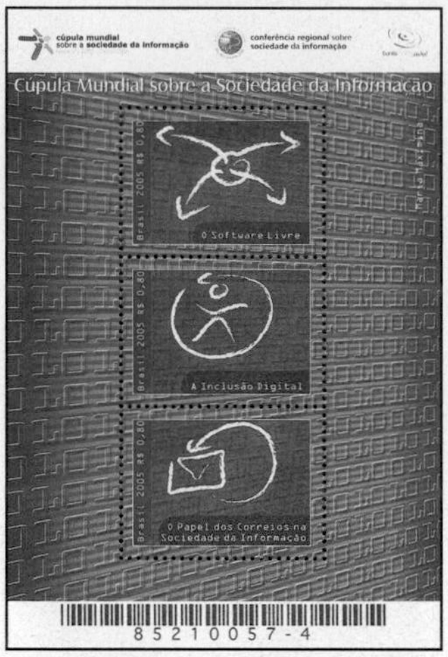

World Summit on the Information Society, Tunis — A1672

No. 2957: a, Circle and arrows. b, Stick figure of person in circle. c, Envelope and arrow.

2005, June 8 **Litho.**
2957 A1672 80c Sheet of 3, #a-c 3.50 3.50

Brazil Year in France A1673

No. 2958, 80c: a, Pankararu Indians. b, Musicians.
No. 2959, 80c: a, Contemporary Dance. b, Vivaldo Lima Stadium
No. 2960, 80c: a, "String" literature. b, Pato na Tucupi and Açai.

2005, June 15 ***Perf. 11½x12***
Pairs, #a-b
2958-2960 A1673 Set of 3 7.25 7.25

Erico Veríssimo (1905-75), Writer — A1674

2005, July 9 ***Perf. 11½x11***
2961 A1674 1.25r multi 1.25 1.25

Mario Quintana (1906-94), Poet A1675

2005, July 30 **Engr.** ***Perf. 11½***
2962 A1675 80c green .80 .80

America Issue — Fight Against Poverty — A1676

2005, Aug. 10 **Litho.** ***Perf. 12x11½***
2963 A1676 80c multi .80 .80

19th Congress of the Postal Union of the Americas, Spain and Portugal — A1677

2005, Aug. 10 ***Die Cut Perf. 12x12¼***
Self-Adhesive
2964 A1677 (85c) multi .75 .75

Royal Road — A1678

No. 2965: a, Map, miner. b, Hikers and cyclist. c, People on horseback, hills and food.

Litho., Litho. & Embossed (#2965a)
2005, Aug. 13 ***Perf. 11½***
2965 A1678 80c Horiz. strip of 3, #a-c 2.25 2.25

Samba Dancer A1679

2005, Aug. 15 **Litho.** ***Perf. 11½x12***
2966 A1679 55c multi .60 .60

Dances — A1680

Parrot and: No. 2967, 80c, Son dancers and Cuban flag. No. 2968, 80c, Samba dancers and Brazilian flag.

2005, Aug. 16 **Litho.** ***Perf. 12x11½***
2967 A1680 80c multi .60 .60
2968 A1680 80c multi .60 .60
a. Pair, #2967-2968 1.45 1.45

See Cuba No. 4497-4498.

Sao Francisco River Basin A1681

2005, Sept. 2 ***Perf. 11½x12***
2969 A1681 80c multi .70 .70

Army Staff and Command School, Cent. A1682

2005, Sept. 22
2970 A1682 80c multi .70 .70

Teacher's Day — A1683

Die Cut Perf. 12x12¼
2005, Oct. 15 **Litho.**
Self-Adhesive
2971 A1683 (55c) multi .50 .50

Christmas A1684

2005, Oct. 25 **Litho.** ***Die Cut***
2972 A1684 (55c) multi .90 .90

Souvenir Sheet

Adoration of the Shepherds, by Oscar Pereira da Silva — A1685

2005, Nov. 24 **Litho.** ***Perf. 12x11½***
2973 A1685 2.90r multi 3.00 3.00

Christmas.

Women's Soccer A1686

2005, Oct. 30 **Litho.** ***Perf. 11½x12***
2974 A1686 85c multi .90 .90

Souvenir Sheet

Salminus Maxillosus — A1687

Litho. & Embossed

2005, Nov. 3 ***Perf. 11¾***

2975 A1687 3.10r multi 3.25 3.25

Brazilian Furniture and Furnishings Design — A1688

No. 2976: a, Ceiling light fixtures, by Fernando Prado. b, Ceiling fan, by Indio da Costa Design. c, Chair, by Humberto and Fernando Campana. d, Desk, by Ivan Rezende.

2005, Dec. 12 **Litho.** ***Perf. 11¾***

2976 A1688 85c Block of 4, #a-d 3.50 3.50

Hans Christian Andersen (1805-75), Author A1689

2005, Dec. 14 ***Perf. 11½x12***

2977 A1689 55c multi .70 .70

Occupations A1690

Die Cut Perf. 12x12¼

2005, Dec. 19 **Photo.**

Self-Adhesive

2978 A1690 5c Seamstress .25 .25
 a. Die cut perf. 12x12¼ syncopated ('11) .25 .25
2979 A1690 20c Shoemaker .25 .25
 a. Die cut perf. 12x12¼ syncopated ('11) .25 .25
2980 A1690 85c Shoe polisher .70 .70
 Nos. 2978-2980 (3) 1.20 1.20

See Nos. 2997-2998, 3020A-3020B.

Graffiti Artists — A1691

Designs: No. 2981, Man with paint sprayer. No. 2982, Man wearing hat, wavy lines. No. 2983, Man with cap and spray paint can, horiz.

Perf. 12x11½, 11½x12

2006, Mar. 27 **Litho.**

2981 A1691 55c multi .35 .35
2982 A1691 55c multi .35 .35
2983 A1691 55c multi .35 .35
 a. Strip of 3, #2981-2983 1.90 1.90

Lubrapex 2006, Rio. See No. 2993.

Brazilian Space Agency — A1692

No. 2984: a, Alberto Santos-Dumont's 14bis airplane. b, Soyuz spacecraft. c, Intl. Space Station.

2006, Apr. 3 ***Perf. 11½***

2984 A1692 85c Horiz. strip of 3, #a-c 2.50 2.50

Brazilians in flight, cent.

2006 World Cup Soccer Championships, Germany — A1693

2006, Apr. 19

2985 A1693 85c multi 1.75 1.75

Bidu Sayao (1902-99), Opera Singer A1694

2006, May 11

2986 A1694 55c multi .60 .60

World Day of Cultural Diversity for Dialogue and Development A1695

2006, May 21 ***Perf. 11½x11***

2987 A1695 1.90r multi 2.00 2.00

2007 Pan American Games, Rio — A1696

2006-07 ***Serpentine Die Cut 10¾***

Self-Adhesive

2988 A1696 (85c) multi 1.75 1.75

Perf. 12x11½

2988A A1696 60c multi + label 2.75 2.75

Issued: No. 2988, 8/8/06, No. 2988A, 2007.

No. 2988A was issued in sheets of 12 + 12 labels that could be personalized. Sheets sold for 25r.

Brazilian Paralympic Committee, 11th Anniv. — A1697

2006, Aug. 16 ***Perf. 11½x12***

2989 A1697 55c multi .80 .80

Viola de Cocho A1698

2006, Aug. 22

2990 A1698 1.35r multi 1.50 1.50

National Parks and Reserves — A1699

No. 2991: a, Emas National Park. b, Mamirauá Reserve. c, Chapada dos Veadeiros National Park. d, Itatiaia National Park.

Litho. & Embossed

2006, Sept. 4 ***Perf. 11½***

2991 A1699 85c Block of 4, #a-d 3.75 3.75

Souvenir Sheet

Cashews — A1700

2006, Sept. 11 **Litho.** ***Die Cut***

2992 A1700 2.90r multi 3.75 3.75

Graffiti Type of 2006

Souvenir Sheet

No. 2993: a, Like #2981. b, Like #2982.

2006, Sept. 11 ***Perf. 12x11½***

2993 A1691 1.60r Sheet of 2, #a-b 3.50 3.50

Lubrapex 2006, Rio.

Fernando de Noronha Archipelago A1701

2006, Sept. 27 ***Perf. 11½***

2994 A1701 2.50r multi 3.25 3.25

First Flight of Alberto Santos-Dumont's 14bis Airplane, Cent. — A1702

2006, Oct. 23 **Litho.** ***Perf. 11½x12***

2995 A1702 (90c) multi .90 .90

Christmas A1703

2006, Oct. 27 **Litho.** ***Die Cut***

Self-Adhesive

2996 A1703 (60c) multi .65 .65

Glitter was applied to portions of the stamp.

Occupation Type of 2005

Die Cut Perf. 12x12¼

2006, Nov. 6 **Photo.**

Self-Adhesive

2997 A1690 1c Popcorn vendor .30 .30
 a. Die cut perf. 12x12¼ syncopated ('11) .25 .25
2998 A1690 1r Manicurist 1.10 1.10
 a. Die cut perf. 12x12¼ syncopated ('11) 1.10 1.10

Souvenir Sheet

Christmas — A1704

No. 2999: a, Shepherds and sheep (25x35mm). b, Angel with horn (36x41mm). c, Holy Family (25x35mm).

Serpentine Die Cut 11½x11

2006, Nov. 9 **Litho.**

2999 A1704 1.60r Sheet of 3, #a-c 5.75 5.75

A shiny varnish was applied to portions of the design.

America Issue, Energy Conservation — A1705

2006, Nov. 22 ***Perf. 11½x12***

3000 A1705 1.75r multi 1.90 1.90

Souvenir Sheet

Sharks — A1706

No. 3001: a, Isurus oxyrinchus and Sphyrna lewini. b, Mustelus schmitti.

Litho., Litho. & Embossed (#3001b)

2006, Nov. 26 *Perf. 11½*

3001 A1706 1.90r Sheet of 2, #a-b 4.75 4.75

Christmas — A1707

2006, Oct. 30 Litho. *Perf. 12x11½*

3002 A1707 (55c) multi + label *7.25 7.25*

No. 3002 was printed in sheets of 12 stamps + 12 labels that could be personalized. Sheets sold for 21r.

A1708

Flag and Map of Brazil — A1708a

2007 Litho. *Perf. 11½x12*

3003 A1708 (90c) multi + label *7.25 7.25*

Perf. 12x11½

3003A A1708a (90c) multi + label *7.25 7.25*

Issued: No. 3003, 2/14; No. 3003A, 10/30. Nos. 3003 and 30003A each were printed in sheets of 12 stamps + 12 labels that could be personalized. Each sheet sold for 25r. See Nos. 3080M-3080N for similar stamps without year date.

Praia Vermelha (Red Beach) — A1708b

Cable Car, Sugarloaf Mountain — A1708c

Guanabara Bay, Sugarloaf Mountain — A1708d

Candelária Church — A1708e

Christ the Redeemer Statue — A1708f

Arcos da Lapa (Carioca Aqueduct) — A1708g

2007, Sept. 24 Litho. *Perf. 12x12¾*

3003B Block of 6 + 6 labels *16.00 16.00*
- *c.* A1708b (90c) multi + label *2.40 2.40*
- *d.* A1708c (90c) multi + label *2.40 2.40*
- *e.* A1708d (90c) multi + label *2.40 2.40*
- *f.* A1708e (90c) multi + label *2.40 2.40*
- *g.* A1708f (90c) multi + label *2.40 2.40*
- *h.* A1708g (90c) multi + label *2.40 2.40*

Rio de Janeiro tourist attractions. No. 3003B was printed in sheets containing 12 stamps +12 labels, two of each stamp, that could be personalized. Sheets sold for 25r.

2007 Pan American Games, Rio A1709

Designs: No. 3004, (85c), Indoor soccer, bright blue background. No. 3005, (85c), Diving, orange background. No. 3006, (85c), Water polo, blue violet background. No. 3007, (85c), Swimming, yellow orange background. No. 3008, (85c), Synchronized swimming, green background.

Serpentine Die Cut 11

2007, Jan. 19 Litho.

Self-Adhesive

3004 A1709 (85c) multi	.85	.85
3005 A1709 (85c) multi	.85	.85
3006 A1709 (85c) multi	.85	.85
3007 A1709 (85c) multi	.85	.85
3008 A1709 (85c) multi	.85	.85
a. Strip of 5, #3004-3008	24.00	24.00

Dances A1710

No. 3009: a, Carimbo. b, Frevo.

2007, Feb. 8 *Perf. 11½*

3009 A1710 Vert. pair, #a-b 1.75 1.75
- *a.* (55c) multi .55 .55
- *b.* (55c) multi .55 .55

Intl. Polar Year — A1711

No. 3010: a, Ship Ary Rongel. b, Commander Ferraz Antarctic Station. c, Emperor penguin, map of Antarctica.

2007, Mar. 13 *Perf. 11½x12*

3010 A1711 (90c) Horiz. strip of 3, #a-c 3.00 3.00

Path of Father José de Anchieta — A1712

No. 3011: a, Our Lady of the Assumption Church. b, Father José de Anchieta. c, Metropolitan Cathedral, Vitória.

2007, Mar. 19 *Perf. 12x11½*

3011 A1712 90c Horiz. strip of 3, #a-c 3.00 3.00

Soccer Stadiums — A1713

Designs: 60c, Mangueirao Stadium, Belem. 90c, Serra Dourada Stadium, Goiania. No. 3014, 2.60r, Maracana Stadium, Rio. No. 3015, 2.60r, Pacaembu Stadium, Sao Paulo.

2007, Mar. 25 *Perf. 11x11½*

3012-3015 A1713 Set of 4 7.00 7.00

Juscelino Kubitschek Bridge, Brasilia A1714

2007, Apr. 21 *Perf. 11½x12*

3016 A1714 (90c) multi 1.10 1.10

Scouting, Cent. — A1715

2007, Apr. 23 *Perf. 12x11½*

3017 A1715 2r multi 2.25 2.25

Pope Benedict XVI A1716

2007, May 9 *Perf. 11½x12*

3018 A1716 90c multi 1.25 1.25

Souvenir Sheet

Shells — A1717

No. 3019: a, Cochlespira elongata. b, Charonia variegata. c, Chicoreus beauii.

Litho. & Embossed

2007, June 5 *Perf. 12x11½*

3019 A1717 2r Sheet of 3, #a-c 6.75 6.75

Portions of the design were applied by a thermographic process producing a shiny, raised effect.

Diplomatic Relations Between Brazil and Canada, 140th Anniv. — A1718

2007, June 27 Litho. *Perf. 12¾x12*

3020 A1718 90c multi .95 .95

Occupations Type of 2005

Die Cut Perf. 12x12¼

2007, July 4 **Photo.**

Self-Adhesive

3020A A1690 60c Barber .65 .65

3020B A1690 90c Carpenter .95 .95

Giuseppe Garibaldi (1807-82), Italian Leader A1719

Designs: No. 3021, 1.40r, Ship, Garibaldi on horseback. No. 3022, 1.40r, Garibaldi, ship.

2007, July 4 *Perf. 12x12¾*

3021-3022 A1719 Set of 2 3.25 3.25

3022a Horiz. pair, #3021-3022 3.25 3.25

See Uruguay Nos. 2196-2197.

Rail Transport A1720

Designs: 1.40r, Rio de Janeiro Metro car. 1.45r, Baroneza steam locomotive. 1.60r, Tram, Santa Teresa.

2007, July 6
3023-3025 A1720 Set of 3 4.75 4.75

Teófilo Ottoni (1807-69), Leader of 1842 Uprising A1721

2007, Aug. 23 Litho. *Perf. 12x12¾*
3026 A1721 60c multi .75 .75

America Issue, Education for All A1722

2007, Sept. 8
3027 A1722 60c multi .75 .75

Souvenir Sheet

Rose Varieties — A1723

No. 3028: a, High & Magic. b, Caballero. c, Avalanche.

2007, Sept. 29 *Perf. 12¾x12*
3028 A1723 2.60r Sheet of 3, #a-c 8.75 8.75

Zoo Animals A1724

No. 3029: a, African elephant. b, Tiger. c, Giraffes. d, Parrot. e, African lion. f, Chimpanzee.

2007, Oct. 5 Litho. *Perf. 12x12¾*
3029 Block or horiz. strip of 6 4.25 4.25
a.-f. A1724 60c Any single .65 .65

Christmas
A1725 A1726

Die Cut Perf. 12x12¼
2007, Oct. 11 Photo.
Self-Adhesive
3030 A1725 (60c) multi .70 .70
3031 A1726 (90c) multi 1.00 1.00

Arrival of Portuguese Royal Family in Brazil, 200th Anniv. — A1727

No. 3032: a, King John VI and ships. b, Royal family and ship.

2008, Jan. 22 Litho. *Perf. 12x12¾*
3032 A1727 2r Horiz. pair, #a-b 4.50 4.50

See Portugal No. 2973.

Bank of Brazil, 200th Anniv. A1728

2008, Jan. 28
3033 A1728 (90c) multi 1.10 1.10

Opening of Brazilian Ports to Friendly Nations, 200th Anniv. A1729

2008, Jan. 28
3034 A1729 (90c) multi 1.10 1.10

Foreign Trade, 200th Anniv. A1730

2008, Jan. 28
3035 A1730 (90c) multi 1.10 1.10

America Issue - Dancer and Musicians A1731

Die Cut Perf. 12¼x12
2008, Feb. 1 Photo.
Self-Adhesive
3036 A1731 (60c) multi .75 .75

Medical Faculty Bicentenaries — A1732

Buildings at: No. 3037, (90c), Federal University of Bahia. No. 3038, (90c), Federal University of Rio de Janeiro.

2008, Feb. 18 Litho. *Perf. 12x12¾*
3037-3038 A1732 Set of 2 2.25 2.25

First National Youth Conference, Brasilia — A1733

Die Cut Perf. 12x12¼
2008, Feb. 27 Photo.
Self-Adhesive
3039 A1733 (90c) multi 1.10 1.10

Naval Fusiliers Corps, 200th Anniv. A1734

2008, Mar. 7 Litho. *Perf. 12x12¾*
3040 A1734 (90c) multi 1.10 1.10

Souvenir Sheet

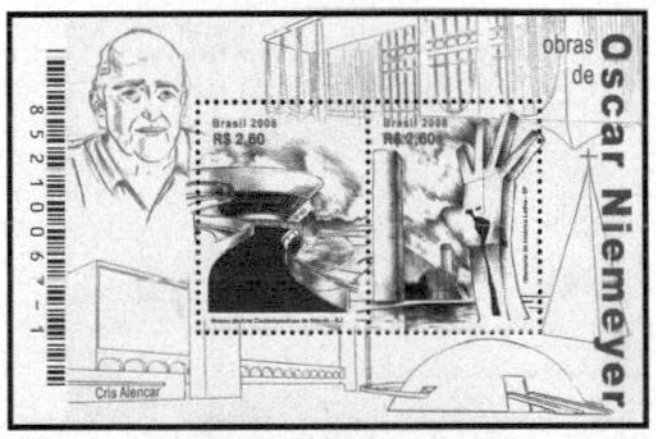
Architecture of Oscar Niemeyer — A1735

No. 3041: a, Museum of Contemporary Art, Niterói. b, Latin America Memorial, Sao Paolo.

Litho. & Embossed
2008, Mar. 18 *Perf. 12x11½*
3041 A1735 2.60r Sheet of 2, #a-b 6.25 6.25

Independent Judiciary, 200th Anniv. — A1736

2008, Mar. 27 Litho. *Perf. 12¾x12*
3042 A1736 (90c) multi 1.10 1.10

Military Justice in Brazil, 200th Anniv. A1737

2008, Apr. 1 *Perf. 12x12¾*
3043 A1737 (90c) multi 1.10 1.10

Brazilian Press Association, Cent. — A1738

2008, Apr. 7
3044 A1738 (90c) multi 1.10 1.10

Brazilian Heroes — A1739

No. 1739: a, Dom Pedro I (1798-1834). b, Marshal Manuel Deodoro da Fonseca (1827-92). c, Duque de Caxias (1803-80), soldier and politician. d, Admiral Francisco Manuel Barroso (1804-82). e, Admiral Joaquim Marques de Tamandaré (1807-97). f, José Bonifácio (1763-1838), statesman. g, Alberto Santos-Dumont (1873-1932), aviation pioneer. h, Zumbi dos Palmares (1655-95), fugitive slave leader. i, Tiradentes (1746-92), Brazilian independence leader. j, José Plácido de Castro (1873-1908), Acrean Army leader.

2008, Apr. 21 *Perf. 12x11½*
3045 A1739 (90c) Block of 10, #a-j 14.00 14.00

Police, 200th Anniv. A1740

2008, May 10 *Perf. 12x12¾*
3046 A1740 (90c) multi 1.10 1.10

Independence Dragoons, 200th Anniv. — A1741

2008, May 10 *Perf. 12¾x12*
3047 A1741 (90c) multi 1.10 1.10

National Printing Office, 200th Anniv. — A1742

2008, May 10
3048 A1742 (90c) multi 1.10 1.10

Souvenir Sheet

Fauna of Serra do Japi Region — A1743

No. 3049: a, Tangara cayana cayana. b, Consul fabius drurii.

2008, May 16 *Perf. 11½x12*
3049 A1743 2r Sheet of 2, #a-b 5.00 5.00

Rio de Janeiro Botanical Gardens, 200th Anniv. — A1744

2008, June 13 *Perf. 12¾x12*
3050 A1744 (60c) multi .75 .75

Souvenir Sheet

Japanese Immigration to Brazil, Cent. — A1745

No. 3051: a, Map of Brazil, ship Kasato-Maru. b, Flags of Brazil and Japan, origami crane.

Litho. With Foil Application
2008, June 18 *Perf. 12x11½*
3051 A1745 3.50r multi 8.75 8.75

See Japan No. 3028.

French and Brazilian Landscapes — A1746

No. 3052: a, Glacier, France. b, Amazonian forest, Brazil.

2008, June 21 Litho. *Perf. 11½x12*
3052 Horiz. pair 5.00 5.00
a.-b. A1746 2r Either single 2.50 2.50

Joao Guimaraes Rosa (1908-67), Novelist — A1747

Litho. & Embossed
2008, June 27 *Perf. 12x11½*
3053 A1747 60c multi .75 .75

Agriculture Ministry, 200th Anniv. — A1748

2008, June 30 Litho. *Perf. 12¾x12*
3054 A1748 (90c) multi 1.10 1.10

2008 Summer Olympics, Beijing — A1749

No. 3055: a, Mascot Beibei, rhythmic gymnastics. b, Mascot Jingjing, equestrian. c, Mascot Huanhuan, swimming. d, Mascots Nini and Yingying, emblem of 2008 Summer Olympics.

Litho. & Embossed
2008, July 4 *Perf. 11½*
3055 A1749 65c Block of 4, #a-d 3.25 3.25

Brazilian Cuisine A1750

2008, Aug. 8 Litho. *Perf. 11½x12*
3056 A1750 90c multi 1.10 1.10

Endangered Animals of the Amazon Region — A1751

Designs: No. 3057, 1r, Pteronura brasiliensis. No. 3058, 1r, Lontra longicaudis. No. 3059, 1r, Trichechus inunguis.

2008, Sept. 5 *Perf. 11½x12*
3057-3059 A1751 Set of 3 3.50 3.50

Birds — A1752

Designs: No. 3060, Strix virgata. No. 3060A, Celeus obrieni.

2008, Oct. 10 *Perf. 12x11½*
3060 A1752 1.40r multi 1.25 1.25
3060A A1752 1.40r multi 1.25 1.25

Christmas
A1753 A1754

Die Cut Perf. 12x12¼
2008, Oct. 17 **Photo.**
Self-Adhesive
3061 A1753 (65c) multi .60 .60
3062 A1754 (1r) multi .95 .95

Convent of St. Anthony, 400th anniv. (No. 3061), Franciscan Movement, 800th anniv. (in 2009) (No. 3062).

Provisional Regulations of General Administration of the Posts, 200th Anniv. — A1755

2008, Nov. 22 Litho. *Perf. 11½x12*
3063 A1755 1r multi .85 .85

Louis Braille (1809-52), Educator of the Blind — A1756

2009, Jan. 4 Litho. & Embossed
3064 A1756 2.20r multi 2.00 2.00

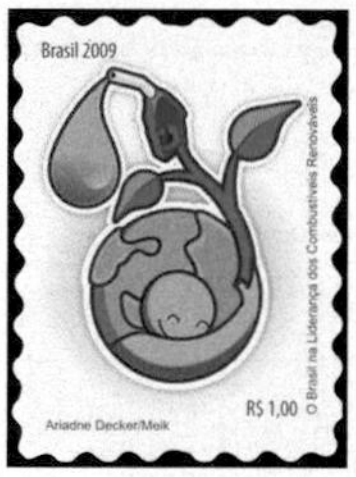

Brazilian Leadership in Production of Fuels From Renewable Resources A1757

Serpentine Die Cut 4¾x5
2009, Jan. 13 **Litho.**
Self-Adhesive
3065 A1757 1r multi .85 .85

New Year 2009 (Year of the Ox) — A1758

Litho. & Embossed With Foil Application
2009, Jan. 15 *Perf. 11½x12*
3066 A1758 2.35r multi 2.00 2.00

Souvenir Sheets

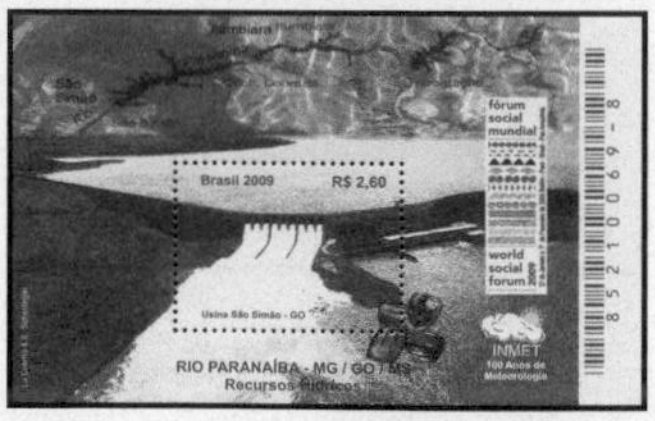

Rivers — A1759

Designs: No. 3067, 2.60r, Sao Simao Hydroelectric Plant, Paranaíba River. No. 3068, 3.85r, Cichla mirianae, Sao Benedito River.

2009, Jan. 27 **Litho.**
3067-3068 A1759 Set of 2 8.00 8.00

Archbishop Helder Camara (1909-99) A1760

2009, Feb. 7 Litho. *Perf. 11½x12*
3069 A1760 1r multi .85 .85

Map, Flag and Scenes of Pernambuco — A1761

2009, Feb. 21
3070 A1761 (1r) multi + label *2.60 2.60*

No. 3070 was printed in sheets of 12 stamps + 12 labels that could be personalized. Sheets sold for 26r.

Intl. Polar Year — A1762

No. 3071: a, Hydrurga leptonyx. b, Ursus maritimus.

Perf. 11½x11¾
2009, Mar. 18 **Litho.**
3071 A1762 1r Horiz. pair, #a-b 1.90 1.90

Postman A1763

Die Cut Perf. 12¼x12
2009, Mar. 20 **Photo.**
Self-Adhesive
3072 A1763 65c multi .60 .60

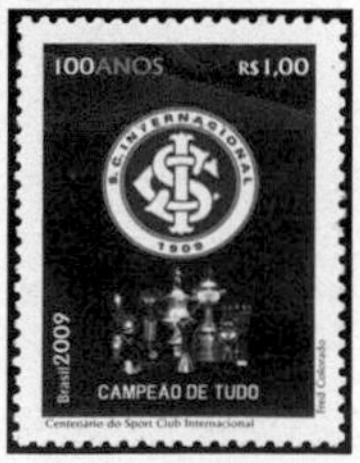

Sport Club Internacional Soccer Team, Cent. — A1764

2009, Apr. 4 Litho. *Perf. 12x11½*
3073 A1764 1r multi .95 .95

Diplomatic Relations Between Brazil and Thailand
A1765

Flowers and buildings: No. 3074, 2.35r, Rhynchostylis gigantea, Grand Palace, Bangkok. No. 3075, 2.35r, Aechmea disticantha, Sao Pedro de Alcântara Cathedral, Petrópolis, Brazil.

2009, Apr. 17

3074-3075 A1765 Set of 2 4.50 4.50

Hercílio Luz Bridge, Florianópolis — A1766

Serra do Rio do Rastro — A1766a

Blumenau — A1766b

Balneário Camboriú — A1766c

Santa Marta Lighthouse, Laguna — A1766d

Windmill, Joinville — A1766e

2009, Apr. 17 Litho. ***Perf. 11½x12***

3076 Block of 6 + 6 labels *40.00 40.00*
a. A1766 (1r) multi + label *6.50 6.50*
b. A1766a (1r) multi + label *6.50 6.50*
c. A1766b (1r) multi + label *6.50 6.50*
d. A1766c (1r) multi + label *6.50 6.50*
e. A1766d (1r) multi + label *6.50 6.50*
f. A1766e (1r) multi + label *6.50 6.50*

Santa Catarina tourist attractions. No. 3076 was printed in sheets containing 12 stamps +12 labels, two of each stamp, that could be personalized. Sheets sold for 26r.

Miniature Sheet

Zebu Expo — A1767

No. 3077: a, Bos taurus indicus Indubrasil. b, Bos taurus indicus Nelore Mocho. c, Bos taurus indicus Sindi. d, Bos taurus indicus Tabapua. e, Bos taurus indicus Brahman. f, Bos taurus indicus Nelore. g, Bos taurus indicus Guzerá. h, Bos taurus indicus Gir Leiteiro. i, Zebu Breeders Association of Brazil Headquarters (Sede ABCZ). j, Bos taurus indicus Gir Mocho. k, Bos taurus indicus Gir Dupla Aptidao. l, Zebu Breeders Association of Brazil Exposition Park.

2009, May 3

3077 A1767 Sheet of 12 + 12 labels *65.00 65.00*
a.-l. (1r) Any single + label *7.25 7.25*

No. 3077 sold for 26r. Labels could be personalized.

Miniature Sheet

Tocantins Tourist Attractions — A1768

No. 3078: a, Morro da Catedral, Jalapao. b, Our Lady of Mercy Cathedral, Porto Nacional. c, Registro Waterfall, Natividade. d, Matriz Church, Natividade. e, Owl, Palmas. f, Araguatins Quay, Araguatins. g, Flower, Palmas. h, Tartaruga Beach, Peixe. i, Velha Waterfall, Jalapao. j, Rafting on Rio Novo, Jalapao. k, Jalapao. l, Graciosa Beach, Palmas.

2009, May 14

3078 A1768 Sheet of 12 + 12 labels *40.00 40.00*
a.-l. (1r) Any single + label *3.00 3.00*

No. 3078 sold for 26r. Labels could be personalized.

Planes and Coastline — A1769

Two Planes — A1769a

Plane and Smoke — A1769b

Plane and Sun — A1769c

Plane Over Water — A1769d

Planes Over Forest — A1769e

2009, May 15 Litho. ***Perf. 11½x12***

3079 Block of 6 + 6 labels *16.00 16.00*
a. A1769 (1r) multi + label *2.40 2.40*
b. A1769a (1r) multi + label *2.40 2.40*
c. A1769b (1r) multi + label *2.40 2.40*
d. A1769c (1r) multi + label *2.40 2.40*
e. A1769d (1r) multi + label *2.40 2.40*
f. A1769e (1r) multi + label *2.40 2.40*

Aerobatics Squadron. No. 3079 was printed in sheets containing 12 stamps +12 labels, two of each stamp, that could be personalized. Sheets sold for 26r.

Miniature Sheet

Rio Grande do Norte Tourist Attractions — A1770

No. 3080: a, Genipabu Beach, Natal. b, Castelo Zé dos Montes, Sítio Novo. c, Pipa Beach, Tibau do Sul. d, Fortalez dos Reis Magos, Natal. e, Rodolfo Fernandes Square, Mossoró. f, Alberto Maranhao Theater, Natal. g, Mae Luiza Lighthouse, Natal. h, Newton Navarro Bridge, Natal. i, Three WIse Men Statue, Natal. j, Ponta Negra Beach, Natal. k, Barra de Cunhaú Beach, Canguaretama. l, Matriz Church, Martins.

2009, July 27

3080 A1770 Sheet of 12 + 12 labels *40.00 40.00*
a.-l. (1r) Any single + label *3.00 3.00*

No. 3080 sold for 26r. Labels could be personalized.

A1770a

Flag and Map of Brazil — A1770b

2009, Aug. 6 ***Perf. 11½x12***

3080M A1770a (1r) multi + label *4.00 4.00*

Perf. 12x11½

3080N A1770b (1r) multi + label *4.00 4.00*

Nos. 3080M and 3080N each were printed in sheets of 12 stamps + 12 labels that could be personalized. Each sheet sold for 26r.

Miniature Sheet

Ceará Tourist Attractions — A1771

No. 3081: a, West Coast, Lagoinha. b, Ipú Waterfall. c, Dragao do Mar Arts and Culture Center, Fortaleza. d, José de Alencar Theater, Fortaleza. e, Iracema Statue, Fortaleza. f, Ubajara National Park. g, Statue of Padre Cícero, Juazerio do Norte. h, West Coast, Jericoacara. i, Beira Mar Avenue, Fortaleza. j, Fortim. k, Cedro Dam and Galinha Choco rock, Quixadá. l, Canoa Quebrada.

2009, Aug. 18 ***Perf. 11½x12***

3081 A1771 Sheet of 12 + 12 labels *75.00 75.00*
a.-l. (1r) Any single + label *4.00 4.00*

No. 3081 sold for 26r. Labels could be personalized.

Books, Khalil Gibran (1883-1931), Poet, and His House in Beirut, Lebanon — A1772

2009, May 5 Litho. ***Perf. 11½x12***

3082 A1772 2.35r multi 2.40 2.40

Telegram
A1773

Die Cut Perf. 12¼x12

2009, Mar. 20 Photo.

Self-Adhesive

3083 A1773 1r multi .90 .90
a. With blue outline of denomination, year and country name ('10) 1.25 1.25

Brazilian Kickboxing
A1774

Die Cut Perf. 12

2009, May 25 Litho.

Self-Adhesive

3084 A1774 65c multi .70 .70

Edésio Fernandes School of Justice — A1775

2009, May 29 ***Perf. 12x11½***

3085 A1775 1r multi 1.10 1.10

Cooperation in Space Projects With Russia — A1776

2009, June 12 *Perf. 11½x12*
3086 A1776 2.35r multi 2.50 2.50

Municipal Theater, Rio de Janeiro, Cent. A1777

Litho. With Foil Application

2009, July 14 *Perf. 11½x11¾*
3087 A1777 (1r) multi 1.10 1.10

Commercial Association of Rio de Janeiro, Bicent. A1778

2009, July 15 Litho. *Perf. 11½x12*
3088 A1778 1r multi 1.10 1.10

Fruit — A1779

No. 3092: a, Vitis labrusca (purple). b, Prunus persica. c, Prunus salicina. d, Malpighia glabra. e, Vitis labrusca (green). f, Fragaria x ananassa. g, Passiflora edulis. h, Vitis spp. i, Ficus carica. j, Diospyros kaki.

2009, July 23 Litho. *Perf. 12x11½*
3089 Block of 10 17.00 17.00
a.-j. A1779 (1r) Any single 1.50 1.50

Miniature Sheet

Dutch Presence in Brazil — A1780

No. 3090: a, Prince John Maurice of Nassau-Siegen ("The Brazilian") (1604-79), governor general of Dutch possessions in Brazil. b, Dutch ship Zutphen. c, Dutch pipes. d, Palácio de Friburgo, Recife. e, Palácio do Campo das Princesas, Recife. f, Dutch houses on Rua Aurora, Recife.

2009, Aug. 4 Litho. *Perf. 12x11½*
3090 A1780 2.20r Sheet of 6, #a-f 14.50 14.50

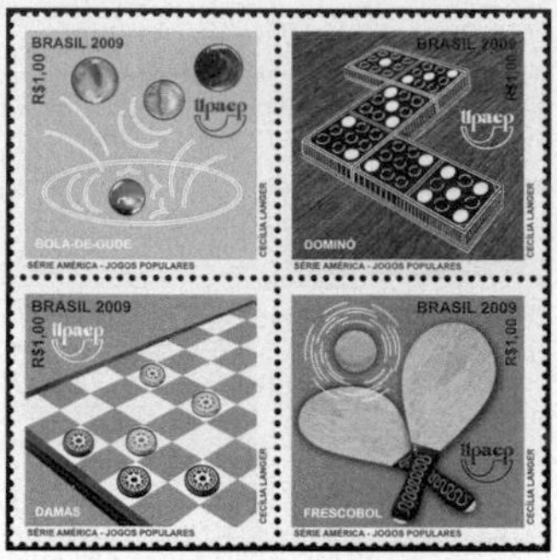

America Issue, Traditional Games — A1781

No. 3091: a, Marbles (bola-de-gude). b, Dominoes. c, Checkers. d, Paddleball.

Litho. & Embossed

2009, Aug. 18 *Perf. 11½*
3091 A1781 1r Block of 4, #a-d 4.25 4.25

A1782

Minas Gerais Flag and Map, Church in Serro — A1783

2009, Aug. 21 *Perf. 11½x12*
3092 A1782 (1r) multi + label *4.00 4.00*

Perf. 12x11½

3093 A1783 (1r) multi + label *4.00 4.00*

Nos. 3092 and 3093 each were printed in sheets of 12 samps + 12 labels that could be personalized. Each sheet sold for 26r.

Miniature Sheet

A1784

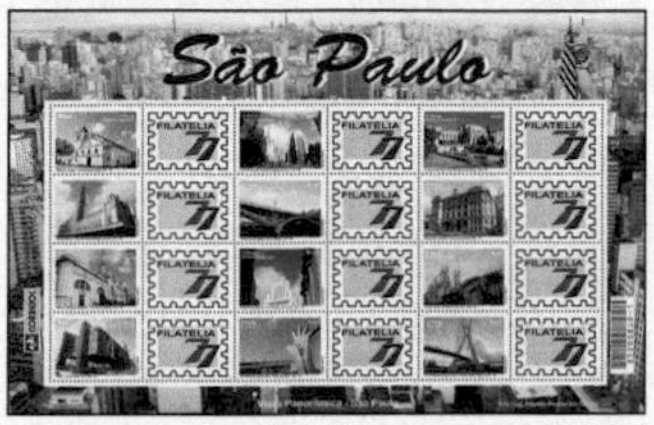

Sao Paulo Tourist Attractions — A1785

Nos. 3094 and 3095: a, Pateo do Collegio. b, Paulista Avenue. c, Ipiranga Museum. d, Luz Station. e, Santa Ifigênia Viaduct. f, Post Office (Palácio dos Correios). g, Mercado Municipal Paulistano. h, Altino Arantes Building. i, Sao Paulo Cathedral (Catedral da Sé). j, Sao Paulo Museum of Art (MASP). k, Latin America Memorial. l, Octávio Frias de Oliveira Bridge. Stamps from No. 3094 are vertical and from No. 3095, horizontal.

2009, Aug. 29 *Perf. 12x11½*
3094 A1784 Sheet of 12 + 12 labels *50.00 50.00*
a.-l. (1r) Any single + label *4.00 4.00*

Perf. 11½x12

3095 A1785 Sheet of 12 + 12 labels *50.00 50.00*
a.-l. (1r) Any single + label *4.00 4.00*

Nos. 3094 and 3095 each sold for 26r. Labels could be personalized.

Federal Educational, Professional and Technological Network, Cent. — A1786

Litho. & Embossed

2009, Sept. 23 *Perf. 11½x12*
3096 A1786 (1r) multi 1.10 1.10

Redrawn With White Border

3096A A1786 (1r) multi + label *7.25 7.25*

No. 3096A was printed in sheets of 12 stamps + 12 labels that could be personalized. Sheets sold for 26r.

Buildings, Historic Center of Sao Luís UNESCO World Heritage Site A1787

2009, Sept. 25 **Litho.**
3097 A1787 (1r) multi 1.10 1.10

Miniature Sheet

Birds — A1788

No. 3098: a, Paroaria coronata. b, Rupicola rupicola. c, Chlorophonia cyanea. d, Porphyrospiza caerulescens. e, Tangara cyanocephala. f, Amblyramphus holosericeus.

2009, Oct. 2
3098 A1788 1r Sheet of 6, #a-f 6.75 6.75

Lubrapex 2009, Evora, Portugal; Birdpex 2010, Antwerp, Belgium.

Carmen Miranda (1909-55), Actress — A1789

2009, Oct. 6 *Perf. 12x11½*
3099 A1789 2.20r multi 2.60 2.60

Souvenir Sheet

France Year in Brazil — A1790

No. 3100: a, Le Corbusier (1887-1965), architect. b, Brazilian Indian.

Litho. & Engr. (#3100a), Litho. & Embossed (#3100b)

2009, Oct. 7 *Perf. 11½*
3100 A1790 2.20r Sheet of 2, #a-b 5.25 5.25

Postman on Motorcycle A1791

Mail Bag — A1792

Die Cut Perf. 12¼x12

2009, Oct. 9 **Photo.**

Self-Adhesive

3101 A1791 (65c) multi .75 .75
a. Die cut perf. 12¼x12 syncopated ('11) .70 .70

Die Cut Perf. 12x12¼

3102 A1792 (1r) multi 1.25 1.25
a. Die cut perf. 12x12¼ syncopated ('11) 1.10 1.10

Coritiba Soccer Club, Cent. — A1793

2009, Oct. 12 Litho. *Perf. 12x11½*
3103 A1793 1.05r multi 1.25 1.25

Sport Club International Soccer Team, Cent. — A1794

2009, Oct. 13
3104 A1794 (1r) multi + label *2.60 2.60*

No. 3104 was printed in sheets of 12 stamps + 12 labels that could be personalized. Sheets sold for 26r.

Souvenir Sheet

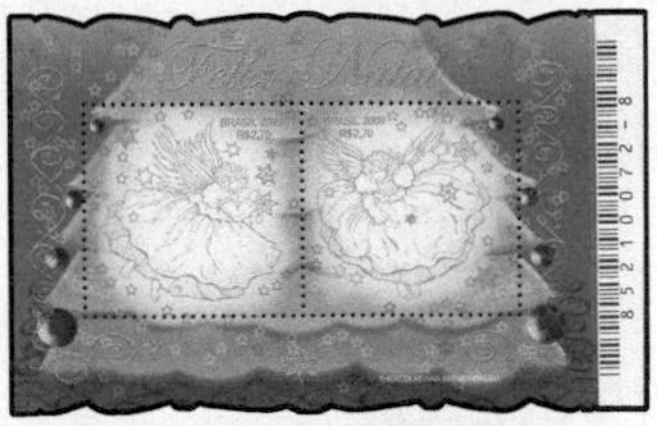

Christmas — A1795

No. 3105 — Angel with denomination at: a, UR. b, UL.

Litho. & Engr.

2009, Oct. 16 ***Perf. 11½***

3105 A1795 2.70r Sheet of 2, #a-b 6.50 6.50

A1796

A1797

A1798

A1799

A1800

A1801

Christmas A1802

Die Cut Perf. 12

2009, Oct. 16 **Litho.**

Self-Adhesive

3106	A1796 (65c) multi	.75	.75
3107	A1797 (65c) multi	.75	.75
3108	A1798 (65c) multi	.75	.75
3109	A1799 (65c) multi	.75	.75
3110	A1800 (65c) multi	.75	.75
3111	A1801 (65c) multi	.75	.75
a.	Horiz. strip of 6, #3106-3111	4.50	

Die Cut

3112	A1802 (1r) multi	1.25	1.25
	Nos. 3106-3112 (7)	5.75	5.75

Bridges — A1803

No. 3113: a, Incheon Bridge, South Korea (denomination at UR). b, Octavio Frias de Oliveira Bridge, Brazil (denomination at UL).

2009, Oct. 30 ***Perf. 11½x11***

3113 A1803 1.05r Horiz. pair, #a-b 2.50 2.50

See South Korea No. 2324.

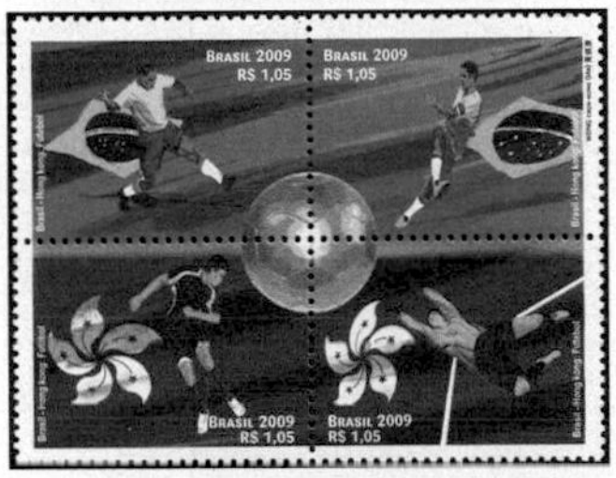

Soccer — A1804

No. 3114 — Soccer player from: a, Brazil, denomination at UR. b, Brazil, denomination at UL. c, Hong Kong, denomination at LR. d, Hong Kong, denomination at LL.

2009, Nov. 5

3114 A1804 1.05r Block of 4, #a-d 5.00 5.00

See Hong Kong Nos. 1372-1375.

Flag, Map and Scenes of Rondônia — A1805

2009, Dec. 29 Litho. ***Perf. 11½x12***

3115 A1805 (1.05r) multi + label *4.00 4.00*

No. 3115 was printed in sheets of 12 stamps + 12 labels that could be personalized. Sheets sold for 26r.

Miniature Sheet

Rio de Janeiro Beach Scenes — A1806

No. 3116 — Flag of Brazil and: a, Praia Vermelha (Red Beach). b, Barra da Tijuca. c, Copacabana. d, Leblon. e, Botafogo. f, Flamengo. g, Ipanema. h, Arpoador. i, Recreio dos Bandeirantes. j, Praia da Reserva. k, Leme. l, Sao Conrado.

2009, Dec. 29

3116	A1806 Sheet of 12 + 12 labels	*50.00*	*50.00*
a.-l.	(1.05r) Any single + label	*4.00*	*4.00*

No. 3116 sold for 26r. Labels could be personalized.

Corrida de Reis Race, Cuiabá — A1807

2010, Jan. 10 Litho. ***Perf. 11½x12***

3117 A1807 70c multi .75 .75

Miniature Sheet

Brasília Tourist Attractions — A1808

No. 3118: a, Cathedral. b, Palácio da Justiça (Palace of Justice. c, Palácio do Planalto (Palace of the Highlands). d, National Congress. e, Our Lady of Fátima Church. f, Federal Supreme Tribunal Building. g, Museum of the Republic. h, Dois Candangos sculpture. i, Juscelino Kubitschek Bridge. j, Ipé tree on the Esplenade. k, Juscelino Kubitschek Memorial. l, Interior of Cathedral.

2010, Feb. 5

3118	A1808 Sheet of 12 + 12 labels	*35.00*	*35.00*
a.-l.	(1.05r) Any single + label	*2.75*	*2.75*

No. 3118 sold for 26r. Labels could be personalized.

Pres. Tancredo de Almeida Neves (1910-85) — A1809

2010, Mar. 10 Litho. ***Perf. 11x11½***

3119 A1809 1.05r multi 1.25 1.25

Zilda Arns (1934-2010), Pediatrician and Aid Worker — A1810

2010, Mar. 25 ***Perf. 11½x12***

3120 A1810 1.45r multi 1.75 1.75

Francisco Cândido Xavier (1910-2002), Medium and Writer — A1811

2010, Apr. 2 ***Perf. 12x11½***

3121 A1811 (1.05r) multi 1.25 1.25

Architecture and Monuments of Brasília — A1812

No. 3122: a, Juscelino Kubitschek Memorial. b, Dois Candangos Monument. c, Cathedral of Brasília, horiz. d, Our Lady of Fatima Chapel (Igrejinha), horiz. e, Sculpture at Alvorada Palace. f, National Congress Buildings and ipê tree blossoms.

Perf. 12x11½, 11½x12 (#3122c, 3122d)

2010, Apr. 21

3122	Strip of 6	7.50	7.50
a.-f.	A1812 (1.05r) Any single	1.25	1.25

St. Benedict's Monastery, Sorocaba, Paintign by Sonia Vrubleski A1813

2010, Apr. 23 ***Perf. 12x11½***

3123 A1813 (1.05r) multi 1.25 1.25

St. Benedict's Monastery, 350th Anniv.

Souvenir Sheet

Amerigo Vespucci (1454-1512), Navigator — A1814

No. 3124 — Map and ship with: a, Vespucci. b, Vespucci and silhouette of building.

2010, May 10 ***Perf. 11½x12***

3124 A1814 2.40r Sheet of 2, #a-b 5.25 5.25

Fifth World Military Games, Rio A1815

2010, May 12

3125 A1815 2r multi 2.25 2.25

Souvenir Sheet

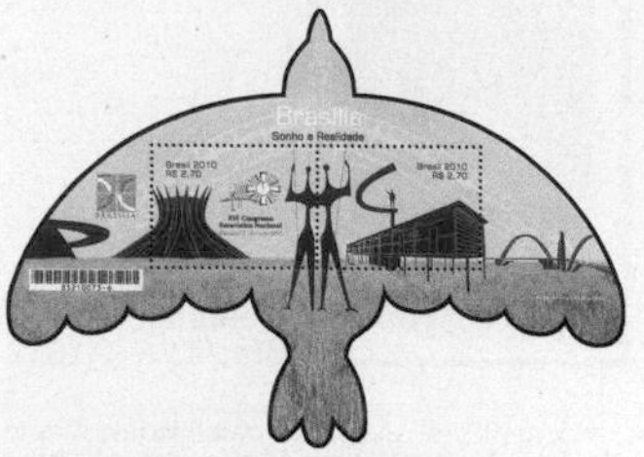

16th National Eucharistic Congress, Brasília — A1816

No. 3126: a, Congress emblem, Cathedral of Brasília, half of Dois Candangos Monument. b, Half of Dois Candangos Monument, Juscelino Kubitschek Moument, Catetinho (first home of Pres. Kubitschek and first building in Brasília).

2010, May 13
3126 A1816 2.70r Sheet of 2, #a-b 6.00 6.00

Church of Our Lady of the Rosary and St. Benedict's Chapel, Cuiabá — A1817

2010, June 4 **Litho.**
3127 A1817 1.10r multi 1.25 1.25

Feast of the Divine Eternal Father, Trinidade A1818

2010, June 6 ***Perf. 12x11½***
3128 A1818 70c multi .80 .80

2010 World Cup Soccer Championships, South Africa — A1819

2010, June 11 ***Perf. 11½***
3129 A1819 2.55r multi 3.00 3.00

Values are for stamps with surrounding selvage.

Miniature Sheet

Brasília Tourist Attractions — A1820

No. 3130: a, Juscelino Kubitschek Memorial. b, Brazilian flag on flagpole. c, Catetinho Building. d, Dois Candangos sculpture. e, National Museum. f, Wall of tiles of Athos Bulcao. g, National Congress. h, Television tower. i, Juscelino Kubitschek Bridge. j, Palácio de Alvorada (President's residence). k, Panteao da Pátria (Pantheon of the Fatherland). l, Cathedral.

2010, June 11
3130 A1820 Sheet of 12 + 12 labels *26.00 26.00*
a.-l. (1.10r) Any single + label *2.10 2.10*

No. 3130 sold for 26r. Labels could be personalized.

Peter Lund (1801-80), Paleontologist — A1821

2010, June 14 **Litho.** ***Perf. 11½x12***
3131 A1821 1.05r multi 1.25 1.25

Historical and Tourism Sites of Brazil and Syria — A1822

2010, June 28 ***Perf. 11½x12***
3132 A1822 2r multi 2.25 2.25

See Syria No. 1677.

Iguaçu Falls and Flags of Brazil and State of Paraná — A1823

2010, June 29
3133 A1823 (1.10r) multi + label *4.00 4.00*

No. 3133 was printed in sheets of 12 stamps + 12 labels that could be personalized. Sheets sold for 26r.

Miniature Sheet

Pará Tourist Attractions — A1824

No. 3134: a, Atalaia Dunes, Salinópolis. b, Buildings, Belém. c, Mosqueiro Beach Entranceway, Belém. d, Ver-o-Peso Market Complex, Belém. e, Mangal das Garças Park, Belém. f, Docks Station (Estaçao das Docas), Belém. g, António Lemos Palace, Belém. h, Paz Theater, Belém. i, Açai berries and paste. j, House of Eleven Windows (Casa das Onze Janelas), Belém. k, Hangar, Convention Center and Amazon Fair, Belém. l, Our Lady of Nazareth Basilica, Belém.

2010, June 29 **Litho.** ***Perf. 11½x12***
3134 A1824 Sheet of 12 + 12 labels *40.00 40.00*
a.-l. (1.10r) Any single + label *3.00 3.00*

No. 3134 sold for 26r. Labels could be personalized.

Souvenir Sheet

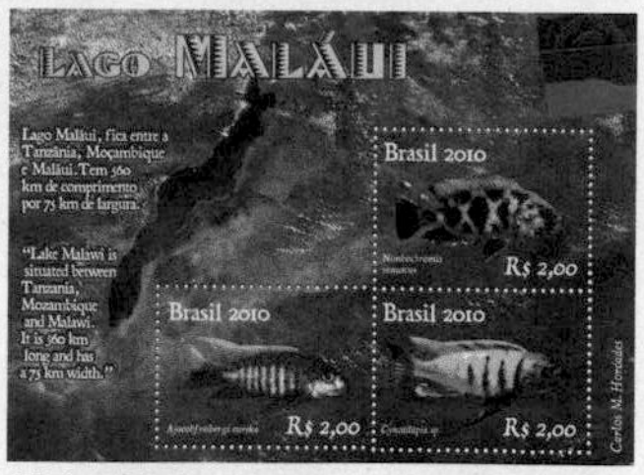

Fish of Lake Malawi, Africa — A1825

No. 3135: a, Nimbochromis venustus. b, Ajacobfreibergi eureka. c, Cynotilapia sp.

2010, July 6
3135 A1825 2r Sheet of 3, #a-c 7.00 7.00

English Village in Paranapiacaba — A1826

2010, July 17
3136 A1826 1.05r multi 1.25 1.25

Temple of Abu Simbel, Egypt A1827

2010, July 22
3137 A1827 1.05r multi 1.25 1.25

Ministry of Agriculture, Livestock and Food Supply, 150th Anniv. — A1828

2010, July 28 ***Perf. 12x11½***
3138 A1828 1.05r multi 1.25 1.25

Irineu Evangelista de Sousa, Viscount of Mauá (1813-89), Railroad Entrepreneur — A1829

2010, July 28 ***Perf. 11½x12***
3139 A1829 1.05r multi 1.25 1.25

Ministry of Transportation, 150th anniv.

Victoria Regia — A1830

Victoria Regia Flower — A1831

Parrots — A1832

Jaguar — A1833

Ipé Tree — A1834

Caiman — A1835

Jabiru — A1836

2010, June 26 **Litho.** ***Perf. 11½x12***
3140 Sheet of 12, #a-b, 2 each #c-g, + 12 labels *45.00 45.00*
a. A1830 (1.05r) multi *3.00 3.00*
b. A1831 (1.05r) multi *3.00 3.00*
c. A1832 (1.05r) multi *3.00 3.00*
d. A1833 (1.05r) multi *3.00 3.00*
e. A1834 (1.05r) multi *3.00 3.00*
f. A1835 (1.05r) multi *3.00 3.00*
g. A1836 (1.05r) multi *3.00 3.00*

Pantanal flora and fauna. No. 3140 sold for 30r. Labels could be personalized.

Textile Crops — A1837

No. 3141: a, Gossypium hirsutum (cotton). b, Cocos nucifera (coir). c, Corchorus capsularis (jute).d, Agave sisalana (sisal).

2010, Aug. 12 **Litho. & Engr.**
3141 A1837 2r Block of 4, #a-d 9.25 9.25

Miniature Sheet

Espírito Santo Tourist Attractions — A1838

No. 3142: a, O Frade e a Freira rock formations. b, Moqueca Capixaba (seafood stew). c, Itaúnas Dunes. d, Ponte da Passagem, Vitória. e, Palácio Anchuieta. f, Penha Convent, Vila Velha. g, Caparaó National Park. h, Pedra Azul. i, Pedra da Cebola. j, Guarapari Beach. k, Port of Vitória. l, Curva da Jurema Beach.

2010, Aug. 16 Litho. *Perf. 11½x12*

3142 A1838 Sheet of 12 + 12 labels 45.00 45.00

a.-l. (1.05r) Any single + label 3.00 3.00

No. 3142 sold for 30r. Labels could be personalized.

A1839

A1840

A1841

Corinthians Paulista Sport Club, Cent. A1842

2010, Sept. 1 Litho. *Perf. 11½x12*

3143 A1839 1.05r multi 1.25 1.25

3144 A1840 (1.05r) multi + label *4.00 4.00*

Perf. 12x11½

3145 A1841 (1.05r) multi + label *4.00 4.00*

Embroidered

Self-Adhesive

Die Cut Perf. 11¾x11½

3146 A1842 8.30r multi 9.75 9.75

Nos. 3144-3145 each were printed in sheets of 12 stamps + 12 labels that sold for 30r. Labels could be personalized.

America Issue, National Symbols — A1843

No. 3147: a, National coat of arms. b, National flag. c, National seal. d, National anthem.

2010, Sept. 7 Litho. *Perf. 11½*

3147 A1843 1.05r Block of 4, #a-d 5.00 5.00

13th Conference of Government Postage Stamp Printers' Association, Rio de Janeiro A1844

Litho. & Embossed

2010, Sept. 20 *Perf. 11½*

3148 A1844 2r multi 2.40 2.40

Souvenir Sheet

Intl. Year of Biodiversity — A1845

No. 3149: a, Tomatoes on vine. b, Organic green vegetables.

2010, Sept. 21 Litho. *Perf. 11½x12*

3149 A1845 2.40r Sheet of 2, #a-b 5.75 5.75

Portugal 2010 World Philatelic Exhibition, Lisbon.

Miniature Sheet

Rio de Janeiro Tourist Attractions — A1846

No. 3150: a, Arcos de Lapa (Lapa Arches), Rio de Janeiro. b, Ponte Estalada (Estalada Bridge), Rio des Ostras. c, Imperial Museum, Petrópolis. d, Monumento dos Pracinhas (World War II Soldier's Monument), Rio de Janeiro. e, Santa Rita Church, Paraty. f, Christ the Redeemer Statue, Rio de Janeiro. g, Serra dos Oragaos, Teresópolis. h, Ponte Rio Niterói (Niterói River Bridge), Rio de Janeiro. i, Crystal Palace, Petrópolis. j, Museum of Contemporary Art, Niterói. k, Sao Tomé Lighthouse, Campos dos Goytacazes. l, Metropolitan Cathedral, Rio de Janeiro.

2010, Sept. 27 *Perf. 12x11½*

3150 A1846 Sheet of 12 + 12 labels *40.00 40.00*

a.-l. (1.05r) Any single + label 3.00 3.00

No. 3150 sold for 30r. Labels could be personalized.

A1847

A1848

Christmas A1849

2010, Oct. 22 *Perf. 11½*

Souvenir Sheet

3151 A1847 2.70r multi 3.25 3.25

Self-Adhesive

Die Cut Perf. 12

3152 A1848 (75c) multi .90 .90

3153 A1849 (1.05r) multi 1.25 1.25

Diplomatic Relations Between Brazil and Zambia — A1850

No. 3154 — Animals and sites in Zambia: a, Leopard. b, Victoria Falls. c, Lion. d, Buffalo. e, Black rhinoceros. f, African elephant.

2010, Oct. 24 *Perf. 11½*

3154 A1850 1.05r Block of 6, #a-f 7.50 7.50

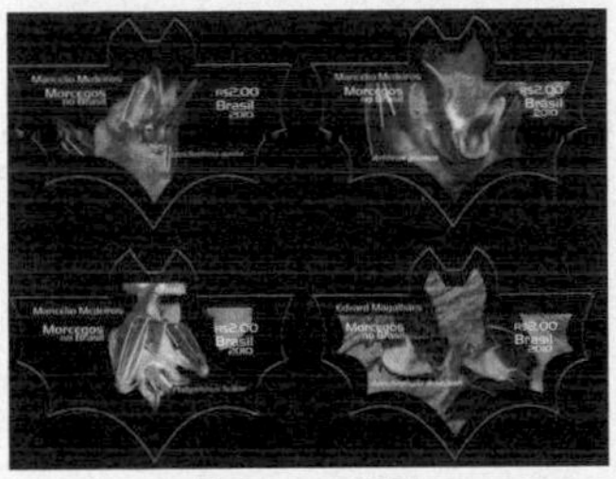

Bats — A1851

No. 3155: a, Lonchorhina aurita. b, Artibeus gnomus. c, Platyrrhinus helleri. d, Lonchophylla dekeyseri.

2010, Oct. 30 *Die Cut*

Self-Adhesive

3155 A1851 Block of 4 9.75

a.-d. 2r Any single 2.40 2.40

A1852

Christmas — A1853

2010, Nov. 30 Litho. *Perf. 11½x12*

3156 A1852 (1.05r) multi + label *2.40 2.40*

Perf. 12x11½

3157 A1853 (1.05r) multi + label *2.40 2.40*

Nos. 3156-3157 each were printed in sheets of 12stamps + 12 labels that sold for 30r. Labels could be personalized.

Miniature Sheet

Goias Tourist Attractions — A1854

No. 3158: a, Vaca Brava Park, Goiânia. b, Waterfalls near Cavalcante. c, Pools, Caldas Novas. d, Rio Quente. e, Praça do Trabalhador (Worker's Square), Goiânia. f, Rio Araguala. g, Mask from Pirenópolis. h, Bosque dos Buritis, Goiânia. i, Waterfalls, Chapada dos Veadeiros National Park. j, Waterfalls, Pirenópolis. k, Basilica, Trinidade. l, Casa de Cora (House of Cora Coralina), Cidade de Goiás.

2010, Dec. 23 *Perf. 11½x12*

3158 A1854 Sheet of 12 + 12 labels *24.00 24.00*

a.-l. (1.05r) Any single + label 2.00 2.00

No. 3158 sold for 30r. Labels could be personalized.

End of Term of Pres. Luiz Inácio Lula da Silva — A1855

2011, Jan. 1 *Perf. 12x11½*

3159 A1855 2r mulyi 2.40 2.40

Federal Savings Bank, 150th Anniv. A1856

2011, Jan. 12 Litho. *Perf. 11½x12*

3160 A1856 (1.05r) multi 1.25 1.25

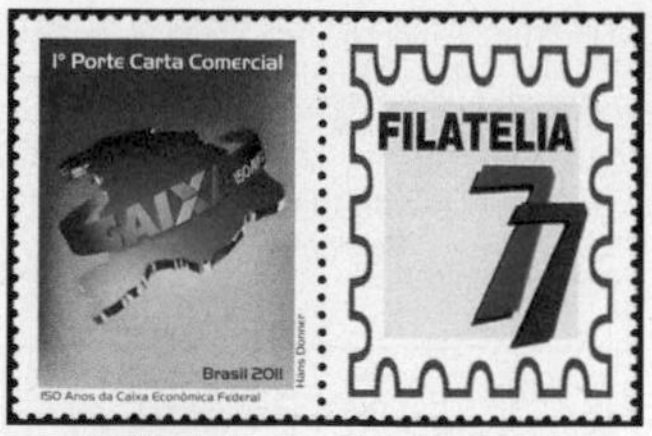

Federal Savings Bank, 150th Anniv. — A1857

2011, Jan. 12 ***Perf. 12x11½***
3161 A1857 (1.05r) multi + label 3.00 3.00

No. 3161 was printed in sheets of 12 stamps + 12 labels that sold for 30r. Labels could be personalized.

Father Roberto Landell de Moura (1861-1928), Radio Pioneer — A1858

2011, Jan. 21 ***Perf. 11½x12***
3162 A1858 (1.05r) multi 1.25 1.25

Postal Union of the Americas, Spain and Portugal (UPAEP), Cent. A1859

2011, Mar. 23 ***Perf. 11½***
3163 A1859 1.25r multi 1.60 1.60

Guarani Soccer Team, Cent. — A1860

2011, Apr. 2 ***Perf. 12x11½***
3164 A1860 (1.10r) multi 1.40 1.40

Mariana, 300th Anniv. — A1861

2011, Apr. 8 ***Perf. 11½x12***
3165 A1861 1.10r multi 1.40 1.40

Military Academy of Agulhas Negras, 200th Anniv. A1862

2011, Apr. 15
3166 A1862 1.10r multi 1.40 1.40

Railway Stations A1863

Designs: No. 3167, Luz Station, Sao Paolo. No. 3168, Júlio Prestes Station, Sao Paolo. No. 3169, Central do Brasil Station, Rio de Janeiro, vert.

2011, Apr. 30 ***Perf. 11½x12***
3167 A1863 1.10r multi 1.40 1.40
3168 A1863 1.10r multi 1.40 1.40

Self-Adhesive

Die Cut Perf. 12

3169 A1863 1.10r multi 1.40 1.40

Itaipu Dam A1864

2011, May 6 ***Perf. 11½x12***
3170 A1864 1.10r multi 1.40 1.40

Paraguayan independence, bicent.

Miniature Sheet

Marine Life — A1865

No. 3171: a, Pelagia sp., Phyllorhiza punctata. b, Sepioteuthis sepioidea. c, Octopus insularis. d, Oreaster reticulatus.

2011, June 5
3171 A1865 2.70r Sheet of 4, #a-d 13.50 13.50

PhilaNippon 2011 Intl. Philatelic Exhibition, Yokohama, Japan.

Intl. Elder Abuse Awareness Day — A1866

2011, June 15 ***Perf. 12x11½***
3172 A1866 1.10r multi 1.40 1.40

Assembly of God Churches in Brazil, Cent. — A1867

2011, June 18 ***Perf. 11½x12***
3173 A1867 (1.10r) multi + label *3.25 3.25*

No. 3173 was printed in sheets of 12 stamps + 12 labels that sold for 30r. Labels could be personalized.

Souvenir Sheet

Flora and Fauna of Tijuca National Park — A1868

No. 3174: a, Tangara seledon, Hadrolaelia lobata. b, Thalurania glaucopis, Coendou insidiosus.

2011, July 6 **Litho.**
3174 A1868 5r Sheet of 2, #a-b 13.00 13.00

Intl. Year of Forests, Brasiliana 2013 Intl. Philatelic Exhibition, Rio de Janeiro.

Ouro Preto, 300th Anniv. — A1869

2011, July 8
3175 A1869 1.10r multi 1.40 1.40

Regional Labor Court, Fortaleza — A1870

2011, July 11 ***Perf. 11½x12***
3176 A1870 (1.10r) multi + label *3.25 3.25*

No. 3176 was printed in sheets of 12 stamps + 12 labels that sold for 30r. Labels could be personalized.

Bahia Commercial Association, 200th Anniv. — A1871

2011, July 15 ***Perf. 12x11½***
3177 A1871 1.10r multi 1.40 1.40

Paulo Gracindo (1911-95), Actor — A1872

2011, July 16 ***Perf. 11½x12***
3178 A1872 1.85r multi 2.40 2.40

Sabará, 300th Anniv. — A1873

2011, July 17
3179 A1873 1.10r multi 1.40 1.40

Brazilian Folklore — A1874

Nos. 3180 and 3181: a, Curupira on boar, logger with chainsaw. b, Mother-of-gold (mae-do-ouro), gold panner. c, Dolphin (boto), pregnant woman. d. Headless mule (mula-sem-cabeça), church.

2011, July 23 ***Perf. 11½***
3180 A1874 (1.10r) Block of 4, #a-d 5.50 5.50

Souvenir Sheet

3181 A1874 1.10r Sheet of 4, #a-d 5.50 5.50

Nos. 3180a-3180d are each inscribed "1 Porte Carta Nao Comercial." Brapex 2011, Recife (No. 3181).

Carta Social — A1875

Die Cut Perf. 12¼x12 Syncopated

2011, Aug. 5 **Self-Adhesive**
3182 A1875 (1c) dk grnsh gray & org brn .25 .25

No. 3182 was for use by impoverished people in the Bolsa Família program on a maximum of five hand-addressed domestic letters weighing no more than 10 grams. Stamps were applied to letters by postal clerks upon verification of the sender's involvement in the program and were not intended for direct sale to customers. The stamp was valid until Sept. 30, 2011.

Diplomatic Relations Between Brazil and Ukraine — A1876

2011, Aug. 24 ***Perf. 11x11½***
3183 A1876 2.55r multi 3.00 3.00

Mogi das Cruzes, 400th Anniv. — A1877

2011, Sept. 1 ***Perf. 11½x12***
3184 A1877 1.10r multi 1.25 1.25

Delivery of Registered Letter — A1878

Die Cut Perf. 12 Syncopated

2011, Sept. 2 Self-Adhesive

3185 A1878 (2.80r) multi 3.25 3.25

Sao Paolo Municipal Theater, Cent. — A1879

2011, Sept. 12 ***Perf. 11½x12***

3186 A1879 2r multi 2.40 2.40

Miniature Sheet

Piauí Tourist Attractions — A1880

No. 3187: a, Parnaíba River Delta. b, Rock arch, Serra da Capivara National Park, Sao Raimundo Nonato. c, Metálica Bridge, Teresina. d, Our Lady of Victory Church, Oeiras. e, Carved wooden statues, Teresina. f, Ferry approaching dock, Parnaiba. g, Master Isidoro França Bridge, Teresina. h, Opal jewelry, Pedro II. i, Rio Poty Canyon, Buriti dos Montes. j, Sete Cidades National Park, Piracuruca. k, Barra Grande Beach, Cajueiro da Praia. l, Monument to the Battle of Jenipapo, Campos Maior.

2011, Sept. 12

3187 A1880 Sheet of 12 + 12 labels 45.00 45.00

a.-l. (1.10r) Any single + label *3.00 3.00*

No. 3187 sold for 30r. Labels could be personalized.

Coelho Rodrigues Court House, Teresina — A1881

2011, Oct. 1 ***Perf. 11½x12***

3188 A1881 (1.10r) multi + label *7.25 7.25*

No. 3188 was printed in sheets of 12 stamps + 12 labels that sold for 30r. Labels could be personalized.

Trees of Brazil — A1882

Nos. 3189 and 3190: a, Tree with small branches and few leaves, text above tree starting with "As árvores nascem." b, Larger tree, text above tree starting with "copas abertas." c, Larger tree, text above tree starting with "devolvendo." d, No text above large tree.

2011, Oct. 3 ***Perf. 11½***

Stamps With White Frames

3189 A1882 (1.10r) Block of 4, #a-d 5.00 5.00

Miniature Sheet

Stamps Without White Frames

3190 A1882 2.70r Sheet of 4, #a-d, + 5 labels 12.50 12.50

On No. 3190, a square of cedar wood is affixed to the back of the central label. The four numbered corner labels illustrate how the stamps can be folded to show the square of cedar wood through the die cut openings replacing the tree trunks that were made in Nos. 3190a-3190c. Two of the corner labels depict stamps from No. 3190, but these labels are not valid for postage.

Mail Recipient Signing for Registered Letter — A1883

Die Cut Perf. 12 Syncopated

2011, Oct. 7 Self-Adhesive

3191 A1883 (5.60r) multi 6.50 6.50

America Issue — A1884

No. 3192: a, Imperial era mailbox. b, Republic era mailbox. c, Department of Mail and Telegraphs (DCT) mailbox. d, Mailbox in current use.

Litho. & Engr., Litho. & Embossed (#3192d)

2011, Oct. 9 ***Perf. 11½***

3192 A1884 2r Block of 4, #a-d 9.25 9.25

Diplomatic Relations Between Brazil and Italy — A1885

2011, Oct. 12 Litho. ***Perf. 12x11½***

3193 A1885 2.10r multi 2.40 2.40

A1886

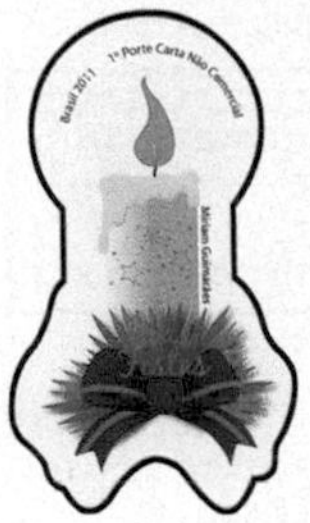

A1887

Christmas A1888

No. 3194: a, Open Bible. b, Closed Bible.

No. 3196 — Ornament color: a, Dark red. b, Purple. c, Green. d, Yellow. e, Blue. f, Red violet.

2011, Oct. 21 ***Perf. 11½***

3194 A1886 2.70r Souvenir sheet of 2, #a-b 6.25 6.25

Self-Adhesive

Die Cut

3195 A1887 (75c) multi .85 .85

3196 Block of 6 7.50

a.-f. A1888 (1.10r) Any single 1.25 1.25

People and Postal Direct Marketing Emblem A1889

Die Cut Perf. 12 Syncopated

2011, Oct. 24 Self-Adhesive

3197 A1889 2r multi 2.25 2.25

Writers — A1890

No. 3198: a, Ivo Andric (1892-1975), Yugoslavian writer, and Nobel medal. b, Rachel de Queiroz (1910-2003), Brazilian writer.

2011, Oct. 26 ***Perf. 11½x12***

3198 A1890 2.55r Horiz. pair, #a-b 6.00 6.00

See Serbia Nos. 570-571.

Diplomatic Relations Between Belgium and Brazil — A1891

Designs: Nos, 3199, 3201a, 2.55r, Flag bearer and master of ceremonies at Carnaval. Nos. 3200, 3201b, 2.55r, Acarajé de Lansan, No Ilê Oxumarê, painting by Carybé.

2011, Oct. 29 ***Perf. 11x11½***

Stamps With White Frames

3199-3200 A1891 Set of 2 5.75 5.75

Souvenir Sheet

Stamps With Gray Frames

3201 A1891 2.55r Sheet of 2, #a-b 5.75 5.75

Brazilian Philatelic Society, Cent. — A1893

Litho. & Engr.

2011, Nov. 18 ***Perf. 12x11½***

3202 A1893 2.55r copper & black 3.00 3.00

No. 3202 was printed in sheets of 28 stamps + 2 labels.

Dawn in Parana Area, Cyanocorax Caeruleus — A1894

Tree and Cyanocorax Caeruleus — A1895

2011, Nov. 25 Litho. ***Perf. 11½x12***

3203 A1894 (1.10r) multi + label *3.25 3.25*

Perf. 12x11½

3204 A1895 (1.10r) multi + label *3.25 3.25*

Nos. 3203-3204 each were printed in sheets of 12 stamps + 12 labels that sold for 30r. Labels could be personalized.

Mário Lago (1911-2002), Actor — A1896

Litho. & Engr.

2011, Nov. 26 ***Perf. 11½x12***

3205 A1896 1.85r black & bronze 2.10 2.10

Campaign for Prevention of AIDS — A1897

No. 3206: a, Heart, condom, man and woman. b, Condom. c, Hypodermic needle. d, Man and woman looking up. e, Condom, man and woman embracing. f, Heart in hourglass frame. g, AIDS ribbons. h, Condoms and hearts.

2011, Dec. 1 Litho. *Perf. 11½*

3206 A1897 (1.10r) Block of 8, #a-h 10.00 10.00

Diplomatic Relations Between Brazil and Qatar — A1898

Litho. & Embossed

2011, Dec. 19 *Perf. 12x11½*

3207 A1898 2.70r multi 3.00 3.00

Rio de Janeiro Presbyterian Church, 150th Anniv. — A1899

2012, Jan. 12

3208 A1899 1.60r multi 1.90 1.90

Lula Oil Field — A1900

2012, Jan. 17 Litho.

3209 A1900 (1.10r) multi 1.25 1.25

Bahia Medical Faculty, 200th Anniv. — A1901

2012, Jan. 19 *Perf. 11½x12*

3210 A1901 (1.10r) multi + label *4.00 4.00*

No. 3210 was printed in sheets of 12 stamps + 12 labels that sold for 30r. Labels could be personalized.

Minas Gerais Flag — A1902

Minas Gerais Flag — A1903

2012, Jan. 19 *Perf. 12x11½*

3211 A1902 (1.10r) multi + label *4.00 4.00*

Perf. 11½x12

3212 A1903 (1.10r) multi + label *4.00 4.00*

Nos. 3211-3212 each were printed in sheets of 12 stamps + 12 labels that sold for 30r. Labels could be personalized.

Miniature Sheet

Santa Catarina Tourist Attractions — A1904

No. 3213: a, Hercílio Luz Bridge, Florianópolis. b, Rock arch, Pedra Furada, Urubici. c, Rua des Palmeiras, Joinville. d, Morro dos Conventos, Araranguá. e, Sao Francisco do Sul. f, Monument to Explorers, Chapecó. g, Whale near Siriú Beach, Garopaba. h, Santa Paulina Sanctuary, Nova Trento. i, Balneário Camboriú. j, German Village, Blumenau. k, Port of Itajaí. l, Railroad Museum, Tubarao.

2012, Jan. 19 *Perf. 11½x12*

3213 A1904 Sheet of 12 + 12 labels *45.00 45.00*

a.-l. (1.10r) Any single + label *3.00 3.00*

No. 3213 sold for 30r. Labels could be personalized.

Souvenir Sheet

Dorina Nowill Foundation for the Blind — A1905

No. 3214: a, Blind boy. b, Nowill (1919-2010), philantropist.

Litho., Litho. & Embossed (#3214b)

2012, Mar. 11 *Perf. 12x11½*

Without Gum

3214 A1905 2.80r Sheet of 2, #a-b 6.25 6.25

Santos Soccer Team, Cent. — A1906

2012, Apr. 14 Litho. *Perf. 12x11½*

3215 A1906 (1.10r) black & gold 1.25 1.25

América Soccer Team, Cent. — A1907

2012, Apr. 30

3216 A1907 (1.10r) multi 1.25 1.25

Traditional Foods of Brazil and Mexico — A1908

No. 3217: a, Milho e mandioca. b, Pozole.

2012, June 1 *Perf. 11½*

3217 A1908 2.30r Horiz. pair, #a-b 4.75 4.75

See Mexico Nos. 2784-2785.

A1909

Rio + 20 United Nations Conference on Sustainable Development, Rio de Janeiro — A1910

No. 3218: a, Monkey, crocodile, birds, butterflies and armadillo in forest. b, Irrigation of fields near house and water tanks. c, People and dog approaching school building. d, Rio + 20 conference emblem. e, Bird, ecotourists, guide, kayaker. f, Farmers harvesting crops from irrigated field, house, water tank, truck. g, Truck at produce market. h, Garbage truck near apartment buildings and park. i, Bulldozer, logs, man planting saplings. j, Dam, dyanmo, electric power lines and towers. k, Cars at gas station and electric recharging station. l, Train, cable cars, bicycles. m, Green factory, electric train, forklift and crates. n, Swimmer in river, scientists testing water. o, Bus on road, electric train on bridge. p, Handicapped people at telephone, bus stop and crosswalk. q, Indigenous people, boar, fish. r, Garbage trucks at recycling center. s, Birds and crabs in mangrove swamp. t, People on beach, solar panels. u, Wind generators. v, Electric train, ship and shipping containers at port. w, Wildlife warden and fishermen in boats. x, Scuba diver, whale, turtle, jellyfish and marine life.

No. 3219: a, City in droplet, sun, birds, tree, ship, whale, shark and dolphins. b, Bird, fish, bicycle, windmill and hand. c, Earth and city in flower.

2012, June 1 *Perf. 11½x12*

3218 Sheet of 24 26.50 26.50

a.-x. A1909 (1.10r) Any single 1.10 1.10

Souvenir Sheet

Self-Adhesive

Die Cut Perf. 12

3219 A1910 2r Sheet of 3, #a-c 6.00 6.00

Wild Cats A1911

No. 3220: a, Puma yagouaroundi. b, Leopardus pardalis.

2012, June 5 *Perf. 11½*

3220 A1911 (1.10r) Pair, #a-b 2.25 2.25

Wind Turbines A1912

2012, June 15 ***Perf. 11x11½***
3221 A1912 1.85r multi 1.90 1.90

21st LUBRAPEX Philatelic Exhibition, Sao Paolo — A1913

Litho. & Engr.
2012, Aug. 1 ***Perf. 12x11½***
3222 A1913 2.75r silver & blk 2.75 2.75

Medicinal Plants — A1914

No. 3223: a, Carapa guianensis. b, Copaifera martii. c, Ptychopetalum olacoides. d, Uncaria guianensis.

2012, Aug. 5 **Litho.** ***Perf. 11½***
3223 A1914 (1.20r) Block of 4, #a-d 4.75 4.75

America Issue A1915

No. 3224 — Legend of origin of: a, Guaraná. b, Cassava.

2012, Aug. 22
3224 A1915 1.85r Vert. pair, #a-b 3.75 3.75

A1916

Poets — A1917

No. 3225: a, Fernando Pessoa (1888-1935). b, Poetry by Pessoa, ship.
No. 3226: a, Joao da Cruz e Sousa (1861-98). b, Poetry by Cruz e Sousa, bird in flight.

2012, Sept. 7 ***Perf. 12x11½***
3225 A1916 2r Horiz. pair, #a-b 4.00 4.00
3226 A1917 2r Horiz. pair, #a-b 4.00 4.00

LUBRAPEX 2012, Sao Paolo. See Portugal Nos. 3437-3438.

Sao Luís Cathedral, Palace of the Lions, Sao Luís — A1918

2012, Sept. 8 ***Perf. 11½x12***
3227 A1918 1.20r multi 1.25 1.25

Sao Luís, 400th anniv.

Holy Family — A1919

Choir — A1920

Gifts in Post Office Box — A1921

No. 3228: a, Jesus and Virgin Mary. b, St. Joseph.

Litho. With Foil Application
2012, Oct. 17 ***Perf. 12x11½***
Souvenir Sheet
3228 A1919 3.85r Sheet of 2, #a-b 7.75 7.75

Litho.
Die Cut
Self-Adhesive
3229 A1920 (80c) multi .80 .80
3230 A1921 (1.20r) multi 1.25 1.25

Christmas.

Emblems of Postal Bank, Bank of Brazil and Brazilian Postal Service — A1922

Die Cut Perf. 12 Syncopated
2012, Oct. 22 **Litho.**
Self-Adhesive
3231 A1922 (1.20r) multi 1.25 1.25

Souvenir Sheet

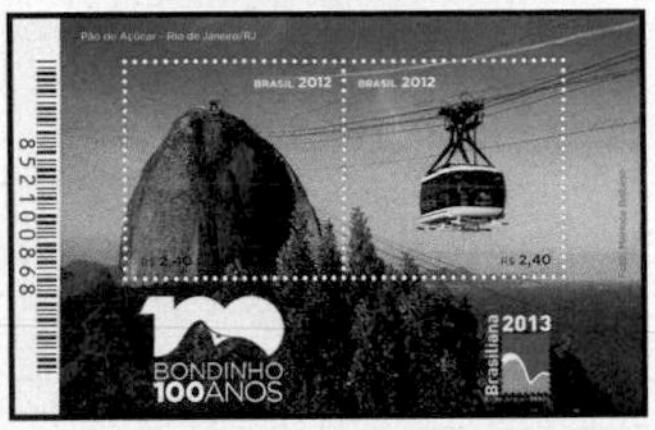

Sugarloaf Mountain Aerial Cable Car, Cent. — A1923

No. 3232: a, Sugarloaf Mountain. b, Cable car.

2012, Oct. 27 ***Perf. 11½***
3232 A1923 2.40r Sheet of 2, #a-b 4.75 4.75

Brasiliana 2013 Intl. Philatelic Exhibition, Rio de Janeiro.

Jorge Amado (1912-2001), Writer A1924

2012, Nov. 10
3233 A1924 1.20r multi 1.25 1.25

LUBRAPEX 2012, Sao Paolo.

Quilombo dos Palmares Memorial Park, Uniao dos Palmares — A1925

2012, Nov. 19 ***Perf. 11x11½***
3234 A1925 (1.20r) multi 1.25 1.25

Chinese Immigration to Brazil, 200th Anniv. — A1926

No. 3235: a, Dragon and ship. b, Dragon dancers.

2012, Dec. 10 ***Perf. 11½x12***
3235 A1926 2.90r Horiz. pair, #a-b 5.75 5.75

Luiz Gonzaga (1912-89), Musician A1927

Litho. & Embossed
2012, Dec. 13 ***Perf. 11½***
3236 A1927 (1.20r) multi 1.25 1.25

Sports and Their Venues A1928

No. 3237: a, Horse racing, Gávea Horse Racing Track, Rio de Janeiro. b, Go-karting, Ayrton Senna Kart Track, Interlagos. c, Volleyball, Journalist Felipe Drummond Stadium, Belo Horizonte. d, Auto racing, Nelson Piquet International Racetrack, Brasilia. e, Cycling, Velodrome, Maringá.

2012, Dec. 14 **Litho. & Engr.**
3237 Horiz. strip of 5 10.00 10.00
a.-e. A1928 2r Any single 2.00 2.00

Federal University of Paraná, Cent. — A1929

2012, Dec. 19 **Litho.** ***Perf. 11x11½***
3238 A1929 1.20r multi 1.25 1.25

Miniature Sheet

Brazilian Postal Services, 350th Anniv. — A1930

No. 3239: a, Ship (first postal activities in Brazil, 1663). b, Mail delivery by horseback. c, Building (first postal administration in Brazil, 1798). d, Court postman making delivery, 1835. e, Issuance of Brazil #1, 2 and 3, 1843. f, Issuance of Brazil #7, 8, 9, 10 and 13, 1844. g, Mail collection box, 1845, Brazil #3192a and 3192b. h, Baron Capanema (1824-1908), installer of first electric telegraph system in Brazil, 1852. i, Dial of Bréguet telegraph. j, Workers constructing telegraph line. k, Equipment in telegraph office. l, Issuance of Brazil #59, 1866. m, Construction of first post office in Rio de Janeiro, 1878. n, Pneumatic post mail, 1910. o, Sao Paolo Post Office, 1922. p, Badges (creation of Department of Posts and Telegraphs,1931). q, Mechanical sorting of mail, 1940. r, Postman with bicycle, emblem of Brazil Posts and Telegraphs Company (creation of Brazilian Posts and Telegraphs Company, 1969). s, Postal workers at electronic sorting equipment, 1972. t, Brazil Postal Headquarters, 1978. u, Participation of postal workers in social and environmental projects. v, Mail sorters, postmen, motorcycle, ship. w, Mail deliverers, postal truck (presence of postal service in all towns, 2001). x, 350th anniv. emblem, Brazil Post emblem (2013).

2013, Jan. 25 **Litho.** ***Perf. 11½x12***
3239 A1930 Sheet of 24 30.00 30.00
a.-x. (1.20r) Any single 1.25 1.25

Campaign Against Racial Discrimination — A1931

2013, Mar. 21 **Litho.** ***Perf. 11½x12***
3240 A1931 2r multi 2.00 2.00

America issue.

Souvenir Sheet

Intl. Year of Water Cooperation — A1932

No. 3241 — Half of stylized globe, water stream and: a, Hand. b, Open mouth.

Litho. & Embossed

2013, Mar. 22 *Perf. 12x11½*

3241 A1932 2.75r Sheet of 2, #a-b 5.50 5.50

World Youth Day, Rio de Janeiro — A1933

2013, Mar. 23 Litho. *Perf. 12x11½*

3242 A1933 1.20r multi 1.25 1.25

Telegraph Key, Smartphone and Map of South America — A1934

2013, May 17 Litho. *Perf. 11x11½*

3243 A1934 2r multi 1.90 1.90

Diplomatic Relations Between Brazil and Georgia — A1935

No. 3244: a, Woodcutter, by Antonio Rafael Pinto Bandeira, Brazilian flag. b, Fisherman in a Red Shirt, by Pirosmani, Georgian flag.

2013, May 26 Litho. *Perf. 11½*

3244 A1935 2.90r Horiz. pair, #a-b 5.50 5.50

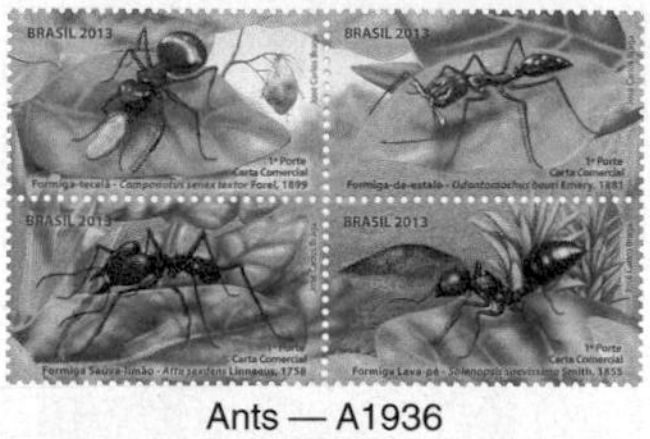

Ants — A1936

No. 3245: a, Camponotus senex textor. b, Odontomachus bauri. c, Atta sexdens. d, Solenopsis saevissima.

2013, June 5 Litho. *Perf. 11x11½*

3245 A1936 (1.20r) Block of 4, #a-d 4.50 4.50

Souvenir Sheet

2013 FIFA Confederations Cup Soccer Tournament, Brazil — A1937

No. 3246: a, 2013 Confederations Cup Tournament emblem. b, Confederations Cup trophy.

2013, June 6 Litho. *Perf. 11½*

3246 A1937 2.75r Sheet of 2, #a-b 5.25 5.25

Diplomatic Relations Between Brazil and Czech Republic — A1938

No. 3247 — Scene from final match of 1962 World Cup soccer tournament: a, Players. b, Players, Brazilian and Czech flags.

2013, June 13 Litho. *Perf. 11½*

3247 A1938 2.75r Horiz. pair, #a-b 5.25 5.25

The Flotilla Commanded by Jerônimo de Albuquerque, by Carlos Kirovsky — A1939

2013, June 26 Litho. *Perf. 11½x12*

3248 A1939 (1.20r) multi 1.10 1.10

Albuquerque's command of flotilla, 400th anniv,

Ilê Axé Opô Afonjá, Brazilian-African Religious Cult — A1940

2013, July 13 Litho. *Perf. 11½x12*

3249 A1940 (1.20r) multi 1.10 1.10

Pope Francis A1941

2013, July 23 Litho. *Perf. 11½x12*

3250 A1941 1.80r multi 1.60 1.60

2013 World Youth Day, Rio de Janeiro.

Brasiliana 2013 Intl. Philatelic Exhibition, Rio de Janeiro — A1942

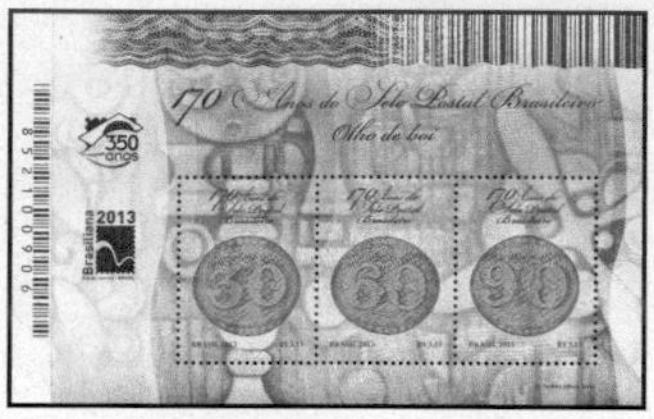

Brazilian Postage Stamps, 170th Anniv. — A1943

No. 3252: a, Brazil #1. b, Brazil #2. c, Brazil #3.

Litho. & Engr.

2013, Aug. 1 *Perf. 12x11½*

3251 A1942 2.90r gold & blk 2.50 2.50

Souvenir Sheet

3252 A1943 3.15r Sheet of 3, #a-c 8.25 8.25

No. 3251 was printed in sheets of 28 + 2 labels. Under magnification, "170" can be seen in the stamp engravings of Brazil #1-3 on Nos. 3252a-3252c.

Serra da Lua Rock Art A1944

2013, Aug. 12 Litho. *Perf. 11½x12*

3253 A1944 (1.20r) multi 1.10 1.10

Cemeteries — A1945

No. 3254: a, Gateway to Arez Cemetery. b, Santa Isabel Cemetery, Mucugê. c, Batalho Cemetery, Campo Maior. d, Head of statue, Soledade Cemetery, Belém.

2013, Aug. 17 Litho. *Perf. 11½*

3254 A1945 2r Block of 4, #a-d 7.00 7.00

Equatorial Monument, Macapá — A1946

2013, Sept. 22 Litho. *Perf. 12x11½*

3255 A1946 (1.20r) multi 1.10 1.10

Miniature Sheet

Diplomatic Relations Between Brazil and Germany — A1947

No. 3256: a, German architecture in Bosque do Alemao Park, Curitiba, Our Lady of Lourdes Cathedral, Canela. b, Wind generators, solar panels, computer, woman reading book. c, Ship, gears, Volkswagen Beetle. d, Hermann Blumenau (1819-99), founder of city of Blumenau, bridge and building in Blumenau. e, Performer on stage, Bertolt Brecht (1898-1956), playwright.

2013, Oct. 3 Litho. *Perf. 11½x12*

3256 A1947 2.75r Sheet of 5, #a-e 13.00 13.00

Souvenir Sheet

Brazilian Postal Services, 350th Anniv. — A1948

No. 3257: a, Caravel, map of coast of Brazil, 1663. b, Telegraph office, 1852. c, Child in doorway, postal sorting machinery, 2013.

2013, Nov. 19 Litho. *Perf. 12x11½*

3257 A1948 3r Sheet of 3, #a-c 7.75 7.75

Personalized Stamp A1949

2013, Nov. 20 Litho. *Perf. 11½*

3258 A1949 (1.20r) multi *2.75 2.75*

No. 3258 was printed in sheets of 12 that sold for 38r. The image portion of the stamp could be personalized, as shown in the illustration. Numerous stamps with generic images were also printed and sold by Brazil Post.

Vinicius de Moraes (1913-80), Composer A1950

2013, Nov. 20 Litho. *Perf. 11½*

3259 A1950 2.75r blk & gold 2.40 2.40

a. Tete-beche pair 4.80 4.80

A1951

A1952

Christmas — A1953

No. 3260: a, Woman with white blouse and red skirt in center of front row of people. b, Man with light green shirt in center of front row of people.

Litho., Sheet Margin Litho. With Foil Application

2013, Dec. 2 ***Perf.***

Souvenir Sheet

3260 A1951 4.15r Sheet of 2, #a-b 7.25 7.25

Litho.

Self-Adhesive

Die Cut

3261 A1952 (80c) multi .70 .70
3262 A1953 (1.20r) multi 1.10 1.10

Diplomatic Relations Between Brazil and Kenya — A1954

No. 3263: a, Ipu Falls, Brazil. b, Grevy's zebras, Kenya.

2013, Dec. 12 Litho. ***Perf. 11½***

3263 A1954 2.90r Horiz. pair, #a-b 5.00 5.00

Souvenir Sheet

Mauritia Flexuosa — A1955

No. 3264: a, Palm crown and fruit. b, Parrots and grove of trees.

2013, Dec. 19 Litho. ***Perf. 11½***

3264 A1955 2.45r Sheet of 2, #a-b 4.25 4.25

Official Posters for Host Cities of the 2014 World Cup Soccer Tournament A1956

No. 3265 — Poster for: a, Belo Horizonte. b, Brasília. c, Cuiabá. d, Curitiba. e, Fortaleza. f, Manaus. g, Natal. h, Porto Alegre. i, Recife. j, Rio de Janeiro. k, Salvador. l, Sao Paolo.

2014, Jan. 30 Litho. ***Perf. 11½***

3265 Block of 12 12.00 12.00
a.-l. A1956 1.20r Any single 1.00 1.00

Paysandú Sports Club, Cent. — A1957

2014, Feb. 2 Litho. ***Perf. 12x11½***

3266 A1957 (1.20r) multi 1.00 1.00

Autism Awareness — A1958

2014, Apr. 2 Litho. ***Perf. 12x11½***

3267 A1958 2r multi 1.75 1.75

Souvenir Sheet

2014 World Cup Soccer Tournament, Brazil — A1959

No. 3268: a, Mascot. b, World Cup trophy. c, Emblem.

2014, Apr. 21 Litho. ***Perf. 12x11½***

3268 A1959 2.75r Sheet of 3, #a-c 7.50 7.50

Miniature Sheet

Monica's Gang, Comic Strip by Mauricio de Sousa — A1960

No. 3269 — Various comic book covers depicting: a, Monica, turtle, man in car. b, Monica playing drum and elephant. c, Monica with rabbits in holsters. d, Monica and stars. e, Monica on ground, Jimmy standing above Her with fists clenched. f, Monica holding rabbit by ears. g, Monica, other characters, man with birthday cake. h, Monica on swing. i, Monica wearing dress inscribed "10 anos," holding rabbit by ears. j, Monica holding rabbit, elephant, stacks of comic books. k, Monica, other characters banner. l, 50th anniv. emblem ("5" with teeth, "0" as rabbit's head).

2014, Apr. 21 Litho. ***Perf. 12x11½***

3269 A1960 Sheet of 12 + 12 labels 30.00 30.00
a.-l. (1.20r) Any single + label 2.50 2.50

No. 3269 sold for 33r. Labels could be personalized.

Child With Soccer Ball A1961

No. 3270 — Various depictions of child and soccer ball with name of 2014 World Cup host city at bottom: a, Belo Horizonte. b, Fortaleza. c, Recife. d, Brasília. e, Manaus. f, Rio de Janeiro. g, Cuiabá. h, Natal. i, Salvador. j, Curitiba. k, Porto Alegre. l, Sao Paolo.

Die Cut Perf. 12 Syncopated

2014, Apr. 29 Litho.

Self-Adhesive

3270 Block of 12 13.50
a.-l. A1961 (1.20r) Any single 1.10 1.10

Dorival Caymmi (1914-2008), Singer — A1962

2014, Apr. 30 Litho. ***Perf. 12x11½***

3271 A1962 1.20r black 1.10 1.10

Portuguese Language, 800th Anniv. A1963

2014, May 5 Litho. ***Perf. 11½x12***

3272 A1963 3r multi 2.75 2.75

New Emblem of Brazilian Post A1964

2014, May 6 Litho. ***Perf. 11½x12***

3273 A1964 (1.20r) multi 1.10 1.10

Zélio Fernandino de Moraes (1891-1975), Founder of Umbanda Branca Religion — A1965

2014, May 13 Litho. ***Perf. 11½x12***

3274 A1965 (1.20r) multi 1.10 1.10

Ceará Sporting Club, Cent. A1966

2014, June 2 Litho. ***Perf. 11½x12***

3275 A1966 (1.20r) black 1.10 1.10

Intl. Year of Family Farming — A1967

No. 3276: a, Farmers with basket of harvested crops, farmer on tractor. b, House, farmers with livestock and wheelbarrow of harvested crops.

2014, June 3 Litho. ***Perf. 11½***

3276 A1967 1.50r Horiz. pair, #a-b 2.75 2.75

Brazilian Olympic Committee, Cent. — A1968

2014, June 8 Litho. ***Perf. 12x11½***

3277 A1968 2.30r multi 2.10 2.10

Diplomatic Relations Between Brazil and the Philippines — A1969

No. 3278: a, Urubitinga coronata, part of Brazilian flag. b, Pithecophaga jeffreyi, part of Philippines flag.

2014, June 10 Litho. ***Perf. 11½x11***

3278 A1969 2.90r Horiz. pair, #a-b 5.25 5.25

Brazilian National Soccer Team, Cent. — A1970

No. 3279: a, 1914 team, emblem inscribed "FBS." b, Brazilian flag, player, goalie making save, emblem inscribed "CBD." c, Brazilian flag, player dribbling ball, emblem inscribed "CBF."

2014, July 21 Litho. ***Perf. 12x11½***

3279 A1970 2r Horiz. strip of 3, #a-c 5.50 5.50

Diplomatic Relations Between Brazil and Peru — A1971

No. 3280: a, Machu Picchu, Peru. b, Rio de Janeiro, Brazil.

2014, July 29 Litho. *Perf. 11½*
3280 A1971 2.20r Horiz. pair, #a-b 4.00 4.00

Sergio Vieira de Mello (1948-2003), United Nations Special Representative for Iraq — A1972

2014, Aug. 19 Litho. *Perf. 12x11½*
3281 A1972 2.45r multi 2.25 2.25

Sociedade Esportiva Palmeiras Soccer Team, Cent. A1973

2014, Aug. 26 Litho. *Perf. 11½*
3282 A1973 (1.30r) multi 1.25 1.25

Syngonanthus Nitens — A1974

No. 3283: a, Map of State of Tocantins, field of Syngonanthus nitens grass. b, Grass harvester. c, Hands making table mat from grass. d, Brazilian flag, hat, vase of Syngonanthus nitens.

Litho., Litho. & Embossed With Foil Application (#3283d)

2014, Sept. 12 *Perf. 12x11½*
3283 A1974 1.80r Block of 4, #a-d 6.00 6.00

People of Kalunga Community, Santa Barbara Waterfall — A1975

2014, Sept. 27 Litho. *Perf. 11½x12*
3284 A1975 1.30r multi 1.10 1.10

Prehistoric Animals — A1976

No. 3285: a, Prionosuchus plummeri, vert. b, Oxalaia quilomboensis, vert. c, Pycnonemosaurus nevesi. d, Eremotherium laurillardi.

2014, Oct. 12 Litho. *Perf. 11½x12*
3285 A1976 1.30r Block of 4, #a-d 4.25 4.25

The prehistoric animals were covered with a smooth varnish on Nos. 3285a and 3285d, and a rough varnish on Nos. 3285b and 3285c.

Diplomatic Relations Between Brazil and Croatia — A1977

No. 3286: a, Map of Brazil, Mario Schenberg (1914-90), physicist. b, Map of Croatia, Nikola Tesla (1856-1943), inventor.

2014, Oct. 28 Litho. *Perf. 11½*
3286 A1977 2.95r Horiz. pair, #a-b 4.75 4.75

Kusiwa Wajapi Indigenous Art — A1978

2014, Nov. 3 Litho. *Perf. 11½*
3287 A1978 (1.30r) multi 1.00 1.00

A1979

A1980

Christmas A1981

No. 3288 — St. Nicholas and: a, Shoes filled with coins. b, People in tub.

2014 Litho. *Perf. 11½*
Souvenir Sheet
3288 A1979 3r Sheet of 2, #a-b 4.50 4.50

Self-Adhesive
Die Cut Perf. 12 Syncopated
3289 A1980 (90c) multi .70 .70
3290 A1981 (1.30r) multi 1.00 1.00

Issued: No. 3288, 12/5; Nos. 3289-3290, 11/7.

Souvenir Sheet

Saints Peter and Paul Archipelago — A1982

No. 3291: a, Belmonte Island Scientific Station (denomination at UR). b, Belmonte Island Lighthouse (denomination at LL).

2014, Dec. 12 Litho. *Perf. 11½x12*
3291 A1982 2.50r Sheet of 2, #a-b 3.75 3.75

Souvenir Sheet

Oscar Niemeyer (1907-2012), Architect — A1983

No. 3292: a, Niemeyer holding pen. b, Design for Palacio do Planalto.

2014, Dec. 12 Litho. *Perf. 11½x12*
3292 A1983 3.50r Sheet of 2, #a-b 5.25 5.25

Transition from 2012 Olympics to 2016 Olympics — A1984

Transition from 2012 Paralympics to 2016 Paralympics — A1985

No. 3293 — Olympic Rings and: a, London skyline, Tower Bridge, Union Jack. b, Tower Bridge, Sugarloaf Mountain and birds. c, Christ the Redeemer statue, Brazilian flag.

No. 3294 — Paralympics emblem and: a, London skyline, Tower Bridge, Union Jack. b, Tower Bridge, Sugarloaf Mountain and birds. c, Christ the Redeemer statue, Brazilian flag.

2015, Jan. 30 Litho. *Perf. 11½x12*
3293 Horiz. strip of 3 3.00 3.00
a.-c. A1984 (1.30r) Any single 1.00 1.00
3294 Horiz. strip of 3 3.00 3.00
a.-c. A1985 (1.30r) Any single 1.00 1.00

Though Nos. 3293-3294 are dated "2012" and first day covers bearing these stamps have July 27, 2012 cancels, the strips were not put on sale until Jan. 30, 2015.

Souvenir Sheets

Transition from 2012 Olympics to 2016 Olympics — A1985a

Transition from 2012 Paralympics to 2016 Paralympics — A1985b

No. 3294D — Olympic rings and: f, Big Ben, Tower Bridge, London. g, Sugarloaf Mountain and cable car, Rio de Janeiro.

No. 3294E — Paralympics emblem and: h, London Eye. i, Christ the Redeemer Statue, Rio de Janeiro.

2015, Feb. 2 Litho. *Perf. 11½*
3294D A1985a 2.60r Sheet of 2, #f-g 4.00 4.00
3294E A1985b 2.60r Sheet of 2, #h-i 4.00 4.00

Though Nos. 3294D-3294E are dated "2012" and first day covers bearing the stamps are dated Dec. 28, 2012, the stamps were not put on sale until Feb. 2, 2015.

2015 WorldSkills Professional Education Competition, Sao Paulo — A1986

2015, Feb. 3 Litho. *Perf. 11½x12*
3295 A1986 3.15r multi 2.10 2.10

Rio de Janeiro, 450th Anniv. — A1987

No. 3296 — Stylized head with: a, Musical symbols and hat. b, Streamers and dots. c, Green, blue and yellow hair. d, Hair of black curved lines.

2015, Mar. 1 Litho. *Perf. 11½*
3296 A1987 (1.30r) Block of 4, #a-d 3.50 3.50

World Summit on Disaster Risk Reduction, Sendai, Japan — A1988

No. 3297: a, Desertification, tornado, rain storms. b, Flood, forest fire, landslide.

2015, Mar. 14 Litho. *Perf. 11½*
3297 A1988 1.80r Horiz. pair, #a-b 2.40 2.40

Miniature Sheet

Sports of the 2016 Summer Olympics and Paralympics, Rio de Janeiro — A1989

No. 3298: a, Basketball (orange area at LL). b, Paralympic racing (orange areas at LL and UR). c, Basketball (light green area at LL). d, Paralympic racing (dark orange area at LL, light green area at UR). e, Rugby (green area at LL). f, Archery (dark orange area at LL, light green area at UR). g, Rugby (deep orange area at LL). h, Archery (light green areas at LL and UR). i, Weight lifting (dark blue area at LL). j, Cycling (deep orange across top). k, Weight lifting (light green area at LL). l, Cycling (light green area at UL). m, Rowing (dark blue in central area). n, Badminton (green and blue background colors). o, Rowing (light green area at UL). p, Badminton (orange in central area). q, Aquatic sports (dark blue in central area). r, Wrestling (blue area across bottom). s, Aquatic sports (light green behind symbol). t, Wrestling (light green area at LR).

2015, Mar. 24 Litho. *Perf. 11x11½*
3298 A1989 (1.30r) Sheet of 20, #a-t 17.00 17.00

World Games of Indigenous Peoples, Palmas — A1990

2015, Apr. 16 Litho. *Perf. 12x11½*
3299 A1990 (1.40r) multi .95 .95

Intl. Association of Portuguese-Speaking Countries, 25th Anniv. — A1991

2015, Apr. 27 Litho. *Perf. 12x11½*
3300 A1991 3.15r multi 2.10 2.10

See Angola No. , Cape Verde No. 1004, Guinea-Bissau No. , Macao No. 1440, Mozambique No. , Portugal Nos. 3694-3695, St. Thomas & Prince Islands No. 2954, and Timor No.

Sustainable Minimum Wages — A1992

2015, Apr. 30 Litho. *Perf. 11x11½*
3301 A1992 (1.40r) multi .95 .95

Marshal Cândido Mariano da Silva Rondon (1865-1958), First Director of Indian Protection Bureau — A1993

No. 3302 — Rondon and: a, Birthplace. b, Surveyor's transit, Praia Vermelha Military School. c, Margarida Telegraph Office. d, Boat and map. e, Indigenous people. f, Automobile used to inspect borders and military badge.

2015, May 5 Litho. *Perf. 11½x12*
3302 A1993 (1.40r) Block of 6, #a-f 5.50 5.50

International Telecommunication Union, 150th Anniv. — A1994

No. 3303 — Background color: a, Blue. b, Green. c, Orange brown. d, Red orange.

2015, May 17 Litho. *Perf. 11½x12*
3303 A1994 3.25r Block of 4, #a-d 8.25 8.25

Miniature Sheet

Bees — A1995

No. 3304: a, Paratrigona lineata. b, Plebeia flavocincta. c, Melipona rufiventris. d, Melipona subnitida. e, Melipona quinquefasciata. f, Nannotrigona testaceicornis.

2015, May 27 Litho. *Perf. 11½x12*
3304 A1995 2.50r Sheet of 6, #a-f 9.50 9.50

Diplomatic Relations Between Brazil and Azerbaijan — A1996

No. 3305: a, Três Poderes Square, Brasília, arms of Brazil. b, National Flag Square, Baku, arms of Azerbaijan.

2015, May 27 Litho. *Perf. 11½x12*
3305 A1996 3.45r Horiz. pair, #a-b 4.50 4.50

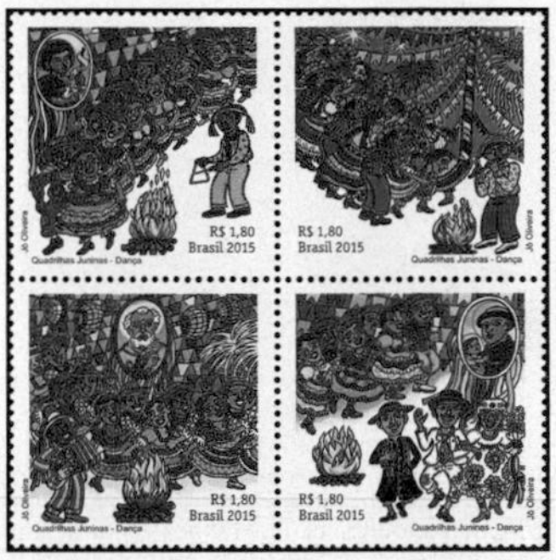

Quadrilha Dancers — A1997

No. 3306 — Dancers and fire with: a, Triangle player, inset of saint at UL. b, Flautist, decorated pole. c, Accordion player, inset of saint at top center. d, Inset of saint at UR.

2015, June 1 Litho. *Perf. 12¾*
3306 A1997 1.80r Block of 4, #a-d 4.75 4.75

Miniature Sheet

Sports of the 2016 Summer Olympics and Paralympics, Rio de Janeiro — A1998

No. 3307: a, Boxing (green area at LR). b, Paralympic judo (green area at LL). c, Boxing (blue area at LR). d, Paralympic judo (violet blue area at LL). e, Fencing (green area at UR). f, Soccer (green area at LL). g, Fencing (light blue area at UR). h, Soccer (light blue area at LL). i, Kayaking (violet blue stripe at LR corner). j, Golf (light blue area at UR). k, Kayaking (two violet blue arcs across stamp). l, Golf (green area at UR). m, Triathlon (green area at LR). n, Table tennis (green area at LL). o, Triathlon (bright purple and blue areas at LR). p, Table tennis (bright purple and violet blue areas at LL). q, Taekwondo (green area at LL). r, Handball (blue area at LL). s, Taekwondo (light blue area at LL). t, Handball (orange area at LL).

2015, June 8 Litho. *Perf. 11x11½*
3307 A1998 (1.40r) Sheet of 20, #a-t 18.00 18.00

Young Apprentice A1999

Campaign to Reduce Carbon Dioxide Emissions A2000

Die Cut Perf. 12 Syncopated
2015, June 10 Photo.
Self-Adhesive
3308 A1999 (95c) multi .60 .60
3309 A2000 (1.40r) multi .90 .90

Campaign Against Human Trafficking — A2001

2015, July 30 Litho. *Perf. 12x11½*
3310 A2001 3.25r blue 1.90 1.90

America Issue.

St. John Bosco (1815-88) — A2002

No. 3311 — Inscription at top: a, Presença Salesiana no Brasil. b, Santuário Dom Bosco Brasília. c, Cultura e Arte. d, Ressocializaçao. e, Amazônia. f, Sonho de Brasília.

2015, Aug. 16 Litho. *Perf. 11½x12*
3311 A2002 (95c) Block of 6, #a-f 3.25 3.25

A2003

Christmas A2004

No. 3312: a, Bird, woman, child, horse, blind man, guide dog and puppy. b, Family. c, People with gifts.

No. 3313, (95c), Elderly man and girl hugging. No. 3314 (1.40r), Woman and child with gift hugging.

2015, Oct. 1 Litho. *Perf. 11½x11*
Souvenir Sheet
3312 A2003 2.50r Sheet of 3, #a-c 4.00 4.00
Self-Adhesive
Die Cut Perf. 12 Syncopated
3313-3314 A2004 Set of 2 1.25 1.25

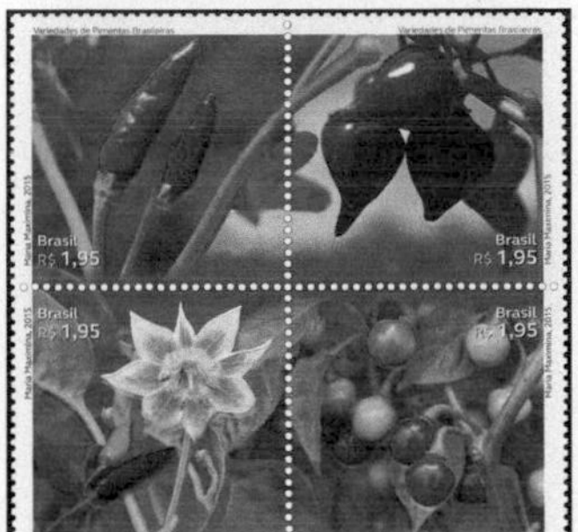

Pepper Varieties — A2005

No. 3315: a, Malagueta peppers (denomination at LL). b, Dedo-de-moça peppers (denomination at LR). c, Bode peppers and flower (denomination at UL). d, Biquinho peppers (denomination at UR).

Litho. & Embossed

2015, Oct. 16 ***Perf. 12¾***

3315 A2005 1.95r Block of 4, #a-d 4.00 4.00

Waters of Minas Gerais — A2006

No. 3316 — Views of: a, Baependi. b, Cambuquira. c, Campanha. d, Carmo de Minas. e, Caxambu. f, Conceiçao do Rio Verde. g, Lambari. h, Maria da Fé. i, Soledade de Minas. j, Três Coraçoes.

2015, Nov. 9 **Litho.** ***Perf. 11½x12***

3316 A2006 (1.40r) Block of 10, #a-j 7.25 7.25

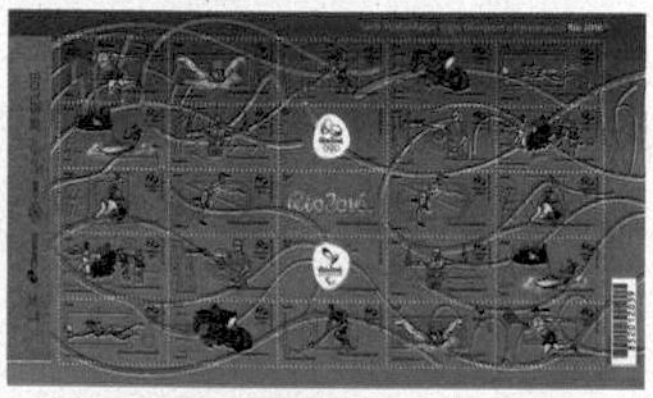

Sports and Emblems of the 2016 Summer Olympics and Paralympics — A2007

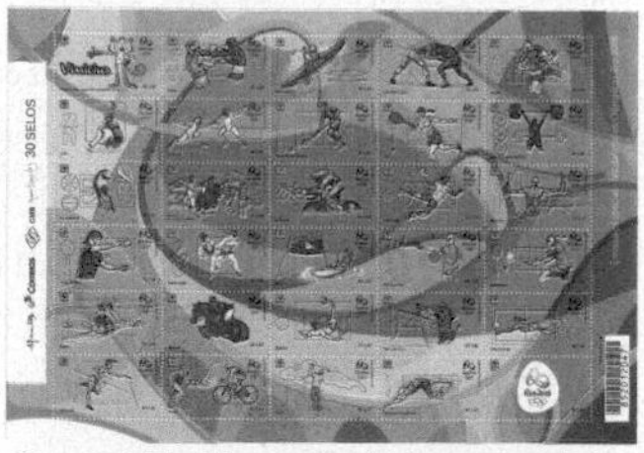

Sports, Emblems and Mascots of the 2016 Summer Olympics — A2008

Vinicius, Mascot of 2016 Summer Olympics — A2009

Tom, Mascot of 2016 Summer Paralympics — A2010

No. 3317: a, Women's tennis, dark blue background. b, Paralympic swimming, dark blue background. c, Field hockey, dark blue background. d, Equestrian, dark blue background. e, Women's beach volleyball, dark blue backgrouund. f, Sailing, dark blue background at top. g, Men's rings, dark blue background at top. h, Rio 2016 Summer Olympics emblem. i, Shooting, dark blue background at top. j, Modern pentathlon, blue background at top. k, Judo, curved bister lines at UL, UR and bottom. l, Women's high jump, one curved bister line. m, "Rio 2016." n, As "l," curved bister lines at top and lower corners. o, As "k," bifurcating bister lines connected in middle. p, As "j," green blue background at bottom. q, As "i," green blue background at bottom. r, Rio 2016 Summer Paralympics emblem. s, As "g," green blue background at bottom. t, As "f," green blue background at bottom. u, As "e," green blue background. v, As "d," green blue background. w, As "c," green blue background. x, As "b," green blue background. y, As "a," green blue background.

No. 3318 — Brazilian flag and: a, Mascot Vinicius. b, Boxing. c, Kayaking. d, Wrestling. e, Rugby. f, Judo. g, Fencing. h, Field hockey. i, Women's tennis. j, Weight lifting. k, Basketball. l, Modern pentathlon. m, Cycling. n, Handball. o, Men's rings. p, Table tennis. q, Taekwondo. r, Sailing. s, Shooting. t, Badminton. u, Rowng. v, Equestrian. w, Soccer. x, Archery. y, Women's beach volleyball. z, Women's high jump. aa, Triathlon. ab, Golf. ac, Aquatic sports. ad, Rio 2016 Summer Olympics emblem.

No. 3319 — Vinicius with: a, Arm extended to left. b, Arm raised.

No. 3320 — Tom: a, Holding tambourine. b, Dancing.

2015 **Litho.** ***Perf. 11x11½***

3317 A2007 (1.40r) Sheet of 25, #a-y 17.50 17.50

3318 A2008 1.40r Sheet of 30, #a-ad 21.00 21.00

Souvenir Sheets

Litho. & Embossed

Perf. 11½

3319 A2009 3.25r Sheet of 2, #a-b 3.25 3.25

3320 A2010 3.25r Sheet of 2, #a-b 3.25 3.25

Issued: Nos. 3317, 3319, 3320, 12/12; No. 3318, 12/15.

Sculptures Depicting Eve — A2011

No. 3321 — Sculpture by: a, Victor Brecheret, Brazil. b, Gheorghe Leonida, Romania.

2015, Dec. 21 **Litho.** ***Perf. 11½***

3321 A2011 3.25r Horiz. pair, #a-b 3.25 3.25

See Romania Nos. 5743-5744.

Miniature Sheet

Belém, 400th Anniv. — A2012

No. 3322: a, 400th anniv. emblem. b, Theatro da Paz. c, Círio de Nazaré. d, Ver o Peso. e, Açai berries. f, Forte do Castelo. g, Costumed Carimbó dancers. h, Estaçao das Docas.

2016, Jan. 12 **Litho.** ***Perf. 11½x12***

3322 A2012 (1.50r) Sheet of 8, #a-h 6.00 6.00

Poets — A2013

No. 3323: a, Rubén Darío (1867-1916), Nicaraguan poet. b, Manoel de Barros (1916-2014), Brazilian poet.

2016, Feb. 25 **Litho.** ***Perf. 11½***

3323 A2013 2.95r Horiz. pair, #a-b 3.00 3.00

French Artistic Mission in Brazil, 200th Anniv. — A2014

No. 3324: a, Joachim Lebreton (1760-1819), leader of mission. b, Auguste-Henri-Victor Grandjean de Montigny (1776-1850), architect. c, Nicholas Antoine Taunay (1755-1830), landscape painter. d, Jean-Baptiste Debret (1768-1848), painter.

2016, Mar. 26 **Litho.** ***Perf. 11x11½***

3324 A2014 3.55r Block of 4, #a-d 8.00 8.00

Souvenir Sheet

Lubrapex Philatelic Exhibitions, 50th Anniv. — A2015

No. 3325: a, Feathered headdress. b, Heart-shaped pendant.

2016, Apr. 26 **Litho.** ***Perf. 11½x12***

3325 A2015 3.55r Sheet of 2, #a-b 4.25 4.25

See Portugal Nos. 3783-3785.

Brazilian Sciences Academy, Cent. — A2016

2016, May 3 **Litho.** ***Perf. 11½x12***

3326 A2016 (1.50r) multi .85 .85

Consumption of Water and Electricity — A2017

Consumption of: No. 3327, 2.10r, Electricity. No. 3328, 2.10r, Water.

Die Cut Perf. 12 Syncopated

2016, June 15 **Litho.**

Self-Adhesive

3327-3328 A2017 Set of 2 2.60 2.60

Horses — A2018

No. 3329, 3.55r: a, Mangalarga Marchador horse, Brazil. b, Lipicanec horse, Slovenia.

2016, June 21 **Litho.** ***Perf. 12x11½***

3329 A2018 Vert. pair, #a-b 4.50 4.50

Souvenir Sheet

2013 World Championship Trophy of Brazilian Women's Handball Team — A2019

Litho. & Embossed

2016, June 26 ***Perf. 11x11½***

3330 A2019 4.25r multi 2.75 2.75

Miniature Sheet

Olympic Sports and Values — A2020

No. 3331 — Winning art in stamp design contest by: a, Alicia Teberga. b, André Paiva. c, Anne Beth. d, Athos Spilborghs. e, Danielle Martins. f, Fernando Degrossi. g, Gabriel Trindade. h, Girlan Quidute. i, Hegildo Alencar. j, Hemilly Pereira. k, Ivan Mola (torch bearer). l, Mola (wheelchair athlete). m, Larissa Mazza. n, Mateus Kuwer. o, Samara Brum. p, Valéria Boelter.

Die Cut Syncopated

2016, June 27 **Litho.**

Self-Adhesive

3331 A2020 Sheet of 16 15.50

a.-p. (1.50r) Any single .95 .95

Serro do Mar Paranaense Railway — A2021

No. 3332: a, Train on Carvalho Viaduct. b, Train approaching Sao Joao Viaduct. c, Train in Marumbi State Park. d, Train on bridge in Serra do Mar Mountains.

2016, July 26 Litho. *Perf. 11½x11¾*

3332 A2021 (1.70r) Block of 4, #a-d 4.25 4.25

Stadiums Used For 2016 Summer Olympics and Paralympics — A2022

No. 3333: a, Estádio Olímpico (Olympic Stadium). b, Velódromo Olímpico do Rio (Olympic Velodrome). c, Arena da Juventude (Youth Arena). d, Maracana Stadium. e, Sambódromo. f, Estádio da Lagoa (Lagoa Stadium).

Litho. & Embossed

2016, Aug. 1 *Perf. 11½x12*

3333 A2022 3.75r Sheet of 6, #a-f 14.00 14.00

g. As No. 3333, with 2016 Paralympics emblem and text in sheet margin 14.00 14.00

America issue. No. 3333 has 2016 Summer Olympics emblem and text in sheet margin.

Souvenir Sheets

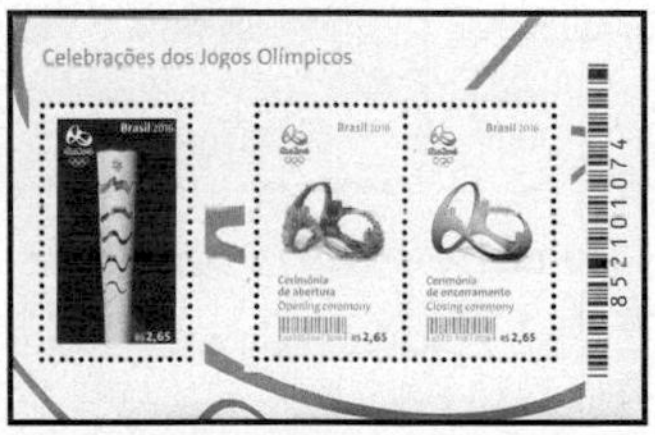

Torch and Emblems of 2016 Summer Olympics — A2023

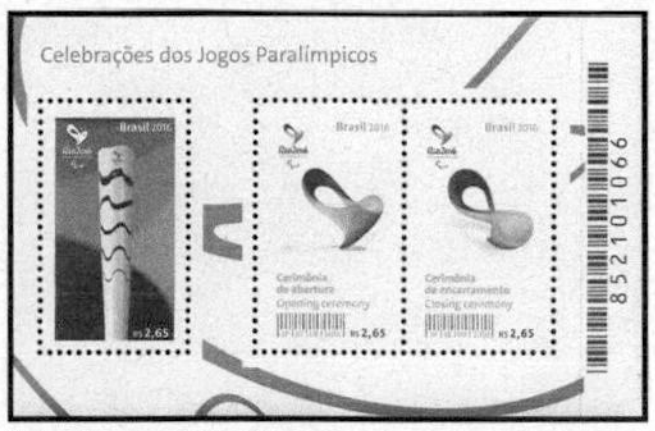

Torch and Emblems of 2016 Summer Paralympics — A2024

No. 3334 — Olympics: a, Torch. b, Opening ceremony emblem. c, Closing ceremony emblem.

No. 3335 — Paralympics: a, Torch. b, Opening ceremony emblem. c, Closing ceremony emblem.

2016, Aug. 5 Litho. *Perf. 11½x11*

3334 A2023 2.65r Sheet of 3, #a-c 5.00 5.00

3335 A2024 2.65r Sheet of 3, #a-c 5.00 5.00

School of Fine Arts, Rio de Janeiro, 200th Anniv. — A2025

No. 3336: a, School building. b, Head of David.

2016, Aug. 12 Litho. *Perf. 12x11½*

3336 A2025 1.70r Horiz. pair, #a-b 2.10 2.10

Brazilian Naval Aviation, Cent. A2026

Perf. 10¾x11½

2016, Aug. 23 Litho.

3337 A2026 (1.70r) multi 1.10 1.10

A2027

A2028

A2029

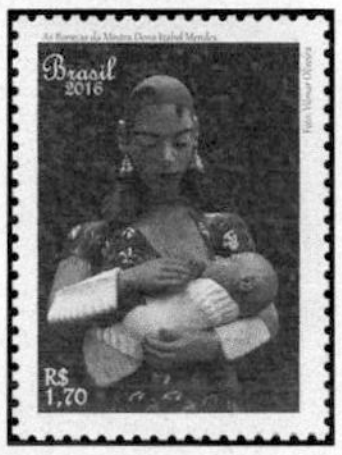

A2030

Dolls Made by Izabel Mendes da Cunha (1924-2014) A2031

2016, Aug. 31 Litho. *Perf. 12x11½*

3338 Horiz. strip of 5 5.50 5.50

a. A2027 1.70r multi 1.10 1.10

b. A2028 1.70r multi 1.10 1.10

c. A2029 1.70r multi 1.10 1.10

d. A2030 1.70r multi 1.10 1.10

e. A2031 1.70r multi 1.10 1.10

A2032

Fruit — A2033

No. 3339: a, Ananas ananassoides. b, Pouteria ramiflora. c, Miconia albicans. d, Byrsonima verbascifolia. e, Alibertia edulis. f, Hancornia speciosa.

No. 3340: a, Anacardium humile. b, Campomanesia adamantium. c, Eugenia klotzschiana. d, Eugenia dysenterica. e, Passiflora setacea. f, Salacia crassifolia. g, Annona crassiflora. h, Dipteryx alata. i, Caryocar brasiliense.

2016, Sept. 11 Litho. *Perf. 11½*

3339 A2032 (1.70r) Block of 6 6.75 6.75

a.-f. (1.70r) Any single 1.10 1.10

Miniature Sheet

Self-Adhesive

Die Cut Perf. 11¼x11½ Syncopated

3340 A2033 Sheet of 9 13.50

a.-i. (2.35r) Any single 1.50 1.50

Employee's Severence Indemnity Fund, 50th Anniv. — A2034

2016, Sept. 13 Litho. *Perf. 12x11½*

3341 A2034 (1.70r) multi 1.10 1.10

Sustainable Transportation A2035

No. 3342: a, Train, bus, people with skateboard, wheelchair, stroller. b, Car, bicycle, people walking, entrance to Metro station.

2016, Sept. 22 Litho. *Perf. 11½x11*

3342 A2035 1.70r Vert. pair, #a-b 2.10 2.10

A2036

Christmas A2037

Litho. & Embossed With Foil Application

2016, Oct. 4 *Perf. 12x11½*

3343 A2036 2.40r gold & multi 1.50 1.50

Litho.

Self-Adhesive

Die Cut Perf. 12¼ Syncopated

3344 A2037 (1.70r) multi 1.10 1.10

João Carlos de Oliveira (1954-99), Olympic Triple Jump Bronze Medalist — A2038

2016, Oct. 15 Litho. *Perf. 11½x11*

3345 A2038 (1.70r) multi 1.10 1.10

Miniature Sheets

A2039

Butterflies — A2040

No. 3346: a, Aricoris middletoni. b, Evenus gabriela. c, Parides bunichus bunichus. d, Melete lycimnia. e, Myscelia orsis. f, Mimoniades versicolor.

No. 3347: a, Udranomia spitzi. b, Marpesia petreus. c, Emesis fatimella. d, Protesilaus sp. e, Junonia evarete. f, Anartia amathea. g, Heliconius sara apseudes. h, Lasaia agesilas. i, Vanessa myrinna. j, Crocozona coecias. k, Siproeta stelenes. l, Urbanus esmeraldus. m, Phocides sp. n, Echydna punctata. o, Chorinea licursis. p, Chamaelimnas briola.

2016, Oct. 20 Litho. *Perf. 11½*

3346 A2039 Sheet of 6 6.75 6.75
a.-f. 1.70r Any single 1.10 1.10

Perf. 11x11½

3347 A2040 Sheet of 16 18.00 18.00
a.-p. (1.70r) Any single 1.10 1.10

Miniature Sheet

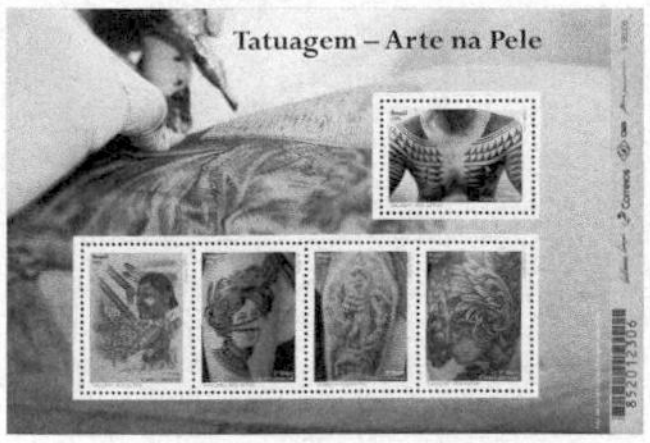

Tattoos — A2041

No. 3348: a, Tattoo on man's chest, shoulders and arms, horiz. b, Man's tattooed face, map and tattooing tools. c, Tattoo depicting split face of woman wearing hat. d, Tattoo depicting helmeted man with spear and chain. e, Tattoo depicting flowers and woman wearing mask.

Perf. 11½x12 (#3348a), 12x11½
2016, Nov. 11 Litho.

3348 A2041 Sheet of 5 5.00 5.00
a.-e. (1.70r) Any single 1.00 1.00

Fossils of Insects From Araripe Geopark — A2042

No. 3349 — Fossil of: a, Dragonfly (libélula). b, Emperor moth (mariposa).

2016, Nov. 21 Litho. *Perf. 11½x12*

3349 A2042 (1.70r) Horiz. pair, #a-b 2.00 2.00

Miguel Arraes (1916-2005), Politician A2043

2016, Dec. 14 Litho. *Perf. 12x11½*

3350 A2043 (1.70r) multi 1.10 1.10

Martin Luther (1483-1546), Religious Reformer — A2044

2017, Apr. 13 Litho. *Perf. 11x11½*

3351 A2044 4.15r multi 2.60 2.60

Protestant Reformation, 500th anniv. See Germany No. 2962.

A2045

Birds A2046

Nos. 3352 and 3353: a, Pararu-espelho (purple-winged ground dove). b, Rolinha-do-planalto (blue-eyed ground dove). c, Soldadinho-do-araripe (Araripe manakin).

2017, June 19 Litho. *Perf. 12x11½*

3352 Horiz. strip of 3 2.25 2.25
a.-c. A2045 1.25r Any single .75 .75

Self-Adhesive

Die Cut Perf. 12¼ Syncopated

3353 Horiz. strip of 3 2.25
a.-c. A2046 (1.25r) Any single .75 .75

Souvenir Sheet

First Samba Recording, Cent. — A2047

2017, June 23 Litho. *Perf. 12½*

3354 A2047 (1.80r) multi 1.10 1.10

Salvador Metro Train A2048

2017, July 28 Litho. *Perf. 11x11½*

3355 A2048 1.50r multi 1.00 1.00

Statues — A2049

No. 3356: a, O Laçador (The Lassoer), Porto Alegre. b, Equestrian Statue of Dom Pedro I, Rio de Janeiro. c, Abertura dos Portos (Monument to the Opening of the Amazon Province Ports to Foreign Nations), Manaus.

2017, Aug. 11 Litho. *Perf. 11½*

3356 Horiz. strip of 3 3.75 3.75
a.-c. A2049 1.80r Any single 1.25 1.25

Araraquara, 200th Anniv. — A2050

2017, Aug. 22 Litho. *Perf. 11½x11*

3357 A2050 (1.80r) multi 1.25 1.25

Revolution of Pernambuco, 200th Anniv. — A2051

2017, Aug. 31 Litho. *Perf. 11½x12*

3358 A2051 1.80r multi 1.25 1.25

Souvenir Sheet

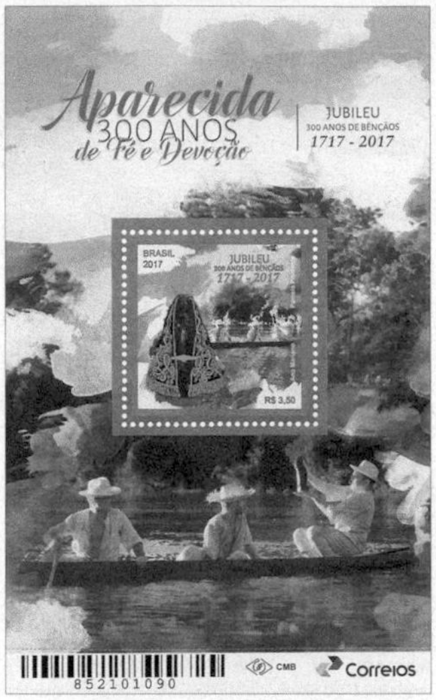

Our Lady of Aparecida Statue, 300th Anniv. — A2052

Litho. & Embossed With Foil Application

2017, Sept. 12 *Perf. 11½*

3359 A2052 3.50r multi 2.25 2.25

Our Lady of Aparecida Statue, 300th Anniv. A2053

Die Cut Perf. 12x11½ Syncopated
2017, Sept. 12 Litho.

Self-Adhesive

3360 A2053 (1.80r) multi 1.25 1.25

Flowers — A2054

No. 3361: a, Begonia. b, Anthurium (Antúrio). c, White ipê (Ipê-branco). d, Pink ipê (Ipê-rosa).

2017, Sept. 22 Litho. *Perf. 11½x12*

3361 A2054 2.55r Block of 4, #a-d 6.50 6.50

No. 3361 is impregnated with a floral scent.

Flowers A2055

Die Cut Perf. 12x11½ Syncopated

2017, Sept. 22 Litho.

Self-Adhesive

3362 A2055 (1.80r) multi 1.25 1.25

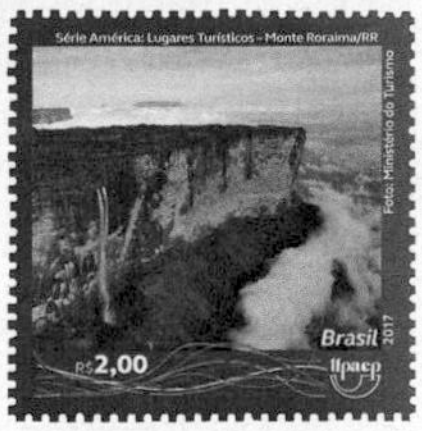

Tourist Attractions A2056

No. 3363: a, Mt. Roraima. b, Maragogi. c, Waterfall, Chapada dos Veadeiros National Park. d, Iguaçu Falls. e. Armaçao dos Búzios.

2017, Sept. 27 Litho. *Perf. 12¾*

3363 Horiz. strip of 5 7.00 7.00
a.-e. A2056 2r Any single 1.40 1.40

Miniature Sheet

Bicycles — A2057

No. 3364: a, 1890 bicycle. b, 1910 bicycle. c, 1940 bicycle. d, 1930 bicycle. e, Front wheel of 1940 bicycle, handlebars and seat of 1950 bicycle. f, Front wheel of 1930 bicycle, handlebars and seat of 1960 bicycle (no date shown). g, Wheels and gears of 1950 bicycle (no date shown). h, Wheels and gears of 1960 bicycle.

2017, Oct. 22 Litho. *Perf. 11x11½*

3364 A2057 1.25r Sheet of 8, #a-h 6.25 6.25

Miniature Sheet

Brasilia as UNESCO World Heritage Site, 30th Anniv. — A2058

No. 3365: a, Playground at Sarah Kubitschek Park. b, National Museum of Brazil. c, Dom Bosco Sanctuary. d, Brazilian Army Headquarters (QG). e, Television tower and fountain. f, Cruzeiro Square (Praça do Cruzeiro). g, Brasilia Palace Hotel. h, Mané Garrincha Stadium. i, Cloverleaf in residential neighborhood (Tesourinha). j, Structural details on apartment building (Cobogó).

2017, Oct. 24 Litho. *Perf. 11½x12*

3365 A2058 2r Sheet of 10, #a-j 12.50 12.50

Miniature Sheet

Plays by William Shakespeare (1564-1616) — A2059

No. 3366: a, Romeo and Juliet. b, A Midsummer Night's Dream (Sonho de uma Noite de Verao). c, Hamlet. d, Othello. e, King Lear. f, Macbeth.

Litho. & Embossed

2017, Oct. 26 *Perf. 12x11½*

3366 A2059 4.20r Sheet of 6, #a-f 15.50 15.50

Arrival in Brazil of Maria Leopoldina of Austria (Wife-to-be of Emperor Pedro I), 200th Anniv. — A2060

Litho. & Engr.

2017, Nov. 7 *Perf. 11½x11*

3367 A2060 4.20r multi 2.60 2.60

Christmas A2061

2017, Nov. 10 Litho. *Perf. 11½*

3368 A2061 2.55r multi 1.60 1.60

Christmas A2062

No. 3369 — Characters from *The Steadfast Tin Soldier*, by Hans Christian Andersen: a, Tin soldier. b, Dancer. c, Goblin. d, Fish.

Die Cut Perf. 12x11¾ Syncopated

2017, Nov. 10 Litho.

Self-Adhesive

3369 Horiz. strip of 4 5.00
a.-d. A2062 (1.85r) Any single 1.25 1.25

Violeta Parra (1917-67), Folk Music Composer — A2063

2017, Nov. 21 Litho. *Perf. 11½x11*

3370 A2063 3.15r multi 2.00 2.00

Souvenir Sheet

Sculpture of St. Francis, Church of the Thrid Order of St. Francis, Bahia — A2064

Litho., Sheet Margin Litho. & Embossed With Foil Application

2017, Dec. 1 *Perf. 11½*

3371 A2064 2.55r gold & multi 1.60 1.60

Eighth World Water Forum, Brasilia A2066

2018, Mar. 19 Litho. *Perf. 11½*

3373 A2066 (1.25r) multi .75 .75

Values are for stamps with surrounding selvage.

Animal Protection — A2067

2018, Mar. 19 Litho. *Perf. 11½x11*

3374 A2067 (1.85r) multi 1.25 1.25

Campaign Against Foot-and-Mouth Disease in Cattle — A2068

2018, Apr. 2 Litho. *Perf. 12x11½*

3375 A2068 (1.85r) multi 1.25 1.25

Items in Postal Library, Brasilia A2069

2018, May 4 Litho. *Perf. 11½x12*

3376 A2069 1.55r multi .85 .85

Acclamation of John VI as King, 200th Anniv. — A2070

Litho. & Engr.

2018, May 16 *Perf. 11½x11*

3377 A2070 2.05r multi 1.10 1.10

2018 World Cup Soccer Championships, Russia — A2071

No. 3378 — Tourist attractions of Russian cities hosting Brazil team's group play games: a, St. Petersburg, Rostov-on-Don. b, Moscow.

2018, June 9 Litho. *Perf. 11½x11*

3378 A2071 2.25r Horiz. pair, #a-b 2.40 2.40

Diplomatic Relations Between Brazil and India, 70th Anniv. — A2072

2018, Oct. 2 Litho. *Perf. 11½x12*

3379 A2072 1.85r multi 1.00 1.00

Mohandas K. Gandhi (1869-1948), Indian Nationalist Leader — A2073

2018, Oct. 2 Litho. *Perf. 12x11½*

3380 A2073 1.85r multi 1.00 1.00

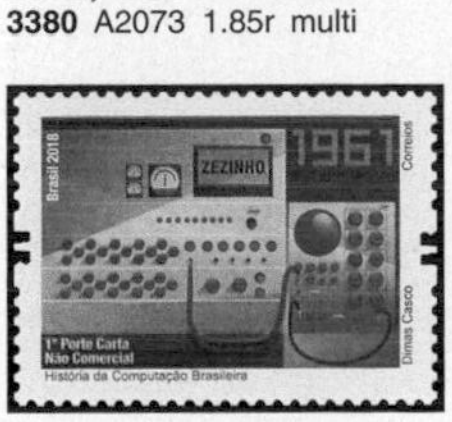

Zezinho Computer, 1961 A2074

Pato Feio Computer, 1971 A2075

Cobra 530 Computer, 1980 A2076

Die Cut Perf. 12x11¼ Syncopated

2018, Oct. 15 **Litho.**

Self-Adhesive

3381	A2074 (1.25r) multi	.70	.70
3382	A2075 (1.25r) multi	.70	.70
a.	Horiz. pair, #3381-3382	1.40	
3383	A2076 (1.25r) multi	.70	.70
a.	Horiz. pair, #3382-3383	1.40	
	Nos. 3381-3383 (3)	2.10	2.10

Nos. 3381-3383 were printed in sheets of 24 containing eight examples of each stamp.

Pets — A2077

No. 3384: a, Dog named Perola. b, Dog named Bela. c, Dog named Bono. d, Dog named Arthur. e, Dog named Foton. f, Dog named Rocco. g, Dog named Joaquim. h, Dog named Elvis. i, Dog named Nadir. j, Dogs named Lotus and Ghana. k, Dog named Chanel. l, Dog named Draco. m, Dogs named Nega, Tobby, and Kika. n, Dog named Amora. o, Dog named Rick-Valente. p, Cat named Caetano. q, White cat named Nina. r, Cat named Hayana. s, Cat named Bárbara. t, Cat named Angel. u, Cat named Dexter. v, Cat named Natan. w, Cat named Pequeno. x, Gray cat named Nina. y, Cats named Mimosa, Tuquinho, Titinho, and Petty. z, Rabbit named Orelhinha. aa, Fish named Morfeu. ab, Chicken named Bela. ac, Parakeets named Blue, Meio e Meio, and Bikinho. ad, Cockatoo named Everest.

2018, Nov. 6 **Litho.** ***Perf. 12x11½***

3384	Sheet of 30	24.00	24.00
a.-ad.	A2077 1.55r Any single	.80	.80

Souvenir Sheet

Hot Air Ballooning — A2078

2018, Nov. 10 **Litho.** ***Perf. 12x11½***

3385	A2078 4.25r multi	2.25	2.25

Visit of Queen Elizabeth II to Brazil, 50th Anniv. — A2079

2018, Nov. 16 **Litho.** ***Perf. 11½x11***

3386	A2079 1.85r multi	1.00	1.00

Opening of First Resident Embassy of Luxembourg in Brasilia — A2080

2018, Nov. 20 **Litho.** ***Perf. 11½x11***

3387	A2080 4.50r multi	2.40	2.40

Republica, by Manoel Lopes Rodrigues (1860-1917) A2081

2018, Nov. 23 **Litho.** ***Perf. 11½***

3388	A2081 3.10r multi	1.60	1.60

Bahia Museum of Art, cent.

Ronald Golias (1929-2005), Comedian A2082

Die Cut Perf. 12¼ Syncopated

2018, Nov. 30 **Litho.**

Self-Adhesive

3389	A2082 (1.25r) multi	.65	.65

National Museum of Rio de Janeiro, 200th Anniv. A2083

2018, Dec. 4 **Litho.** ***Perf. 11½***

3390	A2083 3.10r multi	1.60	1.60

A2085

A2086

Christmas — A2087

Designs: Nos. 3392a, 3394, Franz Xaver Gruber (1787-1863), composer, and Joseph Mohr (1792-1848), lyricist of Christmas song, "Silent Night." Nos. 3392b, 3393, Silent Night Chapel, Oberndorf, Austria.

Litho. & Engr, Sheet Margin Litho. With Foil Application

2018, Dec. 6 ***Perf. 12x11½***

3392	A2085 4.25r Souvenir sheet of 2, #a-b	4.50	4.50

Litho.

Self-Adhesive

Die Cut

3393	A2086 (1.30r) multi	.70	.70
3394	A2087 (1.95r) multi	1.00	1.00

"Silent Night," 200th anniv.

Nelson Mandela (1918-2013), President of South Africa A2088

2018, Dec. 10 **Litho.** ***Perf. 11½***

3395	A2088 2.35r multi	1.25	1.25

Scientists — A2089

No. 3396: a, Cesar Lattes (1924-2005), physicist. b, Johanna Döbereiner (1924-2000), agronomist.

2018, Dec. 11 **Litho.** ***Perf. 11x11½***

3396	A2089 1.85r Horiz. pair, #a-b	2.00	2.00

Miniature Sheet

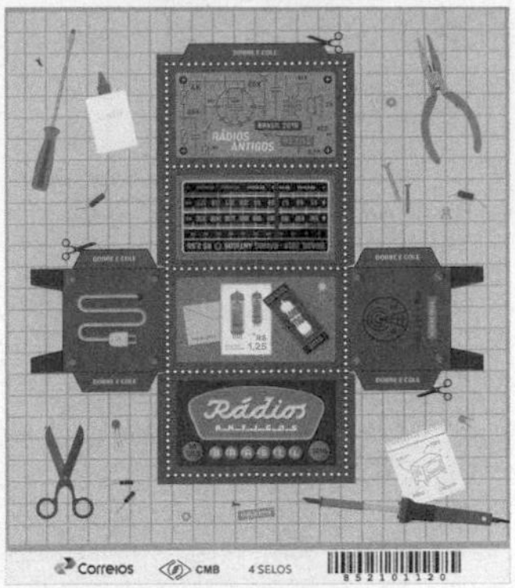

Old Radio — A2090

No. 3397: a, Radio vacuum tubes. b, Speaker cover and selector buttons. c, Electrical diagram of radio. d, Two-band radio dial.

Litho. & Embossed (#3397a, 3397b), Litho. & Engr. (#3397c), Litho. (#3397d)

2018, Dec. 14 ***Perf. 11x11½***

3397	A2090 Sheet of 4	4.00	4.00
a.	1.25r multi	.65	.65
b.	1.85r multi	.95	.95
c.	1.95r multi	1.00	1.00
d.	2.55r multi	1.40	1.40

Souvenir Sheets

Fortaleza Canyon — A2091

Itaimbezinho Canyon — A2092

2018, Dec. 17 **Litho.** ***Perf. 11x11½***

3398	A2091 2.55r multi	1.40	1.40

Perf. 11½x11

3399	A2092 2.55r multi	1.40	1.40

Fernando Figueira (1919-2003), Pediatrician A2093

2019, Feb. 4 **Litho.** ***Perf. 11½x11***

3400	A2093 (1.95r) multi	1.10	1.10

Signs of the Zodiac A2094

2019 Litho. *Perf. 11½*

3401	A2094	(1.30r)	Aries	.70	.70
3402	A2094	(1.30r)	Taurus	.70	.70
3403	A2094	(1.30r)	Gemini	.70	.70
3404	A2094	(1.30r)	Cancer	.70	.70
3405	A2094	(1.30r)	Leo	.70	.70
3406	A2094	(1.30r)	Virgo	.65	.65
3407	A2094	(1.30r)	Libra	.65	.65
3408	A2094	(1.30r)	Scorpio	.65	.65
3409	A2094	(1.30r)	Sagittarius	.65	.65
3410	A2094	(1.30r)	Capricorn	.65	.65
	Nos. 3401-3410 (10)			6.75	6.75

Issued: No. 3401, 3/21; No. 3402, 4/21; No. 3403, 5/21; No. 3404, 6/21; No. 3405, 7/22; No. 3406, 8/23; No. 3407, 9/23; No. 3408, 10/23; No. 3409, 11/22; No. 3410, 12/22.

Souvenir Sheet

Renato Russo (1960-96), Rock Musician — A2095

Litho., Sheet Margin Litho. & Engr.

2019, Mar. 27 *Perf. 11½*

3413 A2095 (2.70r) black 1.40 1.40

Souvenir Sheet

Sao Paolo Philatelic Society, Cent. — A2096

No. 3414: a, Detail of postcard commemorating Mario Martins de Almeida, Euclides Miragaia, Dráusio Marcondes de Sousa and Antonio Camargo de Andrade, students killed in 1932 Paulista Uprising. b, William Edward Lee, founder and first president of Sao Paolo Philatelic Society. c, Emblem of Sao Paolo Philatelic Society.

2019, Apr. 30 Litho. *Perf. 11½*

3414	A2096 Sheet of 3	2.40	2.40
a.-b.	1.30r Either single	.70	.70
c.	1.95r multi	1.00	1.00

2019 Brazilian Philatelic Exhibition, Sao Paulo.

Astronomical Observations of May 29, 1919 Solar Eclipse at Sobral, Cent. — A2097

2019, May 29 Litho. *Perf. 11½x12*

3415 A2097 2.15r multi 1.10 1.10

Geastrum Violaceum A2098

Laetiporus Gilbertsonii A2099

Oudemansiella Cubensis — A2100

Clathrus Chrysomycelinus A2101

Hydnopolyporus Fimbriatus A2102

Clathrus Columnatus A2103

Perf. 11½x12 (#3416a-3416c), 12x11½ (#3416d-3416f)

2019, June 5 Litho.

3416	Block of 6	5.25	5.25
a.	A2098 1.60r multi	.85	.85
b.	A2099 1.60r multi	.85	.85
c.	A2100 1.60r multi	.85	.85
d.	A2101 1.60r multi	.85	.85
e.	A2102 1.60r multi	.85	.85
f.	A2103 1.60r multi	.85	.85

Mushrooms.

Return to Brazil of José Bonifácio de Andrada e Silva (1763-1838), Scientist and Poet, 200th Anniv. — A2104

2019, June 13 Litho. *Perf. 11½x11*

3417 A2104 2.15r multi 1.10 1.10

Nelson Gonçalves (1919-98), Singer — A2105

2019, June 21 Litho. *Perf. 12x11½*

3418 A2105 (1.30r) multi .70 .70

Joaquim Nabuco (1849-1910), Diplomat, and Joaquim Machado e Assis (1839-1908), First President of Brazilian Academy of Letters — A2106

2019, July 20 Litho. *Perf. 11½*

3419 A2106 (2.10r) multi 1.10 1.10

First Man on the Moon, 50th Anniv. — A2107

2019, July 20 Litho. *Perf. 11½x11*

3420 A2107 3.75r black 2.00 2.00

Elza Soares, Singer — A2108

2019, July 23 Litho. *Perf. 11½x11*

3421 A2108 (1.95r) multi 1.00 1.00

Postmarked Covers and Postmarking Device of Brazilian Empire — A2109

2019, Aug. 1 Litho. *Imperf.*

3422 A2109 8r multi 4.25 4.25

A row of rouletting separates stamp from bottom tab.

Hortência Marcari, Basketball Player — A2110

2019, Aug. 15 Litho. *Perf. 11½x11*

3423 A2110 (1.95r) multi .95 .95

Sertoes Rally Vehicles — A2111

No. 3424 — Map of rally route and: a, Mitsubishi ASX automobile. b, Quadricycle. c, Utility vehicle (UTV). d, Motorcycle.

2019, Aug. 23 Litho. *Perf. 11x11½*

3424 A2111 (1.95r) Block of 4, #a-d 3.75 3.75

Stairs — A2112

Sculpture Depicting Angel and Job — A2113

Altar A2114

Archbishop Duarte Leopoldo e Silva (1867-1938) A2115

Sculpture of Angel and St. Jerome A2116

Stairs A2117

2019, Sept. 5 Litho. *Perf. 11½x11*

3425	Horiz. strip of 6	4.00	4.00
a.	A2112 (1.30r) multi	.65	.65
b.	A2113 (1.30r) multi	.65	.65
c.	A2114 (1.30r) multi	.65	.65
d.	A2115 (1.30r) multi	.65	.65
e.	A2116 (1.30r) multi	.65	.65
f.	A2117 (1.30r) multi	.65	.65

Crypt of the Metropolitan Cathedral of Sao Paolo, cent.

Hebe Camargo (1929-2012), Television Host — A2118

2019, Sept. 19 Litho. *Perf. 11½x11*
3426 A2118 (1.95r) multi .95 .95

Fauna — A2119

No. 3427: a, Cupinzeiro luminoso (bioluminescnt termite mounds). b, Preguiça-de-coleira (maned sloth). c, Mico-leao-preto (black lion tamarin).

2019, Sept. 23 Litho. *Perf. 11x11½*
3427 A2119 (2.70r) Vert. strip of 3, #a-c 4.00 4.00

Carolina Maria de Jesus (1914-77), Writer — A2120

2019, Oct. 4 Litho. *Perf. 11½x11*
3428 A2120 (1.95r) multi 1.00 1.00

Miniature Sheet

America Issue — A2121

No. 3429 — Traditional dishes: a, Açaí com açúcar e farinha (Açaí with sugar and flour). b, Ambrosia e bolo de milho (Ambrosia and corn cakes). c, Arroz com feijao na panelinha (Rice and beans). d, Bolo de milho com doce de leite (Corn cake with dulce de leche). e, Bolo de rolo (roll cake). f, Cuscuz com carne de sol e molho (Couscous with sun-dried meat and sauce). g, Cuscuz Paulista (Molded meat and vegetable cake). h, Doce de abóbora (Pumpkin compote). i, Feijoada (Bean stew). j, Filé à Oswaldo Aranha (Beef with garlic). k, Goiabada com queijo (Guava with cheese). l, Jambuçoba (Jambu, cabbage and meat stew). m, Moqueca capixaba mista (Seafood stew). n, Paçoca e amendoins (Peanut candy). o, Pamonha de milho verde (Green corn tamales). p, Pao de queijo com café (Cheese bread and coffee). q, Pastéis com caldo de cana (Pastries with sugar cane juice). r, Prato feito (Rice, beans, fried potato, beef and egg). s, Pudim de leite condensado (Condensed milk pudding). t, Tapioca de banana de terra (Plantain tapioca).

2019, Oct. 9 Litho. *Perf. 11½*
3429 A2121 Sheet of 20 20.00 20.00
a.-t. (1.95r) Any single 1.00 1.00

Maria da Penha, Biopharmacist and Campaigner for Rights of Abused Women — A2122

2019, Nov. 4 Litho. *Perf. 11½x11*
3430 A2122 (1.95r) multi .95 .95

Matterhorn and Sugarloaf Mountain — A2123

2019, Nov. 25 Litho. *Perf. 11½x12*
3431 A2123 2.15r multi 1.10 1.10

Swiss immigrants in Brazil, 200th anniv.

Diplomatic Relations Between Brazil and Finland, Cent. — A2125

2019, Dec. 3 Litho. *Perf. 11½x12*
3433 A2125 2.15r multi 1.10 1.10

SEMI-POSTAL STAMPS

National Philatelic Exhibition Issue

SP1

Thick Paper

Wmk. Coat of Arms in Sheet (236)

1934, Sept. 16 Engr. *Imperf.*
B1 SP1 200r + 100r dp claret .40 *2.00*
B2 SP1 300r + 100r ver .40 *2.00*
B3 SP1 700r + 100r brt bl 4.00 *24.00*
B4 SP1 1000r + 100r blk 5.00 *24.00*
Nos. B1-B4 (4) 9.80 *52.00*

The surtax was to help defray the expenses of the exhibition. Issued in sheets of 60, inscribed "EXPOSICAO FILATELICA NACIONAL."

Red Cross Nurse and Soldier SP2

Wmk. 222

1935, Sept. 19 Typo. *Perf. 11*
B5 SP2 200r + 100r pur & red 1.20 .40
B6 SP2 300r + 100r ol brn & red 1.60 .40
B7 SP2 700r + 100r turq bl & red 10.00 5.00
Nos. B5-B7 (3) 12.80 5.80

3rd Pan-American Red Cross Conf. Exist imperf.

Three Wise Men and Star of Bethlehem — SP3

Angel and Child — SP4

Southern Cross and Child — SP5

Mother and Child — SP6

Wmk. 249

1939-40 Litho. *Perf. 10½*
B8 SP3 100r + 100r chlky bl & bl blk .60 .25
a. Horiz. or vert. pair, imperf. between 40.00
B9 SP4 200r + 100r brt grnsh bl .80 .40
a. Horizontal pair, imperf. between 40.00
B10 SP5 400r + 200r ol grn & ol .60 .25
B11 SP6 1200r + 400r crim & brn red 2.00 .25
a. Vertical pair, imperf. between 40.00
Nos. B8-B11 (4) 4.00 1.15

Dates of issue: #B8, 12/20/39; #B9-B11, 2/26/40.
Surtax for charitable institutions.
For surcharges see Nos. C55-C59.

Catalogue values for unused stamps in this section, from this point to the end of the section, are for Never Hinged items.

In 1980 three stamps that were intended to be semi-postals were issued as postage stamps at the total combined face value. See Nos. 1681-1683.

Children and Citizenship — SP7

Designs: a, Cutouts of children forming pyramid. b, Man and woman's hands holding onto girl. c, Children going into school. d, Pregnant woman in front of house. e, Children flying paper doves. f, Parent working in garden, child writing letters, doves. g, Breastfeeding. h, Father holding birth certificate, mother holding infant. i, Disabled child on wheelchair ramp. j, Mother, father with sick child. k, Stylized child, pencil, letters. l, Hands above and below pregnant woman. m, Two families of different races. n, Small child playing large guitar. o, People looking to baby on pedestal. p, Children, book, "Statute of Children and Adolescent."

1997, Nov. 20 Litho. *Perf. 12x11½*
B12 Sheet of 16 12.50 12.50
a.-p. SP7 22c +8c any single .70 .70

Surcharge for Natl. Fund for Children and Adolescents.

Stampin' the Future Children's Stamp Design Contest Winners — SP8

Art by: a, Jonas Sampaio de Freitas. b, Clarissa Cazane. c, Caio Ferreira Guimaraes de Oliveira. d, Milena Karoline Ribeiro Reis.

2000, Jan. 1 Litho. *Perf. 11½x12*
B13 SP8 22c + 8c Block of 4, #a-d 6.00 6.00

Children's Hope SP9

Designs: No. B14, Child and family activities. No. B15, Children reading, painting, dancing.

2002, July 26 Litho. *Perf. 11½x12*
B14 SP9 (80c) +10c multi .85 .85
B15 SP9 (80c) +10c multi .85 .85
a. Pair, #B14-B15 3.75 3.75

AIR POST STAMPS

Nos. O14-O29 Surcharged

1927, Dec. 28 Unwmk. *Perf. 12*

C1	O2	50r on 10r	.40	.25
a.		Inverted surcharge	250.00	225.00
b.		Top ornaments missing	60.00	40.00
C2	O2	200r on 1000r	2.25	*4.25*
a.		Double surcharge	250.00	
C3	O2	200r on 2000r	1.25	*9.50*
a.		Double surcharge	575.00	
b.		Double surcharge, one inverted	575.00	
C4	O2	200r on 5000r	1.60	1.20
a.		Double surcharge	250.00	225.00
b.		Double surcharge, one inverted	250.00	
c.		Triple surcharge	350.00	
C5	O2	300r on 500r	1.60	2.00
a.		Double surcharge	275.00	—
C6	O2	300r on 600r	.80	.60
b.		Pair, one without surch.	3,750.	
c.		Double surcharge	1,000.	
C6A	O2	500r on 10r	*400.00*	*425.00*
C7	O2	500r on 50r	1.60	.60
a.		Double surcharge	225.00	—
b.		Red surcharge	80.00	—
c.		Inverted surcharge	1,200.	
C8	O2	1000r on 20r	1.20	.25
a.		Double surcharge	*250.00*	*250.00*
C9	O2	2000r on 100r	2.50	1.75
a.		Pair, one without surcharge	2,000.	
b.		Double surcharge	250.00	
C10	O2	2000r on 200r	2.75	1.75
C11	O2	2000r on 10,000r	2.50	.60
C12	O2	5000r on 20,000r	8.75	4.00
C13	O2	5000r on 50,000r	8.75	4.00
C14	O2	5000r on 100,000r	24.00	30.00
C15	O2	10,000r on 500,000r	27.50	20.00
C16	O2	10,000r on 1,000,000r	25.00	25.00
		Nos. C1-C6,C7-C16 (16)	112.45	105.75

Nos. C1, C1b, C6A, C7, C8 and C9 have small diamonds printed over the numerals in the upper corners.

Monument to de Gusmao — AP1

Santos-Dumont's Airship — AP2

Augusto Severo's Airship "Pax" — AP3

Santos-Dumont's Biplane "14 Bis" — AP4

Ribeiro de Barros's Seaplane "Jahu" — AP5

Perf. 12½x13, 13x13½

1929 Typo. Wmk. 206

C17	AP1	50r blue grn	.35	.25
C18	AP2	200r red	.40	.25
C19	AP3	300r brt blue	.40	.25
C20	AP4	500r red violet	1.60	.25
C21	AP5	1000r orange brn	9.50	.25
		Nos. C17-C21 (5)	12.25	1.25

Perf. 11

C17a	AP1	50r blue grn	1.00	.25
C18a	AP2	200r red	1.60	.25
C19a	AP3	300r brt blue	2.00	1.60
C20a	AP4	500r red violet	2.00	.25
C21a	AP5	1000r orange brn	7.50	.40
		Nos. C17a-C21a (5)	14.10	2.75

See Nos. C32-C36. For surcharges see Nos. C26-C27.

Bartholomeu de Gusmao — AP6

Augusto Severo — AP7

Alberto Santos-Dumont AP8

Perf. 11-12

1929-30 Engr. Wmk. 101

C22	AP6	2000r lt green ('30)	7.50	.40
C23	AP7	5000r carmine	10.00	.60
C24	AP8	10,000r olive grn	10.00	.80
		Nos. C22-C24 (3)	27.50	1.80

Perf. 9

C22a	AP6	2000r lt green	20.00	.80
C23a	AP7	5000r carmine	40.00	6.25
C24a	AP8	10,000r olive grn	40.00	2.75
		Nos. C22a-C24a (3)	100.00	9.80

Perf. 11x9, 9x11

C23b	AP7	5000r carmine	100.00	47.50
C24b	AP8	10,000r olive grn	200.00	25.00

Nos. C23-C24 exist imperf.
See Nos. C37, C40.

Allegory: Airmail Service between Brazil and the US — AP9

1929 Typo. Wmk. 206 *Perf. 11-12*

C25	AP9	3000r violet	10.00	2.00
a.		Perf. 9	10.00	2.00
b.		Perf. 9x11, 11x9	10.00	1.60
c.		Perf. 9, 11, compound	10.00	1.60

Exists imperf. See Nos. C38, C41. For surcharge see No. C28.

Nos. C18-C19 Surcharged in Blue or Red

1931, Aug. 16 *Perf. 12½x13½*

C26	AP2	2500r on 200r (Bl)	16.00	18.00
C27	AP3	5000r on 300r (R)	20.00	24.00

No. C25 Surcharged

1931, Sept. 2 *Perf. 11*

C28	AP9	2500r on 3000r vio	20.00	20.00
a.		Inverted surcharge	160.00	425.00
b.		Surch. on front and back	160.00	

Regular Issues of 1928-29 Surcharged

1932, May Wmk. 101

C29	A89	3500r on 5000r gray lil	12.00	14.00
C30	A72	7000r on 10,000r rose	12.00	14.00
b.		Horiz. pair, imperf. between	*750.00*	
c.		Perf. 11½	30.00	40.00

Imperforates

Since 1933, imperforate or partly perforated sheets of nearly all of the airmail issues have become available.

Flag and Airplane AP10

1933, June 7 Wmk. 222 Typo.

C31	AP10	3500r grn, yel & dk bl	4.75	1.25

See Nos. C39, C42.

1934 Wmk. 222

C32	AP1	50r blue grn	1.25	1.25
C33	AP2	200r red	.80	.25
C34	AP3	300r brt blue	2.40	.60
C35	AP4	500r red violet	.80	.25
C36	AP5	1000r orange brn	5.00	.25
		Nos. C32-C36 (5)	10.25	2.60

1934 Wmk. 236 Engr. *Perf. 12x11*

Thick Laid Paper

C37	AP6	2000r lt green	2.50	1.25

Types of 1929, 1933

Perf. 11-12

1937-40 Typo. Wmk. 249

C38	AP9	3000r violet	25.00	2.25
C39	AP10	3500r grn, yel & dk bl	2.50	1.25

Engr.

C40	AP7	5000r ver ('40)	9.00	2.00
		Nos. C38-C40 (3)	36.50	5.50

Watermark note after No. 501 also applies to No. C40.

Types of 1929-33

Perf. 11, 11½x12

1939-40 Typo. Wmk. 256

C41	AP9	3000r violet	1.25	1.25
C42	AP10	3500r bl, dl grn & yel ('40)	1.25	.75

Map of the Western Hemisphere Showing Brazil — AP11

1941, Jan. 14 Engr. *Perf. 11*

C43	AP11	1200r dark brown	2.50	.40
		Never hinged	8.00	

5th general census of Brazil.

No. 506A Overprinted in Carmine

1941, Nov. 10 Wmk. 264 *Rouletted*

C45	A180	5400r slate grn	3.75	1.20
		Never hinged	10.00	
a.		Overprint inverted	100.00	100.00
		Never hinged	200.00	
b.		Wmk. 249	1,200.	1,650.
		Never hinged	2,200.	
c.		Pair, one without overprint	1,000.	
		Never hinged	1,500.	
d.		Double overprint	600.00	
e.		Dbl. ovpt., one inverted	215.00	215.00
		Never hinged	470.00	
f.		As "c," wmk. 249	1,500.	
		Never hinged	3,000.	

President Varges' new constitution, 4th anniv.

Nos. 506A and 508 Surcharged in Black

1942, Nov. 10 Wmk. 264

C47	A180	5.40cr on 5400r sl grn	4.50	2.25
		Never hinged	13.00	
a.		Wmk. 249	130.00	130.00
		Never hinged	225.00	
b.		Surcharge inverted	80.00	80.00
		Never hinged	175.00	
c.		Double surcharge	110.00	110.00
		Never hinged	220.00	

President Vargas' new constitution, 5th anniv.

Southern Cross and Arms of Paraguay AP12

Wmk. 270

1943, May 11 Engr. *Perf. 12½*

C48	AP12	1.20cr lt gray blue	.80	.25
		Never hinged	8.00	

Issued in commemoration of the visit of President Higinio Morinigo of Paraguay.

Map of South America — AP13

1943, June 30 Wmk. 271 *Perf. 12½*

C49	AP13	1.20cr multi	.80	.25
		Never hinged	4.00	

Visit of President Penaranda of Bolivia.

Numeral of Value AP14

1943, Aug. 7

C50	AP14	1cr blk & dull yel	1.00	.50
a.		Double impression	30.00	
C51	AP14	2cr blk & pale grn	2.00	.50
a.		Double impression	40.00	
C52	AP14	5cr blk & pink	2.75	.80
		Nos. C50-C52 (3)	5.75	1.80
		Set, never hinged	19.50	

Centenary of Brazil's first postage stamps.

Souvenir Sheet

AP15

Without Gum *Imperf.*

C53 AP15 Sheet of 3 50.00 50.00
- *a.* 1cr black & dull yellow 15.00 15.00
- *b.* 2cr black & pale green 15.00 15.00
- *c.* 5cr black & pink 15.00 15.00

100th anniv. of the 1st postage stamps of Brazil and the 2nd Phil. Exposition (Brapex). Printed in panes of 6 sheets, perforated 12½ between. Each sheet is perforated on two or three sides. Size approximately 155x155mm. Issued without gum.

Law Book — AP16

1943, Aug. 13 *Perf. 12½*

C54 AP16 1.20cr rose & lil rose .60 .25
Never hinged 2.25

2nd Inter-American Conf. of Lawyers.

No. B10 Surcharged in Red, Carmine or Black

1944, Jan. 3 **Wmk. 249** *Perf. 10½*

C55 SP5 20c on 400r+200r (R) 2.00 .50
C56 SP5 40c on 400r+200r (Bk) 2.75 .50
C57 SP5 60c on 400r+200r (C) 3.50 .50
C58 SP5 1cr on 400r+200r (Bk) 4.75 .50
C59 SP5 1.20cr on 400r+200r (C) 9.50 .50
Nos. C55-C59 (5) 22.50 2.50
Set, never hinged 75.00

No. C59 is known with surcharge in black but its status is questioned.

Bartholomeu de Gusmao and the "Aerostat" — AP17

Wmk. 268

1944, Oct. 23 **Engr.** *Perf. 12*

C60 AP17 1.20cr rose carmine .40 .25
Never hinged 2.00

Week of the Wing.

L. L. Zamenhof AP18

1945, Apr. 16 **Litho.** *Perf. 11*

C61 AP18 1.20cr dull brown .45 .30
Never hinged 2.00

Esperanto Congress held in Rio, Apr. 14-22.

Map of South America — AP19

Baron of Rio Branco — AP20

1945, Apr. 20

C62 AP19 1.20cr gray brown .75 .30
Never hinged 3.00
C63 AP20 5cr rose lilac 1.75 .30
Never hinged 5.00

Centenary of the birth of José Maria de Silva Paranhos, Baron of Rio Branco.

Nos. C62-C63 exist without watermark and gum. Value $75 each.

Dove and Flags of American Republics AP21

Perf. 12x11

1947, Aug. 15 **Engr.** **Unwmk.**

C64 AP21 2.20cr dk blue green .35 .25
Never hinged 1.50

Inter-American Defense Conference at Rio de Janeiro August-September, 1947.

Santos-Dumont Monument, St. Cloud, France — AP22

1947, Nov. 15 **Typo.** *Perf. 11x12*

C65 AP22 1.20cr org brn & ol .50 .30
Never hinged 1.60

Issued to commemorate the Week of the Wing and to honor the Santos-Dumont monument which was destroyed in World War II.

Catalogue values for unused stamps in this section, from this point to the end of the section, are for Never Hinged items.

Bay of Rio de Janeiro and Rotary Emblem — AP23

1948, May 16 **Engr.** *Perf. 11*

C66 AP23 1.20cr deep claret 1.25 .30
C67 AP23 3.80cr dull violet 3.75 .30

39th convention of Rotary Intl., Rio.

Hotel Quitandinha, Petropolis — AP24

1948, July 10 **Litho.** **Wmk. 267**

C68 AP24 1.20cr org brn .75 .30
C69 AP24 3.80cr violet 2.00 .30

International Exposition of Industry and Commerce, Petropolis, 1948.

Musician and Singers AP25

1948, Aug. 13 **Engr.** **Unwmk.**

C70 AP25 1.20cr blue 1.75 .30

National School of Music, cent.

Luis Batlle Berres AP26

1948, Sept. 2 **Typo.**

C71 AP26 1.70cr blue .75 .25

Visit of President Luis Batlle Berres of Uruguay, September, 1948.

Merino Ram AP27

Perf. 12x11

1948, Oct. 10 **Wmk. 267**

C72 AP27 1.20cr dp orange 2.00 .40

Intl. Livestock Exposition at Bagé.

Eucharistic Congress Seal — AP28

Unwmk.

1948, Oct. 23 **Engr.** *Perf. 11*

C73 AP28 1.20cr dk car rose .75 .25

5th Natl. Eucharistic Cong., Porto Alegre, Oct. 24-31.

Souvenir Sheet

AP28a

1948, Dec. 14 **Engr.** *Imperf.*

Without Gum

C73A AP28a Sheet of 3 90.00 *150.00*

No. C73A contains one each of Nos. 674-676. Issued in honor of President Eurico Gasper Dutra and the armed forces. Exists both with and without number on back. Measures 130x75mm. Issued without gum.

Church of Prazeres, Guararapes — AP29

Perf. 11½x12

1949, Feb. 15 **Litho.** **Wmk. 267**

C74 AP29 1.20cr pink 5.00 .80

Second Battle of Guararapes, 300th anniv.

Thomé de Souza Meeting Indians — AP30

Perf. 11x12

1949, Mar. 29 **Engr.** **Unwmk.**

C75 AP30 1.20cr blue 1.25 .30

Founding of the City of Salvador, 400th anniv.

A souvenir folder, issued with No. C75, has an engraved 20cr red brown postage stamp portraying John III printed on it, and a copy of No. C75 affixed to it and postmarked. Paper is laid, and size of folder front is 100x150mm. Value, $5. Also exists on parchment paper in blue, black and red. Value, each $500.

Franklin D. Roosevelt AP31

1949, May 20 **Unwmk.** *Imperf.*

C76 AP31 3.80cr deep blue 2.50 .60
- *a.* Souvenir sheet 35.00 35.00

No. C76a measures 85x110mm, with deep blue inscriptions in upper and lower margins. It also exists unwatermarked or with papermaker's watermark. Value, $25. Souvenir sheet issued without gum.

Joaquim Nabuco (1849-1910), Lawyer and Writer — AP32

1949, Aug. 30 *Perf. 12*

C77 AP32 3.80cr rose lilac 2.00 .25
- *a.* Wmk. 256, imperf. *25.00*

Maracanã Stadium AP33

Soccer Player and Flag — AP34

Perf. 11x12, 12x11

1950, June 24 Litho. Wmk. 267
C78 AP33 1.20cr ultra & salmon 2.00 .40
C79 AP34 5.80cr bl, yel grn & yel 7.50 .55

4th World Soccer Championship, Rio.

AP35

Symbolical of Brazilian population growth.

1950, July 10 ***Perf. 12x11***
C80 AP35 1.20cr red brown 1.25 .25

Issued to publicize the 6th Brazilian census.

AP36

Design: J. B. Marcelino Champagnat.

1956, Sept. 8 Engr. ***Perf. 11½***
C81 AP36 3.30cr rose lilac .25 .25

50th anniversary of the arrival of the Marist Brothers in Northern Brazil.

Santos-Dumont's 1906 Plane — AP37

1956 Photo.
C82 AP37 3cr dk blue grn .80 .25
C83 AP37 3.30cr brt ultra .35 .25
C84 AP37 4cr dp claret .50 .25
C85 AP37 6.50cr red brown .35 .25
C86 AP37 11.50cr orange red 1.25 .35
Nos. C82-C86 (5) 3.25 1.35

Souvenir Sheet

C86A AP37 Sheet of 4 22.50 5.75
b. 3cr dark carmine 2.50 .40

1st flight by Santos-Dumont, 50th anniv. Issued: No. C86A, 10/14; others 10/16.

Lord Baden-Powell AP38

1957, Aug. 1 Unwmk.

Granite Paper

C87 AP38 3.30cr deep red lilac .50 .25

Centenary of the birth of Lord Baden-Powell, founder of the Boy Scouts.

UN Emblem, Soldier and Map of Suez Canal Area AP39

Wmk. 267

1957, Oct. 24 Engr. ***Perf. 11½***
C88 AP39 3.30cr dark blue .25 .25

Brazilian contingent of the UN Emergency Force.

Basketball Player — AP40

1959, May 30 Photo. ***Perf. 11½***
C89 AP40 3.30cr brt red brn & bl .50 .30

Brazil's victory in the World Basketball Championships of 1959.

Symbol of Flight AP41

1959, Oct. 21 Wmk. 267
C90 AP41 3.30cr deep ultra .25 .25

Issued to publicize Week of the Wing.

Caravelle AP42

1959, Dec. 18 ***Perf. 11½***
C91 AP42 6.50cr ultra .25 .25

Inauguration of Brazilian jet flights.

Pres. Adolfo Lopez Mateos — AP43

1960, Jan. 19 Photo. Wmk. 267
C92 AP43 6.50cr brown .25 .25

Issued to commemorate the visit of President Adolfo Lopez Mateos of Mexico.
Exists unwatermarked. Value $150.

Pres. Dwight D. Eisenhower AP44

1960, Feb. 23 ***Perf. 11½***
C93 AP44 6.50cr deep orange .25 .25

Visit of Pres. Dwight D. Eisenhower.

World Refugee Year Emblem — AP45

1960, Apr. 7 Wmk. 268
C94 AP45 6.50cr blue .25 .25

WRY, July 1, 1959-June 30, 1960.

Type of Regular Issue and

Tower at Brasilia — AP46

Designs: 3.30cr, Square of the Three Entities. 4cr, Cathedral. 11.50cr, Plan of Brasilia.

Perf. 11x11½, 11½x11

1960, Apr. 21 Photo. Wmk. 267
C95 A436 3.30cr violet .25 .25
C96 A436 4cr blue .30 .25
C97 AP46 6.50cr rose carmine .30 .25
C98 A436 11.50cr brown .30 .25
Nos. C95-C98 (4) 1.15 1.00

Inauguration of Brazil's new capital, Brasilia, Apr. 21, 1960.

Chrismon and Oil Lamp AP47

1960, May 16 ***Perf. 11x11½***
C99 AP47 3.30cr lilac rose .25 .25

7th Natl. Eucharistic Congress at Curitiba.

Cross, Sugarloaf Mountain and Emblem — AP48

1960, July 1 Wmk. 267
C100 AP48 6.50cr brt blue .25 .25

10th Cong. of the World Baptist Alliance, Rio.

Boy Scout — AP49

1960, July 23 ***Perf. 11½x11***
C101 AP49 3.30cr orange ver .30 .25

Boy Scouts of Brazil, 50th anniversary.

Caravel — AP50

1960, Aug. 5 Engr. Wmk. 268
C102 AP50 6.50cr black .25 .25

Prince Henry the Navigator, 500th death anniv.

Maria E. Bueno AP51

1960, Dec. 15 Photo. ***Perf. 11x11½***
C103 AP51 60cr pale brown .30 .25

Victory at Wimbledon of Maria E. Bueno, women's singles tennis champion.

War Memorial, Sugarloaf Mountain and Allied Flags — AP52

1960, Dec. 22 Wmk. 268
C104 AP52 3.30cr lilac rose .25 .25

Reburial of Brazilian servicemen of WW II.

Power Line and Map — AP53

1961, Jan. 20 ***Perf. 11½x11***
C105 AP53 3.30cr lilac rose .25 .25

Inauguration of Three Marias Dam and hydroelectric station in Minas Gerais.

Malaria Eradication Emblem — AP54

1962, May 24 Wmk. 267 Engr.

C106	AP54	21cr dark blue	.25	.25

WHO drive to eradicate malaria.

F. A. de Varnhagen — AP55

1966, Feb. 17 Photo. Wmk. 267

C107	AP55	45cr red brown	.25	.25

Francisco Adolfo de Varnhagen, Viscount of Porto Seguro (1816-1878), historian and diplomat.

Map of the Americas and Alliance for Progress Emblem
AP56

1966, Mar. 14 ***Perf. 11x11½***

C108	AP56	120cr grnsh bl & vio bl	.30	.25

5th anniv. of the Alliance for Progress.

A souvenir card contains one impression of No. C108, imperf. Size: 113x160mm.

Nun and Globe — AP57

1966, Mar. 25 Photo. ***Perf. 11½x11***

C109	AP57	35cr violet	.25	.25

Centenary of the arrival of the teaching Sisters of St. Dorothea.

Face of Jesus from Shroud of Turin — AP58

1966, June 3 Photo. Wmk. 267

C110	AP58	45cr brown org	.30	.25

Issued to commemorate Vatican II, the 21st Ecumenical Council of the Roman Catholic Church, Oct. 11, 1962-Dec. 8, 1965.

A souvenir card contains one impression of No. C110, imperf. Size: 100x39mm.

Admiral Mariz e Barros — AP59

1966, June 13 Photo. Wmk. 267

C111	AP59	35cr red brown	.25	.25

Death centenary of Admiral Antonio Carlos Mariz e Barros, who died in the Battle of Itaperu.

"Youth" by Eliseu Visconti — AP60

1966, July 31 ***Perf. 11½x11***

C112	AP60	120cr red brown	.55	.25

Birth centenary of Eliseu Visconti, painter.

SPECIAL DELIVERY STAMPS

No. 191 Surcharged

1930 Unwmk. ***Perf. 12***

E1	A62	1000r on 200r dp blue	6.50	1.25
a.		Inverted surcharge	700.00	
b.		Red surcharge	450.00	

POSTAGE DUE STAMPS

D1

1889 Unwmk. Typo. ***Rouletted***

J1	D1	10r carmine	2.00	1.40
J2	D1	20r carmine	2.40	2.00
J3	D1	50r carmine	4.00	4.00
J4	D1	100r carmine	2.00	1.40
J5	D1	200r carmine	60.00	20.00
J6	D1	300r carmine	5.25	*7.25*
J7	D1	500r carmine	5.25	*7.25*
J8	D1	700r carmine	8.75	*12.00*
J9	D1	1000r carmine	8.75	8.75
		Nos. J1-J9 (9)	98.40	64.05

Counterfeits are common.

1890

J10	D1	10r orange	.65	.25
J11	D1	20r ultra	.65	.25
J12	D1	50r olive	1.40	.25
J13	D1	200r magenta	5.25	.60
J14	D1	300r blue green	2.75	1.50
J15	D1	500r slate	4.00	2.75
J16	D1	700r purple	4.00	*8.00*
J17	D1	1000r dk violet	5.25	4.75
		Nos. J10-J17 (8)	23.95	18.35

Counterfeits are common.

D2

1895-1901 ***Perf. 11x11½***

J18	D2	10r dk blue ('01)	2.00	1.25
J19	D2	20r yellow grn	21.00	2.75
J20	D2	50r yellow grn ('01)	8.75	5.25
J21	D2	100r brick red	5.50	1.25
a.		Double impression	1,200.	1,200.
J22	D2	200r violet	5.50	.60
J23	D2	300r dull blue	2.75	2.25
J24	D2	2000r brown	13.00	13.00
		Nos. J18-J24 (7)	58.50	26.35

Perf. 13

J18c	D2	10r dk blue	20.00	2.50
J19c	D2	20r yellow grn	10.00	2.50
J20c	D2	50r yellow grn	15.00	11.00
J21c	D2	100r brick red	10.00	4.50
J22c	D2	200r gray lilac	20.00	4.50

Perf. 13x11

J19d	D2	20r yellow grn	11.00	10.00
J20d	D2	50r yellow grn	10.00	10.00
J23d	D2	300r bluish gray	37.50	14.00
J24d	D2	2000r brn, perf. 13x11x11x11	37.50	37.50

Perf. 11

Thick Paper

J21e	D2	100r brick red	8.00	2.75
J22e	D2	200r gray lilac	5.25	1.75

1906 Wmk. 97

J25	D2	100r brick red	4.75	2.00

Wmk. (97? or 98?)

J26	D2	200r violet	8.75	*15.00*
a.		Wmk. 97	350.00	125.00
b.		Wmk. 98	15.00	*47.50*

D3

1906-10 Unwmk. Engr. ***Perf. 12***

J28	D3	10r slate	.25	.25
J29	D3	20r brt violet	.25	.25
J30	D3	50r dk green	.30	.25
J31	D3	100r carmine	1.40	.60
J32	D3	200r dp blue	1.00	.25
J33	D3	300r gray blk	.75	*1.25*
J34	D3	400r olive grn	1.40	.60
J35	D3	500r dk violet	35.00	35.00
J36	D3	600r violet ('10)	1.40	*2.50*
J37	D3	700r red brown	35.00	35.00
J38	D3	1000r red	2.25	*3.25*
J39	D3	2000r green	4.75	*5.50*
J40	D3	5000r choc ('10)	1.50	*37.50*
		Nos. J28-J40 (13)	85.25	122.20

D4

1919-23 Typo. ***Perf. 12½***

J41	D4	5r red brown	.60	.45
J42	D4	10r violet	.60	.45
J43	D4	20r olive gray	3.00	3.00
J44	D4	50r green ('23)	.25	.25
J45	D4	100r red	5.00	2.00
J46	D4	200r blue	15.00	2.10
J47	D4	400r brown ('23)	1.75	1.60
		Nos. J41-J47 (7)	26.20	9.85

Perf. 11x10½

J43a	D4	20r olive gray	.25	.25
J44a	D4	50r green	.25	.25
J45a	D4	100r red	1.60	.25
J46a	D4	200r blue	7.50	2.00

Perf. 12½ (J48-J49), 12½x13½

1924-35 Wmk. 100

J48	D4	5r red brown	.25	.25
J49	D4	100r carmine	.85	*1.50*
J50	D4	200r slate bl ('29)	1.25	.50
J51	D4	400r dp brn ('29)	1.25	1.25
J52	D4	600r dk vio ('29)	1.40	1.25
J53	D4	600r orange ('35)	.60	.60
		Nos. J48-J53 (6)	5.60	5.35

1924 Wmk. 193 ***Perf. 11x10½***

J54	D4	100r red	55.00	55.00
J55	D4	200r slate blue	6.00	6.00

1925-27 Wmk. 101 ***Perf. 11x10½***

J56	D4	20r olive gray	.25	.25
J57	D4	100r red, perf. 13x13½	1.25	1.25
J58	D4	200r slate blue	10.00	3.75
a.		Perf. 13x13½	3.75	1.75
J59	D4	400r brown	3.25	2.00
J60	D4	600r dk violet	5.50	5.50
		Nos. J56-J60 (5)	20.25	12.75

Wmk. E U BRASIL Multiple (218)

1929-30 ***Perf. 12½x13½***

J61	D4	100r light red	.50	.50
J62	D4	200r blue black	1.75	1.75
J63	D4	400r brown	1.75	1.75
J64	D4	1000r myrtle green	1.75	1.75
		Nos. J61-J64 (4)	5.75	5.75

1931-36 Wmk. 222 ***Perf. 11***

J65	D4	10r lt violet ('35)	.25	.25
J66	D4	20r black ('33)	.75	.75
a.		Perf. 12½x13½	.25	.25
J67	D4	50r blue grn ('35)	.75	.50
J68	D4	100r rose red ('35)	.75	.50
J69	D4	200r sl blue ('35)	2.00	1.25
J70	D4	400r blk brn ('35)	3.25	1.50
J71	D4	600r dk violet	.75	.50
J72	D4	1000r myrtle grn	1.25	1.00
a.		Perf. 12½x13½	.65	.85
J73	D4	2000r brown ('36)	1.25	1.25
J74	D4	5000r indigo ('36)	1.75	1.75
		Nos. J65-J74 (10)	12.75	9.25

1938 Wmk. 249 ***Perf. 11***

J75	D4	200r slate blue	2.75	1.25

1940 Typo. Wmk. 256

J76	D4	10r light violet	1.10	1.10
J77	D4	20r black	1.10	1.10
J79	D4	100r rose red	1.10	1.10
J80	D4	200r myrtle green	2.40	1.10
		Nos. J76-J80 (4)	5.70	4.40

1942 Wmk. 264

J81	D4	10r lt violet	.25	.25
J82	D4	20r olive blk	.25	.25
J83	D4	50r lt blue grn	.25	.25
J84	D4	100r vermilion	1.10	1.10
J85	D4	200r gray blue	1.75	1.75
J86	D4	400r claret	1.10	1.10
J87	D4	600r rose vio	.75	.50
J88	D4	1000r dk bl grn	.75	.50
J89	D4	2000r dp yel brn	1.75	1.75
J90	D4	5000r indigo	.90	.90
		Nos. J81-J90 (10)	8.85	8.35

1949 Wmk. 268

J91	D4	10c pale rose lilac	1.40	1.40
J92	D4	20r black	20.00	20.00

No. J92 exists in shades of gray ranging to gray olive.

OFFICIAL STAMPS

Pres. Affonso Penna — O1

Unwmk.

1906, Nov. 15 Engr. ***Perf. 12***

O1	O1	10r org & grn	1.00	.25
O2	O1	20r org & grn	1.25	.25
O3	O1	50r org & grn	1.90	.25
O4	O1	100r org & grn	1.00	.25
O5	O1	200r org & grn	1.25	.25
O6	O1	300r org & grn	4.00	.40
O7	O1	400r org & grn	7.25	2.00
O8	O1	500r org & grn	4.00	1.40
O9	O1	700r org & grn	4.75	2.75
O10	O1	1000r org & grn	4.75	.80
O11	O1	2000r org & grn	6.50	1.60
O12	O1	5000r org & grn	12.00	1.40
O13	O1	10,000r org & grn	12.00	1.00
		Nos. O1-O13 (13)	61.65	12.60

The portrait is the same but the frame differs for each denomination of this issue.

Pres. Hermes da Fonseca — O2

1913, Nov. 15 Center in Black

O14	O2	10r gray	.25	*.40*
O15	O2	20r ol grn	.25	*.40*
O16	O2	50r gray	.25	*.40*
O17	O2	100r ver	.60	.25
O18	O2	200r blue	1.40	.25
O19	O2	500r orange	2.75	.60
O20	O2	600r violet	4.00	2.50
O21	O2	1000r blk brn	4.00	1.75
O22	O2	2000r red brn	7.00	2.00
O23	O2	5000r brown	8.75	3.50

O24 O2 10,000r black 14.00 7.25
O25 O2 20,000r blue 26.00 26.00
O26 O2 50,000r green 50.00 50.00
O27 O2 100,000r org red 200.00 200.00
O28 O2 500,000r brown 325.00 325.00
O29 O2 1,000,000r dk brn 325.00 325.00
Nos. O14-O29 (16) 969.25 945.30

The portrait is the same on all denominations of this series but there are eight types of the frame.

Pres. Wenceslau Braz — O3

Perf. 11, 11½

1919, Apr. 11 **Wmk. 100**
O30 O3 10r olive green .40 *5.50*
O31 O3 50r green 1.00 1.00
O32 O3 100r rose red 2.00 .60
O33 O3 200r dull blue 2.50 .60
O34 O3 500r orange 7.00 *40.00*
Nos. O30-O34 (5) 12.90 47.70

The official decree called for eleven stamps in this series but only five were issued.
For surcharges see Nos. 293-297.

NEWSPAPER STAMPS

N1

Rouletted

1889, Feb. 1 **Unwmk.** **Litho.**
P1 N1 10r yellow 5.00 5.00
a. Pair, imperf. between 180.00 180.00
P2 N1 20r yellow 12.00 12.00
P3 N1 50r yellow 18.00 15.00
P4 N1 100r yellow 7.50 3.00
P5 N1 200r yellow 3.00 3.00
P6 N1 300r yellow 3.00 3.00
P7 N1 500r yellow 60.00 15.00
P8 N1 700r yellow 6.00 *24.00*
P9 N1 1000r yellow 6.00 *24.00*
Nos. P1-P9 (9) 120.50 104.00

For surcharges see Nos. 125-127.

1889, May 1
P10 N1 10r olive 3.00 1.50
P11 N1 20r green 3.00 1.50
P12 N1 50r brn yel 3.00 1.50
P13 N1 100r violet 4.50 3.00
P14 N1 200r black 4.50 3.00
P15 N1 300r carmine 21.00 21.00
P16 N1 500r green 82.50 *90.00*
P17 N1 700r pale blue 50.00 *55.00*
P18 N1 1000r brown 21.00 *82.50*
Nos. P10-P18 (9) 192.50 259.00

For surcharges see Nos. 128-135.

N2

White Wove Paper Thin to Thick

1890 **Typo.** ***Perf. 12½-14***
P19 N2 10r blue 22.50 12.00
P20 N2 20r emerald 70.00 21.00
P21 N2 100r violet 22.50 22.50
Nos. P19-P21 (3) 115.00 55.50

Perf. 11-11½
P19b N2 10r blue 50.00 20.00
P20b N2 20r emerald 425.00 125.00
P21b N2 100r violet 135.00 37.50

Perf. 11-11½x12½-14
P19c N2 10r blue — 1,500.
P20c N2 20r emerald 300.00 27.50
P21c N2 100r violet 20.00 20.00

For surcharge see No. 137.
No. P19-P21 exist on medium and thick papers.

N3

1890-93 ***Perf. 11-11½***
P22 N3 10r ultramarine 7.50 5.50
P23 N3 10r ultra, *buff* 7.50 3.00
P24 N3 20r green 10.00 3.00
f. 20r grn, perf. 11 50.00 20.00
h. 20r grn, perf. 13 50.00 22.00
j. 20r grn, perf. 11x13 40.00 15.00
P25 N3 50r yel grn ('93) 40.00 15.00
Nos. P22-P25 (4) 65.00 26.50

Perf. 12½-14
P22e N3 10r ultra 3.00 2.00
P23e N3 10r blue, *buff* 3.00 2.00
P24e N3 20r blue green 8.00 4.00

For surcharges see Nos. 136, 138-139.

POSTAL TAX STAMPS

Icarus from the Santos-Dumont Monument at St. Cloud, France — PT1

Perf. 13½x12½

1933, Oct. 1 **Typo.** **Wmk. 222**
RA1 PT1 100r deep brown .75 .25
a. Perf. 11 1.30 .25

Honoring the Brazilian aviator, Santos-Dumont. Its use was obligatory as a tax on all correspondence sent to countries in South America, the US and Spain. Its use on correspondence to other countries was optional. The funds obtained were used for the construction of airports throughout Brazil.

Catalogue values for unused stamps in this section, from this point to the end of the section, are for Never Hinged items.

Father Joseph Damien and Children PT2

Perf. 12x11

1952, Nov. 24 **Litho.** **Wmk. 267**
RA2 PT2 10c yellow brown 1.00 .25

1953, Nov. 30
RA3 PT2 10c yellow green 1.00 .25

Father Bento Dias Pacheco — PT3

1954, Nov. 22 **Photo.** ***Perf. 11½***
RA4 PT3 10c violet blue .25 .25

1955-69, Nov. 24
RA5 PT3 10c dk car rose .25 .25
RA6 PT3 10c org red ('57) .25 .25
RA7 PT3 10c dp emer ('58) .25 .25
RA8 PT3 10c rod lilac ('61) .25 .25
RA9 PT3 10c choc ('62) .25 .25
RA10 PT3 10c slate ('63) .25 .25
RA11 PT3 2cr dp mag ('64) .25 .25
RA12 PT3 2cr violet ('65) .25 .25
RA13 PT3 2cr orange ('66) .30 .25
RA14 PT3 5c brt yel grn ('68) 4.00 1.20
RA15 PT3 5c deep plum ('69) .80 .30

Issued: 11/25, No. RA14; 11/28, No. RA15; others, 11/24.

Eunice Weaver — PT4

1971-73, Nov. 24
RA16 PT4 10c slate green .35 .25
RA17 PT4 10c brt rose lil ('73) .50 .30

Father Nicodemos — PT5

1975, Nov. 24 **Litho.** **Unwmk.**
RA18 PT5 10c sepia .40 .40

Father Vicente Borgard (1888-1977) — PT6

1983, Nov. 24 **Photo.** ***Perf. 11½***
RA19 PT6 10cr brown 2.75 2.00

Father Bento Dias Pacheco — PT7

1984, Nov. 24 **Photo.** ***Perf. 11½***
RA20 PT7 30cr deep blue .60 .40

1985, Nov. 24 **Litho.**
RA21 PT7 100cr lake .40 .25

1986, Nov. 24 **Litho.**
RA22 PT7 10c gray brown .30 .25

1987, Nov. 24 **Photo.**
RA23 PT7 30c sage green .30 .25

Father Santiago Uchoa — PT8

1988, Nov. 24 **Litho.**
RA24 PT8 1.30cz dull red brn .40 .35

See Nos. RA29-RA30.

Fr. Joseph Damien — PT9

1989-92 **Photo.** ***Perf. 11½***
RA25 PT9 2c deep lilac rose .30 .25
RA26 PT9 50c blue .25 .25

Perf. 12½
RA27 PT9 3cr green .25 .25
RA28 PT9 30cr brown .25 .25
Nos. RA25-RA28 (4) 1.05 1.00

Issued: 2c, Nov. 24; 50c, Nov. 24, 1990; 3cr, Nov. 24, 1991; 30cr, Nov. 24, 1992.

Father Santiago Uchoa Type of 1988

1993, Nov. 24 **Photo.** ***Perf. 12½***
RA29 PT8 50c blue .25 .25

1994, Nov. 24
RA30 PT8 1c dull lake .25 .25

The tax was for the care and treatment of lepers.
Use of Nos. RA2-RA30 was required for one week.

POSTAL TAX SEMI-POSTAL STAMP

Catalogue values for unused stamps in this section are for Never Hinged items.

Icarus — PTSP1

Wmk. 267

1947, Nov. 15 **Typo.** ***Perf. 11***
RAB1 PTSP1 40c + 10c brt red .80 .50
a. Pair, imperf. between *350.00*

Aviation Week, November 15-22, 1947, and compulsory on all domestic correspondence during that week.

BRITISH ANTARCTIC TERRITORY

'bri-tish ˌant-'ärk-tik 'ter-ə-ˌtōr-ē

LOCATION — South Atlantic Ocean between 20-80 degrees longitude and south of 60 degrees latitude
GOVT. — British territory
POP. — About 300 scientific staff at research stations.

This territory includes Graham Land (Palmer Peninsula), South Shetland Islands and South Orkney Islands. Formerly part of Falkland Islands Dependency.

12 Pence = 1 Shilling
20 Shillings = 1 Pound
100 Pence = 1 Pound (1971)

Catalogue values for all unused stamps in this country are for Never Hinged items.

M. V. Kista Dan — A1

1p, Skiers hauling load. 1½p, Muskeg (tractor). 2p, Skiers. 2½p, Beaver seaplane. 3p, R.R.S. John Biscoe. 4p, Camp scene. 6p, H.M.S. Protector. 9p, Dog sled. 1sh, Otter skiplane. 2sh, Huskies & aurora australis. 2sh6p, Helicopter. 5sh, Snocat (truck). 10sh, R.R.S. Shackleton. £1, Map of Antarctica.

Perf. 11x11½

1963, Feb. 1 Engr. Wmk. 314

1	A1	½p dark blue	1.00	*1.75*
2	A1	1p brown	1.25	.85
3	A1	1½p plum & red	1.40	1.40
4	A1	2p rose violet	1.50	.85
5	A1	2½p dull green	2.75	1.30
6	A1	3p Prus blue	2.75	1.40
7	A1	4p sepia	2.25	1.50
8	A1	6p dk blue & olive	4.00	2.25
9	A1	9p olive	3.00	2.00
10	A1	1sh steel blue	3.25	1.25
11	A1	2sh dl vio & bis	20.00	9.00
12	A1	2sh6p blue	19.00	12.00
13	A1	5sh rose red & org	22.50	17.50
14	A1	10sh grn & vio bl	42.50	24.00
15	A1	£1 black & blue	45.00	45.00
		Nos. 1-15 (15)	172.15	122.05

See No. 24. For surcharges see Nos. 25-38.

Common Design Types pictured following the introduction.

Churchill Memorial Issue
Common Design Type

1966, Jan. 24 Photo. *Perf. 14*

16	CD319	½p bright blue	.95	3.25
17	CD319	1p green	3.75	3.25
18	CD319	1sh brown	17.50	5.50
19	CD319	2sh violet	19.00	6.00
		Nos. 16-19 (4)	41.20	18.00

Lemaire Channel, Iceberg and Adelie Penguins A2

Designs: 6p, Weather sonde and operator. 1sh, Muskeg (tractor) pulling tent equipment. 2sh, Surveyors with theodolite.

1969, Feb. 6 Litho.

20	A2	3½p blue, vio bl & blk	3.25	2.50
21	A2	6p emer, blk & dp org	1.00	*1.75*
22	A2	1sh ultra, blk & ver	1.00	*1.60*
23	A2	2sh grnsh bl, blk & och	1.00	*2.25*
		Nos. 20-23 (4)	6.25	*8.10*

25 years of continuous scientific work in the Antarctic.

Type of 1963
£1, H.M.S. Endurance and helicopter.

1969, Dec. 1 Engr. *Perf. 11x11½*

24	A1	£1 black & rose red	160.00	140.00

Nos. 1-14 Surcharged in Decimal Currency; Three Bars Overprinted

1971, Feb. 15 Wmk. 314

25	A1	½p on ½p	.65	*3.50*
26	A1	1p on 1p	1.00	1.00
27	A1	1½p on 1½p	1.25	.80
28	A1	2p on 2p	1.25	.50
29	A1	2½p on 2½p	3.25	2.50
30	A1	3p on 3p	2.25	.80
31	A1	4p on 4p	2.50	.80
32	A1	5p on 6p	4.50	3.50
33	A1	6p on 9p	16.00	8.00
34	A1	7½p on 1sh	17.00	9.25
35	A1	10p on 2sh	17.00	12.00
36	A1	15p on 2sh6p	17.00	12.00
37	A1	25p on 5sh	20.00	15.00
38	A1	50p on 10sh	30.00	30.00
		Nos. 25-38 (14)	133.65	99.65

Map of Antarctica, Aurora Australis, Explorers — A3

Map of Antarctica, Aurora Australis and: 4p, Sea gulls. 5p, Seals. 10p, Penguins.

Litho. & Engr.

1971, June 23 *Perf. 14x13*

39	A3	1½p multicolored	6.00	2.00
40	A3	4p multicolored	15.00	5.00
41	A3	5p multicolored	10.00	8.50
42	A3	10p multicolored	22.50	10.00
		Nos. 39-42 (4)	53.50	25.50

10th anniv. of the Antarctic Treaty pledging peaceful uses of and scientific cooperation in Antarctica.

Silver Wedding Issue, 1972
Common Design Type

Design: Queen Elizabeth II, Prince Philip, seals and emperor penguins.

1972, Dec. 13 Photo. *Perf. 14x14½*

43	CD324	5p rose brn & multi	2.75	2.40
44	CD324	10p olive & multi	3.75	3.25

Capt. Cook and "Resolution" — A4

Polar Explorers and their Crafts: 1p, Thaddeus von Bellingshausen and "Vostok." 1½p, James Weddell and "Jane." 2p, John Biscoe and "Tula." 2½p, J. S. C. Dumont d'Urville and "Astrolabe." 3p, James Clark Ross and "Erebus." 4p, C. A. Larsen and "Jason." 5p, Adrien de Gerlache and "Belgica." 6p, Otto Nordenskjöld and "Antarctic." 7½p, W. S. Bruce and "Scotia." 10p, Jean-Baptiste Charcot and "Pourquoi Pas?" 15p, Ernest Shackleton and "Endurance." 25p, Hubert Wilkins and airplane "San Francisco." 50p, Lincoln Ellsworth and airplane "Polar Star." £1, John Rymill and "Penola."

Wmk. 373

1975-80 Litho. *Perf. 14½*

45	A4	½p multi	.90	*3.00*
46	A4	1p multi ('78)	.75	*2.50*
47	A4	1½p multi ('78)	.75	*2.50*
48	A4	2p multi ('79)	2.50	*3.50*
49	A4	2½p multi ('79)	2.50	*3.50*
50	A4	3p multi ('79)	3.00	*3.75*
52	A4	5p multi ('79)	3.00	*4.00*
55	A4	10p multi ('79)	2.25	*3.75*
56	A4	15p multi ('79)	1.50	*2.50*
57	A4	25p multi ('79)	1.50	1.60
58	A4	50p multi ('79)	2.40	3.25
59	A4	£1 multi ('78)	5.00	2.50
		Nos. 45-59 (12)	26.05	36.35

1973, Feb. 14 Wmk. 314

45a	A4	½p multi	*1.50*	*2.75*
46a	A4	1p multi	*2.75*	*4.25*
47a	A4	1½p multi	*11.50*	*5.50*
48a	A4	2p multi	2.50	2.25
49a	A4	2½p multi	2.00	*2.25*
50a	A4	3p multi	1.10	*2.25*
51a	A4	4p multi	1.10	*2.25*
52a	A4	5p multi	1.25	*2.25*
53a	A4	6p multi	1.50	*2.25*
54a	A4	7½p multi	1.75	*3.00*
55a	A4	10p multi	3.00	*3.50*
56a	A4	15p multi	6.00	5.00
57a	A4	25p multi	3.75	*5.00*
58a	A4	50p multi	3.00	*5.50*
59a	A4	£1 multi	5.25	*9.50*
		Nos. 45a-59a (15)	47.95	57.50

1980 Wmk. 373 *Perf. 12*

51	A4	4p multi	.65	*2.00*
53	A4	6p multi	1.00	*3.50*
54	A4	7½p multi	1.50	*4.00*
55b	A4	10p multi	.75	*3.50*
56b	A4	15p multi	.75	*3.50*
57b	A4	25p multi	1.25	*3.00*
58b	A4	50p multi	2.40	*3.00*
59b	A4	£1 multi	4.75	*4.50*
		Nos. 51-59b (8)	13.05	27.00

Princess Anne's Wedding Issue
Common Design Type

1973, Nov. 14 Wmk. 314 *Perf. 14*

60	CD325	5p ocher & multi	.30	.30
61	CD325	15p blue grn & multi	.80	.80

Wedding of Princess Anne and Capt. Mark Phillips, Nov. 14, 1973. Nos. 60-61 were not available locally until Dec. 23, 1973, and first-day covers bear that date.

Churchill and Map of Churchill Peninsula A5

Design: 15p, Churchill and "Trepassey" of Operation Tabarin, 1943.

1974, Nov. 30 Litho. *Perf. 14*

62	A5	5p multicolored	1.50	1.50
63	A5	15p multicolored	2.50	2.50
a.		Souvenir sheet of 2, #62-63	12.50	12.50

Sir Winston Churchill (1874-1965).

Humpback Whale — A6

Wmk. 373

1977, Jan. 4 Litho. *Perf. 14*

64	A6	2p Sperm whale	6.00	4.50
65	A6	8p Fin whale	7.00	5.00
66	A6	11p shown	7.25	5.00
67	A6	25p Blue whale	8.00	6.75
		Nos. 64-67 (4)	28.25	21.25

Conservation of whales.

Prince Philip in Antarctica, 1956-57 — A7

Designs: 11p, Coronation oath. 33p, Queen before taking oath.

1977, Feb. 7 *Perf. 13½x14*

68	A7	6p multicolored	.65	.50
69	A7	11p multicolored	.75	.60
70	A7	33p multicolored	1.90	.80
		Nos. 68-70 (3)	3.30	1.90

25th anniv. of the reign of Elizabeth II.

Elizabeth II Coronation Anniversary Issue
Common Design Types
Souvenir Sheet

Unwmk.

1978, June 2 Litho. *Perf. 15*

71		Sheet of 6	6.00	6.00
a.		CD326 25p Black bull of Clarence	1.00	1.00
b.		CD327 25p Elizabeth II	1.00	1.00
c.		CD328 25p Emperor penguin	1.00	1.00

No. 71 contains 2 se-tenant strips of Nos. 71a-71c, separated by horizontal gutter with commemorative and descriptive inscriptions and showing central part of coronation procession with coach.

Macaroni Penguins — A8

Perf. 13½x14

1979, Jan. 14 Litho. Wmk. 373

72	A8	3p shown	10.00	10.00
73	A8	8p Gentoo	3.00	3.00
74	A8	11p Adelie	3.25	3.25
75	A8	25p Emperor	4.25	4.25
		Nos. 72-75 (4)	20.50	20.50

John Barrow, Tula, Society Emblem A9

Royal Geographical Society Sesquicentennial (Past Presidents and Expedition Scenes): 7p, Clement Markham 11p, Lord Curzon. 15p, William Goodenough. 22p, James Wordie. 30p, Raymond Priestley.

Wmk. 373

1980, Dec. 1 Litho. *Perf. 13½*

76	A9	3p multicolored	.25	.25
77	A9	7p multicolored	.25	.25
78	A9	11p multicolored	.30	.30
79	A9	15p multicolored	.35	.35
80	A9	22p multicolored	.55	.55
81	A9	30p multicolored	.70	.70
		Nos. 76-81 (6)	2.40	2.40

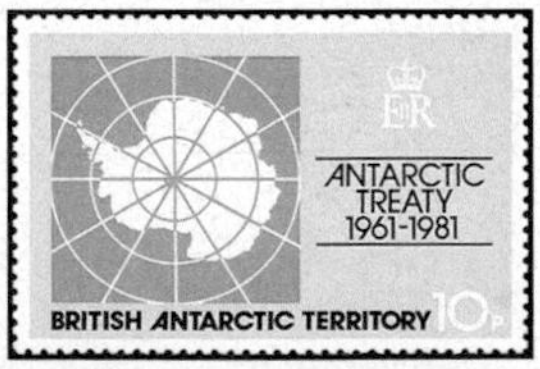

20th Anniv. of Antarctic Treaty — A10

10p, Map. 13p, Conservation research. 25p, Satellite image mapping. 26p, Global geophysics.

1981, Dec. 1 *Perf. 13½x14*

82	A10	10p multicolored	.25	*.65*
83	A10	13p multicolored	.35	*.75*
84	A10	25p multicolored	.60	*.80*
85	A10	26p multicolored	.65	*.80*
		Nos. 82-85 (4)	1.85	3.00

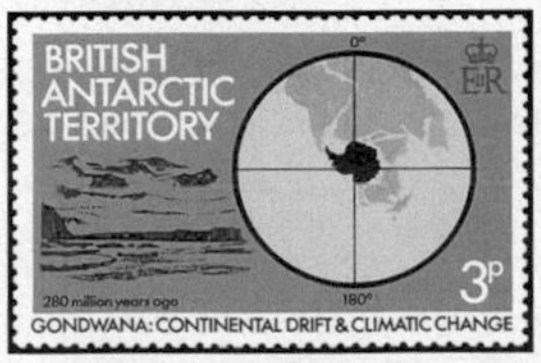

Continental Drift and Climatic Change — A11

1982, Mar. 8 Litho. *Perf. 13½x14*

86	A11	3p Land, water	.30	*.35*
87	A11	6p Shrubs	.30	*.45*
88	A11	10p Dinosaur	.30	*.55*
89	A11	13p Volcano	.45	*.65*

90	A11	25p	Trees	.60	*.75*
91	A11	26p	Penguins	.60	*.75*
			Nos. 86-91 (6)	2.55	3.50

Princess Diana Issue
Common Design Type

5p, Arms. 17p, Diana, by Bryan Organ. 37p, Wedding. 50p, Portrait.

1982, July 1 Litho. *Perf. 14½x14*

92	CD333	5p	multi	.35	.25
93	CD333	17p	multi	.70	.70
94	CD333	37p	multi	1.20	1.00
95	CD333	50p	multi	2.00	1.50
			Nos. 92-95 (4)	4.25	3.45

10th Anniv. of Convention for Conservation of Antarctic Seals — A12

1983, Jan. 3 Litho.

96	A12	5p	shown	.30	*.35*
97	A12	10p	Weddell seals	.45	*.50*
98	A12	13p	Elephant seals	.50	*.60*
99	A12	17p	Fur seals	.65	*.75*
100	A12	25p	Ross seal	.70	*.80*
101	A12	34p	Crabeater seals	1.20	*1.40*
			Nos. 96-101 (6)	3.80	*4.40*

Corethron Criophilum — A13

1p, shown. 2p, Desmonema gaudichaudi. 3p, Tomopteris carpenteri. 4p, Pareuchaeta antarctica. 5p, Antarctomysis maxima. 6p, Antarcturus signiensis. 7p, Serolis comuta. 8p, Parathemisto gaudichaudii. 9p, Bovallia gigantea. 10p, Euphausia superba. 15p, Colossendeis australis. 20p, Todarodes sagittatus. 25p, Notothenia neglecta. 50p, Chaenocephalus aceratus. £1, Lobodon carcinophagus. £3, Antarctic marine food chain.

1984, Mar. 15 Litho. *Perf. 14*

102	A13	1p	multicolored	.85	*1.60*
103	A13	2p	multicolored	.90	*1.60*
104	A13	3p	multicolored	.90	*1.60*
105	A13	4p	multicolored	1.00	*1.60*
106	A13	5p	multicolored	1.00	*1.60*
107	A13	6p	multicolored	1.00	*1.60*
108	A13	7p	multicolored	1.00	*1.60*
109	A13	8p	multicolored	1.00	*1.60*
110	A13	9p	multicolored	1.00	*1.60*
110A	A13	10p	multicolored	1.00	*1.60*
111	A13	15p	multicolored	1.00	*1.60*
112	A13	20p	multicolored	1.10	*1.60*
113	A13	25p	multicolored	1.10	*1.60*
114	A13	50p	multicolored	1.75	*2.00*
115	A13	£1	multicolored	2.25	*2.50*
116	A13	£3	multicolored	6.00	6.00
			Nos. 102-116 (16)	22.85	*31.30*

Manned Flight Bicentenary — A14

5p, De Havilland Twin Otter. 13p, De Havilland Single Otter. 17p, Consolidated Canso. 50p, Lockheed Vega.

1983, Dec. 17 Wmk. 373

117	A14	5p	multicolored	.25	*.30*
118	A14	13p	multicolored	.45	*.55*
119	A14	17p	multicolored	.55	*.70*
120	A14	50p	multicolored	1.50	*1.90*
			Nos. 117-120 (4)	2.75	*3.45*

British-Graham Land Expedition, 1934-1937 — A15

Designs: 7p, M. Y. Penola in Stella Creek. 22p, Northern base, Winter Island. 27p, D. H. Fox Moth at southern base, Barry Island. 54p, Dog team near Ablation Point, George VI Sound.

1985, Mar. 23 Litho. *Perf. 14½*

121	A15	7p	multicolored	.50	*.60*
122	A15	22p	multicolored	.80	*.95*
123	A15	27p	multicolored	1.00	*1.20*
124	A15	54p	multicolored	1.90	*2.25*
			Nos. 121-124 (4)	4.20	*5.00*

A16

Naturalists, fauna and flora: 7p, Robert McCormick (1800-1890), Catharacta Skua Maccormicki. 22p, Sir Joseph Dalton Hooker (1817-1911), Deschampsea antarctica. 27p, Jean Rene C. Quoy (1790-1869), Lagenorhynchus cruciger. 54p, James Weddell (1787-1834), Leptonychotes weddelli.

1985, Nov. 4 Litho. *Perf. 14½*

125	A16	7p	multicolored	1.75	*1.50*
126	A16	22p	multicolored	2.25	*1.90*
127	A16	27p	multicolored	2.50	*2.10*
128	A16	54p	multicolored	3.25	*2.75*
			Nos. 125-128 (4)	9.75	*8.25*

A17

Halley's comet: 7p, Edmond Halley. 22p, Halley Station. 27p, Trajectory, 1531. 54p, Giotto space probe.

1986, Jan. 6 Wmk. 373 *Perf. 14*

129	A17	7p	multi	1.40	*1.50*
130	A17	22p	multi	1.75	*2.75*
131	A17	27p	multi	2.00	*3.25*
132	A17	54p	multi	2.60	*5.25*
			Nos. 129-132 (4)	7.75	12.75

Intl. Glaciological Society, 50th Anniv. — A18

Different snowflakes.

1986, Dec. 6 Wmk. 384 *Perf. 14½*

133	A18	10p	dp blue & lt bl	.60	*1.00*
134	A18	24p	blue grn & lt bl grn	.80	*1.50*
135	A18	29p	dp rose lil & lt lil	.85	*1.75*
136	A18	58p	dp vio & pale vio blue	1.90	*2.75*
			Nos. 133-136 (4)	4.15	7.00

Capt. Robert Falcon Scott, CVO RN (1868-1912) A19

Designs: 24p, The Discovery at Hut Point, 1902-1904. 29p, Cape Evans Hut, 1911-1913. 58p, South Pole, 1912.

1987, Mar. 19 Litho. Wmk. 373

137	A19	10p	multicolored	.70	*.95*
138	A19	24p	multicolored	1.25	*2.00*
139	A19	29p	multicolored	1.35	*2.40*
140	A19	58p	multicolored	2.00	*3.25*
			Nos. 137-140 (4)	5.30	8.60

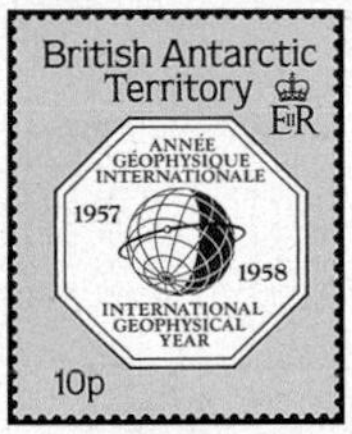

Intl. Geophysical Year, 30th Anniv. — A20

1987, Dec. 25 Wmk. 384

141	A20	10p	Emblem	.50	*.70*
142	A20	24p	Port Lockroy	.75	*1.40*
143	A20	29p	Argentine Islands	1.00	*1.60*
144	A20	58p	Halley Bay	2.00	*2.60*
			Nos. 141-144 (4)	4.25	6.30

Commonwealth Trans-Antarctic Expedition — A21

10p, Aurora over South Ice. 24p, Otter aircraft. 29p, Seismic ice-depth sounding. 58p, Sno-cat over crevasse.

1988, Mar. 19 *Perf. 14*

145	A21	10p	multicolored	.30	*.40*
146	A21	24p	multicolored	.70	*.90*
147	A21	29p	multicolored	.85	*1.05*
148	A21	58p	multicolored	1.75	*2.10*
			Nos. 145-148 (4)	3.60	*4.45*

Lichens A22

10p, Xanthoria elegans. 24p, Usnea aurantiaco-atra. 29p, Cladonia chlorophaea. 58p, Umbilicaria antarctica.

1989, Mar. 25 Wmk. 373

149	A22	10p	multicolored	1.00	*1.15*
150	A22	24p	multicolored	2.00	*2.25*
151	A22	29p	multicolored	2.40	*3.00*
152	A22	58p	multicolored	3.50	*4.50*
			Nos. 149-152 (4)	8.90	*10.90*

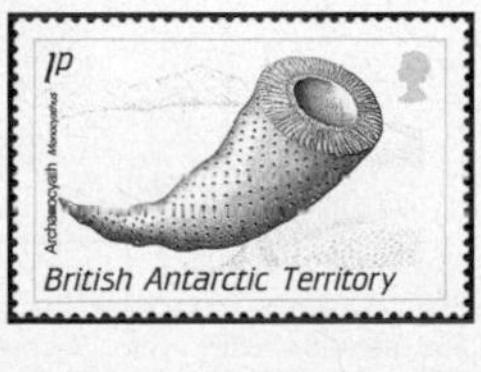

Fossils A23

1p, Archaeocyath. 2p, Brachiopod. 3p, Trilobite (Triplagnostus). 4p, Trilobite (Lyriaspis). 5p, Gymnosperm. 6p, Fern. 7p, Belemnite. 8p, Ammonite (Sanmartinoceras). 9p, Bivalve (Pinna). 10p, Bivalve (Aucellina). 20p, Bivalve (Trigonia). 25p, Gastropod. 50p, Ammonite (Ainoceras). £ 1, Ammonite (Gunnarites). £ 3, Crayfish.

1990, Apr. 2 Litho. Wmk. 384

153	A23	1p	multicolored	1.50	1.50
154	A23	2p	multicolored	1.50	1.50
155	A23	3p	multicolored	1.60	1.60
156	A23	4p	multicolored	1.75	1.75
157	A23	5p	multicolored	1.75	1.75
158	A23	6p	multicolored	1.75	1.75
159	A23	7p	multicolored	1.75	1.90
160	A23	8p	multicolored	1.75	1.90
161	A23	9p	multicolored	1.75	1.90
162	A23	10p	multicolored	1.75	1.90
163	A23	20p	multicolored	3.00	*3.50*
164	A23	25p	multicolored	3.00	*3.50*
165	A23	50p	multicolored	4.00	*5.00*
166	A23	£1	multicolored	7.00	*9.00*
167	A23	£3	multicolored	10.00	*12.00*
			Nos. 153-167 (15)	43.85	*50.45*

Queen Mother, 90th Birthday
Common Design Types

26p, Wedding portrait, 1923. £ 1, Family portrait, 1940.

1990, Aug. 4 Wmk. 384 *Perf. 14x15*

170	CD343 26p	multicolored	1.25	1.25

Perf. 14½

171	CD344 £1	multicolored	4.75	4.75

Age of Dinosaurs A24

12p, Late Cretaceous forest. 26p, Hypsilophodont dinosaur. 31p, Frilled shark. 62p, Mosasaur, plesiosaur.

1991, Mar. 27 Wmk. 373 *Perf. 14*

172	A24	12p	multicolored	1.50	1.50
173	A24	26p	multicolored	2.50	2.50
174	A24	31p	multicolored	2.75	2.75
175	A24	62p	multicolored	4.75	4.75
			Nos. 172-175 (4)	11.50	11.50

Antarctic Ozone Hole — A25

12p, Launching weather balloon. 26p, Measuring ozone. 31p, Ozone hole over Antarctica. 62p, Airplane, chemical studies.

1991, Mar. 30 *Perf. 14½x14*

176	A25	12p	multicolored	1.10	*1.90*
177	A25	26p	multicolored	1.75	*3.00*
178	A25	31p	multicolored	2.25	*3.25*
179	A25	62p	multicolored	4.00	*5.00*
			Nos. 176-179 (4)	9.10	*13.15*

Antarctic Treaty, 30th Anniv. — A26

12p, Dry valley. 26p, Mapping ice sheet. 31p, BIOMASS emblem. 62p, Ross seal.

1991, June 24 *Perf. 14½*

180	A26	12p	multicolored	1.35	1.35
181	A26	26p	multicolored	2.00	2.00
182	A26	31p	multicolored	2.50	2.50
183	A26	62p	multicolored	4.00	4.00
			Nos. 180-183 (4)	9.85	9.85

Royal Research Ship James Clark Ross — A27

Designs: 12p, HMS Erebus and Terror in Antarctic by John W. Carmichael. 26p, Launch of RRS James Clark Ross. 62p, Scientific research.

1991, Dec. 10 ***Perf. 14x14½***

184 A27 12p multicolored 1.15 1.75
185 A27 26p multicolored 2.00 3.00
186 A27 31p shown 2.40 3.50
187 A27 62p multicolored 4.00 5.25
Nos. 184-187 (4) 9.55 13.50

Inscribed in Blue

1991, Dec. 24

188 A27 12p like #184 1.60 2.25
189 A27 26p like #185 2.00 3.25
190 A27 31p like #186 2.50 4.25
191 A27 62p like #187 4.25 5.25
Nos. 188-191 (4) 10.35 15.00

Seals and Penguins A28

4p, Ross seal. 5p, Adelie penguin. 7p, Weddell seal. 29p, Emperor penguin. 34p, Crabeater seal. 68p, Chinstrap penguin.

1992, Oct. 20 ***Perf. 13½***

192 A28 4p multi 1.50 1.75
193 A28 5p multi 1.50 1.75
194 A28 7p multi 1.50 1.75
195 A28 29p multi 3.25 3.75
196 A28 34p multi 3.00 3.75
197 A28 68p multi 3.75 4.25
Nos. 192-197 (6) 14.50 17.00

World Wildlife Fund.

Lower Atmospheric Phenomena A29

14p, Sun pillar at Faraday. 29p, Halo with iceberg. 34p, Lee wave cloud. 68p, Nacreous clouds.

Perf. 14x14½

1992, Dec. 22 **Litho.** **Wmk. 373**

198 A29 14p multi 1.10 1.75
199 A29 29p multi 2.00 2.25
200 A29 34p multi 2.50 3.00
201 A29 68p multi 4.00 5.00
Nos. 198-201 (4) 9.60 12.00

Research Ships A30

1p, SS Fitzroy. 2p, HMS William Scoresby. 3p, SS Eagle. 4p, MV Trepassey. 5p, RRS John Biscoe (I). 10p, MV Norsel. 20p, HMS Protector. 30p, MV Oluf Sven. 50p, RRS John Biscoe (II), RRS Shackleton. £ 1, MV Tottan. £ 3, MV Perla Dan. £ 5, HMS Endurance (I).

Wmk. 373

1993, Dec. 13 **Litho.** ***Perf. 14***

202 A30 1p multi 1.60 2.50
203 A30 2p multi 2.40 2.50
204 A30 3p multi 2.40 2.50
205 A30 4p multi 2.40 2.50
206 A30 5p multi 2.40 2.50
207 A30 10p multi 2.75 3.25
208 A30 20p multi 3.50 4.00
209 A30 30p multi 4.00 4.75
210 A30 50p multi 5.00 6.00
a. Souvenir sheet of 1 4.50 5.25
211 A30 £1 multi 6.75 7.25
a. Souvenir sheet of 1 7.00 8.00
212 A30 £3 multi 14.00 17.00
213 A30 £5 multi 26.00 29.00
Nos. 202-213 (12) 73.20 83.75

No. 210a for Hong Kong '97. Issued 2/3/97.
No. 211a for return of Hong Kong to China. Issued 7/1/97.

Operation Taberin, 50th Anniv. — A31

Designs: 15p, Bransfield House and Post Office, Port Lockroy. 31p, Survey team, Hope Bay. 36p, Dog team, Hope Bay. 72p, SS Fitzroy, HMS William Scoresby at sea.

Wmk. 373

1994, Mar. 19 **Litho.** ***Perf. 14***

214 A31 15p multicolored 1.60 2.25
215 A31 31p multicolored 2.75 3.25
216 A31 36p multicolored 3.25 3.75
217 A31 72p multicolored 4.25 5.00
Nos. 214-217 (4) 11.85 14.25

Old and New Transportation — A32

Designs: 15p, Huskies. 24p, DeHavilland DHC-2 Turbo Beaver, British Antarctic Survey. 31p, Dogs, cargo being taken from aircraft. 36p, DHC-6 Twin Otter, sled team. 62p, DHC-6 in flight. 72p, DHC-6 taxiing down runway.

1994, Mar. 21

218 A32 15p multicolored 1.25 1.25
219 A32 24p multicolored 1.75 1.75
220 A32 31p multicolored 2.00 2.25
221 A32 36p multicolored 2.25 2.50
222 A32 62p multicolored 3.00 3.50
223 A32 72p multicolored 3.75 4.00
Nos. 218-223 (6) 14.00 15.25

Ovptd. with Hong Kong '94 Emblem

1994, Feb. 18

224 A32 15p on #218 1.50 1.50
225 A32 24p on #219 2.00 2.00
226 A32 31p on #220 2.25 2.50
227 A32 36p on #221 2.50 2.75
228 A32 62p on #222 3.50 3.75
229 A32 72p on #223 4.25 4.50
Nos. 224-229 (6) 16.00 17.00

Antarctic Food Chain — A33

a, Crabeater seals. b, Blue whale. c, Wandering albatross. d, Mackeral icefish. e, Krill. f, Squid.

1994, Nov. 29

230 A33 35p Sheet of 6, #a-f 16.00 16.00

Geological Structures A34

Designs: 17p, Hauberg Mountains, folded sedimentary rocks. 35p, Arrowsmith Peninsula, dikes cross-cutting granite. 40p, Colbert Mountains, columnar jointing in volcanic rocks. 76p, Succession Cliffs, flat-lying sedimentary rocks.

Perf. 14x14½

1995, Nov. 28 **Litho.** **Wmk. 373**

231 A34 17p multicolored 2.00 2.00
232 A34 35p multicolored 3.25 3.25
233 A34 40p multicolored 3.50 4.00
234 A34 76p multicolored 5.25 6.00
Nos. 231-234 (4) 14.00 15.25

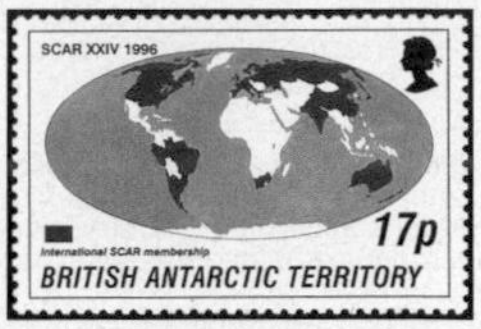

Scientific Committee on Antarctic Research (SCAR) — A35

Designs: 17p, World map showing SCAR member countries. 35p, Earth sciences. 40p, Atmospheric sciences. 76p, Life sciences. £1, Cambridge, August 1996.

Wmk. 384

1996, Mar. 23 **Litho.** ***Perf. 14***

235 A35 17p multicolored 1.60 1.60
236 A35 35p multicolored 2.50 2.50
237 A35 40p multicolored 2.75 2.75
238 A35 76p multicolored 4.00 4.00
Nos. 235-238 (4) 10.85 10.85

Souvenir Sheet

239 A35 £1 multicolored 8.50 8.50

Queen Elizabeth II, 70th Birthday

Common Design Type

Various portraits of Queen: 17p, Pink outfit. 35p, In formal dress, tiara. 40p, Blue outfit. 76p, Red coat.

Wmk. 384

1996, Nov. 25 **Litho.** ***Perf. 14½***

240 CD354 17p multicolored 1.60 .90
241 CD354 35p multicolored 2.10 1.50
242 CD354 40p multicolored 2.25 2.25
243 CD354 76p multicolored 3.50 3.50
Nos. 240-243 (4) 9.45 8.15

Whales A36

Wmk. 373

1996, Nov. 25 **Litho.** ***Perf. 14***

244 A36 17p Killer whale 1.35 1.00
245 A36 35p Sperm whale 2.00 1.50
246 A36 40p Minke whale 3.50 2.50
247 A36 76p Blue whale 4.25 4.00
Nos. 244-247 (4) 11.10 9.00

Souvenir Sheet

248 A36 £1 Humpback whale 9.50 9.50

Christmas — A37

Penguins in snow: 17p, Sledding. 35p, Caroling. 40p, Throwing snowballs. 76p, Ice skating.

Wmk. 384

1997, Dec. 22 **Litho.** ***Perf. 14½***

249 A37 17p multicolored 3.00 1.90
250 A37 35p multicolored 4.75 3.25
251 A37 40p multicolored 5.25 4.75
252 A37 76p multicolored 6.75 7.25
Nos. 249-252 (4) 19.75 17.15

History of Mapping — A38

Maps of Antarctic and: 16p, Surveyor looking through theodolite, 1902-03. 30p, Cartographer, 1949. 35p, Man using radar rangefinder, 1964. 40p, Satellite, 1981. 65p, Tripod, hand held remote control device, 1993.

Wmk. 373

1998, Mar. 19 **Litho.** ***Perf. 14***

253 A38 16p multicolored 2.50 2.25
254 A38 30p multicolored 3.00 2.50
255 A38 35p multicolored 3.75 3.00
256 A38 40p multicolored 4.00 3.25
257 A38 65p multicolored 5.00 5.00
Nos. 253-257 (5) 18.25 16.00

Diana, Princess of Wales (1961-97)

Common Design Type

a, Wearing sun glasses. b, In white top. c, Up close. d, Wearing blue-green blazer.

1998, Mar. 31 ***Perf. 14½x14***

258 CD355 35p Sheet of 4, #a-d 5.50 5.50

No. 258 sold for £1.40 + 20p, with surtax and 50% of profit from total sales being donated to the Princess Diana Memorial Fund.

Antarctic Clothing Through the Ages — A39

Man outfitted for cold weather: 30p, Holding shovel, sailing ship, 1843. 35p, With dog, sailing ship, 1900. 40p, With sketch pad, tripod, dog, steamer ship, 1943. 65p, Wearing red suit, penguins, ship, 1998.

Perf. 14½x14

1998, Nov. 30 **Litho.** **Wmk. 373**

259 A39 30p multicolored 4.00 4.00
260 A39 35p multicolored 4.25 4.25
261 A39 40p multicolored 4.50 4.50
262 A39 65p multicolored 6.75 6.75
Nos. 259-262 (4) 19.50 19.50

Birds A40

Designs: 1p, Sheathbill. 2p, Antarctic prion. 5p, Adelie penguin. 10p, Emperor penguin. 20p, Antarctic tern. 30p, Black bellied storm petrel. 35p, Antarctic fulmar. 40p, Blue eyed shag. 50p, McCormick's skua. £1, Kelp gull. £3, Wilson's storm petrel. £5, Brown skua.

1998 ***Perf. 14***

263 A40 1p multicolored 1.25 1.25
264 A40 2p multicolored 1.25 1.25
265 A40 5p multicolored 1.45 1.45
266 A40 10p multicolored 1.60 1.60
267 A40 20p multicolored 1.75 1.75
268 A40 30p multicolored 2.25 2.25
269 A40 35p multicolored 2.50 2.50
270 A40 40p multicolored 3.00 3.00
271 A40 50p multicolored 4.00 4.00
272 A40 £1 multicolored 5.00 5.00
273 A40 £3 multicolored 10.00 10.00
274 A40 £5 multicolored 16.00 16.00
Nos. 263-274 (12) 50.05 50.05

Fish — A41

Wmk. 373

1999, Nov. 14 Litho. *Perf. 13½*

275	A41	10p	Mackerel icefish	2.40	1.75
276	A41	20p	Toothfish	3.50	2.40
277	A41	25p	Borch	4.00	2.75
278	A41	50p	Marbled notothen	6.00	4.00
279	A41	80p	Bernach	7.00	7.00
			Nos. 275-279 (5)	22.90	17.90

Survey Discoveries — A42

15p, Map of crustal microplates of West Antarctica. 30p, Lead levels in ice. 35p, Gigantism in marine invertebrates. 40p, Ozone hole. 70p, Electric field associated with aurora.

Wmk. 373

1999, Dec. 18 Litho. *Perf. 14*

280	A42	15p	multi, vert.	3.75	2.00
281	A42	30p	multi, vert.	4.00	2.75
282	A42	35p	multi	4.25	3.00
283	A42	40p	multi	4.50	3.25
284	A42	70p	multi	6.00	6.00
			Nos. 280-284 (5)	22.50	17.00

Sir Ernest Shackleton (1874-1922), Polar Explorer — A43

Designs: 35p, Wreck of the Endurance. 40p, Ocean Camp on ice floe. 65p, Launching the James Caird from Elephant Island.

2000, Feb. 10 Wmk. 373

285	A43	35p	multi	7.00	3.50
286	A43	40p	multi	7.50	3.50
287	A43	65p	multi	8.50	5.50
			Nos. 285-287 (3)	23.00	12.50

See Falkland Islands Nos. 758-760, South Georgia and South Sandwich Islands Nos. 254-256.

The Stamp Show 2000, London — A44

Commonwealth Trans-Antarctic Exhibition of 1955-58: a, Map of route. b, Expedition at South Pole, 1958. c, MV Magga Dan. d, Sno-cat repair camp. e, Sno-cat over crevasse. f, Seismic explosion.

Perf. 13¼x13¾

2000, May 22 Litho. Wmk. 373

288 A44 37p Sheet of 6, #a-f 70.00 70.00

Survey Ships A45

Designs: 20p, RRS Bransfield unloading near Halley, vert. 33p, Supply boat Tula and RRS Ernest Shackleton, vert. 37p, RRS Bransfield. 43p, RRS Ernest Shackleton.

Wmk. 373

2000, Nov. 30 Litho. *Perf. 14*

289-292 A45 Set of 4 26.00 26.00

Composing of Antarctic Symphony, by Sir Peter Maxwell Davies — A46

Designs: No. 293, 37p, RRS James Clark Ross and track cut through ice. No. 294, 37p, Iceberg. No. 295, 43p, Camp on Jones Ice Shelf. No. 296, 43p, Iceberg, diff.

2000, Dec. 4

293-296 A46 Set of 4 24.00 24.00

Port Lockroy — A47

Designs: 33p, Visitors near building, penguins, flagpole, 2001. 37p, Visitors on rocks below building, ship in water, 2001. 43p, Port Lockroy building, 1945. 65p, Laboratory interior, 1945.

Perf. 13¾x14

2001, Nov. 29 Litho. Wmk. 373

297-300 A47 Set of 4 26.50 26.50

British National Antarctic Expedition of 1901-04, Cent. A48

Designs: 33p, Map of expedition's route, vert. 37p, Capt. Robert Falcon Scott (1868-1912), vert. 43p, First Antarctic balloon ascent, 1902. 65p, Emperor penguin chick, vert. 70p, Ernest Shackleton, Scott, Edward Adrian Wilson, sleds at southernmost point of expedition. 80p, Discovery trapped in ice.

2001, Dec. 5 Wmk. 384 *Perf. 14*

301-306 A48 Set of 6 25.00 25.00

Reign Of Queen Elizabeth II, 50th Anniv. Issue

Common Design Type

Designs: Nos. 307, 311a, 20p, Princess Elizabeth making first broadcast. Nos. 308, 311b, 37p, At Garter ceremony, 1998. Nos. 309, 311c, 43p, In 1952. Nos. 310, 311d, 50p, In 1996. No. 311e, 50p, 1955 portrait by Annigoni (38x50mm).

Perf. 14¼x14½, 13¾ (#311e)

2002, Feb. 6 Litho. Wmk. 373

With Gold Frames

307	CD360	20p	multicolored	1.25	1.25
308	CD360	37p	multicolored	2.50	2.50
309	CD360	43p	multicolored	2.75	2.75
310	CD360	50p	multicolored	3.50	3.50
			Nos. 307-310 (4)	10.00	10.00

Souvenir Sheet

Without Gold Frames

311 CD360 Sheet of 5, #a-e 13.00 13.00

Queen Mother Elizabeth (1900-2002)

Common Design Type

Designs: 40p, Without hat (sepia photograph). 45p, Wearing blue green hat.

No. 314: a, 70p, Wearing feathered hat (black and white photograph). b, 95p, Wearing dark blue hat.

Wmk. 373

2002, Aug. 5 Litho. *Perf. 14¼*

With Purple Frames

312	CD361	40p	multicolored	3.00	3.00
313	CD361	45p	multicolored	3.25	3.25

Souvenir Sheet

Without Purple Frames

Perf. 14½x14¼

314 CD361 Sheet of 2, #a-b 12.50 12.50

Commission for the Conservation of Antarctic Marine Living Resources, 20th Anniv. — A49

No. 315: a, Map of Antarctica, vessel monitoring satellite. b, Wandering albatross, fishing boat. c, Icefish, toothfish and crabeater seal. d, Krill and phytoplankton.

Perf. 13½x13¾

2002, Oct. 22 Litho. Wmk. 373

315 Vert. strip of 4 16.00 16.00
a.-d. A49 37p Any single 3.75 3.75

Scottish National Antarctic Expedition, 1902-04 — A50

Designs: 30p, Map of oceanographic cruises of the Scotia, vert. 40p, Bagpiper Gilbert Kerr and Emperor penguin. 45p, SY Scotia, vert. 70p, Meteorological observations, cent. 95p, William Speirs Bruce, vert. £1, Omond House, Laurie Island.

Wmk. 373

2002, Dec. 5 Litho. *Perf. 14*

316-321 A50 Set of 6 32.50 32.50

Head of Queen Elizabeth II

Common Design Type

Wmk. 373

2003, June 2 Litho. *Perf. 13¾*

322 CD362 £2 multi 9.50 9.50

Coronation of Queen Elizabeth II, 50th Anniv.

Common Design Type

Designs: Nos. 323, 40p, 325a, Queen in carriage. Nos. 324, 45p, 325b, 95p, Queen and family on Buckingham Palace balcony.

Perf. 14¼x14½

2003, June 2 Litho. Wmk. 373

Vignettes Framed, Red Background

323	CD363	40p	multicolored	3.75	3.75
324	CD363	45p	multicolored	4.25	4.25

Souvenir Sheet

Vignettes Without Frame, Purple Panel

325 CD363 95p Sheet of 2, #a-b 15.00 15.00

Worldwide Fund for Nature (WWF) A51

Blue whale: 40p, Underwater. No. 327, 45p, Tail above water. No. 328, 45p, Two whales underwater. 70p, Two whales at surface.

Wmk. 373

2003, Dec. 5 Litho. *Perf. 14*

326-329 A51 Set of 4 9.50 9.50
329a Sheet, 4 each #326-329 40.00 40.00

Bases and Postmarks A52

Bases: 1p, G, Admiralty Bay. 2p, B, Deception Island. 5p, D, Hope Bay. 22p, F, Argentine Islands. 25p, E, Stonington Island. 40p, A, Port Lockroy. 45p, H, Signy. 50p, N, Anvers Island. 95p, R, Rothera. £1, T, Adelaide Island. £3, Y, Horseshoe Island. £5, Z, Hailey Bay.

2003, Dec. 8 Wmk. 373 *Perf. 14*

330	A52	1p	multi	.40	.40
331	A52	2p	multi	.50	.50
332	A52	5p	multi	.60	.60
333	A52	22p	multi	1.00	1.00
334	A52	25p	multi	1.10	1.10
335	A52	40p	multi	1.75	1.75
336	A52	45p	multi	2.00	2.00
337	A52	50p	multi	2.10	2.10
338	A52	95p	multi	4.00	4.00
339	A52	£1	multi	4.25	4.25
340	A52	£3	multi	12.50	12.50
341	A52	£5	multi	20.00	20.00
			Nos. 330-341 (12)	50.20	50.20

Climate Change A53

No. 342, 24p: a, Map of Antarctica showing annual temperature trends since 1950. b, Larsen Ice Shelf.

No. 343, 42p: a, Graph of ice core age and warmth. b, Ice core drilling.

No. 344, 50p: a, Graph of rise of mean summer air temperatures at Faraday Station. b, Pearlwort.

Wmk. 373

2004, Dec. 9 Litho. *Perf. 14*

Vert. Pairs, #a-b

342-344 A53 Set of 3 20.00 20.00

Petrels A54

Designs: 25p, Cape petrel. 42p, Snow petrel. 75p, Wilson's storm petrel. £1, Antarctic petrel.

No. 349 — Southern giant petrel: a, In flight, name at right. b, In flight, name at left. c, Close-up of head, bird in flight. d, With wings extended above nest. e, Adult and chick. f, Chick.

2005, Jan. 23 *Perf. 13¾*

345-348 A54 Set of 4 19.00 19.00

Souvenir Sheet

349 A54 50p Sheet of 6, #a-f 25.00 25.00

Ships Named Endurance A55

Designs: 42p, Endurance, 1914-15. 50p, HMS Endurance, 1968-90. £1, HMS Endurance, 1991-present.

2005, Jan. 24 *Perf. 14¾x14*

350-352 A55 Set of 3 17.50 17.50

Falkland Islands and Dependencies Aerial Survey Expedition, 50th Anniv. — A56

Designs: 45p, Deception Island. 55p, Hunting Lodge. 80p, Bell 47 helicopter. £1, Canso Flying Boat.

Wmk. 373

2005, Dec. 19 Litho. *Perf. 14*

353-356 A56 Set of 4 19.00 19.00

Halley VI Research Station Design Competition — A57

Designs: No. 357, 45p, Concept of Faber Maunsell. No. 358, 45p, Concept of Buro Hoppold. 55p, Concept by Hopkins. 80p, Laws Building of Halley V Research Station.

Wmk. 373

2005, Dec. 22 Litho. *Perf. 14*

357-360 A57 Set of 4 16.00 16.00

Dogs of Sir Ernest Shackleton — A58

Designs: No. 361, 45p, Shackleton and puppies. No. 362, 45p, Samson, Shakespeare and Surley, horiz. 55p, Ice kennels around ship, Endurance, horiz. £1, Training on sea ice.

2005, Dec. 22

361-364 A58 Set of 4 19.00 19.00

Antarctic Treaty Consultative Meeting Scottish Children's Stamp Design Competition A59

Winning designs by: No. 365, 45p, Erica Currie. No. 366, 45p, Meghan Joyce. 55p, Lorna MacDonald. £1, Danielle Dalgleish.

2006, Feb. 26

365-368 A59 Set of 4 15.00 15.00

Queen Elizabeth II, 80th Birthday A60

Queen: 45p, As child. Nos. 370, 373a, 55p, Wearing crown. Nos. 371, 373b, 80p, Wearing red hat. £1, Without head covering.

Wmk. 373

2006, Apr. 21 Litho. *Perf. 14*

With White Frames

369-372 A60 Set of 4 18.00 18.00

Souvenir Sheet

Without White Frames

373 A60 Sheet of 2, #a-b 10.00 10.00

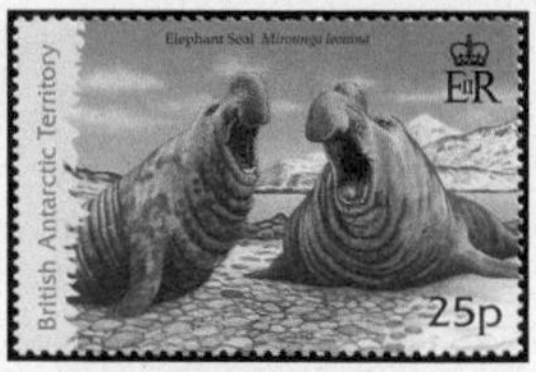

Seals A61

Designs: 25p, Elephant seals. 50p, Crabeater seals. 60p, Weddell seals. £1.05, Leopard seal.

Perf. 14¼x14¾

2006, Dec. 16 Litho. Wmk. 373

374-377 A61 Set of 4 20.00 20.00

Icebergs A62

Various icebergs: 25p, 50p, 60p, £1.05.

Wmk. 373

2007, Nov. 14 Litho. *Perf. 13¾*

378-381 A62 Set of 4 14.50 14.50

Marine Invertebrates — A63

Designs: 25p, Sea lemon. 50p, Antarctic sea anemone. 60p, Sea spider. £1.05, Sea star.

2007, Nov. 14 *Perf. 14*

382-385 A63 Set of 4 14.00 14.00

Souvenir Sheet

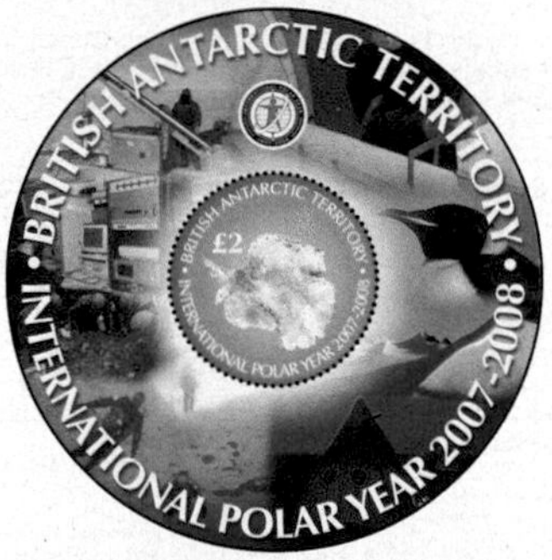

Intl. Polar Year — A64

2007, Nov. 14 *Perf.*

386 A64 £2 multi 10.00 10.00

Explorers and Ships A65

Designs: 1p, James Weddell (1787-1834), Jane and Beaufoy. 2p, Sir James Clark Ross (1800-62), Erebus and Terror. 5p, Neil Alison Mackintosh (1900-74), Discovery II. 27p, Sir Douglas Mawson (1882-1958), Discovery. 55p, Captain James Cook (1728-79), Resolution. Nos. 392, 399a, Captain Egeberg Borchgrevink (1864-1934), Southern Cross. Nos. 393, 399b, Dr. William Speirs Bruce (1867-1921), Scotia. Nos. 394, 399c, Captain Robert Falcon Scott (1868-1912), Discovery. Nos. 395, 399d, Sir Ernest Shackleton (1874-1922), Endurance. £1.10, John Riddoch Rymill (1905-68), Penola. £2.50, Captain Victor Marchesi (1914-2006), William Scoresby. £5, Sir Vivian Fuchs (1908-99), Magga Dan.

Wmk. 406

2008, Nov. 17 Litho. *Perf. 14*

387	A65	1p	multi	.25	.25
388	A65	2p	multi	.25	.25
389	A65	5p	multi	.25	.25
390	A65	27p	multi	.90	.90
391	A65	55p	multi	1.75	1.75
392	A65	65p	multi	2.10	2.10
393	A65	65p	multi	2.10	2.10
394	A65	65p	multi	2.10	2.10
395	A65	65p	multi	2.10	2.10
396	A65	£1.10	multi	4.25	4.25
397	A65	£2.50	multi	8.25	8.25
398	A65	£5	multi	16.50	16.50
	Nos. 387-398 (12)			40.80	40.80

Souvenir Sheet

399 Sheet of 4 8.00 8.00

a.-d. A65 (65p) Any single 2.00 2.00

Nos. 399a-399d are inscribed "Airmail Letter."

A66

A67

A68

A69

Aurora Australis A70

2008, Nov. 17 Wmk. 373

400 Horiz. strip of 5 20.00 20.00

a.	A66 65p multi	4.00	4.00
b.	A67 65p multi	4.00	4.00
c.	A68 65p multi	4.00	4.00
d.	A69 65p multi	4.00	4.00
e.	A70 65p multi	4.00	4.00

Fossil Ferns A71

Map of Antarctica and: 55p, Lophosoria cupulatus. 65p, Cladophlebis oblonga. No. 403, £1.10, Pachypteris indica. No. 404, £1.10, Aculea acicularis.

2008, Nov. 17 *Perf. 14*

401-404 A71 Set of 4 16.00 16.00

Naval Aviation, Cent. A72

Designs: No. 405, 10p, Fairey Seafox. No. 406, 10p, Westland Lynx helicopter. No. 407, 90p, Supermarine Walrus. No. 408, 90p, Westland Wasp helicopter.

£2, HMA No. 1 Mayfly airship.

Wmk. 406

2009, Jan. 1 Litho. *Perf. 14*

405-408 A72 Set of 4 10.50 10.50

Souvenir Sheet

409 A72 £2 multi 11.00 11.00

Worldwide Fund for Nature (WWF) — A73

Crabeater seal: 27p, On ice. 65p, Head poking through hole in ice. £1.10, Two seals on ice. £1.50, Underwater.

Wmk. 406

2009, Nov. 6 Litho. *Perf. 14*

410-413 A73 Set of 4 13.00 13.00

413a Sheet of 16, 4 each #410-413 52.00 52.00

Antarctic Treaty, 50th Anniv. — A74

No. 414, 27p: a, Antarctic fur seal. b, Humpback whale.

No. 415, 55p: a, Southern giant petrel. b, Gentoo penguins.

No. 416, 65p: a, Giant squid. b, Jellyfish.

2009, Nov. 6 *Perf. 14*

Horiz. Pairs, #a-b

414-416 A74 Set of 3 13.00 13.00

Miniature Sheet

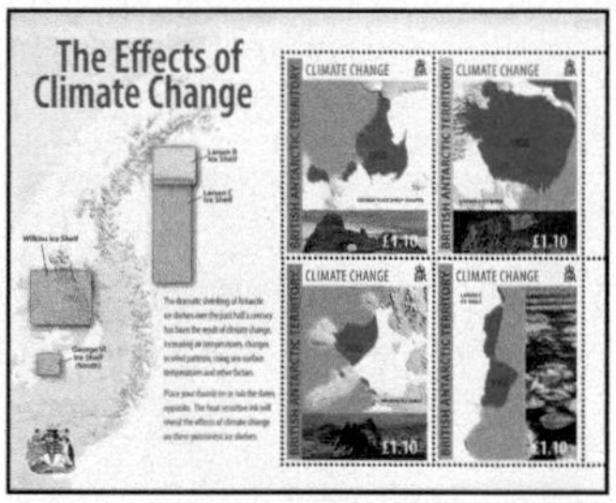

Effects of Climate Change — A75

No. 417 — Maps showing present day and 1950 extents of: a, George VI Ice Shelf (South). b, Larsen B Ice Shelf. c, Wilkins Ice Shelf. d, Larsen C Ice Shelf.

2009, Nov. 26 *Perf. 13¼x13½*

417 A75 £1.10 Sheet of 4, #a-d 17.50 17.50

Marine Life A76

Designs: No. 418, 27p, Polychaete worm. No. 419, 27p, Button worm. No. 420, 27p, Sponge. No. 421, 27p, Amphipod.

No. 422: a, Solitary coral. b, Amphipod, diff. c, Comb jellyfish. d, Basket star.

Wmk. 406

2010, Dec. 3 Litho. *Perf. 14*

418-421 A76 Set of 4 4.50 4.50

Souvenir Sheet

Perf. 13¼

422 A76 £1.15 Sheet of 4, #a-d 17.50 17.50

No. 422 contains four 36x36mm stamps.

Birds — A77

No. 423, 27p: a, South polar skua. b, Adélie penguin.

No. 424, 70p: a, Gray-headed albatross. b, Emperor penguin.

No. 425, £1.15: a, Kelp gull. b, Antarctic petrel.

2010, Dec. 3 ***Perf. 14***

Horiz. Pairs, #a-b

423-425	A77	Set of 3	21.00	21.00

Miniature Sheets

Photographs of 1910-13 British Antarctic Expedition — A78

No. 426, 27p: a, Ship, Terra Nova, on horizon. b, Ponies. c, Cavern in iceberg. d, "Tenements" bunks in Winterquarters hut. e, Capt. Robert Falcon Scott's birthday dinner. f, Observing at the weather station. g, Capt. Scott writing in his journal. h, Terra Nova in the ice.

No. 427, 60p: a, Terra Nova in harbor. b, Lieutenant Rennick leading pony. c, Matterhorn Berg. d, Nelson at work in the lab. e, Capt. Scott on skis. f, Chris (dog) and gramophone. g, Motorized tractor and load passing Inaccessible Island. h, Polar party at the South Pole.

2010, Dec. 3 ***Perf. 13¼***

Sheets of 8, #a-h

426-427	A78	Set of 2	25.00	25.00

Miniature Sheets

A79

Filming in British Antarctic Territrory of *Frozen Planet* Television Series — A80

No. 428: a, Close-up of head of seal. b, Seal with head on rock. c, Head of seal on back in snow. d, Seal in water. e, Dorsal fin of killer whales. f, Head of killer whale and four other killer whales with heads below water. g, Two killer whales with heads abovve water. h, Dorsal fins of two killer whales.

No. 429: a, Adult and juvenile penguin. b, Three penguins walking. c, Four penguins, one with beak open. d, Adult penguin feeding juvenile. e, Juvenile penguin on rock facing left. f, Penguin and ship. g, Group of penguins jumping from water to ice. h, Chinstrap penguin facing forward.

2011, Nov. 17

428	A79	27p Sheet of 8, #a-h		6.75	6.75
429	A80	60p Sheet of 8, #a-h		15.00	15.00

Miniature Sheets

A81

A82

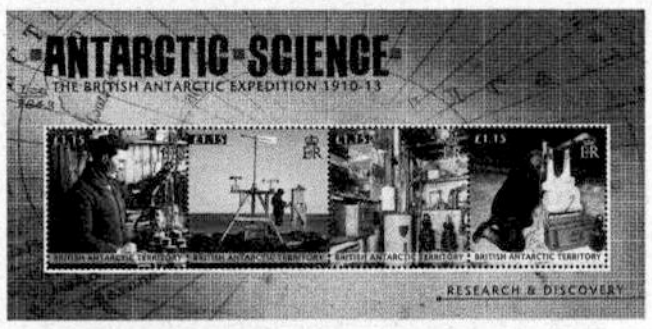

Science in the Antarctic — A83

No. 430: a, Building (sepia-toned). b, Building (color). c, Scientists preparing weather balloon for flight (sepia-toned), vert. d, Scientist preparing weather ballon for flight (color), vert. e, Two scientists on boat preparing equipment (sepia-toned), vert. f, Scientific equipment on cable (color), vert. g, Two skiers, iceberg (sepia-toned). h, Scientists in small boat (color).

No. 431 (color images): a, Airplane. b, Scientist spraying water into air. c, Scientist opening weather station. d, British Antarctic Survey Advanced Ionospheric Sounder.

No. 432 (sepia-toned images): a, Scientist, microscope and bottles. b, Scientist at weather station. c, Equipment in storage. d, Scientist looking through telescope.

2011, Nov. 17 ***Perf. 14***

430 A81	27p	Sheet of 8, #a-h	7.25	7.25
431 A82	70p	Sheet of 4, #a-d	9.25	9.25
432 A83	£1.15	Sheet of 4, #a-d	16.00	16.00
		Nos. 430-432 (3)	32.50	32.50

A84

A85

A86

A87

A88

A89

A90

A91

A92

Glaciers and Icesheets A93

2012, Dec. 21 ***Perf. 13¾***

433		Horiz. strip of 5	10.00	10.00
a.	A84	65p multi	2.00	2.00
b.	A85	65p multi	2.00	2.00
c.	A86	65p multi	2.00	2.00
d.	A87	65p multi	2.00	2.00
e.	A88	65p multi	2.00	2.00
434		Horiz. strip of 5	12.00	12.00
a.	A89	75p multi	2.40	2.40
b.	A90	75p multi	2.40	2.40
c.	A91	75p multi	2.40	2.40
d.	A92	75p multi	2.40	2.40
e.	A93	75p multi	2.40	2.40

British Graham Land Expedition, 75th Anniv. — A94

No. 435, 40p: a, Boat on shore with three crew members. b, Two boats on dock.

No. 436, 40p: a, Dog. b, Dog and expedition member.

No. 437, 50p: a, Airplane, dog, expedition members. b, Airplane on water.

No. 438, 50p: a, Ship, denomination in white at LR. b, Ship, denomination in black at UR. £1.20, Ship "Penola."

2012, Dec. 21 ***Perf. 13¾***

Horiz. Pairs, #a-b

435-438	A94	Set of 4	12.00	12.00

Souvenir Sheet

Perf. 14x14¾

439	A94	£1.20 multi	5.25	5.25

No. 439 contains one 49x33mm stamp.

Souvenir Sheet

HMS Protector — A95

2012, Dec. 21 ***Perf. 14¼x15***

440	A95	£3.50 multi	11.50	11.50

Souvenir Sheet

Naming of Queen Elizabeth Land — A96

2013, Mar. 18 ***Perf. 14¾x14***

441	A96	£3 multi	9.50	9.50

British Antarctic Territory Postage Stamps, 50th Anniv. A97

British Antarctic Territory stamps issued from 1963-69: 1p, #1. 2p, #2. 5p, #3. 10p, #4. 30p, #5. 40p, #6. 50p, #7. 65p, #8. 75p, #9. 85p, #10. 95p, #11. £1, #12. £1.20, #13. £2, #14. £3.50, #15. £5, #24.

Wmk. 406

2013, Nov. 27 **Litho.** ***Perf. 14***

442	A97	1p multi	.25	.25
443	A97	2p multi	.25	.25
444	A97	5p multi	.25	.25
445	A97	10p multi	.30	.30
446	A97	30p multi	.90	.90
447	A97	40p multi	1.25	1.25
448	A97	50p multi	1.45	1.45
449	A97	65p multi	1.90	1.90
450	A97	75p multi	2.25	2.25
451	A97	85p multi	2.50	2.50
452	A97	95p multi	2.75	2.75
453	A97	£1 multi	3.00	3.00
454	A97	£1.20 multi	3.50	3.50
455	A97	£2 multi	6.00	6.00
456	A97	£3.50 multi	10.00	10.00
457	A97	£5 multi	14.50	14.50
		Nos. 442-457 (16)	51.05	51.05

Bransfield House, 70th Anniv. A98

Designs: 65p, Penguins outside of Bransfield House. 75p, Laboratory. 85p, Bransfield House and storage building. £1.20, Kitchen.

Wmk. 406

2013, Nov. 27 **Litho.** ***Perf. 14***

458-461	A98	Set of 4	10.00	10.00

Halley VI Research Station A99

Station: 75p, In daylight. 85p, At night. 95p, In daylight, diff. £1.20, At night, diff.

Wmk. 406

2013, Nov. 27 Litho. *Perf. 14*
462-465 A99 Set of 4 11.00 11.00

Penguins — A100

No. 466, 40p: a, Adult Gentoo penguin (denomination at UR). b, Juvenile Gentoo penguin (denomination at UL).
No. 467, 50p: a, Adult Adélie penguin (denomination at UR). b, Juvenile Adélie penguins (denomination at UL).
No. 468, 75p: a, Adult Chinstrap penguin (denomination at UR). b, Juvenile Chinstrap penguins (denomination at UL).
No. 469, £1.20: a, Adult Emperor penguins (denomination at UR). b, Juvenile Emperor penguins (denomination at UL).

Wmk. 406

2013, Nov. 27 Litho. *Perf. 13¾*
Horiz. Pairs, #a-b
466-469 A100 Set of 4 17.00 17.00

Miniature Sheet

Imperial Trans-Antarctic Expedition, Cent. (in 2014) — A101

No. 470: a, 65p, Sir Ernest Shackleton and his wife. b, 65p, Expedition members How, Barr, Irvine, Macloed, and Macaulay. c, 65p, Lieutenant A. E. Mackintosh and Frank Wild. d, 75p, Departure from Millwall Docks. e, 75p, Shackleton on board the Endurance. f, 75p, SS Endurance setting sail.

Wmk. 406

2013, Nov. 27 Litho. *Perf. 14*
470 A101 Sheet of 6, #a-f 13.00 13.00

See Nos. 471-476, 490-495.

Imperial Trans-Antarctic Expedition Type of 2013

Designs: No. 471, 65p, Endurance in full sail in ice. No. 472, 65p, Endurance trapped in ice and capsizing. No. 473, 75p, Ernest Shackleton and Frank Wild at Ocean Camp. No. 474, 75p, Shackleton and Frank Hurley at Patience Camp. No. 475, £1, Expedition members dragging the James Caird across the ice. No. 476, £1, Expedition members landing on Elephant Island.

2014, Nov. 19 Litho. *Perf. 14*
471-476 A101 Set of 6 13.00 13.00

iStar Ice Stability Program A102

Designs: 65p, Twin Otter airplane in flight. 75p, Surface radar. £1, RRS James Clark Ross. £1.20, Autosub.

2014, Nov. 19 Litho. *Perf. 14*
477-480 A102 Set of 4 10.50 10.50

Antarctic Marine Food Web A103

Designs (without arrows): No. 481, 65p, Phytoplankton. 75p, Krill and squid. £1, Penguins and flying birds. £1.20, Leopard seal.
No. 485, 65p — Designs with arrows: a, Penguins and flying birds. b, Fish. c, Smaller toothed whale. d, Leopard seal. e, Krill and squid. f, Seals. g, Baleen whale. h, Zooplankton. i, Phytoplankton.

2014, Nov. 19 Litho. *Perf. 14*
481-484 A103 Set of 4 10.50 10.50

Miniature Sheet

485 A103 65p Sheet of 9, #a-i 16.50 16.50

Queen Elizabeth II, Longest-Reigning British Monarch — A104

Queen Elizabeth II and events during her reign: 66p, Publications reporting on her coronation, 1953. 76p, Satellite that discovered hole in ozone layer over Antarctica, 1985. £1.01, RSS James Clark Ross, 1990. £1.22, Map of Queen Elizabeth Land, 2012.

2015, Sept. 9 Litho. *Perf. 14*
486-489 A104 Set of 4 10.00 10.00

Imperial Trans-Antarctic Expedition Type of 2013

Designs: No. 490, 66p, Launching the James Caird. No. 491, 66p, Digging a cave for shelter, Elephant Island. No. 492, 76p, The Snuggery, Elephant Island. No. 493, 76p, Crossing the South Georgia Mountains. No. 494, £1.01, The Yelcho rescuing the crew from Elephant Island. No. 495, £1.01, The Yelcho with crew arrives in Chile.

2015, Nov. 17 Litho. *Perf. 14*
490-495 A101 Set of 6 14.00 14.00

Wildlife and Huts — A105

Designs: No. 496, 66p, Weddell seals, Damoy Hut, Dorian Bay. No. 497, 66p, Adélie penguins, Base W, Detaille Island. 76p, Skua, Base Y, Horseshoe Island. £1.01, Blue-eyed shag, Base E, Stonington Island. £1.22, Orca, Base F, Wordie House, Winter Island.

2015, Nov. 17 Litho. *Perf. 14*
496-500 A105 Set of 5 13.00 13.00

Whales — A106

Designs: No. 501, 66p, Antarctic minke whale. No. 502, 66p, Blue whale. No. 503, 66p, Sperm whales. No. 504, 66p, Killer whale. No. 505, 66p, Southern bottlenose whales. No. 506, 66p, Humpback whales.

Perf. 13¼x13½

2015, Nov. 17 Litho.
501-506 A106 Set of 6 11.00 11.00

Queen Elizabeth II, 90th Birthday — A107

Photographs of Queen Elizabeth from: 66p, 1948. 76p, 1972. £1.01, 1962. £1.22, 2009. £3, Queen Elizabeth II in 2008.

2016, Apr. 21 Litho. *Perf. 14*
507-510 A107 Set of 4 9.50 9.50

Souvenir Sheet

511 A107 £3 multi 7.50 7.50

International Association of Antarctic Tour Operators, 25th Anniv. — A108

Emblem and: 66p, Zodiac boat and icebergs. 76p, Tents lit at night. £1.01, Kayakers. £1.22, Penguins and ship.

2016, Nov. 13 Litho. *Perf. 13¼*
512-515 A108 Set of 4 8.25 8.25

Protocol on Environmental Protection to the Antarctic Treaty, 25th Anniv. — A109

Designs: No. 516, 66p, Krill. No. 517, 66p, Emperor penguin. No. 518, 76p, Weddell seal. No. 519, 76p, Humpback whale. No. 520, £1.01, Halley VI Station. No. 521, £1.01, South Pole.

2016, Nov. 13 Litho. *Perf. 14*
516-521 A109 Set of 6 11.50 11.50

A110

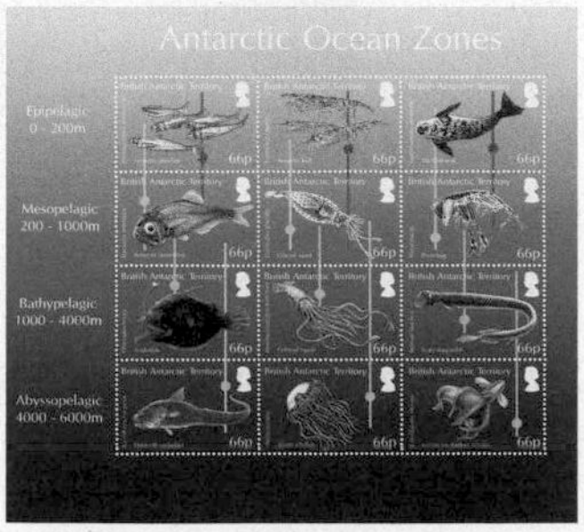

Marine Life of Antarctic Ocean Zones — A111

Designs: No. 522, 66p, Antarctic silverfish. 76p, Glacial squid. £1.01, Anglerfish. £1.22, Cirrate octopus.
No. 526: a, Antarctic silverfish, diff. b, Antarctic krill. c, Weddell seal. d, Antarctic lanternfish. e, Glacial squid, diff. f, Pram bug. g, Anglerfish, diff. h, Colossal squid. i, Scaly dragonfish. j, Dogtooth grenadier. k, Alarm jellyfish. l, Cirrate octopus, diff.

Perf. 13¼x13½

2016, Nov. 13 Litho.
522-525 A110 Set of 4 8.25 8.25

Miniature Sheet

526 A111 66p Sheet of 12, #a-l 20.00 20.00

Murals of Actresses by Evan Watson in Bransfield House, Port Lockroy — A112

Mural of: 66p, Diana Dors. 76p, Jane Russell. £1.01, Jayne Mansfield. £1.22, Sophia Loren.

Perf. 13½x13¼

2017, Nov. 25 Litho.
527-530 A112 Set of 4 9.00 9.00

70th Wedding Anniversary of Queen Elizabeth II and Prince Philip A113

Photograph of Queen Elizabeth II and Prince Philip from: 66p, 1947. 76p, 1961. £1.01, 1972. £1.22, 2015.

2017, Nov. 25 Litho. *Perf. 13¼x13*
531-534 A113 Set of 4 9.00 9.00

Royal Research Ships A114

Designs: No. 535, 76p, RRS John Biscoe (1), 1947-56. No. 536, 76p, RRS Shackleton, 1955-69. No. 537, 76p, RRS John Biscoe (2), 1956-91. No. 538, 76p, RRS Bransfield, 1970-99. No. 539, 76p, RRS James Clark Ross, 1991-present. No. 540, 76p, RRS Ernest Shackleton, 1999-present.

Perf. 13¼x13½

2017, Nov. 25 Litho.
535-540 A114 Set of 6 11.50 11.50

Corals A115

Designs: No. 541, 66p, Anthomastus sp. 76p, Flabellum sp. £1.01, Fannyella sp. £1.22, Stylasteridae (light red brown side panel).
No. 545, 66p: a, Balanophyllia sp. b, Like #542. c, Stylasteridae (orange brown side panel). d, Umbellula. e, Desmophyllum dianthus. f, Like #543. g, Stylasteridae (dark gray side panel). h, Like #544.

Perf. 13¼x13½

2017, Nov. 25 Litho.
541-544 A115 Set of 4 9.00 9.00

Miniature Sheet

545 A115 66p Sheet of 9, #541, 545a-545h 14.50 14.50

Wedding of Prince Harry and Meghan Markle
A116

Various photographs of couple, 66p, 76p, £1.01, £1.22.
£3, Couple, vert.

2018, July 23 Litho. *Perf. 13¼x13½*

546-549	A116	Set of 4	9.75	9.75

Souvenir Sheet

Perf. 13½x13¼

550	A116	£3 multi	8.00	8.00

Penguins — A117

Designs: 1p, Adélie penguin chick. 5p, Macaroni penguin chick. 10p, Chinstrap penguin chick. 20p, Gentoo penguin chick. 50p, King penguin chick. 66p, Emperor penguin chick. 76p, Head of Adélie penguin, horiz. £1, Head of Macaroni penguin, horiz. £1.20, Head of Chinstrap penguin, horiz. £2, Head of Gentoo penguin, horiz. £3.50, Head of King penguin, horiz. £5, Head of Emperor penguin, horiz.

2018, Nov. 1 Litho. *Perf. 13½x13¼*

551	A117	1p multi	.25	.25
552	A117	5p multi	.25	.25
553	A117	10p multi	.25	.25
554	A117	20p multi	.50	.50
555	A117	50p multi	1.40	1.40
556	A117	66p multi	1.75	1.75

Perf. 13¼x13½

557	A117	76p multi	2.00	2.00
558	A117	£1 multi	2.60	2.60
559	A117	£1.20 multi	3.25	3.25
560	A117	£2 multi	5.25	5.25
561	A117	£3.50 multi	9.00	9.00
562	A117	£5 multi	13.00	13.00
		Nos. 551-562 (12)	39.50	39.50

Construction of the RSS Sir David Attenborough — A118

Designs: 66p, Scaffolding around ship. 76p, Moving of ship's hull into water. £1.01, Placement of ship's bridge. £1.22, Ship at sea.

2018, Nov. 1 Litho. *Perf. 13¼x13½*

563-566	A118	Set of 4	9.50	9.50

Landscapes — A119

Designs: 66p, Port Lockroy, Goudier Island. 76p, Paradise Harbor. £1.01, Gould Bay, Weddell Sea. £1.22, Neumayer Channel, Port Lockroy.

2018, Nov. 1 Litho. *Perf. 13¼x13½*

567-570	A119	Set of 4	9.50	9.50

Migratory Seals
A120

No. 571 — Antarctic fur seal and map of: a, 66p, South Georgia and South Sandwich Islands, southern tip of South America. b, 76p, Adelaide Island and Antarctica.

No. 572 — Leopard seal and map of: a, £1.22, Falkland Islands, South Georgia and South Sandwich Islands, southern tip of South America. b, £1.50, Antarctica.

2018, Nov. 1 Litho. *Perf. 13¼x13½*

Vert. pairs, #a-b

571-572	A120	Set of 2	11.00	11.00

Members of Sir Ernest Shackleton Imperial Trans-Antarctic Expedition and Their World War I Medals — A121

No. 573, 76p: a, Alexander Macklin (1889-1967). b, Military Cross.

No. 574, £1.22: a, Joseph Stenhouse (1887-1941). b, Distinguished Service Order and Distinguished Service Cross.

2018, Nov. 4 Litho. *Perf. 13¾x13¼*

Horiz. Pairs, #a-b

573-574	A121	Set of 2	10.00	10.00

Scott Polar Research Center, Cent.
A122

Designs: No. 575, £1.75, Captain Robert Falcon Scott (1868-1912), Antarctic explorer, and his ship, Terra Nova, No. 576, £1.75, Exterior of Scott Polar Research Institute, Cambridge, United Kingdom and bust of Scott.

2019, Nov. 18 Litho. *Perf. 13*

575-576	A122	Set of 2	9.00	9.00

Discovery of Antarctica, 200th Anniv.
A123

Designs: No. 577, £1.26, Williams, the ship of William Smith, discoverer of South Shetland Islands in 1819. No. 578, £1.26, Members of 1901 Discovery Expedition. No. 579, £1.26, Emperor penguins.

2019, Nov. 18 Litho. *Perf. 13*

577-579	A123	Set of 3	9.75	9.75

Establishment of Port Lockroy Station A, 75th Anniv. — A124

Designs: No. 580, 68p, Arrival of British military at Port Lockroy, 1944. No. 581, 68p, Post office, 1944. No. 582, 68p, Base A, 1944. No. 583, 78p, Nissen Hut. No. 584, 78p, Boatshed. No. 585, 78p, Bransfield House.

Perf. 13¼x13½

2019, Nov. 18 Litho.

580-585	A124	Set of 6	11.50	11.50

A125

A126

A127

A128

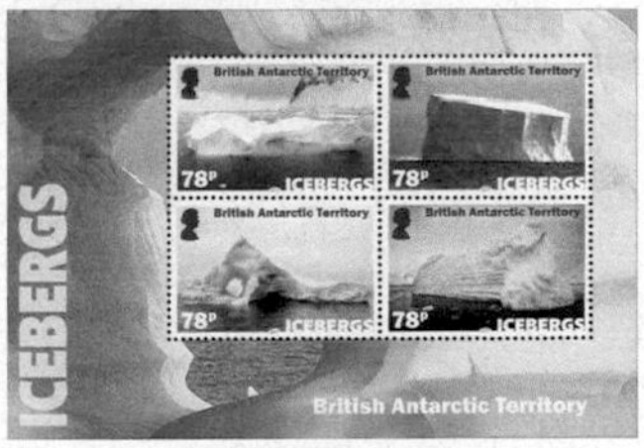

Icebergs — A129

No. 590: a, Ice field. b, Large iceberg with flat tilted top. c, Iceberg with hole. d, Iceberg with horizontal striations.

Perf. 13¼x13½

2019, Nov. 18 Litho.

586	A125	68p multi	1.75	1.75
587	A126	78p multi	2.00	2.00
588	A127	£1.04 multi	2.75	2.75
589	A128	£1.26 multi	3.25	3.25
		Nos. 586-589 (4)	9.75	9.75

Souvenir Sheet

590	A129	78p Sheet of 4, #a-d	8.00	8.00

SEMI-POSTAL STAMPS

Antarctic Heritage
SP1

Designs: 17p+3p, Capt. James Cook, HMS Resolution. 35p+15p, Sir James Clark Ross, HMS Erebus, HMS Terror. 40p+10p, Capt. Robert Falcon Scott. 76p+4p, Sir Ernest Shackleton, HMS Endurance trapped in ice.

Wmk. 384

1994, Nov. 23 Litho. *Perf. 14½*

B1	SP1	17p + 3p multi	2.25	2.25
B2	SP1	35p + 15p multi	3.25	3.25
B3	SP1	40p + 10p multi	3.25	3.25
B4	SP1	76p + 4p multi	6.00	6.00
		Nos. B1-B4 (4)	14.75	14.75

Surtax for United Kingdom Antarctic Heritage Trust.

AIR POST STAMPS

Penguins — AP1

No. C1: a, Two Emperors. b, Macaroni. c, Adult Gentoo. d, Two Adelies. e, Adult Chinstrap. f, Juvenile Gentoo. g, Two emperors, horizon. h, Juvenile Chinstrap. i, Seven Adelies. j, Adult and juvenile Gentoos. k, Two Macaronis. l, Emperor.

Wmk. 373

2003, Dec. 8 Litho. *Perf. 13¼*

C1	AP1 (40p)	Sheet of 12, #a-l	40.00	40.00

Penguins — AP2

Nos. C2 and C3: a, Chinstrap chick. b, Head of Emperor. c, Adelie with wings extended. d, Head of Chinstrap. e, Head of Macaroni, red country name. f, Gentoo adult feeding juvenile. g, Emperor chick. h, Adelie on nest. i, Two Emperors and mountain. j, Gentoo. k, Two Adelies. l, Two Emperor juveniles.

Wmk. 373

2006, Nov. 8 Litho. *Perf. 13¼*

C2	AP2 (50p)	Sheet of 12, #a-l	29.00	29.00

Self-Adhesive

Unwmk.

Die Cut Perf. 9x9½

C3	AP2 (50p)	Booklet pane of 12, #a-l	29.00	29.00

Miniature Sheet

Penguins — AP3

No. C4: a, Head of Chinstrap. b, Adult Gentoo and two chicks. c, Macaroni with open beak. d, Chinstrap with open beak and wings extended. e, Two Emperors. f, Adelie chicks. g, Chinstrap with wings extended. h, Gentoo with open beak. i, Macaroni. j, Adult Emperor and chick. k, Two Adelies. l, Emperor chick.

Wmk. 373

2008, Nov. 17 Litho. *Perf. 13¼*

C4	AP3 (55p) Sheet of 12, #a-l		30.00	30.00

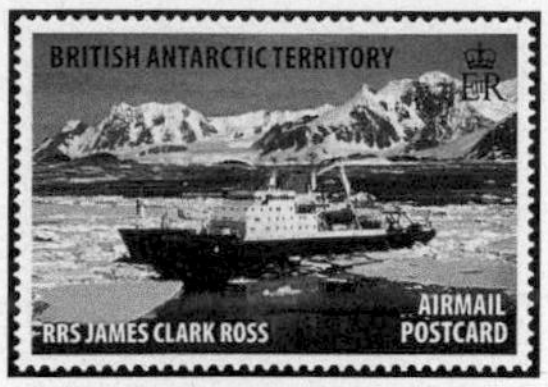

RRS James Clark Ross — AP4

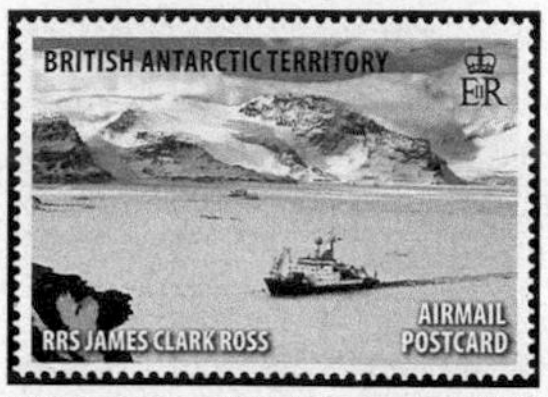

RRS James Clark Ross — AP5

RRS Bransfield — AP6

RRS Bransfield — AP7

RRS Ernest Shackleton — AP8

RRS Ernest Shackleton — AP9

Design: £1.15, RRS James Clark Ross and penguin.

Perf. 14¼x14¾

2011, Nov. 17 Wmk. 406

C5	AP4	(60p) multi		2.10	2.10
C6	AP5	(60p) multi		2.10	2.10
C7	AP6	(60p) multi		2.10	2.10
C8	AP7	(60p) multi		2.10	2.10
C9	AP8	(60p) multi		2.10	2.10
C10	AP9	(60p) multi		2.10	2.10
		Nos. C5-C10 (6)		12.60	12.60

Souvenir Sheet

Perf. 13¼

C11	AP4	£1.15 multi	3.75	3.75

Coil Stamps
Self-Adhesive
Size: 33x22mm

Unwmk.

Die Cut Perf. 13¼x12¾

C12	AP4	(60p) multi	2.00	2.00
C13	AP5	(60p) multi	2.00	2.00
C14	AP6	(60p) multi	2.00	2.00
C15	AP7	(60p) multi	2.00	2.00
C16	AP8	(60p) multi	2.00	2.00
C17	AP9	(60p) multi	2.00	2.00
a.		Horiz. coil strip of 6, #C12-C17	12.00	
		Nos. C12-C17 (6)	12.00	12.00

Gentoo Penguins AP10

Adelie Penguin AP11

Chinstrap Penguin AP12

Adelie Penguin AP13

Gentoo Penguin — AP14

Die Cut Perf. 13¼x13½

2012, Nov. 16 Self-Adhesive

Coil Stamps

C18	AP10	(65p) multi	2.60	2.60
C19	AP11	(65p) multi	2.60	2.60
C20	AP12	(65p) multi	2.60	2.60
C21	AP13	(65p) multi	2.60	2.60
C22	AP14	(65p) multi	2.60	2.60
a.		Vert. strip of 5, #C18-C22	13.00	
		Nos. C18-C22 (5)	13.00	13.00

Penguins AP15

Designs: Nos. C23, C28, Macaroni penguins. Nos. C24, C29, Adelie penguins. Nos. C25, C30, Chinstrap penguins. Nos. C26, C31, Gentoo penguins. Nos. C27, C32, Emperor penguins.

2014, Nov. 19 Litho. *Perf. 13¾*

Inscribed "Airmail Letter"

C23	AP15	(75p) multi	2.40	2.40
C24	AP15	(75p) multi	2.40	2.40
C25	AP15	(75p) multi	2.40	2.40
C26	AP15	(75p) multi	2.40	2.40
C27	AP15	(75p) multi	2.40	2.40
		Nos. C23-C27 (5)	12.00	12.00

Coil Stamps
Self-Adhesive
Size: 22x28mm
Inscribed "Airmail Postcard"

Die Cut Perf. 13½

C28	AP15	(65p) multi	2.10	2.10
C29	AP15	(65p) multi	2.10	2.10
C30	AP15	(65p) multi	2.10	2.10
C31	AP15	(65p) multi	2.10	2.10
C32	AP15	(65p) multi	2.10	2.10
a.		Horiz. strip of 5, #C28-C32	10.50	
		Nos. C28-C32 (5)	10.50	10.50

AP16

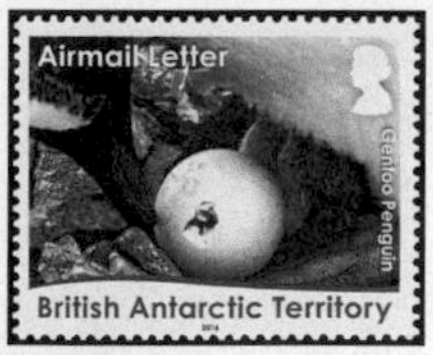

AP17

AP18

AP19

AP20

Gentoo Penguins AP21

Perf. 13½x13¾

2016, Nov. 13 Litho.

C33	AP16	(76p) multi	1.75	1.75
C34	AP17	(76p) multi	1.75	1.75
C35	AP18	(76p) multi	1.75	1.75

Perf. 13¾x13½

C36	AP19	(76p) multi	1.75	1.75
C37	AP20	(76p) multi	1.75	1.75
C38	AP21	(76p) multi	1.75	1.75
		Nos. C33-C38 (6)	10.50	10.50

Coil Stamps
Self-Adhesive
Country Name in Purple
Inscribed "Airmail Postcard"
Size: 25x21mm

Die Cut Perf. 13½

C39	AP17	(66p) multi	1.60	1.60
C40	AP18	(66p) multi	1.60	1.60

Size: 21x25mm

C41	AP19	(66p) multi	1.60	1.60
C42	AP20	(66p) multi	1.60	1.60
C43	AP21	(66p) multi	1.60	1.60
a.		Coil strip of 5, #C39-C43	8.00	
		Nos. C39-C43 (5)	8.00	8.00

BRITISH CENTRAL AFRICA

'bri-tish 'sen-trəl 'a-fri-kə

LOCATION — Central Africa, on the west shore of Lake Nyassa

GOVT. — British territory, under charter to the British South Africa Company

AREA — 37,800 sq. mi.

POP. — 1,639,329

CAPITAL — Zomba

In 1907 the name was changed to Nyasaland Protectorate, and stamps so inscribed replaced those of British Central Africa.

12 Pence = 1 Shilling
20 Shillings = 1 Pound

Rhodesia Nos. 2, 4-19 Overprinted in Black

1891-95 Unwmk. *Perf. 14*

1	A1	1p black	12.00	*14.00*
2	A2	2p gray green & ver	13.00	*5.00*
a.		Half used as 1p on cover ('95)		*7,500.*
3	A2	4p red brn & blk	18.00	*7.50*
4	A1	6p ultramarine	60.00	24.00
5	A1	6p dark blue	21.00	*12.00*
6	A2	8p rose & blue	21.00	*35.00*
7	A1	1sh bis brown	32.50	19.00
8	A1	2sh vermilion	50.00	*60.00*
9	A1	2sh6p gray lilac	90.00	*105.00*
10	A2	3sh brn & grn ('95)	90.00	*90.00*
11	A2	4sh gray & ver ('93)	110.00	*110.00*
12	A1	5sh yellow	110.00	*120.00*
13	A1	10sh green	200.00	*230.00*
14	A3	£1 blue	1,300.	*800.00*
15	A3	£2 rose red	1,400.	*1,600.*
16	A3	£5 yel green	2,250.	—
17	A3	£10 red brown	4,500.	*6,500.*
		Nos. 1-13 (13)	827.50	*831.50*

High values with fiscal cancellation are fairly common and can be purchased at a small fraction of the above values. This applies to subsequent issues also. The most common fiscal marking consists of an undated double-circle cancel with the words "BRITISH CENTRAL AFRICA" between the circles, and a town name in the center. This cancel exists in various sizes and is usually applied in black.

For surcharge see No. 20.

Rhodesia Nos. 13-14 Surcharged in Black

1892-93

18	A2	3sh on 4sh gray & ver ('93)	400.00	400.00
19	A1	4sh on 5sh yellow	100.00	*110.00*

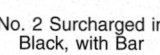

No. 2 Surcharged in Black, with Bar

1895

20	A2	1p on 2p	45.00	*70.00*
a.		Double surcharge	*11,000.*	*8,000.*

A double surcharge, without period after "Penny," and measuring 16mm instead of 18mm, is from a trial printing made at Blantyre. Value, $650.

A4

Coat of Arms of the Protectorate — A5

1895 Unwmk. Typo. *Perf. 14*

21	A4	1p black	23.50	18.50
22	A4	2p grn & blk	55.00	14.50
23	A4	4p org & blk	90.00	52.50
24	A4	6p ultra & blk	95.00	10.00
25	A4	1sh rose & blk	120.00	42.50
26	A5	2sh6p vio & blk	375.00	375.00
27	A5	3sh yel & blk	225.00	65.00

28	A5	5sh ol & blk	300.00	275.00
29	A5	£1 org & blk	1,450.	800.00
30	A5	£10 ver & blk	*8,000.*	*5,500.*
31	A5	£25 bl grn & blk	*16,000.*	*16,000.*
		Nos. 21-28 (8)	1,284.	853.00

1896 **Wmk. 2**

32	A4	1p black	4.25	*13.50*
33	A4	2p green & black	24.00	7.00
34	A4	4p org brown & blk	42.50	*21.00*
35	A4	6p ultra & black	50.00	19.00
36	A4	1sh rose & black	50.00	30.00

Wmk. 1 Sideways

37	A5	2sh6p vio rose & blk	200.00	*160.00*
38	A5	3sh yel & black	225.00	75.00
39	A5	5sh olive & blk	275.00	*275.00*
40	A5	£1 blue & blk	1,350.	650.00
41	A5	£10 ver & blk	*11,000.*	*6,000.*
42	A5	£25 bl grn & blk	*26,000.*	—
		Nos. 32-39 (8)	870.75	*600.50*

A6

A7

1897-1901 **Wmk. 2**

43	A6	1p ultra & blk	4.00	1.50
44	A6	1p rose & vio ('01)	3.50	.80
45	A6	2p yel & black	4.25	2.50
46	A6	4p car rose & blk	8.00	2.25
47	A6	4p ol grn & vio ('01)	16.00	*13.50*
48	A6	6p grn & blk	60.00	5.25
49	A6	6p red brn & vio ('01)	14.00	6.50
50	A6	1sh gray lil & blk	13.50	8.50

Wmk. 1

51	A7	2sh6p ultra & blk	100.00	*50.00*
52	A7	3sh gray grn & blk	350.00	*375.00*
53	A7	4sh car rose & blk	130.00	*100.00*
54	A7	10sh ol & blk	325.00	*325.00*
55	A7	£1 dp vio & blk	500.00	275.00
56	A7	£10 org & black	*8,500.*	*2,750.*
		Nos. 43-54 (12)	1,028.	*890.80*

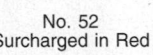

No. 52 Surcharged in Red

1897

57	A7	1p on 3sh	15.00	*22.50*
a.		"PNNEY"	10,000.	7,500.
b.		"PENN"	5,500.	4,500.
c.		Double surcharge	800.00	1,300.

A8

Type I — The vertical framelines are not continuous between stamps.

Type II — The vertical framelines are continuous between stamps.

1898, Mar. 11 **Unwmk.** ***Imperf.***

Type I

Control on Reverse

58	A8	1p ver & ultra	—	145.00
a.		1p ver & deep ultra	5,500.	150.00
b.		No control on reverse	6,500.	220.00
c.		Control double		525.00
d.		Control on front		*3,900.*
e.		Pair, one without oval	*32,500.*	

Type II

Control on Reverse

f.	1p ver & ultra	—	800.00

No Control on Reverse

g.	1p grayish blue & ver, initials on back	16,000.	1,100.
h.	No initials	7,500.	
i.	Oval inverted	32,500.	
j.	Oval double	—	
k.	Pair, with 3 ovals	—	

Perf. 12

Type I

Control on Reverse

59	A8	1p ver & ultra	6,500.	35.00
a.		1p ver & deep ultra	—	47.50
b.		Two diff. controls on reverse	—	850.00

No Control on Reverse

d.	1p ver & ultra	6,000.	115.00

There are 30 types of each setting of Nos. 58-59.

No. 58 issued without gum.

Control consists of figures or letters.

Initials are of Postmaster General (J.G. or J.T.G.).

A9

King Edward VII — A10

1903-04 **Wmk. 2**

60	A9	1p car & black	9.50	2.25
61	A9	2p vio & dull vio	4.50	2.25
62	A9	4p blk & gray green	3.25	*11.00*
63	A9	6p org brn & blk	4.00	*4.00*
64	A9	1sh pale blue & blk ('04)	5.00	*17.50*

Wmk. 1

65	A10	2sh6p gray green	70.00	*110.00*
66	A10	4sh vio & dl vio	115.00	*105.00*
67	A10	10sh blk & gray green	200.00	*300.00*
68	A10	£1 scar & blk	360.00	250.00
69	A10	£10 ultra & blk	*8,000.*	*4,750.*
		Nos. 60-68 (9)	771.25	*802.00*

1907 **Wmk. 3**

70	A9	1p car & black	12.00	3.50
71	A9	2p vio & dull vio	*19,000.*	
72	A9	4p blk & gray grn	*19,000.*	
73	A9	6p org brn & blk	52.50	*60.00*

Nos. 71-72 were not issued.

British Central Africa stamps were replaced by those of Nyasaland Protectorate in 1908.

BRITISH EAST AFRICA

'bri-tish 'ēst 'a-fri-kə

LOCATION — East coast of Africa; modern Kenya. Included all of the territory in East Africa under British control.

Postage stamps were issued by the Imperial British East Africa Company (IBEAC) in May 1900. Transferred to the Crown as a Protectorate July 1, 1895. Postal administration amalgamated with Uganda in 1901 with new stamps issued in July 1903 inscribed 'East Africa and Uganda Protectorates.'

16 Annas = 1 Rupee

A1

A2

Queen Victoria — A3

1890 **Wmk. 30** ***Perf. 14***

1	A1	½a on 1p lilac	350.00	240.00

Beware of forgeries.

2	A2	1a on 2p grn & car rose	575.00	350.00
3	A3	4a on 5p lilac & bl	600.00	375.00

A4

Sun and Crown Symbolical of "Light and Liberty" — A5

1890-94 **Unwmk.** **Litho.** ***Perf. 14***

14	A4	½a bister brown	1.25	*15.00*
b.		½a deep brown	1.00	*10.00*
c.		As "b," horiz. pair, imperf. btwn.	*1,925.*	775.00
d.		As "b," vert. pair, imperf. btwn.	1,400.	600.00
15	A4	1a blue green	9.50	*15.00*
16	A4	2a vermilion	5.00	*6.50*
17	A4	2½a black, *yel* ('93)	6.25	*9.50*
a.		Horiz. pair, imperf. btwn.	8,000.	
18	A4	3a black, *red* ('91)	5.50	*12.00*
b.		Horiz. pair, imperf. btwn.	1,400.	525.00
c.		Vert. pair, imperf. btwn.	1,400.	600.00
19	A4	4a yellow brown	3.00	*14.00*
20	A4	4½a brn vio ('91)	3.00	*24.00*
b.		4½a gray violet ('91)	42.50	22.50
c.		Horiz. pair, imperf. btwn.	2,100.	1,200.
d.		Vert. pair, imperf. btwn.	1,200.	600.00
21	A4	5a blk, *blue* ('94)	1.50	*13.00*
22	A4	7½a black ('94)	1.50	*19.00*
23	A4	8a blue	6.75	*11.50*
24	A4	8a gray	350.00	*350.00*
25	A4	1r rose	7.50	*11.00*
26	A4	1r gray	275.00	275.00
27	A5	2r brick red	17.00	*50.00*
28	A5	3r gray violet	14.00	*60.00*
29	A5	4r ultra	15.00	*60.00*
30	A5	5r gray green	37.50	*85.00*
		Nos. 14-30 (17)	759.25	*1,031.*

Some of the paper used for this issue had a papermaker's watermark and parts of it often can be seen on the stamps.

Values for Nos. 14c, 14d, 18b, 18c, 20c, 20d, unused, are for examples with little or no original gum. Stamps with natural straight edges are almost as common as fully perforated stamps from the early printings of Nos. 14-30, and for all printings of the rupee values. Values about the same.

For surcharges and overprints see Nos. 31-53.

1890-93 ***Imperf.***

Values for Pairs except No. 19b.

14a	A4	½a bister brown	1,200.	450.
14c	A4	½a deep brown	1,700.	725.
15a	A4	1a blue green	4,750.	1,200.
16a	A4	2a vermilion	4,500.	1,300.
17d	A4	2½a blk, *brt yel*	1,200.	550.
18a	A4	3a black, *red*	1,200.	500.
19a	A4	4a yel brown	4,750.	1,600.
19b	A4	4a gray	1,500.	1,700.
20a	A4	4½a dull violet	2,000.	550.
23a	A4	8a blue	10,000.	1,400.
25a	A4	1r rose	15,000.	1,600.

A6

Handstamped Surcharges

1891 ***Perf. 14***

31	A6	½a on 2a ver ("A.D.")	14,000.	1,100.
a.		Double surcharge		*13,000.*
32	A6	1a on 4a yel brn ("A.B.")	21,000.	2,300.

Validation initials are shown in parentheses. See note below No. 35.

Manuscript Surcharges

1891-95

33	A6	½a on 2a ver ("A.B.")	17,000.	1,100.
a.		"½ Annas" ("A.B.")		1,200.
b.		Initialed "A.D."		6,500.
34	A6	½a on 3a blk, *red* ("T.E.C.R.")	700.	60.
b.		Initialed "A.B."	18,000.	2,750.
34A	A6	1a on 3a blk, *red* ("V.H.M.")	16,000.	2,250.
c.		Initialed "T.E.C.R."	23,000.	3,250.
35	A6	1a on 4a yel brn ("A.B.")	12,000.	2,200.

The manuscript initials on Nos. 31-35, given in parentheses, stand for Andrew Dick, Archibald Brown, Victor H. Mackenzie (1891) and T.E.C. Remington (1895).

Three persons applied the surcharge to No. 33, and two persons applied the surcharge to No. 35, resulting in different types.

A7

1894 **Printed Surcharges**

36	A7	5a on 8a blue	85.00	*110.00*
37	A7	7½a on 1r rose	85.00	*110.00*

Stamps of 1890-94 Handstamped in Black

1895

38	A4	½a deep brown	90.00	35.00
b.		Inverted overprint		*6,000.*
39	A4	1a blue green	200.00	135.00
40	A4	2a vermilion	220.00	115.00
41	A4	2½a black, *yel*	220.00	67.50
42	A4	3a black, *dull red*	105.00	60.00
43	A4	4a yel brown	72.50	47.50
44	A4	4½a gray violet	250.00	120.00
a.		4½a brown violet	1,450.	1,150.
45	A4	5a black, *blue*	300.00	170.00
b.		Inverted overprint		*5,000.*
46	A4	7½a black	150.00	100.00
47	A4	8a blue	115.00	90.00
b.		Inverted overprint	*8,000.*	
48	A4	1r rose	67.50	60.00
49	A5	2r brick red	550.00	325.00
50	A5	3r gray violet	275.00	160.00
b.		Inverted overprint		
51	A5	4r ultra	250.00	200.00
52	A5	5r gray green	525.00	*325.00*
		Nos. 38-52 (15)	3,390.	2,010.

Forgeries exist.

Double Overprints

38a	A4	½a	550.	525.
39a	A4	1a	750.	550.
40a	A4	2a	850.	575.
41a	A4	2½a	850.	525.
43a	A4	4a	600.	550.
44b	A4	4½a gray violet	900.	675.
44c	A4	4½a brown violet	3,300.	2,400.
45a	A4	5a	1,100.	1,000.
46a	A4	7½a	850.	675.
47a	A4	8a	750.	725.
48a	A4	1r	700.	675.
50a	A5	3r	1,200.	1,100.
51a	A5	4r	1,100.	1,000.
52a	A5	5r	1,600.	1,600.

Surcharged in Red

1895

53	A4	2½a on 4½a gray vio	225.00	90.00
a.		Double overprint (#44b)	1,200.	1,050.

Stamps of India 1874-95 Overprinted or Surcharged

a

b

c

1895 **Wmk. Star (39)**

54 A17 ½a green 8.50 *6.75*
55 A19 1a maroon 8.00 *7.25*
56 A20 1a6p bister brn 5.25 *5.00*
57 A21 2a ultra 10.00 3.75
58 A28 2a6p green 17.50 3.25
59 A20(a) 2½a on 1a6p bis brn 120.00 57.50
a. "½" without fraction line 135.00
d. As "a," "1" of "½" invtd. 1,200. 725.00
62 A22 3a orange 26.00 *13.50*
63 A23 4a ol grn 50.00 42.50
a. 4a slate green 32.00 26.00
64 A25 8a red violet 35.00 *60.00*
a. 8a red lilac 110.00 85.00
65 A26 12a vio, *red* 27.50 *40.00*
66 A27 1r gray 115.00 80.00
67 A29 1r car & grn 55.00 *160.00*
a. Dbl. ovpt., one sideways 525.00 1,100.
68 A30 2r bis & rose 120.00 *180.00*
69 A30 3r grn & brn 170.00 *200.00*
70 A30 5r vio & ultra 175.00 *240.00*
a. Double overprint 2,750.

Wmk. Elephant's Head (38)

71 A14 6a bister 50.00 *60.00*
Nos. 54-59,62-71 (16) 992.75 *1,160.*

Varieties of the overprint include "Brit1sh," "Br1tish," "Afr1ca," inverted "a" for "t," "Eas" for "East," and letter "B" handstamped. See the *Scott Specialized Catalogue of Stamps and Covers* for detailed listings.

No. 59 is surcharged in bright red; surcharges in brown red were prepared for the UPU, but not regularly issued as stamps. See note following No. 93.

Queen Victoria and British Lions — A8

1896-1901 Engr. Wmk. 2 *Perf. 14*

72 A8 ½a yel green 6.50 1.00
73 A8 1a carmine 17.50 .50
a. 1a red 16.00 .50
74 A8 1a dp rose ('01) 32.50 5.00
75 A8 2a chocolate 13.00 8.50
76 A8 2½a dark blue 18.00 2.50
77 A8 3a gray 10.00 *15.00*
78 A8 4a deep green 8.50 5.00
79 A8 4½a orange 17.50 *20.00*
80 A8 5a dk ocher 9.25 8.00
81 A8 7½a lilac 11.00 *27.00*
82 A8 8a olive gray 11.00 7.00
83 A8 1r ultra 140.00 80.00
a. 1r pale blue 80.00 30.00
84 A8 2r red orange 80.00 35.00
85 A8 3r deep violet 80.00 40.00
86 A8 4r lake 72.50 85.00
87 A8 5r dark brown 70.00 50.00
Nos. 72-87 (16) 597.25 389.50

Zanzibar Nos. 38-40, 44-46 Overprinted in Black

1897 **Wmk. Rosette (71)**

88 A2 ½a yel grn & red 67.50 55.00
89 A2 1a indigo & red 115.00 110.00
90 A2 2a red brn & red 50.00 26.00
91 A2 4½a org & red 60.00 37.50
92 A2 5a bister & red 67.50 50.00
93 A2 7½a lilac & red 70.00 50.00
a. Ovptd. on front and back —
Nos. 88-93 (6) 430.00 328.50

The 1a with red overprint, which includes a period after "Africa", was sent to the UPU, but never placed in use. Nos. 88, 90-93 and 95-100 also exist with period (in black) in sets sent to the UPU. Some experts consider these essays.

Black Ovpt. on Zanzibar #39, 42 New Value Surcharged in Red

1897

95 A2(a) 2½a on 1a 135.00 80.00
a. Black overprint double 7,800.
96 A2(b) 2½a on 1a 325.00 130.00
97 A2(c) 2½a on 1a 160.00 90.00
a. Black overprint double 7,800.
98 A2(a) 2½a on 3a 135.00 67.50
99 A2(b) 2½a on 3a 325.00 120.00
100 A2(c) 2½a on 3a 160.00 75.00
Nos. 95-100 (6) 1,240. 562.50

A special printing of the 2½a surcharge on the 1a and 3a stamps was made for submission to the U.P.U. Stamps have a period after "Africa" in the overprint, and the surcharges included a "2" over "1" error in the fraction of the surcharge. These stamps were never placed in use. The fraction error appears on both the 1a and 3a stamps. Value, each, $1,500.

A10

1898 **Wmk. 1** **Engr.**

102a A10 1r 1r dull blue ('01) 120.00 50.00
103 A10 2r orange 140.00 150.00
104 A10 3r dk violet 180.00 *190.00*
105 A10 4r carmine 500.00 *550.00*
106 A10 5r black brown 450.00 *550.00*
107 A10 10r bister 450.00 *600.00*
108 A10 20r yel green 1,200. *2,500.*
109 A10 50r lilac 2,500. *9,000.*
Nos. 102a-107 (6) 1,840. *2,090.*

Nos. 102-109 are often found with fiscal or Court Fee cancels. Stamps with these cancels can be purchased at a fraction of these values.

The stamps of this country were superseded by the stamps of East Africa and Uganda Protectorate.

BRITISH GUIANA

'bri-tish gē-'a-nə, -'ä-nə

LOCATION — On the northeast coast of South America
GOVT. — British Crown Colony
AREA — 83,000 sq. mi.
POP. — 628,000 (estimated 1964)
CAPITAL — Georgetown

British Guiana became the independent state of Guyana May 26, 1966.

100 Cents = 1 Dollar

Catalogue values for unused stamps in this country are for Never Hinged items, beginning with Scott 242 in the regular postage section and Scott J1 in the postage due section.

Values for unused stamps are for examples with original gum except for Nos. 6-12 and 35-53, which are valued without gum. Very fine examples of all stamps from No. 6 on will have four clear margins. Inferior examples sell at much reduced prices, depending on the condition of the individual stamp.

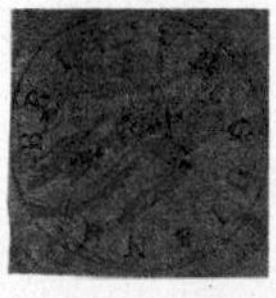

A1

1850-51 Typeset Unwmk. *Imperf.*

1 A1 2c blk, *pale rose,* cut to shape ('51) *325,000.*
2 A1 4c black, *orange* *100,000.*
Cut to shape *16,000.*
a. 4c black, *yellow* *130,000.*
Cut to shape *24,000.*
3 A1 4c blk, *yellow* (pelure) *135,000.*
Cut to shape *26,000.*
4 A1 8c black, *green* *70,000.*
Cut to shape *16,000.*
5 A1 12c black, *blue* *35,000.*
Cut to shape *11,000.*
a. 12c black, *pale blue* *40,000.*
Cut to shape *14,000.*
b. 12c black, *indigo* *45,000.*
Cut to shape *13,000.*
c. "1" of "12" omitted, cut to shape *250,000.*

These stamps were initialed before use by the Deputy Postmaster General or by one of the clerks of the Colonial Postoffice at Georgetown. The following initials are found: — E. T. E. D(alton); E. D. W(ight); G. B. S(mith); H. A. K(illikelley); W. H. L(ortimer). As these stamps are type-set there are several types of each value.

Ship and Motto of Colony — A2

1852 **Litho.**

6 A2 1c black, *magenta* *15,000.* *7,000.*
7 A2 4c black, *blue* *25,000.* *13,000.*

Both 1c and 4c are found in two types. Examples with paper cracked or rubbed sell for much less.

Some examples are initialed E. D. W(ight).

The reprints are on thicker paper and the colors are brighter. They are perforated 12½ and imperforate. Value $20 each.

Seal of the Colony — A3

Without Line above Value

1853-59 ***Imperf.***

8 A3 1c vermilion 8,000. 1,750.

A proof of No. 8 exists in reddish brown, value about $1,600.

Full or Partial White Line Above Value

9 A3 1c red (I) 7,750. 2,250.
10 A3 4c blue 3,250. 850.
a. 4c dark blue 6,000. 1,200.
b. 4c pale blue 2,250. 750.

On No. 9, "ONE CENT" varies from 11 to 13mm in width.

No. 10 Retouched; White Line above Value Removed

11 A3 4c blue 4,750. 1,100.
a. 4c dark blue 8,500. 1,750.
b. 4c pale blue 3,500. 1,100.

Reprints of Nos. 8 and 10 are on thin paper, perf. 12½ or imperf. The 1c is orange red, the 4c sky blue.

1860

Numerals in Corners Framed

12 A3 4c blue 7,500. 850.00

A4

1856 **Typeset** ***Imperf.***

13 A4 1c black, *mag* *9,500,000.*
14 A4 4c black, *mag* *100,000.* *25,000.*
a. 4c black, *rose carmine* *50,000.* *40,000.*
15 A4 4c black, *blue* *150,000.*
16 A4 4c black, *blue, paper colored through* *225,000.*

These stamps were initialed before being issued and the following initials are found: — E. T. E. D.; E. D. W.; W. H. L.; C. A. W. No. 13 is unique.

A5

Wide space between value and "Cents"

1860-61 **Litho.** ***Perf. 12***

Thick Paper

17 A5 1c brown red ('61) 500.00 125.00
18 A5 1c pink 3,500. 300.00
19 A5 2c orange 350.00 65.00
20 A5 8c rose 825.00 130.00
21 A5 12c gray 750.00 55.00
a. 12c lilac 850.00 55.00
22 A5 24c green 1,700. 85.00

All denominations of type A5 above four cents are expressed in Roman numerals.

Bisects and trisects are found on covers. These were not officially authorized.

The reprints of the 1c pink are perforated 12½; the other values have not been reprinted.

1862-65 **Thin Paper**

23 A5 1c brown 950.00 275.00
24 A5 1c black ('63) 175.00 65.00
25 A5 2c orange 165.00 65.00
26 A5 8c rose ('63) 340.00 85.00
27 A5 12c lilac 450.00 55.00
28 A5 24c green 1,850. 110.00

Perf. 12½ and 13

29 A5 1c black 80.00 25.00
30 A5 2c orange 95.00 27.50
31 A5 8c rose 350.00 97.50
32 A5 12c lilac 1,200. 150.00
33 A5 24c green 875.00 80.00

Medium Paper

33A A5 1c black ('64) 70.00 55.00
33B A5 2c dp org ('64) 90.00 32.50
33C A5 8c pink ('64) 300.00 80.00
33D A5 12c lilac ('65) 1,250. 130.00
33E A5 24c green ('64) 375.00 65.00
f. 24c deep green 450.00 90.00

Perf. 10

34 A5 12c gray lilac 875.00 97.50

Imperfs. are proofs. See Nos. 44-62.

A6

A7

A8

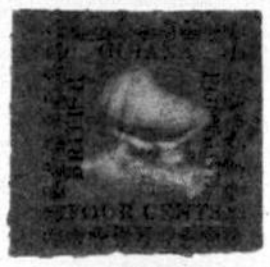

A9

A10

A11

1862 **Typeset** ***Rouletted***

35 A6 1c black, *rose* *5,750.* *850.*
Unsigned 650.
36 A7 1c black, *rose* *7,500.* *1,400.*
Unsigned 750.
37 A8 1c black, *rose* *9,750.* *1,500.*
Unsigned 1,300.
38 A6 2c black, *yellow* *5,750.* *450.*
Unsigned 2,600.
39 A7 2c black, *yellow* *7,500.* *575.*
Unsigned 3,000.
40 A8 2c black, *yellow* *9,750.* *925.*
Unsigned 3,750.
41 A9 4c black, *blue* *8,000.* *1,400.*
Unsigned 1,400.
42 A10 4c black, *blue* *11,000.* *2,000.*
Unsigned —
a. Without inner lines *8,000.* *1,400.*
As "a," unsigned 1,300.
43 A11 4c black, *blue* *6,500.* *1,100.*
Unsigned 1,300.

Nos. 35-43 were typeset, in sheets of 24 each. They were initialed before use "R. M. Ac. R. G.," being the initials of Robert Mather, Acting Receiver General.

The initials are in black on the 1c and in red on the 2c. An alkali was used on the 4c stamps, which, destroying the color of the paper, caused the initials to appear to be written in white.

Uninitialed stamps are remainders, few sheets having been found.

Stamps with roulette on all sides are valued higher.

Narrow space between value and "Cents"

1860 Thick Paper Litho. *Perf. 12*

No.	Type	Description	Unused	Used
44	A5	4c blue	450.00	80.00
c.		4c deep blue	800.00	120.00

Thin Paper

No.	Type	Description	Unused	Used
44A	A5	4c pale blue	150.00	42.50
d.		4c blue	175.00	55.00

Perf. 12½ and 13

No.	Type	Description	Unused	Used
44B	A5	4c blue	115.00	32.50

Medium Paper

1863-68 *Perf. 12½ and 13*

No.	Type	Description	Unused	Used
45	A5	1c black ('66)	80.00	40.00
46	A5	2c orange	85.00	10.00
47	A5	4c gray blue ('64)	100.00	25.00
48	A5	8c rose ('68)	425.00	27.50
49	A5	12c lilac ('67)	650.00	50.00
		Nos. 45-49 (5)	1,340.	152.50

1866-71 *Perf. 10*

No.	Type	Description	Unused	Used
50	A5	1c black	25.00	8.50
51	A5	2c orange	65.00	5.00
52	A5	4c blue	130.00	11.00
a.		Half used as 2c on cover		7,500.
53	A5	8c rose	300.00	37.50
a.		Diagonal half used as 4c on cover		—
54	A5	12c lilac	300.00	27.50
a.		Third used as 4c on cover		—
		Nos. 50-54 (5)	820.00	89.50

1875-76 *Perf. 15*

No.	Type	Description	Unused	Used
58	A5	1c black	65.00	9.00
59	A5	2c orange	195.00	17.00
60	A5	4c blue	350.00	120.00
61	A5	8c rose	400.00	110.00
62	A5	12c lilac	925.00	100.00
		Nos. 58-62 (5)	1,935.	356.00

Seal of Colony — A12

1863 *Perf. 12*

No.	Type	Description	Unused	Used
63	A12	24c yellow green	275.00	15.50
a.		24c green	350.00	25.00

Perf. 12½ to 13

No.	Type	Description	Unused	Used
64	A12	6c blue	200.00	72.50
65	A12	24c green	275.00	16.00
66	A12	48c deep red	425.00	80.00
a.		48c rose	450.00	80.00
		Nos. 63-66 (4)	1,175.	184.00

1866 *Perf. 10*

No.	Type	Description	Unused	Used
67	A12	6c blue	200.00	40.00
a.		6c ultramarine	215.00	67.50
68	A12	24c yellow green	275.00	9.00
a.		24c green	375.00	11.00
69	A12	48c rose red	425.00	37.50
		Nos. 67-69 (3)	900.00	86.50

For surcharges see Nos. 83-92.

1875 *Perf. 15*

No.	Type	Description	Unused	Used
70	A12	6c ultra	1,150.	150.00
71	A12	24c yellow green	850.	42.50
a.		24c deep green	1,600.	120.00

Seal of Colony — A13

1876 Typo. Wmk. 1 *Perf. 14*

No.	Type	Description	Unused	Used
72	A13	1c slate	3.25	1.75
a.		Perf. 14x12½		225.00
73	A13	2c orange	92.50	4.00
74	A13	4c ultra	150.00	15.00
a.		Perf. 12½	1,450.	250.00
75	A13	6c chocolate	110.00	14.00
76	A13	8c rose	160.00	1.00
77	A13	12c lilac	80.00	2.50
78	A13	24c green	90.00	4.00
79	A13	48c red brown	160.00	50.00
80	A13	96c bister	575.00	325.00
		Nos. 72-80 (9)	1,421.	417.25

See Nos. 107-111. For surcharges see Nos. 93-95, 98-101.

Stamps Surcharged by Brush-like Pen Lines

Type a

Type b

Type c

Type d

Surcharge Types:
Type a — Two horiz. lines.
Type b — Two lines, one horiz., one vert.
Type c — Three lines, two horiz., one vert.
Type d — One horiz. line.

On Nos. 75 and 67

1878 *Perf. 10, 14*

No.	Type	Description	Unused	Used
82	A13(a)	(1c) on 6c choc	52.50	150.00
83	A12(b)	(1c) on 6c blue	250.00	90.00
84	A13(b)	(1c) on 6c choc	450.00	135.00

On Nos. O3, O8-O10

No.	Type	Description	Unused	Used
85	A13(c)	(1c) on 4c ultra	425.00	120.00
a.		Type b	50,000.	6,000.
86	A13(c)	(1c) on 6c choc	725.00	135.00
87	A5(c)	(2c) on 8c rose	5,250.	400.00
88A	A13(b)	(2c) on 8c rose	600.00	240.00

On Nos. O1, O3, O6-O7

No.	Type	Description	Unused	Used
89	A5(d)	(1c) on 1c blk	325.00	90.00
89A	A5(d)	(2c) on 8c rose		
90	A13(d)	(1c) on 1c sl	220.00	80.00
91	A13(d)	(2c) on 2c org	450.00	80.00

The provisional values of Nos. 82 to 91 were established by various official decrees. The horizontal lines crossed out the old value, "OFFICIAL," or both.

The existence of No. 89A has been questioned by specialists. The editors would like to see authenticated evidence of its existence.

Nos. 69 and 80 Surcharged with New Values in Black

No. 92

No. 93

No. 94

No. 95

1881

No.	Type	Description	Unused	Used
92	A12	1c on 48c red	55.00	7.00
93	A13	1c on 96c bister	6.00	14.00
94	A13	2c on 96c bister	24.00	27.50
95	A13	2c on 96c bister	85.00	160.00
		Nos. 92-95 (4)	170.00	208.50

Nos. O4, O5 and Unissued Official Stamps Surcharged with New Values

No. 96

No. 97

Nos. 98, 100

Nos. 99, 101

No. 102

1881

No.	Type	Description	Unused	Used
96	A5	1c on 12c lilac (#O4)	155.00	85.00
97	A13	1c on 48c red brn	225.00	140.00
98	A13	2c on 12c lilac	750.00	500.00
99	A13	2c on 12c lilac	110.00	70.00
a.		"2" inverted		
b.		"2" double	950.00	550.00
100	A13	2c on 24c green	1,000.	950.00
101	A13	2c on 24c green	110.00	70.00
a.		"2" inverted		
d.		Double surcharge	1,325.	
102	A12	2c on 24c green (#O5)	400.00	200.00

A27

Typeset

ONE AND TWO CENTS.
Type I — Ship with three masts.
Type II — Brig with two masts.

"SPECIMEN" Perforated Diagonally across Stamp

1882 Unwmk. *Perf. 12*

No.	Type	Description	Unused	Used
103	A27	1c black, *lil rose,* I	80.00	35.00
a.		Horiz. pair, imperf between		10,000.
104	A27	1c black, *lil rose,* II	80.00	35.00
a.		Without "Specimen"	1,500.	600.00
105	A27	2c black, *yel,* I	115.00	60.00
a.		Without "Specimen"	1,300.	700.00
b.		Diagonal half used as 1c on cover		—
106	A27	2c black, *yel,* II	110.00	65.00
a.		Without "Specimen"	1,300.	700.00
		Nos. 103-106 (4)	385.00	195.00

Nos. 103-106 were typeset, 12 to a sheet, and, to prevent fraud on the government, the word *"Specimen"* was perforated across them before they were issued. There were 2 settings of the 1c and 3 settings of the 2c, thus there are 24 types of the former and 36 of the latter.

Type of 1876

1882 Typo. Wmk. 2 *Perf. 14*

No.	Type	Description	Unused	Used
107	A13	1c slate	20.00	.50
108	A13	2c orange	60.00	.35
a.		"2 CENTS" double		11,500.
109	A13	4c ultra	110.00	6.50
110	A13	6c brown	6.00	8.00
111	A13	8c rose	140.00	1.00
		Nos. 107-111 (5)	336.00	16.35

"INLAND REVENUE" Overprint and Surcharged in Black

A28

Type I

Type II

4 CENTS and $4
Type I — Figure "4" is 3mm high.
Type II — Figure "4" is 3½mm high.
6 CENTS
Type I — Top of "6" is flat.
Type II — Top of "6" turns downward.

1889

No.	Type	Description	Unused	Used
112	A28	1c lilac	3.00	.55
113	A28	2c lilac	3.50	3.50
114	A28	3c lilac	2.25	.40
115	A28	4c lilac, I	13.00	.45
116	A28	4c lilac, II	24.00	7.50
117	A28	6c lilac, I	23.00	8.50
118	A28	6c lilac, II	15.00	6.50
119	A28	8c lilac	2.75	.65
120	A28	10c lilac	8.50	3.25
121	A28	20c lilac	27.50	22.50
122	A28	40c lilac	52.50	35.00
123	A28	72c lilac	85.00	72.50
124	A28	$1 green	575.00	650.00
125	A28	$2 green	275.00	300.00
126	A28	$3 green	275.00	300.00
127	A28	$4 green, I	650.00	775.00
127A	A28	$4 green, II	2,400.	3,000.
128	A28	$5 green	400.00	450.00
		Nos. 112-128 (18)	4,835.	5,636.

For surcharges see Nos.129, 148-151B.

No. 113 Surcharged in Red

1889

No.	Type	Description	Unused	Used
129	A29	2c on 2c lilac	6.50	.55

Inverted and double surcharges of "2" were privately made.

A30

1889-1903 **Typo.**

No.	Type	Description	Unused	Used
130	A30	1c lilac & gray	11.00	3.50
131	A30	1c green ('90)	1.10	.25
131A	A30	1c gray grn ('00)	2.10	*6.75*
132	A30	2c lilac & org	8.50	.25
133	A30	2c lil & rose ('00)	4.00	.40
134	A30	2c vio & blk, *red* ('01)	2.00	.25
135	A30	4c lilac & ultra	5.50	4.00
a.		4c lilac & blue	25.00	4.00
136	A30	5c ultra ('91)	4.50	.25
137	A30	6c lilac & mar	8.50	*25.00*
a.		6c lilac & brown	42.50	27.50
138	A30	6c gray blk & ultra ('02)	8.00	*13.50*
139	A30	8c lilac & rose	24.00	4.00
140	A30	8c lil & blk ('90)	13.00	3.25
141	A30	12c lilac & vio	10.00	4.00
142	A30	24c lilac & grn	7.50	4.00
143	A30	48c lilac & ver	42.50	13.00
144	A30	48c dk gray & lil brn ('01)	35.00	35.00
a.		48c gray & purple brown	60.00	50.00
145	A30	60c gray grn & car ('03)	75.00	*250.00*
146	A30	72c lil & org brn	34.00	*55.00*
a.		72c lilac & yellow brown	77.50	90.00
147	A30	96c lilac & carmine	80.00	*85.00*
a.		96c lilac & rose	90.00	*100.00*
		Nos. 130-147 (19)	376.20	*507.40*

Stamps of the 1889-1903 issue with pen or revenue cancellation sell for a small fraction of the above quotations.

See Nos. 160-177.

A31

1890 **Red Surcharge**

No.	Type	Description	Unused	Used
148	A31	1c on $1 grn & blk	3.50	.50
a.		Double surcharge	*300.00*	*170.00*
149	A31	1c on $2 grn & blk	2.50	1.40
a.		Double surcharge	*120.00*	—
150	A31	1c on $3 grn & blk	4.00	1.40
a.		Double surcharge	*160.00*	—
151	A31	1c on $4 grn & blk, type I	7.50	*17.50*
a.		Double surcharge	*150.00*	
151B	A31	1c on $4 grn & blk, type II	15.00	*50.00*
c.		Double surcharge		
		Nos. 148-151B (5)	32.50	*70.80*

Mt. Roraima A32

Kaieteur (Old Man's) Falls — A33

1898 **Wmk. 1** **Engr.**

No.	Type	Description	Unused	Used
152	A32	1c car & gray blk	10.00	2.50
153	A33	2c indigo & brn	40.00	4.75
a.		Horiz. pair, imperf. between	*16,500.*	
b.		2c blue & brown	45.00	4.75
154	A32	5c brown & grn	57.50	6.50
155	A33	10c red & blue blk	30.00	32.50
156	A32	15c blue & red brn	37.50	26.00
		Nos. 152-156 (5)	175.00	72.25

60th anniv. of Queen Victoria's accession to the throne.

Nos. 154-156 Surcharged in Black

1899

No.	Type	Description	Unused	Used
157	A32	2c on 5c brn & grn	4.00	3.25
a.		Without period	185.00	140.00
158	A33	2c on 10c red & bl black	4.50	2.75
a.		"GENTS"	70.00	*92.50*
b.		Inverted surcharge	*750.00*	*875.00*
c.		Without period	25.00	*65.00*
159	A32	2c on 15c bl & red brown	4.50	1.50
a.		Without period	80.00	*80.00*
b.		Double surcharge	*1,100.*	*1,500.*
c.		Inverted surcharge	*875.00*	*1,100.*
		Nos. 157-159 (3)	13.00	7.50

There are many slight errors in the setting of this surcharge, such as: small "E" in "CENTS"; no period and narrow "C"; comma between "T" and "S"; dash between "TWO" and "CENTS"; comma between "N" and "T."

Ship Type of 1889-1903

1905-10 **Wmk. 3**

Chalky Paper

No.	Type	Description	Unused	Used
160	A30	1c gray green	12.00	1.35
a.		Booklet pane of 6		
161	A30	2c vio & blk, *red*	6.50	.25
162	A30	4c lilac & ultra	9.00	*15.00*
163	A30	5c lil & blue, *bl*	4.25	*8.00*
164	A30	6c gray black & ultra	18.00	*50.00*
165	A30	12c lilac & vio	27.50	*55.00*
166	A30	24c lil & grn ('06)	4.50	*5.50*
167	A30	48c gray & vio brn	17.00	*27.50*
168	A30	60c gray grn & car rose	17.00	*110.00*
169	A30	72c lil & org brn ('07)	42.50	*85.00*
170	A30	96c blk & red, *yel*('06)	42.50	*55.00*
		Nos. 160-170 (11)	200.75	*412.60*

The 2c-60c exist on ordinary paper. See *Scott Classic Specialized Catalogue of Stamps and Covers.*

A34

Black Overprint

No.	Type	Description	Unused	Used
171	A34	$2.40 grn & vio	*210.00*	*500.00*

Ship Type of 1889-1903

Type I

Type II

TWO CENTS

Type I — Only the upper right corner of the flag touches the mast.

Type II — The entire right side of the flag touches the mast.

1907-10 **Ordinary Paper**

No.	Type	Description	Unused	Used
171A	A30	1c blue green ('10)	16.00	3.00
172	A30	2c red, type I	21.00	1.10
b.		2c red, type II	10.50	.25
174	A30	4c brown & vio	3.50	1.35
175	A30	5c blue	18.50	6.00
176	A30	6c gray & black	16.00	8.50
177	A30	12c orange & vio	5.00	6.50
		Nos. 171A177 (6)	80.00	26.45

George V — A35

1913-17 ***Perf. 14***

No.	Type	Description	Unused	Used
178	A35	1c green	5.00	1.00
a.		bl grn ('17)	2.25	.30
179	A35	2c scarlet	3.75	.25
a.		2c carmine	1.60	.25
180	A35	4c brn & red vio	7.50	.40
181	A35	5c ultra	2.25	1.25
182	A35	6c gray & black	3.75	2.75
183	A35	12c org & vio	1.75	1.25

Chalky Paper

No.	Type	Description	Unused	Used
184	A35	24c dl vio & grn	4.25	*5.00*
185	A35	48c blk & vio brn	30.00	*21.00*
186	A35	60c grn & car	20.00	*60.00*
187	A35	72c dl vio & org brn	60.00	*100.00*

Surface Colored Paper

No.	Type	Description	Unused	Used
188	A35	96c blk & red, *yel*	32.50	*65.00*

Paper Colored Through

No.	Type	Description	Unused	Used
189	A35	96c blk & red, *yel* ('16)	22.50	*65.00*
		Nos. 178-189 (12)	193.25	*322.90*

The 72c and late printings of the 2c and 5c are from redrawn dies. The ruled lines behind the value are thin and faint, making the tablet appear lighter than before. The shading lines in other parts of the stamps are also lighter. Several paper shades of No. 189 exist.

1921-27 **Wmk. 4**

No.	Type	Description	Unused	Used
191	A35	1c green	5.75	.40
192	A35	2c rose red	7.75	.30
193	A35	2c dp vio ('23)	3.00	.25
194	A35	4c brn & vio	5.75	.25
195	A35	6c ultra	3.75	.40
196	A35	12c org & vio	3.50	2.00

Chalky Paper

No.	Type	Description	Unused	Used
197	A35	24c dl vio & grn	2.75	*5.50*
198	A35	48c blk & vio brn ('26)	12.00	4.50
199	A35	60c grn & car ('26)	12.50	*57.50*
200	A35	72c dl vio & brn org	37.50	*80.00*
201	A35	96c blk & red, *yel* ('27)	35.00	*55.00*
		Nos. 191-201 (11)	129.25	*206.10*

Plowing a Rice Field — A36

Indian Shooting Fish — A37

Kaieteur Falls — A38

Georgetown, Public Buildings A39

1931, July 21 **Engr.** ***Perf. 12½***

No.	Type	Description	Unused	Used
205	A36	1c blue green	2.25	1.10
206	A37	2c dk brown	1.75	.25
207	A38	4c car rose	2.25	.40
208	A39	6c ultra	2.25	*1.10*
209	A38	$1 violet	50.00	*60.00*
		Nos. 205-209 (5)	58.50	*62.85*
		Set, never hinged	100.00	

Cent. of the union of Berbice, Demerara and Essequibo to form the Colony of British Guiana.

A40

A41

Gold Mining — A42

Kaieteur Falls — A43

Shooting Logs over Falls — A44

Stabroek Market — A45

Sugar Cane in Punts — A46

Forest Road — A47

Victoria Regia Lilies — A48

Mt. Roraima — A49

Sir Walter Raleigh and Son — A50

Botanical Gardens
A51

1934, Oct. 1 *Perf. 12½*
210 A40 1c green .60 *2.00*
211 A41 2c brown 1.50 1.75
212 A42 3c carmine .40 .25
b. Perf. 12½x13½ ('43) 1.00 *1.00*
c. Perf. 13x13½ ('49) 2.00 1.00
213 A43 4c vio black 2.25 3.50
a. Vert. pair, imperf. horiz. *20,000. 20,000.*
214 A44 6c dp ultra 8.00 *7.00*
215 A45 12c orange .45 *.25*
a. Perf. 13½x13 ('51) .60 *1.00*
216 A46 24c rose violet 4.00 *15.00*
217 A47 48c black 12.00 *10.00*
218 A43 50c green 18.00 *25.00*
219 A48 60c brown 30.00 *32.00*
220 A49 72c rose violet 2.25 *3.50*
221 A50 96c black 42.50 *47.50*
222 A51 $1 violet 52.50 50.00
Nos. 210-222 (13) 174.45 *197.75*
Set, never hinged 290.00

See Nos. 236, 238, 240.

Common Design Types pictured following the introduction.

Silver Jubilee Issue
Common Design Type

1935, May 6 *Perf. 13½x14*
223 CD301 2c gray blk & ultra .35 .25
224 CD301 6c blue & brown 2.00 *5.50*
225 CD301 12c indigo & grn 7.50 *9.75*
226 CD301 24c brt vio & ind 12.50 *20.00*
Nos. 223-226 (4) 22.35 35.50
Set, never hinged 32.50

Coronation Issue
Common Design Type

1937, May 12 *Perf. 13½x14*
227 CD302 2c brown .25 .25
228 CD302 4c gray black .65 .65
229 CD302 6c bright ultra .55 *2.15*
Nos. 227-229 (3) 1.45 3.05
Set, never hinged 1.60

A52

A53

A54

A55

A56

A57

A58

Victoria Regia Lilies and Jacanas — A59

1938-52 Engr. Wmk. 4 *Perf. 12½*
230 A52 1c green .25 .25
b. Perf. 14x13 ('49) .85 *1.00*
231 A53 2c violet blk, perf. 13x14 ('49) .40 .25
b. Perf. 12½ .50 .25
232 A54 4c black & rose, perf. 13x14 ('52) .90 .25
a. Perf. 12½ .65 .35
c. Vert. pair, imperf. between *40,000. 35,000.*
233 A55 6c deep ultra, perf. 13x14 ('49) 1.60 .40
a. Perf. 12½ 1.50 .25
234 A56 24c deep green 2.75 .25
a. Wmk. upright 20.00 10.00
235 A53 36c purple 3.50 .25
a. Perf. 13x14 ('51) 1.75 .30
236 A47 48c orange yel 1.40 .90
a. Perf. 14x13 ('51) 1.25 2.50
237 A57 60c brown 12.50 9.50
238 A50 96c brown vio 7.50 *3.25*
a. Perf. 12½x13½ ('44) 8.75 *13.00*
239 A58 $1 deep violet 17.50 .35
a. Perf. 14x13 ('51) 300.00 *600.00*
240 A49 $2 rose vio ('45) 12.50 *27.50*
a. Perf. 14x13 ('50) 16.00 *37.50*
241 A59 $3 org brn ('45) 27.50 *40.00*
a. Perf. 14x13 ('52) 29.50 *55.00*
Nos. 230-241 (12) 88.30 *83.15*
Set, never hinged 135.00

The watermark on No. 234 is sideways.

Catalogue values for unused stamps in this section, from this point to the end of the section, are for Never Hinged items.

Peace Issue
Common Design Type

1946, Oct. 21 *Perf. 13½x14*
242 CD303 3c carmine .25 *.45*
243 CD303 6c deep blue .80 *.95*

Silver Wedding Issue
Common Design Types

1948, Dec. 20 Photo. *Perf. 14x14½*
244 CD304 3c scarlet .25 *.45*

Engr.
Perf. 11½x11
245 CD305 $3 orange brown 24.00 *28.00*

UPU Issue
Common Design Types
Engr.; Name Typo. on 6c and 12c
Perf. 13½, 11x11½

1949, Oct. 10 **Wmk. 4**
246 CD306 4c rose carmine .25 *.55*
247 CD307 6c indigo 2.00 2.00
248 CD308 12c orange .25 *.75*
249 CD309 24c blue green .25 *.90*
Nos. 246-249 (4) 2.75 4.20

University Issue
Common Design Types

1951, Feb. 16 Engr. *Perf. 14x14½*
250 CD310 3c carmine & black .55 *.55*
251 CD311 6c dp ultra & black .55 *.70*

Coronation Issue
Common Design Type

1953, June 2 *Perf. 13½x13*
252 CD312 4c car & blk .45 .25

G. P. O., Georgetown
A60

Victoria Regia Lilies and Jacanas — A60a

Indian Shooting Fish — A60b

Map — A60c

Felling Greenheart Tree — A60d

Bauxite Mining — A60e

Mt. Roraima — A60f

Kaieteur Falls — A60g

Arapaima, Fish — A60h

Toucan — A60i

Coat of Arms — A60j

Designs: 2c, Botanical gardens. 6c, Rice combine. 8c, Sugar cane entering factory. $2, Dredging gold.

Engr., Center Litho. on $1
Perf. 12½x13, 13

1954, Dec. 1 **Wmk. 4**
253 A60 1c black .25 .25
254 A60 2c dark green .25 .25
255 A60a 3c red brn & ol 3.75 .25
256 A60b 4c violet 1.50 .25
257 A60c 5c black & red 1.75 .25
258 A60 6c yellow green 1.40 .25
259 A60 8c ultramarine 1.25 .25
260 A60d 12c brown & black 1.40 .30
261 A60e 24c orange & black 5.50 .25
262 A60f 36c black & rose 10.00 1.00
263 A60g 48c red brn & ultra 2.00 *1.00*
264 A60h 72c emerald & rose 20.00 2.50
265 A60i $1 blk, yel, grn & sal 20.00 3.50
266 A60 $2 magenta 30.00 8.00
267 A60j $5 black & ultra 25.00 *35.00*
Nos. 253-267 (15) 124.05 *53.30*

See Nos. 279-287.

Clasped Hands — A62

Perf. 14½x14
1961, Oct. 23 Photo. Wmk. 314
268 A62 5c sal pink & brown .25 .25
269 A62 6c lt blue grn & brown .25 .25
270 A62 30c lt orange & brown .55 .40
Nos. 268-270 (3) 1.05 .90

Fourth annual History and Culture Week.

Freedom from Hunger Issue
Common Design Type

1963, July 22 *Perf. 14x14½*
271 CD314 20c lilac .45 .25

Red Cross Centenary Issue
Common Design Type
Wmk. 314

1963, Sept. 2 Litho. *Perf. 13*
272 CD315 5c black & red .25 .25
273 CD315 20c ultra & red .60 .35

Queen Types of 1954
Engr.; Center Litho. on $1
Perf. 12½x13, 13

1963-65 **Wmk. 314**
279 A60 3c red brn & ol ('65) 5.00 2.00
280 A60 5c black & red ('64) 1.10 .25
281 A61 12c brown & blk ('64) 2.00 .25
282 A60 24c orange & black 4.00 .25
283 A60 36c black & rose 1.60 .25
284 A61 48c red brn & ultra 2.95 *1.95*
285 A61 72c emerald & rose 5.00 *22.50*
286 A60 $1 blk, yel, grn & sal 10.00 1.00
287 A60 $2 magenta 16.00 *15.00*
Nos. 279-287 (9) 47.65 *43.45*

Weight Lifter
A63

1964, Oct. 1 Photo. *Perf. 13x13½*
290 A63 5c orange .25 .25
291 A63 8c blue .25 .25
292 A63 25c carmine rose .25 .40
Nos. 290-292 (3) .75 .90

18th Olympic Games, Tokyo, Oct. 10-25.

ITU Issue
Common Design Type
Perf. 11x11½

1965, May 17 Litho. Wmk. 314
293 CD317 5c emerald & olive .25 .25
294 CD317 25c lt blue & brt pink .25 .25

Intl. Cooperation Year Issue
Common Design Type

1965, Oct. 25 Wmk. 314 *Perf. 14½*
295 CD318 5c blue grn & claret .25 .25
296 CD318 25c lt vio & green .30 .25

Winston Churchill and St. George's Cathedral, Georgetown — A64

1966, Jan. 24 Photo. *Perf. 14x14½*
297 A64 5c multicolored 1.00 .25
298 A64 25c dp blue, blk & gold 2.40 .50

Sir Winston Leonard Spencer Churchill (1874-1965), statesman and WWII leader.

Royal Visit Issue
Common Design Type

1966, Feb. 4 Litho. *Perf. 11x12*
299 CD320 3c violet blue .85 .25
300 CD320 25c dark car rose 1.50 .60

POSTAGE DUE STAMPS

> **Catalogue values for unused stamps in this section are for Never Hinged items.**

D1

Perf. 13½x14

1940-55 Typo. Wmk. 4
J1 D1 1c green, *chalky paper* ('52) 1.75 *22.50*
  a. Wmk. 4a (error) 150.00
J2 D1 2c black, *chalky paper* ('52) 4.00 *10.00*
  a. Wmk. 4a (error) 145.00
J3 D1 4c ultra ('52) 1.00 *14.00*
  a. Wmk. 4a (error) 145.00
J4 D1 12c carmine, *chalky paper* ('55) 17.50 *45.00*
  Nos. J1-J4 (4) 24.25 *91.50*

The 1940 printings of Nos. J1-J2 and J4 are on ordinary paper. For detailed listings, see the Scott Classic Specialized catalogue.

WAR TAX STAMP

Regular Issue No. 179 Overprinted

1918, Jan. 4 Wmk. 3 *Perf. 14*
MR1 A35 2c scarlet 1.50 .25

The relative positions of "War" and "Tax" vary throughout the sheet.

OFFICIAL STAMPS

> Counterfeit overprints exist.

No. 50 Overprinted in Red

1875 Unwmk. *Perf. 10*
O1 A5 1c black 75.00 26.00
  a. Horiz. pair, imperf btwn. 25,000.

Nos. 51, 53-54, 68 Overprinted in Black

O2 A5 2c orange 450.00 15.00
O3 A5 8c rose 375.00 150.00
O4 A5 12c lilac 3,500. 500.00
O5 A12 24c green 2,750. 300.00

For surcharges see Nos. 87, 89, 89A, 96, 102.

Nos. 72-76 Overprinted "OFFICIAL" Similar to #O2-O5

1877 Wmk. 1 *Perf. 14*
O6 A13 1c slate 350.00 70.00
  a. Vert. pair, imperf btwn. 27,500.
O7 A13 2c orange 160.00 18.00
O8 A13 4c ultramarine 140.00 35.00
O9 A13 6c chocolate 6,000. 600.00
O10 A13 8c rose 2,400. 500.00

The type A13 12c lilac, 24c green and 48c red brown overprinted "OFFICIAL" were never placed in use. A few examples of the 12c and 24c have been seen but the 48c is only known surcharged with new value for provisional use in 1881. See Nos. 97-101.

For surcharges see #85-86, 88A, 90-91.

BRITISH HONDURAS

'bri-tish hän-'dur-əs

LOCATION — Central America bordering on Caribbean on east, Mexico on north and Guatemala on west.
GOVT. — British Crown Colony
AREA — 8,867 sq. mi.
POP. — 130,000 (est. 1972)
CAPITAL — Belmopan

Before British Honduras became a colony (subordinate to Jamaica) in 1862, it was a settlement under British influence. In 1884 it became an independent colony. In 1973 the colony changed its name to Belize.

12 Pence = 1 Shilling
100 Cents = 1 Dollar (1888)

> **Catalogue values for unused stamps in this country are for Never Hinged items, beginning with Scott 127 in the regular postage section, Scott J1 in the postage due section.**

Values for unused stamps are for examples with original gum as defined in the catalogue introduction. Very fine examples of Nos. 1-37 will have perforations touching the design on at least one side due to the narrow spacing of the stamps on the plates. Stamps with perfs clear of the design on all four sides are extremely scarce and will command higher prices.

Queen Victoria — A1

1866 Unwmk. Typo. *Perf. 14*
1 A1 1p pale blue 72.50 72.50
  a. Horiz. pair, imperf. btwn.
2 A1 6p rose 425.00 195.00
3 A1 1sh green 400.00 145.00

The 6p and 1sh were printed only in a sheet with the 1p. The 1p was later printed in sheets without the 6p and 1sh. The 1sh is known in se-tenant gutter pairs with the 1p and the 6p.

1872 Wmk. 1 *Perf. 12½*
4 A1 1p pale blue 100.00 42.50
5 A1 3p reddish brn 180.00 90.00
6 A1 6p rose 450.00 55.00
7 A1 1sh green 725.00 50.00
  a. Horiz. pair, imperf. btwn. *27,500.*

For surcharges see Nos. 18-19.
No. 7a is unique and has faults.

1877-79 *Perf. 14*
8 A1 1p blue 87.50 40.00
  a. Horiz. strip of 3, imperf. btwn. *28,000.*
9 A1 3p brown 170.00 32.50
10 A1 4p violet ('79) 300.00 10.00
11 A1 6p rose ('78) 500.00 225.00
12 A1 1sh green 325.00 14.50

For surcharges see Nos. 20-21, 29.

1882-87 Wmk. 2
13 A1 1p blue ('84) 75.00 25.00
14 A1 1p rose ('84) 25.00 18.50
  a. Diagonal half used as ½p on cover —
  b. 1p carmine 60.00 35.00
15 A1 4p violet 100.00 5.75
16 A1 6p yellow ('85) 325.00 240.00
17 A1 1sh gray ('87) 300.00 200.00

For surcharges see Nos. 22-26, 28-35.

Stamps of 1872-87 Surcharged in Black

1888 Wmk. 1 *Perf. 12½*
18 A1 2c on 6p rose 350.00 275.00
19 A1 3c on 3p brown *20,000.* *6,500.*

Perf. 14
20 A1 2c on 6p rose 190.00 180.00
  a. Diagonal half used as 1c on cover *300.00*
  b. Double surcharge 2,700. —
  c. "2" with curved tail 3,500. —
21 A1 3c on 3p brown 110.00 *110.00*

Wmk. 2
22 A1 2c on 1p rose 16.50 *50.00*
  a. Diagonal half used as 1c on cover 220.00
  b. Double surcharge 1,100. 1,100.
  c. Inverted surcharge 9,000. 5,500.
23 A1 10c on 4p violet 70.00 20.00
  a. Inverted surcharge
24 A1 20c on 6p yellow 32.50 *55.00*
25 A1 50c on 1sh gray 475.00 *725.00*

No. 25 with Additional Surcharge in Red or Black

26 A1 2c (R) on 50c on 1sh gray 60.00 *115.00*
  a. "TWO" in black *18,750.* *15,000.*
  b. "TWO" double (Blk + R) *18,750.* *16,000.*
  c. Diagonal half used as 1c on cover 350.00

Stamps of 1872-87 Srchd. in Black — c

1888-89
28 A1 2c on 1p rose 1.25 *1.75*
  a. Diagonal half used as 1c on cover 110.00
29 A1 3c on 3p brown 7.25 1.75
30 A1 10c on 4p violet 27.50 1.00
  a. Double surcharge *3,500.*
31 A1 20c on 6p yel ('89) 19.00 15.00
32 A1 50c on 1sh gray 40.00 *105.00*
  Nos. 28-32 (5) 95.00 *124.50*

For other examples of this surcharge see Nos. 36, 47. For overprint see No. 51.

No. 30 with Additional Surcharge in Black or Red

1891
33 A1 6c (Blk) on 10c on 4p 4.00 2.25
  a. "6" and bar inverted *4,500.* *1,200.*
  b. "6" only inverted *6,500.*
34 A1 6c (R) on 10c on 4p 1.90 *2.50*
  a. "6" and bar inverted *725.00* *725.00*
  b. "6" only inverted *6,500.*

Stamps similar to No. 33 but with "SIX" instead of "6," both with and without bar, were prepared but not regularly issued.
See No. 37.

No. 29 with Additional Surcharge in Black

35 A1 5c on 3c on 3p brown 1.60 *2.00*
  a. Double surcharge of "Five" and bar 450.00 *850.00*

Black Surcharge, Type "c"
36 A1 6c on 3p blue 6.00 *25.00*

No. 36 with Additional Surcharge like Nos. 33-34 in Red

1891
37 A1 15c (R) on 6c on 3p blue 20.00 *35.00*
  a. Double surcharge —

A8

1891-98 Wmk. 2 *Perf. 14*
38 A8 1c green 2.75 1.50
39 A8 2c carmine rose 4.25 .25
40 A8 3c brown 10.00 4.75
41 A8 5c ultra ('95) 12.00 1.25
42 A8 6c ultramarine 15.00 2.00
43 A8 10c vio & grn ('95) 14.00 *19.00*
44 A8 12c vio & green 2.50 *3.50*
45 A8 24c yellow & blue 7.00 *23.00*
46 A8 25c red brn & grn ('98) 95.00 *150.00*
  Nos. 38-46 (9) 162.50 *205.25*

Numeral tablet on Nos. 43-46 has lined background with colorless value and "c."
For overprints see Nos. 48-50.

Type of 1866 Surcharged Type "c"

1892
47 A1 1c on 1p green 1.00 *1.90*

Regular Issue Overprinted in Black

1899 Overprint 12mm Long
48 A8 5c ultramarine 28.00 3.00
  a. "BEVENUE" 180.00 *180.00*
49 A8 10c lilac & green 19.00 *25.00*
  a. "BEVENUE" 350.00 *425.00*
  c. "REVENU" 725.00
50 A8 25c red brn & grn 4.25 *42.50*
  a. "BEVENUE" 200.00 *425.00*
  c. "REVE UE" 2,700.
51 A1 50c on 1sh gray (No. 32) 275.00 450.00
  a. "BEVENUE" 5,500. 6,500.
  Nos. 48-51 (4) 326.25 *520.50*

Two lengths of the overprint are found on the same pane: 12mm (43 to the pane) and 11mm (17 to the pane). The "U" is found in both a tall, narrow type and the more common small type. The tall variety is found in row 1, position 5. The BEVENUE vaiety is found in row 6, position 4.

A9

1899-1901

52 A9 5c gray blk & ultra, *bl* ('00) 22.50 3.50
53 A9 10c vio & grn ('01) 11.00 *10.00*
54 A9 50c grn & car rose 30.00 *72.50*
55 A9 $1 grn & car rose 95.00 *155.00*
56 A9 $2 green & ultra 150.00 *200.00*
57 A9 $5 green & black 325.00 *475.00*
Nos. 52-57 (6) 633.50 *916.00*

Numeral tablet on Nos. 53-54 has lined background with colorless value and "c."

King Edward VII — A10

1902-04 Typo. Wmk. 2

58 A10 1c gray grn & grn ('04) 2.50 *27.50*
59 A10 2c vio & blk, *red* 2.75 .30
60 A10 5c gray blk & ultra, *blue* 22.50 .35
61 A10 20c dl vio & vio ('04) 15.00 *18.00*
Nos. 58-61 (4) 42.75 *46.15*

1904-06 Chalky Paper Wmk. 3

62 A10 1c green 4.00 *2.75*
63 A10 2c vio & blk, *red* 2.75 *.40*
64 A10 5c blk & ultra, *bl* ('05) 2.25 .25
65 A10 10c vio & grn ('06) 5.25 *18.00*
67 A10 25c vio & org ('06) 12.00 *60.00*
68 A10 50c grn & car rose ('06) 35.00 *110.00*
69 A10 $1 grn & car rose ('06) 80.00 *125.00*
70 A10 $2 grn & ultra ('06) 160.00 *275.00*
71 A10 $5 grn & blk ('06) 375.00 *450.00*
Nos. 62-71 (9) 676.25 *1,041.*

The 1c and 2c exist also on ordinary paper.

1909 Ordinary Paper

72 A10 2c carmine 17.50 .25
73 A10 5c ultramarine 3.25 .25

1911

74 A10 25c black, *green* 8.50 *50.00*

Numeral tablet on Nos. 61, 65-68, 74 has lined background with colorless value and "c."

King George V
A11 A12

1913-17 Wmk. 3 *Perf. 14*

75 A11 1c green 5.00 1.25
76 A11 2c scarlet 6.50 1.25
Complete booklet of 100 #76, in blocks of 10 (5x2) 4,500.
a. 2c carmine 6.50 1.25
77 A11 3c orange ('17) 2.00 .25
Complete booklet of 100 #77, in blocks of 10 (5x2) —
78 A11 5c ultra 3.50 1.10

Chalky Paper

79 A12 10c dl vio & ol grn 6.50 *8.00*
80 A12 25c blk, *gray grn* 1.50 *13.00*
a. 25c black, *emerald* 2.10 *35.00*
b. 25c blk, *bl grn*, olive back 6.00 *13.50*
81 A12 50c vio & ultra, *bl* 32.50 *17.50*
82 A11 $1 black & scar 35.00 *75.00*
83 A11 $2 grn & dull vio 90.00 *120.00*
84 A11 $5 vio & blk, *red* 290.00 *350.00*
Nos. 75-84 (10) 472.50 *587.35*

See No. 91. For overprints see Nos. MR2-MR5.

With Moire Overprint in Violet

1915

85 A11 1c green 4.75 *24.00*
a. 1c yellow green .65 *21.00*
86 A11 2c carmine 4.25 .50
87 A11 5c ultramarine .40 *6.00*
Nos. 85-87 (3) 9.40 *30.50*

For 'War' overprint see No. MR1.

Peace Commemorative Issue

Seal of Colony and George V
A13

1921, Apr. 28 Engr.

89 A13 2c carmine 5.50 .75
Never hinged 11.50

Similar to A13 but without "Peace Peace"

1922 Wmk. 4

90 A13 4c dark gray 12.00 .75
Never hinged 25.00

Type of 1913-17

1921 Typo. Wmk. 4

91 A11 1c green 9.00 *13.00*

A14

1922-33 Typo. Wmk. 4

92 A14 1c green ('29) 19.00 6.50
93 A14 2c dark brown 2.00 2.00
Complete booklet of 100 #93, in blocks of 10 (5x2) —
94 A14 2c rose red ('27) 12.00 2.00
Complete booklet of 100 #94, in blocks of 10 (5x2) —
95 A14 3c orange ('33) 37.50 5.00
96 A14 4c gray ('29) 22.50 1.00
97 A14 5c ultramarine 2.00 .70

Chalky Paper

98 A14 10c olive grn & lil 4.00 .40
99 A14 25c black, *emerald* 3.25 *9.00*
100 A14 50c ultra & vio, *bl* 8.00 *16.00*
101 A14 $1 scarlet & blk 22.50 *30.00*
102 A14 $2 red vio & grn 50.00 *130.00*

Wmk. 3

103 A14 25c black, *emerald* 8.50 *55.00*
104 A14 $5 blk & vio, *red* 225.00 *300.00*
Nos. 92-104 (13) 416.25 *557.60*

For surcharges see Nos. B1-B5.

Common Design Types pictured following the introduction.

Silver Jubilee Issue
Common Design Type
Perf. 11x12

1935, May 6 Engr. Wmk. 4

108 CD301 3c black & ultra 2.00 .60
109 CD301 4c indigo & grn 4.50 4.25
110 CD301 5c ultra & brn 2.25 *2.50*
111 CD301 25c brn vio & ind 6.50 *9.00*
Nos. 108-111 (4) 15.25 *16.35*
Set, never hinged 24.00

Coronation Issue
Common Design Type

1937, May 12 *Perf. 13½x14*

112 CD302 3c deep orange .25 .25
113 CD302 4c gray black .35 .25
114 CD302 5c bright ultra .60 *1.90*
Nos. 112-114 (3) 1.20 2.40
Set, never hinged 2.00

Mayan Figures
A15

Chicle Tapping — A16

Cohune Palm — A17

Local Products
A18

Grapefruit Industry
A19

Mahogany Logs in River — A20

Sergeant's Cay — A21

Dory — A22

Chicle Industry
A23

Court House, Belize — A24

Mahogany Cutting — A25

Seal of Colony — A26

1938 *Perf. 11x11½, 11½x11*

115 A15 1c green & violet .25 *1.00*
116 A16 2c car & black .50 *.70*
a. Perf. 12 ('47) 1.90 1.25
117 A17 3c brown & dk vio .80 *1.25*
118 A18 4c green & black .75 *.50*
119 A19 5c slate bl & red vio 1.25 1.25
120 A20 10c brown & yel grn 1.60 .45
121 A21 15c blue & brown 3.00 1.00
122 A22 25c green & ultra 1.75 1.40
123 A23 50c dk vio & blk 13.50 3.25
124 A24 $1 ol green & car 18.00 7.00
125 A25 $2 rose lake & ind 20.00 *28.00*
126 A26 $5 brn & carmine 19.00 *42.50*
Nos. 115-126 (12) 80.40 *88.30*
Set, never hinged 180.00

Issued: 3c-5c, 1/10; 1c, 2c, 10c-50c, 2/14; $1-$5, 2/28.

Catalogue values for unused stamps in this section, from this point to the end of the section, are for Never Hinged items.

Peace Issue
Common Design Type
Perf. 13½x14

1946, Sept. 9 Engr. Wmk. 4

127 CD303 3c brown .25 .25
128 CD303 5c deep blue .25 .25

Silver Wedding Issue
Common Design Types

1948, Oct. 1 Photo. *Perf. 14x14½*

129 CD304 4c dark green .25 *.70*

Engraved; Name Typographed
Perf. 11½x11

130 CD305 $5 light brown 25.00 *52.50*

St. George's Cay — A27

H.M.S. Merlin — A28

1949, Jan. 10 Engr. *Perf. 12½*

131 A27 1c green & ultra .25 *1.25*
132 A27 3c yel brn & dp blue .25 *1.50*
133 A27 4c purple & brn ol .25 *1.75*
134 A28 5c dk blue & brown 2.00 .75
135 A28 10c vio brn & blue grn 2.00 .45
136 A28 15c ultra & emerald 2.00 .45
Nos. 131-136 (6) 6.75 6.15

Battle of St. George's Cay, 150th anniv.

UPU Issue
Common Design Types
Perf. 13½, 11x11½

1949, Oct. 10 Engr. Wmk. 4

137 CD306 4c blue green .40 1.25
138 CD307 5c indigo 1.60 .60
139 CD308 10c chocolate .55 3.75
140 CD309 25c blue .75 .75
Nos. 137-140 (4) 3.30 6.35

University Issue
Common Design Types

1951, Feb. 16 Engr. *Perf. 14x14½*

141 CD310 3c choc & purple .70 1.75
142 CD311 10c choc & green .70 .45

Coronation Issue
Common Design Type

1953, June 2 *Perf. 13½x13*

143 CD312 4c dk green & black .60 .40

Arms — A29

Maya — A30

Designs: 2c, Tapir. 3c, Legislative Council Chamber and mace. 4c, Pine industry. 5c,

Spiny lobster. 10c, Stanley Field Airport. 15c, Mayan frieze. 25c, Blue butterfly. $1, Armadillo. $2, Hawkesworth Bridge. $5, Pine Ridge orchid.

1953-57 Engr. *Perf. 13½*

144 A29 1c gray blk & green .25 *.35*
a. Perf. 13½x13 2.75 2.25
145 A29 2c gray blk & brn, perf. 14 ('57) 2.50 .50
a. Perf. 13½ 1.50 2.75
b. Perf. 13½x13 2.75 1.75
146 A29 3c mag & rose lil, perf. 14 ('57) .25 .25
a. Perf. 13½ .40 .40
b. Perf. 13½x13 13.00 24.00
147 A29 4c grn & dk brn 1.30 .30
148 A29 5c car & ol brn, perf. 14 ('57) 2.00 .25
a. Perf. 13½ .85 .25
149 A29 10c ultra & bl gray 1.75 .25
a. Perf. 13½x13 1.75 .25
150 A29 15c vio & yel grn .60 .25
151 A29 25c brown & ultra 6.50 3.50
152 A30 50c purple & brown 17.50 3.50
153 A29 $1 red brn & sl bl 9.50 4.50
154 A29 $2 gray & car 9.50 4.00
155 A30 $5 blue gray & pur 42.50 15.00
Nos. 144-155 (12) 94.15 32.65

Issued: 5c, 5/15; 2c, 3c, 9/18, perf. 13½, 9/2.
For overprints see Nos. 159-166.

View of Belize, 1842 — A31

Designs: 10c, Public seals, 1860 and 1960. 15c, Tamarind Tree, Newtown Barracks.

Perf. 11½x11

1960, July 1 Wmk. 314

156 A31 2c green .55 *1.10*
157 A31 10c carmine .55 .25
158 A31 15c blue .55 .30
Nos. 156-158 (3) 1.65 1.65

Cent. of the establishment of a local PO.

Nos. 145-146, 149-150 Overprinted

1961, Mar. 1 Wmk. 4 *Perf. 14, 13*

159 A29 2c gray black & brn .30 .50
160 A29 3c mag & rose lilac .40 .50
161 A29 10c ultra & blue gray .40 .25
162 A29 15c violet & yel green .40 .25
Nos. 159-162 (4) 1.50 1.50

Nos. 144, 149, 151-152 Overprinted

1962, Jan. 15 *Perf. 13*

163 A29 1c gray black & green .25 *1.10*
164 A29 10c ultra & blue gray .30 .25
165 A29 25c brown & ultra 1.90 .60
166 A30 50c purple & brown .75 *1.10*
Nos. 163-166 (4) 3.20 3.05

Hurricane Hattie struck Belize, Oct. 31, 1961.

Great Curassow A32

Birds: 2c, Red-legged honeycreeper. 3c, American jacana. 4c, Great kiskadee. 5c, Scarlet-rumped tanager. 10c, Scarlet macaw. 15c, Massena trogon. 25c, Redfooted booby. 50c, Keel-billed toucan. $1, Magnificent frigatebird. $2, Rufous-tailed jacamar. $5, Montezuma oropendola.

Perf. 14x14½

1962, Apr. 2 Photo. Wmk. 314

Birds in Natural Colors; Black Inscriptions

167 A32 1c yellow 1.25 .60
168 A32 2c gray 1.60 .25
a. Green omitted *850.00*
169 A32 3c lt yel green 3.75 2.50
a. Dark grn (legs) omitted *850.00*
170 A32 4c lt gray 3.00 3.25
171 A32 5c buff 2.25 .25
172 A32 10c beige 3.75 .25
a. Blue omitted *900.00*
173 A32 15c pale lemon 1.25 .25
174 A32 25c bluish gray & pink 3.75 .25
175 A32 50c pale blue 5.00 .30
b. Blue (beak & claw) omitted 1,250. 1,250.
176 A32 $1 blue 7.50 1.75
177 A32 $2 pale gray 19.50 5.75
178 A32 $5 light blue 23.00 15.00
Nos. 167-178 (12) 75.60 30.40

For overprints see Nos. 182-186, 195-199.

1967 Wmk. 314 Sideways

Colors as 1962 Issue

167a A32 1c .25 *.50*
168b A32 2c .25 *1.00*
170a A32 4c 2.75 *2.75*
171a A32 5c .45 .25
172b A32 10c .30 .25
173a A32 15c .30 .25
175a A32 50c 2.25 *3.50*
Nos. 167a-175a (7) 6.55 *8.50*

Issued: 1, 4, 5, 50c, 2/16; 2, 10, 15c, 11/28.

Freedom from Hunger Issue

Common Design Type

1963, June 4 *Perf. 14x14½*

179 CD314 22c green .60 .25

Red Cross Centenary Issue

Common Design Type

Wmk. 314

1963, Sept. 2 Litho. *Perf. 13*

180 CD315 4c black & red .25 *1.25*
181 CD315 22c ultra & red .75 *1.25*

Nos. 167, 169, 170, 172 and 174 Overprinted

1964 Photo. *Perf. 14x14½*

182 A32 1c multicolored .25 .40
a. Yellow omitted *300.00*
183 A32 3c multicolored .75 .40
184 A32 4c multicolored .75 .40
185 A32 10c multicolored .75 .25
186 A32 25c multicolored 1.00 .75
Nos. 182-186 (5) 3.50 2.20

Attainment of self-government.

ITU Issue

Common Design Type

Perf. 11x11½

1965, May 17 Litho. Wmk. 314

187 CD317 2c ver & green .25 .25
188 CD317 50c yel & red lilac .50 .50

Intl. Cooperation Year Issue

Common Design Type

1965, Oct. 25 *Perf. 14½*

189 CD318 1c bl grn & claret .25 .25
190 CD318 22c lt violet & green .35 .30

Churchill Memorial Issue

Common Design Type

1966, Jan. 24 Photo. *Perf. 14*

Design in Black, Gold and Carmine Rose

191 CD319 1c bright blue .25 .50
192 CD319 4c green .50 .25
193 CD319 22c brown .80 .25
194 CD319 25c violet .90 .30
Nos. 191-194 (4) 2.45 1.30

Bird Type of 1962 Overprinted

Wmk. 314 Sideways

1966, July 1 *Perf. 14x14½*

195 A32 1c multicolored .25 .45
a. Yellow omitted *400.00*
196 A32 3c multicolored .60 .45
197 A32 4c multicolored .60 .45
198 A32 10c multicolored .60 .30
199 A32 25c multicolored .90 .40
Nos. 195-199 (5) 2.95 2.05

Citrus Grove — A33

10c, Half Moon Cay & Lighthouse Reef. 22c, Hidden Valley Falls & Mountain Pine Ridge. 25c, Xunantunich Mayan ruins in Cayo district.

Perf. 14x14½

1966, Oct. 1 Photo. Wmk. 314

200 A33 5c multicolored .25 .25
201 A33 10c multicolored .25 .25
202 A33 22c multicolored .25 .25
203 A33 25c multicolored .25 .50
Nos. 200-203 (4) 1.00 1.25

1st British Honduras stamp issue, cent.

International Tourist Year — A34

1967, Dec. 4 *Perf. 12½*

204 A34 5c Sailfish .25 .30
205 A34 10c Deer .25 .25
206 A34 22c Jaguar .40 .25
207 A34 25c Tarpon .40 .50
Nos. 204-207 (4) 1.30 1.30

Schomburgkia Tibicinis — A35

Orchids: 10c, Maxillaria tenuifolia. 22c, Bletia purpurea. 25c, Sobralia macrantha.

Inscribed: "20th Anniversary of E.C.L.A."

Perf. 14½x14

1968, Apr. 16 Photo. Wmk. 314

208 A35 5c violet & multi .60 .55
209 A35 10c green & multi .75 .35
210 A35 22c multicolored .90 .35
211 A35 25c olive & multi 1.20 .75
Nos. 208-211 (4) 3.45 2.00

20th anniv. of the Economic Commission for Latin America. See Nos. 226-229, 255-258.

Belizean Patriots' Memorial, Belize City, and Human Rights Flame — A36

Design: 50c, Mayan motif stele, monument at new capital site and Human Rights flame.

Perf. 13x13½

1968, July 15 Litho. Wmk. 314

212 A36 22c multicolored .25 .25
213 A36 50c multicolored .25 .25

International Human Rights Year.

Jewfish A37

Designs: 2c, White-lipped peccary. 3c, Grouper (sea bass). 4c, Collared anteater. 5c, Bonefish. 10c, Paca. 15c, Dolphinfish. 25c, Kinkajou. 50c, Yellow-and-green-banded muttonfish. $1, Tayra. $2, Great barracudas. $5, Mountain lion.

Perf. 13x12½

1968, Oct. 15 Litho. Unwmk.

214 A37 1c yellow & multi .40 .25
215 A37 2c brt yel & multi .25 .25
216 A37 3c pink & multi .25 .25
217 A37 4c brt grn & multi .25 1.25
218 A37 5c brick red & multi .25 1.25
219 A37 10c lilac & multi .25 .25
220 A37 15c org yel & multi 2.00 .25
221 A37 25c multicolored .40 .50
222 A37 50c bl grn & multi .85 1.25
223 A37 $1 ocher & multi 2.75 1.50
224 A37 $2 violet & multi 2.75 2.50
225 A37 $5 ultra & multi 14.00 7.00
Nos. 214-225 (12) 24.40 16.50

See Nos. 234-240, Belize 327-339.
For overprints see Nos. 251-254, 281-282.

Orchid Type of 1968

Inscribed "Orchids of Belize"

Designs: 5c, Rhyncholaetia digbyana. 10c, Cattleya bowringiana. 22c, Lycaste cochleatum. 25c, Coryanthes speciosum.

Perf. 14½x14

1969, Apr. 9 Photo. Wmk. 314

226 A35 5c Prus blue & multi .90 .30
227 A35 10c olive bis & multi 1.00 .25
228 A35 22c yellow grn & multi 1.50 .25
229 A35 25c violet blue & multi 1.60 1.75
Nos. 226-229 (4) 5.00 2.55

Hardwood Trees — A38

1969, Sept. 1 Litho. *Perf. 14*

230 A38 5c Ziricote .25 .25
231 A38 10c Rosewood .25 .25
232 A38 22c Mayflower .25 .25
233 A38 25c Mahogany .35 .35
Nos. 230-233 (4) 1.10 1.10

Timber industry of British Honduras. Issued in sheets of 9 (3x3) on simulated wood background.

Fish-Animal Type of 1968

Designs: ½c, Crana (fish). Others as before.

Wmk. 314 Sideways (½c, 2c, $5), Upright (3c, 5c, 10c)

1969-72 Litho. *Perf. 13x12½*

234 A37 ½c vio bl, yel & blk .25 .25
235 A37 ½c citron, blk & bl ('71) 2.00 2.00
236 A37 2c brt yel, blk & grn ('72) 5.25 3.75
237 A37 3c pink & multi ('72) 5.25 3.75
a. Wmk. sideways ('72) 4.00 6.00
238 A37 5c brick red & multi ('72) 5.25 3.75
239 A37 10c lilac & multi ('72) 5.25 3.75
a. Wmk. sideways ('72) 4.00 7.00
240 A37 $5 ultra & multi ('70) 2.00 6.00
Nos. 234-240 (7) 25.25 23.25

For overprints see Nos. 251-252.

Virgin and Child, by Giovanni Bellini — A39

Christmas: 22c, 25c, Adoration of the Kings, by Veronese.

1969, Nov. 1 Litho. *Perf. 14*

247	A39	5c multicolored	.25	.25
248	A39	15c dp orange & multi	.25	.25
249	A39	22c lilac rose & multi	.25	.25
250	A39	25c emerald & multi	.25	.25
		Nos. 247-250 (4)	1.00	1.00

Nos. 238-239 and Type of 1968 Overprinted

Wmk. 314 Sideways

1970, Feb. 2 Photo. *Perf. 13x12½*

251	A37	5c brick red & multi	.25	.25
252	A37	10c lilac & multi	.25	.25
253	A37	15c org yel & multi	.30	.25
254	A37	25c multicolored	.30	.25
		Nos. 251-254 (4)	1.10	1.00

Orchid Type of 1968 Inscribed: "Orchids of Belize"

Wmk. 314

1970, Apr. 2 Litho. *Perf. 14*

255	A35	5c Black	.65	.25
256	A35	15c White butterfly	1.00	.25
257	A35	22c Swan	1.30	.25
258	A35	25c Butterfly	1.30	.75
		Nos. 255-258 (4)	4.25	1.50

Santa Maria Tree and Wood (Calophyllum Brasiliense) — A40

Hardwood Trees and Woods: 15c, Nargusta (terminalia amazonia). 22c, Cedar (cedrela mexicana). 25c, Sapodilla (achras sapota).

1970, Sept. 7 *Perf. 14*

259	A40	5c multicolored	.40	.25
260	A40	15c multicolored	.65	.25
261	A40	22c multicolored	.80	.25
262	A40	25c multicolored	.80	.65
		Nos. 259-262 (4)	2.65	1.40

Nativity, by Arthur Hughes — A41

Christmas: 5c, 15c, 50c, Mystic Nativity, by Botticelli.

1970, Nov. 2 *Perf. 14*

263	A41	½c black & multi	.25	.25
264	A41	5c brown & multi	.25	.25
265	A41	10c multicolored	.25	.25
266	A41	15c slate bl & multi	.25	.25
267	A41	22c dk green & multi	.30	.25
268	A41	50c black & multi	.40	.40
		Nos. 263-268 (6)	1.70	1.65

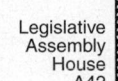

Legislative Assembly House A42

Designs: 5c, View of South Side of Belize. 10c, Government Plaza, Belmopan. 22c, Magistrates' Court. 25c, Police Headquarters. 50c, New General Post Office.

1971, Jan. 30 Litho. *Perf. 13½x14*

Size: 59x22mm

269	A42	5c multicolored	.25	.25
270	A42	10c multicolored	.25	.25

Size: 37x21½mm

271	A42	15c multicolored	.25	.25
272	A42	22c multicolored	.30	.25
273	A42	25c multicolored	.35	.25
274	A42	50c multicolored	.40	.40
		Nos. 269-274 (6)	1.80	1.65

New capital at Belmopan.

Tabebuia Chrysantha — A43

Flowers: 5c, 22c, Hymenocallis littoralis. 10c, 25c, Hippeastrum equestre. 15c, like ½c.

1971, Mar. 27 Litho. *Perf. 14*

275	A43	½c vio blue & multi	.25	.25
276	A43	5c olive & multi	.25	.25
277	A43	10c violet & multi	.25	.25
278	A43	15c multicolored	.25	.25
279	A43	22c multicolored	.25	.25
280	A43	25c lt brown & multi	.25	.25
		Nos. 275-280 (6)	1.50	1.50

Easter.

Type of 1968 Overprinted: "RACIAL EQUALITY / YEAR — 1971"

Perf. 13x12½

1971, June 14 Litho. Wmk. 314

281	A37	10c lilac & multi	.45	.25
282	A37	50c blue green & multi	1.30	.30

Intl. year against racial discrimination.

Tubroos (Enterolobium Cyclocarpum) A44

Hardwood Trees of Belize: 15c, Yemeri (Vochysia hondurensis). 26c, Billyweb (Sweetia panamensis). 50c, Logwood (Haematoxylum campechiaum).

Queen's Head in Silver

1971, Aug. 16 *Perf. 14*

283	A44	5c green, brn & blk	.80	.25
284	A44	15c multicolored	1.10	.35
285	A44	26c multicolored	1.50	.35
286	A44	50c multicolored	2.40	*4.75*
a.		Souvenir sheet of 4, #283-286	7.00	7.00
		Nos. 283-286 (4)	5.80	5.70

Verrazano-Narrows Bridge, New York, and Quebec Bridge, Canada — A45

Bridges of the World: ½c, Hawksworth Bridge connecting San Ignacio and Santa Helena and Belcan Bridge, Belize, Br. Honduras. 26c, London Bridge in 1871, and at Lake Havasu City, Ariz., in 1971. 50c, Belize-Mexico Bridge and Belize Swing Bridge.

1971, Sept. 23 Litho.

287	A45	½c multicolored	.25	.35
288	A45	5c multicolored	.40	.25
289	A45	26c multicolored	1.10	.25
290	A45	50c multicolored	1.25	1.50
		Nos. 287-290 (4)	3.00	2.35

Petrae Volubis — A46

Wild Flowers: 15c, Vochysia hondurensis. 26c, Tabebuia pentaphylla. 50c, Erythrina americana.

1972, Feb. 28

Flowers in Natural Colors; Black Inscriptions

292	A46	6c lilac & yellow	.25	.25
293	A46	15c lt blue & pale grn	.40	.30
294	A46	26c pink & lt blue	.70	.50
295	A46	50c orange & lt grn	1.10	1.40
		Nos. 292-295 (4)	2.45	2.45

Easter.

Seated Jade Figure — A47

Mayan Carved Jade, 4th-8th centuries: 6c, Dancing priest. 16c, Sun god's head, horiz. 26c, Priest on throne and sun god's head. 50c, Figure and mask.

Perf. 14x13½, 13½x14

1972, May 22 Unwmk.

296	A47	3c rose red & multi	.35	.25
297	A47	6c vio bl & multi	.35	.25
298	A47	16c brown & multi	.60	.25
299	A47	26c ol grn & multi	.85	.25
300	A47	50c purple & multi	1.60	2.50
		Nos. 296-300 (5)	3.75	3.50

Black inscription with details of designs on back of stamps.

Banak (Virola Koschnyi) — A48

Hardwood Trees of Belize: 5c, Quamwood (Schizolobium parahybum). 16c, Waika chewstick (Symphonia globulifera). 26c, Mammee-apple (Mammea americana). 50c, My lady (Aspidosperma megalocarpon).

1972, Aug. 21 Wmk. 314 *Perf. 14*

Queen's Head in Gold

301	A48	3c brt pink & multi	.25	.25
302	A48	5c gray & multi	.25	.25
303	A48	16c green & multi	.60	.25
304	A48	26c lemon & multi	.80	.25
305	A48	50c lt violet & multi	1.75	2.00
		Nos. 301-305 (5)	3.65	3.00

Silver Wedding Issue, 1972

Common Design Type

Design: Queen Elizabeth II, Prince Philip and Belize orchids.

1972, Nov. 20 Photo. *Perf. 14x14½*

306	CD324	26c slate grn & multi	.30	.30
307	CD324	50c violet & multi	.50	.50

Baron Bliss Day A49

Festivals of Belize: 10c, Labor Day boat race. 26c, Carib Settlement Day dance. 50c, Pan American Day parade.

1973, Mar. 9 Litho. *Perf. 14½*

308	A49	3c dull blue & black	.25	.25
309	A49	10c red & multi	.25	.25
310	A49	26c ver & multi	.50	.40
311	A49	50c black & multi	1.00	1.00
		Nos. 308-311 (4)	2.00	1.90

SEMI-POSTAL STAMPS

Regular Issue of 1921-29 Surcharged in Black or Red

1932 Wmk. 4 *Perf. 14*

B1	A14	1c + 1c green	3.00	*15.00*
B2	A14	2c + 2c rose red	3.00	*15.00*
B3	A14	3c + 3c orange	3.00	*32.50*
B4	A14	4c + 4c gray (R)	10.00	*35.00*
B5	A14	5c + 5c ultra	7.50	*15.00*
		Nos. B1-B5 (5)	26.50	*112.50*

The surtax was for a fund to aid sufferers from the destruction of the city of Belize by a hurricane in Sept. 1931.

POSTAGE DUE STAMPS

Catalogue values for unused stamps in this section are for Never Hinged items.

D1

1923-64 Typo. Wmk. 4 *Perf. 14*

J1	D1	1c black	3.25	*15.00*
J2	D1	2c black	3.25	*8.00*
J3	D1	4c black	2.50	*7.00*
		Nos. J1-J3 (3)	9.00	*30.00*

Nos. J1-J3 were re-issued on chalky paper in 1956. Values shown are for the 1956 issue. The 1923 issue, on yellowish thin ordinary paper, sells for $7.25 unused, $42.50 used. The 1c was reprinted in 1964 on white, ordinary paper. Value, $37.50 unused, $45 used.

Perf. 13½x13, 13½x14

1965-72 Wmk. 314

J4	D1	2c black ('72)	4.00	*7.50*
J5	D1	4c black	2.00	*7.50*

WAR TAX STAMPS

Nos. 85, 75 and 77 Overprinted

1916-17 **Wmk. 3** *Perf. 14*

With Moire Overprint

MR1	A11 1c green	.25	3.00
a.	"WAR" inverted	300.00	*350.00*

Without Moire Overprint

MR2	A11 1c green ('17)	1.75	*5.50*
MR3	A11 3c orange ('17)	5.50	*14.00*
a.	Double overprint	425.00	425.00
	Nos. MR1-MR3 (3)	7.50	22.50

Nos. 75 and 77 Overprinted

1918

MR4	A11 1c green	.25	*.40*
MR5	A11 3c orange	1.00	*4.00*

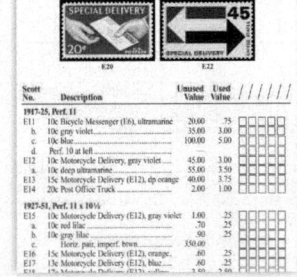

BRITISH INDIAN OCEAN TERRITORY

ˈbri-tish ˈin-dē̤n ˈō-chən
ˈter-ə-ˌtōr-ē

LOCATION — Indian Ocean
GOVT. — British Dependency
POP. — 0

B.I.O.T. was established Nov. 8, 1965. This island group lies 1,180 miles north of Mauritius. It consisted of Chagos Archipelago (chief island: Diego Garcia), Aldabra, Farquhar and Des Roches Islands until June 23, 1976, when the last three named islands were returned to Seychelles.

There is no permanent population on the islands. There are military personnel located there.

100 Cents = 1 Rupee
100 Pence = 1 Pound (1990)

Catalogue values for all unused stamps in this country are for Never Hinged items.

Seychelles Nos. 198-202, 204-212 Overprinted

Perf. 14½x14, 14x14½

1968, Jan. 17 Photo. Wmk. 314

Size: 24x31, 31x24mm

No.	Type	Denomination / Color	Unused	Used
1	A17	5c multicolored	1.40	*1.75*
2	A17	10c multicolored	.25	.25
3	A17	15c multicolored	.25	.25
4	A17	20c multicolored	.25	.25
5	A17	25c multicolored	.25	.25
6	A18	40c multicolored	.35	.25
7	A18	45c multicolored	.35	.35
8	A17	50c multicolored	.35	.35
9	A17	75c multicolored	.85	.45
10	A18	1r multicolored	1.00	.45
11	A18	1.50r multicolored	2.50	1.75
12	A18	2.25r multicolored	4.00	*4.50*
13	A18	3.50r multicolored	4.00	*5.25*
14	A18	5r multicolored	14.00	8.00

Perf. 13x14

Size: 22½x39mm

No.	Type	Denomination / Color	Unused	Used
15	A17	10r multicolored	26.00	20.00
		Nos. 1-15 (15)	55.80	44.10

Lascar A1

Marine Fauna: 10c, Hammerhead shark, vert. 15c, Tiger shark. 20c, Sooty eagle ray. 25c, Butterflyfish, vert. 30c, Robber crab. 40c, Green carangue. 45c, Needlefish, vert. 50c, Barracuda. 60c, Spotted pebble crab. 75c, Parrotfish. 85c, Rainbow runner (fish). 1r, Giant hermit crab. 1.50r, Humphead. 2.25r, Rock cod. 3.50r, Black marlin. 5r, Whale shark, vert. 10r, Lionfish.

Perf. 14x13½, 13½x14; 14 (30c, 60c, 85c)

1968-73 Litho. Wmk. 314

No.	Type	Denomination / Color	Unused	Used
16	A1	5c multicolored	1.00	*2.25*
a.		Wmk. upright ('73)	1.40	5.50
17	A1	10c multicolored	.40	*1.10*
18	A1	15c multicolored	.40	*1.60*
19	A1	20c multicolored	.40	*.90*
20	A1	25c multicolored	.90	.90
21	A1	30c multi ('70)	4.25	3.75
22	A1	40c multicolored	1.10	.35
23	A1	45c multicolored	2.50	2.50
24	A1	50c multicolored	1.10	.65
25	A1	60c multi ('70)	4.25	4.25
26	A1	75c multicolored	2.75	2.50
27	A1	85c multi ('70)	5.25	4.25
28	A1	1r multicolored	1.75	.55
29	A1	1.50r multicolored	2.75	2.75
30	A1	2.25r multicolored	13.50	11.00
31	A1	3.50r multicolored	4.25	4.00
32	A1	5r multicolored	13.50	15.00
33	A1	10r multicolored	10.00	7.50
		Nos. 16-33 (18)	70.05	65.80

No. 16 has watermark sideways.

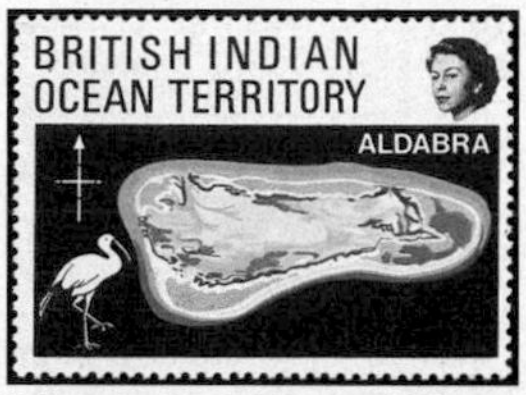

Aldabra Atoll and Sacred Ibis — A2

1969, July 10 Litho. *Perf. 13½x13*

No.	Type	Denomination / Color	Unused	Used
34	A2	2.25r vio blue & multi	2.25	1.75

Outrigger Canoe — A3

75c, Beaching canoe. 1r, Merchant ship Nordvaer. 1.50r, Yacht, Isle of Farquhar.

Perf. 13½x14

1969, Dec. 15 Litho. Wmk. 314

No.	Type	Denomination / Color	Unused	Used
35	A3	45c multicolored	.35	.35
36	A3	75c multicolored	.65	.65
37	A3	1r multicolored	1.00	1.00
38	A3	1.50r multicolored	1.50	1.50
		Nos. 35-38 (4)	3.50	3.50

Giant Land Tortoise — A4

Designs: 75c, Aldabra lily. 1r, Aldabra tree snail. 1.50r, Dimorphic egrets.

1971, Feb. 1 Litho. Wmk. 314

No.	Type	Denomination / Color	Unused	Used
39	A4	45c multicolored	2.75	2.50
40	A4	75c multicolored	3.25	2.50
41	A4	1r multicolored	3.75	2.50
42	A4	1.50r multicolored	13.00	11.00
		Nos. 39-42 (4)	22.75	18.50

Aldabra Nature Reserve.

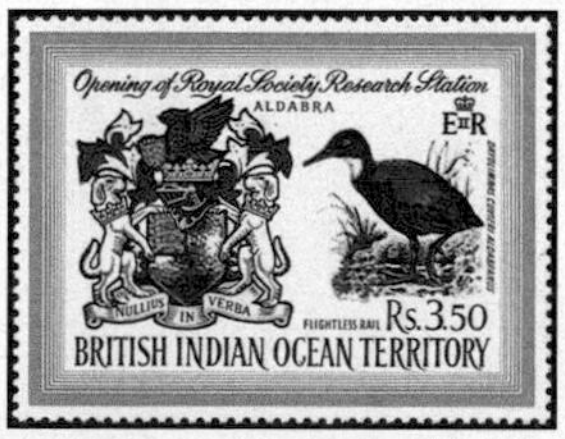

Society Coat of Arms and Flightless Rail — A5

1971, June 30 Litho. *Perf. 13½*

No.	Type	Denomination / Color	Unused	Used
43	A5	3.50r multicolored	16.50	11.00

Opening of Royal Society Research Station at Aldabra.

Acropora Formosa A6

Corals: 60c, Goniastrea pectinata. 1r, Fungia fungites. 1.75r, Tubipora musica.

1972, Mar. 1

No.	Type	Denomination / Color	Unused	Used
44	A6	40c blue & multi	3.75	3.75
45	A6	60c brt pink & multi	4.25	4.25
46	A6	1r blue & multi	4.25	4.25
47	A6	1.75r brt pink & multi	5.75	5.75
		Nos. 44-47 (4)	18.00	18.00

Common Design Types pictured following the introduction.

Silver Wedding Issue, 1972

Common Design Type

Design: Queen Elizabeth II, Prince Philip, flightless rail and sacred ibis.

1972, Nov. 20 Photo. *Perf. 14x14½*

No.	Type	Denomination / Color	Unused	Used
48	CD324	95c multicolored	1.00	.50
49	CD324	1.50r violet & multi	1.00	.50

Crucifixion, 17th Century — A7

Paintings, Ethiopian Manuscripts, 17th Century: 75c, 1.50r, Joseph and Nicodemus burying Jesus. 1r, Like 45c.

1973, Apr. 9 Litho. *Perf. 14*

No.	Type	Denomination / Color	Unused	Used
50	A7	45c buff & multi	.25	*.40*
51	A7	75c buff & multi	.30	*.55*
52	A7	1r buff & multi	.35	*.60*
53	A7	1.50r buff & multi	.65	*.70*
a.		Souvenir sheet of 4, #50-53	2.40	*3.50*
		Nos. 50-53 (4)	1.55	*2.25*

Easter.

Upsidedown Jellyfish — A8

1973, Nov. 12 Litho. Wmk. 314

No.	Type	Denomination / Color	Unused	Used
54	A8	50c shown	3.75	3.50
55	A8	1r Butterflies	4.25	3.50
56	A8	1.50r Spider	4.50	3.50
		Nos. 54-56 (3)	12.50	10.50

Nordvaer and July 14, 1969 Cancel — A9

2.50r, Nordvaer offshore and cancel.

1974, July 14

No.	Type	Denomination / Color	Unused	Used
57	A9	85c multicolored	1.00	.85
58	A9	2.50r multicolored	2.00	1.50

Nordvaer traveling post office, 5th anniv.

Terebra Maculata and Terebra Subulata — A10

Sea Shells: 75c, Turbo marmoratus. 1r, Drupa rubusidaeus. 1.50r, Cassis rufa.

1974, Nov. 12 Litho. *Perf. 13½x14*

No.	Type	Denomination / Color	Unused	Used
59	A10	45c multicolored	2.50	1.40
60	A10	75c multicolored	2.75	1.60
61	A10	1r multicolored	3.00	1.90
62	A10	1.50r multicolored	3.25	2.10
		Nos. 59-62 (4)	11.50	7.00

Aldabra Drongo — A11

Birds: 10c, Malagasy coucal. 20c, Red-headed forest fody. 25c, Fairy tern. 30c, Crested tern. 40c, Brown booby. 50c, Noddy tern. 60c, Gray heron. 65c, Blue-faced booby. 95c, Malagasy white-eye. 1r, Green-backed heron. 1.75r, Lesser frigate bird. 3.50r, White-tailed tropic bird. 5r, Souimanga sunbird. 10r, Malagasy turtledove. Nos. 69, 71-77 horiz.

1975, Feb. 28 Wmk. 314 *Perf. 14*

No.	Type	Denomination / Color	Unused	Used
63	A11	5c buff & multi	1.50	*3.25*
64	A11	10c lt ultra & multi	1.50	*3.25*
65	A11	20c dp yel & multi	1.50	*3.25*
66	A11	25c ultra & multi	1.50	*3.25*
67	A11	30c dl yel & multi	1.50	*3.25*
68	A11	40c bis & multi	1.50	*3.25*
69	A11	50c lt blue & multi	1.50	*3.50*
70	A11	60c yel & multi	1.50	*3.50*
71	A11	65c yel grn & multi	1.50	*3.50*
72	A11	95c citron & multi	1.50	*3.50*
73	A11	1r bister & multi	1.50	*3.50*
74	A11	1.75r yel & multi	2.50	*8.50*
75	A11	3.50r blue & multi	3.25	*8.50*
76	A11	5r pale sal & multi	4.50	*7.50*
77	A11	10r brt yel & multi	8.50	*13.00*
		Nos. 63-77 (15)	35.25	*74.50*

Grewia Salicifolia — A12

Native Plants: 65c, Cassia aldabrensis. 1r, Hypoestes aldabrensis. 1.60r, Euphorbia pyrifolia.

1975, July 10 Litho. Wmk. 314

No.	Type	Denomination / Color	Unused	Used
78	A12	50c multicolored	.65	*1.10*
79	A12	65c multicolored	.70	*1.25*
80	A12	1r multicolored	.85	*1.25*
81	A12	1.60r multicolored	1.10	*1.75*
		Nos. 78-81 (4)	3.30	*5.35*

Nature protection.

Aldabra and Compass Rose — A13

Maps of Islands: 1r, Desroches. 1.50r, Farquhar. 2r, Diego Garcia.

1975, Nov. 8 Litho. *Perf. 13½x14*

No.	Type	Denomination / Color	Unused	Used
82	A13	50c blk, blue & grn	1.00	1.00
83	A13	1r green & multi	1.10	1.10
84	A13	1.50r blk, ultra & grn	1.40	1.40
85	A13	2r blk, lilac & grn	1.50	1.50
a.		Souvenir sheet of 4, #82-85	9.50	*14.00*
		Nos. 82-85 (4)	5.00	5.00

British Indian Ocean Territory, 10th anniv.

Crimson Speckled Moth — A14

Insects: 1.20r, Dysdercus fasciatus. 1.50r, Sphex torridus. 2r, Oryctes rhinoceros.

1976, Mar. 22 Litho. Wmk. 373

86 A14 65c multicolored	1.25	1.25
87 A14 1.20r multicolored	1.50	1.50
88 A14 1.50r multicolored	1.75	1.75
89 A14 2r multicolored	1.75	1.75
Nos. 86-89 (4)	6.25	6.25

Exhibition Emblem and No. 37 — A15

1990, May 3 Wmk. 373 *Perf. 14*

90 A15 15p No. 62	6.25	5.75
91 A15 20p No. 89	6.75	6.00
92 A15 34p No. 85	10.00	8.25
93 A15 54p shown	12.00	10.00
Nos. 90-93 (4)	35.00	30.00

Stamp World London '90.

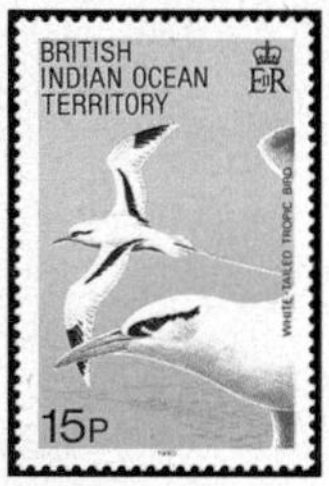

Birds — A16

15p, White-tailed tropic birds. 20p, Turtle doves. 24p, Greater frigate birds. 30p, Little green herons. 34p, Greater sand plovers. 41p, Crab plovers. 45p, Crested terns. 54p, Lesser crested terns. 62p, Fairy terns. 71p, Red-footed boobies. 80p, Indian mynahs. £ 1, Madagascar fodies.

1990, May 3 Wmk. 384 *Perf. 14*

94 A16 15p multicolored	1.30	*2.25*
95 A16 20p multicolored	1.40	*2.25*
96 A16 24p multicolored	2.50	*2.25*
97 A16 30p multicolored	1.90	*2.50*
98 A16 34p multicolored	2.10	*2.50*
99 A16 41p multicolored	2.10	*2.50*
100 A16 45p multicolored	4.00	*3.00*
101 A16 54p multicolored	3.00	*3.75*
102 A16 62p multicolored	3.00	*3.75*
103 A16 71p multicolored	3.25	*3.75*
104 A16 80p multicolored	3.25	*4.50*
105 A16 £1 multicolored	4.50	*4.75*
Nos. 94-105 (12)	32.30	*37.75*

For overprints see Nos. 145-146.

Queen Mother, 90th Birthday
Common Design Types

Designs: 24p, Lady Elizabeth Bowes-Lyon, 1923. £1, Queen, Princesses Elizabeth & Margaret, 1940.

1990, Aug. 4 Wmk. 384 *Perf. 14x15*

106 CD343 24p multicolored	7.00	6.50

Perf. 14½

107 CD344 £1 brown & black	11.00	12.00

British Indian Ocean Territory, 25th Anniv. — A17

1990, Nov. 8 Litho. *Perf. 14*

108 A17 20p Flag	5.75	5.75
109 A17 24p Coat of arms	5.75	5.75

Souvenir Sheet

110 A17 £1 Map	13.50	13.50

Govt. Services A18

20p, Postal service. 24p, Royal Marines. 34p, Police station, officers. 54p, Customs service.

Wmk. 373

1991, June 3 Litho. *Perf. 14*

111 A18 20p multi	2.25	2.25
112 A18 24p multi	3.50	2.50
113 A18 34p multi	4.00	4.00
114 A18 54p multi	5.50	5.50
Nos. 111-114 (4)	15.25	14.25

Visiting Ships A19

20p, Survey ship Experiment, 1786. 24p, US Brig Pickering, 1819. 34p, SMS Emden, 1914. 54p, HMS Edinburgh, 1988.

1991, Nov. 8

115 A19 20p multicolored	3.00	3.00
116 A19 24p multicolored	3.25	3.25
117 A19 34p multicolored	4.25	4.25
118 A19 54p multicolored	5.25	5.25
Nos. 115-118 (4)	15.75	15.75

Queen Elizabeth II's Accession to the Throne, 40th Anniv.
Common Design Type

Wmk. 373

1992, Feb. 6 Litho. *Perf. 14*

119 CD349 15p multicolored	3.25	2.75
120 CD349 20p multicolored	4.00	3.00
121 CD349 24p multicolored	5.50	4.00
122 CD349 34p multicolored	5.00	4.75
123 CD349 54p multicolored	5.00	4.75
Nos. 119-123 (5)	22.75	19.25

Aircraft A20

Wmk. 384

1992, Oct. 23 Litho. *Perf. 14*

124 A20 20p Catalina	1.75	*2.50*
125 A20 24p Nimrod	2.25	*2.50*
126 A20 34p P-3 Orion	2.75	*3.25*
127 A20 54p B-52	3.75	*4.50*
Nos. 124-127 (4)	10.50	*12.75*

Christmas — A21

Paintings: 5p, The Mystical Marriage of St. Cathrin, by Correggio. 24p, Madonna and Child by unknown artist. 34p, Madonna and Child by unknown artist, diff. 54p, The Birth of Jesus, by Kaspar Jele.

1992, Nov. 27 *Perf. 14½*

128 A21 5p multicolored	.75	.75
129 A21 24p multicolored	1.50	1.50
130 A21 34p multicolored	2.00	2.00
131 A21 54p multicolored	2.50	2.50
Nos. 128-131 (4)	6.75	6.75

Coconut Crab A22

No. 132, Crab, coconut. No. 133, Large crab. No. 134, Two crabs. No. 135, Crab on tree trunk.

Wmk. 384

1993, Mar. 3 Litho. *Perf. 14*

132 A22 10p multi	2.10	2.10
133 A22 10p multi	2.10	2.10
134 A22 10p multi	2.10	2.10
135 A22 15p multi	2.50	2.50
Nos. 132-135 (4)	8.80	8.80

World Wildlife Fund.

Royal Air Force, 75th Anniv.
Common Design Type

Airplanes: No. 136, Vickers Virginia. 24p, Bristol Bulldog. 34p, Short Sunderland. 54p, Bristol Blenheim IV.

No. 140: a, Douglas Dakota. b, Gloster Javelin. c, Blackburn Beverley. d, Vickers VC10.

1993, Apr. 1 Wmk. 373

136 CD350 20p multicolored	1.10	1.10
137 CD350 24p multicolored	1.40	1.40
138 CD350 34p multicolored	1.60	1.60
139 CD350 54p multicolored	3.00	3.00
Nos. 136-139 (4)	7.10	7.10

Souvenir Sheet of 4

140 CD350 20p #a.-d.	9.00	9.00

Flowers — A23

Christmas: 20p, Stachytarpheta urticifolia. 24p, Ipomea pes-caprae. 34p, Sida pusilla. 54p, Catharanthus roseus.

Wmk. 373

1993, Nov. 22 Litho. *Perf. 14½*

141-144 A23 Set of 4	7.00	7.00

Nos. 96, 105 Ovptd. with Hong Kong '94 Emblem

Wmk. 384

1994, Feb. 18 Litho. *Perf. 14*

145 A16 24p multicolored	5.50	3.00
146 A16 £1 multicolored	8.00	*8.50*

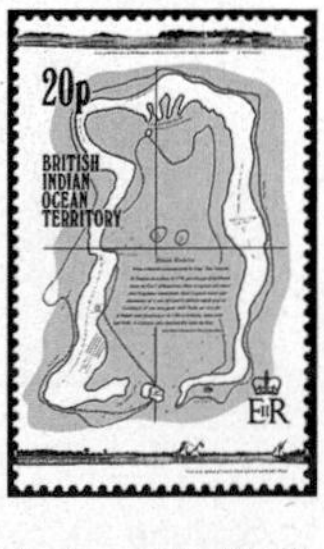

A24

18th Cent. Maps and Charts: a, 20p, Sketch of Diego Garcia. b, 24p, Plan of harbor, Chagos Island or Diego Garcia, by Lt. Archibald Blair. c, 34p, Chart of Chagos Archipelago, by Lt. Blair. d, 44p, Plan of part of Chagos Island or Diego Garcia, from survey made by the Drake. e, 54p, Plan of Chagos Island or Diego Garcia, by M. Aa Fontaine.

1994, June 1 Wmk. 373

147 A24 Strip of 5, #a.-e.	6.75	6.75

Butterflies — A25

24p, Junonia villida. 30p, Petrelaea dana. 56p, Hypolimnas misippus.

1994, Aug. 16 Wmk. 384

148 A25 24p multi	2.50	2.50
149 A25 30p multi	3.00	3.00
150 A25 56p multi	4.00	4.00
Nos. 148-150 (3)	9.50	9.50

Sharks A26

15p, Nurse. 20p, Silver tip. 24p, Black tip reef. 30p, Oceanic white tip. 35p, Black tip. 41p, Smooth hammerhead. 46p, Lemon. 55p, White tip reef. 65p, Tiger. 74p, Indian sand tiger. 80p, Great hammerhead. £ 1, Great white.

1994, Nov. 1 Wmk. 373

151 A26 15p multicolored	4.75	3.50
152 A26 20p multicolored	4.75	3.50
153 A26 24p multicolored	5.50	3.75
154 A26 30p multicolored	6.25	4.75
155 A26 35p multicolored	7.50	6.00
156 A26 41p multicolored	7.50	6.00
157 A26 46p multicolored	7.50	6.00
158 A26 55p multicolored	9.00	6.25
159 A26 65p multicolored	9.00	6.25
a. Souvenir sheet of 1	5.25	5.25
160 A26 74p multicolored	9.25	7.25
a. Souvenir sheet of 1	7.25	7.25
161 A26 80p multicolored	10.50	8.00
162 A26 £1 multicolored	11.50	9.00
Nos. 151-162 (12)	93.00	70.25

No. 159a for Hong Kong '97. Issued 2/3/97.

No. 160a for return of Hong Kong to China. Issued 7/1/97.

End of World War II, 50th Anniv.
Common Design Types

20p, War graves, memorial cross, Diego Garcia. 24p, 6-inch naval gun, Cannon Point. 30p, Sunderland flying boat, 230 Squadron. 56p, HMIS Clive.

£1, Reverse of War Medal 1939-45.

Wmk. 373

1995, May 8 Litho. *Perf. 14*

163 CD351 20p multicolored	2.00	2.00
164 CD351 24p multicolored	2.25	2.25
165 CD351 30p multicolored	2.75	2.75
166 CD351 56p multicolored	3.75	3.75
Nos. 163-166 (4)	10.75	10.75

Souvenir Sheet

167 CD352 £1 multicolored	5.50	5.50

Game Fish A27

1995, Oct. 6 Wmk. 384

168 A27 20p Dolphinfish	2.10	2.10
169 A27 24p Sailfish	2.10	2.10
170 A27 30p Wahoo	3.00	3.00
171 A27 56p Striped marlin	4.25	4.25
Nos. 168-171 (4)	11.45	11.45

Sea Shells A28

20p, Terebra crenulata. 24p, Bursa bufonia. 30p, Nassarius papillosus. 56p, Lopha cristagalli.

1996, Jan. 8 Wmk. 373 *Perf. 14*

172 A28 20p multicolored	2.00	2.00
173 A28 24p multicolored	2.10	2.10
174 A28 30p multicolored	2.50	2.50
175 A28 56p multicolored	4.50	4.50
Nos. 172-175 (4)	11.10	11.10

Queen Elizabeth II, 70th Birthday
Common Design Type

Various portraits of Queen, scenes of British Indian Ocean Territory: 20p, View to north from south end of lagoon. 24p, Manager's House, Peros Banhos. 30p, Wireless station, Peros Banhos. 56p, Sunset scene.
£1, Wearing crown, formal dress.

Perf. 14x14½

1996, Apr. 22 Wmk. 384

176 CD354 20p multicolored	.95	.95
177 CD354 24p multicolored	1.10	1.10
178 CD354 30p multicolored	1.20	1.20
179 CD354 56p multicolored	2.00	2.00
Nos. 176-179 (4)	5.25	5.25

Souvenir Sheet

180 CD354 £1 multicolored 6.25 6.25

Turtles A29

1996, Sept. 2 Wmk. 373

181 A29 20p Loggerhead	1.90	1.90
182 A29 24p Leatherback	2.00	2.00
183 A29 30p Hawksbill	2.75	2.75
184 A29 56p Green	3.50	3.50
Nos. 181-184 (4)	10.15	10.15

Uniforms — A30

Designs: 20p, British representative. 24p, Royal Marine officer. 30p, Royal Marine in camouflage. 56p, Police dog handler, female police officer.

1996, Dec. *Perf. 14*

185 A30 20p multicolored	1.40	1.40
186 A30 24p multicolored	1.90	1.90
187 A30 30p multicolored	2.25	2.25
188 A30 56p multicolored	3.00	3.00
Nos. 185-188 (4)	8.55	8.55

Queen Elizabeth II and Prince Philip, 50th Wedding Anniv. — A31

No. 189, Queen up close. No. 190, 4-horse team fording river. No. 191, Queen riding in open carriage. No. 192, Prince Philip up close. No. 193, Prince driving 4-horse team, Prince, Queen near jeep. No. 194, Queen on horseback, castle in distance.
£1.50, Queen, Prince riding in open carriage.

1997, July 10 *Perf. 14½x14*

189 A31 20p multicolored	1.75	1.75
190 A31 20p multicolored	1.75	1.75
a. Pair, #189-190	3.50	3.50
191 A31 24p multicolored	1.75	1.75
192 A31 24p multicolored	1.75	1.75
a. Pair, #191-192	3.50	3.50
193 A31 30p multicolored	1.75	1.75
194 A31 30p multicolored	1.75	1.75
a. Pair, #193-194	3.50	3.50
Nos. 189-194 (6)	10.50	10.50

Souvenir Sheet

195 A31 £1.50 multicolored 11.50 11.50

Ocean Wave '97, Naval Exercise — A32

Designs: a, HMS Richmond, HMS Beaver. b, HMS Illustrious. c, HMS Beaver. d, RFA Sir Percivale, HMY Britannia, HMS Beaver. e, HMY Britannia. f, HMS Richmond, HMS Beaver, HMS Gloucester. g, HMS Richmond. h, HMS Illustrious (aerial view). i, HMS Sheffield. j, RFA Diligence, HMS Trenchant. k, HMS Illustrious, RFA Fort George, HMS Gloucester. l, HMS Richmond, HMS Beaver, HMS Gloucester.

1997, Dec. 1 Litho. *Perf. 14x14½*

196 A32 24p Sheet of 12, #a.-l. 22.50 22.50

Diana, Princess of Wales (1961-97)
Common Design Type

Various portraits: a, 26p, shown. b, 26p, Close-up. c, 34p. d, 60p.

1998, Mar. 31 *Perf. 14½x14*

197 CD355 Sheet of 4, #a.-d. 5.50 5.50

No. 197 sold for £1.46 + 20p, with surtax and 50% of profits from total sale being donated to the Princess Diana Memorial Fund.

Royal Air Force, 80th Anniv.
Common Design Type of 1993 Re-inscribed

Designs: 26p, Blackburn Iris, 1930-34. 34p, Gloster Gamecock, 1926-33. 60p, North American Sabre F86, 1953-56. 80p, Avro Lincoln, 1945-55.
No. 202: a, Sopwith Baby, 1915-19. b, Martinsyde Elephant, 1916-19. c, De Havilland Tiger Moth, 1932-55. d, North American Mustang III, 1943-47.

1998, Apr. 1 Wmk. 384 *Perf. 14*

198 CD350 26p multicolored	1.60	1.60
199 CD350 34p multicolored	1.90	1.90
200 CD350 60p multicolored	3.25	3.25
201 CD350 80p multicolored	4.25	4.25
Nos. 198-201 (4)	11.00	11.00

Souvenir Sheet

202 CD350 34p Sheet of 4, #a.-d. 10.50 10.50

Intl. Year of the Ocean A33

Dolphins and whales: No. 203, Striped dolphin. No. 204, Bryde's whale. No. 205, Pilot whale. No. 206, Spinner dolphin.

Wmk. 373

1998, Dec. 7 Litho. *Perf. 14*

203 A33 26p multicolored	4.00	4.00
204 A33 26p multicolored	4.00	4.00
205 A33 34p multicolored	4.00	4.00
206 A33 34p multicolored	4.00	4.00
Nos. 203-206 (4)	16.00	16.00

Sailing Ships — A34

2p, Bark "Westminster," 1837. 15p, "Sao Cristovao," Spain, 1589. 20p, Clipper ship "Sea Witch," US, 1849. 26p, HMS "Royal George," 1778. 34p, Clipper ship "Cutty Sark," 1883. 60p, British East India Co. ship "Mentor," 1789. 80p, HM brig "Trinculo," 1809. £1, Paddle steamer "Enterprise," 1825. £1.15, Privateer "Confiance," France, 1800. £2, British East India Co. ship "Kent," 1820.

Wmk. 373

1999, Feb. 1 Litho. *Perf. 14*

207 A34 2p multicolored	.65	.65
208 A34 15p multicolored	1.25	1.25
209 A34 20p multicolored	1.50	1.50
210 A34 26p multicolored	1.75	1.75
211 A34 34p multicolored	2.25	2.25
212 A34 60p multicolored	3.50	3.50
213 A34 80p multicolored	4.25	4.25
214 A34 £1 multicolored	5.25	5.25
215 A34 £1.15 multicolored	5.75	5.75
216 A34 £2 multicolored	9.00	9.00
Nos. 207-216 (10)	35.15	35.15

Tea Race, 1872 A35

a, Cutty Sark (up close). b, Thermopylae (in distance).

Wmk. 384

1999, Mar. 19 Litho. *Perf. 14*

217 A35 60p Sheet of 2, #a.-b. 11.00 11.00

Australia '99 World Stamp Expo.

The Stamp Show 2000, London — A36

Winning photos in photography contest: a, 26p, Field vole by Colin Sargent. b, 34p, Puffin, by P. J. Royal. c, 55p, Red fox, by Jim Wilson. d, £1, Robin, by Harry Smith.

Perf. 14½x14¼

2000, May 22 Litho. Wmk. 373

218 A36 Sheet of 4, #a-d 13.00 13.00

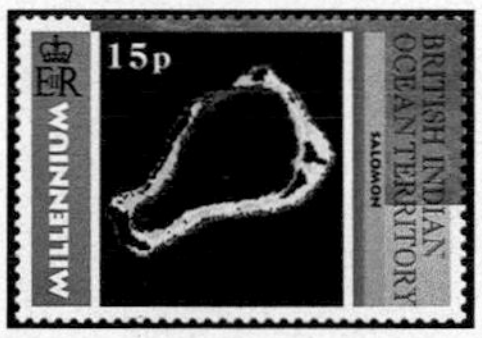

Satellite Images A37

Designs: 15p, Salomon Atoll. 20p, Egmont Atoll. 60p, Blenheim Reef. 80p, Diego Garcia.

Wmk. 373

2000, July 3 Litho. *Perf. 14*

219-222 A37 Set of 4 11.00 11.00

Queen Mother, 100th Birthday — A38

Designs: 26p, Blue hat. 34p, Blue green hat.
No. 225: a, 55p, Blue hat. £1, Yellow hat.

2000, Aug. 4 Wmk. 373 *Perf. 13¾*

223-224 A38 Set of 2 4.50 4.50

Souvenir Sheet

225 A38 Sheet of 2, #a-b 9.00 9.00

Flowers — A39

Designs: 26p, Delonix regia. 34p, Barringtonia asiatica. 60p, Zephyranthes rosea.

2000, Dec. 4 *Perf. 14½x14¼*

226-228 A39 Set of 3 10.00 10.00

Souvenir Sheet

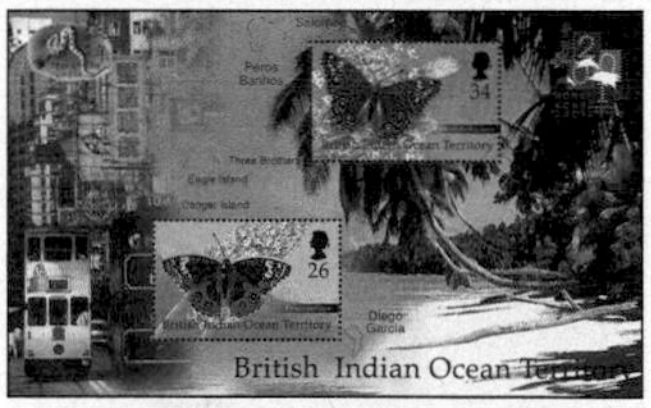

New Year 2001 (Year of the Snake) — A40

Butterflies: a, 26p, Precis orithya. b, 34p, Junonia villida chagoensis.

Perf. 14 ¼

2001, Feb. 1 Litho. Wmk. 373

229 A40 Sheet of 2, #a-b 6.50 6.50

Hong Kong 2001 Stamp Exhibition.

Souvenir Sheet

Royal Navy Submarines, Cent. — A41

No. 230: a, 26p, HMS Turbulent. b, 26p, HMS Churchill. c, 34p, HMS Resolution. d, 34p, HMS Vanguard. e, 60p, HMS Otter. f, 60p, HMS Oberon. Size of Nos. 230e-230f: 75x30mm.

Perf. 14¼x14½

2001, May 28 Litho. Wmk. 373

230 A41 Sheet of 6, #a-f 17.00 17.00

Worldwide Fund for Nature (WWF) A42

Starfish: 15p, Cushion star. 26p, Azure sea star. 34p, Crown-of-thorns. 56p, Banded bubble star.

Wmk. 373

2001, Aug. 1 Litho. *Perf. 13¾*

231-234 A42 Set of 4	9.00	9.00
234a Strip, #231-234	10.00	10.00

Plants — A43

Designs: 10p, Catharanthus roseus, horiz. 26p, Scadoxus mutiflora. 34p, Striga asiatica. 60p, Argusia argentia, horiz. 70p, Euphorbia cyathophora, horiz.

2001, Sept. 24 ***Perf. 13¾x14¼***

235 A43 26p multi 3.00 3.00
a. Perf. 14½ 3.00 3.00
236 A43 34p multi 3.25 3.25
a. Perf. 14½ 3.25 3.25

Souvenir Sheet

Perf. 14½

237 Sheet, #a-c, 235a, 236a 12.00 12.00
a. A43 10p multi .70 .70
b. A43 60p multi 3.00 3.00
c. A43 70p multi 3.50 3.50

Souvenir Sheet

Birdlife International World Bird Festival — A44

Crab plover: a, Resting. b, Eating crab, vert. c, Close-up of head, vert. d, In flight. e, Standing on one leg.

2001, Oct. 1 ***Perf. 14½***

238 A44 50p Sheet of 5, #a-e 13.00 13.00

Reign Of Queen Elizabeth II, 50th Anniv. Issue

Common Design Type

Designs: Nos. 239, 243a, 10p, Princess Elizabeth, 1943. Nos. 240, 243b, 25p, In 1967. Nos. 241, 243c, 35p, With Prince Philip, 1947. Nos. 242, 243d, 55p, Wearing tiara. No. 243e, 75p, 1955 portrait by Annigoni (38x50mm).

Perf. 14¼x14½, 13¾ (#243e)

2002, Feb. 6 **Litho.** **Wmk. 373**

With Gold Frames

239 CD360 10p multicolored .65 .65
240 CD360 25p multicolored 1.75 1.75
241 CD360 35p multicolored 2.50 2.50
242 CD360 55p multicolored 4.00 4.00
Nos. 239-242 (4) 8.90 8.90

Souvenir Sheet

Without Gold Frames

243 CD360 Sheet of 5, #a-e 10.50 10.50

Souvenir Sheet

Red-footed Booby — A45

No. 244: a, Head of bird with brown feathers. b, Bird in flight, vert. c, Bird on nest, vert. d, Close-up of bird with white and black feathers. e, Chick.

Wmk. 373

2002, June 17 **Litho.** ***Perf. 14½***

244 A45 50p Sheet of 5, #a-e 14.50 14.50

Queen Mother Elizabeth (1900-2002)

Common Design Type

Designs: 26p, Wearing hat (sepia photograph). No. 246, £1, Wearing blue green hat.
No. 247: a, £1, Wearing feathered hat (black and white photograph). b, £1, Wearing royal blue hat.

Wmk. 373

2002, Aug. 5 **Litho.** ***Perf. 14¼***

With Purple Frames

245 CD361 26p multicolored 1.10 1.10
246 CD361 £1 multicolored 4.75 4.75

Souvenir Sheet

Without Purple Frames

Perf. 14½x14¼

247 CD361 Sheet of 2, #a-b 11.50 11.50

Friends of the Chagos, 10th Anniv. — A46

Various reef fish: 2p, 15p, 26p, 34p, 58p, £1. £1.90, Fish.

Perf. 14¼x14½

2002, Oct. 3 **Litho.** **Wmk. 373**

248-253 A46 Set of 6 14.50 14.50

Souvenir Sheet

254 A46 £1.90 multi 12.00 12.00

No. 254 is a parcel post stamp.

Sea Slugs — A47

Designs: 2p, Halgerda tesselata. 15p, Notodoris minor. 26p, Nembrotha lineolata. 50p, Chromodoris quadricolor. 76p, Glossodoris cincta. £1.10, Chromodoris cf. leopardus.

Wmk. 373

2003, Mar. 17 **Litho.** ***Perf. 13¼***

255-260 A47 Set of 6 14.50 14.50

Head of Queen Elizabeth II

Common Design Type

Wmk. 373

2003, June 2 **Litho.** ***Perf. 13¾***

261 CD362 £2.50 multi 11.00 11.00

Coronation of Queen Elizabeth II, 50th Anniv.

Common Design Type

Designs: Nos. 262, 264a, £1, Queen wearing crown. Nos. 263, 264b, £2, Queen with family.

Perf. 14¼x14½

2003, June 2 **Litho.** **Wmk. 373**

Vignettes Framed, Red Background

262 CD363 £1 multicolored 5.00 5.00
263 CD363 £2 multicolored 9.00 9.00

Souvenir Sheet

Vignettes Without Frame, Purple Panel

264 CD363 Sheet of 2, #a-b 14.00 14.00

Prince William, 21st Birthday

Common Design Type

No. 265: a, William on polo pony at right. b, William with Prince Charles at left.

Wmk. 373

2003, June 21 **Litho.** ***Perf. 14¼***

265 Horiz. pair 8.00 8.00
a. CD364 50p multi 3.00 3.00
b. CD364 £1 multi 4.50 4.50

Powered Flight, Cent. — A48

Designs: No. 266, 34p, De Havilland Mosquito. No. 267, 34p, Avro Lancaster Dambuster. No. 268, 58p, Supermarine Spitfire. No. 269, 58p, Hawker Hurricane. No. 270, 76p, Lockheed C-130 Hercules. No. 271, 76p, Vickers Armstrong Wellington.
No. 272: a, Boeing E-3A Sentry AWACS. b, Boeing B-17 Flying Fortress. c, Lockheed P3 Orion. d, Consolidated B-24 Liberator. e, Lockheed C-141 Starlifter. f, Supermarine Walrus. g, Short Sunderland. h, Supermarine Stranraer. i, PBY Catalina. j, Supermarine Sea Otter.
Illustration reduced.

Wmk. 373

2003, July 18 **Litho.** ***Perf. 14***

Stamp + Label

266-271 A48 Set of 6 15.00 15.00

Miniature Sheet

272 A48 26p Sheet of 10, #a-j 15.00 15.00

Fisheries Patrol — A49

No. 273: a, 34p, M. V. Pacific Marlin. b, 34p, Marlin. c, 58p, Skipjack tuna. d, 58p, Yellowfin tuna. e, 76p, Swordfish. f, 76p, Bigeye tuna.

Wmk. 373

2004, Feb. 16 **Litho.** ***Perf. 14¼***

273 A49 Sheet of 6, #a-f 17.00 17.00

Birds A50

Designs: 2p, Madagascar fody. 14p, Barred ground dove. 20p, Indian mynah. 26p, Cattle egret. 34p, Fairy tern. 58p, Masked booby. 76p, Greater frigatebird. 80p, White-tailed tropicbird. £1.10, Little green heron. £1.34, Pacific golden plover. £1.48, Garganey teal. £2.50, Bar-tailed godwit.

Wmk. 373

2004, June 21 **Litho.** ***Perf. 14***

274 A50 2p multi .30 .30
275 A50 14p multi .65 .65
276 A50 20p multi .95 .95
277 A50 26p multi 1.10 1.10
278 A50 34p multi 1.50 1.50
279 A50 58p multi 2.50 2.50
280 A50 76p multi 3.25 3.25
281 A50 80p multi 3.50 3.50
282 A50 £1.10 multi 5.00 5.00
283 A50 £1.34 multi 6.00 6.00
284 A50 £1.48 multi 7.25 7.25
285 A50 £2.50 multi 11.00 11.00
Nos. 274-285 (12) 43.00 43.00

Crabs A51

Designs: 26p, Coconut crab. 34p, Land crab. 76p, Rock crab. £1.10, Ghost crab.

Wmk. 373

2004, Dec. 20 **Litho.** ***Perf. 14***

286-289 A51 Set of 4 13.00 13.00

Turtles A52

Designs: No. 290, 26p, Green turtle hatchling. No. 291, 26p, Hawksbill turtle hatchlings. No. 292, 34p, Hawksbill turtle's head. No. 293, 34p, Green turtle's head. 76p, Hawksbill turtle swimming. £1.10, Green turtle swimming. £1.70, Like £1.10.

2005, Feb. 14

290-295 A52 Set of 6 14.00 14.00

Souvenir Sheet

296 A52 £1.70 multi 9.00 9.00

Battle of Trafalgar, Bicent. — A53

Designs: No. 297, 26p, HMS Phoebe. No. 298, 26p, Tower Sea Service pistol, 1796. No. 299, 34p, HMS Harrier. No. 300, 34p, Royal Navy Boatswain, 1805. No. 301, 76p, Portrait of Adm. Horatio Nelson. No. 302, 76p, HMS Victory, horiz.
No. 303: a, HMS Minotaur, ship in distance. b, HMS Spartiate.

Wmk. 373, Unwmkd. (#302)

2005, May 6 ***Perf. 13¼***

297-302 A53 Set of 6 18.00 18.00

Souvenir Sheet

303 A53 £1.10 Sheet of 2, #a-b 12.00 12.00

No. 302 has particles of wood from the HMS Victory embedded in the areas covered by a thermographic process that produces a raised, shiny effect.

Miniature Sheet

End of World War II, 60th Anniv. — A54

No. 304: a, 26p, HMAS Wollongong. b, 26p, Dutch tanker Ordina, HMIS Bengal attacked by Japanese surface raiders. c, 26p, HMS Pathfinder arrives at Diego Garcia. d, 26p, HMS Lossie rescues 112 survivors from Australian freighter Nellore. e, 26p, US Liberty Ship Jean Nicolet sunk by HIJMS I-8. f, 34p, Gen. Douglas MacArthur. g, 34p, Gen. Bernard L. Montgomery. h, 34p, Gen. George S. Patton. i, 34p, British Prime Minister Winston Churchill. j, 34p, Pres. Franklin D. Roosevelt.

Wmk. 373

2005, June 26 **Litho.** ***Perf. 13¾***

304 A54 Sheet of 10, #a-j 18.00 18.00

Sharks and Rays A55

Designs: No. 305, 26p, Blacktip reef shark. No. 306, 26p, Gray reef shark. No. 307, 34p, Silvertip shark. No. 308, 34p, Spotted eagle ray. No. 309, 34p, Tawny nurse shark. No. 310, 34p, Manta ray. 76p, Porcupine ray. £2, Feathertail stingray.

2005, Aug. 15 ***Perf. 13½x13¾***

305-312 A55 Set of 8 26.00 26.00

Battle of Trafalgar, Bicent. — A56

Designs: 26p, HMS Victory. 34p, Ships in battle, horiz. £2, Admiral Horatio Nelson.

Perf. 13¼

2005, Oct. 18 Litho. Unwmk.
313-315 A56 Set of 3 13.00 13.00

Miniature Sheet

British Indian Ocean Territory, 40th Anniv. — A57

No. 316: a, Crab, palm fronds. b, Two crabs. c, White birds. d, Black bird, map of Indian Ocean area. e, Fish, blue starfish. f, Two triggerfish, corals. g, Angelfish, corals. h, Turtle, map of British Indian Ocean Territory.

Perf. 14¾x14¼

2005, Nov. 8 Wmk. 373
316 A57 34p Sheet of 8, #a-h 17.00 17.00

Queen Elizabeth II, 80th Birthday A58

Queen: 26p, As young woman, wearing military cap. 34p, As young woman, diff. 76p, Wearing tiara. £1.10, Wearing kerchief.
No. 321: a, Like 34p. b, Like 76p.

Wmk. 373

2006, Apr. 21 Litho. *Perf. 14*
317-320 A58 Set of 4 13.00 13.00

Souvenir Sheet

321 A58 £1 Sheet of 2, #a-b 10.00 10.00

Miniature Sheet

Angelfish — A59

No. 322: a, 26p, Dusky angelfish. b, 26p, Twospined angelfish. c, 26p, Bicolor angelfish. d, 34p, Orangeback angelfish. e, 34p, Emperor angelfish. £2, Threespot angelfish.
No. 323: a, 26p, Melon butterflyfish. b, 26p, Raccoon butterflyfish. c, 26p, Scrawled butterflyfish. d, 34p, Longnose butterflyfish. e, 34p, Threadfin butterflyfish. f, £2, Masked bannerfish.
No. 324: a, 54p, Common parrotfish. b, 54p, Daisy parrotfish. c, 54p, Bicolor parrotfish. d, 54p, Bridled parrotfish. e, 90p, Indian Ocean steephead parrotfish. f, 90p, Male and female ember parrotfish.

2006-07
322 A59 Sheet of 6, #a-f 19.00 19.00
323 A59 Sheet of 6, #a-f 15.00 15.00
324 A59 Sheet of 6, #a-f 18.00 18.00

Issued: No. 322, 5/29; No. 323, 7/31; No. 324, 3/29/07.

Miniature Sheet

BirdLife International — A60

No. 325: a, 26p, Great frigatebird. b, 26p, Black-naped terns. c, 26p, Yellow-billed tropicbirds. d, 26p, White terns. e, 26p, Brown noddies. f, £2, Red-footed boobies.

2006, Oct. 6 *Perf. 13¾*
325 A60 Sheet of 6, #a-f 16.00 16.00

Wedding of Queen Elizabeth II and Prince Philip, 60th Anniv. — A61

Designs: No. 326, 54p, Couple. No. 327, 54p, Coach in procession. No. 328, 90p, Couple, diff. No. 329, 90p, Wedding ceremony.
£2.14, Couple, diff.

Wmk. 373

2007, June 1 Litho. *Perf. 13¾*
326-329 A61 Set of 4 12.00 12.00

Souvenir Sheet

Perf. 14

330 A61 £2.14 multi 9.00 9.00

No. 330 contains one 43x58mm stamp.

Charles Darwin (1809-82), Naturalist A62

Designs: No. 331, 54p, Darwin and wildlife. No. 332, 54p, HMS Beagle. No. 333, 90p, Coral reef. No. 334, 90p, Turtles.

Wmk. 373

2007, July 23 Litho. *Perf. 13¼*
331-334 A62 Set of 4 14.00 14.00

BirdLife International — A63

Designs: No. 335, 54p, Pomarine skua chasing white-tailed tropic bird. No. 336, 54p, Two Pomarine skuas in flight. No. 337, 54p, Two Pomarine skuas on beach. No. 338, 54p, Pomarine skua attacking red-footed booby in flight, boobies on land. No. 339, 90p, Pomarine skua attacking black-necked terns in flight. No. 340, Pomarine skua on water.

2007, Oct. 1 *Perf. 12½x13*
335-340 A63 Set of 6 19.00 19.00

Miniature Sheet

Damselfish — A64

No. 341: a, 54p, One-spot demoiselle. b, 54p, Banded sergeant. c, 54p, Johnston Island damsel. d, 54p, Chagos anemonefish. e, 90p, Black-axil chromis. f, 90p, Caerulean damsel.

Wmk. 373

2008, Jan. 30 Litho. *Perf. 14*
341 A64 Sheet of 6, #a-f 18.00 18.00

Military Uniforms — A65

Designs: No. 342, 27p, Royal Marines. No. 343, 27p, Royal Engineers. No. 344, 54p, Officer, East India Company Army. No. 345, 54p, Sepoys, East India Company Army. No. 346, 54p, Sergeant, Royal Military Police. No. 347, 54p, Artillery Corps.

2008, Mar. 3
342-347 A65 Set of 6 11.00 11.00

A66

Royal Air Force, 90th Anniv. — A67

Designs: No. 348, 27p, Avro 504. No. 349, 27p, Short Sunderland. No. 350, 27p, Vickers VC10. No. 351, 27p, De Havilland Mosquito. 54p, English Electric Canberra.
£1.72, King George V, Marshal of the Royal Air Force.

Wmk. 373

2008, Apr. 1 Litho. *Perf. 14*
348-352 A66 Set of 5 7.50 7.50

Souvenir Sheet

353 A67 £1.72 black 9.00 9.00

Nos. 348-352 each were printed in sheets of 8 + central label. Value, set of five singles with labels $9.50.

End of World War I, 90th Anniv. — A68

Soldiers and their letters home: No. 354, 50p, Sergeant Major Francis Proud. No. 355, 50p, Second Lieutenant Eric Heaton. No. 356, 50p, Private Dennis Harry Wilson. No. 357, 50p, Second Lieutenant Eric Rose. No. 358, 50p, Second Lieutenant Charles Roberts. No. 359, 50p, Private Harry Lamin.
£1, Wreath of Remembrance.

Wmk. 406

2008, Sept. 16 Litho. *Perf. 14*
354-359 A68 Set of 6 14.00 14.00

Souvenir Sheet

360 A68 £1 multi 5.00 5.00

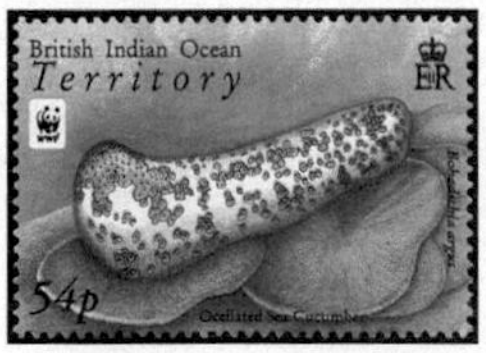

Worldwide Fund For Nature (WWF) — A69

Designs: No. 361, 54p, Ocellated sea cucumber. No. 362, 54p, Pineapple sea cucumber. No. 363, 90p, Graeffe's sea cucumber. No. 364, 90p, Dark green sea cucumber.

Wmk. 373

2008, Dec. 1 Litho. *Perf. 14*
361-364 A69 Set of 4 11.00 11.00
a. Sheet of 16, 4 each #361-364 44.00 44.00

Ships A70

Vasco da Gama (c. 1460-1524), Explorer — A71

Designs: No. 365, 54p, HMS Victory. No. 366, 54p, HMS Endeavour. No. 367, 54p, HMS Beagle. No. 368, 54p, SS Windsor Castle. No. 369, 54p, HMS Edinburgh. No. 370, 54p, SMS Fürst Bismarck.

Wmk. 406

2009, Mar. 9 Litho. *Perf. 14*
365-370 A70 Set of 6 13.00 13.00

Souvenir Sheet

371 A71 £1.30 multi 5.25 5.25

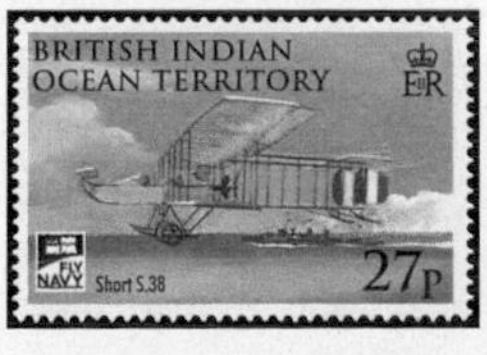

Naval Aviation, Cent. A72

Royal Navy aircraft: No. 372, 27p, Short S.38 and ship. No. 373, 27p, Sopwith Pup. No. 374, 54p, Supermarine Scimitar and ship. No. 375, 54p, Westland Wessex helicopter and ship.

£1.72, Squadron Commander E. H. Dunning landing airplane on HMS Furious, 1917.

2009, Apr. 17
372-375 A72 Set of 4 7.50 7.50

Souvenir Sheet

376 A72 £1.72 multi 7.50 7.50

Nos. 372-375 each were printed in sheets of 8 + central label. Value, set of four singles with labels $10.

Space Exploration A73

Designs: No. 377, 54p, Early rockets Corporal and Private. No. 378, 54p, Flying Bedstead, 1964. No. 379, 54p, Apollo launch site, 1969. No. 380, 54p, Space Shuttle STS-71 launch, 1995. 90p, ESA Columbus laboratory, STS-122, 2008.
£1.50, Astronaut on Moon, painting by Capt. Alan Bean, vert.

2009, July 20 ***Perf. 13¼***
377-381 A73 Set of 5 15.00 15.00

Souvenir Sheet
Perf. 13x13¼

382 A73 £1.50 multi 7.75 7.75

No. 382 contains one 40x60mm stamp. Nos. 377-381 each were printed in sheets of 6.

Flora, Fauna and Sites — A74

Designs: 1p, Two-band anemonefish. 2p, Angelfish. 5p, Royal poinciana flowers. 12p, Beach morning glories. 27p, Bay cedar flowers. 45p, Scaevola bush flowers. 54p, Madagascan red fodies. 90p, Greater frigatebirds. £1.30, Sharks Cove. £1.72, Turtle Cove. £2.64, Hawksbill turtles. £3.02 Sticklefin lemon sharks.

Wmk. 406
2009, Oct. 5 **Litho.** ***Perf. 13¾***

383 A74 1p multi .30 .30
384 A74 2p multi .30 .30
385 A74 5p multi .30 .30
386 A74 12p multi .50 .50
387 A74 27p multi 1.10 1.10
388 A74 45p multi 1.75 1.75
389 A74 54p multi 2.10 2.10
390 A74 90p multi 3.50 3.50
391 A74 £1.30 multi 5.25 5.25
392 A74 £1.72 multi 7.00 7.00
393 A74 £2.64 multi 10.50 10.50
394 A74 £3.02 multi 12.00 12.00
a. Sheet of 12, #383-394 45.00 45.00
Nos. 383-394 (12) 44.60 44.60

Fungi — A75

Designs: No. 395, 54p, Entoloma sp. No. 396, 54p, Lentinus sp. No. 397, 90p, Leucocoprinus sp. No. 398, 90p, Pycnoporus sp.

2009, Dec. 7 ***Perf. 13¼***
395-398 A75 Set of 4 14.50 14.50

Battle of Britain, 70th Anniv. — A76

British leaders and aces: No. 399, 50p, Mike Crossley. No. 400, 50p, Bob Doe. No. 401, 50p, Sir Hugh Dowding. No. 402, 50p, Ginger Lacey. No. 403, 50p, Eric Lock. No. 404, 50p, Bob Stanford Tuck.
£1.50, Sir Douglas Bader.

Perf. 12¾x13
2010, Mar. 18 **Litho.** **Wmk. 406**
399-404 A76 Set of 6 11.00 11.00

Souvenir Sheet

405 A76 £1.50 black & gray 7.00 7.00

Nos. 399-405 each were printed in sheets of 6.

Souvenir Sheet

Great Britain No. 161 — A77

2010, May 8 ***Perf. 14***
406 A77 £1.50 multi 7.00 7.00

Accession to throne of King George V, cent.; London 2010 Intl. Stamp Exhibition.

Battles and Sieges A78

Designs: No. 407, 50p, Battle of Hastings, 1066. No. 408, 50p, Battle of Agincourt, 1415. No. 409, 50p, Battle of Bosworth, 1485. No. 410, 50p, Battle of Naseby, 1645. No. 411, 50p, Battle of Culloden, 1746. No. 412, 50p, Battle of Waterloo, 1815. No. 413, 50p, Battle of the Alma, 1854. No. 414, 50p, Battle of Rorke's Drift, 1879. No. 415, 50p, Siege of Mafeking, 1899. No. 416, 50p, Battle of the Somme, 1916. No. 417, 50p, Battle of El Alamein, 1942. No. 418, 50p, Normandy Landings, 1944.

Wmk. 406
2010, Sept. 30 **Litho.** ***Perf. 13¼***
407-418 A78 Set of 12 24.00 24.00

Service of Queen Elizabeth II and Prince Philip — A79

Designs: No. 419, 54p, Queen Elizabeth II. No. 420, 54p, Queen and Prince Philip, black-and-white photograph, Queen at left. No. 421, 54p, Queen and Prince Philip, black-and-white photograph, Queen at right. No. 422, 54p, Queen and Prince Philip, color photograph, Queen at left. No. 423, 54p, Queen and Prince Philip, color photograph, Queen at right. No. 424, 54p, Prince Philip.
£3.02, Queen and Prince Philip, diff.

Perf. 13¼
2011, Mar. 1 **Litho.** **Unwmk.**
419-424 A79 Set of 6 12.00 12.00
424a Sheet of 6, #419-424, + 3 labels 12.00 12.00

Souvenir Sheet

425 A79 £3.02 multi 11.00 11.00

Souvenir Sheet

Wedding of Prince William and Catherine Middleton — A80

Perf. 14¾x14
2011, Apr. 29 **Wmk. 406**
426 A80 £3 multi 11.00 11.00

Wedding of Prince William and Catherine Middleton — A81

Designs: No. 427, 54p, Couple in carriage waving. No. 428, 54p, Couple kissing, vert. No. 429, 90p, Couple in car after wedding. No. 430, 90p, Couple holding hands, vert.

Wmk. 406
2011, Aug. 1 **Litho.** ***Perf. 12½***
427-430 A81 Set of 4 9.50 9.50

Royal British Legion, 90th Anniv. A82

Poppy at left and: No. 431, 50p, Poppies on crosses. No. 432, 50p, Lines from poem "In Flanders Fields," poppy field. No. 433, 50p, Shadow of soldier, Glorious Dead Cenotaph, London. No. 434, 50p, War graves. No. 435, 50p, Poppy drop. No. 436, 50p, Poppy appeal. No. 437, 50p, Ex-servicemen. No. 438, 50p, Festival of Remembrance. £1.50, Soldiers and sailors at attention.

Perf. 13¼x13½
2011, Nov. 11 **Wmk. 406**
431-438 A82 Set of 8 12.50 12.50

Souvenir Sheet

439 A82 £1.50 multi 4.75 4.75

Reign of Queen Elizabeth II, 60th Anniv. — A83

Queen Elizabeth II wearing: No. 440, 54p, Pearl necklace, no tiara (black-and-white photograph). No. 441, 54p, Blue hat (color photograph). No. 442, 54p, Red dress (color photograph). No. 443, 54p, Tiara and necklace (color photograph). No. 444, 54p, Tiara (black-and-white photograph). No. 445, 54p, Eyeglasses (color photograph).
£3.02, Queen Elizabeth II wearing red dress, diff.

2012, Feb. 6 ***Perf. 13¼***
440-445 A83 Set of 6 10.50 10.50
445a Souvenir sheet of 6, #440-445 10.50 10.50

Souvenir Sheet

446 A83 £3.02 multi 9.75 9.75

Coronation of Queen Elizabeth II, 60th Anniv. — A84

Various photographs of Queen Elizabeth II with panel colors of: 34p, Dark red. 54p, Green. 90p, Purple. £1.10, Dark blue.

Wmk. 406
2013, Dec. 2 **Litho.** ***Perf. 13½***
447-450 A84 Set of 4 9.50 9.50

Coat of Arms A85

No. 451: a, Left half of coat of arms (denomination at left). b, Right half of coat of arms (denomination at right).
£2, Entire coat of arms.

Wmk. 406
2014, June 9 **Litho.** ***Perf. 13¼***
451 A85 54p Horiz. pair, #a-b 3.75 3.75

Souvenir Sheet

452 A85 £2 multi 7.00 7.00

No. 452 contains one 45x45mm stamp.

Miniature Sheet

Sharks — A86

No. 453: a, Tiger shark. b, Silvertip shark. c, Silky shark. d, Gray reef shark. e, Shortfin mako shark. f, Tawny nurse shark.

Wmk. 406
2016, Feb. 12 **Litho.** ***Perf. 14***
453 A86 50p Sheet of 6, #a-f 8.50 8.50

Queen Elizabeth II, 90th Birthday A87

Photograph of Queen Elizabeth II in: No. 454, 54p, Black-and-white, as child. No. 455, 54p, Color, as adult. No. 456, 90p, Black-and-white, as adult. No. 457, 90p, Color, as adult, diff.

Wmk. 406

2016, Apr. 21 Litho. *Perf. 13¼*
454-457 A87 Set of 4 8.50 8.50

Writers and Characters from Their Works — A88

Designs: No. 458, 54p, William Shakespeare (1564-1616), Romeo and Juliet. No. 459, 54p, Beatrix Potter (1866-1943), Peter Rabbit. No. 460, 90p, Charlotte Bronte (1816-55), Jane Eyre. No. 461, 90p, Roald Dahl (1916-90), Fantastic Mr. Fox.

Wmk. 406

2016, July 28 Litho. *Perf. 14*
458-461 A88 Set of 4 7.75 7.75

Sea Turtles A89

Designs: No. 462, 60p, Green turtle hatchling. No. 463, 60p, Hawksbill turtle hatchling. No. 464, £1, Green turtle swimming. No. 465, £1, Hawksbill turtle swimming. £3, Green turtle on sea floor. £5, Hawksbill turtle eating.

Perf. 13¼x13½

2016, Nov. 15 Litho. Wmk. 406
462-467 A89 Set of 6 28.50 28.50
467a Souvenir sheet of 1 #467 13.00 13.00

World War I Aircraft A90

Designs: No. 468, 60p, Royal Aircraft Factory F. E. 2b. No. 469, 60p, Nieuport 11 (Bébé). No. 470, 60p, Sopwith Camel. No. 471, £1, Bristol F.2B. No. 472, £1, Royal Aircraft Factory S. E. 5a. £1.50, Handley Page H.P. O/400.

Perf. 13¼x13½

2017, Mar. 6 Litho. Wmk. 406
468-473 A90 Set of 6 13.50 13.50

Fish A91

Designs: 60p, Sailfish. £1, Reef manta ray. No. 476, £1.50, Oceanic whitetip shark. No. 477, £1.50, Blue marlin. £2, Sunfish. £3, Whale shark.

Wmk. 406

2017, June 8 Litho. *Perf. 13¼*
474-479 A91 Set of 6 25.00 25.00

Miniature Sheet

Corals — A92

No. 480: a, 60p, Acropora cytherea. b, £1, Porites evermanni. c, £1.50, Turbinaria reniformis. d, £2, Ctenella chagius. e, £2.50, Fungia repanda. f,£3, Pocillopora damicornis.

Wmk. 406

2017, Sept. 5 Litho. *Perf. 14¼*
480 A92 Sheet of 6, #a-f 28.00 28.00

70th Wedding Anniversary of Queen Elizabeth II and Prince Philip — A93

Designs: £1, Engagement photograph. £1.50, Wedding photograph. No. 483, £2, Photograph of middle-aged Queen and Prince. No. 484, £2, Photograph of elderly Queen and Prince.

Wmk. 406

2017, Nov. 20 Litho. *Perf. 14¼*
481-484 A93 Set of 4 17.50 17.50

Women's Royal Naval Service, Cent. — A94

No. 485, £1: a, Mine clearance diver. b, World War I Wrens.
No. 486, £1: a, First female submariners on HMS Vigilant, 2014. b, Radar plotter on HMS Dryad.
No. 487, £1: a, Ops room warfare specialist. b, World War II boat crew.

Perf. 13¼x13½

2017, Nov. 28 Litho. Wmk. 406
Horiz. pairs, #a-b
485-487 A94 Set of 3 16.50 16.50

Miniature Sheet

Flowers — A95

No. 488: a, 60p, Barringtonia asiatica. b, 60p, Guettarda speciosa. c, 60p, Intsia bijuga. d, £1, Cordia subcordata. e, £1, Calophyllum inophyllum. f, £2.50, Ipomoea pes-caprae.

Wmk. 406

2018, May 2 Litho. *Perf. 13*
488 A95 Sheet of 6, #a-f 17.00 17.00

Wedding of Prince Harry and Meghan Markle — A96

Designs: £1, Bride, groom and Archbishop of Canterbury. £1.50, Couple kissing. No. 491, £2, Heads of bride and groom. No. 492, £2, Bride and groom holding hands.

Wmk. 406

2018, July 27 Litho. *Perf. 14*
489-492 A96 Set of 4 17.00 17.00

Winning Designs in International Year of the Reef Children's Art Contest — A97

Art by: No. 493, £2, Kyle Irvine. No. 494, £2, Megan Lee Yit May. No. 495, £2, Laura Gilbert. No. 496, £2, Ailis Law.

Wmk. 406

2018, Sept. 4 Litho. *Perf. 14*
493-496 A97 Set of 4 20.50 20.50

End of World War I, Cent. — A98

Poppy and: 60p, Soldiers and large gun. £1, Tank. £2, Soldier on horseback. £3, Soldiers carrying wounded comrade on litter.

Perf. 13¾x13¼

2018, Nov. 11 Litho. Wmk. 406
497-500 A98 Set of 4 17.00 17.00

Christmas A99

Designs: No. 501, 60p, Santa Claus, gifts and Christmas trees. No. 502, 60p, Reindeer and Christmas tree. No. 503, £1, Snowman. No. 504, £1, Robin wearing stocking cap. No. 505, £1.50, Gifts on sleigh. No. 506, £1.50, Penguin wearing stocking cap.

Wmk. 406

2018, Nov. 21 Litho. *Perf. 13¼*
501-506 A99 Set of 6 16.00 16.00

BRUNEI

ˈbrü-ˌnī

LOCATION — On the northwest coast of Borneo
GOVT. — Independent state sultanate
AREA — 2,226 sq. mi.
POP. — 422,675 (2014 est.)
CAPITAL — Bandar Seri Begawan

Brunei became a British protectorate in 1888. A treaty between the sultan and the British Government in 1979 provided for independence in 1983.

100 Cents (Sen) = 1 Dollar

Catalogue values for unused stamps in this country are for Never Hinged items, beginning with Scott 62.

See the *Scott Classic Specialized Catalogue of Stamps and Covers* for the 1895 issue.

Watermarks

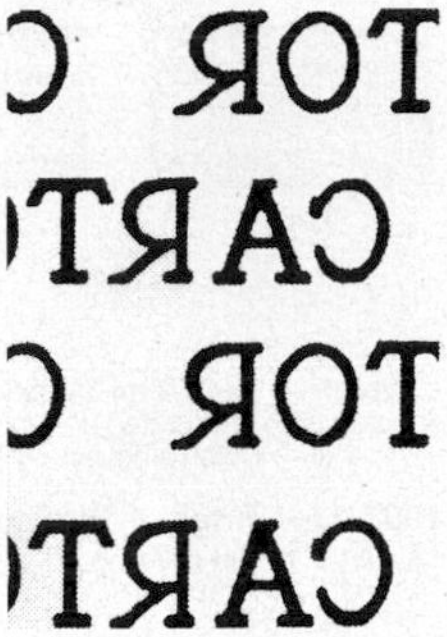

Wmk. 385 — CARTOR

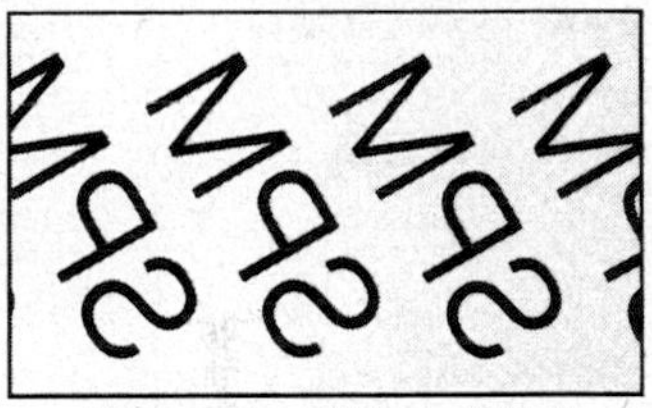

Wmk. 388 — Multiple "SPM"

Syncopated Perforation

Type A (first stamp #555): On 2 longer sides, oval holes equal in width to 3 holes which are the 11th hole from the top and 10th hole from the bottom.

Labuan Stamps of 1902-03 Overprinted or Surcharged in Red

1906 Unwmk. *Perf. 12 to 16*

1	A38	1c violet & blk	50.00	*65.00*
a.		Black overprint	*2,500.*	*3,000.*
2	A38	2c on 3c brn & blk	7.00	*21.00*
a.		"BRUNEI." double	*4,500.*	*3,000.*
b.		"TWO CENTS." double	*6,500.*	
3	A38	2c on 8c org & blk	32.50	*80.00*
a.		"TWO CENTS." double	*14,000.*	
b.		"TWO CENTS." omitted, in pair with normal	*15,000.*	
4	A38	3c brown & blk	38.50	*100.00*
5	A38	4c on 12c yel & black	8.50	*6.00*
6	A38	5c on 16c org brn & green	55.00	*90.00*
7	A38	8c orange & blk	15.00	*37.50*
8	A38	10c on 16c org brn & green	7.75	*26.00*
9	A38	25c on 16c org brn & green	125.00	*150.00*
10	A38	30c on 16c org brn & green	125.00	*150.00*
11	A38	50c on 16c org brn & green	125.00	*150.00*
12	A38	$1 on 8c org & blk	125.00	*150.00*
		Nos. 1-12 (12)	714.25	*1,026.*

The 25c surcharge reads: "25 CENTS."

Scene on Brunei River — A1

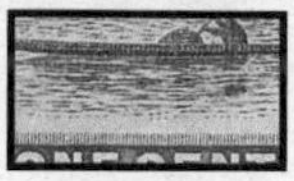

Type I

Type II

Two Types of 1908 1c, 3c:
Type I — Dots form bottom line of water shading. (Double plate.)
Type II — Dots removed. (Single plate.)

1907-21 Engr. Wmk. 3 *Perf. 14*

13	A1	1c yel green & blk	2.75	13.00
14	A1	1c green (II) ('11)	.70	2.50
a.		Type I ('19)	1.00	2.75
15	A1	2c red & black	3.25	4.25
16	A1	2c brn & blk ('11)	4.75	1.50
17	A1	3c red brn & blk	12.50	26.00
18	A1	3c car (I) ('08)	8.00	1.50
a.		Type II ('17)	130.00	45.00
19	A1	4c lilac & blk	9.00	8.00
20	A1	4c claret ('12)	8.00	.90
21	A1	5c ultra & blk	60.00	110.00
22	A1	5c org & blk ('08)	8.50	8.50
23	A1	5c orange ('16)	26.00	25.00
24	A1	8c orange & blk	9.00	27.50
25	A1	8c blue & indigo blue ('08)	8.50	13.00
26	A1	8c ultra ('16)	8.00	32.50
27	A1	10c dk green & blk	5.25	5.00
28	A1	10c violet, *yel* ('12)	10.00	2.10
29	A1	25c yel brn & blue	37.50	57.50
30	A1	25c violet ('12)	11.00	30.00
31	A1	30c black & pur	30.00	25.00
32	A1	30c org & red vio ('12)	17.50	20.00
33	A1	50c brown & grn	18.00	25.00
34	A1	50c blk, *grn* ('12)	40.00	75.00
35	A1	50c blk, *grnsh bl* ('21)	11.00	42.50
36	A1	$1 slate & red	72.50	110.00
37	A1	$1 red & blk, *bl* ('12)	30.00	57.50
38	A1	$5 lake, *grn* ('08)	200.00	350.00
39	A1	$25 blk, *red* ('08)	650.00	1,350.
		Nos. 13-38 (26)	651.70	1,074.
		Set, never hinged	1,500.	

Used value for No. 39 is for a canceled-to-order example dated before December 1941. CTOs dated later are worth about half the value given.

Some stamps in this set exist with watermark reversed or inverted; values are two to five times those shown.

Stamps of 1908-21 Overprinted in Four Lines in Black

1922

14b	A1	1c green	12.00	55.00
16a	A1	2c brown & black	13.00	50.00
18b	A1	3c carmine	14.00	60.00
20a	A1	4c claret	20.00	60.00
23a	A1	5c orange	27.50	65.00
28a	A1	10c violet, *yellow*	12.00	65.00
30a	A1	25c violet	16.00	85.00
35a	A1	50c greenish blue	47.50	160.00
37a	A1	$1 red & black, *blue*	80.00	200.00
		Nos. 14b-37a (9)	242.00	800.00
		Set, never hinged	600.00	

Industrial fair, Singapore, Mar. 31-Apr. 15

Type of 1907 Issue

1924-37 Wmk. 4

43	A1	1c black ('26)	1.25	.90
44	A1	2c deep brown	1.25	11.00
45	A1	2c green ('33)	2.40	1.25
46	A1	3c green	2.00	7.75
47	A1	4c claret brown	3.25	1.50
48	A1	4c orange ('29)	2.40	1.25
49	A1	5c orange	16.00	2.00
50	A1	5c lt gray ('31)	25.00	14.00
51	A1	5c brown ('33)	25.00	1.20
52	A1	8c ultra ('27)	7.25	6.00
53	A1	8c gray ('33)	19.00	.90
54	A1	10c violet, *yel* ('37)	40.00	32.50
55	A1	25c dk violet ('31)	24.00	15.00
56	A1	30c org & red vio ('31)	25.00	19.00
57	A1	50c black, *grn* ('31)	20.00	17.50
58	A1	$1 red & blk, *bl* ('31)	29.00	90.00
		Nos. 43-58 (16)	242.80	221.75

For overprints see Nos. N1-N20.

Dwellings in Town of Brunei A2

1924-31

59	A2	6c black	17.00	12.00
60	A2	6c red ('31)	13.00	12.50
61	A2	12c blue	5.50	11.00
		Nos. 59-61 (3)	35.50	35.50

See note after Nos. N1-N19.

Catalogue values for unused stamps in this section, from this point to the end of the section, are for Never Hinged items.

Types of 1907-24

1947-51 Engr. *Perf. 14*

62	A1	1c brown	.65	2.50
63	A1	2c gray	.75	6.00
a.		Perf. 14½x13½ ('50)	2.40	5.25
64	A2	3c dark green	1.50	8.00
65	A1	5c deep orange	1.00	1.75
a.		Perf. 14½x13½ ('50)	4.75	22.00
66	A2	6c gray black	1.25	6.75
67	A1	8c scarlet	.60	1.50
a.		Perf. 13 ('51)	.65	13.00
68	A1	10c violet	2.25	.40
a.		Perf. 14½x13½ ('50)	3.75	6.50
69	A1	15c brt ultra	2.10	.90
70	A1	25c red violet	3.25	1.25
a.		Perf. 14½x13½ ('51)	4.50	16.00
71	A1	30c dp org & gray blk	3.00	1.25
a.		Perf. 14½x13½ ('51)	3.50	22.00
72	A1	50c black	6.50	1.00
a.		Perf. 13 ('50)	2.10	22.00
73	A1	$1 scar & gray blk	16.00	2.50
74	A1	$5 red org & grn ('48)	22.50	25.00
75	A1	$10 dp claret & gray blk ('48)	110.00	35.00
		Nos. 62-75 (14)	171.35	93.80

Sultan Ahmed and Pile Dwellings A3

1949, Sept. 22 Wmk. 4 *Perf. 13*

76	A3	8c car & black	1.50	1.50
77	A3	25c red orange & pur	1.50	2.10
78	A3	50c blue & black	1.50	2.10
		Nos. 76-78 (3)	4.50	5.70

25th anniv. of the reign of Sultan Ahmed Tajudin Akhazul Khair Wad-din.

Common Design Types pictured following the introduction.

UPU Issue

Common Design Types

Engr.; Name Typo. on 15c and 25c

1949, Oct. 10 *Perf. 13½, 11x11½*

79	CD306	8c rose car	1.40	1.75
80	CD307	15c indigo	3.50	2.10
81	CD308	25c red lilac	2.00	2.00
82	CD309	50c slate	2.60	2.60
		Nos. 79-82 (4)	9.50	8.45

Sultan Omar Ali Saifuddin — A4

River Kampong A5

Perf. 13½x13

1952, Mar. 1 Engr. Wmk. 4

Center in Black

83	A4	1c black	.25	.25
84	A4	2c red orange	.25	.25
85	A4	3c red brown	.25	.25
86	A4	4c green	.25	.25
87	A4	6c gray	.25	.25
88	A4	8c carmine	.30	.25
89	A4	10c olive brown	.25	.25
90	A4	12c violet	4.25	.25
91	A4	15c blue	3.00	.25
92	A4	25c purple	3.00	.25
93	A4	50c ultramarine	3.00	.30

Perf. 13

94	A5	$1 dull green	4.00	1.20
95	A5	$2 red	6.75	3.00
96	A5	$5 deep plum	28.00	12.00
		Nos. 83-96 (14)	53.80	19.00

See Nos. 101-114.

Mosque and Sultan Omar A6

1958, Sept. 24 Wmk. 314 *Perf. 13*

Center in Black

97	A6	8c dull green	.30	.45
98	A6	15c carmine rose	.45	.45
99	A6	35c rose violet	.60	.65
		Nos. 97-99 (3)	1.35	1.55

Opening of the Brunei Mosque.

Freedom from Hunger Issue

Common Design Type with Portrait of Sultan Omar

1963, June 4 Photo. *Perf. 14x14½*

100	CD314	12c sepia	3.25	2.25

Types of 1952
On Ordinary Paper

Wmk. 314 Upright

1964-70 Engr. *Perf. 13½x13*

Center in Black

101	A4	1c black	.25	.25
102	A4	2c red orange	.25	.25
103	A4	3c red brown	.25	.25
104	A4	4c green	.45	.25
105	A4	6c gray	1.10	.25
c.		6c black ('69)	3.50	1.20
106	A4	8c dk carmine	.75	.25
107	A4	10c olive brown	.50	.25
108	A4	12c violet	1.75	.25
109	A4	15c blue	1.30	.25
110	A4	25c purple	2.60	.25
111	A4	50c ultramarine	3.00	.50
b.		50c bright ultra ('69)	10.50	1.00

Perf. 13

112	A5	$1 dull green ('68)	12.00	4.00
		Nos. 101-112 (12)	24.20	7.00

On Whiter, Glazed Paper

Wmk. 314 Upright

1969-72 *Perf. 13½x13*

Center in Black

101a	A4	1c black ('69)	.70	.70
c.		1c slate gray ('72)	.25	.25
102a	A4	2c red org ('70)	.30	.25
103a	A4	3c red brn ('70)	.30	.25
104a	A4	4c green ('70)	.45	.25
c.		4c emerald & black ('71)	1.00	.35
105a	A4	6c gray ('69)	.55	.25
106a	A4	8c dk carmine ('70)	.70	.25
c.		8c brownish red & black ('71)	2.25	.75
107a	A4	10c olive brn ('70)	2.25	.25
c.		10c pale brn & gray ('71)	3.00	.35
108a	A4	12c violet ('70)	8.50	.30
109a	A4	15c blue ('69)	.75	.25
110a	A4	25c purple ('70)	10.00	.85
c.		Reddish violet & black ('71)	13.00	2.00
111a	A4	50c br ultra ('70)	10.00	.25
c.		50c indigo & gray ('71)	11.00	1.00

Perf. 13

112a	A5	$1 dull green ('70)	7.00	4.25
113	A5	$2 red ('70)	37.50	22.50
114	A5	$5 deep plum ('70)	42.50	35.00
		Nos. 101a-114 (14)	121.50	65.60

Wmk. 314 Sideways

1972-73 *Perf. 13½x13*

Center in Black

102b	A4	2c red orange	1.75	.85
103b	A4	3c red brown	2.00	.25
104b	A4	4c green	.60	.25
105b	A4	6c black	3.25	.30
106b	A4	8c dark carmine	3.00	2.50
107b	A4	10c olive brown	1.00	.25
108b	A4	12c violet	1.75	1.00
109b	A4	15c blue	2.00	1.00
		Nos. 102b-109b (8)	15.35	6.40

Issue dates: 2c, 8c, May 9, 1973, others, Nov. 17, 1972.

The following six sets are Common Design Types but with the portrait of Sultan Omar.

ITU Issue

Perf. 11x11½

1965, May 17 Litho. Wmk. 314

116	CD317	4c red lil & org brn	.35	.35
117	CD317	75c orange & emer	1.40	1.40

Intl. Cooperation Year Issue

1965, Oct. 25 *Perf. 14½*

118	CD318	4c blue grn & claret	.25	.25
119	CD318	15c lt violet & grn	.60	.60

Churchill Memorial Issue

1966, Jan. 24 Photo. *Perf. 14*

120	CD319	3c multicolored	.25	.25
121	CD319	10c multicolored	1.00	.80
122	CD319	15c multicolored	1.90	1.50
123	CD319	75c multicolored	4.50	4.00
		Nos. 120-123 (4)	7.65	6.55

World Cup Soccer Issue

1966, July 4 Litho. *Perf. 14*

124	CD321	4c multicolored	.30	.30
125	CD321	75c multicolored	1.00	.95

WHO Headquarters Issue

1966, Sept. 20 Litho. *Perf. 14*

126	CD322	12c multicolored	.45	.45
127	CD322	25c multicolored	.90	.90

UNESCO Anniversary Issue

1966, Dec. 1 Litho. Wmk. 314

128	CD323	4c "Education"	.40	.40
129	CD323	15c "Science"	1.00	1.00
130	CD323	75c "Culture"	3.25	4.00
		Nos. 128-130 (3)	4.65	5.40

State Religious Building and Sultan Hassanal Bolkiah A7

1967, Dec. 19 Photo. *Perf. 12½*

131	A7	4c violet & multi	.25	.25
132	A7	10c red & multi	.25	.25
133	A7	25c orange & multi	.30	.30
134	A7	50c lt violet & multi	.45	.45
		Nos. 131-134 (4)	1.25	1.25

A three-stamp set (12c, 25c, 50c) showing views of the new Language and Communications Headquarters was prepared and announced for release in April, 1968. The Crown Agents distributed sample sets, but the stamps were not issued. Later, Nos. 144-146 were issued instead.

Sultan Hassanal Bolkiah, Brunei Mosque and Flags A8

Sultan Hassanal Bolkiah Installation: 12c, Sultan, Mosque and flags, horiz.

Perf. 13x14, 14x13

1968, July 9 Photo. Unwmk.

135	A8	4c green & multi	.25	.25
136	A8	12c dp bister & multi	.50	.50
137	A8	25c violet & multi	.65	*.75*
		Nos. 135-137 (3)	1.40	1.50

Sultan Hassanal Bolkiah A9

Wmk. 314

1968, July 15 Litho. *Perf. 12*

138	A9	4c multicolored	.25	.25
139	A9	12c multicolored	.25	.25
140	A9	25c multicolored	.50	.50
		Nos. 138-140 (3)	1.00	1.00

Sultan Hassanal Bolkiah's birthday.

Coronation of Sultan Hassanal Bolkiah, Aug. 1, 1968 — A10

1968, Aug. 1 Photo. *Perf. 14½x14*

141	A10	4c Prus blue & multi	.25	.25
142	A10	12c rose lilac & multi	.25	.25
143	A10	25c multicolored	.50	.50
		Nos. 141-143 (3)	1.00	1.00

A11

Hall of Language and Culture — A12

Perf. 13½, 12½x13½ (A12)

1968, Sept. 29 Photo. Wmk. 314

144	A11	10c blue grn & multi	.25	.25
145	A12	15c ocher & multi	.25	.25
146	A12	30c ultra & multi	.60	.60
		Nos. 144-146 (3)	1.10	1.10

Opening of the Hall of Language and Culture and of the Broadcasting and Information Department Building. Nos. 144-146 are overprinted "1968" and 4 bars over the 1967 date. They were not issued without this overprint.

Human Rights Flame and Struggling Man — A13

Unwmk.

1968, Dec. 16 Litho. *Perf. 14*

147	A13	12c green, yel & blk	.25	.25
148	A13	25c ultra, yel & blk	.30	.30
149	A13	75c dk plum, yel & blk	.60	.60
		Nos. 147-149 (3)	1.15	1.15

International Human Rights Year.

Sultan and WHO Emblem A14

1968, Dec. 19 Litho. *Perf. 14*

150	A14	4c lt blue, org & blk	.30	.30
151	A14	15c brt purple, org & blk	.45	.45
152	A14	25c olive, org & blk	.90	.90
		Nos. 150-152 (3)	1.65	1.65

20th anniv. of the WHO.

Sultan Hassanal Bolkiah, Pengiran Shahbandar and Oil Rig — A15

Perf. 14x13

1969, July 10 Photo. Wmk. 314

153	A15	12c green & multi	.75	.75
154	A15	40c dk rose brn & multi	1.00	1.00
155	A15	50c violet & multi	1.90	1.90
		Nos. 153-155 (3)	3.65	3.65

Installation of Pengiran Shahbandar as Second Minister (Di-Galong Sahibol Mal).

Royal Assembly Hall and Council Chamber — A16

Design: 50c, Front view of buildings.

Unwmk.

1969, Sept. 23 Litho. *Perf. 15*

156	A16	12c multicolored	.25	.25
157	A16	25c multicolored	.35	.35
158	A16	50c violet & pink	.70	.70
		Nos. 156-158 (3)	1.30	1.30

Opening of the Royal Assembly Hall and Council Chamber.

Youth Center — A17

1969, Dec. 20 Litho. Wmk. 314

159	A17	6c lt org, blk & dull vio	.25	.25
160	A17	10c cit, blk & dl Prus grn	.25	.25
161	A17	30c yel green, blk & brn	.70	.70
		Nos. 159-161 (3)	1.20	1.20

Opening of Youth Center, Mar. 15, 1969.

Helicopter and Emblem — A18

Designs: 10c, Soldier and emblem, vert. 75c, Patrol boat and emblem.

1971, May 31 Litho. *Perf. 14*

162	A18	10c green & multi	.75	.75
163	A18	15c Prus blue & multi	1.80	1.80
164	A18	75c lt ultra & multi	4.75	4.75
		Nos. 162-164 (3)	7.30	7.30

10th anniv. of Royal Brunei Malay Reg.

50th Anniv. of the Royal Brunei Police Force — A19

1971, Aug. 14 *Perf. 14½*

165	A19	10c Superintendent	.50	.50
166	A19	15c Constable	.75	.75
167	A19	50c Traffic policeman	2.75	2.75
		Nos. 165-167 (3)	4.00	4.00

Sultan, Heir Apparent and View of Brunei — A20

Portraits and: 25c, View of Brunei with Mosque. 50c, Mosque and banner.

1971, Aug. 27 Litho. Wmk. 314

168	A20	15c multicolored	.75	.60
169	A20	25c multicolored	1.00	.85
170	A20	50c multicolored	2.00	2.75
		Nos. 168-170 (3)	3.75	4.20

Installation of Sultan Hassanal Bolkiah's brother Muda Omar Ali Saifuddin as heir apparent (Perdana Wazir).

Brass and Copper Goods A21

Designs: 12c, Basketware. 15c, Leather goods. 25c, Silverware. 50c, Brunei Museum.

1972, Feb. 29 *Perf. 13½x14*

Size: 37x21mm

Portrait in Black

171	A21	10c brn, sal & yel grn	.30	.30
172	A21	12c org, yel & green	.50	.50
173	A21	15c dk grn, emer & org	.65	.65
174	A21	25c brown, org & slate	1.60	1.60

Size: 58x21mm

175	A21	50c dull blue & multi	2.90	2.90
		Nos. 171-175 (5)	5.95	5.95

Opening of Brunei Museum.

Queen Elizabeth II, Sultan and View — A22

Queen Elizabeth II, Sultan Hassanal Bolkiah and: 15c, View of Brunei. 25c, Mosque and barge. 50c, Royal Assembly Hall.

1972, Feb. 29 Photo. *Perf. 13x13½*

176	A22	10c lt brown & multi	.35	.35
177	A22	15c lt blue & multi	1.40	1.40
178	A22	25c lt green & multi	2.40	2.40
179	A22	50c dull purple & multi	4.00	4.00
		Nos. 176-179 (4)	8.15	8.15

Visit of Queen Elizabeth II, Feb. 29.

Bangunan Secretariat (Government Buildings) — A23

Sultans Omar Ali Saifuddin and Hassanal Bolkiah: 15c, Istana Darul Hana (Sultan's residence). 25c, View of capital. 50c, View of new Mosque.

1972, Oct. 4 Litho. *Perf. 13½*

180	A23	10c org, blk & green	.30	.30
181	A23	15c green & multi	.45	.45
182	A23	25c ultra & multi	.90	.90
183	A23	50c rose red & multi	1.35	1.35
		Nos. 180-183 (4)	3.00	3.00

Change of capital's name from Brunei to Bandar Seri Begawan, Oct. 4, 1970.

Beverley Plane Landing — A24

Design: 25c, Blackburn Beverley plane dropping supplies by parachute, vert.

Perf. 14x13½, 13½x14

1972, Nov. 15 Litho.

184	A24	25c blue & multi	2.25	2.25
185	A24	75c ultra & multi	4.50	4.50

Opening of Royal Air Force Museum, Hendon, London.

Silver Wedding Issue, 1972

Common Design Type

Design: Queen Elizabeth II, Prince Philip; girl and boy with traditional gifts.

1972, Nov. 20 Photo. *Perf. 14x14½*

186	CD324	12c multi	.25	.25
187	CD324	75c multi	.45	.45

INTERPOL Emblem and Headquarters, Paris — A25

Design: 50c, similar to 25c.

1973, Sept. 7 Litho. *Perf. 14x14½*

188	A25	25c emerald & multi	1.90	1.90
189	A25	50c multicolored	1.90	1.90

50th anniv. of Intl. Criminal Police Org. (INTERPOL).

Princess Anne and Mark Phillips — A26

1973, Nov. 14 Litho. *Perf. 13½*
190 A26 25c vio blue & multi .25 .25
191 A26 50c red lilac & multi .40 .40

Wedding of Princess Anne and Capt. Mark Phillips, Nov. 14, 1973.

Churchill Painting Outdoors — A27

Design: 50c, Churchill making "V" sign.

Perf. 14x13½
1973, Dec. 31 Litho. Wmk. 314
192 A27 12c car rose & multi .35 .35
193 A27 50c dk green & multi .50 .50

Winston Churchill Memorial Exhibition.

Sultan Hassanal Bolkiah — A28

Wmk. 314 Sideways
1974, July 15 Photo. *Perf. 13x15*
194 A28 4c blue grn & multi .25 .25
195 A28 5c dull blue & multi .25 .25
196 A28 6c olive grn & multi .75 .75
197 A28 10c lt violet & multi .25 .25
b. Watermark upright ('76) 3.00 .50
198 A28 15c brown & multi .25 .25
199 A28 20c buff & multi .25 .25
b. Watermark upright ('76) 2.50 .75
200 A28 25c olive & multi .25 .25
b. Watermark upright ('76) 3.50 1.00
201 A28 30c multicolored .30 .25
202 A28 35c gray & multi .40 .25
203 A28 40c multicolored .40 .25
204 A28 50c yel brn & multi .45 .25
205 A28 75c multicolored .90 1.00
206 A28 $1 dull org & multi 1.50 1.25
207 A28 $2 multicolored 3.00 1.25
208 A28 $5 silver & multi 4.00 *6.25*
209 A28 $10 gold & multi 11.00 10.00
Nos. 194-209 (16) 24.20 23.00

Issue date: Nos. 197b-200b, Apr. 12.

1975, Aug. 13 Wmk. 373
194a A28 4c .25 .25
195a A28 5c .25 .25
196a A28 6c 6.00 1.00
197a A28 10c .25 .25
Complete booklet, 4 x #195a, 8 x #197a 7.25
198a A28 15c .60 .25
199a A28 20c .60 .25
200a A28 25c .65 .25
201a A28 30c .35 .25
202a A28 35c .45 .30
203a A28 40c .55 .25
204a A28 50c .90 .25
205a A28 75c .85 *1.10*
206a A28 $1 1.75 1.10
207a A28 $2 4.75 4.75
208a A28 $5 6.50 *17.50*
209a A28 $10 24.00 *35.00*
Nos. 194a-209a (16) 48.70 63.00

For surcharge see No. 225.
CTO examples of Nos. 208a and 209a sell for less. Values: $6.50 and $24, respectively.

Brunei Airport A29

Design: 75c, Sultan Hassanal Bolkiah in uniform and jet over airport.

Perf. 14x14½, 12½x13 (75c)
1974, July 18 Litho. Wmk. 314
Size: 44x28mm
215 A29 50c multicolored 1.60 1.60
Size: 47x36mm
216 A29 75c multicolored 1.90 1.90

Opening of Brunei Airport.

UPU Emblem A30

1974, Oct. 28 *Perf. 14½*
217 A30 12c orange & multi .30 .30
218 A30 50c blue & multi .70 .70
219 A30 75c emerald & multi 1.00 1.00
Nos. 217-219 (3) 2.00 2.00

Centenary of Universal Postal Union.

Winston Churchill A31

Design: 75c, Churchill smoking cigar.

1974, Nov. 30 Wmk. 373 *Perf. 14*
220 A31 12c vio blue, blue & gold .40 .40
221 A31 75c dk grn, blk & gold 1.00 1.00

Sir Winston Churchill (1874-1965).

Boeing 737 Planes at Airport A32

Designs: 35c, Boeing 737 over Bandar Seri Begawan Mosque. 75c, Boeing 737 in flight. All planes with crest of Royal Brunei Airlines.

Perf. 12½x12
1975, May 14 Unwmk.
222 A32 12c multicolored .60 .60
223 A32 35c multicolored 1.50 1.50
224 A32 75c multicolored 3.50 3.50
Nos. 222-224 (3) 5.60 5.60

Inauguration of Royal Brunei Airlines.

No. 196a Surcharged in Silver

Perf. 13x15
1976, Aug. 16 Photo. Wmk. 373
225 A28 10c on 6c multicolored 3.00 3.00
a. 10c on 6c, wmk 314 sideways (#196) 3.25 3.25

British Royal Coat of Arms — A33

20c, Imperial State Crown. 75c, Elizabeth II.

Wmk. 373
1977, June 7 Litho. *Perf. 14*
226 A33 10c dk blue & multi .25 .25
227 A33 20c purple & multi .25 .25
228 A33 75c yellow & multi .65 .65
Nos. 226-228 (3) 1.15 1.15

25th anniv. of the reign of Elizabeth II.

Coronation of Elizabeth II A34

20c, Elizabeth II with coronation regalia. 75c, Departure from Westminster Abbey (coach).

1978, June 2 Litho. *Perf. 13½x13*
229 A34 10c multicolored .25 .25
230 A34 20c multicolored .25 .25
231 A34 75c multicolored .60 .60
Nos. 229-231 (3) 1.10 1.10

25th anniv. of coronation of Elizabeth II.

Sultan's Coat of Arms — A35

Coronation of Sultan Hassanal Bolkiah, 10th Anniv.: 20c, Ceremony. 75c, Royal crown.

1978, Aug. 1 Wmk. 373 *Perf. 12*
232 A35 10c multicolored .25 .25
233 A35 20c multicolored .30 .30
234 A35 75c multicolored 1.25 1.25
a. Souvenir sheet of 3, #232-234 19.00 19.00
Nos. 232-234 (3) 1.80 1.80

Struggling Man, Human Rights Flame — A36

1978, Dec. 10 Litho. *Perf. 14*
235 A36 10c red, black & yel .25 .25
236 A36 20c violet, black & yel .25 .25
237 A36 75c olive, black & yel 1.00 1.00
Nos. 235-237 (3) 1.50 1.50

Universal Declaration of Human Rights, 30th anniversary.

Children and IYC Emblem A37

1979, June 30 Wmk. 373 *Perf. 14*
238 A37 10c shown .25 .25
239 A37 $1 IYC emblem 1.40 1.40

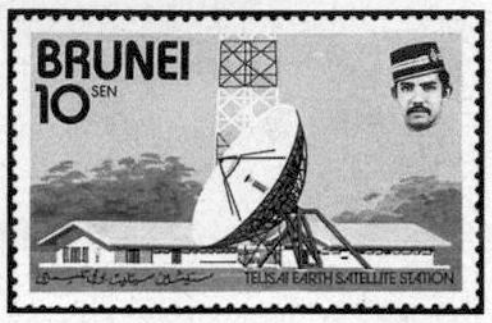

Telisai Earth Satellite Station A38

Designs: 20c, Radar screen and satellite. 75c, Cameraman, telex operator, telephone.

1979, Sept. 23 Litho. *Perf. 14½x14*
240 A38 10c multicolored .25 .25
241 A38 20c multicolored .30 .30
242 A38 75c multicolored 1.00 1.00
Nos. 240-242 (3) 1.55 1.55

Hajeer Emblem — A39

1979, Nov. 21
243 A39 10c multicolored .25 .25
244 A39 20c multicolored .25 .25
245 A39 75c multicolored 1.10 1.10
a. Souvenir sheet of 3, #243-245 5.75 5.75
Nos. 243-245 (3) 1.60 1.60

Hegira, 1400th anniversary.

A set of four depicting the opening of ports and harbors was prepared for use but not issued. A small number of sets exist in collector hands.

A40

No. 246, Installation ceremony. No. 247, Ceremony, diff. No. 248, Jefri Bolkiah. No. 249, Sufri Bolkiah.

1980 Litho. *Perf. 14*
Color of Panels at Top and Bottom
246 A40 10c brt blue .25 .25
247 A40 10c dark green .25 .25
248 A40 75c brt blue 1.00 1.00
249 A40 75c dark green 1.00 1.00
Nos. 246-249 (4) 2.50 2.50

Installation of Jefri Bolkiah and Sufri Bolkiah as Wizars (Ministers of State for Royalty) 1st anniv. Issued: Nos. 246, 248, 11/8; others, 12/6.

A41

1981, Jan. 19 Litho. *Perf. 12x11½*

255 A41 10c Umbrella .25 .25
256 A41 15c Dagger, shield .35 .35
257 A41 20c Spears .45 .45
258 A41 30c Gold pouch .60 .60

Size: 22½x40mm

Perf. 14x13½

259 A41 50c Headdress 1.15 1.15
a. Souvenir sheet of 5, #255-259 6.00 6.00
Nos. 255-259 (5) 2.80 2.80

A42

1981, May 17 Litho. *Perf. 13x13½*

260 A42 10c car rose & black .35 .35
261 A42 75c dp violet & black 2.50 2.50

13th World Telecommunications Day.

A43

Perf. 12½x12, 12 (75c)

1981, July 15 Litho.

Deep Rose Lilac Background

262 A43 10c Dagger, case .25 .25
263 A43 15c Rifle, powder pouch .25 .25
264 A43 20c Spears .25 .25
265 A43 30c Sword, tunic, shield .50 .50
266 A43 50c Horns 1.00 1.00

Size: 28½x45mm

267 A43 75c Gold bowl, table 1.50 1.50
Nos. 262-267 (6) 3.75 3.75

See Nos. 278-289.

Royal Wedding Issue

Common Design Type

1981, July 29 *Perf. 14*

268 CD331 10c Bouquet .25 .25
269 CD331 $1 Charles .65 *1.50*
270 CD331 $2 Couple 1.25 *2.75*
Nos. 268-270 (3) 2.15 *4.50*

World Food Day — A44

1981, Oct. 16 Litho. *Perf. 12*

271 A44 10c Fishermen .75 .75
272 A44 $1 Produce 6.00 6.00

Intl. Year of the Disabled — A45

1981, Dec. 16 Wmk. 373 *Perf. 12*

273 A45 10c Blind man .60 .60
274 A45 20c Sign language 1.10 1.10
275 A45 75c Man in wheelchair 4.00 4.00
Nos. 273-275 (3) 5.70 5.70

TB Bacillus Centenary — A46

1982, Mar. 24 *Perf. 12, 13½ (75c)*

276 A46 10c Lungs .45 .45
277 A46 75c Bacillus, microscope 3.50 3.50

Type of 1981

1982, May 31 Litho. *Perf. 12½x12*

Deep Magenta Background

278 A43 10c shown .25 .25
279 A43 15c Pedestal urn .25 .25
280 A43 20c Silver bowl .25 .25
281 A43 30c Candle .50 .50
282 A43 50c Gold pipe 1.00 1.00

Size: 28x44mm

Perf. 13½

283 A43 75c Silver pointer 1.50 1.50
Nos. 278-283 (6) 3.75 3.75

1982, July 15 Litho. *Perf. 12½x12*

Violet Background

284 A43 10c Urn .30 .30
285 A43 15c Crossed banners .35 .35
286 A43 20c Golden fan .50 .50
287 A43 30c Lid 1.00 1.00
288 A43 50c Sword, sheath 1.50 1.50

Size: 28x44mm

Perf. 12

289 A43 75c Golden chalice pole 2.00 2.00
Nos. 284-289 (6) 5.65 5.65

A47

10c, Flag. 20c, Omar Ali Saifuddin Mosque. 75c, Oil well. $2, Sultan Bolkiah.

1983, Mar. 14 Litho. *Perf. 13½*

290 A47 10c multi .25 .25
291 A47 20c multi .25 .25
292 A47 75c multi 1.20 1.20
293 A47 $2 multi 3.00 3.00
a. Block or strip of 4, #290-293 4.50 4.50

Commonwealth Day.

World Communications Year — A48

10c, Mail delivery. 75c, Teletype, phone. $2, Dish antenna, satellite, TV.

1983, July 15 Litho. *Perf. 13½*

294 A48 10c multi .25 .25
295 A48 75c multi 1.15 1.15
296 A48 $2 multi 2.75 2.75
Nos. 294-296 (3) 4.15 4.15

Opening of Hassanal Bolkiah National Stadium — A49

1983, Sept. 23 Litho. *Perf. 12*

297 A49 10c Soccer, vert. .40 .40
298 A49 75c Runners, vert. 2.00 2.00
299 A49 $1 shown 4.00 4.00
Nos. 297-299 (3) 6.40 6.40

Size, Nos. 297-298: 26x33mm.

Fishing Industry — A50

1983, Sept. 23 Litho. *Perf. 13½*

300 A50 10c Shrimp, lobster .50 .50
301 A50 50c Pacific jacks 3.00 3.00
302 A50 75c Parrotfish, flatfish 4.75 4.75
303 A50 $1 Tuna 5.75 5.75
Nos. 300-303 (4) 14.00 14.00

State Assembly Building — A51

Map of Southeast Asia, Flag — A52

Sultan Hassanal Bolkiah — A53

20c, State Secretariat building. 35c, New Law Court. 50c, Liquid natural gas well. 75c, Omar Ali Saifuddin Mosque. $1, Sultan's Palace.

1984, Jan. 1 Litho. *Perf. 13*

304 A51 10c shown .25 .25
305 A51 20c multicolored .40 .40
306 A51 35c multicolored .75 .75
307 A51 50c multicolored 1.50 1.50
308 A51 75c multicolored 2.00 2.00
309 A51 $1 multicolored 2.75 2.75
310 A52 $3 shown 7.75 7.75
a. Souvenir sheet of 7, #304-310 16.50 16.50
Nos. 304-310 (7) 15.40 15.40

Souvenir Sheets

311 A53 Sheet of 4, Constitution signing, 1959 3.50 3.50
a.-d. 25c any single .75 .75
312 A53 Sheet of 4, Brunei U.K. Friendship Agreement, 1979 3.50 3.50
a.-d. 25c any single .75 .75

Forestry Resources — A54

10c, Forests, enrichment planting. 50c, Water resources. 75c, Recreation forest. $1, Wildlife.

1984, Apr. 21 Litho. *Perf. 13½*

313 A54 10c multi 1.50 1.50
314 A54 50c multi 3.00 3.00
315 A54 75c multi 4.50 4.50
316 A54 $1 multi 6.00 6.00
Nos. 313-316 (4) 15.00 15.00

Philakorea 1984 — A55

Litho. & Engr.

1984, Oct. 22 *Perf. 13*

317 A55 10c No. 93 .75 .75
a. Souvenir sheet of 1 .90 .90
318 A55 75c No. 27 2.00 2.00
a. Souvenir sheet of 1 2.25 2.25
319 A55 $2 1895 local stamp 4.00 4.00
a. Souvenir sheet of 1 4.50 4.50
Nos. 317-319 (3) 6.75 6.75

Brunei Admission to Intl. Organizations A56

1985, Sept. 23 Litho. *Perf. 13*

320 A56 50c UN 1.00 1.00
321 A56 50c Commonwealth 1.00 1.00
322 A56 50c ASEAN 1.00 1.00
323 A56 50c OIC 1.00 1.00
a. Souv. sheet, #320-323 + label 6.25 6.25
Nos. 320-323 (4) 4.00 4.00

Intl. Youth Year A57

75c, Industry, education. $1, Public Service.

1985, Oct. 17 *Perf. 12*

324 A57 10c shown 1.25 1.25
325 A57 75c multi 5.50 5.50
326 A57 $1 multi 6.75 6.75
Nos. 324-326 (3) 13.50 13.50

Intl. Day of Solidarity with the Palestinian People A58

1985, Nov. 29 *Perf. 12x12½*

327 A58 10c lt blue & multi 1.50 1.50
328 A58 50c pink & multi 4.75 4.75
329 A58 $1 lt green & multi 7.75 7.75
Nos. 327-329 (3) 14.00 14.00

Natl. Scout Jamboree, Dec. 14-20 — A59

1985, Dec. 14 *Perf. 13½*

330 A59 10c Scout handshake .45 .45
331 A59 20c Semaphore .90 .90
332 A59 $2 Jamboree emblem 4.50 4.50
Nos. 330-332 (3) 5.85 5.85

Sultan Hassanal Bolkiah — A60

1985-86 Wmk. 233 *Perf. 13½x14½*

333	A60	10c multi	.25	.25
334	A60	15c multi	.25	.25
		Complete booklet, 4 ea. #333, 334	3.00	
335	A60	20c multi	.25	.25
336	A60	25c multi	.30	.30
337	A60	35c multi ('86)	.40	.40
338	A60	40c multi ('86)	.45	.45
339	A60	50c multi ('86)	.55	.55
340	A60	75c multi ('86)	.75	.75

Size: 35x42mm

Perf. 14

341	A60	$1 multi ('86)	1.25	1.25
342	A60	$2 multi ('86)	2.75	2.75
343	A60	$5 multi ('86)	6.50	6.50
344	A60	$10 multi ('86)	12.00	12.00
		Nos. 333-344 (12)	25.70	25.70

Issued: Nos. 333-336, Dec. 23; Nos. 337-340, Jan. 15; Nos. 341-343, Feb. 23; No. 344, Mar. 29.

Admission to Intl. Organizations A61

Wmk. Cartor (385)

1986, Apr. 30 Litho. *Perf. 13*

345	A61	50c WMO	.75	.75
346	A61	50c ITU	.75	.75
347	A61	50c UPU	.75	.75
348	A61	50c ICAO	.75	.75
a.		Souv. sheet, #345-348 + label	6.00	6.00
		Nos. 345-348 (4)	3.00	3.00

Royal Brunei Armed Forces, 25th Anniv. A62

1986, May 31 Unwmk. *Perf. 13½*

349	Strip of 4	25.00	25.00
a.	A62 10c In combat	4.75	4.75
b.	A62 20c Communications	5.25	5.25
c.	A62 50c Air and sea defense	6.75	6.75
d.	A62 75c On parade, Royal Palace	8.25	8.25

Royal Ensigns — A63

No. 350, Tunggul charok buritan, Pisang-pisang, Alam bernaga, Sandaran. No. 351, Dadap, Tunggul kawan, Ambal, Payong ubor-ubor, Sapu-sapu ayeng and Rawai lidah. No. 352, Ula-ula besar, Payong haram, Sumbu layang. No. 353, Payong ubor-ubor tiga ringkat and Payong tinggi. No. 354, Panji-panji, Chogan istiadat, Chogan ugama. No. 355, Lambang duli yang maha mulia and Mahligai.

1986 Litho. *Perf. 12½*

350	A63	10c multicolored	.35	.35
351	A63	10c multicolored	.35	.35
352	A63	75c multicolored	1.75	1.75
353	A63	75c multicolored	1.75	1.75
354	A63	$2 multicolored	3.00	3.00
355	A63	$2 multicolored	3.00	3.00
		Nos. 350-355 (6)	10.20	10.20

Intl. Peace Year — A64

1986, Oct. 24 Litho. *Perf. 12*

356	A64	50c Peace doves	1.00	1.00
357	A64	75c Hands	1.50	1.50
358	A64	$1 Peace symbols	2.00	2.00
		Nos. 356-358 (3)	4.50	4.50

Natl. Anti-Drug Campaign Posters — A65

1987, Mar. 15 Litho. *Perf. 12*

359	A65	10c Jail	1.35	1.35
360	A65	75c Noose	4.50	4.50
361	A65	$1 Execution	6.50	6.50
		Nos. 359-361 (3)	12.35	12.35

Brass Artifacts — A66

1987, July 15

362	A66	50c Kiri (kettle)	.90	.90
363	A66	50c Langguai (bowl)	.90	.90
364	A66	50c Badil (cannon)	.90	.90
365	A66	50c Pelita (lamp)	.90	.90
		Nos. 362-365 (4)	3.60	3.60

See Nos. 388-391.

Dewan Bahasa Dan Pustaka, 25th Anniv. — A67

1987, Sept. 29 *Perf. 13½x13*

366	A67	Strip of 3	3.75	3.75
a.		10c multicolored	.25	.25
b.		50c multicolored	.75	.75
c.		$2 multicolored	2.75	2.75

Language and Literature Bureau.

ASEAN, 20th Anniv. — A68

1987, Aug. 8 Litho. *Perf. 14x13½*

367	A68	20c Map	.55	.55
368	A68	50c Year dates	.80	.80
369	A68	$1 Flags, emblem	1.90	1.90
		Nos. 367-369 (3)	3.25	3.25

World Food Day A70

Fruit: a, Artocarpus odoratissima. b, Canarium odontophyllum mig. c, Litsea garciae. d, Mangifera foetida lour.

1987, Oct. 31 *Perf. 12½*

370	Strip of 4	4.50	4.50
a.-d.	A70 50c any single	1.10	1.10

See Nos. 374, 405, 423, 457-460.

Intl. Year of Shelter for the Homeless A71

Various houses.

1987, Nov. 28 Litho. *Perf. 13*

371	A71	50c multi	.65	.65
372	A71	75c multi, diff.	.95	.95
373	A71	$1 multi, diff.	1.90	1.90
		Nos. 371-373 (3)	3.50	3.50

Fruit Type of 1987 Without FAO Emblem, Dated 1988

Fruit: a, Durio. b, Durio oxleyanus. c, Durio graveolens (cross section at L). d, Durio graveolens (cross section at R).

1988, Jan. 30 Litho. *Perf. 12*

374	Strip of 4	4.50	4.50
a.-d.	A70 50c, any single	1.10	1.10

Opening of Malay Technology Museum — A72

10c, Wooden lathe. 75c, Water wheel, buffalo. $1, Bird caller in blind.

1988, Feb. 29 *Perf. 12½x12*

375	A72	10c multi	.25	.25
376	A72	75c multi	1.10	1.10
377	A72	$1 multi	2.25	2.25
		Nos. 375-377 (3)	3.60	3.60

Handwoven Cloth — A73

Designs: 10c, Kain Beragi Bunga Sakah-Sakah Dan Bunga Cengkih. 20c, Kain Jong Sarat. 25c, Kain Si Pugut. 40c, Kain Si Pugut Bunga Berlapis. 75c, Kain Si Lobang Bangsi Bunga Belitang Kipas.

1988, Apr. 30 Litho. *Perf. 12*

378	A73	10c multicolored	.25	.25
379	A73	20c org brown & blk	.25	.25
380	A73	25c multicolored	.25	.25
381	A73	40c multicolored	.55	.55
382	A73	75c multicolored	1.40	1.40
a.		Souvenir sheet of 5, #378-382 + label	4.25	4.25
		Nos. 378-382 (5)	2.70	2.70

1988, Sept. 29 Litho. *Perf. 12*

Designs: 10c, Kain Beragi. 20c, Kain Bertabur. 25c, Kain Sukma Indra. 40c, Kain Si Pugut Bunga Bersusup. 75c, Kain Beragi Si Lobang Bangsi Bunga Cendera Kesuma.

383	A73	10c multicolored	.25	.25
384	A73	20c multicolored	.25	.25
385	A73	25c multicolored	.55	.55
386	A73	40c multicolored	.80	.80
387	A73	75c multicolored	1.10	1.10
a.		Souvenir sheet of 5, #383-387	4.25	4.25
		Nos. 383-387 (5)	2.95	2.95

Brass Artifacts Type of 1987

No. 388, Celapa (repousse box). No. 389, Gangsa (footed plate). No. 390, Periok (lidded pot). No. 391, Lampong (candlestick).

1988, June 30 Litho. *Perf. 12*

388	A66	50c multicolored	.80	.80
389	A66	50c multicolored	.80	.80
390	A66	50c multicolored	.80	.80
391	A66	50c multicolored	.80	.80
		Nos. 388-391 (4)	3.20	3.20

Coronation of Sultan Hassanal Bolkiah, 20th Anniv. — A74

75c, Reading from the Koran. $2, In full regalia.

1988, Aug. 1 Litho. *Perf. 14*

392	A74	20c shown	.30	.30
393	A74	75c multicolored	1.10	1.10

Size: 26x62mm

Perf. 12½x13

394	A74	$2 multicolored	2.50	2.50
a.		Souvenir sheet of 3, #392-394	4.50	4.50
		Nos. 392-394 (3)	3.90	3.90

Eradicate Malaria, WHO 40th Anniv. — A75

25c, Mosquito. 35c, Extermination. $2, Microscope, infected blood cells.

1988, Dec. 17 Litho. *Perf. 14x13½*

395	A75	25c multicolroed	1.20	1.20
396	A75	35c multicolored	1.60	1.60
397	A75	$2 multicolored	4.00	4.00
		Nos. 395-397 (3)	6.80	6.80

Natl. Day A76

20c, Sultan Bolkiah, officials. 30c, Honor guard. 60c, Fireworks, palace, vert. $2, Religious ceremony.

1989, Feb. 23 Litho. *Perf. 12*

Size of 60c: 22x54½mm

398	A76	20c multicolored	.25	.25
399	A76	30c multicolored	.50	.50
400	A76	60c multicolored	1.00	1.00
401	A76	$2 multicolored	2.50	2.50
a.		Souvenir sheet of 4, #398-401	6.25	6.25
		Nos. 398-401 (4)	4.25	4.25

Independence from Britain, 5th anniv.

Solidarity with the Palestinians — A77

1989, Apr. 1 Litho. *Perf. 13½*

402	A77	20c shown	.75	.75
403	A77	75c Map, flag	2.25	2.25
404	A77	$1 Dome of the Rock	3.00	3.00
		Nos. 402-404 (3)	6.00	6.00

Fruit Type of 1987 Without FAO Emblem, Dated 1989

Designs: a, Daemonorops fissa. b, Eleiodoxa conferia. c, Salacca zalacca. d, Calamus ornatus.

1989, Oct. 31 Litho. *Perf. 12*
405 Strip of 4 9.75 9.75
a.-d. A70 60c any single 2.25 2.25

Oil and Gas Industry, 60th Anniv. A79

1989, Dec. 28 *Perf. 13½*
406 A79 20c Oil well pump 1.50 1.50
407 A79 60c Tanker 4.00 4.00
408 A79 90c Offshore rig 4.00 4.00
409 A79 $1 Rail transport 7.75 7.75
410 A79 $2 Offshore platform 11.00 11.00
Nos. 406-410 (5) 28.25 28.25

Brunei Museum, 25th Anniv. A80

30c, Exhibits. 60c, Official opening, 1965. $1, Museum exterior.

1990, Jan. 1 Litho. *Perf. 12x12½*
411 A80 30c multicolored 1.75 1.75
412 A80 60c multicolored 3.25 3.25
413 A80 $1 multicolored 4.50 4.50
Nos. 411-413 (3) 9.50 9.50

Intl. Literacy Year A81

1990, July 15 Litho. *Perf. 12x12½*
414 A81 15c multicolored 1.00 1.00
415 A81 90c multicolored 3.00 3.00
416 A81 $1 multicolored 4.00 4.00
Nos. 414-416 (3) 8.00 8.00

Tarsier — A82

1990, Sept. 29 Litho. *Perf. 12*
417 A82 20c shown 1.20 1.20
418 A82 60c Eating leaves 3.50 3.50
419 A82 90c Climbing tree 4.75 4.75
Nos. 417-419 (3) 9.45 9.45

Fight Against AIDS — A83

30c, AIDS transmission. 90c, Tombstone, skulls.

1990, Dec. 1 Litho. *Perf. 13*
420 A83 20c shown 2.50 2.50
421 A83 30c multicolored 6.00 6.00
422 A83 90c multicolored 11.00 11.00
Nos. 420-422 (3) 19.50 19.50

Fruit Type of 1987 Without FAO Emblem, Dated 1990

Fruit: a, Willoughbea (uncut core). b, Willoughbea (core cut in half). c, Willoughbea angustifolia.

1990, Dec. 31 *Perf. 12½*
423 Strip of 3 9.50 9.50
a.-c. A70 60c any single 3.00 3.00

Proboscis Monkey, World Wildlife Fund — A84

1991, Mar. 30 Litho. *Perf. 13½x14*
424 A84 15c shown 1.50 1.50
425 A84 20c Head, facing 1.75 1.75
426 A84 50c Sitting on branch 3.75 3.75
427 A84 60c Adult with young 5.25 5.25
Nos. 424-427 (4) 12.25 12.25

Teacher's Day A85

Design: 90c, Teacher at blackboard.

1991, Sept. 23 Litho. *Perf. 13½x14*
428 A85 60c multicolored 3.25 3.25
429 A85 90c multicolored 3.75 3.75

Brunei Beauty A86

1991, Oct. 1 Litho. *Perf. 13*
430 A86 30c Three immature 1.50 1.50
431 A86 60c Female 3.00 3.00
432 A86 $1 Adult male 4.25 4.25
Nos. 430-432 (3) 8.75 8.75

Happy Family Campaign — A87

20c, Family, graduating son. 60c, Mothers, children. 90c, Adults, children, heart.

1991, Nov. 30 Litho. *Perf. 13*
433 A87 20c multicolored .90 .90
434 A87 60c multicolored 2.25 2.25
435 A87 90c multicolored 3.50 3.50
Nos. 433-435 (3) 6.65 6.65

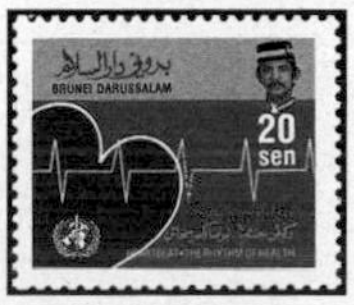

World Health Day — A88

1992, Apr. 7 Litho. *Perf. 13*
436 A88 20c multicolored 1.25 1.25
437 A88 50c multi, diff. 3.50 3.50

Size: 48x28mm

438 A88 75c multi, diff. 5.25 5.25
Nos. 436-438 (3) 10.00 10.00

Brunei-Singapore and Brunei-Malaysia-Philippines Fiber Optic Submarine Cables — A89

1992, Apr. 28 Litho. *Perf. 12*
439 A89 20c Map 1.75 1.75
440 A89 30c Diagram 2.25 2.25
441 A89 90c Submarine cable 7.00 7.00
Nos. 439-441 (3) 11.00 11.00

Visit ASEAN Year — A90

Designs: a, 20c, Sculptures. b, 60c, Judo exhibition. c, $1, Sculptures, diff.

1992, June 30 Litho. *Perf. 13½x14*
442 A90 Strip of 3, #a.-c. 8.25 8.25

ASEAN, 25th Anniv. — A91

60c, Building. 90c, Views of member states.

1992, Aug. 8 Litho. *Perf. 14*
443 A91 20c shown 1.25 1.25
444 A91 60c multicolored 3.50 3.50
445 A91 90c multicolored 3.50 3.50
Nos. 443-445 (3) 8.25 8.25

A92

Sultan in various forms of dress and: No. 446a, Coronation procession. b, Airport. c, New Law Court, Sultan's Palace. d, Ship and Brunei University. e, Mosque, buildings.

1992, Oct. 5 *Perf. 14x13½*
446 A92 25c Strip of 5, #a.-e. 8.50 8.50

Sultan Hassanal Bolkiah's Accession to the Throne, 25th Anniv.

Birds A93

Designs: No. 447, Crested wood partridge, vert. No. 448, Long tailed parakeet, vert. No. 449, Chestnut-breasted malkoha. No. 450, Asian paradise flycatcher, vert. No. 451, Magpie robin, vert. No. 452, White-rumped shama. No. 453, Great argus pheasant, vert. No. 454, Malay lorikeet, vert. No. 455, Black and red broadbill, vert.

Perf. 14x13½, 13½x14

1992-93 Litho.
447 A93 30c multicolored 1.20 1.20
448 A93 30c multicolored 1.20 1.20
449 A93 30c multicolored 1.20 1.20
450 A93 60c multicolored 2.40 2.40
451 A93 60c multicolored 2.40 2.40
452 A93 60c multicolored 2.40 2.40
453 A93 $1 multicolored 2.75 2.75
454 A93 $1 multicolored 2.75 2.75
455 A93 $1 multicolored 2.75 2.75
Nos. 447-455 (9) 19.05 19.05

Issued: Nos. 447, 450, 453, 12/30/92; Nos. 448, 451, 454, 1/27/93; others, 5/3/93.

Natl. Day, 10th Anniv. — A94

10th anniv. emblem and: a, 10c, Natl. flag. b, 20c, Hands supporting inscription. c, 30c, Natl. day emblems, 1985-93. d, 60c, Emblem with star, crossed swords.

1994, June 16 Litho. *Perf. 13*
456 A94 Strip of 4, #a.-d. 5.50 5.50

Fruit Type of 1987 Without FAO Emblem, Dated 1994

No. 457, Nephelium mutabile. No. 458, Nephelium xerospermoides. No. 459, Nephelium spp. No. 460, Nephelium macrophyllum.

1994, Aug. 8 Litho. *Perf. 13½x13*
457 A70 60c multicolored 1.40 1.40
458 A70 60c multicolored 1.40 1.40
459 A70 60c multicolored 1.40 1.40
460 A70 60c multicolored 1.40 1.40
Nos. 457-460 (4) 5.60 5.60

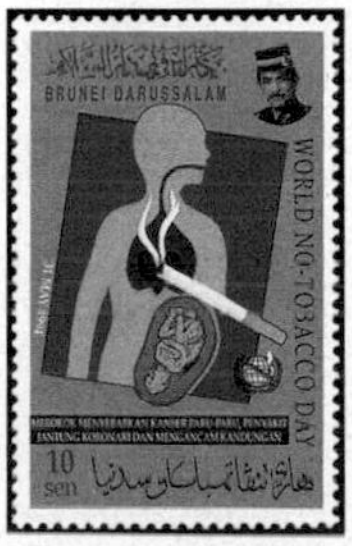

A95

World Stop Smoking Day: 10c, Cigarette, lung, fetus over human figure. 15c, People throwing away tobacco, cigarettes, pipe. $2, Arms around world crushing out cigarettes.

1994, Sept. 1 Litho. *Perf. 13½x13*
461 A95 10c multicolored .50 .50
462 A95 15c multicolored 1.00 1.00
463 A95 $2 multicolored 4.75 4.75
Nos. 461-463 (3) 6.25 6.25

A96

Girl Guides in Brunei, 40th anniv.: a, Leader. b, Girl receiving award. c, Girl reading. d, Girls in various costumes. e, Girls camping out.

1994, Oct. 7 *Perf. 13½*
464 A96 40c Strip of 5, #a.-e. 10.00 10.00

Royal Brunei Airlines, 20th Anniv. A97

Airplanes: 10c, Twin-engine propeller. 20c, Passenger jet attached to tow bar. $1, Passenger jet in air.

1994, Nov. 18 Litho. *Perf. 13½*

465	A97	10c multicolored	.85	.85
466	A97	20c multicolored	1.40	1.40
467	A97	$1 multicolored	3.50	3.50
		Nos. 465-467 (3)	5.75	5.75

Intl. Day Against Drug Abuse — A98

Healthy people wearing traditional costumes: 20c, 60c, $1.

1994, Dec. 30 Litho. *Perf. 13½*

468	A98	Strip of 3, #a.-c.	6.25	6.25

No. 468 is a continuous design.

City of Bandar Seri Begawan, 25th Anniv. A100

Aerial view of city: 30c, In 1970. 50c, In 1980, with details of significant buildings. $1, In 1990.

1995, Oct. 4 Litho. *Perf. 13½*

481	A100	30c multicolored	1.00	1.00
482	A100	50c multicolored	2.00	2.00
483	A100	$1 multicolored	2.75	2.75
		Nos. 481-483 (3)	5.75	5.75

A101

UN headquarters: 20c, Delegates in General Assembly. 60c, Security Council. 90c, Exterior.

1995, Oct. 24 *Perf. 14½x14*

484	A101	20c multicolored	.35	.35
485	A101	60c multicolored	1.40	1.40

Size: 27x44mm

486	A101	90c multicolored	2.00	2.00
		Nos. 484-486 (3)	3.75	3.75

UN, 50th anniv.

A102

University of Brunei, 10th Anniv.: 30c, Students in classroom. 50c, Campus buildings. 90c, Sultan in procession.

1995, Oct. 28 *Perf. 13x13½*

487	A102	30c multicolored	1.00	1.00
488	A102	50c multicolored	1.00	1.00
489	A102	90c multicolored	1.60	1.60
		Nos. 487-489 (3)	3.60	3.60

A103

Royal Brunei Police, 75th Anniv.: 25c, Policemen in various uniforms. 50c, Various tasks performed by police. 75c, Sultan reviewing police.

1996, Feb. 10 Litho. *Perf. 13½x13*

490	A103	25c multicolored	1.00	1.00
491	A103	50c multicolored	2.00	2.00
492	A103	75c multicolored	3.00	3.00
		Nos. 490-492 (3)	6.00	6.00

A104

World Telecommunications Day: 20c, Cartoon telephone, cordless telephone. 35c, Globe, telephone dial surrounded by communication devices. $1, Signals transmitting from earth, people communicating.

1996, May 17 Litho. *Perf. 13½*

493	A104	20c multicolored	1.00	1.00
494	A104	35c multicolored	1.50	1.50
495	A104	$1 multicolored	2.50	2.50
		Nos. 493-495 (3)	5.00	5.00

A105

Sultan: No. 496, Among people, in black attire. No. 497, Waving, in yellow attire. No. 498, In blue shirt. No. 499, Among people, wearing cream-colored robe.

$1, Hand raised in yellow attire.

1996, July 15 Litho. *Perf. 13*

496	A105	50c multicolored	1.50	1.50
497	A105	50c multicolored	1.50	1.50
498	A105	50c multicolored	1.50	1.50
499	A105	50c multicolored	1.50	1.50
		Nos. 496-499 (4)	6.00	6.00

Souvenir Sheet

500	A105	$1 multicolored	3.75	3.75

Sultan Paduka Seri Baginda, 50th birthday.

A souvenir sheet of five $50 stamps exists. Value $650.

Terns — A106

20c, Black-naped tern. 30c, Roseate tern. $1, Bridle tern.

1996, Nov. 11 Litho. *Perf. 13½*

501	A106	20c multi	1.10	1.10
502	A106	30c multi	1.10	1.10
503	A106	$1 multi	2.75	2.75
		Nos. 501-503 (3)	4.95	4.95

No. 502 is spelled "Roslate" on stamp.

Sultan Hassanal Bolkiah
A107 A108

Perf. 14x13½

1996, Oct. 9 Litho. Wmk. 387

Background Color

504	A107	10c yellow green	.25	.25
505	A107	15c pale pink	.25	.25
506	A107	20c lilac pink	.30	.25
507	A107	30c salmon	.35	.25
508	A107	50c yellow	.60	.25
509	A107	60c pale green	.65	.25
510	A107	75c blue	.90	.30
511	A107	90c lilac	1.00	.65
512	A108	$1 pink	1.25	.65
513	A108	$2 orange yellow	3.00	.65
514	A108	$5 light blue	7.50	2.25
515	A108	$10 bright yellow	13.50	9.75
		Nos. 504-515 (12)	29.55	15.75

Flowers A109

20c, Acanthus ebracteatus. 30c, Lumnitzera littorea. $1, Nypa fruticans.

1997, May 29 Litho. *Perf. 12*

516	A109	20c multicolored	.45	.45
517	A109	30c multicolored	.70	.70
518	A109	$1 multicolored	1.90	1.90
		Nos. 516-518 (3)	3.05	3.05

Marine Life A110

Designs: No. 519, Bohadschia argus. No. 520, Oxycomanthus bennetti. No. 521, Heterocentrotus mammillatus. No. 522, Linckia laevigata.

1997, Dec. 15 Litho. *Perf. 12*

519	A110	60c multicolored	.95	.95
520	A110	60c multicolored	.95	.95
521	A110	60c multicolored	.95	.95
522	A110	60c multicolored	.95	.95
		Nos. 519-522 (4)	3.80	3.80

Asian and Pacific Decade of Disabled Persons (1993-2002) — A111

Designs: 20c, Silhouettes of people, hands finger spelling "Brunei," children. 50c, Fireworks over city, blind people participating in arts, crafts, music. $1, Handicapped people playing sports.

1998, Mar. 31 Litho. *Perf. 13x13½*

523	A111	20c multicolored	.45	.45
524	A111	50c multicolored	1.10	1.10
525	A111	$1 multicolored	2.00	2.00
		Nos. 523-525 (3)	3.55	3.55

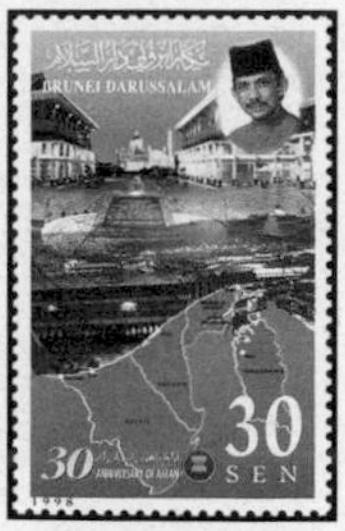

ASEAN, 30th Anniv. — A112

Designs: No. 526, Night scene of Sultan's Palace, buildings, map of Brunei. No. 527, Flags of ASEAN nations. No. 528, Daytime scenes of Sultan's Palace, transportation methods, buildings in Brunei.

1998, Aug. 8 Litho. *Perf. 13½*

526	A112	30c multicolored	1.25	1.25
527	A112	30c multicolored	1.25	1.25
528	A112	30c multicolored	1.25	1.25
		Nos. 526-528 (3)	3.75	3.75

Sultan Hassanal Bolkiah, 30th Anniv. of Coronation — A113

Designs: 60c, In procession, saluting, on throne. 90c, Sultan Omar Ali Saifuddin standing, Sultan Hassanal Bolkiah on throne. $1, Procession.

1998, Aug. 1 Litho. *Perf. 12*

529	A113	60c multicolored	1.00	1.00
530	A113	90c multicolored	1.50	1.50
531	A113	$1 multicolored	1.50	1.50
a.		Souvenir sheet, #529-531	5.00	5.00
		Nos. 529-531 (3)	4.00	4.00

A114

Investiture of Crown Prince Al-Muhtadee Billah: $1, Signing document. $2, Formal portrait. $3, Arms of the Crown Prince.

1998, Aug. 10

532	A114	$1 multicolored	1.25	1.25
533	A114	$2 multicolored	2.50	2.50
534	A114	$3 multicolored	3.75	3.75
a.		Souvenir sheet, #532-534	8.00	8.00
		Nos. 532-534 (3)	7.50	7.50

A115

30c, Hands clasped, woman, man. 60c, Dollar sign over book, arrows, "7.45AM." 90c, Silhouettes of people seated at table, standing, scales.

1998, Sept. 29 *Perf. 13x13½*

535	A115	30c multicolored	.70	.70
536	A115	60c multicolored	1.05	1.05
537	A115	90c multicolored	1.75	1.75
		Nos. 535-537 (3)	3.50	3.50

Civil Sevice Day, 5th anniv.

Kingfishers A116

20c, Blue-eared. 30c, Common. 60c, White-collared. $1, Stork-billed.

1998, Nov. 11 Litho. *Perf. 13½x13*

538	A116 20c multi	.75	.75
539	A116 30c multi	1.10	1.10
540	A116 60c multi	1.75	1.75
541	A116 $1 multi	3.00	3.00
	Nos. 538-541 (4)	6.60	6.60

A117

National Day, 15th Anniv.: 20c, Boat docks, residential area. 60c, Methods of communications. 90c, Buildings, roadways, tower, oil rig.

1999, Feb. 23 Litho. *Perf. 13*

542	A117 20c multicolored	.35	.35
543	A117 60c multicolored	1.25	1.25
544	A117 90c multicolored	2.00	2.00
a.	Souvenir sheet, #542-544	4.25	4.25
	Nos. 542-544 (3)	3.60	3.60

20th Sea Games, 1999 — A119

No. 549, 20c: a, Field hockey, cycling. b, Basketball, soccer. c, Tennis, track and field. d, Billiards. e, Bowling.

No. 550, 20c: a, Shooting. b, Golf, squash. c, Boxing. d, Kick fighting, badminton, ping pong. e, Swimming, rowing.

$1, Shooting, tennis, running, soccer, cycling, basketball.

1999, Aug. 7 Litho. *Perf. 14¼*

Strips of 5, #a.-e.

549-550	A119 Set of 2	6.00	6.00

Souvenir Sheet

551	A119 $1 multicolored	3.50	3.50

No. 551 contains one 35x35mm stamp.

UPU, 125th Anniv. — A120

20c, Handshake, globe, letters. 30c, Emblems of UPU, Brunei Post. 75c, Postal workers & services.

1999, Oct. 9 Litho. *Perf. 14*

552	A120 20c multicolored	.35	.35
553	A120 30c multicolored	.70	.70
554	A120 75c multicolored	1.75	1.75
	Nos. 552-554 (3)	2.80	2.80

Millennium — A121

No. 555: a, Building with clock, children at computer. b, Building with red roof, man and woman at computer. c, Building with gray roof, mosque. d, Map of park. e, Airplane and ships. f, Satellite dishes.

Perf. 13¾x13½ Syncopated Type A

2000, Feb. 1 Litho.

555	A121 20c Strip of 6, #a-f	3.75	3.75
g.	Souvenir sheet, #555	4.25	4.25

Flowers A122

Designs: 30c, Rafflesia pricei. 50c, Rhizanthes lowi. 60c, Nepenthes rafflesiana.

2000, Oct. 2 Litho. *Perf. 14¼x14*

556-558	A122 Set of 3	3.50	3.50

Asia-Pacific Economic Cooperation A123

Designs: 20c, Satellite dish, people at computers. 30c, Food processing enterprises. 60c, Eco-tourism (flower and bridge).

2000, Nov. 15 *Perf. 13½x13*

559	A123 20c multi	.50	.50
a.	Booklet pane of 1	.50	
560	A123 30c multi	1.00	1.00
a.	Booklet pane of 1	1.00	
561	A123 60c multi	1.50	1.50
a.	Booklet pane of 1	1.50	
	Booklet, #559a-561a	3.00	
b.	Souvenir sheet, #559-561	3.50	3.50

The 20th Century — A124

No. 562 — Scenes from: a, 1901-20. b, 1921-40. c, 1941-60. d, 1961-80. e, 1981-99.

Perf. 13¾x13½ Syncopated Type A

2000, Feb. 23 Litho.

562	Strip of 5	5.00	5.00
a.-e.	A124 30c Any single	.90	.90

Turtles A125

No. 563: a, Green turtle. b, Hawksbill turtle. c, Olive Ridley turtle.

2000, Nov. 16 *Perf. 13¼x13*

563	Strip of 3	4.00	4.00
a.-c.	A125 30c Any single	.75	.75

Sultans — A126

No. 564: a, Hashim Jalilul Alam. b, Muhammad Jamalul Alam II. c, Ahmed Tajudin. d, Haji Omar Ali Saifuddin. e, Haji Hassanal Bolkiah.

2000, July 15 Litho. *Perf. 13¾*

564	Horiz. strip of 5	8.00	8.00
a.-e.	A126 60c Any single	1.40	1.40
f.	Souvenir sheet, #564, perf. 14¼x14	7.50	7.50
g.	Booklet pane of 1, #564a	2.75	
h.	Booklet pane of 1, #564b	2.75	
i.	Booklet pane of 1, #564c	2.75	
j.	Booklet pane of 1, #564d	2.75	
k.	Booklet pane of 1, #564e	2.75	
	Booklet, #564g-564k	24.00	

Visit Brunei Year — A127

Designs: 20c, People in boat. 30c, Houses on pilings. 60c, Shown.

2001, Mar. 14 *Perf. 14¼x13¾*

565-567	A127 Set of 3	4.25	4.25

Sultan Hassanal Bolkiah, 55th Birthday — A128

No. 568: a, Navy blue uniform. b, Light blue uniform. c, Robes. d, Camouflage uniform. e, White uniform.

No. 569, Casual shirt.

Perf. 12¼

2001, July 15 Litho. Unwmk.

568	Horiz. strip of 5	4.00	4.00
a.-e.	A128 55c Any single	.75	.75

Souvenir Sheet

Perf. 12

569	A128 55c multi	4.00	4.00

No. 569 contains one 40x70mm stamp.

International Youth Camp 2001 — A129

No. 570: a, Scout, administering first aid. b, Girls, tents. c, Scouts and leader.

2001, Aug. 5 Wmk. 388 *Perf. 12¼*

570	Horiz. strip of 3	2.75	2.75
a.-c.	A129 30c Any single	.75	.75
d.	Souvenir sheet, #570	4.25	4.25

First Intl. Islamic Expo A130

No. 571: a, Jewelry, cane. b, Mosque exterior. c, Computer, satellite dishes. d, Mosque interior.

2001, Aug. 18 Wmk. 388 *Perf. 12*

571	Horiz. strip of 4	2.40	2.40
a.-d.	A130 20c Any single	.60	.60

Visit Brunei Year A131

No. 572: a, Bridge. b, Waterfall. c, Aerial view of city. d, Dock.

Perf. 13¼x13½

2001, Sept. 1 Unwmk.

572	Horiz. strip of 4	3.00	3.00
a.-d.	A131 20c Any single	.80	.80

Year of Dialogue Among Civilizations A132

No. 573: a, Emblem. b, Two abstract heads. c, Cubist-style head, native. d, Multicolored leaves.

2001, Oct. 9 Unwmk. *Perf. 12*

573	Horiz. strip of 4	3.50	3.50
a.-d.	A132 30c Any single	.80	.80

Worldwide Fund for Nature (WWF) — A133

No. 574 — Bulwer's pheasant: a, Male and female. b, Male. c, Female and chicks. d, Female.

2001, Nov. 1 Wmk. 388 *Perf. 12*

574	Horiz. strip of 4	3.50	3.50
a.-d.	A133 30c Any single	.80	.70

Jabatan Telekom Brunei, 50th Anniv. — A134

No. 575: a, People, old telecommunications equipment. b, Anniversary emblem. c, Women, computer, new services.

2002 Litho. *Perf. 12¼*

575	A134 50c Horiz. strip of 3, #a-c	3.00	3.00
a.-c.	50c Any single	.90	.90

Survey Department, 50th Anniv. — A135

No. 576: a, "50." b, Headquarters. c, Surveyor.

2002, July **Litho.** ***Perf. 12¼***
576 Horiz. strip of 3 3.00 3.00
a.-c. A135 50c Any single .90 .90

Yayasan Sultan Haji Hassanal Bolkiah, 10th Anniv. — A136

No. 577: a, Stilt house community. b, Mosque. c, School and children. d, Buildings.

2002, Oct. 5 ***Perf. 12¾x12½***
577 Horiz. strip of 4 2.00 2.00
a.-d. A136 10c Any single .45 .45

Anti-Corruption Bureau, 20th Anniv. — A137

No. 578: a, Anti-Corruption Bureau buildings. b, City skyline. c, Posters.

2002, Nov. 19 **Litho.** ***Perf. 13***
578 Horiz. strip of 3 2.25 2.25
a.-c. A137 20c Any single .65 .65

Medicinal Plants — A138

No. 579: a, Melastoma malabathricum. b, Etlingera solaris. c, Dillenia suffruticosa. d, Costus speciosus.

2003 ***Perf. 12¾x12½***
579 Horiz. strip of 4 3.25 3.25
a.-d. A138 20c Any single .75 .75

ASEAN - Japan Exchange Year — A139

No. 580: a, Drums. b, Tops. c, Kites.

2003, Dec. 13 **Litho.** ***Perf. 13***
580 Horiz. strip of 3 2.00 2.00
a.-c. A139 20c Any single .45 .45

National Day, 20th Anniv. — A140

No. 581: a, Sultan Hassanal Bolkiah at UN. b, Military officer. c, Man reading from scroll. d, Emblem.

2004, Feb. 23 ***Perf. 12¼***
581 Horiz. strip of 4 2.25 2.25
a.-d. A140 20c Any single .65 .65
e. Souvenir sheet, #581 3.00 3.00

Brunei National Philatelic Society — A141

No. 582: a, Magnifying glass, #A1. b, Magnifying glass, tongs, perforation gauge, stamps. c, Brunei stamps and cancels

2004, Mar. 27 ***Perf. 12¾x12½***
582 Horiz. strip of 3 2.00 2.00
a.-c. A141 25c Any single .45 .45

Wedding of Crown Prince Haji al-Muhtadee Billah and Sarah Salleh — A142

No. 583: a, Dark shadows on background below and to right of Sultan Bolkiah's picture and between picture frames. b, Dark shadows on background below "Darussalam" and to left of Crown Prince's picture frame.

2004, Sept. 9 **Litho.** ***Perf. 12***
583 A142 99c Horiz. pair, #a-b, + central label 3.00 3.00

Sultan Hassanal Bolkiah, 60th Birthday — A143

No. 584 — Photographs of Sultan at various activities with panel color of: a, Red violet. b, Rose (women at LL). c, Orange. d, Red (men at LL). e, Green. f, Prussian blue.
$60, Sultan at activities.

2006, July 15 **Litho.** ***Perf. 12½***
584 Horiz. strip of 6 5.25 5.25
a.-f. A143 60c Any single .85 .85
g. Souvenir sheet, #584 5.25 5.25

Souvenir Sheet

Perf. 13¾x13½

585 A143 $60 black 150.00 150.00

No. 585 contains one 100x91mm stamp.

A144

Brunei Postal Service, Cent. — A145

No. 586: a, General Post Office, Bandar Seri Begawan. b, Kuala Belait Post Office. c, Tutong Post Office. d, Bangar Post Office, Temburong.
No. 587 — Children's drawings: a, Airplane, mailbox, letters, packages, globe. b, Postal worker, Postal Service, emblem, post office scenes. c, Cycle of mail delivery. d, Postal worker, letters, buildings, mailbox. e, Globe, letter with wings, children. f, Globe, flags, airplane.

2006, Oct. 11 **Litho.** ***Perf. 13¾x13¼***
586 Horiz. strip of 4 5.75 5.75
a.-d. A144 100c Any single 1.40 1.40
e. Souvenir sheet, #586a-586d 6.00 6.00
587 A145 100c Sheet of 6, #a-f 9.50 9.50

Marine Life — A146

Designs: No. 588, 60c, Orange-striped triggerfish. No. 589, 60c, Leaf scorpionfish.
No. 590: a, Chambered nautilus. b, Spotted boxfish.

Perf. 13½x12x13½x13½

2007, Feb. 6
588-589 A146 Set of 2 2.50 2.50

Souvenir Sheet

Perf. 13½x13¼

590 A146 $1 Sheet of 2, #a-b 3.25 3.25

Dated 2006. See Malaysia Nos. 1139-1141.

Sultan Hassanal Bolkiah
A147 A148

2007, Feb. 23 ***Perf. 13¼***

Background Color

591 A147 10c light blue .25 .25
592 A147 15c bright green .25 .25
593 A147 20c lilac .25 .25
594 A147 30c blue .35 .25
595 A147 50c orange .60 .30
596 A147 60c red .70 .55
597 A147 75c green 1.00 .75
598 A147 90c brt yel grn 1.40 .90

Perf. 13¼x13¾

599 A148 $1 blue 1.75 .55
600 A148 $2 purple 3.50 1.90
601 A148 $5 green 6.75 6.25
602 A148 $10 yellow 17.00 12.00
Nos. 591-602 (12) 33.80 24.20

Bubungan Dua Belas (House of 12 Roofs), Bukit Subok, Cent. — A149

Designs: 30c, House from foot of hill. 60c, Aerial view of house. $1, Early black-and-white picture of house.

2007, July 23 **Litho.** ***Perf. 13½x13¼***
603-605 A149 Set of 3 3.25 3.25
605a Souvenir sheet of 3, #603-605 3.50 3.50

Bubungan Dua Belas was the residence of the British High Commissioner.

Public Works Department, Cent. — A150

No. 606: a, Modern building. b, Riverfront building. c, Centenary emblem.

2007, Aug. 30 ***Perf. 13¼***
606 A150 75c Horiz. strip of 3, #a-c 3.50 3.50

Miniature Sheet

Association of South East Asian Nations (ASEAN), 40th Anniv. — A151

No. 607: a, Secretariat Building, Bandar Seri Begawan, Brunei. b, Yangon Post Office, Myanmar. c, National Museum of Cambodia. d, Malacañang Palace, Philippines. e, Fatahillah Museum, Jakarta, Indonesia. f, National Museum of Singapore. g, Typical house, Laos. h, Vimanmek Mansion, Bangkok, Thailand. i, Malayan Railway Headquarters Building, Kuala Lumpur, Malaysia. j, Presidential Palace, Hanoi, Viet Nam.

2007, Nov. 21
607 A151 20c Sheet of 10, #a-j *3.25 3.25*

See Burma No. 370, Cambodia No. 2339, Indonesia Nos. 2120-2121, Laos Nos. 1717-1718, Malaysia No. 1170, Philippines Nos. 3103-3105, Singapore No. 1265, Thailand No. 2315, and Viet Nam Nos. 3302-3311.

Movement of Capital From Kampong Air to Bandar Seri Begawan, Cent. — A152

Designs: 20c, Istana Majlis. 30c, Istana Kota. 60c, Bandar Brunei. 100c, Bandar Seri Begawan.

2008, Apr. 24 Litho. *Perf. 13¼*
608-611 A152 Set of 4 3.25 3.25

Coronation of Sultan Hassanal Bolkiah, 40th Anniv. — A153

No. 612 — Coronation ceremony: a, Sultan with hand raised. b, Parade. c, Crowning of Sultan. d, Sultan wearing crown.
$40, Parade, diff.

2008, Aug. 1 *Perf. 12¾x12½*
612 Horiz. strip of 4 2.40 2.40
a.-d. A153 40c Any single .60 .60

Souvenir Sheet

Perf. 12

613 A153 $40 multi 55.00 55.00

No. 613 contains one 45x70mm stamp.

Omar Ali Saifuddien Mosque, 50th Anniv. — A154

No. 614: a, Opening ceremony (green panels). b, Sultan Hassanal Bolkiah (blue panels). c, Worshipers (orange panels). d, Aerial view of mosque (red violet panels).
$50, Mosque, diff.

2008, Sept. 26 *Perf. 14½x14*
614 Horiz. strip of 4 2.75 2.75
a.-d. A154 50c Any single .65 .65
e. Souvenir sheet of 4, #614a-614d 2.75 2.75

Souvenir Sheet

Litho. With Foil Application

Perf. 13¾x13½

615 A154 $50 multi 60.00 60.00

No. 615 contains one 44x72mm stamp.

Health Services, Cent. — A155

Designs: No. 616, 10c, Pediatric examination. No. 617, 10c, Magnetic resonance imaging machine, operating room. $1, First government hospital in Brunei town.

2008, Oct. 9 Litho. *Perf. 13¼*
616-618 A155 Set of 3 1.75 1.75

25th National Day — A156

Nos. 619 and 620: a, Buildings, blue sky. b, Buildings, green sky. c, Buildings, military parade, red sky. d, Buildings, buff sky. e, Oil facilities, blue violet sky. f, People with flags, red violet sky. g, Buildings, airplane, satellite dish, brown orange sky. h, Emblem.
$25, Sultans Hassanal Bolkiah and Omar Ali Saifuddin, horiz.

2009, Feb. 23 *Perf. 13¼*

Stamps With Blue Frames

619 A156 25c Sheet of 8, #a-h 2.60 2.60

Stamps With White Frames

620 A156 25c Sheet of 8, #a-h 2.60 2.60

Souvenir Sheet

621 A156 $25 multi 35.00 35.00

No. 621 contains one 102x72mm stamp.

Orchids — A157

No. 622: a, Dendrobium secundum. b, Bulbophyllum sp. c, Phalaenopsis cornucervi.
No. 623: a, Bulbophyllum beccarii. b, Vanda hastifera. c, Corybas pictus.

Litho. & Embossed

2009, Dec. 9 *Perf. 14*
622 Horiz. strip of 3 1.90 1.90
a. A157 10c multi .25 .25
b. A157 20c multi .30 .30
c. A157 $1 multi 1.40 1.40
623 Horiz. strip of 3 1.90 1.90
a. A157 10c multi .25 .25
b. A157 20c multi .30 .30
c. A157 $1 multi 1.40 1.40

Modern Land Administration, Cent. — A158

No. 624: a, People at Land Administration office. b, Surveyors at construction site. c, Two men, house.

2010, June 23 Litho. *Perf. 13½*
624 Horiz. strip of 3 1.90 1.90
a. A158 10c multi .25 .25
b. A158 20c multi .30 .30
c. A158 $1 multi 1.40 1.40

Liquid Natural Gas, 40th Anniv. of Production (in 2009) — A159

No. 625: a, Tanker in harbor. b, Control rooms. c, Workers and pipelines.

2010, July 7 *Perf. 13½x14*
625 Horiz. strip of 3 1.75 1.75
a.-c. A159 40c Any single .55 .55

Miniature Sheet

Sultan Hassanal Bolkiah, 65th Birthday — A160

No. 626 — Sultan and other people with panel color of: a, Dull violet. b, Golden brown. c, Green. d, Blue green. e, Dark brown. f, Rose.

2011, July 15 *Perf. 14x14¼*
626 A160 65c Sheet of 6, #a-f 6.50 6.50

A $65 souvenir sheet was sold only with special packaging for more than face value.

Dewan Bahasa Dan Pustaka Library, 50th Anniv. A161

2011, Sept. 17 *Perf. 12¾*
627 Horiz. strip of 3 2.75 2.75
a. A161 20c Books .35 .35
b. A161 50c Libraries .80 .80
c. A161 $1 Men 1.60 1.60
d. Souvenir sheet of 3, #627a-627c 2.75 2.75

Farmers and Fishermen Day — A162

No. 628: a, Fishermen at work. b, Farm products.

2011, Nov. 1
628 A162 20c Horiz. pair, #a-b .65 .65

A163

Rice Production A164

No. 629 — Inscription "Towards Self-Sufficiency In Rice Production 20%" and: a, Rice plants, arrow with "20%." b, Sultan Hassanal Bolkiah. c, Sultan in rice field.
No. 630 — Inscription "To Commemorate Large Scale Rice Planting" and: a, Sultan driving motorized farm equipment. b, Rice field. c, Sultan planting rice.

2011, Nov. 1 *Perf. 12¾*
629 Horiz. strip of 3 1.10 1.10
a.-c. A163 20c Any single .35 .35
630 Horiz. strip of 3 1.10 1.10
a.-c. A164 20c Any single .35 .35

Royal Brunei Armed Forces, 50th Anniv. (in 2011) — A165

No. 631 — Sultan Hassanal Bolkiah in various uniforms with frame color of: a, Golden brown. b, Dark gray. c, Red. d, Light gray. e, Blue.
$50, Sultan Hassanal Bolkiah and soldiers.

2012, May 31 *Perf. 13¼*
631 Horiz. strip of 5 4.00 4.00
a.-e. A165 50c Any single .80 .80

Souvenir Sheet

Litho., Margin Litho. With Foil Application

Perf. 14½x14¼

632 A165 $50 multi 80.00 80.00

No. 632 contains one 40x72mm stamp dated "2011."

Currency Interchangeability Agreement Between Brunei and Singapore, 45th Anniv. — A166

Designs: $1, Images from Brunei banknotes issued in1967, 1989, 1996 and 2007. $2, Singapore skyline, and mosque, Brunei.

2012, Nov. 27 Litho. *Perf. 12¾*
633-634 A166 Set of 2 5.00 5.00

See Singapore Nos. 1585-1587.

Butterflies — A167

Designs: 10c, Trogonoptera troides brookiana. 20c, Graphium macareus. $1, Graphium delesserti.
$2, Graphium agamemnon.

2012, Dec. 24 Litho. *Perf. 14*
635-637 A167 Set of 3 2.25 2.25
Complete booklet, #635-637 2.25

Souvenir Sheet

638 A167 $2 multi 3.25 3.25

See Nos. 639-641, 645-648, 651-654.

Butterflies Type of 2012

Designs: 10c, Papilio helenus. 20c, Ideopsis juventa. $1, Charaxes solon echo.
$2, Papilio demoleus.

2013, Feb. 28 Litho. *Perf. 14*
639-641 A167 Set of 3 2.10 2.10

Souvenir Sheet

642 A167 $2 multi 3.25 3.25

ASEAN Summit, Bandar Seri Begawan A168

No. 643 — Summit emblem and: a, Brunei Prime Minister's Office. b, Flags of ASEAN member nations. c, International Convention Center, Bandar Seri Begawan.
$23, Buildings in Bandar Seri Begawan, vert.

2013, Oct. 9 Litho. *Perf. 12¾*

643 Horiz. strip of 3 4.80 4.80
a.-c. A168 $1 Any single 1.60 1.60
Complete booklet, #643 4.80

Souvenir Sheet

Perf. 13¾

644 A168 $23 multi 37.00 37.00

No. 644 contains one 57x78mm stamp.

Butterflies Type of 2012

Designs: 10c, Hypolimnas misippus. 20c, Paduca fasciata. $1, Junonia orithya. $2, Graphium delesserti.

2013, Dec. 12 Litho. *Perf. 14*

645-647 A167 Set of 3 2.10 2.10

Souvenir Sheet

648 A167 $2 multi 3.25 3.25

30th National Day — A169

No. 649: a, Ship, combine, fishermen and crates of fish, finished products (light blue stripes). b, Soldiers, Airline personnel (lilac pink stripes). c, People and mosques (light green stripes). d, Emblem (orange stripes).
$30, Sultan Hassanal Bolkiah and National Day emblems, horiz.

2014, Feb. 23 Litho. *Perf. 12¾*

649 Horiz. strip of 4 4.25 4.25
a.-b. A169 30c Either single .50 .50
c.-d. A169 $1 Either single 1.60 1.60

Litho. & Embossed

Souvenir Sheet

650 A169 $30 multi 47.50 47.50

No. 650 contains one 150x74mm stamp.

Butterflies Type of 2012

Designs: 10c, Chilasa paradoxa telesicles. 20c, Hypolimnas anomala. $1, Parthenos sylvia.
$2, Troides andromacha.

2014, Apr. 20 Litho. *Perf. 14*

651-653 A167 Set of 3 2.10 2.10
Complete booklet, #651-653 2.10

Souvenir Sheet

654 A167 $2 multi 3.25 3.25

Formal Education in Brunei, Cent. A170

No. 655: a, Students of 2014. b, Schools. c, Students and teacher in black-and-white photograph. d, Centenary emblem.

2014, Oct. 9 Litho. *Perf. 13¼*

655 Horiz. strip of 4 3.75 3.75
a. A170 10c multi .25 .25
b. A170 20c multi .30 .30
c.-d. A170 $1 Either single 1.60 1.60
e. Souvenir sheet of 4, #655a-655d 3.75 3.75

Flags and Emblem of Association of Southeast Asian Nations A171

2015, Aug. 8 Litho. *Perf. 13*

656 A171 60c multi .85 .85
Complete booklet, #656 .85

See Burma Nos. 417-418, Cambodia No. 2428, Indonesia No. 2428, Laos No. , Malaysia No. 1562, Philippines No. 3619, Singapore No. 1742, Thailand No. 2875, Viet Nam No. 3529.

United Nations, 70th Anniv. A172

No. 657: a, 70th anniv. emblem. b, United Nations emblem. c, United Nations Headquarters.

2015, Oct. 24 Litho. *Perf. 13¼*

657 Horiz. strip of 3 3.00 3.00
a.-c. A172 70c Any single 1.00 1.00
d. Souvenir sheet of 3, #657a-657c 3.00 3.00

Royal Brunei Navy, 50th Anniv. — A173

No. 658: a, Ceremony, docked ship and sailors, Sultan Hassanal Bolkiah saluting. b, Sailors, flag of Brunei, Sultan Hassanal Bolkiah wearing white uniform. c, Ships at sea, Sultan Hassanal Bolkiah wearing beret.

2015, Oct. 30 Litho. *Perf. 12¾*

658 A173 50c Horiz. strip of 3, #a-c 2.25 2.25

A174

A175

A176

A177

Sultan Hassanal Bolkiah, 70th Birthday A178

2016, July 15 Litho. *Perf. 13¾*

659 Vert. strip of 5 5.50 5.50
a. A174 70c multi 1.10 1.10
b. A175 70c multi 1.10 1.10
c. A176 70c multi 1.10 1.10
d. A177 70c multi 1.10 1.10
e. A178 70c multi 1.10 1.10
f. Souvenir sheet of 5, #659a-659e 5.50 5.50
Complete booklet, #659 5.50

A $70 souvenir sheet depicting Sultan Hassanal Bolkiah was produced in limited quantities.

A179

A180

A181

A182

Reign of Sultan Hassanal Bolkiah, 50th Anniv. A183

2017, Oct. 5 Litho. *Perf. 12¾*

661 Horiz. strip of 5 3.75 3.75
a. A179 50c multi .75 .75
b. A180 50c multi .75 .75
c. A181 50c multi .75 .75
d. A182 50c multi .75 .75
e. A183 50c multi .75 .75
Complete booklet, #661 3.75

Brunei Man and Woman in Traditional Costumes — A184

2019, Aug. 8 Litho. *Perf. 14x14½*

662 A184 20c multi .30 .30

OCCUPATION STAMPS

Issued under Japanese Occupation

Stamps and Types of 1908-37 Hstmpd. in Violet, Red Violet, Blue or Red

Perf. 14, 14x11½ (#N7)

1942-44 Wmk. 4

N1	A1	1c black	11.00	*28.00*
N2	A1	2c green	65.00	*125.00*
N3	A1	2c dull orange	9.50	*10.00*
N4	A1	3c green	37.50	*60.00*
N5	A1	4c orange	6.00	*16.50*
N6	A1	5c brown	8.75	*16.00*
N7	A2	6c slate gray	60.00	*300.00*
N8	A2	6c red	800.00	775.00
N9	A1	8c gray (RV)	1,000.	950.00
N10	A2	8c carmine	12.50	*13.50*
N11	A1	10c violet, *yel*	11.00	*20.00*
N12	A2	12c blue	35.00	20.00
N13	A2	15c ultra	25.00	20.00
N14	A1	25c dk violet	25.00	*55.00*
N15	A1	30c org & red vio	105.00	*200.00*
N16	A1	50c blk, *green*	42.50	*65.00*
N17	A1	$1 red & blk, *bl*	75.00	70.00

Wmk. 3

N18	A1	$5 lake, *green*	1,100.	*3,500.*
N19	A1	$25 black, *red*	1,100.	*3,500.*

Overprints vary in shade. Nos. N3, N7, N10 and N13 without overprint are not believed to have been regularly issued.

No. N1 Surcharged in Red

1944 Wmk. 4 *Perf. 14*

N20 A1 $3 on 1c black *8,750.* 8,750.
a. On No. 43 10,000. —

BULGARIA

ˌbəl-ˈgar-ē-ə

LOCATION — Southeastern Europe bordering on the Black Sea on the east and the Danube River on the north

GOVT. — Republic

AREA — 42,855 sq. mi.

POP. — 8,194,772 (1999 est.)

CAPITAL — Sofia

In 1885 Bulgaria, then a principality under the suzerainty of the Sultan of Turkey, was joined by Eastern Rumelia. Independence from Turkey was obtained in 1908.

100 Centimes = 1 Franc

100 Stotinki = 1 Lev (1881)

Catalogue values for unused stamps in this country are for Never Hinged items, beginning with Scott 293 in the regular postage section, Scott B1 in the semi-postal section, Scott C15 in the airpost section, Scott CB1 in the airpost semi-postal section, Scott E1 in the special delivery section, Scott J47 in the postage due section, Scott O1 in the officials section, and Scott Q1 in the parcel post section.

Watermarks

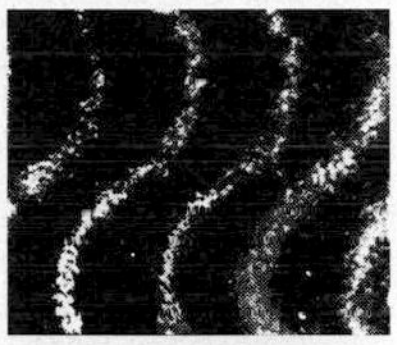

Wmk. 145 — Wavy Lines

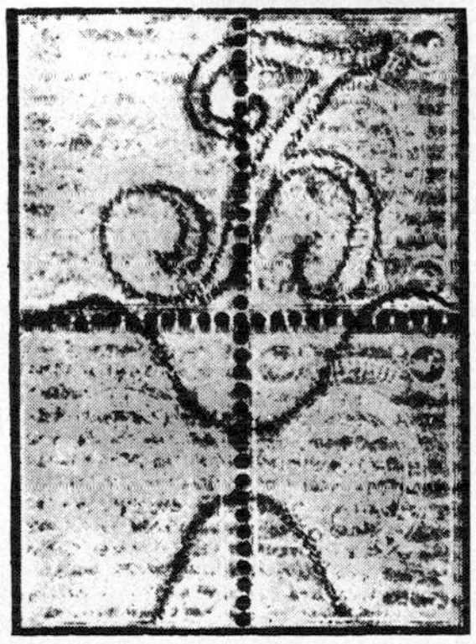

Wmk. 168 — Wavy Lines and EZGV in Cyrillic

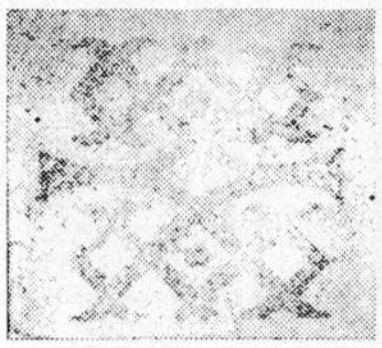

Wmk. 275 — Entwined Curved Lines

Lion of Bulgaria

A1 A2 A3

Perf. 14½x15

1879, May 1 Wmk. 168 Typo.

Laid Paper

1	A1	5c black & orange	150.00	40.00
2	A1	10c black & green	650.00	150.00
3	A1	25c black & violet	400.00	35.00
a.		Imperf.	5,600.	
4	A1	50c black & blue	575.00	120.00
5	A2	1fr black & red	100.00	35.00

1881, Apr. 10

6	A3	3s red & silver	27.50	5.50
7	A3	5s black & orange	27.50	5.50
a.		Background inverted	2,200.	*2,200.*
8	A3	10s black & green	160.00	17.50
9	A3	15s dp car red & green	175.00	17.50
10	A3	25s black & violet	650.00	75.00
11	A3	30s blue & fawn	27.50	14.00

1882, Dec. 4

12	A3	3s orange & yel	1.40	.70
a.		Background inverted	*3,500.*	*2,500.*
13	A3	5s green & pale green	10.50	1.00
a.		5s rose & pale rose (error)	*2,500.*	*2,500.*
14	A3	10s rose & pale rose	14.00	1.00
15	A3	15s red vio & pale lil	14.00	1.00
16	A3	25s blue & pale blue	12.50	1.40
17	A3	30s violet & grn	12.50	1.00
18	A3	50s blue & pink	12.50	1.00
		Nos. 12-18 (7)	77.40	7.10

See Nos. 207-210, 286.

Surcharged in Black, Carmine or Vermilion

A4

A5

1884, May 1 Typo. Surcharge

19	A4	3s on 10s rose (Bk)	210.00	70.00
20	A4	5s on 30s blue & fawn (C)	140.00	90.00
20A	A4	5s on 30s bl & fawn (Bk)	*2,800.*	*2,250.*
21	A5	15s on 25s blue (C)	175.00	100.00

On some values the surcharge may be found inverted or double.

1885, Apr. 5 Litho. Surcharge

21B	A4	3s on 10s rose (Bk)	70.00	70.00
21C	A4	5s on 30s bl & fawn (V)	70.00	70.00
21D	A5	15s on 25s blue (V)	130.00	95.00
22	A5	50s on 1fr blk & red (Bk)	500.00	325.00

Forgeries of Nos. 19-22 are plentiful.

Word below left star in oval has 5 letters

A6

Third letter below left star is "A"

A7

1885, May 25

23	A6	1s gray vio & pale gray	25.00	8.50
24	A7	2s sl grn & pale gray	25.00	5.50

Word below left star has 4 letters

A8

Third letter below left star is "b" with cross-bar in upper half

A9

A10

1886-87

25	A8	1s gray vio & pale gray	1.75	.35
26	A9	2s sl grn & pale gray	1.75	.35
27	A10	1 l black & red ('87)	50.00	6.50
		Nos. 25-27 (3)	53.50	7.20

For surcharge see No. 40.

A11

Perf. 10½, 11, 11½, 13, 13½

1889 Wove Paper Unwmk.

28	A11	1s lilac	1.40	.35
29	A11	2s gray	2.10	1.00
30	A11	3s bister brown	.70	.35
31	A11	5s yellow green	17.50	.30
a.		Vert. pair, imperf. btwn.		
32	A11	10s rose	10.00	.70
33	A11	15s orange	60.00	.70
34	A11	25s blue	10.00	.70
35	A11	30s dk brown	12.00	.70
36	A11	50s green	.70	.35
37	A11	1 l orange red	.70	.70
		Nos. 28-37 (10)	115.10	5.85

The 10s orange is a proof.

Nos. 28-34 exist imperforate. Value, set $350.

See Nos. 39, 41-42. For overprints and surcharges see Nos. 38, 55-56, 77-81, 113.

No. 35 Surcharged in Black

1892, Jan. 26

38	A11	15s on 30s brn	35.00	1.40
a.		Inverted surcharge	*95.00*	*95.00*

1894 *Perf. 10½, 11, 11½*

Pelure Paper

39	A11	10s red	5.25	1.75
a.		Imperf.	*57.50*	

No. 26 Surcharged in Red

Wmk. Wavy Lines (168)

1895, Oct. 25 *Perf. 14½x15*

Laid Paper

40	A9	1s on 2s	1.00	.35
a.		Inverted surcharge	8.00	6.50
b.		Double surcharge	*62.50*	*62.50*
c.		Pair, one without surcharge	*250.00*	*210.00*

The surcharge on No. 24 is a proof. Value, $400.

Wmk. Coat of Arms in the Sheet

1896, Apr. 30 *Perf. 11½, 13*

Wove Paper

41	A11	2 l rose & pale rose	2.75	2.10
42	A11	3 l black & buff	4.25	5.00

Coat of Arms — A14

1896, Feb. 2 *Perf. 13*

43	A14	1s blue green	.35	.25
44	A14	5s dark blue	.35	.25
45	A14	15s purple	.35	.40
46	A14	25s red	5.75	2.00
		Nos. 43-46 (4)	6.80	2.90

Baptism of Prince Boris.

Examples of Nos. 41-46 from sheet edges show no watermark.

Nos. 43, 45-46 were also printed on rough unwatermarked paper.

Cherry Wood Cannon — A15

1901, Apr. 20 Litho. Unwmk.

53	A15	5s carmine	1.00	1.25
54	A15	15s yellow green	1.00	1.25

Insurrection of Independence in April, 1876, 25th anniversary.

Exist imperf. Forgeries exist.

Nos. 30 and 36 Surcharged in Black

1901, Mar. 24 Typo.

55	A11	5s on 3s bister brn	2.00	1.25
a.		Inverted surcharge	45.00	45.00
b.		Pair, one without surcharge	*70.00*	*70.00*
56	A11	10s on 50s green	2.00	1.25
a.		Inverted surcharge	50.00	50.00
b.		Pair, one without surcharge	*72.50*	*72.50*

Tsar Ferdinand — A17

Type I

Type II

ONE LEV:

Type I — The numerals in the upper corners have, at the top, a sloping serif on the left side and a short straight serif on the right.

Type II — The numerals in the upper corners are of ordinary shape without the serif at the right.

1901, Oct. 1-1905 Typo. *Perf. 12½*

57	A17	1s vio & gray blk	.25	.25
58	A17	2s brnz grn & ind	.35	.25
a.		Imperf.		
59	A17	3s orange & ind	.35	.25
60	A17	5s emerald & brn	1.40	.25
61	A17	10s rose & blk	2.00	.25
62	A17	15s claret & gray blk	1.00	.25
63	A17	25s blue & blk	1.00	.25
64	A17	30s bis & gray blk	22.50	.30
65	A17	50s dk blue & brn	1.40	.25
66	A17	1 l red org & brnz grn, type I	3.50	.30
67	A17	1 l brn red & brnz grn, II ('05)	75.00	3.00
68	A17	2 l carmine & blk	7.00	1.00
69	A17	3 l slate & red brn	7.00	5.00
		Nos. 57-69 (13)	122.75	11.60

For surcharges see Nos. 73, 83-85, 87-88.

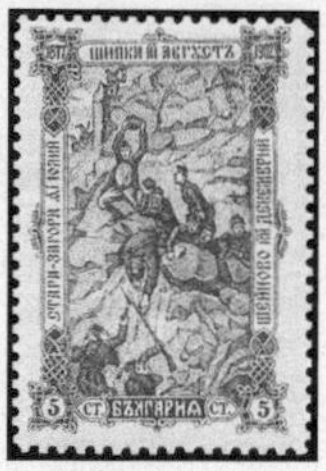
Fighting at Shipka Pass — A18

1902, Aug. 29 Litho. *Perf. 11½*

70	A18	5s lake	2.10	.70
71	A18	10s blue green	2.10	.70
72	A18	15s blue	8.00	3.50
		Nos. 70-72 (3)	12.20	4.90

Battle of Shipka Pass, 1877.
Imperf. copies are proofs.
Excellent forgeries of Nos. 70 to 72 exist.

No. 62 Surcharged in Black

1903, Oct. 1 *Perf. 12½*

73	A17	10s on 15s	3.50	.70
a.		Inverted surcharge	*57.50*	*50.00*
b.		Double surcharge	*57.50*	*50.00*
c.		Pair, one without surcharge	*100.00*	*100.00*
d.		10s on 10s rose & black	*700.00*	*700.00*

Ferdinand in 1887 and 1907 — A19

1907, Aug. 12 Litho. *Perf. 11½*

74	A19	5s deep green	15.00	1.40
75	A19	10s red brown	21.00	1.40
76	A19	25s deep blue	60.00	3.00
		Nos. 74-76 (3)	96.00	5.80

Accession to the throne of Ferdinand I, 20th anniversary.
Nos. 74-76 imperf. are proofs. Nos. 74-76 exist in pairs imperforate between. Values: 5s, $70; 10s, $100; 25s, $140.

Stamps of 1889 Overprinted

1909

77	A11	1s lilac	.65	.60
a.		Inverted overprint	21.00	17.50
b.		Double overprint, one inverted	24.00	24.00
78	A11	5s yellow green	1.60	.60
a.		Inverted overprint	25.00	25.00
b.		Double overprint	25.00	25.00

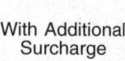

With Additional Surcharge

79	A11	5s on 30s brown (Bk)	2.00	.50
a.		"5" double		
b.		"1990" for "1909"	*700.00*	*550.00*
80	A11	10s on 15s org (Bk)	2.00	.60
a.		Inverted surcharge	17.50	17.50
b.		"1909" omitted	*27.50*	*27.50*
81	A11	10s on 50s dk grn (R)	2.00	.60
a.		"1990" for "1909"	100.00	100.00
b.		Black surcharge	52.50	52.50

Nos. 62 & 64 Surcharged with Value Only

83	A17	5s on 15s (Bl)	1.50	.65
a.		Inverted surcharge	21.00	21.00
84	A17	10s on 15s (Bl)	4.00	.55
a.		Inverted surcharge	21.00	21.00
85	A17	25s on 30s (R)	8.00	1.25
a.		Double surcharge	75.00	75.00
b.		"2" of "25" omitted	87.50	87.50
c.		Blue surcharge	*650.00*	*450.00*

Nos. 59 and 62 Surcharged in Blue

1910, Oct.

87	A17	1s on 3s	3.00	1.25
a.		"1910" omitted	21.00	
88	A17	5s on 15s	3.00	1.00

Tsar Assen's Tower (Crown over lion) A20

Tsar Ferdinand A21

City of Trnovo A22

Tsar Ferdinand A23

Ferdinand A24

Isker River A25

Ferdinand A26

Rila Monastery (Crown at UR) A27

Tsar and Princes — A28

Ferdinand in Robes of Ancient Tsars — A29

Monastery of Holy Trinity — A30

View of Varna — A31

1911, Feb. 14 Engr. *Perf. 12*

89	A20	1s myrtle green	.25	.25
90	A21	2s car & blk	.25	.25
91	A22	3s lake & blk	.35	.25
92	A23	5s green & blk	1.00	.25
93	A24	10s dp red & blk	1.60	.25
94	A25	15s brown bister	4.75	.25
95	A26	25s ultra & blk	.35	.25
96	A27	30s blue & blk	4.75	.25
97	A28	50s ocher & blk	26.00	.25
a.		Center inverted		*4,250.*
98	A29	1 l chocolate	8.00	.25
99	A30	2 l dull pur & blk	2.25	.50
100	A31	3 l blue vio & blk	13.00	4.75
		Nos. 89-100 (12)	62.55	7.75

See Nos. 114-120, 161-162. For overprints and surcharges see Nos. 104-112, 188, B8, Greece N167-N178, N182-N187, Thrace 16-21, Romania 2N1-2N4.

Tsar Ferdinand — A32

1912, Aug. 2 Typo. *Perf. 12½*

101	A32	5s olive green	3.00	1.00
a.		5s pale green	*975.00*	*225.00*
102	A32	10s claret	4.00	1.75
103	A32	25s slate	5.00	3.00
		Nos. 101-103 (3)	12.00	5.75

25th year of reign of Tsar Ferdinand.

Nos. 89-95 Overprinted in Various Colors

1913, Aug. 6 Engr.

104	A20	1s myrtle grn (C)	.35	.25
105	A21	2s car & blk (Bl)	1.25	.25
107	A22	3s lake & blk (Bl Bk)	1.25	.25
108	A23	5s grn & blk (R)	.35	.25
109	A24	10s dp red & blk (Bk)	.35	.25
110	A25	15s brown bis (G)	1.50	1.00
111	A26	25s ultra & blk (R)	4.50	1.75
		Nos. 104-111 (7)	9.55	4.00

Victory over the Turks in Balkan War of 1912-1913.

No. 95 Surcharged in Red

1915, July 6

112	A26	10s on 25s	.75	.25
a.		Pair, one without surcharge	160.00	160.00

No. 28 Surcharged in Green

113	A11	3s on 1s lilac	4.50	3.00

Types of 1911 Re-engraved

1915, Nov. 7 *Perf. 11½, 14*

114	A20	1s dk bl grn	.25	.25
115	A23	5s grn & brn vio	2.75	.25
116	A24	10s red brn & brnsh blk	.25	.25
117	A25	15s olive green	.25	.25
118	A26	25s indigo & blk	.25	.25
119	A27	30s ol grn & red brn	.25	.25
120	A29	1 l dark brown	.35	.25
		Nos. 114-120 (7)	4.35	1.75

Widths: No. 114 is 19½mm; No. 89, 18½mm. No. 118 is 19¼mm; No. 95, 18¼mm. No. 120 is 20mm; No. 98, 19mm. The re-engraved stamps also differ from the 1911 issue in many details of design. Nos. 114-120 exist imperforate. Values, each $11-$22.50.

The 5s exists in two types: I, 20x29.3mm, green and brown violet; II, 19.5x29mm, dark green and brown. There are a number of minor design differences between the two types. The editors would welcome any information that Bulgarian specialists can provide on this and similar varieties on stamps of this period.

The 5s and 10s exist perf. 14x11½.

For Nos. 114-116 and 118 overprinted with Cyrillic characters and "1916-1917," see Romania Nos. 2N1-2N4.

Coat of Arms — A33

Peasant and Bullock — A34

Soldier and Mt. Sonichka — A35

View of Nish — A36

Town and Lake Okhrida — A37

Demir-Kapiya (Iron Gate) — A37a

View of Gevgeli — A38

Perf. 11½, 12½x13, 13x12½

1917-19 Typo.

122	A33	5s green	.40	.25
123	A34	15s slate	.25	.25
124	A35	25s blue	.25	.25
125	A36	30s orange	.25	.25
126	A37	50s violet	.75	.60
126A	A37a	2 l brn org ('19)	.75	.50
127	A38	3 l claret	1.25	1.25
		Nos. 122-127 (7)	3.90	3.35

Liberation of Macedonia. A 1 l dark green was prepared but not issued. Value $1.65.
For surcharges see Nos. B9-B10, B12.

View of Veles — A39

Monastery of St. Clement at Okhrida — A40

1918 *Perf. 13x14*

128	A39	1s gray	.35	.25
129	A40	5s green	.35	.25

Tsar Ferdinand — A41

1918, July 1 *Perf. 12½x13*

130	A41	1s dark green	.70	.25
131	A41	2s dark brown	.70	.25
132	A41	3s indigo	1.40	.35
133	A41	10s brown red	.70	.35
		Nos. 130-133 (4)	3.50	1.20

Ferdinand's accession to the throne, 30th anniv. Nos. 131-133 exist on a thin gray paper.

Plowing with Oxen — A42

1919 *Perf. 13½x13*

134	A42	1s gray	.25	.25

Sobranye Palace — A43

1919 *Perf. 11½x12, 12x11½*

135	A43	1s black	.25	.25
137	A43	2s olive green	.25	.25

For surcharges see Nos. 186, B1.

Tsar Boris III — A44

1919, Oct. 3

138	A44	3s orange brn	.30	.25
139	A44	5s green	.30	.25
140	A44	10s rose red	.30	.25
141	A44	15s violet	.30	.25
142	A44	25s deep blue	.30	.25
143	A44	30s chocolate	.30	.25
144	A44	50s yellow brn	.30	.25
		Nos. 138-144 (7)	2.10	1.75

1st anniv. of enthronement of Tsar Boris III.
Nos. 135-144 exist imperforate.
For surcharges see Nos. 187, B2-B7.

Birthplace of Vazov at Sopot and Cherrywood Cannon — A47

"The Bear Fighter"-a Character from "Under the Yoke" — A48

Ivan Vazov in 1870 and 1920 A49

Vazov — A50

Homes of Vazov at Plovdiv and Sofia A51

The Monk Paisii — A52

1920, Oct. 20 **Photo.** *Perf. 11½*

147	A47	30s brown red	.25	.25
148	A48	50s dark green	.35	.25
149	A49	1 l drab	.50	.35
150	A50	2 l light brown	1.25	.60
151	A51	3 l black violet	2.00	.90
152	A52	5 l deep blue	2.50	1.50
		Nos. 147-152 (6)	6.85	3.85

70th birthday of Ivan Vazov (1850-1921), Bulgarian poet and novelist.
Several values of this series exist imperforate and in pairs imperforate between.

Tsar Ferdinand
A53 A54

Mt. Shar — A55

Bridge over Vardar River — A56

View of Ohrid — A57

Perf. 13x14, 14x13

1921, June 11 **Typo.**

153	A53	10s claret	.25	.25
154	A54	10s claret	.25	.25
155	A55	10s claret	.25	.25
156	A56	10s rose lilac	.25	.25
157	A57	20s blue	.50	.25
		Nos. 153-157 (5)	1.50	1.25

Nos. 153-157 were intended to be issued in 1915 to commemorate the liberation of Macedonia. They were not put in use until 1921. A 50s violet was prepared but never placed in use. Value $1.75.

View of Sofia — A58

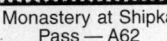

"The Liberator," Monument to Alexander II A59

Monastery at Shipka Pass — A62

Tsar Boris III — A63

Harvesting Grain — A64

Tsar Assen's Tower (No crown over lion) — A65

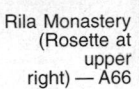

Rila Monastery (Rosette at upper right) — A66

1921-23 **Engr.** *Perf. 12*

158	A58	10s blue gray	.25	.25
159	A59	20s deep green	.25	.25
160	A63	25s blue grn ('22)	.25	.25
161	A22	50s orange	.25	.25
162	A22	50s dk blue ('23)	3.00	1.75
163	A62	75s dull vio	.25	.25
164	A62	75s dp blue ('23)	.25	.25
165	A63	1 l carmine	.25	.25
166	A63	1 l dp blue ('22)	.30	.25
167	A64	2 l brown	.30	.25
168	A65	3 l brown vio	.60	.25
169	A66	5 l lt blue	2.75	.30
170	A63	10 l violet brn	7.00	1.75
		Nos. 158-170 (13)	15.70	6.30

For surcharge see No. 189.

Bourchier in Bulgarian Costume A67

James David Bourchier A68

View of Rila Monastery A69

1921, Dec. 31

171	A67	10s red orange	.25	.25
172	A67	20s orange	.25	.25
173	A68	30s dp gray	.25	.25
174	A68	50s bluish gray	.25	.25
175	A68	1 l dull vio	.25	.25
176	A69	1½ l olive grn	.25	.25
177	A69	2 l deep green	.25	.25
178	A69	3 l Prus blue	.50	.25
179	A69	5 l red brown	.80	.50
		Nos. 171-179 (9)	3.05	2.50

Death of James D. Bourchier, Balkan correspondent of the London Times.
For surcharges see Nos. B13-B16.

Postage Due Stamps of 1919-22 Surcharged — a

1924

182	D6	10s on 20s yellow	.25	.25
183	D6	20s on 5s gray grn	.25	.25
a.		20s on 5s emerald	*30.00*	*30.00*
184	D6	20s on 10s violet	.25	.25
185	D6	20s on 30s orange	.25	.25
		Nos. 182-185 (4)	1.00	1.00

Nos. 182 to 185 were used for ordinary postage.

Regular Issues of 1919-23 Surcharged in Blue or Red

b

c

186	A43 (a)	10s on 1s black (R)	.25	.25
187	A44 (b)	1 l on 5s emer (Bl)	.25	.25
188	A22 (c)	3 l on 50s dk bl (R)	.25	.25
189	A63 (b)	6 l on 1 l car (Bl)	.60	.25
		Nos. 186-189 (4)	1.35	1.00

The surcharge of No. 188 comes in three types: normal, thick and thin.
Nos. 182, 184-189 exist with inverted surcharge.

Lion of Bulgaria
A70 A71

Tsar Boris III — A72

New Sofia Cathedral — A73

Harvesting A74

1925 **Typo.** *Perf. 13, 11½*

191	A70	10s red & bl, *pink*	.30	.25
192	A70	15s car & org, *blue*	.30	.25
193	A70	30s blk & buff	.30	.25
a.		Cliche of 15s in plate of 30s		
194	A71	50s choc, *green*	.30	.25
195	A72	1 l dull green	.70	.25
196	A73	2 l dk grn & buff	1.50	.25
197	A74	4 l lake & yellow	1.50	.25
		Nos. 191-197 (7)	4.90	1.75

Several values of this series exist imperforate and in pairs imperforate between.
See Nos. 199, 201. For overprint see No. C2.

Cathedral of Sveta Nedelya, Sofia, Ruined by Bomb — A75

1926 *Perf. 11½*

198	A75	50s gray black	.25	.25

A76

A77

Type A72 Re-engraved. (Shoulder at left does not touch frame)

1926

199	A76	1 l gray	.45	.25
a.		1 l green	.45	.25
201	A76	2 l olive brown	.70	.25

Center Embossed

202	A77	6 l dp bl & pale lemon	1.50	.25
203	A77	10 l brn blk & brn org	3.50	1.75
		Nos. 199-203 (4)	6.15	2.50

For overprints see Nos. C1, C3-C4.

Christo Botev — A78

1926, June 2

204	A78	1 l olive green	.55	.30
205	A78	2 l slate violet	1.20	.30
206	A78	4 l red brown	1.20	1.60
		Nos. 204-206 (3)	2.95	2.20

Botev (1847-76), Bulgarian revolutionary, poet.

Lion Type of 1881 Redrawn

1927-29 *Perf. 13*

207	A3	10s dk red & drab	.25	.25
208	A3	15s blk & org ('29)	.25	.25
209	A3	30s dk bl & bis brn ('28)	.25	.25
a.		30s indigo & buff	.25	.25
210	A3	50s blk & rose red ('28)	.25	.25
		Nos. 207-210 (4)	1.00	1.00

Scott 207-210 have less detailed scrollwork surrounding the central lion, which is also less detailed than Scott 1-18.

Tsar Boris III — A79

1928, Oct. 3 *Perf. 11½*

211	A79	1 l olive green	.90	.25
212	A79	2 l deep brown	1.00	.25

St. Clement A80

Konstantin Miladinov A81

George S. Rakovski A82

Drenovo Monastery A83

Paisii — A84

Tsar Simeon — A85

Lyuben Karavelov A86

Vassil Levski A87

Georgi Benkovski A88

Tsar Alexander II A89

1929, May 12

213	A80	10s dk violet	.25	.25
214	A81	15s violet brn	.25	.25
215	A82	30s red	.25	.25
216	A83	50s olive grn	.30	.25
217	A84	1 l orange brn	.80	.25
218	A85	2 l dk blue	.80	.25
219	A86	3 l dull green	2.00	.60
220	A87	4 l olive brown	3.50	.25
221	A88	5 l brown	3.00	.75
222	A89	6 l Prus green	3.50	1.50
		Nos. 213-222 (10)	14.65	4.60

Millenary of Tsar Simeon and 50th anniv. of the liberation of Bulgaria from the Turks.

Royal Wedding Issue

Tsar Boris and Fiancee, Princess Giovanna A90

Queen Ioanna and Tsar Boris — A91

1930, Nov. 12 *Perf. 11½*

223	A90	1 l green	.35	.40
224	A91	2 l dull violet	.35	.40
225	A90	4 l rose red	.35	.40
226	A91	6 l dark blue	.35	.40
		Nos. 223-226 (4)	1.40	1.60

Fifty-five copies of a miniature sheet incorporating one each of Nos. 223-226 were printed and given to royal, governmental and diplomatic personages.

Tsar Boris III
A92 A93

Perf. 11½, 12x11½, 13

1931-37 **Unwmk.**

227	A92	1 l blue green	.25	.25
228	A92	2 l carmine	.40	.25
229	A92	4 l red org ('34)	.75	.25
230	A92	4 l yel org ('37)	.25	.25
231	A92	6 l deep blue	.70	.25
232	A92	7 l dp bl ('37)	.25	.25
233	A92	10 l slate blk	8.75	.70
234	A92	12 l lt brown	.40	.25
235	A92	14 l lt brn ('37)	.30	.25
236	A93	20 l claret & org brn	1.00	.45
		Nos. 227-236 (10)	13.05	3.15

Nos. 230-233 and 235 have outer bars at top and bottom as shown on cut A92; Nos. 227-229 and 234 are without outer bars.

See Nos. 251, 279-280, 287. For surcharge see No. 252.

Balkan Games Issues

Gymnast A95

Soccer — A96

Riding — A97

Swimmer A100

"Victory" A101

Designs: 6 l, Fencing. 10 l, Bicycle race.

1931, Sept. 18 *Perf. 11½*

237	A95	1 l lt green	1.25	1.00
238	A96	2 l garnet	1.75	1.40
239	A97	4 l carmine	3.25	1.60
240	A95	6 l Prus blue	7.50	4.50
241	A95	10 l red org	17.50	7.00
242	A100	12 l dk blue	55.00	20.00
243	A101	50 l olive brn	60.00	45.00
		Nos. 237-243 (7)	146.25	80.50

1933, Jan. 5

244	A95	1 l blue grn	1.60	2.75
245	A96	2 l blue	2.50	3.00
246	A97	4 l brn vio	4.00	4.00
247	A95	6 l brt rose	8.00	7.00
248	A95	10 l olive brn	65.00	45.00
249	A100	12 l orange	110.00	70.00
250	A101	50 l red brown	300.00	*375.00*
		Nos. 244-250 (7)	491.10	*506.75*

Nos. 244-250 were sold only at the philatelic agency.

Boris Type of 1931 Outer Bars at Top and Bottom Removed

1933 *Perf. 13*

251	A92	6 l deep blue	.80	.25

Type of 1931 Surcharged in Blue

1934

252	A92	2 (l) on 3 l ol brn	6.00	.60

Soldier Defending Shipka Pass A102

Shipka Battle Memorial A103

Color-Bearer A104

Veteran of the War of Liberation, 1878 — A105

Widow and Orphans — A106

Perf. 10½, 11½

1934, Aug. 26 **Wmk. 145**

253	A102	1 l green	.70	.70
254	A103	2 l pale red	.55	.35
255	A104	3 l bister brn	1.75	2.00
256	A105	4 l dk carmine	1.25	.70
257	A104	7 l dk blue	2.50	2.50
258	A106	14 l plum	9.00	12.50
		Nos. 253-258 (6)	15.75	18.75

Shipka Pass Battle memorial unveiling.

An unwatermarked miniature sheet incorporating one each of Nos. 253-258 was put on sale in 1938 in five cities at a price of 8,000 leva. Printing: 100 sheets. Value: $1,500.

1934, Sept. 21

259	A102	1 l bright green	.70	.70
260	A103	2 l dull orange	.55	.35
261	A104	3 l yellow	1.75	2.00
262	A105	4 l rose	1.25	.70
263	A104	7 l blue	2.50	2.50
264	A106	14 l olive bister	9.00	12.50
		Nos. 259-264 (6)	15.75	18.75

An unwatermarked miniature sheet incorporating one each of Nos. 259-263 was issued. Value: $1,500.

Velcho A. Djamjiyata A108

Capt. G. S. Mamarchev A109

1935, May 5 *Perf. 11½*

265	A108	1 l deep blue	1.50	.60
266	A109	2 l maroon	1.50	.90

Bulgarian uprising against the Turks, cent.

Soccer Game — A110

Cathedral of Alexander Nevski — A111

Soccer Team — A112

Symbolical of Victory — A113

Player and Trophy — A114

The Trophy — A115

1935, June 14

267	A110	1 l green	8.00	7.00
268	A111	2 l blue gray	8.00	7.00
269	A112	4 l crimson	8.00	7.00
270	A113	7 l brt blue	8.00	7.00
271	A114	14 l orange	8.00	7.00
272	A115	50 l lilac brn	175.00	*200.00*
		Nos. 267-272 (6)	215.00	*235.00*

5th Balkan Soccer Tournament.

Gymnast on Parallel Bars A116

Youth in "Yunak" Costume A117

Girl in "Yunak" Costume A118

Pole Vaulting A119

Stadium, Sofia — A120

Yunak Emblem — A121

1935, July 10

273	A116	1 l green	4.00	7.00
274	A117	2 l lt blue	4.00	7.00
275	A118	4 l carmine	4.00	7.00
276	A119	7 l dk blue	4.00	7.00
277	A120	14 l dk brown	4.00	7.00
278	A121	50 l red	125.00	*140.00*
		Nos. 273-278 (6)	145.00	*175.00*

8th tournament of the Yunak Gymnastic Organization at Sofia, July 12-14.

Boris Type of 1931

1935 Wmk. 145 *Perf. 12½, 13*

279	A92	1 l green	.55	.25
280	A92	2 l carmine	20.00	.25

Janos Hunyadi A122

King Ladislas Varnenchik A123

Varna Memorial A124

King Ladislas III — A125

Battle of Varna, 1444 — A126

1935, Aug. 4 *Perf. 10½, 11½*

281	A122	1 l brown org	2.00	1.50
282	A123	2 l maroon	2.00	1.50
283	A124	4 l vermilion	12.50	6.00
284	A125	7 l dull blue	2.00	1.50
285	A126	14 l green	2.00	1.50
		Nos. 281-285 (5)	20.50	12.00

Battle of Varna, and the death of the Polish King, Ladislas Varnenchik (1424-44). Nos. 281-285 exist imperf. Value, set $50.

Lion Type of 1881

1935 Wmk. 145 *Perf. 13*

286	A3	10s dk red & drab	.40	.25

Boris Type of 1933 Outer Bars at Top and Bottom Removed

1935

287	A92	6 l gray blue	.65	.25

Dimitr Monument A127

Haji Dimitr — A128

Haji Dimitr and Stefan Karaja A129

Taking the Oath — A130

Birthplace of Dimitr A131

1935, Oct. 1 Unwmk. *Perf. 11½*

288	A127	1 l green	1.75	1.10
289	A128	2 l brown	2.75	1.75
290	A129	4 l car rose	6.75	4.00
291	A130	7 l blue	9.00	7.00
292	A131	14 l orange	11.00	7.00
		Nos. 288-292 (5)	31.25	20.85

67th anniv. of the death of the Bulgarian patriots, Haji Dimitr and Stefan Karaja. Nos. 288-292 exist imperf.

Catalogue values for unused stamps in this section, from this point to the end of the section, are for Never Hinged items.

A132

A133

1936-39 *Perf. 13x12½, 13*

293	A132	10s red org ('37)	.35	.25
294	A132	15s emerald	.35	.25
295	A133	30s maroon	.35	.25
296	A133	30s yel brn ('37)	.35	.25
297	A133	30s Prus bl ('37)	.35	.25
298	A133	50s ultra	.35	.25
299	A133	50s dk car ('37)	.35	.25
300	A133	50s slate grn ('39)	.35	.25
		Nos. 293-300 (8)	2.80	2.00

Meteorological Station, Mt. Moussalla A134

Peasant Girl A135

Town of Nessebr A136

1936, Aug. 16 Photo. *Perf. 11½*

301	A134	1 l purple	3.00	1.50
302	A135	2 l ultra	3.00	1.50
303	A136	7 l dark blue	6.00	3.00
		Nos. 301-303 (3)	12.00	6.00

4th Geographical & Ethnographical Cong., Sofia, Aug. 1936.

Sts. Cyril and Methodius A137

Displaying the Bible to the People A138

1937, June 2

304	A137	1 l dk green	.55	.25
305	A137	2 l dk plum	.55	.25
306	A138	4 l vermilion	.55	.25
307	A137	7 l dk blue	3.00	1.60
308	A138	14 l rose red	3.00	1.90
		Nos. 304-308 (5)	7.65	4.25

Millennium of Cyrillic alphabet.

Princess Marie Louise — A139

1937, Oct. 3

310	A139	1 l yellow green	.50	.25
311	A139	2 l brown red	.50	.25
312	A139	4 l scarlet	.50	.40
		Nos. 310-312 (3)	1.50	.90

Issued in honor of Princess Marie Louise.

Tsar Boris III — A140

1937, Oct. 3

313	A140	2 l brown red	.80	.35

19th anniv. of the accession of Tsar Boris III to the throne. See No. B11.

National Products Issue

Peasants Bundling Wheat A141

Sunflower A142

Wheat — A143

Chickens and Eggs — A144

Cluster of Grapes — A145

Rose and Perfume Flask — A146

Strawberries A147

Girl Carrying Grape Clusters A148

Rose — A149

Tobacco Leaves — A150

1938 *Perf. 13*

316	A141	10s orange	.25	.25
317	A141	10s red org	.25	.25
318	A142	15s brt rose	.35	.25
319	A142	15s deep plum	.35	.25
320	A143	30s golden brn	.30	.25
321	A143	30s copper brn	.30	.25
322	A144	50s black	.75	.25
323	A144	50s indigo	.75	.25
324	A145	1 l yel grn	.75	.25
325	A145	1 l green	.75	.25
326	A146	2 l rose pink	.75	.25
327	A146	2 l rose brn	.75	.25
328	A147	3 l dp red lil	1.40	.65
329	A147	3 l brn lake	1.40	.65
330	A148	4 l plum	1.00	.35
331	A148	4 l golden brn	1.00	.35
332	A149	7 l vio blue	2.10	.65
333	A149	7 l dp blue	2.10	.65
334	A150	14 l dk brown	3.50	1.40
335	A150	14 l red brn	3.50	1.40
		Nos. 316-335 (20)	22.30	9.10

Several values of this series exist imperforate.

Crown Prince Simeon
A151 A153

Designs: 2 l, Same portrait as 1 l, value at lower left. 14 l, similar to 4 l, but no wreath.

1938, June 16

336	A151	1 l brt green	.25	.25
337	A151	2 l rose pink	.25	.25
338	A153	4 l dp orange	.30	.25
339	A151	7 l ultra	1.00	.50
340	A153	14 l dp brown	1.00	.50
		Nos. 336-340 (5)	2.80	1.75

First birthday of Prince Simeon.
Nos. 336-340 exist imperf. Value, set $15.

Tsar Boris III
A155 A156

Various Portraits of Tsar.

1938, Oct. 3

341	A155	1 l lt green	.25	.25
342	A156	2 l rose brown	.85	.25
343	A156	4 l golden brn	.30	.25
344	A156	7 l brt ultra	.45	.45
345	A156	14 l deep red lilac	.45	.45
		Nos. 341-345 (5)	2.30	1.65

Reign of Tsar Boris III, 20th anniv.
Nos. 341-345 exist imperf. Value, set $40.

Early Locomotive A160

Designs: 2 l, Modern locomotive. 4 l, Train crossing bridge. 7 l, Tsar Boris in cab.

1939, Apr. 26

346	A160	1 l yel green	.35	.25
347	A160	2 l copper brn	.35	.25
348	A160	4 l red orange	2.00	1.00
349	A160	7 l dark blue	6.50	3.00
		Nos. 346-349 (4)	9.20	4.50

50th anniv. of Bulgarian State Railways.

Post Horns and Arrows — A164

Central Post Office, Sofia — A165

1939, May 14 **Typo.**

350	A164	1 l yellow grn	.35	.25
351	A165	2 l brt carmine	.35	.25

Establishment of the postal system, 60th anniv.

Gymnast on Bar — A166

Yunak Emblem — A167

Discus Thrower — A168

Athletic Dancer — A169

Weight Lifter — A170

1939, July 7 **Photo.**

352	A166	1 l yel grn & pale grn	.35	.35
353	A167	2 l brt rose	.35	.35
354	A168	4 l brn & gldn brn	.75	.35
355	A169	7 l dk bl & bl	2.00	1.00
356	A170	14 l plum & rose vio	10.50	8.50
		Nos. 352-356 (5)	13.95	10.55

9th tournament of the Yunak Gymnastic Organization at Sofia, July 4-8.

Tsar Boris III — A171

1940-41 **Typo.**

356A	A171	1 l dl grn ('41)	.70	.25
357	A171	2 l brt crimson	.70	.25

Bulgaria's First Stamp — A172

20 l, Similar design, scroll dated "1840-1940."

1940, May 19 **Photo.** *Perf. 13*

358	A172	10 l olive black	2.25	1.75
359	A172	20 l indigo	2.25	1.75

Cent. of 1st postage stamp.
Nos. 358-359 exist imperf. Value, set $100.

Peasant Couple and Tsar Boris — A174

Flags over Wheat Field and Tsar Boris — A175

Tsar Boris and Map of Dobrudja A176

1940, Sept. 20

360	A174	1 l slate green	.25	.25
361	A175	2 l rose red	.25	.25
362	A176	4 l dark brown	.35	.25
363	A176	7 l dark blue	.75	.60
		Nos. 360-363 (4)	1.60	1.35

Return of Dobrudja from Romania.

Fruit A177

Bees and Flowers A178

Plowing A179

Shepherd and Sheep A180

Tsar Boris III — A181

1940-44 **Typo.** **Unwmk.** *Perf. 13*

364	A177	10s red orange	.25	.25
365	A178	15s blue	.25	.25
366	A179	30s olive brn ('41)	.25	.25
367	A180	50s violet	.25	.25
368	A181	1 l brt green	.25	.25
a.		Perf 10 ¼ ('44)	1.75	.50
b.		Perf 10 ¼x11 ½ ('44)	.25	.25
c.		Perf 11 ½x10 ¼	35.00	35.00
d.		Perf 11 ½ ('44)	.25	.25
369	A181	2 l rose car	.25	.25
a.		Perf 10 ¼ ('44)	1.10	.25
b.		Perf 10 ¼x11 ½ ('44)	.25	.25
c.		Perf 11 ½x10 ¼	25.00	25.00
d.		Perf 11 ½ ('44)	.25	.25
370	A181	4 l red orange	.25	.25
a.		Perf. 11 ½ ('41)	3.50	3.00
371	A181	6 l red vio ('44)	.35	.25
372	A181	7 l blue	.25	.25
373	A181	10 l blue grn ('41)	.35	.25
		Nos. 364-373 (10)	2.70	2.50

See Nos. 373A-377, 440. For overprints see Nos. 455-463, C31-C32.

1940-41 **Wmk. 145** *Perf. 13*

373A	A180	50s violet ('41)	.25	.25
374	A181	1 l brt grn	1.00	.25
375	A181	2 l rose car	.35	.25
376	A181	7 l dull blue	.35	.25
377	A181	10 l blue green	.35	.25
		Nos. 373A-377 (5)	2.30	1.25

Watermarked vertically or horizontally.
Nos. 374-375 exist imperf. Value, each $15.

P. R. Slaveikov A182

Sofronii, Bishop of Vratza A183

Saint Ivan Rilski — A184

Martin S. Drinov — A185

Hrabar The Monk — A186

Kolio Ficheto — A187

1940, Sept. 23 Photo. Unwmk.

378	A182	1 l brt bl grn	.25	.25
379	A183	2 l brt carmine	.25	.25
380	A184	3 l dp red brn	.25	.25
381	A185	4 l red orange	.25	.25
382	A186	7 l deep blue	1.60	1.60
383	A187	10 l red brn	2.40	1.60
		Nos. 378-383 (6)	5.00	4.20

Liberation of Bulgaria from the Turks in 1878.

Johannes Gutenberg A188

N. Karastoyanov, 1st Bulgarian Printer A189

1940, Dec. 16

384	A188	1 l slate green	.35	.25
385	A189	2 l orange brown	.35	.25

500th anniv. of the invention of the printing press and 100th anniv. of the 1st Bulgarian printing press.

Christo Botev — A190

Monument to Botev — A192

Botev with his Insurgent Band — A191

1941, May 3

386	A190	1 l dark blue green	.25	.25
387	A191	2 l crimson rose	.35	.25
388	A192	3 l dark brown	.90	.70
		Nos. 386-388 (3)	1.50	1.20

Christo Botev, patriot and poet.

Palace of Justice, Sofia — A193

20 l, Workers' hospital. 50 l, National Bank.

1941-43 Engr. *Perf. 11½*

389	A193	14 l lt gray brn ('43)	.60	.35
390	A193	20 l gray grn ('43)	.60	.35
391	A193	50 l lt bl gray	2.60	1.50
		Nos. 389-391 (3)	3.80	2.20

Macedonian Woman — A196

City of Okhrida — A200

Outline of Macedonia and Tsar Boris III A197

View of Aegean Sea — A198

Poganovski Monastery A199

1941, Oct. 3 Photo. *Perf. 13*

392	A196	1 l slate grn	.25	.25
393	A197	2 l crimson	.25	.25
394	A198	2 l red org	.25	.25
395	A199	4 l org brn	.25	.25
396	A200	7 l dp gray bl	.65	.45
		Nos. 392-396 (5)	1.65	1.45

Issued to commemorate the acquisition of Macedonian territory from neighboring countries.

Peasant Working in a Field — A201

Designs: 15s, Plowing. 30s, Apiary. 50s, Women harvesting fruit. 3 l, Shepherd and sheep. 5 l, Inspecting cattle.

1941-44

397	A201	10s dk violet	.25	.25
398	A201	10s dk blue	.25	.25
399	A201	15s Prus blue	.25	.25
400	A201	15s dk ol brn	.25	.25
401	A201	30s red orange	.25	.25
402	A201	30s dk slate grn	.25	.25
403	A201	50s blue vio	.25	.25
404	A201	50s red lilac	.25	.25
405	A201	3 l henna brn	.35	.25
406	A201	3 l dk brn ('44)	1.25	.75
407	A201	5 l sepia	1.00	.50
408	A201	5 l vio bl ('44)	1.25	.75
		Nos. 397-408 (12)	5.85	4.25

Girls Singing — A207

Boys in Camp — A208

Raising Flag — A209

Folk Dancers — A211

Camp Scene A210

1942, June 1 Photo.

409	A207	1 l dk bl grn	.25	.25
410	A208	2 l scarlet	.25	.25
411	A209	4 l olive gray	.30	.25
412	A210	7 l deep blue	.40	.25
413	A211	14 l fawn	.45	.25
		Nos. 409-413 (5)	1.65	1.25

National "Work and Joy" movement.

Wounded Soldier — A212

Soldier's Farewell A213

4 l, Aiding wounded soldier. 7 l, Widow & orphans at grave. 14 l, Tomb of Unknown Soldier. 20 l, Queen Ioanna visiting wounded.

1942, Sept. 7

414	A212	1 l slate grn	.30	.25
415	A213	2 l brt rose	.30	.25
416	A213	4 l yel org	.30	.25
417	A213	7 l dark blue	.30	.25
418	A213	14 l brown	.30	.25
419	A213	20 l olive blk	.65	.25
		Nos. 414-419 (6)	2.15	1.50

Issued to aid war victims. No. 419 was printed in sheets of 50, alternating with 50 labels.

Legend of Kubrat — A218

Cavalry Charge — A219

Designs: 30s, Rider of Madara. 50s, Christening of Boris I. 1 l, School, St. Naum. 2 l, Crowning of Tsar Simeon by Boris I. 3 l, Golden era of Bulgarian literature. 4 l, Sentencing of the Bogomil Basil. 5 l, Proclamation of 2nd Bulgarian Empire. 7 l, Ivan Assen II at Trebizond. 10 l, Deporting the Patriarch Jeftimi. 14 l, Wandering minstrel. 20 l, Monk Paisii. 30 l, Monument, Shipka Pass.

1942, Oct. 12

420	A218	10s bluish blk	.25	.25
421	A219	15s Prus grn	.25	.25
422	A219	30s dk rose vio	.25	.25
423	A219	50s indigo	.25	.25
424	A219	1 l slate grn	.25	.25
425	A219	2 l crimson	.25	.25
426	A219	3 l brown	.25	.25
427	A219	4 l orange	.25	.25
428	A219	5 l grnsh blk	.25	.25
429	A219	7 l dk blue	.25	.25
430	A219	10 l brown blk	.25	.25
431	A219	14 l olive blk	.25	.25
432	A219	20 l henna brn	.70	.50
433	A219	30 l black	1.25	.75
		Nos. 420-433 (14)	4.95	4.25

Tsar Boris III A234

Designs: Various portraits of Tsar.

Perf. 13, Imperf.

1944, Feb. 28 Photo. Wmk. 275

Frames in Black

434	A234	1 l olive grn	.25	*.40*
435	A234	2 l red brown	.25	*.40*
436	A234	4 l brown	.25	*.40*
437	A234	5 l gray vio	.50	*1.00*
438	A234	7 l slate blue	.60	*1.25*
		Nos. 434-438 (5)	1.85	*3.45*

Tsar Boris III (1894-1943).

Tsar Simeon II — A239

Unwmk.

1944, June 12 Typo. *Perf. 13*

439	A239	3 l red orange	.25	.25
a.		Perf 11½	.35	.25

Shepherd Type of 1940

1944

440	A180	50s yellow green	.25	.25

Parcel Post Stamps of 1944 Overprinted in Black or Orange

1945, Jan. 25 *Perf. 11½*

448	PP5	1 l dk carmine	.25	.25
449	PP5	7 l rose lilac	.25	.25
450	PP5	20 l org brn	.25	.25
451	PP5	30 l dk brn car	.30	.25
452	PP5	50 l red orange	.50	.25
453	PP5	100 l blue (O)	.75	.25

Overprint reads: "Everything for the Front."

No. 448 with Additional Surcharge of New Value in Black

454	PP5	4 l on 1 l dk car	.25	.25
		Nos. 448-454 (7)	2.55	1.75

Nos. 368 to 370 Overprinted in Black

1945, Mar. 15 *Perf. 11½, 13*

455	A181	1 l brt green, perf 13	.30	.30
456	A181	2 l rose carmine, perf 11½	1.10	.30
a.		Perf 10¾	2.50	3.50
b.		Perf 11½x10¾	40.00	19.50
457	A181	4 l red orange, perf 13	.75	.30

Overprint reads: "Collect old iron."

Overprinted in Black

458	A181	1 l brt green, perf 13	.25	.30
a.		Perf 11½	.25	.30
459	A181	2 l rose carmine, perf 11½	.65	.30
a.		Perf 10¾	12.00	9.00
460	A181	4 l red orange, perf. 13	.95	.30
a.		Perf 11½	4.50	3.00

Overprint reads: "Collect discarded paper."

Overprinted in Black

461	A181	1 l brt green, perf 11½	.25	.25
a.		Perf 13	.30	.30
462	A181	2 l rose carmine, perf 11½	1.10	.25
a.		Perf 10¾	12.00	9.00
b.		Perf 11½x10¾	30.00	18.00
463	A181	4 l red orange, perf 13	.95	.25
		Nos. 455-463 (9)	6.30	2.55

Overprint reads: "Collect all kinds of rags."

Oak Tree — A245

Imperf., Perf. 11½.

1945 Litho. Unwmk.

464	A245	4 l vermilion	.25	.25
465	A245	10 l blue	.25	.25

Imperf

466	A245	50 l brown lake	.35	.35
		Nos. 464-466 (3)	.85	.85

Slav Congress, Sofia, March, 1945.

A246

A247

A248

A249

A251

A252

A253

A254

2 l and 4 l:

Type I. Large crown close to coat of arms.
Type II. Smaller crown standing high.

1945-46 Photo. *Perf. 13*

469	A246	30s yellow grn	.25	.25
470	A247	50s peacock grn	.25	.25
471	A248	1 l dk green	.25	.25
472	A249	2 l choc (I)	.25	.25
a.		Type II	.25	.25
473	A249	4 l dk blue (I)	.25	.25
a.		Type II	.25	.25
475	A251	5 l red violet	.25	.25
476	A251	9 l slate gray	.25	.25
477	A252	10 l Prus blue	.25	.25
478	A253	15 l brown	.25	.25
479	A254	20 l carmine	.35	.25
480	A254	20 l gray blk	.35	.25
		Nos. 469-480 (11)	2.95	2.75

Breaking Chain — A255

1 Lev Coin — A256

Water Wheel — A257

Coin and Symbols of Agriculture and Industry — A258

Unwmk.

1945, June 4 Litho. *Imperf.*

Laid Paper

481	A255	50 l brn red, *pink*	.25	.25
482	A255	50 l org, *pink*	.25	.25
483	A256	100 l gray bl, *pink*	.25	.25
484	A256	100 l brn, *pink*	.25	.25
485	A257	150 l dk ol gray, *pink*	.85	.25
486	A257	150 l dl car, *pink*	.85	.25
487	A258	200 l dp bl, *pink*	1.25	.70
488	A258	200 l ol grn, *pink*	1.25	.70
		Nos. 481-488 (8)	5.20	2.90

Souvenir Sheets

489		Sheet of 4	6.00	9.00
a.		A255 50 l violet blue	.60	.25
b.		A256 100 l violet blue	.60	.25
c.		A257 150 l violet blue	.60	.25
d.		A258 200 l violet blue	.60	.25
490		Sheet of 4	6.00	9.00
a.		A255 50 l brown orange	.60	.25
b.		A256 100 l brown orange	.60	.25
c.		A257 150 l brown orange	.60	.25
d.		A258 200 l brown orange	.60	.25

Publicizing Bulgaria's Liberty Loan.

Olive Branch — A260

1945, Sept. 1 Typo. *Perf. 13*

491	A260	10 l org brn & yel grn	.25	.25
492	A260	50 l dull red & dp grn	.40	.25

Victory of Allied Nations, World War II.

September 9, 1944 — A261

Numeral, Broken Chain — A262

1945, Sept. 7

493	A261	1 l gray green	.25	.25
494	A261	4 l deep blue	.25	.25
495	A261	5 l rose lilac	.25	.25
496	A262	10 l lt blue	.25	.25
497	A262	20 l brt car	.25	.25
498	A261	50 l brt bl grn	.70	.25
499	A261	100 l orange brn	.80	.50
		Nos. 493-499 (7)	2.75	2.00

1st anniv. of Bulgaria's liberation.

Old Postal Savings Emblem — A263

Child Putting Coin in Bank — A265

First Bulgarian Postal Savings Stamp A264

Postal Savings Building, Sofia — A266

1946, Apr. 12

500	A263	4 l brown org	.25	.25
501	A264	10 l dk olive	.25	.25
502	A265	20 l ultra	.25	.25
503	A266	50 l slate gray	.90	.90
		Nos. 500-503 (4)	1.65	1.65

50th anniv. of Bulgarian Postal Savings.

Refugee Children A267

Nurse Assisting Wounded Soldier A269

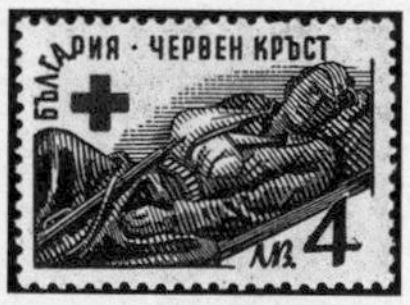

Wounded Soldier A268

35 l, 100 l, Red Cross hospital train.

1946, Apr. 4 Cross in Carmine

504	A267	2 l dk olive	.25	.25
505	A268	4 l violet	.25	.25
506	A267	10 l plum	.25	.25
507	A268	20 l ultra	.25	.25
508	A269	30 l brown org	.25	.25
509	A268	35 l gray blk	.25	.25
510	A269	50 l violet brn	.45	.35
511	A268	100 l gray brn	1.10	1.40
		Nos. 504-511 (8)	3.05	3.25

See Nos. 553-560.

Advancing Troops A271

Grenade Thrower — A272

Attacking Planes — A274

Designs: 5 l, Horse-drawn cannon. 9 l, Engineers building pontoon bridge. 10 l, 30 l, Cavalry charge. 40 l, Horse-drawn supply column. 50 l, Motor transport column. 60 l, Infantry, tanks and planes.

1946, Aug. 9 Typo. Unwmk.

512	A271	2 l dk red vio	.25	.25
513	A272	4 l dk gray	.25	.25
514	A271	5 l dk org red	.25	.25
515	A274	6 l black brn	.25	.25
516	A271	9 l rose lilac	.25	.25
517	A271	10 l dp violet	.25	.25
518	A271	20 l dp blue	.45	.25
519	A271	30 l red org	.45	.25
520	A271	40 l dk ol bis	.50	.25
521	A271	50 l dk green	.55	.25
522	A271	60 l red brown	.85	.50
		Nos. 512-522 (11)	4.30	3.00

Bulgaria's participation in World War II.

Arms of Russia and Bulgaria — A279

1946, May 23

523	A279	4 l red orange	.25	.25
525	A279	20 l turq green	.30	.30

Congress of the Bulgarian-Soviet Association, May 1946. The 4 l exists in dk car rose and 20 l in blue. Value, set $12.

Lion Rampant — A280

1946, May 25 *Imperf.*

526	A280	20 l blue	.60	.30

Day of the Postage Stamp, May 26, 1946.

Alexander Stamboliski (1879-1923), Prime Minister — A281

1946, June 13 *Perf. 12*

527	A281	100 l	red orange	6.25	6.25

Flags of Albania, Romania, Bulgaria and Yugoslavia — A282

1946, July 6 *Perf. 11½*

528	A282	100 l	black brown	1.20	1.20

1946 Balkan Games.

Sheet of 100 arranged so that all stamps are tete beche vert. and horiz., except 2 center rows in left pane which provide 10 vert. pairs that are not tete beche vert.

St. Ivan Rilski — A283

A286

A284

A285

Views of Rila Monastery A287

1946, Aug. 26

529	A283	1 l	red brown	.25	.25
530	A284	4 l	black brn	.25	.25
531	A285	10 l	dk green	.25	.25
532	A286	20 l	dp blue	.35	.25
533	A287	50 l	dk red	1.25	.80
			Nos. 529-533 (5)	2.35	1.80

Millenary of Rila Monastery.

People's Republic

A288

1946, Sept. 15 **Typo.**

534	A288	4 l	brown lake	.25	.25
535	A288	20 l	dull blue	.25	.25
536	A288	50 l	olive bister	.35	.35
			Nos. 534-536 (3)	.85	.85

No. 535 is inscribed "BULGARIA" in Latin characters.

Referendum of Sept. 8, 1946, resulting in the establishment of the Bulgarian People's Republic.

Partisan Army — A289

Snipers — A290

Soldiers: Past and Present — A291

Design: 30 l, Partisans advancing.

1946, Dec. 2

537	A289	1 l	violet brn	.25	.25
538	A290	4 l	dull grn	.25	.25
539	A291	5 l	chocolate	.25	.25
540	A290	10 l	crimson	.25	.25
541	A289	20 l	ultra	.30	.25
542	A290	30 l	olive bister	.35	.25
543	A291	50 l	black	.50	.35
			Nos. 537-543 (7)	2.15	1.85

Relief Worker and Children — A294

Child with Gift Parcels — A295

Waiting for Food Distribution A296

Mother and Child A297

1946, Dec. 30

545	A294	1 l	dk vio brn	.25	.25
546	A295	4 l	brt red	.25	.25
547	A295	9 l	olive bis	.25	.25
548	A294	10 l	slate gray	.25	.25
549	A296	20 l	ultra	.25	.25
550	A297	30 l	dp brn org	.25	.25
551	A296	40 l	maroon	.25	.25
552	A294	50 l	peacock grn	.50	.50
			Nos. 545-552 (8)	2.25	2.25

"Bulgaria" is in Latin characters on No. 548.

Red Cross Types of 1946

1947, Jan. 31 **Cross in Carmine**

553	A267	2 l	olive bister	.25	.25
554	A268	4 l	olive black	.25	.25
555	A267	10 l	blue grn	.25	.25
556	A268	20 l	brt blue	.25	.25
557	A269	30 l	yellow grn	.50	.50
558	A268	35 l	grnsh gray	.50	.50
559	A269	50 l	henna brn	.85	.85
560	A268	100 l	dark blue	1.25	1.25
			Nos. 553-560 (8)	4.10	4.10

Laurel Branch, Allied and Bulgarian Emblems A298

Dove of Peace A299

1947, Feb. 28

561	A298	4 l	olive	.25	.25
562	A299	10 l	brown red	.25	.25
563	A299	20 l	deep blue	.25	.25
			Nos. 561-563 (3)	.75	.75

Return to peace at the close of World War II. "Bulgaria" in Latin characters on No. 563.

A302

Guerrilla Fighters
A303 A304

1947, Jan. 21 *Perf. 11½*

567	A302	10 l	choc & brn org	.55	.40
568	A303	20 l	dk bl & bl	.55	.40
569	A304	70 l	dp claret & rose	45.00	42.50
			Nos. 567-569 (3)	46.10	43.30

Issued to honor the anti-fascists.

Hydroelectric Station A305

Miner — A306

Symbols of Industry — A307

Tractor A308

1947, Aug. 6

570	A305	4 l	olive green	.25	.25
571	A306	9 l	red brown	.25	.25
572	A307	20 l	deep blue	.30	.25
573	A308	40 l	olive brown	.75	.55
			Nos. 570-573 (4)	1.55	1.30

Exhibition Building A309

Former Home of Alphonse de Lamartine A310

Symbols of Agriculture and Horticulture A311

Perf. 11x11½, 11½x11

1947, Aug. 31 **Litho.** **Unwmk.**

574	A309	4 l	scarlet	.25	.25
575	A310	9 l	brown lake	.25	.25
576	A311	20 l	brt ultra	.30	.30
			Nos. 574-576 (3)	.80	.80

Plovdiv Intl. Fair, 1947. See No. C54.

Basil Evstatiev Aprilov — A312

1947, Oct. 19 **Photo.** *Perf. 11*

577	A312	40 l	brt ultra	.60	.30

Cent. of the death of Basil Evstatiev Aprilov, educator and historian. See No. 603.

Bicycle Race — A313

Basketball A314

Chess A315

Balkan Games: 20 l, Soccer players. 60 l, Four flags of participating nations.

1947, Sept. 29 **Typo.** *Perf. 11½*

578	A313	2 l	plum	.25	.25
579	A314	4 l	dk olive grn	.25	.25
580	A315	9 l	orange brn	1.00	.45
581	A315	20 l	brt ultra	1.25	.50
582	A315	60 l	violet brn	3.00	1.50
			Nos. 578-582 (5)	5.75	2.95

People's Theater, Sofia A316

National Assembly A317

Central Post Office, Sofia
A318

Presidential Mansion
A319

1947-48 **Typo.** ***Perf. 12½***

583 A316 50s yellow grn .25 .25
584 A317 50s yellow grn .25 .25
585 A318 1 l green .25 .25
586 A319 1 l green .25 .25
587 A316 2 l brown lake .25 .25
588 A317 2 l lt brown .25 .25
589 A316 4 l deep blue .25 .25
590 A317 4 l deep blue .25 .25
591 A316 9 l carmine .35 .25
592 A317 20 l deep blue .75 .30
Nos. 583-592 (10) 3.10 2.55

On Nos. 583-592 inscription reads "Bulgarian Republic." No. 592 is inscribed in Latin characters.

Redrawn

Added to inscription

593 A318 1 l green .25 .25
594 A318 2 l brown lake .25 .25
595 A318 4 l deep blue .25 .25
Nos. 593-595 (3) .75 .75

Cyrillic inscription beneath design on Nos. 593-595 reads "Bulgarian People's Republic."

Geno Kirov — A320

Actors' Portraits: 1 l, Zlatina Nedeva. 2 l, Ivan Popov. 3 l, Athanas Kirchev. 4 l, Elena Snejina. 5 l, Stoyan Bachvarov.

Perf. 10½

1947, Dec. 8 **Unwmk.** **Litho.**

596 A320 50s bister brn .25 .25
597 A320 1 l lt blue grn .25 .25
598 A320 2 l slate green .25 .25
599 A320 3 l dp blue .25 .25
600 A320 4 l scarlet .25 .25
601 A320 5 l red brown .25 .25
Nos. 596-601,B22-B26 (11) 3.80 3.25

National Theater, 50th anniversary.

Merchant Ship "Fatherland" — A321

1947, Dec. 19

602 A321 50 l Prus bl, *cream* .80 .60

B. E. Aprilov — A322

1948, Feb. 19 ***Perf. 11***

603 A322 4 l brn car, *cream* .25 .25

Centenary of the death of Basil Evstatiev Aprilov, educator and historian.

Worker — A323

1948, Feb. 29 **Photo.** ***Perf. 11½x12***

604 A323 4 l dp blue, *cream* .25 .25

2nd Bulgarian Workers' Congress.

Self-education
A324

Accordion Player — A325

Factory Recess — A326

Girl Throwing Basketball — A327

1948, Mar. 31 **Photo.**

605 A324 4 l red .25 .25
606 A325 20 l deep blue .25 .25
607 A326 40 l dull green .50 .25
608 A327 60 l brown .85 .60
Nos. 605-608 (4) 1.85 1.35

Nicholas Vaptzarov — A328

Portraits: 9 l, P. K. Iavorov. 15 l, Christo Smirnenski. 20 l, Ivan Vazov. 45 l, P. R. Slaveikov.

1948, May 18 **Litho.** ***Perf. 11***
Cream Paper

611 A328 4 l brt ver .25 .25
612 A328 9 l lt brown .25 .25
613 A328 15 l claret .25 .25
614 A328 20 l deep blue .30 .30
615 A328 45 l green .40 .40
Nos. 611-615 (5) 1.45 1.45

Soviet Soldier — A329

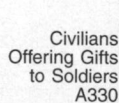

Civilians Offering Gifts to Soldiers
A330

Designs: 20 l, Soldiers, 1878 and 1944. 60 l, Stalin and Spasski Tower.

1948, July 5 **Photo.** **Cream Paper**

616 A329 4 l brown org .25 .25
617 A330 10 l olive grn .25 .25
618 A330 20 l dp blue .25 .25
619 A329 60 l olive brn 1.00 .85
Nos. 616-619 (4) 1.75 1.60

The Soviet Army.

Demeter Blagoev — A331

Monument to Bishop Andrey
A332

9 l, Gabriel Genov. 60 l, Marching youths.

1948, Sept. 6 **Litho.** **Cream Paper**

620 A331 4 l dk brown .25 .25
621 A331 9 l brown org .25 .25
622 A332 20 l dp blue .25 .25
623 A332 60 l brown .80 .60
Nos. 620-623 (4) 1.55 1.35

No. 623 is inscribed in Cyrillic characters.
Natl. Insurrection of 1923, 25th anniv.

Christo Smirnenski — A333

1948, Oct. 2 **Photo.** ***Perf. 11½***
Cream Paper

624 A333 4 l blue .25 .25
625 A333 16 l red brown .25 .25

Christo Smirnenski, poet, 1898-1923.

Battle of Grivitza, 1877 — A334

1948, Nov. 1

626 A334 20 l blue .25 .25
Nos. 626,C56-C57 (3) 1.50 1.45

Romanian-Bulgarian friendship.

Bath, Gorna Banya — A335

Bath, Bankya — A336

Mineral Bath, Sofia
A337

Maliovitza
A338

1948-49 **Typo.** ***Perf. 12½***

627 A335 2 l red brown .25 .25
628 A336 3 l red orange .25 .25
629 A337 4 l deep blue .25 .25
630 A338 5 l violet brown .25 .25
631 A336 10 l red violet .30 .25
632 A338 15 l olive grn ('49) .75 .25
633 A335 20 l deep blue 1.40 .25
Nos. 627-633 (7) 3.45 1.75

Latin characters on No. 633. See No. 653.

Emblem of the Republic — A339

1948-50

634 A339 50s red orange .25 .25
634A A339 50s org brn ('50) .25 .25
635 A339 1 l green .25 .25
636 A339 9 l black .40 .25
Nos. 634-636 (4) 1.15 1.00

Botev's Birthplace, Kalofer
A340

Christo Botev — A341

Designs: 9 l, Steamer "Radetzky." 15 l, Kalofer village. 20 l, Botev in uniform. 40 l, Botev's mother. 50 l, Pen, pistol and wreath.

Cream Paper

Perf. 11x11½, 11½

1948, Dec. 21 **Photo.**

638 A340 1 l dk green .25 .25
639 A341 4 l violet brn .25 .25
640 A340 9 l violet .25 .25
641 A340 15 l brown .25 .25
642 A341 20 l blue .25 .25
643 A340 40 l red brown .50 .25
644 A341 50 l olive blk .65 .50
Nos. 638-644 (7) 2.40 2.00

Botev, Bulgarian natl. poet, birth cent.

Lenin — A342

Lenin Speaking — A343

1949, Jan. 24 **Unwmk.** ***Perf. 11½***
Cream Paper

645 A342 4 l brown .35 .25
646 A343 20 l brown red .50 .25

25th anniversary of the death of Lenin.

Road Construction
A344

Designs: 5 l, Tunnel construction. 9 l, Locomotive. 10 l, Textile worker. 20 l, Female tractor driver. 40 l, Workers in truck.

1949, Apr. 6 *Perf. 10½*

Inscribed: "CHM"

Cream Paper

647	A344	4 l dark red	.25	.25
648	A344	5 l dark brown	.25	.25
649	A344	9 l dk slate grn	.50	.25
650	A344	10 l violet	.50	.25
651	A344	20 l dull blue	.85	.65
652	A344	40 l brown	1.75	.85
		Nos. 647-652 (6)	4.10	2.50

Honoring the Workers' Cultural Brigade.

Type of 1948 Redrawn Country Name and "POSTA" in English Characters

1949 **Typo.** *Perf. 12½*

653	A337	20 l deep blue	2.00	.25

Miner — A345

1949 *Perf. 11x11½*

654	A345	4 l dark blue	.25	.25

A347

Prime Minister George Dimitrov, 1882-1949
A348

1949, July 10 **Photo.**

656	A347	4 l red brown	.25	.25
657	A348	20 l dark blue	1.00	.25

Power Station — A349

Grain Towers — A350

Farm Machinery — A351

Tractor Parade A352

Agriculture and Industry A353

1949, Aug. 5 *Perf. 11½x11, 11x11½*

658	A349	4 l olive green	.25	.25
659	A350	9 l dark red	.25	.25
660	A351	15 l purple	.35	.25
661	A352	20 l blue	1.00	.65
662	A353	50 l orange brn	3.00	1.40
		Nos. 658-662 (5)	4.85	2.80

Bulgaria's Five Year Plan.

Grenade and Javelin Throwers — A354

Hurdlers A355

Motorcycle and Tractor A356

Boy and Girl Athletes — A357

1949, Sept. 5

663	A354	4 l brown orange	.50	.25
664	A355	9 l olive green	1.40	.45
665	A356	20 l violet blue	2.00	1.10
666	A357	50 l red brown	5.25	2.25
		Nos. 663-666 (4)	9.15	4.05

A358

Frontier Guards — A359

1949, Oct. 31

667	A358	4 l chestnut brn	.35	.35
668	A359	20 l gray blue	1.10	.55

See No. C60.

George Dimitrov — A360

Allegory of Labor — A361

Laborers of Both Sexes — A362

Workers and Flags of Bulgaria and Russia — A363

Perf. 11½

1949, Dec. 13 **Photo.** **Unwmk.**

669	A360	4 l orange brn	.25	.25
670	A361	9 l purple	.75	.45
671	A362	20 l dull blue	.75	.45
672	A363	50 l red	.75	.45
		Nos. 669-672 (4)	2.50	1.60

Joseph V. Stalin — A364

Stalin and Dove — A365

1949, Dec. 21

673	A364	4 l deep orange	.35	.25
674	A365	40 l rose brown	1.10	.80

70th anniv. of the birth of Joseph V. Stalin.

Kharalamby Stoyanov — A366

Railway Strikers A367

Communications Strikers — A368

1950, Feb. 15

675	A366	4 l yellow brown	.35	.25
676	A367	20 l violet blue	.35	.25
677	A368	60 l brown olive	1.10	.70
		Nos. 675-677 (3)	1.80	1.20

30th anniv. (in 1949) of the General Railway and Postal Employees' Strike of 1919.

Miner — A369

Locomotive A370

Shipbuilding — A371

Tractor A372

Stalin Central Heating Plant — A374

Textile Worker — A375

Farm Machinery A373

1950-51 *Perf. 11½, 13*

678	A369	1 l olive	.25	.25
679	A370	2 l gray blk	.25	.25
680	A371	3 l gray blue	.25	.25
681	A372	4 l dk blue grn	2.25	.60
682	A373	5 l henna brn	.45	.25
682A	A373	9 l gray blk ('51)	.25	.25
683	A374	10 l dp plum ('51)	.30	.25
684	A375	15 l dk car ('51)	.50	.25
685	A375	20 l dk blue ('51)	.80	.25
		Nos. 678-685 (9)	5.30	2.60

No. 685 is inscribed in Latin characters. See Nos. 750-751A.

Vassil Kolarov (1877-1950) — A377

1950, Mar. 6 *Perf. 11½*

Size: 21½x31½mm

686	A377	4 l red brown	.25	.25

Size: 27x39½mm

687	A377	20 l violet blue	.70	.70

No. 687 has altered frame and is inscribed in Latin characters.

Stanislav Dospevski, Self-portrait A378

King Kaloyan and Desislava A379

Plowman Resting, by Christo Stanchev A380

Statue of Dimtcho Debelianov, by Ivan Lazarov — A381

"Harvest," by V. Dimitrov — A382

Design: 9 l, Nikolai Pavlovich, self-portrait.

1950, Apr. 15 *Perf. 11½*

688	A378	1 l	dk olive grn	.30	.25
689	A379	4 l	dk red	1.25	.45
690	A378	9 l	chocolate	1.75	.45
691	A380	15 l	brown	2.50	.60
692	A380	20 l	deep blue	4.00	1.75
693	A381	40 l	red brown	5.00	1.25
694	A382	60 l	deep orange	4.00	2.00
			Nos. 688-694 (7)	18.80	6.75

Latin characters on No. 692.

Ivan Vazov (1850-1921), Poet and Birthplace A383

1950, June 26

695	A383	4 l	olive green	.25	.25

Road Building A384

Men of Three Races and "Stalin" Flag — A385

Perf. 11½x11, 11x11½

1950, Sept. 19

696	A384	4 l	brown red	.25	.25
697	A385	20 l	violet blue	.65	.25

2nd National Peace Conference.

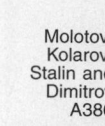

Molotov, Kolarov, Stalin and Dimitrov A386

Spasski Tower and Flags — A387

Russian and Bulgarian Women — A388

Loading Russian Ship — A389

Perf. 11½

1950, Oct. 10 **Unwmk.** **Photo.**

698	A386	4 l	brown	.25	.25
699	A387	9 l	rose carmine	.25	.25
700	A388	20 l	gray blue	.35	.30
701	A389	50 l	dk grnsh blue	1.75	.75
			Nos. 698-701 (4)	2.60	1.55

2nd anniversary of the Soviet-Bulgarian treaty of mutual assistance.

St. Constantine Sanatorium — A390

2 l, 10 l, Children at seashore. 5 l, Rest home.

1950 **Typo.**

702	A390	1 l	dark green	.25	.25
703	A390	2 l	carmine	.25	.25
704	A390	5 l	deep orange	.25	.25
705	A390	10 l	deep blue	.40	.25
			Nos. 702-705 (4)	1.15	1.00

Originally prepared in 1945 as "Sunday Delivery Stamps," this issue was released for ordinary postage in 1950. Compare with Nos. RA16-RA18.

Runners — A393

1950, Aug. 21 **Photo.** *Perf. 11½*

706	A393	4 l	shown	.70	.40
707	A393	9 l	Cycling	.70	.50
a.			Perf 10¾	1.75	1.40
708	A393	20 l	Shot put	1.00	.85
a.			Perf 10¾	2.00	1.75
b.			Perf 11½x10¾	3.50	3.00
709	A393	40 l	Volleyball	2.00	2.00
a.			Perf 10¾	4.25	3.50
			Nos. 706-709 (4)	4.40	3.75

Marshal Fedor I. Tolbukhin — A394

Natives Greeting Tolbukhin A395

Perf. 11½x11, 11x11½

1950, Dec. 10 **Photo.** **Unwmk.**

710	A394	4 l	claret	.30	.25
711	A395	20 l	dk blue	1.10	.25

The return of Dobrich and part of the province of Dobruja from Romania to Bulgaria.

Dimitrov's Birthplace A396

George Dimitrov
A397 A398

Various Portraits, Inscribed

Design: 2 l, Dimitrov Museum, Sofia.

1950, July 2 *Perf. 10½*

712	A396	50s	olive grn	.30	.25
713	A397	50s	brown	.30	.25
714	A397	1 l	redsh brn	.30	.25
715	A396	2 l	gray	.30	.25
716	A397	4 l	claret	.60	.25
717	A397	9 l	red brown	1.00	.50
718	A398	10 l	brown red	1.50	.70
719	A396	15 l	olive gray	1.50	.70
720	A396	20 l	dark blue	2.50	.80
			Nos. 712-720,C61 (10)	13.80	6.70

1st anniversary of the death of George Dimitrov, statesman. No. 720 is inscribed in Latin characters.

A. S. Popov — A400

1951, Feb. 10

722	A400	4 l	red brown	.40	.25
723	A400	20 l	dark blue	.90	.25

No. 723 is inscribed in Latin characters.

Arms of Bulgaria
A401 A402

1950 **Unwmk.** **Typo.** *Perf. 13*

724	A401	2 l	dk brown	.25	.25
725	A401	3 l	rose	.25	.25
726	A402	5 l	carmine	.25	.25
727	A402	9 l	aqua	.25	.25
			Nos. 724-727 (4)	1.00	1.00

Nos. 724-727 were prepared in 1947 for official use but were issued as regular postage stamps Oct. 1, 1950.

Heroes Chankova, Antonov-Malchik, Dimitrov and Dimitrova — A403

Stanke Dimitrov-Marek A404

George Kirkov A405

George Dimitrov at Leipzig A406

Natcho Ivanov and Avr. Stoyanov A407

9 l, Anton Ivanov. 15 l, Christo Michailov.

1951, Mar. 25 **Photo.** *Perf. 11½*

728	A403	1 l	red violet	.25	.25
729	A404	2 l	dk red brn	.25	.25
730	A405	4 l	car rose	.25	.25
731	A405	9 l	orange brn	.80	.25
732	A405	15 l	olive brn	1.75	.65
733	A406	20 l	dark blue	1.75	.90
734	A407	50 l	olive gray	4.25	1.50
			Nos. 728-734 (7)	9.30	4.05

First Bulgarian Tractor A408

First Steam Roller — A409

First Truck — A410

Bulgarian Embroidery — A411

15 l, Carpet. 20 l, Tobacco & roses. 40 l, Fruits.

Perf. 11x10½

1951, Mar. 30 **Photo.** **Unwmk.**

735	A408	1 l	olive brn	.25	.25
736	A409	2 l	violet	.30	.25
737	A410	4 l	red brown	.50	.25
738	A411	9 l	purple	.75	.25
739	A409	15 l	deep plum	1.60	.55
740	A411	20 l	violet blue	3.00	.55
741	A410	40 l	deep green	4.25	1.25

Perf. 13

Size: 23x18½mm

742	A408	1 l purple	.25	.25
743	A409	2 l Prus green	.25	.25
744	A410	4 l red brown	.25	.25
		Nos. 735-744 (10)	11.40	4.10

For surcharges, see Nos. 894, 973.

Turkish Attack on Mt. Zlee Dol A412

Designs: 4 l, Georgi Benkovski speaking to rebels. 9 l, Cherrywood cannon of 1876 and Russian cavalry, 1945. 20 l, Rebel, 1876 and partisan, 1944. 40 l, Benkovski and Dimitrov.

1951, May 3 *Perf. 10½*

Cream Paper

745	A412	1 l redsh brown	.45	.25
746	A412	4 l dark green	.50	.25
747	A412	9 l violet brown	.75	.60
748	A412	20 l deep blue	1.10	1.00
749	A412	40 l dark red	1.50	1.25
		Nos. 745-749 (5)	4.30	3.35

75th anniv. of the "April" revolution.

Industrial Types of 1950

1951 *Perf. 13*

750	A369	1 l violet	.25	.25
a.		Perf 10¾	35.00	17.50
b.		Perf 11½	25.00	11.00
751	A370	2 l dk brown	.35	.35
a.		Perf 10¾	42.50	11.00
b.		Perf 11½	17.50	7.00
c.		Perf 11½x10¾	40.00	18.00
751A	A372	4 l dk yel grn	.55	.25
b.		Perf 10¾	27.50	8.50
c.		Perf 11½	35.00	11.00
		Nos. 750-751A (3)	1.15	.85

Demeter Blagoev Addressing 1891 Congress at Busludja — A413

1951 **Photo.** *Perf. 11*

752	A413	1 l purple	.40	.25
753	A413	4 l dark green	.70	.25
754	A413	9 l deep claret	1.40	.60
		Nos. 752-754 (3)	2.50	1.10

60th anniversary of the first Congress of the Bulgarian Social-Democratic Party.

See Nos. 1174-1176.

Day Nursery A414

Designs: 4 l, Model building construction. 9 l, Playground. 20 l, Children's town.

1951, Oct. 10 **Unwmk.**

755	A414	1 l brown	.25	.25
756	A414	4 l deep plum	.45	.25
757	A414	9 l blue green	1.00	.40
758	A414	20 l deep blue	2.00	1.25
		Nos. 755-758 (4)	3.70	2.15

Children's Day, Sept. 25, 1951.

Order of Labor

A415 A416

1952, Feb. 1 *Perf. 13*

Reverse of Medal

759	A415	1 l red brown	.25	.25
760	A415	4 l blue green	.25	.25
761	A415	9 l dark blue	.45	.25

Obverse of Medal

762	A416	1 l carmine	.25	.25
763	A416	4 l green	.25	.25
764	A416	9 l purple	.45	.25
		Nos. 759-764 (6)	1.90	1.50

No. 764 has numeral at lower left and different background.

Workers and Symbols of Industry — A417

Design: 4 l, Flags, Dimitrov, Chervenkov.

Inscribed: "16 XII 1951"

1951, Dec. 29 *Perf. 11*

765	A417	1 l olive black	.25	.25
766	A417	4 l chocolate	.35	.25

Third Congress of Bulgarian General Workers' Professional Union.

Dimitrov and Chemical Works — A418

George Dimitrov and V. Chervenkov — A419

Portrait: 80s, Dimitrov.

Unwmk.

1952, June 18 **Photo.** *Perf. 11*

767	A418	16s brown	.60	.35
768	A419	44s brown carmine	1.00	.55
769	A418	80s brt blue	1.75	1.00
		Nos. 767-769 (3)	3.35	1.90

70th anniv. of the birth of George Dimitrov.

Vassil Kolarov Dam — A420

1952, May 16 *Perf. 13*

770	A420	4s dark green	.25	.25
771	A420	12s purple	.25	.25
772	A420	16s red brown	.25	.25
773	A420	44s rose brown	.65	.25
774	A420	80s brt blue	2.75	.35
		Nos. 770-774 (5)	4.15	1.35

No. 774 is inscribed in Latin characters.

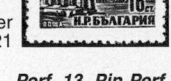

Republika Power Station — A421

1952, June 30 *Perf. 13, Pin Perf.*

775	A421	16s dark brown	.40	.25
a.		Perf 10¾	25.00	10.00
b.		Perf 11½	32.50	20.00
776	A421	44s magenta	1.25	.25
a.		Perf 10¾	25.00	10.00
b.		Perf 11½	32.50	20.00

Nikolai I. Vapzarov A422

Designs: Various portraits.

1952, July 23 *Perf. 10½*

777	A422	16s rose brown	.25	.25
778	A422	44s dk red brn	1.75	.25
779	A422	80s dk olive brn	3.75	1.25
		Nos. 777-779 (3)	5.75	1.75

10th anniversary of the death of Nikolai I. Vapzarov, poet and revolutionary.

Dimitrov and Youth Conference — A423

16s, Resistance movement incident. 44s, Frontier guards & industrial scene. 80s, George Dimitrov & young workers.

1952, Sept. 1 *Perf. 11x11½*

780	A423	2s brown carmine	.25	.25
781	A423	16s purple	.25	.25
782	A423	44s dark green	.85	.55
783	A423	80s dark brown	1.75	1.10
		Nos. 780-783 (4)	3.10	2.15

40th anniv. of the founding conference of the Union of Social Democratic Youth.

Assault on the Winter Palace — A424

Designs: 8s, Volga-Don Canal. 16s, Symbols of world peace. 44s, Lenin and Stalin. 80s, Himlay hydroelectric station.

Perf. 11½

1952, Nov. 6 **Unwmk.** **Photo.**

Dated: "1917-1952"

784	A424	4s red brown	.35	.25
785	A424	8s dark green	.35	.25
786	A424	16s dark blue	1.00	.35
787	A424	44s brown	1.00	.35
788	A424	80s olive brown	2.00	1.60
		Nos. 784-788 (5)	4.70	2.80

35th anniv. of the Russian revolution.

Vassil Levski — A425

Design: 44s, Levski and comrades.

1953, Feb. 19 *Perf. 11*

Cream Paper

789	A425	16s brown	.25	.25
790	A425	44s brown blk	.45	.25

80th anniv. of the death of Levski, patriot.

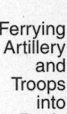

Ferrying Artillery and Troops into Battle A426

Soldier — A427

Designs: 44s, Victorious soldiers. 80s, Soldier welcomed. 1 l, Monuments.

1953, Mar. 3 *Perf. 10½*

791	A426	8s Prus green	.25	.25
792	A427	16s dp brown	.30	.25
793	A426	44s dk slate grn	.70	.25
794	A426	80s dull red brn	2.00	1.00
795	A426	1 l black	2.25	2.00
		Nos. 791-795 (5)	5.50	3.75

Bulgaria's independence from Turkey, 75th anniv.

Mother and Children — A428

1953, Mar. 9

796	A428	16s slate green	.25	.25
797	A428	16s bright blue	.25	.25

Women's Day.

Woodcarvings at Rila Monastery

A429 A430

Designs: 12s, 16s, 28s, Woodcarvings, Rila Monastery. 44s, Carved Ceilings, Trnovo. 80s, 1 l, 4 l, Carvings, Pasardjik.

1953 **Unwmk.** **Photo.** *Perf. 13*

798	A429	2s gray brown	.25	.25
799	A430	8s dk slate grn	.25	.25
800	A430	12s brown	.25	.25
801	A430	16s rose lake	.50	.25
802	A429	28s dk olive grn	.70	.25
803	A430	44s dk brown	1.00	.25
804	A430	80s ultra	1.20	.25
805	A430	1 l violet blue	2.50	.40
806	A430	4 l rose lake	3.25	1.50
		Nos. 798-806 (9)	9.90	3.65

For surcharge see No. 1204.

Karl Marx — A431

"Das Kapital" — A432

1953, Apr. 30 *Perf. 10½*

807 A431	16s bright blue	.35	.25
808 A432	44s deep brown	.70	.50

70th anniversary of the death of Karl Marx.

Labor Day Parade — A433

1953, Apr. 30 *Perf. 13*

809 A433	16s brown red	.35	.35

Labor Day, May 1, 1953.

Joseph V. Stalin — A434

1953, May 23 *Perf. 13x13½*

810 A434	16s dark gray	.65	.25
811 A434	16s dark brown	.35	.25

Death of Joseph V. Stalin, Mar. 5, 1953.

Georgi Delchev — A435

Battle Scene — A436

Peasants Attacking Turkish Troops A437

1953, Aug. 8 *Perf. 13*

812 A435	16s dark brown	.25	.25
813 A436	44s purple	.55	.35
814 A437	1 l deep claret	.80	.60
	Nos. 812-814 (3)	1.60	1.20

50th anniv. of the Ilinden Revolt (Nos. 812, 814) and the Preobrazhene Revolt (No. 813).

Soldier and Rebels A438

44s, Soldier guarding industrial construction.

1953, Sept. 18

815 A438	16s deep claret	.35	.25
816 A438	44s greenish blue	.75	.25

Army Day.

George Dimitrov and Vassil Kolarov A439

Designs: 16s, Citizens in revolt. 44s, Attack.

1953, Sept. 22

817 A439	8s olive gray	.25	.25
818 A439	16s dk red brn	.30	.25
819 A439	44s cerise	1.00	.25
	Nos. 817-819 (3)	1.55	.75

September Revolution, 30th anniversary.

Demeter Blagoev — A440

Portraits: 44s, G. Dimitrov and D. Blagoev.

1953, Sept. 21

820 A440	16s brown	.35	.25
821 A440	44s red brown	1.00	.25

50th anniversary of the formation of the Social Democratic Party.

Railway Viaduct A441

Pouring Molten Metal — A442

Designs: 16s, Welder and storage tanks. 80s, Harvesting machine.

1953, Oct. 17

826 A441	8s brt blue	.25	.25
827 A441	16s grnsh blk	.25	.25
828 A442	44s brown red	.70	.25
829 A441	80s orange	.70	.50
	Nos. 826-829 (4)	1.90	1.25

Month of Bulgarian-Russian friendship.

Belladonna — A443

Medicinal Flowers: 4s, Jimson weed. 8s, Sage. 12s, Dog rose. 16s, Gentian. 20s, Poppy. 28s, Peppermint. 40s, Bear grass. 44s, Coltsfoot. 80s, Cowslip. 1 l, Dandelion. 2 l, Foxglove.

1953 Unwmk. Photo. *Perf. 13*
White or Cream Paper

830 A443	2s dull blue	.25	.25
831 A443	4s brown org	.25	.25
832 A443	8s blue grn	.25	.25
833 A443	12s brown org	.25	.25
834 A443	12s blue grn	.25	.25
835 A443	16s violet blue	.35	.25
836 A443	16s dp red brn	.35	.25
837 A443	20s car rose	.70	.25
838 A443	28s dk gray grn	.55	.25
839 A443	40s dark blue	.35	.35
840 A443	44s brown	1.00	.45
841 A443	80s yellow brn	1.40	.80
842 A443	1 l henna brn	2.75	1.40
843 A443	2 l purple	5.50	2.75
a.	Souvenir sheet	40.00	40.00
	Nos. 830-843 (14)	14.20	8.00

No. 843a contains 12 stamps, one of each denomination above, printed in dark green. Size: 161x172mm. Sold for 6 leva.

Nos. 830-843 exist perf 10¾, 10¾x11½, 12¾, 12¾x10¾, 13¼x12½ and 13¼.

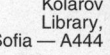

Kolarov Library, Sofia — A444

1953, Dec. 16

854 A444	44s brown	.45	.25

75th anniversary of the founding of the Kolarov Library, Sofia.

Singer and Accordionist A445

1953, Dec. 26

855 A445	16s shown	.25	.25
856 A445	44s Dancers	.50	.30

Lenin and Stalin — A446

Designs: 44s, Lenin statue. 80s, Lenin mausoleum, Moscow. 1 l, Lenin.

1954, Mar. 13 **Cream Paper**

857 A446	16s brown	.25	.25
858 A446	44s rose brown	.50	.25
859 A446	80s blue	.70	.30
860 A446	1 l dp olive grn	1.40	1.00
	Nos. 857-860 (4)	2.85	1.80

30th anniversary of the death of Lenin.

Demeter Blagoev and Followers A447

Design: 44s, Blagoev at desk.

1954, Apr. 28 **Cream Paper**

861 A447	16s dp red brn	.25	.25
862 A447	44s black brn	.50	.25

30th anniv. of the death of Demeter Blagoev.

George Dimitrov — A448

Dimitrov and Refinery A449

1954, June 11

863 A448	44s lake, *cream*	.35	.25
864 A449	80s brown, *cream*	.75	.50

5th anniv. of the death of George Dimitrov.

Train Leaving Tunnel — A450

1954, July 30

865 A450	44s dk grn, *cream*	1.00	.50
866 A450	44s blk brn, *cream*	1.00	.50

Day of the Railroads, Aug. 1, 1954.

Miner at Work — A451

1954, Aug. 19

867 A451	44s grnsh blk, *cream*	.35	.25

Miners' Day.

Academy of Science A452

1954, Oct. 27

868 A452	80s black, *cream*	1.00	.55

85th anniversary of the foundation of the Bulgarian Academy of Science.

Horsemanship — A454

16s, 44s, 2 l, vert.

1954, Dec. 21

869 A454	16s Gymnastics	1.00	.30
870 A454	44s Wrestling	1.20	.65
871 A454	80s shown	2.50	1.25
872 A454	2 l Skiing	4.00	2.75
	Nos. 869-872 (4)	8.70	4.95

Welcoming Liberators A455

Soldier's Return — A456

28s, Refinery. 44s, Dimitrov & Workers. 80s, Girl & boy. 1 l, George Dimitrov.

1954, Oct. 4 **Cream Paper**

873 A455	12s brown car	.25	.25
874 A456	16s dp carmine	.25	.25
875 A455	28s indigo	.25	.25
876 A455	44s redsh brn	.40	.25
877 A456	80s deep blue	.90	.35
878 A456	1 l dark green	1.00	.45
	Nos. 873-878 (6)	3.05	1.80

10th anniversary of Bulgaria's liberation.

Recreation at Workers' Rest Home — A457

Metal Worker and Furnace — A458

80s, Dimitrov, Blagoev, Kirkov.

Unwmk.

1954, Dec. 28 Photo. *Perf. 13*

Cream Paper

879 A457 16s dark green .25 .25
880 A458 44s brown orange .35 .25
881 A457 80s dp violet blue .85 .25
Nos. 879-881 (3) 1.45 .75

50th anniversary of Bulgaria's trade union movement.

Geese — A459

Designs: 4s, Chickens. 12s, Hogs. 16s, Sheep. 28s, Telephone building. 44s, Communist party headquarters. 80s, Apartment buildings. 1 l, St. Kiradgieff Mills.

1955-56

882 A459 2s dk blue grn .25 .25
883 A459 4s olive green .25 .25
884 A459 12s dk red brn .45 .25
885 A459 16s brown orange .75 .25
886 A459 28s violet blue .45 .25
887 A459 44s lil red, *cream* 3.50 .75
a. 44s brown red 6.75 2.50
888 A459 80s dk red brown 1.10 .35
889 A459 1 l dk blue green 1.50 .75
Nos. 882-889 (8) 8.25 3.10

Issued: No. 887, 4/20/56; others, 2/19/55.
Nos. 882-889 exist perf 10¾, 11½, 10¾x13, 12¾, 13½ and 13x11½.

Textile Worker A460

Mother and Child — A461

Design: 16s, Woman feeding calf.

1955, Mar. 5

890 A460 12s dark brown .25 .25
891 A460 16s dark green .25 .25
892 A461 44s dk car rose .85 .25
893 A461 44s blue .85 .25
Nos. 890-893 (4) 2.20 1.00

Women's Day, Mar. 8, 1955.

No. 744 Surcharged in Blue

Type I

Type II

Two overprint types: I, overprint in blue-black, "16" 4mm high, thin font; II, overprint in blue, "16" 5mm high, thick font.

1955, Mar. 8 *Perf. 13*

894 A410 16s on 4 l red brown, Type I 1.50 .35
a. Type II 1.50 .35

May Day Demonstration of Workers — A462

Design: 44s, Three workers and globe.

1955, Apr. 23 Photo.

895 A462 16s car rose .25 .25
896 A462 44s blue .50 .25

Labor Day, May 1, 1955.

Sts. Cyril and Methodius A463

Designs: 8s, Paisii Hilendarski. 16s, Nicolas Karastoyanov's printing press. 28s, Christo Botev. 44s, Ivan Vazov. 80s, Demeter Blagoev and socialist papers. 2 l, Blagoev printing plant, Sofia.

1955, May 21 Cream Paper

897 A463 4s deep blue .25 .25
898 A463 8s olive .25 .25
899 A463 16s black .25 .25
900 A463 28s henna brn .25 .25
901 A463 44s brown .60 .25
902 A463 80s rose red 1.10 .25
903 A463 2 l black 3.00 .95
Nos. 897-903 (7) 5.70 2.45

Creation of the Cyrillic alphabet, 1100th anniv. Latin lettering at bottom on Nos. 901-903.

Sergei Rumyantzev — A464

16s, Christo Jassenov. 44s, Geo Milev.

1955, June 30 Unwmk. *Perf. 13*

Cream Paper

904 A464 12s orange brn .30 .25
905 A464 16s lt brown .30 .25
906 A464 44s grnsh blk 1.10 .70
Nos. 904-906 (3) 1.70 1.20

30th anniv. of the deaths of Sergei Rumyanchev, Christo Jassenov and Geo Milev. Latin lettering at bottom of No. 906.

Mother and Children — A465

1955, July 30

907 A465 44s brn car, *cream* .75 .25

World Congress of Mothers in Lausanne, 1955.

Young People of Three Races — A466

1955, July 30

908 A466 44s blue, *cream* .75 .25

5th World Festival of Youth in Warsaw, July 31-Aug. 14.

Friedrich Engels and Book — A467

1955, July 30

909 A467 44s brown .75 .25

60th anniv. of the death of Friedrich Engels.

Entrance to Fair, 1892 — A468

Statuary Group at Fair, 1955 — A469

Designs: 44s, "Fruit of our Land." 80s, Woman holding Fair emblem.

1955, Aug. 31 Cream Paper

910 A468 4s deep brown .25 .25
911 A469 16s dk car rose .25 .25
912 A468 44s olive blk .35 .25
913 A469 80s deep blue .90 .30
Nos. 910-913 (4) 1.75 1.05

16th International Plovdiv Fair. Latin lettering on Nos. 912-913.

Friedrich von Schiller — A470

44s, Adam Mickiewicz. 60s, Hans Christian Andersen. 80s, Baron de Montesquieu. 1 l, Miguel de Cervantes. 2 l, Walt Whitman.

1955, Oct. 31 Cream Paper

914 A470 16s brown .40 .25
915 A470 44s brown red .80 .25
916 A470 60s Prus blue 1.00 .25
917 A470 80s black 1.40 .45
918 A470 1 l rose violet 2.75 1.10
919 A470 2 l olive green 3.50 2.50
Nos. 914-919 (6) 9.85 4.80

Various anniversaries of famous writers. Nos. 918 and 919 are issued in sheets alternating with labels without franking value. The labels show title pages for Leaves of Grass and Don Quixote in English and Spanish, respectively. Latin lettering on Nos. 915-919.

A471

A472

A473

2s, Karl Marx Industrial Plant. 4s, Alekandr Stamboliski Dam. 16s, Bridge over Danube. 44s, Friendship Monument. 80s, I. V. Michurin. 1 l, Vladimir V. Mayakovsky.

1955, Dec. 1 Unwmk.

920 A471 2s slate blk .25 .25
921 A471 4s deep blue .25 .25
922 A471 16s dk blue grn .25 .25
923 A472 44s red brown .25 .25
924 A473 80s dark green .85 .25
925 A473 1 l gray blk .90 .40
Nos. 920-925 (6) 2.75 1.65

Russian-Bulgarian friendship.

Library Seal — A474

Krusto Pishurka A475

Portrait: 44s, Bacho Kiro.

1956, Feb. 10 *Perf. 11x10½*

926 A474 12s car lake, *cream* .25 .25
927 A475 16s dp brn, *cream* .25 .25
928 A475 44s slate blk, *cream* .85 .25
Nos. 926-928 (3) 1.35 .75

100th anniversary of the National Library. Latin lettering at bottom of No. 928.

Canceled to Order

Beginning about 1956, some issues were sold in sheets canceled to order. Values in second column when much less than unused are for "CTO" examples. Postally used stamps are valued at slightly less than, or the same as, unused.

Quinces — A476

8s, Pears. 16s, Apples. 44s, Grapes.

1956 Photo. *Perf. 13*

929 A476 4s carmine 1.60 .25
930 A476 8s blue green .75 .25
931 A476 16s lilac rose 1.25 .25
932 A476 44s deep violet 1.50 .45
Nos. 929-932 (4) 5.10 1.20

Latin lettering on No. 932. See Nos. 964-967. For surcharge see No. 1364.

Cherrywood Cannon A477

1956, Apr. 28 *Perf. 11x10½*

933 A477 16s shown .35 .25
934 A477 44s Cavalry attack .35 .25

April Uprising against Turkish rule, 80th anniv.

Demeter Blagoev (1856-1924), Writer, Birthplace A478

1956, May 30 *Perf. 11*

935 A478 44s Prus blue 1.00 .50

Cherries — A479

1956 **Unwmk.** *Perf. 13*

936 A479 2s shown .25 .25
937 A479 12s Plums .25 .25
938 A479 28s Peaches .25 .25
939 A479 80s Strawberries 1.00 .25
Nos. 936-939 (4) 1.75 1.00

Latin lettering on No. 939.

Gymnastics A480

Pole Vaulting A481

Designs: 12s, Discus throw. 44s, Soccer, 80s, Basketball. 1 l, Boxing.

Perf. 11x10½, 10½x11

1956, Aug. 29

940 A480 4s brt ultra .40 .25
941 A480 12s brick red .50 .25
942 A481 16s yellow brn .55 .25
943 A481 44s dark green 1.00 .45
944 A480 80s dark red brn 1.60 .85
945 A481 1 l deep magenta 2.25 1.00
Nos. 940-945 (6) 6.30 3.05

Latin lettering on Nos. 943-945.
16th Olympic Games at Melbourne, Nov. 22-Dec. 8, 1956.

Tobacco, Rose and Distillery — A482

1956, Sept. 1 *Perf. 13*

946 A482 44s deep carmine 1.00 .40
947 A482 44s olive green 1.00 .40

17th International Plovdiv Fair.

People's Theater A483

Design: 44s, Dobri Woinikoff and Sawa Dobroplodni, dramatists.

1956, Nov. 16 **Unwmk.**

948 A483 16s dull red brown .25 .25
949 A483 44s dark blue green .50 .25

Bulgarian Theater centenary.

Benjamin Franklin — A484

Portraits: 20s, Rembrandt. 40s, Mozart. 44s, Heinrich Heine. 60s, Shaw. 80s, Dostoevski. 1 l, Ibsen. 2 l, Pierre Curie.

1956, Dec. 29

950 A484 16s dark olive grn .25 .25
951 A484 20s brown .25 .25
952 A484 40s dark car rose .25 .25
953 A484 44s dark violet brn .60 .25
954 A484 60s dark slate .75 .25
955 A484 80s dark brown 1.10 .25
956 A484 1 l bluish grn 1.75 .75
957 A484 2 l Prus green 4.00 1.25
Nos. 950-957 (8) 8.95 3.50

Great personalities of the world.

Cyclists, Palms and Pyramids — A485

1957, Mar. 6 **Photo.** *Perf. 10½*

958 A485 80s henna brown 1.00 .50
959 A485 80s Prus green 1.00 .50

Fourth Egyptian bicycle race.

Woman Technician A486

Designs: 16s, Woman and children. 44s, Woman feeding chickens.

1957, Mar. 8

960 A486 12s deep blue .25 .25
961 A486 16s henna brown .25 .25
962 A486 44s slate green .45 .25
Nos. 960-962 (3) .95 .75

Women's Day. Latin lettering on 44s.

"New Times" Review — A487

1957, Mar. 8 **Unwmk.**

963 A487 16s deep carmine .35 .35

60th anniversary of the founding of the "New Times" review.

Fruit Type of 1956

4s, Quinces. 8s, Pears. 16s, Apples. 44s, Grapes.

1957 **Photo.** *Perf. 13*

964 A476 4s yellow green .25 .25
965 A476 8s brown orange .25 .25
966 A476 16s rose red .25 .25
967 A476 44s orange yellow .90 .25
Nos. 964-967 (4) 1.65 1.00

Latin lettering on No. 967. For surcharge see No. 1364.

Sts. Cyril and Methodius — A488

1957, May 22 *Perf. 11*

968 A488 44s olive grn & buff .90 .25

Centenary of the first public veneration of Sts. Cyril and Methodius, inventors of the Cyrillic alphabet.

Basketball A489

1957, June 20 **Photo.** *Perf. 10½x11*

969 A489 44s dark green 1.50 .50

10th European Basketball Championship at Sofia.

Dancer and Spasski Tower, Moscow — A490

1957, July 18 *Perf. 13*

970 A490 44s blue .60 .25

Sixth World Youth Festival in Moscow.

George Dimitrov (1882-1949) — A491

1957, July 18

971 A491 44s deep carmine 1.10 .25

Vassil Levski — A492

1957, July 18 *Perf. 11*

972 A492 44s grnsh black .75 .25

120th anniversary of the birth of Vassil Levski, patriot and national hero.

No. 742 Surcharged in Carmine

1957 **Unwmk.** *Perf. 13*

973 A408 16s on 1 l purple .25 .25

Trnovo and Lazarus L. Zamenhof A493

1957, July 27

974 A493 44s slate green 1.00 .25

50th anniv. of the Bulgarian Esperanto Society and the 70th anniv. of Esperanto.
For surcharge see No. 1235.

Bulgarian Veteran of 1877 War and Russian Soldier — A494

Design: 44s, Battle of Shipka Pass.

1957, Aug. 13

975 A494 16s dk blue grn .25 .25
976 A494 44s brown .50 .25

80th anniversary of Bulgaria's liberation from the Turks. Latin lettering on No. 976.

Woman Planting Tree — A495

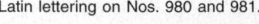

Red Deer in Forest — A496

16s, Dam, lake and forest. 44s, Plane over forest. 80s, Fields on edge of forest.

1957, Sept. 16 **Photo.** *Perf. 13*

977 A495 2s deep green .25 .25
978 A496 12s dark brown .25 .25
979 A496 16s Prus blue .25 .25
980 A496 44s Prus green .50 .25
981 A496 80s yellow green .85 .25
Nos. 977-981 (5) 2.10 1.25

Latin lettering on Nos. 980 and 981.

Lenin — A497

Designs: 16s, Cruiser "Aurora." 44s, Dove over map of communist area. 60s, Revolutionaries and banners. 80s, Chemical plant.

1957, Oct. 29 *Perf. 11*

982 A497 12s chocolate .85 .25
983 A497 16s Prus green 1.75 .55
984 A497 44s deep blue 2.40 1.10

985 A497 60s dk car rose 4.00 1.50
986 A497 80s dark green 6.25 2.00
Nos. 982-986 (5) 15.25 5.40

40th anniv. of the Communist Revolution. Latin lettering on Nos. 984-985.

Globes A498

1957, Oct. 4 ***Perf. 13***
987 A498 44s Prus blue .60 .25

4th Intl. Trade Union Cong., Leipzig, 10/4-15.

Vassil Kolarov Hotel A499

Bulgarian Health Resorts: 4s, Skis and Pirin Mountains. 8s, Old house at Koprivspitsa. 12s, Rest home at Velingrad. 44s, Momin-Prochod Hotel. 60s, Nesebr Hotel, shoreline and peninsula. 80s, Varna beach scene. 1 l, Hotel at Varna.

1958 **Photo.** ***Perf. 13***
988 A499 4s blue .25 .25
989 A499 8s orange brn .25 .25
990 A499 12s dk green .25 .25
991 A499 16s green .25 .25
992 A499 44s dk blue grn .25 .25
993 A499 60s deep blue .25 .25
994 A499 80s fawn .60 .25
995 A499 1 l dk red brn .80 .25
Nos. 988-995 (8) 2.90 2.00

Latin lettering on 44s, 60s, 80s, and 1 l.
Issue dates: Nos. 991-994, 1/20; others, 7/5.
For surcharges see Nos. 1200, 1436.

Mikhail I. Glinka — A500

Portraits: 16s, Jan A. Komensky (Comenius). 40s, Carl von Linné. 44s, William Blake. 60s, Carlo Goldoni. 80s, Auguste Comte.

1957, Dec. 30
996 A500 12s dark brown .50 .25
997 A500 16s dark green .50 .25
998 A500 40s Prus blue 1.25 .30
999 A500 44s maroon 1.25 .35
1000 A500 60s orange brown 1.40 .50
1001 A500 80s deep plum 2.00 2.00
Nos. 996-1001 (6) 6.90 3.65

Famous men of other countries. Latin lettering on Nos. 999-1001.

Young Couple, Flag, Dimitrov — A501

1957, Dec. 28 ***Perf. 11***
1002 A501 16s carmine rose .25 .25

10th anniversary of Dimitrov's Union of the People's Youth.

People's Front Salute — A502

1957, Dec. 28
1003 A502 16s dk violet brn .25 .25

15th anniversary of the People's Front.

Hare A503

12s, Red deer (doe), vert. 16s, Red deer (stag). 44s, Chamois. 80s, Brown bear. 1 l, Wild boar.

Perf. 10½
1958, Apr. 5 **Unwmk.** **Photo.**
1004 A503 2s lt & dk ol grn .45 .25
1005 A503 12s sl grn & red brn .65 .25
1006 A503 16s bluish grn & dk red brn 1.00 .30
1007 A503 44s blue & brown 1.20 .55
1008 A503 80s bis & dk brn 1.40 .50
1009 A503 1 l stl bl & dk brn 1.75 1.50
Nos. 1004-1009 (6) 6.45 3.35

Value, imperf. set $11.

Marx and Lenin A504

Designs: 16s, Marchers and flags. 44s, Lenin blast furnaces.

1958, July 2 ***Perf. 11***
1010 A504 12s dark brown .30 .25
1011 A504 16s dark carmine .50 .25
1012 A504 44s dark blue 1.00 .65
Nos. 1010-1012 (3) 1.80 1.15

Bulgarian Communist Party, 7th Congress.

Wrestlers — A505

1958, June 20 ***Perf. 10½***
1013 A505 60s dk carmine rose 1.40 1.00
1014 A505 80s deep brown 1.60 1.40

World Wrestling Championship, Sofia.

Chessmen and Globe A506

Perf. 10½
1958, July 18 **Unwmk.** **Photo.**
1015 A506 80s grn & yel grn 9.00 7.50
a. Horiz. pair, imperf. btwn. 80.00

5th World Students' Chess Games, Varna.

Conference Emblem A507

1958, Sept. 24
1016 A507 44s blue .65 .25

World Trade Union Conference of Working Youth, Prague, July 14-20.

Swimmer A508

1958 Students' Games: 28s, Dancer, vert. 44s, Volleyball, vert.

1958, Sept. 19 ***Perf. 11x10½***
1017 A508 16s bright blue .25 .25
1018 A508 28s brown orange .40 .25
1019 A508 44s bright green .65 .25
Nos. 1017-1019 (3) 1.30 .75

Onions — A509

Vegetables: 12s, Garlic. 16s, Peppers. 44s, Tomatoes. 80s, Cucumbers. 1 l, Eggplant.

1958, Sept. 20 ***Perf. 13***
1020 A509 2s orange brown .25 .25
1021 A509 12s Prus blue .25 .25
1022 A509 16s dark green .25 .25
1023 A509 44s deep carmine .30 .25
1024 A509 80s deep green .80 .25
1025 A509 1 l brt purple 1.10 .30
Nos. 1020-1025 (6) 2.95 1.55

Value, imperf. set $7.
See No. 1072. For surcharge see No. 1201.

Plovdiv Fair Building A510

1958, Sept. 14 **Unwmk.** ***Perf. 11***
1026 A510 44s deep carmine .65 .25

18th International Plovdiv Fair.

Attack — A511

44s, Fighter dragging wounded man.

1958, Sept. 23 **Photo.** ***Perf. 11***
1027 A511 16s orange ver .25 .25
1028 A511 44s lake .60 .25

35th anniv. of the September Revolution.

Emblem, Brussels Fair — A512

1958, Oct. 13 ***Perf. 11***
1029 A512 1 l blk & brt blue 7.50 7.50

Brussels World's Fair, Apr. 17-Oct. 19.
Exists imperf. Value, $55.

Runner at Finish Line — A513

Woman Throwing Javelin A514

60s, High jumper. 80s, Hurdler. 4 l, Shot putter.

1958, Nov. 30
1030 A513 16s red brn, *pnksh* .60 .30
1031 A514 44s olive, *yelsh* .65 .40
1032 A514 60s dk bl, *bluish* 1.10 .50
1033 A514 80s dp grn, *grnsh* 1.40 .65
1034 A513 4 l dp rose cl, *pnksh* 8.00 5.50
Nos. 1030-1034 (5) 11.75 7.35

1958 Balkan Games.
Latin lettering on Nos. 1032-1033.

Christo Smirnenski A515

1958, Dec. 22
1035 A515 16s dark carmine .30 .25

Christo Smirnenski (1898-1923), poet.

Girls Harvesting — A516

Girl Tending Calves A517

16s, Boy & girl laborers. 40s, Boy pushing wheelbarrow. 44s, Headquarters building.

1958, Nov. 29 **Photo.**
1036 A516 8s dk olive green .25 .25
1037 A517 12s redsh brown .25 .25
1038 A516 16s violet brown .25 .25

1039	A517	40s Prus blue		.25	.25
1040	A516	44s deep carmine		.75	.25
		Nos. 1036-1040 (5)		1.75	1.25

4th Congress of Dimitrov's Union of People's Youth.

UNESCO Building, Paris
A518

1959, Mar. 28 Unwmk. *Perf. 11*

1041 A518 2 l dp red lilac, *cream* 2.25 1.50

Opening of UNESCO Headquarters, Paris, Nov. 3, 1958. Value imperf. $5.

Skier — A519

1959, Mar. 28 *Perf. 11*

1042 A519 1 l blue, *cream* 1.50 .75

Forty years of skiing in Bulgaria.

Soccer Players — A520

1959, Mar. 25

1043 A520 2 l chestnut, *cream* 2.50 1.50

1959 European Youth Soccer Championship.

Russian Soldiers Installing Telegraph Wires — A521

First Bulgarian Postal Coach
A522

Designs: 60s, Stamp of 1879. 80s, First Bulgarian automobile. 1 l, Television tower. 2 l, Strike of railroad and postal workers, 1919.

1959, May 4

1044	A521	12s dk grn & cit	.25	.25
1045	A522	16s deep plum	.35	.25
1046	A521	60s dk brn & yel	.65	.35
1047	A522	80s hn brn & sal	.65	.35
1048	A521	1 l blue	1.60	.40
1049	A522	2 l dk red brown	3.25	1.50
		Nos. 1044-1049 (6)	6.75	3.10

80th anniv. of the Bulgarian post. Latin lettering on Nos. 1046-1049.

Two imperf. souvenir sheets exist with olive borders and inscriptions. One contains one copy of No. 1046 in black & ocher, and measures 92x121mm. The other sheet contains one copy each of Nos. 1044-1045 and 1047-1048 in changed colors: 12s, olive green & ocher; 16s, deep claret & ocher; 80s, dark red & ocher; 1 l, olive & ocher. Each sheet sold for 5 leva. Value, each $45.

Great Tits
A523

Birds: 8s, Hoopoe. 16s, Great spotted woodpecker, vert. 45s, Gray partridge, vert. 60s, Rock partridge. 80s, European cuckoo.

1959, June 30 Photo.

1050	A523	2s olive & sl grn	.25	.25
1051	A523	8s dp orange & blk	.55	.25
1052	A523	16s chestnut & dk brn	.55	.25
1053	A523	45s brown & blk	1.25	.60
1054	A523	60s dp blue & gray	2.25	.85
1055	A523	80s dp bl grn & gray	3.25	1.50
		Nos. 1050-1055 (6)	8.10	3.70

Bagpiper — A524

12s, Acrobats. 16s, Girls exercising with hoops. 20s, Male dancers. 80s, Ballet dancers. 1 l, Ceramic pitcher. 16s, 20s, 80s are horiz.

1959, Aug. 29 Unwmk. *Perf. 11*
Surface-colored Paper

1056	A524	4s dk olive	.25	.25
1057	A524	12s scarlet	.25	.25
1058	A524	16s maroon	.25	.25
1059	A524	20s dk blue	.35	.25
1060	A524	80s brt green	1.10	.45
1061	A524	1 l brown org	1.10	.70
		Nos. 1056-1061 (6)	3.30	2.15

7th International Youth Festival, Vienna. Latin inscriptions on Nos. 1060-1061.

Partisans in Truck
A525

Designs: 16s, Partisans and soldiers shaking hands. 45s, Steel mill. 60s, Tanks. 80s, Harvester. 1.25 l, Children with flag, vert.

1959, Sept. 8

1062	A525	12s red & Prus grn	.25	.25
1063	A525	16s red & dk pur	.25	.25
1064	A525	45s red & int bl	.25	.25
1065	A525	60s red & ol grn	.25	.25
1066	A525	80s red & brn	.60	.25
1067	A525	1.25 l red & dp brn	1.20	.50
		Nos. 1062-1067 (6)	2.80	1.75

15th anniversary of Bulgarian liberation.

Soccer
A526

1959, Oct. 10 Unwmk. *Perf. 11*

1068 A526 1.25 l dp green, *yel* 5.25 5.25

50 years of Bulgarian soccer.
Stamp exists imperf in changed colors. Value $15 unused or used.

Batak Defenders
A527

1959, Aug. 8

1069 A527 16s deep claret .35 .25

300th anniv. of the settlement of Batak.

Post Horn and Letter — A528

Design: 1.25 l, Dove and letter.

1959, Nov. 23

1070	A528	45s emerald & blk	.45	.25
1071	A528	1.25 l lt blue, red & blk	.85	.25

Intl. Letter Writing Week Oct. 5-11.

Type of 1958 Surcharged in Dark Blue

Design: Tomatoes.

1959 Photo. *Perf. 13*

1072 A509 45s on 44s scarlet 1.00 .25

Bird-shaped Lyre — A529

1960, Feb. 23 Unwmk. *Perf. 10½*

1073	A529	80s shown	.65	.25
1074	A529	1.25 l Lyre	1.00	.25

50th anniv. of Bulgaria's State Opera.

N. I. Vapzarov — A530

1959, Dec. 14 *Perf. 11*

1075 A530 80s yel grn & red brn .65 .25

Vapzarov, poet and patriot, 50th birth anniv.

Parachute and Radio Tower — A531

1959, Dec. 3 Photo.

1076 A531 1.25 l dp grnsh bl & yel 2.25 1.10

3rd Cong. of Voluntary Participants in Defense.

Cotton Picker — A532

Harvester Combine
A533

Designs: 2s, Kindergarten. 4s, Woman doctor and child. 10s, Woman milking cow. 12s, Woman holding tobacco leaves. 15s, Woman working loom. 16s, Industrial plants, Dimitrovgrad. 25s, Rural electrification. 28s, Woman picking sunflowers. 40s, "Cold-well" hydroelectric dam. 45s, Miner. 60s, Foundry worker. 80s. Woman harvesting grapes. 1 l, Worker and peasant with cogwheel. 1.25 l, Industrial worker. 2 l, Party leader.

1959-61 Photo. *Perf. 13*

1077	A533	2s brn org ('60)	.25	.25
1077A	A532	4s gldn brn ('61)	.25	.25
1078	A532	5s dk green	.25	.25
1079	A533	10s red brn ('61)	.25	.25
1080	A532	12s red brown	.25	.25
1081	A532	15s red lil ('60)	.25	.25
1082	A533	16s dp vio ('60)	.25	.25
1083	A533	20s orange	.25	.25
1084	A532	25s brt blue ('60)	.25	.25
1085	A532	28s brt green	.25	.25
1086	A533	40s brt grnsh bl	.35	.25
1087	A532	45s choc ('60)	.25	.25
1088	A533	60s scarlet	.65	.25
1089	A532	80s olive ('60)	1.20	.25
1090	A532	1 l maroon	.65	.25
1090A	A533	1.25 l dull bl ('61)	2.00	.50
1091	A532	2 l dp car ('60)	1.25	.40
		Nos. 1077-1091 (17)	8.85	4.65

Early completion of the 5-year plan (in 1959).
For surcharges see Nos. 1192-1199, 1202-1203.

L. L. Zamenhof
A534

1959, Dec. 5 Unwmk. *Perf. 11*

1092 A534 1.25 l dk grn & yel grn 1.00 .65

Lazarus Ludwig Zamenhof (1859-1917), inventor of Esperanto.

Path of Lunik 3 — A535

1960, Mar. 28 *Perf. 11*

1093 A535 1.25 l Prus bl & brt yel 6.50 4.75

Flight of Lunik 3 around moon. Value, imperf. $9

Skier A536

1960, Apr. 15 **Litho.**
1094 A536 2 l ultra, blk & brn 1.00 1.00

8th Winter Olympics, Squaw Valley, CA, Feb. 18-29. Value, imperf. $2.75 unused or used.

Vela Blagoeva A537

Portraits: 28s, Anna Maimunkova. 45s, Vela Piskova. 60s, Rosa Luxemburg. 80s, Klara Zetkin. 1.25 l, N. K. Krupskaya.

1960, Apr. 27 **Photo.** ***Perf. 11***
1095 A537 16s rose & red brn .25 .25
1096 A537 28s citron & olive .25 .25
1097 A537 45s ol grn & sl grn .25 .25
1098 A537 60s lt bl & Prus bl .35 .25
1099 A537 80s red org & dp brn .55 .25
1100 A537 1.25 l dull yel & olive .70 .25
Nos. 1095-1100 (6) 2.35 1.50

International Women's Day, Mar. 8, 1960.

Lenin — A538

1960, May 12
1101 A538 16s shown 1.50 .45
1102 A538 45s Lenin sitting 2.75 1.00

90th anniversary of the birth of Lenin.

A539

1960, June 3 ***Perf. 11***
1103 A539 1.25 l yel & slate grn 1.40 .65

Seventh European Women's Basketball championships.

A541

1960, June 29 **Litho.**
1105 A541 16s Parachutist .35 .35
1106 A541 1.25 l Parachutes 2.25 .65

5th International Parachute Championships.

Yellow Gentian — A542

5s, Tulips. 25s, Turk's-cap lily. 45s, Rhododendron. 60s, Lady's-slipper. 80s, Violets.

1960, July 27 **Photo.** ***Perf. 11***
1107 A542 2s beige, grn & yel .25 .25
1108 A542 5s yel grn, grn & car rose .60 .25
1109 A542 25s pink, grn & org .75 .25
1110 A542 45s pale lil, grn & rose lil .75 .25
1111 A542 60s yel, grn & org 1.50 .25
1112 A542 80s gray, grn & vio bl 1.50 .85
Nos. 1107-1112 (6) 5.35 2.10

Soccer A543

12s, Wrestling. 16s, Weight lifting. 45s, Woman gymnast. 80s, Canoeing. 2 l, Runner.

1960, Aug. 29 **Unwmk.** ***Perf. 11***
Athletes' Figures in Pink
1113 A543 8s brown .25 .25
1114 A543 12s violet .25 .25
1115 A543 16s Prus blue .25 .25
1116 A543 45s deep plum .35 .25
1117 A543 80s blue .85 .25
1118 A543 2 l deep green 1.10 .60
Nos. 1113-1118 (6) 3.05 1.85

17th Olympic Games, Rome, 8/25-9/11. Value, set imperf. in changed colors, $8.50.

Globes — A544

Unwmk.
1960, Oct. 12 **Photo.** ***Perf. 11***
1125 A544 1.25 l blue & ultra .75 .25

15th anniversary of the World Federation of Trade Unions.

Alexander Popov A545

1960, Oct. 12
1126 A545 90s blue & blk 1.10 .25

Centenary of the birth of Alexander Popov, radio pioneer.

Bicyclists A546

1960, Sept. 22
1127 A546 1 l yel, red org & blk 1.50 .85

The 10th Tour of Bulgaria Bicycle Race.

Jaroslav Vésin A547

1960, Nov. 22 **Unwmk.** ***Perf. 11***
1128 A547 1 l brt citron & ol grn 3.50 1.10

Birth centenary of Jaroslav Vesin, painter.

UN Headquarters A548

1961, Jan. 14 **Photo.** ***Perf. 11***
1129 A548 1 l brown & yel 1.75 1.00
a. Souvenir sheet 12.00 12.00

15th anniv. of the UN. No. 1129 sold for 2 l. Value, imperf. $6.

No. 1129a sold for 2.50 l and contains one copy of No. 1129, imperf, in dark olive and pink.

Costume of Kyustendil — A549

Regional Costumes: 16s, Pleven. 28s, Sliven. 45s, Sofia. 60s, Rhodope. 80s, Karnobat.

1961, Jan. 28
1130 A549 12s sal, sl grn & yel .25 .25
1131 A549 16s pale lil, brn vio & buff .25 .25
1132 A549 28s pale grn, sl grn & rose .30 .25
1133 A549 45s blue & red .45 .25
1134 A549 60s grnsh bl, Prus bl & yel 1.00 .25
1135 A549 80s yel, sl grn & pink 1.00 .45
Nos. 1130-1135 (6) 3.25 1.70

Theodor Tiro (Fresco) A550

Designs: 60s, Boyana Church. 1.25 l, Duchess of Dessislava (fresco).

1961, Jan. 28 **Photo.**
1136 A550 60s yel grn, blk & grn .75 .35
1137 A550 80s yel, sl grn & org 1.10 .35
1138 A550 1.25 l yel grn, hn brn & buff 1.50 .75
Nos. 1136-1138 (3) 3.35 1.45

700th anniv. of murals in Boyana Church.

Clock Tower, Vratsa — A551

Wooden Jug — A552

Designs: 12s, Clock tower, Bansko. 20s, Anguchev House, Mogilitsa. 28s, Oslekov House, Koprivspitsa, horiz. 40s, Pasha's house. Melnik, horiz. 45s, Lion sculpture. 60s, Man on horseback, Madara. 80s, Fresco, Bratchkovo monastery. 1 l, Tsar Assen coin.

1961, Feb. 25 **Unwmk.** ***Perf. 11***
Denomination and Stars in Vermilion
1139 A551 8s olive grn .25 .25
1140 A551 12s lt violet .25 .25
1141 A552 16s dk red brn .25 .25
1142 A551 20s brt blue .25 .25
1143 A551 28s grnsh blue .25 .25
1144 A551 40s red brown .30 .25
1145 A552 45s olive gray .35 .25
1146 A552 60s slate .50 .25
1147 A552 80s dk olive gray .90 .25
1148 A552 1 l green .50 .25
Nos. 1139-1148 (10) 3.80 2.50

Capercaillie A553

Birds: 4s, Dalmatian pelican. 16s, Ring-necked pheasant. 80s, Great bustard. 1 l, Lammergeier. 2 l, Hazel hen.

1961, Mar. 31
1149 A553 2s blk, sal & Prus grn .25 .25
1150 A553 4s blk, yel grn & org .25 .25
1151 A553 16s brn, lt grn & org .35 .25
1152 A553 80s brn, bluish grn & yel 2.40 1.85
1153 A553 1 l blk, lt bl & yel 3.00 1.40
1154 A553 2 l brn, bl & yel 3.50 1.50
Nos. 1149-1154 (6) 9.75 5.50

Radio Tower and Winged Anchor A554

1961, Apr. 1 **Unwmk.** ***Perf. 11***
1155 A554 80s brt green & blk .75 .25

50th anniv. of the Transport Workers' Union.

T. G. Shevchenko A555

1961, Apr. 27
1156 A555 1 l olive & blk 4.75 3.50

Centenary of the death of Taras G. Shevchenko, Ukrainian poet.

Water Polo — A556

Designs: 5s, Tennis. 16s, Fencing. 45s, Throwing the discus. 1.25 l, Sports Palace. 2 l, Basketball. 5 l, Sports Palace, different view. 5s, 16s, 45s and 1.25 l, are horizontal.

1961, May 15 Black Inscriptions

1157 A556 4s lt ultra .25 .25
1158 A556 5s orange ver .25 .25
1159 A556 16s olive grn .25 .25
1160 A556 45s dull blue .40 .25
1161 A556 1.25 l yellow brn 1.50 .25
1162 A556 2 l lilac 1.50 .85
Nos. 1157-1162 (6) 4.15 2.10

Souvenir Sheet

Imperf

1163 A556 5 l yel grn, dl bl & yel 12.50 12.50

1961 World University Games, Sofia, Aug. 26-Sept. 3.

Value, Nos. 1157-1162 in changed colors, imperf. $7.50.

Monk Seal A557

Black Sea Fauna: 12s, Jellyfish. 16s, Dolphin. 45s, Black Sea sea horse, vert. 1 l, Starred sturgeon. 1.25 l, Thornback ray.

1961, June 19 ***Perf. 11***

1164 A557 2s green & blk .25 .25
1165 A557 12s Prus grn & pink .25 .25
1166 A557 16s ultra & vio bl .25 .25
1167 A557 45s lt blue & brn 1.00 .70
1168 A557 1 l yel grn & Prus grn 2.75 1.10
1169 A557 1.25 l lt vio bl & red brn 3.00 1.50
Nos. 1164-1169 (6) 7.50 4.05

Hikers — A558

Designs: 4s, "Sredetz" hostel, horiz. 16s, Tents. 1.25 l, Mountain climber.

1961, Aug. 25 Litho. ***Perf. 11***

1170 A558 4s yel grn, yel & blk .25 .25
1171 A558 12s lt bl, cr & blk .25 .25
1172 A558 16s green, cr & blk .25 .25
1173 A558 1.25 l bister, cr & blk .65 .25
Nos. 1170-1173 (4) 1.40 1.00

"Know Your Country" campaign.

Demeter Blagoev Addressing 1891 Congress at Busludja — A559

1961, Aug. 5 Photo.

1174 A559 45s dk red & buff .25 .25
1175 A559 80s blue & pink .55 .25
1176 A559 2 l dk brn & pale cit 1.20 .50
Nos. 1174-1176 (3) 2.00 1.00

70th anniversary of the first Congress of the Bulgarian Social-Democratic Party.

The Golden Girl A560

Fairy Tales: 8s, The Living Water. 12s, The Golden Apple. 16s, Krali-Marko, hero. 45s, Samovila-Vila, Witch. 80s, Tom Thumb.

1961, Oct. 10 Unwmk. ***Perf. 11***

1177 A560 2s blue, blk & org .25 .25
1178 A560 8s rose lil, blk & gray .25 .25
1179 A560 12s bl grn, blk & pink .25 .25
1180 A560 16s red, blk, bl & gray .75 .25
1181 A560 45s ol grn, blk & pink 1.75 .50
1182 A560 80s ocher, blk & dk car 1.75 .60
Nos. 1177-1182 (6) 5.00 2.10

Caesar's Mushroom A561

Designs: Various mushrooms.

1961, Dec. 20 Photo. ***Perf. 11***

Denominations in Black

1183 A561 2s lemon & red .25 .25
1184 A561 4s ol grn & red brn .25 .25
1185 A561 12s bister & red brn .25 .25
1186 A561 16s lilac & red brn .25 .25
1187 A561 45s car rose & yel .45 .25
1188 A561 80s brn org & sepia .55 .45
1189 A561 1.25 l vio & dk brn .80 .40
1190 A561 2 l org brn & brn 1.10 .90
Nos. 1183-1190 (8) 3.90 3.00

Value, denomination in dark grn, imperf set $10 unused or canceled.

Miladinov Brothers and Title Page — A562

1961, Dec. 21 Unwmk. ***Perf. 10½***

1191 A562 1.25 l olive & blk 1.10 .50

Publication of "Collected Folksongs" by the Brothers Miladinov, Dimitri and Konstantin, cent.

Nos. 1079-1085, 1087, 992, 1023, 1090-1091 and 806 Surcharged

In Black — No. 1192

In Black — No. 1193

In Red — No. 1195

In Red — No. 1197

In Violet — No. 1204

1962, Jan. 1

1192 A533 1s on 10s red brn .25 .25
1193 A532 1s on 12s red brn .25 .25
1194 A532 2s on 15s red lilac .25 .25
1195 A533 2s on 16s dp vio (R) .25 .25
1196 A533 2s on 20s orange .25 .25
a. "2 CT." on 2 lines .25 .25
1197 A532 3s on 25s brt bl (R) .25 .25
a. Black surcharge 12.00 12.00
1198 A532 3s on 28s brt grn (R) .25 .25
1199 A532 5s on 45s choc .35 .25
1200 A499 5s on 44s dk bl grn (R) .25 .25
1201 A509 5s on 44s dp car (V) .25 .25
1202 A532 10s on 1 l maroon .45 .25
1203 A532 20s on 2 l dp car .85 .55
1204 A430 40s on 4 l rose lake (V) 2.10 1.10
Nos. 1192-1204 (13) 6.00 4.40

Freighter "Varna" A563

Designs: 5s, Tanker "Komsomoletz." 20s, Liner "G. Dimitrov."

1962, Mar. 1 Photo. ***Perf. 10½***

1205 A563 1s lt grn & brt bl .25 .25
1206 A563 5s lt blue & grn .35 .25
1207 A563 20s gray bl & grnsh bl .90 .25
Nos. 1205-1207 (3) 1.50 .75

Dimitrov Working as Printer — A564

13s, Griffin, emblem of state printing works.

1962, Mar. 19 Unwmk.

1208 A564 2s ver, blk & yel .25 .25
1209 A564 13s red org, blk & yel .55 .25

80th anniversary (in 1961) of the George Dimitrov state printing works.

Roses — A565

1962, Mar. 28

Various Roses in Natural Colors

1210 A565 1s deep violet .25 .25
1211 A565 2s salmon & dk car .25 .25
1212 A565 3s gray & car .30 .25
1213 A565 4s dark green .40 .25
1214 A565 5s ultra .75 .25
1215 A565 6s bluish grn & dk car .75 .35
1216 A565 8s citron & car 2.00 .75
1217 A565 13s blue 3.50 2.50
Nos. 1210-1217 (8) 8.20 4.85

For overprint and surcharges see Nos. 1281-1283.

Malaria Eradication Emblem and Mosquito A566

Design: 20s, Malaria eradication emblem.

1962, Apr. 19

1218 A566 5s org brn, yel & blk .45 .25
1219 A566 20s emerald, yel & blk 1.50 .60

WHO drive to eradicate malaria.

Value, imperf. $5 unused, $1.50 canceled.

Lenin and First Issue of Pravda A567

1962, May 4 Unwmk. ***Perf. 10***

1220 A567 5s deep rose & slate 1.50 .95

50th anniversary of Pravda, Russian newspaper founded by Lenin.

Blackboard and Book — A568

1962, May 21 Photo.

1221 A568 5s Prus bl, blk & yel .40 .25

The 1962 Teachers' Congress.

Soccer Player and Globe A569

1962, May 26 ***Perf. 10½***

1222 A569 13s brt grn, blk & lt brn 1.40 .65

World Soccer Championship, Chile, May 30-June 17. Value, imperf. in changed colors, $4 unused or canceled.

George Dimitrov A570

1962, June 18 Photo.

1223 A570 2s dark green .35 .25
1224 A570 5s turq blue .70 .25

80th anniv. of the birth of George Dimitrov (1882-1949), communist leader and premier of the Bulgarian Peoples' Republic.

Bishop — A571

1962, July 7 Unwmk. *Perf. 10½*

1225	A571	1s shown	.25	.25
1226	A571	2s Rook	.25	.25
1227	A571	3s Queen	.25	.25
1228	A571	13s Knight	1.40	.55
1229	A571	20s Pawn	1.75	.85
		Nos. 1225-1229 (5)	3.90	2.15

15th Chess Olympics, Varna. Nos. 1225-1229 were also issued imperf in changed colors. Value, $6.50 unused.

An imperf. souvenir sheet contains one 20s horizontal stamp showing five chessmen. Size: 75x66mm. Value, $13 unused.

Rila Mountain A572

Designs: 2s, Pirin mountain. 6s, Nesebr, Black Sea. 8s, Danube. 13s, Vidin Castle. 1 l, Rhodope mountain.

1962-63 *Perf. 13*

1230	A572	1s dk blue grn	.25	.25
1231	A572	2s blue	.25	.25
1232	A572	6s grnsh blue	.25	.25
1233	A572	8s lilac	.25	.25
1234	A572	13s yellow grn	1.25	.25
1234A	A572	1 l dp green ('63)	5.00	1.40
		Nos. 1230-1234A (6)	7.25	2.65

No. 974 Surcharged in Red

1962, July 14 *Perf. 13*

1235	A493	13s on 44s slate grn	3.50	2.50

25th Bulgarian Esperanto Congress, Burgas, July 14-16.

Girl and Festival Emblem A573

Design: 5s, Festival emblem.

1962, Aug. 18 Photo. *Perf. 10½*

1236	A573	5s green, lt bl & pink	.25	.25
1237	A573	13s lilac, lt bl & gray	.75	.25

8th Youth Festival for Peace and Friendship, Helsinki, July 28-Aug. 6, 1962.

Parnassius Apollo — A574

1962, Sept. 13

Various Butterflies in Natural Colors

1238	A574	1s pale cit & dk grn	.25	.25
1239	A574	2s rose & brown	.25	.25
1240	A574	3s buff & red brn	.25	.25
1241	A574	4s gray & brown	.25	.25
1242	A574	5s lt gray & brn	.35	.25
1243	A574	6s gray & black	.70	.25
1244	A574	10s pale grn & blk	2.50	.75
1245	A574	13s buff & red brn	3.00	1.75
		Nos. 1238-1245 (8)	7.55	4.00

Planting Machine — A575

2s, Electric locomotive. 3s, Blast furnace. 13s, Blagoev, Dimitrov & Communist flag.

1962, Nov. 1 *Perf. 11½*

1246	A575	1s bl grn & dk ol grn	.25	.25
1247	A575	2s bl & Prus bl	.25	.25
1248	A575	3s carmine & brn	.25	.25
1249	A575	13s plum, red & blk	.85	.25
		Nos. 1246-1249 (4)	1.60	1.00

Bulgarian Communist Party, 8th Congress.

Title Page of "Slav-Bulgarian History" — A576

Paisii Hilendarski Writing History A577

1962, Dec. 8 Unwmk. *Perf. 10½*

1250	A576	2s olive grn & blk	.25	.25
1251	A577	5s brown org & blk	.25	.25

200th anniv. of "Slav-Bulgarian History."

Aleco Konstantinov (1863-1897), Writer A578

1963, Mar. 5 Photo. *Perf. 11½*

1252	A578	5s red, grn & blk	.50	.25

Printed with alternating red brown and black label showing Bai Ganu, hero from Konstantinov's books.

A579

Sofia University — A580

No. 1255, Levski Stadium, Sofia. No. 1256, Arch, Nissaria. No. 1257, Parachutist.

1963, Feb. 20 Unwmk. *Perf. 10*

1253	A579	1s brown red	.25	.25
1254	A580	1s red brown	.25	.25
1255	A580	1s blue green	.25	.25
1256	A580	1s dark green	.25	.25
1257	A580	1s brt blue	.25	.25
		Nos. 1253-1257 (5)	1.25	1.25

Vassil Levski A581

1963, Apr. 11 Photo.

1258	A581	13s grnsh blue & buff	1.40	.45

90th anniversary of the death of Vassil Levski, revolutionary leader in the fight for liberation from the Turks.

Boy, Girl and Dimitrov — A582

13s, Girl with book & boy with hammer.

1963, Apr. 25 Unwmk. *Perf. 11½*

1259	A582	2s org, ver, red brn & blk	.25	.25
1260	A582	13s bluish grn, brn & blk	.55	.25

10th Congress of Dimitrov's Union of the People's Youth.

Red Squirrel — A583

2s, Hedgehog. 3s, European polecat. 5s, Pine marten. 13s, Badger. 20s, Otter. 2s, 3s, 5s, 13s, horiz.

1963, Apr. 30 Red Numerals

1261	A583	1s grn & brn, *grnsh*	.25	.25
1262	A583	2s grn & blk, *yel*	.25	.25
1263	A583	3s grn & brn, *bis*	.35	.25
1264	A583	5s vio & red brn, *lil*	.70	.25
1265	A583	13s red brn & blk, *pink*	2.50	.70
1266	A583	20s blk & brn, *blue*	2.50	1.40
		Nos. 1261-1266 (6)	6.55	3.10

Sun Coast Promenade A584

Black Sea Resorts: 2s, 3s, 13s, Views of Gold Sand. 5s, 20s, Sun Coast.

1963, Mar. 12 Unwmk. *Perf. 13*

1267	A584	1s blue	.25	.25
1268	A584	2s vermilion	.25	.25
1269	A584	2s car rose	2.50	1.25
1270	A584	3s ocher	.25	.25
1271	A584	5s lilac	.25	.25
1272	A584	13s blue green	1.25	.25
1273	A584	20s green	1.25	.25
		Nos. 1267-1273 (7)	6.00	2.75

Freestyle Wrestling A585

Design: 20s, Freestyle wrestling, horiz.

1963, May 31 *Perf. 11½*

1274	A585	5s yel bister & blk	.35	.25
1275	A585	20s org brn & blk	1.25	.25

15th International Freestyle Wrestling Competitions, Sofia.

"Women for Peace" A586

1963, June 24 Unwmk. *Perf. 11½*

1276	A586	20s blue & blk	1.10	.25

World Congress of Women, Moscow, June 24-29.

Esperanto Emblem and Arms of Sofia — A587

1963, June 29 Photo.

1277	A587	13s multicolored	1.00	.25

48th World Esperanto Congress, Sofia, Aug. 3-10.

Moon, Earth and Lunik 4 — A588

2s, Radar equipment. 3s, Satellites and moon.

1963, July 22

1278	A588	1s ultra	.25	.25
1279	A588	2s red lilac	.25	.25
1280	A588	3s greenish blue	.25	.25
		Nos. 1278-1280 (3)	.75	.75

Russia's rocket to the moon, Apr. 2, 1963.

Nos. 1211-1212 and 1215 Ovptd. or Srchd. in Green, Ultra or Black

1963, Aug. 31 *Perf. 10½*

1281	A565	2s (G)	.35	.25
1282	A565	5s on 3s (U)	.75	.25
1283	A565	13s on 6s	1.40	.35
		Nos. 1281-1283 (3)	2.50	.85

Intl. Stamp Fair, Riccione, Aug. 31.

Women's Relay Race — A589

2s, Hammer thrower. 3s, Women's long jump. 5s, Men's high jump. 13s, Discus thrower.

Perf. 11½

1963, Sept. 13 Photo. Unwmk.

Flags in National Colors

1284	A589	1s	slate green	.25	.25
1285	A589	2s	purple	.25	.25
1286	A589	3s	Prus blue	.25	.25
1287	A589	5s	maroon	.70	.25
1288	A589	13s	chestnut brn	2.75	2.10
			Nos. 1284-1288 (5)	4.20	3.10

Balkan Games. A multicolored, 50s, imperf. souvenir sheet shows design of women's relay race. Size: 74x70mm. Value, $5 unused.

"Slav-Bulgarian History" — A590

1963, Sept. 19 ***Perf. 10½***

1289 A590 5s sal pink, slate & yel .40 .40

5th International Slavic Congress.

Revolutionists A591

1963, Sept. 22 ***Perf. 11½***

1290 A591 2s brt red & blk .25 .25

40th anniv. of the September Revolution.

Christo Smirnenski A592

1963, Oct. 28 ***Perf. 10½***

1291 A592 13s pale lilac & indigo .70 .25

Christo Smirnenski, poet, 65th birth anniv.

Columbine A593

1963, Oct. 9 Photo. ***Perf. 11½***

1292	A593	1s	shown	.25	.25
1293	A593	2s	Edelweiss	.25	.25
1294	A593	3s	Primrose	.25	.25
1295	A593	5s	Water lily	.25	.25
1296	A593	6s	Tulips	.25	.25
1297	A593	8s	Larkspur	.75	.25
1298	A593	10s	Alpine clematis	1.50	.25
1299	A593	13s	Anemone	2.75	.60
			Nos. 1292-1299 (8)	6.25	2.35

Horses — A594

Designs: 2s, Charioteer and chariot. 3s, Trumpeters. 5s, Woman carrying tray with food. 13s, Man holding bowl. 20s, Woman in armchair. Designs are from a Thracian tomb at Kazanlik.

1963, Dec. 28 Unwmk. ***Perf. 10½***

1300	A594	1s	gray, org & dk red	.25	.25
1301	A594	2s	gray, ocher & pur	.25	.25
1302	A594	3s	gray, dl yel & sl grn	.25	.25
1303	A594	5s	pale grn, ocher & brn	.30	.25
1304	A594	13s	pale grn, bis & blk	.75	.35
1305	A594	20s	pale grn, org & dk car	1.50	.55
			Nos. 1300-1305 (6)	3.30	1.90

World Map and Emblem A595

Designs: 2s, Blood transfusion. 3s, Nurse bandaging injured wrist. 5s, Red Cross nurse. 13s, Henri Dunant.

1964, Jan. 27 ***Perf. 10½***

1306	A595	1s	lem, blk & red	.25	.25
1307	A595	2s	ultra, blk & red	.25	.25
1308	A595	3s	gray, sl, blk & red	.25	.25
1309	A595	5s	brt bl, blk & red	.25	.25
1310	A595	13s	org yel, blk & red	.80	.25
			Nos. 1306-1310 (5)	1.80	1.25

Centenary of International Red Cross.

Speed Skating A596

Sports: 2s, 50s, Women's figure skating. 3s, Cross-country skiing. 5s, Ski jump. 10s, Ice hockey goalkeeper. 13s, Ice hockey players.

1964, Feb. 21 Unwmk. ***Perf. 10½***

1311	A596	1s	grnsh bl, ind & ocher	.25	.25
1312	A596	2s	brt pink, ol grn & dk sl grn	.25	.25
1313	A596	3s	dl grn, dk grn & brn	.25	.25
1314	A596	5s	bl, blk & yel brn	.25	.25
1315	A596	10s	gray, org & blk	.70	.25
1316	A596	13s	lil, blk & lil rose	.70	.25
			Nos. 1311-1316 (6)	2.40	1.50

Miniature Sheet

Imperf

1317 A596 50s gray, Prus grn & pink 3.75 3.75

9th Winter Olympic Games, Innsbruck, Jan. 29-Feb. 9, 1964.

Mask of Nobleman, 2nd Century A597

2s, Thracian horseman. 3s, Ceramic jug. 5s, Clasp & belt. 6s, Copper kettle. 8s, Angel. 10s, Lioness. 13s, Scrub woman, contemporary sculpture.

1964, Mar. 14 Photo. ***Perf. 10½***

Gray Frame

1318	A597	1s	dp green & red	.25	.25
1319	A597	2s	ol gray & red	.25	.25
1320	A597	3s	bister & red	.25	.25
1321	A597	5s	indigo & red	.25	.25
1322	A597	6s	org brn & red	.45	.25
1323	A597	8s	brn red & red	.70	.25
1324	A597	10s	olive & red	.75	.25
1325	A597	13s	gray ol & red	.90	.45
			Nos. 1318-1325 (8)	3.80	2.20

2,500 years of Bulgarian art.

"The Unborn Maid" A598

Fairy Tales: 2s, Grandfather's Glove. 3s, The Big Turnip. 5s, The Wolf and the Seven Kids. 8s, Cunning Peter. 13s, The Wheat Cake.

1964, Apr. 17 Unwmk. ***Perf. 10½***

1326	A598	1s	bl grn, red & org brn	.25	.25
1327	A598	2s	ultra, ocher & blk	.25	.25
1328	A598	3s	cit, red & blk	.25	.25
1329	A598	5s	dp rose, brn & blk	.25	.25
1330	A598	8s	yel grn, red & blk	.40	.25
1331	A598	13s	lt vio bl, grn & blk	1.25	.25
			Nos. 1326-1331 (6)	2.65	1.50

Ascalaphus Otomanus A599

Insects: 2s, Nemoptera coa., vert. 3s, Saga natalia (grasshopper). 5s, Rosalia alpina, vert. 13s, Anisoplia austriaca, vert. 20s, Scolia flavitrons.

1964, May 16 Photo. ***Perf. 11½***

1332	A599	1s	brn org, yel & blk	.25	.25
1333	A599	2s	dl bl grn, bis & blk	.25	.25
1334	A599	3s	gray, grn & blk	.25	.25
1335	A599	5s	lt ol grn, blk & vio	.65	.25
1336	A599	13s	vio, bis & blk	1.25	.40
1337	A599	20s	gray bl, yel & blk	2.25	.85
			Nos. 1332-1337 (6)	4.90	2.25

Soccer — A600

Designs: 13s, Women's volleyball. 60s, Map of Europe and European Women's Volleyball Championship Cup (rectangular, size: 60x69mm).

1964, June 8 Unwmk. ***Perf. 11½***

1338	A600	2s	bl, dk bl, ocher & red	.25	.25
1339	A600	13s	bl, dk bl, ocher & red	.90	.40

Miniature Sheet

Imperf

1340 A600 60s ultra, ocher, red & gray 3.00 3.00

Levski Physical Culture Assoc., 50th anniv.

Peter Beron and Title Page of Primer — A601

1964, June 22 ***Perf. 11½***

1341 A601 20s red brn & dk brn, *grysh* 1.75 1.75

140th anniversary of the publication of the first Bulgarian primer.

Robert Stephenson's "Rocket" Locomotive, 1825 — A602

Designs: 2s, Modern steam locomotive. 3s, Diesel locomotive. 5s, Electric locomotive. 8s, Freight train on bridge. 13s, Diesel locomotive and tunnel.

1964, July 1 Photo. ***Perf. 11½***

1342	A602	1s	multicolored	.25	.25
1343	A602	2s	multicolored	.25	.25
1344	A602	3s	multicolored	.25	.25
1345	A602	5s	multicolored	.25	.25
1346	A602	8s	multicolored	1.00	.25
1347	A602	13s	multicolored	1.00	.25
			Nos. 1342-1347 (6)	3.00	1.50

German Shepherd — A603

1964, Aug. 22 **Photo.**

1348	A603	1s	shown	.25	.25
1349	A603	2s	Setter	.25	.25
1350	A603	3s	Poodle	.30	.25
1351	A603	4s	Pomeranian	.35	.25
1352	A603	5s	St. Bernard	.50	.25
1353	A603	6s	Terrier	.70	.35
1354	A603	10s	Pointer	2.75	1.25
1355	A603	13s	Dachshund	3.50	2.25
			Nos. 1348-1355 (8)	8.60	5.10

Partisans — A604

Designs: 2s, People welcoming Soviet army. 3s, Russian aid to Bulgaria. 4s, Blast furnace, Kremikovski. 5s, Combine. 6s, Peace demonstration. 8s, Sentry. 13s, Demeter Blagoev and George Dimitrov.

1964, Sept. 9 Unwmk. ***Perf. 11½***

Flag in Red

1356	A604	1s	lt & dp ultra	.25	.25
1357	A604	2s	ol bis & dp ol	.25	.25
1358	A604	3s	rose lil & mar	.25	.25
1359	A604	4s	lt vio & vio	.25	.25
1360	A604	5s	org & red brn	.25	.25
1361	A604	6s	bl & dp bl	.25	.25
1362	A604	8s	lt grn & grn	.25	.25
1363	A604	13s	fawn & red brn	.65	.25
			Nos. 1356-1363 (8)	2.40	2.00

20th anniv. of People's Government of Bulgaria.

No. 967 Surcharged

1964, Sept. 13 ***Perf. 13***

1364 A476 20s on 44s org yel 1.50 .50

International Plovdiv Fair.

Gymnast on Parallel Bars — A606

Sports: 2s, Long jump. 3s, Woman diver. 5s, Soccer. 13s, Women's volleyball. 20s, Wrestling.

1964, Oct. 10 ***Perf. 11½***
1366 A606 1s pale grn, grn & red .25 .25
1367 A606 2s pale vio, vio bl & red .25 .25
1368 A606 3s bl grn, brn & red .25 .25
1369 A606 5s pink, pur & red .25 .25
1370 A606 13s bl, Prus grn & red .85 .25
1371 A606 20s yel, grn & red .85 .45
Nos. 1366-1371 (6) 2.70 1.70

18th Olympic Games, Tokyo. Oct. 10-25. See No. B27.

Vratcata Mountain Road — A607

Bulgarian Views: 2s, Ritlite mountain road. 3s, Pines, Maliovica peak. 4s, Pobitite rocks. 5s, Erkupria. 6s, Rhodope mountain road.

1964, Oct. 26 **Photo.** ***Perf. 12½x13***
1372 A607 1s dk slate grn .25 .25
1373 A607 2s brown .25 .25
1374 A607 3s grnsh blue .25 .25
1375 A607 4s dk red brn .25 .25
1376 A607 5s deep green .25 .25
1377 A607 6s blue violet .60 .25
Nos. 1372-1377 (6) 1.85 1.50

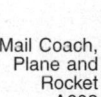

Mail Coach, Plane and Rocket A608

1964, Oct. 3 **Unwmk.** ***Perf. 11½***
1378 A608 20s greenish blue 1.50 .50

First national stamp exhibition, Sofia, Oct. 3-18. Issued in sheets of 12 stamps and 12 labels (woman's head and inscription, 5x5) arranged around one central label showing stylized bird design. No. 1378 with label, value $2.50.
Exists imperf.

Students Holding Book — A609

1964, Dec. 30 **Photo.**
1379 A609 13s lt blue & blk .75 .35

8th Intl. Students' Congress, Sofia.

500-Year-Old Walnut Tree at Golemo Drenovo — A610

Designs: Various old trees.

1964, Dec. 28
1380 A610 1s blk, buff & cl brn .25 .25
1381 A610 2s blk, pink & dp cl .25 .25
1382 A610 3s blk, yel & dk brn .25 .25
1383 A610 4s blk, lt bl & Prus bl .25 .25
1384 A610 10s blk, pale grn & grn .60 .25
1385 A610 13s blk, pale bis & dk ol grn .90 .25
Nos. 1380-1385 (6) 2.50 1.50

Soldiers' Monument A611

1965, Jan. 1 **Unwmk.**
1386 A611 2s red & black .40 .40

Bulgarian-Soviet friendship.

Olympic Medal Inscribed "Olympic Glory" A612

1965, Jan. 27 **Photo.** ***Perf. 11½***
1387 A612 20s org brn, gold & blk 1.10 .50

Bulgarian victories in the 1964 Olympic Games.

"Victory Over Fascism" A613

13s, "Fight for Peace" (dove and globe).

1965, Apr. 16 ***Perf. 11½***
1388 A613 5s gray, blk & ol bis .25 .25
1389 A613 13s gray, blk & blue .60 .25

Victory over Fascism, 5/9/45, 20th anniv.

Vladimir M. Komarov and Section of Globe — A614

Designs: 2s, Konstantin Feoktistov. 5s, Boris B. Yegorov. 13s, Komarov, Feoktistov and Yegorov. 20s, Spaceship Voskhod.

1965, Feb. 15 **Photo.**
1390 A614 1s pale lil & dk bl .25 .25
1391 A614 2s lt bl, ind & dl vio .25 .25
1392 A614 5s pale grn, grn & ol grn .25 .25
1393 A614 13s pale pink, dp rose & mar .65 .25
1394 A614 20s lt bl, vio bl, grnsh bl & yel 1.10 .25
Nos. 1390-1394 (5) 2.50 1.25

Russian 3-man space flight, Oct. 12-13, 1964.
Imperfs in changed colors. Four low values se-tenant. Value, set $4 unused, $2 canceled.

Bullfinch — A615

Birds: 2s, European golden oriole. 3s, Common rock thrush. 5s, Barn swallow. 8s, European roller. 10s, European goldfinch. 13s, Rosy pastor starling. 20s, Nightingale.

1965, Apr. 20 **Unwmk.** ***Perf. 11½***
Birds in Natural Colors
1395 A615 1s blue green .25 .25
1396 A615 2s rose lilac .25 .25
1397 A615 3s rose .25 .25
1398 A615 5s brt blue .50 .25
1399 A615 8s citron .55 .45
1400 A615 10s gray 2.10 .55
1401 A615 13s lt vio blue 2.10 1.00
1402 A615 20s emerald 3.00 2.25
Nos. 1395-1402 (8) 9.00 5.25

Black Sea Fish A616

1965, June 10 **Photo.** ***Perf. 11½***
Gray Frames
1403 A616 1s Sting ray .25 .25
1404 A616 2s Belted bonito .25 .25
1405 A616 3s Hogfish .25 .25
1406 A616 5s Gurnard .35 .25
1407 A616 10s Scad 1.50 .25
1408 A616 13s Turbot 2.00 .50
Nos. 1403-1408 (6) 4.60 1.75

Plane, Bus, Train, Ship and Whale A617

1965, Apr. 30
1409 A617 13s multicolored 1.10 .65

4th Intl. Conf. of Transport, Dock and Fishery Workers, Sofia, May 10-14.

ITU Emblem and Communications Symbols — A618

1965, May 17
1410 A618 20s multicolored 1.10 .60

Centenary of the ITU.

Col. Pavel Belyayev and Lt. Col. Alexei Leonov — A619

Design: 20s, Leonov floating in space.

1965, May 20 **Unwmk.**
1411 A619 2s gray, dull bl & dk brn .35 .25
1412 A619 20s multicolored 2.75 .85

Space flight of Voskhod 2 and the first man floating in space, Lt. Col. Alexei Leonov.

ICY Emblem A620

1965, May 15 **Photo.**
1413 A620 20s org, ol & blk 1.10 .35

International Cooperation Year, 1965.

Corn — A621

1965, Apr. 1 ***Perf. 12½x13***
1414 A621 1s shown .25 .25
1415 A621 2s Wheat .25 .25
1416 A621 3s Sunflowers .25 .25
1417 A621 4s Sugar beet .25 .25
1418 A621 5s Clover .25 .25
1419 A621 10s Cotton .35 .25
1420 A621 13s Tobacco 1.10 .25
Nos. 1414-1420 (7) 2.70 1.75

Marx and Lenin — A622

1965, June ***Perf. 10½***
1421 A622 13s red & dk brn 1.50 .25

6th Conference of Postal Ministers of Communist Countries, Peking, June 21-July 15.

Film and UNESCO Emblem A623

1965, June 30
1422 A623 13s dp bl, blk & lt gray .75 .25

Balkan Film Festival, Varna.

Ballerina — A624

1965, July 10 **Photo.**

1423 A624 5s dp lil rose & blk 1.60 .75

2nd Intl. Ballet Competition, Varna.

Map of Balkan Peninsula and Dove with Letter A625

Col. Pavel Belyayev and Lt. Col. Alexei Leonov — A626

2s, Sailboat and modern buildings. 3s, Fish and plants. 13s, Symbolic sun and rocket. 40s, Map of Balkan Peninsula and dove with letter (like 1s).

1965 ***Perf. 10½***

1424 A625 1s sil, dp ultra & yel .25 .25
1425 A625 2s sil, pur & yel .25 .25
1426 A625 3s gold, grn & yel .25 .25
1427 A625 13s gold, hn brn & yel .90 .90
1428 A626 20s sil, bl & brn 1.50 1.50
Nos. 1424-1428 (5) 3.15 3.15

Miniature Sheet

Imperf

1429 A625 40s gold & brt bl 3.75 2.10

Balkanphila 1965 Philatelic Exhibition, Varna, Aug. 7-15, and visit of Russian astronauts Belyayev and Leonov.

Value, No. 1428 imperf. in changed colors, $1.75.

Issued: 20s, 40s, 8/7; others, 7/23.

Woman Gymnast — A627

Designs: 2s, Woman gymnast on parallel bars. 3s, Weight lifter. 5s, Automobile and chart. 10s, Women basketball players. 13s, Automobile and map of rally.

1965, Aug. 14 ***Perf. 10½***

1430 A627 1s crim, brn & blk .25 .25
1431 A627 2s rose vio, dp cl & blk .25 .25
1432 A627 3s dp car, brn & blk .25 .25
1433 A627 5s fawn, red brn & blk .35 .25
1434 A627 10s dp lil rose, dp cl & blk .65 .25
1435 A627 13s lilac, claret & blk .90 .25
Nos. 1430-1435 (6) 2.65 1.50

Sports events in Bulgaria during May-June, 1965.

No. 989 Surcharged

1965, Aug. 12 ***Perf. 13***

1436 A499 2s on 8s orange brn, surcharge 36mm wide 1.50 1.50
a. Surcharge 32mm wide 6.00 4.00

1st Natl. Folklore Competition, Aug. 12-15.

Escaping Prisoners — A628

1965, July 23 ***Perf. 10½***

1437 A628 2s slate .40 .40

40th anniversary of the escape of political prisoners from Bolshevik Island.

Fruit — A629

1965, July 1 ***Perf. 13***

1438 A629 1s Apples .25 .25
1439 A629 2s Grapes .25 .25
1440 A629 3s Pears .25 .25
1441 A629 4s Peaches .25 .25
1442 A629 5s Strawberries .25 .25
1443 A629 6s Walnuts .30 .25
Nos. 1438-1443 (6) 1.55 1.50

Horsemanship — A630

1965, Sept. 30 **Unwmk.** ***Perf. 10½***

1444 A630 1s Dressage .25 .25
1445 A630 2s Three-day test .25 .25
1446 A630 3s Jumping .25 .25
1447 A630 5s Race .45 .25
1448 A630 10s Steeplechase 2.00 .75
1449 A630 13s Hurdle race 2.25 1.10
Nos. 1444-1449 (6) 5.45 2.85

See No. B28.

Smiling Children — A631

Designs: 2s, Two girl Pioneers. 3s, Bugler. 5s, Pioneer with model plane. 8s, Two singing girls in national costume. 13s, Running boy.

1965, Oct. 24 **Photo.**

1450 A631 1s dk bl grn & yel grn .25 .25
1451 A631 2s vio & deep rose .25 .25
1452 A631 3s olive & lemon .25 .25
1453 A631 5s dp blue & bister .25 .25
1454 A631 8s olive bister & org .60 .25
1455 A631 13s rose car & vio .90 .35
Nos. 1450-1455 (6) 2.50 1.60

Dimitrov Pioneer Organization.

U-52 Plane over Trnovo A632

2s, 1L-14 over Plovdiv. 3s, Mi-4 Helicopter over Dimitrovgrad. 5s, Tu-104 over Ruse. 13s, IL-18 over Varna. 20s, Tu-114 over Sofia.

1965, Nov. 25 ***Perf. 10½***

1456 A632 1s gray, blue & red .25 .25
1457 A632 2s gray, lilac & red .25 .25
1458 A632 3s gray, grnsh bl & red .25 .25
1459 A632 5s gray, org & red .30 .25
1460 A632 13s gray, bister & red .90 .25
1461 A632 20s gray, lt grn & red 1.50 .45
Nos. 1456-1461 (6) 3.45 1.70

Development of Bulgarian Civil Air Transport.

IQSY Emblem, and Earth Radiation Zones A633

Designs (IQSY Emblem and): 2s, Sun with corona. 13s, Solar eclipse.

1965, Dec. 15 **Photo.** ***Perf. 10½***

1462 A633 1s grn, yel & ultra .25 .25
1463 A633 2s yel, red lil & red .25 .25
1464 A633 13s bl, yel & blk .75 .25
Nos. 1462-1464 (3) 1.25 .75

International Quiet Sun Year, 1964-65.

"North and South Bulgaria" A634

1965, Dec. 6

1465 A634 13s brt yel grn & blk .70 .45

Union of North and South Bulgaria, cent.

"Martenitsa" Emblem — A635

"Spring" in Folklore: 2s, Drummer. 3s, Bird ornaments. 5s, Dancer "Lazarka." 8s, Vase with flowers. 13s, Bagpiper.

1966, Jan. 10 **Photo.** ***Perf. 10½***

1466 A635 1s rose lil, vio bl & gray .25 .25
1467 A635 2s gray, blk & crim .25 .25
1468 A635 3s red, vio & gray .25 .25
1469 A635 5s lil, blk & crimson .25 .25
1470 A635 8s rose lil, brn & pur .50 .25
1471 A635 13s bl, blk & rose lilac .85 .25
Nos. 1466-1471 (6) 2.35 1.50

Church of St. John the Baptist, Nessebr A636

Designs: 1s, Christ, fresco from Bojana Church. 2s, Ikon "Destruction of Idols," horiz. 3s, Bratchkovo Monastery. 4s, Zemen Monastery, horiz. 13s, Nativity, ikon from Arbanassi. 20s, Ikon "Virgin and Child," 1342.

1966, Feb. 25 **Litho.** ***Perf. 11½***

1472 A636 1s gray & multi *5.00 1.75*
1473 A636 2s gray & multi .35 .25
1474 A636 3s multicolored .35 .25
1475 A636 4s multicolored .35 .25
1476 A636 5s multicolored .35 .25
1477 A636 13s gray & multi .70 .25
1478 A636 20s multicolored 1.40 .50
Nos. 1472-1478 (7) *8.50 3.50*

2,500 years of art in Bulgaria.

Georgi Benkovski and T. Kableshkov — A637

1s, Proclamation of April Uprising, Koprivstitsa. 3s, Dedication of flag, Panaguriste. 5s, V. Petleshkov, Z. Dyustabanov. 10s, Botev landing at Kozlodui. 13s, P. Volov, Ilarion Dragostinov.

1966, Mar. 3 **Photo.** ***Perf. 10½***

Center in Black

1479 A637 1s red brn & gold .25 .25
1480 A637 2s brt red & gold .25 .25
1481 A637 3s ol grn & gold .25 .25
1482 A637 5s steel bl & gold .25 .25
1483 A637 10s brt rose lil & gold .55 .25
1484 A637 13s lt vio & gold .55 .25
Nos. 1479-1484 (6) 2.10 1.50

April Uprising against the Turks, 90th anniv.

Sofia Zoo Animals A638

1966, May 23 **Litho.**

1485 A638 1s Elephant .25 .25
1486 A638 2s Tiger .25 .25
1487 A638 3s Chimpanzee .25 .25
1488 A638 4s Siberian ibex .25 .25
1489 A638 5s Polar bear .65 .25
1490 A638 8s Lion .80 .50
1491 A638 13s Bison 2.25 1.25
1492 A638 20s Kangaroo 3.00 1.90
Nos. 1485-1492 (8) 7.70 4.90

WHO Headquarters, Geneva — A639

1966, May 3 **Photo.**

1493 A639 13s deep blue & silver .80 .35

Inauguration of the WHO Headquarters, Geneva.

Worker A640

1966, May 9 Photo. *Perf. 10½*

1494	A640	20s gray & rose	1.00	.50

Sixth Trade Union Congress.

Yantra River Bridge, Biela — A641

No. 1496, Maritsa River Bridge, Svilengrad. No. 1497, Fountain, Samokov. No. 1498, Ruins of Fort, Kaskovo. 8s, Old Fort, Ruse. 13s, House, Gabrovo.

1966, Feb. 10 Photo. *Perf. 13*

1495	A641	1s Prus blue	.25	.25
1496	A641	1s brt green	.25	.25
1497	A641	2s olive green	.25	.25
1498	A641	2s dk red brown	.25	.25
1499	A641	8s red brown	.35	.25
1500	A641	13s dark blue	.65	.25
		Nos. 1495-1500 (6)	2.00	1.50

Souvenir Sheet

Moon Allegory — A642

1966, Apr. 29 *Imperf.*

1501	A642	60s blk, plum & sil	4.25	3.50

1st Russian soft landing on the moon by Luna 9, Feb. 3, 1966.

Steamer Radetzky and Bugler — A643

1966, May 28 *Perf. 10½*

1502	A643	2s multicolored	.25	.25

90th anniv. of the participation of the Danube steamer Radetzky in the uprising against the Turks.

Standard Bearer Nicola Simov-Kuruto A644

1966, May 30

1503	A644	5s bister, green & olive	.35	.25

Hero of the Turkish War.

UNESCO Emblem A645

1966, June 8

1504	A645	20s buff, blk & ver	.85	.35

20th anniv. of UNESCO.

Youth Federation Badge — A646

1966, June 6 Photo. *Perf. 10½*

1505	A646	13s silver, bl & blk	.75	.25

7th Assembly of the Intl. Youth Federation.

Soccer — A647

Various soccer scenes. 50s, Jules Rimet Cup.

1966, June 27

1506	A647	1s gray, yel brn & blk	.25	.25
1507	A647	2s gray, crim & blk	.25	.25
1508	A647	5s gray, ol bis & blk	.25	.25
1509	A647	13s gray, ultra & blk	.70	.25
1510	A647	20s gray, Prus bl & blk	.80	.25
		Nos. 1506-1510 (5)	2.25	1.25

Miniature Sheet

Imperf

1511	A647	50s gray, dp lil rose & gold	3.75	2.50

World Soccer Cup Championship, Wembley, England, July 11-30. Size of No. 1511: 60x64mm.

Woman Javelin Thrower — A648

No. 1513, Runner. No. 1514, Young man and woman carrying banners, vert.

1966 Photo. *Perf. 10½*

1512	A648	2s grn, yel & ver	.25	.25
1513	A648	13s dp grn, yel & sal pink	.60	.25
1514	A648	13s bl, lt bl & salmon	.60	.25
		Nos. 1512-1514 (3)	1.45	.75

Nos. 1512-1513: 3rd Spartacist Games; issued Aug. 10. No. 1514: 3rd congress of the Bulgarian Youth Federation; issued May 25.

Wrestlers Nicolas Petrov and Dan Kolov — A649

1966, July 29

1515	A649	13s bis brn, dk brn & lt ol grn	.75	.35

3rd International Wrestling Championships.

Map of Balkan Countries, Globe and UNESCO Emblem — A650

1966, Aug. 26 *Perf. 10½x11½*

1516	A650	13s ultra, lt grn & pink	.75	.25

First Congress of Balkanologists.

Children with Building Blocks A651

2s, Bunny & teddy bear with book. 3s, Children as astronauts. 13s, Children with pails & shovel.

1966, Sept. 1 *Perf. 10½*

1517	A651	1s dk car, org & blk	.25	.25
1518	A651	2s emerald, blk & red brn	.25	.25
1519	A651	3s ultra, org & blk	.25	.25
1520	A651	13s blue, rose & blk	1.10	.25
		Nos. 1517-1520 (4)	1.85	1.00

Children's Day.

Yuri A. Gagarin and Vostok 1 — A652

Designs: 2s, Gherman S. Titov, Vostok 2. 3s, Andrian G. Nikolayev, Pavel R. Popovich, Vostoks 3 & 4. 5s, Valentina Tereshkova, Valeri Bykovski, Vostoks 5 & 6. 8s, Vladimir M. Komarov, Boris B. Yegorov, Konstantin Feoktistov, Voskhod 1. 13s, Pavel Belyayev, Alexei Leonov, Voskhod 2.

1966, Sept. 29 Photo. *Perf. 11½x11*

1521	A652	1s slate & gray	.25	.25
1522	A652	2s plum & gray	.25	.25
1523	A652	3s yel brn & gray	.25	.25
1524	A652	5s brn red & gray	.25	.25
1525	A652	8s ultra & gray	.30	.25
1526	A652	13s Prus bl & gray	.80	.25
		Nos. 1521-1526,B29 (7)	3.50	1.95

Russian space explorations.

St. Clement, 14th Century Wood Sculpture A653

1966, Oct. 27 Photo. *Perf. 11½x11*

1527	A653	5s red, buff & brown	.70	.35

1050th anniversary of the birth of St. Clement of Ochrida.

Metodi Shatorov A654

Portraits: 3s, Vladimir Trichkov. 5s, Valcho Ivanov. 10s, Raiko Daskalov. 13s, General Vladimir Zaimov.

1966, Nov. 8 *Perf. 11x11½*

Gold Frame, Black Denomination

1528	A654	2s crimson & bl vio	.25	.25
1529	A654	3s magenta & blk	.25	.25
1530	A654	5s car rose & dk bl	.25	.25
1531	A654	10s orange & olive	.45	.25
1532	A654	13s red & brown	.55	.25
		Nos. 1528-1532 (5)	1.75	1.25

Fighters against fascism.

George Dimitrov — A655

Steel Worker — A656

1966, Nov. 14 Photo. *Perf. 11½x11*

1533	A655	2s magenta & blk	.25	.25
1534	A656	20s fawn, gray & blk	.90	.25

Bulgarian Communist Party, 9th Congress.

Deer's Head Drinking Cup A667

Gold Treasure: 2s, 6s, 10s, Various Amazon's head jugs. 3s, Ram's head cup. 5s, Circular plate. 8s, Deer's head cup. 13s, Amphora. 20s, Ram drinking horn.

1966, Nov. 28 *Perf. 12x11½*

Vessels in Gold and Brown; Black Inscriptions

1535	A667	1s gray & violet	.25	.25
1536	A667	2s gray & green	.25	.25
1537	A667	3s gray & dk bl	.25	.25
1538	A667	5s gray & red brn	.25	.25
1539	A667	6s gray & Prus bl	.25	.25
1540	A667	8s gray & brn ol	.90	.25
1541	A667	10s gray & sepia	.90	.25
1542	A667	13s gray & dk vio bl	1.10	.35
1543	A667	20s gray & vio brn	1.90	.55
		Nos. 1535-1543 (9)	6.05	2.65

The gold treasure from the 4th century B.C. was found near Panagyurishte in 1949.

Tourist House, Bansko — A668

Tourist Houses: No. 1545, Belogradchik. No. 1546, Triavna. 20s, Rila.

1966, Nov. 29 Photo. *Perf. 11x11½*

1544	A668	1s dark blue	.25	.25
1545	A668	2s dark green	.25	.25
1546	A668	2s brown red	.25	.25
1547	A668	20s lilac	.65	.25
		Nos. 1544-1547 (4)	1.40	1.00

Decorated Tree
A669

Design: 13s, Jug with bird design.

1966, Dec. 12 *Perf. 11*

1548 A669 2s grn, pink & gold .25 .25
1549 A669 13s brn lake, rose, emer & gold .65 .25

New Year, 1967.

Pencho Slaveikov, Author — A670

Portraits: 2s, Dimcho Debeljanov, author. 3s, P. H. Todorov, author. 5s, Dimitri Dobrovich, painter. 8s, Ivan Markvichka, painter. 13s, Ilya Bezhkov, painter.

1966, Dec. 15 *Perf. 10½x11*

1550 A670 1s blue, olive & org .25 .25
1551 A670 2s org, brn & gray .25 .25
1552 A670 3s olive, bl & org .25 .25
1553 A670 5s gray, red brn & org .25 .25
1554 A670 8s lilac, dk gray & bl .40 .25
1555 A670 13s blue, vio & lil .55 .25
Nos. 1550-1555 (6) 1.95 1.50

Dahlia — A671

Flowers: No. 1557, Clematis. No. 1558, Foxglove. No. 1559, Narcissus. 3s, Snowdrop. 5s, Petunia. 13s, Tiger lily. 20s, Bellflower.

Flowers in Natural Colors

1966, Dec. 29

1556 A671 1s gray & lt brn .25 .25
1557 A671 1s gray & dull bl .25 .25
1558 A671 2s gray & dull lil .25 .25
1559 A671 2s gray & brown .25 .25
1560 A671 3s gray & dk grn .35 .25
1561 A671 5s gray & dp ultra .45 .25
1562 A671 13s gray & brown 1.00 .25
1563 A671 20s gray & ultra 1.00 .35
Nos. 1556-1563 (8) 3.80 2.10

Ringnecked Pheasant — A672

Game: 2s, Rock partridge. 3s, Gray partridge. 5s, Hare. 8s, Roe deer. 13s, Red deer.

1967, Jan. 28 *Perf. 11x10½*

1564 A672 1s lt ultra, dk brn & ocher .25 .25
1565 A672 2s pale yel grn & dk grn .25 .25
1566 A672 3s lt bl, blk & cr .25 .25
1567 A672 5s lt grn & blk .65 .35
1568 A672 8s pale bl, dk brn & ocher 2.00 .65
1569 A672 13s bl & dk brn 2.50 1.10
Nos. 1564-1569 (6) 5.90 2.85

Bulgaria No. 1, 1879 — A673

1967, Feb. 4 **Photo.** *Perf. 10½*

1570 A673 10s emerald, blk & yel 1.75 1.00

Bulgarian Philatelic Union, 10th Congress.

Thracian Coin, 6th Century, B.C. — A674

Coins: 2s, Macedonian tetradrachma, 2nd cent. B.C. 3s, Tetradrachma of Odessus, 2nd cent. B.C. 5s, Philip II of Macedonia, 4th cent., B.C. 13s, Thracian King Seuthus VII, 4th cent., B.C., obverse and reverse. 20s, Apollonian coin, 5th cent., B.C., obverse and reverse.

1967, Mar. 30 *Perf. 11½x11*

Size: 25x25mm

1571 A674 1s brn, blk & sil .25 .25
1572 A674 2s red lil, blk & sil .25 .25
1573 A674 3s grn, blk & sil .25 .25
1574 A674 5s brn org, blk & sil .40 .30

Size: 37½x25mm

1575 A674 13s brt bl, blk & brnz 1.10 .60
1576 A674 20s vio, blk & sil 2.00 1.00
Nos. 1571-1576 (6) 4.25 2.65

Partisans Listening to Radio — A675

Design: 20s, George Dimitrov addressing crowd and Bulgarian flag.

1967, Apr. 20 *Perf. 11x11½*

1577 A675 1s red, gold, buff & sl grn .25 .25
1578 A675 20s red, gold, dl red, grn & blk .85 .25

25th anniversary of the Union of Patriotic Front Organizations.

Nikolas Kofardjiev A676

2s, Petko Napetov. 5s, Petko D. Petkov. 10s, Emil Markov. 13s, Traitcho Kostov.

1967, Apr. 24 *Perf. 11½x11*

1579 A676 1s brn red, gray & blk .25 .25
1580 A676 2s ol grn, gray & blk .25 .25
1581 A676 5s brn, gray & blk .25 .25
1582 A676 10s dp bl, gray & blk .25 .25
1583 A676 13s mag, gray & blk .75 .25
Nos. 1579-1583 (5) 1.75 1.25

Fighters against fascism.

Symbolic Flower and Flame — A677

1967, May 18 **Photo.** *Perf. 11x11½*

1584 A677 13s gold, yel & lt grn .70 .25

First Cultural Congress, May 18-19.

Gold Sand Beach and ITY Emblem A678

20s, Hotel, Pamporovo. 40s, Nessebr Church.

1967, June 12 **Photo.** *Perf. 11x11½*

1585 A678 13s ultra, yel & blk .35 .25
1586 A678 20s Prus bl, blk & buff .75 .30
1587 A678 40s brt grn, blk & ocher 1.90 .55
Nos. 1585-1587 (3) 3.00 1.10

International Tourist Year, 1967.

Angora Cat — A679

Cats: 2s, Siamese, horiz. 3s, Abyssinian. 5s, Black European. 13s, Persian, horiz. 20s, Striped domestic.

Perf. 11½x11, 11x11½

1967, June 19

1588 A679 1s dl vio, dk brn & buff .25 .25
1589 A679 2s ol, sl & brt bl .25 .25
1590 A679 3s dull blue & brn .35 .25
1591 A679 5s grn, blk & yel 1.00 .25
1592 A679 13s dl red brn, sl & org 1.40 .25
1593 A679 20s gray grn, brn & buff 1.75 .45
Nos. 1588-1593 (6) 5.00 1.70

Scene from Opera "The Master of Boyana" by K. Iliev A680

Songbird on Keyboard — A681

1967, June 19

1594 A680 5s gray, vio bl & dp car .30 .25
1595 A681 13s gray, dp car & dk bl .55 .25

3rd Intl. Competition for Young Opera Singers.

George Kirkov (1867-1919), Revolutionist — A682

1967, June 24 *Perf. 11x11½*

1596 A682 2s rose red & dk brn .25 .25

Symbolic Tree and Stars — A683

1967, July 28 **Photo.** *Perf. 11½x11*

1597 A683 13s dp bl, car & blk .75 .25

11th Congress of Dimitrov's Union of the People's Youth.

Roses and Distillery A684

Designs: No. 1599, Chick and incubator. No. 1600, Cucumbers and hothouse. No. 1601, Lamb and sheep farm. 3s, Sunflower and oil mill. 4s, Pigs and pig farm. 5s, Hops and hop farm. 6s, Corn and irrigation system. 8s, Grapes and Bolgar tractor. 10s, Apples and cultivated tree. 13s, Bees and honey. 20s, Bee, blossoms and beehives.

1967 *Perf. 11x11½*

1598 A684 1s multicolored .25 .25
1599 A684 1s dk car, yel & blk .25 .25
1600 A684 2s vio, lt grn & blk .25 .25
1601 A684 2s brt grn, gray & blk .25 .25
1602 A684 3s yel grn, yel & blk .25 .25
1603 A684 4s brt pur, yel & blk .25 .25
1604 A684 5s ol bis, yel grn & blk .25 .25
1605 A684 6s ol, brt grn & blk .25 .25
1606 A684 8s grn, bis & blk .35 .25
1607 A684 10s multicolored .35 .25
1608 A684 13s grn, bis brn & blk .70 .25
1609 A684 20s grnsh bl, brt pink & blk .70 .25
Nos. 1598-1609 (12) 4.10 3.00

Issue dates: Nos. 1598-1601, 1607, 1609, July 15; Nos. 1602-1606, 1608, July 24.

Map of Communist Countries, Spasski Tower A685

2s, Lenin speaking to soldiers. 3s, Fighting at Wlodaja, 1918. 5s, Marx, Engels & Lenin. 13s, Oil refinery. 20s, Vostok communication satellite.

1967, Aug. 25 *Perf. 11*

1610 A685 1s multicolored .25 .25
1611 A685 2s magenta & olive .25 .25
1612 A685 3s mag & dull vio .25 .25
1613 A685 5s magenta & red .25 .25
1614 A685 13s magenta & ultra .50 .25
1615 A685 20s magenta & blue .80 .25
Nos. 1610-1615 (6) 2.30 1.50

Russian October Revolution, 50th anniv.

Rod, "Fish" and Varna
A686

1967, Aug. 29 Photo. *Perf. 11*
1616 A686 10s multicolored .60 .25

7th World Angling Championships, Varna.

Skiers and Winter Olympics' Emblem — A687

Sports and Emblem: 2s, Ski jump. 3s, Biathlon. 5s, Ice hockey. 13s, Figure skating couple.

1967, Sept. 20 Photo. *Perf. 11*
1617 A687 1s dk bl grn, red & blk .25 .25
1618 A687 2s ultra, blk & ol .25 .25
1619 A687 3s vio brn, bl & blk .25 .25
1620 A687 5s green, yel & blk .25 .25
1621 A687 13s vio bl, blk & buff .75 .25
Nos. 1617-1621,B31 (6) 3.75 1.85

10th Winter Olympic Games, Grenoble, France, Feb. 6-18, 1968.

Mountain Peaks — A688

1967, Sept. 25 Engr. *Perf. 11½*
1622 A688 1s Bogdan .25 .25
1623 A688 2s Czerny .25 .25
1624 A688 3s Ruen, vert. .25 .25
1625 A688 5s Persenk .25 .25
1626 A688 10s Botev .25 .25
1627 A688 13s Rila, vert. .35 .25
1628 A688 20s Vlhren .65 .25
Nos. 1622-1628 (7) 2.25 1.75

George Rakovski
A689

1967, Oct. 20 Photo. *Perf. 11*
1629 A689 13s yellow grn & blk .75 .35

Centenary of the death of George Rakovski, revolutionary against Turkish rule.

Yuri A. Gagarin, Valentina Tereshkova and Alexei Leonov — A690

Designs: 2s, Lt. Col. John H. Glenn, Jr., and Maj. Edward H. White. 5s, Earth and Molniya 1. 10s, Gemini 6 and 7. 13s, Luna 13 moon probe. 20s, Gemini 10 and Agena rocket.

1967, Nov. 25
1630 A690 1s Prus bl, blk & yel .25 .25
1631 A690 2s dl bl, blk & dl yel .25 .25
1632 A690 5s vio bl, grnsh bl & blk .25 .25
1633 A690 10s dk bl, blk & red .70 .25
1634 A690 13s grnsh bl, brt yel & blk .85 .25
1635 A690 20s dl bl, blk & red .85 .25
Nos. 1630-1635 (6) 3.15 1.50

Achievements in space exploration.

Various Views of Trnovo
A691

1967, Dec. 5 Photo. *Perf. 11*
1636 A691 1s multicolored .25 .25
1637 A691 2s multicolored .25 .25
1638 A691 3s multicolored .25 .25
1639 A691 5s multicolored .25 .25
1640 A691 13s multicolored .50 .25
1641 A691 20s multicolored .65 .25
Nos. 1636-1641 (6) 2.15 1.50

Restoration of the ancient capital Veliko Trnovo.

Ratchenitza Folk Dance, by Ivan Markvichka — A692

1967, Dec. 9
1642 A692 20s gold & gray grn 1.60 .85

Belgo-Bulgarian Philatelic Exposition, Brussels, Dec. 9-10. Printed in sheets of 8 stamps and 8 labels. No. 1642 with label, value $2.

Cosmos 186 and 188 Docking — A693

40s, Venera 4 and orbits around Venus.

1968, Jan.
1643 A693 20s multi .75 .25
1644 A693 40s multi, horiz. 1.75 .50

Docking maneuvers of the Russian spaceships Cosmos 186 and Cosmos 188, Nov. 1, 1967, and the flight to Venus of Venera 4, June 12-Nov. 18, 1967.

Crossing the Danube, by Orenburgski — A694

Paintings: 2s, Flag of Samara, by J. Veschin, vert. 3s, Battle of Pleven by Orenburgski. 13s, Battle of Orlovo Gnezdo, by N. Popov, vert. 20s, Welcome for Russian Soldiers, by D. Gudienov.

1968, Jan. 25 Photo. *Perf. 11*
1645 A694 1s gold & dk green .25 .25
1646 A694 2s gold & dk blue .25 .25
1647 A694 3s gold & chocolate .25 .25
1648 A694 13s gold & dk vio .80 .25
1649 A694 20s gold & Prus grn 1.10 .25
Nos. 1645-1649 (5) 2.65 1.25

90th anniv. of the liberation from Turkey.

Shepherds, by Zlatyn Boyadjiev — A695

Paintings: 2s, Wedding dance, by V. Dimitrov, vert. 3s, Partisans' Song, by Ilya Petrov. 5s, Portrait of Anna Penchovich, by Nikolai Pavlovich, vert. 13s, Self-portrait, by Zachary Zograf, vert. 20s, View of Old Plovdiv, by T. Lavrenov. 60s, St. Clement of Ochrida, by A. Mitov.

1967, Dec. Litho. *Perf. 11½*
Size: 45x38mm, 38x45mm
1650 A695 1s gray & multi .25 .25
1651 A695 2s gray & multi .25 .25
Size: 55x35mm
1652 A695 3s gray & multi .30 .25
Size: 38x45mm, 45x38mm
1653 A695 5s gray & multi .70 .25
1654 A695 13s gray & multi 1.40 .30
1655 A695 20s gray & multi 1.75 .70
Nos. 1650-1655 (6) 4.65 2.00

Miniature Sheet
Size: 65x84mm
Imperf
1656 A695 60s multicolored 3.50 2.00

Marx Statue, Sofia — A696

1968, Feb. 20 Photo. *Perf. 11*
1657 A696 13s black & red .70 .25

150th anniversary of birth of Karl Marx.

Maxim Gorky — A697

1968, Feb. 20
1658 A697 13s ver & grnsh blk .70 .25

Maxim Gorky (1868-1936), Russian writer.

Folk Dancers — A698

5s, Runners. 13s, Doves. 20s, Festival poster, (head, flowers, birds). 40s, Globe & Bulgaria No. 1 under magnifying glass.

1968, Mar. 20
1659 A698 2s multicolored .25 .25
1660 A698 5s multicolored .25 .25
1661 A698 13s multicolored .70 .25
1662 A698 20s multicolored .70 .25
1663 A698 40s multicolored 1.20 .65
Nos. 1659-1663 (5) 3.10 1.65

9th Youth Festival for Peace and Friendship, Sofia, July 28-Aug. 6.

Bellflower — A699

1968, Apr. 25 *Perf. 11*
1664 A699 1s shown .25 .25
1665 A699 2s Gentian .25 .25
1666 A699 3s Crocus .25 .25
1667 A699 5s Iris .35 .25
1668 A699 10s Dog-tooth violet .50 .25
1669 A699 13s Sempervivum 1.00 .25
1670 A699 20s Dictamnus 1.00 .35
Nos. 1664-1670 (7) 3.60 1.85

"The Unknown Hero," Tale by Ran Bosilek
A700

Design: 20s, The Witch and the Young Man (Hans Christian Andersen fairy tale.)

1968, Apr. 25 Photo. *Perf. 10½*
1671 A700 13s black & multi .35 .25
1672 A700 20s black & multi .70 .50

Bulgarian-Danish Philatelic Exhibition.

Memorial Church, Shipka — A701

1968, May 3
1673 A701 13s multi + label .85 .25

Bulgarian Stamp Exhibition in Berlin. No. 1673 with label, value $1.25.

Show Jumping
A702

Olympic Rings and: 1s, Gymnast on bar. 3s, Fencer. 10s, Boxer. 13s, Woman discus thrower.

1968, June 24 Photo. *Perf. 10½*
1674 A702 1s red & black .25 .25
1675 A702 2s gray, blk & rose brn .25 .25
1676 A702 3s mag, gray & blk .25 .25
1677 A702 10s grnsh bl, blk & lem .50 .25
1678 A702 13s vio bl, gray & pink 1.00 .35
Nos. 1674-1678,B33 (6) 3.65 1.80

19th Olympic Games, Mexico City, 10/12-27.

Battle of Buzluja A703

Design: 13s, Haji Dimitr and Stefan Karaja.

1968, July 1

1679 A703 2s silver & red brn .25 .25
1680 A703 13s gold & sl grn .55 .25

Centenary of the death of the patriots Haji Dimitr and Stefan Karaja.

Lakes of Smolian — A704

Bulgarian Scenes: 2s, Ropotamo Lake. 3s, Erma-Idreloto mountain pass. 8s, Isker River dam. 10s, Slanchev Breg (sailing ship). 13s, Cape Caliacra. 40s, Old houses, Sozopol. 2 l, Chudnite Skali ("Strange Mountains").

1968 Photo. *Perf. 13*

1681 A704 1s Prus green .25 .25
1682 A704 2s dark green .25 .25
1683 A704 3s dark brown .25 .25
1684 A704 8s olive green .30 .25
1685 A704 10s redsh brown .35 .25
1686 A704 13s dk olive grn .25 .25
1687 A704 40s Prus blue 1.10 .40
1688 A704 2 l sepia 3.75 1.25
Nos. 1681-1688 (8) 6.50 3.15

Sofia Zoo, 80th Anniv. — A705

1968, July 29 *Perf. 10½*

1689 A705 1s Cinereous vulture .25 .25
1690 A705 2s Crowned crane .25 .25
1691 A705 3s Zebra .25 .25
1692 A705 5s Cheetah .35 .25
1693 A705 13s Indian python 2.10 .90
1694 A705 20s African crocodile 2.75 1.50
Nos. 1689-1694 (6) 5.95 3.40

Human Rights Flame — A706

1968, July 8

1695 A706 20s dp blue & gold .90 .35

International Human Rights Year, 1968.

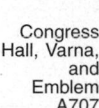

Congress Hall, Varna, and Emblem A707

1968, Sept. 17 Photo. *Perf. 10½*

1696 A707 20s bister, grn & red .70 .25

56th International Dental Congress, Varna.

Flying Swans A708

Rose A709

Designs: 2s, Jug. 20s, Five Viking ships.

1968 Photo. *Perf. 10½*

1697 A709 2s green & ocher 1.10 1.10
1698 A708 5s dp blue & gray 1.10 1.10
1699 A709 13s dp plum & lil rose 1.10 1.10
a. Pair, #1698, 1699 + label 2.50 2.50
1700 A708 20s dp vio & gray 1.00 1.00
a. Pair, #1697, 1700 + label 2.50 2.50
Nos. 1697-1700 (4) 4.30 4.30

Cooperation with the Scandinavian countries. Issued: 5s, 13s, Sept. 12; 2s, 20s, Nov. 22.

Stag Beetle — A710

No. 1702, Ground beetle (Procerus scabrosus). No. 1703, Ground beetle (Calosoma sycophania). No. 1704, Scarab beetle, horiz. No. 1705, Saturnid moth, horiz.

Perf. 12½x13, 13x12½

1968, Aug. 26

1701 A710 1s brown olive .25 .25
1702 A710 1s dark blue .25 .25
1703 A710 1s dark green .25 .25
1704 A710 1s orange brown .25 .25
1705 A710 1s magenta .25 .25
Nos. 1701-1705 (5) 1.25 1.25

Turks Fighting Insurgents, 1688 — A711

1968, Aug. 22 *Perf. 10½*

1706 A711 13s multicolored .75 .25

280th anniversary of the Tchiprovtzi insurrection.

Christo Smirnenski (1898-1923), Poet — A712

1968, Sept. 28 Litho. *Perf. 10½*

1707 A712 13s gold, red org & blk .75 .25

Dalmatian Pelican — A713

Birds: 2s, Little egret. 3s, Crested grebe. 5s, Common tern. 13s, European spoonbill. 20s, Glossy ibis.

1968, Oct. 28 Photo.

1708 A713 1s silver & multi .25 .25
1709 A713 2s silver & multi .35 .25
1710 A713 3s silver & multi .35 .25
1711 A713 5s silver & multi .65 .25
1712 A713 13s silver & multi 1.60 1.25
1713 A713 20s silver & multi 3.25 1.50
Nos. 1708-1713 (6) 6.45 3.75

Srebirna wild life reservation.

Carrier Pigeon A714

1968, Oct. 19

1714 A714 20s emerald .90 .75
a. Sheet of 4 + labels 7.00 3.50

2nd Natl. Stamp Exhib. in Sofia, Oct. 25-Nov. 15. No. 1714a contains 4 No. 1714 and 5 labels. No. 1714 with label, value $1.50.

An imperforate sheet similar to No. 1714a contains stamps in a different color that are not valid for postage.

Man and Woman from Silistra A715

Regional Costumes: 2s, Lovech. 3s, Yambol. 13s, Chirpan. 20s, Razgrad. 40s, Ihtiman.

1968, Nov. 20 Litho. *Perf. 13½*

1715 A715 1s dp org & multi .25 .25
1716 A715 2s Prus bl & multi .25 .25
1717 A715 3s multicolored .25 .25
1718 A715 13s multicolored .50 .25
1719 A715 20s multicolored .90 .40
1720 A715 40s green & multi 2.00 .50
Nos. 1715-1720 (6) 4.15 1.90

St. Arsenius A716

10th cent. Murals & Icons: 2s, Procession with relics of St. Ivan Rilsky, horiz. 3s, St. Michael Torturing the Soul of the Rich Man. 13s, St. Ivan Rilski. 20s, St. John. 40s, St. George. 1 l, Procession meeting relics of St. Ivan Rilsky, horiz.

Perf. 11½x12½, 12½x11½

1968, Nov. 25 Photo.

1721 A716 1s gold & multi .25 .25
1722 A716 2s gold & multi .25 .25
1723 A716 3s gold & multi .25 .25
1724 A716 13s gold & multi .85 .25
1725 A716 20s gold & multi 1.25 .55
1726 A716 40s gold & multi 2.00 .85
Nos. 1721-1726 (6) 4.85 2.40

Souvenir Sheet

Imperf

1727 A716 1 l gold & multi 3.50 3.00

Millenium of Rila Monastery. No. 1727 also: Sofia 1969 Intl. Phil. Exhib., May 31-June 8, 1969. No. 1727 contains one stamp, size: 57x51mm.

Medlar A717

Herbs: No. 1729, Camomile. 2s, Lily-of-the-valley. 3s, Belladonna. 5s, Mallow. 10s, Buttercup. 13s, Poppies. 20s, Thyme.

1969, Jan. 2 Litho. *Perf. 10½*

1728 A717 1s blk, grn & org red .25 .25
1729 A717 1s black, grn & yel .25 .25
1730 A717 2s blk, emer & grn .25 .25
1731 A717 3s black & multi .25 .25
1732 A717 5s black & multi .25 .25
1733 A717 10s black, grn & yel .50 .25
1734 A717 13s black & multi .55 .25
1735 A717 20s black, lil & grn .85 .25
Nos. 1728-1735 (8) 3.15 2.00

Silkworms and Spindles A718

Designs: 2s, Silkworm, cocoons and pattern. 3s, Cocoons and spinning wheel. 5s, Cocoons, woof-and-warp diagram. 13s, Silk moth, Cocoon and spinning frame. 20s, Silk moth, eggs and shuttle.

1969, Jan. 30 Photo. *Perf. 10½*

1736 A718 1s bl, grn, sl & blk .25 .25
1737 A718 2s dp car, sil & blk .25 .25
1738 A718 3s Prus bl, sil & blk .25 .25
1739 A718 5s pur, ver, sil & blk .25 .25
1740 A718 13s red lil, ocher, sil & blk .40 .25
1741 A718 20s grn, org, sil & blk .70 .25
Nos. 1736-1741 (6) 2.10 1.50

Bulgarian silk industry.

Attack and Capture of Emperor Nicephorus A719

Designs (Manasses Chronicle): No. 1742, 1s, Death of Ivan Asen. No. 1746, 3s, Khan Kroum feasting after victory. No. 1748, 13s, Invasion of Bulgaria by Prince Sviatoslav of Kiev. No. 1750, 20s, Russian invasion and campaigns of Emperor John I Zimisces, c. 972 A.D. No. 1752, 40s, Tsar Ivan Alexander, Jesus and Constantine Manasses.

Horizontal designs: No. 1743, 1s, Kings Nebuchadnezzar, Balthazar, Darius and Cyrus. No. 1745, 2s, Kings Cambyses, Gyges and Darius. No. 1747, 5s, King David and Tsar Ivan Alexander. No. 1749, 13s, Persecution of Byzantine army after battle of July 26, 811. No. 1751, 20s, Christening of Bulgarian Tsar Boris, 865. No. 1753, 60s, Arrival of Tsar Simeon in Constantinople and his succeeding surprise attack on that city.

1969 Photo. *Perf. 14x13½, 13½x14*

1742 A719 1s multicolored .25 .25
1743 A719 1s multicolored .25 .25
1744 A719 2s multicolored .25 .25
1745 A719 2s multicolored .25 .25
1746 A719 3s multicolored .25 .25
1747 A719 5s multicolored .25 .25

1748	A719 13s multicolored	.55	.25
1749	A719 13s multicolored	.55	.25
1750	A719 20s multicolored	1.10	.25
1751	A719 20s multicolored	1.10	.25
1752	A719 40s multicolored	1.75	.55
1753	A719 60s multicolored	2.50	.55
	Nos. 1742-1753 (12)	9.05	3.60

Sts. Cyril and Methodius, Mural, Troian Monastery A720

1969, Mar. 23

1754	A720 28s gold & multi	1.40	.60

Post Horn — A721

Designs: 13s, Bulgaria Nos. 1 and 534. 20s, Street fighting at Stackata, 1919.

1969, Apr. 15 Photo. *Perf. 10½*

1755	A721 2s green & yel	.25	.25
1756	A721 13s multicolored	.50	.25
1757	A721 20s dk bl & lt bl	.85	.25
	Nos. 1755-1757 (3)	1.60	.75

Bulgarian postal administration, 90th anniv.

The Fox and the Rabbit A722

Puppet theater characters and illustrations from children's books: 2s, Boy reading to hedgehog and squirrel. 13s, Two birds and frog singing together.

1969, Apr. 21

1758	A722 1s emer, org & blk	.25	.25
1759	A722 2s org, lt bl & blk	.25	.25
1760	A722 13s lt bl, ol & blk	.40	.25
	Nos. 1758-1760 (3)	.90	.75

Issued for Week of Children's Books and Arts.

ILO Emblem — A723

1969, Apr. 28

1761	A723 13s dull grn & blk	.50	.25

50th anniv. of the ILO.

St. George and SOFIA 69 Emblem A724

Designs: 2s, Virgin Mary and St. John Bogoslov. 3s, Archangel Michael. 5s, Three Saints. 8s, Jesus Christ. 13s, Sts. George and Dimitrie. 20s, Christ, the Almighty. 40s, St. Dimitrie. 60s, The 40 Martyrs. 80s, The Transfiguration.

1969, Apr. 30 *Perf. 11x12*

1762	A724 1s gold & multi	.25	.25
1763	A724 2s gold & multi	.25	.25
1764	A724 3s gold & multi	.25	.25
1765	A724 5s gold & multi	.30	.25
1766	A724 8s gold & multi	.30	.25
1767	A724 13s gold & multi	.50	.25
1768	A724 20s gold & multi	.75	.30
1769	A724 40s gold & multi	1.40	1.00
a.	Sheet of 4	9.00	7.75
1770	A724 60s gold & multi	2.00	1.50
1771	A724 80s gold & multi	3.00	1.75
	Nos. 1762-1771 (10)	9.00	6.05

Old Bulgarian art from the National Art Gallery. No. 1769a contains 4 of No. 1769 with center gutter showing Alexander Nevski Shrine. See note on SOFIA 69 after Nos. C112-C120.

St. Cyril Preaching A725

Design: 28s, St. Cyril and followers.

1969, June 20 Litho. *Perf. 10½*

1772	A725 2s sil, grn & red	.25	.25
1773	A725 28s sil, dk bl & red	1.25	.45

St. Cyril (827-869), apostle to the Slavs, inventor of Cyrillic alphabet. Issued in sheets of 25 with se-tenant labels; Cyrillic inscription on label of 2s, Glagolitic inscription on label of 28s.

St. Sophia Church — A726

Sofia Through the Ages: 1s, Roman coin with inscription "Ulpia Serdica." 2s, Roman coin with Aesculapius Temple. 4s, Bojana Church. 5s, Sobranie Parliament. 13s, Vasov National Theater. 20s, Alexander Nevski Shrine. 40s, Clement Ochrida University. 1 l, Coat of arms.

1969, May 25 *Perf. 13x12½*

1774	A726 1s gold & blue	.25	.25
1775	A726 2s gold & ol grn	.25	.25
1776	A726 3s gold & red brn	.25	.25
1777	A726 4s gold & purple	.25	.25
1778	A726 5s gold & plum	.25	.25
1779	A726 13s gold & brt grn	.35	.25
1780	A726 20s gold & vio bl	.55	.25
1781	A726 40s gold & dp car	1.10	.30
	Nos. 1774-1781 (8)	3.25	2.05

Souvenir Sheet

Imperf

1782	A726 1 l grn, gold & red	3.50	2.25

Historic Sofia in connection with the International Philatelic Exhibition, Sofia, 5/31-6/8.

No. 1782 contains one 43½x43½mm stamp. Emblems of 8 preceding philatelic exhibitions in metallic ink in margin; gold inscription.

No. 1782 was overprinted in green "IBRA 73" and various symbols, and released May 4, 1973, for the Munich Philatelic Exhibition. Value $150. The overprint also exists in gray. Value $50.

St. George A727

1969, June 9 Litho. *Perf. 11½*

1783	A727 40s sil, blk & pale rose	1.75	.75

38th FIP Congress, June 9-11.

Hand Planting Sapling A728

1969, Apr. 28 Photo. *Perf. 11*

1784	A728 2s ol grn, blk & lilac	.25	.25

25 years of the reforestation campaign.

Partisans — A729

Designs: 2s, Combine harvester. 3s, Dam. 5s, Flutist and singers. 13s, Factory. 20s, Lenin, Dimitrov, Russian and Bulgarian flags.

1969, Sept. 9

1785	A729 1s blk, pur & org	.25	.25
1786	A729 2s blk, ol bis & org	.25	.25
1787	A729 3s blk, bl grn & org	.25	.25
1788	A729 5s blk, brn red & org	.25	.25
1789	A729 13s blk, bl & org	.50	.25
1790	A729 20s blk, brn & org	.85	.25
	Nos. 1785-1790 (6)	2.35	1.50

25th anniversary of People's Republic.

Women Gymnasts — A730

1969, Sept. Photo. *Perf. 11*

1791	A730 2s shown	.25	.25
1792	A730 20s Wrestlers	.70	.30

Third National Spartakiad.

Tchanko Bakalov Tcherkovski, Poet. Birth Cent. — A731

1969, Sept. 6

1793	A731 13s multicolored	.60	.25

Woman Gymnast A732

2s, Two women with hoops. 3s, Woman with hoop. 5s, Two women with spheres.

1969, Oct.

Gymnasts in Light Gray

1794	A732 1s green & dk blue	.25	.25
1795	A732 2s blue & dk blue	.25	.25
1796	A732 3s emer & sl grn	.25	.25
1797	A732 5s orange & pur	.25	.25
	Nos. 1794-1797,B35-B36 (6)	2.80	1.75

World Championships for Artistic Gymnastics, Varna.

The Priest Rilski, by Zachary Zograf A733

Paintings from the National Art Gallery. 2s, Woman at Window, by Vasil Stoilov. 3s, Workers at Rest, by Nenko Balkanski, horiz. 4s, Woman Dressing (Nude), by Ivan Nenov. 5s, Portrait of a Woman, by N. Pavlovich. 13s, Falstaff, by Duzunov Kr. Sarafov. No. 1804, Portrait of a Woman, by N. Mihajlov, horiz. No. 1805, Workers at Mealtime, by Stojan Sotirov, horiz. 40s, Self portrait, by Tcheno Togorov.

Perf. 11½x12, 12x11½

1969, Nov. 10

1798	A733 1s gold & multi	.25	.25
1799	A733 2s gold & multi	.25	.25
1800	A733 3s gold & multi	.25	.25
1801	A733 4s gold & multi	.25	.25
1802	A733 5s gold & multi	.35	.25
1803	A733 13s gold & multi	.70	.25
1804	A733 20s gold & multi	1.10	.30
1805	A733 20s gold & multi	1.10	.35
1806	A733 40s gold & multi	1.50	.35
	Nos. 1798-1806 (9)	5.75	2.50

Roman Bronze Wolf — A734

Design: 2s, Roman statue of woman, found at Silistra, vert.

1969, Oct. Photo. *Perf. 11*

1807	A734 2s sil, ultra & gray	.25	.25
1808	A734 13s sil, dk grn & gray	.80	.30

City of Silistra's 1,800th anniversary.

Worker and Factory A735

1969 *Perf. 13*

1809 A735 6s ultra & blk .25 .25

25th anniversary of the Engineering Corps.

European Hake — A736

Designs: No. 1811, Deep-sea fishing trawler. Fish: 2s, Atlantic horse mackerel. 3s, Pilchard. 5s, Dentex macrophthalmus. 10s, Chub mackerel. 13s, Otolithes macrognathus. 20s, Lichia vadigo.

1969 *Perf. 11*

1810 A736 1s ol grn & blk .25 .25
1811 A736 1s ultra, ind & gray .25 .25
1812 A736 2s lilac & blk .25 .25
1813 A736 3s vio bl & blk .25 .25
1814 A736 5s rose cl, pink & blk .25 .25
1815 A736 10s gray & blk 1.10 .25
1816 A736 13s ver, sal & blk 1.60 .25
1817 A736 20s ocher & black 2.10 .25
Nos. 1810-1817 (8) 6.05 2.00

Marin Drinov A737

1969, Nov. 10 **Litho.** *Perf. 11*

1818 A737 20s black & red org .30 .25

Centenary of the Bulgarian Academy of Science, founded by Marin Drinov.

Trapeze Artists — A738

Circus Performers: 2s, Jugglers. 3s, Jugglers with loops. 5s, Juggler and bear on bicycle. 13s, Woman and performing horse. 20s, Musical clowns.

1969 **Photo.** *Perf. 11*

1819 A738 1s dk blue & multi .25 .25
1820 A738 2s dk green & multi .25 .25
1821 A738 3s dk violet & multi .25 .25
1822 A738 5s multicolored .25 .25
1823 A738 13s multicolored .50 .25
1824 A738 20s multicolored 1.10 .25
Nos. 1819-1824 (6) 2.60 1.50

Pavel Bania Sanatorium A739

Health Resorts: 5s, Chisar Sanatorium. 6s, Kotel Children's Sanatorium. 20s, Narechen Polyclinic.

1969, Dec. **Photo.** *Perf. 10½-14*

1825 A739 2s blue .25 .25
1826 A739 5s ultra .25 .25
1827 A739 6s green .25 .25
1828 A739 20s emerald .55 .25
Nos. 1825-1828 (4) 1.30 1.00

G. S. Shonin, V. N. Kubasov and Spacecraft A740

Designs: 2s, A. V. Filipchenko, V. N. Volkov, V. V. Gorbatko and spacecraft. 3s, Vladimir A. Shatalov, Alexei S. Yeliseyev and spacecraft. 28s, Three spacecraft in orbit.

1970, Jan. **Photo.** *Perf. 11*

1829 A740 1s rose car, ol grn & blk .25 .25
1830 A740 2s bl, dl cl & blk .25 .25
1831 A740 3s grnsh bl, vio & blk .25 .25
1832 A740 28s vio bl, lil rose & lt bl 1.00 .25
Nos. 1829-1832 (4) 1.75 1.00

Russian space flights of Soyuz 6, 7 and 8, Oct. 11-13, 1969.

Khan Krum and Defeat of Emperor Nicephorus, 811 — A741

Bulgarian History: 1s, Khan Asparuch and Bulgars crossing the Danube (679). 3s, Conversion of Prince Boris to Christianity, 865. 5s, Tsar Simeon and battle of Akhelo, 917. 8s, Tsar Samuel defeating the Byzantines, 976. 10s, Tsar Kaloyan defeating Emperor Baldwin, 1205. 13s, Tsar Ivan Assen II defeating Greek King Theodore Komnine, 1230. 20s, Coronation of Tsar Ivailo, 1277.

1970, Feb. *Perf. 10½*

1833 A741 1s gold & multi .25 .25
1834 A741 2s gold & multi .25 .25
1835 A741 3s gold & multi .25 .25
1836 A741 5s gold & multi .25 .25
1837 A741 8s gold & multi .25 .25
1838 A741 10s gold & multi .45 .25
1839 A741 13s gold & multi .65 .25
1840 A741 20s gold & multi 1.00 .25
Nos. 1833-1840 (8) 3.35 2.00

See Nos. 2126-2133.

Bulgarian Pavilion, EXPO '70 — A742

1970 *Perf. 12½*

1841 A742 20s brown, sil & org 1.40 .75

EXPO '70 International Exposition, Osaka, Japan, Mar. 15-Sept. 13, 1970.

Soccer — A743

Designs: Various views of soccer game.

1970, Mar. 4 **Photo.** *Perf. 12½*

1842 A743 1s blue & multi .25 .25
1843 A743 2s rose car & multi .25 .25
1844 A743 3s ultra & multi .25 .25
1845 A743 5s green & multi .25 .25
1846 A743 20s emerald & multi 1.20 .25
1847 A743 40s red & multi 1.50 .45
Nos. 1842-1847 (6) 3.70 1.70

9th World Soccer Championships for the Jules Rimet Cup, Mexico City, May 30-June 21, 1970. See No. B37.

Lenin (1870-1924) — A744

1970, Apr. 22

1848 A744 2s shown .25 .25
1849 A744 13s Portrait .55 .25
1850 A744 20s Writing 1.20 .25
Nos. 1848-1850 (3) 2.00 .75

Tephrocactus Alexanderi V. Bruchii — A745

Cacti: 2s, Opuntia drummondii. 3s, Hatiora cilindrica. 5s, Gymnocalycium vatteri. 8s, Heliantho cereus grandiflorus. 10s, Neochilenia andreaeana. 13s, Peireskia vargasii v. longispina. 20s, Neobesseya rosiflora.

1970 **Photo.** *Perf. 12½*

1851 A745 1s multicolored .25 .25
1852 A745 2s dk green & multi .25 .25
1853 A745 3s multicolored .25 .25
1854 A745 5s blue & multi .25 .25
1855 A745 8s brown & multi .35 .30
1856 A745 10s vio bl & multi 1.75 .40
1857 A745 13s brn red & multi 1.75 .75
1858 A745 20s purple & multi 2.10 .75
Nos. 1851-1858 (8) 6.95 3.20

Rose — A746

Designs: Various Roses.

1970, June 5 **Litho.** *Perf. 13½*

1859 A746 1s gray & multi .25 .25
1860 A746 2s gray & multi .25 .25
1861 A746 3s gray & multi .25 .25
1862 A746 4s gray & multi .35 .25
1863 A746 5s gray & multi .35 .25
1864 A746 13s gray & multi .65 .30
1865 A746 20s gray & multi 1.40 .65
1866 A746 28s gray & multi 2.50 .95
Nos. 1859-1866 (8) 6.00 3.15

Gold Bowl A747

Designs: Various bowls and art objects from Gold Treasure of Thrace.

1970, June 15 **Photo.** *Perf. 12½*

1867 A747 1s blk, bl & gold .25 .25
1868 A747 2s blk, lt vio & gold .25 .25
1869 A747 3s blk, ver & gold .25 .25
1870 A747 5s blk, yel grn & gold .25 .25
1871 A747 13s blk, org & gold 1.10 .25
1872 A747 20s blk, lil & gold 1.40 .25
Nos. 1867-1872 (6) 3.50 1.50

EXPO Emblem, Rose and Bulgarian Woman — A748

Designs (EXPO Emblem and): 2s, Three women. 3s, Woman and fruit. 28s, Dancers. 40s, Mt. Fuji and pavilions.

1970, June 20

1873 A748 1s gold & multi .25 .25
1874 A748 2s gold & multi .25 .25
1875 A748 3s gold & multi .25 .25
1876 A748 28s gold & multi 1.10 .30
Nos. 1873-1876 (4) 1.85 1.05

Miniature Sheet

Imperf

1877 A748 40s gold & multi 1.40 .85

EXPO '70 International Exposition, Osaka, Japan, Mar. 15-Sept. 13. No. 1877 contains one stamp with simulated perforations.

Ivan Vasov A749

1970, Aug. 1 **Photo.** *Perf. 12½*

1878 A749 13s violet blue .75 .25

Ivan Vasov, author, 120th birth anniv.

UN Emblem — A750

1970, Aug. 1

1879 A750 20s Prus bl & gold .75 .25

25th anniversary of the United Nations.

George Dimitrov — A751

1970, June 8

1880 A751 20s blk, gold & org 1.10 .25

BZNC (Bulgarian Communist Party), 70th anniv.

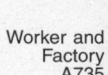

Retriever
A752

Dogs: 1s, Golden retriever, horiz. 3s, Great Dane. 4s, Boxer. 5s, Cocker spaniel. 13s, Doberman pinscher. 20s, Scottish terrier. 28s, Russian greyhound, horiz.

1970 Photo. *Perf. 12½*

1881	A752	1s multicolored	.25	.25
1882	A752	2s multicolored	.25	.25
1883	A752	3s multicolored	.25	.25
1884	A752	4s multicolored	.40	.25
1885	A752	5s multicolored	.40	.25
1886	A752	13s multicolored	1.10	.40
1887	A752	20s multicolored	2.10	.75
1888	A752	28s multicolored	2.50	1.10
		Nos. 1881-1888 (8)	7.25	3.50

Volleyball
A753

No. 1890, Two women players. No. 1891, Woman player. No. 1892, Man player.

1970, Sept. Photo. *Perf. 12½*

1889	A753	2s dk red brn, bl & blk	.25	.25
1890	A753	2s ultra, org & blk	.25	.25
1891	A753	20s Prus bl, yel & blk	.90	.25
1892	A753	20s grn, yel & blk	.90	.25
		Nos. 1889-1892 (4)	2.30	1.00

World Volleyball Championships.

Enrico Caruso and "I Pagliacci" by Ruggiero Leoncavallo — A754

Opera Singers and Operas: 2s, Christina Morfova and "The Bartered Bride" by Bedrich Smetana. 3s, Peter Reitchev and "Tosca" by Giacomo Puccini. 10s, Svetana Tabakova and "The Flying Dutchman" by Richard Wagner. 13s, Katia Popova and "The Masters" by Paroshkev Hadjev. 20s, Feodor Chaliapin and "Boris Godunov" by Modest Musorgski.

1970, Oct. 15 Photo. *Perf. 14*

1893	A754	1s black & multi	.25	.25
1894	A754	2s black & multi	.25	.25
1895	A754	3s black & multi	.25	.25
1896	A754	10s black & multi	.25	.25
1897	A754	13s black & multi	.35	.25
1898	A754	20s black & multi	1.60	.25
		Nos. 1893-1898 (6)	2.95	1.50

Honoring opera singers in their best roles.

Ivan Assen II Coin — A755

Coins from 14th Century with Ruler's Portrait: 2s, Theodor Svetoslav. 3s, Mikhail Chichman. 13s, Ivan Alexander and Mikhail Assen. 20s, Ivan Sratsimir. 28s, Ivan Chichman (initials).

1970, Nov. *Perf. 12½*

1899	A755	1s buff & multi	.25	.25
1900	A755	2s gray & multi	.25	.25
1901	A755	3s multicolored	.25	.25
1902	A755	13s multicolored	.35	.25
1903	A755	20s lt blue & multi	1.00	.25
1904	A755	28s multicolored	1.40	.40
		Nos. 1899-1904 (6)	3.50	1.65

Fire Protection
A756

1970 Litho. *Perf. 12½*

1905	A756	1s Fireman	.25	.25
1906	A756	3s Fire engine	.25	.25

Bicyclists
A757

1970 Photo.

1907	A757	20s grn, yel & pink	.75	.25

20th Bulgarian bicycle race.

Congress Emblem — A758

1970

1908	A758	13s gold & multi	.60	.25

7th World Congress of Sociology, Varna, Sept. 14-19.

Ludwig van Beethoven
A759

1970

1909	A759	28s lil rose & dk bl	2.10	1.10

Beethoven (1770-1827), composer.

Friedrich Engels — A760

1970 Photo. *Perf. 12½*

1910	A760	13s ver, tan & brn	.75	.25

Friedrich Engels (1820-1895), German socialist, collaborator of Karl Marx.

Miniature Sheets

Luna 16
A761

Russian moon mission: 80s, Lunokhod 1, unmanned vehicle on moon, horiz.

1970 Photo. *Imperf.*

1911	A761	80s plum, sil, blk & bl	4.25	4.25
1912	A761	1 l vio bl, sil & red	5.00	4.00

No. 1911 , Lunokhod 1, Nov. 10-17. No. 1912, Luna 16 mission, Sept. 12-24.
Issue dates: 80s, Dec. 18; 1 l, Nov. 10.

Snowflake — A762

1970, Dec. 15 Photo. *Perf. 12½x13*

1913	A762	2s ultra & multi	.25	.25

New Year 1971.

Birds and Flowers
A763

Folk Art: 2s, Bird and flowers. 3s, Flying birds. 5s, Birds and flowers. 13s, Sun. 20s, Tulips and pansies.

1971, Jan. 25 *Perf. 12½x13½*

1914	A763	1s multicolored	.25	.25
1915	A763	2s multicolored	.25	.25
1916	A763	3s multicolored	.25	.25
1917	A763	5s multicolored	.25	.25
1918	A763	13s multicolored	.25	.25
1919	A763	20s multicolored	.75	.25
		Nos. 1914-1919 (6)	2.00	1.50

Spring 1971.

Girl, by Zeko Spiridonov
A764

Modern Bulgarian Sculpture: 2s, Third Class (people looking through train window), by Ivan Funev. 3s, Bust of Elin Pelin, by Marko Markov. 13s, Bust of Nina, by Andrej Nikolov. 20s, Monument to P. K. Yavorov (kneeling woman), by Ivan Lazarov. 28s, Engineer, by Ivan Funev. 1 l, Refugees, by Sekul Krimov, horiz.

1970, Dec. 28 *Perf. 12½*

1920	A764	1s gold & vio	.25	.25
1921	A764	2s gold & dk ol grn	.25	.25
1922	A764	3s gold & rose brn	.25	.25
1923	A764	13s gold & dk grn	.50	.25
1924	A764	20s gold & red brn	.90	.25
1925	A764	28s gold & dk brn	1.00	.25
		Nos. 1920-1925 (6)	3.15	1.50

Souvenir Sheet

Imperf

1926	A764	1 l gold, dk brn & buff	2.25	2.25

Runner
A765

Design: 20s, Woman putting the shot.

1971, Mar. 13 Photo. *Perf. 12½x13*

1927	A765	2s brown & multi	.25	.25
1928	A765	20s dp grn, org & blk	1.40	.35

2nd European Indoor Track and Field Championships.

Bulgarian Secondary School, Bolgrad — A766

Educators: 20s, Dimiter Mitev, Prince Bogoridi and Sava Radoulov.

1971, Mar. 16 *Perf. 12½*

1929	A766	2s silver, brn & grn	.25	.25
1930	A766	20s silver, brn & vio	1.10	.25

First Bulgarian secondary school, 1858, in Bolgrad, USSR.

Communards — A767

1971, Mar. 18 Photo. *Perf. 12½x13*

1931	A767	20s rose mag & blk	.75	.25

Centenary of the Paris Commune.

Dimitrov Facing Goering, Quotation, FIR Emblem — A768

1971, Apr. 11 *Perf. 12½*

1932	A768	2s grn, gold, blk & red	.25	.25
1933	A768	13s plum, gold, blk & red	1.10	.25

Intl. Fed. of Resistance Fighters (FIR), 20th anniv.

George S. Rakovski (1821-1867), Revolutionary Against Turkish Rule — A769

1971, Apr. 14
1934 A769 13s olive & blk brn .60 .25

Edelweiss Hotel, Borovets A770

2s, Panorama Hotel, Pamporovo. 4s, Boats at Albena, Black Sea. 8s, Boats at Rousalka. 10s, Shtastlivetsa Hotel, Mt. Vitosha.

1971 ***Perf. 13***
1935 A770 1s brt green .25 .25
1936 A770 2s olive gray .25 .25
1937 A770 4s brt blue .25 .25
1938 A770 8s blue .25 .25
1939 A770 10s bluish green .45 .25
Nos. 1935-1939 (5) 1.45 1.25

Technological Progress — A771

Designs: 1s, Mason with banner, vert. 13s, Two men and doves, vert.

1971, Apr. 20 **Photo.** ***Perf. 12½***
1940 A771 1s gold & multi .25 .25
1941 A771 2s gray blue & multi .25 .25
1942 A771 13s lt green & multi .85 .25
Nos. 1940-1942 (3) 1.35 .75

10th Cong. of Bulgarian Communist Party.

Panayot Pipkov and Anthem A772

1971, May 20
1943 A772 13s sil, blk & brt grn .75 .25

Panayot Pipkov, composer, birth cent.

Mammoth A773

Prehistoric Animals: 2s, Bear, vert. 3s, Hipparion (horse). 13s, Platybelodon. 20s, Dinotherium, vert. 28s, Saber-tooth tiger.

1971, May 29 ***Perf. 12½***
1944 A773 1s dull bl & multi .25 .25
1945 A773 2s lilac & multi .25 .25
1946 A773 3s multicolored .25 .25
1947 A773 13s multicolored 1.40 .40
1948 A773 20s dp grn & multi 2.10 1.00
1949 A773 28s multicolored 2.50 1.25
Nos. 1944-1949 (6) 6.75 3.40

Khan Asparuch Crossing Danube, 679 A.D., by Boris Angelushev — A774

Historical Paintings: 3s, Reception at Trnovo, by Ilya Petrov. 5s, Chevartov's Troops at Benkovsky, by P. Morozov. 8s, Russian Gen. Gurko and People in Sofia, 1878, by D. Gudjenko. 28s, People Greeting Red Army, by S. Venov.

1971, Mar. 6 ***Perf. 13½x14***
1950 A774 2s gold & multi .25 .25
1951 A774 3s gold & multi .25 .25
1952 A774 5s gold & multi .35 .25
1953 A774 8s gold & multi .70 .25
a. Souv. sheet of 4, #1950-1953 1.40 .85
1954 A774 28s gold & multi 2.75 1.10
Nos. 1950-1954 (5) 4.30 2.10

In 1973, No. 1953a was surcharged 1 lev and overprinted "Visitez la Bulgarie," airline initials and emblems, and, on the 5s stamp, "Par Avion."

Freed Black, White and Yellow Men — A775

1971, May 20 **Photo.** ***Perf. 12½***
1955 A775 13s blue, blk & yel .75 .25

Intl. Year against Racial Discrimination.

Map of Europe, Championship Emblem — A776

"XXX" Supporting Barbell — A777

1971, June 19
1956 A776 2s lt blue & multi .25 .25
1957 A777 13s yellow & multi .90 .25

30th European Weight Lifting Championships, Sofia, June 19-27.

Facade, Old House, Koprivnica — A778

Designs: Decorated facades of various old houses in Koprivnica.

1971, July 10 **Photo.** ***Perf. 12½***
1958 A778 1s green & multi .25 .25
1959 A778 2s brown & multi .25 .25
1960 A778 6s violet & multi .25 .25
1961 A778 13s dk red & multi .65 .25
Nos. 1958-1961 (4) 1.40 1.00

Frontier Guard and German Shepherd A779

1971, July 31 ***Perf. 13***
1962 A779 2s green & ol grn .25 .25

25th anniversary of the Frontier Guards.

Congress of Busludja, Bas-relief — A780

1971, July 31 ***Perf. 12½***
1963 A780 2s dk red & ol grn .25 .25

80th anniversary of the first Congress of the Bulgarian Social Democratic party.

Young Woman, by Ivan Nenov — A781

Paintings: 2s, Lazarova in Evening Gown, by Stefan Ivanov. 3s, Performer in Dress Suit, by Kyril Zonev. 13s, Portrait of a Woman, by Detchko Uzunov. 20s, Woman from Kalotina, by Vladimir Dimitrov. 40s, Gorjanin (Mountain Man), by Stoyan Venev.

1971, Aug. 2 ***Perf. 14x13½***
1964 A781 1s green & multi .25 .25
1965 A781 2s green & multi .25 .25
1966 A781 3s green & multi .25 .25
1967 A781 13s green & multi .70 .25
1968 A781 20s green & multi 1.00 .50
1969 A781 40s green & multi 1.40 .90
Nos. 1964-1969 (6) 3.85 2.40

National Art Gallery.

Wrestlers A782

Designs: 13s, Wrestlers.

1971, Aug. 27 ***Perf. 12½***
1970 A782 2s green, blk & bl .25 .25
1971 A782 13s red org, blk & bl .65 .25

European Wrestling Championships.

Young Workers — A783

1971 **Photo.** ***Perf. 13***
1972 A783 2s dark blue .25 .25

25th anniv. of the Young People's Brigade.

Post Horn Emblem A784

1971, Sept. 15 ***Perf. 12½***
1973 A784 20s dp green & gold .75 .35

8th meeting of postal administrations of socialist countries, Varna.

FEBS Waves Emblem — A785

1971, Sept. 20
1974 A785 13s black, red & mar .75 .35

7th Congress of European Biochemical Association (FEBS), Varna.

Statue of Republic A786

Design: 13s, Bulgarian flag.

1971, Sept. 20 ***Perf. 13x12½***
1975 A786 2s gold, yel & dk red .25 .25
1976 A786 13s gold, grn & red .60 .25

Bulgarian People's Republic, 25th anniv.

Cross Country Skiing and Winter Olympics Emblem A787

Sport and Winter Olympics Emblem: 2s, Downhill skiing. 3s, Ski jump and skiing. 4s, Women's figure skating. 13s, Ice hockey. 28s, Slalom skiing. 1 l, Torch and stadium.

1971, Sept. 25 ***Perf. 12½***
1977 A787 1s dk green & multi .25 .25
1978 A787 2s vio blue & multi .25 .25
1979 A787 3s ultra & multi .25 .25
1980 A787 4s dp plum & multi .25 .25
1981 A787 13s dk blue & multi .60 .25
1982 A787 28s multicolored 1.25 .55
Nos. 1977-1982 (6) 2.85 1.80

Miniature Sheet
Imperf

1983 A787 1 l multicolored 3.50 1.60

11th Winter Olympic Games, Sapporo, Japan, Feb. 3-13, 1972.

Factory, Botevgrad A788

Industrial Buildings: 2s, Petro-chemical works, Pleven, vert. 10s, Chemical works, Vratsa. 13s, Maritsa-Istok Power Station, Dimitrovgrad. 40s, Electronics works, Sofia.

1971 **Photo.** ***Perf. 13***

1984 A788 1s violet .25 .25
1985 A788 2s orange .25 .25
1986 A788 10s deep purple .25 .25
1987 A788 13s lilac rose .40 .25
1988 A788 40s deep brown 1.25 .25
Nos. 1984-1988 (5) 2.40 1.25

UNESCO Emblem A789

1971, Nov. 4 ***Perf. 12½***

1989 A789 20s lt bl, blk, gold & red .75 .25

25th anniv. of UNESCO.

Soccer Player, by Kyril Zonev (1896-1971) A790

Paintings by Kyril Zonev: 2s, Landscape, horiz. 3s, Self-portrait. 13s, Lilies. 20s, Landscape, horiz. 40s, Portrait of a Young Woman.

1971, Nov. 10 ***Perf. 11x12***

1990 A790 1s gold & multi .25 .25
1991 A790 2s gold & multi .25 .25
1992 A790 3s gold & multi .25 .25
1993 A790 13s gold & multi .70 .25
1994 A790 20s gold & multi 1.00 .40
1995 A790 40s gold & multi 1.40 .50
Nos. 1990-1995 (6) 3.85 1.90

Salyut Space Station — A791

Astronauts Dobrovolsky, Volkov and Patsayev — A792

Designs: 13s, Soyuz 11 space transport. 40s, Salyut and Soyuz 11 joined.

1971, Dec. 20 ***Perf. 12½***

1996 A791 2s dk grn, yel & red .25 .25
1997 A791 13s multicolored .35 .25
1998 A791 40s dk blue & multi 1.75 .45
Nos. 1996-1998 (3) 2.35 .95

Souvenir Sheet
Imperf

1999 A792 80s multicolored 2.25 1.50

Salyut-Soyuz 11 space mission, and in memory of the Russian astronauts Lt. Col. Georgi T. Dobrovolsky, Vladislav N. Volkov and Victor I. Patsayev, who died during the Soyuz 11 space mission, June 6-30, 1971.

Oil Tanker Vihren — A793

1972, Jan. 8 **Photo.** ***Perf. 12½***

2000 A793 18s lil rose, vio & blk 1.00 .35

Bulgarian shipbuilding industry.

Goce Delchev A794

5s, Jan Sandanski. 13s, Damjan Gruev.

1972, Jan. 21 **Photo.** ***Perf. 12½***

2001 A794 2s brick red & blk .25 .25
2002 A794 5s green & blk .25 .25
2003 A794 13s lemon & blk .35 .25
Nos. 2001-2003 (3) .85 .75

Centenary of the births of Bulgarian patriots Delchev (1872-1903) and Sandanski, and of Macedonian Gruev (1871-1906).

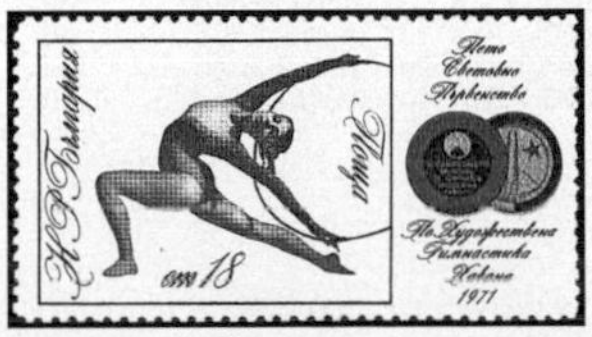

Gymnast with Hoop, Medals — A795

13s, Gymnast with ball, medals. 70s, Gymnasts with hoops, medals.

1972, Feb. 10

2004 A795 13s multicolored .70 .25
2005 A795 18s multicolored 1.00 .25

Miniature Sheet
Imperf

2006 A795 70s multicolored 3.25 2.50

5th World Women's Gymnastic Championships, Havana, Cuba.

View of Melnik, by Petar Mladenov — A796

Paintings from National Art Gallery: 2s, Plower, by Pencho Georgiev. 3s, Funeral, by Alexander Djendov. 13s, Husband and Wife, by Vladimir Dimitrov. 20s, Nursing Mother, by Nenko Balkanski. 40s, Paisii Hilendarski Writing History, by Koio Denchev.

1972, Feb. 20 ***Perf. 13½x14***

2007 A796 1s green & multi .25 .25
2008 A796 2s green & multi .25 .25
2009 A796 3s green & multi .25 .25
2010 A796 13s green & multi 1.25 .25
2011 A796 20s green & multi 1.25 .25
2012 A796 40s green & multi 1.25 .55
Nos. 2007-2012 (6) 4.50 1.80

Paintings from National Art Gallery.

Worker — A797

1972, Mar. 7 ***Perf. 12½***

2013 A797 13s silver & multi .60 .30

7th Bulgarian Trade Union Congress.

Singing Harvesters A798

Designs: Paintings by Vladimir Dimitrov. 3s, 13s, horiz.

1972, Mar. 31 ***Perf. 11½x12, 12x11½***

2014 A798 1s shown .25 .25
2015 A798 2s Harvester .25 .25
2016 A798 3s Women Diggers .25 .25
2017 A798 13s Fabric Dyers .35 .25
2018 A798 20s "My Mother" 1.40 .25
2019 A798 40s Self-portrait 1.40 .45
Nos. 2014-2019 (6) 3.90 1.70

Vladimir Dimitrov, painter, 90th birth anniv.

"Your Heart is your Health" — A799

1972, Apr. 30 ***Perf. 12½***

2020 A799 13s red, blk & grn 1.10 .50

World Health Day.

St. Mark's Basilica and Wave — A800

Design: 13s, Ca' D'Oro and wave.

1972, May 6 ***Perf. 13x12½***

2021 A800 2s ol grn, bl grn & lt bl .25 .25
2022 A800 13s red brn, vio & lt grn .90 .25

UNESCO campaign to save Venice.

Dimitrov in Print Shop, 1901 — A801

Life of George Dimitrov: 2s, Dimitrov as leader of 1923 uprising. 3s, Leipzig trial, 1933. 5s, As Communist functionary, 1935. 13s, As leader and teacher, 1948. 18s, Addressing youth rally, 1948. 28s, With Pioneers, 1948. 40s, Mausoleum. 80s, Portrait.

1972, May 8 **Photo.** ***Perf. 12½***

2023 A801 1s shown .25 .25
2024 A801 2s multicolored .25 .25
2025 A801 3s multicolored .25 .25
2026 A801 5s multicolored .25 .25
2027 A801 13s multicolored .35 .25
2028 A801 18s multicolored .35 .25
2029 A801 28s multicolored .75 .25
2030 A801 40s multicolored 1.50 .45
2031 A801 80s multicolored 4.25 .70
a. Souvenir sheet 4.50 3.50
Nos. 2023-2031 (9) 8.20 2.90

90th anniversary of the birth of George Dimitrov (1882-1949), communist leader.

No. 2031a contains one imperf. stamp similar to No. 2031, but in different colors.

Value, No. 2031 imperf. in slightly changed colors, $8.50.

Paisii Hilendarski A802

Design: 2s, Flame and quotation.

1972, May 12

2032 A802 2s gold, grn & brn .25 .25
2033 A802 13s gold, grn & brn .85 .25

Paisii Hilendarski (1722-1798), monk, writer of Bulgarian-Slavic history.

Canoeing, Motion and Olympic Emblems — A803

Designs (Motion and Olympic emblems and): 2s, Gymnastics. 3s, Swimming, women's. 13s, Volleyball. 18s, Jumping. 40s, Wrestling. 80s, Stadium and sports.

1972, June 25

Figures of Athletes in Silver & Black

2034 A803 1s lt blue & multi .25 .25
2035 A803 2s orange & multi .25 .25
2036 A803 3s multicolored .25 .25
2037 A803 13s yellow & multi .35 .25
2038 A803 18s multicolored .70 .25
2039 A803 40s pink & multi 1.40 .40
Nos. 2034-2039 (6) 3.20 1.65

Miniature Sheet

Imperf

Size: 62x60mm

2040 A803 80s gold, ver & yel 3.00 2.00

20th Olympic Games, Munich, 8/26-9/11.

Angel Kunchev A804

1972, June 30 Photo. *Perf. 12½*

2041 A804 2s mag, dk pur & gold .30 .30

Centenary of the death of Angel Kunchev, patriot and revolutionist.

Zlatni Pyassatsi A805

1972, Sept. 16

2042 A805 1s shown .25 .25
2043 A805 2s Drouzhba .25 .25
2044 A805 3s Slunchev Bryag .25 .25
2045 A805 13s Primorsko .50 .25
2046 A805 28s Roussalka 1.10 .35
2047 A805 40s Albena 1.50 .45
Nos. 2042-2047 (6) 3.85 1.80

Bulgarian Black Sea resorts.

Bronze Medal, Olympic Emblems, Canoeing — A806

Olympic Emblems and: 2s, Silver medal, broad jump. 3s, Gold medal, boxing. 18s, Gold medal, wrestling. 40s, Gold medal, weight lifting.

1972, Sept. 29

2048 A806 1s Prus bl & multi .25 .25
2049 A806 2s dk green & multi .25 .25
2050 A806 3s org brn & multi .25 .25
2051 A806 18s olive & multi 1.25 .25
2052 A806 40s multicolored 1.25 .55
Nos. 2048-2052 (5) 3.25 1.55

Bulgarian victories in 20th Olympic Games. For overprint see No. 2066.

Stoj Dimitrov — A807

Resistance Fighters: 2s, Cvetko Radoinov. 3s, Bogdan Stivrodski. 5s, Mirko Aliev. 13s, Nedelyo Nikolov.

1972, Oct. 30 Photo. *Perf. 12½x13*

2053 A807 1s olive & multi .25 .25
2054 A807 2s multicolored .25 .25
2055 A807 3s multicolored .25 .25
2056 A807 5s multicolored .25 .25
2057 A807 13s multicolored .45 .25
Nos. 2053-2057 (5) 1.45 1.25

"50 Years USSR" A808

1972, Nov. 3 Photo. *Perf. 12½x13*

2058 A808 13s gold, red & yel .60 .25

50th anniversary of Soviet Union.

Turk's-cap Lily — A809

Protected Plants: 2s, Gentian. 3s, Sea daffodil. 4s, Globe flower. 18s, Primrose. 23s, Pulsatilla vernalis. 40s, Snake's-head.

1972, Nov. 25 *Perf. 12½*

Flowers in Natural Colors

2059 A809 1s olive bister .25 .25
2060 A809 2s olive bister .25 .25
2061 A809 3s olive bister .25 .25
2062 A809 4s olive bister .25 .25
2063 A809 18s olive bister .55 .25
2064 A809 23s olive bister 1.00 .30
2065 A809 40s olive bister 1.40 .50
Nos. 2059-2065 (7) 3.95 2.05

No. 2052 Overprinted in Red

1972, Nov. 27

2066 A806 40s multicolored 1.75 .55

Bulgarian weight lifting Olympic gold medalists.

Dobri Chintulov A810

1972, Nov. 28 Photo. *Perf. 12½*

2067 A810 2s gray, dk & lt grn .30 .25

Chintulov, writer, 150th birth anniv.

Forehead Band — A811

Designs (14th-19th Century Jewelry): 2s, Belt buckles. 3s, Amulet. 8s, Pendant. 23s, Earrings. 40s, Necklace.

1972, Dec. 27 Engr. *Perf. 14x13½*

2068 A811 1s red brn & blk .25 .25
2069 A811 2s emerald & blk .25 .25
2070 A811 3s Prus bl & blk .25 .25
2071 A811 8s dk red & blk .35 .25
2072 A811 23s red org & multi .90 .35
2073 A811 40s violet & blk 1.40 .80
Nos. 2068-2073 (6) 3.40 2.15

Skin Divers A812

Designs: 2s, Shelf-1 underwater house and divers. 18s, Diving bell and diver, vert. 40s, Elevation balloon and divers, vert.

1973, Jan. 24 Photo. *Perf. 12½*

2074 A812 1s lt bl, blk & yel .25 .25
2075 A812 2s blk, bl & org yel .25 .25
2076 A812 18s blk, Prus bl & dl org .60 .25
2077 A812 40s blk, ultra & bister 1.40 .45
Nos. 2074-2077 (4) 2.50 1.20

Bulgarian deep-sea research in the Black Sea.

A souvenir sheet of four contains imperf. 20s stamps in designs of Nos. 2074-2077 with colors changed. Sold for 1 l. Value $5.50 unused, $3 canceled.

Execution of Levski, by Boris Angelushev A813

20s, Vassil Levski, by Georgi Danchev.

1973, Feb. 19 *Perf. 13x12½*

2078 A813 2s dull rose & Prus grn .25 .25
2079 A813 20s dull grn & brn 1.25 .25

Centenary of the death of Vassil Levski (1837-1873), patriot, executed by the Turks.

Kukersky Mask, Elhovo Region — A814

Kukersky Masks at pre-Spring Festival: 2s, Breznik. 3s, Hissar. 13s, Radomir. 20s, Karnobat. 40s, Pernik.

1973, Feb. 26 *Perf. 12½*

2080 A814 1s dp rose & multi .25 .25
2081 A814 2s emerald & multi .25 .25
2082 A814 3s violet & multi .25 .25
2083 A814 13s multicolored .45 .25
2084 A814 20s multicolored .65 .25
2085 A814 40s multicolored 3.25 1.75
Nos. 2080-2085 (6) 5.10 3.00

Nicolaus Copernicus — A815

1973, Mar. 21 Photo. *Perf. 12½*

2086 A815 28s ocher, blk & clar 1.90 1.00

500th anniversary of the birth of Nicolaus Copernicus (1473-1543), Polish astronomer.

Vietnamese Worker and Rainbow A816

1973, Apr. 16

2087 A816 18s lt blue & multi .60 .25

Peace in Viet Nam.

Wild Flowers — A817

1973, May Photo. *Perf. 13*

2088 A817 1s Poppy .25 .25
2089 A817 2s Daisy .25 .25
2090 A817 3s Peony .25 .25
2091 A817 13s Centaury .45 .25
2092 A817 18s Corn cockle 4.50 2.50
2093 A817 28s Ranunculus 1.25 .75
Nos. 2088-2093 (6) 6.95 4.25

A818

1973, June 2

2094 A818 2s pale grn, buff & brn .25 .25
2095 A818 18s pale brn, gray & grn 1.00 .55

Christo Botev (1848-1876), poet.

Asen Halachev and Revolutionists — A819

2s, "Suffering Worker."

1973, June 6 Photo. *Perf. 13*

2096 A819 1s gold, red & blk .25 .25
2097 A819 2s gold, org & dk brn .25 .25

50th anniversary of Pleven uprising.

Muskrat
A820

Perf. 12½x13, 13x12½

1973, June 29 **Litho.**

2098 A820 1s shown .25 .25
2099 A820 2s Racoon .25 .25
2100 A820 3s Mouflon, vert. .25 .25
2101 A820 12s Fallow deer, vert. .45 .25
2102 A820 18s European bison 1.25 .60
2103 A820 40s Elk 4.50 2.25
Nos. 2098-2103 (6) 6.95 3.85

Aleksandr Stamboliski — A821

1973, June 14 **Photo.** ***Perf. 12½***

2104 A821 18s dp brown & org .35 .25
a. 18s orange 3.50 1.40

Aleksandr Stamboliski (1879-1923), leader of Peasants' Party and premier.

Trade Union
Emblem — A822

1973, Aug. 27 **Photo.** ***Perf. 12½***

2105 A822 2s yellow & multi .25 .25

8th Congress of World Federation of Trade Unions, Varna, Oct. 15-22.

Stylized Sun,
Olympic
Rings — A823

28s, Emblem of Bulgarian Olympic Committee & Olympic rings. 80s, Soccer, emblems of Innsbruck & Montreal 1976 Games, horiz.

1973, Aug. 29 ***Perf. 13***

2106 A823 13s multicolored 1.25 .60
2107 A823 28s multicolored 1.60 .80

Souvenir Sheet

2108 A823 80s multicolored 4.00 2.50

Olympic Congress, Varna. No. 2108 contains one stamp. It also exists imperf, Value $18; also with violet margin, imperf, Value $80.

Revolutionists with Communist Flag — A824

Designs: 5s, Revolutionists on flatcar blocking train. 13s, Raising Communist flag, vert. 18s, George Dimitrov and Vassil Kolarov.

1973, Sept. 22 **Photo.** ***Perf. 12½***

2109 A824 2s magenta & multi .25 .25
2110 A824 5s magenta & multi .25 .25
2111 A824 13s magenta & multi .40 .25
2112 A824 18s magenta & multi 1.00 .40
Nos. 2109-2112 (4) 1.90 1.15

50th anniv. of the September Revolution.

Warrior
Saint
A825

Murals from Boyana Church: 1s, Tsar Kaloyan and 2s, his wife Dessislava. 5s, "St. Wystratti." 10s, Tsar Constantine Assen. 13s, Deacon Laurentius. 18s, Virgin Mary. 20s, St. Ephraim. 28s, Jesus. 80s, Jesus in the Temple, horiz.

1973, Sept. 24

2113 A825 1s gold & multi .25 .25
2114 A825 2s gold & multi .25 .25
2115 A825 3s gold & multi .25 .25
2116 A825 5s gold & multi .40 .25
2117 A825 10s gold & multi .65 .30
2118 A825 13s gold & multi .65 .40
2119 A825 18s gold & multi 1.00 .60
2120 A825 20s gold & multi 1.00 .70
2121 A825 28s gold & multi 3.25 1.10
Nos. 2113-2121 (9) 7.70 4.10

Miniature Sheet

Imperf

2122 A825 80s gold & multi 6.75 6.75

No. 2122 contains one stamp with simulated perforations.

Christo Smirnenski — A826

1973, Sept. 29 **Photo.** ***Perf. 12½***

2123 A826 1s multicolored .25 .25
2124 A826 2s vio blue & multi .25 .25

Christo Smirnenski (1898-1923), poet.

Human Rights
Flame — A827

1973, Oct. 10

2125 A827 13s dk bl, red & gold .50 .25

Universal Declaration of Human Rights, 25th anniv.

Bulgarian History Type

1s, Tsar Theodor Svetoslav receiving Byzantine envoys. 2s, Tsar Mihail Shishman's army in battle with Byzantines. 3s, Tsar Ivan Alexander's victory at Russocastro. 4s, Patriarch Euthimius at the defense of Turnovo. 5s, Tsar Ivan Shishman leading horsemen against the Turks. 13s, Momchil attacking Turks at Umour. 18s, Tsar Ivan Stratsimir meeting King Sigismund's crusaders. 28s, The Boyars Balik, Theodor & Dobrotitsa, meeting ship bringing envoys from Anne of Savoy.

1973, Oct. 23 ***Perf. 13***

Silver and Black Vignettes

2126 A741 1s olive bister .25 .25
2127 A741 2s Prus blue .25 .25
2128 A741 3s lilac .25 .25
2129 A741 4s green .25 .25
2130 A741 5s violet .25 .25
2131 A741 13s orange & brn .45 .25
2132 A741 18s olive green .65 .25
2133 A741 28s yel brn & brn 1.60 .85
Nos. 2126-2133 (8) 3.95 2.60

Finn
Class — A828

Sailboats: 2s, Flying Dutchman. 3s, Soling class. 13s, Tempest class. 20s, Class 470. 40s, Tornado class.

1973, Oct. 29 **Litho.** ***Perf. 13***

2134 A828 1s ultra & multi .25 .25
2135 A828 2s green & multi .25 .25
2136 A828 3s dk blue & multi .25 .25
2137 A828 13s dull vio & multi .45 .25
2138 A828 20s gray bl & multi .65 .45
2139 A828 40s dk blue & multi 3.00 2.50
Nos. 2134-2139 (6) 4.85 3.95

Value, set imperf. in changed colors, $13.

Village, by Bencho Obreshkov — A829

Paintings: 2s, Mother and Child, by Stoyan Venev. 3s, Rest (woman), by Tsenko Boyadjiev. 13s, Flowers in Vase, by Sirak Skitnik. 18s, Meri Kuneva (portrait), by Ilya Petrov. 40s, Winter in Plovdiv, by Zlatyu Boyadjiev. 13s, 18s, 40s, vert.

Perf. 12½x12, 12x12½

1973, Nov. 10

2140 A829 1s gold & multi .25 .25
2141 A829 2s gold & multi .25 .25
2142 A829 3s gold & multi .25 .25
2143 A829 13s gold & multi .45 .25
2144 A829 18s gold & multi .65 .25
2145 A829 40s gold & multi 3.00 1.25
Nos. 2140-2145 (6) 4.85 2.50

Souvenir Sheet

Paintings by Stanislav Dospevski: a, Domnica Lambreva. b, Self-portrait. Both vert.

2146 Sheet of 2 4.50 2.50
a. A829 50s gold & multi 1.40 1.00
b. A829 50s gold & multi 1.40 1.00

Bulgarian paintings. No. 2146 commemorates the 150th birth anniv. of Stanislav Dospevski.

Souvenir Sheet

Soccer — A830

1973, Dec. 10 **Photo.** ***Perf. 13***

2147 A830 28s multicolored 4.50 3.50

No. 2147 sold for 1 l. Exists overprinted for Argentina 78. Value $9.50.

Angel and
Ornaments
A831

1s, Attendant facing right. 2s, Passover table and lamb. 3s, Attendant facing left. 8s, Abraham and ornaments. 13s, Adam and Eve. 28s, Expulsion from Garden of Eden.

1974, Jan. 21 **Photo.** ***Perf. 13***

2148 A831 1s fawn, yel & brn .25 .25
2149 A831 2s fawn, yel & brn .25 .25
2150 A831 3s fawn, yel & brn .25 .25
a. Strip of 3, #2148-2150 .50 .25
2151 A831 5s slate grn & yel .25 .25
2152 A831 8s slate grn & yel .25 .25
a. Pair, #2151-2152 .65 .50
2153 A831 13s lt brown, yel & ol .30 .25
2154 A831 28s lt brown, yel & ol .50 .30
a. Pair, #2153-2154 1.60 .70
Nos. 2148-2154 (7) 2.05 1.80

Woodcarvings from Rozhen Monastery, 19th century.

Lenin, by N. Mirtchev — A832

18s, Lenin visiting Workers, by W. A. Serov.

1974, Jan. 28 **Litho.** ***Perf. 12½x12***

2155 A832 2s ocher & multi .25 .25
2156 A832 18s ocher & multi .65 .30

50th anniversary of the death of Lenin.

1974, Jan. 28

Demeter Blagoev at Rally, by G. Kowachev.

2157 A832 2s multicolored .25 .25

50th anniversary of the death of Demeter Blagoev, founder of Bulgarian Communist Party.

Domestic Animals A833

1974, Feb. 1	Photo.		Perf. 13	
2158 A833	1s Sheep		.25	.25
2159 A833	2s Goat		.25	.25
2160 A833	3s Pig		.25	.25
2161 A833	5s Cow		.25	.25
2162 A833	13s Buffalo cow		.80	.25
2163 A833	20s Horse		2.00	.75
	Nos. 2158-2163 (6)		3.80	2.00

Comecon Emblem A834

1974, Feb. 11 Photo. *Perf. 13*

2164 A834 13s silver & multi .55 .25

25th anniversary of the Council of Mutual Economic Assistance.

Soccer — A835

Designs: Various soccer action scenes.

1974, Mar.	Photo.	Perf. 13	
2165 A835	1s dull grn & multi	.25	.25
2166 A835	2s brt green & multi	.25	.25
2167 A835	3s slate grn & multi	.25	.25
2168 A835	13s olive & multi	.25	.25
2169 A835	28s blue grn & multi	.70	.30
2170 A835	40s emerald & multi	1.75	.75
	Nos. 2165-2170 (6)	3.45	2.05

Souvenir Sheet

2171 A835 1 l green & multi 3.75 2.00

World Soccer Championship, Munich, June 13-July 7. No. 2171 exists imperf. Value $70.

Salt Production A836

Children's Paintings: 1s, Cosmic Research for Peaceful Purposes. 3s, Fire Dancers. 28s, Russian-Bulgarian Friendship (train and children). 60s, Spring (birds).

1974, Apr. 15	Photo.	Perf. 13	
2172 A836	1s lilac & multi	.25	.25
2173 A836	2s lt green & multi	.25	.25
2174 A836	3s blue & multi	.25	.25
2175 A836	28s slate & multi	2.00	1.25
	Nos. 2172-2175 (4)	2.75	2.00

Souvenir Sheet

Imperf

2176 A836 60s blue & multi 2.75 2.00

Third World Youth Philatelic Exhibition, Sofia, May 23-30. No. 2176 contains one stamp with simulated perforations.

No. 2176 exists in blue with gray inscriptions, but was not valid for postage. Value $50.

Folk Singers — A837

Designs: 2s, Folk dancers (men). 3s, Bagpiper and drummer. 5s, Wrestlers. 13s, Runners (women). 18s, Gymnast.

1974, Apr. 25		Perf. 13	
2178 A837	1s vermilion & multi	.25	.25
2179 A837	2s org brn & multi	.25	.25
2180 A837	3s brn red & multi	.25	.25
2181 A837	5s blue & multi	.25	.25
2182 A837	13s ultra & multi	.90	.30
2183 A837	18s violet bl & multi	.45	.25
	Nos. 2178-2183 (6)	2.35	1.55

4th Amateur Arts and Sports Festival

Flowers A838

1974, May	Photo.	Perf. 13	
2184 A838	1s Aster	.25	.25
2185 A838	2s Petunia	.25	.25
2186 A838	3s Fuchsia	.25	.25
2187 A838	18s Tulip	.50	.25
2188 A838	20s Carnation	.75	.25
2189 A838	28s Pansy	2.25	.85
	Nos. 2184-2189 (6)	4.25	2.10

Souvenir Sheet

2190 A838 80s Sunflower 2.00 1.00

Automobiles and Emblems — A839

1974, May 15 Photo. *Perf. 13*

2191 A839 13s multicolored .50 .25

International Automobile Federation (FIA) Spring Congress, Sofia, May 20-24.

Old and New Buildings, UNESCO Emblem A840

1974, June 15

2192 A840 18s multicolored .50 .25

UNESCO Executive Council, 94th Session, Varna.

Postrider A841

Designs: 18s, First Bulgarian mail coach. 28s, UPU Monument, Bern.

1974, Aug. 5

2193 A841 2s ocher, blk & vio .25 .25

2194 A841 18s ocher, blk & grn .50 .25

Souvenir Sheet

2195 A841 28s ocher, blk & bl 2.10 1.50

UPU cent. No. 2195 exists imperf. Value $60.

Pioneer and Komsomol Girl — A842

Designs: 2s, Pioneer and birds. 60s, Emblem with portrait of George Dimitrov.

1974, Aug. 12

2196 A842 1s green & multi .25 .25

2197 A842 2s blue & multi .25 .25

Souvenir Sheet

2198 A842 60s red & multi 2.00 1.50

30th anniversary of Dimitrov Pioneer Organization, Septemvrilche.

"Bulgarian Communist Party" — A843

Symbolic Designs: 2s, Russian liberators. 5s, Industrialization. 13s, Advanced agriculture and husbandry. 18s, Scientific and technical progress.

1974, Aug. 20			
2199 A843	1s blue gray & multi	.25	.25
2200 A843	2s blue gray & multi	.25	.25
2201 A843	5s gray & multi	.25	.25
2202 A843	13s gray & multi	.40	.25
2203 A843	18s gray & multi	.65	.25
	Nos. 2199-2203 (5)	1.80	1.25

30th anniversary of the People's Republic.

Gymnast on Parallel Bars — A844

Design: 13s, Gymnast on vaulting horse.

1974, Oct. 18 Photo. *Perf. 13*

2204 A844 2s multicolored .25 .25

2205 A844 13s multicolored .40 .25

18th Gymnastic Championships, Varna.

Souvenir Sheet

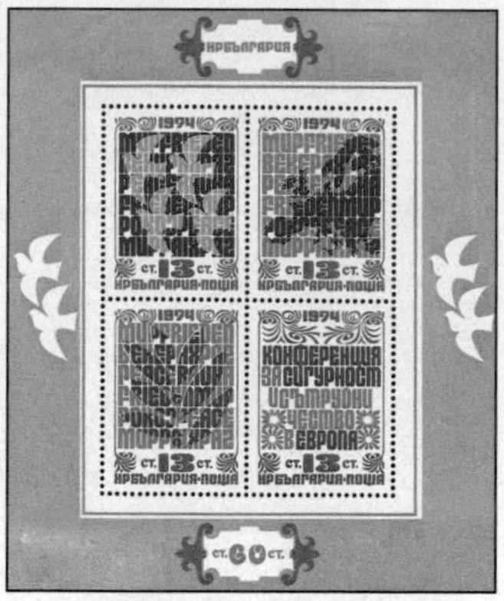
Symbols of Peace — A845

1974, Oct. 29 Photo. *Perf. 13*

2206 A845	Sheet of 4	2.50	2.50
a.	13s Doves	.25	.25
b.	13s Map of Europe	.25	.25
c.	13s Olive Branch	.25	.25
d.	13s Inscription	.25	.25

1974 European Peace Conference. "Peace" in various languages written on Nos. 2206a-2206c. Sold for 60s. Exists imperf. Value $85.

No. 2206 was overprinted "Europa" and various cities and dates in 1979. Value $60.

Nib and Envelope — A846

1974, Nov. 20

2207 A846 2s yellow, blk & grn .25 .25

Introduction of postal zone numbers.

Flowers A847

1974, Dec. 5

2208 A847 2s emerald & multi .25 .25

St. Todor, Ceramic Icon — A848

Designs: 2s, Medallion, Veliko Turnovo. 3s, Carved capital. 5s, Silver bowl. 8s, Goblet. 13s, Lion's head finial. 18s, Gold plate with Cross. 28s, Breastplate with eagle.

1974, Dec. 18	Photo.	Perf. 13	
2209 A848	1s orange & multi	.25	.25
2210 A848	2s pink & multi	.25	.25
2211 A848	3s blue & multi	.25	.25
2212 A848	5s lt vio & multi	.25	.25
2213 A848	8s brown & multi	.25	.25
2214 A848	13s multicolored	.35	.25
2215 A848	18s red & multi	.50	.25
2216 A848	28s ultra & multi	1.40	.65
	Nos. 2209-2216 (8)	3.50	2.40

Art works from 9th-12th centuries.

Fruit Tree Blossoms — A849

1975, Jan. Photo. *Perf. 13*

2217	A849	1s Apricot	.25	.25
2218	A849	2s Apple	.25	.25
2219	A849	3s Cherry	.25	.25
2220	A849	19s Pear	.40	.25
2221	A849	28s Peach	1.00	.25
		Nos. 2217-2221 (5)	2.15	1.25

Tree and Book A850

1975, Mar. 25 Photo. *Perf. 13*

2222 A850 2s gold & multi .25 .25

Forestry High School, 50th anniversary.

Souvenir Sheet

Farmers' Activities (Woodcuts) — A851

1975, Mar. 25

2223 A851 Sheet of 4 1.00 .50
- *a.* 2s Farmer with ax and flag
- *b.* 5s Farmers on guard
- *c.* 13s Dancing couple
- *d.* 18s Woman picking fruit

Bulgarian Agrarian Peoples Union, 75th anniv.

Michelangelo, Self-portrait A852

13s, Night, horiz. 18s, Day, horiz. Both designs after sculptures from Medici Tomb, Florence.

1975

2224	A852	2s plum & dk blue	.25	.25
2225	A852	13s vio bl & plum	.40	.25
2226	A852	18s brown & green	.80	.25
		Nos. 2224-2226 (3)	1.45	.75

Souvenir Sheet

2227 A852 2s olive & red 1.75 1.75

Michelangelo Buonarotti (1475-1564), Italian sculptor, painter and architect. No. 2227 issued to publicize ARPHILA 75 Intl. Phil. Exhib., Paris, June 6-16. Sheet sold for 60s.

Issued: Nos. 2224-2226, 3/28; No. 2227, 3/31.

Souvenir Sheet

Spain No. 1 and España 75 Emblem — A853

1975, Apr. 4

2228 A853 40s multicolored 5.00 4.00

Espana 75 International Philatelic Exhibition, Madrid, Apr. 4-13.

Gabrov Costume A854

Regional Costumes: 3s, Trnsk. 5s, Vidin. 13s, Gocedelchev. 18s, Risen.

1975, Apr. Photo. *Perf. 13*

2229	A854	2s blue & multi	.25	.25
2230	A854	3s emerald & multi	.25	.25
2231	A854	5s orange & multi	.25	.25
2232	A854	13s olive & multi	.65	.25
2233	A854	18s multicolored	1.25	.40
		Nos. 2229-2233 (5)	2.65	1.40

Red Star and Arrow — A855

Design: 13s, Dove and broken sword.

1975, May 9

2234	A855	2s red, blk & gold	.25	.25
2235	A855	13s blue, blk & gold	.45	.25

Victory over Fascism, 30th anniversary.

Standard Kilogram and Meter — A856

1975, May 9 *Perf. 13x13½*

2236 A856 13s silver, lil & blk .25 .25

Cent. of Intl, Meter Convention, Paris, 1875.

IWY Emblem, Woman's Head — A857

1975, May 20 Photo. *Perf. 13*

2237 A857 13s multicolored .35 .25

International Women's Year 1975.

Ivan Vasov — A858

Design: 13s, Ivan Vasov, seated.

1975, May

2238	A858	2s buff & multi	.25	.25
2239	A858	13s gray & multi	.35	.25

125th birth anniversary of Ivan Vasov.

Nikolov and Sava Kokarechkov — A859

2s, Mitko Palaouzov, Ivan Vassilev. 5s, Nicolas Nakev, Stevtcho Kraychev. 13s, Ivanka Pashkoulova, Detelina Mintcheva.

1975, May 30

2240	A859	1s multicolored	.25	.25
2241	A859	2s multicolored	.25	.25
2242	A859	5s multicolored	.25	.25
2243	A859	13s multicolored	.30	.25
		Nos. 2240-2243 (4)	1.05	1.00

Teen-age resistance fighters, killed during World War II.

Mother Feeding Child, by John E. Millais A861

Etchings: 2s, The Dead Daughter, by Goya. 3s, Reunion, by Beshkov. 13s, Seated Nude, by Renoir. 20s, Man in a Fur Hat, by Rembrandt. 40s, The Dream, by Daumier, horiz. 1 l, Temptation, by Dürer.

Photogravure and Engraved

1975, Aug. *Perf. 12x11½, 11½x12*

2248	A861	1s yel grn & multi	.25	.25
2249	A861	2s orange & multi	.25	.25
2250	A861	3s lilac & multi	.25	.25
2251	A861	13s lt blue & multi	.35	.25
2252	A861	20s ocher & multi	.50	.25
2253	A861	40s rose & multi	1.75	.45
		Nos. 2248-2253 (6)	3.35	1.70

Souvenir Sheet

2254 A861 1 l emerald & multi 2.50 1.50

World Graphics Exhibition.

Letter "Z" from 12th Century Manuscript A862

Initials from Illuminated Manuscripts: 2s, "B" from 17th cent. prayerbook. 3s, "V" from 16th cent. Bouhovo Gospel. 8s, "B" from 14th cent. Turnovo collection. 13s, "V" from Dobreisho's Gospel, 13th cent. 18s, "E" from 11th cent. Enina book of the Apostles.

1975, Aug. Litho. *Perf. 11½*

2255	A862	1s multicolored	.25	.25
2256	A862	2s multicolored	.25	.25
2257	A862	3s multicolored	.25	.25
2258	A862	8s multicolored	.25	.25
2259	A862	13s multicolored	.45	.25
2260	A862	18s multicolored	1.25	.25
		Nos. 2255-2260 (6)	2.70	1.50

Bulgarian art.

Whimsical Globe — A863

1975, Aug. Photo. *Perf. 13*

2261 A863 2s multicolored .25 .25

Festival of Humor and Satire.

Lifeboat Dju IV and Gibraltar-Cuba Route — A864

1975, Aug. 5 Photo. *Perf. 13*

2262 A864 13s multicolored .35 .25

Oceanexpo 75, 1st Intl. Ocean Exhib., Okinawa, July 20, 1975-Jan. 18, 1976.

Sts. Cyril and Methodius — A865

Sts. Constantine and Helena — A866

St. Sophia Church, Sofia, Woodcut by V. Zahriev — A867

1975, Aug. 21

2263 A865 2s ver, yel & brn .25 .25
2264 A866 13s green, yel & brn .40 .25

Souvenir Sheet

2265 A867 50s orange & multi 1.40 1.10

Balkanphila V, philatelic exhibition, Sofia, Sept. 27-Oct. 5.

Peace Dove and Map of Europe — A868

1975, Nov. Photo. *Perf. 13*

2266 A868 18s ultra, rose & yel .60 .35

European Security and Cooperation Conference, Helsinki, Finland, July 30-Aug. 1. No. 2266 printed in sheets of 5 stamps and 4 labels, arranged checkerwise.

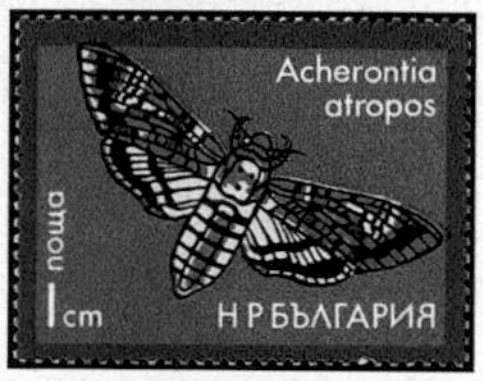

Acherontia Atropos — A869

Moths: 1s, Acherontia atropos. 2s, Daphnis nerii. 3s, Smerinthus ocellata. 10s, Deilephila nicea. 13s, Choerocampa elpenor. 18s, Macroglossum fuciformis.

1975 Photo. *Perf. 13*

2267 A869 1s multicolored .25 .25
2268 A869 2s multicolored .25 .25
2269 A869 3s multicolored .25 .25
2270 A869 10s multicolored .35 .25
2271 A869 13s multicolored .70 .30
2272 A869 18s multicolored 1.40 .50
Nos. 2267-2272 (6) 3.20 1.80

Soccer Player — A870

1975, Sept. 21

2273 A870 2s multicolored .25 .25

8th Inter-Toto (soccer pool) Soccer Championships, Varna.

Constantine's Rebellion Against the Turks, 1403 — A871

Designs (Woodcuts): 2s, Campaign of Vladislav III, 1443-1444. 3s, Battles of Turnovo, 1598 and 1686. 10s, Battle of Liprovsko, 1688. 13s, Guerrillas, 17th century. 18s, Return of exiled peasants.

1975, Nov. 27 Photo. *Perf. 13*

2274 A871 1s bister, grn & blk .25 .25
2275 A871 2s blue, car & blk .25 .25
2276 A871 3s yellow, lil & blk .25 .25
2277 A871 10s orange, grn & blk .25 .25
2278 A871 13s green, lil & blk .40 .25
2279 A871 18s pink, grn & blk .75 .25
Nos. 2274-2279 (6) 2.15 1.50

Bulgarian history.

Red Cross and First Aid — A872

Design: 13s, Red Cross and dove.

1975, Dec. 1

2280 A872 2s red brn, red & blk .25 .25
2281 A872 13s bl grn, red & blk .40 .25

90th anniversary of Bulgarian Red Cross.

Egyptian Galley A873

Historic Ships: 2s, Phoenician galley. 3s, Greek trireme. 5s, Roman galley. 13s, Viking longship. 18s, Venetian galley.

1975, Dec. 15 Photo. *Perf. 13*

2282 A873 1s multicolored .25 .25
2283 A873 2s multicolored .25 .25
2284 A873 3s multicolored .25 .25
2285 A873 5s multicolored .25 .25
2286 A873 13s multicolored .40 .25
2287 A873 18s multicolored .85 .25
Nos. 2282-2287 (6) 2.25 1.50

See Nos. 2431-2436, 2700-2705.

Souvenir Sheet

Ethnographical Museum, Plovdiv — A874

1975, Dec. 17

2288 A874 Sheet of 3 6.00 3.50
a. 80s grn, yel & dark brn 1.75 1.00

European Architectural Heritage Year. No. 2288 contains 3 stamps and 3 labels showing stylized bird.

Dobri Hristov — A875

1975, Dec. *Perf. 13*

2289 A875 5s brt grn, yel & brn .25 .25

Dobri Hristov, musician, birth centenary.

United Nations Emblem — A876

1975, Dec.

2290 A876 13s gold, blk & mag .35 .25

United Nations, 30th anniversary.

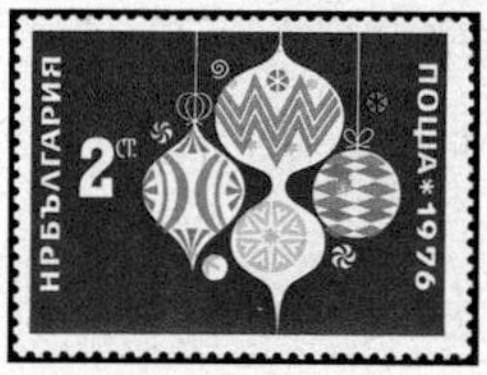

Glass Ornaments — A877

13s, Peace dove, decorated ornament.

1975, Dec. 22 Photo. *Perf. 13*

2291 A877 2s brt violet & multi .25 .25
2292 A877 13s gray & multi .25 .25

New Year 1976.

Downhill Skiing — A878

Designs (Winter Olympic Games Emblem and): 2s, Cross country skier, vert. 3s, Ski jump. 13s, Biathlon, vert. 18s, Ice hockey, vert. 23s, Speed skating, vert. 80s, Figure skating, pair, vert.

1976, Jan. 30 *Perf. 13½*

2293 A878 1s silver & multi .25 .25
2294 A878 2s silver & multi .25 .25
2295 A878 3s silver & multi .25 .25
2296 A878 13s silver & multi .40 .25
2297 A878 18s silver & multi .40 .25
2298 A878 23s silver & multi 1.25 .25
Nos. 2293-2298 (6) 2.80 1.50

Souvenir Sheet

2299 A878 80s silver & multi 2.50 1.50

12th Winter Olympic Games, Innsbruck, Austria, Feb. 4-15.

Electric Streetcar, Sofia, 1976 — A879

Design: 13s, Streetcar and trailer, 1901.

1976, Jan. 12 Photo. *Perf. 13½x13*

2300 A879 2s gray & multi .25 .25
2301 A879 13s gray & multi .55 .25

75th anniversary of Sofia streetcars.

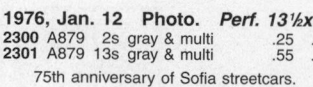

Stylized Bird — A880

5s, Dates "1976," "1956" & star. 13s, Hammer & sickle. 50s, George Dimitrov.

1976, Mar. 1 *Perf. 13*

2302 A880 2s gold & multi .25 .25
2303 A880 5s gold & multi .25 .25
2304 A880 13s gold & multi .25 .25
Nos. 2302-2304 (3) .75 .75

Souvenir Sheet

2305 A880 50s gold & multi 1.75 3.00

11th Bulgarian Communist Party Congress.

A. G. Bell and Telephone, 1876 — A881

1976, Mar. 10

2306 A881 18s dk brn, yel & ocher .50 .25

Centenary of first telephone call by Alexander Graham Bell, Mar. 10, 1876.

Mute Swan — A882

Waterfowl: 2s, Ruddy shelduck. 3s, Common shelduck. 5s, Garganey teal. 13s, Mallard. 18s, Red-crested pochard.

1976, Mar. 27 Litho. *Perf. 11½*

2307 A882 1s vio bl & multi .25 .25
2308 A882 2s yel grn & multi .25 .25
2309 A882 3s blue & multi .25 .25
2310 A882 5s multicolored 1.10 .25
2311 A882 13s purple & multi 1.10 .55
2312 A882 18s green & multi 2.75 1.75
Nos. 2307-2312 (6) 5.70 3.30

Guerrillas — A883

Designs (Woodcuts by Stoev): 2s, Peasants with rifle and proclamation. 5s, Raina Knaginia with horse and guerrilla. 13s, Insurgents with cherrywood cannon.

1976, Apr. 5 Photo. *Perf. 13*

2313 A883 1s multicolored .25 .25
2314 A883 2s multicolored .25 .25
2315 A883 5s multicolored .25 .25
2316 A883 13s multicolored .25 .25
Nos. 2313-2316 (4) 1.00 1.00

Centenary of uprising against Turkey.

Guard and Dog
A884

13s, Men on horseback, observation tower.

1976, May 15

2317 A884 2s multicolored .25 .25
2318 A884 13s multicolored .25 .25

30th anniversary of Border Guards.

Construction Worker — A885

1976, May 20

2319 A885 2s multicolored .25 .25

Young Workers Brigade, 30th anniversary.

Busludja, Bas-relief
A886

Design: 5s, Memorial building.

1976, May 28 Photo. *Perf. 13*

2320 A886 2s green & multi .25 .25
2321 A886 5s violet bl & multi .25 .25

First Congress of Bulgarian Social Democratic Party, 85th anniversary.

Memorial Building — A887

2s, AES Complex. 8s, Thermal power plant. 10s, Chemical plant. 13s, Chemical plant (diff.). 20s, Hydroelectric station.

1976, Apr. 7

2322 A887 5s green .25 .25
2323 A887 8s maroon .25 .25
2324 A887 10s green .25 .25
2325 A887 13s violet .55 .25
2326 A887 20s brt green .65 .25
Nos. 2322-2326 (5) 1.95 1.25

Five-year plan accomplishments.

Children Playing Around Table — A888

Kindergarten Children: 2s, with doll carriage & hobby horse. 5s, playing ball. 23s, in costume.

1976, June 15

2327 A888 1s green & multi .25 .25
2328 A888 2s yellow & multi .25 .25
2329 A888 5s lilac & multi .25 .25
2330 A888 23s rose & multi .40 .25
Nos. 2327-2330 (4) 1.15 1.00

Demeter Blagoev — A889

1976, May 28

2331 A889 13s bluish blk, red & gold .50 .25

Demeter Blagoev (1856-1924), writer, political leader, 120th birth anniversary.

Christo Botev — A890

1976, May 25

2332 A890 13s ocher & slate grn .60 .25

Christo Botev (1848-1876), poet, death centenary. Printed se-tenant with yellow green and ocher label, inscribed with poem.

Boxing, Montreal Olympic Emblem — A891

Designs (Montreal Olympic Emblem): 1s, Wrestling, horiz. 3s, 1 l, Weight lifting. 13s, One-man kayak. 18s, Woman gymnast. 28s, Woman diver. 40s, Woman runner.

1976, June 25

2333 A891 1s orange & multi .25 .25
2334 A891 2s multicolored .25 .25
2335 A891 3s lilac & multi .25 .25
2336 A891 13s multicolored .25 .25
2337 A891 18s multicolored .50 .25
2338 A891 28s blue & multi .70 .25
2339 A891 40s lemon & multi 1.00 .50
Nos. 2333-2339 (7) 3.20 2.00

Souvenir Sheet

2340 A891 1 l orange & multi 1.75 1.25

21st Olympic Games, Montreal, Canada, July 17-Aug. 1.

Belt Buckle — A892

Thracian Art (8th-4th Centuries): 2s, Brooch. 3s, Mirror handle. 5s, Helmet cheek cover. 13s, Gold ornament. 18s, Lion's head (harness decoration). 20s, Knee guard. 28s, Jeweled pendant.

1976, July 30 Photo. *Perf. 13*

2341 A892 1s gold & multi .25 .25
2342 A892 2s blue & multi .25 .25
2343 A892 3s multicolored .25 .25
2344 A892 5s claret & multi .25 .25
2345 A892 13s purple & multi .35 .25
2346 A892 18s multicolored .40 .25
2347 A892 20s multicolored .55 .25
2348 A892 28s multicolored .55 .25
Nos. 2341-2348 (8) 2.85 2.00

Souvenir Sheet

Composite of Bulgarian Stamp Designs — A893

1976, June 5

2349 A893 50s red & multi 2.75 1.25

International Federation of Philately (F.I.P.), 50th anniversary and 12th Congress.

Partisans at Night, by Ilya Petrov — A894

Paintings: 5s, Old Town, by Tsanko Lavrenov. 13s, Seated Woman, by Petrov, vert. 18s, Seated Boy, by Petrov, vert. 28s, Old Plovdiv, by Lavrenov, vert. 80s, Ilya Petrov, self-portrait, vert.

1976, Aug. 11 Photo. *Perf. 14*

2350 A894 2s multicolored .25 .25
2351 A894 5s multicolored .25 .25
2352 A894 13s ultra & multi .35 .25
2353 A894 18s multicolored .65 .25
2354 A894 28s multicolored .80 .25
Nos. 2350-2354 (5) 2.30 1.25

Souvenir Sheet

2354A A894 80s multicolored 1.60 1.25

Souvenir Sheet

Olympic Sports and Emblems — A895

1976, Sept. 6 Photo. *Perf. 13*

2355 A895 Sheet of 4 2.00 1.50
a. 25s Weight Lifting .35 .25
b. 25s Rowing .35 .25
c. 25s Running .35 .25
d. 25s Wrestling .35 .25

Medalists, 21st Olympic Games, Montreal.

Souvenir Sheet

Fresco and UNESCO Emblem — A896

1976, Dec. 3

2356 A896 50s red & multi 1.75 1.00

UNESCO, 30th anniv.

"The Pianist" by Jendov — A897

Designs (Caricatures by Jendov): 5s, Imperialist "Trick or Treat." 13s, The Leader, 1931.

1976, Sept. 30 Photo. *Perf. 13*

2357 A897 2s green & multi .25 .25
2358 A897 5s purple & multi .25 .25
2359 A897 13s magenta & multi .30 .25
Nos. 2357-2359 (3) .80 .75

Alex Jendov (1901-1953), caricaturist.

Fish and Hook — A898

1976, Sept. 21 Photo. *Perf. 13*

2360 A898 5s multicolored .25 .25

World Sport Fishing Congress, Varna.

St. Theodore
A899

Frescoes: 3s, St. Paul. 5s, St. Joachim. 13s, Melchizedek. 19s, St. Porphyrius. 28s, Queen. 1 l, The Last Supper.

1976, Oct. 4 Litho. *Perf. 12x12½*

2361 A899 2s gold & multi .25 .25
2362 A899 3s gold & multi .25 .25
2363 A899 5s gold & multi .25 .25
2364 A899 13s gold & multi .45 .25

2365 A899 19s gold & multi .50 .25
2366 A899 28s gold & multi .70 .25
Nos. 2361-2366 (6) 2.40 1.50

Miniature Sheet

Perf. 12

2367 A899 1 l gold & multi 1.75 1.25

Zemen Monastery frescoes, 14th cent.

Document A900

1976, Oct. 5
2368 A900 5s multicolored .25 .25

State Archives, 25th anniversary.

Cinquefoil A901

1976, Oct. 14 Photo. *Perf. 13*
2369 A901 1s Chestnut .25 .25
2370 A901 2s Cinquefoil .25 .25
2371 A901 5s Holly .25 .25
2372 A901 8s Yew .25 .25
2373 A901 13s Daphne .35 .25
2374 A901 23s Judas tree .85 .25
Nos. 2369-2374 (6) 2.20 1.50

Dimitri Polianov — A902

1976, Nov. 19
2375 A902 2s dk purple & ocher .25 .25

Dimitri Polianov (1876-1953), poet.

Christo Botev, by Zlatyu Boyadjiev A903

Paintings: 2s, Partisan Carrying Cherrywood Cannon, by Ilya Petrov. 3s, "Necklace of Immortality" (man's portrait), by Detchko Uzunov. 13s, "April 1876," by Georgi Popoff. 18s, Partisans, by Stoyan Venev. 60s, The Oath, by Svetlin Ruseff.

1976, Dec. 8
2376 A903 1s bister & multi .25 .25
2377 A903 2s bister & multi .25 .25
2378 A903 3s bister & multi .25 .25
2379 A903 13s bister & multi .25 .25
2380 A903 18s bister & multi .35 .25
Nos. 2376-2380 (5) 1.35 1.25

Souvenir Sheet

Imperf

2381 A903 60s gold & multi 1.50 1.00

Uprising against Turkish rule, centenary.

"Pollution" and Tree A904

Design: 18s, "Pollution" obscuring sun.

1976, Nov. 10 *Perf. 13*
2382 A904 2s ultra & multi .25 .25
2383 A904 18s blue & multi .40 .25

Protection of the environment.

Congress Emblem — A904a

Flags — A904b

1976, Nov. 28 Photo. *Perf. 13*
2384 A904a 2s multicolored .25 .25
2384A A904b 13s multicolored .40 .25

33rd BSIS Cong. (Bulgarian Socialist Party).

Tobacco Workers, by Stajkov A905

Paintings by Stajkov: 2s, View of Melnik. 13s, Shipbuilder.

1976, Dec. 16 Photo. *Perf. 13*
2385 A905 1s multicolored .25 .25
2386 A905 2s multicolored .25 .25
2387 A905 13s multicolored .30 .25
Nos. 2385-2387 (3) .80 .75

Veselin Stajkov (1906-1970), painter.

Snowflake — A906

1976, Dec. 20
2388 A906 2s silver & multi .25 .25

New Year 1977.

Zachary Stoyanov (1851-1889), Historian — A907

1976, Dec. 30
2389 A907 2s multicolored .25 .25

Bronze Coin of Septimus Severus — A908

Roman Coins: 2s, 13s, 18s, Bronze coins of Caracalla, diff. 23s, Copper coin of Diocletian.

1977, Jan. 28 Photo. *Perf. 13½x13*
2390 A908 1s gold & multi .25 .25
2391 A908 2s gold & multi .25 .25
2392 A908 13s gold & multi .25 .25
2393 A908 18s gold & multi .40 .25
2394 A908 23s gold & multi .60 .25
Nos. 2390-2394 (5) 1.75 1.25

Coins struck in Serdica (modern Sofia).

Skis and Compass — A909

1977, Feb. 14 *Perf. 13*
2395 A909 13s ultra, red & lt bl .25 .25

2nd World Ski Orienteering Championships.

Tourist Congress Emblem — A910

1977, Feb. 24 Photo. *Perf. 13*
2396 A910 2s multicolored .25 .25

5th Congress of Bulgarian Tourist Organization.

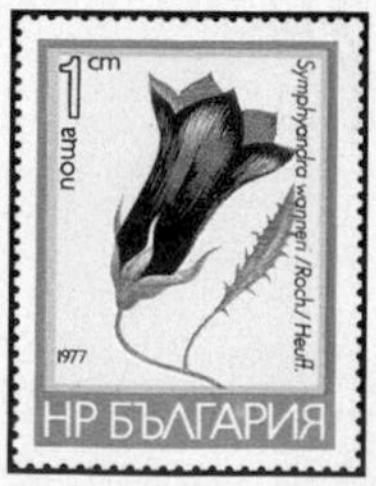

Bellflower A911

Designs: Various bellflowers.

1977, Mar. 2
2397 A911 1s yellow & multi .25 .25
2398 A911 2s rose & multi .25 .25
2399 A911 3s lt blue & multi .25 .25
2400 A911 13s multicolored .40 .25
2401 A911 43s yellow & multi 1.50 .30
Nos. 2397-2401 (5) 2.65 1.30

Vasil Kolarov — A912

1977, Mar. 21 Photo. *Perf. 13*
2402 A912 2s blue & black .25 .25

Vasil Kolarov (1877-1950), politician.

Union Congress Emblem — A913

1977, Mar. 25
2403 A913 2s multicolored .25 .25

8th Bulgarian Trade Union Cong., Apr. 4-7.

Wolf — A914

Wild Animals: 2s, Red fox. 10s, Weasel. 13s, European wildcat. 23s, Jackal.

1977, May 16 Litho. *Perf. 12½x12*
2404 A914 1s multicolored .25 .25
2405 A914 2s multicolored .25 .25
2406 A914 10s multicolored .30 .25
2407 A914 13s multicolored .55 .40
2408 A914 23s multicolored 1.25 .60
Nos. 2404-2408 (5) 2.60 1.75

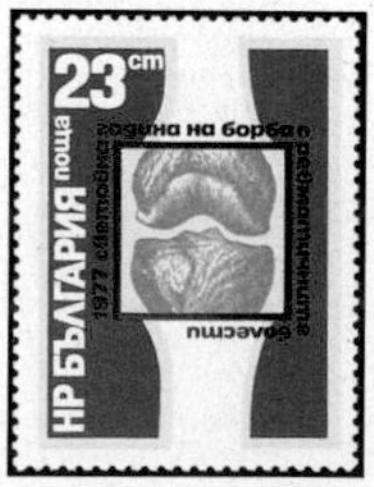

Diseased Knee — A915

1977, Mar. 31 Photo. *Perf. 13*
2409 A915 23s multicolored .60 .25

World Rheumatism Year.

Writers' Congress Emblem A916

1977, June 7

2410 A916 23s lt bl & yel grn 1.00 .50

International Writers Congress: "Peace, the Hope of the Planet." No. 2410 printed in sheets of 8 stamps and 4 labels with signatures of participating writers.

Old Testament Trinity, Sofia, 16th Century A917

Icons: 1s, St. Nicholas, Nessebur, 13th cent. 3s, Annunciation, Royal Gates, Veliko Turnovo, 16th cent. 5s, Christ Enthroned, Nessebur, 17th cent. 13s, St. Nicholas, Elena, 18th cent. 23s, Presentation of the Virgin, Rila Monastery, 18th cent. 35s, Virgin and Child, Tryavna, 19th cent. 40s, St. Demetrius on Horseback, Provadia, 19th cent. 1 l, The 12 Holidays, Rila Monastery, 18th cent.

1977, May 10 **Photo.** ***Perf. 13***

2411	A917	1s black & multi	.25	.25
2412	A917	2s green & multi	.25	.25
2413	A917	3s brown & multi	.25	.25
2414	A917	5s blue & multi	.25	.25
2415	A917	13s olive & multi	.35	.25
2416	A917	23s maroon & multi	.60	.25
2417	A917	35s green & multi	.85	.35
2418	A917	40s dp ultra & multi	1.60	.55
		Nos. 2411-2418 (8)	4.40	2.40

Miniature Sheet

Imperf

2419 A917 1 l gold & multi 3.25 3.25

Bulgarian icons. See Nos. 2615-2619.

Souvenir Sheet

St. Cyril — A918

1977, June 7 **Photo.** ***Perf. 13***

2420 A918 1 l gold & multi 2.50 2.50

St. Cyril (827-869), reputed inventor of Cyrillic alphabet.

Congress Emblem — A919

1977, May 9

2421 A919 2s red, gold & grn .25 .25

13th Komsomol Congress.

Newspaper Masthead — A920

1977, June 3 **Photo.** ***Perf. 13***

2422 A920 2s multicolored .25 .25

Cent. of Bulgarian daily press and 50th anniv. of Rabotnichesko Delo newspaper.

Patriotic Front Emblem — A921

1977, May 26

2423 A921 2s gold & multi .25 .25

8th Congress of Patriotic Front.

Weight Lifting — A922

1977, June 15

2424 A922 13s dp brown & multi .35 .25

European Youth Weight Lifting Championships, Sofia, June.

Women Basketball Players — A923

1977, June 15 ***Perf. 13***

2425 A923 23s multicolored .75 .25

7th European Women's Basketball Championships.

Wrestling — A924

Games Emblem and: 13s, Running. 23s, Basketball. 43s, Women's gymnastics.

1977, Apr. 15

2426	A924	2s multicolored	.25	.25
2427	A924	13s multicolored	.25	.25
2428	A924	23s multicolored	.65	.25
2429	A924	43s multicolored	1.00	.40
		Nos. 2426-2429 (4)	2.15	1.15

UNIVERSIADE '77, University Games, Sofia, Aug. 18-27.

No. 2427 exists imperf. Value, $200.

TV Tower, Berlin — A925

1977, Aug. 12 **Litho.** ***Perf. 13***

2430 A925 25s blue & dk blue .75 .25

SOZPHILEX 77 Philatelic Exhibition, Berlin, Aug. 19-28.

Ship Type of 1975

Historic Ships: 1s, Hansa cog. 2s, Santa Maria, caravelle. 3s, Golden Hind, frigate. 12s, Santa Catherina, carrack. 13s, La Corone, galleon. 43s, Mediterranean galleass.

1977, Aug. 29 **Photo.** ***Perf. 13***

2431	A873	1s multicolored	.25	.25
2432	A873	2s multicolored	.25	.25
2433	A873	3s multicolored	.25	.25
2434	A873	12s multicolored	.30	.25
2435	A873	13s multicolored	.30	.25
2436	A873	43s multicolored	1.25	.30
		Nos. 2431-2436 (6)	2.60	1.55

Ivan Vasov National Theater A926

Buildings, Sofia: 13s, Party Headquarters. 23s, House of the People's Army. 30s, Clement Ochrida University. 80s, National Gallery. 1 l, National Assembly.

1977, Aug. 30 **Photo.** ***Perf. 13***

2437	A926	12s red, *gray*	.25	.25
2438	A926	13s red brn, *gray*	.35	.25
2439	A926	23s blue, *gray*	.55	.25
2440	A926	30s olive, *gray*	.80	.30
2441	A926	80s violet, *gray*	1.25	.70
2442	A926	1 l claret, *gray*	1.75	.90
		Nos. 2437-2442 (6)	4.95	2.65

Map of Europe A927

1977, June 10

2443 A927 23s brown, bl & grn .60 .25

21st Congress of the European Organization for Quality Control, Varna.

Union of Earth and Water, by Rubens A928

Rubens Paintings: 23s, Venus and Adonis. 40s, Pastoral Scene (man and woman). 1 l, Portrait of a Lady in Waiting.

1977, Sept. 23 **Litho.** ***Perf. 12***

2444	A928	13s gold & multi	.40	.25
2445	A928	23s gold & multi	.80	.25
2446	A928	40s gold & multi	1.40	.35
		Nos. 2444-2446 (3)	2.60	.85

Souvenir Sheet

2447 A928 1 l gold & multi 2.50 2.00

Peter Paul Rubens (1577-1640).

George Dimitrov A929

1977, June 17 **Photo.** ***Perf. 13***

2448 A929 13s red & deep claret .50 .25

George Dimitrov (1882-1947).

Flame with Star — A930

1977, May 17

2449 A930 13s gold & multi .35 .25

3rd Bulgarian Culture Congress.

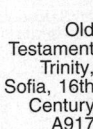

Smart Pete on Donkey, by Ilya Beshkov — A931

1977, May 19

2450 A931 2s multicolored .25 .25

11th National Festival of Humor and Satire Gabrovo.

Elin Pelin — A932

Writers: 2s, Pelin (Dimitur Ivanov Stojanov, (1877-1949). 5s, Peju K. Jaworov (1878-1914).

Artists: 13s, Boris Angelushev (1902-1966), 23s, Ceno Todorov (Ceno Todorov Dikov, 1877-1953). Each printed with label showing scenes from authors' works or illustrations by the artists.

1977, Aug. 26 **Photo.** ***Perf. 13***

2451	A932	2s gold & brown	.25	.25
2452	A932	5s gold & gray grn	.25	.25
2453	A932	13s gold & claret	.30	.30
2454	A932	23s gold & blue	.70	.35
		Nos. 2451-2454 (4)	1.50	1.15

13th Canoe World Championships — A933

1977, Sept. 1 Photo. *Perf. 13*

2455	A933	2s shown	.25	.25
2456	A933	23s 2-man canoe	.65	.25

Albena, Black Sea — A933a

1977, Oct. 5 Photo. *Perf. 13*

2456A	A933a	35s shown	.85	.35
2456B	A933a	43s Rila Monastery	.85	.35

Sheet contains 4 each plus label.

Dr. Pirogov — A934

1977, Oct. 14 Photo. *Perf. 13*

2457	A934	13s olive, ocher & brn	.35	.25

Centenary of visit by Russian physician N. J. Pirogov during war of liberation from Turkey.

Peace Decree, 1917 — A935

13s, Lenin, 1917. 23s, "1917" as a flame.

1977, Oct. 21

2458	A935	2s black, buff & red	.25	.25
2459	A935	13s multicolored	.40	.25
2460	A935	23s multicolored	.75	.25
		Nos. 2458-2460 (3)	1.40	.75

60th anniv. of Russian October Revolution.

Old Soldier with Grandchild A936

Designs (Festival Posters): 13s, "The Bugler." 23s, Liberation Monument, Sofia (detail). 25s, Samara flag.

1977, Sept. 30

2461	A936	2s multicolored	.25	.25
2462	A936	13s multicolored	.30	.25
2463	A936	23s multicolored	.70	.25
2464	A936	25s multicolored	.70	.30
		Nos. 2461-2464 (4)	1.95	1.05

Liberation from Turkish rule, centenary.

Souvenir Sheet

Games' and Sports Emblems — A937

1977, Aug. 10 Photo. *Perf. 13½x13*

2465	A937	1 l multicolored	2.25	1.75

University Games '77, Sofia.

Conference Building — A938

1977, Sept. 12 *Perf. 13½*

2466	A938	23s multicolored	.65	.25

64th Interparliamentary Union Conf., Sofia.

Bulgarian Worker's Newspaper, Anniversaries A939

1977, Sept. 12 Photo. *Perf. 13*

2467	A939	2s yel grn, blk & red	.25	.25

Ornament A940

New Year 1978: 13s, Different ornament.

1977, Dec. 1

2468	A940	2s gold & multi	.25	.25
2469	A940	13s silver & multi	.40	.25

Railroad Bridge — A941

1977, Nov. 9

2470	A941	13s green, yel & gray	.60	.25

Transport Organization, 50th anniversary.

A942

1977, Nov. 15

2471	A942	8s gold & vio brn	.50	.50

Petko Ratchev Slaveikov (1827-95), poet, birth sesquicentennial. No. 2471 printed in sheets of 8 stamps and 8 labels in 4 alternating vertical rows.

A943

Designs: 23s, Soccer player and Games' emblem. 50s, Soccer players.

1978, Jan. 30 Photo. *Perf. 13*

2472	A943	13s multicolored	.50	.25
2473	A943	23s multicolored	.70	.25

Souvenir Sheet

2474	A943	50s ultra & multi	1.75	1.40

11th World Cup Soccer Championship, Argentina, June 1-25.

Todor Zhivkov and Leonid I. Brezhnev A944

1977, Sept. 7 Photo. *Perf. 13*

2475	A944	18s gold, car & brn	.65	.45

Bulgarian-Soviet Friendship. No. 2475 issued in sheets of 3 stamps and 3 labels.

Ostankino Tower, Moscow, Bulgarian Post Emblem — A945

1978, Mar. 1

2476	A945	13s multicolored	.35	.25

Comecon Postal Organization (Council of Mutual Economic Assistance), 20th anniv.

Leo Tolstoy — A946

Shipka Pass Monument — A947

5s, Fedor Dostoevski. 13s, Ivan Sergeevich Turgenev. 23s, Vasili Vasilievich Vereshchagin. 25s, Giuseppe Garibaldi. 35s, Victor Hugo.

1978, Mar. 28 Photo. *Perf. 13*

2477	A946	2s yellow & dk grn	.25	.25
2478	A946	5s lemon & brown	.25	.25
2479	A946	13s tan & sl grn	.25	.25
2480	A946	23s gray & vio brn	.35	.25
2481	A946	25s yel grn & blk	.35	.25
2482	A946	35s lt bl & vio bl	.95	.50
		Nos. 2477-2482 (6)	2.40	1.75

Souvenir Sheet

2483	A947	50s multicolored	1.10	.80

Bulgaria's liberation from Ottoman rule, cent.

Bulgarian and Russian Colors A948

1978, Mar. 18

2484	A948	2s multicolored	.25	.25

30th anniv. of Russo-Bulgarian co-operation.

Heart and WHO Emblem A949

1978, May 12

2485	A949	23s gray, red & org	.75	.25

World Health Day, fight against hypertension.

Goddess A950

Ceramics (2nd-4th Cent.) & Exhibition Emblem: 5s, Mask of bearded man. 13s, Vase. 23s, Vase. 35s, Head of Silenus. 53s, Cock.

1978, Apr. 26

2486	A950	2s green & multi	.25	.25
2487	A950	5s multicolored	.25	.25
2488	A950	13s multicolored	.35	.25
2489	A950	23s multicolored	.55	.25
2490	A950	35s multicolored	.80	.45
2491	A950	53s carmine & multi	2.50	.55
		Nos. 2486-2491 (6)	4.70	2.00

Philaserdica Philatelic Exhibition.

Nikolai Roerich, by Svyatoslav Roerich — A951

"Mind and Matter," by Andrei Nikolov — A952

1978, Apr. 5

2492 A951 8s multicolored .25 .25
2493 A952 13s multicolored .35 .25

Nikolai K. Roerich (1874-1947) and Andrei Nikolov (1878-1959), artists.

Bulgarian Flag and Red Star — A953

1978, Apr. 18

2494 A953 2s vio blue & multi .25 .25

Bulgarian Communist Party Congress.

Young Man, by Albrecht Dürer A954

Paintings: 23s, Bathsheba at Fountain, by Rubens. 25s, Portrait of a Man, by Hans Holbein the Younger. 35s, Rembrandt and Saskia, by Rembrandt. 43s, Lady in Mourning, by Tintoretto. 60s, Old Man with Beard, by Rembrandt. 80s, Knight in Armor, by Van Dyck.

1978, June 19 Photo. *Perf. 13*

2495 A954 13s multicolored .25 .25
2496 A954 23s multicolored .35 .25
2497 A954 25s multicolored .40 .25
2498 A954 35s multicolored .55 .25
2499 A954 43s multicolored .65 .25
2500 A954 60s multicolored .85 .40
2501 A954 80s multicolored 2.00 .65
Nos. 2495-2501 (7) 5.05 2.30

Dresden Art Gallery paintings.

Doves and Festival Emblem — A955

1978, May 31

2502 A955 13s multicolored .35 .25

11th World Youth Festival, Havana, 7/28-8/5.

Fritillaria Stribrnyi — A956

Rare Flowers: 2s, Fritillaria drenovskyi. 3s, Lilium rhodopaeum. 13s, Tulipa urumoffii. 23s, Lilium jankae. 43s, Tulipa rhodopaea.

1978, June 27

2503 A956 1s multicolored .25 .25
2504 A956 2s multicolored .25 .25
2505 A956 3s multicolored .25 .25
2506 A956 13s multicolored .35 .25
2507 A956 23s multicolored .40 .25
2508 A956 43s multicolored 1.25 .50
Nos. 2503-2508 (6) 2.75 1.75

Yacht Cor Caroli and Map of Voyage A957

1978, May 19 Photo. *Perf. 13*

2509 A957 23s multicolored 1.40 .25

First Bulgarian around-the-world voyage, Capt. Georgi Georgiev, 12/20/76-12/20/77.

Market, by Naiden Petkov — A958

Views of Sofia: 5s, Street, by Emil Stoichev. 13s, Street, by Boris Ivanov. 23s, Tolbukhin Boulevard, by Nikola Tanev. 35s, National Theater, by Nikola Petrov. 53s, Market, by Anton Mitov.

1978, Aug. 28 Litho. *Perf. 12½x12*

2510 A958 2s multicolored .25 .25
2511 A958 5s multicolored .25 .25
2512 A958 13s multicolored .25 .25
2513 A958 23s multicolored .40 .25
2514 A958 35s multicolored .75 .25
2515 A958 53s multicolored 1.00 .40
Nos. 2510-2515 (6) 2.90 1.65

Miniature Sheet

Sleeping Venus, by Giorgione — A959

1978, Aug. 7 Photo. *Imperf.*

2516 A959 1 l multicolored 1.75 .85

View of Varna — A960

1978, July 13 Photo. *Perf. 13*

2517 A960 13s multicolored .60 .30

63rd Esperanto Cong., Varna, 7/29-8/5.

Black Woodpecker A961

Woodpeckers: 2s, Syrian. 3s, Three-toed. 13s, Middle spotted. 23s, Lesser spotted. 43s, Green.

1978, Sept. 1

2518 A961 1s multicolored .25 .25
2519 A961 2s multicolored .25 .25
2520 A961 3s multicolored .25 .25
2521 A961 13s multicolored .60 .30
2522 A961 23s multicolored .90 .50
2523 A961 43s multicolored 2.40 1.25
Nos. 2518-2523 (6) 4.65 2.80

"September 1923" — A962

1978, Sept. 5

2524 A962 2s red & brn .25 .25

55th anniversary of September uprising.

Souvenir Sheet

A963

a, National Theater, Sofia. b, Festival Hall, Sofia. c, Charles Bridge, Prague. d, Belvedere Palace, Prague.

Photogravure and Engraved

1978, Sept. 1 *Perf. 12x11½*

2525 A963 Sheet of 4 2.50 1.00
a.-d. 40s any single .60 .25

PRAGA '78 and PHILASERDICA '79 Philatelic Exhibitions

Black and White Hands, Human Rights Emblem — A964

1978, Oct. 3 Photo. *Perf. 13x13½*

2526 A964 13s multicolored .35 .25

Anti-Apartheid Year.

Gotse Deltchev — A965

1978, Aug. 1 Photo. *Perf. 13*

2527 A965 13s multicolored .40 .25

Gotse Deltchev (1872-1903), patriot.

Bulgarian Calculator — A966

1978, Sept. 3

2528 A966 2s multicolored .25 .25

International Sample Fair, Plovdiv.

Guerrillas — A967

1978, Aug. 1

2529 A967 5s blk & rose red .25 .25

Ilinden and Preobrazhene revolts, 75th anniv.

"Pipe Line" and Flags A968

1978, Oct. 3

2530 A968 13s multicolored .35 .25

Construction of gas pipe line from Orenburg to Russian border.

A969

1978, Oct. 4 *Perf. 13x13½*
2531 A969 13s Three acrobats .35 .25

3rd World Acrobatic Championships, Sofia, Oct. 6-8.

A970

1978, Sept. 18 **Photo.** ***Perf. 13***
2532 A970 2s dp claret & ocher .30 .50

Christo G. Danov (1828-1911), 1st Bulgarian publisher. No. 2532 printed with se-tenant label showing early printing press.

Insurgents, by Todor Panajotov — A971

1978, Sept. 20
2533 A971 2s multicolored .25 .25

Vladaja mutiny, 60th anniversary.

A972

1978, Oct. 11 **Photo.** ***Perf. 13***
2534 A972 13s dk brn & org red .35 .25

Salvador Allende (1908-1973), president of Chile.

Human Rights Flame — A973

1978, Oct. 18
2535 A973 23s multicolored .70 .25

Universal Declaration of Human Rights, 30th anniversary.

A974

Burgarian Paintings: 1s, Levski and Matei Mitkaloto, by Kalina Tasseva. 2s, "Strength for my Arm" by Zlatyu Boyadjiev. 3s, Rumena, woman military leader, by Nikola Mirchev, horiz. 13s, Kolju Ficeto, by Elza Goeva. 23s, Family, National Revival Period, by Naiden Petkov.

Perf. 12x12½, 12½x12

1978, Oct. 25 **Litho.**
2536 A974 1s multicolored .25 .25
2537 A974 2s multicolored .25 .25
2538 A974 3s multicolored .25 .25
2539 A974 13s multicolored .35 .25
2540 A974 23s multicolored .65 .25
Nos. 2536-2540 (5) 1.75 1.25

1300th anniversary of Bulgaria (in 1981).

From late 1978 to 1991, imperf varieties, some overprinted, exist for many sets and souvenir sheets. These were distributed in limited numbers and are described in footnotes following the listed issues.

Souvenir Sheet

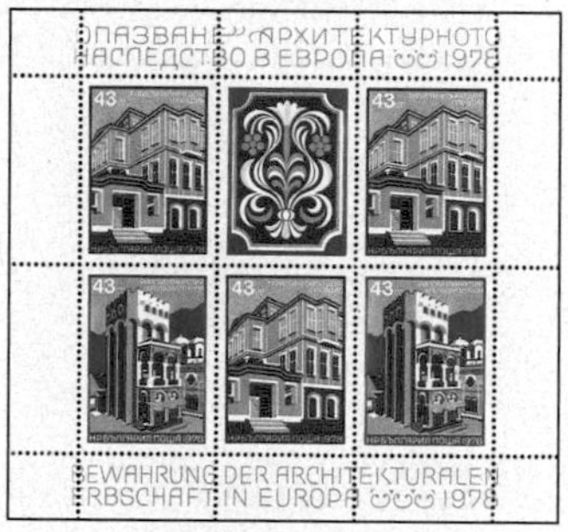

A975

Designs: a, Tourism building, Plovdiv. b, Chrelo Tower, Rila Cloister.

1978, Nov. 1 **Photo.** ***Perf. 13***
2541 A975 Sheet of 5 + label 4.00 2.00
a.-b. 43s any single .85 .35

Conservation of European architectural heritage. No. 2541 contains 3 No. 2541a & 2 No. 2541b.

Exists overprinted "Essen 1978." Value $32.50.

Ferry, Map of Black Sea with Route A976

1978, Nov. 1 **Photo.** ***Perf. 13***
2542 A976 13s multicolored .40 .25

Opening of Ilychovsk-Varna Ferry.

Bird, from Marble Floor, St. Sofia Church — A977

1978, Nov. 20
2543 A977 5s multicolored .35 .25

3rd Bulgaria '78, National Philatelic Exhibition, Sofia. Printed se-tenant with label showing emblems of Bulgaria '78 and Philaserdica '79.

Initial, 13th Century Gospel — A978

Designs: 13s, St. Cyril, miniature, 1567. 23s, Book cover, 16th century. 80s, St. Methodius, miniature, 13th century.

1978, Dec. 15 **Photo.** ***Perf. 13***
2544 A978 2s multicolored .25 .25
2545 A978 13s multicolored .30 .25
2546 A978 23s multicolored .65 .25
Nos. 2544-2546 (3) 1.20 .75

Souvenir Sheet

2547 A978 80s multicolored 1.60 1.00

Cent. of the Cyril and Methodius Natl. Library.

Bulgaria No. 53 A979

Bulgarian Stamps: 13s, #534. 23s, #968. 35s, #1176, vert. 53s, #1223, vert. 1 l, #1.

1978, Dec. 30
2548 A979 2s ol grn & red .25 .25
2549 A979 13s ultra & rose car .25 .25
2550 A979 23s rose lil & ol grn .35 .25
2551 A979 35s brt bl & blk .65 .25
2552 A979 53s ver & sl grn 1.10 .35
Nos. 2548-2552 (5) 2.60 1.35

Souvenir Sheet

2553 A979 1 l multicolored 1.75 1.25

Philaserdica '79, International Philatelic Exhibition, Sofia, May 18-27, 1979, and centenary of Bulgarian stamps. No. 2553 exists imperf. Value $16.

A larger (63mmx61mm) souvenir sheet was issued in 1979, containing one 1 l stamp, perf 13. Value $4.50. A second souvenir sheet (92mmx125mm), containing one 5 l stamp, perf 13, with reproductions of many stamps of the first Bulgarian issue, was also issued in 1979. Value $35.

See Nos. 2560-2564.

St. Clement of Ochrida — A980

1978, Dec. 8
2554 A980 2s multicolored .25 .25

Clement of Ochrida University, 90th anniv.

Ballet Dancers A981

1978, Dec. 22
2555 A981 13s multicolored .35 .25

Bulgarian ballet, 50th anniversary.

Nikola Karastojanov — A982

1978, Dec. 12
2556 A982 2s multicolored .35 .25

Nikola Karastojanov (1778-1874), printer. No. 2556 printed se-tenant with label showing printing press.

Christmas Tree Made of Birds — A983

1978, Dec. 22
2557 A983 2s shown .25 .25
2558 A983 13s Post horn .25 .25

New Year 1979.

COMECON Building, Moscow, Members' Flags — A984

1979, Jan. 25 **Photo.** ***Perf. 13***
2559 A984 13s multicolored .35 .25

Council for Mutual Economic Aid (COMECON), 30th anniversary.

Philaserdica Type of 1978
Designs as Before

1979, Jan. 30
2560 A979 2s brt bl & red .25 .25
2561 A979 13s grn & dk car .25 .25
2562 A979 23s org brn & multi .45 .25
2563 A979 35s dl red & blk .70 .35
2564 A979 53s vio & dk ol .90 .55
Nos. 2560-2564 (5) 2.55 1.65

Philaserdica '79.

Bank Building, Commemorative Coin — A985

1979, Feb. 13
2565 A985 2s yel, gray & silver .25 .25

Centenary of Bulgarian People's Bank.

Aleksandr Stamboliski A986

1979, Feb. 28
2566 A986 2s orange & dk brn .25 .25

Aleksandr Stamboliski (1879-1923), leader of peasant's party and premier.

Flower with Child's Face, IYC Emblem — A987

1979, Mar. 8
2568 A987 23s multicolored .65 .25

International Year of the Child.

Stylized Heads, World Association Emblem — A988

1979, Mar. 20
2569 A988 13s multicolored .35 .25

8th World Cong. for the Deaf, Varna, June 20-27.

"75" and Trade Union Emblem — A989

1979, Mar. 20
2570 A989 2s slate grn & org .25 .25

75th anniversary of Bulgarian Trade Unions.

Souvenir Sheet

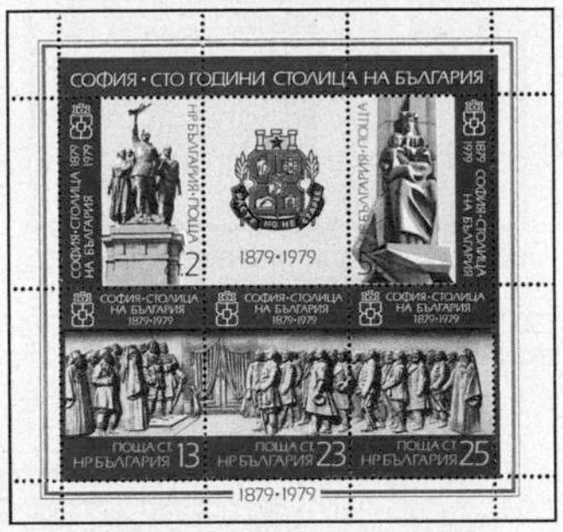

Sculptures in Sofia — A990

Designs: 2s, Soviet Army Monument (detail). 5s, Mother and Child, Central Railroad Station. 13s, 23s, 25s, Bas-relief from Monument of the Liberators.

1979, Apr. 2 **Photo.** ***Perf. 13***
2571 A990 Sheet of 5 + label 1.50 1.00
a. 2s multicolored .25 .25
b. 5s multicolored .25 .25
c. 13s multicolored .35 .25
d. 23s multicolored .45 .25
e. 25s multicolored .50 .25

Centenary of Sofia as capital.

Rocket Launch, Space Flight Emblems A991

Intercosmos & Bulgarian-USSR Flight Emblems and: 25s, Link-up, horiz. 35s, Parachute descent. 1 l, Globe, emblems & orbit, horiz.

1979, Apr. 11
2572 A991 12s multicolored .25 .25
2573 A991 25s multicolored .70 .25
2574 A991 35s multicolored .90 .40
Nos. 2572-2574 (3) 1.85 .90

Souvenir Sheet

2575 A991 1 l multicolored 1.75 1.00

1st Bulgarian cosmonaut on Russian space flight.

A slightly larger imperf. sheet similar to No. 2575 with control numbers at bottom and rockets at sides exists. $100.

Georgi Ivanov A992

Design: 13s, Rukavishnikov and Soviet cosmonaut Georgi Ivanov.

1979, May 14 **Photo.** ***Perf. 13***
2576 A992 2s multicolored .25 .25
2577 A992 13s multicolored .50 .25

Col. Rukavishnikov, 1st Bulgarian astronaut.

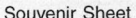

Souvenir Sheet

Thracian Gold-leaf Collar — A993

1979, May 16
2578 A993 1 l multicolored 3.50 2.25

48th International Philatelic Federation Congress, Sofia, May 16-17.

Post Horn, Carrier Pigeon, Jet, Globes and UPU Emblem — A994

Designs (Post Horn, Globes and ITU Emblem): 5s, 1st Bulgarian and modern telephones. 13s, Morse key and teleprinter. 23s, Old radio transmitter and radio towers. 35s, Bulgarian TV tower and satellite. 50s, Ground receiving station

1979, May 8 ***Perf. 13½x13***
2579 A994 2s multicolored .25 .25
2580 A994 5s multicolored .25 .25
2581 A994 13s multicolored .35 .25
2582 A994 23s multicolored .50 .25
2583 A994 35s multicolored .70 .30
Nos. 2579-2583 (5) 2.05 1.30

Souvenir Sheet

Perf. 13

2584 A994 50s vio, blk & gray 2.00 1.40

Intl. Telecommunications Day and cent. of Bulgarian Postal & Telegraph Services. Size of stamp in No. 2584: 39x28mm. No. 2584 exists imperf. Value $15.

Hotel Vitosha-New Otani — A996

1979, May 20
2586 A996 2s ultra & pink .25 .25

Philaserdica '79 Day.

Horseman Receiving Gifts, by Karellia and Boris Kuklievi — A997

1979, May 23
2587 A997 2s multicolored .25 .25

Bulgarian-Russian Friendship Day.

A998

Man on Donkey, by Boris Angeloushev.

1979, May 23 **Photo.** ***Perf. 13½***
2588 A998 2s multicolored .25 .25

12th National Festival of Humor and Satire, Gabrovo.

Durer Engravings A999

13s, Four Women. 23s, Three Peasants. 25s, The Cook and his Wife. 35s, Portrait of Helius Eobanus Hessus. 80s, Rhinoceros, horiz.

Lithographed and Engraved

1979, May 31 ***Perf. 14x13½***
2589 A999 13s multicolored .35 .25
2590 A999 23s multicolored .45 .25
2591 A999 25s multicolored .60 .25
2592 A999 35s multicolored .90 .25
Nos. 2589-2592 (4) 2.30 1.00

Souvenir Sheet

Imperf

2593 A999 80s multicolored 1.75 1.25

Albrecht Durer (1471-1528), German engraver and painter.

R. Todorov (1879-1916) — A1000

Bulgarian Writers: No. 2595, Dimitri Dymov (1909-66). No. 2596, S. A. Kostov (1879-1939).

1979, June 26 **Photo.** ***Perf. 13***
2594 A1000 2s multicolored .25 .65
2595 A1000 2s slate grn & yel grn .25 .65
2596 A1000 2s dp claret & yel .25 .65
Nos. 2594-2596 (3) .75 1.95

Nos. 2594-2596 each printed se-tenant with label showing title page or character from writer's work.

Moscow '80 Emblem, Runners A1001

Moscow '80 Emblem and: 13s, Pole vault, horiz. 25s, Discus. 35s, Hurdles, horiz. 43s, High jump, horiz. 1 l, Long jump.

1979, May 15 *Perf. 13*

2597	A1001	2s multicolored	.25	.25
2598	A1001	13s multicolored	.35	.25
2599	A1001	25s multicolored	1.00	.25
2600	A1001	35s multicolored	1.00	.35
2601	A1001	43s multicolored	1.40	.45
2602	A1001	1 l multicolored	2.50	.95
		Nos. 2597-2602 (6)	6.50	2.50

Souvenir Sheet

2602A A1001 2 l multicolored 7.00 4.00

22nd Summer Olympic Games, Moscow, July 19-Aug. 3, 1980.

Rocket — A1002

5s, Flags of USSR and Bulgaria. 13s, "35."

1979, Sept. 4 **Photo.**

2603 A1002	2s multicolored	.25	.25
2604 A1002	5s multicolored	.25	.25
2605 A1002	13s multicolored	.25	.25
	Nos. 2603-2605 (3)	.75	.75

35th anniversary of liberation.

Moscow '80 Emblem, Gymnast A1003

Moscow '80 Emblem & gymnasts.

1979, July 31 **Photo.** *Perf. 13*

2606 A1003	2s multi	.25	.25
2607 A1003	13s multi, horiz.	.25	.25
2608 A1003	25s multi	.40	.25
2609 A1003	35s multi	.80	.35
2610 A1003	43s multi	.80	.35
2611 A1003	1 l multi	2.50	1.00
	Nos. 2606-2611 (6)	5.00	2.45

Souvenir Sheet

2612 A1003 2 l multicolored 7.75 4.00

22nd Summer Olympic Games, Moscow, July 19-Aug. 3, 1980.

A1004

1979, July 8 **Photo.** *Perf. 13*

2613 A1004 13s ultra & blk .30 .25

Theater Institute, 18th Congress.

A1005

1979, July 17

2614 A1005 8s multicolored .25 .25

Journalists' Vacation House, Varna, 20th Anniv.

Icon Type of 1977

Virgin and Child from: 13s, 23s, Nesebar, 16th cent., diff. 35s, 43s, Sozopol, 16th cent., diff. 53s, Samokov, 19th cent. Inscribed 1979.

1979, Aug. 7 **Litho.** *Perf. 12½*

2615 A917	13s multicolored	.60	.25
2616 A917	23s multicolored	.60	.25
2617 A917	35s multicolored	.60	.25
2618 A917	43s multicolored	.60	.25
2619 A917	53s multicolored	1.20	.45
	Nos. 2615-2619 (5)	3.60	1.45

Anton Besenschek A1006

1979, Aug. 9 **Photo.** *Perf. 13x13½*

2620 A1006 2s multi .25 .25

Bulgarian stenography centenary.

A1007

1979, Aug. 28 *Perf. 13*

2621 A1007 2s multicolored .25 .25

Bulgarian Alpine Club, 50th anniv.

Public Health Ordinance — A1008

1979, Aug. 31 *Perf. 13½*

2622 A1008 2s multicolored .25 .25

Public Health Service centenary. No. 2622 printed with label showing Dimitar Mollov, founder.

Isotope Measuring Device — A1009

1979, Sept. 8 *Perf. 13½x13*

2623 A1009 2s multicolored .25 .25

International Sample Fair, Plovdiv.

Games' Emblem A1010

1979, Sept. 20 *Perf. 13*

2624 A1010 5s multicolored .25 .25

Universiada '79, World University Games, Mexico City, Sept.

Sofia Locomotive Sports Club, 50th Anniversary — A1011

1979, Oct. 2

2625 A1011 2s blue & org red .25 .25

Ljuben Karavelov (1837-1879), Poet and Freedom Fighter — A1012

1979, Oct. 4 **Photo.** *Perf. 13*

2626 A1012 2s blue & slate grn .25 .25

A1013

1979, Oct. 20

2627 A1013	2s Biathlon	.25	.25
2628 A1013	13s Speed skating	.30	.25
2629 A1013	23s Downhill skiing	.50	.25
2630 A1013	43s Luge	1.25	.40
	Nos. 2627-2630 (4)	2.30	1.15

Souvenir Sheet

Imperf

2631 A1013 1 l Slalom 2.00 1.25

13th Winter Olympic Games, Lake Placid, NY, Feb. 12-24.

No. 2631 exists overprinted "Lake Placid 1980," with serial number. Value $100.

A1014

Decko Uzunov, 80th Birthday: 12s, Apparition in Red. 13s, Woman from Thrace. 23s, Composition.

1979, Oct. 31 *Perf. 14*

2632 A1014	12s multicolored	.30	.25
2633 A1014	13s multicolored	.30	.25
2634 A1014	23s multicolored	.85	.25
	Nos. 2632-2634 (3)	1.45	.75

Swimming, Moscow '80 Emblem — A1016

2s, Two-man kayak, vert. 13s, Swimming, vert. 35s, One-man kayak. 43s, Diving, vert. 1 l, Diving, vert., diff.
2 l, Water polo, vert.

1979, Nov. 30 **Photo.** *Perf. 13*

2636 A1016	2s multicolored	.25	.25
2637 A1016	13s multicolored	.40	.25
2638 A1016	25s shown	1.10	.25
2639 A1016	35s multicolored	1.10	.25
2640 A1016	43s multicolored	1.50	.60
2641 A1016	1 l multicolored	2.25	1.00
	Nos. 2636-2641 (6)	6.60	2.60

Souvenir Sheet

2642 A1016 2 l multicolored 7.75 4.00

22nd Summer Olympic Games, Moscow, July 19-Aug. 3, 1980.

Nikola Vapzarov — A1017

1979, Dec. 7 **Photo.** *Perf. 13*

2643 A1017 2s claret & rose .30 .30

Vapzarov (1909-1942), poet and freedom fighter. No. 2643 printed with label showing smokestacks.

The First Socialists, by Bojan Petrov — A1018

Paintings: 13s, Demeter Blagoev Reading Newspaper, by Demeter Gjudshenov, 1892. 25s, Workers' Party March, by Sotir Sotirov, 1917. 35s, Dawn in Plovdiv, by Johann Leviev, vert.

Perf. 12½x12, 12x12½

1979, Dec. 10 **Litho.**

2644	A1018	2s	multicolored	.25	.25
2645	A1018	13s	multicolored	.30	.25
2646	A1018	25s	multicolored	.60	.25
2647	A1018	35s	multicolored	.85	.25
	Nos. 2644-2647 (4)			2.00	1.00

Sharpshooting, Moscow '80 Emblem A1019

13s, Judo, horiz. 25s, Wrestling, horiz. 35s, Archery. 43s, Fencing, horiz. 1 l, Fencing. 2 l, Boxing.

1979, Dec. 22 **Photo.** ***Perf. 13***

2648	A1019	2s	shown	.25	.25
2649	A1019	13s	multi	.35	.25
2650	A1019	25s	multi	1.00	.25
2651	A1019	35s	multi	1.00	.35
2652	A1019	43s	multi	1.40	.75
2653	A1019	1 l	multi	2.10	1.40
	Nos. 2648-2653 (6)			6.10	3.25

Souvenir Sheet

2654	A1019	2 l	multi	7.75	5.00

Procession with Relics, 11th Century Fresco A1020

Frescoes of Sts. Cyril and Methodius, St. Clement's Basilica, Rome: 13s, Reception by Pope Hadrian II. 23s, Burial of Cyril the Philosopher, 18th century. 25s, St. Cyril. 35s, St. Methodius.

1979, Dec. 25

2655	A1020	2s	multicolored	.25	.25
2656	A1020	13s	multicolored	.25	.25
2657	A1020	23s	multicolored	.45	.25
2658	A1020	25s	multicolored	.55	.25
2659	A1020	35s	multicolored	.85	.25
	Nos. 2655-2659 (5)			2.35	1.25

Bulgarian Television Emblem — A1021

1979, Dec. 29 ***Perf. 13½***

2660	A1021	5s	violet bl & lt bl	.30	.30

Bulgarian television, 25th anniversary. No. 2660 printed with label showing Sofia television tower.

Doves in Girl's Hair A1022

Design: 2s, Children's heads, mosaic, vert.

1979 ***Perf. 13***

2661	A1022	2s	multicolored	.25	.25
2662	A1022	13s	multicolored	.30	.25

International Year of the Child. Issue dates: 2s, July 17; 13s, Dec. 14.

Puppet on Horseback, IYC Emblem — A1023

1980, Jan. 22 **Photo.** ***Perf. 13***

2663	A1023	2s	multicolored	.25	.25

UNIMA, Intl. Puppet Theater Organization, 50th anniv. (1979); Intl. Year of the Child (1979).

Thracian Rider, Votive Tablet, 3rd Century — A1024

National Archaeological Museum Centenary; 13s, Deines stele, 5th century B.C.

1980, Jan. 29 **Photo.** ***Perf. 13x13½***

2664	A1024	2s	brown & gold	.25	.25
2665	A1024	13s	multicolored	.25	.25

A miniature sheet was issued March 27, 1980, containing six 13s stamps, perf 13, which spelled out "EUROPA." Size 130mmx118mm. Value $30.

Dimitrov Meeting Lenin in Moscow, by Alexander Poplilov A1026

1980, Mar. 28 ***Perf. 12x12½***

2667	A1026	13s	multicolored	.30	.25

Lenin, 110th birth anniversary.

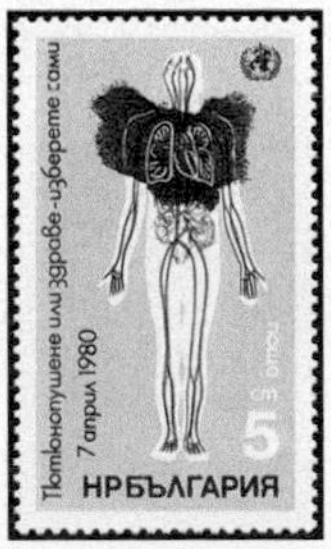

A1027

Circulatory system, lungs enveloped in smoke.

1980, Apr. 7 ***Perf. 13***

2668	A1027	5s	multicolored	.25	.25

World Health Day fight against cigarette smoking.

A1027a

1980, Apr. 10 **Photo.** ***Perf. 13***

2669	A1027a	2s	Basketball	.25	.25
2670	A1027a	13s	Soccer	.35	.25
2671	A1027a	25s	Hockey	1.10	.35
2672	A1027a	35s	Cycling	1.10	.55
2673	A1027a	43s	Handball	1.50	.75
2674	A1027a	1 l	Volleyball	2.25	1.10
	Nos. 2669-2674 (6)			6.55	3.25

Souvenir Sheet

2675	A1027a	2 l	Weightlifting	7.50	5.00

22nd Summer Olympic Games, Moscow, July 19-Aug. 3, 1980.

Souvenir Sheet

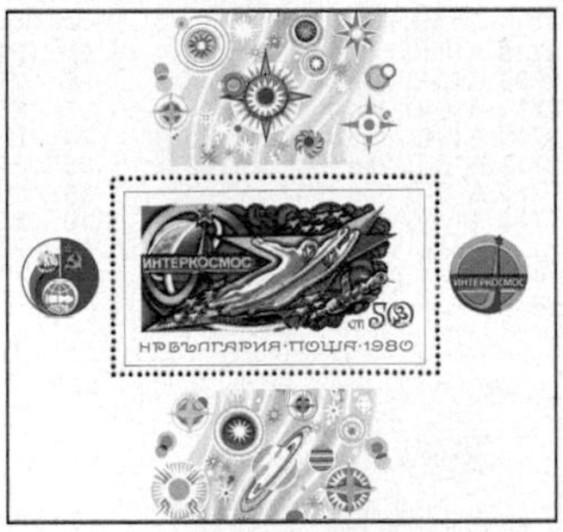

Intercosmos Emblem, Cosmonauts — A1028

1980, Apr. 22 ***Perf. 12***

2676	A1028	50s	multicolored	1.40	.80

Intercosmos cooperative space program.

Penio Penev (1930-1959), Poet — A1029

1980, Apr. 22 **Photo.** ***Perf. 13***

2677	A1029	5s	multicolored	.25	.25

Se-tenant with label showing quote from author's work.

Penny Black — A1030

1980, Apr. 24 ***Perf. 13***

2678	A1030	25s	dark red & sepia	.85	.60

London 1980 International Stamp Exhibition, May 6-14; printed se-tenant with label showing Rowland Hill between every two stamps.

No. 2678 was overprinted "UPU 1984" in 1982. Value $3.

Demeter H. Tchorbadjiiski, Self-portrait — A1031

1980, Apr. 29

2679	A1031	5s	shown	.25	.25
2680	A1031	13s	"Our People"	.25	.25

Nikolai Giaurov — A1032

1980, Apr. 30

2681	A1032	5s	multicolored	.50	.50

Nikolai Giaurov (b. 1930), opera singer; printed se-tenant with label showing Boris Godunov.

Raising Red Flag Reichstag Building, Berlin — A1033

Armistice, 35th Anniversary: 13s, Soviet Army memorial, Berlin-Treptow.

1980, May 6 ***Perf. 13x13½***

2682	A1033	5s	multicolored	.25	.25
2683	A1033	13s	multicolored	.25	.25

Numeral — A1034

1979 ***Perf. 14***

2684	A1034	2s	ultra	.25	.25
2685	A1034	5s	rose car	.25	.25

A1034a

1980, May 12 **Photo.** ***Perf. 13***

2685A	A1034a	5s	multicolored	.25	.25

75th Anniv. of Teachers' Union.

Warsaw Pact, 25th Anniv. — A1035

1980, May 14 **Photo.** ***Perf. 13***

2686	A1035	13s multicolored	.35	.25

Statues A1036

1980, June 10

2687	A1036	2s multicolored	.25	.25
2688	A1036	13s multicolored	.35	.35
2689	A1036	25s multicolored	1.00	.50
2690	A1036	35s multicolored	1.00	.60
2691	A1036	43s multicolored	1.40	.80
2692	A1036	1 l multicolored	2.10	1.25
		Nos. 2687-2692 (6)	6.10	3.75

Souvenir Sheet

2693	A1036	2 l multicolored	7.50	3.50

22nd Summer Olympic Games, Moscow, July 19-Aug. 3.

In 1981 a souvenir sheet was issued, containing one 50s stamp, perf 13, depicting Olympic medal and lion. Size 100x105mm. Value $18.50.

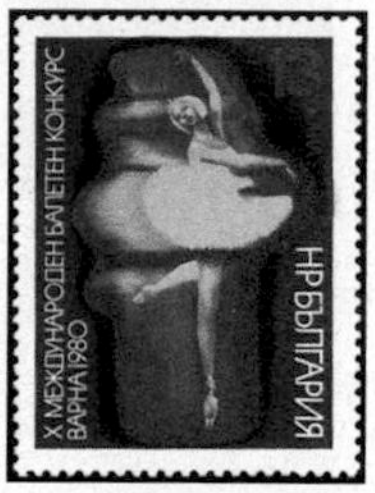

A1037

1980, Sept. **Photo.** ***Perf. 13***

2694	A1037	13s multicolored	.35	.25

10th Intl. Ballet Competition, Varna.

Hotel Europa, Sofia A1038

Hotels: No. 2696, Bulgaria, Burgas, vert. No. 2697, Plovdiv, Plovdiv. No. 2698, Riga, Russe, vert. No. 2699, Varna, Djuba.

1980, July 11

2695	A1038	23s lt ultra & multi	.45	.25
2696	A1038	23s orange & multi	.45	.25
2697	A1038	23s gray & multi	.45	.25
2698	A1038	23s blue & multi	.45	.25
2699	A1038	23s yellow & multi	.45	.25
		Nos. 2695-2699 (5)	2.25	1.25

See No. 2766.

Ship Type of 1975

Ships of 16th, 17th Centuries: 5s, Christ of Lubeck, galleon. 8s, Roman galley. 13s, Eagle, Russian galleon. 23s, Mayflower. 35s, Maltese galley. 53s, Royal Louis, galleon.

1980, July 14

2700	A873	5s multicolored	.25	.25
2701	A873	8s multicolored	.25	.25
2702	A873	13s multicolored	.25	.25
2703	A873	23s multicolored	.45	.25
2704	A873	35s multicolored	.80	.25
2705	A873	53s multicolored	1.10	.40
		Nos. 2700-2705 (6)	3.10	1.65

On Aug. 28, 1980, a miniature sheet of six stamps, denominated 5s to 45s, perf 13, was issued. Size: 115mmx135mm. Inscribed "ESSEN 1980" in selvage and serially numbered. Value $40.

Int'l Year of the Child, 1979 — A1040

Designs: Children's drawings and IYC emblem. 43s, Tower. 5s, 25s, 43s, vert.

Perf. 12½x12, 12x12½

1980, Sep. 1 **Litho.**

2708	A1040	3s multicolored	.25	.25
2709	A1040	5s multicolored	.25	.25
2710	A1040	8s multicolored	.25	.25
2711	A1040	13s multicolored	.25	.25
2712	A1040	25s multicolored	.35	.25
2713	A1040	35s multicolored	.55	.25
2714	A1040	43s multicolored	1.10	.25
		Nos. 2708-2714 (7)	3.00	1.75

Helicopter, Missile Transport, Tank — A1041

1980, Sept. 23 **Photo.** ***Perf. 13***

2715	A1041	3s shown	.25	.25
2716	A1041	5s Jet, radar, rocket	.25	.25
2717	A1041	8s Helicopter, ships	.25	.25
		Nos. 2715-2717 (3)	.75	.75

Bulgarian People's Army, 35th anniversary.

St. Anne, by Leonardo da Vinci A1042

Da Vinci Paintings: 8s, 13s, Annunciation (diff.). 25s, Adoration of the Kings. 35s, Lady with the Ermine. 50s, Mona Lisa.

1980, Oct. 10

2718	A1042	5s multicolored	.25	.25
2719	A1042	8s multicolored	.25	.25
2720	A1042	13s multicolored	.25	.25
2721	A1042	25s multicolored	.50	.25
2722	A1042	35s multicolored	.80	.25
		Nos. 2718-2722 (5)	2.05	1.25

Souvenir Sheet

Imperf

2723	A1042	50s multicolored	1.25	.40

International Peace Conference, Sofia — A1043

1980, Sept. 4 **Photo.** ***Perf. 13***

2724	A1043	25s multicolored	.45	.25

Yordan Yovkov (1880-1937), Writer — A1044

1980, Sept. 19

2725	A1044	5s multicolored	.25	.25

Se-tenant with label showing scene from Yovkov's work.

International Samples Fair, Plovdiv — A1045

1980, Sept. 24 ***Perf. 13½x13***

2726	A1045	5s multicolored	.25	.25

On Oct. 1, 1980, a souvenir sheet containing one perf 13 50s stamp depicting a map of Europe and dove, was issued. Size: 80mmx80mm). Serially numbered. Value $30.

Blooming Cacti — A1045a

1980, Nov. 4 **Photo.** ***Perf. 13***

2726A	A1045a	5s multicolored	.25	.25
2726B	A1045a	13s multicolored	.25	.25
2726C	A1045a	25s multicolored	.55	.25
2726D	A1045a	35s multicolored	.85	.45
2726E	A1045a	53s multicolored	1.75	.55
		Nos. 2726A-2726E (5)	3.65	1.75

Souvenir Sheet

25th Anniv. of Bulgarian UN Membership — A1045b

1980, Nov. 25

2726F	A1045b	60s multicolored	2.50	2.00

World Ski Racing Championship, Velingrad — A1046

1981, Jan. 17 **Photo.** ***Perf. 13***

2727	A1046	43s multicolored	.85	.40

Hawthorn A1047

Designs: Medicinal herbs.

1981, Jan.

2728	A1047	3s shown	.25	.25
2729	A1047	5s St. John's wort	.25	.25
2730	A1047	13s Common elder	.35	.25
2731	A1047	25s Blackberries	.65	.25
2732	A1047	35s Lime	.85	.25
2733	A1047	43s Wild briar	1.25	.45
		Nos. 2728-2733 (6)	3.60	1.70

Slalom — A1048

1981, Feb. 27 **Photo.** ***Perf. 13***

2734	A1048	43s multicolored	.90	.40

Evian Alpine World Ski Cup Championship, Borovets.

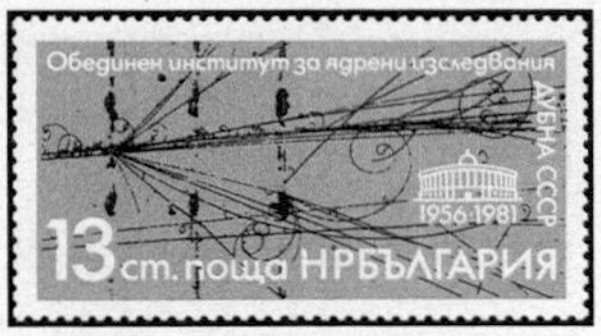

Nuclear Traces, Research Institute — A1049

1981, Mar. 10 *Perf. 13½x13*
2735 A1049 13s gray & blk .30 .25

Nuclear Research Institute, Dubna, USSR, 25th anniversary.

Congress Emblem — A1050

13s, Stars. 23s, Teletape.
50s, Demeter Blagoev, George Dimitrov.

1981, Mar. 12 *Perf. 13½*
2736 A1050 5s shown .25 .25
2737 A1050 13s multicolored .30 .25
2738 A1050 23s multicolored .40 .30
Nos. 2736-2738 (3) .95 .80

Souvenir Sheet

2739 A1050 50s multicolored 1.00 .75

12th Bulgarian Communist Party Congress. Nos. 2736-2738 each printed se-tenant with label.

Paintings by Zachary Zograf — A1050a

1981, Mar. 23 Photo. *Perf. 12x12½*
2739A A1050a 5s multicolored .25 .25
2739B A1050a 13s multicolored .40 .25
2739C A1050a 23s multicolored .60 .25
2739D A1050a 25s multicolored .75 .25
2739E A1050a 35s multicolored 1.10 .25
Nos. 2739A-2739E (5) 3.10 1.25

Nos. 2739A-2739C are vert.

EXPO '81, Plovdiv — A1050b

1981, Apr. 7
2739F A1050b 5s multicolored .25 .25
2739G A1050b 8s multicolored .35 .25
2739H A1050b 13s multicolored .50 .25
2739J A1050b 25s multicolored 1.20 .25
2739K A1050b 53s multicolored 2.25 .70
Nos. 2739F-2739K (5) 4.55 1.70

Centenary of Bulgarian Shipbuilding — A1050c

35s, Georgi Dimitrov, liner. 43s, 5th from RMS, freighter. 53s, Khan Asparuch, tanker.

1981, Apr. 15 Photo. *Perf. 13*
2739L A1050c 35s multi .75 .25
2739M A1050c 43s multi 1.10 .25
2739N A1050c 53s multi 1.50 .35
Nos. 2739L-2739N (3) 3.35 .85

On May 15, 1980, a souvenir sheet commemorating the 125th anniv. of the European Danube Commission was issued. It contains two 25s stamps depicting ships, perf 13, was issued. Size: 90mmx124mm. Serially numbered. Value $24.

A miniature sheet containing eight perf 13 35s stamps depicting ships, was issued Sept. 25, 1981. Size: 109mmx176mm. Value $24.

Arabian Horse A1051

Various breeds.

1980, Nov. 27 Litho. *Perf. 12½x12*
2740 A1051 3s multicolored .25 .25
2741 A1051 5s multicolored .25 .25
2742 A1051 13s multicolored .45 .25
2743 A1051 23s multicolored 1.20 .25
2744 A1051 35s multicolored 2.40 .25
Nos. 2740-2744 (5) 4.55 1.25

Vassil Stoin, Ethnologist, Birth Centenary — A1052

1980, Dec. 5 Photo. *Perf. 13½x13*
2745 A1052 5s multicolored .25 .25

12th Bulgarian Communist Party Congress — A1052a

1980, Dec. 26 Photo. *Perf. 13x13½*
2745A A1052a 5s Party symbols .25 .25

New Year A1053

1980, Dec. 8 *Perf. 13*
2746 A1053 5s shown .25 .25
2747 A1053 13s Cup, date .25 .25

Culture Palace, Sofia A1053a

1981, Mar. 13 Photo. *Perf. 13*
2747A A1053a 5s multicolored .25 .25

Vienna Hofburg Palace A1054

1981, May 15 Photo. *Perf. 13*
2748 A1054 35s multicolored .75 .25

WIPA 1981 Intl. Philatelic Exhibition, Vienna, May 22-31.

34th Farmers' Union Congress — A1055

1981, May 18 *Perf. 13½*
2749 A1055 5s shown .25 .25
2750 A1055 8s Flags .25 .25
2751 A1055 13s Flags, diff. .25 .25
Nos. 2749-2751 (3) .75 .75

Wild Cat — A1056

1981, May 27
2752 A1056 5s shown .25 .25
2753 A1056 13s Boar .35 .25
2754 A1056 23s Mouflon .65 .30
2755 A1056 25s Mountain goat .80 .40
2756 A1056 35s Stag 1.00 .40
2757 A1056 53s Roe deer 1.60 .65
Nos. 2752-2757 (6) 4.65 2.25

Souvenir Sheet

Perf. 13½x13

2758 A1056 1 l Stag, diff. 2.00 1.50

EXPO '81 Intl. Hunting Exhibition, Plovdiv. Nos. 2752-2757 each se-tenant with labels showing various hunting rifles. No. 2758 contains one stamp, size: 48½x39mm.

25th Anniv. of UNESCO Membership A1057

1981, June 11 *Perf. 13*
2759 A1057 13s multicolored .30 .25

Hotel Type of 1980

23s, Veliko Tirnovo Hotel.

1981, July 13 Photo. *Perf. 13*
2766 A1038 23s multi .45 .25

Flying Figure, Sculpture by Velichko Minekov — A1059

Bulgarian Social Democratic Party Buzludja Congress, 90th Anniv. (Minkov Sculpture): 13s, Advancing Female Figure.

1981, July 16 *Perf. 13½*
2767 A1059 5s multicolored .25 .25
2768 A1059 13s multicolored .25 .25

Kukeri, by Georg Tschapkanov A1060

1981, May 28 Photo. *Perf. 13*
2769 A1060 5s multicolored .25 .25

13th Natl. Festival of Humor and Satire.

Statistics Office Centenary A1061

1981, June 9
2770 A1061 5s multicolored .25 .25

Gold Dish A1063

Designs: Goldsmiths' works, 7th-9th cent.

1981, July 21
2772 A1063 5s multicolored .25 .25
2773 A1063 13s multicolored .25 .25
2774 A1063 23s multicolored .40 .25
2775 A1063 25s multicolored .45 .35
2776 A1063 35s multicolored .45 .40
2777 A1063 53s multicolored 1.25 .60
Nos. 2772-2777 (6) 3.05 2.10

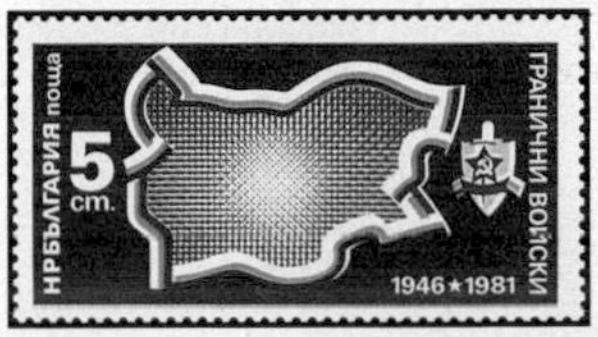

35th Anniv. of Frontier Force — A1064

1981, July 28 *Perf. 13½x13*
2778 A1064 5s multicolored .25 .25

1300th Anniv. of First Bulgarian State — A1065

Designs: No. 2779, Sts. Cyril and Methodius. No. 2780, 9th cent. bas-relief. 8s, Floor plan, Round Church, Preslav, 10th cent. 12s, Four Evangelists of King Ivan Alexander, miniature, 1356. No. 2783, King Ivan Asen II memorial column. No. 2784, Warriors on horseback. 16s, April uprising, 1876. 23s, Russian liberators, Tirnovo. 25s, Social Democratic Party founding, 1891. 35s, September uprising, 1923. 41s, Fatherland Front. 43s, Prime Minister George Dimitrov, 5th Communist Party Congress, 1948. 50s, Lion, 10th cent. bas-relief. 53s, 10th Communist Party Congress. 55s, Kremikovski Metalurgical Plant. 1 l, Brezhnev, Gen. Todor Zhivkov.

1981, Aug. 10

2779	A1065	5s multicolored	.25	.25
2780	A1065	5s multicolored	.25	.25
2781	A1065	8s multicolored	.25	.25
2782	A1065	12s multicolored	.25	.25
2783	A1065	13s multicolored	.25	.25
2784	A1065	13s multicolored	.30	.25
2785	A1065	16s multicolored	.30	.25
2786	A1065	23s multicolored	.45	.25
2787	A1065	25s multicolored	.55	.25
2788	A1065	35s multicolored	.70	.25
2789	A1065	41s multicolored	.85	.45
2790	A1065	43s multicolored	1.00	.45
2791	A1065	53s multicolored	1.00	.50
2792	A1065	55s multicolored	1.00	.50
		Nos. 2779-2792 (14)	7.40	4.40

Souvenir Sheets

2793	A1065	50s multicolored	.90	.75
2794	A1065	1 l multicolored	2.00	1.50

European Volleyball Championship A1066

1981, Sept. 16 *Perf. 13*

2795	A1066	13s multicolored	.30	.25

Pegasus, Bronze Sculpture (Word Day) — A1067

1981, Oct. 2

2796	A1067	5s olive & cream	.25	.25

World Food Day — A1068

1981, Oct. 16

2797	A1068	13s multicolored	.30	.25

Professional Theater Centenary A1069

1981, Oct. 30

2798	A1069	5s multicolored	.25	.25

Anti-Apartheid Year — A1070

1981, Dec. 2

2799	A1070	5s multicolored	.25	.25

Espana '82 World Cup Soccer — A1071

Designs: Various soccer players.

1981, Dec.

2800	A1071	5s multicolored	.25	.25
2801	A1071	13s multicolored	.25	.25
2802	A1071	43s multicolored	.70	.25
2803	A1071	53s multicolored	.85	.35
		Nos. 2800-2803 (4)	2.05	1.10

Heritage Day A1072

1981, Nov. 21 **Photo.** *Perf. 13*

2804	A1072	13s multicolored	.25	.25

Souvenir Sheet

2804A	A1072	60s multicolored	4.00	1.90

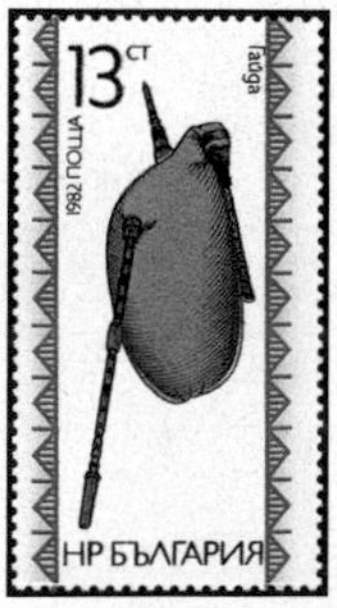

Bagpipe — A1073

1982, Jan. 14

2805	A1073	13s shown	.25	.25
2806	A1073	25s Flutes	.40	.25
2807	A1073	30s Rebec	.50	.25
2808	A1073	35s Flute, recorder	.55	.25
2809	A1073	44s Mandolin	.75	.30
		Nos. 2805-2809 (5)	2.45	1.30

Public Libraries and Reading Rooms, 125th Anniv — A1074

1982, Jan. 20

2810	A1074	5s dk grn	.25	.25

Souvenir Sheet

Intl. Decade for Women (1975-1985) — A1075

1982, Mar. 8

2811	A1075	1 l multicolored	1.75	1.00

New Year 1982 A1076

1981, Dec. 22 **Photo.** *Perf. 13*

2812	A1076	5s Ornament	.25	.25
2813	A1076	13s Ornament, diff.	.25	.25

The Sofia Plains, by Nicolas Petrov (1881-1916) — A1077

13s, Girl Embroidering. 30s, Fields of Peshtera.

1982, Feb. 10 *Perf. 12½*

2814	A1077	5s shown	.25	.25
2815	A1077	13s multicolored	.25	.25
2816	A1077	30s multicolored	.60	.25
		Nos. 2814-2816 (3)	1.10	.75

35th Anniv. of UNICEF (1981) — A1078

Mother and Child Paintings: No. 2817, Vladimir Dimitrov. No. 2818, Basil Stoilov. No. 2819, Ivan Milev. No. 2820, Liliana Russeva.

1982, Feb. 25 *Perf. 14*

2817	A1078	53s multi	1.00	.35
2818	A1078	53s multi	1.00	.35
2819	A1078	53s multi	1.00	.35
2820	A1078	53s multi	1.00	.35
		Nos. 2817-2820 (4)	4.00	1.40

Figures, by Vladamir Dimitrov (1882-1961) — A1079

8s, Landscape. 13s, View of Istanbul. 25s, Harvesters, vert. 30s, Woman in a Landscape, vert. 35s, Peasant Woman, vert.
50s, Self-portrait.

1982, Mar. 8 **Litho.**

2821	A1079	5s shown	.25	.25
2822	A1079	8s multicolored	.25	.25
2823	A1079	13s multicolored	.35	.25
2824	A1079	25s multicolored	.40	.25
2825	A1079	30s multicolored	.40	.25
2826	A1079	35s multicolored	.75	.30
		Nos. 2821-2826 (6)	2.40	1.55

Souvenir Sheet

2827	A1079	50s multicolored	1.00	.75

No. 2827 contains one stamp, size: 54x32mm.

Trade Union Congress — A1080

No. 2828, Dimitrov reading union paper. No. 2829, Culture Palace.

1982, Apr. 8 **Photo.** *Perf. 13½*

2828	A1080	5s multicolored	.25	.25
2829	A1080	5s multicolored	.25	.25

Nos. 2828-2829 se-tenant with label showing text.

Medicinal Plants — A1081

3s, Marsh snowdrop. 5s, Chicory. 8s, Chamaenerium angustifolium. 13s, Solomon's seal. 25s, Violets. 35s, Centaury.

1982, Apr. 10 **Photo.** *Perf. 13*

2830	A1081	3s shown	.25	.25
2831	A1081	5s multi	.25	.25
2832	A1081	8s multi	.25	.25

2833	A1081	13s multi		.35	.25
2834	A1081	25s multi		.65	.25
2835	A1081	35s multi		1.00	.35
		Nos. 2830-2835 (6)		2.75	1.60

Cosmonauts' Day — A1082

13s, Salyut-Soyuz link-up.

1982, Apr. 12 *Perf. 13½*

2836	A1082	13s multi	.25	.25

Se-tenant with label showing K.E. Tsiolkovsky (space pioneer).

Souvenir Sheet

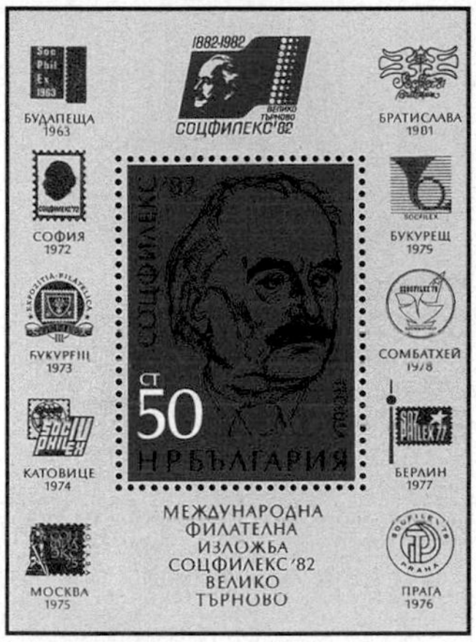

SOZFILEX Stamp Exhibition — A1083

50s, Dimitrov, emblems.

1982, May 7 *Perf. 13*

2837	A1083	50s multi	2.25	1.25

Exists imperf. Value, $60.

14th Komsomol Congress (Youth Communists) — A1084

1982, May 25

2838	A1084	5s multicolored	.25	.25

PHILEXFRANCE '82 Intl. Stamp Exhibition, Paris, June 11-21 — A1085

42s, France #1, Bulgaria #1.

1982, May 28

2839	A1085	42s multi	.75	.30

19th Cent. Fresco A1086

Designs: Various floral pattern frescoes.

1982, June 8 *Perf. 11½*

2840	A1086	5s red & multi	.25	.25
2841	A1086	13s green & multi	.25	.25
2842	A1086	25s violet & multi	.35	.25
2843	A1086	30s ol grn & multi	.45	.25
2844	A1086	42s blue & multi	.70	.30
2845	A1086	60s brown & multi	1.40	.45
		Nos. 2840-2845 (6)	3.40	1.75

Souvenir Sheet

George Dimitrov (1882-1949), First Prime Minister — A1087

1982, June 15 *Perf. 13*

2846	A1087	50s multicolored	1.00	.50

9th Congress of the National Front — A1088

1982, June 21 **Photo.** *Perf. 13*

2847	A1088	5s Dimitrov	.25	.25

35th Anniv. of Balkan Bulgarian Airline — A1089

1982, June 28 *Perf. 13½x13*

2848	A1089	42s multicolored	.65	.50

Nuclear Disarmament A1090

1982, July 15 *Perf. 13*

2849	A1090	13s multicolored	.35	.25

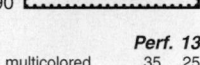

A1091

1982, July **Photo.** *Perf. 13*

2850	A1091	5s multicolored	.25	.25
2851	A1091	13s multicolored	.25	.25

Souvenir Sheet

2852	A1091	1 l multicolored	1.50	.75

Ludmila Zhivkova (b. 1942), artist.

5th Congress of Bulgarian Painters — A1092

1982, July 27 *Perf. 13½*

2853	A1092	5s multicolored	.35	.25

Se-tenant with label showing text.

Flag of Peace Youth Assembly — A1093

Various children's drawings, Frame & inscriptions: 3s, Concert. 5s, Ice Skating. 8s, Children. 13s, Two children celebrating holiday.
50s, In hot air ballon, vert.

1982, Aug. 10 *Perf. 14*

2853A	A1093	3s pink & multi	.25	.25
2853B	A1093	5s blue & multi	.25	.25
2853C	A1093	8s blue grn & multi	.25	.25
2853D	A1093	13s bister & multi	.25	.25
		Nos. 2853A-2853D (4)	1.00	1.00

Souvenir Sheet

Perf. 14

2853E	A1093	50s org & multi	1.50	.35
a.		Imperf.	2.50	1.00

See Nos. 2864-2870, 3052-3058, 3321-3327.

10th Anniv. of UN Conference on Human Environment, Stockholm — A1093a

1982, Nov. 10 *Perf. 13*

2854	A1093a	13s dk blue & grn	.35	.35

A1094

Designs: No. 2855, Park Hotel Moskva, Sofia. No. 2856, Tchernomore, Varna.

1982, Oct. 20 **Photo.** *Perf. 13*

2855	A1094	32s lt blue & multi	.60	.25
2856	A1094	32s pink & multi	.60	.25

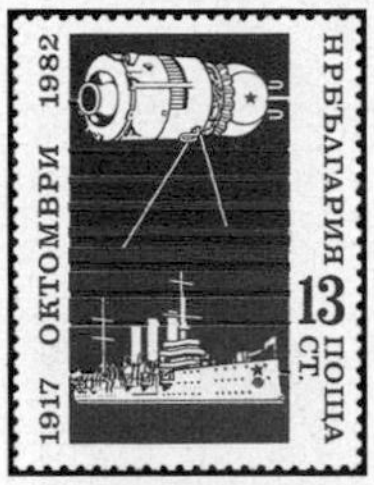

Cruiser Aurora, Vostok I — A1095

1982, Nov. 4

2857	A1095	13s multicolored	.30	.25

October Revolution, 65th anniv.

60th Anniv. of Institute of Communications A1096

1982, Dec. 9

2858	A1096	5s ultra	.30	.25

60th Anniv. of USSR A1097

1982, Dec. 9

2859	A1097	13s multicolored	.35	.35

The Piano, by Pablo Picasso (1881-1973) A1098

30s, Portrait of Jacqueline. 42s, Maternity. 1 l, Self-portrait.

Perf. 11½x12½

1982, Dec. 24 **Litho.**

2860	A1098	13s shown	.40	.25
2861	A1098	30s multi	.40	.25
2862	A1098	42s multi	1.25	.45
		Nos. 2860-2862 (3)	2.05	.95

Souvenir Sheet

2863	A1098	1 l multi	2.00	.75

Children's Drawings Type of 1982

Various children's drawings: 3s, Friends. 5s, Town. 8s, Fairy Tales, vert. 13s, Birds, vert. 25s, Women. 30s, Lion.
50s, Shaking Hands, vert.

1982, Dec. 28 *Perf. 14*

2864	A1093	3s pale vio & multi	.25	.25
2865	A1093	5s org & multi	.25	.25
2866	A1093	8s blue grn & multi	.25	.25
2867	A1093	13s pink & multi	.25	.25
2868	A1093	25s bister & multi	.50	.25
2869	A1093	30s pale grn & multi	.60	.25
		Nos. 2864-2869 (6)	2.10	1.50

Souvenir Sheet

Perf. 14

2870	A1093	50s turq blue & multi	1.50	.35
a.		Imperf.	2.00	.75

New Year
A1100

1982, Dec. 28 **Photo.** ***Perf. 13***

2872	A1100	5s multicolored	.25	.25
2873	A1100	13s multicolored	.25	.25

A1101

No. 2874, Robert Koch. No. 2875, Simon Bolivar. No. 2876, Rabindranath Tagore (1861-1941).

1982, Dec. 28

2874	A1101	25s multicolored	.45	.25
2875	A1101	30s multicolored	.45	.25
2876	A1101	30s multicolored	.45	.25
		Nos. 2874-2876 (3)	1.35	.75

No. 2874 also for TB bacillus cent.

A1102

1983, Feb. 10 **Photo.** ***Perf. 13x13½***

2877	A1102	5s olive & brown	.25	.25

Vassil Levski (1837-73), revolutionary.

Universiade Games — A1103

1983, Feb. 15 ***Perf. 13***

2878	A1103	30s Downhill skiing	.60	.25

Fresh-water Fish — A1104

1983, Mar. 24 **Photo.** ***Perf. 13½x13***

2879	A1104	3s Pike	.25	.25
2880	A1104	5s Sturgeon	.25	.25
2881	A1104	13s Chub	.25	.25
2882	A1104	25s Perch	.55	.25
2883	A1104	30s Catfish	.60	.25
2884	A1104	42s Trout	1.50	.55
		Nos. 2879-2884 (6)	3.40	1.80

Karl Marx (1818-1883)
A1105

1983, Apr. 5 ***Perf. 13x13½***

2885	A1105	13s multicolored	.30	.25

Jaroslav Hasek (1883-1923) — A1106

1983, Apr. 20 **Photo.** ***Perf. 13***

2886	A1106	13s multicolored	.30	.25

Martin Luther (1483-1546)
A1107

1983, May 10

2887	A1107	13s multicolored	.45	.25

55th Anniv. of Komsomol Youth Movement — A1108

1983, May 13

2888	A1108	5s "PMC"	.25	.25

National Costumes
A1109

1983, May 17 **Litho.** ***Perf. 14***

2889	A1109	5s Khaskovo	.25	.25
2890	A1109	8s Pernik	.25	.25
2891	A1109	13s Burgas	.25	.25
2892	A1109	25s Tolbukhin	.55	.25
2893	A1109	30s Blagoevgrad	.60	.25
2894	A1109	42s Topolovgrad	1.60	.25
		Nos. 2889-2894 (6)	3.50	1.50

A1111

6th Intl. Satire and Humor Biennial, Gabrovo: Old Man Feeding Chickens.

1983, May 20

2900	A1111	5s multicolored	.25	.25

Christo Smirnensky (1898-1983), Poet — A1112

1983, May 25

2901	A1112	5s multicolored	.25	.25

17th Intl. Geodesists' Congress
A1113

1983, May 27

2902	A1113	30s Emblem	.50	.25

Interarch '83 Architecture Exhibition, Sofia — A1114

1983, June 6

2903	A1114	30s multicolored	.60	.25

8th European Chess Championships, Plovdiv
A1115

13s, Chess pieces, map of Europe.

1983, June 20 **Photo.** ***Perf. 13***

2904	A1115	13s multi	.35	.25

Souvenir Sheet

BRASILIANA '83 Philatelic Exhibition — A1116

Brazilian and Bulgarian stamps

1983, June 24

2905	A1116	1 l multicolored	1.75	1.25

Social Democratic Party Congress of Russia, 80th Anniv. — A1118

Design: Lenin addressing congress.

1983, July 29 **Photo.** ***Perf. 13***

2907	A1118	5s multicolored	.25	.25

Ilinden-Preobrazhensky Insurrection, 80th Anniv. — A1119

5s, Gun, dagger, book.

1983, July 29

2908	A1119	5s multi	.25	.25

Institute of Mining and Geology, Sofia, 30th Anniv. — A1120

1983, Aug. 10

2909	A1120	5s multicolored	.25	.25

60th Anniv. of September 1923 Uprising — A1121

1983, Aug. 19

2910	A1121	5s multicolored	.25	.25
2911	A1121	13s multicolored	.25	.25

Angora Cat
A1123

1983, Sept. 26 ***Perf. 13***

2917	A1123	5s shown	.25	.25
2918	A1123	13s Siamese	.35	.25
2919	A1123	20s Abyssinian, vert.	.45	.25
2920	A1123	25s Persian	.65	.25
2921	A1123	30s European, vert.	.80	.45
2922	A1123	42s Indochinese	1.25	.55
		Nos. 2917-2922 (6)	3.75	2.00

Animated Film Festival — A1124

1983, Sept. 15 Photo. *Perf. 14x13½*
2923 A1124 5s Articulation layout .25 .25

Trevethick's Engine, 1804 — A1125

Locomotives: 13s, Blenkinsop's Prince Royal, 1810. 42s, Hedley's Puffing Billy, 1812. 60s, Adler (first German locomotive), 1835.

1983, Oct. 20 *Perf. 13*

2924	A1125	5s	multicolored	.25	.25
2925	A1125	13s	multicolored	.35	.25
2926	A1125	42s	multicolored	1.40	.70
2927	A1125	60s	multicolored	2.40	.80
	Nos. 2924-2927 (4)			4.40	2.00

See Nos. 2983-2987.

Souvenir Sheet

Liberation Monument, Plovdiv — A1126

1983, Nov. 4
2928 A1126 50s multicolored 1.00 .75

Philatelic Federation, 90th anniv.

Sofia Opera, 75th Anniv. — A1127

1983, Dec. 2 *Perf. 13x13½*
2929 A1127 5s Mask, lyre, laurel .25 .25

Composers' Assoc., 50th Anniv. — A1128

Composers: 5s, Ioan Kukuzel (14th cent.) 8s, Atanasov. 13s, Petko Stainov. 20s, Veselin Stodiov. 25s, Liubomir Pipkov. 30s, Pancho Vladigerov. Se-tenant with labels showing compositions.

1983, Dec. 5

2930	A1128	5s	multicolored	.25	.25
2931	A1128	8s	multicolored	.25	.25
2932	A1128	13s	multicolored	.25	.25
2933	A1128	20s	multicolored	.35	.25
2934	A1128	25s	multicolored	.35	.25
2935	A1128	30s	multicolored	.45	.30
	Nos. 2930-2935 (6)			1.90	1.55

New Year 1984 A1129

1983, Dec. 10 *Perf. 13*
2936 A1129 5s multicolored .25 .25

Angelo Donni, by Raphael A1130

13s, Cardinal. 30s, Baldassare Castiglioni. 42s, Donna Belata. 1 l, Sistine Madonna.

1983, Dec. 22 *Perf. 14*

2937	A1130	5s	shown	.25	.25
2938	A1130	13s	multicolored	.25	.25
2939	A1130	30s	multicolored	.45	.25
2940	A1130	42s	multicolored	.70	.30
	Nos. 2937-2940 (4)			1.65	1.05

Souvenir Sheet

2941 A1130 1 l multicolored 1.75 1.25

Bat, World Wildlife Emblem — A1131

Various bats and rodents.

1983, Dec. 30 *Perf. 13*

2942	A1131	12s	multicolored	.35	.25
2943	A1131	13s	multicolored	.50	.25
2944	A1131	20s	multicolored	.80	.25
2945	A1131	30s	multicolored	1.25	.25
2946	A1131	42s	multicolored	2.50	.50
	Nos. 2942-2946 (5)			5.40	1.50

Dmitri Mendeleev (1834-1907), Russian Chemist — A1132

1984, Mar. 14
2947 A1132 13s multicolored .30 .25

Ljuben Karavelov, Poet and Freedom Fighter, Birth Sesquicentenary A1133

1984, Jan. 31 *Perf. 13x13½*
2948 A1133 5s multicolored .25 .25

Tanker Gen. V.I. Zaimov A1137

13s, Mesta. 25s, Veleka. 32s, Ferry. 42s, Cargo ship Rossen.

1984, Mar. 22 *Perf. 13½*

2959	A1137	5s	shown	.25	.25
2960	A1137	13s	multi	.30	.25
2961	A1137	25s	multi	.55	.25
2962	A1137	32s	multi	.55	.25
2963	A1137	42s	multi	1.10	.35
	Nos. 2959-2963 (5)			2.75	1.35

Souvenir Sheet

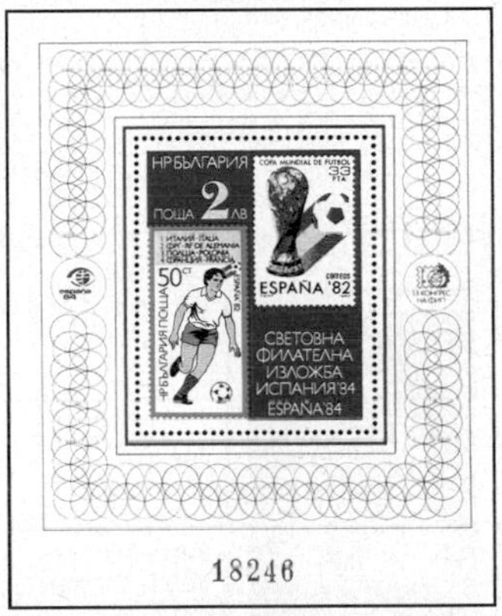

World Cup Soccer Commemorative of 1982, Spain No. 2281 — A1137a

1984, Apr. 18 Photo. *Perf. 13x13½*
2963A A1137a 2 l multicolored 5.00 4.00

ESPANA '84.

Dove with Letter over Globe — A1138

1984, Apr. 24 *Perf. 13*
2964 A1138 5s multicolored .25 .25

World Youth Stamp Exhibition, Pleven, Oct. 5-11.

Berries — A1139

1984, May 5

2965	A1139	5s	Cherries	.25	.25
2966	A1139	8s	Strawberries	.25	.25
2967	A1139	13s	Blackberries	.25	.25
2968	A1139	20s	Raspberries	.40	.25
2969	A1139	42s	Currants	1.20	.30
	Nos. 2965-2969 (5)			2.35	1.30

Athlete, Doves — A1140

1984, May 23
2970 A1140 13s multicolored .35 .35

6th Republican Spartikiade games,

Folk Singer, Drum — A1142

1984, June 12
2972 A1142 5s multicolored .25 .25

6th amateur art festival.

Bulgarian-Soviet Relations, 50th Anniv. — A1143

1984, June 27
2973 A1143 13s Initialed seal .30 .25

Doves and Pigeons A1144

1984, July 6 Litho. *Perf. 14*

2974	A1144	5s	Rock dove	.25	.25
2975	A1144	13s	Stock dove	.25	.25
2976	A1144	20s	Wood pigeon	.40	.25
2977	A1144	30s	Turtle dove	.65	.25
2978	A1144	42s	Domestic pigeon	.85	.35
	Nos. 2974-2978 (5)			2.40	1.35

1st Natl. Communist Party Congress, 60th Anniv. — A1145

1984, May 18 Photo. *Perf. 13½x13*
2979 A1145 5s multicolored .25 .25

Souvenir Sheet

Intl. Stamp Exhibition, Essen, May 26-31 — A1146

Europa Conf. stamps: a, 1980. b, 1981.

1984, May 22 *Perf. 13x13½*

2980	A1146	Sheet of 2	*6.00*	*5.00*
a.-b.		1.50 l multi	*3.00*	*2.50*

Mount Everest A1147

1984, May 31 *Perf. 13*

2981	A1147	5s multicolored	.25	.25

1st Bulgarian Everest climbing expedition, Apr. 20-May 9.

Souvenir Sheet

UPU Congress, Hamburg — A1148

1984, June 11 *Perf. 13½x13*

2982	A1148	3 l Sailing ship	*5.00*	*4.00*

Locomotives Type of 1983

13s, Best Friend of Charleston, 1830, US. 25s, Saxonia, 1836, Dresden. 30s, Lafayette, 1837, US. 42s, Borsig, 1841, Germany. 60s, Philadelphia, 1843, Austria.

1984, July 31 *Perf. 13*

2983	A1125	13s multicolored	.25	.25
2984	A1125	25s multicolored	.45	.25
2985	A1125	30s multicolored	.60	.25
2986	A1125	42s multicolored	.85	.35
2987	A1125	60s multicolored	1.40	.50
		Nos. 2983-2987 (5)	3.55	1.60

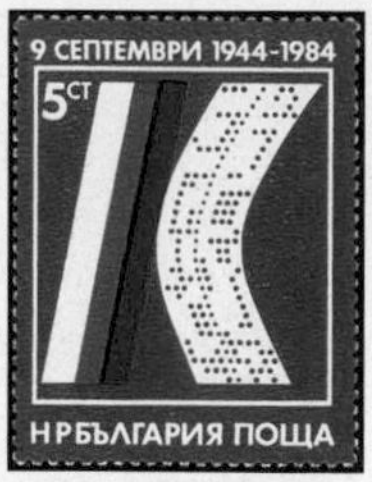

September 9 Revolution, 40th Anniv. — A1149

5s, K, production quality emblem. 20s, Victory Monument, Sofia. 30s, Star, "9".

1984, Aug. 4

2988	A1149	5s multicolored	.25	.25
2989	A1149	20s multicolored	.40	.25
2990	A1149	30s multicolored	.60	.45
		Nos. 2988-2990 (3)	1.25	.95

Paintings by Nenko Balkanski (1907-1977) — A1150

5s, Boy Playing Harmonica, vert. 30s, A Paris Window, vert. 42s, Double Portrait. 1 l, Self-portrait, vert.

1984, Sept. 17 *Perf. 14*

2991	A1150	5s multicolored	.25	.25
2992	A1150	30s multicolored	.60	.25
2993	A1150	42s multicolored	1.10	.35
		Nos. 2991-2993 (3)	1.95	.85

Souvenir Sheet

2994	A1150	1 l multicolored	1.75	1.25

MLADPOST '84 International Youth Stamp Exhibition, Pleven — A1151

Buildings in Pleven: 5s, Mausoleum to Russian soldiers, 1877-78 Russo-Turkish War. 13s, Panorama Building.

1984, Sept. 20 *Perf. 13*

2995	A1151	5s multicolored	.25	.25
2996	A1151	13s multicolored	.30	.25

Septembrist Young Pioneers Org., 40th Anniv. — A1152

1984, Sept. 21 **Photo.** *Perf. 13*

2997	A1152	5s multicolored	.25	.25

Nikola Vapzarov A1153

1984, Oct. 2

2998	A1153	5s mar & pale yel	.25	.25

Natl. Soccer, 75th Anniv. A1154

1984, Oct. 3

2999	A1154	42s multicolored	.75	.35

Souvenir Sheet

MLADPOST '84 — A1155

1984, Oct. 5 **Photo.** *Perf. 13*

3000	A1155	50s multicolored	.90	.50

Bridges and Maps — A1156

5s, Devil's Bridge, Arda River. 13s, Koljo-Fitscheto, Bjala. 30s, Asparuchow, Warna. 42s, Bebresch Highway Bridge, Botevgrad. 1 l, Bridge of Friendship, Russia.

1984, Oct. 5 **Photo.** *Perf. 13½x13*

3001	A1156	5s multicolored	.25	.25
3002	A1156	13s multicolored	.40	.25
3003	A1156	30s multicolored	.60	.55
3004	A1156	42s multicolored	1.40	.75
		Nos. 3001-3004 (4)	2.65	1.80

Souvenir Sheet

3005	A1156	1 l multicolored	5.25	2.50

Intl. Olympic Committee, 90th Anniv. — A1158

1984, Oct. 24 **Photo.** *Perf. 13*

3007	A1158	13s multicolored	.30	.25

Pelecanus Crispus A1159

1984, Nov. 2

3008	A1159	5s Adult, young	.35	.25
3009	A1159	13s Two adults	.70	.30
3010	A1159	20s Adult in water	1.10	.70
3011	A1159	32s In flight	2.50	1.00
		Nos. 3008-3011 (4)	4.65	2.25

World Wildlife Fund.

A1160

1984, Nov. 2

3012	A1160	5s multicolored	.25	.25

Anton Ivanov (1884-1942), labor leader.

Women's Socialist Movement, 70th Anniv. — A1161

1984, Nov. 9

3013	A1161	5s multicolored	.25	.25

Telecommunication Towers — A1162

1984, Nov. 23

3014	A1162	5s Snezhanka	.25	.25
3015	A1162	1 l Orelek	1.60	.75

Snowflakes, New Year 1985 — A1163

5s, Doves, posthorns. 13s, Doves, blossom.

1984, Dec. 5

3016	A1163	5s multicolored	.25	.25
3017	A1163	13s multicolored	.25	.25

Paintings by Stoyan Venev (b. 1904) — A1164

5s, September Nights. 30s, Man with Three Medals. 42s, The Best.

1984, Dec. 10 **Litho.**

3018	A1164	5s multicolored	.25	.25
3019	A1164	30s multicolored	.65	.30
3020	A1164	42s multicolored	1.00	.35
		Nos. 3018-3020 (3)	1.90	.90

Butterflies A1165

13s, Inachis io. 25s, Papilio machaon. 30s, Brintesia circe. 42s, Anthocaris cardamines. 60s, Vanessa atalanta.
1 l, Limenitis populi.

1984, Dec. 14 *Perf. 11½*

3021	A1165	13s multicolored	.25	.25
3022	A1165	25s multicolored	.45	.25
3023	A1165	30s multicolored	.60	.30
3024	A1165	42s multicolored	.85	.35
3025	A1165	60s multicolored	1.50	.50
		Nos. 3021-3025 (5)	3.65	1.65

Souvenir Sheet

3026	A1165	1 l multicolored	1.50	.75

A1166

1984, Dec. 18 Photo. *Perf. 13x13½*

3027	A1166	13s multicolored	.30	.25

Cesar Augusto Sandino (1895-1934), Nicaraguan freedom fighter.

A1167

5s, The Three Graces. 13s, Cupid and the Graces. 30s, Original Sin. 42s, La Fornarina.
1 l, Galatea.

1984, Dec. 28 Litho. *Perf. 14*

3028	A1167	5s multicolored	.25	.25
3029	A1167	13s multicolored	.35	.25
3030	A1167	30s multicolored	.70	.35
3031	A1167	42s multicolored	1.00	.50
		Nos. 3028-3031 (4)	2.30	1.35

Souvenir Sheet

3032	A1167	1 l multicolored	1.75	1.00

Raphael, 500th birth anniv. (1983).

Cruise Ship Sofia, Maiden Voyage — A1168

1984, Dec. 29 Photo. *Perf. 13*

3033	A1168	13s blue, dk bl & yel	.30	.25

Predators A1170

13s, Conepatus leuconotus. 25s, Prionodon linsang. 30s, Ictonix striatus. 42s, Hemigalus derbyanus. 60s, Galidictis fasciata.

1985, Jan. 17

3035	A1170	13s multicolored	.25	.25
3036	A1170	25s multicolored	.45	.25
3037	A1170	30s multicolored	.55	.25
3038	A1170	42s multicolored	.80	.35
3039	A1170	60s multicolored	1.25	.60
		Nos. 3035-3039 (5)	3.30	1.70

Nikolai Liliev (1885-1960), Poet, UNESCO Emblem — A1171

1985, Jan. 25

3040	A1171	30s multicolored	.50	.30

Zviatko Radojnov (1895-1942), Labor Leader — A1172

1985, Jan. 29

3041	A1172	5s dk red & dk brn	.25	.25

Dr. Assen Zlatarov (1885-1936), Chemist A1173

1985, Feb. 14

3042	A1173	5s multicolored	.25	.25

Souvenir Sheet

Akademik, Research Vessel — A1174

1985, Mar. 1

3043	A1174	80s multicolored	1.50	1.00

UNESCO Intl. Oceanographic Commission, 25th anniv.

Souvenir Sheet

Lenin — A1175

1985, Mar. 12

3044	A1175	50s multicolored	.85	.65

A1176

1985, Mar. 19

3045	A1176	13s multicolored	.25	.25

Warsaw Treaty Org., 30th anniv.

Composers A1177

1985, Mar. 25

3046	A1177	42s Bach	.90	.45
3047	A1177	42s Mozart	.90	.45
3048	A1177	42s Tchaikovsky	.90	.45
3049	A1177	42s Mussorgsky	.90	.45
3050	A1177	42s Verdi	.90	.45
3051	A1177	42s Kutev	.90	.45
		Nos. 3046-3051 (6)	5.40	2.70

Children's Drawings Type of 1982

Various children's drawings: 5s, Girl with bird and rooster. 8s, Children painting. 13s, Girl, bird & flowers. 20s, Two adults, three children. 25s, People with join hands around the globe. 30s, Nurse with stethoscope.
50s, Children dancing, vert.

1985, Mar. 26 Litho. *Perf. 14*

3052	A1093	5s red & multi	.25	.25
3053	A1093	8s blue & multi	.25	.25
3054	A1093	13s bister & multi	.25	.25
3055	A1093	20s pale vio & multi	.35	.25
3056	A1093	25s blue grn & multi	.45	.25
3057	A1093	30s ochre & multi	.50	.30
		Nos. 3052-3057 (6)	2.05	1.55

Souvenir Sheet

3058	A1093	50s pale grn & multi	1.50	.75

Inscribed 1985. 3rd Flag of Peace Intl. Assembly, Sofia.
No. 3058 exists imperf. with blue control number, same value.

St. Methodius, 1100th Death Anniv. — A1179

1985, Apr. 6 Photo. *Perf. 13*

3059	A1179	13s multicolored	.50	.25

Victory Parade, Moscow, 1945 — A1180

13s, 11th Infantry on parade, Sofia. 30s, Soviet soldier, orphan. 50s, Soviet flag-raising, Berlin.

1985, Apr. 30 *Perf. 13½*

3060	A1180	5s multicolored	.25	.25
3061	A1180	13s multicolored	.25	.25
3062	A1180	30s multicolored	.60	.25
		Nos. 3060-3062 (3)	1.10	.75

Souvenir Sheet

Perf. 13

3063	A1180	50s multicolored	1.10	.50

Defeat of Nazi Germany, end of World War II, 40th anniv. Nos. 3060-3062 printed se-tenant with labels picturing Soviet (5s, 30s) and Bulgarian medals of honor.

7th Intl. Humor and Satire Biennial — A1181

1985, Apr. 30 *Perf. 13½*

3064	A1181	13s yel, sage grn & red	.25	.25

No. 3064 printed se-tenant with label picturing Gabrovo Cat emblem.

Intl. Youth Year — A1182

1985, May 21 *Perf. 13*

3065	A1182	13s multicolored	.25	.25

Ivan Vazov (1850-1921), Poet — A1183

1985, May 30 *Perf. 13½*
3066 A1183 5s tan & sepia .25 .25

No. 3066 printed se-tenant with label picturing Vasov's birthplace in Sopot.

Soviet War Memorial, Haskovo City Arms A1184

1985, June 1 *Perf. 13*
3067 A1184 5s multicolored .25 .25

Haskovo millennium.

12th World Youth Festival, Moscow — A1185

1985, June 25
3068 A1185 13s multicolored .25 .25

Indira Gandhi (1917-1984), Prime Minister of India — A1186

1985, June 26
3069 A1186 30s org yel, sep & ver .50 .25

Vasil Aprilov, Founder — A1187

1985, June 30
3070 A1187 5s multicolored .25 .25

1st secular school, Gabrovo, 150th anniv.

INTERSTENO '85 — A1188

1985, June 30
3071 A1188 13s multicolored .25 .25

Congress for the Intl. Union of Stenographers and Typists, Sofia.

Alexander Nevski Cathedral A1189

1985, July 9
3072 A1189 42s multicolored .65 .35

World Tourism Org., general assembly, Sofia.

UN, 40th Anniv. A1190

1985, July 16
3073 A1190 13s multicolored .25 .25

A1191

1985, July 16
3074 A1191 13s multicolored .25 .25

Admission of Bulgaria to UN, 30th anniv.

Roses — A1192

5s, Rosa damascena. 13s, Rosa trakijka. 20s, Rosa radiman. 30s, Rosa marista. 42s, Rosa valentina. 60s, Rosa maria.

1985, July 20 **Litho.**
3075 A1192 5s multi .25 .25
3076 A1192 13s multi .25 .25
3077 A1192 20s multi .35 .25
3078 A1192 30s multi .40 .25
3079 A1192 42s multi .65 .30
3080 A1192 60s multi 1.00 .35
a. Min. sheet of 6, #3075-3080 3.00 2.00
Nos. 3075-3080 (6) 2.90 1.65

Helsinki Conference, 10th Anniv. — A1193

1985, Aug. 1 **Photo.**
3081 A1193 13s multicolored .35 .25

European Swimming Championships, Sofia — A1194

5s, Butterfly stroke. 13s, Water polo, vert. 42s, Diving, vert. 60s, Synchronized swimming.

1985, Aug. 2 **Litho.** *Perf. 12½*
3082 A1194 5s multi .25 .25
3083 A1194 13s multi .25 .25
3084 A1194 42s multi .85 .35
3085 A1194 60s multi 1.40 .35
Nos. 3082-3085 (4) 2.75 1.20

The 60s exists with central design inverted.

Natl. Tourism Assoc., 90th Anniv. A1195

1985, Aug. 15 **Photo.** *Perf. 13*
3086 A1195 5s multicolored .25 .25

1986 World Cup Soccer Championships, Mexico A1196

Various soccer plays.

1985, Aug. 29 *Perf. 13*
3087 A1196 5s multicolored .25 .25
3088 A1196 13s multicolored .25 .25
3089 A1196 30s multicolored .55 .25
3090 A1196 42s multicolored .30 .45
Nos. 3087-3090 (4) 1.35 1.20

Souvenir Sheet

3091 A1196 1 l multi, horiz. 1.75 1.00

Union of Eastern Rumelia and Bulgaria, 1885 — A1197

1985, Aug. 29 *Perf. 14x13½*
3092 A1197 5s multicolored .25 .25

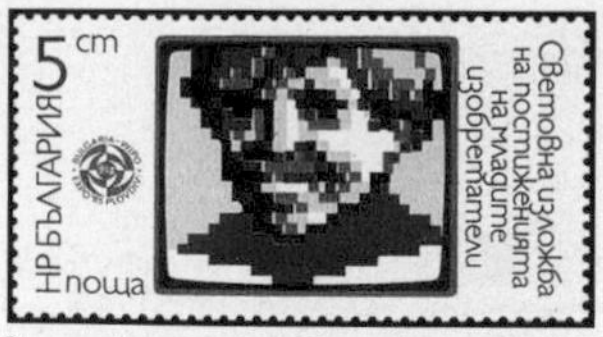

Computer Design Portraits — A1198

1985, Sept. 23 *Perf. 13*
3093 A1198 5s Boy .25 .25
3094 A1198 13s Youth .25 .25
3095 A1198 30s Cosmonaut .50 .30
Nos. 3093-3095 (3) 1.00 .80

Intl. Exhibition of the Works of Youth Inventors, Plovdiv.

St. John the Baptist Church, Nessebar A1199

Natl. restoration projects: 13s, Tyrant Hreljo Tower, Rila Monastery. 35s, Soldier, fresco, Ivanovo Rock Church. 42s, Archangel Gabriel, fresco, Bojana Church. 60s, Thracian Woman, fresco, Tomb of Kasanlak, 3rd century B.C. 1 l, The Horseman of Madara, basrelief.

1985, Sept. 25 **Litho.** *Perf. 12½*
3096 A1199 5s multicolored .25 .25
3097 A1199 13s multicolored .25 .25
3098 A1199 35s multicolored .65 .30
3099 A1199 42s multicolored .80 .35
3100 A1199 60s multicolored 1.25 .35
Nos. 3096-3100 (5) 3.20 1.50

Souvenir Sheet

Imperf

3101 A1199 1 l multicolored 1.75 .90

UNESCO, 40th anniv.

Souvenir Sheet

Ludmila Zhishkova Cultural Palace, Sofia — A1200

1985, Oct. 8 *Perf. 13*
3102 A1200 1 l multicolored 1.60 1.00

UNESCO 23rd General Assembly, Sofia.

Colosseum, Rome — A1201

1985, Oct. 15 Photo. *Perf. 13½*

3103 A1201 42s multicolored .50 .25

ITALIA '85. No. 3103 printed se-tenant with label picturing the exhibition emblem.

Souvenir Sheet

Cultural Congress, Budapest — A1202

Designs: No. 3104a, St. Cyril, patron saint of Europe. No. 3104b, Map of Europe. No. 3104c, St. Methodius, patron saint of Europe.

Perf. 13, 13 Vert. (#3104b)

1985, Oct. 22 Photo.

3104 A1202 Sheet of 3 2.00 1.25
a.-c. 50s, any single .65 .40

Helsinki Congress, 10th anniv.

Exists imperf with serial number. Value $27.50.

Flowers — A1203

No. 3105, Gladiolus hybridy. No. 3106, Iris germanica. No. 3107, Convolvulus tricolor.

1985, Oct. 22 Photo. *Perf. 13x13½*

3105 A1203 5s rose & rose car .25 .25
3106 A1203 5s gray blue & dk blue .25 .25
3107 A1203 5s pale vio & vio .25 .25
Nos. 3105-3107 (3) .75 .75

See Nos. 3184-3186.

Historic Sailing Ships A1204

5s, Dutch. 12s, Sea Sovereign, Britain. 20s, Mediterranean. 25s, Royal Prince, Britain. 42s, Mediterranean. 60s, British battleship.

1985, Oct. 28 Photo. *Perf. 13*

3108 A1204 5s multicolored .25 .25
3109 A1204 12s multicolored .25 .25
3110 A1204 20s multicolored .30 .25
3111 A1204 25s multicolored .40 .25
3112 A1204 42s multicolored .75 .40
3113 A1204 60s multicolored 1.25 .45
Nos. 3108-3113 (6) 3.20 1.85

Souvenir Sheet

PHILATELIA '85, Cologne — A1205

Designs: a, Cologne Cathedral. b, Alexander Nevski Cathedral, Sofia.

1985, Nov. 4 *Imperf.*

3114 A1205 Sheet of 2 1.00 .50
a.-b. 30s, any single .45 .25

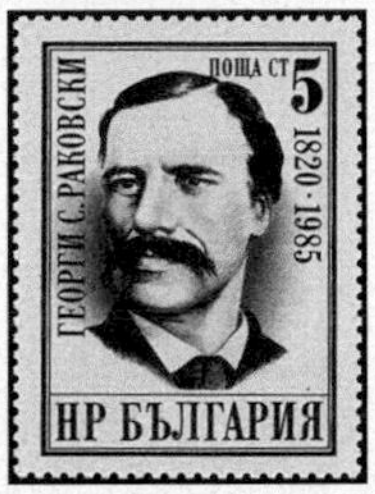

Conspiracy to Liberate Bulgaria from Turkish Rule, 150th Anniv. — A1206

Freedom fighters and symbols: No. 3115, Georgi Stojkov Rakowski (1820-76). No. 3116, Batscho Kiro (1835-76). No. 3117, Sword, Bible & hands.

1985, Nov. 6 *Perf. 13*

3115 A1206 5s multicolored .25 .25
3116 A1206 5s multicolored .25 .25
3117 A1206 13s multicolored .25 .25
Nos. 3115-3117 (3) .75 .75

Liberation from Byzantine Rule, 800th Anniv. — A1207

Paintings: 5s, The Revolt 1185, by G. Bogdanov. 13s, The Revolt 1185, by Alexander Tersiev. 30s, Battle Near Klokotnitza, by B. Grigorov and M. Ganowski. 42s, Velika Tarnovo Town Wall, by Zanko Lawrenov. 1 l, St. Dimitriev Church, 12th cent.

1985, Nov. 15 Litho.

3118 A1207 5s multicolored .25 .25
3119 A1207 13s multicolored .30 .25
3120 A1207 30s multicolored .35 .25
3121 A1207 42s multicolored .35 .55
Nos. 3118-3121 (4) 1.25 1.30

Souvenir Sheet

Imperf

3122 A1207 1 l multicolored 1.60 .80

Souvenir Sheet

BALKANPHILA '85 — A1208

1985, Nov. 29 Photo. *Perf. 13*

3123 A1208 40s Dove, posthorn .75 .50

Intl. Post and Telecommunications Development Program — A1209

1985, Dec. 2

3124 A1209 13s multicolored .25 .25

Anton Popov (1915-1942), Freedom Fighter — A1210

1985, Dec. 11 Photo. *Perf. 13*

3125 A1210 5s lake .25 .25

New Year 1986 A1211

5s, Doves, snowflake. 13s, Doves.

1985, Dec. 11 Photo. *Perf. 13*

3126 A1211 5s multi .25 .25
3127 A1211 13s multi .25 .25

Hunting Dogs and Prey — A1212

5s, Pointer, partridge. 8s, Irish setter, pochard. 13s, English setter, mallard. 20s, Cocker spaniel, woodcock. 25s, German pointer, rabbit. 30s, Balkan hound, boar. 42s, Shorthaired dachshund, fox.

1985, Dec. 27 Litho. *Perf. 13x12½*

3128 A1212 5s multicolored .25 .25
3129 A1212 8s multicolored .25 .25
3130 A1212 13s multicolored .25 .25
3131 A1212 20s multicolored .25 .25
3132 A1212 25s multicolored .40 .25
3133 A1212 30s multicolored .55 .25
3134 A1212 42s multicolored 1.10 .35
Nos. 3128-3134 (7) 3.05 1.85

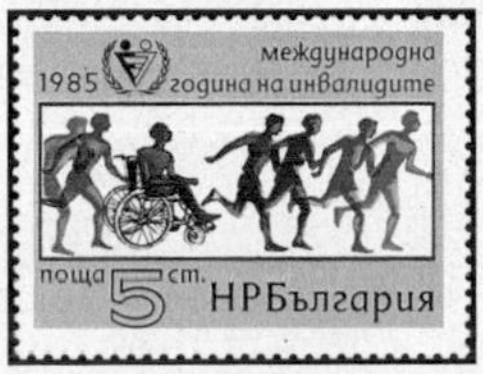

Intl. Year of the Handicapped — A1213

1985, Dec. 30 Photo. *Perf. 13*

3135 A1213 5s multicolored .25 .25

George Dimitrov (1882-1949) — A1214

1985, Dec. 30 Photo. *Perf. 13*

3136 A1214 13s brn lake .30 .25

7th Intl. Communist Congress, Moscow.

UN Child Survival Campaign — A1215

1986, Jan. 21 Photo. *Perf. 13*

3137 A1215 13s multicolored .30 .25

UNICEF, 40th anniv.

Demeter Blagoev (1856-1924) A1216

1986, Jan. 28 Photo. *Perf. 13*

3138 A1216 5s dk lake, car & dk red .25 .25

Intl. Peace Year A1217

1986, Jan. 31 *Perf. 13½*

3139 A1217 5s multicolored .25 .25

Orchids — A1218

5s, Dactylorhiza romana. 13s, Epipactis palustris. 30s, Ophrys cornuta. 32s, Limodorum abortivum. 42s, Cypripedium calceolus. 60s, Orchis papilionacea.

1986, Feb. 12 Litho. *Perf. 13x12½*

3140 A1218 5s multicolored .25 .25
3141 A1218 13s multicolored .25 .25
3142 A1218 30s multicolored .30 .25
3143 A1218 32s multicolored .35 .25
3144 A1218 42s multicolored .55 .25
3145 A1218 60s multicolored 1.10 .25
a. Min. sheet of 6, #3140-3145 2.75 1.25
Nos. 3140-3145 (6) 2.80 1.50

Nos. 3140-3145 exist imperf. Value, $7.50.

Hares and Rabbits
A1219

1986, Feb. 24 *Perf. 12½x12*

3146 A1219 5s multicolored .25 .25
3147 A1219 25s multicolored .45 .25
3148 A1219 30s multicolored .50 .25
3149 A1219 32s multicolored .55 .25
3150 A1219 42s multicolored .70 .25
3151 A1219 60s multicolored .75 .25
Nos. 3146-3151 (6) 3.20 1.50

Exist imperf. Value, set $8.

Bulgarian Eagle, Newspaper, 140th Anniv. — A1220

Front page of 1st issue & Ivan Bogorov, journalist.

1986, Feb. 2 **Photo.** *Perf. 13*

3152 A1220 5s multicolored .25 .25

Souvenir Sheet

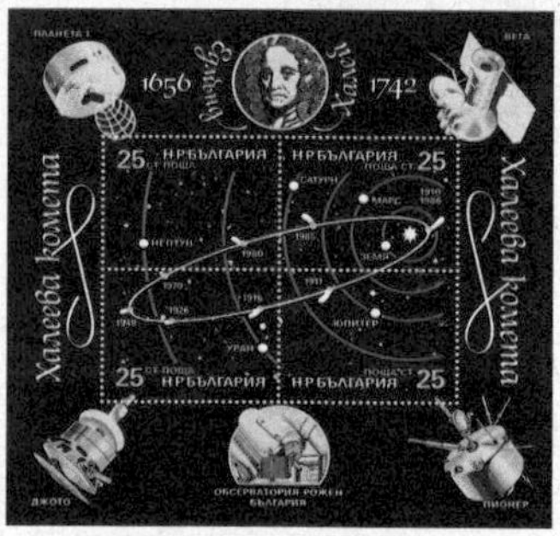

Halley's Comet — A1221

Comet's orbit in the Solar System: a, 1980. b, 1910-86. c, 1916-70. d, 1911.

1986, Mar. 7 *Perf. 13½x13*

3153 A1221 Sheet of 4 1.50 1.10
a.-d. 25s, any single .35 .25

Exists imperf. Value $15.

A1222

1986, Mar. 12 *Perf. 13x13½*

3154 A1222 5s dp bl & bl .25 .25

Vladimir Bachev (1935-1967), poet.

A1223

1986, Mar. 17 *Perf. 13*

3155 A1223 5s Wavy lines .25 .25
3156 A1223 8s Star .25 .25
3157 A1223 13s Worker .25 .25
Nos. 3155-3157 (3) .75 .75

Souvenir Sheet
Imperf

3158 A1223 50s Scaffold, flags .60 .40

13th Natl. Communist Party Congress.

Souvenir Sheet

1st Manned Space Flight, 25th Anniv. — A1224

Designs: a, Vostok I, 1961. b, Yuri Gagarin (1934-68), Russian cosmonaut.

1986, Mar. 28 *Perf. 13½x13*

3159 A1224 Sheet of 2 1.25 1.00
a.-b. 50s, any single .60 .50

Exists imperf. Value $12.

April Uprising against the Turks, 110th Anniv. — A1225

Monuments: 5s, 1876 Uprising monument, Panagjuriste. 13s, Christo Botev, Vraca.

1986, Mar. 30 *Perf. 13*

3160 A1225 5s multicolored .25 .25
3161 A1225 13s multicolored .25 .25

A1225a

Levsky-Spartak Sports Club, 75th Anniv. — A1226

50s, Rhythmic gymnastics.

1986 *Perf. 13*

3161A A1225a 5s multicolored .25 .25

Souvenir Sheet
Imperf

3162 A1226 50s multicolored .60 .40

Issue dates: 5s, Dec. 50s, May 12.

A1227

5s, Congress emblem. 8s, Emblem on globe. 13s, Flags.

1986, May 19 *Perf. 13*

3163 A1227 5s multicolored .25 .25
3164 A1227 8s multicolored .25 .25
3165 A1227 13s multicolored .25 .25
Nos. 3163-3165 (3) .75 .75

35th Congress of Bulgarian farmers, Sofia.

A1228

1986, May 27 *Perf. 13x13½*

3166 A1228 13s multicolored .25 .25

Conference of Transport Ministers from Socialist Countries.

17th Intl. Book Fair, Sofia — A1229

1986, May 28

3167 A1229 13s blk, brt red & grysh blk .25 .25

1986 World Cup Soccer Championships, Mexico — A1230

Various soccer plays; attached labels picture Mexican landmarks.

1986, May 30 *Perf. 13½*

3168 A1230 5s multi, vert. .25 .25
3169 A1230 13s multicolored .25 .25
3170 A1230 20s multicolored .30 .25
3171 A1230 30s multicolored .50 .25
3172 A1230 42s multicolored .70 .25
3173 A1230 60s multi, vert. 1.40 .25
Nos. 3168-3173 (6) 3.40 1.50

Souvenir Sheet
Perf. 13

3174 A1230 1 l Azteca Stadium 1.25 .75

Exist imperf. Value: set $6; souvenir sheet $10.

Treasures of Preslav — A1231

Gold artifacts: 5s, Embossed brooch. 13s, Pendant with pearl cross, vert. 20s, Crystal and pearl pendant. 30s, Embossed shield. 42s, Pearl and enamel pendant, vert. 60s, Enamel shield.

1986, June 7 *Perf. 13½x13, 13x13½*

3175 A1231 5s multicolored .25 .25
3176 A1231 13s multicolored .25 .25
3177 A1231 20s multicolored .30 .25
3178 A1231 30s multicolored .50 .25
3179 A1231 42s multicolored .70 .30
3180 A1231 60s multicolored .70 .30
Nos. 3175-3180 (6) 2.70 1.60

World Fencing Championships, Sofia, July 25-Aug. 3 — A1232

1986, July 25 **Photo.** *Perf. 13*

3181 A1232 5s Head cut, lunge .25 .25
3182 A1232 13s Touche .25 .25
3183 A1232 25s Lunge, parry .45 .25
Nos. 3181-3183 (3) .95 .75

Flower Type of 1985

No. 3184, Ipomoea tricolor. No. 1385, Anemone coronaria. No. 1386, Lilium auratum.

1986, July 29 *Perf. 13x13½*

3184 A1203 8s multi .25 .25
3185 A1203 8s multi .25 .25
3186 A1203 32s multi .45 .25
Nos. 3184-3186 (3) .95 .75

A1233

1986, Aug. 25

3187 A1233 42s sepia, sal brn & lake .45 .30

STOCKHOLMIA '86. No. 3187 printed in sheets of 3 + 3 labels picturing folk art.

Miniature Sheet

A1234

Environmental Conservation: a, Ciconia ciconia. b, Nuphar lutea. c, Salamandra salamandra. d, Nymphaea alba.

1986, Aug. 25 **Litho.** *Perf. 14*

3188 A1234 Sheet of 4 + label 3.00 2.50
a.-d. 30s any single .50 .35

No. 3188 is a miniature sheet containing a center label picturing the oldest oak tree in Bulgaria, Granit Village.
Exists imperf. Value $14.

Natl. Arms, Building of the Sobranie — A1235

1986, Sept. 13 Photo. *Perf. 13*

3189	A1235	5s Prus grn, yel grn & red	.25	.25

People's Republic of Bulgaria, 40th anniv.

15th Postal Union Congress — A1236

1986, Sept. 24

3190	A1236	13s multicolored	.25	.25

Natl. Youth Brigade Movement, 40th Anniv. — A1237

1986, Oct. 4

3191	A1237	5s multicolored	.25	.25

Intl. Organization of Journalists, 10th Congress A1238

1986, Oct. 13

3192	A1238	13s blue & dark blue	.25	.25

Sts. Cyril and Methodius, Disciples — A1239

1986, Oct. 28 *Perf. 13½*

3193	A1239	13s dark brown & buff	.25	.25

Sts. Cyril and Methodius in Bulgaria, 1100th anniv. No. 3193 se-tenant with inscribed label.

Telephones in Bulgaria, Cent. — A1240

1986, Nov. 5 *Perf. 13*

3194	A1240	5s multicolored	.25	.25

World Weight Lifting Championships — A1241

1986, Nov. 6

3195	A1241	13s multicolored	.25	.25

Ships A1242

5s, King of Prussia. 13s, East Indiaman, 18th cent. 25s, Shebek, 18th cent. 30s, St Paul. 32s, Topsail schooner, 18th cent. 42s, Victory.

1986, Nov. 20

3196	A1242	5s multicolored	.25	.25
3197	A1242	13s multicolored	.25	.25
3198	A1242	25s multicolored	.35	.25
3199	A1242	30s multicolored	.35	.25
3200	A1242	32s multicolored	.50	.30
3201	A1242	42s multicolored	1.10	.10
		Nos. 3196-3201 (6)	2.80	1.70

European Security and Cooperation Congress, Vienna — A1243

Various buildings and emblems: a, Bulgaria. b, Austria. c, Donau Park, UN.

Perf. 13, Imperf. x13 (#3202b)

1986, Nov. 27

3202	A1243	Souvenir sheet of 3	2.75	1.25
a.-c.		50s any single	.75	.40

Exists imperf. bearing control number. Value $22.50.

Rogozen Thracian Pitchers A1244

1986, Dec. 5 *Perf. 13*

3203	A1244	10s Facing left	.25	.25
3204	A1244	10s Facing right	.25	.25
a.		Block, #3203-3204 + 2 labels	.65	.65

Union of Bulgarian Philatelists, 14th Congress.

Exist imperf. Value, block $1.

New Year 1987 A1245

1986, Dec. 9

3205	A1245	5s shown	.25	.25
3206	A1245	13s Snow flakes	.25	.25

Home Amateur Radio Operators in Bulgaria, 60th Anniv. — A1246

1986, Dec. 10

3207	A1246	13s multicolored	.25	.25

Miniature Sheet

Paintings by Bulgarian Artists — A1247

a, Red Tree, by Danail Dechev (1891-1962). b, Troopers Confront Two Men, by Ilya Beshkov (1901-58). c, View of Melnik, by Veselin Stajkov (1906-70). d, View of Houses through Trees, by Kyril Zonev (1896-1961).

1986, Dec. 10 Litho. *Perf. 14*

3208	A1247	Sheet of 4	1.75	1.00
a.-b.		25s any single	.40	.25
c.-d.		30s any single	.45	.30

Sofia Academy of Art, 90th anniv.

Augusto Cesar Sandino (1893-1934), Nicaraguan Revolutionary, and Flag — A1248

1986, Dec. 16 Photo. *Perf. 13*

3209	A1248	13s multicolored	.25	.25

Sandinista movement in Nicaragua, 25th anniv.

Smoyan Mihylovsky (b. 1856), Writer — A1249

Ran Bossilek (b. 1886) A1250

Title Page from Bulgarian Folk Songs of the Miladinov Brothers — A1251

Annivs. and events: No. 3211, Pentcho Slaveyckov (b. 1861), writer. No. 3212, Nickola Atanassov (b. 1886), musician.

1986, Dec. 17

3210	A1249	5s multicolored	.25	.25
3211	A1249	5s multicolored	.25	.25
3212	A1249	8s multicolored	.25	.25
3213	A1250	8s multicolored	.25	.25
3214	A1251	10s multicolored	.25	.25
		Nos. 3210-3214 (5)	1.25	1.25

Paintings by Titian — A1252

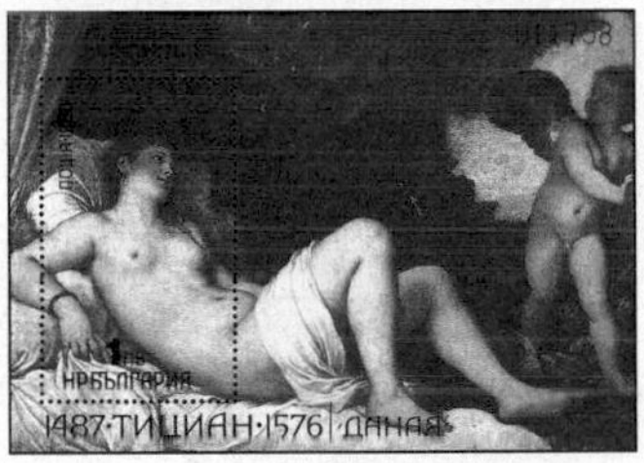

A1253

Various portraits.

1986, Dec. 23 Litho. *Perf. 14*

3215	A1252	5s multicolored	.25	.25
3216	A1252	13s multicolored	.25	.25
3217	A1252	20s multicolored	.30	.25
3218	A1252	30s multicolored	.35	.25
3219	A1252	32s multicolored	.55	.25
3220	A1252	42s multicolored	.90	.30
a.		Min. sheet of 6, #3215-3220	2.25	1.25
		Nos. 3215-3220 (6)	2.60	1.55

Souvenir Sheet

3221	A1253	1 l multicolored	2.00	.75

Rayko Daskalov (b. 1886), Politician A1254

1986, Dec. 23 Photo. *Perf. 13*

3222	A1254	5s deep claret	.25	.25

Sports Cars — A1255

1986, Dec. 30 **Litho.** ***Perf. 13½***

3223 A1255 5s 1905 Fiat .25 .25
3224 A1255 10s 1928 Bugatti .25 .25
3225 A1255 25s 1936 Mercedes .35 .25
3226 A1255 32s 1952 Ferrari .45 .25
3227 A1255 40s 1985 Lotus .55 .30
3228 A1255 42s 1986 McLaren .90 .30
Nos. 3223-3228 (6) 2.75 1.60

Varna Railway Inauguration, 120th Anniv. — A1257

1987, Jan. 19 **Photo.** ***Perf. 13½***

3229 A1257 5s multicolored .25 .25
a. Perf. 11 .40 .40

Dimcho Debelianov (1887-1916), Poet — A1258

1987, Jan. 20 **Photo.** ***Perf. 13***

3230 A1258 5s blue, dull yel & dp blue .25 .25

L.L. Zamenhof, Creator of Esperanto — A1259

1987, Feb. 12

3231 A1259 13s multicolored .25 .25

Mushrooms A1260

5s, Amanita rubescens. 20s, Boletus regius. 30s, Leccinum aurantiacum. 32s, Coprinus comatus. 40s, Russula vesca. 60s, Cantharellus cibarius.

1987, Feb. 6 **Litho.** ***Perf. 11½***

3232 A1260 5s multicolored .25 .25
3233 A1260 20s multicolored .25 .25
3234 A1260 30s multicolored .25 .25
3235 A1260 32s multicolored .35 .25
3236 A1260 40s multicolored .45 .25
3237 A1260 60s multicolored .55 .35
a. Min. sheet of 6, #3232-3237 2.50 2.50
Nos. 3232-3237 (6) 2.10 1.60

10th Natl. Trade Unions Congress A1261

1987, Mar. 20 **Photo.** ***Perf. 13***

3238 A1261 5s dark red & violet .25 .25

Rogozen Thracian Treasure A1262

Embossed and gilded silver artifacts: 5s, Plate, Priestess Auge approaching Heracles. 8s, Pitcher, lioness attacking stag. 20s, Plate, floral pattern. 30s, Pitcher, warriors on horseback dueling. 32s, Urn, decorative pattern. 42s, Pitcher (not gilded), winged horses.

1987, Mar. 31

3239 A1262 5s multicolored .25 .25
3240 A1262 8s multicolored .25 .25
3241 A1262 20s multicolored .25 .25
3242 A1262 30s multicolored .25 .25
3243 A1262 32s multicolored .35 .25
3244 A1262 42s multicolored .45 .25
Nos. 3239-3244 (6) 1.80 1.50

Miniature Sheet

Modern Architecture — A1263

Designs: a, Ludmila Zhivkova conf. center, Varna. b, Ministry of Foreign Affairs, Sofia. c, Interpred Building, Sofia. d, Hotel, Sandanski.

1987, Apr. 7 ***Perf. 13½x13***

3245 A1263 Sheet of 4 1.50 1.00
a.-d. 30s any single .35 .25

Exists imperf. with black control number. Value $12.

European Freestyle Wrestling Championships A1264

1987, Apr. 22 ***Perf. 13***

3246 A1264 5s multicolored .25 .25
3247 A1264 13s multi, diff. .25 .25

CAPEX '87, Toronto A1265

1987, Apr. 24

3248 A1265 42s multicolored .60 .30

10th Congress of the Natl. Front — A1266

1987, May 11

3249 A1266 5s multicolored .25 .25

15th Communist Youth Congress — A1267

1987, May 13

3250 A1267 5s George Dimitrov .25 .25

8th Intl. Humor and Satire Biennial, Gabrovo — A1268

1987, May 15 ***Perf. 13x13½***

3251 A1268 13s multicolored .25 .25

13th World Rhythmic Gymnastics Championships, Varna — A1269

Gymnasts: 5s, Maria Gigova. 8s, Iliana Raeva. 13s, Anelia Ralenkova. 25s, Pilyana Georgieva. 30s, Lilia Ignatova. 42s, Bianca Panova.

1 l, Neshka Robeva, coach.

1987, Aug. 5 **Photo.** ***Perf. 13***

3252 A1269 5s multicolored .25 .25
3252A A1269 8s multicolored .25 .25
3252B A1269 13s multicolored .25 .25
3252C A1269 25s multicolored .35 .25
3252D A1269 30s multicolored .45 .25
3252E A1269 42s multicolored .55 .25
Nos. 3252-3252E (6) 2.10 1.50

Souvenir Sheet

Perf. 13x13½

3252F A1269 1 l multi 1.50 1.25

Exists imperf. with black control number. Value $7.

Vassil Kolarov — A1270

1987, June 3 ***Perf. 13***

3253 A1270 5s dk red, yel & dk bl .25 .25

Stela Blagoeva (b. 1887) — A1271

1987, June 4

3254 A1271 5s pink & sepia .25 .25

Rabotnichesko Delo Newspaper, 60th Anniv. — A1272

1987, May 28

3255 A1272 5s black & lake .25 .25

Deer A1273

5s, Capreolus capreolus, vert. 10s, Alces alces. 32s, Dama dama, vert. 40s, Cervus nippon, vert. 42s, Cervus elaphus. 60s, Rangifer tarandus, vert.

1987, June 23 **Litho.**

3256 A1273 5s multicolored .25 .25
3257 A1273 10s multicolored .25 .25
3258 A1273 32s multicolored .45 .25
3259 A1273 40s multicolored .50 .25
3260 A1273 42s multicolored .55 .30
3261 A1273 60s multicolored .80 .35
a. Min. sheet, #3256-3261, imperf 3.00 2.50
Nos. 3256-3261 (6) 2.80 1.65

Vassil Levski (1837-73) A1274

Various portraits.

1987, June 19 **Photo.**

3262 A1274 5s red brn & dark grn .25 .25
3263 A1274 13s dark grn & red brn .25 .25

Namibia Day A1275

1987, July 8

3264 A1275 13s org, blk & dark red .25 .25

Georgi Kirkov (1867-1919), Revolutionary A1276

1987, July 17 *Perf. 13x13½*

3265	A1276	5s clar & dp clar	.25	.25

Bees and Plants — A1277

5s, Phacelia tanacetifolia. 10s, Helianthus annuus. 30s, Robinia pseudoacacia. 32s, Lavandula vera. 42s, Tilia parvifolia. 60s, Onobrychis sativa.

1987, July 29 **Litho.** *Perf. 13*

3266	A1277	5s multicolored	.25	.25
3267	A1277	10s multicolored	.25	.25
3268	A1277	30s multicolored	.35	.25
3269	A1277	32s multicolored	.35	.25
3270	A1277	42s multicolored	.50	.30
3271	A1277	60s multicolored	.70	.35
a.		Min. sheet of 6, #3266-3271	2.50	2.00
		Nos. 3266-3271 (6)	2.40	1.65

BULGARIA '89 — A1278

1987, Sept. 3 *Perf. 13½x13*

3272	A1278	13s No. 1	.25	.25

HAFNIA '87 — A1279

1987, Sept. 8 *Perf. 13*

3273	A1279	42s multicolored	.45	.25

No. 3273 issued in sheets of 3 plus 2 labels picturing emblems of the HAFNIA '87 and BULGARIA '89 exhibitions, and 1 label with background similar to Denmark Type A32 with castle instead of denomination.

Portrait of a Girl, by Stefan Ivanov — A1280

Paintings in the Sofia City Art Galler: 8s, Grape-gatherer, by Bencho Obreshkov. 20s, Portrait of a Lady with a Hat, by David Perets. 25s, Listeners of Marimba, by Kiril Tsonev. 32s, Boy with an Harmonica, by Nenko Balkanski. 60s, Rumyana, by Vasil Stoilov.

1987, Sept. 15 **Litho.** *Perf. 14*

3274	A1280	5s shown	.25	.25
3275	A1280	8s multicolored	.25	.25
3276	A1280	20s multicolored	.25	.25
3277	A1280	25s multicolored	.30	.25
3278	A1280	32s multicolored	.35	.25
3279	A1280	60s multicolored	.80	.25
		Nos. 3274-3279 (6)	2.20	1.50

Intl. Atomic Energy Agency, 30th Anniv. A1281

1987, Sept. 15 **Photo.** *Perf. 13½x13*

3280	A1281	13s red, lt blue & emer	.25	.25

Songbirds A1282

5s, Troglodytes troglodytes. 13s, Emberiza citrinella. 20s, Sitta europaea. 30s, Turdus merula. 42s, Coccothraustes coccothraustes. 60s, Cinclus cinclus.

1987, Oct. 12 **Litho.** *Perf. 12½x12*

3281	A1282	5s multicolored	.25	.25
3282	A1282	13s multicolored	.25	.25
3283	A1282	20s multicolored	.30	.25
3284	A1282	30s multicolored	.45	.25
3285	A1282	42s multicolored	.65	.30
3286	A1282	60s multicolored	.90	.35
a.		Min. sheet of 6, #3281-3286	3.00	2.00
		Nos. 3281-3286 (6)	2.80	1.65

Balkan War, 75th Anniv. A1283

1987, Sept. 15 **Photo.** *Perf. 13½*

3287	A1283	5s buff, blk & brt org	.25	.25

Newspaper Anniversaries — A1283a

1987, Sept. 24 **Photo.** *Perf. 13*

3287A	A1283a	5s multicolored	.25	.25

Rabotnik, 95th anniv.; Rabotnicheski Vstnik, 90th anniv. and Rabotnichesko Delo, 60th anniv.

October Revolution, Russia, 70th Anniv. — A1284

Lenin and: 5s, Revolutionary. 13s, Cosmonaut.

1987, Oct. 27 **Photo.** *Perf. 13*

3288	A1284	5s rose brn & red org	.25	.25
3289	A1284	13s brt ultra & red org	.25	.25

1988 Winter Olympics, Calgary A1285

5s, Biathlon. 13s, Slalom. 30s, Women's figure skating. 42s, 4-Man bobsled.
1 l, Ice hockey.

1987, Oct. 27 **Litho.** *Perf. 13x13½*

3290	A1285	5s multi	.25	.25
3291	A1285	13s multi	.25	.25
3292	A1285	30s multi	.35	.25
3293	A1285	42s multi	.50	.35
		Nos. 3290-3293 (4)	1.35	1.10

Souvenir Sheet

3294	A1285	1 l multi	1.50	1.25

No. 3294 exists imperf. Value $7.

Souvenir Sheet

Soviet Space Achievements, 1957-87 — A1286

Designs: No. 3295a, Vega probe. No. 3295b, Mir-Soyuz Space Station.

1987, Dec. 24 **Photo.** *Perf. 13½x13*

3295	A1286	Sheet of 2	2.00	1.50
a.-b.		50s any single	1.25	.75

Exists imperf. Value $12.

New Year 1988 A1287

Sofia stamp exhibition emblem within folklore patterns.

1987, Dec. 25 *Perf. 13*

3296	A1287	5s multicolored	.25	.25
3297	A1287	13s multi, diff.	.25	.25

Souvenir Sheet

European Security Conferences — A1288

Conferences held in Helsinki, 1973, and Vienna, 1987: a, Helsinki Conf. Center. b, Map of Europe. c, Vienna Conf. Center.

Perf. 13x13½ on 2 or 4 Sides

1987, Dec. 30

3298	A1288	Sheet of 3	3.00	2.50
a.-c.		50s any single	1.00	.75

Exists imperf. Value $14.

A1289

1988, Jan. 20

3299	A1289	5s multicolored	.25	.25

Christo Kabaktchiev (b. 1878), party leader.

Marine Flowers A1290

5s, Scilla bythynica. 10s, Geum rhodopaeum. 13s, Caltha polypetala. 25s, Nymphoides peltata. 30s, Cortusa matthioli. 42s, Stratiotes aloides.

1988, Jan. 25 **Litho.** *Perf. 12*

3300	A1290	5s multicolored	.25	.25
3301	A1290	10s multicolored	.25	.25
3302	A1290	13s multicolored	.25	.25
3303	A1290	25s multicolored	.25	.25
3304	A1290	30s multicolored	.40	.25
3305	A1290	42s multicolored	.60	.45
a.		Min. sheet of 6, #3300-3305	1.75	1.50
		Nos. 3300-3305 (6)	2.00	1.70

Liberation of Bulgaria, 110th Anniv. A1291

1988, Feb. 15 **Photo.** *Perf. 13*

3306	A1291	5s Officer, horse	.25	.25
3307	A1291	13s Soldiers	.25	.25

8th Intl. Civil Servants Congress, Sofia — A1292

1988, Mar. 22 **Photo.** *Perf. 13*

3308	A1292	13s multicolored	.25	.25

State Railways, Cent. — A1293

Locomotives: 5s, Jantra, 1888. 13s, Christo Botev, 1905. 25s, 0-10-1, 1918. 32s, 4-12-1 heavy duty, 1943. 42s, Diesel, 1964. 60s, Electric, 1979.

1988, Mar. 25 Litho. *Perf. 11*

3309	A1293	5s multicolored	.25	.25
3310	A1293	13s multicolored	.25	.25
3311	A1293	25s multicolored	.35	.25
3312	A1293	32s multicolored	.45	.25
3313	A1293	42s multicolored	.55	.30
3314	A1293	60s multicolored	.90	.35
a.		Min. sheet of 6, #3309-3314	3.00	1.75
		Nos. 3309-3314 (6)	2.75	1.65

Ivan Nedyalkov (1880-1925) A1294

Postal workers, heroes of socialism: 8s, Delcho Spasov (1918-43). 10s, Nikola Ganchev (1915-43). 13s, Ganka Stoyanova Rasheva (1921-44).

1988, Mar. 31 Photo. *Perf. 13½x13*

3315	A1294	5s buff & dk rose brn	.25	.25
3316	A1294	8s pale ultra & vio blue	.25	.25
3317	A1294	10s pale ol grn & ol grn	.25	.25
3318	A1294	13s pale pink & lake	.25	.25
		Nos. 3315-3318 (4)	1.00	1.00

Georgi Traikov (b. 1898), Statesman A1295

1988, Apr. 8 Litho. *Perf. 13x13½*

3319 A1295 5s orange & brn .25 .25

Intl. Red Cross and Red Crescent Organizations, 125th Annivs. — A1296

1988, Apr. 26 Photo. *Perf. 13*

3320 A1296 13s multicolored .25 .25

Children's Drawings Type of 1982

Designs: 5s, Girl wearing a folk costume, vert. 8s, Painter at easel, vert. 13s, Children watching clown. 20s, Children releasing doves. 32s, Melodica player, vert. 42s, Cosmonaut, vert. 50s, Assembly emblem.

1988, Apr. 28 Litho. *Perf. 14*

3321	A1093	5s pink & multi	.25	.25
3322	A1093	8s blue grn & multi	.25	.25
3323	A1093	13s red & multi	.25	.25
3324	A1093	20s apple grn & multi	.30	.25
3325	A1093	32s blue & multi	.40	.25
3326	A1093	42s pale vio & multi	.50	.25
		Nos. 3321-3326 (6)	1.95	1.50

Souvenir Sheet

3327 A1093 50s red & multi 1.00 .50

4th Intl. Children's Assembly, Sofia.
No. 3327 exists imperf. Value $2.50.

Karl Marx A1297

1988, May 5 *Perf. 13*

3328 A1297 13s multicolored .25 .25

Birds — A1297a

Designs: No. 3328A, Ciconia ciconia. No. 3328B, Larus argentatus. No. 3328C, Ardea cinerea. No. 3328D, Corvus corone cornix. 10s, Accipiter gentillis. 42s, Bubo bubo.

1988, May 6 Litho. *Perf. 13x13½*

3328A	A1297a	5s multicolored	.25	.25
3328B	A1297a	5s multicolored	.25	.25
3328C	A1297a	8s multicolored	.25	.25
3328D	A1297a	8s multicolored	.25	.25
3328E	A1297a	10s multicolored	.40	.25
3328F	A1297a	42s multicolored	1.20	.30
		Nos. 3328A-3328F (6)	2.60	1.55

Dated 1987.

Sofia Zoo A1298

5s, Loxodonta africana. 13s, Ceratotherium simum. 25s, Lycaon pictus. 30s, Pelecanus onocrotalus. 32s, Bucorvus abissinicus. 42s, Nyctea scandiaca.

1988, May 20

3329	A1298	5s multicolored	.25	.25
3330	A1298	13s multicolored	.25	.25
3331	A1298	25s multicolored	.35	.25
3332	A1298	30s multicolored	.45	.25
3333	A1298	32s multicolored	.50	.25
3334	A1298	42s multicolored	.65	.25
a.		Min. sheet of 6, #3329-3334	2.50	1.50
		Nos. 3329-3334 (6)	2.45	1.50

FINLANDIA '88 — A1299

1988, June 7

3335 A1299 30s Finland No. 1 .50 .35

No. 3335 printed in miniature sheets of 3 plus 3 labels picturing skyline, SOFIA '89 and FINLANDIA '88 exhibition emblems.
Exists imperf. Value $.90

2nd Joint USSR-Bulgaria Space Flight — A1300

1988, June 7

3336	A1300	5s shown	.25	.25
3337	A1300	13s Rocket, globe	.25	.25

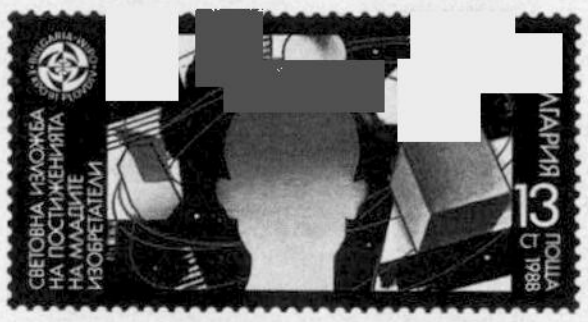

EXPO '91, Plovdiv — A1301

1988, June 7 *Perf. 13½x13*

3338 A1301 13s multicolored .25 .25

1988 European Soccer Championships — A1302

5s, Corner kick. 13s, Heading the ball. 30s, Referee, player. 42s, Player holding trophy.
1 l, Stadium.

1988, June 10 *Perf. 13*

3339	A1302	5s multi	.25	.25
3340	A1302	13s multi	.25	.25
3341	A1302	30s multi	.40	.25
3342	A1302	42s multi	.55	.25
		Nos. 3339-3342 (4)	1.45	1.00

Souvenir Sheet

3343 A1302 1 l multi 1.25 1.00

No. 3343 exists imperf. Value $12.50.

Paintings by Dechko Usunov (1899-1986) A1303

Designs: 5s, Portrait of a Young Girl. 13s, Portrait of Maria Wassilewa. 30s, Self-portrait.

1988, June 14 *Perf. 13x13½*

3344	A1303	5s multicolored	.25	.25
3345	A1303	13s multicolored	.25	.25
3346	A1303	30s multicolored	.40	.25
		Nos. 3344-3346 (3)	.90	.75

Souvenir Sheet

1st Woman in Space, 25th Anniv. — A1304

1988, June 16 *Perf. 13½x13*

3347 A1304 1 l multicolored 1.50 1.00

Valentina Tereshkova's flight, June 16-19, 1963.
Exists imperf. Value $13.50.

Kurdzhali Region Religious Art — A1305

Designs: 5s, St. John the Baptist, 1592. 8s, St. George Slaying the Dragon, 1841.

1988, June 27 *Perf. 13x13½*

3348	A1305	5s multicolored	.25	.25
3349	A1305	8s multicolored	.25	.25

1988 Summer Olympics, Seoul — A1306

5s, High jump. 13s, Weight lifting. 30s, Greco-Roman wrestling. 42s, Rhythmic gymnastics.
1 l, Volleyball.

1988, July 25 Litho. *Perf. 13*

3350	A1306	5s multicolored	.25	.25
3351	A1306	13s multicolored	.25	.25
3352	A1306	30s multicolored	.35	.25
3353	A1306	42s multicolored	.55	.25
		Nos. 3350-3353 (4)	1.40	1.00

Souvenir Sheet

3354 A1306 1 l multicolored 1.50 1.00

No. 3354 exists imperf. Value $12.50.

Dimitr and Karaja A1307

1988, July 25 Litho. *Perf. 13*

3355 A1307 5s blk, dark olive bister & grn .25 .25

120th anniv. of the deaths of Haji Dimitr and Stefan Karaja, patriots killed during the Balkan Wars.

Problems of Peace and Socialism, 30th Anniv. — A1308

1988, July 26 Photo.

3356 A1308 13s multicolored .25 .25

Paintings in the Ludmila Zhivkova Art Gallery
A1309

Paintings: No. 3357, Harbor, Algiers, by Albert Marquet (1875-1947). No. 3358, Portrait of Hermine David in the Studio, by Jules Pascin (1885-1930). No. 3359, Madonna with Child and Sts. Sebastian and Rocco, by Giovanni Rosso (1494-1540). No. 3360, The Barren Tree, by Roland Oudot (1879-1982).

1988, July 27 Litho. *Perf. 14*
3357 A1309 30s multicolored .35 .25
3358 A1309 30s multicolored .35 .25
3359 A1309 30s multicolored .35 .25
3360 A1309 30s multicolored .35 .25
Nos. 3357-3360 (4) 1.40 1.00

St. Clement of Ohrid University, Sofia, 100th Anniv. — A1310

1988, Aug. 22 *Perf. 13*
3361 A1310 5s blk & pale yel .25 .25

PRAGA '88
A1311

25s, Czechoslovakia #2 in vermilion.

1988, Aug. 22
3362 A1311 25s multi .40 .30

Printed in miniature sheets of 3 plus 3 labels picturing skyline, PRAGA '88 and SOFIA '89 exhibition emblems.
Exists imperf.

OLYMPHILEX '88 — A1312

1988, Sept. 1
3363 A1312 62s Korea No. 1 1.25 .75

Printed in miniature sheets of 3 plus 3 labels picturing skyline, OLYMPHILEX '88 and SOFIA '89 exhibition emblems.
Exists imperf.

A1313

1988, Sept. 15
3364 A1313 5s dp bl, lt bl & red .25 .25

Kremikovtsi steel mill, 25th anniv.

A1314

1988, Sept. 16 *Perf. 13½x13*
3365 A1314 13s dark red & ultra .25 .25

80th Interparliamentary Conference.

Transportation Commission 80th Congress — A1315

1988, Oct. 17
3366 A1315 13s deep lil rose & blk .25 .25

Kurdzhali Region Artifacts
A1316

5s, Earthenware bowl, 13th-14th cent. 8s, Medieval fortification, Gorna Krepost Village, vert.

1988, Sept. 20 *Perf. 13*
3367 A1316 5s multicolored .25 .25
3368 A1316 8s multicolored .25 .25

Chiprovo Uprising, 300th Anniv. — A1317

1988, Sept. 23
3369 A1317 5s multicolored .25 .25

Bears
A1318

Designs: 5s, Ursus arctos. 8s, Thalassarctos maritimus. 13s, Melursus ursinus. 20s, Helarctos malayanus. 32s, Selenarctos thibetanus. 42s, Tremarctos ornatus.

1988, Sept. 26 *Perf. 12½*
3370 A1318 5s multicolored .25 .25
3371 A1318 8s multicolored .25 .25
3372 A1318 13s multicolored .25 .25
3373 A1318 20s multicolored .30 .25
3374 A1318 32s multicolored .45 .25
3375 A1318 42s multicolored .70 .25
a. Min. sheet of 6, #3370-3375 2.00 1.50
Nos. 3370-3375 (6) 2.20 1.50

ECOFORUM for Peace — A1319

1988, Oct. 29 *Perf. 13*
3376 A1319 20s multicolored .30 .25

PLOVDIV '88 — A1320

Design: Amphitheater ruins, PRAGA '88 and PLOVDIV '88 emblems.

1988, Nov. 2
3377 A1320 5s multicolored .25 .25

Exists in imperf. sheet of six.

Radio & Television Authority, 25th Anniv. — A1321

1988, Nov. 17 Litho. *Perf. 13*
3378 A1321 5s multicolored .25 .25

BULGARIA '89 — A1321a

1988, Nov. 22 Litho. *Perf. 13*
3379 A1321a 42s No. 1 .50 .45

Printed in miniature sheets of 3+3 labels picturing exhib. emblem and conf. center.
Exists imperf.

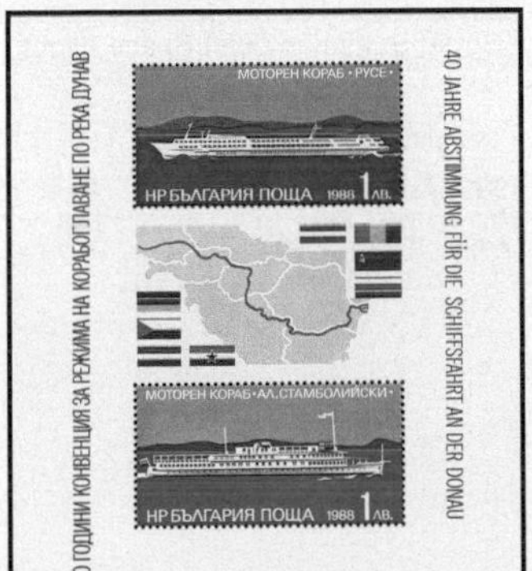

Danube Cruise Excursion Industry, 40th Anniv. — A1321b

1988, Nov. 25 *Perf. 13½x13*
3380 A1321b Sheet of 2 2.50 2.00
a. 1 l *Russia* 1.25 1.00
b. 1 l *Aleksandr Stamboliski* 1.25 1.00

Exists imperf. Value $18.

Traffic Safety — A1321c

1988, Nov. 28
3381 A1321c 5s multicolored .25 .25

New Year 1989 — A1321d

1988, Dec. 20 *Perf. 13*
3382 A1321d 5s shown .25 .25
3383 A1321d 13s multi, diff. .25 .25

Hotels in Winter
A1322

1988, Dec. 19 Litho. *Perf. 13½x13*
3384 A1322 5s shown .25 .25
3385 A1322 8s multi, diff. .25 .25
3386 A1322 13s multi, diff. .25 .25
3387 A1322 30s multi, diff. .30 .25
Nos. 3384-3387 (4) 1.05 1.00

Souvenir Sheet

Soviet Space Shuttle Energija-Buran
A1322a

1988, Dec. 28 *Perf. 13½x13*
3387A A1322a 1 l dark blue 1.50 1.00

Exists imperf. Value $12.50.

BULGARIA '89 — A1322b

Traditional modes of postal conveyance.

1988, Dec. 29 *Perf. 13½x13*
3387B A1322b 25s Mail coach .35 .25
3387C A1322b 25s Biplane .35 .25
3387D A1322b 25s Truck .35 .25
3387E A1322b 25s Steam packet .35 .25
Nos. 3387B-3387E (4) 1.40 1.00

Philatelic Exhibitions — A1323

1989 Litho. *Perf. 13*

3388 A1323 42s France No. 1	.75	.60
3389 A1323 62s India No. 200	.75	.60

BULGARIA '89 and PHILEXFRANCE '89 (42s) or INDIA '89 (62s).

Nos. 3388-3389 each printed in sheets of 3 + 3 labels picturing skylines, BULGARIA '89 and PHILEXFRANCE or INDIA exhibition labels. Exist in sheets of 4 also. Exist imperf.

Issue dates: 42s, Feb. 23; 62s, Jan. 14.

Souvenir Sheet

Universiade Winter Games, Sofia — A1324

Designs: a, Downhill skiing. b, Ice hockey. c, Cross-country skiing. d, Speed skating.

1989, Jan. 30 Litho. *Imperf.*
Simulated Perforations

3390 A1324 Sheet of 4	1.50	.75
a.-d. 25s multicolored	.35	.25

No. 3390 exists imperf. without simulated perforations and containing black control number. Value $12.

Humor and Satire Festival, Gabrovo A1325

1989, Feb. 7 *Perf. 13½x13*

3391 A1325 13s Don Quixote	.25	.25

Endangered Plant Species — A1326

Designs: 5s, Ramonda serbica. 10s, Paeonia maskula. 25s, Viola perinensis. 30s, Dracunculus vulgaris. 42s, Tulipa splendens. 60s, Rindera umbellata.

1989, Feb. 22 *Perf. 13x13½*

3392 A1326 5s multicolored	.25	.25
3393 A1326 10s multicolored	.25	.25
3394 A1326 25s multicolored	.30	.25
3395 A1326 30s multicolored	.40	.25
3396 A1326 42s multicolored	.60	.30
3397 A1326 60s multicolored	.75	.35
a. Min. sheet of 6, #3392-3397	2.75	1.75
Nos. 3392-3397 (6)	2.55	1.65

World Wildlife Fund A1327

Bats: 5s, Nyctalus noctula. 13s, Rhinolophus ferrumequinum. 30s, Myotis myotis. 42s, Vespertilio murinus.

1989, Feb. 27 *Perf. 13*

3398 A1327 5s multicolored	.25	.25
3399 A1327 13s multicolored	.25	.25
3400 A1327 30s multicolored	.75	.30
3401 A1327 42s multicolored	1.25	.90
a. Min. sheet of 4, #3398-3401	3.50	2.50
Nos. 3398-3401 (4)	2.50	1.70

Aleksandr Stamboliski (1879-1923), Premier — A1328

1989, Mar. 1 *Perf. 13½x13*

3402 A1328 5s brt org & blk	.25	.25

Souvenir Sheet

Soviet-Bulgarian Joint Space Flight, 10th Anniv. — A1329

Designs: a, Liftoff. b, Crew.

1989, Apr. 10 *Perf. 13*

3403 A1329 Sheet of 2	2.40	1.25
a.-b. 50s any single	1.10	.60

Exists imperf. Value $15.

EXPO '91 Young Inventors Exhibition, Plovdiv — A1330

1989, Apr. 20 *Perf. 13½x13*

3404 A1330 5s multicolored	.25	.25

Petko Enev (b. 1889) A1331

Stanke Dimitrov Marek (b. 1889) — A1332

1989, Apr. 28 *Perf. 13½x13, 13x13½*

3405 A1331 5s scarlet & black	.25	.25
3406 A1332 5s scarlet & black	.25	.25

Icons — A1333

Paintings by Bulgarian artists: No. 3407, Archangel Michael, by Dimiter Molerov. No. 3408, Mother and Child, by Toma Vishanov. No. 3409, St. John, by Vishanov. No. 3410, St. Dimitri, by Ivan Terziev.

1989, Apr. 28 *Perf. 13x13½*

3407 A1333 30s multicolored	.35	.25
3408 A1333 30s multicolored	.35	.25
3409 A1333 30s multicolored	.35	.25
3410 A1333 30s multicolored	.35	.25
Nos. 3407-3410 (4)	1.40	1.00

Nos. 3408, 3410 exist in sheets of four. Nos. 3407-3410 exist in souvenir sheets of four and together in one sheet of four, imperf.

Photocopier A1334

1989, May 5

3411 A1334 5s shown	.25	.25
3412 A1334 8s Computer	.25	.25
3413 A1334 35s Telephone	.40	.30
3414 A1334 42s Dish receiver	.55	.35
Nos. 3411-3414 (4)	1.45	1.15

Bulgarian Communications, 110th anniv. Nos. 3411-3413 exist in imperf. sheets of six.

Souvenir Sheet

58th FIP Congress — A1335

1989, May 22

3415 A1335 1 l Charioteer	1.50	.75

Exists imperf. Value $12.

1st Communist Party Congress in Bulgaria, 70th Anniv. — A1336

1989, June 15

3416 A1336 5s mar, blk & dk red	.25	.25

Famous Men — A1337

No. 3417, Ilya Blaskov. No. 3418, Sofronii, Bishop of Vratza. No. 3419, Vassil Aprilov (b. 1789), educator, historian. No. 3420, Christo Jassenov (1889-1925). No. 3421, 10s, Stoyan Zagorchinov (1889-1969).

1989

3417 A1337 5s black & gray ol	.25	.25
3418 A1337 5s blk, brn blk & pale green	.25	.25
3419 A1337 8s lt blue, blk & vio blk	.30	.25
3420 A1337 8s tan, blk & dark red brown	.25	.25
3421 A1337 10s blk, pale pink & gray blue	.30	.25
Nos. 3417-3421 (5)	1.35	1.25

Issued: Nos. 3417-3418, June 15; No. 3419, Aug. 1; No. 3420, Sept. 25; 10s, Aug. 5.

French Revolution, Bicent. — A1338

1989, June 26 *Perf. 13½x13*

3422 A1338 13s Anniv. emblem	.25	.25
3423 A1338 30s Jean-Paul Marat	.35	.25
3424 A1338 42s Robespierre	.50	.25
Nos. 3422-3424 (3)	1.10	.75

7th Army Games — A1339

1989, June 30 *Perf. 13*

3425	A1339	5s	Gymnast	.25	.25
3426	A1339	13s	Equestrian	.25	.25
3427	A1339	30s	Running	.35	.25
3428	A1339	42s	Shooting	.50	.30
			Nos. 3425-3428 (4)	1.35	1.05

22nd World Canoe and Kayak Championships, Plovdiv — A1340

1989, Aug. 11 **Litho.** *Perf. 13*

3429	A1340	13s	Woman paddling	.25	.25
3430	A1340	30s	Man rowing	.45	.25

Photography, 150th Anniv. — A1341

1989, Aug. 29 *Perf. 13½x13*

3431	A1341	42s	blk, buff & yel	.75	.30

September 9 Revolution, 45th Anniv. — A1342

5s, Revolutionaries. 8s, Couple embracing. 13s, Faces in a crowd.

1989, Aug. 30 *Perf. 13*

3432	A1342	5s	multicolored	.25	.25
3433	A1342	8s	multicolored	.25	.25
3434	A1342	13s	multicolored	.25	.25
			Nos. 3432-3434 (3)	.75	.75

Natural History Museum, Cent. A1343

1989, Aug. 31

3435	A1343	13s	multicolored	.25	.25

Postal Workers Killed in World War II — A1343a

Designs: 5s, L.D. Dardjikov. 8s, I.B. Dobrev. 10s, N.P. Antonov.

1989, Sept. 22 **Litho.** *Perf. 13*

3436	A1343a	5s	multicolored	.25	.25
3437	A1343a	8s	multicolored	.25	.25
3438	A1343a	13s	multicolored	.25	.25
			Nos. 3436-3438 (3)	.75	.75

12th Shipping Unions Congress (FIATA) — A1344

1989, Sept. 25 **Litho.** *Perf. 13½x13*

3439	A1344	42s	lt blue & dk blue	.65	.40

Jawaharlal Nehru, 1st Prime Minister of Independent India — A1346

1989, Oct. 10

3440	A1346	13s	blk, pale yel & brn	.25	.25

Souvenir Sheet

European Ecology Congress — A1347

1989, Oct. 12 *Perf. 13*

3441	A1347	Sheet of 2	2.75	2.75
a.		50s multicolored	.75	.65
b.		1 l multicolored	1.50	1.10

Souvenir sheet exists imperf. Value $15.

Snakes A1368

Designs: 5s, Eryx jaculus turcicus. 10s, Elaphe longissima. 25s, Elaphe situla. 30s, Elaphe quatuorlineata. 42s, Telescopus fallax. 60s, Coluber rubriceps.

1989, Oct. 20 **Litho.** *Perf. 13*

3491	A1368	5s	multicolored	.25	.25
3492	A1368	10s	multicolored	.25	.25
3493	A1368	25s	multicolored	.35	.25
3494	A1368	30s	multicolored	.45	.30
3495	A1368	42s	multicolored	.65	.35
3496	A1368	60s	multicolored	.85	.45
a.			Min. sheet of 6, #3491-3496	3.00	2.00
			Nos. 3491-3496 (6)	2.80	1.85

Intl. Youth Science Fair, Plovdiv, 1989 — A1369

1989, Nov. 4

3497	A1369	13s	multicolored	.25	.25

1990 World Soccer Championships, Italy — A1370

Various athletes: No. 3502a, Athletes facing right. No. 3502b, Athletes facing left.

1989, Dec. 1

3498	A1370	5s	shown	.25	.25
3499	A1370	13s	multi, diff.	.25	.25
3500	A1370	30s	multi, diff.	.35	.25
3501	A1370	42s	multi, diff.	.85	.35
			Nos. 3498-3501 (4)	1.70	1.10

Souvenir Sheet

3502		Sheet of 2	1.50	.85
a.-b.	A1370	50s any single	.75	.40

No. 3502 exists imperf. Value $12.50.

Air Sports A1371

1989, Dec. 8

3503	A1371	5s	Glider planes	.25	.25
3504	A1371	13s	Hang glider	.25	.25
3505	A1371	30s	Sky diving	.55	.30
3506	A1371	42s	Three sky divers	.55	.30
			Nos. 3503-3506 (4)	1.60	1.10

82nd General conference of the FAI, Varna.

Traffic Safety A1372

1989, Dec. 12

3507	A1372	5s	multicolored	.25	.25

New Year 1990 — A1373

1989, Dec. 25 **Litho.** *Perf. 13*

3508	A1373	5s	Santa's sleigh	.25	.25
3509	A1373	13s	Snowman	.25	.25

Cats A1374

No. 3510, Persian. No. 3511, Tiger. 8s, Tabby. No. 3513, Himalayan. No. 3514, Persian, diff. 13s, Siamese. Nos. 3511, 3514-3515 vert.

Perf. 13½x13, 13x13½

1989, Dec. 26 **Background Color**

3510	A1374	5s	gray	.25	.25
3511	A1374	5s	yellow	.25	.25
3512	A1374	8s	orange	.25	.25
3513	A1374	10s	blue	.25	.25
3514	A1374	10s	brown orange	.25	.25
3515	A1374	13s	red	.30	.25
			Nos. 3510-3515 (6)	1.55	1.50

Explorers and Their Ships — A1375

1990, Jan. 17 *Perf. 13*

3516	A1375	5s	Columbus	.25	.25
3517	A1375	8s	da Gama	.25	.25
3518	A1375	13s	Magellan	.25	.25
3519	A1375	32s	Drake	.45	.30
3520	A1375	42s	Hudson	.70	.45
3521	A1375	60s	Cook	.90	.45
a.			Min. sheet of 6, #3516-3521	3.00	2.25
			Nos. 3516-3521 (6)	2.80	1.95

Natl. Esperanto Movement, Cent. — A1376

1990, Feb. 23 **Litho.** *Perf. 13*

3522	A1376	10s	multicolored	.25	.25

Paintings by Foreign Artists in the Natl. Museum A1377

Artists: No. 3523, Suzanna Valadon (1867-1938). No. 3524, Maurice Brianchon (1899-1978). No. 3525, Moise Kisling (1891-1953). No. 3526, Giovanni Beltraffio (1467-1516).

1990, Mar. 23 *Perf. 14*

3523	A1377	30s	multicolored	.55	.30
3524	A1377	30s	multicolored	.55	.30
3525	A1377	30s	multicolored	.55	.30
3526	A1377	30s	multicolored	.55	.30
			Nos. 3523-3526 (4)	2.20	1.20

1990 World Soccer Championships, Italy — A1378

Various athletes.

1990, Mar. 26 *Perf. 13*

3527	A1378	5s	multicolored	.25	.25
3528	A1378	13s	multi, diff.	.25	.25
3529	A1378	30s	multi, diff.	.45	.25
3530	A1378	42s	multi, diff.	.75	.30
			Nos. 3527-3530 (4)	1.70	1.05

Souvenir Sheet

3531		Sheet of 2	1.75	1.00
a.	A1378	50s Three players	.85	.40
b.	A1378	50s Two players	.85	.40

No. 3531 exists imperf. Value $10.

Bavaria No. 1 A1379

1990, Apr. 6 Litho. *Perf. 13*

3532 A1379 42s vermilion & blk .65 .45

ESSEN '90, Germany, Apr. 12-22. No. 3532 printed in sheets of 3 + 3 labels.

Souvenir Sheet

Penny Black, 150th Anniv. — A1380

1990, Apr. 10

3533 A1380 Sheet of 2 2.00 1.00
a. 50s Great Britain #1 1.00 .50
b. 50s Sir Rowland Hill 1.00 .50

Cooperative Farming in Bulgaria, Cent. — A1381

1990, Apr. 17

3534 A1381 5s multicolored .25 .25

Dimitar Chorbadjiski-Chudomir (1890-1967) — A1382

1990, Apr. 24

3535 A1382 5s multicolored .25 .25

Labor Day, Cent. — A1383

1990, May 1 *Perf. 13x13½*

3536 A1383 10s multicolored .25 .25

ITU, 125th Anniv. — A1384

1990, May 13 Litho. *Perf. 13½x13*

3537 A1384 20s bl, red & blk .35 .25

Belgium No. 1 A1385

1990, May 23 *Perf. 13*

3538 A1385 30s multicolored .60 .35

Belgica '90. No. 3538 printed in sheets of 3 + 3 labels.

Lamartine (1790-1869), French Poet — A1386

1990, June 15 *Perf. 13½x13*

3539 A1386 20s multicolored .35 .25

Dinosaurs — A1387

5s, Brontosaurus. 8s, Stegosaurus. 13s, Edaphosaurus. 25s, Rhamphorhynchus. 32s, Protoceratops. 42s, Triceratops.

1990, June 19 *Perf. 12½*

3540 A1387 5s multi .25 .25
3541 A1387 8s multi .25 .25
3542 A1387 13s multi .25 .25
3543 A1387 25s multi .45 .30
3544 A1387 32s multi .60 .35
3545 A1387 42s multi .90 .45
a. Min. sheet of 6, #3540-3545 3.00 1.60
Nos. 3540-3545 (6) 2.70 1.85

1992 Summer Olympic Games, Barcelona — A1388

1990, July 13 *Perf. 13½x13*

3546 A1388 5s Swimming .25 .25
3547 A1388 13s Handball .25 .25
3548 A1388 30s Hurdling .45 .30
3549 A1388 42s Cycling .75 .30
Nos. 3546-3549 (4) 1.70 1.10

Souvenir Sheet

3550 Sheet of 2 2.00 1.00
a. A1388 50s Tennis, forehand 1.00 .50
b. A1388 50s Tennis, backhand 1.00 .50

No. 3550 exists imperf. Value $10.

Butterflies A1389

5s, Zerynthia Polyxena. 10s, Panaxia quadripunctaria. 20s, Proserpinus proserpina. 30s, Hyles lineata. 42s, Thecla betulae. 60s, Euphydryas cynthia.

1990, Aug. 8 Litho. *Perf. 13*

3551 A1389 5s multicolored .25 .25
3552 A1389 10s multicolored .25 .25
3553 A1389 20s multicolored .25 .25
3554 A1389 30s multicolored .45 .25
3555 A1389 42s multicolored .50 .25
3556 A1389 60s multicolored .85 .45
a. Min. sheet of 6, #3551-3556 3.00 1.75
Nos. 3551-3556 (6) 2.55 1.70

Airplanes — A1390

1990, Aug. 30 Litho. *Perf. 13½x13*

3557 A1390 5s Airbus A-300 .25 .25
3558 A1390 10s Tu-204 .25 .25
3559 A1390 25s Concorde .35 .25
3560 A1390 30s DC-9 .35 .30
3561 A1390 42s Il-86 .50 .35
3562 A1390 60s Boeing 747 .85 .55
a. Min. sheet of 6, #3557-3562 3.00 2.00
Nos. 3557-3562 (6) 2.55 1.95

Exarch Joseph I (1840-1915), Religious Leader — A1391

1990, Sept. 27 *Perf. 13*

3563 A1391 5s blk, pur & grn .25 .25

Intl. Traffic Safety Year A1392

1990, Oct. 9 Litho. *Perf. 13*

3564 A1392 5s multicolored .25 .25

Olymphilex '90, Varna — A1393

1990, Oct. 16 *Perf. 13x13½*

3565 A1393 5s Shot put .25 .25
3566 A1393 13s Discus .25 .25
3567 A1393 42s Hammer throw .55 .35
3568 A1393 60s Javelin .75 .60
a. Souv. sheet of 4, #3565-3568, imperf. 8.00 6.00
Nos. 3565-3568 (4) 1.80 1.45

Space Exploration — A1394

Designs: 5s, Sputnik, 1957, USSR. 8s, Vostok, 1961, USSR. 10s, Voshkod 2, 1965, USSR. 20s, Apollo-Soyuz, 1975, US-USSR. 42s, Space Shuttle Columbia, 1981, US. 60s, Galileo, 1989-1996, US. 1 l, Apollo 11 Moon landing, 1969, US.

1990, Oct. 22 *Perf. 13½x13*

3569 A1394 5s multicolored .25 .25
3570 A1394 8s multicolored .25 .25
3571 A1394 10s multicolored .25 .25
3572 A1394 20s multicolored .30 .25
3573 A1394 42s multicolored .70 .35
3574 A1394 60s multicolored .85 .55
Nos. 3569-3574 (6) 2.60 1.90

Souvenir Sheet

3575 A1394 1 l multicolored 1.75 1.25

No. 3575 exists imperf. Value $7.50.

St. Clement of Ohrid — A1395

1990, Nov. 29 Litho. *Perf. 13*

3576 A1395 5s multicolored .25 .25

Christmas A1396

1990, Dec. 25 Litho. *Perf. 13*

3577 A1396 5s Christmas tree .25 .25
3578 A1396 20s Santa Claus .30 .25

European Figure Skating Championships, Sofia — A1397

1991, Jan. 18 *Perf. 13½x13*

3579 A1397 15s multicolored .25 .25

Farm Animals
A1398

1991-92 *Perf. 14x13½*

3581	A1398	20s	Sheep	.25	.25
3582	A1398	25s	Goose	.25	.25
3583	A1398	30s	Hen, chicks	.25	.25
3584	A1398	40s	Horse	.25	.25
3585	A1398	62s	Goat	.35	.30
3586	A1398	86s	Sow	.50	.30
3587	A1398	95s	Goat	.35	.25
3588	A1398	1 l	Donkey	.50	.35
3589	A1398	2 l	Bull	1.00	.75
3590	A1398	5 l	Turkey	1.75	1.00
3591	A1398	10 l	Cow	3.50	1.00
			Nos. 3581-3591 (11)	8.95	4.95

Issued: 20s, 25s, 40s, 86s, 1 l, 8/21; 10 l, 2/22; 95s, 5/5/92; others, 2/11/91.

Mushrooms
A1399

5s, Amanita phalloides. 10s, Amanita verna. 20s, Amanita pantherina. 32s, Amanita muscaria. 42s, Gyromitra esculenta. 60s, Boletus satanas.

1991, Mar. 19 *Perf. 12½x13*

3597	A1399	5s	multicolored	.25	.25
3598	A1399	10s	multicolored	.25	.25
3599	A1399	20s	multicolored	.25	.25
3600	A1399	32s	multicolored	.25	.25
3601	A1399	42s	multicolored	.30	.25
3602	A1399	60s	multicolored	.70	.25
a.			Min. sheet of 6, #3597-3602	2.00	1.50
			Nos. 3597-3602 (6)	2.00	1.50

French Impressionists
A1400

Designs: 20s, Good Morning, by Gauguin. 43s, Madame Dobini, by Degas. 62s, Peasant Woman, by Pissarro. 67s, Woman with Black Hair, by Manet. 80s, Blue Vase, by Cezanne. 2 l, Jeanny Samari, by Renoir. 3 l, Self portrait, by Van Gogh.

1991, Apr. 1 *Perf. 13*

3603	A1400	20s	multicolored	1.10	.35
3604	A1400	43s	multicolored	.25	.25
3605	A1400	62s	multicolored	.25	.25
3606	A1400	67s	multicolored	.25	.25
3607	A1400	80s	multicolored	.40	.35
3608	A1400	2 l	multicolored	1.10	.35
			Nos. 3603-3608 (6)	3.35	1.80

Miniature Sheet

3609	A1400	3 l	multicolored	2.00	1.50

Swiss Confederation, 700th Anniv. — A1401

1991, Apr. 11

3610	A1401	62s	multicolored	.60	.35

Philatelic Review, Cent. — A1402

1991, May 7 **Litho.** *Perf. 13*

3611	A1402	30s	multicolored	.25	.25

Europa — A1403

1991, May 10 *Perf. 13x13½*

3612	A1403	43s	Meteosat	*.70*	*.40*
3613	A1403	62s	Ariane rocket	*1.00*	*.55*

Horses — A1404

5s, Przewalski's horse. 10s, Tarpan. 25s, Arabian. 35s, Arabian. 42s, Shetland pony. 60s, Draft horse.

1991, May 21 *Perf. 13x12½*

3614	A1404	5s	multi	.25	.25
3615	A1404	10s	multi	.25	.25
3616	A1404	25s	multi	.25	.25
3617	A1404	35s	multi	.25	.25
3618	A1404	42s	multi	.30	.25
3619	A1404	60s	multi	.70	.35
a.			Min. sheet of 6, #3614-3619	2.50	1.50
			Nos. 3614-3619 (6)	2.00	1.60

EXPO 91, Plovdiv — A1405

1991, June 6 **Litho.** *Perf. 13½x13*

3620	A1405	30s	multicolored	.25	.25

Wolfgang Amadeus Mozart
A1406

1991, July 2 *Perf. 13*

3621	A1406	62s	multicolored	.50	.30

Space Shuttle Missions, 10th Anniv.
A1407

12s, Columbia. 32s, Challenger. 50s, Discovery. 86s, Atlantis, vert. 1.50 l, Buran, vert. 2 l, Atlantis, diff., vert.
3 l, US shuttle, earth.

1991, July 23 **Litho.** *Perf. 13*

3622	A1407	12s	multi	.25	.25
3623	A1407	32s	multi	.25	.25
3624	A1407	50s	multi	.40	.25
3625	A1407	86s	multi	.40	.25
3626	A1407	1.50 l	multi	1.10	.30
3627	A1407	2 l	multi	1.10	.35
			Nos. 3622-3627 (6)	3.50	1.65

Souvenir Sheet

3628	A1407	3 l	multi	2.00	1.00

No. 3628 exists imperf. Value $6.25.

1992 Winter Olympics, Albertville
A1408

30s, Luge. 43s, Slalom skiing. 67s, Ski jumping. 2 l, Biathlon.
3 l, Two-man bobsled.

1991, Aug. 7 **Litho.** *Perf. 13x13½*

3629	A1408	30s	multi	.25	.25
3630	A1408	43s	multi	.30	.25
3631	A1408	67s	multi	.45	.30
3632	A1408	2 l	multi	1.50	.90
			Nos. 3629-3632 (4)	2.50	1.70

Souvenir Sheet

3633	A1408	3 l	multi	2.00	1.00

No. 3633 exists imperf. Value $6.50.

Sheraton Sofia Hotel Balkan
A1409

1991, Sept. 6 **Litho.** *Perf. 13*

3634	A1409	62s	multicolored	.40	.30

Printed in sheets of 3 + 3 labels.

Dogs — A1410

30s, Japanese. 43s, Chihuahua. 62s, Pinscher. 80s, Yorkshire terrier. 1 l, Chinese. 3 l, Pug.

1991, Oct. 11 *Perf. 13x13½*

3635	A1410	30s	multi	.25	.25
3636	A1410	43s	multi	.25	.25
3637	A1410	62s	multi	.40	.25
3638	A1410	80s	multi	.40	.25
3639	A1410	1 l	multi	.55	.35
3640	A1410	3 l	multi	1.50	.75
a.			Min. sheet of 6, #3635-3640	4.00	2.75
			Nos. 3635-3640 (6)	3.35	2.10

Cologne '91, Intl. Philatelic Exhibition
A1411

1991, Oct. 21 *Perf. 13*

3641	A1411	86s	multicolored	.60	.45

Printed in sheets of 3 + 3 labels.

Souvenir Sheet

Brandenburg Gate, Bicent. — A1412

1991, Oct. 23

3642	A1412	4 l	multicolored	1.75	1.75

Exists imperf. Value $7.50.

Phila Nippon '91
A1413

1991, Nov. 11

3643	A1413	62s	Japan #1	.45	.35

Printed in sheets of 3 + 3 labels.

Bulgarian Railroad, 125th Anniv. — A1414

1991, Nov. 30

3644	A1414	30s	Locomotive	.25	.25
3645	A1414	30s	Passenger car	.25	.25

Medicinal Plants — A1415

Designs: 30s, Pulsatilla vernalis. 40s, Pulsatilla pratensis. 55s, Pulsatilla halleri. 60s, Aquilegia nigricans. 1 l, Hippophae rhamnoides. 2 l, Ribes nigrum.

1991, Nov. 20 **Litho.** *Perf. 13*

3646	A1415	30s	+15s label	.25	.25
3647	A1415	40s	multicolored	.25	.25
3648	A1415	55s	multicolored	.25	.25
3649	A1415	60s	multicolored	.25	.25
3650	A1415	1 l	multicolored	.40	.25
3651	A1415	2 l	multicolored	.80	.30
a.			Min. sheet of 6, #3646-3651	2.50	1.00
			Nos. 3646-3651 (6)	2.20	1.55

No. 3646 printed se-tenant with label. No. 3651a sold for 5 l, but does not contain the 15s label printed with No. 3646.

Basketball, Cent. A1416

1991, Dec. 6 *Perf. 13½x13*

3652 A1416 43s Ball below rim .25 .25
3653 A1416 62s Ball at rim .30 .25
3654 A1416 90s Ball in cylinder .35 .25
3655 A1416 1 l Ball in basket .45 .30
Nos. 3652-3655 (4) 1.35 1.05

El Greco, 450th Birth Anniv. — A1417

Paintings: 43s, Christ Carrying the Cross. 50s, Holy Family with St. Anne. 60s, St. John the Evangelist and St. John the Baptist. 62s, St. Andrew and St. Francis. 1 l, Holy Family with St. Mary Magdalene. 2 l, Cardinal Nino de Guevara. 3 l, Holy Family with St. Anne (detail).

1991, Dec. 13 *Perf. 13*

3656 A1417 43s multicolored .25 .25
3657 A1417 50s multicolored .25 .25
3658 A1417 60s multicolored .30 .25
3659 A1417 62s multicolored .35 .25
3660 A1417 1 l multicolored .45 .25
3661 A1417 2 l multicolored .75 .25
Nos. 3656-3661 (6) 2.35 1.50

Souvenir Sheet

3662 A1417 3 l multicolored 1.25 .75

No. 3662 contains one 43x53mm stamp.

Christmas — A1418

30s, Snowman, candle, bell, heart. 62s, Star, angel, flower, house, tree.

1991, Dec. 18

3663 A1418 30s multicolored .25 .25
3664 A1418 62s multicolored .30 .25

Marine Mammals — A1419

Designs: 30s, Phogophoca graenlandica. 43s, Orcinus orca. 62s, Odobenus rosmarus. 68s, Tursiops truncatus. 1 l, Monachus monachus. 2 l, Phocaena phocaena.

1991, Dec. 24

3665 A1419 30s multicolored .25 .25
3666 A1419 43s multicolored .25 .25
3667 A1419 62s multicolored .25 .25
3668 A1419 68s multicolored .25 .25
3669 A1419 1 l multicolored .45 .25
3670 A1419 2 l multicolored .75 .30
a. Min. sheet of #3665-3670 2.10 .75
Nos. 3665-3670 (6) 2.20 1.55

Settlement of Jews in Bulgaria, 500th Anniv. — A1420

1992, Mar. 5 **Litho.** *Perf. 13*

3671 A1420 1 l multicolored .40 .25

Gioacchino Rossini (1792-1868), Composer — A1421

1992, Mar. 11

3672 A1421 50s multicolored .25 .25

Plovdiv Fair, Cent. A1422

1992, Mar. 25

3673 A1422 1 l buff & black .40 .25

Fiat Croma — A1423

Automobiles.

1992, Mar. 26 *Perf. 13½x13*

3674 A1423 30s Volvo 740 .25 .25
3675 A1423 45s Ford Escort .25 .25
3676 A1423 50s shown .25 .25
3677 A1423 50s Mercedes 600 .25 .25
3678 A1423 1 l Peugeot 605 .55 .25
3679 A1423 2 l BMW 316 1.00 .30
Nos. 3674-3679 (6) 2.55 1.55

Francisco de Orellana A1424

Explorers: No. 3681, Vespucci. No. 3682, Magellan. No. 3683, Gonzalo Jimenez de Quesada (1500-1579). 2 l, Drake. 3 l, Pedro de Valdivia (1500-1553). 4 l, Columbus.

1992, Apr. 22 **Litho.** *Perf. 13*

3680 A1424 50s multicolored .25 .25
3681 A1424 50s multicolored .25 .25
3682 A1424 1 l multicolored .35 .25
3683 A1424 1 l multicolored .45 .25
3684 A1424 2 l multicolored .75 .35
3685 A1424 3 l multicolored 1.10 .35
Nos. 3680-3685 (6) 3.15 1.70

Souvenir Sheet

3686 A1424 4 l multicolored 1.75 1.00

Granada '92 A1425

1992, Apr. 23

3687 A1425 62s multicolored .30 .30

No. 3687 printed in sheets of 3 + 3 labels.

Discovery of America, 500th Anniv. — A1426

1992, Apr. 24

3688 1 l Ships, map .90 .45
3689 2 l Columbus, ship 1.75 .65
a. A1426 Pair, #3688-3689 3.00 1.50

Europa.

SOS Children's Village A1427

1992, June 15 **Litho.** *Perf. 13*

3690 A1427 1 l multicolored .45 .25

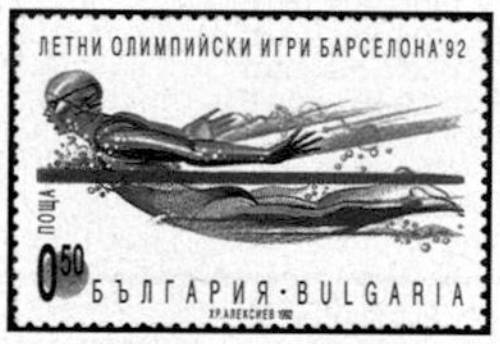

1992 Summer Olympics, Barcelona — A1428

1992, July 15 *Perf. 13½x13*

3691 A1428 50s Swimming .25 .25
3692 A1428 50s Long jump .25 .25
3693 A1428 1 l High jump .35 .25
3694 A1428 3 l Gymnastics 1.10 .35
Nos. 3691-3694 (4) 1.95 1.10

Souvenir Sheet

Perf. 13x13½

3695 A1428 4 l Torch, vert. 1.50 1.00

Motorcycles — A1429

Designs: 30s, 1902 Laurin & Klement. No. 3697, 1928 Puch 200 Luxus. No. 3698, 1931 Norton CS1. 70s, 1950 Harley Davidson. 1 l, 1986 Gilera SP 01. 2 l, 1990 BMW K1.

1992, July 30 *Perf. 13*

3696 A1429 30s multicolored .25 .25
3697 A1429 50s multicolored .25 .25
3698 A1429 50s multicolored .25 .25
3699 A1429 70s multicolored .45 .25
3700 A1429 1 l multicolored .30 .25
3701 A1429 2 l multicolored .85 .30
Nos. 3696-3701 (6) 2.35 1.55

Genoa '92 Intl. Philatelic Exhibition A1430

1992, Sept. 18 *Perf. 13*

3702 A1430 1 l multicolored .45 .25

This is a developing set. Numbers may change.

Insects A1431

1 l, Dragonfly. 2 l, Mayfly. 3 l, Locust. 4 l, Stag beetle. 5 l, Carrion beetle. 7 l, Ant. 20 l, Bee. 50 l, Praying mantis.

1992 **Litho.** *Perf. 14x13½*

3710 A1431 1 l multi *.25*
3711 A1431 2 l multi *.45*
3712 A1431 3 l multi *.55*
3713 A1431 4 l multi *.80*
3714 A1431 5 l multi *1.00*
3715 A1431 7 l multi *1.50*
3716 A1431 20 l multi *3.50*
3717 A1431 50 l multi *10.50*
Nos. 3710-3717 (8) *18.55*

Issued: 7, 20 l, 9/25; 3, 50 l, 11/30; 1, 2, 4, 5 l, 12/15/93.

A1432

1992, Sept. 30 *Perf. 13*

3719 A1432 1 l blk, pink & rose .45 .25

Higher Institute of Architecture and Building, 50th anniv.

Trees — A1433

No. 3720, Quercus mestensis. No. 3721, Aesculus hippocastanum. No. 3722, Quercus thracica. No. 3723, Pinus peuce. 2 l, Acer heldreichii. 3 l, Pyrus bulgarica.

1992, Oct. 16 **Litho.** *Perf. 13*

3720 A1433 50s multicolored .25 .25
3721 A1433 50s multicolored .25 .25
3722 A1433 1 l multicolored .35 .25
3723 A1433 1 l multicolored .35 .25
3724 A1433 2 l multicolored .85 .25
3725 A1433 3 l multicolored 1.10 .30
Nos. 3720-3725 (6) 3.15 1.55

Ethnographical Museum, Cent. — A1434

1992, Oct. 23

3726 A1434 1 l multicolored .45 .25

Tanker Bulgaria — A1435

30s, Freighter Bulgaria. 50s, Castor. 1 l, Hero of Sevastopol. 2 l, Aleko Constantinov. 3 l, Varna.

1992, Oct. 30 Litho. *Perf. 13*

3727	A1435 30s multicolored		.25	.25
3728	A1435 50s multicolored		.25	.25
3729	A1435 1 l multicolored		.45	.25
3730	A1435 2 l shown		.45	.25
3731	A1435 2 l multicolored		.45	.25
3732	A1435 3 l multicolored		1.10	.45
	Nos. 3727-3732 (6)		2.95	1.70

Bulgarian Merchant Fleet, Cent.

Bulgaria, Member of the Council of Europe — A1436

1992, Nov. 6 Litho. *Perf. 13*

3733 A1436 7 l multicolored 2.50 1.50

Souvenir Sheet

4th World Congress of Popular Sports, Varna — A1437

1992, Nov. 17 Litho. *Perf. 13*

3734 A1437 4 l multicolored *1.50* 1.50

Christmas A1438

1992, Dec. 1 *Perf. 13½x13*

3735	A1438 1 l Santa Claus	.40	.25
3736	A1438 7 l Madonna & Child	2.25	.90

Wild Cats — A1439

No. 3737, Panthera pardus. No. 3738, Acinonyx jubatus. No. 3739, Panthera onca. No. 3740, Panthera tigris. No. 3741, Felis concolor. No. 3742, Panthera leo.

1992, Dec. 18 Litho. *Perf. 13*

3737	A1439 50s multicolored	*.25*	.25
3738	A1439 50s multicolored	*.25*	.25
3739	A1439 1 l multicolored	*.45*	.25
3740	A1439 2 l multicolored	*.90*	.40
3741	A1439 2 l multicolored	*.90*	.40
3742	A1439 3 l multicolored	*1.20*	.45
	Nos. 3737-3742 (6)	*3.95*	2.00

Sports A1440

1992, Dec. 18

3743	A1440 50s Baseball	*.25*	.25
3744	A1440 50s Cricket	*.25*	.25
3745	A1440 1 l Polo	*.50*	.25
3746	A1440 1 l Harness racing	*.50*	.25
3747	A1440 2 l Field hockey	*.80*	.45
3748	A1440 3 l Football	*1.20*	.60
	Nos. 3743-3748 (6)	*3.50*	2.05

Owls A1441

No. 3749, Aegolius funereus. No. 3750, Strix aluco. No. 3751, Asio otus. No. 3752, Otus scops. No. 3753, Asio flammeus. No. 3754, Tyto alba.

1992, Dec. 23

3749	A1441 30s multi	*.25*	.25
3750	A1441 50s multi	*.25*	.25
3751	A1441 1 l multi	*.45*	.25
3752	A1441 2 l multi	*.90*	.35
3753	A1441 2 l multi	*.90*	.35
3754	A1441 3 l multi	*1.40*	.45
	Nos. 3749-3754 (6)	*4.15*	1.90

Nos. 3749, 3751, 3753-3754 are vert.

Paintings Depicting History of Bulgaria A1442

Artists: 50s, Dimiter Gyudzhenov. 1 l, 3 l, Nikolai Pavlovich. 2 l, Dimiter Panchev. 4 l, Mito Ganovski.

1992, Dec. 28

3755	A1442 50s multicolored	*.25*	.25
3756	A1442 1 l multicolored	*.45*	.25
3757	A1442 2 l multicolored	*.70*	.35
3758	A1442 3 l multicolored	*1.10*	.45
	Nos. 3755-3758 (4)	*2.50*	1.30

Souvenir Sheet

3759 A1442 4 l multi, vert. *1.50* 1.50

Archeological Museum, Cent. — A1443

1993, Jan. 1 Litho. *Perf. 13x13½*

3760 A1443 1 l multicolored *.45* .25

1993 World Biathlon Championships, Borovetz — A1444

1 l, Woman aiming rifle. 7 l, Skiing.

1993, Feb. 5

3761	A1444 1 l multi	*.35*	.25
3762	A1444 7 l multi	*2.75*	1.20

Neophit Rilski, Birth Bicent. A1445

1993, Apr. 22 Litho. *Perf. 13½x13*

3763 A1445 1 l hen brn & ol bis *.45* .25

Contemporary Art — A1446

Europa: 3 l, Sculpture of centaur, by Georgi Chapkinov. 8 l, Painting of geometric forms, by D. Bujukliski.

1993, Apr. 29 *Perf. 13x13½*

3764	A1446 3 l multicolored	*1.00*	.40
3765	A1446 8 l multicolored	*1.75*	1.00

Fish A1447

No. 3766, C.a.j. bicaudatus. No. 3767, Mollienesia velifera. No. 3768, Aphyosemion bivittatum. No. 3769, Pterophyllum eimekei. No. 3770, Symphysodon discus. No. 3771, Trichogaster leeri.

1993, June 29 Litho. *Perf. 13*

3766	A1447 1 l multicolored	*.25*	.25
3767	A1447 2 l multicolored	*.30*	.25
3768	A1447 3 l multicolored	*.45*	.25
3769	A1447 3 l multicolored	*.45*	.25
3770	A1447 4 l multicolored	*.65*	.25
3771	A1447 8 l multicolored	*1.25*	.45
	Nos. 3766-3771 (6)	*3.35*	1.70

Fruit — A1448

No. 3772, Malus domestica. No. 3773, Pyrus sativa. No. 3774, Persica vulgaris. No. 3775, Cydonia oblonga. No. 3776, Punica granatum. No. 3777, Ficus carica.

1993, July 8 *Perf. 13x13½*

3772	A1448 1 l multicolored	*.25*	.25
3773	A1448 2 l multicolored	*.30*	.25
3774	A1448 2 l multicolored	*.30*	.25
3775	A1448 3 l multicolored	*.45*	.25
3776	A1448 5 l multicolored	*.85*	.25
3777	A1448 7 l multicolored	*1.25*	.35
	Nos. 3772-3777 (6)	*3.40*	1.60

Claudio Monteverdi (1567-1643), Composer — A1449

1993, July 20 Litho. *Perf. 13½x13*

3778 A1449 1 l multicolored *.25* .25

17th World Summer Games for the Deaf A1450

1993, July 20 *Perf. 13*

3779	A1450 1 l shown	*.25*	.25
3780	A1450 2 l Swimming	*.30*	.25
3781	A1450 3 l Cycling	*.55*	.25
3782	A1450 4 l Tennis	*.55*	.25
	Nos. 3779-3782 (4)	*1.65*	1.00

Souvenir Sheet

3783 A1450 5 l Soccer *.75* .75

Miniature Sheet

A1451

Council of Preslav, Cyrillic Alphabet in Bulgaria, 1100th Anniv.: a, Baptism of Christian convert. b, Tsar Boris I (852-889). c, Tsar Simeon (893-927). d, Battle between Bulgarians and Byzantines.

1993, Sept. 16 Litho. *Perf. 13½x13*

3784 A1451 5 l Sheet of 4, #a.-d. *3.00* 3.00

Alexander of Battenberg (1857-93), Prince of Bulgaria — A1452

1993, Sept. 23 *Perf. 13x13½*

3785	A1452	3 l	multicolored	.45	.25

Peter I. Tchaikovsky (1840-93) A1453

1993, Sept. 30 *Perf. 13½x13*

3786	A1453	3 l	multicolored	.45	.25

Small Arms — A1454

No. 3787, Crossbow, 16th cent. No. 3788, Pistol, 18th cent. No. 3789, Luger, 1908. No. 3790, Pistol, 1873. No. 3791, Rifle, 1938. No. 3792, Kalashnikov, 1947.

1993, Oct. 22 Litho. *Perf. 13½x14*

3787	A1454	1 l	multicolored	.25	.25
3788	A1454	2 l	multicolored	.30	.25
3789	A1454	3 l	multicolored	.45	.25
3790	A1454	3 l	multicolored	.45	.25
3791	A1454	5 l	multicolored	.80	.25
3792	A1454	7 l	multicolored	1.10	.45
			Nos. 3787-3792 (6)	3.35	1.70

Isaac Newton (1643-1727) A1455

1993, Oct. 29 *Perf. 13½x13*

3793	A1455	1 l	multicolored	.25	.25

Organized Philately in Bulgaria, Cent. A1456

1993, Nov. 16

3794	A1456	1 l	multicolored	.25	.25

Ecology A1457

1993, Nov. 17

3795	A1457	1 l	shown	.25	.25
3796	A1457	7 l	Ecology	1.10	.45

Game Animals A1458

No. 3797, Anas platrhynchos. No. 3798, Phasianus colchicus. No. 3799, Vulpes vulpes. No. 3800, Capreolus capreolus. No. 3801, Lepus europaeus. No. 3802, Sus scrofa.

1993, Nov. 25

3797	A1458	1 l	multicolored	.25	.25
3798	A1458	1 l	multicolored	.25	.25
3799	A1458	2 l	multicolored	.25	.25
3800	A1458	3 l	multicolored	.40	.25
3801	A1458	6 l	multicolored	.80	.30
3802	A1458	8 l	multicolored	1.20	.50
			Nos. 3797-3802 (6)	3.15	1.80

Christmas A1459

Signs of Zodiac on sundial: No. 3803a, Taurus, Gemini, Cancer. b, Libra, Virgo, Leo.
No. 3804a, Aquarius, Pisces, Aries. b, Capricorn, Sagittarius, Scorpio.

1993, Dec. 1

3803	A1459	1 l	Pair, #a.-b.	.45	.25
3804	A1459	7 l	Pair, #a.-b.	1.75	.70

When placed together, Nos. 3803-3804 form a complete sundial.

Regional Folk Costumes for Men

A1460 A1461

1993, Dec. 16 Litho. *Perf. 13½x14*

3805	A1460	1 l	Sofia	.25	.25
3806	A1461	1 l	Plovdiv	.25	.25
3807	A1460	2 l	Belogradchik	.25	.25
3808	A1460	3 l	Shumen	.30	.25
3809	A1461	3 l	Oryakhovitsa	.30	.25
3810	A1461	8 l	Kurdzhali	.90	.40
			Nos. 3805-3810 (6)	2.25	1.65

1994 Winter Olympics, Lillehammer A1462

1994, Feb. 8 *Perf. 13*

3811	A1462	1 l	Freestlye skiing	.25	.25
3812	A1462	2 l	Speed skating	.25	.25
3813	A1462	3 l	2-Man luge	.40	.25
3814	A1462	4 l	Hockey	.65	.25
			Nos. 3811-3814 (4)	1.55	1.00

Souvenir Sheet

3815	A1462	5 l	Downhill skiing	.65	.65

Nikolai Pavlovich (1835-94) A1463

1994, Feb. 16 *Perf. 13½x13*

3816	A1463	3 l	multicolored	.50	.25

Dinosaurs — A1464

No. 3817, Plesiosaurus. No. 3818, Iguanodon. No. 3819, Archaeopteryx. No. 3820, Edmontonia. No. 3821, Styracosaurus. No. 3822, Tyrannosaurus Rex.

1994, Apr. 27 Litho. *Perf. 13*

3817	A1464	2 l	multi	.25	.25
3818	A1464	3 l	multi	.40	.25
3819	A1464	3 l	multi	.40	.25
3820	A1464	4 l	multi	.50	.30
3821	A1464	5 l	multi	.60	.30
3822	A1464	7 l	multi	.90	.45
			Nos. 3817-3822 (6)	3.05	

1994 World Cup Soccer Championships, US — A1465

Players in championships of: 3 l, Chile, 1962. 6 l, England, 1966. 7 l, Mexico, 1970. 9 l, West Germany, 1974. No. 3827a, Mexico, 1986, vert. b, US, 1994.

1994, Apr. 28

3823	A1465	3 l	multicolored	.35	.25
3824	A1465	6 l	multicolored	.75	.25
3825	A1465	7 l	multicolored	.85	.30
3826	A1465	9 l	multicolored	1.10	.45
			Nos. 3823-3826 (4)	3.05	1.25

Souvenir Sheet

3827	A1465	5 l	Sheet of 2, #a.-b.	1.40	.70

For No. 3827 with inscription reading up along the left margin, see No. 3851.

Europa A1466

European Discoveries: 3 l, Axis of symmetry. 15 l, Electrocardiogram.

1994, Apr. 29 Litho. *Perf. 13½*

3828	A1466	3 l	multicolored	.70	.30
3829	A1466	15 l	multicolored	2.50	1.00

Boris Hristov (1914-93) — A1467

1994, May 18 Litho. *Perf. 13*

3830	A1467	3 l	brown & bister	.40	.25

Cricetus Cricetus A1468

Designs: 3 l, In nest. 7 l, Emerging from burrow. 10 l, Standing on hind legs. 15 l, Finding berry.

1994, Sept. 23 Litho. *Perf. 13*

3831	A1468	3 l	multicolored	.35	.25
3832	A1468	7 l	multicolored	.75	.40
3833	A1468	10 l	multicolored	1.20	.55
3834	A1468	15 l	multicolored	1.75	.85
			Nos. 3831-3834 (4)	4.05	2.05

World Wildlife Fund.

Space Program — A1469

1994, Nov. 4 Litho. *Perf. 13*

3835	A1469	3 l	multicolored	.40	.25

Intl. Olympic Committee, Cent. — A1470

1994, Nov. 7

3836	A1470	3 l	multicolored	.40	.25

Icons — A1471

2 l, Christ. 3 l, Christ, the healer. 5 l, Crucifixion. 7 l, Archangel Michael. 8 l, Sts. Cyril, Methodius. 15 l, Madonna & Child.

1994, Nov. 24 Litho. *Perf. 13x13½*

3837	A1471	2 l	multicolored	.25	.25
3838	A1471	3 l	multicolored	.40	.25
3839	A1471	5 l	multicolored	.40	.25
3840	A1471	7 l	multicolored	.75	.30
3841	A1471	8 l	multicolored	.90	.35
3842	A1471	15 l	multicolored	1.90	.35
			Nos. 3837-3842 (6)	4.60	1.75

Christmas A1472

1994, Dec. 1

3843	A1472	3 l	Ancient coin	.35	.25
3844	A1472	15 l	Coin, diff.	2.00	1.00

Roses A1473

1994, Dec. 12 *Perf. 13*

Color of Rose

3845	A1473	2 l	yellow	.25	.25
3846	A1473	3 l	rose red	.35	.25
3847	A1473	5 l	white	.55	.25
3848	A1473	7 l	salmon	.85	.40
3849	A1473	10 l	carmine	1.20	.40
3850	A1473	15 l	orange & yellow	1.90	.40
			Nos. 3845-3850 (6)	5.10	1.95

No. 3827 with Addtl. Inscription in Left Sheet Margin

1994, Dec. 15 Litho. *Perf. 13*
Souvenir Sheet

3851 A1465 5 l Sheet of 2, #a.-b. *14.00 14.00*

Trams — A1474

1994, Dec. 29

3852 A1474 1 l Model 1912 .25 .25
3853 A1474 2 l Model 1928 .25 .25
3854 A1474 3 l Model 1931 .35 .25
3855 A1474 5 l Model 1942 .55 .25
3856 A1474 8 l Model 1951 1.10 .45
3857 A1474 10 l Model 1961 1.20 .50
Nos. 3852-3857 (6) 3.70 1.95

Vassil Petleshkov (1845-76), Revolutionary — A1475

1995, Feb. 27 Litho. *Perf. 13½x13*
3858 A1475 3 l multicolored .40 .25

End of World War II, 50th Anniv. — A1476

Europa: 15 l, Dove holding olive branch standing on gun barrel.

1995, May 3 Litho. *Perf. 13*
3859 A1476 3 l multicolored .75 .35
3860 A1476 15 l multicolored 2.50 1.00

Men's World Volleyball League, Cent. — A1477

Designs: a, 10 l, Player digging ball. b, 15 l, Player spiking ball, vert.

1995, May 25 Litho. *Perf. 13*
3861 A1477 Sheet of 2, #a.-b. *2.75* 1.25

Souvenir Sheet

European Nature Conservation Year — A1478

Designs: a, 10 l, Pancratium maritimum. b, 15 l, Aquila heliaca.

1995, June 23 Litho. *Perf. 13*
3862 A1478 Sheet of 2, #a.-b. 3.00 3.00

Antarctic Wildlife — A1479

1 l, Euphausia superba. 2 l, Chaenocephalus. 3 l, Physeter catodon. 5 l, Leptonychotes weddelli. 8 l, Stercorarius skua. 10 l, Aptenodytes forsteri, vert.

1995, June 29

3863 A1479 1 l multicolored .25 .25
3864 A1479 2 l multicolored .25 .25
3865 A1479 3 l multicolored .30 .25
3866 A1479 5 l multicolored .55 .25
3867 A1479 8 l multicolored .90 .45
3868 A1479 10 l multicolored 1.10 .55
Nos. 3863-3868 (6) 3.35 2.00

Stephan Stambolov (1854-95), Revolutionary Leader, Politician — A1480

1995, July 6 Litho. *Perf. 13*
3869 A1480 3 l multicolored .40 .25

1996 Summer Olympics, Atlanta A1481

Designs: 3 l, Pole vault. 7 l, High jump. 10 l, Women's long jump. 15 l, Track.

1995, July 17

3870 A1481 3 l multicolored .30 .25
3871 A1481 7 l multicolored .70 .35
3872 A1481 10 l multicolored 1.10 .35
3873 A1481 15 l multicolored 1.60 .35
Nos. 3870-3873 (4) 3.70 1.30

Legumes — A1482

No. 3874, Pisum sativum. No. 3875, Glicine. No. 3876, Cicer arietinum. No. 3877, Spinacia oleracea. No. 3878, Arachis hypogaea. No. 3879, Lens esculenta.

1995, July 31

3874 A1482 2 l multicolored .55 .35
3875 A1482 3 l multicolored .25 .25
3876 A1482 3 l multicolored .25 .25
3877 A1482 4 l multicolored .55 .30
3878 A1482 5 l multicolored .55 .30
3879 A1482 15 l multicolored 1.50 .40
Nos. 3874-3879 (6) 3.65 1.85

Organized Tourism in Bulgaria, Cent. — A1483

1995, Aug. 21 Litho. *Perf. 13*
3880 A1483 3 l multicolored .40 .25

Vassil Zahariev (1895-1971), Graphic Artist — A1484

Designs: 2 l, Woodcut of a man. 3 l, Woodcut of building in valley. 5 l, Self-portrait. 10 l, Carving of two women.

1995, Sept. 4 Litho. *Perf. 13*
3881 A1484 2 l multicolored .25 .25
3882 A1484 3 l multicolored .35 .25
3883 A1484 5 l multicolored .55 .30
3884 A1484 10 l multicolored 1.10 .55
Nos. 3881-3884 (4) 2.25 1.35

UN, 50th Anniv. A1485

1995, Sept. 12
3885 A1485 3 l multicolored .40 .25

Airplanes — A1486

1995, Sept. 26 Litho. *Perf. 13*
3886 A1486 3 l PO-2 .30 .25
3887 A1486 5 l Li-2 .55 .25
3888 A1486 7 l JU52-3M .75 .35
3889 A1486 10 l FV-58 1.10 .35
Nos. 3886-3889 (4) 2.70 1.20

Motion Pictures, Cent. — A1487

Designs: 2 l, Charlie Chaplin, Mickey Mouse. 3 l, Marilyn Monroe, Marlene Dietrich. 5 l, Humphrey Bogart. 8 l, Sophia Loren, Liza Minnelli. 10 l, Toshiro Mifune. 15 l, Katya Paskaleva.

1995, Oct. 16

3890 A1487 2 l multicolored .25 .25
3891 A1487 3 l multicolored .30 .25
3892 A1487 5 l multicolored .40 .25
3893 A1487 8 l multicolored 1.00 .25
3894 A1487 10 l multicolored 1.10 .25
3895 A1487 15 l multicolored 1.50 .50
Nos. 3890-3895 (6) 4.55 1.75

Minerals A1488

1995, Nov. 20 Litho. *Perf. 13*
3896 A1488 1 l Agate .25 .25
3897 A1488 2 l Sphalerite .25 .25
3898 A1488 5 l Calcite .60 .25
3899 A1488 7 l Quartz .75 .25
3900 A1488 8 l Pyromorphite .90 .25
3901 A1488 10 l Almandine 1.20 .40
Nos. 3896-3901 (6) 3.95 1.65

Christmas A1489

1995, Dec. 8 Litho. *Perf. 13*
3902 A1489 3 l shown .40 .25
3903 A1489 15 l Magi 1.90 .25

Southern Fruit, by Cyril Tsonev (1896-1961) — A1490

1996, Jan. 25 Litho. *Perf. 13*
3904 A1490 3 l multicolored .40 .25

Martin Luther (1483-1546) — A1491

1996, Feb. 5

3905 A1491 3 l multicolored *.40* .25

Historic Buildings A1492

Monasteries: 3 l, Preobragenie. 5 l, Arapovsky. 10 1, Drianovo. 20 l, Bachkovo. 25 l, Troyan. 40 l, Zografski.

1996, Feb. 28 ***Perf. 14x13½***

3906 A1492 3 l green *.25* .25
3907 A1492 5 l red *.25* .25
3908 A1492 10 l blue *.30* .25
3909 A1492 20 l yellow orange *.75* .30
3910 A1492 25 l brown *.90* .40
3911 A1492 40 l purple *1.50* .65
Nos. 3906-3911 (6) *3.95* 2.10

5th Meeting of European Bank for Reconstruction and Development A1493

1996, Apr. 15 **Litho.** ***Perf. 13***

3912 A1493 7 l shown *.35* .25
3913 A1493 30 l Building, diff. *1.25* .50

Conifers A1494

Designs: 5 l, Taxus baccata. 8 l, Abies alba. 10 l, Picea abies. 20 l, Pinus silvestris. 25 l, Pinus heldreichii. 40 l, Juniperus excelsa.

1996, Apr. 23 ***Perf. 13½x13***

3914 A1494 5 l multicolored *.25* .25
3915 A1494 8 l multicolored *.30* .25
3916 A1494 10 l multicolored *.40* .25
3917 A1494 20 l multicolored *.75* .25
3918 A1494 25 l multicolored *.90* .25
3919 A1494 40 l multicolored *1.50* .50
Nos. 3914-3919 (6) *4.10* 1.75

A1495

10 l, People in distress. 40 l, Khristo Botev (1848-1876), poet, patriot, horiz.

1996, May 1 ***Perf. 13***

3920 A1495 10 l multicolored *.40* .25
3921 A1495 40 l multicolored *1.60* .85

April Uprising, death of Khristo Botev, 120th anniv.

A1496

Uniforms: 5 l, Light brown dress uniform. 8 l, Brown combat, helmet. 10 l, Brown uniform, holding gun with fixed bayonet. 20 l, Early red, blue dress uniform. 25 l, Officer's early green dress uniform. 40 l, Soldier's green uniform.

1996, May 6

3922 A1496 5 l multicolored *.90* .25
3923 A1496 8 l multicolored *.25* .25
3924 A1496 10 l multicolored *.25* .25
3925 A1496 20 l multicolored *.60* .30
3926 A1496 25 l multicolored *.75* .35
3927 A1496 40 l multicolored *1.20* .50
Nos. 3922-3927 (6) *3.95* 1.90

Republic of Bulgaria, 50th Anniv. — A1497

1996, May 13 **Litho.** ***Perf. 13½***

3928 A1497 10 l multicolored *.35* .25

Famous Women A1498

Europa: 10 l, Elisaveta Bagriana (1893-1990), poet. 40 l, Katia Popova (1924-66), opera singer.

1996, May 29 **Litho.** ***Perf. 13***

3929 A1498 10 l multicolored *1.25* .75
Complete booklet, 5 #3929 *8.25*
3930 A1498 40 l multicolored *2.00* 1.00
Complete booklet, 5 #3930 *12.00*

Souvenir Sheet

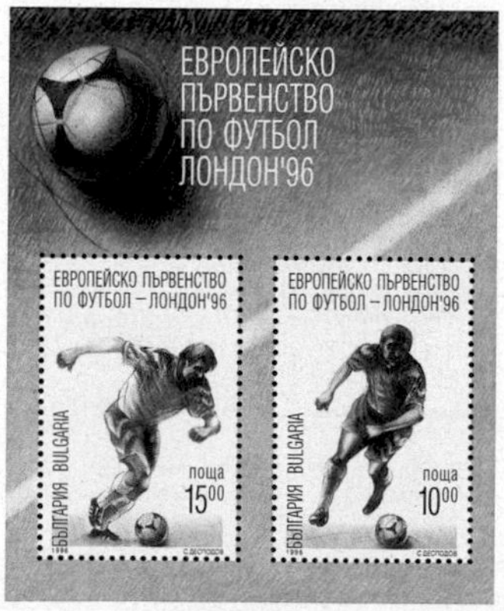

A1499

10 l, Soccer player. 15 l, Soccer player, diff.

1996, June 4

3931 A1499 Sheet of 2, #a.-b. *1.75* .85

Euro '96, European Soccer Championships, Great Britain.

A1500

5 l, Wrestling. 8 l, Boxing. 10 l, Women's shot put. 25 l, Women sculling. 15 l, Pierre de Coubertin.

1996, July 4

3932 A1500 5 l multicolored *.25* .25
3933 A1500 8 l multicolored *.30* .25
3934 A1500 10 l multicolored *.50* .25
3935 A1500 25 l multicolored *1.00* .35
Nos. 3932-3935 (4) *2.05* 1.10

Souvenir Sheet

3936 A1500 15 l multicolored *1.00* .75

1996 Summer Olympic Games, Atlanta. Olymphilex '96 (No. 3936).

Crabs A1501

Designs: 5 l, Gammarus arduus. 10 l, Asellus aquaticus. 12 l, Astacus astacus. 25 l, Palaemon serratus. 30 l, Cumella limicola. 40 l, Carcinus mediterraneus.

1996, July 30

3937 A1501 5 l multicolored *2.00* .75
3938 A1501 10 l multicolored *.35* .25
3939 A1501 12 l multicolored *.35* .25
3940 A1501 25 l multicolored *.35* .25
3941 A1501 30 l multicolored *.35* .25
3942 A1501 40 l multicolored *.35* .25
Nos. 3937-3942 (6) *3.75* 2.00

Francisco Goya (1746-1828) A1502

Entire paintings or details: 8 l, Young Woman with a Letter. 26 l, The Third of May, 1808. 40 l, Neighboring Women on a Balcony.
No. 3947: a, 10 l, The Clothed Maja. b, 15 l, The Naked Maja.

1996, July 9 **Litho.** ***Perf. 13***

3943 A1502 5 l multicolored *.25* .25
3944 A1502 8 l multicolored *.40* .25
3945 A1502 26 l multicolored *1.00* .45
3946 A1502 40 l multicolored *1.50* .75
Nos. 3943-3946 (4) *3.15* 1.70

Souvenir Sheet

Perf. 13½x13

3947 A1502 Sheet of 2, #a.-b. *1.25* 1.25

No. 3947 contains two 54x29mm stamps.

Souvenir Sheet

St. John of Rila (876-946), Founder of Rila Monastery — A1503

1996, Sept. 3

3948 A1503 10 l multicolored *.65* .65

Bulgarian Renaissance Houses A1504

Various multi-level houses.

1996, Sept. 12 **Litho.** ***Perf. 14x13½***

Background Color

3949 A1504 10 l buff *.25* .25
3950 A1504 15 l orange yellow *.30* .25
3951 A1504 30 l yellow green *.60* .25
3952 A1504 50 l red lilac *1.10* .25
3953 A1504 60 l apple green *1.40* .75
3954 A1504 100 l green blue *2.25* 1.10
Nos. 3949-3954 (6) *5.90* 2.85

Steam Locomotives — A1505

1996, Sept. 24 ***Perf. 13***

3955 A1505 5 l 1836 *.25* .25
3956 A1505 10 l 1847 *.40* .25
3957 A1505 12 l 1848 *.50* .25
3958 A1505 26 l 1876 *1.00* .35
Nos. 3955-3958 (4) *2.15* 1.10

Natl. Gallery of Art, Cent. A1506

1996, Oct. 14 **Litho.** ***Perf. 13***

3959 A1506 15 l multicolored *.60* .25

Defeat of Byzantine Army by Tsar Simeon, 1100th Anniv. — A1507

10 l, Sword hilt, soldiers on horseback. 40 l, Sword blade, dagger, fallen soldiers.

1996, Oct. 21

3960 A1507 10 l multicolored .40 .25
3961 A1507 40 l multicolored 1.60 .25
a. Pair, #3960-3961 2.00 2.00

No. 3961 is a continuous design.

UNICEF, 50th Anniv. — A1508

Children's drawings: 7 l, Diver, fish. 15 l, Circus performers. 20 l, Boy, artist's pallete. 60 l, Women seated at table.

1996, Nov. 18 Litho. ***Perf. 13***

3962 A1508 7 l multicolored .30 .25
3963 A1508 15 l multicolored .60 .30
3964 A1508 20 l multicolored .85 .35
3965 A1508 60 l multicolored 2.50 1.20
Nos. 3962-3965 (4) 4.25 2.10

Christmas A1509

1996, Nov. 26

3966 A1509 15 l Candles on tree .50 .25
3967 A1509 60 l Church 2.10 1.00

A1510

Painting of Old Bulgarian Town, by Tsanko Lavrenov (1896-1978).

1996, Dec. 11 Litho. ***Perf. 13***

3968 A1510 15 l multicolored .50 .25

Puppies A1511

1997, Feb. 25 Litho. ***Perf. 13***

3969 A1511 5 l Pointer .25 .25
3970 A1511 7 l Chow chow .25 .25
3971 A1511 25 l Carakachan dog .80 .30
3972 A1511 50 l Basset hound 1.60 .65
Nos. 3969-3972 (4) 2.90 1.45

Alexander Graham Bell (1847-1922) — A1512

1997, Mar. 10

3973 A1512 30 l multicolored .65 .35

Ivan Milev (1897-1927), Painter — A1513

Paintings: 5 l, Boy drinking from jar. 15 l, Person with head bowed holding up hand. 30 l, Woman. 60 l, Woman carrying child.

1997, Mar. 20

3974 A1513 5 l multicolored .25 .25
3975 A1513 15 l multicolored .25 .25
3976 A1513 30 l multicolored .60 .25
3977 A1513 60 l multicolored 1.50 .45
Nos. 3974-3977 (4) 2.60 1.20

Stories and Legends — A1514

Europa: 120 l, "March" lady in folk costume, symbol of spring. 600 l, St. George.

1997, Apr. 14

3978 A1514 120 l multicolored 1.25 .75
3979 A1514 600 l multicolored 1.00 .75

Konstantin Kissimov (1897-1965), Actor — A1515

1997, Apr. 16

3980 A1515 120 l multicolored .25 .25

A1516

1997, Apr. 21

3981 A1516 60 l multicolored .25 .25

Heinrich von Stephan (1831-97).

A1517

Historical Landmarks: 80 l, Nessebar. 200 l, Ivanovo Rock Churches. 300 l, Boyana Church. 500 l, Madara horseman. 600 l, Tomb of Sveshtari. 1000 l, Tomb of Kazanlak.

1997, May 2 ***Perf. 13½***

3982 A1517 80 l brn & multi .25 .25
3983 A1517 200 l pur & multi .25 .25
3984 A1517 300 l bis & multi .30 .25
3985 A1517 500 l grn & multi .45 .25
3986 A1517 600 l yel & multi .75 .30
3987 A1517 1000 l org & multi 1.00 .40
Nos. 3982-3987 (6) 3.00 1.70

Composers — A1518

Designs: a, Gaetano Donizetti (1797-1848). b, Franz Schubert (1797-1828). c, Felix Mendelssohn (1809-1847). d, Johannes Brahms (1833-1897).

1997, May 29 Litho. ***Perf. 13½x13***

3988 A1518 120 l Sheet of 4, #a.-d. 1.50 1.10

Plants in Bulgaria's Red Book — A1519

Designs: 80 l, Trifolium rubens. 100 l, Tulipa hageri. 120 l, Inula spiraeifolia. 200 l, Paeonia tenuifolia.

1997, June 24 ***Perf. 13***

3989 A1519 80 l multicolored .25 .25
3990 A1519 100 l multicolored .25 .25
3991 A1519 120 l multicolored .25 .25
3992 A1519 200 l multicolored .75 .25
Nos. 3989-3992 (4) 1.50 1.00

A1520

1997, June 29 Litho. ***Perf. 13***

3993 A1520 120 l multicolored .25 .25

Civil aviation in Bulgaria, 50th anniv.

A1521

1997, July 3

3994 A1521 120 l multicolored .25 .25

Evlogy Georgiev (1819-97), banker, philanthopist.

Sofia '97, Modern Pentathlon World Championship — A1522

60 l, Equestrian cross-country, running. 80 l, Fencing, swimming. 100 l, Running, women's fencing. 120 l, Men's shooting, diving. 200 l, Equestrian jumping, women's shooting.

1997, July 25

3995 A1522 60 l multicolored .40 .35
3996 A1522 80 l multicolored .40 .35
3997 A1522 100 l multicolored .40 .35
3998 A1522 120 l multicolored .40 .35
3999 A1522 200 l multicolored .40 .35
Nos. 3995-3999 (5) 2.00 1.75

City of Moscow, 850th Anniv. — A1523

1997, July 30

4000 A1523 120 l multicolored .60 .60

No. 4000 is printed se-tenant with label for Moscow '97 Intl. Philatelic Exhibition.

Diesel Engine, Cent. A1524

1997, Sept. 8 Litho. ***Perf. 13½x13***

4001 A1524 80 l Boat .25 .25
4002 A1524 100 l Tractor .25 .25
4003 A1524 120 l Truck .50 .25
4004 A1524 200 l Forklift .80 .25
Nos. 4001-4004 (4) 1.80 1.00

43rd General Assembly of Atlantic Club of Bulgaria — A1525

Designs: a, Goddess Tyche. b, Eagle on sphere. c, Building, lion statue, denomination UL. d, Building, denomination UR.

1997, Oct. 2 ***Perf. 13***

4005 A1525 120 l Sheet of 4, #a.-d. 1.25 .90

Miguel de Cervantes (1547-1616) — A1526

1997, Oct. 15

4006 A1526 120 l multicolored .45 .45

Asen Raztsvetnikov (1897-1951), Poet, Writer — A1527

1997, Nov. 5

4007 A1527 120 l multicolored .25 .25

Tsar Samuel (d. 1014), Ascension to Throne, 1000th Anniv. A1528

1997, Nov. 18 *Perf. 13½x13*

4008	A1528	120 l	Inscription	*.25*	.25
4009	A1528	600 l	Tsar, soldiers	*1.50*	.65
a.			Pair, #4008-4009	*1.75*	.90

Christmas A1529

Designs: 120 l, Snow-covered houses, stars inside shape of Christmas tree, animals. 600 l, Nativity scene.

1997, Dec. 8 *Perf. 13x13½*

4010	A1529	120 l	multicolored	*.35*	.25
4011	A1529	600 l	multicolored	*1.40*	.65

1998 Winter Olympic Games, Nagano A1530

Designs: 60 l, Speed skating. 80 l, Skiing. 120 l, Biathlon. 600 l, Pairs figure skating.

1997, Dec. 17 *Perf. 13½x13*

4012	A1530	60 l	multicolored	*.25*	.25
4013	A1530	80 l	multicolored	*.25*	.25
4014	A1530	120 l	multicolored	*.25*	.25
4015	A1530	600 l	multicolored	*1.75*	1.00
			Nos. 4012-4015 (4)	*2.50*	1.75

For overprint see No. 4029.

Coat of Arms of Bulgaria A1531

1997, Dec. 22 **Litho.** *Perf. 13½x13*

4016	A1531	120 l	multicolored	*.25*	.25

Souvenir Sheet

Bulgarian Space Program, 25th Anniv. — A1532

1997, Dec. 22 *Perf. 13*

4017	A1532	120 l	multicolored	*.85*	.85

Christo Botev (1848-76), Revolutionary, Poet — A1533

1998, Jan. 6 **Litho.** *Perf. 13*

4018	A1533	120 l	multicolored	*.25*	.25

Bertolt Brecht (1898-1956), Playwright A1534

1998, Feb. 10

4019	A1534	120 l	multicolored	*.25*	.25

Bulgarian Telegraph Agency, Cent. A1535

1998, Feb. 13

4020	A1535	120 l	multicolored	*.25*	.25

Illustrations by Alexander Bozhinov (1878-1968) A1536

Designs: a, Bird wearing bonnet. b, Black bird wearing hat. c, Grandfather Frost, children. d, Girl among flowers looking upward at rain.

1998, Feb. 24 *Perf. 13½x13*

4021	A1536	120 l	Sheet of 4, #a.-d.	*1.25*	.50

Prince Alexander A1537

1998, Feb. 27 *Perf. 13*

4022	A1537	120 l	multicolored	*.25*	.25
4023	A1537	600 l	Monument	*1.40*	.40
a.			Pair, #4022-4023	*1.60*	.80

Bulgarian independence from Turkey, 120th anniv.

Easter — A1538

1998, Mar. 27 **Litho.** *Perf. 13*

4024	A1538	120 l	multicolored	*.25*	.25

Bulgarian Olympic Committee, 75th Anniv. — A1539

1998, Mar. 30

4025	A1539	120 l	multicolored	*.25*	.25

PHARE (Intl. Post and Telecommunications Program) — A1540

1998, Apr. 24 **Litho.** *Perf. 13*

4026	A1540	120 l	multicolored	*.25*	.25

National Days and Festivals — A1541

Europa: 120 l, Girls with flowers, "Enyovden." 600 l, Masked men with bells, "Kukery."

1998, Apr. 27

4027	A1541	120 l	multicolored	*.50*	.25
4028	A1541	600 l	multicolored	*1.75*	1.50

No. 4014 Overprinted

1998, Apr. 29 *Perf. 13½x13*

4029	A1530	120 l	multicolored	*2.25*	1.50

Dante and Virgil in Hell, by Eugene Delacroix (1798-1863) A1542

1998, Apr. 30

4030	A1542	120 l	multicolored	*.25*	.25

A1543

1998, May 15 *Perf. 13*

4031	A1543	120 l	multicolored	*.25*	.25

Soccer Team of Central Sports Club of the Army, 50th anniv.

Cats — A1544

60 l, European tabby. 80 l, Siamese. 120 l, Exotic shorthair. 600 l, Birman.

1998, May 25

4032	A1544	60 l	multicolored	*.25*	.25
4033	A1544	80 l	multicolored	*.25*	.25
4034	A1544	120 l	multicolored	*.25*	.25
4035	A1544	600 l	multicolored	*1.25*	.60
			Nos. 4032-4035 (4)	*2.00*	1.35

Are You Jealous?, by Paul Gauguin (1848-1903) — A1545

1998, June 4

4036	A1545	120 l	multicolored	*.25*	.25

Neophit Hylendarsky-Bozvely (1745-1848), Priest, Author — A1546

1998, June 4

4037	A1546	120 l	multicolored	*.25*	.25

1998 World Cup Soccer Championships, France — A1547

Lion mascot with soccer ball, various stylized soccer plays.

1998, June 10

4038	A1547	60 l	multicolored	*.25*	.25
4039	A1547	80 l	multicolored	*.25*	.25
4040	A1547	120 l	multicolored	*.35*	.25
4041	A1547	600 l	multicolored	*1.60*	.60
			Nos. 4038-4041 (4)	*2.45*	1.35

Souvenir Sheet

4042	A1547	120 l	Mascot, Eiffel Tower	*.75*	.75

A. Aleksandrov's Flight on Mir, 10th Anniv. — A1548

1998, June 17 **Litho.** ***Perf. 13***
4043 A1548 120 l multicolored *.35* .25

Lisbon '98 — A1549

Designs: a, Map showing route around Cape of Good Hope, Vasco da Gama (1460-1524). b, Sailing ship, map of Africa.

1998, June 23
4044 A1549 600 l Sheet of 2, #a.-b. + 2 labels *3.50* 2.25

Helicopters — A1550

80 l, Focke Wulf FW61, 1937. 100 l, Sikorsky R-4, 1943. 120 l, Mil Mi-12 (V-12), 1970. 200 l, McDonnell-Douglas MD-900, 1995.

1998, July 7 **Litho.** ***Perf. 13***
4045 A1550 80 l multicolored *.25* .25
4046 A1550 100 l multicolored *.30* .30
4047 A1550 120 l multicolored *.40* .40
4048 A1550 200 l multicolored *.55* .55
Nos. 4045-4048 (4) *1.50* 1.50

Souvenir Sheet

Intl. Year of the Ocean — A1551

Monachus monachus.

1998, July 14 **Litho.** ***Perf. 13***
4049 A1551 120 l multicolored *1.25* *1.00*

Dimitr Talev (1898-1966), Writer — A1552

1998, Sept. 14
4050 A1552 180 l multicolored *.45* *.25*

A1553

1998, Sept. 22
4051 A1553 180 l multicolored *.45* *.25*

Declaration of Bulgarian Independence, 90th anniv.

A1554

Butterflies, flowers. 60 l, Limenitis rodukta, ligularia sibirica. 180 l, Vanessa cardui, anthemis macrantha. 200 l, Vanessa atalanta, trachelium jacquinii. 600 l, Anthocharis gruneri, geranium tuberosum.

1998, Sept. 24
4052 A1554 60 l multicolored *.25* *.25*
4053 A1554 180 l multicolored *.40* *.25*
4054 A1554 200 l multicolored *.50* *.50*
4055 A1554 600 l multicolored *1.60* *1.60*
Nos. 4052-4055 (4) *2.75* *2.60*

Christo Smirnenski (1898-1923), Poet — A1555

1998, Sept. 29
4056 A1555 180 l multicolored *.45* *.25*

Universal Declaration of Human Rights, 50th Anniv. — A1556

1998, Oct. 26 **Litho.** ***Perf. 13***
4057 A1556 180 l multicolored *.45* *.25*

Giordano Bruno (1548-1600), Philosopher — A1557

1998, Oct. 26
4058 A1557 180 l multicolored *.45* *.25*

Greetings Stamps A1558

No. 4059, Man diving through flaming heart, "I Love You." No. 4060, Baby emerging from chalice, "Happy Birthday." No. 4061, Grape vine, bird, wine coming from vat, "Happy Holiday." No. 4062, Waiter carrying tray with glass & ttle of wine, "Happy Name Day."

1998, Nov. 11
4059 A1558 180 l multi *.50* *.25*
4060 A1558 180 l multi, vert. *.50* *.25*
4061 A1558 180 l multi, vert. *.50* *.25*
4062 A1558 180 l multi, vert. *.50* *.25*
Nos. 4059-4062 (4) *2.00* *1.00*

See No. 4628.

Christmas A1559

1998, Dec. 2 **Litho.** ***Perf. 13½x13***
4063 A1559 100 l multicolored *.45* *.25*

Ivan Geshov (1849-1924), Finance Minister — A1560

1999, Feb. 8 **Litho.** ***Perf. 13***
4064 A1560 180 l multicolored .35 .25

Third Bulgarian State, 120th Anniv. — A1561

Designs: a, Reflection of National Assembly. b, Men, paper, Council of Ministers. c, Scales of Justice, Supreme Court of Appeal. d, Coins, Bulgarian Natl. Bank. e, Soldiers, Bulgarian Army. f, Llon, lightpost, Sofia, capital of Bulgaria.

1999, Feb. 10
4065 A1561 180 l Sheet of 6, #a.-f. 2.50 1.25

Bulgarian Culture and Art — A1562

180 l, Georgy Karakashev (1899-1970), set designer. 200 l, Bencho Obreshkov (1899-1970), artist. 300 l, Assen Naydenov (1899-1995), conductor. 600 l, Pancho Vladiguerov (1899-1978), composer.

1999, Mar. 12 **Litho.** ***Perf. 13***
4066 A1562 180 l multicolored .25 .25
4067 A1562 200 l multicolored .25 .25
4068 A1562 300 l multicolored .75 .75
4069 A1562 600 l multicolored 1.50 .85
Nos. 4066-4069 (4) 2.75 2.10

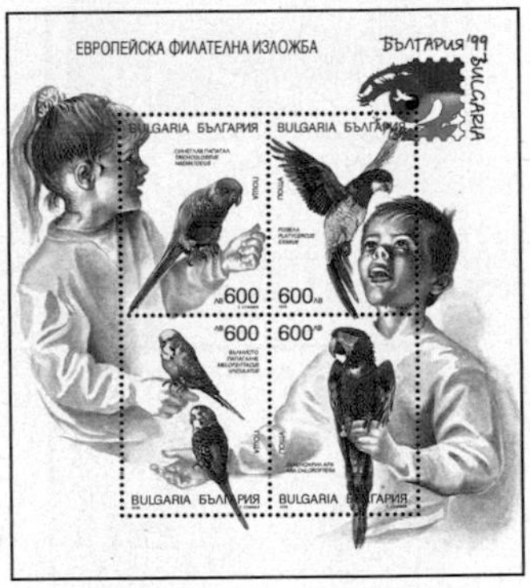

Bulgaria '99 — A1562a

Parrots: a, Trichoglossus haematodus. b, Platycercus eximius. c, Melopsittacus undulatus. d, Ara chloroptera.

1999, Mar. 15 **Litho.** ***Perf. 13x13¼***
4069A A1562a 600 l Sheet of 4, #a.-d. 7.50 *7.50*

NATO, 50th Anniv. — A1563

1999, Mar. 29 **Litho.** ***Perf. 13***
4070 A1563 180 l multicolored .35 .25

Easter A1564

1999, Apr. 1
4071 A1564 180 l multicolored .35 .25

National Parks and Nature Preserves — A1565

Europa: 180 l, Duck, pond, Ropotamo Preserve. 600 l, Ibex, waterfall, Central Balkan Natl. Park.

1999, Apr. 13 **Litho.** ***Perf. 13***
4072 A1565 180 l multicolored *.65* *.25*
4073 A1565 600 l multicolored *1.60* *.85*

IBRA '99, Intl. Philatelic Exhibition, Nuremberg — A1566

1999, Apr. 15

4074 A1566 600 l multicolored 1.50 .75

No. 4074 is divided in half by vert. simulated perfs. and was issued in sheets of 3 + 3 labels.

Council of Europe, 50th Anniv. — A1567

1999, May 5 **Litho.** ***Perf. 13***

4075 A1567 180 l multicolored 1.00 .50

Foreign Culture and Art — A1567a

Designs: 180 l, Honoré de Balzac (1799-1850), novelist. 200 l, Johann Wolfgang von Goethe (1749-1832), poet. 250 l, Aleksandr Pushkin (1799-1837), poet. 600 l, Diego Velázquez (1599-1660), painter.

1999, May 18

4076 A1567a 180 l multi .35 .25
4077 A1567a 200 l multi .70 .25
4078 A1567a 300 l multi .70 .30
4078A A1567a 600 l multi 1.25 .65
Nos. 4076-4078A (4) 3.00 1.45

Bicycles — A1568

Designs: 180 l, Large front-wheeled bicycle, 1867. 200 l, Multi-gear bicycle. 300 l, BMX racing bike. 600 l, Mountain racing bike.

1999, June 1 **Litho.** ***Perf. 13¼***

4079 A1568 180 l multicolored .25 .25
4080 A1568 200 l multicolored .25 .25
4081 A1568 300 l multicolored .85 .25
4082 A1568 600 l multicolored 1.50 .50
Nos. 4079-4082 (4) 2.85 1.25

Sts. Cyril and Methodius — A1569

Various paintings of Sts. Cyril and Methodius standing side by side with denomination at: a, UL. b, UR. c, LL. d, LR.

1999, June 15 **Litho.** ***Perf. 13¼***

4083 A1569 600 l Sheet of 4, #a.-d. 10.00 10.00

Bulgaria '99, European Philatelic Exhibition.

Flowers A1570

a, Oxytropis urumovii. b, Campanula transsilvanica. c, Iris reichenbachii. d, Gentiana punctata.

1999, July 20

4084 A1570 60s Sheet of 4, #a.-d. 12.00 12.00

Bulgaria '99, European Philatelic Exhibition.

Mushrooms — A1571

Designs: a, 10s, Russula virescens. b, 18s, Agaricus campestris. c, 20s, Hygrophorus russula. d, 60s, Lepista nuda.

1999, July 27

4085 A1571 Sheet of 4, #a.-d. 2.75 2.75

Souvenir Sheet

Total Solar Eclipse, Aug. 11, 1999 — A1572

1999, Aug. 10 ***Perf. 13***

4086 A1572 20s multicolored 1.50 1.50

A1573

1999, Sept. 23 **Litho.** ***Perf. 13***

4087 A1573 18s multicolored .25 .25

Organized agrarian movement in Bulgaria, 100th anniv.

Souvenir Sheet

A1574

Lion (portion) and: a, No. J2. b, Dove and letter. c, Eastern hemisphere. d, Western hemisphere.

1999, Oct. 5 ***Perf. 13x13½***

4088 A1574 60s Sheet of 4, #a.-d. 6.00 6.00

Bulgaria '99, UPU 125th anniv.

Birds, Eggs and Nests — A1575

8s, Lanius minor. 18s, Turdus viscivorus. 20s, Prunella modularis. 60s, Emberiza hortulana.

1999, Oct. 6 ***Perf. 13***

4089 A1575 8s multicolored .25 .25
4090 A1575 18s multicolored .25 .25
4091 A1575 20s multicolored .25 .25
4092 A1575 60s multicolored 1.90 1.90
Nos. 4089-4092 (4) 2.65 2.65

Endangered Turtles — A1576

10s, Testudo graeca. 18s, Emys orbicularis. 30s, Testudo hermanni. 60s, Mauremys caspica.

1999, Oct. 8 ***Perf. 13***

4093 A1576 10s multicolored .25 .25
4094 A1576 18s multicolored .25 .25
4095 A1576 30s multicolored .85 .85
4096 A1576 60s multicolored 1.50 1.50
Nos. 4093-4096 (4) 2.85 2.85

Olympic Sports A1577

1999, Oct. 10

4097 A1577 10s Boxing .25 .25
4098 A1577 20s High jump .25 .25
4099 A1577 30s Weight lifting .85 .85
4100 A1577 60s Wrestling 1.50 1.50
Nos. 4097-4100 (4) 2.85 2.85

Fountains — A1578

Fountains from: 1s, Sopotski Monastery. 8s, Karlovo. 10s, Koprivshchitsa. 18s, Sandanski. 20s, Karlovo. 60s, Sokolski Monastery.

1999 **Litho.** ***Perf. 13½x14***

Fountain Color

4101 A1578 1s bister .25 .25
4102 A1578 8s green .25 .25
4103 A1578 10s brown .25 .25
4104 A1578 18s light blue .30 .30
4105 A1578 20s dark blue .35 .35
4109 A1578 60s brown 1.00 1.00
Nos. 4101-4109 (6) 2.40 2.40

Issued: 8s, 60s, 11/22/99; others, 1999.

2003, Mar. ***Perf. 12¾ Syncopated***

4101a A1578 1s .25 .25
4102a A1578 8s .25 .25
4103a A1578 10s .25 .25
4104a A1578 18s .25 .25
4105a A1578 20s .25 .25
4109a A1578 60s .65 .65
Nos. 4101a-4109a (6) 1.90 1.90

Police Trade Unions' European Council, 10th Anniv. — A1579

1999, Nov. 8 **Litho.** ***Perf. 13***

4113 A1579 18s multi .35 .25

A1580

Various gold artifacts from Panagyurishte.

1999, Nov. 15 ***Perf. 13½x14***

4114 A1580 2s multi .25 .25
4115 A1580 3s multi .25 .25
4116 A1580 5s multi .25 .25
4117 A1580 30s multi .45 .25
4118 A1580 1 l multi 1.50 1.25
Nos. 4114-4118 (5) 2.70 2.25

Perf. Perf. 12¾ Syncopated

2003, Mar.

4114a A1580 2s .25 .25
4115a A1580 3s .25 .25
4116a A1580 5s .25 .25
4117a A1580 30s .30 .30
4118a A1580 1 l 1.10 1.10
Nos. 4114a-4118a (5) 2.15 2.15

A1581

1999, Nov. 22 ***Perf. 13***

4119 A1581 18s Icon, 1600 .35 .35
4120 A1581 60s Icon, 1607 1.25 1.25

Scouting A1582

10s, Scout, campfire. 18s, Scout assisting another. 30s, Salute. 60s, Scouts, cross.

1999, Dec. 6

4121 A1582 10s multi .25 .25
4122 A1582 18s multi .40 .40
4123 A1582 30s multi .65 .65
4124 A1582 60s multi 1.25 1.25
Nos. 4121-4124 (4) 2.55 2.55

Expo 2005, Japan — A1583

1999, Dec. 21 ***Perf. 13***

4125 A1583 18s multi .30 .25

Start of Negotiations for Bulgaria's Entry into European Community — A1584

2000, Feb. 15 **Litho.** ***Perf. 13***

4126 A1584 18s multi 1.00 1.00

Souvenir Sheet

Ciconia Ciconia — A1585

2000, Mar. 22

4127 A1585 60s multi 2.00 1.25

Petar Beron (1800-71), Scientist — A1586

Zakhari Stoyanov (1850-89), Writer — A1586a

Kolyo Ficheto (1800-81), Architect — A1586b

2000, Mar. 30 **Litho.** ***Perf. 13¼***

4128 A1586 10s multi .25 .25
4129 A1586a 20s multi .45 .45
4130 A1586b 50s multi 1.10 1.10
Nos. 4128-4130 (3) 1.80 1.80

Europa A1587

60s, Madonna and child at right.

2000, Apr. 26 **Litho.** ***Perf. 13***

4131 A1587 18s shown *.60 .40*
4132 A1587 60s multicolored *1.40 1.40*

2000 Summer Olympics, Sydney — A1588

2000, Apr. 28 ***Perf. 13¼x13***

4133 A1588 10s Judo .25 .25
4134 A1588 18s Tennis .30 .30
4135 A1588 20s Shooting .40 .35
4136 A1588 60s Long jump 1.10 1.00
Nos. 4133-4136 (4) 2.05 1.90

Bulgarian Art A1589

Designs: No. 4137, Friends, by Assen Vassilev (1900-81). No. 4138, Landscape from Veliko Turnovo, by Ivan Hristov (1900-87). No. 4139, At the Fountain, sculpture by Ivan Funev (1900-83). No. 4140, All Souls' Day, by Pencho Georgiev (1900-40).

2000, May 23 ***Perf. 13***

4137 A1589 18s multi .40 .40
4138 A1589 18s multi .40 .40
4139 A1589 18s multi .40 .40
4140 A1589 18s multi .40 .40
Nos. 4137-4140 (4) 1.60 1.60

Souvenir Sheet

Fairy Tales — A1590

Designs: a, Puss in Boots, by Charles Perrault. b, Little Red Riding Hood, by the Brothers Grimm. c, Thumbelina, by Hans Christian Andersen.

2000, May 23 ***Perf. 13¼x13***

4141 A1590 18s Sheet of 3, #a-c + 3 labels 1.50 1.50

Expo 2000, Hanover — A1591

2000, May 31 ***Perf. 13***

4142 A1591 60s multi + label 1.25 .50

Birth and Death Anniversaries — A1592

Designs: 10s, Johann Gutenberg, inventor of movable type (c. 1400-68). 18s, Johann Sebastian Bach, composer (1685-1750). 20s, Guy de Maupassant, writer (1850-93). 60s, Antoine de Saint-Exupéry, writer (1900-44).

2000, June 20

4143 A1592 10s multi .25 .25
4144 A1592 18s multi .40 .40
4145 A1592 20s multi .50 .50
4146 A1592 60s multi 1.40 1.40
Nos. 4143-4146 (4) 2.55 2.55

Airships — A1593

Designs: 10s, Le Jaune over Paris. 18s, LZ-13 Hansa over Cologne. 20s, N-1 Norge over Rome. 60s, Graf Zeppelin over Sofia.

2000, July 3 **Litho.** ***Perf. 13¼***

4147 A1593 10s multi .25 .25
4148 A1593 18s multi .25 .25
4149 A1593 20s multi .50 .25
4150 A1593 60s multi 1.50 .45
Nos. 4147-4150 (4) 2.50 1.20

Ivan Vazov (1850-1921), Writer — A1594

2000, July 9

4151 A1594 18s multi .40 .25

Souvenir Sheet

European Security and Cooperation Conference, Helsinki, 25th Anniv. — A1595

No. 4152: a, Hands. b, Three "e's."

2000, July 19 **Litho.** ***Perf. 13***

4152 A1595 20s Sheet of 2, #a-b 2.00 1.50

Churches A1596

Panel colors: 22s, Blue. 24s, Red violet. 50s, Bister. 65s, Bright green. 3 l, Brown. 5 l, Red.

2000, Sept. 1 ***Perf. 14x13¾***

4153-4158 A1596 Set of 6 14.00 4.50

Perf. Perf. 12¾ Syncopated

2003, Mar.

4153a A1596 22s .25 .25
4154a A1596 24s .55 .55
4155a A1596 50s .55 .55
4156a A1596 65s .75 .75
Nos. 4153a-4156a (4) 2.10 2.10

Animals A1597

Designs: 10s, Capra ibex. 22s, Ovis ammon. 30s, Bison bonasus. 65s, Bos grunniens.

2000, Sept. 25 ***Perf. 13***

4159-4162 A1597 Set of 4 2.75 1.60

Flowers — A1598

Designs: 10s, Gladiolus segetum. 22s, Hepatica nobilis. 30s, Adonis vernalis. 65s, Anemone pavonina.

2000, Oct. 17 ***Perf. 13x13¼***

4163-4166 A1598 Set of 4 2.50 .80

European Convention on Human Rights, 50th Anniv. A1599

2000, Nov. 3 Litho. ***Perf. 13¼x13***
4167 A1599 65s multi 1.60 .80

Bulgarian Orders — A1600

Designs: 12s, Bravery. 22s, St. Alexander. 30s, Citizen's merit. 65s, Sts. Cyril and Methodius.

2000, Nov. 28 ***Perf. 13***
4168-4171 A1600 Set of 4 2.75 .80

Souvenir Sheet

Christianity, 2000th Anniv. — A1601

No. 4172: a, 22s, St. Boris Michael (2000 at UL). b, 22s, St. Sofroni Vrachanski (2000 at LL). c, 65s, Madonna and Child (2000 at UL). d, 65s, Exarch Antim I (2000 at LL).

2000, Nov. 28 ***Perf. 13¼x13***
4172 A1601 Sheet of 4, #a-d 4.00 4.00

First Bulgarian Law, 120th Anniv. — A1602

2000, Dec. 8 ***Perf. 13x13¼***
4173 A1602 22s multi .50 .25

Advent of New Millennium — A1603

2001, Jan. 8 ***Perf. 13x12¾***
4174 A1603 22s multi .50 .50

Souvenir Sheet

Electrified City Transport in Bulgaria, Cent. — A1604

No. 4175: a, 22s, Streetcar. b, 65s, Two streetcars.

2001, Jan. 12 ***Perf. 13***
4175 A1604 Sheet, 2 each #4175a-4175b 4.00 4.00

Viticulture A1605

Wine glass, wine grapes and buildings: 12s, Muscat, Evxinograd Palace. 22s, Gumza, Baba Vida Fortress. 30s, Wide Melnik, houses in Melnik. 65s, Mavroud, Assenova Fortress.

2001, Feb. 7
4176-4179 A1605 Set of 4 2.75 1.00

Souvenir Sheet

Bulgaria and the Information Society — A1606

No. 4180: a, 22s, Circuits, "@" character. b, 65s, Letters, Dr. John Atanasov (1903-95), computer pioneer.

2001, Mar. 1 ***Perf. 13¼x13***
4180 A1606 Sheet of 2, #a-b 7.50 6.50

Souvenir Sheet

"Atlantic" Values, 10th Anniv. — A1607

2001, Apr. 4 ***Perf. 13x12¾***
4181 A1607 65s multi 4.00 4.00

Europa A1608

Designs: 22s, Aerial view of Rila Lakes. 65s, Rock bridges, Rhodope Mountains.

2001, Apr. 18 ***Perf. 12¾x13***
4182-4183 A1608 Set of 2 *14.00 10.00*

Todor Kableshkov (1851-1876), Organizer of 1876 April Uprising — A1609

2001, May 1 ***Perf. 13***
4184 A1609 22s multi .50 .25

Protected Species Neophron Percnopterus — A1610

Designs: 12s, Juvenile in flight. 22s, Juvenile with mouth open. 30s, Adult and chick. 65s, Adult and eggs.

2001, May 21 Litho. ***Perf. 13***
4185-4188 A1610 Set of 4 2.75 2.75

Souvenir Sheet

Athletes — A1611

No. 4189: a, 22s, Georgi Asparuchov (1943-71), soccer player. b, 30s, Dan Kolov (1892-1940), wrestler. c, 65s, Krum Lekarski (1898-1981), equestrian.

2001, June 29
4189 A1611 Sheet of 3, #a-c, + 3 labels 3.00 3.00

UN High Commissioner for Refugees, 50th Anniv. — A1612

2001, July 11
4190 A1612 65s multi 1.50 1.40

Writers A1613

Designs: 22s, Aleksandr Zhendov (1901-53). 65s, Ilya Beshkov (1901-58).

2001, July 24
4191-4192 A1613 Set of 2 2.00 2.00

Constitutional Court, 10th Anniv. — A1614

2001, Oct. 3
4193 A1614 25s multi .50 .25

Souvenir Sheet

Sofia Summit 2001 — A1615

Flags of various countries: a, 12s. b, 24s. c, 25s. d, 65s.

2001, Oct. 5 ***Perf. 13¼x13***
4194 A1615 Sheet of 4, #a-d 3.00 3.00

Year of Dialogue Among Civilizations A1616

2001, Oct. 9 ***Perf. 13***
4195 A1616 65s multi 1.50 .50

Souvenir Sheet

Intl. Black Sea Preservation Day — A1617

2001, Oct. 31
4196 A1617 65s multi 1.60 1.60

Christmas A1618

2001, Nov. 19
4197 A1618 25s multi .50 .25

Lighthouses A1619

Designs: 25s, Shabla. 32s, Kaliakra.

2001, Nov. 19 ***Perf. 14x13½***
4198-4199 A1619 Set of 2 1.10 .50

2003, Mar. ***Perf. 12¾ Syncopated***
4198a-4199a A1619 Set of 2 1.00 1.00

A souvenir sheet containing Nos. 4198a and 4199a dated "2013" and 2 labels was produced in limited quantities and released 8/15/13.

Souvenir Sheet

Zograf Monastery, Mount Athos, Greece — A1620

No. 4200: a, 25s, Monastery. b, 65s, Icon of St, George.

2001, Nov. 27
4200 A1620 Sheet of 2, #a-b 2.50 2.50

Cartoons — A1621

2001, Dec. 12 Litho. ***Perf. 13¼x13***
4201 A1621 25s multi + label .60 .60

Printed in sheets of 3 stamps and labels.

Vincenzo Bellini (1801-35), Italian Composer — A1622

2001, Dec. 17 ***Perf. 13***
4202 A1622 25s multi .60 .25

Builders of the Bulgarian State — A1623

Designs: 10s, Ancient Bulgarian calendar. 25s, Khans Kubrat (632-51) and Asparukh (681-700). 30s, Khans Krum (803-14) and Omurtag (814-31). 65s, King Boris I (852-89) and Tsar Simeon I (893-927).

2001, Dec. 21
4203-4206 A1623 Set of 4 3.00 1.20

Introduction of Euro Currency in 12 European Nations — A1624

2002, Jan. 3
4207 A1624 65s multi 1.50 1.50

UN Disarmament Committee, 50th Anniv. — A1625

2002, Jan. 23
4208 A1625 25s multi .60 .60

Souvenir Sheet

Balkanmax 2002 — A1626

No. 4209: a, 25s, Natural bridge. b, 65s, Buteo rufinus.

2002, Jan. 29
4209 A1626 Sheet of 2, #a-b 17.50 17.50

2002 Winter Olympics, Salt Lake City A1627

Designs: 25s, Figure skater. 65s, Speed skater.

2002, Feb. 5 ***Perf. 13¼x13***
4210-4211 A1627 Set of 2 2.00 2.00

10th Natl. Antarctic Expedition — A1628

2002, Mar. 20
4212 A1628 25s multi + label .60 .60

Issued in sheets of 3 stamps and 3 different labels.

Europa A1629

Circus performers: 25s, Elephant trainer. 65s, Clown.

2002, Mar. 22 ***Perf. 13***
4213-4214 A1629 Set of 2 *2.50 2.50*

See No. 4629 for clown stamp without "Europa" inscription..

Famous Bulgarians — A1630

Designs: 25s, Veselin Stoyanov (1902-69), composer. 34s, Angel Karaliichev (1902-72), writer.

2002, Mar. 27 ***Perf. 13¼x13***
4215-4216 A1630 Set of 2 1.25 1.25

Paintings — A1631

Designs: 10s, Industrial Landscape, by Vasil Barakov, vert. 25s, Illustration for book *Under the Yoke*, by Boris Angelushev. 65s, The Balcony and the Canary, by Ivan Nenov, vert.

2002, Apr. 17 ***Perf. 13***
4217-4219 A1631 Set of 3 2.25 2.25

Stamp Designers A1632

Designs: 25s, Stefan Kanchev (1915-2001). 65s, Alexander Popilov (1916-2001).

2002, Apr. 26 ***Perf. 13¼x13***
4220-4221 A1632 Set of 2 2.00 2.00

Fruits and Vegetables A1633

Designs: 10s, Cucumis melo. 25s, Citrullus lanatus. 27s, Cucurbita pepo. 65s, Lagenaria siceraria.

2002, May 8 Litho. ***Perf. 13¼x13***
4222-4225 A1633 Set of 4 2.75 2.75

Roosters A1634

Designs: 10s, Bankivski, vert. 20s, Leghorn. 25s, Bergich Crower. 65s, Plymouth Rock, vert.

2002, May 10 ***Perf. 13x13¼, 13¼x13***
4226-4229 A1634 Set of 4 2.75 2.75

Visit of Pope John Paul II to Bulgaria A1635

2002, May 24 Litho. ***Perf. 13***
4230 A1635 65s multi 1.25 1.25

Souvenir Sheet

Chess — A1636

No. 4231: a, 25s, Chess pieces. b, 65s, Hand moving piece.

2002, May 27
4231 A1636 Sheet of 2, #a-b 2.00 2.00

Admission to Council of Europe, 10th Anniv. A1637

2002, May 29
4232 A1637 25s multi .60 .60

Carvings by Peter Kushlev A1638

Designs: 6s, Rabbit and fawn. 12s, Deer. 36s, Bird. 44s, Boar.

Perf. 13¾x13½

2002, Aug. 12 **Litho.**

4233-4236 A1638 Set of 4 2.00 2.00

Perf. Perf. 12¾ Syncopated

2003, Mar.

4233a-4236a A1638 Set of 4 1.75 1.75

Ships A1639

Designs: 12s, Maria Luisa. 36c, Percenk. 49c, Kaliakra. 65c, Sofia.

2002, Oct. 18 ***Perf. 13¼x13***

4237-4240 A1639 Set of 4 3.25 2.75

Christmas A1640

2002, Nov. 20

4241 A1640 36s multi .75 .75

Souvenir Sheet

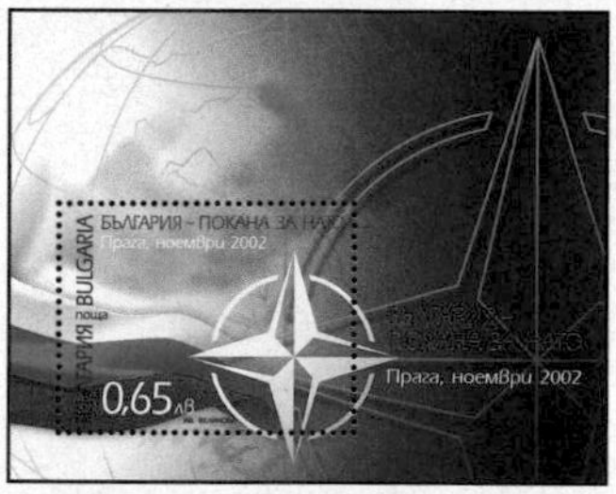

Invitation to Join NATO — A1641

2002, Nov. 21 ***Perf. 13***

4242 A1641 65s multi 1.25 1.25

Souvenir Sheet

Start of European Security and Cooperation Negotiations, 30th Anniv. — A1642

2002, Nov. 22 ***Perf. 13¼x13***

4243 A1642 65s multi 2.00 2.00

Tsars A1643

Designs: 18s, Samuel (d. 1014). 36s, Peter II (d. 1197), Assen (d. 1196). 49s, Kaloyan (d. 1207). 65s, Ivan Assen II (d. 1241).

2002, Dec. 6 **Litho.** ***Perf. 13¼x13***

4244-4247 A1643 Set of 4 3.50 3.50

See Nos. 4272, 4288-4290.

Europalia, European Culture Festival — A1644

2003, Jan. 10 **Litho.** ***Perf. 13***

4248 A1644 65s multi 1.25 1.25

Paintings A1645

Designs: 18s, Rose Pickers, by Stoyan Sotirov (1903-84). 36s, The Blind Rebec Player, by Ilya Petrov (1903-75). 65s, Pig Tender, by Zlatyo Boyadjiev (1903-76).

2003, Jan. 28

4249-4251 A1645 Set of 3 2.25 2.25

Souvenir Sheet

Science Fiction — A1646

2003, Feb. 7

4252 A1646 65s multi 1.25 1.25

Re-establishment of the Bulgarian State, 125th Anniv. — A1647

2003, Feb. 28 **Litho.** ***Perf. 13***

4253 A1647 36s multi .65 .65

Rescue of Bulgarian Jews, 60th Anniv. — A1648

2003, Mar. 10

4254 A1648 36s multi .80 .80

Europa — A1649

No. 4255: a, 36s, Woman and birds. b, 65s, Legs, chicken, pig and dog.

2003, Mar. 17

4255 A1649 Vert. pair, #a-b *2.00 2.00*

Souvenir Sheet

Vincent van Gogh (1853-90), Painter — A1650

2003, Mar. 19 ***Perf. 13x13¼***

4256 A1650 65s multi 1.40 1.40

Prehistoric Animals A1651

2003, Apr. 24 ***Perf. 13***

4257 Horiz. strip of 4 3.75 3.75
- *a.* A1651 30s Pterodactylus .60 .60
- *b.* A1651 36s Gorgosaurus .75 .75
- *c.* A1651 49s Mesosaurus 1.00 1.00
- *d.* A1651 65s Monoclonius 1.40 1.40
- Booklet, #4257 5.00

Bulgaria 2003 Philatelic Exhibition — A1652

2003, May 15

4258 A1652 36s multi .80 .80

Bees A1653

Designs: 20s: Apis mellifera. 30s, Anthidium manicatum. 36s, Bombus subterraneus. 65s, Xylocopa violacea.

2003, June 17 **Litho.** ***Perf. 13¼x13***

4259-4262 A1653 Set of 4 3.00 3.00

Water Plants — A1654

Designs: 20s, Butomus umbellatus. 36s, Sagittaria sagittifolia. 50s, Menyanthes trifoliata. 65s, Iris pseudacorus.

2003, July 25 **Litho.** ***Perf. 13***

4263-4266 A1654 Set of 4 3.50 3.50

Goce Delchev (1872-1903), Patriot — A1655

2003, Aug. 1

4267 A1655 36s multi .75 .75

Ilinden and Preobrazhene Revolts, cent.

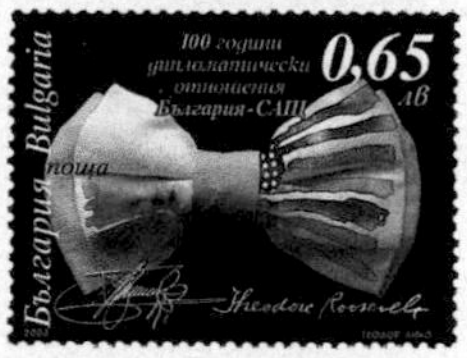

Bulgaria — United States Diplomatic Relations, Cent. A1656

2003, Sept. 19 **Litho.** ***Perf. 13***

4268 A1656 65s multi 1.25 1.25

Intl Years of Fresh Water, Mountains and Ecotourism — A1657

2003, Sept. 19

4269 A1657 65s multi + label 1.50 1.50

Printed in sheets of 3 + 3 different labels.

John Atanassov (1903-95), Computer Pioneer — A1658

2003, Oct. 3 **Litho.** ***Perf. 13***

4270 A1658 65s multi + label 1.25 1.25

2003 European Team Chess Championships, Plovdiv — A1659

2003, Oct. 10

4271 A1659 65s multi 1.40 1.40

Tsar Type of 2002

Design: Tsar Ivan Shishman (d. 1396).

2003, Oct. 18
4272 A1643 65s multi 1.40 1.40

Bulgarian Olympic Committee, 80th Anniv. — A1660

New Olympic sports: 20s, Taekwondo. 36s, Mountain biking. 50s, Softball. 65s, Canoe slalom.

2003, Oct. 18
4273-4276 A1660 Set of 4 3.50 3.50

Christmas A1661

2003, Nov. 24 ***Perf. 13x13¼***
4277 A1661 65s multi 1.25 1.25

Coaches — A1662

Designs: 30s, Man and coach. 36s, Man and woman in coach. 50s, Woman, dog and coach. 65s, Man, woman and coach.

2003, Nov. 28 ***Perf. 13***
4278-4281 A1662 Set of 4 3.50 3.50

FIFA (Fédération Internationale de Football Association), Cent. (in 2004) — A1663

Designs: 20s, FIFA emblem. 25s, Soccer match. 36s, Soccer match, rules. 50s, FIFA Fair Play Trophy, vert. 65s, FIFA World Player Trophy, vert.

2003, Dec. 12
4282-4286 A1663 Set of 5 4.00 4.00

Re-establisment of Masons in Bulgaria, 10th Anniv. — A1664

2003, Dec. 22 **Litho.** ***Perf. 13***
4287 A1664 80s multi 1.60 1.60

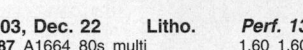

Tsar Type of 2002

Designs: 30s, Tsar Ivan Alexander (r. 1331-71). 45s, Despot Dosrotitsa (r. 1360-85). 80s, Tsar Ivan Strazhimir (r. 1371-96).

2003, Dec. 23
4288-4290 A1643 Set of 3 3.00 3.00

Butterflies A1665

Designs: 40s, Noctua tertia. 45s, Rethera komarovi. 55s, Symtomis marjana. 80s, Arctia caja.

2004, Jan. 15 ***Perf. 12¾ Syncopated***
4291-4294 A1665 Set of 4 4.00 4.00

Perf. 14x13½
4291a-4294a A1665 Set of 4 30.00 30.00

Issued: Nos 4291a-4294a, Oct.

A souvenir sheet containing Nos. 4291-4294 with inscriptions commemorating the Australia 2013 and Thailand 2013 World Stamp Exhibitions was produced in limited quantities.

Intl. Masquerade Festival, Pernik — A1666

2004, Jan. 23 ***Perf. 13***
4295 A1666 80s multi + label 1.60 1.60

Printed in sheets of 3 +3 labels.

Bulgarian Chairmanship of Organization for Security and Cooperation in Europe — A1667

2004, Jan. 30
4296 A1667 80s multi 1.50 1.50

Ivan Vazov National Theater, Cent. — A1668

2004, Feb. 19
4297 A1668 45s multi + label 1.00 1.00

Famous Men A1669

Designs: 45s, Atanas Dalchev (1904-78), poet. 80s, Lubomir Pipkov (1904-74), composer.

2004, Mar. 25
4298-4299 A1669 Set of 2 2.50 2.50

Admission to NATO — A1670

2004, Apr. 2
4300 A1670 80s multi 1.75 1.75

Souvenir Sheet

Flight of Georgi Ivanov, First Bulgarian in Space, 25th Anniv. — A1671

2004, Apr. 15
4301 A1671 80s multi 1.50 1.50

Souvenir Sheet

Turnovo Constitution and Restoration of Bulgarian State, 125th Anniv. — A1672

2004, Apr. 16
4302 A1672 45s multi 4.00 4.00

"Bulgarian Dream" Program A1673

2004, May 3
4303 A1673 45s multi .90 .90

Souvenir Sheet

Salvador Dali (1904-89), Artist — A1674

2004, May 12 **Litho.** ***Perf. 13***
4304 A1674 80s multi 2.00 2.00

Artists — A1675

Designs: 45s, Boris Ivanov (1904-93) and Lyuben Dimitrov (1904-2000). 80s, Vassil Stylov (1904-90) and Stoyan Venev (1904-89).

2004, May 21
4305-4306 A1675 Set of 2 2.50 2.50

Europa — A1676

Designs: 45s, Skiers on mountain. 80s, Parachutist near seaside resort.

2004, May 27
4307-4308 A1676 Set of 2 *2.50 2.50*
4308a Booklet pane, 2 each #4307-4308 *5.00* —
Complete booklet, 2 #4308a *10.00*

Complete booklet contains one pane with illustrated margins at right and one pane with illustrated margins at left.

Soccer Players — A1677

No. 4309: a, Christo Stoychkov wearing collared shirt, player holding trophy. b, Georgi Asparuchov wearing uncollared shirt, players wearing green and black shorts. c, Krassimir Balakov wearing collared shirt, players wearing white and yellow shirts. d, Nilola Kotkov wearing uncollared shirt, players wearing white shorts.

2004, June 2
4309 A1677 45s Block of 4, #a-d 3.75 3.75

Souvenir Sheet

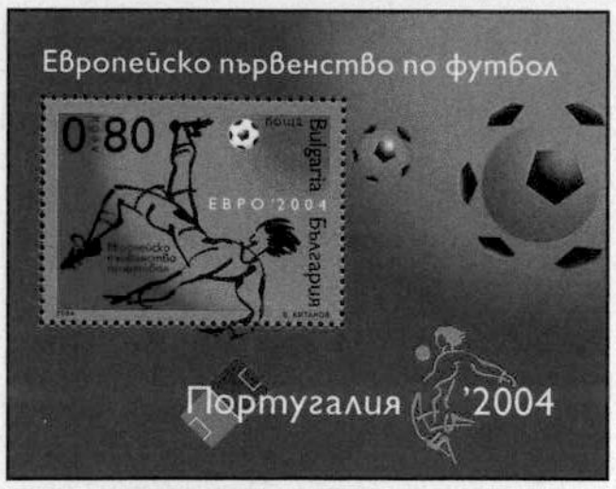

European Soccer Championships, Portugal — A1678

2004, June 11
4310 A1678 80s multi 1.50 1.50

Bulgaria — Austria Diplomatic Relations, 125th Anniv. — A1679

2004, June 23 Litho. *Perf. 13*
4311 A1679 80s multi 1.50 1.50

Interior Ministry, 125th Anniv. — A1680

2004, June 26
4312 A1680 45s multi 1.00 1.00

Souvenir Sheet

Bulgarian Postal Service, 125th Anniv. — A1681

2004, July 16
4313 A1681 45s multi + label 4.00 4.00

Souvenir Sheet

Ecology — A1682

No. 4314: a, 45s, Milvus milvus. b, 80s, Blennius ocellaris.

2004, July 28
4314 A1682 Sheet of 2, #a-b 3.25 3.25

2004 Summer Olympics, Athens — A1683

Olympic rings, torch bearer, torch, map of Bulgaria showing route of torch bearers going to Olympics in: 10s, Berlin, 1936. 20s, Munich, 1972. 45s, Moscow, 1980. 80s, Athens, 2004.

2004, Aug. 5
4315-4318 A1683 Set of 4 3.25 3.25

Bulgarian Navy, 125th Anniv. — A1684

Designs: 10s, Steamer "Krum." 25s, Torpedo boat "Druski." 45s, Mine sweeper "Christo Botev." 80s, Frigate "Smeli."

2004, Aug. 6
4319-4322 A1684 Set of 4 3.25 3.25

Masons in Bulgaria, 125th Anniv. A1685

2004, Sept. 20 Litho. *Perf. 13*
4323 A1685 45s multi 5.50 5.50

Famous Bulgarians — A1686

Designs: 10s, Patriarch Ephtimius Turnovski (1327-1402). 20s, Princes Fruzhin (1393-1460) and Constantine (1396-1422). 45s, Georgi Peyachevich (1655-1725) and Peter Partchevich (1612-74), uprising leaders. 80s, Paisii Hilendarski (1722-73), historian.

2004, Nov. 15
4324-4327 A1686 Set of 4 3.00 3.00

Miniature Sheet

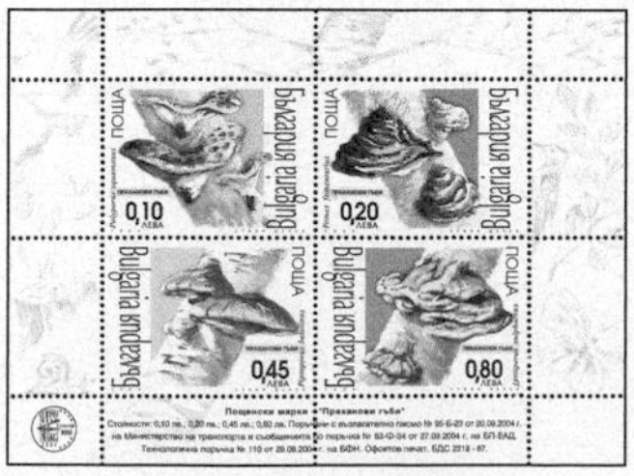

Mushrooms — A1687

No. 4328: a, 10s, Polyporus squamosus. b, 20s, Fomes fomentarius. 45s, Piptoporus betulinus. 80s, Laetiporus sulphureus.

2004, Nov. 17
4328 A1687 Sheet of 4, #a-d 3.50 3.50

Worldwide Fund for Nature (WWF) — A1688

No. 4329: a, Two fish, blue background. b, One fish, yellow green background. c, One fish, light blue background. d, Large fish eating small fish, green background.

2004, Nov. 18
4329 Horiz. strip of 4 7.50 7.50
a.-d. A1688 80s Any single 1.60 1.60
Complete booklet, 2 #4329 16.00

Christmas — A1689

2004, Nov. 24
4330 A1689 45s multi 1.00 1.00

Souvenir Sheet

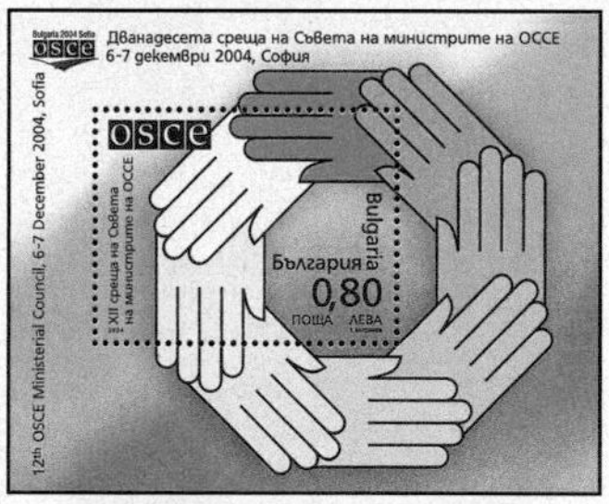

Organization for Security and Cooperation in Europe Ministerial Council Meeting, Sofia — A1690

2004, Dec. 6 Litho. *Perf. 13*
4331 A1690 80s multi 1.50 1.50

Self-Portrait of Geo Milev (1895-1925), Artist, Writer — A1691

2005, Jan. 17
4332 A1691 45s multi 1.00 1.00

Rotary International, Cent. — A1692

2005, Feb. 23
4333 A1692 80s multi 1.60 1.60

Souvenir Sheet

Cinema History — A1693

No. 4334: a, 10s, Charlie Chaplin in "The Gold Rush." b, 20s, "The Battleship Potemkin." c, 45s, Marlene Dietrich in "The Blue Angel." d, 80s, Vassil Ghendov in "Bulgaran is a Gallant Man."

2005, Feb. 25 *Perf. 13x13¼*
4334 A1693 Sheet of 4, #a-d 3.00 3.00

Souvenir Sheet

Bulgarian Exarchate, 135th Anniv. — A1694

2005, Mar. 11 *Perf. 13*
4335 A1694 45s multi 1.00 1.00

Volunteers for Europe A1695

2005, Mar. 16
4336 A1695 80s multi 1.60 1.60

Panayot Hitov (1830-1912) and Philip Totyo (1830-1907), Revolutionaries A1696

2005, Mar. 21
4337 A1696 45s multi 1.00 1.00

Souvenir Sheet

Polar Explorers — A1697

No. 4338: a, 45s, Admiral Robert Peary (1856-1920). b, 80s, Roald Amundsen (1872-1928).

2005, Mar. 23
4338 A1697 Sheet of 2, #a-b 2.50 2.50

Souvenir Sheet

Fire Trucks — A1698

No. 4339: a, 10s, 1936 Peugeot. b, 20s, 1935 Mercedes. 45s, 1934 Magirus. 80s, 1925 Renault.

2005, Apr. 2 Litho. ***Perf. 13***
4339 A1698 Sheet of 4, #a-d 3.25 3.25

Souvenir Sheet

Hans Christian Andersen (1805-75), Author — A1699

2005, May 20
4340 A1699 80s multi 1.60 1.60

Souvenir Sheet

Introduction of Cyrillic Alphabet to European Union — A1700

2005, May 24
4341 A1700 80s multi 1.60 1.60

Souvenir Sheet

Trains — A1701

No. 4342: a, 45s, Series 46 locomotive. b, 80s, DMV Series 10.

2005, May 26
4342 A1701 Sheet, 2 each #4342a-4342b 5.00 5.00

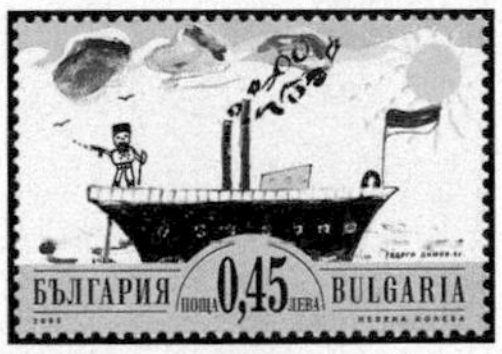

Child's Drawing of the Radetski A1702

2005, May 27 Litho. ***Perf. 13***
4343 A1702 45s multi 1.00 1.00

Europa A1703

No. 4344: a, Plates of food, apple, gourd. b, Plates of food, wine glass, tomato, scallions.

2005, May 28

4344	Pair	*1.75*	*1.75*
a.	A1703 45s green & multi	*.75*	*.75*
b.	A1703 80s red & multi	*1.00*	*1.00*
c.	Booklet pane, 2 each #4344a-4344b	*3.50*	3.50
	Complete booklet, 2 #4344c	*7.50*	

European Philatelic Cooperation, 50th Anniv. (in 2006) — A1704

Designs: 45s, Two stylized people. 80s, Rectangle of stylized people.

2005, May 28
4345-4346 A1704 Set of 2 2.50 2.50

Europa stamps, 50th anniv. (in 2006).

Dragonflies A1705

Designs: 10s, Cordulegaster bidentata. 20s, Erythromma najas, horiz. 45s, Sympetrum pedemontanum, horiz. 80s, Brachytron pratense.

2005, June 29
4347-4350 A1705 Set of 4 3.25 3.25

Elias Canetti (1905-94), 1981 Nobel Laureate in Literature — A1706

2005, July 25
4351 A1706 80s multi 1.75 1.75

Spiders A1707

Designs: 10s, Synema globosum. 20s, Argiope bruennichi. 45s, Eresus cinnaberinus. 80s, Araneus diadematus.

2005, July 29
4352-4355 A1707 Set of 4 3.25 3.25

Organized Tourism in Bulgaria, 110th Anniv. — A1708

2005, Aug. 26 Litho. ***Perf. 13***
4356 A1708 45s multi .90 .90

Union of Bulgaria and Eastern Rumelia, 120th Anniv. — A1709

2005, Sept. 6
4357 A1709 45s multi .90 .90

Women's Folk Costumes A1710

Clothing from region of: 20s, Sofia. 25s, Pleven. 45s, Sliven. 80s, Stara Zagora.

2005, Oct. 15 Litho. ***Perf. 13***
4358-4361 A1710 Set of 4 3.50 3.50

Souvenir Sheet

Stamen Grigoroff (1878-1945) and Microscope — A1711

2005

4362	A1711 80s multi + label	1.25	1.25
a.	As #4362, with owl added in UR of stamp, imperf.	12.00	12.00

Grigoroff's discovery of Lactobacillus bulgaricus grigoroff, cent.

Issued: No. 4362, 10/21; No. 4362a, 12/2.

No. 4362a has simulated perforations and a perforated serial number.

Antoaneta Stefanova, Female World Chess Champion — A1712

2005, Nov. 10
4363 A1712 80s multi 1.25 1.25

Christmas — A1713

2005, Nov. 30
4364 A1713 45s multi .90 .90

Souvenir Sheet

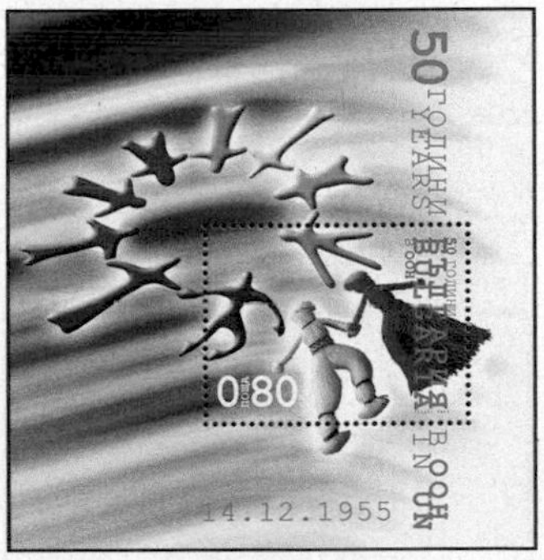

Admission to the United Nations, 50th Anniv. — A1714

2005, Dec. 14 Litho. ***Perf. 13***
4365 A1714 80s multi 1.50 1.50

Builders of the Bulgarian State — A1715

Designs: 10s, Illarion Makariopolski (1812-75) and Antim I (1816-88), religious leaders. 20s, Georgi Rakovski (1821-67) and Vassil Levski (1837-73), revolutionaries. 45s, Ljuben

Karavelov (1834-79) and Christo Botev (1848-76), poets. 80s, Panayot Volov (1850-76) and Pavel Bobekov (1852-77), revolutionaries.

2005, Dec. 20
4366-4369 A1715 Set of 4 3.00 3.00

Roses — A1716

Designs: 54s, Rosa pendulina. 1.50 l, Rosa gallica. 2 l, Rosa spinosissima. 10 l, Rosa arvenis.

Perf. 13x12¾ Syncopated

2006, Jan. 23 **Litho.**

4370	A1716	54s multi	.85	.50
4371	A1716	1.50 l multi	2.40	1.25
4372	A1716	2 l multi	3.25	1.75
4373	A1716	10 l multi	15.00	10.00
	Nos. 4370-4373 (4)		21.50	13.50

Wolfgang Amadeus Mozart (1756-91), Composer — A1717

2006, Jan. 27 ***Perf. 13***
4374 A1717 1 l multi + label 2.50 2.50

Famous Bulgarian Philatelists — A1718

Designs: 35s, Ellin Pellin (1877-1949), novelist. 55s, Lazar Dobrich (1881-1970), circus performer. 60s, Boris Christov (1914-93), opera singer. 1 l, Bogomil Nonev (1920-2002), writer.

2006, Jan. 31 **Litho.**
Stamp + Label
4375-4378 A1718 Set of 4 3.75 3.75

Souvenir Sheet

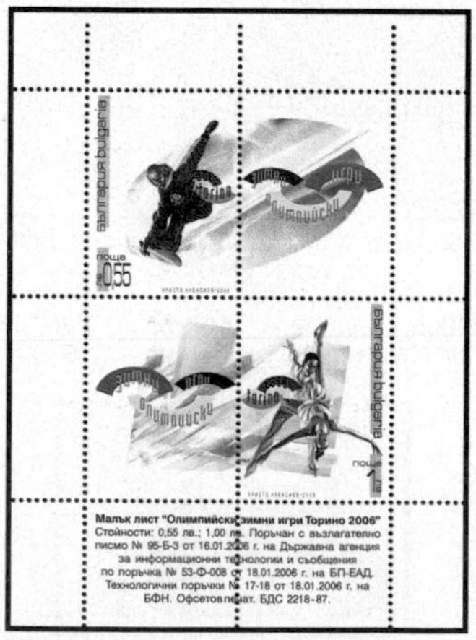

2006 Winter Olympics, Turin — A1719

No. 4379: a, 55s, Snowboarding. b, 1 l, Figure skating.

2006, Feb. 10 ***Perf. 13x13¼***
4379 A1719 Sheet of 2, #a-b 2.50 2.50

Souvenir Sheet

Bulgarian Antarctic Cartography, 10th Anniv. — A1720

2006, Feb. 28 ***Perf. 13***
4380 A1720 1 l multi 1.75 1.75

Battle of Nicopolis, 610th Anniv. — A1721

2006, Mar. 14
4381 A1721 1.50 l multi 2.75 2.75

Souvenir Sheet

Ecology — A1722

No. 4382: a, 55s, Martes martes. b, 1.50 l, Ursus arctos.

2006, Mar. 28 ***Perf. 13½x13¼***
4382 A1722 Sheet of 2, #a-b + label 3.75 3.75

Europa A1723

Designs: 55c, Person holding star. 1 l, Flower.

Perf. 12¾x13 Syncopated

2006, Apr. 25

4383	A1723	55c multi	1.00	1.00
4384	A1723	1 l multi	2.00	2.00

Booklet Stamps

Perf. 13

4385	A1723	55c multi	3.00	3.00
4386	A1723	1 l multi	8.00	8.00
a.		Booklet pane, 4 each #4385-4386	55.00	—
		Complete booklet, #4386a	57.50	
	Nos. 4383-4386 (4)		14.00	14.00

Souvenir Sheet

Meeting of NATO Foreign Ministers, Sofia — A1724

2006, Apr. 27 ***Perf. 13***
4387 A1724 1.50 l multi 2.50 2.50

Trud Newspaper, 70th Anniv. — A1725

2006, Apr. 28
4388 A1725 55s multi 1.25 1.25

Souvenir Sheet

Vesselin Topalov, World Chess Champion — A1726

2006, May 4 ***Perf. 13***
4389 A1726 1.50 l multi 2.50 2.50

Exists imperf. with perforated serial number. Value $12.

Palace of Culture, Sofia, 25th Anniv. — A1727

2006, May 5 ***Perf. 13¼x13***
4390 A1727 55s multi + label 1.25 1.25

Birds A1728

Designs: 10s, Circus aeruginosus. 35s, Circus cyaneus. 55s, Circus macrourus. 1 l, Circus pygargus.

2006, May 9 ***Perf. 13***
4391-4394 A1728 Set of 4 3.75 3.75

Nikola Vaptsarov Naval Academy, 125th Anniv. — A1729

2006, May 20 ***Perf. 13¼x13***
4395 A1729 55s multi 1.00 1.00

Souvenir Sheet

2006 World Cup Soccer Championships, Germany — A1730

2006, June 9
4396 A1730 1 l multi 1.75 1.75

Bulgarian Membership in UNESCO, 50th Anniv. — A1731

2006, June 29 ***Perf. 13***
4397 A1731 1 l multi .50 .50

Gena Dimitrova (1941-2005), Opera Singer — A1732

2006, July 18 **Litho.** ***Perf. 13¼***
4398 A1732 1 l multi 2.00 2.00

Flowers A1733

No. 4399: a, Saponaria stranjensis. b, Trachystemon orientalis. c, Hypericum calycinum. d, Rhododendron ponticum.

2006, July 28 ***Perf. 13***

4399		Horiz. strip of 4	3.00	3.00
a.		A1733 10s multi	.25	.25
b.		A1733 35s multi	.45	.45
c.		A1733 55s multi	.70	.70
d.		A1733 1 l multi	1.40	1.40

No. 4399 printed in sheets of 2 strips which are tete-beche.

Bulgarian Automobiles — A1734

Designs: 10s, 1995 Rover Maestro. 35s, 1967 Moskvich. 55s, 1967 Bulgaralpine. 1 l, 1967 Bulgarrenault.

2006, Sept. 29 Litho. *Perf. 13*
4400-4403 A1734 Set of 4 3.00 3.00

Souvenir Sheet

Return of the Prodigal Son, by Rembrandt (1606-69) — A1735

2006, Oct. 25
4404 A1735 1 l multi 2.00 2.00

Paintings by Bulgarian Artists — A1736

Designs: 10s, All Souls Day, by Ivan Murkvitchka. 35s, Sozopol - Houses, by Veselin Staykov. 55s, Sofia in Winter, by Nikola Petrov. 1 l, Portrait of T. Popova, by Georgi Popov.

2006, Oct. 27 *Perf. 13x13¼*
4405-4408 A1736 Set of 4 3.25 3.25

World Sambo Championships, Sofia — A1737

2006, Nov. 3 *Perf. 13*
4409 A1737 55s multi .90 .90

Souvenir Sheet

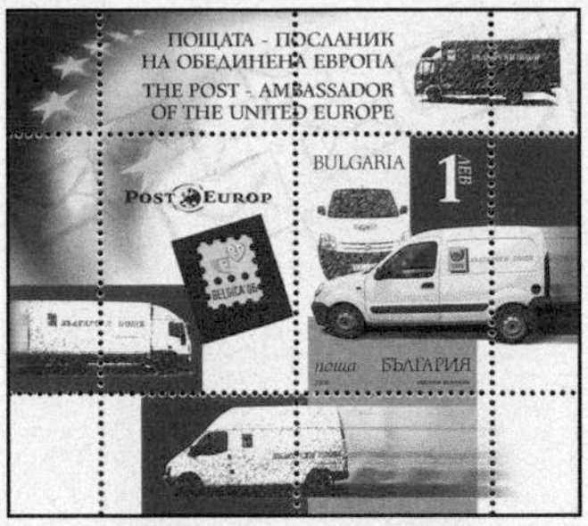

Postal Vans — A1738

2006, Nov. 17 *Perf. 13¼*
4410 A1738 1 l multi + label 4.00 4.00

Christmas — A1739

2006, Nov. 24 *Perf. 13¼x13*
4411 A1739 55s multi .90 .90

2007 Admission of Bulgaria and Romania into European Union — A1740

Designs: 55s, Flags of Bulgaria and Romania, map of Europe, European Union ballot box. 1.50 l, "EU" in colors of Bulgarian and Romanian flags.

2006, Nov. 29 *Perf. 13*
4412-4413 A1740 Set of 2 3.25 3.25
4413a Souvenir sheet, #4412-4413 3.25 3.25

See Bulgaria Nos.

Peter Dimkov (1886-1981), Naturopath — A1741

2006, Dec. 20
4414 A1741 55s multi .90 .90

Builders of the Bulgarian State — A1742

Designs: 10s, Gen. Danail Nikolaev (1852-1942), Gen. Racho Petrov (1861-1942). 35s, Petko Karavelov (1843-1903), Marin Drinov (1838-1906). 55s, Dr. Konstantin Stoylov (1853-1901), Stefan Stambolov (1854-95). 1 l, Prince Alexander I (1857-93).

2006, Dec. 21
4415-4418 A1742 Set of 4 3.25 3.25

Souvenir Sheet

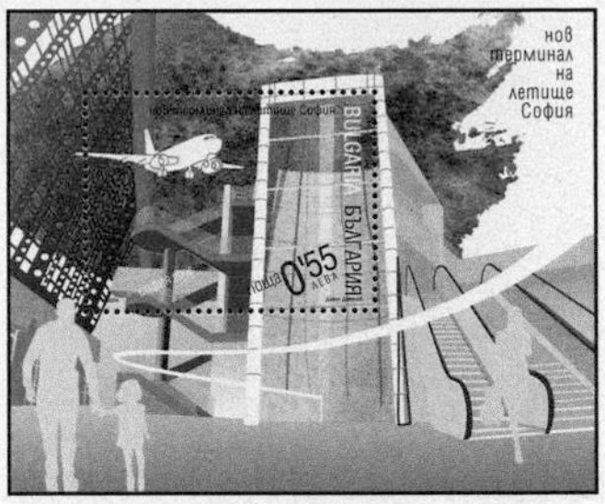

Opening of New Terminal at Sofia Airport — A1743

2006, Dec. 27 Litho.
4419 A1743 55s multi 1.25 1.25

Exists imperf. with perforated serial number. Value, $15.

Souvenir Sheet

Admission to European Union — A1744

2007, Jan. 31 *Perf. 13¼*
4420 A1744 1.50 l multi 2.00 2.00

Emilian Stanev (1907-79), Novelist — A1745

2007, Feb. 28 *Perf. 13*
4421 A1745 55s multi + label 1.00 1.00

Treaty of Rome, 50th Anniv. A1746

2007, Mar. 23 *Perf. 13¼x13*
4422 A1746 1 l multi 1.60 1.60

Stage Actors — A1747

Designs: 10s, Ivan Dimov (1897-1965). 55s, Sava Ognyanov (1876-1933). 1 l, Krustyo Sarafov (1876-1952).

2007, Mar. 27 *Perf. 13*
4423-4425 A1747 Set of 3 2.50 2.50

Souvenir Sheet

Launch of Sputnik 1, 50th Anniv. — A1748

2007, Apr. 25 Litho. *Perf. 13¼x13*
4426 A1748 1 l multi 1.40 1.40

Europa — A1749

Nos. 4427 and 4428: a, 55s, Scouts around campfire. b, 1.50 l, Scouts reading map.

2007, Apr. 26 *Perf. 13 Syncopated*
Size: 39x28mm
4427 A1749 Pair, #a-b 3.25 3.25

Booklet Stamps
Size: 31x23mm
Perf. 13

4428 A1749 Pair, #a-b 4.50 4.50
c. Booklet pane, 4 each #4428a-4428b 18.00 —
Complete booklet, #4428c 18.00

Scouting, cent.

Military Aircraft A1750

Designs: 10s, DAR 3, 1937. 35s, DAR 9, 1939. 55s, KB 309, 1939. 1 l, KB 11A, 1940

2007, Apr. 27 *Perf. 13¼x13*
4429-4432 A1750 Set of 4 3.00 3.00

Death of King Boris I, 1100th Anniv. A1751

2007, May 2
4433 A1751 55s multi 1.00 1.00

Poets and Painters A1752

Designs: 10s, Dimcho Debelyanov (1887-1916), poet. 35s, Nenko Balkanski (1907-77), painter. 55s, Vera Lukova (1907-74), painter. 1 l, Theodor Trayanov (1882-1945), poet.

2007, May 23 *Perf. 13*
4434-4437 A1752 Set of 4 3.00 3.00

European Conference of Transportation Ministers, Sofia — A1753

2007, May 30 *Perf. 13x13¼*
4438 A1753 1 l multi 1.60 1.60

Monasteries — A1754

Designs: 63s, Lozenski Monastery. 75s, Obradovski Monastery. 1.20 l, Kremikovski Monastery. 2.20 l, Chepinski Monastery.

Perf. 12½x12¾ Syncopated
2007, May 30
Color Behind Denomination

4439	A1754	63s	yel orange	.90	.90
4440	A1754	75s	green	1.25	1.25
4441	A1754	1.20 l	red	1.90	1.90
4442	A1754	2.20 l	blue	3.50	3.50
	Nos. 4439-4442 (4)			7.55	7.55

Souvenir Sheet

Diplomatic Relations Between Bulgaria and Azerbaijan, 15th Anniv. — A1755

2007, June 1 *Perf. 13*
4443 A1755 1 l multi 1.60 1.60

Excavations of San Clemente Basilica, Rome, 150th Anniv. — A1756

2007, May 21 **Litho.** *Perf. 13*
4444 A1756 1 l multi 1.60 1.60

Flowers — A1757

Designs: 10s, Onosma thracica. 45s, Astracantha aitosensis. 55s, Veronica krumovii. 1 l, Verbascum adrianopolitanum.

Perf. 13x12½ Syncopated
2007, July 6
4445-4448 A1757 Set of 4 3.50 3.50

Vassil Levski (1837-73), Patriot — A1758

2007, July 18 *Perf. 13*
4449 A1758 55s multi 1.00 1.00

World Youth 470 Class Yachting Championships, Bourgas A1759

2007, July 21
4450 A1759 1 l multi 2.00 2.00

Battle of Stara Zagora, 130th Anniv. — A1760

2007, July 31
4451 A1760 55s multi 1.00 1.00

2007 Rugby World Cup, France A1761

2007, Sept. 5 *Perf. 13¼*
4452 A1761 55s multi 1.00 1.00

Souvenir Sheet

Ropotamo Reserve, 15th Anniv. — A1762

No. 4453: a, 55s, Lutra lutra. b, 1 l, Haliaeetus albicilla.

2007, Sept. 10
4453 A1762 Sheet of 2, #a-b 2.50 2.50

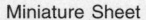

Miniature Sheet

Endangered Birds — A1763

No. 4454: a, 10s, Alcedo atthis. b, 35s, Tichodroma muraria. c, 55s, Bombycilla garrulus. d, 1 l, Phoenicopterus ruber.

2007, Sept. 11 *Perf. 13*
4454 A1763 Sheet of 4, #a-d 3.25 3.25

Great Lodge of the Old Freemasons of Bulgaria, 10th Anniv. — A1764

2007, Sept. 21
4455 A1764 55s multi 1.75 1.75

Souvenir Sheet

Bulgaria Post Exchange and Sorting Center, Sofia — A1765

2007, Oct. 9 **Litho.** *Perf. 13¼*
4456 A1765 55s multi 1.00 1.00

World Post Day.

Ivan Hadjiiski (1907-44), Psychologist A1766

2007, Oct. 12 *Perf. 13*
4457 A1766 55s multi 1.00 1.00

Christmas A1767

2007, Nov. 27 **Litho.** *Perf. 13*
4458 A1767 55s multi 1.00 1.00

Sports Champions A1768

Designs: 10s, Rumyana Neykova, European 2000-meter skiff rowing champion. 35s, Stanka Zlateva, world freestyle wrestling champion. 1 l, Stefka Kostadinova, women's world record-holder in high jump.

2007, Dec. 19 *Perf. 13½x13*
4459-4461 A1768 Set of 3 2.25 2.25

Military Reconnaisance in Bulgaria, Cent. — A1769

2007, Dec. 20 *Perf. 13x13¼*
4462 A1769 55s multi 1.00 1.00

Christo Botev (1848-76), Poet — A1770

2008, Jan. 6 **Litho.** *Perf. 13*
4463 A1770 55s multi 1.00 1.00

Souvenir Sheet

Intl. Polar Year — A1771

No. 4464: a, 55s, Polar bear. b, 1 l, Penguins.

2008, Jan. 30 *Perf. 13¼*
4464 A1771 Sheet of 2, #a-b, + 2 labels 2.40 2.40

Bulgarian Antarctic expeditions, 20th anniv.

Souvenir Sheet

2008 Summer Olympics, Beijing — A1772

No. 4465: a, 55s, One volleyball player. b, 1 l, Two volleyball players.

2008, Feb. 25 Litho. ***Perf. 13***
4465 A1772 Sheet of 2, #a-b 2.40 2.40

Independence, 130th Anniv. — A1773

2008, Feb. 29
4466 A1773 55s multi 1.10 1.10

Europa — A1774

Cover with stamp and: Nos. 4467, 4468, Postman. Nos. 4469, 4470, Bird.

2008, Apr. 22

4467 A1774 55s grn & multi		1.00	1.00
4468 A1774 55s lilac & multi		1.00	1.00
a. Booklet pane of 4		4.00	—
4469 A1774 1 l blue & multi		2.00	2.00
4470 A1774 1 l org yel & multi		3.00	3.00
a. Booklet pane of 4		12.00	—
Complete booklet, #4468a, 4470a		13.00	
Nos. 4467-4470 (4)		7.00	7.00

Stamps in booket panes are tete-beche.

Military Aviators — A1775

No. 4471 — Airplane and: a, 55s, Capt. Dimitri Spisarevski (1918-43). b, 1 l, Gen. Stoyan Stoyanov (1913-97).

2008, Apr. 25
4471 A1775 Horiz. pair, #a-b 2.75 2.75

Art — A1776

Designs: 10s, Painting by Boris Kotsev (1908-59). 35s, Nude, by Eliezer Alsheh (1908-78). 55s, Nude, by Vera Nedkova (1908-96). 1 l, Sculpture by Asen Peikov (1908-73).

2008, May 7
4472-4475 A1776 Set of 4 3.75 3.75

Sofia Zoo, 120th Anniv. — A1777

No. 4476: a, 10s, Csalithrix geoffroyi. b, 20s, Hippopotamus amphibius. c, 35s, Camelus bactrianus. d, 55s, Suricata suricata. e, 60s, Ara ararauna. f, 1 l, Lynx lynx.
No. 4477, Like No. 4476d.

2008, May 14 ***Perf. 13***
4476 A1777 Sheet of 6, #a-f 5.00 5.00

Souvenir Sheet

Imperf

4477 A1777 55s multi *22.50 22.50*

No. 4477 has simulated perforations. Bulgaria 2009 European Philatelic Exhibition.

Souvenir Sheet

Central Sports Club of the Army (CSKA) Soccer Team, 60th Anniv. — A1778

2008, May 7 Litho. ***Perf. 13½x13¼***
4478 A1778 55s multi 1.00 1.00

Souvenir Sheet

Space Flight of Alexander Alexandrov, 20th Anniv. — A1779

2008, June 9 Litho. ***Perf. 13***
4479 A1779 1 l multi 1.75 1.75

Union of Bulgarian Philatelists, 70th Anniv. — A1780

2008, June 16 Litho. ***Perf. 13***

Stamp With White Border

4480 A1780 60s multi 1.00 1.00

An imperforate souvenir sheet containing No. 4480 with a colored background sold for well above face value. Value, $20.

Souvenir Sheet

Wildlife of Strandzha Nature Park — A1781

No. 4481: a, 60s, Canis aureus. b, 1.50 l, Aquila pomarina, vert.

2008, July 21 Litho. ***Perf. 13¼***
4481 A1781 Sheet of 2, #a-b 3.50 3.50

Relations Between Bulgaria and European Economic Community, 20th Anniv. — A1782

2008, July 30 ***Perf. 13***
4482 A1782 1 l multi 1.75 1.75

Railroad Anniversaries — A1783

No. 4483: a, Orient Express passenger car, coat of arms of Paris, Munich and Vienna. b, Locomotive of Bulgarian State Railways, coat of arms of Belgrade, Sofia and Istanbul.

2008, Sept. 11

4483	Pair	3.50	3.50
a.	A1783 60s multi	1.00	1.00
b.	A1783 1.50 l multi	2.40	2.40

Orient Express and Bulgarian State Railways, 130th anniv. No. 4483 printed in sheets containing four of each stamp + one label.

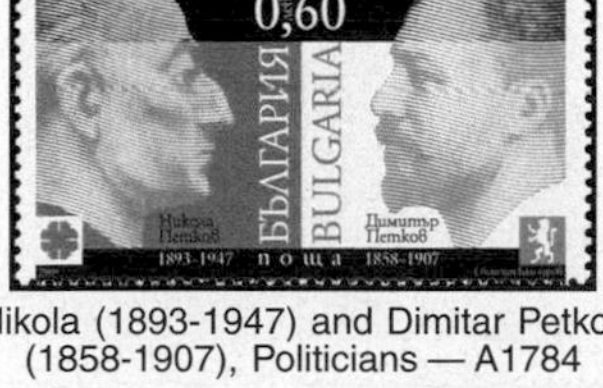

Nikola (1893-1947) and Dimitar Petkov (1858-1907), Politicians — A1784

2008, Sept. 18 Litho. ***Perf. 13***
4484 A1784 60s multi 1.20 1.20

Souvenir Sheet

Tsar Ferdinand (1861-1948) — A1785

2008, Sept. 22 ***Perf. 13x13¼***
4485 A1785 60s multi 1.20 1.20

Proclamation of Bulgarian independence, cent.

Destruction of the Knights Templar, 700th Anniv. — A1786

2008, Sept. 30 ***Perf. 13***
4486 A1786 1 l multi 2.00 2.00

Ferrari Race Cars — A1787

2008, Oct. 16

4487	Pair	20.00	20.00
a.	A1787 60s 2008 Ferrari	7.00	7.00
b.	A1787 1 l 1952 Ferrari	10.00	10.00

An imperforate souvenir sheet of the 60s stamp with simulated perforations exists.

Red Cross in Bulgaria, 130th Anniv. — A1788

2008, Oct. 24
4488 A1788 60s multi 1.20 1.20

Christmas A1789

2008, Nov. 21

4489 A1789 60s multi 1.20 1.20

Monastery Icons — A1790

No. 4490 — Madonna and Child icons from: a, Rila Monastery, 12th cent. b, Troyan Monastery, 18th cent. c, Bachkovo Monastery, 14th cent.

2008, Nov. 21

4490 Horiz. strip of 3 20.00 20.00
a. A1790 50s multi 3.50 3.50
b. A1790 60s multi 7.00 7.00
c. A1790 1 l multi 9.00 9.00

An imperf. souvenir sheet of the 60s stamp with simulated perforations exists.

Sofia St. Clement of Ohrid University, 120th Anniv. — A1791

2008, Nov. 25

4491 A1791 60s multi 1.20 1.20

Famous Men — A1792

No. 4492: a, Andranik Ozanian (1865-1927), Armenian general who particpated in Balkan Wars. b, Peyo Yavorov (1878-1914), Bulgarian poet.

2008, Dec. 10

4492 Horiz. pair 4.00 4.00
a. A1792 60s multi 1.25 1.25
b. A1792 1.50 l multi 2.50 2.50

See Armenia No. 789.

Bulgaria 2009 European Stamp Exhibition A1793

2009, Jan. 23

4493 A1793 60s multi 1.20 1.20

Famous Men Born in 1809 — A1794

Designs: 10s, Abraham Lincoln (1809-65), US President. 50s, Nikolai Gogol (1809-52), writer. 60s, Charles Darwin (1809-82), naturalist. 1 l, Edgar Allan Poe (1809-49), writer.

2009, Feb. 6

4494-4497 A1794 Set of 4 4.00 4.00

An imperf. souvenir sheet of No. 4496 with simulated perforations exists.

Birds — A1795

Designs: Nos. 4498a, 4499a, 60s, Scolopax rusticola. Nos. 4498b, 4499b, 1 l, Monticola saxatilis.

2009, Mar. 2 ***Perf. 13***

4498 A1795 Horiz. pair, #a-b 3.00 3.00

Souvenir Sheet

Imperf

4499 A1795 Sheet of 2, #a-b 3.00 3.00

No. 4499 has simulated perforations. See Serbia Nos. 457-458.

Amethyst A1796

2009, Mar. 24 **Litho.** ***Perf. 13x13¼***

4500 A1796 60s multi 1.20 1.20

Natl. Museum of Natural History, 120th anniv. An imperf. souvenir sheet with simulated perforations exists. Value, $20.

Hagia Sofia Church and St. Alexander Nevsky Cathedral, Sofia — A1797

2009, Mar. 25 ***Perf. 13***

4501 A1797 60s multi 1.00 1.00

Sofia as Bulgarian capital, 130th anniv.

Souvenir Sheet

Preservation of Polar Regions and Glaciers — A1798

No. 4502: a, 60s, Penguins, head of narwhal. b, 1.50 l, Body of narwhal, polar bear, seal, white-tailed eagle, icebreaker.

2009, Mar. 27

4502 A1798 Sheet of 2, #a-b 4.00 4.00

NATO Anniversaries — A1799

No. 4503 — NATO emblem and flags making up number: a, 60s, "60" (60th anniv. of NATO). b, 1.50s, "5" (5th anniv. of Bulgarian membership in NATO).

2009, Mar. 30

4503 A1799 Horiz. pair, #a-b 4.00 4.00

Bicycles A1800

Various bicycles.

2009, Mar. 31

4504 Horiz. strip of 4 4.00 4.00
a. A1800 10s multi .25 .25
b. A1800 50s multi .70 .70
c. A1800 60s multi .90 .90
d. A1800 1 l multi 1.40 1.40

An imperf. souvenir sheet of the 60s with simulated perforations exists. Value, $20.

Souvenir Sheet

Space Flight of First Bulgarian Cosmonaut Georgi Ivanov, 30th Anniv. — A1801

2009, Apr. 9 ***Perf. 13¼x13***

4505 A1801 60s multi 1.20 1.20

Souvenir Sheet

Restoration of the Bulgarian State, 130th Anniv. — A1802

No. 4506 — Arms of: a, 60s, 1879. b, 1 l, 1997.

2009, Apr. 15

4506 A1802 Sheet of 2, #a-b 2.75 2.75

Cacti — A1803

No. 4507: a, 10s, Rathbunia alamosensis. b, 50s, Mammilaria pseudoperbella. c, 60s, Obregonia degenerii. d, 1.50 l, Astrophitum mayas.

2009, Apr. 24 ***Perf. 13***

4507 A1803 Horiz. strip of 4, #a-d 5.00 5.00

An imperf souvenir sheet of the 60s with simulated perforations exists. Value, $20.

Europa A1804

Designs: Nos. 4508, 4510, 60s, IC342 galaxy. Nos. 4509, 4511, 1.50 l, M31 (Andromeda galaxy).

2009, Apr. 28 ***Perf. 13 Syncopated***

Size: 28x40mm

4508-4509 A1804 Set of 2 4.00 4.00

Size: 25x36mm

Perf. 13x13¼

4510-4511 A1804 Set of 2 4.00 4.00
4511a Souvenir sheet, 2 each #4510-4511 8.00 8.00
4511b Booklet pane of 4, #4510, 3 #4511 13.00 —
4511c Booklet pane of 4, #4511, 3 #4510 8.00 —
Complete booklet, #4511b, 4511c 24.00

Intl. Year of Astronomy. Nos. 4508-4509 were printed in sheets of 5 + label.

Introduction of the Euro, 10th Anniv. — A1805

2009, May 20 ***Perf. 13***

4512 A1805 1 l multi 2.00 2.00

Art — A1806

Designs: 10s, Landscape, by Vassil Ivanov (1909-75). 50s, Three Vases, by Georgi Kolarov (1909-96). 60s, The Black Sea, by Alexander Mutaffov (1879-1957). 1 l, Cast Shadows, by Konstantin Sturkelov (1889-1961).

2009, May 27 **Litho.**

4513-4516 A1806 Set of 4 4.00 4.00

Lokomotiv Sofia Soccer Team, 80th Anniv. — A1807

2009, May 28 *Perf. 13¼x13*
4517 A1807 60s multi 1.20 1.20

Owls — A1808

No. 4518: a, 10s, Bubo bubo. b, 50s, Athene noctua. c, 60s, Strix uralensis. d, 1.50 l, Glaucidium passerinum.

2009, May 30 *Perf. 13x13¼*
4518 A1808 Horiz. strip or block of 4, #a-d 5.00 5.00

Souvenir Sheet

Supermoto European Cup, Plovon A1809

2009, June 16
4519 A1809 60s multi 1.20 1.20

Captain Petko Voivoda (1844-1900), Hajduk Leader — A1810

2009, June 17 *Perf. 13*
4520 A1810 60s multi 1.20 1.20

Todor Burmov (1834-1906), First Bulgarian Prime Minister — A1811

2009, June 26
4521 A1811 60s multi 1.20 1.20

Ministry of Internal Affairs, 130th anniv.

Souvenir Sheet

Bulgarian Post and Communications Department, 130th Anniv. — A1812

No. 4522 — Hands: a, 60s, Opening air mail letter. b, 1 l, Holding telephone.

2009, June 29 *Perf. 13¼x13*
4522 A1812 Sheet of 2, #a-b 3.00 3.00

Souvenir Sheet

First Man on the Moon, 40th Anniv. — A1813

2009, July 20
4523 A1813 60s multi 1.20 1.20

Bulgarian Academy of Science, 140th Anniv. — A1814

2009, Oct. 9 **Litho.** *Perf. 13*
4524 A1814 60s multi 1.20 1.20

Souvenir Sheet

Diplomatic Relations Between Bulgaria and Italy, 130th Anniv. — A1815

2009, Oct. 15 *Perf. 13¼x13*
4525 A1815 1 l multi 2.00 2.00

See Italy No. 2970.

Souvenir Sheet

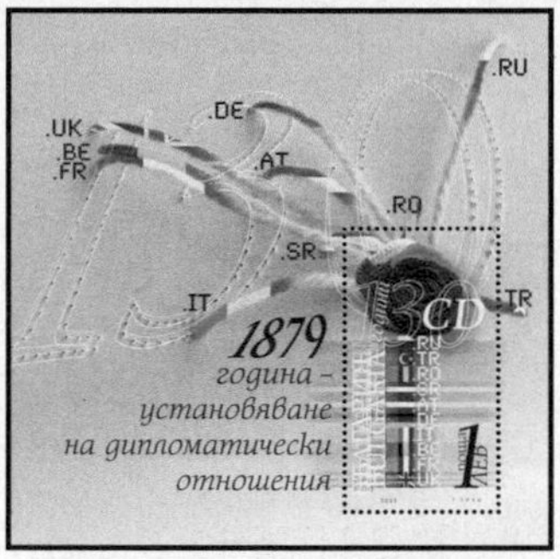

First Establishment of Diplomatic Relations With Foreign Countries, 130th Anniv. — A1816

2009, Nov. 1 *Perf. 13x13¼*
4526 A1816 1 l multi 2.00 2.00

Bulgarian National Television, 50th Anniv. — A1817

2009, Nov. 14 *Perf. 13¼x13*
4527 A1817 60s multi 1.20 1.20

Military Aviation — A1818

No. 4528: a, Fokker E. III and Capt. Marko Parvanov (1892-1962). b, Assen Jordanoff (1896-1967), aeronautical engineer, and Jordanoff 1.

2009, Nov. 18 *Perf. 13*
4528 Horiz. pair 3.00 3.00
a. A1818 60s multi 1.00 1.00
b. A1818 1 l multi 1.75 1.75

Nikola Vapzarov (1909-42), Poet — A1819

2009, Nov. 20
4529 A1819 60s multi 1.20 1.20

Christmas A1820

2009, Nov. 20
4530 A1820 60s multi 1.20 1.20

Dimitar Miladinov (1810-62), Poet — A1821

2010, Jan. 7 **Litho.** *Perf. 13*
4531 A1821 60s multi 1.20 1.20

Bulgarian National Radio, 75th Anniv. — A1822

2010, Jan. 25 *Perf. 13x13¼*
4532 A1822 60s multi 1.20 1.20

Souvenir Sheet

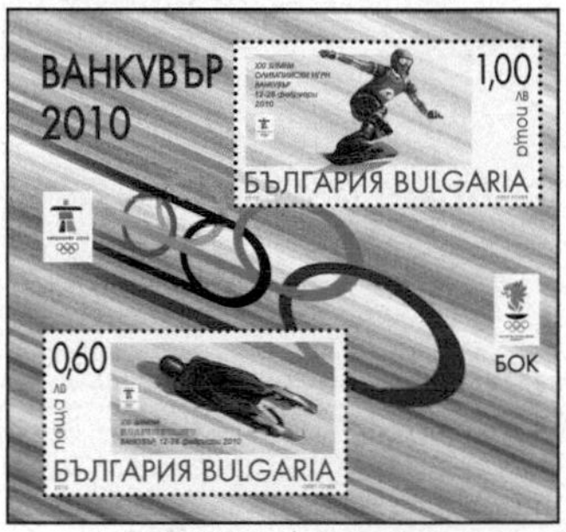

2010 Winter Olympics, Vancouver — A1823

No. 4533: a, 60s, Luge. b, 1 l, Snowboarding.

2010, Feb. 5 *Perf. 13½x13*
4533 A1823 Sheet of 2, #a-b 3.00 3.00

Souvenir Sheet

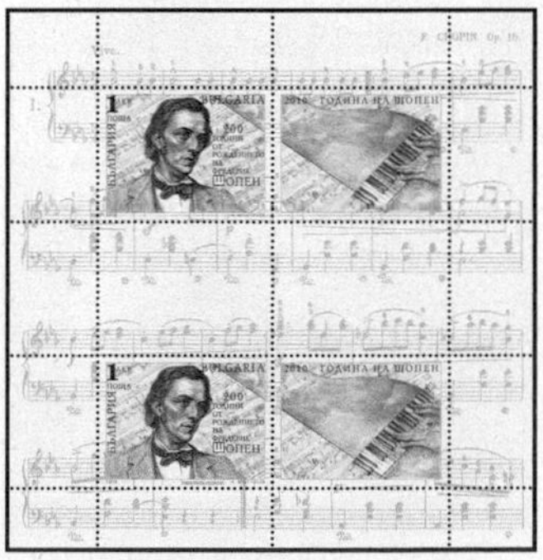

Frédéric Chopin (1810-49), Composer — A1824

No. 4534 — Chopin with: a, G line of musical staff below blue frame line at bottom. b, Beam connecting four notes below blue frame line below Chopin's tie and lapel.

2010, Mar. 1 *Perf. 13*
4534 A1824 1 l Sheet of 2, #a-b, + 4 labels 4.00 4.00

Souvenir Sheet

Peonies — A1825

No. 4535: a, Paeonia suffruticosa subsp. rockii. b, Paeonia officinalis "Rubra Plena."

2010, Mar. 23
4535 A1825 60s Sheet of 2, #a-b 2.25 2.25

Miniature Sheet

Military Commanders — A1826

No. 4536: a, General Georgi Vazov (1860-1934), denomination at left. b, General Ivan Fichev (1860-1931). c, General Stilyan Kovachev (1860-1939). d, Colonel Vladimir Serafimov (1860-1934), denomination at right. e, General Dimitar Geshev (1860-1922).

2010, Mar. 26
4536 A1826 60s Sheet of 5, #a-e, + label 5.75 5.75

Souvenir Sheet

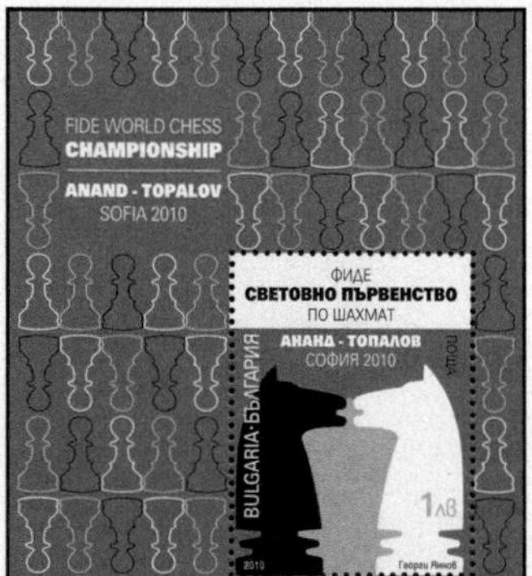

FIDE World Chess Championship Match, Sofia — A1827

2010, Apr. 22
4537 A1827 1 l multi 2.00 2.00

Europa A1828

Children's book, tree and: 60s, House, flowers, bird. 1.50s, Rabbit, insect, owl.

2010, Apr. 23 Litho. *Perf. 13*
4538 Horiz. pair 4.00 4.00
a. A1828 60s multi, 29x40mm, with white frame 1.10 1.10
b. A1828 1.50 l multi, 29x40mm, with white frame 2.75 2.75

Perf. 13x13¼

4539 Booklet pane of 2 + central label *4.00 4.00*
a. A1828 60s multi, 25x36mm, with white frame *1.10 1.10*
b. A1828 1.50 l multi, 25x36mm, with white frame *2.75 2.75*
Complete booklet, 4 #4539 *16.00*

Souvenir Sheet

Perf. 13

4540 Sheet of 2 4.00 4.00
a. A1828 60s multi, 32x43mm, without white frame 1.10 1.10
b. A1828 1.50 l multi, 32x43mm, without white frame 2.75 2.75

Expo 2010, Shanghai — A1829

2010, Apr. 30 Litho. *Perf. 13*
4541 A1829 1.40 l multi 2.75 2.75

Diplomatic Relations Between Bulgaria and Spain, Cent. A1830

2010, May 4 *Perf. 13½x13*
4542 A1830 1 l multi 2.00 2.00

Souvenir Sheet

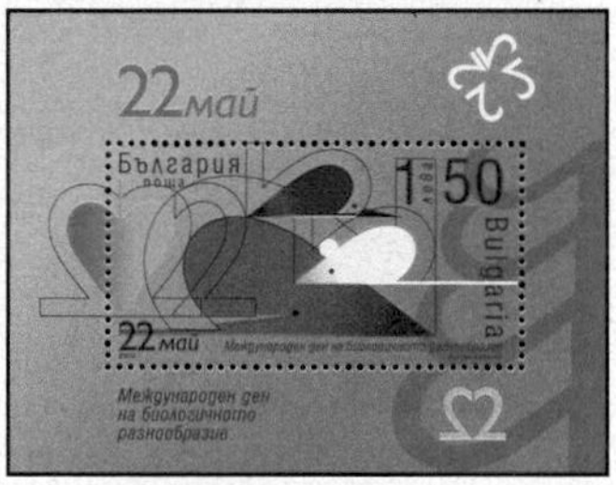

Intl. Day of Biological Diversity — A1831

2010, May 21 *Perf. 13¼x13*
4543 A1831 1.50 l multi 3.00 3.00

Souvenir Sheets

Emanuil Manolov (1860-1902), Composer — A1832

Robert Schumann (1810-56), Composer — A1833

No. 4544 — Manolov with: a, Notes above blue frame line at top and below blue frame line at bottom. b, No notes above blue frame line at top, tails of quarter notes below blue frame line at bottom.

No. 4545 — Schumann with: a, F line of musical staff below blue frame line at bottom. b, Lines of musical staff and notes below blue frame line at bottom.

2010, June 8 Litho. *Perf. 13*
4544 A1832 1 l Sheet of 2, #a-b, + 4 labels 4.00 4.00
4545 A1833 1 l Sheet of 2, #a-b, + 4 labels 4.00 4.00

Souvenir Sheet

Bulgarian Shepherd — A1834

2010, June 9 *Imperf.*
4546 A1834 60s multi *14.00 14.00*

Balkanfila Philatelic Exhibition, Plovdiv.

Souvenir Sheet

2010 World Cup Soccer Championships, South Africa — A1835

2010, June 10 *Perf. 13¼x13*
4547 A1835 2.10 l multi 4.00 4.00

St. Prokopi Varnenski, 200th Anniv. of Death — A1836

2010, June 16 *Perf. 13*
4548 A1836 60s multi 1.20 1.20

Paintings by Jaroslav Veshin (1860-1915) — A1837

No. 4549: a, Maneuvers, 1899. b, Returning from the Market, 1898.

2010, July 23 *Perf. 13¼x13*
4549 A1837 1 l Vert. pair, #a-b, + central label 4.00 4.00

Souvenir Sheet

Alphonse Mucha (1860-1939), Illustrator — A1838

No. 4550: a, Summer, Autumn (denomination at left). b, Winter, Spring (denomination at right).

2010, July 23 *Perf. 13¼*
4550 A1838 1 l Sheet of 2, #a-b, + central label 4.00 4.00

Youth Olympics, Singapore A1839

2010, July 30 *Perf. 13*
4551 A1839 1.40 l multi 2.75 2.75

Unification of Bulgaria, 125th Anniv. — A1840

2010, Sept. 3 Litho. *Perf. 13*
4552 A1840 60s multi 1.00 1.00

These imperforate souvenir sheets with simulated perforations, released in late 2010, were produced in limited quantities.

Miniature Sheet

Pandas — A1841

No. 4553: a, 10s, Head of Ailuropoda melanoleuca. b, 60s, Ailuropoda melanoleuca. c, 1 l, Ailurus fulgens. d, 1.50 l, Head of Ailurus fulgens.

2010, Oct. 28 **Litho.** ***Perf. 13***
4553 A1841 Sheet of 4, #a-d 7.50 7.50

Military Aircraft — A1842

Designs: 50s, Yak-23. 65s, MiG-15. 1 l, MiG-29.

2010, Nov. 12
4554-4556 A1842 Set of 3 4.00 4.00

Christmas — A1843

2010, Nov. 19
4557 A1843 65s multi 1.25 1.25

Miniature Sheet

Tourist Attractions of Northeastern Bulgaria — A1844

No. 4558: a, 10s, Carvings from Thracian Tomb of Sveshtari. b, 50s, Balchik Palace. c, 65s, Srebarna Nature Reserve. d, 1 l, Pobiti Kamani Geological Formation.

2010, Nov. 24 ***Perf. 13x13¼***
4558 A1844 Sheet of 4, #a-d 4.25 4.25

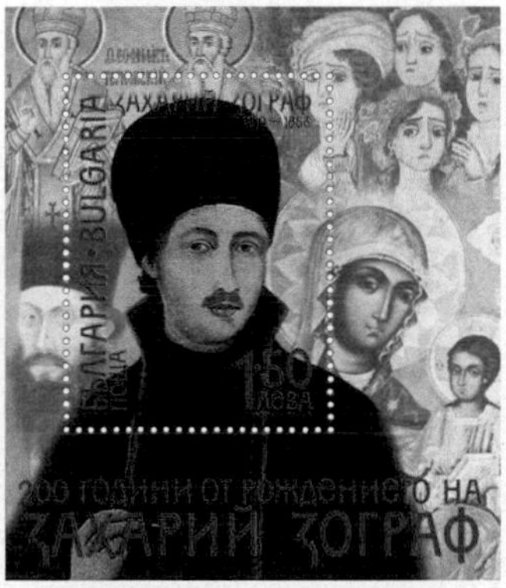

Zachary Zograf (1810-53), Painter — A1845

2010, Nov. 26 ***Perf. 13***
4559 A1845 1.50 l multi 3.00 3.00

Diplomatic Relations Between Bulgaria and Cuba, 50th Anniv. — A1846

No. 4560: a, 65s, Cuban flag, San Cristobal Church, Havana. b, 1.40 l, Bulgarian flag, St. Alexander Nevsky Cathedral, Sofia.

2010, Dec. 10
4560 A1846 Horiz. pair, #a-b 4.00 4.00

Hydrurga Leptonyx and Map of Antarctica A1847

2011, Jan. 7 ***Perf. 12¾ Syncopated***
4561 A1847 58s multi 1.00 1.00

A souvenir sheet containing 2 stamps + 2 labels was printed in 2013 in limited quantities.

Princess Clementine and 9th Plovdiv Infantry Regiment — A1848

2011, Jan. 24 ***Perf. 13***
4562 A1848 65s multi + label 1.25 1.25

9th Plovdiv Infantry Regiment, 125th anniv. Printed in sheets of 4 + 4 labels.

Vanga (Vangelia Pandeva Dimitrova) (1911-96), Mystic A1849

2011, Jan. 31 **Litho.**
4563 A1849 65s multi 1.25 1.25

April Fools' Day — A1850

2011, Apr. 1
4564 A1850 65s multi + label 1.25 1.25

Fictional discovery of the Planet of Gabrovo, 35th anniv. Gabrovo is Bulgarian town hosting a humor festival. Printed in sheets of 4 stamps + 4 labels. Horizontal stamp + label strips are tete-beche within the sheet.

Souvenir Sheet

Atlantic Club of Bulgaria, 20th Anniv. — A1851

2011, Apr. 11
4565 A1851 1 l multi 2.00 2.00

Souvenir Sheet

Space Achievements of the Soviet Union, 50th Anniv. — A1852

No. 4566: a, 65s, First manned space flight by Yuri Gagarin. b, 1.50 l, First probe to Venus, Venera 1.

2011, Apr. 12 ***Perf. 13x13¼***
4566 A1852 Sheet of 2, #a-b 4.00 4.00

Europa — A1853

Forest and: 65s, Capreolus capreolus in winter. 1.50 l, Scolopax rusticola.

2011, Apr. 28 **Litho.** ***Perf. 13***
Size: 29x54mm

4567 A1853 65s multi 1.25 1.25
4568 A1853 1.50 l multi 3.50 3.50
a. Souvenir sheet, #4567-4568, perf. 13x13¼ 5.00 5.00

Booklet Stamps
Size: 24x44mm
Perf. 13

4569 A1853 65s multi 1.50 1.50
4570 A1853 1.50 l multi 3.75 3.75
a. Booklet pane of 4, 2 each #4569-4570 10.00 —
Complete booklet, 2 #4570a 20.00

Intl. Year of Forests

Souvenir Sheet

Serdica Edict of Religious Toleration, 1700th Anniv. — A1854

2011, Apr. 30 ***Perf. 13¼x13***
4571 A1854 65s multi 1.25 1.25

Competition Protection Commission, 20th Anniv. — A1855

2011, May 2 ***Perf. 13x12¾***
4572 A1855 65s multi 1.25 1.25

This imperforate souvenir sheet with simulated perforations, released in May 2011, was produced in limited quantities. Value, $15.
Compare with Type A1905.

Miniature Sheet

Tourist Attractions of North Central Bulgaria — A1856

No. 4573: a, 65s, Bear and Woodpecker, Boatin Reserve. b, 65s, Gold ring of Tsar Kaloyan, Church of the Forty Holy Martyrs, Veliko Turnovo. c, 1 l, Glozhene Monastery. d, 1 l, Woman at Etar Architectural and Ethnographic Complex, Gabrovo.

2011, June 10 ***Perf. 13x13¼***
4573 A1856 Sheet of 4, #a-d 6.00 6.00

Miniature Sheet

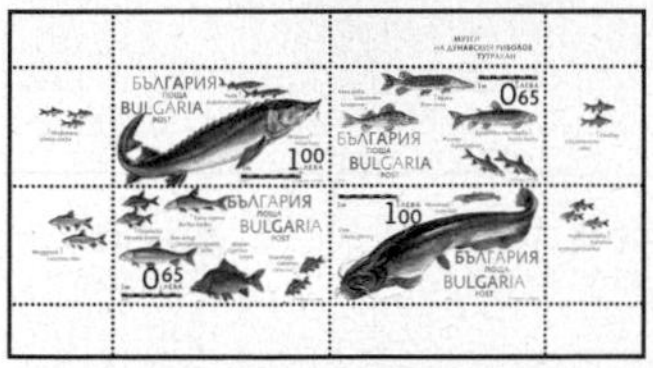

Fish of the Danube River — A1857

No. 4574: a, 65s, Stizostedion lucioperca, Esox lucius, Aspius aspius, Hucho hucho. b, 65s, Abramis brama, Barbus barbus, Ctenopharyngodon idella, Cyprinus carpio, Carassius carassius. c, 1 l, Acipenser ruthenus, Huso huso. d, 1 l, Silurus glanis, Lota lota.

2011, June 29 ***Perf. 13¼x13***
4574 A1857 Sheet of 4, #a-d 6.00 6.00

Victory of Khan Krum at Battle of Pliska, 1200th Anniv. A1858

2011, July 26
4575 A1858 65s multi 1.25 1.25

Miniature Sheet

Poisonous Mushrooms — A1859

No. 4576: a, 65s, Rhodophyllus sinuatus. b, 65s, Inocybe patouillardii. c, 1 l, Russula emetica. d, 1 l, Omphalotus olearius.

2011, July 29 ***Perf. 13***
4576 A1859 Sheet of 4, #a-d 6.00 6.00

Souvenir Sheet

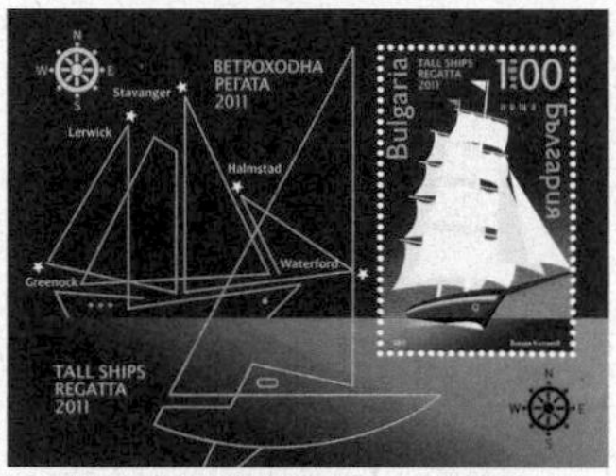

Waterford, Ireland to Halmstad, Sweden Tall Ships Regatta — A1860

2011, Aug. 25 ***Perf. 13¼***
4577 A1860 1 l multi 2.00 2.00

Souvenir Sheet

Fridtjof Nansen (1861-1930), Arctic Explorer — A1861

2011, Oct. 10 Litho. ***Perf. 13x13¼***
4578 A1861 1 l multi 2.00 2.00

Franz Liszt (1811-86), Composer — A1862

2011, Oct. 21 ***Perf. 13***
4579 A1862 1 l multi + label 4.00 4.00

Printed in sheets of 2 + 2 labels.

Souvenir Sheet

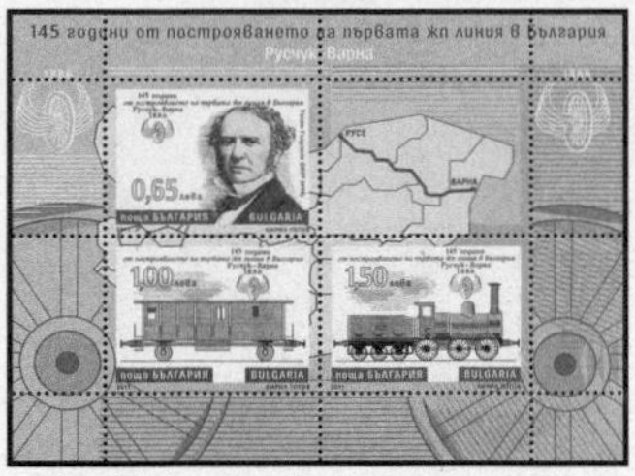

First Bulgarian Railway Line, 145th Anniv. — A1863

No. 4580: a, 65s, William Gladstone (1809-98), British prime minister. b, 1 l, Rail carriage. c, 1.50 l. Locomotive.

2011, Oct. 27 ***Perf. 13¼x13***
4580 A1863 Sheet of 3, #a-c, + label 6.00 6.00

Miniature Sheet

Dogs Launched Into Space — A1864

No. 4581: a, 65s, Laika (Nov. 3, 1957). b, 65s, Belka and Strelka (Aug. 19, 1960). c, 1 l, Chernushka (Mar. 9, 1961). d, 1 l, Zvezdochka (Mar. 25, 1961).

2011, Oct. 28 ***Perf. 13¼x13***
4581 A1864 Sheet of 4, #a-d 6.00 6.00

A souvenir sheet containing an imperforate example of No. 4581a exists from a limited printing. Value, $19.

First Bulgarians in Dakar Rally, South America — A1865

2011, Oct. 29 ***Perf. 13***
4582 A1865 1.50 l multi + label 5.50 5.50

Printed in sheets of 2 + 2 labels.

Souvenir Sheet

Intl. Black Sea Action Day — A1866

No. 4583: a, Scomber scombrus. b, Mytilus galloprovincialis.

2011, Oct. 31 ***Perf. 13x13¼***
4583 A1866 1 l Sheet of 2, #a-b 4.00 4.00

Yosif Tsankov (1911-71), Composer — A1867

2011, Nov. 7 Litho. ***Perf. 13¼x13***
4584 A1867 65s multi + label 1.25 1.25

Christmas A1868

2011, Nov. 17 ***Perf. 13x13¼***
4585 A1868 65s multi 1.25 1.25

Military Medical Academy, 120th Anniv. — A1869

2011, Dec. 1 ***Perf. 13¼x13***
4586 A1869 65s multi 1.25 1.25

Flowers A1870

Designs: 65s, Shown. 1 l, Flowers, diff., vert.

2012, Mar. 16 ***Perf. 13 Syncopated***
4587-4588 A1870 Set of 2 1.25 1.25

Disbanding of the Knights Templar, 700th Anniv. — A1871

2012, Mar. 22 ***Perf. 13¼x13***
4589 A1871 65s multi 1.25 1.25

No. 4589 was printed in sheets of 5 + label.

Famous People — A1872

Designs: No. 4590, 65s, Dimcho Debelyanov (1887-1916), poet. No. 4591, 65s, Anton Mitov (1862-1930), painter. No. 4592, 1 l, Yana Yazova (1912-74), writer. No. 4593, 1 l, Petya Dubarova (1962-79), poet.

2012, Mar. 28 ***Perf. 13x13¼***
4590-4593 A1872 Set of 4 6.00 6.00

Europa
A1873

Landmarks in Veliko Turnovo: Nos. 4594, 4596a, 65s, Baldwin Tower. Nos. 4595, 4596b, 1.50 l, Patriarchal Cathedral of Tsaravets.

Perf. 13 Syncopated

2012, Apr. 4 **Litho.**

4594-4595 A1873 Set of 2 4.00 4.00

Souvenir Sheet

Perf. 13

4596 A1873 Sheet of 2, #a-b 4.00 4.00

c. Booklet pane of 4, #4596a, perf. 13 on 3 sides *8.00* —

d. Booklet pane of 4, #4596b, perf. 13 on 3 sides *21.00* —

Complete booklet, #4596c-4596d *30.00* —

20th National Antarctic Expedition — A1874

2012, Apr. 7 ***Perf. 13¼x13***

4597 A1874 1.40 l multi + label 5.50 5.50

No. 4597 was printed in sheets of 2 + 2 labels. A 65s imperf. souvenir sheet with simulated perfoations was produced in limited quantities. Value, $15.

Souvenir Sheet

Sinking of the Titanic, Cent. — A1875

2012, Apr. 10

4598 A1875 1.40 l multi 2.50 2.50

Airplane Bombardment of Edirne Railway Station, Cent. — A1876

2012, Apr. 12 ***Perf. 13x13¼***

4599 A1876 65s multi 1.75 1.75

Parashkev Hadjiev (1912-92), Composer — A1877

2012, Apr. 27 ***Perf. 13¼x13***

4600 A1877 65s multi + label 1.25 1.25

Bulgarian Admission to Council of Europe, 20th Anniv. — A1878

2012, May 7 ***Perf. 13x13¼***

4601 A1878 1 l multi 2.00 2.00

Stara Zagora Stone Relief Lion, 9th-11th Cent. A1879

2012, May 16 ***Perf. 13***

4602 A1879 65s multi 1.25 1.25

Souvenir Sheet

Association of Bulgarian Enterprises for Intl. road Transport and Roads, 50th Anniv. — A1880

2012, May 30 ***Perf. 13¼x13***

4603 A1880 2.10 l multi 4.00 4.00

Souvenir Sheet

2012 European Soccer Championships, Poland and Ukraine — A1881

2012, June 8 **Litho.** ***Perf. 13¼***

4604 A1881 1 l multi 1.75 1.75

Miniature Sheet

Thorny Plants — A1882

No. 4605: a, 65s, Silybum marianum and butterfly. b, 65s, Carduus acanthoides and bee. c, 1 l, Centaurea solstitialis and ladybug. d, 1 l, Dipsacus laciniatus and beetle.

2012, June 14 ***Perf. 13***

4605 A1882 Sheet of 4, #a-d 6.00 6.00

A1883

2012, June 22

4606 A1883 65s multi 1.25 1.25

Slavonic-Bulgarian History, by St. Paisios of Hilandar, 250th Anniv. of Publication.

Miniature Sheet

Tourist Attractions of Northwestern Bulgaria — A1884

No. 4607: a, 65s, Plate and goblet from Rogozen Treasure archaeological find. b, 65s, Drawings from Magura Cave. c, 1 l, Meshchiite Tower, Vratsa. d, 1 l, Baba Vida Fortress, Vidin.

2012, July 12 ***Perf. 13x13¼***

4607 A1884 Sheet of 4, #a-d 6.00 6.00

Souvenir Sheet

2012 Summer Olympics, London — A1885

2012, July 16 ***Perf. 13¼x13***

4608 A1885 1.50 l multi 3.00 3.00

Vassil Levski (1837-73), National Hero — A1886

2012, July 18

4609 A1886 65s multi 1.25 1.25

Claude Debussy (1862-1918), Composer — A1887

2012, Aug. 22 ***Perf. 13***

4610 A1887 1 l multi + label 2.00 2.00

Plovdiv Fair, 120th Anniv. — A1888

2012, Sept. 24

4611 A1888 65s multi 1.25 1.25

Ivan Stoyanovich (1862-1947), Revolutionary Leader A1889

2012, Sept. 25

4612 A1889 65s multi 1.25 1.25

Monument of Liberty, Ruse, by Arnoldo Zocchi (1862-1940)
A1890

2012, Oct. 10 ***Perf. 13x13¼***

4613 A1890 1 l blue 2.00 2.00

Souvenir Sheet

Flora and Fauna of Parangalitsa Preserve — A1891

No. 4614: a, 65s, Primula deorum. b, 1.50 l, Felis silvestris silvestris.

2012, Oct. 18 ***Perf. 13***

4614 A1891 Sheet of 2, #a-b 4.25 4.25

Miniature Sheet

Railroad Mail Cars — A1892

No. 4615: a, 65s, First mail car (blue and red), ships on river. b, 65s, Green and red mail car used from 1888-1904, post offices. c, 1 l, Brown mail car used from 1895-1930, picture postcard depicting Plovdiv area costumes. d, 1 l, Green mail car used from 1909-35, railway map.

2012, Oct. 22

4615 A1892 Sheet of 4, #a-d, + 2 labels 6.00 6.00

This imperforate souvenir sheet with simulated perforations, released in October 2012, was produced in limited quantities. Value, $15.

A1893

Horses — A1894

No. 4616: a, 65s, Andalusian horse. b, 1 l, Arabian horse.

No. 4617: a, 65s, Irish tinker horse. b, 1 l, Haflinger pony.

2012, Oct. 28

4616 A1893 Pair, #a-b 3.00 3.00

4617 A1894 Pair, #a-b 3.00 3.00

Nos. 4616-4617 each were printed in sheets containing two horizontal pairs and 2 labels.

Ministry of Railways, Posts and Telegraph, Cent. — A1895

2012, Oct. 30

4618 A1895 65s multi 1.25 1.25

Discovery of Artifacts From Grave of Khan Kubrat, Cent. — A1896

2012, Nov. 7

4619 A1896 1 l multi 2.00 2.00

Christmas
A1897

2012, Nov. 20

4620 A1897 65s multi 1.25 1.25

Intl. Year of Chemistry — A1898

2012, Nov. 28 **Litho.**

4621 A1898 65s multi 1.40 1.40

Diplomatic Relations Between Bulgaria and Kazakhstan, 20th Anniv. — A1899

No. 4622: a, 65s, Gold rhyton with design of deer's head, 4th cent. B.C. b, 1.40 l, Gold buckle depicting bird and deer, 8th-7th cent. B.C.

2012, Dec. 12

4622 A1899 Pair, #a-b 4.00 4.00

Printed in sheets containing 3 pairs. See Kazakhstan No. 689.

Souvenir Sheet

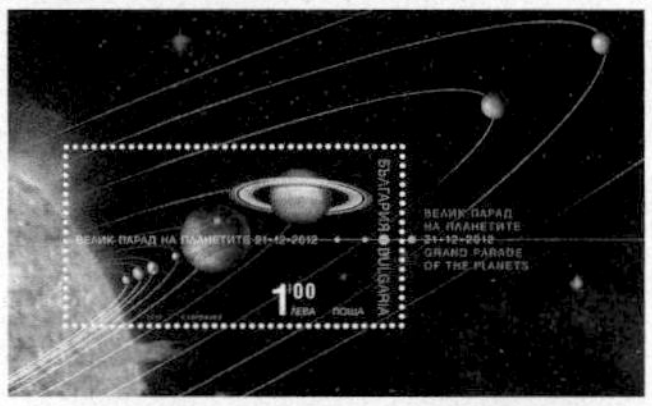

Planetary Alignment of Dec. 21, 2012 — A1900

2012, Dec. 21 ***Perf. 13¼x13***

4623 A1900 1 l multi 2.00 2.00

Tourism
A1901

2013, Jan. 4 ***Perf. 13***

4624 A1901 1 l multi 2.00 2.00

Maritime Administration, 130th Anniv. — A1902

2013, Feb. 28 ***Perf. 13¼x13***

4625 A1902 65s multi + label 1.25 1.25

Souvenir Sheet

General M. D. Skobelev on Horse, by N. D. Dimitriev-Orenburgsky — A1903

2013, Mar. 5 ***Perf. 13x13¼***

4626 A1903 1.40 l multi 2.75 2.75

End of Russo-Turkish War, 135th anniv. See Russia No. 7436.

An 65s imperforate sheet of type A1903 was printed in limited quantities and issued on Oct. 25. Value, $15.

Salvation of Bulgarian Jews, 70th Anniv. — A1904

2013, Mar. 10

4627 A1904 1.40 l multi + label 2.75 2.75

Printed in sheets containing 2 stamps + 2 labels.

Bird, Grapes and Wine Vat Greetings Type of 1998

Perf. 13 Syncopated

2013, Mar. 29 **Litho.**

4628 A1558 65s multi 1.50 1.50

No. 4214 Redrawn With Bulgarian Inscription at Lower Left Instead of "Europa"

2013, Mar. 29 ***Perf. 13 Syncopated***

4629 A1629 65s multi 1.50 1.50

Rabbit Mail Carrier
A1905

2013, Mar. 29 ***Perf. 13 Syncopated***

4630 A1905 65s multi 1.25 1.25

See footnote after No. 4572.

Bells — A1906

2013, Mar. 29
4631 A1906 1 l multi 2.00 2.00

A souvenir sheet produced in limited quantities containing No. 4631and 3 labels was issued on Dec. 12, 2018.

Cherno More Soccer Team, Cent. — A1907

2013, Mar. 29 ***Perf. 13¼x13***
4632 A1907 65s multi 1.25 1.25

No. 4632 was printed in sheets of 3 + label.

Slavia Soccer Team, Cent. — A1908

2013, Apr. 5 ***Perf. 13¼x13***
4633 A1908 65s multi 1.25 1.25

No. 4633 was printed in sheets of 3 + label.

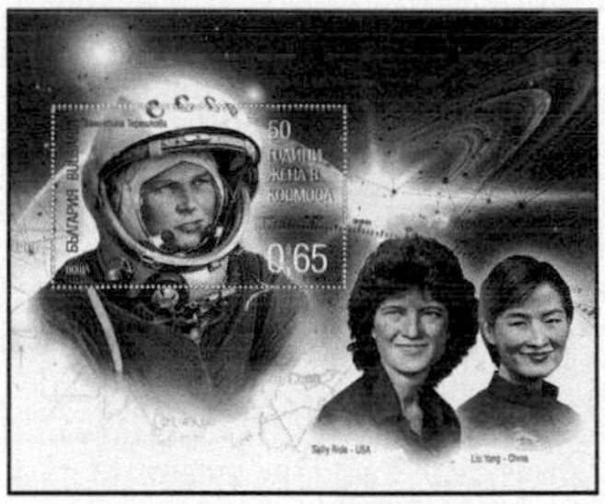

This Imperforate souvenir sheet with simulated perforations, released in Apr. 2013, was produced in limited quantities. Value, $15.

Miniature Sheet

Balkan Wars, Cent. — A1909

Designs: a, 65s, Bulgairan Army in battle. b, 65s, Victory Arch. c, 1 l, Surrender of Adrianople, Mar. 13, 1913. d, 1 l, Tsar Ferdinand on horse.

2013, Apr. 16 Litho. ***Perf. 13¼x13***
4634 A1909 Sheet of 4, #a-d 6.25 6.25

CSKA Soccer Team, 65th Anniv. — A1910

2013, Apr. 23
4635 A1910 65s multi 1.50 1.50

No. 4635 was printed in sheets of 3 + label.

Europa — A1911

Bulgarian postal van: Nos. 4636, 4640a, 65s, Facing lower left corner, area in red behind denomination. Nos. 4637, 4640b, 1.50 l, Facing lower right corner, with red triangle at lower left. No. 4638, Like No. 4636, with olive green area behind denomination. No. 4639, Like No. 4637, with blue triangle at lower left.

2013, Apr. 24 ***Perf. 13x13¼***

Stamps With White Frames

4636 A1911 65s multi 1.25 1.25
4637 A1911 1.50 l multi 3.00 3.00

Booklet Stamps

Perf. 13 on 3 Sides

4638 A1911 65s multi 1.50 1.50
a. Booklet pane of 4 6.00 —
4639 A1911 1.50 l multi 3.50 3.50
a. Booklet pane of 4 14.00 —
Complete booklet, #4638a, 4639a 21.00

Souvenir Sheet

Stamps Without White Frame

Perf. 13x13¼

4640 A1911 Sheet of 2, #a-b 4.25 4.25

Souvenir Sheet

Bulgarian State Railways, 125th Anniv. — A1912

2013, May 14 ***Perf. 13***
4641 A1912 1.40 l multi + label 2.75 2.75

Richard Wagner (1813-83), Composer — A1913

2013, May 22 ***Perf. 13¼x13***
4642 A1913 1 l multi + label 2.00 2.00

Souvenir Sheet

Birds in Mantaritsa Nature Reserve — A1914

2013, May 22 **Litho.**
4643 A1914 1.50 l multi 3.00 3.00

St. Ivan Rilski University of Mining and Geology, 60th Anniv. — A1915

2013, May 28 ***Perf. 13x13¼***
4644 A1915 65s multi 1.25 1.25

SOS Children's Villages — A1916

2013, May 30 ***Perf. 13***
4645 A1916 65s multi 1.25 1.25

Souvenir Sheet

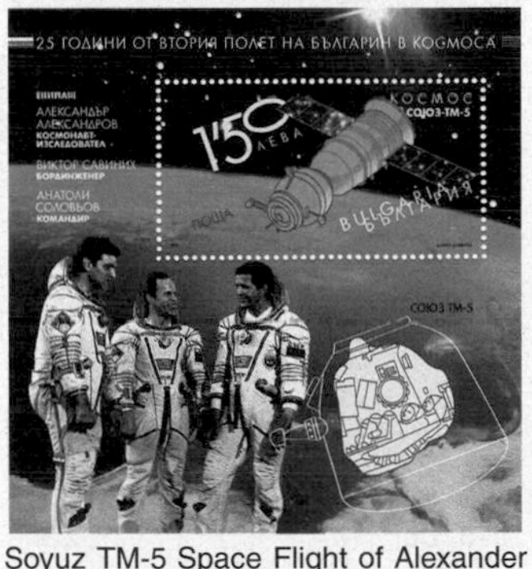

Soyuz TM-5 Space Flight of Alexander Alexandrov, 25th Anniv. — A1917

2013, May 30 ***Perf. 13¼x13***
4646 A1917 1.50 l multi 3.00 3.00

Souvenir Sheet

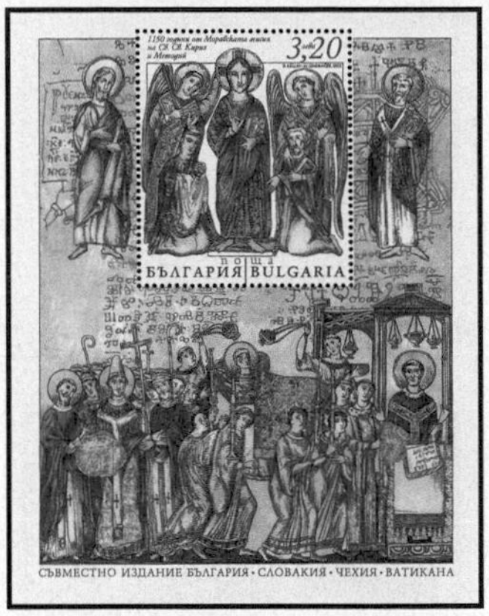

Mission of Sts. Cyril and Methodius to Slavic Lands, 1150th Anniv. — A1918

2013, June 12 ***Perf. 13x13¼***
4647 A1918 3.20 l multi 6.25 6.25

See Czech Republic No. 3573, Slovakia No. 666 and Vatican City No. 1536.

Miniature Sheet

Tourist Attractions in Southwestern Bulgaria — A1919

No. 4648: a, 65s, Building in Kovachevitsa. b, 65s, Wildlife in Skakavitsa Reserve. c, 1 l, Fresco, Zemen Monastery. d, 1 l, Church of St. Petka of the Saddlers, Vassil Levski (1837-73), national hero.

2013, June 17
4648 A1919 Sheet of 4, #a-d 6.25 6.25

Souvenir Sheet

Tsar Boris III (1894-1943) — A1920

2013, Aug. 30 **Litho.** ***Perf. 13¼***
4649 A1920 1.50 l multi 3.00 3.00

Diplomatic Relations Between Bulgaria and the United States, 110th Anniv. — A1921

2013, Sept. 12 Litho. *Perf. 13¼x13*
4650 A1921 1.40 l multi 2.75 2.75

Botev-Plovdiv Soccer Team, Cent — A1922

2013, Oct. 25 Litho. *Perf. 13*
4651 A1922 65s multi 1.25 1.25

No. 4651 was printed in sheets of 3 + label.

Cat Breeds — A1923

No. 4652: a, 65s, Siamese. b, 1 l, Birman.
No. 4653, horiz.: a, 65s, Scottish Fold. b, 1 l, Somali.

Perf. 13¼x13, 13x13¼
2013, Oct. 26 Pairs, #a-b Litho.
4652-4653 A1923 Set of 2 6.25 6.25

Miniature Sheet

Orchids — A1924

No. 4654: a, 65s, Cymbidium tridioides. b, 65s, Dendrobium fimbriatum var. occulatum. c, 1 l, Epidendrum radicans. d, 1 l, Dendrobium nobile.

2013, Oct. 26 Litho. *Perf. 13*
4654 A1924 Sheet of 4, #a-d 6.25 6.25

Souvenir Sheet

Green Balkans Association, 25th Anniv. — A1925

2013, Oct. 27 Litho. *Perf. 13½x13¼*
4655 A1925 1 l multi 2.00 2.00

Sofia Metro, 15th Anniv. A1926

No. 4656 — Metro cars and: a, Serdika Fortress, Sofia coat of arms. b, Lion's Bridge Station. c, Station, Sofia coat of arms.

2013, Nov. 22 Litho. *Perf. 13x13¼*

4656	Booklet pane of 3 + label	6.25	—
a.	A1926 65s multi	1.25	1.25
b.	A1926 1 l multi	1.75	1.75
c.	A1926 1.50 l multi	2.75	2.75
	Complete booklet, #4656	6.25	

Christmas — A1927

2013, Nov. 22 Litho. *Perf. 13x13¼*
4657 A1927 65s multi 1.25 1.25

Thracian Artifacts from 4th Cent., B.C. A1928

Designs: No. 4658, 1 l, Silver vial with griffin ornamentation. No. 4659, 1 l, Rhyton with galloping horse.

Perf. 13x12¾ Syncopated
2013, Dec. 18 Litho.
4658-4659 A1928 Set of 2 3.75 3.75

Souvenir Sheet

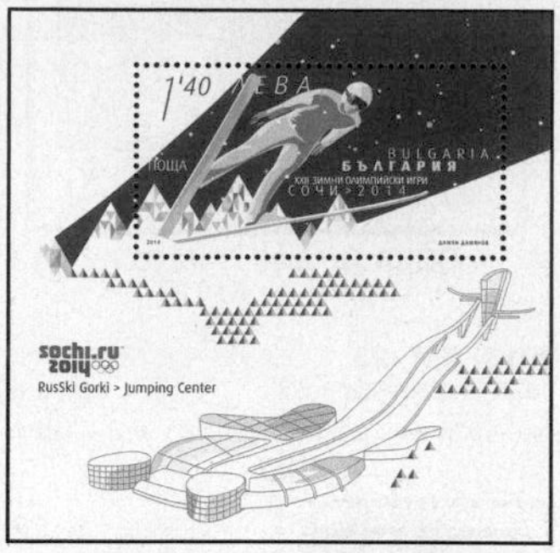

2014 Winter Olympics, Sochi, Russia — A1929

2014, Jan. 31 Litho. *Perf. 13¼x13*
4660 A1929 1.40 l multi 2.75 2.75

Mushrooms A1930

Dersigns: 10s, Boletus pinophilus. 20s, Coprinus picaceus. 50s, Amanita citrina. 1 l, Russula virescens.

Perf. 12¾x12½ Syncopated
2014, Feb. 10 Litho.

4661	A1930 10s multi	.35	.35
4662	A1930 20s multi	.50	.50
4663	A1930 50s multi	1.00	1.00
4664	A1930 1 l multi	2.00	2.00
	Nos. 4661-4664 (4)	3.85	3.85

PFC Levski Sofia Soccer Team, Cent. — A1931

2014, Feb. 21 Litho. *Perf. 13¼x13*
4665 A1931 65s multi, dated "2013" 1.25 1.25
a. Dated "2014" 1.25 1.25

Nos. 4665 and 4665a were each printed in sheets of 3 + label.

Galileo Galilei (1564-1642), Astronomer — A1932

2014, Feb. 21 Litho. *Perf. 13¼x13*
4666 A1932 1 l multi 2.00 2.00

No. 4666 was printed in sheets of 4.

Diplomatic Relations Between Bulgaria and Romania, 135th Anniv. — A1933

2014, Mar. 7 Litho. *Perf. 13*
4667 A1933 80s multi 1.60 1.60

Souvenir Sheet

Diplomatic Relations Between Bulgaria and People's Republic of China, 65th Anniv. — A1934

2014, Mar. 14 Litho. *Perf. 13*
4668 A1934 2.10 l multi 4.00 4.00

St. Sophronius of Vratsa (1739-1813), Bishop — A1935

2014, Mar. 17 Litho. *Perf. 13*
4669 A1935 65s multi 1.40 1.40

A1936

Bulgarian Parliamentarism, 135th Anniv. — A1937

No. 4670: a, 10s, Turnovo Constitution. b, 20s, Exarch Anthim I (1816-88). c, 30s, Copper bell of 1879 Parliament. d, 65s, 1991 Bulgarian Constitution and current bell of Parliament.
1 l, Exarch Anthim I, diff.

2014, Apr. 3 Litho. *Perf. 13¼x13*
4670 A1936 Sheet of 4, #a-d 2.50 2.50

Souvenir Sheet

4671 A1937 1 l multi 2.00 2.00

Miniature Sheet

Famous Men — A1938

No. 4672: a, 65s, Taras Shevchenko (wearing hat) (1814-61), writer. b, 65s, Richard Strauss (1864-1949), composer. c, 1 l, William

Shakespeare (1564-1616), writer. d, 1 l, Mikhail Lermontov (1814-41), writer.

2014, Apr. 5 Litho. *Perf. 13*
4672 A1938 Sheet of 4, #a-d 6.25 6.25

Balkanfila 2014 Intl. Philatelic Exhibition, Vidin.

Zaria Masonic Lodge, Sofia, Cent. — A1939

2014, Apr. 15 Litho. *Perf. 13¼x13*
4673 A1939 65s multi 1.25 1.25
a. Souvenir sheet of 4 3.80 3.80

Launch of STV Kaliakra, 30th Anniv. — A1940

2014, Apr. 17 Litho. *Perf. 13¼x13*
4674 A1940 65s multi + label 1.25 1.25

No. 4674 was printed in sheets of 2 + 2 labels.

Europa A1941

Dancers and musicians playing: 65s, Drum. 1.50 l, Shepherd's pipe.

Perf. 13 Syncopated
2014, Apr. 29 Litho.
Stamps With White Frames

4675 A1941 65s multi 1.25 1.25
4676 A1941 1.50 l multi 3.00 3.00

Souvenir Sheet
Stamps Without White Frame
Perf. 13

4677 Sheet of 2 4.25 4.25
a. A1941 65s multi 1.25 1.25
b. A1941 1.50 l multi 3.00 3.00

Size: 29x39mm
Stamps With White Frames

4678 Booklet pane of 6 + label 17.00 —
a. A1941 65s multi, perf. 13 vert. 2.50 2.50
b. A1941 65s multi, perf. 13 at left 2.50 2.50
c. A1941 65s multi, imperf. 2.50 2.50
d. A1941 1.50 l multi, perf. 13 vert. 4.50 4.50
e. A1941 1.50 l multi, perf. 13 at left 4.50 4.50
f. A1941 1.50 l multi, imperf. 4.50 4.50
Complete booklet, #4678 17.00

Souvenir Sheet

Ulmus Minor — A1942

2014, May 12 Litho. *Perf. 13x13¼*
4679 A1942 1 l multi 2.50 2.50

Souvenir Sheet

Stephan Parushev (1850-95), First Postmaster of Bulgarian Post — A1943

2014, May 14 Litho. *Perf. 13*
4680 A1943 1 l multi 2.00 2.00

Bulgarian Post, 135th anniv.

Kozloduy Nuclear Power Plant, 40th Anniv. — A1944

2014, May 20 Litho. *Perf. 13¼x13*
4681 A1944 65s multi 1.25 1.25

Souvenir Sheet

2014 World Cup Soccer Championships, Brazil — A1945

2014, June 12 Litho. *Perf. 13¼x13*
4682 A1945 2.10 l multi 4.50 4.50

Journalism in Bulgaria, 170th Anniv. — A1946

2014, June 17 Litho. *Perf. 13¼x13*
4683 A1946 65s multi 1.25 1.25

Diplomatic Relations Between Bulgaria and Russia, 135th Anniv. A1947

2014, July 7 Litho. *Perf. 13*
4684 A1947 1.40 l multi 2.75 2.75

See Russia No. 7542.

Prince Alexander I (1857-93) and National Guards — A1948

2014, July 10 Litho. *Perf. 13*
4685 A1948 65s multi 1.25 1.25

National Guard Unit of Bulgaria, 135th anniv.

Souvenir Sheet

Peter Deunov (1864-1944), Spiritual Leader — A1949

2014, July 11 Litho. *Perf. 13x13¼*
4686 A1949 1.50 l multi 3.00 3.00

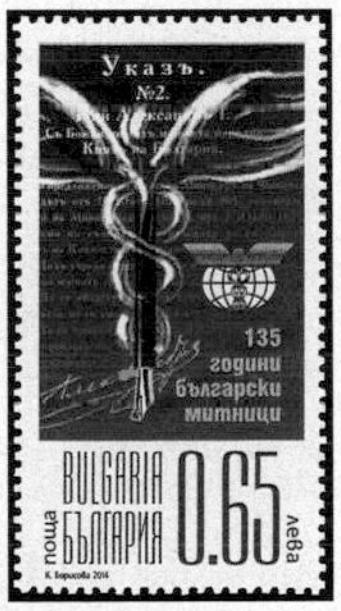

Bulgarian Customs Department, 135th Anniv. — A1950

2014, Aug. 8 Litho. *Perf. 13x13¼*
4687 A1950 65s multi 1.25 1.25

Trams A1951

Tram from: 30s, Berlin, 1900. 65s, Glasgow, 1930. 80s, Melbourne, 1945. 1 l, Sofia, 2014.

2014, Oct. 24 Litho. *Perf. 13*
4688-4691 A1951 Set of 4 5.25 5.25
4691a Souvenir sheet of 4, #4688-4691 5.25 5.25

Birds — A1952

Designs: 30s, Bombycilla garrulus. 50s, Erythropygia galactotes. 1 l, Melanocorypha yeltoniensis. 1.50 l, Hippolais icterina.

2014, Oct. 25 Litho. *Perf. 13¼x13*
4692-4695 A1952 Set of 4 6.00 6.00
4695a Souvenir sheet of 4, #4692-4695 6.00 6.00

Miniature Sheet

Tourist Attractions of South Central Bulgaria — A1953

No. 4696: a, 65s, Gold coin found at Perperikon archaeological site. b, 65s, Plovdiv Regional Ethnographic Museum. c, 1 l, Bulgarian National Astronomical Observatory, Rozhon. d, 1 l, Flora and fauna of Kupona Nature Reserve.

2014, Oct. 25 Litho. *Perf. 13x13¼*
4696 A1953 Sheet of 4, #a-d 6.25 6.25

This imperforate souvenir sheet with simulated perforations, released in Oct. 2014, was produced in limited quantities. Value, $17.50.

Alexandrovska Hospital, Sofia, 135th Anniv. — A1954

2014, Oct. 31 Litho. *Perf. 13¼x13*
4697 A1954 65s multi 1.25 1.25

Souvenir Sheet

King Wladyslaw III of Poland (1424-44) — A1955

2014, Nov. 10 Litho. *Perf. 13*
4698 A1955 1.50 l multi 3.00 3.00

Battle of Varna, 570th anniv.

Diplomatic Relations Between Bulgaria and the Sovereign Military Order of Malta, 20th Anniv. — A1956

2014, Nov. 11 Litho. *Perf. 13x13¼*
4699 A1956 1.50 l multi 3.00 3.00

Christmas A1957

2014, Nov. 20 Litho. *Perf. 13x13¼*
4700 A1957 65s multi 1.25 1.25

Souvenir Sheet

Tsar Samuel of Bulgaria — A1958

2014, Nov. 25 Litho. *Perf. 13x13¼*
4701 A1958 65s multi 1.40 1.40

Battle of Belasitsa, 1000th anniv.

Consecration of Church of St. Nicholas the Miracle Maker, Sofia, Cent. — A1959

2014, Dec. 5 Litho. *Perf. 13x13¼*
4702 A1959 65s multi 1.25 1.25

Artists — A1960

Designs: 30s, Konstantin Sturkelov (1889-1961), painter. 65s, Nikolai Rainov (1889-1954), painter. 80s, Mikhail Katz (1889-1964), sculptor. 1 l, Ivan Lazarov (1889-1952), sculptor.

2014, Dec. 5 Litho. *Perf. 13¼x13*
4703-4706 A1960 Set of 4 5.25 5.25

Petar Uvaliev (1915-98), Writer and Radio Commentator — A1961

2015, Jan. 12 Litho. *Perf. 13*
4707 A1961 65s multi 1.25 1.25

Bulgarian Cinema, Cent. A1962

2015, Jan. 13 Litho. *Perf. 13¼x13*
4708 A1962 65s multi 1.25 1.25

Old Clocks and Watches A1963

Designs: 5s, Astronomical clock. 30s, Table clock. 80s, Pocket watch.

Perf. 12¾x12½ Syncopated

2015, Feb. 20 Litho.

4709 A1963 5s multi	.35	.35
a. Perf. 13 horiz.	.60	.60
4710 A1963 30s multi	1.25	1.25
a. Perf. 13 horiz.	.40	.40
4711 A1963 80s multi	.90	.90
Nos. 4709-4711 (3)	2.50	2.50

Bandung 2017 World Stamp Exhibition, Indonesia (Nos. 4709a, 4710a). Issued: Nos. 4709a, 4710a, 7/27/17. Nos. 4709a and 4710a were printed together in sheets of four containing two of each stamp.

Souvenir Sheet

Apollo-Soyuz Joint Space Flight, 40th Anniv. — A1964

2015, Feb. 20 Litho. *Perf. 13*
4712 A1964 65s multi 1.25 1.25

Imperforate examples of No. 4712 exist from a limited printing.

Disabled Soldiers' Union, Cent. — A1965

2015, Mar. 27 Litho. *Perf. 13*
4713 A1965 65s multi 1.25 1.25

Europa A1966

Toys: 65s, Rocking horse. 1.50 l, Doll.

Perf. 13 Syncopated

2015, Apr. 20 Litho.

4714 A1966 65s	1.25	1.25
4715 A1966 1.50 l multi	3.00	3.00

Souvenir Sheet

Perf. 13

4716 Sheet of 2	4.25	4.25
a. A1966 65s multi	1.25	1.25
b. A1966 1.50 l multi	2.75	2.75

Booklet Stamps
Size: 29x39mm
Perf. 13 on 1 Side

4717 A1966 65s	*1.25*	*1.25*
a. Booklet pane of 4	*5.00*	—
4718 A1966 1.50 l multi	*3.00*	*3.00*
a. Booklet pane of 4	*12.00*	—
Complete booklet, #4717a, 4718a	17.00	

This imperforate souvenir sheet with simulated perforations, released in April 2015, was produced in limited quantities. Value, $15.

Souvenir Sheet

Ecology and Forestry — A1967

2015, May 7 Litho. *Perf. 13¼x13*
4719 A1967 1 l multi 2.00 2.00

Medical University of Plovdiv, 70th Anniv. — A1968

2015, May 14 Litho. *Perf. 13¼x13*
4720 A1968 65s multi 1.25 1.25

International Telecommunication Union, 150th Anniv. — A1969

2015, May 18 Litho. *Perf. 13¼x13*
4721 A1969 1 l multi 1.75 1.75

Marek Soccer Team, Cent. — A1970

2015, May 25 Litho. *Perf. 13*
4722 A1970 65s multi 1.25 1.25

No. 4722 was printed in sheets of 3 + label.

Souvenir Sheet

First European Games, Baku — A1971

2015, May 29 Litho. *Perf. 13¼x13*
4723 A1971 1.40 l multi 2.75 2.75

Oncology Hospital, 65th Anniv. — A1972

2015, June 17 Litho. *Perf. 13¼x13*

4724 A1972 65s multi 1.25 1.25

Baby, Princess Marie Louise and Maichin Dom Gynecological Hospital, Sofia — A1973

2015, Aug. 6 Litho. *Perf. 13x13¼*

4725 A1973 65s multi 1.25 1.25

Souvenir Sheet

Stephan Kunchev (1915-2001), Stamp Designer — A1974

2015, Aug. 6 Litho. *Perf. 13*

4726 A1974 1.50 l multi 3.00 3.00

An imperforate souvenir sheet containing a 65s stamp of this design was produced in limited quantities.

Folk Art — A1975

People in costumes at Koprivstitsa Folk Festival: 50s, Men and women. 65s, Men. 1 l, Women.

2015, Aug. 6 Litho. *Perf. 13¼x13*

4727-4729 A1975 Set of 3 4.25 4.25

4729a Souvenir sheet of 3, #4727-4729 + 3 labels 4.25 4.25

Miniature Sheet

Tourist Attractions of Southeastern Bulgaria — A1976

No. 4730: a, 65s, St. Anastasia Island. b, 65s, Artifact from Kabyle Archaeological Reserve. c, 1 l, Nestinarstvo dancer on hot coals. d, 1 l, Grapes and glass of wine.

2015, Aug.15 Litho. *Perf. 13x13¼*

4730 A1976 Sheet of 4, #a-d 6.25 6.25

Book A1977

Dove A1978

Ferris Wheel — A1979

Trophy A1980

Bird on Branch and Ladybugs A1981

Perf. 13 Syncopated

2015, Sept. 16 Litho.

4731 A1977 65s multi 1.25 1.25
4732 A1978 65s multi 1.25 1.25
4733 A1979 65s multi 1.25 1.25
4734 A1980 1 l multi 2.00 2.00
4735 A1981 1 l multi 2.00 2.00
Nos. 4731-4735 (5) 7.75 7.75

Alphonse de Lamartine (1790-1869), Writer — A1982

2015, Oct. 21 Litho. *Perf. 13x13¼*

4736 A1982 1.50 l multi 3.00 3.00

No. 4736 was printed in sheets of 4 + 2 labels.

Worldwide Fund for Nature (WWF) — A1983

Canis lupus lupus: Nos. 4737, 4741a, 65s, Adult and three pups. Nos. 4738, 4741b, 80s, Wolf with head lowered. Nos. 4739, 4741c, 1.40 l, Wolf with head raised. Nos. 4740, 4741d, 3 l, Four wolves.

2015, Oct. 23 Litho. *Perf. 13*

4737-4740 A1983 Set of 4 11.50 11.50

4740a Block or horiz. strip of 4, #4737-4740 11.50 11.50

Souvenir Sheet

Perf. 13¼

4741 A1983 Sheet of 4, #a-d 11.50 11.50

No. 4741 contains four 39x29mm stamps. Nos. 4737-4740 were each printed in sheets containing 20 stamps + 5 labels. No. 4740a was printed in a sheet containing two blocks or strips.

An imperforate souvenir sheet with simulated perforations containing a 30s stamp depicting Roald Amundsen and a 40s stamp depicting Robert Peary, released Oct. 23, 2015, was produced in limited quantities.

Flowers — A1984

Designs: 10s, Viola rhodopeia. 50s, Veronica kellereri. 65s, Papaver degenii. 1 l, Colchicum borisii.

2015, Nov. 6 Litho. *Perf. 13x13¼*

4742-4745 A1984 Set of 4 4.50 4.50

4745a Souvenir sheet of 4, #4742-4745 4.50 4.50

National Philatelic Exhibition, Veliko Turnovo (#4745a).

Souvenir Sheet

Uprising of Peter and Assen, 830th Anniv. — A1985

2015, Nov. 8 Litho. *Perf. 13½x13¼*

4746 A1985 1.50 l multi 2.75 2.75

Locomotives and Railroad Stations — A1986

No. 4747: a, 65s, 1891 locomotive, Ruse and Kaspichan stations. b, 1 l, 1897 locomotive, Kaspichan and Varna stations. c, 1.50 l, 1887 locomotive, Tsaribrod and Sofia stations. d, 2 l, 1890 locomotive, Sofia and Saranbei stations.

2015, Nov. 18 Litho. *Perf. 13¼x13*

4747 A1986 Sheet of 4, #a-d 10.00 10.00

Opening of Sofia Tech Park — A1987

2015, Dec. 1 Litho. *Perf. 13x13¼*

4748 A1987 1 l multi 2.00 2.00

Christmas — A1988

2015, Dec. 2 Litho. *Perf. 13*

4749 A1988 1 l multi 1.75 1.75

Souvenir Sheet

Plovdiv, 2019 European Capital of Culture — A1989

2015, Dec. 21 Litho. *Perf. 13¼*
4750 A1989 1 l multi 2.00 2.00

Emil Dimitrov (1940-2005), Singer — A1990

2015, Dec. 23 Litho. *Perf. 13*
4751 A1990 65s multi 1.25 1.25

Postcrossing — A1991

2015, Dec. 23 Litho. *Perf. 13*
4752 A1991 1 l multi 2.00 2.00

Souvenir Sheet

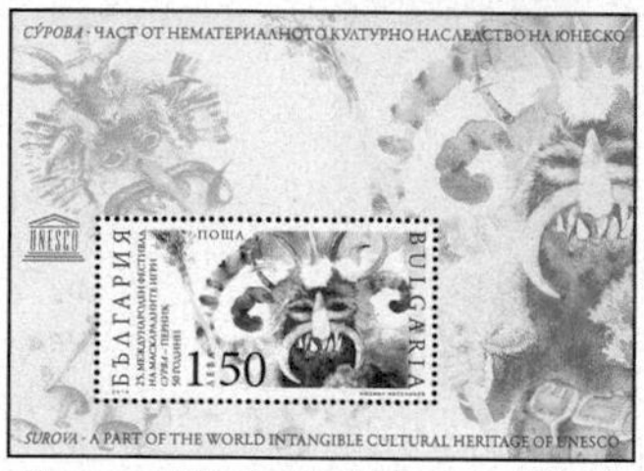

Surova Folk Festival Mask — A1992

2016, Jan. 28 Litho. *Perf. 13¼x13*
4753 A1992 1.50 l multi 3.00 3.00

This imperforate souvenir sheet with simulated perforations, released in Feb. 2016, was produced in limited quantities. Value, $17.50.

Assen Stareyshiski (1936-91), Artist — A1993

2016, Mar. 30 Litho. *Perf. 13*
4754 A1993 65s multi 1.25 1.25

A1994

Europa A1995

Perf. 13 Syncopated

2016, Apr. 26 Litho.
4755 A1994 1 l multi 2.00 2.00
4756 A1995 2 l multi 4.00 4.00

Souvenir Sheet

Perf. 13

4757 Sheet of 2 6.00 6.00
a. A1994 1 l multi 2.00 2.00
b. A1995 2 l multi 4.00 4.00

Size: 47x29mm

Perf. 13¼ on 2 Sides

4758 A1994 1 l multi 2.00 2.00
a. Tete-beche pair 4.00 4.00
4759 A1995 2 l multi 4.00 4.00
a. Tete-beche pair 8.00 8.00

Think Green Issue.

Nos. 4758 and 4759 were each printed in sheets of 4, with one stamp tete-beche in relation to the other stamps. The stamps include an imperforate margin at left or right. The sheets were sold with, but unattached to, a booklet cover.

Pencho Slaveykov (1866-1912), Poet — A1996

2016, Apr. 27 Litho. *Perf. 13*
4760 A1996 65s multi 1.25 1.25

New Year 2016 (Year of the Monkey) — A1997

2016, Apr. 28 Litho. *Perf. 13*
4761 A1997 2 l multi 4.00 4.00

An imperforate souvenir sheet of type A1997, with the emblem for World Stamp Show 2016 in the upper corner was produced in limited quantities. Value, $17.50.

St. George's Church, Kavarna A1998

Perf. 12¾ Syncopated

2016, May 5 Litho.
4762 A1998 65s multi 1.25 1.25

Ancient Thracian Coins — A1999

Designs: 65s, Silver coin depicting Tsar Sitalk, 444-424 B.C. 1 l, Silver coin depicting Tsar Metok, 407-389 B.C. 1.50 l, Silver coin depicting Hebrizelm, 405-383 B.C. 2 l, Bronze coin depicting Kotis, 383-359 B.C.

2016, May 10 Litho. *Perf. 13*
4763-4766 A1999 Set of 4 10.00 10.00
4766a Sheet of 4, #4763-4766, + 4 labels 10.00 10.00

Nos. 4763-4766 were each issued in sheets of 50 and sheets of 20 + 20 labels.

Alexander Poplilov (1916-2001), Painter — A2000

2016, May 12 Litho. *Perf. 13¼x13*
4767 A2000 65s multi 1.25 1.25

Beroe Soccer Team, Cent. — A2001

2016, May 16 Litho. *Perf. 13*
4768 A2001 65s multi 1.25 1.25
a. Souvenir sheet of 4 3.50 3.50

Hristo Botev (1848-76), Poet, and Steamship Radetski — A2002

2016, May 18 Litho. *Perf. 13*
4769 A2002 65s multi 1.25 1.25

Hijacking of the Radetski by Botev and followers to enter Bulgaria, 140th anniv.

Port of Ruse, 150th Anniv. A2003

2016, May 26 Litho. *Perf. 13¼x13*
4770 A2003 1 l multi 1.50 1.50

Souvenir Sheet

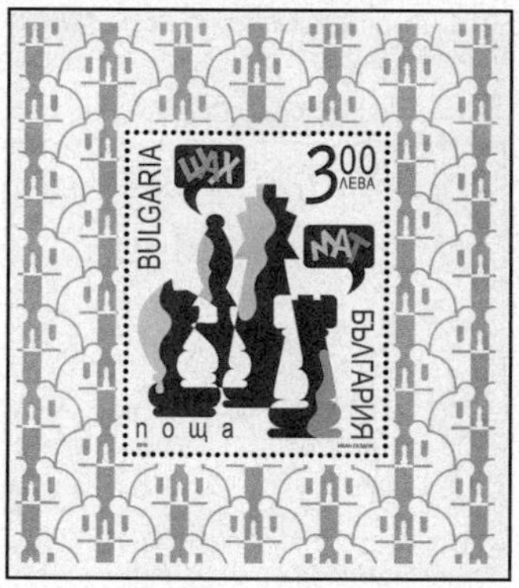

Chess — A2004

2016, July 12 Litho. *Perf. 13x13¼*
4771 A2004 3 l multi 6.25 6.25

White Storks, Flags of Bulgaria and Israel A2005

2016, Sept. 13 Litho. *Perf. 13*
4772 A2005 2.20 l multi 4.50 4.50

See Israel No. 2115.

Exarch Anthim I (1816-88), Chairman of National Assembly of Bulgaria — A2006

2016, Sept. 15 Litho. *Perf. 13¼x13*
4773 A2006 65s multi 1.00 1.00

Souvenir Sheet

Restoration of Trapezitsa Architectural Museum Reserve, Veliko Tarnovo — A2007

2016, Sept. 22 Litho. ***Perf. 13¼x13***
4774 A2007 1.50 l multi 3.00 3.00

See Azerbaijan No. 1119.

Wiki Loves Earth International Photography Contest — A2008

2016, Oct. 7 Litho. ***Perf. 13¼x13***
4775 A2008 2 l multi 2.75 2.75

A souvenir sheet containing 4 No. 4775 was prduced in limited quantities.

"Great Is Our Soldier," Bulgarian Army Anthem, Cent. — A2009

2016, Oct. 7 Litho. ***Perf. 13¼x13***
4776 A2009 2 l multi 4.00 4.00

Worldwide Fund for Nature (WWF) — A2010

Testudo graeca: Nos. 4777, 4781a, 65s, Laying eggs. Nos. 4778, 4781b, 80s, Eggs hatching. Nos. 4779, 4781c, 1.40 l, Adult. Nos. 4780, 4781d, 3 l, Two adults.

2016, Oct. 21 Litho. ***Perf. 13***
4777-4780 A2010 Set of 4 6.75 6.75
4780a Block of 4, #4777-4780, perf. 13 syncopated 6.75 6.75

Souvenir Sheet
Perf. 13¼
4781 A2010 Sheet of 4, #a-d 6.75 6.75

No. 4781 contains four 39x29mm stamps.

An imperforate souvenir sheet with simulated perforations containing a 65s stamp depicting a cat, released Oct. 10, 2016, was produced in limited quantities.

Motorcycles — A2011

Designs: 65s, BMW R 1200 GS. 1.50 l, Suzuki V-Strom 1000. 2 l, Honda VFR800X Crossrunner. 3 l, Suzuki Multistrada 1200S.

2016, Oct. 22 Litho. ***Perf. 13***
4782-4785 A2011 Set of 4 8.25 8.25
4785a Souvenir sheet of 4, #4782-4785, perf. 13¼ 8.25 8.25

An imperforate souvenir sheet containing No. 4782 with simulated perforations was produced in limited quantities.

Bulgarian Antarctic Expedition, 25th Anniv. — A2012

2016, Nov. 14 Litho. ***Perf. 13***
4786 A2012 65s multi .70 .70

Flags of Bulgaria and Switzerland, Louis-Emil Eyer (1865-1916), Physical Education Teacher and Coach — A2013

2016, Nov. 16 Litho. ***Perf. 13***
4787 A2013 1 l multi 1.10 1.10

Diplomatic relations between Bulgaria and Switzerland, cent.

Christmas A2014

2016, Nov. 16 Litho. ***Perf. 13x13¼***
4788 A2014 1 l multi 1.10 1.10

Souvenir Sheet

Paintings by Dimitar Dobrovich (1816-1905) — A2015

No. 4789: a, 65s, Self-portrait. b, 2 l, The Spinner Woman.

2016, Nov. 17 Litho. ***Perf. 13x13¼***
4789 A2015 Sheet of 2, #a-b, + 2 labels 3.00 3.00

Konstantin Velichkov (1855-1907), Writer and Co-Founder of National Academy of Arts — A2016

2016, Nov. 22 Litho. ***Perf. 13¼x13***
4790 A2016 65s multi .70 .70

National Academy of Arts, 120th anniv.

Vasil Yonchev (1916-85), Typographer — A2017

2016, Nov. 22 Litho. ***Perf. 13¼x13***
4791 A2017 65s multi .70 .70

Georgi Bonchev (1866-1955), Geologist A2018

2016, Dec. 7 Litho. ***Perf. 13x13¼***
4792 A2018 65s multi .70 .70

National Palace of Culture, Sofia, 35th Anniv. — A2019

2016, Dec. 9 Litho. ***Perf. 13¼x13***
4793 A2019 1.50 l multi + label 1.60 1.60

Souvenir Sheet

Gen. Vladimir Stoychev (1892-1990) Riding Horse — A2020

2017, Feb. 28 Litho. ***Perf. 13***
4794 A2020 2 l multi 2.25 2.25

An imperforate souvenir sheet with simulated perforations containing a 65s stamp depicting a rooster, released Feb. 28, 2017, was produced in limited quantities.

Bulgarian Civil Aviation, 70th Anniv. — A2021

2017, Mar. 22 Litho. ***Perf. 13***
4795 A2021 65s multi + label .70 .70

Rotary Foundation, Cent. — A2022

2017, Apr. 4 Litho. ***Perf. 13¼x13***
4796 A2022 2 l multi 2.25 2.25

Varna, 2017 European Youth Capital — A2023

2017, Apr. 7 Litho. ***Perf. 13***
4797 A2023 1 l multi 1.10 1.10

Souvenir Sheet

Plovdiv, 2019 European Capital of Culture — A2024

No. 4798 — Mosaic from Plovdiv depicting: a, 1 l, Pears. b, 1.50 l, Bird.

2017, Apr. 11 Litho. ***Perf. 13x13¼***
4798 A2024 Sheet of 2, #a-b, + 2 labels 3.00 3.00

Souvenir Sheet

Ella Fitzgerald (1917-96), Jazz Singer — A2025

2017, Apr. 28 Litho. *Perf. 13¼x13*
4799 A2025 2 l multi 2.25 2.25

Imperforate examples of No. 4799 with simulated perforations and the emblem of the Finlandia 2017 Philatelic Exhibition in the sheet margin were printed in limited quantities.

Bulgarian Marine Aviation, Cent. — A2026

2017, Apr. 29 Litho. *Perf. 13¼x13*
4800 A2026 65s multi .75 .75

Arturo Toscanini (1867-1957), Conductor — A2027

2017, May 4 Litho. *Perf. 13*
4801 A2027 1 l multi + label 1.25 1.25

Europa A2028

Designs: 65s, Euxinograd Palace, Varna. 2.10 l, Asen's Fortress.

Perf. 13 Syncopated
2017, May 4 Litho.
4802 A2028 65s multi .75 .75
4803 A2028 2.10 l multi 2.40 2.40

Booklet Stamps
Perf. 13¼ on 2 or 3 Sides
4804 A2028 65s multi .75 .75
a. Booklet pane of 4 3.00 —
4805 A2028 2.10 l multi 2.40 2.40
a. Booklet pane of 4 9.75 —
Complete booklet, #4804a, 4805a 13.00

Souvenir Sheet
Perf. 13¼
4806 Sheet of 2 3.25 3.25
a. A2028 65s multi .75 .75
b. A2028 2.10 l multi 2.40 2.40

No. 4806 contains two 39x29mm stamps.

Souvenir Sheet

Battle of Doiran, Cent. — A2029

2017, May 9 Litho. *Perf. 13x13¼*
4807 A2029 1.50 l multi 1.75 1.75

Souvenir Sheet

Black Sea Marine Life — A2030

No. 4808: a, 65s, Delphinus delphis ponticus. b, 2 l, Barnea candida.

2017, May 22 Litho. *Perf. 13*
4808 A2030 Sheet of 2, #a-b 3.00 3.00

See Ukraine No. 1094.

Grigor Vachkov (1932-80), Actor — A2031

2017, May 26 Litho. *Perf. 13¼x13*
4809 A2031 65s multi .75 .75

Rose Festival, Kazanlak — A2032

2017, June 2 Litho. *Perf. 13x13¼*
4810 A2032 65s multi .75 .75

Carl Djerassi (1923-2015), Chemist — A2033

2017, June 8 Litho. *Perf. 13x13¼*
4811 A2033 1 l multi 1.25 1.25

Tsar Simeon II, Chairman of Union of Bulgarian Philatelists — A2034

2017, June 16 Litho. *Perf. 13x13¼*
4812 A2034 1.50 l multi + label 1.75 1.75
a. Souvenir sheet of 2 + 2 labels 3.50 3.50

Union of Bulgarian Philatelists, 80th anniv. (in 2018).

Lighthouses A2035

Designs: 65s, Akhtopol Lighthouse. 1 l, Shabla Lighthouse. 1.50 l, Burgas Lighthouse. 2 l, Galata Lighthouse.

2017, June 22 Litho. *Perf. 13*
4813-4816 A2035 Set of 4 6.00 6.00
4816a Souvenir sheet of 4, #4813-4816 6.00 6.00

The Ninth Wave, by Ivan Aivazovsky (1817-1900) — A2036

2017, July 26 Litho. *Perf. 13*
4817 A2036 1 l multi 1.25 1.25
a. Souvenir sheet of 4 5.00 5.00

Rayna Knyaginya (1856-1917), Seamstress of Flag of the Uprising of April 1876 — A2037

2017, July 28 Litho. *Perf. 13*
4818 A2037 1 l multi 1.25 1.25

Rayko Raychev, Pathologist, Cent. of Birth — A2038

2017, Aug. 8 Litho. *Perf. 13*
4819 A2038 65s multi .80 .80

Souvenir Sheet

International Year of Sustainable Tourism for Development — A2039

2017, Aug. 28 Litho. *Perf. 13½x13*
4820 A2039 2.10 l multi 2.60 2.60

Sofia Airport, 80th Anniv. — A2040

2017, Sept. 13 Litho. *Perf. 13*
4821 A2040 65s multi .80 .80

Souvenir Sheet

Bulgarian Astronautics Society, 60th Anniv. — A2041

2017, Oct. 9 Litho. *Perf. 13*
4822 A2041 65s multi .80 .80

Souvenir Sheet

80th Birthday of Dimitar Trendafilov, Painter and Graphic Artist — A2042

2017, Oct. 11 Litho. *Perf. 13¼x13½*
4823 A2042 65s multi + label .80 .80

Printed in sheets of 2 stamps + 2 labels.

Souvenir Sheet

Brazil 2017 World Philatelic Exhibition, Brasilia — A2043

Perf. 13¼ Horiz.

2017, Oct. 20 **Litho.**
4824 A2043 1 l multi + label 1.25 1.25

Sparrows A2044

Designs: 65s, Passer hispaniolensis. 1 l, Passer montanus. 1.50 l, Passer domesticus. 2 l, Passer petronia.

2017, Oct. 21 **Litho.** ***Perf. 13***
4825-4828 A2044 Set of 4 5.00 5.00
4828a Sheet of 4, #4825-4828, without light gray frame 5.00 5.00

Alternative Transportation — A2045

Designs: 65s, Rollerblades. 1.40 l, Hoverboard. 1.50 l, Skateboard. 2 l, Scooter.

2017, Oct. 21 **Litho.** ***Perf. 13½x13***
4829-4832 A2045 Set of 4 6.75 6.75
4832a Sheet of 4, #4829-4832 6.75 6.75

First Bulgarian Presidency of the Council of the European Union — A2046

2017, Nov. 1 **Litho.** ***Perf. 13***
4833 A2046 1 l multi 1.25 1.25

Communication Regulation Commission, 20th Anniv. — A2047

2017, Nov. 2 **Litho.** ***Perf. 13¼x13***
4834 A2047 65s multi .80 .80

Christmas A2048

2017, Nov. 16 **Litho.** ***Perf. 13***
4835 A2048 1 l multi 1.25 1.25

Julio Palencia (1884-1952), Spanish Diplomat in Sofia Who Rescued Jews in World War II — A2049

2017, Nov. 28 **Litho.** ***Perf. 13***
4836 A2049 1.50 l multi 1.90 1.90

Boys Eating Grapes and Melon, by Bartolomé Esteban Murillo (1617-82) — A2050

2017, Dec. 14 **Litho.** ***Perf. 13***
4837 A2050 1 l multi 1.25 1.25

This souvenir sheet, released Dec. 14, 2017, was produced in limited quantities.

Dan Kolov (1892-1940), Wrestler — A2051

2017, Dec. 19 **Litho.** ***Perf. 13***
4838 A2051 65s multi .80 .80

Sofia, 2018 European Capital of Sports — A2052

2018, Feb. 20 **Litho.** ***Perf. 13***
4839 A2052 1.50 l multi + label 1.90 1.90

This souvenir sheet, released Feb. 23, 2018, was produced in limited quantities.

Souvenir Sheet

CSKA Sofia Soccer Team, 70th Anniv. — A2053

2018, Mar. 7 **Litho.** ***Perf. 13***
4840 A2053 1.50 l multi 1.90 1.90

Sheets with perforated numbers are without gum.

Souvenir Sheet

Liberation of Bulgaria and End of Russo-Turkish War, 140th Anniv. — A2054

No. 4841: a, 1 l, Eduard Ivanovich Totleben (1818-84), Russian general b,1.80 l, Nikolai Grigoryevich Stoletov (1831-1912), Russian commander.

2018, Mar. 20 **Litho.** ***Perf. 13***
4841 A2054 Sheet of 2, #a-b 3.75 3.75

See Russia No. 7904.

Souvenir Sheet

Knights Templar, 900th Anniv. (in 2019) — A2055

2018, Apr. 17 **Litho.** ***Perf. 13x13¼***
4842 A2055 2.50 l multi 3.25 3.25

Souvenir Sheet

Plovdiv Philately Association, 125th Anniv. — A2056

2018, Apr. 20 **Litho.** ***Perf. 13x13¼***
4843 A2056 1.50 l multi 1.90 1.90

Europa A2057

Designs: Nos. 4844a, 4845, 95s, Covered Bridge, Lovech. Nos. 4844b, 4846, 2 l, Kadin Bridge, Nevestono.

2018, Apr. 25 **Litho.** ***Perf. 13***
4844 A2057 Vert. pair, #a-b 3.75 3.75
c. Souvenir sheet of 2, #4844a-4844b 3.75 3.75

Booklet Stamps
Black Bridges and White Background

Perf. 13 Horiz.

4845 A2057 95s brown & black 1.25 1.25
a. Booklet pane of 4 5.00 —
4846 A2057 2 l dk grn & blk 2.50 2.50
a. Booklet pane of 4 10.00 —
Complete booklet, #4845a, 4846a 15.00

No. 4844 was printed in sheets containing 4 pairs + 2 labels.

Souvenir Sheet

Georgi Asparuhov (1943-71), Soccer Player — A2058

2018, May 4 **Litho.** ***Perf. 13¼x13***
4847 A2058 2 l multi 2.40 2.40

Bulgarian Presidency of the Council of the European Union — A2059

2018, May 16 Litho. *Perf. 13*
4848 A2059 1.50 l multi 1.90 1.90

United Grand Masonic Lodge of Bulgaria, 25th Anniv. — A2060

2018, May 19 Litho. *Perf. 13*
4849 A2060 65s multi .80 .80

Souvenir Sheet
Perf. 13x13¼

4850 A2060 2.50 l multi 3.00 3.00

Souvenir Sheet

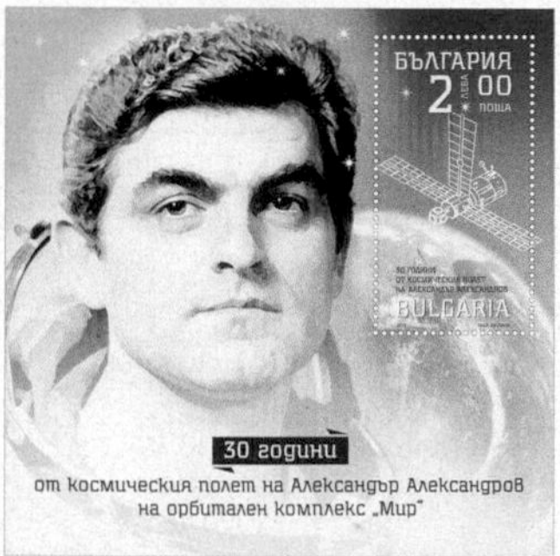

Alexander Alexandrov's Space Flight to Mir Space Station, 30th Anniv. — A2061

2018, June 5 Litho. *Perf. 13x13¼*
4851 A2061 2 l multi 2.40 2.40

2018 World Cup Soccer Championships, Russia — A2062

Designs: 1 l, Soccer player approaching ball. 2 l, Soccer ball in space.

2018, June 14 Litho. *Perf. 13*
4852-4853 A2062 Set of 2 3.75 3.75
4853a Souvenir sheet of 2, #4852-4853 3.75 3.75

Souvenir Sheet

Bulgarian Army, 140th Anniv. — A2063

2018, July 20 Litho. *Perf. 13¼x13*
4854 A2063 1.50 l multi 1.90 1.90

This souvenir sheet, released in July 2018 to commemorate the 80th anniversary of the Union of Bulgarian Philatelists, was produced in limited quantities.

Souvenir Sheet

End of the Siege of Constantinople Following Bulgar Khanate's Victory Over Arab Forces, 1300th Anniv. — A2064

2018, Aug. 15 Litho. *Perf. 13¼x13*
4855 A2064 2 l multi 2.40 2.40

Bulgarian State Railways, 130th Anniv. A2065

Designs: Nos. 4856, 4860a, 65s, Train emerging from tunnel and traversing bridge, train behind bridge. Nos. 4857, 4860b, 1.20 l, Steam locomotive on bridge, horse pulling rail wagon. Nos. 4858, 4860c, 1.50 l, People and steam locomotive at station. Nos. 4859, 4860d, 2 l, People, steam locomotive, passenger coach and bus at station.

2018, Sept. 26 Litho. *Perf. 13*
Stamps With White Frames

4856-4859 A2065 Set of 4 6.50 6.50

Souvenir Sheet
Stamps Without White Frames

4860 A2065 Sheet of 4, #a-d 6.50 6.50

Port of Lom, 180th Anniv. — A2066

2018, Oct. 18 Litho. *Perf. 13*
4861 A2066 95s multi 1.10 1.10

Extinct Animals and Their Skeletons — A2067

Designs: Nos. 4862, 4866a, 65s, Bos primigenius. Nos. 4863, 4866b, 1.20 l, Hydrodamalis gigas. Nos. 4864, 4866c, 1.50 l, Thylacinus cynocephalus. Nos. 4865, 4866d, 2 l, Pinguinus impennis.

2018, Oct. 19 Litho. *Perf. 13*
Stamps With Tinted Backgrounds

4862-4865 A2067 Set of 4 6.25 6.25

Souvenir Sheet
Stamps With White Backgrounds

4866 A2067 Sheet of 4, #a-d 6.25 6.25

Examples of No. 4866 without gum were printed in limited quantities, as was a gummed souvenir sheet containing No. 4866a.

Famous Men A2068

Designs: No. 4867, 65s, Thomas Mayne Reid (1818-83), writer. No. 4868, 65s, Charles-François Gounod (1818-93), composer. No. 4869, 1.50 l, Jacopo Tintoretto (1518-94), painter. No. 4870, 1.50 l, Ingmar Bergman (1918-2007), film director.

2018, Oct. 19 Litho. *Perf. 13*
4867-4870 A2068 Set of 4 5.00 5.00

Sheets of 4 containing one each of Nos. 4867-4870 were printed in limited quantities.

Souvenir Sheet

Fire Dancing As UNESCO Intangible Cultural Heritage, 10th Anniv. — A2069

2018, Oct. 20 Litho. *Perf. 13x13¼*
4871 A2069 2 l multi 2.40 2.40

A horizontal pair of No. 4871 was printed in limited quantities.

Souvenir Sheet

Accession to the Throne of Tsar Boris III (1894-1943), Cent. — A2070

2018, Nov. 20 Litho. *Perf. 13¼x13*
4872 A2070 2 l multi 2.40 2.40

A vertical pair of No. 4872 was printed in limited quantities.

Christmas A2071

2018, Nov. 28 Litho. *Perf. 13*
4873 A2071 1.50 l multi 1.75 1.75

Saints Cyril and Methodius National Library, Sofia, 140th Anniv. — A2072

2018, Dec. 5 Litho. *Perf. 13*
4874 A2072 1.50 l multi + label 1.75 1.75

National Gallery of Art, Sofia, 70th Anniv. — A2073

2018, Dec. 5 Litho. *Perf. 13*
4875 A2073 1.50 l multi 1.75 1.75

St. Clement of Ohrid Sofia University, 130th Anniv. — A2074

2018, Dec. 8 Litho. *Perf. 13*
4876 A2074 85s multi + label 1.00 1.00

Space Exploration A2075

2018, Dec. 21 Litho. *Perf. 13¼x13*
4877 A2075 1 l multi 1.25 1.25

Glagolithic Script — A2076

Perf. 13 Syncopated
2019, Jan. 17 Litho.
4878 A2076 1.50 l multi 1.75 1.75

Embroidery Pattern — A2077

Perf. 13 Syncopated
2019, Jan. 17 Litho.
4879 A2077 1.50 l multi 1.75 1.75

Fauna A2078

Designs: 65s, Podiceps cristatus. 1 l, Egretta garzetta. 1.50 l, Pelecanus onocrotalus. 2 l, Phalacrocorax pygmeus.

Perf. 13 Syncopated
2019, Feb. 1 Litho.
4880-4883 A2078 Set of 4 6.00 6.00
4883a Souvenir sheet of 4, #4880-4883 6.00 6.00

An ungummed souvenir sheet of 8 containing 2 each Nos. 4880-4883 was printed in limited quantities.

Souvenir Sheet

Turnovo Constitution and Constituent Assembly, 140th Anniv. — A2079

2019, Feb. 8 Litho. *Perf. 13¼x13*
4884 A2079 2 l multi 2.40 2.40

Souvenir Sheet

Bulgarian Air Traffic Services Authority, 50th Anniv. — A2080

2019, Feb. 15 Litho. *Perf. 13¼x13*
4885 A2080 2 l multi 2.40 2.40

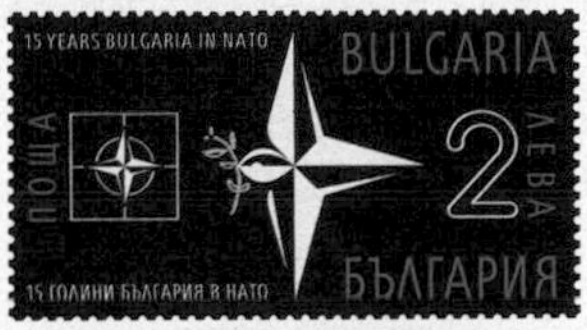

Bulgaria in North Atlantic Treaty Organization, 15th Anniv. — A2081

2019, Feb. 20 Litho. *Perf. 13¼x13*
4886 A2081 2 l multi 2.40 2.40
a. Souvenir sheet of 2 + central label 5.00 5.00

This souvenir sheet, released with gum and without gum in February 2019 to commemorate Antarctic explorer Robert Falcon Scott, was produced in limited quantities.

Alexander Stamboliski (1879-1923), Prime Minister — A2082

2019, Mar. 1 Litho. *Perf. 13*
4887 A2082 65s multi .75 .75

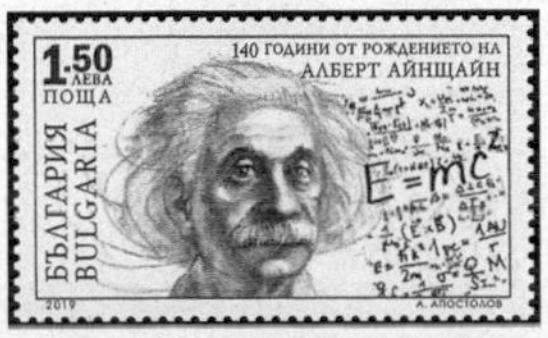

Albert Einstein (1879-1955), Physicist — A2083

2019, Mar. 20 Litho. *Perf. 13*
4888 A2083 1.50 l multi 1.75 1.75

No. 4888 was printed in sheets of 2 + central label.

Pancho Vladigerov (1899-1978), Composer — A2084

2019, Mar. 21 Litho. *Perf. 13*
4889 A2084 65s multi .75 .75

Souvenir Sheet

Icon of Jesus Holding Cathedral of St. Sophia — A2085

2019, Apr. 2 Litho. *Perf. 12¾*
4890 A2085 1.50 l multi 1.75 1.75

Sofia as capital of Bulgaria, 140th anniv.

Space Flight of Cosmonaut Georgi Ivanov, 40th Anniv. — A2086

2019, Apr. 10 Litho. *Perf. 13x13¼*
4891 A2086 1.50 l multi 1.75 1.75

This souvenir sheet, released in April 2019 to commemorate the Akhal-Teke horse, was produced in limited quantities. It was issued with and without gum, with differences in the inscriptions.

Europa A2087

Designs: 95s, Falco biarmicus. 2 l, Bonasa bonasia.

2019, Apr. 24 Litho. *Perf. 13¼*
4892 A2087 95s multi 1.10 1.10
4893 A2087 2 l multi 2.40 2.40
a. Souvenir sheet of 2, #4892-4893 3.50 3.50

Booklet Stamps
Size: 39x26mm
Perf. 13¼ at Left

4894 A2087 95s multi 1.10 1.10
a. Imperf. 1.10 1.10
b. Booklet pane of 4, 2 each #4894, 4894a 4.50 —
4895 A2087 2 l multi 2.40 2.40
a. Imperf. 2.40 2.40
b. Booklet pane of 4, 2 each #4895, 4895a 9.75 —
Complete booklet, #4894b, 4895b 14.50

Nos. 4892-4893 were each printed in sheets of 5 + label.

Visit of Pope Francis to Bulgaria — A2088

2019, May 3 Litho. *Perf. 13*
4896 A2088 2 l multi 2.40 2.40

No. 4896 was printed in sheets of 3 + label.

Souvenir Sheet

Bulgarian Postal Service, 140th Anniv. — A2089

2019, May 16 Litho. *Perf. 13*
4897 A2089 1.50 l multi 1.75 1.75

Self-portrait of Stefan Gruev (1944-2017), Graphic Artist — A2090

2019, May 21 Litho. *Perf. 13*
4898 A2090 1 l multi + label 1.25 1.25

Bulgarian Diplomacy, 140th Anniv. — A2091

2019, May 29 Litho. *Perf. 13*
4899 A2091 1.50 l multi 1.75 1.75

Souvenir Sheet

Council of Europe, 70th Anniv. and European Court of Human Rights, 60th Anniv. — A2092

2019, May 31 Litho. *Perf. 13¼x13*
4900 A2092 2 l multi 2.40 2.40

Souvenir Sheet

Ministry of the Interior, 140th Anniv. — A2093

2019, June 10 Litho. *Perf. 13*
4901 A2093 1.50 l multi 1.75 1.75

Zonta International, Cent. — A2094

2019, June 14 Litho. *Perf. 13*
4902 A2094 1 l multi 1.25 1.25
a. Souvenir sheet of 2 + central label 2.50 2.50

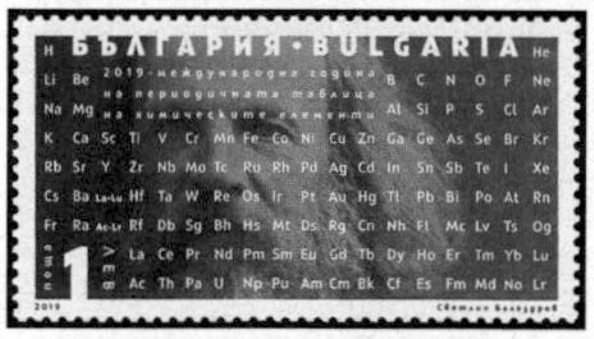

International Year of the Periodic Table — A2095

2019, June 24 Litho. *Perf. 13*
4903 A2095 1 l multi 1.25 1.25

Souvenir Sheet

Addition of MiG-29 Airplanes to Bulgarian Air Force, 30th Anniv. — A2096

2019, June 28 Litho. *Imperf.*
4904 A2096 2 l multi 2.40 2.40

No. 4904 has simulated rouletting.

Diplomatic Relations Between Bulgaria and Russia, 140th Anniv. — A2097

2019, July 9 Litho. *Perf. 13*
4905 A2097 1.50 l multi 1.75 1.75

Ministry of Finance, 140th Anniv. — A2098

2019, July 12 Litho. *Perf. 13*
4906 A2098 1 l multi 1.25 1.25

Grape Harvesting — A2099

No. 4907 — Woman with basket of: a, Floral (green) grapes. b, Ruby Kaliskin (purple) grapes.

2019, July 15 Litho. *Perf. 13*
4907 A2099 1.50 l Horiz. pair, #a-b 3.50 3.50

Stamps without gum were issued in limited quantities. See Russia No. 8038.

Souvenir Sheet

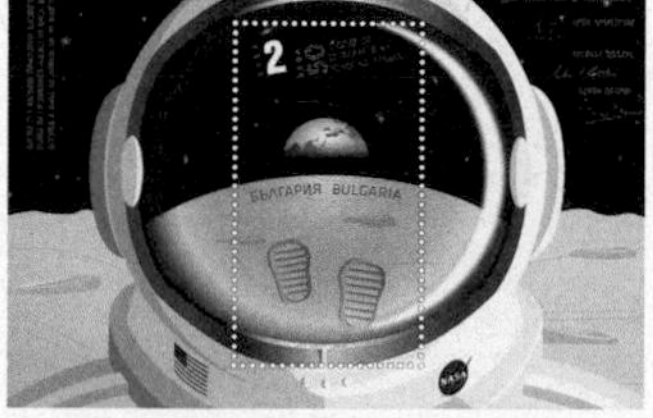

First Man on the Moon, 50th Anniv. — A2100

2019, July 19 Litho. *Perf. 13x13¼*
4908 A2100 2 l multi 2.25 2.25

Bulgarian Customs, 140th Anniv. A2101

2019, July 24 Litho. *Perf. 13*
4909 A2101 65s multi .75 .75

Bulgarian Navy, 140th Anniv. A2102

2019, Aug. 8 Litho. *Perf. 13*
4910 A2102 65s multi .75 .75

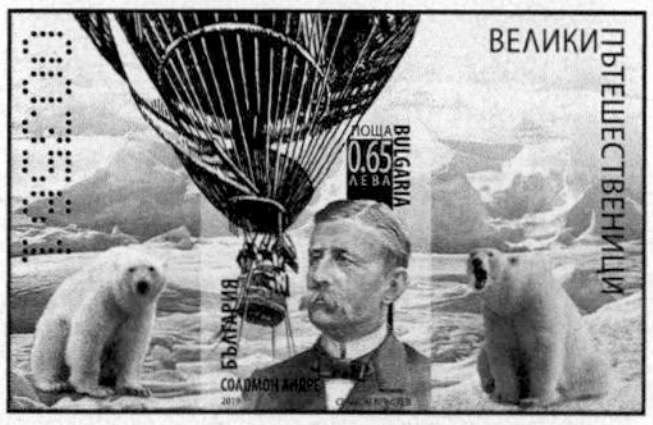

This souvenir sheet, released in August 2019 to commemorate polar explorer Solomon Andree, was produced in limited quantities. It was issued with and without gum with differences in the inscriptions.

Souvenir Sheet

29th Congress of the World Association of Breast and Cardiovascular Surgeons, Sofia — A2103

2019, Sept. 5 Litho. *Perf. 13¼x13*
4911 A2103 1.50 l multi 1.75 1.75

Energy and Water Regulatory Commission, 20th Anniv. A2104

2019, Sept. 10 Litho. *Perf. 13¼x13*
4912 A2104 1 l multi 1.10 1.10

Mohandas K. Gandhi (1869-1948), Indian Nationalist Leader — A2105

2019, Sept. 30 Litho. *Perf. 13¼x13*
4913 A2105 1.50 l multi 1.75 1.75

Bulgarian Academy of Sciences, 150th Anniv. — A2106

2019, Oct. 7 Litho. *Perf. 13*
4914 A2106 65s multi .75 .75

Ivan Vazov National Library, Plovdiv, 140th Anniv. — A2107

2019, Oct. 15 Litho. *Perf. 13*
4915 A2107 1.50 l multi + label 1.75 1.75

Souvenir Sheets

Ships — A2108

No. 4916: a, 65s, Chinese junk, 8th cent. B.C. b, 1.50 l, Byzatntine dromon, 9th cent.
No. 4917: a, 1 l, Greek bireme, 6th cent. B.C. b, 2 l, English galley, 17th cent.

2019, Oct. 17 Litho. *Perf. 13¼x13*
4916 A2108 Sheet of 2, #a-b 2.50 2.50
c. As "a," perf. 13 syncopated .75 .75
d. As "b," perf. 13 syncopated 1.75 1.75
4917 A2108 Sheet of 2, #a-b 3.50 3.50
c. As "a," perf. 13 syncopated 1.25 1.25
d. As "b," perf. 13 syncopated 2.25 2.25
e. Sheet of 4, #4916c, 4916d, 4917c, 4917d 6.00 6.00

Souvenir Sheet

Drawings by Leonardo da Vinci (1452-1519) — A2109

2019, Oct. 17 Litho. *Perf. 13¼x13*
4918 A2109 1.50 l multi 1.75 1.75

Nikolay Haytov (1919-2002), Writer — A2110

2019, Oct. 18 Litho. *Perf. 13¼x13*
4919 A2110 1.50 l multi 1.75 1.75

A sheet of 4 of No. 4919 was produced in limited quantities.

This souvenir sheet, released in October 2019 to commemorate the otter, was produced in limited quantities. It was issued with and without gum with differences in the inscriptions.

Souvenir Sheet

Various Folk Costumes — A2111

2019, Oct. 20 Litho. *Perf. 13¼x13*
4920 A2111 2 l multi 2.40 2.40

Plovdiv Phila 2019 Philatelic Exhibition, Plovdiv.

Alexandrovska University Hospital, Sofia, 140th Anniv. — A2112

2019, Nov. 7 Litho. *Perf. 13*
4921 A2112 65s multi .75 .75

Georgi Ovcharov (1889-1953), Architect, and Sofia University Faculty of Agriculture Building — A2113

2019, Nov. 11 Litho. *Perf. 13*
4922 A2113 65s purple brn .75 .75

Nikola Ganushev (1889-1958) and Nikola Marinov (1879-1948), Painters — A2114

2019, Nov. 11 Litho. *Perf. 13¼x13*
4923 A2114 1.50 l multi 1.75 1.75

Souvenir Sheet

Bulgaria's Signing of Convention on the Rights of the Child, 30th Anniv. — A2115

2019, Nov. 18 Litho. *Perf. 13x13¼*
4924 A2115 2.30 l multi 2.60 2.60

Christmas A2116

2019, Nov. 22 Litho. *Perf. 13*
4925 A2116 1.50 l multi 1.75 1.75

Diplomatic Relations Between Bulgaria and the Sovereign Military Order of Malta, 25th Anniv. — A2117

2019, Dec. 12 Litho. *Perf. 13¼x13*
4926 A2117 2.30 l gold & multi 2.75 2.75
a. Sheet of 2 + central label 5.50 5.50

Diplomatic Relations Between Bulgaria and People's Republic of China, 70th Anniv. — A2118

2019, Dec. 17 Litho. *Perf. 13*
4927 A2118 2 l multi 2.40 2.40

Souvenir Sheet

New Year 2020 (Year of the Rat) — A2119

2020, Jan. 29 Litho. *Perf. 13x13¼*
4928 A2119 3 l multi 3.50 3.50

Imperforate souvenir sheets with simulated perforations, perforated serial numbers, and different design details in the sheet margin were issued with and without gum in limited quantities.

Bulgarian Exarchate, 150th Anniv. — A2121

2020, Feb. 28 Litho. *Perf. 13¼x13*
4930 A2121 1.70 l multi 2.00 2.00

Souvenir Sheet

Ludwig van Beethoven (1770-1827), Composer — A2122

2020, May 20 Litho. *Perf. 13x13¼*
4931 A2122 3 l multi 3.50 3.50

Souvenir Sheet

City Coats of Arms — A2124

No. 4935 — Coat of arms of: a, Burgas, 1994. b, Haskovo, 1995.

2020, June 24 Litho. *Perf. 13x13¼*
4935 A2124 2.30 l Sheet of 2, #a-b, + central label 5.25 5.25

United Nations, 75th Anniv. — A2125

2020, June 26 Litho. *Perf. 13x13¼*
4936 A2125 2.30 l multi 2.60 2.60

Bulgarian membership in United Nations, 65th anniv.

Ivan Vazov (1850-1921), Writer — A2126

2020, June 27 Litho. *Perf. 13*
4937 A2126 1.10 l multi 1.25 1.25

SEMI-POSTAL STAMPS

Catalogue values for unused stamps in this section are for Never Hinged items.

Regular Issues of 1911-20 Surcharged

a

b

c

Perf. 11½x12, 12x11½

1920, June 20 Unwmk.

B1	A43 (a)	2s + 1s ol grn	.25	.25
B2	A44 (b)	5s + 2½s grn	.25	.25
B3	A44 (b)	10s + 5s rose	.25	.25
B4	A44 (b)	15s + 7½s vio	.25	.25
B5	A44 (b)	25s + 12½s dp bl	.25	.25
B6	A44 (b)	30s + 15s choc	.25	.25
B7	A44 (b)	50s + 25s yel brn	.25	.25
B8	A29 (c)	1 l + 50s dk brn	.45	.25
B9	A37a (a)	2 l + 1 l brn org	.45	.40
B10	A38 (a)	3 l + 1½ l claret	1.20	.80
		Nos. B1-B10 (10)	3.85	3.20

Surtax aided ex-prisoners of war. Value, Nos. B1-B7 imperf., $7.75.

Tsar Boris Type of 1937

Souvenir Sheet

1937, Nov. 22 Photo. *Imperf.*
B11 A140 2 l + 18 l ultra 10.00 *20.00*

19th anniv. of the accession of Tsar Boris III to the throne.

Stamps of 1917-21 Surcharged in Black

1939, Oct. 22 ***Perf. 12½, 12***

B12	A34	1 l + 1 l on 15s slate	.25	.25
B13	A69	2 l + 1 l on 1½ l ol grn	.25	.35
B14	A69	4 l + 2 l on 2 l dp grn	.25	.35
B15	A69	7 l + 4 l on 3 l Prus bl	.80	*1.10*
B16	A69	14 l + 7 l on 5 l red brn	1.00	*2.00*
		Nos. B12-B16 (5)	2.55	*4.05*

Surtax aided victims of the Sevlievo flood. The surcharge on #B13-B16 omits "leva."

Map of Bulgaria SP2

1947, June 6 **Typo.** ***Perf. 11½***

B17	SP2	20 l + 10 l dk brn red & grn	.75	.75

30th Jubilee Esperanto Cong., Sofia, 1947.

Postman — SP3

Radio Towers — SP6

#B19, Lineman. #B20, Telephone operators.

1947, Nov. 5

B18	SP3	4 l + 2 l ol brn	.25	.25
B19	SP3	10 l + 5 l brt red	.25	.25
B20	SP3	20 l + 10 l dp ultra	.25	.25
B21	SP6	40 l + 20 l choc	1.00	1.00
		Nos. B18-B21 (4)	1.75	1.75

Christo Ganchev — SP7

Actors' Portraits: 10 l+6 l, Adriana Budevska. 15 l+7 l, Vasil Kirkov. 20 l+15 l, Sava Ognianov. 30 l+20 l, Krostyu Sarafov.

1947, Dec. 8 **Litho.** ***Perf. 10½***

B22	SP7	9 l + 5 l Prus grn	.25	.25
B23	SP7	10 l + 6 l car lake	.25	.25
B24	SP7	15 l + 7 l rose vio	.35	.25
B25	SP7	20 l + 15 l ultra	.35	.25
B26	SP7	30 l + 20 l vio brn	1.10	.75
		Nos. B22-B26 (5)	2.30	1.75

National Theater, 50th anniversary.

Souvenir Sheet

Olympic Emblem — SP8

1964, Oct. 10 **Litho.** ***Imperf.***

B27	SP8	40s + 20s bis, red & bl	4.00	1.75

18th Olympic Games, Tokyo, Oct. 10-25.

Horsemanship Type of 1965

Miniature Sheet

1965, Sept. 30 **Photo.** ***Imperf.***

B28	A630	40s + 20s Hurdle race	4.00	1.75

Space Exploration Type of 1966

Designs: 20s+10s, Yuri A. Gagarin, Alexei Leonov and Valentina Tereshkova. 30s+10s, Rocket and globe.

1966, Sept. 29 **Photo.** ***Perf. 11½x11***

B29	A652	20s + 10s pur & gray	1.40	.45

Miniature Sheet

Imperf

B30	A652	30s + 10s gray, fawn & blk	3.00	1.10

Winter Olympic Games Type of 1967

Sports and Emblem: 20s+10s, Slalom. 40s+10s, Figure skating couple.

1967, Sept. **Photo.** ***Perf. 11***

B31	A687	20s + 10s multi	2.00	.60

Souvenir Sheet

Imperf

B32	A687	40s + 10s multi	2.75	.85

Type of Olympic Games Issue, 1968

Designs: 20s+10s, Rowing. 50s+10s, Stadium, Mexico City, and communications satellite.

1968, June 24 **Photo.** ***Perf. 10½***

B33	A702	20s + 10s vio bl, gray & pink	1.40	.45

Miniature Sheet

Imperf

B34	A702	50s + 10s gray, blk & Prus bl	3.00	1.50

Sports Type of Regular Issue, 1969

Designs: 13s+5s, Woman with ball. 20s+10s, Acrobatic jump.

Gymnasts in Light Gray

1969, Oct. **Photo.** ***Perf. 11***

B35	A732	13s + 5s brt rose & vio	.80	.35
B36	A732	20s + 10s citron & bl grn	1.00	.40

Miniature Sheet

Soccer Ball — SP9

1970, Mar. 4 **Photo.** ***Imperf.***

B37	SP9	80s + 20s multi	3.00	1.75

9th World Soccer Championships for the Jules Rimet Cup, Mexico City, May 30-June 21, 1970.

Souvenir Sheet

Yuri A. Gagarin — SP10

1971, Apr. 12 **Photo.** ***Imperf.***

B38	SP10	40s + 20s multi	3.00	1.10

10th anniversary of the first man in space.

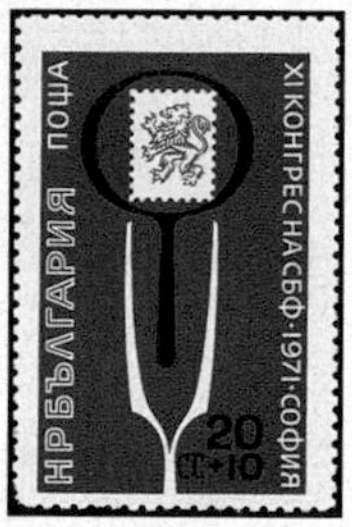

SP11

Bulgarian lion, magnifying glass, stamp tongs

1971, July 10 **Photo.** ***Perf. 12½***

B39	SP11	20s + 10s brn org, blk & gold	1.25	.40

11th Congress of Bulgarian Philatelists, Sofia, July, 1971.

SP12

Toys: a, Skateboarding. b, Doll, ball. c, Rope. d, Train set.

Souvenir Sheet

1989, Nov. 10 **Litho.** ***Perf. 13x13½***

B40		Sheet of 4	2.75	1.40
a.-d.		SP12 30s +15s any single	.55	.35

For the benefit of the Children's Foundation. Exists imperf. Value $8.75.

AIR POST STAMPS

Regular Issues of 1925-26 Overprinted in Various Colors

1927-28 **Unwmk.** ***Perf. 11½***

C1	A76	2 l ol (R) ('28)	1.40	1.40
C2	A74	4 l lake & yel (Bl)	2.00	1.50
C3	A77	10 l brn blk & brn org (G) ('28)	55.00	15.00

Overprinted Vertically and Surcharged with New Value

C4	A77	1 l on 6 l dp bl & pale lem (C)	1.40	1.40
a.		Inverted surcharge	*340.00*	*275.00*
b.		Pair, one without surcharge	*440.00*	
		Nos. C1-C4 (4)	59.80	19.30

Nos. C2-C4 overprinted in changed colors were not issued, value set $14.

Dove Delivering Message — AP1

1931, Oct. 28 **Typo.**

C5	AP1	1 l dk green	.40	.25
C6	AP1	2 l maroon	.40	.25
C7	AP1	6 l dp blue	.50	.35
C8	AP1	12 l carmine	1.00	.35
C9	AP1	20 l dk violet	1.00	.60
C10	AP1	30 l dp orange	2.00	.75
C11	AP1	50 l orange brn	2.75	1.50
		Nos. C5-C11 (7)	8.05	4.05

Counterfeits exist. See Nos. C15-C18.

Junkers Plane, Rila Monastery — AP2

1932, May 9

C12	AP2	18 l blue grn	40.00	25.00
C13	AP2	24 l dp red	27.50	20.00
C14	AP2	28 l ultra	15.00	17.50
		Nos. C12-C14 (3)	82.50	62.50

Catalogue values for unused stamps in this section, from this point to the end of the section, are for Never Hinged items.

Types of 1931

1938, Dec. 27

C15	AP1	1 l violet brown	.30	.25
C16	AP1	2 l green	.35	.25
C17	AP1	6 l deep rose	1.00	.45
C18	AP1	12 l peacock blue	1.25	.45
		Nos. C15-C18 (4)	2.90	1.40

Counterfeits exist.

Mail Plane — AP3

Plane over Tsar Assen's Tower — AP4

Designs: 4 l, Plane over Bachkovski Monastery. 6 l, Bojurishte Airport, Sofia. 10 l, Plane, train and motorcycle. 12 l, Planes over Sofia Palace. 16 l, Plane over Pirin Valley. 19 l, Plane over Rila Monastery. 30 l, Plane and Swallow. 45 l, Plane over Sofia Cathedral. 70 l, Plane over Shipka Monument. 100 l, Plane and Royal Cipher.

1940, Jan. 15 **Photo.** ***Perf. 13***

C19	AP3	1 l	dk green	.25	.25
C20	AP4	2 l	crimson	2.00	.25
C21	AP4	4 l	red orange	.25	.25
C22	AP3	6 l	dp blue	.35	.25
C23	AP4	10 l	dk brown	.40	.25
C24	AP3	12 l	dull brown	.80	.35
C25	AP3	16 l	brt bl vio	1.10	.50
C26	AP3	19 l	sapphire	1.25	.75
C27	AP4	30 l	rose lake	2.00	1.00
C28	AP4	45 l	gray violet	5.25	1.25
C29	AP4	70 l	rose pink	4.00	2.50
C30	AP4	100 l	dp slate bl	12.00	5.00
			Nos. C19-C30 (12)	29.65	12.60

Nos. 368 and 370 Overprinted in Black

1945, Jan. 26

C31	A181	1 l	bright green	.25	.25
C32	A181	4 l	red orange	.25	.25

A similar overprint on Nos. O4, O5, O7 and O8 was privately applied.

Type of Parcel Post Stamps of 1944 Surcharged or Overprinted in Various Colors

Imperf

C37	PP5	10 l	on 100 l dl yel (Bl)	.25	.25
C38	PP5	45 l	on 100 l dl yel (C)	.30	.25
C39	PP5	75 l	on 100 l dl yel (G)	1.00	.25
C40	PP5	100 l	dl yel (V)	1.00	.35
			Nos. C37-C40 (4)	2.55	1.10

Plane and Sun — AP16

Pigeon with Letter — AP17

Plane, Letter AP18

Wings, Posthorn AP19

Winged Letter — AP20

Plane, Sun — AP21

Pigeon, Posthorn AP22

Mail Plane AP23

Conventionalized Figure Holding Pigeon — AP24

1946, July 15 **Litho.** ***Perf. 13***

C41	AP16	1 l	dull lilac	.25	.25
C42	AP16	2 l	slate gray	.25	.25
C43	AP17	4 l	violet blk	.25	.25
C44	AP18	6 l	blue	.25	.25
C45	AP19	10 l	turq green	.25	.25
C46	AP19	12 l	yellow brn	.25	.25
C47	AP20	16 l	rose violet	.25	.25
C48	AP19	19 l	carmine	.25	.25
C49	AP21	30 l	orange	.25	.25
C50	AP22	45 l	lt ol grn	.25	.25
C51	AP22	75 l	red brown	.60	.25
C52	AP23	100 l	slate blk	1.60	.60
C53	AP24	100 l	red	1.60	.60
			Nos. C41-C53 (13)	6.30	3.95

No. C47 exists imperf. Value $90.

People's Republic

Plane over Plovdiv AP25

1947, Aug. 31 **Photo.** ***Imperf.***

C54	AP25	40 l	dull olive grn	1.20	1.20

Plovdiv International Fair, 1947.

Baldwin's Tower — AP26

1948, May 23 **Litho.** ***Perf. 11½***

C55	AP26	50 l	ol brn, *cr*	1.50	1.50

Stamp Day and the 10th Congress of Bulgarian Philatelic Societies, June 1948.

Romanian and Bulgarian Parliament Buildings AP27

Romanian and Bulgarian Flags, Bridge over Danube AP28

1948, Nov. 3 **Photo.**

C56	AP27	40 l	ol gray, *cr*	.35	.30
C57	AP28	100 l	red vio, *cr*	.90	.90

Romanian-Bulgarian friendship.

Mausoleum of Pleven — AP29

1949, June 26

C58	AP29	50 l	brown	3.00	3.00

7th Congress of Bulgarian Philatelic Associations, June 26-27, 1949.

Symbols of the UPU — AP30

1949, Oct. 10 ***Perf. 11½***

C59	AP30	50 l	violet blue	2.00	2.00

75th anniv. of the UPU.

Frontier Guard and Dog — AP31

1949, Oct. 31

C60	AP31	60 l	olive black	3.00	3.00

Dimitrov Mausoleum AP32

1950, July 3 ***Perf. 10½***

C61	AP32	40 l	olive brown	5.50	2.75

1st anniv. of the death of George Dimitrov.

Belogradchic Rocks — AP33

Air View of Plovdiv Fair — AP34

Designs: 16s, Beach, Varna. 20s, Harvesting grain. 28s, Rila monastery. 44s, Studena dam. 60s, View of Dimitrovgrad. 80s, View of Trnovo. 1 l, University building, Sofia. 4 l, Partisans' Monument.

1954, Apr. 1 **Unwmk.** ***Perf. 13***

C62	AP33	8s	olive black	.25	.25
C63	AP34	12s	rose brown	.25	.25
C64	AP33	16s	brown	.25	.25
C65	AP33	20s	brn red, *cream*	.25	.25
C66	AP33	28s	dp bl, *cream*	.30	.25
C67	AP33	44s	vio brn, *cream*	.35	.25
C68	AP33	60s	red brn, *cream*	.65	.25
C69	AP34	80s	dk grn, *cream*	.70	.30
C70	AP33	1 l	dk bl grn, *cream*	2.25	.65
C71	AP34	4 l	deep blue	3.75	1.50
			Nos. C62-C71 (10)	9.00	4.20

Glider on Mountainside AP35

60s, Glider over airport. 80s, Three gliders.

1956, Oct. 15 **Photo.**

C72	AP35	44s	brt blue	.35	.25
C73	AP35	60s	purple	.35	.25
C74	AP35	80s	dk blue grn	1.00	.70
			Nos. C72-C74 (3)	1.70	1.20

30th anniv. of glider flights in Bulgaria.

Passenger Plane — AP36

1957, May 21 **Unwmk.** ***Perf. 13***

C75	AP36	80s	deep blue	1.00	.45

10th anniv. of civil aviation in Bulgaria.

Sputnik 3 over Earth AP37

1958, Nov. 28 ***Perf. 11***

C76	AP37	80s	brt grnsh blue	4.50	3.50

International Geophysical Year, 1957-58. Value, imperf. $12.50.

Lunik 1 Leaving Earth for Moon — AP38

1959, Mar. ***Perf. 10½***

C77	AP38	2 l	brt blue & ocher	7.00	7.00

Launching of 1st man-made satellite to orbit moon. Value, imperf. in slightly different colors, $12.50 unused, $5 canceled.

Statue of Liberty and Tu-110 Airliner AP39

Perf. 10½

1959, Nov. 11 **Photo.** **Unwmk.**

C78	AP39	1 l	violet bl & pink	3.00	2.50

Visit of Khrushchev to US. Value, imperf. $7.50.

Lunik 2 and Moon — AP40

1960, June 23 **Litho.** ***Perf. 11***

C79	AP40	1.25 l	blue, blk & yel	5.00	3.00

Russian rocket to the Moon, Sept. 12, 1959.

Sputnik 5 and Dogs Belka and Strelka — AP41

1961, Jan. 14 Photo. *Perf. 11*

C80	AP41 1.25 l brt grnsh bl & org	5.00	3.50

Russian rocket flight of Aug. 19, 1960.

Maj. Yuri A. Gagarin and Vostok 1 AP42

1961, Apr. 26 Unwmk.

C81	AP42 4 l grnsh bl, blk & red	4.00	3.00

First manned space flight, Apr. 12, 1961.

Soviet Space Dogs AP43

1961, June 28 *Perf. 11*

C82	AP43 2 l slate & dk car	3.50	2.50

Venus-bound Rocket — AP44

1961, June 28

C83	AP44 2 l brt bl, yel & org	7.00	4.50

Soviet launching of the Venus space probe, 2/12/61.

Maj. Gherman Titov AP45

Design: 1.25 l, Spaceship Vostok 2.

1961, Nov. 20 Photo. *Perf. 11x10½*

C84	AP45 75s dk ol grn & gray grn	2.25	1.75
C85	AP45 1.25 l vio bl, lt bl & pink	2.75	2.00

1st manned space flight around the world, Maj. Gherman Titov of Russia, 8/6-7/61.

Iskar River Narrows AP46

Designs: 2s, Varna and sailboat. 3s, Melnik. 10s, Trnovo. 40s, Pirin mountains.

1962, Feb. 3 Unwmk. *Perf. 13*

C86	AP46 1s bl grn & gray bl	.25	.25
C87	AP46 2s blue & pink	.25	.25
C88	AP46 3s brown & ocher	.25	.25
C89	AP46 10s black & lemon	.50	.25
C90	AP46 40s dk green & green	1.90	.40
	Nos. C86-C90 (5)	3.15	1.40

Ilyushin Turboprop Airliner AP47

1962, Aug. 18 *Perf. 11*

C91	AP47 13s blue & black	1.10	.35

15th anniversary of TABSO airline.

Konstantin E. Tsiolkovsky and Rocket Launching — AP48

Design: 13s, Earth, moon and rocket on future flight to the moon.

1962, Sept. 24 *Perf. 11*

C92	AP48 5s dp green & gray	3.50	1.25
C93	AP48 13s ultra & yellow	1.50	.75

13th meeting of the International Astronautical Federation.

Maj. Andrian G. Nikolayev — AP49

Designs: 2s, Lt. Col. Pavel R. Popovich. 40s, Vostoks 3 and 4 in orbit.

1962, Dec. 9 Photo. Unwmk.

C94	AP49 1s bl, sl grn & blk	.25	.25
C95	AP49 2s bl grn, grn & blk	.50	.25
C96	AP49 40s dk bl grn, pink & blk	2.75	1.75
	Nos. C94-C96 (3)	3.50	2.25

First Russian group space flight of Vostoks 3 and 4, Aug. 12-15, 1962.

Spacecraft "Mars 1" Approaching Mars — AP50

Design: 13s, Rocket launching spacecraft, Earth, Moon and Mars.

1963, Mar. 5 Unwmk. *Perf. 11*

C97	AP50 5s multicolored	.70	.35
C98	AP50 13s multicolored	1.40	.70

Launching of the Russian spacecraft "Mars 1," Nov. 1, 1962.

Lt. Col. Valeri F. Bykovski AP51

Designs: 2s, Lt. Valentina Tereshkova. 5s, Globe and trajectories.

1963, Aug. 26 Unwmk. *Perf. 11½*

C99	AP51 1s pale vio & Prus bl	.25	.25
C100	AP51 2s citron & red brn	.25	.25
C101	AP51 5s rose & dk red	.35	.25
	Nos. C99-C101 (3)	.85	.75

The space flights of Valeri Bykovski, June 14-19, and Valentina Tereshkova, first woman cosmonaut, June 16-19, 1963. An imperf. souvenir sheet contains one 50s stamp showing Spasski tower and globe in lilac and red brown. Light blue border with red brown inscription. Size: 77x67mm. Value $4. See No. CB3.

Nos. C99-C100 Surcharged in Magenta or Green

1964, Aug. 22

C102	AP51 10s on 1s (M)	.35	.25
C103	AP51 20s on 2s	1.00	.40

International Space Exhibition in Riccione, Italy. Overprint in Italian on No. C103.

St. John's Monastery, Rila — AP52

13s, Notre Dame, Paris; French inscription.

1964, Dec. 22 Photo. *Perf. 11½*

C104	AP52 5s pale brn & blk	.35	.25
C105	AP52 13s lt ultra & sl bl	.90	.35

The philatelic exhibition at St. Ouen (Seine) organized by the Franco-Russian Philatelic Circle and philatelic organizations in various People's Democracies.

Paper Mill, Bukijovtz AP53

10s, Metal works, Plovdiv. 13s, Metal works, Kremikovtsi. 20s, Oil refinery, Stara-Zagora. 40s, Fertilizer plant, Stara-Zagora. 1 l, Rest home, Meded.

1964-68 Unwmk. *Perf. 13*

C106	AP53 8s grnsh blue	.35	.25
C107	AP53 10s red lilac	.50	.25
C108	AP53 13s brt violet	.45	.25
C109	AP53 20s slate blue	1.00	.25
C110	AP53 40s dk olive grn	1.50	.25
C111	AP53 1 l red ('68)	2.75	.55
	Nos. C106-C111 (6)	6.55	1.80

Issue dates: 1 l, May 6. Others, Dec. 7.

Three-master AP54

Means of Communication: 2s, Postal coach. 3s, Old steam locomotive. 5s, Early cars. 10s, Montgolfier balloon. 13s, Early plane. 20s, Jet planes. 40s, Rocket and satellites. 1 l, Postrider.

1969, Mar. 31 Photo. *Perf. 13x12½*

C112	AP54 1s gray & multi	.25	.25
C113	AP54 2s gray & multi	.25	.25
C114	AP54 3s gray & multi	.25	.25
C115	AP54 5s gray & multi	.25	.25
C116	AP54 10s gray & multi	.25	.25
C117	AP54 13s gray & multi	.45	.25
C118	AP54 20s gray & multi	.75	.30
C119	AP54 40s gray & multi	1.40	.60
	Nos. C112-C119 (8)	3.85	2.40

Miniature Sheet

Imperf

C120	AP54 1 l gold & org	2.75	2.00

SOFIA 1969 Philatelic Exhibition, Sofia, May 31-June 8.

Veliko Turnovo — AP55

Designs: Historic buildings in various cities.

1973, July 30 Photo. *Perf. 13*

C121	AP55 2s shown	.25	.25
C122	AP55 13s Roussalka	.50	.25
C123	AP55 20s Plovdiv	2.75	1.50
C124	AP55 28s Sofia	.70	.40
	Nos. C121-C124 (4)	4.20	2.40

Aleksei A. Leonov and Soyuz AP56

Designs: 18s, Thomas P. Stafford and Apollo. 28s, Apollo and Soyuz over earth. 1 l, Apollo Soyuz link-up.

1975, July 15

C125	AP56 13s blue & multi	.35	.25
C126	AP56 18s purple & multi	.75	.25
C127	AP56 28s multicolored	1.50	.45
	Nos. C125-C127 (3)	2.60	.95

Souvenir Sheet

C128	AP56 1 l violet & multi	3.25	2.00

Apollo Soyuz space test project (Russo-American cooperation), launching July 15; link-up July 17.

Balloon Over Plovdiv — AP57

1977, Sept. 3

C129	AP57 25s yellow, brn & red	.75	.25

Alexei Leonov Floating in Space — AP58

Designs: 25s, Mariner 6, US spacecraft. 35s, Venera 4, USSR Venus probe.

1977, Oct. 14 Photo. *Perf. 13½*

C130 AP58 12s multicolored .35 .25
C131 AP58 25s multicolored .70 .25
C132 AP58 35s multicolored 1.00 .35
Nos. C130-C132 (3) 2.05 .85

Space era, 20 years.

TU-154, Balkanair Emblem AP59

1977 *Perf. 13*

C133 AP59 35s ultra & multi 1.25 .40

30th anniv. of Bulgarian airline, Balkanair. Issued in sheets of 6 stamps + 3 labels (in lilac) with inscription and Balkanair emblem.

Baba Vida Fortress AP60

Design: 35s, Peace Bridge, connecting Rousse, Bulgaria, with Giurgiu, Romania.

1978 Photo. *Perf. 13*

C134 AP60 25s multicolored .50 .50
C135 AP60 35s multicolored .75 .75

The Danube, European Intercontinental Waterway. Issued in sheets containing 5 each of Nos. C134-C135 and 2 labels, one showing course of Danube, the other hydrofoil and fish.

Red Cross AP61

1978, Mar. Photo. *Perf. 13*

C136 AP61 25s multicolored .75 .30

Centenary of Bulgarian Red Cross.

AP62

Clock towers.

1979, June 5 Litho. *Perf. 12x12½*

C137 AP62 13s Byalla Cherkva .50 .25
C138 AP62 23s Botevgrad .50 .25
C139 AP62 25s Pazardgick .50 .25
C140 AP62 35s Grabovo .50 .25
C141 AP62 53s Tryavna 1.10 .50
Nos. C137-C141 (5) 3.10 1.50

1980, Oct. 22 Photo. *Perf. 12x12½*

C142 AP62 13s Bjala .25 .25
C143 AP62 23s Rasgrad .35 .25
C144 AP62 25s Karnabat .40 .25
C145 AP62 35s Serlievo .65 .35
C146 AP62 53s Berkovitza 1.25 .55
Nos. C142-C146 (5) 2.90 1.65

AP63

1980

C147 AP63 13s shown .25 .25
C148 AP63 25s Parachutist .60 .25

15th World Parachute Championships, Kazanluk.

DWVY-1 Aircraft — AP64

1981, June 27 Litho. *Perf. 12½*

C149 AP64 5s shown .25 .25
C150 AP64 12s LAS-7 .25 .25
C151 AP64 25s LAS-8 .55 .25
C152 AP64 35s DAR-1 .75 .25
C153 AP64 45s DAR-3 .85 .35
C154 AP64 55s DAR-9 1.10 .45
Nos. C149-C154 (6) 3.75 1.80

AP65

1983, June 28

C155 Sheet of 2 2.00 1.25
a. AP65 50s Valentina Tereshkova 1.00 .60
b. AP65 50s Svetlana Savitskaya 1.00 .60

Women in space, 20th anniv.

AP66

5s, TV tower, Tolbukhin. 13s, Postwoman. 30s, TV tower, Mt. Botev.

1983, July 20 Photo. *Perf. 13*

C156 AP66 5s multi .25 .25
C157 AP66 13s multi .30 .25
C158 AP66 30s multi .45 .25
a. Strip of 3, #C156-C158 1.25 .85

World Communications Year. Emblems of World Communications Year, Bulgarian Post, UPU and ITU on attached margins.

Souvenir Sheet

Geophysical Map of the Moon, Russia's Luna I, II and III Satellites — AP67

1984, Oct. 24 Photo. *Perf. 13*

C159 AP67 1 l multicolored 2.00 1.25

Conquest of Space.

Intl. Civil Aviation Org., 40th Anniv. — AP68

42s, Balkan Airlines jet.

1984, Dec. 21 Photo. *Perf. 13*

C160 AP68 42s multi .75 .35

Balkan Airlines — AP69

Design: Helicopter MU-8, passenger jet TU-154 and AN-21 transport plane.

1987, Aug. 25 Photo.

C161 AP69 25s multicolored .50 .30

2nd Joint Soviet-Bulgarian Space Flight — AP70

Cosmonauts: A. Aleksandrov, A. Solovov and V. Savinich.

1989, June 7 Litho. *Perf. 13½x13*

C162 AP70 13s multicolored .35 .25

AIR POST SEMI-POSTAL STAMPS

Catalogue values for unused stamps in this section are for Never Hinged items.

Statue of Liberty, Plane and Bridge SPAP1

Perf. 11½.

1947, May 24 Unwmk. Litho.

CB1 SPAP1 70 l + 30 l red brn 1.50 1.50

5th Philatelic Congress, Trnovo, and CIPEX, NYC, May, 1947.

Bulgarian Worker SPAP2

1948, Feb. 28 Photo. *Perf. 12x11½.*

CB2 SPAP2 60 l henna brn, *cream* .55 .45

2nd Bulgarian Workers' Congress, and sold by subscription only, at a premium of 16 l over face value.

Type of Air Post Stamps, 1963

Valeri Bykovski & Valentina Tereshkova.

1963, Aug. 26 Unwmk. *Perf. 11½*

CB3 AP51 20s + 10s pale bluish grn & dk grn 1.75 .45

See note after No. C101.

SPECIAL DELIVERY STAMPS

Catalogue values for unused stamps in this section are for Never Hinged items.

Postman on Bicycle SD1

Postman on Motorcycle SD3

Mail Car — SD2

1939 Unwmk. Photo. *Perf. 13*

E1 SD1 5 l deep blue 1.20 .25
E2 SD2 6 l copper brn .25 .25
E3 SD3 7 l copper brn .35 .25
E4 SD2 8 l red orange 1.20 .25
E5 SD1 20 l bright rose 2.50 .40
Nos. E1-E5 (5) 5.50 1.40

POSTAGE DUE STAMPS

D1

Large Lozenge Perf. 5½ to 6½

1884 Typo. Unwmk.

J1 D1 5s orange 600.00 75.00
J2 D1 25s lake 325.00 55.00
J3 D1 50s blue 45.00 35.00
Nos. J1-J3 (3) 970.00 165.00

1886 *Imperf.*

J4 D1 5s orange 375.00 17.50
J5 D1 25s lake 550.00 16.00
J6 D1 50s blue 19.00 16.00
Nos. J4-J6 (3) 944.00 49.50

1887 *Perf. 11½*

J7 D1 5s orange 57.50 6.00
J8 D1 25s lake 20.00 6.00
J9 D1 50s blue 20.00 15.00
Nos. J7-J9 (3) 97.50 27.00

Same, Redrawn
24 horizontal lines of shading in upper part instead of 30 lines

1892 ***Perf. 10½, 11, 11½***
J10 D1 5s orange 37.50 6.00
J11 D1 25s lake 20.00 6.00

D2

1893 **Pelure Paper**
J12 D2 5s orange 47.50 15.00

D3

1895 ***Imperf.***
J13 D3 30s on 50s blue 22.50 9.00
Perf. 10½, 11½
J14 D3 30s on 50s blue 27.50 9.00

D4

Wmk. Coat of Arms in the Sheet
1896 ***Perf. 13***
J15 D4 5s orange 27.50 2.50
J16 D4 10s purple 11.00 3.25
J17 D4 30s green 9.00 2.50
Nos. J15-J17 (3) 47.50 8.25

Nos. J15-J17 are also known on unwatermarked paper from the edges of sheets. Values about 40% less.

In 1901 a cancellation, "T" in circle, was applied to Nos. 60-65 and used provisionally as postage dues.

D5

1901-04 **Unwmk.** ***Perf. 11½***
J19 D5 5s dl rose .70 .40
J20 D5 10s yel grn 1.40 .40
J21 D5 20s dl bl ('04) 10.00 .40
J22 D5 30s vio brn 3.50 .40
J23 D5 50s org ('02) 8.50 8.50
Nos. J19-J23 (5) 24.10 10.10

Nos. J19-J23 exist imperf. and in pairs imperf. between. Value, imperf., $250.

D6

Thin Semi-Transparent Paper
1915 **Unwmk.** ***Perf. 11½***
J24 D6 5s green .45 .25
J25 D6 10s purple .45 .25
J26 D6 20s dl rose .45 .25
J27 D6 30s dp org 2.50 .60
J28 D6 50s dp bl .85 .35
Nos. J24-J28 (5) 4.70 1.70

1919-21 ***Perf. 11½, 12x11½***
J29 D6 5s emerald .70 .25
a. 5s gray green ('21) .30 .25
J30 D6 10s violet .70 .25
a. 10s light violet ('21) .25 .25
J31 D6 20s salmon .70 .25
a. 20s yellow .25 .25
J32 D6 30s orange .70 .25
a. 30s red orange ('21) .65 .65
J33 D6 50s blue 1.40 .25
J34 D6 1 l emerald ('21) .25 .25
J35 D6 2 l rose ('21) .25 .25
J36 D6 3 l brown org ('21) .35 .25
Nos. J29-J36 (8) 5.05 2.00

Stotinki values of the above series surcharged 10s or 20s were used as ordinary postage stamps. See Nos. 182-185.

The 1919 printings are on thicker white paper with clean-cut perforations, the 1921 printings on thicker grayish paper with rough perforations.

Most of this series exist imperforate and in pairs imperforate between.

Heraldic Lion — D7

1932, Aug. 15 **Thin Paper**
J37 D7 1 l olive bister .75 .85
J38 D7 2 l rose brown .75 .85
J39 D7 6 l brown violet 1.50 1.00
Nos. J37-J39 (3) 3.00 2.70

Lion of Trnovo — D8

National Arms — D9

1933, Apr. 10
J40 D8 20s dk brn .25 .25
J41 D8 40s dp bl .25 .25
J42 D8 80s car rose .25 .25
J43 D9 1 l org brn .80 .30
J44 D9 2 l olive .80 .50
J45 D9 6 l dl vio .40 .30
J46 D9 14 l ultra 1.00 .50
Nos. J40-J46 (7) 3.75 2.35

Catalogue values for unused stamps in this section, from this point to the end of the section, are for Never Hinged items.

National Arms — D10

1947, June **Typo.** ***Perf. 10½***
J47 D10 1 l chocolate .25 .25
J48 D10 2 l deep claret .25 .25
J49 D10 8 l deep orange .30 .25
J50 D10 20 l blue .85 .25
Nos. J47-J50 (4) 1.65 1.00

Arms of the People's Republic — D11

1951 ***Perf. 11½x10½***
J51 D11 1 l chocolate .25 .25
J52 D11 2 l claret .25 .25
J53 D11 8 l red orange .45 .35
J54 D11 20 l deep blue 1.10 .90
Nos. J51-J54 (4) 2.05 1.75

OFFICIAL STAMPS

Catalogue values for unused stamps in this section are for Never Hinged items.

Bulgarian Coat of Arms
O1 O2

1942 **Unwmk.** **Typo.** ***Perf. 13***
O1 O1 10s yel grn .25 .25
O2 O1 30s red .25 .25
O3 O1 50s bister .25 .25
O4 O2 1 l vio bl .25 .25
O5 O2 2 l dk grn .25 .25
O6 O2 3 l lilac .25 .25
O7 O2 4 l rose .25 .25
O8 O2 5 l carmine .35 .25
Nos. O1-O8 (8) 2.10 2.00

1944 ***Perf. 10½x11½***
O9 O2 1 l blue .90 .35
O10 O2 2 l brt red .90 .35

Lion Rampant
O3 O4

O5

1945 ***Imperf.***
O11 O5 1 l pink .25 .25
Perf. 10½x11½, Imperf.
O12 O3 2 l blue green .25 .25
O13 O4 3 l bister brown .25 .25
O14 O4 4 l light ultra .25 .25
O15 O5 5 l brown lake .25 .25
Nos. O11-O15 (5) 1.25 1.25

In 1950, four stamps prepared for official use were issued as regular postage stamps. See Nos. 724-727.

PARCEL POST STAMPS

Catalogue values for unused stamps in this section are for Never Hinged items.

Weighing Packages — PP1

Parcel Post — PP2

Designs: 3 l, 8 l, 20 l, Parcel post truck. 4 l, 6 l, 10 l, Motorcycle.

Perf. 12½x13½, 13½x12½
1941-42 **Photo.** **Unwmk.**
Q1 PP1 1 l slate grn .25 .25
Q2 PP2 2 l crimson .25 .25
Q3 PP2 3 l dull brn .25 .25
Q4 PP2 4 l red org .25 .25
Q5 PP1 5 l deep blue .35 .25
Q6 PP1 5 l slate grn ('42) .25 .25
Q7 PP2 6 l red vio .35 .25
Q8 PP2 6 l henna brn ('42) .25 .25
Q9 PP1 7 l dark blue .35 .25
Q10 PP1 7 l dk brn ('42) .25 .25
Q11 PP2 8 l brt bl grn .35 .25
Q12 PP2 8 l green ('42) .25 .25
Q13 PP2 9 l olive gray .35 .25
Q14 PP2 9 l dp olive ('42) .35 .25
Q15 PP2 10 l orange .65 .25
Q16 PP2 20 l gray vio .65 .25
Q17 PP2 30 l dull blk 1.25 .25
Q18 PP2 30 l sepia ('42) .90 .25
Nos. Q1-Q18 (18) 7.55 4.50

Arms of Bulgaria — PP5

1944 **Litho.** ***Imperf.***
Q21 PP5 1 l dk carmine .25 .25
Q22 PP5 3 l blue grn .25 .25
Q23 PP5 5 l dull bl grn .25 .25
Q24 PP5 7 l rose lilac .25 .25
Q25 PP5 10 l deep blue .25 .25
Q26 PP5 20 l orange brn .25 .25
Q27 PP5 30 l dk brn car .25 .25
Q28 PP5 50 l red orange .30 .25
Q29 PP5 100 l blue .50 .25
Nos. Q21-Q29 (9) 2.55 2.25

For overprints and surcharges see Nos. 448-454, C37-C40.

POSTAL TAX STAMPS

The use of stamps Nos. RA1 to RA18 was compulsory on letters, etc., to be delivered on Sundays and holidays. The money received from their sale was used toward maintaining a sanatorium for employees of the post, telegraph and telephone services.

View of Sanatorium PT1

Sanatorium, Peshtera PT2

1925-29 **Unwmk.** **Typo.** ***Perf. 11½***
RA1 PT1 1 l blk, *grnsh bl* 2.75 .25
RA2 PT1 1 l chocolate ('26) 2.75 .25
RA3 PT1 1 l orange ('27) 3.00 .30
RA4 PT1 1 l pink ('28) 4.50 .30
RA5 PT1 1 l vio, *pnksh* ('29) 4.75 .30
RA6 PT2 2 l blue green .35 .25
RA7 PT2 2 l violet ('27) .35 .25
RA8 PT2 5 l deep blue 3.00 .80
RA9 PT2 5 l rose ('27) 3.75 .40
Nos. RA1-RA9 (9) 25.20 3.10

St. Constantine Sanatorium PT3

1930-33
RA10 PT3 1 l red brn & ol grn 4.00 .25
RA11 PT3 1 l ol grn & yel ('31) .50 .25
RA12 PT3 1 l red vio & ol brn ('33) .50 .25
Nos. RA10-RA12 (3) 5.00 .75

Trojan Rest Home PT4

Sanatorium
PT5

1935 **Wmk. 145** ***Perf. 11, 11½***

RA13	PT4	1 l choc & red org	.30	.25
RA14	PT4	1 l emer & indigo	.30	.25
RA15	PT5	5 l red brn & indigo	1.40	.35
		Nos. RA13-RA15 (3)	2.00	.85

St.
Constantine
Sanatorium
PT6

2 l, Children at seashore. 5 l, Rest home.

1941 **Unwmk.** **Photo.** ***Perf. 13***

RA16	PT6	1 l dark olive green	.25	.25
RA17	PT6	2 l red orange	.25	.25
RA18	PT6	5 l deep blue	.30	.25
		Nos. RA16-RA18 (3)	.80	.75

See Nos. 702-705 for same designs in smaller size issued as regular postage.

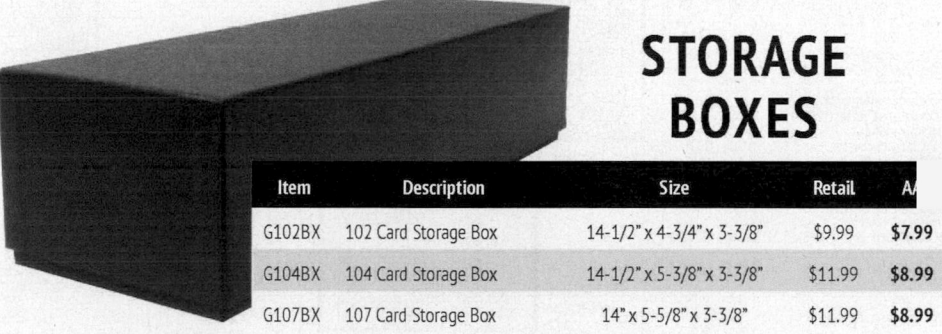

BURKINA FASO

bur-'kē-nə-'fä-sō

Upper Volta

LOCATION — Northwestern Africa, north of Ghana
GOVT. — Republic
AREA — 105,869 sq. mi.
POP. — 11,575,898 (1999 est.)
CAPITAL — Ouagadougou

In 1919 the French territory of Upper Volta was detached from the southern section of Upper Senegal and Niger and made a separate colony. In 1933 the colony was divided among its neighbors: French Sudan, Ivory Coast, and Niger Territory. The Republic of Upper Volta was proclaimed December 11, 1958; the name was changed to Burkina Faso on August 4, 1984.

100 Centimes = 1 Franc

Catalogue values for unused stamps in this country are for Never Hinged items, beginning with Scott 70 in the regular postage section, Scott B1 in the semi-postal section, Scott C1 in the air-post section, Scott J21 in the postage due section, and Scott O1 in the official section.

See French West Africa Nos. 67, 84 for additional stamps inscribed "Haute Volta" and "Afrique Occidentale Francaise."

Stamps and Types of Upper Senegal and Niger, 1914-17, Overprinted in Black or Red

1920-28 Unwmk. *Perf. 13½x14*

1	A4	1c brn vio & vio	.25	.50
2	A4	2c gray & brn vio (R)	.25	.50
3	A4	4c blk & bl	.30	.60
4	A4	5c yel grn & bl grn	1.00	1.00
5	A4	5c ol brn & dk brn ('22)	.25	.50
6	A4	10c red org & rose	2.00	2.00
7	A4	10c yel grn & bl grn ('22)	.25	.50
		Complete booklet, 20 #7	—	
8	A4	10c claret & bl ('25)	1.00	1.00
a.		Overprint omitted	240.00	
9	A4	15c choc & org	1.00	1.00
		Complete booklet, 20 #9	—	
10	A4	20c brn vio & blk (R)	1.50	1.50
11	A4	25c ultra & bl	2.00	1.40
12	A4	25c blk & bl grn ('22)	1.00	1.00
a.		Overprint omitted	200.00	
13	A4	30c ol brn & brn (R)	4.00	*4.50*
14	A4	30c red org & rose ('22)	2.00	2.50
15	A4	30c vio & brn red ('25)	1.50	2.00
16	A4	30c dl grn & bl grn ('27)	1.50	2.00
17	A4	35c car rose & vio	1.00	2.00
18	A4	40c gray & car rose	1.00	2.00
19	A4	45c bl & brn (R)	1.00	2.00
20	A4	50c blk & grn	3.50	4.50
21	A4	50c ultra & bl ('22)	1.50	2.50
22	A4	50c red org & bl ('25)	1.50	2.00
a.		Double surcharge, one inverted	1,275.	1,400.
23	A4	60c org red ('26)	1.00	1.50
24	A4	65c bis & pale bl ('28)	2.00	3.00
25	A4	75c org & brn	2.00	2.00
26	A4	1fr brn & brn vio	1.50	*2.50*
27	A4	2fr grn & bl	2.50	*3.00*
28	A4	5fr vio & blk (R)	5.00	*7.00*
		Nos. 1-28 (28)	43.30	56.50

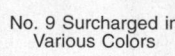

No. 9 Surcharged in Various Colors

1922

29	A4	0,01c on 15c (Bk)	1.10	1.40
a.		Double surcharge	175.00	250.00
30	A4	0,02c on 15c (Bl)	1.10	1.40
31	A4	0,05c on 15c (R)	1.20	1.50
		Nos. 29-31 (3)	3.40	4.30

Type of 1920 Surcharged

1922

32	A4	60c on 75c vio, *pnksh*	.75	1.15

Stamps and Types of 1920 Surcharged with New Value and Bars

1924-27

33	A4	25c on 2fr grn & bl	.80	*1.00*
34	A4	25c on 5fr vio & blk	.80	*1.00*
35	A4	65c on 45c bl & brn ('25)	1.50	1.50
36	A4	85c on 75c org & brn ('25)	1.60	*2.40*
37	A4	90c on 75c brn red & sal pink ('27)	2.25	2.25
38	A4	1.25fr on 1fr dp bl & lt bl (R) ('26)	1.50	*2.00*
39	A4	1.50fr on 1fr dp bl & ultra ('27)	3.00	*3.50*
40	A4	3fr on 5fr dl red & brn org ('27)	4.50	*5.50*
41	A4	10fr on 5fr ol grn & lil rose ('27)	15.00	*18.50*
42	A4	20fr on 5fr org brn & vio ('27)	22.50	*28.00*
		Nos. 33-42 (10)	53.45	*65.65*

Hausa Chief — A5

Hausa Woman — A6

Hausa Warrior A7

1928 Typo. *Perf. 13½x14*

43	A5	1c indigo & grn	.40	.40
44	A5	2c brn & lil	.40	.40
45	A5	4c blk & yel	.40	.75
46	A5	5c indigo & gray bl	.40	.75
47	A5	10c indigo & pink	1.15	1.15
48	A5	15c brn & bl	1.50	*2.25*
49	A5	20c brn & grn	1.50	*1.60*
50	A6	25c brn & yel	1.90	*2.40*
51	A6	30c dp grn & grn	1.90	*2.40*
52	A6	40c blk & pink	1.90	*2.25*
53	A6	45c brn & blue	3.00	*3.75*
54	A6	50c blk & grn	2.25	*2.40*
55	A6	65c indigo & bl	3.00	*3.75*
56	A6	75c blk & lil	2.40	*3.00*
57	A6	90c brn red & lil	3.00	*3.75*

Perf. 14x13½

58	A7	1fr brn & grn	2.40	*2.75*
59	A7	1.10fr indigo & lil	3.00	*4.00*
60	A7	1.50fr ultra & grysh	3.75	*4.50*
61	A7	2fr blk & bl	4.00	*4.75*
62	A7	3fr brn & yel	4.00	*5.25*
63	A7	5fr brn & lil	4.00	*5.25*
64	A7	10fr blk & grn	20.00	*26.00*
65	A7	20fr blk & pink	30.00	*32.50*
		Nos. 43-65 (23)	96.25	*116.00*

Common Design Types pictured following the introduction.

Colonial Exposition Issue

Common Design Types

1931 Engr. *Perf. 12½*

Country Name Typo. in Black

66	CD70	40c dp grn	4.00	4.00
67	CD71	50c violet	4.75	4.75
68	CD72	90c red org	4.75	4.75
69	CD73	1.50fr dull blue	5.50	5.50
		Nos. 66-69 (4)	19.00	19.00

Catalogue values for unused stamps in this section, from this point to the end of the section, are for Never Hinged items.

Republic

President Ouezzin Coulibaly — A8

1959 Unwmk. Engr. *Perf. 13*

70	A8	25fr black & magenta	.55	.40

1st anniv. of the proclamation of the Republic; Ouezzin Coulibaly, Council President, who died in December, 1958.

Imperforates

Most Upper Volta stamps from 1959 onward exist imperforate in issued and trial colors (values two to four times regularly issued stamps), and also in small presentation sheets in issued colors (values four to five times regularly issued stamps).

Deer Mask and Deer — A9

Animal Masks: 1fr, 2fr, 4fr, Wart hog. 5fr, 6fr, 8fr, Monkey. 10fr, 15fr, 20fr, Buffalo. 25fr, Coba (antelope). 30fr, 40fr, 50fr, Elephant. 60fr, 85fr, Secretary bird.

1960

71	A9	30c rose & violet	.25	.25
72	A9	40c buff & dp claret	.25	.25
73	A9	50c bl grn & gray ol	.25	.25
74	A9	1fr red, blk & red brn	.25	.25
75	A9	2fr emer, yel grn & dk grn	.25	.25
76	A9	4fr bl, vio & ind	.25	.25
77	A9	5fr ol bis, red & brn	.25	.25
78	A9	6fr grnsh bl & vio brn	.25	.25
79	A9	8fr org & red brn	.25	.25
80	A9	10fr lt yel grn & plum	.25	.25
81	A9	15fr org, ultra & brn	.40	.25
82	A9	20fr green & ultra	.40	.35
83	A9	25fr bl, emer & dp clar	.60	.35
84	A9	30fr dk bl grn, blk & brn	.75	.35
85	A9	40fr ultra, ind & dk car	1.00	.50
86	A9	50fr brt pink, brn & grn	1.25	.50
87	A9	60fr org brn & bl	1.50	.65
88	A9	85fr gray ol & dk bl	2.25	1.00
		Nos. 71-88 (18)	10.65	6.45

C.C.T.A. Issue

Common Design Type

1960 Engr. *Perf. 13*

89	CD106	25fr vio bl & slate	.65	.40

Emblem of the Entente — A9a

1960 Photo. *Perf. 13x13½*

90	A9a	25fr multicolored	.65	.40

Council of the Entente.

Pres. Maurice Yameogo — A10

1960, May 1 Engr. *Perf. 13*

91	A10	25fr dk vio brn & slate	.55	.25

Flag, Village and Couple — A11

1960, Aug. 5 Unwmk. *Perf. 13*

92	A11	25fr red brn, blk & red	.65	.40

Proclamation of independence, Aug. 5, 1960.

World Meteorological Organization Emblem — A12

1961, May 4

93	A12	25fr blk, bl & red	.90	.45

First World Meteorological Day.

Arms of Republic — A13

1961, Dec. 8 Photo. *Perf. 12x12½*

94	A13	25fr multicolored	.65	.40

The 1961 independence celebrations.

WMO Emblem, Weather Station and Sorghum Grain — A14

1962, Mar. 23 Unwmk. *Perf. 13*

95	A14	25fr dk bl, emer & brn	.70	.45

UN 2nd World Meteorological Day, Mar. 23.

Hospital and Nurse — A15

1962, June 23 *Perf. 13x12*

96	A15	25fr multicolored	.90	.55

Founding of Upper Volta Red Cross.

Buffalos at Water Hole — A16

Designs: 10fr, Lions, horiz. 15fr, Defassa waterbuck. 25fr, Arly reservation, horiz. 50fr, Diapaga reservation, horiz. 85fr, Buffon's kob.

Perf. 12½x12, 12x12½

1962, June 30 **Engr.**

97	A16	5fr sepia, bl & grn	.40	.25
98	A16	10fr red brn, grn & yel	.55	.35
99	A16	15fr sepia, grn & yel	1.45	.50
100	A16	25fr vio brn, bl & grn	.95	.70
101	A16	50fr vio brn, bl & grn	1.90	1.65
102	A16	85fr red brn, bl & grn	4.50	2.75
		Nos. 97-102 (6)	9.75	6.20

Abidjan Games Issue

Common Design Type

Designs: 20fr, Soccer. 25fr, Bicycling. 85fr, Boxing. All horiz.

1962, July 21 **Photo.** *Perf. 12½x12*

103	CD109	20fr multicolored	.55	.35
104	CD109	25fr multicolored	.75	.55
105	CD109	85fr multicolored	1.50	.85
		Nos. 103-105 (3)	2.80	1.75

African-Malgache Union Issue

Common Design Type

1962, Sept. 8 **Unwmk.**

106	CD110	30fr red, bluish grn & gold	1.10	.75

Weather Map and UN Emblem A17

1963, Mar. 23 *Perf. 12x12½*

107	A17	70fr multicolored	1.45	.70

3rd World Meteorological Day, Mar. 23.

Friendship Games, Dakar, Apr. 11-21 — A18

1963, Apr. 11 **Engr.** *Perf. 13*

108	A18	20fr Basketball	.40	.30
109	A18	25fr Discus	.60	.30
110	A18	50fr Judo	1.25	.55
		Nos. 108-110 (3)	2.25	1.15

Amaryllis A19

Flowers: 50c, Hibiscus. 1fr, Oldenlandia grandiflora. 1.50fr, Rose moss (portulaca). 2fr, Tobacco. 4fr, Morning glory. 5fr, Striga senegalensis. 6fr, Cowpea. 8fr, Lepidagathis heudelotiana. 10fr, Spurge. 25fr, Argyreia nervosa. 30fr, Rangoon creeper. 40fr, Water lily. 50fr, White plumeria. 60fr, Crotalaria retusa. 85fr, Hibiscus.

1963 **Photo.**

111	A19	50c multi, vert.	.25	.25
112	A19	1fr multi, vert.	.25	.25
113	A19	1.50fr multi, vert.	.25	.25
114	A19	2fr multi, vert.	.25	.25
115	A19	4fr multi, vert.	.25	.25
116	A19	5fr multi, vert.	.30	.25
117	A19	6fr multi, vert.	.35	.25
118	A19	8fr multi, vert.	.35	.25
119	A19	10fr multi, vert.	.35	.25
120	A19	15fr multi	.40	.35
121	A19	25fr multi	.55	.35
122	A19	30fr multi	.75	.35
123	A19	40fr multi	1.25	.50
124	A19	50fr multi	1.40	.50
125	A19	60fr multi	1.75	.80
126	A19	85fr multi	2.25	1.00
		Nos. 111-126 (16)	10.95	6.10

Centenary Emblem and Globe — A20

1963, Oct. 21 **Unwmk.** *Perf. 12*

127	A20	25fr multicolored	1.00	.75

Centenary of International Red Cross.

Scroll — A21

1963, Dec. 10 **Photo.** *Perf. 13x12½*

128	A21	25fr dp claret, gold & bl	.80	.50

15th anniv. of the Universal Declaration of Human Rights.

Sound Wave Patterns A22

1964, Jan. 16 *Perf. 12½x13*

129	A22	25fr multicolored	.65	.35

Upper Volta's admission to the ITU.

Recording Rain Gauge and WMO Emblem A23

1964, Mar. 23 **Engr.** *Perf. 13*

130	A23	50fr dk car rose, grn & bl	1.20	.80

4th World Meteorological Day, Mar. 23.

World Connected by Letters and Carrier Pigeon — A24

60fr, World connected by letters and jet plane.

1964, Mar. 29 **Photo.** *Perf. 13x12*

131	A24	25fr gray brn & ultra	.65	.35
132	A24	60fr gray brn & org	1.10	.90

Upper Volta's admission to the UPU.

IQSY Emblem and Seasonal Allegories — A25

1964, Aug. 17 **Engr.** *Perf. 13*

133	A25	30fr grn, ocher & car	.90	.65

International Quiet Sun Year.

Cooperation Issue

Common Design Type

1964, Nov. 7 **Unwmk.** *Perf. 13*

134	CD119	70fr dl bl grn, dk brn & car	1.25	.75

Hotel Independance, Ouagadougou — A26

1964, Dec. 11 **Litho.** *Perf. 12½x13*

135	A26	25fr multicolored	1.90	.90

Pigmy Long-tailed Sunbird — A27

15fr, Olive-bellied Sunbird. 20fr, Splendid Sunbird.

1965, Mar. 1 **Photo.** *Perf. 13x12½*

Size: 22x36mm

136	A27	10fr shown	.90	.35
137	A27	15fr multi	1.10	.50
138	A27	20fr multi	2.00	.90
		Nos. 136-138,C20 (4)	24.00	9.25

Comoe Waterfall — A28

25fr, Great Waterfall of Banfora, horiz.

1965 **Engr.** *Perf. 13*

139	A28	5fr yel grn, bl & red brn	.35	.25
140	A28	25fr dk red, brt bl & grn	.85	.30
		Nos. 139-140 (2)	1.20	.55

Soccer — A29

Designs: 25fr, Boxing gloves and ring. 70fr, Tennis rackets, ball and net.

1965, July 15 **Unwmk.** *Perf. 13*

141	A29	15fr brn, red & dk grn	.40	.25
142	A29	25fr pale org, bl & brn	.60	.35
143	A29	70fr dk car & brt grn	1.50	.80
		Nos. 141-143 (3)	2.50	1.40

1st African Games, Brazzaville, July 18-25.

Abraham Lincoln — A30

1965, Nov. 3 **Photo.** *Perf. 13x12½*

144	A30	50fr green & multi	.90	.45

Centenary of death of Abraham Lincoln.

Pres. Maurice Yameogo — A31

1965, Dec. 11 **Photo.** *Perf. 13x12½*

145	A31	25fr multicolored	.60	.30

Mantis A32

Wart Hog — A33

1fr, Nemopistha imperatrix. 2fr, Ball python. 4fr, Grasshopper. 6fr, Scorpion. 8fr, Green monkey. 10fr, Dromedary. 15fr, Leopard. 20fr, Cape buffalo. 25fr, Hippopotamus. 30fr, Agama lizard. 45fr, Common puff adder. 50fr, Chameleon. 60fr, Ugada limbata. 85fr, Elephant.

1966 *Perf. 13x12½, 12½x13*

146	A33	1fr multi	.25	.25
147	A33	2fr multi	.25	.25
148	A32	3fr shown	.35	.25
149	A32	4fr multi	.35	.25
150	A33	5fr shown	.35	.25
151	A32	6fr multi	.55	.25
152	A33	8fr multi	.65	.25
153	A32	10fr multi	.50	.25
154	A33	15fr multi	1.00	.35
155	A32	20fr multi	1.35	.45
156	A33	25fr multi	1.55	.50
157	A32	30fr multi	1.10	.60
158	A33	45fr multi	2.25	.80
159	A33	50fr multi	2.50	1.00
160	A33	60fr multi	2.75	.90
161	A33	85fr multi	3.50	1.25
		Nos. 146-161 (16)	19.25	7.85

Headdress — A34

25fr, Plumed headdress. 60fr, Male dancer.

1966, Apr. 9 Photo. ***Perf. 13x12½***
162 A34 20fr yel grn, choc & red .60 .25
163 A34 25fr multicolored .65 .30
164 A34 60fr org, dk brn & red 1.50 .60
Nos. 162-164 (3) 2.75 1.15

Intl. Negro Arts Festival, Dakar, Senegal, 4/1-24.

Pô Church A35

Design: No. 166, Bobo-Dioulasso Mosque.

1966, Apr. 15 ***Perf. 12½x13***
165 A35 25fr multicolored .60 .35
166 A35 25fr bl, cream & red brn .60 .35

The Red Cross Helping the World — A36

1966, June Photo. ***Perf. 13x12½***
167 A36 25fr lemon, blk & car .80 .40

Issued to honor the Red Cross.

Boy Scouts in Camp A37

15fr, Two Scouts on a cliff exploring the country.

1966, June 15 ***Perf. 12½x13***
168 A37 10fr multicolored .50 .25
169 A37 15fr blk, bis brn, & dl yel .50 .25

Issued to honor the Boy Scouts.

Cow Receiving Injection A38

1966, Aug. 16 Photo. ***Perf. 12½x13***
170 A38 25fr yel, blk & blue 1.40 .60

Campaign against cattle plague.

Plowing with Donkey A39

Design: 30fr, Crop rotation, Kamboince Experimental Station.

1966, Sept. 15 Photo. ***Perf. 12½x13***
171 A39 25fr multicolored .60 .30
172 A39 30fr multicolored .60 .30

Natl. and rural education; 3rd anniv. of the Kamboince Experimental Station (No. 172).

UNESCO Emblem and Map of Africa A40

UNICEF Emblem and Children A41

1966, Dec. 10 Engr. ***Perf. 13***
173 A40 50fr brt bl, blk & red .90 .60
174 A41 50fr dk vio, dp lil & dk red .90 .50

20th anniv. of UNESCO and of UNICEF.

Arms of Upper Volta — A42

1967, Jan. 2 Photo. ***Perf. 12½x13***
175 A42 30fr multicolored .75 .25

Europafrica Issue

Symbols of Agriculture, Industry, Men and Women — A43

1967, Feb. 4 Photo. ***Perf. 12½***
176 A43 60fr multicolored 1.40 .60

Scout Handclasp and Jamboree Emblem A44

5fr, Jamboree emblem, Scout holding hat.

1967, June 8 Photo. ***Perf. 12½x13***
177 A44 5fr multicolored .40 .25
178 A44 20fr multicolored .85 .50

12th Boy Scout World Jamboree, Farragut State Park, Idaho, Aug. 1-9. See No. C41.

Bank Book and Hands with Coins A45

1967, Aug. 22 Engr. ***Perf. 13***
179 A45 30fr slate grn, ocher & olive .60 .30

National Savings Bank.

Mailman on Bicycle — A46

1967, Oct. 15 Engr. ***Perf. 13***
180 A46 30fr dk bl, emer & brn .90 .45

Stamp Day.

Monetary Union Issue
Common Design Type

1967, Nov. 4 Engr. ***Perf. 13***
181 CD125 30fr dk vio & dl bl .65 .35

View of Nizier A47

Olympic Emblem and: 50fr, Les Deux-Alps, vert. 100fr, Ski lift and view of Villard-de-Lans.

1967, Nov. 28
182 A47 15fr brt bl, grn & brn .45 .25
183 A47 50fr brt bl & slate grn .80 .40
184 A47 100fr brt bl, grn & red 2.00 1.00
Nos. 182-184 (3) 3.25 1.65

10th Winter Olympic Games, Grenoble, France, Feb. 6-18, 1968.

White and Black Men Holding Human Rights Emblem A48

1968, Jan. 2 Photo. ***Perf. 12½x13***
185 A48 20fr brt bl, gold & dp car .60 .25
186 A48 30fr grn, gold & dp car .75 .35

International Human Rights Year.

Administration School and Student — A49

1968, Feb. 2 Engr. ***Perf. 13***
187 A49 30fr ol bis, Prus bl & brt grn .65 .35

National School of Administration.

WHO Emblem and Sick People A50

1968, Apr. 8 Engr. ***Perf. 13***
188 A50 30fr ind, brt bl & car rose .65 .30
189 A50 50fr brt bl, sl grn & lt brn .95 .50

WHO, 20th anniversary.

Telephone Office, Bobo-Dioulasso — A51

1968, Sept. 30 Photo. ***Perf. 12½x12***
190 A51 30fr multicolored .90 .45

Opening of the automatic telephone office in Bobo-Dioulasso.

Weaver A52

1968, Oct. 30 Engr. ***Perf. 13***
Size: 36x22mm
191 A52 30fr mag, brn & ocher .70 .30

See No. C58.

Grain Pouring over World, Plower and FAO Emblem — A53

1969, Jan. 7 Engr. ***Perf. 13***
192 A53 30fr slate, vio bl & maroon .70 .35

UNFAO world food program.

Automatic Looms and ILO Emblem A54

1969, Mar. 15 Engr. ***Perf. 13***
193 A54 30fr brt grn, mar & indigo .75 .45

ILO, 50th anniversary.

Smith A55

1969, Apr. 3 Engr. ***Perf. 13***
Size: 36x22mm
194 A55 5fr magenta & blk .35 .25

See No. C64.

Blood Donor A56

1969, May 15 Engr. ***Perf. 13***
195 A56 30fr blk, bl & car 1.00 .50

League of Red Cross Societies, 50th anniv.

Nile Pike — A57

Fish: 20fr, Nannocharax gobioides. 25fr, Hemigrammocharax polli. 55fr, Alestes luteus. 85fr, Micralestes voltae.

1969 Engr. ***Perf. 13***
Size: 36x22mm
196 A57 20fr brt bl, brn & yel 1.25 .40
197 A57 25fr slate, brn & dk brn 1.25 .45
198 A57 30fr dk olive & blk 1.50 .75
199 A57 55fr dk grn, yel & ol 2.00 .90
200 A57 85fr slate brn & pink 3.50 1.75
Nos. 196-200,C66-C67 (7) 15.75 7.00

Development Bank Issue
Common Design Type

1969, Sept. 10 Engr. ***Perf. 13***
201 CD130 30fr sl grn, grn & ocher .65 .30

Millet A58

Design: 30fr, Cotton.

1969, Oct. 30 Photo. *Perf. 12½x13*
202 A58 15fr dk brn, grn & yel .50 .25
203 A58 30fr dp claret & brt bl .80 .35
Nos. 202-203,C73-C74 (4) 5.80 2.10

ASECNA Issue
Common Design Type

1969, Dec. 12 Engr. *Perf. 13*
204 CD132 100fr brown 1.75 1.00

Niadale Mask — A59

Carvings from National Museum: 30fr, Niaga. 45fr, Man and woman, Iliu Bara. 80fr, Karan Weeba figurine.

1970, Mar. 5 Engr. *Perf. 13*
207 A59 10fr dk car rose, org & dk brn .30 .25
209 A59 30fr dk brn, brt vio & grnsh bl .50 .25
211 A59 45fr yel grn, brn & bl 1.00 .45
212 A59 80fr pur, rose lil & brn 1.75 .70
Nos. 207-212 (4) 3.55 1.65

African Huts and European City — A60

1970, Apr. 25 Engr. *Perf. 13*
213 A60 30fr dk brn, red & bl .85 .45

Issued for Linked Cities' Day.

Mask for Nebwa Gnomo Dance A61

Designs: 8fr, Cauris dancers, vert. 20fr, Gourmantchés dancers, vert. 30fr, Larllé dancers.

1970, May 7 Photo. *Perf. 13*
214 A61 5fr lt brn, vio bl & blk .55 .25
215 A61 8fr org brn, car & blk .55 .25
216 A61 20fr dk brn, sl grn & ocher .85 .25
217 A61 30fr dp car, dk gray & brn 1.05 .35
Nos. 214-217 (4) 3.00 1.10

Education Year Emblem, Open Book and Pupils A62

Design: 90fr, Education Year emblem, telecommunication and education symbols.

1970, May 14 *Perf. 12½x12*
218 A62 40fr black & multi .60 .25
219 A62 90fr olive & multi 1.40 .60

International Education Year.

UPU Headquarters Issue

Abraham Lincoln, UPU Headquarters and Emblem — A63

1970, May 20 Engr. *Perf. 13*
220 A63 30fr dk car rose, ind & red brn .70 .25
221 A63 60fr dk bl grn, vio & red brn 1.25 .50

See note after CD133, Common Design section.

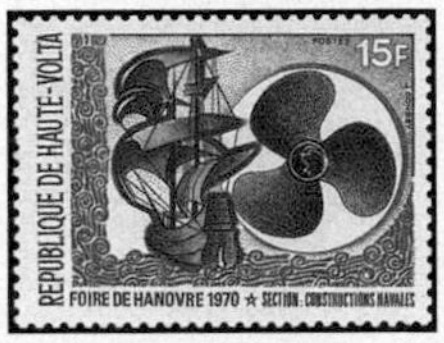

Ship-building Industry — A64

45fr, Chemical industry. 80fr, Electrical industry.

1970, June 15
222 A64 15fr brt pink, red brn & blk .90 .40
223 A64 45fr emerald, dp bl & blk 1.00 .40
224 A64 80fr red brn, claret & blk 2.00 .70
Nos. 222-224 (3) 3.90 1.50

Hanover Fair.

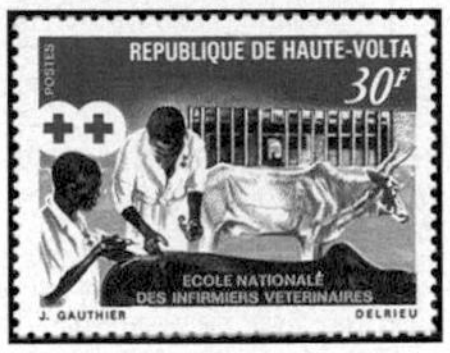

Cattle Vaccination A65

1970, June 30 Photo. *Perf. 13*
225 A65 30fr Prus bl, yel & sepia 1.00 .50

National Veterinary College.

Vaccination and Red Cross — A66

1970, Aug. 28 Engr. *Perf. 12½x13*
226 A66 30fr chocolate & car 1.00 .50

Issued for the Upper Volta Red Cross.
For surcharge see No. 252.

Europafrica Issue

Nurse with Child, by Frans Hals — A67

Paintings: 30fr, Courtyard of a House in Delft, by Pieter de Hooch. 150fr, Christina of Denmark, by Hans Holbein. 250fr, Courtyard of the Royal Palace at Innsbruck, Austria, by Albrecht Dürer.

1970, Sept. 25 Litho. *Perf. 13x14*
227 A67 25fr multicolored .80 .25
228 A67 30fr multicolored .95 .45
229 A67 150fr multicolored 3.25 1.25
230 A67 250fr multicolored 5.00 1.75
Nos. 227-230 (4) 10.00 3.70

Citroen A68

Design: 40fr, Old and new Citroen cars.

1970, Oct. 16 Engr. *Perf. 13*
231 A68 25fr ol brn, mar & sl grn 1.40 .50
232 A68 40fr brt grn, plum & sl 1.75 .85

57th Paris Automobile Salon.

Professional Training Center A69

1970, Dec. 10 Engr. *Perf. 13*
233 A69 50fr grn, bis & brn .75 .40

Opening of Professional Training Center under joint sponsorship of Austria and Upper Volta.

Upper Volta Arms and Soaring Bird — A70

1970, Dec. 10 Photo.
234 A70 30fr lt blue & multi .55 .25

Tenth anniversary of independence, Dec. 11.

Political Maps of Africa — A71

1970, Dec. 14 Litho. *Perf. 13½*
235 A71 50fr multicolored .80 .45

10th anniv. of the declaration granting independence to colonial territories and countries.

Beingolo Hunting Horn — A72

Musical Instruments: 15fr, Mossi guitar, vert. 20fr, Gourounsi flutes, vert. 25fr, Lunga drums.

1971, Mar. 1 Engr. *Perf. 13*
236 A72 5fr blue, brn & car .45 .30
237 A72 15fr grn, crim rose & brn .90 .30
238 A72 20fr car rose, bl & gray 1.45 .30
239 A72 25fr brt grn, red brn & ol gray 1.65 .60
Nos. 236-239 (4) 4.45 1.50

Voltaphilex I, National Phil. Exhibition.

Four Races — A73

1971, Mar. 21 Engr. *Perf. 13*
240 A73 50fr rose cl, lt grn & dk brn 1.60 .50

Intl. year against racial discrimination.

Telephone and Globes A74

1971, May 17 Engr. *Perf. 13*
241 A74 50fr brn, gray & dk pur 1.00 .40

3rd World Telecommunications Day.

Cane Field Worker, Banfora Sugar Mill — A75

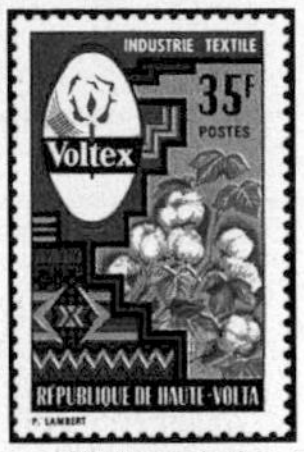

Cotton and Voltex Mill Emblem — A76

1971, June 24 Photo. *Perf. 13*
242 A75 10fr multicolored .25 .25
243 A76 35fr multicolored .50 .25

Industrial development.

Gonlmbrasia Hecate — A77

Butterflies and Moths: 2fr, Hamanumida daedalus. 3fr, Ophideres materna. 5fr, Danaus chyrsippus. 40fr, Hypolimnas misippus. 45fr, Danaus petiverana.

1971, June 30
244 A77 1fr blue & multi .30 .25
245 A77 2fr lt lilac & multi .60 .25
246 A77 3fr multicolored .70 .25
247 A77 5fr gray & multi 1.40 .35
248 A77 40fr ocher & multi 6.00 1.65
249 A77 45fr multicolored 11.00 2.10
Nos. 244-249 (6) 20.00 4.85

Kabuki Actor — A78

40fr, African mask and Kabuki actor.

1971, Aug. 12 Photo. *Perf. 13*
250 A78 25fr multicolored .50 .25
251 A78 40fr multicolored .70 .35

Philatokyo 71, Philatelic Exposition, Tokyo, Apr. 19-29.

No. 226 Surcharged

1971 Engr. *Perf. 12½x13*
252 A66 100fr on 30fr choc & car 1.60 .85

10th anniversary of Upper Volta Red Cross.

Seed Preparation A79

Designs: 75fr, Old farmer with seed packet, vert. 100fr, Farmer in rice field.

1971, Sept. 30 Photo. *Perf. 13*

253 A79	35fr ocher & multi	.45	.25
254 A79	75fr lt blue & multi	.80	.30
255 A79	100fr brown & multi	1.00	.45
	Nos. 253-255 (3)	2.25	1.00

National campaign for seed protection.

Outdoor Classroom A80

Design: 50fr, Mother learning to read.

1971, Oct. 14

256 A80	35fr multicolored	.60	.25
257 A80	50fr multicolored	.80	.45

Women's education.

Joseph Dakiri, Soldiers Driving Tractors — A81

40fr, Dakiri & soldiers gathering harvest.

1971, Oct. 13 *Perf. 12x12½*

258 A81	15fr blk, yel & red brn	.60	.25
259 A81	40fr blue & multi	.80	.45

Joseph Dakiri (1938-1971), inaugurator of the Army-Aid-to-Agriculture Program.

Spraying Lake, Fly, Man Leading Blind Women A82

1971, Nov. 26 Photo. *Perf. 13*

260 A82	40fr dk brn, yel & bl	.90	.50

Drive against onchocerciasis, roundworm infestation.

For surcharge see No. 295.

Children and UNICEF Emblem — A84

1971, Dec. 11 *Perf. 13*

262 A84	45fr red, bister & blk	.75	.50

UNICEF, 25th anniv.

Peulh House A85

Upper Volta Houses: 20fr, Gourounsi house. 35fr, Mossi houses. 45fr, Bobo house, vert. 50fr, Dagari house, vert. 90fr, Bango house, interior.

Perf. 13x13½, 13½x13

1971-72 Photo.

263 A85	10fr ver & multi	.25	.25
264 A85	20fr multicolored	.45	.25
265 A85	35fr brt grn & multi	.60	.45
266 A85	45fr multi ('72)	.70	.25
267 A85	50fr multi ('72)	.85	.45
268 A85	90fr multi ('72)	1.40	.60
	Nos. 263-268 (6)	4.25	2.25

Town Halls of Bobo-Dioulasso and Chalons-sur-Marne — A86

1971, Dec. 23 *Perf. 13x12½*

269 A86	40fr yellow & multi	.80	.50

Kinship between the cities of Bobo-Dioulasso, Upper Volta, and Chalons-sur-Marne, France.

Louis Armstrong — A87

1972, May 17 *Perf. 14x13*

270 A87	45fr multicolored	4.50	1.00

Black musician. See No. C104.

Red Crescent, Cross and Lion Emblems A88

1972, June 23 *Perf. 13x14*

271 A88	40fr yellow & multi	.75	.50

World Red Cross Day. See No. C105.

Coiffure of Peulh Woman — A89

Designs: Various hair styles.

1972, July 23 Litho. *Perf. 13*

272 A89	25fr blue & multi	.40	.25
273 A89	35fr emerald & multi	.70	.25
274 A89	75fr yellow & multi	1.50	.50
	Nos. 272-274 (3)	2.60	1.00

Classroom A90

15fr, Clinic. 20fr, Factory. 35fr, Cattle. 40fr, Plowers.

1972, Oct. 30 Engr. *Perf. 13*

275 A90	10fr sl grn, lt grn & choc	.25	.25
276 A90	15fr brt grn, brn org & brn	.25	.25
277 A90	20fr bl, lt brn & grn	.45	.25
278 A90	35fr grn, brn & brt bl	.80	.25
279 A90	40fr choc, pink & sl grn	.80	.25
	Nos. 275-279,C106 (6)	3.55	2.05

2nd Five-Year Plan.

West African Monetary Union Issue

Common Design Type

1972, Nov. 2

280 CD136	40fr brn, bl & gray	.60	.25

Lottery Office and Emblem A91

1972, Nov. 6 Litho.

281 A91	35fr multicolored	.80	.40

5th anniversary of National Lottery.

Domestic Animals — A92

1972, Dec. 4 Litho. *Perf. 13½x12½*

282 A92	5fr Donkeys	.25	.25
283 A92	10fr Geese	1.00	.25
284 A92	30fr Goats	1.50	.35
285 A92	50fr Cow	1.90	.50
286 A92	65fr Dromedaries	2.75	.70
	Nos. 282-286 (5)	7.40	2.05

Mossi Woman's Hair Style, and Village — A93

1973, Jan. 24 Engr. *Perf. 13*

287 A93	5fr slate grn, org & choc	.25	.25
288 A93	40fr bl, org & chocolate	.70	.25

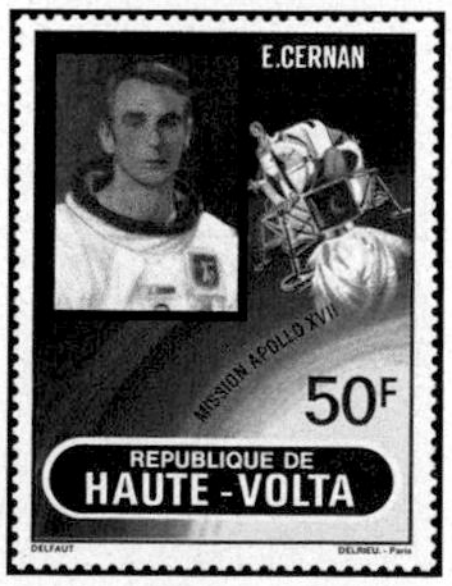

Eugene A. Cernan and Lunar Module A94

65fr, Ronald E. Evans & splashdown. 100fr, Capsule, in orbit & interior, horiz. 150fr, Harrison H. Schmitt & lift-off. 200fr, Conference & moon-buggy. 500fr, Moon-buggy & capsule, horiz.

Perf. 12½x13½, 13½x12½

1973, Mar. 29 Litho.

289 A94	50fr multi	.50	.25
290 A94	65fr multi	.70	.25
291 A94	100fr multi	1.00	.40
292 A94	150fr multi	1.20	.45
293 A94	200fr multi	1.50	.65
	Nos. 289-293 (5)	4.90	2.00

Souvenir Sheet

294 A94	500fr multi	4.50	3.50

Apollo 17 moon mission.

No. 260 Srchd. in Red

1973, Apr. 7 Photo. *Perf. 13*

295 A82	45fr on 40fr multi	.75	.45

WHO, 25th anniversary.

Scout Bugler A95

1973, July 18 Litho. *Perf. 12½x13*

296 A95	20fr multicolored	.40	.25
	Nos. 296,C160-C163 (5)	4.30	2.25

African Postal Union Issue

Common Design Type

1973, Sept. 12 Engr. *Perf. 13*

297 CD137	100fr brt red, mag & dl yel	1.25	.70

Pres. Kennedy, Saturn 5 on Assembly Trailer A96

Pres. John F. Kennedy (1917-1963) and: 10fr, Atlas rocket carrying John H. Glenn. 30fr, Titan 2 rocket and Gemini 3 capsule.

1973, Sept. 12 Litho. *Perf. 12½x13*

298 A96	5fr multicolored	.25	.25
299 A96	10fr multicolored	.25	.25
300 A96	30fr multicolored	.40	.25
	Nos. 298-300,C167-C168 (5)	4.40	2.60

Cross-examination — A97

Designs: 65fr, "Diamond Ede." 70fr, Forensic Institute. 150fr, Robbery scene.

1973, Sept. 15 *Perf. 13x12½*

301 A97	50fr multicolored	.70	.25
302 A97	65fr multicolored	.70	.25
303 A97	70fr multicolored	.85	.35
304 A97	150fr multicolored	1.40	.60
	Nos. 301-304 (4)	3.65	1.45

Interpol, 50th anniversary. See No. C170.

Market Place, Ouagadougou — A98

40fr, Swimming pool, Hotel Independence.

1973, Sept. 30

305 A98 35fr multicolored .45 .25
306 A98 40fr multicolored .60 .35
Nos. 305-306,C171 (3) 2.45 1.40

Tourism. See No. C172.

Protestant Church — A99

Design: 40fr, Ouahigouya Mosque.

1973, Sept. 28 ***Perf. 13x12½***

307 A99 35fr multicolored .35 .25
308 A99 40fr multicolored .45 .25
Nos. 307-308,C173 (3) 3.20 1.70

Houses of worship. See. No. C173.

Kiembara Dancers A100

Folklore: 40fr, Dancers.

1973, Nov. 30 Litho. ***Perf. 12½x13***

309 A100 35fr multicolored .40 .25
310 A100 40fr multicolored .50 .25
Nos. 309-310,C174-C175 (4) 4.25 1.95

Yuri Gagarin and Aries — A101

Famous Men and their Zodiac Signs: 10fr, Lenin and Taurus. 20fr, John F. Kennedy, rocket and Gemini. 25fr, John H. Glenn, orbiting capsule and Cancer. 30fr, Napoleon and Leo. 50fr, Goethe and Virgo. 60fr, Pelé and Libra. 75fr, Charles de Gaulle and Scorpio. 100fr, Beethoven and Sagittarius. 175fr, Conrad Adenauer and Capricorn. 200fr, Edwin E. Aldrin, Jr. (Apollo XI) and Aquarius. 250fr, Lord Baden-Powell and Pisces.

1973, Dec. 15 Litho. ***Perf. 13x14***

311 A101 5fr multicolored .25 .25
312 A101 10fr multicolored .25 .25
313 A101 20fr multicolored .25 .25
314 A101 25fr multicolored .25 .25
315 A101 30fr multicolored .35 .25
316 A101 50fr multicolored .35 .25
317 A101 60fr multicolored .55 .25
318 A101 75fr multicolored .85 .35
319 A101 100fr multicolored .85 .35
320 A101 175fr multicolored 1.40 .55
321 A101 200fr multicolored 1.75 .55
322 A101 250fr multicolored 2.25 .70
Nos. 311-322 (12) 9.35 4.25

See Nos. C176-C178.

Rivera with Italian Flag and Championship '74 Emblem — A102

40fr, World Cup, soccer ball, World Championship '74 emblem & Pelé with Brazilian flag.

1974, Jan. 15 ***Perf. 13x12½***

323 A102 5fr multicolored .25 .25
324 A102 40fr multicolored .45 .25
Nos. 323-324,C179-C181 (5) 4.10 1.80

10th World Cup Soccer Championship, Munich, June 13-July 7.

Charles de Gaulle A103

40fr, De Gaulle memorial. 60fr, Pres. de Gaulle.

1974, Feb. 4 Litho. ***Perf. 12½x13***

325 A103 35fr multicolored .80 .25
326 A103 40fr multicolored 1.15 .25
327 A103 60fr multicolored 1.30 .35
a. Strip of 3, Nos. 325-327 3.25 .85
Nos. 325-327,C183 (4) 6.75 2.60

Gen. Charles de Gaulle (1890-1970), president of France. See No. C184.

N'Dongo and Cameroun Flag A104

World Cup, Emblems and: 20fr, Kolev and Bulgarian flag. 50fr, Keita and Mali flag.

1974, Mar. 19

328 A104 10fr multicolored .25 .25
329 A104 20fr multicolored .25 .25
330 A104 50fr multicolored .45 .25
Nos. 328-330,C185-C186 (5) 4.30 2.10

10th World Cup Soccer Championship, Munich, June 13-July 7.

Map and Flags of Members A105

1974, May 29 Photo. ***Perf. 13x12½***

331 A105 40fr blue & multi .85 .50

15th anniversary of the Council of Accord.

UPU Emblem and Mail Coach — A106

1974, July 23 Litho. ***Perf. 13½***

332 A106 35fr Mail coach .40 .25
333 A106 40fr Steamship .50 .25
334 A106 85fr Mailman .65 .40
Nos. 332-334,C189-C191 (6) 6.30 3.40

Universal Postal Union centenary.
For overprints see Nos. 339-341, C197-C200.

Soccer Game, Winner Italy, in France, 1938 — A107

World Cup, Game and Flags: 25fr, Uruguay, in Brazil, 1950. 50fr, West Germany, in Switzerland, 1954.

1974, Sept. 2 Litho. ***Perf. 13½***

335 A107 10fr multicolored .25 .25
336 A107 25fr multicolored .25 .25
337 A107 50fr multicolored .40 .25
Nos. 335-337,C193-C195 (6) 5.70 3.30

World Cup Soccer winners.

Map and Farm Woman — A108

1974, Oct. 2 Litho. ***Perf. 13x12½***

338 A108 35fr yellow & multi .75 .50

Kou Valley Development.

Nos. 332-334 Overprinted in Red

1974, Oct. 9

339 A106 35fr multicolored .75 .25
340 A106 40fr multicolored 1.00 .35
341 A106 85fr multicolored 1.15 .55
Nos. 339-341,C197-C199 (6) 9.75 3.95

Universal Postal Union centenary.

Flowers, by Pierre Bonnard A109

Flower Paintings by: 10fr, Jan Brueghel. 30fr, Jean van Os. 50fr, Van Brussel.

1974, Oct. 31 Litho. ***Perf. 12½x13***

342 A109 5fr multicolored .25 .25
343 A109 10fr multicolored .25 .25
344 A109 30fr multicolored .25 .25
345 A109 50fr multicolored .45 .25
Nos. 342-345,C201 (5) 4.70 2.10

Churchill as Officer of India Hussars — A110

Churchill: 75fr, As Secretary of State for Interior. 100fr, As pilot. 125fr, meeting with Roosevelt, 1941. 300fr, As painter. 450fr, and "HMS Resolution."

1975, Jan. 11 ***Perf. 13½***

346 A110 50fr multicolored .50 .25
347 A110 75fr multicolored .60 .25
348 A110 100fr multicolored .90 .35
349 A110 125fr multicolored 1.00 .45
350 A110 300fr multicolored 2.75 1.25
Nos. 346-350 (5) 5.75 2.55

Souvenir Sheet

351 A110 450fr multicolored 4.75 1.75

Sir Winston Churchill, birth centenary.

US No. 619 and Minutemen — A111

US Stamps: 40fr, #118 and Declaration of Independence. 75fr, #798 and Signing the Constitution. 100fr, #703 and Surrender at Yorktown. 200fr, #1003 and George Washington. 300fr, #644 and Surrender of Burgoyne at Saratoga. 500fr, #63, 68, 73, 157, 179, 228 and 1483a.

1975, Feb. 17 Litho. ***Perf. 11***

352 A111 35fr multicolored .45 .25
353 A111 40fr multicolored .45 .25
354 A111 75fr multicolored .80 .25
355 A111 100fr multicolored 1.00 .35
356 A111 200fr multicolored 2.00 .60
357 A111 300fr multicolored 3.00 .95
Nos. 352-357 (6) 7.70 2.65

Souvenir Sheet

Imperf

358 A111 500fr multicolored 7.50 2.25

American Bicentennial.

"Atlantic" No. 2670, 1904-12 — A112

Locomotives from Mulhouse, France, Railroad Museum: 25fr, No. 2029, 1882. 50fr, No. 2129, 1882.

1975, Feb. 28 Litho. *Perf. 13x12½*

359 A112 15fr multicolored .50 .25
360 A112 25fr multicolored .80 .25
361 A112 50fr multicolored 1.40 .25
Nos. 359-361,C203-C204 (5) 6.95 1.75

French Flag and Renault Petit Duc, 1910 — A113

Flags and Old Cars: 30fr, US and Ford Model T, 1909. 35fr, Italy and Alfa Romeo "Le Mans," 1931.

1975, Apr. 6 *Perf. 14x13½*

362 A113 10fr multicolored .25 .25
363 A113 30fr multicolored .45 .25
364 A113 35fr multicolored .50 .25
Nos. 362-364,C206-C207 (5) 5.20 1.95

Washington and Lafayette — A114

American Bicentennial: 40fr, Washington reviewing troops at Valley Forge. 50fr, Washington taking oath of office. 500fr, British surrender at Yorktown.

1975, May 6 Litho. *Perf. 14*

365 A114 30fr multicolored .25 .25
366 A114 40fr multicolored .35 .25
367 A114 50fr multicolored .60 .25
Nos. 365-367,C209-C210 (5) 5.60 2.90

Souvenir Sheet

367A A114 500fr multicolored 4.75 2.25

Schweitzer and Pelicans — A115

15fr, Albert Schweitzer and bateleur eagle.

1975, May 25 Litho. *Perf. 13½*

368 A115 5fr multicolored .30 .25
369 A115 15fr multicolored .50 .25
Nos. 368-369,C212-C214 (5) 7.05 2.75

Albert Schweitzer, birth centenary.

Apollo and Soyuz Orbiting Earth — A116

Design: 50fr, Apollo and Soyuz near link-up.

1975, July 18

370 A116 40fr multicolored .35 .25
371 A116 50fr multicolored .45 .25
Nos. 370-371,C216-C218 (5) 5.80 2.40

Apollo-Soyuz space test project, Russo-American cooperation, launched July 15, link-up July 17.

Maria Picasso Lopez, Artist's Mother A117

Paintings by Pablo Picasso (1881-1973): 60fr, Self-portrait. 90fr, First Communion.

1975, Aug. 7

372 A117 50fr multicolored .45 .25
373 A117 60fr multicolored .70 .25
374 A117 90fr multicolored .90 .40
Nos. 372-374,C220-C221 (5) 8.30 2.60

Expo '75 Emblem and Tanker, Idemitsu Maru — A118

Oceanographic Exposition, Okinawa: 25fr, Training ship, Kaio Maru. 45fr, Firefighting ship, Hiryu. 50fr, Battleship, Yamato. 60fr, Container ship, Kamakura Maru.

1975, Sept. 26 Litho. *Perf. 11*

375 A118 15fr multicolored .25 .25
376 A118 25fr multicolored .35 .25
377 A118 45fr multicolored .50 .25
377A A118 50fr multicolored .65 .25
378 A118 60fr multicolored .85 .30
Nos. 375-378,C223 (6) 4.60 1.90

Woman, Globe and IWY Emblem — A119

1975, Nov. 20 Photo. *Perf. 13*

379 A119 65fr multicolored .90 .60

International Women's Year.

Msgr. Joanny Thevenoud and Cathedral — A120

65fr, Father Guillaume Templier & Cathedral.

1975, Nov. 20 Engr. *Perf. 13x12½*

380 A120 55fr grn, blk & dl red .90 .45
381 A120 65fr blk, org & dl red 1.00 .60

75th anniv. of the Evangelization of Upper Volta.

Farmer's Hat, Hoe and Emblem A121

1975, Dec. 10 Photo. *Perf. 13x13½*

382 A121 15fr buff & multi .25 .25
383 A121 50fr lt green & multi .80 .45

Development of the Volta valleys.

Sledding and Olympic Emblem — A122

Innsbruck Background, Olympic Emblem and: 45fr, Figure skating. 85fr, Skiing.

1975, Dec. 16 Litho. *Perf. 13½*

384 A122 35fr multicolored .40 .25
385 A122 45fr multicolored .60 .25
386 A122 85fr multicolored .80 .40
Nos. 384-386,C225-C226 (5) 4.50 2.05

12th Winter Olympic Games, Innsbruck, Austria, Feb. 4-15, 1976.

Gymnast and Olympic Emblem — A123

1976, Mar. 17

387 A123 40fr Gymnastics .30 .25
388 A123 50fr Sailing .45 .25
389 A123 100fr Soccer 1.00 .45
Nos. 387-389,C228-C229 (5) 4.25 1.85

21st Olympic Games, Montreal, Canada, July 17-Aug. 1.

Olympic Emblem and Sprinters A124

Olympic Emblem and: 55fr, Equestrian. 75fr, Hurdles.

1976, Mar. 25 Litho. *Perf. 11*

390 A124 30fr multicolored .30 .25
391 A124 55fr multicolored .45 .25
392 A124 75fr multicolored .60 .25
Nos. 390-392,C231-C232 (5) 4.25 1.80

21st Olympic Games, Montreal.

For overprints see nos. 420-422, C245-C247.

Blind Woman and Man — A125

1976, Apr. 7 Engr. *Perf. 13*

393 A125 75fr dk brn, grn & org 1.00 .45
394 A125 250fr dk brn, ocher & org 2.75 1.50

Drive against onchocerciasis, roundworm infestation.

"Deutschland" over Friedrichshafen — A126

Airships: 40fr, "Victoria Louise" over sailing ships. 50fr, "Sachsen" over German countryside.

1976, May 11 Litho. *Perf. 11*

395 A126 10fr multicolored .25 .25
396 A126 40fr multicolored .40 .25
397 A126 50fr multicolored .70 .30
Nos. 395-397,C234-C236 (6) 7.10 3.20

75th anniversary of the Zeppelin.

Viking Lander and Probe on Mars — A127

Viking Mars project: 55fr, Viking orbiter in flight. 75fr, Titan rocket start for Mars, vert.

1976, June 24 *Perf. 13½*

398 A127 30fr multicolored .25 .25
399 A127 55fr multicolored .50 .25
400 A127 75fr multicolored .75 .25
Nos. 398-400,C238-C239 (5) 6.15 1.95

World Map, Arms of Upper Volta A128

Design: 100fr, World map, arms and dove.

1976, Aug. 19 Litho. *Perf. 12½*

401 A128 55fr brown & multi .55 .25
402 A128 100fr blue & multi 1.25 .60

5th Summit Conference of Non-aligned Countries, Colombo, Sri Lanka, Aug. 9-19.

Bicentennial, Interphil 76 Emblems and Washington at Battle of Trenton — A129

90fr, Bicentennial, Interphil 76 emblems, Seat of Government, Pennsylvania.

1976, Sept. 30 *Perf. 13½*

403 A129 60fr multicolored	.65	.25
404 A129 90fr multicolored	.80	.25
Nos. 403-404,C241-C243 (5)	6.30	2.30

American Bicentennial, Interphil 76, Philadelphia, Pa., May 29-June 6.

UPU and UN Emblems — A130

1976, Dec. 8 **Engr.** *Perf. 13*

405 A130 200fr red, olive & blue	2.25	1.25

UN Postal Administration, 25th anniv.

Arms of Tenkodogo A131

Coats of Arms: 20fr, 100fr, Ouagadougou.

1977, May 2 **Litho.** *Perf. 13*

406 A131 10fr multicolored	.25	.25
407 A131 20fr multicolored	.25	.25
408 A131 65fr multicolored	.70	.25
409 A131 100fr multicolored	.90	.45
Nos. 406-409 (4)	2.10	1.20

Bronze Statuette — A132

Design: 65fr, Woman with bowl, bronze.

1977, June 13 **Photo.** *Perf. 13*

410 A132 55fr multicolored	.60	.25
411 A132 65fr multicolored	1.00	.35

Nos. 410-411 issued in sheets and coils with black control number on every 5th stamp.

Granaries A133

1977, June 20 **Photo.** *Perf. 13½x13*

412 A133 5fr Samo	.25	.25
413 A133 35fr Boromo	.35	.25
414 A133 45fr Banfora	.55	.25
415 A133 55fr Mossi	.75	.25
Nos. 412-415 (4)	1.90	1.00

Handbags A134

1977, June 20

416 A134 30fr Gouin	.35	.25
417 A134 40fr Bissa	.35	.25
418 A134 60fr Lobi	.60	.25
419 A134 70fr Mossi	.60	.35
Nos. 416-419 (4)	1.90	1.10

Nos. 390-392 Overprinted in Gold

(a)

(b)

(c)

1977, July 4 **Litho.** *Perf. 11*

420 A124 (a) 30fr multicolored	.30	.25
421 A124 (b) 55fr multicolored	.50	.45
422 A124 (c) 75fr multicolored	.70	.60
Nos. 420-422,C245-C246 (5)	4.25	3.00

Winners, 21st Olympic Games.

Crinum Ornatum — A135

Haemanthus Multiflorus A136

Hannoa Undulata A137

Flowers, flowering branches and wild fruits: 2fr, Cordia myxa. 3fr, Opilia celtidifolia. 15fr, Crinum ornatum. 25fr, Haemanthus multiflorus. 50fr, Hannoa undulata. 90fr, Cochlospermum planchonii. 125fr, Clitoria ternatea. 150fr, Cassia alata. 175fr, Nauclea latifolia, horiz. 300fr, Bombax costatum, horiz. 400fr, Eulophia cucullata.

1977 **Litho.** *Perf. 12½*

423 A137 2fr multicolored	.25	.25
424 A137 3fr multicolored	.35	.25
425 A135 15fr multicolored	.55	.25
426 A136 25fr multicolored	.60	.25
427 A137 50fr multicolored	.90	.45
428 A135 90fr multicolored	1.40	.55
429 A135 125fr multicolored	2.25	.60
430 A136 150fr multicolored	2.00	1.25
431 A136 175fr multicolored	2.25	1.40
432 A136 300fr multicolored	3.50	1.75
433 A135 400fr multicolored	5.25	2.00
Nos. 423-433 (11)	19.30	9.00

Issued: 25fr, 150fr, 175fr, 300fr, 8/1; 2fr, 3fr, 50fr, 8/8; 15fr, 90fr, 125fr, 400fr, 8/23.

De Gaulle and Cross of Lorraine A138

Designs: 200fr, King Baudouin of Belgium.

1977, Aug. 16 *Perf. 13½x14*

434 A138 100fr multicolored	2.50	.75
435 A138 200fr multicolored	1.75	.65

Elizabeth II A139

Designs: 300fr, Elizabeth II taking salute. 500fr, Elizabeth II after Coronation.

1977, Aug. 16

436 A139 200fr multicolored	1.75	.65
437 A139 300fr multicolored	2.50	.80

Souvenir Sheet

438 A139 500fr multicolored	4.25	2.00

25th anniv. of reign of Queen Elizabeth II. For overprints see Nos. 478-480.

Lottery Tickets, Cars and Map of Upper Volta in Flag Colors — A140

1977, Sept. 16 **Photo.** *Perf. 13*

439 A140 55fr multicolored	.70	.50

10th anniversary of National Lottery.

Selma Lagerlof, Literature — A141

Nobel Prize Winners: 65fr, Guglielmo Marconi, physics. 125fr, Bertrand Russell, literature. 200fr, Linus C. Pauling, chemistry. 300fr, Robert Koch, medicine. 500fr, Albert Schweitzer, peace.

1977, Sept. 22 **Litho.** *Perf. 13½*

440 A141 55fr multicolored	.80	.25
441 A141 65fr multicolored	.50	.30
442 A141 125fr multicolored	1.10	.40
443 A141 200fr multicolored	1.75	.65
444 A141 300fr multicolored	3.25	.95
Nos. 440-444 (5)	7.40	2.55

Souvenir Sheet

445 A141 500fr multicolored	5.00	2.00

The Three Graces, by Rubens A142

Paintings by Peter Paul Rubens (1577-1640): 55fr, Heads of Black Men, horiz. 85fr, Bathsheba at the Fountain. 150fr, The Drunken Silenus. 200fr, 300fr, Life of Maria de Medicis, diff.

1977, Oct. 19 **Litho.** *Perf. 14*

446 A142 55fr multicolored	.55	.25
447 A142 65fr multicolored	.65	.25
448 A142 85fr multicolored	.75	.25
449 A142 150fr multicolored	1.50	.55
450 A142 200fr multicolored	1.90	.70
451 A142 300fr multicolored	3.00	1.00
Nos. 446-451 (6)	8.35	3.00

Lenin in His Office A143

85fr, Lenin Monument, Kremlin. 200fr, Lenin with youth. 500fr, Lenin & Leonid Brezhnev.

1977, Oct. 28 Litho. *Perf. 12*

452	A143	10fr multicolored	*.45*	*.25*
453	A143	85fr multicolored	*1.55*	*.75*
454	A143	200fr multicolored	*3.50*	*1.75*
455	A143	500fr multicolored	*7.50*	*3.75*
		Nos. 452-455 (4)	*13.00*	*6.50*

Russian October Revolution, 60th anniv.

Stadium and Brazil No. C79 — A144

Stadium and: 65fr, Brazil #1144. 125fr, Gt. Britain #458. 200fr, Chile #340. 300fr, Switzerland #350. 500fr, Germany #1147.

1977, Dec. 30 Litho. *Perf. 13½*

456	A144	55fr multicolored	.35	.25
457	A144	65fr multicolored	.50	.25
458	A144	125fr multicolored	1.00	.35
459	A144	200fr multicolored	1.60	.50
460	A144	300fr multicolored	2.25	.85
		Nos. 456-460 (5)	5.70	2.20

Souvenir Sheet

461	A144	500fr multicolored	4.25	1.90

11th World Cup Soccer Championship, Argentina.

For overprints see Nos. 486-491.

Jean Mermoz and Seaplane — A145

History of Aviation: 75fr, Anthony H. G. Fokker. 85fr, Wiley Post. 90fr, Otto Lilienthal, vert. 100fr, Concorde. 500fr, Charles Lindbergh and "Spirit of St. Louis."

1978, Jan. 2 Litho. *Perf. 13½*

462	A145	65fr multicolored	.65	.25
463	A145	75fr multicolored	.65	.25
464	A145	85fr multicolored	.75	.25
465	A145	90fr multicolored	.95	.25
466	A145	100fr multicolored	1.10	.50
		Nos. 462-466 (5)	4.10	1.50

Souvenir Sheet

467	A145	500fr multicolored	5.00	1.90

Crataeva Religiosa — A146

1978, Feb. 28 Litho. *Perf. 12½*

468	A146	55fr Spider tree	.70	.40
469	A146	75fr Fig tree	.90	.60

Souvenir Sheet

Virgin and Child, by Rubens — A147

1978, May 24 Litho. *Perf. 13½x14*

470	A147	500fr multicolored	5.75	1.90

Peter Paul Rubens (1577-1640).

Antenna and ITU Emblem A148

1978, May 30 *Perf. 13*

471	A148	65fr silver & multi	.70	.50

10th World Telecommunications Day.

Fetish Gate of Bobo — A149

1978, July 10 Litho. *Perf. 13½*

472	A149	55fr Bobo fetish	.70	.35
473	A149	65fr Mossi fetish	.90	.50

Capt. Cook and "Endeavour" — A150

Capt. James Cook (1728-1779) and: 85fr, Death on Hawaiian beach. 250fr, Navigational instruments. 350fr, "Resolution."

1978, Sept. 1 Litho. *Perf. 14½*

474	A150	65fr multicolored	.60	.25
475	A150	85fr multicolored	.75	.25
476	A150	250fr multicolored	1.75	.70
477	A150	350fr multicolored	2.75	1.00
		Nos. 474-477 (4)	5.85	2.20

Nos. 436-438 Overprinted in Silver

1978, Oct. 24 Litho. *Perf. 13½x14*

478	A139	200fr multicolored	1.75	1.00
479	A139	300fr multicolored	2.50	1.40

Souvenir Sheet

480	A139	500fr multicolored	4.75	4.25

25th anniversary of Coronation of Queen Elizabeth II. Overprint in 3 lines on 200fr, in 2 lines on 300fr and 500fr.

Nos. 478-480 exist with overprint in metallic red.

Trent Castle, by Dürer — A151

Paintings by Albrecht Durer (1471-1528): 150fr, Virgin and Child with St. Anne, vert. 250fr, Sts. George and Eustachius, vert. 350fr, Hans Holzschuher, vert.

Perf. 14x13½, 13½x14

1978, Nov. 20 Litho.

481	A151	65fr multicolored	.70	.25
482	A151	150fr multicolored	1.30	.45
483	A151	250fr multicolored	2.25	.90
484	A151	350fr multicolored	3.25	1.25
		Nos. 481-484 (4)	7.50	2.85

Human Rights Emblem A152

1978, Dec. 10 Litho. *Perf. 12½*

485	A152	55fr multicolored	.65	.25

Universal Declaration of Human Rights, 30th anniv.

Nos. 456-461 Overprinted in Silver

(a)

(b)

(c)

(d)

(e)

(f)

1979, Jan. 4 Litho. *Perf. 13½*

486	A144(a)	55fr multicolored	.45	.25
487	A144(b)	65fr multicolored	.60	.45
488	A144(c)	125fr multicolored	1.00	.70
489	A144(d)	200fr multicolored	1.40	.95
490	A144(e)	300fr multicolored	2.25	1.10
		Nos. 486-490 (5)	5.70	3.45

Souvenir Sheet

491	A144(f)	500fr multicolored	4.50	3.50

Winners, World Soccer Cup Championships 1950-1978.

Radio Station A153

Design: 65fr, Mail plane at airport.

1979, Mar. 30 Litho. *Perf. 12½*

492	A153	55fr multicolored	.45	.25
493	A153	65fr multicolored	.70	.40

Post and Telecommunications Org., 10th anniv.

Teacher and Pupils, IYC Emblem — A154

1979, Apr. 9 *Perf. 13½*

494	A154	75fr multicolored	1.00	.60

International Year of the Child.

Telecommunications — A155

1979, May 17 Litho. *Perf. 13*

495 A155 70fr multicolored .70 .45

11th Telecommunications Day.

Basketmaker and Upper Volta No. 111 — A156

Design: No. 497, Map of Upper Volta, Concorde, truck and UPU emblem.

1979, June 8 Photo.

496 A156 100fr multicolored 3.50 2.40
497 A156 100fr multicolored 3.50 2.40

Philexafrique II, Libreville, Gabon, June 8-17. Nos. 496, 497 each printed in sheets of 10 and 5 labels showing exhibition emblem.

Synodontis Voltae A157

Fresh-water Fish: 50fr, Micralestes comoensis. 85fr, Silurus.

1979, June 10 Litho. *Perf. 12½*

498 A157 20fr multicolored .75 .25
499 A157 50fr multicolored 1.50 .25
500 A157 85fr multicolored 2.00 .60
Nos. 498-500 (3) 4.25 1.10

Rowland Hill, Train and Upper Volta No. 60 — A158

Sir Rowland Hill (1795-1879), originator of penny postage, Trains and Upper Volta Stamps: 165fr, #59. 200fr, #57. 300fr, #56. 500fr, #55.

1979, June Litho. *Perf. 13½*

501 A158 65fr multicolored .65 .25
502 A158 165fr multicolored 1.50 .55
503 A158 200fr multicolored 1.90 .65
504 A158 300fr multicolored 3.25 1.00
Nos. 501-504 (4) 7.30 2.45

Souvenir Sheet

505 A158 500fr multicolored 5.00 1.90

Wildlife Fund Emblem and Protected Animals — A159

30fr, Waterbuck. 40fr, Roan antelope. 60fr, Caracal. 100fr, African bush elephant. 175fr, Hartebeest. 250fr, Leopard.

1979, Aug. 30 Litho. *Perf. 14½*

506 A159 30fr multicolored 1.40 .25
507 A159 40fr multicolored 2.00 .25
508 A159 60fr multicolored 2.75 .30
509 A159 100fr multicolored 3.75 .80
510 A159 175fr multicolored 6.00 1.00
511 A159 250fr multicolored 14.00 1.25
Nos. 506-511 (6) 29.90 3.85

Adult Students and Teacher — A160

Design: 55fr, Man reading book, vert.

1979, Sept. 8 *Perf. 12½x13, 13x12½*

512 A160 55fr multicolored .50 .45
513 A160 250fr multicolored 2.50 1.50

World Literacy Day.

Map of Upper Volta, Telephone Receiver and Lines, Telecom Emblem — A161

1979, Sept. 20 *Perf. 13x12½*

514 A161 200fr multicolored 1.90 .95

3rd World Telecommunications Exhibition, Geneva, Sept. 20-26.

King Vulture — A162

1979, Oct. 26 Litho. *Perf. 13*

515 A162 5fr King vulture 1.00 .25
516 A162 10fr Hoopoe 1.00 .25
517 A162 15fr Bald vulture 1.10 .25
518 A162 25fr Egrets 1.75 .35
519 A162 35fr Ostrich 2.50 .45
520 A162 45fr Crowned crane 3.00 .55
521 A162 125fr Eagle 7.00 1.90
Nos. 515-521 (7) 17.35 4.00

Control Tower, Emblem, Jet — A163

1979, Dec. 12 Photo. *Perf. 13x12½*

522 A163 65fr multicolored .90 .60

ASECNA (Air Safety Board), 20th anniv.

Central Bank of West African States — A164

1979, Dec. 28 Litho. *Perf. 12½*

523 A164 55fr multicolored .70 .45

Eugene Jamot, Map of Upper Volta, Tsetse Fly — A165

1979, Dec. 28 *Perf. 13x13½*

524 A165 55fr multicolored 2.25 .80

Eugene Jamot (1879-1937), discoverer of sleeping sickness cure.

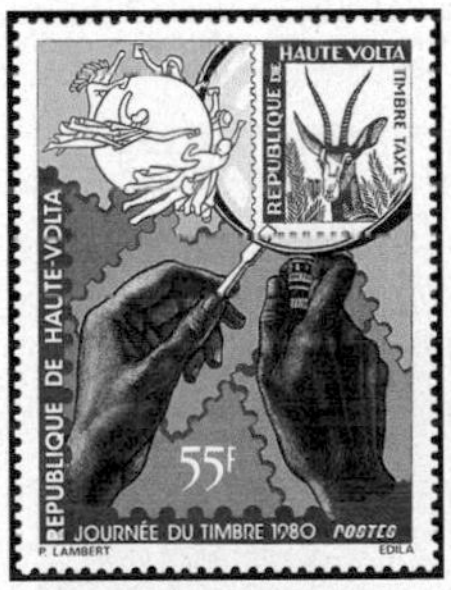

UPU Emblem, Upper Volta Type D4 under Magnifier A166

1980, Feb. 26 Litho. *Perf. 12½x13*

525 A166 55fr multicolored .80 .35

Stamp Day.

World Locomotive Speed Record, 25th Anniversary A167

1980, Mar. 30 Litho. *Perf. 12½*

526 A167 75fr multicolored 2.00 .60
527 A167 100fr multicolored 2.75 1.25

Pres. Sangoule Lamizana, Pope John Paul II, Cardinal Pau Zoungrana, Map of Upper Volta — A168

1980, May 10 Litho. *Perf. 12½*

528 A168 65fr multicolored 2.50 .60

Size: 21x36mm

529 A168 100fr Pope John Paul II 3.25 1.50

Visit of Pope John Paul II to Upper Volta.

A169

1980, May 17 *Perf. 13x12½*

530 A169 50fr multicolored .60 .35

12th World Telecommunications Day.

Solar Energy — A170

65fr, Sun and earth. 100fr, Statue, hills.

1980, June 12 Litho. *Perf. 13*

531 A170 65fr multicolored .60 .35
532 A170 100fr multicolored 1.00 .45

Downhill Skiing, Lake Placid '80 Emblem — A171

65fr, Downhill skiing. 100fr, Women's downhill. 200fr, Figure skating. 350fr, Slalom, vert. 500fr, Speed skating.

1980, June 26 *Perf. 14½*

533 A171 65fr multi .50 .25
534 A171 100fr multi .75 .30
535 A171 200fr multi 1.60 .50
536 A171 350fr multi 2.75 1.00
Nos. 533-536 (4) 5.60 2.05

Souvenir Sheet

537 A171 500fr multi 4.50 1.90

12th Winter Olympic Game Winners, Lake Placid, NY, Feb. 12-24.

Europafrica Issue

Map of Europe and Africa, Jet — A172

1980, July 14 Litho. *Perf. 13*

538 A172 100fr multicolored 1.20 .60

Hand Holding Back Sand Dune — A173

Operation Green Sahel: 55fr, Hands holding seedlings.

1980, July 18

539	A173	50fr multicolored	.65	.25
540	A173	55fr multicolored	.85	.45

Gourmantche Chief Initiation — A174

30fr, Gourmantche chief initiation. 55fr, Moro Naba, Mossi Emperor. 65fr, Princess Guimbe Quattara, vert.

1980, Sept. 12 **Litho.** ***Perf. 14***

541	A174	30fr multicolored	.40	.25
542	A174	55fr multicolored	.60	.30
543	A174	65fr multicolored	.85	.30
		Nos. 541-543 (3)	1.85	.85

A175

Gourounsi mask, conference emblem.

1980, Oct. 6 ***Perf. 13½x13***

544	A175	65fr multicolored	.80	.45

World Tourism Conf., Manila, Sept. 27.

A176

1980, Nov. 5 **Litho.** ***Perf. 12½***

545	A176	55fr Agriculture	.40	.25
546	A176	65fr Transportation	.50	.35
547	A176	75fr Dam, highway	.60	.35
548	A176	100fr Industry	1.00	.50
		Nos. 545-548 (4)	2.50	1.45

West African Economic Council, 5th anniv.

20th Anniv. of Independence — A177

1980, Dec. 11 ***Perf. 13***

549	A177	500fr multicolored	5.25	3.00

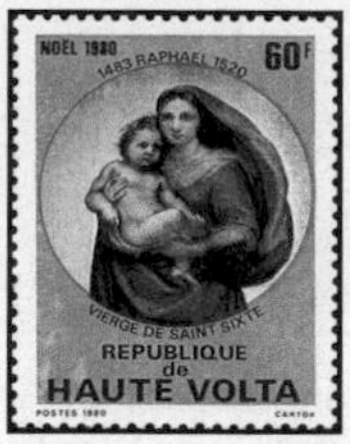

Madonna and Child, by Raphael — A178

Christmas: Paintings of Madonna and Child, by Raphael.

1980, Dec. 22 ***Perf. 12½***

550	A178	60fr multicolored	.50	.25
551	A178	150fr multicolored	1.40	.50
552	A178	250fr multicolored	2.25	.80
		Nos. 550-552 (3)	4.15	1.55

West African Postal Union, 5th Anniv. — A179

1980, Dec. 24 **Photo.** ***Perf. 13½***

553	A179	55fr multicolored	.75	.45

Dung Beetle A180

5fr, Dung beetle. 10fr, Crickets. 15fr, Termites. 20fr, Praying mantis, vert. 55fr, Emperor moth. 65fr, Locust, vert.

Perf. 13x13½, 13½x13

1981, Mar. 10 **Litho.**

554	A180	5fr multicolored	.55	.25
555	A180	10fr multicolored	.55	.25
556	A180	15fr multicolored	1.15	.25
557	A180	20fr multicolored	2.25	.25
558	A180	55fr multicolored	3.75	.45
559	A180	65fr multicolored	4.00	.55
		Nos. 554-559 (6)	12.25	2.00

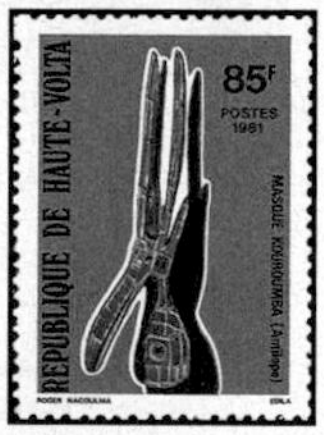

Antelope Mask, Kouroumba A181

Designs: Various ceremonial masks.

1981, Mar. 20 **Litho.** ***Perf. 13***

560	A181	45fr multicolored	.50	.25
561	A181	55fr multicolored	.60	.30
562	A181	85fr multicolored	.90	.50
563	A181	105fr multicolored	1.25	.60
		Nos. 560-563 (4)	3.25	1.65

Notre Dame of Kologh' Naba College, 25th Anniv. A182

1981, Mar. 30

564	A182	55fr multicolored	.60	.25

Heinrich von Stephan, UPU Founder, Birth Sesquicentennial — A183

1981, May 4 **Litho.** ***Perf. 13***

565	A183	65fr multicolored	.75	.45

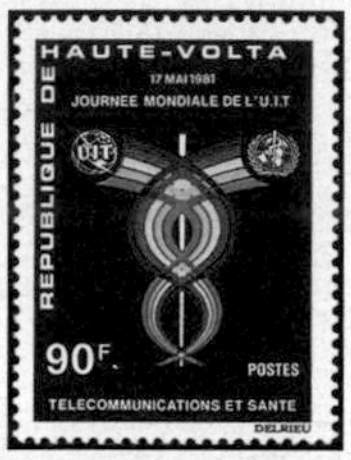

13th World Telecommunications Day — A184

1981, May 17 ***Perf. 13½x13***

566	A184	90fr multicolored	.80	.50

Diesel Train, Abidjan-Niger Railroad — A185

Designs: Trains.

1981, July 6 **Litho.** ***Perf. 13***

567	A185	25fr Diesel train	.40	.25
568	A185	30fr Gazelle	.70	.25
569	A185	40fr Belier	.80	.35
		Nos. 567-569 (3)	1.90	.85

Tree Planting Month A186

1981, July 15

570	A186	70fr multicolored	1.10	.50

Natl. Red Cross, 20th Anniv. A187

1981, July 31 ***Perf. 12½x13***

571	A187	70fr multicolored	1.00	.50

Intl. Year of the Disabled — A188

1981, Aug. 20 **Litho.** ***Perf. 13x12½***

572	A188	70fr multicolored	1.00	.45

View of Koudougou A189

1981, Sept. 3 **Litho.** ***Perf. 12½***

573	A189	35fr Koudougou	.40	.25
574	A189	45fr Toma	.50	.25
575	A189	85fr Volta Noire	1.00	.30
		Nos. 573-575 (3)	1.90	.80

World Food Day — A190

1981, Oct. 16 ***Perf. 13***

576	A190	90fr multicolored	1.10	.70

Elephant A191

Designs: Various protected species.

1981, Oct. 21 **Photo.** ***Perf. 14***

577	A191	5fr multicolored	.45	.25
578	A191	15fr multicolored	.70	.25
579	A191	40fr multicolored	1.20	.35
580	A191	60fr multicolored	2.25	.65
581	A191	70fr multicolored	2.25	.90
		Nos. 577-581 (5)	6.85	2.40

Fight Against Apartheid — A192

1981, Dec. 9 **Litho.** ***Perf. 12½***

582	A192	90fr red orange	1.00	.50

Mangoes — A193

20fr, Papayas, horiz. 35fr, Fruits, vegetables, horiz. 75fr, Mangoes, vert. 90fr, Melons, horiz.

1981, Dec. 15 ***Perf. 13x13½, 13½x13***

583	A193	20fr multicolored	.60	.25
584	A193	35fr multicolored	.55	.25
585	A193	75fr multicolored	.90	.50
586	A193	90fr multicolored	1.00	.70
		Nos. 583-586 (4)	3.05	1.70

Guinea Hen — A194

Breeding animals. 10fr, 25fr, 70fr, 250fr, 300fr horiz.

1981, Dec. 22 *Perf. 13*

587 A194 10fr Donkey .25 .25
588 A194 25fr Pig .35 .25
589 A194 70fr Cow .90 .25
590 A194 90fr Guinea hen 1.00 .45
591 A194 250fr Rabbit 2.75 1.10
Nos. 587-591 (5) 5.25 2.30

Souvenir Sheet

592 A194 300fr Sheep 4.25 4.00

West African Rice Development Assoc., 10th Anniv. — A195

1981, Dec. 29

593 A195 90fr multicolored 1.10 .50

20th Anniv. of World Food Program — A196

1982, Jan. 18

594 A196 50fr multicolored .60 .25

Traditional Houses — A197

30fr, Morhonaba Palace, vert. 70fr, Bobo. 100fr, Gourounsi. 200fr, Peulh. 250fr, Dagari.

1982, Apr. 23 **Litho.** *Perf. 12½*

595 A197 30fr multicolored .35 .25
596 A197 70fr multicolored .70 .25
597 A197 100fr multicolored 1.10 .35
598 A197 200fr multicolored 2.00 .75
599 A197 250fr multicolored 2.00 .90
Nos. 595-599 (5) 6.15 2.50

14th World Telecommunications Day — A198

1982, May 17

600 A198 125fr multicolored 1.20 .60

Water Lily — A199

25fr, Water lily. 40fr, Kapoks. 70fr, Frangipani. 90fr, Cochlospermum planchonii. 100fr, Cotton.

1982, Sept. 22 *Perf. 13x12½*

601 A199 25fr multi .25 .25
602 A199 40fr multi .50 .25
603 A199 70fr multi .85 .25
604 A199 90fr multi 1.10 .45
605 A199 100fr multi 1.20 .60
Nos. 601-605 (5) 3.90 1.80

African Postal Union A200

1982, Oct. 7

606 A200 70fr multicolored .60 .25
607 A200 90fr multicolored 1.00 .50

25th Anniv. of Cultural Aid Fund — A201

1982, Nov. 10 *Perf. 12½x13*

608 A201 70fr multicolored .80 .45

Map, Hand Holding Grain, Steer Head A202

1982 *Perf. 12½*

609 A202 90fr multicolored .95 .45

Traditional Hairstyle A203

1983, Jan. **Litho.** *Perf. 12½*

610 A203 90fr lt green & multi .90 .35
611 A203 120fr lt blue & multi 1.25 .45
612 A203 170fr pink & multi 1.90 .70
Nos. 610-612 (3) 4.05 1.50

For overprints see Nos. 884-886.

8th Film Festival, Ouagadougou — A204

90fr, Scene. 500fr, Filmmaker Dumarou Ganda.

1983, Feb. 10 **Litho.** *Perf. 13x12½*

613 A204 90fr multi 1.40 .80
614 A204 500fr multi 7.00 3.50

UN Intl. Drinking Water and Sanitation Decade, 1981-90 — A205

1983, Apr. 21 **Litho.** *Perf. 13½x13*

615 A205 60fr Water drops .50 .25
616 A205 70fr Carrying water 1.00 .50

Manned Flight Bicentenary A206

Portraits and Balloons: 15fr, J.M. Montgolfier, 1783. 25fr, Etienne Montgolfier's balloon, 1783, Pilatre de Rozier. 70fr, Charles & Roberts flight, 1783, Jacques Charles. 90fr, Flight over English Channel, John Jeffries. 100fr, Testu-Brissy's horseback flight, Wilhemine Reichardt. 250fr, Andree's Spitzbergen flight, 1897, S.A. Andree. 300fr, Piccard's stratosphere flight, 1931, August Piccard.

No. 623A, J. M. and J. E. Montgolfier, balloon, horiz. No. 623B, John Wise, balloon.

1983, Apr. 15 **Litho.** *Perf. 13½*

617 A206 15fr multicolored .25 .25
618 A206 25fr multicolored .25 .25
619 A206 70fr multicolored .70 .25
620 A206 90fr multicolored .90 .30
621 A206 100fr multicolored 1.10 .35
622 A206 250fr multicolored 2.25 .80
Nos. 617-622 (6) 5.45 2.20

Souvenir Sheet

623 A206 300fr multicolored 3.50 1.25

Size: 57x39mm

623A A206 1500fr gold & multi 18.00 18.00

Souvenir Sheet

623B A206 1500fr gold & multi 25.00 25.00

No. 623 contains one stamp 38x47mm. Nos. 621-623 airmail.

No. 623B contains one 39x57mm stamp. Nos. 623A-623B are airmail.

World Communications Year — A207

30fr, Man reading letter. 45fr, Aircraft over stream. 90fr, Girl on telephone.

1983, May 26 **Litho.** *Perf. 12½*

624 A207 30fr multi .25 .25
625 A207 35fr Like No. 624 .45 .25
626 A207 45fr multi .65 .25
627 A207 90fr multi .90 .40
Nos. 624-627 (4) 2.25 1.15

Fishing Resources A208

20fr, Synadontis gambiensis. 30fr, Palmotochromis. 40fr, Boy fishing, vert. 50fr, Fishing with net. 75fr, Fishing with basket.

1983, July 28 **Litho.** *Perf. 13*

628 A208 20fr multicolored .60 .25
629 A208 30fr multicolored .80 .25
630 A208 40fr multicolored 1.00 .35
631 A208 50fr multicolored 1.10 .35
632 A208 75fr multicolored 1.75 .45
Nos. 628-632 (5) 5.25 1.65

Anti-deforestation — A209

10fr, Planting saplings. 50fr, Tree nursery. 100fr, Prevent forest fires. 150fr, Woman cooking. 200fr, Prevent felling, vert.

1983, Sept. 13 **Litho.** *Perf. 13*

633 A209 10fr multicolored .25 .25
634 A209 50fr multicolored .50 .25
635 A209 100fr multicolored 1.10 .25
636 A209 150fr multicolored 2.00 .60
637 A209 200fr multicolored 2.25 .90
Nos. 633-637 (5) 6.10 2.25

Fresco Detail, by Raphael — A210

Paintings: 120fr, Self-portrait, by Pablo Picasso, 1901, vert. 185fr, Self-portrait at the palette, by Manet, 1878, vert. 350fr, Fresco Detail, diff., by Raphael. 500fr, Goethe, by George Oswald May, 1779, vert.

1983, Nov. **Litho.** *Perf. 13*

638 A210 120fr multicolored 1.50 .45
639 A210 185fr multicolored 1.75 .55
640 A210 300fr multicolored 2.50 .75
641 A210 350fr multicolored 2.75 1.00
642 A210 500fr multicolored 4.50 1.50
Nos. 638-642 (5) 13.00 4.25

25th Anniv. of the Republic A211

1983, Dec. 9 **Litho.** *Perf. 14*

643 A211 90fr Arms .70 .25
644 A211 500fr Family, flag 4.00 1.50

A212

1984, May 29 **Litho.** *Perf. 12½*

645 A212 90fr multicolored .80 .30
646 A212 100fr multicolored .90 .40

Council of Unity, 25th anniv.

Flowers and Fungi — A213

25fr, Polystictus leoninus. 185fr, Pterocarpus Lucens. 200fr, Phlebopus colossus sudanicus. 250fr, Cosmos sulphureus. 300fr, Trametes versicolor. 400fr, Ganoderma lucidum.

600fr, Leucocoprinus cepaestipes.

1984, June 15 **Litho.** *Perf. 13½*

647 A213 25fr multicolored .40 .25
648 A213 185fr multicolored 3.00 .60
649 A213 200fr multicolored 3.25 .70
650 A213 250fr multicolored 4.75 .75

651 A213 300fr multicolored 4.00 .80
652 A213 400fr multicolored 6.00 1.10
Nos. 647-652 (6) 21.40 4.20

Souvenir Sheet

653 A213 600fr multicolored 6.25 2.25

Nos. 647-653 have Scouting emblem. Nos. 651-653 are airmail. For overprints see Nos. 669-674.

Wildlife
A214

Wildlife — A215

15fr, Cheetah, four cubs. 35fr, Two adults. 90fr, One adult. 120fr, Cheetah, two cubs. 300fr, Baboons. 400fr, Vultures.
1000fr, Antelopes.

1984, July 19

654 A214 15fr multicolored .50 .25
655 A214 35fr multicolored 1.10 .50
656 A214 90fr multicolored 2.75 .70
657 A214 120fr multicolored 3.00 1.00
658 A214 300fr multicolored 3.50 1.10
659 A214 400fr multicolored 3.50 1.15
Nos. 654-659 (6) 14.35 4.70

Souvenir Sheet

660 A215 1000fr multicolored 10.00 2.00

World Wildlife Fund (Nos. 654-657); Rotary Intl. (Nos. 658, 660); Natl. Boy Scouts (No. 659). Nos. 658-660 are airmail.

Sailing Ships and Locomotives — A216

1984, Aug. 14 *Perf. 12½*

661 A216 20fr Maiden Queen .25 .25
662 A216 40fr CC 2400 ch .45 .25
663 A216 60fr Scawfell .70 .25
664 A216 100fr PO 1806 1.00 .25
665 A216 120fr Harbinger 1.25 .45
666 A216 145fr Livingstone 1.40 .60
667 A216 400fr True Briton 4.25 1.50
668 A216 450fr Pacific C51 4.50 1.10
Nos. 661-668 (8) 13.80 4.65

Burkina Faso

Natl. Defense — A216a

Design: 120fr, Capt. Sankara, crowd, horiz.

1984, Nov. 21 **Litho.** *Perf. 13½*

668A A216a 90fr multicolored *45.00* —
668B A216a 120fr multicolored *65.00* —

No. 635 Overprinted

Methods and Perfs As Before

1984

668C A209 100fr multi *80.00 75.00*

Nos. 647-652 Overprinted

1985, Mar. 5 **Litho.** *Perf. 13½*

669 A213 25fr multicolored *.50 .25*
670 A213 185fr multicolored *3.25 1.10*
671 A213 200fr multicolored *5.00 1.50*
672 A213 250fr multicolored *4.50 1.60*
673 A213 300fr multicolored *6.00 2.25*
674 A213 400fr multicolored *7.50 3.00*
Nos. 669-674 (6) 26.75 9.70

A217

Designs: 5fr, 120fr, Flag. 15fr, 150fr, Natl. Arms, vert. 90fr, 185fr, Map.

1985, Mar. 8 **Litho.** *Perf. 12½*

675 A217 5fr multicolored .45 .25
676 A217 15fr multicolored .65 .30
677 A217 90fr multicolored 2.10 .80
678 A217 120fr multicolored 1.40 .60
679 A217 150fr multicolored 2.00 .75
680 A217 185fr multicolored 2.25 .90
Nos. 675-680 (6) 8.85 3.60

Nos. 678-680 are airmail.

1986 World Cup Soccer Championships, Mexico — A218

Various soccer plays and Aztec artifacts.

1985, Apr. 20 **Litho.** *Perf. 13*

681 A218 25fr multicolored .25 .25
682 A218 45fr multicolored .30 .25
683 A218 90fr multicolored .55 .25
684 A218 100fr multicolored .60 .30
685 A218 150fr multicolored .90 .55
686 A218 200fr multicolored 1.25 .85
687 A218 250fr multicolored 1.60 1.00
Nos. 681-687 (7) 5.45 3.45

Souvenir Sheet

688 A218 500fr multicolored 6.75 1.25

Nos. 681-685 vert. No. 684-688 are airmail. No. 688 contains one 40x32mm stamp.

Motorcycle, Cent. — A220

50fr, Steam tricycle, G.A. Long. 75fr, Pope. 80fr, Manet-90. 100fr, Ducati. 150fr, Jawa. 200fr, Honda. 250fr, B.M.W.

1985, May 26

689 A220 50fr multi .35 .25
690 A220 75fr multi .50 .25
691 A220 80fr multi .60 .25
692 A220 100fr multi .80 .30
693 A220 150fr multi 1.10 .45
694 A220 200fr multi 1.60 .65
695 A220 250fr multi 1.75 .80
Nos. 689-695 (7) 6.70 2.95

Nos. 692-695 are airmail.

Reptiles
A221

5fr, Chamaeleon dilepis. 15fr, Agama stellio. 35fr, Lacerta Lepida. 85fr, Hiperolius marmoratus. 100fr, Echis leucogaster. 150fr, Kinixys erosa. 250fr, Python regius.

1985, June 20

696 A221 5fr multicolored .25 .25
697 A221 15fr multicolored .25 .25
698 A221 35fr multicolored .50 .25
699 A221 85fr multicolored 1.40 .30
700 A221 100fr multicolored 1.50 .30
701 A221 150fr multicolored 1.80 .45
702 A221 250fr multicolored 2.90 .60
Nos. 696-702 (7) 8.60 2.40

Nos. 696-697 vert. Nos. 700-702 are airmail.

A222

Queen Mother, 85th Birthday
A222a

75fr, On pony bobs. 85fr, Wedding, 1923. 500fr, Holding infant Elizabeth, 1926. 600fr, Coronation of King George VI, 1937. 1000fr, Christening of Prince William, 1982. No. 707A, Christening of Prince Harry, 1985.

1985, June 21 *Perf. 13½*

703 A222 75fr multicolored .90 .45
704 A222 85fr multicolored 1.00 .45
705 A222 500fr multicolored 4.00 1.50
706 A222 600fr multicolored 5.25 1.75
Nos. 703-706 (4) 11.15 4.15

Litho. & Embossed

Perf. 13¼

706A A222a 1500fr gold & multi 12.50 —

Souvenir Sheets

Litho.

707 A222 1000fr multi 10.00 10.00

Litho. & Embossed

707A A222a 1500fr gold & multi 12.50 —

Nos. 705-707A are airmail.

Vintage Autos and Aircraft — A223

5fr, Benz Victoria, 1893. 25fr, Peugeot 174, 1927. 45fr, Louis Bleriot. 50fr, Breguet 14. No. 712, Bugatti Coupe Napoleon T41 Royale. No. 713, Airbus A300-P4. No. 714, Mercedes-Benz 540K, 1938. No. 715, Airbus A300B.
No. 716, Louis Bleriot, Karl Benz.

1985, June 21

708 A223 5fr multicolored .25 .25
709 A223 25fr multicolored .45 .25
710 A223 45fr multicolored .60 .25
711 A223 50fr multicolored .60 .25
712 A223 500fr multicolored 5.00 1.00
713 A223 500fr multicolored 4.00 1.00
714 A223 600fr multicolored 5.00 1.25
715 A223 600fr multicolored 5.00 1.25
Nos. 708-715 (8) 20.90 5.50

Souvenir Sheet

716 A223 1000fr multicolored 9.50 2.25

Automobile, cent. Nos. 712-716 are airmail.

Audubon Birth Bicent.
A224

Illustrations of No. American bird species by Audubon and scouting trefoil: 60fr, Aix sponsa. 100fr, Mimus polyglotos. 300fr, Icterus galbula. 400fr, Sitta carolinensis. 500fr, Asyndesmus lewis. 600fr, Buteo cagopus.
1000fr, Columba leucocephala.

1985, June 21

717 A224 60fr multicolored .55 .25
718 A224 100fr multicolored .85 .30
719 A224 300fr multicolored 2.75 .80
720 A224 400fr multicolored 3.50 1.00
721 A224 500fr multicolored 3.75 1.00
722 A224 600fr multicolored 4.50 1.25
Nos. 717-722 (6) 15.90 4.60

Souvenir Sheet

723 A224 1000fr multicolored 11.00 2.25

Nos. 721-723 are airmail.

ARGENTINA '85, Buenos Aires — A225

Various equestrians: 25fr, Gaucho, piebald. 45fr, Horse and rider, Andes Mountains. 90fr, Rodeo. 100fr, Hunting gazelle. 150fr, Gauchos, 3 horses. 200fr, Rider beside mount. 250fr, Contest.
500fr, Foal.

1985, July 5 *Perf. 13*

724 A225 25fr multicolored .40 .25
725 A225 45fr multicolored .65 .25
726 A225 90fr multicolored 1.15 .25
727 A225 100fr multicolored .80 .25
728 A225 150fr multicolored 1.20 .25
729 A225 200fr multicolored 1.60 .40
730 A225 250fr multicolored 2.25 .60
Nos. 724-730 (7) 8.05 2.25

Souvenir Sheet

731 A225 500fr multicolored 4.50 1.40

Nos. 727-731 are airmail.

Locomotives — A226

50fr, 105-30 electric, tank wagon. 75fr, Diesel shunting locomotive. 80fr, Diesel locomotive. 100fr, Diesel railcar. 150fr, No. 6093. 200fr, No. 105 diesel railcar. 250fr, Diesel, passenger car.

1985, July 23

732	A226	50fr multicolored	.70	.25
733	A226	75fr multicolored	.95	.25
734	A226	80fr multicolored	1.10	.25
735	A226	100fr multicolored	.80	.25
736	A226	150fr multicolored	1.20	.30
737	A226	200fr multicolored	1.60	.45
738	A226	250fr multicolored	2.10	.60
		Nos. 732-738 (7)	8.45	2.35

Nos. 735-738 are airmail.

Artifacts — A227

Designs: 10fr, 4-legged jar, Tikare. 40fr, Lidded pot with bird handles, P. Bazega. 90fr, Mother and child, bronze statue, Ouagadougou. 120fr, Drummer, bronze statue, Ouagadougou.

1985, July 27 ***Perf. 13x12½***

739-742	A227	Set of 4	4.00	1.50

No. 742 is airmail.

Fungi — A228

15fr, Philiota mutabilis. 20fr, Hypholoma (nematoloma) fasciculare. 30fr, Ixocomus granulatus. 60fr, Agaricus campestris. 80fr, Trachypus scaber. 150fr, Armillaria mellea. 250fr, Marasmius scorodonius.

1985, Aug. 8 ***Perf. 13***

743	A228	15fr multicolored	.25	.25
744	A228	20fr multicolored	.25	.25
745	A228	30fr multicolored	.30	.25
746	A228	60fr multicolored	.60	.25
747	A228	80fr multicolored	1.00	.30
748	A228	150fr multicolored	2.10	.45
749	A228	250fr multicolored	2.25	.60
		Nos. 743-749 (7)	6.75	2.35

No. 748 is airmail.

ITALIA '85 A228a

Paintings by Botticelli: 25fr, Virgin and Child. 45fr, Portrait of a Man. 90fr, Mars and Venus. 100fr, Birth of Venus. 150fr, Allegory of the Calumny. 200fr, Pallas and the Centaur. 250fr, Allegory of Spring. 500fr, The Virgin of Melagrana.

1985, Oct. 25 Litho. ***Perf. 12½x13***

749A	A228a	25fr multicolored	.35	.25
749B	A228a	45fr multicolored	.60	.25
749C	A228a	90fr multicolored	1.20	.30
749D	A228a	100fr multicolored	.75	.30
749E	A228a	150fr multicolored	.85	.30
749F	A228a	200fr multicolored	1.50	.45
749G	A228a	250fr multicolored	2.00	.70
		Nos. 749A-749G (7)	7.25	2.55

Souvenir Sheet

749H	A228a	500fr multicolored	3.00	1.50

No. 749D-749H are airmail.

Intl. Red Cross in Burkina Faso, 75th Anniv. A229

40f, Helicopter. 85fr, Ambulance. 150fr, Henri Dunant. 250fr, Physician, patient.

1985, Nov. 10

750	A229	40f multi	1.55	.35
751	A229	85fr multi	3.25	.40
752	A229	150fr multi	.85	.35
753	A229	250fr multi	1.25	.40
		Nos. 750-753 (4)	6.90	1.50

Nos. 752-753 are vert. and airmail.

Child Survival A230

1986, Jan. 6

754	A230	90fr Breast-feeding	1.25	.50

Dated 1985.

Dodo Carnival — A231

20fr, Three children, drummer. 25fr, Lion, 4 dancers. 40fr, Two dancers, two drummers. 45fr, Three dancers. No. 759, Zebra, ostrich, dancers. No. 760, Elephant, dancer.

1986, Jan. 6 ***Perf. 12½***

755	A231	20fr multicolored	.25	.25
756	A231	25fr multicolored	.25	.25
757	A231	40fr multicolored	.45	.25
758	A231	45fr multicolored	.50	.25
759	A231	90fr multicolored	1.10	.45
760	A231	90fr multicolored	1.10	.45
		Nos. 755-760 (6)	3.65	1.90

Dated 1985.

Christopher Columbus (1451-1506) — A232

Columbus: 250fr, At Court of King of Portugal, the Nina. 300fr, Using astrolable, the Santa Maria. 400fr, Imprisonment at Hispanola, 1500, the Santa Maria. 450fr, At San Salvador, 1492, the Pinta. 1000fr, Fleet departing Palos harbor, 1492.

1986, Feb. 10 ***Perf. 13½***

761	A232	250fr multicolored	2.25	.60
762	A232	300fr multicolored	2.40	.75
763	A232	400fr multicolored	3.25	.90
764	A232	450fr multicolored	3.50	1.50
		Nos. 761-764 (4)	11.40	3.75

Souvenir Sheet

765	A232	1000fr multicolored	6.50	2.25

Nos. 764-765 are airmail. Dated 1985.

Railroad Construction — A233

90fr, Man, woman carrying rail. 120fr, Laying rails. 185fr, Diesel train on new tracks. 500fr, Adler locomotive, 1835.

1000fr, Electric train, Series 290 diesel.

1986, Feb. 10

766	A233	90fr multicolored	1.00	.45
767	A233	120fr multicolored	1.10	.50
768	A233	185fr multicolored	1.60	.60
769	A233	500fr multicolored	4.75	1.50
		Nos. 766-769 (4)	8.45	3.05

Souvenir Sheet

770	A233	1000fr multicolored	9.00	2.25

German Railways, sesquicentennial. Nos. 769-770 are airmail. Dated 1985.

Intl. Peace Year — A234

1986, Oct. 10 Photo. ***Perf. 12½x13***

771	A234	90fr blue	1.50	.45

World Health by the Year 2000 — A235

Designs: 100fr, Primary care medicine. 150fr, Mass inoculations.

1986, Aug. 8 Litho. ***Perf. 13***

772	A235	90fr multicolored	1.10	.40

Size: 26x38mm

Perf. 12½x13

773	A235	100fr multicolored	1.10	.50
774	A235	120fr multicolored	1.50	.55
		Nos. 772-774 (3)	3.70	1.45

Insects — A236

15fr, Phryneta aurocinta. 20fr, Sternocera interrupta. 40fr, Prosoprocera lactator. 45fr, Gonimbrasia hecate. 85fr, Charaxes epijasius.

1986, Sept. 10 Litho. ***Perf. 12½x13***

775	A236	15fr multicolored	.35	.25
776	A236	20fr multicolored	.35	.25
777	A236	40fr multicolored	.90	.35
778	A236	45fr multicolored	.95	.35
778A	A236	85fr multicolored	1.90	.70
		Nos. 775-778A (5)	4.45	1.90

World Post Day — A237

1986, Oct. 9 ***Perf. 13***

779	A237	120fr multicolored	1.50	.45

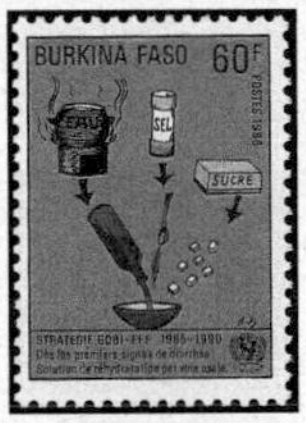

UN Child Survival Campaign — A238

Designs: 30fr, Mother feeding child. 60fr, Adding medicines to food. 90fr, Nurse vaccinating child. 120fr, Nurse weighing child.

1986, Oct. 8 Litho. ***Perf. 11½x12***

780	A238	30fr multicolored	.50	.25
781	A238	60fr multicolored	.80	.35
782	A238	90fr multicolored	1.10	.50
783	A238	120fr multicolored	1.60	.60
		Nos. 780-783 (4)	4.00	1.70

Mammals A239

Designs: 50fr, Warthog. 65fr, Hyena. 90fr, Antelope. 100fr, Gazelle. 120fr, Bushbuck. 145fr, Kudu. 500fr, Gazelle, diff.

1986, Nov. 3 Litho. ***Perf. 13x12½***

784	A239	50fr multicolored	.50	.25
784A	A239	65fr multicolored	.60	.30
784B	A239	90fr multicolored	.75	.40
784C	A239	100fr multicolored	.75	.50
784D	A239	120fr multicolored	.85	.55
784E	A239	145fr multicolored	1.15	.65
784F	A239	500fr multicolored	4.00	2.00
		Nos. 784-784F (7)	8.60	4.65

Traditional Dances — A240

Designs: 10fr, Namende. 25fr, Mouhoun. 90fr, Houet. 105fr, Seno. 120fr, Ganzourgou.

1986, Nov. 3 Litho. ***Perf. 12½x13***

785	A240	10fr multicolored	.35	.25
785A	A240	25fr multicolored	.50	.25
785B	A240	90fr multicolored	1.75	.45
785C	A240	105fr multicolored	1.75	.45
785D	A240	120fr multicolored	2.25	.60
		Nos. 785-785D (5)	6.60	2.00

Hairstyles A241

1986, Nov. 4 Litho. *Perf. 12½x13*

788 A241 35fr Peul	.35	.25
789 A241 75fr Dafing	.90	.40
790 A241 90fr Peul, diff.	1.40	.50
791 A241 120fr Mossi	1.75	.65
792 A241 185fr Peul, diff.	2.50	.90
Nos. 788-792 (5)	6.90	2.70

10th African Film Festival — A242

90fr, Maps, cameras. 120fr, Jolson, cameramen. 185fr, Charlie Chaplin.

1987, Feb. 21 Litho. *Perf. 12x12½*

793 A242 90fr multi	1.25	.60
794 A242 120fr multi	2.25	.90
795 A242 185fr multi	3.25	1.40
Nos. 793-795 (3)	6.75	2.90

60th Anniv. of the film *The Jazz Singer* (120fr); 10th anniv. of the death of Charlie Chaplin (185fr).

Intl Women's Day — A243

1987, Mar. 8 *Perf. 13½*

796 A243 90fr multicolored	1.00	.40

Flora — A244

70fr, Calotropis procera. 75fr, Acacia seyal. 85fr, Parkia biglobosa. 90fr, Sterospernum kunthianum. 100fr, Dichrostachys cinerea. 300fr, Combretum paniculatum.

1987, June 6 Litho. *Perf. 12½x13*

797 A244 70fr multicolored	1.00	.35
798 A244 75fr multicolored	1.00	.35
799 A244 85fr multicolored	1.25	.55
800 A244 90fr multicolored	1.25	.55
801 A244 100fr multicolored	1.60	.55
802 A244 300fr multicolored	3.75	1.00
Nos. 797-802 (6)	9.85	3.35

Fight Against Leprosy — A245

Raoul Follereau (1903-1977) and: 90fr, Doctors examining African youth. 100fr, Laboratory research. 120fr, Gerhard Hansen (1841-1912), microscope, bacillus under magnification. 300fr, Follereau embracing cured leper.

1987, Aug. 6 *Perf. 13*

803 A245 90fr multicolored	1.15	.45
804 A245 100fr multicolored	1.20	.45
805 A245 120fr multicolored	1.40	.60
806 A245 300fr multicolored	3.25	1.50
Nos. 803-806 (4)	7.00	3.00

World Environment Day — A246

1987, Aug. 18 Litho. *Perf. 13x12½*

807 A246 90fr shown	1.10	.50
808 A246 145fr Emblem, huts	1.65	.75

Pre-Olympic Year — A247

75fr, High jump. 85fr, Tennis, vert. 90fr, Ski jumping. 100fr, Soccer. 145fr, Running. 350fr, Pierre de Coubertin, tennis, vert.

1987, Aug. 31 *Perf. 12½*

809 A247 75fr multicolored	.90	.45
810 A247 85fr multicolored	1.00	.45
811 A247 90fr multicolored	1.00	.60
812 A247 100fr multicolored	1.10	.60
813 A247 145fr multicolored	1.60	.75
814 A247 350fr multicolored	3.75	1.60
Nos. 809-814 (6)	9.35	4.45

Pierre de Coubertin (1863-1937).

World Post Day — A248

1987, Oct. 5 Litho. *Perf. 12½x13*

815 A248 90fr multicolored	1.00	.45

Fight Against Apartheid — A249

100fr, Luthuli, book, 1962.

1987, Nov. 11 Litho. *Perf. 13*

816 A249 90fr shown	1.00	.45
817 A249 100fr multicolored	1.20	.45

Albert John Luthuli (1898-1967), South African reformer, author and 1960 Nobel Peace Prize winner. No. 817 incorrectly inscribed "1899-1967."

Traditional Costumes — A250

1987, Dec. 4 Litho. *Perf. 11½x12*

818 A250 10fr Dagari	.25	.25
819 A250 30fr Peul	.30	.25
820 A250 90fr Mossi	.75	.25
821 A250 200fr Senoufo	1.60	.90
822 A250 500fr Mossi	4.00	2.10
Nos. 818-822 (5)	6.90	3.75

Traditional Musical Instruments A251

20fr, Xylophone. 25fr, 3-Stringed lute, vert. 35fr, Zither. 90fr, Conical drum. 1000fr, Calabash drum, vert.

Perf. 12x11½, 11½x12

1987, Dec. 4 Litho.

823 A251 20fr multicolored	.30	.25
824 A251 25fr multicolored	.30	.25
825 A251 35fr multicolored	.40	.25
826 A251 90fr multicolored	1.00	.45
827 A251 1000fr multicolored	10.00	4.00
Nos. 823-827 (5)	12.00	5.20

Intl. Year of Shelter for the Homeless — A252

1987, Dec. 4 Litho. *Perf. 13*

828 A252 90fr multicolored	1.00	.45

Five-year Natl. Development Plan — A253

40fr, Small businesses. 55fr, Agriculture. 60fr, Constructing schools. 90fr, Transportation and communications. 100fr, Literacy. 120fr, Animal husbandry.

1987, Dec. 15 *Perf. 13½*

829 A253 40fr multicolored	.40	.25
830 A253 55fr multicolored	.65	.25
831 A253 60fr multicolored	.65	.25
832 A253 90fr multicolored	1.00	.30
833 A253 100fr multicolored	1.10	.55
834 A253 120fr multicolored	1.40	.60
Nos. 829-834 (6)	5.20	2.20

World Health Organization, 40th Anniv. — A254

1988, Mar. 31 Litho. *Perf. 12½x13*

835 A254 120fr multicolored	1.25	.45

1988 Summer Olympics, Seoul A255

1988, May 5 *Perf. 13x12½*

836 A255 30fr shown	.25	.25
837 A255 160fr Torch, vert.	1.25	.60
838 A255 175fr Soccer	1.50	.70
839 A255 235fr Volleyball, vert.	2.00	1.00
840 A255 450fr Basketball, vert.	3.50	2.00
Nos. 836-840 (5)	8.50	4.55

Souvenir Sheet

Perf. 12½x13

841 A255 500fr Runners	6.50	5.25

No. 841 contains one stamp, size: 40x52mm plus two labels.

Ritual Masks A256

10fr, Epervier, Houet. 20fr, Jeunes Filles, Oullo. 30fr, Bubale, Houet. 40fr, Forgeron, Mouhoun. 120fr, Nounouma, Ouri. 175fr, Chauve-souris, Ouri.

1988, May 30 Litho. *Perf. 13*

842 A256 10fr multicolroed	.25	.25
843 A256 20fr multicolored	.25	.25
844 A256 30fr multicolored	.30	.25
845 A256 40fr multicolored	.35	.25
846 A256 120fr multicolored	1.00	.45
847 A256 175fr multicolored	1.50	.75
Nos. 842-847 (6)	3.65	2.20

Nos. 842-846 vert.

Handicrafts A257

5fr, Kieriebe ceramic pitcher, vert. 15fr, Mossi basket. 25fr, Gurunsi chair. 30fr, Bissa basket. 45fr, Ougadougou leather box. 85fr, Ougadougou bronze statue, vert. 120fr, Ougadougou leather valise.

1988, Aug. 22 Litho. *Perf. 13½*

848 A257 5fr multicolored	.25	.25
849 A257 15fr multicolored	.25	.25
850 A257 25fr multicolored	.25	.25
851 A257 30fr multicolored	.30	.25
852 A257 45fr multicolored	.50	.25
853 A257 85fr multicolored	.80	.35
854 A257 120fr multicolored	1.25	.55
Nos. 848-854 (7)	3.60	2.15

World Post Day — A258

1988, Oct. 9 Litho. *Perf. 13*

855 A258 120fr multicolored	1.35	.45

Aquatic Fauna A259

1988, Oct. 31 *Perf. 12*

856 A259 70fr Angler martin	.80	.25
857 A259 100fr Mormyrus rume	1.10	.45
858 A259 120fr Frog	1.50	.55
859 A259 160fr Duck	2.10	.70
Nos. 856-859 (4)	5.50	1.95

Civil Rights and Political Activists A260

Designs: 80fr, Mohammed Ali Jinnah (1876-1948), 1st Governor General of Pakistan.

120fr, Mahatma Gandhi (1869-1948), India. 160fr, John F. Kennedy. 235fr, Martin Luther King, Jr.

1988, Nov. 22 Litho. *Perf. 14*

860	A260	80fr multicolored	.80	.35
861	A260	120fr multicolored	1.25	.55
862	A260	160fr multicolored	1.75	.70
863	A260	235fr multicolored	2.25	1.10
		Nos. 860-863 (4)	6.05	2.70

No. 863 is airmail.

Christmas — A261

Stained-glass windows: 120fr, Adoration of the shepherds. 160fr, Adoration of the Magi. 450fr, Madonna and child. 1000fr, Flight into Egypt.

1988, Dec. 2 *Perf. 12*

864	A261	120fr multicolored	1.25	.45
865	A261	160fr multicolored	1.50	.65
866	A261	450fr multicolored	4.50	1.80
867	A261	1000fr multicolored	9.50	4.50
		Nos. 864-867 (4)	16.75	7.40

A262

No. 869, Ababacar Makharam. No. 870, Jean Tchissoukou. No. 871, Paulin Vieyra.

1989, Feb. 25 LItho. *Perf. 14*

868	A262	75fr shown	1.10	.35
869	A262	500fr muticolored	5.00	1.75
870	A262	500fr multicolored	5.00	1.75
871	A262	500fr multicolored	5.00	1.75
		Nos. 868-871 (4)	16.10	5.60

Souvenir Sheet

872		Sheet of 3	16.00	14.00
a.-c.		A262 500fr like #869-871, inscribed in gold	4.00	1.75

Panafrican Film Festival (FESPACO), 20th anniv. Nos. 869-872 are airmail.

World Fight Against AIDS A263

1989, Apr. 7 Litho. *Perf. 13*

873	A263	120fr multicolored	1.25	.50

Council for Rural Development, 30th Anniv. — A264

1989, May 3 Litho. *Perf. 15x14*

874	A264	75fr multicolored	.90	.45

Parasitic Plants — A265

Legumes and cereals: 20fr, Striga generiodes. 50fr, Striga hermonthica. 235fr, Striga aspera. 450fr, Alectra vogelii.

1989, Oct. 9 Litho. *Perf. 11½*

Granite Paper

875	A265	20fr multicolored	.25	.25
876	A265	50fr multicolored	.35	.25
877	A265	235fr multicolored	1.75	1.10
878	A265	450fr multicolored	3.00	1.50
		Nos. 875-878 (4)	5.35	3.10

Dogs A266

1989, Oct. 9 *Perf. 15x14½*

879	A266	35fr Sahel	.55	.25
880	A266	50fr Puppy	.65	.25
881	A266	60fr Hunting dog	.90	.25
882	A266	350fr Guard dog	4.00	2.00
		Nos. 879-882 (4)	6.10	2.75

Solidarity with the Palestinian People — A267

1989, Nov. 15 *Perf. 13*

883	A267	120fr Monument, Place de la Palestine	1.50	.45

Nos. 610-612 Overprinted

1988, Dec. 21 Litho. *Perf. 12½*

884	A203	90fr multicolored	.90	.30
885	A203	120fr multicolored	1.10	.30
886	A203	170fr multicolored	1.75	.50
		Nos. 884-886 (3)	3.75	1.10

Visit of Pope John Paul II A268

120fr, Our Lady of Yagma. 160fr, Pope, crowd.

1990, Jan. 1 Litho. *Perf. 15x14*

887	A268	120fr multi	1.25	.55
888	A269	160fr multi	1.75	.90

150th Anniv. of the Postage Stamp A269

500fr, Penny Black, ship.

1990, Mar. 20 Litho. *Perf. 15x14*

889	A269	120fr multicolored	1.40	.60

Souvenir Sheet

Perf. 14x15

890	A269	500fr multicolored	4.75	4.25

Stamp World London '90.

World Cup Soccer Championships, Italy — A270

1990, Apr. 26 Litho. *Perf. 11½*

891	A270	30fr multicolored	.30	.25
892	A270	150fr multi, diff.	2.10	.70

Souvenir Sheet

893	A270	1000fr multi, horiz.	10.00	8.50

Intl. Literacy Year A271

1990, July 10 Litho. *Perf. 13*

894	A271	40fr multicolored	.50	.25
895	A271	130fr multicolored	1.45	.60

Mushrooms — A272

10fr, Cantharellus cibarius. 15fr, Psalliota bispora. 60fr, Amanita caesarea. 190fr, Boletus badius.

1990, May 17 Litho. *Perf. 11½*

896	A272	10fr multicolored	.30	.25
897	A272	15fr multicolored	.50	.25
898	A272	60fr multicolored	1.10	.80
899	A272	190fr multicolored	3.50	1.75
a.		Souv. sheet of 4, #896-899	19.50	6.25
		Nos. 896-899 (4)	5.40	3.05

Intl. Exposition of Handicrafts — A273

35fr, Masks, fans, vert. 270fr, Rattan chair, vert.

1990, Sept. 25 Litho. *Perf. 13*

900	A273	35fr multi	.30	.25
901	A273	45fr shown	.40	.25
902	A273	270fr multi	2.50	1.00
		Nos. 900-902 (3)	3.20	1.50

Gen. Charles de Gaulle (1890-1970) A274

1990, Nov. 22 Litho. *Perf. 13*

903	A274	200fr multicolored	2.25	.90

Minerals A275

1991, Feb. 4 Litho. *Perf. 15x14*

904	A275	20fr Quartz	.35	.25
905	A275	50fr Granite	.60	.25
906	A275	280fr Amphibolite	3.25	1.40
		Nos. 904-906 (3)	4.20	1.90

African Film Festival — A276

1991, Feb. 20 *Perf. 11½*

907	A276	150fr multicolored	2.00	.90

Souvenir Sheet

908	A276	1000fr Award	14.00	10.00

Fight Against Drugs — A277

1991, Feb. 20

909	A277	130fr multicolored	1.35	.60

Samuel F.B. Morse (1791-1872), Inventor — A278

1991, May 17 Litho. *Perf. 13*

910	A278	200fr multicolored	2.00	.90

Native Girl — A279

1991-94 Litho. *Perf. 14½x15*

911	A279	5fr gray & multi	.25	.25
912	A279	10fr yellow & multi	.25	.25
913	A279	25fr lilac rose & multi	.25	.25
914	A279	50fr red lilac & multi	.25	.25
915	A279	130fr blue & multi	1.25	.55
916	A279	150fr multicolored	1.50	.60

920 A279 200fr multicolored 1.90 .80
922 A279 330fr orange & multi 3.25 1.40
Nos. 911-922 (8) 8.90 4.35

Issued: 150fr, 200fr, 6/20/91; 130fr, 330fr, 1/15/93; 5-50fr, 5/3/94.

Flowers — A280

5fr, Grewia tenax. 15fr, Hymenocardia acide. 60fr, Cassia sieberiana, vert. 100fr, Adenium obesum. 300fr, Mitragyna inermis.

1991, July 31 Litho. *Perf. 11½*
926 A280 5fr multicolored .25 .25
927 A280 15fr multicolored .25 .25
928 A280 60fr multicolored .65 .25
929 A280 100fr multicolored 1.00 .40
930 A280 300fr multicolored 3.00 1.25
Nos. 926-930 (5) 5.15 2.40

Traditional Dance Costumes — A281

1991, Aug. 20 *Perf. 12½*
931 A281 75fr Warba .90 .40
932 A281 130fr Wiskamba 1.35 .70
933 A281 280fr Pa-zenin 3.50 1.50
Nos. 931-933 (3) 5.75 2.60

World Post Day — A282

1991, Oct. 9 *Perf. 13½*
934 A282 130fr multicolored 1.35 .50

Cooking Utensils — A283

45fr, Pancake fryer. 130fr, Cooking pot, vert. 310fr, Mortar & pestle, vert. 500fr, Ladle, calabash.

1992, Jan. 8 Litho. *Perf. 11½*
935 A283 45fr multicolored .50 .25
936 A283 130fr multicolored 1.50 .45
937 A283 310fr multicolored 3.50 1.25
938 A283 500fr multicolored 5.50 2.00
Nos. 935-938 (4) 11.00 3.95

1992 African Soccer Championships, Senegal — A284

50fr, Yousouf Fofana. 100fr, Francois-Jules Bocande.
500fr, Trophy.

1992, Jan. 17 *Perf. 13½*
939 A284 50fr multicolored .65 .25
940 A284 100fr multicolored 1.25 .40

Souvenir Sheet
Perf. 13x12½
941 A284 500fr multicolored 5.50 2.00

UN Decade For the Handicapped — A285

1992, Mar. 31 Litho. *Perf. 12½*
942 A285 100fr multicolored 1.10 .40

World Health Day — A286

1992, Apr. 7 *Perf. 13*
943 A286 330fr multicolored 5.00 1.40

Discovery of America, 500th Anniv. — A287

50fr, Columbus, Santa Maria. 150fr, Ships, natives. 350fr, Map.

1992, Aug. 12 Litho. *Perf. 12½*
944 A287 50fr multicolored 1.00 .25
945 A287 150fr multicolored 2.50 .65

Souvenir Sheet
946 A287 350fr multicolored 4.75 1.50

Genoa '92. No. 946 contains one 52x31mm stamp.

Insects — A288

20fr, Dysdercus voelkeri. 40fr, Rhizopertha dominica. 85fr, Orthetrum microstigma. 500fr, Apis mellifera.

1992, Aug. 17 *Perf. 15x14*
947 A288 20fr multicolored .25 .25
948 A288 40fr multicolored .55 .25
949 A288 85fr multicolored 1.10 .35
950 A288 500fr multicolored 6.50 2.25
Nos. 947-950 (4) 8.40 3.10

A289

Christmas: 10fr, Boy, creche. 130fr, Children decorating creche. 1000fr, Boy holding painting of Madonna and Child.

1992, Dec. 21 Litho. *Perf. 11½*
951 A289 10fr multicolored .25 .25
952 A289 130fr multicolored 1.40 .50
953 A289 1000fr multicolored 10.00 4.00
Nos. 951-953 (3) 11.65 4.75

Invention of the Diesel Engine, Cent. — A290

1993, Jan. 25 Litho. *Perf. 11½*
954 A290 1000fr multicolored 11.50 4.00

Paris '94, Philatelic Exhibition — A291

1993, July 15
955 A291 400fr multicolored 5.00 1.75
956 A291 650fr multi, diff. 7.00 2.75

African Film Festival — A292

Designs: 250fr, Monument to the cinema. 750fr, M. Douta (1919-1991), comedian, horiz.

Perf. 11½x12, 12x11½
1993, Feb. 16 Litho.
957 A292 250fr multicolored 2.75 1.00
958 A292 750fr multicolored 8.25 3.00

Birds — A293

100fr, Mycteria ibis. 200fr, Leptoptilos crumeniferus. 500fr, Ephippiorhynchus senegalensis.

1993, Mar. 31 *Perf. 11½x12*
959 A293 100fr multicolored 1.00 .40
960 A293 200fr multicolored 2.00 .80
961 A293 500fr multicolored 5.25 2.00
a. Souvenir sheet of 3, #959-961 13.00 4.75
Nos. 959-961 (3) 8.25 3.20

No. 961a sold for 1200fr.

1994 World Cup Soccer Championships, U.S. — A294

1000fr, Players, US flag.

1993, Apr. 8 *Perf. 15*
962 A294 500fr shown 6.50 2.00
963 A294 1000fr multi 13.50 4.00

Fruit Trees — A295

150fr, Saba senegalensis, vert. 300fr, Butyrospermum parkii. 600fr, Adansonia digitata, vert.

1993, June 2 Litho. *Perf. 11½*
964 A295 150fr multicolored 1.75 .95
965 A295 300fr multicolored 3.50 1.90
966 A295 600fr multicolored 7.50 4.00
Nos. 964-966 (3) 12.75 6.85

Traditional Jewelry — A296

200fr, Ring for hair. 250fr, Agate necklace, vert. 500fr, Bracelet.

1993, Sept. 25 Litho. *Perf. 11½*
967 A296 200fr multi 1.75 .85
968 A296 250fr multi 2.25 1.00
969 A296 500fr multi 4.50 2.00
Nos. 967-969 (3) 8.50 3.85

Gazella Rufifrons — A297

1993, Dec. 10 Litho. *Perf. 14½*
970 A297 30fr shown 1.15 .25
971 A297 40fr Two facing left 1.15 .25
972 A297 60fr Two standing 2.25 .75
973 A297 100fr Young gazelle 4.50 1.25
a. Souvenir sheet, #970-973 8.00 6.50
Nos. 970-973 (4) 9.05 2.50

World Wildlife Fund (Nos. 970-973). No. 973a sold for 400fr.

Kingfishers — A298

600fr, Halcyon senegalensis. 1200fr, Halcyon chelicuti. 2000fr, Ceyx picta.

1994, Mar. 8 Litho. *Perf. 11½*
974 A298 600fr multicolored 4.00 1.75
975 A298 1200fr multicolored 8.50 3.75

Souvenir Sheet
976 A298 2000fr multicolored 17.00 9.75

1994 World Cup Soccer Championships, U.S. — A299

1000fr, Players, US map. 1800fr, Soccer ball, players.

1994, Mar. 28
977 A299 1000fr multicolored 5.00 2.00
978 A299 1800fr multicolored 8.00 4.00
a. Souvenir sheet of 1 10.00 8.50

No. 978a sold for 2000fr.

First Manned Moon Landing, 25th Anniv. — A300

No. 979, Astronaut, flag. No. 980, Lunar module, earth.

1994, July 15 Litho. *Perf. 11½*

979 A300 750fr multi	3.25	1.90
980 A300 750fr multi	3.25	1.90
a. Pair, #979-980	7.00	3.75

No. 980a is a continuous design.

First Stamp Exhibition, Paris, 1994 A301

1994, Apr. 28

981 A301 1500fr Dogs	7.25	3.75
a. Souvenir sheet of 1	10.00	8.25

Legumes — A302

40fr, Hibiscus sabdariffa. 45fr, Solanum aethiopicum. 75fr, Solanum melongena. 100fr, Hibiscus esculentus.

1994 Litho. *Perf. 11½*

982 A302 40fr multicolored	.25	.25
983 A302 45fr multicolored	.35	.25
984 A302 75fr multicolored	.60	.25
985 A302 100fr multicolored	.75	.25
Nos. 982-985 (4)	1.95	1.00

Intl. Olympic Committee, Cent. — A303

1994, Oct. 10 *Perf. 15*

986 A303 320fr multicolored	1.90	.80

Domestic Animals — A304

150fr, Pig, horiz. 1000fr, Capra hircus. 1500fr, Ovis aries, horiz.

1994, Oct. 10 *Perf. 11½*

987 A304 150fr multi	.75	.35
988 A304 1000fr multi	4.75	2.50
989 A304 1500fr multi	7.00	3.00
Nos. 987-989 (3)	12.50	5.85

Elvis Presley (1935-77) A305

A305a

Portraits in feature films: 300fr, Loving You. 500fr, Jailhouse Rock. 1000fr, Blue Hawaii. 1500fr, Marilyn Monroe, Presley.

1995 Litho. *Perf. 13½*

990-992 A305 Set of 3	10.00	4.75

Souvenir Sheets

993 A305 1500fr multi	7.50	6.50

Litho. & Embossed

993A A305a 3000fr gold & multi	17.50	11.00

Nos. 990-992 exist in souvenir sheets of one. No. 993 contains one 51x42mm stamp with continuous design. No. 993A, exists in souvenir sheets of silver & multi with different designs in sheet margin.

Issued: No. 993A, 2/24/95.

See Nos. 1012-1015A.

Crocodile — A306

1995, Feb. 6 Litho. *Perf. 15x14½*

994 A306 10fr brown & multi	.25	.25
995 A306 20fr lilac & multi	.25	.25
996 A306 25fr olive brn & multi	.25	.25
997 A306 30fr green & multi	.25	.25
998 A306 40fr red brn & multi	.25	.25
999 A306 50fr gray & multi	.25	.25
1000 A306 75fr gray vio & multi	.35	.25
1001 A306 100fr gray brn & multi	.50	.25
1002 A306 150fr olive & multi	.75	.40
1003 A306 175fr gray bl & multi	.90	.45
1004 A306 250fr brn lake & multi	1.25	.65
1005 A306 400fr bl grn & multi	1.50	1.00
Nos. 994-1005 (12)	6.75	4.50

World Tourism Organization, 20th Anniv. A307

Designs: 150fr, Man riding donkey, vert. 350fr, Bobo-Dioulasso railroad station. 450fr, Grand Mosque, Bani. 650fr, Gazelle, map.

1995, Jan. 26 Litho. *Perf. 11½*

1006 A307 150fr multicolored	.75	.40
1007 A307 350fr multicolored	1.75	.90
1008 A307 450fr multicolored	2.25	1.10
1009 A307 650fr multicolored	3.25	1.60
Nos. 1006-1009 (4)	8.00	4.00

FESPACO '95 — A308

Motion pictures: 150fr, "Rabi," Gaston Kabore. 250fr, "Tilai," Idrissa Ouedraogo.

1995 *Perf. 13½*

1010 A308 150fr multicolored	.80	.40
1011 A308 250fr multicolored	1.40	.70

Nos. 1010-1011 exist in souvenir sheets of one. Motion pictures, cent.

Traditional Houses A308a

1995 Litho. *Perf. 13½*

1011A A308a 70fr Mossi	.30	.25
1011B A308a 100fr Kassena	.55	.25
1011C A308a 200fr Bobo	1.00	.40
1011D A308a 250fr Peulh	1.50	.60
Nos. 1011A-1011D (4)	3.35	1.50

Stars of Motion Pictures Type of 1995

Marilyn Monroe in feature films: 400fr, The Joyful Parade. 650fr, The Village Tramp. 750fr, Niagara.

1500fr, The Seven Year Itch. 3000fr, Marilyn Monroe (1926-62).

1995 Litho. *Perf. 13½*

1012-1014 A305 Set of 3	9.00	3.25

Souvenir Sheets

1015 A305 1500fr multi	8.25	4.00

Litho. & Embossed

1015A A305a 3000fr gold & multi	17.50	11.00

Nos. 1012-1014 exist in souvenir sheets of 1. No. 1015 contains one 42x51mm stamp with continuous design. No. 1015A exists in souvenir sheets of silver & multi with different designs in sheet margin.

Birds — A309

Designs: 450fr, Laniarius barbarus. 600fr, Estrilda bengala. 750fr, Euplectes afer.

1995, Apr. 5 Litho. *Perf. 11½*

1016 A309 450fr multicolored	2.25	.75
1017 A309 600fr multicolored	3.25	1.40
1018 A309 750fr multicolored	4.00	1.75
a. Souv. sheet, #1016-1018	9.75	4.50
Nos. 1016-1018 (3)	9.50	3.90

No. 1018a sold for 2000fr.

Reptiles A310

Designs: 450fr, Psammophis sibilans. 500fr, Eryx muelleri. 1500fr, Turtle.

1995, Dec. 31

1019 A310 450fr multicolored	3.00	1.00
1020 A310 500fr multicolored	3.00	1.10
1021 A310 1500fr multicolored	9.00	3.50
Nos. 1019-1021 (3)	15.00	5.60

1996 Summer Olympics, Atlanta A311

150fr, Basketball. 250fr, Baseball. 650fr, Tennis. 750fr, Table tennis.

1500fr, Equestrian event. 3000fr, Tennis, diff.

1995, Sept. 20 Litho. *Perf. 13½*

1022 A311 150fr multi	.65	.25
1023 A311 250fr multi	1.00	.30
1024 A311 650fr multi	2.50	.60
1025 A311 750fr multi	3.50	1.25
a. Souv. sheet, #1022-1025	*50.00*	—
Nos. 1022-1025 (4)	7.65	2.40

Souvenir Sheets

1026 A311 1500fr multi	7.75	7.00

Litho. & Embossed

1026A A311 3000fr gold & multi	16.00	10.00

No. 1026A also exists as a silver & multi souvenir sheet with different design in sheet margin. Both the gold & silver stamps also exist together in a souvenir sheet of 2.

Sports Figures A312

Ayrton Senna (1960-94), World Driving Champion — A313

Designs: 300fr, Juan Manuel Fangio, race car driver, 1955 Mercedes W 196. 400fr, Andre Agassi, US tennis player. 500fr, Ayrton Senna (1960-94), race car driver, McLaren MP 4/6 Honda. 1000fr, Michael Schumacher, race car driver, 1995 Benetton B 195.

1500fr, Enzo Ferrari, 412 TR, F40.

1995, Sept. 20

1027 A312 300fr multi	1.50	1.00
1028 A312 400fr multi	1.65	.50
1029 A312 500fr multi	2.25	.50
1030 A312 1000fr multi	4.25	1.00
a. Souvenir sheet of 3, #1027, 1029-1030	13.00	7.25
Nos. 1027-1030 (4)	9.65	3.00

Souvenir Sheets

1031 A312 1500fr multicolored	7.25	6.00

Litho. & Embossed

1032 A313 3000fr gold & multi	15.00	10.00

Nos. 1027-1030 exist in souvenir sheets of 1. No. 1031 contains one 55x48mm stamp.

No. 1032 also exists as a silver & multi souvenir sheet with different design in sheet margin. Both the gold and silver stamps also exist together in a souvenir sheet of 2.

For surcharge see No. 1078.

Souvenir Sheets

John Lennon (1940-1980) — A314

Designs: No. 1033, With guitar, circular pattern with name "LENNON," portrait. No. 1034, With guitar, emblem, portrait.

1995 Litho. & Embossed *Perf. 13½*

1033 A314 3000fr gold & multi	15.00	6.00
1034 A314 3000fr gold & multi	15.00	6.00

Nos. 1033-1034 each exist in souvenir sheets of silver & multi. Souvenir sheets of one gold and one silver exist in same designs and one of each design.

1995 Boy Scout Jamboree, Holland A315

Mushrooms: 150fr, Russula nigricans. 250fr, Lepiota rhacodes. 300fr, Xerocomus subtomentos. 400fr, Boletus erythropus. 500fr, Russula sanguinea. 650fr, Amanita rubescens. 750fr, Amanita vaginata. 1000fr, Geastrum sessil.

No. 1043, 1500fr, Amanita muscaria. No. 1044, 1500fr, Morchella esculenta.

1996, Feb. 20 Litho. *Perf. 13½*

1035-1042	A315	Set of 8	17.50	8.00
1041a		Sheet of 4, #1035, 1037, 1040-1041	15.00	12.50
1042a		Sheet of 4, #1036, 1038-1039, 1042	15.00	12.50

Souvenir Sheets

1043-1044	A315	Set of 2	15.00	6.00

Mushrooms — A316

Designs: 175fr, Hygrophore perroquet. 250fr, Pleurote en huitre. 300fr, Pezize (oreille d'ane). 450fr, Clavaire jolie.

1996, Jan. 24

1045-1048	A316	Set of 4	6.50	2.25
1048a		Souv. sheet, #1045-1048	16.00	2.25

Nos. 1045-1048 each exist in souv. sheets of 1.

UN, 50th Anniv. A317

Designs: 500fr, UN headquarters, New York. 1000fr, UN emblem, people, vert.

1995, Dec. 20 *Perf. 11½*

1049	A317	500fr multicolored	2.50	1.25
1050	A317	1000fr multicolored	4.50	2.25

Christmas A318

Designs: 150fr, Christmas tree, children pointing to picture of nativity scene. 450fr, Yagma Grotto. 500fr, Flight into Egypt. 1000fr, Adoration of the Magi.

1995, Dec. 18

1051	A318	150fr multicolored	.80	.40
1052	A318	450fr multicolored	2.40	1.25
1053	A318	500fr multicolored	2.75	1.40
1054	A318	1000fr multicolored	5.00	2.25
		Nos. 1051-1054 (4)	10.95	5.30

Entertainers — A319

Portraits: 150fr, Michael Jackson. 250fr, Prince. 300fr, Madonna. 400fr, Mick Jagger. 500fr, Bob Marley. 650fr, The Beatles. 750fr, Marilyn Monroe. 1000fr, Elvis Presley wearing black jacket. No. 1062, Elvis Presley, smiling. No. 1063, 1500fr, Presley, hand under chin. No. 1064, 1500fr, Stevie Wonder.

1996, May 14 Litho. *Perf. 13½*

1055	A319	150fr multi	.80	.25
1056	A319	250fr multi	1.25	.25
1057	A319	300fr multi	1.50	.35
1058	A319	400fr multi	2.00	.35
1059	A319	500fr multi	2.50	.50
1060	A319	650fr multi	2.50	.50
1061	A319	750fr multi	4.00	.60
1061A	A319	1000fr multi	5.00	.60
		Nos. 1055-1061A (8)	19.55	3.40

Souvenir Sheets

1062-1064	A319	Set of 3	*20.00*	*10.00*

Dated 1995.

Butterflies and Insects A320

100fr, Epiphora bauhiniae. 150fr, Kraussella amabile. 175fr, Charaxes epijasius. 250fr, Locusta migratoria.

1996 Litho. *Perf. 13½*

1065	A320	100fr multi, vert.	.50	.25
1066	A320	150fr multi, vert.	.85	.35
1067	A320	175fr multi, vert.	.85	.35
1068	A320	250fr multi	1.10	.50
		Nos. 1065-1068 (4)	3.30	1.45

Two souvenir sheets containing Nos. 1065, 1067 and Nos. 1066, 1068, respectively, exist.

Butterflies A321

Designs: 150fr, Morpho rega. 250fr, Hypolymnas misippus. 450fr, Pseudacraea boisduvali. 600fr, Charaxes castor. 1500fr, Antanartia delius.

1996, June 28 Litho. *Perf. 13½*

1069	A321	150fr multicolored	.80	.35
1070	A321	250fr multicolored	1.25	.55
1071	A321	450fr multicolored	2.25	1.00
1072	A321	600fr multicolored	3.25	2.75
		Nos. 1069-1072 (4)	7.55	4.65

Souvenir Sheet

1073	A321	1500fr multicolored	8.25	6.00
a.		Ovptd. in sheet margin	8.25	5.50

Overprint in silver in sheet margin of No. 1073a contains Hong Kong '97 Exhibition emblem and two line inscription in Chinese. Issued in 1997.

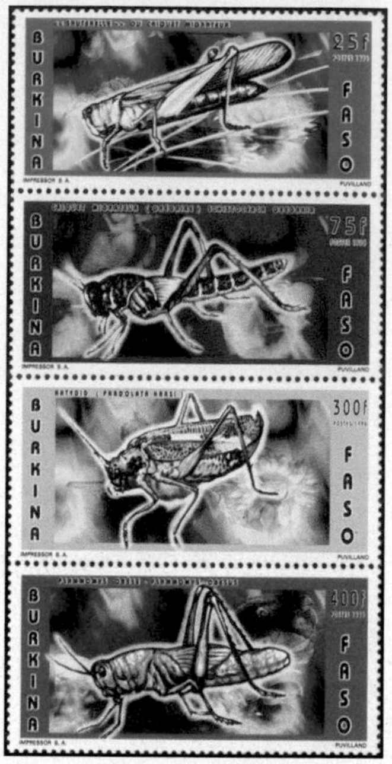

Insects — A321a

c, 25fr, Sauterelle. d, 75fr, Schistocerca gregaria. e, 300fr, Pardolata haasi. f, 400fr, Psammomys obesus.

1996, June 28 Litho. *Perf. 13½*

1073B	A321a	Strip of 4, #c.-f.	4.25	1.40

1998 World Cup Soccer Championships, France — A322

Various soccer plays.

1996 Litho. *Perf. 13*

1074	A322	50fr multi	.25	.25
1075	A322	150fr multi, vert.	.90	.25
1076	A322	250fr multi, vert.	1.10	.50
1077	A322	450fr multi, vert.	2.25	1.00
		Nos. 1074-1077 (4)	4.50	2.00

No. 1028 Ovptd. in Metallic Red

1996 Litho. *Perf. 13½*

1078	A312	400fr multicolored	*8.25*	*.80*

No. 1078 exists in souvenir sheet of 1.

Wild Cats — A323

Designs: 100fr, Panthera leo. 150fr, Acinonyx jubatus. 175fr, Lynx caracal. 250fr, Panthera pardus.

1996 *Perf. 12½x12*

1079	A323	100fr multicolored	.75	.25
1080	A323	150fr multicolored	.85	.30
1081	A323	175fr multicolored	.90	.35
1082	A323	250fr multicolored	1.50	.40
		Nos. 1079-1082 (4)	4.00	1.30

Summit of France and African Nations, Ouagadougou A323a

1996 Litho. *Perf. 11¾*

1082A	A323a	150fr pink & multi	—	*1.00*
1082B	A323a	250fr yel & multi	—	*1.50*

Orchids — A324

Various orchids.

1996, Aug. 30 Litho. *Perf. 12½x13*

1083	A324	100fr blue & multi	.75	.25
1084	A324	175fr lilac & multi	1.10	.30
1085	A324	250fr orange & multi	1.50	.40
1086	A324	300fr olive & multi	2.00	.75
		Nos. 1083-1086 (4)	5.35	1.70

UNICEF, 50th Anniv. — A324a

Design: 70fr, Child drinking near water pump, horiz. 75fr, Child reading book. 150fr, Mother nursing child. 250fr, Vaccination of child.

1996 Litho. *Perf. 11¾*

1086A	A324a	70fr multi	*4.00*	*2.00*
1086B	A324a	75fr multi	*4.00*	*2.00*
1086C	A324a	150fr multi	*4.00*	*2.00*
1086D	A324a	250fr multi	*8.00*	*5.00*
		Nos. 1086A-1086D (4)	*20.00*	*11.00*

Birds — A325

Designs: 500fr, Falco peregrinus. 750fr, Crossoptilon mantchuricum. 1000fr, Branta canadensis. 1500fr, Pelecanus crispus.

1996, June 25 *Perf. 12½x12*

1087	A325	500fr multicolored	1.90	.80
1088	A325	750fr multicolored	2.60	1.00
1089	A325	1000fr multicolored	3.25	1.50
1090	A325	1500fr multicolored	5.25	2.00
		Nos. 1087-1090 (4)	13.00	5.30

Nos. 1087-1090 each printed se-tenant with labels.

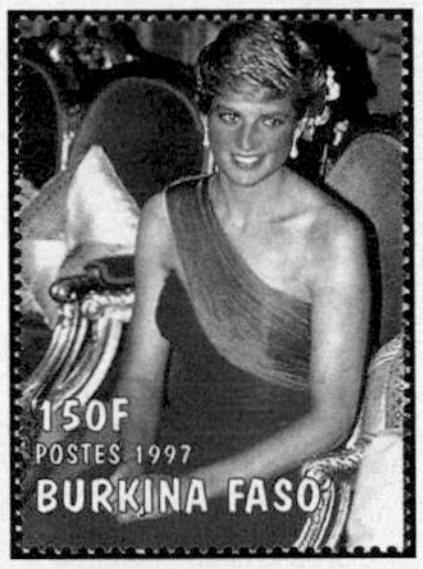

Diana, Princess of Wales (1961-97) — A325a

Various portraits, color of sheet margin: No. 1090A, blue. No. 1090K, deep pink.

No. 1090U, 2000fr, In yellow. No. 1090V, 2000fr, Wearing tiara.

Sheets of 9

1997 Litho. *Perf. 13½*

1090A A325a 150fr #Ab-Aj 6.75 2.40
1090K A325a 180fr #Kl-Kt 8.25 3.00

Souvenir Sheets

1090U-1090V A325a Set of 2 25.00 7.00

Nos. 1090U-1090V each contain one 41x46mm stamp.

See Nos. 1125U-1128.

Flowers — A325b

Design: 150fr, Cienfuegosia digitata, vert. 175fr, Costus pectabilis. 250fr, Cerathoteca sesamoides, vert. 400fr, Crotalaria retusa, vert.

Perf. 13¼x13, 13x13¼

1997, Dec. 22 Litho.

1090W A325b 150fr multi *3.50 1.50*
1090X A325b 175fr multi *4.00 1.50*
1090Y A325b 250fr multi *6.00 1.50*
1090Z A325b 400fr multi *9.50 1.50*
Nos. 1090W-1090Z (4) 23.00 6.00

A326

Various portraits, color of sheet margin: No. 1091, Pale pink. No. 1092, Pale blue. No. 1093, Pale yellow.

No. 1094, 1500fr, In white dress, serving food to child (in sheet margin). No. 1095, 1500fr, Wearing wide-brimmed hat.

Sheets of 6

1998 Litho. *Perf. 14*

1091 A326 425fr #a.-f. 11.00 4.50
1092 A326 530fr #a.-f. 13.00 5.50
1093 A326 590fr #a.-f. 15.00 6.00

Souvenir Sheets

1094-1095 A326 Set of 2 18.00 5.00

Diana, Princess of Wales (1961-97).

A327

1998 Litho. *Perf. 14*

1096 A327 260fr shown 1.80 .30

Souvenir Sheet

1097 A327 1500fr Portrait, diff. 10.00 2.50

Mother Teresa (1910-97). No. 1096 was issued in sheets of 6. Nos. 1096-1097 have birth date inscribed "1907."

Birds — A328

5fr, White-winged triller. 10fr, Golden sparrow. 100fr, American goldfinch. 170fr, Red-legged thrush. 260fr, Willow warbler. 425fr, Blue grosbeak.

No. 1104: a, Bank swallow. b, Kirtland's warbler. c, Long-tailed minivet. d, Blue-gray gnatcatcher. e, Reed-bunting. f, Black-collared apalis. g, American robin. h, Cape long-claw. i, Wood thrush.

No. 1105: a, Song sparrow. b, Dartford warbler. c, Eastern bluebird. d, Rock thrush. e, Northern mockingbird. f, Northern cardinal. g, Eurasian goldfinch. h, Varied thrush. i, Northern oriole.

No. 1106, 1500fr, Golden whistler. No. 1107, 1500fr, Barn swallow, horiz.

1998, Oct. 1 Litho. *Perf. 13½*

1098-1103 A328 Set of 6 7.00 2.00

Sheets of 9

1104 A328 260fr #a.-i. 13.50 4.50
1105 A328 425fr #a.-i. 20.00 8.00

Souvenir Sheets

1106-1107 A328 Set of 2 18.00 6.00

Butterflies and Moths A329

No. 1108: a, Arctia caja. b, Nymphalis antiopa. c, Brahmaea wallichii. d, Issoria lathonia. e, Speyeria cybele. f, Vanessa virginiensis. g, Rothchildia orizaba. h, Cethosia hypsea. i, Marpesia petreus.

No. 1109: a, Agraulis vanillae. b, Junonia coenia. c, Danaus gilippus. d, Polygonia comma. e, Anthocharis cardamines. f, Heliconius aoede. g, Atlides halesus. h, Mesosemia croseus. i, Automeris io.

No. 1110, 1500fr, Papilio xuthus. No. 1111, 1500fr, Pterourus multicaudatus. No. 1112, 1500fr, Pterourus troilus. No. 1113, 1500fr, Papilio machaon.

1998, Oct. 25 Sheets of 9

1108 A329 170fr #a.-i. 9.00 3.75
1109 A329 530fr #a.-i. 24.00 9.00

Souvenir Sheets

1110-1113 A329 Set of 4 36.00 12.00

Nos. 1110-1113 each contain one 56x42mm stamp.

Christmas — A330

Fauna, flora with Christmas items: 100fr, Tersina viridis, holly, vert. 170fr, Citherias menander, present, vert. 260fr, Chrysanthemum, reindeer, sleigh, vert. 425fr, Swallowtail butterfly, greeting card. 530fr, European bee eater, Santa Claus, snowman.

No. 1119, 1500fr, Anthemis tinctoria, sleigh. No. 1120, 1500fr, Papilio ulysses, greeting card.

1998, Dec. 1 Litho. *Perf. 14*

1114-1118 A330 Set of 5 7.75 2.75

Souvenir Sheets

1119-1120 A330 Set of 2 18.00 5.50

Handicrafts A330a

Design: No. 1120A, Wooden carved stool, vert. No. 1120B, Stool with carved heads. 50fr, Peul hat. 70fr, Basket with handle, vert. 75fr, Bronze figurine of woman milk seller and child, vert. No. 1120F, Bronze figurine of Mossi chief on horseback. No. 1120G, Dagari stool. 150fr, Basket, vert. 170fr, Wooden statue, Pasoré region, vert. 260fr, Wooden statue, Kaya region, vert.

1996-98 Litho. *Perf. 11¾*

1120A A330a 25fr multi *6.00 1.50*
1120B A330a 25fr multi *6.00 1.50*
1120C A330a 50fr multi *6.00 1.50*
1120D A330a 70fr multi *6.00 1.50*
1120E A330a 75fr multi *6.00 1.50*
1120F A330a 100fr multi *6.00 1.50*
1120G A330a 100fr multi *6.00 1.50*
1120H A330a 150fr multi *6.00 1.50*
1120I A330a 170fr multi *6.00 1.50*
1120J A330a 260fr multi *6.00 1.50*
Nos. 1120A-1120J (10) 60.00 15.00

Issued: No. 1120A, 50fr, 70fr, 75fr, No. 1120F, 150fr, 11/13/96. No. 1120B, 1120G, 170fr, 260f, 6/20/98.

34th Organization for African Unity Summit, Ouagadougou — A330b

1998, May 20 Litho. *Perf. 13x13¼*

1120K A330b 170fr red & multi *1.75 .40*
1120L A330b 425fr blue & multi *4.25 1.00*

Protected Wildlife — A330c

Designs: 170fr, Leptoptilos crumeniferus. 200fr, Acionyx jubatus. 260fr, Orycteropus afer. 530fr, Struthio camulus. 590fr, Hippopotamus amphibus, horiz.

Perf. 13¼x13, 13x13¼

1998, May 20 Litho.

1120M A330c 170fr multi *1.00 .40*
1120N A330c 200fr multi *1.00 .50*
1120O A330c 260fr multi *1.25 .60*
1120P A330c 530fr multi *2.75 1.25*
1120Q A330c 590fr multi *3.00 1.50*
Nos. 1120M-1120Q (5) 9.00 4.25

15th FESPACO Film Festival — A330d

Film: 150fr, Enfance et Jeunesse. 250fr, Etalon de Yennega.

1997, Feb. 5 Litho. *Perf. 11½x11¾*

1120R A330d 150fr multi *.90 .40*
1120S A330d 250fr multi *1.50 .50*

Wild Animals — A330e

Design: 25fr, Redunca. 50fr, Cob Defassa (Defassa waterbuck). 150fr, Bubale. 250fr, Buffle (buffalo).

Perf. 11½x11¾

1997, Mar. 20 Litho.

1120T A330e 25fr multi *.25 .25*
1120U A330e 50fr multi *— .25*
1120V A330e 150fr multi *.70 .45*
1120W A330e 250fr multi *— .75*
x. Souvenir sheet, #1120T-1120W *— 2.50*

No. 1120Wx sold for 500fr.

Heinrich Von Stephan (1831-97), Founder of UPU — A320f

1997, Apr. 8 Litho. *Perf. 11¾*

1120Y A320f 250fr multi *13.00 1.50*

Trains — A331

No. 1121: a, CDR No. 19, Ireland. b, EMD "F" Series Bo-Bo, US. c, Class 72000, France. d, Class AE 4/4 Bo-Bo, Switzerland. e, Class 277, Spain. f, ET 403 four car train, West Germany. g, Class EM2 Co-Co, UK. h, Europe Dutch Swiss Tee.

No. 1122: a, DF 4 East Wind IV Co-Co, China. b, Union Pacific Railroad, US. c, No. 3.641, Norway. d, Class GE 4/4 Bo-bo, Switzerland. e, Class GE Bo-Bo, South Africa. f, WDM-2 Co-Co, India. g, Kraus Mafeei Co-Co, US. h, RTG Four-car transit, France.

No. 1123, 1500fr, ETR 401 Pendolino, Italy. No. 1124, 1500fr, No. 12 Sarah Siddons, UK.

1998, Nov. 10 Sheets of 8

1121 A331 170fr #a.-h. 8.00 3.00
1122 A331 425fr #a.-h. 21.00 8.00

Souvenir Sheets

1123-1124 A331 Set of 2 18.00 7.50

Intl. Fund for Agricultural Development, 20th Anniv. — A331a

Design: 150fr, Restoration of degraded soils. 400fr, "20," wheat stalk.

Perf. 13½x13¼

1998, Mar. 20 Litho.

1124A A331a 150fr multi *.70 .30*
1125 A331a 400fr multi *1.75 .80*

Masks — A331b

Design: 75fr, Buffalo mask, vert. 150fr, Duck mask. 200fr, Kob mask. 250fr, Mask with panels, vert.

1997, May 20 Litho. *Perf. 13¼*

1125A	A331b	75fr multi		6.50	1.50
1125B	A331b	150fr multi		13.00	2.00
1125C	A331b	200fr multi		18.00	3.00
1125D	A331b	250fr multi		22.50	3.00
	Nos. 1125A-1125D (4)			*60.00*	*9.50*

Ceramics — A331c

Design: 100fr, Millet container. 150fr, Decorated covered baking pot. 250fr, Beer mug. 450fr, Vase.

Perf. 11½x11¾

1997, Sept. 11 Litho.

1125E	A331c	100fr multi	—	.50
1125F	A331c	150fr multi	—	.75
1125G	A331c	250fr multi	—	1.00
1125H	A331c	450fr multi	*2.75*	*1.50*

Fish — A331d

Design: 100fr, Aplocheiolichthys pfaffi. 150fr, Fundulosoma thierryi. 175fr, Sarotherodon galilaeus. 250fr, Epiplatys spilargyreius.

1997, Nov. 20 Litho. *Perf. 13¼*

1125I	A331d	100fr multi	*.45*	*.25*
1125J	A331d	150fr multi	—	—
1125K	A331d	175fr multi		—
1125L	A331d	250fr multi		—

African Soccer Championships — A331e

Design: 175fr, Goalie making save. 150fr, Four players. 250fr, Soccer player, stylized person holding food bowl, vert. 500fr, Soccer ball, trophy, map of Africa, vert.

Perf. 13x13¼, 13¼x13

1998, Jan. 20 Litho.

1125M	A331e	150fr multi	*.70*	*.30*
1125N	A331e	175fr multi	*.85*	*.30*
1125O	A331e	250fr multi		—
1125P	A331e	500fr multi		—

No. 1125P is dated 1997.

Traditional Costumes — A331f

Design: 150fr, Peulh (Togore). 175fr, Mossi (Banague). 250fr, Peulh (Boodi). 450fr, Bissa (Gangadruku).

1998, Feb. 20 Litho. *Perf. 13½x13*

1125Q	A331f	150fr multi	*3.00*	*.25*
1125R	A331f	175fr multi	4.00	.50
1125S	A331f	250fr multi	*5.00*	*.75*
1125T	A331f	450fr multi	*6.00*	*1.00*
	Nos. 1125Q-1125T (4)		*18.00*	*2.50*

Diana, Princess of Wales Type

Designs: 260fr, Diana wearing tiara. 425fr, Diana in white blouse. 590fr, Diana with Pope John Paul II. No. 1127A: various portraits, color of sheet margin is violet.

1500fr, Diana speaking, American Red Cross emblem in sheet margin. 2000fr, Diana wearing Japanese kimono.

1997 Litho. *Perf. 13½*

1125U	A325a	260fr multi		—
1126	A325a	425fr multi	1.60	1.60
1127	A325a	590fr multi	2.25	1.10
		Sheet of 9		
1127A	A325a	180fr #b-j	6.00	3.00
		Souvenir Sheets		
1127K	A325a	1500fr multi	11.00	2.75
1128	A325a	2000fr multi	12.00	3.75

No. 1127 was issued in sheets of 9. No. 1127K contains one 41x46mm stamp.

Airplanes A332

No. 1129: a, Sukhoi Su-24. b, Yakovlev Yak-38. c, Tupolev Blackjack. d, Antonov An-26. e, Antonov An-22 Anteus. f, Antonov An-124.

1000fr, Ilyushin Il-76T.

1999, Sept. 8 Litho. *Perf. 14*

1129	A332	425fr Sheet of 6, #a.-f.	12.50	6.00
		Souvenir Sheet		
1130	A332	1000fr multicolored	6.00	4.00

No. 1130 contains one 57x43mm stamp.

Ships A333

No. 1131: a, Portland. b, Goethe. c, Fulton.

No. 1132: a, CSS Nashville. b, Cutty Sark. c, Brilliant. d, Eagle. e, Red Jacket. f, USS Columbia. g, HMS Rose. h, Resolution. i, 1000-ton paquebot. j, Mayflower.

No. 1133: a, USS Tennessee. b, HMS Alacrity. c, Bismarck. d, Yamoto. e, Aurora. f, Iowa class battleship. g, Liberty Ship. h, F209. i, Star. j, Big Eagle.

Each 1000fr: No. 1134, Batavia. No. 1135, Grand Voilier.

1999, Sept. 8 Sheets of 3 and 10

1131	A333	170fr #a.-c.	2.75	1.75
1132	A333	100fr #a.-j.	5.75	3.25
1133	A333	200fr #a.-j.	12.50	6.50
		Souvenir Sheets		
1134-1135	A333	Set of 2	12.00	6.50

Domesticated Animals — A334

5fr, Tabby cat, vert. 10fr, Chinchilla. 20fr, Yorkshire terriers. 25fr, Cocker spaniels.

No. 1140, vert.: a, Afghan hound. b, Fox terrier. c, Pug. d, Dalmatian. e, Boston terrier. f, Cocker spaniel.

No. 1141: a, American wirehaired. b, Tabby. c, Blue Burmese. d, Abyssinian. e, Lilac Burmese. f, Siamese.

No. 1142, 1000fr, Persian. No. 1143, 1000fr, Japanese bobtail, vert. No. 1144, 1000fr, Labrador retriever, vert. No. 1145, 1000fr, Labrador retrievers, vert.

1999, Oct. 4

1136-1139	A334	Set of 4	1.25	.80
		Sheets of 6		
1140	A334	260fr #a.-f.	7.75	3.00
1141	A334	530fr #a.-f.	16.00	10.00
		Souvenir Sheets		
1142-1145	A334	Set of 4	22.00	12.00

Domesticated Animals — A335

No. 1146 — Horses: a, Gelderlander. b, Trait lourd. c, Vladimir. d, Percheron. e, Sumba. f, Dartmoor.

No. 1147 — Dogs: a, French bulldog. b, Bernese. c, Griffon. d, King Charles spaniel. e, Spitz. f, Yorkshire terrier.

No. 1148 — Cats: a, American wirehaired. b, Japanese bobtail. c, Himalayan. d, LaPerm. e, Lilac Siamese colorpoint. f, Norwegian forest cat.

No. 1149, 1000fr, Shetland pony, vert. No. 1150, 1000fr, Basset hound, vert. No. 1151, 1000fr, Japanese bobtail, diff., vert.

1999, Oct. 4 Sheets of 6

1146	A335	170fr #a.-f.	5.25	3.50
1147	A335	425fr #a.-f.	11.00	9.00
1148	A335	590fr #a.-f.	15.00	13.00
		Souvenir Sheets		
1149-1151	A335	Set of 3	16.50	9.00

Fight Against Hunger — A337

1999, Dec. Litho. *Perf. 14*

1157	A337	350fr multi	1.75	1.00

Issued in sheets of 5.

FESPACO '99 Film Festival A338

Award winning film: 170fr, Tilai, by Idrissa Ouédraogo. 260fr, Map of Africa, camera, clapper board, vert. 425fr, Buud Yam, by Gaston Kaboré.

1999 Litho. *Perf. 13x13¼, 13¼x13*

1158	A338	170fr multi	*.70*	*.30*
1159	A338	260fr multi	*1.25*	*.45*
1159A	A338	425fr multi	*2.00*	*.75*

Issued: 1159A, 2/22/99.

Council of the Entente, 40th Anniv. A338a

Denomination color: 170fr, Black. 260fr, Green.

1999, May 5 Litho. *Perf. 13x13¼*

1160-1161	A338a	Set of 2	*1.90*	*.75*

Lions A338b

Panel colors: 170fr, blue; 260fr, red; 425fr, green; 530fr, orange; 590fr, purple.

1999, May 26 Litho. *Perf. 13x13¼*

1161A-1161E	A338b	Set of 5	*28.00*	*3.50*

Philex France 99.

Orchids — A339

No. 1162, each 260fr: a, Angraecum orchid cape. b, Disa kirstenbosck pride. c, Disa blackii. d, Angraecum long icalear. e, Bulbophyllum falcatum. f, Phragmipedium schlimii (two flowers). g, Polystachya affinis. h, Jumellea sagittata (with leaves).

No. 1163, each 260fr: a, Angraecum sesquipedale. b, Oeceoclades maculata. c, Ancistrochilus childianus. d, Polystachyabella. e, Bulbophyllum lepidum. f, Vanilla imperialis. g, Tridactyle tridactylites. h, Eulophia guineensis.

No. 1164, each 260fr: a, Ansellia africana. b, Aerangis luteo-alba. c, Disa uniflora. d, Angraecum distichum. e, Bulbophyllum falcatum. f, Phragmepedium schlimii (pink flower). g, Polystachya affinis. h, Jumellea sagittata (without leaves).

No. 1165, 1500fr, Disa tripetaloides, horiz. No. 1166, 1500fr, Liparis guineensis, horiz. No. 1167, 1500fr, Bolusiella talbotii, horiz.

2000, Jan. 10 Litho. *Perf. 14*

Sheets of 8, #a.-h.

1162-1164	A339	Set of 3	35.00	20.00
		Souvenir Sheets		
1165-1167	A339	Set of 3	27.50	16.00

Space Exploration A340

No. 1168: a, Robert H. Goddard and 1926 rocket. b, Sputnik 1. c, X-15. d, Chinese, inventors of rockets. e, V-2. f, Explorer 1.

No. 1169: a, Vostok 1. b, Friendship 7. c, Soyuz 1. d, Freedom 7. e, Gemini 4. f, Apollo 7.

No. 1170, horiz.: a, Gemini 8. b, Agena target vehicle. c, Soyuz 11. d, Salyut 1. e, Apollo 18. f, Soyuz 19.

No. 1171, 1500fr, Tacsat satellite. No. 1172, 1500fr, Hubble Space Telescope. No. 1173, 1500fr, Viking Lander, horiz.

2000, Jan. 10 Sheets of 6

1168	A340	350fr #a.-f.	12.50	7.50
1169	A340	425fr #a.-f.	14.50	9.00
1170	A340	530fr #a.-f.	19.00	11.00
		Souvenir Sheets		
1171-1173	A340	Set of 3	18.00	13.00

No. 1173 contains one 57x42mm stamp.

Peter Pan — A341

Designs: a, 75fr, Fairy, red flowers. b, 75fr, Parrot. c, 75fr, Moon, Wendy, Michael, John. d, 75fr, White flower. e, 80fr, Fairy, pink flower. f, 80fr, Butterflies. g, 80fr, Peter Pan. h, 80fr, Fairy. i, 90fr, Red flower. j, 90fr, Butterflies. k, 90fr, Egret. l, 90fr, White flower. m, 100fr, Mermaid. n, 100fr, Pirate ship, crocodile's tail. o, 100fr, Crocodile's head. p, 100fr, Captain Hook.

2000, Jan. 10 *Perf. 12¼*

1174	A341	Sheet of 16, #a.-p.	8.25	4.25

2000 Summer Olympics, Sydney — A343

No. 1191: a, Hannes Kohlemainen. b, Runner. c, US flag, Fulton County Stadium, Atlanta. d, Discus thrower.

2000, Nov. 12 Litho. *Perf. 14*

1191	A343	350fr Sheet of 4, #a-d	8.00	3.75

First Zeppelin Flight, Cent. — A344

No. 1192, 350fr: a, LZ-1, b, LZ-2 (dark gray at left). c, LZ-2 (white at left) d, LZ-5. e, LZ-8. f, LZ-7.

No. 1193, 350fr: a, LZ-9. b, LZ-10. c, LZ-11. d, LZ-127. e, LZ-129. f, LZ-130.

No. 1194, 1500fr, LZ-1. No. 1195, 1500fr, LZ-4.

2000, Nov. 12 Sheets of 6, #a-f

1192-1193	A344	Set of 2	23.00	11.00

Souvenir Sheets

1194-1195	A344	Set of 2	18.00	8.00

Berlin Film Festival, 50th Anniv. — A345

No. 1196: a, Le Grand Blond Avec Une Chaussure Noire. b Ruy Guerra. c, Mario Monicelli. d, Mudhur Jaffrey. e, Orökbefogadás. f, Palermo Oder Wolfsburg.

2000, Nov. 12 Litho. *Perf. 14*

Sheet of 6

1196	A345	420fr #a-f	14.00	7.00

Souvenir Sheet

1197	A345	1500fr Platoon	9.25	4.50

Souvenir Sheets

Public Railways, 175th Anniv. — A346

No. 1198: a, George Stephenson, Locomotion No. 1. b, Stourbridge Lion.

No. 1199: a, George Stephenson, Brusselton inclined plane. b, Robert Stephenson, turnpike crossing near Darlington. c, Locomotive built by George Stephenson. d, Experiment passenger coach built by Robert Stephenson.

2000, Nov. 12 Sheets of 2 and 4

1198	A346	550fr #a-b	7.00	3.25
1199	A346	800fr #a-d	17.00	9.25

Fruits — A347

95fr, Parkia biglobosa. 100fr, Baobab. 170fr, Tamarind, horiz. 425fr, Vitellaria paradoxa.

2000 Litho. *Perf. 14¾*

1200	A347	95fr multicolored	2.75	.25
1201	A347	100fr multicolored	2.75	.25
1202	A347	170fr multicolored	5.00	.30
1203	A347	425fr multicolored	12.00	.60
		Nos. 1200-1203 (4)	22.50	1.40

Elephants A348

2000, Mar. 22 Litho. *Perf. 14¾*

1204	A348	200fr Facing left	9.00	1.00
1205	A348	425fr multi, vert.	19.00	1.25
1206	A348	500fr Facing right	26.00	1.50
		Nos. 1204-1206 (3)	54.00	3.75

National Culture Week — A349

Designs: 120fr, Sidari Troupe, Sidéradougou, vert. 130fr, Dancer and drummer, vert. 260fr, Dancer and xylophone player, vert. 425fr, Dancers and drummer. 530fr, Musicians. 590fr, Dancers.

2000 Litho. *Perf. 13½x13, 13x13½*

1207	A349	120fr multi	3.00	.50
1208	A349	130fr multi	3.00	.50
1209	A349	260fr multi	6.50	1.00
1210	A349	425fr multi	10.00	1.50
1211	A349	530fr multi	12.50	2.00
1212	A349	590fr multi	14.00	2.00
		Nos. 1207-1212 (6)	49.00	7.50

Molluscs and Crustaceans A350

Designs: 30fr, Limnaea natalensis. 170fr, Caelastura teretiscula. 250fr, Achatina achatina. 260fr, Biomphalaria pfeifferi. 425fr, Potamonautes macleay.

2000, Apr. 28 Litho. *Perf. 13x13¼*

1213	A350	30fr multi	.65	.25
1214	A350	170fr multi	6.00	.40
1215	A350	250fr multi	9.00	.75
1216	A350	260fr multi	9.50	.75
1217	A350	425fr multi	15.00	1.00
		Nos. 1213-1217 (5)	40.15	3.15

Belem-Yegre Museum — A351

Designs: 170fr, Dougui mask, vert. 260fr, Main entrance. 425fr, Monuments. 530fr, Tombstone, vert.

2000 Litho. *Perf. 15x14¾, 14¾x15*

1218	A351	170fr multi	3.75	.50
1219	A351	260fr multi	6.00	.60
1220	A351	425fr multi	10.00	1.00
1221	A351	530fr multi	12.50	1.25
		Nos. 1218-1221 (4)	32.25	3.35

Items in National Museum — A352

Designs: 170fr, Kurumba statuettes. 260fr, Mossi statuette. 425fr, Loulouka pot. 530fr, Mossi du Kourwéogo statuette. 590fr, San statuette.

2001 Litho. *Perf. 13¼x13*

1222	A352	170fr multi	4.00	.40
1223	A352	260fr multi	7.00	.50
1224	A352	425fr multi	10.00	1.00
1224A	A352	530fr multi	13.00	1.25
1225	A352	590fr multi	15.00	1.75
		Nos. 1222-1225 (5)	49.00	4.90

Birds A353

Designs: 25fr, Anaplectes rubriceps. 50fr, Dendrocygna viduata. 95fr, Ploceus cucullatus, vert. 170fr, Bubulcus ibis, vert. 425fr, Campethera masculosa, vert. 590fr, Francolinus bicalcaratus, vert.

2001 Litho. *Perf. 13x13¼, 13¼x13*

1226	A353	25fr multi	1.25	.25
1227	A353	50fr multi	1.75	.25
1227A	A353	95fr multi	3.75	.25
1228	A353	170fr multi	6.75	.50
1228A	A353	425fr multi	17.50	1.00
1229	A353	590fr multi	24.00	1.50
		Nos. 1226-1229 (6)	55.00	3.75

Tourism A354

Designs: 170fr, Karfiguéla Waterfall, vert. 260fr, Sand dune, Oursi. 425fr, Laongo granite sculptures, vert. 530fr, Decorated homes, Tiébélé. 590fr, Sindou Peaks.

2001 Litho. *Perf. 13¼x13, 13x13¼*

1230	A354	170fr multi	3.75	.50
1231	A354	260fr multi	7.00	.75
1232	A354	425fr multi	10.00	1.00
1233	A354	530fr multi	12.00	1.25
1234	A354	590fr multi	14.00	1.50
		Nos. 1230-1234 (5)	46.75	5.00

Fish A355

Designs: 25fr, Gymnarchus niloticus. 40fr, Bagrus docmak. 50fr, Hemisynedontis membranenceus. 170fr, Oreochromis niloticus niloticus. 425fr, Lates niloticus. 530fr, Heterotis niloticus.

2001 Litho. *Perf. 13x13½*

1235	A355	25fr multi	1.40	.50
1236	A355	40fr multi	1.75	.75
1237	A355	50fr multi	1.90	1.00
1238	A355	170fr multi	6.50	1.25
1239	A355	425fr multi	17.00	1.50
1240	A355	530fr multi	21.00	2.00
		Nos. 1235-1240 (6)	49.55	7.00

Insects A356

Designs: 5fr, Helicoverpa armigera. 10fr, Poekilocerus bufonius hieroglyphicus. 20fr, Diopsis thoracica. 100fr, Psalydolitta sp. 170fr, Ptinus fur, vert. 200fr, Bruchidius atralineatus, vert. 260fr, Dysdercus sp., vert. 500fr, Lygus lineolaris. 1000fr, Doryphora. 1500fr, Acantbosceiides obtectus say, vert.

Perf. 13x13½, 13½x13

2002, Apr. 4 Litho.

1241	A356	5fr multi	1.00	.25
1242	A356	10fr multi	1.00	.25
1243	A356	20fr multi	1.00	.25
1244	A356	100fr multi	3.00	.75
1245	A356	170fr multi	3.50	.80
1246	A356	200fr multi	4.00	1.00
1247	A356	260fr multi	5.00	1.25
1248	A356	500fr multi	10.00	2.50
1249	A356	1000fr multi	20.00	5.00
1250	A356	1500fr multi	24.00	2.25
		Nos. 1241-1250 (10)	72.50	14.30

Crafts — A357

Design: 100fr, Long-headed Pouni mask. 170fr, Figurine of Mossi tom-tom player. 425fr, Calao Pouni mask, horiz.

2003, June 30 Litho. *Perf. 13½x13*

1251	A357	100fr multi	2.50	.75
1252	A357	170fr multi	4.00	1.00

Perf. 13x13½

1253	A357	425fr multi	13.00	3.50

Intl. Fund for Agricultural Development, 25th Anniv. — A358

2003, Sept. 20 Litho. *Perf. 13x13¼*

1254	A358	170fr multi	*5.00*	*1.25*

Burkina Faso - Taiwan Cooperation — A359

Designs: 5fr, 10fr, 20fr, 100fr, 170fr, Kou Valley rice farm. 200fr, 260fr, 425fr, 530fr, 590fr, Bagré Aqueduct.

2003, Oct. 10 Litho. *Perf. 13x13½*

Frame Color

1255	A359	5fr red	.50	.25
1256	A359	10fr blue	.50	.25
1257	A359	20fr brown	.50	.25
1258	A359	100fr blue	1.75	.25
1259	A359	170fr black	2.75	.25
1260	A359	200fr dark red	3.50	.55
1261	A359	260fr blue	4.50	.60
1262	A359	425fr brown	8.00	1.00
1263	A359	530fr blue	9.50	1.25
1264	A359	590fr black	11.00	1.50
		Nos. 1255-1264 (10)	42.50	6.15

Musical Instruments A360

Design: 30fr, Bwaba balaphone, horiz. 40fr, Nouni flute. 75fr, Mossi flute. 150fr, Mossi funerary drum, horiz.

2004, Mar. 27 Litho. *Perf. 13½x13*

1265	A360	30fr multi	1.00	1.00
1266	A360	40fr multi	1.50	1.50
1267	A360	75fr multi	2.00	2.00
1268	A360	150fr multi	3.00	3.00
		Nos. 1265-1268 (4)	7.50	7.50

National Pardon Day — A361

2004, Mar. 30 Litho. *Perf. 13¼x13*

1269	A361	170fr tan & multi	2.00	2.00
1270	A361	530fr red & multi	5.00	5.00

Tenth Francophone Summit, Ouagadougou A362

2004, Nov. 1 Litho. *Perf. 13½x13*

1271	A362	425fr lil, brn & multi	*3.25*	*2.75*
1272	A362	530fr red, grn & multi	*4.00*	*3.50*
1273	A362	590fr blue & multi	*5.00*	*4.50*
		Nos. 1271-1273 (3)	*12.25*	*10.75*

Mediator of Faso, 10th Anniv. — A363

2005, Jan. 20 Litho. *Perf. 13½x13*

1274	A363	100fr grn & multi	*1.00*	*1.00*
1275	A363	200fr grn & multi	*2.00*	*2.00*
1276	A363	330fr blue & multi	*3.50*	*3.50*
1277	A363	690fr blue & multi	*7.00*	*7.00*
		Nos. 1274-1277 (4)	13.50	13.50

Hoes — A363a

Designs: 5p, Peulh hoe, Dou, vert. 10fr, Dagari hoe, eastern region. 30fr, Dagari hoe. 70fr, Mossi plateau hoe. 100fr, Mossi hoe, Zitenga, horiz.

Perf. 13½x13, 13x13½

2005, Nov. 16 Litho.

1276B	A363a	5fr multi	*3.25*	*1.00*
1276C	A363a	10fr multi	*3.25*	*1.00*
1276D	A363a	30fr multi	*3.25*	*1.00*
1276E	A363a	70fr multi	*3.25*	*1.00*
1276F	A363a	100fr multi	*3.25*	*1.00*
		Nos. 1276B-1276F (5)	*16.25*	*5.00*

Hats — A363b

Designs: 265fr, Peulh du Seno hat, horiz. 300fr, Mossi chief's hat. 500fr, Yatenga banded hat. 690fr, Crooked Yatenga hat.

2005, Nov. 16 Litho. *Perf. 13½x13*

1276G	A363b	265fr multi	*2.50*	*1.50*
1276H	A363b	300fr multi	*3.00*	*1.50*
1276I	A363b	500fr multi	*4.50*	*1.50*
1276J	A363b	690fr multi	*6.75*	*1.50*
		Nos. 1276G-1276J (4)	*16.75*	*6.00*

See Nos. 1285-1291.

Léopold Sédar Senghor (1906-2001), First President of Senegal — A364

2006, Mar. 2 Litho. *Perf. 13x13½*

1277	A364	100fr red & multi	*.75*	*.75*
1278	A364	200fr bl grn & multi	*1.50*	*1.50*
1279	A364	1000fr pur & multi	*7.50*	*7.50*
		Nos. 1277-1279 (3)	*9.75*	*9.75*

Cooperation Between Burkina Faso and Germany — A365

2006 Litho. *Perf. 13x13¼*

1280	A365	200fr multi	*2.50*	*2.50*

Burkina EMS Chronopost, 5th Anniv. — A366

2006, June 9 Litho. *Perf. 13½x13*

1281	A366	200fr org & multi	*2.00*	*2.00*
1282	A366	330fr red brn & multi	*3.00*	*3.00*
1283	A366	690fr red vio & multi	*5.00*	*5.00*

Hats Type of 2005

Design: 5fr, 10fr, 20fr, 40fr, 50fr, 75fr, 1000fr, 1500fr, Peulh du Seno hat, horiz.

2006, Nov. 6 Litho. *Perf. 13x13¼*

1284	A363b	5fr rose & multi	*1.00*	*1.00*
1285	A363b	10fr lt blue & multi	*1.00*	*1.00*
1286	A363b	20fr org & multi	*1.00*	*1.00*
1287	A363b	40fr blue & multi	*1.00*	*1.00*
1288	A363b	50fr green & multi	*1.00*	*1.00*
1289	A363b	75fr lt blue & multi	*1.25*	*1.25*
1290	A363b	1000fr ol & multi	*10.00*	*10.00*
1291	A363b	1500fr yel brn & multi	*15.00*	*15.00*
		Nos. 1284-1291 (8)	31.25	31.25

Dated 2006.

Lions International, 90th Anniv. — A367

Denomination color: 330fr, Blue; 690fr, Pink.

2007 Litho. *Perf. 13¼*

1292	A367	330fr multi	*3.00*	*3.00*
1293	A367	690fr multi	*7.00*	*7.00*

Wrestling A368

Designs: 5fr, Parade of wrestlers. 30fr, Wrestlers in attack position. 200fr, Wrestlers grabbing each other's thighs, vert. 690fr, Wrestler grabbing opponent's leg.

2008, Mar. 17 Litho. *Perf. 13x13¼*

1294	A368	5fr multi	*.25*	*.25*
1295	A368	30fr multi	*.30*	*.25*
1296	A368	200fr multi	*2.00*	*.50*
1297	A368	690fr multi	*6.50*	*2.00*
		Nos. 1294-1297 (4)	*9.05*	*3.00*

Safari Animals and Shelters A369

Designs: 10fr, Nerwaya Safari hut, lion. 25fr, Express Safari hut, duck. 75fr, Sahel shelter, bird, vert. 100fr, Safari Chasse hut, leopard.

Perf. 13x13¼, 13¼x13

2008, June 6 Litho.

1298	A369	10fr multi	*1.25*	*1.00*
1299	A369	25fr multi	*1.50*	*1.00*
1300	A369	75fr multi	*3.25*	*1.50*
1301	A369	100fr multi	*4.50*	*2.00*
1302	A369	200fr multi	*9.50*	*4.00*
		Nos. 1298-1302 (5)	*20.00*	*9.50*

Dances — A370

Designs: 50fr, Bissa dance. 200fr, Gourmatché dance. 500fr, Mossi Kiegba dance. 690fr, Kassena dance.

2008, July 1 Litho. *Perf. 13¼x13*

1303	A370	50fr multi	*.35*	*.25*
1304	A370	200fr multi	*1.40*	*.50*
1305	A370	500fr multi	*3.50*	*1.50*
1306	A370	690fr multi	*5.00*	*1.75*
		Nos. 1303-1306 (4)	*10.25*	*4.00*

Burkina Faso Federation of Associations for Promotion of the Handicapped — A371

2008, Oct. 31 Litho. *Perf. 13x13¼*

1307	A371	200fr blue & multi	*3.00*	*1.00*
1308	A371	690fr green & multi	*12.00*	*3.00*

Independence, 48th Anniv. — A372

2008, Dec. 5 Litho. *Perf. 13¼x13*

1309	A372	200fr green & multi	*4.00*	*1.00*
1310	A372	690fr blue & multi	*16.00*	*4.00*

FESPACO 2009 Film Festival A373

Designs: 690fr, Sembene Ousmane (1923-2007), writer and film director. 1000fr, 40th anniversary emblem.

2009, Feb. 20 *Perf. 13x13¼*

Granite Paper

1311-1312	A373	Set of 2	*13.00*	*13.00*

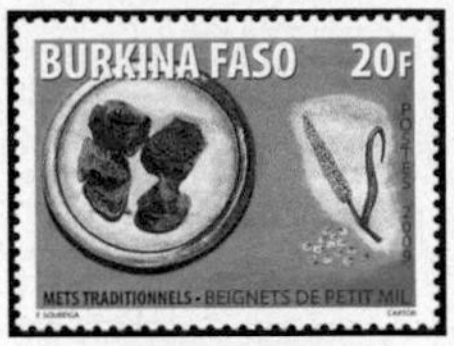

Traditional Foods A374

Designs: 20fr, Millet fritters. 300fr, Tô de mais. 1500fr, Bean fritters.

2009 Litho. Granite Paper
1313-1315 A374 Set of 3 *15.00 7.50*

Agricultural Work A375

Designs: 200fr, Planting. 690fr, Hoeing. 1000fr, Millet harvesting.

2009 Litho. *Perf. 13x13¼*
1316-1318 A375 Set of 3 *20.00 10.00*

Traditional Occupations — A376

Designs: 40fr, Blacksmith. 200fr, Weaver. 1500fr, Cotton spinner.

2009 Litho. *Perf. 13x13¼*
Granite Paper
1319-1321 A376 Set of 3 *20.00 10.00*

Loropéno Ruins UNESCO World Heritage Site A377

Designs: 200fr, Wall. 500fr, Wall and overgrown foliage. 690fr, Wall, vert.

2009 Litho. *Perf. 13x13¼*
1322 A377 200fr multi — —
1323 A377 500fr multi —

Perf. 13¼x13
1324 A377 690fr multi — —

Transportation — A378

Designs: 30fr, Woman on bicycle. 70fr, Man on donkey cart.

2010, Aug. 16 Litho. *Perf. 13x13¼*
1325-1326 A378 Set of 2 *5.00 2.50*

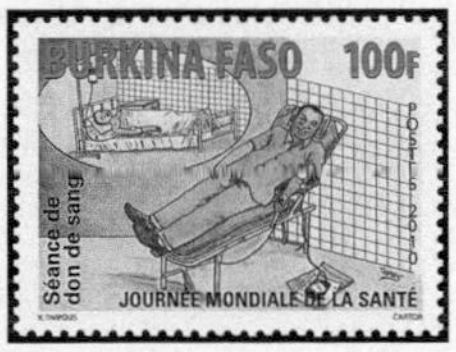

World Health Day A379

Designs: 100fr, Blood donation. 160fr, Campaign against malaria.

2010, Oct. 15 Granite Paper
1327-1328 A379 Set of 2 *7.00 2.50*

Domesticated Animals — A381

Designs: 100fr, Donkey. 265fr, Horse. 300fr, Dromedary.

2011, Feb. 1 Litho. *Perf. 13x13¼*
1331-1333 A381 Set of 3 3.50 1.75

Dated 2010.

Campaign Against AIDS, 30th Anniv. A382

Designs: 200fr, Man, woman, letter carrier with Post Office AIDS campaign poster. 690fr, People in post office, Post Office AIDS campaign poster.

2011, Aug. 8
1334-1335 A382 Set of 2 5.25 2.75

Poultry A383

Designs: 100fr, Ducks (canard). 160fr, Turkeys (dindon). 265fr, Rooster and hen (coq).

2011, Oct. 12
1336-1338 A383 Set of 3 3.50 1.75

Vegetable Cultivation A384

Designs: 30fr, Onions. 70fr, Cabbages. 100fr, Carrots.

2011, Nov. 7
1339-1341 A384 Set of 3 3.50 1.75

Cooperation Between Burkina Faso and Germany, 50th Anniv. — A385

Background color: 200fr, Blue. 690fr, Yellow orange.

2011, Dec. 23 *Perf. 14½x14¼*
1342-1343 A385 Set of 2 7.00 3.50

National Assembly, 20th Anniv. A386

Background color: 200fr, Blue. 690fr, Brown.

2012, Apr. 20 Litho. *Perf. 13x13¼*
1344-1345 A386 Set of 2 5.50 3.00

Everyday Life in Ouagadougou — A387

Designs: 100fr, Street traffic. 330fr, Roadside restaurant.

2012, Oct. 16 Litho. *Perf. 13x13¼*
1346-1347 A387 Set of 2 3.50 3.50

Cooking Implements A388

Designs: 500fr, Portable hearth for cooking pancakes. 690fr, Hearth for preparing millet beer.

2012, Nov. 30 Litho. *Perf. 13x13¼*
1348-1349 A388 Set of 2 10.00 10.00

Riches of the Forest A389

Designs: 100fr, Jujubes. 200fr, Detarium microcarpa. 500fr, Karité (shea nuts). 1500fr, Plums.

2012, Nov. 30 Litho. *Perf. 13x13¼*
1350-1353 A389 Set of 4 19.50 19.50

Village Life A390

Designs: 200fr, Women at water pump. 330fr, Women cooking. 690fr, Women at grain mill. 1000fr, Women crushing millet.

2012, Dec. 13 Litho. *Perf. 13x13¼*
1354-1357 A390 Set of 4 19.00 19.00

Food Storage Containers A391

Designs: 200fr, Gourd. 690fr, Canari (pot).

2012, Dec. 18 Litho. *Perf. 13x13¼*
1358-1359 A391 Set of 2 7.50 7.50

Environmental Protection — A392

Designs: 5fr, Collection of plastic bags. 10fr, Planting of trees. 20fr, Campaign against excessive tree cutting. 50fr, Campaign against brushfires.

2013, Sept. 19 Litho. *Perf. 13x13¼*
1360-1363 A392 Set of 4 — —

Monuments A393

Designs: 200fr, Place de la Nation, Ouagadougou. 1000fr, Place de la Femme, Bobo-Dioulasso.

2013, Oct. 1 Litho. *Perf. 13x13¼*
1364-1365 A393 Set of 2 *15.00 15.00*

Villagers Around Fire A395

2013, Oct. 9 Litho. *Perf. 13x13¼*
1367 A395 40fr multi —

An additional stamp was issued in this set. The editors would like to examine any example of it.

Drums A395

Design: 50fr, Tambour. 200fr, Tambour d'aisselle. 690fr, Tam-tam.

2013, Nov. 11 Litho. *Perf. 13x13¼*
1368 A395 50fr multi — —
1369 A395 200fr multi — —
1370 A395 690fr multi —

Traditional Communication — A396

2013, Nov. 11 Litho. *Perf. 13x13¼*
1371 A396 330fr multi *3.00 3.00*

St. Camillus de Lellis (1550-1614), Patron Saint of the Sick — A397

Background color: 200fr, White. 690fr, Brown.

Perf. 14¼x14½
2014, Aug. 10 Litho.
1372-1373 A397 Set of 2 *12.00 4.25*

Postman on Bicycle A398

2014, Aug. 10 Litho. *Perf. 13x13¼*
1374 A398 690fr multi *8.75 3.00*

Pres. Saye Zerbo (1932-2013), and Flag of Upper Volta — A399

Perf. 14¼x14½
2014, Aug. 10 Litho.
1375 A399 200fr multi *5.75 3.00*

National Coat of Arms — A400

Perf. 14½x14¼
2014, Aug. 10 Litho.
1376 A400 690fr multi *7.00 2.50*

United Nations, 70th Anniv. A401

2015, Oct. 24 Litho. *Perf. 13x13¼*
1377 A401 690fr multi *7.00 3.00*

Economic Community of West African States, 40th Anniv. A402

2015, Dec. 17 Litho. *Perf. 13x13¼*
1378 A402 200fr multi *5.00 —*

African Philatelic Hub — A403

2016, Sept. 23 Litho. *Perf. 13¼x13*
1379 A403 690fr multi *10.00 10.00*

Old Tenkodogo Post Office A404

2016, Oct. 5 Litho. *Perf. 13x13¼*
1380 A404 200fr multi *4.00 —*

Tour de Faso Bicycle Race A405

2016, Oct. 27 Litho. *Perf. 13x13¼*
1381 A405 200fr multi *— —*

Bomavé Konate, Sculptor — A406

2016, Dec. 2 Litho. *Perf. 13¼x13*
1382 A406 690fr multi *11.00 4.00*

Gnassogoni Troglodyte Village — A407

2016, Dec. 17 Litho. *Perf. 13¼x13*
1383 A407 500fr multi *11.00 4.00*

Lobi Statuette — A408

2017, Oct. 9 Litho. *Perf. 13¼x13*
1384 A408 500fr multi *6.00 —*

Campaign Against Breast Cancer A409

2017, Oct. 9 Litho. *Perf. 13x13¼*
1385 A409 830fr multi *7.00 4.00*

National Internet Week — A410

2017 Litho. *Perf. 13¼x13*
1386 A410 670fr multi *6.00 —*

National Heroes Monument and Martyr's Steles, Ouagadougou A411

2017 Litho. *Perf. 13¼x13*
1387 A411 830fr multi *7.00 —*

Nelson Mandela (1918-2013), President of South Africa — A412

2018, July 18 Litho. *Perf. 13¼*
1388 A412 1000fr multi *— —*

SEMI-POSTAL STAMPS

Catalogue values for unused stamps in this section are for Never Hinged items.

Anti-Malaria Issue
Common Design Type
Perf. 12½x12
1962, Apr. 7 Engr. Unwmk.
B1 CD108 25fr + 5fr red org .75 .70

Freedom from Hunger Issue
Common Design Type
1963, Mar. 21 *Perf. 13*
B2 CD112 25fr + 5fr dk grn, bl & brn .75 .70

CAN '96 (African Nations) Soccer Championships — SP1

Designs: 150fr+25fr, Stallions, soccer ball. 250fr+25fr, Map of Africa, soccer player.

1996, Jan. 2 Litho. *Perf. 11½*
B3 SP1 150fr +25fr multi 1.25 .50
a. Souvenir sheet of 1 2.75 2.00
B4 SP1 250fr +25fr multi 2.50 .90

No. B3a sold for 500fr.

AIR POST STAMPS

Catalogue values for unused stamps in this section are for Never Hinged items.

Plane over Map Showing Air Routes — AP1

200fr, Plane at airport, Ouagadougou. 500fr, Champs Elysees, Ouagadougou.

Unwmk.
1961, Mar. 4 Engr. *Perf. 13*
C1 AP1 100fr multicolored 1.45 .70
C2 AP1 200fr multicolored 4.50 1.40
C3 AP1 500fr multicolored 10.50 4.00
Nos. C1-C3 (3) 16.45 6.10

Air Afrique Issue
Common Design Type
1962, Feb. 17
C4 CD107 25fr brt pink, dk pur & lt grn 3.50 1.75

UN Emblem and Upper Volta Flag — AP2

Perf. 13½x12½
1962, Sept. 22 Photo.
C5 AP2 50fr multicolored .75 .40
C6 AP2 100fr multicolored 1.75 .80

Admission to UN, second anniversary.

Post Office, Ouagadougou — AP3

1962, Dec. 11 *Perf. 13x12*
C7 AP3 100fr multicolored 1.50 .70

Jet Over Map AP4

1963, June 24
C8 AP4 200fr multicolored 5.00 1.50

First jet flight, Ouagadougou to Paris. For surcharge see No. C10.

African Postal Union Issue
Common Design Type
1963, Sept. 8 Unwmk. *Perf. 12½*
C9 CD114 85fr dp vio, ocher & red 1.50 .75

No. C8 Surcharged in Red

1963, Nov. 19 *Perf. 13x12*
C10 AP4 50fr on 200fr multi 1.40 .80

See note after Mauritania No. C26.

Europafrica Issue
Common Design Type

50fr, Sunburst & Europe linked with Africa.

1964, Jan. 6 *Perf. 12x13*
C11 CD116 50fr multicolored 1.50 .80

Ramses II, Abu Simbel — AP5

1964, Mar. 8 **Engr.** *Perf. 13*
C12 AP5 25fr dp green & choc .75 .50
C13 AP5 100fr brt bl & brn 2.75 2.00

UNESCO world campaign to save historic monuments of Nubia.

Greek Sculptures AP6

15fr, Greek Portrait Head. 25fr, Seated boxer. 85fr, Victorious athlete. 100fr, Venus of Milo.

1964, July 1 **Unwmk.** *Perf. 13*
C14 AP6 15fr multicolored .45 .25
C15 AP6 25fr multicolored .60 .25
C16 AP6 85fr multicolored 1.40 1.00
C17 AP6 100fr multicolored 2.00 1.10
a. Min. sheet of 4, #C14-C17 10.00 10.00
Nos. C14-C17 (4) 4.45 2.60

18th Olympic Games, Tokyo, Oct. 10-25.

West African Gray Woodpecker AP7

1964, Oct. 1 **Engr.** *Perf. 13*
C18 AP7 250fr multicolored 10.00 5.00

President John F. Kennedy (1917-1963) AP8

1964, Nov. 25 **Photo.** *Perf. 12½*
C19 AP8 100fr orange, brn & lil 2.25 1.50
a. Souvenir sheet of 4 10.00 8.00

Bird Type of Regular Issue, 1965

1965, Mar. 1 **Photo.** *Perf. 13*
Size: 27x48mm
C20 A27 500fr Abyssinian roller 20.00 7.50

Earth and Sun — AP9

1965, Mar. 23 **Engr.**
C21 AP9 50fr multicolored .85 .45

5th World Meteorological Day.

Hughes Telegraph, ITU Emblem and Dial Telephone — AP10

1965, May 17 **Unwmk.** *Perf. 13*
C22 AP10 100fr red, sl grn & bl grn 1.90 1.00

ITU, centenary.

Intl. Cooperation Year — AP10a

1965, June 21 **Photo.** *Perf. 13*
C23 AP10a 25fr multicolored .45 .25
C24 AP10a 100fr multicolored 1.40 .50
a. Min. sheet, 2 each #C23-C24 3.75 3.00

Sacred Sabou Crocodile — AP11

1965, Aug. 9 **Engr.** *Perf. 13*
C25 AP11 60fr shown 3.00 1.00
C26 AP11 85fr Lion, vert. 3.75 1.10

Early Bird Satellite over Globe — AP12

1965, Sept. 15 **Unwmk.** *Perf. 13*
C27 AP12 30fr brt bl, brn & brn red .75 .30

Space communications.

Tiros Satellite and Weather Map — AP13

1966, Mar. 23 **Engr.** *Perf. 13*
C28 AP13 50fr dk car, brt bl & blk .90 .60

6th World Meteorological Day.

FR-1 Satellite over Ouagadougou Space Tracking Station — AP14

1966, Apr. 28 *Perf. 13*
C29 AP14 250fr mag, ind & org brn 4.75 2.50

Inauguration of WHO Headquarters, Geneva — AP15

1966, May 3 **Photo.**
C30 AP15 100fr yel, blk & bl 2.00 .95

Air Afrique Issue
Common Design Type

1966, Aug. 31 **Photo.** *Perf. 13*
C31 CD123 25fr tan, blk & yel grn .75 .50

Sir Winston Churchill, British Lion and "V" Sign — AP16

1966, Nov. 5 **Engr.** *Perf. 13*
C32 AP16 100fr slate grn & car rose 2.00 .85

Sir Winston Spencer Churchill (1874-1965), statesman and WWII leader.

Pope Paul VI, Peace Dove, UN General Assembly and Emblem — AP17

1966, Nov. 5
C33 AP17 100fr dk blue & pur 2.00 .85

Pope Paul's appeal for peace before the UN General Assembly, Oct. 4, 1965.

Blind Man and Lions Emblem — AP18

1967, Feb. 28 **Engr.** *Perf. 13*
C34 AP18 100fr dk vio bl, brt bl & dk brn 2.00 .85

50th anniversary of Lions Intl.

UN Emblem and Rain over Landscape AP19

1967, Mar. 23 **Engr.** *Perf. 13*
C35 AP19 50fr ultra, dk grn & bl grn 1.10 .60

7th World Meteorological Day.

Diamant Rocket — AP20

French Spacecraft: 20fr, FR 1 satellite, horiz. 30fr, D1-C satellite. 100fr, D1-D satellite, horiz.

1967, Apr. 18 **Engr.** *Perf. 13*
C36 AP20 5fr brt bl, sl grn & org .25 .25
C37 AP20 20fr lilac & slate blue .50 .25
C38 AP20 30fr red brn, brt bl & emer .75 .25
C39 AP20 100fr emer & dp claret 1.50 .85
Nos. C36-C39 (4) 3.00 1.60

For overprint see No. C69.

Albert Schweitzer (1875-1965), Medical Missionary and Organ Pipes — AP21

1967, May 12 Engr. *Perf. 13*
C40 AP21 250fr claret & blk 4.75 2.50

World Map and 1967 Jamboree Emblem — AP22

1967, June 8 Photo.
C41 AP22 100fr multicolored 1.75 .85

12th Boy Scout World Jamboree, Farragut State Park, Idaho, Aug. 1-9.

Madonna and Child, 15th Century AP23

Paintings: 20fr, Still life by Paul Gauguin. 50fr, Pietà, by Dick Bouts. 60fr, Anne of Cleves, by Hans Holbein the Younger. 90fr, The Money Lender and his Wife, by Quentin Massys (38x40mm). 100fr, Blessing of the Risen Christ, by Giovanni Bellini. 200fr, The Handcart, by Louis Le Nain, horiz. 250fr, The Four Evangelists, by Jacob Jordaens.

Perf. 12½x12, 12x12½, 13½ (90fr)
1967-68 Photo.
C42 AP23 20fr multi ('68) .45 .35
C43 AP23 30fr multi .70 .35
C44 AP23 50fr multi 1.00 .50
C45 AP23 60fr multi ('68) .85 .60
C46 AP23 90fr multi ('68) 1.25 .95
C47 AP23 100fr multi 1.50 1.00
C48 AP23 200fr multi ('68) 2.75 2.10
C49 AP23 250fr multi 4.25 2.50
Nos. C42-C49 (8) 12.75 8.35

See Nos. C70-C72.

African Postal Union Issue, 1967
Common Design Type

1967, Sept. 9 Engr. *Perf. 13*
C50 CD124 100fr multicolored 1.80 .70

Caravelle "Ouagadougou" — AP24

1968, Feb. 29 Engr. *Perf. 13*
C51 AP24 500fr bl, dp cl & blk 10.00 5.50

WMO Emblem, Sun, Rain, Wheat — AP25

1968, Mar. 23 Engr. *Perf. 13*
C52 AP25 50fr dk red, ultra & gray grn 1.10 .50

8th World Meteorological Day.

Europafrica Issue

Clove Hitch — AP25a

1968, July 20 Photo. *Perf. 13*
C53 AP25a 50fr yel bis, blk & dk red .90 .50

See note after Niger No. C89.

Vessel in Form of Acrobat with Bells, Colima Culture — AP26

Mexican Sculptures: 30fr, Ballplayer, Veracruz, vert. 60fr, Javelin thrower, Colima, vert. 100fr, Seated athlete with cape, Jalisco.

1968, Oct. 14 Engr. *Perf. 13*
C54 AP26 10fr dk red, ocher & choc .55 .25
C55 AP26 30fr bl grn, brt grn & dk brn .70 .25
C56 AP26 60fr ultra, ol & mar 1.40 .55
C57 AP26 100fr brt grn, bl & mar 1.90 .90
Nos. C54-C57 (4) 4.55 1.95

19th Olympic Games, Mexico City, 10/12-27.

Artisan Type of Regular Issue

1968, Oct. 30 Engr. *Perf. 13*
Size: 48x27mm
C58 A52 100fr Potter 1.60 .75

PHILEXAFRIQUE Issue

Too Late or The Letter, by Armand Cambon AP27

1968, Nov. 22 Photo. *Perf. 12½*
C59 AP27 100fr multicolored 3.50 3.00

PHILEXAFRIQUE, Phil. Exhib., Abidjan, Feb. 14-23, 1969. Printed with alternating rose claret label.

Albert John Luthuli — AP28

Design: No. C61, Mahatma Gandhi.

1968, Dec. 16 Photo. *Perf. 12½*
C60 AP28 100fr dk grn, yel grn & blk 1.50 1.25
C61 AP28 100fr dk grn, yel & blk 1.50 1.00
a. Min. sheet, 2 each #C60-C61 9.00 9.00

Exponents of non-violence.

2nd PHILEXAFRIQUE Issue
Common Design Type

50fr, Upper Volta #59, dancers & musicians.

1969, Feb. 14 Engr. *Perf. 13*
C62 CD128 50fr pur, bl car & brn 4.00 3.25

Weather Sonde, WMO Emblem, Mule and Cattle in Irrigated Field — AP29

1969, Mar. 24 Engr. *Perf. 13*
C63 AP29 100fr dk brn, brt bl & grn 3.25 2.00

9th World Meteorological Day.

Artisan Type of Regular Issue

Design: 150fr, Basket weaver.

1969, Apr. 3 Engr. *Perf. 13*
Size: 48x27mm
C64 A55 150fr brn, bl & blk 2.75 1.25

Lions Emblem, Eye and Blind Man — AP30

1969, Apr. 30 Photo.
C65 AP30 250fr red & multi 3.50 1.75

12th Congress of District 403 of Lions Intl., Ouagadougou, May 2-3.

Fish Type of Regular Issue

Designs: 100fr, Phenacogrammus pabrensis. 150fr, Upside-down catfish.

1969 Engr. *Perf. 13*
Size: 48x27mm
C66 A57 100fr slate, pur & yel 2.25 1.00
C67 A57 150fr org brn, gray & slate 4.00 1.75

Earth and Astronaut — AP31

Embossed on Gold Foil

1969 *Die-cut Perf. 10½x10*
C68 AP31 1000fr gold 25.00 25.00

Apollo 8 mission, which put the first man into orbit around the moon, Dec. 21-27, 1968.

No. C39 Overprinted in red with Lunar Landing Module and

1969, July 25 Engr. *Perf. 13*
C69 AP20 100fr emer & dp claret 4.00 4.00

See note after Mali No. C80.

Painting Type of 1967-68

Paintings: 50fr, Napoleon Crossing Great St. Bernard Pass, by Jacques Louis David. 150fr, Napoleon Awarding the First Cross of the Legion of Honor, by Jean-Baptiste Debret. 250fr, Napoleon Before Madrid, by Carle Vernet.

1969, Aug. 18 Photo. *Perf. 12½x12*
C70 AP23 50fr carmine & multi 2.25 1.00
C71 AP23 150fr violet & multi 5.75 2.50
C72 AP23 250fr green & multi 8.00 4.50
Nos. C70-C72 (3) 16.00 8.00

Napoleon Bonaparte (1769-1821).

Agriculture Type of Regular Issue

1969, Oct. 30 Photo. *Perf. 12½x13*
Size: 47½x27mm
C73 A58 100fr Peanuts 1.25 .50
C74 A58 200fr Rice 3.25 1.00

AP32

Tree of Life, symbols of science, agriculture and industry.

1969, Nov. 21 Photo. *Perf. 12x13*
C75 AP32 100fr multicolored 1.10 .80

See note after Mauritania No. C28.

AP33

Designs: 20fr, Lenin. 100fr, Lenin Addressing Revolutionaries in Petrograd, by V. A. Serov, horiz.

1970, Apr. 22 Photo. *Perf. 12½*
C76 AP33 20fr ocher & brn .80 .50
C77 AP33 100fr blk, lt grn & red 1.90 1.25

Lenin (1870-1924), Russian communist leader.

Pres. Roosevelt with Stamp Collection — AP34

10fr, Franklin Delano Roosevelt, vert.

1970, June 4 Photo. *Perf. 12½*

C78 AP34	10fr dk brn, emer & red brn	.25	.25
C79 AP34	200fr vio bl, gray & dk car	2.25	1.10

Soccer Game and Jules Rimet Cup — AP35

100fr, Goalkeeper catching ball, globe.

1970, June 4 Engr. *Perf. 13*

C80 AP35	40fr olive, brt grn & brn	.60	.45
C81 AP35	100fr blk, lil, brn & grn	1.50	.80

9th World Soccer Championships for the Jules Rimet Cup, Mexico City, 5/30-6/21/70.

EXPO Emblem, Monorail and "Cranes at the Seashore" AP36

Design: 150fr, EXPO emblem, rocket, satellites and "Geisha."

1970, Aug. 7 Photo. *Perf. 12½*

C82 AP36	50fr multicolored	1.60	.80
C83 AP36	150fr green & multi	2.60	1.00

Issued to publicize EXPO '70 International Exhibition, Osaka, Japan, Mar. 15-Sept. 13.

UN Emblem, Dove and Star — AP37

250fr, UN emblem and doves, horiz.

1970, Oct. 2 Engr. *Perf. 13*

C84 AP37	60fr dk bl, bl & grn	.50	.35
C85 AP37	250fr dk red brn, vio bl & ol	3.25	1.25

25th anniversary of the United Nations.

Holy Family — AP38

Silver Embossed

1970, Nov. 27 *Die-Cut Perf. 10*

C86 AP38	300fr silver	8.00	8.00

Gold Embossed

C87 AP38	1000fr gold	20.00	20.00

Christmas.

Family and Upper Volta Flag — AP39

Litho.; Gold Embossed

1970, Dec. 10 *Perf. 12½*

C88 AP39	500fr gold, blk & red	6.00	3.00

10th anniversary of independence, Dec. 11.

UN "Key to a Free World" — AP40

1970, Dec. 14 Engr. *Perf. 13*

C89 AP40	40fr red, bister & blue	.90	.50

UN Declaration of Independence for Colonial Peoples, 10th anniv.

Gamal Abdel Nasser — AP41

1971, Jan. 30 Photo. *Perf. 12½*

C90 AP41	100fr green & multi	1.10	.50

Nasser (1918-1970), president of Egypt.

Herons, Egyptian Art, 1354 — AP42

250fr, Page from Koran, Egypt, 1368-1388.

1971, May 13 Photo. *Perf. 13*

C91 AP42	100fr multi	1.25	.80
C92 AP42	250fr multi, vert.	3.25	2.00

Olympic Rings and Various Sports — AP43

1971, June 10 Engr. *Perf. 13*

C93 AP43	150fr vio bl & red	3.25	1.60

Pre-Olympic Year.

Boy Scout and Buildings — AP44

1971, Aug. 12 Photo. *Perf. 12½*

C94 AP44	45fr multicolored	1.10	.60

13th Boy Scout World Jamboree, Asagiri Plain, Japan, Aug. 2-10.

De Gaulle, Map of Upper Volta, Cross of Lorraine — AP45

Charles de Gaulle — AP46

1971, Nov. 9 Photo. *Perf. 13x12*

C95 AP45	40fr lt brn, grn & blk	.90	.50

Lithographed; Gold Embossed

Perf. 12½

C96 AP46	500fr gold & grn	11.00	10.00

Gen. Charles de Gaulle (1890-1970), president of France.

African Postal Union Issue, 1971

Common Design Type

Design: 100fr, Mossi dancer and UAMPT building, Brazzaville, Congo.

1971, Nov. 13 Photo. *Perf. 13x13½*

C97 CD135	100fr bl & multi	1.50	.70

Gen. Sangoule Lamizana AP47

1971, Dec. 11 *Perf. 12½*

C98 AP47	35fr sep, blk, gold & ultra	.90	.60

Inauguration of 2nd Republic of Upper Volta.

Kabuki Actor and Ice Hockey — AP48

1972, Feb. 15 Engr. *Perf. 13*

C99 AP48	150fr red, bl & pur	2.50	1.25

11th Winter Olympic Games, Sapporo, Japan, Feb. 3-13.

Music, by Pietro Longhi AP49

Design: 150fr, Gondolas and general view, by Ippolito Caffi, horiz.

1972, Feb. 28 Photo. *Perf. 13*

C100 AP49	100fr gold & multi	2.25	1.00
C101 AP49	150fr gold & multi	3.25	1.50

UNESCO campaign to save Venice.

Running and Olympic Rings — AP50

Design: 200fr, Discus and Olympic rings.

1972, May 5 Engr. *Perf. 13*

C102 AP50	65fr dp bl, brn & grn	.70	.60
C103 AP50	200fr dp bl & brn	2.25	1.50
a.	Min. sheet of 2, #C102-C103	3.00	3.00

20th Olympic Games, Munich, 8/26-9/10.

Musician Type of Regular Issue

Design: 500fr, Jimmy Smith and keyboard.

1972, May 17 Photo. *Perf. 14x13*

C104 A87	500fr green & multi	9.00	4.75

Red Crescent Type of Regular Issue

1972, June 23 *Perf. 13x14*

C105 A88	100fr yellow & multi	1.40	.60

2nd Plan Type of Regular Issue

Design: 85fr, Road building machinery.

1972, Oct. 30 Engr. *Perf. 13*

C106 A90	85fr brick red, bl & blk	1.00	.80

Presidents Pompidou and Lamizana — AP51

Design: 250fr, Presidents Pompidou and Lamizana, different design.

1972, Nov. 20 Photo. *Perf. 13*
Size: 48x37mm

C107 AP51 40fr gold & multi 2.00 2.00

Photogravure; Gold Embossed
Size: 56x36mm

C108 AP51 250fr yel grn, dk grn & gold 7.00 6.25

Visit of Pres. Georges Pompidou of France, Nov. 1972.

Skeet-shooting, Scalzone, Italy — AP52

Gold-medal Winners: 40fr, Pentathlon, Peters, Great Britain. 45fr, Dressage, Meade, Great Britain. 50fr, Weight lifting, Talts, USSR. 60fr, Boxing, light-weight, Seales, US. 65fr, Fencing, Ragno-Lonzi, Italy. 75fr, Gymnastics, rings, Nakayama, Japan. 85fr, Gymnastics, Touritcheva, USSR. 90fr, 110m high hurdles, Milburn, US. 150fr, Judo, Kawaguchi, Japan. 200fr, Sailing, Finn class, Maury, France. 250fr, Swimming, Spitz, US (7 gold). 300fr, Women's high jump, Meyfarth, West Germany. 350fr, Field Hockey, West Germany. 400fr, Javelin, Wolfermann, West Germany. No. C124, Women's diving, King, US. No. C125, Cycling, Morelon, France. No. C126, Individual dressage, Linsenhoff, West Germany.

1972-73 Litho. *Perf. 12½*

C109 AP52 35fr multi ('73) .40 .25
C110 AP52 40fr multi .40 .25
C111 AP52 45fr multi ('73) .45 .30
C112 AP52 50fr multi ('73) .40 .30
C113 AP52 60fr multi ('73) .65 .45
C114 AP52 65fr multi .65 .45
C115 AP52 75fr multi ('73) .65 .55
C116 AP52 85fr multi .95 .55
C117 AP52 90fr multi ('73) .70 .55
C118 AP52 150fr multi ('73) 1.15 .70
C119 AP52 200fr multi 1.75 .80
C120 AP52 250fr multi ('73) 2.00 .80
C121 AP52 300fr multi 3.00 1.50
C122 AP52 350fr multi ('73) 2.60 1.50
C123 AP52 400fr multi ('73) 3.50 1.50
Nos. C109-C123 (15) 19.25 10.45

Souvenir Sheets

C124 AP52 500fr multi 7.50 5.00
C125 AP52 500fr multi ('73) 7.50 5.00
C126 AP52 500fr multi ('73) 7.50 5.00

20th Olympic Games, Munich.

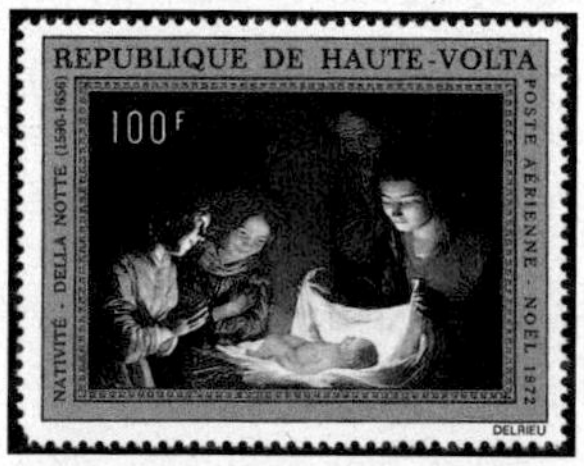

Nativity, by Della Notte — AP53

Christmas: 200fr, Adoration of the Kings, by Albrecht Dürer.

1972, Dec. 23 Photo. *Perf. 13*

C127 AP53 100fr gold & multi 1.25 .90
C128 AP53 200fr gold & multi 2.75 2.00

Madonna and Child, by Albrecht Dürer AP54

Christmas: 75fr, Virgin Mary, Child and St. John, by Joseph von Führich. 100fr, The Virgin of Grand Duc, by Raphael. 125fr, Holy Family, by David. 150fr, Madonna and Child, artist unknown. 400fr, Flight into Egypt, by Gentile da Fabriano, horiz.

1973, Mar. 22 Litho. *Perf. 12½x13*

C129 AP54 50fr multi .45 .25
C130 AP54 75fr multi .60 .35
C131 AP54 100fr multi .90 .45
C132 AP54 125fr multi 1.10 .55
C133 AP54 150fr multi 1.40 .55
Nos. C129-C133 (5) 4.45 2.15

Souvenir Sheet

C134 AP54 400fr multi 5.25 4.00

Manned Lunar Buggy on Moon — AP55

Moon Exploration: 65fr, Lunakhod, Russian unmanned vehicle on moon. 100fr, Lunar module returning to orbiting Apollo capsule. 150fr, Apollo capsule in moon orbit. 200fr, Space walk. 250fr, Walk in Sea of Tranquillity.

1973, Apr. 30 Litho. *Perf. 13x12½*

C135 AP55 50fr multi .45 .25
C136 AP55 65fr multi .70 .25
C137 AP55 100fr multi 1.00 .45
C138 AP55 150fr multi 1.25 .60
C139 AP55 200fr multi 2.00 .80
Nos. C135-C139 (5) 5.40 2.35

Souvenir Sheet

C140 AP55 250fr multi 3.50 2.50

Giraffes AP56

African Wild Animals: 150fr, Elephants. 200fr, Leopard, horiz. 250fr, Lion, horiz. 300fr, Rhinoceros, horiz. 500fr, Crocodile, horiz.

Perf. 12½x13, 13x12½
1973, May 3 Litho.

C141 AP56 100fr multi 1.00 .30
C142 AP56 150fr multi 1.50 .60
C143 AP56 200fr multi 2.00 1.10
C144 AP56 250fr multi 2.25 1.10
C145 AP56 500fr multi 5.00 2.75
Nos. C141-C145 (5) 11.75 5.85

Souvenir Sheet

C146 AP56 300fr multi 4.00 4.00

Europafrica Issue

Girl Reading Letter, by Jan Vermeer AP57

Paintings: 65fr, Portrait of a Lady, by Roger van der Weyden. 100fr, Young Lady at her Toilette, by Titian. 150fr, Jane Seymour, by Hans Holbein. 200fr, Mrs. Williams, by John Hoppner. 250fr, Milkmaid, by Jean-Baptiste Greuze.

1973, June 7 Litho. *Perf. 12½x13*

C147 AP57 50fr multi .45 .25
C148 AP57 65fr multi .70 .25
C149 AP57 100fr multi 1.00 .45
C150 AP57 150fr multi 1.25 .60
C151 AP57 200fr multi 2.00 .80
Nos. C147-C151 (5) 5.40 2.35

Souvenir Sheet

C152 AP57 250fr multi 3.75 1.50

For overprint see No. C165-C166.

Africa Encircled by OAU Flags AP58

1973, June 7

C153 AP58 45fr multi .75 .40

10th anniv. of Org. for African Unity.

Locomotive "Pacific" 4546, 1908 — AP59

Locomotives from Railroad Museum, Mulhouse, France: 40fr, No. 242, 1927. 50fr, No. 2029, 1882. 150fr, No. 701, 1885-92. 250fr, "Coupe-Vent" No. C145, 1900. 350fr, Buddicomb No. 33, Paris to Rouen, 1884.

1973, June 30 *Perf. 13x12½*

C154 AP59 10fr multi .35 .25
C155 AP59 40fr multi .55 .25
C156 AP59 50fr multi .60 .25
C157 AP59 150fr multi 1.75 .60
C158 AP59 250fr multi 3.00 .90
Nos. C154-C158 (5) 6.25 2.25

Souvenir Sheet

C159 AP59 350fr multi 4.00 2.75

Boy Scout Type of 1973

40fr, Flag signaling. 75fr, Skiing. 150fr, Cooking. 200fr, Hiking. 250fr, Studying stars.

1973, July 18 Litho. *Perf. 12½x13*

C160 A95 40fr multi .45 .25
C161 A95 75fr multi .70 .45
C162 A95 150fr multi 1.25 .60
C163 A95 200fr multi 1.50 .70
Nos. C160-C163 (4) 3.90 2.00

Souvenir Sheet

C164 A95 250fr multi 4.00 1.25

Nos. C148 and C150 Surcharged in Silver

1973, Aug. 16

C165 AP57 100fr on 65fr multi 1.75 1.50
C166 AP57 200fr on 150fr multi 3.50 2.25

Drought relief.

Kennedy Type, 1973

John F. Kennedy and: 200fr, Firing Saturn 1 rocket, Apollo program. 300fr, First NASA manned space capsule. 400fr, Saturn 5 countdown.

1973, Sept. 12 Litho. *Perf. 12½x13*

C167 A96 200fr multi 1.40 .80
C168 A96 300fr multi 2.10 1.05

Souvenir Sheet

C169 A96 400fr multi 4.25 2.50

10th death anniv. of Pres John F. Kennedy.

Interpol Type of 1973
Souvenir Sheet

Design: Victim in city street.

1973, Sept. 15 *Perf. 13x12½*

C170 A97 300fr multi 3.25 1.10

Tourism Type of 1973

1973, Sept. 30

C171 A98 100fr Waterfalls 1.40 .80

Souvenir Sheet

C172 A98 275fr Elephant 4.25 1.25

House of Worship Type of 1973

Cathedral of the Immaculate Conception.

1973, Sept. 28

C173 A99 200fr multi 2.40 1.20

Folklore Type of 1973

100fr, 225fr, Bobo masked dancers, diff.

1973, Nov. 30 Litho. *Perf. 12½x13*

C174 A100 100fr multi 1.35 .50
C175 A100 225fr multi 2.00 .95

Zodiac Type of 1973
Souvenir Sheets

Zodiacal Light and: No. C176, 1st 4 signs of Zodiac. No. C177, 2nd 4 signs. No. C178, Last 4 signs.

1973, Dec. 15 *Perf. 13x14*

C176 A101 250fr multi 3.00 1.10
C177 A101 250fr multi 3.00 1.10
C178 A101 250fr multi 3.00 1.10

Nos. C176-C178 have multicolored margin showing night sky and portraits: No. C176, Louis Armstrong; No. C177, Mahatma Gandhi; No. C178, Martin Luther King.

Soccer Championship Type, 1974

Championship '74 emblem and: 75fr, Gento, Spanish flag. 100fr, Bereta, French flag. 250fr, Best, British flag. 400fr, Beckenbauer, West German flag.

1974, Jan. 15 Litho. *Perf. 13x12½*

C179 A102 75fr multi .60 .25
C180 A102 100fr multi .90 .25
C181 A102 250fr multi 1.90 .80
Nos. C179-C181 (3) 3.40 1.30

Souvenir Sheet

C182 A102 400fr multi 8.00 3.25

De Gaulle Type, 1974

300fr, De Gaulle, Concorde, horiz. 400fr, De Gaulle, French space shot.

Perf. 13x12½, 12½x13
1974, Feb. 4 Litho.

C183 A103 300fr multi 3.50 1.75

Souvenir Sheet

C184 A103 400fr multi 7.00 1.90

Soccer Cup Championship Type, 1974

World Cup, Emblems and: 150fr, Brindisis, Argentinian flag. No. C186, Kenko, Zaire flag. No. C187, Streich, East German flag. 400fr, Cruyff, Netherlands flag.

1974, Mar. 19 *Perf. 12½x13*

C185 A104 150fr multi 1.10 .45
C186 A104 300fr multi 2.25 .90

Souvenir Sheets

C187 A104 300fr multi 4.00 1.50
C188 A104 400fr multi 4.00 1.50

UPU Type, 1974

UPU Emblem and: 100fr, Dove carrying mail. 200fr, Air Afrique 707. 300fr, Dish antenna. 500fr, Telstar satellite.

1974, July 23 *Perf. 13½*

C189 A106 100fr multi 1.00 .50
C190 A106 200fr multi 1.50 .75
C191 A106 300fr multi 2.25 1.25
Nos. C189-C191 (3) 4.75 2.50

Souvenir Sheet

C192 A106 500fr multi 4.75 1.90

For overprint see No. C197-C200.

Soccer Cup Winners Type, 1974

World Cup, Game and Flags: 150fr, Brazil, in Sweden, 1958. 200fr, Brazil, in Chile, 1962. 250fr, Brazil, in Mexico, 1970. 450fr, England, in England, 1966.

1974, Sept. 2

C193 A107 150fr multi 1.05 .55
C194 A107 200fr multi 1.50 .75
C195 A107 250fr multi 2.25 1.25
Nos. C193-C195 (3) 4.80 2.55

Souvenir Sheet

C196 A107 450fr multi 4.00 1.90

Nos. C189-C192 Overprinted in Red

1974, Oct. 9

C197 A106 100fr multi 1.35 .60
C198 A106 200fr multi 2.00 .90
C199 A106 300fr multi 3.50 1.30
Nos. C197-C199 (3) 6.85 2.80

Souvenir Sheet

C200 A106 500fr multi 4.00 1.90

Universal Postal Union, centenary.

Flower Type of 1974

Flower Paintings by: 300fr, Auguste Renoir. 400fr, Carl Brendt.

1974, Oct. 31 Litho. *Perf. 12½x13*

C201 A109 300fr multi 3.50 1.10

Souvenir Sheet

C202 A109 400fr multi 5.25 1.60

Locomotive Type of 1975

Locomotives from Railroad Museum. Mulhouse, France: 100fr, Crampton No. 80, 1852. 200fr, No. 701, 1885-92. 300fr, "Forquenot," 1882.

1975, Feb. 28 Litho. *Perf. 13x12½*

C203 A112 100fr multi 1.50 .35
C204 A112 200fr multi 2.75 .65

Souvenir Sheet

C205 A112 300fr multi 5.25 2.25

Old Cars Type, 1975

Flags and Old Cars: 150fr, Germany and Mercedes-Benz, 1929. 200fr, Germany and Maybach, 1936. 400fr, Great Britain and Rolls Royce Silver Ghost, 1910.

1975, Apr. 6 *Perf. 14x13½*

C206 A113 150fr multi 1.75 .50
C207 A113 200fr multi 2.25 .70

Souvenir Sheet

C208 A113 400fr multi 3.75 1.75

American Bicentennial Type

200fr, Washington crossing Delaware. 300fr, Hessians Captured at Trenton.

1975, May 6 Litho. *Perf. 14*

C209 A114 200fr multi 2.00 .90
C210 A114 300fr multi 2.40 1.25

Schweitzer Type of 1975

Albert Schweitzer and: 150fr, Toucan. 175fr, Vulturine guinea fowl. 200fr, King vulture. 450fr, Crested corythornis.

1975, May 25 Litho. *Perf. 13½*

C212 A115 150fr multi 1.50 .60
C213 A115 175fr multi 2.00 .70
C214 A115 200fr multi 2.75 .95
Nos. C212-C214 (3) 6.25 2.25

Souvenir Sheet

C215 A115 450fr multi 6.25 2.25

Apollo Soyuz Type of 1975

100fr, Apollo, Soyuz near link-up. 200fr, Cosmonauts Alexei Leonov, Valeri Kubasov. 300fr, Astronauts Donald K. Slayton, Vance Brand, Thomas P. Stafford. 500fr, Apollo Soyuz emblem, U.S., USSR flags.

1975, July 18 Litho. *Perf. 13½*

C216 A116 100fr multi 1.00 .25
C217 A116 200fr multi 1.50 .65
C218 A116 300fr multi 2.50 1.00
Nos. C216-C218 (3) 5.00 1.90

Souvenir Sheet

C219 A116 500fr multi 5.00 2.25

Picasso Type of 1975

Picasso Paintings: 150fr, El Prado, horiz. 350fr, Couple in Patio. 400fr, Science and Charity.

1975, Aug. 7

C220 A117 150fr multi 2.25 .70
C221 A117 350fr multi 4.00 1.00

Souvenir Sheet

C222 A117 400fr multi 3.50 1.60

EXPO '75 Type of 1975

Expo '75 emblem and: 150fr, Passenger liner Asama Maru. 300fr, Future floating city Aquapolis.

1975, Sept. 26 Litho. *Perf. 11*

C223 A118 150fr multi 2.00 .60

Souvenir Sheet

Perf. 13½

C224 A118 300fr multi 3.75 1.25

Winter Olympic Games Type of 1975

Innsbruck Background, Olympic Emblem and: 100fr, Ice hockey. 200fr, Ski jump. 300fr, Speed skating.

1975, Dec. 15 *Perf. 13½*

C225 A122 100fr multi .95 .45
C226 A122 200fr multi 1.75 .70

Souvenir Sheet

C227 A122 300fr multi 4.25 1.50

Olympic Games Type of 1976

Olympic Emblem and: 125fr, Heavyweight judo. 150fr, Weight lifting. 500fr, Sprint.

1976, Mar. 17 Litho. *Perf. 13½*

C228 A123 125fr multi 1.00 .35
C229 A123 150fr multi 1.50 .55

Souvenir Sheet

C230 A123 500fr multi 4.25 2.25

Summer Olympic Games Type of 1976

Olympic emblem and: 150fr, Pole vault. 200fr, Gymnast on balance beam. 500fr, Two-man sculls.

1976, Mar. 25 *Perf. 11*

C231 A124 150fr multi 1.15 .45
C232 A124 200fr multi 1.75 .60

Souvenir Sheet

C233 A124 500fr multi 4.25 2.25

For overprint see No. C245-C247.

Zeppelin Type of 1976

Airships: 100fr, Graf Zeppelin over Swiss Alps. 200fr, LZ-129 over city. 300fr, Graf Zeppelin. 500fr, Zeppelin over Bodensee.

1976, May 11

C234 A126 100fr multi 1.00 .45
C235 A126 200fr multi 2.00 .75
C236 A126 300fr multi 2.75 1.20
Nos. C234-C236 (3) 5.75 2.40

Souvenir Sheet

C237 A126 500fr multi 4.75 2.25

Viking Mars Type of 1976

Designs: 200fr, Viking lander assembly. 300fr, Viking orbiter in descent on Mars. 450fr, Viking in Mars orbit.

1976, June 24 Litho. *Perf. 13½*

C238 A127 200fr multi 1.90 .45
C239 A127 300fr multi 2.75 .75

Souvenir Sheet

C240 A127 450fr multi 4.25 2.25

American Bicentennial Type

Bicentennial and Interphil '76 Emblems and: 100fr, Siege of Yorktown. 200fr, Battle of Cape St. Vincent. 300fr, Peter Francisco's bravery. 500fr, Surrender of the Hessians.

1976, Sept. 30 Litho. *Perf. 13½*

C241 A129 100fr multi 1.00 .35
C242 A129 200fr multi 1.60 .65
C243 A129 300fr multi 2.25 .80
Nos. C241-C243 (3) 4.85 1.80

Souvenir Sheet

C244 A129 500fr multi 6.50 2.25

Nos. C231-C233 Overprinted in Gold

a. VAINQUEUR 1976 / TADEUSZ SLUSARSKI / POLOGNE
b. VAINQUEUR 1976 / NADIA COMANECI / ROUMANIE

(c)

1977, July 4 Litho. *Perf. 11*

C245 A124(a) 150fr multi 1.00 .70
C246 A124(b) 200fr multi 1.75 1.00

Souvenir Sheet

C247 A124(c) 500fr multi 4.25 2.25

Winners, 21st Olympic Games.

UPU Emblem over Globe — AP60

1978, Aug. 8 Litho. *Perf. 13*

C248 AP60 350fr multi 3.50 2.00

Congress of Paris, establishing UPU, cent.

Jules Verne, Apollo 11 Emblem, Footprint on Moon, Neil Armstrong — AP61

Space Conquest: 50fr, Yuri Gagarin and moon landing. 100fr, Montgolfier hot air balloon and memorial medal, 1783; Bleriot's monoplane, 1909.

1978, Sept. 27 Litho. *Perf. 13x12½*

C249 AP61 50fr multi .55 .25
C250 AP61 60fr multi .60 .25
C251 AP61 100fr multi 1.10 .55
Nos. C249-C251 (3) 2.25 1.05

Anti-Apartheid Year — AP62

1978, Oct. 12 Litho. *Perf. 13*

C252 AP62 100fr blue & multi 1.10 .60

Philexafrique II-Essen Issue

Common Design Types

No. C253, Hippopotamus, Upper Volta #C18. No. C254, Kingfisher, Hanover #1.

1978, Nov. 1 Litho. *Perf. 12½*

C253 CD138 100fr multi 2.40 1.40
C254 CD139 100fr multi 2.40 1.40

Nos. C253-C254 printed se-tenant.

Sun God Horus with Sun — AP63

300fr, Falcon with cartouches, UNESCO emblem.

1978, Dec. 4

C255 AP63 200fr multi 1.75 .80
C256 AP63 300fr multi 2.50 1.25

UNESCO Campaign to safeguard monuments at Philae.

Jules Verne and Balloon — AP64

1978, Dec. 10 Engr. *Perf. 13*

C257 AP64 200fr multi 2.50 1.40

Verne (1828-1905), science fiction writer.

Bicycling, Olympic Rings — AP65

Designs: Bicycling scenes.

1980				*Perf. 14½*	
C258	AP65	65fr	multi	.70	.25
C259	AP65	150fr	multi, vert.	1.25	.50
C260	AP65	250fr	multi	2.50	.80
C261	AP65	350fr	multi	3.50	1.25
	Nos. C258-C261 (4)			7.95	2.80

Souvenir Sheet

C262	AP65	500fr	multi	6.00	1.90

22nd Summer Olympic Games, Moscow, July 19-Aug. 3.

Nos. C258-C262 Overprinted with Name of Winner and Country

1980, Nov. 22		Litho.		*Perf. 14½*	
C263	AP65	65fr	multi	.70	.40
C264	AP65	150fr	multi, vert.	1.60	.85
C265	AP65	250fr	multi	2.75	1.50
C266	AP65	350fr	multi	3.50	1.75
	Nos. C263-C266 (4)			8.55	4.50

Souvenir Sheet

C267	AP65	500fr	multi	6.00	3.50

1982 World Cup — AP66

Designs: Various soccer players.

1982, June 22		Litho.		*Perf. 13½*	
C268	AP66	70fr	multi	.60	.25
C269	AP66	90fr	multi	.80	.35
C270	AP66	150fr	multi	1.40	.50
C271	AP66	300fr	multi	2.50	1.00
	Nos. C268-C271 (4)			5.30	2.10

Souvenir Sheet

C272	AP66	500fr	multi	4.75	1.60

Anniversaries and Events — AP67

90fr, Space Shuttle. 120fr, World Soccer Cup. 300fr, Cup, diff. 450fr, Royal Wedding. 500fr, Prince Charles, Lady Diana.

1983, June		Litho.		*Perf. 13½*	
C273	AP67	90fr	multicolored	.80	.25
C274	AP67	120fr	multicolored	1.10	.45
C275	AP67	300fr	multicolored	2.50	.80
C276	AP67	450fr	multicolored	3.50	1.10
	Nos. C273-C276 (4)			7.90	2.60

Souvenir Sheet

C277	AP67	500fr	multicolored	4.75	1.75

Pre-Olympics, 1984 Los Angeles — AP68

90fr, Sailing. 120fr, Type 470. 300fr, Wind surfing. 400fr, Wind surfing, diff. 500fr, Soling Class, Wind surfing.

1983, Aug. 1		Litho.		*Perf. 13*	
C278	AP68	90fr	multicolored	.90	.25
C279	AP68	120fr	multicolored	1.10	.35
C280	AP68	300fr	multicolored	2.90	.80
C281	AP68	400fr	multicolored	3.75	1.00
	Nos. C278-C281 (4)			8.65	2.40

Souvenir Sheet

C282	AP68	500fr	multicolored	6.00	1.75

Christmas AP69

Rubens Paintings: 120fr, Adoration of the Shepherds. 350fr, Virgin of the Garland. 500fr, Adoration of the Kings.

1983		Litho.		*Perf. 13*	
C283	AP69	120fr	multicolored	1.00	.45
C284	AP69	350fr	multicolored	3.00	.90
C285	AP69	500fr	multicolored	4.00	1.40
	Nos. C283-C285 (3)			8.00	2.75

1984 Summer Olympics — AP70

1984, Mar. 26		Litho.		*Perf. 12½*	
C286	AP70	90fr	Handball, vert.	.70	.25
C287	AP70	120fr	Volleyball, vert.	1.00	.35
C288	AP70	150fr	Handball, diff.	1.40	.45
C289	AP70	250fr	Basketball	2.25	.60
C290	AP70	300fr	Soccer	2.75	1.00
	Nos. C286-C290 (5)			8.10	2.65

Souvenir Sheet

C291	AP70	500fr	Volleyball, diff.	4.75	1.75

Local Birds — AP71

90fr, Phoenicopterus roseus. 185fr, Choriotis kori, vert. 200fr, Buphagus erythrorhynchus, vert. 300fr, Bucorvus leadbeateri.

1984, May 14		Litho.		*Perf. 12½*	
C292	AP71	90fr	multicolored	1.40	.55
C293	AP71	185fr	multicolored	2.50	1.25
C294	AP71	200fr	multicolored	2.50	1.40
C295	AP71	300fr	multicolored	3.50	2.25
	Nos. C292-C295 (4)			9.90	5.45

AP72

Famous Men — AP73

Designs: 5fr, Houari Boumediene (1927-1978), president of Algeria 1965-78. 125fr, Gottlieb Daimler (1834-1900), German automotive pioneer, and 1886 Daimler. 250fr, Louis Bleriot (1872-1936), French aviator, first to fly the English Channel in a heavier-than-air craft. 300fr, Abraham Lincoln. 400fr, Henri Dunant (1828-1910), founder of the Red Cross. 450fr, Auguste Piccard (1884-1962), Swiss physicist, inventor of the bathyscaphe Trieste, 1948. 500fr, Robert Baden-Powell (1856-1941), founder of Boy Scouts. 600fr, Anatoli Karpov, Russian chess champion. 1000fr, Paul Harris (1868-1947), founder of Rotary Intl.

1984, May 21		Litho.		*Perf. 13½*	
C296	AP72	5fr	multi	.25	.25
C297	AP72	125fr	multi	1.10	.35
C298	AP72	250fr	multi	2.25	.60
C299	AP72	300fr	multi	2.75	.80
C300	AP72	400fr	multi	3.50	1.00
C301	AP72	450fr	multi	4.00	1.00
C302	AP72	500fr	multi	4.50	1.25
C303	AP72	600fr	multi	4.75	1.50
	Nos. C296-C303 (8)			23.10	6.75

Souvenir Sheet

C304	AP73	1000fr	multi	9.00	2.00

No. C304 contains one 51x30mm stamp.

Burkina Faso

Butterflies — AP73a

10fr, Graphium pylades. 120fr, Hypolimnas misippus. 400fr, Danaus chrysippus. 450fr, Papilio demodocus.

1984, May 23				*Perf. 13½*	
C305	AP73a	10fr	multicolored	.25	.25
C306	AP73a	120fr	multicolored	1.75	.60
C307	AP73a	400fr	multicolored	5.50	2.25
C308	AP73a	450fr	multicolored	5.75	2.50
	Nos. C305-C308 (4)			13.25	5.60

Philexafrica '85, Lome — AP74

No. C309, Solar & wind energy. No. C310, Children.

1985, May 20		Litho.		*Perf. 13*	
C309	AP74	200fr	multi	2.40	1.25
C310	AP74	200fr	multi	2.40	1.25
a.	Pair, #C309-C310 + label			5.00	2.50

PHILEXAFRICA '85, Lome — AP75

National development: No. C311, Youth. No. C312, Communications and transportation.

1985, Nov. 16		Litho.		*Perf. 13*	
C311	AP75	250fr	multi	4.25	1.50
C312	AP75	250fr	multi	4.25	1.50
a.	Pair, #C311-C312 + label			10.50	4.00

Intl. Youth Year (No. C311).

French Revolution, Bicent. — AP76

Designs: 150fr, *Oath of the Tennis Court,* by David. 200fr, *Storming of the Bastille,* by Thevenin. 600fr, *Rouget de Lisle Singing La Marseillaise,* by Pils.

1989, May 3		Litho.		*Perf. 13*	
C313	AP76	150fr	multi	1.75	.70
C314	AP76	200fr	multi	2.10	1.00
C315	AP76	600fr	multi	7.00	2.75
	Nos. C313-C315 (3)			10.85	4.45

PHILEXFRANCE '89.

POSTAGE DUE STAMPS

Postage Due Stamps of Upper Senegal and Niger, 1914, Overprinted in Black or Red

1920		Unwmk.		*Perf. 14x13½*	
J1	D2	5c	green	.40	.80
J2	D2	10c	rose	.40	.80
J3	D2	15c	gray	.75	.80
J4	D2	20c	brown (R)	.75	.80
J5	D2	30c	blue	.75	.80
J6	D2	50c	black (R)	1.25	1.60
J7	D2	60c	orange	1.25	1.60
J8	D2	1fr	violet	2.25	2.25
	Nos. J1-J8 (8)			7.80	9.45

Type of 1914 Issue Surcharged

1927					
J9	D2	2fr on 1fr	lilac rose	3.50	3.50
J10	D2	3fr on 1fr	orange brn	6.00	4.50

D3

1928				Typo.	
J11	D3	5c	green	.40	.80
J12	D3	10c	rose	.80	.80
J13	D3	15c	dark gray	1.25	1.60
J14	D3	20c	dark brown	1.25	1.60
J15	D3	30c	dark blue	1.75	2.50
J16	D3	50c	black	3.50	4.00
J17	D3	60c	orange	4.00	4.75
J18	D3	1fr	dull violet	6.50	7.25

J19	D3	2fr lilac rose		11.00	11.00
J20	D3	3fr orange brn		15.00	19.00
		Nos. J11-J20 (10)		45.45	53.30

Catalogue values for unused stamps in this section, from this point to the end of the section, are for Never Hinged items.

Republic

D4

1962, Jan. 31 ***Perf. 14x13½***

Denomination in Black

J21	D4	1fr bright blue	.25	.25
J22	D4	2fr orange	.25	.25
J23	D4	5fr brt vio blue	.25	.25
J24	D4	10fr red lilac	.35	.35
J25	D4	20fr emerald	.80	.80
J26	D4	50fr rose red	1.75	1.75
		Nos. J21-J26 (6)	3.65	3.65

OFFICIAL STAMPS

Catalogue values for unused stamps in this section are for Never Hinged items.

Elephant — O1

Perf. 12½

1963, Feb. 1 **Unwmk.** **Photo.**

Center in Sepia

O1	O1	1fr red brown	.25	.25
O2	O1	5fr yel green	.25	.25
O3	O1	10fr deep vio	.25	.25
O4	O1	15fr red org	.35	.35
O5	O1	25fr brt rose lilac	.80	.80
O6	O1	50fr brt green	1.25	1.25
O7	O1	60fr brt red	1.40	1.40
O8	O1	85fr dk slate grn	2.25	2.25
O9	O1	100fr brt blue	3.50	3.50
O10	O1	200fr bright rose	5.25	5.25
		Nos. O1-O10 (10)	15.55	15.55

BURMA

ˈbər-mə

Myanmar

LOCATION — Bounded on the north by China; east by China, Laos and Thailand; south and west by the Bay of Bengal, Bangladesh and India.
GOVT. — Republic
AREA — 261,228 sq. mi.
POP. — 60,584,850 (2012 est.)
CAPITAL — Naypyidaw Myodaw

Burma was part of India from 1826 until April 1, 1937, when it became a self-governing unit of the British Commonwealth and received a constitution. On January 4, 1948, it achieved full independence as the Union of Burma. In 1989 it became known as the Republic of the Union of Myanmar.

12 Pies = 1 Anna
16 Annas = 1 Rupee
100 Pyas = 1 Kyat (1953)

Catalogue values for unused stamps in this country are for Never Hinged items, beginning with Scott 35 in the regular postage section and Scott O28 in the official section.

Myanmar postal authorities have declared overprints of No. 362 with Burmese inscriptions for the 2006 World Cup to be illegal.

Watermarks

Wmk. 196 — Multiple Stars

Wmk. 254 — Elephant Heads

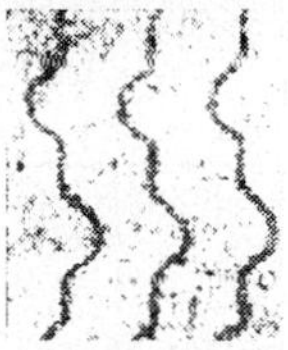

Wmk. 257 — Curved Wavy Lines

George V Stamps of India 1926-36 Overprinted in Black

Wmk. 196

1937, Apr. 1 **Typo.** ***Perf. 14***

1	A46	3p slate	1.25	.25
2	A71	½a green	.65	.25
3	A68	9p dark green	.65	.25
4	A72	1a dark brown	2.75	.25
5	A49	2a ver	.65	.25
6	A57	2a6p buff	.55	.25
7	A51	3a carmine rose	2.75	.50
8	A70	3a6p deep blue	4.25	.25
9	A52	4a olive green	.75	.25
10	A53	6a bister	.75	.60
11	A54	8a red violet	2.25	.25
12	A55	12a claret	8.50	3.50

Overprint is at the bottom on No. 7.

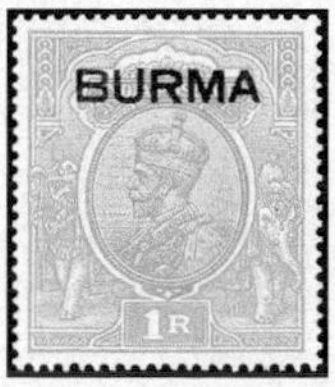

Overprinted in Black

13	A56	1r green & brown	35.00	5.50
14	A56	2r brn org & car rose	29.00	27.50
15	A56	5r dk violet & ultra	32.50	30.00
16	A56	10r car & green	135.00	110.00
17	A56	15r ol grn & ultra	450.00	225.00
18	A56	25r blue & ocher	750.00	525.00
		Nos. 1-18 (18)	1,457.	929.85
		Set, never hinged	2,600.	

For overprints see Nos. O1-O14, 1N1-1N3, 1N25-1N26, 1N47.

King George VI
A1 A2

Royal Barge — A3

Elephant Moving Teak Log — A4

Farmer Plowing Rice Paddy — A5

Sailboat on Irrawaddy River — A6

George VI and Peacock — A7

George VI — A8

Perf. 13½x14

1938-40 **Litho.** **Wmk. 254**

18A	A1	1p red org ('40)	2.25	2.00
19	A1	3p violet	.25	*3.00*
20	A1	6p ultramarine	.65	.25
21	A1	9p yel green	1.50	*2.00*
22	A2	1a brown violet	.25	.25
23	A2	1½a turq grn	1.20	*3.75*
24	A2	2a carmine	2.25	1.00
		Perf. 13		
25	A3	2a6p rose lake	10.00	3.75
26	A4	3a dk violet	10.00	3.75
27	A5	3a6p dp bl & brt bl	2.50	*9.50*
28	A2	4a slate blue, perf. 13½x14	2.40	.25
29	A6	8a slate green	2.75	.50
		Perf. 13½		
30	A7	1r brt ultra & dk violet	3.00	1.00
31	A7	2r dk vio & red brown	16.00	6.00
32	A8	5r car & dull vio	42.50	*55.00*
33	A8	10r gray grn & brn	47.50	*80.00*
		Nos. 18A-33 (16)	145.00	172.00
		Set, never hinged	240.00	

See Nos. 51-65. For overprints and surcharges see Nos. 34-50, O15-O27, 1N4-1N11, 1N28-1N30, 1N37-1N46, 1N48-1N49.

No. 25 Surcharged in Black

1940, May 6 ***Perf. 13***

34	A3	1a on 2a6p rose lake	3.00	2.50
		Never hinged	4.50	

Centenary of first postage stamp.

Catalogue values for unused stamps in this section, from this point to the end of the section, are for Never Hinged items.

Nos. 18A to 33 Overprinted in Black

a

b

1945

35	A1(a)	1p red orange	.25	.25
a.		Pair, one without overprint	1,850.	
36	A1(a)	3p violet	.25	*1.60*
37	A1(a)	6p ultramarine	.25	*.35*
38	A1(a)	9p yel green	.35	*1.40*
39	A2(a)	1a brown violet	.25	.25
40	A2(a)	1½a turq green	.25	.25
41	A2(a)	2a carmine	.25	.25
42	A3(b)	2a6p rose lake	1.75	2.50
43	A4(b)	3a dk violet	1.00	.25
44	A5(b)	3a6p dp bl & brt bl	.25	*.85*
45	A2(a)	4a slate blue	.25	*.85*
46	A6(b)	8a slate green	.25	*1.60*
47	A7(b)	1r brt ultra & dk vio	.60	.70
48	A7(b)	2r dk vio & red brown	.60	*1.50*
49	A8(b)	5r car & dull vio	.65	*1.50*
50	A8(b)	10r gray grn & brn	.65	*1.50*
		Nos. 35-50 (16)	7.85	*15.60*

Types of 1938

Perf. 13½x14

1946, Jan. 1 **Litho.** **Wmk. 254**

51	A1	3p brown	.25	*3.75*
52	A1	6p violet	.25	*.40*
53	A1	9p dull green	.25	*5.75*
54	A2	1a deep blue	.25	.25
55	A2	1½a salmon	.25	.25
56	A2	2a rose lake	.25	*.60*
		Perf. 13		
57	A3	2a6p greenish blue	3.25	*6.75*
58	A4	3a blue violet	7.00	*9.50*
59	A5	3a6p ultra & gray blk	2.25	*4.50*
60	A2	4a rose lil, perf. 13½x14	.60	*1.00*
61	A6	8a deep magenta	2.00	*6.25*
		Perf. 13½		
62	A7	1r dp mag & dk vio	2.10	*3.25*
63	A7	2r sal & red brn	9.00	6.25
64	A8	5r red brn & dk grn	10.00	*25.00*
65	A8	10r dk vio & car	25.00	*37.50*
		Nos. 51-65 (15)	62.70	*111.00*

For overprints see Nos. 70-84, O28-O42.

Burmese Man — A9

Burmese Woman — A10

Mythological Leogyph Chinthe — A11

Elephant Hauling Teak — A12

1946, May 2 *Perf. 13*

66	A9	9p peacock green	.30	.25
67	A10	1½a brt violet	.30	.25
68	A11	2a carmine	.30	.25
69	A12	3a6p ultramarine	.60	.50
		Nos. 66-69 (4)	1.50	1.25

Victory of the Allied Nations in WWII.

Nos. 51-65 Overprinted in Black

1947, Oct. 1 *Perf. 13½x14, 13, 13½*

70	A1	3p brown	1.75	.85
71	A1	6p violet	.25	*.40*
72	A1	9p dull green	.25	*.40*
a.		Inverted overprint	26.00	*37.50*
73	A2	1a deep blue	.25	*.40*
74	A2	1½a salmon	2.40	.25
75	A2	2a rose lake	.40	.30
76	A3	2a6p greenish bl	2.40	1.75
77	A4	3a blue violet	4.50	2.00
78	A5	3a6p ultra & gray blk	1.75	*3.50*
79	A2	4a rose lilac	2.50	.50
80	A6	8a dp magenta	2.50	3.50
81	A7	1r dp mag & dk vio	8.25	3.75
82	A7	2r sal & red brn	8.25	8.25
83	A8	5r red brn & dk grn	8.25	8.00
84	A8	10r dk vio & car	5.50	*8.00*
		Nos. 70-84 (15)	49.20	*41.85*

The overprint is slightly larger on Nos. 76 to 78 and 80 to 84. The Burmese characters read "Interim Government."

Other denominations are known with the overprint inverted or double.

Issues of the Republic

Bogyoke (Major General) Aung San Map and Chinze — A13

Perf. 12½x12

1948, Jan. 6 **Litho.** **Unwmk.**

85	A13	½a emerald	.25	.25
86	A13	1a deep rose	.25	.25
87	A13	2a carmine	.35	.25
88	A13	3½a blue	.55	.25
89	A13	8a lt chocolate	.85	.25
		Nos. 85-89 (5)	2.25	1.25

Attainment of independence, Jan. 4, 1948.

Martyrs' Memorial — A14

1948, July 19 **Engr.** *Perf. 14x13½*

90	A14	3p ultramarine	.25	.25
91	A14	6p green	.25	.25
92	A14	9p dp carmine	.25	.25
93	A14	1a purple	.25	.25
94	A14	2a lilac rose	.25	.25
95	A14	3½a dk slate green	.35	.25
96	A14	4a yel brown	.45	.25
97	A14	8a orange red	.50	.25
98	A14	12a claret	.70	.25
99	A14	1r blue green	1.25	.25
100	A14	2r deep blue	2.00	.35
101	A14	5r chocolate	5.50	.80
		Nos. 90-101 (12)	12.00	3.65

1st anniv. of the assassination of Burma's leaders in the fight for independence.

Ball Game (Chin-lone) A15

Bell A16

Mythical Duck (Shwe hintha) — A17

Rice Planting A18

Royal Palace — A18a

Cutting Teak — A18b

Royal Throne — A19

Designs: 6p, Dancer. 9p, Musician. 3a, Spinning. 8a, Plowing rice field.

Perf. 12½ (A15-A17), 12x12½ (A18), 13 (A19)

1949, Jan. 4

102	A15	3p ultramarine	1.90	.45
103	A15	6p green	.25	.25
104	A15	9p brn lake	.25	.25
105	A16	1a red orange	.40	.25
106	A17	2a orange	1.00	.25
107	A18	2a6p brt purple	.40	.25
108	A18	3a violet	.40	.25
109	A18a	3a6p dk grn	.65	.25
110	A18b	4a chocolate	.65	.25
111	A18	8a car ver	.85	.25
112	A19	1r blue green	1.60	.25
a.		Perf. 14	6.00	4.00
113	A19	2r deep blue	2.90	.60
114	A19	5r chocolate	6.25	1.50
115	A19	10r orange red	12.50	2.75
		Nos. 102-115 (14)	30.00	7.80

See Nos. 122-135, 139-152.
For overprints see O56-O67.

UPU Monument, Bern — A20

1949, Oct. 9 **Unwmk.** *Perf. 13*

116	A20	2a orange	.45	.40
117	A20	3½a olive grn	.55	.40
118	A20	6a lilac	.80	.40
119	A20	8a crimson	1.10	1.00
120	A20	12½a ultra	2.00	1.25
121	A20	1r blue green	2.40	1.90
		Nos. 116-121 (6)	7.30	5.35

75th anniv. of the UPU.

Types of 1949

Designs as before.

Perf. 13½x14, 14x13½, 13

1952-53 **Litho.** **Wmk. 254**

122	A15	3p brown orange	1.00	.40
123	A15	6p deep plum	.25	.25
124	A15	9p blue	.25	.25
125	A16	1a violet bl	.25	.25
126	A17	2a green ('52)	.90	.25
127	A18	2a6p green	.35	.25
128	A18	3a sal pink ('52)	.40	.25
129	A18	3a6p brown orange	.65	.25
130	A16	4a vermilion	.65	.25
131	A18	8a lt blue ('52)	.80	.50
132	A19	1r rose violet	1.00	.75
133	A19	2r yel green	2.00	.85
134	A19	5r ultramarine	5.75	2.00
135	A19	10r aquamarine	12.00	4.50
		Nos. 122-135 (14)	26.25	11.00

Map of Burma and Monument — A21

1953, Jan. 4 *Perf. 14*

136	A21	14p green	.85	.25

Perf. 13

Size: 36½x26mm

137	A21	20p salmon pink	1.10	.30
138	A21	25p ultramarine	1.25	.40

Fifth anniversary of independence.
For surcharge see No. 166.

Types of 1949

Designs: 2p, Dancer. 3p, Female musician. 20p, Spinning. 25p, Royal Palace. 30p, Cutting teak. 50p, Plowing rice field.

1954, Jan. 4 *Perf. 14x13½, 13, 14*

139	A15	1p brown orange	1.40	.25
140	A15	2p plum	.25	.25
141	A15	3p blue	.25	.25
142	A16	5p ultramarine	.25	.25
143	A18	10p yel green	.25	.25
144	A17	15p green	.65	.25
145	A18	20p vermilion	.45	.25
146	A18	25p lt red org	.45	.25
147	A16	30p vermilion	.65	.25
148	A18	50p blue	.75	.25
149	A19	1k rose violet	1.60	.50
150	A19	2k green	2.75	.75
151	A19	5k ultramarine	7.00	1.00
152	A19	10k light blue	17.50	1.50
		Nos. 139-152 (14)	34.20	6.25

For overprints and surcharges see Nos. 163-165, 173-175, O68-O79, O80-O81, O83, O85, O87.

Peace Pagoda, Monks' Hostels and Meeting-cave — A22

Designs: 10p, Sangha (community) of Cambodia. 15p, Sangha of Burma — Kuthodaw Pagoda, Mandalay, council meeting. 35p, Kaba Aye Pagoda and meeting cave, Yangon. 50p, Sangha of Thailand — Wat Arun, Bangkok. 1k, Sangha of Ceylon — Sri Dalada Maligawa, Kandy. 2k, Sangha of Laos — Pha That Luang, Vientiane.

1954 **Typo.** *Perf. 13*

153	A22	10p deep blue	.25	.25
154	A22	15p deep claret	.30	.25
155	A22	35p dark brown	.60	.25
156	A22	50p green	.80	.25
157	A22	1k carmine	1.75	.70
158	A22	2k violet	3.00	1.30
		Nos. 153-158 (6)	6.70	3.00

6th Buddhist Council, Rangoon, 1954-56.

Marble Markers of 5th Buddhist Council A23

Designs: 40p, Thatbyinnyu Pagoda. 60p, Shwedagon Pagoda, Rangoon. 1.25k, Aerial View of 6th Buddhist Council, Yegu.

Perf. 11x11½

1956, May 24 **Litho.** **Unwmk.**

159	A23	20p blue & gray olive	.45	.25
160	A23	40p blue & brt yel grn	.75	.30
161	A23	60p green & lemon	1.10	.50
162	A23	1.25k gray blue & yel	2.25	.90
		Nos. 159-162 (4)	4.55	1.95

2500th anniv. of the Buddhist Era.

Nos. 146, 149-150 Srchd. or Ovptd.

1959, Nov. 9 **Wmk. 254** *Perf. 13, 14*

163	A18	15p on 25p lt red org	.50	.25
164	A19	1k rose violet	1.50	1.00
165	A19	2k green	3.00	1.75
		Nos. 163-165 (3)	5.00	3.00

Centenary of Mandalay, former capital.
The two lines of overprint are 4mm apart on No. 163; 7mm on Nos. 164-165.

No. 136 Surcharged

1961, June *Perf. 14*

166	A21	15p on 14p green	3.00	.40

Children playing hurdles — A24

Unwmk.

1961, Dec. 11 **Litho.** *Perf. 13*

167	A24	15p claret & rose claret	1.25	.25

15th anniversary of UNICEF.

Runner with Torch — A25

Soccer, Pole Vault and Shot Put — A26

Designs: 50p, Women runners. 1k, Hurdling, weight lifting, boxing, bicycling and swimming.

Perf. 14x13, 13x14

1961, Dec. 11 Photo.

168	A25	15p red & ultra	.35	.25
169	A26	25p dk green & ocher	.60	.25
170	A26	50p vio blue & pink	1.10	.35
171	A25	1k brt green & yel	1.75	.75
		Nos. 168-171 (4)	3.80	1.60

2nd South East Asia Peninsular Games, Rangoon.

Map and Flag of Burma — A27

1963, Mar. 2 Engr. *Perf. 13*

172 A27 15p red 2.75 .25

First anniversary of new government.

Nos. 143 and 148 Ovptd. in Violet or Red

1963, Mar. 21 Wmk. 254 Litho.

173	A18 10p yel green (V)	2.00	.60
174	A18 50p blue (R)	4.00	1.25

FAO "Freedom from Hunger" campaign. No. 173 is known with a red overprint.

No. 145 Overprinted

1963, May 1 Wmk. 254

175 A18 20p vermilion 2.50 .50

Issued for May Day.

White-browed Fantail Flycatcher — A28

Indian Roller — A29

Birds: 20p, Red-whiskered bulbul. 25p, Crested serpent eagle. 50p, Sarus crane. 1k, Oriental pied hornbill. 2k, Kalij pheasant. 5k, Green peafowl.

Perf. 13½

1964, Apr. 16 Unwmk. Photo.

Size: 25x21mm

176	A28	1p gray	.55	.25
177	A28	2p carmine rose	.65	.25
178	A28	3p blue green	.65	.25

Size: 22x26½mm

Perf. 13½x13, 13 (#182)

179	A29	5p violet blue	.75	.30
180	A29	10p orange brn	.85	.30
181	A29	15p olive	1.00	.45

Size: 35x25mm

182 A28 20p rose & brn 1.25 .45

Size: 27x36½mm, 36½x27mm

183	A29	25p yel & brown	1.40	.45
184	A29	50p red, blk & gray	2.25	.65
185	A29	1k gray, ind & yel	6.00	1.50
186	A28	2k pale ol, ind & red	12.50	4.00
187	A29	5k citron, dk bl & red	27.50	10.00
		Nos. 176-187 (12)	55.35	18.85

See Nos. 197-208. For overprints see Nos. O82, O84, O86, O88-O93, O94-O115.

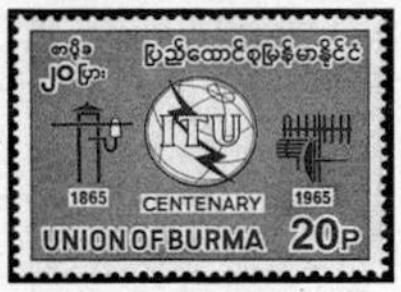

ITU Emblem, Old and New Communication Equipment — A30

1965, May 17 Litho. *Perf. 15*

Size: 32x22mm

188 A30 20p bright pink 2.50 .25

Perf. 13

Size: 34x24½mm

189 A30 50p dull green 3.50 .50

Centenary of the ITU.

ICY Emblem A31

1965, July 1 Unwmk. *Perf. 13*

190	A31	5p violet blue	.90	.25
191	A31	10p brown orange	1.40	.25
192	A31	15p olive	3.00	.50
		Nos. 190-192 (3)	5.30	1.00

International Cooperation Year.

Rice Farmer — A32

1966, Mar. 2 *Perf. 13½x13*

193 A32 15p multicolored 4.25 .40

Issued for Farmers' Day.

Cogwheel and Hammer — A33

1967, May 1 Litho. Unwmk.

194 A33 15p lt blue, yel & black 4.25 .50

Issued for Labor Day, May 1.

Bogyoke (Major General) Aung San, Tractor and Farmers A34

1968, Jan. 4 Unwmk. *Perf. 13½*

195 A34 15p sky bl, blk & ocher 4.25 .40

20th anniversary of independence.

Largest Burmese Pearl — A35

1968, Mar. 4 Litho. *Perf. 13½*

196 A35 15p blue, ultra, gray & yel 7.50 .40

4th Burmese Gems and Pearls Emporium

Bird Types of 1964 in Changed Sizes

Designs as before.

Unwmk.

1968, July 1 Photo. *Perf. 14*

Size: 21x17mm

197	A28	1p gray	.65	.30
198	A28	2p carmine rose	.65	.30
199	A28	3p blue green	.70	.40

Size: 23½x28mm

200	A29	5p violet blue	.70	.40
201	A29	10p orange brown	.75	.55
202	A29	15p olive	.95	.60

Size: 38½x21, 21x38½mm

203	A28	20p rose & brown	1.10	.60
204	A29	25p yel & brown	1.50	1.25
205	A29	50p ver, blk, & gray	2.50	1.25
206	A29	1k gray, ind & yel	17.50	1.25
207	A28	2k dull cit, ind & red	15.00	3.25
208	A29	5k yel, dk blue & red	30.00	14.00
		Nos. 197-208 (12)	72.00	24.15

For overprints see Nos. O92-O102.

Paddy Rice — A36

1969, Mar. 2 Litho. *Perf. 13*

209 A36 15p blue, emerald & yel 4.25 .30

Issued for Peasant's Day.

ILO Emblem A37

1969, Oct. 29 Photo.

210	A37	15p dk blue grn & gold	.75	.25
211	A37	50p dp carmine & gold	1.75	.55

50th anniv. of the ILO.

Soccer — A38

Designs: 25p, Runner, horiz. 50p, Weight lifter. 1k, Women's volleyball.

Perf. 12½x13, 13x12½

1969, Dec. 1 Litho.

212	A38	15p brt olive & multi	.40	.25
213	A38	25p brown & multi	.60	.25
214	A38	50p brt green & multi	1.30	.30
215	A38	1k blue, yel grn & blk	2.40	.50
		Nos. 212-215 (4)	4.70	1.30

5th South East Asia Peninsular Games, Rangoon.

Burmese Flags and Marching Soldiers — A39

1970, Mar. 27 *Perf. 13*

216 A39 15p multicolored 2.50 .30

Issued for Armed Forces Day.

Solar System and UN Emblem A40

1970, June 26 Photo. Unwmk.

217 A40 15p lt ultra & multi 4.25 .40

25th anniversary of the United Nations.

Scroll, Marchers, Peacock Emblem — A41

Designs: 25p, Students' boycott demonstration. 50p, Banner and marchers at Shwedagon Camp.

1970, Nov. 23 Litho. *Perf. 13*

218	A41	15p ultra & multi	.75	.25
219	A41	25p multicolored	1.25	.25
220	A41	50p lt blue & multi	2.00	.50
		Nos. 218-220 (3)	4.00	1.00

50th National Day (Students' 1920 uprising).

Workers, Farmers, Technicians — A42

15p, Burmese of various races, & flags. 25p, Hands holding document. 50p, Red party flag.

1971, June 28 Litho. *Perf. 13½*

221	A42	5p blue & multi	.75	.25
222	A42	15p blue & multi	1.25	.25
223	A42	25p blue & multi	1.50	.30
224	A42	50p blue & multi	2.00	.50
a.		Souvenir sheet of 4, #221-224	22.50	22.50
		Nos. 221-224 (4)	5.50	1.30

1st Congress of Burmese Socialist Program Party.

Child Drinking Milk — A43

UNICEF, 25th Anniv.: 50p, Marionettes.

1971, Dec. 11 *Perf. 14½*

225	A43	15p lt ultra & multi	1.25	.30
226	A43	50p emerald & multi	2.00	.60

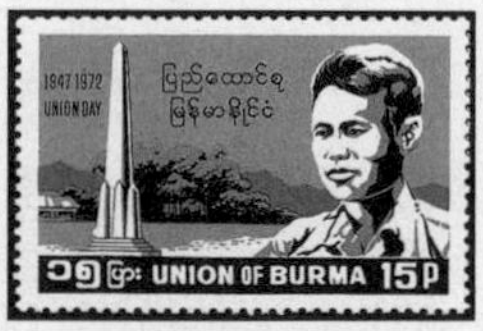

Aung San, Independence Monument, Panglong — A44

Union Day, 25th Anniv.: 50p, Bogyoke Aung San and people in front of Independence Monument. 1k, Map of Burma with flag pointing to Panglong, vert.

1972, Feb. 12 *Perf. 14*

227 A44 15p ocher & multi .85 .25
228 A44 50p blue & multi 1.45 .50
229 A44 1k green, ultra & red 3.75 .75
Nos. 227-229 (3) 6.05 1.50

Burmese and Double Star A45

1972 **Litho.** *Perf. 14*

230 A45 15p bister & multi 2.10 .25

Revolutionary Council, 10th anniversary.

"Your Heart is your Health" — A46

1972, Apr. 7 *Perf. 14x14½*

231 A46 15p yellow, red & black 2.40 .30

World Health Day.

Burmese of Various Ethnic Groups A47

1973, Feb. 12 **Litho.** *Perf. 14*

232 A47 15p multicolored 2.40 .45

1973 census.

In 1973, the Government Security Printing Works located at Wazi assumed control of tthe production of Burma's postage stamps and bank notes. Unless otherwise mentioned, all subsequent issues were printed at that location. Collectors should note that the printing is often poor and the gauge of perforations may vary from the gauge stated in the catalogue listings.

Casting Vote — A48

Natl. Referendum: 10p, Voters holding map of Burma. 15p, Farmer & soldier holding ballots.

Perf. 14x14½, 14½x14

1973, Dec. 15 **Litho.**

233 A48 5p deep org & black .80 .25
234 A48 10p blue & multi .85 .30
235 A48 15p blue & multi, vert. .90 .45
Nos. 233-235 (3) 2.55 1.00

Open-air Meeting A49

Designs: 15p, Regional flags. 1k, Scales of justice and Burmese emblem.

1974, Mar. 2 **Photo.** *Perf. 13½*

Size: 80x26mm

236 A49 15p blue & multi 1.10 .30

Size: 37x25mm

237 A49 50p blue & multi 1.75 .50
238 A49 1k lt blue, bis & blk 2.65 .95
Nos. 236-238 (3) 5.50 1.75

First meeting of People's Assembly.

Carrier Pigeon and UPU Emblem A50

UPU Cent.: 20p, Mother reading letter to child, vert. 50p, Simulated block of stamps, vert. 1k, Burmese doll, vert. 2k, Mailman delivering letter to family.

1974, May 22 *Perf. 13x13½, 13½x13*

239 A50 15p grn, lt grn & org .75 .25
240 A50 20p multicolored 1.00 .25
241 A50 50p green & multi 1.75 .40
242 A50 1k ultra & multi 2.75 .75
243 A50 2k blue & multi 5.00 1.50
Nos. 239-243 (5) 11.25 3.15

Kachins A51

Bamar (Burmese) Couple A52

Designs: 3p, Karennis woman. 5p, 15p, Karin couple. 10p, Chin couple (like 1p). 50p, Mon woman with fan. 1k, Seated Rakhine woman. 5k, Shan drummer.

Inscribed: Socialist Republic of the Union of Burma

Perf. 13, 13x13½ (#248-251)

1974-78 **Photo.**

244 A51 1p rose & lilac rose .55 .25
245 A51 3p dk brown & pink .70 .25
246 A51 5p pink & violet .75 .25
246A A51 10p Prus blue ('76) 1.00 .25
247 A51 15p lt grn & ol ('75) 1.00 .25
248 A52 20p lt blue & multi 1.50 .25
249 A52 50p ocher & multi 2.50 .50
250 A52 1k brt rose & multi 5.00 1.25
251 A52 5k ol green & multi 16.00 5.00
Nos. 244-251 (9) 29.00 8.25

For different country names see Nos. 298-303.

IWY Emblem, Woman and Globe A53

IWY: 2k, Symbolic flower, globe and IWY emblem, vert.

1975, Dec. 15 **Photo.** *Perf. 13*

252 A53 50p green & black *1.00* .30
253 A53 2k black & blue *3.75* 1.10

Burmese with Raised Fists A54

Constitution Day: 50p, Demonstrators with banners and emblem. 1k, People and map of Burma, emblem.

1976, Jan. 3 *Perf. 14*

254 A54 20p blue & black 1.30 .25
255 A54 50p blue, blk & brn 1.70 .50

Size: 56x20mm

256 A54 1k blue & multi 4.00 1.00
Nos. 254-256 (3) 7.00 1.75

Students, Campaign Emblem — A55

Abacus A56

Intl. Literacy Year: 50p, Campaign emblem. 1k, Emblem, book and globe.

1976, Sept. 8 **Photo.** *Perf. 14*

257 A55 10p salmon & black .65 .30
258 A56 15p blue grn & multi .85 .45
259 A56 50p ultra, org & blk 2.00 .75
260 A55 1k multicolored 3.50 1.50
Nos. 257-260 (4) 7.00 3.00

Steam Locomotive A57

Diesel Train Emerging from Tunnel — A58

Cent. of Burma's Railroad: 20p, Early train and oxcart. 25p, Old and new trains approaching station. 50p, Railroad bridge.

1977, May 1 *Perf. 13½*

261 A57 15p multicolored 11.00 1.75

Size: 38x26, 26x38mm

262 A57 20p multicolored 3.50 .60
263 A57 25p multicolored 5.25 .85
264 A57 50p multicolored 6.50 1.75
265 A58 1k multicolored 15.00 2.50
Nos. 261-265 (5) 41.25 7.45

Karaweik Pagoda A59

Design: 1k, Karaweik Pagoda, front view.

1977

266 A59 50p light brown 1.75 .55

Size: 78x25mm

267 A59 1k multicolored 4.25 .95

Jade Dragon — A60

Precious Jewelry: 20p, Gold bird with large pear in beakl. 50p, Hand holding pearl necklace with pendant. 1k, Gold dragon, horiz.

1978 **Photo.** *Perf. 13*

268 A60 15p green & yel grn 1.00 .25
269 A60 20p multicolored 2.00 .35
270 A60 50p multicolored 4.00 .75

Size: 55x20mm

Perf. 14

271 A60 1k multicolored 9.00 1.50
Nos. 268-271 (4) 16.00 2.85

16th Gem Emporium.

Satellite over Map of Asia A61

1979, Feb., 12 **Photo.** *Perf. 13*

272 A61 25p multicolored 4.25 .60

Introduction of satellite communications system.

IYC Emblem in Map of Burma — A62

1979, Dec. **Photo.** *Perf. 13½*

273 A62 25p multicolored 1.25 .30
274 A62 50p multicolored 3.25 .60

International Year of the Child.

Weather Balloon, WMO Emblem — A63

50p, Weather satellite, cloud.

1980, Mar. 23 **Photo.** *Perf. 13½*

275 A63 25p shown 1.25 .25
276 A63 50p red, grn & blk 2.75 .45

World Meteorological Day.

Weight Lifting, Olympic Rings A64

1980, Dec. **Litho.** *Perf. 14*

277 A64 20p Weight lifting .85 .25
278 A64 50p Boxing 1.50 .40
279 A64 1k Soccer 2.40 .65
Nos. 277-279 (3) 4.75 1.30

22nd Summer Olympic Games, Moscow, July 19-Aug. 3.

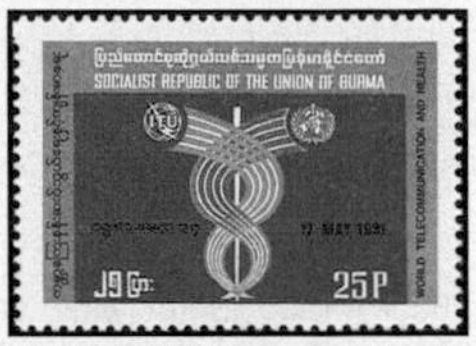

13th World Telecommunications Day — A65

1981, May 17 Photo. *Perf. 13½*
280 A65 25p orange & black 3.75 .40

World Food Day A66

25p, Livestock, produce. 50p, Farmer, rice, produce. 1k, Emblems.

1981, Oct. 16 Photo. *Perf. 13½*
281 A66 25p multi 1.50 .25
282 A66 50p multi 3.00 .50
283 A66 1k multi 3.75 .90
Nos. 281-283 (3) 8.25 1.65

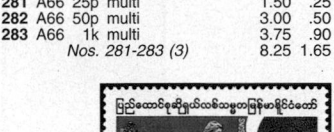

Intl. Year of the Disabled A67

1981, Dec. 12
284 A67 25p multicolored 3.00 .35

World Communications Year — A68

1983, Sept. 15 Litho. *Perf. 14½x14*
285 A68 15p pale blue & black 1.00 .30
286 A68 25p dull lake & black 2.00 .50
287 A68 50p grn, pale grn, blk & lake 5.00 1.25
288 A68 1k buff, blk, beige & yel grn 8.00 2.00
Nos. 285-288 (4) 16.00 4.05

Fish, Ship, Globe, FAO Emblem — A69

1983, Oct. 16 Photo. *Perf. 14x14½*
289 A69 15p brt blue, bister & blk 1.50 .40
290 A69 25p yel grn, pale org & blk 2.50 .85
291 A69 50p org, pale grn & blk 5.50 1.75
292 A69 1k yel, ultra & black 9.00 3.00
Nos. 289-292 (4) 18.50 6.00

World Food Day.

Stylized Trees, Hemispheres and Log — A70

1984, Oct. 16 *Perf. 14½x14*
293 A70 15p org, black & blue 1.60 .50
294 A70 25p pale yel, blk & lt vio 2.40 1.00
295 A70 50p pale pink, blk & lt grn 4.00 1.60
296 A70 1k yel, blk & lt rose vio 9.00 3.60
Nos. 293-296 (4) 17.00 6.70

World Food Day.

Intl. Youth Year — A71

1985, Oct. 15 *Perf. 14x14½*
297 A71 15p multicolored 2.40 .30

Types of 1974
Inscribed: Union of Burma

1989 Photo. *Perf. 13½*
298 A51 15p olive & lt green .80 .30
298A A52 20p lt blue & multi *37.50* —
299 A52 50p violet & brown 1.90 .75
300 A52 1k multicolored 3.00 1.25
Nos. 298,299-300 (3) 5.70 2.30

Issued: 15p, 6/26; 50p, 6/12; 1k, 9/6.

No. 298A was prepared but not issued. A quantity was accidentally supplied to the Shan State post office in July 1995, and these stamps were sold to the public. A limited quantity was subsequently made available to collectors in Yangon.

UNION OF MYANMAR
Inscribed: Union of Myanmar

1990-91 Photo. *Perf. 13½*
301 A51 15p olive & lt green .80 .30
301A A52 20p brn, grnsh blue & blk ('91) *27.50* —
302 A52 50p violet & brown 2.00 .55
303 A52 1k multicolored 3.00 1.25

Issued: 15p, May 26; 50p, May 12.

Fountain, Natl. Assembly Park — A74

1990, May 27 Litho. *Perf. 14½x14*
304 A74 1k multicolored 5.25 1.25

State Law and Order Restoration Council.

A75

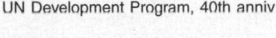

1990, Dec. 20 Litho. *Perf. 14x14½*
305 A75 2k multicolored 6.00 1.75

UN Development Program, 40th anniv.

Nawata Ruby — A76

1991, Jan. 26
306 A76 50p multi 7.00 1.25

Myanmar Gems and Jade Enterprise Emporium.

Painting of Freedom Fighters — A77

Bronze Statue — A78

1992, Jan. 4 Litho. *Perf. 14x14½*
307 A77 50p multicolored 1.00 .60
308 A78 2k multicolored 3.50 2.00

44th anniversary of independance.

National Sports Festival — A79

1992, Apr. 10 Litho. *Perf. 14x14½*
309 A79 50p multicolored 2.25 .60

A80

1992, Dec. 1 Litho. *Perf. 14x14½*
310 A80 50p red 2.75 .50

World Campaign Against AIDS.

A81

1992, Dec. 5 Litho. *Perf. 14x14½*
Background Color
311 A81 50p pink .60 .30
312 A81 1k yellow 1.00 .50
313 A81 3k orange 2.60 1.25
314 A81 5k green 5.00 2.50
Nos. 311-314 (4) 9.20 4.55

Intl. Conference on Nutrition, Rome.

Artifacts — A82

1993, Sept. 1 Litho. *Perf. 14x14½*
315 A82 5k Golden goose (Hintha) 3.00 1.50
316 A82 10k Lawkanatt 6.00 3.00

Natl. Constitutional Convention A83

1993, Jan. 1 Litho. *Perf. 14x14½*
317 A83 50p multicolored .75 .30
318 A83 3k multicolored 3.75 1.50

Equestrian Festival — A84

1993, Oct. 23 Litho. *Perf. 14½x14*
319 A84 3k multicolored 4.00 1.50

Environment Day — A85

1994, June 5 Litho. *Perf. 14*
320 A85 4k multicolored 5.00 2.00

A86

1994, Sept. 15 Litho. *Perf. 14*
321 A86 3k multicolored 4.25 2.00

Union of Solidarity & Development, 1st anniv.

Armed Forces, 50th Anniv. A87

1995, Mar. 27 Litho. ***Perf. 14½x14***
322 A87 50p multicolored 1.50 .50

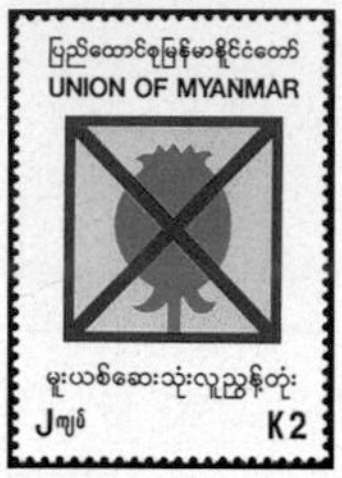

Prevent Drug Abuse — A88

1995, June 26 Litho. ***Perf. 14***
323 A88 2k multicolored 3.00 1.50

A89

1995, Oct. 17 Litho. ***Perf. 14x14½***
324 A89 50p multicolored 1.60 .50

Myanmar motion pictures, 60th anniv.

UN, 50th Anniv. — A90

1995, Oct. 24
325 A90 4k multicolored 5.00 2.50

A91

1995, Nov. 1
326 A91 50p pink & multi .80 .50
327 A91 2k green & multi 3.25 1.75

University of Yangon (Rangoon), 75th anniv.

Visit Myanmar Year A92

Designs: 50p, Couple in boat on Inlay Lake with food bowl for Buddha, Buddhist monks. 4k, Decorated royal barge on Kandawgyi (Royal Lake), Yangoon. 5k, Royal moat, entrance of Yadanabon (Mandalay), vert.

Perf. 14½x14, 14x14½
1996, Mar. 1 **Litho.**
328 A92 50p multicolored .75 .50
329 A92 4k multicolored 5.25 2.75
330 A92 5k multicolored 6.50 3.25
Nos. 328-330 (3) 12.50 6.50

UNICEF, 50th Anniv. — A93

Stylized designs: 1k, Mother breastfeeding. 2k, Vaccinating child. 4k, Girls going to school.

1996, Dec. 11 Litho. ***Perf. 14x14½***
331 A93 1k multicolored 1.00 .75
332 A93 2k multicolored 1.90 1.00
333 A93 4k multicolored 4.00 2.00
Nos. 331-333 (3) 6.90 3.75

Intl. Letter Writing Week A94

Designs: 2k, Men in canoe. 5k, Stylized figures forming pyramid, flag, map, vert.

1996, Oct. 7 ***Perf. 14½x14, 14x14½***
334 A94 2k multicolored 1.75 1.20
335 A94 5k multicolored 3.50 2.40

A95

1997, July 24 Litho. ***Perf. 14x14½***
336 A95 1k blue & multi 1.25 1.25
337 A95 2k yellow & multi 2.75 2.75

Assoc. of Southeast Asian Nations (ASEAN), 30th anniv.

A96

1998, Jan. 4 Litho. ***Perf. 14x14½***
338 A96 2k multicolored 3.00 3.00

Independence, 50th anniv.

Musical Instruments A97

5k, Xylophone. 10k, Mon brass gongs. 20k, Rakhine (drum). 30k, Harp. 50k, Shan pot drum. 100k, Kachin brass gong.

1998-2001 Photo. ***Perf. 13¼***
339 A97 5k multicolored *.75* *.50*
340 A97 10k multicolored *1.10* *.90*
341 A97 20k multicolored *1.90* *1.60*
342 A97 30k multicolored *3.00* *2.50*
343 A97 50k multicolored *5.75* *4.75*
344 A97 100k multicolored *7.50* *6.00*
Nos. 339-344 (6) 20.00 16.25

Caution: Market prices for Nos. 339-344 have been speculative for the past 10 years.

Issued: 5k, 8/28; 10k, 10/9; 20k, 2/12/99; 30k, 4/18/01; 50k, 11/15/99; 100k, 2/12/00.

See No. 413.

Compare type A97 with type A163.

Asian & Pacific Decade of Disabled Persons (1993-2002) A98

1999, Jan. 10 Litho. ***Perf. 14***
345 A98 2k yellow & multi 1.75 1.50
346 A98 5k apple green & multi 3.25 2.75

UPU, 125th Anniv. — A99

1999, Dec. 20 Litho. ***Perf. 14x14¼***
347 A99 2k blue & multi 2.00 1.50
348 A99 5k purple & multi 4.00 3.50

Independence, 52nd Anniv. — A100

2000, Jan. 4
349 A100 2k multi 3.00 3.00

World Meteorological Day — A101

Perf. 14x14¼, 14¼x14
2000, Mar. 23 **Photo.**
350 A101 2k Anemometer, vert. 1.90 1.90
351 A101 5k shown 4.75 4.75
352 A101 10k Cloud, sun 8.50 8.50
Nos. 350-352 (3) 15.15 15.15

World Meteorological Organization, 50th anniv.

Diplomatic Relations with People's Republic of China, 50th Anniv. — A102

2000, June 8 Litho. ***Perf. 14¼x14***
353 A102 5k multi 4.50 4.50

Myanmar postal officials have declared as "illegal" the following items inscribed "Union of Myanmar."

Sheets of nine stamps of various denominations depicting:

Personalities of the 20th Century, Musical stars, Orchids with Rotary emblems, Mushrooms with Rotary emblems, Cats and dogs with Scout emblems, Chess, Fish, Owls, and Trains (two different).

Sheets of six stamps of various denominations depicting:

Bruce Lee, Horror movie scenes, and Marilyn Monroe (two different).

Souvenir sheets of two stamps of various denominations depicting:

Formula 1 race cars (two different), Golfers (six different), and Classic cars (eight different).

Souvenir sheets of one depicting:

Dutch royal wedding, Bruce Lee (three different), Tiger Woods (three different), Impressionist paintings (six different), Elvis Presley (six different), and Chess (twelve different).

Campaign Against Drugs — A103

2000, June 26 Litho. ***Perf. 14x14¼***
354 A103 2k multi 3.75 3.75

Independence, 53rd Anniv. — A104

2001, Jan. 4
355 A104 2k multi 3.00 3.00

Independence, 54th Anniv. — A105

Inscriptions in: (2k), Burmese. 30k, English.

2002, Jan. 4
356-357 A105 Set of 2 *10.00 10.00*

Independence, 55th Anniv. — A106

Inscriptions in: (2k), Burmese. 30k, English.

2003, Jan. 4
358-359 A106 Set of 2 *11.00 11.00*

Flora — A107

Designs: No. 360, 30k, Black orchide. No. 361, 30k, Mango.

2004, Feb. 11
360-361 A107 Set of 2 *9.00 9.00*

FIFA (Fédération Internationale de Football Association), Cent. — A108

2004, May 5 ***Perf. 14¼x14***
362 A108 2k multi *4.00 4.00*

Myanmar postal authorities have declared overprints of No. 362 with Burmese inscriptions for the 2006 World Cup to be illegal.

World Buddhist Summit — A109

Designs: 5k, Emblem, temples. 30k, Emblem, temples, diff.

2004, Dec. 9 Litho. ***Perf. 14¼x14***
363-364 A109 Set of 2 6.25 6.25

Independence, 59th Anniv. — A110

Statues, star and: (2k), Flag, Burmese inscriptions. 5k, Map, English inscriptions.

2007, Jan. 4 Litho. ***Perf. 14x14¼***
365-366 A110 Set of 2 *3.75 3.75*

A111

A112

National Convention — A113

2007, Aug. 13 Litho. ***Perf. 14¼x14***
367 A111 20k multi *.90 .90*
368 A112 30k multi *1.60 1.60*
369 A113 50k multi *2.00 2.00*
Nos. 367-369 (3) 4.50 4.50

Miniature Sheet

Association of South East Asian Nations (ASEAN), 40th Anniv. — A114

No. 370: a, Secretariat Building, Bandar Seri Begawan, Brunei. b, National Museum of Cambodia. c, Fatahillah Museum, Jakarta, Indonesia. d, Typical house, Laos. e, Malayan Railway Headquarters Building, Kuala Lumpur, Malaysia. f, Yangon Post Office, Myanmar. g, Malacañang Palace, Philippines. h, National Museum of Singapore. i, Vimanmek Mansion, Bangkok, Thailand. j, Presidential Palace, Hanoi, Viet Nam.

2007, Oct. 19
370 A114 50k Sheet of 10, #a-j *11.00 11.00*

See Brunei No. 607, Cambodia No. 2339, Indonesia Nos. 2120-2121, Laos Nos. 1717-1718, Malaysia No. 1170, Philippines Nos. 3103-3105, Singapore No. 1265, Thailand No. 2315, and Viet Nam Nos. 3302-3311.

A115

Independence, 60th Anniv. — A116

2008, Jan. 4 Litho. ***Perf. 14¼x14***
371 A115 50k multi *1.75 1.75*
372 A116 100k multi *3.00 3.00*

Constitutional Referendum — A117

Designs: No. 373, 100k, Map of Burma, people, statues, ballot box. No. 374, 100k, Line of people casting ballots, statues. 200k, Map of Burma, hand depositing ballot, vert.

Perf. 14¼x14, 14x14¼

2008, May 9 Litho.
373-375 A117 Set of 3 *5.50 5.50*

A118

Independence, 61st Anniv. — A119

2009, Jan. 4 Litho. ***Perf. 14¼x14***
376 A118 200k multi *2.00 2.00*
377 A119 300k multi *3.00 3.00*

The values for the stamps are based on official exchange rates set by the Myanmar government. Actual exchange rates appear to differ significantly.

A120

Independence, 62nd Anniv. — A121

2010, Jan. 4 Litho. ***Perf. 14¼x14***
378 A120 100k multi *5.00 5.00*
379 A121 200k multi *5.00 5.00*

Diplomatic Relations Between Myanmar and People's Republic of China, 60th Anniv. — A122

2010, June 8 Litho. ***Perf. 14¼x14***
380 A122 100k multi *2.00 2.00*

General Elections — A123

2010, Nov. 7
381 A123 500k multi *3.00 3.00*

Souvenir Sheet

Vienna Convention for the Protection of the Ozone Layer, 25th Anniv. — A124

2010, Nov. 18
382 A124 100k multi *3.00 3.00*

Independence, 63rd Anniv. — A125

2011, Jan. 4 Litho. ***Perf. 14¼x14***
383 A125 100k multi *3.00 3.00*

Union Assembly Building — A126

President's Office Building — A127

2011, June 16 Litho. ***Perf. 14¼x14***
384 A126 500k multi *3.50 3.50*
385 A127 500k multi *3.50 3.50*

Celebrating the renaming of the country as the Republic of the Union of Myanmar.

A128

Independence, 64th Anniv. — A129

2012, Jan. 4
386 A128 500k multi *1.50 1.50*
387 A129 1200k multi *3.50 3.50*

Miniature Sheet

11th ASEAN Telecommunications and Information Technology Ministers Meeting, Nay Pyi Taw — A130

No. 388: a, 100k, Line of flags, emblem, building. b, 100k, Circle of flags around emblem, building. c, 100k, Emblem, buildings in circle. d, 200k, Like #388a. e, 200k, Like #388b. f, 200k, Like #388c.

2012, Mar. 19

388 A130	Sheet of 6, #a-f	*6.75*	*6.75*
a.-c.	Any single	*.75*	*.75*
d.-f.	Any single	*1.50*	*1.50*

A131

Second Leaders Retreat of Asian Telecommunications Senior Officials and Asian Telecommunications Regulators Council, Bangkok, Thailand — A132

2012, Oct. 1

389 A131	500k multi	*3.75*	*3.75*
390 A132	500k multi	*3.75*	*3.75*

A133

Independence, 65th Anniv. — A134

2013, Jan. 4

391 A133	100k multi	*2.75*	*2.75*
392 A134	100k multi	*2.75*	*2.75*

Diplomatic Relations Between Myanmar and Russia, 65th Anniv. — A135

2013, Apr. 10

393 A135	500k multi	*3.50*	*3.50*

Miniature Sheet

27th South East Asia Games, Naypyidaw — A136

No. 394: a, 100k, Emblem of 2013 Games. b, 100k, Owl holding torch. c, 100k, Two owls. d, 100k, Six owls. e, 500k, Like #394a. f, 500k, Like #394b. g, 500k, Like #394c. h, 500k, Like #394d.

2013, Sept. 2 Litho. *Perf. 14¼x14*

394 A136	Sheet of 8, #a-h	*11.50*	*11.50*
a.-d.	Any single	*.45*	*.45*
e.-h.	Any single	*2.40*	*2.40*

A137

A138

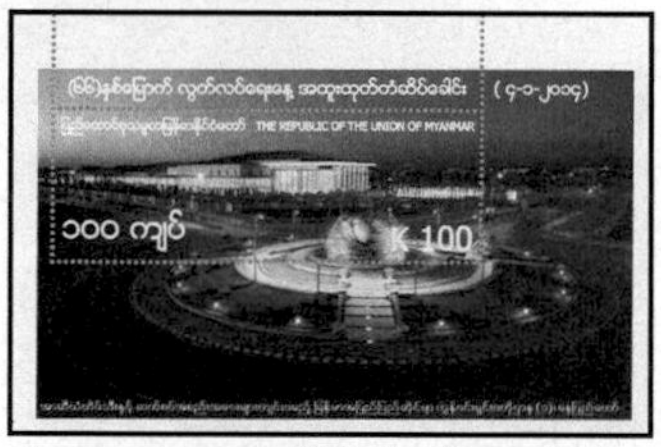

Independence, 66th Anniv. — A139

2014, Jan. 4 Litho. *Perf. 14¼x14*

395 A137	100k multi	*1.25*	*1.25*
396 A138	200k multi	*2.25*	*2.25*

Souvenir Sheet

397 A139	100k multi		*2.75*

A140

A141

Census — A142

2014, Feb. 24 Litho. *Perf. 14¼x14*

398 A140	200k multi	*1.00*	*1.00*

English Text

399 A141	200k green & multi	*1.00*	*1.00*
400 A141	200k blue & multi	*1.00*	*1.00*

Burmese Text

401 A142	200k green & multi	*1.00*	*1.00*
402 A142	200k blue & multi	*1.00*	*1.00*
	Nos. 398-402 (5)	*5.00*	*5.00*

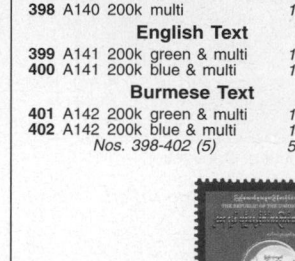

A143

A144

A145

Census A146

2014, Mar. 10 Litho. *Perf. 14x14¼*

403 A143	100k multi	*1.00*	*1.00*

Perf. 14¼x14

404 A144	100k multi	*1.00*	*1.00*

English Text

405 A145	100k green & multi	*1.00*	*1.00*
406 A145	100k blue & multi	*1.00*	*1.00*

Burmese Text

407 A146	100k green & multi	*1.00*	*1.00*
408 A146	100k blue & multi	*1.00*	*1.00*
	Nos. 403-408 (6)	6.00	*6.00*

A147

2014 ASEAN Summit, Naypyidaw — A148

2014, May 8 Litho. *Perf. 14¼x14*

409 A147	100k multi	*2.00*	*2.00*
410 A148	100k multi	*2.00*	*2.00*

Issued to commemorate Myanmar taking the ASEAN chair.

Announcement of Five Principles of Peaceful Co-existence Between Burma, China and India, 60th Anniv. — A149

Temple, Myanmar, Great Wall of China and Taj Mahal with background color of: 100k, Green. 500k, Orange brown.

2014, June 28 Litho. *Perf. 14¼x14*

411-412 A149	Set of 2	*4.50*	*4.50*

Musical Instrument Type of 1998-2000 Inscribed "Republic of the Union of Myanmar"

2014 ? Litho. *Perf. 14x14¼*

413 A97	100k Kachin brass gong	*1.40*	*1.40*

A150

A151

Independence, 67th Anniv. — A152

2015, Jan. 4 Litho. *Perf. 14¼x14*

414 A150	100k multi	*1.00*	*1.00*
415 A151	100k multi	*1.00*	*1.00*
416 A152	200k multi	*2.00*	*2.00*
	Nos. 414-416 (3)	*4.00*	*4.00*

ASEAN Emblem and Flags — A153

Denominations: 100k, 500k.

2015, Aug. 8 Litho. *Perf. 14¼x14*

417-418 A153	Set of 2	*5.00*	*5.00*

See Brunei No. 656, Cambodia No. 2428, Indonesia No. 2428, Laos No. , Malaysia No. 1562, Philippines No. 3619, Singapore No. 1742, Thailand No. 2875, Viet Nam No. 3529.

A154

A155

Independence, 68th Anniv. — A156

2016, Jan. 4 Litho. *Perf. 14¼x14*

419 A154 100k multi	1.75	1.75
420 A155 100k multi	1.75	1.75
421 A156 200k multi	3.50	3.50
Nos. 419-421 (3)	7.00	7.00

A157

A158

Union Peace Conference, Naypyidaw — A159

2016, Aug. 29 Litho. *Perf. 14¼x14*

422 A157 100k multi	1.25	1.25
423 A158 200k multi	2.40	2.40
424 A159 500k multi	6.25	6.25
Nos. 422-424 (3)	9.90	9.90

Bogyoke Aung San (1915-47), Politician — A162

2017, Mar. 17 Litho. *Perf. 14x14¼*

428 A162 500k multi	6.00	6.00

Ministry of Foreign Affairs, 70th anniv.

Musical Instruments A163

Designs: No. 429, Rakhine auspicious drum. No. 430, Shan pot drum. No. 431, Kachin brass gong. No. 432, Mon brass gongs. 1000k, Myanmar xylophone. 2500k, Myanmar harp.

2017 Litho. *Perf. 14x14¼*

429 A163 200k multi	.60	.60
430 A163 200k multi	.60	.60
431 A163 500k multi	1.50	1.50
432 A163 500k multi	1.50	1.50
433 A163 1000k multi	3.00	3.00
434 A163 2500k multi	7.50	7.50
Nos. 429-434 (6)	14.70	14.70

Issued: 1000k, 2500k, 7/27; others, 9/14. Compare type A163 with type A97.

A165

A166

Independence, 70th Anniv. — A167

2018, Jan. 4 Litho. *Perf. 14¼x14*

436 A165 100k multi	1.40	1.40
437 A166 100k multi	—	—
438 A167 100k multi	—	—

Yangon Post Office Building, 110th Anniv. A168

2018, Sept. 20 Litho. *Perf. 14¼x14*

439 A168 200k multi	2.10	2.10

A169

A170

Independence, 71st Anniv. — A171

2019, Jan. 4 Litho. *Perf. 14¼x14*

440 A169 100k multi	1.40	1.40
441 A170 100k multi	1.40	1.40
442 A171 100k multi	1.40	1.40
Nos. 440-442 (3)	4.20	4.20

Festivals — A172

Designs: No. 443, Equestrian Festival. No. 444, Htamanè Festival. No. 445, Sand Pagodas Festival. No. 446, Thingyan Water Festival. No. 447, Bodhi Tree Water Pouring Festival. No. 448, Religious Examination Festival. No. 449, Buddhist Ordination Festival. No. 450, Sayedanmè Festival. No. 451, Boat Racing Festival. No. 452, Thidingyut Festival of Lights. No. 453, Kathina Robe Offering Festival. No. 454, Myanmar Literature Festival.

2019 Litho. *Perf. 14¼x14*

443 A172 200k multi	2.10	2.10
444 A172 200k multi	2.10	2.10
445 A172 200k multi	2.10	2.10
446 A172 200k multi	2.10	2.10
447 A172 200k multi	2.10	2.10
448 A172 200k multi	2.10	2.10
449 A172 200k multi	2.10	2.10
450 A172 200k multi	2.10	2.10
451 A172 200k multi	2.10	2.10
452 A172 200k multi	2.10	2.10
453 A172 200k multi	2.10	2.10
454 A172 200k multi	2.10	2.10
Nos. 443-454 (12)	25.20	25.20

Issued: No. 443, 1/6; No. 444, 2/5; No. 445, 3/6; No. 446, 4/5; No. 447, 5/4; No. 448, 6/3; No. 449, 7/3; No. 450, 8/1. No. 451, 8/30; No. 452, 9/29; No. 453, 10/28: No. 454, 11/27.

Miniature Sheets

Dancers From Ethnic Groups — A173

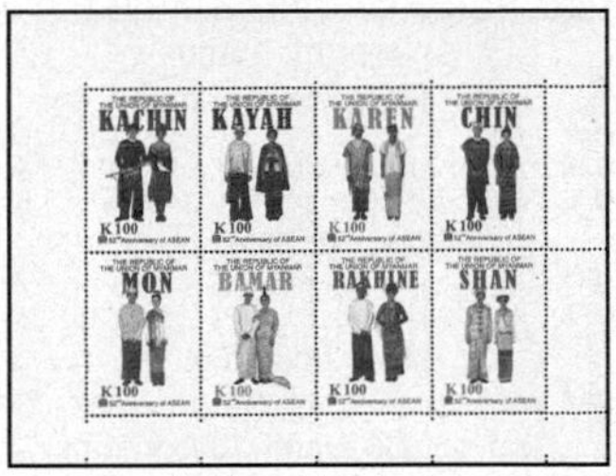

People From Ethnic Groups Standing — A174

Nos. 455 and 456 — Ethnic group: a, Kachin. b, Kayah. c, Karen. d, Chin. e, Mon. f, Bamar. g, Rakhine. h, Shan.

2019, Aug. 8 Litho. *Perf. 14x14¼*

455 A173 100k Sheet of 8, #a-h	8.25	8.25
456 A174 100k Sheet of 8, #a-h	8.25	8.25

Association of Southeast Asian Nations, 52nd anniv.

Mohandas K. Gandhi (1869-1948), Indian Nationalist Leader — A175

2019, Oct. 2 Litho. *Perf. 14¼x14*

457 A175 100k multi	1.10	1.10

Universal Postal Union, 145th Anniv. A176

2019, Oct. 9 Litho. *Perf. 14¼x14*

458 A176 200k multi	2.10	2.10

OFFICIAL STAMPS

Stamps of India, 1926-34, Overprinted in Black

1937 Wmk. 196 *Perf. 14*

O1	A46	3p gray	4.50	.25
O2	A71	½a green	17.50	.30
O3	A68	9p dark green	5.00	2.00
O4	A72	1a dark brown	9.50	.35
O5	A49	2a vermilion	18.00	1.00
O6	A57	2a6p buff	12.00	3.75
O7	A52	4a olive grn	12.00	.35
O8	A53	6a bister	10.00	*20.00*
O9	A54	8a red violet	12.00	4.00
O10	A55	12a claret	12.50	*20.00*

Overprinted

O11	A56	1r green & brown	35.00	12.00
O12	A56	2r buff & car rose	50.00	*65.00*
O13	A56	5r dk vio & ultra	200.00	*90.00*
O14	A56	10r car & green	600.00	*300.00*
		Nos. O1-O14 (14)	998.00	*519.00*
		Set, never hinged	1,475.	

For overprint see No. 1N27.

Regular Issue of 1938 Overprinted in Black

1939 Wmk. 254 *Perf. 14*

O15	A1	3p violet	.30	.30
O16	A1	6p ultramarine	.30	.30
O17	A1	9p yel green	3.50	3.50
O18	A2	1a brown violet	.30	.35
O19	A2	1½a turquoise green	3.25	2.00
O20	A2	2a carmine	1.00	.30
O21	A2	4a slate blue	3.50	3.50

Overprinted

Perf. 13½x13

O22	A3	2a6p rose lake	17.00	17.00
O23	A6	8a slate green	15.00	5.00

Perf. 14

O24	A7	1r brt ultra & dk vio	15.00	6.00
O25	A7	2r dk vio & red brn	30.00	15.00
O26	A8	5r car & dull vio	25.00	*40.00*
O27	A8	10r gray grn & brn	110.00	*50.00*
		Nos. O15-O27 (13)	224.15	143.25
		Set, never hinged	375.00	

For overprints see Nos. 1N12-1N16, 1N31-1N36, 1NO1.

Catalogue values for unused stamps in this section, from this point to the end of the section, are for Never Hinged items.

Nos. 51-56, 60 Overprinted Like Nos. O15-O21

1946 *Perf. 13½x14*

O28	A1	3p brown	3.75	*2.75*
O29	A1	6p violet	2.75	2.00
O30	A1	9p dull green	.70	*3.50*
O31	A2	1a deep blue	.30	*2.25*
O32	A2	1½a salmon	.30	.35
O33	A2	2a rose lake	.35	*2.25*
O34	A2	4a rose lilac	.35	.90

Nos. 57, 61-65 Ovptd. Like Nos. O22-O27

Perf. 13, 13½

O35	A3	2a6p greenish blue	2.50	*4.75*
O38	A6	8a deep magenta	4.50	*2.50*
O39	A7	1r dp mag & dk vio	1.90	*3.75*
O40	A7	2r salmon & red brn	10.00	*35.00*
O41	A8	5r red brn & dk grn	19.00	*45.00*
O42	A8	10r dk violet & car	20.00	*65.00*
		Nos. O28-O42 (13)	66.40	*170.00*

Nos. O28 to O42 Overprinted in Black

1947

O43	A1	3p	brown	2.00	.45
O44	A1	6p	violet	4.00	.25
O45	A1	9p	dull green	7.00	1.20
O46	A2	1a	deep blue	7.00	1.00
O47	A2	1½a	salmon	10.00	.40
O48	A2	2a	rose lake	7.00	.30
O49	A3	2a6p	greenish bl	35.00	15.00
O50	A2	4a	rose lilac	24.00	.50
O51	A6	8a	dp magenta	24.00	4.50
O52	A7	1r	dp mag & dk vio	*20.00*	3.00
O53	A7	2r	sal & red brn	20.00	*22.50*
O54	A8	5r	red brn & dk grn	20.00	*22.50*
O55	A8	10r	dk vio & car	20.00	*35.00*
			Nos. O43-O55 (13)	200.00	106.60

The overprint is slightly larger on Nos. O49 and O51 to O55. The Burmese characters read "Interim Government."

Issues of the Republic

Nos. 102-106, 109-115 Overprinted in Carmine or Black

a. Overprint 13mm long.
b. Overprint 15mm long.

1949 Unwmk. *Perf. 12½, 13*

O56	A15(a)	3p	ultra (C)	1.25	.25
O57	A15(a)	6p	green (C)	.50	.25
O58	A15(a)	9p	carmine	.50	.25
O59	A16(a)	1a	red orange	.50	.25
O60	A17(a)	2a	orange	.60	.25
O61	A18(b)	3a6p	dk sl grn (C)	.60	.25
O62	A16(a)	4a	chocolate	.60	.25
O63	A18(b)	8a	carmine	.60	.25
O64	A19(b)	1r	blue green (C)	1.25	.25
O65	A19(b)	2r	dp blue (C)	2.60	1.00
O66	A19(b)	5r	chocolate	8.00	2.50
O67	A19(b)	10r	orange red	22.50	6.00
			Nos. O56-O67 (12)	39.50	11.75

Same Overprint in Black on Nos. 139-142, 144-152

Perf. 14x13½, 13, 14

1954-57 Wmk. 254

O68	A15(a)	1p	brown org	.30	.25
O69	A15(a)	2p	plum	.30	.25
O70	A15(a)	3p	blue	.30	.25
O71	A16(a)	5p	ultra	.30	.25
O72	A17(a)	15p	green	.30	.25
O72A	A18(b)	20p	ver ('57)	.50	.25
O73	A18(b)	25p	lt red org	.50	.25
O74	A16(a)	30p	vermilion	.50	.25
O75	A18(b)	50p	blue	1.25	.30
O76	A19(b)	1k	rose violet	1.75	.40
O77	A19(b)	2k	green	4.25	.75
O78	A19(b)	5k	ultra	7.00	1.25
O79	A19(b)	10k	light blue	22.50	3.50
			Nos. O68-O79 (13)	39.75	8.20

No. 141 Ovptd. Service

1964 Litho. *Perf. 14*

O80	A15	3p	blue	*20.00*	*12.50*

Nos. 139, 141-142, 144, 177-179, 181, 183 Ovptd.

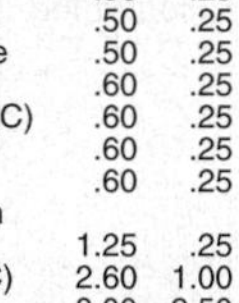

1964-65 Overprint: 11½mm

O81	A15	1p	brown orange	*8.00*	*1.00*
O82	A28	2p	carmine rose ('65)	*7.00*	*1.00*
O83	A15	3p	blue	*8.00*	*1.00*
O84	A28	3p	blue green ('65)	*7.00*	*1.00*
O85	A16	5p	ultramarine	*8.00*	*1.00*
O86	A28	5p	violet blue ('65)	*7.00*	*1.00*
O87	A17	15p	green	*8.00*	*1.00*
O88	A28	15p	olive ('65)	*7.00*	*1.00*
O89	A29	25p	yel & brn ('65)	*8.00*	*1.00*
			Nos. O81-O89 (9)	*68.00*	*9.00*

Nos. 176-178 Ovptd.

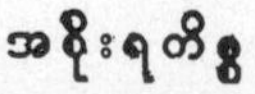

No. 181 Overprinted

1966 Overprint: 15mm

O90	A28	1p	gray	11.00	3.00
O91	A28	2p	carmine rose	11.00	3.00
O92	A28	3p	blue green	11.00	3.00

Overprint: 12mm

O93	A29	15p	olive	11.00	3.00

Nos. 176-179, 181-187 Overprinted in Black or Red

1967 Unwmk. Photo. *Perf. 13½*

Overprint: 15mm

Size: 25x21mm

O94	A28	1p	gray	.50	.40
O95	A28	2p	carmine rose	.90	.50
O96	A28	3p	blue green	.90	.65

Size: 22x26½mm

O97	A29	5p	violet blue	1.10	.70
O98	A29	15p	olive	1.10	.80

Size: 35x25mm

O99	A28	20p	rose & brown	2.00	.90

Size: 27x36½mm, 36½x27mm

O100	A29	25p	yel & brown (R)	2.50	1.00
O101	A29	50p	red, blk & gray	4.00	1.25
O102	A29	1k	gray, ind & yel (R)	9.25	1.90
O103	A28	2k	pale ol, ind & red (R)	15.50	3.00
O104	A29	5k	cit, dk bl & red (R)	40.00	15.00
			Nos. O94-O104 (11)	77.75	26.10

Similar Overprint on Nos. 197-200, 202-208 in Black or Red

1968 Unwmk. *Perf. 14*

Size: 21x17mm

Overprint: 13mm

O105	A28	1p	gray	.50	.25
O106	A28	2p	carmine rose	1.00	.25
O107	A28	3p	blue green	1.10	.40

Size: 23½x28mm

Overprint: 15mm

O108	A29	5p	violet blue	1.25	.40
O109	A29	15p	olive	1.25	.40

Size: 38½x21mm, 21x38½mm

Overprint: 14mm

O110	A28	20p	rose & brn	2.00	.50
O111	A29	25p	yel & brown (R)	4.00	.50
O112	A29	50p	ver, blk & gray	5.00	.75
O113	A29	1k	gray, ind & yel (R)	7.75	1.00
O114	A28	2k	dl cit, ind & red (R)	12.50	2.00
O115	A29	5k	yel, dk bl & red (R)	19.00	5.75
			Nos. O105-O115 (11)	55.35	12.20

OCCUPATION STAMPS

Issued by Burma Independence Army (in conjunction with Japanese occupation officials)

Henzada Issue

Stamps of Burma, 1937-40, Overprinted in Black Blue, or Red; Nos. 1, 3, 5 Overprinted in Blue or Black

Henzada Type I

1942, May Wmk. 196 *Perf. 14*

1N1	A46	3p	slate	5.00	*25.00*
1N2	A68	9p	dark green	30.00	*80.00*
1N3	A49	2a	vermilion	130.00	*225.00*

On 1938-40 George VI Issue

Perf. 13½x14

Wmk. 254

1N4	A1	1p	red orange	275.00	*400.00*
1N5	A1	3p	violet	47.50	*95.00*
1N6	A1	6p	ultra	30.00	*65.00*
1N7	A1	9p	yel green	1,100.	
1N8	A2	1a	brown violet	11.00	*50.00*
1N9	A2	1½a	turq green	25.00	*85.00*
1N10	A2	2a	carmine	25.00	*85.00*
1N11	A2	4a	slate blue	50.00	*120.00*

On Official Stamps of 1939

1N12	A1	3p	violet	150.00	*300.00*
1N13	A1	6p	ultra	175.00	*300.00*
1N14	A2	1½a	turq green	200.00	*350.00*
1N15	A2	2a	carmine	425.00	550.00
1N16	A2	4a	slate blue	1,350.	

Authorities believe this overprint was officially applied only to postal stationery and that the adhesive stamps existing with it were not regularly issued. It has been called "Henzada Type II."

Myaungmya Issue

1937 George V Issue Overprinted in Black

Myaungmya Type I

1942, May Wmk. 196 *Perf. 14*

1N25	A68	9p	dk green	130.00	
1N26	A70	3a6p	deep blue	85.00	

On Official Stamp of 1937, No. O8

1N27	A53	6a	bister	95.00	

On 1938-40 George VI Issue

Perf. 13½x14

Wmk. 254

1N28	A1	9p	yel green	175.00	
1N29	A2	1a	brown vio	650.00	
1N30	A2	4a	sl blue (blk ovpt. over red)	190.00	

On Official Stamps of 1939

1N31	A1	3p	violet	42.50	*110.00*
1N32	A1	6p	ultra	27.00	*80.00*
1N33	A2	1a	brown vio	28.00	*65.00*
1N34	A2	1½a	turq green	900.00	*1,350.*
1N35	A2	2a	carmine	40.00	*120.00*
1N36	A2	4a	slate blue	40.00	*95.00*

1938-40 George VI Issue Overprinted

Myaungmya Type II

1942, May

1N37	A1	3p	violet	22.00	*90.00*
1N38	A1	6p	ultra	60.00	*130.00*
1N39	A1	9p	yel green	27.00	*85.00*
1N40	A2	1a	brown vio	17.50	*80.00*
1N41	A2	2a	carmine	32.50	*100.00*
1N42	A2	4a	slate blue	60.00	*130.00*

Nos. 30-31 Overprinted

Myaungmya Type III

1N43	A7	1r	brt ultra & dk vio	450.00	*750.00*
1N44	A7	2r	dk vio & red brn	275.00	*550.00*

Pyapon Issue

No. 5 and 1938-40 George VI Issue Overprinted

1942, May

1N45	A1	6p	ultra	100.00	
1N46	A2	1a	brown vio	120.00	*300.00*
1N47	A49	2a	vermilion	100.00	
1N48	A2	2a	carmine	160.00	*350.00*
1N49	A2	4a	slate blue	850.00	850.00
			Nos. 1N45-1N49 (5)	1,330.	

Nos. 1N47-1N49 are valued in faulty condition.

Counterfeits of the peacock overprints exist.

OCCUPATION OFFICIAL STAMP

Myaungmya Issue

Burma No. O23 Overprinted in Black

1942, May Wmk. 254 *Perf. 13*

1NO1	A6	8a	slate green	110.00	*300.00*

Overprint characters translate: "Office use." Two types of overprint differ mainly in base of peacock which is either 5mm or 8mm.

ISSUED UNDER JAPANESE OCCUPATION

Yano Seal — OS1

Wmk. ABSORBO DUPLICATOR and Outline of Elephant in Center of Sheet

Handstamped

1942, June 1 *Perf. 12x11*

Without Gum

2N1	OS1	1(a)	vermilion	75.00	*120.00*

This stamp is the handstamped impression of the personal chop or seal of Shizuo Yano, chairman of the committee appointed to re-establish the Burmese postal system. It was prepared in Rangoon on paper captured from the Burma Government Offices. Not every stamp shows a portion of the watermark.

Farmer Plowing — OS2

Vertically Laid Paper Without Gum

Wmk. ELEPHANT BRAND and Outline of Trumpeting Elephant Covering Several Stamps

1942, June 15 Litho. *Perf. 11x12*

2N2	OS2	1a	scarlet	30.00	*35.00*

See illustration OS4.

Same, Surcharged with New Value

1942, Oct. 15

2N3	OS2	5c on 1a	scarlet	26.00	*30.00*

Stamps of Japan, 1937-42, as shown, Handstamp Surcharged with New Value in Black

½A. 1R.

Rice Harvest A83

General Nogi A84

Power Plant A85

Admiral Togo A86

Diamond Mountains, Korea — A89

Meiji Shrine, Tokyo — A90

Yomei Gate, Nikko — A91

Mount Fuji and Cherry Blossoms A94

Torii of Miyajima Shrine — A96

1942, Sept. Wmk. 257 *Perf. 13*

2N4	A83 ¼a on 1s fawn	50.00	*52.50*
2N5	A84 ½a on 2s crim	55.00	*55.00*
2N6	A85 ¾a on 3s green	85.00	*90.00*
2N7	A86 1a on 5s brn lake	82.50	72.50
2N8	A89 3a on 7s dp green	130.00	*150.00*
2N9	A86 4a on 4s dk green	65.00	*72.50*
a.	4a on 4s + 2s dk green (#B5)	190.00	*200.00*
2N10	A90 8a on 8s dk pur & pale vio	180.00	180.00
a.	Red surcharge	300.00	*325.00*
2N11	A91 1r on 10s lake	29.00	*37.50*
2N12	A94 2r on 20s ultra	60.00	60.00
a.	Red surcharge	60.00	60.00
2N13	A96 5r on 30s pck bl	19.00	*32.50*
a.	Red surcharge	30.00	*37.50*
	Nos. 2N4-2N13 (10)	755.50	*802.50*

Numerous double, inverted, etc., surcharges exist.

Re-surcharged in Black

15 C.

1942, Oct. 15

2N14	A83 1c on ¼a on 1s	65.00	65.00
2N15	A84 2c on ½a on 2s	65.00	65.00
2N16	A85 3c on ¾a on 3s	65.00	65.00
a.	"3C." in blue	225.00	
2N17	A86 5c on 1a on 5s	90.00	77.50
2N18	A89 10c on 3a on 7s	170.00	150.00
2N19	A86 15c on 4a on 4s	55.00	*60.00*
2N20	A90 20c on 8a on 8s (#2N10)	900.00	750.00
a.	On #2N10a	400.00	200.00
	Nos. 2N14-2N20 (7)	1,410.	1,233.

No. 2N16a was issued in the Shan States.

Done locally, numerous different handstamps of each denomination can exist.

Stamps of Japan, 1937-42, Handstamp Surcharged with New Value in Black

15C.

1942, Oct. 15

2N21	A83 1c on 1s fawn	40.00	24.00
2N22	A84 2c on 2s crim	65.00	45.00
2N23	A85 3c on 3s green	100.00	65.00
a.	"3C." in blue	110.00	*120.00*
2N24	A86 5c on 5s brn lake	100.00	60.00
a.	"5C." in violet	180.00	*200.00*
2N25	A89 10c on 7s dp grn	140.00	82.50
2N26	A86 15c on 4s dk grn	30.00	*30.00*
2N27	A90 20c on 8s dk pur & pale vio	210.00	110.00
	Nos. 2N21-2N27 (7)	685.00	*416.50*

Nos. 2N23a and 2N24a were issued in the Shan States.

Burma State Government Crest — OS3

Unwmk.

1943, Feb. 15 Litho. *Perf. 12*

Without Gum

2N29	OS3 5c carmine	29.00	*35.00*
a.	Imperf.	29.00	*35.00*

This stamp was intended to be used to cover the embossed George VI envelope stamp and generally was sold affixed to such envelopes. It is also known used on private envelopes.

Farmer Plowing — OS4

1943, Mar. Typo. Without Gum

2N30	OS4 1c deep orange	6.00	10.00
2N31	OS4 2c yel green	1.50	*1.20*
2N32	OS4 3c blue	5.00	1.20
a.	Laid paper	24.00	40.00
2N33	OS4 5c carmine	4.00	*8.00*
a.	Small "5c"	32.00	*21.00*
b.	Imperf, pair	130.00	
2N34	OS4 10c violet brown	9.50	*9.50*
2N35	OS4 15c red violet	.75	*4.50*
a.	Laid paper	7.25	*25.00*
2N36	OS4 20c dull purple	.75	*1.20*
2N37	OS4 30c blue green	1.25	*3.00*
	Nos. 2N30-2N37 (8)	28.75	*38.60*

Small "c" in Nos. 2N34 to 2N37.

Burmese Soldier Carving "Independence" OS5

Farmer Rejoicing OS6

Boy with Burmese Flag OS7

Hyphen-hole Perf., Pin-Perf. x Hyphen-hole Perf.

1943, Aug. 1 Typo.

2N38	OS5 1c orange	1.50	*2.10*
a.	Perf. 11	15.00	*20.00*
2N39	OS6 3c blue	3.00	*4.00*
a.	Perf. 11	15.00	*20.00*
2N40	OS7 5c rose	3.50	*4.25*
a.	Perf. 11	23.00	11.00
	Nos. 2N38-2N40 (3)	8.00	*10.35*

Declaration of the independence of Burma by the Ba Maw government, Aug. 1, 1943.

Burmese Girl Carrying Water Jar — OS8

Elephant Carrying Teak Log — OS9

Watch Tower of Mandalay Palace — OS10

1943, Oct. 1 Litho. *Perf. 12½*

2N41	OS8 1c dp salmon	24.00	18.00
2N42	OS8 2c yel green	1.00	*2.40*
2N43	OS8 3c violet	1.00	*2.75*
2N44	OS9 5c rose	1.00	*1.00*
2N45	OS9 10c blue	2.25	1.25
2N46	OS9 15c vermilion	1.20	*3.50*
2N47	OS9 20c yel green	1.20	*2.10*
2N48	OS9 30c brown	1.20	*2.40*
2N49	OS10 1r vermilion	.75	*2.40*
2N50	OS10 2r violet	.75	*2.75*
	Nos. 2N41-2N50 (10)	34.35	*38.55*

No. 2N49 exists imperforate. Canceled to order examples of Nos. 2N42-2N50 same values as unused.

Bullock Cart OS11

Shan Woman OS12

1943, Oct. 1 *Perf. 12½*

2N51	OS11 1c brown	45.00	*47.50*
2N52	OS11 2c yel green	50.00	*47.50*
2N53	OS11 3c violet	8.00	*14.00*
2N54	OS11 5c ultra	3.50	*8.50*
2N55	OS12 10c blue	18.00	*22.50*
2N56	OS12 20c rose	47.50	22.50
2N57	OS12 30c brown	27.50	*75.00*
	Nos. 2N51-2N57 (7)	199.50	*237.50*

For use only in the Shan States. Perak No. N34 also used in Shan States. Canceled-to-order stamps are valued at ½ used value.

Surcharged in Black

1944, Nov. 1

2N58	OS11 1c brown	5.00	*10.00*
2N59	OS11 2c yel green	1.00	*6.50*
a.	Inverted surcharge	500.00	*850.00*
2N60	OS11 3c violet	2.75	*8.50*
2N61	OS11 5c ultra	3.00	*4.00*
2N62	OS12 10c blue	4.00	3.00
2N63	OS12 20c rose	.85	*2.00*
2N64	OS12 30c brown	1.50	*2.25*
	Nos. 2N58-2N64 (7)	18.10	*36.25*

Top line of surcharge reads: "Bama naing ngan daw" (Burma State). Bottom line repeats denomination in Burmese. Surcharge applied when the Shan States came under Burmese government administration, Dec. 24, 1943. Canceled-to-order stamps same value as unused.

BURUNDI

bu-'rün-dē

LOCATION — Central Africa, adjoining the ex-Belgian Congo Republic, Rwanda and Tanzania
GOVT. — Republic
AREA — 10,759 sq. mi.
POP. — 5,735,937 (1999 est.)
CAPITAL — Bujumbura

Burundi was established as an independent country on July 1, 1962. With Rwanda, it had been a UN trusteeship territory (Ruanda-Urundi) administered by Belgium. A military coup overthrew the monarchy November 28, 1966.

100 Centimes = 1 Franc

Catalogue values for all unused stamps in this country are for Never Hinged items.

Flower Issue of Ruanda-Urundi, 1953 Overprinted

Perf. 11½

1962, July 1 Unwmk. Photo.

Flowers in Natural Colors

1	A27 25c dk grn & dull org	.25	.25
2	A27 40c grn & salmon	.25	.25
3	A27 60c blue grn & pink	.45	.40
4	A27 1.25fr dk grn & blue	19.00	19.00
5	A27 1.50fr vio & apple grn	.65	.55
6	A27 5fr dp plum & lt bl grn	1.60	1.10
7	A27 7fr dk grn & fawn	2.50	1.90
8	A27 10fr dp plum & pale ol	5.00	3.25
	Nos. 1-8 (8)	29.70	26.70

Animal Issue of Ruanda-Urundi, 1959-61 with Similar Overprint or Surcharge in Black or Violet Blue

Size: 23x33mm, 33x23mm

9	A29 10c multicolored	.25	.25
10	A30 20c multicolored	.25	.25
11	A29 40c multicolored	.25	.25
12	A30 50c multicolored	.25	.25
a.	Larger overprint and bar	4.50	1.75
b.	As "a," ovpt. "Royume du Royaume"	12.50	
13	A29 1fr multicolored	.25	.25
14	A30 1.50fr multi (VB)	.25	.25
15	A29 2fr multicolored	.25	.25
16	A30 3fr multicolored	.25	.25
17	A30 3.50fr on 3fr multi	.25	.25
18	A30 4fr on 10fr multi ("XX" 6mm wide)	.45	.25
a.	"XX" 4mm wide	1.40	.60
19	A30 5fr multicolored	.30	.25
20	A30 6.50fr multicolored	.30	.25
a.	Ovpt. "Royume du Royaume"	15.00	
21	A30 8fr multicolored	1.00	.35
a.	Violet blue overprint	4.00	1.40
22	A30 10fr multicolored	1.00	.50

Size: 45x26½mm

23	A30 20fr multicolored	2.50	.80
24	A30 50fr multi (ovpt. bars 2mm wide)	6.00	1.25
a.	Overprint bars 4mm wide	9.00	2.25
	Nos. 9-24 (16)	13.80	5.90

On No. 12a, "Burundi" is 13mm long; bar is continuous line across sheet. On No. 12, "Burundi" is 10mm; bar is 29mm. No. 12a was issued in 1963.

Two types of overprint exist on 10c, 40c, 1fr and 2fr: I, "du" is below "me"; bar 22½mm. II, "du" below "oy"; bar 20mm.

The 50c and 3fr exist in two types, besides the larger 50c overprint listed as No. 12: I, "du" is closer to "Royaume" than to "Burundi"; bar is less than 29mm; wording is centered above bar. II, "du" is closer to "Burundi"; bar is more than 30mm; wording is off-center leftward.

King Mwami Mwambutsa IV and Royal Drummers — A1

Flag and Arms of Burundi — A2

2fr, 8fr, 50fr, Map of Burundi and King.

Unwmk.

1962, Sept. 27 Photo. *Perf. 14*

25	A1	50c dull rose car & dk brn	.25	.25
26	A2	1fr dk grn, red & emer	.25	.25
27	A1	2fr brown ol & dk brn	.25	.25
28	A1	3fr vermilion & dk brn	.25	.25
29	A2	4fr Prus bl, red & emer	.25	.25
30	A1	8fr violet & dk brn	.25	.25
31	A1	10fr brt green & dk brn	.25	.25
32	A2	20fr brown, red & emer	.60	.25
33	A1	50fr brt pink & dk brn	1.75	.25
		Nos. 25-33 (9)	4.10	2.25

Burundi's independence, July 1, 1962.
Exist imperf. Value set, $20.
See Nos. 47-50. For overprints see Nos. 45-46, 51-52.

Ruanda-Urundi Nos. 151-152 Srchd.

Photogravure, Surcharge Engraved

1962, Oct. 31 *Perf. 11½*

Inscription in French

34	A31	3.50fr on 3fr ultra & red	.25	.25
35	A31	6.50fr on 3fr ultra & red	.30	.25
36	A31	10fr on 3fr ultra & red	.65	.35

Inscription in Flemish

37	A31	3.50fr on 3fr ultra & red	.30	.25
38	A31	6.50fr on 3fr ultra & red	.50	.30
39	A31	10fr on 3fr ultra & red	.65	.35
		Nos. 34-39 (6)	2.65	1.75

Dag Hammarskjold, Secretary General of the United Nations, 1953-61.

King Mwami Mwambutsa IV, Map of Burundi and Emblem — A3

1962, Dec. 10 Photo. *Perf. 14*

40	A3	8fr yel, bl grn & blk brn	.50	.25
41	A3	50fr gray grn, bl grn & blk brn	2.00	.75

WHO drive to eradicate malaria.
Exist imperf. Value set, $24.
Stamps of type A3 without anti-malaria emblem are listed as Nos. 27, 30 and 33.

Sowing Seed over Africa — A4

1963, Mar. 21 *Perf. 14x13*

42	A4	4fr olive & dull pur	.25	.25
43	A4	8fr dp org & dull pur	.25	.25
44	A4	15fr emerald & dull pur	.30	.25
		Nos. 42-44 (3)	.80	.75

FAO "Freedom from Hunger" campaign.
Exist imperf. Value set, $25.

Nos. 27 and 33 Overprinted in Dark Green

1963, June 19 Unwmk. *Perf. 14*

45	A1	2fr brn olive & dk brn	2.25	2.25
46	A1	50fr brt pink & dk brn	3.50	3.50

Conquest and peaceful use of outer space.

Types of 1962 Inscribed: "Premier Anniversaire" in Red or Magenta

1963, July 1 Photo.

47	A2	4fr olive, red & emer (R)	.25	.25
48	A1	8fr orange & dk brn (M)	.25	.25
49	A1	10fr lilac & dk brn (M)	.30	.25
50	A2	20fr gray, red & emer (R)	1.00	.25
		Nos. 47-50 (4)	1.80	1.00

First anniversary of independence.
Exist imperf. Value set, $12.

Nos. 26 and 32 Surcharged in Brown

1963, Sept. 24 Unwmk. *Perf. 14*

51	A2	6.50fr on 1fr multi	.55	.25
52	A2	15fr on 20fr multi	.90	.25

Red Cross Flag over Globe with Map of Africa — A5

1963, Sept. 26 *Perf. 14x13*

53	A5	4fr emer, car & gray	.25	.25
54	A5	8fr brn ol, car & gray	.40	.25
55	A5	10fr blue, car & gray	.70	.25
56	A5	20fr lilac, car & gray	1.60	.50
		Nos. 53-56 (4)	2.95	1.25

Centenary of International Red Cross.
Exist imperf. Value set, $17.50.
See No. B7.

"1962", Arms of Burundi, UN and UNESCO Emblems — A6

UN Agency Emblems: 8fr, ITU. 10fr, World Meteorological Organization. 20fr, UPU. 50fr, FAO.

1963, Nov. 4 Unwmk. *Perf. 14*

57	A6	4fr yel, ol grn & blk	.25	.25
58	A6	8fr pale lil, Prus bl & blk	.35	.25
59	A6	10fr blue, lil & blk	.45	.25
60	A6	20fr yel grn, grn & blk	.90	.25
61	A6	50fr yel, red brn & blk	1.50	.35
a.		Souvenir sheet of 2	5.00	5.00
		Nos. 57-61 (5)	3.45	1.35

1st anniv. of Burundi's admission to the UN. Exist imperf. Value set, $20. No. 61a contains two imperf. stamps with simulated perforations similar to Nos. 60-61. The 20fr stamp shows the FAO and the 50fr the WMO emblems.

UNESCO Emblem, Scales and Map — A7

Designs: 3.50fr, 6.50fr, Scroll, scales and "UNESCO." 10fr, 20fr, Abraham Lincoln, broken chain and scales.

1963, Dec. 10 Litho. *Perf. 14x13½*

62	A7	50c pink, lt bl & blk	.25	.25
63	A7	1.50fr org, lt bl & blk	.25	.25
64	A7	3.50fr fawn, lt grn & blk	.25	.25
65	A7	6.50fr lt vio, lt grn & blk	.25	.25
66	A7	10fr blue, bis & blk	.30	.25
67	A7	20fr pale brn, ocher, bl & blk	.55	.25
		Nos. 62-67 (6)	1.85	1.50

15th anniv. of the Universal Declaration of Human Rights and the cent. of the American Emancipation Proclamation (Nos. 66-67). Exist imperf. Value set, $5.

Ice Hockey — A8

3.50fr, Women's figure skating. 6.50fr, Torch. 10fr, Men's speed skating. 20fr, Slalom.

Unwmk.

1964, Jan. 25 Photo. *Perf. 14*

68	A8	50c olive, blk & gold	.25	.25
69	A8	3.50fr lt brown, blk & gold	.25	.25
70	A8	6.50fr pale gray, blk & gold	.60	.25
71	A8	10fr gray, blk & gold	1.50	.30
72	A8	20fr tan, blk & gold	2.00	.50
		Nos. 68-72 (5)	4.60	1.55

Issued to publicize the 9th Winter Olympic Games, Innsbruck, Jan. 29-Feb. 9, 1964. Exist imperf. Value set, $80.

A souvenir sheet contains two stamps (10fr+5fr and 20fr+5fr) in tan, black and gold. Value: perf, $12, unused or used; imperf $12, unused or used.

Canceled to Order

Starting about 1964, values in the used column are for "canceled to order" stamps. Postally used stamps sell for much more.

Impala — A9

Animals: 1fr, 5fr, Hippopotamus, horiz. 1.50fr, 10fr, Giraffe. 2fr, 8fr, Cape buffalo, horiz. 3fr, 6.50fr, Zebra, horiz. 3.50fr, 15fr, Defassa waterbuck. 20fr, Cheetah. 50fr, Elephant. 100fr, Lion.

Perf. 14x13, 13x14

1964, Feb. 10 Litho.

Size: 21½x35mm, 35x21½mm

73	A9	50c multi	.25	.25
74	A9	1fr multi	.25	.25
75	A9	1.50fr multi	.25	.25
76	A9	2fr multi	.35	.25
77	A9	3fr multi	.50	.25
78	A9	3.50fr multi	.60	.25

Size: 26x42mm, 42x26mm

79	A9	4fr multi	.25	.25
80	A9	5fr multi	.35	.25
81	A9	6.50fr multi	.40	.35
82	A9	8fr multi	.50	.35
83	A9	10fr multi	.80	.40
84	A9	15fr multi	1.00	.50

Perf. 14

Size: 53x33mm

85	A9	20fr multi	1.75	.50
86	A9	50fr multi	3.50	.80
87	A9	100fr multi	7.00	1.10
		Nos. 73-87,C1-C7 (22)	30.25	8.70

Exist imperf. Value set (22), $48.

Burundi Dancer — A10

Designs: Various Dancers and Drummers.

Unwmk.

1964, Aug. 21 Litho. *Perf. 14*

Dancers Multicolored

88	A10	50c gold & emerald	.25	.25
89	A10	1fr gold & vio blue	.25	.25
90	A10	4fr gold & brt blue	.25	.25
91	A10	6.50fr gold & red	.30	.25
92	A10	10fr gold & brt blue	.45	.25
93	A10	15fr gold & emerald	.60	.25
94	A10	20fr gold & red	.85	.50
a.		Souvenir sheet of 3, #92-94	4.25	4.25
		Nos. 88-94 (7)	2.95	2.00

Exist imperf. Value set, $7.50; souvenir sheet, $4.50.

1964, Sept. 10

Dancers Multicolored

88a	A10	50c	silver & emerald	.25	.25
89a	A10	1fr	silver & violet blue	.25	.25
90a	A10	4fr	silver & bright blue	.25	.25
91a	A10	6.50fr	silver & red	.30	.25
92a	A10	10fr	silver & bright blue	.45	.25
93a	A10	15fr	silver & emerald	.60	.25
94b	A10	20fr	silver & red	.85	.50
c.			Souvenir sheet of 3, #92a-94b	4.25	4.25
			Nos. 88a-94b (7)	2.95	2.00

New York World's Fair, 1964-65.

Exist imperf. Value set, $7.50; souvenir sheet, $4.50.

Pope Paul VI and King Mwami Mwambutsa IV — A11

22 Sainted Martyrs — A12

4fr, 14fr, Pope John XXIII and King Mwami.

1964, Nov. 12 Photo. *Perf. 12*

95	A11	50c	brt bl, gold & red brn	.25	.25
96	A12	1fr	mag, gold & slate	.25	.25
97	A11	4fr	pale rose lil, gold & brn	.25	.25
98	A12	8fr	red, gold & brn	.30	.25
99	A11	14fr	lt grn, gold & brn	.60	.25
100	A11	20fr	red brn, gold & grn	.90	.35
			Nos. 95-100 (6)	2.55	1.60

Canonization of 22 African martyrs, 10/18/64. Exist imperf. Value set, $12.50.

Shot Put — A13

Sports: 1fr, Discus. 3fr, Swimming. 4fr, Running. 6.50fr, Javelin, woman. 8fr, Hurdling. 10fr, Broad jump. 14fr, Diving, woman. 18fr, High jump. 20fr, Vaulting.

3fr, 8fr, 10fr, 18fr, 20fr are horiz.

1964, Nov. 18 Litho. *Perf. 14*

101	A13	50c	olive & multi	.25	.25
102	A13	1fr	brt pink & multi	.25	.25
103	A13	3fr	multi	.25	.25
104	A13	4fr	multi	.25	.25
105	A13	6.50fr	multi	.25	.25
106	A13	8fr	lt bl & multi	.40	.25
107	A13	10fr	multi	.45	.25
108	A13	14fr	multi	.60	.25
109	A13	18fr	bister & multi	.85	.35
110	A13	20fr	gray & multi	.90	.60
			Nos. 101-110 (10)	4.45	2.95

18th Olympic Games, Tokyo, Oct. 10-25, 1964. Exist imperf. Value set, $12.50. See No. B8.

African Purple Gallinule — A14

Birds: 1fr, 5fr, Little bee eater. 1.50fr, 6.50fr, Secretary bird. 2fr, 8fr, Yellow-billed stork. 3fr, 10fr, Congo peacock. 3.50fr, 15fr, African anhinga. 20fr, Saddle-billed stork. 50fr, Abyssinian ground hornbill. 100fr, Crowned crane.

Birds in Natural Colors

1965 Unwmk. *Perf. 14*

Size: 21x35mm

111	A14	50c	tan, grn & blk	.25	.25
112	A14	1fr	pink, mag & blk	.25	.25
113	A14	1.50fr	blue & blk	.25	.25
114	A14	2fr	yel grn, dk grn & blk	.25	.25
115	A14	3fr	yellow, brn & blk	.25	.25
116	A14	3.50fr	yel grn, dk grn & blk	.35	.25

Size: 26x43mm

117	A14	4fr	tan, grn & blk	.45	.25
118	A14	5fr	pink, mag & blk	.55	.25
119	A14	6.50fr	blue & blk	.70	.25
120	A14	8fr	yel grn, dk grn & blk	.90	.25
121	A14	10fr	yel, brn & blk	1.10	.30
122	A14	15fr	yel grn, dk grn & blk	1.75	.30

Size: 33x53mm

123	A14	20fr	rose lilac & blk	2.25	.40
124	A14	50fr	yellow, brn & blk	4.50	.75
125	A14	100fr	green, yel & blk	9.00	1.25
			Nos. 111-125 (15)	22.80	5.50

Issue dates: Nos. 111-116, Mar. 31. Nos. 117-122, Apr. 16. Nos. 123-125, Apr. 30.

For overprints see Nos. 174-184, C35A-C35I.

Relay Satellite and Morse Key — A15

3fr, Telstar & old telephone handpiece. 4fr, Luna satellite & old wall telephone. 6.50fr, Orbiting Geophysical Observatory & radar screen. 8fr, Telstar II & headphones. 10fr, Sputnik II & radar aerial. 14fr, Syncom & transmission aerial. 20fr, Interplanetary Explorer & tracking aerial.

1965, July 3 Litho. *Perf. 13*

126	A15	1fr	multi	.25	.25
127	A15	3fr	multi	.25	.25
128	A15	4fr	multi	.25	.25
129	A15	6.50fr	multi	.25	.25
130	A15	8fr	multi	.25	.25
131	A15	10fr	multi	.25	.25
132	A15	14fr	multi	.25	.25
133	A15	20fr	multi	.30	.25
			Nos. 126-133 (8)	2.05	2.00

Cent. of the ITU. Exist imperf, Value, set $6.

Perf. and imperf. souv. sheets of 2 contain Nos. 131, 133. Size: 120x86mm. Value, both sheets, $6 unused or used.

Globe and ICY Emblem — A16

Designs: 4fr, Map of Africa and UN development emblem. 8fr, Map of Asia and Colombo Plan emblem. 10fr, Globe and UN emblem. 18fr, Map of the Americas and Alliance for Progress emblem. 25fr, Map of Europe and EUROPA emblems. 40fr, Map of Outer Space and satellite with UN wreath.

1965, Oct. 1 Litho. *Perf. 13*

134	A16	1fr	ol green & multi	.25	.25
135	A16	4fr	dull blue & multi	.25	.25
136	A16	8fr	pale yellow & multi	.25	.25
137	A16	10fr	lilac & multi	.25	.25
138	A16	18fr	salmon & multi	.45	.25
139	A16	25fr	gray & multi	.75	.25
140	A16	40fr	blue & multi	1.25	.25
a.			Souvenir sheet of 3, #138-140	4.00	4.00
			Nos. 134-140 (7)	3.45	1.75

International Cooperation Year.

Exist imperf. Values: set $6; souvenir sheet $4.

Protea A17

Flowers: 1fr, 5fr, Crossandra. 1.50fr, 6.50fr, Ansellia. 2fr, 8fr, Thunbergia. 3fr, 10fr, Schizoglossum. 3.50fr, 15fr, Dissotis. 4fr, 20fr, Protea. 50fr, Gazania. 100fr, Hibiscus. 150fr, Markhamia.

1966 Unwmk. *Perf. 13½*

Size: 26x26mm

141	A17	50c	multi	.25	.25
142	A17	1fr	multi	.25	.25
143	A17	1.50fr	multi	.25	.25
144	A17	2fr	multi	.25	.25
145	A17	3fr	multi	.25	.25
146	A17	3.50fr	multi	.25	.25

Size: 31x31mm

147	A17	4fr	multi	.25	.25
148	A17	5fr	multi	.35	.25
149	A17	6.50fr	multi	.45	.25
150	A17	8fr	multi	.90	.25
151	A17	10fr	multi	1.00	.25
152	A17	15fr	multi	1.10	.25

Size: 39x39mm

153	A17	20fr	multi	1.60	.25
154	A17	50fr	multi	3.50	.30
155	A17	100fr	multi	5.25	.50
156	A17	150fr	multi	7.50	.70
			Nos. 141-156,C17-C25 (25)	39.60	8.10

Issue dates: Nos. 141-147, Feb. 28; Nos. 148-153, May 18; Nos. 154-156, June 15.

Exist imperf. Value set (25), $55.

For overprints see Nos. 159-173, C27-C35.

Souvenir Sheets

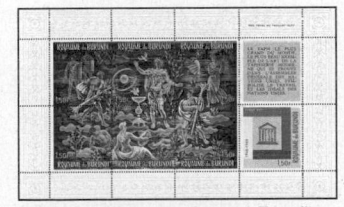

Allegory of Prosperity and Equality Tapestry by Peter Colfs — A18

1966, Nov. 4 Litho. *Perf. 13½*

157	A18	Sheet of 7 (1.50fr)	2.75	.95
a.-g.		Any single	.25	.25
158	A18	Sheet of 7 (4fr)	4.50	1.50
a.-g.		Any single	.25	.25

20th anniv. of UNESCO. Each sheet contains 6 stamps showing a reproduction of the Colfs tapestry from the lobby of the General Assembly Building, NYC, and one stamp with the UNESCO emblem plus a label. The labels on Nos. 157-158 and C26 are inscribed in French or English. The 3 sheets with French inscription have light blue marginal border. The 3 sheets with English inscription have pink border. See No. C26.

Exist imperf. Value each sheet, $15.

Republic

Nos. 141-152, 154-156 Overprinted

1967 Litho. *Perf. 13½*

Size: 26x26mm

159	A17	50c	multi	.25	.25
160	A17	1fr	multi	.25	.25
161	A17	1.50fr	multi	.25	.25
162	A17	2fr	multi	.25	.25
163	A17	3fr	multi	.25	.25
164	A17	3.50fr	multi	.25	.25

Size: 31x31mm

165	A17	4fr	multi	1.60	.30
166	A17	5fr	multi	.25	.25
167	A17	6.50fr	multi	.35	.25
168	A17	8fr	multi	.35	.25
169	A17	10fr	multi	.60	.25
170	A17	15fr	multi	.80	.25

Size: 39x39mm

171	A17	50fr	multi	3.50	.90
172	A17	100fr	multi	11.00	2.75
173	A17	150fr	multi	11.00	2.75
			Nos. 159-173,C27-C35 (24)	57.30	14.95

Nos. 111, 113, 116, 118-125 Overprinted "REPUBLIQUE DU BURUNDI" and Horizontal Bar

1967 Litho. *Perf. 14*

Birds in Natural Colors

Size: 21x35mm

174	A14	50c	multi	2.75	2.75
175	A14	1.50fr	blue & black	.60	.60
176	A14	3.50fr	multi	.75	.75

Size: 26x43mm

177	A14	5fr	multi	.90	.90
178	A14	6.50fr	blue & black	1.00	1.00
179	A14	8fr	multi	1.25	1.25
180	A14	10fr	yel, brn & blk	1.75	1.75
181	A14	15fr	multi	2.25	2.25

Size: 33x53mm

182	A14	20fr	multi	4.00	4.00
183	A14	50fr	multi	7.00	7.00
184	A14	100fr	multi	12.00	12.00
			Nos. 174-184 (11)	34.25	34.25

Haplochromis Multicolor — A19

Various Tropical Fish.

1967 Photo. *Perf. 13½*

Size: 42x19mm

186	A19	50c	multi	.25	.25
187	A19	1fr	multi	.25	.25
188	A19	1.50fr	multi	.25	.25
189	A19	2fr	multi	.30	.25
190	A19	3fr	multi	.30	.25
191	A19	3.50fr	multi	.40	.25

Size: 50x25mm

192	A19	4fr	multi	.60	.25
193	A19	5fr	multi	.75	.25
194	A19	6.50fr	multi	.85	.25
195	A19	8fr	multi	1.40	.25
196	A19	10fr	multi	2.25	.25
197	A19	15fr	multi	2.75	.25

Size: 59x30mm

198	A19	20fr	multi	4.00	.35
199	A19	50fr	multi	6.75	.45
200	A19	100fr	multi	11.00	.65
201	A19	150fr	multi	15.00	1.00
			Nos. 186-201,C46-C54 (25)	96.60	8.25

Issue Dates: Nos. 186-191, Apr. 4; Nos. 192-197, Apr. 28; Nos. 198-201, May 18.

Ancestor Figures, Ivory Coast — A20

African Art: 1fr, Seat of Honor, Southeast Congo. 1.50fr, Antelope head, Aribinda Region. 2fr, Buffalo mask, Upper Volta. 4fr, Funeral figures, Southwest Ethiopia.

1967, June 5 Photo. *Perf. 13½*

202	A20	50c silver & multi	.25	.25
203	A20	1fr silver & multi	.25	.25
204	A20	1.50fr silver & multi	.25	.25
205	A20	2fr silver & multi	.25	.25
206	A20	4fr silver & multi	.25	.25
		Nos. 202-206,C36-C40 (10)	3.70	2.80

Exists imperf. Value set, $7.

Scouts on Hiking Trip — A21

Designs: 1fr, Cooking at campfire. 1.50fr, Lord Baden-Powell. 2fr, Boy Scout and Cub Scout giving Scout sign. 4fr, First aid.

1967, Aug. 9 Photo. *Perf. 13½*

207	A21	50c silver & multi	.25	.25
208	A21	1fr silver & multi	.35	.25
209	A21	1.50fr silver & multi	.50	.25
210	A21	2fr silver & multi	.65	.25
211	A21	4fr silver & multi	.80	.25
		Nos. 207-211,C41-C45 (10)	12.80	2.65

60th anniv. of the Boy Scouts and the 12th Boy Scout World Jamboree, Farragut State Park, Idaho, Aug. 1-9.

Exists imperf. Value set, $20.

The Gleaners, by Francois Millet A22

Paintings Exhibited at EXPO '67: 8fr, The Water Carrier of Seville, by Velazquez. 14fr, The Triumph of Neptune and Amphitrite, by Nicolas Poussin. 18fr, Acrobat Standing on a Ball, by Picasso. 25fr, Marguerite van Eyck, by Jan van Eyck. 40fr, St. Peter Denying Christ, by Rembrandt.

1967, Oct. 12 Photo. *Perf. 13½*

212	A22	4fr multi	.25	.25
213	A22	8fr multi	.25	.25
214	A22	14fr multi	.45	.25
215	A22	18fr multi	.50	.25
216	A22	25fr multi	.80	.25
217	A22	40fr multi	1.00	.25
a.		Souvenir sheet of 2, #216-217	2.25	2.25
		Nos. 212-217 (6)	3.25	1.50

EXPO '67 International Exhibition, Montreal, Apr. 28-Oct. 27. Printed in sheets of 10 stamps and 2 labels inscribed in French or English.

Exists imperf. Value: set $6; souvenir sheet $2.25.

Place de la Revolution and Pres. Michel Micombero — A23

Designs: 5fr, President Michel Micombero and flag. 14fr, Formal garden and coat of arms. 20fr, Modern building and coat of arms.

1967, Nov. 23 *Perf. 13½*

218	A23	5fr multi	.25	.25
219	A23	14fr multi	.40	.25
220	A23	20fr multi	.70	.25
221	A23	30fr multi	.90	.25
		Nos. 218-221 (4)	2.25	1.00

First anniversary of the Republic.

Exists imperf. Value set, $4.

Madonna by Carlo Crivelli — A24

Designs: 1fr, Adoration of the Shepherds by Juan Bautista Mayno. 4fr, Holy Family by Anthony Van Dyck. 14fr, Nativity by Maitre de Moulins.

1967, Dec. 7 Photo. *Perf. 13½*

222	A24	1fr multi	.25	.25
223	A24	4fr multi	.25	.25
224	A24	14fr multi	.60	.25
225	A24	26fr multi	1.00	.30
a.		Sheetlet of 4, #222-225	3.00	3.00
		Nos. 222-225 (4)	2.10	1.05

Christmas 1967. Exists imperf. Value: set $4; souvenir sheet, $3.

Printed in sheets of 25 and one corner label inscribed "Noel 1967" and giving name of painting and painter.

Slalom — A25

10fr, Ice hockey. 14fr, Women's skating. 17fr, Bobsled. 26fr, Ski jump. 40fr, Speed skating. 60fr, Hand holding torch, and Winter Olympics emblem.

1968, Feb. 16 Photo. *Perf. 13½*

226	A25	5fr silver & multi	.25	.25
227	A25	10fr silver & multi	.30	.25
228	A25	14fr silver & multi	.55	.25
229	A25	17fr silver & multi	.65	.25
230	A25	26fr silver & multi	.95	.25
231	A25	40fr silver & multi	1.20	.25
232	A25	60fr silver & multi	1.65	.25
a.		Souvenir sheet of 2, types of #231-232 inscribed "Poste Aerienne"	3.00	2.25
		Nos. 226-232 (7)	5.55	1.75

Issued to publicize the 10th Winter Olympic Games, Grenoble, France, Feb. 6-18. Issued in sheets of 10 stamps and label.

Exists imperf. Values: set, $10; souvenir sheet, $3.

The Lacemaker, by Vermeer A26

Paintings: 1.50fr, Portrait of a Young Man, by Botticelli. 2fr, Maja Vestida, by Goya, horiz.

1968, Mar. 29 Photo. *Perf. 13½*

233	A26	1.50fr gold & multi	.25	.25
234	A26	2fr gold & multi	.25	.25
235	A26	4fr gold & multi	.30	.25
		Nos. 233-235,C59-C61 (6)	3.05	2.05

Issued in sheets of 6.

Exists imperf. Value set, $4.

Moon Probe A27

Designs: 6fr, Russian astronaut walking in space. 8fr, Mariner satellite, Mars. 10fr, American astronaut walking in space.

1968, May 15 Photo. *Perf. 13½*

Size: 35x35mm

236	A27	4fr silver & multi	.25	.25
237	A27	6fr silver & multi	.30	.25
238	A27	8fr silver & multi	.40	.25
239	A27	10fr silver & multi	.50	.25
		Nos. 236-239,C62-C65 (8)	5.50	2.35

Issued to publicize peaceful space explorations. Exist imperf. Value, set $8.

A souvenir sheet contains one 25fr stamp in Moon Probe design and one 40fr in Mariner satellite design. Stamp size: 41x41mm. Value: $4, perf or imperf.

Salamis Aethiops A28

Butterflies: 1fr, 5fr, Graphium ridleyanus. 1.50fr, 6.50fr, Cymothoe. 2fr, 8fr, Charaxes eupale. 3fr, 10fr, Papilio bromius. 3.50fr, 15fr, Teracolus annae. 20fr, Salamis aethiops. 50fr, Papilio zonobia. 100fr, Danais chrysippus. 150fr, Salamis temora.

1968 Size: 30x33½mm

240	A28	50c gold & multi	.25	.25
241	A28	1fr gold & multi	.25	.25
242	A28	1.50fr gold & multi	.35	.25
243	A28	2fr gold & multi	.45	.25
244	A28	3fr gold & multi	.60	.25
245	A28	3.50fr gold & multi	.75	.25

Size: 33½x37½mm

246	A28	4fr gold & multi	.90	.25
247	A28	5fr gold & multi	1.10	.25
248	A28	6.50fr gold & multi	1.60	.25
249	A28	8fr gold & multi	2.00	.25
250	A28	10fr gold & multi	2.75	.30
251	A28	15fr gold & multi	3.50	.35

Size: 41x46mm

252	A28	20fr gold & multi	4.50	.40
253	A28	50fr gold & multi	7.75	.60
254	A28	100fr gold & multi	15.00	1.00
255	A28	150fr gold & multi	20.00	1.50
		Nos. 240-255,C66-C74 (25)	117.10	12.85

Issue dates: Nos. 240-245, June 7; Nos. 246-251, June 28; Nos. 252-255, July 19.

Women, Along the Manzanares, by Goya — A29

Paintings: 7fr, The Letter, by Pieter de Hooch. 11fr, Woman Reading a Letter, by Gerard Terborch. 14fr, Man Writing a Letter, by Gabriel Metsu.

1968, Sept. 30 Photo. *Perf. 13½*

256	A29	4fr multi	.25	.25
257	A29	7fr multi	.25	.25
258	A29	11fr multi	.40	.25
259	A29	14fr multi	.50	.25
		Nos. 256-259,C84-C87 (8)	8.05	2.40

International Letter Writing Week.

Exists imperf. Value set, $9.

Soccer — A30

1968, Oct. 24

260	A30	4fr shown	.25	.25
261	A30	7fr Basketball	.25	.25
262	A30	13fr High jump	.25	.25
263	A30	24fr Relay race	.35	.25
264	A30	40fr Javelin	.75	.30
		Nos. 260-264,C88-C92 (10)	8.45	3.00

19th Olympic Games, Mexico City, Oct. 12-27. Printed in sheets of 8.

Exists imperf. Value set, $12.50.

Virgin and Child, by Fra Filippo Lippi — A31

Paintings: 5fr, The Magnificat, by Sandro Botticelli. 6fr, Virgin and Child, by Albrecht Durer. 11fr, Madonna del Gran Duca, by Raphael.

1968, Nov. 26 Photo. *Perf. 13½*

265	A31	3fr multi	.25	.25
266	A31	5fr multi	.25	.25
267	A31	6fr multi	.25	.25
268	A31	11fr multi	.35	.25
a.		Souvenir sheet of 4, #265-268	1.60	1.25
		Nos. 265-268,C93-C96 (8)	3.75	2.25

Christmas 1968. Exist imperf. Value: set (8) $4; souvenir sheet $4.

For overprints see Nos. 272-275, C100-C103.

WHO Emblem and Map of Africa — A32

1969, Jan. 22

269 A32 5fr gold, dk grn & yel .25 .25
270 A32 6fr gold, vio & ver .35 .25
271 A32 11fr gold, pur & red lil .50 .25
Nos. 269-271 (3) 1.10 .75

20th anniv. of WHO in Africa. Exist imperf. Value set, $2.

Nos. 265-268 Overprinted in Silver

1969, Feb. 17 Photo. *Perf. 13½*

272 A31 3fr multi .25 .25
273 A31 5fr multi .25 .25
274 A31 6fr multi .35 .25
275 A31 11fr multi .55 .25
Nos. 272-275,C100-C103 (8) 4.15 2.30

Man's 1st flight around the moon by the US spacecraft Apollo 8, Dec. 21-27, 1968. Exist imperf. Value set (8), $6.

Map of Africa, and CEPT Emblem A33

Designs: 14fr, Plowing with tractor. 17fr, Teacher and pupil. 26fr, Maps of Europe and Africa and CEPT (Conference of European Postal and Telecommunications Administrations) emblem, horiz.

1969, Mar. 12 Photo. *Perf. 13*

276 A33 5fr multi .25 .25
277 A33 14fr multi .45 .25
278 A33 17fr multi .55 .25
279 A33 26fr multi .90 .25
Nos. 276-279 (4) 2.15 1.00

5th anniv. of the Yaounde (Cameroun) Agreement, creating the European and African-Malgache Economic Community. Exist imperf. Value set, $3.

Resurrection, by Gaspard Isenmann — A34

Paintings: 14fr, Resurrection by Antoine Caron. 17fr, Noli me Tangere, by Martin Schongauer. 26fr, Resurrection, by El Greco.

1969, Mar. 24

280 A34 11fr gold & multi .35 .25
281 A34 14fr gold & multi .45 .25
282 A34 17fr gold & multi .60 .25
283 A34 26fr gold & multi .75 .25
a. Souvenir sheet of 4, #280-283 2.25 2.25
Nos. 280-283 (4) 2.15 1.00

Easter 1969. Exist imperf. Values: set $3; souvenir sheet $2.25.

Potter — A35

ILO Emblem and: 5fr, Farm workers. 7fr, Foundry worker. 10fr, Woman testing corn crop.

1969, May 17 Photo. *Perf. 13½*

284 A35 3fr multicolored .25 .25
285 A35 5fr multicolored .25 .25
286 A35 7fr multicolored .25 .25
287 A35 10fr multicolored .35 .25
Nos. 284-287 (4) 1.10 1.00

50th anniv. of the ILO. Exist imperf. Value set, $2.

Industry and Bank's Emblem A36

African Development Bank Emblem and: 17fr, Communications. 30fr, Education. 50fr, Agriculture.

1969, July 29 Photo. *Perf. 13½*

288 A36 10fr gold & multi .30 .25
289 A36 17fr gold & multi .50 .25
290 A36 30fr gold & multi .80 .40
291 A36 50fr gold & multi 1.40 .75
a. Souvenir sheet of 4, #288-291 4.00 4.00
Nos. 288-291 (4) 3.00 1.65

African Development Bank, 5th anniv. Exist imperf. Values: set $5; souvenir sheet $3.50.

Girl Reading Letter, by Vermeer A37

Paintings: 7fr, Graziella (young woman), by Auguste Renoir. 14fr, Woman writing a letter, by Gerard Terborch. 26fr, Galileo Galilei, painter unknown. 40fr, Ludwig van Beethoven, painter unknown.

1969, Oct. 24 Photo. *Perf. 13½*

292 A37 4fr multicolored .25 .25
293 A37 7fr multicolored .25 .25
294 A37 14fr multicolored .45 .25
295 A37 26fr multicolored .75 .25
296 A37 40fr multicolored 1.10 .25
a. Souvenir sheet of 2, #295-296 2.50 2.50
Nos. 292-296 (5) 2.80 1.25

Intl. Letter Writing Week, Oct. 7-13. Exist imperf. Values: set $4; souvenir sheet $2.50.

Rocket Launching A38

Moon Landing: 6.50fr, Rocket in space. 7fr, Separation of landing module from capsule. 14fr, 26fr, Landing module landing on moon. 17fr, Capsule in space. 40fr, Neil A. Armstrong leaving landing module. 50fr, Astronaut on moon.

1969, Nov. 6 Photo. *Perf. 13½*

297 A38 4fr blue & multi .25 .25
298 A38 6.50fr vio blue & multi .25 .25
299 A38 7fr vio blue & multi .50 .25
300 A38 14fr black & multi 1.00 .25
301 A38 17fr vio blue & multi 1.75 .30
Nos. 297-301,C104-C106 (8) 12.00 2.55

Souvenir Sheet

302 Sheet of 3 12.00 12.00
a. A38 26fr multicolored 1.50 1.50
b. A38 40fr multicolored 2.00 2.00
c. A38 50fr multicolored 3.00 3.00

Exist imperf. Values: set $12; souvenir sheet $15.

See note after Algeria No. 427.

Madonna and Child, by Rubens — A39

Paintings: 6fr, Madonna and Child with St. John, by Giulio Romano. 10fr, Magnificat Madonna, by Botticelli.

1969, Dec. 2 Photo.

303 A39 5fr gold & multi .25 .25
304 A39 6fr gold & multi .25 .25
305 A39 10fr gold & multi .40 .25
a. Souvenir sheet of 3, #303-305 4.00 4.00
Nos. 303-305,C107-C109 (6) 5.60 1.60

Christmas 1969. Exist imperf. Values: set (6) $7; souvenir sheets (2) $6.

Sternotomis Bohemani — A40

Designs: Various Beetles and Weevils.

1970 Size: 39x28mm *Perf. 13½*

306 A40 50c multicolored .25 .25
307 A40 1fr multicolored .25 .25
308 A40 1.50fr multicolored .25 .25
309 A40 2fr multicolored .25 .25
310 A40 3fr multicolored .30 .25
311 A40 3.50fr multicolored .40 .25

Size: 46x32mm

312 A40 4fr multicolored .50 .25
313 A40 5fr multicolored .65 .25
314 A40 6.50fr multicolored .75 .25
315 A40 8fr multicolored .90 .25
316 A40 10fr multicolored 1.50 .25
317 A40 15fr multicolored 2.00 .30

Size: 52x36mm

318 A40 20fr multicolored 3.25 .40
319 A40 50fr multicolored 6.00 .50
320 A40 100fr multicolored 10.50 .75
321 A40 150fr multicolored 15.00 1.00
Nos. 306-321,C110-C118 (25) 78.70 9.90

Issue dates: Nos. 306-313, Jan. 20; Nos. 314-318, Feb. 17; Nos. 319-321, Apr. 3.

Jesus Condemned to Death — A41

Stations of the Cross, by Juan de Aranoa y Carredano: 1.50fr, Jesus carries His Cross. 2fr, Jesus falls the first time. 3fr, Jesus meets His mother. 3.50fr, Simon of Cyrene helps carry the cross. 4fr, Veronica wipes the face of Jesus. 5fr, Jesus falls the second time.

1970, Mar. 16 Photo. *Perf. 13½*

322 A41 1fr gold & multi .25 .25
323 A41 1.50fr gold & multi .25 .25
324 A41 2fr gold & multi .25 .25
325 A41 3fr gold & multi .25 .25
326 A41 3.50fr gold & multi .25 .25
327 A41 4fr gold & multi .25 .25
328 A41 5fr gold & multi .25 .25
a. Souv. sheet, #322-328 + label 1.60 1.60
Nos. 322-328,C119-C125 (14) 7.65 4.15

Easter 1970. Exists imperf. Values: set (14) $11; souvenir sheets (2) $10.

Parade and EXPO '70 Emblem — A42

Designs (EXPO '70 Emblem and): 6.50fr, Aerial view. 7fr, African pavilions. 14fr, Pagoda, vert. 26fr, Recording pavilion and pool. 40fr, Tower of the Sun, vert. 50fr, Flags of participating nations.

1970, May 5 Photo. *Perf. 13½*

329 A42 4fr gold & multi .25 .25
330 A42 6.50fr gold & multi .25 .25
331 A42 7fr gold & multi .25 .25
332 A42 14fr gold & multi .40 .25
333 A42 26fr gold & multi .80 .25
334 A42 40fr gold & multi 1.10 .25
335 A42 50fr gold & multi 1.25 .30
Nos. 329-335 (7) 4.30 1.80

EXPO '70 Intl. Exhibition, Osaka, Japan, Mar. 15-Sept. 13, 1970. Exists imperf. Value $5.50.

See No. C126.

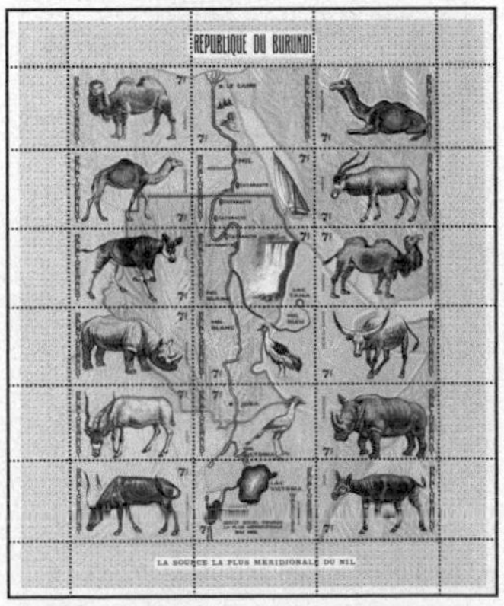

Fauna and Map of the Nile — A43

Fauna: a, i, Camel. c, d, Dromedary. g, r, Okapi. f, m, Addax. j, o, Rhinoceros. l, p, Burundi cow (each animal in 2 different poses).

Map of the Nile: b, Delta and pyramids. e, dhow. h, Falls. k, Blue Nile and crowned crane. n, Victoria Nile and secretary bird. q, Lake Victoria and source of Nile on Mt. Gikizi. Continuous design.

1970, July 8 Photo. *Perf. 13½*

No.	Type	Description	Unused	Used
336	A43	Sheet of 18	45.00	24.50
a.-r.		7fr any single	2.50	.35

Publicizing the southernmost source of the Nile on Mt. Gikizi in Burundi. Exists imperf. Value $50.

See No. C127.

Winter Wren, Firecrest, Skylark and Crested Lark — A44

Birds: 2fr, 3.50fr, 5fr, vert.; others horiz.

1970, Sept. 30 Photo. *Perf. 13½*
Stamp Size: 44x33mm

No.	Type	Description	Unused	Used
337	A44	Block of 4	2.50	.60
a.		2fr Northern shrike	.60	.25
b.		2fr European starling	.60	.25
c.		2fr Yellow wagtail	.60	.25
d.		2fr Bank swallow	.60	.25
338	A44	Block of 4	3.00	.70
a.		3fr Winter wren	.65	.25
b.		3fr Firecrest	.65	.25
c.		3fr Skylark	.65	.25
d.		3fr Crested lark	.65	.25
339	A44	Block of 4	4.00	.80
a.		3.50fr Woodchat shrike	.75	.25
b.		3.50fr Common rock thrush	.75	.25
c.		3.50fr Black redstart	.75	.25
d.		3.50fr Ring ouzel	.75	.25
340	A44	Block of 4	5.50	1.00
a.		4fr European Redstart	1.00	.25
b.		4fr Hedge sparrow	1.00	.25
c.		4fr Gray wagtail	1.00	.25
d.		4fr Meadow pipit	1.00	.25
341	A44	Block of 4	6.50	1.10
a.		5fr Eurasian hoopoe	1.15	.25
b.		5fr Pied flycatcher	1.15	.25
c.		5fr Great reed warbler	1.15	.25
d.		5fr Eurasian kingfisher	1.15	.25
342	A44	Block of 4	7.75	1.25
a.		6.50fr House martin	1.50	.30
b.		6.50fr Sedge warbler	1.50	.30
c.		6.50fr Fieldfare	1.50	.30
d.		6.50fr European Golden oriole	1.50	.30
		Nos. 337-342,C132-C137 (12)	152.25	19.20

Nos. 337-342 are printed in sheets of 16.

Exists imperf. Value: set of 12 blocks, $1,700.

Library, UN Emblem — A45

Designs: 5fr, Students taking test, and emblem of University of Bujumbura. 7fr, Students in laboratory and emblem of Ecole Normale Superieure of Burundi. 10fr, Students with electron-microscope and Education Year emblem.

1970, Oct. 23

No.	Type	Description	Unused	Used
343	A45	3fr gold & multi	.25	.25
344	A45	5fr gold & multi	.25	.25
345	A45	7fr gold & multi	.30	.25
346	A45	10fr gold & multi	.50	.25
		Nos. 343-346 (4)	1.30	1.00

Issued for International Education Year. Exists imperf. Value set, $1.50.

Pres. and Mrs. Michel Micombero — A46

Designs: 7fr, Pres. Michel Micombero and Burundi flag. 11fr, Pres. Micombero and Revolution Memorial.

1970, Nov. 28 Photo. *Perf. 13½*

No.	Type	Description	Unused	Used
347	A46	4fr gold & multi	.25	.25
348	A46	7fr gold & multi	.35	.25
349	A46	11fr gold & multi	.45	.25
a.		Souvenir sheet of 3	1.25	1.25
		Nos. 347-349 (3)	1.05	.75

4th anniv. of independence. No. 349a contains 3 stamps similar to Nos. 347-349, but inscribed "Poste Aerienne."

Exist imperf. Value: set $1.25; souvenir sheet, $1.25.

See Nos. C140-C142.

Lenin with Delegates A47

Designs (Lenin, Paintings): 5fr, addressing crowd. 6.50fr, with soldier and sailor. 15fr, speaking from balcony. 50fr, Portrait.

1970, Dec. 31 Photo. *Perf. 13½*
Gold Frame

No.	Type	Description	Unused	Used
350	A47	3.50fr dk red brown	.55	.25
351	A47	5fr dk red brown	.70	.25
352	A47	6.50fr dk red brown	.85	.25
353	A47	15fr dk red brown	1.40	.40
354	A47	50fr dk red brown	3.50	.50
		Nos. 350-354 (5)	7.00	1.65

Lenin's birth centenary (1870-1924). Exist imperf. Value set, $8.

Lion — A48

1971, Mar. 19 Photo. *Perf. 13½*
Size: 38x38mm

No.	Type	Description	Unused	Used
355		Strip of 4	2.50	.80
a.	A48	1fr Lion	.35	.25
b.	A48	1fr Cape buffalo	.35	.25
c.	A48	1fr Hippopotamus	.35	.25
d.	A48	1fr Giraffe	.35	.25
356		Strip of 4	3.00	.90
a.	A48	2fr Hartebeest	.45	.25
b.	A48	2fr Black rhinoceros	.45	.25
c.	A48	2fr Zebra	.45	.25
d.	A48	2fr Leopard	.45	.25
357		Strip of 4	4.00	1.00
a.	A48	3fr Grant's gazelles	.55	.25
b.	A48	3fr Cheetah	.55	.25
c.	A48	3fr African white-backed vultures	.55	.25
d.	A48	3fr Johnston's okapi	.55	.25
358		Strip of 4	4.50	1.10
a.	A48	5fr Chimpanzee	.60	.25
b.	A48	5fr Elephant	.60	.25
c.	A48	5fr Spotted hyenas	.60	.25
d.	A48	5fr Beisa	.60	.25
359		Strip of 4	5.50	1.50
a.	A48	6fr Gorilla	.95	.30
b.	A48	6fr Gnu	.95	.30
c.	A48	6fr Wart hog	.95	.30
d.	A48	6fr Cape hunting dog	.95	.30
360		Strip of 4	7.50	1.75
a.	A48	11fr Sable antelope	1.10	.35
b.	A48	11fr Caracal lynx	1.10	.35
c.	A48	11fr Ostriches	1.10	.35
d.	A48	11fr Bongo	1.10	.35
		Nos. 355-360,C146-C151 (12)	102.50	15.70

Nos. 355a-355d, 356a-356d, 357a-357d, 358a-358d and 359a-359d exist with gold line under country name.

For overprints and surcharges see Nos. C152, CB15-CB18.

The Resurrection, by Il Sodoma — A49

Paintings: 6fr, Resurrection, by Andrea del Castagno. 11fr, Noli me Tangere, by Correggio.

1971, Apr. 2

No.	Type	Description	Unused	Used
361	A49	3fr gold & multi	.25	.25
362	A49	6fr gold & multi	.25	.25
363	A49	11fr gold & multi	.50	.25
a.		Souvenir sheet of 3, #361-363	1.75	1.75
		Nos. 361-363,C143-C145 (6)	5.60	1.60

Easter 1971. Exist imperf. Value: set (6) $4.75; souvenir sheets, $5.75.

Young Venetian Woman, by Dürer — A50

Dürer Paintings: 11fr, Hieronymus Holzschuher. 14fr, Emperor Maximilian I. 17fr, Holy Family, from Paumgartner Altar. 26fr, Haller Madonna. 31fr, Self-portrait, 1498.

1971, Sept. 20

No.	Type	Description	Unused	Used
364	A50	6fr multicolored	.25	.25
365	A50	11fr multicolored	.30	.25
366	A50	14fr multicolored	.45	.25
367	A50	17fr multicolored	.75	.40
368	A50	26fr multicolored	1.00	.50
369	A50	31fr multicolored	1.25	.60
a.		Souvenir sheet of 2, #368-369	3.00	3.00
		Nos. 364-369 (6)	4.00	2.25

International Letter Writing Week. Albrecht Dürer (1471-1528), German painter and engraver.

Exist imperf. Values: set $9; souvenir sheet $3.

Nos. 364-369, 369a Overprinted in Black and Gold: "VIème CONGRES / DE L'INSTITUT INTERNATIONAL / DE DROIT D'EXPRESSION FRANCAISE"

1971, Oct. 8

No.	Type	Description	Unused	Used
370	A50	6fr multicolored	.25	.25
371	A50	11fr multicolored	.30	.25
372	A50	14fr multicolored	.45	.25
373	A50	17fr multicolored	.65	.25
374	A50	26fr multicolored	1.00	.25
375	A50	31fr multicolored	1.25	.25
a.		Souvenir sheet of 2	2.50	2.50
		Nos. 370-375 (6)	3.90	1.50

6th Cong. of the Intl. Legal Institute of the French-speaking Area, Bujumbura, 8/10-19.

Exists imperf. Values: set $9; souvenir sheet $2.50.

Madonna and Child, by Il Perugino — A51

Paintings of the Madonna and Child by: 5fr, Andrea del Sarto. 6fr, Luis de Morales.

1971, Nov. 2 Photo. *Perf. 13½*

No.	Type	Description	Unused	Used
376	A51	3fr dk green & multi	.30	.25
377	A51	5fr dk green & multi	.30	.25
378	A51	6fr dk green & multi	.35	.25
a.		Souvenir sheet of 3, #376-378	4.50	4.50
		Nos. 376-378,C153-C155 (6)	3.85	1.60

Christmas 1971.

Exist imperf. Value: set (6) $4.50; souvenir sheets, $9.

For surcharges see Nos. B49-B51, CB19-CB21.

Lunar Orbiter A52

Designs: 11fr, Vostok. 14fr, Luna 1. 17fr, Apollo 11 astronaut on moon. 26fr, Soyuz 11. 40fr, Lunar Rover (Apollo 15).

1972, Jan. 15

No.	Type	Description	Unused	Used
379	A52	6fr gold & multi	.25	.25
380	A52	11fr gold & multi	.40	.25
381	A52	14fr gold & multi	.60	.25
382	A52	17fr gold & multi	.70	.25
383	A52	26fr gold & multi	1.25	.30
384	A52	40fr gold & multi	2.00	.50
a.		Souvenir sheet of 6	5.50	5.50
		Nos. 379-384 (6)	5.20	1.80

Conquest of space.

No. 384a contains one each of Nos. 379-384 inscribed "APOLLO 16."

Exist imperf. Value: set $11; souvenir sheet, $11.

See No. C156.

Slalom and Sapporo '72 Emblem — A53

Sapporo '72 Emblem and: 6fr, Figure skating, pairs. 11fr, Figure skating, women's. 14fr, Ski jump. 17fr, Ice hockey. 24fr, Speed skating, men's. 26fr, Snow scooter. 31fr, Downhill skiing. 50fr, Bobsledding.

1972, Feb. 3

No.	Type	Description	Unused	Used
385	A53	5fr silver & multi	.25	.25
386	A53	6fr silver & multi	.25	.25
387	A53	11fr silver & multi	.35	.25
388	A53	14fr silver & multi	.45	.25
389	A53	17fr silver & multi	.60	.25
390	A53	24fr silver & multi	.75	.25
391	A53	26fr silver & multi	.90	.25
392	A53	31fr silver & multi	1.00	.25
393	A53	50fr silver & multi	1.75	.30
		Nos. 385-393 (9)	6.30	2.30

11th Winter Olympic Games, Sapporo, Japan, Feb. 3-13. Printed in sheets of 12. See No. C157.

Exists imperf. Value: set $35.

Issued: Nos. 385-390, 2/1; Nos. 391-393, 2/21.

Ecce Homo, by Quentin Massys — A54

Paintings: 6.50fr, Crucifixion, by Rubens. 10fr, Descent from the Cross, by Jacopo da Pontormo. 18fr, Pieta, by Ferdinand Gallegos. 27fr, Trinity, by El Greco.

1972, Mar. 20 Photo. *Perf. 13½*
394 A54 3.50fr gold & multi .25 .25
395 A54 6.50fr gold & multi .45 .25
396 A54 10fr gold & multi .65 .25
397 A54 18fr gold & multi 1.25 .25
398 A54 27fr gold & multi 1.50 .25
a. Souv. sheet, #394-398 + label 7.00 7.00
Nos. 394-398 (5) 4.10 1.25

Easter 1972. Printed in sheets of 8 with label.
Exist imperf. Value: set $6; souvenir sheet $7.

Gymnastics, Olympic Rings and "Motion" A55

1972, May 19
399 A55 5fr shown .25 .25
400 A55 6fr Javelin .35 .25
401 A55 11fr Fencing .70 .25
402 A55 14fr Bicycling .90 .25
403 A55 17fr Pole vault 1.10 .25
Nos. 399-403,C158-C161 (9) 11.50 2.60

Souvenir Sheet
404 Sheet of 2 4.00 3.75
a. A55 31fr Discus 1.50 1.50
b. A55 40fr Soccer 1.50 1.50

20th Olympic Games, Munich, 8/26-9/11.
Exist imperf. Values: set (9) $9; souvenir sheet $5.

Prince Rwagasore, Pres. Micombero, Burundi Flag, Drummers A56

7fr, Rwagasore, Micombero, flag, map of Africa, globe. 13fr, Micombero, flag, globe.

1972, Aug. 24 Photo. *Perf. 13½*
405 A56 5fr silver & multi .25 .25
406 A56 7fr silver & multi .25 .25
407 A56 13fr silver & multi .45 .25
a. Souvenir sheet of 3, #405-407 2.00 .90
Nos. 405-407,C162-C164 (6) 2.65 1.70

10th anniversary of independence.
Exist imperf. Values: set $3; souvenir sheets $2.

Madonna and Child, by Andrea Solario — A57

Paintings of the Madonna and Child by: 10fr, Raphael. 15fr, Botticelli.

1972, Nov. 2
408 A57 5fr lt blue & multi .30 .25
409 A57 10fr lt blue & multi .60 .25
410 A57 15fr lt blue & multi 1.10 .25
a. Souvenir sheet of 3, #408-410 2.75 2.75
Nos. 408-410,C165-C167 (6) 8.00 1.65

Christmas 1972. Sheets of 20 stamps + label.
Exist imperf. Values: set (6) $8; souvenir sheets $8.
For surcharges see Nos. B56-B58, CB26-CB28.

Orchids — A58

50c, Platycoryne Crocea. 1fr, Cattleya trianaei. 2fr, Eulophia cucullata. 3fr, Cymbidium hamsey. 4fr, Thelymitra pauciflora. 5fr, Miltassia. 6fr, Miltonia.

1972 Size: 33x33mm
411 A58 50c shown .40 .25
412 A58 1fr multicolored .50 .25
413 A58 2fr multicolored .60 .25
414 A58 3fr multicolored .75 .25
415 A58 4fr multicolored .90 .25
416 A58 5fr multicolored 1.25 .25
417 A58 6fr multicolored 1.50 .25

Size: 38x38mm
418 A58 7fr Like 50c 1.75 .25
419 A58 8fr Like 1fr 2.00 .25
420 A58 9fr Like 2fr 2.50 .25
421 A58 10fr Like 3fr 3.00 .25
Nos. 411-421,C168-C174 (18) 41.90 5.35

Issued: Nos. 411-417, 11/6; Nos. 418-421, 11/29.

Henry Morton Stanley — A59

Designs: 7fr, Porters, Stanley's expedition. 13fr, Stanley entering Ujiji.

1973, Mar. 19 Photo. *Perf. 13½*
422 A59 5fr gold & multi .35 .25
423 A59 7fr gold & multi .50 .25
424 A59 13fr gold & multi .85 .25
Nos. 422-424,C175-C177 (6) 5.05 1.60

Exploration of Africa by David Livingstone (1813-1873) and Henry Morton Stanley (John Rowlands; 1841-1904).
Exist imperf. Values: set (6) $3.50; souvenir sheets $3.50.

Crucifixion, by Roger van der Weyden — A60

Easter (Paintings): 5fr, Flagellation of Christ, by Caravaggio. 13fr, The Burial of Christ, by Raphael.

1973, Apr. 10
425 A60 5fr gold & multi .25 .25
426 A60 7fr gold & multi .35 .25
427 A60 13fr gold & multi .65 .25
a. Souvenir sheet of 3, #425-427 3.75 3.00
Nos. 425-427,C178-C180 (6) 5.80 1.65

Exist imperf. Values: set (6) $6; souvenir sheets $6.

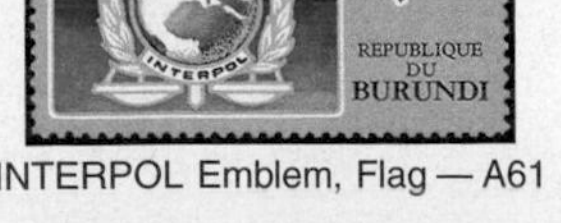

INTERPOL Emblem, Flag — A61

Design: 10fr, INTERPOL flag and emblem. 18fr, INTERPOL Headquarters and emblem.

1973, May 19 Photo. *Perf. 13½*
428 A61 5fr silver & multi .25 .25
429 A61 10fr silver & multi .35 .25
430 A61 18fr silver & multi .60 .25
Nos. 428-430,C181-C182 (5) 4.05 1.55

Intl. Criminal Police Organization, 50th anniv.
Exist imperf. Value set, $5.50.

Signs of the Zodiac, Babylon — A62

Designs: 5fr, Greek and Roman gods representing planets. 7fr, Ptolemy (No. 433a) and Ptolemaic solar system. 13fr, Copernicus (No. 434a) and heliocentric system.
a, UL. b, UR. c, LL. d, LR.

1973, July 27 Photo. *Perf. 13½*
431 A62 3fr Block of 4, #a.-d. 1.10 .40
432 A62 5fr Block of 4, #a.-d. 1.75 .60
433 A62 7fr Block of 4, #a.-d. 2.50 .60
434 A62 13fr Block of 4, #a.-d. 3.50 1.00
e. Souvenir sheet of 4, #431-434 35.00 35.00
Nos. 431-434,C183-C186 (8) 31.60 7.60

500th anniversary of the birth of Nicolaus Copernicus (1473-1543), Polish astronomer.
Exist imperf. Values: set (8) $40; souvenir sheets $95.

Flowers and Butterflies — A63

Block of 4 containing 2 flower & 2 butterfly designs. The 1fr, 2fr, 5fr and 11fr have flower designs listed as "a" and "d" numbers, butterflies as "b" and "c" numbers; the arrangement is reversed for the 3fr and 6fr.

1973, Sept. 3 Photo. *Perf. 13*
Stamp Size: 34x41½mm
435 A63 Block of 4 2.50 .40
a. 1fr Protea cynaroides .30 .25
b. 1fr Precis octavia .30 .25
c. 1fr Epiphora bauhiniae .30 .25
d. 1fr Gazania longiscapa .30 .25
436 A63 Block of 4 5.00 .40
a. 2fr Kniphofia .60 .25
b. 2fr Cymothoe coccinata .60 .25
c. 2fr Nudaurelia zambesina .60 .25
d. 2fr Freesia refracta .60 .25
437 A63 Block of 4 6.50 .40
a. 3fr Calotis eupompe .90 .25
b. 3fr Narcissus .90 .25
c. 3fr Cineraria hybrida .90 .25
d. 3fr Cyrestis camillus .90 .25
438 A63 Block of 4 10.00 .40
a. 5fr Iris tingitana 1.50 .25
b. 5fr Pappilio demodocus 1.50 .25
c. 5fr Catopsilia avelaneda 1.50 .25
d. 5fr Nerine sarniensis 1.50 .25
439 A63 Block of 4 12.00 .45
a. 6fr Hypolimnas dexithea 1.75 .25
b. 6fr Zantedeschia tropicalis 1.75 .25
c. 6fr Sandersonia aurantiaca 1.75 .25
d. 6fr Drurya antimachus 1.75 .25
440 A63 Block of 4 14.00 .50
a. 11fr Nymphaea capensis 2.00 .25
b. 11fr Pandoriana pandora 2.00 .25
c. 11fr Precis orythia 2.00 .25
d. 11fr Pelargonium domestica 2.00 .25
Nos. 435-440,C187-C192 (12) 134.00 7.10

Virgin and Child, by Giovanni Bellini — A64

Virgin and Child by: 10fr, Jan van Eyck. 15fr, Giovanni Boltraffio.

1973, Nov. 13 Photo. *Perf. 13*
441 A64 5fr gold & multi .50 .25
442 A64 10fr gold & multi 1.00 .25
443 A64 15fr gold & multi 1.25 .25
a. Souvenir sheet of 3, #441-443 2.50 2.00
Nos. 441-443,C193-C195 (6) 7.50 1.55

Christmas 1973.
Exist imperf. Values: set $8; souvenir sheets $8.
For surcharges see Nos. B59-B61, CB29-CB31.

Pietá, by Paolo Veronese — A65

Paintings: 10fr, Virgin and St. John, by van der Weyden. 18fr, Crucifixion, by van der Weyden. 27fr, Burial of Christ, by Titian. 40fr, Pietá, by El Greco.

1974, Apr. 19 Photo. *Perf. 14x13½*
444 A65 5fr gold & multi .25 .25
445 A65 10fr gold & multi .40 .25
446 A65 18fr gold & multi 1.10 .25
447 A65 27fr gold & multi 1.60 .25
448 A65 40fr gold & multi 2.50 .35
a. Souvenir sheet of 5, #444-448 4.50 4.50
Nos. 444-448 (5) 5.85 1.35

Easter 1974.
Exist imperf. Values: set $6.50; souvenir sheet $4.50.

Fish — A66

1974, May 30 Photo. *Perf. 13*
Stamp Size: 35x35mm
449 A66 Block of 4 4.50 .50
a. 1fr Haplochromis multicolor .80 .25
b. 1fr Pantodon buchholzi .80 .25
c. 1fr Tropheus duboisi .80 .25
d. 1fr Distichodus sexfasciatus .80 .25
450 A66 Block of 4 6.00 .40
a. 2fr Pelmatochromis kribensis .90 .25
b. 2fr Nannaethiops tritaeniatus .90 .25
c. 2fr Polycentropsis abbreviata .90 .25
d. 2fr Hemichromis bimaculatus .90 .25
451 A66 Block of 4 6.50 .55
a. 3fr Ctenopoma acutirostre 1.00 .25
b. 3fr Synodontis angelicus 1.00 .25
c. 3fr Tilapia melanopleura 1.00 .25
d. 3fr Aphyosemion bivittatum 1.00 .25
452 A66 Block of 4 10.00 .60
a. 5fr Monodactylus argenteus 1.60 .25
b. 5fr Zanclus canescens 1.60 .25
c. 5fr Pygoplites diacanthus 1.60 .25
d. 5fr Cephalopholis argus 1.60 .25
453 A66 Block of 4 12.50 .65
a. 6fr Priacanthus arenatus 2.25 .25
b. 6fr Pomacanthus arcuatus 2.25 .25
c. 6fr Scarus guacamaia 2.25 .25
d. 6fr Zeus faber 2.25 .25
454 A66 Block of 4 25.00 1.60
a. 11fr Lactophrys quadricornis 4.50 .45
b. 11fr Balistes vetula 4.50 .45

c. 11fr Acanthurus bahianus 4.50 .45
d. 11fr Holocanthus ciliaris 4.50 .45
Nos. 449-454,C207-C212 (12) 144.00 10.35

Soccer and Cup A67

Designs: Various soccer scenes and cup.

1974, July 4 Photo. *Perf. 13*

455 A67 5fr gold & multi .30 .25
456 A67 6fr gold & multi .40 .25
457 A67 11fr gold & multi .75 .25
458 A67 14fr gold & multi 1.10 .30
459 A67 17fr gold & multi 1.50 .30
a. Souvenir sheet of 3 6.00 6.00
Nos. 455-459,C196-C198 (8) 10.05 2.65

World Soccer Championship, Munich, June 13-July 7. No. 459a contains 3 stamps similar to Nos. C196-C198 without "Poste Aerienne."

Exist imperf. Values: set (8) $8; souvenir sheet $10.

Flags over UPU Headquarters, Bern — A68

No. 460b, G.P.O., Bujumbura. No. 461a, Mailmen ("11F" in UR). No. 461b, Mailmen ("11F" in UL). No. 462a, UPU emblem. No. 462b, Means of transportation. No. 463a, Pigeon over globe showing Burundi. No. 463b, Swiss flag, pigeon over map showing Bern. Pairs are continuous designs.

1974, July 23

460 A68 6fr Pair, #a.-b. .85 .25
461 A68 11fr Pair, #a.-b. 1.25 .25
462 A68 14fr Pair, #a.-b. 1.75 .25
463 A68 17fr Pair, #a.-b. 2.10 .25
c. Souvenir sheet of 8, #460-463 20.00 20.00
Nos. 460-463,C199-C202 (8) 19.95 3.35

Cent. of UPU.
Exist imperf. Value set, $30.

St. Ildefonso Writing Letter, by El Greco A69

Paintings: 11fr, Lady Sealing Letter, by Chardin. 14fr, Titus at Desk, by Rembrandt. 17fr, The Love Letter, by Vermeer. 26fr, The Merchant G. Gisze, by Holbein. 31fr, Portrait of Alexandre Lenoir, by David.

1974, Oct. 1 Photo. *Perf. 13*

468 A69 6fr gold & multi .35 .25
469 A69 11fr gold & multi .60 .30
470 A69 14fr gold & multi .70 .35
471 A69 17fr gold & multi 1.00 .35
472 A69 26fr gold & multi 1.10 .45
473 A69 31fr gold & multi 1.50 .60
a. Souvenir sheet of 2, #472-473 4.00 4.00
Nos. 468-473 (6) 5.25 2.30

International Letter Writing Week, Oct. 6-12.
Exist imperf. Values: set $7; souvenir sheet $4.

Virgin and Child, by Bernaert van Orley — A70

Paintings of the Virgin and Child: 10fr, by Hans Memling. 15fr, by Botticelli.

1974, Nov. 7 Photo. *Perf. 13*

474 A70 5fr gold & multi .65 .25
475 A70 10fr gold & multi 1.20 .25
476 A70 15fr gold & multi 1.50 .25
a. Souvenir sheet of 3, #474-476 4.00 4.00
Nos. 474-476,C213-C215 (6) 8.75 1.75

Christmas 1974. Sheets of 20 stamps and one label.
Exist imperf. Values: set (6) $7.50; souvenir sheets $9.

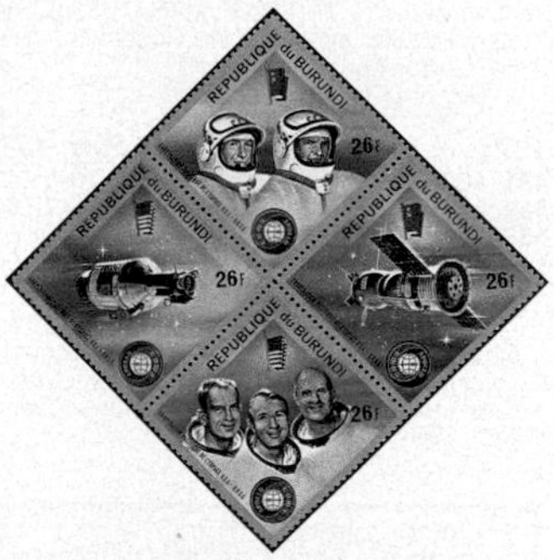

Apollo-Soyuz Space Mission and Emblem — A71

1975, July 10 Photo. *Perf. 13*

477 A71 Block of 4 4.00 2.75
a. 26fr A.A. Leonov, V.N. Kubasov, Soviet flag .65
b. 26fr Soyuz and Soviet flag .65
c. 26fr Apollo and American flag .65
d. 26fr D.K. Slayton, V.D. Brand, T.P. Stafford, American flag .65
478 A71 Block of 4 5.00 3.25
a. 31fr Apollo-Soyuz link-up .95
b. 31fr Apollo, blast-off .95
c. 31fr Soyuz, blast-off .95
d. 31fr Kubasov, Leonov, Slayton, Brand, Stafford .95
Nos. 477-478,C216-C217 (4) 18.00 12.00

Apollo Soyuz space test project (Russo-American cooperation), launching July 15; link-up, July 17.
Exist imperf. Value set, $16.

Addax — A72

1975, July 31 Photo. *Perf. 13½*

479 Strip of 4 1.50 .65
a. A72 1fr shown .30 .25
b. A72 1fr Roan antelope .30 .25
c. A72 1fr Nyala .30 .25
d. A72 1fr White rhinoceros .30 .25
480 Strip of 4 2.40 .65
a. A72 2fr Mandrill .45 .25
b. A72 2fr Eland .45 .25
c. A72 2fr Salt's dik-dik .45 .25
d. A72 2fr Thomson's gazelles .45 .25
481 Strip of 4 4.00 .65
a. A72 3fr African small-clawed otter .65 .25
b. A72 3fr Reed buck .65 .25
c. A72 3fr Indian civet .65 .25
d. A72 3fr Cape buffalo .65 .25
482 Strip of 4 6.00 1.10
a. A72 5fr White-tailed gnu 1.10 .25
b. A72 5fr African wild asses 1.10 .25
c. A72 5fr Black-and-white colobus monkey 1.10 .25
d. A72 5fr Gerenuk 1.10 .25
483 Strip of 4 8.75 1.10
a. A72 6fr Dama gazelle 1.60 .25
b. A72 6fr Black-backed jackal 1.60 .25
c. A72 6fr Sitatungas 1.60 .25
d. A72 6fr Zebra antelope 1.60 .25
484 Strip of 4 12.00 1.10
a. A72 11fr Fennec 2.25 .25
b. A72 11fr Lesser kudus 2.25 .25
c. A72 11fr Blesbok 2.25 .25
d. A72 11fr Serval 2.25 .25
Nos. 479-484,C218-C223 (12) 94.90 11.30

For overprints see Nos. C224-C227.

Jonah, by Michelangelo — A73

Paintings from Sistine Chapel: No. 485b, Libyan Sybil. No. 486a, Prophet Isaiah. No. 486b, Delphic Sybil. No. 487a, Daniel. No. 487b, Cumaean Sybil.

1975, Dec. 3 Photo. *Perf. 13*

485 A73 5fr Pair, #a.-b. 1.50 .25
486 A73 13fr Pair, #a.-b. 3.50 .35
487 A73 27fr Pair, #a.-b. 6.00 .50
c. Souvenir sheet of 6, #485-487 12.00 9.00
Nos. 485-487,C228-C230 (6) 30.50 2.95

Michelangelo Buonarotti (1475-1564), Italian sculptor, painter and architect. Printed in sheets of 18 stamps + 2 labels.
Exist imperf. Values: set (6) $30; souvenir sheets $28.
For surcharges see Nos. B65-B67, CB35-CB37.

Speed Skating — A74

Designs (Innsbruck Games Emblem and): 24fr, Figure skating, women's. 26fr, Two-man bobsled. 31fr, Cross-country skiing.

1976, Jan. 23 Photo. *Perf. 14x13½*

491 A74 17fr dp bl & multi .70 .25
492 A74 24fr multi 1.00 .25
493 A74 26fr multi 1.25 .25
494 A74 31fr plum & multi 1.50 .35
a. Souvenir sheet of 3, perf. 13½ 5.50 3.50
Nos. 491-494,C234-C236 (7) 9.35 2.50

12th Winter Olympic Games, Innsbruck, Austria, Feb. 4-15.
No. 494a contains stamps similar to Nos. C234-C236, without "POSTE AERIENNE."
Exist imperf. Values: set (7) $12; souvenir sheets $12.

Basketball — A75

Montreal Games Emblem and: Nos. 495a, 498b, 499c, Basketball. Nos. 495b, 497a, 499b, Pole vault. Nos. 496a, 497b, 499d, Running. Nos. 496b, 498a, 499a, Soccer.

1976, May 3 Litho. *Perf. 13½*

495 A75 14fr Pair, #a.-b. 1.50 1.00
496 A75 17fr Pair, #a.-b. 2.25 1.50
497 A75 28fr Pair, #a.-b. 3.50 2.25
498 A75 40fr Pair, #a.-b. 9.00 4.00
Nos. 495-498,C237-C239 (7) 34.25 20.90

Souvenir Sheet

499 Sheet of 4 13.50 13.50
a. A75 14fr red & multi 3.00 3.00
b. A75 17fr olive & multi 3.00 3.00
c. A75 28fr blue & multi 3.00 3.00
d. A75 40fr magenta & multi 3.00 3.00

21st Olympic Games, Montreal, Canada, July 17-Aug. 1.
Exist imperf. Values: set (7) $30; souvenir sheets $50.

Virgin and Child, by Dirk Bouts — A76

Virgin and Child by: 13fr, Giovanni Bellini. 27fr, Carlo Crivelli.

1976, Oct. 18 Photo. *Perf. 13½*

504 A76 5fr gold & multi .85 .25
505 A76 13fr gold & multi 1.10 .25
506 A76 27fr gold & multi 2.00 .25
a. Souvenir sheet of 3, #504-506 4.00 3.50
Nos. 504-506,C250-C252 (6) 11.20 1.75

Christmas 1976. Sheets of 20 stamps and descriptive label.
Exist imperf. Values: set (6) $10; souvenir sheets $11.
For surcharges see Nos. B71-B73, CB41-CB43.

St. Veronica, by Rubens A77

Paintings by Rubens: 21fr, Christ on the Cross. 27fr, Descent from the Cross. 35fr, The Deposition.

1977, Apr. 5 Photo. *Perf. 13*

507 A77 10fr gold & multi 1.50 1.50
508 A77 21fr gold & multi 3.00 3.00
509 A77 27fr gold & multi 3.25 3.25
510 A77 35fr gold & multi 4.00 4.00
a. Souvenir sheet of 4 10.00 10.00
Nos. 507-510 (4) 11.75 11.75

Easter 1977. Sheets of 30 stamps and descriptive label. No. 510a contains 4 stamps similar to Nos. 507-510 inscribed "POSTE AERIENNE."
Exist imperf. Values: set $14; souvenir sheet $12.

A78

No. 511a, Alexander Graham Bell. Nos. 511b, Intelsat Satellite, Modern & Old Telephones. No. 512a, Switchboard operator, c. 1910, wall telephone. No. 512b, Intelsat, radar. No. 513a, A.G. Bell, 1st telephone. No. 513b, Satellites around globe, videophone.

1977, May 17 Photo. *Perf. 13*

511 A78 10fr Pair, #a.-b. 1.25 1.00
512 A78 17fr Pair, #a.-b. 2.50 2.00
513 A78 26fr Pair, #a.-b. 4.50 4.00
Nos. 511-513,C253-C254 (5) 13.90 12.65

Centenary of first telephone call by Alexander Graham Bell, Mar. 10, 1876.
Exist imperf. Value set (5), $9.

Wildlife — A80

1977, Aug. 22 Photo. *Perf. 14x14½*

517 A80 Strip of 4 2.25 .25
a. 2fr Buffon's Kob .50 .25
b. 2fr Marabous .50 .25
c. 2fr Brindled gnu .50 .25
d. 2fr River hog .50 .25

518 A80 Strip of 4 3.75 .50
a. 5fr Zebras .75 .25
b. 5fr Shoebill .75 .25
c. 5fr Striped hyenas .75 .25
d. 5fr Chimpanzee .75 .25
519 A80 Strip of 4 6.00 .60
a. 8fr Flamingos 1.25 .25
b. 8fr Nile crocodiles 1.25 .25
c. 8fr Green mamba 1.25 .25
d. 8fr Greater kudus 1.25 .25
520 A80 Strip of 4 12.00 .70
a. 11fr Hyrax 2.25 .25
b. 11fr Cobra 2.25 .25
c. 11fr Jackals 2.25 .25
d. 11fr Verreaux's eagles 2.25 .25
521 A80 Strip of 4 17.50 1.00
a. 21fr Honey badger 3.25 .25
b. 21fr Harnessed antelopes 3.25 .25
c. 21fr Secretary bird 3.25 .25
d. 21fr Klipspringer 3.25 .25
522 a80 Strip of 4 22.50 1.50
a. 27fr African big-eared fox 4.75 .30
b. 27fr Elephants 4.75 .30
c. 27fr Vulturine guineafowl 4.75 .30
d. 27fr Impalas 4.75 .30
Nos. 517-522,C258-C263 (12) 184.50 13.45

Exist imperf.

The Goose Girl, by Grimm — A81

Fairy Tales: 5fr, by Grimm Brothers. 11fr, by Aesop. 14fr, by Hans Christian Andersen. 17fr, by Jean de La Fontaine. 26fr, English fairy tales.

1977, Sept. 14 *Perf. 14*
523 Block of 4 5.50 .65
a. A81 5fr shown 1.00 .25
b. A81 5fr The Two Wanderers 1.00 .25
c. A81 5fr The Man of Iron 1.00 .25
d. A81 5fr Snow White and Rose Red 1.00 .25
524 Block of 4 11.50 .65
a. A81 11fr The Quarreling Cats 2.00 .25
b. A81 11fr The Blind and the Lame 2.00 .25
c. A81 11fr The Hermit and the Bear 2.00 .25
d. A81 11fr The Fox and the Stork 2.00 .25
525 Block of 4 14.50 .65
a. A81 14fr The Princess and the Pea 2.50 .25
b. A81 14fr The Old Tree Mother 2.50 .25
c. A81 14fr The Ice Maiden 2.50 .25
d. A81 14fr The Old House 2.50 .25
526 Block of 4 18.00 1.00
a. A81 17fr The Oyster and the Suitors 3.50 .25
b. A81 17fr The Wolf and the Lamb 3.50 .25
c. A81 17fr Hen with the Golden Egg 3.50 .25
d. A81 17fr The Wolf as Shepherd 3.50 .25
527 Block of 4 24.00 1.25
a. A81 26fr Three Heads in the Well 4.00 .25
b. A81 26fr Mother Goose 4.00 .25
c. A81 26fr Jack and the Beanstalk 4.00 .25
d. A81 26fr Alice in Wonderland 4.00 .25
Nos. 523-527 (5) 73.50 4.20

Exist imperf. Value (set), $80.

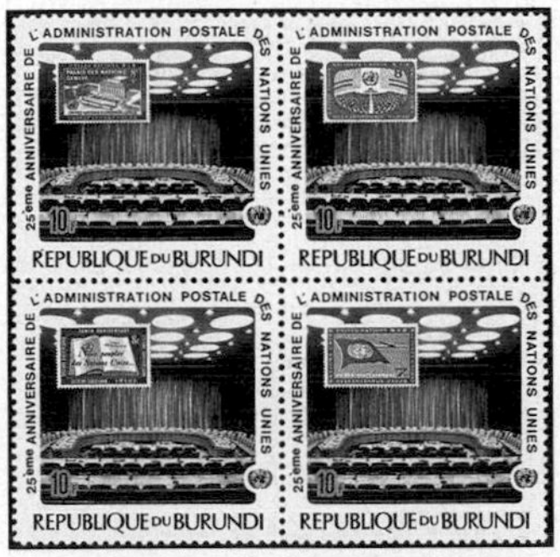

Security Council Chamber, UN Nos. 28, 46, 37, C7 — A82

UN Stamps and: 8fr, UN General Assembly, interior. 21fr, UN Meeting Hall.

1977, Oct. 10 Photo. *Perf. 13½*
528 A82 Block of 4 3.50 2.50
a. 8fr No. 25 .90 .50
b. 8fr No. C5 .90 .50
c. 8fr No. 23 .90 .50
d. 8fr No. 2 .90 .50
529 A82 Block of 4 5.25 3.50
a. 10fr No. 28 1.00 .75
b. 10fr No. 46 1.00 .75
c. 10fr No. 37 1.00 .75
d. 10fr No. C7 1.00 .75
530 A82 Block of 4 8.75 6.00
a. 21fr No. 45 1.60 1.25
b. 21fr No. 42 1.60 1.25
c. 21fr No. 17 1.60 1.25
d. 21fr No. 13 1.60 1.25
e. Souvenir sheet of 3 4.00 4.00
Nos. 528-530,C264-C266 (6) 41.00 35.50

25th anniv. (in 1976) of the UN Postal Administration. No. 530e contains 8fr in design of No. 529d, 10fr in design of No. 530b, 21fr in design of No. 528c.
Exist imperf. Value (set), $55.

Virgin and Child — A83

Paintings of the Virgin and Child: 5fr, By Meliore Toscano. 13fr, By J. Lombardos. 27fr, By Emmanuel Tzanes, 1610-1680.

1977, Oct. 31 Photo. *Perf. 14x13*
531 A83 5fr multicolored 1.10 .30
532 A83 13fr multicolored 2.25 .60
533 A83 27fr multicolored 3.25 .75
a. Souvenir sheet of 3, #531-533 6.00 6.00
Nos. 531-533,C267-C269 (6) 14.60 6.65

Christmas 1977. Sheets of 24 stamps with descriptive label.
Exist imperf. Values: set (6) $15; souvenir sheets $9.
For surcharges see Nos. B74-B76, CB44-CB46.

Cruiser Aurora, Russia Nos. 211, 303, 1252, 187 — A84

Russian Stamps and: 8fr, Kremlin, Moscow. 11fr, Pokrovski Cathedral, Moscow. 13fr, Labor Day parade, 1977 and 1980 Olympic Games emblem.

1977, Nov. 14 Photo. *Perf. 13*
534 A84 Block of 4 4.00 .60
a. 5fr No. 211 .85 .25
b. 5fr No. 303 .85 .25
c. 5fr No. 1252 .85 .25
d. 5fr No. 187 .85 .25
535 A84 Block of 4 7.75 .60
a. 8fr No. 856 1.25 .25
b. 8fr No. 1986 1.25 .25
c. 8fr No. 908 1.25 .25
d. 8fr No. 2551 1.25 .25
536 A84 Block of 4 10.50 .60
a. 11fr No. 3844b 1.75 .25
b. 11fr No. 3452 1.75 .25
c. 11fr No. 3382 1.75 .25
d. 11fr No. 3837 1.75 .25
537 A84 Block of 4 13.00 .90
a. 13fr No. 4446 2.10 .25
b. 13fr No. 3497 2.10 .25
c. 13fr No. 2926 2.10 .25
d. 13fr No. 2365 2.10 .25
Nos. 534-537 (4) 35.25 2.70

60th anniv. of Russian October Revolution.
Exist imperf. Value (set), $30.00.

Ship at Dock, Arms and Flag — A85

Burundi Arms and Flag and: 5fr, Men at lathes. 11fr, Male leopard dance. 14fr, Coffee harvest. 17fr, Government Palace.

1977, Nov. 25 Photo. *Perf. 13½*
538 A85 1fr sil & multi .25 .25
539 A85 5fr sil & multi .25 .25
540 A85 11fr sil & multi .70 .25
541 A85 14fr sil & multi 1.10 .25
542 A85 17fr sil & multi 1.40 .30
Nos. 538-542 (5) 3.70 1.30

15th anniversary of independence.
Exist imperf. Value (set), $4.

A86

Paintings of the Virgin and Child by: 13fr, Rubens. 17fr, Solario. 27fr, Tiepolo. 31fr, Gerard David. 40fr, Bellini.

1979, Feb. Photo. *Perf. 14x13*
543 A86 13fr multi 1.75 1.10
544 A86 17fr multi 2.10 1.25
545 A86 27fr multi 3.50 2.10
546 A86 31fr multi 4.50 2.75
547 A86 40fr multi 6.00 3.75
Nos. 543-547 (5) 17.85 10.95

Christmas 1978. See Nos. B77-B81, C270, CB47.
Exist imperf. Value (set), $19.

Birds — A87

Designs: 1fr, Buceros abyssinicus. 2fr, Anhinga rufa. 3fr, Melittophagus pusillus. 5fr, Phoeniconais minor. 8fr, Afropavo congenis. 10fr, Porphyrio alba. 20fr, Polemaethus bellicosus. 27fr, Ibis ibis. 50fr, Ephippiorhynchus senegalensis.

1979 Photo. *Perf. 13½x13*
548 A87 1fr multicolored .60 .60
549 A87 2fr multicolored .65 .65
550 A87 3fr multicolored .75 .75
551 A87 5fr multicolored 1.10 1.00
552 A87 8fr multicolored 1.90 1.75
553 A87 10fr multicolored 2.25 2.00
554 A87 20fr multicolored 4.75 4.50
555 A87 27fr multicolored 5.25 5.00
556 A87 50fr multicolored 10.50 10.00
Nos. 548-556,C273-C281 (18) 91.50 65.90

See Nos. 585A-585L.

Mother and Infant, IYC Emblem A88

IYC Emblem and: 20fr, Infant. 27fr, Girl with doll. 50fr, Children in Children's Village.

1979, July 19 Photo. *Perf. 14*
557 A88 10fr multi .90 .90
558 A88 20fr multi 2.10 1.75
559 A88 27fr multi 2.75 2.75
560 A88 50fr multi 4.25 4.25
Nos. 557-560 (4) 10.00 9.65

Exist imperf. Value set, $10.
See No. B82.

A89

Virgin and Child by: 20fr, del Garbo. 27fr, Giovanni Penni. 31fr, G. Romano. 50fr, Jacopo Bassano.

1979, Oct. 12
561 A89 20fr multi 2.00 1.00
562 A89 27fr multi 3.75 2.00
563 A89 31fr multi 5.25 2.50
564 A89 50fr multi 6.50 2.75
Nos. 561-564,B83-B86 (8) 39.50 16.50

Christmas 1979. See Nos. C271, CB48.
Exist imperf. Value set (8), $35.

A90

Designs: 20fr, Rowland Hill, Penny Black. Stamps of Burundi: 27fr, German East Africa Nos. 17, N17. 31fr, Nos. 4, 24. 40fr, Nos. 29, 294. 60fr, Heinrich von Stephan, No. 462.

1979, Nov. 6
565 A90 20fr multi 1.35 .75
566 A90 27fr multi 1.90 1.00
567 A90 31fr multi 2.10 1.10
568 A90 40fr multi 3.50 1.90
569 A90 60fr multi 5.00 2.75
Nos. 565-569 (5) 13.85 7.50

Sir Rowland Hill (1795-1879), originator of penny postage.
Exist imperf. Vale, set $14.
See No. C272.

A91

No. 570: a, 110-meter hurdles. b, Hurdles, Thomas Munkelt. c, Hurdles, R.D.A.
No. 571: a, Discus. b, Discus, V. Rasshchupkin. c, Discus, U.R.S.S.
No. 572: a, Soccer (player preparing to kick ball) b, Soccer (ball in air) c, Soccer, (ball being blocked by hands).

1980, Oct. 24 Photo. *Perf. 13x13½*
570 A91 20fr Strip of 3, #a.-c. 10.00 4.00
571 A91 30fr Strip of 3, #a.-c. 16.00 6.00
572 A91 40fr Strip of 3, #a.-c. 23.00 9.50
Nos. 570-572 (3) 49.00 19.50

22nd Summer Olympic Games, Moscow, July 19-Aug. 3.
Exist imperf. Value set, $49.
See No. C282.

Virgin and Child, by Mainardi A92

Christmas 1980 (Paintings): 30fr, Holy Family, by Michelangelo. 40fr, Virgin and Child, by di Cosimo. 45fr, Holy Family, by Fra Bartolomeo.

1980, Dec. 12 Photo. *Perf. 13½x13*

579	A92	10fr multi	1.50	.65
580	A92	30fr multi	3.00	1.25
581	A92	40fr multi	6.50	3.00
582	A92	45fr multi	9.00	4.00
		Nos. 579-582,B87-B90 (8)	42.10	17.80

Exist imperf. Value set, $45.
See No. CB49.

UPRONA Party National Congress, 1979 — A93

1980, Dec. 29 *Perf. 14x13½*

583	A93	10fr multi	.90	.65
584	A93	40fr multi	2.75	2.10
585	A93	45fr multi	3.00	2.40
		Nos. 583-585 (3)	6.65	5.15

Exist imperf. Value set, $6.50.

Birds Type of 1979

Designs: 5fr, Buceros abyssinicus. 10fr, Anhinga rufa. 30fr, Melittophagus pusillus. 40fr, Phoeniconaias minor. 45fr, Afropavo congensis. 50fr, Porphyrio alba.

1980 Photo. *Perf. 13½x13*

Brown Frame

585A	A87	5fr multi	*75.00*	—
585B	A87	10fr multi	*75.00*	
585C	A87	30fr multi	*75.00*	—
585D	A87	40fr multi	*75.00*	—
585E	A87	45fr multi	*75.00*	
585F	A87	50fr multi	*75.00*	—

Metallic Blue Frame

585G	A87	5fr Like #585A	*80.00*	
585H	A87	10fr Like #585B	*80.00*	
585I	A87	30fr Like #585C	*80.00*	
585J	A87	40fr Like #585D	*80.00*	
585K	A87	45fr Like #585E	*80.00*	
585L	A87	50fr Like #585F	*80.00*	—

Nos. 585A-585L exist imperf. Value $600.

Johannes Kepler, Dish Antenna A94

1981, Feb. 12 *Perf. 14*

586	A94	10fr shown	2.75	1.00
587	A94	40fr Satellite	6.00	1.90
588	A94	45fr Satellite, diff.	8.25	2.50
a.		Souvenir sheet of 3, #586-588	17.50	13.00
		Nos. 586-588 (3)	17.00	5.40

350th death anniv. of Johannes Kepler and 1st earth satellite station in Burundi.
Exist imperf. Values: set $16; souvenir sheet $19.

Lion A95

3fr, Giraffes. 5fr, Rhinoceros. 10fr, Cape buffalo. 20fr, Elephant. 25fr, Hippopotamus. 30fr, Zebra. 50fr, Warthog. 60fr, Oryx. 65fr, Wild dog. 70fr, Cheetah. 75fr, Wildebeest. 85fr, Hyena.

1983, Apr. 22 Photo. *Perf. 13*

589	A95	2fr shown	*4.50*	*8.00*
590	A95	3fr multi	*4.50*	*8.00*
591	A95	5fr multi	*6.00*	*8.00*
592	A95	10fr multi	*7.50*	*10.00*
593	A95	20fr multi	*11.00*	*10.00*
594	A95	25fr multi	*15.00*	*21.00*
595	A95	30fr multi	*22.50*	*21.00*
596	A95	50fr multi	*30.00*	*37.50*
597	A95	60fr multi	*15.00*	*40.00*
598	A95	65fr multi	*19.00*	*52.50*
599	A95	70fr multi	*22.50*	*65.00*
600	A95	75fr multi	*30.00*	*80.00*
601	A95	85fr multi	*1,100.*	*375.00*
		Nos. 589-601 (13)	*1,288.*	*736.00*

Nos. 589-601 Overprinted in Silver with World Wildlife Fund Emblem

1983 Photo. *Perf. 13*

589a	A95	2fr multi	*10.00*	*5.00*
590a	A95	3fr multi	*10.00*	*6.00*
591a	A95	5fr multi	*10.00*	*6.50*
592a	A95	10fr multi	*10.00*	*15.00*
593a	A95	20fr multi	*25.00*	*22.50*
594a	A95	25fr multi	*40.00*	*27.50*
595a	A95	30fr multi	*50.00*	*40.00*
596a	A95	50fr multi	*75.00*	*60.00*
597a	A95	60fr multi	*90.00*	*67.50*
598a	A95	65fr multi	*110.00*	*75.00*
599a	A95	70fr multi	*130.00*	*80.00*
600a	A95	75fr multi	*180.00*	*90.00*
601a	A95	85fr multi	*260.00*	*100.00*
		Nos. 589a-601a (13)	*1,000.*	*595.00*

Apparently there is speculation in these two sets. Both sets exist imperf, offered at prices 5-7 times the values shown above.

20th Anniv. of Independence, July 1, 1982 — A96

Flags, various arms, map or portrait.

1983 *Perf. 14*

602	A96	10fr multi	1.00	.60
603	A96	25fr multi	3.25	2.00
604	A96	30fr multi	3.75	2.25
605	A96	50fr multi	5.25	3.00
606	A96	65fr multi	6.75	4.50
		Nos. 602-606 (5)	20.00	12.35

Exist imperf. Value set, $20.

Christmas 1983 — A97

Virgin and Child paintings: 10fr, by Luca Signorelli (1450-1523). 25fr, by Esteban Murillo (1617-1682). 30fr, by Carlo Crivelli (1430-1495). 50fr, by Nicolas Poussin (1594-1665).

1983, Oct. 3 Litho. *Perf. 14½x13½*

607	A97	10fr multi	4.50	1.00
608	A97	25fr multi	6.50	1.40
609	A97	30fr multi	12.00	2.75
610	A97	50fr multi	17.00	7.25
		Nos. 607-610,B91-B94 (8)	89.50	24.80

Exist imperf. Value set, $110.
See Nos. C285, CB50.

Butterflies — A98

No. 611a, Cymothoe coccinata. No. 611b, Papilio zalmoxis. No. 612a, Asterope pechueli. No. 612b, Papilio antimachus. No. 613a, Papilio hesperus. No. 613b, Bebearia mardania. No. 614a, Euphaedra neophron. No. 614b, Euphaedra perseis. No. 615a, Euphaedra imperialis. No. 615b, Pseudocraea striata.

1984, June 29 Photo. *Perf. 13*

611	A98	5fr Pair, #a.-b.	13.00	3.75
612	A98	10fr Pair, #a.-b.	22.00	4.50
613	A98	30fr Pair, #a.-b.	62.50	18.00
614	A98	35fr Pair, #a.-b.	67.50	29.00
615	A98	65fr Pair, #a.-b.	150.00	50.00
		Nos. 611-615 (5)	315.00	105.25

Exist imperf. Value set, $1,600.
For surcharges see No. 654D.

19th UPU Congress, Hamburg A99

UPU emblem and: 10fr, German East Africa, #17, N17. 30fr, #4, 24. 35fr, #294, 595. 65fr, Dr. Heinrich von Stephan, #464-465.

1984, July 14 Litho. *Perf. 13x13½*

621	A99	10fr multi	2.75	.55
622	A99	30fr multi	6.00	2.50
623	A99	35fr multi	7.25	3.50
624	A99	65fr multi	8.75	4.00
		Nos. 621-624 (4)	24.75	10.55

Exist imperf. Value set, $27.50.
See No. C286.

1984 Summer Olympics — A100

Gold medalists: 10fr, Jesse Owens, US, track and field, Berlin, 1936. 30fr, Rafer Johnson, US, decathlon, 1960. 35fr, Bob Beamon, US, long jump, 1968. 65fr, Kipchoge Keino, Kenya, 3000-meter steeplechase, 1972.

1984, Aug. 6 *Perf. 13½x13*

625	A100	10fr multi	2.50	.90
626	A100	30fr multi	6.50	2.75
627	A100	35fr multi	8.00	3.00
628	A100	65fr multi	13.00	6.00
		Nos. 625-628 (4)	30.00	12.65

Exist imperf. Value set, $30.
See No. C287.

Christmas 1984 — A101

Paintings: 10fr, Rest During the Flight into Egypt, by Murillo (1617-1682). 25fr, Virgin and Child, by R. del Garbo. 30fr, Virgin and Child, by Botticelli (1445-1510). 50fr, The Adoration of the Shepherds, by Giacomo da Bassano (1517-1592).

1984, Dec. 15 *Perf. 13½*

629	A101	10fr multi	3.25	1.00
630	A101	25fr multi	7.50	2.50
631	A101	30fr multi	9.00	3.00
632	A101	50fr multi	13.00	4.75
		Nos. 629-632,B95-B98 (8)	60.75	22.50

Exist imperf. Value set (8), $65.
See Nos. C288, CB51.

Flowers — A102

1986, July 31 Photo. *Perf. 13x13½*

633	A102	2fr Thunbergia	.50	.40
634	A102	3fr Saintpaulia	.75	.50
635	A102	5fr Clivia	1.25	.75
636	A102	10fr Cassia	3.25	1.60
637	A102	20fr Strelitzia	6.50	4.00
638	A102	35fr Gloriosa	9.75	5.75
		Nos. 633-638,C289-C294 (12)	120.00	77.50

For surcharges see Nos. 654A-654B.

Intl. Peace Year — A103

10fr, Rockets as housing. 20fr, Atom as flower. 30fr, Handshake. 40fr, Globe, chicks.

1986, May 1 Litho. *Perf. 14*

639	A103	10fr multicolored	1.00	.45
640	A103	20fr multicolored	2.00	.85
641	A103	30fr multicolored	3.25	1.60
642	A103	40fr multicolored	4.75	2.25
a.		Souvenir sheet of 4, #639-642	11.50	5.00
		Nos. 639-642 (4)	11.00	5.15

No. 642a exists imperf. Value $11.

Great Lake Nations Economic Community (CEPGI), 10th Anniv. — A104

Outline maps of Lake Tanganyika, CEPGI emblem and: 5fr, Aviation. 10fr, Agriculture. 15fr, Industry. 25fr, Electrification. 35fr, Flags of Burundi, Rwanda and Zaire.

1986, May 1 Photo. *Perf. 13½x14½*

643	A104	5fr multi	2.75	.50
644	A104	10fr multi	6.50	1.75
645	A104	15fr multi	10.50	2.25
646	A104	25fr multi	14.50	3.50
647	A104	35fr multi	21.00	7.50
a.		Souv. sheet, #643-647 + label	70.00	27.50
		Nos. 643-647 (5)	55.25	15.50

No. 647a exists imperf. Value $70.

Intl. Year of Shelter for the Homeless A105

10fr, Hovel. 20fr, Drain pipe shelter. 80fr, Shoveling sand. 150fr, Children, house model.

1987, June Litho. *Perf. 14*

648	A105	10fr multicolored	2.50	.55
649	A105	20fr multicolored	4.50	1.25
650	A105	80fr multicolored	10.00	4.50
651	A105	150fr multicolored	18.00	7.75
a.		Souvenir sheet of 4, #648-651	35.00	15.00
		Nos. 648-651 (4)	35.00	14.05

Exist imperf. Values: set $35; souvenir sheet $35.

A106

1987(?) Litho. *Perf. 14*

652	A106	5fr shown	1.45	.40
653	A106	20fr Skull, lungs	9.00	2.00
654	A106	80fr Cigarette, face	24.00	6.50
		Nos. 652-654 (3)	34.45	8.90

WHO Anti-smoking campaign.
Exist imperf. Value set, $35.

Nos. 633-634, and C294 Srchd. in Silver and Black

Methods and Perfs As Before

1989

654A A102 20fr on 2fr #633 —
654B A102 20fr on 3fr #634 —
654C A102 20fr on 150fr #C294 — —

Nos. 613-615 Surcharged

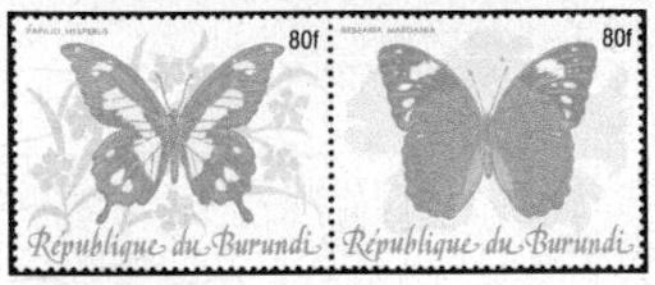

1989 **Photo.** ***Perf. 13***

654D A98 80fr on 30fr, Pair, #e.-f. — *125.00*
654G A98 80fr on 35fr, Pair, #h.-i. *125.00*
654J A98 80fr on 65fr, Pair, #k.-l. *250.00 125.00*

The original value is obscured.

Visit of Pope John Paul II — A107

1990 **Litho.** ***Perf. 14***

655 A107 5fr red lil & multi 1.15 .30
656 A107 10fr blue & multi 1.75 .50
657 A107 20fr gray & multi 3.25 1.25
658 A107 30fr ol grn & multi 5.25 2.25
659 A107 50fr brt blue & multi 7.25 3.25
660 A107 80fr grn bl & multi 11.50 5.50
a. Souv. sheet of 6, #655-660, perf. 13½ 30.00 15.00
Nos. 655-660 (6) 30.15 13.05

No. 660a exists imperf. Value $37.50.

Animals A108

5fr, Hippopotamus. 10fr, Chickens. 20fr, Lion. 30fr, Elephant. 50fr, Guinea fowl. 80fr, Crocodile.

1991, Oct. 4 **Litho.** ***Perf. 14***

661 A108 5fr multicolored 1.10 .40
662 A108 10fr multicolored 1.40 .65
663 A108 20fr multicolored 3.00 1.90
664 A108 30fr multicolored 4.25 2.00
665 A108 50fr multicolored 6.00 3.50
666 A108 80fr multicolored 12.00 4.75
a. Souv. sheet of 6, #661-666, perf. 13½ 27.50 17.50
Nos. 661-666 (6) 27.75 13.20

No. 666a exists imperf. Value $30.

Flowers — A108a

15fr, Impatiens petersiana. 20fr, Lachenalia aloides. 30fr, Nymphaea lotus. 50fr, Clivia miniata.

1992, June 2 **Litho.** ***Perf. 14***

666B A108a 15fr multicolored 3.00 .70
666C A108a 20fr multicolored 4.25 1.40
666D A108a 30fr multicolored 6.75 1.75
666E A108a 50fr multicolored 8.50 3.00
f. Souvenir sheet of 4, #666B-666E, perf. 13½ 22.50 6.00
Nos. 666B-666E (4) 22.50 6.85

No. 666Ef exists imperf. Value $22.50.

A109

Native Music and Dancing A110

15fr, Native drummer. 30fr, Two dancers. 115fr, Drummers. 200fr, Five dancers.

1992, Apr. 2 **Litho.** ***Perf. 14***

667 A109 15fr multicolored 1.25 .40
668 A109 30fr multicolored 2.00 .85
669 A110 115fr multicolored 7.75 2.50
670 A110 200fr multicolored 11.50 4.50
a. Souvenir sheet 22.50 8.00
Nos. 667-670 (4) 22.50 8.25

No. 670a contains one each of Nos. 667-668, perf. 13x13½, and Nos. 669-670, perf. 13½x13.

No. 670a exists imperf. Value $22.50.

Independence, 30th Anniv. — A111

30fr, 140fr, People with flag. 85fr, 115fr, Natl. flag. 110fr, 200fr, Monument. 120fr, 250fr, Map.

1992, June 30 **Litho.** ***Perf. 15***

671 A111 30fr multi .50 .30
672 A111 85fr multi 1.75 1.10
673 A111 110fr multi, vert. 2.00 1.50
674 A111 115fr multi 2.50 1.90
675 A111 120fr multi, vert. 2.75 2.00
676 A111 140fr multi 3.00 2.25
677 A111 200fr multi, vert. 4.25 3.00
678 A111 250fr multi, vert. 5.25 4.25
Nos. 671-678 (8) 22.00 16.30

Discovery of America, 500th Anniv. A112

Columbus' fleet, globe and: 200fr, Pre-Columbian artifacts. 400fr, Fruits and vegetables.

1992, Oct. 12 **Litho.** ***Perf. 15***

679 A112 200fr multicolored 6.50 3.25
680 A112 400fr multicolored 11.00 7.00

Felis Serval A113

130fr, Two seated. 200fr, One standing, one lying. 220fr, Two faces.

1992, Oct. 16

681 A113 30fr shown 1.10 .50
682 A113 130fr multi 5.75 3.25
683 A113 200fr multi 8.00 4.25
684 A113 220fr multi 10.00 5.50
Nos. 681-684 (4) 24.85 13.50

World Wildlife Fund.

Each stamp in this set was issued in 1997 with a 50fr surcharge and overprinted 'CAROLOPHILEX 97.' Value, set $100.

Mushrooms A114

Designs: 10fr, Russula ingens. 15fr, Russula brunneorigida. 20fr, Amanita zambiana. 30fr, Russula subfistulosa. 75fr, 85fr, Russula meleagris. 100fr, Russula immaculata. 110fr, like No. 685. 115fr, like No. 686. 120fr, 130fr, Russula sejuncta. 250fr, Afroboletus luteolus.

1992-93 ***Perf. 11½x12***

Granite Paper

685 A114 10fr multicolored .25 .25
686 A114 15fr multicolored .40 .25
687 A114 20fr multicolored .45 .30
688 A114 30fr multicolored 1.00 .90
689 A114 75fr multicolored 2.50 1.90
690 A114 85fr multicolored 3.00 2.50
691 A114 100fr multicolored 4.00 2.75
691A A114 110fr multicolored 3.50 2.50
691B A114 115fr multicolored 4.50 3.25
692 A114 120fr multicolored 5.25 3.25
693 A114 130fr multicolored 6.50 3.75
694 A114 250fr multicolored 12.50 7.75
Nos. 685-694 (12) 43.85 29.35

Issued: 110fr, 115fr, 1993; others, 9/30/92.

For surcharges see Nos. 781-783.

1992 Summer Olympics, Barcelona A115

1992, Nov. 6 ***Perf. 15***

695 A115 130fr Runners 3.50 1.75
696 A115 500fr Hurdler 12.00 7.50

A116

Christmas (Details of Adoration of the Kings, by Gentile da Fabriano): a, 100fr, Crowd, horses. b, 130fr, Kings. c, 250fr, Nativity scene.

1992, Dec. 7 **Litho.** ***Perf. 11½***

697 A116 Strip of 3, #a.-c. 10.00 4.50
d. Souvenir sheet of 3, #697a-697c 11.50 5.50

Nos. 697a-697c have white border. No. 697d has continuous design and sold for 580fr.

A116a

Designs: 200fr, Emblems. 220fr, Profile of person made from fruits and vegetables.

1992, Dec. 5 **Litho.** ***Perf. 15***

697E A116a 200fr multicolored 6.50 3.00
697F A116a 220fr multicolored 7.50 4.00

Intl. Conference on Nutrition, Rome.

European Common Market A117

Designs: 130fr, Flags, stars. 500fr, Europe, Africa, clasped hands, stars.

1993, Mar. 29 **Litho.** ***Perf. 15***

698 A117 130fr multicolored 2.25 1.10
699 A117 500fr multicolored 8.75 5.75

1994 World Cup Soccer Championships, US — A118

Players, stadium, US flag and: 130fr, Statue of Liberty. 200fr, Golden Gate Bridge.

1993, July 5 **Litho.** ***Perf. 15***

700 A118 130fr multicolored 4.00 1.75
701 A118 200fr multicolored 5.25 2.50

Traditional Musical Instruments — A119

1993, Apr. 30 **Litho.** ***Perf. 15***

702 A119 200fr Indonongo 2.75 2.50
703 A119 220fr Ingoma 3.00 2.75
704 A119 250fr Ikembe 3.50 3.00
705 A119 300fr Umuduri 5.25 4.50
Nos. 702-705 (4) 14.50 12.75

A120

130fr, Papilio bromius. 200fr, Charaxes eupale. 250fr, Cymothoe caenis. 300fr, Graphium ridleyanus.

1993, June 4 Litho. *Perf. 11½*

706	A120 130fr multicolored	2.50	2.25
707	A120 200fr multicolored	4.00	3.25
708	A120 250fr multicolored	5.00	4.50
709	A120 300fr multicolored	5.50	4.50
a.	Souvenir sheet of 4, #706-709	19.00	19.00
	Nos. 706-709 (4)	17.00	14.50

No. 709a sold for 980fr.

Farm Animals — A121

1993, Dec. 9 *Perf. 14*

710	A121 100fr Cattle	1.50	1.25
711	A121 120fr Sheep	1.75	1.60
712	A121 130fr Pigs	2.25	1.75
713	A121 250fr Goats	3.75	3.00
	Nos. 710-713 (4)	9.25	7.60

Christmas — A122

Natives adoring Christ Child: a, 100fr, Woman carrying baby, two people kneeling. b, 130fr, With Christ Child. 250fr, c, Woman carrying baby, three other people.

1993, Dec. 10 *Perf. 11½*

714	A122 Strip of 3, #a.-c.	9.00	9.00
d.	Souvenir sheet of 3, #714a-714c	9.00	9.00

Nos. 714a-714c have white border. No. 714d has continuous design and sold for 580fr.

Rock Stars — A123

60fr, Elvis Presley. 115fr, Mick Jagger. 120fr, John Lennon. 200fr, Michael Jackson.

1994 Litho. *Perf. 15*

715	A123 60fr multi	1.50	1.25
716	A123 115fr multi	3.00	2.50
717	A123 120fr multi	3.00	2.50
718	A123 200fr multi	5.00	4.50
a.	Souvenir sheet, #715-718	12.50	12.50
	Nos. 715-718 (4)	12.50	10.75

No. 718a sold for 600fr.

A124

1994, Oct. 10 Litho. *Perf. 15*

719	A124 150fr multicolored	10.00	10.00

Intl. Olympic Committee, cent.

A125

Christmas (Madonna and Child): a, 115fr, Chinese. b, 120fr, Japanese. c, 250fr, Polish.

1994, Dec. 14 Photo. *Perf. 15*

720	A125 Strip of 3, #a.-c.	12.50	12.50
d.	Souvenir sheet of 1, #720c	9.00	9.00

A126

115fr, FAO, 50th anniv. 120fr, UN, 50th anniv.

1995, Feb. 21 Litho. *Perf. 11½*

721	A126 115fr multicolored	3.00	3.00
722	A126 120fr multicolored	3.00	3.00

A127

Flowers: 15fr, Cassia didymobotrya. 20fr, Mitragyna rubrostipulosa. 30fr, Phytolacca dodecandra. 85fr, Acanthus pubescens. 100fr, Bulbophyllum comatum. 110fr, Angraecum evradianum. 115fr, Eulophia burundiensis. 120fr, Habenaria adolphii.

Granite Paper

1995 Litho. *Perf. 11½*

723	A127 15fr multicolored	.25	.25
724	A127 20fr multicolored	.45	.25
725	A127 30fr multicolored	.85	.45
726	A127 85fr multicolored	2.00	1.40
727	A127 100fr multicolored	2.50	1.60
728	A127 110fr multicolored	2.75	2.10
729	A127 115fr multicolored	3.50	2.75
730	A127 120fr multicolored	4.25	3.25
	Nos. 723-730 (8)	16.55	12.05

Transportation Methods — A128

30fr, Otraco bus. 115fr, Transintra semi truck. 120fr, Arnolac tugboat. 250fr, Air Burundi airplane.

1995, Nov. 16 Litho. *Perf. 11½*

731	A128 30fr multicolored	.50	.35
732	A128 115fr multicolored	2.10	1.60
733	A128 120fr multicolored	2.40	1.90
734	A128 250fr multicolored	5.00	4.25
	Nos. 731-734 (4)	10.00	8.10

A129

Christmas (African sculpture): a, 100fr, Boy with panga, basket on head. b, 130fr, Boy carrying sheaf of wheat. c, 250fr, Mother, children.

1995, Dec. 26 Litho. *Perf. 11½x12*

735	A129 Strip of 3, #a.-c.	7.50	7.50
d.	Souvenir sheet of 3, #735a-735c	10.00	10.00

A130

Athlete, national flag: 130fr, Venuste Niyongabo. 500fr, Arthemon Hatungimana.

1996, June 28 Litho. *Perf. 14*

736	A130 130fr multicolored	1.75	1.60
737	A130 500fr multicolored	6.00	5.00

1996 Summer Olympic Games, Atlanta.

Birds A131

Designs: 15fr, Hagedashia hagedash. 20fr, Alopochen aegyptiacus. 30fr, Haliaeetus vocifer. 120fr, Ardea goliath. 165fr, Balearica regulorum. 220fr, Actophilornis africana.

1996 Litho. *Perf. 14*

740	A131 15fr multicolored	.30	.30
741	A131 20fr multicolored	.45	.45
742	A131 30fr multicolored	.50	.50
743	A131 120fr multicolored	1.25	1.25
744	A131 165fr multicolored	2.50	2.50
745	A131 220fr multicolored	3.25	3.25
	Nos. 740-745 (6)	8.25	8.25

Fish of Lake Tanganyika A132

Designs: 30fr, Julidochromis malieri. 115fr, Cyphotilapia frontosa. 120fr, Lamprologus brichardi. 250fr, Synodonis petricola.

1996, June 4 Litho. *Perf. 11¾x11½*

746	A132 30fr multicolored	.55	.45
747	A132 115fr multicolored	1.75	1.60
748	A132 120fr multicolored	2.10	1.75
749	A132 250fr multicolored	4.00	4.00
a.	Souv. sheet, #746-749, perf 11¾	10.00	10.00
	Nos. 746-749 (4)	8.40	7.80

No. 749a sold for 615fr.

Although ostensibly issued in 1996, this set was not available in the philatelic marketplace until 1999.

SOS Children's Village, 50th Anniv. A133

100fr, Children in Village. 250fr, Children, flags. 270fr, Children around flagpole.

1998, Dec. 26 Litho. *Perf. 14*

750	A133 100fr multicolored	.85	.85
751	A133 250fr multicolored	1.90	1.90
752	A133 270fr multicolored	2.00	2.00
	Nos. 750-752 (3)	4.75	4.75

Christmas — A134

Various paintings of Madonna and Child.

1999, Jan. 19 *Perf. 11¾*

Frame color

753	A134 100fr green	1.20	1.20
754	A134 130fr yellow brown	1.60	1.60
755	A134 250fr rose	3.00	3.00
a.	Souvenir sheet of 3, #753-755	7.00	7.00
	Nos. 753-755 (3)	5.80	5.80

Nos. 753-755 are dated "1996," "1997," and "1998," respectively.

No. 755a sold for 580fr.

Diana, Princess of Wales (1961-97) A135

Denominations: a, 100fr. b, 250fr. c, 300fr.

1999, Sept. 30 *Perf. 13¾*

756	A135 Sheet of 6, 2 each #a.-c.		12.00 12.00

Fight Against Hunger — A136

2000, Feb. 28 Litho. *Perf. 14*

757	A136 350fr Danny Kaye	2.50	2.50

Issued in sheets of 5.

Second Republic, 10th Anniv. (in 1986) — A136a

Designs: 70fr, Coffee pickers, statue. 80fr, Pres. Jean-Baptiste Bagaza, arms of Burundi. 200fr, Children at school, statue.

2000 ? Photo. *Perf. 13¾x14*

757B	A136a 200fr multi	—
757C	A136a 70fr multi	—
757D	A136a 80fr multi	—

Nos. 757B-757D were originally scheduled for issue, July 31, 1986. However they were not issued at the time, and became available sometime during or before the year 2000. Another design was prepared with this set, the editors would like to evidence of postal usage. The other design is: 5 fr, barges, airplane, and statue.

Space — A137

No. 758, horiz.: a, Space plane (2003). b, Reuseable space plane. c, Future space ship. d, Galileo. e, Space telescope. f, Space platform. g, Satellite launched Feb. 17, 1996. h, Cassini. i, Solar probe. j, Vehicle without fenders. k, Vehicle with fenders. l, Spacecraft for Mars.

1500fr, Newton's telescope.

2000, July 24 Litho. *Perf. 14*

758 A137	165fr Sheet of 12, #a-l	20.00	20.00

Souvenir Sheet

759 A137	1500fr multi	20.00	20.00

Flowers — A138

Design: 150fr, Dodecatheon. 200fr, Fremontodendron. 250fr, Rudbeckia laciniata. 300fr, Tagetes erecta. 350fr, Helianthus amnus. 400fr, Lilium longiflorum.

2002, Apr. 4 Litho. *Perf. 13x12¾*

760 A138	150fr multi	2.50	2.50
761 A138	200fr multi	3.00	3.00
762 A138	250fr multi	4.00	4.00
763 A138	300fr multi	4.50	4.50
764 A138	350fr multi	5.00	5.00
765 A138	400fr multi	6.00	6.00
	Nos. 760-765 (6)	25.00	25.00

Orchids, Mushrooms, Birds and Butterflies — A139

No. 766, 650fr — Orchids: a, Angraceum eburnum. b, Disa cardinalis. c, Bulbophyllum guttulatum. d, Aerangis luteoalba. e, Disa diores. f, Disa kirstenbosch.

No. 767, 650fr, horiz. — Mushrooms: a, Stropharia aerugirosa. b, Inocybe rimosa. c, Cortinarius alboviolaceus. d, Hypholoma fasciculare. e, Cortinarius purpurascens. f, Hebeloma crustuliniforme.

No. 768, 650fr — Birds: a, Phalacrocorax carbo. b, Threskiornis aethiopicus. c, Nycticorax nycticorax. d, Phoeniconaias minor. e, Balaeniceps rex. f, Balearica regulorum.

No. 769, 650fr, horiz. — Butterflies: a, Papilio antenor. b, Graphium policenes. c, Papilio bromius. d, Graphium ridleyanus. e, Eurytides xanticles. f, Papilio gallienus.

No. 770, 2500fr, Aerangis citrata. No. 771, 2500fr, Coprinus picaceus. No. 772, 2500fr, Dendrocygna viduata. No. 773, 2500fr, Papilio dardanus, horiz.

2004, Nov. 8 Litho. *Perf. 14*

Sheets of 6, #a-f

766-769 A139	Set of 4	70.00	70.00

Souvenir Sheets

770-773 A139	Set of 4	60.00	60.00

Worldwide Fund for Nature (WWF) — A140

No. 774 — Sitatunga: a, Pair, both without horns. b, One, with horns. c, One, without horns. d, Pair, one with horns.

2004, Nov. 8 *Perf. 13¼*

774 A140	500fr Block or strip of 4, #a-d	15.00	15.00
e.	Sheet, 2 each #774a-774d	25.00	25.00

Frames vary.

No. 774e exists imperf. Value $90.

Tourism A141

Designs: 150fr, Source of the Nile River (Luvironza River). 250fr, Monument to Burton and Speke, Nyanza. 500fr, Shanga Waterfall, Karera. 1000fr, Monument to Stanley and Livingstone, Mugere.

2007, May 8 Litho. *Perf. 13x13½*

775-778 A141	Set of 4	18.00	18.00

24th UPU Congress A142

2007, Oct. 16 Litho. *Perf. 13x13½*

779 A142	730fr multi	9.00	9.00
780 A142	730fr +20fr multi	13.00	13.00

The 24th UPU Congress was moved to Geneva from Nairobi because of political unrest.

No. 692 Surcharged in White and Black

Methods and Perfs As Before

2007

781 A114	1200fr on 120fr #692	*12.00*	*12.00*
782 A114	1300fr on 120fr #692	*13.00*	*13.00*
783 A114	2500fr on 120fr #692	*25.00*	*25.00*
	Nos. 781-783 (3)	*50.00*	*50.00*

2008 Summer Olympics, Beijing — A144

2008, Aug. 1 Litho. *Perf. 13½x13*

787 A144	500fr multi	*6.00*	*6.00*

Flowers and Birds A145

Designs: 90fr, Erythrina flowers. 150fr, Maracuja flower. 500fr, Werner flowers, vert. 810fr, Heron, vert. 1000fr, Aigle royal (bateluer), vert.

2008, Dec. 24 *Perf. 13x13½, 13½x13*

788-792 A145	Set of 5	*45.00*	*45.00*

Birds A146

Designs: 290fr, Hieraaetus spilogaster. 295fr, Falco eleonorae. 505fr, Falco subbuteo. 515fr, Falco biarmicus. 555fr, Bubo africanus. 590fr, Milvus migrans aegyptius. 710fr, Haliaeetus vocifer. 730fr, Trigonoceps occipitalis. 810fr, Gypohierax angolensis.

2009, July 6 Litho. *Perf. 13x13½*

Granite Paper

793-801 A146	Set of 9	*50.00*	*50.00*
801a	Sheet of 9, #793-801	*50.00*	*50.00*

Owls — A147

Various owls: 860fr, 1010fr, 1030fr, 1100fr.

2009, July 8 *Perf. 13½x13*

Granite Paper

802-805 A147	Set of 4	*45.00*	*45.00*
805a	Souvenir sheet of 4, #802-805	*45.00*	*45.00*

A148

A149

A150

A151

A152

A153

A154

A155

Butterflies A156

2009, July 13 *Perf. 13x13½*

Granite Paper

806 A148	500fr multi	*6.00*	*6.00*
807 A149	500fr multi	*6.00*	*6.00*
808 A150	500fr multi	*6.00*	*6.00*
809 A151	500fr multi	*6.00*	*6.00*
810 A152	500fr multi	*6.00*	*6.00*
811 A153	500fr multi	*6.00*	*6.00*
812 A154	500fr multi	*6.00*	*6.00*
813 A155	500fr multi	*6.00*	*6.00*
814 A156	500fr multi	*6.00*	*6.00*
a.	Sheet of 9, #806-814	*55.00*	*55.00*
	Nos. 806-814 (9)	*54.00*	*54.00*

Miniature Sheet

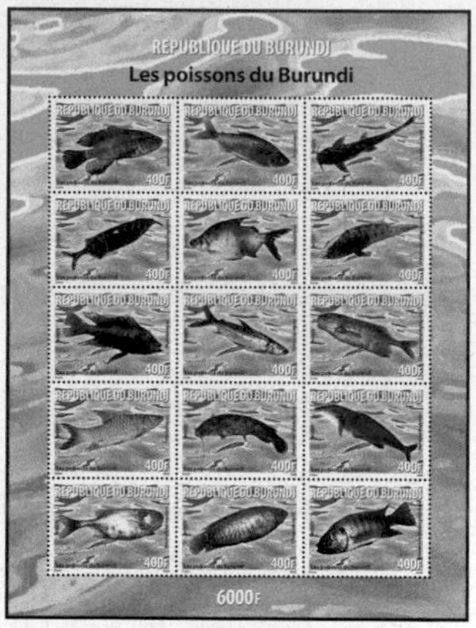

Fish — A157

No. 815: a, Astatoreochromis straeleni. b, Brycinus imberi. c, Amphilius jacksonii. d, Gnathonemus longibarbis. e, Citharinus gibbosus. f, Orthochromis malagaraziensis. g, Hapiochromis sp. h, Hydrocynus vittatus. i, Hippopotamyrus dischorhynchus. j, Labeobarbus sp. k, Malapterurus tanganyikaensis. l, Mormyrus longirostris. m, Petrocephalus catastoma. n, Ctenopoma muriei. o, Oreochromis niloticus eduardianus.

2009, Aug. 1 **Granite Paper**
815 A157 400fr Sheet of 15, #a-o *70.00 70.00*

Miniature Sheet

Traditional Hairstyles — A158

No. 816: a, Close-up of bearded man. b, Man with neckerchief and bag with letter "A." c, Bearded man, hand holding stick in background. d, Man with back of head shaved, with pipe in mouth, facing right. e, Man wearing patterned neckerchief with pipe in mouth, facing right. f, Man with necklace and bracelet.

2010, Jan. 1 ***Perf. 13¾x13¼***
816 A158 500fr Sheet of 6, #a-f *25.00 25.00*

Souvenir Sheet

Traditional Houses — A159

No. 817: a, Family and house. b, House.

2010, Jan. 1 ***Perf. 13¼x13¾***
817 A159 500fr Sheet of 2, #a-b *10.00 10.00*

Miniature Sheet

Art and Culture — A160

No. 818: a, Dancers. b, Busts. c, Two women, spears, sculpture, flowers. d, Woman with bowls and containers. e, Large decorated pot. f, Man with stick and pot. g, Woman with head on hand, vert. h, Sculptures. i, Woman with necklace and headcovering, vert.

Perf. 13x13½, 13½x13 (#818g, 818i)
2010, June 1 **Granite Paper**
818 A160 500fr Sheet of 9, #a-i *35.00 35.00*

Pan-African Postal Union, 30th anniv.

Primates A161

Designs: 730fr, Chimpanzee. 1000fr, Baboons. 2500, Gorillas.

2011, Mar. 15 ***Perf. 13x13¼***
819-821 A161 Set of 3 *25.00 25.00*
821a Souvenir sheet of 3, #819-821 *25.00 25.00*

Animals A162

Hippopotamus amphibius: 1000fr, Three animals. 1020fr, Three animals, diff. No. 824, 3000fr, Three animals with open mouths. No. 825, 3000fr, Two animals.
No. 826: a, 1090fr, One animal facing right. b, 1090fr, One animal facing left. c, 3000fr, One animal facing forward. d, 3000fr, One animal facing left.

2011, Dec. 1 ***Perf. 13x13½***
822-825 A162 Set of 4 *15.00 15.00*

Miniature Sheet

Perf. 13½
826 A162 Sheet of 4, #a-d *15.00 15.00*

Primates

Designs: 1020fr, Pan troglodytes. No. 828, 1090fr, Papio anubis. No. 829, 3000fr, Two Colobus angolensis. No. 830, 3000fr, Two Chlorocebus pygerythrus.
No. 831: a, 1090fr, Two Chlorocebus pygerythrus, diff. b, 1090fr, Pan troglodytes, diff. c, 3000fr, Papio anubis, diff. d, 3000fr, Adult, juvenile and head of Colobus angolensis.

Perf. 13x13½
827-830 A162 Set of 4 *15.00 15.00*

Miniature Sheet

Perf. 13½
831 A162 Sheet of 4, #a-d *15.00 15.00*

Rhinoceroses

Designs: No. 832, 1090fr, Diceros bicornis. No. 833, 1090fr, Ceratotherium simum. No. 834, 3000fr, Diceros bicornis facing right. No. 835, 3000fr, Ceratotherium simum facing left.
No. 836: a, 1020fr, Ceratotherium simum, diff. b, 1120fr, Diceros bicornis, diff. c, 3000fr, Adult and juvenile Ceratotherium simum. d, 3000fr, Diceros bicornis facing left.

832-835 A162 Set of 4 *15.00 15.00*

Miniature Sheet

Perf. 13½
836 A162 Sheet of 4, #a-d *15.00 15.00*

Bats

Designs: No. 837, 1020fr, Epomops franqueti. No. 838, 1020fr, Nyctalus noctula. No. 839, 3000fr, Desmodus rotundus. No. 840, 3000fr, Plecotus austriacus, name at LR.
No. 841: a, 1000fr, Nyctalus noctula, diff. b, 1120fr, Rhinolophus hipposideros. c, 3000fr, Plecotus austriacus, name at UL. d, 3000fr, Nyctophilus corbeni.

Perf. 13x13½
837-840 A162 Set of 4 *15.00 15.00*

Miniature Sheet

Perf. 13½
841 A162 Sheet of 4, #a-d *15.00 15.00*

Cats

Designs: 1000fr, Acinonyx jubatus. No. 843, 1090fr, Leptailurus serval. No. 844, 3000fr, Panthera pardus facing left. No. 845, 3000fr, Panthera leo.
No. 846: a, 1020fr, Acinonyx jubatus, diff. b, 1090fr, Panthera leo, diff. c, 3000fr, Felis silvestris. d, 3000fr, Panthera pardus facing right.

Perf. 13x13½
842-845 A162 Set of 4 *15.00 15.00*

Miniature Sheet

Perf. 13½
846 A162 Sheet of 4, #a-d *15.00 15.00*

Elephants

Loxodonta afrciana: No. 847, 1000fr, Adult and juvenile. 1120fr, Adult facing right. No. 849, 3000fr, Adult facing left, animal name at UR. No. 850, 3000fr, Adult and juvenile, diff.
No. 851: a, 1000fr, Adult, animal name at left. b, 1000fr, Adult, animal name at UR. c, 3000fr, Adult facing right, animal name at LR. d, 3000fr, Adult facing left, animal name at LL.

Perf. 13x13½
847-850 A162 Set of 4 *15.00 15.00*

Miniature Sheet

Perf. 13½
851 A162 Sheet of 4, #a-d *15.00 15.00*

Dolphins

Designs: No. 852, 1020fr, Lagenorhynchus albirostris. 1090fr, Grampus griseus. No. 854, 3000fr, Delphinus delphis. No. 855, 3000fr, Lagenorhynchus cruciger.
No. 856: a, 1000fr, Tursiops truncatus. b, 1020fr, Stenella attenuata. c, 3000fr, Stenella longirostris. d, 3000fr, Stenella frontalis.

Perf. 13x13½
852-855 A162 Set of 4 *15.00 15.00*

Miniature Sheet

Perf. 13½
856 A162 Sheet of 4, #a-d *15.00 15.00*

Whales

Designs: No. 857, 1020fr, Balaenoptera musculus. No. 858, 1020fr, Balaenoptera physalus. No. 859, 3000fr, Orcinus orca. No. 860, 3000fr, Eschrichtius robustus.
No. 861: a, 1000fr, Eschrichtius robustus, diff. b, 1000fr, Balaenoptera musculus, diff. c, 3000fr, Megaptera novaeangliae. d, 3000fr, Delphinopterus leucas.

Perf. 13x13½
857-860 A162 Set of 4 *15.00 15.00*

Miniature Sheet

Perf. 13½
861 A162 Sheet of 4, #a-d *15.00 15.00*

Birds of Prey

Designs: 1000fr, Gypohierax angolensis. No. 863, 1090fr, Pandion haliaetus. No. 864, 3000fr, Torgos tracheliotos. No. 865, 3000fr, Aquila wahlbergi.
No. 866: a, 1020fr, Lophaetus occiptialis. b, 1090fr, Necrosyrtes monachus. c, 3000fr, Falco tinnunculus. d, 3000fr, Polemaetus bellicosus.

Perf. 13x13½
862-865 A162 Set of 4 *15.00 15.00*

Miniature Sheet

Perf. 13½
866 A162 Sheet of 4, #a-d *15.00 15.00*

Birds

Designs: 1000fr, Pelecanus onocrotalus. 1090fr, Phalacrocorax carbo. No. 869, 3000fr, Podiceps cristatus. No. 870, 3000fr, Mycteria ibis.
No. 871: a, 1020fr, Microcarbo africanus. b, 1020fr, Nettapus auritus. c, 3000fr, Phoenicopterus minor. d, 3000fr, Balaeniceps rex.

Perf. 13x13½
867-870 A162 Set of 4 *15.00 15.00*

Miniature Sheet

Perf. 13½
871 A162 Sheet of 4, #a-d *15.00 15.00*

Parrots

Designs: No. 872, 1000fr, Agapornis fischeri. No. 873, 1000fr, Poicephalus meyeri. No. 874, 3000fr, Psittacus erithacus, name at UL. No. 875, 3000fr, Poicephalus robustus, name at right.
No. 876: a, 1000fr, Agapornis pullarius. b, 1090fr, Agapornis fischeri, diff. c, 3000fr, Poicephalus robustus, name at left. d, 3000fr, Psittacus erithacus, name at right.

Perf. 13x13½
872-875 A162 Set of 4 *15.00 15.00*

Miniature Sheet

Perf. 13½
876 A162 Sheet of 4, #a-d *15.00 15.00*

Owls

Designs: No. 877, 1090fr, Tyto alba. No. 878, 1090fr, Tyto capensis. No. 879, 3000fr, Asio capensis, name at top. No. 880, 3000fr, Bubo africanus.
No. 881: a, 1020fr, Tyto capensis, diff. b, 1090fr, Bubo africanus, diff. c, 3000fr, Asio capensis, name at LR. d, 3000fr, Otus scops.

Perf. 13x13½
877-880 A162 Set of 4 *15.00 15.00*

Miniature Sheet

Perf. 13½
881 A162 Sheet of 4, #a-d *15.00 15.00*

Bees

Designs: 1000fr, Bombus mixtus. 1090fr, Xylocopa virginica. No. 884, 3000fr, Bombus lapidarius. No. 885, 3000fr, Thyreus nitidulus.
No. 886: a, 1020fr, Osmia ribifloris. b, 1020fr, Apis mellifera. c, 3000fr, Anthidium florentinum. d, 3000fr, Apis mellifera scutellata.

Perf. 13x13½
882-885 A162 Set of 4 *15.00 15.00*

Miniature Sheet

Perf. 13½
886 A162 Sheet of 4, #a-d *15.00 15.00*

Butterflies

Designs: 1090fr, Papilio torquatus. No. 888, 1120fr, Boloria dia. No. 889, 3000fr, Lasiommata megera. No. 890, 3000fr, Papilio menatius.
No. 891: a, 1020fr, Salamis temora. b, 1120fr, Charaxes castor. c, 3000fr, Acraea acrita. d, 3000fr, Papilio demodocus.

Perf. 13x13½
887-890 A162 Set of 4 *15.00 15.00*

Miniature Sheet

Perf. 13½
891 A162 Sheet of 4, #a-d *15.00 15.00*

Fish and Marine Life

Designs: No. 892, 1000fr, Rhinobatos lentiginosus. 1090fr, Anoplogaster cornuta. No. 894, 3000fr, Stegostoma fasciatum. No. 895, 3000fr, Ocypode quadrata.
No. 896: a, 1000fr, Carcharhinus limbatus. b, 1020fr, Myliobatis californica. c, 3000fr, Hippocampus ingens. d, 3000fr, Mola mola.

Perf. 13x13½
892-895 A162 Set of 4 *15.00 15.00*

Miniature Sheet

Perf. 13½
896 A162 Sheet of 4, #a-d *15.00 15.00*

Turtles

Designs: No. 897, 1020fr, Pelusios sinuatus. 1120fr, Stigmochelys pardalis. No. 899, 3000fr, Pelusios subniger. No. 900, 3000fr, Pelomedusa subrufa, name at UL.
No. 901: a, 1000fr, Stigmochelys pardalis, diff. b, 1020fr, Pelusios subniger, diff. c, 3000fr, Pelomedusa subrufa, name at UR. d, 3000fr, Pelusios sinuatus, diff.

Perf. 13x13½
897-900 A162 Set of 4 *15.00 15.00*

Miniature Sheet

Perf. 13½
901 A162 Sheet of 4, #a-d *15.00 15.00*

Frogs

Designs: 1020fr, Leptopelis kivuensis. 1090fr, Hyperolius discodactylus. No. 904, 3000fr, Phrynobatrachus versicolor. No. 905, 3000fr, Hyperolius castaneus.

No. 906: a, 1000fr, Hyperolius viridiflavus. b, 1120fr, Bubbling kassina. c, 3000fr, Common plantannia. d, 3000fr, Hyperolius marmoratus.

Perf. 13x13½

902-905 A162 Set of 4 *15.00 15.00*

Miniature Sheet

Perf. 13½

906 A162 Sheet of 4, #a-d *15.00 15.00*

Prehistoric Crocodiles

Designs: No. 907, 1020fr, Shansisuchus. 1090fr, Desmatosuchus. No. 909, 3000fr, Luperosuchus. No. 910, 3000fr, Araripesuchus.

No. 911: a, 1020fr, Baurusuchus. b, 1120fr, Champsosaurus. c, 3000fr, Dokosaursus. d, 3000fr, Geosaurus.

Perf. 13x13½

907-910 A162 Set of 4 *15.00 15.00*

Miniature Sheet

Perf. 13½

911 A162 Sheet of 4, #a-d *15.00 15.00*

Dinosaurs

Designs: No. 912, 1090fr, Giganotosaurus. No. 913, 1090fr, Ankylosaurus. No. 914, 3000fr, Temnodontosaurus. No. 915, 3000fr, Triceratops.

No. 916: a, 1000fr, Stegosaurus. b, 1120fr, Pterosaur. c, 3000fr, Chasmatosaursus. d, 3000fr, Scutosaurus.

Perf. 13x13½

912-915 A162 Set of 4 *15.00 15.00*

Miniature Sheet

Perf. 13½

916 A162 Sheet of 4, #a-d *15.00 15.00*

Worldwide Fund for Nature (WWF) A163

Laniarius mufumbiri: No. 917, 1120fr, Three birds. No. 918, 1120fr, One bird facing right. No. 919, 3000fr, One bird, facing left. No. 920, 3000fr, Two birds.

2011, Dec. 1 ***Perf. 13x13½***

917-920 A163 Set of 4 *15.00 15.00*

920a Souvenir sheet of 4, #917-920, perf. 13½ *15.00 15.00*

Organizations, People and Events — A164

Scouting: No. 921, 1020fr, Six Scouts, purple emblem at LR. No. 922, 1020fr, Five scouts hunting and examining butterflies, green emblem at UR. No. 923, 3000fr, Scouts starting fire, green emblem at LR. No. 924, 3000fr, Kenyan Scouts, purple emblem at UL.

No. 925: a, 1000fr, Lord Robert Baden-Powell, scouts on rope bridge. b, 1090fr, Scout saluting, Scouts cooking, purple emblem at UL. c, 1090fr, Scouts around pile of sticks for campfire, green emblem at LR. d, 3000fr, Scout examining flower, Scouts in tower, purple emblem at LR.

2011, Dec. 30 Litho. ***Perf. 13x13½***

921-924 A164 Set of 4 *15.00 15.00*

Miniature Sheet

Perf. 13½

925 A164 Sheet of 4, #a-d *15.00 15.00*

Humanitarian Organizations

Designs: No. 926, 1020fr, International Red Cross emblem, relief efforts in Obo, Central African Republic. No. 927, 1020fr, Rotary International emblem, Rotary recruitment, Méru, Kenya. No. 928, 3000fr, Lions International emblem, planting of trees in China. No. 929, 3000fr, UNICEF emblem, relief efforts to Pakistan flood victims.

No. 930: a, 1020fr, Lions International emblem, food distribution to Philippine typhoon victims. b, 1120fr, UNICEF emblem, Vietnamese school children. c, 3000fr, International Red Cross emblem, first aid, Rio de Janeiro. d, 3000fr, Rotary International emblem, Saint Jude School, Tanzania.

Perf. 13x13½

926-929 A164 Set of 4 *15.00 15.00*

Miniature Sheet

Perf. 13½

930 A164 Sheet of 4, #a-d *15.00 15.00*

Pope John Paul II

Pope John Paul II and: 1000fr, Sisters Marie Simon Pierre and Tobianna carrying relics of Pope John Paul II. 1020fr, Crowd holding banners. No. 933, 3000fr, Pope Benedict XVI holding infant. No. 929, 3000fr, Beatification ceremony for Pope John Paul II.

No. 935 — Pope John Paul II and: a, 1090fr, Pope Benedict XVI blessing crowd. b, 1090fr, Crowd holding banners, diff. c, 3000fr, Crowd holding banners and United States flag. d, 3000fr, Pope John Paul II waving to crowd.

Perf. 13x13½

931-934 A164 Set of 4 *15.00 15.00*

Miniature Sheet

Perf. 13½

935 A164 Sheet of 4, #a-d *15.00 15.00*

Pope Benedict XVI

Pope Benedict XVI and works by Michelangelo: 1000fr, Ezekiel. 1120fr, Christ Carrying the Cross. No. 938, 3000fr, Zacharias. No. 939, 3000fr, Delphic Sybil.

No. 940 — Pope Benedict and works by Michelangelo: a, 1090fr, Libyan Sibyl. b, 1090fr, Joel. c, 3000fr, Creation of the Earth, Moon and Planets. d, 3000fr, Last Judgment.

Perf. 13x13½

936-939 A164 Set of 4 *15.00 15.00*

Miniature Sheet

Perf. 13½

940 A164 Sheet of 4, #a-d *15.00 15.00*

Pierre-Auguste Renoir

Renoir and his works: No. 941, 1000fr, The Laundrywoman, 1891. No. 942, 1000fr, The Seine at Asnières, 1897. No. 943, 3000fr, Coucher de Soleil sur la Mer, 1879. No. 944, 3000fr, The Children of Monsieur Caillebotte, 1895.

No. 945 — Renoir and his works: a, 1000fr, Children on a Guernsey Beach, 1883. b, 1020fr, Oarsmen at Chatou, 1879. c, 1090fr, La Grenouillère, 1869. d, 3000fr, Luncheon of the Boating Party, 1880-81.

Perf. 13x13½

941-944 A164 Set of 4 *15.00 15.00*

Miniature Sheet

Perf. 13½

945 A164 Sheet of 4, #a-d *15.00 15.00*

Pablo Picasso

Picasso and his works: No. 946, 1090fr, Child with a Dove, 1901. No. 947, 1090fr, Lecture, 1932. No. 948, 3000fr, Mother and Child, 1905. No. 949, 3000fr, Seated Woman in a Garden, 1938.

No. 950 — Picasso and his works: a, 1090fr, Guitar (I Love Eva), 1912. b, 1120fr, Head of a Woman, 1960. c, 3000fr, Jacqueline with Flowers, 1954. d, 3000fr, At the Lapin Agile, 1905.

Perf. 13x13½

946-949 A164 Set of 4 *15.00 15.00*

Miniature Sheet

Perf. 13½

950 A164 Sheet of 4, #a-d *15.00 15.00*

Film Actors and Actresses

Designs: No. 951, 1000fr, James Dean. 1090fr, Marlene Dietrich. No. 953, 3000fr, Grace Kelly. No. 954, 3000fr, Clark Gable.

No. 955: a, 1000fr, John Wayne. b, 1120fr, Elizabeth Taylor. c, 3000fr, Romy Schneider. d, 3000fr, Marlon Brando.

Perf. 13x13½

951-954 A164 Set of 4 *15.00 15.00*

Miniature Sheet

Perf. 13½

955 A164 Sheet of 4, #a-d *15.00 15.00*

Marilyn Monroe

Monroe: No. 956, 1020fr, With legs crossed. No. 957, 1020fr, With arms extended and leg raised. No. 958, 3000fr, With child on lap. No. 959, 3000fr, Holding drink.

No. 960: a, 1000fr, Seated, wearing gown . b, 1120fr, Seated on pilings, wearing bathing suit. c, 3000fr, Playing guitar. d, 3000fr, With skirt blowing up.

Perf. 13x13½

956-959 A164 Set of 4 *15.00 15.00*

Miniature Sheet

Perf. 13½

960 A164 Sheet of 4, #a-d *15.00 15.00*

Elvis Presley

Presley: No. 961, 1090fr, Holding microphone, denomination at UL. No. 962, 1090fr, No microphone, denomination at UR. No. 963, 3000fr, Two images, microphone on stand, denomination at UR. No. 964, 3000fr, Two images, holding microphone, denomination at UR.

No. 965 — Presley: a, 1020fr, No microphone. b, 1120fr, Holding microphone. c, 3000fr, Three images, holding microphone, denomination at UR. d, 3000fr, Three images, no microphone, denomination at UL.

Perf. 13x13½

961-964 A164 Set of 4 *15.00 15.00*

Miniature Sheet

Perf. 13½

965 A164 Sheet of 4, #a-d *15.00 15.00*

Singers

Designs: No. 966, 1090fr, Jimi Hendrix. No. 967, 1090fr, Paul McCartney. No. 968, 3000fr, Mick Jagger. No. 969, 3000fr, Ray Charles.

No. 970: a, 1020fr, Bob Marley. b, 1090fr, Tina Turner. c, 3000fr, Fats Domino. d, 3000fr, Stevie Wonder.

Perf. 13x13½

966-969 A164 Set of 4 *15.00 15.00*

Miniature Sheet

Perf. 13½

970 A164 Sheet of 4, #a-d *15.00 15.00*

Composers

Designs: No. 971, 1000fr, Wolfgang Amadeus Mozart and memorial to Mozart, Vienna. 1090fr, Ludwig van Beethoven and Beethoven Monument, Bonn. No. 973, 3000fr, Antonio Vivaldi, and St. John the Baptist Church, Venice. No. 974, 3000fr, Frédéric Chopin, violin and bow.

No. 975: a, 1000fr, Mozart and keyboard. b, 1020fr, Beethoven and pipe organ. c, 3000fr, Vivaldi holding violin, churches. d, 3000fr, Chopin and piano.

Perf. 13x13½

971-974 A164 Set of 4 *15.00 15.00*

Miniature Sheet

Perf. 13½

975 A164 Sheet of 4, #a-d *15.00 15.00*

Table Tennis Players

Designs: 1000fr, Wang Hao. 1120fr, Zhang Yining. No. 978, 3000fr, Guo Yue. No. 979, 3000fr, Werner Schlager.

No. 980: a, 1020fr, Ding Ning. b, 1090fr, Zhang Jike. c, 3000fr, Wang Liqin. d, 3000fr, Wang Nan.

Perf. 13x13½

976-979 A164 Set of 4 *15.00 15.00*

Miniature Sheet

Perf. 13½

980 A164 Sheet of 4, #a-d *15.00 15.00*

Soccer Players

Designs: No. 981, 1000fr, Wayne Rooney, Municipal Stadium, Wroclaw, Poland. 1020fr, Bastian Schweinsteiger, National Stadium, Warsaw, Poland. No. 983, 3000fr, Samuel Eto'o, Poznan Stadium, Poznan, Poland. No. 984, 3000fr, Karim Benzema, Olympic Stadium, Kyiv, Ukraine.

No. 985: a, 1000fr, Cristiano Ronaldo, Olympic Stadium, Kyiv. b, 1090fr, Lionel Messi, Metalist Stadium, Kharkiv, Ukraine. c, 3000fr, Kaká, PGE Arena, Gdansk. d, 3000fr, Manuel Neuer, Donbass Arena, Donetsk, Ukraine.

Perf. 13x13½

981-984 A164 Set of 4 *15.00 15.00*

Miniature Sheet

Perf. 13½

985 A164 Sheet of 4, #a-d *15.00 15.00*

Chess Players

Designs: 1020fr, Stan Vaughan. 1120fr, Emanuel Lasker. No. 988, 3000fr, Paul Morphy. No. 989, 3000fr, Alexandra Kosteniuk.

No. 990: a, 1090fr, François-André Danican Philidor. b, 1090fr, Domenico Ercole Del Rio. c, 3000fr, Howard Staunton. d, 3000fr, Johannes Zukertort.

Perf. 13x13½

986-989 A164 Set of 4 *15.00 15.00*

Miniature Sheet

Perf. 13½

990 A164 Sheet of 4, #a-d *15.00 15.00*

Famous Africans

Designs: No. 991, 1020fr, Bishop Desmond Tutu. 1090fr, Wangari Maathai and Salamis temora butterfly. No. 993, 3000fr, Patrice Lumumba and Aerangis modesta flowers. No. 994, 3000fr, Kofi Annan.

No. 995: a, 1020fr, Nelson Mandela and Malachite. b, 1020fr, Léopold Sédar Senghor and Acraea acrita butterfly. c, 3000fr, Albert Lutuli and Precis sophia butterfly. d, 3000fr, Maathai and Fluorite.

Perf. 13x13½

991-994 A164 Set of 4 *15.00 15.00*

Miniature Sheet

Perf. 13½

995 A164 Sheet of 4, #a-d *15.00 15.00*

Aviators

Designs: No. 996, 1020fr, Orville Wright and Wright biplane. No. 997, 1020fr, Adolphe Pégoud and Blériot monoplane. No. 998, 3000fr, Bert Hinkler and Puss Moth. No. 999, 3000fr, Richard E. Byrd and Curtiss-Wright biplane.

No. 1000: a, 1000fr, William Boeing, Boeing 787 and Boeing 80. b, 1090fr, Louis Blériot and Blériot XI. c, 3000fr, Charles Lindbergh and Spirit of St. Louis. d, 3000fr, Anthony Fokker and Fokker F-27 and Fokker Spin.

Perf. 13x13½

996-999 A164 Set of 4 *15.00 15.00*

Miniature Sheet

Perf. 13½

1000 A164 Sheet of 4, #a-d *15.00 15.00*

Wedding of Prince William and Catherine Middleton

Prince William, Catherine Middleton and: 1090fr, Arms, British flag. No. 1002, 1120fr, Couple walking. No. 1003, 3000fr, Arms and Prince Harry. No. 1004, 3000fr, British flag, denomination at UR.

No. 1005 — Prince William, Catherine Middleton and: a, 1020fr, British flag, diff. b, 1120fr, British flag, diff. c, 3000fr, British flag, denomination at UL. d, 3000fr, British flag, denomination at UR, Prince wearing military cap.

Perf. 13x13½

1001-1004 A164 Set of 4 *15.00 15.00*

Miniature Sheet

Perf. 13½

1005 A164 Sheet of 4, #a-d *15.00 15.00*

The Titanic

Titanic: No. 1006, 1000fr, At sea, denomination at UR in black. 1120fr, Near tugboats. No. 1008, 3000fr, Striking iceberg, denomination at UR in white, "Titanic" at UL in white. No. 1009, 3000fr, With Captain Edward Smith in ship's wheel, denomination at UR in black, "Titanic" at UL in black.

No. 1010 — Titanic: a, 1000fr, Sinking near lifeboat and iceberg. b, 1020fr, Sending up distress flares. c, 3000fr, At sea, denomination at UR in white, "Titanic" at UR in white. d, 3000fr, At sea, denomination at UR in black, "Titanic" at UR in black.

Perf. 13x13½

1006-1009 A164 Set of 4 *12.50 12.50*

Miniature Sheet

Perf. 13½

1010 A164 Sheet of 4, #a-d *12.00 12.00*

Christmas

Paintings: No. 1011, 1020fr, Adoration of the Shepherds, by Gerrit van Honthorst. No. 1012, 1020fr, Adoration of the Shepherds, by Louis Le Nain. No. 1013, 3000fr, Nativity, by Georges de La Tour. No. 1014, 3000fr, Adoration of the Shepherds, by Bartolomé Esteban Murillo.

No. 1015: a, 1000fr, The Third Joyful Mystery, by Lorenzo Lotto. b, 1000fr, Adoration of the Child, by van Honthorst. c, 3000fr, Song of the Angels, by William Adolphe Bouguereau. d, 3000fr, Holy Family, by Lorenzo Costa.

Perf. 13x13½

1011-1014 A164 Set of 4 *12.50 12.50*

Miniature Sheet

Perf. 13½

1015 A164 Sheet of 4, #a-d *12.00 12.00*

New Year 2012 (Year of the Dragon)

Dragon color: No. 1016, 1020fr, Red, tail at left. No. 1017, 1020fr, Green, tail at right. No.

1018, 3000fr, Blue, tail at UR. No. 1019, 3000fr, Brown, tail at LR.
No. 1020: a, 1090fr, Red, tail at left. b, 1090fr, Red and green, tail at right. c, 3000fr, Green and red, tail at right. d, 3000fr, Blue and red, tail at UL.

Perf. 13x13½

1016-1019 A164 Set of 4 *12.50 12.50*

Miniature Sheet

Perf. 13½

1020 A164 Sheet of 4, #a-d *12.50 12.50*

A165

Sports Personalities — A166

No. 1021 — Muhammad Ali and scenes from fights with: a, 1070fr, Floyd Patterson. b, 1070fr, Doug Jones. c, 3000fr, Sonny Liston. d, 3000fr, Leon Spinks
No. 1022: a, 1070fr, He Chong, diving. b, 1070fr, Jordyn Marie Wieber, gymnastics. c, 1070fr, Olha Saladukha, triple jump. d, 5000fr, Pawel Wojciechowski, pole vault.
No. 1023: a, 1070fr, Lance Armstrong, cyclist. b, 1070fr, Martina Navratilova, tennis. c, 1070fr, Brian Lara, cricket. d, 5000fr, Pelé, soccer.
No. 1024: a, 1070fr, Lionel Messi, soccer. b, 1070fr, Novak Djokovic, tennis. c, 1070fr, Martin Kaymer, golf. d, 5000fr, Usain Bolt, track.
No. 1025, 7500fr, Muhammad Ali and Joe Frazier. No. 1026, 7500fr, Eric Guay, skiing. No. 1027, 7500fr, Carl Lewis, track. No. 1028, 7500fr, Magnus Carlsen, chess.

2012, Mar. 30 Litho. *Perf. 13¼*

Sheets of 4, #a-d

1021-1024 A165 Set of 4 *50.00 50.00*

Souvenir Sheets

1025-1028 A166 Set of 4 *47.50 47.50*

A167

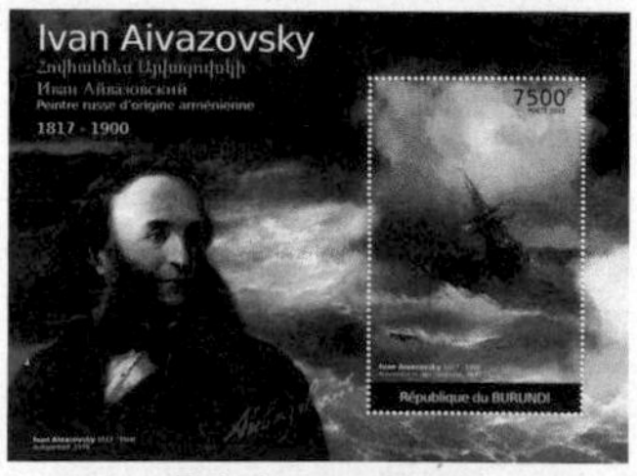

Paintings — A168

No. 1029 — Paintings of Ivan Aivazovsky: a, 1070fr, Portrait of the Fleet on the Northern Sea, 1849. b, 1070fr, The Great Roads at Kronstadt, 1836, vert. c, 3000fr, Brig Mercury Attacked by Two Turkish Ships, 1892. d, 3000fr, The Battle in the Chios Channel, 1848, vert.
No. 1030 — Paintings of Camille Pissarro: a, 1070fr, Pont Boieldieu at Sunset, 1896. b, 1070fr, Woman Hanging Laundry, 1887, vert. c, 3000fr, Boulevard Montmartre on a Cloudy Morning, 1897. d, 3000fr, The Old Market in Rouen, 1898, vert.
No. 1031 — Paintings of Edgar Degas: a, 1070fr, Hall of the Opera Ballet, 1874. b, 1070fr, Dance Examination, 1880, vert. c, 3000fr, Dance School, 1873. d, 3000fr, Singer with a Glove, 1878, vert.
No. 1032 — Paintings of Paul Cézanne: a, 1070fr, Rideau, Couchon et Compotier, 1893-94. b, 1070fr, The Village of Gardanne, 1886, vert. c, 3000fr, The Card Players, 1893-96. d, 3000fr, Forest Near the Rocky Caves Above the Chateau Noir, 1904, vert.
No. 1033 — Paintings of Claude Monet: a, 1070fr, Arrival of the Normandy Train, Gare Saint-Lazare, 1877. b, 1070fr, The Boat Studio, 1876, vert. c, 3000fr, Impression, Sunrise, 1872. d, 3000fr, Woman with Parasol, 1875, vert.
No. 1034 — Paintings of Frédéric Bazille: a, 1070fr, Family Reunion, 1867. b, 1070fr, The Rose Dress, 1864, vert. c, 3000fr, The Banks of the Lez, 1870. d, 3000fr, La Diseuse de Bonne Aventure, 1869, vert.
No. 1035 — Paintings of Berthe Morisot: a, 1070fr, Interior, 1872. b, 1070fr, At the Ball, 1875, vert. c, 3000fr, Lady at her Toilette, 1875. d, 3000fr, Young Girl with Cage, 1885, vert.
No. 1036 — Paintings of Armand Guillaumin: a, 1070fr, Sunset at Ivry, 1873. b, 1070fr, Hollow in the Snow, 1869, vert. c, 3000fr, La Place Valhubert, 1875. d, 3000fr, Outskirts of Paris, 1875, vert.
No. 1037 — Paintings of Gustave Caillebotte: a, 1070fr, The Boating Party, 1877-78. b, 1070fr, Interior, 1880, vert. c, 3000fr, The Floor Scrapers, 1875. d, 3000fr, A Balcony, 1880, vert.
No. 1038 — Paintings of Edouard Manet: a, 1070fr, Racecourse in the Bois du Boulogne, 1872. b, 1070fr, Café Concert, 1878, vert. c, 3000fr, Bar at the Folies-Bergère, 1881-82. d, 3000fr, Portrait of Irma Brunner, 1882, vert.
No. 1039 — Paintings of Ivan Shishkin: a, 1070fr, Rye Field, 1869. b, 1070fr, Bratzevo, 1869, vert. c, 1070fr, Morning in a Pine Forest, 1886 (bears on trees, title incorrect on stamp). d, 5000fr, Birch Grove, 1896, vert.
No. 1040 — Paintings of Alfred Sisley: a, 1070fr, Flood at Port-Marly, 1876. b, 1070fr, Snow at Louveciennes, 1874, vert. c, 1070fr, The Seine at Port-Marly Sand Piles, 1875. d, 5000fr, Street in Ville d'Avray, 1873, vert.
No. 1041 — Paintings of Pierre-Auguste Renoir: a, 1070fr, Moulin de la Galette, 1876 (artist and title omitted on stamp). b, 1070fr, Two Sisters on the Terrace, 1881, vert. c, 1070fr, Madame Charpentier and Her Children, 1878. d, 5000fr, The Theater Box, 1874, vert.
No. 1042 — Paintings of Mary Cassatt: a, 1070fr, Cup of Tea, 1879 (title omitted on stamp). b, 1070fr, Portrait of a Lady of Seville, 1873, vert. c, 1070fr, A Woman and a Girl Driving, 1881. d, 5000fr, Spanish Dancer Wearing a Lace Mantilla Box, 1873, vert.
No. 1043 — Tingatina paintings by: a, 1070fr, Saidi Omary. b, 1070fr, Noel Kapanda, vert. c, 1070fr, George Lilanga. d, 5000fr, Iddi Issa, vert.
No. 1044 — Paintings depicting Joan of Arc: a, 1070fr, Joan of Arc Kissing the Sword of Deliverance, by Dante Gabriel Rossetti, 1863. b, 1070fr, Joan of Arc During the Siege of Orleans, by Jules Eugene Lenepveu, 1889, vert. c, 1070fr, Capture of Joan of Arc, by Adolphe Alexandre Dillens, 1850. d, 5000fr, Joan of Arc at the Coronation of Charles VII in the Cathedral of Reims, by Jean Auguste Dominique Ingres, 1854, vert.
No. 1045, 7500fr, A Ship in the Stormy Sea, 1887, by Aivazovsky. No. 1046, 7500fr, The Poultry Market at Pontoise, 1882, by Pissarro. No. 1047, 7500fr, The Green Dancer, 1879, by Degas. No. 1048, 7500fr, Harlequin, 1888-90, by Cézane. No. 1049, 7500fr, Rouen Cathedral, Magic in Blue, 1894, by Monet. No. 1050, 7500fr, Village View, 1868, by Bazille. No. 1051, 7500fr, In the Dining Room, 1875, by Morisot. No. 1052, 7500fr, Vase of Chrysanthemums, 1885, by Guillaumin. No. 1053, 7500fr, Young Man at His Window, 1876, by Caillebotte. No. 1054, 7500fr, Spring (Jeanne de Marsy), 1881, by Manet. No. 1055, 7500fr, Evening, 1892, by Shishkin. No. 1056, 7500fr, Grande Rue, Argenteuil, 1872, by Sisley. No. 1057, 7500fr, In the Garden, 1885, by Renoir. No. 1058, 7500fr, Woman with a Pearl Necklace in a Theater Box, 1879, by Cassatt. No. 1059, 7500fr, Paon sur un Baobab, 1972, by Edward Saidi Tingatinga. No. 1060, 7500fr, Joan of Arc in Battle, 1843, by Hermann Anton Stilke.

2012, Mar. 30 *Perf. 13¼*

Sheets of 4, #a-d

1029-1044 A167 Set of 16 *200.00 200.00*

Souvenir Sheets

1045-1060 A168 Set of 16 *190.00 190.00*

Transportation and Space Flight — A169

No. 1061 — Boats: a, 1070fr, Anna Tunnicliffe sailing boat in 2008 Olympics. b, 1070fr, Yacht in Yarmouth Regatta. c, 3000fr, Europa, horiz. d, 3000fr, Colvin Gazelle, horiz.
No. 1062 — Steam trains: a, 1070fr, Venezia Santa Lucia. b, 1070fr, Class A4 Silver Fox. c, 3000fr, Flying Scotsman Express, horiz. d, 3000fr, Denver, Leadville and Gunnison train, horiz.
No. 1063 — French trains: a, 1070fr, TGV-PSE. b, 1070fr, Z-TER (Z 21561). c, 3000fr, Thalys PBKA, horiz. d, 3000fr, La Gironde and Joseph Eugène Schneider, horiz.
No. 1064 — German trains: a, 1070fr, ICE TD (Class 605). b, 1070fr, DB Class 614. c, 3000fr, RS-1 Regio Shuttle, horiz. d, 3000fr, Saxonia and Johann Andreas Schubert, horiz.
No. 1065 — Japanese trains: a, 1070fr, JRW Shinkansen Series 500 W1. b, 1070fr, Tobu 100. c, 3000fr, Shinkansen Superexpress Series 700, horiz. d, 3000fr, Shinkansen Series E5, horiz.
No. 1066 — Chinese trains: a, 1070fr, CRH5. b, 1070fr, CRH2. c, 3000fr, CRH2A, horiz. d, 3000fr, CRH3C, horiz.
No. 1067 — Bicycles: a, 1070fr, Mountain biker climbing hill. b, 1070fr, Mountain bikers descending hill. c, 3000fr, Road cycling (cyclisme sur route), horiz. d, 3000fr, Track cycling (cyclisme sur piste), horiz.
No. 1068 — Formula 1 race cars and drivers: a, 1070fr, AT&T Williams team car, Ayrton Senna, Brazilian flag. b, 1070fr, Mercedes GP Petronas team car, Michael Schumacher, German flag. c, 3000fr, Alfa Romeo 158, Giuseppe Farina, Italian flag, horiz. d, 3000fr, Mercedes-Benz W 196 R, Juan Manuel Fangio, Argentine flag, horiz.
No. 1069 — Helicopters: a, 1070fr, Boeing AH-64 Apache. b, 1070fr, Boeing CH-47 Chinook. c, 3000fr, Bell UH-1, horiz. d, 3000fr, MBB/Kawasaki BK 117 C2, horiz.
No. 1070 — Concorde: a, 1070fr, Two airplanes, line drawing of aiplane's nose. b, 1070fr, Two airplanes, line drawing of airplane's tail. c, 3000fr, Denomination at UR, horiz. d, 3000fr, Denomination at UL, horiz.
No. 1071 — Ships and Amerigo Vespucci: a, 1070fr, Vespucci at right, horiz. b, 1070fr, Vespucci at left. c, 1070fr, Vespucci at right. d, 5000fr, Vespucci at right, horiz.
No. 1072 — Horses and carriages: a, 1070fr, Lewis Tompkins driving carriage, horiz. b, 1070fr, Queen Elizabeth II and Prince Philip in carriage. c, 1070fr, Horse's head and omnibus carriage. d, 5000fr, Horse-drawn ambulance, horiz.
No. 1073 — Balloons and their creators: a, 1070fr, Balloon of Francesco Lana de Terzi, horiz. b, 1070fr, Balloon of Jean-Pierre Blanchard. c, 1070fr, Balloon of André-Jacques Garnerin, ascending. d, 5000fr, Balloon of Garnerin descending, horiz.
No. 1074 — The Hindenburg and Ferdinand von Zeppelin: a, 1070fr, Hindenburg in flight, horiz. b, 1070fr, Hindenburg and Empire State Building. c, 1070fr, Hindenburg on fire. d, 5000fr, People around Hindenburg, horiz.
No. 1075 — Centenary of London to Paris flight of Henri Salmet: a, 1070fr, Salmet in cockpit of Blériot monoplane, plane in flight facing left, horiz. b, 1070fr, Salmet at left, post card depicting his plane in flight. c, 1070fr, Salmet at right, post card depicting his plane on ground. d, 5000fr, Salmet in cockpit, plane in flight facing right, horiz.
No. 1076 — Opel Automobile Company, 150th Anniv.: a, 1070fr, Adam Opel, Opel emblem, sewing machine, horiz. b, 1070fr, Fritz Opel on Opel bicycle, bicycle emblem. c, 1070fr, 1899 Opel automobile, automobile emblem. d, 5000fr, 1935 Opel Olympia and emblem, horiz.
No. 1077 — Fire-fighting vehicles: a, 1070fr, 1870 Tozer pumper, horiz. b, 1070fr, 1883 Valiant pumper. c, 1070fr, Ladder truck and motorcycle with sidecar. d, 5000fr, Ladder truck, horiz.
No. 1078 — Soviet space pioneers and vehicles: a, 1070fr, Dogs Belka and Strelka, horiz. b, 1070fr, Alexei Leonov. c, 1070fr, Valentina Tereshkova. d, 5000fr, Lunokhod 1, horiz.
No. 1079 — Sergei Krikalev and space vehicles: a, 1070fr, Space Shuttle Endeavour, horiz. b, 1070fr, Soyuz TM-7, denomination at UL. c, 1070fr, Soyuz TM-7, denomination at UR. d, 5000fr, Space Shuttle Flight STS-60 landing, horiz.
No. 1080, 7500fr, Viking drakkar, horiz. No. 1081, 7500fr, LNER Class A4 locomotive, Mallard commemorative plaque, horiz. No. 1082, 7500fr, TGV Duplex train, France, horiz. No. 1083, 7500fr, ICE 3 (Class 407), Germany, horiz. No. 1084, 7500fr, SL Yamaguchi C571 locomotive, Japan, horiz. No. 1085, 7500fr, CRH1 train, China, horiz. No. 1086, 7500fr, Arthur Zimmerman, world champion cyclist, 1893, horiz. No. 1087, 7500fr, Red Bull Formula 1 race cars, Sebastian Vettel, flag of Germany, horiz. No. 1088, 7500fr, Sikorsky S-70A Firehawk helicopter, horiz. No. 1089, 7500fr, Concorde, horiz. No. 1090, 7500fr, Ship and Vespucci, horiz. No. 1091, 7500fr, United States horse-drawn mail wagon, 1911, horiz. No. 1092, 7500fr, Balloon of Jacues Etienne Montgolfier, horiz. No. 1093, 7500fr, Zeppelin, Hindenburg in flight, horiz. No. 1094, 7500fr, Salmet in cockpit, plane in flight, horiz. No. 1095, 7500fr, 2011 Opel RAK e concept automobile, horiz. No. 1096, 7500fr, Firemen and pumper, 1903, horiz. No. 1097, 7500fr, Yuri Gagarin and Vostok 1, horiz. No. 1098, 7500fr, Krikalev and Mir Space Station, horiz.

2012, May 30 Litho.

Sheets of 4, #a-d

1061-1079 A169 Set of 19 *225.00 225.00*

Souvenir Sheets

1080-1098 A169 Set of 19 *200.00 200.00*

Miniature Sheets

Leaders of Burundi — A170

No. 1099 — King Mwambutsa IV Bangiricenge (1912-77): a, 270fr. b, 550fr. c, 1090fr. d, 2050fr.
No. 1100 — Prince Louis Rwagasore (1932-61), Prime Minister: a, 270fr. b, 550fr. c, 1090fr. d, 2050fr.
No. 1101 — Charles Ndizeye (King Ntare V) (1947-72): a, 270fr. b, 550fr. c, 1090fr. d, 2050fr.
No. 1102 — President Michel Micombero (1940-83): a, 270fr. b, 550fr. c, 1090fr. d, 2050fr.
No. 1103 — President Jean-Baptiste Bagaza: a, 270fr. b, 550fr. c, 1090fr. d, 2050fr.
No. 1104 — President Pierre Buyoya: a, 270fr. b, 550fr. c, 1090fr. d, 2050fr.
No. 1105 — President Melchior Ndadaye (1953-93): a, 270fr. b, 550fr. c, 1090fr. d, 2050fr.
No. 1106 — President Cyprien Ntaryamira (1955-94): a, 270fr. b, 550fr. c, 1090fr. d, 2050fr.
No. 1107 — President Sylvestre Ntibantunganya: a, 270fr. b, 550fr. c, 1090fr. d, 2050fr.
No. 1108 — President Domitien Ndayizeye: a, 270fr. b, 550fr. c, 1090fr. d, 2050fr.
No. 1109 — President Pierre Nkurunziza: a, 270fr. b, 550fr. c, 1090fr. d, 2050fr.

2012, Aug. 1 *Perf. 13¼*

Sheets of 4, #a-d

1099-1109 A170 Set of 11 *62.50 62.50*

Nos. 1099c and 1099d lack king's name.

Nature Protection — A171

No. 1110 — Commerce in endangered wild animals: a, 1070fr, Two Panthera tigris in cage. b, 1070fr, Pongo pygmaeus abelii. c, 3000fr, Nycticebus sp. d, 3000fr, Gavialis gangeticus.

No. 1111 — Deforestation: a, 1070fr, Agalychnis callidryas. b, 1070fr, Harpia harpyja. c, 3000fr, Pongo pygmaeus. d, 3000fr, Ramphastos sulfuratus.

No. 1112 — Habitat fragmentation: a, 1070fr, Ceratotherium simum. b, 1070fr, Ursus arctos. c, 3000fr, Camelus dromedarius. d, 3000fr, Panthera leo and vans.

No. 1113 — Destruction of the Antarctic ozone layer: a, 1070fr, Orcinus orca, map of Antarctica. b, 1070fr, Balaenoptera musculus, scientific balloon launch. c, 3000fr, Megaleledone setebos, Antarctic research station. d, 3000fr, Leptonychotes weddellii, map of Antarctica.

No. 1114 — Warming of the climate: a, 1070fr, Bubo scandiacus. b, 1070fr, Sterna paradisaea. c, 3000fr, Pygoscelis adeliae. d, 3000fr, Odobenus rosmarus.

No. 1115 — Sea of plastic waste in North Pacific: a, 1070fr, Fish in net. b, 1070fr, Oceanographic vessel Kaisei and rubber raft. c, 3000fr, Map of Pacific Ocean, turtles ensnared in plastic packaging. d, 3000fr, Seals and plastic waste.

No. 1116 — Species extinct or threatened in the wild: a, 1070fr, Gallirallus owstoni. b, 1070fr, Nectophrynoides asperginis. c, 3000fr, Elaphurus davidianus. d, 3000fr, Brachylagus idahoensis.

No. 1117 — Endangered mammals: a, 1070fr, Panthera tigris facing right. b, 1070fr, Panthera leo on ground and in tree. c, 3000fr, Equus quagga. d, 3000fr, Adult and juvenile Ceratotherium simum.

No. 1118 — Sharks and pinnipeds: a, 1070fr, Carcharodon carcharias, Phocidae, "Phocidae" in black. b, 1070fr, Carcharodon carcharias, Phocidae, "Phocidae" in white. c, 3000fr, Carcharodon carcharias, name in black. d, 3000fr, Carcharodon carcharias, Phocidae, names in white.

No. 1119 — Dolphins: a, 1070fr, Stenella frontalis. b, 1070fr, Tursiops truncatus. c, 3000fr, Tursiops truncatus, denomination at UL. d, 3000fr, Tursiops truncatus, denomination at UR.

No. 1120 — Orcinus orca and Carcharodon carcharias with denomination in: a, 1070fr, White. b, 1070fr, Black. c, 3000fr, White. d, 3000fr, Black.

No. 1121 — Whales: a, 1070fr, Physeter macrocephalus. b, 1070fr, Megaptera novaeangliae. c, 3000fr, Eschrichtius robustus. d, 3000fr, Balaenoptera acutorostrata.

No. 1122 — Birds and air pollution: a, 1070fr, Cuculus canorus. b, 1070fr, Grus americana. c, 3000fr, Crax rubra. d, 3000fr, Carduelis cucullata.

No. 1123 — Endangered birds: a, 1070fr, Anodorhynchus hyacintinus, Ara militaris. b, 1070fr, Merops orientalis. c, 3000fr, Aquila rapax. d, 3000fr, Strix nebulosa.

No. 1124 — Endangered plants and insects: a, 1070fr, Lobelia bridgesii, Cerambyx dux. b, 1070fr, Begonia samhaensis, Chlorophorus aegyptiacus. c, 3000fr, Sarracenia flava, Ampedus cardinalis. d, 3000fr, Echinocactus grusonii, Magicicada cassini.

No. 1125 — Endangered butterflies: a, 1070fr, Papilio palinurus. b, 1070fr, Idea iasonia. c, 3000fr, Parides hahneli. d, 3000fr, Euphaedra themis.

No. 1126 — Endangered fish: a, 1070fr, Cheilochromis euchilus. b, 1070fr, Pomacanthus imperator. c, 3000fr, Apolemichthys xanthotis. d, 3000fr, Cephalopholis miniata.

No. 1127 — Endangered reptiles: a, 1070fr, Calumma tarzan. b, 1070fr, Astrochelys yniphora. c, 3000fr, Crotalus catalinensis. d, 3000fr, Acanthodactylus beershebensis.

No. 1128 — Dinosaurs: a, 1070fr, Pachyrhinosaurus. b, 1070fr, Tropeognathus. c, 3000fr, Lystrosaurus. d, 3000fr, Arrhinoceratops.

No. 1129 — Acid rain and mushrooms: a, 1070fr, Gyromitra esculenta. b, 1070fr, Calvatia gigantea. c, 3000fr, Chorioactis. d, 3000fr, Hydnellum peckii.

No. 1130, 7500fr, Nycticebus pygmaeus. No. 1131, 7500fr, Danaus plexippus. No. 1132, 7500fr, Odocoileus virginianus clavium. No. 1133, 7500fr, Aptenodytes forsteri, airplanes over iceberg, globe. No. 1134, 7500fr, Ursus maritimus. No. 1135, 7500fr, Zalophus californianus ensnared in net. No. 1136, 7500fr, Oryx dammah. No. 1137, 7500fr, Cebus flavius. No. 1138, 7500fr, Carcharodon carcharias, Otariidae, vert. No. 1139, 7500fr, Delphinus delphis. No. 1140, 7500fr, Orcinus orca and Carhcharodon carcharias, diff. No. 1141, 7500fr, Megaptera novaeangliae, diff. No. 1142, 7500fr, Cacatua sulphurea citrinocristata. No. 1143, 7500fr, Strix occidentalis. No. 1144, 7500fr, Latania loddegesii, Buprestis splendens. No. 1145, 7500fr, Diaethria eluina. No. 1146, 7500fr, Pomacanthus maculosus. No. 1147, 7500fr, Glyptemys insculpta. No. 1148, 7500fr, Compsognathus. No. 1149, 7500fr, Entoloma hochstetteri and acid rain.

2012, Aug. 31 — Litho.

Sheets of 4, #a-d

1110-1129 A171 Set of 20 *225.00 225.00*

Souvenir Sheets

1130-1149 A171 Set of 20 *210.00 210.00*

Egg House, Moscow, and Fabergé Eggs — A172

No. 1150 — Egg House and: a, Red egg with three portraits of Emperor Nicholas II and two daughters at top. b, Jeweled frame with portraits of Emperor Nicholas II and Empress Alexandra. c, Egg with portrait of Emperor Nicholas II. d, Egg with portrait of Empress Alexandra at top. e, Egg with mounted horseman. f, Ship inside open egg.

No. 1151, 5000fr, Egg House, egg and coach. No. 1152, 5000fr, Egg House, blue egg, 12 pendants.

2012, Oct. 15 Litho. *Perf. 12¾x13¼*

1150 A172 1190fr Sheet of 6, #a-f *9.75 9.75*

Souvenir Sheets

1151-1152 A172 Set of 2 *13.50 13.50*

Rossica 2013 Intl. Philatelic Exhibition, Moscow.

A173

No. 1153 — George Carlin (1937-2008), comedian, mask and text in French beginning with: a, 1180fr, "La seule bonne chose. . ." b, 1190fr, "J'ai finalement accepté Jésus. . ." c, 3000fr, "La religion est en quelque sorte. . ." d, 3000fr, "Nous avons créé Dieu. . ."

No. 1154 — Neil Armstrong (1930-2012), first man to walk on Moon, and: a, 1180fr, Apollo 11 emblem. b, 1190fr, Apollo command and service modules. c, 3000fr, Apollo 11 command, service and lunar modules. d, 3000fr, Astronaut and flag.

No. 1155 — Exploration of Mars: a, 1180fr, Artist's conception of Mars Exploration Hover. b, 1190fr, Curiosity rover. c, 3000fr, Satellite orbiting Mars. d, 3000fr, Sojourner rover.

No. 1156 — Impressionists and their paintings: a, 1180fr, The Soda Fountain, by William Glackens. b, 1190fr, In a Daisy Field, by Theodore Robinson. c, 3000fr, The Ballet Dancers, by William Metcalf. d, 3000fr, Portrait of a Woman, by Albert Henry Collings.

No. 1157 — Alexander Graham Bell (1847-1922), inventor of the telephone, and: a, 1180fr, AEA Silver Dart airplane. b, 1190fr, Examination of the wounded Pres. James A. Garfield. c, 3000fr, Magneto telephone. d, 3000fr, Columbia gramophone.

No. 1158 — Scenes from films adapted from works written by Ray Bradbury (1920-2012): a, 1180fr, *Moby Dick* (television play), 1956. b, 1190fr, *The Illustrated Man* (movie), 1969. c, 3000fr, *Something Wicked This Way Comes* (movie), 1983. d, 3000fr, *The Beast from 20,000 Fathoms* (movie), 1953.

No. 1159 — Marilyn Monroe (1926-62), actress, and: a, 1180fr, Arthur Miller (1915-2005), playwright and Monroe's husband. b, 1190fr, Second image of Monroe. c, 3000fr, Brooklyn Bridge, Pres. John F. Kennedy (1917-63). d, 3000fr, Frank Sinatra (1915-98), singer.

No. 1160 — Musicians: a, 1180fr, B.B. King. b, 1190fr, Stevie Ray Vaughan. c, 3000fr, Tina Turner. d, 3000fr, Cher.

No. 1161 — Khadja Nin, musician: a, 1180fr, Two images of Nin. b, 1190fr, One image of Nin. c, 3000fr, Stevie Wonder. d, 3000fr, Montserrat Caballe.

No. 1162 — Princess Diana (1961-97), and: a, 1180fr, Prince William. b, 1190fr, Land mine sign. c, 3000fr, Princes William and Harry. d, 3000fr, Princes Charles and William.

No. 1163 — Pope John Paul II (1920-2005): a, 1180fr, And dove flying to right. b, 1190fr, And dove flying to left. c, 3000fr, Praying, dove at LL . d, 3000fr, With hand raised.

No. 1164 — Sergio Pininfarina (1926-2012), automobile designer and: a, 1180fr, Peugeot 504 Cabriolet. b, 1190fr, Lancia Montecarlo. c, 3000fr, Rolls-Royce Hyperion. d, 3000fr, Ferrari F40.

No. 1165 — Sports of the 2012 Summer Olympics, London: a, 1180fr, Judo. b, 1190fr, Soccer. c, 3000fr, Table tennis. d, 3000fr, Cycling.

No. 1166 — Minerals: a, 1180fr, Tanzanite and Vanadinite. b, 1190fr, Diamond and Vanadinite. c, 3000fr, Liddicoatite tourmaline and Tanzanite. d, 3000fr, Liddicoatite tourmaline.

No. 1167 — Pigeons, with inscription: a, 1180fr, Pigeon Hirondelle. b, 1190fr, Le "Cravaté Africain." c, 3000fr, "Le Dragon." d, 3000fr, Le Pigeon Souabe.

No. 1168 — Somniosus microcephalus, with diagonal line running from: a, 1180fr, UL to LR. b, 1190fr, LL to UR. c, 3000fr, LL to UR. d, 3000fr, UL to LR.

No. 1169 — Festivals: a, 1180fr, Diwali, India. b, 1190fr, New Year, China. c, 3000fr, Octoberfest, Germany. d, 3000fr, Feast of San Fermin, Spain.

No. 1170 — Burundi coffee production: a, 1180fr, Hands holding coffee cherries, coffee bean sorters. b, 1190fr, Harvesters, bags of coffee beans. c, 3000fr, Women drinking coffee. d, 3000fr, Harvester with basket, hands holding coffee cherries.

No. 1171 — Royal Drummers and Dancers of Burundi, with diagonal line running from: a, 1180fr, UL to LR. b, 1190fr, LL to UR. c, 3000fr, LL to UR. d, 3000fr, UL to LR.

No. 1172, 7500fr, Carlin and mask. No. 1173, 7500fr, Armstrong and bald eagle from Apollo 11 emblem. No. 1174, 7500fr, Curiosity landing on Mars. No. 1175, 7500fr, Portrait of Miss Dora Wheeler, by William Merritt Chase. No. 1176, 7500fr, First telephone invented by Bell. No. 1177, 7500fr, Bradbury and scene from miniseries adapted from *The Martian Chronicles*. No. 1178, 7500fr, Monroe and Joe DiMaggio (1914-99), baseball player and Monroe's husband. No. 1179, 7500fr, Bob Marley (1945-81), musician. No. 1180, 7500fr, Nin and Wonder. No. 1181, 7500fr, Princess Diana and Red Cross flag. No. 1182, 7500fr, Pope John Paul II and dove, diff. No. 1183, 7500fr, Pininfarina and Maserati GranTurismo 5. No. 1184, 7500fr, Swimmer. No. 1185, 7500fr, Tanzanite and Vanadinite, diff. No. 1186, 7500fr, Two pigeons. No. 1187, 7500fr, Somniosus microcephalus, diff. No. 1188, 7500fr, Carnaval, Rio de Janeiro. No. 1189, 7500fr, Woman, coffee bush and beans. No. 1190, 7500fr, Royal Drummers and Dancers of Burundi, diff.

2012, Oct. 15 Litho. *Perf. 13¼*

Sheets of 4, #a-d

1153-1171 A173 Set of 19 *220.00 220.00*

Souvenir Sheets

1172-1190 A173 Set of 19 *195.00 195.00*

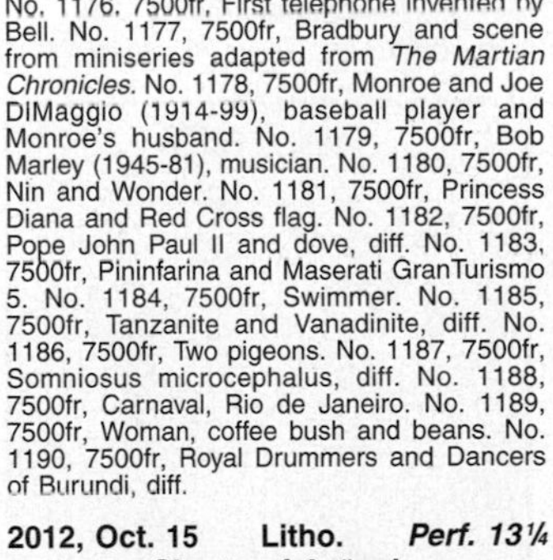

A174

No. 1191 — Hystrix africaeaustralis: a, 1180fr, Facing left. b, 1190fr, Facing right. c, 3000fr, Facing right, diff. d, 3000fr, Facing left, diff.

No. 1192 — Pangolins: a, 1180fr, Manis temminckii. b, 1190fr, Manis gigantea. c, 3000fr, Manis javanica. d, 3000fr, Manis temminckii, diff.

No. 1193 — Gorilla gorilla: a, 1180fr, Walking. b, 1190fr, Sitting. c, 3000fr, On back, denomination in black. d, 3000fr, Head, denomination in white.

No. 1194 — Pan troglodytes: a, 1180fr, On one tree branch. b, 1190fr, Holding two trees. c, 3000fr, Adult and juvenile. d, 3000fr, Adult.

No. 1195 — Lions International emblem and Panthera leo: a, 1180fr, Two females. b, 1190fr, Male running. c, 3000fr, Male walking. d, 3000fr, Male and female.

No. 1196 — Loxodonta africana: a, 1180fr, Adult and juvenile. b, 1190fr, Adult. c, 3000fr, Adults, animal name in black. d, 3000fr, Adult, animal name in white.

No. 1197 — Dolphins: a, 1180fr, Cephalorhynchus hectori maui. b, 1190fr, Lipotes vexillifer. c, 3000fr, Delphinus delphis . d, 3000fr, Orcaella brevirostris.

No. 1198 — Whales: a, 1180fr, Caperea marginata. b, 1190fr, Physeter catodon. c, 3000fr, Balaeniptera physalus. d, 3000fr, Balaenoptera musculus.

No. 1199 — Birds of prey: a, 1180fr, Elanus caeruleus. b, 1190fr, Milvus aegypticus. c, 3000fr, Haliaeetus vocifer. d, 3000fr, Milvus milvus.

No. 1200 — Owls: a, 1180fr, Bubo virginianus. b, 1190fr, Bubo africanus. c, 3000fr, Bubo bubo, Bubo africanus. d, 3000fr, Otus asio, Ptilopsis leucotis.

No. 1201 — Vultures: a, 1180fr, Vultur gryphus. b, 1190fr, Sarcogyps calvus. c, 3000fr, Necrosyrtes monachus. d, 3000fr, Gypaetus barbatus.

No. 1202 — Parrots: a, 1180fr, Psittacus erithacus. b, 1190fr, Agapornis fischeri. c, 3000fr, Poicephalus robustus. d, 3000fr, Agapornis personatus.

No. 1203 — Chrysolophus pictus: a, 1180fr, In flight. b, 1190fr, Two males. c, 3000fr, Male and female, denomination at LR. d, 3000fr, Two males and female, denomination at LL.

No. 1204 — Bees and wasps: a, 1180fr, Apis cerana. b, 1190fr, Vespula germanica. c, 3000fr, Apis mellifera. d, 3000fr, Vespa orientalis.

No. 1205 — Draogonflies: a, 1180fr, Trithemis arteriosa. b, 1190fr, Trithemis arteriosa, diff. c, 3000fr, Orthetrum chrysostigma. d, 3000fr, Schnura senegalensis.

No. 1206 — Butterflies: a, 1180fr, Belenois calypso. b, 1190fr, Graphium angolanus. c, 3000fr, Graphium ridleyanus. d, 3000fr, Papilio dardanus antinorii.

No. 1207 — Butterflies: a, 1180fr, Papilio demodocus. b, 1190fr, Cymothoe mabillei. c, 3000fr, Eurema hecabe. d, 3000fr, Euphaedra janetta.

No. 1208 — Goldfish breeds: a, 1180fr, Panda Moor. b, 1190fr, Celestial Eye. c, 3000fr, Bubble Eye. d, 3000fr, Black Moor.

No. 1209 — Fish: a, 1180fr, Pelvicachromis pulcher. b, 1190fr, Neochromis omnicaeruleus. c, 3000fr, Ptyochromis sp. d, 3000fr, Paralabidochromis sp.

No. 1210 — Shells: a, 1180fr, Chlamyis varia, Cardita calcyculata. b, 1190fr, Jujubinus exasperatus, Marmarostoma. c, 3000fr, Ovula ovum, Cymathium rubeculum. d, 3000fr, Epitonium commune, Solemya togata.

No. 1211 — Sea turtles: a, 1180fr, Dermochelys coriacea. b, 1190fr, Caretta caretta. c, 3000fr, Natator depressus. d, 3000fr, Eretmochelys imbricata.

No. 1212 — Cacti and animals: a, 1180fr, Euphorbia trigona, Varanus albigularis. b, 1190fr, Opuntia ficu-indica, hyaena hyaena. c, 3000fr, Euphorbia tortilis, Suricata suricatta. d, 3000fr, Euphorbia trigona var. rubra, Naja haje.

No. 1213 — Edible mushrooms: a, 1180fr, Amanita rubescens. b, 1190fr, Morchella conica. c, 3000fr, Cantharellus cibarius. d, 3000fr, Boletus edulis.

No. 1214 — Poisonous mushrooms: a, 1180fr, Entoloma sinuatum. b, 1190fr, Amanita verna, Amanita muscaria. c, 3000fr, Russula emetica. d, 3000fr, Amanita phalloides, Paxillus involutus.

No. 1215 — Minerals: a, 1180fr, Orthose. b, 1190fr, Agate. c, 3000fr, Galena. d, 3000fr, Topaz.

No. 1216, 7500fr, Hystrix africaeaustralis, diff. No. 1217, 7500fr, Manis tricuspis. No. 1218, 7500fr, Gorilla gorilla gorilla. No. 1219, 7500fr, Pan troglodytes, diff. No. 1220, 7500fr, Lions International emblem and Panthera leo, diff. No. 1221, 7500fr, Loxodonta africana, diff. No. 1222, 7500fr, Platanista gangetica. No. 1223, 7500fr, Delphinapterus leucas. No. 1224, 7500fr, Haliaeetus vocifer, diff. No. 1225, 7500fr, Tyto alba. No. 1226, 7500fr, Sarcoramphus papa. No. 1227, 7500fr, Poicephalus meyeri. No. 1228, 7500fr, Chrysolophus pictus, diff. No. 1229, 7500fr, Apis mellifera, diff. No. 1230, 7500fr, Crocothemis erythraea. No. 1231, 7500fr, Papilio dardanus cenea. No. 1232, 7500fr, Hypolycaena antifaunus. No. 1233, 7500fr, Pearlscale goldfish. No. 1234, 7500fr,

Lithochromis rufus. No. 1235, 7500fr, Melo aethiopicus, Hippopus hippopus. No. 1236, 7500fr, Caretta caretta, diff. No. 1237, 7500fr, Opuntia robusta, Vulpes zerda. No. 1238, 7500fr, Amanita caesarea. No. 1239, 7500fr, Boletus satanas. No. 1240, 7500fr, Calcite.

2012, Dec. 21 Litho. *Perf. 13¼*

Sheets of 4, #a-d

1191-1215 A174 Set of 25 *275.00 275.00*

Souvenir Sheets

1216-1240 A174 Set of 25 *245.00 245.00*

Transportation and Space — A175

No. 1241 — Dog and sleds: a, 1180fr, Dogs, sled and driver. b, 1190fr, Dogs, sled and driver, diff. c, 3000fr, Sled dog, statue of Balto. d, 3000fr, Two dogs and sled.

No. 1242 — Paintings of horses and wagons by: a, 1180fr, Charles Cooper Henderson. b, 1190fr, James Pollard. c, 3000fr, Pollard, diff. d, 3000fr, John Nost Sartorius.

No. 1243 — Medieval ships: a, 1180fr, Norman ship, 11th cent. b, 1190fr, Venetian merchant ship, 1250. c, 3000fr, Galley, 1280. d, 3000fr, Nostra Senora, 1275.

No. 1244 — Discovery of America by Christopher Columbus, 520th anniv.: a, 1180fr, Columbus Before the Queen, painting by Emanuel Gottlieb Leutze. b, 1190fr, Columbus Landing at Guanahani, painting by John Vanderlyn. c, 3000fr, Columbus and ship, Santa Maria. d, 3000fr, The Death of Columbus, painting by Louis Prang.

No. 1245 — Steamboats, 225th anniv.: a, 1180fr, John Fitch and his steamboat. b, 1190fr, James Watt and steam engine. c, 3000fr, Robert Fulton and diagram of steamboat. d, 3000fr, Steamboat Washington.

No. 1246 — Warships: a, 1180fr, Prinz Eugen. b, 1190fr, Bismarck. c, 3000fr, Yamato. d, 3000fr, Georgy Pobedonosets.

No. 1247 — Invention of the locomotive: a, 1180fr, Limmat 4-2-2. b, 1190fr, The General 4-4-0. c, 3000fr, Statue of Richard Trevithick, Trevithick's 1804 locomotive. d, 3000fr, Statue of George Stephenson, Stockton & Darlington Railroad locomotive.

No. 1248 — Aerotrains: a, 1180fr, Prototype #02. b, 1190fr, Prototype Rohr. c, 3000fr, Experimental train 01. d, 3000fr, I-80 HV.

No. 1249 — Snowmobiles: a, 1180fr, BRP Ski-Doo Rev XP. b, 1190fr, Arctic Cat ProClimb M1100 Sno Pro Limited. c, 3000fr, Yamaha FX Nytro RMX. d, 3000fr, Polaris RMK 700.

No. 1250 — Fire trucks: a, 1180fr, 1915 American La France. b, 1190fr, 1985 Pierce Arrow. c, 3000fr, 2002 Pierce. d, 3000fr, 1946 Bickle Seagrave.

No. 1251 — Buses: a, 1180fr, 1940 Greyhound. b, 1190fr, 1954 Bristol double-decker. c, 3000fr, JCK 892. d, 3000fr, 1940 General American Autocoach.

No. 1252 — Automobiles: a, 1180fr, 1906 Mercedes-Benz race car. b, 1190fr, Mercedes-Benz W196 race car. c, 3000fr, 1935 Mercedes-Benz Roadster. d, 3000fr, 1923 Lancia Lambda Torpedo.

No. 1253 — Taxis: a, 1180fr, Coco taxi, Havana, Cuba. b, 1190fr, 1834 fiacre, England. c, 3000fr, 1912 Unic taxi, London. d, 3000fr, Maybach taxi, Moscow.

No. 1254 — Stock cars and NASCAR drivers: a, 1180fr, 2012 Chevrolet, Tony Stewart. b, 1190fr, 1983 Ford, Dale Earnhardt. c, 3000fr, 2012 Dodge, Brad Keselowski. d, 3000fr, 1957 Oldsmobile, Richard Petty.

No. 1255 — Harley-Davidson motorcycles: a, 1180fr, 2012 FLTRX Road Glide Custom. b, 1190fr, 1942 WLA. c, 3000fr, 2010 CVO Fat Bob FXDFSE2. d, 3000fr, 2010 VRSCB V-Rod.

No. 1256 — Disappearance of Amelia Earhart (1897-1937), pilot: a, 1180fr, Earhart sitting on nose of plane. b, 1190fr, Earhart parachuting. c, 3000fr, Earhart in front of plane,denomination in white. d, Earhart in front of plane, denomination in black.

No. 1257 — Supersonic aircraft: a, 1180fr, Tupolev Tu-144, flying right. b, 1190fr, British Airways Concorde. c, 3000fr, Air France Concorde. d, 3000fr, Tupolev Tu-144, flying left.

No. 1258 — Air ambulances: a, 1180fr, Victoria Hawker Beechcraft B200C King Air. b, 1190fr, LAHAK MBB Bo-105CBS-4 helicopter. c, 3000fr, Eurocopter-Kawasaki EC-145 (BK-117C-2) helicopter. d, 3000fr, King Air B350.

No. 1259 — Military aircraft: a, 1180fr, Boeing B-52H Stratofortress. b, 1190fr, Boeing Bird of Prey, Boeing F/A-18E. c, 3000fr, Lockheed YF-117A Nighthawk, Lockheed F-117A Nighthawk. d, 3000fr, Northrop YB-35.

No. 1260 — American X-Planes: a, 1180fr, Northrup Grumman X-47A Pegasus. b, 1190fr, Boeing X-50 Dragonfly. c, 3000fr, McDonnell Douglas/Boeing X-36. d, 3000fr, Grumman X-29.

No. 1261 — Space tourism: a, 1180fr, White Knight One. b, 1190fr, Virgin Atlantic Global Flyer. c, 3000fr, Richard Branson and SpaceShip One. d, 3000fr, White Knight Two.

No. 1262 — Voyager 2, 35th anniv.: a, 1180fr, Voyager 2 and Neptune. b, 1190fr, Voyageer 2 and Saturn. c, 3000fr, Voyager 2 and Uranus. d, 3000fr, Storms on Jupiter, Jupiter's moons Callisto and Io.

No. 1263 — Mail transportation: a, 1180fr, Vespa scooter. b, 1190fr, Pacific Air Transport 840 biplane. c, 3000fr, Panhard Dyna van. d, 3000fr, 1931 Ford postal truck.

No. 1264 — Cargo transportation: a, 1180fr, Airbus Skylink A-300 B4-608ST Beluga. b, 1190fr, Cargo ship Irina Trader. c, 3000fr, Scania R620 trucks. d, 3000fr, Class 7100 electric locomotive.

No. 1265 — Electric vehicles: a, 1180fr, Heathrow Airport transport pods. b, 1190fr, Policeman on Segway personal transporter. c, 3000fr, Series 500 Shinkansen train. d, 3000fr, 2009 Nisan Denki concept vehicle.

No. 1266, 7500fr, Dogs, sled and driver, diff. No. 1267, 7500fr, Painting of Royal Mail coach by John Frederick Herring, Sr. No. 1268, 7500fr, Fortune, 1300 (ship). No. 1269, 7500fr, Santa Maria, statue of Columbus, Madrid. No. 1270, 7500fr, John Fitch and 1790 steamboat model. No. 1271, 7500fr, German battleship Scharnhorst. No. 1272, 7500fr, Stephenson's Rocket, 1829. No. 1273, 7500fr, Aerotrain I-80 HV on bridge. No. 1274, 7500fr, Arctic Cat Firecat F7 snowmobile. No. 1275, 7500fr, Pierce 105-foot rear mount ladder firetruck. No. 1276, 7500fr, 1951 Bristol Royal Blue LL6B bus. No. 1277, 7500fr, 1886 Benz automobile. No. 1278, 7500fr, London taxi, 1950-82. No. 1279, 7500fr, Chevrolet and Jimmie Johnson. No. 1280, 7500fr, 2008 Harley-Davidson VRSCA V-Rod motorcycle. No. 1281, 7500fr, Earhart airplane wing and compass rose, vert. No. 1282, 7500fr, Tupolev Tu-144, diff. No. 1283, 7500fr, Canadair CL-600-2B16 Challenger 604 air ambulance. No. 1284, 7500fr, Lockheed F-117A Nighthawk, diff. No. 1285, 7500fr, NASA X-38. No. 1286, 7500fr, SpaceShip Two. No. 1287, 7500fr, Antenna of Voyager 2. No. 1288, 7500fr, Royal Air Mail automobile. No. 1289, 7500fr, Cargo ship Angeln. No. 1290, 7500fr, Solar Impulse solar-powered airplane.

2012, Dec. 28 Litho. *Perf. 13¼*

Sheets of 4, #a-d

1241-1265 A175 Set of 25 *275.00 275.00*

Souvenir Sheets

1266-1290 A175 Set of 25 *245.00 245.00*

Famous People — A176

No. 1291 — Frank Sinatra (1915-98), singer: a, 90fr, Wearing hat. b, 1180fr, Holding microphone. c, 3000fr, Standing near microphone. d, 3000fr, Wearing hat, diff.

No. 1292 — Johann Sebastian Bach (1685-1750), composer: a, 90fr, Wearing blue cravat. b, 1190fr, Playing organ. c, 3000fr, With cello and bow. d, 3000fr, Wearing red cravat.

No. 1293 — Robert Schumann (1810-56), composer: a, 90fr, Wearing blue jacket. b, 1190fr, Reviewing score. c, 3000fr, At piano. d, 3000fr, Wearing blue jacket, diff.

No. 1294 — Georges Lemmen (1865-1916), painter: a, 90fr, Lemmen. b, 1190fr, The Carousel, by Lemmen, 1896. c, 3000fr, Houses at La Hulpe, by Lemmen, 1888. d, 3000fr, Plage à Heist, by Lemmen, 1891.

No. 1295 — Paul Signac (1863-1935), painter: a, 90fr, Signac. b, 1190fr, Woman at her Toilette Wearing a Purple Corset, by Signac, 1893. c, 3000fr, Lighthouse at Grox, by Signac, 1923. d, 3000fr, Portrait of Félix Fénéon, by Signac, 1890.

No. 1296 — Brigitte Bardot, actress: a, 90fr, Wearing hat. b, 1190fr, Holding mask. c, 3000fr, Without hat. d, 3000fr, Scene from *Viva Maria!*

No. 1297 — Ludwig van Beethoven (1770-1827), composer: a, 1020fr, Wearing red cravat. b, 1180fr, As conductor. c, 3000fr, Holding paper. d, 3000fr, Wearing white cravat.

No. 1298 — Wolfgang Amadeus Mozart (1756-91), composer: a, 1020fr, Playing harpsichord. b, 1180fr, Portrait. c, 3000fr, Playing violin. d, 3000fr, Playing harpsichord with woman.

No. 1299 — Franz Schubert (1797-1828), composer: a, 1020fr, Wearing blue shirt. b, 1180fr, Playing piano. c, 3000fr, Playing guitar. d, 3000fr, Wearing red cravat.

No. 1300 — Richard Wagner (1813-83), composer: a, 1020fr, Facing right, wearing red cravat. b, 1180fr, Playing piano. c, 3000fr, Writing at desk. d, 3000fr, Facing forward, wearing red cravat.

No. 1301 — Charlie Chaplin (1889-1977), actor: a, 1020fr, Wearing cap. b, 1180fr, With dog. c, 3000fr, Holding "Little Tramp" doll. d, 3000fr, Without hat.

No. 1302 — John Wayne (1907-79), actor: a, 1020fr, Wearing red neckerchief. b, 1180fr, On horse. c, 3000fr, Holding rifle, wearing badge. d, 3000fr, Wearing hat.

No. 1303 — Greta Garbo (1905-90), actress: a, 1020fr, With Herbert Marshall in *The Painted Veil*. b, 1180fr, Wearing blue dress. c, 3000fr, With Conrad Nagel in *The Mysterious Lady*. d, 3000fr, Wearing crown.

No. 1304 — Marilyn Monroe (1926-62), actress: a, 1020fr, Wearing yellow dress and red scarf. b, 1180fr, Wearing top hat. c, 3000fr, Seated, wearing blue dress. d, 3000fr, Holding money.

No. 1305 — Georges Seurat (1859-91), painter: a, 1020fr, Seurat. b, 1190fr, Chahut, by Seurat, 1889-90. c, 3000fr, The Eiffel Tower, by Seurat, 1889. d, 3000fr, Bathers at Asnières, by Seurat, 1884.

No. 1306 — Paul Sérusier (1864-1927), painter: a, 1020fr, Sérusier. b, 1190fr, The Flowered Barrier, by Sérusier, 1889. c, 3000fr, The Garland of Roses, by Sérusier, 1898. d, 3000fr, L'Averse, by Sérusier, 1893.

No. 1307 — Grace Kelly (1929-82), actress and princess: a, 1090fr, Wearing fur stole. b, 1180fr, Seated, wearing white gown. c, 3000fr, Wearing white blouse and blue pants. d, 3000fr, Wearing white dress.

No. 1308 — James Dean (1931-55), actor: a, 1090fr, With Julie Harris in *East of Eden*. b, 1180fr, Wearing dark shirt and jacket. c, 3000fr, Wearing t-shirt and jacket. d, 3000fr, With Elizabeth Taylor in *Giant*.

No. 1309 — Jane Fonda, actress: a, 1090fr, Holding weapon. b, 1180fr, Wearing striped blouse. c, 3000fr, Wearing nurse's cap. d, 3000fr, Saluting, holding space helmet.

No. 1310 — Paul Gauguin (1843-1903), painter: a, 1090fr, Gauguin. b, 1190fr, Agony in the Garden, by Gauguin, 1889. c, 3000fr, Picking Lemons, by Gauguin, 1891. d, 3000fr, Peasant Woman and Cows in a Landscape, by Gauguin, 1890.

No. 1311 — Vincent van Gogh (1853-90), painter: a, 1090fr, Van Gogh. b, 1190fr, Olive Picking, by van Gogh, 1889. c, 3000fr, The Good Samaritan, by van Gogh, 1890. d, 3000fr, Avenue of Poplars in Autumn, by van Gogh, 1884.

No. 1312 — Henri de Toulouse-Lautrec (1864-1901), painter: a, 1090fr, Toulouse-Lautrec. b, 1190fr, At the Circus Fernando - The Rider, by Toulouse-Lautrec, 1888. c, 3000fr, Woman with an Umbrella, by Toulouse-Lautrec, 1889. d, 3000fr, The Clowness Cha U Ka O at the Moulin Rouge, by Toulouse-Lautred, 1895.

No. 1313 — Félix Vallotton (1865-1925), painter: a, 1090fr, Vallotton. b, 1190fr, Woman Reading, by Vallotton, 1922. c, 3000fr, Still Life with Flowers, by Vallotton, 1925. d, 3000fr, Still Life with Marigolds and Tangerines, by Vallotton, 1924.

No. 1314 — Pierre Bonnard (1867-1947), painter: a, 1090fr, Bonnard. b, 1190fr, Woman with a Parrot, by Bonnard, 1910. c, 3000fr, View of Cannet, by Bonnard, 1927. d, 3000fr, Jeune Fillesà la Mouette, by Bonnard, 1917.

No. 1315 — Elvis Presley (1935-77), musician: a, 1090fr, With guitar. b, 1190fr, Wearing white shirt and blue jacket. c, 3000fr, Wearing striped jacket and green shirt. d, 3000fr, In Hawaiian shirt playing ukulele.

No. 1316, 7500fr, Sinatra, diff. No. 1317, 7500fr, Bach, diff. No. 1318, 7500fr, Schumann, diff. No. 1319, 7500fr, Lemmen, diff. No. 1320, 7500fr, Signac, diff. No. 1321, 7500fr, Bardot and Lino Ventura in *Rum Runners*. No. 1322, 7500fr, Beethoven, diff. No. 1323, 7500fr, Mozart, diff. No. 1324, 7500fr, Schubert, diff. No. 1325, 7500fr, Wagner, diff. No. 1326, 7500fr, Chaplin, diff. No. 1327, 7500fr, Wayne, diff. No. 1328, 7500fr, Garbo, diff. No. 1329, 7500fr, Monroe, diff. No. 1330, 7500fr, Seurat, diff. No. 1331, 7500fr, Sérusier, diff. No. 1332, 7500fr, Kelly, diff. No. 1333, 7500fr, Dean with Natalie Wood in *Rebel Without a Cause*. No. 1334, 7500fr, Fonda, diff. No. 1335, 7500fr, Gauguin, diff. No. 1336, 7500fr, Van Gogh, diff. No. 1337, 7500fr, Toulouse-Lautred, diff. No. 1338, 7500fr, Vallotton, diff. No. 1339, 7500fr, Bonnard, diff. No. 1340, 7500fr, Presley, diff.

2013, July 5 Litho. *Perf. 13¼*

Sheets of 4, #a-d

1291-1315 A176 Set of 25 *260.00 260.00*

Souvenir Sheets

1316-1340 A176 Set of 25 *245.00 245.00*

A177

No. 1341 — Intl. Red Cross, 150th anniv.: a, 90fr, Rescue dog. b, 1180fr, Red Cross doctor examining patient. c, 3000fr, Red Cross worker giving food box to child. d, 3000fr, Rescue dog, diff.

No. 1342 — Paul P. Harris (1868-1947), founder of Rotary International: a, 90fr, Rotary emblem, Harris, Laeliocattleya ridolfiana. b, 1180fr, Rotary and Rotary Foundation emblems, owl, books, mortarboard and diploma. c, 3000fr, Rotary emblem, needle with polio vaccine, brain of boy. d, 3000fr, Rotary emblem, Harris, Selenipedium grande.

No. 1343 — Edvard Munch (1863-1944), painter, and: a, 90fr, The Haymaker, 1917. b, 1180fr, The Scream, 1893. c, 3000fr, Red and White, 1899-1900. d, 3000fr, Self-portrait with a Wine Bottle, 1906.

No. 1344 — 50th anniv. of space flight of Valentina Tereshkova, first woman in space: a, 90fr, Tereshkova in space suit, space capsule. b, 1190fr, Tereshkova on wheel, Tereshkova in military uniform. c, 3000fr, Tereshkova in space suit, Tershkova in military uniform. d, 3000fr, Tereshkova being examined by technicians, Tereshkova in space suit.

No. 1345 — Haroun Tazieff (1914-88), geologist and vulcanologist: a, 90fr, Tazieff and Nyiragongo Volcano, Congo. b, 1190fr, Tyrannosaurus and Redoubt Volcano, Alaska. c, 3000fr, Compsognathus and Ulawun Volcano, Papua New Guinea. d, 3000fr, Tazieff and Mount Etna, Sicily.

No. 1346 — Magnus Carlsen, chess grand master: a, 1020fr, Wearing red suit. b, 1180fr, Playing against Garry Kasparov. c, 3000fr, Playing against Levon Aronian. d, 3000fr, Wearing red suit, diff.

No. 1347 — Shenzhou 10: a, 1020fr, Astronaut Nie Haisheng. b, 1180fr, Astronaut Wang Yaping. c, 3000fr, Astronaut Zhang Xiaoguang. d, 3000fr, Shenzhou 10 docking with Tiangong 1.

No. 1348 — Butterflies and Scouts: a, 1020fr, Ornithoptera paradisea, Lord Robert Baden-Powell (1857-1941), founder of Scouting movement. b, 1190fr, Chrysiridia rhipheus, Scout hiking. c, 3000fr, Appias nero, Scout leaning on walking stick. d, 3000fr, Rhetus periander, Baden-Powell.

No. 1349 — Campaign against malaria: a, 1020fr, Line of people, malaria detection test strip. b, 1190fr, Campaign emblem, man receiving package. c, 3000fr, Red Cross workers. d, 3000fr, World Malaria Day emblem, Anopheles stephensi.

No. 1350 — Joan Miró (1893-1983), painter, and: a, 1020fr, Still Life II - The Carbide Lamp, 1922-23. b, 1190fr, Vineyards and Olive Trees, 1919. c, 3000fr, Abstract painting, 1933. d, 3000fr, The Smile of the Flamboyant Wings, 1953.

No. 1351 — Paintings in Rijksmuseum, Amsterdam: a, 1020fr, The Windmill at Wijk-bij-Duurstede, by Jacob van Ruysdael. b, 1190fr, Children of the Sea, by Jozef Israels. c, 3000fr, The Damrak in Amsterdam, by George Hendrik Breitner. d, 3000fr, The Art Gallery of Jan Gildemeester, by Adriaan de Lelie.

No. 1352 — Resignation of Pope Benedict XVI: a, 1020fr, Pope Benedict XVI holding censer, statue of angel holding cross. b, 1190fr, Pope Benedict XVI with clasped hands, St. Peter's Basilica. c, 3000fr, Pope Benedict XVI waving, St. Peter's Basilica. d, 3000fr, Pope Benedict XVI wearing miter and holding cross, statue of angel.

No. 1353 — Election of Pope Francis: a, 1090fr, Pope Francis waving. b, 1180fr, Pope Francis consecrating host. c, 3000fr, Pope Francis with children. d, 3000fr, Popes Francis and Benedict XVI.

No. 1354 — Coronation of Queen Elizabeth II, 60th anniv: a, 1090fr, Queen Elizabeth II as young woman on throne. b, 1180fr, Queen Elizabeth II as older woman on throne. c,

3000fr, Queen Elizabeth II with attendant lifting cape. d, 3000fr, Queen Elizabeth II and Prince Philip.

No. 1355 — Miles Joseph Berkeley (1803-89), mycologist: a, 1090fr, Boletus appendiculatus, Uroglaux dimorpha. b, 1180fr, Berkeley, Cortinarius caperatus. c, 3000fr, Berkeley, Amanita muscaria. d, 3000fr, Hypholoma faciculare, Tyto alba.

No. 1356 — Pierre de Coubertin (1863-1937), founder of International Olympic Committee: a, 1090fr, Coubertin, cycling. b, 1180fr, Diving, running. c, 3000fr, Hurdling, women's gymnastics. d, 3000fr, Men's gymnastics, rhythmic gymnastics.

No. 1357 — New Year 2014 (Year of the Horse: a, 1090fr, Horse leaping. b, 1180fr, Head of horse. c, 3000fr, Head of horse, diff. d, 3000fr, Horse galloping.

No. 1358 — Airships: a, 1090fr, Early propellor-driven dirigible. b, 1190fr, 2005 dirigible concept. c, 3000fr, High-altitude dirigible. d, 3000fr, Hindenburg.

No. 1359 — Mohandas K. Gandhi (1869-1948), Indian nationalist leader, and butterflies: a, 1090fr, Troides aeacus. b, 1190fr, Teinopalpus imperialis. c, 3000fr, Papilio krishna. d, 3000fr, Junonia almana.

No. 1360 — Diplomatic relations between Burundi and the People's Republic of China, 50th anniv.: a, 1090fr, Flags of China and Burundi, Mao Zedong and King Mwambutsa IV. b, 1190fr, Jia Qinglin meeting with Gabriel Ntisezerana, 2012. c, 3000fr, Jia Qinglin and Pierre Nkurunziza shaking hands, 2006. d, 3000fr, Flags of China and Burundi, Mao Zedong and King Mwambutsa IV, diff.

No. 1361, 7500fr, Red Cross worker holding child, Henry Dunant, founder of Red Cross. No. 1362, 7500fr, Rotary emblems throughout the years. No. 1363, 7500fr, Munch and Evening on the Avenue Karl-Johan, 1892. No. 1364, 7500fr, Tereshkova and Yuri Gagarin. No. 1365, 7500fr, Tazieff, Mount Etna, Pteranodon. No. 1366, 7500fr, Carlsen playing Viswanathan Anand. No. 1367, 7500fr, Shenzhou 10 astronauts in capsule. No. 1368, 7500fr, Hebomoia leucippe, group of Scouts. No. 1369, 7500fr, Red Cross patient, Anopheles stephensi. No. 1370, 7500fr, Miró and Burnt Canvas I, 1973. No. 1371, 7500fr, Still Life, by Floris van Dyck. No. 1372, 7500fr, Pope Benedict XVI and his coat of arms. No. 1373, 7500fr, Pope Francis and his coat of arms, St. Peter's Basilica. No. 1374, 7500fr, Queen Elizabeth II, Buckingham Palace. No. 1375, 7500fr, Berkeley, Boletus regineus, Boletus edulis. No. 1376, 7500fr, Discus and high jump. No. 1377, 7500fr, Horse galloping, diff. No. 1378, 7500fr, Ferdinand von Zeppelin (1838-1917), airship manufacturer, and Graf Zeppelin. No. 1379, 7500fr, Gandhi and Parnassius maharaja. No. 1380, 7500fr, Hospital in Bubanza, Burundi, flags of Burundi and China.

2013, Aug. 5 Litho. *Perf. 13¼*
Sheets of 4, #a-d

1341-1360 A177 Set of 20 *210.00 210.00*

Souvenir Sheets

1361-1380 A177 Set of 20 *195.00 195.00*

Rossica 2013 Intl. Philatelic Exhibition, Moscow (#1344, 1364); 2013 China Intl. Collection Expo, Beijing (#1360, 1380).

A178

No. 1381 — African animals: a, 90fr, Loxodonta africana. b, 1180fr, Panthera onca. c, 3000fr, Giraffa camelopardalis. d, 3000fr, Gorilla gorilla gorilla.

No. 1382 — Wild dogs and cacti: a, 90fr, Lycaon pictus, Opuntia ovata. b, 1190fr, Canis lupus dingo, Ferocactus echidne. c, 3000fr, Canis lupus dingo, Ferocactus pileus. d, 3000fr, Cuon alpinus, Cylindropuntia fulgida.

No. 1383 — Fish: a, 90fr, Sphaeramia nematoptera. b, 1190fr, Pterapogon kauderni. c, 3000fr, Balistapus undulatus. d, 3000fr, Synchiropus splendidus.

No. 1384 — Snakes: a, 90fr, Elaphe obsoleta quadrivittata. b, 1190fr, Lampropeltis triangulum. c, 3000fr, Diadophis punctatus. d, 3000fr, Opheodrys vernalis.

No. 1385 — Minerals: a, 90fr, Brazilian carnelian agate. b, 1190fr, Malachite. c, 3000fr, Spirit quartz (amethyst). d, 3000fr, Blue azurite.

No. 1386 — Pope John Paul II (1920-2005), and: a, 90fr, His coat of arms. b, 1190fr, St. Peter's Basilica. c, 3000fr, Colonnades in St. Peter's Square. d, 3000fr, Doves.

No. 1387 — Cat breeds: a, 1020fr, Bambino. b, 1180fr, Persian. c, 3000fr, Sphynx. d, 3000fr, Abyssinian.

No. 1388 — Birds: a, 1020fr, Buteo augur. b, 1180fr, Gyps africnus. c, 3000fr, Aquila verreauxii. d, 3000fr, Aquila nipalensis.

No. 1389 — Dinosaurs: a, 1020fr, Tyrannosaurus rex. b, 1180fr, Nasutoceratops. c, 3000fr, Stegosaurus. d, 3000fr, Plateosaurus.

No. 1390 — Human ancestors: a, 1020fr, Homo erectus hunting. b, 1180fr, Homo neanderthalensis drawing on cave wall. c, 3000fr, Homo neanderthalensis, drawing of mammoth. d, 3000fr, Homo floresiensis hunting.

No. 1391 — Impressionist paintings: a, 1020fr, A Cloudy Day, by Julian Onderdonk. b, 1180fr, Woman Reading in the Garden, by Richard E. Miller. c, 3000fr, Summer Fragrance, by Edward Alfred Cucuel. d, 3000fr, Out to Sea, by Guy Rose.

No. 1392 — Giuseppe Verdi (1813-1901), composer, and costumes from: a, 1020fr, Aida. b, 1180fr, Rigoletto. c, 3000fr, Aida, diff. d, 3000fr, Don Carlos.

No. 1393 — Mao Zedong (1893-1976), Chinese communist leader: a, 1020fr, At desk. b, 1180fr, With arm raised. c, 3000fr, With hands together. d, 3000fr, Reading newspaper and giving speech.

No. 1394 — 95th birthday of Nelson Mandela, President of South Africa: a, 1020fr, Mandela with Mother Teresa. b, 1180fr, Mandela waving. c, 3000fr, Mandela with hands together. d, 3000fr, Mandela with Pope John Paul II.

No. 1395 — Turtles: a, 1020fr, Rhinoclemmys funerea, Leucocephalon yuwonoi. b, 1190fr, Heosemys spinosa. c, 3000fr, Eretmochelys imbricata. d, 3000fr, Chelonia mydas.

No. 1396 — Cricket players: a, 1020fr, Travis Birt. b, 1190fr, Graeme Swann. c, 3000fr, M. S. Dhoni. d, 3000fr, Misbah-ul-Haq.

No. 1397 — Dolphins: a, 1090fr, Sotalia fluviatilis. b, 1180fr, Stenella coeruleoalba. c, 3000fr, Steno bredanensis. d, 3000fr, Lagenorhynchus obscurus.

No. 1398 — Bees and flowers: a, 1090fr, Apis mellifera mellifera, Camellia japonica. b, 1180fr, Apis cerana, Primula sinensis. c, 3000fr, Apis mellifera, Rhododendron maximum. d, 3000fr, Apis florea, Syringa vulgaris.

No. 1399 — Fire trucks: a, 1090fr, Mercedes-Benz Atego LF 10/6 Ziegler. b, 1180fr, Ford F-350. c, 3000fr, Kronenburg MAC 11. d, 3000fr, Scania P270 FJ 07 ANP.

No. 1400 — Visit of Pope Francis to Brazil: a, 1090fr, Pope Francis, flag of Brazil, youth, World Youth Day emblem. b, 1180fr, Pope Francis, flag of Brazil, Aparecida Cathedral. c, 3000fr, Pope Francis, World Youth Day emblem and stage. d, 3000fr, Pope Francis, World Youth Day emblem, Christ the Redeemer statue, flags.

No. 1401 — Owls: a, 1090fr, Asio otus. b, 1190fr, Pseudoscops clamator. c, 3000fr, Asio flammeus. d, 3000fr, Strix aluco aluco.

No. 1402 — Endangered animals: a, 1090fr, Cercopithecus hamlyni. b, 1190fr, Eidolon helvum. c, 3000fr, Phataginus tricuspis. d, 3000fr, Felis margarita.

No. 1403 — Shells and lighthouses: a, 1090fr, Chicoreus palmarosae, Boca Chita Lighthouse, Florida. b, 1190fr, Lobatus gigas, Peggys Point Lighthouse, Nova Scotia. c, 3000fr, Cardium costatum, La Martre Lighthouse, Quebec. d, 3000fr, Columbarium pagoda pagoda, Maota Pagoda Lighthouse, China.

No. 1404 — Paintings by Pablo Picasso (1881-1973): a, 1090fr, Dying Bull, 1934. b, 1190fr, Mandolin and Guitar, 1924. c, 3000fr, Interior with a Girl Drawing, 1935. d, 3000fr, Les Demoiselles d'Avignon, 1907.

No. 1405 — High-speed trains: a, 1180fr, SNCF TGV Atlantique. b, 1190fr, BR Class 395 Javelin. c, 3000fr, NTV Alstom AGV ETR 575. d, 3000fr, Hitachi Super Express.

No. 1406, 7500fr, Ceratotherium simum. No. 1407, 7500fr, Cuon alpinus, Hylocereus undatus. No. 1408, 7500fr, Nemateleotris magnifica. No. 1409, 7500fr, Regina rigida sinicola. No. 1410, 7500fr, Variscite. No. 1411, 7500fr, Pope John Paul II, statue. No. 1412, 7500fr, Siberian cat. No. 1413, 7500fr, Terathopius ecaudatus. No. 1414, 7500fr, Dolludon. No. 1415, 7500fr, Homo neanderthalensis drawing on cave wall, diff. No. 1416, 7500fr, The Bowdoin, Monhegan Island, by Edward Willis Redfield. No. 1417, 7500fr, Verdi and scene from Aida. No. 1418, 7500fr, Mao Zedong and Chinese writing. No. 1419, 7500fr, Mandela, map of Africa. No. 1420, 7500fr, Psammobates geometricus. No. 1421, 7500fr, Adam Gilchrist. No. 1422, 7500fr, Cephalorhynchus commerssonii. No. 1423, 7500fr, Vespula germanica, Hydrangea macrophylla. No. 1424, 7500fr, Rosenbauer fire truck. No. 1425, 7500fr, Pope Francis, youths raising cross, flag of Brazil. No. 1426, 7500fr, Bubo virginianus. No. 1427, 7500fr, Varecia rubra. No. 1428, 7500fr, Charonia tritonis, Sambro Island Lighthouse, Nova Scotia. No. 1429, The Old Guitarist, by Picasso, 1903. No. 1430, 7500fr, Siemens Velaro ICE 3DB Class 407.

2013, Aug. 20 Litho. *Perf. 13¼*
Sheets of 4, #a-d

1381-1405 A178 Set of 25 *260.00 260.00*

Souvenir Sheets

1406-1430 A178 Set of 25 *245.00 245.00*

Brasiliana 2013 Intl. Philatelic Exhibition, Rio (#1400, 1425).

SEMI-POSTAL STAMPS

Prince Louis Rwagasore — SP1

Prince and Stadium SP2

Nos. B3, B6, Prince, memorial monument.

Perf. 14x13, 13x14

1963, Feb. 15 Photo. Unwmk.

B1 SP1 50c + 25c brt vio .25 .25
B2 SP2 1fr + 50c red org & dk bl .25 .25
B3 SP2 1.50fr + 75c lem & dk vio .25 .25
B4 SP1 3.50fr + 1.50fr lil rose .25 .25
B5 SP2 5fr + 2fr rose pink & dk bl .25 .25
B6 SP2 6.50fr + 3fr gray ol & dk vio .25 .25
Nos. B1-B6 (6) 1.50 1.50

Issued in memory of Prince Louis Rwagasore (1932-61), son of King Mwami Mwambutsa IV and Prime Minister. The surtax was for the stadium and monument in his honor.

Exist imperf. Value set, $18.

Red Cross Type of Regular Issue
Souvenir Sheet

1963, Sept. 26 Litho. *Imperf.*

B7 Sheet of 4 5.00 5.00
a. A5 4fr + 2fr fawn, red & black 1.00 1.00
b. A5 8fr + 2fr green, red & black 1.00 1.00
c. A5 10fr + 2fr gray, red & black 1.00 1.00
d. A5 20fr + 2fr ultra, red & black 1.00 1.00

Surtax for Red Cross work in Burundi.

Olympic Type of Regular Issue
Souvenir Sheet

Designs: 18fr+2fr, Hurdling, horiz. 20fr+5fr, Vaulting, horiz.

1964, Nov. 18 *Perf. 13½*

B8 Sheet of 2 9.00 9.00
a. A13 18fr + 2fr yel grn & multi 4.00 3.00
b. A13 20fr + 5fr brt pink & multi 4.00 3.00

Exists imperf. Value $9.

Scientist with Microscope and Map of Burundi — SP3

Lithographed and Photogravure

1965, Jan. 28 Unwmk. *Perf. 14½*

B9 SP3 2fr + 50c multi .25 .25
B10 SP3 4fr + 1.50fr multi .25 .25
B11 SP3 5fr + 2.50fr multi .30 .25
B12 SP3 8fr + 3fr multi .40 .25
B13 SP3 10fr + 5fr multi .65 .30
Nos. B9-B13 (5) 1.85 1.30

Souvenir Sheet
Perf. 13x13½

B14 SP3 10fr + 10fr multi 1.50 1.50

Issued for the fight against tuberculosis.

Exist imperf. Values: set $5; souvenir sheet $2.

Coat of Arms, 10fr Coin, Reverse SP4

Designs (Coins of Various Denominations): 4fr+50c, 8fr+50c, 15fr+50c, 40fr+50c, King Mwambutsa IV, obverse.

Lithographed; Embossed on Gilt Foil

1965, Aug. 9 *Imperf.*

Diameter: 39mm

B15 SP4 2fr + 50c crim & org .25 .25
B16 SP4 4fr + 50c ultra & ver .30 .30

Diameter: 45mm

B17 SP4 6fr + 50c org & gray .50 .50
B18 SP4 8fr + 50c bl & mag .65 .65

Diameter: 56mm

B19 SP4 12fr + 50c lt grn & red lil .95 .95
B20 SP4 15fr + 50c yel grn & lt lil 1.10 1.10

Diameter: 67mm

B21 SP4 25fr + 50c vio bl & buff 2.10 2.10
B22 SP4 40fr + 50c brt pink & red brn 4.00 4.00
Nos. B15-B22 (8) 9.85 9.85

Stamps are backed with patterned paper in blue, orange and pink engine-turned design.

Prince Louis Rwagasore and Pres. John F. Kennedy SP5

4fr+1fr, 20fr+5fr, Prince Louis, memorial. 20fr+2fr, 40fr+5fr, Pres. John F. Kennedy, library shelves. 40fr+2fr, King Mwambutsa IV at Kennedy grave, Arlington, vert.

1966, Jan. 21 Photo. *Perf. 13½*

B23 SP5 4fr + 1fr gray bl & dk brn .25 .25
B24 SP5 10fr + 1fr pale grn, ind & brn .25 .25
B25 SP5 20fr + 2fr lil & dp grn .50 .25
B26 SP5 40fr + 2fr gray grn & dk brn 1.10 .55
Nos. B23-B26 (4) 2.10 1.30

Souvenir Sheet

B27 Sheet of 2 3.25 3.25
a. SP5 20fr + 5fr gray bl & dk brn 1.50 1.50
b. SP5 40fr + 5fr lilac & dp grn 1.50 1.50

Issued in memory of Prince Louis Rwagasore and President John F. Kennedy.

Exist imperf. Values: set $6; souvenir sheet $3.50.

Republic

Winston Churchill and St. Paul's, London SP6

Designs: 15fr+2fr, Tower of London and Churchill. 20fr+3fr, Big Ben and Churchill.

1967, Mar. 23 Photo. *Perf. 13½*

B28	SP6	4fr + 1fr multi	.30	.25
B29	SP6	15fr + 2fr multi	.50	.25
B30	SP6	20fr + 3fr multi	.65	.40
		Nos. B28-B30 (3)	1.45	.90

Issued in memory of Sir Winston Churchill (1874-1965), statesman and World War II leader.

Exist imperf. Value $4.50.

A souvenir sheet contains one airmail stamp, 50fr+5fr, with Churchill portrait centered. Size: 80x80mm. Exists perf and imperf. Value, each sheet, $2.

Nos. B28-B30 Overprinted

1967, July 14 Photo. *Perf. 13½*

B31	SP6	4fr + 1fr multi	.70	.25
B32	SP6	15fr + 2fr multi	1.00	.40
B33	SP6	20fr + 3fr multi	1.25	.50
		Nos. B31-B33 (3)	2.95	1.15

50th anniversary of Lions International.

Exist with dates transposed. Value, set $30.

Both the regular set imperf and the souvenir sheets described below No. B30 also received this Lions overprint.

Value: set $8.50; souvenir sheet, each $3.50. Also exists imperf. Value, set $50.

Blood Transfusion and Red Cross — SP7

Designs: 7fr+1fr, Stretcher bearers and wounded man. 11fr+1fr, Surgical team. 17fr+1fr, Nurses tending blood bank.

1969, June 26 Photo. *Perf. 13½*

B34	SP7	4fr + 1fr multi	.25	.25
B35	SP7	7fr + 1fr multi	.35	.25
B36	SP7	11fr + 1fr multi	.40	.25
B37	SP7	17fr + 1fr multi	.60	.25
		Nos. B34-B37,CB9-CB11 (7)	5.55	2.25

League of Red Cross Societies, 50th anniv.

Exist imperf. Value set (7), $9.

Pope Paul VI and Map of Africa — SP8

3fr+2fr, 17fr+2fr, Pope Paul VI. 10fr+2fr, Flag made of flags of African Nations. 14fr+2fr, View of St. Peter's, Rome. 40fr+2fr, 40fr+5fr, Martyrs of Uganda. 50fr+2fr, 50fr+5fr, Pope on Throne.

1969, Sept. 12 Photo. *Perf. 13½*

B38	SP8	3fr + 2fr multi, vert.	.25	.25
B39	SP8	5fr + 2fr multi	.25	.25
B40	SP8	10fr + 2fr multi	.35	.25
B41	SP8	14fr + 2fr multi	.75	.25
B42	SP8	17fr + 2fr multi, vert.	1.25	.30
B43	SP8	40fr + 2fr multi	1.75	.60
B44	SP8	50fr + 2fr multi	2.00	.65
		Nos. B38-B44 (7)	6.60	2.55

Souvenir Sheet

B45		Sheet of 2	4.50	4.50
a.		SP8 40fr + 5fr multi	2.00	2.00
b.		SP8 50fr + 5fr multi	2.00	2.00

Visit of Pope Paul VI to Uganda, 7/31-8/2.

Exist imperf. Values: set $10; souvenir sheet $4.50.

Virgin and Child, by Albrecht Dürer — SP9

Christmas (Paintings): 11fr+1fr, Madonna of the Eucharist, by Sandro Botticelli. 20fr+1fr, Holy Family, by El Greco.

1970, Dec. 14 Photo. *Perf. 13½*

Gold Frame

B46	SP9	6.50fr + 1fr multi	.70	.25
B47	SP9	11fr + 1fr multi	1.00	.25
B48	SP9	20fr + 1fr multi	1.25	.35
a.		Souv. sheet of 3, #B46-B48	3.50	3.50
		Nos. B46-B48,CB12-CB14 (6)	6.95	2.15

Exist imperf. Values: set (6) $6.50; souvenir sheets $6.75.

Nos. 376-378 Surcharged in Gold and Black

1971, Nov. 27

B49	A51	3fr + 1fr multi	.25	.25
B50	A51	5fr + 1fr multi	.65	.25
B51	A51	6fr + 1fr multi	.75	.25
a.		Souvenir sheet of 3	4.00	4.00
		Nos. B49-B51,CB19-CB21 (6)	5.45	1.80

UNICEF, 25th anniv. No. B51a contains 3 stamps similar to Nos. B49-B51 with 2fr surtax each.

Exist imperf. Values: set (6) $5.50; souvenir sheets $8.

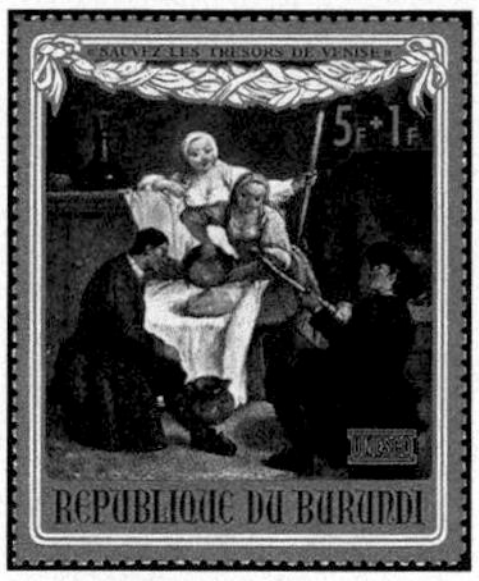

"La Polenta," by Pietro Longhi SP10

Designs: 3fr+1fr, Archangel Michael, Byzantine icon from St. Mark's 6fr+1fr, "Gossip," by Pietro Longhi. 11fr+1fr, "Diana's Bath," by Giovanni Batista Pittoni. All stamps inscribed UNESCO.

1971, Dec. 27

B52	SP10	3fr + 1fr gold & multi	.25	.25
B53	SP10	5fr + 1fr gold & multi	.40	.25
B54	SP10	6fr + 1fr gold & multi	.50	.25
B55	SP10	11fr + 1fr gold & multi	1.00	.25
a.		Souvenir sheet of 4	4.00	4.00
		Nos. B52-B55,CB22-CB25 (8)	6.20	2.20

The surtax was for the UNESCO campaign to save the treasures of Venice. No. B55a contains 4 stamps similar to Nos. B52-B55, but with 2fr surtax.

Exist imperf. Values: set (8) $8.50; souvenir sheets $15.

Nos. 408-410 Surcharged in Silver

1972, Dec. 12 Photo. *Perf. 13½*

B56	A57	5fr + 1fr multi	.55	.25
B57	A57	10fr + 1fr multi	1.00	.25
B58	A57	15fr + 1fr multi	1.60	.25
a.		Souvenir sheet of 3	3.00	3.00
		Nos. B56-B58,CB26-CB28 (6)	8.40	1.95

Christmas 1972. No. B58a contains 3 stamps similar to Nos. B56-B58, but with 2fr surtax.

Exist imperf. Values: set (6) $10; souvenir sheets $16.

Nos. 441-443 Surcharged "+1F" in Silver

1973, Dec. 14 Photo. *Perf. 13*

B59	A64	5fr + 1fr multi	1.00	.25
B60	A64	10fr + 1fr multi	1.50	.25
B61	A64	15fr + 1fr multi	1.50	.25
a.		Souvenir sheet of 3	4.50	4.50
		Nos. B59-B61,CB29-CB31 (6)	7.90	1.95

Christmas 1973. No. B61a contains 3 stamps similar to Nos. B59-B61 with 2fr surtax each.

Exist imperf. Values: set (6) $8.50; souvenir sheets $8.

Christmas Type of 1974

1974, Dec. 2 Photo. *Perf. 13*

B62	A70	5fr + 1fr multi	1.00	.25
B63	A70	10fr + 1fr multi	1.40	.30
B64	A70	15fr + 1fr multi	2.10	.40
a.		Souvenir sheet of 3	5.50	5.50
		Nos. B62-B64,CB32-CB34 (6)	10.10	2.85

No. B64a contains 3 stamps similar to Nos. B62-B64 with 2fr surtax each.

Exist imperf. Values: set (6) $11; souvenir sheets $17.

Nos. 485-487 Surcharged "+ 1F" in Silver and Black

1975, Dec. 22 Photo. *Perf. 13*

Pairs, #a.-b.

B65	A73	5fr + 1fr #485	3.25	.25
B66	A73	13fr + 1fr #486	6.50	.30
B67	A73	27fr + 1fr #487	10.00	.60
c.		Souvenir sheet of 6	17.50	17.50
		Nos. B65-B67,CB35-CB37 (6)	41.50	2.55

Michelangelo Buonarroti (1475-1564), 500th birth anniversary. No. B67c contains 6 stamps similar to Nos. B65a-B67b with 2fr surcharge each.

Exist imperf. Values: set (6) $50; souvenir sheets $37.50.

Nos. 504-506 Surcharged "+1f" in Silver and Black

1976, Nov. 25 Photo. *Perf. 13½*

B71	A76	5fr + 1fr multi	.95	.25
B72	A76	13fr + 1fr multi	1.50	.25
B73	A76	27fr + 1fr multi	3.00	.60
a.		Souvenir sheet of 3	5.50	5.50
		Nos. B71-B73,CB41-CB43 (6)	12.55	2.35

Christmas 1976. No. B73a contains 3 stamps similar to Nos. B71-B73 with 2fr surtax each.

Exist imperf. Values: set (6) $11; souvenir sheets $10.

Nos. 531-533 Surcharged "+1fr" in Silver and Black

1977 Photo. *Perf. 14x13*

B74	A83	5fr + 1fr multi	.90	.25
B75	A83	13fr + 1fr multi	2.50	.25
B76	A83	27fr + 1fr multi	3.00	.50
a.		Souvenir sheet of 3	6.50	6.50
		Nos. B74-B76,CB44-CB46 (6)	14.40	2.25

Christmas 1977. No. B76a contains 3 stamps similar to Nos. B74-B76 with 2fr surtax each.

Exist imperf. Values: set (6) $12; souvenir sheets $13.

Christmas Type of 1979

1979, Feb. Photo. *Perf. 14x13*

B77	A86	13fr + 1fr multi	1.50	1.25
B78	A86	17fr + 1fr multi	1.90	1.60
B79	A86	27fr + 1fr multi	3.50	2.50
B80	A86	31fr + 1fr multi	4.00	3.50
B81	A86	40fr + 1fr multi	5.25	4.50
		Nos. B77-B81 (5)	16.15	13.35

Exist imperf. Value $12.

IYC Type of 1979

1979, July 19 Photo. *Perf. 14*

B82		Sheet of 4	11.00	11.00
a.		A88 10fr + 2fr like #557	2.50	2.50
b.		A88 20fr + 2fr like #558	2.50	2.50
c.		A88 27fr + 2fr like #559	2.50	2.50
d.		A88 50fr + 2fr like #560	2.50	2.50

Exist imperf. Value $12.50.

Christmas Type of 1979

1979, Dec. 10 Photo. *Perf. 13½*

B83	A89	20fr + 1fr like #561	2.50	1.00
B84	A89	27fr + 1fr like #562	4.75	2.00
B85	A89	31fr + 1fr like #563	6.50	2.50
B86	A89	50fr + 2fr like #564	8.25	2.75
		Nos. B83-B86 (4)	22.00	8.25

Christmas Type of 1980

1981, Jan. 16 Photo. *Perf. 13½x13*

B87	A92	10fr + 1fr like #579	1.60	.65
B88	A92	30fr + 1fr like #580	3.25	1.25
B89	A92	40fr + 1fr like #581	7.25	3.00
B90	A92	50fr + 1fr like #582	10.00	4.00
		Nos. B87-B90 (4)	22.10	8.90

Christmas Type of 1983

1983, Nov. 2 Litho. *Perf. 14½x13½*

B91	A97	10fr + 1fr like #607	5.50	1.00
B92	A97	25fr + 1fr like #608	8.00	1.40
B93	A97	30fr + 1fr like #609	15.00	2.75
B94	A97	50fr + 1fr like #610	21.00	7.25
		Nos. B91-B94 (4)	49.50	12.40

Christmas Type of 1984

1984, Dec. 15 *Perf. 13½*

B95	A101	10fr + 1fr like #629	2.75	1.00
B96	A101	25fr + 1fr like #630	6.50	2.50
B97	A101	30fr + 1fr like #631	7.75	3.00
B98	A101	50fr + 1fr like #632	11.00	4.75
		Nos. B95-B98 (4)	28.00	11.25

Multi-party Elections, 1st Anniv.
SP11 SP12

30fr+10fr, Pres. Buyoya handing Baton of Power to Pres. Ndadaye. 110fr+10fr, Pres. Ndadaye giving inauguration speech. 115fr+10fr, Arms, map of Burundi. 120fr+10fr, Warrior, flag of Burundi, trees, map of Burundi.

1994, Oct. 20 Litho. *Perf. 15*

B99	SP11	30fr +10fr multi	1.00	.75
B100	SP11	110fr +10fr multi	3.50	2.75
B101	SP12	115fr +10fr multi	4.00	2.75
B102	SP12	120fr +10fr multi	4.00	2.75
		Nos. B99-B102 (4)	12.50	9.00

AIR POST STAMPS

Animal Type of Regular Issue

6fr, Zebra. 8fr, Cape buffalo (bubalis). 10fr, Impala. 14fr, Hippopotamus. 15fr, Defassa waterbuck. 20fr, Cheetah. 50fr, Elephant.

Unwmk.

1964, July 2 Litho. *Perf. 14*

Size: 42x21mm, 21x42mm

C1	A9	6fr multi	.40	.25
C2	A9	8fr multi	.50	.25
C3	A9	10fr multi, vert.	.70	.25
C4	A9	14fr multi	1.05	.30
C5	A9	15fr multi, vert.	1.35	.40

Size: 53x32½mm

C6	A9	20fr multi	2.50	.50
C7	A9	50fr multi	6.00	.75
		Nos. C1-C7 (7)	12.50	2.70

Exists imperf.

Bird Type of Regular Issue

Birds: 6fr, Secretary bird. 8fr, African anhinga. 10fr, African peacock. 14fr, Bee eater. 15fr, Yellow-billed stork. 20fr, Saddle-billed stork. 50fr, Abyssinian ground hornbill. 75fr, Martial eagle. 130fr, Lesser flamingo.

1965, June 10 Litho. *Perf. 14*

Size: 26x43mm

C8 A14 6fr multi .25 .25
C9 A14 8fr multi .35 .25
C10 A14 10fr multi .45 .25
C11 A14 14fr multi .75 .30
C12 A14 15fr multi .95 .40

Size: 33x53mm

C13 A14 20fr multi 1.90 .45
C14 A14 50fr multi 3.00 .65
C15 A14 75fr multi 4.50 1.00
C16 A14 130fr multi 7.75 1.60
Nos. C8-C16 (9) 19.90 5.15

For overprints see Nos. C35A-C35I.

Flower Type of Regular Issue

Flowers: 6fr, Dissotis. 8fr, Crossandra. 10fr, Ansellia. 14fr, Thunbergia. 15fr, Schizoglossum. 20fr, Gazania. 50fr, Protea. 75fr, Hibiscus. 130fr, Markhamia.

1966, Oct. 10 Unwmk. *Perf. 13½*

Size: 31x31mm

C17 A17 6fr multi .35 .25
C18 A17 8fr multi .50 .25
C19 A17 10fr multi .60 .25
C20 A17 14fr multi .75 .25
C21 A17 15fr multi 1.00 .25

Size: 39x39mm

C22 A17 20fr multi 1.25 .25
C23 A17 50fr multi 2.25 .35
C24 A17 75fr multi 3.50 .50
C25 A17 130fr multi 6.00 1.00
Nos. C17-C25 (9) 16.20 3.35

For overprints see Nos. C27-C35.

Tapestry Type of Regular Issue
Souvenir Sheet

1966, Nov. 4 Unwmk. *Perf. 13½*

C26 A18 Sheet of 7 (14fr) 9.00 6.50

See note after No. 158.

REPUBLIC

Nos. C17-C25 Overprinted

1967 Litho. *Perf. 13½*

Size: 31x31mm

C27 A17 6fr multi .25 .25
C28 A17 8fr multi .35 .25
C29 A17 10fr multi .50 .25
C30 A17 14fr multi .75 .25
C31 A17 15fr multi 1.00 .25

Size: 39x39mm

C32 A17 20fr multi 2.00 .35
C33 A17 50fr multi 5.00 .90
C34 A17 75fr multi 8.00 1.50
C35 A17 130fr multi 8.50 1.50
Nos. C27-C35 (9) 26.35 5.50

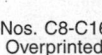

Nos. C8-C16 Overprinted

1967 Litho. *Perf. 14*

Size: 26x43mm

C35A A14 6fr multi *.50* .40
C35B A14 8fr multi *1.00* .50
C35C A14 10fr multi *1.50* .60
C35D A14 14fr multi *2.00* .75
C35E A14 15fr multi *2.75* .90

Size: 33x53mm

C35F A14 20fr multi *4.00* 2.00
C35G A14 50fr multi *8.50* 4.00
C35H A14 75fr multi *12.50* 5.00
C35I A14 130fr multi *18.00* 7.50
Nos. C35A-C35I (9) 50.75 21.65

African Art Type of Regular Issue

10fr, Spirit of Bakutu figurine, Equatorial Africa. 14fr, Pearl throne of Sultan of the Bamum, Cameroun. 17fr, Bronze head of Mother Queen of Benin, Nigeria. 24fr, Statue of 109th Bakouba king, Kata-Mbula, Central Congo. 26fr, Baskets and lances, Burundi.

1967, June 5 Photo. *Perf. 13½*

C36 A20 10fr gold & multi .25 .25
C37 A20 14fr gold & multi .30 .25
C38 A20 17fr gold & multi .45 .25
C39 A20 24fr gold & multi .55 .30
C40 A20 26fr gold & multi .90 .50
Nos. C36-C40 (5) 2.45 1.55

Boy Scout Type of Regular Issue

10fr, Scouts on hiking trip. 14fr, Cooking at campfire. 17fr, Lord Baden-Powell. 24fr, Boy Scout & Cub Scout giving Scout sign. 26fr, First aid.

1967, Aug. 9 *Perf. 13½*

C41 A21 10fr gold & multi 1.25 .25
C42 A21 14fr gold & multi 1.50 .25
C43 A21 17fr gold & multi 1.75 .25
C44 A21 24fr gold & multi 2.75 .25
C45 A21 26fr gold & multi 3.00 .40
Nos. C41-C45 (5) 10.25 1.40

A souvenir sheet of 2 contains one each of Nos. C44-C45 and 2 labels in the designs of Nos. 208-209 with commemorative inscriptions was issued 1/8/68. Size: 100x100mm. Value, $8 unused, $5 used.

Fish Type of Regular Issue

Designs: Various Tropical Fish

1967, Sept. 8 Photo. *Perf. 13½*

Size: 50x23mm

C46 A19 6fr multi .95 .25
C47 A19 8fr multi 1.40 .25
C48 A19 10fr multi 1.90 .25
C49 A19 14fr multi 2.25 .25
C50 A19 15fr multi 2.00 .25

Size: 58x27mm

C51 A19 20fr multi 3.75 .25
C52 A19 50fr multi 7.75 .30
C53 A19 75fr multi 11.50 .35
C54 A19 130fr multi 18.00 .65
Nos. C46-C54 (9) 49.50 2.80

Boeing 707 of Air Congo and ITY Emblem — AP1

Designs: 14fr, Boeing 727 of Sabena over lake. 17fr, Vickers VC10 of East African Airways over lake. 26fr, Boeing 727 of Sabena over airport.

1967, Nov. 3 Photo. *Perf. 13*

C55 AP1 10fr blk, yel brn & sil .35 .25
C56 AP1 14fr blk, org & sil .55 .25
C57 AP1 17fr blk, brt bl & sil .60 .30
C58 AP1 26fr blk, brt rose lil & sil 1.25 .55
Nos. C55-C58 (4) 2.75 1.35

Opening of the jet airport at Bujumbura and for International Tourist Year, 1967.
Exist imperf. Value set, $6.50.

Paintings Type of Regular Issue

Paintings: 17fr, Woman with Cat, by Renoir. 24fr, The Jewish Bride, by Rembrandt, horiz. 26fr, Pope Innocent X, by Velazquez.

1968, Mar. 29 Photo. *Perf. 13½*

C59 A26 17fr multi .50 .25
C60 A26 24fr multi .75 .30
C61 A26 26fr multi 1.00 .75
Nos. C59-C61 (3) 2.25 1.30

Issued in sheets of 6.

Space Type of Regular Issue

14fr, Moon Probe. 18fr, Russian astronaut walking in space. 25fr, Mariner satellite, Mars. 40fr, American astronaut walking in space.

1968, May 15 Photo. *Perf. 13½*

Size: 41x41mm

C62 A27 14fr sil & multi .60 .25
C63 A27 18fr sil & multi .80 .25
C64 A27 25fr sil & multi .90 .25
C65 A27 40fr sil & multi 1.75 .60
Nos. C62-C65 (4) 4.05 1.35

Butterfly Type of Regular Issue

Butterflies: 6fr, Teracolus annae. 8fr, Graphium ridleyanus. 10fr, Cymothoe. 14fr, Charaxes eupale. 15fr, Papilio bromius. 20fr, Papilio zenobia. 50fr, Salamis aethiops. 75fr, Danais chrysippus. 130fr, Salamis temora.

1968, Sept. 9 Photo. *Perf. 13½*

Size: 38x42mm

C66 A28 6fr gold & multi 1.10 .25
C67 A28 8fr gold & multi 2.00 .25
C68 A28 10fr gold & multi 2.25 .30
C69 A28 14fr gold & multi 2.75 .40
C70 A28 15fr gold & multi 3.00 .50

Size: 44x49mm

C71 A28 20fr gold & multi 4.25 .75
C72 A28 50fr gold & multi 7.50 1.00
C73 A28 75fr gold & multi 12.50 1.25
C74 A28 130fr gold & multi 20.00 1.50
Nos. C66-C74 (9) 55.35 6.20

Painting Type of Regular Issue

Paintings: 17fr, The Letter, by Jean H. Fragonard. 26fr, Young Woman Reading Letter, by Jan Vermeer. 40fr, Lady Folding Letter, by Elisabeth Vigée-Lebrun. 50fr, Mademoiselle Lavergne, by Jean Etienne Liotard.

1968, Sept. 30 Photo. *Perf. 13½*

C84 A29 17fr multi .65 .30
C85 A29 26fr multi 1.25 .30
C86 A29 40fr multi 2.00 .40
C87 A29 50fr multi 2.75 .40
Nos. C84-C87 (4) 6.65 1.40

A souvenir sheet containing examples of Nos. C86-C87 with changed colors exists perf and imperf. Value, each $6.50.

Olympic Games Type

1968, Oct. 24

C88 A30 10fr Shot put .25 .25
C89 A30 17fr Running .45 .25
C90 A30 26fr Hammer throw .90 .25
C91 A30 50fr Hurdling 1.75 .40
C92 A30 75fr Broad jump 3.25 .55
Nos. C88-C92 (5) 6.60 1.70

Christmas Type of 1968

Paintings: 10fr, Virgin and Child, by Correggio. 14fr, Nativity, by Federigo Baroccio. 17fr, Holy Family, by El Greco. 26fr, Adoration of the Magi, by Maino.

1968, Nov. 26 Photo. *Perf. 13½*

C93 A31 10fr multi .35 .25
C94 A31 14fr multi .45 .25
C95 A31 17fr multi .60 .25
C96 A31 26fr multi 1.25 .50
a. Souv. sheet of 4, #C93-C96 3.00 2.25
Nos. C93-C96 (4) 2.65 1.25

For overprints see Nos. C100-C103.

Human Rights Flame, Hand and Globe — AP2

1969, Jan. 22

C97 AP2 10fr multi .35 .25
C98 AP2 14fr multi .55 .25
C99 AP2 26fr lil & multi .90 .25
Nos. C97-C99 (3) 1.80 .75

International Human Rights Year, 1968.
Exist imperf. Value set, $4.50.

Nos. C93-C96 Overprinted in Silver

1969, Feb. 17 Photo. *Perf. 13½*

C100 A31 10fr multi .45 .25
C101 A31 14fr multi .60 .25
C102 A31 17fr multi .70 .30
C103 A31 26fr multi 1.00 .50
Nos. C100-C103 (4) 2.75 1.30

Man's 1st flight around the moon by the US spacecraft Apollo 8, Dec. 21-27, 1968.

Moon Landing Type of 1969

Designs: 26fr, Neil A. Armstrong leaving landing module. 40fr, Astronaut on moon. 50fr, Splashdown in the Pacific.

1969, Nov. 6 Photo. *Perf. 13½*

C104 A38 26fr gold & multi 1.75 .30
C105 A38 40fr gold & multi 2.50 .45
C106 A38 50fr gold & multi 4.00 .50
Nos. C104-C106 (3) 8.25 1.25

Christmas Type of 1969

Paintings: 17fr, Madonna and Child, by Benvenuto da Garofalo. 26fr, Madonna and Child, by Jacopo Negretti. 50fr, Madonna and Child, by Il Giorgione. All horizontal.

1969, Dec. 2 Photo.

C107 A39 17fr gold & multi .70 .25
C108 A39 26fr gold & multi 1.25 .25
C109 A39 50fr gold & multi 2.75 .35
a. Souv. sheet of 3, #C107-C109 4.25 3.50
Nos. C107-C109 (3) 4.70 .85

Insect Type of Regular Issue

Designs: Various Beetles and Weevils.

1970 Size: 46x32mm *Perf. 13½*

C110 A40 6fr gold & multi .65 .25
C111 A40 8fr gold & multi .80 .25
C112 A40 10fr gold & multi 1.00 .25
C113 A40 14fr gold & multi 1.25 .25
C114 A40 15fr gold & multi 1.50 .25

Size: 52x36mm

C115 A40 20fr gold & multi 3.00 .40
C116 A40 50fr gold & multi 5.75 .55
C117 A40 75fr gold & multi 8.50 .75
C118 A40 130fr gold & multi 13.50 1.25
Nos. C110-C118 (9) 35.95 4.20

Issued: Nos. C110-C115, 1/20; Nos. C116-C118, 2/27.

Easter Type of 1970

Stations of the Cross, by Juan de Aranoa y Carredano: 8fr, Jesus meets the women of Jerusalem. 10fr, Jesus falls a third time. 14fr, Jesus stripped. 15fr, Jesus nailed to the cross. 18fr, Jesus dies on the cross. 20fr, Descent from the cross. 50fr, Jesus laid in the tomb.

1970, Mar. 16 Photo. *Perf. 13½*

C119 A41 8fr gold & multi .30 .25
C120 A41 10fr gold & multi .40 .25
C121 A41 14fr gold & multi .55 .25
C122 A41 15fr gold & multi .65 .25
C123 A41 18fr gold & multi .90 .30
C124 A41 20fr gold & multi 1.00 .40
C125 A41 50fr gold & multi 2.10 .70
a. Souv. sheet of 7, #C119-C125 + label 7.25 6.00
Nos. C119-C125 (7) 5.90 2.40

EXPO '70 Type of Regular Issue
Souvenir Sheet

Designs: 40fr, Tower of the Sun, vert. 50fr, Flags of participating nations, vert.

1970, May 5 Photo. *Perf. 13½*

C126 Sheet of 2 3.00 3.00
a. A42 40fr multi 1.00 1.00
b. A42 50fr multi 1.25 1.25

Rhinoceros Type of Regular Issue

Fauna: a, i, Camel. c, d, Dromedary. g, r, Okapi. f, m, Addax. j, o, Rhinoceros. l, p, Burundi cow (each animal in 2 different poses).

Map of the Nile: b, Delta and pyramids. e, dhow. h, Falls. k, Blue Nile and crowned crane. n, Victoria Nile and secretary bird. q, Lake Victoria and source of Nile on Mt. Gikizi. Continuous design.

1970, July 8 Photo. *Perf. 13½*

C127 Sheet of 18 50.00 25.00
a.-r. A43 14fr any single 2.00 .35

Publicizing the southernmost source of the Nile on Mt. Gikizi in Burundi.

UN Emblem and Headquarters, NYC — AP3

25th Anniv. of the UN (UN Emblem and): 11fr, Security Council and mural by Per Krohg. 26fr, Pope Paul VI and U Thant. 40fr, Flags in front of UN Headquarters, NYC.

1970, Oct. 23 Photo. *Perf. 13½*

C128 AP3 7fr gold & multi .25 .25
C129 AP3 11fr gold & multi .35 .25
C130 AP3 26fr gold & multi .85 .25
C131 AP3 40fr gold & multi 1.10 .40
a. Souvenir sheet of 2 3.75 3.75
Nos. C128-C131 (4) 2.55 1.15

No. C131a contains 2 stamps similar to Nos. C130-C131 but without "Poste Aerienne."
Exist imperf. Values: set $4; souvenir sheet $7.

Bird Type of Regular Issue

8fr, 14fr, 30fr, vert.; 10fr, 20fr, 50fr, horiz.

1970 Photo. *Perf. 13½*
Stamp size: 52x44mm

C132 A44 Block of 4 13.50 1.50
a. 8fr Northern shrike 2.75 .25
b. 8fr European starling 2.75 .25
c. 8fr Yellow wagtail 2.75 .25
d. 8fr Bank swallow 2.75 .25
C133 A44 Block of 4 16.50 1.75
a. 10fr Winter wren 3.25 .30
b. 10fr Firecrest 3.25 .30
c. 10fr Skylark 3.25 .30
d. 10fr Crested lark 3.25 .30
C134 A44 Block of 4 20.00 2.00
a. 14fr Woodchat shrike 4.00 .35
b. 14fr Common rock thrush 4.00 .35
c. 14fr Black redstart 4.00 .35
d. 14fr Ring ouzel 4.00 .35
C135 A44 Block of 4 18.00 2.25
a. 20fr European redstart 3.75 .40
b. 20fr Hedge sparrow 3.75 .40
c. 20fr Gray wagtail 3.75 .40
d. 20fr Meadow pipit 3.75 .40
C136 A44 Block of 4 22.50 2.75
a. 30fr Eurasian hoopoe 4.50 .45
b. 30fr Pied flycatcher 4.50 .45
c. 30fr Great reed warbler 4.50 .45
d. 30fr Eurasian kingfisher 4.50 .45
C137 A44 Block of 4 32.50 3.50
a. 50fr House martin 7.00 .60
b. 50fr Sedge warbler 7.00 .60
c. 50fr Fieldfare 7.00 .60
d. 50fr European Golden oriole 7.00 .60
Nos. C132-C137 (6) 123.00 13.75

Queen Fabiola and King Baudouin of Belgium AP4

Designs: 20fr, Pres. Michel Micombero and King Baudouin. 40fr, Pres. Micombero and coats of arms of Burundi and Belgium.

1970, Nov. 28 Photo. *Perf. 13½*

C140 AP4 6fr multicolored 1.25 .25
C141 AP4 20fr multicolored 3.50 .65
C142 AP4 40fr multicolored 6.25 1.10
a. Souvenir sheet of 3 11.00 11.00
Nos. C140-C142 (3) 11.00 2.00

Visit of the King and Queen of Belgium. No. C142a contains 3 stamps similar to Nos. C140-C142, but without "Poste Aerienne."
Exist imperf. Values: set $10; souvenir sheet $9.

Easter Type of Regular Issue

Paintings of the Resurrection: 14fr, by Louis Borrassá. 17fr, Piero della Francesca. 26fr, Michel Wohlgemuth.

1971, Apr. 2 Photo. *Perf. 13½*

C143 A49 14fr gold & multi .95 .25
C144 A49 17fr gold & multi 1.25 .25
C145 A49 26fr gold & multi 2.40 .35
a. Souv. sheet of 3, #C143-C145 5.00 5.00
Nos. C143-C145 (3) 4.60 .85

Easter 1971.

Animal Type of Regular Issue

1971 Photo. *Perf. 13½*
Size: 44x44mm

C146 Strip of 4 9.00 .85
a. A48 10fr Lion 1.60 .25
b. A48 10fr Cape buffalo 1.60 .25
c. A48 10fr Hippopotamus 1.60 .25
d. A48 10fr Giraffe 1.60 .25
C147 Strip of 4 10.00 1.00
a. A48 14fr Hartebeest 1.90 .25
b. A48 14fr Black rhinoceros 1.90 .25
c. A48 14fr Zebra 1.90 .25
d. A48 14fr Leopard 1.90 .25
C148 Strip of 4 12.00 1.00
a. A48 17fr Grant's gazelles 2.10 .25
b. A48 17fr Cheetah 2.10 .25
c. A48 17fr African white-backed vultures 2.10 .25
d. A48 17fr Johnston's okapi 2.10 .25
C149 Strip of 4 13.50 1.50
a. A48 24fr Chimpanzee 2.25 .30
b. A48 24fr Elephant 2.25 .30
c. A48 24fr Spotted Hyenas 2.25 .30
d. A48 24fr Beisa 2.25 .30
C150 Strip of 4 15.00 1.90
a. A48 26fr Gorilla 2.50 .40
b. A48 26fr Gnu 2.50 .40
c. A48 26fr Warthog 2.50 .40
d. A48 26fr Cape hunting dog 2.50 .40
C151 Strip of 4 16.00 2.40
a. A48 31fr Sable antelope 3.00 .50
b. A48 31fr Caracal lynx 3.00 .50
c. A48 31fr Ostriches 3.00 .50
d. A48 31fr Bongo 3.00 .50
Nos. C146-C151 (6) 75.50 8.65

For overprint and surcharges see Nos. C152, CB15-C18.

No. C146 Overprinted in Gold and Black

1971, July 20 Photo. *Perf. 13½*

C152 Strip of 4 6.00 3.00
a. A48 10fr Lion 1.10 .25
b. A48 10fr Cape buffalo 1.10 .25
c. A48 10fr Hippopotamus 1.10 .25
d. A48 10fr Giraffe 1.10 .25

Intl. Year Against Racial Discrimination.

Christmas Type of Regular Issue

Paintings of the Madonna and Child by: 14fr, Cima de Conegliano. 17fr, Fra Filippo Lippi. 31fr, Leonardo da Vinci.

1971, Nov. 2 Photo. *Perf. 13½*

C153 A51 14fr red & multi .60 .25
C154 A51 17fr red & multi .80 .25
C155 A51 31fr red & multi 1.50 .35
a. Souv. sheet of 3, #C153-C155 3.00 3.00
Nos. C153-C155 (3) 2.90 .85

Christmas 1971.
For surcharges see Nos. CB19-CB21.

Spacecraft Type of Regular Issue
Souvenir Sheet

1972, Jan. 15 Photo. *Perf. 13½*

C156 Sheet of 6 7.00 7.00
a. A52 6fr Lunar Orbiter .75 .75
b. A52 11fr Vostok .75 .75
c. A52 14fr Luna I .75 .75
d. A52 17fr Apollo 11 astronaut on moon .75 .75
e. A52 26fr Soyuz 11 .75 .75
f. A52 40fr Lunar rover (Apollo 15) .75 .75

Sapporo '72 Type of Regular Issue
Souvenir Sheet

Emblem and: 26fr, Snow scooter. 31fr, Downhill skiing. 50fr, Bobsledding.

1972, Feb. 3

C157 Sheet of 3 6.00 5.00
a. A53 26fr silver & multi 1.50 1.25
b. A53 31fr silver & multi 1.50 1.25
c. A53 50fr silver & multi 1.50 1.25

Olympic Games Type of 1972

1972, July 24 Photo. *Perf. 13½*

C158 A55 24fr Weight lifting 1.60 .25
C159 A55 26fr Hurdles 1.75 .25
C160 A55 31fr Discus 2.10 .40
C161 A55 40fr Soccer 2.75 .45
Nos. C158-C161 (4) 8.20 1.35

Independence Type of 1972

Designs: 15fr, Prince Rwagasore, Pres. Micombero, Burundi flag, drummers. 18fr, Rwagasore, Micombero, flag, map of Africa, globe. 27fr, Micombero, flag, globe.

1972, Aug. 24 Photo. *Perf. 13½*

C162 A56 15fr gold & multi .40 .25
C163 A56 18fr gold & multi .50 .30
C164 A56 27fr gold & multi .80 .40
a. Souv. sheet of 3, #C162-C164 2.00 2.00
Nos. C162-C164 (3) 1.70 .95

Christmas Type of 1972

Paintings of the Madonna and Child by: 18fr, Sebastiano Mainardi. 27fr, Hans Memling. 40fr, Lorenzo Lotto.

1972, Nov. 2 Photo. *Perf. 13½*

C165 A57 18fr dk car & multi 1.50 .25
C166 A57 27fr dk car & multi 1.75 .25
C167 A57 40fr dk car & multi 2.75 .40
a. Souv. sheet of 3, #C165-C167 6.00 4.75
Nos. C165-C167 (3) 6.00 .90

For surcharges see Nos. CB26-CB28.

Orchid Type of Regular Issue

13fr, Thelymitra pauciflora. 14fr, Miltassia. 15fr, Miltonia. 18fr, Platycoryne crocea. 20fr, Cattleya trinaei. 27fr, Eulophia cucullata. 36fr, Cymbidium hamsey.

1973, Jan. 18 Photo. *Perf. 13½*
Size: 38x38mm

C168 A58 13fr multi 2.50 .25
C169 A58 14fr multi 2.75 .25
C170 A58 15fr multi 3.00 .30
C171 A58 18fr multi 3.50 .35
C172 A58 20fr multi 4.00 .40
C173 A58 27fr multi 5.00 .45
C174 A58 36fr multi 6.00 .60
Nos. C168-C174 (7) 26.75 2.60

African Exploration Type of 1973

Designs: 15fr, Livingstone writing his diary. 18fr, "Dr. Livingstone, I presume." 27fr, Livingstone and Stanley discussing expedition.

1973, Mar. 19 Photo. *Perf. 13½*

C175 A59 15fr gold & multi .85 .25
C176 A59 18fr gold & multi 1.00 .25
C177 A59 27fr gold & multi 1.50 .35
a. Souv. sheet of 3 4.00 4.00
Nos. C175-C177 (3) 3.35 .85

No. C177a contains 3 stamps similar to Nos. C175-C177, but without "Poste Aerienne."

Easter Type of 1973

Paintings: 15fr, Christ at the Pillar, by Guido Reni. 18fr, Crucifixion, by Mathias Grunewald. 27fr, Descent from the Cross, by Caravaggio.

1973, Apr. 10

C178 A60 15fr gold & multi 1.25 .25
C179 A60 18fr gold & multi 1.40 .30
C180 A60 27fr gold & multi 1.90 .35
a. Souv. sheet of 3, #C178-C180 4.75 3.75
Nos. C178-C180 (3) 4.55 .90

INTERPOL Type of Regular Issue

Designs: 27fr, INTERPOL emblem and flag. 40fr, INTERPOL flag and emblem.

1973, May 19 Photo. *Perf. 13½*

C181 A61 27fr gold & multi 1.25 .30
C182 A61 40fr gold & multi 1.60 .50

Copernicus Type of Regular Issue

Designs: 15fr, Copernicus (C183a), Earth, Pluto, and Jupiter. 18fr, Copernicus (No. C184a), Venus, Saturn, Mars. 27fr, Copernicus (No. C185a), Uranus, Neptune, Mercury. 36fr, Earth and various spacecraft.
a, UL. b, UR. c, LL. d, LR.

1973, July 27 Photo. *Perf. 13½*

C183 A62 15fr Block of 4, #a.-d. 3.50 1.75
C184 A62 18fr Block of 4, #a.-d. 4.25 .75
C185 A62 27fr Block of 4, #a.-d. 6.50 1.25
C186 A62 36fr Block of 4, #a.-d. 8.50 1.25
e. Souv. sheet, #C183-C186 25.00 25.00
Nos. C183-C186 (4) 22.75 5.00

Flower-Butterfly Type of 1973

Designs: Each block of 4 contains 2 flower and 2 butterfly designs. The 10fr, 14fr, 24fr and 31fr have flower designs listed as "a" and "d" numbers, butterflies as "b" and "c" numbers; the arrangement is reversed for the 17fr and 26fr.

1973, Sept. 28 Photo. *Perf. 13*
Stamp Size: 35x45mm

C187 A63 Block of 4 15.00 .40
a. 10fr Protea cynaroides 3.00 .25
b. 10fr Precis octavia 3.00 .25
c. 10fr Epiphora bauhiniae 3.00 .25
d. 10fr Gazania longiscapa 3.00 .25
C188 A63 Block of 4 10.00 .40
a. 14fr Kniphofia 2.00 .25
b. 14fr Cymothoe coccinata 2.00 .25
c. 14fr Nudaurelia zambesina 2.00 .25
d. 14fr Freesia refracta 2.00 .25
C189 A63 Block of 4 12.00 .75
a. 17fr Calotis eupompe 2.25 .25
b. 17fr Narcissus 2.25 .25
c. 17fr Cineraria hybrida 2.25 .25
d. 17fr Cyrestis camillus 2.25 .25
C190 A63 Block of 4 14.00 .75
a. 24fr Iris tingitana 2.50 .25
b. 24fr Papilio demodocus 2.50 .25
c. 24fr Catopsilia avelaneda 2.50 .25
d. 24fr Nerine sarniensis 2.50 .25
C191 A63 Block of 4 15.00 1.00
a. 26fr Hypolimnas dexithea 2.75 .25
b. 26fr Zantedeschia tropicalis 2.75 .25
c. 26fr Sandersonia aurantiaca 2.75 .25
d. 26fr Drurya antimachus 2.75 .25
C192 A63 Block of 4 18.00 1.25
a. 31fr Nymphaea capensis 3.00 .25
b. 31fr Pandoriana pandora 3.00 .25
c. 31fr Precis orythia 3.00 .25
d. 31fr Pelargonium domestica 3.00 .25
Nos. C187-C192 (6) 84.00 4.55

Christmas Type of 1973

Virgin and Child by: 18fr, Raphael. 27fr, Pietro Perugino. 40fr, Titian.

1973, Nov. 19

C193 A64 18fr gold & multi .85 .25
C194 A64 27fr gold & multi 1.50 .25
C195 A64 40fr gold & multi 2.40 .30
a. Souv. sheet of 3, #C193-C195 5.00 4.50
Nos. C193-C195 (3) 4.75 .80

For surcharges see Nos. CB239-CB31.

Soccer Type of Regular Issue

Designs: Various soccer scenes and cup.

1974, July 4 Photo. *Perf. 13*

C196 A67 20fr gold & multi 1.50 .30
C197 A67 26fr gold & multi 1.75 .45
C198 A67 40fr gold & multi 2.75 .55
Nos. C196-C198 (3) 6.00 1.30

For souvenir sheet see No. 459a.

UPU Type of 1974

No. C199a, Flags over UPU Headquarters, Bern. No. C199b, G.P.O., Bujumbura. No. C200a, Mailmen ("26F" in UR). No. C200b, Mailmen ("26F" in UL). No. C201a, UPU emblem. No. C201b, Means of transportation. No. C202a, Pigeon over globe showing Burundi. No. C202b, Swiss flag, pigeon over map showing Bern.

1974, July 23

C199 A68 24fr Pair, #a.-b. 2.75 .50
C200 A68 26fr Pair, #a.-b. 3.00 .50
C201 A68 31fr Pair, #a.-b. 3.25 .60
C202 A68 40fr Pair, #a.-b. 5.00 .75
c. Souv. sheet, #C199-C202 27.50 27.50
Nos. C199-C202 (4) 14.00 2.35

Fish Type of 1974

1974, Sept. 9 Photo. *Perf. 13*
Size: 35x35mm

C207 A66 Block of 4 4.75 .40
a. 10fr Haplochromis multicolor .90 .25
b. 10fr Pantodon buchholzi .90 .25
c. 10fr Tropheus duboisi .90 .25
d. 10fr Distichodus sexfasciatus .90 .25
C208 A66 Block of 4 7.75 .60
a. 14fr Pelmatochromis kribensis 1.50 .25
b. 14fr Nannaethiops tritaeniatus 1.50 .25
c. 14fr Polycentropsis abbreviata 1.50 .25
d. 14fr Hemichromis bimaculatus 1.50 .25
C209 A66 Block of 4 10.50 .85
a. 17fr Ctenopoma acutirostre 1.90 .25
b. 17fr Synodontis angelicus 1.90 .25
c. 17fr Tilapia melanopleura 1.90 .25
d. 17fr Aphyosemion bivittatum 1.90 .25
C210 A66 Block of 4 14.50 1.10
a. 24fr Monodactylus argenteus 2.75 .30
b. 24fr Zanclus canescens 2.75 .30
c. 24fr Pygoplites diacanthus 2.75 .30
d. 24fr Cephalopholis argus 2.75 .30
C211 A66 Block of 4 18.00 1.50
a. 26fr Priacanthus arenatus 3.50 .35
b. 26fr Pomacanthus arcutus 3.50 .35
c. 26fr Scarus guacamaia 3.50 .35
d. 26fr Zeus faber 3.50 .35
C212 A66 Block of 4 24.00 1.60
a. 31fr Lactophrys quadricornis 4.50 .45
b. 31fr Balistes vetula 4.50 .45
c. 31fr Acanthurus bahianus 4.50 .45
d. 31fr Holocanthus ciliaris 4.50 .45
Nos. C207-C212 (6) 79.50 6.05

Christmas Type of 1974

Paintings of the Virgin and Child: 18fr, by Hans Memling. 27fr, by Filippino Lippi. 40fr, by Lorenzo di Gredi.

1974, Nov. 7 Photo. *Perf. 13*

C213 A70 18fr gold & multi 1.25 .25
C214 A70 27fr gold & multi 1.75 .30
C215 A70 40fr gold & multi 2.40 .45
a. Souv. sheet of 3, #C213-C215 5.00 4.00
Nos. C213-C215 (3) 5.40 1.00

Christmas 1974. Sheets of 20 stamps and one label.

Apollo-Soyuz Type of 1975

1975, July 10 Photo. *Perf. 13*

C216 A71 Block of 4 4.00 2.75
a. 27fr A.A. Leonov, V.N. Kubasov, Soviet flag .65
b. 27fr Soyuz and Soviet flag .65
c. 27fr Apollo and American flag .65
d. 27fr Slayton, Brand, Stafford, American flag .65
C217 A71 Block of 4 5.00 3.25
a. 40fr Apollo-Soyuz link-up .95
b. 40fr Apollo, blast-off .95
c. 40fr Soyuz, blast-off .95
d. 40fr Kubasov, Leonov, Slayton, Brand, Stafford .95

Nos. C216-C217 are printed in sheets of 32 containing 8 blocks of 4.

Animal Type of 1975

1975, Sept. 17 Photo. *Perf. 13½*

C218 Strip of 4 5.00 .35
a. A72 10fr Addax .90 .25
b. A72 10fr Roan antelope .90 .25
c. A72 10fr Nyala .90 .25
d. A72 10fr White rhinoceros .90 .25
C219 Strip of 4 6.75 .65
a. A72 14fr Mandrill 1.25 .25
b. A72 14fr Eland 1.25 .25
c. A72 14fr Salt's dik-dik 1.25 .25
d. A72 14fr Thomson's gazelles 1.25 .25
C220 Strip of 4 10.00 .65
a. A72 17fr African small-clawed otter 1.75 .25
b. A72 17fr Reed buck 1.75 .25
c. A72 17fr Indian civet 1.75 .25
d. A72 17fr Cape buffalo 1.75 .25
C221 Strip of 4 11.50 1.40
a. A72 24fr White-tailed gnu 2.00 .30
b. A72 24fr African wild asses 2.00 .30
c. A72 24fr Black-and-white colobus monkey 2.00 .30
d. A72 24fr Gerenuk 2.00 .30
C222 Strip of 4 13.00 1.40
a. A72 26fr Dama gazelle 2.25 .30
b. A72 26fr Black-backed jackal 2.25 .30
c. A72 26fr Sitatungas 2.25 .30
d. A72 26fr Zebra antelope 2.25 .30
C223 Strip of 4 14.00 1.00
a. A72 31fr Fennec 2.50 .35
b. A72 31fr Lesser kudus 2.50 .35
c. A72 31fr Blesbok 2.50 .35
d. A72 31fr Serval 2.50 .35
Nos. C218-C223 (6) 60.25 6.05

Nos. C218-C219 Ovptd. in Black & Silver

1975, Nov. 19 Photo. *Perf. 13½*

C224 Strip of 4 4.50 2.50
a. A72 10fr Addax .85 .40
b. A72 10fr Roan antelope .85 .40
c. A72 10fr Nyala .85 .40
d. A72 10fr White rhinoceros .85 .40
C225 Strip of 4 7.00 4.50
a. A72 14fr Mandrill 1.50 .75
b. A72 14fr Oryx 1.50 .75
c. A72 14fr Dik-dik 1.50 .75
d. A72 14fr Thomson's gazelles 1.50 .75

International Women's Year 1975.

Nos. C222-C223 Ovptd. in Black and Silver

1975, Nov. 19

C226 Strip of 4 13.00 12.00
a. A72 26fr Dama gazelle 2.25 2.00
b. A72 26fr Wild dog 2.25 2.00
c. A72 26fr Sitatungas 2.25 2.00
d. A72 26fr Striped duiker 2.25 2.00
C227 Strip of 4 17.00 15.00
a. A72 31fr Fennec 3.00 2.50
b. A72 31fr Lesser kudus 3.00 2.50
c. A72 31fr Blesbok 3.00 2.50
d. A72 31fr Serval 3.00 2.50

United Nations, 30th anniversary.

Michelangelo Type of 1975

Paintings from Sistine Chapel: No. C228a, Zachariah. No. C228b, Joel. No. C229a, Erythrean Sybil. No. C229b, Prophet Ezekiel. No. C230a, Persian Sybil. No. C230b, Prophet Jeremiah.

1975, Dec. 3 Photo. *Perf. 13*

C228 A73 18fr Pair, #a.-b. 4.50 .45
C229 A73 31fr Pair, #a.-b. 6.00 .65
C230 A73 40fr Pair, #a.-b. 9.00 .75
c. Souv. sheet of 6, #C228-C230 16.00 12.00
Nos. C228-C230 (3) 19.50 1.85

Printed in sheets of 18 stamps + 2 labels.
For surcharges see Nos. CB35-CB37.

Olympic Games Type, 1976

Designs (Olympic Games Emblem and): 18fr, Ski jump. 36fr, Slalom. 50fr, Ice hockey.

1976, Jan. 23 Photo. *Perf. 14x13½*

C234 A74 18fr ol brn & multi .90 .25
C235 A74 36fr grn & multi 1.75 .50
C236 A74 50fr pur & multi 2.25 .65
a. Souvenir sheet of 4 5.00 4.00
Nos. C234-C236 (3) 4.90 1.40

No. C236a contains 4 stamps similar to Nos. 491-494, perf. 13½, inscribed "POSTE AERIENNE."

21st Olympic Games, Montreal, Canada, July 17-Aug. 1 — AP5

Montreal Games Emblem and: Nos. C237b, C239a, C240b, High jump. Nos. C238a, C239b, C240a, Athlete on rings. Nos. C237a, C238b, C240c, Hurdles.

1976, May 3 Litho. *Perf. 13½*

C237 AP5 27fr Pair, #a.-b. 3.75 2.40
C238 AP5 31fr Pair, #a.-b. 4.75 3.25
C239 AP5 50fr Pair, #a.-b. 9.50 6.50
Nos. C237-C239 (3) 18.00 12.15

Souvenir Sheet

C240 AP5 Sheet of 3, #a.-c. 13.50 13.50

Battle of Bunker Hill, by John Trumbull — AP6

Paintings: 26fr, Franklin, Jefferson and John Adams. 36fr, Declaration of Independence, by John Trumbull.

1976, July 16 Photo. *Perf. 13*

C244 AP6 18fr Pair, #a.-b. 2.00 .35
C245 AP6 26fr Pair, #a.-b. 3.00 .45
C246 AP6 36fr Pair, #a.-b. 3.75 .85
c. Souv. sheet of 6, #C244-C246 9.00 9.00
Nos. C244-C246 (3) 8.75 1.65

American Bicentennial.
Exist imperf. Values: set $11; souvenir sheet $10.

Christmas Type of 1976

Paintings: 18fr, Virgin and Child with St. Anne, by Leonardo da Vinci. 31fr, Holy Family with Lamb, by Raphael. 40fr, Madonna of the Basket, by Correggio.

1976, Oct. 18 Photo. *Perf. 13½*

C250 A76 18fr gold & multi 1.75 .25
C251 A76 31fr gold & multi 2.25 .30
C252 A76 40fr gold & multi 3.25 .45
a. Souv. sheet of 3, #C250-C252 7.50 5.00
Nos. C250-C252 (3) 7.25 1.00

Christmas 1976. Sheets of 20 stamps and descriptive label.
For surcharges see Nos. CB41-CB40.

A.G. Bell Type of 1977

10fr, A.G. Bell and 1st telephone. No. C253a, 17fr, A.G. Bell speaking into microphone. Nos. C253b, C255e, Satellites around globe, videophone. No. C254a, Switchboard operator, c.1910, wall telephone. No. C254b, 26fr, Intelsat satellite, modern & old telephones. No. C255c, Intelsat, radar.

1977, May 17 Photo. *Perf. 13*

C253 A78 18fr Pair, #a.-b. 1.90 1.90
C254 A78 36fr Pair, #a.-b. 3.75 3.75
C255 Sheet of 5 7.00 7.00
a. A78 10fr multi 1.00 1.00
b. A78 17fr multi 1.00 1.00
c. A79 18fr multi 1.00 1.00
d. A79 26fr multi 1.00 1.00
e. A79 36fr multi 1.00 1.00

#C255c, C255e are air post stamps.

Animal Type of 1977

1977, Aug. 22 Photo. *Perf. 14x14½*

C258 A80 Strip of 4 5.00 .35
a. 9fr Buffon's kob .95 .25
b. 9fr Marabous .95 .25
c. 9fr Brindled gnu .95 .25
d. 9fr River hog .95 .25
C259 A80 Strip of 4 7.50 .80
a. 13fr Zebras 1.40 .25
b. 13fr Shoebill 1.40 .25
c. 13fr Striped hyenas 1.40 .25
d. 13fr Chimpanzee 1.40 .25
C260 A80 Strip of 4 12.00 1.50
a. 30fr Flamingos 2.25 .25
b. 30fr Nile Crocodiles 2.25 .25
c. 30fr Green mamba 2.25 .25
d. 30fr Greater kudus 2.25 .25
C261 A80 Strip of 4 21.00 1.75
a. 35fr Hyrax 4.00 .35
b. 35fr Cobra 4.00 .35
c. 35fr Jackals 4.00 .35
d. 35fr Verreaux's eagles 4.00 .35
C262 A80 Strip of 4 30.00 2.00
a. 54fr Honey badger 6.00 .45
b. 54fr Harnessed antelopes 6.00 .45
c. 54fr Secretary bird 6.00 .45
d. 54fr Klipspringer 6.00 .45
C263 A80 Strip of 4 45.00 2.50
a. 70fr African big-eared fox 8.50 .55
b. 70fr Elephants 8.50 .55
c. 70fr Vulturine guineafowl 8.50 .55
d. 70fr Impalas 8.50 .55
Nos. C258-C263 (6) 120.50 8.90

UN Type of 1977

Designs (UN Stamps and): 24fr, UN buildings by night. 27fr, UN buildings and view of Manhattan. 35fr, UN buildings by day.

1977, Oct. 10 Photo. *Perf. 13½*

C264 A82 Block of 4 6.00 6.00
a. 24fr No. 77 1.20 1.20
b. 24fr No. 78 1.20 1.20
c. 24fr No. 40 1.20 1.20
d. 24fr No. 32 1.20 1.20
C265 A82 Block of 4 7.00 7.00
a. 27fr No. 50 1.40 1.40
b. 27fr No. 21 1.40 1.40
c. 27fr No. 30 1.40 1.40
d. 27fr No. 44 1.40 1.40
C266 A82 Block of 4 10.50 10.50
a. 35fr No. C6 2.00 2.00
b. 35fr No. 105 2.00 2.00
c. 35fr No. 4 2.00 2.00
d. 35fr No. 1 2.00 2.00
e. Souvenir sheet of 3 1.40
Nos. C264-C266 (3) 23.50 23.50

No. C266e contains 24fr in design of No. C265b, 27fr in design of No. C266a, 35fr in design of No. C264c.

Christmas Type of 1977

Paintings of the Virgin and Child: 18fr, Master of Moulins. 31fr, Workshop of Lorenzo de Credi. 40fr, Palma Vecchio.

1977, Oct. 31 Photo. *Perf. 14x13*

C267 A83 18fr multi 1.75 1.00
C268 A83 31fr multi 2.75 1.75
C269 A83 40fr multi 3.50 2.25
a. Souv. sheet of 3, #C267-C269 6.00 6.00
Nos. C267-C269 (3) 8.00 5.00

Sheets of 24 stamps and descriptive label.
For surcharges see Nos. CB44-CB46.

Christmas 1978 Type of 1979

Souvenir Sheet

1979, Feb. Photo. *Perf. 14x13½*

C270 Sheet of 5 12.00 10.00
a. A86 13fr like #543 2.00 2.00
b. A86 17fr like #544 2.00 2.00
c. A86 27fr like #545 2.00 2.00
d. A86 31fr like #546 2.00 2.00
e. A86 40fr like #547 2.00 2.00

Christmas Type of 1979

Souvenir Sheet

1979, Oct. 12 *Perf. 13½*

C271 Sheet of 4 12.50 12.50
a. A89 20fr like #561 2.50 2.50
b. A89 27fr like #562 2.50 2.50
c. A89 31fr like #563 2.50 2.50
d. A89 50fr like #564 2.50 2.50

Hill Type of 1979

Souvenir Sheet

1979, Nov. 6

C272 Sheet of 5 11.00 8.00
a. A90 20fr like #565 2.00 1.40
b. A90 27fr like #566 2.00 1.40
c. A90 31fr like #567 2.00 1.40
d. A90 40fr like #568 2.00 1.40
e. A90 60fr like #569 2.00 1.40

Bird Type of 1979

1979 Photo. *Perf. 13½x3*

C273 A87 6fr like #548 1.25 .65
C274 A87 13fr like #549 2.25 1.50
C275 A87 18fr like #550 3.75 2.00
C276 A87 26fr like #551 5.00 3.00
C277 A87 31fr like #552 5.75 4.00
C278 A87 36fr like #553 7.25 5.00
C279 A87 40fr like #554 9.00 6.00
C280 A87 54fr like #555 13.00 7.50
C281 A87 70fr like #556 16.50 10.00
Nos. C273-C281 (9) 63.75 39.65

Olympic Type of 1980

Souvenir Sheet

1980, Oct. 24 Photo. *Perf. 13½*

C282 Sheet of 9 35.00 25.00
a. A91 20fr like #570a 3.50 2.00
b. A91 20fr like #570b 3.50 2.00
c. A91 20fr like #570c 3.50 2.00
d. A91 30fr like #571a 3.50 2.00
e. A91 30fr like #571b 3.50 2.00
f. A91 30fr like #571c 3.50 2.00
g. A91 40fr like #572a 3.50 2.00
h. A91 40fr like #572b 3.50 2.00
i. A91 40fr like #572c 3.50 2.00

Christmas Type of 1980

Souvenir Sheet

1980, Dec. 12 Photo. *Perf. 13½x13*

C283 Sheet of 4 22.00 10.00
a. A92 10fr like #579 4.00 2.00
b. A92 30fr like #580 4.00 2.00
c. A92 40fr like #581 4.00 2.00
d. A92 45fr like #582 4.00 2.00

UPRONA Type of 1980

Souvenir Sheet

1980, Dec. 29 *Perf. 14½x13½*

C284 Sheet of 3 6.50 4.50
a. A93 10fr like #583 1.60 1.00
b. A93 40fr like #584 1.60 1.00
c. A93 45fr like #585 1.60 1.00

Christmas Type of 1983

Souvenir Sheet

1983, Oct. 3 Litho. *Perf. 14½x13½*

C285 Sheet of 4 75.00 75.00
a. A97 10fr like #607 15.00 15.00
b. A97 25fr like #608 15.00 15.00
c. A97 30fr like #609 15.00 15.00
d. A97 50fr like #610 15.00 15.00

UPU Congress Type of 1984

Souvenir Sheet

1984, July 14 *Perf. 13x13½*

C286 Sheet of 4 25.00 25.00
a. A99 10fr like #621 5.00 5.00
b. A99 30fr like #622 5.00 5.00
c. A99 35fr like #623 5.00 5.00
d. A99 65fr like #624 5.00 5.00

Summer Olympics Type of 1984

Souvenir Sheet

1984, Aug. 6 *Perf. 13½x13*

C287 Sheet of 4 30.00 30.00
a. A100 10fr like #625 6.25 6.25
b. A100 30fr like #626 6.25 6.25
c. A100 35fr like #627 6.25 6.25
d. A100 65fr like #628 6.25 6.25

Christmas Type of 1984

Souvenir Sheet

1984, Dec. 15 *Perf. 13½*

C288 Sheet of 4 30.00 12.00
a. A101 10fr like #629 6.00 2.40
b. A101 25fr like #630 6.00 2.40
c. A101 30fr like #631 6.00 2.40
d. A101 50fr like #632 6.00 2.40

Flower Type of 1986 with Dull Lilac Border

1986, July 31 Photo. *Perf. 13x13½*

C289 A102 70fr like #633 11.50 8.50
C290 A102 75fr like #634 13.00 9.00
C291 A102 80fr like #635 14.00 10.00
C292 A102 85fr like #636 15.50 11.00
C293 A102 100fr like #637 18.00 12.00
C294 A102 150fr like #638 26.00 14.00
Nos. C289-C294 (6) 98.00 64.50

Animals AP8

100fr, M. nemestrina. 115fr, Equus grevyi. 200fr, Long horn cattle. 220fr, Pelecanus onocrotalus.

1992, June 2 Litho. *Perf. 14*

C298	AP8 100fr multicolored		3.50	2.25
C299	AP8 115fr multicolored		4.50	2.50
C300	AP8 200fr multicolored		10.00	6.00
C301	AP8 220fr multicolored		12.00	7.00
	a. Souvenir sheet of 4, #C298-C301, perf. 13½		30.00	
	Nos. C298-C301 (4)		30.00	17.75

No. C301a exists imperf. Value, $30.

AIR POST SEMI-POSTAL STAMPS

Coin Type of Semi-Postal Issue

Designs (Coins of Various Denominations): 3fr+1fr, 11fr+1fr, 20fr+1fr, 50fr+1fr, Coat of Arms, reverse. 5fr+1fr, 14fr+1fr, 30fr+1fr, 100fr+1fr, King Mwambutsa IV, obverse.

Lithographed; Embossed on Gilt Foil

1965, Nov. 15 *Imperf.*

Diameter: 39mm

CB1	SP4	3fr + 1fr lt & dk vio	.25	.25
CB2	SP4	5fr + 1fr pale grn & red	.35	.35

Diameter: 45mm

CB3	SP4	11fr + 1fr org & lilac	.55	.55
CB4	SP4	14fr + 1fr red & emer	.70	.70

Diameter: 56mm

CB5	SP4	20fr + 1fr ultra & blk	.90	.90
CB6	SP4	30fr + 1fr dp org & mar	1.25	1.25

Diameter: 67mm

CB7	SP4	50fr + 1fr bl & vio bl	2.50	2.50
CB8	SP4	100fr+ 1fr rose & dp cl	4.50	4.50
		Nos. CB1-CB8 (8)	11.00	11.00

Stamps are backed with patterned paper in blue, orange, and pink engine-turned design.

Red Cross Type of Semi-Postal Issue

Designs: 26fr+3fr, Laboratory. 40fr+3fr, Ambulance and thatched huts. 50fr+3fr, Red Cross nurse with patient.

1969, June 26 Photo. *Perf. 13½*

CB9	SP7 26fr + 3fr multi	.95	.25
CB10	SP7 40fr + 3fr multi	1.25	.40
CB11	SP7 50fr + 3fr multi	1.75	.60
	Nos. CB9-CB11 (3)	3.95	1.25

Perf. and imperf. souvenir sheets exist containing 3 stamps similar to Nos. CB9-CB11, but without "Poste Aerienne." Size: 90½x97mm

Christmas Type of Semi-Postal Issue

Paintings: 14fr+3fr, Virgin and Child, by Velázquez. 26fr+3fr, Holy Family, by Joos van Cleve. 40fr+3fr, Virgin and Child, by Rogier van der Weyden.

1970, Dec. 14 Photo. *Perf. 13½*

CB12	SP9 14fr + 3fr multi	.75	.25
CB13	SP9 26fr + 3fr multi	1.25	.45
CB14	SP9 40fr + 3fr multi	2.00	.60
	a. Souv. sheet of 3, #CB12-CB14	4.00	4.00
	Nos. CB12-CB14 (3)	4.00	1.30

No. C147 Surcharged in Gold and Black

1971, Aug. 9 Photo. *Perf. 13½*

CB15	Strip of 4	11.00	4.00
	a. A48 14fr+2fr Hartebeest	2.40	.25
	b. A48 14fr+2fr Black rhinoceros	2.40	.25
	c. A48 14fr+2fr Zebra	2.40	.25
	d. A48 14fr+2fr Leopard	2.40	.25

UNESCO campaign against illiteracy.

No. C148 Surcharged in Gold and Black

1971, Aug. 9

CB16	Strip of 4	15.00	5.00
	a. A48 17fr+1fr Grant's gazelles	3.00	.25
	b. A48 17fr+1fr Cheetah	3.00	.25
	c. A48 17fr+1fr African white-backed vultures	3.00	.25
	d. A48 17fr+1fr Johnston's okapi	3.00	.25

International help for refugees.

Nos. C150-C151 Surcharged in Black and Gold

a

b

1971, Aug. 16

CB17	Strip of 4	14.00	4.00
	a. A48(a) 26fr+1fr Gorilla	3.00	.90
	b. A48(a) 26fr+1fr Gnu	3.00	.90
	c. A48(a) 26fr+1fr Warthog	3.00	.90
	d. A48(a) 26fr+1fr Cape hunting dog	3.00	.90
CB18	Strip of 4	17.50	5.00
	a. A48(b) 31fr+1fr Sable antelope	3.50	1.10
	b. A48(b) 31fr+1fr Caracal lynx	3.50	1.10
	c. A48(b) 31fr+1fr Ostriches	3.50	1.10
	d. A48(b) 31fr+1fr Bongo	3.50	1.10

75th anniv. of modern Olympic Games (#CB17); Olympic Games, Munich, 1972 (#CB18).

Nos. C153-C155 Surcharged

1971, Nov. 27 Photo. *Perf. 13½*

CB19	A51 14fr + 1fr multi	.80	.35
CB20	A51 17fr + 1fr multi	1.25	.35
CB21	A51 31fr + 1fr multi	1.75	.35
	Nos. CB19-CB21 (3)	3.80	1.05
	a. Souvenir Sheet of 3	4.00	3.25

25th anniv. of UNICEF.

No. CB21a contains 3 stamps similar to #CB19-CB21 with 2 fr surcharge each.

Casa D'Oro, Venice SPAP1

Views in Venice: 17fr+1fr, Doge's Palace. 24fr+1fr, Church of Sts. John and Paul. 31fr+1fr, Doge's Palace and Piazzetta at Feast of Ascension, by Canaletto.

1971, Dec. 27

CB22	SPAP1 10fr + 1fr multi	.45	.25
CB23	SPAP1 17fr + 1fr multi	.80	.25
CB24	SPAP1 24fr + 1fr multi	1.20	.35
CB25	SPAP1 31fr + 1fr multi	1.60	.35
	a. Souvenir sheet of 4	6.00	6.00
	Nos. CB22-CB25 (4)	4.05	1.20

Surtax for the UNESCO campaign to save the treasures of Venice. No. CB25a contains 4 stamps similar to Nos. CB22-CB25, but with 2fr surtax.

Nos. CB22-CB25a exist imperf. Value: set $6.50; souvenir sheet $8.

Nos. C165-C167, C193-C195 Srchd. in Silver

1972, Dec. 12 Photo. *Perf. 13½*

CB26	A57 18fr + 1fr multi	1.00	.25
CB27	A57 27fr + 1fr multi	1.75	.35
CB28	A57 40fr + 1fr multi	2.50	.60
	a. Souvenir sheet of 3	6.00	5.00
	Nos. CB26-CB28 (3)	5.25	1.20

Christmas 1972. No. CB28a contains 3 stamps similar to Nos. CB26-CB28 but with 2fr surtax.

1973, Dec. 14 Photo. *Perf. 13*

CB29	A64 18fr + 1fr multi	.90	.30
CB30	A64 27fr + 1fr multi	1.25	.40
CB31	A64 40fr + 1fr multi	1.75	.50
	a. Souvenir sheet of 3	4.50	4.00
	Nos. CB29-CB31 (3)	3.90	1.20

Christmas 1973. No. CB31a contains 3 stamps similar to Nos. CB29-CB31 with 2fr surtax each.

Christmas Type of 1974

1974, Dec. 2 Photo. *Perf. 13*

CB32	A70 18fr + 1fr multi	1.10	.30
CB33	A70 27fr + 1fr multi	1.75	.60
CB34	A70 40fr + 1fr multi	2.75	1.00
	a. Souvenir sheet of 3	6.00	6.00
	Nos. CB32-CB34 (3)	5.60	1.90

Christmas 1974. No. CB34a contains 3 stamps similar to Nos. CB32-CB34 with 2fr surtax.

Nos. C228-C230 Srchd. in Silver and Black

1975, Dec. 22 Photo. *Perf. 13*

CB35	A73 18fr +1fr Pair, #a-b	5.00	.30
CB36	A73 31fr +1fr Pair, #a-b	6.75	.50
CB37	A73 40fr +1fr Pair, #a-b	10.00	.60
	c. Souvenir sheet of 6	20.00	20.00
	Nos. CB35-CB37 (3)	21.75	1.40

Michelangelo Buonarroti (1475-1564). No. CB37c contains 6 stamps similar to Nos. CB35-CB37 with 2fr surtax each.

Nos. C250-C252 Surcharged "+1f" in Silver and Black

1976, Nov. 25 Photo. *Perf. 13½*

CB41	A76 18fr + 1fr multi	1.60	.25
CB42	A76 31fr + 1fr multi	2.25	.35
CB43	A76 40fr + 1fr multi	3.25	.65
	a. Souvenir sheet of 3	7.00	7.00
	Nos. CB41-CB43 (3)	7.10	1.25

Christmas 1976. No. CB43a contains 3 stamps similar to Nos. CB41-CB43 with 2fr surtax each.

Nos. C267-C269 Surcharged "+1fr" in Silver and Black

1977 Photo. *Perf. 14x13*

CB44	A83 18fr + 1fr multi	1.50	.30
CB45	A83 31fr + 1fr multi	2.75	.40
CB46	A83 40fr + 1fr multi	3.75	.55
	a. Souvenir sheet of 3	12.00	12.00
	Nos. CB44-CB46 (3)	8.00	1.25

Christmas 1977. No. CB46a contains 3 stamps similar to Nos. CB44-CB46 with 2fr surtax each.

Christmas 1978 Type

Souvenir Sheet

1979, Feb. Photo. *Perf. 14x13*

CB47	Sheet of 5	22.00	12.00
	a. A86 13fr + 2fr multi	3.75	1.75
	b. A86 17fr + 2fr multi	3.75	1.75
	c. A86 27fr + 2fr multi	3.75	1.75
	d. A86 31fr + 2fr multi	3.75	1.75
	e. A86 40fr + 2fr multi	3.75	1.75

Christmas Type of 1979

Souvenir Sheet

1979, Dec. 10 Photo. *Perf. 13½*

CB48	Sheet of 4	22.00	12.00
	a. A89 20fr + 2fr like #561	3.75	2.00
	b. A89 27fr + 2fr like #562	3.75	2.00
	c. A89 31fr + 2fr like #563	3.75	2.00
	d. A89 50fr + 2fr like #564	3.75	2.00

Exists imperf. Value $13.

Christmas Type of 1980

Souvenir Sheet

1981, Jan. 16 Photo. *Perf. 13½x13*

CB49	Sheet of 4	22.00	22.00
	a. A92 10fr + 2fr like #579	3.75	3.75
	b. A92 30fr + 2fr like #580	3.75	3.75
	c. A92 40fr + 2fr like #581	3.75	3.75
	d. A92 50fr + 2fr like #582	3.75	3.75

Exists imperf. Value $13.

Christmas Type of 1983

Souvenir Sheet

1983, Nov. 2 Litho. *Perf. 14½x13½*

CB50	Sheet of 4	16.00	16.00
	a. A97 10fr + 2fr like #607	1.25	1.00
	b. A97 25fr + 2fr like #608	2.00	1.75
	c. A97 30fr + 2fr like #609	4.00	3.50
	d. A97 50fr + 2fr like #610	5.50	5.00

Exists imperf. Value $13.

Christmas Type of 1984

Souvenir Sheet

1984, Dec. 15 *Perf. 13½*

CB51	Sheet of 4	15.00	15.00
	a. A101 10fr + 2fr like #629	3.00	3.00
	b. A101 25fr + 2fr like #630	3.00	3.00
	c. A101 30fr + 2fr like #631	3.00	3.00
	d. A101 50fr + 2fr like #632	3.00	3.00

BUSHIRE

bü-'shir

LOCATION — On Persian Gulf

Bushire is an Iranian port that British troops occupied Aug. 8, 1915.

20 Chahis (or Shahis) = 1 Kran
10 Krans = 1 Toman

Watermark

Wmk. 161 — Lion

ISSUED UNDER BRITISH OCCUPATION

Basic Iranian Designs

Iranian Stamps of 1911-13 Overprinted in Black

Perf. 11½, 11½x11
Typo. & Engr.

1915, Aug. 15 **Unwmk.**

N1	A32	1c green & org	200.00	*160.00*
N2	A32	2c red & sepia	200.00	160.00
N3	A32	3c gray brn & grn	250.00	*190.00*
N4	A32	5c brown & car	1,600.	*1,400.*
N5	A32	6c green & red brn	250.00	190.00
N6	A32	9c yel brn & vio	300.00	*250.00*
a.		Double overprint		
N7	A32	10c red & org brn	350.00	*300.00*
N8	A32	12c grn & ultra	400.00	*300.00*
N9	A32	1k ultra & car	400.00	300.00
a.		Double overprint	7,500.	
N10	A32	24c vio & grn	350.00	300.00
N11	A32	2k grn & red vio	800.00	700.00
N12	A32	3k vio & blk	850.00	*750.00*
N13	A32	5k red & ultra	750.00	650.00
N14	A32	10k ol bis & cl	750.00	650.00
		Nos. N1-N14 (14)	7,450.	6,300.

Nos. N1-N14, except No. N4, exist without period after "Occupation." This variety sells for more. See the *Scott Classic Catalogue of Stamps and Covers* for listings.

Forged overprints exist of Nos. N1-N29.

The Bushire overprint exists on Iran No. 537 but is considered a forgery.

On Iranian Stamps of 1915

No. N15

No. N26

No. N29

Perf. 11, 11½

1915, Sept. **Wmk. 161**

N15	A33	1c car & indigo	2,000.	2,000.
N16	A33	2c blue & car	25,000.	*25,000.*
N17	A33	3c dk grn	2,500.	*2,500.*
N18	A33	5c red	25,000.	*25,000.*
N19	A33	6c ol grn & car	10,000.	*10,000.*
N20	A33	9c yel brn & vio	*3,000.*	3,000.
N21	A33	10c bl grn & yel brn	4,000.	*4,000.*
N22	A33	12c ultra	5,000.	*5,000.*
N23	A34	1k sil, yel brn & gray	2,500.	2,500.
N24	A33	24c yel brn & dk brn	2,500.	2,500.
N25	A34	2k sil, bl & rose	2,500.	2,500.
N26	A34	3k sil, vio & brn	2,500.	2,500.
N27	A34	5k sil, brn & grn	3,000.	3,000.
a.		Inverted overprint	—	*35,000.*
N28	A35	1t gold, pur & blk	3,500.	*3,500.*
N29	A35	3t gold, cl & red brn	9,000.	*9,000.*

Persia (Iran) resumed administration of Bushire post office Oct. 16, 1915.

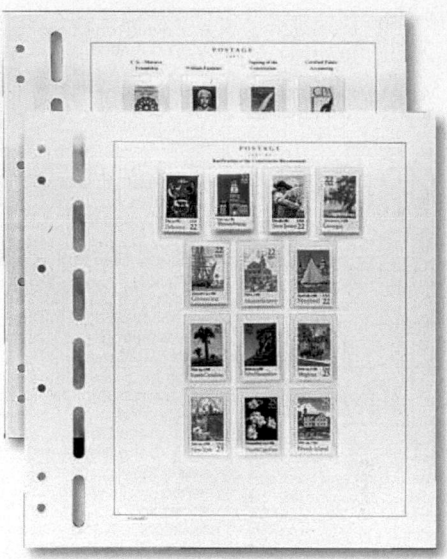

INDEX AND IDENTIFIER

All page numbers shown are those in this Volume 1B.

Postage stamps that do not have English words on them are shown in the Scott *Stamp Illustrated Identifier*. To purchase it visit AmosAdvantage.com or call Amos Media at 800-572-6885.

Vols. 1A-1B number additions, deletions and changes

Number in 2021 Catalogue	Number in 2022 Catalogue
United States	
new	527d
new	1384t
new	2150c
new	2216q
new	5335c
Semi-postal Stamps	
new	B5b
Official Stamps	
new	O136b
Confederate Postmasters' Provisionals	
new	153XU1
Afghanistan	
4	deleted
4A	4
Aitutaki	
642	641
641	642
Albania	
new	18a
new	19a
new	19b
new	19c
new	J1a
new	J1b
new	J2a
new	J2b
new	J3a
Argentina	
new	C20a
O129	deleted
Australian States – New South Wales	
new	71b
Belgium	
new	82a
new	J17a
new	J18a
new	J19a
new	J21a
Bolivia	
new	450a

INDEX TO ADVERTISERS
2022 VOLUME 1B

2022
VOLUME 1B
DEALER DIRECTORY
YELLOW PAGE LISTINGS

This section of your Scott Catalogue contains advertisements to help you conveniently find what you need, when you need it...!

Albania

WORLDSTAMPS/ FRANK GEIGER PHILATELISTS
PO Box 4743
Pinehurst, NC 28374
PH: 910-295-2048
Frank@WorldStamps.com
www.WorldStamps.com

Andorra

WORLDSTAMPS/ FRANK GEIGER PHILATELISTS
PO Box 4743
Pinehurst, NC 28374
PH: 910-295-2048
Frank@WorldStamps.com
www.WorldStamps.com

Appraisals

DR. ROBERT FRIEDMAN & SONS STAMP & COIN BUYING CENTER
2029 W. 75th St.
Woodridge, IL 60517
PH: 800-588-8100
FAX: 630-985-1588
stampcollections@drbobstamps.com
www.drbobfriedmanstamps.com

MILLER'S STAMP COMPANY
P.O. Box 1011
Niantic, CT 06357
www.millerstamps.com
PH: 860-908-6200

Auctions

DUTCH COUNTRY AUCTIONS
The Stamp Center
4115 Concord Pike
Wilmington, DE 19803
PH: 302-478-8740
FAX: 302-478-8779
auctions@dutchcountryauctions.com
www.dutchcountryauctions.com

Australia

COLONIAL STAMP COMPANY
5757 Wilshire Blvd. PH #8
Los Angeles, CA 90036
PH: 323-933-9435
FAX: 323-939-9930
info@colonialstamps.com
www.colonialstamps.com

WORLDSTAMPS/ FRANK GEIGER PHILATELISTS
PO Box 4743
Pinehurst, NC 28374
PH: 910-295-2048
Frank@WorldStamps.com
www.WorldStamps.com

Austria

HENRY GITNER PHILATELISTS, INC.
PO Box 3077-S
Middletown, NY 10940
PH: 845-343-5151
PH: 800-947-8267
FAX: 845-343-0068
hgitner@hgitner.com
www.hgitner.com

WORLDSTAMPS/ FRANK GEIGER PHILATELISTS
PO Box 4743
Pinehurst, NC 28374
PH: 910-295-2048
Frank@WorldStamps.com
www.WorldStamps.com

Bangkok

COLONIAL STAMP COMPANY
5757 Wilshire Blvd. PH #8
Los Angeles, CA 90036
PH: 323-933-9435
FAX: 323-939-9930
info@colonialstamps.com
www.colonialstamps.com

Belgium

WORLDSTAMPS/ FRANK GEIGER PHILATELISTS
PO Box 4743
Pinehurst, NC 28374
PH: 910-295-2048
Frank@WorldStamps.com
www.WorldStamps.com

Bermuda

COLONIAL STAMP COMPANY
5757 Wilshire Blvd. PH #8
Los Angeles, CA 90036
PH: 323-933-9435
FAX: 323-939-9930
info@colonialstamps.com
www.colonialstamps.com

Bhutan

WORLDSTAMPS/ FRANK GEIGER PHILATELISTS
PO Box 4743
Pinehurst, NC 28374
PH: 910-295-2048
Frank@WorldStamps.com
www.WorldStamps.com

British Asia

THE STAMP ACT
PO Box 1136
Belmont, CA 94002
PH: 650-703-2342
thestampact@sbcglobal.net

British Commonwealth

COLLECTORS EXCHANGE ORLANDO STAMP SHOP
1814A Edgewater Drive
Orlando, FL 32804
PH: 407-620-0908
PH: 407-947-8603
FAX: 407-730-2131
jlatter@cfl.rr.com
www.OrlandoStampShop.com

ARON R. HALBERSTAM PHILATELISTS, LTD.
PO Box 150168
Van Brunt Station
Brooklyn, NY 11215-0168
PH: 718-788-3978
arh@arhstamps.com
www.arhstamps.com

ROY'S STAMPS
PO Box 28001
600 Ontario Street
St. Catharines, ON
CANADA L2N 7P8
Phone: 905-934-8377
Email: roystamp@cogeco.ca
www.roysstamps.com

THE STAMP ACT
PO Box 1136
Belmont, CA 94002
PH: 650-703-2342
thestampact@sbcglobal.net

British Commonwealth

WORLDSTAMPS/ FRANK GEIGER PHILATELISTS
PO Box 4743
Pinehurst, NC 28374
PH: 910-295-2048
Frank@WorldStamps.com
www.WorldStamps.com

British E. Africa

COLONIAL STAMP COMPANY
5757 Wilshire Blvd. PH #8
Los Angeles, CA 90036
PH: 323-933-9435
FAX: 323-939-9930
info@colonialstamps.com
www.colonialstamps.com

British Guiana

COLONIAL STAMP COMPANY
5757 Wilshire Blvd. PH #8
Los Angeles, CA 90036
PH: 323-933-9435
FAX: 323-939-9930
info@colonialstamps.com
www.colonialstamps.com

Buying

DR. ROBERT FRIEDMAN & SONS STAMP & COIN BUYING CENTER
2029 W. 75th St.
Woodridge, IL 60517
PH: 800-588-8100
FAX: 630-985-1588
stampcollections@drbobstamps.com
www.drbobfriedmanstamps.com

Canada

CANADA STAMP FINDER
PO Box 92591
Brampton, ON L6W 4R1
PH: 514-238-5751
Toll Free in North America: 877-412-3106
FAX: 323-315-2635
canadastampfinder@gmail.com
www.canadastampfinder.com

ROY'S STAMPS
PO Box 28001
600 Ontario Street
St. Catharines, ON
CANADA L2N 7P8
Phone: 905-934-8377
Email: roystamp@cogeco.ca
www.roysstamps.com

China - PRC

THE STAMP ACT
PO Box 1136
Belmont, CA 94002
PH: 650-703-2342
thestampact@sbcglobal.net

Collections

DR. ROBERT FRIEDMAN & SONS STAMP & COIN BUYING CENTER
2029 W. 75th St.
Woodridge, IL 60517
PH: 800-588-8100
FAX: 630-985-1588
stampcollections@drbobstamps.com
www.drbobfriedmanstamps.com

British Commonwealth

British Empire
1840 - 1935

Aden to Zululand Mint & Used
Most complete stock in North America

For over 40 years, we have built some of the world's finest collections. Our expert ***Want List Services*** can do the same for you. Over 50 volumes filled with singles, sets and rare stamps, we are sure we have what you need. We welcome your Want Lists in Scott or Stanley Gibbons numbers.

Put our expertise to work for you today!
You'll be glad you did!

Colonial Stamp Company
"Rarity and quality are remembered ...long after price is forgotten."
5757 Wilshire Blvd., Penthouse 8
Los Angeles, CA 90036 USA
Tel: +1 (323) 933-9435 Fax: +1 (323) 939-9930
Email: *Info@ColonialStamps.com*
www.ColonialStamps.com

Ask for your free Public Auction Catalogue today!

Collectors Club New York

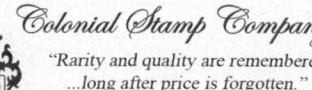

Ducks

MICHAEL JAFFE
PO Box 61484
Vancouver, WA 98666
PH: 360-695-6161
PH: 800-782-6770
FAX: 360-695-1616
mjaffe@brookmanstamps.com
www.brookmanstamps.com

Europe-Western

HENRY GITNER PHILATELISTS, INC.
PO Box 3077-S
Middletown, NY 10940
PH: 845-343-5151
PH: 800-947-8267
FAX: 845-343-0068
hgitner@hgitner.com
www.hgitner.com

German Colonies

COLONIAL STAMP COMPANY
5757 Wilshire Blvd. PH #8
Los Angeles, CA 90036
PH: 323-933-9435
FAX: 323-939-9930
info@colonialstamps.com
www.colonialstamps.com

Great Britain

COLONIAL STAMP COMPANY
5757 Wilshire Blvd. PH #8
Los Angeles, CA 90036
PH: 323-933-9435
FAX: 323-939-9930
info@colonialstamps.com
www.colonialstamps.com

New Issues

DAVIDSON'S STAMP SERVICE
Personalized Service since 1970
PO Box 36355
Indianapolis, IN 46236-0355
PH: 317-826-2620
ed-davidson@earthlink.net
www.newstampissues.com

WORLDSTAMPS/ FRANK GEIGER PHILATELISTS
PO Box 4743
Pinehurst, NC 28374
PH: 910-295-2048
Frank@WorldStamps.com
www.WorldStamps.com

Stamp Stores

California

COLONIAL STAMP COMPANY
5757 Wilshire Blvd. PH #8
Los Angeles, CA 90036
PH: 323-933-9435
FAX: 323-939-9930
info@colonialstamps.com
www.colonialstamps.com

Connecticut

MILLER'S STAMP COMPANY
P.O. Box 1011
Niantic, CT 06357
www.millerstamps.com
PH: 860-908-6200

Delaware

DUTCH COUNTRY AUCTIONS
The Stamp Center
4115 Concord Pike
Wilmington, DE 19803
PH: 302-478-8740
FAX: 302-478-8779
auctions@dutchcountryauctions.com
www.dutchcountryauctions.com

Florida

DR. ROBERT FRIEDMAN & SONS STAMP & COIN BUYING CENTER
PH: 800-588-8100
FAX: 630-985-1588
stampcollections@drbobstamps.com
www.drbobfriedmanstamps.com

Illinois

DR. ROBERT FRIEDMAN & SONS STAMP & COIN BUYING CENTER
2029 W. 75th St.
Woodridge, IL 60517
PH: 800-588-8100
FAX: 630-985-1588
stampcollections@drbobstamps.com
www.drbobfriedmanstamps.com

New Jersey

BERGEN STAMPS & COLLECTIBLES
306 Queen Anne Rd.
Teaneck, NJ 07666
PH: 201-836-8987
bergenstamps@gmail.com

Stamp Stores

New Jersey

TRENTON STAMP & COIN
Thomas DeLuca
Store: Forest Glen Plaza
1804 Highway #33
Hamilton Square, NJ 08690
Mail: PO Box 8574
Trenton, NJ 08650
PH: 609-584-8100
FAX: 609-587-8664
TOMD4TSC@aol.com
www.trentonstampandcoin.com

New York

CK STAMPS
42-14 Union St. # 2A
Flushing, NY 11355
PH: 917-667-6641
ckstampsllc@yahoo.com

Ohio

HILLTOP STAMP SERVICE
Richard A. Peterson
PO Box 626
Wooster, OH 44691
PH: 330-262-8907 (O)
PH: 330-201-1377 (H)
hilltopstamps@sssnet.com
www.hilltopstamps.com

Supplies

BROOKLYN GALLERY COIN & STAMP, INC.
8725 4th Ave.
Brooklyn, NY 11209
PH: 718-745-5701
FAX: 718-745-2775
info@brooklyngallery.com
www.brooklyngallery.com

Topicals

E. JOSEPH McCONNELL, INC.
PO Box 683
Monroe, NY 10949
PH: 845-783-9791
FAX: 845-782-0347
ejstamps@gmail.com
www.EJMcConnell.com

WORLDSTAMPS/ FRANK GEIGER PHILATELISTS
PO Box 4743
Pinehurst, NC 28374
PH: 910-295-2048
Frank@WorldStamps.com
www.WorldStamps.com

Topicals - Columbus

MR. COLUMBUS
PO Box 1492
Fennville, MI 49408
PH: 269-543-4755
David@MrColumbus1492.com
www.MrColumbus1492.com

United Nations

BRUCE M. MOYER
Box 12031
Charlotte, NC 28220
PH: 908-237-6967
moyer@unstamps.com
www.unstamps.com

United States

ACS STAMP COMPANY
2914 W 135th Ave
Broomfield, Colorado 80020
303-841-8666
www.ACSStamp.com

BROOKMAN STAMP CO.
PO Box 90
Vancouver, WA 98666
PH: 360-695-1391
PH: 800-545-4871
FAX: 360-695-1616
info@brookmanstamps.com
www.brookmanstamps.com

HENRY GITNER PHILATELISTS, INC.
PO Box 3077-S
Middletown, NY 10940
PH: 845-343-5151
PH: 800-947-8267
FAX: 845-343-0068
hgitner@hgitner.com
www.hgitner.com

MILLER'S STAMP COMPANY
P.O. Box 1011
Niantic, CT 06357
www.millerstamps.com
PH: 860-908-6200

WORLDSTAMPS/ FRANK GEIGER PHILATELISTS
PO Box 4743
Pinehurst, NC 28374
PH: 910-295-2048
Frank@WorldStamps.com
www.WorldStamps.com

Supplies

United States

U.S. Classics/Moderns

BARDO STAMPS
PO Box 7437
Buffalo Grove, IL 60089
PH: 847-634-2676
jfb7437@aol.com
www.bardostamps.com

HENRY GITNER PHILATELISTS, INC.
PO Box 3077-S
Middletown, NY 10940
PH: 845-343-5151
PH: 800-947-8267
FAX: 845-343-0068
hgitner@hgitner.com
www.hgitner.com

U.S.-Collections Wanted

DUTCH COUNTRY AUCTIONS
The Stamp Center
4115 Concord Pike
Wilmington, DE 19803
PH: 302-478-8740
FAX: 302-478-8779
auctions@dutchcountryauctions.com
www.dutchcountryauctions.com

DR. ROBERT FRIEDMAN & SONS STAMP & COIN BUYING CENTER
2029 W. 75th St.
Woodridge, IL 60517
PH: 800-588-8100
FAX: 630-985-1588
stampcollections@drbobstamps.com
www.drbobfriedmanstamps.com

MILLER'S STAMP COMPANY
P.O. Box 1011
Niantic, CT 06357
www.millerstamps.com
PH: 860-908-6200

Want Lists - British Empire 1840-1935 German Cols./Offices

COLONIAL STAMP COMPANY
5757 Wilshire Blvd. PH #8
Los Angeles, CA 90036
PH: 323-933-9435
FAX: 323-939-9930
info@colonialstamps.com
www.colonialstamps.com

Want Lists - U.S.

HENRY GITNER PHILATELISTS, INC.
PO Box 3077-S
Middletown, NY 10940
PH: 845-343-5151
PH: 800-947-8267
FAX: 845-343-0068
hgitner@hgitner.com
www.hgitner.com

Wanted - Worldwide Collections

DUTCH COUNTRY AUCTIONS
The Stamp Center
4115 Concord Pike
Wilmington, DE 19803
PH: 302-478-8740
FAX: 302-478-8779
auctions@dutchcountryauctions.com
www.dutchcountryauctions.com

Wanted - U.S.

HENRY GITNER PHILATELISTS, INC.
PO Box 3077-S
Middletown, NY 10940
PH: 845-343-5151
PH: 800-947-8267
FAX: 845-343-0068
hgitner@hgitner.com
www.hgitner.com

Websites

ACS STAMP COMPANY
2914 W 135th Ave
Broomfield, Colorado 80020
303-841-8666
www.ACSStamp.com

MILLER'S STAMP COMPANY
P.O. Box 1011
Niantic, CT 06357
www.millerstamps.com
PH: 860-908-6200

Wholesale - Dealers

HENRY GITNER PHILATELISTS, INC.
PO Box 3077-S
Middletown, NY 10940
PH: 845-343-5151
PH: 800-947-8267
FAX: 845-343-0068
hgitner@hgitner.com
www.hgitner.com

Worldwide

GUILLERMO JALIL
Maipu 466, local 4
1006 Buenos Aires
Argentina
guillermo@jalilstamps.com
philatino@philatino.com
www.philatino.com (worldwide stamp auctions)
www.jalilstamps.com (direct sale, worldwide stamps)

Worldwide-Collections

DR. ROBERT FRIEDMAN & SONS STAMP & COIN BUYING CENTER
2029 W. 75th St.
Woodridge, IL 60517
PH: 800-588-8100
FAX: 630-985-1588
stampcollections@drbobstamps.com
www.drbobfriedmanstamps.com